THE COLUMBIA
GRANGER'S®
INDEX TO POETRY

THE COLUMBIA GRANGER'S® INDEX TO POETRY

TENTH EDITION, COMPLETELY REVISED

INDEXING ANTHOLOGIES

PUBLISHED THROUGH JUNE 3, 1993

EDITED BY

EDITH P. HAZEN

COLUMBIA UNIVERSITY PRESS

NEW YORK

THE COLUMBIA GRANGER'S ® INDEX TO POETRY

COPYRIGHT 1904, 1918, 1929, 1940, 1945, 1953, © 1957, 1962
1973, 1978, 1982, 1986, 1990, 1994

BY COLUMBIA UNIVERSITY PRESS

TENTH EDITION, COMPLETELY REVISED

LIBRARY OF CONGRESS CATALOGING-IN-PUBLICATION DATA

Hazen, Edith P.
    The Columbia Granger's index to poetry. 10th ed.,
competely rev., indexing anthologies published through
June 3, 1993 / edited by Edith P. Hazen.
    p. cm.
ISBN 0-231-08408-0
    1. Poetry — Indexes. 2. English poetry — Indexes.
I. Granger, Edith. Index to poetry. II. Title.
PN1022.H39 1994
016.80881 — dc20   93-39161
                                              CIP

CASEBOUND EDITIONS OF COLUMBIA UNIVERSITY PRESS BOOKS ARE
PRINTED ON PERMANENT AND DURABLE ACID-FREE PAPER.

PRINTED IN THE UNITED STATES OF AMERICA

C 10 9 8 7 6 5 4 3 2

PREFACE TO THE TENTH EDITION

The publication of the tenth edition of THE COLUMBIA GRANGER'S® INDEX TO POETRY, or "Granger's®," ninety years after publication of the first edition, is an appropriate moment not only to celebrate the introduction of two new features, indexing by last line and author dating, but to explain some policies, principles, and procedures that have gone toward making this work the solid institution that it is.

First, the important new feature: last lines. In this edition, we have indexed 12,500 last lines, without dropping any feature of Granger's®, and without reducing the number of anthologies we index or poems we cite. We have chosen to index the last lines of the 12,500 poems that have been anthologized most frequently. These are the poems reprinted most often, circulated most often, most likely to be present on library shelves, and therefore most likely to be remembered and searched for. Questions about quotations from other lines in a poem may be answered by consulting THE COLUMBIA GRANGER'S® DICTIONARY OF POETRY QUOTATIONS (1992), which has a full keyword index, or by consulting THE COLUMBIA GRANGER'S® WORLD OF POETRY ON CD-ROM.

As for how and why we compile Granger's® in the way we do, we aim simply to index the anthologies that are likely to be on library shelves. We collect all the anthologies that have appeared since the most recent edition of Granger's®, and we select among them with the help of our board of consultants. For the tenth edition, our consultants are:

— William Katz, a compiler and reviewer of many library reference works, including THE COLUMBIA GRANGER'S® GUIDE TO POETRY ANTHOLOGIES;

— John Frederick Nims and Dana Gioia, two poets who are also anthologists and accomplished translators of poetry;

— Mary Biggs, a Dean of Libraries who has written a book about the publishing of contemporary poetry;

— James Shapiro, an Associate Professor of English at Columbia University and author.

These consultants helped the Press decide which 150 new anthologies should be indexed in this edition, which 150 anthologies in the last edition should be dropped in order to make space for the new ones, and which 40 anthologies should be singled out for library purchase — one star for thirty we consider especially important and two stars for those we consider outstanding.

The criteria we employ to select and star an anthology include the excellence of the poems chosen in it; the originality, beauty, or strength of their ordering; the quality of the introduction and notes; the quality of illustration; the presence of a table of contents and indexes; and the overall design and physical quality of the book. For full descriptions and evaluations of all anthologies indexed in the seventh, eighth, ninth, and tenth editions of Granger's®, we refer librarians to THE COLUMBIA GRANGER'S® GUIDE TO POETRY ANTHOLOGIES, Second Edition 1994.

Staff of the Press read every poem in every chosen anthology to give each a subject (or sometimes two or more subjects), and then to index titles, first lines, last lines, authors, and subjects. In doing this, we provide a service not only to librarians and their patrons but to the original publishers, none of whom give their poems subjects — unless of course their entire anthology is arranged around a subject or subjects. Granger's® is the only poetry reference work that includes a genuine subject index.

We often index anthologies better than their own editors do. Many anthologies, provide only a first line index, or only an author index, or only a title index. We give all three — and last lines, and subjects. There are times when we provide five times the amount of access provided by the original anthology. We provide the correct names of authors attributed in anthologies to the wrong author or described in anthologies as "unknown." We now provide dates for authors, wherever we have been able to find them (our second new feature in this edition), giving the most complete source of such dates in any reference work. And we provide the original titles for poems, showing as different variants any titles given to them in anthologies. In the detailed care of its preparation, Granger's® can be regarded as a meticulous and historic reference work.

In this tenth edition of Granger's®, there are:
— 79,000 poems, of which 21,000 are indexed for the first time
— located 120,000 times (see below)
— in 400 anthologies, of which 150 are new
— by 11,000 authors, of whom 900 are new
— and 4,000 subjects.

The second figure in the list above is particularly significant. We are able to lead searchers to particular poems in particular anthologies 120,000 times, which is, we believe, a measure of the overall convenience of Granger's®. Granger's® maximizes the chances of a person finding the poem he or she wants in an anthology, because all the possible anthologies are listed after the poem's title and first line. We have located Blake's "The Tiger" not merely in one anthology but in over fifty anthologies. So the Granger's® system provides the maximum amount of access to any library's anthology collection.

The anthologies indexed include general anthologies of poetry in English; general anthologies of American poetry; general anthologies of British poetry; many anthologies of poetry in translation; anthologies of poetry by women, by ethnic Americans, by poets of many different periods, on many different themes; anthologies of ballads, limericks, hymns, and poetry for children.

These anthologies constitute a very large world of poetry. Inasmuch as anthologies are by definition endorsements of poems by publishers who did not originally publish them, this large world of poetry is, we believe, the right one to index. To put it another way, this collection of anthologies, rather than, for instance, a collection of periodicals that include poetry or a collection of poetry by individual poets, can best claim to constitute at any one time "poetry in English." In this our tenth edition of Granger's®, we are proud to be providing again the best key to it.

James Raimes

HOW TO USE THE COLUMBIA GRANGER'S® INDEX TO POETRY

The poems, authors, and subjects indexed in the tenth edition of THE CO-LUMBIA GRANGER'S® INDEX TO POETRY are contained in the 400 anthologies listed on pages XIII-XXX. But searchers arrive at that list after they have asked one of several questions, and the easiest way to explain how the book works is to show in detail how it answers some of these typical questions.

Title, First Line, and Last Line Indexes

Where can I find a poem called "Out of Sight, Out of Mind"? If you go to the Title, First Line, and Last Line Index, which forms the great bulk of Granger's®, you will find it listed there, with the name of its author, Barnabe Googe, and with the letters ElL and InPS after it. These are the symbols for the anthologies in which "Out of sight, Out of Mind" can be found. You then look up the symbols in the List of Anthologies, where the symbols rather than the anthologies themselves are arranged alphabetically. There you will learn that you can read "Out of Sight, Out of Mind" in *Elizabethan Lyrics*, edited by Norman Ault, published by Wiliam Sloane Associates, and also in *An Introduction to Poetry*, edited by Louis Simpson, the third edition of which was published by St. Martin's Press in 1986.

What is the title of the poem that begins "When I was a bachelor I lived all alone"? That question is also answered in the Title, First Line, and Last Index of Granger's®. The poem's title is "The Foggy, Foggy Dew." This index also tells you that its author is unknown and that it can be found in seven anthologies.

Who wrote the poem that begins "In the cold, cold parlor"? The Title, First Line, and Last Line Index tells you that Elizabeth Bishop wrote it. It also tells you that the poem's title is "First Death in Nova Scotia" and that it can found in five anthologies.

What poem ends with the line "I am a lady young in beauty waiting"? Again, the Title, First Line, and Last Line Index tells you that it is the last line (LL) of "Piazza Piece" by John Crowe Ransom and that it can be found in 17 anthologies.

Author Index

What poems can I find by May Swenson? The Author index lists 18 poems in this edition of Granger's®.

Did Edna St. Vincent Millay write under a pseudonym? The Author Index tells you that she used the pen-name Nancy Boyd and also that she lived from 1892 to 1950.

Subject Index

Where can I find some poems about Paris, France? The Subject Index is an especially valuable tool for poetry searchers, and we have again increased its value considerably in this tenth edition. It tells you that there are 19 poems about Paris, by such authors as Apollinaire, Kenneth Koch, Ezra Pound, and Thackeray. Citations for all these poems can be found in the Title, First Line, and Last Line Index.

What books of religious poetry can my church add to its library? The Subject Index, under Religious Verse, lists 19 anthologies that are exclusively about God or religion or religious life.

List of Anthologies

Among these four hundred anthologies, which should I buy first? In the List of Anthologies we have starred 40 anthologies: one star to 30 antholgies we consider especially important, two stars to those we consider outstanding.

The Columbia Granger's® Index to Poetry
Tenth Edition

PUBLISHER
JOHN D. MOORE

EDITORIAL DIRECTOR, REFERENCE DIVISION
JAMES RAIMES

DIRECTOR OF DESIGN AND PRODUCTION
AUDREY SMITH

EDITOR
EDITH P. HAZEN

STAFF

THERESA ALVIAR
WILLIAM MATTHEW ANDERSON
IAN CUNNINGHAM
JENNIFER FIORE
NICHOLAS FRANKOVICH
KEITH W. FROME
DANIAL M. KAUFMAN
FRANCES KIM
ISHMAEL KLEIN
DAVID M. LARZELERE
BRIAN M. LENNON
POLLY C. MEYERS

ELLEN S. MILLER
RONALD MOORE
EMILY RAIMES
LUCY RAIMES
LEAH SCHANZER
OLIVIA SCHANZER
GREG M. SHAW
CATHERINE F. VILLA
GEORGIA WINSTON
MAX WINTER
JOHN S. WYETH, JR.
SHELINA SHARIFF ZIA

CONTENTS

LIST OF ANTHOLOGIES

Anthologies starred with two asterisks (**) are recommended for priority acquisition by small libraries, one star (*) for further acquisition. Anthologies marked with a dagger (†) have been translated into English. See PREFACE *for fuller explanation.*

AAP	African-American Poetry of the Nineteenth Century; an Anthology. *Joan R. Sherman, ed.* (1992) University of Illinois Press
AAS	Anchor Anthology of Sixteenth-Century Verse, The. *Richard S. Sylvester, ed.* (1974) Doubleday/Anchor Books (Also published in 1984 by W. W. Norton & Company as English Sixteenth-Century Verse)
AfAz	After Aztlan: Latino Poets of the Nineties. *Ray González, ed.* (1992) David R. Godine
AH	American Hymns Old and New, Vols. I–II. Vol. I, with music; Vol. II, notes on the hymns and biographies of the authors and composers. *Albert Christ-Janer, Charles W. Hughes, and Carleton Sprague Smith, eds.* (1980) Columbia University Press
AiP	America in Poetry. *Charles Sullivan, ed.* (1988) Harry N. Abrams
AIW	†Ain't I a Woman! a Book of Women's Poetry from around the World. *Illona Linthwaite, ed.* (1988) Peter Bedrick Books
AmFP	American Folk Poetry; an Anthology. *Duncan Emrich, ed.* (1974) Little, Brown and Company
AmPA	American Poetry Anthology, The. *Daniel Halpern, ed.* (1975) Avon Books
AmPP	American Poetry and Prose. *Norman Foerster, Norman S. Grabo, Russel B. Nye, E. Fred Carlisle, and Robert Falk, eds.* (5th ed., 1970) Houghton Mifflin Company
AmWP	American Women Poets of the Nineteenth Century; an Anthology. *Cheryl Walker, ed.* (1992) Rutgers University Press
AnAmPo	Anthology of American Poetry. *George Gesner, ed.* (1983) Avenel Books
AnAn	Antaeus Anthology, The. *Daniel Halpern, ed.* (1986) Bantam Books
AngWe	Anglo-Welsh Poetry, 1480-1980. *Raymond Garlick and Roland Mathias, eds.* (1984) Poetry Wales Press
AnOE	Anthology of Old English Poetry, An. *Charles W. Kennedy, tr.* (1960) Oxford University Press
AnRep	†Another Republic; 17 European & South American Writers. *Charles Simic and Mark Strand, eds.* (1976) Ecco Press
APAS	Anthology of Poems on Affairs of State; Augustan Satirical Verse, 1600–1714. *George deF. Lord, ed.* (1975) Yale University Press
ArLo	Art & Love; an Illustrated Anthology of Love and Poetry. *Kate Farrell, ed.* (1990) The Metropolitan Museum of Art and Bulfinch Press
ArNa	Art & Nature; an Illustrated Anthology of Nature Poetry. *Kate Farrell, ed.* (1992) The Metropolitan Museum of Art and Bulfinch Press

ArOW   Articles of War; a Collection of American Poetry about World War II. *Leon Stokesbury, ed.* (1990) University of Arkansas Press

ArPe   †Arabic & Persian Poems in English. *Omar S. Pound, comp.* (1970) New Directions

AS   American Songbag, The. *Carl Sandburg, comp.* (1927) Harcourt, Brace & Company

ASW   Anglo-Saxon World, The; an Anthology. *Kevin Crossley-Holland, ed. and tr.* (1991) Oxford University Press

AWP   Anthology of World Poetry, An. *Mark Van Doren, ed.* (Rev. and enl. ed., 1936) Reynal & Hitchcock

BAP-89   Best American Poetry, 1989. *Donald Hall, ed.* (1989) Macmillan Publishing Company

BAP-90   Best American Poetry, 1990, The. *Mark Strand, ed.* (1990)Collier Books

BAP-91   Best American Poetry, 1991, The. *Mark Strand, ed.* (1991) Collier Books

BCF   Before Columbus Foundation Poetry, The; Selections from the American Book Awards, 1980–1990. *J. J. Phillips, Ishmael Reed, Gundars Strads, and Shawn Wong, eds.* (1992) W. W. Norton & Company

BeJo   Ben Jonson and the Cavalier Poets; *Hugh Maclean, ed.* (1974) W. W. Norton & Company

BeLS   Best Loved Story Poems. *Walter E. Thwing, ed.* (1941) Garden City Publishing Company

BiHa   Bitter Harvest; an Anthology of Contemporary Irish Verse. *John Montague, ed.* (1989) Charles Scribner's Sons

BIrV   Book of Irish Verse, The; an Anthology of Irish Poetry from the Sixth Century to the Present. *John Montague, ed.* (1974) Macmillian Publishing Company (Also published as The Faber Book of Irish Verse)

BLPA   **Best Loved Poems of the American People, The. *Hazel Felleman, ed.* (1936) Doubleday & Company

BLPL   Best-Loved Poems in Large Print. *Virginia S. Reiser, ed.* (1983) G. K. Hall & Company

BLRP   Best Loved Religious Poems, The. *James Gilchrist Lawson, comp.* (1933) Fleming H. Revell Company

BlSi   Black Sister; Poetry by Black American Women, 1746–1980. *Erlene Stetson, ed.* (1981) Indiana University Press

BOEP   Book of English Poetry, A: Chaucer to Rossetti. *G. B. Harrison, ed.* (New, enl. ed., 1950) Penguin Books

BoLoP   Book of Love Poetry, A. *Jon Stallworthy, ed.* (1974) Oxford University Press (Published in Great Britain as The Penguin Book of Love Poetry)

BoNaP   Book of Nature Poems, A. *William Cole, comp.* (1969) The Viking Press

BoTP   Book of a Thousand Poems, The; a Family Treasury. *J. Murray Macbain, ed.* (1983) Peter Bedrick Books

BoWoP   *Book of Women Poets from Antiquity to Now, A. *Aliki Barnstone and Willis Barnstone, eds.* (1980) Schocken Books

BPo   **Black Poets, The. *Dudley Randall, ed.* (1971) Bantam Books

LIST OF ANTHOLOGIES

BrRo	Bread and Roses; an Anthology of Nineteenth- and Twentieth-Century Poetry by Women Writers. *Diana Scott, ed.* (1982) Virago Press
BTR	Blood to Remember; American Poets on the Holocaust. *Charles Fishman, ed.* (1991) Texas Tech University Press
BXAP	Brand-X Anthology of Poetry, The: Burnt Norton Edition. *William Zaranka, ed.* (1981) Apple-Wood Books
CaPo	Cavalier Poets; Selected Poems. *Thomas Clayton, ed.* (1978) Oxford University Press
CAPP	Contemporary American Poetry. *A. Poulin, Jr., ed.* (4th ed., 1985) Houghton Mifflin Company
CBAP	Collins Book of Australian Poetry, The. *Rodney Hall, comp.* (1981, 1984) Fontana/Collins
CBCK	Chatto Book of Cabbages and Kings, The; Lists in Literature. *Francis Spufford, ed.* (1989) Chatto & Windus
CBLP	Chatto Book of Love Poetry, The. *John Fuller, ed.* (1990) Chatto & Windus
CBNP	Chatto Book of Nonsense Poetry, The. *Hugh Haughton* (1988) Chatto & Windus
CBWP 1-4	*Collected Black Women's Poetry, Vols. I–IV. *Joan R. Sherman, ed.* (1988) Oxford University Press
CDC	Caroling Dusk; an Anthology of Verse by Negro Poets. *Countee Cullen, ed.* (1927) Harper & Brothers
CDW	Carriers of the Dream Wheel; Contemporary Native American Poetry. *Duane Niatum, ed.* (1975) Harper & Row
CH	*Come Hither; a Collection of Rhymes & Poems for the Young of All Ages. *Walter de la Mare, comp.* (3d ed., 1957) Alfred A. Knopf
ChIV 1-2	Chapters into Verse; Poetry in English Inspired by the Bible, Vols. I–II. Vol. I: Genesis to Malachi; Vol. II: Gospels to Revelation. *Robert Atwan and Laurance Wieder, eds.* (1993) Oxford University Press
ChTr	Cherry-Tree, The. *Geoffrey Grigson, comp.* (1959) Phoenix House
CIP	Contemporary Irish Poetry; an Anthology. *Anthony Bradley, ed.* (New and rev. ed., 1988) University of California Press
ClHu	Classic Hundred, The; All-Time Favorite Poems. *William Harmon, ed.* (1990) Columbia University Press
CMoP	*Chief Modern Poets of Britain and America. *Gerald DeWitt Sanders, John Herbert Nelson, and M. L. Rosenthal, eds.* (5th ed., 1970) Macmillian Publishing Company
CoAP	Contemporary American Poets, The; American Poetry since 1940. *Mark Strand, ed.* (1969) New American Library
CoGr	Common Ground; an Anthology. *Marghanita Laski, ed.* (1989) Carcanet Press
CoMu	Common Muse, The; an Anthology of Popular British Ballad Poetry, XVth–XXth Century. *Vivian de Sola Pinto and Allan Edwin Rodway, eds.* (1957) Philosophical Library
CRH	Cat Will Rhyme with Hat; a Book of Poems. *Jean Chapman, comp.* (1986) Charles Scribner's Sons
CRP	Contemporary Religious Poetry. *Paul Ramsey, ed.* (1987) Paulist Press
CrSp	Cries of the Spirit; a Celebration of Women's Sprituality. *Marilyn Sewell, ed.* (1991) Beacon Press

CTC   Confucius to Cummings; an Anthology of Poetry. *Ezra Pound and Marcella Spann, eds.* (1964) New Directions

DiPo   Direction of Poetry, The; an Antholgly of Rhymed and Metered Verse Written in the English Language since 1975. *Robert Richman, ed.* (1988) Houghton Mifflin Company

DL   Death in Literature. *Robert F. Weir, ed.* (1980) Columbia University Press

DT   Dancing the Tightrope; New Love Poems by Women. *Barbara Burford, Lindsay MacRae, and Sylvia Paskin, eds.* (1988) Peter Bedrick Books

EAP   Early American Poetry. *Jane Donahue Eberwein, ed.* (1978) University of Wisconsin Press

EaPr   Earth Prayers from Around the World: 365 Prayers, Poems, and Invocations for Honoring the Earth. *Elizabeth Roberts and Elias Amidon, eds.* (1991) HarperCollins

EBEV   Everyman's Book of English Verse. *John Wain, ed.* (1981) J. M. Dent & Sons

EBEvV   Everyman's Book of Evergreen Verse. *David Herbert, ed.* (1984) J. M. Dent & Sons

EBNV   Everyman Book of Narrative Verse, The. *David Herbert, ed.* (1991) J. M. Dent & Sons

EBVV   Everyman's Book of Victorian Verse. *J. R. Watson, ed.* (1982) J. M. Dent & Sons

EBVVPR   Everyman Book of Victorian Verse, The; the Post- Romantics. *Donald Thomas, ed.* (1992) J. M. Dent & Sons

ECEV   Eighteenth-Century English Verse. *Dennis Davison, ed.* (1988) Penguin Books

ECWP   Eighteenth Century Women Poets; an Oxford Anthology. *Roger Lonsdale, ed.* (1989) Oxford University Press

ElL   Elizabethan Lyrics. *Norman Ault, ed.* (3d ed., 1949) William Sloane Associates (Paperback edition of 1960 published by G. P. Putnam's Sons)

EnlH   Enlightened Heart, The; an Anthology of Sacred Poetry. *Stephen Mitchell, ed.* (1989) Harper & Row

ELP   English Lyric Poems, 1500–1900. *C. Day Lewis, ed.* (1961) Appleton-Century-Crofts

EnLoPo   English Love Poems. *John Betjeman and Geoffrey Taylor, comps.* (1957; paperback 1964) Faber and Faber

EnRePo   English Renaissance Poetry; a Collection of Shorter Poems from Skelton to Jonson. *John Williams, ed.* (2d ed., 1990) University of Arkansas Press

EnRP   English Romantic Poetry and Prose. *Russell Noyes, ed.* (1956) Oxford University Press

EnSB   English and Scottish Ballads. *Robert Graves, ed.* (1957) William Heinemann

    English Sixteenth-Century Verse; an Anthology. (1984) W. W. Norton & Company (This book is the same as The Anchor Anthology of Sixteenth-Century Verse [AAS]; see above.)

EnVB   English Verse, 1300–1500. *John Burrow, ed.* (1977) Longman

EnVR   English Verse, 1830–1890. *Bernard Richards, ed.* (1980) Longman

LIST OF ANTHOLOGIES

FaBoPV	Faber Book of Political Verse, The. *Tom Paulin, ed.* (1986) Faber and Faber
	Faber Book of Popular Verse, The. (1971) Faber and Faber (This book is the same as The Gambit Book of Popular Verse [GBP]; see below.)
FaBoRV	Faber Book of Reflective Verse, The. *Geoffrey Grigson, ed.* (1984) Faber and Faber
FaBoTw	Faber Book of Twentieth-Century Verse, The. *John Heath-Stubbs and David Wright, eds.* (3d ed., 1975) Faber and Faber
FaBoUs	Faber Book of Useful Verse, The. *Simon Brett, ed.* (1981) Faber and Faber
FaBoVe	Faber Book of Vernacular Verse, The. *Tom Paulin, ed.* (1990) Faber and Faber
FaBoWP	Faber Book of 20th Century Women's Poetry, The. *Fleur Adcock, ed.* (1987) Faber and Faber
FaBV	Family Book of Verse, The. *Lewis Gannett, ed.* (1961) Harper & Row
FaPoB	Family Poetry Book, The. Foreward by Felicity Kendal (1990) Michael Joseph
FaPON	Favorite Poems Old and New. *Helen Ferris, ed.* (1957) Doubleday & Company
FaPoR	Faber Popular Reciter, The. *Kingsley Amis, ed.* (1978) Faber and Faber
FF	Fine Frenzy; Enduring Themes in Poetry. *Robert Baylor and Brenda Stokes, eds.* (2d ed., 1978) McGraw-Hill Book Company
FHYEP	Five Hundred Years of English Poetry: Chaucer to Arnold. *Barbara Lloyd-Evans, ed.* (1989) Peter Bedrick Books
FiBHP	Fireside Book of Humorous Poetry, The. *William Cole, ed.* (1959) Simon and Schuster
FM	Fellow Mortals; an Anthology of Animal Verse. *Roy Fuller, comp.* (1981) Macdonald and Evans
FoLa	Forgotten Language, The; Contemporary Poets and Nature. *Christopher Merrill, ed.* (1991) Gibbs-Smith Publisher
FYAP	Fifty Years of American Poetry; Anniversary Volume for the Academy of American Poets. Introduction by Robert Penn Warren. (1984) Harry N. Abrams
GBL	Gambit Book of Love Poems, The. *Geoffrey Grigson, ed.* (1975) Gambit (Originally published in Great Britain by Faber and Faber as The Faber Book of Love Poems)
GBP	Gambit Book of Popular Verse, The. *Geoffrey Grigson, ed.* (1971) Gambit (Also published in Great Britain as The Faber Book of Popular Verse)
GeHe	George Herbert and the Seventeenth-Century Religious Poets. *Mario A. di Cesare, ed.* (1978) W. W. Norton & Company
GePo	†German Poetry from the Beginnings to 1750. *Ingrid Walsøoe-Engel, ed.* (1992) The Continuum Publishing Company
GGP	Gift of Great Poetry, The. *Lucien Stryk, ed.* (1992) Regnery Gateway
GLP	*Gay & Lesbian Poetry in Our Time; an Anthology. *Carl Morse and Joan Larkin, eds.* (1988) St. Martin's Press

LIST OF ANTHOLOGIES

GN   Golden Numbers. *Kate Douglas Wiggin and Nora Archibald Smith, eds*. (1902) Doubleday, Doran & Company

GOA   Gift Outright, The; America to Her Poets. *Helen Plotz, ed*. (1977) Greenwillow Books

GoJo   Golden Journey, The; Poems for Young People. *Louise Bogan and William Jay Smith, comps*. (1990) Contemporary Books (Edition of 1965 published by Reilly & Lee Company)

GoYe   Golden Year, The; the Poetry Society of America Anthology (1910–1960). *Melville Cane, John Farrar, and Louise Townsend Nicholl, eds*. (1960) The Fine Editions Press

GOYP   Going Over to Your Place; Poems for Each Other. *Paul B. Janeczko, comp*. (1987) Bradbury Press

GrAn   †Greek Anthology and Other Ancient Epigrams, The; a Selection in Modern Verse Translations. *Peter Jay, ed*. (Rev. ed., 1981) Penguin Books

GrPl   Green Place, A; Modern Poems. *William Jay Smith, comp*. (1982) Delacorte Press/Seymour Lawrence

GTBS   Golden Treasury of the Best Songs and Lyrical Poems in the English Language. *Francis Turner Palgrave, comp*. (1991, ed. by Christopher Ricks) Penguin Books (Edition of 1929 published by Oxford University Press)

GTBS-P   *Golden Treasury of the Best Songs & Lyrical Poems in the English Language. *Francis Turner Palgrave, comp*. With a fifth book selected by John Press*. (5th ed., 1964) Oxford University Press

HAP   *Harper Anthology of Poetry, The. *John Fredrick Nims, ed*. (1981) Harper & Row

HATNAP   *Harper's Anthology of 20th Century Native American Poetry. *Duane Niatum, ed*. (1988) Harper & Row

HBAPE   Heinemann Book of African Poetry in English, The. *Adewale Maja-Pearce, comp*. (1990) Heinemann

HCAP   **Harvard Book of Contemporary American Poetry, The. *Helen Vendler, ed*. (1985) The Belknap Press of Harvard University Press

HeIL   Heath Introduction to Literature, The. *Alice S. Landy, ed*. (4th ed., 1992) D. C. Heath and Company

HeIP   Heath Introduction to Poetry, The. *Joseph de Roche, ed*. (4th ed., 1992) D. C. Heath and Company

HePo   †Hellenistic Poetry; an Anthology. *Barbara Hughes Fowler, ed. and tr*. (1990) The University of Wisconsin Press

HoPM   *How Does a Poem Mean? *John Ciardi and Miller Williams, eds*. (2d ed., 1975) Houghton Mifflin Company

HSix   †Horse Has Six Legs, The; an Anthology of Serbian Poetry. *Charles Simic, ed. and tr*. (1992) Graywolf Press

IB   Inherited Boundaries, The; Younger Poets of the Republic of Ireland. *Sebastian Barry, ed*. (1986) The Dolmen Press

IBB   Illustrated Border Ballads, The. *John Marsden, ed*. (1990) Macmillan London

IHMS   I Hear My Sisters Saying; Poems by Twentieth-Century Women. *Carol Konek and Dorothy Walters, eds*. (1976) Thomas Y. Crowell Company

IHNG	I Have No Gun But I Can Spit; an Anthology of Satirical and Abusive Verse. *Kenneth Baker, ed.* (1980) Faber and Faber
IIP	*Ireland in Poetry. *Charles Sullivan, ed.* (1990) Harry N. Abrams
ImGa	Imaginary Gardens; American Poetry and Art for Young People. *Charles Sullivan* (1989) Harry N. Abrams
ImPo	Immortal Poems of the English Language; an Anthology. *Oscar Williams, ed.* (1952) Simon & Schuster
IMW	In the Midst of Winter; Selections from the Literature of Mourning. *Mary Jane Moffat, ed.* (1992) Vintage Books
InMo	†Infinite Moment, The; Poems from Ancient Greek. *Sam Hamill, tr.* (1992) New Directions
InPK	Introduction to Poetry, An. *X. J. Kennedy, ed.* (6th ed., 1986) Little, Brown & Company
InPS	Introduction to Poetry, An. *Louis Simpson, ed.* (3d ed., 1986) St. Martin's Press
InvP	Invitation to Poetry; a Round of Poems from John Skelton to Dylan Thomas. *Lloyd Frankenberg, ed.* (1956) Doubleday & Company
IPY	Irish Poetry after Yeats; Seven Poets. *Maurice Harmon, ed.* (1979) Little, Brown and Company
ISE	I Saw Esau; the Schoolchild's Pocket Book. *Iona Opie and Peter Opie, eds.* (1992) Candlewick Press (Original edition published 1947 by Williams and Northgate)
Jaz	Jazz Poetry Anthology, The. *Sascha Feinstein and Yusef Komunyakaa, eds.* (1991) Indiana University Press
JB	Jump Bad; a New Chicago Anthology *Gwendolyn Brooks, ed.* (1971) Broadside Press
JCP	Jacobean and Caroline Poetry; an Anthology. *T. G. S. Cain, ed.* (1981) Methuen
KTR	Kissing the Rod; an Anthology of Seventeenth-Century Women's Verse. *Germaine Greer, Susan Hastings, Jeslyn Medoff, and Melinda Sansone, eds.* (1988) Farrar Straus Giroux
LCAP	Longman Anthology of Contemporary American Poetry, The. *Stuart Friebert and David Young, eds.* (2d ed., 1989) Longman
LHF	†Literature of the Hundred Flowers. Vol. II: Poetry and Fiction. *Hualing Nieh, ed.* (1981) Columbia University Press
LiTA	Little Treasury of American Poetry, A. *Oscar Williams, ed.* (1948) Charles Scribner's Sons
LiTB	Little Treasury of British Poetry, A. *Oscar Williams, ed.* (1951) Charles Scribner's Sons
LiTM	Little Treasury of Modern Poetry, A: English and American. *Oscar Williams, ed.* (3d ed., 1970) Charles Scribner's Sons
LoHo	Looking for Home; Women Writing about Exile. *Deborah Keenan and Roseann Lloyd, eds.* (1990) Milkweed Editions
LPA	Loving: Poetry and Art. *Charles Sullivan, ed.* (1992) Harry N. Abrams
MAT	Messages; a Thematic Anthology of Poetry. *X. J. Kennedy, ed.* (1973) Little, Brown & Company
MDDM	Mother to Daughter, Daughter to Mother; Mothers on Mothering. *Tillie Olsen, ed.* (1984) The Feminist Press

MeEL	Medieval English Lyrics; a Critical Anthology. *R. T. Davies, ed.* (1964) Northwestern University Press
MeLP	Metaphysical Lyrics & Poems of the Seventeenth Century; Donne to Butler. *Herbert J. C. Grierson, ed.* (1921; reissue, 1947) Oxford University Press
MeMAP	Mentor Book of Major American Poets, The. *Oscar Williams and Edwin Honig, eds.* (1962) New American Library
MeMBP	Mentor Book of Major British Poets, The. *Oscar Williams, ed.* (1963) New American Library
Mes	Messages; a Book of Poems. *Naomi Lewis, comp.* (1985) Faber and Faber
MHP	†Modern Hebrew Poetry; a Bilingual Anthology. *Ruth Finer Mintz, ed. and tr.* (1966) University of California Press
MiEL	Middle English Lyrics: From Virgil to Milton. *Maxwell S. Luria and Richard L. Hoffman, eds.* (1974) W. W. Norton & Company
MLL	†More Latin Lyrics. *Dame Felicitas Corrigan, ed.* (1977) W. W. Norton & Company
MoAB	Modern American & British Poetry. *Louis Untermeyer, ed., with Karl Shapiro and Richard Wilbur.* (Rev., shorter ed., c.1955) Harcourt, Brace and Company
MoAmPo	Modern American Poetry. *Louis Untermeyer, ed.* (8th rev. ed., 1962) Harcourt, Brace & World
MoBrPo	Modern British Poetry. *Louis Untermeyer, ed.* (7th rev. ed., 1962) Harcourt, Brace & World
MoBS	Modern Ballads and Story Poems. *Charles Causley, ed.* (1965) Franklin Watts (Published in Great Britain in 1964 by Brockhampton Press with title Rising Early.)
MoCV	Modern Canadian Verse. *A. J. M. Smith, ed.* (1967) Oxford University Press
MoP	Modern Poems; an Introduction to Poetry. *Richard Ellmann and Robert O'Clair, eds.* (1976) W. W. Norton & Company
MoShBr	Moon Is Shining Bright as Day, The; an Anthology of Good-Humored Verse. *Ogden Nash, ed.* (1953) J. B. Lippincott Company
MT	Made Thing, The; an Anthology of Contemporary Southern Poetry. *Leon Stokesbury, ed.* (1987) The University of Arkansas Press
NAAL 1-2	Norton Anthology of American Literature, The, Vols. I–II. *Nina Baym and others, eds.* (2d ed., 1985) W. W. Norton & Company
NAEL 1-2	*Norton Anthology of English Literature, The, Vols. I–II. *M. H. Abrams, general ed.* (5th ed., 1986) W. W. Norton & Company
NALW	**Norton Anthology of Literature by Women, The; the Tradition in English. *Sandra M. Gilbert and Susan Gubar, eds.* (1985) W. W. Norton & Company
NAmP	New American Poets of the 80's. *Jack Myers and Roger Weingarten, eds.* (1984) Wampeter Press
NAmP90	New American Poets of the '90s. *Jack Myers and Roger Weingarten, eds.* (1991) David R. Godine
NaP	Naked Poetry; Recent American Poetry in Open Forms. *Stephen Berg and Robern Mezey, eds.* (1969) The Bobbs-Merrill Company
NAs	Naked Astronaut, The; Poems on Birth and Birthdays. *René Graziani, ed.* (1983) Faber and Faber

NAWM 1-2   Norton Anthology of World Masterpieces, The, Vols. I–II. *Maynard Mack, general ed.* (5th ed., 1985) W. W. Norton & Company

NBLV   Norton Book of Light Verse, The. *Russell Baker, ed.* (1986) W. W. Norton & Company

NBrP   New British Poetry, 1968–88, The. *Gillian Allnutt, Fred D'Aguiar, Ken Edwards, and Eric Mottram, eds.* (1988) Grafton Books

NBV   New Black Voices; an Anthology of Contemporary Afro-American Literature. *Abraham Chapman, ed.* (1972) Penguin Books/Mentor

NeAP   New American Poetry, The. *Donald M. Allen, ed.* (1960) Grove Press

NegPo   †Negritude Poets, The; an Anthology of Translations from the French. *Ellen Conroy Kennedy, ed.* (1989) Thunder's Mouth Press

NeIt   †New Italian Poets. *Dana Gioia and Michael Palma, eds.* (1991) Story Line Press

NGP   New Geography of Poets, A. *Edward Field, Gerald Locklin, and Charles Stetler, eds.* (1992) University of Arkansas Press

NIP   Norton Introduction to Poetry, The. *J. Paul Hunter, ed.* (4th ed., 1991) W. W. Norton & Company

NMM   No More Masks! an Anthology of Poems by Women. *Florence Howe and Ellen Bass, eds.* (1973) Doubleday/Anchor Books

NNaP   New Naked Poetry, The; Recent American Poetry in Open Forms. *Stephen Berg and Robert Mezey, eds.* (1976) The Bobbs-Merrill Company

NoAM   *Norton Anthology of Modern Poetry, The. *Richard Ellmann and Robert O'Clair, eds.* (2d ed., 1988) W. W. Norton & Company

NOBA   *New Oxford Book of American Verse, The. *Richard Ellmann, ed.* (1976) Oxford University Press

NOBAu   New Oxford Book of Australian Verse. *Les Murray, ed.* (Expanded ed., 1991) Oxford University Press

NOBC   *New Oxford Book of Canadian Verse in English, The. *Margaret Atwood, comp.* (1982) Oxford University Press

NOBE   *New Oxford Book of English Verse, The, 1250–1950 *Helen Gardner, ed.* (1972) Oxford University Press

NOBL   *New Oxford Book of English Light Verse, The. *Kingsley Amis, comp.* (1978) Oxford University Press

NOBVV   New Oxford Book of Victorian Verse, The. *Christopher Ricks, ed.* (1987) Oxford University Press

NOCV   New Oxford Book of Christian Verse, The. *Donald Davie, ed.* (1981) Oxford University Press

NOEC   **New Oxford Book of Eighteenth Century Verse, The. *Roger Lonsdale, ed.* (1984) Oxford University Press

NOIV   New Oxford Book of Irish Verse, The. *Thomas Kinsella, ed. and tr.* (1986) Oxford University Press

NoP   Norton Anthology of Poetry, The. *Alexander W. Allison and others, eds.* (3d ed., 1983) W. W. Norton & Company

NOSC   **New Oxford Book of Seventeenth Century Verse, The. *Alastair Fowler, ed.* (1991) Oxford University Press

NOSiC   **New Oxford Book of Sixteenth Century Verse, The. *Emrys Jones, ed.* (1991) Oxford University Press

LIST OF ANTHOLOGIES

NSI   Never Such Innocence; a New Anthology of Great War Verse. *Martin Stephen, ed.* (1991) J. M. Dent & Sons

NTCP   New Treasury of Children's Poetry, A; Old Favorites and New Discoveries. *Joanna Cole, comp.* (1984) Doubleday & Company

NTP   New Treasury of Poetry, A. *Neil Philip, ed.* (1990) Stewart, Tabori & Chang

NU   News of the Universe; Poems of Twofold Consciousness. *Robert Bly, comp.* (1980) Sierra Club Books

NWP   New Women Poets. *Carol Rumens, ed.* (1990) Bloodaxe Books

NYBP   New Yorker Book of Poems, The. (1969) The Viking Press

OAEL 1-2*   Oxford Anthology of English Literature, The, Vols. I–II. Vol. I: The Middle Ages through the Eighteenth Century; Vol. II: 1800 to the Present. *Frank Kermode and John Hollander, general eds.* (1973) Oxford University Press (Also published as six paperback vols.: Medieval English Literature, *J. B. Trapp, ed.;* The Literature of Renaissance England, *John Hollander and Frank Kermode, eds.;* The Restoration and the Eighteenth Century, *Martin Price, ed.;* Romantic Poetry and Prose, *Harold Bloom and Lionel Trilling, eds.;* Victorian Prose and Poetry, *Lionel Trilling and Harold Bloom, eds.;* Modern British Literature, *Frank Kermode and John Hollander, eds.*)

OBAL   Oxford Book of American Light Verse, The. *William Harmon, ed.* (1979) Oxford University Press

OBAP   Oxford Book of Animal Poems, The. *Michael Harrison and Christopher Stuart-Clark, eds.* (1992) Oxford University Press

OBCA   Oxford Book of Children's Verse in America, The. *Donald Hall, ed.* (1985) Oxford University Press

OBCP   Oxford Book of Christmas Poems, The. *Michael Harrison and Christopher Stuart-Clark, eds.* (1983) Oxford University Press

OBD   Oxford Book of Death, The. *D. J. Enright, ed.* (1987) Oxford University Press

OBET   Oxford Book of English Traditional Verse, The. *Frederick Woods, ed.* (1983) Oxford University Press

OBEV   Oxford Book of English Verse, The, 1250–1918. *Sir Arthur Quiller-Couch, ed.* (New ed., rev. and enl., 1939) Oxford University Press

OBF   Oxford Book of Friendship, The. *D. J. Enright and David Rawlinson, eds.* (1991) Oxford University Press

OBMV   Oxford Book of Modern Verse, The, 1892–1935. *William Butler Yeats, comp.* (1936) Oxford University Press

OBNC   Oxford Book of Nineteenth-Century English Verse, The. *John Hayward, ed.* (1964; reprinted, with corrections, 1965) Oxford University Press

OBNV   Oxford Book of Narrative Verse, The. *Iona Opie and Peter Opie, eds.* (1983) Oxford University Press

OBSP   Oxford Book of Story Poems, The. *Michael Harrison and Christopher Stuart-Clark, eds.* (1990) Oxford University Press

OBSV   Oxford Book of Satirical Verse, The. *Geoffrey Grigson, comp.* (1980) Oxford University Press

OBTV   Oxford Book of Travel Verse, The. *Kevin Crossley-Holland, ed.* (1986) Oxford University Press

Poems of Classical Tamil. *A. K. Ramanujan, comp. and tr.* (1985) Columbia University Press

PNI   Poets from the North of Ireland. *Frank Ormsby, ed.* (New ed., 1990) The Blackstaff Press

PoA   *Poetry Anthology, The, 1912–1977. *Daryl Hine and Joseph Parisi, eds.* (1978) Houghton Mifflin Company

PoBA   Poetry of Black America, The; Anthology of the 20th Century. *Arnold Adoff, ed.* (1973) Harper & Row

PoBeRe   Portable Beat Reader, The. *Ann Charters, ed.* (1992) Viking Penguin

PoE   Poetry in English; an Anthology. *M. L. Rosenthal, general ed.* (1987) Oxford University Press

PoEL 1-5   Poets of the English Language, Vols. I–V. Vol. I: Langland to Spenser; Vol. II: Marlowe to Marvell; Vol. III: Milton to Goldsmith; Vol. IV: Blake to Poe; Vol. V: Tennyson to Yeats. *W. H. Auden and Norman Holmes Pearson, eds.* (1950) The Viking Press (Vol. IV reissued, 1978, as The Portable Poets: Blake to Poe)

Poetr   Poetry. *Jill P. Baumgaertner, ed.* (1990) Harcourt, Brace, Jovanovich

Poetsp   Poetspeak; In Their Work, about Their Work. *Paul B. Janeczko, ed.* (1991) Collier Books

PoLF   Poems That Live Forever. *Hazel Felleman, ed.* (1965) Doubleday & Company

PoM   Postmoderns, The; the New American Poetry Revised. *Donald Allen and George F. Butterick, eds.* (1982) Grove Press

PoNe   Poetry of the Negro, The, 1746–1970. *Langston Hughes and Arna Bontemps, eds.* (Rev. ed., 1970) Doubleday & Company

PoRA   Poems to Read Aloud. *Edward Hodnett, ed.* (Rev. ed., 1967) W. W. Norton & Company

PoSu   †Poetry of Survival,The; Post-War Poets of Central and Eastern Europe. *Daniel Weissbort, ed.* (1991) Anvil Press Poetry

PoToHe   Poems That Touch the Heart. *A. L. Alexander, ed.* (New, enl. ed., 1956) Doubleday

PoWW   Poetry of the World Wars. *Michael Foss, ed.* (1990) Peter Bedrick Books

PPP   Poetry: Past and Present. *Frank Brady and Martin Price, eds.* (1974) Harcourt Brace Jovanovich

PRA   Paris Review Anthology, The. *George Plimpton, ed.* (1990) W. W. Norton & Company

Prf   Preferences; 51 American Poets Choose Poems from Their Own Work and from the Past. *Richard Howard, ed.* (1974) The Viking Press

PrIm   Practical Imagination, The; an Introduction to Poetry. *Northrop Frye, Sheridan Baker, and George Perkins.* (1983) Harper & Row

PWE   Poetry with an Edge. *Neil Astley, ed.* (1988) Bloodaxe Books

PWR   Poetry Worth Remembering; an Anthology of Poetry. *Roy W. Watson, comp.* (1986) Brunswick Publishing Company

PYC   Poems for Young Children. *Caroline Royds, comp.* (1986) Doubleday & Company

Portable Romantic Poets, The: Blake to Poe. (1978) (This book is the same as Poets of the English Language, Vol. IV: Blake to Poe [PoEL-4]; see above.)

RaBo   Rag and Bone Shop of the Heart, The; Poems for Men. *Robert Bly, James Hillman, and Michael Meade, eds.* (1992) HarperCollins

RB   Rattle Bag, The; an Anthology of Poetry. *Seamus Heaney and Ted Hughes, comps.* (1982) Faber and Faber

ReMoGo   *Real Mother Goose, The. (1944) Checkerboard Press

RFM   Room for Me and a Mountain Lion; Poetry of Open Space. *Nancy Larrick, comp.* (1974) M. Evans and Company

RiWo   Ring of Words, The; an Anthology of Song Texts. *Philip L. Miller, comp. and tr.* (1973) W. W. Norton & Company

RoPo   Rocket in My Pocket, A; the Rhymes and Chants of Young Americans. *Carl Withers, comp.* (1948) Henry Holt and Company

SAmP   Six American Poets; an Anthology. *Joel Conarroe, ed.* (1991) Random House

SCAP   Seventeenth-Century American Poetry. *Harrison T. Meserole, ed.* (1968) Doubleday/Anchor Books

SCBI   Some Contemporary Poets of Britain and Ireland; an Anthology. *Michael Schmidt, ed.* (1983) Carcanet Press

ScCV   Scottish Collection of Verse to 1800, The. *Eileen Dunlop and Antony Kamm, eds.* (1985) Rich and Drew

SCGP   Six Centuries of Great Poetry. *Robert Penn Warren and Albert Erskine, eds.* (1955) Dell Publishing

SCV   Six Centuries of Verse. *Anthony Thwaite, ed.* (1984) Thames Methuen

SeCP   Seventeenth Century Poetry; the Schools of Donne and Jonson. *Hugh Kenner, ed.* (1964) Holt, Rinehart and Winston

SeCV 1-2   Seventeenth-Century Verse and Prose, Vols. I–II. Vol. I: 1600–1660; Vol. II: 1660–1700. *Helen C. White, Ruth C. Wallerstein, and Ricardo Quintana, eds.* (1951, 1952) The Macmillan Company

ShDr   Shadowed Dreams; Women's Poetry of the Harlem Renaissance. *Maureen Honey, ed.* (1989) Rutgers University Press

SiPS   Silver Poets of the Sixteenth Century. *Gerald Bullett, ed.* (1947) J. M. Dent & Sons

SiPSBD   Silver Poets of the Sixteenth Century. *Douglas Brooks-Davies, ed.* (New ed., 1992) J. M. Dent & Sons

SiSoPo   Sing a Song of Popcorn; Every Child's Book of Poems. *Beatrice Schenk de Regniers, Eva Moore, Mary Michaels White, and Jan Carr, comps.* (1988) Scholastic

SM   Strong Measures; Contemporary American Poetry in Traditional Forms. *Philip Dacey and David Jauss, eds.* (1986) Harper & Row

SoCa   Sophisticated Cat, The; a Gathering of Stories, Poems, and Miscellaneous Writings about Cats. *Joyce Carol Oates and Daniel Halpern, comps.* (1992) Dutton

Son   Sonnet, The; an Anthology. *Robert M. Bender and Charles L. Squier, eds.* (1987) Washington Square Press/Pocket Books

SoSe   Sound and Sense; an Introduction to Poetry. *Laurence Perrine and Thomas R. Arp, eds.* (8th ed., 1992) Harcourt Brace Jovanovich

SOTW   Sleeping on the Wing; an Anthology of Modern Poetry with Essays on

LIST OF ANTHOLOGIES

WPC   †Women Poets of China. *Kenneth Rexroth and Ling Chung, eds. and trs.* (1982) New Directions (Also published 1972 by The Seabury Press as The Orchid Boat)

WPE   Women Poets in English, The; an Anthology. *Ann Stanford, ed.* (1972) McGraw-Hill Book Company

WPJ   †Women Poets of Japan. *Kenneth Rexroth and Ikuko Atsumi, eds. and trs.* (1982) New Directions (Also published 1977 by The Seabury Press as The Burning Heart)

WPOW   *Women Poets of the World. *Joanna Bankier and Deirdre Lashgari, eds.* (1983) Macmillan Publishing Company

WTO   †World Treasury of Oral Poetry, A. *Ruth Finnegan, ed.* (1978) Indiana University Press

ZA   Zooful of Animals, A. *William Cole, comp.* (1992) Houghton Mifflin Company

ABBREVIATIONS

abr.	abridged	*mod.*	modernized *or* modern
ad.	adapted	*N.T.*	New Testament
add.	additional	*O.T.*	Old Testament
arr.	arranged	*orig.*	original
at.	attributed	*par.*	paraphrase *or* paraphrased
Bk.	book	*pr.*	prose
br.	brief	*Pt.*	part
ch.	chapter	*rev.*	revised
comp.	complied *or* compiler	*sc.*	scene
comps.	compliers	*Sec.*	section
cond.	condensed	*sel.*	selection
diff.	different	*sels.*	selections
fr.	from	*sl.*	slightly
frag.	fragment	*st.*	stanza
incl.	included *or* including	*sts.*	stanzas
introd.	introduction *or* introductory	*tr.*	translator, translation, *or* translated
ll.	lines	*trs.*	translators *or* translations
LL.	last line	*var.*	various
med.	medieval	*vers.*	version *or* versions
misc.	miscellaneous	*wr.*	wrong *or* wrongly

TITLE, FIRST LINE, AND LAST LINE INDEX

Titles, first lines, and last lines are arranged in one alphabetical listing in the Title, First Line, and Last line Index. Titles are distinguished by initial capital letters on the important words. All first line entries are followed by the title of the poem, if there is a title. When the title and first line of a poem are identical, or nearly so, only the title is listed, although occasionally, for purposes of clarity, the first line has been added in quotation marks and in parentheses to the title entry.

Anthology codes are listed after titles, first lines, and last lines. Last lines are distinguished from first lines by the symbol (LL). However, more complete information as to translators, acts and scenes, abridgments, and variant titles is given in the first line entry.

Indented listings below an entry have the following significance: a single indentation indicates a selection from the above work; double indentation, within parentheses, signifies a variant title or variant first line as used in the anthologies that follow.

Mother Goose rhymes are listed by first line only, rather than by the numerous arbitrary titles assigned to them by anthologists.

Generic title entries, such as Ode, Song, Sonnet, are followed by the first line in quotation marks for easy identification. Such entries, of course, may also be located by first line listing.

Titles and first lines beginning with "O" and "Oh" are filed separately, with cross-references where necessary. Names beginning "Mac," "Mc," and "M'" are filed as if all were spelled "Mac."

A-sleepin' at length on the sand. The Sea Serpent. Wallace Irwin. FiBHP

A soun tres chere et special. *Unknown. Fr.* Lines from Love Letters. OBEV

A-spreading out-of-doors. (*LL*) Rudolph Is Tired of the City. Gwendolyn Brooks. PDV

A. Stands for Absolutely Anything. Noël Coward. *Fr.* Little Ones' A. B. C., The. NBLV

A stands for Archibald who told no lies. Hilaire Belloc. *Fr.* Moral Alphabet, A. NoAM

A-swell within her billowed skirts. The Mad Woman of Punnet's Town. L. A. G. Strong. MoBrPo

A' things created have their uses. Strictures on the Economy of Nature. George Outram. FaBoCo

A to Amerous, to Adventurous, ne Angre the not to moche. The Alphabet of Aristotle. Mayster Benet. FaBoUs

A-traipsin' from a shindig, I unsaddles. Agamemnon before Troy. John Frederick Nims. Son

A tumbled down, and hurt his Arm, against a bit of wood. Alphabet. Edward Lear. FaBoNo

"Like Grandpa Paul/ The water is all of my mind." ChIV-1

A, U, A. (*LL*) A, U, Hinny Burd. *Unknown.* GBP

A, U, Hinny Burd. *Unknown.* GBP

A-Waitin' for me — with a knife and fork. (*LL*) The Constant Cannibal Maiden. Wallace Irwin. AnAmPo; OBAL

A-walking and a-talking. The Cuckoo. *Unknown.* OBET, (B *vers.*)

A was an apple pie, B bit it, C cut it. Mother Goose. FaBoUs; OxNR

A was an archer, who shot at a frog. *Unknown.* FaBoUs; OxBChV; OxNR

A was an Army, to settle disputes. A Single-Rhyme Alphabet. *Unknown.* FaBoUs

A was once an apple-pie. An Alphabet. Edward Lear. OxBChV

A-zellen meat-weare I shall get noo meat. Shop o' Meat-Weare. William Barnes. NOBVV

Aa the skippers of bonny Lothen. Young Allan. *Unknown.* ESPB

Aa this while, Peter wis doun ablò i the yaird. Bible, *N.T., Par. by* William Laughton Lorimer. *Fr.* St. Mark. FaBoVe

Aa went te Blaydon Races, 'twas on the ninth o' June. Blaydon Races. *Unknown.* ELP

Aaron. George Herbert. ChIV-1; GeHe; MeLP; NOSC; OAEL-1; PeECV

Aaron Burr's Wooing. Edmund Clarence Stedman. PAH

Aaron Hatfield. Edgar Lee Masters. *Fr.* Spoon River Anthology. LiTA

Aaron Nicholas, Almost Ten. Janet Campbell Hale. VoR

Aaron Stark. E. A. Robinson. MeMAP; MoAB; MoAmPo; Son

Aa's a broken-hairted keelman and Aa's ower heid in love. Cushie Butterfield. George Ridley. FaBoVe

Ab no, not these! Parentage. Alice Meynell. PeVV

Abalone. *Unknown.* AS

Abalone, like inkfish. The Relaxed Abalone. Rosemarie Waldrop. InPK

Abandon then the base and viler clown; Spenser. *Fr.* Shepherd's Garden, The. EPCY

Abandonado, El. *Unknown, tr. fr. Spanish by* Frank J. Dobie. AS

Abandon'd Day, why dost thou now appear? On My Wedding Day. Sarah Fyge. KTR

Abandoned, The. Nathan Alterman, *tr. fr. Hebrew by* Ruth Finer Mintz. MHP

Abandoned, The. Zbigniew Herbert, *tr. fr. Polish by* Michael March *and* Jaroslaw Anders. PoSu

Abandoned camps/ pineapple breasts untouched. The Rake. Abu Nuwas, *tr. fr. Arabic by* Omar S. Pound. ArPe

Abandoned Farmhouse. Ted Kooser. WeW

Abandoned Schoolhouse on Long Branch. Fred Chappell. NGP

Abandoned the world. (*LL*) Time of Waiting in Amsterdam. Ingrid Jonker. BoWoP

Abandoning the Plans of Visiting West Lake. Hsü Wei, *tr. fr. Chinese by* Irving Y. Lo. SuSp

Abandoning Your Car in a Snowstorm: Rosslyn, Virginia. Michael C. Blumenthal. NoAM

Abandonment, The. Wesley McNair. BAP-89

Abandonment of Autos. Bruce Dawe. CBAP

Abate, fair fugitive, abate thy speed. Daphne and Apollo. Ovid, *tr. by* Matthew Prior. *Fr.* Metamorphoses. NOEC

Abbey Church at Bath, The. Henry Harington. FaBoEE

Abbey Cwmhir. Harri Webb. AngWe

Abbot John. Fulbert of Chartres, *tr. fr. Latin by* Helen Waddell. MLL

Abbot John, in stature small, The. Abbot John. Fulbert of Chartres, *tr. fr. Latin by* Helen Waddell. MLL

Abbot of Inisfalen, The. William Allingham. GN; TIRV

Abbreviated Interviews with a Few Disgruntled Literary Celebrities. Reed Whittemore. FiBHP

ABC, An. *Unknown. See* In Adam's fall/ We sinned all.

ABC From the Store. Harry Mathews. *Fr.* Plaque. CBCK

A.B.C. of Devotion, An. *Unknown.* MeEL

Abdelazer, *sels.* Aphra Behn.

"Love in fantastic [*or* fantastique] triumph sat [*or* sate *or* satt]." NOBE; WPE

(Love Armed.) NALW

(Song: Love Armed.) NOSC; Poetr; WeW

(Song: "Love in fantastic triumph sate.") OBEV; OxAEP-1; TrGrPo

Abdelfatteh. E. A. Lacey. PeHV

Abdication of Noman, The. Richard Henry Stoddard. AnAmPo

Abduction, The. Stanley Kunitz. CAPP; SV; WeW

Abdul. *Unknown.* NSI

Abdul, the Bulbul Ameer. *Unknown.* AS

Abel. Demetrios Capetanakis. GTBS-P

Abel. John Wheelwright. ChIV-1

Abelard was: God is. Sic et Non. Sir Herbert Read. FaBoTw

Abel's Blood. Henry Vaughan. OBWVE

Abel's Bride. Denise Levertov. FaBoWP; NALW; VGW

Abenamar, Abenamar. *Unknown, tr. fr. Spanish by* Robert Southey. AWP

Aberdarcy: The Chaucer Road. Kingsley Amis. *Fr.* Evans Country, The. FaBoBl; NOBL

Aberdarcy: The Main Square. Kingsley Amis. *Fr.* Evans Country, The. NoAM; NOBL; OxBTC

Aberdare, Llanwynno through. Glyn Cynon Wood. *Unknown, tr. fr. Welsh by* Gwyn Williams. OBWVE

Abhor, and spew out all neutralities. (*LL*) Neutrality Loathsome. Robert Herrick. ChIV-1; LiTB; NoP

Abhorrent to all natural joys. Epigram: To Philaenis. Martial, *tr. fr. Latin.* PeHV

Abide, gud men, and hald your pays. *Unknown.* MiEL

Abide in Me, O Lord, and I in Thee. Harriet Beecher Stowe. AH

Abide Not in the Realm of Dreams. William Henry Burleigh. AH

Abide with Me. Henry Francis Lyte. BLRP; EBVV; FaBoBe; FaPoR; NOCV; PIP; PWR; TIRV; WBLP; WGRP

Abiding Love, The. John White Chadwick. BLPA; FaBoBe; WGRP

Abigail's Lamentation for the Loss of Mr. Harley. William Walsh. APAS

Abiku. J. P. Clark Bekedereme. HBAPE

Abiku. Wole Soyinka. PBA

Abilene. Victoria Kohn. UTF

Abishag. Jacob Fichman, *tr. fr. Hebrew by* Sholom J. Kahn. TrJP

Abishag. Jacob Fichman, *tr. fr. Hebrew.* TrJP, *tr. by* Robert Friend

Abishag. Shirley Kaufman. CrSp

Abishag. Rainer Maria Rilke, *tr. fr. German by* Jethro Bithell. AWP

Abishag. André Spire, *tr. fr. French by* Emanuel Eisenberg. TrJP

Abla. Antar, *tr. by* E. Powys Mathers. *Fr.* Mu'allaqat, The. AWP

Able at last to stop. Old People on the Nursing Home Porch. Mark Strand. CAPP

Abnegation. Adrienne Rich. WPE

Abner Silver's "Pu-leeze! Mr. Hemingway!" Ring Lardner, OBAL

Abnormal Is Not Courage, The. Jack Gilbert. CoAP

Aboard at a Ship's Helm. Walt Whitman. NOBA; OxBA

Abode of the nightingale is bare, The. Alone. Walter de la Mare. CBLP; ChTr; EnLoPo

Abolitionist Hymn, The. *Unknown.* SWP

Abomination Of Evil, The. "Angelus Silesius," *tr. fr. German. Fr.* Cherubical Wanderer, The. GePo, *tr. by* George C. Schoolfield

Abominations break above the river. Customize the Grass. Peter Finch. NBrP

Aborigine. Hugo Williams. OBTV

Abortion. Ai. BoWoP

Abortion, The. Anne Sexton. CAPP; IHMS; LCAP; MAT; NMM; Poetr; SM; VGW

Abortion, The. Anne Sexton. CAPP

Abortion, An. Liz Lochhead. NBrP

Abortion, An. Frank O'Hara. TAP

Abortions will not let you forget. The Mother. Gwendolyn Brooks. *Fr.* Street in Bronzeville, A. BlSi; BPo; CAPP; CrSp; FaBoWP; MDDM; NALW; NMM

Abou Ben Adhem. Leigh Hunt. BeLS; BLPA; EBEvV; EnRP; FaBoBe; FaBV; FaPoR; NOBE; NTP; OBEV; OxAEP-2; PIP; PWR; TFi; WBLP; WGRP

Abou Ben Adhem and the Angel. Leigh Hunt. *See* Abou Ben Adhem (may his tribe increase!).

Abou Ben Adhem (may his tribe increase!). Abou Ben Adhem. Leigh Hunt. BeLS; BLPA; EBEvV; EnRP; FaBoBe; FaBV; FaPoR; NOBE; NTP; OBEV; OxAEP-2; PIP; PWR; TFi; WBLP; WGRP

(Abou Ben Adhem and the Angel.) FaBoRV; FaPON; GN

Above the Pages. Allen Grossman. *Fr.* Ether Dome (an Entertainment), The. BAP-91

Above the pages. . . . Above the table in the room. Above the Pages. Allen Grossman. *Fr.* Ether Dome (an Entertainment), The. BAP-91

Above the pines the moon was slowly drifting. Dickens in Camp. Bret Harte. AnAmPo

Above the place where children play. A Sussex Legend. Charles Dalmon. BoTP

Above the Pool. John Montague. NOIV

Above the pools, above the valley of fears. Élévation. Baudelaire, *tr. fr. French by* Arthur Symons. AWP

Above the quiet dock in midnight. Above the Dock. T. E. Hulme. FaBoMo; GTBS-P; NTP

Above the quiet valley and unrippled lake. Spring Oak. Galway Kinnell. BoNaP

Above the rocking heads of the mothers. Nelly Sachs, *tr. fr. German by* Ruth Mead *and* Matthew Mead. PBWP

Above the sound of the flooding waterfalls. (*LL*) Bird and Waterfall Music. Wang Wei. OHMPC

Above the violent park. A Star. George MacBeth. NYBP

Above the voiceful windings of a river. At the Grave of Henry Vaughan. Siegfried Sassoon. CMoP; GTBS-P

Above the waste allotments the dawn halts. (*LL*) Light Breaks Where No Sun Shines. Dylan Thomas. CMoP; ErPo; FaBoMo; ImPo; LiTB; LPA; MoAB; MoBrPo; OxAEP-2; OxBTC; PIP

Above These Cares. Edna St. Vincent Millay. NoP

Above this bramble-overarched long lane. The Clearing. Robert Graves. NYBP

Above, through lunar woods a goddess flees. The Lovers. William Jay Smith. MoAmPo

Above us, numbering all our dreams with tales. The Chain. Peter Scupham. SCBI

Above us, stars. Beneath us, constellations. Flying at Night. Ted Kooser. InPK; PBCAP

Above yon sombre swell of land. The Plough. Richard Henry Horne. OBEV

Above, you paint the sky. How to Paint a Perfect Christmas. Miroslav Holub, *tr. fr. Czech by* George Theiner *and* Ian Milner. OBCP

Abraham. George Bogin. GOYP

Abraham. Edwin Muir. ChIV-1

Abraham. Delmore Schwartz. ChIV-1

Abraham and Isaac. Else Lasker-Schüler, *tr. fr. German.* BoWoP, *tr. by* Rosemarie Waldrop

Abraham built a town of sod. Abraham and Isaac. Else Lasker-Schüler, *tr. fr. German.* BoWoP, *tr. by* Rosemarie Waldrop

Abraham Davenport. Whittier. AmPP; NoP

Abraham Lincoln. A. S. Ames. OHIP

Abraham Lincoln. Henry Howard Brownell. GN

Abraham Lincoln. Bryant. *See* Oh [*or* O], slow to smite and swift to spare.

Abraham Lincoln. Alice Cary. AmWP

Abraham Lincoln. Samuel Valentine Cole. OHIP

Abraham Lincoln. Edmund Clarence Stedman. PAH

Abraham Lincoln. Richard Henry Stoddard. AnAmPo; FaBoBe; GN; OHIP; PAH

Abraham Lincoln. Tom Taylor. PAH

Abraham Lincoln, the Dear President. The Dear President. John James Piatt. PAH

Abraham Lincoln, the Master. Thomas Curtis Clark. OHIP

Abraham Lincoln Walks at Midnight. Vachel Lindsay. AmPP; CMoP; FaBV; FaPON; GOA; LiTA; MeMAP; MoAmPo; NOBA; OHIP; OxBA; PAH; TAP; TFi; VGW

Abraham to kill him. Emily Dickinson. ChIV-1; SoSe

Abraham was the name. Abraham. George Bogin. GOYP

Abraham's children played with shells. Hagar and Ishmael. Else Lasker-Schüler, *tr. fr. German.* BoWoP, *tr. by* Rosemarie Waldrop

Abraham's Madness. Bink Noll. ChIV-1

Abraham's Sacrifice of Isaac. Sir John Stradling. NOSC

Abram Bailey he'd three sons. Sir Lionel. *Unknown.* AmFP

Abram Brown. *Unknown.* OxNR

Abroad as I Was Walking. *Unknown.* OBET

Abroad as I was walking/ All on a summer's day. Young Barnswell. *Unknown.* OBET

Abroad in the meadows to see the young lambs. Innocent Play. Isaac Watts. NOEC

Abroad on a winter's night there ran. A Christmas Legend. Frank Sidgwick. OHIP

Abroad Thoughts. Edward Blishen. NOBL

Abruptly All the Palm Trees. William Jay Smith. PoA

Absalom and Achitophel, Pt. I. Dryden. NoP; OAEL-1; SeCV-2 *Sels.*

Achitophel: The Earl of Shaftsbury. NOBE

"From hence began that Plot, the nation's curse." FaBoEH

"In pious times ere [*or* e'r] priest-craft did begin." EBEvV; FaBoPV; FHYEP; HAP; NOSC; PoE

"In the first rank of these did Zimri stand." HAP

"Of these the false Achitophel was first." FaBoEH; HAP; InPS; PoEL-3

(Achitophel: The Earl of Shaftsbury.) NOBE

(Achitophel.) AWP

(Shaft[e]sbury.) NOSC; 09OBS

"Some by their friends, more by themselves thought wise." ChIV-1; OBSV

"Some of their chiefs were princes of the land." EBEV; SCV

(On the Duke of Buckingham.) IHNG

(Zimri: "Some of their chiefs were princes of the land.") AWP

"Sunk were his eyes, his voice was harsh and loud." FaBoEH

"With all these loads of injuries opprest." EBEV

Zimri: The Duke of Buckingham. NOBE; OBSV

(Zimri: "Numerous host of dreaming saints succeed.") AWP

Absalom and Achitophel, Pt. II, *sels.* John Dryden *and* Nahum Tate.

"Doeg, though without knowing how or why." FHYEP; PoEL-3

"Next These, a troop of busy [*or* buisy] spirits press." PPP; SeCV-2

Og [and Doeg]. AWP

Thomas Shadwell the Poet. ChTr

"To make quick way I'll leap o'er heavy blocks." OBSV

Absence. Matthew Arnold. *Fr.* Switzerland. EnVR

Absence. Théophile Gautier, *tr. fr. French by* Philip L. Miller. RiWo

Absence. *At.* to John Hoskyns, *sometimes at.* to John Donne. MeLP; OPOP

Absence. Richard Jago. OBEV

Absence, *sels.* Fanny Kemble. What Shall I Do? PoToHe

Absence. Elizabeth Knies. GOYP

Absence. Walter Savage Landor. *Fr.* Ianthe. EnRP

Absence. Walter Savage Landor. *See* Ianthe! you resolve [*or* are called] to cross the sea!

Absence, The. Denise Levertov. NaP

Absence. Claude McKay. CDC

Absence. Charlotte Mew. MoAB; MoBrPo

Absence. Shakespeare. *See* Being your slave, what should I do[e] but tend.

Absence. Sir Philip Sidney. SiPS

Absence, The. Sylvia Townsend Warner. MoBrPo

Absence absenting causeth me to complain. Sir Thomas Wyatt. SiPS; SiPSBD

Absence, alas,/ Causeth me pass. Sir Thomas Wyatt. SiPSBD

Absence/ Can you imagine. Can You Imagine. Artur Miedzyrzecki, *tr. fr. Polish by* Stanislaw Barańczak *and* Clare Cavanagh. PoSu

Absence, hear thou my [*or* heare my] protestation. Absence. *At.* to John Hoskyns, *sometimes at.* to John Donne. MeLP; OPOP

(Ode: "Absence, Hear Thou My Protestation.") SCGP

Absence of heart — as in public buildings. The Chimeras. W. H. Auden. MeMAP

Absence, the noble truce. Fulke Greville. *Fr.* Caelica. EnRePo; PoEL-1

Absences. Donald Justice. ArNa

Absent, The. Edwin Muir. MeMBP; NoAM

Absent Daughter. Barend Toerien, *tr. fr. Afrikaans by the author.* PeSA

Absent Friends. Anne Bloch. *Fr.* Separation. Mes

Absent from thee, I languish still. The Earl of Rochester. BoLoP; ELP; EnLoPo; GBL; SeCV-2

(Return.) NOBE; OBEV

Absent Lover. *Unknown, tr. fr. Xhosa by* A. C. Jordan. PBA

Absent, this morning. Aube Provençale. Marilyn Hacker. AmPA

Absentmindedly. 529 1983. Gerda Mayer. Spl

Absinthe-Drinker, The. Arthur Symons. FaBoTw; NOBVV

Absolute, An/ patience. The Breathing. Denise Levertov. NaP; RFM

Absolute and Abitofhell. Ronald Arbuthnott Knox. FaBoCo

Absolute straight line across the pond. Champagne. Kenward Elmslie. UL

Absolute zero: the locust sings. Summer. Conrad Aiken. NoAM; Poetr

Absolutely Abstemious Ass, The. Twenty-Six Nonsense Rhymes. Edward Lear. CBNP; RB

Absolutely Ordinary Rainbow, An. Les A. Murray. CBAP; FaBoMA

Absolvers, The. Robert Southey. *Fr.* Vision of Judgement, A. EnRP

Absorption of Rock. Maxine Hong Kingston. OpBo

Abstinence. Kenneth Rosen. AmPA

Abstinence Sows Sand All Over. Blake. *Fr.* Gnomic Verses. EBEV; FaBoEE; FF; GBL; MeMBP; OxBM; TrGrPo

Abstracted, sour, as he reaches across a dish. Scylla and Charybdis. Thomas Kinsella. OxBTC

Abstruse Buddhahood and Taoist immortality are both unattainable. Mixed Emotions. Huang Ching-jen, *tr. fr. Chinese by* Chang Yin-nan *and* Lewis C. Walmsley. SuSp

Abt Vogler. Robert Browning. FHYEP; NAEL-2; OAEL-2; TOF; WGRP

Abu. Dudley Randall. BPo

Abu Nowas for the Barmacides. *Unknown, tr. fr. Arabic by* E. Powys Mathers. *Fr.* Thousand and One Nights, The. AWP

Abukbo. Jim Barnes. *Fr.* Four Things Choctaw. HATNAP

Abuse, but the girl's. Case Study. Gayle Kaune. LoHo

Abysmal corners will dis (be) located. Vitality. Maria Amalia Fonte Boa, *tr. fr. Portuguese by* Willis Barnstone *and* Nelson Cerqueira. BoWoP

Academia; or The Humours of the University of Oxford, *sels.* Alicia D'Anvers.
  "I ask'd a young Youth what it mean'd." KTR
  "Next, who 'as leave to domineer, The." KTR
  "Now being arrived at his Colledge." KTR
  "There's some are fat, and some are lean." KTR
  To the University. KTR; NOSC

Academic. Theodore Roethke. FaBoEE; OBAL

Acadia, *sels.* Joseph Howe.

Acadian Lane. David St. John. SM

Accept from me not silence. Edouard J. Maunick, *tr. fr. French by* Ellen Conroy Kennedy. *Fr.* As Far as Yoruba Land. NegPo

Accept, much honoured shade! the artless lays. On the Death of Mrs. Rowe. Elizabeth Carter. ECWP

Accept My Full Heart's Thanks. Ella Wheeler Wilcox. PoToHe

Accept, my God, the praises which I bring. The Offering: Part One. Mary Lee, Lady Chudleigh. WPE

Accept my love, and leave this copy out. *(LL)* To His Honored Friend Thomas Stanley Esquire, Upon His Elegant Poems. James Shirley. BeJo

Accept, my love, as true a heart. Les Estreines. Matthew Prior. OxBSP

Accept this indent, Sweet, from me. Chloe. Sir Edward de Stein. NSI

Accept this song that I have made for you. *(LL)* Moschus Moschiferus. A. D. Hope. CBAP; GrPl

Acceptance. Robert Frost. CMoP; OxBA

Acceptance Speech. Marvin Bell. AmPA

Acceptation. Margaret Junkin Preston. PAH

Access, The. Henry Kanabus. UL

Accident. Nina Cassian, *tr. fr. Romanian by* Fleur Adcock. VBLP

Accident, The. Liz Rosenberg. PBCAP

Accident Has Occurred, The. Margaret Atwood. NMM

"Accident" is what he calls the time, The. Dancing with Poets. Ellen Bryant Voigt. CrSp

Accident of memory reversed, An. Rumaucourt. Elizabeth Garrett. NWP

Accident or the gods. Subplot. Jack Butler. MT

Accidental Meeting with an Old Friend While Traveling at Night, An. Tai Shu-lun, *tr. fr. Chinese by* William H. Nienhauser. SuSp

Accidents of Birth. William Meredith. NoP

Accidents will happen — still, in time. A Bedtime Story. Robert Mezey. (If I Should Die Before I Wake.) NYBP

Acclaim the dawn of Mother's Day! Mother's Day. Edwin Becker. PWR

Acclaim the sun. *(LL)* A Black November Turkey. Richard Wilbur. LCAP; MoAB; NAAL-2

Accommodating Lion, An. Tudor Jenks. OBCA

Accompani'd with thine. *(LL)* The Soldier Going to the Field. Sir William Davenant. NOBE; OBWP

Accompanying a Gift ("From thy patient, who while here"). L. A. J. Moorer. CBWP-3

Accompanying a Gift ("One whose love will never end.") L. A. J. Moorer. CBWP-3

Accomplices, The. Conrad Aiken. NOBA

Accomplices. Bei Dao, *tr. fr. Chinese by* Donald Finkel *with* Chen Xueliang. SpMi

Accordance. Henry Kanabus. UL

According as his will is. *(LL)* Christ, My Beloved. William Baldwin. EIL; ELP; NOCV

According to Brueghel. Landscape with the Fall of Icarus. William Carlos Williams. *Fr.* Pictures from Brueghel. LCAP; NAAL-2; NoAM; PPP

According to Einstein. A Special Theory of Relativity. Alan Bold. FaBoBl

According to metaphysical creed. Her Education. Thomas Hood. *Fr.* Miss Kilmansegg and Her Precious Leg. EBVV

According to old Sigmund Freud. *Unknown.* PeLi

According to some learn'd opinions. Irish Antiquities. Thomas Moore. FaBoEE

According to the impeccable calibrations. Now and Then. David Chaloner. VaA

According to the Mighty Working. Thomas Hardy. CMoP

According to the silence, winter has arrived. Shepherd. William Stafford. PoA

According to the word of the Eternal Being. L'Imprévisibilité. Zinaida Hippius, *tr. fr. Russian by* Temira Pachmuss. PBWP

Accordingly, on weighty business bound. Robert Browning. *Fr.* Red Cotton Night-Cap Country. EBVVPR, (III)

Account of the Cruelty of the Papists, An. Benjamin Harris. SCAP

Account of the Greatest English Poets, An, *sels.* Joseph Addison.
  "But Milton next, with high and haughty stalks." EPCY
  "Great Cowley then, a mighty genius, wrote." EPCY

Accountability. Paul Laurence Dunbar. PoLF

Accountability. William Stafford. LCAP; NoP

Accountant in His Bath, The ("The accountant dried his imperfect back"). Adrian Mitchell. NYBP

Accountants hover over the earth like helicopters. A Dream of Suffocation. Robert Bly. NaP

Accounted our commodities. A Quiet Neighbour. John Heywood. NoSic

Accounting Cat, The. John Clarke. UV

Accross the fallow clods at early morn. Pewits Nest. John Clare. FaBoVe

Accumulation of reefs, The. The Distances. PoA

Accursed power which stands on Privilege, The. On a General Election. Hilaire Belloc. FaBoCo; FaBoEE; NOBE; NOBL; OBSV; OxBTC (On a Great Election.) OxBoLi

Accursed [or Accurst] the man, whom fate ordains, in spite. The Pains of Education. Charles Churchill. *Fr.* Author, The. FaBoCo

Accusation. Utahania, *tr. fr. Eskimo.* WTO

Accusation of the Inward Man, The. Edward Taylor. LiTA; MeMAP

Accused though I be without desert. Sir Thomas Wyatt. SiPS (Epigram: "Accused though I be without desert.") SiPSBD

Acer. Peter Finch. AngWe

Achaian Invasion of Sparta, The. *Unknown, tr. fr. Greek by* Peter Jay. GrAn

Ache of it, The. *(LL)* The Ache of Marriage. Denise Levertov. FF; InPK; NALW; NoAM; NOBA; Poetr; PoM; PWE; TAP; VCAP

Ache of love! *(LL)* On the Beach at Fontana. James Joyce. MoBrPo; OBMV; PoA; RaBo; RB

Ache of Marriage, The. Denise Levertov. FF; InPK; NALW; NoAM; NOBA; Poetr; PoM; PWE; TAP; VCAP

Achievements of the Fat. Les A. Murray. *Fr.* Quintets for Robert Morley. CBCK

Achieving Perspective. Pattiann Rogers. MT

Achill. Derek Mahon. BiHa; PBCIP; PNI

Achill Woman, The. Eavan Boland. BiHa

Achilles, *sels.* John Gay.
  "Soldier, think before you marry." PeLV
  "Think of dress in every light." InvP
  (Song: "Think of dress in every light.") OxBSP

Achilles and the Tortoise. Miroslav Holub, *tr. fr. Czech by* Stuart Friebert *and* Dana Hábová. PoSu

Achilles' baneful wrath resound, O goddess, that imposed. Proposition and Invocation. Homer, *tr. fr. Greek. Fr.* Iliad, The. NOSC

Achilles in Scyros., *sels.* Philip Bainbrigge.
  Chorus of Scyrian Maidens. PeHV

Achilles with wild fury in his heart. Homer, *tr. by* Robert Fitzgerald. *Fr.* Iliad, The. OBWP

Achitophel. Dryden. *See* Of these the false Achitophel was first.

Achitophel: The Earl of Shaftsbury. Dryden. *See* Of these the false Achitophel was first.

Achitophel: The Earl of Shaftsbury. Dryden. *Fr.* Absalom and Achitophel, Pt. I. NOBE; NoP; OAEL-1; SeCV-2

Achtung. Sappho, *tr. fr. Greek by* Thomas Hardy. CTC; OBVE

Achtung! Achtung! Mary Hacker. PAW

Achziv, *sels.* Yehuda Amichai, *tr. fr. Hebrew by* Warren Bargad *and* Stanley F. Chyet.

Acis and Galatea, *sels.* John Gay.
  "I rage, I melt, I burn." NAEL-1
  Love in Her Eyes. ELP
  "O ruddier than the cherry!" CBLP; EBEvV; ELP; NAEL-1; NOEC (Song: "O ruddier than the cherry.") NOBE

Acka, bacca, soda cracka. *Unknown.* RoPo

Acme and Septimius. Catullus, *tr. by* Abraham Cowley. AWP

Acne blossoms scarlet on their cheeks. Porirua Friday Night. Sam Hunt. PeNZ

Acolyte, The. Denise Levertov. CrSp

Acoma. William Oandasan. HATNAP

Acon. Hilda Doolittle ("H. D."). VGW

Aconite, The. A. M. Graham. BoTP

Acorn, The. *Unknown.* BoTP

Acquaint thyself with God, if thou wouldst taste. William Cowper. *Fr.* Winter Morning Walk, The. OxAEP-1

Acquainted with Grief. Helen Hunt Jackson. AmWP

Acquainted with the Night. Robert Frost. ChTr; CMoP; HAP; LiTM; MeMAP; MoAmPo; MoP; NoAM; NOBA; PDV; PoE; Poetr; PoLF; PPP; SAmP; Son; TAP; TFi; TRP; TwCP; VGW; WeW

Acre of Grass, An. W. B. Yeats. CMoP; NoAM

Acres of Clams. *Unknown.* SWP

Acrobat from Xanadu disdained all nets, The. Dan Georgakas. FF

Acrobat on the border of the sea, An. The Woman That Had More Babies than That. Wallace Stevens. LiTA

Acropolis. Lawrence Durrell. OxAEP-2

Across a city from you, I'm with you. Adrienne Rich. *Fr.* Twenty-one Love Poems. GLP; PeHV

Across a hairy leaf. (*LL*) Only My Opinion. Monica Shannon. FaPON

Across a limpid stream white birds aslant. On the River. Ku K'uang, *tr. fr. Chinese by* Irving Y. Lo. SuSp

Across a wound. (*LL*) Gallery. Duo Duo. SpMi

Across daubed rock evacuates its dead. (*LL*) Requiem for the Plantagenet Kings. Geoffrey Hill. FaBoEH; NAEL-2; NoAM

Across from two men and a boy. By the Pump Dry-eyed. Janet Fisher. NWP

Across Kansas. William Stafford. CAPP

Across North Wales. Dafydd ap Gwilym Resents the Winter. Rolfe Humphries. NYBP

Across Roblin Lake, two shores away. Wilderness Gothic. Alfred W. Purdy. HeIP; MoCV; NOBC; NoP

Across Space and Time. Charles Olson. PoM

Across the ages they come thundering. Say This of Horses. Minnie Hite Moody. PoLF

Across the Bay. Donald Davie. NoAM

Across the brook of Time man leaping goes. Laus Mariae. Sidney Lanier. Son

Across the channel, Mare Island welders cut. Bird-Watching. Dennis Schmitz. LCAP

Across the correct perspective to the painted sky. Landscape. David Gascoyne. FaBoMo

Across the Delaware. Will M. Carleton. PAH

Across the desk. Crocodiles. Mira Teru Kurka. UL

Across the dewy lawn she treads. Paean. Jonathan Henderson Brooks. CDC

Across the Eastern sky has glowed. The Crowing of the Red Cock. Emma Lazarus. AmWP

Across the expedient and wicked stones. (*LL*) Auto Wreck. Karl Shapiro. CMoP; FF; LiTM; NIP; RB; VGW

Across the flesh and feeling of soledad. Orisha. Jayne Cortez. BlSi

Across the floor flits the mechanical toy. Cirque d'Hiver. Elizabeth Bishop. InPS; LiTA

Across the footpath tidy. Mercy. Andrew Lansdown. NOBAu

Across the frozen Bering Sea is the invisible border. Nine Below. Joy Harjo. VBLP

Across the lonely beach we flit. The Sandpiper. Celia Laighton Thaxter. ImGa

Across the millstream below the bridge. The Blue Swallows. Howard Nemerov. NoP; Poetr

Across the mist flowers and grass appear far and hazy. Gathering Lotus. Chu Ch'ing-yu, *tr. fr. Chinese by* Irving Y. Lo. SuSp

Across the narrow beach we flit. The Sandpiper. Celia Laighton Thaxter. FaBoBe; FaPON; GN; OBCA; OxBChV; PWR; WBLP

Across the night. From Creature to Ghost. Pauline Hanson. TAP

Across the ocean to her unknown lover. (*LL*) Latin as a Foreign Language. Michael O'Loughlin. IB

Across the open countryside. The Unsettled Motorcyclist's Vision of His Death. Thom Gunn. PoA

Across the page of history. Lincoln Leads. Minna Irving. OHIP

Across the road. Flock. Lance Henson. VoR

Across the round field, under the dark male tower. The Lovers. Alex Comfort. PoA

Across the sand I saw a black man stride. Jamaican Fisherman. Philip Sherlock. PBCV

Across the Sea, Along the Shore. Arthur Hugh Clough. ChIV-2

Across the sea will come Adze-head. Adze-Head. *Unknown, tr. fr. Irish by* James Carney. BIrV

Across the sky. (*LL*) Sometimes/ I go about pitying myself. *Unknown.* EaPr

Across the sky run streaks of white light, aching. Before Olympus. John Gould Fletcher. MoAmPo

Across the sky the daylight crept. Coventry Patmore. *Fr.* Angel in the House, The. GBL

Across the snow the silver bells. Silver Bells. Hamish Hendry. BoTP

Across the snowy pastures of the estate. The Fox Who Watched for the Midnight Sun. Norman Dubie. LCAP

Across the Stony Mountains, o'er the desert's drouth and sand. The Crisis. Whittier. PAH

Across the street — the freeway. Beneath the Shadow of the Freeway. Lorna Dee Cervantes. BCF; PBCAP

Across the Swamp. Olav H. Hauge, *tr. fr. Norwegian by* Robert Bly. RaBo

Across the swamps and marshlands of the hours. A Sea-Change: For Harold. Joseph Langland. LiTM

Across the tracks in Cheyenne, behind the biggest billboard. A Long Way outside Yellowstone. Thomas McGrath. VGW

Across the Western Ocean. (*LL*) Across the Western Ocean *or* Leave Her, Bullies, Leave Her. *Unknown.* AS; OxBSS

Across the Western Ocean *or* Leave Her, Bullies, Leave Her. *Unknown.* AS; OxBSS

Across this dream of seas blue mountains fall. Between Seasons. Anne Welsh. PeSA

Across to the Peloponnese. James Welch. CDW

Across upon this undulated board of verdure chequered bright. David Jones. *Fr.* In Parenthesis. NAEL-2; NoAM

Acrostic, An. Lucretia Davidson. AmWP

Acrostic on Wharton, An. *Unknown.* FaBoEH; OBSV

Acrostick on Mrs. Elizabeth Hull, An. John Saffin. SCAP

Acrostick on Mrs. Winifret Griffin, An. John Saffin. SCAP

Acrostics. George Moses Horton. AAP

Act, The. William Carlos Williams. ArNa; SAmP; SOTW; VGW

Act, An. Kenneth Rosen. AmPA

Act. Indifferent, she takes no part in the mourning. (*LL*) Jade, or the Medea within Us. Patrizia Vicinelli. VBLP

Act like a crazy dog. Wear sashes & other fine clothes, carry a. Crazy Dog Events. Jerome Rothenberg. RaBo

Act of Love, The. Robert Creeley. HAP

Act of Love. Vernon Scannell. ErPo

Act I/ Orlando hails. The Five-Minute Orlando Macbeth. George MacBeth. NOBL; PeLV

Act Six. Peter Goldsworthy. NOBAu

Actaeon. Rayner Heppenstall. FaBoTw

Acteon. Ovid, *tr. by* Arthur Golding. *Fr.* Metamorphoses. CTC

Acting, dear Thornton, its perfection draws. Robert Lloyd. *Fr.* Actor, The. ECEV

Action. James Oppenheim. TrJP

Action of Electricity, The. Erasmus Darwin. *Fr.* Economy of Vegetation, The. FaBoUs

Action of Invisible Ink, The. Erasmus Darwin. *Fr.* Economy of Vegetation, The. FaBoUs

Action Rhyme. E. H. Adams. BoTP

Action runs left to right, The. Movies, Left to Right. Robert Sward. NYBP

Action Would Kill It/ A Gamble. Robert Adamson. CBAP; FaBoMA

Actions. Marcel Schwob, *tr. fr. French by* William Brown Meloney. TrJP

"Active balls?" said an old man of Stoneham. C. D. Cudmore. PeLi

Acton Beauchamp, Herefordshire. *Unknown.* FaBoPP; GBP

Actor, The, *sels.* Robert Lloyd.
 "Acting, dear Thornton, its perfection draws." ECEV

Actor, The. Thomas Snapp. NYBP

Actors, The, *sels.* Nizar Qabbani, *tr. fr. Arabic by* Diana Der Hovanessian *and* Lena Jayyusi.

Actors in the theatre. Written at Hsiang-kuo Temple on the Occasion of Watching Actors in the Hsing-hsiang Garden of the T'ung-t'ien-chieh Tao-ch'ang. Wang An-shih, *tr. fr. Chinese by* Jan W. Walls. SuSp

Acts of my life swarm down the street like Puerto Rican kids, The. My Acts. William Meredith. *Fr.* Consequences. VCAP

Acts passed beyond the boundary of mere wishing. Stephen Spender. OxBTC

Actual Vision of Morning's Extrusion. Alan Dugan. PPP

Actually: it's the balls I look for, always. Balls. Anne MacNaughton. RaBo

Actually: it's the balls I look for, always. Teste Moanial. Anne MacNaughton. BAP-89

Acum/ minature minat minet. Acer. Peter Finch. AngWe

Ad. Kenneth Fearing. BTR

Ad Amicam. Francis Thompson. Son

Ad Auroram, Ne Properet. Ovid, *tr. fr. Latin by* Christopher Marlowe. *Fr.* Amores. NoSic

Ad Coelum. William Pattison. OxBSP

Ad Coelum. Harry Romaine. BLPA; FaBoBe

Ad-dressing of Cats, The. T. S. Eliot. FM; PFP

Ad Finem. Heine, *tr. fr. German by* Elizabeth Barrett Browning. AWP

Ad Finem. Ella Wheeler Wilcox. BLPA

Ad Henricum Wottonem. Thomas Bastard. FaBoEE; FaBoPP

Ad Infinitum. Joan Aronsten. NOBAu

Ad Johannuelem Leporem, Lepidissimum, Carmen Heroicum. *Unknown.* CBNP; FaBoNo

Ad Leuconoen. Horace. *See* Seek not, Leuconöe, to know how long you're going to live yet.

Ad Librum. Samuel Danforth, Jr. SCAP

Ad Limina. Joseph Campbell. BIrV

Ad Patriam, *sels.* Dudley Foulke.

Ad Patriam. Clinton Scollard. PAH

Ad Tusserum. *Unknown.* FaBoUs

Adage: "Gardener's rule applies to youth and age, The." Henry James Byron. FaBoUs; NBLV

Adam. *Unknown. See* Adam Lay ybounden [*or* i-bounden], bounded in a bond.

Adam, a brown old vulture in the rain. Ancient History. Siegfried Sassoon. ChIV-1; Mes

Adam and Eve. Itsik Manger, *tr. fr. Yiddish by* Jacob Sonntag. TrJP

Adam and Eve, *sels.* Karl Shapiro.
Exile. CRP
Recognition of Eve, The. ChIV-1; MoAB
Sickness of Adam, The. CRP; MoAB

Adam and Eve. C. H. Sisson. FaBoTw

Adam and Eve and Pinch-me. *Unknown.* ISE; RoPo

Adam and Eve, like us. A Circle. Theodore Spencer. NYBP

Adam and God. Anne Wilkinson. MoCV

Adam Bel [*or* Bell], Clym [*or* Clim] of the Clough[e], and Wyllam [*or* William] of Cloudesle [*or* Cloudesly]. *Unknown.* ESPB; OxBB

Adam Birkett took his gun. Birkett's Eagle. Dorothy S. Howard. Mes; MoBS

Adam Confesses an Infidelity to Eve. David Constantine. PWE

Adam Fallen. Milton. *See* Descended, Adam to the bower where Eve.

Adam Fallen. Milton. *See* He ended, and they both descend the hill.

Adam/ Had 'em. On the Antiquity of Microbes. Strickland W. Gillilan. NBLV

Adam/ Had 'em. Poem to Answer the Question: How Old Are Fleas? *Unknown.* Spl

Adam, indignant, would not eat with Eve. Paradise Saved. A. D. Hope. OxBC

Adam Lay Bound. *Unknown. See* Adam Lay ybounden [*or* i-bounden], bounded in a bond.

Adam Lay in Bondage. *Unknown. See* Adam Lay ybounden [*or* i-bounden], bounded in a bond.

Adam Lay Y-Bounden. *Unknown. See* Adam Lay ybounden [*or* i-bounden], bounded in a bond.

Adam Lay yBounden [*or* I-bounden]. *Unknown.* ChIV-2; ChTr; CTC; EnVB; HAP; InPS; MiEL; NOBE; NOCV; NoP; OAEL-1; OxBLMV; OxBoLi; PoE; PoEL-1; TFi; TOF; TRP; WeW
(Adam Lay Bound.) NAEL-1
(Adam Lay in Bondage.) MeEL
(Adam Lay Y-Bounden.) PeLV
(Adam.) CH

Adam on His Way Home. Robert Pack. ErPo

Adam Posed. The Countess of Winchilsea. ChIV-1; ECWP

Adam Says See, *sels.* Julia Randall.
"How shall we walk naked when." CrSp

Adam scrivein [*or* scrivain], if ever it thee bifalle. To Adam, His Scribe. Chaucer. OAEL-1
(To His Scribe Adam.) NAEL-1
(Unto Adam, His Own Scriveyn.) OxBSP

Adam Smith. E. C. Bentley. *Fr.* Clerihews. FaBoCo

Adam Speaks. Milton. *See* Oh, why did God,/ Creator wise.

Adam the goodliest man of men since born. Milton. *Fr.* Paradise Lost. EPCY
(Scene in Paradise, A.) GN

Adam Unfallen. Milton. *See* O favorable spirit, propitious guest.

Adam was de first man and Eve was de udder. *Unknown. Fr.* Metrical Version of the Bible, Said to Have Been Composed by a Negro Christian in the State of Massachusetts, and Published in Louisville, Kentucky, in 1858, A. FaBoUs

Adam was my grandfather. For All Blasphemers. Stephen Vincent Benét. OxBA

Adam was no fool. He knew that at his age. A Family Matter. Allen Curnow. *Fr.* Trees, Effigies, Moving Objects. PeNZ

Adams and Liberty. Robert Treat Paine. PAH

Adam's Commentary After the Fall. Aidan Carl Mathews. IB

Adam's Complaint. Denise Levertov. BoWoP; NNaP

Adam's Curse. W. B. Yeats. BIrV; CMoP; NAEL-2; NoAM; NoP; OAEL-2; PFP; SOTW; TEP; WeW

Adam's Dying. Ridgely Torrence. FYAP

Adam's Footprint. Vassar Miller. MT

Adam's Hymn in Paradise. Joost van den Vondel, *tr. fr. Dutch by* Sir John Bowring. WGRP

Adam's Morning Hymn. Milton. *See* These are thy glorious works, Parent of good.

Adam's Song of the Visible World, *much abr.* Ridgely Torrence. TrPWD

Adam's Task. John Hollander. NIP; NoP; PPP

Adapt Thyself. Shem-Tob ben Joseph Palquera, *tr. fr. Hebrew by* J. Chotzner. TrJP

Add a picture of his factory. · (*LL*) The Advertising Agency Song. *Unknown.* FaBoUs; NBLV

Adder's Epigrams. Colin Ellis. FaBoEE

Addict, The. Larry Rubin. GoYe

Addiction to the exceptional event. Barbarossa. Hubert Witheford. PeNZ

Addition to Kipling's "The Dead King (Edward VII), 1910." Max Beerbohm. FaBoEE; IHNG

Additional Poem, An. John Ashbery. FaBoMo

Additional Verses to Hail Columbia. Oliver Wendell Holmes. PAH

Address. Andrew Geddes Bain. PeSAV

Address. Bruce Smith. *Fr.* In My Father's House. Son

Address to a Bachelor on a Delicate Occasion. Priscilla Pointon. ECWP

Address to a Child during a Boisterous Winter Evening. Dorothy Wordsworth. NTP; OxBChV; WoRP

Address to Children. Theodore Hook. *See* My little dears, who learn to read, pray early learn to shun.

Address to Ethiopia. Priscilla Jane Thompson. CBWP-2

Address to Her Husband. Mehetabel Wright. ECWP

Address to Lady ———, Who Asked What the Passion of Love Was? Charles Morris. NOEC

Address to Miss Phillis Wheatley, An, *sels.* Jupiter Hammon.
"O come you pious youth! adore." AmPP

Address to Mr. Cross, of Exeter 'Change, on the Death of the Elephant. Thomas Hood. FM

Address to My Infant Daughter, *sels.* Wordsworth.

Address to My Malay Krees. John Leyden. OBTV

Address to My Soul. Elinor Wylie. AWP; LiTM; OxBA

Address to the Deil. Burns. EnRP; NOEC; OAEL-1; OxBS; PoEL-4

Address to the King, An, *sels.* John Gower.
"O worthi noble kyng, Henry the ferthe." FaBoEH

Address to the Muses, An, *sels.* Joanna Baillie.
"Ye are the spirits who preside." ECWP

Address to the Plebeians, An, *sels.* John Learmont.
"Poor crawlin' bodies, sair neglectit." NOEC

Address to the Refugees. John Malcolm Brinnin. GOA

Address to the Scholars of New England. John Crowe Ransom. GOA; LiTM; MeMAP

Address to the Soul Occasioned by a Rain, An. Edward Taylor. MeMAP; NAAL-1; NOBA; OxBA; PoEL-3

Address to the Unco Guid, or the Rigidly Righteous. Burns. ChIV-1; EnRP; NOBE; NOCV; NoP; OxBS; TrGrPo

Address to the Vacationers at Cape Lookout, An. William Stafford. NYBP

Address to Venus. Lucretius, *tr. fr. Latin. Fr.* De Rerum Natura (On the Nature of Things). AWP, *tr. by* Spenser

Address to Venus. Spenser. *Fr.* Faerie Queene, The. AWP

Addressed to ———. Lady Mary Wortley Montagu. ECWP

Addressed to a Beech Tree. Christian Carstairs. ECWP

Addressed to a Koto-player. Su Man-shu, *tr. fr. Chinese by* Wu-chi Liu. SuSp

Addressed to a Young Lady. William Cowper. *See* Sweet stream, that winds through [*or* thro'] yonder glade.

Addressed to Haydon. Keats. *See* Great Spirits Now on Earth.

Addressing the Comet. Ivan V. Lalic, *tr. fr. Serbo-Croatian by* Charles Simic. HSix

Adela Cathcart., *sels.* George Macdonald.
Sir Lark and King Sun; a Parable. GN

Adelaide! (*LL*) Adelaide. Friedrich von Matthison. RiWo

Adelaide. Friedrich von Matthison, *tr. fr. German by* Philip L. Miller. RiWo

Adelaide's Dream. Christopher Middleton. FaBoBl; PeLV

Adelina Patti. Adah Isaacs Menken. CBWP-1

Adelita ("Adelita's the name of the lady"). *Unknown, tr. fr. Spanish by* F. S. Curtis, Jr. AS

Adepts, The. Lawrence Durrell. *Fr.* Eight Aspects of Melissa. ErPo

Adequate of Hell, The. (*LL*) Remorse is memory awake. Emily Dickinson. NAAL-1; NOBA; NOCV; NoP; SAmP

Adeste Fideles. *Unknown. See* O Come, All Ye Faithful.

Adew, my King, court, cuntrey, and my kin. To Henry Constable and Henry Keir. Alexander Montgomerie. OxBS

Adhesive Autopsy of Walt Whitman, The. Jonathan Williams. PoM

Adhesive: For Earlene. Robert Hass. NGP

Adieu. Charles-Jean Grandmougin, *tr. fr. French by* Philip L. Miller. *Fr.* Poem of a Day. RiWo

Adieu. Mary E. Tucker. CBWP-1

Adieu, Adieu! *(LL)* Fairy Song. Keats. FaPON

Adieu, Adieu, Forever. Priscilla Jane Thompson. CBWP-2

Adieu, blind fortune, with thy miserable purse. Adieu, to Fortune. Henry Francis Fynn. PeSAV

Adieu, dear life! here am I left alone. On My Late Dear Wife. Jonathan Richardson. NOEC

Adieu, dear name which birth and nature gave. An Elegy on a Maiden Name. Jane Cave. ECWP

Adieu, Farewell, Earth's Bliss[e]. Thomas Nashe. *Fr.* Summer's Last Will and Testament. CH; CoGr; EBEV; EIL; ELP; HAP; HeIP; InvP; NoSic; PIP; TEP; TFi; TRP

Adieu, farwell earth's bliss. Thomas Nashe. *See* Adieu, Farewell, Earth's Bliss[e].

Adieu Love, Untrue Love. *Unknown. See* While that the sun with his beams hot.

Adieu My Lovely Nancy. *Unknown.* OBET

"Adieu!" she cries; and waves her lily hand. *(LL)* Sweet William's Farewell to Black-eyed [or ey'd] Susan. John Gay. AmFP, *(folk vers.)*; BeLS; BoLoP; CBLP; NOEC

Adieu Sirocco, Sun, and Sweat. Byron. *See* Adieu, ye joys of La Valette!

Adieu, sweet Angus, Maeve and Fand. The Passing of the Shee. J. M. Synge. BIrV; FaBoEE

Adieu the woods and waters' side. Lines on Leaving a Scene in Bavaria. Thomas Campbell. OBNC

Adieu, the years are a broken song. *Unknown.* NOBAu

Adieu to Belashanny [or Ballyshannon]! where I was bred and born. The Winding Banks of Erne [or Adieu to Belashanny]. William Allingham. PeIV

Adieu, to Fortune. Henry Francis Fynn. PeSAV

Adieu to My Landlady, An. George Farewell. NOEC

Adieu to the pleasure of murder and whoring. Sir Thomas Armstrong's Last Farewell to the World. *Unknown.* APAS

Adieu, ye joys of La Valette! Farewell to Malta. Byron. OBTV (Adieu Sirocco, Sun, and Sweat.) CBCK

Adieu, you haughty maiden! Adieu, Adieu, Forever. Priscilla Jane Thompson. CBWP-2

Adiew, madam my mother dear. Lord Maxwell's Last Goodnight. *Unknown.* ESPB

Adina. Harold Milton Telemaque. TTY

Adjectives. Moishe Nadir, *tr. fr. Yiddish by* Joseph Leftwich. TrJP

Adjuration. Charles Enoch Wheeler. PoNe

Adjustment. Whittier. WGRP

Adlatts parke is wyde and broad. Will Stewart and John. *Unknown.* ESPB

Adler. Gerald Stern. BTR

Adlestrop. Edward Thomas. CH; EBEvV; FaBoPP; FaPoB; GGP; GoJo; HAP; LiTB; NAEL-2; NOBE; OBEV; OxBTC; PlP; UV

Adman into Toad. Frank Polite. UL

Administrator, The. Marilyn Chin. LoHo

Administrator, An. Geoffrey Grigson. FaBoEE

Admiral. John Alexander Allen. NYBP

Admiral Benbow. *Unknown. See* Come, all ye seamen [or you sailors] bold.

Admiral Byng. *Unknown.* OxBSS

Admiral Dugout. Cicely Fox Smith. NSI

Admiral Hosier's Ghost. Richard Glover. NOEC

Admiral, the prisoner of your giant's. Admiral. John Alexander Allen. NYBP

Admirals All. Sir Henry Newbolt. FaPoR

Admiral's Caravan, The, *sels.* Charles Edward Carryl.
Song of the Camel, The. OTCP
(Camel's Complaint, The.) OBCA; OxBChV
(Plaint of the Camel, The.) FaPON

Admiration. Josephine D. Henderson Heard. CBWP-4

Admire Cranmer! Stevie Smith. NoAM

Admire the face of plastered stone. Quebec Farmhouse. John Glassco. NOBC

Admire the old man, admire him, admire him. Admire Cranmer! Stevie Smith. NoAM

Admire the watered silky gap. Anointed Vessel. Paul Verlaine, *tr. fr. French by* Alistair Elliot. FaBoBl

Admire thy wreath? And wherefore should I not. To a Plagiarist. Moses ibn Ezra, *tr. fr. Hebrew by* Solomon Solis-Cohen. TrJP

Admire, when you come here, the glimmering hair. Vuillard: "The Mother and Sister of the Artist." W. D. Snodgrass. CoAP

Admirer's Lament of Chaucer, An. Thomas Hoccleve. *Fr.* Regement of Princes. EPCY

Admirers of the Little Box, The. Vasco [or Vasko] Popa, *tr. fr. Serbo-Croatian by* Charles Simic. HSix

Admission. Henry Vaughan *and* Thomas Stanley. ESCV

Admit them, admit them. *(LL)* Not I, not I, but the wind that blows through me! D. H. Lawrence. CMoP; FaBoMo; GTBS-P; InPS; LiTM; MeMBP; OxBTC; PeFWW; PoE; RaBo; TRP

Admonition. Philip Stack. BLPA

Admonition to a Traveller. Wordsworth. GTBS; GTBS-P

Admonition to Montgomerie. James I, King of England. GTBS; GTBS-P; OxBS

Admonition to the Muse. Geoffrey Taylor. FaBoEE

Admonitions. Lucille Clifton. BPo; CAPP; NALW; NMM

Ado. Mary Ursula Bethell. ArNa

Adolescence. W. H. Auden. *See* By landscape reminded once of his mother's figure.

Adolescence. Gregory Orr. Poetsp

Adolescence — I. Rita Dove. NoAM; VBLP

Adolescence — II. Rita Dove. AmPA; HCAP; NoAM; VCAP

Adolescence — III. Rita Dove. NoAM

Adolescent night, breath of the town, The. Midsummer. Robert Fitzgerald. PoA

Adolicus; that's a creeper rug, its small. "Robin Hyde." *Fr.* Houses, The. PeNZ

Adonais; an Elegy on the Death of John Keats. (I weep for Adonais — he is dead.) Shelley. EBEV; EnRP; FHYEP; HoPM; ImPo; MeMBP; NoP; OAEL-2; PoEL-4; TrGrPo
Sels.
Song of the Camel, The. OTCP
Go Thou to Rome. ChTr
(Grave of Keats, The.) FaBoPP
"He is made one with Nature; there is heard." EPCY; WGRP
"Most musical of mourners, weep again!" EPCY
"One remains, the many change and pass, The." SCV
"Peace, peace! he is not dead, he doth not sleep." OBD
(Elegy on the Death of John Keats, An.) OBNC
(Mourn Not for Adonais.) NOBE

Adonis. Hilda Doolittle ("H. D."). AWP; LiTA

Adonis. Theocritus [or Theokritus], *tr. fr. Greek.* NoSic

Adonis, Dying. Praxilla, *tr. fr. Greek by* Richard Lattimore. PBWP; WPOW

Adonis Theater. Mark Doty. NAmP90

Adoramus Te, Christe. David O'Bruadair, *tr. fr. Irish by* Thomas Kinsella. NOIV

Adoration. Mme Guyon. WGRP

Adoration. Jane Miller. BAP-90

Adoration. Christopher Smart. GGP

Adoration of the Anchor. Laura Jensen. LCAP

Adoration of the Disk by King Akhnaten and Princess Nefer Neferiu Aten. *Unknown, tr. fr. Egyptian by* Robert Hillyer. *Fr.* Book of the Dead. AWP

Adoration of the Magi, The. Christopher Pilling. OBCP

Adore November's sacred seventeenth day. Morris Kyffin. *Fr.* Blessednes of Brytaine, The. AngWe

Adore the lifted standard of the Cross. On the Cross. Alcuin, *tr. fr. Latin by* Helen Waddell. MLL

Adore we the Lord. *Unknown.* NOIV

Adown the Heights of Ages. Priscilla Jane Thompson. CBWP-2

Adrian Block's Song. Edward Everett Hale. PAH

Adrian Henri's Talking after Christmas Blues. Adrian Henri. PeLV

Adriani Morientis ad Animam Suam. Emperor Hadrian, *tr. by* Matthew Prior. OBVE; OxBSP

Adriano; or, The First of June. James Hurdis. ECEV
Sels.
Student, The.

Adrift. Elizabeth Dickinson Dowden. WGRP

Adrift on an oil-drum raft. Michael Anania. *Fr.* Riversongs of Arion, The. NoAM

Adrowse, my pen trailed on, and a voice spoke. Prehistories. Peter Scupham. SCBI

Adulescentia, *sels.* Robert Fitzgerald.

Adult Lullaby, An. *Unknown. See* Lollay, lollay, littel child, why wepestow so sore?

Adulterers and customers of whores. Womanisers. John Press. BoLoP; ErPo

(My Love Is Dead.) WiR

(Mynstrelle's Songe ("O! synge untoe mie roundelaie").) EnLoPo; EnRP; NOEC; OxAEP-1

(Song: "O sing into my roundelay.") OBEV

Aeneas at Washington. Allen Tate. FYAP; LiTA; NoAM; NOBA; OxBA

Aeneas built, in days of yore. Edward B. Goodwin. *Fr.* Roman History in Rhyme. FaBoUs

Aeneas Sees Italy. Virgil, *tr.* by Gavin Douglas. *Fr.* Aeneid [*or* Eneados], The. NAWM-1; OxBLMV

Aeneid [*or* Eneados], The. (I sing of warfare and a man at war.) Virgil, *tr. fr. Latin* by Robert Fitzgerald. NAWM-1
Sels.
Aeneas Sees Italy. OxBLMV
"Affrayit, I glistnyt of sleip, and stert on feit." OBVE
"Amyd the wod his modir met thame tway." OBVE
"And now Aeneas charges straight at Turnus." OBWP
"And now we gan draw near unto the gate." NoSic, *tr.* by Henry Howard, Earl of Surrey; SiPSBD, *tr.* by Henry Howard, Earl of Surrey.
"And oft the owle with rufull song complaind." OBVE
"And Turnus than, quhar he at erth dyd ly." OBVE
"Arms, and the man I sing, who forc'd by fate." OBVE
"As, sum tyme, dois the curser stert and ryn." OBVE
"As this convine and ordinance was mayd." OBVE
"As when a fragment, from a mountain torn." OBVE
"Attentively he heard us, while we spoke." OBVE
"Batellis [*or* Batalis] and the man I will descrive." OBVE
(Batalis and the Man, The.) CTC
"Belive Eneas membris schuk for cald." ScCV
"Bot now the haisty, egir, and wild Dido." OBVE
"But lo, Polites, one of Priam's sons." SiPSBD, *tr.* by Henry Howard, Earl of Surrey.
"But now the wounded queen with heavy care." SiPSBD, *tr.* by Henry Howard, Earl of Surrey.
"But trembling Dido eagerly now bent." SiPSBD, *tr.* by Henry Howard, Earl of Surrey.
"Come is the ending day, Troy's hour is come." MLL, *tr.* by Helen Waddell.
"Dear Sister, my resentment had not been." OBVE
Destruction of Troy, The. SeCV-1
"Eneas wonderit the greitnes of Cartiage." OBVE
Euryalus and Nisus Meet Their Deaths. NoSic
"Exulting in his strength, he seems to dare." OBVE
"Greeks' chieftains, all irked with the war, The." OAEL-1
"Heaven, the earth, and all the liquid main [*or* mayne], The." OBVE; SiPSBD
"Hesperia the Grecians call the place." SiPSBD, *tr.* by Sir Walter Ralegh.
"How hard a fate enthrals the wretched maid." ECWP, *tr.* by Elizabeth Tollet.
"In the main sea the isle of Crete doth lie." SiPSBD, *tr.* by Sir Walter Ralegh.
"It was the time when, granted from the gods." NAEL-1; SiPSBD
"It was then night: the sound[e] and quiet sleep [*or* slepe]." OAEL-1; PoEL-1; SiPSBD
"Loe! formest of a rout that followd him." OBVE
"Loud report through Lybian cities goes, The." OBVE
"Now manhood and garbroyls I chaunt." BIrV; OBVE
"O boys, O strong of heart in vain." MLL, *tr.* by Helen Waddell.
"Onto the hallowit steid bryng in, thai cry." OBVE
Polyphemus. NoSic
"Prince, with wonder, sees the stately tow'rs, The." OBVE
Prologue to Book VII, The. OxBLMV; OxBS
Queen Dido Rides Out Hunting. OxBLMV
"Quhen thou art careit to that cuntree." OBVE
Sixth Book of the Aeneis, The. SeCV-2
"There Charon stands, who rules the dreary coast." OBVE
"They wished [*or* whisted] all, with fixèd face attent." LiTB; SiPS; SiPSBD
"Thir riveris and thir watteris kepit war." OBVE
"Thus fell the King, who yet surviv'd the state." OBVE
"To my prowd foe thus, sister, humble saye." OBVE
"Wee leave Creete Country; and our sayls unwrapped uphoysing." OBVE
"Whom when I saw assembled in such wise." PoE

Aenigma on the Six Cases. *Unknown.* FaBoUs

Aeolian Harp, The. Herman Melville. AmPP

Aeons of history float. Prisoner. Marguerite George. GoYe

Aerial, The. Reiner Kunze, *tr. fr. German* by Ewald Osers. PoSu

Aerogrammes. Russell Leong. OpBo

Aerophorion, *sels.* Henry James Pye.
Air Balloon, The. NOEC

Aeroplane, The. Jeannie Kirby. BoTP

Aeroplane. Pudjipangu, *tr. fr. Aborigine* by Georg von Brandenstein. NOBAu

[Aesoe] Isope myn auctor makis mencioun. Robert Henryson. *See* Aesop, mine author, makis mention.

Aesop at Play. Phaedrus, *tr. fr. Latin* by Christopher Smart. AWP

Aesop, mine author, makis mention. The Tale of the Upland Mouse and the Burgess Mouse. Robert Henryson. OBNV
([Aesoe] Isope myn auctor makis mencioun.) EnVB
(Tale of the Country Mouse and the Town Mouse, The.) ScCV
(Tale of the Uplandis Mous and the Borowstown Mous, The.) EnVB

Aesop's Fable of the Frogs. La Fontaine, *tr. fr. French* by John Hookham Frere. OBVE

Aestas. Joshua Sylvester. NOSC

Aesthete, The. W. S. Gilbert. *See* If you're anxious for to shine in the high aesthetic line as a man of culture rare.

Aesthete to the Rose, The. *Unknown.* BXAP

Aesthete Weasel, The. Christian Morgenstern, *tr. fr. German* by Geoffrey Grigson. FaBoNo

Aesthetic. Norman Rosten. PoA

Aesthetic Point of View, The. W. H. Auden. *See* As the poets have mournfully sung.

Aestivation [an Unpublished Poem, by My Late Latin Tutor]. Oliver Wendell Holmes. *Fr.* Autocrat of the Breakfast Table, The. NOBL; OBAL

Aeterna Poetae Memoria. Archibald MacLeish. Son

Æthelstan [the] King, lord of eorls [*or* ruler of earls]. *Unknown, tr. fr. Anglo-Saxon. Fr.* Battle of Brunanburh. AnOE, *tr.* by Charles W. Kennedy; ASW, *tr.* by Kevin Crossley-Holland; OBVE, *tr.* by Tennyson; OBWP, *tr.* by Tennyson; TrGrPo, *tr.* by Tennyson

Aetherials have no sex, said Fielding. Penelope Sets Up House with Odysseus. Jane Oliensis. UTF

Afar in the desert I love to ride. A War (?) in the Desert. *Unknown.* PeSAV

Afetr a pretty amorous discourse. The Imperfect Enjoyment. Sir George Etherege *and to* William Walsh. NOSC

Affable irregular, An. The Road at My Door. W. B. Yeats. *Fr.* Meditations in Time of Civil War. BIrV; LiTB; NOBE; PoE

Affair of Honour. George Whalley. MoCV

Affectionate Shepherd, The. Richard Barnfield. NoSic

Affectionate Shepherd, The, *sels.* Richard Barnfield.
"As it fell upon a day." GBL
(Nightingale, The.) AWP; GTBS; GTBS-P
(Ode, An: "As it fell upon a day.") EiL
(Philomel.) CH; NOBE; OBEV
Daphnis to Ganymede. EiL

Affections Must Not. Denise Riley. NBrP; VBLP

Affections must not support the rent. (*LL*) Affections Must Not. Denise Riley. NBrP; VBLP

Affinity, The. Anna Wickham. NALW

Afflicted by order, the minimalist disease. To the Islands. Howard Moss. SM

Affliction. Bible, *O.T. Fr.* Lamentations. TrJP

Affliction. Sir John Davies. *Fr.* Nosce Teipsum. NOBE; NoSic, abr.; SiPS

Affliction ("Broken in pieces all asunder"). George Herbert. ESCV; GeHe; JCP; NOSC

Affliction ("Kill me not every day"). George Herbert. NOSC; TEP

Affliction of Margaret, The. Wordsworth. EnRP; GTBS; GTBS-P; PoEL-4

Affliction shall advance the flight in me. (*LL*) Easter Wings. George Herbert. AngWe; ChIV-1; ESCV; FHYEP; GeHe; HAP; HeIP; InPK; InPS; LiTB; MeLP; NAEL-1; NIP; NoP; NOSC; OAEL-1; PoE; PoEL-2; Poetr; PPP; SeCP; TEP; TFi; TOF; TrCP; TRP; WeW

Affliction ("When first thou didst entice to thee my heart"). George Herbert. ESCV; FHYEP; GeHe; JCP; LiTB; MeLP; NAEL-1; NOBE; NoP; NOSC; SeCP

Affliction ("When My Heart Did Heave, and There Came Forth, 'O God!'"). George Herbert. NOSC

Afforestation. E. A. Wodehouse. FiBHP

Affrayit, I glistnyt of sleip, and stert on feit. Virgil, *tr.* by Gavin Douglas. *Fr.* Aeneid [*or* Eneados], The. NAWM-1; OBVE

Afoot and light-hearted I take to the open road. Walt Whitman. *Fr.* Song of the Open Road. NOBA; RFM

Afore ye tak in hand this beuk. Lines Written in the Front of a Well-read Copy of Burns's *Songs:* To the Reader. *Unknown.* FaBoUs

Afraid of the sun [*or* sunlight]. Advice to a Neighbour Girl. Yü Hsüan-chi, *tr. fr. Chinese.* PBWP, *tr.* by Kenneth Rexroth *and* Ling Chung; WPC (For a Neighbor Girl.) BoWoP, *tr.* by Geoffrey R. Waters

Afraid! Of whom am I afraid? Emily Dickinson. OHIP; PoE

Afraid to find love's shakey equilibrium. (*LL*) Declaration of Independence, II. Jane Oliensis. UTF

Africa. Lewis Alexander. CDC

Africa. Maya Angelou. NIP; WoWa

Africa. Change Is Not Always Progress. Don L. Lee. TAP

Africa. David Diop, *tr. fr. French.* NegPo, *tr. by* Ellen Conroy Kennedy; PBA, *tr. by* Ulli Beier; TTY, *tr. by* Ulli Beier

Africa. James Russell Grant. OBTV

Africa. Maria White Lowell. AmWP

Africa. Claude McKay. Son

Africa. L. A. J. Moorer. CBWP-3

Africa. Adèle Naudé. PeSA

Africa and the Caribbean. Jennifer Brown, *tr. fr. Romanian by* Laura Schiff. AIW

Africa — London — Africa. Tony Harrison. *Fr.* Zeg-Zeg Postcards, The. FaBoBl

Africa, my Africa. Africa. David Diop, *tr. fr. French.* NegPo, *tr. by* Ellen Conroy Kennedy; PBA, *tr. by* Ulli Beier; TTY, *tr. by* Ulli Beier

Africa Sky. Kojo Laing. HBAPE

Africa Thing, The. Adam David Miller. NBV

Africa, you were once just a name to me. The Meaning of Africa. Abioseh Nicol. PBA

African. Peter Tosh. PBCV

African Affair, The. Bruce McM. Wright. PoBA; PoNe

African Beauty. Taiwo Olaleye-Oruene. AIW

African Chief, The. Bryant. BLPA; VPP

African China. Melvin B. Tolson. PoBA

African Christmas. John Press. OBCP

African Dance. Langston Hughes. FaPON

African Day. Gloria de Sant'Ana, *tr. fr. Portuguese by* Allan Francovich *and* Kathleen Weaver. PBWP

African Dirge. M. J. Chapman. PBCV

African Dream. Bob Kaufman. PoBA

African Easter. Abioseh Nicol. PBA

African Elegy, An. Robert Duncan. NoAM

African Images, *much abr.* Alice Walker. InPS

African in Louisiana. Kojo Gyinaye Kyei. PBA

African Lion, The. A. E. Housman. CBNP

African Poems, *sels.* Don L. Lee.

African Student. Noel H. Brettell. PeSAV

African Sunday. Maureen Owen. UL

African Trader's Complaint, The. Dennis C. Osadebay. PBA

African Tramp, The. Geoffrey Haresnape. PeSA

Africa's Plea. Roland Tombekai Dempster. TTY

Afrique Accidentale. Ted Joans. PoBeRe

Aft on the poop deck and walking about. Strike the Bell. *Unknown.* OxBSS

Aft' them white trash any mo'. *(LL)* Mrs. Johnson Objects. Clara Ann Thompson. AIW; BISi; CBWP-2

After. Anthony Barnett. VaA

After. Robert Browning. TrGrPo

After. Caroline Grayson. BLRP

After. Ralph Hodgson. MoBrPo

After. Philip Bourke Marston. NOBVV

After/ the Moratorium Reading. Nigel Roberts. NOBAu

After a Bath. Aileen Fisher. OTCP

After a bourbon. My Cheap Lifestyle. Eileen Myles. UL

After a Death. Sandra M. Gilbert. IMW

After a Death. Gregory Orr. AnAn

After a Death. Jennifer Strauss. FaBoMA

After a dozen years of death. Poem to My Grandmother in Her Death. Michele Murray. CrSp; IMW

After a Dream. Romain Bussine, *tr. fr. French by* Philip L. Miller. RiWo

After a dream in which your love's fullness. The Sapphire. W. S. Merwin. PoA

After A. E. Housman. Peter Titheradge. *Fr.* Teatime Variations. FaBoPa

After a fall of rain. *(LL)* In Time of Grief. Lizette Woodworth Reese. AmWP

After a fearful maze where doubt. Chimera. Barbara Howes. TwCP

After a friend has gone I like the feel of it. Nocturne. Eavan Boland. NBrP

After a Friendship. Robert Minhinnick. AngWe

After a Game of Squash. Samuel L. Albert. GoYe

After a hundred years. Emily Dickinson. AWP; OxBA

After a Journey. Thomas Hardy. CBLP; CMoP; EBEV; ELP; EnLoPo; FaBoPP; GBL; GTBS-P; MeMBP; OBNC; OxAEP-2; OxBTC; PoE; PoEL-5

After a little I could not have told. The Song of the Tortured Girl. John Berryman. CAPP; CoAP

After a long flight to his cote. *(LL)* I remember. William Carlos Williams. MeMAP

After a long winter, giving/ each other nothing. Chiyojo, *tr. fr. Japanese by* David Ray. BoWoP

After a month and a half without rain. August Rain. Robert Bly. LCAP; SV

After a Parting. Alice Meynell. NOBVV

After a Passage in Baudelaire. Robert Duncan. CMoP; PoA; PoE

After a soiree, with his dark head bent. Hazlitt Sups. Katharine Day Little. GoYe

After a Spring meeting in their nineteenth-century fastness at. Irish Hierarchy Bans Colour Photography. Paul Durcan. BiHa; PBCIP

After a Storm, Going a Hawking. George Daniel. NOSC

After a Sultry Morning. Rodney Hall. *Fr.* Owner of My Face, The. CBAP

After a Summer Fire. Lance Henson. ETG

After a Thirties Poet. Peter Titheradge. *Fr.* Teatime Variations. FaBoPa

After a throbbing night, the house still dark, pull. Those of Pure Origin. Roy Fuller. FaBoMo

After a Visit to the Natural History Museum. Laura E. Richards. ImGa

After a War. Michael Hamburger. PAW

After a war the boys play soldier with real weapons. After the War. Karl Shapiro. ArOW

After a week of physical anguish. An Evening Lull. Walt Whitman. NAAL-1

After a while it dawns on us. Historical Museum, Manitoulin Island. Lisel Mueller. PoA

After a wife's death a man may talk. The Possibilities. Beckian Fritz Goldberg. NAmP90

After/ a winding walk. A Flower from Robert Kennedy's Grave. Edward Sanders. BCF

After Algernon Charles Swinburne. Peter Titheradge. *Fr.* Teatime Variations. FaBoPa

After All. Donald Jeffrey Hayes. CDC

After all and after all. After All. Donald Jeffrey Hayes. CDC

After all, Charlie, we shall see them go. Longshore Intellectual. Sean Lucy. CIP

After all the late suppers of that faraway. Nineteen Fifty-five. Sherod Santos. NAmP90

After all the wit. Oscar Wilde. Ulick O'Connor. PeIV

After all, there's only one world for us. Love Story. Bei Dao, *tr. fr. Chinese by* Donald Finkel *with* Chen Xueliang. SpMi

After all these years. Picture from the Blitz. Lois Clark. PAW

After all those years. Accomplices. Bei Dao, *tr. fr. Chinese by* Donald Finkel *with* Chen Xueliang. SpMi

After an age when thunderbolts and hail. Louise Labé, *tr. fr. French by* Willis Barnstone. BoWoP

After an hundred and thirty years' nap. On the Erection of Shakespeare's Statue in Westminster Abbey. Pope. FaBoEE

After Anacreon. Lew Welch. *Fr.* Taxi Suite. NeAP; PoBeRe; PoM

After Annunciation. Anna Wickham. MoBrPo

After Apple-picking. Robert Frost. AmPP; AnAmPo; CMoP; InPS; LiTA; MeMAP; MoAB; MoAmPo; MoP; NAAL-2; NoAM; NOBA; NTP; NU; OxBA; PoE; Poetr; PPP; PrIm; SAmP; SoSe; TAP; TFi; TRP; UnPo

After Arguing against the Contention That Art Must Come from Discontent. William Stafford. NoAM

After Aughrim. Arthur G. Geoghegan. PeIV

After Aughrim. Emily Lawless. OBEV; PeIV

After Babel. Peter Goldsworthy. NOBAu

After Being in Love, the Next Responsibility. Jalal al-Din Rumi, *tr. fr. Persian by* John Moyne *and* Coleman Barks. UnAS

After Blenheim. Robert Southey. *See* 'Twas [*or* It was] a summer [*or* summer's] evening.

After breakfast and you'd left for school. Divorce. Bink Noll. MAT

After Brecht. D. J. Enright. AnAn

After centuries of dissecting. Lesbian Poem. Robin Morgan. IHMS

After Christmas. W. H. Auden. *See* Well so that is that. Now we must dismantle the tree.

After Christmas. Michael Richards. OBCP

After Christopher Wood. John James. NBrP; VaA

After Church. Samuel Alfred Beadle. AAP

After class Thursday nights, the students. The Philosopher's Club. Kim Addonizio. NGP

After Claude Lanzmann's Shoah. Liliane Richman. BTR

After Clouds and Rain. Sam Hamill. ArNa

After Dark. Adrienne Rich. LCAP; LiTM; VGW

After dark, I came in. Strange Filth. Harry Clifton. IB

After dark/ Near the South Dakota border. Having Lost My Sons, I Confront the Wreckage of the Moon: Christmas, 1960. James Wright. CoAP; HCAP; NAAL-2

After Dark Vapours. Keats. EnRP; FaBoRV; TEP

After days of putting down my poem. January. Ellen Bryant Voigt. NoP

After Death. Fanny Parnell. IIP

After Death. Christina Rossetti. GBL; NAEL-2; NALW; TEP

After Death. Swinburne. NOBVV; PeVV

After death, and clean as a finishing line. (LL) The Crafty Butcher. Susan Hampton. NOBAu

After Death in Arabia. Sir Edwin Arnold. WGRP

After death nothing is, and nothing, death. Seneca, tr. fr. Latin by the Earl of Rochester. Fr. Troades. EBEV; OBD; OBVE

After death, suppose we were judged by animals: The Tribunal. Chris Wallace-Crabbe. ChIV-2

After Dilettante Concetti. Henry Duff Traill. BXAP; FaBoCo

After dinner sit awhile. Unknown. FaBoUs

After dreaming some hours of the land of Cockaigne. Thomas Moore. Fr. Fudge Family in Paris, The. BIrV

After Drinking All Night with a Friend, We Go Out in a Boat at Dawn to See Who Can Write the Best Poem. Robert Bly. ArLo; NaP

After each quake. Crack in the Wall Holds Flowers. Adam David Miller. PoBA

After Eden. James Simmons. PNI

After Edgehill, 1642. Gladys Mary Coles. FaBoEH

After Elegies. Jean Valentine. LCAP

After 11 years. The Most Beautiful Woman at My Highschool Reunion. Ellen Marie Bissert. GLP; PeHV

After Ever Happily [or, The Princess and the Woodcutter]. Ian Serraillier. OBSP

After Experience Taught Me. W. D. Snodgrass. ArOW; CAPP; CoAP; OBWP; PPP; TAP

After explanations and regulations, he. A WASP Woman Visits a Black Junkie in Prison. Etheridge Knight. NBV

After extremity. To the Linen Hall. Tom Paulin. SCBI

After fifteen months you fly in. Visitation Rights. Heather Wishik. GLP

After fifty years, nearly, I remember. The King's Horses. John Hewitt. IIP

After Five Years. Augustus Young. BIrV

After Floods on the Wharfe. Andrew Marvell. Fr. Upon Appleton House, to My Lord Fairfax. FaBoPP; SeCP; SeCV-1

After Forty Years. Carolyne Wright. BTR

After fourteen hours clearing they came to him. London, 1940. Frank Thompson. FaBoEH

After Frost. Brian Patten. EBEV

After Galen. Oliver St. John Gogarty. FaBoEE; OBMV; PoRA

After-Glow, The. Mathilde Blind. OBNC

After-Glow of Pain, The. Clara Ann Thompson. CBWP-2

After Goliath. Kingsley Amis. NOBL; OxBTC

After Grave Deliberation. Elizabeth Flynn. NBLV

After great pain, a formal feeling comes. Emily Dickinson. AmPP; BoWoP; GGP; HAP; HeIP; IMW; InPS; LiTA; MoAB; MoAmPo; NAAL-1; NALW; NAWM-2; NIP; NoAM; NOBA; NoP; PoE; Poetr; PrIm; SAmP; TAP; TFi; TRP; UnPo

After great storms the calm returns. Sir Thomas Wyatt. SiPS; SiPSBD

After Greece. James Merrill. CAPP; NOBA; NYBP; TRP

After Grey Vigils. George Santayana. Fr. Sonnets. AnAmPo

After grey vigils, sunshine in the heart. After Grey Vigils. George Santayana. Fr. Sonnets. AnAmPo

After Grief. Stanley Plumly. AmPA; LCAP

After hangin' Danny Deever in the mornin'! (LL) Danny Deever. Kipling. CoGr; EBEvV; EBVV; FaBoBa; FaPoR; GTBS-P; InPS; LiTB; MoBrPo; NAEL-2; NoAM; NOBE; NOBVV; OHCV; OxBoLi; OxBTC; PeVV; PlP; PoLF; SCGP; SCV; TEP; TFi; TrGrPo; UnPo

After having slain very many beasts. Louise Labé, tr. fr. French by Willis Barnstone. BoWoP

After Haymaking. Robert Wells. SCBI

After He Had Gone. Sylvia Townsend Warner. MoBrPo

After he had several adventures, the potato boy took the. Potchikoo Marries. Louise Erdrich. Fr. Old Man Potchikoo. HATNAP

After he stripped off my clothes. Villana, tr. fr. Sanskrit by Willis Barnstone. AIW; BoWoP

After Her Husband Died, Doña Carlota Was So Alone. Leroy V. Quintana. AfAz

After her husband died, Zita decided to get the face-lift. Distance from Loved Ones. James Tate. BAP-90

After her pills the girl slept and counted. Tally. Josephine Miles. NoAM

After Hilaire Belloc. Max Beerbohm. UV

After Hilary, Age 5. Faye Kicknosway. UL

After His Death. Norman MacCaig. CBNP

After his ham & cheese in the drape factory cafeteria. Torque. David Rivard. PBCAP

After his head's pull'd off, to find it out. (LL) Convert's but a fly, that turns about, A. Samuel Butler. FaBoEE

After his talking destroyed her. Antarctica. R. A. Simpson. CBAP

After Horace. Alfred Denis Godley. NOBL

After hot loveless nights, when cold winds stream. The Sisters. Roy Campbell. BoLoP; ErPo; FaBoTw; LPA; OBMV

After Hours. Robert Mezey. NaP

After I died I could not close my eyes. Departure. Van K. Brock. MT

After I had cut off my hands. Intrusion. Denise Levertov. CAPP; VCAP

After I Had Worked All Day. Charles Reznikoff. Fr. Five Groups of Verse. PrIm; VGW

After I Have Voted. Laura Jensen. AmPA

After its end. (LL) The Tale About a Tale. Vasco [or Vasko] Popa. AnRep, tr. by Charles Simic; HSix

After Jericho. R. S. Thomas. OxBC

After Jill died they remembered how she liked this chair. Jill's Death. George Buchanan. PNI

After John Keats. Peter Titheradge. Fr. Teatime Variations. FaBoPa

After Johnny wear mi clothes. Johnny Tek Away Mi Wife. Slim Beckford and Sam Blackwood. PBCV

After kicking on the swing. Li Ch'ing-chao. See Ride in the swing.

After kicking on the swing. Li Ch'ing-chao, tr. fr. Chinese by Kenneth Rexroth and Ling Chung. BoWoP
(To the Tune "I Paint My Lips Red.") WPC
(Tune: Crimson Lips Adorned.) PBWP, tr. by C. H. Kwôck and Vincent McHugh

After late evenings. After Touch. Jan Clausen. GLP

After Laughter. Grace Buchanan Sherwood. GoYe

After Li Ch'ing-chao. Anne Waldman. UL

After life there must be life. (LL) After the Grand Perhaps. Lucie Brock-Broido. UTF

After listening to Monk. Tom Dent. Jaz

After Long Busyness. Robert Bly. CAPP; PoA

After long journey in sun. Ear Is Not Deaf. Irene Dayton. GoYe

After Long Rain. Wang Wei, tr. fr. Chinese by Robert Payne. TAL

After Long Silence. W. B. Yeats. BoLoP; CMoP; EnLoPo; HeIP; HoPM; LiTM; NAEL-2; OAEL-2; OBMV; PPP; PrIm; UnPo

After long trouble in a taedious way. Mary Sidney Wroth, Countess of Montgomery. Fr. Urania. KTR; WPE

After Longfellow. Unknown. See Lives of great men all remind us/ As their pages o'er we turn.

After Lorca. Robert Creeley. InPS; LCAP; NaP

After Lorca. Ted Hughes. PoA

After Love. Maxine W. Kumin. CrSp; NMM; TAP; VBLP

After Love. John Stone. MT

After lunch the old Duchess of Teck. Unknown. PeLi

After Making Love We Hear Footsteps. Galway Kinnell. InPS; NIP; NoAM; RaBo; VCAP

After many scornes [or scorns] like these. What He(e) Suffered. Ben Jonson. Fr. Celebration of Charis in Ten Lyric[k] Peeces [or pieces], A. BeJo; OxAEP-1; SeCP

After many strange thoughts. After Working. Robert Bly. NaP

After Margrave died, nothing. History of a Literary Movement. Howard Nemerov. PoE

After Mass. "Michael Field." WPE

After Mass. Tony Flynn. PWE

After melon. Unknown. FaBoUs

After Midnight. Louis Simpson. CAPP; NoAM

After Midnight. Charles Vildrac, tr. fr. French by Jethro Bithell. AWP

After midnight I heard a scream. By Night. Robert Francis. VGW

After Midsummer. E. J. Scovell. OxBTC

After Mr. Mayhew's Visit. Ken Smith. PWE

After much driving. 1974 — The Sounds. Christina Beer. PeNZ

After my bath. After a Bath. Aileen Fisher. OTCP

After My Grandmother's Death. Michele Roberts. AIW

After nestling champagne splits in ice. Maquillage. Lynda Hull. UTF

After night, the waking knowledge. Awaking. Stephen Spender. NYBP

After night there comes the day. Still He Sings. Allan Taylor. OBET

After Nightfall. William Renton. NOBVV

After night's thunder far away had rolled. Haymaking. Edward Thomas. MoAB; MoBrPo

After noon, in the plaza, cries, shrill yells, running and breaking. Memorial Day. Josephine Miles. NoP

After one moment when I bowed my head. The Convert. G. K. Chesteron. ChIV-2

After One of the 19 Famous Han Poems. Pao Ling-hui, tr. fr. Chinese by Kenneth Rexroth and Ling Chung. WPC

After our damp skins slid apart. Definition. Lauren Shakely. FYAP

After our Epilogue this crowd dismisses. Congreve. *Fr.* Way of the World, The. NAEL-1

After our fierce loving. The Profile on the Pillow. Dudley Randall. BPo; PoBA; TAP

After Passing the Examination. Meng Chiao, *tr. fr. Chinese by* Irving Y. Lo. SuSp

After Plotinus. William Stafford. PoA

After Publication of Under the Volcano. Malcolm Lowry. FaBoTw

After rain. Mountain Study. Peter van Toorn. NOBC

After Rain. P. K. Page. NOBC; PoE

After rain a bright moon appears. Written beneath Hui Mountain, When Tsou Liu-yi Comes by for a Visit. Wang Shih-chieng, *tr. fr. Chinese by* Richard John Lynn. SuSp

After rain, through afterglow, the unfolding fan. Train Ride. John Wheelwright. VGW

After Reading a Child's Guide to Modern Physics. W. H. Auden. NYBP

After Reading Bryant's Lines to a Waterfowl. Eloise Bibb Thompson. ShDr

After Reading *Country of the Pointed Firs, The.* Jean Garrigue. VCAP

After Reading in a Letter Proposals for Building a Cottage. John Clare. OxAEP-2

After Reading "Lead, Kindly Light." Paul Laurence Dunbar. TrPWD

After Reading St. John the Divine. Gene Derwood. ImPo; LiTM; WPE

After Reading Sylvia Plath. Alta. IHMS

After Reading the Life of Mrs. Catherine Stubbs in Isaac Ambrose's "War with the Devils." Isaac Hann. NOCV

After Reading the Poems of Master Han Shan, *sels.* Wang Chiu-ssu, *tr. fr. Chinese by* Jonathan Chaves.

After St. Augustine. Mary Elizabeth Coleridge. TrPWD

After scanning its face again and again. John Muir on Mt. Ritter. Gary Snyder. *Fr.* Myths and Texts. NeAP; NOBA; PoM

After School. Liz Cashdan. NWP

After Seeing Paintings in a Small Book by T. C. Cannon (1946-1978). Alice Sadongei. HATNAP

After Shakespeare. Alex Comfort. ErPo

After sharp words from the fine mind. The Flowering Bars. Charles Donnelly. CIP

After she drives her younger daughter to school, struggling. The Woman with the Wild-Grown Hair Relaxes after Another Long Day. Nita Penfold. CrSp

After she/ had complained about. The Proposition. Paul Blackburn. ErPo

After six little spaces of chill, and six of burning. (*LL*) Here Lies a Lady. John Crowe Ransom. AWP; CMoP; HAP; InvP; LiTM; MeMAP; MoAB; MoAmPo; MoP; NAAL-2; NoAM; PoRA; RB; TAP; VGW

After so long an absence. The Meeting. Longfellow. OBF

After so many deaths to breathe again. Variations on a Theme by George Herbert. Marya Zaturenska. TrPWD

After so many decades of . . . of what? To Whom It May Concern. J. V. Cunningham. FYAP

After so much battering of fire and steel. Butchers and Tombs. Ivor Gurney. PeFWW

After some years Bohemian came to this. J. V. Cunningham. VGW

After-Song. Richard Watson Gilder. TrPWD

After Speaking of One Dead a Long Time. Padraic Colum. GoYe

After Stroke. Bill Griffiths. NBrP

After stumbling around for months. Blue Tango. Michael van Walleghen. NAmP90

After such words. Pitchipoi. George Bogin. BTR

After such years of dissension and strife. Dust to Dust. Thomas Hood. NBLV

(Natural Tears.) FiBHP

After sudden rain, a clear autumn night. Stars and Moon on the Yangtse. Tu Fu, *tr. fr. Chinese by* A. C. Graham. PLT

After sundown the clouds start to burn. Thunderstorm. Sam Mitchell, *tr. fr. Aborigine by* Georg von Brandenstein. NOBAu

After surmounting three-score and ten. My 71st Year. Walt Whitman. NAs

After Tempest. Percy MacKaye. FYAP

After ten years, I try the veil. Girl Warrior. Mary E. O'Donnell. NWP

After Tennyson. Edward Lear. FaBoNo

After Tennyson. Edward Lear. FaBoNo

After that hervest inned had his sheves. Thomas Hoccleve. *Fr.* Hoccleve's Complaint. EnVB

After That Time. Harriet Susskind. BTR

After the act of stabbing and. Stone Wall and Celebration. János Pilinszky, *tr. fr. Hungarian by* Peter Jay. PoSu

After the air of summer. (*LL*) Roman Fountain. Louise Bogan. NoP; WPOW

After the all been done and i. Island Mary. Lucille Clifton. NALW

After the Anonymous Swedish. James Harrison. VGW

After the Apocalypse., *sels.* Samih al-Qasim, *tr. fr. Arabic by* Sharif Elmusa *and* Naomi Shihab Nye.

After the Ball. Amiri Baraka. NAAL-2

After the baths and bowl-work, he was dead. Old Relative. Gwendolyn Brooks. *Fr.* Notes from the Childhood and the Girlhood. LCAP

After the Battle. A. P. Herbert. NSI

After the Battle. George Sylvester Viereck. GoYe

After the blast of lightning from the East. The End. Wilfred Owen. CH; ChIV-1; FaBoRV; PAW

After the Blitz, 1941. J. R. Ackerley. PeHV

After the brief bivouac of Sunday. The Stenographers. P. K. Page. HeIP; LiTM; NALW; NoAM; NoP

After the bronzed, heroic traveller. The Mapmaker on His Art. Howard Nemerov. NYBP

After the Burial. James Russell Lowell. UnPo

After the burial-parties leave. The Hyaenas [*or* Hyenas]. Kipling. NAEL-2; OBSV

After the Camanches. Rose Terry Cooke. AmWP; PAH

After the Centennial. Christopher Pearse Cranch. PAH

After the centers' naked files, the basic line. The Lines. Randall Jarrell. ArOW

After the Chinese. Tess Gallagher. NAmP90

After the cloud embankments. Reconnaissance. Arna Bontemps. BPo

After the Convention. Robert Lowell. NoAM

After the darkness and storm. After. Caroline Grayson. BLRP

After the day's great sun. (*LL*) At Nightfall. Charles Hanson Towne. BLPA; FaBoBe

After the Death of an Elder Klallam. Duane Niatum. CDW

After the Death of Her Daughter in Child-birth. Lady Izumi Shikibu, *tr. fr. Japanese by* Edwin A. Cranston. PBWP

After the Deluge. Wole Soyinka. HBAPE

After the doctor checked to see. First Practice. Gary Gildner. AmPA; PBCAP

After the door shuts and the footsteps die. A Hunt in the Black Forest. Randall Jarrell. CoAP; LCAP

After the dread tales and red yarns of the Line. First Time In. Ivor Gurney. FaBoVe

After the dreadful Flood was past. The Tower of Babel. Nathaniel Crouch. OxBChV

After the drink, after dinner, after the half-hour idiot kids' cartoon. The Mistress. C. K. Williams. PWE

After the end of the world. In the Middle of Life. Tadeusz Rózewicz, *tr. fr. Polish by* Czeslaw Milosz.
(In the Midst of Life.) PoSu, *tr. by* Adam Czerniawski

After the evening's music comes a storm. After the Music. John Riley. VaA

After the event the rockslide. Clarity. A. R. Ammons. HCAP; TAP

After the explosion or cataclysm, that big. The Eternal City. A. R. Ammons. CAPP; HCAP

After the eyes that looked, the lips that spake. Lincoln at Gettysburg. Bayard Taylor. *Fr.* Gettysburg Ode, The. OHIP; PAH

After the Fair. Thomas Hardy. *Fr.* At Casterbridge Fair. CMoP; HAP

After the Fall. Gloria Escoffery. PBCV

After the fall drive, the last. Montana Eclogue. William Stafford. NYBP

After the fallen sun the wind was sad. Moonrise Over Battlefield. Edgell Rickword. NSI; PoWW

After the feast, my Shapcott, see. Oberon's Palace. Robert Herrick. CaPo

After the fierce midsummer all ablaze. Friendship After Love. Ella Wheeler Wilcox. AmWP

After the fiercest pangs of hot desire. A Song. Richard Duke. BoLoP; ECEV

After the Fire. Oliver Wendell Holmes. PAH

After the First Communion. Sunday Afternoon. Denise Levertov. IHMS

After the first death, there is no other. (*LL*) A Refusal to Mourn the Death, by Fire, of a Child in London. Dylan Thomas. BLPL; CMoP; EBEV; FaBoMo; FF; GTBS-P; HeIP; HoPM; ImPo; LiTB; LiTM; MeMBP; MoAB; MoBrPo; MoP; NoAM; NOBE; NoP; OAEL-2; OBWVE; OxAEP-2; OxBTC; PAW; PoE; PoWW; TEP; TFi; TwCP; UnPo

After the First Frost. Lew Blockcolski. VoR

After the first powerful plain manifesto. The Express. Stephen Spender. CMoP; GoJo; HeIP; LiTM; MoAB; MoBrPo; MoP; NoAM; TwCP

After the first shallows have dropped away. Daily the Ocean between Us. Patricia Goedicke. TAP

After the Flight of the Earls. Fearflatha O'Gnive. NOIV

After the Flood. John Foulcher. NOBAu

After the Flood. Sir David Lindsay. *Fr.* Monarche, The. ChIV-1; OxBS

After the Flood. Rimbaud, *tr.* by Enid Rhodes Peschal. *Fr.* Illuminations. SOTW

After the Funeral. Dylan Thomas. AngWe; CMoP; FaBoMo; MeMBP; NAEL-2; NoP; OAEL-2; OBWVE; OxAEP-2

After the funeral, mule praises, brays. After the Funeral. Dylan Thomas. AngWe; CMoP; FaBoMo; MeMBP; NAEL-2; NoP; OAEL-2; OBWVE; OxAEP-2
(In Memory of Ann Jones.) ImPo

After the Funerals. Felice Picano. PFL

After the funerals, the questions arise. After the Funerals. Felice Picano. PFL

After the Ghanaian dancing, we fought. Grief. Maureen Seaton. LoHo

After the Golden Wedding, *sels.* James Kenneth Stephen.
"She's not a faultless woman; no!." EBVV; NOBVV; OxBM

After the Grand Perhaps. Lucie Brock-Broido. UTF

After the Holocaust, No Poetry. David Koenig. BTR

After the horrors of Heathrow. 747 (London-Chicago). Robert Conquest. OxBC

After the Hunt. Detlev von Liliencron, *tr. fr. German* by Ludwig Lewisohn. AWP

After the Hurricane. Samuel Hazo. GrPl

After the Impossible Dream. Tracey Herd. NWP

After the Industrial Revolution, All Things Happen at Once. Robert Bly. CoAP

After the Inscription on a Greek Stele of a Woman Holding Her Grandchild on Her Knees. *Unknown, tr. fr. Greek* by Stephen Spender. GrAn

After the Irish of Egan O'Rahilly. Egan O'Rahilly. *See* Without flocks or cattle or the curved horns.

After the Japanese. Mae V. Cowdery. ShDr

After the Last Bulletins. Richard Wilbur. CoAP; MoAB; MoAmPo; NYBP; TrGrPo

After the Last Dynasty. Stanley Kunitz. TAP

After the Last Practice. Edward Hirsch. NAmP90

After the Laws of Good-Bye & Autumn, *sels.* Eddy van Vliet, *tr. fr. Dutch* by James S. Holmes.

After the leaves have fallen, we return. The Plain Sense of Things. Wallace Stevens. HCAP; NoAM

After the leg is lost, the pain remains as an emblem. Phantom Pain. Maxine Chernoff. EOEF

After the legshows and the brandies. Night Club. Louis MacNeice. OxBSP

After the light has set. The Return. George MacBeth. NYBP

After the long infirmity of love. (*LL*) As someone on his back for months of illness. Ausiàs March. STV

After the market crash, everyone. Luck – 1932. Lucien Stryk. NGP

After the Massacre. Musaemura Bonus Zimunya. PeSAV

After the midnight unfolding of the White Rose. The Feast of Stephen. Kevin Nichols. OBCP

After the midwinter marriages – the bride of snow. John Hollander. *Fr.* Powers of Thirteen. VCAP

After the milk-white hounds of the moon. (*LL*) Madman's Song. Elinor Wylie. MoAB; MoAmPo; PoRA

After the murder. The Last Quatrain of the Ballad of Emmett Till. Gwendolyn Brooks. LCAP; PoBA; WPE

After the Music. John Riley. VaA

After the Night. Mang Ke, *tr. fr. Chinese* by Donald Finkel *with* Li Guohua. SpMi

After the Night Hunt. James Dickey. PoA

After the noose, and the black diary deeds. Casement's Funeral. Richard Murphy. *Fr.* Battle of Aughrim, The. NOIV; PBCIP

After the official exchange, when all. Climbing Out of the Cage. *Unknown.* BAP-90

After the Pangs of a Desperate Lover. Dryden. *Fr.* Evening's Love, An. ELP; PeLV

After the paradiso and the milky way and the kosmos, seeming. Yolanda Meets the Wild Boys. Jessica Hagedorn. OpBo

After the Party. Luigi Fontanella, *tr. fr. Italian* by W. S. Di Piero. NeIt

After the Party. William Wise. FaPON

After the people and the flowers. Leaving Town after the Funeral. Richard Jones. NAmP90

After the Persian. Louise Bogan. NYBP; PoA

After the planes unloaded, we fell down. The Dead in Europe. Robert Lowell. LiTM; OxBA; OxBC

After the Pleasure Party. Herman Melville. NAAL-1; PoEL-5

After the ploughshare and the stumbling team. (*LL*) As the Team's Head-Brass. Edward Thomas. GTBS-P; NAEL-2; NSI; OBWP; OxAEP-2; OxBTC; PeFWW; PoE; RB

After the Poem. Sydney Clouts. PeSAV

After the poem the coastline took. After the Poem. Sydney Clouts. PeSAV

After the Pow-Wow., *sels.* Harold Littlebird.

After the Quarrel. Paul Laurence Dunbar. AnAmPo; CDC

After the Quarrel. Barbara Gibson. FF

After the Quarrel. Priscilla Jane Thompson. CBWP-2

After the Rain. Edward A. Collier. BLRP

After the rain of stars. At the Gate of the Valley. Zbigniew Herbert, *tr. fr. Polish by* Czeslaw Milosz. PoSu

After the rapture comes, and everyone goes away. March Journal. Charles Wright. LCAP

After the rare arch-poet Jonson died. Upon [Mr.] Ben Jonson: Epigram. Robert Herrick. CaPo
(Upon Master Ben Jonson: Epigram.) BeJo

After the red leaf and the gold have gone. A Spell before Winter. Howard Nemerov. LiTM

After the red-rose-bordered hem. (*LL*) To Ireland in the Coming Times. W. B. Yeats. NoAM; NOIV; PeIV

After the Revolution. Marilyn Hacker. AmPA

After the Revolution for Jesus the Associate Professor [*or a* Secular Man] Prepares His Final Remarks. Miller Williams. MT

After the ribboning fever of interstate. Frugal Repasts. Lynda Hull. NAmP90

After the rooster falls from the hen. Final Soliloquy on a Randy Rooster (in a Key of Yellow). Robert Peters. BXAP

After the sagittal and lateral cuts. Threshold. Dean Young. NAmP90

After the satyr's twilight in the park. Homecoming – Massachusetts. John Ciardi. NYBP

After the sea, the harbor. Sequence. Edgar Daniel Kramer. BLRP

After the Second Operation. Patricia Goedicke. TAP

After the Seizer there were ten chiefs, and there was much warfare south and east. *Unknown, tr.* by Daniel G. Brinton. *Fr.* Walam [*or* Wallum] Olum; or, Red Score. OBVE

After the sentence. Letters to Martha. Dennis Brutus. PeSAV

After the silence of the centuries? (*LL*) The Man with the Hoe. Edwin Markham. AnAmPo; BLPA; BLPL; LiTA; MoAmPo; PrIm; TFi; TrGrPo; WBLP; WGRP

After the stars were all hung separately. The Book of How. Merrill Moore. MoAmPo

After the Storm. Elizabeth Bartlett. GoYe

After the Storm. Edmond Yi-Teh Chang. OpBo

After the Storm. H. Cordelia Ray. AmWP; CBWP-3

After the storm. The Living Mirror. Jason Shinder. UTF

After the sun's eclipse. Teresa. Richard Wilbur. NoAM

After the Supper and Talk. Walt Whitman. MoAmPo; NAAL-1

After the Surprising Conversions. Robert Lowell. AmPP; HAP; NAAL-2; NoAM; NoP; PPP; TRP

After the sweat of swathes and the sinking madder sun. A Drink of Spring. John Ennis. CIP; PBCIP

After the test they sent an expert. School Days. William Stafford. LCAP

After the third evening roud. Be Seeing You. Vasco [*or* Vasko] Popa, *tr. fr. Serbo-Croatian. Fr.* Raw Flesh. PoSu, *tr.* by Anne Pennington

After the thorns I came to the first page. The Sleeping Beauty; Variation of the Prince. Randall Jarrell. PoA

After the tide's long gear-shifting gesture. Landscape. Robert Gray. FaBoMA

After the tiff there was stiff silence, till. The Lovers. W. R. Rodgers. BIrV; OxBSP; PNI

After the tumult and the blood. At Vshchizh. Fyodor Tyutchev, *tr. fr. Russian* by Charles Tomlinson. OBWP

After the uprising of the 17th June. The Solution. Bertolt Brecht, *tr. fr. German* by Dereck Bowman. PoSu

After the Visit. Thomas Hardy. NOBE; OBNC

After the War. Douglas Dunn. OxBC

After the War. Richard Le Gallienne. PAH

After the War. Karl Shapiro. ArOW

After the war – I hear men ask – what then? After the War. Richard Le Gallienne. PAH

After the whey-faced anonymity. South Country. Kenneth Slessor. CBAP; FaBoMA

After the whoosh of doors slid shut. At Lansdowne Bridge. Arthur Nortje. HBAPE

After the Winter. Claude McKay. PoBA; PoNe

After the words of the magnificence and doom. Country Burial. Janet Lewis. CRP

After these things should be. (*LL*) The New House. Edward Thomas. EBEV; MoAB; MoBrPo; NOBE; OBEV; OBWVE

After these words the Weather-Geat prince. Beowulf's Fight with Grendel's Mother. *Unknown, tr.* by Michael Alexander. *Fr.* Beowulf. ASW, *tr.* by Kevin Crossley-Holland; WTO

Against Homosexuality. Thomas Gilbert. *Fr.* View of the Town, A. In an Epistle to a Friend. NOEC

Against Hope. Abraham Cowley. *Fr.* Mistress, The. LiTB; MeLP; NOSC; SeCV-1

Against Hurt. J. H. Prynne. VaA

Against Idleness and Mischief. Isaac Watts. *See* How doth the little busy bee.

Against Indifference. Charles Webbe. OBEV

Against its waiting window, open still! (*LL*) Ad Amicam. Francis Thompson. Son

Against Jealousie. Ben Jonson. CBLP

Against Love. Katherine Philips. BoWoP; WPE

Against Marriage to His Mistress. William Walsh. FaBoUs; GGP

Against Meaning. Andrei Codrescu. UL

Against Minoan sunlight. Wishes for Her. Denis Devlin. CIP; NOIV

Against Modesty in Love. Matthew Prior. ErPo

Against pain. (*LL*) The Ice Queen's Calla Lily Fingers. Diane Wakoski. SRLS

Against Paradise. Jonathan Holden. NAmP90

Against Parting. Natan Zach, *tr. fr. Hebrew by* Jon Silkin. PoSu, *tr. by* Peter Everwine *and* Shulamit Yasny-Starkman

Against Proud Poor Phryna. John Davies of Hereford. FaBoEE

Against Romanticism. Kingsley Amis. NoAM

Against Seasons. Robert Mezey. NYBP

Against Simple Reading. Meredith Stricker. LoHo

Against Slavery. William Cowper. *See* Oh for a lodge in some vast wilderness.

Against Sodomy. Charles Churchill. *See* Go where we will, at ev'ry time and place.

Against Still Life. Margaret Atwood. MoCV; NMM

Against Te Rauparaha. Alistair Campbell. *Fr.* Sanctuary of Spirits. PeNZ

Against that time, if ever that time come. Shakespeare. *Fr.* Sonnets. OxAEP-1

Against the Baron's Enemies. *Unknown.* MeEL

Against the Baron's Enemies. *Unknown. See* Sitteth alle stille and herkneth to me.

Against the burly air I strode. Genesis. Geoffrey Hill. ChIV-1; HAP; OAEL-2; OxBC; PeECV; PRA; TOF

Against the Dark. James McAuley. FaBoMA

Against the dark of night. (*LL*) Pete at the Zoo. Gwendolyn Brooks. PDV; TLR

Against the enemy's decoding, against simple reading. (*LL*) Against Simple Reading. Meredith Stricker. LoHo

Against the Evidence. David Ignatow. CAPP; NNaP

Against the evidence, I live by choice. (*LL*) Against the Evidence. David Ignatow. CAPP; NNaP

Against the Fear of Death. Lucretius, *tr. by* Rolfe Humphries. *Fr.* De Rerum Natura (On the Nature of Things). DL, *abr.*

Against the guide of Truth. *Unknown. tr. fr. Hebrew. Fr.* Duel with Verses over a Great Man. TrJP

Against the King. William Drummond of Hawthornden. NOSC

Against the king, sir, now why would ye fight? Against the King. William Drummond of Hawthornden. NOSC

Against the lamp I sit by the south window. Sitting at Night. Po Chü-i, *tr. fr. Chinese by* Robert Payne. TAL

Against the Love of Great Ones. Richard Lovelace. CBLP

Against the Magpie. *Unknown.* GBP

Against the paper sands of the paper shore! (*LL*) The Katzenjammer Kids. James Reaney. MoCV

Against the potent poison of your hate. (*LL*) The White House. Claude McKay. AmPP; NIP; PoBA

Against the pure, reflective tiles. My Six Toothbrushes. Phyllis McGinley. GoYe

Against the rubber tongues of cows and the hoeing hands of men. Thistles. Ted Hughes. FaBoVe; NoAM; OxBSP; OxBTC; SoSe

Against the Silences to Come. Ron Loewinsohn. PoM

Against the snow, the rain. Restless Love. Goethe, *tr. fr. German by* Philip L. Miller. RiWo

Against the sun — the world of flowers and dreams. (*LL*) Lines Written Near San Francisco. Louis Simpson. PRA

Against the wall. (*LL*) It's No Secret. Medaksé. VBLP

Against the Wall. Judith Wright. FaBoMA

Against the Wind. Amir Gilboa, *tr. fr. Hebrew by* Bernhard Frank. MHP, *tr. by* Ruth Finer Mintz

Against the window pane. Summer Rain. Sir Herbert Read. LiTM

Against Them Who Lay Unchastity to the Sex of Women. William Habington. *Fr.* Castara. BeJo; JCP; SeCP

Against these turbid turquoise skies. Les Ballons. Oscar Wilde. NOBVV

Against what light. Black Dada Nihilismus. Amiri Baraka. PoM

Against Witches. *Unknown.* GBP

Against Women, *sels. Unknown., tr. fr. Welsh by* Gwyn Williams. "Woman is by aptitude." OBWVE

Against Women. *Unknown.* MeEL

Against your ear. (*LL*) The Distant Drum. Calvin C. Hernton. FF; TTY

Agamemnon. Aeschylus, *tr. by* Louis MacNeice. NAWM-1

Agamemnon (Dear gods, set me free from all the pain). Aeschylus, *tr. fr. Greek by* Robert Fagles. NAWM-1
Sels.
"Great Fortune is an hungry thing." AWP
Hymn to Zeus. WGRP
Signal Fire, The. CTC

Agamemnon before Troy. John Frederick Nims. Son

Agamemnon's Tomb (Tomb/ A hollow hateful world). Sacheverell Sitwell. LiTB; OBMV
Sels.
"One by one, as harvesters, all heavy laden." MoBrPo

Agape the sooty collier stands. John Dalton. *Fr.* Descriptive Poem, Addressed to Two Ladies at Their Return from Viewing the Mines, near Whitehaven, A. NOEC

Agatha Christie and Beatrix Potter. John Updike. AnAmPo

Agatha Christie to. Said. George Starbuck. OBAL

Agathon, *sels.* George Edward Woodberry.

Agbor Dancer. John Pepper Clark. PBA

Age. Abraham Cowley. AWP

Age. Rae Desmond Jones. CBAP

Age. Walter Savage Landor. FaBoEE; NOBVV; PoEL-4

Age. Philip Larkin. CMoP

Age, The. Osip Mandelstam, *tr. fr. Russian by* Peter Russell. AnAn

Age. Sir Thomas More. *Fr.* Pageant Verses. EnRePo

Age after age our bird through incense flies. Bird, Bird. Gene Derwood. LiTA

Age, An. Laura Jensen. LCAP

Age, and the deaths, and the ghosts. He Resigns. John Berryman. OxBSP; SM; WeW

Age and Youth. Shakespeare. *See* Crabbed age and youth cannot live together.

Age cannot reach me where the veils of God. Immortality. Susan Langstaff Mitchell. TIRV

Age Cannot Wither Her. Shakespeare. *Fr.* Antony and Cleopatra. ImPo

Age cannot wither her, nor custom stale. Age Cannot Wither Her. Shakespeare. *Fr.* Antony and Cleopatra. ImPo

Age demanded an image, The. Ezra Pound. *Fr.* Hugh Selwyn Mauberly. (Life and Contacts). AmPP; CMoP; HAP; InPS; LiTA; LiTM; MoAmPo; NoAM; NOBA; NoP; TAP; VGW

Age grips the body but the heart stays young. Love Is Bitter. *Unknown.* PeSA

Age in her embraces passed [*or* pass'd, *or* past], An. Mistress, The: A Song. The Earl of Rochester. EBEV; NOBE; NOSC (Mistress, The.) OxAEP-1

Age in Prospect. Robinson Jeffers. MoAB; MoAmPo

Age instinct with wisdom, love, bends towards. Rembrandt's Return of the Prodigal Son. Dick Davis. SCBI

Age is a quality of mind. How Old Are You? H. S. Fritsch. PoLF; PoToHe

Age is dull and mean, The. Men creep. For Righteousness' Sake. Whittier. PoEL-4

Age Is Great and Strong, The. Victor Hugo, *tr. fr. French by* W. J. Robertson. WGRP

Age is when to a man. Samuel Beckett. *Fr.* Words and Music. BIrV

Age Looks Back at Youth. Thomas, Lord Vaux. *See* When I look back and in myself behold.

Age might but take the things Youth needed not! (*LL*) A Lesson. Wordsworth. GTBS; GTBS-P

Age ("Most explicit"). Robert Creeley. BAP-89

Age of a Dream, The. Lionel Johnson. OBMV

Age of Animals, The. *Unknown.* FaBoUs

Age of Bronze, The, *sels.* Byron.
"Alas, the country! how shall tongue or pen." OBSV

Age of Bronze awoke now in brutality, The. John Heath-Stubbs. *Fr.* Artorius. EBEV

Age of Gold. Pietro Metastasio, *tr. fr. Italian by* Ezra Pound. CTC

Age of Innocence, The. Steve Ellis. PWE

Age of Innocence. Graham Hough. PoRA

Age of Reason, The. *mod. by* Donald Attwater. William Langland. *Fr.* Vision of Piers Plowman, The. NOCV

Age of Reason, The. Michael van Walleghen. NAmP90

Age of Sheen, The. Dorothy Hughes. NYBP

Age, The/ requires this task. A Different Image. Dudley Randall. BPo; FF; TAP

Aged, Aged Man, The. "Lewis Carroll." *See* I'll tell thee everything I can.

Aged, bittersweet, in salt crusted, the pink meat. Smithfield Ham. Dave Jeddie Smith. HCAP

Aged catch their breath, The. W. H. Auden. *Fr.* Sea and the Mirror, The. LiTA

Aged Fisherman. Witter Bynner. GoYe

Aged Lover Discourses in the Flat Style, The. J. V. Cunningham. NoAM; SM

Aged Lover Renounceth Love, The. Thomas, Lord Vaux. EiL; EnRePo; NoSic; OAEL-1; PoEL-1; SCGP

Aged man, that mowes [*or* mows] these fields. A Dialogue betwixt Time and a Pilgrim [*or* Pilgrim]. Aurelian Townshend. NOBE; OAEL-1; PoEL-2; SeCP

Aged Pilot Man, The. "Mark Twain." OBAL

Aged Sophocles, the light of life has dimmed. Sophocles. *Unknown, tr. fr. Greek by* Lee T. Pearcy. GrAn

Aged Stranger, The. Bret Harte. AnAmPo

Aged twenty-six. Birthdays. C. J. Driver. PeSA

Aged Wino's Counsel to a Young Man on the Brink of Marriage, The. X. J. Kennedy. FF

Ageing Hunter, The. Avane, *tr. fr. Eskimo.* WTO

Agelaus was kind to Acestorides. Nicarchus of Alexandria, *tr. fr. Greek by* Peter Porter. GrAn

Agent of Love. A. K. Redwing. VoR

Ages of Man, The. *At. to* Abraham ibn Ezra Abraham Ibn Ezra, *tr. fr. Hebrew by* Nina Davis Salaman. TrJP

Aghadoe. John Todhunter. PeIV

Agincourt. Michael Drayton. *See* Fair [*or* Faire] stood the wind for France.

Agincourt Carol, The. *Unknown.* EBEV; OAEL-1; OBET

Aging. Randall Jarrell. PoA

Aging. Erica Jong. CrSp

Aging Actress Sees Herself a Starlet on the Late Show, The. Miller Williams. MT

Aging old queers are no treat. *Unknown.* PeHV

Aging Poet, on a Reading Trip to Dayton, Visits the Air Force Museum and Discovers There a Plane He Once Flew, The. Richard Snyder. Poetsp

Agitation of the air, An. End of Summer. Stanley Kunitz. CAPP; MoAmPo; Poetsp; VGW

Agitato ma Non Troppo. John Crowe Ransom. OxBA

Aglaura, *sels.* Sir John Suckling.
"No, no, fair heretic[k], it needs must be." BeJo; CaPo; PrIm
Why So Pale and Wan, Fond Lover? AWP; BeJo; ClHu; ELP; FaBV; HAP; HoPM; NOBE; OBEV; OtMeF; PoE; PoRA; TEP; TrGrPo; UnPo
(Encouragements to a Lover.) GTBS; GTBS-P
(Song: "Why so pale and wan, fond lover?") BoLoP; CaPo; ClHu; EBEvV; EnLoPo; HeIP; InPS; JCP; NAEL-1; NBLV; NIP; NOSC; OPOP; OxAEP-1; PlP; PoEL-3; PrIm; SeCP; SeCV-1; TFi

Aglow in Nowhere. James Richard Broughton. NGP

Agnes De Castro, *sels.* Catherine Trotter.
"Ah! She who told me of my Husband's Heart." KTR

Agni full of moisture, come and flood me with splendour. (*LL*) Waters, you are the ones who bring us the life force. *Unknown.* EaPr

Agnosco Veteris Vestigia Flammae. J. V. Cunningham. VGW

Agnosto Theo (To an Unknown God). Thomas Hardy. WGRP

Ago. Elizabeth Jennings. GOYP

Agog, in rain house-deep. Apologia. Jean Garrigue. LiTA

Agon. Branko Miljkovic, *tr. fr. Serbo-Croatian by* Charles Simic. HSix

Agonies confirm His hour. Bahá'u'lláh in the Garden of Ridwan. Robert Hayden. PoBA

Agonizing Memory, The. Pierre Louÿs, *tr. fr. French. Fr.* Chansons de Bilitis. PeHV

Agony. Giuseppe Ungaretti, *tr. fr. Italian by* Charles Tomlinson. PeFWW

Agony, An. As Now. Amiri Baraka. AmPP; BPo; LiTM; NAAL-2; PoE; PPP

Agony in the Garden, The. Felicia Dorothea Hemans. TrCP

Agony [*or* Agonie], The. George Herbert. ESCV; GeHe

Agosu if you go tell them. Kofi Awoonor. HBAPE

Agreeable Monsters. Amy Clampitt. AnAn

Agreed that all these birds. All These Birds. Richard Wilbur. NOBA; Prf

Agreement swerves. Lyn Hejinian. UL

Agricultural Show, Flemington, Victoria, The. Suzanne Gardinier. CBAP

Agriculture, *sels.* Robert Dodsley.
Method of Preserving Hay from Being Mow-Burnt, or Taking Fire, A. FaBoUs
Rustic Courtship. ECEV

Aguinaldo. Bertrand Shadwell. PAH

Ah, all the sands of the earth lead unto heaven. Persian Miniature. William Jay Smith. CoAP

Ah, Are You Digging on My Grave? Thomas Hardy. DL; MoAB; MoBrPo; NAEL-2; OBD; TEP

Ah bar arkh. Fox's Song. Barbara Angell. ImGa

Ah, Ben!/ Say how, or when. An Ode for Ben Jonson. Robert Herrick. AWP; BeJo; EPCY; InvP; OBF; SCGP; SeCP; TrGrPo
(Ode for Him, An.) CaPo; NoP; NOSC; SeCV-1

Ah blackbird, giving thanks. *Unknown.* NOIV

Ah blessed plant! ah lucky creeper! Entwined. *Malay Oral Tradition, tr. by* R. J. Wilkinson *and* R. O. Winstedt. WTO

Ah blow! thou art the last, the last! Broken Heart. H. Cordelia Ray. CBWP-3

Ah Bounce! ah gentle Beast! why wouldst thou dye. Pope. OBF
(Lines on Bounce.) FM

Ah, breathe on it softly — it dies in an hour. (*LL*) 'Twas in heaven pronounced, and 'twas muttered in hell. Catherine Fanshawe. ChTr

Ah, broken is the golden bowl! the spirit flown forever! Lenore. Poe. AmPP; AnAmPo; LiTA

Ah! but the third one, ah! but the third. The Judgment of Paris. *Unknown. Fr.* Goddesses Three. OtMeF

Ah! changed and cold, how changed and very cold! Dead before Death. Christina Rossetti. NAEL-2; NALW

Ah child, no Persian — perfect art. Horace. *See* Boy, I have their empty shouts.

Ah! Chloe, when, my charming fair? (*LL*) Epigram on the First of April. John Winstanley. NOEC

Ah, Christ. Allen Tate. *Fr.* Sonnets at Christmas. HAP; LiTA; LiTM; NOBA; OxBA; PoNe; Son; VGW

Ah Cloris! That I Now Could Sit. Sir Charles Sedley. *Fr.* Mulberry Garden, The. SeCV-2

Ah, comic officer and gentleman. Elegy: E. W. L. E. Sissman. NYBP

Ah! County Guy, the hour is nigh. Serenade. Sir Walter Scott. *Fr.* Quentin Durward. GTBS; GTBS-P
(County Guy.) PFP
(Song: "Ah! County Guy, the hour is nigh.") CH

Ah, cruel maid, because I see. The Cruel Maid. Robert Herrick. CaPo

Ah! curst Ambition, to thy lures we owe. Thomas Tickell. *Fr.* On the Prospect of Peace. ECEV

Ah Dalmatia, if only I could send word of your dear sons. Ante Kosovic, *tr. fr. Maori by* Amelia Batistich *and* Ian Wedde. PeNZ

Ah Dangerous Swain, tell me no more. Delariviere Manley. *Fr.* Lost Lover, The. KTR

Ah Dearest, let us haste us. Martin Opitz, *tr. fr. German by* F. Warnke. GePo

Ah dearest limbs, my life's best joy and stay. Robert Sidney. NoSic

Ah dextrous Chirurgeons, mitigate your plan. On Having Piles. Sir Walter Scott. FaBoEE

Ah, did you once see Shelley plain. Memorabilia. Robert Browning. FHYEP; NAEL-2; NOBVV; NoP; OAEL-2; OBNC; PoE; RB

Ah, Douglass, we have fall'n on evil days. Douglass. Paul Laurence Dunbar. AAP; Son

Ah, dry those tears; they flow too fast. To Miss ———— on the Death of Her Goldfish. Mr. Meredyth. FM

Ah, Fading Joy. Dryden. *Fr.* Indian Emperor, The. ChTr

Ah! fair and lovely bloom the flowers of youth. Youth and Age. Mimnermus, *tr. fr. Greek by* John Addington Symonds. AWP

Ah! fair face gone from sight. Lionel Johnson. *Fr.* In Memory. OBNC; PoEL-5

Ah, fair Zenocrate, divine Zenocrate. Christopher Marlowe. *Fr.* Tamburlaine the Great. EBEV; PoEL-2
(Fair Is Too Foul an Epithet.) LiTB

Ah false Amyntas, can that hour. Aphra Behn. *Fr.* Dutch Lover, The. WPE

Ah, Fate! cannot a man. Fame. Emerson. AnAmPo

Ah, Faustus,/ Now hast thou but one bare hour [*or* hower] to live. Christopher Marlowe. *Fr.* Doctor Faustus. FaBoVe; HeIP; NAEL-1; OAEL-1; PeECV
(End of Doctor Faustus, The.) PoEL-2
(End of Faustus, The.) TrGrPo

Ah, Feare! abortive impe of drouping mind. Fear. Robert Southwell. *Fr.* Saint Peter's Complaint. CBCK

Ah, flow on, flow on. Sail Peacefully Home. Simeon Grigoryevich Frug, *tr. fr. Yiddish.* TrJP

Ah for the throes of a heart sorely wounded! The Damsel. Omar b. Abi Rabi'a, *tr. fr. Arabic by* W. G. Palgrave. AWP

Ah, friend! 'tis true — this truth you lovers know. To Mr. Gay, Who Wrote Him a Congratulatory Letter on the Finishing His House. Pope. NOEC

Ah, friend you have changed; neckless. Friend, Ah You Have Changed! Frank Mkalawile Chipasula. HBAPE

Ah! gentle, fleeting, wav'ring sprite. Emperor Hadrian, *tr. fr. Latin by* Byron. *Fr.* Hadrian's Address to His Soul When Dying. OBD; OBVE

Ah gentle shepherd, thine the lot to tend. John Dyer. *Fr.* Fleece, The. PoEL-3

Ah! Grandmother weaves! Grandmother Sleeps. Liz Sohappy Bahe. CDW

Ah, Guillaume, my friend, and greatest of predecessors, if. To Guillaume Apollinaire. Jim Brodey. UL

Ah! Hannah, why shouldst thou despair. Hope. Christopher Smart. ChIV-1

Ah hapless sex! who bear no charms. To Alexis in Answer to his Poem against Fruition. Aphra Behn. KTR
(To Alexis in Answer to his Poem against Fruition: Ode.) NOSC

Ah, happy who have seen Him, whom the world. Francis William Bourdillon. *Fr.* Lost God, A. WGRP

Ah, happy youths, ah, happy maid. On a Picture by Poussin Representing Shepherds in Arcadia. John Addington Symonds. FaBoBe

Ah hate to see de ev'nin' sun go down. St. Louis Blues. William Christopher Handy. FF

Ah! he is fled! The British [*or* Brittish] Church. Henry Vaughan. ESCV; PeECV

Ah heart, heart, look! I throw myself at your feet. (*LL*) Stormy Night. W. R. Rodgers. PNI

Ah heaven! — what truth to him. (*LL*) The College Colonel. Herman Melville. OBWP

Ah, how poets sing and die! Dunbar. Anne Spencer. CDC

Ah, How Sweet It Is to Love! Dryden. *Fr.* Tyrannic Love. HoPM

Ah! Hoyland, empress of my heart. Ode to Miss Hoyland. Thomas Chatterton. BXAP

Ah! I alone know what makes me suffer! (*LL*) That Old Mulemba. Geraldo Bessa Victor. PeSAV

Ah! I could curse them in my woe. Revenge. Mary E. Tucker. AmWP; CBWP-1

Ah, I know what happiness is! Blanche Taylor Dickinson. CDC

Ah! I remember well (and how can I). Early Love. Samuel Daniel. *Fr.* Hymen's Triumph. ErPo

Ah, if I could, I'd dwell with you tonight. A Message. George Ives. PeHV

Ah! if yee aske (my friendes) why this salt shower. Translation of the Death of a Sparrow, out of Passerat. William Drummond of Hawthornden. ScCV

Ah, in the past, towards rare individuals. Desire. D. H. Lawrence. CBLP

Ah in the thunder air. Trees in the Garden. D. H. Lawrence. CMoP; MoAB; MoBrPo; NoP

Ah, indeed, the sweet man is fond of me. (*LL*) A Sweet Thing Is Marriage. Christine de Pisan. VBLP

Ah, is there no, no place on earth. Weariness. Mary E. Tucker. CBWP-1

Ah, it is so! Women's Rondo. *Unknown, tr. fr. Aborigine.* NOBAu

Ah — it's the skeleton of a lady's sunshade. The Sunshade. Thomas Hardy. OxBTC

Ah, Jesu Kri. María Sabina, *tr. fr. Mazatec Indian by* Henry Munn. *Fr.* Chants, The. STP

Ah, Lenin, you were richt. But I'm a poet. Second Hymn to Lenin. "Hugh MacDiarmid." OAEL-2

Ah, let me look, let me watch, let me wait, unhurried, unprompted! Claude to Eustace ("Ah, Let Me Look"). Arthur Hugh Clough. *Fr.* Amours de Voyage. EnVR; NOBVV

Ah, let your arms about me in the bed. The Frozen Boy. Brian W. Aldiss. OxBM

Ah! light lovely lady with delicate lips aglow. At Mass. *Unknown, tr. fr. Irish by* Robin Flower. BIrV

Ah! little fly, alighting fitfully. Calvus to a Fly. Charles Tennyson Turner. FM; NOBVV

Ah, little road, all whirry in the breeze. The Road. Helene Johnson. BlSi; CDC; PoNe; ShDr

Ah, London! London! our delight. A Ballad of London. Richard Le Gallienne. FaBoPP

Ah, look at all the lonely people! Eleanor Rigby. John Lennon *and* Paul McCartney. PrIm; WTO

Ah, look,/ How sucking their last sweetness from the air. The Divers. Peter Quennell. MoBrPo

Ah Love! could you and I with Him conspire. Omar Khayyám, *tr. fr. Persian by* Edward Fitzgerald. *Fr.* Rubáiyát of Omar Khayyám of Naishápúr, The. AWP; EBVV, *abr.;* FaBoBe; FaBoRV, *abr.;* FaPoR, *abr.;* GGP; HAP, *abr.;* LiTB; NAEL-2; NoP; PoEL-5; PrIm, *abr.;* TrGrPo

Ah! Love, my Master, hear me swear. Of His Death. Meleager, *tr. fr. Greek by* Andrew Lang. AWP

Ah! Lovely Appearance of Death! Charles Wesley. AH

Ah, Lucasta, why so bright. To Lucasta. Richard Lovelace. CaPo

Ah, madness seizes me! (*LL*) Blessed Be the Happy Mother. Paul Johann Ludwig Heyse. RiWo

Ah! Matt.: old age has brought to me. Senex to Matt. Prior. James Kenneth Stephen. *Fr.* Two Epigrams. FiBHP

Ah me! conceiv'd in sin, and born in sorrow. Childhood. Anne Bradstreet. *Fr.* Four Ages of Man, The. KTR

Ah me! How differently th'untutor'd slave. John Singleton. *Fr.* General Description of the West Indian Islands, A. PBCV

Ah me! I cannot sleep at night. Foiled Sleep. "Marie Madelaine," *tr. fr. German by* Ferdinand E. Kappey. PeHV

Ah me, if I grew sweet to man. The Tragic Mary Queen of Scots. "Michael Field." EnLoPo; OBMV

Ah me, my friend! it will not, will not last! William Shenstone. NOEC

Ah me, the aspidistra grows dusty behind the window pane. In North Great George's Street. "Seumas O'Sullivan." BIrV

Ah me! those old familiar bounds! Ode on a Distant Prospect of Clapham Academy. Thomas Hood. BXAP

Ah me! while up the long, long vale of time. The Destruction of the Pequods. Timothy Dwight. *Fr.* Greenfield Hill. EAP

Ah, Melissa, where's your famous golden beauty. Rufinus Domesticus, *tr. fr. Greek by* Sam Hamill. InMo

Ah! might I in some humble Kentish dale. Lines Written at Cambridge, to W. R., Esquire. Phineas Fletcher. *Fr.* To My Ever-honoured Cousin W. R. Esquire. EiL

Ah, more than any priest, O soul, we too believe in God. Walt Whitman. *Fr.* Passage to India. AmPP; PoEL-5; WGRP

Ah my Anthea! must my heart still break? To Anthea. Robert Herrick. CaPo

Ah my daughter, my grandchild! All You Others, Eat. Djurberaui, *tr. fr. Aborigine by* Catherine H. Berndt. NOBAu; WTO

Ah my dear angry [*or* deare angrie] Lord. Bitter-sweet. George Herbert. FHYEP; GeHe; NOBE; NoP; OxBSP; TrPWD

Ah, my dear friend and brother. Keats. *Fr.* Epistle to George Keats. FHYEP

Ah my deare God! though I am clean forgot, Let me not love thee, if I love thee not. (*LL*) Affliction. George Herbert. ESCV; FHYEP; GeHe; JCP; LiTB; MeLP; NAEL-1; NOBE; NoP; NOSC; SeCP

Ah! my heart, ah! what aileth thee? (*LL*) Ah! my heart, ah! what aileth thee. Sir Thomas Wyatt. SiPSBD

Ah! my heart, ah! what aileth thee. Sir Thomas Wyatt. SiPSBD
(To His Heart.) SiPS

Ah my Perilla! do'st thou grieve to see. To Perilla. Robert Herrick. CaPo; SCGP; SeCP; SeCV-1

Ah my Perilla! dost thou grieve to see. To Perilla. Robert Herrick. BeJo; NOSC

Ah, my race. My Race. Helene Johnson. ShDr

Ah, necromancy sweet! Emily Dickinson. NOBA

Ah no, ah no, they weren't all gross and slow. Michael Foley. *Fr.* True Life Love Stories. PNI

Ah, no more! Thou break'st my heart. (*LL*) A Dialogue. George Herbert. GeHe; OBEV; SeCV-1

Ah no; nor I myselfe: though my pure love. Richard Barnfield. *Fr.* Sonnets. PeHV

Ah no! not these! Parentage. Alice Meynell. NALW

Ah! no!/ You are not a soldierly upright row! Upon a Row of Old Books and Shoes in a Pawnbroker's Window. Suzanne Gardinier. CBAP

Ah, nobody knows. Frost. Stella Benson. OxBTC

Ah, not to be cut off. Rainer Maria Rilke, *tr. fr. German by* Stephen Mitchell. EnlH

Ah nuts! It's boring reading French newspapers. Les Luths. Frank O'Hara. NoAM; NOBA; PoBeRe

Ah! on Thanksgiving Day, when from East and from West. The Pumpkin. Whittier. ImGa

Ah, pity love where'er it grows! The Old Man's Complaint. *Unknown.* OxBSP

Ah! poor intoxicated little knave. To a Fly, Taken out of a Bowl of Punch. "Peter Pindar." NOEC

Ah poor Olinda never boast. Elizabeth Taylor. KTR

Ah Posthumus! our years [*or* yeares] hence fly [*or* flye]. His Age, Dedicated to His Peculiar Friend, Master John Wickes, under the Name of Posthumus. Robert Herrick. CaPo; SeCP

Ah Poverties, Wincings, and Sulky Retreats. Walt Whitman. OxBSP

Ah Power that swirls us together. Gary Snyder. EaPr

Ah, ra, chickera. *Unknown.* OxNR

Ah, Raleigh, when thy breath thou didst resign. Britannia and Raleigh. John Ayloffe. APAS

Ah, Robin,/ Jolly Robin. Sir Thomas Wyatt. SiPS; SiPSBD

Ah! sad wer we as we did peace. The Turnstile. William Barnes. CH; NOBVV

Ah, see the fair chivalry come, the companions of Christ! Te Martyrum Candidatus. Lionel Johnson. OBMV; TIRV

Aimless. Louis Palagyi, *tr. fr. Hungarian by* Watson Kirkconnell. TrJP

Ain' Go'n' to Study War No Mo'. *Unknown.* AS

Ain't been on Market Street for nothing. Ballad of the Hoppy-Toad. Margaret Walker. BlSi; HoPM; NBV

Ain't Gonna Rain. *Unknown.* AS

Ain't I a Woman? Sojourner Truth. AIW; BlSi

Ain't It [*or* It's] Fine Today. Douglas Malloch. BLPA; WBLP

Ain't Nature Commonplace! Arthur Guiterman. FiBHP

Ain't No Grave Can Hold My Body Down. *Unknown.* AmFP

Air. Amiri Baraka. SOTW

Air. Philip Dow. BXAP

Air. John Gay. *Fr.* Polly; an Opera. NOEC

Air. W. S. Merwin. CAPP; NaP

Air. Kathleen Raine. MoAB; MoBrPo

Air. Cyn Zarco. BCF

Air a-gittin' cool an' coolah. Signs of the Times. Paul Laurence Dunbar. AnAmPo

Air: "Arise, arise, arise!" Henry Brooke. *Fr.* Jack the Giant Queller; an Antique History. NOEC

Air: "Cat bird singing." Robert Creeley. Prf

Air: "Flaxen-headed cow-boy, as simple as may be, A." John O'Keefe. NOEC

Air: "For often my mammy has told." Henry Brooke. *Fr.* Jack the Giant Queller; an Antique History. NOEC

Air: "Fox may steal your hens, sir, A." John Gay. *Fr.* Beggar's Opera, The. NOEC; OAEL-1
(Lawyer, The.) IHNG
(Soldier and a Sailor, A.) TEP

Air: "I ne'er could any lustre see." Sheridan. *Fr.* Duenna, The. NOEC

Air: "Love of a woman, The." Robert Creeley. VCAP; VGW

Air: "O ruddier than the cherry!" John Gay. *Fr.* Acis and Galatea. CBLP; EBEvV; ELP; NAEL-1; NOEC
(Song: "O ruddier than the cherry.") NOBE

Air: "Since laws were made for ev'ry degree." John Gay. *Fr.* Beggar's Opera, The. NOEC; OAEL-1

Air: "Since laws were made for ev'ry degree." John Gay. *Fr.* Beggar's Opera, The. NOEC; OAEL-1

Air: "So full of courtly reverence." Dudley North. OxBSP

Air: "What a charming thing's a battle!" Isaac Bickerstaffe. *Fr.* Recruiting Serjeant, The. NOEC

Air arcs overhead. Archangel. Kit Robinson. UL

Air as the fuel of owls. Snow. Iowa. Michael Dennis Browne. NYBP

Air Balloon, The. Henry James Pye. *Fr.* Aerophorion. NOEC

Air Base at Châteauroux, France, The. Sherod Santos. NAmP90

Air-borne ants attacked softer parts of the cyclist, measuring. Race on Gathering Bites. Kojo Laing. HBAPE

Air Circus. Carl Sandburg. AnAmPo

Air commented in a whisper, The. (*LL*) Gallantry. Keith Douglas. NAEL-2; NoAM; OBWP

Air, earth and water meet at the sea's edge. A Naked Girl Swimming. A. R. D. Fairburn. PeNZ

Air in Newfound-land [*or* Aire in Newfoundland-land] is wholesome, good, The. The Pleasant Life in Newfoundland. Robert Hayman. NOBC
(Four Elements in Newfound-land, The.) OBTV

Air Is. John Michael Brennan. MAT

Air is a mill of hooks, The. Mystic. Sylvia Plath. NYBP

Air is a smoke-tree, the wind, The. Reviewing Past Lives while Leaf-Burning. Anita Endrezze-Danielson. HATNAP

Air is empty where our speech has been, The. (*LL*) The Mistress to Her Lover. Jan Montefiore. VBLP

Air is gravid with life, The. White Balloon. Maureen Seaton. PFL

Air is high and blue yet, as we drive, The. Coming Home from Abroad. David Holbrook. OBTV

Air is like a butterfly, The. Easter. Joyce Kilmer. PDV

Air is quiet, The. The Coming of Teddy Bears. Dennis Lee. TLR

Air is thick with nerves and smoke, The. University Examinations in Egypt. D. J. Enright. OxBTC; TwCP

Air New Zealand. C. K. Stead. *Fr.* Clodian Songbook. PeNZ

Air of June Sings, The. Edward Dorn. NeAP; PoM

Air of the museum, The. The Frozen Hero. Thomas H. Vance. NYBP

Air Plant, The. Hart Crane. MoAB; MoAmPo; NoP

Air Raid. Peter Wild. Poetsp

Air: Sentir avec Ardeur. Marie-Françoise-Catherine de, Marquise de Boufflers Beauveau, *tr. fr. French by* Ezra Pound. CTC; WPOW

Air stiffens to a crust, the. The Wound. Louise Glück. NoAM

Air that holds the world that was my world. (*LL*) Easter Morning. A. R. Ammons. HCAP; NAAL-2; NoAM; NoP

Air, the dream-inspiring air, The. An Idyl of Spring. H. Cordelia Ray. CBWP-3

Air Travel in Arabia. Sir Charles Johnston. OBTV

Air View of an Industrial Scene. Andrew Hudgins. ArOW

Air was soft, the ground still cold, The. April 5, 1974. Richard Wilbur. HCAP

Air where their ashes have gone, The. For Our Dead. Marilynn Talal. BTR

Air, which is not anything. Elements. Carolyn Wilson Link. GoYe

Air which thy smooth voice doth break, The. Speaking and Kissing. Thomas Stanley. BeJo

Airborne dragonfly, An. Hunter's Moon. Stephen Sandy. NYBP

Air[e] and Angels. John Donne. CBLP; EnRePo; ESCV; JCP; MeLP; NAEL-1; OAELL-1; Prf; SeCP; SeCV-1

Airedale, erect beside the chauffeur of a Rolls-Royce, An. Fashions in Dogs. E. B. White. FiBHP

Airing Cupboard. Robert Walton. AngWe

Airing Linen. Henry Taylor. GoJo

Airline Breakfast, An. William Matthews. AnAn

Airliner. Francis Webb. CBAP; NOBAu

Airly Beacon. Charles Kingsley. EBVV; OBEV

Airman. Stephen Spender. *See* He will watch the hawk with an indifferent eye.

Airman's Breastplate, The. Oliver St. John Gogarty. TIRV

Airman's Virtue. William Meredith. ArOW

Airplane, The ("An airplane has gigantic wings"). Rowena Bastin Bennett. FaPON

Airport. Martin Johnston. CBAP

Airport coffee tastes less of America, The. The Gulf. Derek Walcott. NoP

Air's advice is all, The. Prelude to Commencement. Marie De L. Welch. NYBP

Airs and Distance. Tim Longville. VaA

Airs and Graces. Peter Fallon. PBCIP

Airs from the sea blown back. Ovid on the Dacian Coast. Dunstan Thompson. NYBP

Airs of Pei, sels. Confucius, *tr. fr. Chinese by* Ezra Pound.
Efficient Wife's Complaint, The. CTC

Airs! that wander and murmur round. The Siesta. *Unknown, tr. fr. Spanish by* Bryant. AWP

Airstrip in Essex, 1960, An. Donald Hall. LCAP; LiTM; PAW

Airy Christ, The. Stevie Smith. ChIV-2; NOCV

Airy spirits, you who love. Inscription in a Beautiful Retreat Called Fairy Bower. Hannah More. ECWP

Aishah Schechinah. Robert Stephen Hawker. OBNC

Aisle of a Temple, The. Congreve. OxAEP-1

Aisling. Paul Muldoon. PNI

Aitana, my child, springtime bows. For Aitana. Rafael Alberti, *tr. fr. Spanish by* Perry Higman. ArLo

Ajanta. Muriel Rukeyser. LiTA; LiTM; MoAB; MoAmPo; NNaP

Ajax, sels. Sophocles, *tr. fr. Greek by* Winthrop Mackworth Praed.
"Fair Salamis, the billow's roar." AWP

Ajax, sels. Sophocles.
"Happiest life consists in ignorance, The." IMW

Ajax' Conclusion. Frank Barbour Coffin. AAP

Ajax Samples, The. Laura Jensen. LCAP

Ajax the swift swerv'd never from the side. Homer, *tr. by* William Cowper. *Fr.* Iliad, The. OBVE

Akat'ani/ x'aax'. Tlingit Concrete Poem. Nora Dauenhauer. NIP

Akosua selling palm wine. The Palm Wine Seller. Gladys May Casely Hayford. ShDr

Al Aaraff, sels. Poe.
Song from "Al Aaraaf." AmPP; AnAmPo; OxBA
Sonnet — Science. AmPP; MeMAP; NAAL-1; NoP; OxBA; TAP
Sonnet — To Science. PFP
"Young flowers were whispering in melody." NOBA

Al kynde of man thee holden is to blesse! (*LL*) Balade and Roundel to Master Somer. Thomas Hoccleve. OxBLMV

Al were he mitre, crowne, or diademe. (*LL*) Firste stok, fader of gentilesse, The. Chaucer. MiEL

Ala. Grace Nichols. AIW

Ala, mala, mink, monk. *Unknown.* OxNR

Alabama, The. Maurice Bell. PAH

Alabama. Julia Fields. PoBA; PoNe

Alabama Bus. Will Hairston. FaBoPV

Alabama Centennial. Naomi Long Madgett. BPo

Alack! 'tis melancholy theme to think. The Irish Schoolmaster. Thomas Hood. BXAP

Alack, why am I sent for to a king. Shakespeare. *Fr.* King Richard II. FaBoEH

Alajire, we ask you to be patient. *Yoruba Oral Tradition, tr. by* Ulli Beier. WTO

Alamance. Seymour W. Whiting. PAH

Alaric/ At Danzig/ Saw Pegasus. Three Amphigouris. Jean-Joseph Vade, *tr. fr. French.* CBNP

Alarm, The. Hildebrand Jacob. NOEC

Alarm and time clock still intrude too early. And on This Shore. M. Carl Holman. PoBA; PoNe

Alarmed Skipper, The. James Thomas Fields. AnAmPo; NBLV

Alarming New Development, An. Ron Schreiber. GLP

Alarum. Urszula Koziol, *tr. fr. Polish by* Czeslaw Milosz. WPOW

Alarum, The. Sylvia Townsend Warner. MoBrPo

Alas! Sadi, *tr. by* L. Cranmer-Byng. Fr. Gulistan, The. AWP

Alas, Alack! Walter de la Mare. FaPON; OxBChV

Alas! alas! the while. *Unknown.* MiEL
　(Night with a Holy-Water Clerk, A.) MeEL

Alas! alas! thou turn'st in vain. Claim to Love. Giovanni Battista Guarini, *tr. fr. Italian by* Thomas Stanley. AWP

Alas, alas, well evil I sped! Undo! *Unknown.* NOCV

Alas, all my years, where have they disappeared? Walther von der Vogelweide, *tr. fr. German by* Frederick Goldin. GePo

Alas! and am I born for this. On Liberty and Slavery. George Moses Horton. AAP; PoNe

Alas! and not play too? *(LL)* Alciphron and Leucippe. Walter Savage Landor. OBEV

Alas! behold! how steep! how high! The Road to Shu Is Hard. Li Po, *tr. fr. Chinese by* Irving Y. Lo. SuSp

Alas! Carolina! J. Gordon Coogler. OBAL

Alas, dear Clio, every day. To Clio, from Rome. John Dyer. NOEC

Alas, dear heart! what hope had I. Love Me Again. *Unknown.* EiL

Alas, dear Mother, fairest queen and best. Dialogue Between Old England and New, A; Concerning Their Present Troubles, Anno, 1642. Anne Bradstreet. EAP

Alas, Death. Charles, Duc d'Orléans. OxBLMV

Alas! deceite that in truste is nowe. Trust Only Yourself. *Unknown.* MeEL

Alas, departing is ground of wo! *Unknown.* MiEL

Alas, eheu, one question that sorely vexes. Ezra Pound. *Fr.* L'Homme Moyen Sensuel. OBSV

Alas, England, my own generous mother. General Bloodstock's Lament for England. Robert Graves. IHNG

Alas! England now mourns for her poet that's gone. William McGonagall. *Fr.* Death and Burial of Lord Tennyson. OBD

Alas! for all the pretty women who marry dull men. Meditation at Kew. Anna Wickham. FaBoTw; MoBrPo; NALW

Alas for me, who loved a falcon well! A Lady Laments for Her Lost Lover, by Similitude of a Falcon. *Unknown, tr. fr. Italian by* Dante Gabriel Rossetti. AWP

Alas, for Peter not a helping hand. Peter Grimes at Aldeburgh. George Crabbe. *Fr.* Borough, The. EBNV; ECEV; EnRP; FaBoPP; FHYEP; OBNV; PoEL-4; TEP

Alas! for the South. J. Gordon Coogler. OBAL

Alas for the voyage, O High King of Heaven. Farewell to Ireland. *At. to* St. Columcille Saint Columcille, *tr. by* Douglas Hyde. AWP

Alas! for them, their day is o'er. Indians. Charles Sprague. GN

Alas for this unhappy night! A Song of Instruction. Te Kooti Rikirangi, *tr. fr. Maori by* Margaret Orbell. PeNZ

Alas, for us, who need beware. On Worldly Prelates. Charles Wesley. ChIV-2

Alas for Youth. Firdausi, *tr. fr. Persian by* R. A. Nicholson. AWP

Alas, good friend, what profit can you see. Lines to a Reviewer. Shelley. OxBSP

Alas, have I not pain enough, my friend. Sir Philip Sidney. *Fr.* Astrophel and Stella. AAS; ESo, *(sl. abr.);* GGP; HeIL, *(Sonnets, I–CVIII and 11 Songs);* NoP; NoSic; OAEL-1; Poetr; SCGP, *(Sonnets, I–CVIII and 11 Songs);* SiPS, *(Sonnets, I–CVIII and 11 Songs);* SiPSBD, *(Sonnets, I–CVIII and 11 Songs)*

Alas, his mind is sunk. Boethius, *tr. fr. Latin. Fr.* Consolation of Philosophy, The. MLL, *tr. by* Helen Waddell
　("Heu Quam Praecipih Mersa Profundo.") MLL, *tr. by* Helen Waddell

Alas, how easily things go wrong! Sweet Peril. George Macdonald. BLPA; FaBoBe

Alas! how full of fear. The Fate of the Prophets. Longfellow. *Fr.* Christus; a Mystery. WGRP

Alas How Long ("Alas how long shall I and my maidenhead lie.") *Unknown.* ErPo

Alas! How should I sing? *Unknown.* NOIV

Alas, how soon the hours are over. Plays. Walter Savage Landor. EnRP; NBLV; NoP; OxBoLi; OxBSP; PeLV

Alas! I am seized by the shark, great shark! Love Is a Shark. *Unknown, tr. fr. Hawaiian by* N. B. Emerson. WTO

Alas/ I believe. Three Laments. Diane Di Prima. PoBeRe

Alas, I draw breath heavily. An Old Woman's Song. Akjartoq, *tr. fr. Eskimo into Danish by* Knud Rasmussen; *English vers. by* Tom Lowenstein. WPOW

Alas! I have lost my God. Rejected. Lord Alfred Bruce Douglas. OHCV; PeVV

Alas! if I think of her, my throat becomes. Love. Pierre Louÿs, *tr. fr. French. Fr.* Chansons de Bilitis. PeHV

Alas, is wiser far [*or* farre] than I. *(LL)* The Bait[e]. John Donne. CBLP; CoGr; ErPo; HoPM; InPK; InPS; LPA; NAEL-1; NOSC; OAEL-1; PoRA; RB; TEP

Alas, madam [madame], for stealing [stelying] of a kiss [kysse]. Sir Thomas Wyatt. BoLoP; CBLP
　(Epigram: "Alas, Madam, for Stealing of a Kiss.") SiPSBD

Alas, my brothers. Hilda Doolittle ("H. D."). *Fr.* Helen in Egypt. NOBA

Alas, my God, I know not what. *(LL)* The Thanksgiving. George Herbert. ESCV; GeHe

Alas, my God and we should be. Thomas Shepherd. *Fr.* For Communion with God. TrPWD

Alas, my hart will brek in three. Fearful Death. *Unknown.* MeEL

Alas, my heart is black. The New Heart. *Unknown, tr. fr. Chinese.* WGRP

Alas, my heart! mine eye hath wronged thee. Corydon to His Phyllis. Sir Edward Dyer. EiL

Alas! my love, you [*or* ye] do me wrong. Lady Greensleeves. *Unknown.* GBL; PoEL-2
　(Greensleeves.) EBEvV
　(My Lady Greensleeves.) OxAEP-1
　(New Courtly Sonnet of the Lady Greensleeves, A.) NoSic

Alas, my Purse! how can lean and low! Soliloquy on an Empty Purse. Mary Jones. ECWP

Alas! now o'er the civilized world there hangs a gloom. William McGonagall. *Fr.* Hero of Kharthoum, The. FaBoEH

Alas poor Death, where does thy great strength lye? Meditations for July 25, 1666. Philip Pain. EAP

Alas! poor Fanny! wretched girl, alas! Fanny's Removal in 1714. John Winstanley. NOEC

Alas, poor heart, I pity thee. *Unknown, tr. fr. French by* John Addington Symonds. *Fr.* Medieval Norman Song. AWP

Alas, poor man, what hap have I. Sir Thomas Wyatt. SiPS

Alas! Poor Queen. Marion Angus. FaBoEH

Alas, poor Tom! how oft, with merry heart. On the Death of Mr. Thomas Lancashire, Comedian. Robert Fergusson. ScCV

Alas, shall I not see again. Heinrich von Morungen, *tr. fr. German by* Frederick Goldin. GePo

Alas, So All Things Now. Petrarch. *See* Long[e] love that in my thought doth harbour, The.

Alas, so all things now do hold [*or* thinges nowe doe holde] their peace. The Earl of Surrey, *after* Petrarch. SiPSBD
　(Complaint by Night, A.) SCGP
　(Complaint by Night of the Lover Not Beloved, A.) AAS; AWP; EBEV; EiL; OAEL-1; OBVE; SiPS; TEP; NAEL-1; Son

Alas! So All Things Now Do Hold Their Peace. Petrarch, *tr. fr. Italian. Fr.* Sonnets to Laura. NAEL-1; NoP; OAEL-1; OBVE

Alas, so all things now do hold their peace. Petrarch. *See* Long[e] love that in my thought doth harbour, The.

Alas, that ever that speche was spoken. *Unknown.* EnLoPo

Alas, that I ne had English, rhyme or prose. Chaucer. *Fr.* Legend of Good Women: Prologue, The. EPCY

Alas, that I should be. To My Infant Daughter. Yvor Winters. VGW

Alas, that I should die. Song of a Woman Abandoned by the Tribe. *Unknown, tr. fr. Shoshone Indian by* Mary Austin. AIW; WPE

Alas! that such a soul should taste of death. In Memory of Arthur Clement Williams. Eloise Bibb. CBWP-4

Alas, that wisdom, and youth. Walther von der Vogelweide, *tr. fr. German by* Frederick Goldin. GePo

Alas, the country! how shall tongue or pen. Byron. *Fr.* Age of Bronze, The. OBSV

Alas the grief, and deadly woful smart! Sir Thomas Wyatt. SiPS

Alas, the ignorance of unhappy men. Boethius, *tr. fr. Latin. Fr.* Consolation of Philosophy, The. MLL, *tr. by* Helen Waddell

Alas, the moon should ever beam. The Water Lady. Thomas Hood. CH

Alas! the time has come, old dress. Lines to an Old Dress. Mary E. Tucker. CBWP-1

Alas the while! *(LL)* There was never nothing more me pained [*or* payned]. Sir Thomas Wyatt. AAS; GBL; SiPS; SiPSBD

Alas! they had been friends in youth. The Scars Remaining. Samuel Taylor Coleridge. *Fr.* Christabel. CH, ll. 1-65; EnRP; FHYEP; OAEL-2; OBNC

Alice Corbin Is Gone. Carl Sandburg. PoA

Alice, dear, what ails you. A Frosty Night. Robert Graves. CH; MoAB; MoBrPo; MoBS; OxBTC

Alice Fell; or, Poverty. Wordsworth. BeLS; OBNV

Alice grown lazy, mammoth but not fat. Last Days of Alice. Allen Tate. NAAL-2; NOBA; OxBA; UnPo

Alice is gone and I'm alone. W. H. Auden. CBNP

Alice is tall and upright as a pine. Alice. Charles Cotton. *Fr.* Resolution in Four Sonnets, of a Poetical Question Put to Me by a Friend, Concerning Four Rural Sisters. PoEL-3; Prf; Son; TrGrPo (Two Rural Sisters.) BoLoP; EnLoPo

Alice Lee stood awaiting her lover one night. The Lips That Touch Liquor Shall Never Touch Mine. Harriet A. Glazebrook. VPP

Alice of Daphne, 1799. John Ennis. PBCIP

Alice Zeno Talking, and Her Son George Lewis the Jazz Clarinetist in Attendance. William Matthews. Jaz

Alice's Adventures in Wonderland, *sels.* "Lewis Carroll."
Alice's Recitation. FaBoCo; FaBoNo; NOBL; UV
(Lobster, The, *sl. diff. vers.*) OxBChV
('Tis the Voice of the Lobster.) CBNP; PeLV
"Beautiful Soup, so rich and green."
(Song of the Mock Turtle, The.) UV
(Turtle Soup.) FaBoNo
Evidence Read at the Trial of the Knave of Hearts. FaBoNo; GTBS-P; NOBVV; OxBoLi; PeLV
(Alice's Evidence.) PFP
(Silence in Court.) FaBoCo
(Verses from the Trials of the Knave of Hearts.) CBNP
Father William. BXAP; CBNP; FaBoCo; FaBoNo; FaBoPa; FaPON; FiBHP; GGP; GoJo; HoPM; LiTB; NOBL; NOBVV; OxBChV; PDV; PoLF; PoRA; TFi; TrGrPo; UnPo
("You Are Old, Father William.") PeLV; PIP; UV
Fury Said to a Mouse. NoAM; NoP
(Mouse's Tale, The.) CBNP; FaBoNo
"How doth the little crocodile." CBNP; FaBoCh; FaBoCo; FaBoEE; FaBoNo; FaPON; MoShBr; NBLV; NOBL; NOBVV; RB; TFi; TTTS; UV
(Crocodile, The.) HoPM; TrGrPo
"Speak roughly to your little boy." FaBoCh; FaBoCo; NBLV; UV
(Duchess's Lullaby, The.) CBNP; FaBoNo
"Twinkle, twinkle, little bat!" UV
(Mad Hatter's Concert Song, The.) CBNP
(Mad Hatter's Song, The.) FaBoNo; NOBL
"Will you walk a little faster?" said a [*or* the] whiting to a [*or* the] snail. NoAM; OxAEP-2
(Lobster Quadrille, The.) BoTP; FaPON; MoShBr; OxBChV; PFP; UV
(Mock Turtle's Song, The.) CBNP; ChTr; FaBoNo
"You are old," said the youth, "and your jaws are too weak." OxBM

Alice's Evidence. "Lewis Carroll." *See* "They told me you had been to her."

Alice's Recitation. "Lewis Carroll." *Fr.* Alice's Adventures in Wonderland. FaBoCo; FaBoNo; NOBL; UV

Alien. Gillian Allnutt. NBrP

Alien. Donald Jeffrey Hayes. EaPr

Alien. Nancy Paddock. LoHo

Alien. William Price Turner. OxBS

Alike he thwarts the hospitable end. Homer, *tr. fr. Greek by* Pope. *Fr.* Odyssey. NAWM-1; OBF

Alison. *Unknown.* CBLP; MeEL; MiEL; NAEL-1; NoP; OAEL-1; OBEV; PeLV

Alison and Willie. *Unknown.* ESPB

Alison ("In March and April thereabout.") *Unknown.* HAP

Alison [*or* Allison] Gross. *Unknown.* CH; ESPB; FaBoCh; OxBB

Aliter. Confucius, *tr. fr. Chinese by* Ezra Pound. *Fr.* Songs of Ch'en. CTC

Alive. (*LL*) World War II. Jeni Couzyn. PeSAV

Alive Alive O. Padraic Fiacc. PeIV

Alive, in a slippery grave. (*LL*) Weed Puller. Theodore Roethke. AmPP; HCAP; NAAL-2

Alive, ne'er parted be. (*LL*) Sweetest Love, I Do Not Go. John Donne. AWP; BoLoP; EiL; ELP; EnRePo; ESCV; FHYEP; HeIP; InPS; InvP; JCP; MeLP; NOBE; NoP; NoSic; OAEL-1; PoEL-2; SeCP; SeCV-1; TEP; TFi; TrGrPo

Alive or Not. Alfred W. Purdy. NOBC

Alive, the foe thy dreadful vigour fled. Goldsmith. *Fr.* Stanzas on the Taking of Quebec. FaBoEH

Alive, this man was Manes, a common slave. Anyte, *tr. fr. Greek by* Willis Barnstone. BoWoP
(When this man, Manes, lived, he was a slave.) GrAn, *tr. by* Sally Purcell

Alive Together. Lisel Mueller. IHMS

Alkinoos, king and admiration of men. New Coasts and Poseidon's Son. Homer, *tr. by* Robert Fitzgerald. *Fr.* Odyssey. NAWM-1; WTO

All. Bei Dao, *tr. fr. Chinese by* Donald Finkel *with* Chen Xueliang. SpMi

All. Antoni Slonimski, *tr. fr. Polish by* Wanda Dynowska. TrJP

All a green willow, willow, willow. John Heywood. EiL

All a-tremble she awoke. The Annunciation. Amrita Pritam, *tr. fr. Punjabi by* Khushwant Singh *and* Krishna Gorowara. WPOW

All Abdéra mourned at the funeral pyre. Anacreon, *tr. fr. Greek by* Peter Jay. GrAn

All after pleasures as I rid one day. Christmas. George Herbert. GeHe; NOSC; PeECV; SeCV-1; TOF; TrCP

All, All a-Lonely. *Unknown.* ChTr; OxBoLi

All, all are gone, the old familiar faces. (*LL*) The Old Familiar Faces. Charles Lamb. AWP; BLPA; CoGr; EnRP; FaBoBe; FaBoRV; FaPoR; GTBS; GTBS-P; NOBE; OBEV; OBF; OxAEP-2; PlP; RB

All, all of a piece throughout. All, All of a Piece Throughout. Dryden. *Fr.* Secular Masque, The. ChTr; CoGr; ELP; HAP; ImPo; InPS; NAEL-1; PoE; PoEL-3; PrIm; SCGP; SeCV-2
(Chorus to the Gods.) OxBSP
(Song: "All, all of a piece throughout.") WeW

All, All of a Piece Throughout. Dryden. *Fr.* Secular Masque, The. ChTr; CoGr; ELP; HAP; ImPo; InPS; NAEL-1; PoE; PoEL-3; PrIm; SCGP; SeCV-2

All Alone. Mary E. Tucker. CBWP-1

All alone and unknown, at Edinbro' in an inn. (*LL*) Epitaph on Himself. Samuel Taylor Coleridge. FaBoEE

All alone as I am alone. (*LL*) The Travelling Out. Lucile Adler. IHMS; NYBP

All alone from his dark sanctum the lingam fronts, affronts the sea. Mahabalipuram. Louis MacNeice. OBTV

All alone in my little cell. *Unknown.* NOIV

All alone on the hillside. "Grey Horse Troop," The. Robert W. Chambers. PAH

All alone with my shadow. A Letter to Lady T'ao Ch'iu. Ch'iu Chin, *tr. fr. Chinese by* Kenneth Rexroth *and* Ling Chung. WPC

All along the backwater. Ducks' Ditty. Kenneth Grahame. *Fr.* Wind in the Willows, The. BoTP; FaPON; GoJo; MoShBr; NTCP; OTCP; OxBChV; PDV; WHSW

All along the rail. In Texas Grass. Quincy Troupe. PoBA

All along the valley, stream that flashest white. In the Valley of Cauteretz. Tennyson. BoLoP; NAEL-2; NOBE

All Americans are ambiguous. Shorter American Memory of the American Character According to Santayana. Rosemary Waldrop. EOEF

All are architects of fate. The Builders. Longfellow. AnAmPo; PFP; PWR

All are but parts of one stupendous whole. Pope. *Fr.* Essay on Man, An. FHYEP; WGRP

All are not born to soar — and ah! how few. On Imitation. Samuel Taylor Coleridge. OxBSP

All are nothing but flowers. Nakagawa Soen-Roshi. EaPr

All arms combined magnificently together. (*LL*) The Persian Version. Robert Graves. CMoP; FaBoCo; LiTB; LiTM; MoP; NoAM; NOBL; OBWP; WeW

All around I heard the whispering larches. Forest Song. Shane Leslie. TIRV

All around me. (*LL*) Where I sit is holy. *Unknown.* EaPr

All around me may it be delightful. (*LL*) May it be delightful my house. *Unknown.* EaPr

All around old Chattanooga. Freedom at McNealy's. Priscilla Jane Thompson. CBWP-2

All around, shards of a lost tradition. A Lost Tradition. John Montague. CIP; PBCIP

All around the altar, huge lianas. Reading the Bible Backwards. Eleanor Wilner. BAP-90

All around the butter dish. *Unknown.* RoPo

All around the Town, *sels.* Phyllis McGinley.
"B's the Bus." FaPON
"F is the fighting Firetruck." FaPON
"J's the jumping Jay-walker." FaPON

All Around Us. Constance Urdang. PBCAP

All ashes, all ashes again. (*LL*) On Neal's Ashes. Allen Ginsberg. CAPP; PoM

All beaded with dew. Gary Snyder. *Fr.* Myths and Texts. NaP

All because I think of you. Silhouette. Marc Cohen. EOEF

All-Beethoven night at the Concertgebouw. The Amsterdam Poem. Maxine W. Kumin. BTR

All beginnings start right here. The Move Continuing. Al Young. PoBA

All Being Well. W. W. Gibson. OxBTC

All beneath the white-rose tree. The Three Captains. *Unknown, tr. fr. French by* Andrew Lang. AWP

All fixed: early arrival at the flat. Nothing to Fear. Kingsley Amis. ErPo; OxBC

All flesh and bone are thus betrayed. To the Soldiers of El Salvador Who from 1931 to 1980 Have Ruled the Country through a Military Dictatorship. Lillian Jimenéz, *tr.* by Mary McAnally. WoWa

All Flesh Is Grass. Bible, *O.T. Fr.* Isaiah. TrJP

All Flesh Is Grass, *sels.* Brenda G. Macrow.

All flesh waxeth old as a garment. Bible, Apocrypha. *Fr.* Ecclesiasticus. OBVE

All folks, who pretend to religion and grace. The Place of the Damn'd [*or* Damned]. Swift. CBCK; ChIV-2; FaBoEE; OBSV

All Fools' Day. *Unknown.* BoTP

All for Love. Byron. *See* Oh [*or* O], talk not to me of a name great in story.

All for Love, *sels.* Dryden.

All Frenchmen are of *petit-maître kind.* (*LL*) Epistle to the Right Honourable William Pulteney, Esq. John Gay. OBTV

All Friends Together. R. A. Simpson. NOBAu

All gentlemen and yeomen good. Robin Hood and the Shepherd. *Unknown.* ESPB

All glorious, — yet forlorn. (*LL*) Columbus. Lydia Huntley Sigourney. PAH

All glory cannot vanish from the hills. The Passing of the Forest. William Pember Reeves. PeNZ

All gods and goddesses, all looked up to. Meditation on the Nativity. Elizabeth Jennings. NAs

All god's spades got spades. (*LL*) The Truth. Ted Joans. TTY

All God's spades wear dark shades. Its Curtains. Ted Joans. PoBA

All goes onward and outward, nothing collapses. Walt Whitman. *Fr.* Song of Myself. AmPP; IMW; LiTA; MoAmPo, (*abr.*); NOBA; OxBA; SOTW, (*much abr.*)

All gone,/ the silver-green silk of time. Immigrant Daughter's Song. Mary Ann Larkin. IIP

All good things. The Inner Source. Andrei Codrescu. UL

All grave old men, and souldiers they had bene, but for age. Homer, *tr.* by George Chapman. *Fr.* Iliad, The. OBVE

All great events have harbingers. Nicarchus of Alexandria, *tr. fr. Greek by* Peter Porter. GrAn

All great things crush themselves; such end the gods. Lucan, *tr. fr. Latin by* Christopher Marlowe. *Fr.* Pharsalia. NoSic

All Greece hates. Helen. Hilda Doolittle ("H. D."). AnAmPo; BoWoP; FaBoWP; LiTM; LPA; MoAmPo; NAAL-2; NALW; NoAM; NOBA; NoP; TAP

All hail! Holy Mary, our hope and our joy! Irish Reaper's Harvest Hymn. John Keegan. TIRV

All hail, once pleasing, once inspiring shade. Lines Written in Windsor Forest. Pope. EBEV

(Hymn Written in Windsor Forest, A.) NOEC; OxBSP

All Hail the Power of Jesus' Name. Edward Perronet. NOCV

All hail! thou gorgeous sunset. Sunset. Mary Weston Fordham. CBWP-2

All Hail, Thou Noble Guest. Martin Luther, *tr. fr. German by* Arthur Tozer Russell *and* Catherine Winkworth. TrPWD

All hail! Unfurl the Stripes and Stars! God Save Our President. Francis DeHaes Janvier. PAH

All hallelujahs, Oh ye heav'nly quires. A Poem upon the Triumphant Translation of . . . Mrs. Anne Eliot. John Danforth. SCAP

All Hallows, Louise Glück. AmPA; FoLa; HCAP; NU

All has stilled, Magician Sleep having cast his spell. Those Last, Late Hours of Christmas Eve. Lou Ann Welte. PChr

All he owns is. Squirrel near Library. Genevieve Taggard. WPE

All heavy minds. Sir Thomas Wyatt. SiPS

All he'll get is a kick in the arse. (*LL*) Dinky Di. *Unknown.* NOBAu

All Hellas is his monument, though his bones. Euripides. Thucydides, *tr. fr. Greek by* Peter Jay. GrAn

All her Kamikaze friends admired my aunt. A Family Turn. William Stafford. CAPP

All her life's round. (*LL*) Rain on a Grave. Thomas Hardy. OxAEP-2

All hesitant & dim, anchoring, waiting their time. (*LL*) Childhood. Bruce Beasley. UTF

All his beauty, wit and grace. To Joshua. Alice Thomas Ellis. OBD

All his children in the same house. Job the Father. Richard Shelton. PBCAP

All his hopes were hands, his ventures hands. The Hands. Tony Harrison. FaBoTw

All his life, Mr. George Bernard Shaw. Audrey Herbert. PeLi

All holy influences dwell within. The Children Band. Sir Aubrey De Vere. OBEV

All honor to him, who shall win the fight. For Those Who Fail. Joaquin Miller. PoToHe

All honor to that day which long ago. Washington's Birthday. Arthur J. Burdick. OHIP

All honour to the persevering toil. The Press. Thomas Phipson. PeSAV

All houses wherein men have lived and died. Haunted Houses. Longfellow. PWR

All how silent and how still. Noon. John Clare. OxAEP-2

All human kind on earth. Boethius, *tr. fr. Latin by* Queen Elizabeth I. *Fr.* Consolation of Philosophy, The. NoSic

All human race would fain be wits. Swift. *Fr.* On Poetry; a Rhapsody. HAP; OBSV; PoEL-3

All Human Things. Peter Schroeder. BXAP

All human things are subject to decay. Dryden. *Fr.* MacFlecknoe; or, A Satire [*or* Satyr] upon the True-Blue [*or* -Blew] Protestant Poet T. S. CBNP, (*sl. abr.*); FHYEP; HAP, (*abr.*); NAEL-1; NoP; NOSC, *ll.* 1-30; OAEL-1; OBSV; OxBoLi; PeLV; PoE; Poetr; PPP; SCV; SeCV-2; TEP; TFi; TrGrPo

(Crown Prince of Dullness, The.) NOBE

(Primacy of Dullness, The.) 09OBS

All hung with stars!), there still would be no bear. (*LL*) The Great Bear. John Hollander. LiTM; NoAM; NYBP; TwCP

All hurts. Dear friends. Still Trees. Momcilo Nastasijevic, *tr. fr. Serbo-Croatian by* Charles Simic. HSix

All Hushed and Still within the House. Emily Brontë. FaBoCh; Mes; NOBVV

All I can do is curse, complain. Cassandra's Answer. John Montague. BiHa

All I can dream tonight is an autumn sunset. Boyhood in Tobacco Country. Robert Penn Warren. AnAn

All I can give you is broken-face gargoyles. Broken-Face Gargoyles. Carl Sandburg. AmPP; MoAmPo; OxBA

All I can offer now is a cracked china jug. Winter Offering. D. S. Savage. LiTB

All I could see from where I stood. Edna St. Vincent Millay. *Fr.* Renascence. MoAB; MoAmPo; PDV; PFP

All I know is a door into the dark. The Forge. Seamus Heaney. NAEL-2; OxAEP-2

All I said was — Alexis is gorgeous. Plato, *tr. fr. Greek by* Peter Jay. PeHV

(Alexis.) GrAn

All I want in this creation's. Black-eyed Susie. *Unknown.* AmFP

All I wanted was to brew him rhubarb wine. My First Forty Years. Kevin Ireland. PeNZ

All I wanted/ was your/ love. To Mother and Steve. Mari Evans. BPo; PoBA

All I would say. On a Sea-Grape Leaf. Katherine Garrison Chapin. GrPl

All Ignorance Toboggans into Know. E. E. Cummings. MeMAP; NAAL-2; NOBA; OxBA

All Impelled Onward Alike. Robert Blair. *Fr.* Grave, The. OxAEP-1

All in a Garden Green. W. E. Henley. OBMV

All in a literary parleur. Bootie Black and the Seven Giants. Mike Cook. JB

All in All. Tennyson. *See* In Love, if Love be Love, if Love be ours.

All-in-All seems here a Greek, The. (*LL*) The Attic Landscape. Herman Melville. AnAmPo; NOBA; OBAL

All in Due Time. J. V. Cunningham. NIP

All in good time. (*LL*) How She Operates. Grace Caroline Bridges. LoHo

All in Green Went My Love Riding. E. E. Cummings. CMoP; FaBV; GoJo; HeIL; HeIP; LiTA; LiTM; MoP; NoAM; NoP; OxBA; PoRA

All in June. W. H. Davies. OxBSP

All in Red. Eileen Mathias. BoTP

All in the April evening [morning]. Sheep and Lambs. Katharine Tynan. BoTP; OBEV; TIRV

All in the Downs the fleet was moored [*or* moor'd]. Sweet William's Farewell to Black-eyed [*or* ey'd] Susan. John Gay. AmFP, (*folk vers.*); BeLS; BoLoP; CBLP; NOEC

(Black-eyed Susan.) GTBS; GTBS-P

All in the merry month of May. Barbara Allen's Cruelty ("All in the merry month of May.") *Unknown.* FaBoBe

All in the summery weather. Ballad of Fine Days. Phyllis McGinley. ArOW

All in this pleasant evening, together come are we. Old May Song. *Unknown.* BoTP; CH

All in thy sight my life doth whole depend. Sir Thomas Wyatt. SiPSBD

All in together. *Unknown.* RoPo

All in white shall wait around. (*LL*) Once in Royal David's City. Cecil Frances Alexander. OxBChV; PlP

All Intents. Larry Eigner. VGW

All Ireland's now one vessel's company. Fearghal Og MacWard, *tr. fr. Irish. Fr.* Flight of the Earls, The, 1607. BIrV

All Is Best. Milton. *Fr.* Samson Agonistes. FHYEP; NOBE; NOSC; OAEL-1; OBEV; PoEL-3

All is dying; hearts are breaking. Unchanging Jesus. Karl Johann Philipp Spitta, *tr. fr. German by* R. Massie. BLRP

All is Emptiness, and I Must Spin. Thomas Kinsella. PBCIP

All is fated. All. Bei Dao, *tr. fr. Chinese by* Donald Finkel *with* Chen Xueliang. SpMi

All Is Not So Simple. Shin Shalom. *See* All's Not That Simple.

All is possible. (*LL*) Is It Possible[?]. Sir Thomas Wyatt. ELP; EnRePo; GBL; NoP; NoSic; SiPS; SiPSBD

All is the same still. Earth and heaven locked in. Emily Brontë. C. Day Lewis. GTBS-P

All is upon the earth and all is sacred. (*LL*) Behold This and Always Love It. Meridel Le Sueur. SRLS

All Is Vanity. Andreas Gryphius, *tr. fr. German by* George C. Schoolfield. GePo

All Is Vanity, Saith the Preacher. Byron. ChIV-1; TrCP

All Is Well. Victor Martinez. AfAz

All its indifference is a different rage. (*LL*) Codicil. Derek Walcott. MoP; NoAM

All Jolly Fellows That Follow the Plough. *Unknown.* OBET

All joy to mortals, joy and mirth. Aphra Behn. *Fr.* Emperor of the Moon. WPE

All June I bound the rose in sheaves. One Way of Love. Robert Browning. OtMeF

All kings, and all their favourites [*or* favorites]. The Anniversary [*or* Anniversarie]. John Donne. BoLoP; ESCV; FHYEP; HAP; HoPM; JCP; LiTB; MeLP; NOBE; NoP; NoSic; OAEL-1; OxBM; SCGP; SeCP; SeCV-1; TFi; WeW

All-knowing God, 'Tis Thine to Know. *Unknown.* AH

All Last Night. Lascelles Abercrombie. FaBoTw

All last night I kept speaking in this. Mysteries. Terence Winch. UL

All last week you preened before the mirror. Memory says Yes. Margaret Randall. WoWa

All Legendary Obstacles. John Montague. BIrV; CIP; IPY; NOIV; PBCIP; PNI

All life is star. Slade's Invective. Iain Sinclair. VaA

All life is your own. Starhawk. EaPr

All live in deck chairs on skid row. The Extras. Chris Daly. NGP

All look and likeness caught from earth. Phantom. *Unknown, sometimes at. to* Samuel Taylor Coleridge. MeMBP; NAEL-2; OAEL-2; OxBSP; PoEL-4

All looking down for the love of me. (*LL*) The Mermaid. Tennyson. BoTP, (*ll.* 1–14); FaPON; GN

All looks be pale, hearts cold as stone. A Lamentation. Thomas Campion. CH; OHIP

All love is sacred, and the marriage-tie. Katherine Philips. *Fr.* Friendship. OBF

All love that has not friendship for its base. Upon the Sand. Ella Wheeler Wilcox. AnAmPo

All Lovely Things. Conrad Aiken. AnAmPo; PoRA

All matronly in her stoop, her wings canted. The Black Angel. Henri Coulette. NYBP

All meet here with us, finally. Ostriches and Grandmothers! Amiri Baraka. NeAP

All men are brothers and each people is my own. My Song to the Jewish People. Leib Olitski, *tr. fr. Yiddish by* Jacob Sonntag. TrJP

All men are locked in their cells. Fall Down. Calvin C. Hernton. PoBA

All men are wormes: but this no man. In silke. On Court-Worme. Ben Jonson. SeCP

All men from all lands. Inscription for a Wayside Spring. Frances Cornford. BrRo

All men may hasty-gone happiness find. Shepherd-Song ("All men may hasty-gone happiness find.") Sigmund von Birken, *tr. fr. German by* George C. Schoolfield. GePo

All men wait for battle and when it comes. An Apple Tree and a Pig. Emyr Humphreys. OBWVE

All month a smell of burning, of dry peat. July 1914. "Anna Akhmatova," *tr. fr. Russian by* Stanley Kunitz *and* Max Hayward. PeFWW; WPOW. (*Pt.* I *only, tr. by* Stanley Kunitz)

All Morning. Gregory Orr. TRP

All Morning. Theodore Roethke. EaPr; NaP

All Morning. Terry Stokes. AmPA

All morning! All morning! (*LL*) All Morning. Theodore Roethke. EaPr

All morning, as I sit thinking of you. Monarchs. Sharon Olds. LoHo

All morning long. The Next Story. Pattiann Rogers. NAmP90

All morning the dream lingers. All Morning. Gregory Orr. TRP

All morning you squat in the weeds. Rescue. Ellen Bryant Voigt. NoP

All moves within the visual frame. A Monument. Charles Madge. FaBoMo

All music, sauces, feasts, delights and pleasures. Thomas Traherne. *Fr.* Christian Ethics. OxBSP

All must be used. Barracks Apt. 14. Theodore Weiss. CoAP; TAP

All must have Beauty, else they pine and die. Fabrique of Things Spent. Edith M. Thomas. AmWP

All my dead people. Over the Edge. Fleur Adcock. PeNZ

All my favourite characters have been. Mythology. Lawrence Durrell. OxBTC

All my future plans, dear. The Blue Room. Lorenz Hart. OBAL

All my life I lived in a coconut. Locked In. Ingemar Leckius, *tr. fr. Swedish.* TSaS, *tr. by* May Swenson

All my life so far. Discoveries in Arizona. James Wright. NoP

All my life/ they have told me. To You. Frank Horne. *Fr.* Letters [*or* Notes] Found near a Suicide. BPo; CDC; PoBA; PoNe

All my other lives. (*LL*) Waxwings. Robert Francis. LCAP; NU; RaBo

All my past life is mine no more. Love and Life. The Earl of Rochester. BoLoP; ELP; EnLoPo; FF; GBL; HAP; NOBE; OBEV; PoEL-3; SeCV-2; TrGrPo

(Love and Life: A Song.) NOSC

All my plans for suicide are ridiculous. The Heart's Location. Peter Meinke. GOYP

All My Pretty Ones. Anne Sexton. NAAL-2; NoAM; OPOP

All my pwoblems. Maybe Dats Your Pwoblem Too. Jim Hall. MT

All my senses, like beacon's flame. Fulke Greville. *Fr.* Caelica. EnRePo; InvP; NoSic; PoEL-1

(Sonnet ("All my senses, like beacon's flame").) NOSC

All my sex life, I had been drifting. Royston Ellis. *Fr.* Cherry Boy, The. PeHV

All my sheep/ Gather in a heap. Last Words before Winter. Louis Untermeyer. MoAmPo

All my shortcomings, in this year of grace. Dear Uncle Stranger. Conrad Aiken. NoAM; NOBA

All my spirit is illuminated. (*LL*) Enlightment. Ch'en Yu Yi. OHMPC

All my stars forsake me. Song of the Night at Daybreak. Alice Meynell. CH

All my thoughts always speak to me of Love. Dante, *tr. fr. Italian by* Dante Gabriel Rossetti. *Fr.* Vita Nuova, La. AWP

All Nashville is a chill. And everywhere. A January Dandelion. George Marion McClellan. AAP

All Nature Has a Voice to Tell. James Gilchrist Lawson. BLRP

All Nature is a temple where the alive. Correspondences. Baudelaire, *tr. fr. French by* Allen Tate. AWP

All Nature is but art, unknown to thee. Pope. *Fr.* Essay on Man, An. ECEV

All nature seems at work. Slugs leave their lair. Work without Hope. Samuel Taylor Coleridge. BoNaP; EnRP; MeMBP; NAEL-2; NOBE; NoP; OBEV; OxAEP-2; PFP; Son; TEP

(In Springtime.) BoTP, 4 *ll.*

All Nature's incense rise! (*LL*) The Universal Prayer. Pope. BLPA; FaBoBe; NoP; WGRP

All Nearness Pauses, While a Star Can Grow. E. E. Cummings. NoAM

All Needs Met. J. H. Sammis. BLRP

All night a noise of leaping fish. The Fisher. Roderic Quinn. CBAP

All night and all day the wind roared in the streets. Mid-Country Blow. Theodore Roethke. BoNaP

All Night by the Rose. *Unknown. See* All night by the rose, rose.

All night by the rose, rose. *Unknown.* MiEL

(All Night by the Rose.) GBL; HeIP

(Alnight by the rose.) EnVB

(Rose's Scent, The.) WiR

All night eerily! (*LL*) Voices from Things Growing in a Churchyard. Thomas Hardy. FaBoVe; OBD; OxBTC

All night fell hammers, shock on shock. A London Fete. Coventry Patmore. EBVV; EnVR; FaBoEH; HAP; PeVV

All night from the roof of the chieftain. Or Ever God Created Adam. Malay Oral Tradition, *tr. by* R. J. Wilkinson. WTO

All night had shout of men and cry. Easter Night. Alice Meynell. BrRo; ChIV-2; OHIP

All night he craned with an unbending neck. Bateleur. Douglas Livingstone. PeSAV

All night he galloped alone, in wild excitement, pitilessly spurring. Alone with His Work. Yannis Ritsos, *tr. fr. Greek by* Paul Merchant. AnRep

All night headlamps dazzle. Off the Map. David Malouf. FaBoMA

All night I clatter upon my creed. The Wife Who Would a Wanton Be. *Unknown.* FaBoCo

All night I could not sleep. *Unknown, tr. fr. Chinese. Fr.* Tzu Yeh Songs. BoWoP, *tr. by* Arthur Waley

All night I hear the hammers. The Students of Justice. W. S. Merwin. NaP

All night I lay awake beside you. Marthe Away (She Is Away). Kenneth Rexroth. UnAS

All night I sat reading a book. The Reader. Wallace Stevens. SAmP

All night I walked among your spirits, Richard. A Mourning Letter from Paris. Conrad Kent Rivers. BPo

All night I weep, all day I cry, ay me. Mary Sidney Wroth, Countess of Montgomery. NOSC; WPE

All night in the flue like a trapped thing. January 25th. Maxine W. Kumin. SM

All night It Bullied You. C. K. Stead. Fr. Small Registry of Births and Deaths, A. NAs

All night it humps the air. Cannery Town in August. Lorna Dee Cervantes. NoAM

All night like a star a single bulb. Late, Passing Prairie Farm. William Stafford. GOYP

All Night Long. Unknown. AS

All night long and every night. Young Night Thought. Robert Louis Stevenson. OTCP; PWR

All Night Long Fooling Me. Unknown. AmFP

All night long into my sleeping bag's head pad the blood. The Far Side of Introspection. Alfred M. Lee. CoAP

All night long the hockey pictures. To a Sad Daughter. Michael Ondaatje. GOYP; NoAM

All night long, through the starlit air and the stillness. The Cattle of His Hand. Wilbur Underwood. WGRP

All night sopping up rain. Mynydd Mawr. David Constantine. PWE

All night the blind entrance of the children. Barren Poem. Michael Ryan. AmPA

All night the expensive Sthenelais I laid. Sthenelais. Unknown, tr. fr. Greek by Guy Davenport. GrAn

All night the filaments stayed red. The Night Post. Matthew Sweeney. IB

All night the sound had. The Rain. Robert Creeley. CAPP; CoAP; PoE; RaBo; TRP; VGW

All night the tall young man. Merlin and the Snake's Egg. Leslie Norris. OBSP

All night the west wind cuts the banana leaves. Tune: "Remembering the Prince." Na-lan Hsing-te, tr. fr. Chinese by William Golightly. SuSp

All night the wind. History. Thomas McGrath. FoLa

All night the wind swept over the house. Winter Morning. William Jay Smith. BoNaP

All night they marched, the infantrymen under pack. 1935. Stephen Vincent Benét. MoAmPo

All night they whine upon their ropes and boom. Nocturne of the Wharves. Arna Bontemps. BPo; LPA; PoNe

All night, this headland. Sleepless at Crown Point. Richard Wilbur. InPK; WeW

All night upon the guarded hill. The Defence of Lawrence. Richard Realf. PAH

All night waiting, in an empty house. The Streets of Air. Malcolm Cowley. Fr. Blue Juniata. PoA

All-Night Waitress, The. Maura Stanton. AmPA

All of a Sudden. Teresa de Jesús, tr. fr. Spanish by Maria A. Proser, Arlene Scully and James Scully. WPOW

All of a sudden the big nasturtiums. The Big Nasturtiums. Robert Beverly Hale. BoNaP; GoJo; NYBP

All of a summer's day. (LL) Milton by Firelight. Gary Snyder. CAPP; CoAP; InPS; NAAL-2; PoBeRe; PPP

All of Beauty, All of Us. Tennyson. Fr. Ode Sung at the Opening of the International Exhibition. CBCK

All of our lives. (LL) Phantasia for Elvira Shatayev. Adrienne Rich. NALW

All of our machines need repair. Slightly Old. Bob Rosenthal. UL

All of the loved ones will see love die? (LL) O, Where Were We Before Time Was. Max Dunn. NOBAu

All of them the wind took, all of them the light lured. Alone. Hayyim Nahman Bialik, tr. fr. Hebrew by Jessie Sampter. TrJP

All of These. Denis Glover. PeNZ

All of us always turning away for solace. Delmore Schwartz. OxBA

All of Us Here, sels. Irving Feldman.
    Of Course, We Would Wish. VCAP
    Simple Outlines, Human Shapes. VCAP
    Surely They're Just So Large. VCAP

All of you that pour the bath for Pallas. On the Bath of Pallas. Callimachus, tr. fr. Greek by Barbara Hughes Fowler. Fr. Hymns. HePo

All of your ideas. Andrew Crozier. Fr. High Zero. NBrP

All old women sometimes come to this. Old Women of Toronto. Miriam Waddington. NOBC

All on one summer's evening when the fever were a-dawning. The Grey Cock. Unknown. FaBoBa

All on the road to Alibazan. Alibazan. Laura E. Richards. OBCA

All on the threshold, yet all short of life. (LL) A Triad. Christina Rossetti. NAEL-2; NALW; PBWP

All One in Christ. John Oxenham. BLRP

All or Nothing. Bayard Taylor. BXAP

All other joys of life he strove to warm. George Meredith. Fr. Modern Love. EnVR

All other love is like the mone. Unknown. MiEL

All Other Love Is like the Moon. Unknown. MiEL

All others talked as if. Caedmon. Denise Levertov. NoAM

All our French poets can turn an inspired line. The Nihilist as Hero. Robert Lowell. VCAP

All Our Joy Is Enough. Geoffrey Scott. OBMV

All our pink and gold and blue. V-Winged and Hoary. Henri Cole. UTF

All our roads go nowhere. On Inhabiting an Orange. Josephine Miles. NoAM; PoA

All our stones like as much sun as possible. Forecast. Josephine Miles. NoAM

All out for Illinois Central. Calling Trains. Unknown. AmFP

All out of doors looked darkly in at him. An Old Man's Winter Night. Robert Frost. AWP; HAP; MoAB; MoAmPo; NAAL-2; NoAM; OxBA; VGW

All over America railroads ride through roses. Landscape as Metal and Flowers. Winfield Townley Scott. GoJo

All over America women are burning dinners. What's That Smell in the Kitchen? Marge Piercy. NBLV; NGP; NIP

All over Italy, the saints'. The Reliquary. Bruce Beasley. UTF

All over the plain of the world lovers are being hurt. C. K. Stead. Fr. Quesada. PeNZ

All over the world, I wonder, in lands that I never have trod. Meditations of a Hindu Prince. Sir Alfred Comyn Lyall. WGRP

All over town. (LL) A Poem for Record Players. John Wieners. PoBeRe

All parts in place/ or nearly so. (LL) Cicada. Adrien Stoutenburg. NYBP; RFM

All passes. Art alone. Austin Dobson, after the French of Théophile Gautier. Fr. Ars Victrix. CTC

All paths lead. Winter. John Davies. AngWe

All Paths Lead to You. Blanche Shoemaker Wagstaff. BLPA; FaBoBe

All people like me! (LL) Jonathan Bing. Beatrice Curtis Brown. FaPON; PDV

All people that on earth do dwell. Old Hundredth. William Kethe. FaPoR (Psalm 100. 'O Be Joyful in the Lord, All Ye Lands'.) PeECV (Psalm C.) NOCV (Scotch Te Deum.) WGRP

All perished — brides and infants. Song of a Jewish Boy. "M. J.," tr. fr. Polish by A. Glanz-Leyeles. TrJP

All play and no work makes Jack a mere toy. (LL) All work and no play makes Jack a dull boy. Unknown. OxNR

All Possession Is Theft. Lauris Edmond. PeNZ

All praise be yours through Brother Sun. Paul Winter. EaPr

All Praise to Thee. F. Bland Tucker. AH

All praise to Thee, my God, this night. An Evening Hymn. Thomas Ken. OxBChV

All praise your face, your verses none abuse. Horace Walpole. FaBoEE

All profits disappear: the gain. The Reckoning. Theodore Roethke. PoA

All Quiet along the Potomac. At. to Ethel Lynn Beers, sometimes at. to Lamar Fontaine. AnAmPo; BeLS; FaBoBe; VPP

All right, gentlemen who cry blue murder as always. Draft of a Reparations Agreement. Dan Pagis, tr. fr. Hebrew by Stephen Mitchell. PoSu

All right, I may have lied to you, and about you. Love, 20 Cents the First Quarter Mile. Kenneth Fearing. HAP

All right, I'll die, my spirit is strong. Fear. Vittoria Aganoor Pompili, tr. fr. Italian by Brenda Webster. PBWP

All right now, listen to me right good. Unloading Rails. Unknown. AmFP

All right. Try this. Northern Pike. James Wright. NAAL-2

All right with me,/ Little brown boy. (LL) Little brown boy. Helene Johnson. CDC; PoBA; ShDr

All round about the door of your house. Regret and Refusal. Unknown, tr. fr. Tewa Indian by H. J. Spinden. WTO

All round the Browns stretched forty acres of potatoes. The Brown Family. Colleen Thibaudeau. NOBC

All round the horizon black clouds appear. On a Sea-Storm nigh the Coast. Richard Steere. SCAP

All round the room I waltzed with Ellen Taylor. Ellen Taylor. Unknown. OBET

All Saints' Day, sels. Margherita Guidacci, tr. fr. Italian by Ruth Feldman and Brian Swann.

"All Saints' Day; November sky." PBWP

All Saints' Day; November sky. Margherita Guidacci, tr. fr. *Italian* by Ruth Feldman *and* Brian Swann. *Fr.* All Saints' Day. PBWP

All saints revile her, and all sober men. The White Goddess. Robert Graves. MeMBP; MoBrPo; NAEL-2; OAEL-2; OPOP

All sea is sea. How mad it is to blame. Antipater of Thessalonica, tr. fr. *Greek* by Alistair Elliot. GrAn

All seas, all ships. (*LL*) Song for All Seas, All Ships. Walt Whitman. CH; FaBoBe

All Seasons in One. *Unknown.* GBL; HeIP; TrGrPo

All Seasons Shall Be Sweet. Samuel Taylor Coleridge. BoTP

All seasons shall be sweet to thee. The Silent Icicles. Samuel Taylor Coleridge. *Fr.* Frost at Midnight. BoTP; EBEV; EnRP; FaBoRV; FHYEP; HAP; MeMBP; NAEL-2; NAs; NOBE; NoP; OAEL-2; OBNC; PFP; PoE; PoEL-4; Poetr; PPP; PrIm; TFi; TOF

All-seeing Intellect, The. Phineas Fletcher. *Fr.* Purple Island, The. JCP

All seem to know what is for heaven alone. (*LL*) Love in the Valley. George Meredith. AWP; EBVV; EnVR; ErPo; LiTB; NOBE; OAEL-2; OBEV, *abr.*; TrGrPo

All service ranks the same with God. Service. Robert Browning. *Fr.* Pippa Passes. TrGrPo

All shadows on the wall are blue. Shadows in Llanbadarn. Gillian Clarke. SCBI

All Shams. *Unknown.* APAS

All shiny in your mind! (*LL*) Some People. Rachel Field. FaPON; NTCP; PDV

All silence says music will follow. Onion Bucket. Lorenzo Thomas. PoBA

All songs/ are tattoos. The Singer. Diane Wakoski. HeIP

All sorts of men through various labours presse. Verses Written by Mrs. Hutchinson. Lucy Hutchinson. KTR; NOSC

All Souls'. Ruth Bidgood. AngWe

All Souls. D. H. Lawrence. FaBoRV

All Souls. May Sarton. CrSp; IMW

All Souls' Day. Herman von Gilm zu Rosenegg, tr. fr. *German* by Philip L. Miller. RiWo

All Souls' Day. D. H. Lawrence. OBD

All Souls' Night. Frances Cornford. EnLoPo; OBD; OxBSP; OxBTC

All Souls' Night. W. B. Yeats. *Fr.* Vision, A. OxAEP-2

All souls rest in peace! (*LL*) Litany for All Souls Day. Johann Georg Jacobi. RiWo

All souls that struggle and aspire. Whittier. *Fr.* Shadow and the Light, The. TrPWD

All Splendor on Earth. Karin Kiwus, tr. fr. *German* by Almut McAuley. BoWoP

All Still. William Barnes. NOBVV

All streams meander to the sea. (*LL*) The Promenade. Tchicaya U Tam'si. NegPo

All such proclivities are tabulated. The Quiet Glades of Eden. Robert Graves. BoLoP; ErPo

All-sufficient Christ, The. Bernice W. Lubke. BLRP

All summer I heard them. The Snakes of September. Stanley Kunitz. AnAn; FoLa

All summer long. (*LL*) In Spring. Ernst Konrad Friedrich Schulze. RiWo

All summer long the people knelt. At the President's Grave. Richard Watson Gilder. PAH

All summer long the smartypants. A Poem in Response to Doom. William Hathaway. NAmP90

All summer the sheep were strewn like crumbs. Flanking Sheep in Mosedale. David Scott. PWE

All that blazing day, swift-breasted swallows. Thunderstorm in South Dakota. Kay Boyle. WPE

All that blesses the step of the antelope. Else a Great Prince in Prison Lies. Denise Levertov. NaP; PPP; VGW

All that doth flow we cannot liquid name. What Is Liquid. Margaret Cavendish, Duchess of Newcastle. FaBoUs

All that Friday. An Ulster Unionist Walks the Streets of London. Tom Paulin. PNI

All That Glisters Is Not Gold. Shakespeare. *Fr.* Merchant of Venice, The. CTC

All that have two or but one ear. The Four-legg'd Quaker. *Unknown.* CoMu

All that he is . . . does . . . is attractive. Meleager, tr. fr. *Greek* by Peter Whigham. GrAn

All That I Am. Verna Arvey. AH

All that I do is clumsy and ill timed. The Doppelganger. Daryl Hine. (Double-Goer, The.) MoCV

All that I had I brought. Exchanges. Ernest Dowson. OBMV

All that I have. Handfuls of Wind. Yekhi'el [*or* Yehiel] Mar, tr. fr. *Hebrew* by Ruth Finer Mintz. MHP

All that I have comes from my Mother! Luisah Teish. EaPr

All that I know/ Of a certain star. My Star. Robert Browning. FaPON; TrGrPo

All that I may swynk or swet. Care Away. *Unknown.* OxBoLi

All that I ran from. The Mood. Quandra Prettyman. PoBA

All that I try to save him from. Sleep-Learning. Ruth Fainlight. NMM

All That Is Left. Basho, tr. fr. *Japanese* by Curtis Hidden Page. AWP

All That Is Left. Michael Hartnett. NOIV

All That Is Lovely in Men. Robert Creeley. NaP; RaBo

All that is moulded of iron. Woodworker's Ballad. Herbert Edward Palmer. OBEV

All that it should be. Andrew Crozier. *Fr.* High Zero. NBrP

All that I've never thought of — think of me! (*LL*) A Sick Child. Randall Jarrell. InPK; InvP; OxBC; VGW

All that love me. (*LL*) Lady Moon. Richard Monckton Milnes. BoTP; MoShBr; OxBChV

All That Matters. Walter Sorell. GoYe

All that matters is to be at one with the living God. Pax. D. H. Lawrence. EnlH; PeECV; TrCP

All that night I walked alone and wept. Gethsemane. Arna Bontemps. CDC

All that running water outside. The Marshes. Jane Mayhall. TAP

All That Time. May Swenson. FF

All that was me is gone. (*LL*) Sing me a song of a lad that is gone. Robert Louis Stevenson. NOBE; NTP

All that was mine — I have loved it, and loved it both true and well. Faithful Over a Few Things. Edith M. Thomas. AmWP

All that was promis'd by the Spring. (*LL*) To a Very Young Lady. Edmund Waller. SCGP; SeCP; TrGrPo

All that was there. (*LL*) Mornings. Alice Notley. VBLP

All that we see, about, abroad. On the Universality and Other Attributes of the God of Nature. Philip Freneau. EAP

All That You Have Given Me, Africa. Anoma Kanié, tr. fr. *French* by Kathleen Weaver. AIW; PBWP

All that you have lost, they told me, is yours. Boundaries. José Emilio Pacheco, tr. fr. *Spanish* by John Frederick Nims. STV

All That's Past. Walter de la Mare. ArNa; GoJo; MoAB; NOBE; OAEL-2; OBMV; OtMeF; OxBTC; TrGrPo

All the afternoon there has been a chirping of birds. Free Fantasia on Japanese Themes. Amy Lowell. MoAmPo

All the air quivers, and the east sky glows. (*LL*) A Front. Randall Jarrell. ArOW; OBWP; OxBC; PoWW; VGW

All the bells of heaven may ring. A Child's Laughter. Swinburne. BLPL; NTP; PoLF

All the birds have come again. Spring's Arrival. *Unknown.* FaPON

All the black same I dance my blue head off! (*LL*) King David Dances. John Berryman. ChIV-1; OxBC; OxBSP

All the boys always wanted her, so. Leda's Sister and the Geese. Katharyn Machan Aal. SoSe

All the breath and the bloom of the year in the bag of one bee. Summum Bonum. Robert Browning. OHCV; PFP

All the cages are empty. The Two Selves. Margaret Avison. MoP

All the cattle are resting in the fields. Poem to the Sun ("All the Cattle are resting in the fields.") *Ancient Egyptian Oral Tradition*, tr. by Christopher Wertz. TTTS

All the cautionary tales of strange girls. Mythics. Helen Chasin. IHMS

All the Cilicians are bad. Demodocus, tr. fr. *Greek* by Alistair Elliot. GrAn

All the day I worked and played. A Labourer's Wife. John Davidson. *Fr.* To the Street Piano. EBVV

All the Dead Dears. Sylvia Plath. IHMS

All the Death-Room Needs. Michael Hartnett. CIP

All the flies are reading microscopic books. Serious Readers. Peter Redgrove. OxBC

All the flowers of the spring. John Webster. *Fr.* Devil's Law Case, The. CoGr; EiL; ELP; ImPo; LiTB; NOSC; PoEL-2; PoRA; SCGP (Burial, The.) CH (Nets to Catch the Wind.) TrGrPo (Vanitas Vanitatum.) NOBE; OBEV

All the flowers, wet with dew, have sent. Towards Evening. Andreas Grimelund Jynge, tr. fr. *Norwegian* by Philip L. Miller. RiWo

All the forms are fugitive. Emerson. *Fr.* Woodnotes II ("As sunbeams stream through liberal space"). NOBA; WGRP

All the fruit is ripe, plunged into fire, cooked. Friedrich Hölderlin, tr. fr. *German* by Robert Bly. NU

All the full-moon night in the coomb. In the Night of the Full Moon. Carl Busse, tr. fr. *German* by Jethro Bithell. AWP

All things return, Nietzsche said. The Recurrence. Edwin Muir. MeMBP

All things that are on earth shall wholly pass away. The Love of God. Bernard Rascas, *tr. fr. Provençal by* Bryant. WGRP

All things that go deep enough. The Ice Skin. James Dickey. NYBP

All things that pass. Passing and Glassing. Christina Rossetti. OBNC

All things that Peter saw and felt. Shelley. *Fr.* Peter Bell the Third. EPCY

All things uncomely and broken, all things worn out and old. The Lover Tells of the Rose in His Heart. W. B. Yeats. CMoP (Aedh Tells of the Rose in His Heart.) MoBrPo

All Things Wait upon Thee. Christina Rossetti. GN

All things within this fading world hath end. Before the Birth of One of Her Children. Anne Bradstreet. BoWoP; EAP; KTR; MAT; NAAL-1; NAs; NOBA; OxBM; PeECV; WPE; WPOW

All this — and the housekeeper. Hart Crane. AnAn

All this breaks down to a mental. AIDS and the Art of Living. John Harkness. UnDi

All this indigo, nonviolent light will triumph. Sunday Evenings. John Hollander. NYBP

All this is history, the still disputed fate. Line-up. Dori Katz. BTR

All this is one. My Faith. Ananda Acharya. WGRP

All this is true without deceit. (*LL*) Every lady in this land. Mother Goose. OxNR; ReMoGo

All this travelling around and I've learned. Looking for Angels in New York. Jacqueline Osherow. UTF

All those buffalos have green horns. A Song of the Red & Green Buffalo. *Unknown, tr. fr. Oto Indian by* William Whitman. STP

All those summers, waiting. Waiting for You to Come By. Simon J. Ortiz. CDW

All those treasures that lie in the little bolted box. Slow Movement. William Carlos Williams. PoA

All those who, over the sorrows of strangers, led their spirits to dance and to delight. From All Sides Laughter Shall Strike Them. Amir Gilboa, *tr. fr. Hebrew by* Ruth Finer Mintz. MHP

All those women working. Working. Maxine Scates. PBCAP

All those years. Good Old Body. C.M. Donald. AIW

All those years that you ate and changed. Peasant. W. S. Merwin. NYBP

All thoughts, all passions, all delights. Love. Samuel Taylor Coleridge. BeLS; EnRP; GTBS; GTBS-P; OBEV

All thro' the breathing night there seemed to flow. A Venetian Night. Hugo von Hofmannsthal, *tr. fr. German by* Ludwig Lewisohn. AWP

All thro' the Year. *Unknown.* BLRP

All through spring, nothing but wind and rain. Tune: "Bean Leaves Yellow." Lu Yu, *tr. fr. Chinese by* James J. Y. Liu. SuSp

All through that summer at ease we lay. The Castle. Edwin Muir. LiTB

All through the day, little peach blossoms in the garden. Little Peach Blossoms in the Garden. Li Shang-yin, *tr. fr. Chinese by* Eugene Eoyang *and* Irving Y. Lo. SuSp

All through the garden I went and went. The Butterbean Tent. Elizabeth Madox Roberts. GoJo

All through the march, besides bag and blanket. Crazed Man in Concentration Camp. Agnes Gergely, *tr. fr. Hungarian by* Edwin Morgan. BoWoP; PAW

All through the Night. *Unknown.* FaPON

All through the night my eyes have streamed with rain. Strato, *tr. fr. Greek by* Sydney Oswald. PeHV

All through the night the happy sheep. The Happy Sheep. Wilfrid Thorley. ZA

All through the Stranger's Wood. Isaac Leibush Peretz, *tr. fr. Yiddish by* Joseph Leftwich. TrJP

All through the valley, the people are whispering. Return of the Wolves. Anita Endrezze-Danielson. HATNAP

All through the windless night the clipper rolled. John Masefield. *Fr.* Dauber. CMoP

All time shall hail thee, Europe's noblest Son! (*LL*) Lafayette. Dolley Madison. AiP; PAH

All to Myself. Wilbur D. Nesbit. BLPA

All today I lie in the bottom of the wardrobe. Yoko. Thom Gunn. NoAM

All tongues speak of him, and the bleared sights. Shakespeare. *Fr.* Coriolanus. FaBoPV

All Too Late. *Unknown.* EBEV; OAEL-1

All too late. *Unknown. See* When mine eynen misteth.

All travail of high thought. The Beginnings of Faith. Sir Lewis Morris. WGRP

All travelers [*or* travellers] at first incline. Stella's Birthday, 1721 ("All travelers at first incline"). Swift. NAEL-1; PeIV; PoEL-3 (Stella's Birthday 1720.) OxAEP-1

All trembling in my arms Aminta lay. The Dream. Aphra Behn. *Fr.* Voyage to the Isle of Love, A. PBWP

All Tropic Places Smell of Mold. Karl Shapiro. VGW

All turn to patches of duckweed spreading on the river. (*LL*) Tune: "Song of Picking Mulberry." Wang Kuo-wei. SuSp

All Turns into Yesterday. *Unknown.* MeEL

All under the leaves, the leaves of life. The Seven Virgins. *Unknown.* CH; ChTr; GBP; OBET; OBEV

All upstarts, insolent in place. The Butterfly and the Snail. John Gay. *Fr.* Fables. FM

All Virgil's idylls end in sunsets; pale. The Voice. Edmund Wilson. NYBP

All walking leans to the left. Pencilled by the Rain. Peter Hooper. PeNZ

All was as it is, before the beginning began, before. Jacob. Delmore Schwartz. ChIV-1

All Watched Over by Machines of Loving Grace. Richard Brautigan. MAT

All waters as the shore. (*LL*) Ave atque Vale. Swinburne. NAEL-2; NOBE; OAEL-2; OBEV; OBNC

All We Ask Is Justice. Mrs. Henry Linden. CBWP-4

All we make is enough. All Our Joy Is Enough. Geoffrey Scott. OBMV

All we were going strong last night this time. John Berryman. FaBoMo

All week long. Sunday. Ludwig Uhland, *tr. fr. German by* Philip L. Miller. RiWo

All week she watched. The Silos. Nancy Paddock. LoHo

All week, the maid tells me, bowing. A Walk in Kyoto. Earle Birney. GoYe

All were to little for the merchauntes hande. George Gascoigne. AAS

All were too little for the merchant's hand. George Gascoigne. *Fr.* Gascoigne's Memories. EnRePo; Son

All what I am, it is you. (*LL*) When, to my deadly [*or* deadlie] pleasure. Sir Philip Sidney. CBLP; EnLoPo; PoEL-1

All wheels; a man breathed fire. The Celebration. James Dickey. VGW

All Which Isn't Singing Is Mere Talking. E. E. Cummings. VGW

All who are sick at heart and cry in bitterness. The Garden of Song. Moses ibn Ezra, *tr. fr. Hebrew by* David Goldstein. TOF

All who have loved, be sure of this from me. Richard Watson Dixon. *Fr.* Love's Consolation. OBNC

All winds died this hot day. *Unknown, tr. by* Michael E. Workman. *Fr.* Tzu-yeh Songs of the Four Seasons. SuSp

All Winter. Linda Hogan. ETG

All winter I have been waiting. Sitting on Zero. Karen Murai. UTF

All winter long. *Unknown.* EaPr

All winter long you listened for the boom. The Stoic: for Laurà von Courten. Edgar Bowers. ArOW; CoAP; MT

All winter through I bow my head. The Scarecrow. Walter de la Mare. MoBrPo; OxBTC

All winter your brute shoulders strained against collars, padding. Names of Horses. Donald Hall. CAPP; FoLa; HAP; InPK; SoSe; TRP

All women are beautiful as they rise. Poem for Easter. Robert Kelly. VGW

All women loved dance in a dying light. They Sing. Theodore Roethke. NYBP

All work and no play makes Jack a dull boy. *Unknown.* OxNR

All worldly shapes shall melt in gloom. The Last Man. Thomas Campbell. EnRP

All/ wrong. Charles Olson. *See* This morning of the small snow.

All ye nations, pause a moment! listen to the Negro's voice. The Voice of the Negro. L. A. J. Moorer. CBWP-3

All ye poets of the age. Namby-Pamby. Henry Carey. CBNP; FaBoNo; FaBoPa; NOEC; OBSV; UV, (*sh. vers.*)

All Ye That Go Astray. Moses ibn Ezra, *tr. fr. Hebrew by* Solomon Solis-Cohen. *Fr.* World's Illusion, The. TrJP

All ye that handle harp and viol. Moses Hayyim Luzzatto, *tr. fr. Hebrew by* Nina Davis Salaman. *Fr.* Unto the Upright Praise. TrJP

All ye that lovely lovers be. Harvester's Song. George Peele. *Fr.* Old Wives' [*or* Wife's] Tale, The. TrGrPo

All ye that pass along Love's trodden way. Dante, *tr. fr. Italian by* Dante Gabriel Rossetti. *Fr.* Vita Nuova, La. AWP

All ye that passe be [*or* by] this holy place. *Unknown.* MiEL (Second Epitaph, A.) MeEL

All ye who do not love her — ye know where ye can go. (*LL*) Edna's Hymn. Barry Humphries. NOBAu

All ye who, far from town, in rural hall. On a Wet Summer. John Codrington Bampfylde. NOEC

All ye woods, and trees, and bowers. The God of Sheep. John Fletcher. *Fr.* Faithful Shepherdess, The. EiL; FaBoCh (To Pan.) TrGrPo

All ye young men, I pray draw near. The Gardener. *Unknown.* GBP

All year in open places, underneath. Dyddgu Replies to Dafydd. Gillian Clarke. SCBI

All Year Long. *Unknown, tr. fr. Chinese by* Kenneth Rexroth. OHMPC

All year, Mozart went under. To a Daughter at Fourteen Forsaking the Violin. Carole Oles. WeW

All year the flax-dam festered in the heart. Death of a Naturalist. Seamus Heaney. HAP; NoAM; OxBC; WeW

All you are doing and saying is to America dangled mirages. To a President. Walt Whitman. NAAL-1

All you big things, bless the Lord. *Unknown.* EaPr

All you can about animals as persons. What You Should Know to Be a Poet. Gary Snyder. NNaP; PoM

All you flowers. Withered Flowers. Wilhelm Müller, *tr. fr. German by* Philip L. Miller. *Fr.* Beautiful Maid of the Mill, The. RiWo

All you lords of Scottland ffaire. Tom Potts. *Unknown.* ESPB

All you made has let the winter in. (*LL*) The Man and the Tree. Philip Mead. NOBAu

All You Others, Eat. Djurberaui, *tr. fr. Aborigine by* Catherine H. Berndt. NOBAu; WTO

All you that are low-spirited, I think it won't be wrong. A New Hunting Song. *Unknown.* OBET

All you that are single and wild in your ways. Old Maids. *Unknown.* AmFP

All you that are mirth inclin'd, come tarry here a little while. The Country Girl's Policy; or, The Cockney Outwitted. *Unknown.* CoMu

All you that delight in a frolicsome song. A New Song, Called the Frolicsome Sea Captain; or, Tit for Tat. *Unknown.* OxBSS

All you that delight to spend some time. Little John a Begging. *Unknown.* ESPB

All you that desire to here of a jest. The Unfortunate Miller; or, The Country Lasses Witty Invention. *Unknown.* CoMu; OxBB

All you that in His house be here. Old Christmas. *Unknown.* OHIP

All you that in the condemned hole do lie. The Condemned Cell at Newgate. *Unknown.* FaBoEH

All you that to feasting and mirth are inclined. Old Christmas Returned. *Unknown.* GN; OHIP

All you violated ones with gentle hearts. For Malcolm X. Margaret Walker. BPo; PoBA; Son

All you young men an' maidens come an' listen to my song. A New Song on the Taxes. *Unknown.* WTO

All young men dream. The Bind. Wayne Brown. PBCV

All your days are holy days. Lullaby for Rachael. James Simmons. PNI

All Your Fortunes We Can Tell Ye. Ben Jonson. *Fr.* Gypsies Metamorphosed, The. ChTr

All your future sorrows and your only blessing. (*LL*) The Horizon. Kevin Hart. NOBAu

All your life you wait around for some damn man! (*LL*) Chant for Dark Hours. Dorothy Parker. VBLP

All yow that crye O hone! O hone! A Lementable New Ballad upon the Earle of Essex Death. *Unknown.* CoMu

Allace depairting, grund of wo. Fairweill. *Unknown.* OxBS

Allace! So Sobir Is the Micht. Mersar. OxBS

Allah ("Allah gives light in darkness.") Siegfried August Mahlmann, *tr. fr. German by* Longfellow. AWP

Allan Ian Og Macleod of Raasay. Macleod's Lament. Neil Munro. NSI

Allansford Pursuit, The. Robert Graves. RB

Allas, deth! Who made thee so hardy. Alas, Death. Charles, Duc d'Orléans. OxBLMV

"Allas," sche seide, "how that this manis mynde." Heu quam precipiti. Boethius, *tr. by* John Walton. *Fr.* Consolation of Philosophy, The. OBMV

Allatoona. *Unknown.* PAH

Alle that beth of herte trewe. The Death of King Edward I. *Unknown.* MeEL

Allegiance is assigned. Choice. J. V. Cunningham. VGW

Allegory. Goethe, *tr. fr. German by* John White. ArNa

Allegory, An. Barcroft Henry Boake. CBAP

Allegory, An. David Ignatow. VGW

Allegory in Black. Carl Clark. JB

Allegory of Death and Night. Frank Stanford. MT

Allegory of the Adolescent and the Adult. George Barker. LiTB; MeMBP

Allegory of the Wolf Boy, The. Thom Gunn. OxBC

Allegro. Tomas Tranströmer, *tr. fr. Swedish by* Robin Fulton. PWE

Allelauder. "Hugh MacDiarmid." FaBoEH

Alleluia!. (*LL*) The Novice. Jakob Nikolaus von Craigher de Jachelutta. RiWo

Alleluia, alleluia,/ Alleluia, now sing we. *Unknown.* MiEL

Alleluia! Christ Is Risen Today. John Henry Hopkins, Jr.. AH

Alleluya. Rubén Darío, *tr. fr. Spanish by* Lysander Kemp. TTY

Allen-a-Dale. Sir Walter Scott. *Fr.* Rokeby. EnRP

Allen Ginsberg. Toi Derricotte. PBCAP

Allen said, I am searching for the true cadence. Gray. Helicon. John Hollander. Poetr

Alley, The. Lorna Dee Cervantes. *Fr.* Lots. ETG

Alley; an Imitation of Spenser, The. Pope. NOEC

Alley Cat. Esther Valck Georges. OTCP; Spl

Alley of granite arkite pillars, The. Stones: Avesbury. Daisy Aldan. PoA

Allie ("Allie, call the birds in.") Robert Graves. FaPON; GoJo; NTP; PeLV

Alligator. Grace Nichols. OBAP

Alligator, The. Beatrice Ravenel. WPE

Alligator's Struggles with the 400 sons. *Unknown, tr. fr. Mayan by* Munro Edmonson. *Fr.* Popol Vuh, The. STP

All – intellectual eye, our solar round. James Thomson. *Fr.* To the Memory of Sir Isaac Newton. NOEC

Alliteration, or the Siege of Belgrade. *At. to* Alaric Alexander Watts. *See* Austrian Army, An.

Allowance. Jim Mitsui. ETG

Alloy. Muriel Rukeyser. NoAM

All's a scattering,/ A shining. (*LL*) Meditation at Oyster River. Theodore Roethke. CAPP; CMoP; MoAmPo; NYBP

All's ill and will be so. The Wind Is Ill. John Malcolm Brinnin. LiTA

All's Not That Simple. Shin Shalom, *tr. fr. Hebrew by* Bernhard Frank.

All's over, then: does truth sound bitter. The Lost Mistress. Robert Browning. BoLoP; NOBE; OBEV; OBNC

All's Right with the World. Gerald Massey. EBVV

All's Vast. Francis Thompson. *See* O nothing in this corporal earth of man.

All's Well. Whittier. OxBSP

All's Well That Ends Well, *sels.* Shakespeare.
"O Lord, sir, let me live, or let me see my death!" OxAEP-1

Allthough the most do with officious heat. On the Death of the Queen of Bohemia. Katherine Philips. KTR

Alluding to the One-armed Bandit. D. C. Berry. BXAP

Allusion to Horace, An, *sels.* The Earl of Rochester.
"Sedley has that prevailing, gentle art." EPCY
"Should I be troubled when the purblind knight." EPCY
"Waller, by nature for the bays designed." EPCY

Allusion to Horace; or, the Tenth Satire of the First Book, An. The Earl of Rochester. APAS

Alma. Tom Lehrer. NBLV

Alma Mater, Forget Me. William Cole. FiBHP

Alma; or, The Progress of the Mind, *sels.* Matthew Prior.
"In Britain's isles, as Heylyn notes." NOEC

Alma, te quiero que tú no eres ni gringa. Santos and Stones. J. Delayne Barber. LoHo

Alma Venus, *sels.* Bernard O'Dowd.

Almada Hill: An Epistle from Lisbon, *sels.* William Julius Mickle.
"While you, my friend, from louring wintry plains." OBTV

Almagest, Last Letter to Zakarias. Siv Cedering. PBCAP

Almanac. May Swenson. NYBP

Almanac Verse. Samuel Danforth. SCAP

Almanac Verse. *Unknown.* SCAP

Almanack for the Year of Our Lord, 1657, An. Samuel Bradstreet. SCAP

Almanac's green vellum skin is rubbed. Peter Scupham. *Fr.* Marginalia. SCBI

Almightie Judge, how shall poore wretches brook. Judgement. George Herbert. ESCV; GeHe; SeCP

Almighty and everlasting God, we thank Thee. Prayer for Every Day. *Unknown, tr. fr. Fanti by* Kweku Martin. PBA

Almighty creator and ruler as well. Hymn to the Creator. John Clare. NOBVV

Almighty father! of high Heaven posses'd! The Lord's Prayer in Verse. Aaron Hill. FaBoUs

Almighty God. (*LL*) Caedmon's Hymn. Caedmon. EBEV, *tr. by* Sally Purcell; OAEL-1, *tr. by* Walter Kendrick; TEP, *tr. by* Walter Kendrick

Almighty God, Fader of Hevene. A Prayer to the Trinity. *Unknown.* MeEL

Almighty God in Being Was. Silas Ballou. AH

Almighty God, Thy Constant Care. Henry Stevenson Washburn. AH

Almighty God, who are mother and father to us all. Helen Weaver. EaPr

Almighty God, who fillest the recesses of the heavens. Bishop Patrick, *tr. fr. Latin.* NOIV

Almighty God, Whose Justice Like a Sun. Hilaire Belloc. TrPWD

Almighty Lord, with One Accord. Melancthon W. Stryker. AH

Almighty Maker God! Isaac Watts. *Fr.* Sincere Praise. TrPWD

Almighty Sovereign of the Skies! Nathan Strong. AH

Almighty Spake, and Gabriel Sped, Th'. George Richards. AH

Almighty! What Is Man? Solomon ibn Gabirol, *tr. fr. Hebrew by* Emma Lazarus. TrJP

Almond Blossom. Sir Edwin Arnold. GN

Almond Blossom. D. H. Lawrence. FaBoPP

Almond flourisheth, the birch trees flow, The. Signs of Spring. Sir Thomas Browne. NOSC

Almond groves of Samarkand, The. The East A-Callin.' Oscar Wilde. Fr. Ave Imperatrix. OtMeF

Almond Tree, The. Jon Stallworthy. NoAM; NoP

Almost always underground dank. A Lyric Meditation on Sour Locker Rooms. Dabney Stuart. Fr. Opposite Field, The. NGP

Almost Aubade. Marilyn Hacker. NoAM

Almost before the princess had grown cold. The True Story of Snow White. Bruce Bennett. SM

Almost believed in. Paul Brown. Fr. De Rebus. NBrP

Almost bought a machete. The Weight of the Sheets. Jon Forrest Glade. NGP

Almost enough. (LL) Femina Contra Mundum. G. K. Chesteron. OxAEP-2

Almost four years, and, though I merely guess. Elegy, An: December, 1970. Edgar Bowers. MT

Almost Going. David Huddle. PBCAP

Almost happy now, he looked at his estate. Voltaire at Ferney. W. H. Auden. LiTA; LiTM

Almost Human. C. Day Lewis. NoAM

Almost I, yes, I hear. W. S. Graham. Fr. Dark Dialogues, The. OxBS

Almost Love. Magaly Sánchez, tr. fr. Spanish by Margaret Randall. AIW

Almost naked like the children of the sea. (LL) Portrait. Antonio Machado Ruiz. RaBo; STV

Almost Persuaded. Philip Paul Bliss. AH

Almost reluctant, we approach the block. Thumbprint. Celeste Turner Wright. Poetsp

Almost sheer fatigue. Early Pregnancy. Penelope Shuttle. BrRo

Almost singing, she stares past the crowd and flies. Old Woman Awaiting the Greyhound Bus. Duane Niatum. CDW

Almost to Jealousy. (LL) So proud she was to die. Emily Dickinson. NOBA; OBD

Almost to Jesus. Michael Burkard. PFL

Almost touching you. (LL) The Porch. Gary Gildner. NGP

Almost twenty years. Drinking Cold Water. Peter Everwine. NNaP

Almost two years now I've been sleeping. After Elegies. Jean Valentine. LCAP

Almswomen. Edmund Blunden. OBMV; OxBTC

Alnight by the rose, rose. Unknown. See All night by the rose, rose.

Alnwick Castle. Fitz-Greene Halleck. AnAmPo

Aloe Plant, The. Henry Harbaugh. BLPA

Aloft in Heavenly Mansions, Doubleyou One. The Playboy of the Demi-World[: 1938]. William Plomer. IHNG; OxBTC; PeHV; UV

Aloft upon an old basaltic crag. Kane. Fitz-James O'Brien. PAH

Aloha Oe. Don Blanding. PoToHe

Alone. "Anna Akhmatova," tr. fr. Russian by Stephen Berg. BoWoP

Alone. Hayyim Nahman Bialik, tr. fr. Hebrew by Jessie Sampter. TrJP

Alone. Chu Shu-chen, tr. by Kenneth Rexroth. BoWoP

Alone. Walter de la Mare. CBLP; ChTr; EnLoPo

Alone. Jonathan Holden. Poetsp

Alone. James Joyce. InvP

Alone. Poe. See From childhood's hour I have not been.

Alone. Sappho, tr. fr. Greek by William Ellery Leonard. AWP

Alone. E. J. Scovell. GBL

Alone. Richard Shelton. NYBP

Alone. Celia Laighton Thaxter. AmWP

Alone. Tomas Transtromer, tr. fr. Swedish by Robin Fulton. PWE

Alone. Carolyn Wells. PoToHe

Alone am I, and alone I wish to be. Christine de Pisan, tr. fr. French by Julie Allen. BoWoP

Alone and Godless, stopped by the sudden edge. Patrick MacDonogh. Fr. Escape to Love. BIrV

Alone at night. 1951. Frank O'Hara. LCAP

Alone at night, afraid to move. Grave Stone. Tim Longville. VaA

Alone, at night, with all the world. Evil Nigger Waits for Lightnin.' Amiri Baraka. NOBA

Alone far in the wilds and mountains I hunt. Walt Whitman. Fr. Song of Myself. AmPP; LiTA; MoAmPo, (abr.); NOBA; OxBA; SAmP; SOTW, (much abr.)

Alone for the evening. Bringing Flowers. Roberta Spear. AmPA

Alone God sufficeth. (LL) Lines Written in Her Breviary. St. Theresa of Avila. AWP

Alone, he came to his decision. Felo de Se. Vernon Scannell. OBD

Alone, I live alone. Unknown. MiEL

Alone I sat; the summer day. Emily Brontë. NALW

Alone I stand in autumn cold. "Spring in Ch'in's Garden." Mao Tse-tung, tr. fr. Chinese by Eugene Eoyang. SuSp

Alone I tiptoe through the stars. Star Journey. Naomi Long Madgett. BPo

Alone in a cold autumn I stood. Midstream. Mao Tse-tung, tr. fr. Chinese by Earle Birney. MoCV

Alone in an Inn at Southampton, April the 25th, 1737. Aaron Hill. NOEC

Alone in greenwood must I roam. Hollin, Green Hollin. Unknown. GBP

Alone In Her Beauty. Tu Fu, tr. fr. Chinese by Witter Bynner. ArLo

Alone in the atoning belfry how I grieve. Giotto's Campanile. Guy Butler. PeSA

Alone in the Fields. Hermann Allmers, tr. fr. German by Philip L. Miller. RiWo

Alone in the great storm. (LL) Presaging. Rainer Maria Rilke. AWP; TrJP

Alone in the night. Stars. Sara Teasdale. FaPON

Alone in this desert under the cold moon. If I Forget Thee. Emanuel Litvinoff. TrJP

Alone is delicious. Alone. Jonathan Holden. Poetsp

Alone Is the Hunter. Harold Littlebird. VoR

Alone, Musing. Sir Thomas Wyatt. SiPSBD

Alone of gods death has no love for gifts. Aeschylus, tr. fr. Greek by C. M. Bowra. Fr. Niobe. OBD

Alone on Lykaion since man hath been. Mount Lykaion. Trumbull Stickney. Fr. Sonnets from Greece. OxBA; Son; TrGrPo

Alone on our porch swing, I hear the Future. Late Fall Night. William Trowbridge. NGP

Alone on the hill of storms. Battle of the Stars. Adah Isaacs Menken. CBWP-1

Alone on the hill-top, sadly and silently. Banishment. Mairi MacLeod, tr. fr. Gaelic by Rev. Thomas Pattison. ScCV

Alone on the jagged rock. November Day at McClure's. Robert Bly. NU

Alone on the lawn. The Dancing Cabman. J. B. Morton. MoShBr; NOBL

Alone on the shore in the pause of the nighttime. The Full Heart. Robert Nichols. BoNaP

Alone on the tower. Diver. R. A. Simpson. CBAP

Alone one noon on a sheet of igneous rock. Myths. Guy Butler. PeSA

Alone she feeds the white swans. The Swans of Vadstena. Ralph Gustafson. MoCV

Alone the pallid cuckoo now. Pallid Cuckoo. David Campbell. CBAP

Alone together, enraptured, singing! In the Abbey Ruins. Victor Hugo, tr. fr. French by Philip L. Miller. RiWo

Alone up here on the mountain. Unknown. NOIV

Alone, upon the broad low bench, he sits. To Borglum's Seated Statue of Abraham Lincoln. Charlotte Brewster Jordan. OHIP

Alone upon the housetops to the North. The Love Song of Har Dyal. Kipling. OtMeF

Alone walking,/ In thought pleining. Wishing My Death. Unknown. MeEL

Alone with God for one sweet, solemn hour. The Quiet Hour. Louise Hollingsworth Bowman. BLRP

Alone with His Work. Yannis Ritsos, tr. fr. Greek by Paul Merchant. AnRep

Along a river-side, I know not where. The Washers of the Shroud. James Russell Lowell. PAH

Along Ancona's hills the shimmering heat. Poppies in the Wheat. Helen Hunt Jackson.
(Poppies on the Wheat.) AmWP

Along come that F.F.V., the swiftest on the line. George Allen. Unknown. AmFP

Along East River and the Bronx. Ode to Walt Whitman. Federico García Lorca, tr. fr. Spanish. PeHV

Along Highway 40, blare. The Shape of Autumn. Virginia Russ. GoYe

Along History. Muriel Rukeyser. NALW; NNaP

Along how many Main Streets have I walked. The Eternal Return. Robert Silliman Hillyer. AiP; NYBP

Along Hsi-ling Lake under the cypress trees. (LL) A Song of Hsi-ling Lake. Su Hsiao-hsiao. WPC

Along that footpath, shepherd, past the oaks. Theocritus [or Theokritus], tr. fr. Greek by Anthony Holden. GrAn

Along the alleys I can hear the love songs. The One. Gillian Conoley. Jaz

Along the avenue of cypresses. Giorno dei Morti. D. H. Lawrence. FaBoRV; NOBE

Along the Banks. Joel Barlow. AH; ChIV-1

Along the banks where Babel's current flows. Along the Banks. Joel Barlow. AH; ChIV-1

Along the blushing borders bright with dew. Spring Flowers. James Thomson. Fr. Seasons, The. NOBE

Along the brook many little flowers grow. The Miller's Flowers. Wilhelm Müller, *tr. fr. German by* Philip L. Miller. *Fr.* Beautiful Maid of the Mill, The. RiWo

Along the caravan routes go the camels tall. Camels in Persia. Dorothy Wellesley. OBTV

Along the cement walkway I pick up. Markings. Frank Steele. Poetsp

Along the dark, and silent night. The Bell-Man. Robert Herrick. BeJo

Along the dark bank of the river. After the Night Hunt. James Dickey. PoA

Along the Field as We Came By. A. E. Housman. *Fr.* Shropshire Lad, A. FaPoB; HAP; MoAB; MoBrPo; WeW

Along the garden terrace, under which. George Meredith. *Fr.* Modern Love. NOBVV

Along the great coast south of Bordeaux. The Bunkers. Michael O'Loughlin. *Fr.* Shards, The. IB; PBCIP

Along the lake the bugle rings. Echo Reverie. H. Cordelia Ray. CBWP-3

Along the line of smoky hills. Indian Summer. Wilfred Campbell. NOBC

Along the path of ghosts, the ashen path. Package for Another World. Jemal Sharah. NOBAu

Along the path that skirts the wood. The Three Musicians. Aubrey Beardsley. NOBVV; OBTV; PeVV

Along the Quay. Sully-Prudhomme, *tr. fr. French by* Philip L. Miller. RiWo

Along the quay the great ships. Along the Quay. Sully-Prudhomme, *tr. fr. French by* Philip L. Miller. RiWo

Along the Road. Robert Browning Hamilton. BLPA; BLPL

Along the road all shapes must travel by. Prolonged Sonnet: In the Last Days of the Emperor Henry VII. Simone dall' Antella, *tr. fr. Italian by* Dante Gabriel Rossetti. AWP

Along the roadside, like the flowers of gold. Whittier. *Fr.* Among the Hills. NAAL-1; OxBA; PoEL-4

Along the sprawled body of the derailed. Outside Fargo, North Dakota. James Wright. LCAP; NNaP

Along the Strand. Alfred Mombert, *tr. fr. German by* Jethro Bithell. TrJP

Along the street a post-horn sounds. The Mail-Coach. Wilhelm Müller, *tr. fr. German by* Philip L. Miller. *Fr.* Winter's Journey, The. RiWo

Along the thousand roads of France. The Good Joan. Lizette Woodworth Reese. FaPON; MoShBr

Along the walks the sweet queens walk their dogs. Central Park West. Jack Spicer. PeHV

Along the water the small invisible owls. Dawn near an Old Battlefield, in a Time of Peace. James Wright. AnAn

Along those roads we cannot hear him bark. (*LL*) The Tramp. Ben King. AnAmPo

Along thy dead indifference of walls. (*LL*) The Berg. Herman Melville. AmPP; LiTA; NOBA; NoP; PoEL-5; TAP

Along with the wraggle taggle gipsies, O! (*LL*) The Wraggle Taggle Gipsies. *Unknown.* BoTP; CH; FaPON; WiR

Alons au bois le may cueillir. Charles, Duc d'Orléans, *tr. fr. French by* W. E. Henley. AWP

Aloof. Christina Rossetti. *See* Irresponsive silence of the land, The.

Aloof, as if a thing of mood and whim. The Schreckhorn. Thomas Hardy. OAEL-2

Aloofe, aloofe, and come no neare. Sea Marke. John Smith. SCAP

Alow and aloof. The Windy Night. Thomas Buchanan Read. GN

Alpaca pictures of the previous past. Confounded Nonsense. Tom Hood. CBNP; FaBoNo

Alpha and Omega, God, my God! Prayer to God the Father. Hildebert, *tr. fr. Latin by* Helen Waddell. MLL

Alpha, Beta, Gamma, Delta. Greek Alphabet. *Unknown.* ISE

Alpha November Golf Sierra Tango. Tom Clark. UL

Alphabet. Edward Lear. FaBoNo

Alphabet, The. Karl Shapiro. NoAM; PoA

Alphabet, The. *Unknown.* ReMoGo

Alphabet ("A, B, C, D, E, F, G.") *Unknown.* FaBoUs

Alphabet, An. Edward Lear. OxBChV

Alphabet by the Pool on a Sunday Afternoon, The. Lusia Slomkowska. LoHo

Alphabet Calendar of Amergin, The. *Unknown, tr. fr. Irish by* Robert Graves. BIrV

Alphabet ("Great A was alarmed at B's bad behavior"). *Unknown.* FaBoUs; OxNR

Alphabet of Aristotle, The. Mayster Benet. FaBoUs

Alphabet of Fishes. Bob Cobbing. NBrP

Alphabet of, The/ the trees. The Botticellian Trees. William Carlos Williams. AmPP; LiTA

Alphabetical Song on the Corn Law Bill. *Unknown.* OxBoLi

Alphabets. Seamus Heaney. NoAM

Alphonse arrives as a fifth season. A Visit from Alphonse. Paul Zimmer. GOYP

Alphonso of Castile. Emerson. NOBA

Alpine. R. S. Thomas. BoNaP; RFM

Alpine Spirit's Song. Thomas Lovell Beddoes. OBNC; OBTV

Already Autumn, and from the belt of Boötes. To Epicles. Antipater of Thessalonica, *tr. fr. Greek by* Tony Harrison. GrAn

Already autumn begins here in the mossy rocks. Thinking of "The Autumn Fields." Robert Bly. NNaP

Already blushes on thy cheek. Nemesis. Emerson. NOBA

Already Embraced by the Arm of Heavenly Solace. Nelly Sachs, *tr. fr. German by* Michael Roloff. PoSu

Already fallen plum-bloom stars the green. The Poor Man's Pig. Edmund Blunden. MoBrPo

Already forfeit, now for ever lost. (*LL*) Dad. Elaine Feinstein. AIW

Already He has done. (*LL*) Creation. Robin Gurr. NOBAu

Already I am no longer looked at with lechery or love. A Sunset of the City. Gwendolyn Brooks. FaBoWP; LCAP; LPA; PBWP

Already it bore the scars of secret tears. (*LL*) Complaint of a Neglected Wife. Meng Chiao. PLT

Already it's late summer. Sunbathers go. The Divine Insect. John Hall Wheelock. GoYe; NYBP

Already marked out for death. (*LL*) The Secular. Chris Wallace-Crabbe. NOBAu

Already old age is wrinkling my. Sappho, *tr. fr. Greek by* Josephine Balmer. AIW

Already one day has detached itself from all the rest up ahead. Reunion. Charles Wright. CAPP

Already prepared in the golden chamber. Antipater of Sidon, *tr. fr. Greek by* Tony Harrison. GrAn

"Already," Said My Host. Michael Roberts. OBD

Already she seems bone thin. A Poem about Breasts. James Wright. TAP

Already sleek with narrow eyes. (*LL*) Surfers at Santa Cruz. Paul Goodman. FF

Already something of a stranger now. Epil y Filiast. Harri Webb. AngWe

Already swallows build their homes of mud. Thyillos, *tr. fr. Greek by* Adrian Wright. GrAn

Already the ducklings resemble their aunts and uncles. Andrew Crozier. VaA

Already the field, fair with leaves, in her fruitful bringing to birth. Theaitetos, *tr. fr. Greek by* John Heath-Stubbs *and* Carol A. Whiteside. GrAn

Already the old men at the kraal are sharpening their knives! (*LL*) The Praises of the Canna. *Unknown.* PeSAV

Already the past's/ a touched-up picture. End of Term. Prunella Power. Mes

Already we are both fans of the green and golden dragon. A Natural History of Unicorns and Dragons My Daughter and I Have Known. William Pitt Root. SM

Already yesterday's lips have broken. Lan Ling. *Fr.* White Color of Nearness, The. WPC

Als I me rode this endre day. The Singing Maid. *Unknown.* MeEL

Also All. Shu Ting, *tr. fr. Chinese by* Donald Finkel *with* Yi Jinsheng. SpMi

Also an old image has a moment's birth. Moon. Nathan Alterman, *tr. fr. Hebrew by* Ruth Finer Mintz. MHP

Also for little ones, just like me. The Blade of Grass Sings to the Stream. Leah Goldberg, *tr. fr. Hebrew by* Ruth Finer Mintz. *Fr.* Songs of the Stream. MHP

Also glisten, and the world is mine. (*LL*) Rain Downriver. Philip Levine. VCAP

Also in sleep I see you, comprehend. The Fire in the Stone. Tuvia Rivner, *tr. fr. Hebrew by* Ruth Finer Mintz. MHP

Also it could prove serious for the pool. Sugar Loaf. David Campbell. FaBoMA

Also scripture saithe, woo be to that regyon. *Unknown.* FaBoEH

Also Ulysses once — that other war. Kilroy. Peter Viereck. ArOW; FF; MoAmPo

(Kilroy Was Here.) PoRA

Altaforte. Ezra Pound. CMoP; FaBoTw; ImPo; LiTA; MoAB; MoAmPo; NOBA; SOTW

Altamira. William Hart-Smith. FaBoMA

Altar, The. George Herbert. AngWe; ChIV-1; ESCV; GeHe; HoPM; InPS; JCP; NAEL-1; NOSC; OAEL-1; Poetr; SeCP; SeCV-1; TrCP; TrGrPo

Altar boy from a Mass for the dead, The. Alive Alive O. Padraic Fiacc. PeIV

Altar boy marches up the altar steps, The. Soldiers. Padraic Fiacc. PNI

Altar of glasses behind the bar, The. The Drinking Art. Robert Minhinnick. AngWe

Altar Prayers. *Unknown, tr. fr. Hawaiian by* N. B. Emerson. WTO

Altars in the Street, The. Denise Levertov. CAPP

Altarwise by Owl-Light. Dylan Thomas. LiTM

Sels.

  "While you, my friend, from louring wintry plains." OBTV

  "Altarwise by owl-light in the half-way house." CMoP; FaBoMo; MoAB; Son

  "Death is all metaphors, shape in one history." CMoP; MoAB; Son

  "First there was the lamb on knocking knees." CMoP

  "From the oracular archives and the parchment." CMoP

  "Let the tale's sailor from a Christian voyage." CMoP; FaBoMo; OAEL-2

  "Now stamp the Lord's Prayer on a grain of rice." FaBoMo

  "This was the crucifixion on the mountain." CMoP

  "What is the metre of the dictionary?" CMoP; FaBoMo

Altarwise by owl-light in the half-way house. Dylan Thomas. *Fr.* Altarwise by Owl-Light. CMoP; FaBoMo; LiTM; MoAB; Son

Altazor, sels. Vincente Huidobro.

  "At the horislope of the mountizon." TSaS, *tr. by* Eliot Weinberger

Alter or mend eternal fact. (*LL*) The Past. Emerson. FaBoCh; LiTA; MeMAP; PoEL-4; TAP

Alter! When the hills do. Emily Dickinson. AmPP; CBLP; FaBoBe; SoSe; VBLP

Altered look about the hills, An. Emily Dickinson. OxBA; PPP; SoSe

Alternative Endings to an Unwritten Ballad. Paul Dehn. FiBHP

Alternatives. Kingsley Amis. OxBC

Alternatives. Peter Cooley. AmPA

Altho' a slave me is born and bred. J. B. Moreton. PBCV

Although a poor blind boy! (*LL*) The Blind Boy. Colley Cibber. GTBS; GTBS-P; NOEC; OxBChV

Although accustomed to picking them, it always. The Woman and the Aloe. Perseus Adams. PeSA

Although art is autonomous. On This Day I Complete My Fortieth Year. Peter Porter. NAs

Although at first it was single. The Trace. Roy Fisher. VaA

Although crowds gathered once if she but showed her face. Fallen Majesty. W. B. Yeats. PoA

Although, great Queen, thou now in silence lie. In Honour of That High and Mighty Princess Queen Elizabeth of Happy Memory. Anne Bradstreet. NALW

Although he has no form. Mukta Bai, *tr. fr. Marathi by* Willis Barnstone. BoWoP

Although [*or* Altho'] I be the basest of mankind. St. Simeon Stylites. Tennyson. NOBVV; OAEL-2

Although I can see him still. The Fisherman. W. B. Yeats. CMoP; HAP; NoAM

Although I come to you constantly. Ono no Komachi, *tr. fr. Japanese by* Kenneth Rexroth *and* Ikuko Atsumi. WPJ

Although I Conquer All the Earth. *Unknown.* ArLo; TTTS

Although I cry and though my eyes still shed. Louise Labé, *tr. fr. French.* BoWoP, *tr. by* Willis Barnstone

Although I do not hope to turn again. T. S. Eliot. *Fr.* Ash Wednesday. LiTA; MoAB; MoAmPo; NoAM; NOBA; OxBA; VGW

Although I do not know. Saigyo, *tr. fr. Japanese by* Arthur Waley. AWP

Although I had a check. The Earl of Surrey. SiPS

Although I leave Braglu, I am close to it. I Djanggawul, am paddling. Djanggawul Song-Cycle. *Aborigine Oral Tradition*, *tr. by* R. M. Berndt. WTO

Although I mean it, and project the meaning. The Ice-Cream Wars. John Ashbery. CAPP; PoA

Although I put away his life. Emily Dickinson. MoAmPo

Although I Remember the Sound. Robert Huff. SM

Although I shelter from the rain. The Lamentation of the Old Pensioner. W. B. Yeats. HAP; PeVV; TRP; WeW

Although I was her pupil,/ even I reproach Myrtis. Korinna, *tr. fr. Greek by* Willis Barnstone. BoWoP

Although it is a cold evening. At the Fishhouses. Elizabeth Bishop. CoAP; FaBoWP; HAP; HCAP; LCAP; LiTM; NAAL-2; NALW; NoP; NYBP; Poetr; PoRA; VCAP

Although it is night, I sit in the bathroom, waiting. Adolescence — II. Rita Dove. AmPA; HCAP; NoAM; VCAP

Although it is not plainly visible to the eye. Fujiwara no Toshiyuki, *tr. by* Arthur Waley. *Fr.* Kokin Shu. AWP

Although it may appear archaic. Eppur Si Muove? Robert Silliman Hillyer. GoYe

Although it's cold no clothes I wear. *Unknown.* GBP

Although lamps burn along the silent streets. James Thomson ("B.V."). *Fr.* City of Dreadful Night, The. EBVV; OBNC

Although Michaelmas Daisies bloom for a very long time. Gather Ye Rosebuds. Laurence Fowler. BXAP

Although my claws weaken. Sweetness. *Unknown, tr. fr. Irish by* John Montague. BIrV

Although my house floats on a lawn. Blues for John Coltrane, Dead at 41. William Matthews. Jaz

Although only a fool would mock. Queen Mother to New Queen. Robert Graves. OBSV

Although propriety be crossed. A New Year's Gift. William Cartwright. BeJo

Although she feeds me bread of bitterness. America. Claude McKay. CDC; MoP; NIP; NoAM; PoBA; PoNe; TAP; TTY

Although she's a girl, Dorkion. Asclepiades, *tr. fr. Greek by* Kenneth Rexroth. GrAn; PGA

Although some are afraid that to speak of a spade as a spade is a social mistake. Rigoletto. Newman Levy. OBAL

Although the aepyornis. He "Digesteth Harde Yron." Marianne Moore. CMoP; NoAM

Although the field lay cut in swaths. Timothy. Timothy Steele. InPK

Although the sign says. The Wild Horses of Assateague Island. John Bensko. MT; NGP

Although the snow still lingers. Last Snow. Andrew Young. OxBTC

Although there is yet. Ray A. Young Bear. *Fr.* Three translated Poems for October. ETG

Although they have tightly bound my arms and legs. On the Way. Ho Chi Minh. EaPr, *tr. by* Christopher Jenkins, Tran Khanh Tuget, *and* Hugh Sanh Thong

Although, those years, we squandered. A Plaint of Flowers. Ernest Sandeen. CRP

Although thy blood be frozen, and thy scalp. To a Covetous Churl. Edward May. FaBoEE

Although thy hand and faith, and good work[e]s too. Change. John Donne. *Fr.* Elegies. CBLP; EBEV

Although Tormented. Kalonymos ben Judah, *tr. fr. Hebrew.* TrJP

Although We Do Not All the Good We Love. John Davies of Hereford. *Fr.* Holy Rood, The. Son

Although what glitters. Two Paintings by Gustav Klimt. Jorie Graham. SV

Although you sit in a room that is gray. Gray Room. Wallace Stevens. ArLo

Although your ears must be plentifully occupied. Julius Polyaenus, *tr. fr. Greek by* John Heath-Stubbs *and* Carol A. Whiteside. GrAn

Although your white bones waste in. On a Hound. Simonides, *tr. fr. Greek by* Kenneth Rexroth. PGA

Altitudes. Richard Wilbur. CMoP

Alton Locke, *sels.* Charles Kingsley.

  Sands of Dee, The. BeLS; CH; EBEvV; EBVV; FaBoPP; FaPON; FaPoR; GN; OxAEP-2; PlP; WBLP

Alumnus Football. Grantland Rice. PoLF

Aluqa, the demon who swims underwater in streams. Meadow Bug. Rossana Ombres, *tr. fr. Italian by* Ruth Feldman. NeIt

Always. Mark Strand. CAPP; Poetr; TRP

Always a third one's there. The Uninvited. Dorothy Livesay. NOBC

Always afraid to say more than it meant. (*LL*) The Letter. W. H. Auden. FaBoTw; MoP; NoAM

Always at dusk, the same tearless experience. The Eyes of My Regret. Angelina Weld Grimké. CDC

Always be kind to animals. John Gardner. ZA

Always before, we sped in the same direction. The Queen. Kenneth Pitchford. NYBP

Always before Your Voice My Soul. E. E. Cummings. LiTA; MoAmPo

Always Begin Where You Are. Thomas Hornsby Ferril. PrIm; VGW

Always driven, always in the bite of the blast. And Yet We Are Here! Karl Wolfskehl, *tr. fr. German by* Carol North Valhope *and* Ernst Morowitz. TrJP

Always expecting the winter. In Dream: The Privacy of Sequence. Ray A. Young Bear. CDW

Always Finish. *Unknown.* BLPA; FaBoBe; WBLP

Always first to rise. In My Father's House. George Barlow. Jaz

Always for thirty years now. Fish Peddler and Cobbler. Kenneth Rexroth. NNaP

Always, from My First Boyhood. John Peale Bishop. VGW

Always he sits in his accustomed place. Habitué. Helen Frith Stickney. GoYe

Always I have meant to write of Apollo Café. Apollo Café. Stephen Gray. PeSAV

Always I have searched for the mislaid tin spoon. One Fine Day. János Pilinszky, *tr. fr. Hungarian by* Peter Jay. PoSu

Always I lay upon the brink of love. Judas. Vassar Miller. ChIV-2; MoAmPo

Always — I tell you this they learned. House Fear. Robert Frost. *Fr.* Hill Wife, The. CMoP; HAP; InPS; LiTM; NoP; NTP; VGW

Always I thought they suffered, the way they huffed. On the Bearing of Waitresses. Rodney Jones. BAP-90

Always/ in the middle. Love, Maybe. Audre Lorde. Poetr

Always in the Parting Year. Else Lasker-Schüler, *tr. fr. German by* Ralph Manheim. TrJP

Always it happens when we are not there. Metamorphosis. May Sarton. ArNa

Always it was a summer afternoon. The House of Broughton Street. Mary Ann Larkin. AiP

Always it was going on. Today Is Friday. Ramon Guthrie. PoE

Always just one demon in the attic. Interferon. Miroslav Holub, *tr. by* Ewald Osers. PWE

Always on Monday, God's name is in the morning papers. The Day after Sunday. Phyllis McGinley. MoAmPo; OBSV; UnPo

Always pruning, always cropping? Matthew 9.12. Francis Quarles. ChIV-2

Always she goes like a captured wild bird. Sappho. Jack Cope. PeSA

Always She Moves from Me. Shirley Kaufman. WPE

Always so late in the day. Always. Mark Strand. CAPP; Poetr; TRP

Always the arriving winds of words. Words. W. R. Rodgers. OxBSP; PNI

Always the Following Wind. W. H. Auden. MoBrPo

Always the same: watching. Watching War Movies. Lucien Stryk. ArOW; CAPP

Always the same, when on a fated night. The Onset. Robert Frost. CMoP; MoAB; MoAmPo; OxBA; PPP

Always the setting forth was the same. Odysseus. W. S. Merwin. NOBA; NoP

Always to want to. The Tortoise. Cid Corman. InPK; SM; VGW

Always too eager for the future, we. Next, Please. Philip Larkin. MoBrPo

Always True to You in My Fashion, *sels*. Cole Porter. "If a custom-tailored vet." NBLV

Always with love, with love. (*LL*) The Letter. Elizabeth Riddell. FaBoMA; NOBAu

Always/ with magpies' flights. Memorial for a Fisherman. Johannes Bobrowski, *tr. fr. German by* Don Bogen. AnAn

Always wonderful of this world, The. (*LL*) Black Love. Gwendolyn Brooks. VBLP

Always wondering what's left besides us. To GB from Tuscany. Paul Monette. PFL

Always you are there — standing. The Anima Has a Predilection. Michael Harlow. *Fr.* Poem Then, for Love. PeNZ

Always your body like a foreign country. Location. Knute Skinner. MAT

Alzheimer's: The Wife. C. K. Williams. VCAP

Am Belisarius? (*LL*) Belisarius. Longfellow. PoEL-5; WiR

Am, by being dead, immortal, Can ghosts die? (*LL*) The Computation. John Donne. CBNP; NoSic; OxBSP; SoSe

Am I a king, that I should call my own. From My Arm-Chair. Longfellow. BLPA

Am I a stone and not a sheep. Good Friday. Christina Rossetti. ChIV-2; MeMBP; PoEL-5

Am I alone,/ And unobserved? I am! If You're Anxious for to Shine in the High Aesthetic Line. W. S. Gilbert. *Fr.* Patience. NAEL-2; NBLV

Am I alone — or is it you, my friend? Toussaint L'Ouverture. E. A. Robinson. PoNe

Am I despised because you say. To a Gentlewoman Objecting to Him His Grey Hairs. Robert Herrick. BeJo; CaPo; JCP

Am I failing? For no longer can I cast. George Meredith. *Fr.* Modern Love. EnVR; GBL; SCGP

Am I mad, O noble Festus. The Distracted Puritan. Richard Corbett [*or* Corbet]. BeJo; OxBoLi

Am I sadly cast aside. The Slave's Complaint. George Moses Horton. AAP

Am I the slave they say. Soggarth Aroon. John Banim. TIRV

Am i there with the strawberry vanilla oozing down my face. A Maze of Decades. Martha Sansom. UnDi

Am I thus conquered? Have I lost the powers. Mary Sidney Wroth, Countess of Montgomery. *Fr.* Urania. NAEL-1; WPE
(Sonnet: "Am I thus conquered? Have I lost the powers.") NOSC

Am I thy gold? Or purse, Lord, for thy wealth. Edward Taylor. *Fr.* Preparatory Meditations Before My Approach to the Lord's Supper. EAP; LiTA; MeMAP; NOSC; OxBA; TAP

Am I to be blamed for the state of it now? — Surely not. Clio's. Mick Imlah. CBLP

Am I to become profligate as if I were a blonde? Meditations in an Emergency. Frank O'Hara. CAPP; TAP; VCAP

Am I to blame the drink or the downpour? Antipater of Thessalonica, *tr. fr. Greek by* Tony Harrison. GrAn

Am I to Lose You? Louisa S. Guggenberger. NOBVV

Am I too dangerous, that no man can let. D. B. Wyndham Lewis. *Fr.* If So the Man You Are. OBSV

Am I your only love — in the whole world — now? Tell Me Again. Nigâr Hanim, *tr. fr. Turkish by* Tâlat S. Halman. PBWP

Am not I in blessed case. My Dear Lady. *Unknown.* EIL

Ama Credo. Margaret Reckord. AIW

Amadu I live alone inside four walls of books. Letter to a Tormented Playwright. Syl Cheney-Coker. HBAPE

Amagansett Beach Revisited. John Hall Wheelock. NYBP

Amanda! Robin Klein. OTCP

Amanda Barker. Edgar Lee Masters. *Fr.* Spoon River Anthology. NoAM

Amang the holtis hair. (*LL*) Robin [*or* Robene] and Makyne. Robert Henryson. OBEV; PeLV; PoEL-1

Amang the lily flower. (*LL*) The Birth of Robin Hood. *Unknown.* OAEL-1; OxBB

Amantium Irae. Richard Edwards. *See* In going to my naked bed, as one that would have slept.

Amantium Irae Amoris Redintegratio. Richard Edwards. EIL; OBEV

Amarantha sweet and fair. To Amarantha, That She Would Dishevel Her Hair. Richard Lovelace. BeJo; HoPM; NoP; OBEV; SeCP; SeCV-1; TrGrPo
(Song: To Amarantha, That She Would Dishevel Her Hair.) CaPo; NOSC; PoE

Amateur, The. Russell Edson. LCAP

Amateur and muddled, as their sex goes. The Professionals. Geoffrey Grigson. PoA

Amateur Flute, The. *Unknown.* BXAP

Amateurs of Heaven, The. Howard Nemerov. SoSe

Amateurs, we gathered mushrooms. Fall. Robert Hass. AmPA

Amazed we read of Nature's early throes. Man the Monarch. Mary Leapor. ECWP

Amazing Grace. Anselm Hollo. PoM

Amazing, how the young man who empties. Wing Road. Eamon Grennan. PBCIP

Amazing how this world manages to be all of a piece. Lesson in "A Waltz for Debby," The. Rosemary Catacalos. AfAz

Amazing, how we waited for his call. (*LL*) The Iceman. Gordon Challis. PeNZ

Amazing monster! that, for aught I know. A Fish Answers. Leigh Hunt. *Fr.* Fish, the Man, and the Spirit, The. ChTr; EnRP; FiBHP; FM; GGP; HAP; NBLV; NOBL; NTP; OBEV; PoEL-4; SCGP
(Fish Replies, A.) PeLV
(Fish to Man.) MoShBr

Amazing Sight! The Saviour Stands. Henry Alline. *Fr.* Christ Inviting Sinners to His Grace. AH

Amazing thing happened to me, An. Daniil Kharms, *tr. fr. Russian by* George Gibian. FaBoNo

Amazons, The, *sels*. Marie-Anne du Boccage, *tr. fr. French by* Dorothy Backer.

Amazons. Louise Glück. NAmP90

Ambarvalia, *sels*. Arthur Hugh Clough. Pont-y-Wern. FaBoPP

Ambassador, The. Stevie Smith. Mes

Ambassador Puser the ambassador. Memorial Rain. Archibald MacLeish. AmPP; CMoP; LiTA; MeMAP; MoAB; MoAmPo; OBWP

Amber Bead, The. Robert Herrick. BeJo; CaPo; ChTr

Amber husk/ fluted with gold. Sea Poppies. Hilda Doolittle ("H. D."). NALW

Ambition. Mary Astell. KTR

Ambition. W. H. Davies. MoBrPo; TrGrPo

Ambition. John Fletcher *and* William Shakespeare. *Fr.* King Henry VIII. TrGrPo

Ambition. Robert Herrick. CaPo

Ambition. Maggie Pogue Johnson. CBWP-4

Ambition. H. Cordelia Ray. AmWP; CBWP-3

Ambition. Joachim Ringelnatz, *tr. fr. German by* C. Middleton. OBD

Ambition. Nathaniel Parker Willis. OBCA

Ambition of Ghosts, The. Rosemarie Waldrop. UL

Ambitious. Jim Gustafson. UL

Ambitious Ant, The. Amos R. Wells. OBCA; OBSP

Ambitious ant would a-travelling go, The. The Ambitious Ant. Amos R. Wells. OBCA; OBSP

Amboyna; or, The Cruelties of the Dutch to the English Merchants, *sels*. Dryden.
"As needy gallants in the scriv'ners' hands." OBSV

Ambrose is an Old Etonian and he. Fiction: The House Party. Gavin Ewart. PeLV

Ambrosia. William Hart-Smith. FaBoMA

Ambrosia, brought safe. Leonidas of Tarentum, *tr. fr. Greek by* Kenneth Rexroth. GrAn

Ambrosia of Dionysus and Semele, The. Robert Graves. NYBP

Ambulance men touched her cold, The. The Death of Marilyn Monroe. Sharon Olds. HeIP

Ambulance Train. W. W. Gibson. NSI

Ambulances. Philip Larkin. FaBoTw; NAEL-2; OxBC

Ambulando. Charles Brasch. PeNZ

Ambushed by Angels. Gustav Davidson. GoYe

Ambushed myself discovered. Humility. Marie Luise Kaschnitz, tr. fr. German by Michael Hamburger. WPOW

Amelia Mixed the Mustard. A. E. Housman. FaBoNo

Amen. Frederick G. Browning. BLRP

Amen. (LL) Everywhere is the green of new growth. Unknown. EaPr

Amen. (LL) For the marvelous grace of Your Creation. Unknown. EaPr

Amen. (LL) Grace after Dinner. Burns. FaBoEE

Amen. Richard W. Thomas. PoBA

Amen. (LL) Wyatt Resteth Here. The Earl of Surrey. NoP

Amen! Amen! (LL) Holy Willie's Prayer. Burns. EBEV; FaBoBl; NOEC; OBSV; OxBS; PoE; PoEL-4; PPP; TFi

"Amen! Amen!" (LL) The Bells. Saul Tchernichowsky. MHP

"Amen, amen," dicentes. (LL) Tutivillus, the Devil. Unknown. EBEV; MeEL

Amen. The casket like a spaceship bears her. Annie Hill's Grave. James Merrill. WeW

Amen, who scared off my girl. (LL) The Rattle Bag. Dafydd ap Gwilym. NBLV; RB

Amendis to the Telyouris and Sowtaris for the Turnament Maid on Thame, The. William Dunbar. OBSV

Amendment. Thomas Traherne. SeCV-2

Amends for Ladies, sels. Nathaniel Field.
  Rise, Lady Mistress, Rise! EIL

Amends to the Tailors and Shoemakers. William Dunbar. See Betuix twell houris and ellevin.

Amergin's Songs. Amergin. NOIV
  Sels.
  "Fish-teeming sea."
  "I am wind on sea."
  "I call the land of Ireland."

America. Maya Angelou. WoWa

America. Kofi Awoonor. HBAPE

America, sels. Blake.
  Prophecy, A. FaBoEH

America. Arthur Cleveland Coxe. PAH

America. Robert Creeley. MAT

America. Lucretia Davidson. AmWP

America. Henry Dumas. PoBA

America. Allen Ginsberg. CAPP; CoAP; HCAP; InPS; NaP; NoAM; PoBeRe; PoE; Poetr; PoM; PPP; TRP

America. Claude McKay. CDC; MoP; NIP; NoAM; PoBA; PoNe; TAP; TTY

America. John Newlove. NOBC

America. Wendy Rose. CDW

America. Samuel Francis Smith. AiP; AnAmPo; EBEvV; FaBoBe; FaPON; PoLF; WBLP

America. Walt Whitman. GOA

America; a Prophecy. (Shadowy daughter of Urthona stood before red Orc.) Blake. OAEL-2
  Sels.
  Empire Is No More. EnRP

America always! American Feuillage. Walt Whitman. CBCK

America America. Owed to America. Lawrence Durrell. OBTV

America Bleeds. Angelo Lewis. PoBA

America! dear brother land! Greeting from England. Unknown. PAH

America for Me. Henry van Dyke. BLPA; BLPL; WBLP

America Greets an Alien. Unknown.

America, here is your son, born of your iron heel. The True American. Georgia Douglas Johnson. ShDr

America, I Love You. Bert Kalmar and Harry Ruby. FiBHP

America I'm putting my queer shoulder to the wheel. (LL) America. Allen Ginsberg. CAPP; CoAP; HCAP; InPS; NaP; NoAM; PoBeRe; PoE; Poetr; PoM; PPP; TRP

America Is Hard to See. Robert Frost. AiP

America, it is to thee. From America. James M. Whitfield. BPo

America I've given you all and now I'm nothing. America. Allen Ginsberg. CAPP; CoAP; HCAP; InPS; NaP; NoAM; PoBeRe; PoE; Poetr; PoM; PPP; TRP
  (On America.) IHNG

America, my own! National Song. William Henry Venable. PAH

America, O Power benign, great hearts revere your name. Land of the Free. Arthur Nicholas Hosking. BLPA

America the Beautiful. Katharine Lee Bates. BLPA; EaPr, st. 1 only; EBEvV; FaBoBe; FaBV; FaPON; FaPON; GOA; TAP; WBLP; WGRP

America! thou fractious nation. A Proclamation. Unknown. PAH

America Was Promises, sels. Archibald MacLeish.

America, watch out! Flesh Coupon. Jeff Wright. UL

America, you are luckier. The United States. Goethe, tr. fr. German by Robert Bly. AiP

America, you ode for reality! America. Robert Creeley. MAT

American blacks are known. Anti Apart Hate Art. Michelle T. Clinton. AIW

American Boyhood, An. Jonathan Holden. Poetsp

American Change. Allen Ginsberg. HCAP

American Dream, The, sels. Johnie Scott.

American Dreams. Louis Simpson. CAPP

American Eagle, The. D. H. Lawrence. OAEL-2

American Experiment has entered, The. My Friends the Pigeons. Richard Katrovas. NAmP90

American Falls. Greg Keeler. SM

American Farm, 1934. Genevieve Taggard. VGW

American Feuillage. Walt Whitman. CBCK

American Flag, The. Joseph Rodman Drake. AnAmPo; FaBoBe; GN; PAH; VPP; WBLP

American frigate, a frigate of fame, An. Paul Jones's Victory. Unknown. AmFP

American frigate from Baltimore came, An. Paul Jones. Unknown. PAH

American girl in Versailles, An. C. K. B. PeLi

American Heartbreak. Langston Hughes. AmPP; BPo; LiTM

American Heritage. Robert Sward. OBAL

American hero must triumph over, The. Eisenhower's Visit to Franco, 1959. James Wright. NaP

American History. Michael S. Harper. BPo; HCAP; NoAM

American History. W. R. Moses. LiTA

American Independence. Francis Hopkinson. PAH

American Indian, The. Unknown. FaBoCo; FiBHP; NBLV

American jump, American jump. Unknown. OxNR

American Landscape with Clouds & a Zoo. Jon Anderson. AnAn

American Letter. Archibald MacLeish. AmPP; OxBA

American Lights, Seen from Off Abroad. John Berryman. LCAP; OBAL

American Memory of Africa, An. Kofi Awoonor. HBAPE

American Names. Stephen Vincent Benét. GOA; OBAL; OxBA

American Patriot's Prayer, The. Unknown. PAH

American Plan. John Malcolm Brinnin. GOA

American Poet, The — "But Since It Came to Good." William Hathaway. UL

American Poetry. Louis Simpson. CAPP; MoP; NoAM; NOBA; TAP

American Portrait: Old Style. Robert Penn Warren. FYAP; Poetr

American Primitive. William Jay Smith. FF; InPK; MoAmPo; OxBSP; RaBo; TwCP

American Rain. Marilyn Chin. OpBo

American Rhapsody. Kenneth Fearing. MoAmPo

American Scenes (1904). Donald Justice. MT

American Soldier, The. Philip Freneau. TAP

American Soldier's Hymn, The. Unknown. PAH

American Sonnet, The. Frederick Seidel. Fr. AIDS Days. BAP-90

American Traveller, The. "Orpheus C. Kerr." FaBoCo; OBAL

American Twilights, 1957. James Wright. CoAP

American Vineyard. Mildred Cousens. GoYe

Americana IX. Unknown. InPS

Americanized. Bruce Dawe. CBAP

American's a hustler, for he says so, The. A Ballad of Abbreviations. G. K. Chesteron. NOBL

Americans, rejoice. Old Song Written during Washington's Life. Unknown. OHIP

America's Answer. R. W. Lilliard. BLPA

America's Wailing Wall. Naomi Quinonez. AfAz

America's Welcome Home. Henry van Dyke. AiP

America's Wounded Knee. Phillip William George. VoR

Ametas and Thestylis Making Hay-Ropes. Andrew Marvell. InvP; SeCP

Amhrán na mBréag. Pearse Hutchinson. PBCIP

Amid a downfall of dampish towels. (LL) At the Wrong Door. Christopher Reid. CBLP

Amid curled leaves and green. Peach Tree with Fruit. Padraic Colum. BoNaP

Amid my bale I bathe in bliss. A Straunge [or Strange] Passion of a Lover. George Gascoigne. AAS; EnRePo

Amid rows of tvs, screens blank as postcards from cemeteries. Utopia TV Store. Maxine Chernoff. UL

Amid the bitterness of things occult. (*LL*) For "Our Lady of the Rocks." Dante Gabriel Rossetti. EBEV

Amid the cares of married strife. Tell Her So. *Unknown*. PoToHe

Amid the Derringers I Ride. Edward Blishen. NTP

Amid the desolation of a city. The Tower of Famine. Shelley. Poetr

Amid the shimmer of the mirroring waves. A Song to be Sung on the Water. Friedrich Leopold Graf zu Stolberg, *tr. fr. German by* Philip L. Miller. RiWo

Amid the turbulent waters. The Turbulent Water. *Unknown, tr. fr. Chinese by* Robert Payne. TAL

Amid this fearful trance, a thundering sound. William Falconer. *Fr.* Shipwreck, The. ECEV

Amid this hot green glowing gloom. Interlude. Edith Sitwell. MoAB; MoBrPo

Amid Tibetan snows the ancient lama. What Hath Man Wrought Exclamation Point. Morris Bishop. NYBP

Amids my help, and helpless doth remain. (*LL*) Fruit of all the service that I serve, The. Sir Thomas Wyatt. SiPS; SiPSBD

Aminta, *sels.* Tasso, *tr. fr. Italian.*
    "O lovely age of gold!." OBVE, *tr. by* Leigh Hunt
    (Golden Age, The.) AWP, *tr. by* Leigh Hunt
    (Pastoral[l], A: "Oh [*or* O] happy golden age.") OAEL-1, *tr. by* Samuel Daniel; PoEL-2, *tr. by* Samuel Daniel

Amintas and Claudia; or, The Merry Shepherdess. *Unknown*. CoMu

Amish, The. John Updike. OBAL

Amish Rug, An. Michael Longley. CIP; PNI

Amnesia. David Lehman. EOEF

Amnesiac. Sylvia Plath. NYBP

Amo, Amas. John O'Keefe. ChTr; GBL

Amo, amas,/ I had a little lass. *Unknown*. ISE

Amo, amas,/ I love a lass. *Unknown*. ISE

Amo, amas,/ I loved a lass, and she was tall and slender. *Unknown*. ISE

Amoeba named Sam, and his brother, An. *Unknown*. PeLi

Amoebaean Eclogues, *sels.* John Scott of Amwell.
    How to Fertilize Soil. FaBoUs

Among All Lovely Things My Love Had Been. Wordsworth. CoGr; GBL

Among bloody candles I welcomed winter 1254. Notation in Gold. Ljubomir Simovic, *tr. fr. Serbo-Croatian by* Charles Simic. HSix

Among branches. Gray Glove. Roo Borson. NOBC

Among death-protected creatures in a case. Killing Time. Tony Harrison. *Fr.* Art & Extinction. SCBI

Among Elms and Maples, Morgantown, West Virginia, August 1935. Maggie Anderson. ETG

Among green leaves and blossoms sweet. (*LL*) The Birds. Blake. CH

Among green shades and flowering ghosts, the remembrances of love. The Two Fires. Judith Wright. MoBrPo

Among Hawks. Lance Henson. VoR

Among His Books. E. Nesbit. NOBVV

Among His Books. Robert Southey. *See* My days among the dead are past.

Among Iron Fragments. Tuvia Ruebner, *tr. fr. Hebrew by* Robert Friend. UnAS

Among left trucks, mailbags, churns. Homing Pigeons. Ted Walker. NYBP

Among men who do not love her, liner here. (*LL*) Composed by the Seaside, near Calais, August, 1802. Wordsworth. EnRP; Son

Among men who play Rugger. On the Ambivalence of Male Contact Sports. Gavin Ewart. FaBoBl

Among/ of/ green. The Locust Tree in Flower. William Carlos Williams. SOTW; Spl; TTTS

Among our hills and valleys, I have known. The Old Man's Counsel. Bryant. EAP

Among our young lassies there's Muirland Meg. Muirland Meg. Burns. ErPo

Among Pelagian travellers. On the Circuit. W. H. Auden. NOBL; OxBTC

Among Philistines. R. S. Gwynn. MT

Among School Children. W. B. Yeats. BLPL; CMoP; GTBS-P; HAP; ImPo; InPS; LiTB; LiTM; MeMBP; MoAB; MoBrPo; MoP; NAEL-2; NAWM-2; NIP; NoAM; NOBE; NoP; OAEL-2; OxBTC; PoE; Poetr; PPP; PrIm; SCGP; TFi; TrGrPo; TRP

Among Sharks. Alfred M. Lee. AmPA

Among snake-patterned swords Weland tasted sorrow. Deor. *Unknown, tr. fr. Anglo-Saxon.* EBEV, *tr. by* John Wain; TEP, *tr. by* Walter Kendrick

Among snake-patterned swords Weland tasted sorrow. *Unknown. See* Weland, that dauntless man, well learned to bear [*or* well knew about exile].

Among some hills there dwelt in parody. The Song of Absinthe Granny. Ruth Stone. NALW

Among Strangers. William Stafford. NNaP

Among Tall Buildings. Molly Peacock. WoWa

Among the ancient tombs both high and low. On an Ancient Tomb East of the Village. Po Chü-i, *tr. fr. Chinese by* Robert Payne. TAL

Among the beautiful pictures. Among the Beautiful Pictures. Alice Cary. BLPA
    (Pictures of Memory.) AmWP

Among the Beautiful Pictures. Alice Cary. BLPA

Among the Berkshire Hills. H. Cordelia Ray. CBWP-3

Among the birds in the sky above. Nature in Couplets. Charlton Ogburn. GrPl

Among the blessed in endless joys remain. (*LL*) On My Dear Grandchild Simon Bradstreet, [Who Died on 16 November, 1669, Being But A Month, And One Day Old]. Anne Bradstreet. EAP; KTR; NAAL-1; SCAP

Among the coffee cups and soup toureens walked Beauty. Jack Spicer. PeHV

Among the dead we come. *Unknown, tr. fr. Greek by* Kenneth Rexroth. PGA

Among the dear old friends we people cherish. Memory of Lincoln and the Yankees. James Ephriam McGirt. AAP

Among the drinking doves, Galla Placidia. Afternoon Hours. Rossana Ombres, *tr. fr. Italian by* Robert McCracken *and* Pietro Pedace. *Fr.* Excursion to Ravenna of A Young Girl with Her Parents. PeFWW

Among the Ferns. Edward Carpenter. WGRP

Among the Finger Lakes. Robert Wallace. GrPl

Among the Firs. Eugene Lee-Hamilton. NOBVV

Among the greatest plagues, one is the third day ague. Of Scolding Wives and the Third Day Ague. Henricus Selyns. AiP; SCAP

Among the green slim reeds. (*LL*) The Snake Trying. W. W. Eustace Ross. MoCV; NOBC

Among the high-branching, leafless boughs. The View from an Attic Window. Howard Nemerov. CoAP

Among the Hills, *sels.* Whittier.
    "Along the roadside, like the flowers of gold." NAAL-1; OxBA; PoEL-4

Among the iodoform, in twilight-sleep. The Leg. Karl Shapiro. HAP; MoAB; MoAmPo; TrGrPo; UnPo; WeW

Among the later dinosaurs. Pachycephalosaurus. Richard Armour. SiSoPo

Among the leaves the small birds sing. Lauds. W. H. Auden. *Fr.* Horae Canonicae. TrCP

Among the lilies, and forgetting them. (*LL*) The Obscure Night of the Soul. St. John of the Cross. AWP; OBMV

Among the Myriad Voices of the Spring. George Santayana. AnAmPo

Among the Narcissi. Sylvia Plath. FaBoMo; RB; SCV

Among the Nuts. *Unknown*. BoTP

Among the orchard weeds, from every search. Hen's Nest. John Clare. Son

Among the oxen (like an ox I'm slow). The Nativity. C. S. Lewis. ChIV-2; TrCP

Among the plovers and the stonechats. Of Difference Does It Make. Tom Paulin. BiHa

Among the primary rocks. The Forest. Miroslav Holub, *tr. fr. Czech by* George Theiner. PoSu

Among the provisions they carried. Michael Anania. *Fr.* Riversongs of Arion, The. NoAM

Among the rain. The Great Figure. William Carlos Williams. AiP; HeIP; InPK; MoP; NoAM; SAmP; TTTS

Among the red words that drink his voice. (*LL*) Yuba City School. Chitra Divakaruni. LoHo; OpBo

Among the Rocks. Robert Browning. *Fr.* James Lee's Wife. OxBSP

Among the Roman love-poets, possession. Note on Propertius I.5. Fleur Adcock. BoLoP; PeNZ

Among the rout of the drugged oak. The Winter Jacket. Sebastian Barry. IB

Among the rushes lived a mouse. The Needless Alarm. John Ruskin. FM

Among the sayings of our race. We Are Rising. George Clinton Rowe. AAP

Among the shadows of the dead. (*LL*) Someday you will be dead. Sappho. InMo

Among the signs of autumn I perceive. Tall Ambrosia. Thoreau. PoEL-4

Among the smoke and fog of a December afternoon. Portrait of a Lady. T. S. Eliot. TwCP

Among the smooth hills of Manika. Magwere, Who Waits Wondering. Kingsley Fairbridge. PeSAV

Among the snowy gulls and summer spray. (*LL*) The Artist on Penmaenmawr. Charles Tennyson Turner. FaBoPP; OBNC

Among the splendor of torches of darkness, shedding darkness on the lost bride and her groom. (*LL*) Bavarian Gentians. D. H. Lawrence. CMoP; FaBoCh; FaBoMo; GoJo; GTBS-P; HAP; ImPo; InPK; InPS;

LiTB; MeMBP; MoP; NAEL-2; NoAM; NOBE; NoP; OAEL-2, 2 ver.;
PoE; Poetr; SOTW; TFi; TRP; TTTS

Among the springs which flow from Ida's head. *Unknown, formerly at. to
Homer, tr. fr. Greek by* Congreve. *Fr.* Hymn to Venus, The. OBVE

Among the swells, the storm past, surfers sit. At Will Robers Beach.
Timothy Steele. WeW

Among the taller wood with ivy hung. The Vixen. John Clare. OBAP;
RB

Among the white walls we read quietly. House-Rules I: Reading. Alistair
Elliot. CBLP

Among the woebegone sunflowers. *(LL)* Summer. Duo Duo. SpMi

Among the Worst of Men That Ever Lived. Thoreau. PoEL-4

Among them marble where the man may lie. A Thurn. John Berryman.
NOBA

Among these mountains, do you know. For Allan, Who Wanted to See
How I Wrote a Poem. Robert Frost. PChr

Among these othre of Slouthes kinde. John Gower. *Fr.* Confessio
Amantis. EnVB, *sect.* IV

Among these tempests great and manifold. His Hope or Sheet-Anchor.
Robert Herrick. CaPo

Among These Troopes of Christs Souldiers, Came . . . Mr. Roger
Harlackenden. Edward Johnson. SCAP

Among These Turf-Stacks. Louis MacNeice. ImPo; LiTB

Among those joys, 'tis one at eve to sail. Sailing upon the River. George
Crabbe. *Fr.* Borough, The. OBNC

Among Those Killed in the Dawn Raid Was a Man Aged a Hundred. Dylan
Thomas. Son

Among tired men. Urban. Oliver Davies. AngWe

Among trees/ my father was a spruce. Family Photograph. Gerald
Vizenor. VoR

Among twenty snowy mountains. Thirteen Ways of Looking at a
Blackbird. Wallace Stevens. BLPL; CMoP; HCAP; HeIL; HeIP; InPK;
InPS; LiTM; MoP; NAAL-2; NoAM; NOBA; NoP; PoE; Poetr; RB;
SAmP; SOTW; TAP; TFi

Amongest many kings. Desire of Dominion. Timothy Kendall. NoSic

Amongst the Cliffs. Han Yü, *tr. fr. Chinese by* Kenneth Rexroth. OHMPC

Amongst the leaves so green. *(LL)* Robin Hood and Allen [*or* Allin]
-a-Dale. *Unknown.* ESPB; FaBoBe; GBP; MoShBr; OxAEP-1

Amongst the long grass. The Peepshow Girl. Marion Lomax. PWE

Amongst the poets Dacus numbered is. Sir John Davies. *Fr.* Epigrams.
NoSic

Amongst the princely paragons. A Princely Ditty in Praise of the English
Rose. Thomas Deloney. BoTP

Amongst the pure ones all. The Quaker's Song. *Unknown.* CoMu

Amor Loci. W. H. Auden. NOCV

Amor Mundi. Christina Rossetti. MeMBP; NoP; PoEL-5; Poetr

Amor Mysticus. Sister Marcela de Carpio de San Felix, *tr. fr. Spanish by*
John Hay. AWP

Amor Triumphans., *sels.* Arthur Symons.

Amor Vacui. John Fowles. AnAn

Amor Vincit Omnia. Edgar Bowers. VCAP

Amores, *sels.* Ovid, *tr. fr. Latin.*
  Ad Auroram, Ne Properet. NoSic
  Complaisant Swain, The. AWP
  Corinna, Having Tried, with Her Own Hand. NAs
  Corinnae Concubitus, I, 5. EBEV; GBL; OBVE
    (Corinnae Concubitus.) NoSic; OxAEP-1
    (Elegy: "In summer's heat and mid-time of the day.") BoLoP
    (In Summer's Heat.) FaBoBl
  "Cypassis, that a thousand ways trimm'st hair." EBEV
  "Either she was foule, or her attire was bad." OBVE
    (Either She was Foul.) FaBoBl
    (Shameful Impotence.) ErPo
  "Envy, why carp'st thou my time is spent so ill?" NoSic
  "Graecinus (well I wot) thou told'st me once." EBEV
  "Here Tantalus in water weeks for water, and doth miss." SiPSBD, *tr. by*
    Sir Walter Ralegh.
  "I ask but right: let her that caught me late." EBEV
  "I Ovid poet of my wantonnesse." OBVE
  "Now ore the sea from her old love comes she." OBVE
  "Seeing thou art faire, I barre not thy false playing." OBVE
  "Thy husband to a banquet goes with me." NoSic
  To His Mistress. BoLoP; ErPo

Amoret. Mark Akenside. OBEV

Amoretti. Spenser. AAS; ESo, *lacking epigrams* I–IV; HeIL
  Sels.
  By Her That Is Most Assured to Her Self. EnRePo
  "How long shall this like dying life endure." EnRePo
  I. "Happy ye leaves whenas those lily [*or* lilly] hands." EBEV; NAEL-1;
    OAEL-1; PoE; Son
  III. "Soverayne beauty which I doo admire, The." PoEL-1

"Lacking my love, I go from place to place." EIl; NoSic

Like a huntsman. EnRePo; GBL; HeIP; NAEL-1; NoP; PoE; PoEL-1;
Son; TrGrPo

LIV. "Of this world's theatre in which we stay." NAEL-1; NoP; OAEL-1

LV. "So oft as I her beauty do behold." Son; TrGrPo

LVI. "Fair ye be sure, but cruel and unkind." Son

LXI. "Glorious image of the Maker's beauty, The." Son

LXIII. "After long storms and tempests sad assay." OAEL-1

LXIV. "Coming [*or* Comming] to kiss [*or* kisse] her lips [*or* lyps], (such
grace I found)." EBEV; NAEL-1; OAEL-1; Son

LXV. "Doubt which ye misdeeme, fayre love, is vaine, The." NAEL-1

LXX. "Fresh Spring, the herald of love's mighty king." AWP; ChTr; EIl;
FF; HAP; InPS; NoP; OBEV; PoE; Son
  (Fresh Spring, the Herald.) LiTB

LXXI. "I joy to see how, in your drawen work." PoE

LXXII. "Oft when my spirit doth spread her bolder wings." Son

LXXIV. "Most happy letters framed by skilfull trade." NAEL-1

LXXIX. "Men call you fair [*or* fayre], and you do[e] credit it." AWP;
FaBoBe; NAEL-1; NoP; Son
  (Sonnet: "Men call you fair, and you do credit it.") BLPL

LXXVI. "Fair bosom! fraught with virtue's richest treasure." NIP

LXXVII. "Was it a dream, or did I see it plain?" CBLP; NIP

LXXXI. "Fair [*or* Fayre] is my love, when her fair [*or* fayre] golden
heares." EIl; NoP; Son

LXXXII. "Joy of my life, full oft for loving you." HeIP

LXXXIII. "Let not one sparke of filthy lustfull fyre." TEP

LXXXIX. "Like as the culver on the bared bough." FF; GBL; PoE

"Most glorious lord of life that on this day." ChIV-2; EIl; EnRePo; HAP;
InPS; LiTB; NAEL-1; NOCV; NoP; NoSic; PoE; Son; TrPWD
  (Easter Morning.) OHIP
  (Easter.) NOBE; OBEV; PeECV
  (Most Glorious Lord of lyfe, that on this day.) PeECV

My Love Is Like to Ice. ErPo; FF; ImPo; LiTB; TrGrPo

"New year, forth looking out of Janus' gate." NoSic

"One day I wrote her name upon the strand." ArLo; AWP; BLPL;
BoLoP; CBLP; EBEV; EIl; EPCY; GBL; HAP; HeIP; ImPo; InPS;
LiTB; NAEL-1; NoP; NoSic; OAEL-1; PoE; Son; TFi; WeW

Panther, knowing that his spotted hide, The. EnRePo

Since I Have Lacked the Comfort. EnRePo

V. "Rudely thou wrongst my dear heart's desire." EIl

VIII. "More than most fair [*or* fayre], full of the living fire [*or* fyre].
NoP; PoE; Son; TEP; TrGrPo

X. "Unrighteous Lord of love, what law is this." NoP

XIII. "In That proud port, which her so goodly graceth." PoE

XLIV. "When those renowned noble peers of Greece." PoE

XLVII. "Trust not the treason of those smiling looks." TrGrPo

XV. "Ye tradeful merchants that, with weary toil." HeIP; LiTB; NIP;
OAEL-1; Son; TrGrPo

XVI. "One day as I unwarily did gaze." OAEL-1

XXII. "This holy season, fit to fast and pray." PoE

XXVI. "Sweet is the rose, but grows upon a brere." EIl

XXVII. "Fair proud, now tell me, why should fair be proud." Son

XXXIV. "Like as a ship, that through the ocean wide." NAEL-1; PoE

XXXVII. "What guile [*or* guyle] is this, that those her golden tresses."
NAEL-1; NoP; Son; TrGrPo

Amoris Victima, *sels.* Arthur Symons.
"And yet, there was a hunger in your eyes." PeVV

Amorix Exsul, *sels.* Arthur Symons.
In the Bay. OBNC

Amorous Anticipation. Jorge Luis Borges, *tr. fr. Spanish by* Perry Higman.
ArLo

Amorous Dialogue between John and His Mistress, An. *Unknown.* CoMu

Amorous Leander, beautiful and young. Christopher Marlowe. *Fr.* Hero
and Leander. AAS; NoP; PeHV

Amorous maiden antique, An. *Unknown.* PeLi

Amorous Neptune. Christopher Marlowe. *Fr.* Hero and Leander. AAS;
NOBE; NoP

Amorous shepherd lov'd a charming boy, An. Theocritus [*or* Theokritus],
tr. by Thomas Creech. *Fr.* Idylls. PeHV

Amorous Temper, An. John Trumbull. *Fr.* Progress of Dulness, The.
AmPP

Amos, *sels.* Bible, *O.T.*
O Ye That Would Swallow the Needy. TrJP

Amours de Voyage. Arthur Hugh Clough. NOBVV
  Sels.
  Ah, That I Were Far Away. OBNC
    (Upon Apennine Slope.) FaBoPP
  "At last, dearest Louisa, I take up my pen to address you." EBVVPR,
    canto I,iii
  Claude to Eustace. CBLP
  Claude to Eustace ("Ah, Let Me Look"). EnVR
  Claude to Eustace ("I am in love"). EnVR; FaBoVe
  Claude to Eustace ("No, The Christian Faith"). EnVR

"Dear Eustatio, I write that you may write me an answer." EBVV; EBVVPR; FaBoVe; OBTV; OxAEP-2

"Dear Miss Roper, — It seems, George Vernon, before we left Rome, said." FaBoVe

"Dearest Louisa, — Inquire, if you please, about Mr. Claude." FaBoVe

"Dulce it is, and *decorum*, no doubt, for the country to fall." EBVV; EnVR; FaBoPV; OxAEP-2

"Farewell, politics, utterly! What can I do? I can not." FaBoPV

"I am to tell you, you say, what I think of our last new acquaintance." FaBoVe

"I cannot stay at Florence, not even to wait for a letter." EBVVPR, *canto* V, vii

"I have but one chance left, — and that is going to Florence." FaBoVe

"Is it illusion? or does there a spirit from perfecter ages." EBEV; OxAEP-2 (Spirit from Perfecter Ages.) OBNC

Juxtaposition. OBNC
    (Claude to Eustace.) CBLP

"Luther, they say, was unwise; he didn't see how things were going." FaBoVe

"Now supposing the French or the Neopolitan soldier." PeLV

"Oh, 'tisn't manly, of course, 'tisn't manly, this method of/ wooing" EBVVPR, *canto* II, xiv

"Only think, dearest Louisa, what fearful scenes we have witnessed!" EBVV

"Rome disappoints me still; but I shrink and adapt myself to it." EBVV; EBVVPR; OBTV; OxAEP-2
    (Rome.) FaBoPP

Rome ("Rome disappoints me much"). FaBoPP

"Rome will not suit me, Eustace; the priests and soldiers possess/ it." EBVVPR, *canto* V, x

"Shall we come out of it all, some day, as one does from a." EBVVPR, *sect.* V, ix

"So, I have seen a man killed!" EBVV; PeVV

"These are the facts. The uncle, the elder brother, the squire." FaBoVe

"To-morrow we're starting for Florence." EBVVPR, *canto* II, xv

"When God makes a great Man he intends all others to crush him." OBSV

"Wherefore and how I am certain, I can hardly tell; but it [or is so]." EBVVPR, *canto* II, xiii

"Yes, we are fighting at last, it appears." EBVV; OxAEP-2; PeVV

"You have heard nothing; of course I know you can have heard/ nothing." EBVVPR, *canto* V, xi

Amphibious Crocodile. John Crowe Ransom. OBAL

Amphitryon, *sels.* Dryden.
    "Fair Iris I love, and hourly I die." AWP
    (Mercury's Song [to Phaedra].) NOSC; OxBSP; PoEL-3; SeCV-2

Amphora, The. Fyodor Sologub, *tr. fr. Russian by* Babette Deutsch *and* Avrahm Yarmolinsky. AWP

Ample heaven of fabrik sure, The. A Summer's Day. Alexander Hume. CH

Ample make this bed. Emily Dickinson. MoAB; MoAmPo; NAAL-1; OxBA; PoEL-5

Ample, plain snow inhibits detail but frees splendor, The. Naming the House. Ann Lauterbach. PRA

Ample the air above the western peaks. After Nightfall. William Renton. NOBVV

Ampoo is intensely neat, The. The Utter Zoo Alphabet. Edward Gorey. CBNP

Amputee Soldier, The. Philip Dacey. GOYP

Amsterdam. Dermot Bolger. IB

Amsterdam. Jean Garrigue. TAP

Amsterdam. Francis Jammes, *tr. fr. French by* Jethro Bithell. AWP; FaPON, (*ll.* 1–20)

Amsterdam Letter. Jean Garrigue. NYBP; VCAP

Amsterdam Poem, The. Maxine W. Kumin. BTR

Am/Trak. Amiri Baraka. Jaz

Amulet. Ted Hughes. OBAP

Amulet, The, *sels.* Isaac Rosenberg.
    "Slime clung, The." PeFWW

Amurrika! Philip Appleman. BXAP

Amusedly, among the ancient Dead. (*LL*) Oh! Death will find me, long before I tire. Rupert Brooke. PoRA

Amusing Our Daughters. Carolyn Kizer. VCAP; VGW

Amy, dieu vous sauve. Pour demander le chemin. *Unknown. Fr.* Lytell Treatyse for to Lerne Englysshe and Frens, A. OxBLMV

Amy Elizabeth Ermyntrude Annie. Queenie Scott-Hopper. BoTP

Amy Wentworth. Whittier. AnAmPo; BeLS

Amyd the wod his modir met thame tway. Virgil, *tr. by* Gavin Douglas. *Fr.* Aeneid [*or* Eneados], The. NAWM-1; OBVE

Amymone. Rufinus, *tr. fr. Greek by* Alan Marshfield. GrAn

Amyntas Led Me to a Grove. Aphra Behn. *Fr.* Dutch Lover, The. ErPo

An a forkie tailie. (*LL*) The Horny-Goloch. *Unknown.* FaBoCh

An a so de rain a-fall. A Song for England. Andrew Salkey. PBCV

An Charlie &c. (*LL*) Charlie, He's My Darling. Burns. CH; FaBoPV

An' Charlie he's my darling. Charlie He's My Darling. Burns. CH

An de beat well red. Reflection in Red. Oku Onuora. PBCV

An' de walls come tumblin' down. (*LL*) Joshua Fit De [*or* Fought the] Battle of [*or* ob] Jericho. *Unknown.* BPo; NOBA; TAP; TrGrPo

An' dis here white-starched kapje! (*LL*) Katisje's Patchwork Dress. Pauline Smith. PeSAV

An' get hame my rantin laddie. (*LL*) The Baron o [*or* of] Leys. *Unknown.* ESPB; OxBB

An' hankerin' for me. But go! (*LL*) The Drained Cup. D. H. Lawrence. CBLP

An hendy hap etc. (*LL*) Alison. *Unknown.* CBLP; MeEL; MiEL; NAEL-1; NoP; OAEL-1; OBEV; PeLV

An' hey for houghmagandie. (*LL*) Gie the Lass her Fairin.' Burns. CoMu; ErPo

An laughing bout yu antics. (*LL*) Love Story (Part 2). Marsha Prescod. VBLP

An noo he's king ower a' his ain. (*LL*) King Orfeo. *Unknown.* ESPB; OxBB; OxBoLi

An' raise dat rucus to-night. (*LL*) Raise a "Rucus" To-Night. *Unknown.* BPo; TAP

An' so it seems it is reported. A Young Lass's Soliloquy. Rebekah Carmichael. ECWP

An' so ole Tho'nton bounced you. The Turncoat. Priscilla Jane Thompson. CBWP-2

An' the Crucified maun bleed. (*LL*) The Innumerable Christ. "Hugh MacDiarmid." EBEV; NoP; OxAEP-2; OxBS

An' the dawn comes up like thunder outer China 'crost the Bay! (*LL*) Mandalay. Kipling. CoGr; EBEvV; FaBV; LiTB; MoBrPo; NOBE; OBTV; OxAEP-2; TrGrPo

An' there's no discharge in the war! (*LL*) Boots. Kipling. BLPA; FaPoR; MoBrPo

An they'll no be hame till noon. (*LL*) Hush-a-ba birdie [*or* burdie], croon, croon. *Unknown.* GBP; OxNR

An Thou Were My Ain Thing. Allan Ramsay. OxAEP-1

An' Tommy ain't a bloomin' fool — you bet that Tommy sees! (*LL*) Tommy. Kipling. EBEV; FaBoEH; FaBV; FaPoR; MoBrPo; NoP; OBWP; OHCV; OxAEP-2; OxBTC; PAW; PeVV; PFP; PlP; UV, (*ll.* 1–18)

An' we hope that his like we shall ne'er see again. (*LL*) Verses on Daniel Good. *Unknown.* CoMu; OxBB

An' while I went 'ithin a train. William Barnes. *Fr.* Railroad, The. EnVR

Anabasis, *sels.* "St.-John Perse," *tr. fr. French by* T. S. Eliot.
    "Such is the way of the world." OBVE

Anachronism. Oliver St. John Gogarty. FYAP

Anaconda. Doug Macleod. ZA

Anacreon. Johann Wilhelm Ludwig Gleim, *tr. fr. German by* George C. Schoolfield. GePo

Anacreon. Friedrich von Hagedorn, *tr. fr. German by* George C. Schoolfield. GePo

Anacreon, my teacher. Anacreon. Johann Wilhelm Ludwig Gleim, *tr. fr. German by* George C. Schoolfield. GePo

Anacreon's Dove. Samuel Johnson. AWP

Anacreon's Grave. Goethe, *tr. fr. German by* John Frederick Nims. STV

Anacreon's Grave. Goethe, *tr. fr. German by* Philip L. Miller. RiWo

Anacreontic. Austin Clarke. NOIV

Anacreontic. Robert Herrick. CaPo; OxBoLi

Anacreontic. Robert Herrick. CaPo

Anacreontic: Drinking. Abraham Cowley, after the Greek of Anacreon. *See* Thirsty earth soaks up the rain, The.

Anacreontic, on Parting with a Little Child. Samuel Wesley. NOEC

Anacreontic to Flip. Royall Tyler. OABL

Anacreontic Verse. Robert Herrick. PeLV

Anadarko John. Carroll Arnett. VoR

Anaesthesia. Jean Valentine. TAP

Anahorish. Seamus Heaney. PBCIP

Anal erotic named Herman, An. *Unknown.* PeHV

Analogue of Unity in Multeity. Richard Eberhart. Poetr

Analogy. Brian Higgins. FaBoTw

Analysands. Dudley Randall. BPo

Analysis of Baseball. May Swenson. ImGa

Ana(Mary-Army)gram. George Herbert. ChIV-2; GeHe; OAEL-1

Anarchy and grow your own. Durham. Tony Harrison. NoAM

Anastasia McLaughlin. Tom Paulin. PBCIP

Anastasia, the Graces blossom and you were their flower. Julianus of Egypt, *tr. fr. Greek by* W. S. Merwin. GrAn

Anathemata, The, *sels.* David Jones.
    Angle-Land. NoAM

"Did he meet Lud at the Fleet Gate? did count the top." EBEV

Lady of the Pool, The. AngWe

"Ship's master:/ before him, in the waist and before it." FaBoTw

"We already and first of all discern him making this thing other." PeECV

Anatomy of Baseness, The, *sels*. John Andrews.
To the Detracted. EIL

Anatomy of Happiness, The. Ogden Nash. LiTA; TAP

Anatomy of Humor, The. Morris Bishop. NBLV

Anatomy of Melancholy, The, *sels*. Robert Burton.
Authors [*or* Author's] Abstract of Melancholy, The. NOSC

Anatomy [*or* Anatomie] of the World, An[: The First Anniversary], *sels*.
John Donne.
Doth Not a Tenarif, or Higher Hill. ChTr
First Anniversary, The. NAEL-1; SeCV-1
"And new philosophy calls all in doubt." NOSC
"She, she is dead; she's dead: when thou knowest this." JCP
Verse and Fame. FaBoRV

Anaximander Lewis. John C. Tribble. Jaz

Ancestor. Thomas Kinsella. BIrV; NOIV; PBCIP; PoE

Ancestor, The. Dave Jeddie Smith. SM

Ancestor Worship. Emyr Humphreys. AngWe

Ancestors, The. John Peale Bishop. PoA

Ancestors. Raymond Garlick. AngWe

Ancestors. Rowley Habib. PeNZ

Ancestors. Dudley Randall. BPo

Ancestors are not in our blood, but our heads. Robert Brackenbury. Alison Brackenbury. SCBI

Ancestral Faces. Kwesi Brew. PBA

Ancestral Houses. W. B. Yeats. *Fr.* Meditations in Time of Civil War. LiTB; OAEL-2

Ancestral Messengers/Composition 11. Ntozake Shange. SRLS

Ancestral Poem. Olive Senior. PBCV

Ancestral Weight. Alfonsina Storni, *tr. fr. Spanish by* Marti Moody. WPOW

Anchises, Paris, and Adonis too. Spoken by Venus on Seeing Her Statue Done by Praxiteles. *Unknown, tr. fr. Greek*. FaBoEE

Anchor: I must fight with the waves whipped up by the wind. Unknown, formerly at. to Cynewulf, *tr. fr. Anglo-Saxon. Fr.* Riddles (Exeter Book). ASW, *tr. by* Kevin Crossley-Holland

Anchor: "Oft I must strive with wind and wave." Unknown, formerly at. to Cynewulf, *tr. by* Charles W. Kennedy. *Fr.* Riddles (Exeter Book). AnOE

Anchorage. Lavinia Greenlaw. NWP

Anchorage. Joy Harjo. HATNAP

Anchored now to Neptune's temple floor, this. Macedonius, *tr. fr. Greek by* Adrian Wright. GrAn

Anchored on the Chin-huai River, the rain has vanished. Tune: "Magnolia Blossoms, Slow"—Traveling on the Yangtze. Chiang Ch'un-lin, *tr. fr. Chinese by* Bruce Carpenter. SuSp

Anchorsmiths, The. Charles Dibdin. NOEC

Ancient Airs. Li Po, *tr. fr. Chinese by* Joseph J. Lee. SuSp

Ancient and Modern. William Scammell. FaBoEH

Ancient and Modern Rome, *sels*. George Keate.
"What, though oblivion in her sable shroud." OBTV

Ancient and young and begetting. (*LL*) On a Recollected Road. Amir Gilboa. MHP

Ancient annals strewn left and right. Occasional Poem. Han Yü, *tr. fr. Chinese by* Charles Hartman. SuSp

Ancient Barbarossa, the Kaiser Frederick old, The. Barbarossa. Friedrich Rückert, *tr. fr. German by* Elizabeth Craigmyle. AWP

Ancient biologist, Heine, An. Carol Rumens. PeLi

Ancient bridge, and a more ancient tower, An. My House. W. B. Yeats. *Fr.* Meditations in Time of Civil War. LiTB

Ancient chestnut's blossoms threw, An. Alciphron and Leucippe. Walter Savage Landor. OBEV

Ancient Christmas Carol. *Unknown*. OHIP; PChr

Ancient Couple on Lu Mountain, The. Mark Van Doren. VGW

Ancient forests of earth, The. (*LL*) Garden is rich with diversity, The. *Unknown*. EaPr

Ancient Gesture, An. Edna St. Vincent Millay. NALW

Ancient History. Arthur Guiterman. OBCA

Ancient History. Siegfried Sassoon. ChIV-1; Mes

Ancient Lights. Austin Clarke. BIrV; CMoP; IPY

Ancient Mansion, The, *sels*. George Crabbe.
Spring to Winter. ChTr
(In Suffolk.) FaBoPP

Ancient Mariner: The Wedding Guest's Version of the Affair from His Point of View, The. *Unknown*. FaBoPa

Ancient Masters were profound and subtle, The. Lao Tzu, *tr. fr. Chinese. Fr.* Tao Te Ching. EnlH, *vers. by* Stephen Mitchell

Ancient Monuments. John Ormond. AngWe; OBWVE

Ancient Music. Ezra Pound. BXAP; FaBoCo; FaBoPa; FF; HeIL; HeIP; LiTM; NBLV; OBAL; OxBA; PeLV; UV

Ancient nomadic snowman has rolled around. The Snowman. P. K. Page. NOBC

Ancient of Days. William Croswell Doane. AH

Ancient of Days, old friend, no one believes you'll come back. Stone Canyon Nocturne. Charles Wright. HCAP; LCAP; VCAP

Ancient pages of the Talmud. The Talmud. Simeon Grigoryevich Frug, *tr. fr. Yiddish by* Alice Stone Blackwell. TrJP

Ancient Person, for whom I. A Song of a Young Lady to Her Ancient Lover. The Earl of Rochester. BoLoP; EBEV; ErPo; FaBoBl; GBL; NOSC; OPOP; OxAEP-1

Ancient Person of my Heart. (*LL*) A Song of a Young Lady to Her Ancient Lover. The Earl of Rochester. BoLoP; EBEV; ErPo; FaBoBl; GBL; NOSC; OPOP; OxAEP-1

Ancient Pistol, peacock Payne. Tennyson. FaBoEE

Ancient Pistol, sealskin Payne. (*LL*) Ancient Pistol, peacock Payne. Tennyson. FaBoEE

Ancient Portuguese speech of the sea, The. (*LL*) Azure, or Green, or Purple. William Plomer. PeSAV

Ancient Prayer, An. Thomas H. B. Webb. BLPA; FaBoBe

Ancient Prophecy, An. Philip Freneau. PAH

Ancient Prophets ate? The. (*LL*) By what miracle. Judith Morley. EaPr

Ancient saga tells us how, An. Dead Cow Farm. Robert Graves. PlP; PoWW

Ancient Sage, The. Tennyson. WGRP

Ancient Song of a Woman of Fez, An. *Unknown, tr. fr. Arabic by* Willis Barnstone. AIW; BoWoP

Ancient spring year after year abides. Temple of the Orchid Fragrance Goddess. Li Ho, *tr. fr. Chinese by* Michael Fish. SuSp

Ancient story I'll tell you anon, An. King John and the Abbot of Canterbury. *Unknown*. BoTP; EnSB; GN; TrGrPo

Ancient sun, eternally young. *Unknown*. EaPr

Ancient Thought, The. Watson Kerr. WGRP

Ancient to Ancients, An. Thomas Hardy. CMoP; GTBS-P; LiTM; OxBTC; SCGP

Ancient Virgin, An. George Crabbe. *Fr.* Parish Register, The. OAEL-1, *abr.; OBNC*

Ancient Wisdom, Rather Cosmic. Ezra Pound. NOBA

Ancientest of cats, truest. Hoppy. Reginald Gibbons. DiPo; SoCa

Ancientness surrounds me. Death. Patty L. Harjo. VoR

Ancients argued that friendship could never last, The. Quarrelling. Lyall Tao Tschung Yu. OBF

Ancients happily could sing, The. Our Naughty Time. Friedrich von Logau, *tr. fr. German*. GePo, *tr. by* George C. Schoolfield

Ancients lie buried under barren hills, The. A Occasional Poem. Lu Yu, *tr. fr. Chinese by* Chiang Yee. SuSp

Ancients of the World, The. R. S. Thomas. RB

Ancre at Hamel: Afterwards, The. Edmund Blunden. PeFWW

And. Robert Creeley. LCAP

And L for Fifty, I'll tell you. (*LL*) X shall stand for playmates Ten. *Unknown*. OxNR

And a blind seed all. (*LL*) The Road. Edwin Muir. CMoP; ImPo; LiTB; LiTM; MeMBP; Mes

And a clam caught my little finger. The Little Girl That Lost a Finger. Gabriela Mistral, *tr. fr. Spanish by* Muna Lee. FaPON

And a coast as souls are lost on. (*LL*) Boston, Lincolnshire. *Unknown*. FaBoPP; GBP

And a cruel wind blows. (*LL*) End of Summer. Stanley Kunitz. CAPP; MoAmPo; Poetsp; VGW

And a cruel wind blows. (*LL*) The Science of the Night. Stanley Kunitz. MoAmPo; TwCP

And a fair woman walking in the spring. (*LL*) An Old Man Remembers. Frances Horovitz. VBLP

And a G.I. escort. (*LL*) The Year of the Foxes. David Malouf. FaBoMA; NOBAu

And a great blank in its memory. (*LL*) The Day He Died. Ted Hughes. OxAEP-2

And a green gown. (*LL*) Daffy-down-dilly is new come to town [*or* Daffadowndilly has come up to town]. Mother Goose. NTCP; OxNR

And a happier place. (*LL*) At a Concert of Music. Conrad Aiken. MoAB; MoAmPo

And a hateful wish to be empty and tall like you. (*LL*) The Californians. Theodore Spencer. NYBP

And a jolly good bonfire to roast him. (*LL*) The Gunpowder Plot. *Unknown*. FaBoUs

And a kiss from time to time. (*LL*) Autobiography. Gloria Fuertes. AnAn; PBWP

And a man with his back to the East. (*LL*) Unwelcome. Mary Elizabeth Coleridge. CH; CoGr; GGP; OBEV; OBNC; WPE

And a pond edged with grayish leaves. (*LL*) Neutral Tones. Thomas Hardy. CMoP; EBVV; EnVR; HAP; HeIP; InPK; InPS; MeMBP; MoBrPo; MoP; NAEL-2; NoAM; NOBVV; OAEL-2; PPP; TEP; TFi; UnPo

And a profound reactionary sorrow. (*LL*) The Malefic Return. Ramón López Velarde. OBVE

And a singe runs through lace and feather. (*LL*) A Utilitarian View of the *Monitor's* Fight. Herman Melville. AmPP; NAEL-1; UnPo

And a slow dissection. (*LL*) A Small Demand. Karen Murai. UTF

And a smile on the face of the tiger. (*LL*) There was a young lady of Riga. Cosmo Monkhouse. FaBoCo; PeLi

And a soft berth and a smooth course till the long trip ended. (*LL*) Sea-Chill. Arthur Guiterman. BXAP; FaBoPa; UV

And a sprig of the rosemary. (*LL*) The Rock. *Unknown*. ChTr; GBL

And a tenth part of Okeanos is given to dark night. Styx. Robert Duncan. VCAP

And a wig-wag. (*LL*) Four stiff-standers. *Unknown*. ChTr; GBP; OxNR, *diff. vers.*

And able age, to do Thy holy will. (*LL*) On the Instability of Youth. Thomas, Lord Vaux.

And adieu to you, my darlings. (*LL*) Three Knights from Spain. *Unknown*. CH

And adjust, no one to drive the car. (*LL*) To Elsie. William Carlos Williams. CMoP; InPS; MeMAP; NAEL-2; NOBA; OxBA; PoE

And after all a slave sits out the centuries. Ghosts II. Lauris Edmond. PeNZ

And, after all, it is to them we return. Quaint Mazes. Geoffrey Hill. *Fr.* Apology for the Revival of Christian Architecture in England, An. NoAM

And after all your trapesings, child, lie still! (*LL*) A St. Helena Lullaby. Kipling. CoGr; EBEV; FaBoCh; OBMV; OtMeF; PoEL-5

And after singing Psalm the Twelfth. Rochester Extempore. The Earl of Rochester. ChIV-1

And after that, I always get them all mixed up. (*LL*) Pictures in the Smoke. Dorothy Parker. CoGr; NBLV

And after these the Sea Nymphs marched all. The Sea Nymphs. Spenser. *Fr.* Faerie Queene, The. CBCK

And, after this life, to see thy glorious Face. (*LL*) A Prayer to the Father of [*or* in] Heaven. John Skelton. HoPM; TrPWD

And after this quick bash in the dark. Portrait of a Young Girl Raped at a Suburban Party. Brian Patten. OxBTC

And after you have gone. The Two Nights. Nicki Jackowska. DT

And afterwards, after the shedding of mucus. A Talk with My Cousin Alone. Hone Tuwhare. PeNZ

And Again. Humphrey Evans. BXAP

And again I see the long pouring headland. The Return. Alistair Campbell. PeNZ

And again the Spirit of Pity whispered, "Why?" (*LL*) "And There Was a Great Calm." Thomas Hardy. ChTr; CMoP; FaBoRV; LiTM: OAEL-2

And ages drop in it like rain. (*LL*) Two Rivers. Emerson. AmPP; NOBA; OxBA; PoE; TrGrPo

And al is thrugh thy necligence and rape. (*LL*) To Adam, His Scribe. Chaucer. OAEL-1

And all beset with flowers. (*LL*) To the Western Wind. Robert Herrick. CaPo; OBEV; SeCV-1

And all dishevelled wandering stars. (*LL*) Who Goes with Fergus? W. B. Yeats. CMoP; FaBoCh; GoJo; InPK; MoP; NAEL-2; NoAM; NOBE; NOBVV; PeVV; PoE; PoRA; TRP

And all for love of one. (*LL*) I Must Go Walk[e] the Woods So Wild. *At. to* Sir Thomas Wyatt. MeEL; MiEL; SiPSBD

And all her silken flanks with garlands drest. Vlamertinghe; Passing the Château, July 1917. Edmund Blunden. OBWP; PeFWW

And all his island shivered into flowers. (*LL*) Live Blindly. Trumbull Stickney. LiTA

And all his Pictures Faded. (*LL*) Sir Joshua Reynolds. Blake. FaBoCo; FaBoEE; FiBHP; OxBoLi; PeLV

And all I could ever hope to bear. (*LL*) Genealogy. Joan Larkin. LoHo

And all is a tale for thee and me. (*LL*) Fair Is the World. William Morris. FaBoRV

And all is done as I have told. (*LL*) The Mental Traveller. Blake. ChIV-2; EnRP; MeMBP; NAEL-2; OAEL-2; OPOP; PoE; PoEL-4

And all is hushed at Shiloh. (*LL*) Shiloh; a Requiem. Herman Melville. AnAmPo; FF; LiTA; NOBA; NoP; OBWP; OxBA; PAW; SCV; WiR

And all is rolled back in the book of days. (*LL*) The Alphabet. Karl Shapiro. NoAM; PoA

And all is well, tho' faith and form. Tennyson. *Fr.* In Memoriam A. H. H. EBVV, *abr.*; EBVVPR, *sect.* CXXVII; OAEL-2, *abr.*; PeECV, *abr.*

And all is what imagination dreams. (*LL*) How Great unto the Living Seem the Dead! Charles Heavysege.

And all its conscience — through our weeping. (*LL*) We Were Not Likened to Dogs among the Gentiles. Uri Zvi Greenberg. MHP

And all living beings upon it. (*LL*) Gaia's Alchemy: Ruin and Renewal of the Elements. Ralph Metzner. EaPr

And all mankind her creatures are. (*LL*) Laura Sleeping. Charles Cotton. ELP

And all needful blessings you surely shall find. (*LL*) New England's Annoyances. *Unknown*. PAH

And all of their dancing was, "Life, thou art good!" (*LL*) The Daisies. Bliss Carman. AnAmPo; BoNaP

And all of wood. Watch it closely. (*LL*) The Monument. Elizabeth Bishop. HCAP; LiTA; NoAM; NOBA; Poetr; TRP

And all our mourning should be to rejoice. (*LL*) Elegy on Gordon Barber. Gene Derwood.

And all the birds fly out of my scene. (*LL*) The Meeting. Muriel Rukeyser. MoAmPo; TrJP

And all the birds in the air couldn't catch me. (*LL*) I had a little nut-tree,/ nothing would it bear. Mother Goose. BoTP; CH; GBP; MoShBr; NTP; OxBoLi; OxNR

And all the earth trembles when he rushes by. (*LL*) A Modern Dragon. Rowena Bastin Bennett. PDV

And all the great conclusions coming near. (*LL*) Answers. Elizabeth Jennings. OxBSP; OxBTC

And all the playthings come alive. (*LL*) Foreign Lands. Robert Louis Stevenson. BoTP; PFP

And all the rest, but vanity we find. (*LL*) The Vanity of All Worldly Things. Anne Bradstreet. ChIV-1; EAP; NoP; SCAP

And all the rest is literature. (*LL*) Art Poétique. Paul Verlaine. AWP

And all the stars looked down. (*LL*) Christ child lay on Mary's lap, The. G. K. Chesterton. BoTP; OBCP; OHIP

And all the stones have wings. (*LL*) The Small. Theodore Roethke. GrPl

And all the storied, splendid sins. (*LL*) Experience. Lesbia Harford. CBAP

And all the summer through the water saunter. (*LL*) On This Island. W. H. Auden. CMoP; NAEL-2; PAW; PoE

And all the wickedness in this world that man might work or think. God's Mercy. William Langland. *Fr.* Vision of Piers Plowman, The. NOCV

And all the wild sweetness I waked was thy own. (*LL*) Dear Harp of My Country. Thomas Moore. EnRP; NOIV

And all the winters are hidden. (*LL*) The Throstle. Tennyson. BoNaP; FaPON

And all these through her eyes, have stopt her eares. (*LL*) My Picture Left in Scotland. Ben Jonson. BeJo; CBLP; EnRePo; NAEL-1; PoEL-2; SeCP; SeCV-1

And all they had to strike now was the human face. (*LL*) The Jew Wrecked in the German Cell. W. H. Auden.

And all things fair and bright are Thine. (*LL*) The Glory of God in Creation. Thomas Moore. OHIP

And all those horses. What She Said ("And all those horses.") Kapilar, *tr. fr.* Tamil by A. K. Ramanujan. PLW

And all thy great Forefathers were from Homer down to Ben. (*LL*) Destinie. Abraham Cowley. MeLP

And all thy sons, O Nature, learn my tale. (*LL*) Ode to Simplicity. William Collins. EnRP; NOBE; OBEV; OxAEP-1; TEP

And all to inform me so common a thing! (*LL*) The Six Badgers. Robert Graves. GoJo; GrPl

And all we need of hell. (*LL*) My life closed twice before its close. Emily Dickinson. AmPP; BoLoP; BoWoP; EBEvV; GBL; HeIP; ImGa; MeMAP; MoAmPo; MoP; NAAL-1; NIP; NoAM; NOBA; OxBA; OxBSP; Poetr; PPP; SAmP; SCV; TFi; TrGrPo

And all were in the wrong! (*LL*) The Blind Men and the Elephant. John Godfrey Saxe. BLPA; BoTP; FaBoBe; OBCA; OTCP; PoToHe; WBLP

And almost gently asks: are you a Jew? (*LL*) The First Time. Karl Shapiro. ErPo; SM; VGW

And also many other things. (*LL*) Sporting Goods. Philippe Soupault. TTTS

And alter with age. (*LL*) The Lockless Door. Robert Frost. NOBA

And always on the buttered side. (*LL*) I Never Had a Piece of Toast. James Payn. FaBoPa

And am drifting blissfully with them through the eternal spaces. (*LL*) Alone in the Fields. Hermann Allmers. RiWo

"And am no more" — she cried. (*LL*) Silver Wedding. Ralph Hodgson. CBLP; OxBTC; TrGrPo

And am not even sorry that I know nothing/ About fish. (*LL*) On His Queerness. Christopher Isherwood. OxBTC; PeHV

And an old man stand on her pool — alone. (*LL*) The Flying Dutchman. Ian D. Colvin. PeSAV

And another day fresh as a cedar started. (*LL*) After Reading *Country of the Pointed Firs, The.* Jean Garrigue. VCAP

And answer made King Arthur, breathing hard. Tennyson, *incorporated in* Idylls of the King *with changes, as* The Passing of Arthur. Fr. Morte d'Arthur. DL; EBEV; EBVVPR; FaBoBe; FaBoRV; FHYEP; NAEL-2; NIP; NOBVV; OAEL-2; OBNC; OBNV; PeECV; PoEL-5

And antedates our promised Paradise. (*LL*) Correggio's Cupolas at Parma. Aubrey Thomas De Vere. Son

And anthems in new tongues I hear saluting me. (*LL*) Prayer of Columbus. Walt Whitman. AmPP; WGRP

And are gone. (*LL*) Emplumada. Lorna Dee Cervantes. NoAM; PBCAP

And are they dancing: or gazing at the earth. (*LL*) Are They Dancing. Edward Dorn. NeAP; PoM

And are ye sure the news is true? The Sailor's Wife. *At. to* William Julius Mickle, *also at. to* Jean Adam. BeLS; GN; GTBS; GTBS-P (There's Nae Luck about the House.) NOEC; OxAEP-1

And are you sure where you sill lie tonight, woman. (*LL*) Beggar's Serenade. John Heath-Stubbs. BoLoP; ErPo

And argues your wisdom down. (*LL*) After the Burial. James Russell Lowell. UnPo

And art thou grieved, sweet and sacred Dove. Grieve Not the Holy Spirit, &c. George Herbert. ESCV

And art thou he, now "fallen on evil days." In Age. William Lisle Bowles. *Fr.* Milton: On the Busts of Milton, in Youth and Age. Son

And, as anyone can see by reading this, he also destroyed the meter. (*LL*) A Decrepit Old Gasman. *Unknown.*

And, as at first, still lodge him in the manger. (*LL*) Yet if his majesty, our sovereign [*or* soverajn] Lord. *Unknown.* FaBoCh; NoP; PlP; PoRA

And as dawn rises you forsake me limping again? (*LL*) Israel. Yitzhak Lamdan. MHP

And as for me, though that I konne [*or* can] but [*or* my wit be] lyte. Chaucer. *Fr.* Legend of Good Women: Prologue, The. CH; HeIP

And, as he goes, the transient vision mourns. (*LL*) A Winter-Piece. Ambrose Philips. NOEC; OBTV

And as I rise slapping my feet. I Wake Thinking of Myself as a Man. Susan Griffin. GLP

And as in winter time when Jove his cold-sharpe javelines throwes. Homer, *tr.* by George Chapman. *Fr.* Iliad, The. OBVE

And as life is to the living, so death is to the dead. (*LL*) The Two Mysteries. Mary Mapes Dodge. PWR; TrCP; WGRP

And as silently steal away. (*LL*) The Day Is Done. Longfellow. AnAmPo; BLPA; FaBoBe; MeMAP; NOBA; OxBA; PoRA; PWR; TrGrPo

And as soon as it was morning the chief priests. Bible, *N.T. Fr.* St. Mark. DL

And as the war in its fifth spring. The Legend of the Dead Soldier. Bertolt Brecht, *tr. German by* Louis MacNeice. PAW

And as to the meaning, it's what you please. (*LL*) Auld wife sat at her ivied door, The. Charles Stuart Calverley. BXAP; FaBoCo; FiBHP; NBLV; OxAEP-2; UV; WiR

And as we came down the staircase. Valse Oubliée. John Heath-Stubbs. OxBTC

And as when with the West-wind's flawes the sea thrusts up her waves. Homer, *tr.* by George Chapman. *Fr.* Iliad, The. OBVE

And ask him to make a comparison. (*LL*) To the Short Tune "The Magnolias." Li Ch'ing-chao. WPC

And ask them for your name again. (*LL*) "Mystery Boy' Looks for Kin in Nashville." Robert Hayden. NoAM; PoE

And Assemble the engine again.' (*LL*) The Dying Airman. *Unknown.* AS; FaBoNo; OxBoLi; PeLV; RB

And at all times. (*LL*) If I were alone in a desert. *Unknown.* EaPr

And at each shrine I bend my knee in turn. (*LL*) God Scatters Beauty. Walter Savage Landor. EnRP

And at his heels a stone. (*LL*) The Friar of Orders Gray. *Unknown.* NOEC

And at home in the bath I would surface giving the ape-call. (*LL*) Johnny Weissmuller Dead in Acapulco. Clive James. NOBAu

And at Lake Geneva, which is in Wisconsin. At Lake Geneva. Richard Eberhart. LiTA

And at night light upon his back. (*LL*) For Freckle-faced Gerald. Etheridge Knight. BPo

And at night you did not return. (*LL*) Fighting South of the Castle. *Unknown.* AWP

And at the last I cast my mine eye aside. Lady of the Arbour. *Fr.* Flower and the Leaf, The. WPE

And, at the turning point, made fire. (*LL*) Making Camp. David Wagoner. VCAP

And auld Robin Forbes hes gien tem a dance. Auld Robin Forbes. Susanna Blamire. ECWP

And autumn's best of cheer. (*LL*) September [Days Are Here]. Helen Hunt Jackson. FaPON; GoJo; OBCA; PoLF

And avarice be the only outcast thing. (*LL*) Sonnets of the Months: September. Folgore da San Geminiano. AWP

And awake, my heart, to be loved; awake, awake! (*LL*) Awake, My Heart, to Be Loved. Robert Bridges. GTBS-P; MoAB; MoBrPo; NOBE; OBEV

And awakened? Who's to know? (*LL*) Parables, I. Antonio Machado Ruiz. STV

And away I flew. (*LL*) Song of the Murdered Child. *Unknown.* GBP

And away they all flew. (*LL*) What's in the Cupboard? *Unknown.* CH; ChTr; GBP; OxNR

And away went the beggar-men all in a row. (*LL*) Craigbilly Fair. *Unknown.* ChTr; GBP

And azure water hoisting out of wells. (*LL*) In the Elegy Season. Richard Wilbur. InPK; MoAB; NYBP

And Back. Rodney Bennett. BoTP

And — back in love with people. (*LL*) Ill Humor. Goethe. STV

And be a friend to man. (*LL*) The House by the Side of the Road. Sam Walter Foss. AnAmPo; BLPA; BLPL; FaBoBe; WBLP; WGRP

And be a true Whig, while I'm not in game. (*LL*) An Excellent New Song, Being the Intended Speech of a Famous Orator against Peace. Swift. APAS

And be among her cloudy trophies hung. (*LL*) Ode on Melancholy. Keats. EnRP; FHYEP; HAP; ImPo; InPK; InPS; LiTB; MAT; MeMBP; NAEL-2; NAWM-2; NOBE; NoP; OAEL-2; OBEV; OBNC; OxAEP-2; PlP; PoE; PoEL-4; Poetr; PoRA; PPP; PrIm; SCGP; TEP; TFi; TrGrPo

And be anonymous? (*LL*) Our Hunting Fathers. W. H. Auden. FaBoMo; MoP; NoAM

And be buried in the dust of marching feet. (*LL*) For Black Poets Who Think of Suicide. Etheridge Knight. HeIP; InPK; PoBA

And be it said of thee. Michael Drayton. *Fr.* To Henry Reynolds, of Poets and Poesy. EPCY

And be the mistress of Mankind! (*LL*) Upon [His] Leaving His Mistress. The Earl of Rochester. EnLoPo; GBL; NBLV; NOSC; TEP; TrGrPo

And be their wonder, as we were their scorne. (*LL*) To His Late Majesty Concerning the True Form of English Poetry. Sir John Beaumont. JCP

And bearing brilliant an dnobel human beings. (*LL*) To the Tune "The River Is Red." Ch'iu Chin. AiP; BoWoP; PBWP; WPC

And beat him today. (*LL*) Jack. Charles Henry Ross. OxBChV; Spl

And begin to crow. (*LL*) Poland/ 1931 "The Wedding." Jerome Rothenberg. PoM; Prf

And being good for nothing else, be wise. (*LL*) The Disabled Debauchee. The Earl of Rochester. BoLoP; GGP; HAP; NAEL-1; NOBL; OBSV; PPP

And believing she was a maid. The Faithless Wife. Federico García Lorca, *tr. fr. Spanish by* A. L. Lloyd. BoLoP

And bellies of those whose spirits walked before. (*LL*) Return to Mankiller Flats, Oklahoma. Mary Crescenzo Simons. LoHo

And bells beyond the sand. (*LL*) Here We Come a-Piping. *Unknown.* BoTP; CH; CoGr

And bigamy, sir, is a crime. (*LL*) There was an old party of lyme. *At. to* Edward Lear. FaBoCo; FF; OxBoLi

And bird-blood leap within your veins. (*LL*) Interlude. Edith Sitwell. MoAB; MoBrPo

And birds came crying. James Cunningham. *Fr.* Narrator's Trance, The. JB

And bite us again! (*LL*) Octopus. Arthur Clement Hilton. BXAP; FaBoCo; FaBoPa; UV

And black Fate took these stubborn spearmen. On the Thessalians Who Fought at Marathon. Aeschylus, *tr. fr. Greek by* Edwin Morgan. GrAn

And bleached bones lie unclaimed. (*LL*) A Song of Parable. *Unknown.* SuSp

And bless it. (*LL*) Lord Bless Africa. Enoch Sontonga. PeSAV

And bless the gods — I've got a fever. (*LL*) Farewell to Malta. Byron. OBTV

And "Bless you sir" I added as he went to his fate in the rain, dapper Irishman. (*LL*) Uptown. Allen Ginsberg. FF; TwCP

And blessed be the women who get you through. Robin Morgan. *Fr.* Hallowing of Hell, The. GLP

And blew. "Childe Roland to the Dark Tower came". (*LL*) Childe Roland to the Dark Tower Came. Robert Browning. EnVR; NAEL-2; NOBVV; NoP; OAEL-2; OBNV; OtMeF; PeVV; PoE; PPP

And blew the insides out. (*LL*) The Alphabet by the Pool on a Sunday Afternoon. Lusia Slomkowska. LoHo

And bloody Faith the foulest birth of Time. (*LL*) Feelings of a Republican on the Fall of Bonaparte. Shelley. Son

And blow the candle out. (*LL*) Prophecy. Elinor Wylie. BLPL; BoWoP; FaBoWP; NTP; PrIm; VGW

And both are the same thing at last. (*LL*) Somnus, the humble god, that dwells. Sir John Denham. BeJo

And both thy servants be. (*LL*) Man. George Herbert. ESCV; GeHe; ImPo; NAEL-1; NoP; PoEL-2; SeCP; SeCV-1; TrGrPo; TrPWD, *abr*

And bought the New York Times, and went to bed. (*LL*) Hot Night on Water Street. Louis Simpson. CAPP; TwCP

And bowing not knowing to what. (*LL*) For the Anniversary of My Death. W. S. Merwin. CoAP; HCAP; InPK; NAAL-2; NaP; NOBA; Poetr; VCAP

And braves as he may the night Of darkness and tears. (*LL*) Winter Nightfall. Robert Bridges. MoAB; MoBrPo; OBEV; SCGP

And break it shall I never! (*LL*) Come, let me take thee to my breast. Burns. CBLP

And break the hidden snare. (*LL*) The Mouse's Petition. Anna Laetitia Barbauld. ECWP; FM; OxBChV

And break the jam on Gerry's Rocks with their foreman, young Monroe. (*LL*) The Jam on Gerry's Rock. *Unknown.* AmFP; AS; FaBoBa

And break thyself in shivers on her eye. (*LL*) The Bubble; a Song. Robert Herrick. CaPo

And breake before thee. (*LL*) To the Name above Every Name, the Name of Jesus, a Hymn. Richard Crashaw. SeCV-1

And breaks the glass of Time. (*LL*) Nahant. Emerson.

And breed the last from nothing. (*LL*) A Ballad of Hunters. C. J. Driver. PeSAV

And brighter bliss of heaven. (*LL*) I Love Thy Kingdom, Lord. Timothy Dwight. AH

And brighter hope when hope despairs. (*LL*) To Imagination. Emily Brontë. EnVR

And bring about the collapse of the whole empire. (*LL*) Shame. Richard Wilbur. FaBoMo; OxBC

& bring her in. Then a terrific Italian raid begins. (*LL*) Malta. John Forbes. NOBAu

And bring my thoughts to an end. (*LL*) Thoughts about the Person from Porlock. Stevie Smith. FaBoCo; NAEL-2; NoAM; NoP

And bring wine while you're at it. (*LL*) Ted Berrigan. Connie Deanovich. UTF

And broad old cesspools glittered in the sun. (*LL*) Mouse's Nest. John Clare. ChTr; InPK; LiTB; NAEL-2; RB

And, brother, what shall you say? (*LL*) And What Shall You Say? Joseph S. Cotter, Sr.. CDC; PoBA; PoNe

And brothers give you back the sword. (*LL*) Message to Siberia. Pushkin. AWP; TTY

And buggered his wife with the key. (*LL*) There was an old man of Dundee. *Unknown.* PeLi

And build, a new country. (*LL*) The Breezing Dawn of the New Day. Mongane Wally Serote. PeSAV

And build our happy nest again. (*LL*) Child's Talk in April. Christina Rossetti. GN

And built a braver Palace than before. (*LL*) The World. George Herbert. GeHe; NOSC; SeCV-1

And built herself an everlasting name. (*LL*) Godiva. Tennyson. BeLS; FaBoEH

And built the nest in the rock! (*LL*) I Am the Mountainy Singer. Joseph Campbell. MoBrPo

And Burgh under Stanemuir there dwels Dickie. (*LL*) Dick o' the Cow. *Unknown.* ESPB; IBB; OxBB

And buried brother John! (*LL*) The Twins. Henry S. Leigh. FaPON

And buried him where he fell. (*LL*) Vigil Strange I Kept on the Field One Night. Walt Whitman. HeIP; MeMAP; MoAmPo; NAAL-1; NOBA; NoP; OBWP; PeHV; PoE; TAP

And burn thee up, as well as I. (*LL*) To the Rose; a Song. Robert Herrick. SeCP

And burying ground. (*LL*) Traveling Back. Sara Hunter. LoHo

And but a chair. (*LL*) The Pilgrimage. George Herbert. ChTr; ESCV; FaBoRV; GeHe; NAEL-1; NOSC; PoE

And but in darkness is she visible. (*LL*) To an Old Lady. William Empson. FaBoTw; GTBS-P; MoAB; NoAM; NOBE; OxAEP-2

And by that light found out. (*LL*) A Light Left On. May Sarton. VBLP

And by the way, I was the only Nature poet. (*LL*) If, after I Die. Fernando Pessoa. PeSAV

And by what way shall I go back? (*LL*) L'An Trentiesme de Mon Eage. Archibald MacLeish. LiTM; MoP; NOBA

And call her crazed with wrong. (*LL*) Night and Sleep. Coventry Patmore. EBVV

And call this other thing, a/ foxtail pine. (*LL*) Foxtail Pine. Gary Snyder. NaP; NU

And call ye this to utter what is just. Bible, *O.T., paraphrased by* Sir Thomas Wyatt. *See* Do ye indeed speak righteousness, O congregation?

And called for one hot buttered toast. (*LL*) There was an old man of the coast. Edward Lear. MoShBr; OHCV; PeLi

And calling Justice, all things burn. (*LL*) Decay. George Herbert. ESCV; SCGP; SeCP; SeCV-1

And Camelot, and starlit Stonehenge. (*LL*) Channel Firing. Thomas Hardy. CMoP; EBEV; HAP; HeIP; ImPo; LiTB; MeMBP; MoP; NAEL-2; NIP; NoAM; NoP; OAEL-2; OxAEP-2; OxBTC; PeECV; PeFWW; PoE; PoEL-5; Poetr; PoRA; PoWW; PrIm; RB; SoSe; TFi; UnPo

And can I ever bid these joys farewell? Keats. *Fr.* Sleep and Poetry. EnRP; TOF

And can it be, that I should gain. Free Grace. Charles Wesley. NOCV

And can my simple harp be strung. To My Friend and Patron, M —— K ——, Esq. Lucretia Davidson. AmWP

And can return no more. (*LL*) First Love. John Clare. BoLoP; ChTr; EnLoPo; GBL; HAP; NOBVV; NoP

And can the muse reflect her tear-stain'd eye. *Unknown. Fr.* Jamaica, a Poem in Three Parts, Written in That Island in the Year 1776. PBCV

And Can the Physician. *Unknown. See* And can the physician make sick men well?

And can the physician make sick men well? Lily, Germander, and Sops-in-Wine. *Unknown. Fr.* Robin Goodfellow. CBCK

(And Can the Physician.) ELP

(Song: "And can the physician make sick men well?") EIL

& cannot be let go. (*LL*) However heavy the walls of love, or well shored, they. Janet Gray. VBLP

And cannot ease my burning heart. (*LL*) To the Tune "Plucking a Cinnamon Branch." Huang O. WPC

And Canst Thou, Sinner, Slight. Abby Bradley Hyde. AH

And caressed by the rain. (*LL*) Scotland. Sir Alexander Gray. OxBS

And carry away the pitcher. (*LL*) The Pitcher. Hsiung-hung. WPC

And carry you away. (*LL*) For the Courtesan Ch'ing Lin. Wu Tsao. BoWoP; VBLP; WPC; WPOW

And cascades hang noiseless in the mountains, rainbows of jade. (*LL*) The Northern Cold. Li Ho. PLT

And, cast by conscience out, spendsavour salt? (*LL*) The Candle Indoors. Gerard Manley Hopkins. ChIV-2; ImPo; LiTB; LiTM; OxAEP-2; PoEL-5

And ceilings crack. (*LL*) The Boarder. Louis Simpson. InPK; SM

And change his soul for harmony. (*LL*) In Commendation of Music. William Strode. ELP; OBEV

And change with hurried hand has swept these scenes. Frederick Goddard Tuckerman. *Fr.* Sonnets. HAP; NOBA; TAP

And cheer my mind in sorrow. (*LL*) Yarrow Visited. Wordsworth. EnRP; GTBS; GTBS-P

And cherish and shelter us. (*LL*) Sea Gods. Hilda Doolittle ("H. D."). LiTA

And children and a keg of beer and an accordion. (*LL*) Happiness. Carl Sandburg. AnAmPo; OxBA

And Christ comes with a January flower. (*LL*) Advent. Patrick Kavanagh. IIP; TIRV

And Christe receive thy saule. (*LL*) Lyke-Wake Dirge, The [*or* A]. *Unknown.* CH; ChTr; CoGr; EBEvV; FaBoCh; FaBoRV; GBP; HAP; HoPM; NOBE; NoP; NTP; OBEV; OtMeF; PeECV; PoEL-1; ScCV; TFi; WeW

And chucks me on the rubbish heap. (*LL*) Passion. Jena Lengold. VBLP

And Cities — ooze away. (*LL*) A Still — Volcano — Life. Emily Dickinson. TRP

And clasp'd them sobbing, to his aching breast. (*LL*) Eliza. Erasmus Darwin. VPP

And classic bronze of Benin. (*LL*) A Different Image. Dudley Randall. BPo; FF; TAP

And cleans its muzzle after. (*LL*) How It Goes On. Maxine W. Kumin. FoLa

And clearly I recall the second day's end. The Perfect Disc of the Moon. Richard Kenney. Son

And closed her up, as in a tomb. (*LL*) The Funeral Rites of the Rose. Robert Herrick. CaPo; NOSC; OBEV

And closed in with "lisses" of strong piles. (*LL*) Well Pleaseth Me the Sweet Time of Easter. Bertrans de Born. InVP

And closing toward the river. (*LL*) Five Dawn Skies in November. David Wagoner. VCAP

And cluck your children in about your knee! (*LL*) Sonnet to Gath. Edna St. Vincent Millay. BoWoP; CMoP; MoAB; MoAmPo

And cold as any icicle. (*LL*) Parting, without a Sequel. John Crowe Ransom. MeMAP; MoAB; MoAmPo; OxBA; SoSe

And cold, on the pillow's dark side. (*LL*) The Night Mirror. John Hollander. NYBP; PeNM; VCAP

And come and be my guest, — for I am Love's. (*LL*) Epipsychidion. Shelley. EnRP

And come unto my courtship as my prayer. (*LL*) A Devout Lover. Thomas Randolph. HoPM; OBEV

And comes from a country far away as health. (*LL*) Tulips. Sylvia Plath. HAP; NaP; NoP; NYBP; PPP; WeW; WPE

And coming the proud over all o' the birds o' the sea. (*LL*) Sea Change. John Masefield. FaBoTw; OBMV; RB

And conclusions reached. (*LL*) To the Writers' Worship in Zomba. Felix Mnthali. PeSAV

And confident thou'lt raise me with the just. (*LL*) On Himself, upon Hearing What Was His Sentence. James Graham, Marquess of Montrose. NOSC

And consummation comes, and jars two hemispheres. (*LL*) The Convergence of the Twain (Lines on the Loss of the *Titanic*). Thomas Hardy. FaBoEH; FaBoTw; HeIP; InPK; InPS; LiTB; LiTM; MeMBP; MoAB; MoBrPo; MoP; NAEL-2; NIP; NoAM; NoP; OAEL-2; OHCV; OxBTC; PeVV; PFP; Poetr; PrIm; SCGP; TEP; TFi

And continued to knock him about. (*LL*) There was an old man who screamed out. Edward Lear. CBNP; EBEV; NOBVV; OxAEP-2

And corn in valleys grow. (*LL*) Edom. Isaac Watts. AmFP

And could no longer recollect my name. (*LL*) Epigram. J. V. Cunningham. VCAP

And couldn't get up in the morning. (*LL*) It's raining, it's pouring. *Unknown*. ISE; OxNR; RoPo

And couldn't write. (*LL*) A Bookshop Idyll. Kingsley Amis. OxBTC; PeLV

And counterfeit mortality. (*LL*) The Recurrence. Edwin Muir. MeMBP

And covered them with shade. (*LL*) On the Way to the Mission. Duncan Campbell Scott. NOBC

And covered up our names. (*LL*) I died for beauty — but was scarce. Emily Dickinson. AnAmPo; AWP; BLPL; BoWoP; ImPo; LiTA; LiTM; LPA; MeMAP; MoAB; MoAmPo; NAAL-2; NAWM-2; NOBA; NoP; SAmP

And covers my body with petals. (*LL*) Summer Day. Yüan Mei. OHMPC

And crash a grunting cheat that's young. (*LL*) The Maunder's Praise of His Strowling Mort. *Unknown*. CBNP; OxBoLi; PeLV

And cries, "It shall be done sometime, somewhere." (*LL*) Pray without Ceasing. Ophelia Guyon Browning. BLPA; BLPL

And crowd to Stella's at fourscore. (*LL*) Stella's Birthday, 1721 ("All travelers at first incline.") Swift. NAEL-1; PeIV; PoEL-3

And crown with love my ever-during night. (*LL*) My Sweetest Lesbia [Let Us Live and Love]. Thomas Campion, *after the Latin of* Catullus. AAS; AWP; EiL; EnRePo; FF; GBL; HAP; HeIP; InPS; NAEL-1; NoP; NoSic; OAEL-1; OBVE; PoE; PoRA; PrIm; SCGP; TEP; TFi; TrGrPo; WeW

And Cupids yoke the doves. (*LL*) Few Happy Matches. Isaac Watts. NOEC

And curl forever in some far-off farmyard flower. (*LL*) Beehive. Jean Toomer. PoBA; TTY

And curse her yellow teeth with this. (*LL*) Zimmer's Head Thudding against the Blackboard. Paul Zimmer. PBCAP

And curse the men who have misused you. (*LL*) Sausalito,/ Little Willow. Lew Welch. EaPr

And cursing, stumble out like ghosts into the frozen dark. (*LL*) Mess Deck Casualty. Alan Ross.

And custom for the spreading laurel tree. (*LL*) A Prayer for My Daughter. W. B. Yeats. BLPL; CMoP; HAP; LiTB; LiTM; MeMBP; MoAB; MoP; NAEL-2; NAs; NoAM; NoP; OxBTC; PoA; PoLF; PoRA; PrIm; RaBo; TEP; TFi

And cut them and gave them to me / in my hand. (*LL*) The Act. William Carlos Williams. ArNa; SAmP; SOTW; VGW

And dance again when trumpets blow. (*LL*) Epilogue for a Masque of Purcell. Adrienne Rich. NYBP

And dance, and revel then, as we do now. (*LL*) In Answer of an Elegiacal Letter, Upon the Death of the King of Sweden. Thomas Carew. BeJo

And dance with foolish grace to heaven. (*LL*) The Book of Myths. Joy Harjo. SRLS

And dance with me next season. (*LL*) Lines Written for a Blank Page of "The Keepsake." Winthrop Mackworth Praed. CBLP

And darkness. All the old figures. Peter Philpott. VaA

And daunce to th' Musick of your Chaines. (*LL*) The Vintage to the Dungeon. Richard Lovelace. BeJo; CaPo; SeCV-1

And David fled from Naioth in Ramah. Bible, *O.T. Fr.* First Samuel. OBF

And David lamented with this lamentation. Bible, *O.T. Fr.* Second Samuel. OBF

And day and night yield one delight once more? (*LL*) Sudden Light. Dante Gabriel Rossetti. BoLoP; CTC; EBEvV; ELP; NOBE; NOBVV; NoP; OAEL-2; OBNC; OHCV; OPOP; PIP; PoLF; TrGrPo

And dazzled Reason yields as quite undone. (*LL*) Like two proud armies marching in the field. *Unknown*. NoSic

And dear they are, but not so dear. (*LL*) Shut Out. Christina Rossetti. NALW; PFP

And death, after all, was only "another room." (*LL*) Resurrection of Arp. A. J. M. Smith. MoCV; NOBC

And death be strong, yet love is strong as death. (*LL*) Love Me - I Love You. Christina Rossetti. BoTP

And death i think is no parenthesis. (*LL*) Since Feeling Is First. E. E. Cummings. MoAB; MoAmPo; NoP; PrIm

And death is no evil. (*LL*) Night. Robinson Jeffers. AWP; LiTA; MoAmPo; NOBA; OxBA

And death shall have no dominion. (*LL*) And Death Shall Have No Dominion. Dylan Thomas. ChIV-2; CMoP; EBEvV; FaPoB; LiTM; LPA; MeMBP; MoAB; MoBrPo; NoAM; Poetr; RB

And Death Shall Have No Dominion. Dylan Thomas. ChIV-2; CMoP; EBEvV; FaPoB; LiTM; LPA; MeMBP; MoAB; MoBrPo; NoAM; Poetr; RB

And deck the broken stones like saxifrage. (*LL*) She. Richard Wilbur. AmPP

And deep-eyed children cannot long be children. Ballad of the Outer Life. Hugo von Hofmannsthal, *tr. fr. German by* Jethro Bithell. AWP; TrJP

And defecar on those goddam guidebook. (*LL*) Sinalóa. Earle Birney. MoCV; OxBC; PeLV

And dense with happy blood, dark rainbow bliss in the sea. (*LL*) Whales Weep Not! D. H. Lawrence. CMoP; MeMBP; NoAM; NU

And depressed that Young Lady in White. (*LL*) Limerick. Edward Lear. PeLi

And did ever a man go black with sun in a Belgian swamp. Nigger. Karl Shapiro. OxBA

And Did the Animals? Mark Van Doren. VGW

And did these feet, in pre-war days. The New Jerusalem. Allan M. Laing. UV

And Did Those Feet. Blake. *See* And Did Those Feet in Ancient Time.

And Did Those Feet in Ancient Time. Blake. *Fr.* Milton. AWP; ClHu; EBEvV; EnRP; FaBoCh; FaBoPV; FaBV; HAP; HeIP; InPS; MAT; MeMBP; NAEL-2; NAWM-2; NoP; OAEL-2; PeECV; PIP; PoE; PoEL-4; PoRA; PrIm; SCGP; TFi; WGRP

And did we come into our own. Letter to Derek Mahon. Michael Longley. CIP; IIP

And did you get what. Late Fragment. Raymond Carver. ArLo

And did you know. Snowflakes. Clive Sansom. OBCP

And did you not hear of a jolly young waterman. The Jolly Young Waterman. Charles Dibdin. NOEC; OxAEP-1

And did you not hear of a mirth that befell. Away to Twiver, Away, Away! *Unknown*. EiL

And did young Stephen sicken. Emmeline Grangerford's "Ode to Stephen Dowling Bots, Dec'd." "Mark Twain." *Fr.* Adventures of Huckleberry Finn, The. NBLV; OBAL

(Ode to Stephen Dowling Bots, Dec'd.) FiBHP; Poetr

And didn't get back till the Fourth of July. (*LL*) I asked my mother for fifty cents. *Unknown*. ISE; MoShBr; OxBoLi; RoPo

And die a martyr to thy love of light. (*LL*) Calvus to a Fly. Charles Tennyson Turner. FM; NOBVV

And die, or kill. (*LL*) Laurana's Song. Richard Hovey. AnAmPo

And die to Fame an honored martyr. (*LL*) Fame. Emerson. AnAmPo

And died a month later. (*LL*) Colonel. Kate Llewellyn. NOBAu

And dies between three cannibals. (*LL*) The Fly. Karl Shapiro. LiTM; MoP; NoAM; SoSe

And discovered as Keats once said that wood is wooden. (*LL*) This is Not a Poem but a Proem. Edward Vincent Swart. PeSAV

And disembodied bones. (*LL*) The Eagle and the Mole. Elinor Wylie. AWP; BoWoP; LiTA; LiTM; MoAB; MoAmPo; NALW; UnPo

And, disenchanted, I'm momentarily yet. (*LL*) Hearing Russian Spoken. Donald Davie. GTBS-P

And dish water gives back no images. (*LL*) No Images. Waring Cuney. CDC; MAT; NIP; TTY

And dismal darkness then doth smutch the face. (*LL*) Life Is the Body's Light. Robert Herrick. BeJo

And distant from our eyes. (*LL*) Cartography. Louise Bogan. TRP

And dive off in my grave like the old swimmin'-hole. (*LL*) The Old Swimmin'-Hole. James Whitcomb Riley. AnAmPo; BeLS

And do not even own clothing. (*LL*) Salutation. Ezra Pound. HeIP; MeMAP; MoAB; MoAmPo; NOBA; OxBA; TAP; VGW

And do our loves all perish with our frames. Immortality. Richard Henry Dana. WGRP

And do they so? have they a Sense. Rom. Cap. 8 Ver. 19. Henry Vaughan. ESCV; GeHe; MeLP

And does not drift away. (*LL*) Medusa. Louise Bogan. AWP; BoWoP; HoPM; MoAB; MoAmPo; NALW; NoAM; NoP; Poetr; WPE

And does the heart grow old? You know. To My Wife. J. V. Cunningham. VCAP

And Don't Be Deaf to the Singing Beyond. Carter Revard. HATNAP

And don't bother telling me anything. César Vallejo, *tr. fr. Spanish by* Robert Bly. AnAn

And don't you want to hear him, Kate? (*LL*) To Kate, Skating Better than Her Date. David Daiches. FiBHP; NYBP

And dost thou faithlessly abandon me? The Unrealities. Schiller, *tr. fr. German by* James Clarence Mangan. AWP

And down to make a bed for you. (*LL*) Cackle, cackle, Mother Goose. *Unknown.* OxNR

And downstairs, shut. (*LL*) The Time before You. Medbh McGuckian. CBLP

& drank up all my water. (*LL*) My First Memory, Switzerland, Circa 1947. Joan Dobbie. LoHo

And dream my time away.' (*LL*) Expostulation and Reply. Wordsworth. EnRP; FHYEP; NAEL-2; OAEL-2

And dreaming he's dead, he'll forget to awake. (*LL*) Willie the Weeper. *Unknown.* BeLS; BLPA; OBAL

And dreams, Forgetfulness! (*LL*) Forgetfulness. James Russell Lowell. AnAmPo

And dressed me gently in my little clothes. (*LL*) The Boat. Robert Pack. CoAP; SM

And drew her backward home. (*LL*) The Subverted Flower. Robert Frost. CMoP; HAP; MeMAP; MoP; NoAM; NOBA; OxBA; PoE; Poetr

And drives like she is living. She Drives. Sophie Cabot Black. LoHo

And Dromio's denouement of tragic mirth. (*LL*) The Twins. Karl Shapiro. MoAmPo; TrJP

And drop like firebrands on the fragrant hearth. (*LL*) Church Burning: Mississippi. James A. Emanuel. PoBA; PoNe

And drove the first dart deeper more and more. (*LL*) Enemy of life, decayer of all kind, The. Sir Thomas Wyatt. OxBSP; SiPS; SiPSBD

And drunk the milk of Paradise. (*LL*) Kubla Khan; or, A Vision in a Dream. Samuel Taylor Coleridge. AWP; CH; ChTr; ELP; EnRP; FaBoBe; FaBoCh; FaBV; FF; GGP; GN; GoJo; HAP; HeIL; HeIP; HoPM; InPK; InPS; InvP; LiTB; MAT; MeMBP; NAEL-2; NAWM-2; NIP; NOBE; NoP; OAEL-2; OBEV; OBNC; OPOP; OtMeF; PlP; PoE; PoEL-4; Poetr; PoRA; PrIm; SCGP; SCV; SoSe; TEP; TOF; TRP

And dust is for a time. (*LL*) In Distrust of Merits. Marianne Moore. ArOW; LiTA; LiTM; MeMAP; MoAB; MoAmPo; NAAL-2; OBWP; OxBA; TrGrPo

And dying again. (*LL*) When the Moon Is Full. Elaine Equi. UTF

And dying in black and white we fight for what we love, not are. (*LL*) Ode: Salute to the French Negro Poets. Frank O'Hara. GLP; NeAP; NNaP; PoM; PoNe

And each a 2 pence, 2 pence, 2 pence gave him and went away. (*LL*) The Rural Dance about the Maypole. *Unknown.* GBP; OxBoLi

And each anointed sense will see. (*LL*) Extreme Unction. Ernest Dowson. MoBrPo; OAEL-2; OBMV; PeECV; PeVV

And each as silent as a man being shaved. (*LL*) Prolonged Sonnet: When the Troops Were Returning from Milan [*or* When The Troops Were Returning from Milan]. Niccolò degli Albizzi. AWP; OBVE

And earth, sea, man, are all in each. (*LL*) The Sea-Limits. Dante Gabriel Rossetti. EnVR; NAEL-2; OAEL-2; OHCV

And eat him while he's hot. (*LL*) Davy Davy Dumpling. *Unknown.* OxNR

And eats the meadow flowers. (*LL*) The Cow. Robert Louis Stevenson. FaPON; FM; NTCP; OxBChV; PWR; TLR; WHSW

And Elvira to her Ferdinand's irrevocably mated! (*LL*) Ferdinando and Elvira; or, The Gentle Pieman. W. S. Gilbert. FaBoCo; FaBoNo; FiBHP

And embraces his silence again. (*LL*) Tramp. Frank Mkalawile Chipasula. PeSAV

And Emily Geiger's ride. (*LL*) Emily Geiger. *Unknown.* BLPL; PoLF

And empty spaces in the throat. (*LL*) The Evening of the Mind. Donald Justice. VCAP

And enjoy the clear Autumn. (*LL*) To an Old Tune. Hsin Ch'i-chi. OHMPC

And equal to the peaks of our desire. (*LL*) The Road. James Stephens. PlP

And escaped from the people of Basing. (*LL*) There was an old person of Basing. Edward Lear. CBNP; EBEV; OxAEP-2; PeLi

And Ettrick mourns with her their poet dead. (*LL*) Extempore Effusion upon the Death of James Hogg. Wordsworth. EBEV; FaBoRV; NOBE; NoP; OAEL-2; SCV

And Even, Even If They Take Away the Stove. Miron Bialoszewski, *tr. fr. Polish by* Czeslaw Milosz.

"And even our women," lastly grumbles Ben. The Girl of All Periods: An Idyll. Coventry Patmore. EnVR

And eventually sent a telegram. (*LL*) How I Brought the Good News from Aix to Ghent (or Vice Versa). R. J. Yeatman *and* W. C. Sellar. BXAP; FaBoPa; FiBHP; UV

And ever aloft on the palace roof the old banner of England blew. (*LL*) The Defence of Lucknow. Tennyson. BeLS

And Ever is Now. (*LL*) A Pavane for the Nursery. William Jay Smith. GoJo; MoAmPo

And ever more shall be-O. (*LL*) Carol of the Numbers. *Unknown.* AmFP

And evermore be merry! (*LL*) So now is come our joyful'st feast. George Wither.

And evermore of him shall live the best. (*LL*) An Epitaph on Sir Philip Sidney. James I, King of England. Son

And every bird shew'd in his proper kind. Michael Drayton. *Fr.* Owle, The. FM

And every house a folly. (*LL*) For Though the Eaves [*or* Caves] Were Rabbeted [*or* Rabbited]. Thoreau. OxBSP; PoEL-4

And every prodigal greatness. The Flowering Urn. Laura Riding. LiTA

And every wave is charmed. (*LL*) Terminus. Emerson. AmPP; AWP; MeMAP; NOBA; OxBA; PoEL-4; PoLF; TAP

And every year a world my will did deem. George Gascoigne. *Fr.* Gascoigne's Memories. EnRePo; Son

And every yeare a worlde my will did deeme. (*LL*) Before mine eye to feede my greedy will. George Gascoigne. AAS

And every yeare a worlde my will did deeme. George Gascoigne. AAS

And everyone, everyone pointing up and shouting! (*LL*) Child on Top of a Greenhouse. Theodore Roethke. LCAP; VGW

And everyone simply dances away. (*LL*) Slow Dance. David St. John. AmPA; AnAn; LCAP

And everyone wins. (*LL*) Hug o' War. Shel Silverstein. NTCP

And ev'n Devotion! (*LL*) To a Louse [on Seeing One on a Lady's Bonnet at Church]. Burns. BLPA; EnRP; FaBoVe; InvP; LiTB; NAEL-2; NOEC; OxBS; PrIm

And ev'ry thing, save her, who all should grace. (*LL*) Phoebus, Arise. William Drummond of Hawthornden. EIL

And examine my pomegranate flower dress. (*LL*) A Love Song of the Empress Wu. Empress Wu Tse-t'ien. WPC

And explaining again, still clearer. The Pardon of Assisi. Sebastian Barry. IB

And faded kivas of our dreams. (*LL*) The Blessing. Paula Gunn Allen. SRLS

And fades away like morning dew. (*LL*) Waly, Waly ("When cockle shells turn silver bells.") *Unknown.* AmFP

And fainted on the deck! (*LL*) The Main-Truck; or, A Leap for Life. *At. to* George Pope Morris. AnAmPo; BLPL; PoLF; VPP

And faithful Petrarch gloriously crown'd. (*LL*) Keen, Fitful Gusts. Keats. EnRP; PoEL-4; Son; TEP

And fall before thee. (*LL*) Fain Would I Change That Note. *At. to* Tobias Hume. EIL; ELP; PoEL-2

And fall in blood: we bring him even now. (*LL*) Six o'Clock. Trumbull Stickney. AnAmPo; OxBA

& familiar. The dark watermark of your absence, a hush. (*LL*) Hush. David St. John. LCAP

And fate change me to worms. (*LL*) Against Constancy. The Earl of Rochester. GBL; NOSC; OxAEP-1

And fear lit by the breadth of such calmly turns to praise. (*LL*) The City Limits. A. R. Ammons. CAPP; HCAP; MoP; NAAL-2; NoAM; NOBA; NoP; Poetr; VCAP

And fears not portly Azcan nor his hoos. (*LL*) Bantams in Pine-Woods. Wallace Stevens. CMoP; InPS; MeMAP; NoAM; NOBA; OxBA; SAmP; UnPo

And feed the future with its ripeness. (*LL*) The Revolution of the Aged. Njabulo S. Ndebele. PeSAV

& feel good. (*LL*) Get It & Feel Good. Ntozake Shange. VBLP

And feel his little silvery feet. (*LL*) A Garden Song. Thomas Moore. BoNaP

And feel on my forehead the brand of Cain. (*LL*) A War (?) in the Desert. *Unknown.* PeSAV

And fell in love with sin. (*LL*) Elegy for a Puritan Conscience. Alan Dugan. CAPP; SM

And few but pure the words I need. (*LL*) Dedication. N. P. van Wyk Louw. PeSAV

And filled with pollen. (*LL*) Hush, My Little Grandmother. Meridel LeSueur. SRLS

And find Love in Thine eyes. (*LL*) From Thee to Thee. Solomon ibn Gabirol. TrJP

And find the last the best. (*LL*) Emancipation. Maltbie D. Babcock. BLRP; WBLP

And find the same corruption there. (*LL*) I am the only being whose doom. Emily Brontë. MAT; MeMBP; NALW

And finished knowing — then. (*LL*) I Felt a Funeral, in My Brain. Emily Dickinson. AmPP; AnAmPo; BoWoP; CMoP; HeIP; LiTA; MeMAP; NAAL-1; NALW; NOBA; NoP; OxBA; PBWP; PoE; PoEL-5; Poetr; PoRA; RaBo; SCV; SoSe; TAP; TFi

And fire their only future. (*LL*) The Asians Dying. W. S. Merwin. CoAP; HCAP; NaP; NOBA; NYBP; VCAP

And first is Quince the wonder working one. Quince. Nigel Wells. PWE

And five minutes left before the world begins. (*LL*) Possibly. Lesléa Newman. VBLP

And flies with the cloud. (*LL*) Chimes. Alice Meynell. BoTP; CH; MoBrPo; WPE

And flows its sure, slow heart. (*LL*) The Snapper. William Heyen. AmPA

And flung it at the people. (*LL*) There Was a Man and He Was Mad. *Unknown.* GBP; RB

And fly into its boughs. (*LL*) The Knot. Stanley Kunitz. CAPP; HAP

And for a word too much men oft have died. (*LL*) Ku Klux. Madison Cawein. PAH

And for Alice, his wife, pray too. (*LL*) Shameful Death. William Morris. ChTr; GTBS-P; PeVV

And for CHANGE! (*LL*) 'It's Nation Time.' Michael McClure. PoBeRe

And for her sake trip up Death. (*LL*) Little Elegy. X. J. Kennedy. CoAP; GoJo; HoPM

And for thy veil gave me thy FACE. (*LL*) The Hymn of Saint Thomas in Adoration of the Blessed Sacrament. Richard Crashaw.

And for what, except for you, do I feel love? Wallace Stevens. *Fr.* Notes toward a Supreme Fiction. NOBA

And forced the underbrush — and that was all. (*LL*) The Most of It. Robert Frost. EaPr; HAP; NAAL-2; NoP; NU; TOF; TRP; WeW

And Forgetful of Europe. Geoffrey Grigson. OBTV

And Forgive Us Our Trespasses. Aphra Behn. EBEV

And forth they yede togider, twain and twain. A Courtly Scene and a Sudden Storm. *Fr.* Floure and the Leafe, The. OxBLMV

And found it was perfectly true. (*LL*) There was an old man of [*or* from] Peru/ Who dreamt [*or* dreamed] he was eating his shoe. *Unknown.* PDV; SoSe

And foxes stunk and littered in St. Paul's.' (*LL*) On Lord Holland's Seat near Margate, Kent. Thomas Gray. NOEC; OAEL-1; OPOP

And frame from thinking and is realized. (*LL*) To an Old Philosopher in Rome. Wallace Stevens. EnlH; MeMAP; MoP; NoAM; NOBA; Poetr

And free land of the grave. (*LL*) Crossing Alone the Nighted Ferry. A. E. Housman. FaBoRV; GTBS-P; NOBE; NoP; OxBSP

And freed his soul the nearest way. (*LL*) On the Death of Mr. [*or* Dr.] Robert Levet [a Practiser in Physic]. Samuel Johnson. ChIV-2; EBEV; InPS; NAEL-1; NOBE; NOEC; NoP; OAEL-1; OBEV; OxAEP-1; PeECV; PIP; PoE; PoEL-3; PPP; SCGP; SCV; TEP; TFi

And Freedom's banner streaming o'er us! (*LL*) The American Flag. Joseph Rodman Drake. AnAmPo; FaBoBe; GN; PAH; VPP; WBLP

And freedoms birthright from the weak devours. (*LL*) The Fallen Elm. John Clare. FaBoPV; FHYEP

And freely give her Love. (*LL*) The Sound Country Lass. *Unknown.* CoMu; ErPo

And, friend, in your buying, remember poor me! (*LL*) Upon Receipt of a Pound of Coffee in 1863. Mary E. Tucker. AmWP; CBWP-1

And frightened Miss Muffet away. (*LL*) Little Miss Muffet/ Sat on a tuffet. Mother Goose. FaBoBe; OxNR; ReMoGo

And from all troubles rest. (*LL*) For Just Men Light Is Sown. Michael Wigglesworth. AH

And from my bosom find a surer rest. (*LL*) The Earth. Jones Very. AnAmPo; OxBA

And from that hour those Bachelors were never heard of more. (*LL*) The Two Old Bachelors. Edward Lear. BeLS; FiBHP

And from the Citie Tegea there came the Paragone. Ovid, *tr.* by Arthur Golding. *Fr.* Metamorphoses. OBVE

And from the house his mother called his name. (*LL*) Childhood. Edwin Muir. CMoP; HeIP; NoP

And frowzy pores that taint the ambient air. (*LL*) On Jacob Tonson, His Publisher. Dryden. ChTr; FaBoEE; OBSV

And fuck my bloody life away. (*LL*) I Don't Want to Be a Soldier. *Unknown.* NSI; PoWW

And fuddled by my drunkness forget/ — Monangambeeee. (*LL*) Monangamba. Antonio Jacinto. TTY, *tr.* by Alan Ryder

And fullness is never and now. (*LL*) I Saw Her Dancing. Marge Piercy. SRLS

And futile as regret. (*LL*) Bewick Finzer. E. A. Robinson. CMoP; MeMAP; MoAB; MoAmPo; NAAL-2; PPP

And gallop terribly against each other's bodies. (*LL*) Autumn Begins in Martins Ferry, Ohio. James Wright. CAPP; HCAP; HeIP; InPK; InPS; NaP; NoAM; VCAP; WeW

And garland-streams. (*LL*) The Starre. George Herbert. ESCV; MiEL; PeECV

And gather roses, while 'tis called to-day. (*LL*) Of His Lady's Old Age. Pierre de Ronsard. AWP; CTC

And gathering swallows twitter in the skies. (*LL*) To Autumn. Keats. ArNa; AWP; BoNaP; BoTP; CH; ClHu; CoGr; EBEV; EBVV; EnRP; FaBoRV; FaPoB; FF; FHYEP; GTBS; HAP; HeIP; ImPo; InPK; InPS; InvP; LiTB; MeMBP; Mes; NAEL-2; NAWM-2; NIP; NOBE; NoP;

NTP; NU; OAEL-2; OBEV; OBNC; OxAEP-2; PlP; PoE; PoEL-4; Poetr; PoLF; PPP; Prf; PrIm; RaBo; RB; SCGP; SCV; SoSe; TEP; TFi; TRP; UnPo; WeW

And gave her good kirking. (*LL*) Hind Etin. *Unknown.* OxBB

And gave me/ five! (*LL*) The Roach. John Raven. BPo; HoPM

And gaze, and gazing think, how base a thing am I. (*LL*) Arcades Ambo. Charles Stuart Calverley. BXAP

And ghosts hover like circling birds waiting to claim you back. (*LL*) The Ghosts in the Ark. Dermot Bolger. IB

And ghosts then keep their distance; and I know some liberty. (*LL*) Wessex Heights. Thomas Hardy. CMoP; EBVV; FaBoPP; MeMBP; OAEL-2; OBNC; PoEL-5; SCGP

And ginger-bread nuts are smallish. (*LL*) Dawlish Fair. Keats. NTP; PeLV

And give it good thought/ OK? (*LL*) Please Say Something. Tomioka Taeko. WPOW

And give thanks it was not I, nor yet one close to I. (*LL*) The Open Sea. William Meredith. CoAP; GoJo; GrPl; TAP; UnPo

And give to February twenty-nine. (*LL*) Thirty days hath September. Mother Goose. FaBoBe; FaBoUs; OxNR; ReMoGo

And gladly whode helerne, and gladly rechè. (*LL*) A Clerk Ther Was of Cauntebrige Also. W. W. Skeat. BXAP

And gleam again on the shadowy moss. (*LL*) Deep in the Mountain Wilderness. Wang Wei. OHMPC

And glistens like quicksilver. (*LL*) Ballydavid Pier. Thomas Kinsella. BIrV

And glittering eyelids of my soul's desire. (*LL*) Love and Sleep. Swinburne. BoLoP; CBLP

And glory to our Sovereign Lord, King Henry of Navarre! (*LL*) Ivry. Macaulay. FaBV; GN

And go and kiss within the hay. (*LL*) Ametas and Thestylis Making Hay-Ropes. Andrew Marvell. InvP; SeCP

And go away. (*LL*) Angel. John Forbes. NOBAu

And God alone will know his sin upon the judgment day. (*LL*) The Bank Thief. J. R. Farrell. BeLS; BLPA

And God at every gate. (*LL*) Our journey had advanced. Emily Dickinson. LiTA; LiTM; MoAB; NOCV; PoEL-5; SoSe

And God bless me. (*LL*) I See the Moon. *Unknown.* GBP, *diff. vers.*; NTCP; OxNR; PYC

And God looked down at God that day. My God, My God, Look upon Me. Chad Walsh. *Fr.* Psalm of Christ, The. TrCP

And God said, let the waters generate. Milton. *Fr.* Paradise Lost. EPCY (Creation of the Animals.) FM
(Creation.) NOSC, *bk.* VII, *ll.* 387–516

And God saw everything that He had made, and found it very good. *Unknown.* EaPr

And God saw that the wickedness of man was great. Bible, *O.T. Fr.* Genesis. NAWM-1

And God shall hear your words and make them true. (*LL*) Optimism. Ella Wheeler Wilcox. BLPA; BLPL; FaBoBe

And God truly lives in the world. (*LL*) This world is the abode of God. Angad. EaPr

And gods disgusting. — You and I, Cassandra. (*LL*) Cassandra. Robinson Jeffers. HeIP; LiTA; LiTM

And going to the office in the train. (*LL*) Dreamers. Siegfried Sassoon. MoBrPo; NoAM; Son

And gold on my neck the sun. (*LL*) The Collier. Vernon Watkins. FaBoTw; OBWVE

And good-bye to the bar and its moaning. (*LL*) The Three Fishers [Went Sailing]. Charles Kingsley. BeLS; EBVV; FaPoR; GGP; OHCV; OtMeF; PlP; PoLF; PWR; WBLP

And grant his reign over the entire building. (*LL*) Homage to the British Museum. William Empson. CMoP; FaBoMo; LiTM; MoAB; MoBrPo; PoE

And grave by grave we civilize the ground. (*LL*) To the Western World. Louis Simpson. CAPP; CoAP; GOA; LiTM; NOBA; SM; TAP; TRP

And great thy wisdom, Vander Brüin. (*LL*) A Dutch Proverb. Matthew Prior. FaBoEE; NOEC

And greet the anxious reader from the Press. (*LL*) The Press. Thomas Phipson. PeSAV

And greet the dawn with praise. Amen. (*LL*) Morning comes and now is!, The. *Unknown.* EaPr

And gulp from them the dailiness of life. (*LL*) Well Water. Randall Jarrell. InPK; NAAL-2; NOBA; NoP; OxBSP; VCAP; VGW

And Gwydion said to Math, when it was Spring. The Wife of Llew. Francis Ledwidge. PeIV

And habit builds the bridge at last! (*LL*) A Builder's Lesson. John Boyle O'Reilly. PoLF; PoToHe, *St. 1 only*; PWR

And hail Him, blessed Jesus. (*LL*) There Is No Name So Sweet on Earth. George Washington Bethune. AH

And handled with a chain. (*LL*) Much madness is divinest sense. Emily Dickinson. AmPP; BoWoP; CMoP; HeIP; LiTM; MAT; MeMAP; NAAL-1; NALW; NAWM-2; NoAM; NOBA; NoP; OxBA; PFP; Poetr; RaBo; SAmP; SoSe; TFi; TRP; WPE

And hang from implacable boughs. (*LL*) Chagrin. Isaac Rosenberg. MoBrPo

And hang it in the junior college. (*LL*) Digging for Indians. Gary Gildner. AmPA; PBCAP

And Hannah prayed, and said. Hannah's Thanksgiving. Bible, *O.T. Fr.* First Samuel. BoWoP

And haply may forget. (*LL*) When I am dead, my dearest. Christina Rossetti. AWP; BoLoP; CH; CoGr; DL; EBEV; FF; GBL; InPS; MeMBP; NAEL-2; NOBE; NOBVV; NoP; OAEL-2; OBD; OBEV; PlP; Poetr; PoLF; PoRA; SCV; TFi; WPE

And happier than a feather. (*LL*) Sleep My Little Love. Breyten Breytenbach. PeSAV

And happy each at home enjoys his love. (*LL*) Cymon and Iphigenia. Dryden. EPCY; OBNV

And hardly safe from brother traitors there. (*LL*) To Sir Toby. Philip Freneau. NAAL-1; NoP; TAP

And hast thou left old Jemmy in the lurch? A Satire upon the French King. Thomas Brown. APAS

And hastens to you. (*LL*) Memory. Joseph Freiherr von Eichendorff. RiWo

And hate my next-door neighbour. (*LL*) The World State. G. K. Chesterton. IHNG

And haunt the places where their Honour dy'd. (*LL*) When other fair ones [*or* ladies] to the shades [*or* groves] go down. Pope. FaBoEE

& have a party! (*LL*) Up, Up, Home & Away. John Forbes. NOBAu

And have done what they told themselves to do. (*LL*) Metaphor for My Son. John Holmes. ImGa

And have one Titan at a time. (*LL*) The Master. E. A. Robinson. LiTA; LiTM; MoAB; MoAmPo; OHIP

And Have the Bright Immensities. Howard Chandler Robbins. AH

And have we lost another friend? John Close. *Fr.* In Respectful Memory of Mr. Yarker. FaBoCo

And having nothing, yet hath all. (*LL*) The Character of a Happy Life. Sir Henry Wotton. EBEvV; EIL; GTBS; GTBS-P; LiTB; NOBE; NOSC; NTP; OBEV; TrGrPo

And haze, and vista, and the far horizon, fading away. (*LL*) A Farm Picture. Walt Whitman. InPS; TRP

And He Answered Them Nothing. Richard Crashaw. ChIV-2

And he bought a wedding Ring-o! (*LL*) Bingo. *Unknown.* CH; TTTS

And he cannot get it down. (*LL*) Family Life. *Unknown.* FaBoBl

And he couldn't porter. (*LL*) Giles Johnson, Ph.D. Frank Marshall Davis. BPo; PoBA

And he did — nine soliloquies later. (*LL*) Hamlet. Stanley J. Sharpless. BXAP; NBLV; PeLi

And he died on the waters, away, far away! (*LL*) O Brazil, the Isle of the Blest. Gerald Griffin. CH

And he drew one Leg after a great way behind, fa, la, la. (*LL*) A Shepherd Kept Sheep on a Hill So High. Thomas D'Urfey. CoMu; ErPo

And he drove me off without a rap — the stringybark cockatoo. (*LL*) The Stringybark Cockatoo. *Unknown.* NOBAu

And he had lived enough when he had dried her tear. (*LL*) For an Epitaph at Fiesole. Walter Savage Landor. FaBoEE; OBNC

And He hath not forgotten my age. (*LL*) The Old Man's Comforts and How He Gained Them. Robert Southey. EBEvV; HoPM; OxBChV; UnPo; UV; VPP

And he is risen? Well, be it so. A Drizzling Easter Morning. Thomas Hardy. CMoP

And he is the one who has made it all. (*LL*) The Simple Purification. Kabir. EnlH; NU

And he lived over nine hundred years. (*LL*) Methuselah ("Methuselah ate what he found on his plate.") *Unknown.* BLPA; BLPL; FaBoBe

And he ne'er came home again. God bless the Queen! (*LL*) Upon Sir Francis Drake's Return from His Voyage about the World, and the Queen's Meeting Him. *Unknown.* CoMu; EIL; FaBoCh; OxBSS

And he never saw his bonny lady! (*LL*) Annan Water ("Annan's Water's waiding deep.") *Unknown.* CH

And he said, So is the kingdome of God. Bible, *N.T. Fr.* St. Mark. OBVE

And he said, So soule doth magnifie the Lord. Bible, *N.T. Fr.* St. Mark. OBVE

And he showed me a pure river of water of life. There Shall Be No Night. Bible, *N.T. Fr.* Revelation. TrGrPo

And he, "To begin with a swelled head and end with swelled feet." (*LL*) Ezra Pound. Robert Lowell. MoP; NAAL-2; NoAM; NOBA

And he was left lamenting. (*LL*) Lord Ullin's Daughter. Thomas Campbell. BeLS; BoTP; EnRP; FaPON; FaPoR; GN; GTBS; GTBS-P; WBLP

And he was strong — and I was half asleep. (*LL*) Seduced Girl. Hedylos. BoLoP; ErPo

And he went to the chase with a tear on his cheek. (*LL*) The Childless Father. Wordsworth. CH

And he went unto Ramah. There met. The Dance of Saul with the Prophets. Saul Tchernichowsky, *tr. fr. Hebrew by* I. M. Lask. TrJP

And he who fain would find it, first must die. (*LL*) Thou knowest, love, I know that thou dost know. Michelangelo. PeHV

And he will make it plain. (*LL*) God moves in a mysterious way. William Cowper. EBEvV; ELP

And heal each other. (*LL*) Grandfather,/ Look at our brokenness. *Unknown.* EaPr

And heal my troubled breast which cryes/ which dyes. (*LL*) Longing. George Herbert. ESCV; SeCV-1; UV, (*sl. sh. vers.*)

And heap our measures fuller. (*LL*) The Bobolinks. Christopher Pearse Cranch. GN

And hear no more at all. (*LL*) Blows the Wind Today. Robert Louis Stevenson. CH

And hear the thrushes singing in the lilacs round the lawn. (*LL*) A Good Boy. Robert Louis Stevenson. PWR

And heard the sound of rushing wind. (*LL*) The Coming of the Plague. Weldon Kees. ChIV-1; NaP; VGW

And hears an unintelligible prayer. (*LL*) The Feast of Stephen. Anthony Hecht. HAP; NoAM; NoP; VCAP

And heartier loves; that lamp is from the tomb. (*LL*) The Leaders of the Crowd. W. B. Yeats. EBEV; MoAB; MoBrPo; OxAEP-2

And heave the sigh of memory and of love. (*LL*) Go, Valentine. Robert Southey. Son

And Heaven its dews by staying. (*LL*) As We Dance Round. *Unknown.* CH

And Heaven reflected in her face. (*LL*) To a Young Lady. William Cowper. GTBS; GTBS-P

And Heavenly musick, furr'd with praise. (*LL*) Upon a Wasp Chilled [*or* Child] with Cold. Edward Taylor. EAP; GGP; NAAL-1; NOBA; NOCV; PoEL-3

And heed not them that warn or chide thee. Hark! The Rosy Days Are Numbered. Moses ibn Ezra, *tr. fr. Hebrew by* Solomon Solis-Cohen. *Fr.* Wine-Songs. TrJP

And held her in my arms! (*LL*) Politics. W. B. Yeats. CBLP; CMoP; FF; HeIP; InPS; OxBTC; PoE; SCV

And held it trembling there. (*LL*) Twilight at Sea. Amelia B. Welby. AnAmPo

And he'll forgive the past. (*LL*) Attend, Young Friends, While I Relate. *Unknown.* AmFP

And her eyes lightnings and her shoulders wings. (*LL*) In Progress. Christina Rossetti. BoWoP; NAEL-2; WPE

And her long robe trails all about the south. (*LL*) Peace, Be at Peace, O Thou My Heaviness. Baudelaire. InPK

And her right home and her right passion." (*LL*) Lady Lost. John Crowe Ransom. MoAB; MoAmPo; TrGrPo; UnPo

And her shoes were full of feet. (*LL*) In the Night. *Unknown.* FaBoNo; NBLV

And her ways are ways of gentleness and all her paths are peace. (*LL*) I Vow to Thee, My Country. Cecil Arthur Spring-Rice. BoTP; CoGr; NSI

And here face down beneath the sun. You, Andrew Marvell. Archibald MacLeish. AWP; CMoP; FaBV; FYAP; HAP; HeIP; HoPM; LiTA; LiTM; MeMAP; MoAB; MoAmPo; MoP; NAAL-2; NoAM; NOBA; NoP; OxBA; Poetr; PoRA; PPP; PrIm; SoSe; TFi; TrGrPo; TRP; TwCP

And here fair freedom shall forever reign. Leander. Hugh Henry Brackenridge *and* Philip Freneau. *Fr.* Rising Glory of America, The. AiP

And here he lies and still is Knott. (*LL*) Epitaph on John Knott. *Unknown.* ChTr; FaBoEE; SeCV-1

And here I wish my soul died with my breath. Ovid, *tr. by* Henry Vaughan. *Fr.* Tristium. OBVE

And here my ship rides, having anchor cast. (*LL*) The End of His Work. Robert Herrick. CaPo

And here stand I, a suppliant at the door. (*LL*) At the Grave of Henry Vaughan. Siegfried Sassoon. CMoP; GTBS-P

And here the precious dust is laid [*or* layd]. Maria Wentworth. Thomas Carew. CaPo; JCP; MeLP; OBD; PeECV; SeCV-1
(Epitaph for Maria Wentworth.) BeJo
(Inscription on the Tomb[e] of the Lady Mary Wentworth, The.) SCGP

And here we are back. Going Back Patiently. Frank Mkalawile Chipasula. HBAPE

And here's the child's Dad. *Unknown.* OxNR

And here's the house of Stuart. (*LL*) The Battle of Sole Bay. *Unknown.* GBP

And Hermann's a German. (*LL*) Porson on German Scholarship. Richard Porson. FaBoCo; FaBoEE

And hid his face amid a crowd of stars. (LL) When You Are Old. W. B. Yeats, *after the French of* Pierre de Ronsard. ArLo; AWP; BoLoP; ClHu; CMoP; CoGr; CTC; EBEvV; EBVV; FaBV; FaPoB; GBL; GoJo; HeIP; InvP; LiTM; LPA; MeMBP; MoAB; MoBrPo; MoP; NAEL-2; NAWM-2; NoAM; NOBVV; NoP; OBEV; OHCV; OtMeF; OxBM; OxBTC; PoLF; PrIm; TEP; TFi

And hide its face/ for shame. (LL) Death. William Carlos Williams. NAAL-2; OxBA; VGW

And hide the shame!. (LL) Ichabod. Whittier. AnAmPo; LiTA; NAAL-1; NOBA; OxBA; PAH; PoEL-4; TAP

And hide the thrush's skull away. (LL) The Relic. Robert Silliman Hillyer. GoYe

And hiding their tossing manes and their tumultuous feet. (LL) Michael Robartes Bids His Beloved Be at Peace. W. B. Yeats. MoP; NoAM

And him the best o' me. (LL) Reminiscence. Wallace Irwin. FiBHP; NOBL

And his arm lay lightly around my breast — and that night I was happy. (LL) When I Heard at the Close of the Day. Walt Whitman. AmPP; GBL; NAAL-1; NoAM; OxBA; PoE

And his bed father after him. (LL) The Sad Boy. Laura Riding. CBNP; RB

And his breast kindle with a kindred flame! (LL) Colonial Nomenclature. John Dunmore Lang. NOBAu

And his doctrine denounced as barbarian. (LL) There was a great German Grammarian. Thomas Thorneley. PeLi

And his first minute, after noone, is night. (LL) A Lecture upon the Shadow. John Donne. AWP; EnRePo; ESCV; ImPo; NAEL-1; NoSic; SCGP; SeCP; TEP; UnPo

And His graver of frost. (LL) To a Snowflake. Francis Thompson. BoNaP; FaBV; MoAB; MoBrPo; TrGrPo

And his head upon my knees and my lips move over his face. (LL) The Silent Words. Haim Guri. MHP

And his late kingdom, only from the road. (LL) My house, I say. But hark to the sunny doves. Robert Louis Stevenson. FM; NOBVV

and his name was Willy Wood. (LL) Aiken Drum. *Unknown.* FaBoCh; FaBoNo; OxNR

And His own face to see. (LL) The Mystery. Ralph Hodgson. CH; MoAB; MoBrPo; WGRP

And His praise glorified. (LL) Blessed is the spot, and the house. Baha 'U' Lla'h. EaPr

And his shout that gives a hissing sound. (LL) On Shooting Particles beyond the World. Richard Eberhart. LiTA; LiTM

And his son Judas, who was called Maccabeus. (LL) Judas Maccabeus. Bible, Apocrypha. *Fr.* First Maccabees. TrJP

And his thoughts turned back to the place where she said, "I'm growing warmer now." (LL) Young Charlottie or, The Frozen Girl. *Unknown.* AmFP; BeLS; BLPA

And his work its own reward shall be. (LL) Plant a Tree. Lucy Larcom. WBLP

And ho but I love thee dearly! (LL) The Orphan's Song. Sydney Thompson Dobell. CH; ELP; OBNC

And hold love in. (LL) Prayer for This House. Louis Untermeyer. BLPL; FaPON; PoLF; PoToHe

And holiness. (LL) There is religion in everything around us. John Ruskin. EaPr

And home shall never come. (LL) The Twa Brothers. *Unknown.* CH; EBEV; ESPB, (A *vers.*); OxBB

And honour my death with a double encore. (LL) The Broken-hearted Gardener. *Unknown.* ChTr; GBP

And hope was false, but love was true. (LL) Newark Abbey. Thomas Love Peacock. NOBE; OBNC; PIP

And Hope without an object cannot live. (LL) Work without Hope. Samuel Taylor Coleridge. BoNaP; EnRP; MeMBP; NAEL-2; NOBE; NoP; OBEV; OxAEP-2; PFP; Son; TEP

And hopeless. (LL) Spring Night. Chu Shu-chen. WPC

And hoping a little, a little, that either may be. (LL) Blackberry Winter. John Crowe Ransom. AnAmPo; OxBA; PoRA

And hops about like a filly-foal. (LL) As black as ink and isn't ink. *Unknown.* OxNR

And how beguile you? Death has no repose. James Elroy Flecker. *Fr.* Golden Journey to Samarkand, The. CoGr; FaBoRV; OxBTC

And how do you do again? (LL) One misty, moisty morning. Mother Goose. FaBoBe; OxNR

And how I do and did. (LL) Our Lips and Ears. *Unknown.* BLPA; WBLP

And how soft and vulnerable is naked flesh. (LL) Letters to Martha. Dennis Brutus. PeSAV

And how sweet a story it is. Jack Kerouac. *Fr.* Mexico City Blues. PoBeRe

And how young they were, how innocent. (LL) The Taking of the Koppie. Uys Krige. PeSAV

And hurl me to the shark, I shall not die! (LL) The Leg. Karl Shapiro. HAP; MoAB; MoAmPo; TrGrPo; UnPo; WeW

And hurls for him, O half hurls earth for him off under his feet. (LL) Hurrahing in Harvest. Gerard Manley Hopkins. BoNaP; ChTr; CMoP; FaBoPP; InvP; MeMBP; MoAB; MoBrPo; NAEL-2; PeECV; PoE; TOF

And hymn thy favourite name! (LL) Ode to Evening. William Collins. AWP; EBEV; ECEV; EnRP; FaBoBe; GGP; GTBS; GTBS-P; HAP; ImPo; LiTB; NAEL-1; NOBE; NOEC; NoP; OAEL-1; OBEV; OxAEP-1; PoE; PoEL-3; PPP; SCGP; TFi; TrGrPo

And I a beginner. Answer to Yo/ Question. Sonia Sanchez. BPo

And I aimed them at the tideline. (LL) The Lame Waltzer. Matthew Sweeney. IB

And I am in the wilderness alone. (LL) The Prairies. Bryant. AmPP; EAP; NAAL-1; NOBA; OxBA; PoEL-4; TAP

And I am lost in the beautiful white ruins / of America. (LL) Having Lost My Sons, I Confront the Wreckage of the Moon: Christmas, 1960. James Wright. CoAP; HCAP; NAAL-2

And I am lost without you. (LL) They Dream Only of America. John Ashbery. CAPP

And I Am Old to Know. Pauline Hanson. TAP

And I am pregnant too. (LL) A Woman's Prayer. Yehuda Karni. MHP

And I am pure as a babe of one day. (LL) Purity. Avigdor Hame'iri. MHP

And I am sad and lonely. (LL) The Months Go By. *Unknown.* OHMPC

And I am safe and always have been. (LL) Kaddish. David Ignatow. EaPr; NU; RaBo

And I am the Queen of Wands. The Queen of Wands. Judy Grahn. SRLS

And i am turning. (LL) Perhaps. Lucille Clifton. CAPP

And I became alone. (LL) Wind — tapped like a tired man, The. Emily Dickinson. FaBoVe; Mes; MoAB; MoAmPo; TOF

And I bowed [*or* ich bowede] my body and beheld all about [*or* bihelde al aboute]. William Langland. *Fr.* Vision of Piers Plowman, The. CTC (Vision of Nature, A.) PoEL-1

And I can let her go. (LL) Satin Doll. David Wojahn. Jaz; PBCAP

And I can't sleep for thinking on't. (LL) We're A' Dry wi' the Drinkin' O't. *Unknown.* ErPo

And I can't think why! (LL) The Disagreeable Man. W. S. Gilbert. FiBHP

And I content me with my hire. (LL) Once, [*or* Ons] as methought [*or* me thought], fortune me kissed [*or* kist *or* kyst]. Sir Thomas Wyatt. SiPSBD

And I converse with many a shipwrecked crew. (LL) The Fisher's Boy. Thoreau. ChTr

And i could do for many days/ Without eggs. (LL) Egg Thoughts. Russell Hoban. NTCP, (*St.* 1 *only, sl. diff.*); OTCP

And I could fashion it no more! (LL) Sculpture. *Unknown.* BLPL; PoLF

And I don't feel so well myself. (LL) On the Vanity of Earthly Greatness. Arthur Guiterman. BXAP; HeIP; HoPM; OBCA; TrJP

And I don't want no Bail. (LL) Girl Held without Bail. Margaret Walker. BPo; PoBA

And I doubt all. You. Or a violet. (LL) Love Note. Gwendolyn Brooks. VBLP

And I eat men like air. (LL) Lady Lazarus. Sylvia Plath. CAPP; ChIV-2; FaBoWP; HCAP; MAT; MoP; NAAL-2; NALW; NaP; NIP; NoAM; NOBA; NoP; Poetr; PrIm; TAP; TRP; VCAP; VGW

And I fare you well, Lady Ouncebell. Lord Lovel. *Unknown.* ESPB

And I fell in love with a woman so tall that. From the Travels of Gulliver. Suniti Namjoshi. GLP

And I find in its revelation, alas, I am but a man. (LL) Tune: "Sand of Silk-washing Stream." Wang Kuo-wei. SuSp

And i guess nobody ever does. (LL) Legacies. Nikki Giovanni. CrSp

And I hadn't been. (LL) Come In. Robert Frost. AmPP; BoNaP; FaBV; LiTA; LiTM; MoAB; MoAmPo; NOBA; NoP; RaBo; TrGrPo; TRP

And I half bent to throw me down withall. (LL) When Windsor walls sustained [*or* sustain'd] my wearied arm. The Earl of Surrey. SiPS; SiPSBD

And I have broken down before the wind. (LL) Nocturne of the Wharves. Arna Bontemps. BPo; LPA; PoNe

And I have chosen the sea as no man's land. Edouard J. Maunick, *tr. fr. French by* Ellen Conroy Kennedy. *Fr.* As Far as Yoruba Land. NegPo

And I have come upon this place. L'An Trentiesme de Mon Eage. Archibald MacLeish. LiTM; MoP; NOBA
  (In My Thirtieth Year.) MoAmPo

And I have learned how diving's done. Fantasia. Dorothy Livesay. MoCV

And I have only set the same to pen. (LL) To Oxford. Gerard Manley Hopkins. FaBoPP

And I have something to expiate;/ A pettiness. (LL) Snake. D. H. Lawrence. CMoP; EBEvV; EBNV; FaBoMo; HeIP; HoPM; LiTB; LiTM; MeMBP; MoAB; NoAM; NOBE; NoP; NTP; NU; OAEL-2; Poetr; PoRA; PPP; PrIm; SOTW; TFi

And it seemed, while we waited, he began to walk. Geoffrey Hill. *Fr.* Mercian Hymns. NoAM; NoP

And it shall come to pass in the end of days. In the End of Days. Bible, *O.T. Fr.* Isaiah. TrJP

And it shall come to pass when the days shall grow long. When the Days Shall Grow Long. Hayyim Nahman Bialik, *tr. fr. Hebrew by* A. M. Klein. TrJP

And It Was Windy Weather. James Stephens. ArNa

And it would never be over. After that. After That Time. Harriet Susskind. BTR

And it's forty miles to Nicut Hill. Prince Robert. *Unknown.* AmFP

And it's hard to see the mountains. Can I Say. Dolly Bird. WPOW

And it's oh, my good fortune. (*LL*) The Little Drummer. *Unknown.* AmFP

And it's three score and ten boys and men were lost from Grimsby town. Three Score and Ten. *Unknown.* OxBSS

And Jack from Joan, and they shall never marry. (*LL*) Another Song. Donald Justice. VGW

And Jack on the gallows-tree! (*LL*) Gin by Pailfuls. Sir Walter Scott. ChTr

And jest upon their blind forefathers' eyes. (*LL*) Ignotum per Ignotius, or a Furious Hodge-Podge of Nonsense; a Pindaric. *Unknown.* CBNP; NOEC

And Jesus call us to Heaven's perfect peace. (*LL*) Peace, Perfect Peace. Edward H. Bickersteth. BLRP; WGRP

And Jesus saith unto them, All ye shall be offended. Bible, *N.T. Fr.* St. Mark. OBF, *abr.*

And Joseph was brought down to Egypt. Bible, *O.T. Fr.* Genesis. NAWM-1

And joy and strength and courage are with Thee? (*LL*) Lord, what a change within us one short hour. Richard Chenevix Trench. WBLP; WGRP

And joy at last for thee and me. (*LL*) The Voice of Toil. William Morris. OHCV

And joy of snow and snow. (*LL*) Annual Gaiety. Wallace Stevens. MoAB; MoAmPo

And Jude, now you're married, will stretch on the floor. (*LL*) On an Island. J. M. Synge. BIrV; FaBoVe; MoBrPo; OxBSP; PeVV

And just by crossing the short sea. Channel Crossing. George Barker. GTBS-P

And keep them all like gentlemen. (*LL*) Dove says, Coo, coo, The. Mother Goose. BoTP; OxNR; ReMoGo

And keep us through life's wintry days. (*LL*) 'Tis Winter Now. Samuel Longfellow. AH

And kept my spirit with the free. (*LL*) A Vision. John Clare. ChTr; EBVV; FaBoRV; GTBS-P; NAEL-2; NOBVV; NTP; OAEL-2; OBNC; OPOP; PoE; PPP

And kept on drinking. (*LL*) Miniver Cheevy. E. A. Robinson. AmPP; AWP; ChTr; ClHu; CMoP; EBEvV; FaBoCh; FaBV; FF; HeIP; ImPo; LiTA; LiTM; MoAB; MoAmPo; MoP; NAAL-2; NBLV; NoAM; NOBA; NoP; OBSV; OxBA; PeLV; PoEL-5; Poetr; PoLF; PoRA; RaBo; SCV; SoSe; TAP; TFi; TrGrPo

And killed the mice in his father's barn. (*LL*) Ding, dong, bell,/ Pussy's in the well. Mother Goose. OxNR; ReMoGo

And Kingsley goes to Froude for history. (*LL*) A Hymn on Froude and Kingsley. William Stubbs. FaBoEE

And kiss on a grass-green pillow. (*LL*) Where Be You [*or* YE] Going, You [*or* Ye] Devon Maid? Keats. CBLP; ErPo; FHYEP

And kissed my sister instead of me. (*LL*) Trip upon trenchers, and dance upon dishes. Mother Goose. NOBL; OxNR; ReMoGo

And knit again the knot that should not slide. (*LL*) Face that should content me wonders well, A. Sir Thomas Wyatt. CTC; EnLoPo

And knocked it right off his head, head, head. (*LL*) There was a little man,/ And he had a little gun. Mother Goose. OxNR; ReMoGo

And knocked out all their teeth. (*LL*) As I went over the water. *Unknown.* OxNR

And know what Clancy knew. (*LL*) Old Australian Ways. Andrew Barton Paterson. NOBAu

And knows herself in death. (*LL*) The Great Breath. "Æ." MoBrPo; OBEV; OBMV; WGRP

And knows not whether he be first or last. (*LL*) Time, Real and Imaginary. Samuel Taylor Coleridge. EnRP; MeMBP; NOBE; OBEV; OxBSP; PFP

And ladders leaning against damson trees. The Looker-On. Frank Kendon. PAW

And laid me down among the swine. (*LL*) I Saw a Chapel All of Gold. Blake. EnRP; ImPo; LiTB; MeMBP

And laid them away in a box of gold. (*LL*) For a Poet. Countee Cullen. PoNe; TTY

And landscape, into which the traveler might set out. (*LL*) The Parachutist. Jon Anderson. AmPA; NYBP

And Langland told how heaven could not keep love. The Beach. Peter Scupham. SCBI

And last night a man came in. Spring Street Bar. Mei-Mei Berssenbrugge. WPOW

And last of all in an automobile. (*LL*) Listen, my children, and you shall hear. *Unknown.* RoPo

And, laterally / to Adam's pulsing eye. The Cloud. Derek Walcott. ChIV-1

And laughed at the death of crows. (*LL*) Cro-Kill. Anthony Lawrence. NOBAu

And laught out with a ha, ha, ha, ha, ha, ha, ha, ha, ha, ha, ha, ha, ha. (*LL*) Amintas and Claudia; or, The Merry Shepherdess. *Unknown.* CoMu

And leaf-shadow are lost. (*LL*) Evening. Hilda Doolittle ("H. D."). CMoP; FaBoMo; VGW; WPE

And leaning out to look at me. (*LL*) Strange Tree. Elizabeth Madox Roberts. BoNaP; FaPON; GrPl

And learn a style from a despair. (*LL*) This Last Pain. William Empson. CMoP; EBEV; FaBoMo; GTBS-P; LiTM; MoAB; MoBrPo; NoAM; OAEL-2

And learn O voyager to walk. Seafarer. Archibald MacLeish. NoP; Poetr

And learn, with joy, the gulf, the vast, the deep. (*LL*) Putting to Sea. Louise Bogan. LiTM; PoA

And leave its odor there. (*LL*) Had I the Choice. Walt Whitman. Poetr; SoSe

And leave our desert to its peace! (*LL*) Stanzas from the Grande Chartreuse. Matthew Arnold. EBVV; EnVR; NAEL-2; OAEL-2; PoE; PoEL-5; TEP

And leave th' earth to their food. (*LL*) The H. Communion. George Herbert. ChIV-1; ESCV; MiEL

And leave the rest to me. (*LL*) Alibi. Eunice De Souza. VBLP

And leave the world without a soul. (*LL*) Love's Hue and Cry. James Shirley. BeJo

And leave to thee thy true integrity. (*LL*) To Dante [*or* Sonnet: Guido Cavalcanti to Dante]. Cavalcanti. AWP; OBVE

And leave you with them empty bed blues. (*LL*) Empty Bed Blues. Bessie Smith. OBAL; UnPo

And leaves a lonesome place against the sky. (*LL*) Lincoln, the Man of the People. Edwin Markham. MoAmPo; OHIP; PAH; TrGrPo

And leaves his hold and cackles, groans, and dies. (*LL*) Badger. John Clare. EnRP; FHYEP; HAP; LiTB; NoP; NU; OAEL-2; PoEL-4; Poetr; PrIm; SCGP; WiR

And led the flock away. (*LL*) I'll tell you how the sun rose. Emily Dickinson. AmPP; FaBV; MoShBr; PDV; PoEL-5; TAP

And left his body lying. (*LL*) Around the rick, around the rick. *Unknown.* OxNR

And left me no recourse, far from my home. (*LL*) A Dog Named Ego, the Snowflakes as Kisses. Delmore Schwartz. LiTA; LiTM

And left me old, and cold, and grey. (*LL*) May. Christina Rossetti. GBL; NOBVV

And left the vivid air signed with their honour. (*LL*) I Think Continually of Those Who Were Truly Great. Stephen Spender. ChTr; CMoP; EBEvV; HAP; HeIP; ImPo; LiTB; LiTM; MoAB; MoBrPo; NOBE; NoP; OAEL-2; OxBTC; PAW; PoRA; RaBo; TFi; TrGrPo

And left to Heaven the rest. (*LL*) The Happiest Heart. John Vance Cheney. WGRP

And lend a hand. (*LL*) Look Up *or* Lend a Hand. Edward Everett Hale. FaBoBe

And let me die before my death! (*LL*) Regeneration. Henry Vaughan. ChIV-1; ESCV; GeHe; JCP; MeLP; NAEL-1; NoBV; PoE

And let me hear your faithful steel clash once around my board; (*LL*) The Baron's Last Banquet. Albert Gorton Greene. AnAmPo; BeLS

And let me never. William Everson. EaPr

And let that Wine be all for me! (*LL*) A Drinking-Song. Henry Carey. OBEV

And let the ape and tiger die. (*LL*) Contemplate all this work of Time. Tennyson. EBVV, *abr.*; EnVR; FF; OAEL-2, *abr.*; PeECV, *abr.*

And let the king and his men come in. (*LL*) How Many Miles to Babylon? Mother Goose. BoTP; CoGr; FaBoCh; GBP; MoShBr; NTP; OxBoLi; OxBSP; OxNR

And let the plants identify me. (*LL*) Watching gardeners label their plants. Robert Aitken. EaPr

And let them warm with thee. (*LL*) Ah, Robin,/ Jolly Robin. Sir Thomas Wyatt. SiPS; SiPSBD

And let us have a lark instead. (*LL*) To Minerva. Thomas Hood. ChTr; FaBoCo; FaBoNo; FiBHP; NBLV; NOBL; OxBoLi; PeLV

And let you go. (*LL*) To a Squirrel at Kyle-na-no. W. B. Yeats. FaPON; FM; PDV; SiSoPo

And let your full lips laugh at Fate! (*LL*) To a Dark Girl. Gwendolyn B. Bennett. BlSi; CDC; PoBA; ShDr; VBLP

And let your weeds lack dew, and duly sterve. (*LL*) Clear or Cloudy, Sweet as April Showering. *Unknown.* EIL

And lets them live, and takes the wise away. (*LL*) An Epitaph of the Death of Nicholas Grimald. Barnabe Googe. EnRePo; SCGP

And lette the coppe go rounde. (*LL*) Tappster, fille another ale. *Unknown.* MiEL

And letting them out again. (*LL*) The Vacant Lot. Gwendolyn Brooks. NAAL-2; NoAM; NOBA

And lick the grease from his fingers. He Wanted Someone to Cook Chicken. Lavinia Greenlaw. NWP

And lie thou there. Matthew Arnold. *Fr.* Empedocles on Etna. EnVR

And lie with your bride all night. (*LL*) Harry Parry. *Unknown.* GBP; OxNR

And lies down, who was my moon or more. (*LL*) Complaint. James Wright. NOBA; TAP; VGW

And lies with those he never saw. (*LL*) The Chameleon. Matthew Prior. OBSV

And life in the upturned bellies of the fishkill in the creek. (*LL*) Long Island. Marvin Bell. CAPP

And life still smile, like child-hood's hour. (*LL*) To Thine Eternal Arms, O God. Thomas Wentworth Higginson. AH

And life to me wore less. (*LL*) The Subalterns. Thomas Hardy. CMoP; MeMBP; MoAB; MoBrPo; MoP; NoAM; NOBVV; OAEL-2; Poetr; PPP; TEP

And lightly, like the flowers. (*LL*) And Lightly, like the Flowers. Pierre de Ronsard, *tr. fr. French by* W. E. Henley. AWP

And lightly shower again. (*LL*) When Israel out of Egypt Came. A. E. Housman. ChIV-1; LiTB; MeMBP

And, like a bird at rest. National Anthem. Egbert Martin. PBCV

And, like a dying lady, lean and pale. The Waning Moon. Shelley. CH; FHYEP; OxBSP; TrGrPo
  (Moon, The.) FaBoCh; OBEV

And like a river, rises in quiet fury. (*LL*) Beyond Silence. Lan Ling. WPC

And like a thunderbolt he falls. (*LL*) The Eagle. Tennyson. BoTP; CH; ClHu; CoGr; FaBoCh; FaPON; FF; FHYEP; FM; GN; GoJo; GTBS-P; HeIL; HeIP; InPK; MeMBP; NAEL-2; NOBVV; NoP; NTCP; NTP; OAEL-2; OxBSP; PDV; Poetr; PrIm; SCGP; TFi; TrGrPo; TRP; UnPo; WiR

And like bricks fearsome in their everyday squareness. (*LL*) Anniversary. John Wain. TwCP

And, like gold white-heated, I was purified in the crucibley. (*LL*) Poppies. Zalman Schneour. MHP

And like thy father sing in tunefulness. A Barren Soul. Joseph Ezobi, *tr. fr. Spanish by* D. I. Friedmann. *Fr.* Silver Bowl, The. TrJP

And, like thy shadow, follow thee. (*LL*) Compensation. Emerson. AmPP; LiTA; MeMAP; NOBA; TAP

And, like thy shadow, follow thee. (*LL*) Compensation. Emerson. AmPP; NOBA

And listened longer than I did. (*LL*) A Green Cornfield. Christina Rossetti. BoTP

And little Ariadne sleep. (*LL*) Birthright. John Drinkwater. CH; CoGr; OxBTC

And little feel boys o'er their heads can stray. (*LL*) Snowstorm. John Clare. BoNaP; WiR

And little hunted hares. (*LL*) The Bells of Heaven. Ralph Hodgson. BoTP; CoGr; GoJo; LiTM; MoAB; MoBrPo; NOBE; OBEV; OtMeF; OxBSP

And little Miss Montague screams in her ward. (*LL*) A Game of Consequences. Paul Dehn. ErPo; FiBHP; NOBL

And live forever, like the dust. (*LL*) Poem in Three Parts. Robert Bly. CAPP; NaP; NOBA

And live I still to see Relations gone. To the Memory of My Dear Daughter in Law, Mrs. Mercy Bradstreet. Anne Bradstreet. KTR

And live on corn dodgers the rest of my life. (*LL*) Starving to Death on a Government Claim. *Unknown.* AmFP; OBAL

And live three times as long. (*LL*) Fragment in Imitation of Wordsworth. Catherine Fanshawe. FaBoNo; FaBoPa

And lived alone without a husband. (*LL*) The Girl by Green River. *Unknown.* OHMPC

And living stone. (*LL*) Raven Sweat. Rochelle Wallace. EaPr

And lo, amid the watery roar. Thomas Warton the Younger. *Fr.* For the King's Birthday, 1790. FaBoEH

And, lo! Ben Adhem's name led all the rest! (*LL*) Abou Ben Adhem. Leigh Hunt. BeLS; BLPA; EBEvV; EnRP; FaBoBe; FaBV; FaPoR; NOBE; NTP; OBEV; OxAEP-2; PlP; PWR; TFi; WBLP; WGRP

And lo! on the ground Rose Mary lay. Dante Gabriel Rossetti. *Fr.* Rose Mary. Poetr

And lo! the earth was filled with lights. (*LL*) After the Storm. H. Cordelia Ray. AmWP; CBWP-3

And, lo! the long laborious miles of Palace. All of Beauty, All of Us. Tennyson. *Fr.* Ode Sung at the Opening of the International Exhibition. CBCK

And lonesome, very lonesome, is my strand. (*LL*) Autumn. Christina Rossetti. BrRo

And longs to be a dinosaur. (*LL*) The Lizard. Theodore Roethke. GrPl

And look up at the stars. Oh oh the sky is too wide to sleep under! (*LL*) The Clown. Janet Frame. PeNZ

And looked and looked our infant sight away. (*LL*) Over 2000 Illustrations and a Complete Concordance. Elizabeth Bishop. HCAP; LCAP; NAAL-2; NoAM; VCAP

And lordy, give us our share. (*LL*) I Have Three Daughters. Ruth Stone. InPS; NMM

And Los and Enitharmon builded Jerusalem weeping. Vala, Night the Ninth Being the Last Judgment. Blake. *Fr.* Vala; or The Four Zoas. OAEL-2

And lose my everlasting rest. (*LL*) Absent from thee, I languish still. The Earl of Rochester. BoLoP; ELP; EnLoPo; GBL; SeCV-2

And lose the name of authors. (*LL*) Hamlet's Soliloquy Imitated. Richard Jago. BXAP; FaBoCo; FaBoPa

And love, and man's unconquerable mind. (*LL*) To Toussaint L'Ouverture. Wordsworth. EnRP; FaBoPV; InPK; NOBE; OBNC; PoNe; PoRA; PPP; TrGrPo

And love arrived may find us somewhere else. (*LL*) Delay. Elizabeth Jennings. NIP; OxBTC

And love goes too. . .but goes the last. (*LL*) O fond, but fickle and untrue. Walter Savage Landor. CBLP; GBL

And love her as hard as you can. (*LL*) The Way. Robert Creeley. BoLoP; LiTM; NeAP; PPP

And love hung still as crystal over the bed. Louis MacNeice. *Fr.* Trilogy for X. CIP; GBL
  (And Love Hung Still.) MoBrPo

And love in love shall make it fine. (*LL*) Divine Love. *Unknown.* OAEL-1

And Love is fled, to come no more. (*LL*) Early Thoughts of Marriage. Nathaniel Cotton. OxBChV

And love like anger in the night. (*LL*) To My Wife. J. V. Cunningham. VCAP

And love live lovers ought to love? (*LL*) In the middle of the night. Philodemus. PGA

And love the brightest eyes, but love in vain! (*LL*) Lines Written in Windsor Forest. Pope. EBEV

And love with old familiar love. (*LL*) The Convent Threshold. Christina Rossetti. MeMBP; NALW; NoP; PFP

And loved to course with tempests through the night. (*LL*) Horses on the Camargue. Roy Campbell. GTBS-P; OBAP; OBTV; PeSA

And lovely as the night. (*LL*) Secret Love. Joseph Freiherr von Eichendorff. RiWo

And lovers float down from the cliffs like rain. (*LL*) Salvador Dali. David Gascoyne. OxBTC

And loving — ! God above, it's great! (*LL*) The Meeting, the Departure. Goethe. STV

And Lowells speak only to God. (*LL*) Boston. John Collins Bossidy, *also at. to* Samuel C. Bushnell. FaBoCo; FaBoEE; NBLV; OBAL; OxBoLi; PeLV

And maddening--it's all by someone else! Mirabell's Books of Number. James Merrill. *Fr.* Changing Light at Sandover, The. NAAL-2

And made cider inside her inside. (*LL*) Limerick. *Unknown.* PDV

And made much within her. (*LL*) Song of Fixed Accord. Wallace Stevens. InPS; SAmP

And made the appellation hideous. (*LL*) Epitaph on the Late King of the Sandwich Isles. Winthrop Mackworth Praed. FiBHP

And made the kites to whet their beaks clack clack. (*LL*) Captain Carpenter. John Crowe Ransom. CBNP; FaBoMo; HoPM; ImPo; LiTA; LiTM; MeMAP; MoAB; MoAmPo; MoP; NoAM; NOBA; OxBA; TRP; TwCP

And made to go on wings. (*LL*) Firefly. Elizabeth Madox Roberts. GoJo; NTCP; PDV; SiSoPo

And make a dust of their seraphic song. (*LL*) On Some Shells Found Inland. Trumbull Stickney. LiTA; Son

And make her grave green with tear on tear. (*LL*) Autumn; a Dirge. Shelley. CH

And make mankind its hideous secret torch. (*LL*) Radiation Victim. Colin Thiele. NOBAu

And make my sacrifice compleat. (*LL*) O thou who camest from above. Charles Wesley. TrPWD

And make no sound. (*LL*) All Day the Light Is Clear. Tess Gallagher. VBLP

And make them fair in soul as well as face. (*LL*) To a Lady Upon a Looking-Glass Sent. James Shirley. BeJo

And make them rose-like in His name. (*LL*) God's Garden. Richard Burton. WGRP

And make up our defects with His sweet art. (*LL*) Easter ("Rise, heart, thy Lord is risen.") George Herbert. ESCV; GeHe; NAEL-1; NOSC; PeECV; SeCV-1; TrCP

And make up the tale myself. (*LL*) The Dumb Soldier. Robert Louis Stevenson. OxBChV

And make us blest at last. (*LL*) Mistress, The: A Song. The Earl of Rochester. EBEV; NOBE; NOSC

And make us, whilst we pity him, forget our loyalty. (*LL*) Advice to the Painter. Matthew Prior. APAS

And makes a constant sacrament of praise. (*LL*) Peter Quince at the Clavier. Wallace Stevens. AmPP; CMoP; HeIP; InPK; InPS; LiTM; MeMAP; MoAB; MoAmPo; NAWM-2; NoAM; NOBA; OxBA; PoE; PPP; SAmP; TAP; TFi; TrGrPo; TwCP

And makes him bring back one leg. (*LL*) Two legs sat upon three legs. Mother Goose. OxNR

And makes me end where I begun [or begunne]. (*LL*) Valediction, A: Forbidding Mourning. John Donne. BLPL; CBLP; EnRePo; ESCV; FaPoB; FF; FHYEP; HAP; HeIP; HoPM; ImPo; InPS; JCP; LiTB; MeLP; NAEL-1; NOBE; NoP; NOSC; OAEL-1; PoE; PoEL-2; Poetr; PPP; PrIm; SCGP; SeCP; SeCV-1; SoSe; TEP; TFi; UnPo; WeW

And makes the Happiness she does not find. (*LL*) Vanity of Human Wishes, The: The Tenth Satire of Juvenal Imitated. Samuel Johnson. EBEV; ECEV; NOEC; NoP; OAEL-1; OxAEP-1; PoEL-3; PrIm; TEP; TFi

And making Death a Victory. (*LL*) Prometheus. Byron. EnRP; InPS; NOBE; NoP; OAEL-2; OxAEP-2; Poetr

And man became a living soul./ Amen, Amen. (*LL*) The Creation. James Weldon Johnson. CDC; ChIV-1; FaBV; MoAmPo; PoBA; PoRA; TrCP

And Man did just that, which is weird. (*LL*) There was an Old Man with a Beard/ Who said: "I demand to be feared." Roger Woddis. PeLi

And Man is left alone with Man. 'Tis well! At the Worst. Israel Zangwill. WGRP

And man's religion be complete. (*LL*) On the Religion of Nature. Philip Freneau. AmPP; EAP; NAAL-1

And many accidents do wait on war. (*LL*) To Odelia. James Shirley. BeJo

And many voices marshalled in one hymn. Thomas Lovell Beddoes. NOBVV

And Marie Carmichael, and me. (*LL*) Mary Hamilton. *Unknown.* ESPB, A *vers.*; FaBoBa; NoP; SCGP, A *vers.*

And Marie said, My soule doth magnifie the Lord. Bible, *N.T. See* My soul magnifies the Lord.

And marries either's Dust. (*LL*) La Belle Confidente. Thomas Stanley. BeJo; JCP; MeLP

And marvellous to them his works have been. (*LL*) And Truly It Is a Most Glorious Thing. William Bradford. AH

And may he lend her shade to me! (*LL*) Graceful Acacia. Walter Savage Landor. PoEL-4

And may it increase our love. (*LL*) Food which we are about to eat, The. *Unknown.* EaPr

And mayst thou find a home at last in heaven's celestial bowers. (*LL*) Wail of the Divorced. Mary E. Tucker. AmWP; CBWP-1

And me also the most happy. (*LL*) After great storms the calm returns. Sir Thomas Wyatt. SiPS; SiPSBD

And me happiest when I compose poems. The Birth of Tragedy. Irving Layton. MoCV; NoAM; NoP

And me that morning Walter showed the house. Sir Walter Vivian's House. Tennyson. *Fr.* Princess, The. CBCK

And men, coming and going on the earth. (*LL*) Clouds. Rupert Brooke. OBEV; OBMV; OxBTC

And mend my rhyme. (*LL*) Denial. George Herbert. GeHe; JCP; NAEL-1; NOBE; NoP; OAEL-1

And mend your own, by *True's* Behaviour. (*LL*) An Epitaph on True, Her Majesty's Dog. Matthew Prior. FM

And mightier grew the joy to meet full-faced. Swimming. Swinburne. *Fr.* Tristram of Lyonesse. GN

And miles to go before I sleep. (*LL*) Stopping by Woods on a Snowy Evening. Robert Frost. AmPP; BoNaP; ClHu; CMoP; CoGr; FaBoCh; FaBV; FaPON; FF; GGP; GoJo; GrPl; HAP; HeIP; HoPM; ImGa; ImPo; InPK; InPS; LiTA; LiTM; MeMAP; MoAB; MoAmPo; MoP; MoShBr; NAAL-2; NIP; NoAM; NOBA; NoP; NTCP; NTP; OBCA; OxBA; PDV; PIP; PoE; Poetr; PoRA; PrIm; PYC; RB; SAmP; SCV; SiSoPo; SoSe; TAP; TFi; TOF; TRP; TTTS

And mirth was bounty with a humbler name. (*LL*) Prologue to [Hugh Kelly's] "A Word to the Wise." Samuel Johnson. EBEV; FaPoR; OxAEP-1

And Mr. Ferritt. Judith Wright. MoBrPo

And mixed with quartz grains, rose and amethyst. (*LL*) Sandpiper. Elizabeth Bishop. AiP; HeIP; NYBP; RB; TOF

And mocks my loss of liberty. (*LL*) How Sweet I Roamed from Field to Field. Blake. CH; ChTr; EnLoPo; EnRP; LiTB; MeMBP; NAEL-2; NOEC; NoP; OAEL-2; OBNC; PoEL-4; TFi; TrGrPo

And Monelle said: I will speak to you of actions. Actions. Marcel Schwob, *tr. fr.* French by William Brown Meloney. TrJP

And Monelle said: I will speak to you of moments. Moments. Marcel Schwob, *tr. fr.* French by William Brown Meloney. TrJP

And Monelle said: I will speak to you of things dead. Things Dead. Marcel Schwob, *tr. fr.* French by William Brown Meloney. TrJP

And — more — is Nature's Roman, never to be scourged. (*LL*) The House-Top. Herman Melville. LiTA; NAAL-1; NOBA; Prf

And moulder in dust away! (*LL*) The Children's Hour. Longfellow. FaBoBe; FaBV; FaPoB; FaPON; GGP; ImGa; OBAL; OBCA; PoEL-5; PoLF; WBLP; WHSW

And mount *herself*, like *Him*, to' *Eternitie* in *Fire*. (*LL*) The Extasie. Abraham Cowley. SeCP

And mourn'd till Pity's self be dead. (*LL*) A Fidele. William Collins. EnRP; NOEC

And move to space beneath our sky. (*LL*) M., Singing. Louise Bogan. GoJo; LiTA; NoAM

And moves again and flashed again, time flashed again. (*LL*) Martial Cadenza. Wallace Stevens. MeMAP; OxBA; VGW

And Mrs Roebeck will be there. (*LL*) Ballade of Hell and of Mrs. Roebeck. Hilaire Belloc. OBF

And much fruit, the swan. See in the Midst of Fair Leaves. Marianne Moore. MoAB

And muffle that awful band. (*LL*) Cuba Street. Matthew Sweeney. IB

And music must cure you, so pipe it yourself. (*LL*) A Familiar Letter to Several Correspondents. Oliver Wendell Holmes. FaBoUs

And MUSICK shall untune the Sky. (*LL*) A Song for St. Cecilia's Day, 1687. Dryden. AWP; FaBoTw; FHYEP; GGP; GTBS; GTBS-P; HAP; InPS; LiTB; NOSC; OAEL-1; OBEV; OPOP; PoEL-3; PPP; SCGP; SeCV-2; TEP; TFi; TrGrPo

And must have it. (*LL*) Mother's Voice. Robert Creeley. CAPP; Poetr

And must I lose a soul's inheritance? (*LL*) Hélas! Oscar Wilde. MoBrPo; NAEL-2; Son; TEP; TIRV

And must I sing? What subject shall I choose? Ben Jonson. BeJo

And mute as any fish. (*LL*) A New Song of New Similies. John Gay. CBNP; FaBoCo; NOBL

And muttered, "I'm extinct." (*LL*) The Great Auk's Ghost. Ralph Hodgson. MoShBr

And my fear is great that you have taken God from me! (*LL*) Donal[l] Oge [*or* Og]: Grief of a Girl's Heart. *Unknown.* GBL; PBWP; RB

And my good days are done. (*LL*) The Sandgate Girl's Lamentation. *Unknown.* CoMu; ELP

And my heart soars. (*LL*) Beauty of the trees, The. Chief Dan George. EaPr

And my images roared and rose on heaven's hill. (*LL*) I, in My Intricate Image. Dylan Thomas. LiTB; MeMBP

And my mother's tunes are devoured of this music's ravaging glamour. (*LL*) The Piano. D. H. Lawrence. WeW

And my neck from the gallows-tree. (*LL*) The Maid Freed from the Gallows. *Unknown.* AWP; ESPB

And my nineteen years weigh heavily on my feet. (*LL*) October. Patrick Kavanagh. CIP; GTBS-P

And my *Pyramides*. (*LL*) His Poetry His Pillar. Robert Herrick. BeJo; CaPo; JCP; NOSC

And my suit is made of wood. (*LL*) Cowboy Song. Charles Causley. PoRA

And my too heavy care. (*LL*) The Coffin. Heine. AWP

And my whole heart will rise. (*LL*) Canzonetta: He Will Neither Boast nor Lament to His Lady. Jacopo da Lentino. AWP

And my young sweetheart sat at board with me. Alfred Mombert, *tr. fr.* German by Ludwig Lewisohn. AWP

And naked was my pastime in between. (*LL*) Epitaph for Someone or Other. J. V. Cunningham. OBAL; SM; TRP

And Naomi said/ Unto her two daughters-in-law. Naomi and Ruth. Bible, *O.T. Fr.* Ruth. TrJP

And Nature renews it all. (*LL*) Verses for a First Birthday. George Barker. MoAB; MoBrPo

And ne'er the first assault to proffer. (*LL*) Of Scolding Wives and the Third Day Ague. Henricus Selyns. AiP; SCAP

And ne'er was Anna Grace seen again. (*LL*) The Fairy Thorn. Sir Samuel Ferguson. CH; PeIV

And neither awful Voice be heard by thee! (*LL*) Thought [*or* Thoughts] of a Briton on the Subjugation of Switzerland. Wordsworth. EnRP; UV

And never again will he vomit it up. (*LL*) The Eclipse of the Moon. Lu T'ung. PLT

And never brought my babies home. (*LL*) Exiles. Judy F. Ham. LoHo

And never could understand! *(LL)* The Vampire. Kipling. BLPL; CoGr; NOBVV

And never give a thought to night. *(LL)* Two doves upon the selfsame branch. Christina Rossetti. CBLP

And never once gone back to visit you? *(LL)* Insomnia. Lu Yu. OHMPC

And never scent the ground where they will lie. *(LL)* Simple Autumnal. Louise Bogan. MoAB; MoAmPo; Son

And never stain a cheek for it. *(LL)* To His Book[e]. Martial. AWP; OBVE

And never to change you for no new. *(LL)* Sometime I sigh, sometime I sing. Sir Thomas Wyatt. SiPS; SiPSBD

And never went there again. *(LL)* Doctor Foster went to Gloucester [*or* Glo'ster]. Mother Goose. OxBoLi; OxNR; ReMoGo

And new philosophy calls all in doubt. John Donne. *Fr.* Anatomy [*or* Anatomie] of the World, An [: The First Anniversary]. NAEL-1; NOSC; SeCV-1

And night and distant travel; for the train. Last Evening. Rainer Maria Rilke, *tr. fr. German by* J. B. Leishman. OBWP

And night approaches with her shades. *(LL)* Composed upon an Evening of Extraordinary Splendour and Beauty. Wordsworth. EnRP; OAEL-2

And night by night when all is still. Enoch Made Them — Enoch Shall Break Them. *Unknown.* FaBoEH

And night is a dark tower. *(LL)* Early Supper. Barbara Howes. GoJo; GrPl; SM

And night is pierced with stars. *(LL)* Round the Year. Coventry Patmore. BoTP

And Night shall fold him in soft wings. *(LL)* Into Battle. Julian Grenfell. FaPoR; OBEV; OBMV; OBWP; OtMeF; OxBTC; PeFWW

And no birds sing — . *(LL)* La Belle Dame sans Merci. Keats. AWP; BeLS; BLPA; CH; ChTr; ClHu; CoGr; EBEvV; ELP; EnRP; FaBoBe; FaBoCh; FHYEP; GoJo; GTBS; GTBS-P; HAP; HeIP; ImPo; InPS; InvP; LiTB; MeMBP; NAEL-2; NAWM-2; NOBE; NoP; NTP; OAEL-2; OBEV; OBNC; OBSP; OtMeF; OxAEP-2; PoE; PoEL-4; Poetr; PoRA; Prf; PrIm; RB; SCGP; SCV; SoSe; TEP; TFi, *sl. sh. vers.*; TrGrPo; TRP; UnPo; UV, *sl. sh. vers.*

And no blight on her. The Third Generation. Katherine Janowitz. BTR

And no bread in his pocket. *(LL)* The Brother. Peter Everwine. FYAP; NNaP

And no one could tell them from the real thing. *(LL)* The Real Thing. Michael O'Loughlin. IB

And no one shall put salt on their bright tails. *(LL)* The Sea Birds. Van K. Brock. NYBP; SM

And no one to answer the bell. *(LL)* The Dolgelley Hotel. Thomas Hughes. FaBoCo

And no one will remember me any more even here. *(LL)* Far from Home. Joseph Freiherr von Eichendorff. RiWo

And no one will worry a bit. *(LL)* Does It Matter? Siegfried Sassoon. CoGr; MoBrPo; PAW; PeFWW; PoWW

And No Regrets. Lex Banning. NOBAV

And no such darkness. *(LL)* Beasts. Richard Wilbur. AmPP; LCAP; NU; PPP; TwCP

And no visible recompense. *(LL)* But I, Too, Want to Be a Poet. Fanny Howe. VBLP

And Noah was six hundred years old when the flood of waters. Bible, O.T. *Fr.* Genesis. NAWM-1

And nobody buys. *(LL)* No Buyers; a Street Scene. Thomas Hardy. LiTB; MeMBP; NoP

And Nod. *(LL)* Wynken, Blynken, and Nod. Eugene Field. BeLS; BoTP; FaBoBe; FaPON; NBLV; NTCP; OBAL; OBCA; OTCP; OxBChV; PoRA; PYC; TFi

And none has quite escaped my smile. *(LL)* Let No Charitable Hope. Elinor Wylie. LiTA; LiTM; MoAB; MoAmPo; NAAL-2; NALW; OxBA; OxBSP; TrGrPo; VGW

And none of the worlds between! *(LL)* The Poet. Padraic Fiacc. CIP

And none remain'd to give the rest. *(LL)* The Cornelian. Byron. PeHV

And none shall be afraid. *(LL)* It is up to us to receive and transmit our Torah. Rami M. Shapiro. EaPr

And none shall speak his name. *(LL)* Poet. Karl Shapiro. CMoP; LiTM; MoAB; MoAmPo; NoAM

And not afriad to dare. *(LL)* Interim. Clarissa Scott Delany. CDC; PoNe; ShDr

And not be ashamed. *(LL)* April Fool Birthday Poem for Grandpa. Diane Di Prima. PoBeRe

And not commit upon itself this rape. *(LL)* Upon the Lark and the Fowler. Bunyan. CH

And not far off was the churchyard gate. *(LL)* Both Less and More. Richard Watson Dixon. SCGP

And not one of them all seemed to know the name of care. *(LL)* The Idlers. Edmund Blunden. BoTP; CH

"And not," said the room, "go out any more." *(LL)* Green Candles. Humbert Wolfe. MoBrPo

And not the storms or the strife. *(LL)* The Winds of Fate. Ella Wheeler Wilcox. AnAmPo; BLPA; WBLP

And not unblest. *(LL)* From My Window. Mary Elizabeth Coleridge. OBNC

And not waving but drowning. *(LL)* Not Waving but Drowning. Stevie Smith. CoGr; FaBoWP; FaPoB; FF; GTBS-P; HAP; HeIP; MoP; NAEL-2; NALW; NoAM; NOBE; NoP; OAEL-2; OxAEP-2; OxBTC; PoE; Poetr; PPP; PrIm; TEP; TFi; UV; WeW

And not your yellow hair. *(LL)* For Anne Gregory. W. B. Yeats. CMoP; ImPo; LiTM; MeMBP; NAEL-2; OxAEP-2; Poetr; SOTW

And Nothing Moved. Richard C. Raymond. BTR

And nothing, not even the girl you love. Among Tall Buildings. Molly Peacock. WoWa

And nothing permanent. *(LL)* After Twenty Years. Adrienne Rich. TRP

And nothing to do but to pocket my gold! *(LL)* The Laureate. William Edmonstoune Aytoun. BXAP; UV

And nothing to say or do? *(LL)* Gloucester Moors. William Vaughn Moody. AnAmPo; NOBA; OxBA

And nought beyond, oh earth! *(LL)* The Graves of a Household. Felicia Dorothea Hemans. FaPoR; PlP; WBLP; WPE

And nought, when old, enjoy'd, denied the pow'r. *(LL)* On Late-acquired Wealth *or* Riches. *Unknown.* OBVE

And nourishing the long thoughts in my soul. *(LL)* Autumn. Pushkin. AWP

And Now. J. B. Boothroyd. FiBHP

And now a fig for the lower house. Patrick Carey. JCP
(Fig for the Lower House, A.) NOSC

And now Aeneas charges straight at Turnus. Virgil, *tr. by* Allen Mandelbaum. *Fr.* Aeneid [*or* Eneados], The. NAWM-1; OBWP

And now all Nature seem'd in Love. On a Bank [*or* Banck] as I Sate [*or* Sat] a-Fishing; a Description of the Spring. Sir Henry Wotton. NOSC; SeCP
(May Day, A.) CH

And now among them these dark mornings yours. A Brightness to Cast Shadows. David Constantine. PWE

And now an *Epode* to deep ears I sing. *(LL)* And must I sing? What subject shall I choose? Ben Jonson. BeJo

And now begin to weep when they have done. *(LL)* On the Death of Sir Philip Sidney. Henry Constable. EiL; OBEV

And now, behold! as at the approach of the morning. The Celestial Pilot. Dante, *tr. by* Longfellow. *Fr.* Divina Commedia. MeMAP; WGRP

And now Eurynome had bath'd the king. Homer, *tr. by* George Chapman. *Fr.* Odyssey. NAWM-1; OBVE
(Ulysses Reunited with Penelope.) NOSC, *sect.* XXIV

And, now gives Time, her states description. George Chapman. *Fr.* Euthymiae Raptus; or, The Teares of Peace. PoEL-2

And now good night. Good night to this old house. Good Night Near Christmas. Robert Francis. ArNa

And now his blessing is, he can't be curst. *(LL)* Directed to That Inconsiderable Animal Called Husband. *Unknown.* IHNG

And now his well-known bow the master bore. Homer, *tr. by* Pope. *Fr.* Odyssey. NAWM-1; OBVE

And now I am growing old. *(LL)* Autumn Wind. Emperor Wu of Han. OHMPC

And now I live, and now my life is done. *(LL)* Tichborne's Elegy. Chidiock Tichborne. EiL; FaBoRV; FF; HAP; HeIP; InPS; NoP; NoSic; OAEL-1; OBD; TFi

And now I, Meleager, am among them. Meleager, *tr. fr. Greek by* Peter Whigham. GrAn; PeHV

And now I wish to pray and perform. David Ignatow. EaPr

And now I'm engaged to Miss Joan Hunter Dunn. *(LL)* A Subaltern's Love-Song. Sir John Betjeman. BoLoP; EBEvV; HAP; NoAM; NOBL; OxAEP-2; OxBTC; TwCP

And now in turn see Swinburne bent. Lines on Swinburne. Robert Browning. EPCY

And now, it seems, you are fearful. The Dark. Richard Poole. AngWe

And now, kind friends, what I have wrote. Julia A. Moore. FaBoCo; FiBHP

And now, lash'd on by destiny severe. The Ship Is Lost. William Falconer. *Fr.* Shipwreck, The. OxAEP-1

And now let pass a week. Once more behold. Robert Browning. *Fr.* Red Cotton Night-Cap Country. EBVVPR, *sect.* III

And now, like a posy, a pretty one plump in his hands. *(LL)* Catch. Robert Francis. InPK; RaBo

And now love sang: but his was such a song. Willowwood ("And now love sang: but his was such a song.") Dante Gabriel Rossetti. *Fr.* House of Life, The. NAEL-2; OAEL-2

And now man-slaughtering Pallas took in hand. Homer, *tr. by* George Chapman. *Fr.* Odyssey. NAWM-1; OBVE

And now my pampered beast. Epitaph for My Cat. Jean Garrigue. TAP

And now of a Bloody Mary! (*LL*) Gold. Thomas Hood. WBLP

And now — once more to die. (*LL*) The Mystic Magi. Robert Stephen Hawker. ChTr; OBCP

And now one prayer. *Unknown, tr. by* William Morris *and* Eirikr Magnusson. *Fr.* Elder Edda, The. AWP; OBVE

"And now," said the Governor, gazing abroad on the piled-up store. First Thanksgiving Day. Margaret Junkin Preston. PAH

And now shall not. (*LL*) Two Years. Pamela Gillilan. PWE

And now she cleans her teeth into the lake. Camping Out. William Empson. CMoP; FaBoMo; OxBTC

And now she goes on the trapeze. (*LL*) The Man on the Flying Trapeze. *At. to* George Leybourne. BeLS; BLPA; FaBoBe

And now take thought, my sonnet, who is he. Sonnets of the Months: Conclusion. Folgore da San Geminiano, *tr. by* Dante Gabriel Rossetti. AWP

And now th'art set wide ope, the spear's sad art. I Am the Door. Richard Crashaw. GeHe; NAEL-1

And, now that every thing may in the proper place. Michael Drayton. *Fr.* Polyolbion. FM

And now the dark comes on, all full of chitter noise. The Sound of Night. Maxine W. Kumin. BoNaP; SoSe; WPE

And now the falcon is hooded and comforted away. (*LL*) The Falcon and the Dove. Sir Herbert Read. FaBoMo

And now the green household is dark. In the Tree House at Night. James Dickey. NoP

And now the morn arase, when o'er the plain. Timothy Dwight. *Fr.* Triumph of Infidelity, The. EAP

And now the Queene of women had intent. Homer, *tr. by* George Chapman. *Fr.* Odyssey. NAWM-1; OBVE

And now the riverbank. For the last time. Marina Tsvetaeva, *tr. fr. Russian by* Paul Schmidt. *Fr.* Daughter of Jairus, The. BoWoP

And now the riverbank. I cling. Marina Tsvetaeva, *tr. fr. Russian by* Paul Schmidt. *Fr.* Daughter of Jairus, The. BoWoP

And now the sun that through the horizon peeps. Christopher Marlowe. *Fr.* Hero and Leander. AAS; NoP; OAEL-1

And now the trembling light. Shoreham: Twilight Time. Samuel Palmer. OAEL-2

(Twilight Time.) FaBoPP; NTP

And now the words. Mourning Song. Robert Pearl, *tr. fr. Tsimshian Indian by* Armand Schwerner. STP

And Now There Is Nothing Left To Celebrate. George Barker. *Fr.* Pacific Sonnets. LiTM; MeMBP

And now there is the lively sound. Baby's Awake Now. Bill Berkson. UL

And now they keep an oyster-shop for mermaids down below. (*LL*) The Ballad of the Oysterman. Oliver Wendell Holmes. AnAmPo; MoShBr

And now they lien in helle ifere: (*LL*) Ubi Sunt Qui ante Nos Fuerunt? [*or* Contempt of the World]. *Unknown.* NoP

And now they nigh approachèd to the stead. The Mermaids. Spenser. *Fr.* Faerie Queene, The. ChTr

And now thou seest my soul's angelic hue. (*LL*) A "Prize" Poem. Shirley Brooks. FaBoCo; FaBoNo

And now 'tis time; for their officious haste. Heroique Stanzas, Consecrated to the Glorious Memory of His Most Serene and Renowned Highnesse, Oliver, Late Lord Protector of this Common-Wealth. Dryden. SeCV-2

"And now to God the Father," he ends. In Church. Thomas Hardy. *Fr.* Satires of Circumstance. IHNG; InPK; MoAB; MoBrPo; SCV

And now to the abyss I pass. Andrew Marvell. *Fr.* Upon Appleton House, to My Lord Fairfax. OAEL-1; SeCP; SeCV-1

And now, unveiled, the toilet stands displayed. Pope. *Fr.* Rape of the Lock, The. ECEV; FHYEP; HAP; ImPo; NoP; OAEL-1; OBNV; OxAEP-1; PeLV; PoEL-3; TEP; TrGrPo

(Toilet, The.) NOBE

And now was Paris come/ From his high towres. Homer, *tr. by* George Chapman. *Fr.* Iliad, The. OBVE

And now we gan draw near unto the gate. Virgil, *tr. fr. Latin by* Robert Fitzgerald. *Fr.* Aeneid [*or* Eneados], The. NAWM-1; NoSic, *tr. by* Henry Howard, Earl of Surrey; SiPSBD, *tr. by* Henry Howard, Earl of Surrey

And now we three in Euston waiting-room. (*LL*) Parting in Wartime. Frances Cornford. CoGr; FaBoWP; NIP

And now we walked along the solid mire. Dante, *tr. by* Robert Lowell. *Fr.* Divina Commedia. MeMAP; NAWM-1, *tr. by* John Ciardi; OBVE

And now we will count to twelve. Keeping Quiet. Pablo Neruda, *tr. by* Alastair Reed. EaPr

And now what monarch would not gardener be. To Amanda Walking in the Garden. N. Hookes. NOSC

And now where're he sleeps. Richard Crashaw. *See* Hail[e], sister springs!

And now with him she sleeps in Yarrow. (*LL*) The Braes of Yarrow. John Logan. GTBS; GTBS-P; SCGP

And now you comb and braid your hair. Paulus Silentiarius, *tr. fr. Greek by* Sam Hamill. InMo

And now you grudge a spot to me. (*LL*) What Jenner Said on Hearing in Elysium That Complaints Had Been Made of His Having a Statue [in Trafalgar Square]. Shirley Brooks. FaBoEE

And Now You're Ready Who While She Was Here. J. V. Cunningham, *after the Greek of* Skythinos. FaBoBl; OBVE

And now you're ready who while she was here. Scythinus, *tr. fr. Greek by* J. V. Cunningham. GrAn

And nubile/ loving. (*LL*) For My Mother. June Jordan. BoWoP; NMM

And nuzzling each other in the smelly fold. (*LL*) Magnificat. Michele Roberts. BrRo; NBrP; VBLP

And O and O. Song of Spring. Keats. BoTP

And O she was the Sunday/ In every week. (*LL*) The Planter's Daughter. Austin Clarke. CIP; OxBTC

And observed all the ruins of Philae. (*LL*) There was an old person of Philae. Edward Lear. CBNP; FaBoNo

And o'er your happy songs its plaudits rang. (*LL*) Paul Laurence Dunbar. James David Corrothers. PoNe

And of Columbus. Horace Gregory. GOA

And, of its one movement, the depth. (*LL*) The Movement of Fish. James Dickey. NYBP; VGW

And oft the owle with rufull song complaind. Virgil, *tr. by* the Earl of Surrey. *Fr.* Aeneid [*or* Eneados], The. NAWM-1; OBVE

And often swore my lips were sweet. (*LL*) Mother, I Cannot Mind My Wheel. Walter Savage Landor, *first st. paraphrased fr. the Greek of* Sappho. AWP, *st.* 1; BoLoP; EnRP; GBL; NAEL-2; NOBE; OBEV; OBVE; TEP; TrGrPo

And, oh, may no other maiden know such reproach as I! (*LL*) Cashel of Munster. *At. to* William English. BIrV; GBL; OBEV; PeIV

And, oh! 'tis delicious to hate you! (*LL*) When I loved you, I can't but allow. Thomas Moore. EnLoPo; OxBSP

And old men shall drop by the wayside. (*LL*) Shaka, King of the Zulus. *Unknown.* PBA; TTY

And, on a park bench, come to a last decision. (*LL*) The Nameless Ones. Conrad Aiken. AnAmPo; OxBA

And on My Eyes Dark Sleep by Night. "Michael Field." OBMV

And on that day, upon the heavenly scarp. Upon the Heavenly Scarp. A. M. Klein. *Fr.* Psalter of Avram Haktani, The. PoA

And on the bleached bones, when the sun shines, we shall / begin to build. (*LL*) Working Class. Bertram J. Warr. NOBC

And on the fifth day, he was — dead! (*LL*) The Story of Augustus, Who Would Not Have Any Soup. Heinrich Hoffmann. FaBoUs; GoJo; MoShBr; NBLV; OxBChV

And on the magic mountain nothing moved. (*LL*) The Green Shepherd. Louis Simpson. NYBP

And on the mere the wailing died away. (*LL*) So all day long the noise of battle rolled. Tennyson, *incorporated in* Idylls of the King *with changes, as* The Passing of Arthur. DL; EBNV; EBVPR; EnVR; FaBoBe; FaBoRV; NIP; NOBVV; OAEL-2; OBNV; OxAEP-2; PoEL-5

And on the porch, across the upturned chair. The Poet at Seven. Donald Justice. MT; WeW

And on the right the slogan Born To Lose. (*LL*) Black Jackets. Thom Gunn. HeIP; NAEL-2; TwCP

And on the ships at sea. (*LL*) Rain. Robert Louis Stevenson. GoJo; NTCP; SiSoPo

And on the wall was limned a mouldering corse. On the Wall. Immanuel di Roma, *tr. fr. Hebrew by* Solomon Solis-Cohen. TrJP

And on this day, which poets unto thee. Ovid, *tr. by* Henry Vaughan. *Fr.* Tristium. OBVE

And on This Shore. M. Carl Holman. PoBA; PoNe

And once again I was within that house. The Dream. John Peale Bishop. LiTA; LiTM

And one boundless reach of sky. (*LL*) The Builders. Longfellow. AnAmPo; PFP; PWR

And one for the little boy that lives in the lane. (*LL*) Baa, baa, black sheep, have you any wool? Mother Goose. FaBoBe; OxNR; ReMoGo

And one had a pancake sticking to his bum. (*LL*) Children's Rhymes and Parodies. *Unknown.* NOBAu

And one in a velvet gown. (*LL*) Hark, Hark, the Dogs Do Bark. Mother Goose. CoGr; OxNR; ReMoGo

And one light green. (*LL*) Image. Gu Cheng. SpMi

And one morning while in the woods I stumbled suddenly upon the thing. Between the World and Me. Richard Wright. LiTM; MoP; PoBA

And one of them is rather coarse. (*LL*) The Horse. Naomi Royde-Smith. FaBoCo; FiBHP

And One Shall Live in Two. Jonathan Henderson Brooks. PoNe

And onely my loke declareth my hert. (*LL*) Bicause I have the still kept fro lyes and blame. Petrarch. OBVE

And one's game must soon come right. *(LL)* Golf. Matthew Sweeney. IB

And only bitter land was washed away. *(LL)* Childhood. Margaret Walker. IHMS; PBWP; PoBA; Son; WPOW

And only God is with them. *(LL)* Pictures of the Jews. Haim Guri. MHP

And only know I should drown if you laid not your hand on me. *(LL)* Stillness. James Elroy Flecker. CH; GoJo; MoBrPo

And only the heart is withered and sere. *(LL)* Die blauen Veilchen der Äugelein. Heine. AWP

And only then the eye begins to see. *(LL)* The Counterpart. Elizabeth Jennings. LiTM; TOF

And only wake with you! *(LL)* Ah! Why, because the Dazzling Sun. Emily Brontë. BrRo; NALW

And opposite Beersheba's road — we watch. *(LL)* Canaan. Benyamin Galai. MHP

And opposition of the stars. *(LL)* The Definition of Love. Andrew Marvell. BLPL; BoLoP; CBLP; EBEV; ESCV; FHYEP; GBL; GeHe; HoPM; ImPo; InPS; JCP; LiTM; MeLP; NAEL-1; NOBE; NoP; NOSC; OAEL-1; OBEV; PoEL-2; SCGP; SeCP; SeCV-1; TEP; TFi; TrGrPo; UnPo

And other folk should get the ugly ones. *(LL)* Sonnet: Of All He Would Do. Cecco Angiolieri, da Siena. AWP

And other hippopotomusses. *(LL)* Habits of the Hippopotamus. Arthur Guiterman. FaBV; FiBHP; OBCA

And other wond'rous works were done. Ascension of Our Lord Jesus Christ. Christopher Smart. *Fr.* Hymns and Spiritual Songs. NOCV

And others call it God. *(LL)* Each in His Own Tongue. William Herbert Carruth. BLPA; WBLP; WGRP

And our charity is in the children's faces. *(LL)* The Children. William Soutar. PAW

And our eternal home. *(LL)* Our God, Our Help in Ages Past. Isaac Watts. OBVE; PlP; PWR; TOF

And our hands are together as always, and know well what they hold. *(LL)* Teaching to Shoot. Valentine Ackland. VBLP

And our hearts, like thy waters, be mingled in peace. *(LL)* The Meeting of the Waters. Thomas Moore. ArLo; IIP; NOIV; OxBoLi; PoEL-4

And our hem crooked forever? *(LL)* House Guest. Elizabeth Bishop. NYBP; TAP

And our multiple thirsts. *(LL)* When we are like two drunken suns. Yvonne Caroutch.

And our one night flower. *(LL)* Bad Blood. Tchicaya U Tam'si. NegPo

And our ordinary garments decent in the dead one's eyes. *(LL)* Journey to the Place of Ghosts. Jay Wright. VCAP

And our windy sighs to its sails. *(LL)* Parting. Gu Cheng. SpMi

And out doth keep/ All fear[e]. *(LL)* The Gnat. Joseph Beaumont. FM; NOSC

And out of his eyes two great tears rolled, like stones, and he died. *(LL)* Death of a Son. Jon Silkin. FF; GTBS-P; MoP; OxBTC

And out of the swing of the sea. *(LL)* Heaven-Haven. Gerard Manley Hopkins. EBEvV; HeIL; HeIP; MoAB; MoBrPo; MoP; NoAM; NOBE; NOCV; OBEV; OBNC; OxAEP-2; OxBSP; PeECV; RB; SoSe; SOTW; TFi; TOF; TrGrPo

And outside stray rivers course by. *(LL)* A Scriptwriter's Discipline. Matthew Sweeney. IB

And over all the sky — the sky! far, far out of reach, studded, breaking out, the eternal stars. *(LL)* Bivouac on a Mountain Side. Walt Whitman. AiP; ChTr; OxBA; PoLF

And over-read what I have writ. *(LL)* The Departure of the Good Daemon. Robert Herrick. CoGr; FaBoRV

And pain and muteness in me shall sprout purity, this is the lot of man. *(LL)* Reward. Shimon Halkin. MHP

And palms before my feet. *(LL)* The Donkey. G. K. Chesterton. ChIV-2; CoGr; EBEvV; FaBV; FaPoB; FaPoR; InPK; MoBrPo; OBEV; PoLF; RB; WGRP

And panting and panting. *(LL)* Message from a Cross. Max Harris. NOBAu

And Paradise does come. Joy. Gavin Bantock. OxBTC

And pardon this one. *(LL)* Hotel Paradiso e Commerciale. John Malcolm Brinnin. NYBP; TwCP

And Paris be it or Helen dying. A Fragment on Death. Villon, *tr. fr. French by* Swinburne. CTC; PeVV
(Fragment of Death.) AWP

And pass me by. *(LL)* Song of the Rootless People. Chung Ling. WPC

And passionate as the dawn. *(LL)* The Fisherman. W. B. Yeats. CMoP; HAP; NoAM

And pay for the punch beside. *(LL)* The Dorchester Giant. Oliver Wendell Holmes. FaPON

And Peace, and Art, and Labour joined her train. *(LL)* Visit of Hope to Sydney Cove, near Botany-Bay. Erasmus Darwin. ECEV; NOEC; OBTV

And Pergamos,/ City of the Phrygians. Euripides, *tr. fr.* Greek by Hilda Doolittle ("H. D."). *Fr.* Iphigenia [*or* Iphigeneia] in Aulis. AWP; OBVE

And perhaps as well some tasteless specks of salt. *(LL)* Here is. Jean-Joseph Rabéarivelo. NegPo

And perish in our own. *(LL)* Daisy. Francis Thompson. AWP; BeLS; FaBV; MoAB; MoBrPo; OBEV; OBNC

And perish in their infancy. *(LL)* Break of Day. *Unknown, at. to* John Donne. EIL; TrGrPo

And perseveringly collected stamps. *(LL)* King George V. Charles W. Hayward. NOBAu

And Peter turned, and rushed on Rome and death. *(LL)* Domine Quo Vadis? Sir William Watson. WGRP

And Phyllis is some forty-three. *(LL)* Phillis's *or* Phyllis's Age. Matthew Prior. EnLoPo; FaBoEE

And pipes her 'tweet-tut' fears the whole day long. *(LL)* The Firetail's Nest. John Clare. EnRP

And plain old Margaret Fuller died as well. *(LL)* Ballad of Ladies Lost and Found. Marilyn Hacker. VCAP

And ploughs down palaces, and thrones, and towers. *(LL)* The Serf. Roy Campbell. GTBS-P; LiTB; MoBrPo; OBMV

And poetry by this increase grow less. *(LL)* On Mr. Shirley's Poems. Thomas Stanley. BeJo

And point with taper spire to Heaven. *(LL)* A Wish. Samuel Rogers. FaPoR; GGP; GTBS; GTBS-P; NOBE; OBEV; OxAEP-2; PlP

And points us to a better home. *(LL)* West London. Matthew Arnold. FF; OBF; OHCV; SCGP; Son

And poplars stand there still as death. *(LL)* Southern Mansion. Arna Bontemps. AiP; FF; LiTM; PoBA; PoNe; TTY

And port was celestial glory. *(LL)* Epitaph on John Dove. Burns. FaBoCo

And possess the common heritage to which all flesh is heir? *(LL)* The Virgin Martyr. Ada Cambridge. NOBAu

And pour another cup for Cousin Klaas! *(LL)* Oom Gert's Story. C. Louis Leipoldt. PeSAV

And practice drives me mad. *(LL)* Arithmetic. *Unknown.* ISE; ReMoGo; UsP

And praise him who did make and mend our eies. *(LL)* Love. George Herbert. HoPM; SeCV-1; Son

And praise the Lord from west to east. *(LL)* I'm Far From What I Call My Home. John Campbell. PeSAV

And pray for Kharma under the holy mountain. *(LL)* Chard Whitlow. Henry Reed. BXAP; FaBoCo; FaBoNo; FaBoPa; FiBHP; LiTM; MoBrPo; NBLV; NOBL; NoP; OxBTC; PeLV; UnPo; UV

And pray, who are you? The Tax-Gatherer. John Banister Tabb. GN

And prays for love. *(LL)* And If the Angel Should Ask. Hayyim Nahman Bialik. MHP

And pretty maids all in a row. *(LL)* Mary, Mary, quite contrary. Mother Goose. FaBoEH; OxNR; ReMoGo

And pull'd out fourscore. *(LL)* When I Was a Little Boy. *Unknown.* CBNP; OxNR

And pure religion breathing household laws. *(LL)* London, MDCCCII ("O friend! I know not which way I must look.") Wordsworth. GTBS; GTBS-P

And pure religion breathing household laws. *(LL)* Written in London, September, 1802. Wordsworth. FaBoPV; TrGrPo

And purpose of our being here? *(LL)* To spend uncounted years of pain. Arthur Hugh Clough. EnVR; NOBVV; OBNC; OxBSP

And put him into bed? Why don't they come? *(LL)* Disabled. Wilfred Owen. CMoP; FF; InPS; LiTM; MeMBP; MoP; NAEL-2; NoAM; NSI; OBWVE; OxBTC; PoFWW; SCGP

And put in twa een o' tree. *(LL)* Tam Lin. *Unknown.* ESPB; FaBoBa; NOBE; OBEV; OBNV; OxBB; OxBS

And putting it there in a style to stay. *(LL)* God in the Nation's Life. *Unknown.* BLRP; WBLP

And quiet pilgrimage. *(LL)* The Man of Life Upright. Thomas Campion. AAS; CoGr; EIL; EnRePo; NoSic; PoRA

And quiet sleep and a sweet dream when the long trick's over. *(LL)* Sea-Fever. John Masefield. CoGr; EBEvV; FaBoBe; FaBV; FaPON; FaPoR; MoAB; MoBrPo; NTP; OBTV; OtMeF; OxAEP-2; OxBTC; PDV; PoLF; TrGrPo; UV

And raise her children to eternal day. *(LL)* Along the Banks. Joel Barlow. AH; ChIV-1

And raised prize melons. *(LL)* On His Thirty-Third Birthday. Ch'ang Kuo Fan. OHMPC

And raised such a hellabelioux? *(LL)* The Sioux. Eugene Field. FiBHP

And raised thee up to where thou art. *(LL)* The Duke of York's Statue. Walter Savage Landor. FaBoEE

And rattles her crutch, which may put forth a small bloom, perhaps white. *(LL)* Pursuit. Robert Penn Warren. HAP; LiTA; MoAmPo; TwCP

And raving, distracted, he died the next night. *(LL)* The Gosport Tragedy. *Unknown.* AmFP

And rear children. *(LL)* The Two Sisters. *Aborigine Oral Tradition.* NOBAu

And reconciles man to his lot. *(LL)* Verses Supposed to Be Written by Alexander Selkirk during His Solitary Abode on the Island of Juan Fernandez. William Cowper. EBEvV; NOEC; PoEL-3; PoLF

And rest with Thee? *(LL)* Weary in Well-doing. Christina Rossetti. TrPWD

And rested on a drying hill. *(LL)* Sir Gawaine and the Green Knight. Yvor Winters. MoP; NoAM; PoRA; VGW

And retreating, always retreating, behind it. *(LL)* Brazil, January 1, 1502. Elizabeth Bishop. FaBoWP; NoAM; VCAP

And returned on the previous night. *(LL)* There was a young lady named [*or* called] Bright. *At. to* Arthur Buller. NOBL; OxBoLi; PeLi; PeLV

And returned to their homes by another way. *(LL)* The Three Kings. Longfellow. ChIV-2; GN

And revel o'er me, like a soulless sheep. *(LL)* Lunar Stanzas. Henry Coggswell Knight. CBNP; FaBoNo

And rid it out of pain. *(LL)* O Goodly Hand. Sir Thomas Wyatt. InvP; SiPS

And Ride in Triumph through Persepolis. Christopher Marlowe. *Fr.* Tamburlaine the Great. TrGrPo

And rip the edge off any ideal or dream. *(LL)* Among These Turf-Stacks. Louis MacNeice. ImPo; LiTB

And roar in Numbers worthy *Bounce.* *(LL)* Bounce to Fop; an Heroick Epistle from a Dog at Twickenham to a Dog at Court. Pope. FM

And Ronda with the old windows of the posadas. Yes. James Joyce. *Fr.* Ulysses. FF

And rooted in Romance remain. *(LL)* Old Susan. Walter de la Mare. CMoP; MoBrPo

And rose is, and lily, and moon and dove. *(LL)* Rose, die Lilie, die Taube, die Sonne, Die. Heine. AWP

And ruin is the lot of all. *(LL)* The Hurricane. Philip Freneau. EAP; TAP

And Ruth said, Intreat me not to leave. Bible, *O.T. Fr.* Ruth. FF (Ruth to Naomi.) TrGrPo

And sae the Lord be thankit. *(LL)* A Child's Grace. Burns. FaBoCh; FaPON; MoShBr

And sae this ends my sang. *(LL)* Lord Livingston. *Unknown.* ESPB; OxBB

And said he was very well serv'd in his kind. *(LL)* The Unfortunate Miller; or, The Country Lasses Witty Invention. *Unknown.* CoMu; OxBB

And said I that my limbs were old. Love. Sir Walter Scott. *Fr.* Lay of the Last Minstrel, The. OxAEP-2

And said, 'Nay, we are seven!' *(LL)* Simple child, A. Wordsworth. BLPA; BLPL; EnRP; GN; NAEL-2; OBD; OxBChV; TEP; WBLP

And said, "Not yet! in quiet lie." *(LL)* Daybreak. Longfellow. BoTP; PoLF; PWR

And said, What a good boy am I! *(LL)* Little Jack Horner/ Sat in a corner. Mother Goose. FaBoEH; OxNR, *orig. and parody;* ReMoGo; SoSe

And said "You must not ask." *(LL)* My Fairy. "Lewis Carroll." CBNP; FaBoNo

And Samuel sixty-two. *(LL)* The Bards. Walter de la Mare. FaBoNo; NOBL

And sanctify this ALTAR to be thine. *(LL)* The Altar. George Herbert. AngWe; ChIV-1; ESCV; GeHe; HoPM; InPS; JCP; NAEL-1; NOSC; OAEL-1; Poetr; SeCP; SeCV-1; TrCP; TrGrPo

And sank her in the sea. *(LL)* The Demon Lover. *Unknown.* EnSB; HAP; LiTB; MAT; SCGP; TFi; UnPo; WeW

And Satan's self had thoughts of taking orders. *(LL)* Tophet. Thomas Gray. ChIV-1; FaBoEE; NOEC; OxBSP

And Saul said unto his servants. Bible, *O.T. Fr.* First Samuel. OBF

And saved a great cause that heroic day. *(LL)* Opportunity. Edward Rowland Sill. AnAmPo; BLPA; GN; WGRP

And saved the sum of things for pay. *(LL)* Epitaph on an Army of Mercenaries. A. E. Housman. CoGr; EBEvV; NSI; OtMeF; PAW; SCGP; SoSe

And say dat's good enough for nigger. *(LL)* We raise de wheat. *Unknown.* BPo; TAP

And, say! how does it seem to you? *(LL)* Far from the Madding Crowd. Nixon Waterman. BLPA; FaBoBe

And say my glory was I had such freinds. *(LL)* The Municipal Gallery Revisited. W. B. Yeats. GTBS-P; LiTB; MeMBP; OxBTC

And say, *Where God is, all agree.* *(LL)* The Constellation. Henry Vaughan. SeCV-1

And scarce fifteen of age. *(LL)* Bird in a Cage. *Unknown.* AS; GBP

And scattered comets like flowers. *(LL)* Bless the Lord, O my soul. Ernesto Cardenal. EaPr

And scattered vowels of Jerusalem. *(LL)* Anglo-Saxon. Edward Leslie Mayo. BCF

And schoolboys lag with satchels in their hands. *(LL)* A Description of the Morning. Swift. EBEV; ECEV; FF; HAP; HeIP; InPS; NOBE; NOEC; NoP; OAEL-1; OxAEP-1; Poetr; PPP; Prf; SoSe; TEP; TFi

And scratched him in again. *(LL)* The Man of Thessaly. *Unknown.* CBNP; FaBoCo; FaBoNo; OxNR

And sea and air. *(LL)* The Irish Cliffs of Moher. Wallace Stevens. NOBA; RaBo; TOF; VGW

And seal her to the Stranger for his castle in the gloom. *(LL)* Emily Hardcastle, Spinster. John Crowe Ransom. CMoP; MeMAP; OxBSP

And seal the hushèd casket of my soul. *(LL)* To Sleep. Keats. ChTr; EBEvV; EnRP; FaBoRV; MeMBP; NIP; OBEV; PlP; PoEL-4; PrIm; Son; TEP

And seasons, changeless since the day she died. *(LL)* The Cross of Snow. Longfellow. HeIP; MeMAP; NOBA; OxBA; TAP

And see his chariot triumph 'bove his wain. *(LL)* Ode to Himsel[f]e. Ben Jonson. BeJo; NAEL-1; OAEL-1; SeCP

And see how he howls! *(LL)* Teapots and Quails. Edward Lear. CBNP; GoJo

And see no other thing than it I touch. *(LL)* Green Enravishment of Human Life. Sister Juana Inés de la Cruz. WPOW, *tr. by* Samuel Beckett *and* Octavio Paz

And see Odell, the tax-collector, hung. *(LL)* Odell. James Stephens. MoAB; MoBrPo

And see th' expected hour is on the wing. Prospect of the Future Glory of America. John Trumbull. .AmPP

And see the men at play. *(LL)* The Golf Links. Sarah Norcliffe Cleghorn. ImPo; InPK; PoLF

And see you safely through diminished fields. *(LL)* Riding a One-eyed Horse. Henry Taylor. HeIP; InPK

And seeing the multitudes, he went up. Bible, *N.T. Fr.* St. Matthew. NAWM-1

And sell him in Algiers. *(LL)* A Dutch Picture. Longfellow. MoShBr

And sell their country in a closer way. *(LL)* Advice to a Painter. *Unknown.* APAS

And send her back ere noon?' *(LL)* Young Beichan. *Unknown.* ESPB; FaBoBa

And send it a thousand miles, thinking. *(LL)* Exile's Letter. Li Po. CTC; FaBoMo; OxBA

And send it from above! *(LL)* My Spirit Longeth for Thee. John Byrom. BLPL; NOBE

And send you a happy new year. *(LL)* The Moon Shines Bright. *Unknown.* GBP; ISE; OBET

And send you a joyful May. *(LL)* Song of the Mayers [*or* The Mayers' Song]. *Unknown.* CH; GBP

And sent him to take a ground sweat. *(LL)* The Night before Larry Was Stretched. *Unknown.* BIrV; FaBoBa; GBP; NOBL; NOIV; OxBoLi; PeIV

And serve but Him alone. *(LL)* The Nut-brown Maid. *Unknown.* NoSic; OBEV

And set our billie Archie free. *(LL)* Archie o [*or* of] Cawfield. *Unknown.* AmFP; ESPB; OxBS

And settle Satan's kingdom ev'rywhere. *(LL)* The Extravagant Drunkard's Wish. Edward Ward. CBNP; NOEC

And settled upon his eyes in a black soot. *(LL)* "More Light! More Light!" Anthony Hecht. ArOW; BTR; CoAP; HAP; NoAM; NOBA; NoP; OBWP; Poetr; RB; SM; TwCP; UnPo; VCAP; VGW

And several strengths from drowsiness campaigned. The Sermon on the Warpland. Gwendolyn Brooks. BPo; LiTM; NOBA; PoBA

And shaking with silent laughter. *(LL)* The Pointed People. Rachel Field. FaPON

And shall it not fade? *(LL)* And on This Shore. M. Carl Holman. PoBA; PoNe

And Shall Trelawny Die? Robert Stephen Hawker. *See* Good sword and a trusty hand, A!

And shall we ever seek in vain. All Alone. Mary E. Tucker. CBWP-1

And share in my grace. *(LL)* Nature's Praise of God. Christian Fürchtegott Gellert. RiWo

And share them through your generations on earth. *(LL)* Ancient sun, eternally young. *Unknown.* EaPr

And sharp-broken/ Dinner plates. *(LL)* Tinker's Wife. Patrick Kavanagh. CIP; InPS; MoP; NoAM

And shatter your virginity. *(LL)* Corinna in Vendome. Pierre de Ronsard. BoLoP; ErPo

And she aloof to laughter — till I don't know. Big, Fat Summer — and the Lean and Hard. Frederick Bock. NYBP

And she, an avalanche of woe. *(LL)* The Three Voices. "Lewis Carroll." BXAP

And she, being old, fed from a mashed plate. Old Woman. Iain Crichton Smith. FaBoTw; OxBTC

And she can't see. *(LL)* Great A, little a. Mother Goose. CBNP; OxNR

And she compliant to his every wish. *(LL)* Note on Propertius I.5. Fleur Adcock. BoLoP; PeNZ

And she dropt me a curtsey. *(LL)* As I was going up Pippen Hill. Mother Goose. OxNR; ReMoGo

And she has crept under/ The warming pan. *(LL)* Ladybird, Ladybird fly away home. Mother Goose. FaBoVe, *diff. vers.*; FaPON; ISE, *diff. vers.*; OxNR; ReMoGo, *diff. vers.*

And she his murd'ress is, who now is coy. *(LL)* To His Scornful Mistress. William Hammond. CBLP

And she is all alone. *(LL)* Streamers. Sandra McPherson. VCAP

And she is beautiful, our daughter. To Our Daughter. Jennifer Armitage. BrRo

And she laid a white egg in a willow tree root. *(LL)* The Goose and the Gander. *Unknown.* GBP; RB

And she said. 15th March 1939. Gerda Mayer. PAW

And she singeth full like a papejay. *(LL)* A Description of His Ugly Lady. Thomas Hoccleve. MeEL

And she to Paris Green. *(LL)* The Farmer and the Farmer's Wife. P. G. Hiebert. FiBHP; NBLV

And she was smiling to her ears! *(LL)* On Mother's Day. Aileen Fisher. NTCP

And She Washed His Feet with Her Tear[e]s, and Wiped Them with the Hairs of Her Head. Sir Edward Sherburne, *after the Italian of Giambattista Marina.* ChTr; MeLP; NOSC

And sheath their minds in scorn and self-conceit. *(LL)* Another. Thomas Lovell Beddoes. Son

And show that smile on us and sang. *(LL)* Homage to the Empress of the Blues. Robert Hayden. HCAP; Jaz; LCAP; PoBA; PoNe

And shores and strands and naked piers. Henry James at Newport. Weldon Kees. PoA

And should I thank you, my dear skin. Gratitude. Annette Lynch. FF

And shout "God will build" in the light of the great stars! *(LL)* At Your Feet, Jerusalem. Uri Zvi Greenberg. MHP

And shoved in, and driven away. *(LL)* A Note to Olga. Denise Levertov. NALW

And show her own teeth. *(LL)* Celebration. Julia Vinograd. SRLS

And show thy power thereby. *(LL)* Give Me Leave. "A. W." TrGrPo

And show your good conduct by timely possessing. *(LL)* Advice to the Ladies. William Somervile. FaBoUs

And shriek with joy in that place beyond prayer. *(LL)* Parting as Descent. John Berryman. LiTA; MoAmPo

And sick for home. *(LL)* Outside Fargo, North Dakota. James Wright. LCAP; NNaP

And sighing and kissing so close. *(LL)* Sylvia the fair, in the bloom of fifteen. Dryden. EBEV; ErPo

And sighs for the bucket that hung in the well. *(LL)* The Old Oaken Bucket. Samuel Woodworth. AnAmPo; BLPA; FaBoBe; FaPON; WBLP

And silently cut and run. *(LL)* The Day Is Done. Phoebe Cary. AnAmPo; BXAP; OBAL

And since he was Master and Servant in all that we asked him. Kipling. *Fr.* Dead King (Edward VII), 1910, The. FaBoEH

And since thou own'st that praise, I spare thee mine. *(LL)* To Mary Unwin [*or* Sonnet to Mrs. Unwin]. William Cowper. GTBS; GTBS-P; OBEV; TrGrPo

And sing of brave Grace Darling, who nobly saved the crew. *(LL)* Grace Darling. *Unknown.* OBET; OxBSS

And sing that rycht Balulalow. *(LL)* Ane Sang of the Birth of Christ, with the Tune of Baw Lula Low. Martin Luther. ChTr

And sing the centennial song. *(LL)* Immigrant. Arthur Nortje. PeSAV

And sink into the marsh near them. *(LL)* The Widow's Lament in Springtime. William Carlos Williams. CMoP; HAP; IMW; LiTM; MoP; NAAL-2; NoAM; NOBA; PFP; PoE; SAmP; SoSe; TAP

And sink off the Lowlands low. *(LL)* The Golden Vanity. *Unknown.* CH; ELP; FaBoCh; OBET; WiR

And sisters in India, stemming a little violence, among birds. *(LL)* The Jain Bird Hospital in Delhi. William Meredith. VCAP

And sits by your bed, and brings her knitting. *(LL)* Good Luck and Bad ("Good luck is the gayest of all gay girls.") John Milton Hay, *after the German of* Heine. AnAmPo; FaBoEE; NBLV

And six I'll gie to thee. *(LL)* Fair Annie. *Unknown.* CH; ESPB, *A, B, and E vers.*; FaBoBa; OxBB

And sky. *(LL)* Tiller of the Soil. Avraham Shlonsky. MHP

And sleepily resumes his half of heaven. *(LL)* On Spadina Avenue. Emily Grosholz. VBLP

And slow cascading of the paddle wheel. *(LL)* A Simile for Her Smile. Richard Wilbur. HoPM; InPK

And slowly answered Arthur from the barge. Tennyson. *Fr.* Idylls of the King. FaBoEH

And smite a rock. *(LL)* Good Friday. Christina Rossetti. ChIV-2; MeMBP; PoEL-5

And smooth the heads of the hungry children. *(LL)* Prelude to an Evening. John Crowe Ransom. MoAB; MoAmPo; OxBA

And so adieu, I thank thee for thy pain. *(LL)* An Epitaph of Maister Win Drowned in the Sea. George Turberville. FaBoEE

And so an easier life our Cyclops drew. Theocritus [*or* Theokritus], *tr. fr. Greek. Fr.* Idylls. OBVE, *tr. by* Elizabeth Barrett Browning (Cyclops, The ("And so an easier life").) AWP (For love there is no other drug, Nicias.) HePo, *tr. by* Barbara Hughes Fowler

And so are you. *(LL)* Roses are red. *Unknown.* OxNR; RoPo

And so be Constable of *France.* *(LL)* An English Ballad, on the Taking of Namur by the King of Great Britain, 1695. Matthew Prior. PoEL-3

And so briefly we detained him in the hall. The Foreign Element. Greg Johnson. PFL

And so cold. *(LL)* This Is Just to Say. William Carlos Williams. FF; GoJo; HeIP; HoPM; InPK; InPS; NAAL-2; NIP; NoAM; NOBA; NoP; NTP; PFP; Poetr; SOTW; TAP; TRP

And so depart into dark. Homage to Ezra Pound. Gilbert Highet. (Homage.) BXAP

And so did I, and my three friends are dead. *(LL)* Nights of 1964-66: The Old Reliable. Marilyn Hacker. VCAP

And so do I. *(LL)* Round about, round about,/ maggotty pie. *Unknown.* OxNR

And so do I. *(LL)* Weather[s]. Thomas Hardy. BoTP; CH; EBEvV; FaBoCh; FaBV; MoAB; MoBrPo; NTP; OBMV; OtMeF; RB

And, so doing, open ours. *(LL)* Slow Movement. Louis MacNeice. CBLP

And so enjoy her, and none miss her. *(LL)* Absence. *At. to* John Hoskyns, *sometimes at. to* John Donne. MeLP; OPOP

And so for nights. The Night-blooming Cereus. Robert Hayden. CAPP; NoP; NU

And so he will! And so he will! *(LL)* The Wind. James Stephens. BoNaP; InPK; MoP; NoAM

And so I cross into another world. New Heaven and Earth. D. H. Lawrence. CMoP

And so I lay without her. *(LL)* She Lay All Naked in Her Bed. *Unknown.* BoLoP; ErPo

And so I leave to stir him, lest he stink. *(LL)* A Little Shrub Growing By. Ben Jonson. BeJo; EnRePo

And so I love no more. *(LL)* Farewell to Love. Sir John Suckling. CaPo

And so I rest your constant friend. *(LL)* A Letter to the Honourable Lady Miss Margaret Cavendish Holles-Harley. Matthew Prior. NoAM; NOEC; NoP; OxBC; OxBSP

And so I speak/ in place of that primordial cry. Monique Laederach, *tr. fr. French by* Charles Guenther. *Fr.* Penelope. BoWoP

And so I went singing along. *(LL)* As I was going along, long, long. Mother Goose. OxNR; ReMoGo

And so I'm linked to you. Watchers. Robert Pack. FoLa

And so let's all be jolly. *(LL)* Sing, hey! Sing, hey!/ For Christmas Day. *Unknown.* PChr

And so lie down in peace. *(LL)* 'Twas at the Matin Hour. *Unknown.* OHIP

And so live ever — or else swoon to death. *(LL)* Bright Star! Would I Were Steadfast as Thou Art. Keats. ArLo; BLPL; CBLP; EnLoPo; GBL; GTBS; GTBS-P; HAP; ImPo; InPK; InPS; LiTB; MeMBP; NAEL-2; NAWM-2; NIP; OAEL-2; PoE; PPP; PrIm; SCV; Son; TrGrPo

And so must I lose her whose mind. Prothalamium. Donagh MacDonagh. BIrV

And so my wife taught me to say. *(LL)* Inscription in a Garden. George Gascoigne. TrGrPo

And so night after night, God, you come to me. Israel. Yitzhak Lamdan, *tr. fr. Hebrew by* Ruth Finer Mintz. MHP

And so Rome's soldier settles down. The Carthaginian Peace. Horace, *tr. fr. Latin. Fr.* Odes. MLL, *tr. by* Helen Waddell

And so she makes music wherever she goes. *(LL)* Ride a cock-horse [*or* a-cock horse] to Banbury Cross,/ To see a fine lady upon a white horse. Mother Goose. BoTP; FaBoBe; OxBoLi; OxNR

And so the commotion arose at the fair. *(LL)* The Fair at Windgap. Austin Clarke. OxBTC

And so the day beginning. A. J. Seymour. *Fr.* For Christopher Columbus. PBCV

And so the others were the first to leave. After the Party. Luigi Fontanella, *tr. fr. Italian by* W. S. Di Piero. NeIt

And so they all went home again. *(LL)* Three Young Rats. *Unknown.* ChTr; FaBoNo; InvP; OxBoLi; OxNR

And so they buried Lincoln? Strange and vain. Cenotaph of Lincoln. James Thompson McKay. OHIP

And so they lived; and so they died. *(LL)* Interred [*or* Interr'd] beneath this marble stone. Matthew Prior. FaBoEE; NAEL-1; OAEL-1; OBD; OBSV; PoEL-3

And so thirteen rounds out the show/ Lord, I'm done! *(LL)* Lord, I'm done for: now Margot. Vincent Voiture. FiBHP

And so to a chambre full solacious. Dame Music. Stephen Hawes. *Fr.* Pastime of Pleasure, The. PoEL-1

And so we meet again. The Blessing. Paula Gunn Allen. SRLS

And so we two *[or too]* came where the rest have come. The Question. F. T. Prince. BoLoP; GTBS-P; PeSA

And so when he reached my bed. Grand-Père. Robert W. Service. NSI

And so you found that poor room dull. Appearances. Robert Browning. OxBSP

And softened under the cold tap. *(LL)* Keeping Pacific Time. Aidan Carl Mathews. IB

And some chose trade they fared the better. The Entertainment Industry. William Langland. *Fr.* Vision of Piers Plowman, The. NOCV

And Somers has the turtle — turtle disagrees with him. *(LL)* Etiquette. W. S. Gilbert. FaBoCh; FaBoCo; FiBHP

And something else, but what I dare not name. *(LL)* On the Happy Corydon and Phyllis. *At. to* Sir Charles Sedley. BoLoP; CoMu; ErPo; FaBoBl

And something that . . . that is theirs — no longer ours. The Dispossessed. John Berryman. VGW

And sometimes I am sorry when the grass. Peace. Patrick Kavanagh. IIP

And sometimes I bring her a bottle of *Nuit d'Amour*. *(LL)* The Dover Bitch. Anthony Hecht. BXAP; MAT; NBLV; NIP; NOBA; NOBL; OBAL; PeLV; PPP; UnPo; VGW

And sometimes in the cool night I see you are an animal. Ode for Soft Voice. Michael McClure. NeAP

And soon divided and etymologised: Ho là. *(LL)* Christ-in-the-Woods. Sebastian Barry. IB

And sound thy praises everlastingly. *(LL)* For Inspiration. Michelangelo. WGRP

And sound will be my sleep. *(LL)* Sir Hugh; or, The Jew's Daughter. *Unknown.* AmFP; ESPB

And spare his golden bindings. *(LL)* The Book-Worms. Burns. ChTr; FaBoEE; FiBHP

And sped along without shadows. *(LL)* Iron Spike. Seamus Heaney. TRP

And spit whenever we wanted to. *(LL)* Mrs. Trollope in America. Helen Smith Bevington. NBLV; OBAL

And split the tomb. *(LL)* Advent. William Everson. NeAP; TrCP

And spoke: coopers, craftsmen, shepherds. Great God Paused among Men. Daniel Berrigan. MAT

And spoke the feeling for them, which was what they had lacked. *(LL)* Large Red Man Reading. Wallace Stevens. HAP; LCAP

And stand outside these nations and their noise. *(LL)* Braddan Vicarage. Thomas Edward Brown. FaBoPP

And start to die together. *(LL)* My Son, My Executioner. Donald Hall. CAPP; LPA; SM; TRP

And start a worm farm. *(LL)* Nobody Loses All the Time. E. E. Cummings. CMoP; DL; FaBoCo; FF; LiTM; NAAL-2; NBLV; NOBA; RB; TwCP

And started away in surprise. *(LL)* There was a young lady whose eyes. Edward Lear. EBEV

And stay by my cradle till morning is nigh. *(LL)* Away in a Manger. *At. to* Martin Luther. AH

And stayed His hand! *(LL)* What Thomas an Buile Said in a Pub. James Stephens. MoAB; MoBrPo; MoP; PoRA; TrGrPo; WGRP

And steal the bags to hold the crumbs. *(LL)* The Common Cormorant [or Shag]. Christopher Isherwood. ChTr; FaBoCh; FaBoCo; FaBoNo; FiBHP; NBLV; PYC

And steal their poems. *(LL)* I Am 25. Gregory Corso. PoBeRe

And Steinberg, who is off the wagon, by the way, and that insane woman who lives upstairs, and a few reporters, if anything should break. *(LL)* Love, 20 Cents the First Quarter Mile. Kenneth Fearing. HAP

And still, at sea all night, we had a sense. Samos. James Merrill. *Fr.* Scripts for the Pageant. HCAP

And still disappointment is a lucid madness. *(LL)* Double curtains hang deep in the room of Never Grieve. Li Shang-yin. PLT

And still dreams on. *(LL)* If I Had but Two Little Wings. Samuel Taylor Coleridge. BoTP; CH; OHIP

And still I lie here. Song of the Invisible Corpse in the Field. Gregory Orr. AnAn

And still I'm lying in my bed alone. *(LL)* Alone. Sappho. AWP

And still in Rome a pale-faced client be! *(LL)* Country Pleasures. Martial. AWP

And still it is a loom, simply. Spider. Judy Grahn. BCF

And still it seems to last. *(LL)* The Yawn of Yawns. Vasco *[or Vasko]* Popa. AnRep, *tr. by* Charles Simic; PoSu, *tr. by* Anne Pennington

And still no stronger. Swathed in rugs he lingered. A Day in August. Frank Ormsby. IIP; PBCIP; PNI

And still nothing happens. I am not arrested. Entry in an Unknown Hand. Franz Wright. NAmP90

And still our horses rustle like the rain. *(LL)* The Youth Dreams. Rainer Maria Rilke. TrJP

And still strong. *(LL)* The Lonely Land. A. J. M. Smith. NOBC

And still the sea is salt. *(LL)* Stars, I Have Seen Them Fall. A. E. Housman. ChTr; NoP; OxBSP

And still the sun rosies the fronts of houses. Evening of the Whirlwind. Amir Gilboa, *tr. fr. Hebrew by* Ruth Finer Mintz. MHP

And still they come and go: and this is all I know. Picture-Show. Siegfried Sassoon. CMoP; NSI

And still, thro' mercy, may enjoy the smell! *(LL)* The Adventures of Simon Swaugum, a Village Merchant. Philip Freneau. PoEL-4

And still thy white-wing's angels hover dimly in our air. *(LL)* The Angels of Buena Vista. Whittier. BeLS; PAH

And still we wear our uniforms, follow. The Progress. Gwendolyn Brooks. WoWa

And still you lie. We Can Try Again Another Day. Judith Kazantzis. DT

And Stoic independence of mankind. *(LL)* The Filbert. Robert Southey. FM

And straight I called unto mind that it was Christmas Day. *(LL)* The Burning Babe. Robert Southwell. CH; EIL; ESCV; FaBoCh; HAP; HeIP; InPS; LiTB; NAEL-1; NAs; NOBE; NOCV; NoP; NoSic; OAEL-1; OBCP; OBEV; OxAEP-1; PoEL-2; Prf; RB; SCGP; TFi; TOF; TrCP; TrGrPo; TRP

And striking Folly blind. *(LL)* Behold a Wonder Here! *Unknown.* TrGrPo

And stroked all night, with black wing, my wings. *(LL)* The Black Swan. Randall Jarrell. CAPP; CMoP; PoE

And struck the white dove dead. *(LL)* The Dove. Victor James Daley. NOBAu

And such beginnings touch their E N D. *(LL)* Paradise. George Herbert. AngWe; GeHe; ImPo; NOSC; OAEL-1; SeCP; TrGrPo

And suddenly, all turns gray. Gray Moment. Momcilo Nastasijevic, *tr. fr. Serbo-Croatian by* Charles Simic. HSix

And suddenly, and all at once, the rain! *(LL)* Memorial Rain. Archibald MacLeish. AmPP; CMoP; LiTA; MeMAP; MoAB; MoAmPo; OBWP

And Summer mornings the mute child, rebellious. Eleven. Archibald MacLeish. HAP; MeMAP; WeW

And summer turns her head with its dark tangle. Ralegh's Prizes. Robert Pinsky. DiPo; VCAP

And Sunday Morning. Christian McEwen. VBLP

And, sure of Heaven, rides triumphing in. *(LL)* An Elegie on the Lady Jane Pawlet, Marchion: of Winton. Ben Jonson. SeCP

And sustains all life. *(LL)* Water flows from high in the mountains. Thich Nhat Hanh. EaPr

And sweter be the birdin that hangis upon thee. *(LL)* Stedefast *[or Steddefast or Steadfast]* cross[e], inmong *[or among]* alle *[or all]* other. Venantius Fortunatus. MiEL

And swinges the scaly horror of his folded tail. *(LL)* Lizards and Snakes. Anthony Hecht. FaBoMo; TwCP

And swollow you outright. *(LL)* The Cummerbund. Edward Lear. OBTV

And 't was *Jupiter and Io!*. *(LL)* Jupiter and Ten. James Thomas Fields. AnAmPo; OBAL

And take a lesson from this tale of the Spider and the Fly. *(LL)* The Spider and the Fly. Mary Howitt. BeLS; FaPON; OTCP; OxBChV; PWR; UV; WGRP

And take a life immortal from my verse. *(LL)* To the Reverend Shade of His Religious Father. Robert Herrick. CaPo; JCP; SeCV-1

And take short verses. *(LL)* Under Which Lyre, a Reactionary Tract for the Times. W. H. Auden. MoAB; MoBrPo; NOBL; PeLV

And take their walks across the ceiling. *(LL)* The Folk Who Live in Backward Town. Mary Ann Hoberman. OBCA; SiSoPo

And take thy Rest. *(LL)* On This Day I Complete My Thirty-sixth Year. Byron. EnRP; FHYEP; MeMBP; NAs; NoP; OAEL-2; OBWP; PoE

And take up his cold hands. *(LL)* The Legend. Garrett Kaoru Hongo. NAmP90; OpBo; TRP

And take up my place again under my eyelids. *(LL)* The Lover. Solveig von Schoultz. VBLP

And taking the moon and leaving the paper dark. *(LL)* The Prediction. Mark Strand. LCAP; VCAP

And talk back to the time of the night rains on Mount Pa? *(LL)* Night Rains: to my Wife up North. Li Shang-yin. PLT

And tamed the Chaldean lions, is mighty still to save! *(LL)* Cassandra Southwick. Whittier. AnAmPo; PAH

And tamn ta whusky duty! *(LL)* The Massacre of the Macpherson. William Edmonstoune Aytoun. BXAP; ChTr; FaBoCo; OtMeF

And taught his gorgon destinies to sing. *(LL)* Luis de Camões. Roy Campbell. FaBoTw; OxAEP-2; PeSA

And tell stories. *(LL)* Let the trees be consulted. John Wright. EaPr

And tell why I have chosen thee! (*LL*) Plead for Me. Emily Brontë. MeMBP; PoEL-5

And tells the jest without the smile. (*LL*) Youth and Age. Samuel Taylor Coleridge. BLPL; EnRP; GTBS; GTBS-P; OBEV; OBNC; PoLF

And thank him than. (*LL*) Pleasure It Is. William Cornish. CH; MeEL

And thanks grandmother! (*LL*) Let the Bird of Earth, Fly! Meridel LeSueur. SRLS

And that conniving cold. (*LL*) Piccola Commedia. Richard Wilbur. PRA

And that dark other mountain. (*LL*) That Dark Other Mountain. Robert Francis. CRP

And that drums had to be rolling, rolling, rolling. (*LL*) Dry Loaf. Wallace Stevens. MeMAP; NOBA; OxBA; PoRA; RaBo

And that ended the comedy. (*LL*) The Donkey and the Lapdog. La Fontaine. OBVE

And that gentle bard. Gentle Spenser. Wordsworth. *Fr.* Prelude [or, Growth of a Poet's Mind], The. EnRP; EPCY; FaBoPP; HAP; OAEL-2; OxAEP-2, *abr.*

And that has made all the difference. (*LL*) The Road Not Taken. Robert Frost. AiP; AmPP; ChTr; CMoP; EBEvV; FaBoCh; FaPoB; HAP; HeIP; ImPo; LiTA; LiTM; MeMAP; MoAB; MoAmPo; MoP; NAAL-2; NIP; NoAM; NoP; NTP; OxBA; Poetr; PoLF; RFM; SAmP; SoSe; TAP; TFi; TRP; TwCP

And that he has gone away for ever and ever. (*LL*) Now I Do Believe. B. W. Vilakazi. PeSAV

And that is how I came to know. (*LL*) The Duel. Eugene Field. BeLS; FaBoBe; FaPON; MoShBr; OBAL; OBCA; PoLF; PoRA; TFi

And that is life! (*LL*) Life. Paul Laurence Dunbar. AnAmPo; CDC

And that is the only worship of God there is. (*LL*) Wherever you are is home. Wilfred Pelletier *and* Ted Poole. EaPr

And that it's the others who scar me/ not you. (*LL*) The Girl I Call Alma. Linda Gregg. AmPA; AnAn

And that pale sustenance,/ Despair! (*LL*) I cannot live with you. Emily Dickinson. AmPP; MAT; MoAB; MoAmPo; NAAL-1; NOBA; NoP; OxBA; PoEL-5; TRP

And that stands all awry. (*LL*) Peter White will ne'er go right. Mother Goose. OxBoLi; OxNR

And that the same last eddy swallows up. (*LL*) The Orchard-Pit. Dante Gabriel Rossetti. EnLoPo; NAEL-2; OAEL-2; PeVV; PoEL-5; SCV

And that was the end of the monk. (*LL*) Animal Fair. *Unknown.* AS; BLPA; FaBoBe; MoShBr; NTCP; RoPo

And that water these words what can they do what can they do prince. (*LL*) Elegy of Fortinbras. Zbigniew Herbert. FaBoPV; PoSu

And that year. 1945. Bernard S. Mikofsky. BTR

And that, you can be sure, we will survive. (*LL*) Survival. Robin Morgan. VBLP

And that you had it all along. (*LL*) Tulips: A Selected History. Vickie Karp. UTF

And that You'll stand beside us to the last. (*LL*) Christ in Flanders. Lucy Whitmell. NSI

And that's all that you'll be underground. (*LL*) God, A Poem. James Fenton. DiPo; NoAM

And that's how people burn to death in hotel rooms. (*LL*) Life Story. Tennessee Williams. GLP; PeHV

And that's the end of my little pig tale. (*LL*) A Pig Tale. James Reeves. SiSoPo

And that's the end of my song. (*LL*) The Monkey's Wedding. *Unknown.* AS; BLPA

And that's the part to be acted. (*LL*) Up Tails All. Robert Herrick. BeJo

And that's the way they captured him — the wild Colonial boy. (*LL*) The Wild Colonial Boy. *Unknown.* FaBoBa

And that's to keep thy Lent. (*LL*) To Keep a True Lent. Robert Herrick. TrCP

And that's why I'm going to Tilbury Town. (*LL*) John Evereldown. E. A. Robinson. AnAmPo; CMoP; MeMAP; OxBA

And thaws it before the flames. (*LL*) Twenty Below. R. A. D. Ford. NOBC

And the Age Ended. W. H. Auden. *Fr.* In Time of War. Son

And the Americans put Pound in a cage. The Cage. John Berryman. PoA

And the angel, taking some pains, told. Joseph's Suspicion. Rainer Maria Rilke, *tr. fr. German by* J. B. Leishman. TrCP

And the Angels said, 'My! But that was near!' (*LL*) The Fir-Tree of Bosnia. Dante Gabriel Rossetti. FaBoNo

And the apple-blossom is allowed to wither on the bough. (*LL*) Swineherd. Eiléan Ní Chuilleanáin. BIrV; CIP; FaBoWP; WPOW

And the arrogance of lucky races. (*LL*) The Totem. Léopold Sédar Senghor. NegPo

And the back that wears it. (*LL*) The Militance of a Photograph in the Passbook of a Bantu under Detention. Michael S. Harper. VCAP

And the barber kept on shaving. (*LL*) The Owl-Critic. James Thomas Fields. BLPA; OBAL; WBLP

And the *Beacon Light*. (*LL*) A Landing. Aidan Carl Mathews. IB

And the Beatles' first LP. (*LL*) Annus Mirabilis. Philip Larkin. NBLV; NIP; NOBL; OBAL

And the beautiful bride is crying. (*LL*) In the Castle. Joseph Freiherr von Eichendorff. RiWo

And the beetle drones his horn. (*LL*) The Field Mouse. "Fiona Macleod." FaPON; MoShBr

And the best will come back to you. (*LL*) Life's Mirror. "Madeline Bridges." BLPA; FaBoBe; PoToHe; PWR; WBLP

And the bewilder'd chimes. (*LL*) The Fountain. Wordsworth. EnRP; GTBS; GTBS-P; OxAEP-2

And the Bishop said: "The ways of God are strange!" (*LL*) They. Siegfried Sassoon. CMoP; IHNG; NAEL-2; OBSV; OBWP

And the bitter storm augments; the wild winds wage. John Josselyn. SCAP

And the Black Prince goes whimpering to bed. (*LL*) Feigned Courage. Charles Lamb *and* Mary Lamb. GN; OxBChV

And the blackberries a-growing. (*LL*) What's the Railroad to Me? Thoreau. PoEL-4; TAP

And the blood is black upon the unturned leaves. (*LL*) The Soldier Walks under the Trees of the University. Randall Jarrell. OxBA

And the body beginning to swell. (*LL*) Mountain Bride. Robert Morgan. MT

And the Bow was gone. (*LL*) The Rainbow. Walter de la Mare. NTP

And the boy who was half-past three. (*LL*) One, Two, Three. H. C. Bunner. FaPON; PoLF

And the bright oar and the oar spray. (*LL*) Aegean. Louis Simpson. GrPl; NYBP

And the buffaloes are gone. (*LL*) Buffalo Dusk. Carl Sandburg. GOA; OBAP; OBCA; PDV; RFM; SiSoPo

And the bugles that do shine. (*LL*) A New Year Carol. *Unknown.* BoTP; CH; OxBoLi

And the child draws another inscrutable house. (*LL*) September rain falls on the house. Elizabeth Bishop. InPK; LCAP; NoP; PFP; PoE; Poetr; SM

And the Cock Begins to Crow. Richard K. Avery. AH

And the colours have all passed away from her eyes! (*LL*) The Reverie of Poor Susan. Wordsworth. CoGr; EnRP; GTBS; GTBS-P; OxBoLi; WiR

And the Communists have nothing to offer but fat cheeks and eyeglasses and lying policemen. Kral Majales. Allen Ginsberg. PoM

And the compass/ idea/ being/ city/ interim. Compass Poem. Bill Griffiths. NBrP

And the crew of the captain's gig! (*LL*) The Yarn of the *Nancy Bell*. W. S. Gilbert. BeLS; BLPA; EBEvV; EBNV; FaBoBe; FaBoCh; FaBoCo; FaBV; HoPM; MoShBr; NOBL; TFi; TrGrPo; UV, *sh. vers.*

And the Cycles wheel! (*LL*) Just lost, when I was saved! Emily Dickinson. AmPP; NOBA; NOCV; Prf

And the day it 's well return'd again. (*LL*) The Fire of Frendraught. *Unknown.* ESPB; OxBB

And the day the theme was camouflage. (*LL*) A Surrey Morning. Matthew Sweeney. IB

And the Days Are Not Full Enough. Ezra Pound. ArNa; RB; Spl

And the dead begin from their dark to sing in my sleep. (*LL*) Journey to the Interior. Theodore Roethke. LCAP; NYBP; TRP; VGW

And the deep river ran on. (*LL*) As I Walked Out One Evening. W. H. Auden. CBNP; FF; HeIP; InPK; LiTM; NoAM; NOBE; NoP; OxAEP-2; PAW; PrIm; RB; TwCP; UnPo

And the dish ran away with the spoon. (*LL*) Hey [*or* Sing hey], diddle, diddle,/ The cat and the fiddle. Mother Goose. FaBoBe; HoPM; OxBoLi; OxNR

And the donkey is he who can't see the. (*LL*) An Arab and His Donkey. *Unknown.* NBLV

And the dying Negro to moan. (*LL*) Southern Cop. Sterling A. Brown. SoSe

And the earth begins at our heads. (*LL*) Desert. Linda Hogan. SRLS

And the Earth grow young again. (*LL*) Lines Written among the Euganean Hills. Shelley. EnRP; GTBS; GTBS-P; PoEL-4

And the Earth Rebelled. Yuri Suhl, *tr. fr. Yiddish by* Max Rosenfeld. BTR; TrJP

And "the earth under our feet." At Kenneth Burke's Place. William Carlos Williams. NOBA

And the enduring soul holds out. (*LL*) Christine to Her Son. Christine de Pisan. BoWoP

And the euphorbia. December 1974: a Lament. Abdur-Rahman Slade Hopkinson. PBCV

And the façade that we are; this year before it ends. (*LL*) This Year, before It Ends. Eve Langley. NOBAu

And the first murderer lay upon the earth. (*LL*) Imperial Adam. A. D. Hope. CBAP; ChIV-1; ErPo; HAP; NIP; NoAM; NoP

And the first music heard among the trees. (LL) Panope. Edith Sitwell. MoAB; MoBrPo

And the first time I saw him. Jocasta. Janet Fisher. NWP

And the five wounds our Lord did bear. (LL) The Rising in the North. Unknown. ESPB

And the founderig shriek of the gale. (LL) Wild Iron. Allen Curnow. NTP; RB

And the fresh-severed head of it, my head. (LL) The Show. Wilfred Owen. ImPo; LiTB; LiTM; MoAB; MoBrPo; NSI; OBWVE; OxBTC; PeFWW

And the fret lies on me. (LL) The Lamentation of the Old Pensioner. W. B. Yeats. HAP; InPK; NoAM; TRP; WeW

And the general view. (LL) Lady "Rogue" Singleton. Stevie Smith. FaBoWP; OxBSP

And the gentle sounding flute. (LL) My Master Hath a Garden. Unknown. CH; CoGr

And the girls are gone. (LL) The Moving Occupations. Wayne Koestenbaum. UTF

And the girls as sweet as candy. (LL) My Pretty [Little] Pink. Unknown. AmFP; AS

And the glimmering Spirit I kissed in the gloom beside me. (LL) Marriage. W. J. Turner. NOBAu

And the gods shook, they knew not why. (LL) Uriel. Emerson. LiTA; NAAL-1; NOBA; OxBA

And the good that I can do. (LL) What I Live For. George Linnaeus Banks. BLPA; FaBoBe; WBLP

And the graduates can't stand the college-trained staff. Lucky Eugene. Michael Foley. PNI

And the grass on the mountains. (LL) The Grass on the Mountain. Unknown. AWP; FaPON; GOA

And the Greek legends and Andersen. (LL) The Barn-yard. Sheila Cussons. PeSAV

And the green grass growing over me. (LL) The King's Dochter Lady Jean. Unknown. AmFP; ESPB

And the green leaves they grow rarely. (LL) The Cruel Mother. Unknown. AmFP; ESPB, A, B, C, and P vers.; FaBoBa; InPK; OBET; OxBB

And the green silent pastures, yet remain. (LL) Composed at Neidpath Castle, the Property of Lord Queensberry, 1803. Wordsworth. GTBS; GTBS-P

And the ground spoke when she was born. For Alva Benson, and for Those Who Have Learned to Speak. Joy Harjo. HATNAP

And the Haggards Ride no more. (LL) To R. K. James Kenneth Stephen. BXAP; FaBoCo; FaBoEE; FaBoPa; NBLV; NOBL; OtMeF; PeLV; UV

And the harbor's eyes. (LL) Lost. Carl Sandburg. AmPP; CMoP; PDV

And the heat weighs a dreamy load. (LL) A Half-Way Pause. Dante Gabriel Rossetti. NOBVV

And the heavy rain to follow. (LL) Chimes. Dante Gabriel Rossetti. OBNC

And the hills of Ise. (LL) The Snow Party. Derek Mahon. CIP; FaBoPV; OxBC; PBCIP; PNI; SCBI

And the horn may now paw the air howling goodbye. Elegy for Alto. Christopher Okigbo. HBAPE

And the hunter home from the hill. (LL) Under the wide and starry sky. Robert Louis Stevenson. CoGr; DL; EBVV; FaBV; FaPoR; MoBrPo; NBLV; NOBE; NOBVV; OBD; OBEV; OBNC; OHCV; PoLF; PoRA; TrGrPo; WGRP

And the immodest thigh. (LL) The Man Who Married Magdalene. Louis Simpson. MoP; NoAM; SM; TAP

And the jails are too small, sweaty AND STINK! (LL) Fud at Foster's. Philip Lamantia. PoBeRe

And the king o' England's brither. (LL) The Knight and Shepherd's Daughter. Unknown. ESPB

And the King was well and gay. (LL) The Enchanted Shirt. John Milton Hay. BLPA; GN; VPP

And the kings began to sing. (LL) The Wise Men Ask the Children the Way. Heine. OBCP

And the ladies dress in silk. On the High Cost of Dairy Products. James McIntyre. FiBHP

And the lanes half shadow. (LL) A Frisky Lamb. Christina Rossetti. BoTP; WHSW

And the last buds cease blowing. (LL) Bitter for Sweet. Christina Rossetti. GBL

And the leaves have begun to fall. (LL) In its going down, the moon. Robert Hoggra. MoCV

And the light, a wakened heyday of air. November Sunday Morning. Alvin Feinman. CoAP

And the light that fills the world. (LL) And I thought over again. Unknown. EaPr

And the lips like pomegranate blossoms. (LL) Red Sandalwood Mouth. Chao Luan-luan. WPC

And the lips that touch liquor shall never touch mine. (LL) The Lips That Touch Liquor Shall Never Touch Mine. Harriet A. Glazebrook. VPP

And the little cloud blushed in the vast sky. (LL) The Sky Is Vast. Pramila Khadun. TSaS

And the little shoes died. (LL) The Little Shoes That Died. Mary Gilmore. NOBAu

And the little space their fathers leave round them. (LL) The Young. Sebastian Barry. IB

And the Lord God planted a garden eastward in Eden. Bible, O.T. Fr. Genesis. OAEL-1

And the Lord God said: 'Behold, the man is become as one of us.' A Little Knowledge. Bible, O.T. Fr. Genesis. LPA

And the love, whatever it was, an infection. (LL) Wanting to Die. Anne Sexton. IHMS; MoP; NoAM; TAP; TRP; VCAP

And the maidens who were promised still await the absent Smith. (LL) The Smiths. E. G. Murphy. NOBAu

And the message of the yew tree is blackness — blackness and silence. (LL) The Moon and the Yew Tree. Sylvia Plath. CoAP; FaBoMo; FaBoWP; NaP; NYBP; PlP; PPP; VGW; WPE; WPOW

And the midnight message of Paul Revere. (LL) Paul Revere's Ride (The Landlord's Tale). Longfellow. AiP; AnAmPo; BeLS; BLPA; EBEvV; EBNV; FaBoBe; FaBoTw; FaBV; FaPON; FaPoR; ImGa; OBAL; OBCA; OBNV; PAH; PWR; TFi; TrGrPo; WBLP

And the miracle of birth. (LL) To be of the Earth is to know. John Soos. EaPr

And the mist: and the rain in the west: and the wind steady. The Omelet of A MacLeish. Edmund Wilson. NYBP

And the mistaken child that shall not know her father's twisting paths. (LL) To Tarshish. Shimon Halkin. MHP

And the mole crept along the garden. Terraces of Rain. David St. John. NAmP90

And the moss on the shore burning red. (LL) In the Home of the Scholar Wu Su-chiang. Wu Tsao. BoWoP; WPC; WPOW

And the mother, closing the exercise book. Poets Seven Years Old. Rimbaud, tr. fr. French by Kenneth Koch and Georges Guy. SOTW

And the musick shall be praise. (LL) Dooms-Day. George Herbert. GeHe; JCP; OBD; SeCP; SeCV-1

And the name of the man was Elimelech. Bible, O.T. Fr. Ruth. OBF

And the need of a world of men for me. (LL) Parting at Morning. Robert Browning. AWP; EBEvV; EnVR; FaBV; FF; FHYEP; HeIP; ImPo; InPS; NAEL-2; NOBE; OBEV; OBNC; OHCV; OxBSP; PFP; SCGP; SoSe; TFi; UnPo; WiR

And the new gospel verifies the old. (LL) Adjustment. Whittier. WGRP

And the next day begins. Louis MacNeice. Fr. Autumn Journal. FaBoEH

And the night gets sassy again. October 21st, 9 P.M. (Autumn She Don't Waste no Time!). Carmen Tafolla. ETG

And the night passes — and never passes. (LL) A Goodnight. William Carlos Williams. MoAB; MoAmPo

And the old days never will come again. (LL) Adieu, the years are a broken song. Unknown. NOBAu

And the old river rolls on, slowly to the gulf. (LL) Foreclosure. Sterling A. Brown. PoBA; PoNe

And the Old Women Gathered. Mari Evans. BlSi; PoBA

And the ones that got tough. The Inheritors. William Peskett. PNI

And the overseer's bravado as he swaggered it to heaven. (LL) The Black Man's Lament. Léon Damas. NegPo

And the pain you are causing to me? (LL) Red River Valley. Unknown. AS; FaBoBe

And the past. (LL) So you have swept me back. Hilda Doolittle ("H. D."). NALW; VBLP; VGW

And the people are sad. (LL) Gubbinal. Wallace Stevens. NAAL-2; SOTW

And the People's liberty! (LL) Life of Ages, Richly Poured. Samuel Johnson. AH

And the pig got up and slowly walked away. (LL) Judged by the Company One Keeps. Unknown. BLPA; NBLV

And the pimpernel muddles his head. (LL) Come into the orchard, Anne. Swinburne. FaBoNo; UV

And the pins stuck in the wrong way. (LL) There Were Three Jovial Welshmen. Unknown. AngWe; CBNP

And the place of their waiting a long burrow. David Jones. Fr. In Parenthesis. FaBoMo

And the point in the spectrum. Hilda Doolittle ("H. D."). Fr. Tribute to the Angels. NALW

And the poor have all the money. (LL) Tony O! Colin Francis. CH; CoGr; FaBoCo

And the poor, when they're old, have little of peace! (LL) To the Four Courts, Please. James Stephens. BIrV; MoAB; MoBrPo; UnPo

And the pump has frozen tonight. (*LL*) Star-Talk. Robert Graves. BoNaP; GoJo; MoBrPo; OxBTC

And the Queen Anne's lace! (*LL*) Portrait by a Neighbor. Edna St. Vincent Millay. FaPON; MoShBr; OBCA; PDV

And the quiet of love in her feet. (*LL*) The Cap and Bells. W. B. Yeats. ChTr; MoAB; MoBrPo; NoAM; NoP; OtMeF; RB

And the reconstruction of the mind. (*LL*) Planetarium. Adrienne Rich. CAPP; FaBoWP; HCAP; MoP; NAAL-2; NALW; NIP; NoAM; NOBA; Poetr; VCAP

And the red glare on Skiddaw rouse the burghers of Carlisle. (*LL*) The Armada. Macaulay. BeLS; CoGr; FaBoCh; FaBoEH; FaPoR; GN; WBLP

And the rich He hath sent empty away. (*LL*) Our Lady. Mary Elizabeth Coleridge. OBEV; OBMV; WPE

And the roads deep in snow? (*LL*) First Death in Nova Scotia. Elizabeth Bishop. CoAP; FaBoWP; LCAP; NOBA; NYBP

And the rocks they melt by the heat of the sun. (*LL*) The Grey Cock. *Unknown*. ELP; OBET

And the rose wrapped round the briar. (*LL*) Barbara Allen's Cruelty ("All in the merry month of May.") *Unknown*. FaBoBe

And the ruler of the earth the rhinoceros/ Or us. (*LL*) We chant and enchant. Velimir Khlebnikov. CBNP

And the Same Words. David Ignatow. NNaP

And the sawbones will say 'Old One-Finger's dead.' (*LL*) Hallelujah, I'm a Bum. *Unknown*. AS; SWP

And the Scream. Stephen Berg. NAmP90

And the sea that bangs in my throat. (*LL*) The Room of My Life. Anne Sexton. VCAP

And the sea, the moving sea, the sea. / God is cold. (*LL*) A Man Adrift on a Slim Spar. Stephen Crane. NAAL-2

And the sea where it goes. (*LL*) The Buried Life. Matthew Arnold. CBLP; EnVR; FHYEP; MeMBP; NAEL-2; OAEL-2

And the secret names. I Learned That Her Name Was Proverb. Denise Levertov. CrSp

And the separate dictionaries of our heads. (*LL*) After Babel. Peter Goldsworthy. NOBAu

And the sharing of other forms of life. (*LL*) We venerate the Three Treasures. *Unknown*. EaPr

And the shielding tree. (*LL*) Hey! Lean to hear my feeble voice. Black Elk. EaPr

And the short quick quench of the sea. (*LL*) The Raid. William Everson. ArOW; MoP; NoAM; PrIm

And the single pool of the ocean has drained into a cup. (*LL*) A Dream of Heaven. Li Ho. PLT

And the skies were aglow with stars. (*LL*) Over the Steppe. Aleksei Nikolayevich Pleshcheyev. RiWo

And the skyline of hills, after millions of hard year,/ Sitting soft. (*LL*) Ravens. Ted Hughes. InPS; NAs

And the smile on the face of the Tiger. (*LL*) There Was a Young Lady of Niger. *At*. *to* Cosmo Monkhouse. FaPON; InvP; NBLV; PDV; TLR

And the soldiers with their guns. (*LL*) Carrickfergus. Louis MacNeice. FaBoPP; NAEL-2; NoAM; NOIV; PNI

And the soul creeps out of the tree. (*LL*) All Hallows. Louise Glück. AmPA; FoLa; HCAP; NU

And the spinners backward go. (*LL*) The Ropewalk. Longfellow. MeMAP

And the spirit within it /Is gone. (*LL*) Me. Walter de la Mare. FaPON

And the square I live in, measured out with lime. (*LL*) Prothalamion. Maxine W. Kumin. NYBP

And the Squire, and Lady Susan, murmur mildly to me now. (*LL*) Friends Beyond. Thomas Hardy. CoGr; EBVV; FaBoRV; FaBoVe; GTBS-P; NOBVV; OBEV

And the stars going round in my head. (*LL*) Escape at Bedtime. Robert Louis Stevenson. OTCP; TrGrPo

And the storm has ceased to blow. (*LL*) Ye Mariners of England. Thomas Campbell. BLPA; EBEvV; EnRP; FaPoR; GN; GTBS; GTBS-P; NOBE; OBEV; OBWP; OxAEP-2; PAW; PIP

And the streams here, ledge to ledge. Lights among Redwood. Thom Gunn. OBTV

And the strutting ferm lay seeds on the black sill. (*LL*) After the Funeral. Dylan Thomas. AngWe; CMoP; FaBoMo; MeMBP; NAEL-2; NoP; OAEL-2; OBWVE; OxAEP-2

And the stuff I love: slub silk. (*LL*) La Toilette. Seamus Heaney. CBLP

And the style of your prose growing limper and limper. (*LL*) Academic. Theodore Roethke. FaBoEE; OBAL

And the has drunk the perspiration of my blood. (*LL*) Marie Galante. Guy Tirolien. NegPo

And the sun wields mercy. The Sun Wields Mercy. Charles Bukowski. MAT

And the sweet name to my mouth. (*LL*) Italia, Io Ti Saluto. Christina Rossetti. CoGr; OBTV; WPE

And the taste on my lips of bitter mold. (*LL*) Dialogue. Leah Goldberg. MHP

And the tears of the women fall on the doilies. (*LL*) Duchesses. David Campbell. NOBAu

And the things we have seen and have known and have heard of fail us. (*LL*) On a Dead Child. Robert Bridges. CMoP; EBEV; LiTB; LiTM; NoAM; NOBE; NOBVV; OBMV; OBNC; OxAEP-2; SCGP

And the thoughts of youth are long, long thoughts. (*LL*) My Lost Youth. Longfellow. AmPP; AnAmPo; AWP; FaBoBe; FaBV; FaPoR; GoJo; ImGa; LiTA; MeMAP; NAAL-1; NOBA; OBEV; OxBA; PoEL-5; PoLF; PoRA; TAP; TFi

And the tide rises, the tide falls. (*LL*) The Tide Rises, the Tide Falls. Longfellow. AmPP; BLPL; ChTr; ImPo; MeMAP; NOBA; OxBA; PoE; PoRA; TAP

And the tither is a bonny brier. (*LL*) Fair Janet. *Unknown*. ESPB; OxBB

And the tootle, tootle, tooting of its toot. (*LL*) The Amateur Flute. *Unknown*. BXAP

And the top of the morning. (*LL*) Sun has climbed the hill, the day is on the downward slope, The. D. H. Lawrence. EaPr

And the trains that go from Rouen at the ending of the day. (*LL*) Rouen. May Wedderburn Cannan. NAEL-2; OBWP; OxBTC

And the traveller hopes: let me be far from any. Journey to Iceland. W. H. Auden. PoA

And the trees in the rain. (*LL*) Returned American. Kathleen Cain. LoHo

And the trunk: "So sweet those words to me that I." Pier delle Vigne. Dante, *tr*. by John Ciardi. *Fr*. Divina Commedia. HoPM; MeMAP; NAWM-1, *tr*. by John Ciardi

And the truth wailing there like a red babe. (*LL*) If I Could Only Live at the Pitch That Is near Madness. Richard Eberhart. FF; LiTM; MAT; MoAB

And the unknown world. One life, or the faring stars. (*LL*) Now Green, Now Burning. Muriel Rukeyser. LPA

And the Vietnamese boat-people of Portadown. (*LL*) Home. Frank Ormsby. PBCIP; PNI

And the visions too real to see. (*LL*) The Visions. Sebastian Barry. IB

And the voice in my dreaming ear melted away. (*LL*) The Soldier's Dream. Thomas Campbell. BeLS; EnRP; FaPoR; GTBS; GTBS-P; OxAEP-2; PIP

And the voice said: Walk. Little Falls. Robert Hogg. MoCV

And the vulture hath bidden them all to the feast! (*LL*) The Caffer Commando. Thomas Pringle. PeSAV

And the waves flowed above him, and he died. (*LL*) The Death of Cuchulain. W. B. Yeats. ChTr

And the way goes on in the worn earth. Archibald MacLeish. *Fr*. Conquistador. NoAM

And the whole deck put on its leaves again. (*LL*) The Old Ships. James Elroy Flecker. CH; CoGr; FaBoRV; MoBrPo; OBMV; OtMeF; PoRA

And the whole earth was of one language, and of one speech. Bible, *O.T.* *Fr*. Genesis. NAWM-1

And the Whole heart of man. (*LL*) The Landscape of the Heart. Geoffrey Grigson. LiTB

And the wife's face, with or without tears. (*LL*) Adam's Commentary After the Fall. Aidan Carl Mathews. IB

And the wild sheets. O to your bed! (*LL*) Spring. Paul Verlaine. ErPo; PeHV

And the winds be all asleep. (*LL*) The Sheep and the Goat. George Macdonald. EBVV

And the winter called it a dreadful crime. (*LL*) Soft Snow. Blake. FF; SoSe; TEP

And the woman calling. (*LL*) The Voice. Thomas Hardy. BoLoP; CBLP; CMoP; EnLoPo; GBL; GTBS-P; HAP; InPS; MoP; NAEL-2; NoAM; NoP; OAEL-2; OBNC; OxAEP-2; PFP; PoE; PoEL-5; Poetr; TFi

And the woman made for man. (*LL*) Man, Man, Man. *Unknown*. ErPo

And the women warbled: Nothing like us ever was. (*LL*) Four Preludes on Playthings of the Wind. Carl Sandburg. CMoP; MoAB; MoAmPo; NOBA

And the word still is Forward! along the whole line. (*LL*) Kearny at Seven Pines. Edmund Clarence Stedman. AnAmPo; PAH

And the world is destroyed. (*LL*) From All Sides Laughter Shall Strike Them. Amir Gilboa. MHP

And the world is waved away. (*LL*) The Calyx of the Oboe Breaks. Conrad Aiken. NYBP

And the world's danger. (*LL*) I Saw a Stable. Mary Elizabeth Coleridge. ChIV-2; OBCP; OxBSP; PChr

And the young ones picked the bones, oh. (*LL*) The Fox. *Unknown*. OxNR

And thee returning on thy silver wheels. (*LL*) Tithonus. Tennyson. EnVR; HAP; ImPo; LiTB; MeMBP; NAEL-2; NAWM-2; NOBE; NOBVV; NoP; OAEL-2; OBNC; PoE; PoEL-5; PPP; SCGP; TEP

And Thee, the spirit of them all! *(LL)* To the [*or* a] Highland Girl of Inversneyde. Wordsworth. EnRP; GTBS; GTBS-P

And theekit it o'er wi' rashes. *(LL)* Bessy [*or* Bessie] Bell and Mary Gray. *Unknown.* ESPB; OxBB; ScCV

And their built or driven nests. *(LL)* The Hill Wife. Robert Frost. CMoP; HAP; InPS; LiTM; NoP

And their Earth to Earth again. *(LL)* Epitaph of Pyramus and Thisbe. Abraham Cowley. EnLoPo; FaBoEE

And their eyes are burning. *(LL)* O What Is That Sound [Which So Thrills the Ear]. W. H. Auden. FaBoPV; LiTB; MeMAP; PoE

And their judges spoke with one dialect. Tom Leonard. *Fr.* Situations Theoretical and Contemporary. NBrP

And their snuff-laden breath blowing lightly over me in my first sleep. *(LL)* Frau Bauman, Frau Schmidt, and Frau Schwartze. Theodore Roethke. CoAP; MoAB; MoP; NAAL-2; NoAM; NOBA; NYBP; TAP

And their tongues are teasing oil from whales. *(LL)* The Lady in Kicking Horse Reservoir. Richard Hugo. CoAP; LCAP; NAAL-2; NoAM; NoP; VCAP

And then Accept My Prayers. *(LL)* Assist me while I wander here. Caroline Codling. FaBoVe

And then all that has divided us will merge. Judy Chicago. CrSp

And then (and only then) did Aaron laugh. *(LL)* Aaron Stark. E. A. Robinson. MeMAP; MoAB; MoAmPo; Son

And then? Colors and names of colors. No Way of Knowing. John Ashbery. AnAn

And then forever to be gone. *(LL)* The Falling Star. Sara Teasdale. MoShBr; OBCA; PDV

And then he loved her very well. *(LL)* Peter, Peter, pumpkin eater. Mother Goose. FaBoBe; OxNR

And then he would lift this finest. Out-of-the-Body Travel. Stanley Plumly. AmPA; LCAP

And then I pressed the shell. The Shell. James Stephens. BoNaP; BoTP; CH; CMoP; MoAB; MoBrPo; MoShBr

And then I sat me down, and gave the rein. Gustav Rosenhane, *tr. fr. Swedish by* Sir Edmund Gosse. AWP

And then I saw through the swirling. *(LL)* The Gap in the Cedar. Roy Scheele. Poetsp; SM

And then i see the cattle of my own town. My Dream About the Cows. Lucille Clifton. TRP

And then I was in love. *(LL)* Once Did My Thoughts. *Unknown.* EBEV; ELP

And then I'll see my dearie! *(LL)* Cam' Ye By [the Salmon Fishers]. *Unknown.* CH; GBP

And Then It Rained. Mark Van Doren. BoNaP

And then it's all up with the fly. *(LL)* The Gentle Anarchist. Brunton Stephens. NOBAu

And then meet here. *(LL)* His Winding-Sheet. Robert Herrick. CaPo; OBEV

And then, moves on. *(LL)* Fog. Carl Sandburg. AmPP; FaBV; FaPON; HeIL; HeIP; InPK; MoAB; MoAmPo; NAAL-2; OBCA; OFC; PYC; Spl; TAP; TFi; TTTS

And Then No More. Friedrich Rückert, *tr. fr. German by* James Clarence Mangan. BlrV; BLPA; PeIV

And then one day Hershey played by the door. You Are a Jew! Delmore Schwartz. *Fr.* Genesis. TrJP

And then she died and became. Survivors. Chana Bloch. CrSp

And then she'll be a true lover of mine. *(LL)* The Elfin Knight. *Unknown.* AmFP

And then she'll fly away. *(LL)* The Cuckoo. *Unknown.* AmFP; ChTr; NTP; OBET, 2 *vers.*; OxNR

And then start down! *(LL)* Afternoon on a Hill. Edna St. Vincent Millay. AnAmPo; BoTP; FaPON; GrPl; ImGa; NTCP; OBCA; OxBA; PDV; TTTS

And then that last and shortest . . *(LL)* To His Watch. Gerard Manley Hopkins. MoAB; MoBrPo

And then, the curtain. *(LL)* He Abjures Love. Thomas Hardy. CBLP; OBNC

And then the dark fell and "there has never." The Journey. Eavan Boland. BiHa

And then the knife. Song of the Hanged. Eléni Vakaló, *tr. fr. Modern Greek by* James Damaskos. PBWP

And then the old inhabitants, so kind. Fishing Village. Louis Dudek. *Fr.* Provincetown. MoCV

And then the song of each member of these States. *(LL)* From Paumanok Starting I Fly like a Bird. Walt Whitman. GOA

And Then the Water. Milo De Angelis, *tr. fr. Italian by* Lawrence Venuti. NeIt

And then there comes a shutting of the door. *(LL)* Your Body Is Stars. Stephen Spender. CBLP; FaBoTw

And then they died both together. *(LL)* Fair Margaret and Sweet William. *Unknown.* ESPB, B *vers.*; OBET

And then they have their answer home. *(LL)* The Quip. George Herbert. GeHe; JCP; LiTB; NOSC; OxAEP-1; SeCP; SeCV-1

And then they sung a psalm. *(LL)* There was a Presbyterian cat. *Unknown.* FaBoCh

And then to love again. *(LL)* Upon Drinking in a Bowl. The Earl of Rochester. OxBoLi; SeCV-2

And then to weep they both were licensed. *(LL)* Observation. Robert Herrick. ChIV-2

And then went down to the ship. Ezra Pound. *Fr.* Cantos. AmPP; CMoP; LiTA; MeMAP; MoAB; MoAmPo; MoP; NoAM; NoP; OBVE; PoE; TrGrPo; VGW

And then, without his knowing, sweet sleep descended down. The Marriage in Eden. William Williams, *tr. fr. Welsh by* Lewis Saunders *and* Gwyn Jones. *Fr.* View of Christ's Kingdom, A. OBWVE

And then, ye know, boys will be boys, and hosses — well, hosses is hosses! *(LL)* Chiquita. Bret Harte. AnAmPo

And there a clump of houses with a church. *(LL)* The Onset. Robert Frost. CMoP; MoAB; MoAmPo; OxBA; PPP

And/ there/ are. Transcendental Vision: Indigo. Askia Muhammad Touré. BCF

And there are men to buy. *(LL)* Retrospection. Dunstan Shaw. NOB/

And there are other people. *(LL)* Love Story. Bei Dao. SpMi

And there are stars, but none of you, to spare. *(LL)* Sunflower Sonnet Number Two. June Jordan. SM; Son

And there are times truly. An Underdeveloped Country. D. J. Enright. NOBL

And there came two angels to Sodom at even. Bible, *O.T. Fr.* Genesis. HoPM

And there goes the bell for the third month. The Fight of the Year. Robert McGough. OBCP

And there I found a gray and ancient ass. Pegasus Lost. Elinor Wylie. MoAmPo

And there I found myself more truly and more strange. *(LL)* Tea at the Palaz of Hoon. Wallace Stevens. FaBoMo; PoA

And there I was, is how these things begin. World Lines. Howard Nemerov. ArOW

And there I was. Not a dictionary. Northwest Airlines. Fred Chappell. HoPM

And there is dying in an hospital. *(LL)* An Old Man [*or* Old Man Travelling]. Wordsworth. FaBoCh; OBWP

And there is no such thing as a vain look. *(LL)* The Prophets. W. H. Auden. CBLP

And there is nothing at all — neither fear. Natalya Gorbanevskaya, *tr. fr. Russian by* Daniel Weissbort. BoWoP

And there is nothing else. *(LL)* The Black Angel. Henri Coulette. CoAP; NYBP

And there shall come forth a rod out of the stem of Jesse. The Rod of Jesse. Bible, *O.T. Fr.* Isaiah. AWP; OBVE; TrJP

And there she's leand her back to a thorn. The Cruel Mother. *Unknown.* ESPB

And There Was a Great Calm. Thomas Hardy. ChTr; CMoP; FaBoRV; LiTM; OAEL-2

And there was great mourning in Israel in every place. Great Mourning. Bible, *Apocrypha. Fr.* First Maccabees. TrJP

And there was nothing left in the room/ but mercy. *(LL)* Saxophonetyx. Cyn Zarco. UL

And there we two stood, hand clasped; I and she! *(LL)* Once at Swanage. Thomas Hardy. CBLP; FaBoPP

And there were in the same country shepherds abiding in the field. Bible, *N.T. Fr.* St. Luke. PChr

And there were no strings/Attached. *(LL)* Don't Let That Horse. Lawrence Ferlinghetti. CBNP; RB

And There Were Pits. Barbara Helfgott Hyett. BTR

And there were spring-faced cherubs that did sleep. The Sea of Death. *Unknown.* CH

And there will be fresh children once more. Song: Venceremos. Edward Dorn. BCF

And there will be seven half-crowns for me. *(LL)* A-Begging Buttermilk I Will Go. *Unknown.* OBET

And there's an end of bully. *(LL)* The Bully. *At.* to Earl of Rochester *and* to Thomas D'Urfey. InVP

And there's no doing anything about it! *(LL)* The Rum Tum Tugger. T. S. Eliot. FaBoNo; FaBV; FaPON; NTP; PDV; PlP

And thereto trust. *(LL)* It was my choice, it was no chance, Sir Thomas Wyatt. EnRePo; SiPS; SiPSBD

And therfore his evyn on Crystes owyn day. *(LL)* St. Stephen and King Herod. *Unknown.* ESPB, *Middle English vers.*; NoP, *mod. vers.*; OxBoLi, *Middle English vers.*; TrGrPo, *mod. vers.*

And to die. Solitary Acts. Irena Klepfisz. BTR

And to die bleeding — consummate with Life. *(LL)* Fulfillment. Helene Johnson. CDC; PoNe; ShDr

And to do that to birds was why she came. *(LL)* Never Again Would Birds' Song Be the Same. Robert Frost. FYAP; HAP; InPK; NIP; NoAM; NoP; Son; SoSe; VGW

And to Her-Without-Bounds I send. Tribal Memories. Robert Duncan. *Fr. Passages.* NOBA

And to intensify it. *(LL)* The Vow. Galway Kinnell. VCAP

And to look at all beings with eyes of compassion. *(LL)* Waking up this morning, I smile. Thich Nhat Hanh. EaPr

And to my dead heart run them in! *(LL)* The Celestial Surgeon. Robert Louis Stevenson. EBVV; MoBrPo; PoToHe; TrGrPo; TrPWD; WGRP

And to my whole is *JESU.* *(LL)* Jesu. George Herbert. MeLP

And to possess them, honour'd Margaret. *(LL)* To the Lady Margaret Ley. Milton. GTBS; GTBS-P; OBEV

And to Private Ball it came. David Jones. *Fr. In Parenthesis.* OBWVE

And to see the city again and to see it again. Patrizia Cavalli, *tr. fr. Italian by* Judith Baumel. NeIt

And to the hollering sun. *(LL)* My brother the star, my mother the earth. Nancy Wood. EaPr

And to the Young Men. Merrill Moore. MoAmPo

And to those who will return. *(LL)* Diptych. Birago Diop. NegPo

And to wander to the water-hole. *(LL)* Zebra. "Isak Dinesen." GoJo; RFM

And toll your voyage out again again. *(LL)* Frontispiece. May Swenson. CoAP; WPE

And tombstones rewrite names on dead men's graves. *(LL)* Culbin Sands. Andrew Young. GTBS-P; OxBS; OxBTC

And Tommy's dead. *(LL)* Tommy's Dead. Sydney Thompson Dobell. PeVV

And tomorrow the sun will shine again. Tomorrow. John Henry Mackay. *tr. fr. German by* Philip L. Miller. RiWo

And Tomorrow Wend Our Ways. *Malay Oral Tradition, tr. by* R. J. Wilkinson *and* R. O. Winstedt. WTO

And tomorrow's uprising to deeds shall be sweet. *(LL)* The Message of the March Wind. William Morris. OBNC; WiR

And tonight they die. *(LL)* A Crown of Windflowers. Christina Rossetti. OxBChV

And, touched with love like mine, preserve my absent friend. *(LL)* An Ode on the Popular Superstitions of the Highlands of Scotland. William Collins. EnRP; NOEC; OAEL-1; OxAEP-1

And trackless, like the Sea — of Tranquillity. *(LL)* Staying at Ed's Place. May Swenson. VCAP

And treat some rescued Breton as a comrade and a guest. *(LL)* A Ballad for a Boy. William Johnson Cory. FaPoR; OxBChV

And trees yield up their wordless therapy. *(LL)* Catalpa Tree. Miriam Waddington. MoCV

And tremble at its mysteries. *(LL)* The Edge. Rosemary Dobson. NOBAu

And trembling for me. *(LL)* A Zorro Man. Maya Angelou. VBLP

And tribal, intimate revenge. *(LL)* Punishment. Seamus Heaney. FaBoPV; InPS; NAEL-2; NoAM; NoP; OxAEP-2; PBCIP

And trod as if on the four winds. *(LL)* The Nymph and Her Fawn. Andrew Marvell. CH; FaBoCh; FM; HeIP; OAEL-1; PoEL-2; SeCP; SeCV-1

And trodden out the Mills. *(LL)* Brain, within its groove, The. Emily Dickinson. NoAM; NOBA; SAmP

And trouble him; then Death's his Epilogue. *(LL)* De Morte. Sir Henry Wotton. NOSC; OxBSP

And trousers down. *(LL)* Apples Be Ripe. *Unknown.* GBP

And Truly It Is a Most Glorious Thing. William Bradford. AH

And trumpet of your resurrection. *(LL)* Black Rock of Kiltearn. Andrew Young. FaBoTw; RB

And trust the unknown for the known. *(LL)* The Over-Heart. Whittier. ChIV-2; NOCV; WGRP

And Truth diffuse her Radiance from the Stage. *(LL)* Prologue [Spoken by Mr. Garrick] [at the Opening of the Theatre in Drury-Lane, 1747]. Samuel Johnson. EBVV; EPCY, *(ll. 1–8)*; NAEL-1; NOEC; NoP; OxAEP-1

And truth discern, who knew but learning's lore. *(LL)* If with light head erect I sing. Thoreau. AmPP; BLPL; FaBoBe, *(abr.)*; NOBA; OxBA; WGRP, *abr.*

And Truth reveal herself to you. *(LL)* An Insincere Wish Addressed to a Beggar. Mary Elizabeth Coleridge. NOBVV

And Truthe shall deliver, it is no dread. *(LL)* Balade de Bon Conseill. Chaucer. EnVB; MiEL; SCGP; TrGrPo

And try to stack them in a better load. *(LL)* The Armful. Robert Frost. CMoP; OxBSP

And turn once more our *Water* into *Wine!* *(LL)* Religion. Henry Vaughan. ESCV; NOCV; OAEL-1; OxAEP-1; PeECV; TOF

And Turnus than, quhar he at erth dyd ly. Virgil, *tr. by* Gavin Douglas. *Fr. Aeneid [or Eneados],* The. NAWM-1; OBVE

And twenty jangling wires are set at war. *(LL)* The Sage in Unison. Harold Stewart. NOBAu

And two solitudes. *(LL)* Couple. Forugh Farrokhzad. VBLP

And two to bear my soul away. *(LL)* Matthew, Mark, Luke and John. *Unknown.* CoGr, *diff. vers.*; ISE, *diff. vers.*; OxNR; PYC; FaBoCh; NTP

And unawares, just as before, sing *Rise in the Night and Come.* *(LL)* First Month: at Ch'ung-jang House. Li Shang-yin. PLT

And uniforms of snow. *(LL)* To fight aloud is very brave. Emily Dickinson. LiTA; WPE

And universal Queen. *(LL)* Pangloss's Song [A Comic-Opera Lyric]. Richard Wilbur. IHNG; MoP; NBLV; NoAM

And universals/ are not that world. Ron Welburn. NBV

And up and left his yellow bride. *(LL)* Long John Nelson and Sweetie Pie. Margaret Walker. VBLP

And up and till't like fire! *(LL)* The Patriarch. Burns. ChIV-1; CoMu

And upon us will descend the great silence of happiness. *(LL)* Tomorrow. John Henry Mackay. RiWo

And "Ut Pictura Poesis" Is Her Name. John Ashbery. InPS; VCAP

And Vallejo: "Think of the unemployed. Think of the forty million families of the hungry." *(LL)* Rusia en 1931. Robert Hass. AnAn

And venture, and to Guy the oil. *(LL)* Guy. Emerson. NOBA

And very old. *(LL)* When the Saints Come Marching In. Audre Lorde. CrSp

And Virtue lead to endless bliss above. *(LL)* To Stella. Hester Mulso. ECWP

And vowed he'd steal no more. *(LL)* Queen of Hearts, The. Mother Goose. FaBoBe; OxNR

And wait, and tend our agonizing seeds. *(LL)* From the Dark Tower. Countee Cullen. BPo; CDC; LiTM; NAAL-2; PoBA; PoNe; Son

And wait to die. *(LL)* Time of Turtles. Grace Perry. NOBAu

And waits an hour sometimes for such a will. *(LL)* Will. Ella Wheeler Wilcox. BLPA; PoToHe

And waits and looks around him. *(LL)* Eros Turannos. E. A. Robinson. CMoP; GBL; HAP; HeIP; LiTA; LiTM; MeMAP; MoAB; MoAmPo; MoP; NAAL-2; NoAM; NOBA; NoP; OxBA; PoA; PoE; Poetr; TAP; TFi; TRP

And wake up to ourselves, nourished and surprised. *(LL)* For the Sleepwalkers. Edward Hirsch. FYAP

And wake when it is day! *(LL)* The Cottager to Her Infant. Dorothy Wordsworth. CH; NTP; OxBChV; TTTS

And walk the rest of the way. *(LL)* The Draft Horse. Robert Frost. CMoP; HeIP; HoPM; PoE; SAmP; TRP

And walk with you, and talk with you, like any other boy. *(LL)* Rioupéroux. James Elroy Flecker. OBEV; OBTV

And walke her Mourner, in this Black and Whight. *(LL)* An Elegie Made by Mr. Aurelian Townshend in Remembrance of the Ladie Venetia Digby. Aurelian Townshend. SeCP

And war began next Monday on the Danes. *(LL)* Scyros. Karl Shapiro. HoPM; ImPo; LiTA; LiTM

And was helped to a hansom outside. *(LL)* The Arrest of Oscar Wilde at the Cadogan Hotel. Sir John Betjeman. CMoP; EBEV; FaBoEH; InVP; MoBrPo; MoP; NoAM; NoP; OxBTC

And was it not a worthy sight. Song Sung by Egistus and Clytemnestra. John Pickering. *Fr. Horestes.* NoSic

And Was Not Improved. Lerone Bennett, Jr. PoBA

And was obliged to call him woman. *(LL)* A Sonnet on a Monkey. Marjory Fleming. FaBoCo; FiBHP

And wasna he a roguey. The Piper o' Dundee. *Unknown.* OxBS

And watch our love making in the mirror. *(LL)* To the Tune "Intoxicated with Shadows of Flowers." Yü Ch'ing-tseng. WPC

And watch the moon through the clear autumn. *(LL)* Jewel Stairs' Grievance, The ("The jewelled steps are already quite white with dew.") Li Po. NOBA; OBVE

And waters wide and fleet. *(LL)* If thou art sleeping, maiden. Gil Vicente. AWP; CTC

And Wayland's work/ Is worn away. *(LL)* Junk. Richard Wilbur. HAP; NoP; SM; WeW

And we all may look at each other. *(LL)* A Cat May Look at a King. *Unknown.* ISE; OxBoLi

And we all sing. *(LL)* Summer Words of [or for] a Sistuh [or Sister] Addict. Sonia Sanchez. BlSi; BPo; UnPo

And we both shall monarchs prove. *(LL)* Young Love. Andrew Marvell. OxAEP-1

And we call it wisdom. It is pain. *(LL)* 90 North. Randall Jarrell. CAPP; CoAP; FYAP; MoAB; MT; NAAL-2; NoAM; NOBA; TAP; VCAP

And when they asked her what she wanted to be. Vocation. Judith Herzberg, tr. fr. Dutch by Manfred Wolf. WPOW

And when they came together in one place. Homer, tr. by Tennyson. Fr. Iliad, The. OBVE

And when we die at last. Heaven and Hell. Nalungiaq, tr. fr. Eskimo by Edward Field. DL; STP

And when you have forgotten the bright bedclothes. When You Have Forgotten Sunday: The Love Story. Gwendolyn Brooks. BPo; FF; WPOW

And when you sleep you remind me of the dead. (LL) The Dug-out. Siegfried Sassoon. CH; MoBrPo; NSI; OHIP

And Where Do You Stand on the National Question. Tom Paulin. CIP

And where have you been, my Mary? The Fairies of the Caldon-Low. Mary Howitt. BeLS

And where the plankton is falling. Retrieval System. Peter Porter. AnAn

And where thou mad'st an end, there I'le begin. (LL) The Lamp[e]. Henry Vaughan. ChIV-2; ESCV

And — which is more — you'll be a Man, my son! (LL) If. Kipling. BLPA; CoGr; EBEvV; FaBoBe; FaPoB; FaPoR; OtMeF; OxBChV; OxBTC; PlP; PWR; UV; VPP; WBLP

And while he digs thee out, falls in the ditch. (LL) Avarice. George Herbert. FaBoRV; LiTB

And while it lasts, we cannot wholly end. (LL) Palladium. Matthew Arnold. GTBS-P; OAEL-2; OBNC; PPP

And While We Are Waiting. Carolyn M. Rodgers. JB

And while we stay, let us be always warm. (LL) Ben. Johnsons Sociable Rules for the Apollo. Ben Jonson. SeCV-1

And whispers, "Forget me not!" (LL) Moon stands over the mountain, The. Franz Kugler. RiWo

And whistle and I'll be there. (LL) Shake hands, we shall never be friends, all's over. A. E. Housman. CBLP

And whistle and I'll come soon. (LL) Eppie Morrie. Unknown. ESPB; OxBB

And whistle as you leave. (LL) No Welcome. Matthew Sweeney. IB

And whistles a little tune, dreaming of home. (LL) The Chinese Restaurant in Portrush. Derek Mahon. TRP

And white owl's feather! (LL) The Fairies. William Allingham. CH; ChTr; CoGr; FaBoCh; FaBoPP; FaBV; FaPON; Mes; NOBE; NOBVV; OBEV; OTCP; OxBChV; PDV; TFi

And who but Lady Greensleeves. (LL) Greensleeves. Unknown. TTTS

And who directs all things for the good of his children. (LL) We return thanks to our mother, the earth. Unknown. EaPr

And Who Has Seen a Fair Alluring Face. George Peele. ErPo

And who has seen the moon, who has not seen. Moonrise. D. H. Lawrence. LiTM; PoA

And who shall separate the dust. Common Dust. Georgia Douglas Johnson. PoBA; ShDr; TTY

And Who Will Look Upon Our Testimony. Edward Hirsch. PFL

And whoever forces himself to love anybody. Retort to Jesus. D. H. Lawrence. PeECV

And whoever walks a mile full of false sympathy. Retort to Whitman. D. H. Lawrence. MeMBP

And whom I love, I love indeed. (LL) The Pains of Sleep. Samuel Taylor Coleridge. EnRP; FHYEP; NAEL-2; OBNC; TEP

And why. Anacreon, tr. fr. Greek by Sam Hamill. InMo

And why an honoured ragged shirt, that shows. To a Lady with Child that Asked an Old Shirt. Richard Lovelace. NOSC

And why are you pale, my Nora? Growing Rich. Alice Cary. AmWP

And why did you go so soon? (LL) Evening Waterfall. Carl Sandburg. ImPo

And why do I feel no shame kicking the loose gravel home? (LL) White Center. Richard Hugo. NAAL-2; NoP

And why does Gratt teach English? Why, because. Professor Gratt. Donald Hall. OBAL

And why has that invitation been directed to me? (LL) Questionnaire of Sleeplessness. Miodrag Pavlović. HSix

And why is it yet unfound? (LL) Facing West from California's Shores. Walt Whitman. MoAmPo; NAAL-1; TAP

And why so coffined in this vile disguise. John Cleveland. Fr. King's Disguise, The. JCP

And why this vault and tomb? Alike we must. Wiston Vault. Katherine Philips. NOSC

And why to me this, thou lame Lord of fire. An Execration upon Vulcan. Ben Jonson. BeJo; SeCP

And wild for to hold though I seem tame. (LL) Whoso List to Hunt. Sir Thomas Wyatt. AAS; BoLoP; EBEV; EnRePo; GBL; HAP; InvP; NAEL-1; NoP; NoSic; OAEL-1; OBVE; PoE; PoEL-1; Prlm; SCGP; SiPSBD; TFi

And will be and my birthday is. (LL) Your Birthday Comes to Tell Me This. E. E. Cummings. ArLo; NAs

And will be to the day that ye dee. (LL) Lizie Lindsay. Unknown. ESPB

And will he [or a'] not come again? Shakespeare. Fr. Hamlet. ImPo; NAWM-1; NoSic; PoEL-2
(Ophelia's Songs, 2 ("And will he not come again").) TrGrPo

And will not let thee go. (LL) I Will Not Let Thee Go. Robert Bridges. BeLS; BLPL; CMoP; EnLoPo; FaBoBe; OBNC

And will not open again. (LL) Like the Touch of Rain. Edward Thomas. BoLoP; EnLoPo; GBL

And will not scare. (LL) Skunk Hour. Robert Lowell. AmPP; CAPP; CMoP; CoAP; FaBoMo; HAP; HCAP; HeIP; InPK; InPS; LCAP; MoAmPo; MoP; NAAL-2; NIP; NoAM; NOBA; NoP; OPOP; OxBC; PFF; PoE; Poetr; PPP; Prlm; SCV; TAP; TFi; TRP; VCAP

And will the flowers die? Poem from a Three Year Old. Brendan Kennelly. PWE

And will they always be so tender, her. Swift Love, Sweet Motor. Hildegarde Flanner. WPE

And will they cast the altars down. In Portugal, 1912. Alice Meynell. NOCV

And will, while such a lane remain. (LL) Beyond the Last Lamp Near Tooting Common. Thomas Hardy. NOBE; OBNC

And will you cut a stone for him. The Stone. W. W. Gibson. MoBrPo

And Will You Hunt the Loba? Diane Di Prima. Fr. Loba. SRLS

And willows could not hold more steady sound. (LL) Repose of Rivers. Hart Crane. AWP; CMoP; LiTM; MeMAP; MoAB; MoAmPo; NOBA; OxBA; PoE

And Willy, my eldest-born, is gone, you say, little Anne? The Grandmother. Tennyson. PFP

And wilt cast forth no more. (LL) For My Funeral. A. E. Housman. CMoP; TrPWD

And wilt thou have me fashion into speech. Elizabeth Barrett Browning. Fr. Sonnets from the Portuguese. BrRo; EnVR

And Wilt Thou Leave Me Thus? Sir Thomas Wyatt. EBEvV; EIL; EnLoPo; EnRePo; NAEL-1; NoSic; SCGP; SiPS; SiPSBD

And winter pulled a sheet over his head. (LL) The Sleeping Giant. Donald Hall. GoJo; GrPl; NYBP; Poetsp; TwCP

And wipe the tears from my eyes. (LL) Home. Unknown. OHMPC

And wiped his eyes, though they were blind. (LL) Bruton Town. Unknown. EnSB

And wish not for, nor fear thine end. (LL) A Happy Life. Mildmay Fane, 2d Earl of Westmorland. BeJo

And with damp rags she bathes him, brings him. Anna's Grace. Bruce Weigl. NAmP90

And with each motion she ensnared a heart. (LL) On Lydia Distracted. Philip Ayres. EnLoPo; Son

And with God be the rest! (LL) Prospice. Robert Browning. BLPL; DL; FaBV; FHYEP; ImPo; LiTB; MeMBP; NAEL-2; OBD; PlP; PoLF; PoRA; TrCP; TrGrPo; WGRP

And with March a Decade in Bolinas. Joanne Kyger. UL

And with my bowels I his cancers feed. (LL) Ah dearest limbs, my life's best joy and stay. Robert Sidney. NoSic

And with open hands. (LL) It Must Be. Linda Hogan. SRLS

And with the Ape thou art alone/ Do,/ Do. (LL) Though the world has slipped and gone. Edith Sitwell. CMoP; LiTM; NALW

And with the self-same weapon, too! (LL) Jack and Roger. At. to Benjamin Franklin. ChTr; FaBoEE; NOBL

And with what body do they come? Emily Dickinson. OBD

And without the indestructable night I am alone. (LL) Passage over Water. Robert Duncan. NoAM; NOBA

And won't let me sleep for melancholy. (LL) The Autumn Brook. Hsüeh T'ao. WPC

And won't play enny more. (LL) Bobby's First Poem. Norman Gale. FiBHP; MoShBr

And woodthrush calling through the fog/ My daughter. (LL) Marina. T. S. Eliot. CMoP; FaBoMo; GTBS-P; HeIP; LiTA; NAEL-2; NOBE; NOCV; PoE; TOF

And woos the arts with such pure sighs. (LL) Before a Saint's Picture. Walter Savage Landor. OxBChV

And Wordsworth! Ah, pale ghosts, rejoice! Matthew Arnold. Fr. Memorial Verses. EBVVPR; EPCY; NAEL-2; OAEL-2

And worn them tightly on your breasts. (LL) Inanna and the Divine Essences. Enheduanna. VBLP

And worn with vain pursuit, man also dies. (LL) Epitaph on Fop. William Cowper. OBD

And Would It Have Been Worth It? T. S. Eliot. Fr. Love Song of J. Alfred Prufrock, The. LPA

And would suffice. (LL) Fire and Ice. Robert Frost. AmPP; CMoP; EBEvV; FaBoEE; FF; HeIP; HoPM; InPK; LiTA; LiTM; MoAB; MoAmPo; MoP; NAAL-2; NoAM; NOBA; OxBA; Poetr; PPP; Prlm; RaBo; SoSe; TAP; TFi; TrGrPo

And would you gather turds. A History of Love. William Carlos Williams. VGW

And Would You See Your Lover Perish? Paul Johann Ludwig Heyse, *tr. fr. German by* Philip L. Miller. RiWo

And would you sign my copy sir? A Scotch? The Poet at Fifty. Laurence David Lerner. PeSA

And wring your blood out on Hiroshima. (*LL*) The Enemy. Randolph Stow. NOBAu

And write Thy Epitaph in Blood and Wounds! (*LL*) His Metrical Vow. James Graham, Marquess of Montrose. OxBS

And write your name in the corner of the picture. (*LL*) To Paint the [or a] Portrait of a Bird. Jacques Prévert.

And wylde for to hold, though I seme tame. (*LL*) Who so list to hount, I knowe where is an hynde. Sir Thomas Wyatt. CBLP

And wylt thou leve me thus? Sir Thomas Wyatt. *See* And Wilt Thou Leave Me Thus?

And ye maun bide at hame. (*LL*) John Grumlie. Allan Cunningham. GBP; PoLF

And ye shall walk in silk attire. The Siller Croun. Susanna Blamire. ECWP

And ye vaunted your fathomless powers, and ye flaunted your iron pride. Following British Failures Exposed by the Boer War. Kipling. FaBoEH

And, yeah, brothers. Dark Prophecy: I Sing of Shine. Etheridge Knight. BPo; PBCAP

And yes, my friend, we, too. Seamus Heaney. *Fr.* Crossings. BAP-90

And Yet. Arthur B. Rhinow. BLRP

And Yet. Errol B. Sloan. BLRP

And yet a kiss (like blubber)'d blur and slip. Love and Death. John Frederick Nims. HoPM; SM

And yet abide the World! (*LL*) There came a wind like a bugle. Emily Dickinson. CMoP; MeMAP; MoAB; NAAL-1; NAWM-2; NOBA; OPOP; OxBA; RB; SAmP

And yet gaze the everlasting hills to rubble. (*LL*) The Nihilist as Hero. Robert Lowell. VCAP

And yet God has not said a word! (*LL*) Porphyria's Lover. Robert Browning. AWP; BeLS; CBLP; EnVR; FHYEP; HAP; MeMBP; NAEL-2; OBEV; TEP; TrGrPo

And yet hath prayer, the heav'n-breathing foliage of faith. Ethick. Robert Bridges. *Fr.* Testament of Beauty, The. OxBTC

And yet I cannot reprehend the flight. Samuel Daniel. *Fr.* To Delia. ESo; OBEV

And yet I really must complain. The Modern Traveller. Hilaire Belloc. OtMeF

And yet I bare the flower[flour] away. (*LL*) All night by the rose, rose. *Unknown.* MiEL

And yet in some very subtle way. Hilda Doolittle ("H. D."). *Fr.* Tribute to the Angels. NALW

And yet not long ago. *Unknown. Fr.* Vox Populi, Vox Dei. FaBoPV

And yet, not to forget, each night one less vermin in the world. (*LL*) On the Eating of Mice. Russell Edson.

And yet one arrives somehow. Arrival. William Carlos Williams. AnAmPo

And yet, one hates to change. Ten years of intimacy! Declaration of Independence, II. Jane Oliensis. UTF

And yet she hathe but care and woe. (*LL*) A Woman Is a Worthy Thing. *Unknown.* FaBoCo; GBP

And yet so fragrant as you know. (*LL*) Even Little Things. Paul Johann Ludwig Heyse. RiWo

And yet the driving mirror shows me plain. To His Coy Mistress. W. J. Webster. BXAP

And yet the southern whale does some time come. The Whales. Marguerite Young. WPE

And yet, there was a hunger in your eyes. Arthur Symons. *Fr.* Amoris Victima. PeVV

And yet this great wink of eternity. Hart Crane. *Fr.* Voyages (I–VI). AmPP; CMoP; GGP; HAP; ImPo; LiTM; MeMAP; MoAB; MoAmPo; NoAM; NOBA; NoP; OxBA; PoE; PPP; RaBo; TAP; TRP; UnPo; VGW

And Yet We Are Here! Karl Wolfskehl, *tr. fr. German by* Carol North Valhope *and* Ernst Morowitz. TrJP

And yet, where would we be without the American culture. Goodbye Nkrumah. Diane Di Prima. PoM

And yet white. A Sketch for a Modern Love Poem. Tadeusz Rózewicz, *tr. fr. Polish by* Czeslaw Milosz. (Draft of a Modern Love Poem.) PoSu, *tr. by* Magnus J. Krynski.

And yet, who did not. (*LL*) Did Not. Thomas Moore. BoLoP; ErPo; PeLV

And yet you experienced the flames of Hell. Proof. Czeslaw Milosz, *tr. fr. Polish by the author.* TOF

And yonder she sits in my cane-bottom'd chair. (*LL*) The Cane-bottomed [*or* Cane-bottom'd] Chair. Thackeray. VPP

And you above them, wounded and dominant. (*LL*) Messengers. Louise Glück. AnAn; HCAP; VCAP

And you are doomed to hell. (*LL*) The Cruel Mother. *Unknown.* AmFP; OBET

And you are the weaver's bonny. (*LL*) The Devil's Nine Questions. *Unknown.* AmFP

And you as a river will cut your own channels. (*LL*) My Esmeralda. Vijay Seshadri. UTF

And You as Well Must Die, Beloved Dust. Edna St. Vincent Millay. MeMAP; PoLF; PoRA; TAP

And you came back. Samar Attar. *Fr.* Return of the Dead, The. PBWP

And you can't imagine. (*LL*) Dead Horse Bay. Robert Adamson. NOBAu

And you do it! (*LL*) Friendship. Shel Silverstein. NTCP

And You, Helen. Edward Thomas. BoLoP; OBWVE

And you just *know* he knows he knows. (*LL*) The Sloth. Theodore Roethke. AnAmPo; FiBHP; OBAL; OBAP; OBCA; TRP

And you keep quiet and I will go. (*LL*) Keeping Quiet. Pablo Neruda. EaPr

And you know very well whom I mean. (*LL*) A Certain Young Lady. Washington Irving. FaBoBe

And you know who. (*LL*) Jerusalem. Julia Vinograd. SRLS

And you look like hell when they're through with you. (*LL*) The Hearse Song. *Unknown.* AS, *A and B vers.*; OxBoLi; RB

And you my daughter. Daughter. Mary Dorcey. AIW

And you, my earth-mother, you are my own blood. (*LL*) Descendant. Elisaveta Bagriana. VBLP

And you my saint unnamed. (*LL*) Come, You Pretty False-eyed Wanton. Thomas Campion. ELP

And you, O most of all. Enemies. Robert Noble Denison Wilson. PeIV

And you shall still be Lady Clare. (*LL*) Lady Clare. Tennyson. BeLS; FaPON

And you smile up at us — eternally. (*LL*) In Memory of My Mother. Patrick Kavanagh. BIrV; CIP; MoP; NoAM; RaBo

And you too perished long ago, by a bush with matted roots. Anyte, *tr. fr. Greek by* John Heath-Stubbs *and* Carol A. Whiteside. GrAn

And you, whate'er your Fav'rite does, approve. Tibullus, *tr. fr. Latin by* John Dart. *Fr.* Odes. PeHV

And you will be amazed. (*LL*) Instructions to a Princess. Ishmael Reed. PoBA

And you will rank among the sages. (*LL*) Epigrams must be curt, nor seem. Walter Savage Landor. FaBoEE

And you will understand/ My hatred. (*LL*) Hatred. Gwendolyn B. Bennett. BlSi; CDC; PoBA; RaBo; ShDr

And you won't catch me! (*LL*) Ring-a-Ring. Kate Greenaway. FaPON; MoShBr

And you, you . . . you, you utter/ You wait! (*I L*) Beyond Words. Robert Frost. Spl; WeW

And you'll eat in the sweet bye and bye. (*LL*) The Preacher and the Slave. *At. to* Joe Hill. AS; SWP; WTO

And you'll get just what I mean. (*LL*) Embraceable You. Ira Gershwin. CBLP

And you'll hear something! (*LL*) Therese. Gottfried Keller. RiWo

And you'll say a nation totters. G. D. H. Cole. *Fr.* Civil Riot. OxBTC

And your brothers too, I shall ever love. Farewell. (*LL*) Death of a Ram. Sedulius Scottus. NOIV

And your dialect blurred with locality, I think. Vendemmia. Robert Wells. SCBI

And your eyes peel to red mud. (*LL*) Babylon Revisited. Amiri Baraka. BPo; MoP; NoAM

And your fragrance. (*LL*) Gentle Goddess. Lew Welch. EaPr

And your growth into martyrdom. (*LL*) For Malcolm: After Mecca. Gerald William Barrax. PoBA

And your letter melts into melody. (*LL*) The New Cecilia. Thomas Lovell Beddoes. OAEL-2

And your little job is done. (*LL*) Madam Life's a Piece in Bloom. W. E. Henley. EBVV; NAEL-2; OPOP; PeVV

And your love of it will stop midway. (*LL*) A Song of Grief. Pan Chieh-yû. WPC

And your money, too. (*LL*) 50 — 50. Langston Hughes. NoAM; NOBA; PoE

And your true name is Mistress Betty. (*LL*) On a Romantic Lady. Mary Monck. ECWP; NOEC

And you're a damned fool for following me! (*LL*) Archie o Cawfield. *Unknown.* AmFP

And yours the losse and myn the dedly pain. (*LL*) How Oft Have I My Dere and Cruell Foo. Petrarch. AAS; SiPSBD

And you've struck it — on Poverty Flat. (*LL*) Her Letter. Bret Harte. AnAmPo; PoLF

And Zero at the Bone. (*LL*) A Narrow Fellow in the Grass. Emily Dickinson. AmPP; BoWoP; ClHu; CMoP; FM; GoJo; HAP; HeIP; HoPM; LiTM; MeMAP; NAAL-1; NALW; NIP; NoAM; NOBA; NoP; NTP; OBCA; OxBA; PoE; PoEL-5; Poetr; PoLF; PPP; RB; SAmP; SoSe; TAP; TFi; TRP; WeW

And Zimbabwe was born. (*LL*) A Maze of Blood. N. C. G. Mathema. PeSAV

Andalusian merchant, that returns, The. *Unknown. Fr.* Wonders. EiL; FaBoCh

Andante, ma Non Assai. Rufinus Domesticus, *tr. fr. Greek by* Dudley Fitts. ErPo

Andean Flute, The. Derek Mahon. SCBI

And/Mother Why Did You Tell Me. Stephanie Markman. MDDM

Andonis is the spring song, me-na-wah — . (*LL*) Andonis, My Daughter. Thomas Love Peacock. VoR

Andonis, My Daughter. Thomas Love Peacock. VoR

Andraitx — Pomegranate Flowers. D. H. Lawrence. NoP

André Chénier. Marina Tsvetayeva, *tr. fr. Russian by* Tom Paulin. FaBoPV

Andrea del Sarto. Robert Browning. CTC; EnVR; MeMBP; NAEL-2; NOBVV; NoP; OAEL-2; PoE; PoEL-5

Andreas, *sels. Unknown, tr. fr. Anglo-Saxon by* Charles W. Kennedy. St. Andrew's Voyage to Mermedonia. AnOE

Andrée Rexroth. Kenneth Rexroth. PrIm; VGW

André's Request to Washington. *Unknown.* PAH

Andrew and Maudlin, Rebecca and Will. A Ballad of Andrew and Maudlin. *Unknown.* CoMu

Andrew Gear of Sunderland. *Unknown.* FaBoCo

Andrew Lammie. *Unknown. See* At Fyvie's yetts there grows a flower.

Andrew Rose. *Unknown.* OxBSS

Andrew Rykman's Prayer. Whittier. TrPWD
　　Sels.
　　"Make my mortal dreams come true."
　　"Pardon, Lord, the lips that dare."

Andrew M'Crie. Robert Fuller Murray. FaBoCo

Androgynous child whose hair curls into flowers. The Total Influence or Outcome of the Matter: The Sun. Marge Piercy. WPOW

Andromache, *sels.* Euripides, *tr. fr. Greek by* George Allen.

Andromache's Lament for Hector. Homer, *tr. fr. Greek. Fr.* Iliad, The. OxBM

Andromache's lament is still in our ears. Alpheios, *tr. fr. Greek by* Edwin Morgan. GrAn

Andromache's Lamentation. Homer, *tr. by* Congreve. *Fr.* Iliad, The. OBVE

Andromache's Wedding. Sappho, *tr. fr. Greek by* Willis Barnstone. BoWoP

Andromeda. Gerard Manley Hopkins. EBEV; FaBoMo; LiTB; MeMBP; OxAEP-2; SCGP

Andromeda, *sels.* Charles Kingsley.

Andromeda, by Perseus saved and wed. Aspecta Medusa. Dante Gabriel Rossetti. OxBSP

Andromeda/ forgot. Sappho, *tr. fr. Greek by* Willis Barnstone. BoWoP

Andy-Diana DNA Letter. Andrew Weiman. HAP

Ane Godlie Dreame. Elizabeth Melvill, Lady Culross. KTR

Ane Godly Dream, *sels.* Elizabeth Melvill, Lady Culross.
　　"Upon one day as I did mourn full sore." ChIV-1

Ane Sang of the Birth of Christ, with the Tune of Baw Lula Low. Martin Luther, *tr. fr. German by* John Wedderburn. ChTr

Ane Satire [*or* Satyre] of the Three [*or* Thrie] Estaitis, *sels.* Sir David Lindsay.
　　"Bona dies, Bona dies." SeCP
　　"My patent pardouns ye may see." OBSV

Anear the centre of that northern crest. James Thomson ("B.V."). *Fr.* City of Dreadful Night, The. EnVR; GTBS-P; OBNC
　　(City's Queen, The.) NOBE

Anecdote for Fathers. Wordsworth. EnRP

Anecdote from William IV Street. D. J. Enright. OxBC

Anecdote of Love, An. John Clare. NOBVV

Anecdote of the Jar. Wallace Stevens. AmPP; CMoP; HCAP; HeIP; HoPM; InPK; LiTA; MeMAP; MoAB; MoMaPo; MoP; NAAL-2; NAWM-2; NoAM; NOBA; NoP; OxBA; OxBSP; PoA; Poetr; PPP; PrIm; SAmP; SOTW; TAP; TFi; UnPo

Anecdote of the Prince of Peacocks. Wallace Stevens. SOTW

Anemic pictures! Legend. Jules Laforgue, *tr. fr. French by* Louis Simpson. Prf

Anesthetist is singing, The. In the Operating Room. Alden Nowlan. NOBC

Angel, The. Blake. *Fr.* Songs of Experience. CH; EnRP; FHYEP; LiTB

Angel, The. Blake. *See* I asked a thief to steal me a peach.

Angel. Andrew Elliott. PNI

Angel. John Forbes. NOBAu

Angel, The. Alfred Hayes. TrJP

Angel, The. Galway Kinnell. LCAP; NoAM

Angel. Brad Leithauser. DiPo; FYAP

Angel. James Merrill. CAPP; PoA

Angel. Maxine Scates. PBCAP

Angel, *sels.* Ian Wedde.
　　"And this is where." PeNZ

Angel and Stone. Howard Nemerov. NYBP

Angel and the girl are met, The. The Annunciation. Edwin Muir. ChIV-2; CMoP; CRP; NOCV

Angel Boley. Stevie Smith. EBNV

Angel came to me, An. O Simplicitas. Madeleine L'Engle. *Fr.* Three Songs of Mary. OBCP; PChr

Angel came to me and said, An. Memorable Fancy, A ("Angel came to me and said.") Blake. *Fr.* Marriage of Heaven and Hell, The. EnRP; NU; OAEL-2

Angel came to me and stood by my bedside, An. Nightmare, with Angels. Stephen Vincent Benét. MAT

Angel Eye of Memory. John Malcolm Brinnin. PoA

Angel here, the Divel there, An. (*LL*) To Lucasta: Her Reserved Looks. Richard Lovelace. CaPo; SeCV-1

Angel in the House, The, *sels.* Coventry Patmore.
　　"Across the sky the daylight crept." GBL
　　Attainment, The. FaBoEE
　　Cathedral Close, The. EBVV
　　　(Salisbury; the Cathedral Close.) EBVV; FaBoPP
　　County Ball, The. EBVV
　　Going to Church. PeVV
　　"I vow'd unvarying faith; and she." NOBVV
　　　(Constancy Rewarded.) OxBSP
　　In Love, at Stonehenge. FaBoPP
　　Kiss, The. ArLo; BoLoP; EnLoPo; FiBHP; NOBVV
　　Love at Large. EBVV, I, ii; NOBVV, I, ii
　　Love Serviceable. EnLoPo
　　Lover, The. OxAEP-2
　　Love's Perversity. EnVR
　　Married Lover, The. OBEV; OxAEP-2; TrGrPo
　　Perspective. FaBoEE; GBL
　　Rainbow, The. GTBS-P
　　Revelation, The. EnLoPo; GBL; GTBS-P; HAP; OBNC; OxBSP
　　Sahara. EBVV
　　Spirit's Epochs, The. EBEV; GBL; OxBSP
　　Tribute, The. EBEV; OBNC
　　'Twas When the Spousal Time of May. GBL; OxAEP-2
　　"Whirl'd off at last, for speech I sought." GBL

Angel, king of streaming morn. Sun. Henry Rowe. OBEV

Angel of Death, The. *Unknown.* AmFP

Angel of History, The, *sels.* Carolyn Forché.
　　"This is Izieu during the war, Izieu and the neighboring." BTR

Angel of Patience, The. Whittier. WGRP

Angel of Peace, Thou Hast Wandered Too Long. Oliver Wendell Holmes. AH

Angel of poets,/ Tell us how. Prayer for All Poets at This Time. Irwin Edman. TrPWD

Angel [*or* Angell] saith to Joseph mild, The. For Innocents' Day. Luke Wadding. NOIV; TIRV

Angel, robed in spotless white, An. Dawn. Paul Laurence Dunbar. AnAmPo; PoLF; PoNe

Angel said to me, The: "Why are you laughing?" Sarah. Delmore Schwartz. ChIV-1

Angel slide your hand. A Poem in Yellow after Tristan Tzara. Jerome Rothenberg. PoM

Angel Spirits of Sleep. Robert Bridges. CH

Angel Surrounded by Paysans. Wallace Stevens. HCAP; LCAP; PPP

Angel That Presided o'er My Birth, The. Blake. *Fr.* Gnomic Verses. InPK; NAs; OxBSP; RB; TrGrPo

Angel-Thief, The. Oliver Wendell Holmes. AnAmPo

Angel told Mary, An. Harry Behn. PChr

Angel Unawares, An. *Unknown.* BLRP

Angel was tired of heaven, as he lounged in the golden street, An. The Woman and the Angel. Robert W. Service. ChIV-1

Angel with a voice like summer show'rs, An. Repose. H. Cordelia Ray. CBWP-3

Angela Davis. Alice S. Cobb. BlSi

Angela Davis. Jackie Kay. NWP

Angela Honey (she wrote) I would it were not so. From Lois in London. Angela McCabe. AmPA

Angelica has gain'd the dell. Robert Dunbar. *Fr.* Caraguin, The. PBCV

Angelica the Doorkeeper. *Unknown, tr. fr. Serbian by* Anne Pennington. RB

Angelles bee wrogte to bee of neidher kynde. Mynstrelles Songe: "Angelles bee wrogte to bee of neidher kynde." Thomas Chatterton. *Fr.* Aella; a Tragycal Enterlude. EnLoPo

Angelo Orders His Dinner. Bayard Taylor. AnAmPo; BXAP

Angels. Dannie Abse. PoA

Angels, The. William Drummond of Hawthornden. GN

Angels, The. Paul Ramsey. CRP

Angels. Anne Szumigalski. Mes; NOBC

Angels, The. Marguerite Young. WPE

Angels and ministers of grace defend us! Shakespeare. *Fr.* Hamlet. EBEV; NAWM-1; OxAEP-1

Angels are bending, The. W. B. Yeats. NOBVV

Angels, as well as birds, on silent wing. On Angels. W. W. Eustace Ross. MoCV

Angels Came a-Mustering, The. *Unknown, tr. fr. Hebrew by* Israel Zangwill. TrJP

Angels' eyes, whom veils cannot deceive, The. Of the Blessed Sacrament of the Altar. Robert Southwell. OBEV

Angel's Flight. Maxine Scates. PBCAP

Angels, from the realms of glory. Nativity. James Montgomery. NOCV

Angels in Heav'n, as we may say. A Poem upon the Caelestial Embassy. Richard Steere. SCAP

Angels in Winter. Nancy Willard. LCAP

Angels, it seems, don't always know. Lyn Hejinian. UL

Angel's Like a Flea, The. Samuel Taylor Coleridge. CBNP

Angel's Message, The. Clara Ann Thompson. CBWP-2

Angels/ might fall that way. Snowfall: Four Variations. George Amabile. NYBP

Angels of Bethlehem, echo the strain! (*LL*) Angel of Peace, Thou Hast Wandered Too Long. Oliver Wendell Holmes. AH

Angels of Buena Vista, The. Whittier. BeLS; PAH

Angels of 1912 and 1972, The. Richard Jackson. NAmP90

Angel's Song. Charles Causley. OBCP

Angels' Song, The. Edmund Hamilton Sears. *See* It Came upon the Midnight Clear.

Angels Sung a Carol, The. Edward Taylor. AH

Angels take approaches, The. Some enter by root. The Angels. Paul Ramsey. CRP

Angel's Visit, The. Eugene Field. PWR

Angel's Visit, The. Charlotte L. Forten Grimke. AAP

Angels walking under the palm trees. A Little Carol of the Virgin. Lope de Vega. PChr

Angelus inquit pastoribus. Now the Most High Is Born. James Ryman. MeEL

Anger. Robert Creeley. NaP

Anger. Charles Lamb *and* Mary Lamb. FaBoBe

Anger. Julia Vinograd. SRLS

Anger, and the vow are the same. (*LL*) The Bad Old Days. Kenneth Rexroth. NNaP; NoAM

Anger in its time and place. Anger. Charles Lamb *and* Mary Lamb. FaBoBe

Anger Lay by Me All Night Long. Elizabeth Daryush. RB

Anger rises with metal filings, The. A Man All Grown Up Is Supposed To. Terry Stokes. AmPA

Anger shines through me. A Just Anger. Marge Piercy. CrSp

Anger that breaks a man down into boys, The. César Vallejo. *tr. fr. Spanish by* Robert Bly.

(Anger that Breaks the Man into Chidren, The.) RaBo

Angered, may I be near a glass of water. Sapphics against Anger. Timothy Steele. SM

Anger's Freeing Power. Stevie Smith. NTP; OxBC

Anghiari is medieval, a sleeve sloping down. The Journey. James Wright. CAPP; NoAM; PoE

Angilbert's Prayer. Angilbert, *tr. fr. Latin by* Helen Waddell. MLL

Angina. David Campbell. *Fr.* Starting from Central Station. FaBoMA

Angina Pectoris. W. R. Moses. LiTA

Anglais Mort a Florence. Wallace Stevens. SAmP

Angle-Land. David Jones. *Fr.* Anathemata, The. NoAM

Angle of Geese. N. Scott Momaday. CDW; HATNAP

Angle of Vision. Robert Rendall. OxBTC

Angler, The. Thomas Buchanan Read. AnAmPo

Angler's Invitation, The. Thomas Tod Stoddart. GN

Angler's Reveille, The. Henry van Dyke. *Fr.* Toiling of Felix, The. GN

Anglers Song, The, *sels.* William Basse. "As inward love breeds outward talk." (Angler's Song, The.) NOSC

Angler's Song, The. John Dennys. *Fr.* Secrets of Angling, The. ElL

Anglican curate in want, An. Ronald Arbuthnott Knox. FaBoNo

Anglican firelight. The Other Voice. Tom Paulin. PNI

Anglo-Saxon. Edward Leslie Mayo. BCF

Anglo Saxon Street. Earle Birney. HeIP; NOBC

Anglo-Swiss, or a Day among the Alps, *sels.* William Plomer.

Angola independent. (*LL*) We Must Return. Agostinho Neto. PeSAV

Angola Question Mark. Langston Hughes. BPo; TTY

Angrier than my now occasional. A Preface to the Memoirs. James Merrill. NOBA

Angry Dusk. Jack Lindsay. NOBAu

Angry-feathered trees. Late Summer Storm. Christine Churches. FaBoMA

Angry Poet, The. Frank O'Connor, *tr. fr. Irish.* CIP

Angry Samson. Robert Graves. ChIV-1

Angry Summer, The ("From Abertillery and Aberdare.") Idris Davies. AngWe

Angry Summer, The ("Mrs. Evans Fach, You Want Butter Again.") Idris Davies. AngWe

Angry Word, An. Margaret E. Bruner. PoToHe

Angry word is like a boomerang, An. An Angry Word. Margaret E. Bruner. PoToHe

Angry young husband called Bicket, An. John Galsworthy. PeLi

Angst, poetry, urbanized fret. Sydney Bernard Smith. PeLi

Angst-ridden amorist, Fred, An. Love Song of J. Alfred Prufrock, The, J. Walker. BXAP; PeLi

Anguish. Stéphane Mallarmé, *tr. fr. French by* Arthur Symons. AWP

Anguish. Henry Vaughan. OxAEP-1

Anguish is always there, lurking at night. The Kingdom of Kali. May Sarton. *Fr.* Invocation to Kali, The. SRLS

Anguish of a naked body is more terrible, The. A Prayer to the Lord Ramakrishna. James Wright. NNaP

Anima Christi, *sels.* Unknown. "Soul of Earth, sanctify me." EaPr, *ad. by* Jane Pellowski

Anima Has a Predilection, The. Michael Harlow. *Fr.* Poem Then, for Love. PeNZ

Anima quodammodo omnia. Translation. Howard Nemerov. CRP

Anima Urbis. Edith M. Thomas. AmWP

Animal. Max Eastman. FYAP

Animal. Bill Griffiths. NBrP

Animal Acts. Charles Simic. LCAP

Animal bones and some mossy tent rings. Lament for the Dorsets. Alfred W. Purdy. NoAM; NoP

Animal Crackers. Christopher Morley. FaPON

Animal Days. Lee Harwood. NBrP

Animal Fair. *Unknown.* AS; BLPA; FaBoBe; MoShBr; NTCP; RoPo

Animal House, The. Sandy Brechin. Mes

Animal Howl, The. "M. J.," *tr. fr. Polish by* A. Glanz-Leyeles. TrJP

Animal I wanted, The. Kenneth Patchen. VGW

Animal Kingdom. Sydney Clouts. PeSA

Animal kingdom came, The. Cat. Pablo Neruda, *tr. fr. Spanish by* Ben Belitt. SoCa

Animal Magnetism; the Pseudo-Philosopher Baffled. Laurence Hynes Halloran. NOEC

Animal Pictures. Lawrence Locke. GrPl

Animal runs, it passes, it dies, The. And it is the great cold. Death Rites II. *Unknown, tr. by* C. M. Bowra. TTY

Animal Song. Heather McHugh. AnAn

Animal Store, The. Rachel Field. PDV

Animal That Drank Up Sound, The. William Stafford. VGW

Animal, Vegetable and Mineral. Louise Bogan. FM

Animal Weather-Forecasting. *At. to* Thomas Lodge *and to* Robert Greene. NoSic

Animal willows of November. The Willows of Massachusetts. Denise Levertov. NAAL-2

Animals, The. Stephen Berg. NaP

Animals, The. Josephine Jacobsen. GoYe

Animals, The. Robinson Jeffers. NU

Animals, The. W. S. Merwin. VCAP

Animals, The. Edwin Muir. ChIV-1; CMoP; CRP; EBEV; HeIP; MoBrPo; NoP

Animals. Walt Whitman. *See* I think I could turn and live awhile with animals.

Animals are coming, The. Songs to Welcome the Society of the Mystic Animals. *Unknown, tr. fr. Seneca Indian by* Jerome K. Rothenberg *and* Richard Johnny John. STP

Animals Are Passing from Our Lives. Philip Levine. CAPP; CoAP; NOBA; Poetr; RaBo; SM; TAP

Animals' Arrival, The. Elizabeth Jennings. PBWP

Animals' Carol, The. Charles Causley. NAs

Animals do not sleep. At night. The Face of the Horse. Nikolai Alekseevich Zabolotsky, *tr. fr. Russian by* Daniel Weissbort. RB

Animals have no names. A Walk. Nikolai Alekseevich Zabolotsky, *tr. fr. Russian by* Daniel Weissbort. RB

Animals' Houses. James Reeves. OTCP

Animals in That Country, The. Margaret Atwood. NALW; NoAM; NoP

Animals live in the Ark, The. *Unknown. Fr.* Deluge, The. ChTr; GBP

Animals live in darkness, The. World of Darkness. Robert Chatain. PoA

Animals own a fur world. Adults Only. William Stafford. FF

Animals Sick of the Plague, The. Marianne Moore, *ad. fr.* La Fontaine. InPS

Animals that look at us like children, The. The Dying Animals. Gavin Ewart. OBD

Animals That Stand in Dreams, *sels.* Harley Elliott.

Animals we have seen, all marvelous creatures, The. The Park in Milan. William Jay Smith. CoAP

Animism. Birago Diop, *tr. fr. French by* Ellen Conroy Kennedy. NegPo

Animula. T. S. Eliot. CRP; LiTB; NAs

Animula. W. S. Merwin. CAPP

Animula vagula blandula. Conrad Aiken. FaBoNo; OBAL

Animula Vagula, Blandula. Emperor Hadrian, *tr. fr. Latin by* Henry Vaughan. FaBoRV

Anishinabe children sing songs of sleep. For the Children. Thomas Love Peacock. VoR

Anishinabe Grandmothers. Gerald Vizenor. VoR

Anita and Giovanni. H. Cordelia Ray. CBWP-3

Ank'hor Vat. Denis Devlin. BIrV; CIP; IPY; NOIV

Ankle's chief end is exposiery, The. Anthony Euwer. PeLi

Anklet Song. *Unknown, tr. fr. Hawaiian by* N. B. Emerson. WTO

Ankotarinya. *Unknown, tr. fr. Aranda by* T. G. H. Strehlow. CBAP

Ann and the Fairy Song. Walter de la Mare. *Fr.* Child's Day, A. FaBV

Ann, Ann!/ Come! quick as you can! Alas, Alack! Walter de la Mare. FaPON; OxBChV

Ann Arbor Solitary. Lawrence Goldstein. NGP

Ann Griffith. R. S. Thomas. PeECV

Ann Griffiths. Sally Roberts Jones. AngWe

Ann Lee. Lynne McMahon. NAmP90

Anna. Burns. TrGrPo

Anna banana. *Unknown.* RoPo

Anna Elise. *Unknown.* OxNR

Anna Perenna, *sels.* Lucio Piccolo, *tr. fr. Italian by* Charles Tomlinson.

Anna Playing in a Graveyard. Caroline Gilman. OBCA

Anna Speaks of the Childhood of Mary Her Daughter. Lucille Clifton. NALW

Anna Town. Anne Carson. *Fr.* Life of Towns, The. BAP-90

Annabel Lee. Poe. AiP; AmPP; AnAmPo; AWP; BeLS; BLPA; CH; DL; EBEvV; FaPON; HeIL; HeIP; ImPo; LiTA; MeMAP; NAAL-1; NOBA; NoP; OBCA; OBSP; OPOP; OtMeF; OxBA; Prlm; TAP; TFi; TrGrPo; WBLP

Annabell and the Witches. Mick Gowar. OBSP

Annales, *sels.* Quintus Ennius, *tr. fr. Latin by* John Wight.

Annan Water ("Annan's Water's waiding deep.") *Unknown.* CH

Anna's Grace. Bruce Weigl. NAmP90

Anne and the Peacock. Noel Welch. FF

Anne Boleyn. Eloise Bibb. CBWP-4

Anne Frank Huis. Andrew Motion. SCBI

Anne Hutchinson's Exile. Edward Everett Hale. PAH

Anne Playing the Spinet. Clément Marot, *tr. fr. French by* Philip L. Miller. RiWo

Anne Rutledge. Edgar Lee Masters. *Fr.* Spoon River Anthology. CMoP; HAP; ImPo; LiTA; LiTM; MoAmPo; MoP; NoAM; NOBA; OxBA; TFi; TrGrPo

Annette came through the meadows. H. Cordelia Ray. CBWP-3

Annette Myers; or, A Murder in St. James's Park. *Unknown.* OxBoLi

Anniad, The. Gwendolyn Brooks. BlSi

Annie and Rhoda, sisters twain. The Sisters. Whittier. AWP

Annie and Willie's Prayer. Sophia P. Snow. BeLS; BLPA

Annie ate jam. *Unknown.* ISE

Annie Bolanny. *Unknown.* ChTr

Annie Died the Other Day. E. E. Cummings. ErPo

Annie Hill's Grave. James Merrill. WeW

Annie Laurie. William Douglas, *rev. by* Lady Jane Scott. FaBoBe; FaBV; GN; ImPo; ScCV; WBLP

Annie, my first-born, gentle child. To Annie. Mary E. Tucker. CBWP-1

Annie of Tharaw. *Unknown, tr. fr. German by* Henry Wadsworth Longfellow. GePo

Annie of Tharaw, my true love of old. Annie of Tharaw. *Unknown, tr. fr. German by* Henry Wadsworth Longfellow. GePo

Annihilated for ever and ever. *(LL)* Now I Will Only Believe. B. W. Vilakazi. PeSAV

Annihilation. Conrad Aiken. GBL; MoAB; MoAmPo

Annihilation. Elizabeth Oakes Smith. *Fr.* Atheism. AmWP

Anniversary, The. David Bottoms. ArOW

Anniversary, The. William Dickey. GOYP

Anniversary. Heine, *tr. fr. German by* Alistair Elliot. OBD

Anniversary. Ted Kooser. SM

Anniversary. Richmond Lattimore. NYBP

Anniversary. John Wain. TwCP

Anniversary, An. Thomas Hardy. OxBTC

Anniversary Approaches, An; of the Birth of God. David Wright. *Fr.* On the Margin. NAs

Anniversary of Death, An. John Wieners. PoM

Anniversary of Samansa's Death, The. Shiraishi Kazuko, *tr. fr. Japanese by* Kenneth Rexroth *and* Ikuko Atsumi. WPJ

Anniversary on the Hymeneals of My Noble Kinsman, Thomas Stanley, Esquire, An. Richard Lovelace. CaPo

Anniversary on the Island. W. S. Merwin. ArLo

Anniversary [*or* Anniversarie], The. John Donne. BoLoP; ESCV; FHYEP; HAP; HoPM; JCP; LiTB; MeLP; NOBE; NoP; NoSic; OAEL-1; OxBM; SCGP; SeCP; SeCV-1; TFi; WeW

Anniversary Poem, The. Diana Der Hovanessian. BTR

Anniversary Poem Entitled the Progress of Liberty, An, *sels.* James Madison Bell.
   "Bondsman's gloomy night has passed, The." AAP

Anniversary Poem for the Cheyennes Who Fell at Sand Creek. Lance Henson. VoR

Anniversary poem is a glass roofed, The. The Anniversary Poem. Diana Der Hovanessian. BTR

Anniverse; an Elegy, The. Henry King. JCP

Anno Domini, *sels.* Craig Raine.
   Birth. NAs

Anno 1829. Heine, *tr. fr. German by* Charles Stuart Calverley. AWP; OBVE

Annot Lyle's Song. Sir Walter Scott. *Fr.* Legend of Montrose, The. EnRP

Annotations of Auschwitz, *sels.* Peter Porter.
   "London is full of chickens, on electric spits." OxBTC

Annotators agree Composer X. St Cecilia's Day Epigram. Peter Porter. PeLV

Announced by all the trumpets of the sky. The Snow-Storm. Emerson. AmPP; AnAmPo; BLPL; BoNaP; FaBoBe; GN; LiTA; MeMAP; NAAL-1; NOBA; NoP; OxBA; PoE; PoEL-4; PoLF; Prf; TAP; TFi; TrGrPo; UnPo; WiR

Annual Gaiety. Wallace Stevens. MoAB; MoAmPo

Annual Legend. Winfield Townley Scott. CoAP; LiTA; LiTM

Annuity, The. George Outram. PeVV

Annul Wars. Rabbi Nahman of Bratzlav, *tr. fr. Hebrew by* Jacob Sloan. TrJP

Annunciation. John Donne. *Fr.* La Corona. ChIV-2; ESCV; Son; TrCP

Annunciation. Ken Etheridge. AngWe

Annunciation, The. Edwin Muir. ChIV-2; CMoP; CRP; NOCV

Annunciation, The. Amrita Pritam, *tr. fr. Punjabi by* Khushwant Singh *and* Krishna Gorowara. WPOW

Annunciation. Rainer Maria Rilke, *tr. fr. German by* James Blair Leishman. OBVE

Annunciation. Kay Smith. NIP

Annunciation, The. *Unknown.* MeEL

Annunciation over the Shepherds, *sels.* Rainer Maria Rilke, *tr. fr. German by* M. D. Herter Norton.
   "Look up, you men. Men there at the fire." PChr

Annus Mirabilis, *sels.* Dryden.
   "Fire, mean time, walks in a broader gross, The." FaBoEH
   Fire of London, The. ChTr
   New London, The. FaBoCh
   (London after the Great Fire, 1666.) FaBoEH; NOBE
   "Now on their coasts our conquering navy rides." OxAEP-1
   "Now van to van the foremost squadrons meet." OBWP
   "Swell'd with our late successes on the foe." EBEV
   "Yet London, empress of the northern clime." NAEL-1; PeECV

Annus Mirabilis. Philip Larkin. NBLV; NIP; NOBL; OBAL

Another youthful advocate of truth and right has gone. To the Memory of J. Horace Kimball. "Ada." BlSi

Anseo. Paul Muldoon. CIP; FaBoPV; PNI

Answeare to my Lady Alice Edgertons Songe, Of I prethy send mee back my Hart, An. Lady Jane Cavendish *and* Lady Elizabeth Brackley. KTR

Answer, The. Sir Robert Ayton. NOSC

Answer. Bei Dao, *tr. fr. Chinese by* Donald Finkel *with* Chen Xueliang. SpMi

Answer, The. Stephen Berg. IMW

Answer, The. George Herbert. FaBoRV; FaBoVe; TEP

Answer, The. Robinson Jeffers. CMoP; GoYe

Answer, The. John Montague. CIP; TIRV

Answer, The. Sara Teasdale. PoA

Answer, The. Chuck Wachtel. UL

Answer, The. The Countess of Winchilsea. NALW

Answer, An. Perceval Gibbon. PeSAV

Answer for Hope. Richard Crashaw. *See* Dear hope! Earth's dowry and heaven's debt!

Answer in Verse for Someone Studying in Ingolst, An, *sels*. Argula von Grumbach, *tr. fr. German by* Susan L. Cocalis.

Answer is blowin' in the wind, The. (*LL*) Blowin' in the Wind. Bob Dylan. PoBeRe

Answer Is in the Garden, The. Wayne Koestenbaum. PFL

Answer Me. Adah Isaacs Menken. CBWP-1

Answer of Mr. Waller's Painter to His Many New Advisers, The. *Unknown*. APAS

Answer that ye made to me, my dear, The. Sir Thomas Wyatt. SiPS

Answer to a Child's Question. Samuel Taylor Coleridge. ArLo; EnRP; FaBoBe; NTP; OxBChV

Answer to a Kind Enquiry. Mary Holtby. UV

Answer to a Lady Advising Me to Retirement, An. Lady Mary Wortley Montagu. TEP

Answer to a Love-Letter in Verse, An. Lady Mary Wortley Montagu. ECWP

Answer to a Man's Question, "What Can I Do about Women's Liberation?," An. Susan Griffin. GLP

Answer to Another Persuading a Lady to Marriage, An. Katherine Philips. HAP; VBLP; WeW

Answer to Cloe [*or* Chloe] Jealous. Matthew Prior. NOBE

Answer to Dunbar's "After a Visit." Joseph S. Cotter, Sr. AAP

Answer to Marlowe. Sir Walter Ralegh. *See* If all the world and love were young.

Answer to Mr. Ben Jonson's Ode, to Persuade Him Not to Leave the Stage, An. Thomas Randolph. BeJo

Answer to ——'s Professions of Affection. Byron. OxBSP

Answer to the Parson, An. Blake. FaBoEE; MeMBP; NBLV; OxBoLi

Answer to Thomas Barry, An. Pierce Fitzgerald, *tr. fr. Irish by* Joan Keefe. TIRV

Answer to Voznesensky and Evtushenko. Frank O'Hara. LCAP; NNaP; PoM

Answer to Yo/ Question. Sonia Sanchez. BPo

Answer Yes or No. Robert Penn Warren. *Fr.* Tale of Time. LCAP

Answered Prayers. Ella Wheeler Wilcox. PWR

Answerers. William Stafford. CAPP

Answering Li Ying Who Showed Me His Poems about Summer Fishing. Yü Hsüan-chi, *tr. fr. Chinese*. BoWoP, *tr. by* Geoffrey R. Waters

Answering Machine, The. Philip Schultz. NAmP90

Answers, The. Robert Clairmont. OTCP; ZA

Answers. Elizabeth Jennings. OxBSP; OxBTC

Ant, The. Richard Flecknoe. NOSC

Ant, The. Richard Lovelace. CaPo

Ant, The. Ogden Nash. FaBV; OBAL

Ant climbs up a trunk, The. A Short Story. David Escobar Galindo, *tr. fr. Spanish*. TSaS, *tr. by* Jorge D. Piche

Ant Dodger. William Knott. PBCAP

Ant has made himself illustrious, The. The Ant. Ogden Nash. FaBV; OBAL

Ant-Heap, The. A. C. Benson. EBVV

Ant-Hills. "Marian Douglas." OBCA

Ant on the tablecloth, An. Departmental. Robert Frost. GoYe; HeIP; HoPM; MoAB; MoAmPo; NAAL-2; NOBA; NOBL; OBAL; PeLV; SoSe

Ant-seething city, city full of dreams. The Seven Old Men. Baudelaire, *tr. fr. French by* Roy Campbell. OBVE

Ant Trap, The. Joe Rosenblatt. NOBC

Ant Village, The. Marion Edey *and* Dorothy Grider. FaPON

Ant wyht in wode be fleme. (*LL*) Lenten Is [*or* Ys] Come [with Love to Toune]. *Unknown*. HAP; MeEL; MiEL

Antaeus; a Fragment. Wilfred Owen. PeHV

Antarctic Muse, The. Thomas Perry. OBTV

Antarctica. Carole Forman. EaPr

Antarctica. Derek Mahon. PBCIP

Antarctica. R. A. Simpson. CBAP

Antarctica. Great plasterwork of gales. Green Windows. Carol Rumens. PWE

Ante-bellum Negro prayed, The. Must Be Freed. L. A. J. Moorer. CBWP-3

Ante-Bellum Sermon, An. Paul Laurence Dunbar. AAP; BPo

Ante Mortem. Robinson Jeffers. MoAmPo

Ante-natal Dream. Patrick Kavanagh. NAs

Antemasque, The: Witches the Nomber Beinge Five. Lady Jane Cavendish *and* Lady Elizabeth Brackley. *Fr.* Pastorall, A. KTR

Anteroom: Geneva. Denis Devlin. CIP

An'the hull lan' shuddered fer miles aroun.' (*LL*) Jesse James. William Rose Benét. FYAP; MoAmPo; TrGrPo

Anthea bade me tie her shoe. The Shoe-tying. Robert Herrick. CaPo

Anthem: "Let us praise our Maker, with true passion extol Him." W. H. Auden. NOCV

Anthem for Doomed Youth. Raymond Garlick. AngWe

Anthem for Doomed Youth. Wilfred Owen. ChTr; ClHu; CMoP; EBEV; FaBoMo; FaBoRV; FaPoB; GTBS-P; HAP; HeIP; HoPM; ImPo; InPK; InPS; LiTM; MoAB; MoBrPo; MoP; NAEL-2; NoAM; NOBE; NoP; OAEL-2; OBEV; OBWP; OxBTC; PlP; PoE; PPP; SCV; Son; SoSe; TFi; TrGrPo; WeW

Anthem of the ILGWU. *Unknown*. SWP

Anthologistics. Arthur Guiterman. NBLV

Anthology of Nouns. Parker Tyler. PoA

Anthology Poem. Petra von Morstein, *tr. by* Rosemarie Waldrop. BoWoP

Anthropology. Anselm Hollo. UL

Anthropology: Cricket at Kano. Stewart Brown. OBTV

Anthropophagites See a Sign on NC Highway 177 That Looks like Heaven, The. Jonathan Williams. OBAL

Anthropos apteros for days. The Labyrinth. W. H. Auden. LiTA

Anti-aircraft seen from a certain distance. Dam Neck, Virginia. Richard Eberhart. LiTA; MoAB; PoWW

Anti Apart Hate Art. Michelle T. Clinton. AIW

Anti-Love Poems. Elizabeth Brewster. NOBC

Anti-Memoirs. Simon Schuchat. UL

Anti-Racist Person. Marsha Prescod. AIW

Anti-Semanticist, The. Everett Hoagland. BPo; NBV

Anti-Vietnam War Peace Mobilization. Allen Ginsberg. PoBeRe

Antichrist, or the Reunion of Christendom; an Ode. G. K. Chesterton. FaBoCo; IHNG; NOBE; NOBL; OBSV; OxAEP-2

Antichrist, playing his lissome flute and merry. Armageddon. John Crowe Ransom. ChIV-2; LiTA; MeMAP

Anticipation. Emily Brontë. OBNC

Anticipation. Lord De Tabley. ELP

Anticipation. Sheila Richter. LoHo

Anticipation. Joseph Tusiani. GoYe

Anticipation of Sharks. Diane Wakoski. MAT

Antidoted Fanfreluches: or, a Galimatia of Extravagant Conceits Found in an Ancient Monument, The. Rabelais, *tr. fr. French by* Sir Thomas Urquhart. CBNP

Antiginides' two daughters, Melo. Leonidas of Tarentum, *tr. fr. Greek by* Alan Marshfield. GrAn

Antigone. Ileana Malancioui, *tr. fr. Romanian by* Daniela Gioseffi. WoWa

Antigone. (My own flesh and blood — .) Sophocles, *tr. fr. Greek*. NAWM-1, *tr. by* Robert Fagles

Sels.

Antigone and Oedipus. H. Cordelia Ray. AAP; BlSi; CBWP-3

Antigone I. Herbert Martin. PoBA

Antigone VI. Herbert Martin. PoBA

Antigonish. Hughes Mearns. *See* As I was going up the stair.

Antikrates knew the stars. Philodemus, *tr. fr. Greek by* Kenneth Rexroth. PGA

Antimony one. Susan Howe. *Fr.* Hear. BCF

Antiodemis, Aphrodite's pet cherub, from a baby. Antipater of Sidon, *tr. fr. Greek by* Tony Harrison. GrAn

Antipastoral Memory of One Summer, An. Dave Jeddie Smith. MT

Antipathy. Rowland Watkyns, *after the Latin of* Martial. FaBoEE

Antiphanes, son of the same, to Hermes. Dedication of a Torch. Crinagoras, *tr. fr. Greek by* Alistair Elliot. GrAn

Antiphon: "Let all the world in ev'ry corner sing *My God and King*." George Herbert. PeECV

Antiphonal Hymn in Praise of Inanna. Enheduanna, *tr. fr. Sumerian*. BoWoP, *ad. by* Aliki *and* Willis Barnstone

Antiphonal Sonnets, *sels.* Clive Wilmer.
  "Suppose a man were dying and this sound." SCBI
Antiplatonic[k], The. John Cleveland. CBLP; NOSC; SeCP
Antipsalm. Novica Tadic, *tr. fr. Serbo-Croatian* by Charles Simic. HSix
Antiquary, The. Joseph Campbell. OxBTC
Antiquary. John Donne. EBEV; FF; NOSC
Antiquary, The, *sels.* Sir Walter Scott.
  Oyster, The. FaBoCh, 1 *st.*; NTP
  Red Harlaw. OxBB
  Why Sit'st Thou by That Ruin'd Hall. EnRP
Antique Harvesters. John Crowe Ransom. MoAB; MoAmPo; NoP; OxBA
Antique Indian should be Henry James, The. American Plan. John
  Malcolm Brinnin. GOA
Antique Shop. Carl Carmer. FaPON
Antiques. Walter de la Mare. PoA
Antiquity of Freedom, The. Bryant. EAP
Antiseptic Baby and the Prophylactic Pup, The. Strictly Germ-proof.
  Arthur Guiterman. BLPA; TrJP
Antiseptic heart? (*LL*) State of the Union. Aimé Césaire. NegPo
Antlered forests, The. Ank'hor Vat. Denis Devlin. BIrV; CIP; IPY; NOIV
Antlered scarab rolled a dungball, The. Near Damascus. W. S. Di Piero.
  ChIV-2
Antlers butting against the full moon. Twins of a Gazelle Which Feed
  Among the Lilies. Catherine Bowman. BAP-89
Antoine, Doug and Tommy cut logs and pulp right through that winter and
  into spring. Tommy Again, Finally. David Budbill. ETG
Antonio. Laura E. Richards. MoShBr; OBCA; PDV
Antonius, *sels.* The Countess of Pembroke.
  Of Death. EIL
Antony and Cleopatra. William Haines Lytle. *See* I am dying, Egypt,
  dying.
Antony and Cleopatra, *sels.* Shakespeare.
  Age Cannot Wither Her. ImPo
  "Barge she sat in, like a burnish'd throne, The." EBEvV; SCV
    (Cleopatra.) LiTB
    (Cleopatra's Barge.) TrGrPo
  Cleopatra's Lament. UnPo
  Drinking Song, A. NoSic
  "Enobarbus, Antony." OxAEP-1
  "Eros, thou yet behold'st me?" EBEV; OxAEP-1
  "Give me my robe, put on my crown; I have." OxAEP-1
    (Cleopatra's Death.) TrGrPo
    (Immortal Longings.) FaBoRV
  "Go charge Agrippa." OBF
  "How now! is he dead?" OxAEP-1
  "Miserable change now at my end, The." EBEV
  "Most noble empress, you have heard of me?" OxAEP-1
  "My desolation does begin to make." OBD
  "Noblest of men, woo't die?" IMW, *act* V, *sc.* 1; OxAEP-1, *sect.* IV,
    xiii
  "O! bear me witness, night." OxAEP-1
  "Thou hast a sister by the mother's side." OxAEP-1
Antony to Cleopatra. William Haines Lytle. BeLS
Antony's Oration [over Caesar's Body]. Shakespeare. *See* Friends,
  Romans, countrymen, lend me your ears.
Antrim. Robinson Jeffers. BIrV; IIP; NOBA; VGW
Ants. Yusuf al-Sa'igh, *tr. fr. Arabic* by Diana Der Hovanessian *with* Salma
  Khadra Jayyusi. TSaS
Ants and birds trace patterns in the dirt, but these creatures. Rhinoceros.
  Harold Farmer. OBAP
Ants and Others. Adrien Stoutenburg. FYAP; NYBP
Ants are walking under the ground, The. The People. Elizabeth Madox
  Roberts. OBAP
Ants look up as I trot by. Dog's Song. Robert Wallace. TLR
Antwerp, *sels.* Ford Madox Ford.
  "This is Charing Cross." PeFWW
Antwerp and Bruges. Dante Gabriel Rossetti. OBTV
Antwerp: Musée des Beaux-Arts. Alan Ross. NYBP
Antwerp to Ghent. Dante Gabriel Rossetti. *Fr.* Trip to Paris and Belgium,
  A. OBTV; PeVV, *sect.* V
Anvil, The. Kipling. FaBoEH
Anvil — God's Word, The. *At. to* John Clifford. BLPA; BLRP; PoToHe
Anxiety about Dying. Alicia Ostriker. CrSp
Anxiety clears meat chunks out of the stew, carrots, takes. Anxiety's
  Prosody. A. R. Ammons. BAP-89
Anxiety's Prosody. A. R. Ammons. BAP-89
Anxious Dead, The. John McCrae. OHIP
Anxious eyes loom down the damp-black streets. Dawn Walkers. Jenny
  Joseph. PWE
Anxious Farmer, The. Burges Johnson. BoNaP

Any clear thing that blinds us with surprise. Fishnet. Robert Lowell.
  HCAP; VCAP
Any Complaints? Vernon Scannell. OxBTC
Any country is only a way of failing. Considerations. David Helwig.
  NOBC
Any dogsbody can sit up all night. Power Cut. Seamus Deane. PBCIP
Any flowers of Spring. (*LL*) View from the Cliffs. Tu Mu. OHMPC
Any Husband or Wife. Carol Haynes. *See* Let us be guests in one
  another's house.
Any Little Woman. Rod Jellema. *Fr.* Four Voices Ending on Some Lines
  from Old Jazz Records. Jaz
Any Man to His Secretary. Hilary Corke. ErPo
Any Man's Advice to His Son. Kenneth Fearing. CMoP
Any more, any more, any more, never more! (*LL*) The New Vestments.
  Edward Lear. NOBVV
Any niche is my college. A Hedge Schoolmaster. Padraic Fallon. CIP
Any of the several names. Eulogy for Populations. Ron Welburn. PoBA
Any Part of Piggy. Noël Coward. NBLV; PeLV
Any Saint. Francis Thompson. MoBrPo
Any silly little soul. Unknown. ISE
Any Soul to Any Body. Cosmo Monkhouse. NOBVV
Any thing to me. Harke, Despair away. (*LL*) The Bag. George Herbert.
  ESCV; GeHe; SeCP
Any thing — to save our cherries. (*LL*) The Cherries; a Parable. Thomas
  Moore. OBSV
Any Wife or Husband. Carol Haynes. BLPA
Any Wife to Any Husband. Robert Browning. OBNC; OtMeF
Any Woman's Blues. Sherley Anne Williams. Jaz
Anyone could hunt the old dog. The One to Grieve. Rudy Thomas.
  GOYP
Anyone Lived in a Pretty How Town. E. E. Cummings. CMoP; EBEvV;
  HAP; InPK; LiTA; LiTM; MeMAP; MoAB; MoAmPo; NAAL-2;
  NOBA; NoP; PoA; Poetr; PrIm; RB; TAP; TFi; TwCP; VGW
Anyone lived there. (*LL*) The Image, As In a Hexagram. Lew Welch.
  PoBeRe
Anyone with quiet pace who. Walking West. William Stafford. RB
Anys for my saik. (*LL*) The Ballad of Kynd Kittok. William Dunbar.
  OxBoLi; PeLV
Anything, everything! (*LL*) Freaks of Fashion. Christina Rossetti. FM
Anything Goes. Cole Porter. OBAL
Anywhere. (*LL*) I Have Given Fair Warning. Philip Lamantia. PoBeRe
Aodh Ruadh O'Domhnaill. Thomas MacGreevy. CIP; OBMV
Aoibhinn, A Leabhráin, Do Thriall. Unknown, *tr. fr. Irish* by Flann
  O'Brien. BIrV
Apart, and on the sacred hill retired. William Hayley. *Fr.* Essay on Epic
  Poetry, An. EPCY
Apart from my sisters, estranged. Cinderella. Olga Broumas. InPK
Apart possibly from waving hello to the cliff-divers. Johnny Weissmuller
  Dead in Acapulco. Clive James. NOBAu
Apart, thank Heaven, from all to do. The Owl. Walter de la Mare.
  OxBSP
Apartheid 1983 Style. (*LL*) Haanetjie's Morning Dialogue. Essop Patel.
  PeSAV
Apartment Cats. Thom Gunn. GrPl
Ape. George Barker. OBAP
Ape. Russell Edson. RaBo
Ape, Lion, Fox and Ass, An. Unknown. OBET
Apelles' Song. John Lyly. *See* Cupid and my Campaspe played [*or* playd].
Apeneck Sweeney spread his knees. Sweeney among the Nightingales. T.
  S. Eliot. AmPP; AnAmPo; CMoP; FaBoMo; HAP; HeIP; InvP; LiTA;
  LiTM; MoP; NAAL-2; NAEL-2; NoAM; NOBA; NOBE; NoP; OBMV;
  OxBA; Poetr; PPP; TFi; WeW
Apes in Avernus. (*LL*) Hark, All You Ladies. Thomas Campion. EIL
Apes yawn and adore their fleas in the sun, The. The Jaguar. Ted
  Hughes. LiTM
Apex. Nate Salsbury. NBLV
Aphorism. "Novalis," *tr. fr. German* by Charles E. Passage. NU
Aphrodisiac, The. Medbh McGuckian. PBCIP
Aphrodite!/ Aphrodite of the blue sleep. Blue Sleep. Winifred Bryher.
  PoA
Aphrodite,/ my Cape Town lady. To Like, to Love. Anne Sexton. AnAn
Apis Mellifica. Roger McDonald. NOBAu
Apocalypse. D. J. Enright. OBSV
Apocalypse. Francis Ernest Kobina Parkes. PBA
Apocrypha. János Pilinszky, *tr. fr. Hungarian* by Ted Hughes. PoSu
Apocrypha. Charles Simic. AnAn
Apocrypha of Jacques Derrida, The. Norman Dubie. NAmP90
Apodal Stride (Cursive). Anthony Barnett. VaA

Apollo 8. John Berryman. AnAn

Apollo and Daphne. W. R. Rodgers. ErPo; LiTB

Apollo and Daphne, sels. Paul Whitehead.
Hunting Song. OxBoLi

Apollo and Daphne. Yvor Winters. Son

Apollo and Marsyas. Zbigniew Herbert, tr. fr. Polish by Czeslaw Milosz.
PoSu, tr. by John and Bogdana Capenter

Apollo as lately a circuit he made. The Circuit of Apollo. The Countess of
Winchilsea. NALW

Apollo Café. Stephen Gray. PeSAV

Apollo Great. Sir Philip Sidney. Fr. Arcadia. SiPSBD

Apollo great, whose beams the greater world do light. Apollo Great. Sir
Philip Sidney. Fr. Arcadia. SiPSBD

Apollo kept my father's sheep. A Daughter of Admetus. T. Sturge
Moore. FaBoTw

Apollo now, Sol's carman, drives his stud. Evening; an Elegy. Horace
Smith. BXAP

Apollophanes married for an alibi. Lucilius, tr. fr. Greek by Peter Porter.
GrAn

Apollo's first, at last the true God's priest. (LL) An Elegy upon the Death
of the Dean of [St.] Paul's, Dr. John Donne. Thomas Carew. CaPo;
JCP; NoP

Apollyonists, The, sels. Phineas Fletcher.
Cambridge and the Cam. FaBoPP

Apologia. Jean Garrigue. LiTA

Apologia (Nkomati). Wole Soyinka. HBAPE

Apologia pro Poemate Meo. Wilfred Owen. FaBoRV; LiTM; MeMBP;
MoAB; MoBrPo; NAEL-2; NSI; PeFWW

Apologia pro Vita Sua. A. R. Ammons. CAPP; HCAP; NOBA

Apologia Pro Vita Sua. Samuel Taylor Coleridge. EnRP; OxBSP

Apologia pro Vita Sua. Pope. Fr. Epistle to Dr. Arbuthnot. FHYEP;
InPS; NOBE; NoP; OAEL-1; OxAEP-1; PoE; PoEL-3; TFi

Apologia pro Vita Sua. Sedulius Scottus, tr. fr. Latin by Helen Waddell.
BIrV

Apologie for Having Loved Before, An. Edmund Waller. CBLP

Apologie for the Precedent Hymnes on Tereas, An. Richard Crashaw. See
Thus have I back again [or againe] to thy bright name.

Apologies, dear Aphrodite. I. Philodemos the Epicurean, tr. fr. Greek by
Sam Hamill. InMo

Apologist's Evening Prayer, The. C. S. Lewis. TrCP

Apologue. Tony Connor. BoLoP

Apology, An. Anne Bradstreet. KTR

Apology. Anthony Cronin. CIP

Apology, The. Emerson. AmPP; AnAmPo

Apology, An. William Morris. Fr. Earthly Paradise, The. AWP; EBVV;
EnVR; LiTB; NAEL-2; NoP; OAEL-2; OBNC; OPOP

Apology. Duane Niatum. HATNAP

Apology, An. Diane Wakoski. TAP

Apology. William Carlos Williams. OxBA; SAmP

Apology for Actors, An, sels. Thomas Heywood.
Author to His Book[e], The. NOSC

Apology for Bad Dreams. Robinson Jeffers. AmPP; LiTA; MoAB;
MoAmPo; NOBA; OxBA

Apology for the Foregoing Hymn, An. Richard Crashaw. JCP

Apology for the Revival of Christian Architecture in England, An, sels.
Geoffrey Hill.
Idylls of the King. FaBoRV; NoAM; PoE
Laurel Axe, The. NAEL-2; NoAM; NoP; PoE
Quaint Mazes. NoAM

Apology for Understatement. John Wain. OxBTC

Apology of the Young Scientists. Celia Dimmette. GoYe

Apon the midsummer evin, mirriest of nichtis. William Dunbar. Fr. Tretis
of the Tua Mariit Wemen and the Wedo, The. EnVB, ll. 1–149;
OxBS

Apostasy. Aus of Kuraiza, tr. fr. Arabic by Hartwig Hirschfeld. TrJP

Apostasy of One and But One Lady, The. Richard Lovelace. CaPo

Apostate, The. A. E. Coppard. OBMV

Apostle Town. Anne Carson. Fr. Life of Towns, The. BAP-90

Apostles of the hidden sun. The Last Supper. Oscar Williams. ImPo;
LiTA; LiTM

Apostrophe to a Dead Friend. Maxine W. Kumin. CAPP

Apostrophe to Man. Edna St. Vincent Millay. NALW

Apostrophe to the Island of Cuba. James Gates Percival. PAH

Apostrophe to the Ocean. Byron. See There is a pleasure in the pathless
woods.

Apostrophe to the Parret. E. H. Burrington. FaBoPP

Apothegms and Counsels. Colette Inez. EOEF

Apotheosis of the Kitchen Goddess II. Teresa Noelle Roberts. CrSp

Appalachia in Cincinnati. Turner Cassity. NGP

Appalachian Convalescence. Robert Conquest. OxBC

Appalachian Front. Robert Lewis Weeks. NYBP

Appalachian Song. Sharon Doubiago. ETG

Apparel of green woods and meadows gay. On Revisiting Cintra after the
Death of Catarina. Camões, tr. fr. Spanish by Richard Garnett. AWP

Apparent Failure. Robert Browning. EBVVPR; NAEL-2; NOBE

Apparently in the real past tough men dazzled the illiterate tribes. Kelvin
Corcoran. NBrP

Apparently with no surprise. Emily Dickinson. AmPP; NAAL-1; NoP;
Poetr; PPP; SAmP; SoSe; TrGrPo

Apparition, The. John Donne. EnLoPo; EnRePo; ESCV; GBL; HeIP;
NAEL-1; NAWM-1; NOBE; NOBL; NoSic; OAEL-1; OBD; OBEV;
PoE; SCGP; SCV; SeCP; SeCV-1; SoSe; TFi

Apparition. W. E. Henley. Fr. In Hospital. TrGrPo

Apparition, The. Herman Melville. NoP

Apparition, The. Stephen Phillips. OBEV

Apparition of a salsa band, The. Latin Night at the Pawnshop. Martín
Espada. TRP

Apparition of His Mistress[e] Calling Him to Elizium [or Elysium], The.
Robert Herrick. CaPo; SeCP; SeCV-1

Apparition of these faces in the crowd, The. In a Station of the Metro.
Ezra Pound. AmPP; HAP; HeIL; HeIP; InPK; MeMAP; MoAB;
MoAmPo; MoP; NAAL-2; NIP; NoAM; NOBA; NoP; OxBA; PoE;
Poetr; TAP; TFi; UnPo; VGW; WeW

Apparitions. Thomas Bailey Aldrich. AnAmPo

Apparitions, The. W. B. Yeats. CMoP; LiTM; TRP

Appeal, The. Kipling. OBD

Appeal. Noémia da Sousa, tr. fr. Portuguese. TTY, tr. by Dorothy Guedes
and Philippa Rumsey; WPOW, tr. by Alan Ryder

Appeal, An. Unknown. NSI

Appeal by Unemployed Ex-Service Men, An. Unknown. OBET

Appeal to Cats in the Business of Love, An. Thomas Flatman. EnLoPo;
GBL; HAP

Appeal to My Countrywomen, An. Frances E. W. Harper. AmWP; BlSi

Appeal to the Moongod Nanna-Suen to Throw Out Lugalanne. Enheduanna,
tr. fr. Sumerian by Aliki and Willis Barnstone. BoWoP

Appear, O Mother, was the perpetual cry. Wilfred Watson. MoCV

Appearance and Reality. John Hollander. OBAL

Appearances. Robert Browning. OxBSP

Appearances. Ben King. AnAmPo

Appears on the water, then is gone. (LL) Twilight in the River Pavilion.
Chiang Shih-ch'üan. OHMPC

Appendix to the Anniad. Gwendolyn Brooks. BlSi

Appendix to the Vision of Peace, An. Yehuda Amichai, tr. fr. Hebrew by
Glenda Abramson and Tudor Parfitt. PoSu

Applauding youths laughed with young prostitutes. The Harlem Dancer.
Claude McKay. BPo; FF; NIP; NoAM; Son; TAP

Applause. Carol Muske. PFL

Apple, The. Judah Halevi, tr. fr. Hebrew by Robert Mezey. UnAS

Apple, The. At. to Plato, tr. fr. Greek. WeW

Apple, The. Ray Smith. TrCP

Apple a day, An. Health Food. Unknown. FaBoUs

Apple and Cloth. Tim Longville. VaA

Apple-Barrel of Johnny Appleseed, The. Vachel Lindsay. OxBA

Apple Blight. Paul Zimmer. VGW

Apple Blossom. Louis MacNeice. NTP; PeECV; RB

Apple-blossom, a great spread of it. And Where Do You Stand on the
National Question. Tom Paulin. CIP

Apple Blossoms. Henry Adams Parker. BoTP

Apple blossoms look like snow. A Comparison. John Farrar. FaPON;
WHSW

Apple-Culture. John Philips. Fr. Cyder. OxAEP-1

Apple Dumplings. Mary E. Tucker. AmWP; CBWP-1

Apple Dumplings and a King, the. "Peter Pindar." OBSV

Apple Gathering, An. Christina Rossetti. NAEL-2; OBNC

Apple-green west and an orange bar. Frost To-night. Edith M. Thomas.
AmWP

Apple Harvest. Helen Leuty. BoTP

Apple Hell. Mark Van Doren. PoA

Apple of My Eye, sels. Rosalie Sorrels.
"What can I say, but that it's not easy?" MDDM

Apple on a stick. Unknown. RoPo

Apple on its bough is her desire, The. Garden Abstract. Hart Crane.
MeMAP

Apple on the barefaced, The. Apple and Cloth. Tim Longville. VaA

Apple Orchard in the Spring, An. William Martin. GN; PWR

Apple Peeler. Robert Francis. LCAP

Apple-pie, apple-pie. *Unknown.* OxNR

Apple Rhyme, The. Madeleine Nightingale. BoTP

Apple-Seed John. Lydia Maria Child. OHIP

Apple Song. Frances Frost. FaPON

Apple Tree, The. James K. Baxter. OxBC

Apple Tree and a Pig, An. Emyr Humphreys. OBWVE

Apple-Tree Man, The. Charles Causley. OBSP

Apple Trees, The. Louise Glück. HCAP

Apple Wassail. *Unknown.* OBET

Apples. Donald Hall. LCAP

Apples. Shirley Kaufman. CrSp; MDDM; NMM

Apples and oranges, four for a penny. *Unknown.* ISE

Apples are seasoned, The. Apple Song. Frances Frost. FaPON

Apples Be Ripe. *Unknown.* GBP

Apples, bright on the leafless bough. Apple Hell. Mark Van Doren. PoA

Apples in New Hampshire. Marie Emilie Gilchrist. BoNaP

Apples, Normandy, 1944. Frank Ormsby. *Fr. Northern Spring, A.* PNI

Apples of gold, in silver pictures shrined. Edward Taylor. *Fr. Preparatory Meditations Before My Approach to the Lord's Supper.* NAAL-1

Apples, ripen for the dray! (*LL*) The Victoria Markets Recollected in Tranquility. "Furnley Maurice." NOBAu

Apples Ripen Under Yellowing Leaves, The. Thomas Caulfield Irwin. PeIV

Applicant, The. Sylvia Plath. MAT; NAAL-2; NaP; NMM; NOBA; TwCP

Apply for the position (I've forgotten now for what) I had. In Order To. Kenneth Patchen. NaP

Appoggiatura. Donald Jeffrey Hayes. PoBA; PoNe

Appointed Rounds. Louis Jenkins. RaBo

Appointment, The. Maxine W. Kumin. NMM

Appointment, The. L. A. G. Strong. OxBTC

Appointment, A. Chang Shiang-Lua. TSaS, *tr. by* Stephen L. Smith *with* Naomi Shihab Nye.

Appraisal. Sara Teasdale. MoAmPo

Appraise me! — you, Christian of any stock. The Testament of a Vivisector. John Davidson. MeMBP

Apprehend God in all things. *Unknown.* EaPr

Apprehension this spring . . . the leaves, the leaves. Homage and Lament for Ezra Pound in Captivity. Robert Duncan. NOBA

Apprentice — fifteen, ugly, not too thin, The. Low Scene. Paul Verlaine, *tr. fr. French by* Alistair Elliot. FaBoBl

Apprentice Painter, The. Jack Myers. AmPA

Approach, The, *sels.* Thomas Traherne.
　"O Lord, I wonder at thy lov." TrPWD

Approach of the Storm, The. *Unknown, tr. fr. Chippewa Indian by* Frances Densmore. OBVE; TTTS

Approach the Holocaust. Yellow Starred. Sister Mary Philip de Camara. BTR

Approach to a City. William Carlos Williams. PoRA

Approach to Thebes, The. Stanley Kunitz. PoA

Approaches, The. W. S. Merwin. NOBA; Prf

Approaching by the gate (Class of '79). Views of the Favorite Colleges. John Malcolm Brinnin. LiTA; MoAB

Approaching death. William Carlos Williams. *Fr. Asphodel, That Greeny Flower.* FaBoMo

Approaching night her mantle flings. To _____. James M. Whitfield. AAP

Approximate Man, The, *sels.* Tristan Tzara, *tr. fr. French by* Michael Benedikt.

Approximately. Yannis Ritsos, *tr. fr. Greek by* Nikos Stangos. CBCK

Après le Bain. William Carlos Williams. OBAL

Après-midi d'un Faune, L'. Stéphane Mallarmé, *tr. fr. French by* Aldous Huxley. AWP
　Sels.
　"Proud of my music, let me often make." ErPo

Apricot Garden. Yüan Chen, *tr. fr. Chinese by* Angela Jung Palandri. SuSp

Apricot Tree. Magda Isanos, *tr. fr. Romanian by* Willis Barnstone *and* Matei Calinescu. BoWoP

Apricots Die Young, *sels.* Meng Chiao, *tr. fr. Chinese.*
　"Don't let freezing hands play with these pearls." SuSp
　"In vain I gather up these stars from the ground." SuSp
　"It must have been a single thread of tears." SuSp
　"Nipping chill, the frost killed spring." SuSp
　"When I tread the earth, I fear to hurt the ground." SuSp
　"When my son was born, the moon was not bright." SuSp

April. Remy Belleau, *tr. fr. French by* Andrew Lang. AWP

April. Vidame de Chartres, *tr. fr. French by* Swinburne. AWP

April. Linda Pastan. Poetsp

April. Ezra Pound. CMoP

April. H. Cordelia Ray. CBWP-3

April. Sara Teasdale. FaPON; PDV

April. Samuel Thompson. BIrV

April. Jean Valentine. TAP

April. Sir William Watson. *See* April, April,/ Laugh thy girlish laughter.

April. Nathaniel Parker Willis. AnAmPo

April. Yvor Winters. RFM

April. Charles Wright. CAPP; MT

April, and a fool's good day. April Notebook. C. K. Stead. PeNZ

April and May. Emerson. *Fr.* May-Day. GN; OHIP

April, and no one able to calculate. Patrick Kavanagh. *Fr.* Great Hunger, The. IPY

April, April,/ Laugh thy girlish laughter. Sir William Watson. OBEV; TrGrPo
　(April.) BoTP; FaBV
　(Song to April.) GN

April. Bad month. Visit spa. Stanley J. Sharpless. PeLi

April cold with dropping rain. April and May. Emerson. *Fr.* May-Day. GN; OHIP

April Day, An. Joseph S. Cotter, Sr. CDC

April, 1885. Robert Bridges. OxBSP; OxBTC

April 5, 1974. Richard Wilbur. HCAP

April Fool, The. Eugene Field. PWR

April Fool Birthday Poem for Grandpa. Diane Di Prima. PoBeRe

April fool, go to school. *Unknown.* RoPo

April Fool's Day, or St. Mary Egypt. John Berryman. *Fr.* Dream Songs. ChIV-2; NaP

April fool's gone past. *Unknown.* ISE

April Fourth. Robert Mezey. NaP

April Gale. Ivor Gurney. Spl

April Hill, The. Janet Lewis. CRP

April. I have wheeled you to the park. Oradour-sur-Glane. Silence. Lucia Cordell Getsi. LoHo

April in England. Robert Browning. *See* Oh [*or* O] to be in England.

April Inventory. W. D. Snodgrass. CAPP; CoAP; HAP; LiTM; NoAM; NoP; Poetr; TAP; TRP; TwCP; VCAP

April is a very unkind month, I am telling you. The Wasted Land. Edward Pygge. FaBoPa

April is in my mistress' face. All Seasons in One. *Unknown.* GBL; HeIP; TrGrPo

April is the cruellest month, breeding. The Waste Land. T. S. Eliot. AmPP; CMoP; FaBoMo; HAP; LiTA; LiTM; MoAB; MoAmPo; MoP; NAAL-2; NAEL-2; NAWM-2; NoAM; NOBA; NOBE; NoP; OAEL-2; OxAEP-2; OxBA; OxBTC; PoE; TAP; TFi; UnPo

April Mortality. Léonie Adams. MoAB; MoAmPo
　Sels.
　"With all the drifting race of men." TrGrPo

April 1962. Paul Goodman. VGW

April Notebook. C. K. Stead. PeNZ

April, pride of woodland ways. April. Remy Belleau, *tr. fr. French by* Andrew Lang. AWP

April Rain. Robert Loveman. BoTP; TrJP

April Rain Song. Langston Hughes. FaPON; ImGa; NTCP; OBCA; PDV; SiSoPo

April showers/ Bring May flowers. *Unknown.* RoPo

4/13/79. Lewis Warsh. UL

April this year, not otherwise. Song of a Second April. Edna St. Vincent Millay. CMoP; OxBA

April winds are magical, The. Spring. Emerson. OtMeF

April. You hearken, my fellow. Earth's Lyric. Bliss Carman. AnAmPo

Aprill. Spenser. *Fr.* Shepheardes [*or* Shepeards *or* Shepherd's] Calender, The. NAEL-1; PoEL-1

Aprille is of al the months moste dyr. Buriall of the Dede. Martin Fagg. BXAP

Aprilly. Bert Leston Taylor. OBAL

Apron of Flowers, The. Robert Herrick. CaPo; SeCV-1

Apron Strings. Marge Piercy. TAP

Aprons of Silence. Carl Sandburg. NOBA

Apropos of the Falling Sleet. Harry Clifton. IB

Aqua, *sels.* Asger Schnack.
　"Let the poppy unfold itself let it intoxicate." Jaz

Aquarium. George T. Wright. NYBP

Aquarium du Trocadéro. Duncan Bush. AngWe

Arab and His Donkey, An. *Unknown.* NBLV

Arab came to the river side, An. An Arab and His Donkey. *Unknown.* NBLV

Arab Chieftain to His Young Wife, An. Abid ibn al-Abras, *tr. fr. Arabic by* Omar S. Pound. ArPe

Arab Love-Song, An. Francis Thompson. AWP; MoAB; MoBrPo; OtMeF

Arab to His Favorite Steed, The. Caroline E. Norton. BeLS

Arabesque. Fred Johnson. PoBA

Arabesque. "Sagittarius." IHNG

Arabesque: Five Poems for Women without Children, *sels.* Mary Mackey. Grande Jetée. AIW

Arabia. Walter de la Mare. CoGr

Arabia. John Meade Falkner. OxBTC

Arabian Nights. Jack Marshall. UL

Arabic Script. Anthony Thwaite. OBTV

Arabs complain — or so I have been told. For the Rain It Raineth Every Day. Robert Graves. GoJo; NYBP

Arab's Farewell to His Steed, The. Caroline E. Norton. *See* My beautiful! my beautiful! that standest meekly by.

Arachne. William Empson. InvP; OBMV

Arachne. Judith Kazantzis. BrRo

Arac's Song. W. S. Gilbert. *Fr.* Princess Ida. FiBHP

Aranda Song. *Unknown, tr. fr. Aranda by* T. G. H. Strehlow. CBAP

Arawak Prologue. Basil McFarlane. PBCV

Arawata Bill, *sels.* Denis Glover.
   Camp Site. PeNZ
   River Crossing, The. PeNZ
   "With his weapon a shovel." PeNZ

Arbasto, *sels.* Robert Greene.
   Whereat Erewhile I Wept, I Laugh. ElL

Arbeit Macht Frei. Dennis Schmitz. AnAn

Arbor Amoris. Villon, *tr. fr. French by* Andrew Lang. AWP

Arbor Day Tree, An. *Unknown.* OHIP

Arbor Vitae. Coventry Patmore. *Fr.* Unknown Eros, The. OBNC; PeVV

Arbour, The. Anne Brontë. EBVV

Arc. Tom Clark. UL

Arc Inside and Out, The. A. R. Ammons. NoAM; NoP

Arc of an egg, The. Nothing So Wise. Jeanne Lohmann. CrSp

Arcades, *sels.* Milton.
   Nymphs and Shepherds. ELP
   "O'er [*or* O're] the smooth enameled green." OBEV; TrGrPo
   (Song: "O'er The smooth enamelled green.") OxBSP

Arcades Ambo. Charles Stuart Calverley. BXAP

Arcadia, *sels.* Sir Philip Sidney.
   Apollo Great. SiPSBD
   As I Behind a Bush Did Sit. SiPSBD
   "As I my little flock on Ister Bank." SiPSBD
   (Shepherd Song.) SiPS
   Complaint of Love. PoEL-1; SiPS
   Corona. SiPSBD
   Country Song, A. SiPS
   Cupid. SiPS
   (Against Cupid.) SiPSBD
   Echo. SiPS
   (Echo Song.) SiPSBD
   "Fire to see my wrongs for anger burneth, The." SiPSBD
   (Wronged Lover, The.) SiPS
   Geron and Histor. SiPS
   Get Hence Foule Griefe. PoEL-1
   (Contentment.) SiPS
   Graven Thoughts. SiPS
   How Is My Sun. SiPSBD
   In Vain, Mine Eyes. SiPS; SiPSBD
   "Let mother Earth now deck herself in flowers." OxAEP-1; SiPS
   (Epithalamium: "Let mother Earth.") SiPSBD
   "Let not old age disgrace my high desire." SiPSBD
   (Old Age.) SiPS
   Lock Up, Fair Lids. SiPSBD
   (Sleep.) SiPS
   (Sonnet: "Lock up, fair lids, the treasure of my heart.") ElL
   Love and Jealousy. SiPS
   Love and Reason. SiPS
   My Sheep Are Thoughts. NoSic; SiPS; SiPSBD
   "My true love hath my heart, and I have his." BoLoP; CH; EBEvV; FaBoBe; GBL; NoSic; PoE; PoEL-1; SCGP; SiPSBD; TFi; TrGrPo; UV
   (Arcadian Duologue.) SiPS
   (Bargain, The.) NOBE; OBEV; OtMeF; OxAEP-1
   (Ditty, A: "My true love hath my heart, and I have his.") AWP; GTBS; GTBS-P
   (Heart Exchange.) LiTB
   (Sonnet: "My true love hath my heart.") ElL
   (True Love.) ChTr
   "Neighbour mine not long ago there was, A." SiPSBD
   (Tale for Husbands, A.) SiPS
   "O night, the ease of care, the pledge of pleasure." SiPSBD
   (Night.) SiPS
   "O sweet woods, the delight of solitariness." NoSic; SiPSBD
   (Delight of Solitariness, The.) LiTB

   (O Sweet Woods.) FaBoRV; PoEL-1
   (Solitariness.) SCGP; SiPS
   Sweetly Empty Woods. CBCK
   "O words, which fall like summer dew on me!" SiPSBD
   (Rural Poesy.) ElL
   Over These Brooks. SiPSBD
   Pastoral Elegy. SiPSBD
   "Phoebus Farewell." SiPSBD
   "Phoebus farewell, a sweeter saint I serve." SiPSBD
   (Sweeter Saint I Serve, A.) SiPS
   Sapphics. SiPS
   Sestina: "Farewell, O Sun." SiPSBD
   Shepherd's Tale, A. SiPS
   "Since Nature's works be good, and death doth serve." SiPSBD
   (Why Fear to Die?) SiPS
   Since So Mine Eyes. SiPS
   Since That the Stormy Rage. SiPSBD
   Song Contest: Lalus and Dorus. SiPSBD
   This Cave Is Dark. SiPSBD
   What Tongue Can Her Perfections Tell? EnRePo; SiPS; SiPSBD
   When Two Suns Do Appear. EnRePo; SiPS; SiPSBD
   "Who doth desire that chaste his wife should be." SiPSBD
   (Advice to the Same.) SiPS
   "Why dost thou haste away?" NoSic; SiPS
   Ye Goat-herd Gods. HAP; NAEL-1; NOBE; NoP; NoSic; OAEL-1
   (Double Sestine [*or* Sestina].) ImPo; LiTB; PoEL-1; SiPSBD
   You Living Powers. SiPSBD

Arcadian Duologue. Sir Philip Sidney. *See* My true love hath my heart, and I have his.

Arcanum One. Gwendolyn MacEwen. MoCV

Arch film duds. Bee Elk. Clark Coolidge. PRA

Archaeological Picnic, The. Sir John Betjeman. EnLoPo

Archæologist, The. James Simmons. PBCIP

Archaeology of Love, The. Richard Murphy. EnLoPo

Archaic Song of Dr. Tom the Shaman. *Unknown, tr. fr. Nootka Indian by* Jerome K. Rothenberg. STP

Archaic Torso of Apollo. Rainer Maria Rilke, *tr. fr. German.* NAWM-2, *tr. by* Stephen Mitchell; RaBo

Archaic Torso of Apollo. Rainer Maria Rilke, *tr. fr. German by* Robert Bly. NU

Archaic Torso of My Uncle Phil. Mark Cox. NAmP90

Archangel. Kit Robinson. UL

Archbishop is away. The church is gray, The. Gray Stones and Gray Pigeons. Wallace Stevens. SAmP

Archbishop Tait. *Unknown.* ChTr; FaBoNo

Archer, The. Clinton Scollard. FaPON

Archer (acquainted with brilliance), The. The Access. Henry Kanabus. UL

Archer is wake, The! Peace on Earth. William Carlos Williams. LiTA

Archery. Walter de la Mare. FaBoNo

Archibald MacLeish Suspends the Five Little Pigs. Louis Untermeyer. *Fr.* Mother Goose Up-to-Date. MoAmPo

Ar(chibald')s Poetica. Alan Ribback. BXAP

Archie o [*or* of] Cawfield. *Unknown.* AmFP; ESPB; OxBS

Archimedes, the early truth-seeker. Stanley J. Sharpless. PeLi

Archinos, this retsina bottle contains. Rhianus, *tr. fr. Greek by* Peter Jay. GrAn

Archy and Mehitabel, *sels.* Don Marquis.
   Archy at the Zoo. NBLV; OBAL
   Archy Confesses. FiBHP
   Cheerio My Deario. FaBoCo
   Hen and the Oriole, The. FiBHP
   Mehitabel and Her Kittens. SoCa
   Mehitabel Tries Companionate Marriage. OFC
   No Social Stuff for Mehitabel. OFC
   Old Trouper, The. FaBoCo
   Song of Mehitabel, The. FiBHP; OFC; SoCa
   Wail of Archy, The. FiBHP
   Warty Bliggens, the Toad. FiBHP

Archy at the Zoo. Don Marquis. *Fr.* Archy and Mehitabel. NBLV; OBAL

Archy Confesses. Don Marquis. *Fr.* Archy and Mehitabel. FiBHP

Archy, the Cockroach, Speaks. Don Marquis. *Fr.* Certain Maxims of Archy. FaPON; OBAL

Archys Life of Mehitabel, *sels.* Don Marquis.
   Ballade of the Under Side. InvP

ARCS above OXUS. Colin Simms. NBrP

Arctic Convoy. J. K. Annand. OxBS

Arctic Fox, The. Ted Hughes. OBAP

Arctic honey blabbed over the report causing darkness, The. Leaving the Atocha Station. John Ashbery. CAPP

Arctic moon hangs overhead, The. The Wolf Cry. Lew Sarett. FaPON

Arctic Ox, The. Marianne Moore. NYBP

Arctic Tern in a Museum. Mary Effie Lee Newsome. PoNe

Arctic Vision, An. Bret Harte. PAH

Arcturus is his other name. Emily Dickinson. FaBV; NOBA

Arcturus, the bear driver. Night Sky. Louise Erdrich. HATNAP

Arcuconspicilla oves looks for perditas. She Lost Her Sheep. J. Moyr Smith. FaBoNo

Ardan Mór. Francis Ledwidge. See As I was climbing Ardán Mór.

Ardelia's Spiritual Progress. The Countess of Winchilsea. Fr. Fragment, A. CBCK

Arden is not Eden, but Eden's rhyme. In Arden. Charles Tomlinson. OxBC

Ardent in love and cold in charity. A Man's [a] Sliding Mood. Mary Elizabeth Fullerton. CBAP; NOBAu

Ardent lover cannot find, The. Address to Her Husband. Mehetabel Wright. ECWP

Ardour and Memory. Dante Gabriel Rossetti. Fr. House of Life, The. OAEL-2

Are added unto them that have plenty of water. (LL) Green, Green Is El Aghir. Norman Cameron. MoBS; OBWP; OxBTC

Are all growing green in my north country. (LL) The North Country Maid. Unknown. OBET

Are all such off'rings, as are crusht, and bruis'd. Francis Quarles. FaBoEE

Are all these stones. Close-up. A. R. Ammons. PoA

Are always tender. (LL) Sprout. Tuo Ssu. WPC

Are an old family. It was our forebears speaking. (LL) Tongues. Philip Martin. NOBAu

Are blonde. (LL) Racial Memories. Elizabeth Mische John. LoHo

Are blue. The top of the sky/ is too. (LL) Vaquero. Edward Dorn. NeAP; PoM

Are blurred into one face: a child's set face. (LL) A Hunt in the Black Forest. Randall Jarrell. CoAP; LCAP

Are both fair, tall, kind, and witty. (LL) Her Commendation. Francis Davison.

Are bright, as though the sun had set a rainbow in each feather! (LL) Tasmanian Scenes. Louisa Meredith. NOBAu

Are brothers of cinders. (LL) Psalm of Those Who Go Forth before Daylight. Carl Sandburg. MoShBr; OxBA

Are by the sunbeams tickled by degrees. (LL) The Coming of Good Luck. Robert Herrick. FaBoEE; JCP; OxBSP; Spl

Are Cat and Dog, and Rogue and Whore. (LL) Phyllis; or, The Progress of Love. Swift. OAEL-1; OBSV; PoE

Are creatures with wings. (LL) Footpaths Cross in the Rice Field. Lin Ling. WPC

Are dark windows? (LL) The World Outside. Denise Levertov. TRP

Are dim with kisses, day and night? (LL) Darling Shell, where hast thou been. Walter Savage Landor. CBLP

Are Flowers Whores? Elizabeth Smart. VBLP

Are forced, for my greater grief, from me their face to hide. (LL) Psalm 88. The Earl of Surrey. SiPSBD

Are friends delight or pain? Emily Dickinson. OBF

Are full of the voice of the unborn. (LL) The Night of the Shirts. W. S. Merwin. VCAP

Are God Almighty's bow and arrow. (LL) Greed. Unknown. OxNR

Are green and spring up again. (LL) The Unquiet Grave. Unknown. FaBoBa; OBET

Are Holy-Land! (LL) To Helen. Poe. AmPP; AnAmPo; AWP; BoLoP; CH; ChTr; ClHu; FaBoBe; FaBV; GBL; HAP; HelP; HoPM; ImPo; InPS; InvP; LiTA; MeMAP; NAAL-1; NIP; NOBA; NOBE; NoP; OBEV; OtMeF; OxBA; PoE; PoEL-4; PoLF; PoRA; PrIm; TAP; TFi; TrGrPo; WeW

Are indecorums with the modern maid. (LL) On Women ("Britannia's daughters.") Edward Young. ECEV

Are like South Africa. The Hamptons. Kathy Engel. WoWa

Are naked as a line of poetry in a war. (LL) The Song of the Borderguard. Robert Duncan. NeAP; PoM

Are never wrong and I am rhythm to strong medicine. (LL) In My Lifetime. James Welch. CDW

Are not more far apart. (LL) We Never Said Farewell. Mary Elizabeth Coleridge. OxBSP; WPE

Are not such furious boys with blood on their faces. (LL) To the Woman in Bond Street Station. Edward Weismiller. LiTA

Are one. (LL) To Jane. Shelley. FHYEP; Mes; NoP

Are one with all the dead, since she is gone. (LL) The Glory of the Day Was in Her Face. James Weldon Johnson. CDC; PoBA

Are pictures of home, to be admired more stringently. (LL) On Nothing. Unknown. BAP-90

Are ready. (LL) The Oranges Are Ripe. Bei Dao. SpMi

Are shaken with earth's old and weary cry. (LL) The Sorrow of Love. W. B. Yeats. MoAB; MoBrPo; NoAM; NOBVV; OAEL-2; PoEL-5; TEP

Are signs. (LL) Creation Story. Paula Gunn Allen. SRLS

Are sisters under their skins! (LL) The Ladies. Kipling. MoBrPo; NAEL-2

Are sorrows hard to bear, — the ruin. Burdens. Edward Dowden. NOBVV

Are still allow'd to fiddle with the case. (LL) Elinda's [or Ellinda's] Glove. Richard Lovelace. CaPo; CBLP; NOSC

Are sweet like wanton loves because I hate. (LL) The White City. Claude McKay. BPo; NoAM; RaBo; TAP

Are thanks — and from the dead is gratitude. (LL) Cleitagoras. Leonidas of Tarentum. AWP

Are the color of nipples. Worn silk thins to mesh. (LL) Paris Aubade. Susan Ludvigson. VBLP

Are the desolate, dark weeks. These. William Carlos Williams. MoAB; MoAmPo; MoP; NOBA; NoP; OxBA

(These/ are the desolate, dark weeks.) MeMAP

Are the horns of the hall on fire? The Battle of Finnsburg. Unknown. tr. fr. Anglo-Saxon by Charles W. Kennedy. AnOE

Are the tear drops of my mourners. (LL) Cloud Dissects Itself. Lin Ling. WPC

Are the things so strange and marvelous you see or have seen? (LL) Ethiopia Saluting the Colors. Walt Whitman. PAH; PoNe

Are there not twelve whole hours in every day. The Day of Denial. Jones Very. NOBA

Are there others too. What She Said. Venkorran, tr. fr. Tamil by A. K. Ramanujan. PLW

Are these ashes in my hand. Hilda Doolittle ("H. D."). Fr. Sigil. AnAn

Are these mellifluous sheep. Strictly Bucolic. Charles Simic. FoLa

Are these the honors they reserve for me. Columbus in Chains. Philip Freneau. PAH

Are these the pope's grand tools? On the Murder of Sir Edmund Berry Godfrey. Unknown. APAS

Are they blind, the lords of Gaza. Angry Samson. Robert Graves. ChIV-1

Are they clinging to their crosses. Antichrist, or the Reunion of Christendom; an Ode. G. K. Chesteron. FaBoCo; IHNG; NOBE; NOBL; OBSV; OxAEP-2

Are They Dancing. Edward Dorn. NeAP; PoM

Are they exiles here from the rest of the world? What Do the Birds Think? Alfred W. Purdy. MoCV

Are They Not All Ministering Spirits? Robert Stephen Hawker. ArNa; OxAEP-2

Are they shadows that we see? Samuel Daniel. Fr. Tethy's Festival. NOSC

(Are They Shadows [That We See]?) CH; ElL; InvP; NoP

(Shadows.) NOBE

(Song: "Are they shadowes that we see?") PoEL-2

Are thine eyes weary? is thy heart too sick. November. William Morris. Fr. Earthly Paradise, The. EnVR

Are Those Two Stars. Giles Fletcher the Elder. Fr. Licia. Son

Are We Not the People, sels. Al-Samau'al Ibn Adiya, tr. fr. Arabic by Hartwig Hirschfeld.

"Now listen to boasting which leaves the heart dazed." TrJP

Are we now? Do we know anything? (LL) Colloquy. Weldon Kees. NaP; NYBP

Are We Ready for the Jimi Hendrix Story? Connie Deanovich. UTF

Are we to keep Christ writhing on the cross! (LL) Calvary. E. A. Robinson. MoAmPo; Son; WGRP

Are we unfathomable night. Hilda Doolittle ("H. D."). Fr. Sigil. AnAn

Are Ye Right There, Michael? (A Lay of the Wild West Clare.). William Percy French. WTO

Are you? (LL) Forever. Charles Stuart Calverley. NOBL; NOBVV

Are You a Marsupial? John Becker. ZA

Are you a poet? Conversation with a Poet. Miroslav Holub, tr. by Ewald Osers. PWE

Are you a trailor, or are you a trolley? Are You You? Edmund Vance Cooke. PWR

Are you alive? The Pool. Hilda Doolittle ("H. D."). CMoP

Are you almost disgusted with life, little man? How to Be Happy. Unknown. BLPA

Are you awake, Gemelli. Star-Talk. Robert Graves. BoNaP; GoJo; MoBrPo; OxBTC

Are you Content? W. B. Yeats. IIP

Are you dead, Pyrrho? Epitaph in Dialogue on the Sceptic Philosopher Pyrrho. Julianus of Egypt, tr. fr. Greek by Lee T. Pearcy. GrAn

Are You Glad? Mongol Oral Tradition, tr. by C. R. Bawden. WTO

Are you going to Whittingham Fair? Whittingham Fair. Unknown. GBP

Are you he who would assume a place to teach or be a poet here in the States? Walt Whitman. Fr. By Blue Ontario's Shore. FaBoPV

Are you hot there too? Black Muslim Boy in a Hospital. James A. Emanuel. PoNe

Are you looking for me? Mathenge. Marjorie Oludhe Macgoye. HBAPE

Are you looking for me? I am in the next seat! The Breath. Robert Bly. *Fr.* Two Translations from Kabir. PRA

Are you out, woman of the lean pelt. Ire. R. S. Thomas. OxBSP

Are you ready, O Virginia. The Call to the Colors. Arthur Guiterman. PAH

Are you ready? soul said again. Two Trinities. Kenneth Mackenzie. CBAP; FaBoMA

Are you sleeping, are you sleeping, Brother John, Brother John. Brother John. *Unknown.* SWP

Are you so weary? Come to the window. Wind in the Grass. Mark Van Doren. FaBV

Are you standing at "Wit's End Corner." Wit's End Corner. Antoinette Wilson. BLRP

Are you the guy. *Unknown.* RoPo

Are You the New Person Drawn toward Me? Walt Whitman. OxBSP; PPP

Are You There? Strickland W. Gillilan. PoToHe

Are you very weary? Rest a little bit. Rest. *Unknown.* PoToHe

Are you washed in the blood of the Lamb? (*LL*) General William Booth Enters into Heaven. Vachel Lindsay. AmPP; ChIV-2; CMoP; ImPo; LiTA; LiTM; MeMAP; MoAB; MoAmPo; NOBA; OxBA; PoA; PoE; TAP; TrGrPo; WGRP

Are you what your faire lookes expresse? Thomas Campion. AAS

Are you worsted in a fight? Laugh It Off. Henry Rutherford Elliot. WBLP

Are You You? Edmund Vance Cooke. PWR

Are you You or Me or It? Hello Up There. Marge Piercy. NBLV

Are your Delinquent Travellers! (*LL*) The Delinquent Travellers. Samuel Taylor Coleridge. OBTV

Are your sorrows hard to bear? The Length of Life. Amos R. Wells. PWR

Arena dust rusted by four bulls' blood to a dull redness. The Goring. Sylvia Plath. OBTV

Ares. Albert Ehrenstein, *tr. fr. German by* Babette Deutsch *and* Avrahm Yarmolinsky. TrJP

Ares at last has quit the field. Under Which Lyre, a Reactionary Tract for the Times. W. H. Auden. MoAB; MoBrPo; NOBL; PeLV

Arethusa. Shelley. EnRP; GN; WiR

Arethusa, The. Prince Hoare. FaPoR

Argalus and Parthenia, *sels.* Francis Quarles.
   Hos Ego Versiculos. NOSC

Argent Solipsism. Howard Blake. PoA

Argenteuil County. Peter Dale Scott. MoCV

Argentina in one swing of the bell skirt. The Beautiful Train. William Empson. OxAEP-2

Argentine gaucho named Bruno, An. *Unknown.* NOBL

Argoed. T. Gwynn Jones, *tr. fr. Welsh by* Anthony Conran. OBWVE

Argonautica, The. Apollonius Rhodius, *tr. fr. Greek by* Barbara Hughes Fowler. HePo

Argonauts, The. D. H. Lawrence. NoAM

Arguement, The. Anna Hume. *Fr.* Triumphs of Death. KTR

Argument, The. Samuel Butler. *Fr.* Hudibras. EBEV; NAEL-1; OAEL-1; SeCV-2

Argument, An. Thomas Moore. BoLoP; EnLoPo; OxBSP

Argument of Democritus Platonissans, or the Infinitie of Worlds, The. Henry More. SeCV-2

Argument of His Book, The. Robert Herrick. AWP; BeJo; CaPo; EBEV; HAP; ImPo; InvP; JCP; NAEL-1; NoP; NOSC; OAEL-1; OxAEP-1; PeECV; PoE; PoEL-3; PoRA; SeCP; SeCV-1; TEP; TFi; TrGrPo; TTTS

Argument of the Fourth Booke, The. Lucretius, *tr. fr. Latin. Fr.* De Rerum Natura (On the Nature of Things). KTR, *tr. by* Lucy Hutchinson.

Argus. Pope. OBF

Aria. Rolfe Humphries. NYBP

Aria. Delmore Schwartz. ErPo

Aria. Briar Wood. NWP

Aria Senza da Capo. Robert Finch. MoCV

Ariake, Japanese friend, I regard. To Ariake Kambara. Norman Rosten. NYBP

Arid that country and high, anger of sun on the mountains, but. Rattlesnake Country. Robert Penn Warren. NAAL-2; VCAP

Aridity. "Michael Field." OBMV

Ariel. David Campbell. CBAP

Ariel. Sylvia Plath. CMoP; HCAP; HeIP; LCAP; MoP; NAAL-2; NALW; NoAM; NOBA; NoP; PBWP; PoE; Poetr; VCAP

Ariel to Miranda: — Take. With a Guitar, to Jane. Shelley. EnRP; FHYEP; OAEL-2

(To a Lady, with a Guitar.) GTBS; GTBS-P

Ariel was glad he had written his poems. The Planet on the Table. Wallace Stevens. HAP; HCAP; SAmP

Ariel's Dirge. Shakespeare. *See* Full fathom [*or* fadom] five thy father lies.

Ariel's Song: "Come unto these yellow sands." Shakespeare. *See* Come unto these yellow sands.

Ariel's Song: "Full fathom five thy father lies." Shakespeare. *See* Full fathom [*or* fadom] five thy father lies.

Ariel's Song: "Where the bee sucks, there suck I." Shakespeare. *See* Where the bee sucks, there suck I.

Arion. Zbigniew Herbert, *tr. fr. Polish by* Czeslaw Milosz *and* Peter Dale Scott. AnRep

Ariosto. Osip Mandelstam, *tr. fr. Russian by* W. S. Merwin *and* Clarence Brown. OBVE

Arise and go now to the city of slaughter. The City of Slaughter. Hayyim Nahman Bialik, *tr. fr. Hebrew by* A. M. Klein. TrJP

Arise and Pick a Posy. *Unknown.* OBET

Arise and See the Glorious Sun. Francis Hopkinson. AH

Arise, Arise. *Unknown.* OBET

Arise, arise, arise! Henry Brooke. *Fr.* Jack the Giant Queller; an Antique History. NOEC

Arise, arise,/ Dull fancy, from the bed of earth. My Carol. Mildmay Fane, 2d Earl of Westmorland. BeJo

Arise faint Muse bring one heart-melting verse. An Elegie on the Deploreable Departure of the Honered and Truely Religious Chieftain John Hull. John Saffin. SCAP

Arise from your rope-strung bed, Clabe Mott. Clabe Mott. James Still. GrPl

Arise, my soul, on wings enraptured, rise. Thoughts on the Works of Providence. Phillis Wheatley. NAAL-1

Arise, My Soul! With Rapture Rise! Samuel J. Smith. AH

Arise, O Glorious Zion. William G. Mills. AH

Arise, then women of this day! Mother's Day Proclamation of 1870. Julia Ward Howe. CrSp

Arise! thrust in Thy sickle? (*LL*) Corruption. Henry Vaughan. ESCV; GeHe; JCP; NAEL-1; NOCV; NOSC; OAEL-1; Prf; SeCP; SeCV-1

Arise up on thy feet, O Quiet Heart! He Biddeth Osiris to Arise from the Dead. *Unknown, tr. fr. Egyptian by* Robert Hillyer. *Fr.* Book of the Dead. AWP

Arise! we slept, nor of the peril recked. (*LL*) Awake! Walther von der Vogelweide. AWP

Arise ye daughters of a land. The Women's Marseillaise. F. E. M. Macaulay. BrRo

Arise, Ye Saints of Latter Days. *Unknown.* AH

Arise, ye sons of France, to glory! La Marseillaise. Claude Joseph Rouget de Lisle, *tr. fr. French by* Charles H. Kerr. SWP

Aristarchus and the Whale. Martin Johnston. FaBoMA

Aristeides. Antipater of Sidon, *tr. fr. Greek by* Charles Whibley. AWP

Aristocrateia,/ You've crossed the dark stream. Mnasalcas, *tr. fr. Greek by* Edward Lucie-Smith. GrAn

Aristocrats. Keith Douglas. FaBoMo; NAEL-2; NoAM; OBWP

Aristomache loved a drink:/ The old chatterbox was fonder. Argentarius, *tr. fr. Greek by* Fleur Adcock. GrAn

Aristophanes. Plato, *tr. fr. Greek by* Peter Jay. GrAn

Aristophanes' Symposium. Rita Mae Brown. IHMS

Aristotle was a little man with/ eyes like a lizard. Humanities Lecture. William Stafford. NNaP; NoAM

Aristotle's Story. Mother Goose. *See* There were two birds sat on a stone.

Arithmetic. *Unknown.* ISE; ReMoGo; UsP

Arithmetic ("Arithmetic is where numbers fly like pigeons in and out of your head.") Carl Sandburg. FaPON; SiSoPo, *abr.*

Arithmetic on the Frontier. Kipling. OBWP

Arithmetique [*or* Arithmetic] nine digits, and no more. Upon the Loss[e] of His Little Finger. Thomas Randolph. BeJo; NOSC

Arizona. Sharlot M. Hall. PAH

Arizona. *Unknown.* AmFP

Arizona Highways. James Welch. CDW; NoAM

Arizona Nature Myth. James Michie. NOBL

Arjuna said:/ How shall I in battle against Bhisma. *Unknown, tr. by* Franklin Edgerton. *Fr.* Bhagavad-Gita, The. DL

Ark, The. Noah Calwell Cannon. AAP

Ark. Gu Cheng, *tr. fr. Chinese by* Donald Finkel *with* Li Guohua. SpMi

Ark, The, *sels.* Jay Macpherson.
   Ark Anatomical. NOBC
   Ark Apprehensive. NOBC
   Ark Artefact. NOBC
   Ark Articulate. NOBC
   Ark Astonished. NOBC
   Ark Overwhelmed. NOBC

Ark Parting. NOBC
Ark to Noah. NOBC; PoA
Ark Anatomical. Jay Macpherson. *Fr.* Ark, The. NOBC
Ark Apprehensive. Jay Macpherson. *Fr.* Ark, The. NOBC
Ark Artefact. Jay Macpherson. *Fr.* Ark, The. NOBC
Ark Articulate. Jay Macpherson. *Fr.* Ark, The. NOBC
Ark Astonished. Jay Macpherson. *Fr.* Ark, The. NOBC
Ark for Lawrence Durrell, An. Robert Duncan. RaBo
Ark Overwhelmed. Jay Macpherson. *Fr.* Ark, The. NOBC
Ark Parting. Jay Macpherson. *Fr.* Ark, The. NOBC
Ark to Noah. Jay Macpherson. *Fr.* Ark, The. NOBC; PoA
Arkansas Traveller. Charles Wright. MT
Arkheanassa. Asclepiades, *tr. fr. Greek by* Peter Jay. GrAn
Arlington Cemetery Looking toward the Capitol. Winthrop Palmer. GoYe
Arlo Will. Edgar Lee Masters. *Fr.* Spoon River Anthology. LiTA
Arm, Arm, Arm, Arm! John Fletcher. *Fr.* Mad Lover, The. ElL
Arm in Arm. Louis Simpson. PBCV
Arm of bronze outstretched against all evil!, The. *(LL)* Dance of the Macabre Mice. Wallace Stevens. CMoP; NOBA; OxBA
Arm thee with thunder, heavenly muse. The Law Given at Sinai. Isaac Watts. ChIV-1
Arm Wrestling with My Father. Jack Driscoll *and* Bill Meissner. GOYP
Armada, The. (Attend, all ye who list to hear our noble England's praise.) Macaulay. BeLS; CoGr; FaBoCh; FaBoEH; FaPoR; GN; WBLP
Sels.
England's Standard. OtMeF
"Night sank upon the dusky beach, and on the purple sea." EBEvV; OBNC; PeVV
Armada, 1588, The. John Wilson. OxBChV
Armadillo[— Brazil], The. Elizabeth Bishop. CAPP; HCAP; MoP; NAAL-2; NoAM; NOBA; NoP; NYBP; Poetr; SM; TAP; VCAP; VGW
Armageddon. Georgia Douglas Johnson. ShDr
Armageddon. John Crowe Ransom. ChIV-2; LiTA; MeMAP
Arme, Arme, Arme, great Neptune rowze, awake. John Smith of His Friend Master John Taylor. John Smith. SCAP
Armed Vision. N. P. van Wyk Louw, *tr. fr. Afrikaans by* Jack Cope *and* Uys Krige. PeSA
Armed with his crutches, the thief, wolf-like. The Outsider. Syl Cheney-Coker. HBAPE
Armenia, *sels.* Osip Mandelstam.
Azure and Clay. CBCK
Armenian Looking at Newsphotos of the Cambodian Deathwatch, An. Diana Der Hovanessian. WoWa
Armful, The. Robert Frost. CMoP; OxBSP
Armies and lemmings do not go. The New from Ethiopia and the Sudan. J. P. Clark Bekederemo. HBAPE
Armies Enter Cuailnge, The. *Unknown, tr. fr. Irish by* Thomas Kinsella. *Fr.* Táin, The. NOIV
Armies in the Fire. Robert Louis Stevenson. *Fr.* Child's Garden of Verses, A. EBVV
Arming of Pigwiggen, The. Michael Drayton. *See* He quickly arms him for the field.
Arminius, *sels.* Daniel Casper von Lohenstein. GePo
Armistice. Paul Dehn. OxBTC; PAW
Armistice Day. Charles Causley. NAEL-2; OBWP
Armistice Day. William Plomer. IHNG
Armistice Day, 1918. Robert Graves. FaBoEH
Armor. James Dickey. CoAP
Armor. Sharon Olds. InPS
Armor in mêlée. *(LL)* Some prefer a glory of horsemen; warships. Sappho. STV
Armorer-that is I!, The. *(LL)* The Armorer's Song. Harry Bache Smith. OHIP
Armorer's Song, The. Harry Bache Smith. OHIP
Armorial. Ralph Gustafson. MoCV
Armoured dinosaur. Woodlouse. Judith Nicholls. OBAP
Arms and the Boy. Wilfred Owen. CMoP; HAP; ImPo; LiTB; LiTM; MeMBP; MoAB; MoBrPo; OAEL-1; OAEL-2; OxBSP; PoE; Poetr; WeW
Arms and the Man. Samuel Butler. *Fr.* Hudibras. NOSC
Arms, and the man I sing, who forc'd by fate. Virgil, *tr. by* Dryden. *Fr.* Aeneid [*or* Eneados], The. NAWM-1; OBVE
Arms and the Woman. Dorothea MacKellar. NOBAu
Arms at my side like some inadequate sign. Mountain Town — Mexico. Eldon Grier. NOBC
Arms finned-out across the water. The Drowned. David Bottoms. MT
Arms reversed and banners craped. A Dirge for McPherson. Herman Melville. PAH; PoEL-5
Arms seem clumsy at first, The. The Fever Toy. Charles Wright. AmPA

Arms/ spiral/ in clinical. The Dance. Maud Sulter. DT
Arms Which Articulate Nothing. Nick Totton. VaA
Armstrong at Fayal, The. Wallace Rice. PAH
Army. Ciaran Carson. BiHa; PBCIP
Army Corps on the March, An. Walt Whitman. AiP; InPS; PoLF
Army horses, gangs and droves. Meeting the Herdsmen. Mei Yao Ch'en, *tr. fr. Chinese by* Jonathan Chaves. SuSp
Army marched by for days and was admired by all, The. The Decimation before Phraata. Alan Dugan. AnAn
Army, Navy. *Unknown.* OxNR
Army of the Dead, The. Barry Pain. NSI
Army of the Lord. I'm a Soldier in the Army of the Lord. *Unknown.* AmFP
Army of unalterable law, The. *(LL)* Cousin Nancy. T. S. Eliot. AnAmPo; OBAL; OxBSP
Army of unalterable law, The. *(LL)* Lucifer in Starlight. George Meredith. AWP; CH; ChIV-1; EBVV; EnVR; FF; GGP; HAP; ImPo; InPK; LiTB; Mes; NAEL-2; NOBE; NOBVV; NoP; OAEL-2; OBEV; OBNC; PoE; PoEL-5; SCGP; Son; TFi; TrGrPo; UnPo
Army retreated and left, The. Mushroom. Nancy Willard. FoLa
Army was ours that spring, The. Landing in England. North Pickenham. Coman Leavenworth. *Fr.* Norfolk Memorials. LiTA
Arnold at Stillwater. Thomas Dunn English. PAH
Arnold, the Vile Traitor ("Arnold the name, as heretofore.") *Unknown.* PAH
Arnolfinis both sat to Van Eyck. Sir Robert Witt. PeLi
Around, above my bed, the pitch-dark fly. Truth. Howard Nemerov. HoPM; LiTM
Around, around the sun we go. Mother Goose's Garland. Archibald MacLeish. AnAmPo; OBAL
Around existence twine. Basho, *tr. fr. Japanese by* Harold G. Henderson. TAL
Around five in the next garden, a rooster. Likelihood of Snow, The/ The Danger of Fire. Gerald Dawe. PNI
Around her shrine no earthly blossoms blow. La Madonna dell' Acqua. John Ruskin. NOBVV
Around islands of jade and malachite. The Wave Symphony. Arthur Davison Ficke. *Fr.* Four Japanese Paintings. PoA
Around it the furze-clad hills arise. The Mountain Altar. Brian O'Higgins. TIRV
Around me is waste land. *(LL)* O That I Knew the Way Back. Klaus Groth. RiWo
Around me roar and crash the pagan isms. The Pagan Isms. Claude McKay. BPo
Around me the images of thirty years. The Municipal Gallery Revisited. W. B. Yeats. GTBS-P; LiTB; MeMBP; OxBTC
Around my garden the little wall is low. Losing a Slave-Girl. Po Chü-i, *tr. fr. Chinese by* Arthur Waley. AWP
Around My Room. William Jay Smith. TLR
Around stones called precious. Black Meat. Jean Follain, *tr. fr. French by* W. S. Merwin. AnRep
Around the battlements go by. War on the Periphery. George Johnston. NOBC
Around the Campfire. Andrew Hudgins. MT
Around the Corner. Laura Riding. *Fr.* Forgotten Girlhood. RB
Around the Corner ("Around the corner I have a friend.") Charles Hanson Towne. PoLF; PoToHe
Around the Corner from Francis Bacon. Paul Durcan. BiHa
Around the fire addressed its evening hours. *(LL)* Say not of me that weakly I declined. Robert Louis Stevenson. OBNC; PeVV
Around the fire one wintry night. The Beggar Man. Lucy Aikin. OxBChV
Around the fireplace, pointing at the fire. On Falling Asleep by Firelight. William Meredith. ChIV-1; NoAM; NYBP
Around the gleaming map of Europe. Autobahnmotorwayautoroute. Adrian Mitchell. RB
Around the Green Gravel. *Unknown.* ReMoGo
Around the highest village, fields are ploughed. Gran Sasso. Robert Wells. SCBI
Around the house stood an. Grandmothers Land. William Oandasan. HATNAP
Around the house the flakes fly faster. Birds at Winter Nightfall. Thomas Hardy. MoBrPo
Around the little park. Back to Life. Thom Gunn. NoP
Around the quays, kicked off in twos. Fishing Boats in Martigues. Roy Campbell. FaBoEE; FaBoPP; OxBSP
Around the rick, around the rick. *Unknown.* OxNR
Around the Rough and Rugged Rocks the Ragged Rascal Rudely Ran. John Ashbery. InPS

Around the time Charles Darwin had declined. Dark Times. Tony Harrison. *Fr.* Art & Extinction. SCBI

Around the World. Gary Lenhart. UL

Around us, dazing us with its light like snow. (*LL*) After They Have Tired of the Brilliance of Cities. Stephen Spender. FaBoMo; LiTM

Around us summer wrote its last farewell. September Afternoon. Margaret Haley Carpenter. GoYe

Around were all the roses red. Spleen. Paul Verlaine, *tr. fr. French by* Ernest Dowson. AWP

Arouse, arouse, ye friends of right. The World Hymn. James Gilchrist Lawson. WBLP

Arraigned by silence, I recall. The Brethren. Seamus Deane. PNI

Arraignment of a Lover, The. George Gascoigne. AAS

Arraignment of Paris, The, *sels.* George Peele.
   Fair and Fair. EIL; OBEV
   (Oenone and Paris.) NOBE
   O Gentle Love. EIL
   Oenone's Complaint. EIL
   "Welladay, welladay, poor Colin, thou art going to the ground." EIL

Arran. *Unknown, tr. fr. Old Irish.* ChTr, *tr. by* Kenneth Jackson; FaBoCh, *tr. by* Kuno Meyer; FaBoPP, *tr. by* Kenneth Jackson.

Arrange the scene with only a shade of difference. An Incident. Douglas Le Pan. MoCV

Arranged by two's as peaches are. Nine Nectarines and Other Porcelain. Marianne Moore. OxBA

Arranged on the opposite porch is a male. Hilaire Kirkland. *Fr.* Observations. PeNZ

Arrangements with Earth for Three Dead Friends. James Wright. NIP

Arras. P. K. Page. MoCV

Arrest delight, when I my Love embrace. (*LL*) Delay. William Hammond. CBLP

Arrest of Oscar Wilde at the Cadogan Hotel, The. Sir John Betjeman. CMoP; EBEV; FaBoEH; InvP; MoBrPo; MoP; NoAM; NoP; OxBTC

Arria to Poetus. Mary E. Tucker. CBWP-1

Arrival, The. Lan Ling, *tr. fr. Chinese by* Kenneth Rexroth *and* Ling Chung. WPC

Arrival, The. Alexander McLachlan. *Fr.* Emigrant, The. NOBC

Arrival. John Wain. EBEV

Arrival. William Carlos Williams. AnAmPo

Arrival and Departure. Charles Eglington. PeSA

Arrival at Santos. Elizabeth Bishop. FaBoWP; OxBC

Arrival at the Waldorf. Wallace Stevens. HCAP

Arrival in Hell. Ricarda Huch, *tr. fr. German by* Susan C. Strong. PBWP

Arrival, New York Harbor. Robert Peters. GOA

Arrival of the Bee Box, The. Sylvia Plath. FaBoMo; FaBoWP; HCAP; NALW; NaP

Arrival of the Mail. William Cowper. *See* Hark! 'tis the twanging horn o'er yonder bridge.

Arrivals at a Watering-Place. Winthrop Mackworth Praed. NOBL; PeLV

Arrivals, Departures. Philip Larkin. MoBrPo

Arrivants. Musaemura Bonus Zimunya. HBAPE

Arrive. The Ladies from the Ladies' Betterment League. The Lovers of the Poor. Gwendolyn Brooks. CAPP; LCAP; MoP; NAAL-2; NoAM; NOBA; Poetr

Arrived from scattered cities, several lands. Shipment to Maidanek. Ephim G. Fogel. BTR; OBWP; TrJP

Arrived now at our ship, we launched and set. Ulysses Invokes the Dead. Homer, *tr. fr. Greek by* Robert Fitzgerald. *Fr.* Odyssey. NAWM-1; NOSC, *tr. by* George Chapman.

Arrived upon the downs of asphodel. Classic Encounter. "Christopher Caudwell." OxBTC

Arrives like a jinn, instantly. Resuscitation Team. U. A. Fanthorpe. FaBoWP

Arriving. Daniel Halpern. HoPM

Arriving after Rain at the Temple of Heavenly Peace. Wang Shih-chieng, *tr. fr. Chinese by* Richard John Lynn. SuSp

Arriving at North Pond by Stupid Brook on a Morning Walk after the Rain. Liu Tsung-yüan, *tr. fr. Chinese by* Jan W. Walls. SuSp

Arriving was their passion. The Tourists. C. Day Lewis. OBTV

Arrogance. Walter de la Mare. OxBSP

Arrogance Repressed. Sir John Betjeman. FiBHP

Arrow and the Song, The. Longfellow. AnAmPo; MeMAP; PFP; PoToHe; PWR; UV

Arrow of Desire, The. *Gond Oral Tradition, tr. by* V. Elwin *and* S. Hivale. WTO

Arrow pointing three directions, The. Virgule. Donald Britton. PRA

Arrowhead from the Ancient Battlefield of Ch'ang-p'ing, An. Li Ho, *tr. fr. Chinese by* A. C. Graham. PLT

Arrows. William Heyen. SM

Arrows of rain. Dark Dreaming. Dorothy Kruger. ShDr

Arrows of the narrow moon flock down direct, The. Communion of Saints: The Poor Bastard under the Bridge. Marie Ponsot. VGW

Arrowy Dreams. Witter Bynner. GOA

Arroyo. Tom Weatherly. PoBA

Ars. Marina Tsvetayeva, *tr. fr. Russian by* Willis Barnstone *and* Edward Brown. BoWoP

Ars Poetica. Jorge Luis Borges, *tr. fr. Spanish by* Harold Morland. ArNa

Ars Poetica. X. J. Kennedy. ErPo

Ars Poetica. Archibald MacLeish. AmPP; AWP; CMoP; HAP; HeIL; HeIP; HoPM; InPK; LiTA; LiTM; MeMAP; MoAB; MoAmPo; NAAL-2; NIP; NOBA; NoP; OxBA; PoA; Poetr; PoRA; TAP; TFi; WeW

Ars Poetica? Czeslaw Milosz, *tr. fr. Polish by* Lillian Vallee. AnAn

Ars Poetica. Linda Pastan. NIP

Ars Poetica. Victor van Vriesland, *tr. fr. Dutch by* Adriaan J. Barnouw. TrJP

Ars Poetica. Charles Wright. AnAn; FoLa

Ars Poetica about Ultimates. Tram Combs. TwCP

Ars Victrix, *sels.* Austin Dobson, *after the French of* Théophile Gautier.
   "All passes. Art alone." CTC

Arsehole. Craig Raine. FaBoBl

Arsenal at Springfield, The. (This is the arsenal. From floor to ceiling.) Longfellow. AmPP
   Sels.
   Message of Peace, A. WBLP

Arsenic. Howard Moss. CoAP; NYBP

"Arsenio" (she writes to me), "I, breathing gently here." Thrust and Riposte. Eugenio Montale, *tr. fr. Italian by* Gavin Ewart. PeFWW

Art. Théophile Gautier, *tr. fr. French by* George Santayana. AWP

Art. Herman Melville. AmPP; NAAL-1; NOBA

Art, *sels.* James Thomson ("B.V.").
   "Singing is sweet; but be sure of this." NOBVV

Art. *Unknown.* BLPA; NBLV

Art & Extinction, *sels.* Tony Harrison.
   Birds of America: John James Audubon, The. SCBI
   Birds of America, The; Weeki Wachee. SCBI
   Dark Times. SCBI
   Killing Time. SCBI
   Looking Up. SCBI
   Loving Memory. SCBI
   Standards in Hopeful Anticipation of the Bicentenery of the National Emblem of the United States of America. SCBI
   T'ark. SCBI

Art, I. Alfred Noyes. OBEV

Art, II. Alfred Noyes. OBEV

Art above Nature, to Julia. Robert Herrick. BeJo; NOSC

Art and Heart. Ella Wheeler Wilcox. AnAmPo

Art and Reality. James Simmons. PeIV

Art as meagre as a quilt, An. The Spare Quilt. John Peale Bishop. GOA

Art for Art's Sake. Marc Blitzstein. *Fr.* Cradle Will Rock, The. TrJP

Art full of jealousy. (*LL*) The Zebra. *Unknown.* PeSAV

Art has not made our life. The Seventeenth of May. Anthony Barnett. VaA

Art. It cures affliction. As lights go down and. Farewell Performance. James Merrill. PFL

Art McCooey. Patrick Kavanagh. CIP

Art, Nature's Ape. Edward Taylor. *Fr.* Preparatory Meditations Before My Approach to the Lord's Supper. CBCK

Art, natures Ape, hath many brave things done. Art, Nature's Ape. Edward Taylor. *Fr.* Preparatory Meditations Before My Approach to the Lord's Supper. CBCK

Art of Angling, The. Thomas Barker. FaBoUs
   Sels.
   Baits for Various Fish.
   How to Catch Trout.
   Methods of Cooking Trout.

Art of Biography, The. E. C. Bentley. *Fr.* Clerihews. FiBHP; NOBL; NTP; PeLV

Art of Clay, The. Duane Niatum. HATNAP

Art of Cookery, The, *sels.* William King.
   "Far from the parlour have your kitchen placed." ECEV; FaBoUs

Art of Coquetry, The, *sels.* Charlotte Lennox.
   "First form your artful looks with studious care." ECWP

Art of Dancing, The. Soame Jenyns. FaBoUs
   Sels.
   "But let me now my lovely charge remind." ECEV
   "Dare I in such momentous points advise." ECEV
   "Let each fair maid, who fears to be disgraced." ECEV
   "Now haste, my Muse, pursue thy destined way." ECEV

Art of losing isn't hard to master, The. One Art. Elizabeth Bishop. CAPP; DiPo; HAP; NAAL-2; NALW; NoAM; PFP; PoE; SM; SoSe; VCAP

Art of Love, The, *sels.* Kenneth Koch.
"To win the love of women one should first discover." NNaP

Art of Love, The, *sels.* Ovid, *tr. fr. Latin.*
"Attend, ye nymphs, by wedlock unconfin'd." FaBoUs
"Kiss, if you can: Resistance if she make." ErPo
"You, who in Cupid's rolls inscribe your name." FaBoUs

Art of Making Puddings, The, *sels.* William King.
"Sometimes the frugal matron seems in haste." FaBoUs

Art of Poetry, The, *sels.* Horace, *tr. fr. Latin.*
"As woods whose change appears." OBVE
"Should some ill painter, in a wild design." OBVE

Art of Poetry, The. Pope. *Fr.* Essay on Criticism. ECEV; PoEL-3

Art of Poetry, An. James McAuley. NOCV

Art of Politics, The, *sels.* James Bramston.
Time's Changes. NOEC

Art of Preserving Health, The, *sels.* John Armstrong.
Advantages of Washing, The. FaBoUs
Causes of Old Age. ECEV
Dangers of Sexual Excess, The. FaBoUs
Madness. NOEC
Transience. NOEC
Urban Pollution. ECEV; NOEC

Art of Satire, The. Pope. *See* Ask you what provocation I have had?

Art of the Sonnet, *sels.* Gil Orlovitz.
"Night comes. Day runs for its life into my eyes." PoA

Art of War, The, *sels.* Joseph Fawcett.
Feast of Blood, The. NOEC

Art of Wenching, The, *sels. Unknown.*
"Be punctual then to know." NOEC

Art Pepper. Edward Hirsch. NAmP90

Art photographer alone, The. Quantum. Martin Johnston. CBAP

Art Poétique. Paul Verlaine, *tr. fr. French by* Arthur Symons. AWP

Art thou a Statist in the van. A Poet's Epitaph. Wordsworth. EnRP

Art thou afraid the adorer's prayer. Walter Savage Landor. GBL

Art Thou Gone in Haste? *At. to* John Webster *and* William Rowley. *Fr.* Thracian Wonder, The. EiL; ELP; OxBoLi

Art thou gone so far. Ode: The Spirit Wooed. Richard Watson Dixon. OBNC

Art Thou Lonely? John Oxenham. PoToHe

Art thou lonely, O my brother? Art Thou Lonely? John Oxenham. PoToHe

Art thou not hungry for thy children, Zion. To Zion. Judah Halevi, *tr. fr. Hebrew by* Maurice Samuel. AWP

Art thou pale for weariness. To the Moon. Shelley. BoNaP; GTBS; GTBS-P; OxAEP-2; PPP; TrGrPo; TTTS
(Fragment: To the Moon.) EnRP

Art thou playing with Time in thy sweet baby-glee? The Child Playing with a Watch. Frances Sargent Osgood. AmWP

Art thou poor, yet hast thou golden slumbers? Thomas Dekker *and others. Fr.* Pleasant Comedy of Patient Grissell [*or* Grissel *or* Grissill], The. HAP; InPS; NoSic; SCGP; UnPo
(Basket-Maker's Song, The.) TrGrPo
(Happy Heart, The.) GTBS; GTBS-P; RB; SCGP
(Sweet Content.) CH; EiL; GGP; OBEV; OtMeF

Art Thou That She. *Unknown.* OxBSP

Art thou the grave of Charidas? If for Arimmas' son. Callimachus, *tr. fr. Greek. Fr.* Epigrams. OBD

Art Thou, Time, Way, and Wayfarer. (*LL*) "I Am the Way." Alice Meynell. NOBVV; OBMV; OxBSP

Arte Popular. Pat Mora. AfAz

Artemeias, surely when you from the nether world's bark. Antipater of Sidon, *tr. fr. Greek by* Barbara Hughes Fowler. *Fr.* Epigrams. HePo

Artemidora! Gods invisible. The Death of Artemidora. Walter Savage Landor. *Fr.* Pericles and Aspasia. EnRP; OBNC

Artemis. Rita Boumi-Pappas, *tr. fr. Greek by* Eleni Fourtouni. AIW

Artemis. Peter Davison. ErPo

Artemis. Perses, *tr. fr. Greek by* Peter Whigham. GrAn

Artemis. Anne Waldman. SRLS

Artemon once traveled in shadows. Anacreon, *tr. fr. Greek by* Sam Hamill. InMo

Arteries Juicy with Blood. Osip Mandelstam, *tr. fr. Russian by* James Greene. *Fr.* Lines Concerning the Unknown Soldier. NAs

Arthritic farmer and a calf watch Dr. Graves, The. These Obituaries of Rattlesnakes Being Eaten by the Hogs. Roger Weingarten. AmPA

Arthur. Ogden Nash. FiBHP; NoP; PeLi

Arthur is gone . . . Tristram in Careol. Hic Jacet Arthurus Rex Quondam Rexque Futurus. Francis Brett Young. OtMeF

Arthur Mitchell. Marianne Moore. PoNe

Arthur O'Bower has broken his bands [*or* band]. The Wind. *Unknown.* FaBoCh; GBP; OxNR
(High Wind, The.) ChTr

Arthur Ridgewood, M.D. Frank Marshall Davis. BPo

Arthur wes forwunded, wunder ane swithe. The Passing of Arthur. Layamon. *Fr.* Brut, The. PoE

Arthur's Anthology of English Poetry. Laurence David Lerner. PeLV

Arthur's Fight with Orgoglio and Duessa. Spenser. *Fr.* Faerie Queene, The. EBNV

Arthur's Seat, *sels.* Thomas Mercer.
"Where is the gallant race that rose." OxBS

Artichoke. Henry Taylor. MT

Artificer. X. J. Kennedy. TwCP

Artificial Beauty. Lucianus, *tr. fr. Greek by* William Cowper. AWP

Artificial Teeth. Solyman Brown. *Fr.* Dentologia; a Poem on the Diseases of the Teeth and Their Proper Remedies. FaBoUs

Artillerie [*or* Artillery]. George Herbert. GeHe; InPS; NoP; PoEL-2; SeCV-1

Artisan, The. Alice Brown. TrPWD

Artist, The. Frances E. W. Harper. AmWP

Artist, The. Stanley Kunitz. CAPP

Artist, The. *Unknown, tr. fr. Aztec Indian by* Denise Levertov. STP

Artist, The. William Carlos Williams. InPS; LCAP; NYBP; RB; SAmP

Artist, An. Robinson Jeffers. VGW

Artist and Ape. Gordden Link. GoYe

Artist, The: disciple, abundant, multiple, restless. The Artist. *Unknown, tr. fr. Aztec Indian by* Denise Levertov. STP

Artist friend once, An. Poema Como Valentin (or a San Francisco Love Poem). Cherríe Moraga. ETG

Artist in the North, An. Tomas Tranströmer, *tr. fr. Swedish by* Robin Fulton. PWE

Artist is the creator of beautiful things, The. Oscar Wilde. *Fr.* Picture of Dorian Gray, The. NAEL-2

Artist must leave these woods now, The. The Departure. Reed Whittemore. TAP

Artist on Penmaenmawr, The. Charles Tennyson Turner. FaBoPP; OBNC

Artist, that underneath my table. The Spider. Edward Littleton. NOEC

Artist who lived in St. Ives, An. A. G. Prys-Jones. PeLi

Artist who lived near Montmartre, An. Sir John Waller. PeLi

Artists' Letters. Thomas Kinsella. BiHa

Artist's Life, An. Felice Picano. PFL

Artists/ work on the art farm, The. In the Land of Art. Anselm Hollo. NGP

Artorius. John Heath-Stubbs. EBEV
Sels.
"Age of Bronze awoke now in brutality, The."
"It was the virgin Zennora, who dwelt."
"Raft drifted, The." PeECV

Arundel Tomb, An. Philip Larkin. FaBoEH; FaPoB; OxAEP-2; OxBM; PPP

As (& not as). Prefix. Robert Kelly. BCF

As a bathtub lined with white porcelain. The Bathtub [*or* Bath Tub]. Ezra Pound. NIP; TRP; WeW

As a Beauty I Am Not a Star. Anthony Euwer. *Fr.* Limeratomy, The. InVP

As a boy with a richness of needs I wandered. Clifford Dyment. OxBTC

As a child. In This Motherless Geography. Elaine Orr. CrSp

As a child holds a pet. Port Bou. Stephen Spender. OBTV; TwCP

As a child/ I bought a red scarf. Four Sheets to the Wind and a One-Way Ticket to France. Conrad Kent Rivers. BPo; PoBA; PoNe

As a child I was. Woman. Elouise Loftin. PoBA

As a child (in Australia). Strange Adventure. Rossana Ombres, *tr. fr. Italian by* Ruth Feldman. NeIt

As a child of cedar, hemlock, and the sea. No One Remembers [Abandoning] the Village of White Fir. Duane Niatum. CDW; ETG

As a child running loose. Learning to Speak. Peter Everwine. NNaP

As a child, they could not keep me from wells. Personal Helicon. Seamus Heaney. IPY

As a compass for your route. (*LL*) Viaticum. Pao Yu. OHMPC

As a critic the poet Buchanan. On Robert Buchanan, Who Attacked Him under the Pseudonym of "Thomas Maitland." Dante Gabriel Rossetti. FaBoEE

As a dare-gale skylark scanted in a dull cage. The Caged Skylark. Gerard Manley Hopkins. CMoP; FM; LiTM; MeMBP; MoAB; MoBrPo; OBMV; Son; SoSe

As a fond mother, when the day is o'er. Nature. Longfellow. BoNaP; FaBoBe; PoLF; TAP; TrGrPo

As Dick and I. Lines Left at Mr. Theodore Hook's House in June, 1834. "Thomas Ingoldsby." FaBoUs

As did *Methusalem* of old, and so I end my song. (*LL*) An Excellent New Song upon His Grace Our Good Lord Archbishop of Dublin. Swift. CoMu

As did the Outlaw Murray of the forest frie? (*LL*) The Outlaw Murray. *Unknown.* ESPB; OxBB

As Difference Blends into Identity. Josephine Miles. NoAM; Poetr

As doctors give physic by way of prevention. For My Own Monument. Matthew Prior. GGP; OBEV
(For His Own Epitaph.) FaBoEE

As Down a Lone Valley. Timothy Dwight. AH

As down the garden walks we go." (*LL*) Henry and Mary. Robert Graves. GoJo; NTP

As down the rapid Po I chanced to glide. On Descending the River Po. William Parsons. OBTV

As down the torrent of an angry flood. The Story of the Pot and the Kettle. Charles Montagu. APAS

As down through Cupid's garden for pleasure I did walk. The 'Prentice Boy. *Unknown.* AmFP

As down through Moore's field one evening I went. The Silk Weaver's Daughter. *Unknown.* AmFP

As down thru Sally's garden one evening as I chanced to stray. Sally's Garden. *Unknown.* AmFP

As dry fields weep with rain. (*LL*) Earth teach me stillness. *Unknown.* EaPr

As due by many titles I resign[e]. John Donne. *Fr.* Holy Sonnets. ESCV; JCP

As dull as the life of the cloister. *Unknown.* PeLi

As Dungeons are for Criminals prepar'd. A Satyr. Elizabeth Tipper. *Fr.* Pilgrim's Viaticum; or, The Destitute, But Not Forlorn. KTR

As each year might assign. (*LL*) He Never Expected Much. Thomas Hardy. NAEL-2; NAs; NoAM; OxBTC; SCV

As Eenty Feenty Halligolun. *Unknown.* ISE

As empty-handed as I went. (*LL*) Back. Weldon Kees. NaP; PrIm

As, even today, the airman, feeling the plane sweat. Icarus. Valentin Iremonger. BIrV; CIP; PeIV

As evening comes. To the Tune "Picking Mulberries." Li Ch'ing-chao, *tr. fr. Chinese by* Kenneth Rexroth *and* Ling Chung. WPC

As ever in my great Task-Master's eye. (*LL*) How Soon Hath Time [the Subtle Thief of Youth]. Milton. CoGr; FF; HeIP; InPS; LiTB; NAEL-1; NAs; PFP; PoE; SCGP; Son

As everything dies quickly, the rose. Adieu. Charles-Jean Grandmougin, *tr. fr. French by* Philip L. Miller. *Fr.* Poem of a Day. RiWo

As Expected. Thom Gunn. · GLP

As fair as morn, as fresh as May. *Unknown.* GBL

As far as Cho-fu-Sa. (*LL*) River Merchant's Wife, The; a Letter. Li Po. AmPP; AWP; BoLoP; ClHu; FYAP; HAP; HeIP; InPK; InPS; LiTA; LPA, *tr. by* Ezra Pound; MeMAP; MoAB; MoAmPo; MoP; NAAL-2; NIP; NoAM; NOBA; NOBE; NoP; OBMV; OBVE; OxBA; Poetr; PPP; PrIm; RaBo; RB; SOTW; TAP; TFi; TRP; TTTS; TwCP; UnPo; WeW

As far as I am concerned. Journey. Gillian Clarke. SCBI

As far as statues go, so far there's not. From Trollope's Journal. Elizabeth Bishop. FaBoPV; GOA

As Far as Yoruba Land, *sels.* Edouard J. Maunick, *tr. fr. French by* Ellen Conroy Kennedy.
"Accept from me not silence." NegPo
"And I have chosen the sea as no man's land." NegPo
"Enter in the circle." NegPo
"For there is an African virtue of the tree." NegPo
"I am from everywhere." NegPo
"I have mentioned it by name." NegPo
"I have understood nothing." NegPo
"I made the motions of the sacred place." NegPo
"Ofatedo/ seek it out upon the skin of Africa." NegPo
"Point no scornful finger at Yoruba Land." NegPo
"Speaking of Gethsemane in Yoruba Land." NegPo
"This is where the warrior from Ibokun came." NegPo
"Trees were forbidden me, The." NegPo
"Where does this poem come from?" NegPo

As fine a piece of furniture. Central. Ted Kooser. Poetsp

As Firefrorefiddle, the Fiend of the Fell. (*LL*) Gus: The Theatre Cat. T. S. Eliot. OBCA; OxBTC

As first a various, uniformed hint we find. Music and Poetry. Abraham Cowley. *Fr.* Davideis. EPCY

As first he cut her throat and then his own. (*LL*) Faustus. A. D. Hope. NOBAu

As Flows the Rapid River. Samuel Francis Smith. AH

As for him who. Fragment. William Carlos Williams. Spl

As for me I am a child of the god of the mountains. This Poem Is for Bear. Gary Snyder. *Fr.* Myths and Texts. NOBA; NU

As for me/ I have seen Llywelyn. A Day Which Endures Not. A. G. Prys-Jones, *tr. fr. Welsh by* Anthony Conran. OBWVE

As for me, my Nanna ignores me. Condemning the Moongod Nanna. Enheduanna, *ad. by* Aliki *and* Willis Barnstone, *tr. fr. Sumerian.* BoWoP

As for my life, I've led it. A Placid Man's Epitaph. Thomas Hardy. MoBrPo

As for Poets. Gary Snyder. CAPP

A's for the anchor that swings at our bow. The Sailors' Alphabet. *Unknown.* AmFP; OxBSS

As for the Quince. Nuala Ni Dhomhnaill, *tr. fr. Irish by* Paul Muldoon. BiHa; CIP; PBCIP

As for them all I do not thus lament. *At. to* Sir Thomas Wyatt. FaBoEH

As Fowlers Lie in Wait. Bible, *O.T. Fr.* Jeremiah. TrJP

As Freedom Is a Breakfastfood. E. E. Cummings. CMoP; LiTA; LiTM; MAT; NOBA; OxBA; TAP; VGW

As from an [*or* their] ancestral oak. Similes for Two Political Characters of 1819. Shelley. FaBoPV; RB
(To Sidmouth and Castlereagh.) NAEL-2

As from the Dorset shore I travell'd home. The White Horse of Westbury. Charles Tennyson Turner. EBEV; PeVV

As frosty morning's sun, as moonshine night. (*LL*) Alas, why say you I am rich? when I. Robert Sidney. NoSic

As funny as I can. (*LL*) The Height of the Ridiculous. Oliver Wendell Holmes. FiBHP; MoShBr; OBAL; OBCA

As Gentle Dews Distill. George Rogers. AH

As glad to have my body as my mind. (*LL*) The Blossom [*or* Blossome]. John Donne. AWP; ESCV; ImPo; LiTB; MeLP; NAEL-1; SCGP; SeCP; UnPo

As good to write, as for to lie and groan. Sir Philip Sidney. *Fr.* Astrophel and Stella. AAS; ESo, (*sl. abr.*); GGP; HeIL, (*Sonnets,* I–CVIII *and 11 Songs*); NoSic; Poetr; SCGP, (*Sonnets,* I–CVIII *and 11 Songs*); SiPS, (*Sonnets,* I–CVIII *and 11 Songs*); SiPSBD, (*Sonnets,* I–CVIII *and 11 Songs*)

As grit swirls in the wind the word spreads. The Center of Attention. Daniel Hoffman. FYAP; UnPo

As guns pounded on the shore. (*LL*) Europe and America. David Ignatow. NNaP; UnPo

As hang two mighty thunderclouds. The Guns in the Grass. Thomas Frost. PAH

As happy as Cliff Klingenhagen is. (*LL*) Cliff Klingenhagen. E. A. Robinson. AmPP; AnAmPo; MeMAP; MoAB; MoAmPo; Son

As hath been, lo, these many generations. First Travels of Max. John Crowe Ransom. MoAmPo
(In that old house of many generations.) NTP, *diff. vers.*

As He Came near Death. Roy Fisher. FaBoMo; OBD

As he climbs down our hill, my kestrel rises. Esyllt. Glyn Jones. AngWe; OBWVE

As he fattens on larceny. (*LL*) Warrior. Frank Mkalawile Chipasula. PeSAV

As he filled up his order book pp. *Unknown.* PeLi

As he led, so he followed 'em all to the Devil. (*LL*) An Epitaph upon That Profound and Learned Casuist, the Late Ordinary of Newgate. Thomas Brown. OBSV

As he left the ship he saw this, only this. The Descent of the Vulture. Marya Zaturenska. WPE

As he lies in bed. (*LL*) Life in the Palace. Lady Hua Jui. WPC

As he moves the mine-detector. Hunting Civil War Relics at Nimblewill Creek. James Dickey. PoE

As he said vanity, so vain say I. The Vanity of All Worldly Things. Anne Bradstreet. ChIV-1; EAP; NoP; SCAP

As he sang upon a tree! (*LL*) The Rivals. James Stephens. BoTP; FaPON; InvP; OBEV; OBMV

As he sinks two into the chains. (*LL*) Makin' Jump Shots. Michael S. Harper. PoE

As he stood against the fretted hedge, which was like white lace. (*LL*) To a Conscript of 1940. Sir Herbert Read. LiTB; LiTM; NSI; OBWP; PoWW

As he stood in their shop, Mr. Boosey. Jimmy Pearse. PeLi

As he that sees a dark and shady grove. H. Baptism. George Herbert. GeHe

As He, the maker of this Song. (*LL*) A Meditation for His Mistress[e]. Robert Herrick. CaPo; JCP; NOBE; NOSC; OBEV; SeCP

As he trudged along to school. The Story of Johnny Head-in-Air. Heinrich Hoffmann, *tr. fr. German.* OxBChV

As he was a poet sublimer than me. (*LL*) Answer to Cloe [*or* Chloe] Jealous. Matthew Prior. NOBE

As he went on fishing his way. (*LL*) The Lady and the Bear. Theodore Roethke. GoJo; NBLV

As Hermes once took to his feathers light. On a Dream. Keats. EnRP

As hid all measure of the feat. (LL) Character. Emerson. LiTA; OxBSP

As his men were pullin' away in the boat. (LL) Captain Cook. *Aborigine Oral Tradition*. NOBAu

As his own Arthur fared across the mere. The Passing of Tennyson. Ernest Dowson. EPCY

As Holy Kirke makes mind. The Nativity. *Unknown*. MeEL

As honest Jacob on a night. The Patriarch. Burns. ChIV-1; CoMu

As honey in wine/ wine, honey. Meleager, *tr. fr. Greek by* Peter Whigham. GrAn; PeHV

As I am a Rhymer. On My Joyful Departure from the City of Cologne. Samuel Taylor Coleridge. FaBoCo; InvP; OBTV
(On My Joyful Departure from the Same City.) NBLV

As I am,/ I should be able to. Missing Beat. Carolyn M. Rodgers. JB

As I am mine, their sweating selves; but worse. (LL) I Wake and Feel the Fell of Dark Not Day. Gerard Manley Hopkins. EnVR; FaBoVe; MeMBP; OxAEP-2; PeVV; TRP

As I am unhappy. Yosano Akiko, *tr. fr. Japanese by* Glenn Hughes *and* Yozan T. Iwasaki. WPOW

As I beheld a winters evening air. Another ("As I beheld a winters evening air.") Richard Lovelace. SeCP

As I Behind a Bush Did Sit. Sir Philip Sidney. *Fr.* Arcadia. SiPSBD

As I believe that thou and I should be. (LL) Sonnet: To Guido Cavalcanti. Dante. AWP

"As I cam in by boney Glasgow town." Glasgow Peggie. *Unknown*. ESPB

As I cam in by Dunidier. The Battle of Harlaw. *Unknown*. ESPB

As I cam thro the Garrioch land. The Battle of Harlaw. *Unknown*. ESPB

As I came down the Cano'gate. Merry May the Keel Row. *Unknown*. GBP

As I came home through Drury's woods. Cold Fear. Elizabeth Madox Roberts. WPE

As I Came in by Fiddich-Side. *Unknown*. RB

As I Came O'er Cairney Mount. Burns. CoMu

As I came out of the New York Public Library. Nuns in the Wind. Muriel Rukeyser. NNaP

As I came over London Bridge. Geordie. *Unknown*. OBET

As I came over Windy Gap. Running to Paradise. W. B. Yeats. NTP; OxBoLi

As I came round the harbor buoy. The Long White Seam. Jean Ingelow. GN; NOBVV

As I came through the desert thus it was. James Thomson ("B.V."). *Fr.* City of Dreadful Night, The. LiTB; OBNC

As I came through the Valley of Despair. Through the Valley. Ella Wheeler Wilcox. AnAmPo

As I came to the edge of the woods. Come In. Robert Frost. AmPP; BoNaP; FaBV; LiTA; LiTM; MoAB; MoAmPo; NOBA; NoP; RaBo; TrGrPo; TRP

As I closed the bathroom door. (LL) Sure. Hugo Williams. CBLP

As I did the washing one day. The Shirt of a Lad. *Unknown*, *tr. fr. Welsh by* Anthony Conran. OBWVE; VBLP

As I did walk abroad one time. The Mourning Conquest; or, The Woman's Sad Complaint, and Doleful Cry to See Her Love in Fainting Fits to Lye. *Unknown*. CoMu

As I did walke my selfe alone. King James and Brown. *Unknown*. ESPB

As I do now? (LL) Shall I come to see. Lady Ise. PRA; WPJ

As I do now? (LL) The One Furrow. R. S. Thomas. HoPM; OxBC

As I do zew, wi' nimble hand. Lwonesomeness. William Barnes. NOBVV

As I drive my parents home through the snow. Driving My Parents Home at Christmas. Robert Bly. CAPP

As I drive to the junction of lane and highway. At Castle Boterel. Thomas Hardy. EBEV; GTBS-P; NOBE; OBNC; OxAEP-2; PeVV; PoE; SCV

As I Ebb'd with the Ocean of Life. Walt Whitman. AmPP; NAAL-1; NOBA; PrIm; TRP

As I gaed down to Collistown. The Cunning Clerk. *Unknown*. OxBB

As I gaed in by the Duke o' Athole's gates. The Duke o' Athole's Nurse. *Unknown*. OxBB

As I Gird on for Fighting. A. E. Housman. CMoP

As I go down the highway. In Memoriam R. M. Stalker, Missing, September 1916. E.A. Mackintosh. OBF

As I go up to heaven. (LL) Woman. Malangatana Ngwenya. PeSAV

As I Grew Older. Langston Hughes. AmPP

As I grow older. White Dwarf. A. R. Ammons. CAPP

As I have been to mine. (LL) Lady Alice. *Unknown*. ESPB, (A *vers*.)

As I have said, I floated to the earth. Shelley. *Fr.* Prometheus Unbound. EnRP; FHYEP; OAEL-2

As I in hoary [or hoarie] winter's night/ stood [or stoode] shivering in the snow. The Burning Babe. Robert Southwell. CH; EIL; ESCV; FaBoCh; HAP; HeIP; InPS; LiTB; NAEL-1; NAs; NOBE; NOCV; NoP;

NoSic; OAEL-1; OBCP; OBEV; OxAEP-1; PoEL-2; Prf; RB; SCGP; TFi; TOF; TrCP; TrGrPo; TRP

As I lay asleep in Italy. Shelley. *Fr.* Mask [or Masque] of Anarchy. EnRP; FaBoEH; FHYEP; Mes; OBSV; OxAEP-2; RB; SCV

As I lay dreaming, open-eyed. Her Mouth and Mine. W. H. Davies. CBLP

As I lay, fullness of praise. The Rattle Bag. Dafydd ap Gwilym, *tr. fr. Welsh by* Joseph Clancy. NBLV; RB

As I lay in the bath the air was filling with bells. 1940. Sir John Betjeman. PAW

As I lay musing all alone/ upon my resting bed. The Poore [or Poor] Man Payes [or Pays] for All. *Unknown*. CoMu; OBET

As I Lay Musing ("As I lay musing all alone.") *Unknown*. CoMu

As I lay musing in my bed. The Praise of Sailors. *Unknown*. OxBSS

As I Lay Quiet. Margaret Widdemer. GoYe

As I Lay Sleeping. *Unknown*. TrGrPo

As I lay upon a night. *Unknown*. MiEL

As I Lay with My Head in Your Lap Camerado. Walt Whitman. AnAmPo; NAAL-1; OxBA

As I leaned at my window. The Song of Samuel Sweet. Charles Causley. OBNV

As I lie here in the sun. Jonah. Randall Jarrell. ChIV-1

As I listened from a beach-chair in the shade. Their Lonely Betters. W. H. Auden. ArNa; GoJo; NAEL-2; NoAM

As I look from the isle, o'er its billows of green. Sun and Shadow. Oliver Wendell Holmes. AnAmPo

As I look out from the desk window. Laura St. Martin. FF

As I looked, the poplar rose in the shining air. The Deceptive Present, the Phoenix Year. Delmore Schwartz. BoNaP

As I me rod this ender day. *Unknown*. MiEL

As I mused by the hearthside. Comfort. Walter de la Mare. PFP

As I my little flock on Ister Bank. Sir Philip Sidney. *Fr.* Arcadia. SiPSBD
(Shepherd Song.) SiPS

As I one evening [or ev'ning] sat before my cell. Artillerie [or Artillery]. George Herbert. GeHe; InPS; NoP; PoEL-2; SeCV-1

As I one morning shaving sat. The Cat and the Boot; or, An Improvement upon Mirrors. *Unknown*. FaBoUs

As I pass through my incarnations in every age and race. The Gods of the Copybook Headings. Kipling. FaPoR; NoAM; OBSV; OPOP; OxBTC

As I pass'd [or passed] by a river side [or riverside]. The Carnal and the Crane. *Unknown*. ESPB; OBET

As I passed by a willow tree. The Willow Tree. *Unknown*. OBET

As I reach to close each book. Against the Evidence. David Ignatow. CAPP; NNaP

As I rode in to Burrumbeet. The Traveller. C. J. Dennis. NOBAu

As I rode out by Tom Sherman's bar-room. The Dying Cowboy. *Unknown*. FaBoBa

As I roved by the dockside one evening so rare. Fiddler's Green. John Conolly. OxBSS

As I roved out impatiently. In the Ringwood. Thomas Kinsella. CMoP; PBCIP

As I roved out on a May morning. Johnny's the Lad I Love. *Unknown*. OxBoLi

As I roved out on a summer's morning. Castle Hyde. *Unknown*. FaBoPP

As I roved out one summer's morning, speculating most curiously. Colleen Rue. *Unknown*. BIrV

As I rowed out to the light-house. The Light-House Keeper's White-Mouse. John Ciardi. PDV

As I rummaged thro' the attic. My Trundle Bed. J. G. Baker. BLPA; FaBoBe

As I Sat at My Spinning-Wheel. *Unknown*. CoMu

As I sat at the café, I said to myself. Arthur Hugh Clough. *Fr.* Dipsychus *also in* Spectator ab Extra. ELP; EnVR; FaBoCo; FaBoPV; FiBHP; GTBS, 3 *sts*.; NOBVV; OAEL-2; OxBoLi; PeLV; PeVV
(How Pleasant It Is to Have Money.) NOBE

As I sat by my window last evening. Miss Foggerty's Cake. *Unknown*. BLPA; NBLV

As I sat down one evening. The Frozen Logger. *Unknown*. OBAL

As I sat down to breakfast in state. The Country Clergyman's Trip to Cambridge. Macaulay. OBSV; OxBoLi; PeLV

As I sat in a lonesome grove. The Little Dove. *Unknown*. AmFP

As I Sat on a Sunny Bank. *Unknown*. ChTr; OxBoLi, (abr.); OxNR, (abr.)

As I sat on the toilet. Travel Plans. Mary Kathryn Stillwell. PRA

As I sat one evening in sweet meditation. The Twilight Hour. Joshua McCarter Simpson. AAP

As I Sat under a Sycamore Tree. *Unknown*. LiTB

As I sate Musing by my selfe alone. Thoughts Several Be. Margaret Cavendish, Duchess of Newcastle. *Fr.* Dialogue Between Melancholy and Mirth, A. CBCK

As I sd to my/ friend. I Know a Man. Robert Creeley. CAPP; InPS; MAT; NIP; NOBA; OxBSP; PoM; PPP; VCAP

As I should lay alone. (*LL*) Whistle, Daughter, Whistle. *Unknown.* AIW; AmFP; ErPo; OBET; OxNR, (*shorter vers.*); ReMoGo

As I sing this in darkness. (*LL*) Sydney. Robert Harris. NOBAu

As I sit alone at present, dreaming darkly of a Dun. (*LL*) In the Gloaming. Charles Stuart Calverley. BXAP; NOBL; PeLV

As I sit by the ruddy oak fire. Nestle-down Cottage. Mary Weston Fordham. CBWP-2

As I sit looking out of a window of the building. The Instruction Manual. John Ashbery. HAP; InPS; MoP; NeAP; NoAM; NOBA; Poetr; PoM; SOTW

As I Sit Writing Here. Walt Whitman. NAAL-1

As I Step over a Puddle at the End of Winter, I Think of an Ancient Chinese Governor. James Wright. CAPP; NaP

As I stood/ Ling'ring upon the threshold, half-concealed. Xantippe. Amy Levy. BrRo

As I strole the city, oft I. Swift. *Fr.* Legion Club, The. BIrV

As I strolled out one evening just as the sun went down. The Farmer and the Shanty Boy. *Unknown.* AmFP

As I strolled out one evening upon a dark career. The Fire Ship. *Unknown.* OxBSS

As I talk with learned people. A Spade Is Just a Spade. Walter Everette Hawkins. PoBA

As I therein no other's face but yours can view. (*LL*) So well I love thee, as without thee I. Michael Drayton. GBL

As I walk through the streets. F. S. Flint. TrPWD

As I walk'd thinking through a little grove. Catch: On a Wet Day. Franco Sacchetti, *tr. fr. Italian by* Dante Gabriel Rossetti. AWP (On a Wet Day.) BoNaP

As I walked alone. Robert Crowley. FaBoEH

As I walked between Bolton and Bury. The New Bury Loom. *Unknown.* OBET (New Bury Loom, The.) FaBoEH

As I Walked [*or* Walk'd] by Myself. *Unknown.* CBNP; ChTr; FaBoEE; FaBoEH; OxBSP; OxNR; ReMoGo

As I walked down by the river. A Ballad for Katharine of Aragon. Charles Causley. FaBoTw

As I walked down yon meadow, I carelessly did stray. A British Man-of-War. *Unknown.* OBET

As I walked fforth one morninge. Christopher White. *Unknown.* ESPB

As I walked forth one morning fair. The Wanton Seed. *Unknown.* OBET

As I walked forth one summer's morn, all in the month of June. Brave Collier Lads. *Unknown.* OBET

As I walked her down to the river! (*LL*) The Unfaithful Wife. Federico García Lorca. STV

As I walked one May morning. Down by the Riverside. *Unknown.* OBET

As I walked out early. Thomas A. Clark. *Fr.* Sixteen Sonnets. NBrP

As I Walked Out in the Streets of Laredo. *Unknown.* AS

As I Walked Out One Evening. W. H. Auden. CBNP; FF; HeIP; InPK; LiTM; NoAM; NOBE; NoP; OxAEP-2; PAW; PrIm; RB; TwCP; UnPo

As I walked out one evening, all in the month of May. The Banks of Claudy. *Unknown.* AmFP; OBET

As I walked out one evening down by the Strawberry Lane. Captain Wedderburn's Courtship. *Unknown.* AmFP, (A *and* B *vers.*); ESPB, (A *and* B *vers.*)

As I walked out one May morning,/ One May morning betimes. Searching for Lambs. *Unknown.* OBET

As I walked out one May morning,/ One May morning early. Seventeen Come Sunday. *Unknown.* OBET

As I walked out one May morning,/ When May was all in bloom. The Royal Fisherman. *Unknown.* GBP

As I walked out one May morning/ When May was white in bloom. Cupid the Ploughboy. *Unknown.* OBET

As I walked out one May morning,/ When the small birds sang so sweet. The Lover Proved False. *Unknown.* AmFP

As I walked out one midsummer's morning. The Banks of Sweet Primroses. *Unknown.* ELP

As I Walked Out One Morning. *Unknown.* AmFP

As I walked out one morning in May. Archie o Cawfield. *Unknown.* AmFP

As I walked out one morning, just as day was dawning. As I Walked Out One Morning. *Unknown.* AmFP

As I walked out one morning on the fourteenth of July. The Mower. *Unknown.* CoMu; OBET

As I Walked Out One Night. *Unknown.* Mes

As I walked out that sultry night. Full Moon. Robert Graves. NOBE

As I walked over the western plain. Legend. Charles Causley. TOF

As I Walked through the Meadows. *Unknown.* OBET

As I walked with my friend. Columbus. Louis Simpson. Mes

As I wandered in the forest. Wild Flower's Song. Blake. BoTP

As I wandered on the beach. The Great Blue Heron. Carolyn Kizer. CoAP; IMW; WPE

As I wandered round the homestead. My Mother's Prayer. T. C. O'Kane. BLPA; FaBoBe

As I wandrede her by weste. *Unknown.* MiEL

As I was a-going to Strawberry Fair. Strawberry Fair. *Unknown.* OBET

As I was a-gwine down the road. Turkey in the Straw. *Unknown.* AS; GBP

As I was a-hoeing, a-hoeing my lands. The Six Badgers. Robert Graves. GoJo; GrPl

As I was a-roaming for pleasure one day. The Little Mohea. *Unknown.* AmFP

As I was a-roving one morning in spring. The Mantle So Green. *Unknown.* AmFP

As I was a-walkin' down Paradise Street. Blow the Man Down. *Unknown.* AS

As I was a-walking down Wapping. Ratcliffe Highway. *Unknown.* OxBSS

As I was a walking, I cannot tell where. Narcissus, Come Kiss Us! *Unknown.* ErPo

As I was a-walking on Westminster Bridge. *Unknown.* OxNR

As I was a-walking on yon far distant shore. The Indian Lass. *Unknown.* OBET

As I was a-walking one midsummer's morning. The Plains of Waterloo. *Unknown.* OBET

As I was a-walking/ One morning in spring. The Pretty Ploughboy. *Unknown.* GBP (Lark in the Morning, The.) ChTr

As I was a-walking one morning in the spring. The Sign of the Bonny Blue Bell. *Unknown.* OBET

As I was a-walking the other day. The Shoemaker. *Unknown.* FaPON

As I was a-walking to Nottingham Fair. Nottingham Fair. *Unknown.* AmFP

As I was a-walking [*or* walked out] one morning for pleasure. Whoopee-Ti-Yi-Yo. *Unknown.* AS; FaPON; ImGa (Git Along, Little Dogies.) MoShBr

As I was by one brought forth, I would bring forth another. (*LL*) Fain Would I Wed. Thomas Campion. NAEL-1

As I was cast in my ffirst sleepe. Young [*or* Younge] Andrew. *Unknown.* ESPB; OxBB

As I was climbing Ardán Mór. The Herons. Francis Ledwidge. (Ardan Mór.) AWP

As I was crossing Trafalgar Square. Epilogue to an Empire 1600-1900. Jon Stallworthy. FaBoEH

As I was driving my waggon one day. Gee Ho, Dobin. *Unknown.* CoMu

As I was fishing off Pondy Point. Jim Desterland. Hyam Plutzik. RB; VGW

As I was going along, long, long. Mother Goose. OxNR; ReMoGo

As I was going by Charing Cross. *Unknown.* CH; FaBoCh; OxNR (King Charles the First.) GBP

As I was going down the lane. Ballad of No Proper Man. Daniel Hoffman. MAT

As I was going o'er London Bridge. Mother Goose. ISE

As I was going o'er Tipple Tine. *Unknown.* OxNR

As I was going out one day down by the Clarence Dock. Heave Away, My Johnny. *Unknown.* OxBSS

As I was going over Mulberry Mountain. Mulberry Mountain. *Unknown.* AmFP

As I was going through Windy Gap. Windy Gap. David Campbell. NTP

As I was going to Banbury. *Unknown.* OxNR

As I was going to Bethlehem town. Bethlehem Town. Eugene Field. WBLP

As I was going to Derby. The Derby Ram. *Unknown.* CBNP; FaBoNo; GBP; NTP; OxNR; ReMoGo (Wonderful Derby Ram, The.) BoTP

As I was going to Derby. *Unknown. See* Oh, as I went down to Derby Town.

As I was going to Derby, all on a market day. The Wonderful Derby Ram. *Unknown.* BoTP

As I Was Going to Saint Ives. Daniel Hoffman. NYBP

As I was going to St. Ives. Mother Goose. NTCP; OFC; OxNR; ReMoGo

As I was going to sell my eggs. Mother Goose. OxNR (Bandy Legs.) ReMoGo

As I was going to town. Me Alone. Lula Lowe Weeden. CDC

As I was going up Pippen Hill. Mother Goose. OxNR; ReMoGo

As I was going up the hill. *Unknown.* OxNR

(Jack the Piper.) ChTr; GBP

As I was going up the stair. The Little Man Who Wasn't There. Hughes
    Mearns. FaPON
    (Antigonish.) BLPL; NBLV; PoLF
    (Case, A.) FaBoCo
    (Little Man, The.) 09RHPC
    (Man Who Wasn't There, The.) PYC

As I was hiking past the woods, the cool and sleepy summer woods. Out
    There Somewhere. Henry Herbert Knibbs. BLPA

As I Was Laying on the Green. Unknown. FiBHP

As I was letting down my hair. The Lady with Technique. Hughes
    Mearns. Fr. Later Antigonishes. FiBHP

As I was musing by myself alone. Mirth and Melancholy. Margaret
    Cavendish, Duchess of Newcastle. WPE

As I was sitting in my chair. The Perfect Reactionary. Hughes Mearns.
    NTCP

As I Was Standing in the Street. Unknown. NTCP

As I was strolling lonely in the Backs. In the Backs. James Kenneth
    Stephen. NOBVV

As I was travelling toward the city of satisfactions. The City of
    Satisfactions. Daniel Hoffman. Prf

As I was waiting for the bus. Sight Unseen. Kingsley Amis. ErPo;
    NoAM

As I was walkin' an' a-ramblin' one day. The Wild Rippling Water.
    Unknown. FaBoBa

As I Was Walkin' down Wexford Street. Unknown. AS

As I was walkin' the jungle round, a-killin' of tigers an' time. Guy
    Wetmore Carryl. BXAP; NBLV

As I was walking. A Memorable Fancy. Blake. Fr. Marriage of Heaven
    and Hell, The. EnRP; NU; OAEL-2

As I Was Walking. Robert Creeley. RaBo

As I was walking all alane [or alone]. The Twa Corbies. Unknown.
    AWP; CH; CoGr; EBEvV; ELP; EnSB; ESPB; FaBoBa; FaBoCh; GTBS;
    GTBS-P; HAP; InPK; NoP; OBEV; OxBS; PPP; RB; ScCV; SCGP;
    UnPo
    (Two Ravens, The.) SoSe

As I was walking [or wa'king] all alone [or alane]. The Wee Wee Man.
    Unknown. CH; EBEV; ELP; ESPB; FaBoCh; GBP; OAEL-1; OxBB

As I was walking down by the seashore. The Lover's Lament for Her
    Sailor. Unknown. AmFP

As I was walking down Covent Garden. The Buck's Elegy. Unknown.
    OBET

As I was walking in a field of wheat. Unknown. OxNR

As I was walking in the fields last Tuesday of all days. The Slender Lad.
    Unknown, tr. fr. Welsh by Kenneth Hurlstone Jackson. OBWVE

As I was walking mine alane. Archie o [or of] Cawfield. Unknown.
    AmFP; ESPB; OxBS

As I was walking one midsummer morning. O Dear O. Unknown. ErPo

As I was walking one morn at my ease. What's the Life of a Man?
    Unknown. OBET

As I was walking one morning in spring. I Shall Be Married on Monday
    Morning. Unknown. ErPo

As I was walking out one morning, I met a buxom lass. Buxom Lass.
    Unknown. ErPo

As I was walking up the street. O Mally's Meek, Mally's Sweet. Burns.
    GN

As I went a-walking one fine summer's morning. The Shoofly. Felix
    O'Hare. AmFP

As I went by a dyer's door. The Dyer. Unknown. ChTr; OxNR

As I went by St. James's, I heard a bird sing. An Excellent New Ballad
    Called the Prince of Darkness. Unknown. APAS

As I went down that yella bank. Unknown. FaBoVe

As I went down the hill along the wall. Meeting and Passing. Robert
    Frost. OxBA; PFP

As I went down the hill I heard. The Voice. Norman Gale. OHIP

As I went down the village green. Ducks. Norman Ault. BoTP

As I Went Down to David's Town. George Craig Stewart. AH

As I went down to Dymchurch Wall. In Romney Marsh. John Davidson.
    EBVV; FaBoPP; MeMBP; OxBTC

As I went down to the huckleberry picnic. The Kicking Mule. Unknown.
    AmFP

As I went down to the mowin' field. Fod. Unknown. AmFP

As I went on Yol Day. Jankin, the Clerical Seducer. Unknown. MeEL
    (Jolly Jankin.) OxBLMV

As I went out a crow. The Last Word of a Bluebird. Robert Frost.
    FaPON; GoJo; GrPl

As I went out a-walking to breathe the pleasant air. Rolly Trudum.
    Unknown. AmFP

As I went out one May morning. Bird in a Cage. Unknown. AS; GBP

As I went out, so I came in. Unknown. GBP

As I went out walking for pleasure one day. The Little Mohea. Unknown.
    AmFP

As I went over London Bridge. Unknown. ChTr

As I went over the water. Unknown. OxNR

As I went over Tipple Tyne. Unknown. ChTr

As I went owre the Hill o' Hoos. Unknown. GBP

As I went through a field of wheat. Unknown. RoPo

As I went through a guttery gap/ I met a wee man with a red cap.
    Unknown. FaBoVe

As I went through the garden gap. A Cherry. Unknown. ReMoGo

As I went through yon guttery gap/ I met my Uncle Davy. Unknown.
    FaBoVe

As I Went to Bonner. Unknown. CBNP; OxBoLi; OxNR; ReMoGo

As I went to Totnam. The Maid of Tottenham. Unknown. CoMu

As I went up by Ovillers. Ballad of the Three Spectres. Ivor Gurney.
    OBWP

As I went up the Brandy hill. Unknown. OxNR

As I went up the garden. Unknown. BoTP

As I went up the humber jumber. Unknown. FaBoNo

As I went up to Craigbilly Fair. Craigbilly Fair. Unknown. ChTr; GBP

As I wer readen ov a stwone. Readen ov a Head-Stwone. William
    Barnes. CH

As I work at the pump, the wind heavy. Mother. Seamus Heaney. NAs

As idle as a German ship. The Surrender of the Hun Fleet. Unknown.
    NSI

As idlers, — always pity such. (LL) The Mistake. Unknown. VPP

As if a one-room schoolhouse were all we knew. An Amish Rug. Michael
    Longley. CIP; PNI

As If a Phantom Caress'd Me. Walt Whitman. GBL; SAmP

As if by late light shaped of its. Slipped Quadrant. Nathaniel Mackey.
    BAP-90

As if God were an old man. The Task. Denise Levertov. CrSp

As if he'd been really invited. (LL) There was a young man so benighted.
    Frances Parkinson Keyes. PeLi

As if I didn't have enough. Small Aircraft. Bella Akhmadulina, tr. fr.
    Russian by Daniel Halpern. BoWoP; PAW

As if I had committed, against the whole scheme of life, a desecration.
    (LL) Moss-gathering. Theodore Roethke. RFM; VGW

As if in a presence of an intelligence. The Cold. Charles Simic. HCAP

As if in snow you walked. And you walked in snow. A Song of Blue and
    Red. Amir Gilboa, tr. fr. Hebrew by Ruth Finer Mintz. MHP

As if it were a scene made-up by the mind. Often I Am Permitted to Return
    to a Meadow. Robert Duncan. CAPP; CMoP; NOBA; NU

As if it were/ forever that they move, that we. Merritt Parkway. Denise
    Levertov. AmPP; NeAP; PoM

As if my answering machine were a rejection. Phonic. Gail Mazur.
    NAmP90

As if of great happiness to come. (LL) Bewitching Distant Landscape.
    Joseph Freiherr von Eichendorff. RiWo

As if some irremediable poison. London. J. R. Rowland. CBAP

As if somebody ordered it. Tashkent Breaks into Bloom. "Anna
    Akhmatova," tr. fr. Russian by Richard McKane. BoWoP

As if that sax. Coleman Hawkins (d. 1969), RIP. William Matthews. Jaz

As if the Checks were given. (LL) I never saw a moor. Emily
    Dickinson. FaPON; GN; HeIP; ImGa; ImPo; LiTA; LiTM; MeMAP;
    MoAB; MoAmPo; PoLF; SAmP; TAP; TFi; TrGrPo; WGRP

As if the dead hare were soon to awaken! (LL) The Fox Who Watched for
    the Midnight Sun. Norman Dubie. LCAP

As if the trees were not indifferent. Gathered at the River. Denise
    Levertov. CrSp; SV

As if they never called you mine,/ mine, mine. (LL) The Masochist.
    Maxine W. Kumin. IHMS; PoA

As if they were his ripe prize vegetables. (LL) My Father's Garden.
    David Wagoner. DiPo; NIP

As if to hide the horror from God's eye. (LL) By the Potomac. Thomas
    Bailey Aldrich. PAH; Son

As imperceptibly as grief. Emily Dickinson. CMoP; LiTA; NAAL-1;
    NOBA; NoP; PBWP; PoE; PoEL-5; SoSe

As in a dream of flood from which we rose intact but alone. The Break.
    E. N. Sargent. NYBP

As in a duskie [or dusky] and tempestuous night. William Drummond of
    Hawthornden. NOSC; OxAEP-1

As in a pot the milk turns sour. The Shattering of Love. Gond Oral
    Tradition, tr. by V. Elwin and S. Hivale. WTO

As in a Rose-Jar. Thomas Samuel Jones, Jr.. PoLF

As in a thunderstorm at night. Waiting. Robert Pack. GOYP

As in a Watteau fete of rose and silver blue. The Tempest. Marya
    Zaturenska. MoAmPo

As in her ancient mistress' lap. Familiarity Dangerous. William Cowper, tr. fr. Latin by Vincent Bourne. OFC

As in the age of shepherd king and queen. Dans l'Allée. Paul Verlaine, tr. fr. French by Arthur Symons. AWP

As in the cool-air'd road I come by. My Love's Guardian Angel. William Barnes. GBL; PoEL-4

As in the gardens, all through May, the rose. His Lady's Tomb. Pierre de Ronsard, tr. fr. French by Andrew Lang. AWP

As in the house I sate [or sat]. Poverty. Thomas Traherne. Prf; TEP; TrCP

As in the inward suspicious mind. (LL) Written in Her French Psalter. Elizabeth I, Queen of England. PBWP; WPE

As in the midst of battle there is room. George Santayana. Fr. Sonnets. AnAmPo; AWP

As in wild earth a Grecian vase! (LL) A Poor Scholar of the 'Forties. Padraic Colum. NOIV

As innocent as now thou art. (LL) To His Son [or Sonne], Vincent Corbet[t]. Richard Corbett [or Corbet]. BeJo; FaBoCh; NOSC; OxAEP-1; OxBChV; TrGrPo

As into the Garden Elizabeth Ran. A. E. Housman. NBLV

As inward love breeds outward talk. William Basse. Fr. Anglers Song, The.
(Angler's Song, The.) NOSC

As is the sand upon the ocean's shore. One Generation Passeth Away. Jones Very. ChIV-1

As it[t] befel[l] in midsum[m]ertime [or midsumer-time]. Sir Andrew Bart[t]on. Unknown. AmFP, 2 vers.; EnSB; ESPB; OxBB

As it befell on a bright holiday. The Bitter Withy. Unknown. ChTr; FaBoBa; GBP; NOCV; NoP; OBET
(As it fell out upon one day.) OBET

As it befell upon one time. Hughie Grame. Unknown. ESPB
(Hughie Graham.) OxBB

As it comes back, brick by smoky brick. In the Lost Province. Tom Paulin. PBCIP

As it fell on a holy day. John Dory. Unknown. ESPB; OxBSS

As it fell one holy-day [or on a light holyday or high holyday]. Little Musgrave and Lady Barnard. Unknown. ErPo; ESPB; FaBoBa; InvP; OBET; OxBB

As it fell out in a long summer's day. Fair Margaret and Sweet William ("As it fell out in a long summer's day.") Unknown. ESPB, A vers.; OxBB

As it fell out on a holiday. Holy Well, The ("As it fell out on a holiday.") Unknown. OBET

As it fell out on a holy day [or upon a bright holiday or upon one day]. The Bitter Withy. Unknown. FaBoBa; NOCV; NoP

As it fell out one May morning. Holy Well, The ("As it fell out one May morning.") Unknown. FaBoCh; GBP; NOCV

As it fell out upon a day [or one day]. Dives and Lazarus ("As it fell out upon a day.") Unknown. ELP; ESPB; FaBoBa; OBET; OxBB

As it fell out upon one day. The Bitter Withy. Unknown. OBET

As it fell out upon one day. Unknown. See As it befell on a bright holiday.

As it fell upon a day. A Vision of Truth. J. C. Squire. NOBL

As it fell upon a day. Richard Barnfield. Fr. Affectionate Shepherd, The. GBL
(Nightingale, The.) AWP; GTBS; GTBS-P
(Ode, An: "As it fell upon a day.") EIL
(Philomel, The.) CH; NOBE; OBEV

As it fell upon a day. Richard Barnfield. Fr. Passionate Pilgrim, The. GBL
(Nightingale, The.) AWP; GTBS; GTBS-P
(Ode, An.) EIL
(Philomel.) CH; NOBE; OBEV

As it grows dark/ drinking wine. (LL) After Work. Gary Snyder. HoPM; NNaP

As It Happens, sels. Ken Smith.
In the Flats, flat voices. PWE
Remembered City, The. PWE

As It Looked Then. E. A. Robinson. CMoP; MeMAP

As it shone on distant Bingen — fair Bingen on the Rhine. (LL) Bingen on the Rhine. Caroline E. Norton. BeLS; BLPA; WBLP

As It Was. John Mander. Mes

As it was free from wrong. (LL) Upon a Diamond Cut in Form[e] of a Heart . . . Sent in a New Year's [or New-yeares] Gift. Sir Robert Ayton. EIL

As it was in the beginning. Robin Morgan. Fr. Network of the Imaginary Mother, The. CrSp

As It Were an Attendant. J. H. Prynne. VaA

As Jack, the jolly plowboy, was plowing of his land. The Jolly Plowboy. Unknown. AmFP

As Jack walked out of London city. Jack the Jolly Tar. Unknown. AmFP

As Jock the Leg and the merry merchant. Jock the Leg and the Merry Merchant. Unknown. ESPB

As Joe Gould says in. E. E. Cummings. FiBHP

As Joseph Was a-Walking [or a-Waukin']. Unknown. BoTP; OHIP

As Julia once a-slumbering lay. The Captived Bee; or, The Little Filcher. Robert Herrick. CaPo

As Katherine, for the Court's sake, put downe Stewes. (LL) Raderus. John Donne. PeLV

As Kingfishers Catch Fire [Dragonflies Draw Flame]. Gerard Manley Hopkins. CMoP; EBEV; EBVV; EnlH; FaBoMo; LiTM; NAEL-2; NOBVV; NOCV; NoP; PoE; PrIm; RB

As kingfishers catch fire dragonflies dráw fláme. Gerard Manley Hopkins. See As Kingfishers Catch Fire [Dragonflies Draw Flame].

As Lady Marg'ret sat in her bow'r. Sweet William's Ghost. Unknown. ScCV

As Lambs into the Pen. Dorothy Wellesley. FaBoTw

As lamps burn silent, with unconscious light. Modesty. Aaron Hill. OxBSP

As landscapes richen after rain, the eye. Foliage of Vision. James Merrill. VGW

As lark ascending. Praying. P. J. Kavanagh. OxBSP

As late I journey'd o'er the extensive plain. Life. Samuel Taylor Coleridge. EnRP

As lately I travelled towards Gravesend. The Seaman's Compass. Laurence Price. OxBSS

As Sir Launfal made morn through the darksome gate. Sir Launfal and the Leper. James Russell Lowell. Fr. Vision of Sir Launfal, The. GN

As laurel leaves that cease not to be green. The Promise of a Constant Lover. Unknown. EIL

As life improved, their poems. Postscript. R. S. Thomas. FaBoMo; OxBC

As life runs on, the road grows strange. Sixty-eighth Birthday. James Russell Lowell. OxBSP; PoEL-5

As Life What Is So Sweet? Unknown. OxBSP

As little Jenny Wren/ Was sitting by the shed. Mother Goose. OxNR
(Jenny Wren.) ReMoGo

As Lob among his cows one day. Lob's Courtship. Elizabeth Hands. ECWP

As long ago, my love, how long ago. (LL) Echo. Christina Rossetti. BoLoP; CH; EBEvV; EBVV; ELP; GBL; MeMBP; NOBE; NoP; OAEL-2; OBNC; OHCV; PFP; PIP; PoE; PoEL-5; VBLP

As long ago we carried to your knees. Mother. Unknown. PoToHe

As long as I continue weeping. Louise Labé, tr. fr. French by Joan Keefe and Richard Terdiman. PBWP

As long as I go forth on ships that sail. A Seaman's Confession of Faith. Harry Hibbard Kemp. TrPWD

As long as I live. Me. Walter de la Mare. FaPON

As long as it talks I am going to listen. (LL) What a thing it is to sit absolutely alone. Thomas Merton. EaPr

As long as it was still noon and the earth. Callimachus, tr. fr. Greek by Barbara Hughes Fowler. Fr. Hecale. HePo

As long as it watched me. (LL) February Twilight. Sara Teasdale. FaPON; OBCA; PDV

As long as we look forward, all seems free. The Western Approaches. Howard Nemerov. HCAP; TAP

As love and I, late harbour'd in one inn. Michael Drayton. GBL

As Love and I, late harboured in one inn. Michael Drayton. Fr. Idea. ESo; NoSic

As love has me for only you! (LL) Of the Marriage of the Dwarfs. Edmund Waller. CBLP

As loving hind that (hartless) wants her deer. A Letter to Her Husband, Absent upon Public Employment. Anne Bradstreet. OxBA; WPE
(Another.) SCAP

As Lucy Went A-Walking. Walter de la Mare. OBSP

As Lucy went a-walking one morning cold and fine. As Lucy Went A-Walking. Walter de la Mare. OBSP

As mad sexton's bell, tolling. Song on the Water. Thomas Lovell Beddoes. Fr. Death's Jest Book. FaBoCh

As make them think thee Angel without sex. (LL) To Cynthia. Sir Francis Kynaston. CBLP

As makes her seem not fair, nor rich, nor young. (LL) Fair, Rich, and Young. Sir John Harington, after the Latin of Martial. EIL; NIP

As male and female, thrust and ache. (LL) Palais des Arts. Louise Glück. AnAn; VCAP

As man behind his mask still wears a child. (LL) Mask. Stephen Spender. MoAB; MoBrPo

As many red herrings as grow in the wood. (LL) Man in the wilderness asked [of] me [or said to me], The [or A]. Mother Goose. BoTP; CBNP; FaBoCh; FaBoCo; FaBoNo; GBP; OxNR; ReMoGo; Spl

As Mars and Minerva were viewing of some implements. Under the Rose. Unknown. OBET

As May was opening the rosebuds. Birth of the Foal. Ferenc Juhász, *tr. fr. Hungarian* by David Wevill. RB

As me and me marrer was gannin' te work. The Collier's Rant. *Unknown*. OBET

As men, for fear the stars should sleep and nod. Divinity. George Herbert. NOSC

As men from men. Despondency Corrected. Wordsworth. *Fr.* Excursion, The. EnRP

As men, the heavens have their hypocrisy? (*LL*) Fair Days; or, Dawns Deceitful. Robert Herrick. CaPo

As men, turn all to ears. (*LL*) A Canticle to Apollo. Robert Herrick. CaPo

As men who fought for home and child and wife. The Battle of Oriskany. Charles D. Helmer. PAH

As men who see a city fitly planned. Proofs of Buddha's Existence. *Unknown*. WGRP

As monthly meetings once a week and Soirées every morning. (*LL*) Address. Andrew Geddes Bain. PeSAV

As Moses supposes his toeses to be. (*LL*) Moses. *Unknown*. ISE; OxNR

As Mozart composed a sonata. *Unknown*. PeLi

As Much as You Can. C. P. Cavafy, *tr. fr. Greek* by Edmund Keeley *and* Philip Sherrard. RB

As mundane effect of the incendiary veil. The Contours of Indifference. Nick Totton. VaA

As my eyes search the prairie. Spring Song. *Unknown, tr. fr. Chippewa Indian* by Frances Densmore. ArNa; EaPr; OBVE

As my fellows be? (*LL*) How Should I Be So Pleasant. Sir Thomas Wyatt. SiPS

As my imagination rises. Beyond Imagination. David Rokeah, *tr. fr. Hebrew* by Ruth Finer Mintz. MHP

As my last Remembrances. (*LL*) Lyric[k] for Legacies. Robert Herrick. BeJo; FaBoRV; JCP

As my mind in fancy wanders. The Negro Has a Chance. Maggie Pogue Johnson. CBWP-4

As my mind's leaves. Two Movements Which Begin at the Head and End at the Feet. Richard Caddel. NBrP

As my mother ages and becaomes. My Mother in Old Age. Eric Ormsby. NIP

As my new life begins, I start smiling at the people around me. Farewell to Kurdistan. Rosemary Tonks. OxBTC

As my true-hearted Fannie. (*LL*) Fannie ("Fannie has the sweetest foot.") Thomas Bailey Aldrich. AnAmPo; OBAL

As "Name of individual, partnership, or corporation to whom paid." Royalties. D. J. Enright. NOBL; PeLV

As Nature H——'s clay was blending. On a Certain Effeminate Peer. John Winstanley. FaBoEE

As near beauteous Boston lying. A New Song. *Unknown*. PAH

As near Portobello lying. Admiral Hosier's Ghost. Richard Glover. NOEC

As needy gallants in the scriv'ners' hands. *Fr.* Amboyna; or, The Cruelties of the Dutch to the English Merchants. OBSV

As Negro as the Africa they robbed me of. (*LL*) Whitewash. Léon Damas. NegPo

As New and as Old. Martin Carter. PBCV

As Night Comes On. Cecil Cobb Wesley. GoYe

As night drew on, and, from the crest. Winter Night. Whittier. *Fr.* Snowbound; a Winter Idyl [*or* Idyll]. AmPP; GN; NOBA; OxBA; TAP; TrGrPo; WiR

As night was falling slowly on city, town and bush. The Bastard from the Bush. *Unknown*. NOBAu

As Nilus' sudden ebbing here. A Dream Broke. William Cartwright. NOSC

As oceans are to porpoises. The Snowfish. Edward Field. GrPl

As Ocean's Stream. Fyodor Tyutchev, *tr. fr. Russian* by Babette Deutsch *and* Avrahm Yarmolinsky. AWP

As o'er my latest book I pored. Printer's Error. P. G. Wodehouse. FiBHP

As o'er thy loved one now in grief ye bendeth. Solace. Josephine D. Henderson Heard. CBWP-4

As of tears. (*LL*) Blowing Bubbles. William Allingham. GN

As oft as I behold and see. The Earl of Surrey. SiPS

As oft I do record. Jinny. *Unknown*. NOSC

As often as some where before my feet. Francis Daniel Pastorius. SCAP

As on a Darkling Plain. Henry Taylor. MT; Poetr

As on a window late I cast mine eye. Love-Joy. George Herbert. OAEL-1

As on the bank the poor fish lies. The Restless Heart. *Unknown, tr. fr. Marathi*. WGRP

As on the Cross, the Saviour hung. Deep Spring. *Unknown*. AmFP

As on the Heather. Reinmar von Hagenau, *tr. fr. German* by Jethro Bithell. AWP

As on the highway's quiet edge. Coast, The: Norfolk. Frances Cornford. OxBTC

As on two that have no longer much of anything to tell. (*LL*) John Gorham. E. A. Robinson. MoAB; MoAmPo

As once grave Pluto drove his royal wheels. Proserpine's Ragout. Mary Leapor. ECWP

As once, if not with light regard. Ode on the Poetical Character. William Collins. EnRP; NAEL-1; NOEC; OAEL-1; PoE; PoEL-3; TEP

As once in black I disrespected walked. On a Maid [*or* Maide] of Honour Seen by a Scholar in Somerset Garden. Thomas Randolph. JCP

As once in heaven Dante looked back down. The Backward Look. Howard Nemerov. OxBC

As once in her fire-lit heart I felt the furies/ Beating, beating. (*LL*) Lines to a Nasturtium. Anne Spencer. CDC; PoNe; ShDr; VBLP

As once in May. (*LL*) All Souls' Day. Herman von Gilm zu Rosenegg. RiWo

As once the winged energy of delight. Rainer Maria Rilke, *tr. fr. German*. *Fr.* Sonnets to Orpheus. EnlH, *tr.* by Stephen Mitchell

As one abandoned on a barren shore. To Rotenham. August, Graf von Platen, *tr. fr. German* by Reginald Bancroft Cooke. PeHV

As one asked for soup and began to explain. (*LL*) Imagined Arrival. Matthew Sweeney. IB

As one, at midnight, wakened by the call. W. W. Gibson. MoBrPo

As One Non-Combatant to Another. George Orwell. OxBTC

As One Put Drunk into the Packet-Boat. John Ashbery. HAP; HCAP; VCAP

As one that for a weary space has lain. The Odyssey. Andrew Lang. OBEV; OBNC; OtMeF; PoLF; PoRA

As One Who Bears beneath His Neighbor's Roof. Robert Silliman Hillyer. MoAmPo

As one who came with ointments sweet. Spikenard. Laurence Housman. TrPWD

As one who has sailed across an unknown sea. The Solitary. Rainer Maria Rilke, *tr. fr. German* by C. F. MacIntyre. TrJP

As one who, long by wasting sickness worn. Hope. William Lisle Bowles. EnRP

As One Who Wanders into Old Workings. C. Day Lewis. FaBoMo; LiTM

As other fellows do of Trinity. (*LL*) Here lies a Doctor of Divinity. Richard Porson. FaBoEE

As other men, so I myself do muse. Michael Drayton. *Fr.* Idea. ESo; JCP; NOSC; NoSic; Son

As Our Bloods Separate. David Constantine. PWE

As our bloods separate the clock resumes. As Our Bloods Separate. David Constantine. PWE

As our destiny. (*LL*) A World to Come. Bernard Dadié. NegPo

As our good manners required. (*LL*) Manners [for a Child of 1918]. Elizabeth Bishop. GOYP; OxBC; RB

As our king lay musing on his bed. King Henry Fifth's Conquest of France. *Unknown*. ESPB
(Henry V's Conquest of France.) OBET

As over muddy shores a dragon flock. The Fear. Lascelles Abercrombie. OBMV

As Oyster Nan Stood by Her Tub. *Unknown*. CoMu

As Pants the Hart. Nahum Tate. TIRV

As Parmigianino did it, the right hand. Self-Portrait in a Convex Mirror. John Ashbery. HCAP; NAAL-2

As Phyllis the gay, at the break of the day. Edward Moore. ECEV

As pilot well expert in perilous wave. Spenser. *Fr.* Faerie Queene, The. OAEL-1
(Cave of Mammon, The.) PoEL-1

As played by the phantoms of Shrule. Tony Butler. PeLi

As pools beneath stone arches take. John Drinkwater. PoA

As power and wit will me assist. Sir Thomas Wyatt. SiPS

As praiseworthy/ the power of breathing. Lorine Niedecker. VGW

As proper mode of quenching legal lust. Gerald Massey. NOBVV

As proved our strong restorative by's blood. (*LL*) My Carol. Mildmay Fane, 2d Earl of Westmorland. BeJo

As pure at ninety-four as any babe. Aunt Lucy. Jane Gentry. CrSp

As Pyramus did on Thisbe's breast bewail. (*LL*) Divers [*or* Diverse] thy death do diversely bemoan. The Earl of Surrey. SiPSBD

As queens of kings. (*LL*) All Things Wait upon Thee. Christina Rossetti. GN

As Ralph and Nick i'th'field were plowing. The Plowman. *Unknown*. APAS

As red as a starling's his peepers. Opium-Den. *Malay Oral Tradition, tr. by* R. J. Wilkinson *and* R. O. Winstedt. WTO

As Regis asserts they resemble one another. The Murderers of Kings. Zbigniew Herbert, *tr. fr. Polish* by John Carpenter *and* Bogdana Carpenter. AnAn

As reminders to the wise, of duty's call? (*LL*) The Sacred Book. *At. to* Zoroaster. AWP

As riper years approach us. Glimpses of Infancy. Priscilla Jane Thompson. CBWP-2

As rising from the vegetable World. James Thomson. *Fr.* Seasons, The. PoEL-3

As Rochefoucauld his maxims drew. Verses on the Death of Dr. Swift, D.S.P.D., Occasioned by Reading a Maxim in Rochefoucauld. Swift. NOEC; OBF, (*abr.*); PoEL-3; TEP

As round as an apple, as deep as a cup. Mother Goose. OxNR (Well, The.) ReMoGo

As round as an apple, as deep as a pail. *Unknown.* OxNR

As round the rose's heart the golden threads. Soul Incense. H. Cordelia Ray. CBWP-3

As round their dying father's bed. The Father and His Children. *Unknown.* OxBChV

As Sam crumbles lumps of tofu on her tray. Gardens We Have Left. David Mura. OpBo

As sea-foam blown of the winds, as blossom of brine that is drifted. "Home, Sweet Home," with Variations ("As sea-foam blown of the winds, as blossom of brine that is drifted.") H. C. Bunner. *Fr.* Home. OBAL

As seventh sign, the antique heavens show. Feast of the Ram's Horn. Harvey Shapiro. VGW

As Severn lately in her ebbs that sank. The Severn. Michael Drayton. *Fr.* Baron's War, The. ChTr

As Shadows Cast by Cloud and Sun. Bryant. AH

As shall mocke the envious eye. (*LL*) Come and let us live my deare. Catullus. OBVE

As she climbed the cathedral tower. Gargoyles, the. Pauline Stainer. PWE

As she did upon this leaze. (*LL*) In a Eweleaze Near Weatherbury. Thomas Hardy. EnVR

As she liv'd peerless. Shakespeare. *Fr.* Winter's Tale, The. OxAEP-1

As she shook her little fist. The Death of the Novel. David Young. AmPA

As shine by fountains, bubbles, flowers, or snow? (*LL*) A Palinode. Edmund Bolton. ElL; InvP; NoSic; PoEL-2; PrIm

As shines the sunbeam through dark clouds. Hope. Mary E. Tucker. CBWP-1

As ships, becalmed at eve, that lay. Qua Cursum Ventus. Arthur Hugh Clough. EBVVPR; OBEV

As shows the air when with a rainbow graced. Upon Julia's Ribband. Robert Herrick. CaPo

As silent as a mirror is believed. Legend. Hart Crane. InPS; OxBA

As simple an act. Way Out West. Amiri Baraka. NeAP; PoBA; PoBeRe

As since he dares not come within my sight. (*LL*) The Dream[e]. Ben Jonson. BeJo; CBLP; NOBE; NOSC; PoEL-2

As sinewy as biltong, as narrow. My Grandmother. Perseus Adams. PeSA

As Sisyphus against the infernal steep. Byron. *Fr.* English Bards and Scotch Reviewers. OBSV

As slow I climb the cliff's ascending side. At Tynemouth Priory, after a Tempestuous Voyage. William Lisle Bowles. Son

As slow our ship her foamy track. The Journey Onwards. Thomas Moore. GTBS; GTBS-P; OxAEP-2

As slowly and sadly I strayed by the river. Lost Jimmie Whalen. *Unknown.* AmFP

As smell thereof the stynk! (*LL*) The Pilgrims' Sea Voyage and Seasickness. *Unknown.* OBTV

As soft as silk, as white as milk. Mother Goose. GBP; OxNR (Walnut, A.) ReMoGo

As solid-seeming as antiquity. A Marriage in the 'Sixties. Adrienne Rich. TRP

As some brave admiral, in former war. The Disabled Debauchee. The Earl of Rochester. BoLoP; GGP; HAP; NAEL-1; NOBL; OBSV; PPP (Maim[e]'d Debauchee, The.) PoEL-3; SCGP

As some dark stream within a cavern's breast. Love. Anne Lynch Botta. AmWP

As some day it may happen that a victim must be found. Ko-Ko's Song ("As some day it may happen that a victim must be found.") W. S. Gilbert. *Fr.* Mikado, The. LiTB (Lord High Executioner's Song, The.) CBCK (They'll None of 'Em Be Missed.) OHCV

As some fond virgin, whom her mother's care. Epistle to Miss [*or* Miss Teresa] Blount, on Her Leaving the Town after the Coronation. Pope. BoLoP; EBEV; FHYEP; NAEL-1; NOBE; NOEC; NoP; OPOP; PoEL-3; PPP

As some heroes bold, I will unfold, together were conversing. Grand Conversation on Brave Nelson. *Unknown.* OBET

As someone on his back for months of illness. Ausiàs March, *tr. fr. Catalan by* John Frederick Nims. STV

As something worth the giving. (*LL*) After Reading in a Letter Proposals for Building a Cottage. John Clare. OxAEP-2

As sometimes in a dead man's face. As Sometimes in a Dead Man's Face. Tennyson. *Fr.* In Memoriam A. H. H. EBVV, *abr.*; ImPo; LiTB; OAEL-2, *abr.*; PeECV, *abr.*

As Sometimes in a Dead Man's Face. Tennyson. *Fr.* In Memoriam A. H. H. EBVV, *abr.*; ImPo; LiTB; OAEL-2, *abr.*; PeECV, *abr.*

As Sonata in Praes o Molli. Swift. *See* Mollis Abuti.

As soon as April pierces to the root, *mod. vers. by* Theodore Robinson. Chaucer. *See* Whan that Aprill[e] with his shoures [*or* shower] soote.

As soon as he came home, straightway Pygmalion did repair. Pygmalion's Statue Comes to Life. Ovid, *tr. by* Arthur Golding. *Fr.* Metamorphoses. OAEL-1

As soon as I climb into the car. The Hitchhiker. Joseph Bruchac. PRA

As soon as I could I have called you together. The Queen's Speech. Arthur Mainwaring. APAS

As soon as I lie down in my soft bed. Louise Labé, *tr. fr. French by* Willis Barnstone. BoWoP

As soon as I saw I was naked. Will the Real Me Please Stand Up? A. L. Hendricks. PBCV

As soon as I'm in bed at night. Mrs. Brown. Rose Fyleman. BoTP; OxBChV

As soon as my sister and I got out of our. The Sisters of Sexual Treasure. Sharon Olds. PBCAP

As soon as the idea of the Flood had subsided. After the Flood. Rimbaud, *tr. by* Enid Rhodes Peschal. *Fr.* Illuminations. SOTW

As soon it must, from the mountain. (*LL*) Sestina: Here in Katmandu. Donald Justice. SM

As soon they will be happy to desert. (*LL*) Cat Goddesses. Robert Graves. NYBP; OxBSP

As soone as wee to bee begvnne. *Unknown.* OBD

As Spring the Winter Doth Succeed. Anne Bradstreet. AH

As Stealthily. For the New Year. Eduard Friedrich Mörike, *tr. fr. German by* Philip L. Miller. RiWo

As still he envied me, so fair she was! (*LL*) The Bishop Orders His Tomb at Saint Praxed's Church. Robert Browning. EBVV; EBVVPR; EnVR; FHYEP; HAP; HeIP; NAEL-2; NAWM-2; NOBVV; NoP; OAEL-2; OBAL; OtMeF; PoE; Poetr; PPP; PrIm; SCGP; TEP; TFi

As, sum tyme, dois the curser stert and ryn. Virgil, *tr. by* Gavin Douglas. *Fr.* Aeneid [*or* Eneados], The. NAWM-1; OBVE

As summer ends and leaves fall like dust. A Cantor's Dream before the High Holy Days. Martin Robbins. (In white robes I'm joined by a.) BTR

As sure as shooting. From the Brothers Grimm to Sister Sexton to Mother Goose; One Transmogrification. David Cummings. BXAP

As surely as I hold your hand in mine. Brown Boy to Brown Girl. Countee Cullen. PoBA

As swelled from nothing, doth dissolve in nought. (*LL*) This life, which seems so fair. William Drummond of Hawthornden. CH; NOSC; TrGrPo

As swift to me as heavenly light! (*LL*) My Life's Delight. Thomas Campion. ElL; InvP; TrGrPo

As Syllable from Sound. (*LL*) Cause. Emily Dickinson. EnIH; MoAB; MoAmPo; MoP; NAAL-1; NAWM-2; NTP; OxBA; Poetr

As Tam the Chapman on a day. Tam the Chapman. Burns. ScCV

As that Arabian bird (whom all admire). William Browne. *Fr.* Britannia's Pastorals. OAEL-1

As the Allied tanks trod Germany to shard. May, 1945. Peter Porter. OxBC

As the army corps advances. (*LL*) An Army Corps on the March. Walt Whitman. AiP; InPS; PoLF

As the basket comes in procession, greet it, women. Hymn to Demeter. Callimachus, *tr. fr. Greek by* Barbara Hughes Fowler. *Fr.* Hymns. HePo

As the birds come in Spring. The Poet and His Songs. Longfellow. AnAmPo

As the black curtain of the night. Reveille Matin, or Good Morrow to a Friend. Mildmay Fane, 2d Earl of Westmorland. NOSC

As the black storm upon the mountain-top. Residence in London. Wordsworth. *Fr.* Prelude [or, Growth of a Poet's Mind], The. EnRP; HAP, (*short sel.*); OAEL-2; PoEL-4, (*sl. shorter*)

As the body denies the means to look. Pernette de Guillet, *tr. fr. French by* Joan Keefe *and* Richard Terdiman. PBWP

As the cassias blossom. What Her Girl Friend Said ("As the cassias blossom.") Peyanar, *tr. fr. Tamil by* A. K. Ramanujan. *Fr.* Nine on Happy Reunion. PLW

As the cat. William Carlos Williams. FaPON; InPS; InvP; NoP; OFC; PDV; SoCa; SoSe; TTTS

As the chameleon, who is known. The Chameleon. Matthew Prior. OBSV

As the clouds that are so light. The Clouds That Are So Light. Edward Thomas. FaBoTw

As the crescent moon is born from the Western Sea. Ch'en Tzu-ang, *tr. by* William H. Nienhauser. *Fr.* Impressions of Things Encountered. SuSp

As the crest of some slow-arching wave. Lincolnshire Shores. Tennyson. *Fr.* Idylls of the King. FaBoPP

As the Crow Flies, Let Him Fly, *sels.* Samuel Hoffenstein. "Early bird may catch the worm, The." NBLV

As the day stands when the Sun begins to glow. Dante, *tr. fr. Italian. Fr.* Divina Commedia. MeMAP; NAWM-1, *tr. by* John Ciardi

As the days grow longer. Lengthening Days. *Unknown.* ReMoGo

As the Dead Prey upon Us. Charles Olson. NeAP

As the deep blue of heaven brightens into stars. God's Promises. *Unknown.* BLRP

As the deer begin to hide. What He Said ("As the deer begin to hide.") Peyanar, *tr. fr. Tamil by* A. K. Ramanujan. *Fr.* Nine on Happy Reunion. PLW

As the dew flies over the green vallee. (*LL*) The Wife Wrapt in Wether's Skin. *Unknown.* AmFP; ESPB, (F *vers.*)

As the divorced [*or* divorc'd] soul from her body parts. (*LL*) The Surrender. Henry King. BoLoP; CBLP; EBEV; JCP; NOSC; TrGrPo

As the dow flies over the mulberry-tree. (*LL*) The Riddling Knight. *Unknown.* FaBoCh; PoEL-1

As the dry, red sun set we sat and watched. Kinneret. John Hollander. BAP-89

As the Duck and the Kangaroo? (*LL*) The Duck and the Kangaroo. Edward Lear. OxBChV

As the dust from the wet dream of a nation. Written in Unbridled Repugnance near Sioux Falls, Alabama — April 30, 1974. A. K. Redwing. VoR

As the earth. Elizabeth Barrett Browning. *Fr.* Aurora Leigh. EPCY

As the elevator car left our floor. *Unknown.* PeLi

As the eternall monument of me. (*LL*) To Laurels. Robert Herrick. CaPo; SeCV-1

As the Father hath loved me, so have I loved you. Bible, *N.T. Fr.* St. John. OBF

As the first spring mists appear. Lady Ise, *tr. fr. Japanese by* Kenneth Rexroth *and* Ikuko Atsumi. WPJ

As the full moon slowly rose. Sappho, *tr. fr. Greek by* Sam Hamill. InMo

As the gook woman howls. In the Mourning Time. Robert Hayden. BPo

As the green grass glows upwards, strangers in the garden. (*LL*) Trees in the Garden. D. H. Lawrence. CMoP; MoAB; MoBrPo; NoP

As the hand moves over the harp, and the strings speak. Inspiration. *Unknown, tr. fr. Greek by* J. Rendel Harris. *Fr.* Solomon. WGRP

As the hart panteth after the water brooks. Bible, *O.T., paraphrased by* Sir Thomas Wyatt. *Fr.* Psalms. AWP; TrJP (My Soul Thirsteth for God.) TrGrPo (Search, The, XLII *and* XLIII *Moulton, Modern Reader's Bible.*) WGRP

As the harvest moon in a summer sky. (*LL*) Julian of Norwich. Kathleen Jamie. VBLP

As the holly [*or* holy] groweth [*or* grouth] green [*or* grene]. Green Groweth the Holly. *Unknown.* NoSic; OxBLMV

As the image of the sun. Estuary. Ted Walker. NYBP

As the land lifts. In Memory of My Country. Douglas Crase. FoLa

As the lean tree burst into grief. (*LL*) The Mad Scene. James Merrill. CoAP; NOBA; PoA; PoE; TAP

As the lined sheets in life's stern ledger book. (*LL*) An Auditor Thinks about Female Nature. Jamie Grant. NOBAu

As the lovely new flowers. What She Said ('As the lovely new flowers'). Allur Nanmullai, *tr. fr. Tamil by* A. K. Ramanujan. PLW

As the Mist Leaves No Scar. Leonard Cohen. NoP

As the mower. Apodal Stride (Cursive). Anthony Barnett. VaA

As the mute nightingale in closest groves. To the Blessed Virgin Mary. Gerald Griffin. TIRV

As the natives got ready to serve. Ed Cunningham. PeLi

As the observer wills. (*LL*) Study of Two Pears. Wallace Stevens. InPS; NAAL-2; NoAM; NU; OxBA

As the player's breath warms the fipple the tone clears. Basil Bunting. *Fr.* Briggflatts [An Autobiography]. PWE

As the poets have mournfully sung. W. H. Auden. FaBoBl; PeLi (Aesthetic Point of View, The.) NBLV; OBAL (Comprehensive Death.) CBCK

As the poor end of each dead day drew near. He Liked the Dead. Malcolm Lowry. OxBTC

As the primrose spreads so sweetly. (*LL*) The Cruel Brother. *Unknown.* AmFP; ESPB; OxBB

As the Queen and Prince Albert, so buxom and all pert. Old England Forever and Do It No More. *Unknown.* GBP

As the rain is lagging, wayward, in the river. On the Fragile Labyrinth. José Emilio Pacheco, *tr. fr. Spanish by* John Frederick Nims. STV

As the rains of spring. Lady Izumi Shikibu, *tr. fr. Japanese by* Edwin A. Cranston. PBWP

As the season changes. Daughter of Shunzei, *tr. fr. Japanese by* Kenneth Rexroth *and* Ikuko Atsumi. WPJ

As the seed loves the earth enclosing it. (*LL*) The Seed Is the Light of the Earth. Christina Pacosz. LoHo

As the seed waits eagerly watching for its flower and fruit. Night VIII (The Eternal Man). Blake. *Fr.* Vala; or The Four Zoas. PoE

As the single pang of the blow, when the metal is mingled well. Tropic Rain. Robert Louis Stevenson. OBTV

As the slanting sun drowsed lazily. Cape Coloured Batman. Guy Butler. PeSA

As the stars hide in the light before daybreak. Avoiding News by the River. W. S. Merwin. NaP

As the stores close, a winter light. February Evening in New York. Denise Levertov. NoAM

As the sun rises. Early Song. Carroll Arnett. ETG

As the sun sets, the mountain air becomes cool. Sailing along the Tai Stream from Stone Bridge to the Foot of Mo-ho Peak. Wang Shih-chieng, *tr. fr. Chinese by* Chang Yin-nan *and* Lewis C. Walmsley. SuSp

As the sun that lights creation. Africa. L. A. J. Moorer. CBWP-3

As the sunbeams stream through liberal space. Emerson. *Fr.* Woodnotes II ("As sunbeams stream through liberal space"). NOBA; OHIP

As the sunlight in the sky. For the Cultural Campaign. Chimedin Jigmed, *tr. fr. Mongol Oral Tradition by* C. R. Bawden. WTO

As the swamp cooler breathes. A Sale of Smoke. Roberta Spear. AmPA

As the sweet sweat of roses in a still. The Comparison. John Donne. *Fr.* Elegies. PeLV

As the Team's Head-Brass. Edward Thomas. GTBS-P; NAEL-2; NSI; OBWP; OxAEP-2; OxBTC; PeFWW; PoE; RB

As the twig is bent, the tree's inclined. Her Precious Leg. Thomas Hood. *Fr.* Miss Kilmansegg and Her Precious Leg. NOBVV

As the used anger drips from his hands like blood. The Murderer. Paul Petrie. NYBP

As the war-trumpet drowns the rustic flute. Pindar. Antipater of Sidon, *tr. fr. Greek by* John Addington Symonds. AWP

As the Window Darkens. Laura Jensen. LCAP

As the wise men of old brought gifts. The Gift. William Carlos Williams. ChIV-2

As the Word came to prophets of old. Prophets for a New Day. Margaret Walker. BPo

As the youthful morning's light, On S. John the Baptist. Thomas Stanley. ChIV-2

As theirs, I lay, like them, my best gifts on thy shrine!. (*LL*) I love the old melodious lays. Whittier. AnAmPo; NoP; OxBA; TAP

As then I had mine, in the place that was happy and poor. (*LL*) Time's Fool. Ruth Pitter. MoBrPo; OxBTC; PoRA; WPE

As then in death, so now in love. (*LL*) C[h]aritas Nimia; or, The Dear[e] Bargain. Richard Crashaw. ESCV; JCP; NOCV; NOSC

As there, along the elmy hedge, I go. Troubles of the Day. William Barnes. GTBS-P

As there are taped sororal presents and psychological reversals. It Was Miss Scarlet with the Candlestick in the Billiard Room. Bernadette Mayer. UL

As there is now in this of mine. (*LL*) The Dead Marten. Walter Savage Landor. FM

As they came from the East. Kings and Stars. John Erskine. TrCP

As they came in by the Eden side. The Slaughter of the Laird of Mellerstain. *Unknown.* ESPB

As they carry the white paddy of their land. What Her Girl Friend Said to Him, Trying to Dissuade Him from His Long Journey. *Unknown, tr. fr. Tamil by* A. K. Ramanujan. PLW

As they cut the body loose. Jazz Funeral. Maxine Cassin. *Fr.* Three Love Poems by a Native. Jaz

As they sat and talked beneath the boundary trees. Married Love. Sherod Santos. Son

As they toast the archangels in Bundaberg rum. (*LL*) Bundaberg Rum. W. N. Scott. NOBAu

As thin little Proclus was fanning the fire. Lucilius, *tr. fr. Greek by* Peter Porter. GrAn

As things be/come. Word Poem (Perhaps Worth Considering). Nikki Giovanni. PoBA

As this convine and ordinance was mayd. Virgil, *tr. by* Gavin Douglas. *Fr.* Aeneid [*or* Eneados], The. NAWM-1; OBVE

As this in Kew thirst for the Red Dawn. (*LL*) Note on Local Flora. William Empson. EBEV; FaBoMo; OxAEP-2

As Thomas was cudgell'd [*or* cudgel'd] one day by his wife. Swift. FaBoEE (Cudgeled Husband, The.) NBLV

As those we love decay, we die in part. On the Death of a Particular Friend. James Thomson. *Fr.* On the Death of Mr. William Aikman the Painter. OBEV; SCGP

As those who are not athletic at breakfast day by day. Nature Morte. Louis MacNeice. NoAM

As those who pass the Alps do say. To the Queen. Anne Killigrew. KTR

As Thou didst once the Delphian Oracle. (LL) Upon the Times. Mildmay Fane, 2d Earl of Westmorland. BeJo

As thou now sufferest mine. (LL) I prithee let my heart alone. Thomas Stanley. BeJo

As though an aged person were to wear. Elegy for the Monastery Barn. Thomas Merton. VGW

As though forever, his appointed pigeon. (LL) Pigeons. Alastair Reid. NYBP; TwCP

As though his subject had decided to remain a prayer. (LL) The Painter. John Ashbery. HCAP; NOBA; NoP; PoE; SOTW

As though it had been washed. (LL) In the Country. Lu Yu. OHMPC

As though it soared suchwise through heaven too. (LL) Royal Palm. Hart Crane. CMoP; MoAB; MoAmPo; MoP; NoAM; NoP; TrGrPo

As though it were a toy! (LL) Franklin Hyde. Hilaire Belloc. FaBoUs; NBLV

As though it were an altar. (LL) As the full moon slowly rose. Sappho. InMo

As though it were flying home. (LL) Moonlit Night. Joseph Freiherr von Eichendorff. RiWo

As though they did not care. (LL) Old Black Men. Georgia Douglas Johnson. CDC; PoBA; PoNe

As though they were grass. (LL) A Dragonfly. Eleanor Farjeon. FaPON; PDV

As thro' the Land at Eve. Tennyson. Fr. Princess, The. LiTB

As through a mist, the pious prosperous ghosts. (LL) Indian Reservation: Caughnawaga. A. M. Klein. LiTM; NOBC; NoP

As through earth's garden once I strayed. The Crushed Flower. Mary E. Tucker. CBWP-1

As through the Land. Tennyson. See As through the land at eve we went.

As through the land at eve we went. As thro' the Land at Eve. Tennyson. Fr. Princess, The. LiTB
  (As Thro' the Land at Eve We Went.) ImPo
  (As through the Land.) SCGP
  (We Kiss'd Again with Tears.) PoToHe

As thumb is genius of the hand. Objects in Mirror are Closer Than They Appear. Jeffrey Skinner. PBCAP

As thus he spake, each bird and beast behold. Milton. Fr. Paradise Lost. EPCY; OBF

As thus the snows arise, and foul and fierce. Winter ("As thus the snows arise, and foul and fierce.") James Thomson. Fr. Seasons, The.
  (Winter Tragedy, A.) ECEV

As Thy Days. Grant Colfax Tullar. BLRP

As Thy Days So Shall Thy Strength Be. "George Klingle." BLRP

As time one day by me did pass. As Time One Day by Me Did Pass. Henry Vaughan. ESCV; GeHe; MeLP; SeCV-1

As Time One Day by Me Did Pass. Henry Vaughan. ESCV; GeHe; MeLP; SeCV-1

As time turns it will be like this again. (LL) The Water-Colourist. Sebastian Barry. IB

As to Being Alone. James Oppenheim. TrJP

As to harden the unhard and unhard/ the hardened. (LL) It's Here In The. Russell Atkins. PoBA

As to His Choice of Her. Wilfrid Scawen Blunt. Fr. Love Sonnets of Proteus, The. Son

As to kidnap the Congress has long been my aim. General Howe's Letter. Unknown. PAH

As to my heart, that may as well be forgotten. Personal Column. Basil Bunting. ArLo

As to my own concerns, it seems odd, given. Peroration, Concerning Genius. Robert Pinsky. Fr. Essay on Psychiatrists. NoAM

As to our relatives. (LL) Listen to the air. John Lame Deer. EaPr

As to the blooming prime. Edmund Bolton. NoSic

As to thy Crosse reverence we may have. (LL) An A.B.C. of Devotion. Unknown. MeEL

As to thy greater light a sacrifice. (LL) The Glowworm. Thomas Stanley. BeJo; NOSC

As Toilsome I Wander'd Virginia's Woods. Walt Whitman. NAAL-1

As Tom the porter went up Ludgate Hill. Tom the Porter. John Byrom. NOEC

As Tommy Snooks and Bessy Brooks. Mother Goose. OxNR; ReMoGo

As tongueless Echo in the pastoral vale. To the Greek Anthologists. George Rostrevor Hamilton, after the Greek of Satyros. FaBoEE

As t'other night in bed I thinking lay. The Dream of the Cabal; a Prophetical Satire. Unknown. APAS

As tourists inspected the apse. Edward Gorey. PeLi; PeLV

As Tranquil Streams. Marion Franklin Ham. AH

As travellours [or travellers] when the twilight's come. The Pilgrimage. Henry Vaughan. ChIV-2; ESCV

As tree and wheat rise green. Nile the Hermit. Unknown, tr. fr. Greek by Guy Davenport. GrAn

As true as I was born into. Halfway. Maxine W. Kumin. GoYe

As twenty days are now. (LL) To a Butterfly. Wordsworth. EnRP; FM

As two men were a-walking, down by the sea-side. The Duke of Grafton. Unknown. ChTr; GBP

As unpredictable as picnic weather, blue. Guide to the Perplexed. David Malouf. NOBAu

As unto the bow the cord is. Hiawatha's Wooing. Longfellow. Fr. Song of Hiawatha, The. BeLS; EBNV

As usual. (LL) Hope Chest. Elaine Equi. VBLP

As usual, the clock in The Clock Bar was a good few minutes. Hamlet. Ciaran Carson. FaBoVe; PNI

As usual, the clock in the Clock bar was a good few minutes fast. Hamlet. Ciaran Carson. FaBoVe

As usual, the first gate was modest. It is dilapidated. She can't tell. Tan Tien. Mei-Mei Berssenbrugge. OpBo

As usual/ this day is pushed into my room. Reading Matter. Martin Sorescu, tr. fr. Romanian. CBNP

As Venus one day, at her toilet affairs. Venus Attiring the Graces. William Whitehead. ECEV

As vineyards of deathless Cypris. (LL) As honey in wine/ wine, honey. Meleager. GrAn; PeHV

As virtuous men pass [or passe] mildly away. Valediction, A: Forbidding Mourning. John Donne. BLPL; CBLP; EnRePo; ESCV; FaPoB; FF; FHYEP; HAP; HeIP; HoPM; ImPo; InPS; JCP; LiTB; MeLP; NAEL-1; NOBE; NoP; NOSC; OAEL-1; PoE; PoEL-2; Poetr; PPP; PrIm; SCGP; SeCP; SeCV-1; SoSe; TEP; TFi; UnPo; WeW

As vonce I valked by a dismal svamp. The Old Cove. Henry Howard Brownell. PAH

As we are departing. (LL) Taking Leave of a Friend. Li Po. RB; SOTW

As We Are So Wonderfully Done with Each Other. Kenneth Patchen. ErPo; UnAS

As we are together, praying for peace, let us be truly with each other. Thich Nhat Hanh. EaPr

As we came through the gate to look at the few new lambs. Ravens. Ted Hughes. InPS; NAs

As we come marching, marching in the beauty of the day. Bread and Roses. James Oppenheim. SWP

As we crossed the field, I told her. (LL) The Centaur. May Swenson. FaBoWP; GrPl; NMM; NTP; TwCP

As We Dance Round. Unknown. CH

As we drove back, crossing the hill. A Locked House. W. D. Snodgrass. VCAP

As we eat crushed strawberry ice. Seamstress at St. Léon. Gillian Clarke. Fr. Journal from France, A. OBTV

As we get older we do not get any younger. Chard Whitlow. Henry Reed. BXAP; FaBoCo; FaBoNo; FaBoPa; FiBHP; LiTM; MoBrPo; NBLV; NOBL; NoP; OxBTC; PeLV; UnPo; UV

As we go about the toils of life. As We Sow We Shall Reap. Maggie Pogue Johnson. CBWP-4

As We Grow Older. Rollin J. Wells. See Little more tired at the close of the Day, A.

As we have borne the pains. (LL) Mothers. Nikki Giovanni. UnPo

As we have to be. (LL) Hymn to Priapus. D. H. Lawrence. CMoP; MoAB; OBMV; PoE; SCGP

As we lay musing in our beds. The Seamen's Distress. Unknown. OxBSS (Mermaid, The.) ESPB

As we live, we are transmitters of life. We Are Transmitters. D. H. Lawrence. OxBTC

As we pass through the field of purple herbs. Princess Nukada, tr. fr. Japanese by Kenneth Rexroth and Ikuko Atsumi. WPJ

As we rowed from our ships and set foot on the shore. The Savages. Josephine Miles. LiTM

As we rush, as we rush in the train. As We Rush, As We Rush in the Train. James Thomson ("B.V."). Fr. Sunday at Hampstead. OHCV
  (In the Train.) BoTP; OBEV

As We Rush, As We Rush in the Train. James Thomson ("B.V."). Fr. Sunday at Hampstead. OHCV

As we sailed on the water blue. Whisky Johnny. Unknown. AS

As We Sow We Shall Reap. Maggie Pogue Johnson. CBWP-4

As we speed out of youth's sunny station. Life's Journey. Ella Wheeler Wilcox. PWR

As we stood on the crushed stone. A Conversation. Barbara Howes. IHMS

As we stood on the [edge of the crag] or cliff's edge. Against the Wind. Amir Gilboa, tr. fr. Hebrew by Bernhard Frank. MHP, tr. by Ruth Finer Mintz

As we was sailing on the main. The *Caesar's* Victory. *Unknown.* OxBSS

As we went/ I felt a scruple, which I durst not vent. The Poet Questions Peace. George Chapman. *Fr.* Euthymiae Raptus; or, The Teares of Peace. JCP

As we were marching to Quebec. Marching to Quebec. *Unknown.* AmFP

As we wearied pilgrims, once possessed. His Own Epitaph. Robert Herrick. CaPo

As weary-hearted as that hollow moon. (*LL*) Adam's Curse. W. B. Yeats. BIrV; CMoP; NAEL-2; NoAM; NoP; OAEL-2; PFP; SOTW; TEP; WeW

As Weary Pilgrim. Anne Bradstreet. *See* As Weary Pilgrim, Now at Rest.

As Weary Pilgrim, Now at Rest. Anne Bradstreet. NAAL-1; PoEL-3; SCAP

As Well as They Can ("As well as it can, the hooked fish while it dies.") *At. to* A. D. Hope Alec Derwent Hope. GrPl

As well as things. (*LL*) Riprap. Gary Snyder. CAPP; HCAP; NAAL-2; NeAP; NoAM; NOBA; PoBeRe; PoM; VCAP

As well, maybe, that you cannot read our minds. The Enemy. Randolph Stow. NOBAu

As what he loves may never like too much. (*LL*) On My First Son [*or* Sonne]. Ben Jonson. AWP; BeJo; ClHu; CoGr; EBEV; EIL; EnRePo; FaBoEE; FF; HAP; HoPM; IMW; InPK; InPS; JCP; LiTB; NAEL-1; NIP; NoP; NOSC; OAEL-1; OBD; OxBSP; PFP; PoE; PoEL-2; Poetr; RaBo; RB; SCGP; SeCP; SeCV-1; TEP; TFi; TRP; WeW

As, when a beauteous nymph decays. Stella's Birthday, 1725. Swift. NOEC

As When a Child. Charles Lamb. Son

As when a fragment, from a mountain torn. Virgil, *tr. by* Dryden. *Fr.* Aeneid [*or* Eneados], The. NAWM-1; OBVE

As when a ship, that flyes faire under saile. Spenser. *Fr.* Faerie Queene, The. FHYEP

As, when a tree's cut down, the secret root. Prologue to "The Tempest." Dryden. NoP

As when an architect some palace wall. Homer, *tr. by* William Cowper. *Fr.* Iliad, The. OBVE

As when desire, long darkling, dawns, and first. Bridal Birth. Dante Gabriel Rossetti. *Fr.* House of Life, The. Son

As when devouring flames some forest seize. Homer, *tr. by* William Cowper. *Fr.* Iliad, The. OBVE

As when far off the warbled strains are heard. LaFayette. Samuel Taylor Coleridge. EnRP

As when into the garden paths by night. Old Age. Frederick Tennyson. NOBVV

As when it happ'neth that some lovely town. Sonnet: Content and Resolute. William Drummond of Hawthornden. JCP

As when of frequent bees. Homer, *tr. by* George Chapman. *Fr.* Iliad, The. OBVE

As when of old some orator renowed. Milton. *Fr.* Paradise Lost. ChIV-1; EPCY

As when rooting in a bin. Dick, a Maggot. Swift. NBLV

As when some dire usurper Heav'n provides. The Fire of London. Dryden. *Fr.* Annus Mirabilis. ChTr

As When Some Hungry Fledgling Hears and Sees. Vittoria da Colonna, *tr. fr. Italian.* BoWoP, *tr. by* Barbara Howes; PBWP, *tr. by* Lynne Lawner

As when some mighty Hero first appears. To Mrs. Manley, upon Her Tragedy Call'd The Royal Mischief. Mary Pix. KTR

As, when some treasurer lays down the stick. Dryden. *Fr.* Love Triumphant. NOSC

As when some wayfaring man passing a wood. A Devonshire Walk. William Browne. *Fr.* Britannia's Pastorals. FaBoPP

As when the bright Crulean firmament. Sir John Davies. *Fr.* Gulling[e] Sonnets, The. ESo; NoSic; Son

As, when the squire and tinker, Wood. Prometheus. Swift. FaBoPV

As when the winds, ascending by degrees. Homer, *tr. by* Pope. *Fr.* Iliad, The. OBVE

As when, to one who long hath watched, the morn. John Codrington Bampfylde. NOEC

As when two men have loved a woman well. Lost on Both Sides. Dante Gabriel Rossetti. *Fr.* House of Life, The. EnVR; NoP

As when two monarchs of the brindled breed. Paul Whitehead. *Fr.* Gymnasiad, The, or Boxing Match. NOEC

As Whistler heard colors like a stretch of music. For the Sake of Retrieval. Linda Bierds. NAmP90

As white their bark, so white this lady's hours. (*LL*) A Virginal. Ezra Pound. CMoP; MeMAP; MoAB; MoAmPo; NAAL-2; NIP; NOBA; OxBA; Poetr; Son; TAP

As who was not, in laughter, pain, and love. (*LL*) Days of 1964. James Merrill. CoAP; HCAP; NAAL-2; PoE; VCAP

As wild oxen bellowed. What He Said ("As wild oxen bellowed.") Peyanar, *tr. fr. Tamil by* A. K. Ramanujan. *Fr.* Nine on Happy Reunion. PLW

As William and Mary stood by the seaside. William and Mary. *Unknown.* AmFP

As Winter, fleeing. The Fearless. Mortimer J. Adler. PoA

As with Gladness Men of Old. William Chatterton Dix. FaPoR

As with heaped bees at hiving time. Robert Louis Stevenson. NOBVV

As withereth the primrose by the river. A Palinode. Edmund Bolton. EIL; InvP; NoSic; PoEL-2; PrIm

As Women of Our Race. Mrs. Henry Linden. CBWP-4

As woods whose change appeares. Horace, *tr. by* Ben Jonson. *Fr.* Art of Poetry, The. OBVE

As wrestlers use, you must be naked too. (*LL*) Beauty and Denial. William Cartwright. BeJo

As Wulfstan said on another occasion. Speech for the Repeal of the McCarran Act. Richard Wilbur. CMoP; GOA

As ye go through these palm-trees. A Song of the Virgin Mother. Lope de Vega, *tr. fr. Spanish by* Ezra Pound. AWP

As ye said, it shall be sae. . . (*LL*) Earl Mar's Daughter. *Unknown.* GN

As ye see, a mountain[e] lion fare. Sarpedon's Speech. Homer, *tr. by* George Chapman. *Fr.* Iliad, The. NOSC

As years advance, the abated soul, in most. Jabez Hughes. EPCY

As years do grow, so cares increase. To Mistress Anne Cecil, upon Making Her a New Year's Gift, January 1, 1567-8. William Cecil, 1st Baron Burghley. EIL; FaBoEH

As yonder lamp in my vacated room. The Lamp. Charles Whitehead. OBEV

As you advance in years you long. Of Change of Opinions. Victor Plarr. NOBVV

As you all know, tonight is the night of the full moon. 12 o'Clock News. Elizabeth Bishop. OxBC

As you and I walked slowly to the station. (*LL*) Bluebells for Love. Patrick Kavanagh. IPY

As you are big for you. (*LL*) The Little Elf. John Kendrick Bangs. FaBoBe; NTCP; OBCA

As You Came from the Holy Land. John Ashbery. CAPP

As You Came from the Holy Land. Sir Walter Ralegh. CBLP; OxAEP-1
Sels.
"But true love is a durable fire." OBD

As You Came from the Holy Land [of Walsingham]. *Unknown, sometimes at. to* Sir Walter Ralegh. AAS; ChTr; EIL; EnLoPo; GBL; HAP; InPS; NoP; NoSic; NTP; OBEV; PoEL-2; PrIm; RB; SiPSBD; TFi; TrGrPo

As You Come In. Anne Marriott. NOBC

As you drank deep as Thor, did you think of milk or wine? Fish Food. John Wheelwright. LiTA

As you haven't asked me for advice. Plug. Edmund Vance Cooke. PWR

As you lay in sleep. Cartography. Louise Bogan. TRP

As You Leave Me. Etheridge Knight. FF; MT; NNaP

As You Like It., *sels.* Shakespeare.
"All the world's a stage." EBEvV; FaPoR; FF; LiTB; PlP; PoLF; RB; TrGrPo; UV
(Seven Ages of Man, The.) ImPo
"Blow, blow, thou winter wind." AWP; CH; ChTr; EIL; ELP; EnRePo; GBL; GTBS; GTBS-P; ImPo; InPS; LiTB; NAEL-1; NOBE; NoP; NoSic; OAEL-1; OBEV; PrIm; SCGP; TrGrPo; WiR
(Blow, Thou Winter Wind.) 09FaFP; 08TreF
(Song: "Blow, blow, thou winter wind.") CTC; EBEvV; OxAEP-1; PoEL-2
(Songs of the Greenwood: "Blow, blow, thou winter wind.") TrGrPo
"Freeze, freeze, thou bitter sky" OBF
Compound Melancholy, A. CBCK
Good in Everything. PoToHe
"If the scorn of your bright eyne." CTC
"It was a lover and his lass." AWP; CBLP; CH; EIL; ELP; GBL; GTBS; GTBS-P; HeIL; ImPo; InPS; LiTB; NAEL-1; NOBE; NoP; NoSic; OBEV; RB; SCGP; TFi; TTTS
(Country Song.) TrGrPo
(Song: "It was a lover and his lass.") OxAEP-1; EBEvV; CTC; 09FiP
Motley's the Only Wear. TrGrPo
Orlando's Rhymes. CTC
"Under the greenwood tree." AWP; BoNaP; BoTP; CH; EIL; ELP; EnRePo; FaBoBe; FaPON; GN; GTBS; GTBS-P; HoPM; ImPo; InPS; LiTB; NAEL-1; NoP; NoSic; OAEL-1; OBEV; OHIP; PFP; SCGP; TTTS; UnPo; WiR
(Song: "Under the greenwood tree.") EBEvV; CTC; 09FiP
(Songs of the Greenwood.) TrGrPo
"What shall he have that killed the deer?." NoSic
(Song: "What shall he have that kill'd the dear?.") CTC
"What would you have? Your gentleness shall force." OxAEP-1

As You Like It. Theodore Weiss. TAP

As you love me! (*LL*) May Song. Goethe. STV

As you may see on t'other side. (LL) A was an apple pie, B bit it, C cut it. Mother Goose. FaBoUs; OxNR

As you pass by. (LL) On the Slope of Hua Mountain. *Unknown.* WPC

As you plaited the harvest bow. The Harvest Bow. Seamus Heaney. BiHa; NoAM; PBCIP; PNI

As you read, a white bear leisurely. To the Reader. Denise Levertov. AmPP; PoM; VGW

As you walk on your way thinking of other things. Epitaph from Athens. *Unknown, tr. fr. Greek by* Peter Jay. GrAn

As you work, and sleep, and talk, and laugh, and die. (LL) Resurrection. Kenneth Fearing. CMoP; PoE

As you would wish it done. (LL) A Woman Mourned by Daughters. Adrienne Rich. IHMS; IMW; Poetr

As young — as young as she! (LL) The Chaperon. H. C. Bunner. AnAmPo

As Your Eyes Are Blue. Lee Harwood. NBrP

As your true worship. (LL) Be a gardener. Julian of Norwich. EaPr

As yung Awrora with cristall haile. The Fenyeit Freir of Tungland. William Dunbar. OxBLMV

Asante Sana, Te Te. Thadious M. Davis. BlSi

Ascend — ascend — ascend, at my command. (LL) A Charm. Dryden. ChTr

Ascend my shoulders, firmly keep thy seat. Formerly at. to Homer, *tr. fr. Greek by* Thomas Parnell. *Fr.* Battle of the Frogs and Mice, The. OBVE

Ascending pile, The. Mulciber. Milton. *Fr.* Paradise Lost. EPCY; NOSC

Ascending Red Cedar Moon. Duane Niatum. CDW

Ascends the sky. (LL) Morning. Blake. FaBoCh; OAEL-2

Ascension. Denis Devlin. BIrV; ChIV-2

Ascension [or Ascention]. John Donne. *Fr.* La Corona. ChIV-2; ESCV; Son

Ascension-Day. Henry Vaughan. ESCV

Ascension Hymn. Henry Vaughan. *See* They Are All Gone into the World of Light.

Ascension Hymn., sels. Henry Vaughan.
  "Dear, beauteous death! the jewel of the just." OBD

Ascension Hymn ("Dust and clay.") Henry Vaughan. ESCV; GeHe; NOSC; SeCV-1; TrCP

Ascension: 1925, The. John Malcolm Brinnin. InPK

Ascension of Our Lord Jesus Christ. Christopher Smart. *Fr.* Hymns and Spiritual Songs. NOCV

Ascension Thursday. Saunders Lewis, *tr. fr. Welsh by* Gwyn Morgan. OBWVE

Ascensions, The. William Pillen. BTR; RaBo

Ascent into Hell. A. D. Hope. FaBoMA

Ascent of Species. Milton. *Fr.* Paradise Lost. EPCY; NOSC

Ascent of Vasco da Gama, The. Fernando Pessoa, *tr. fr. Portuguese by* F.E.G. Quintanilha. PeSAV

Ascent to the Sierras. Robinson Jeffers. OxBA

Ascetic art student named Josh, An. D. H. Cudmore. PeLi

Ascetic Trove of Responsive Fact, The. Wallace Stevens. *Fr.* Montrachet — le — Jardin. CBCK

Asclepiades the Miser was horrified. Lucilius, *tr. fr. Greek by* Peter Porter. GrAn

Asclepias who loves to love. Meleager, *tr. fr. Greek by* Peter Whigham. GrAn

Asclepius cured the body: to make men whole. On Plato's Grave. *Unknown, tr. fr. Greek by* William J. Philbin. GrAn

Ascot Waistcoat. David McCord. FiBHP; NBLV

Ase I me rod this ender day. The Five Joys of Mary. *Unknown.* MeEL

Asenath. Diana Hume George. ChIV-1

Ash Keys. Michael Longley. PBCIP

Ash on an old man's sleeve. T. S. Eliot. *Fr.* Four Quartets. FaBoMo; FaBoPV; FaBoTw; GTBS-P; MoP; NAEL-2; NAWM-2; NoAM; NOBA; NOBE; OAEL-2; OxAEP-2; OxBTC; PeECV; PrIm; TAP; TFi

Ash Plant, The. Seamus Heaney. BiHa

Ash-tray of the old year. Grit and Snow. Tracey Herd. NWP

Ash Tree on Ching Hill, The. Liu Sha-ho, *tr. fr. Chinese. Fr.* Two Poems of Peking. LHF, *tr. by* Hualing Nieh

Ash Wednesday. T. S. Eliot. LiTA; MoAB; MoAmPo; OxBA; VGW
Sels.
  "Although I do not hope to turn again." NoAM; NOBA
  "At the first turning of the second stair." NOBA
  "Blessed sister, holy mother, spirit of the fountain." EaPr
  "If the lost word is lost, if the spent word is spent." UV

Ash Wednesday. Christina Rossetti. TrCP

Ashen feelers of the frigid morrow, The. The Specter. Ernst Hardt, *tr. fr. German by* Jethro Bithell. AWP

Ashes. Vasco [*or* Vasko] Popa, *tr. fr. Serbo-Croatian by* Anne Pennington. *Fr.* Games. RB

Ashes of Life. Edna St. Vincent Millay. BLPL; FaBoBe

Ashkelon is not cut off with the remnant of a valley. Judith. Adah Isaacs Menken. AmWP; CBWP-1

Ashland Tragedy, The. Elijah Adams. AmFP

Ashtabula Disaster, The. Julia A. Moore. OBAL

Asia. Jean Follain, *tr. fr. French by* Richard Ellmann. AnRep

Asian Desert. Dorothy Wellesley. OBMV

Asian Peace Offers Rejected without Publication. Robert Bly. NaP

Asians Dying, The. W. S. Merwin. CoAP; HCAP; NaP; NOBA; NYBP; VCAP

Aside. Alan Dugan. PoA

Aside. R. S. Thomas. OxBC

Asides on the Oboe. Wallace Stevens. FaBoMo; MoAB; MoAmPo

Ask, and Ye Shall Receive. Mrs. Havens. BLRP

Ask in one life no more. Word by Night. Charles Brasch. PeNZ

Ask, is it well, O thou consumed of fire. The Burning of the Law. Meïr of Rothenburg, *tr. fr. Hebrew by* Nina Davis Salaman. TrJP

Ask Me No More. Tennyson. *See* Ask me no more: the moon may draw the sea.

Ask me no more, my truth to prove. Winter Song. Elizabeth Tollet. ECWP; NOEC

Ask Me No More [the Moon May Draw the Sea]. Tennyson. *Fr.* Princess, The. CBLP; GBL; ImPo; LiTB; MeMBP; NAEL-2; OBNC; PoEL-5; TrGrPo

Ask me no questions. *Unknown.* RoPo

Ask me not for the semblance of my loue. She Dwelt among the Untrodden Ways. J. C. Squire. BXAP

Ask Mummy Ask Daddy. John Agard. OTCP

Ask night how it feels to be dark. To Be Black, to Be Lost. Hannah Kahn. GoYe

Ask no more of me. (LL) Little-Bitty Man. Alfonsina Storni. VBLP

Ask No Return. Horace Gregory. *See* Ask no return for love that's given.

Ask no return for love that's given. Horace Gregory. *Fr.* Chorus for Survival. VGW
  (Ask No Return.) MoAmPo

Ask not overmuch for fair. He That Loves a Rosy Cheek. Heinrich von Rugge, *tr. fr. German by* Jethro Bithell. AWP

Ask not the cause why sullen spring. Song to a Fair Young Lady, Going Out of the Town in the Spring. Dryden. OBEV

Ask not to know this man. If fame should speak. A Little Shrub Growing By. Ben Jonson. BeJo; EnRePo

Ask not why hearts turn magazines of passions. A Funeral Elogy, upon . . . Mrs. Anne Bradstreet. John Norton. SCAP

Ask not why sorrow shades my brow. Song: Montrose. Charles Cotton. NOSC

Ask [*or* Aske] Me No More Where Jove Bestows [*or* Bestowes]. Thomas Carew. AWP; CBLP; ClHu; ELP; HAP; NAEL-1; PoE; PoRA; TEP

Ask [*or* aske] me why I send you here. The Primrose. *At.* to Robert Herrick. CBLP; FaBoUs; OBEV; PFP

Ask the Empresse of the night. The Magnet. Thomas Stanley. NOBE

Ask the Lord of the East, "Where lie the ends of the earth?" Tune: "Song of the Lunar Palace" — Sending Off Spring. Kuan Yun-shih, *tr. fr. Chinese by* Richard John Lynn. SuSp

Ask you what provocation I have had? Pope. *Fr.* Epilogue to the Satires [*or* 1738]. EPCY; OAEL-1; OBSV
  (Art of Satire, The.) ECEV
  (Defence of Satire.) NOEC
  (Power of Ridicule, The.) NOBE

Askal barfas canker dranick. Alphabet of Fishes. Bob Cobbing. NBrP

Askest, "How long thou shalt stay?" The Visit. Emerson. AnAmPo; NOBA

Asking for Ruthie. Judy Grahn. NMM

Asking what, asking what? — all a boy's afternoon. Debate: Question, Quarry, Dream. Robert Penn Warren. VGW

Asleep at the Switch. George Hoey. BeLS; VPP

Asleep in the City. Michael Smith. PBCIP

Asleep, My Love? Shakespeare. *See* Lunatic, the lover, and the poet, The.

Asleep on guard. In the Castle. Joseph Freiherr von Eichendorff, *tr. fr. German by* Philip L. Miller. RiWo

Asleep on the sand, dozing on the water, they form a flock. About Geese. Li Shang-yin, *tr. fr. Chinese by* Eugene Eoyang *and* Irving Y. Lo. SuSp

Asleep upon a chair." (LL) The Ballad of Father Gilligan. W. B. Yeats. EBVV; MoBrPo; PoRA

Asleep while the children howl and the house burns. Goddess. Judith Johnson Sherwin. BoWoP

Asleep, you turn. Hot Bath in an Old Hotel. Paula Rankin. MT

"Fly, fly, my friends, I have my death wound; fly." NoSic; TEP

"Having this day my horse, my hand, my lance." EnRePo; HAP; NAEL-1; PoE; Son

"Highway, since you my chief Parnassus be." EiL; EnRePo
(Highway, The.) LiTB; OBEV; OxAEP-1

"I never drank of Aganippe well." EnRePo; NAEL-1; NoSic; Son

II. "Not at the first sight, nor with a dribbed shot." NAEL-1; OAEL-1

"In a grove most rich of shade." NoSic

"In martial sports I had my cunning tried." NAEL-1; NoSic

"It is most true that eyes are formed to serve." NAEL-1; NoSic; OAEL-1; Son

IX. "Queen Virtue's court, which some call Stella's face." NAEL-1

"Let dainty wits cry on the sisters nine." NoSic; OAEL-1; Son

LII. "Strife is grown between Virtue and Love, A." NAEL-1; NoP

LIX. "Dear, why make you more of a dog than me?" GBL; PrIm

"Loving in truth, and fain[e] in verse my loue to show." AWP; BLPL; EBEV; EPCY; GBL; HAP; ImPo; InPS; LiTB; NAEL-1; NoP; NoSic; OAEL-1; OxAEP-1; PoE; Son; TEP; TFi; TrGrPo

LVI. "Fie, school of patience, fie, your lesson is." NAEL-1

LXI. "Oft with true sighs, oft with uncallèd tears." NAEL-1

LXIII. "O grammar-rules, O now your virtues show."
(Grammar-Rules.) FaBoUs

LXV. "Love, by sure proof I may call thee unkind." Son

LXXII. "Desire, though thou my old companion art." NAEL-1

LXXIII. "Love still a boy and oft a wanton is." Son

LXXXI. "O kiss, which dost those ruddy gems impart." NAEL-1; Son

LXXXII. "Nymph of the garden where all beauties be." InvP; PoE

LXXXIX. "Now that of absence the most irksome night." NAEL-1

LXXXVII. "When I was forced from Stella ever dear." NAEL-1

Ninth Song. NoSic

No More, My Dear, No More These Counsels Try.
(No More, My Dear.) SCGP

"O happie Tems, that didst my *Stella* beare." OxAEP-1

"O joy, too high for my low stile to show." NAEL-1; OxAEP-1; TrGrPo

"Of all the kings that ever here did reign." NoSic

"On Cupid's bow how are my heart-strings bent." NoSic

"Only joy, now here you are." EiL; EnRePo; GBL; HAP; InvP; NAEL-1; NoP; NoSic

Second Song. NoSic

"Some lovers speak, when they their muses entertain." NAEL-1; NoSic; Son

"Stella oft sees the very face of woe." InPS; NAEL-1; NoSic; PoE

"Stella since thou so right a Princess art." NoP; OxAEP-1

"Stella, think not that I by verse seek fame." NoSic

Stella's Kiss. CBCK; NoSic

Third Song. PoEL-1

VII. "When Nature made her chief work, Stella's eyes." NAEL-1; NIP; Son

"When far-spent night persuades each mortal eye." NoSic; PoE; Son

"Whether the Turkish new-moon minded be." NoSic; PoE

Who Is It That This Dark Night. EiL; EnRePo; NAEL-1; PoE; PoEL-1; TEP
(Eleventh Song.) NoSic; OxAEP-1
(Voices at the Window.) NOBE; OBEV; 08PoPle

"Who will in fairest book of Nature know." InPS; NAEL-1; NoP; NoSic; OAEL-1; PoE

"With how sad steps, O Moone, thou climb'st the skies!" AWP; BoLoP; CH; ChTr; EiL; EnLoPo; EnRePo; GBL; HAP; HeIP; InPS; InvP; MAT; NAEL-1; NoP; NoSic; OxAEP-1; PoE; PoEL-1; PoRA; PPP; Son; TEP; TFi; TrGrPo; TRP
(His Lady's Cruelty.) OBEV
(Languishing Moon, The.) BoNaP
(To the Sad Moon.) NOBE

"With what sharp checks I in myself am shent." NAEL-1; NoSic

X. "Reason, in faith thou art well served, that still." NAEL-1

XCI. "Stella, while now by honor's [or honor's] cruel might." NAEL-1; PoE

XCVIII. "Ah bed! the field where joy's peace some do see." EnLoPo

XI. "In truth, O Love, with what a boyish kind." CBLP; EiL; InvP; PoE

XLIX. "I on my horse, and Love on me, doth try." NAEL-1; NoP; OAEL-1; PoE

XLVII. "What, have I thus betrayed my liberty?" GBL; NAEL-1; NoP; PoEL-1
(Yoke of Tyranny, The.) TrGrPo

XLVIII. "Soul's joy, bend not those morning stars from me." NoP

XVI. "In nature apt to like when I did see." NAEL-1

XXII. "In highest way of heaven the Sun did ride." Son

XXV. "Wisest scholar of the wight most wise, The." NoP; OAEL-1

XXVI. "Though dusty wits dare scorn astrology." OAEL-1; Son

XXXIII. "I might — unhappy word — oh me, I might." OAEL-1

XXXVII. "My mouth doth water, and my breast doth swell." NAEL-1; Son

"You that do search for euerie purling spring." NAEL-1; NoSic; OAEL-1; OxAEP-1; Son

"You that with allegory's curious frame." NoSic; OAEL-1

"Your words, my friend, right helpful caustics, blame." NAEL-1; NoSic; PoE; TEP

Asturiana. Manuel de Falla, *tr. fr. Spanish by* Philip L. Miller. RiWo

Astute Melanesians on Munda. *Unknown.* PeLi

Aswelay. Norman Henry, II Pritchard. PoBA

Asylum, The, *sels.* Hayden Carruth.
"Winds; words of the wind; rumor of great walls pierced." SM

Asylum. Ciaran Carson. PNI

Asylum. John Freeman. OBMV

Asylum under my tread all this day. Samuel Beckett. *Fr. Echo's Bones.* NoAM

Asymmetry of the Universe. Fabio Doplicher, *tr. fr. Italian by* Stephen Sartarelli. NeIt

At 8 P.M., each office window. Glass. Vickie Karp. UTF

At a Bach Concert. Adrienne Rich. NIP; SM

At a Calvary Near the Ancre. Wilfred Owen. ChIV-2

At a Child's Baptism. Vassar Miller. GoJo

At a Chinaman's Grave. Wing Tek Lum. BCF

At a Concert of Music. Conrad Aiken. MoAB; MoAmPo

At a Country Fair. John Holmes. MoShBr

At a Country Hotel. Howard Nemerov. PoRA

At a Danse Macabre. Charles Spear. PeNZ

At a Friends' Meeting. Mary Elizabeth Coleridge. WPE

At a Loss. James L. Weil. GoYe

At a Low Mass for Two Hot-Rodders. X. J. Kennedy. NGP; Poetsp

At a Mass Grave. M. Truman Cooper. BTR

At a meadow in Golden Gate Park. Aglow in Nowhere. James Richard Broughton. NGP

At a party I spy a handsome psychiatrist. Afternoon Happiness. Carolyn Kizer. Poetr

At a party of university people. Double Exposure. Ian Young. PeHV

At a Pause in a Country Dance. Thomas Hardy. Mes

At a place in the mountains. The Savior Is Abducted in Puerto Rico. Martín Espada. TRP

At a pleasant evening party I had taken down to supper. Ferdinando and Elvira; or, The Gentle Pieman. W. S. Gilbert. FaBoCo; FaBoNo; FiBHP

At a Potato Digging. Seamus Heaney. CIP; IPY; PeIV

At a Private Showing in 1982. Maxine W. Kumin. SV

At a Queen's Funeral. Arnie Kantrowitz. PFL

At a Reading. Thomas Bailey Aldrich. AnAmPo; OBAL

At a Reading. J. D. McClatchy. DiPo

At a Solemn Music [or Musick]. Milton. GTBS; GTBS-P; HeIP; NOBE; OBEV; PoEL-3
Sels.
"Blest pair of Sirens, pledges of Heaven's joy." EPCY; SCGP

At a springe-well [or springe wel] under a thorn. *Unknown.* MiEL
(Spring under a Thorn, The.) MeEL

At a street corner. Gentle Lamb. Arthur Gregor. NGP

At a summer home in Ningpo, near Shanghai. A Picture of my Mother's Family. Wing Tek Lum. OpBo

At a Summer Hotel. Isabella Gardner. GrPl

At a Vacation Exercise [in the College], *sels.* Milton.
"Hail native language, that by sinews weak." JCP

At a Watering-Place. Thomas Hardy. *Fr. Satires of Circumstance.* CMoP

At a Welsh Waterfall. Gerard Manley Hopkins. *See* It was a hard thing to undo this knot.

At a Window. Carl Sandburg. FaBoBe; PoToHe; TrPWD

At Aberdeen. *At. to* George Macdonald. *See* Here lie I, Martin Elginbrodde.

At alarming bell daybreak, before. Eiléan Ní Chuilleanáin. *Fr. Site of Ambush.* CIP

At Algezir, and will in overplus. Two Centos. William Empson. CBNP

At all. (*LL*) Cousin Ella Goes to Town. George Ella Lyon. ETG

At all, at all, at all. (*LL*) Some One. Walter de la Mare. PYC; TLR

At all that he is: the heart of heartlessness. (*LL*) The Snow-Leopard. Randall Jarrell. CAPP; LiTM; TwCP

At all times I see them. Harbach 1944. János Pilinszky, *tr. fr. Hungarian by* János Csokits *and* Ted Hughes. PoSu

At all times redy to kiss you. (*LL*) 'I pray you, cum kiss me.' *Unknown.* MiEL

At an Exhibition of Historical Paintings, Hobart. Vivian Smith. CBAP; NOBAu

At an Inn. Thomas Hardy. NOBVV

At an Inn in Yü-kan. Liu Ch'ang-ch'ing, *tr. fr. Chinese by* William H. Nienhauser. SuSp

At an open window sitting. Written on Whitsun-Monday, 1795. Matilda Betham-Edwards. ECWP

At Evening Time., *sels.* Hayyim Nahman Bialik, *tr. fr. Hebrew by* Bernhard Frank.

At Evening when Flicker. Shin Shalom, *tr. fr. Hebrew by* Ruth Finer Mintz. MHP

At evening when the lamp is lit. The Land of Story-Books. Robert Louis Stevenson. FaBoBe; FaPON; OHCV; PWR

At every stroke his brazen fins do take. The Whale. John Donne. *Fr.* Progress[e] of the Soul[e], The. ChTr

At Famine's Feast, ye ken, man. (*LL*) Drone v. Worker. Ebenezer Elliot. FaBoPV; OBSV

At Farringford. Tennyson. *Fr.* To the Rev. F. D. Maurice. FaBoPP; GTBS-P

At fifteen I joined the army. Home. *Unknown, tr. fr. Chinese by* Kenneth Rexroth. OHMPC

At fifteen Jean Calvin made a list. Preposterous. Jim Hall. MT

At fifty, I approach myself. In a Dream. David Ignatow. PoA

At First. C. H. Sisson. OxBC

At first blush, discomfiting. Diehard. Judith Moffett. PoA

At first from your verse. To Dennis Brutus. Kofi Awoonor. HBAPE

At first he refused to deliver junk mail because it was stupid, all. Appointed Rounds. Louis Jenkins. RaBo

At first her grief was a grey. The Passing of Sorrow. Mary Jane Moffat. IMW

At first I couldn't remember the name. A Flower for the New Year. Robert Kelly. BAP-91

At first I prayed for Light. The Larger Prayer. Ednah D. Cheney. BLRP; WGRP

At first I thought I would feel. Nothing Could Take Away the Bear-King's Image. Ray A. Young Bear. HATNAP

At first I thought there was a superfine. Fleming Helphenstine. E. A. Robinson. MeMAP

At first I used to read headlines. The Grocery Store. Maura Stanton. NAmP90

At first I was given centuries. Margaret Atwood. HAP; NMM; WPOW

At first I was worried about you. When I Held You to My Chest, You Fit. Jack Myers. AmPA

At first it was as though you had passed. Many Wagons Ago. John Ashbery. HCAP

At first nothing is. Nothing Is. Sun-Ra. PoBA

At first she led them out onto the floor. The Dance. Irene McKinney. PBCAP

At first she thought the lump in the road. Red String. Minnie Bruce Pratt. ETG

At First Sight. Robert Graves. FaBoEE; OxBSP

At first the river's very small. The Growing River. Rodney Bennett. BoTP

At first the surprise. Dancing with God. Stephen P. Dunn. NIP

At first there all sea-water on the topland. On the Creation and Ontogony. *Unknown, tr. fr. by* C. S. Rafinesque. *Fr.* Walam [*or* Wallum] Olum; or, Red Score. LiTA

At first there was nothing. Then a closed space. Endymion. Thomas Kinsella. PBCIP

At first there's a lizard, cradled. My Car Slides Off the Road. Sarah Gorham. VBLP

At first there's greenish flesh until the konb's. Living Color. Laurie Sheck. BAP-91

At first we heard the jingling of her ornaments. Egyptian Dancer at Shubra. Bernard Spencer. NoAM

At first we sat imprisoned in this place. Conversation in Black and White. May Sarton. GoYe

At first we see the tiny leaves. The Strawberry. Maggie Pogue Johnson. CBWP-4

At first when I heard the old song. I Heard the Old Song. B. W. Vilakazi, *tr. fr. Zulu.* PeSA

At first when we saw a girl. Sunday Afternoon. Philip Levine. NaP

At five I knew at twelve. Cherry Bombs. Alice Fulton. NAmP90

At five in the afternoon. Lament for Ignacio Sánchez Mejías. Federico García Lorca, *tr. fr. Spanish.* NAWM-2, *tr. by* Stephen Spender *and* J. L. Gili; OBVE, *tr. by* A. L. Lloyd

At five in the morning, as jolly as any. The Miner's Doom. *Unknown.* AmFP

At five this morn, when Phoebus raised his head. Tunbridge Wells. The Earl of Rochester. FaBoPP; OBSV

At Flores in the Azores Sir Richard Grenville lay. Tennyson. *Fr.* Revenge, The. BeLS; EBEvV; EBNV; EBVV; FaBoCh; FaBoEH; FaPoB; FaPoR; OBWP; PoRA

At forty, a man's not yet old. Inscribed on the Arbor of the Old Drunkard (Tsui-weng-t'ing) at Ch'u-chou. Ou-yang Hsiu, *tr. fr. Chinese by* Irving Y. Lo. SuSp

At Fotheringay. Robert Southwell. PoEL-2

At four in the morning the smoke of the forded river. While We Slept. David Wolff. TrJP

At four o'clock. Roosters. Elizabeth Bishop. ChIV-2; LiTM; NALW

At 4:00 a.m., I drove to American Falls. American Falls. Greg Keeler. SM

At 4:30 AM/ she rose. Ntozake Shange. *Fr.* For Colored Girls Who Have Considered Suicide When the Rainbow Is Enuf. BoWoP

At Francis Allen's on the Christmas eve. The Epic. Tennyson. EnVR; NAEL-2

At Frank 'n' Helen's. Constance Urdang. PBCAP

At Fredericksburg. John Boyle O'Reilly. PAH

At Fyvie's yetts there grows a flower. The Trumpeter of Fyvie. *Unknown.* OxBB

(Andrew Lammie.) ESPB

At Galway Races. W. B. Yeats. IIP

At Gettysburg full anonymity. Yugoslav Cemetery. Celeste Turner Wright. WPE

At Gibraltar. George Edward Woodberry. GN

At Glastonbury. Henry Kingsley. PoRA

At Glendalough lived a young saint. St. Kevin. *At. to* Samuel Lover. WTO

At Golgotha I stood alone. Edwin John Ellis. *Fr.* Himself. OBMV

At Graceland with a Six Year Old, 1985. David Wojahn. *Fr.* Mystery Train: A Sequence. PBCAP

At Grandfather's. Clara Doty Bates. OBCA

At Grass. Philip Larkin. HAP; OxBTC; PlP; RB; WeW

At Great Torrington, Devon. *Unknown.* FaBoCo; FaBoEE

At Guaracara Park. Eric Roach. PBCV

At Gull Lake; August, 1810. Duncan Campbell Scott. NOBC

At Hadleigh, Suffolk. *Unknown.* FaBoCo

At half-past five — the earth cooling. Bachelor Farmer. Roger McDonald. CBAP; FaBoMA

At half past three, a single bird. Emily Dickinson. MoAmPo; NAWM-2; OxBA

At Half Past Three in the Afternoon. Jon Stallworthy. EOEF

At Hallowmas, whan nights grow lang. Hallow-Fair. Robert Fergusson. OxBS

At name it's hard to feel. (*LL*) Parley of Beasts. "Hugh MacDiarmid." ChIV-1; MoBrPo; MoP; NoAM; NoP; OBMV

At Harper's Ferry Just Before the Attack. Edward W. Williams. AAP

At Harvard a randy old Dean. *Unknown.* PeLi

At Henry's bier let some thing fall out well. John Berryman. *Fr.* Dream Songs. NoP

At her departure his disdain return'd. Homer, *tr. by* Dryden. *Fr.* Iliad, The. OBVE

At her doorway Mrs. Mayle. The Lavender Bush. Elizabeth Fleming. BoTP

At Her Fair Hands. Walter Davison. EIL

At Her Grave. Kuthaiyir, *tr. fr. Arabic by* Omar S. Pound. ArPe

At her step the water-hen. Dante Gabriel Rossetti. FM

At his cramped desk. Star-fix. Marilyn Nelson Waniek. NAmP90

At His Execution. Kipling. ChIV-2

At His Father's Grave. John Ormond. FaBoTw; OBD; OBWVE

At his incipient sun. First Love. Stanley Kunitz. GOYP

At Home. Christina Rossetti. OHCV

At home, abroad, and every where,. (*LL*) A Letter to Her Husband, Absent upon Public Employment. Anne Bradstreet. OxBA; WPE

At home, *alone.* (*LL*) Home, Sweet Home, with Variations, III. H. C. Bunner. OBAL

At home alone, O Nomades. Home, Sweet Home, with Variations, III. H. C. Bunner. OBAL

At home at Annika's place. At Annika's Place. Siv Widerberg, *tr. fr. Swedish by* Verne Moberg. NTCP

At home at ease to live in joy. (*LL*) Another of Seafarers, Describing Evil Fortune. *Unknown.* OxBSS

At home I loved to wear old clothes. Wang Chien, *tr. by* William H. Nienhauser. *Fr.* Palace Poems. SuSp

At Home in Dakar. Margaret Danner. BlSi

At Home in Heaven. Robert Southwell. EnVR; ESCV

At home, in my flannel gown, like a bear to its floe. 90 North. Randall Jarrell. CAPP; CoAP; FYAP; MoAB; MT; NAAL-2; NoAM; NOBA; TAP; VCAP

At home in the damp hills of Champagne. M. François le Vaillant Recalls His Travels to the Interior Parts of Africa. Patrick Cullinan. PeSAV

At Home the Green Remains. John Figueroa. PBCV

At Horizon's End, Thinking of Li Po. Tu Fu, *tr. fr. Chinese by* Eugene Eoyang. SuSp

At Ichiyiama/ Boating on Lake Nio. Matsumoto Koyu-Ni, *tr. fr. Japanese by* Kenneth Rexroth *and* Ikuko Atsumi. WPJ

At insular café tables under awnings. Green Coconuts: Rio. Lawrence Durrell. OBTV

At It. R. S. Thomas. OxBC

At Ithaca. Hilda Doolittle ("H. D."). VGW

At its own stable door. (*LL*) I like to see it lap the miles. Emily Dickinson. BoWoP; FaBV; FaPON; HeIL; InPK; LiTA; LiTM; MoAB; MoAmPo; MoShBr; NAAL-1; NAWM-2; NoAM; NOBA; OBAL; OBCA; OxBA; PDV; PrIm; SoSe; TFi

At Jacob's well a stranger sought. Jacob's Well. *Unknown.* OBET

At Jad Gate Pass mountain ridges several thousand-fold. Wang Ch'ang-ling, tr. by Ronald C. Miao. *Fr.* Following the Army on Campaign. SuSp

At Kenneth Burke's Place. William Carlos Williams. NOBA

At Kfar Kana. Charles Causley. TOF

At Kino Viejo, Mexico. Alberto A. Ríos. NoAM

At Kisheneff two wicked men. Russia's Resentment. L. A. J. Moorer. CBWP-3

At Kresge's Diner in Stonefalls, Arkansas. Edward Hirsch. SM

At Lake Geneva. Richard Eberhart. LiTA

At Lansdowne Bridge. Arthur Nortje. HBAPE

At Last. John Montague. PBCIP

At Last. Eileen Myles. PFL

At Last. Whittier. TrPWD; WGRP

At last a juggler is led out under the stars. The Initiate. W. S. Merwin. NNaP

At last a shaft daunted, which his hart did feele. (*LL*) Breake now my heart and dye! Oh no, she may relent. Thomas Campion. AAS

At last, at last, unite them there! (*LL*) Qua Cursum Ventus. Arthur Hugh Clough. EBVVPR; OBEV

At last, dearest Louisa, I take up my pen to address you. Arthur Hugh Clough. *Fr.* Amours de Voyage. EBVVPR, *canto* I,iii; NOBVV

At last earnest sternness is transformed to sweet. Hatred Surely Does Not Kiss. Kaspar Stieler, *tr. fr.* German by George C. Schoolfield. GePo

At last I can figure out the nature of that whisking sound. Fate in Incognito. Michael Benedikt. OBAL

At last I found the monastery. A young. Abstinence. Kenneth Rosen. AmPA

At last I have found myself. (*LL*) I Return to the Place I Was Born. T'ao Ch'ien. OHMPC

At last I have some real enemies. Loving My Enemies. Anna Kamienska, tr. fr. Polish by Susan Bassnett and Piotr Kuhiwzak. VBLP

At last I put off love. He Abjures Love. Thomas Hardy. CBLP; OBNC

At last I've seduced the *au pair*. Cyril Ray. PeLi

At last kooke, kooke, kooke: six kookes to one ko. (*LL*) Of Use. John Heywood. FaBoEE

At last, kooke, kooke, kooke; six kookes to one koo. (*LL*) The Koocoo. *Unknown.* GBP; TTTS

At last love has come. I would be more ashamed. Sulpicia, *tr. fr. Latin by* Aliki *and* Willis Barnstone. BoWoP

At last, my old, inveterate foe. To Melancholy. The Countess of Winchilsea. WPE

At last, O thou serene retreat. To Retirement. Luis de León, *tr. fr. Spanish by* Thomas Walsh. TrJP

At last, on delicate feet. Sappho, *tr. fr. Greek by* Sam Hamill. InMo

At last the beef appears in sight. Edward Chicken. *Fr.* Collier's Wedding, The. NOEC

At last the night comes, stifling the sun. Presences. Michael Dransfield. FaBoMA

At Last the Secret Is Out. W. H. Auden. InPS

At last, the train will lurch in. Return. Mary Dorcey. AIW

At last to be identified! Resurgam. Emily Dickinson. WGRP

At last Wayman gets the girl into bed. Wayman in Love. Tom Wayman. NIP; NOBC

At Last We Killed the Roaches. Lucille Clifton. CAPP

At last withdraw your cruelty. Sir Thomas Wyatt. SiPS

At last you yielded up the album, which. Lines on a Young Lady's Photograph Album. Philip Larkin. EnLoPo; HAP; OAEL-2

At least 100 seabirds attended my grandmother's funeral. My Grandmother's Funeral. Thomas Lux. WeW

At least a hundred times. For Edward Hicks. David Helwig. NOBC

At least as far as he is able. (*LL*) Whole Duty of Children. Robert Louis Stevenson. FaBoUs; NBLV; OxBChV

At least I broke and stole that branch with love. (*LL*) For C. Philip Whalen. NeAP; VGW

At least I can offer that./ Com'mere, boy! (*LL*) Brass Spittoons. Langston Hughes. MoAmPo; NoAM; Poetr

At least I have the flowers of myself. Hilda Doolittle ("H. D."). *Fr.* Eurydice. VBLP

At Leeds. *Unknown.* FaBoCo

At length, by flight, I over-went the Pack. Francis Quarles. *Fr.* Emblems. ESCV

At length, by so much importunity pressed. Lover, The; a Ballad. Lady Mary Wortley Montagu. ECWP; GGP; NAEL-1; NoP

At length, my Lord, I have the bliss. Thomas Moore. *Fr.* Fudge Family in Paris, The. OBSV

At length my soul the fatal union finds. Octavia Walsh. ECWP

At length nigh to the sea they drew. Spenser. *Fr.* Faerie Queene, The. NoP

At Length the Busy Day Is Done. Francis Hopkinson. AH

At length the long-expected morning came. The Voyage. Denis Florence MacCarthy. *Fr.* Voyage of St. Brendan, The. TIRV

At length the soft nocturnal minutes fly. The Bricklayer's Labours. Robert Tatersal. NOEC

At length the year, which marks his course, expires. Lines Addressed to Mr. Jefferson. Philip Freneau. EAP

At length their long kiss severed, with sweet smart. Nuptial Sleep. Dante Gabriel Rossetti. *Fr.* House of Life, The. EBVV; EnVR; NAEL-2; NOBVV

At Length There Dawns the Glorious Day. Ozora Stearns Davis. AH

At length 'tis done, the glorious conflict's done. On the Late Successful Expedition against Louisbourg. Francis Hopkinson. PAH

At length we have settled a pastor. Wanted, a Minister's Wife. *Unknown.* BLPA

At length with jostling, elbowing, and the aid. Byron. *Fr.* Vision of Judgment, The. EnRP; OAEL-2; OBSV; TEP

At liberty I sit and see. The Lover in Liberty Smileth at Them in Thraldom, That Sometime Scorned His Bondage. *Unknown.* EIL

At Licenza. Robert Wells. SCBI

At Lindos. May Sarton. WPE

At Lord's. Francis Thompson. CoGr; EBVV; OxBSP; PeLV

At Loschwitz above the city. The Birch-Tree at Loschwitz. Amy Levy. TrJP

At low tide like this how sheer the water is. The Bight. Elizabeth Bishop. FaBoWP; HCAP; NAAL-2; NYBP; RB; VCAP

At Luca Signorelli's Resurrection of the Body. Jorie Graham. HCAP

At Magnolia Cemetery. Henry Timrod. *See* Sleep sweetly in your humble graves.

At Mass. Vachel Lindsay. VGW

At Mass. *Unknown, tr. fr. Irish by* Robin Flower. BIrV

At Matyne houre in midis of the nicht. Honour with Age. Walter Kennedy. OxBS

At me and giggle. (*LL*) Miss Cho Composes in the Cafeteria. James Tate. SM; WeW

At me — The Sea withdrew. (*LL*) I started early — took my dog. Emily Dickinson. AmPP; HAP; InPK; LiTM; MeMAP; NAAL-1; PoEL-5; WeW

At Melville's Tomb. Hart Crane. HAP; MoAmPo; MoP; NAAL-2; NoAM; NoP; PoA; TAP; UnPo; VGW

At Memphis the horn'd bull told our friend. Tauromancy at Memphis. Diogenes Laertius, *tr. fr. Greek by* Dudley Fitts. GrAn

At Mid-Ocean. Robert Bly. CAPP

At midday the birds doze. The Hermit Picks Berries. Maxine W. Kumin. RFM

At midday they looked up and saw their death. George Barker. *Fr.* Pacific Sonnets. ImPo; LiTM

At Midnight. Ted Kooser. GOYP

At midnight by the stream I roved. Lewti. Samuel Taylor Coleridge. EnRP

At midnight Death dismissed the chancellor. Lines on the Death of Bismarck. John Jay Chapman. PoEL-5

At midnight, flaking down like chromium. Closing Time. David Wagoner. NYBP

At midnight I woke up [*or* awoke]. Clams. Ishigaki Rin, *tr. fr. Japanese by* Hiroaki Sato. PBWP

At midnight, in his guarded tent. Fitz-Greene Halleck. *Fr.* Marco Bozzaris. AnAmPo; BeLS; GN; HoPM; WBLP

At midnight in the alley. The Tom-Cat. Don Marquis. PoRA

At midnight, in the month of June. The Sleeper. Poe. AmPP; AnAmPo; LiTA; MeMAP; NAAL-1; NOBA; OxBA; PoEL-4; TAP; TrGrPo

At Midnight's Hour I Raised My Head. Thoreau. PoEL-4

At midnight's scrawl, the fog has. The Harbor of Illusion. Charles Bernstein. UL

At Midsummer. Norman Dubie. NoAM

At minus tide the music. Poke-Pole Fishing. Dennis Schmitz. AmPA

At Mrs. Alefounder's. Barbara Howes. AnAn

At Monday dawn, I climbed into my skin. Diary. David Wagoner. CoAP

At morning light the ark lay grounded fast. A Problem in History. Robert Wallace. CRP

At morning we all look out. Hedge Life. James Dickey. LCAP
At most [or moost] mischief. My Lute and I. Sir Thomas Wyatt. MeEL; SiPS
At Mt. Auburn Cemetery. Diana Der Hovanessian. LoHo
At my blameless life and shaking its flamelike head? *(LL)* The Faithful. Jane Cooper. SM
At my dear land of Story-books. *(LL)* The Land of Story-Books. Robert Louis Stevenson. FaBoBe; FaPON; OHCV; PWR
At my end of the earth the Atlantic began. Ends. Matthew Sweeney. IB
At My Father's Grave. John Ciardi. SM
At My Father's Grave. "Hugh MacDiarmid." GTBS-P
At my father's wake. Desmet, Idaho, March 1969. Janet Campbell Hale. VoR
At My Mother's Bedside. Marcia Lee Masters. WPE
At My Nativity. Shakespeare. *Fr.* King Henry IV, Pt. I. NAEL-1; NAs
At my window, I pull the curtains wide. A Visitation. W. D. Snodgrass. SM
At my windowpane a bird. That Is All I Heard. "Yehoash," *tr. fr. Yiddish by* Isidore Goldstick. TrJP
At Nature's Shrine. H. Cordelia Ray. CBWP-3
At new age fifty. A Phoenix at Fifty. Lawrence Ferlinghetti. NAs
At Night. Bella Akhmadulina, *tr. fr. Russian by* Daniel Halpern *and* Albert Todd. BoWoP
At Night. Jimmy Santiago Baca. AfAz
At Night. Frances Cornford. MoBrPo
At Night. Margherita Guidacci, *tr. fr. Italian by* Marina La Palma. WPOW
At Night. Elizabeth Jennings. OTCP
At Night. Alice Meynell. CH; OxAEP-2
At Night. Georg Trakl, *tr. fr. German by* Joachim Neugroschel. AnAn
At night a majo comes to my lattice and gazes at me. The Timid Majo. Fernando Periquet Y Zuaznabar, *tr. fr. Spanish by* Philip L. Miller. RiWo
At night, alone. Night and Day. Linda Hogan. BCF
At night, alone, the animals came and shone. The Animals. Josephine Jacobsen. GoYe
At night, as drough the mead I took my way. To Me. William Barnes. PoEL-4
At night at the hairdresser's. At the Hairdresser. Novica Tadic, *tr. fr. Serbo-Croatian by* Charles Simic. HSix
At Night atop Shou-hsiang Citadel, Hearing Tartar Flutes. Li Yi, *tr. fr. Chinese by* Paul Kroll. SuSp
At night, by the fire. Domination of Black. Wallace Stevens. AmPP; MoAB; MoAmPo; OxBA
At night Chinamen jump. Frank O'Hara. CBNP; NoAM; NOBA; SM
At night fart a guinness smell against the wife. You Jane. Carol Ann Duffy. FaBoBl
At night/ he'd lie in bed. Louis B. Russell. Bruce Guernsey. InPK
At night I make her bed. Lullaby for My Mother. Blaga Dimitrova, *tr. fr. Bulgarian by* John Balaban. VBLP
At night in each other's arms. Love's Vision. Edward Carpenter. WGRP
At night in summer. *(LL)* Sea Nocturne. Tchicaya U Tam'si. NegPo
At Night in the Wood. Nancy M. Hayes. BoTP
At night in Vinton County a Satanic cult. Offering. Debra Allbery. PBCAP
At night, late, the men I loved began. Mauve. Leslie Ullman. NAmP90
At night make me one with the darkness. Wendell Berry. EaPr
At night sometimes the big fog roams in tall. What God Used for Eyes Before We Came. William Stafford. PRA
At night, sometimes, when I cannot sleep. 11 rue Daguerre. John Montague. (Chosen Light, A.) IPY
At night the factories. Varick Street. Elizabeth Bishop. VBLP
At night the gold and black slashed bees come. Gold and Black. Michael Ondaatje. NoP
At night the wallpaper shakes. At Night. Margherita Guidacci, *tr. fr. Italian by* Marina La Palma. WPOW
At night they cross the border. The Wreckers. Rafael Zepeda. NGP
At night what things will stalk abroad. Lux in Tenebris. Katharine Tynan. TrPWD
At night when ale is in. Of Drunkenness. George Turberville. NBLV; NoP
At night when dying proceeds to sever all seams. Landscape of Screams. Nelly Sachs, *tr. fr. German by* Michael Roloff. NYBP
At night while. Black Warrior. Norman Jordan. PoBA
At Nightfall. Charles Hanson Towne. BLPA; FaBoBe
At nightfall the autumn woods cry out. Grodek. Georg Trakl, *tr. fr. German by* Michael Hamburger. PeFWW
At Nigitazu we wait for the moon. Princess Nukada, *tr. fr. Japanese by* Kenneth Rexroth *and* Ikuko Atsumi. WPJ

At nine from behind the door. Serenade for Strings. Dorothy Livesay. NAs
At nine I knew what Jesus would do. Uncle. Julia Kasdorf. PBCAP
At nine in the morning there passed a church. Faintheart in a Railway Train. Thomas Hardy. CBLP; CTC; EnLoPo
At noon, I leave my clothes out to dry. Drying Clothes. Yang Wan-li, *tr. fr. Chinese by* Jonathan Chaves. SuSp
At noon, in the dead centre of a faith. Desertmartin. Tom Paulin. CIP; PBCIP; PNI
At noon in the desert a panting lizard. At the Bomb Testing Site. William Stafford. CAPP; CoAP; LiTM; NIP; NoAM; NoP; OBWP; PAW; Poetr; RB
At noon of night, and at the night's pale end. Apparitions. Thomas Bailey Aldrich. AnAmPo
At noon they talk of evening and at evening. Cypresses. Robert Francis. LCAP
At noon, Tithonus, withered by his singing. The Wedding. Conrad Aiken. CMoP; TAP
At noon today, I woke from a nightmare. Mexico, 1940. Ai. NoAM
At North Farm. John Ashbery. HCAP; PoE; Poetr
At once, and he died looking towards my face. *(LL)* Dream. Richard Watson Dixon. EBEV; NOBVV; PeVV; SCGP
At once on th' eastern cliff of paradise. Milton. *Fr.* Paradise Lost. EPCY; PeECV, *ll.* 275–290
At once whatever happened starts receding. Whatever Happened? Philip Larkin. Son
At once with resolution held. John Trumbull. *Fr.* M'Fingal. AmPP
At one glance/ I loved you. Mihri Hatun, *tr. fr. Turkish by* Tâlat S. Halman. PBWP
At 100 Mile House the cowboys ride in rolling. The Cariboo Horses. Alfred W. Purdy. HeIP; NoBC
At one o'clock it was the thin cattle. Pharaoh's Dream. Fiona Hall. NWP
At one the wind rose. Night-Music. Philip Larkin. InPS
At Only That Moment. Alan Ross. ErPo
At Pakiri Beach. David Mitchell. PeNZ
At Paris it was, at the Opera there. Aux Italiens. "Owen Meredith." BeLS; BLPA; BLPL; FaBoBe
At Pavia, a visitation of some sorrow. Boethius' dungeon. Geoffrey Hill. *Fr.* Mercian Hymns. FaBoMo
At Penshurst [Another]. Edmund Waller. BeJo; OAEL-1; SeCV-1
At Penshurst ("While in the park I sing.") Edmund Waller. BeJo
At Perigord near to the wall. A Perigord pres del muralh. Bertrans de Born, *tr. fr. Provençal by* Ezra Pound. CTC
At Piccadilly Circus. Vivian de Sola Pinto. OBMV
At Pina's house. Country Memory. Leticia Herrera Alvarez, *tr. fr. Spanish.* TSaS, *tr. by* Judith Infante
At Pleasure Bay. Robert Pinsky. BAP-89
At Polwart on the Green. Polwart on the Green. Allan Ramsay. NOEC
At Pompeii. Shelley. *Fr.* Ode to Naples. FaBoPP
At Port Royal. Whittier. PAH
  Sels.
  Song of the Negro Boatman. GN
At Port Royal. Whittier. PAH
  Sels.
  Song of the Negro Boatman. GN
At Potterne, Wiltshire. *Unknown.* FaBoCo
At precisely three o'clock Don Pedro arrived at our table. Marvels of the Will. Octavio Paz, *tr. fr. Spanish by* Eliot Weinberger. AnRep
At Quincey's moat the squandering village ends. Almswomen. Edmund Blunden. OBMV; OxBTC
At Rest in the Blast. Marianne Moore. MoAB; MoAmPo
At Robert Fergusson's Grave, October 1962. Robert Garioch. OxBS
At Rochecoart/ Where the hills part. Provincia Deserta. Ezra Pound. OxBA
At Ropley Station the foot of night. The Return. Sebastian Barry. IB
At Rundane. Aasmund Olavsen Vinje, *tr. fr. Norwegian by* Philip L. Miller. RiWo
At Runnymede, at Runnymede. The Reeds of Runnymede. Kipling. FaBoEH
At Sacred Heart, if you said you did it. Catholic Boys. David Kirby. NGP
At Saint Patrick's Purgatory. Donnchadh Mor O'Dala, *tr. fr. Irish by* Sean O'Faolain. TIRV
At Sainte-Marguerite. Trumbull Stickney. LiTA; OxBA
At Saxman, the totems slash down. The Circle of Totems. Peggy Shumaker. PBCAP
At School. Stevie Smith. VBLP
At school, we all had to pick a plague. The Age of Innocence. Steve Ellis. PWE

At see-saw across the gate. (*LL*) Jack and Gill [or Jill] went up the hill. Mother Goose. CBNP; FaBoBe; OxBoLi; OxNR

At Set of Sun. "George Eliot." *See* If you sit down at set of sun.

At seven, when I go to bed. A Child's Thought. Robert Louis Stevenson. BoTP

At several times the speed of light. Gemini Jones. Willard R. Espy. FaBoUs

At Shagger's funeral there wasn't much to say. At Shagger's Funeral. Bruce Dawe. NOBAu

At sight of sparkling bowls or beauteous dames. Verses in Baretti's Commonplace Book. Samuel Johnson. OxAEP-1

At six o'clock we were waiting for coffee. A Miracle for Breakfast. Elizabeth Bishop. LiTA

At six years old I had before mine eyes. Old Man. James Henry. NOBVV

At sixteen I came West, riding. A Living Pearl. Kenneth Rexroth. LiTM

At sixty I, Dionysios of Tarsos, lie here. *Unknown, tr. fr. Greek by* Peter Jay. GrAn

At sixty, it might be well to start. The Collector. Desirée Flynn. BrRo

At slammed door and smoker's cough in the hall. (*LL*) Docker. Seamus Heaney. HeIL; HeIP; IIP; MoP; NOIV; Poetr

At spirit séances in Queen's. Morris Bishop. PeLi

At start of spring I open a trench. Wendell Berry. EaPr

At stated ,ic times. Composed in the Composing Room. Franklin P. Adams. NIP; OBAL

At Su K'wa K'e there used to bloom a flower. Lost Love. *Unknown, tr. fr. Tewa Indian by* H. J. Spinden. WTO

At such high tide, her savoury goose. (*LL*) The Fire. Sir Walter Scott. OBCP

At summer eve, when Heaven's ethereal bow. Thomas Campbell. *Fr.* Pleasures of Hope, The. EnRP

At Sunrise. Rosa Zagnoni Marinoni. PoToHe

At Sunset. Ivy O. Eastwick. BoTP

At Sunset. H. Cordelia Ray. CBWP-3

At Sunset. Margaret E. M. Sangster. PWR

At sunset/ the white horse has disappeared. The Other Side. Linda Hogan. ETG

At Swindon. Reginald Brett. PeHV

At Tara today, in this awful hour. St. Patrick's Hymn before Tara. James Clarence Mangan. EnRP

At Tara today in this fateful hour. St. Patrick. EaPr

At Tauba's death I swore. Lamenting Tauba. Laila Akhyaliyya, *tr. fr. Arabic by* Willis Barnstone. BoWoP

At tea in cocktail weather. Publisher's Party. Phyllis McGinley. OBAL

At ten a clock, when I the fire rake. Francis Daniel Pastorius. SCAP

At ten A.M. the young housewife. The Young Housewife. William Carlos Williams. HeIP; NAAL-2; NoP; TAP

At ten I was wheeled in a chair. The Summer Anniversaries. Donald Justice. AnAn

At That Moment. Raymond R. Patterson. PoBA

At that time. David Diop. *See* In those days/ When civilization kicked us in the face.

At th'Calends, puts all out again. (*LL*) The Praises of a Country Life. Ben Jonson. OBVE; SeCP

At The Abbey Theatre (Imitated from Ronsard). W. B. Yeats. Son

At the Airport. John Malcolm Brinnin. MoAB

At the airport, ready to leave on my little trip. The Fear of Flying. Mona Van Duyn. NMM

At the alder-darkened brink. Hamlen Brook. Richard Wilbur. CAPP; VCAP; WeW

At the Algonquin. Howard Moss. Poetsp

At the Altar. Robert Lowell. *Fr.* Between the Porch and the Altar. InPK

At the Altar-Rail. Thomas Hardy. *Fr.* Satires of Circumstance. MoAB; MoBrPo

At the Aquarium. Max Eastman. FaPON; WGRP

At the back of the houses there is the wood. The House in the Wood. Randall Jarrell. LCAP

At the Back of the North Wind, *sels.* George Macdonald. FaPON
   Baby, The. FaPON
   (At the Back of the North Wind.) VPP
   (Where Did You Come From, [Baby Dear?].) BLPA; OxBChV; WHSW

At the Back of the North Wind. George Macdonald. *See* Where did you come from, baby dear?

At the Badr Trench. Safiya bint Musafir, *tr. fr. Arabic by* Bridget Connelly *and* Deirdre Lashgari. WPOW

At the Ball. A. K. Tolstoy, *tr. fr. Russian by* Philip L. Miller. RiWo

At the Ball! Charles H. Webb. OBAL

At the Ball Game. William Carlos Williams. CMoP; MoP; NoAM; NOBA; OxBA; PoE

At the Band Concert. John Malcolm Brinnin. PoA

At the bar called. Chicago Scene. John Logan. Jaz

At the bar of Judge Conscience stood Reason arraign'd. A Flight of Fancy. Frances Sargent Osgood. AmWP

At the bar two blocks away. Trumpets from the Islands of Their Eviction. Martín Espada. NGP

At the Battery Sea-Wall. Clifford James Laube. GoYe

At the Beach. Kemal Ozer, *tr. fr. Turkish.* TSaS, *tr. by* O. Yalim, W. Fielder, *and* Dionis Riggs

At the beginning I noticed. A Stone Diary. Pat Lowther. NOBC

At the beginning of winter a cold spirit comes. *Unknown, tr. fr. Chinese by* Arthur Waley. BoWoP

At the big trumpet, we must all put on. Rise and Shine. Richmond Lattimore. NYBP; Poetr

At the black canvas of estrangement. The Jewish Bride. Paul Durcan. BiHa

At the black center it bursts. (*LL*) The Watercolor. Carol Moldaw. UTF

At the blackboard I had missed. Zimmer's Head Thudding against the Blackboard. Paul Zimmer. PBCAP

At the boat-yard's dry-dock. A Landing. Aidan Carl Mathews. IB

At the Bomb Testing Site. William Stafford. CAPP; CoAP; LiTM; NIP; NoAM; NoP; OBWP; PAW; Poetr; RB

At the Bottom of the Well. Louis Untermeyer. GoJo

At the break of day I come to an old temple. A Visit to the Broken Hill Temple. Ch'ang Chien, *tr. fr. Chinese by* Joseph J. Lee. SuSp

At the bridal bed of star-crossed Petalê. The Lost Bride. Antiphanes, *tr. fr. Greek by* Dudley Fitts. GrAn

At the Bridge with Rufus. Kenneth McClane. Jaz

At the British Museum. Richard Aldington. MoBrPo

At the British War Cemetery, Bayeux. Charles Causley. NAEL-2; OBWP; OxBC; PAW; PoWW

At the brow of a hill a fair shepherdess dwelt. The Lass of the Hill. Mary Jones. ECWP

At the Cafe. Peter Riley. *Fr.* One Day. VaA

At the Cannon's Mouth. Herman Melville. PAH

At the Carnival. Anne Spencer. BlSi; CDC; PoNe; ShDr

At the Cascade. H. Cordelia Ray. AmWP; CBWP-3

At the Cave. Artur Miedzyrzecki, *tr. fr. Polish by* Stanislaw Barańczak *and* Clare Cavanagh. PoSu

At the Cavour. Arthur Symons. NOBVV; OxBSP

At the Cedars. Duncan Campbell Scott. NOBC

At the Cemetery. Jean Richepin, *tr. fr. French by* Philip L. Miller. RiWo

At the center of the earth. *Unknown, tr. fr. Chippewa Indian by* Jerome K. Rothenberg. STP

At the center of the earth there is a mother. Susan Griffin. EaPr; SRLS

At the ceremony of Emobo. Ceremony. Kattie M. Cumbo. BlSi

At the Chiang-ning River Mouth. Wang An-shih, *tr. fr. Chinese by* Jan W. Walls. SuSp

At the Classics Teacher's. Elizabeth Macklin. BAP-91

At the close of a winter day. The Rhyme of the Three Captains. Kipling. BeLS

At the Corner of Muck and Myer. Paul Violi. UL

At the Corner of the world. Tu Fu, *tr. fr. Chinese by* A. C. Graham. PLT

At the corner of Wood Street, when daylight appears. The Reverie of Poor Susan. Wordsworth. CoGr; EnRP; GTBS; GTBS-P; OxBoLi; WiR

At the Criterion. John Tranter. FaBoMA

At the cross her station keeping. Stabat Mater. *At.* to Jacopone da Todi, *tr. fr. Latin.* WGRP

At the crossroads. Jealousy. Valerie Sinason. DT

At the Crossroads. Thomas Kinsella. NoAM

At the Crossroads. William Knott. PBCAP

At the cry of the first bird. The Crucifixion. *Unknown, tr. fr. Irish by* Kuno Meyer. TIRV

At the Dark Hour. Paul Dehn. BoLoP

At the dark street corner. Guilt, Desire and Love. James Baldwin. GLP

At the dark water. (*LL*) To Flood Stage Again. James Wright. NOBA; Prf

At the dawn I seek Thee. Morning Song. Solomon ibn Gabirol, *tr. fr. Hebrew by* Nina Davis Salaman. TrJP

At the Day-centre. Martin Sorescu, *tr. fr. Romanian by* David Constantine *and* Ioana Russell-Gebbett. PWE

At the demolishing, this seat. To My Lord Fairfax. Andrew Marvell. *Fr.* Upon Appleton House, to My Lord Fairfax. NOSC; SeCP; SeCV-1

At the Discharge of Cannon Rise the Drowned. Hubert Witheford. PeNZ

At the Dog Show. Christopher Morley. MoShBr

At the Door. Lillie Fuller Merriam. PoToHe

At the door of his hut sat Massasoit. The Peace Message. Burton Egbert Stevenson. PAH

At the door of Mercy Sighing. Thomas Mackellar. AH

At the Door of the Native Studies Director. Robert H. Davis. HATNAP

At the door on summer evenings. Longfellow. *See* By the shores of Gitche [*or* Gitchee] Gumee.

At the Doors. "Der Nistor," *tr. fr. Yiddish by* Joseph Leftwich. TrJP

At the Draper's. Thomas Hardy. *Fr.* Satires of Circumstance. MoAB; MoBrPo; OBD; OxBM

At the earliest ending of winter. Not Ideas about the Thing but the Thing Itself. Wallace Stevens. HAP; HCAP; LCAP; MeMAP; SAmP; TAP

At the Edge. Denise Levertov. NAAL-2

At the edge of all the ages. The Song of Finis. Walter de la Mare. MoBrPo

At the edge of the forest. On the Meatwheel. Dick Gallup. UL

At the Edge of the Jungle. Patrick Lane. NOBC

At the edge of the sluice she peels and. Constantly. Adrienne Greer. VBLP

At the edge of the world, a traveler long used to grief. My Boat Moored on a River. Yen Yu, *tr. fr. Chinese by* Irving Y. Lo. SuSp

At the Edge of Town. William Stafford. NNaP

At the Electronic Frontier. Miguel Algarin. BCF

At the end. Doppelgänger. Jason Shinder. UTF

At the End. Richard Ryan. PBCIP

At the end a/ "The Prisoner of Zenda." The Prisoner of Zenda. Richard Wilbur. NBLV

At the end, he listened only to. Late Stravinsky Listening to Late Beethoven. Stephen Spender. AnAn

At the end of a bitter April. East Moors. Gillian Clarke. SCBI

At the end of a long-walled garden. The Cottage Hospital. Sir John Betjeman. GTBS-P; MoBrPo; NoAM; NOBE; OBD; PlP; UnPo

At the end of life paralysis or those creeping teeth. Bog and Candle. Robert David Fitzgerald. CBAP

At the end of my years there is a vat. *Unknown.* ChTr

At the end of October a mallard. The Mallard's Going. John Logan. PRA

At the End of Spring. Po Chü-i, *tr. fr. Chinese by* Arthur Waley. ArLo

At the End of Spring. Yü Hsüan-chi, *tr. fr. Chinese by* Geoffrey R. Waters. BoWoP

At the end of Tarriers' Lane, which was the street. Wm. Brazier. Robert Graves. NOBL

At the End of the Affair. Maxine W. Kumin. TAP

At the end of the bough! Sweet Apple. James Stephens. CMoP

At the end of the familiar. Roy Fisher. *Fr.* Handsworth Liberties. VaA

At the end of the garden. Pumpkins. John Cotton. BoNaP

At the end of the garden walk. The Cold Green Element. Irving Layton. NOBC; NoP

At the end of the journey we built. Journeys. Meg Campbell. PeNZ

At the end of the road, in a drab chapel. Mother Tongue. Jon Stallworthy. NoAM

At the end of the row. The Objection to Being Stepped On. Robert Frost. NBLV

At the end of the third act, poetry gutters down. After Shakespeare. Alex Comfort. ErPo

At the end of the war I arose. The Driver. James Dickey. VGW

At the End of the Weekend. Ted Kooser. PBCAP

At the End of Things. Arthur Edward Waite. WGRP

At the Entrance. Douglas Stewart. CBAP

At the equinox when the earth was veiled in a late rain. Continent's End. Robinson Jeffers. AWP; FaBV

At the Executed Murderer's Grave. James Wright. HCAP; VCAP

At the expense of man?/ Do I?/ It might be so. (*LL*) A Slice of Wedding Cake. Robert Graves. BoLoP; NAEL-2; NOBE; OxBTC; PlP

At the eye, we say, of a hurricane, a. Nine Men's Morris. Peter Philpott. VaA

At the factory I worked. Mexicans Begin Jogging. Gary Soto. NGP

At the far end of a trip north. Nooksack Valley. Gary Snyder. NaP

At the feast of Belshazzar and a thousand of his lords. The Handwriting on the Wall. Knowles Shaw. BLPA

At the feet of those dark city walls. The Gamblers. Ai Ch'ing, *tr. fr. Chinese.* LHF, *tr. by* Hualing Nieh

At the Ferry. U. A. Fanthorpe. FaBoWP

At the Ferry. Vijaya Mukhopadhyay, *tr. fr. Hindi.* TSaS, *tr. by* Mukhopadhyay Vijaya

At the fever of tongues. Michael Palmer. *Fr.* Six Hermetic Songs. BAP-90

At the field's edge. The White Hare. Lilian Bowes-Lyon. OxBTC

At the Fillmore. Philip Levine. NNaP

At the first turning of the second stair. T. S. Eliot. *Fr.* Ash Wednesday. LiTA; MoAB; MoAmPo; NOBA; OxBA; VGW

At the Fishhouses. Elizabeth Bishop. CoAP; FaBoWP; HAP; HCAP; LCAP; LiTM; NAAL-2; NALW; NoP; NYBP; Poetr; PoRA; VCAP

At the foot of the apple-tree. (*LL*) The Planting of the Apple-Tree. Bryant. GN; OHIP

At the foot of the Cathedral of Burgos. Autobiography. Gloria Fuertes, *tr. fr. Spanish by* Philip Levine. AnAn; PBWP

At the foot of yonder mountain where the fountains do flow. The Green Briar Shore. *Unknown.* AmFP

At the ford, while grass-green frogs. Charming the Moon. James DenBoer. MAT

At the Fountain. Marcabrun, *tr. fr. French by* Harriet Waters Preston. AWP

At the frontier the long train slows to a stop. The Frontier. John Hewitt. BIrV

At the full face of the forest lies our little town. To the Red Lory. John Shaw Neilson. NOBAu

At the full length of all their chain. (*LL*) The Unequal Fetters. The Countess of Winchilsea. VBLP

At the Garden Gate. David McCord. FaPON

At the gate of old Granada, when all its bolts are barred. The Lamentation for Celin. *Unknown, tr. fr. Spanish by* John Gibson Lockhart. AWP

At the Gate of the Valley. Zbigniew Herbert, *tr. fr. Polish by* Czeslaw Milosz. PoSu

At the gathered ends of rooty paths. The Island in the Evening. Fairfield Porter. PoA

At the gesticulating/ of the ushers. (*LL*) A Green Lowland of Pianos. Jerzy Harasymowicz. CBNP

At the going rate, your body gave you. The Victor Vanquished. Richard Howard. BAP-90

At the Golden Ball and Lillie's Head. To Saffold's Customers. *At.* to John Case. FaBoUs

At the Grave of Burns. Wordsworth. EnRP

At the Grave of Henry James. W. H. Auden. LiTA; NoP

At the Grave of Henry Vaughan. Siegfried Sassoon. CMoP; GTBS-P

At the Grave of Walker. Joaquin Miller. AnAmPo

At the Great Wall of China. Edmund Blunden. GTBS-P

At the Grey Round of the Hill. W. B. Yeats. RB

At the Hairdresser. Novica Tadic, *tr. fr. Serbo-Croatian by* Charles Simic. HSix

At the Half-Note Café. Ira Sadoff. Jaz; NAmP90

At the Hammersmith Palais. Alan Riddell. NOBAu

At the hands of the Human King. (*LL*) South African Exhibition, 1907. Kingsley Fairbridge. PeSAV

At the head of Wear Water about twelve at noon. The North Country Collier. *Unknown.* OxBSS

At the Heich Kirk-Yaird, *sels.* Alastair MacKie.

At the Heng-ts'ui Pavilion of Fa-hui Monastery. Su Shih, *tr. fr. Chinese by* Irving Y. Lo. SuSp

At the Holi festival of color. Mirabai, *tr. fr. Hindi by* Willis Barnstone *and* Usha Nilsson. BoWoP

At the horislope of the mountizon. Vincente Huidobro, *tr. fr. Spanish. Fr.* Altazor. TSaS, *tr. by* Eliot Weinberger

At the hour I slept. Birds in Their Title Work Freeholds of Straw. Les A. Murray. *Fr.* Walking to the Cattle Place. FaBoMA

At the hour shaped for him Scyld departed. *Unknown. Fr.* Beowulf. ASW, *tr. by* Kevin Crossley-Holland; OBD, *tr. by* Michael Alexander.

At the hour when the heat of the day is overcome. Dante, *tr. by* John Ciardi. *Fr.* Divina Commedia. MeMAP; NAWM-1

At the Indian Killer's Grave. Robert Lowell. NOBA; VGW

At the inn of night for aye. (*LL*) Soldier from the Wars Returning. A. E. Housman. LiTB; OBMV

At the instant of drowning he invoked the three sisters. The Three Fates. Rosemary Dobson. BoWoP

At the Jaffé Memorial Fountain, Botanic Gardens. Frank Ormsby. CIP

At the Jazz Club He Comes on a Ghost. Wanda Coleman. Jaz

At the Jesuits' church, the sexton father's racked. *At.* to Pietro Aretino, *tr. fr. Italian by* Alistair Elliot. *Fr.* Some More Cases of Love with Solutions. FaBoBl

At the Jewish Museum. Olga Cabral. BTR

At the Keyhole. Walter de la Mare. MoAB; MoBrPo

At the king's gate the subtle noon. Coronation. Helen Hunt Jackson. AmWP; BeLS; GN

At the Klamath Berry Festival. William Stafford. InPK

At the large foot of a fair hollow tree. The Country-Mouse. Abraham Cowley, *after the Latin of* Horace. OBVE; SeCP

At the last, tenderly. The Last Invocation. Walt Whitman. GGP; MoAmPo; OBD; OxBA; PoEL-5; TrGrPo; TrPWD

At the Worst. ("And Man is left alone with Man." 'Tis well:.) Israel Zangwill. WGRP
Sels.
At the Worst. Israel Zangwill. WGRP
At the worst place in the hills above the city. The Birthday Dream. James Dickey. NAs
At the Wrong Door. Christopher Reid. CBLP
At the "Ye That Do Truly." Charles Williams. NOCV
At the Zoo. John Davies. AngWe
At the Zoo. A. A. Milne. FaPON
At the Zoo. Thackeray. NTCP; OxBChV
At the Zoo. Israel Zangwill. TrJP
At thee the Mocker sneers in cold derision. The Maid of Orleans. Schiller, *tr. fr. German by* James Clarence Mangan. AWP
At Thermopylae. Simonides.
At thieves I bark; at lovers wag my tail. *Unknown, after the Latin of* Joachim du Bellay. FaBoEE
At Thirteen. Benjamin Saenz. AfAz
At thirteen, I knew what it was to sin. At Thirteen. Benjamin Saenz. AfAz
At thirteen I was reading Oedipus Rex. The Women I Knew. Lois Roma-Deeley. LoHo
At this Adonis smiles as in disdain. Shakespeare. *Fr.* Venus and Adonis. BeLS; EBEV
At this moment in time. They Flee from Me That Sometime Did Me Seek. Gavin Ewart. OxBC
At this point of Interrogation. (*LL*) Metaphysics. Oliver Herford. CBNP
At this th' impatient hero sowrly smil'd. Homer, *tr. by* Dryden. *Fr.* Iliad, The. OBVE
At this time I find the bed very arid. The Reason for Poetry. Nancy Morejón, *tr. fr. Spanish by* Anita Whitney. WPOW
At those who come to my grave with flowers, I can but laugh. One of the Dead Speaks. Cahit Sitki Taranci, *tr. fr. Turkish by* Nermin Menemencioglu. OBD
At 3 a.m. I run my tongue. Death's Head. Phyllis Gotlieb. NOBC
At three in the morning. The Bride's Nights in a Strange Village. Helen Dunmore. PWE; VBLP
At Thurgarton Church, *sels.* George Barker.
At thy nativity a glorious quire. Milton. *Fr.* Paradise Regained [*or* Regain'd]. PChr
At Times. Cheryl Moskowitz. DT
At times I almost believed it: madness. Emily Dickinson's Sestina for Molly Bloom. Barbara F. Lefcowitz. SM
At times I resort, beyond man's discerning. Wind: "At times I resort, beyond man's discerning." *Unknown, formerly at. to* Cynewulf, *tr. fr. Anglo-Saxon. Fr.* Riddles (Exeter Book). AnOE
At times I see it, present. A Bright Day. John Montague. CIP
At times it is like watching a face you have just met. The Way It Sometimes Is. Henry Taylor. MT; Poetr
At times it seemed the country itself was a cloud. England. Mary Jo Salter. DiPo
At Times Spirit Surges. David Shimoni, *tr. fr. Hebrew by* Ruth Finer Mintz. MHP
At times spirit surges up from bodies' prison. At Times Spirit Surges. David Shimoni, *tr. fr. Hebrew by* Ruth Finer Mintz. MHP
At times the heart looks toward open fields. Near Twelve Mile Point. Lance Henson. HATNAP
At times, things close to sprouting. The Corroding Air. Jack Marshall. UL
At Timon's villa let us pass a day. Pope. *Fr.* Moral Essays. NOEC; OAEL-1; OBSV; PoEL-3; PPP
(Of the Use of Riches.) ECEV
(Timon's Villa.) PoE
At Timon's Villa let us pass a day. Timon's Villa. Pope. *Fr.* Epistles to Several Persons, to Richard Boyle, Earl of Burlington: Of the Use of Riches. PoE
At Tripolis. Constance Carrier. WPE
At turn of the tide, with wind blowing us salty weather. (*LL*) The Oyster-Eaters. John Blight. NOBAu
At 12 o'clock in the afternoon. Meleager, *tr. fr. Greek by* Peter Whigham. GrAn; PeHV
At twenty, I loved Lise. She was frail and white. Oswald Durand. *See* Like Lise, moreover, my mother was white.
At twenty-one Jupe ran away. Slave Story. Hodding Carter. PoNe
At twilight I went into the street. Descending Figure. Louise Glück. AnAn; FaBoWP
At two a.m. a thing, jumping out of a manhole. News Report. David Ignatow. ErPo; TwCP
At two P.M. there was a studies class. The Political Studies Class. Mu Tan, *tr. fr. Chinese.* LHF, *tr. by* Hualing Nieh

At Tynemouth Priory, after a Tempestuous Voyage. William Lisle Bowles. Son
At Upton-on-Severn. *Unknown.* FaBoCo; FaBoEE
At Venice. . . (*LL*) The Eve of Saint Mark. Keats. CH; EnRP
At Viscount Nelson's lavish funeral. 1805. Robert Graves. FaBoCh; FaBoEH; OBSV; PeLV; PlP
At Vshchizh. Fyodor Tyutchev, *tr. fr. Russian by* Charles Tomlinson. OBWP
At War. Charles Madge. FaBoMo
At Wednesbury there was a cocking. The Wednesbury Cocking. *Unknown.* EnSB; FaBoBa
At weekends, my father and younger sister. Washing the Money. Rhyll McMaster. FaBoMA
At whiles (yea oftentimes) I muse over. Dante, *tr. fr. Italian by* Dante Gabriel Rossetti. *Fr.* Vita Nuova, La. AWP
At Will Robers Beach. Timothy Steele. WeW
At winter's end. Snowman Sniffles. N. M. Bodecker. TLR
At Woodlawn I heard the dead cry. The Flight. Theodore Roethke. *Fr.* Lost Son, The. HAP; HCAP; LiTM; NAAL-2; RB; TrGrPo; TRP; VGW
At Woodward's Gardens. Robert Frost. PoA
At Work. Artur Miedzyrzecki, *tr. fr. Polish by* Artur Miedzyrzecki *and* John Batki. PoSu
At work his arms wave like a windmill. The Secretary. Peter Redgrove. OxBTC
At Year's End. Richard Wilbur. *See* Now winter downs the dying of the year.
At Ynysddu. Graham Thomas. AngWe
At Yorktown. Charles Olson. BCF
At your entreaty [*or* Intreaty], I at last have writ. Maidenhead. "Ephelia." KTR; WPE
(Maidenhead: Written at the Request of a Friend.) NOSC
At Your Feet, Jerusalem. Uri Zvi Greenberg, *tr. fr. Hebrew by* Ruth Finer Mintz. MHP
At your silver wedding in '64 we gave. Psycho. Peter Olds. PeNZ
At Your Table. Vienna V, 1957. Lisa Ress. BTR
At Yuen Yang Lake. Wu Wei-yeh, *tr. fr. Chinese by* Kenneth Rexroth. OHMPC
Atalanta in Calydon. Swinburne. EnVR
Sels.
Before the Beginning of Years. ImPo; LiTB; NAEL-2; NoP; NTP
(Chorus: "Before the beginning of years.") EBVV; EBVVPR; OBEV
(Man.) TrGrPo
Hounds of Spring, The. AWP; CTC; EBVV; FaBoBe; FaBV; GTBS-P; HAP; LiTB; NAEL-2; NOBE; NoP; OAEL-2; OBEV; PoE; PrIm; SCGP; TEP; TFi; TrGrPo; WeW
(Chorus: "When the hounds of spring are on winter's traces.") EBVVPR
"Maiden, and mistress of the months and stars." PoEL-5
"Who hath given man speech? or what hath set therein." OAEL-2
Atavism. Elinor Wylie. NALW; PoA
Ate me alive day and night these land mines. The Worrying. Paul Monette. BAP-90
Athalie, *sels.* Jean Racine, *tr. fr. French by* Charles Randolph.
"God whose goodness filleth every clime, The." WGRP
Atharva Veda. *Unknown, tr. fr. Sanskrit by* Romesh Dutt. *Fr.* Vedic Hymns. EaPr
Atheism, *sels.* Elizabeth Oakes Smith.
Annihilation. AmWP
Faith. AmWP
Reason. AmWP
Atheist. (*LL*) The Great Mother. Susan Griffin. SRLS
Atheist's Tragedy, The, *sels.* Cyril Tourneur.
Epitaph on a Soldier. EIL
Atheling Grange; or, The Apotheosis of Lotte Nussbaum. William Plomer. OBNV
Athelstan King. Battle of Brunanburh. Tennyson. PeVV
Athelstan the king, captain of earls. Brunanburg. *Unknown, tr. fr. Anglo-Saxon by* Kemp Malone. PoE
Athelstane. Priscilla Jane Thompson. CBWP-2
Athena in the Front Lines. Marge Piercy. SRLS
Athenagoras begot Eubulus — . Chairemon, *tr. fr. Greek by* Richard Evans. GrAn
Athens. Milton. *See* Look once more ere we leave this specular Mount.
Athirst in spirit, through the gloom. The Prophet. Pushkin, *tr. by* Babette Deutsch *and* Avrahm Yarmolinsky. AWP
Athlete, one vacation, An. An Accommodating Lion. Tudor Jenks. OBCA
Athol Brose. Thomas Hood. FaBoCo
Athwart the sky. (*LL*) The Incantation. Sarah Kirsch. VBLP

Athwart the sky a lowly sigh. London. John Davidson. MeMBP; NOBE; OBNC

Atlanta Exposition Ode. Mary Weston Fordham. AAP; CBWP-2

Atlantic. Peter Scupham. SCBI

Atlantic Charter: 1942. Francis Brett Young. OtMeF

Atlantic is a stormy moat, and the Mediterranean, The. The Eye. Robinson Jeffers. GGP; ImPo; LiTA; LiTM; NoAM; NOBA; OxBA

Atlantis. W. H. Auden. OxAEP-2

Atlantis. David Constantine. SCBI

Atlantis. Hart Crane. *Fr.* Bridge, The. LiTA; LiTM; NAAL-2

Atlantis, *sels.* Louis Dudek.
  Marine Aquarium, The. MoCV

Atlantis. John Engman. NAmP90

Atlantis. Slavko Mihalic, *tr. by* Charles Simic. PoSu

Atlas. Heine, *tr. fr. German by* Philip L. Miller. RiWo

Atlas, The, *sels.* Kenneth Slessor.

Atoll in the Mind, The. Alex Comfort. LiTB; LiTM

Atomic Pantoum. Peter Meinke. SM; WeW

Atomic Prayer. Cornelius Eady. NGP

Atomic Psalm. Maurya Simon. FoLa

Atonement. Margaret E. Bruner. PoToHe

Atong. Benilda S. Santos, *tr. fr. Spanish.* TSaS, *tr. by* Ramón C. Sunico

Atong and His Goodbye. Benilda S. Santos, *tr. fr. Spanish.* TSaS, *tr. by* Ramón C. Sunico

Atop a tower I pitched a silken thing. Parachuting Thoor Ballylee. William Zaranka. BXAP

Atrocity . . . And with the star obscure. The Star Obscure. Gueni Zaimof. WoWa

Atropos. Hilaire Kirkland. *Fr.* Clotho, Lachesis, Atropos. PeNZ

Attached itself as a vocabulary of change. (*LL*) The Sorrow Garden. Thomas McCarthy. BiHa; IB

Attack, The. Thomas Buchanan Read. PAH

Attack. Siegfried Sassoon. MoBrPo; NOBE; OxBTC; PlP

Attack me, Father, now. Prayer for Peace. Johnstone G. Patrick. TrPWD

Attack of the Crab Monsters. Lawrence Raab. AmPA; NoP

Attack of the Squash People. Marge Piercy. NBLV

Attainment. Madison Cawein. WGRP

Attainment, The. Coventry Patmore. *Fr.* Angel in the House, The. FaBoEE

Attainment. Ella Wheeler Wilcox. WGRP

Attempt at Jealousy, An. Craig Raine. NoAM

Attempt at Jealousy, An. Marina Tsvetayeva, *tr. fr. Russian by* Robert Perelman *and* Aleksandar Petrov. WPOW

Attempt was brave, how happy our success, Th.' To Mrs. Manley. Catherine Trotter. KTR

Attend my fable if your ears be clean. Roy Campbell. *Fr.* Wayzgoose, The. OBSV; PeSAV

Attend my lays, ye ever honour'd nine. An Hymn to the Morning. Phillis Wheatley. TAP

Attend, my Muse, and, if you can, approve. In Praise of Young Girls. Herbert Asquith. OtMeF

Attend, ye mournful Parents, while. Another to Urania. Benjamin Colman. ChIV-1; SCAP

Attend, ye nymphs, by wedlock unconfin'd. Ovid, *tr. by* Congreve. *Fr.* Art of Love, The. FaBoUs

Attend you and give ear a while, and you shall understand. The Honour of Bristol. *At. to* Laurence Price. OxBSS

Attend, Young Friends, While I Relate. *Unknown.* AmFP

Attention. Adrienne Rich. TAP

Attention was commanded through a simple, unadorned, unexplained, often decentered presence. Jealousy. Mei-Mei Berssenbrugge. BAP-90; OpBo; UL

Attentive eyes, fantastic heed. A Poet. Thomas Hardy. NoAM

Attentively he heard us, while we spoke. Virgil, *tr. by* Dryden. *Fr.* Aeneid [*or* Eneados], The. NAWM-1; OBVE

Atthis hung up the belt with the pompoms. Leonidas of Tarentum, *tr. fr. Greek by* Peter Levi. GrAn

Attibon Legba. René Depestre, *tr. fr. French by* Ellen Conroy Kennedy. *Fr.* Epiphanies of the Voodoo Gods. NegPo

Attic, The. Henri Coulette. PoRA

Attic Landscape, The. Herman Melville. AnAmPo; NOBA; OBAL

Attic maid! with honey fed. To the Swallow. William Cowper, *after the Greek of* Euenus. OBVE

Attic, The ("The attic and the cedar closet — nostalgia!") Richard Eberhart. *Fr.* Burr Oaks. MoAB

Atticus ("Peace to all such! but were there one whose fires.") Pope. *Fr.* Epistle to Dr. Arbuthnot. AWP; FHYEP; InPK; InPS; NOBE; NoP; OAEL-1; OxAEP-1; PoE; PoEL-3; TFi; TRP

Attired in black, spangled with flames of fire. The Spirit of Night. Thomas Rogers. EiL

Attis. Catullus, *tr. fr. Latin by* Peter Whigham. OBVE

Attis (Overseas sped, he, Attis, in the speediest of ships). Catullus, *tr. fr. Latin by* John Frederick Nims. STV

Attractions of a Fashionable Irish Watering-Place, The. Francis Sylvester Mahony. FaBoPP

Attributes, The. Robert Wells. SCBI

Atween the world o' licht. Scotland. William Soutar. OxBS

Au Bout du Temps. Andrei Codrescu. UL

Au Champ d'Honneur. Charles Kenneth Michael Scott Moncrieff. NSI

Au Jardin des Plantes. John Wain. OxBTC

Au Tombeau de Mon Père. Ronald McCuaig. NOBAu

Aubade. Marilyn Chin. NIP

Aubade. Nuala Ni Dhomhnaill, *tr. fr. Irish by* Michael Longley. BiHa; PBCIP

Aubade. *Unknown, at. to* John Donne. *See* Stay, O sweet, and do not rise!

Aubade: "Hark! hark! the lark at heaven's gate sings." Shakespeare. *See* Hark! hark! the lark at heaven's gate sings.

Aubade: "Hours before dawn we were woken by the quake." William Empson. FaBoMo; FaBoTw; LiTB; OxAEP-2; OxBTC

Aubade: "I work all day, and get half drunk at night." Philip Larkin. OPOP; SoSe; TRP

Aubade: "Jane, Jane,/ Tall as a crane." Edith Sitwell. CMoP; MoAB; MoBrPo; MoP; NALW; NoAM; Poetr; PoRA

Aubade: "Lark now leaves his watery [*or* wat'ry] nest, The." Sir William Davenant. *See* Lark Now Leaves His Watery [*or* Wat'ry] Nest.

Aubade: "Million stars are dreaming out, A." Frank O'Hara. SM

Aubade: "Night's ride's over." Anselm Hollo. UL

Aubade: "Today above the gull's call." Louise Glück. AnAn

Aubade: "What dawn is it?" Karl Shapiro. VGW

Aubade: Donna Anna to Juan, Still Asleep. Richard Howard. PoA

Aubade for Hope. Robert Penn Warren. MoAmPo

Aubade: Lake Erie. Thomas Merton. NYBP

Aubade: N.Y.C. Robert Wallace. HoPM

Aubade: The Desert. Frederick Bock. PoA

Aubade Triste. Agnes Mary Frances Robinson. NOBVV

Aube Provençale. Marilyn Hacker. AmPA

Auburn. Paul Verlaine, *tr. fr. French by* Lawrence M. Bensky. ErPo

A.U.C. 334: about this date. Advice to Young Ladies. A. D. Hope. FaBoMA; NoAM; NoP

Aucassin and Nicolette, *sels. Unknown, tr. fr. French by* Andrew Lang. Who Would List. CTC

"Auchanachie Gordon is bonny and braw." Lord Saltoun and Auchanachie. *Unknown.* ESPB

Auction, The, *sels.* Galway Kinnell.
  "My wife lies in another dream." NGP

Auction Extraordinary. Lucretia Davidson. AmWP

Auction Sale, The. Henry Reed. MoBrPo

Auction Sale — Household Furnishings. Adele DeLeeuw. PoToHe

Auctioneer. Carl Sandburg. PDV

Auctioneer of parting, The. Emily Dickinson. PoEL-5

Auctioneer's Handbill, An. William Hall. FaBoUs

Auden at Milwaukee. Stephen Spender. AiP

Auden, MacNeice, Day Lewis, I have read them all. British Leftish Poetry, 1930-40. "Hugh MacDiarmid." CMoP; FaBoTw; NoAM

Auden's Funeral. Stephen Spender. AnAn

Auditor Thinks about Female Nature, An. Jamie Grant. NOBAu

Audley Court. Tennyson. NOBVV; PeVV

Audley Court, *sels.* Tennyson.
  "Sleep, Ellen Aubrey, sleep, and dream of me." CBLP

Audrey Hepburn moons big-eyed on the cover. A Guide to Holland. Peter Sirr. PBCIP

Audubon, *sels.* Robert Penn Warren.
  Tell Me a Story. MT

Audubon, Drafted. Amiri Baraka. PPP; TTY

Auf dem Wasser zu Singen. Stephen Spender. EnLoPo

Auf meiner Herzliebsten Äugelein. Heine, *tr. fr. German by* Richard Garnett. AWP

Auf Wiedersehen. Donald Jeffrey Hayes. CDC

Augher Clogher Fivemiletown. Omagh Post Office Rhyme. *Unknown.* FaBoVe

Augmentation of the Unknown. Yannis Ritsos, *tr. fr. Greek by* Kimon Friar *and* Kostas Myrsiades. AnAn

Augsburg Adoration, The. Randall Jarrell. NYBP

Auguries of Innocence. Blake. BLPL; EBEV; EnRP; FaBoCh; FaBV; FaPoR; FM; LiTB; OAEL-1; OBNC; OxBoLi; PoEL-4; TrGrPo

"I just knew it when we swept above the old roofs of Dijon." PeVV
"I learnt the collects and the catechism." EnVR; TEP
"I mused/ Up and down, up and down, the terraced streets." OBTV
"I think I see my father's sister stand." NALW
"My mother was a Florentine." NALW
"Of writing many books there is no end!" NOBVV
Olives and Mountains. FaBoPP; OBTV
Reading. GN
Sweetness of England, The. OxAEP-2
"Then, land! — then, England! oh, the frosty cliffs." FaBoPP; NAEL-2
"Then, must it be." NALW
"There it is!/ You play beside a death-bed like a child." BrRo
"Truth, so far, in my book; the truth which draws." WGRP
Tuscan Life. FaBoPP
"Without considering whether they were fit." PFP
Auroras of Autumn, The, *sels.* Wallace Stevens.
   "Farewell to an idea . . . A cabin stands." CMoP; HCAP
   "Farewell to an idea . . . The mother's face." CMoP; HCAP
   "Is there an imagination that sits enthroned?" CMoP; HCAP
   "It is a theatre floating through the clouds." CMoP; HCAP
   "This is where the serpent lives, the bodiless." CMoP; PoE
   "Unhappy people in a happy world, An." CMoP
Auschwitz. Harvey Shapiro. BTR
Auschwitz, *sels.* Elizabeth Wyse.
Auschwitz #1. Alfred Van Loen. BTR
Auschwitz #5. Alfred Van Loen. BTR
Auschwitz #6. Alfred Van Loen. BTR
Auschwitz with H and C. Birmingham. Roger McGough. IHNG
Auspex. James Russell Lowell. PoEL-5; TAP
Auspice of Jewels. Laura Riding. LiTA
Austere the Music of My Songs. Fyodor Sologub, *tr. fr. Russian by* Babette
   Deutsch *and* Avrahm Yarmolinsky. AWP
Austerity in Vermont. Terry Hummer. NAmP90
Austerity of Poetry [*or* Jacopone da Todi]. Matthew Arnold. EPCY
Australasia, *sels.* William Charles Wentworth.
Australia. Gary Catalano. NOBAu
Australia. A. D. Hope. NoAM; NoP
Australia, *sels.* Iain Crichton Smith.
   "All day the kookaburra is laughing." OBAP
Australia 1970. Judith Wright. CBAP; NoAM
Australian Dream, The. David Campbell. CBAP
Australian Transcripts. "Fiona Macleod." FM
   Sels.
   Bell-Bird, The.
   Mid-Noon in January.
   Wood-Swallows, The.
Australia's best-kept dead-end road. Women on the Road to Pine Gap.
   Wendy Poussard. AIW
Australorp. Edith Speers. NOBAu
Austrian Army, An. *At. to* Alaric Alexander Watts. FaBoCo; FiBHP;
   NOBL; PeLV
Austrians After Sadowa (1866), The. Michael Hofmann. SCBI
Autant En Emporte le Vent. Marguerite de Navarre, *tr. fr. French by* Aline
   Allard. PBWP
Autet e bas. Daniel Arnaut, *tr. fr. Provençal by* Ezra Pound. CTC
Authentic, The! Shadows of it. Matins. Denise Levertov. AmPP;
   FaBoWP; IHMS; MoP; NoAM; NOBA; Poetr
Author, The, *sels.* Charles Churchill.
   "Gods! with what pride I see the titled slave." OBSV
   Pains of Education, The. FaBoCo
   "When with much pains this boasted learning's got." OBSV
Author Apologizes to a Lady for His Being a Little Man, The. Christopher
   Smart. BoLoP; CBLP
Author Consults a Critic and Sells His Manuscript, The. Francis Hawling.
   Fr. Signal, The; or, A Satire against Modesty. NOEC
Author Loving These Homely Meats. John Davies of Hereford. *Fr.*
   Scourge of Folly, The. CBLP; CBNP; ElL; FaBoNo; Son
Author of *Christine*, The. Richard Howard. CoAP
Author, of His Own Fortune, The. Sir John Harington. FaBoEE
Author of light, revive my dying spright. Thomas Campion. AAS
Author to Her Book, The. Anne Bradstreet. AmPP; AnAmPo; EAP; InPK;
   NAAL-1; NALW; NOBA; NoP; OxBA; PoE; Poetr; SCAP; TAP
Author to His Body on Their Fifteenth Birthday, 29.ii.80, The. Howard
   Nemerov. NAs; NoAM
Author to His Book, The. George Alsop. SCAP
Author to His Book[e], The. Thomas Heywood. *Fr.* Apology for Actors,
   An. NOSC
Author to His Wife, of a Woman's Eloquence, The. Sir John Harington.
   BoLoP; ErPo; LPA; OxBM
Author to the Reader, The. Randall Jarrell. OxBC
Author Unknown. William Montgomerie. OxBS

Authoress, armed with a skewer, An. *Unknown.* PeLi
Authority is a disease, and cure. Samuel Butler. FaBoEE
Authority is afraid. Poor Losers. Keith A. Dodson. NGP
Authors and actors and artists and such. Bohemia. Dorothy Parker.
   AnAmPo; NBLV
Author's Apology for His Book, The, *sels.* Bunyan.
   "When at the first I took my pen in hand." FaBoVe
Author's Epitaph, The. *Unknown.* FiBHP
Author's Epitaph, Made By Himself, The. Sir Walter Ralegh. *See* Even
   such is time, that takes in trust.
Author's Epitaph, Written by Himself, An. Abel Evans. FaBoEE
Authors of Confession, The. Elizabeth Major. *Fr.* Honey on the Rod.
   KTR
Authors of the Town, The, *sels.* Richard Savage.
   "First, let me view what noxious nonsense reigns." OBSV
Authors [*or* Author's] Abstract of Melancholy, The. Robert Burton. *Fr.*
   Anatomy of Melancholy, The. NOSC
Author's Prologue. Dylan Thomas. *See* This day winding down now.
Author's Quietus, The. Henry Carey. FaBoVe
Author's Reply, The. Sir Carr Scroope. APAS
Author's Resolution, The. George Wither. *See* Shall I, Wasting in Despair.
Authorship. James Ball Naylor. *See* King David and King Solomon.
Autistic Poses. Iain Sinclair. VaA
Auto-erotic. *Unknown.* PeLi
Auto Mobile. A. R. Ammons. FF; OBAL
Auto Wreck. Karl Shapiro. CMoP; FF; LiTM; NIP; RB; VGW
Autobahnmotorwayautoroute. Adrian Mitchell. RB
Autobiographia Literaria. Frank O'Hara. CAPP; NNaP; NOBA; TTTS
Autobiographical. A. M. Klein. MoCV; NoAM
Autobiography. Sonja Åkesson, *tr. fr. Swedish by* Ingrid Claréus. BoWoP
Autobiography. Charles Causley. LiTM; Son
Autobiography. Mbella Sonne Dipoko. TTY
Autobiography. Janet Dubé. BrRo
Autobiography. Gloria Fuertes, *tr. fr. Spanish by* Philip Levine. AnAn;
   PBWP
Autobiography. Thom Gunn. NoAM
Autobiography. Louis MacNeice. NOIV; PNI; RB
Autobiography. Dan Pagis, *tr. fr. Hebrew.* PoSu, *tr. by* Stephen Mitchell
Autobiography. Tom Weatherly. NBV
Autobiography, An. Ernest Rhys. *See* Wales England wed; so I was bred.
Autobiography, Chapter XVII: Floating the Big Piney. Jim Barnes.
   HATNAP
Autobiography, Chapter XLII: Three Days in Louisville. Jim Barnes.
   HATNAP
Autobiography: Last Chapter. Jim Barnes. CDW
Autobiography of a Lungworm. Roy Fuller. MoP; NoAM; NoP; OxBC
Autocrat of the Breakfast Table, The, *sels.* Oliver Wendell Holmes.
   Aestivation [an Unpublished Poem, by My Late Latin Tutor]. NOBL;
   OBAL
   (Intramural Aestivation, or Summer in Town, by a Teacher of Latin.)
   ChTr; FaBoNo
   Chambered Nautilus, The. AmPP; FaBoBe; GN; HoPM; ImPo; LiTA;
   NOBA; NoP; PoEL-5; PoLF; PrIm; TFi; WGRP
   Contentment. AmPP; AnAmPo; OxBA; PWR
   Deacon's Masterpiece, The; or, The Wonderful "One-Hoss Shay." AmPP;
   LiTA; MoShBr; NOBA; OBAL; OBCA; OxBA; PoLF; PoRA; TAP; TFi;
   VPP; WBLP
   (Wonderful "One-Hoss Shay," The.) BeLS; FaBoBe
Autograph Book/ Prophecy. Anne Halley. NMM
Autograph on the Soul, The. Adah Isaacs Menken. CBWP-1
Autoincineration of the Right Stuff. Iván Argüelles. UL
Autolycus as Peddler. Shakespeare. *See* Lawn as white as driven snow.
Autolycus Sings. Shakespeare. *See* When Daffodils Begin to Peer.
Autolycus's Song ("When daffodils begin to peer.") Shakespeare. *See*
   When Daffodils Begin to Peer.
Automatic fingers write, The. Séance. Francis King. PoA
Automation. Joseph Glazer. SWP
Automobile, The. Russell Edson. LCAP; RaBo
Automobile Mechanics. Dorothy W. Baruch. FaPON
Automobiles/ In/ a/ row. Stop-Go. Dorothy W. Baruch. FaPON
Autonomous. Mark Van Doren. LiTA
Autopsy. Arthur Nortje. HBAPE
Autosonic Door. Dorothy Brown Thompson. GoYe
Autumn. Bella Akhmadulina, *tr. fr. Russian by* Barbara Einzig. BoWoP
Autumn. D. R. Beeton. PeSA
Autumn. Roy Campbell. GTBS-P; MoBrPo; OBMV; OxBTC
Autumn. William Carpenter. Poetsp
Autumn. Thomas Chatterton. *Fr.* Aella; a Tragycal Enterlude. Mes

Autumn ("I love the fitful gust.") John Clare. BoTP

Autumn ("Thistledown's flying, The.") John Clare. BoNaP; EnVR; HAP; NU; PoEL-4; WeW

Autumn. Walter de la Mare. OxBTC

Autumn. Fan Ch'eng-ta, tr. by Irving Y. Lo. Fr. Seasonal Poems on Fields and Gardens. SuSp

Autumn. Gu Cheng, tr. fr. Chinese by Donald Finkel. SpMi

Autumn. Florence Hoatson. BoTP

Autumn. Thomas Hood. BLPL; ImPo; LiTB; OBEV; OxAEP-2

Autumn. Patricia Hubbell. PDV

Autumn. T. E. Hulme. FaBoMo; NTP

Autumn. Walter Savage Landor. See Mild is the parting year, and sweet.

Autumn. Philip Levine. NNaP

Autumn. Detlev von Liliencron, tr. fr. German by Ludwig Lewisohn. AWP

Autumn. Itsik Manger, tr. fr. Yiddish. TrJP, tr. by Ruth Whitman and Joseph Leftwich

Autumn. Marjorie Marshall. ShDr

Autumn. Thomas Nashe. Fr. Summer's Last Will and Testament. ElL; NoSic; OAEL-1; PlP; SCGP; TrGrPo

Autumn. Ngo Chi Lan, tr. fr. Vietnamese by M. S. Merwin and Nguyen Ngoh Bich. ArNa

Autumn. Pushkin, tr. fr. Russian by Max Eastman. AWP

Autumn. Rainer Maria Rilke, tr. fr. German by C. F. MacIntyre. TrJP

Autumn. Christina Rossetti. BrRo

Autumn. Vernon Scannell. OxBTC

Autumn. Thomas W. Shapcott. CBAP

Autumn. Princess Shikishi, tr. fr. Japanese by Hiroaki Sato. PBWP

Autumn. Paul Armand Silvestre, tr. fr. French by Philip L. Miller. RiWo

Autumn. Stevie Smith. See He Told His Life Story to Mrs Courtly.

Autumn. Spenser. Fr. Faerie Queene, the. GN

Autumn. Rabindranath Tagore. WGRP

Autumn ("List to the sad wind, drearily moaning.") Priscilla Jane Thompson. CBWP-2

Autumn ("Sun shines bright, but sadly, The.") Priscilla Jane Thompson. CBWP-2

Autumn. Unknown. See Woman full of wile.

Autumn ("I at my window sit, and see.") Unknown. NOEC

Autumn. Jean Starr Untermeyer. MoAmPo

Autumn. Wang Wei, tr. fr. Chinese by Kenneth Rexroth. OHMPC

Autumn. Frances Winwar. GoYe

Autumn, sels. Humbert Wolfe.

Autumn. Charles Wright. FoLa

Autumn; a Dirge. Shelley. CH

Autumn and the Sea. Javier Heraud. TSaS, tr. by Javier Heraud

Autumn, and we're still like the will-o'-the wisp. To Li Po. 'Aisha bint Ahmad al-Qurtubiyya, tr. fr. Chinese by Eugene Eoyang. SuSp

Autumn Begins in Martins Ferry, Ohio. James Wright. CAPP; HCAP; HeIP; InPK; InPS; NaP; NoAM; VCAP; WeW

Autumn Brook, The. Hsüeh T'ao, tr. fr. Chinese by Kenneth Rexroth and Ling Chung. WPC

Autumn Chapter in a Novel. Thom Gunn. FaBoMo; OxBTC

Autumn chrysanthemums have beautiful color. T'ao Ch'ien, tr. by Wu-chi Liu. Fr. Drinking Wine. SuSp

Autumn Comes. Li Ho, tr. fr. Chinese by A. C. Graham. PLT

Autumn constellations, The. Moon Festival. Tu Fu, tr. fr. Chinese by Kenneth Rexroth. SuSp

Autumn Cove. Li Po, tr. fr. Chinese by Burton Watson. OBAP; TTTS

Autumn, Crystal Eye. Margot Ruddock. OBMV

Autumn Day. Rainer Maria Rilke, tr. fr. German by C. F. MacIntyre. TrJP

Autumn Day, An. Clara Ann Thompson. CBWP-2

Autumn Day, An — Leisurely Boating on West Lake. Lin Pu, tr. fr. Chinese by Jonathan Chaves. SuSp

Autumn day its course has run, The — the Autumn evening falls. Charlotte Brontë. NOBVV

Autumn eats its leaf out of my hand: we are friends. Paul Celan. See Fall eats its leaf from my hand, The: we are friends.

Autumn eats its leaf out of my hand: we are friends. Corona. Paul Celan. PoSu, tr. by Michael Hamburger

Autumn Equinox. Peter Blue Cloud. Fr. Within the Seasons. HATNAP

Autumn Evening. Robinson Jeffers. ArNa

Autumn Evening. Tu Mu, tr. fr. Chinese by A. C. Graham. PLT

Autumn Fancies. Unknown. FaPON

Autumn feels slowed down, The. Paula Becker to Clara Westhoff. Adrienne Rich. NAAL-2; VCAP

Autumn finds me old and poorer. Meng Chiao, tr. by Irving Y. Lo. Fr. Autumn Meditations. SuSp

Autumn Fires. Robert Louis Stevenson. NTP

Autumn Garden. Dino Campana, tr. fr. Italian by John Frederick Nims. STV

Autumn has turned the dark trees toward the hill. Quail in Autumn. William Jay Smith. Poetsp

Autumn hath all the summer's fruitful treasure. Autumn. Thomas Nashe. Fr. Summer's Last Will and Testament. ElL; NoSic; OAEL-1; PlP; SCGP; TrGrPo

(Autumn Hath All the Summer's Fruitful Treasure.) EnRePo

Autumn Idleness. Dante Gabriel Rossetti. Fr. House of Life, The. GBL; OAEL-2

Autumn Imagined. Donald Davie. PoA

Autumn Impressions, sels. Cha Shen-hsing, tr. fr. Chinese by William Schultz.

Autumn in Hobart. James McAuley. FaBoMA

Autumn is weary, halt, and old. The October Redbreast. Alice Meynell. MoBrPo

Autumn Journal, sels. Louis MacNeice.
"And I remember Spain." OBWP; OxAEP-2
"And the next day begins." FaBoEH
"August is nearly over, the people." CMoP
"Conferences, adjournments, ultimatums." FaBoPV; OxBTC
"Nightmare leaves fatigue." BlrV; CIP; PNI
"Now we are back to normal, now the mind is." OxAEP-2
"Shelley and jazz and lieder and love and hymn-tunes." NOBL
Week to Christmas, A. TIRV

Autumn Leaves. James Schuyler. ArLo

Autumn Leaves. Clara Ann Thompson. CBWP-2

Autumn Leaves. Charles H. Webb. OBAL

Autumn made colors burn, The. Venus Khoury-Gata, tr. fr. French by Willis Barnstone. BoWoP

Autumn Maneuver. Ingeborg Bachmann, tr. by Mark Anderson. PRA

Autumn Meditation. Tu Fu, tr. fr. Chinese by A. C. Graham. PLT

Autumn Meditations, sels. Meng Chiao, tr. fr. Chinese.
"Autumn finds me old and poorer." SuSp
"Bones of the lonely-wretched spend no quiet nights." SuSp
"In autumn moonlight the face turns icy." SuSp
"Old and sick, many strange broodings." SuSp

Autumn met me today as I walked over Castle Hill. The Stand-to. C. Day Lewis. OBWP

Autumn Morning. Adeline White. BoTP

Autumn Morning, An. Unknown. BoTP

Autumn Morning at Cambridge. Frances Cornford. PoRA

Autumn Morning in Shokoku-ji, An. Gary Snyder. Fr. Four Poems for Robin. HAP; MoP; NNaP; NoAM; NOBA; NoP; SOTW; VGW; WeW

Autumn Mushrooms. Kenneth Mackenzie. CBAP

Autumn nightfall. (LL) On a withered branch. Basho. TAL

Autumn, 1939. Alun Lewis. PAW; PoWW

Autumn 1940. W. H. Auden. LiTA

Autumn 1942. Roy Fuller. PoWW

Autumn on Nan-Yueh., sels. William Empson.

Autumn on the Beaches. Sara Teasdale. ArNa

Autumn on the Upper Thames. William Morris. See Fair Is the World.

Autumn-pallid sun looks down, The. The End Is Now. "Marie Madelaine," tr. fr. German by Ferdinand E. Kappey. PeHV

Autumn Psalm of Contentment. Edward Hays. EaPr

Autumn Rain. Kenneth Rexroth. NU

Autumn Refrain. Wallace Stevens. LiTA

Autumn resumes the land, ruffles the woods. The Laurel Axe. Geoffrey Hill. Fr. Apology for the Revival of Christian Architecture in England, An. NAEL-2; NoAM; NoP; PoE

Autumn Rivulets., sels. Walt Whitman.
There Was a Child Went Forth. ImPo; NAAL-1; NTP; SAmP

Autumn Robin, The. John Clare. BoTP

Autumn Scene. Basil Dowling. BoNaP

Autumn Sentiments. Yuan Hao-wen, tr. fr. Chinese by Irving Y. Lo. SuSp

Autumn Sequel, sels. Louis MacNeice.

Autumn Sequence. Adrienne Rich. VGW

Autumn Shade, sels. Edgar Bowers.
"Autumn shade is thin, The. Grey leaves lie faint." MT
"Awakened by some fear, I watch the sky." VCAP
"I drive home with the books that I will read." VCAP
"In nameless warmth, sun light in every corner." VCAP
"Snow and then rain. The roads are wet. A car." VCAP

Autumn shade is thin, The. Grey leaves lie faint. Edgar Bowers. Fr. Autumn Shade. MT

Autumn Song. Margaret Rose. BoTP

Autumn Song. Johann Ludwig Tieck, tr. fr. German by James Clarence Mangan. AWP

Autumn Song on Perry Street. Lloyd Frankenberg. GrPl

Autumn Sonnets, The, *sels.* May Sarton.
"If I could let you go as trees let go." PoSu
Autumn Spring. Hsüeh T'ao, *tr. fr. Chinese by* Eric W. Johnson. SuSp
Autumn Sun over the *t'ung* Tree. Wang An-shih, *tr. fr. Chinese by* Jan W. Walls. SuSp
Autumn Testament., *sels.* James K. Baxter.
"Rata blooms explode, the bow-legged tomcat, The." PeNZ
"Spider crouching on the ledge above the sink, The." PeNZ
"To wish to climb a ladder to the loft." PeNZ
Autumn: the ninth year of Yüan Ho. The Temple. Po Chü-i, *tr. fr. Chinese by* Arthur Waley. OBMV
Autumn Thoughts., *sels.* Han Yü, *tr. fr. Chinese by* Burton Watson.
"Frosty wind harries the *wu-t'ung*, A." PLT
Autumn Thoughts., *sels.* Meng Chiao, *tr. fr. Chinese by* A. C. Graham.
"Face of the autumn moon freezes, The." PLT
"Wind and bamboos strum and speak to each other." PLT
Autumn Thoughts. Ts'en Shen, *tr. fr. Chinese by* C. H. Wang. SuSp
Autumn Thoughts., *sels.* Tu Fu, *tr. fr. Chinese.*
"I have heard the affairs in Ch'ang-an are like a game of chess." SuSp
"Jade dews deeply wilt and wound the maple woods." SuSp
"Waters of K'un-ming Pool recalled the achievements of Han lives, The." SuSp
Autumn Thoughts. Mary E. Tucker. CBWP-1
Autumn Thoughts ("Sumac showing faint traces of red.") Lu Yu, *tr. fr. Chinese by* Burton Watson. SuSp
Autumn-time has come, The. My Triumph. Whittier. NOBA; PFP
Autumn Twilight in the Mountains. Wang Wei, *tr. fr. Chinese by* Kenneth Rexroth. OHMPC
Autumn upon us was rushing, The. Ravings. Tom Hood. BXAP
Autumn Walk, An. Witter Bynner. GoYe
Autumn Warrior. Barney Bush. HATNAP
Autumn Wastes, The. Tu Fu, *tr. fr. Chinese by* A. C. Graham. PLT
Autumn wastes are each day wilder, The. The Autumn Wastes. Tu Fu, *tr. fr. Chinese by* A. C. Graham. PLT
Autumn wheat turns green and lush as spring wheat yellows. Reeling Silk. Fan Ch'eng-ta, *tr. by* Wu-chi Liu. *Fr.* Four Songs in Imitation of Wang Chien. SuSp
Autumn Wind, The. John Clare. BoNaP
Autumn Wind. Ruth Dallas. *Fr.* Letter to a Chinese Poet. PeNZ
Autumn Wind, The. Liu Ch'e, *tr. fr. Chinese by* Ronald C. Miao. SuSp
Autumn Wind. Emperor Wu of Han, *tr. fr. Chinese by* Kenneth Rexroth. OHMPC
Autumn Wind, The ("Autumn wind rises; white clouds fly.") Emperor Wu Ti, *tr. fr. Chinese by* Arthur Waley. FaBoCh
Autumn wind blows across the sea in the deepening twilight, An. Inscribed on Byron's Poetic Works. Su Man-shu, *tr. fr. Chinese by* Wu-chi Liu. SuSp
Autumn wind blows white clouds, The. Autumn Wind. Emperor Wu of Han, *tr. fr. Chinese by* Kenneth Rexroth. OHMPC
Autumn wind came stealing. The Thief. Irene F. Pawsey. BoTP
Autumn wind soughs and sighs, the setting sun is red. Tune: "Song of River Goddess" — Moorinig My Boat at Fen-shui at Night. Huang Shu, *tr. fr. Chinese by* James J. Y. Liu. SuSp
Autumn winds are getting a move on. John Riley. VaA
Autumn winds rise. The Autumn Wind. Liu Ch'e, *tr. fr. Chinese by* Ronald C. Miao. SuSp
Autumn winds whistle sadly, the air grows chill. Song of Yen. Ts'ao P'i, *tr. fr. Chinese by* Ronald C. Miao. SuSp
Autumn with your hazy sky, your heart-breaking horizons. Autumn. Paul Armand Silvestre, *tr. fr. French by* Philip L. Miller. RiWo
Autumnal. Ernest Dowson. EBVV; OBNC
Autumnal Ode. Aubrey Thomas De Vere. OBNC
Autumnal Song. Walter Savage Landor. *See* Very True, the Linnets Sing.
Autumnal[l], The. John Donne. *Fr.* Elegies. InPS; JCP; NOSC; PoEL-2; SeCV-1; TEP
Autumn's a blue country. Autumn. Gu Cheng, *tr. fr. Chinese by* Donald Finkel. SpMi
Autumn's bright moon. Kaga no Chiyo, *tr. fr. Japanese by* R. H. Blyth. PBWP
Autumn's Mirth. Samuel Minturn Peck. GN
Autumn's onset means cooling breezes. Juan Chi, *tr. by* Charles Hartman. *Fr.* Poems Expressing My Feelings. SuSp
Autumn's Processional. Dinah Maria Mulock Craik. GN
Autumn's wind on suthering wings, The. The Autumn Wind. John Clare. BoNaP
Autumnus. Joshua Sylvester. EiL
Aux Italiens. "Owen Meredith." BeLS; BLPA; BLPL; FaBoBe
Avalanche, The. Linda Hogan. FoLa
Avalanche. Adrien Stoutenburg. NYBP

Avant Garde. Louis Dudek. *Fr.* Provincetown. MoCV
Avarice. Anthony Hecht. OxBSP
Avarice. George Herbert. FaBoRV; LiTB
Avast, honest Jack! now, before you get mellow. The Battle of Erie. *Unknown.* PAH
Ave. Diane Di Prima. *Fr.* Loba. SRLS
Ave Atque Vale. *Malay Oral Tradition, tr. by* R. J. Wilkinson *and* R. O. Winstedt. WTO
Ave atque Vale. Swinburne. NAEL-2; NOBE; OAEL-2; OBEV; OBNC
Ave atque Vale. Rosamund Marriott Watson. NOBE; OAEL-2; OBEV; OBNC
Ave Caesar. Robinson Jeffers. FaBoPV; MoP; NoAM; NOBA; OxBA; OxBSP
Ave Imperatrix! Oscar Wilde. PeVV
Ave Imperatrix., *sels.* Oscar Wilde.
East A-Callin', The. OtMeF
Ave Maria. Hart Crane. *Fr.* Bridge, The. LiTA; NAAL-2; NoAM; NOBA
Ave Maria. Barbara Ferland. PBCV
Ave Maria. Frank O'Hara. HCAP; NAAL-2; NNaP; NoP; PoM; VCAP
Ave Maria, Gratia Plena. Oscar Wilde. ChIV-2
Ave Maria! Maiden mild! Hymn to the Virgin. Sir Walter Scott. *Fr.* Lady of the Lake, The. EnRP
Ave Maris Stella ("Ave maris stella, the star of the sea.") *Unknown.* CTC
Ave, Virgo! Gr-r-r — you swine! (*LL*) Soliloquy of the Spanish Cloister. Robert Browning. FaBoCo; FaBoVe; FHYEP; ImPo; InPK; LiTB; MeMBP; NAEL-2; NIP; NOBL; NOBVV; NoP; OAEL-2; OtMeF; PeVV; TEP; TOF; TrGrPo; UV, *sh. vers.*
'Ave you 'eard o' the Widow at Windsor. The Widow at Windsor. Kipling. FaBoEH; NAEL-2; NoAM; NoP
Avenge, O Lord, thy slaughtered [*or* slaughter'd] saints, whose bones. On the Late Massacre [*or* Massacher] in Piedmont [*or* Piemont]. Milton. AWP; GTBS; GTBS-P; HAP; HeIP; LiTB; NAEL-1; NOBE; NoP; OBWP; PAW; PoEL-3; Poetr; PPP; SCGP; Son; TFi; TRP; UnPo; WeW
(Sonnet: "Avenge, O Lord, thy slaughtered saints, whose bones.") OAEL-1
(Sonnet: On the Late Massacre in Piedmont.) JCP; NOCV
Avengers, The. Edwin Markham. MoAmPo
Avenue, The. Paul Muldoon. PBCIP
Avenue Bearing the Initial of Christ into the New World, The, *sels.* Galway Kinnell.
"Behind the Power Station on 14th, the held breath." NaP
"Children set fires in ashbarrels." NaP
"First Sun Day of the year. Tonight." NaP
"Fishmarket closed, the fishes gone into flesh, The." NaP
"In sunlight on the Avenue." LiTM
"In the pushcart market, on Sunday." NaP
"Pcheek pcheek pcheek pcheek pcheek." LiTM
"Promise was broken too freely, The." NaP
Avenue rises toward a city of white marble, The. Sleeping. Donald Hall. PRA
Avenue was green and long, and green, The. A Visit to Castletown House. Michael Hartnett. BiHa; PBCIP
Average Man, The. Margaret E. M. Sangster. WBLP
Average man was Private Flynn, An. The Vision. Katharine Tynan. NSI
Avising the bright beams of these fair eyes. Sir Thomas Wyatt. SiPSBD
Avocado. John Logan. CAPP
Avoid extremes; and shun the fault of such. Pope. *Fr.* Essay on Criticism. FHYEP; PoEL-3
Avoid the reeking herd. The Eagle and the Mole. Elinor Wylie. AWP; BoWoP; LiTA; LiTM; MoAB; MoAmPo; NALW; UnPo
Avoidances. Ron Welburn. PoBA
Avoiding News by the River. W. S. Merwin. NaP
Avondale Mine Disaster, The. *Unknown.* AmFP
Aw was young and lusty. Sair Fyel'd, Hinny. *Unknown.* GBP
Aw wish my lover she was a cherry. A Pitman's Lovesong. *Unknown.* FaBoBl; FaBoVe
Awake! Bible, O.T. *Fr.* Song of Solomon, The. FaPON
Awake! Jack Black. BXAP
Awake! Mary Elizabeth Coleridge. OBNC
Awake! W. R. Rodgers. LiTM
Awake! Walther von der Vogelweide, *tr. fr. German by* Jethro Bithell. AWP
Awake, Aeolian lyre, awake. The Progress of Poesy. Thomas Gray. AWP; EnRP; GTBS; GTBS-P; NOEC; OBEV
Awake all night till the. *Unknown, tr. fr. Greek by* Kenneth Rexroth. PGA
Awake, alone, aware. Insomniac Poem. Ron Loewinsohn. NeAP
Awake, and with attention hear. The 34. Chapter of the Prophet Isaiah. Abraham Cowley. ChIV-1

Awake! arise! Oh, men of my race. Daybreak. George Marion McClellan. AAP

Awake, arise,/ Pull out your eyes. Mother Goose. OxNR

Awake, arise, the hour is come. A Radical War Song. Macaulay. OBSV

Awake! arise, ye men of might! To Arms. Park Benjamin. PAH

Awake, Arise, You Drowsy Sleeper. *Unknown.* AmFP

Awake, awake, good people all. May Carol. *Unknown.* OBET

Awake! awake! my gallant friends. The Battle of Tippecanoe. *Unknown.* PAH

Awake, awake, my little boy! The Land of Dreams. Blake. BeLS; CH

Awake, awake, my Lyre! A Supplication. Abraham Cowley. *Fr.* Davideis. GTBS, III; GTBS-P, III (Music.) OxAEP-1

Awake, awake, O Church of God! The Clarion-Call. *Unknown.* BLRP

Awake, Awake! [Thou Heavy Sprite]. Thomas Campion. ChIV-1; ELP

Awake, awake, ye drowsy souls. New Year's Carol. *Unknown.* OBET

Awake between times and now. Theory. David Chaloner. VaA

Awake! flower of the forest, sky-treading bird of the prairie. Calling One's Own. *Unknown, tr. fr. Ojibwa Indian by* Charles Fenno Hoffman. AnAmPo

Awake! for morning in the bowl of night. Omar Khayyám, *tr. fr. Persian by* Edward Fitzgerald. *Fr.* Rubáiyát of Omar Khayyám of Naishápúr, The. AWP; EBEvV; EBVV, *abr.;* FaBoBe; FaBoRV, *abr.;* FaPoB; FaPoR, *abr.;* HAP, *abr.;* LiTB; Mes; NAEL-2; NOBVV; NoP; OxAEP-2, *abr.;* PeVV, *sect.* I–XII; PlP; PoEL-5; PrIm, *abr.;* TAL; TrGrPo; UV

Awake! for Morning on the Pitch of Night. Strugnell's Rubáiyát. Wendy Cope. UV

Awake! For Sweeney in pyjamas bright. Awake! Jack Black. BXAP

Awake, glad heart! get up, and sing. Christ's Nativity. Henry Vaughan. ESCV

Awake (great Sir) the Sun shines heer. On New-Year's Day 1640, to the King. Sir John Suckling. SeCV-1

Awake I steal what they dream. Sleepers. Branko Miljkovic, *tr. fr. Serbo-Croatian by* Charles Simic. HSix

Awake, like a hippopotamus with eyes bulged. Monday. William Stafford. NYBP

Awake, mine eyes, see Phoebus bright arising. *Unknown.* EIL

Awake, My Fair. Judah Halevi, *tr. fr. Hebrew by* Alice Lucas. TrJP

Awake, My Heart, to Be Loved. Robert Bridges. GTBS-P; MoAB; MoBrPo; NOBE; OBEV

Awake, my heart's delight, awake. A Fair Melody: To Be Sung by Good Christians. Hans Sachs, *tr. fr. German by* Catherine Winkworth. GePo

Awake, My Lute! C. S. Lewis. FaBoNo

Awake my Lute, daughters of Musick come. Mary Astell. KTR

Awake, my St. John! leave all meaner things. Pope. *Fr.* Essay on Man, An. NAEL-1; NoP; PoEL-3 (Wild Garden, The.) PrIm, *ll.* 1–16

Awake, My Soul! Philip Doddridge. WGRP

Awake, My Soul. Moses ibn Ezra, *tr. fr. Hebrew by* Solomon Solis-Cohen. *Fr.* Wine-Songs. TrJP

Awake, my soul, and with the sun. Morning Hymn. Thomas Ken. NOSC

Awake My Soul, Betimes Awake. Isaac Chanler. AH

Awake, My Soul! In Grateful Songs. Andrew Fowler. AH

Awake, my soul; stretch every nerve. Awake, My Soul! Philip Doddridge. WGRP

Awake, O Lord, Awake Thy Saints. Morgan Llwyd. AngWe

Awake, O rain, O sun, O night. Ending. *Unknown, tr. fr. Hawaiian by* K. Luomala. WTO

Awake! Oh, north wind. Awake! Bible, *O.T. Fr.* Song of Solomon, The. FaPON

Awake, oh you young men of England. Oh You Young Men. George Orwell. FaBoEH

Awake sad heart, whom sorrow ever drowns. The Dawning. George Herbert. ESCV; NOSC

Awake sound sleeper! hark, what dismal knells. Upon the Death of His Much Esteemed Friend Mr. Jno Saffin Junr. Grindall Rawson. SCAP

Awake! The day is coming now. Awake! Walther von der Vogelweide, *tr. fr. German by* Jethro Bithell. AWP

Awake, thou best of sense. Upon the Times. Mildmay Fane, 2d Earl of Westmorland. BeJo

Awake to the cold light. March. Hart Crane. BoNaP

Awake, ye nations, slumbering supine. Sonnets Written in the Fall of 1914. George Edward Woodberry. PAH

Awake yee westerne nymphs, arise and sing. Samuel Danforth. SCAP

Awakened by some fear, I watch the sky. Edgar Bowers. *Fr.* Autumn Shade. VCAP

Awakened War God, The. Margaret Widdemer. WGRP

Awakening. Robert Bly. NaP

Awakening, The. Robert Creeley. NeAP

Awakening, The. Angela Morgan. OHIP

Awakening. H. Cordelia Ray. CBWP-3

Awakening. Lucien Stryk. CAPP; SV

Awakening — / Voices of birds. Nelly Sachs, *tr. fr. German by* Ruth Mead *and* Matthew Mead. PBWP

Awakening from Drunkenness on a Spring Day. Li Po, *tr. fr. Chinese by* Robert Payne. TAL

Awakening/ in a moment of peace. Harriet Kofalk. EaPr

Awakening like return to Earth from Moon. Brian Coffey. *Fr.* Advent. CIP

Awakening of Man, The. Robert Browning. *Fr.* Paracelsus. WGRP

Awakening spring: how many leaves! Willow. Li Shang-yin, *tr. fr. Chinese by* Eugene Eoyang *and* Irving Y. Lo. SuSp

Awaking. Stephen Spender. NYBP

Awaking of the Poetic Faculty, The. George Henry Boker. Son

Award. Ray Durem. BPo; PoBA; TTY

Aware. D. H. Lawrence. BoNaP; MoBrPo; NoAM

Aware Aware. Tram Combs. TwCP

Aware that summer baked the water clear. Skykomish River Running. Richard Hugo. PoA

Aware to the dry throat of the wide hell in the world. King David Dances. John Berryman. ChIV-1; OxBC; OxBSP

Awareness. Don L. Lee. PoBA

Away. Walter de la Mare. NoAM

Away. Max Ehrmann. PoToHe

Away! Robert Frost. NOBA

Away. James Whitcomb Riley. BLRP; WGRP

Away above a Harborful. Lawrence Ferlinghetti. *Fr.* Coney Island of the Mind, A. ErPo

Away above a harborful. Lawrence Ferlinghetti. *Fr.* Pictures of a Gone World. BoLoP; ErPo; PoM

Away! Away! (*LL*) Cold, Cold. *Unknown.* EaPr

Away, away. (*LL*) This Is the Key. *Unknown.* CBNP; CH; FaBoCh; MoShBr; NTP; OxBoLi; Prf

Away, away in the Northland. A Legend of the Northland. Phoebe Cary. OBCA; OBSP

Away! away!/ Tempt me no more, insidious Love. The Complaint. Mark Akenside. OBEV

Away, away! You are safer in the tomb. (*LL*) To a Shade. W. B. Yeats. LiTB; NAEL-2; PoEL-5

Away beyond the Jarboe house. Strange Tree. Elizabeth Madox Roberts. BoNaP; FaPON; GrPl

Away, birds, away! The Bird Scarer. *Unknown.* ReMoGo

Away, Delights. Beaumont *and* Fletcher *and* John Fletcher. *Fr.* Captain, The. EIL; NOBE; OBEV

Away despair; my gracious Lord doth heare. The Bag. George Herbert. ESCV; GeHe; SeCP

Away down deep and away up high. At the Playground. William Stafford. TLR

Away down East, away down West. *Unknown.* TLR

Away down into the shadowy depths of the Real I once lived. Myself. Adah Isaacs Menken. CBWP-1

Away, fear, with thy projects, no false fire. William Alabaster. NoSic

Away, for we are ready to a man! James Elroy Flecker. *Fr.* Golden Journey to Samarkand, The. FaBoRV; NOBE

Away from earth and its cares set free. Eternity. Josephine D. Henderson Heard. CBWP-4

Away from Home. *Unknown.* PWR

Away he bore. (*LL*) Death of the Day. Walter Savage Landor. NoP

Away he goes, the hour's delightful hero. She and the Muse. Denise Levertov. CrSp

Away in a Manger. *At. to* Martin Luther. AH

Away; let nought to Love displeasing. Winifreda. *Unknown.* OBEV

Away loose-reined careers of poetry! Urian Oakes. *Fr.* Elegie upon The Death of the Reverend — . Mr. Thomas Shepard, An. NOCV; SCAP

Away, Melancholy. Stevie Smith. OxBTC; PBWP

Away mine ashes, then thy fire doth glow. (*LL*) The Ebb and Flow. Edward Taylor. AmPP; SCAP

Away the horde rode, in a storm of hail. The Uncertain Battle. David Gascoyne. PoWW

Away! the moor is dark beneath the moon. Stanzas — April, 1814. Shelley. EnRP; OBNC; SCGP (Remorse.) OBEV

Away thou fondling motley humourist. A London Street. John Donne. *Fr.* Satires. NoSic

Away to Canada. Joshua McCarter Simpson. AAP

Away to Twiver, Away, Away! *Unknown.* EIL

Away Vane World. Alexander Montgomerie. NOCV

Away! who overtakes us now shall claim thee for his pains! (*LL*) The Arab to His Favorite Steed. Caroline E. Norton. BeLS

Away with all whimsical bubbles of air. Botany Bay. John Freeth. NOEC

Away with silks, away with lawn. Clothes Do but Cheat and Cozen Us. Robert Herrick. CaPo; ErPo

Away with these self-loving lads. Fulke Greville. *Fr.* Caelica. EnRePo (Of His Cynthia.) EIL; ELP; NoP

Away with you, away with you, James de Grant! James Grant. *Unknown*. ESPB

Away, ye gay landscapes, ye gardens of roses! Lachin y Gair. Byron. OxBS

Aweary Am I. Abu-l-Ala al-Maarri, *tr. fr. Arabic* by R. A. Nicholson. AWP

Awesome are the works of God. The Works of God. Moses ibn Ezra, *tr. fr. Hebrew* by Solomon Solis-Cohen. TrJP

Awesome power. (*LL*) Kali, be with us. May Sarton. EaPr

Awful but cheerful. (*LL*) The Bight. Elizabeth Bishop. FaBoWP; HCAP; NAAL-2; NYBP; RB; VCAP

Awful Lot Was Happening, An. Lawrence Joseph. BAP-89

Awful Mother, The. Susan Griffin. MDDM

Awful shadow of some unseen power, The. Hymn to Intellectual Beauty. Shelley. BLPL; EnRP; FHYEP; HAP; HeIP; ImPo; MeMBP; NAEL-2; NoP; OAEL-2; OBNC; PoE; TOF

Awhile in the dead of the winter. Seasons and Times. William Barnes. NOBVV

Awhile she lay all passive to the touch. An Indian Mother about to Destroy Her Child. James Montgomery. VPP

Awkward and milky and beautiful only to hunger. (*LL*) Potato. Richard Wilbur. CAPP; LiTA; MoAB; TrGrPo

Awkward as evolution of flight itself taxis. The Evolution of the Flightless Bird. Richard Kenney. FoLa

Awkward was she yesterday. The Maiden. Peter Hille, *tr. fr. German* by Jethro Bithell. AWP

Awkwardly. (*LL*) Cold. Dennis Brutus. PeSAV

Awkwardly but alive in the unmeasured womb. (*LL*) Art McCooey. Patrick Kavanagh. CIP

Axe angles, An/ From my neighbor's ashcan. Junk. Richard Wilbur. HAP; NoP; SM; WeW

Axe Handles. Gary Snyder. CAPP; NoAM; PoBeRe; VCAP

Axe has cut the forest down, The. Conquest. Elizabeth J. Coatsworth. (Wilderness Is Tamed, The.) FaPON

Axe-Helve, The. Robert Frost. OxBA

Axe rings in the wood, The. Remembered Morning. Janet Lewis. SoSe; WPE

Axehandle, The. Robert Wells. SCBI

Axes/ After whose stroke the wood rings. Words. Sylvia Plath. HCAP; LCAP; NAAL-2; NALW; PoE; Poetr; VCAP

Axle Song. Mairtin O Direain. BiHa

Axolotl, The. David McCord. FiBHP; OBAL

Ay! (*LL*) Polo. Manuel de Falla. RiWo

Ay: A Gift of Elephants. Mutamociyar, *tr. fr. Tamil* by A. K. Ramanujan. PLW

Ay, ay, Oay — the winds that bend the brier! Tristram's Song. Tennyson. *Fr.* Idylls of the King. FaBoRV

Ay, ay, Sir! Stiddy, Sir! Sou'wes'-b'sou'! (*LL*) A Sea Dialogue. Oliver Wendell Holmes. OBAL

Ay [*or* Aye], besherewe yow [*or* beshrew you!] be [*or* by] my fay. Mannerly Margery Mylk and Ale. John Skelton. AAS; FaBoNo; NAEL-1; NoP

Ay[e], but to die, and go we know not where. Shakespeare. *Fr.* Measure for Measure. OBD; RB

Ay, buzz and buzz away. Dost thou suppose. Luther to a Bluebottle Fly. Eugene Lee-Hamilton. *Fr.* Imaginary Sonnets. Son

Ay! drop the treacherous mask! throw by. Butler's Proclamation. Paul Hamilton Hayne. PAH

Ay: His Hill. Mutamociyar, *tr. fr. Tamil* by A. K. Ramanujan. PLW

Ay, his mother was a mad one. The Sad Boy. Laura Riding. CBNP; RB

Ay, it is fitting on this holiday. Ode in Memory of the American Volunteers Fallen for France. Alan Seeger. PAH

Ay, let it rest! And give us peace. The Gospel of Peace. James Jeffrey Roche. PAH

Ay, man, but a'm dead noo. (*LL*) Johnny Dow [*or* Doo]. *Unknown*. FaBoCo; FaBoEE; FiBHP

Ay me, alas, heigh ho, heigh ho! Thomas Weelkes. FaBoCh; OxBoLi

Ay me, alas! the beautiful bright hair. Canzone: His Lament for Selvaggia. Cino da Pistoia, *tr. fr. Italian* by Dante Gabriel Rossetti. AWP

Ay me, ay me, I sigh to see the scythe afield. A Proper Sonnet, How Time Consumeth All Earthly Things. *At. to* Thomas Proctor. FaBoRV (How Time Consumeth All Earthly Things.) ChTr; EiL (Sic Transit.) TrGrPo

Ay me, how many perils doe unfold [*or* enfold]. Spenser. *Fr.* Faerie Queene, The. FHYEP; OAEL-1

Ay me! whilst thee the shores and sounding seas. Milton. *Fr.* Lycidas. AWP; ChTr; ClHu; EBEV; EBEvV; FHYEP; GTBS; GTBS-P; HAP; ImPo; InPS; JCP; LiTB; NOBE; NoP; NOSC; OAEL-1; OBEV; OxAEP-1; PoEL-3; Poetr; PPP; Prf; PrIm; SCGP; TFi; TrGrPo; UnPo; WGRP

Ay, Oliver! I was but seven, and he was eleven. Echo and the Ferry. Jean Ingelow. EBVV

Ay or Nay? Ralph Schomberg. *Fr.* Judgment of Paris, The. TrJP

"Ay!" said Creep. (*LL*) Old Shellover. Walter de la Mare. BoTP; OxBChV

Ay, shout and rave, thou cruel sea. Herndon. Silas Weir Mitchell. PAH

Ay, so, God be wi' ye! Now I am alone. Shakespeare. *Fr.* Hamlet. NAWM-1; OxAEP-1

Ay, so it is in every brain. To a Young Brother. Maria Jane Jewsbury. OxBChV

Ay, tear her tattered ensign down! Old Ironsides. Oliver Wendell Holmes. AiP; AnAmPo; BLPA; EBEvV; FaBoBe; FaPON; GN; GOA; NAAL-1; PAH; PWR; TAP; TFi

Ay, 'Tis Thus. *Unknown*, *tr. fr. Hebrew* by Israel Zangwill. TrJP

Ay Waukin O. Burns. *See* Simmer's a Pleasant Time.

Ay! we come! we come! (*LL*) On the Horizon. Stephen Crane. MeMAP

Ay, Workman. Stephen Crane. MeMAP

Ay, workman, make me a dream. Ay, Workman. Stephen Crane. MeMAP

Ayaiyaja/ This why, I wonder. It Is Hard to Catch Trout. Piuvkaq, *tr. fr. Eskimo*. WTO

Aye, at that time our days wer but vew. Childhood. William Barnes. NOBVV

Aye, aye, lads, we fought 'em. Off Manilly. Edmund Vance Cooke. PAH

Aye ban a farmer in Minnesota. One Happy Swede. Donna Shwarzrock. SWP

Aye! I am a poet and upon my tomb. And Thus in Nineveh. Ezra Pound. VGW

"Aye, squire," said Stevens, "they back him at evens." How We Beat the Favourite. Adam Lindsay Gordon. CBAP; OtMeF; PeVV

Aye, there it is! It wakes to-night. Emily Brontë. NALW

Aye up at the feast, by Melhill's brow. Melhill Feast. William Barnes. OBNC

Aye! What a thing is the passing of Cronos, the angular-minded. John Cowper Powys. *Fr.* Ridge, The. OBWVE

Ayee! Ai! This is heavy earth on our shoulders. Burying Ground by the Ties. Archibald MacLeish. *Fr.* Frescoes for Mr. Rockefeller's City. GOA; MoAmPo; UnPo

Ayii, Ayii,/ I walked on the ice of the sea. *Unknown*, *tr. fr. Eskimo*. RFM

Ayii, Ayii/ The great sea has set me in motion. *Unknown*, *tr. fr. Eskimo*. RFM

Aylmer's Field, *sels.* Tennyson. Leolin and Edith. GN

Ayn't it all a bloody shyme! (*LL*) It's the Syme the Whole World Over. *Unknown*. AS

Ayohu Kanogisdi. Carroll Arnett.

Azalea, The. Coventry Patmore. *Fr.* Unknown Eros, The. ELP; GBL

Azimuth. Gavin Selerie. NBrP

Aziola, The. Shelley. EBEV

Azouou. Mririda n'Ait Attik, *tr. fr. Berber into French by* René Euloge; *English vers.* by Daniel Halpern *and* Paula Paley. WPOW

Azra. The. Heine, *tr. fr. German* by John Hay. AWP

Azure and Clay. Osip Mandelstam, *tr. fr. Russian* by David McDuff. *Fr.* Armenia. CBCK

Azure and Clay, clay and azure. Azure and Clay. Osip Mandelstam. *tr. fr. Russian* by David McDuff. *Fr.* Armenia. CBCK

Azure, I come! from the caves of death withdrawn. Helen, the Sad Queen. Paul Valéry, *tr. fr. French* by Joseph T. Shipley. AWP

Azure, or Green, or Purple. William Plomer. PeSAV

Azure, or green, or purple when the sun. Azure, or Green, or Purple. William Plomer. PeSAV

Azure sky, An. Christmas. "Mary I." BoTP

Azure Striation Swirls beyond the Stones. Marilyn Hacker. *Fr.* La Fontaine de Vaucluse. Son

Azured [*or* Azur'd] vault, the crystal circles bright, The. James I, King of England. EIL (All These the Lord Did Frame.) CBCK (Heaven and Earth.) ChTr

Azzoomm, azzoomm loud and strong. Riding in an Airplane. Dorothy W. Baruch. FaPON

B

B. Larry Eigner. NeAP

B Flat. Douglas Stewart. FaBoMA

Bad Man Ballad. *Unknown.* AmFP

Bad Morning. Langston Hughes. OBAL

Bad Mother, The. Susan Griffin. CrSp

Bad news has come to town, bad news is carried. Montcalm and Wolfe. *Unknown.* AmFP

Bad Old Days, The. Kenneth Rexroth. NNaP; NoAM

Bad Poetry. Pope. *See* Here she beholds the chaos dark and deep.

Bad quartos were my first love. Bibliographer. Josephine Miles. FaBoWP

Bad Run at King's Rest. Douglas Livingstone. PeSAV

Bad Season Makes the Poet Sad, The. Robert Herrick. BeJo; CaPo; LiTB; NAEL-1; PrIm; SCGP

Bad (she said) was. Hymn To a Woman Under Interrogation. Reiner Kunze, *tr. fr. German by* Ewald Osers. PoSu

Bad Shepherd, The. Gwyneth Lewis. NWP

Bad Sleeper, A. Paul Verlaine, *tr. fr. French by* François Pirou. PeHV

Bad Time for Poetry. Bertolt Brecht, *tr. fr. German by* John Willett *and* Ralph Manheim. PoSu

Badger and the hare, The. *(LL)* The Passing of the Shee. J. M. Synge. BIrV; FaBoEE

Badger ("When midnight comes a host of dogs and men.") John Clare. EnRP; FHYEP; HAP; LiTB; NoP; NU; OAEL-2; PoEL-4; Poetr; PrIm; SCGP; WiR

Sels.
  Badger ("Badger grunting on his woodland track, The"). FaBoVe; FM; InPS

Badger grunting on his woodland track, The. Badger. John Clare. *Fr.* Badger ("When midnight comes a host of dogs and men"). EnRP; FaBoVe; FHYEP; FM; HAP; InPS; LiTB; NoP; NU; OAEL-2; PoEL-4; Poetr; PrIm; SCGP; WiR

Badgers, The. Eden Phillpotts. BoTP

Badman of the Guest Professor. Ishmael Reed. BPo

Badminton. Sir Alfred Comyn Lyall. *Fr.* Studies at Delhi, 1876. OBTV; PeVV

Badminton at Great Barrington, The. Michael Benedikt. PRA

Baedeker for Metaphysicians. Brian Higgins. FaBoTw

Baffled Knight, The. *Unknown.* ESPB

Bag, The. George Herbert. ESCV; GeHe; SeCP

Bag of Tools, A. R. L. Sharpe. BLPA; PoToHe

Bag Woman. Dudley Randall. NoAM

Bagel, The. David Ignatow. CAPP; FF; TwCP

Bagel Shop Jazz. Bob Kaufman. Jaz

Baggot Street Deserta. Thomas Kinsella. CIP; CMoP; IPY; NoAM

Bagpipe Music. "Hugh MacDiarmid." OAEL-2

Bagpipe Music. Louis MacNeice. CMoP; EBEvV; GTBS-P; ImPo; LiTB; LiTM; MoP; NAEL-2; NBLV; NoAM; NOBE; NOBL; NoP; OAEL-2; OBSV; OxBTC; PeLV; PIP; RB; TFi; UV, *abr.*

Bags of Meat. Thomas Hardy. FM; RB

Bags Packed and We Expected This. Ramona Wilson. VoR

Bah! I have sung women in three cities. Cino. Ezra Pound. VGW

Bah! there's not a colour in the bottom of the dish. *(LL)* The Digger's Song. Barcroft Henry Boake. NOBAu

Bahamas. George Oppen. NYBP

Bahá'u'lláh in the Garden of Ridwan. Robert Hayden. PoBA

Baii. Jim Barnes. *Fr.* Four Things Choctaw. HATNAP

Bailey Beareth the Bell Away, The. *Unknown. See* Maidens Came, The.

Bailey Gatzert: The First Grade, 1945. Lonny Kaneko. ETG

Bailiff's Daughter of Islington, The. *Unknown.* ESPB; FaBoBa; GN; OBET; OxBB; OxBoLi

Bailiff's Daughter of Islington, The. *Unknown.* AmFP; ESPB; FaBoBa; GN; OBET; OxBB; OxBoLi

Bairnies cuddle doon at nicht, The. Cuddle Doon. Alexander Anderson. GN

Bait, The. Eric Chock. OpBo

Bait[e], The. John Donne. CBLP; CoGr; ErPo; HoPM; InPK; InPS; LPA; NAEL-1; NOSC; OAEL-1; PoRA; RB; TEP

Baith Gud and Fair and Womanlie [*or* Womanly]. *Unknown.* OxBS

Baith gude and fair and womanly. *(LL)* Baith Gud[e] and Fair and Womanlie [*or* Womanly]. *Unknown.* OxBS

Baits for Various Fish. Thomas Barker. *Fr.* Art of Angling, The. FaBoUs

Baja. Gerald Stern. SV

Bajan Litany. Bruce St. John. PBCV

Bakchos the wine-god/ dissolver of limbs. *Unknown, tr. fr. Greek by* Peter Jay. GrAn

Baked and cleaned. Grandmother. Siv Cedering. PBCAP

Baked the day she suddenly dropped dead. Book Ends. Tony Harrison. *Fr.* School of Eloquence, The. DiPo; NAEL-2; NoAM; SCBI

Baker's Boy, The. Mary Effie Lee Newsome. CDC; ShDr

Baker's boy delivers loaves, The. The Baker's Boy. Mary Effie Lee Newsome. CDC; ShDr

Baker's Dozen of Wild Beasts, A. Carolyn Wells. OBCA
  Sels.
  Bath-Bunny, The.
  Corn-Pone-y, The.
  Cream-Puffin, The.
  Mince-Python, The.

Baker's Duzzen uv Wize Sawz, A. Edward Rowland Sill. FaBoBe

Baker's Tale, The. "Lewis Carroll." *Fr.* Hunting of the Snark, The. CBNP; EBEV; EBEvV, (*Pt.* 1 *only*); FaBoNo; FiBHP, *much abr.*; NAEL-2; OBNC; OBNV; OxAEP-2; PoEL-5

Bakerwoman God. Alla Renee Bozarth. EaPr

Bakerwoman God, remake. *(LL)* Bakerwoman God. Alla Renee Bozarth. EaPr

Balaam. Charles Causley. EBNV

Balaam. John Keble. OBNC

Balaam's Blessing. Bible, *O.T. Fr.* Numbers. TrGrPo

Balaclava. *Unknown.* OBET

Balade: "Hide [*or* Hyd], Absalon, thy gilte tresses clere." Chaucer. *Fr.* Legend of Good Women: Prologue, The. AWP; ChTr; EBEV; EnVB; GBL; HAP; ImPo; NOBE; OAEL-1; OBEV; SCGP
  (Lady without Paragon, A.) MeEL

Balade and Roundel to Master Somer. Thomas Hoccleve. OxBLMV

Balade de Bon Conseill. Chaucer. EnVB; MiEL; SCGP; TrGrPo

Balade Simple. John Lydgate. GBL

Balalaika. Norman Dubie. AmPA

Balance, The. Alma Villanueva. AfAz

Balance. Marilyn Nelson Waniek. NAmP90

Balanced a row of peas on it. My Grandaddy Mostly with His Knife. David Huddle. GrPl

Balankin was as gude a mason. Lamkin. *Unknown.* ESPB

Balboa. Nora Perry. PAH

Balboa, the Entertainer. Amiri Baraka. NoAM

Bald. Bill Zavatsky. UL

Bald-bare, bone-bare, and ivory yellow: skull. The U. S. Sailor with the Japanese Skull. Winfield Townley Scott. ArOW; LiTM

Bald Cavalier, The. *Unknown.* OxBChV

Bald heads forgetful of their sins. The Scholars. W. B. Yeats. CMoP; NoP; OAEL-2; PoA

Balder, *sels.* Sydney Thompson Dobell.
  Chanted Calendar, A. BoTP; OBEV
  (Procession of the Flowers, The.) GN

Balder Dead, *sels.* Matthew Arnold.
  "But when the Gods and Heroes heard, they brought." PeVV
  "Forth from the east, up the ascent of Heaven." PeVV

Baldpate Pond. E. F. Weisslitz. NYBP

Balearic Idyll. Frederick Packard. FiBHP

Baleful phantoms underground, The. *(LL)* Low Barometer. Robert Bridges. CMoP; LiTB; MoP; NoAM; NOCV; OBNC; Poetr; SCGP

Balena, The. *Unknown.* OxBSS

Balgu Song. *Unknown, tr. fr. Balgu by* Clancy McKenna. CBAP

Balin and Balan. Tennyson. *Fr.* Idylls of the King.

Balkis was in her marble town. Lascelles Abercrombie. *Fr.* Judith. MoBrPo

Ball, almost, The. Basketball. Ronald Wallace. PBCAP

Ball is pockmarked & depressable, The. Golf. Matthew Sweeney. IB

Ball of Kirriemuir, The, *sels. Unknown.*
  "Four and twenty virgins." FaBoBl

Ball Poem, The. John Berryman. CoAP; FF; MoAmPo; NoAM; NOBA; NoP; Poetr

Ball will bounce, but less and less, A. Juggler. Richard Wilbur. CMoP; LiTM; MoAB; NYBP; TAP

Ballad: "Altho' a slave me is born and bred." J. B. Moreton. PBCV

Ballad: "As I was walkin' the jungle round, a-killin' of tigers an' time." Guy Wetmore Carryl. BXAP; NBLV

Ballad: "Auld wife sat at her ivied door, The." Charles Stuart Calverley. BXAP; FaBoCo; FiBHP; NBLV; OxAEP-2; UV; WiR

Ballad: "Der noble Ritter Hugo." Charles Godfrey Leland. VPP

Ballad: "He went with another." Gabriela Mistral, *tr. fr. Spanish by* Muriel Kittel. AIW

Ballad: "I put my hat upon my head." Samuel Johnson. CBNP; NOBL; OxAEP-1; UV

Ballad: "I therefore pray thee, Renny dear," Samuel Johnson. OxAEP-1

Ballad: "If the man who turnips cries." Samuel Johnson. OxAEP-1

Ballad: "I'll tell you a story/ concerning John and Joan." Peter Reading. PeLV

Ballad: "It was Earl Haldan's daughter." Charles Kingsley. GN

Ballad: "Knight went down to the river's rim, A." Gerda Mayer. OBSP

Ballad of the Conemaugh Flood, A. Hardwick Drummond Rawnsley. PAH

Ballad of the Cool Fountain. *Unknown, tr. fr. Spanish by* Edwin Honig. BoWoP

Ballad of the Courtier and the Country Clown, A. *Unknown.* CoMu

Ballad of the D-Day Dodgers. *Unknown.* WTO

Ballad of the Dark Ladie, The. Samuel Taylor Coleridge. EnRP

Ballad of the Days of the Messiah. A. M. Klein. TrJP

Ballad of the Despairing Husband. Robert Creeley. NeAP; NoP; OBAL; RaBo; SM

Ballad of the Dreamy Girl. Edith Roseveare, *tr. fr. Chinese.* Mes

Ballad of the Drinker in His Pub. N. P. van Wyk Louw, *tr. fr. Afrikaans by* Uys Krige, Jack Cope, *and* Ruth Miller. PeSA

Ballad of the Electric Eel. Wayne Brown. PBCV

Ballad of the Emeu, The. Bret Harte. NBLV

Ballad of the Ferocious Tiger. Hsü Pen, *tr. fr. Chinese by* Jonathan Chaves. OBAP

Ballad of the Flood. Edwin Muir. MoBS

Ballad of the French Fleet, A. Longfellow. PAH

Ballad of the Frozen Field, The. Dabney Stuart. MT

Ballad of the Gibbet. Villon, *tr. fr. French by* Andrew Lang. AWP

Ballad of the Girl Whose Name is Mud. Langston Hughes. SAmP

Ballad of the Good Lord Nelson, A. Lawrence Durrell. ErPo; FaBoBl; ImPo; LiTM; PeLV

Ballad of the Goodly Fere. Ezra Pound. ChIV-2; CMoP; ImPo; LiTA; LiTM; MeMAP; MoAB; MoAmPo; MoBS; PoRA; TrCP; TrGrPo

Ballad of the Hidden Dragon. *Unknown, tr. fr. Chinese.* WTO

Ballad of the Homing Man, The. Ernest Rhys. AngWe

Ballad of the Hoppy-Toad. Margaret Walker. BlSi; HoPM; NBV

Ballad of the Icondic. John Ciardi. OBAL

Ballad of the Landlord. Langston Hughes. HCAP; NOBA

Ballad of the Late Annie, The. Gwendolyn Brooks. *Fr.* Notes from the Childhood and the Girlhood. LCAP

Ballad of the Little Cart, A. Ch'en Tzu-lung, *tr. fr. Chinese by* Wu-chi Liu. SuSp

Ballad of the Londoner. James Elroy Flecker. EnLoPo

Ballad of the Long-legged Bait. Dylan Thomas. MeMBP

Ballad of the Lords of Old Time. Villon, *tr. fr. French by* Swinburne. AWP; PeVV

Ballad of the Man Who's Gone. Langston Hughes. SAmP

Ballad of the Mermaid. Charles Godfrey Leland. *See* Noble Ritter Hugo, Der.

Ballad of the Morning Streets. Amiri Baraka. SOTW; TTTS

Ballad of the Mouse. Robert Wallace. NYBP

Ballad of the Oedipus Complex. Lawrence Durrell. FaBoCo

Ballad of the Orioles in the Fields. Ts'ao Chih, *tr. fr. Chinese by* Hans H. Frankel. SuSp

Ballad of the Outer Life. Hugo von Hofmannsthal, *tr. fr. German by* Jethro Bithell. AWP; TrJP

Ballad of the Oysterman, The. Oliver Wendell Holmes. AnAmPo; MoShBr

Ballad of the Scarecrow Christ. Elder Olson. ChIV-2

Ballad of the Stonegut Sugar Works. James K. Baxter. PeNZ

Ballad of the Strange and Wonderful Storm of Hail, A. *Unknown.* CoMu

Ballad of the Tempest. James Thomas Fields. AnAmPo; BeLS; BLPL; FaBoBe; PoLF

Ballad of the Ten Casino Dancers. Cecília Meireles, *tr. fr. Portuguese by* James Merrill. BoWoP

Ballad of the Three Spectres. Ivor Gurney. OBWP

Ballad of the Tinker's Wife, The. Sigerson Clifford. IIP; PeIV

Ballad of the Two Tapsters. Vernon Watkins. MoBS

Ballad of the White Horse, The, *sels.* G. K. Chesteron. "Northmen came about our land, The." FaBoEH

Ballad of the Women of Paris. Villon, *tr. fr. French by* Swinburne. AWP

Ballad of the Yorkshire Ripper, The, *sels.* Blake Morrison. "Ower t'ills o Bingley." FaBoVe

Ballad of Trees and the Master, A. Sidney Lanier. AnAmPo; ChIV-2; LiTA; NOBA; OxBA; PoEL-5; PoLF; WGRP

Ballad of Villon and Fat Madge, The. Villon, *tr. fr. French by* Swinburne. FaBoBl; OBVE

Ballad of William Bloat, The. *Unknown.* NOBL; PeLV

Ballad of William Sycamore, The. Stephen Vincent Benét. MoAmPo; PoRA

Ballad of Yukon Jake, The. Edward E. Paramore, Jr. BeLS; BLPA

Ballad on the Taxes, A. *At. to* Edward Ward. OxBoLi

Ballad on the Times, A. *At. to* Edward Ward. *See* Good people, what, will you of all be bereft.

Ballad [*or* Ballade] upon a Wedding, A. (I tell thee, Dick, where I have been.) Sir John Suckling. BeJo; CaPo; CoMu; EBEV; EBNV; FaBoBa; InvP; JCP; NoP; OxBM; SeCP; SeCV-1

Sels.

Bride, The. TrGrPo

Ballad-Singer, The. Thomas Hardy. *Fr.* At Casterbridge Fair. BoLoP

Ballad: Sun Had Grown on Lessening Day, The. John Clare. EnVR

Ballad: Time of Roses. Thomas Hood. *See* It Was Not in the Winter.

Ballad to a Traditional Refrain. Maurice James Craig. BIrV; TIRV

Ballad to Mrs. Catherine Fleming in London from Malshanger Farm in Hampshire, A. The Countess of Winchilsea. ECWP

Ballad to Queen Elizabeth, A. Austin Dobson.

Ballad to the Tune of Bateman, A. Sir Charles Sedley. CoMu

Ballad upon the Popish Plot, A. John Gadbury. CoMu

Ballad Which Anne Askew Made and Sang When She Was in Newgate, The. Anne Askew. NoSic; WPE

Ballad Written for a Bridegroom. Villon, *tr. fr. French by* Swinburne. AWP

Ballade: "Lone am I, and would be." Christine de Pisan, *tr. fr. French by* Tom Vaughan. AIW

Ballade: "Pretty maid she died, she died, in love-bed as she lay, The." Paul Fort, *tr. fr. French by* Frederick York Powell. AWP

(Pretty Maid, The.) OBMV

Ballade: "Tell me where, in what country, where." Villon, *tr. fr. French by* John Frederick Nims. STV

Ballade: "Wisdom, innocently the sun rises." Branko Miljkovic, *tr. fr. Serbo-Croatian by* Charles Simic. HSix

Ballade by the Fire. E. A. Robinson. AnAmPo

Ballade de Marguerite. *Unknown, tr. fr. French by* Oscar Wilde. AWP

Ballade des Belles Milatraisses. Rosalie Jonas. BlSi

Ballade d'une Grande Dame. G. K. Chesteron. OxBoLi

Ballade Made in the Hot Weather. W. E. Henley. MoBrPo

Ballade of Boys Bathing. Frederick William Rolfe. PeHV

Ballade of Dead Actors. W. E. Henley. EBVV; OBMV

Ballad[e] of Dead Ladies. Villon, *tr. fr. French by* Dante Gabriel Rossetti. AWP; CTC; HelL; OBVE; PoRA; PrIm

Ballade of England. Louis MacNeice. NYBP

Ballade of Evolution, A. Grant Allen. EBVV

Ballade of Expansion. Hilda Johnson. PAH

Ballade of Genuine Concern. Hilaire Belloc. EBEvV

Ballade of Good Counsel. Chaucer. *See* Flee from [*or* Fle fro] the press [*or* prees *or* pres] and dwelle with soothfastnesse [*or* sothefastnesse *or* sothfastnesse].

Ballade of Hell and of Mrs. Roebeck. Hilaire Belloc. OBF

Ballad[e] of Ladies' Love, Number Two. Villon, *tr. by* John Payne. ErPo

Ballade of Liquid Refreshment. E. C. Bentley. FaBoCo

Ballade of Lost Objects. Phyllis McGinley. CRP; NBLV; PoRA

Ballade of Sayings. W. S. Merwin. NNaP

Ballade of Suicide, A. G. K. Chesteron. CoGr; FiBHP; NBLV

Ballade of the Armada, A. Austin Dobson. *See* King Philip had vaunted his claims.

Ballade of the Back Road. Ron Block. SM

Ballade of the Grindstones. Judith Johnson Sherwin. SM

Ballade of the Poetic Life. J. C. Squire. OBMV

Ballade of the Scottyshe Kynge, A. John Skelton. CoMu; FaBoBa

Ballade of the Under Side. Don Marquis. *Fr.* Archys Life of Mehitabel. InvP

Ballade of the Women of Paris. Villon, *tr. fr. French by* Philip L. Miller. RiWo

Ballade of Villon to His Love. Villon, *tr. fr. French by* Philip L. Miller. RiWo

Ballade on Eschatology. Sister Mary Madeleva. GoYe

Ballade to His Mistress. Villon, *tr. fr. French by* Norman Cameron. WeW

Ballade to My Psychoanalyst. Kenneth Lillington. FiBHP

Ballade to Rosamund. Chaucer. *See* Madame, ye been [*or* ben] of alle [*or* all *or* al] beautee [*or* beaute] shrine [*or* shryne].

Ballade Tragique à Double Refrain. Max Beerbohm. IHNG; OBSV

Ballade un Peu Banale. A. J. M. Smith. MoCV

Ballade which Villon Made. Donagh MacDonagh. TIRV

Ballade Which Villon Wrote at the Request of His Mother to Pray to Our Lady. Villon, *tr. fr. French by* Philip L. Miller. RiWo

Ballata V: "Light do I see within my Lady's eyes." Cavalcanti, *tr. fr. Italian by* Ezra Pound. CTC

Ballata: Concerning a Shepherd-Maid. Cavalcanti, *tr. fr. Italian by* Dante Gabriel Rossetti. AWP

Ballata: He Reveals, in a Dialogue, His Increasing Love for Mandetta. Cavalcanti, *tr. fr. Italian by* Dante Gabriel Rossetti. AWP

Ballata: He Will Gaze upon Beatrice. Dante, *tr. fr. Italian by* Dante Gabriel Rossetti. AWP

Ballata: His Talk with Certain Peasant Girls. Franco Sacchetti, *tr. fr. Italian by* Dante Gabriel Rossetti. AWP

Ballata: In Exile at Sarzana. Cavalcanti, *tr. fr. Italian by* Dante Gabriel Rossetti. AWP

Ballat o the Hingit. Villon, *tr. fr. French by* Tom Scott. OBVE

Ballat o the Leddies o Langsyne. Villon, *tr. fr. French by* Tom Scott. OBVE

Ballata: Of a Continual Death in Love. Cavalcanti, *tr. fr. Italian by* Dante Gabriel Rossetti. AWP

Ballata: Of His Lady among Other Ladies. Cavalcanti, *tr. fr. Italian by* Dante Gabriel Rossetti. AWP

Ballata: Of True and False Singing. *Unknown, tr. fr. Italian by* Dante Gabriel Rossetti. AWP

Ballata: One Speaks of the Beginning of His Love. *Unknown, tr. fr. Italian by* Dante Gabriel Rossetti. AWP

Ballatetta. Ezra Pound. VGW

Ballet Blanc. Katha Pollitt. SM

Ballet [*or* Ballit] of de Boll Weevil, De. *Unknown.* AS; NOBA

Ballet of the Fifth Year, The. Delmore Schwartz. MoAB; OxBA; TwCP

Ballinderry. *Unknown.* WTO

Balliol Rhymes, sels. *Var. authors.*
"First come I. My name is Jowett." FaBoCo; FaBoEE; ISE; NOBL; PeLV
"I am Branson; Nature's laws." FaBoEE
"I am featly-tripping Lee." FaBoEE
"I am rather tall and stately." FaBoEE; NOBL
"I am the Dean, and this is Mrs. Liddell." FaBoEE
"I am the Dean of Christ Church, Sir." FaBoCo; FaBoEE; NOBL
"I'm the great Sir William Anson." FaBoEE
"My name is George Nathaniel Curzon." FaBoCo; FaBoEE; NOBL; PeLV
"Positivists ever talk in s-/Uch an epic style as Dawkins." FaBoEE

Ballistical student named Raffity, A. D. H. Cudmore. PeLi

Ballit of de Boll Weevil, De. *Unknown.* NOBA

Ballocky Bill the Sailor. Gavin Ewart. *Fr.* Variations and Excerpts. FaBoBl

Balloon, The. Karla Kuskin. PDV

Balloon, The. Mother Goose. *See* What's the news of the day.

Balloon, A! My Daddy brought for me. Surprise. Bible, Apocrypha, *tr. fr. Spanish.* TSaS, *tr. by* Aurelio Major

Balloon Faces. Carl Sandburg. CMoP; PoE

Balloon Man, The. Rose Fyleman. BoTP

Balloon Man, The. E. Herbert. BoTP

Balloon Seller, The. Elizabeth Fleming. BoTP

Balloons. Sylvia Plath. FaBoWP; PoE

Balloons hang on wires in the Marigold Gardens, The. Balloon Faces. Carl Sandburg. CMoP; PoE

Ballot and the Bullet, The. Chris Van Wyk. PeSAV

Ballot, The/ This means voting. The Ballot and the Bullet. Chris Van Wyk. PeSAV

Ballroom Dancing Class. Phyllis McGinley. MoShBr

Balls. Anne MacNaughton. RaBo

Ball's Bluff. Herman Melville. OBWP

Balls in an over, six you know. Aids for Latin. Gordon Perry. FaBoUs

Ballydavid Pier. Thomas Kinsella. BIrV

Ballygrand Widow. Deborah Randell. VBLP

Ballynahinch. George Canning. FaBoCo

Ballyshannon foundered off the coast of Cariboo, The. Etiquette. W. S. Gilbert. FaBoCh; FaBoCo; FiBHP

Balme. Spenser. *Fr.* Faerie Queene, The. CH

Balmoral balconies are tossed in gloom. Death of a Comic Opera Composer. Peter Porter. *Fr.* Baroque Quatrains. AnAn

Balmy as summer. It won't last. Sunday Morning Through Binoculars. Eamon Grennan. PBCIP

Balow, my Babe, weep not for me. The New Balow. *Unknown.* CoMu

Balsham Bells. Kenrick Prescot. NOEC

Balulalow. John James *and* Robert Wedderburn. OBEV

Bam, Bam, Bam. Eve Merriam. PDV

Bambini picking daisies in the new spring grass. Daisies of Florence. Kathleen Raine. NYBP

Bamboo. William Plomer. PeSA

Bamboo. Eric Rolls. NOBAu

Bamboo Branch Song, sels. Liu Yu Hsi, *tr. fr. Chinese.*
"Gorges of Wu are hoary and im in the season of mist and rain, The." SuSp
"Up in the hills are bank on bank of blossoming peach and plum trees." SuSp

Bamboo by Li Ch'e Yun's Window, The. Po Chü-i, *tr. fr. Chinese by* Kenneth Rexroth. OHMPC

Bamboo Elegy: Two. Edmond Yi-Teh Chang. OpBo

Bamboo Shaded Pool, The. Chang Wên-chi, *tr. fr. Chinese by* Kenneth Rexroth *and* Ling Chung. WPC

Bamboo's chill creeps into the chamber. A Tired Night. Tu Fu, *tr. fr. Chinese by* Jan W. Walls. SuSp

Bamboos rustle, the wind in battle array. Written While Lying on My Pillow in the Morning on the Twelfth Day of the Eleventh Month. Fan Ch'eng-ta, *tr. fr. Chinese by* Wu-chi Liu. SuSp

Banana. Charles G. Bell. ErPo

Banana leaves are burning. "Containing Communism." Charlie Cobb. PoBA

Bananas down at the Safeway, The. The High-Class Bananas. Gary Gildner. PBCAP

Bananas ripe and green, and ginger-root. The Tropics in New York. Claude McKay. ArNa; NoAM; PoBA; PoNe; TTY

Banbury Fair. Edith G. Millard. BoTP

Band comes booming down the street, The. Here Comes the Band. William Cole. SiSoPo

Band of Gideon, The. Joseph S. Cotter, Sr. CDC

Band of the bold were gathered together, The. The Parting of the Red Sea. *Unknown, tr. fr. Anglo-Saxon by* Charles W. Kennedy. *Fr.* Exodus. AnOE

Band Played On, The. John F. Palmer. OBAL

Band Played Waltzing Matilda, The. Eric Bogle. OBET

Banded Cobra, The. C. Louis Leipoldt, *tr. fr. Afrikaans by* Uys Krige, Jack Cope, *and* Ruth Miller. PeSA

Bands of black men seem to be drifting in the air. The Sick Man. Wallace Stevens. Jaz

Bands of kings. (*LL*) The Permanent City. Matthew Sweeney. IB

Bandy Legs. Mother Goose. *See* As I was going to sell my eggs.

Bang, bang, bang. The History of the Flood. John Heath-Stubbs. MoBS; NTP; OxBTC

Bangkok. F. R. Scott. MoCV

Baning Summer. Thomas Nashe. *See* Fair summer droops, droop men and beasts therefore.

Banished, dispossessed dead, The. Litany of the Rooms of the Dead. Franz Werfel, *tr. fr. German by* Edith Abercrombie Snow. TrJP

Banished Duke of Grantham, The. *Unknown.* EnSB

Banished Gods, The. Derek Mahon. OxBC

Banishment. Mairi MacLeod, *tr. fr. Gaelic by* Rev. Thomas Pattison. ScCV

Banishment, The. Milton. *See* So spake our Mother Eve, and Adam heard.

Banishment from Ur. Enheduanna, *tr. fr. Sumerian by* W. W. Hallo *and* J. J. A. van Dijk. BoWoP

Banjo, The. Robert Winner. FF

Banjo Player, The. Fenton Johnson. PoNe

Banjo Song, A. Paul Laurence Dunbar. AnAmPo

Bank-manager's rapid signature, A. At the Wrong Door. Christopher Reid. CBLP

Bank may sweat about the debt — I'm on the Gravy Train, The. (*LL*) The Gravy Train. R. R. Davidson. NOBAu

Bank of fine grass and light breeze, A. Night Thoughts aboard a Boat. Tu Fu, *tr. fr. Chinese by* James J. Y. Liu *and* Irving Y. Lo. SuSp

Bank Thief, The. J. R. Farrell. BeLS; BLPA

Bank to bank, the stream is wide. T'ao Ch'ien, *tr. by* Eugene Eoyang. *Fr.* Seasons Come and Go, The. SuSp

Bankers Are Just like Anybody Else, except Richer. Ogden Nash. IHNG; LiTA

Banking Coal. Jean Toomer. PoNe

Bankis of Helicon, The, sels. *Unknown.*
"Declair, ye bankis of Helicon." OxBS

Bankrupt. Cortlandt W. Sayres. PoLF; PoToHe

Banks are empty: not a trace, The. Windstorm on the Han River. Ts'ai Ch'i-chiao, *tr. fr. Chinese.* *Fr.* Han River, The. LHF, *tr. by* Hualing Nieh

Banks fou, braes fou. *Unknown.* GBP

Banks O' Doon, The. Burns. *See* Ye banks and braes o' Bonnie Doon.

Banks of Champlain, The. *Unknown.* AmFP

Banks of Claudy, The. *Unknown.* AmFP; OBET

Banks of Dee, The. *Unknown.* AmFP

Banks of Doon, The. Burns. BoLoP; GTBS; GTBS-P; NOBE; NOEC; OBEV; PrIm; TrGrPo; WBLP

Banks of Newfoundland, The. *Unknown.* GBP

Banks of Newfoundland, The ("Oh may you bless your happy lot that lies secure on shore"). *Unknown.* OxBSS

Banks of Newfoundland, The ("You rambling boys of Liverpool I'll have you to beware"). *Unknown.* OxBSS

Banks of Sacramento, The. *Unknown.* AS

Banks of Sweet Dundee, The. *Unknown.* AmFP

Banks of Sweet Primroses, The. *Unknown.* ELP

Banks of the Condamine, The. *Unknown.* FaBoBa; GBP; NOBAu

Banks of the Gaspereaux, The. *Unknown.* AmFP

Banks of the Nile, The. *Unknown.* OBET
Banks of Wye, The. Robert Bloomfield. OBNC
Sels.
Coracle Fishers, The.
Meandering Wye.
Banneker. Rita Dove. LCAP; NoAM
Banner of England, not for a season, O banner of Britain, hast thou. The Defence of Lucknow. Tennyson. BeLS
Banner of Freedom high floated unfurled, The. The *United States* and *Macedonian*. *Unknown.* PAH
Banner of the Jew, The. Emma Lazarus. AmWP; TrJP
Banquet, The. George Herbert. ESCV; GeHe
Banquet, The. Milton. *Fr.* Paradise Regained [*or* Regain'd]. NOSC
Banquet, A. Sotades, *tr. fr. Greek by* Charles Duke Yonge. FaBoUs
Bantams in Pine-Woods. Wallace Stevens. CMoP; InPS; MeMAP; NoAM; NOBA; OxBA; SAmP; UnPo
Banyan Tree, The. Ts'ai Ch'i-chiao, *tr. fr. Chinese.* LHF, *tr. by* Hualing Nieh
Baobab Fruit Picking; or, Development in Monkey Bay. Jack A. Mapanje. PeSAV
Baptism. Claude McKay. PBCV; PoNe
Baptism. Dale Zieroth. NOBC
Baptist, The. William Drummond of Hawthornden. *See* Last and greatest herald of Heaven's King, The.
Bar, The. *Unknown.* PoToHe
Bar close as you can, and bolt fast too your door. No Lock against Lechery. Robert Herrick. CaPo
Bar Giamaica, 1959-60. Charles Wright. EOEF
Bar is closed and I come, The. Night on Clinton. Robert Mezey. AmPA; NaP
Bar Kochba. Emma Lazarus. TrJP
Bar Light. Ammon Wrigley. UnDi
Bar of steel — it is only, A. Carl Sandburg. *Fr.* Smoke and Steel. AiP
Bar on the Piccola Marina, A. Noël Coward. NBLV
Bar Room Conversation. James K. Baxter. *Fr.* Cressida. PeLV
Bar-Room Matins. Louis MacNeice. NYBP
Barabbas, Judas Iscariot. The Morning After. Dorothy Wellesley. OBMV
Barbadoes. M. J. Chapman. PBCV
Sels.
"Still sparkles here the glory of the west."
"While the noon-lustre o'er the land is spread."
Barbados. Nathaniel Weekes. PBCV
Sels.
"Virtues of the cane must now be sung, The."
"When frequent rains, and gentle show'rs descend."
Barbara Allan ("It was about the Martinmas time.") *Unknown.* EnSB
Barbara Allen. *Unknown.* EBEvV; EBNV
Barbara Allen ("Down in London where I was raised.") *Unknown.* FaBoBa
Barbara Allen ("In London City where once I did dwell.") *Unknown.* BeLS
Barbara Allen ("Twas early in the month of May.") *Unknown.* OBET
Barbara Allen's Cruelty ("All in the merry month of May.") *Unknown.* FaBoBe
Barbara Allen's Cruelty. *Unknown.* See In Scarlet town, where I was born [*or* bound].
Barbara Frietchie. Whittier. AiP; AnAmPo; BeLS; BoTP; CTC; EBNV; FaBoBe; FaBV; FaPON; FaPoR; FF; GN; NOBA; OBAL; OBCA; PAH; PoLF; TFi; TrGrPo; VPP; WBLP
Barbara Palmer, Duchess of Cleveland. The Earl of Rochester. FaBoEH
Barbarian Suite. Marilyn Chin. OpBo
Barbarians. John Fowles. AnAn
Barbarians. Jovan Hristic, *tr. fr. Serbo-Croatian by* Charles Simic. HSix
Barbarossa. Friedrich Rückert, *tr. fr. German by* Elizabeth Craigmyle. AWP
Barbarossa. Hubert Witheford. PeNZ
Barb'd blossoms of the guarded gorse. A Song of Winter. Emily Jane Pfeiffer. OBWVE
Barbecue Service. James Applewhite. MT
Barbed Wire Fence Meditates upon the Goldfinch, A. Don McKay. NOBC
Barber, The. John Gray. NOBVV
Barber, barber, shave a pig. Mother Goose. OxNR; ReMoGo
Barber is cutting the hair, A. Self-Portrait at Thirty-Nine. Ted Kooser. PBCAP
Barber shaved the mason, The. *Unknown.* OxNR
Barber's, The. Walter de la Mare. FaBoNo
Barbie Doll. Marge Piercy. CAPP; NIP; Poetr
Barbie's Ferrari. Lynne McMahon. BAP-90; NAmP90
Barbourville Jail, The. (LL) Down in the Valley. *Unknown.* AS; WTO
Barbra Allen. *Unknown.* See In London City where I once did dwell, there's where I got my learning.

Barbury Camp. Charles Hamilton Sorley. NSI
Barbus Vulgaris. Matt Simpson. PWE
Barcan, its urging windslope in motion. ARCS above OXUS. Colin Simms. NBrP
Bard. Gavin Bantock. FaBoTw
Bard, The. Blake. *See* Hear the voice of the Bard!
Bard, The. Thomas Gray. EnRP; GTBS; GTBS-P; NOBE; NOEC; OAEL-1
Sels.
"Ruin seize thee, ruthless King!" FaBoEH
Bard, The. James Shirley. ErPo
Bard, The. Elizabeth Oakes Smith. AmWP
Bard, The; A Pindaric Ode. Thomas Gray. EnRP; GTBS; GTBS-P; NOBE; NOEC; OAEL-1; OxAEP-1
Bard is buried here, not strong, but sweet, A. The Epitaph of Eusthenes. Edward Cracroft Lefroy, *after the Greek of* Theocritus. *Fr.* Echoes from Theocritus. AWP
Bard of *The Fleece* whose skilful genius made. To the Poet, John Dyer. Wordsworth. EPCY
Bard whom pilf'red pastorals reknown, The. Pope. *Fr.* Epistle to Dr. Arbuthnot. FHYEP; InPS; NoP; OAEL-1; OBSV; OxAEP-1; PoE; PoEL-3; TFi
Bards, The. Walter de la Mare. FaBoNo; NOBL
Bards, The. Robert Graves. MeMBP
Bards falter in shame, their running verse, The. The Bards. Robert Graves. MeMBP
Bard's Family, A. Peruncittiranar, *tr. fr. Tamil by* A. K. Ramanujan. PLW
Bards of passion and of mirth. Keats. EnRP; OBEV
(Ode on the Poets.) GTBS; GTBS-P
(Ode.) FHYEP; OxAEP-2
Bare Almond-Trees. D. H. Lawrence. FaBoPP; FaBoVe; OBTV
Bare Arms of Trees, The. John Tagliabue. Poetsp
Bare branches tremble, The. Tzu Yeh, *tr. fr. Chinese by* Kenneth Rexroth *and* Ling Chung. WPC; WPOW
Bare bulb, a scatter of nails, The. An Ulster Twilight. Seamus Heaney. CIP; PBCIP
Bare Fig-trees. D. H. Lawrence. FaBoVe
Bare-handed, I hand the combs. Stings. Sylvia Plath. NALW; NaP
Bare root of the bean is pink, The. What She Said. Allur Nanmullai, *tr. fr. Tamil by* A. K. Ramanujan. PLW
Bare skin is my wrinkled sack. The Shrouded Stranger. Allen Ginsberg. NeAP
Bare Tree, The. Samuel Menashe. ArNa
Bare trees, The/ alternate. Larry Eigner. PoM
Barefaced baby with the three minute dream. Miss Penelope Burgess, Balling the Jack. Thomas McGrath. BCF
Barefoot and ragged, with neglected hair. On a Fair Beggar. Philip Ayres. EnLoPo
Barefoot Boy, The. Whittier. FaBoBe; GGP; GN; LiTA; OBAL; OBCA; PoLF; WBLP, *abr*
Sels.
"Blessings on thee, little man." FaPON
"Oh for boyhood's painless play." AiP
Barefoot Days. Rachel Field. FaPON
Barefoot I went and made no sound. The Viper. Ruth Pitter. FaBoTw
Barefoot, in unaccustomed clouts or skirts of raw muslin. The New Saddhus. Robert Pinsky. NAmP90
Barefoot is how I always used to be. Was Fun Running 'Round Descalza. Evangelina Vigil. BCF
Barefoot through the bazaar. Sindhi Woman. Jon Stallworthy. OxBC
Barefoot without a stitch she walks. Dance with Banderillas. Richard Duerden. NeAP
Barely a twelvemonth after. Horses, The ("Barely a twelvemonth after.") Edwin Muir. CMoP; GGP; HAP; HeIP; MoBrPo; MoP; NoAM; NOBE; NoP; OAEL-2; OxBTC; PAW; PoE; Poetr; RB; TEP; TRP; WeW
Barely anything to say, everything said. But you break. Michael Palmer. UL
Barely, rarely, comest thou. Shelley. *See* Rarely, rarely, comest thou.
Barely tolerated, living on the margin. Soonest Mended. John Ashbery. HCAP; NAAL-2; Prf; VCAP
Barely twelve years old. In Memory of My Arab Grandmother. Evelyn Arcad Zerbe. WPOW
Bargain. Lizette Woodworth Reese. AmWP
Bargain. The. Sir Philip Sidney. *See* My true love hath my heart, and I have his.
Bargain Sale, A. Samuel Ellsworth Kiser. PoToHe
Barge glided, The. Vision. Israel Zangwill. TrJP
Barge she sat in, like a burnish'd throne, The. Shakespeare. *Fr.* Antony and Cleopatra. EBEvV; SCV

(Cleopatra.) LiTB

(Cleopatra's Barge.) TrGrPo

Barges on the Hudson. Babette Deutsch. WPE

Bark leaps love-fraught from the land, The. The Thousand Islands. Charles Sangster. *Fr.* St. Lawrence and the Saguenay. NOBC

Bark smells like pineapple. Foxtail Pine. Gary Snyder. NaP; NU

Barking sound the shepherd hears, A. Fidelity. Wordsworth. FM

Barks the melancholy dog. Wakeful in the Township. Elizabeth Riddell. NOBAu

Barley-Break, A. Sir John Suckling. CaPo; SeCV-1

Barley-Break; or, Last in Hell. Robert Herrick. CaPo

Barley field/ spreading a brittle wing. The Open Gate. Tracey Herd. NWP

Barley straw's good fodder. *Unknown.* FaBoUs

Barman vaulted the counter, The. A True Story Ending in False Hope. Pearse Hutchinson. PBCIP

Barmenissa's Song. Robert Greene. FaBoRV

Barn, The. Edmund Blunden. MoBrPo

Barn, The. Elizabeth J. Coatsworth. OBCP

Barn, The. Peter Didsbury. PWE

Barn, The. Seamus Heaney. HAP

Barn, The. Stephen Spender. CMoP

Barn Fire. Thomas Lux. LCAP

Barn Owl, The. Jean Follain, *tr. fr. French* by W. S. Merwin. AnRep

Barn Owl. Leslie Norris. AngWe

Barn-yard, The. Sheila Cussons, *tr. fr. Afrikaans* by Johann de Lange. PeSAV

Barney Bodkin broke his nose. *Unknown.* OxNR

Barney Google. Billy Rose. OBAL

Barney McGee! (*LL*) Barney McGee. Richard Hovey. AnAmPo; OBAL

Barney McGee. Richard Hovey. AnAmPo; OBAL

Barney's Invitation. Philip Freneau. PAH

Barns huddle over the horns. November Harvest. Anita Endrezze-Danielson. HATNAP

Barnsley and District. Donald Davie. NoAM; OxBC

Barnyard, The. *Unknown.* AmFP

Barnyard Melodies. Fred Emerson Brooks. OBAL

Baron has decided to make the monster, The. The Bride of Frankenstein. Edward Field. CoAP; HeIP

Baron o [*or* of] Leys, The. *Unknown.* ESPB; OxBB

Baron of Brackley, The. *Unknown.* ESPB, A *and* B *vers.*

Baron of Braikley, The. *Unknown.* OxBB

Baron of Braikley, The. *Unknown.* See Inverey cam doun Deeside, whistlin and playin.

Baron of Buchlyvie. Buchlyvie. *Unknown.* GBP

Baron of Smaylho'me rose with day, The. The Eve of Saint John. Sir Walter Scott. EnRP; PoEL-4

Baron of the sea, the great tropic, A. The Marvel. Keith Douglas. RB

Baron Renfrew's Ball. Charles Graham Halpine. PAH

Barones as burgeises and bondemen als. William Langland. *Fr.* Vision of Piers Plowman, The. FaBoVe

Barones and burgieses and bandemen als. William Langland. *Fr.* Vision of Piers Plowman, Prologue, The. FaBoVe

Baroness Mu Impeded in Her Wish to Help Famine Victims in Wei. Confucius, *tr. fr. Chinese* by Ezra Pound. *Fr.* Yung Wind. CTC

Baron's Last Banquet, The. Albert Gorton Greene, *tr. by* Alice C. Fletcher. AnAmPo; BeLS

Baron's War, The, *sels.* Michael Drayton.
Severn, The. ChTr

Baroque Quatrains. Peter Porter. AnAn
Sels.
Death of a Comic Opera Composer.
Queer Assayers of the Frontier, The.

Baroque Wall-Fountain in the Villa Sciarra, A. Richard Wilbur. AmPP; CAPP; NAAL-2; NoP; NYBP; Poetr; TwCP; VCAP

Barques we ride on over the sea. The Trees. Bill Manhire. PeNZ

Barquisimeto, Venezuela, October 27, 1561. Ai. *Fr.* Gilded Man, The. AnAn

Barracks Apt. 14. Theodore Weiss. CoAP; TAP

Barracks-square, washed clean with rain, The. In Barracks. Siegfried Sassoon. FaBoTw

Barre Lizzy hates. Tom Weatherly. UL

Barred owls scream in the black pines, The. Owls. Louise Erdrich. TRP

Barrel Organ, The. Daniel Mark Epstein. *Fr.* Homage to Mallarmé. DiPo

Barrel-Organ, The. Alfred Noyes. BLPL; BoTP; FaBV; MoBrPo; PoRA

Barrel-Organ, The. Arthur Symons. NOBVV

Barrels of blue potato-spray, The. Spraying the Potatoes. Patrick Kavanagh. BIrV; IIP; IPY; NoP

Barren. Rachel, *tr. fr. Hebrew* by L. V. Snowman. TrJP

Barren Poem. Michael Ryan. AmPA

Barren Shore, The. Coventry Patmore. GBL

Barren soil, the evil men, the slag and hideous rot, The. (*LL*) "Rounded Catalogue Divine Complete, The." Walt Whitman. NAAL-1

Barren Soul, A. Joseph Ezobi, *tr. fr. Spanish* by D. I. Friedmann. *Fr.* Silver Bowl, The. TrJP

Barren Spring. Dante Gabriel Rossetti. *Fr.* House of Life, The. EBVV; IMW; NoP; OAEL-2; OBNC; PoEL-5

Barren Tree, The, *sels.* Llewelyn Wyn Griffith.
"From his own solitude to the world unheeding." OBWVE

Barren Woman. Sylvia Plath. OxBSP

Barricade — a wall — a stronghold, A. The Breech. Michael McClure. NeAP

Barricades. Michael S. Harper. PoBA

Barrier, The. Louis Lavater. NOBAu

Barrier stone has rolled away, The. Easter. Edwin L. Sabin. OHIP

Barrier we may neither breach nor overpass, A. (*LL*) The Barrier. Louis Lavater. NOBAu

Barrister's Dream, The. "Lewis Carroll." *See* They sought it with thimbles, they sought it with care.

Barry Island. John Idris Jones. AngWe

Bars. Nicolás Guillén, *tr. fr. Spanish* by Perry Higman. ArLo

Bar's Fight, August 28, 1746. Lucy Terry. BISi; BPo; PoNe

Bars on Eighth Avenue in Harlem, The. Harlem Gallery: From the Inside. Larry Neal. BPo; NBV

Barter. Marie Blake. PoToHe

Barter. Sara Teasdale. FaBV; FaPON; SoSe

Barter. Margaret Widdemer. WGRP

Bartholdi Statue, The. Whittier. PAH

Barthram's Dirge. *Unknown.* FaBoRV

Bartleme Fair. George Alexander Stevens. ELP; NOEC

Bartley Costello, eighty years old. Gaeltacht. Pearse Hutchinson. BIrV; PBCIP

Bartow Black. Timothy Thomas Fortune. AAP

Baruch, *sels.* Bible, Apocrypha.
Path of Wisdom, The. TrJP

Baryshnikov leaps higher than your heart. Ballet Blanc. Katha Pollitt. SM

Bas Bleu, The; or, Conversation, *sels.* Hannah More.
Cold Ceremony. ECWP

Base Details. Siegfried Sassoon. FF; MoBrPo; OxBSP; PeFWW; PIP

Base metal hanger by your master's thigh! One Writing against His Prick. *Unknown.* NOSC

Base Stealer, The. Robert Francis. GoJo; NTCP

Base Words Are Uttered. W. H. Auden. OxBSP

Base words are uttered only by the base. Base Words Are Uttered. W. H. Auden. OxBSP

(Words.) PeLV

Baseball. Frank Dempster Sherman. OBCA

Baseball and Writing. Marianne Moore. BoWoP

Bashert, *sels.* Irena Klepfisz.

Bashful Earthquake, The, *sels.* Oliver Herford.

Bashful young fellow of Brighton, A. E. O. Parrott. PeLi

Basho, coming. The Snow Party. Derek Mahon. CIP; FaBoPV; OxBC; PBCIP; PNI; SCBI

Basia, *sels.* Johannes Secundus, *tr. fr. Latin* by Thomas Stanley.
"Not alwayes give a melting kiss." OBVE

Basic. Ray Durem. PoNe

Basic Con, The. Lew Welch. PoBeRe

Basil. Gibbons Ruark. MT

Basket-Maker's Song, The. Thomas Dekker *and others. See* Art thou poor, yet hast thou golden slumbers?

Basket of dirty clothes, A. Repetition of Words and Weather. Ruth Stone. BoWoP

Basket Of Summer Fruit, A. Charles Harpur. NOBAu

Basketball. Ronald Wallace. PBCAP

Baskets of ripe fruit in air. Gardener Janus Catches a Naiad. Edith Sitwell. MoAB; MoBrPo

Bass Culture. Linton Kwesi Johnson. PBCV

Basta! D. H. Lawrence. CBLP

Bastard, The, *sels.* Richard Savage.
"In gayer hours, when high my fancy ran." NOEC; OBSV

Bastard from the Bush, The. *Unknown.* NOBAu

Bastard God!, A. (*LL*) To the Christians. Francis Lauderdale Adams. ChIV-2; OxBS; WGRP

Bastille Day. Maxine Cassin. *Fr.* Three Love Poems by a Native. Jaz

Bat, The. Ted Hughes. OBAP

Bat, The. Jane Kenyon. CrSp

Bat. D. H. Lawrence. GTBS-P; HAP; OAEL-1; OAEL-2; OBTV

Battle of Gettysburg, The. Stephen Vincent Benét. *Fr.* John Brown's Body. BeLS

Battle of Harlaw, The. *Unknown.* ESPB

Battle of Harlaw, The (B *vers.*). *Unknown.* ESPB

Battle of Hohenlinden, The. Thomas Campbell. *See* On Linden, when the sun was low.

Battle of India and Europe. Aleksei Kruchenykh, *tr. fr. Russian by* Vladimir Markov. CBNP

Battle of Ivry, The. Macaulay. *See* Now glory to the Lord of Hosts, from whom all glories are!

Battle of King's Mountain, The. *Unknown.* PAH

Battle of La Prairie, The. William Douw Schuyler-Lighthall. PAH

Battle of Lake Champlain, The. Philip Freneau. PAH

Battle of Lookout Mountain, The. George Henry Boker. PAH

Battle of Lovell's Pond, The. Longfellow. PAH

Battle of Maldon, The. *Unknown, tr. fr. Anglo-Saxon by* Charles W. Kennedy. AnOE, *tr. by* Kevin Crossley-Holland; OAEL-1, *tr. by* Kevin Crossley-Holland; OBWP, *tr. by* Kevin Crossley-Holland

Battle of Maldon, The. *Unknown, tr. fr. Anglo-Saxon by* Kevin Crossley-Holland. FaBoEH

Battle of Maldon, The. *Unknown, tr. fr. Anglo-Saxon by* Kevin Crossley-Holland. ASW; OBWP

Battle of Manila, The. Richard Hovey. PAH

Battle of Monmouth, The. Thomas Dunn English. PAH

Battle of Monmouth, The. "R. H." PAH

Battle of Morris' Island, The. *Unknown.* PAH

Battle of Murfreesboro, The. Kinahan Cornwallis. PAH

Battle of Muskingum; or, The Defeat of the Burrites, The. William Harrison Safford. PAH

Battle of Naseby, The. Macaulay. FaBoEH; OtMeF; OxAEP-2

Battle of Navarino, The. *Unknown.* CoMu

Battle of New Orleans, The. Thomas Dunn English. PAH

Battle of New Orleans, The. *Unknown.* AmFP

Battle of Oriskany, The. Charles D. Helmer. PAH

Battle of Otterbourne, The, *sels. Unknown.*
Fey. OtMeF, C *vers.*

Battle of Otterburn [*or* Oterborne], The. *Unknown.* ESPB; IBB, *sl. diff.*; OxBS; ScCV, *sl. diff.*

Battle of Philiphaugh, The. *Unknown.* ESPB

Battle of Plattsburg, The. *Unknown.* PAH

Battle of Plattsburg Bay, The. Clinton Scollard. PAH

Battle of Queenstown, The. William Banker, Jr. PAH

Battle of Sedgemoor. Come and bring your friends. Return to Sedgemoor. Patricia Beer. PAW

Battle of Shiloh, The. *Unknown.* AmFP

Battle of Similes. *Malay Oral Tradition, tr. by* R. J. Wilkinson *and* R. O. Winstedt. WTO

Battle of Sole Bay, The. *Unknown.* GBP

Battle of Somerset. Cornelius C. Cullen. PAH

Battle of Stonington on the Seaboard of Connecticut, The. Philip Freneau. PAH

Battle of the Baltic. Thomas Campbell. EnRP; FaPoR; GN; GTBS; GTBS-P; OBEV

Battle of the *Bonhomme Richard* and the *Serapis.* Walt Whitman. *See* Would You Hear of an Old-Time [*or* Old-Fashioned] Sea Fight?

Battle of the Cowpens, The. Thomas Dunn English. PAH

Battle of the Falkland Isles. I. C. NSI

Battle of the Frogs and Mice, The, *sels.* Formerly at. to Homer, *tr. fr. Greek by* Thomas Parnell.
"Ascend my shoulders, firmly keep thy seat." OBVE

Battle of the Kegs, The. Francis Hopkinson. AnAmPo; OBAL

Battle of the King's Mill. Thomas Dunn English. PAH

Battle of the Lake Regillus, The, *sels.* Macaulay.
Death of Herminius, The. OtMeF
Fight in the Centre, The. OtMeF

Battle of the Stars. Adah Isaacs Menken. CBWP-1

Battle of Tippecanoe, The. *Unknown.* PAH

Battle of Trenton, The. *Unknown.* PAH

Battle of Valparaiso, The. *Unknown.* PAH

Battle of Waun Gaseg, The. Llywelyn ab y Moel, *tr. fr. Welsh by* H. Idris Bell. OBWVE

Battle of Wills Disguised, A. Marge Piercy. HeIP

Battle on the Blackbird's Field, The. Vasco [*or* Vasko] Popa, *tr. fr. Serbo-Croatian. Fr.* Blackbird's Field, The. PoSu, *tr. by* Anne Pennington

Battle [*or* Battel] of the Summer-Islands, The, *sels.* Edmund Waller.
"Aid me Bellona, while the dreadful fight." BeJo; SeCV-1

Battle Pledge. *Somali Oral Tradition, tr. by* M. Laurence. WTO

Battle Problem. William Meredith. NYBP

Battle rent a cobweb diamond-strung, The. Range-finding. Robert Frost. MoP; NIP; NoAM; NoP; OBWP; Poetr; RB

Battle Report. Bob Kaufman. Jaz; TTY

Battle Royal between Dr. Sherlock, Dr. South, and Dr. Burnet, The. William Pittis. APAS

Battle Scene. Aricil Kilar, *tr. fr. Tamil by* A. K. Ramanujan. PLW

Battle Song. Ebenezer Elliot. OxAEP-2

Battle Song. Macuilxochitl, *tr. fr. Nahuatl Indian by* Catherine Rodriguez-Nieto. WPOW

Battle Song. Shaka, King of the Zulus, *tr. fr. Zulu by* Henry Francis Fynn. PeSAV

Battle Song. Robert Burns Wilson. PAH

Battle-Song of the *Oregon. Wallace Rice. PAH*

Battle Songs of the King Tshaka. *Unknown, tr. fr. Zulu.* PeSA

Battle waged strong, The. The Release. Adah Isaacs Menken. CBWP-1

Battle Within [*or* Who Shall Deliver Me?], The. Christina Rossetti.

Battle Won Is Lost. Phillip William George. GrPl

Battledore. John Gray. NOBVV

Battlefield. Richard Aldington. OBWP

Battlefield. August Stramm, *tr. fr. German by* Michael Hamburger. PeFWW

Battle's set 'twixt Envy, Greed, and Pride, The. On a General Election. W. B. Yeats. IHNG

Battling to the death for what is his. (*LL*) Gamecock. James Dickey. HoPM; UnPo

Battue of Berlin, The, *sels.* Harry Graham.
"It was a winter's morning." UV

Batuschka. Thomas Bailey Aldrich. AnAmPo

Batyushkov. Osip Mandelstam, *tr. fr. Russian by* W. S. Merwin *and* Clarence Brown. OBVE

Baucis. Erinna, *tr. fr. Greek by* Richard Garnett. AWP

Baucis and Philemon. Dick Davis. SCBI

Baucis and Philemon. Katherine Hoskins. PoA

Baucis and Philemon. Ovid, *tr. fr. Latin by* Dryden. *Fr.* Metamorphoses. NOSC

Baucis and Philemon; Imitated from the Eighth Book of Ovid. Swift. GN; NOEC; OAEL-1

Baudelaire. Delmore Schwartz. TwCP; VGW

Baudelaire in Brussels. Anthony Cronin. BIrV

Baudelaire took the train. Radiant Silhouette III. John Yau. OpBo

Bavarian Gentians. D. H. Lawrence. CMoP; FaBoCh; FaBoMo; GoJo; GTBS-P; HAP; ImPo; InPK; InPS; LiTB; MeMBP; MoP; NAEL-2; NoAM; NOBE; NoP; OAEL-2, 2 *ver.*; PoE; Poetr; SOTW; TFi; TRP; TTTS

Baxter Bickerbone of Burlington. On Learning to Adjust to Things. John Ciardi. OBCA

Bay, The. James K. Baxter. PeNZ

Bay Fight, The. Henry Howard Brownell. PAH

Bay is cold, heavy under a north wind, The. Whitecaps. Betsy Sholl. CrSp

Bay is not blue but somber yellow, The. Self-Criticism in February. Robinson Jeffers. AmPP

Bay of Biscay, The. *Unknown.* AmFP

Bay of Tsunu, The. Hitomaro, *tr. fr. Japanese by* Kenneth Rexroth. UnAS

Bay Poem. Lance Henson. VoR

Bay Psalm Book, The, *sels. Unknown.*
"Heavens doe declare/ The majesty of God, The." SCAP
"I to the hills lift up mine eyes." OBCA
"Lord to me a shepherd is, The." OBCA
"O Blessed man, that in th'advice." SCAP
"O Give yee thanks unto the Lord." SCAP
"O Thou my soule, Jehovah blesse." SCAP

Bay steed of your stable could not be caught in a portrait, The. A Song of the Bay Steed of Governor Wei. Ts'en Shen, *tr. fr. Chinese by* Daniel Bryant. SuSp

Bayonne Turnpike to Tuscarora. Allen Ginsberg. NNaP

B.C. William Stafford. FoLa

BC:AD. U. A. Fanthorpe. OBCP

Be a gardener. Julian of Norwich. EaPr

Be a loafer/ Wash off the dust of fame and gain in the vast waves. Lu Chih, *tr. by* Sherwin S. S. Fu. *Fr.* Tune: "Pleasure in Front of the Hall." SuSp

Be a workhouse grave. (*LL*) Little Willie. Gerald Massey. VPP

Be Absolute for Death. Shakespeare. *Fr.* Measure for Measure. FaBoRV

Be against all sorts of mortmain. (*LL*) Commission. Ezra Pound. BoLoP; OPOP; TwCP

Be ahead of all parting, as though it already were. Rainer Maria Rilke, *tr. fr. German. Fr.* Sonnets to Orpheus. EnlH

Be always in time. *Unknown.* OxNR

Be assured, the Dragon is not dead. Vanity. Robert Graves. GTBS-P

Be Attentive. Natan Zach, *tr. fr. Hebrew by* Peter Everwine *and* Shulamit Yasny-Starkman. PoSu

Be-Bop Boys. Langston Hughes. OBAL

Be Born a Saint. Pearse Hutchinson. PBCIP

Be born a saint; or keep. Be Born a Saint. Pearse Hutchinson. PBCIP

Be Careful. *Unknown.* NBLV

Be Careful. Natan Zach. PoSu

Be careful! Be careful! Ome Shushiki, *tr. fr. Japanese by* Kenneth Rexroth *and* Ikuko Atsumi. WPJ

Be careful. Open your life. Be Careful. Natan Zach. PoSu

Be careful, then, and be gentle about death. All Souls' Day. D. H. Lawrence. OBD

Be careful what/ You say or do. Zoo Manners. Eileen Mathias. BoTP

Be cheerful, sir: Shakespeare. *Fr.* Tempest, The. EnlH; OAEL-1

Be composed — be at ease with me — I am Walt Whitman. To a Common Prostitute. Walt Whitman. MoAmPo

Be Cool, Baby. Rob Penny. PoBA

Be Daedalus. Nanina Alba. PoBA; PoNe

Be dark enough thy shades, and be thou there content. *(LL)* Did I my lines intend for public[k] view. The Countess of Winchilsea. NAEL-1; NALW; WPOW

Be Different [*or* Deferent] to Trees. Mary Carolyn Davies. FaPON; OHIP

Be dumb ye infant chimes, thump not the metal. Great Tom. Richard Corbett [*or* Corbet]. OxBoLi

Be ever meek and humble, nor essay. The Meek and the Proud. Abraham ibn Chasdai, *tr. fr. Hebrew by* J. Chotzner. TrJP

Be extra careful by this door. The Whisperer. Mark Van Doren. MoAmPo

Be found a gem on God's great sorting table. *(LL)* Epitaph on a Diamond Digger. Albert Brodrick. PeSAV

Be Frugal. Richard Church. OxBSP; OxBTC

Be glad, of all maidens floure. *Unknown.* MiEL

Be glaid, al ye that luvaris bene. Four May Poems: "Be glaid, al ye that luvaris bene." *Unknown.* OxBS

Be Glorified Eternally. Balthasar Hoffman, *tr. fr. German by* Sheema Z. Buehne. AH

Be gone, have done! Down, wanton, down! *(LL)* Down, Wanton, Down! Robert Graves. BoLoP; CBLP; CMoP; ErPo; FaBoBl; FaBoTw; HeIP; InPK; LiTM; MeMBP; MoP; NAEL-2; NoAM; NoP; OAEL-2; PoE; Poetr; TEP

Be good. For Starters. Victoria McCabe. CRP

Be good to those who come after us. *(LL)* Eavesdropper. Breyten Breytenbach. PeSAV

Be governour baith guid and gratious. To the Queen. Lord Darnley. OxBS

Be happy for me, girls,/ my mother-in-law is dead! *Unknown*, *tr. fr. Arabic by* Willis Barnstone. BoWoP
(Traditional Women's Song of Algeria.) IMW

Be his memory forever green and rich. Baal Shem Tov. A. M. Klein. TrJP

Be Hopeful. Strickland W. Gillilan. PoToHe

Be hopeful, friend, when clouds are dark and days are. Be Hopeful. Strickland W. Gillilan. PoToHe

Be horrid Chimpanzees to-day. *(LL)* The Chimpanzee. Oliver Herford. FaBV; FiBHP

Be hushed, all voices and untimely laughter. A Dead March. Mary C. Gillington. PeVV

Be in me as the eternal moods. Doria. Ezra Pound. MoAB; MoAmPo

Be it right or wrong, these men among. The Nut-brown Maid. *Unknown.* NoSic; OBEV

Be it so, for I submit; his doom is fair. Milton. *Fr.* Paradise Lost. EPCY; NAWM-1

Be Judge your self, I'll bring it to the test. The Earl of Rochester. *Fr.* Satire [*or* Satyre] against [Reason and] Mankind, A. NoP; NOSC; OAEL-1; OBSV; PlP; PoEL-3; SCV; SeCV-2
(On Man.) IHNG

Be just (domestick monarchs) unto them. George Alsop. SCAP

Be Kind. Margaret Courtney. PoToHe

Be kind and tender to the Frog. The Frog. Hilaire Belloc. FaBoBe; FaBV; FaPON; FiBHP; GoJo; MoShBr; NTCP; OxBChV

Be kind, good sir, and I'll lift my sark. Confucius, *tr. fr. Chinese by* Ezra Pound. *Fr.* Songs of Cheng. CTC

Be kind to her. To End Her Fear. John Freeman. OBMV

Be kind to me. Sappho, *tr. fr. Greek by* Mary Barnard. PeHV

Be kind to the three babes I've born to thee. *(LL)* Jamie Douglas. *Unknown.* ESPB

Be kind to thy father: for when you were young. Be Kind. Margaret Courtney. PoToHe

Be kind to yourself, it is only one. Who Be Kind To. Allen Ginsberg. NNaP

Be less like the wild gods, love. *(LL)* From You I Have Understood. Eunice De Souza. VBLP

Be life what it has been, and let us hold. To His Wife. Ausonius, *tr. fr. Latin by* Terrot Reaveley Glover. AWP

Be like a tree in pursuit of your cause. *Unknown.* EaPr

Be like the Bird. Victor Hugo, *tr. fr. French.* FaPON; Spl

Be, like the wind that fans it, free. *(LL)* The Abolitionist Hymn. *Unknown.* SWP

Be literal a moment. Recollect. Seamus Heaney. *Fr.* Crossings. BAP-90

Be mean with an onion. Recipe: Pastime for the Unemployed. Tom Pickard. NBrP

Be Merry. *Unknown.* RB

Be near me when my light is low. Be Near Me (When My Light Is Low). Tennyson. *Fr.* In Memoriam A. H. H. EBVV, *abr.*; EBVVPR; ELP; EnVR; HAP; HeIP; LiTB; MeMBP; NOCV; NoP; OAEL-2, *abr.*; PeECV, *abr.*; PoEL-5; SCGP; SCV

Be near to me, O white shadowless Light of my soul's swift venture. Psalm to the Holy Spirit. A. M. Sullivan. TrPWD

Be Never Discouraged. Daniel C. Colesworthy. PWR

Be not afeard: the isle is full of noises. Shakespeare. *Fr.* Tempest, The. OAEL-1; OxAEP-1; RB
(To Dream Again.) IHNG

Be not afraid of every stranger. A Spell. George Peele. *Fr.* Old Wives' [*or* Wife's] Tale, The. ChTr

Be not afraid of my body. *(LL)* As Adam Early in the Morning. Walt Whitman. ChIV-1; OxBA; SAmP

Be not dismayed, whate'er betide. God's Goodness. C. D. Martin. WBLP

Be not frighted with our fashion. All Your Fortunes We Can Tell Ye. Ben Jonson. *Fr.* Gypsies Metamorphosed, The. ChTr

Be not proud, but now incline. The Changes to Corinna. Robert Herrick. JCP

Be not proud of your sweet body. *Gond Oral Tradition*, *tr. by* V. Elwin *and* S. Hivale. WTO

Be Not Silent. David ben Meshullam, *tr. fr. Hebrew.* TrJP

Be not thou so foolish nice. Invitation to Dalliance. *Unknown.* FaBoEE

Be not too certain, life! The Hill. Horace Holley. WGRP

Be not too wise, nor too foolish. Instructions of King Cormac. King of Cashel Cormac. PoToHe

Be of good cheer, spirit of Myrrha! To a Courtesan a Thousand Years Dead. Paul Eldridge. PoA

Be Off! Stevie Smith. OxBC

Be on guard — keep alert and vigilant! *(LL)* Twilight. Joseph Freiherr von Eichendorff. RiWo

Be one, and one anothers All. *(LL)* Lovers' Infiniteness[e]. John Donne. EIL; ESCV; LiTB; MeLP; NOSC; OAEL-1; PoEL-2; SeCP; SeCV-1

Be Patient. "George Klingle." PoToHe

Be, patient, Morning Star, with Love; though close. Macedonius, *tr. fr. Greek by* Adrian Wright. GrAn

Be patient, solemn nose. Precious Five. W. H. Auden. PeECV

Be peace the crowning gem. *(LL)* O Beautiful, My Country. Frederick L. Hosmer. AH

Be pitiful, my God! Mea Culpa. "Ethna Carbery." TrPWD

Be plain in dress and sober in your diet. Lady Mary Wortley Montagu. FaBoEE

Be praise and glory evermore. *(LL)* Old Hundredth. William Kethe. FaPoR

Be praised, my God, by all your creation which tells of new life. *(LL)* Be praised, my God, by butterfly and dragonfly wings exercising. Mary Goergen. EaPr

Be praised, my God, by butterfly and dragonfly wings exercising. Mary Goergen. EaPr

Be praised my lord with all your creatures. St. Francis of Assisi. EaPr

Be Present at Our Table, Lord. *At. to* John Cennick. BLRP

Be proud as Spaniards! Leap for pride ye fleas! On Donne's Poem "To a Flea." Samuel Taylor Coleridge. FM

Be punctual then to know. *Unknown. Fr.* Art of Wenching, The. NOEC

Be Quiet, Sir! *Unknown.* ErPo

Be, rather than be called, a child of God. On an Infant Which Died before Baptism. Samuel Taylor Coleridge. OBD

Be reasonable, my pain, and think with more detachment. Inward Conversation. Baudelaire, *tr. fr. French by* Robert Bly. InPK

Be reckon'd but with herbs and flowers! *(LL)* The Garden. Andrew Marvell. AWP; BLPL; ClHu; ESCV; GeHe; HAP; ImPo; InPS; InvP; JCP; LiTB; MeLP; NAEL-1; NIP; NOBE; NoP; NOSC; OAEL-1; PoE; PoEL-2; Poetr; PoLF; PoRA; PPP; SCGP; SeCP; SeCV-1; TEP; TFi; TOF; TrGrPo; TRP

Be Sad, My Heart. Francis Quarles. NIP

Be satisfied — or I shall find a worse. (*LL*) Aesop's Fable of the Frogs. La Fontaine. OBVE

Be seated, pray. "A grave appeal?" A Virtuoso. Austin Dobson. PeVV

Be Seeing You. Vasco [*or* Vasko] Popa, *tr. fr. Serbo-Croatian.* Fr. Raw Flesh. PoSu, *tr. by* Anne Pennington

Be silent, you still music of the spheres. On a Gentlewoman that Sung and Played upon a Lute. William Strode. NOSC

Be so ashamed of thee. (*LL*) What soft — Cherubic Creatures. Emily Dickinson. AmPP; HAP; MeMAP; MoAB; MoAmPo; NALW; WPE

Be Still. William Ward Ayer. BLRP

Be still: be still: nor dare. A Holy Hill. "Æ." AWP

Be Still Heart. Nilene O. A. Foxworth. AIW

Be still, my soul, be still; the arms you bear are brittle. A. E. Housman. *Fr.* Shropshire Lad, A. FaPoB; MoAB; MoBrPo; NOBVV; OAEL-2; OBNC; SCGP; TrGrPo

Be still O green cliffs of the Dryads. Inscription for a Statue of Pan. *Unknown, tr. fr. Greek by* Dudley Fitts. GrAn

Be still, refrain thyself, and wait. (*LL*) Put forth thy leaf, thou lofty plane. Arthur Hugh Clough. EBEV; EnVR

Be still, sweet babe, no harm shall reach thee. To an Unborn Infant. Isabella Kelly. ECWP

Be Still. The Hanging Gardens Were a Dream. Trumbull Stickney. LiTA

Be still, while the music rises about us: the deep enchantment. At a Concert of Music. Conrad Aiken. MoAB; MoAmPo

Be Strong. Maltbie D. Babcock. AH; BLPA; FaBoBe; PWR; SoSe; WBLP

Be sure you paint. Alluding to the One-armed Bandit. D. C. Berry. BXAP

Be Swift O Sun. R. A. K. Mason. PeNZ

Be Thankful unto Him. Bible, *O.T., paraphrased by* Sir Thomas Wyatt. *See* Make a joyful noise unto the Lord, all ye lands.

Be the Best of Whatever You Are. Douglas Malloch. BLPA

Be the mistress of my choice. What Kind of Mistress He Would Have. Robert Herrick. CaPo; TrGrPo

Be then your counsels, as your subject, great. To the Federal Convention. Timothy Dwight. PAH

Be thou at peace this night. Edward Davison. CH

Be Thou My Guide. Florence Earle Coates. TrPWD

Be thou my vision, O Lord of my heart. *Unknown, tr. fr. Irish by* Eleanor Hull. TIRV

Be thou praised, my Lord, with all Thy creatures. Praise of Created Things. St. Francis of Assisi. FaPON

Be thou then my beauty named. Thomas Campion. AAS

Be told with truth save New south Wales? (*LL*) There Is a Place in Distant Seas. Richard, Archbishop Whately. NOBAu

Be True [*or* Be True Thyself]. Horatius Bonar. FaBoBe; GN; PWR

Be True to Your Condition in Life. John Audelay [*or* Awdelay]. MeEL

Be Useful. George Herbert. GN

Be wary, lad; the road up which you go. To a Negro Boy Graduating. Eugene T. Maleska. PoNe

Be what you were than what you are. (*LL*) Epigram: On a Slanderer. Martial. PeHV

Be wise as thou art cruel; do not press. Shakespeare. *Fr.* Sonnets. NoSic

Be with me, Beauty, for the fire is dying. On Growing Old. John Masefield. CMoP; ImPo; LiTB; LiTM; MoAB; MoBrPo; PoLF; PoRA

Be With Me, Lord. George Macdonald. *Fr.* Diary of an Old Soul. TrCP

Be with me, Luis de San Angel, now. Ave Maria. Hart Crane. *Fr.* Bridge, The. LiTA; NAAL-2; NoAM; NOBA

Be with us, Lord, at eventide. Grace at Evening. Edwin McNeill Poteat. TrPWD

Be You. Norman Jordan. NBV

Be you all pleased? Your pleasures grieve me not. Mary Sidney Wroth, Countess of Montgomery. *Fr.* Urania. NOSC; WPE

Be you to others kind and true. Our Saviour's Golden Rule. Isaac Watts. OxBChV

Be your highest good. (*LL*) Woman's Love and Life. Adelbert von Chamisso. RiWo

Be your words made, good sir, of Indian ware. Sir Philip Sidney. *Fr.* Astrophel and Stella. AAS; ESo, *sl. abr.*; GGP; HeIL, *Sonnets, I–CVIII and 11 Songs*; NoSic; Poetr; SCGP, *Sonnets, I–CVIII and 11 Songs*; SiPS, *Sonnets, I–CVIII and 11 Songs*; SiPSBD, *Sonnets, I–CVIII and 11 Songs*

Beach, The. Robert Graves. OxBSP

Beach, The. Peter Scupham. SCBI

Beach Burial. Kenneth Slessor. CBAP; FaBoMA; PAW

Beach Glass. Amy Clampitt. FaBoWP; NoAM; VCAP

Beach Homos, The. Forrest Anderson. PeHV

Beach in August, The. Weldon Kees. VGW

Beach on Aegina is a bit tawdry, although, The. Happening on Aegina. John Logan. CAPP

Beach Talk. Norman MacCaig. PoA

Beachcomber. George Mackay Brown. NTP; OxBC

Beaches, The, *sels.* "Robin Hyde."
"Close under here, I watched two lovers once." FaBoWP; PeNZ
"Cool and certain, their oars will be lifted in dusk." PeNZ

Beaches are full of dirty nails after rain. Coming Back. Ellsworth McGranaham Keane. PBCV

Beachy Head, *sels.* Charlotte Smith.
"I once was happy, when, while yet a child." WPE

Beacons from the abode where the Eternal are. (*LL*) Adonais; an Elegy on the Death of John Keats. Shelley. EBEV; EnRP; FHYEP; HoPM; ImPo; MeMBP; NoP; OAEL-2; PoEL-4; TrGrPo

Beadle's Testimony, The. Jerome Rothenberg. NNaP

Beads around/ my neck. African Images. Alice Walker. InPS

Beagles. W. R. Rodgers. FaBoTw

Beaks of Eagles, The. Robinson Jeffers. NOBA

Beale Street. Langston Hughes. PPP

Beams. Audre Lorde. NoAM

Bean Eaters, The. Gwendolyn Brooks. AIW; BlSi; GrPl; HAP; HeIL; HeIP; LCAP; MAT; NALW; NoP; PoBA; PoE; Poetr; PrIm; TAP; TRP; TTY; WeW

Beanfield, The. John Clare. BoTP

Beans, Bacon, and Gravy. *Unknown.* SWP

Beans in blossom with their spots of jet, The. Field Path. John Clare. OxBSP

Beanstalk, Meditated Later, The. Judith Wright. NoAM

Beanstalks, in any breeze, are a slack church parade. The Broad Bean Sermon. Les A. Murray. FaBoMA

Bear, The. Robert Frost. MoAB; MoAmPo; NoAM

Bear, The. Ted Hughes. FaBoMo

Bear, The. Galway Kinnell. CAPP; CoAP; InPS; NNaP; RFM; TAP; TRP; VCAP; VGW

Bear, The. N. Scott Momaday. CDW; HATNAP

Bear: A Totem Dance As Seen by Raven. Peter Blue Cloud. HATNAP

Bear and the Garden Lover, The. Jean De la Fontaine. OBF

Bear and the Squirrels, The. Christopher Pearse Cranch. OBCA

Bear cub, chained and tethered to a stake, A. Squaring the Circle. Louis O. Coxe. NYBP

Bear down under the cliff, A. Gary Snyder. *Fr.* Myths and Texts. HCAP; NaP; NOBA; NU

Bear him, comrades, to his grave. Burial of Barber. Whittier. PAH

Bear Hunt, The. Margaret Widdemer. FaPON

Bear Hunting. Aua, *tr. fr. Eskimo.* WTO

Bear in mind. Catmint. Eric Clough Taylor. CRH

Bear in mind. Drum. Langston Hughes. MoAmPo

Bear it, O matcht unequally, you must. To One Unequally Matched. Walter Savage Landor. CBLP

Bear me to Dictaeus. Acon. Hilda Doolittle ("H. D."). VGW

Bear on the Delhi Road, The. Earle Birney. HeIP; MoCV; NoAM; NOBC; NoP; NYBP; PrIm

Bear part with me most straight and pleasant tree. Morea's Sonnet. Mary Sidney Wroth, Countess of Montgomery. *Fr.* Urania. WPE

Bear puts both arms around the above her, The. The Bear. Robert Frost. MoAB; MoAmPo; NoAM

Bear sleeps in a cellar hole, A. New Hampshire. Donald Hall. LCAP

Bear Song, *sels.* Sándor Rákos, *tr. fr. Hungarian by* Jascha Kessler.

Bear [*or* Bare] that breath[e]s [*or* breaks] the northern blast, The. Upon a Wasp Chilled [*or* Child] with Cold. Edward Taylor. EAP; GGP; NAAL-1; NOBA; NOCV; PoEL-3

Bear Trees, The. Kate Barnes. EaPr

Bear us on to the ultimate night. (*LL*) Exile. Ernest Dowson. BoLoP

Bear went over the mountain, The. Song Without End. *Unknown.* RoPo

Bear who eats with a silver spoon, A. Animal Acts. Charles Simic. LCAP

Bear with me, Master, when I turn from Thee. Edith Lovejoy Pierce. TrPWD

Beard-wagging stick-waving beggarman Cynic, A. Lucianus, *tr. fr. Greek by* Edwin Morgan. GrAn

Bearded Oaks. Robert Penn Warren. LiTM; MoAmPo; MoP; NAAL-2; NoAM; NOBA; PoA; PoE; TAP; TwCP

Bearded Woman, by Ribera, The. Paul Muldoon. BiHa

Bearer of Evil Tidings, The. Robert Frost. MoP; NoAM; SAmP

Bearer of finches and clouds, pale atmosphere. Oxygen. Joan Swift. NYBP

Bearing a lifeless body in his arms. (*LL*) The Abdication of Noman. Richard Henry Stoddard. AnAmPo

With the Green Lute-Ribbon.
Withered Flowers.
Beautiful man and his wife, The. Window Dressing. William Peskett. PNI
Beautiful Meals. T. Sturge Moore. BoTP
Beautiful Melite, in the throes of middle age. Agathias, *tr. fr. Greek by* Sam Hamill. InMo
Beautiful mortals of the glowing earth. Wild Flowers. John Clare. ArNa
Beautiful mother is bending, The. Nativity Song. Jacopone da Todi, *tr. fr. Latin by* Sophia Jewett. OHIP
Beautiful must be the mountains whence ye come. Nightingales. Robert Bridges. CMoP; GGP; ImPo; LiTB; LiTM; MoAB; MoBrPo; NOBE; OAEL-2; OBEV; OBMV; OBNC; SCGP; TFi; TrGrPo; UnPo
Beautiful, my delight. To Be Sung on the Water. Louise Bogan. PrIm; VGW
Beautiful natural blossoms. To a Beautiful Pear Tree. James Wright. HAP
Beautiful Necessity, The, *sels.* Claude Bragdon.
Beautiful Ohio. James Wright. CAPP
Beautiful over all things and human hope. (*LL*) Yes to the Earth. "Sibilla Aleramo." WoWa
Beautiful person awakes, A. Sacrificial Victim. Yoshiyuki Rie, *tr. fr. Japanese by* Kenneth Rexroth *and* Ikuko Atsumi. WPJ
Beautiful place is the town of Lo-yang, A. Lo-yang. Emperor Ch'ien Wen-ti, *tr. fr. Chinese by* Arthur Waley. AWP
Beautiful Railway Bridge of the Silv'ry Tay! William McGonagall. *Fr.* Tay Bridge Disaster, The. UV
Beautiful rain falls, the unheeded angel, The. In Time. Kathleen Raine. WPE
Beautiful Ruined Orchard, The. Daniel Berrigan. FYAP
Beautiful Sea, The. Mary E. Tucker. CBWP-1
Beautiful! Sir, you may say so. Thar is n't her match in the country. Chiquita. Bret Harte. AnAmPo
Beautiful Snow, The. John Whittaker Watson. BLPA; WBLP
Beautiful snow falls on a bed, A. Philip Dacey. SM
Beautiful Soup, so rich and green. "Lewis Carroll." *Fr.* Alice's Adventures in Wonderland.
(Song of the Mock Turtle, The.) UV
(Turtle Soup.) FaBoNo
Beautiful star in heav'n so bright. Star of the Evening. James M. Sayles. UV, *sl. sh. vers.*
Beautiful sun that giveth us light. Beautiful. William Allen Bixler. WBLP
Beautiful Sunday. "Jake Falstaff." BoNaP
Beautiful Swimmer, The. Walt Whitman. PeHV
Beautiful, tender, wasting away for sorrow. Luscious and Sorrowful. Christina Rossetti. PoEL-5
Beautiful thing/ I saw you. William Carlos Williams. *Fr.* Paterson. CMoP
Beautiful Things. Ellen Palmer Allerton. BLPA; PWR; WBLP
Beautiful Toilet, The. Ezra Pound, *after the Chinese.* OBVE
Beautiful, tragical faces. Piccadilly. Ezra Pound. AnAmPo
Beautiful trail, her. (*LL*) Now Talking God. *Unknown.* EaPr
Beautiful Train, The. William Empson. OxAEP-2
Beautiful Urinals of Paris, The. Charles David Wright. MT
Beautiful was the appearance of Cormac in that assembly. Cormac Mac Airt Presiding at Tara. *Unknown, tr. fr. Irish by* Douglas Hyde. BIrV
Beautiful, The! what is not perfect here below. The Beautiful. Mary E. Tucker. CBWP-1
Beautiful Woman. Dale Zieroth. NOBC
Beautiful woman, a cup of wine, and a garden, A. Joy of Life. Moses ibn Ezra, *tr. fr. Hebrew by* Solomon Solis-Cohen. *Fr.* Book of Tarshish, The. TrJP
Beautiful woman, you crown the hours. Beautiful Woman. Dale Zieroth. NOBC
Beautiful World, The. W. Lomax Childress. OHIP
Beautiful you rise upon the horizon of heaven. The Hymn to the Sun. Akhenaton, *tr. fr. Egyptian by* J. E. Manchip White. ArNa, *sh. vers.*; TTY
Beautiful Young Nymph Going to Bed, A. Swift. ECEV; NOEC; OPOP
Beautifully Janet slept. Janet Waking. John Crowe Ransom. CMoP; InPK; MeMAP; MoAB; MoAmPo; MoP; NAAL-2; NoAM; NoP; OBD; PoE; Poetr; RB; TAP
Beauty. Laurence Binyon. MoBrPo
Beauty. Abraham Cowley. ImPo; LiTB; PoEL-2; TrGrPo
Beauty. "E-Yeh-Shure." FaPON
Beauty. Sir Richard Fanshawe, *after the Italian of* Giovanni Battista Guarini. *See* Let us use it while [or whilst] we may.
Beauty. Peter Hille, *tr. fr. German by* Jethro Bithell. AWP
Beauty. Christopher Marlowe. *Fr.* Tamburlaine the Great. ChTr; TrGrPo
Beauty. Yannis Ritsos, *tr. fr. Greek by* Minas Sarras. AnRep
Beauty. Isaac Rosenberg. TrJP
Beauty. Thomas Stanley, *after the Greek of* Anacreon. AWP; OBVE

Beauty. Walt Whitman. WeW
Beauty. Elinor Wylie. NAAL-2; OxBA
Beauty. Octavia Beatrice Wynbush. ShDr
Beauty, A. John Ash. SCBI
Beauty — a beam, nay, flame. Fading Beauty. Giovanni Battista Marino, *tr. fr. Italian by* Samuel Daniel. AWP
Beauty, Alas, Where Wast Thou Born. *At. to* Thomas Lodge *and to* Robert Greene. EIL
Beauty and Denial. William Cartwright. BeJo
Beauty and Love. Andrew Young. GBL
Beauty and Sadness. Cathy Song. NoAM
Beauty and silence of the great migrations, The. (*LL*) Monarchs. Sharon Olds. LoHo
Beauty and Terror. Lesbia Harford. CBAP
Beauty and the Beast. Rita Dove. NoAM
Beauty and the Bird. Dante Gabriel Rossetti. FM
Beauty [or Beautie], and the life, The. William Drummond of Hawthornden. EIL; PoEL-2
(Her Passing.) OBEV
Beauty, Arise! Thomas Dekker *and others. Fr.* Pleasant Comedy of Patient Grissell [or Grissel or Grissill], The. EIL
Beauty as a Shield. Elsie Robinson. BLPA; PoToHe
Beauty Bathing. Anthony Munday. *See* Beauty sat bathing by a spring.
Beauty — be not caused — it is. Emily Dickinson. TAP
Beauty clear and fair. John Fletcher. *Fr.* Elder Brother, The. NOSC; OBEV
Beauty does not walk through lovely days. Beauty and Terror. Lesbia Harford. CBAP
Beauty Extoll'd. *At. to* Henry Noel *and to* William Strode. ChTr; ELP
Beauty his transient eyes descried. (*LL*) The Image-Maker. Oliver St. John Gogarty. OBEV; OBMV; PoRA
Beauty in Trouble. Robert Graves. NYBP
Beauty in woman; the high will's decree. Sonnet: He Compares All Things with His Lady, and Finds Them Wanting. Cavalcanti, *tr. fr. Italian by* Dante Gabriel Rossetti. AWP
Beauty Is a Witch. Shakespeare. *Fr.* Much Ado about Nothing. TrGrPo
Beauty is never satisfied. Mythmaking. Kathleen Spivack. NMM
Beauty Is Not Bound. Thomas Campion. *See* Give beauty all her right.
Beauty is not caused — it is. Emily Dickinson. LiTA
Beauty is seen. Beauty. "E-Yeh-Shure." FaPON
Beauty Is the Straw. Amy Witting. NOBAu
Beauty is the straw I clutch at, but to say straw. Beauty Is the Straw. Amy Witting. NOBAu
Beauty Kills. Charlie Smith. PFL
Beauty kissed your mouth, and gave the petals. Macedonius, *tr. fr. Greek by* Adrian Wright. GrAn
Beauty no more the subject be. Thomas Nabbes. NOSC
Beauty no other thing is than a beam. The Definition of Beauty. Robert Herrick. BeJo; CaPo
Beauty of Israel is slain [or slaine] upon thy high places, The. Bible, *O.T. Fr.* Second Samuel. OBVE; OBWP
(David's Lament for Saul and Jonathan.) AWP
(David's Lament over Saul.) PAW
(David's Lament.) ChTr, I: 19–27; FF, I: 19–27; TrGrPo, I: 19–27; TrJP, I: 19–27
Beauty of Job's Daughters, The. Jay Macpherson. ChIV-1; MoCV; NOBC
Beauty of manhole covers, The — what of that? Manhole Covers. Karl Shapiro. GoJo; NoAM
Beauty of the Earth, The. (*LL*) All praise be yours through Brother Sun. Paul Winter. EaPr
Beauty of the Friend it was that taught me, The. Makhfi, *tr. fr. Farsi by* Paul Whalley. WPOW
Beauty of the Stars, The. Moses ibn Ezra, *tr. fr. Hebrew by* Solomon Solis-Cohen. TrJP
Beauty of the trees, The. Chief Dan George. EaPr
Beauty of the unused, The. Unspeakable. Margaret Avison. NOBC
Beauty of their walls, The. (*LL*) The Walls of Carthage. Harry Clifton. IB
Beauty of Things, The. Robinson Jeffers. PoA
Beauty out of sight, A. (*LL*) Orara. Henry Clarence Kendall. CBAP
Beauty Rohtraut. Eduard Friedrich Mörike, *tr. fr. German by* George Meredith. AWP; OBVE
Beauty sat bathing by a spring. Anthony Munday. *Fr.* Primaleon of Greece. EBEvV
(Beauty Bathing.) NOBE; OBEV
(Beauty Sat Bathing by a Spring.) EIL
(Colin.) GTBS; GTBS-P
Beauty screws her new. Rewrite. E. A. Markham. PBCV

Bedtime. Eleanor Farjeon. OTCP

Bedtime. Denise Levertov. IHMS; NaP; SM; TwCP

Bedtime. *Unknown.* ReMoGo

Bedtime Story. Lou Lipsitz. VGW

Bedtime Story. George MacBeth. MoP; SoSe

Bedtime Story. Lilian Moore. NTCP

Bedtime Story. Charles Simic. AnAn

Bedtime Story. Nayo-Barbara Watkins. NBV

Bedtime Story, A. Robert Mezey.

Bedtime tears/ and evening sorrow. Small Rains. N. M. Bodecker. Spl

Bee, The. Emily Dickinson. GN; MoAB; MoAmPo

Bee, The. John Fandel. GoYe

Bee, The. Charles Fitz-Geffry. *Fr.* Sir Francis Drake. ElL

Bee. X. J. Kennedy. OBCA; Spl

Bee and the Petunia, The. Katherine Hoskins. ErPo

Bee buzz round and round, The. *(LL)* These Several Selves . . . Joanne Kyger. VBLP

Bee committed parricide, The. *(LL)* Fuscara, or the Bee Errant. John Cleveland. CBLP

Bee Dice Game, The. Paule Barton, *tr. fr. Creole* by Howard Norman. PRA

Bee Elk. Clark Coolidge. PRA

Bee his burnished carriage, A. Emily Dickinson. NOBA

Bee! I'm expecting you! Letter to Bee. Emily Dickinson. SAmP; SOTW; TLR; TTTS

Bee-keeper kissed me, The. *Unknown, tr. fr. Spanish* by W. S. Merwin. BoWoP

Bee Meeting, The. Sylvia Plath. HCAP; InPS; NALW; Poetr; PPP; WPE

Bee Mother. Meredith Stricker. LoHo

Bee-Orchis, The. Andrew Young. ChTr

Bee Song. Carl Sandburg. PDV

Bee Target on His Shoulder, The. J. H. Prynne. VaA

Bee, the Ant, and the Sparrow, The. Nathaniel Cotton. OxBChV

Bee upon a briar-rose hung, A. The Flesh-Fly and the Bee. Coventry Patmore. FaBoEE

Bee Wassail. *Unknown.* OBET

Bee-Wisp, The. Charles Tennyson Turner. FM

Bee ye my fictions; But her story. *(LL)* Wishes to His Supposed Mistress[e]. Richard Crashaw. BoLoP; EBEV; ImPo; MeLP; NOSC; OBEV; OxAEP-1; PoEL-2; SeCP; SeCV-1

Beech, The. Andrew Young. BoNaP

Beech amid the forest lives, The. *(LL)* Trees. Sara Coleridge. BoTP; OHIP; OxBChV

Beech boles whiten in the swollen stream, The. Autumn, 1939. Alun Lewis. PAW; PoWW

Beech leaves caught in a moment gust, The. Departure. Edmund Blunden. OxBSP

Beechwoods at Knole. V. Sackville-West. NTP

Beef and bacon's out of season. *Unknown.* RoPo

Beehive. Jean Toomer. PoBA; TTY

Beehive Cell. Richard Murphy. CIP

Beehould a cluster to itt selfe a vine. William Alabaster. *Fr.* Divine Meditations. ESCV; Son

Beekeeper's Daughter, The. Sylvia Plath. IHMS

Sir Beelzebub. Edith Sitwell. *Fr.* Façade. BoWoP; FaBoWP; HoPM; MoAB; MoBrPo; NALW; OxBTC; PrIm

Beeman Cliton hews/ From the flower fed hive. Apollonides, *tr. fr. Greek* by Peter Whigham. GrAn

Been in the Pen So Long. *Unknown.* AS

Been in the wire-wood — have! So Spring. Nigel Wells. PWE

Been on the hummer since ninety-four. A. R. U. *Unknown.* AS

Been out in the lifeboat often? Ay, ay, sir, oft enough. The Lifeboat. George R. Sims. VPP

Beeny Cliff. Thomas Hardy. OBNC; OxAEP-2; RB

BEEP . . . bEEP/ joy . . ./ BEEP! *(LL)* Christmas 1959 et Cetera. Gerald William Barrax. PChr

Beer. George Arnold. OBAL

Beer. Charles Stuart Calverley. BXAP; FaBoCo

Sels.
    "But hark! a sound is stealing on my ear." FiBHP

Beer. Julianus, *tr. fr. Greek* by Peter Jay. GrAn

Beer Bottle. Ted Kooser. SM

Beer Drops. Melba Joyce Boyd. BlSi

Bees, The. Lola Ridge. FaPON

Bees and a honeycomb in the dried head of a horse. In Tall Grass. Carl Sandburg. PoA

Bees and lilies there were. Bring the Day! Theodore Roethke. CRP

Bees are black, with gilt surcingles. Emily Dickinson. NAAL-1

Bees, bees of paradise. Bee Wassail. *Unknown.* OBET

Bees build around red liver. A Poor Christian Looks at the Ghetto. Czeslaw Milosz, *tr. fr. Polish by the author.* AnRep; PoSu

Bees build in the crevices, The. The Stare's Nest by My Window. W. B. Yeats. *Fr.* Meditations in Time of Civil War. BIrV; GTBS-P; InPS; LiTB; NOBE

(Bees in the crevices, The.) FaBoPV

Bees in the crevices, The. W. B. Yeats. *See* Bees build in the crevices, The.

Bees in the late summer sun. Bee Song. Carl Sandburg. PDV

Bee's Last Journey to the Rose, The. Brian Patten. OTCP

Bees over the gooseberry bushes. The Bees. Lola Ridge. FaPON

Bees rode the scalloped air of the garden. In the Middle of Things, Begin. Beckian Fritz Goldberg. NAmP90

Bees, six tiny legs and wings all lovely. What She Said ("Bees, six tiny legs and wings all lovely.") Orampokiyar, *tr. fr. Tamil* by A. K. Ramanujan. *Fr.* Five on the Riverside Cane. PLW

Bees that have been hiving above the church pond, The. James K. Baxter. *Fr.* Jerusalem Sonnets. PeNZ

Beeth hevy again, or elles moot I die. *(LL)* The Complaint of Chaucer to His Empty Purse. Chaucer. MiEL; MIS; NAEL-1; SCGP

Beethoven. Bob Cobbing. *Fr.* Beethoven Today. NBrP

Beethoven. Zbigniew Herbert, *tr. fr. Polish* by John Carpenter *and* Bogdana Carpenter. AnAn

Beethoven. H. Cordelia Ray. CBWP-3

Beethoven. John Hall Wheelock. PoA

Beethoven, Opus 111. Amy Clampitt. NIP

Beethoven Today, *sels.* Bob Cobbing.
    "Beethoven." NBrP

Beethoven's Death Mask. Stephen Spender. OxBTC

Beetle, The, *sels.* James Whitcomb Riley.
    "Shrilling locust slowly sheathes, The." FaPON

Beetle loves his unpretending track, The. Wordsworth. *Fr.* Liberty. FaBoCo; FiBHP

Beetle on the Shasta Daylight. Shirley Kaufman. NYBP; WPE

Beetles. Lorna Dee Cervantes. ETG

Before. W. E. Henley. *Fr.* In Hospital. MoBrPo

Before a mirror at midnight I compose myself. Self-Portrait as Van Gogh. Peter Cooley. NAmP90

Before a Pack of deep-mouth'd Lusts I flee. Francis Quarles. *Fr.* Emblems. ESCV

Before a Saint's Picture. Walter Savage Landor. OxBChV

Before Action. Leon Gellert. CBAP

Before Action. William Noel Hodgson. PAW; WGRP

Before Agincourt. Shakespeare. *See* Now entertain conjecture of a time.

Before Agincourt. Shakespeare. *See* O! that we now had here.

Before an audible sound, an almost recognizable. Prelude to Memorial Song: 100 Years Later. Phillip William George. VoR

Before/ and After. Jewel C. Latimore. JB

Before and After Marriage. Anne Campbell. PoToHe

Before any match was struck. In the Forest Without Leaves. John Haines. FoLa

Before Bannockburn. John Barbour. *Fr.* Bruce, The. OxBS

Before Bannockburn. Burns. *See* Scots, wha hae wi' Wallace bled.

Before, before he was aware. Comrades; an Episode. Robert Nichols. NSI

Before, behind, above. *(LL)* Interruption. Robert Graves. ImPo; LiTB; LiTM; MeMBP

Before Breakup on the Chena outside Fairbanks. David McElroy. Poetsp

Before Dawn. Horace Hamilton. NYBP

Before dawn i rose thirsty. Other. Lance Henson. VoR

Before Day. Siegfried Sassoon. WGRP

Before daybreak, before dew breaks. Youth. Barend Toerien, *tr. fr. Afrikaans by the author.* PeSA

Before Disaster. Yvor Winters. HoPM

Before dusk on the lake, the moon just full. Chang Chih-ho, *tr. by* Hellmut Wilhelm. *Fr.* Fisherman's Songs. SuSp

Before Gereint, foe's affliction. Gereint ab Erbin. *Unknown, tr. fr. Welsh* by Joseph P. Clancy. OBWVE

Before God's footstool to confess. Henry Cole. PoToHe

(Thy Best.) PWR

Before God's last *Put out the Light* was spoken. *(LL)* Once by the Pacific. Robert Frost. CMoP; HAP; HeIP; LiTA; LiTM; MeMAP; MoAB; MoAmPo; NAAL-2; NOBA; PrIm; Son; TRP; VGW; WeW

Before he died. Equena, *tr. fr. Tlinglit Indian* by James Koller. STP

Before he leaves on his fated journey. Bede's Death Song. *At. to* The Venerable Bede, *tr. fr. Anglo-Saxon* by Kevin Crossley-Holland. ASW

Before he went to feed with owls and bats. Nebuchadnezzar's Dream. Keats. ChIV-1

Before the old gentleman missed her. (*LL*) There was an old soldier of Bicester. *Unknown.* FaBoNo; OxBChV

Before the Pacific. Blanca Varela, *tr. fr. Spanish by* Willis Barnstone. BoWoP

Before the Paling of the Stars. Christina Rossetti. TrCP

Before the Peak of Returning Joy the sand was like snow. A Song of War. Li Po, *tr. fr. Chinese by* Robert Payne. TAL

Before the plums fell asleep. On the Way to Mind. Milo De Angelis, *tr. fr. Italian by* Lawrence Venuti. NeIt

Before the Poetry Reading. Louis Simpson. OxBC

Before the prayer begun. (*LL*) Lady Maisry. *Unknown.* ESPB, A *and* B vers.; OBET; OxBB

Before the press scarce one could see. To His Book ("Before the press . . . .") Robert Herrick. OxBSP

Before the Rain. Thomas Bailey Aldrich. GN

[Before the Rape]. Shakespeare. *Fr.* Rape of Lucrece, The. BeLS; NoSic

Before the Roman came to Rye or Caesar conquered Gaul. The Rolling Chinese Wall. Roger Woddis. UV

Before the Roman came to Rye or out to Severn strode. The Rolling English Road. G. K. Chesterton. CoGr; FaBoCh; NOBE; NOBL; OBEV; OBMV; OtMeF; OxAEP-2; OxBTC; PlP; UV

Before the seas again divide. Walter Adolphe Roberts. PBCV

Before the sixth day of the next new year. On the Cards and Dice. Sir Walter Ralegh. ChIV-2; EnRePo; RB (Prognostication upon Cards and Dice, A.) SiPS; SiPSBD

Before the Statue of Apollo. Saul Tchernichowsky, *tr. fr. Hebrew by* L. V. Snowman. TrJP

Before the Storm. Richard Dehmel, *tr. fr. German by* Ludwig Lewisohn. AWP

Before the Storm. Kenneth O. Hanson. CoAP

Before the Stuff Comes Down. Gary Snyder. HeIP

Before the sun goes down. Astrid Hjertenaes Andersen, *tr. fr. Norwegian by* Nadia Christensen. BoWoP

Before the thing begins we have. Poetry Reading. Vernon Scannell. NOBL

Before the Wall. Roberta Hill Whiteman. ETG

Before the war. From Our Album. Lawson Fusao Inada. AmPA

Before the War. Marilyn Hacker. AmPA

Before the world, I hold that none of these. Albery Allson Whitman. *Fr.* Octoroon, The. AAP

Before the world was made. (*LL*) Before the World Was Made. W. B. Yeats. CBLP; GTBS-P

Before the World Was Made. W. B. Yeats. CBLP; GTBS-P

Before there was a trace of this world of men. Bibi Hayati, *tr. fr. Persian by* Jane Hirshfield. EnIH

Before there was any water there were tides of fire, both our tones flow from the older fountain. (*LL*) Continent's End. Robinson Jeffers. AWP; FaBV

Before They Made Things Be Alive They Spoke. Lucario Cuevish, *tr. fr. Luiseño Indian by* Jerome K. Rothenberg. STP

Before they ripen into diffused spirits. Katerina Anghelaki-Rooke, *tr. fr. Modern Greek by* Kimon Friar. NU

Before they saw through it and found me. (*LL*) The Diggers. W. S. Merwin. CBNP

Before this fever of the almost cold. Mirror. Peter De Vries. PoA

Before this longing. Her Longing. Theodore Roethke. NAAL-2; NU

Before this tyme in Kentschire it befell. The Unicornis Tale. *Unknown.* Fr. Talis of the Fyve Bestis, The. OxBLMV

Before thy door too long of late. III, 10. Extremum Tanain. Horace, *tr. fr. Latin by* Austin Dobson. *Fr.* Odes. AWP, *tr. by* Austin Dobson

Before Vespasian's regal throne. Death of Gaudentis. "Harriet Annie." WBLP

Before Vicksburg. George Henry Boker. PAH

Before Waterloo. Thomas Hardy. *See* Eyelids of eve fall together at last, The.

Before we go! (*LL*) The Deserter's Lamentation. John Philpot Curran. FaBoRV

Before we go to Paradise by way of Kensal Green. (*LL*) The Rolling English Road. G. K. Chesteron. CoGr; FaBoCh; NOBE; NOBL; OBEV; OBMV; OtMeF; OxAEP-2; OxBTC; PlP; UV

Before we shall again behold. Endimion Porter and Olivia. Sir William Davenant. MeLP; NOBE (Song: "Before we shall again behold.") MeLP (Song: "Endimion Porter and Olivia.") NOSC

Before when you left you would always forget. Patrizia Cavalli, *tr. fr. Italian by* Judith Baumel. NeIt

Before which we may not speak or sing or ever stop. (*LL*) Rain Forest. Dave Jeddie Smith. HCAP; MT

Before you can learn the trees, you have to learn. Learning the Trees. Howard Nemerov. VCAP

Before you fade. Paul Verlaine, *tr. fr. French by* Philip L. Miller. RiWo

Before you have kissed the first star? (*LL*) On This Day. Leah Goldberg. MHP

Before you know the years are lost. "Yvonne." *Fr.* Iwilla/Scourge. ETG

Before you left for the Lucky Strike. The Waitress's Kid. Peggy Shumaker. PBCAP

Before you praise Spring's advent note. Tu Fu, *tr. fr. Chinese by* Robert Payne. TAL

Before you run out into the street and they shoot. (*LL*) At first I was given centuries. Margaret Atwood. HAP; NMM; WPOW

Before you step out. I Hope I Don't Have You Next Semester, But. Edwin S. Godsey. HoPM

Before you thought of Spring. Emily Dickinson. SAmP

Before you were conceived. The Miracle. Maureen Hawkins. AIW

Before your cry. Budded with Child. Meridel Le Sueur. ETG

Before your hair was ever cut. *Unknown, tr. fr. Greek by* Alistair Elliot. GrAn

Before your mouth was fringed with hair. Epigram: On a Slanderer. Martial, *tr. fr. Latin.* PeHV

Before Your Waking. Anna Gréki, *tr. fr. French by* Anita Barrows. WPOW

Before Your Wonders I Stand, My World. Shimon Halkin, *tr. fr. Hebrew by* Ruth Finer Mintz. MHP

Beg a ten cent mista. Version. Dennis Scott. PBCV

Beg for mercy. (*LL*) Follow, follow. Thomas Campion. EnLoPo

Beg-Innish. J. M. Synge. MoBrPo; PeIV

Beg Parding. *Unknown.* ChTr

Begats, The. Bible, *O.T. Fr.* First Chronicles. CBCK

Begetting. Dorothea Spears. PeSA

Beggar, The. Margaret E. Bruner. PoToHe

Beggar, The. Adrian Mitchell. FaBoTw

Beggar, The. Thomas Moss. NOEC

Beggar, The. *Unknown.* OBET

Beggar at the Gate, The. Ian Wedde. PeNZ

Beggar Boy, The. Cecil Frances Alexander. OxBChV

"Beggar," he sayes. Little John a Begging. *Unknown.* ESPB

Beggar-Laddie, The. *Unknown.* ESPB

Beggar Maid, The. Tennyson. BeLS; BoTP

Beggar Man, The. Lucy Aikin. OxBChV

Beggar shouts his martial wares, The. The Beggar. Adrian Mitchell. FaBoTw

Beggar to Beggar Cried. W. B. Yeats. CMoP; NoAM; OxAEP-2

Beggar to Burgher. A. R. D. Fairburn. PeNZ

Beggar to Mab, the Fairy [*or* Fairie] Queen, The. Robert Herrick. CaPo

Beggar to the graveyard hied, A. Poverty. *Unknown, tr. fr. Sanskrit by* Arthur Ryder. *Fr.* Panchatantra, The. AWP

Beggar Wind, The. Mary Austin. BoNaP

Beggar Woman, The. William King. ECEV; NOEC

Beggarly Bat, a cut out, scattily, The. The Bat. Ted Hughes. OBAP

Beggarman's Song, A, *sels. Unknown, tr. fr. Gaelic by* Frank O'Connor. "Would God that I and my darling." WTO

Beggars. Francis Davidson. CH

Beggars and Kings. W. S. Merwin. AnAn

Beggars Are Coming to Town, The. Mother Goose. *See* "Hark, Hark, the Dogs Do Bark."

Beggar's Bush, *sels.* John Fletcher.
   Beggar's Holiday, The. NOSC

Beggars have changed places, but the lash goes on, The. (*LL*) The Great Day. W. B. Yeats. BIrV; CMoP; FF; IHNG; OxBSP

Beggar's Holiday, The. John Fletcher. *Fr.* Beggar's Bush. NOSC

Beggar's Opera, The. (If poverty be a title to poetry, I am sure nobody can dispute mine.) John Gay. OAEL-1
Sels.
   "Before the barn-door crowing." ErPo; OxBSP; PoEL-3
   "Can love be controlled by advice?" OxBSP
   Employments of Life, The. PeLV
   "Fox may steal your hens, sir, A." NOEC
      (Lawyer, The.) IHNG
      (Soldier and a Sailor, A.) TEP
   Highwaymen, The. WiR
   "If any wench Venus's girdle wear." PeLV; PoEL-3
   "If the heart of a man is deprest [*or* depressed] with cares." ELP; EnLoPo; NAEL-1
      (Would You Have a Young Virgin?) TEP
   "O Polly, you might have toy'd and kist." EnLoPo
   Packington's Pound. OBF
   "Since laws were made for ev'ry degree." NOEC
   "Since laws were made for ev'ry degree." NOEC
   "Thus I stand like the Turk, with his doxies around." PeLV
   "Thus when the swallow, seeking prey." PoEL-3

"'Tis woman that seduces all mankind!" PeLV

"Were I laid on Greenland's coast." CBLP; EBEvV, *sect.* I, *pt.* i; EnLoPo; NAEL-1; OxBoLi; PeLV; PoEL-3 (Macheath and Polly.) NOEC
(Over the Hills and Far Away.) NOBE; PrIm

What Shall I Do to Show How Much I Love Her? TEP

Youth's the Season. WiR
(Youth and Love.) NOBE

Beggar's Serenade. John Heath-Stubbs. BoLoP; ErPo

Begge thou wouldst take thy Tenants Rent. (*LL*) My God, thou that didst dye for me. Henry Vaughan *and* Thomas Stanley. ESCV

Begging. Henry Vaughan *and* Thomas Stanley. ESCV

Begging Another, on Colour of Mending the Former. Ben Jonson. *Fr.* Celebration of Charis in Ten Lyric[k] Peeces [*or* pieces], A. BeJo; CBLP; OxAEP-1; PoEL-2; SeCP

Begging for Food. T'ao Ch'ien, *tr. fr. Chinese by* Wu-chi Liu. SuSp

Begging the Question. Daryl Hine. PFL

Begin and never cease! (*LL*) While Shepherds Watched [Their Flocks by Night]. Nahum Tate. AmFP, 1 *st.*; GN; NOCV; NOSC; PIP; TIRV; UV, *Sts.* I *and* II *only*

Begin, and the rest will follow. (*LL*) The Source. David Wagoner. VCAP

Begin before birth with swept-back fins. The Matin Pandemoniums. Richard Eberhart. NYBP

Begin by parting your hair. Parting; a Game. Lynn Sukenick. NMM

Begin, ephebe, by perceiving the idea. Wallace Stevens. *Fr.* Notes toward a Supreme Fiction. NOBA

Begin Summer. Ingrid Jonker, *tr. fr. Afrikaans by* Jack Cope *and* Uys Krige. PeSA

Begin to charm, and as thou strok'st mine ears. To Music. Robert Herrick. CaPo

Begin to gleam across the mournful plain? (*LL*) The Raven Days. Sidney Lanier. AnAmPo; OxBA

Begin to talk/ of HYenaaaAAS. (*LL*) Hospital/Poem. Sonia Sanchez. BPo; PoBA

Begin unto my God with timbrels. With Timbrels. Bible, Apocrypha. *Fr.* Judith. TrJP

Begin with a kiss. Up Tails All. Robert Herrick. BeJo

Begin with the last and unrecorded scene. Elegies for Etsuko. Mary Jo Salter. UTF

Beginner, The. Kipling. *Fr.* Epitaphs of the War, 1914–1918. FaBoTw; NoP; OBWP

Beginner/ Perpetual beginner. What Can I Tell My Bones? Theodore Roethke. AmPP; NOBA

Beginners. Denise Levertov. CrSp

Beginning. Cynthia Fuller. NWP

Beginning. Alden Nowlan. NOBC

Beginning, The. Wallace Stevens. VGW

Beginning. James Wright. VCAP

Beginning again and again. Ken Smith. *Fr.* Fox Running. PWE

Beginning by Example, *sels.* Christopher Gilbert.
Blue. FYAP

Beginning from you, Phoebus, I shall tell the glory. The Argonautica. Apollonius Rhodius, *tr. fr. Greek by* Barbara Hughes Fowler. HePo

Beginning in half darkness. The Morning Track. Edward Parone. NYBP

Beginning my fortieth year. Beyond the Presidency. Morgan Gibson. FF

Beginning My Studies. Walt Whitman. NAAL-1; OxBA

Beginning of a lizard, The. Lizard. Bundgård Povlsen, *tr. fr. Danish by* Poul Borum. TSaS

Beginning of a Long Poem on Why I Burned the City, The. Lawrence Benford. TTY

Beginning of an Undergraduate Poem. *Unknown.* FaBoCo

Beginning of the End, The. Jon Stallworthy. OxBC

Beginning on Paper. Ruth Krauss. SiSoPo

Beginning, The: Some landscape & words about nature. Kirk Lonergren's Home Movie Taking Place Just North of Prince George, with Sound. Sharon Thesen. NOBC

Beginning the Year at Rosebud, S.D. Roberta Hill Whiteman. CDW

Beginning to dangle beneath. In the Marble Quarry. James Dickey. NoP

Beginning to Squall. May Swenson. RFM

Beginning with a Stain. Alice Notley. VBLP

Beginning with a stain, as the universe did perhaps. Beginning with a Stain. Alice Notley. VBLP

Beginnings, *sels.* Robert Hayden.

Beginnings. Peter Sirr. PBCIP

Beginnings. *Unknown, tr. fr. Mayan by* Munro Edmonson. *Fr.* Popol Vuh, The. STP

Beginnings. Michael S. Weaver. PBCAP

Beginnings of Faith, The. Sir Lewis Morris. WGRP

Begins the crying. Guitar. Federico García Lorca, *tr. fr. Spanish by* Keith Waldrop. InPK

Begins the long and painful process of letting go. (*LL*) Meet the Supremes. David Trinidad. UL; UTF

Begins with the *ooo ooo* of a mourning dove. Holy Thursday. Charles Wright. AnAn

Begonia's soil is rich and wet, The. Collusion. Medbh McGuckian. BiHa

Begot by butchers, but by bishops bred. On Cardinal Wolsey. *Unknown.* FaBoCo

Begotten by the meeting of rock with rock. Sea Holly. Conrad Aiken. LiTM

Begotten of the Spleen. Charles Simic. LCAP

Begun before Easter . . . / Sign of the Fish. Thomas McGrath. *Fr.* Letter to an Imaginary Friend, Part Two. NNaP

Behavior of Mirrors on Easter Island, The. Julio Cortázar, *tr. by* Paul Blackburn. AnRep

Behaviorally. Anselm Hollo. UL

Behaviorist, The. Van K. Brock. ArOW

Behaviour of Fish in an Egyptian Tea Garden. Keith Douglas. FaBoMo; OBTV; RB

Behaviour of Money. Bernard Spencer. LiTB

Behind a vermilion gate, on the eve of the Skills Festival. Autumn. Fan Ch'eng-ta, *tr. by* Irving Y. Lo. *Fr.* Seasonal Poems on Fields and Gardens. SuSp

Behind a web of bottles, bales. The Gombeen. Joseph Campbell. BIrV

Behind Bars, *sels.* Fadwa Tuqan, *tr. fr. Arabic by* Hatem Hussaini. "My mother's phantom hovers here." TSaS

Behind bars you stand. Ese Chicano. Jimmy Santiago Baca. ETG

Behind Calyx Hall's towers the sun has just set. On a Painting of the Radiant Emperor's Night Revels by Candlelight. Kao Ch'i, *tr. fr. Chinese by* Irving Y. Lo. SuSp

Behind drawn curtains in reflecting shades. Existentialist. Janet Fisher. NWP

Behind glass, my room is neat. Out of Chaos Out of Order Out. Michele Roberts. BrRo

Behind her not the quivering of a leaf. Circe. A. D. Hope. PPP

Behind him a picture. Class Room. Virginia A. Houston. ShDr

Behind him lay the gray Azores. Columbus. Joaquin Miller. AnAmPo; BeLS; EBEvV; FaBoBe; FaPON; GN; PAH; PPP; VPP

Behind him the hotdogs split and drizzled. Suicide off Egg Rock. Sylvia Plath. PPP

Behind his dinner jacket. He's Doing Natural Life. Conyus. PoBA

Behind King's Chapel what the earth has kept. At the Indian Killer's Grave. Robert Lowell. NOBA; VGW

Behind me, and will not go away. (*LL*) Follower. Seamus Heaney. IIP; IPY; PNI

Behind me — dips eternity. Emily Dickinson. PBWP

Behind me, the folly of my flight. (*LL*) The Cywdd to Morvydd. Dafydd ap Gwilym. NOEC

Behind secluded screens the hush of daytime scenes. Summertime. Su Shun-ch'in, *tr. fr. Chinese by* Michael E. Workman. SuSp

Behind shut doors, in shadowy quarantine. The First Time. Karl Shapiro. ErPo; SM; VGW

Behind, sun, before, shadow! Silhouette. Annette M'Baye, *tr. fr. French by* Kathleen Weaver. PBWP

Behind the Falls. William Stafford. RFM

Behind the Glass Wall. Harold Norse. PeHV

Behind the granite church. Fugue. Constance Carrier. GoYe

Behind the house the upland falls. After the Pleasure Party. Herman Melville. NAAL-1; PoEL-5

Behind the Lights. Jeremy Hooker. SCBI

Behind the Log, *sels.* E. J. Pratt. "There is a language in a naval log." MoCV

Behind the moth-eaten curtain, 'stead of press. Mary Davys. *Fr.* Modern Poet, The. ECWP

Behind the Power Station on 14th, the held breath. Galway Kinnell. *Fr.* Avenue Bearing the Initial of Christ into the New World, The. NaP

Behind the Veil. Andrew Lansdown. NOBAu

Behind their mortgaged houses. (*LL*) Men at Forty. Donald Justice. CAPP; MT; NoAM; Poetr; PPP; Prf; VCAP

Behind thin curtains, sun rising. Dark Mothers. Anne Cluysenaar. VBLP

Behind you/ a riot of pallid orphans. Small Country. Claribel Alegría, *tr. fr. Spanish by* Aliki *and* Willis Barnstone. BoWoP

Behind you, now. Schwerner, Chaney, Goodman. Raymond R. Patterson. NBV

Behold. *Unknown, tr. fr. Hawaiian by* M. K. Pukui. WTO

Behold! a giant am I! The Windmill. Longfellow. MoShBr

Behold! A Proof of Irish Sense! *Unknown.* CBNP

Behold, a silly [*or* little] tender babe. New Prince, New Pomp[e]. Robert Southwell. ELP; ESCV; GN; NOBE; NOCV; NoSic; OHIP; TrCP

Behold, a virgin shall conceive. The Messiah. Bible, *O.T. Fr.* Isaiah. AWP

Behold a woman! The Justified Mother of Men. Walt Whitman. OHIP

Behold a Wonder Here! *Unknown.* TrGrPo

Behold, four Kings in majesty rever'd. The Playing Cards. Pope. *Fr.* Rape of the Lock, The. ChTr; FHYEP; HAP; ImPo; NoP; OAEL-1; OBNV; PeLV; PoEL-3; TEP; TrGrPo

Behold from sluggish winter's arm. Primo Vere. Giosuè Carducci, *tr. fr. Italian by* John Bailey. AWP

Behold he comes to make thy people groan. Pasquin to the Queen's Statue at St. Paul's. William Shippen. APAS

Behold her lip, how thin it is; her nose. The Shrew. Rowland Watkyns. AngWe

Behold her seven hills loom white. Resurge San Francisco. Joaquin Miller. PAH

Behold her, single in the field. The Solitary Reaper. Wordsworth. AWP; BLPL; CH; ClHu; EBEvV; EnRP; FaBoCh; FaPoB; FaPoR; FHYEP; GN; HAP; HeIP; ImPo; InPS; LiTB; MeMBP; NAEL-2; NOBE; NoP; OAEL-2; OBEV; OBNC; OxAEP-2; PoEL-4; Poetr; PoRA; PPP; SCGP; SCV; SoSe; TEP; TFi; TrGrPo; UnPo; WeW (Reaper, The.) GTBS; GTBS-P

Behold her there in the evening sun. Unwedded. Lucy Larcom. AmWP

Behold him now his genuine colours wear. Sonnet: To the Departing Spirit of an Alienated Friend. Anna Seward. PeHV

Behold, how eager this our little boy. Of the Boy and Butterfly. Bunyan. OxBChV

Behold how every man, drawn with delight. Samuel Daniel. *Fr.* Musophilus; or, Defence of All Learning. NoSic

Behold, how good and how pleasant it is. Bible, *O.T., paraphrased by* Sir Thomas Wyatt. *Fr.* Psalms. AWP (Psalm CXXXIII: "Beholde, how good and joyfull a thinge it is.") OBVE, *tr. by* Miles Coverdale (To Dwell Together in Unity.) TrJP

Behold I see the haven nigh at hand. Spenser. *Fr.* Faerie Queene, The. FHYEP

Behold! in various throngs the scribbling crew. Byron. *Fr.* English Bards and Scotch Reviewers. EnRP; OAEL-2

Behold, love. (*LL*) Behold, love, thy power how she despiseth! Sir Thomas Wyatt. GBL; SiPSBD

Behold, love, thy power how she despiseth! Sir Thomas Wyatt. GBL; SiPSBD

Behold me waiting — waiting for the knife. Before. W. E. Henley. *Fr.* In Hospital. MoBrPo

Behold, my brothers, the spring has come. Sitting Bull. EaPr

Behold, my dearest, how the fragrant rose. To Her Love. Edward May. FaBoEE

Behold My Mother! Abu Dolama, *tr. fr. Arabic by* Omar S. Pound. ArPe

Behold, my servant shall deal prudently. The Song of The Suffering Servant. Bible, *O.T. Fr.* Isaiah. NAWM-1

Behold, O Aspasia! I Send You Verses. Walter Savage Landor. *Fr.* Pericles and Aspasia. OBNC; SCGP

Behold, O Man. Spenser. *Fr.* Faerie Queene, The. EiL

Behold, One of Several Little Christs. Kenneth Patchen. NaP

Behold! Our Mother Earth is lying here. *Unknown, tr. fr. Pawnee Indian.* EaPr

Behold that tree, in Autumn's dim decay. Anna Seward. *Fr.* Sonnets. WoRP

Behold the birds of heaven. God Provides. Bible, *N.T. Fr.* St. Matthew. BLRP

Behold the brand of beauty tossed! The Dancer. Edmund Waller. CBLP; TrGrPo

Behold the child, by Nature's kindly law. Pope. *Fr.* Essay on Man, An. ECEV; FaBoRV

Behold the Deeds! H. C. Bunner. NBLV

Behold the dental artist's bright array. Artificial Teeth. Solyman Brown. *Fr.* Dentologia; a Poem on the Diseases of the Teeth and Their Proper Remedies. FaBoUS

Behold the duck. The Duck. Ogden Nash. MoShBr; RB; SiSoPo

Behold the ever-tim'rous hare. April. Samuel Thompson. BIrV

Behold the fatal day arrive! Swift. *Fr.* Verses on the Death of Doctor Swift [D.S.P.D., Occasioned by Reading a Maxim in Rochefoucauld]. PeLV; SCV

Behold the flag! Is it not a flag? "Orpheus C. Kerr." *Fr.* Rejected "National Hymns," The. OBAL

Behold, the Grave of a Wicked Man. Stephen Crane. *Fr.* Black Riders, The. TAP

Behold, the grave of a wicked man. Why? Stephen Crane. *Fr.* Black Riders, The. MeMAP

Behold the hippopotamus! The Hippopotamus. Ogden Nash. FaBV

Behold the house of Sir William Forbes. The Pentland Hills. *Unknown.* GBP

Behold the man alive in me. Ecce Homo. Witter Bynner. WGRP

Behold the Manly Mesomorph. W. H. Auden. OxBSP

Behold, the Meads. Guillaume de Poitiers, *tr. fr. French by* Harriet Waters Preston. AWP

Behold the politician. On American Politicians. *Unknown.* IHNG

Behold the ravens on the trees. Contentment. Benjamin Schlipf. BLRP

Behold, the Shade of Night Is Now Receding. St. Gregory the Great, *tr. fr. Latin by* Ray Palmer. AH

Behold the tormented and the fallen angel. Beethoven. John Hall Wheelock. PoA

Behold the works of William Morris! (*LL*) Behold the works of William Morris. *Unknown.* BXAP

Behold the works of William Morris. *Unknown.* BXAP

Behold This and Always Love It. Meridel Le Sueur. SRLS

Behold this brief hexagonal. Text. Audrey Wurdemann. FYAP

Behold this fleeting world, how all things fade. An Epitaph of the Death of Nicholas Grimald. Barnabe Googe. EnRePo; SCGP

Behold this little volume here enrolled. On the Bible. *Unknown.* NOSC

Behold this needle when the arctic stone. On the Needle of a Sundial. Francis Quarles. TrGrPo

Behold this ruin! 'Twas a skull. To a Skeleton. Anna Jane Vardhill. BLPA

Behold those wingèd images. A Legend of the Hive. Robert Stephen Hawker. EBVV

Behold, thou art fair. Bible, *O.T. Fr.* Song of Solomon, The. OxBM; TrJP

Behold three Kings come from the East. For Twelfth Day. Luke Wadding. TIRV

Behold through the veil of distance a pleasing image. Jonathan. Rachel, *tr. fr. Hebrew by* L. V. Snowman. TrJP

Behold thy darling, which thy lustfull care. Francis Quarles. *Fr.* Emblems. ESCV

Behold thy slave, all day that walks these woods unknown! (*LL*) I Would I Were Actaeon. *At. to* — — — Bewe. EiL; NoSic

Behold, we have gathered together our battleships, near and afar. Mene, Mene, Tekel, Upharsin. Madison Cawein. PAH

Behold, where Dryden's less presumptuous car. Thomas Gray. *Fr.* Progress of Poesy, The. EPCY

Behold with Joy. Elhanan Winchester. AH

Behold, within the leafy shade. The Sparrow's Nest. Wordsworth. EnRP

Behold! wood into bird and bird to wood again. Boomerang. William Hart-Smith. NOBAu; NTP

Behold yon breathing prospect bids the Muse. Spring ("Behold yon breathing prospect bids the muse.") James Thomson. *Fr.* Seasons, The. PoE

Behold yon hill, how it is swell'd with pride. Describes the Place Where Cynthia Is Sporting Herself. Philip Ayres. EnLoPo

Behold young Raphael coming back. Raphael. Priscilla Jane Thompson. CBWP-2

Beholde me, I pray thee, with all thine whole reson. Wofully Araide. *Unknown.* MeEL

Beholding element, in whose pure eye. The Aspen and the Stream. Richard Wilbur. NYBP

Bei-shung. Gerard Benson. OBAP

Bei Tai-He Beach. Shu Ting, *tr. fr. Chinese by* Carolyn Kizer *with* Y.H. Zhao. SpMi

Beija-Flor. Diane Ackerman. NIP

Being a bachelor is crazy business. In Mazatlán. Luis Omar Salinas. AfAz

Being a boy from the hills, brought up. The Welshman in Exile Speaks. T. Harri Jones. AngWe; OBWVE

Being a friend means,/ After all. (*LL*) Love. *At. to* Roy Croft. BLPA; FaBoBe

Being a Giant. Robert Mezey. GrPl

Being a woman, I am. The Wife Speaks. Mary Stanley. PeNZ

Being always/ Poor. (*LL*) Ennui. Langston Hughes. OBAL; OBCA

Being asked by an intimate party. His Answer to "Her Letter." Bret Harte. AnAmPo

Being Aware. Dennis Cooper. ETG; GLP; UL

Being black in America. Lonely Eagles. Marilyn Nelson Waniek. NAmP90

Being Born Is Important. Carl Sandburg. NAs

Being Called For. Rosemary Dobson. CBAP; Mes

Being Children. Marilynn Talal. BTR

Being double dead: going, and bidding go[e]. (*LL*) The Expiration. John Donne. CBLP; EiL; MeLP; OxBSP; SeCP

Being drawn again. Some Loss. Roy Fisher. VaA

Being drunk upstairs and listening. Green Revolutions. Barbara Guest. FaBoWP

Being Forsaken of His Friend He Complaineth. "E. S." ElL

Being his resting place. A Dog Sleeping on My Feet. James Dickey. NAAL-2

Being Human. Ruth Stone. IMW

Being in thought of love, I chanced to see. Ballata: He Reveals, in a Dialogue, His Increasing Love for Mandetta. Cavalcanti, tr. fr. Italian by Dante Gabriel Rossetti. AWP

Being menial, how can we let vastnesses strike through. The Fractal Lanes. Alice Fulton. BAP-91

Being mighty a master, being a father and fond. (LL) In the Valley of the Elwy. Gerard Manley Hopkins. EnVR; ImPo; MeMBP; NOBVV; NOCV; OxAEP-2; PiP; TOF

Being myself so corrupted. Expecting the Lord. Ann Griffiths, tr. fr. Welsh by Tony Conran. VBLP

Being neither white nor black? (LL) Cross. Langston Hughes. LiTM; PoBA; PoLF; SAmP; SoSe; TAP

Being, not doing, is my first job. (LL) I thirst by day. I watch by night. Theodore Roethke. EaPr

Being one day at my window all alone. The Visions. Petrarch, tr. fr. Italian. Fr. Sonnets to Laura. AWP

Being Proteus, he never dreamed at all. (LL) The Shape-Changer. Chris Wallace-Crabbe. NOBAu

Being roused, uncurled. Beginning. Cynthia Fuller. NWP

Being set in order, to conduct a life. Permanent Wave. Andrew Crozier. NBrP

Being set on the idea. Atlantis. W. H. Auden. OxAEP-2

Being slowly lifted up, thou long black arm. On Seeing a Piece of Our Artillery Brought into Action. Wilfred Owen. MeMBP

Being Somebody. Edwin Honig. TAP

Being the Third Song of Urias. Ken Smith. PWE

Being through weakness to the house confin'd. The Preface to Divine Songs and Meditacions. Anne Collins. KTR

Being to Timelessness as It's to Time. E. E. Cummings. HAP; UnAS

Being too young to go to the show at night alone. (LL) A Dim View of Berkeley in the Spring. Philip Whalen. PoBeRe

Being very religious, she devoted most of her time to fear. Episode of Decay. Witter Bynner. OxBM

Being, whose flesh dissolves. To the Unseeable Animal. Wendell Berry. ArNa

Being with you. Margaret Atwood. Fr. Circle Game, The. MoCV

Being witless it said no prayer. The Death of an Angel. Russell Edson. LCAP

Being you, you cut your poetry from wood. The Egg Boiler. Gwendolyn Brooks. PoBA

Being your slave, what should I do[e] but tend. Shakespeare. Fr. Sonnets. HAP; NoSic; OBEV; PeHV; PoEL-2 (Absence.) GTBS; GTBS-P

Beinn Naomh, sels. Kathleen Raine. Summit, The. OxBS

Beirut, sels. Mahmoud Darwish, tr. fr. Arabic by Lena Jayyusi and Christopher Middleton.

Beirut-Hell Express, The, sels. Etel Adnan. "Human race is going to the cemetery, The." WPOW

Bel m'es quan lo vens m'alena. Arnaut Daniel, tr. fr. French by Harriet Waters Preston. AWP

Belden Hollow. Leslie Nelson Jennings. GoYe

Beleaguered City, The. Longfellow. AnAmPo

Belfast. Louis MacNeice. PeECV

Belfast. Donald Revell. SM

Belfast Confetti. Ciaran Carson. BiHa; CIP; PNI; PWE

Belfast Linen. Unknown. See In a mean abode in [or on] the Shankill Road.

Belfast Lough. Unknown, tr. fr. Irish by John Montague. BIrV

Belfry, The. Laurence Binyon. CH

Belief. A. R. Ammons. GOA

Belief. "Angelus Silesius," tr. fr. German. Fr. Cherubical Wanderer, The. GePo, tr. by George C. Schoolfield

Belief. Josephine Miles. FaBoWP; MoP; NoAM; TAP

Belief. Ella Wheeler Wilcox. PWR

Belief, and the love, and the truth, The. (LL) My child, we were two children. Heine. OBVE

Belief and Unbelief. Robert Browning. Fr. Bishop Blougram's Apology. EBVVPR; FaBV; OBNC; OtMeF; PoEL-5

Belief/ As unbelief before, Shakes us by fits. Belief and Unbelief. Robert Browning. Fr. Bishop Blougram's Apology. EBVVPR; FaBV; OBNC; OtMeF; PoEL-5

Belief, great mustard seed, sends mountains to the sea. Belief. "Angelus Silesius," tr. fr. German. Fr. Cherubical Wanderer, The. GePo, tr. by George C. Schoolfield

Belief to regulate. (LL) Last night that she lived, The. Emily Dickinson. BoWoP; CMoP; HeIP; LiTA; MeMAP; NAAL-1; OxBA; PoEL-5; SOTW

Believe and leave to wonder. (LL) God and Yet a Man, A? Unknown. HAP; MiEL

Believe It. John Logan. AnAn; CAPP

Believe it or Not. Nicolai Kantchev, tr. fr. Bulgarian. TSaS, tr. by Alexander Shurbanov

Believe me, every hour e'en yet I dream. To Schmidlein. August, Graf von Platen, tr. fr. German by Reginald Bancroft Cooke. PeHV

Believe me, I loved you. (LL) Farewell to My Scooter. Mbuyiseni Oswald Mtshali. PeSAV

Believe Me, If All Those Endearing Young Charms. Thomas Moore. BLPA; ELP; EnRP; FaBoBe; FaBV; ImPo; LiTB; NAEL-2; OBNC; PiP; PoEL-4; TEP; WBLP

Believe me, knot of gristle, I bleed like a tree. Give Way, Ye Gates. Theodore Roethke. CMoP

Believe me, Love, this vagrant life. To Cordelia. Joseph Stansbury. NOBC

Believe me, sir, I'd like to spend whole days. Martial, tr. fr. Latin by J. V. Cunningham. OBVE

Believe Not. Isaac Leibush Peretz, tr. fr. Yiddish by Solomon Liptzin. TrJP

Believe not that the world is for naught, made. Believe Not. Isaac Leibush Peretz, tr. fr. Yiddish by Solomon Liptzin. TrJP

Believers' Best Buy. Roger Woddis. UV

Believe't, I will. (LL) How should I love my best? Lord Herbert of Cherbury. PoEL-2; SeCP

Believing against all evidence, no one will take this away. (LL) Foreigners. Meredith Stricker. LoHo

Believing in Those Inexorable Laws. Muriel Rukeyser. Son

Belinda lived in a little white house. The Tale of Custard the Dragon. Ogden Nash. FaPON; OBCA; OTCP; PoRA; PYC

Belisarius. Longfellow. PoEL-5; WiR

Belive Eneas membris schuk for cald. Virgil, tr. by Gavin Douglas. Fr. Aeneid [or Eneados], The. NAWM-1; ScCV

Bell, The. Richard Jones. NAmP90

Bell & Capitol. Daniel Halpern. BAP-90

Bell-Bird, The. "Fiona Macleod." Fr. Australian Transcripts. FM

Bell-Birds. Henry Clarence Kendall. NOBAu

Bell does. (LL) I Saw Myself. Lew Welch. PoBeRe

Bell horses, bell horses, what time of day? Mother Goose. BoTP; OxNR; ReMoGo

Bell-Man, The. Robert Herrick. BeJo

Bell-rope that gathers God at dawn, The. The Broken Tower. Hart Crane. AmPP; CMoP; LiTM; MeMAP; MoAB; MoAmPo; NoAM; NOBA; NoP; OxBA; Poetr; TrGrPo

Bell Speech. Richard Wilbur. MoAB; MoAmPo

Bell strikes one: we take no note of time. Edward Young. Fr. Night Thoughts.

Bell-that swings slowly and slowly over. (LL) Still and All. Burns Singer. OxBS

Bell Tower. Léonie Adams. MoAB; MoAmPo

Bell wakes me at half past a pale spring dawn, The. Letter from Pretoria Central Prison. Arthur Nortje. HBAPE

Bella was young and Bella was fair. Unhappy Bella. Unknown. ErPo

Belle de Jour. George Melly. FaBoPa

Belle Isle, 1949. Philip Levine. VCAP

Belle of the Balkans, The. Newman Levy. FiBHP

Belle of the Ball-Room, The. Winthrop Mackworth Praed. Fr. Every-Day Characters. EnRP; FaBoCo

Bellerophon, sels. Euripides, tr. fr. Greek by John Addington Symonds.

Bellflower spilling a candlesnuffer's dark hints. Of. Debora Greger. EOEF

Bellies bitter with drinking the/ Weak tears. Final Chorus. Archibald MacLeish. Fr. Panic. MoAmPo

Bellman, The. Robert Herrick. CaPo; CH

Bellman's Song, The. Unknown. EBEV; EIL; SCGP

Bellona the fierce, who held man in disdain. On a Lady, Preached into the Colic, by One of Her Lovers. Aaron Hill. ECEV

Bellow of good Master Bull, The. Ballade un Peu Banale. A. J. M. Smith. MoCV

Bellower with the antlers. Suibne Geilt. NOIV

Bellows Maker of Oxford, The. John Hoskyns. FaBoEE

Bellows: O wise man, weigh your words. Unknown, formerly at. to Cynewulf, tr. fr. Anglo-Saxon. Fr. Riddles (Exeter Book). ASW, tr. by Kevin Crossley-Holland

Beneath both the feet of Boötes you may see. Aratus, tr. fr. Greek by Barbara Hughes Fowler. Fr. Phaenomena. HePo

Beneath each black duck. Morning: The World in the Lake. Linda Hogan. SRLS

Beneath her very feet. (LL) The Violet. Goethe. STV

Beneath him with new wonder now he views. Milton. Fr. Paradise Lost. EPCY; PPP

Beneath my feet the pier shifts. Redondo. Ron Koertge. NGP

Beneath my feet when Flora cast. The Rose. Elizabeth Tollet. ECWP

Beneath my palm-trees, by the riverside. Song of the Indian Maid, The ("Beneath my palm-trees, by the riverside.") Keats. Fr. Endymion [a Poetic Romance]. NOBE

Beneath our consecrated elm. The New-come Chief. James Russell Lowell. Fr. Under the Old Elm. PAH

Beneath our eaves the moonbeams play. Moon and Candle-light. William Renton. NOBVV

Beneath our feet, the shuddering bogs. On Yes Tor. Sir Edmund Gosse. CH

Beneath the better part. (LL) Apple Dumplings. Mary E. Tucker. AmWP; CBWP-1

Beneath the blaze of a tropical sun the mountain peaks are the Thrones of. The Blossoming of the Solitary Date-Tree. Samuel Taylor Coleridge. CBLP

Beneath the blistering tropical sun. Wheeler's Brigade at Santiago. Wallace Rice. PAH

Beneath the branch of the green may. Unknown, tr. fr. French by John Addington Symonds. Fr. Medieval Norman Song. AWP

Beneath the brushed wing of the mallard. Lint. Rita Dove. TRP

Beneath the Cypress Shade. Thomas Love Peacock. See I dug, beneath the cypress shade.

Beneath the drear November trees. (LL) Autumnal. Ernest Dowson. EBVV; OBNC

Beneath the Good how far — but far above the Great. (LL) The Progress of Poesy. Thomas Gray. AWP; EnRP; GTBS; GTBS-P; NOEC; OBEV

Beneath the hazel tree. (LL) The Lapful of Nuts. Sir Samuel Ferguson. PeIV

Beneath the Hollin Tree. (LL) The Bonny Hind. Unknown. ESPB

Beneath the Malebolge lies Hastings Street. Christ Walks in This Infernal District Too. Malcolm Lowry. MoCV; NOBC

Beneath the mocking, loving tones. (LL) The Family Cat. Roy Fuller. OxBC; TEP

Beneath the myrtle's secret shade. The Progress of Love. Robert Dodsley. ECEV

Beneath the one white covering, breathing and dead? (LL) Seventy-five Are My Abyssed Forests. Shimon Halkin. MHP

Beneath the poinsettia's red in war December. (LL) Flame-Heart. Claude McKay. CDC; PoNe

Beneath the Pole of Proud Raven. Jana Harris. SRLS

Beneath the Radar — for the RAF and All Low Flying Aircraft. Geraldine Monk. NBrP

Beneath the sagging roof. Ezra Pound. Fr. Hugh Selwyn Mauberly. (Life and Contacts.) AmPP; CMoP; InPS; LiTA; LiTM; MoAmPo; NoAM; NOBA; NoP; TAP

Beneath the shadow of dawn's aerial cope. Hope and Fear. Swinburne. FaBoBe

Beneath the Shadow of the Freeway. Lorna Dee Cervantes. BCF; PBCAP

Beneath the shadow of Tongariro mountain. A Song of Yearning. Kohine Whakarua Ponika, tr. fr. Maori by the author. PeNZ

Beneath the sky, the cone-shaped drum is rumbling. Sacrifice. Léon Laleau, tr. fr. French by Ellen Conroy Kennedy. Fr. Black Music. NegPo

Beneath the small peach branches. Tune: "Telling of Innermost Feelings" — Wandering in Spring. Ch'en Tzu-lung, tr. fr. Chinese by Bruce Carpenter. SuSp

Beneath the turf that I have often trod. (LL) Winter Walk at Noon, A [or The]. William Cowper. EnRP; FHYEP; TEP

Beneath the umbrageous shadow of a shade. A Pastoral; in the Modern Style. "Worcester." NOEC

Beneath the waning moon I walk at night. The Journey of Life. Bryant. EAP

Beneath the willow wound round with ivy. Hops. Boris Pasternak, tr. fr. Russian by Jon Stallworthy and Peter France. BoLoP; TTTS

Beneath their brown lashes. (LL) Verse Written in the Album of Mademoiselle. Pierre Dalcour. PoNe; TTY

Beneath their flames, cities of candelabra. The Chestnut Avenue at Alton House. Charles Tomlinson. FaBoTw

Beneath these alien stars. Pioneer Woman. Vesta Pierce Crawford. AiP

Beneath these fruit-tree boughs that shed. The Green Linnet. Wordsworth. EnRP; GTBS; GTBS-P

Beneath these plains. West of Chicago. John Dimoff. RFM

Beneath these poppies buried deep. Epitaph on Robert Southey. Thomas Moore. FaBoCo; FaBoEE

Beneath these shades, beside yon winding steam. On Visiting the Graves of Hawthorne and Thoreau. Jones Very. TAP

Beneath these trembling hands. (LL) Back from the Word-Processing Course, I Say to My Old Typewriter. Michael C. Blumenthal. GOYP; NoAM

Beneath this smooth stone by the bone of his bone. Unknown. FaBoEE

Beneath this sod lie the remains. Epitaph on a Young Poet Who Died before Having Achieved Success. Amy Lowell. OBAL

Beneath this stone a Poet Laureate lies. Epitaph on William Whitehead. Unknown. FaBoEE

Beneath this stone does William Hazlitt lie. W. H. Eheu! Samuel Taylor Coleridge. FaBoEE

Beneath this stone in hopes of Zion. At Upton-on-Severn. Unknown. FaBoCo; FaBoEE
(Advertising Epitaph: From Upton-on-Severn, Gloustershire.) FaBoUs

Beneath this stone lies the body of Hengist. Hengest Cyning. Jorge Luis Borges, tr. fr. Spanish by Norman Thomas di Giovanni. NYBP

Beneath this tent, clutching this glass of beer. Blues for an Old Blue. Walker Gibson. NYBP

Beneath those parts, where stretching to its bound. Claude Quillet, tr. fr. Latin by George Sewell. Fr. Callipaedia; or, The Art of Getting Beautiful Children. ECEV; FaBoUs

Beneath Thy Wing. Hayyim Nahman Bialik, tr. fr. Hebrew by Helena Frank. TrJP

Beneath Time's roaring cannon. When the Mississippi Flowed in Indiana. Vachel Lindsay. CMoP

Beneath yon birch with silver bark. The Ballad of the Dark Ladie. Samuel Taylor Coleridge. EnRP

Beneath yon larkspur's azure bells. The Blue-Bird. Herman Melville. BLPL; NOBA

Beneath yon ruin'd abbey's moss-grown piles. Thomas Warton the Younger. Fr. Pleasures of Melancholy, The. NOEC; OxAEP-1

Beneath your cooling coverlet you lie. Radiation Victim. Colin Thiele. NOBAu

Benedicite, What Dreamed I This Night? Unknown. HAP; PoEL-1

Benedick's Complaints: Much Ado about Nothing. Gary Mitchner. BAP-91

Benediction. Bible, O.T. Fr. Numbers. TrGrPo

Benediction. Donald Jeffrey Hayes. EaPr; PoNe

Benediction. Bob Kaufman. PoNe

Benediction. Stanley Kunitz. VGW

Benediction. Mark Turbyfill. PoA

Benediction for the Felt. Mongol Oral Tradition, tr. by C. R. Bawden. WTO

Benediction for the Tent. Mongol Oral Tradition, tr. by C. R. Bawden. WTO

Benedicto: May your trails be crooked, winding, lonesome. Edward Abbey. EaPr

Benefactors of the Little Box, The. Vasco [or Vasko] Popa, tr. fr. Serbo-Croatian by Charles Simic. HSix

Beneficent but blind, my blood. The Prayer of the Arab Physician. Monk Gibbon. TIRV

Benefiecent, believe me./ His Eccentricities. (LL) Bat is dun, with wrinkled wings, The. Emily Dickinson. FM; NAAL-1

Benefits and Abuse of Alcohol, The. Eubulus, tr. fr. Greek by Richard Cumberland. FaBoUs; NBLV

Benefits of Sorrow. L. A. J. Moorer. CBWP-3

Benicasim. Sylvia Townsend Warner. OBWP

Benign Neglect/ Mississippi, 1970. Primus St. John. PoBA

Benjamin. Ogden Nash. PeLi

Benjamin Banneker Sends His Almanac to Thomas Jefferson. Jay Wright. VCAP

Benjamin Franklin 1706-1790. Rosemary and Stephen Vincent Benét. FaPON

Benjamin Franklin Hazard. Edgar Lee Masters. Fr. New Spoon River, The. GOA

Benjamins' Lamentation for Their Sad Loss at Sea, by Storms and Tempests, The. Unknown. OxBSS

Bennington. William Henry Babcock. PAH

Benny. Fran Adler. BTR

Bent. Martin Carter. PBCV

Bent double, like old beggars under sacks. Dulce et Decorum Est. Wilfred Owen. CMoP; DL; FaBoEH; FaBoPV; FaBoTw; FaBV; FaPoB; FF; HeIL; HeIP; HoPM; InPK; InvP; LiTB; LiTM; MeMBP; MoAB; MoBrPo; NAEL-2; NIP; NoAM; NoP; OAEL-2; OBWP; PAW; PeFWW; PoE; Poetr; PoWW; PPP; PrIm; RaBo; TFi; TRP; UnPo

Bent old men and women and dirty children scavenging. Environment. Lionel Kearns. NOBC

Best? Siv Widerberg, *tr. fr. Swedish by* Verne Moberg. NTCP

Best and brightest, come away. The Invitation. Shelley. GTBS; GTBS-P; OBEV
(Invitation, to Jane, The.) CH
(To Jane: The Invitation.) NAEL-2

Best-Beloved, The. Francis Quarles. OxBM

Best Cowboy Movie, The. Elizabeth Smither. PeNZ

Best dance is the dance of the eastern clans, The. *Somali Oral Tradition, tr. by* B. W. Andrzejewski *and* I. M. Lewis. WTO

Best days are the first, The/ To flee. (*LL*) Mantova. James Wright. NNaP

Best Friend, The. W. H. Davies. OBMV

Best-loved Night!, The. (*LL*) Hymn to the Night. Longfellow. BLPL; MeMAP; NOBA; OxBA; PWR; TAP; TrGrPo

Best Loved of Africa. Margaret Danner. PoBA; PoNe

Best Man in the Vield, The, *sels.* William Barnes.
Sam and Bob. PeVV, *tr. by* Hualing Nieh, *Eclogue*

Best of All, The. Fanny Crosby. BLRP

Best of All, The. Margaret G. Rhodes. BoTP

Best of All. *Unknown.* WBLP

Best of All. J. M. Westrup. BoTP

Best of both worlds being got, The. Poets' Corner. Robert Graves. FaBoEE

Best of thy sex! if sacred friendship can. To Phylocles, Inviting Him to Friendship. "Ephelia." KTR; NOSC; WPE

Best Old Fellow in the World, The. *Unknown.* AmFP

Best Religion, The. Heine, *tr. fr. German by* Emma Lazarus. *Fr.* Tannhäuser. TrJP

Best slave, The. Alcestis on the Poetry Circuit. Erica Jong. AmPA; NALW

Best Slow Dancer, The. David Wagoner. NoAM; VCAP

Best Thing in the World, The. Elizabeth Barrett Browning. *See* What's the best thing in the world?

Best Time for Conception, The. Claude Quillet, *tr. fr. Latin by* George Sewell. *Fr.* Callipaedia; or, The Art of Getting Beautiful Children. FaBoUs

"Best way to go, The," said my muffled-up friend. March Hares. Walter de la Mare. FaBoNo

Bestiary, The, *sels. Unknown, tr. fr. Middle English.*
Whale, The. CRP

Bestiary, A. (Man who found the aardvark, The.) Kenneth Rexroth. OBAL
Sels.
Deer. HoPM
Fox. NNaP
Herring. HoPM
Horse. NNaP
Lion. HoPM
Raccoon. NNaP; ZA
(Racoon.) FiBHP
Vulture. NNaP
Wolf. NNaP
You. HoPM

Bestiary for the Fingers of My Right Hand. Charles Simic. AmPA; LCAP

Bestow this day on us the grace. The Festival of the Nativity. Richard de Ledrede, *tr. fr. Latin by* Robert Wyse Jackson. TIRV

Bête Humaine. Francis Brett Young. CH

Beth Gêlert. William Robert Spencer. BeLS

Beth Gêlert; or, The Grave of the Greyhound. William Robert Spencer. *See* Spearmen heard the bugle sound, The.

Bethel. A. J. H. Duganne. PAH

Bethel, Horeb, Engedi, Soar. Exile: Welsh Service from Daventry. Llewelyn Wyn Griffith. AngWe

Bethlehem. William Canton. *See* When the herd[s] were watching.

Bethlehem Town. Eugene Field. WBLP

Bethou me, said sparrow, to the crackled blade. Wallace Stevens. *Fr.* Notes toward a Supreme Fiction. LiTM

Bethsabe Bathing. George Peele. *See* Hot sun [*or* sunne], cool[e] fire, tempered with sweet air[e].

Bethsabe's Song. George Peele. *Fr.* David and [Fair] Bethsabe. ChIV-1; EnRePo; GBL; NOBE; NoP; NoSic; OxBoLi; OxBSP; PoEL-2; RB; TEP

Betjeman at the Post Office. Stanley J. Sharpless. FaBoPa

Betjeman, 1984. Charles Causley. FaBoCo; NOBL; OxBTC; PeLV; UV

Betony. Mary Mackey. SRLS

Betray no surprise. Whisper in Agony. Jules Supervielle, *tr. fr. French by* D. J. Enright. OBD

Betray what they have found? (*LL*) M. François le Vaillant Recalls His Travels to the Interior Parts of Africa. Patrick Cullinan. PeSAV

Betrayal. Léon Laleau, *tr. fr. French by* Ellen Conroy Kennedy. *Fr.* Black Music. NegPo

Betrayed by a maid in her teens. (*LL*) The Man on the Flying Trapeze. *Unknown.* BLPA; OxBoLi

Betrayed by friend dragged from the garden hailed. Ecce Homunculus. R. A. K. Mason. PeNZ

Betrayed her own own leaders, one by one. (*LL*) Ladies and gents, you are here assembled. James Joyce. IIP

Betrayed Maiden, The. *Unknown.* OBET

Betrothal, A. E. J. Scovell. GBL

Betrothed. Louise Bogan. CrSp

Betsey and I Are Out. Will M. Carleton. VPP

Betsy Baker. *Unknown.* OxNR

Betsy, if pencil erasers could sing. 110 Year Old House. Ed Ochester. Poetsp

Betsy's Battle Flag. Minna Irving. PAH

Bette Davis. Jackie Kay. NWP

Better a day in Oxbridge. Stanley J. Sharpless. BXAP

Better Answer to Cloe [*or* Chloe] Jealous, A. Matthew Prior. *See* Dear Cloe [*or* Chloe], how blubbered is that pretty face!

Better Books to Burn. Ben Jonson. *Fr.* Exercration Upon Vulcan, An. CBCK

Better born than married, misled. The Grandmother. Wendell Berry. MT

Better Come Drink Wine with Me, *sels.* Po Chü-i, *tr. fr. Chinese by* Burton Watson.

Better disguised than the leaf-insect. The Lake. Ted Hughes. FaBoTw; NYBP

Better it were had you borne black earth, o mother, rather than me. Mother of Man. Vesna Parun, *tr. fr. Croatian by* Mary Coote. PBWP

Better, my lover, dead. (*LL*) The Farmer's Wife. Anne Sexton. HoPM; LiTM

Better never trouble Trouble. Trouble. David Keppel. PoLF; WBLP

Better not go to these deep woods. The Great Fountains. Anne Hébert, *tr. fr. French by* Willis Barnstone. BoWoP

Better not to go back to the village. The Malefic Return. Ramón López Velarde, *tr. fr. Spanish by* Samuel Beckett. OBVE

Better one thin frail line of friendship in a letter. The Letter. John Blight. CBAP

Better quit fooling, fooling me. (*LL*) All Night Long Fooling Me. *Unknown.* AmFP

Better Resurrection, A. Christina Rossetti. NOBVV; TrPWD

Better than a closet martinet. What Happened? John Wieners. PoM

Better than grandeur, better than gold. Better than Gold. Abram Joseph Ryan. PoToHe

Better than granite, Spoon River. Aaron Hatfield. Edgar Lee Masters. *Fr.* Spoon River Anthology. LiTA

Better the book against the rock. Three Poems about Children. Austin Clarke. CIP

Better they never learned to read! The Misogynist. Jean Morgan. FF

Better Things. George Macdonald. PWR

Better to close the book and say good-night. The Double Autumn. James Reeves. OxBSP

Better to live as a rogue and a bum. Mahsati, *tr. fr. Farsi by* Deirdre Lashgari. AIW; WPOW

Better to see your cheek grown hollow. Madman's Song. Elinor Wylie. MoAB; MoAmPo; PoRA

Better to smell the violet cool than sip. Better Things. George Macdonald. PWR

Better trust all and be deceived. Faith. Fanny Kemble. FaBoBe

Better Way, The. Walter Leaf. FaBoCo

Better, Wiser and Happier. Ella Wheeler Wilcox. WBLP

Better yet, if called by a panther,/ Don't anther. (*LL*) The Panther. Ogden Nash. FaPON; MoShBr; OBAL; OBCA

Betty at the Party. *Unknown.* BoTP

Betty Blue. Mother Goose. OxNR; ReMoGo

Betty Boop,/ Isn't she cute? *Unknown.* RoPo

Betty Botter bought some butter. *Unknown.* OTCP; OxNR

Betty by the Sea. Ronald McCuaig. NOBAu

Betty Fuller cried and said, Hit me. A Local Man Remembers Betty Fuller. James Whitehead. MT

Betty Pringle's Pig. Mother Goose. OxNR

Betty Zane. Thomas Dunn English. PAH

Betuix twell houris and ellevin. The Amendis to the Telyouris and Sowtaris for the Turnament Maid on Thame. William Dunbar. OBSV
(Amends to the Tailors and Shoemakers.) ScCV

Between. Vladimir Holan, *tr. fr. Czech by* Ian Milner *and* Jarmila Milner. PoSu

Between a Contractor and His Wife. *Unknown.* NOEC

Between a sleep and a sleep. (*LL*) Before the Beginning of Years. Swinburne. EnVR; ImPo; LiTB; NAEL-2; NoP; NTP

Between a sunny bank and the sun. Two Houses. Edward Thomas. FaBoCh

Between a Tyrant and a King. The Difference Between a King and a Tyrant. Timothy Kendall. NoSic

Between adventures the picaro must lie down. Picaro. Harry Clifton. IB

Between an Unemployed Artist and His Wife. *Unknown.* NOEC

Between Awajishima and Suma. *Unknown, tr. fr. Japanese* by Kenneth Rexroth *and* Ikuko Atsumi. WPJ

Between Battles. Zhimin Zhang. PAW

Between Botallack and the light. A Ballad of a Mine. Robin Skelton. MoBS

Between Cellini's Perseus and the Sabine Rape. More Nudes for Florence. Harold Witt. ErPo

Between each layer of tattered, broken flesh. Burial Detail. Andrew Hudgins. MT

Between Ebb and Flow. Fadwa Tuqan, *tr. fr. Arabic.* TSaS, *tr. by* Salma Khadra Jayyusi *and* Naomi Shihab Nye

Between fields of popcorn. "America, I Love You." Bert Kalmar *and* Harry Ruby. FiBHP

Between five and fifty. Praise. Jane Cooper. TAP

Between four and five. (*LL*) Ding dang, bell rang. *Unknown.* OxNR

Between great coloured vanes the butterflies. Wings. Judith Wright. CBAP; NOBAu

Between her breasts is my home, between her breasts. Song of a Man Who Is Loved. D. H. Lawrence. OxBM

Between Here and Illinois. Ralph Pomeroy. Poetsp

Between him and me, I feel. Bi-Lingual. Sylvia Paskin. DT

Between hunger and love? (*LL*) Mundus et Infans. W. H. Auden. LiTB; LiTM; MeMAP; MoAB; MoBrPo; NAs; NoAM

Between living and dreaming. Antonio Machado Ruiz, *tr. fr. Spanish* by Robert Bly. EnlH

Between Love and Death. Frank Stanford. MT

Between Me and Anyone Who Can Understand. Sharon Scott. JB

Between me and the rising sun. Cobwebs. E. L. M. King. BoTP

Between me and the sunset, like a dome. The Man against the Sky. E. A. Robinson. AmPP; CMoP; LiTA; OxBA

Between me and the wood. Ark Artefact. Jay Macpherson. *Fr.* Ark, The. NOBC

Between me and thy spirit. (*LL*) O my brothers of the wilderness. Mary Austin. EaPr

Between my finger and my thumb. Digging. Seamus Heaney. BIrV; CIP; IIP; InPS; IPY; NAEL-2; TwCP

Between myself and thee! (*LL*) My Playmate. Whittier. AnAmPo; NOBA; PFP

Between Ourselves. Audre Lorde. WPOW

Between rebellion as a private study and the public. Last Poem. Charles Donnelly. BIrV
(Poem: "Between rebellion as a private study and the public.") CIP; IIP

Between Rivers and Seas. Lance Henson. VoR

Between sea-foam and the tide. To a Boy. Nancy Morejón, *tr. fr. Spanish* by Kathleen Weaver. AIW

Between Seasons. Li-Young Lee. TRP

Between Seasons. Anne Welsh. PeSA

Between statements I. In the Sweet Dark. John Seed. VaA

Between the avenues of cypresses. Service of All the Dead. D. H. Lawrence. NSI

Between the clod and the midnight. The Interim. Robert Penn Warren. *Fr.* Tale of Time. LCAP

Between the conscious and the unconscious, the mind has put up a swing. Kabir, *tr. fr. Hindi* by Robert Bly. EnlH

Between the dark and the daylight. If. Franklin P. Adams. OBAL

Between the dark and the daylight. The Children's Hour. Longfellow. FaBoBe; FaBV; FaPoB; FaPON; GGP; ImGa; OBAL; OBCA; PoEL-5; PoLF; WBLP; WHSW

Between the dark silent trees. Dionysius. Sophia de Mello Breyner Andresen, *tr. fr. Portuguese* by Allan Francovich. PBWP

Between the fosse and inner wall. The Defender. Arthur M. Sampley. GoYe

Between the GARDENING and the COOKERY. A Bookshop Idyll. Kingsley Amis. OxBTC; PeLV

Between the Haunted House. Barry Island. John Idris Jones. AngWe

Between the idea and the word. Between. Vladimir Holan, *tr. fr. Czech* by Ian Milner *and* Jarmila Milner. PoSu

Between the midnight and the morn. The Secret Muse. Roy Campbell. PeSA

Between the perfect. Somewhere the Equation Breaks Down. Daniel Berrigan. NYBP

Between the Porch and the Altar. (Meeting his mother makes him lose ten years.) *sels.* Robert Lowell.

At the Altar. InPK

Between the railway and the mine. The Blackberry. Norman Nicholson. MoBrPo

Between the River and the Sea. Tim Longville. VaA

Between the rose-bud and the cherry. (*LL*) Of a Spider. Wilfred Thornley. FaPON; PDV

Between the rows. How Early Fall Came This Year. John Z. Guzlowski. BTR

Between the ship's side and the quay, a gap. Day Trip. Evan Gwyn Williams. AngWe

Between the sunset and the eucalyptus tree. Home. Nasima Aziz, *tr. fr. Hindi.* TSaS

Between the Traveller and the Setting Sun. Thoreau. PoEL-4

Between the under and the upper blue. Seagulls. Robert Francis. RFM

Between the walls, the brim. Terce. James McMichael. PoA

Between the Wars. Robert Hass. VCAP

Between the wet trees and the sorry steeple. W. H. Louise Imogen Guiney. AmWP

Between the World and Me. Richard Wright. LiTM; MoP; PoBA

Between thirty and forty, one is distracted by the five lusts. On Being Sixty. Po Chü-i, *tr. fr. Chinese* by Arthur Waley. AWP

Between town and the. The Quarry Pool. Denise Levertov. VGW

Between two fires. (*LL*) The Conflict. C. Day Lewis. LiTB; LiTM; MoAB; MoBrPo; NoP

Between Two Furious Oceans, *sels.* Dick Diespecker. MT

Between two golden tufts of summer grass. Lying in the Grass. Sir Edmund Gosse. EBVV

Between two mighty hills a sheer. The Eagle. "Fiona Macleod." *Fr.* Transcripts from Nature. FM

Between two rivers. Island. Langston Hughes. HCAP

Between Two Worlds. Rosemary Thomas. NYBP

Between Us. Stephen Berg. NaP

Between Us. James Merrill. PoE

Between Vicksburg and Rolling Fork. Road. D. C. Berry. MT

Between vistas painted into vastness. The Next Act. Debora Greger. *Fr.* Afterlife, The. BAP-91

Between Walls. William Carlos Williams. HoPM; SOTW; TAP; VGW

Between weapon and buffcoat seldom a letter comes. (*LL*) Midnight. Tu Fu. PLT

Between You and Me. Samuel Hazo. GOYP

Between you and me on the overlook. Two in Twilight. Eugenio Montale, *tr. fr. Italian* by William Arrowsmith. AnAn

Between yourself and me. (*LL*) She's All My Fancy Painted Him. "Lewis Carroll." FaBoNo

Betweenpie mountains — lights a lovely mile. (*LL*) My Own Heart Let Me More Have Pity On. Gerard Manley Hopkins. EnVR; FaBoMo; InPS; LiTM; MeMBP; MoAB; MoBrPo; NOBVV; NoP; TOF

Betwixt the stirrop and the ground. Camden's Remains. *Unknown.* OtMeF

Betwixt traffic and trains, boats on the tide. In the Flats, flat voices. Ken Smith. *Fr.* As It Happens. PWE

Betwixt two ridges of plowed-[ploughed] land sat [lay] Wat. The Hunting of the Hare. Margaret Lucas, Duchess of Newcastle. FaBoVe; FM; KTR; NOSC

BE2c is my 'bus; therefore I shall want, The. The Pilot's Psalm. *Unknown.* NSI; PoWW

Beverley Maid and the Tinker, The. *Unknown.* CoMu

Beverly Hills, Chicago. Gwendolyn Brooks. Poetr; VGW

Bewail not much, my parents! me, the prey. Lucianus, *tr. fr. Latin* by William Cowper. OBD

Bewailing in my chamber thus allone. He Sees His Beloved. James I, King of Scotland. *Fr.* Kingis Quair, The. PoEL-1

Bewar, squier, yeman, and page. A Warning to Those Who Serve Lords. *Unknown.* MeEL

Beware. (*LL*) Beneath the Pole of Proud Raven. Jana Harris. SRLS

Beware: Do Not Read This Poem. Ishmael Reed. BPo; NIP; NoP; PoBA

Beware Fair Maide. *At.* to Joshua Sylvester. GGP

Beware, My Child. Shel Silverstein. PDV

Beware, my friend, of fiends and their grimaces. Beware of Kittens. Heine, *tr. fr. German* by Alma Strettell. SoCa

Beware of Dogmas. Ebenezer Elliot. FaBoEE

Beware of doubt — faith is the subtle chain. Faith. Elizabeth Oakes Smith. *Fr.* Atheism. AmWP

Beware of Figs. Nicophon, *tr. fr. Greek* by Charles Duke Yonge. FaBoUs

Beware of Kittens. Heine, *tr. fr. German* by Alma Strettell. SoCa

Beware of Ruins. A. D. Hope. NoAM

Beware of the man who denounces ambition. Seventeen Warnings in Search of a Feminist Poem. Erica Jong. AmPA

Beware of thinking nothing's there. Virtual Particles. Frank Wilczek. NBLV

Beware the Cuckoo. Ernest G. Moll. NOBAu

Beware the cuckoo, though she bring. Beware the Cuckoo. Ernest G. Moll. NOBAu

Beware! The Israelite of old, who tore. The Warning. Longfellow. ChIV-1

Beware. There are fawns. Kydios, *tr. fr. Greek by* Sam Hamill. InMo

Beware! therfore: the blind eteth many a fly. *(LL)* Against Women. *Unknown.* MeEL

Bewick and Graham. *Unknown.* ESPB

Bewick and the Graeme, The. *Unknown.* OxBB

Bewick Finzer. E. A. Robinson. CMoP; MeMAP; MoAB; MoAmPo; NAAL-2; PPP

Bewildered in our buying throng. Patrum Propositum. Robert Fitzgerald. GOA

Bewildered tonight, how often. Elegy for a Five Year Old. Aidan Carl Mathews. IB

Bewildered with the broken tongue. Words in Time. Archibald MacLeish. PoRA

Bewilderingly, from wildly shaken cloud. Internal Firesides. Mathilde Blind. FM

Bewilderment at the Entrance of the Fat Boy into Eden, A. Daryl Hine. NOBC

Bewitching Distant Landscape. Joseph Freiherr von Eichendorff, *tr. fr. German by* Philip L. Miller. RiWo

Bewitching the blossoms of the spring grove. *Unknown, tr. by* Ronald C. Miao. *Fr.* Tzu-yeh Songs of the Four Seasons. SuSp

Bewley's Oriental Café, Westmoreland Street. Paul Durcan. CIP

Bewteis of the Fute-Ball, The. *Unknown.* FaBoCo; OxBS; ScCV

Bewty of hir amorus ene, The. Off Womanheid Ane Flour Delice. *Unknown.* OxBS

Beyond. *Unknown.* PWR

Beyond all this, the wish to be alone. Wants. Philip Larkin. GTBS-P; NoP

Beyond, beneath, within, wherever blood. A Quintina of Crosses. Chad Walsh. TrCP

Beyond Fear. Odia Ofeimun. HBAPE

Beyond Imagination. David Rokeah, *tr. fr. Hebrew by* Ruth Finer Mintz. MHP

Beyond its own sweet will! *(LL)* Amy Wentworth. Whittier. AnAmPo; BeLS

Beyond Kerguelen. Henry Clarence Kendall. NOBAu

Beyond Knowledge. Alice Meynell. ChIV-1

Beyond Magdalen and by the Bridge, on a place called there the Plain. By Magdalen Bridge, Oxford. Gerard Manley Hopkins. FaBoPP

Beyond Melody. Nathan Alterman, *tr. fr. Hebrew by* Ruth Finer Mintz. MHP

Beyond my window in the night. A Town Window. John Drinkwater. BoTP

Beyond Nagel's Funeral Parlor. "Elizabethans Called It Dying, The." James Schuyler. NeAP; PoM

Beyond Religion. Lucretius, *tr. fr. Latin by* William Ellery Leonard. AWP

Beyond Silence. Lan Ling, *tr. fr. Chinese by* Kenneth Rexroth *and* Ling Chung. WPC

Beyond that next turning of the canyon walls. *(LL)* Benedicto: May your trails be crooked, winding, lonesome. Edward Abbey. EaPr

Beyond the Alps. Robert Lowell. LCAP; NOBA

Beyond the Atlas roams a glutton. The Glutton. Robert Graves. CMoP

Beyond the bamboo fence, cooking fire and smoke. Liu Tsung-yüan, *tr. by* Jan W. Walls. *Fr.* Farmers. SuSp

Beyond the Beaten Way. George Sands Johnson. PWR

Beyond the Chagres. James Stanley Gilbert. PoLF

Beyond the choric gestures of the olive. Greece. Derek Walcott. AnAn

Beyond the dry rustling cornstalks. *(LL)* Once Again. Liz Sohappy Bahe. CDW

Beyond the East Gate. *Unknown, tr. fr. Chinese by* Robert Payne. TAL

Beyond the edge of the sepia. Lament for a Cricket Eleven. Kenneth Allott. OxBTC

Beyond the End. Denise Levertov. NeAP; VGW

Beyond the fence she hesitates. Midwife Cat. Mark Van Doren. CRH

Beyond the foot of the bed: a seascape whose ocean. On Motel Walls. David Wagoner. DiPo

Beyond the fuselage. *(LL)* Night Flight. Marion Alexopoulos. NOBAu

Beyond the gate the cormorant had gone and not returned. Tu Fu, *tr. fr. Chinese by* Jerome P. Seaton. SuSp

Beyond the Grave. Margaret E. Bruner. PoToHe

Beyond the great valley an odd instinctive rising. Ascent to the Sierras. Robinson Jeffers. OxBA

Beyond the hour we counted rain that fell. Old Countryside. Louise Bogan. HAP; LiTA; WPE

Beyond the Hunting Woods. Donald Justice. NYBP

Beyond the inmost barriers of the brain. The Owl. Edward Davison. PoA

Beyond the last gate, where I made my first halt. On Scafell Pike. Ted Walker. NYBP

Beyond the last horizon's rim. The Hills of Rest. Albert Bigelow Paine. WGRP

Beyond the last house, where home was. American Portrait: Old Style. Robert Penn Warren. FYAP; Poetr

Beyond the Last Lamp Near Tooting Common. Thomas Hardy. NOBE; OBNC

Beyond the mountain passes. Crossing Han River. Li P'in, *tr. fr. Chinese by* Kenneth Rexroth. OHMPC

Beyond the murk that swallows me. Irene Rutherford McLeod. *Fr.* Rebel. WGRP

Beyond the Nigger ("Beyond the outstretched hands.") Sterling Plumpp. PoBA

Beyond the Potomac. Paul Hamilton Hayne. PAH

Beyond the Presidency. Morgan Gibson. FF

Beyond the Profit of Today. *Unknown.* PoToHe

Beyond the rapture and the dread? *(LL)* The Abduction. Stanley Kunitz. CAPP; SV; WeW

Beyond the seas to the infinite? *(LL)* At Day's End. Hayyim Nahman Bialik. MHP

Beyond the sphere which spreads to widest space. Dante, *tr. fr. Italian by* Dante Gabriel Rossetti. *Fr.* Vita Nuova, La. AWP; CTC

Beyond the stone wall. Jug Brook. Ellen Bryant Voigt. MT

Beyond the stream at Seta stretches an endless view. Liu Ya-tzu, *tr. by* Wu-chi Liu. *Fr.* Miscellaneous Poems on Lake Biwa. SuSp

Beyond the Tapestries. Norma Farber. GoYe

Beyond the vague Atlantic deep. Our Mother Tongue. Richard Monckton Milnes. GN

Beyond the view of crossroads ringed with breath. Rubaiyat. Mimi Khalvati. NWP

Beyond the waste of commerce there are hills. Office Window. Llewelyn Wyn Griffith. AngWe

Beyond time, the one message she knew. *(LL)* Package for Another World. Jemal Sharah. NOBAu

Beyond Wars. David Morton. PAH

Beyond Words. Robert Frost. Spl; WeW

Bhagavad-Gita, The, *sels. Unknown, tr. fr. Sanskrit.*
    "Arjuna said:/ How shall I in battle against Bhisma." DL
    "Hear father yet thou Long-Armed Lord! these latest words I say." TAL
    "Learn from me, Son of Kunti! also this." TOF
    "Learn now, dear Prince! how, if thy soul be set." TAL
    "Nay, but of such an one." TOF
    "Now will I open unto thee — whose heart." TAL
    "Sovereign soul, The/ Of him who lives self-governed and at peace." TOF
    "Steadfast a lamp burns sheltered from the wind." TOF
    "Therefore, who doeth work rightful to do." TAL
    "This, for my soul's peace, have I heard from Thee." TAL
    "Those who realize true wisdom." EnlH, (*vers. by* Stephen Mitchell).
    "Who is that BRAHMA? What that Soul of Souls." TAL
    "Yet hard/ The travail is for such as bend their minds." TOF

Bi-lingual. Maria Jastrzebska. NBrP

Bi-Lingual. Sylvia Paskin. DT

Biafra. L. V. Mack. PoBA

Bialik tradition back home was, A. Earrings. Annette Bialik Harchik. BTR

Bianca. Arthur Symons. OHCV; PeVV

Bianca among the Nightingales. Elizabeth Barrett Browning. BrRo; GTBS-P

Bible, The, *sels.* David Levi, *tr. fr. Italian by* Mary A. Craig.
    "Thou, Zion, old and suffering." TrJP

Bible, The. L. A. J. Moorer. CBWP-3

Bible, The. Sir Walter Scott. *See* Within this [*or* that] ample volume lies.

Bible, The. Thomas Traherne. PeECV

Bible Bob Responds to a Jesus Honker. D. H. Lloyd. NGP

Bible is a book of race, The. White. Gerald William Barrax. *Fr.* Old Gory, The. NBV

Bible is an antique volume, The. Emily Dickinson. ChIV-1; NAAL-1; NoP

Bible says Sennacherib's campaign was spoiled, The. C. S. Lewis. TrCP

Bible soothes the harried soul, The. Travelling Companions. Richard Armour. GrPl

Bible Story. Charles Causley. TOF

Bibles sold as cheap as these. *(LL)* From a London Bookshop. *Unknown.* FaBoUs; NBLV

Bibliographer. Josephine Miles. FaBoWP

Bibliolaters, *sels.* James Russell Lowell.
    God Is Not Dumb. ChIV-1; WGRP

Bile Them Cabbage Down. *Unknown*. AmFP

Bill. Peter Kocan. CBAP

Bill 'Awkins. Kipling. CBLP

Bill Bailey, Won't You Please Come Home. Hughie Cannon. OBAL

Bill, Bill, can't sit still. *Unknown*. RoPo

Bill Bubble in a bowler hat. All the Way Back. Laura Riding. *Fr.* Forgotten Girlhood. RB

Bill/ exists. A Personality Sketch: Bill. Ronda Davis. JB

Bill Jones had been the shining star upon his college team. Alumnus Football. Grantland Rice. PoLF

Bill the Bachelor lived by himself. Bachelors' Buttons. Maud Morin. BoTP

Bill/ Was ill. Careless Talk. Mark Hollis. FiBHP; NBLV

Billboard Song, The. *Unknown*. CBNP

Billiard Table, The. Roy Fisher. VaA

Billie Holiday's burned voice. Canary. Rita Dove. VCAP

Billie Pierce used to sing to me. Billie Pierce's Jazz Funeral. Lee Meitzen Grue. Jaz

Billie Pierce's Jazz Funeral. Lee Meitzen Grue. Jaz

Billowy headlands swiftly fly, The. Battle-Song of the *Oregon*. Wallace Rice. PAH

Bill's Story. Mark Doty. PFL

Billy. Harry Graham. *See* Billy in one of his nice new sashes.

Billy Batter. Dennis Lee. TLR

Billy, Billy. *Unknown*. ReMoGo

Billy, Billy, strong and able. *Unknown*. RoPo

Billy Boy. Dorothy King. BoTP

Billy Boy. *Unknown*. OBET

Billy Boy. *Unknown*. AmFP; BLPA; HoPM; OBET

Billy Budd, Foretopman, *sels*. Herman Melville.
　Billy in the Darbies. HAP; NAAL-1; NAWM-2; NOBA; OxBoLi; PoEL-5

Billy Goat Gruff. The Troll to her Children. Jane Yolen. OTCP

Billy Grimes. *Unknown*. AmFP

Billy in one of his nice new sashes. Tender-Heartedness. Harry Graham. *Fr.* Some Ruthless Rhymes. CBNP; NBLV; PeLV

(Billy.) FaBoCo

Billy in the Darbies. Herman Melville. *Fr.* Billy Budd, Foretopman. HAP; NAAL-1; NAWM-2; NOBA; OxBoLi; PoEL-5

Billy the Kid. *Unknown*. FaBoBe

Billy's dead, and gone to glory — so is Billy's sister Nell. Billy's Rose. George R. Sims. VPP

Billy's Rose. George R. Sims. VPP

Bim Bam. Dorothy Rosenberg. PoNe

Binary mathematician, A. *Unknown*. PeLi

Bind, The. Wayne Brown. PBCV

Bind-Weed. "Susan Coolidge." GN

Bind your straight hair. Thessalian. Winifred Bryher. PoA

Binds us together with you. (*LL*) Chorus of the Rescued. Nelly Sachs. PoSu; WPOW, *tr. by* Ruth Mead *and* Matthew Mead

Bingen on the Rhine. Caroline E. Norton. BeLS; BLPA; WBLP

Bingo. *Unknown*. CH; TTTS

Binnorie; or, The Two Sisters. *Unknown*. OBEV; PoE; TrGrPo

Binoculars. Fleur Adcock. PWE

Binsey Poplars (Felled 1879). Gerard Manley Hopkins. BoNaP; EBVV; ELP; EnVR; FaBoPP; InPS; Mes; NAEL-2; NoAM; NoP; RB

Biodrama. Miroslav Holub, *tr. fr. Czech by* Ewald Osers. CBNP

Biographical Notes. Al Robles. ETG

Biography. Amiri Baraka. TAP

Biography, *sels*. Ernst Jandl.

Biography. A. M. Klein. TrJP

Biography, *sels*. John Masefield.
　"Other bright days of action have seemed great." OxBTC

Biography. Michael Ondaatje. NoAM

Biography for Traman, *sels*. Winfield Townley Scott.
　"Let us record/ The evenings when we were innocents of twenty." ErPo

Biography of an Agnostic. Louis Ginsberg. TrJP

Biography of Southern Rain. Kenneth Patchen. VGW

Biological Light. Primus St. John. ETG

Biology Teacher. Zbigniew Herbert, *tr. fr. Polish by* John Carpenter *and* Bogdana Carpenter. PoSu

Biplane, The. Steve Orlen. GOYP

Birch begins to crack its outer sheath, The. A Young Birch. Robert Frost. BoNaP; LiTA; SAmP

Birch-Tree at Loschwitz, The. Amy Levy. TrJP

Birch Trees. John Richard Moreland. OHIP

Birches. Robert Frost. AmPP; CMoP; FaBoVe; FaBV; HeIL; HeIP; ImGa; LiTA; LiTM; MeMAP; MoAB; MoAmPo; MoP; NAAL-2; NoAM; NoP; OxBA; Poetr; PoLF; PoRA; RB; SAmP; SoSe; TAP; TFi; TrGrPo; TRP

Birches stand in their beggar's row, The. February; the Boy Breughel. Norman Dubie. LCAP

Birches that dance on the top of the hill, The. Parenthood. John Farrar. OHIP

Bird, The. Robert Greacen. PNI

Bird, The. Moyshe-Leyb Halpern, *tr. fr. Yiddish by* John Hollander. PPP

Bird, The. Samuel Hoffenstein. FiBHP

Bird, The. Max Michelson. TrJP

Bird, The. Edwin Muir. ArNa

Bird. Agnes Nemes Nagy, *tr. fr. Hungarian by* Bruce Berlind. BoWoP; PoSu

Bird, The. Charles Simic. AmPA

Bird, The. Louis Simpson. ArOW; BTR

Bird, The. Henry Vaughan. ESCV; FM; GeHe; OBEV; PoE; PoEL-2; SeCV-1

Bird, A. Emily Dickinson. *See* Bird came down the walk, A.

Bird and beast. What She Said ("Bird and Beast.") Nannakaiyar, *tr. fr. Tamil by* A. K. Ramanujan. PLW

Bird and the Muse. Marya Zaturenska. PoA

Bird and the Tree, The. Ridgely Torrence. PoNe

Bird and Waterfall Music. Wang Wei. OHMPC

Bird Appeal. Asa Benveniste. NBrP

Bird at Dawn, The. Harold Monro. BoTP; MoBrPo

Bird at Night. Marion Ethel Hamilton. GoYe

Bird Bath, The. Florence Hoatson. BoTP

Bird, Bird. Gene Derwood. LiTA

Bird, bird don't edge me in. The Reply. Theodore Roethke. NoP; NYBP

Bird calls me, A. The Bird. Charles Simic. AmPA

Bird came down the walk, A. Emily Dickinson. AmPP; BLPL; CMoP; FaPON; FF; FM; GoJo; HeIP; InvP; LiTA; LiTM; MeMAP; Mes; MoAmPo; NAAL-1; NoAM; NOBA; NoP; NTCP; OBAL; OBCA; OxBA; PDV; PoLF; PoRA; SAmP; TFi

(Bird, A.) SiSoPo

Bird came with a crutch under his wing, A. The Bird. Moyshe-Leyb Halpern, *tr. fr. Yiddish*. PPP, *tr. by* John Hollander

Bird Catcher, The. *Unknown, tr. fr. Egyptian by* Ulli Beier. TTY

Bird comes, A/ delicately as a little girl. Yosano Akiko, *tr. fr. Japanese by* Kenneth Rexroth *and* Ikuko Atsumi. WPJ; WPOW

Bird Cried, A. Vilhelm Andreas Wexels Krag, *tr. fr. Norwegian by* Philip L. Miller. RiWo

Bird cried over the desolate sea, A. A Bird Cried. Vilhelm Andreas Wexels Krag, *tr. fr. Norwegian by* Philip L. Miller. RiWo

Bird flew tangent-wise to the open window, A. The Bird. Robert Greacen. PNI

Bird flies and I gum it to a concept, A. Letter to Anne Ridler. G. S. Fraser. OxBS

Bird flies yonder o'er the Field, The. (*LL*) My Little Bird. Bunyan.

Bird flying past my head said previous previous, the. Conrad Aiken. *Fr.* Time in the Rock [or, Preludes to Definition]. VGW

Bird had come to the very end of its song, The. The End of the World. Miroslav Holub, *tr. by* Ewald Osers. PWE

Bird in a Cage. *Unknown*. AS; GBP

Bird in the Cage, The. Mary Effie Lee Newsome. ShDr

Bird in the Hand, A. Vassar Miller. CRP

Bird in the House. Jim Wayne Miller. ETG

Bird is calling from the willow, A. *Unknown*. *Fr.* Four Glosses. NOIV

Bird is lost, The. Yardbird's Skull. Owen Dodson. Jaz; PoBA; VGW

Bird is my neighbor, a whimsical fellow and dim, The. The Crane Is My Neighbor. John Shaw Neilson. CBAP

Bird is tangled in a tree, A. Wilhelm Busch. OBD

Bird kept saying that birds had once been men, The. On an Old Horn. Wallace Stevens. LiTA

"Bird Lives": Charles Parker [in St. Louis]. Michael S. Harper. AmPA; Jaz

Bird of Dawning, The. Shakespeare. *See* Some say that ever 'gainst that season comes.

Bird of Endless Time, The. James Laughlin. WeW

Bird of Glass. Rhyll McMaster. FaBoMA

Bird of Night, The. Randall Jarrell. RFM

Bird of Paradise, The. W. H. Davies. NSI

Bird of Power. Jim Tollerud. VoR

Bird of the bitter bright grey golden morn. A Ballad of François Villon. Swinburne. PoEL-5; PoRA

Bird of the moths! that radiant wing. The Butterfly. Robert Stephen Hawker. EBVV

Bird of the wilderness. The Skylark. James Hogg. GN

Bird of the woodland, sing me a song. To the Mock-Bird. Mary Weston Fordham. AmWP; CBWP-2

Black Bourgeoisie. Amiri Baraka. BPo

Black Boy. Norman Rosten. TrJP

Black boy/ let me get up from the white man's table of fifty sounds. Melvin B. Tolson. PoBA

Black boy, the night hides you. Black Boy. Norman Rosten. TrJP

Black Bread. Tom Paulin. CIP; SCBI

Black brother, think you life so sweet. Time to Die. Ray Garfield Dandridge. PoBA

Black Bud. Michael Smith. PBCV

Black Buoy. Robert H. Davis. HATNAP

Black, carved writing desk, the two silver candlesticks, The. The Poet's Place. Yannis Ritsos, tr. fr. Greek by Paul Merchant. AnRep

Black cat, sweet brother. For James Baldwin. Kay Boyle. NMM

Black cat yawns, The. Cat. Mary Britton Miller. CRH; TLR; WHSW

Black Cloud, The. W. H. Davies. RB

Black cock crowed, The. Two o'Clock. Katharine Pyle. Fr. Wonder Clock, The. OBCA

Black Cottage, The. Robert Frost. VGW

Black Crispus Attucks taught. Dark Symphony. Melvin B. Tolson. PoNe

Black Cross. Reed Whittemore. ArOW

Black currant, red currant, raspberry tart. Unknown. ISE

Black Dada Nihilismus. Amiri Baraka. PoM

Black Dog. Ray A. Young Bear. CDW

Black Draftee from Dixie, The. Carrie Williams Clifford. BlSi

Black Earth. Marianne Moore. FaBoMo

Black education, A. (LL) A Few Blue Words to the Wise. Ted Joans. PoBeRe

Black-eyed Susan. John Gay. See All in the Downs the fleet was moored [or moor'd].

Black-eyed Susie. Unknown. AmFP

Black eyes if you seem dark. To Her Eyes. Lord Herbert of Cherbury. JCP

Black-faced house will love, A. (LL) On the Baptized Ethiopian (or Aethiopian). Richard Crashaw. ChIV-2; FaBoEE; NoP; SeCV-1

Black Faced Sheep, The. Donald Hall. LCAP; SV

Black Faces. Anita Scott Coleman. ShDr

Black Finger, The. Angelina Weld Grimké. PoBA; ShDr

Black flies kept nagging in the heat, The. Tao and Unfitness at Inistiogue on the River Nore. Thomas Kinsella. PBCIP

Black fool, why winter here? These frozen skies. Advice to a Raven in Russia [December, 1812]. Joel Barlow. AmPP; NAAL-1; NOBA; OBWP; OxBA

Black fox loped out of the hills, The. Dream of a Black Fox. Brendan Kennelly. PBCIP

Black, frost-cold distance, sparsely honey-combed. Space. Edward Rowland Sill. AnAmPo

Black girl black girl. Blackberry Sweet. Dudley Randall. HAP; InPS; SoSe; WeW

(Black Magic.) PoBA

Black Girl, De. Unknown. GBP

Black Girl Goes By, A. Emile Roumer, tr. fr. French by Edna Worthley Underwood. TTY

Black Gold, blackgold . . . aint no oil. Blackgoldblueswoman. Kirk Hall. NBV

Black greyed into white a nightmare of bicycling. That Which We Call a Rose. Michael Dransfield. CBAP; NOBAu

Black grows the sudden sky, betokening rain. Sudden Shower. John Clare. OxAEP-2

Black Hairs, The. Heinz Pasman, tr. fr. German by Robert Bly. RaBo

Black Hat, The. Clayton Eshleman. VGW

Black heart of the witch. (LL) Black Soap. Sandra McPherson. VCAP

Black Hen, The. Mother Goose. See Hickety, pickety.

Black Henry. Tejumola Ologboni. NBV

Black Hills Survival Gathering, 1980. Linda Hogan. WoWa

Black history. The Living Truth. Sterling Plumpp. PoBA

Black Horseman. Branko Miljkovic, tr. fr. Serbo-Croatian by Charles Simic. HSix

Black Hose, The. Bruce Weigl. NAmP90

Black I am and much admired. Mother Goose. OxNR

Black in blazonry means. The Buffalo. Marianne Moore. PoA

Black iron fence closes the graves in, A. Visiting Emily Dickinson's Grave with Robert Francis. Robert Bly. LCAP

Black Is a Soul. Joseph Blanco White. PoBA

Black is beautiful. Ron Welburn. NBV

Black Is Best. Larry Thompson. PoBA

Black is; slavery was; I am. This Child Is the Mother. Gloria C. Oden. BlSi

Black is the beauty of the brightest day. To Entertain Divine Zenocrate. Christopher Marlowe. Fr. Tamburlaine the Great. ChTr

Black Is the Color. Unknown. FF

Black Is the Colour. Unknown. GBP

Black is the first nail I ever stepped on. Negritude. James A. Emanuel. BPo

Black is the night. What Is Black? Mary O'Neill. NTCP

Black is what the prisons are. The African Affair. Bruce McM. Wright. PoBA; PoNe

Black Island. Charles Pressoir, tr. fr. French by Ellen Conroy Kennedy. NegPo

Black Jack Davey. Unknown. See There were three gipsies a-come to my door.

Black Jackets. Thom Gunn. HeIP; NAEL-2; TwCP

Black Jam for Dr. Negro. Mari Evans. BPo; PoBA

Black Java Pepper. Arthur Sze. OpBo

Black Jess. Peter Kane Dufault. NYBP

Black Jewel, The. W. S. Merwin. CAPP; LCAP

Black key. White key. No. Unrelenting Flood. William Matthews. Jaz

Black Lace Fan My Mother Gave Me, The. Eavan Boland. BiHa

Black lake, black boat, two black, cut-paper people. Crossing the Water. Sylvia Plath. CAPP; HCAP; RB

Black leather streets are polished by the fog. Two in Search of Dawn. Andrew Taylor. FaBoMA

Black lie the hills; swiftly doth daylight flee. Land-locked. Celia Laighton Thaxter. AmWP

Black like me. (LL) Dream Variation [or Variations]. Langston Hughes. CDC; HAP; NAAL-2; NOBA; PoBA; PoNe

Black, long-tailed, The. The Yellow Season. William Carlos Williams. MoAB; MoAmPo

Black Love. Gwendolyn Brooks. VBLP

Black luggie, lammer bead. Against Witches. Unknown. GBP

Black Madonna, The. Albert Rice. CDC

Black Magic. Dudley Randall. See Black girl black girl.

Black Magic. Sonia Sanchez. BPo

Black Maid to the Fair Boy, The. Henry Reynolds. NOSC

Black Mail. Alice Walker. AmPA

Black Majesty. Countee Cullen. PoBA; VGW

Black Man, 13th Floor. James A. Emanuel. NBV

Black Man, A. Sam Cornish. PoBA

Black Man Go Back To The Old Country. High Modes: Vision as Ritual: Confirmation. Michael S. Harper. NBV

Black Man Talks of Reaping, A. Arna Bontemps. BPo; CDC; PoBA; PoNe

Black Man's Feast. Sarah Webster Fabio. PoBA; PoNe

Black Man's Lament, The. Léon Damas, tr. fr. French by ELlen Conroy Kennedy. NegPo

Black Man's Son, The. Oswald Durand, tr. fr. French by Edna Worthley Underwood. TTY, tr. by Ellen Conroy Kennedy

Black Maps. Mark Strand. PoA

Black Mare. Lynda Hull. UTF

Black Marigolds. At. to Bilhana, formerly at. to Chauras, tr. fr. Sanskrit by E. Powys Mathers. AWP; ErPo, abr.

Black Meat. Jean Follain, tr. fr. French by W. S. Merwin. AnRep

Black men are the tall trees that remain. Portraiture. Anita Scott Coleman. ShDr

Black men with outasight afros. (LL) Beautiful Black Men. Nikki Giovanni. BPo; NMM

Black Mesa, The. James Merrill. PoA

Black milk of dawn [or daybreak] we drink it at dusk [or nightfall]. Death Fugue. Paul Celan, tr. fr. German. AnRep, tr. by Clement Greenberg; PoSu, tr. by John Felstiner; TrJP, tr. by Clement Greenberg (Fugue of Death.) AnRep, tr. by Christopher Middleton; OBVE, tr. by Christopher Middleton

Black Money. Tess Gallagher. NGP

Black Mood. Rosalía de Castro, tr. fr. Galician by John Frederick Nims. STV

Black Mood. Rosalía de Castro. WeW

Black Mother Woman. Audre Lorde. CrSp; MDDM; Poetr

Black Music, sels. Léon Laleau, tr. fr. French by Ellen Conroy Kennedy.
Betrayal. NegPo
Cannibal. NegPo
Legacies. NegPo
Sacrifice. NegPo
Voodoo. NegPo

Black Muslim Boy in a Hospital. James A. Emanuel. PoNe

Black Narcissus. Gerald William Barrax. PoBA

Black Night./ White snow. Alexander Blok, tr. fr. Russian by Babette Deutsch and Avrahm Yarmolinsky. Fr. Twelve, The. AWP

Black November Turkey, A. Richard Wilbur. LCAP; MoAB; NAAL-2

Blackleg Miners, The. *Unknown.* GBP; OBET

Black'm saut'm rough'm glower'm saw. *Unknown.* FaBoVe

Blackout Sonnets. Joan Larkin. ETG

Blackpool Breezes. *Unknown.* CoMu

Blacks in frame houses. Song: I Want a Witness. Michael S. Harper. CAPP

Blackshaw 289: the Replies. Peter Riley. VaA

Blackshawled women of New Mexico, The. Old Women beside a Church. Keith Wilson. Poetsp

Blacksmith. B. K. Pyke. BoTP

Blacksmith, The. Ludwig Uhland, *tr. fr. German by* Philip L. Miller. RiWo

Blacksmith, The ("A blacksmith, courted me, nine months and better.") *Unknown.* OBET

Blacksmith Pain. Otto Julius Bierbaum, *tr. fr. German by* Jethro Bithell. AWP

Blacksmiths, The. *Unknown.* RB; WiR

Blacksmiths. *Unknown.* WiR

Blacksmith's boy went out with a rifle, The. Legend. Judith Wright. NOBAu; NTP; PAW; RB

Blacksmith's quite a logical man, The. Palladas, *tr. fr. Greek by* Tony Harrison. GrAn

Blacksmith's Song, The. *Unknown.* GBP

Blackstone Rangers, The. Gwendolyn Brooks. NoAM; PoBA

Blackthorn. Euros Bowen, *tr. fr. Welsh by the author.* OBWVE

Blackwater Mountain. Charles Wright. CAPP

Blade better, A. Waldere 2. *Unknown, tr. fr. Anglo-Saxon by* Kevin Crossley-Holland. ASW

Blade licks out and acts, A. Thomas Kinsella. *Fr.* Technical Supplement, A. BiHa

Blade of a knife, The. Richard Murphy. IPY

Blade of Grass Sings to the River, The. Leah Goldberg, *tr. by* Robert Friend. *Fr.* Songs of the Stream. TrJP

Blade of Grass Sings to the Stream, The. Leah Goldberg, *tr. fr. Hebrew by* Ruth Finer Mintz. *Fr.* Songs of the Stream. MHP

Blades of Grass, The. Stephen Crane. *Fr.* Black Riders, The. MoAmPo

Bladyn's Song of Cloten. Charles Montague Doughty. *Fr.* Dawn in Britain, The. PoEL-5

Blaen Cwrt. Gillian Clarke. AngWe

Blah, Blah, Blah. Ira Gershwin. OBAL

Blair Peach died with a broken head. Paul Evans. *Fr.* Sofa Book, The. NBrP

Blake Leads a Walk on the Milky Way. Nancy Willard. OBCA

Blake Mistake, The. Sandie Castle. UL

Blake or Yeats Slept with You. Anthony Barnett. VaA

Blake shuts his eyes. Life Mask. Charles Brasch. PeNZ

Blakeney people, The. The People of Blakeney. *Unknown.* GBP

Blam! Blam! Blam! Pow! Blam! Pow! For a Black Poet. Gerald William Barrax. NBV

Blame me not, Sweet, if here and there. Alibi. Arthur Guiterman. BXAP

Blame Nor My Lute. Sir Thomas Wyatt. *See* Blame not my lute, for he must sssnd [*or* Sownde].

Blame not my cheeks, though pale with love they be. Thomas Campion. AAS; SCGP; UnPo

Blame not my lute. (*LL*) Blame not my lute, for he must sssnd [*or* Sownde]. Sir Thomas Wyatt. AAS; EBEV; EIL; NAEL-1; OAEL-1; PoE; SiPS; SiPSBD

Blame Not My Lute. Sir Thomas Wyatt. *See* Blame not my lute, for he must sssnd [*or* Sownde].

Blame not my lute, for he must sssnd [*or* Sownde]. Sir Thomas Wyatt. AAS; EBEV; EIL; NAEL-1; OAEL-1; PoE; SiPS; SiPSBD
(Blame Nor My Lute.) EnRePo
(Blame Not My Lute.) SCGP

"Blame not thyself too much," I said, "nor blame." Tennyson. *Fr.* Princess, The. NAEL-2

Blancheflour and Jellyflorice. *Unknown.* ESPB

Blank Book Letter, The. Samuel Greenberg. LiTA

Blank though the dalehead and the bony face. (*LL*) William Wordsworth. Sidney Keyes. OxBTC

Blank Verse Written on the Sea Shore. Hannah Cowley. ECWP

Blanket Hog. Paul B. Janeczko. TLR

Blanket, its weight, while we were growing, The. In the Lungs. Milo De Angelis, *tr. fr. Italian by* Lawrence Venuti. NeIt

Blantyre Explosion, The. *Unknown.* OBET; SWP

Blarney castle. Francis Sylvester Mahony. IIP

Blason, A. A. D. Hope. NOBAu

Blasphemy. Yoshihara Sachiko, *tr. fr. Japanese by* Kenneth Rexroth *and* Ikuko Atsumi. WPJ

Blasphemy, A. Rodney Jones. WeW

Blast Furnace, The. Luis J. Rodriguez. AfAz

Blast of triumph o'er thy grave, The. (*LL*) The Battle-Field. Bryant. AnAmPo; PoLF

Blast of War, The. Shakespeare. *See* Once more unto the breach, dear friends, once more.

Blast of wind, a momentary breath, A. Barnabe Barnes. *Fr.* Divine Century of Spiritual Sonnets, A. EBEV
(Life of Man, The.) CBCK

Blasted Herb, The. Meshech Weare. PAH

Blasted with sighs, and surrounded with tears. Twicknam [*or* Twickenham] Garden. John Donne. EBEV; EnLoPo; ESCV; FaBoPP; MeLP; OPOP; PoE; PoEL-2; SCGP; SeCP; TEP

Blasting from Heaven. Philip Levine. CoAP

Blasts rip newspaper grey Mannahatta's mid day air spires. Friday the Thirteenth. Allen Ginsberg. NNaP

Blatant as factory buildings. Marina Tsvetayeva, *tr. fr. Russian by* Elaine Feinstein *and* Angela Livingstone. *Fr.* Poem of the End. PBWP

Blatherskite. Tom Weatherly. UL

Blatz was drafted, act of God and neighbors. White Cross. Reed Whittemore. ArOW

Blaydon Races. *Unknown.* ELP

Blaze of promise everywhere, The. (*LL*) Always. Mark Strand. CAPP; Poetr; TRP

Blaze two red eyes as hot as cooking-coals. (*LL*) Dog. John Crowe Ransom. InPS; LiTA; OBAL

Blazing fire, and Christmas treat. (*LL*) The Garden Year. Sara Coleridge. FaBoBe; OTCP

Blazing in gold and quenching in purple. Emily Dickinson. NTP

Blazing noon, fierce, unrelenting noon!, The. William Hosack. *Fr.* Isle of Streams; or, the Jamaica Hermit, The. PBCV

Blazing stanchions and the corporate lights — , The. Euclid Avenue. Harry Clifton. PBCIP

Blazon Columbia's emblem. Columbia's Emblem. Edna Dean Proctor. GN

Bleach in the foot-bathtub. Sunday Morning, 1950. Irene McKinney. PBCAP

Bleached wood massed in bone piles. Kalaloch. Carolyn Forché. AmPA; AnAn; NoAM

Bleak season was it, turbulent and bleak. The Sunbeam Said, Be Happy. Wordsworth. *Fr.* Recluse, The. FaBoRV

Bleak the February light. Kingdom of Heaven. Léonie Adams. MoAB; MoAmPo

Bleat of Protest. Mildred Weston. FiBHP

Bled/ holding on/ to details. Monogram 23. Martina Werner, *tr. fr. German by* Rosemarie Waldrop. BoWoP

Bleeberrying. Jonathan Denwood. MoBS

Bleecker Street. Jean Garrigue. TAP

Bleeding. May Swenson. NALW

Bleeding hearts talk of happy days. Today Is Not Like They Said. Kirk Hall. NBV

Bleeding to death. The counter-attack had failed. (*LL*) Counter-Attack. Siegfried Sassoon. MoBrPo; OxAEP-2; PeFWW; PoWW

Bleeds with its death-wound, its wound of love for thee! (*LL*) Sweet in her green dell the flower of beauty slumbers. George Darley. OBEV

Blenheim, *sels.* John Philips.
War Poetry. NOEC

Blennerhassett's Island. Thomas Buchanan Read. *Fr.* New Pastoral, The. PAH

Blesing be thine, green Apple-tree!, A. (*LL*) Mine Host of "The Golden Apple." Thomas Westwood. GN; OHIP

Bless Adonai. Rami M. Shapiro. EaPr

Bless earth with Thine Advent, O Saviour Christ! *Unknown, tr. fr. Anglo-Saxon by* Charles W. Kennedy. *Fr.* Christ 1. AnOE

Bless God for Christ, that kept them all. (*LL*) The Ten Commandments. *Unknown.* FaBoUs; BoSChV

Bless Him ("Bless Him, O constant companions.") *Unknown, tr. fr. Hebrew by* Israel Abrahams. TrJP

Bless me! this is pleasant, riding on the rail! (*LL*) Rhyme of the Rail[s]. John Godfrey Saxe. AnAmPo; MoShBr; PoLF

Bless the four corners of this house. House Blessing. Arthur Guiterman. TrPWD

Bless the Lord, O my soul. Ernesto Cardenal. EaPr

Bless the Lord, O my soul: and all that is within me. Bible, *O.T.*, *paraphrased by* Sir Thomas Wyatt. *Fr.* Psalms. AWP
(Psalm CIII: "Praise the Lord, O my soul," *paraphrased by* Henry Francis Lyte.) NOCV
(O Thou my soule, Jehovah blesse, *Bay Psalm Book*.) SCAP

Bless the Lord, O my soul/ O Lord my God. Bible, *O.T.*, *paraphrased by* Sir Thomas Wyatt. *Fr.* Psalms. NAWM-1; OHIP, *abr.*; TrJP
(Hymn of the World Without.) WGRP

(Unnamable God, you are fathomless.) EnlH

Bless the love of the holy one within us. (*LL*) Blessing of galaxies, blessing of stars. *Unknown.* EaPr

Bless the meat. *Unknown.* ISE

Bless Thee, O Lord, for the living arc of the sky over me this morning. Carl Sandburg. EaPr

Bless Thou this year, O Lord! A Prayer for a Happy New Year. Andrew Stuart Currie Clarke. BLRP

Bless you, bless you. The Price of Giving Too Much. Vanparanar, *tr. fr. Tamil by* A. K. Ramanujan. PLW

Bless you, bless you, burnie-bee [*or* bonnie-bee]. Mother Goose. BoTP; OxNR

Bless you, earth. Earth's Bounty. Auvaiyar, *tr. fr. Tamil by* A. K. Ramanujan. PLW

Bless you, friend. Listen. What She Said to Her Girl Friend When She Returned from the Hills. Kapilar, *tr. fr. Tamil by* A. K. Ramanujan. PLW

Bless you. Listen to me. What She Said to Her Girl Friend, Her Foster-Mother within Earshot. Kapilar, *tr. fr. Tamil by* A. K. Ramanujan. PLW

Bless you, Mother. On the Appeal from the Race of Sheba: II. Léopold Sédar Senghor, *tr. fr. French by* John Reed *and* Clive Wake. TTY

Bless you, Mother, but listen. What Her Friend Said to the Foster Mother. Kapilar, *tr. fr. Tamil by* A. K. Ramanujan. PLW

Bless you, the ass replied. (*LL*) Balaam. Charles Causley. EBNV

Bless'd art Thou, O Lord of all. Prayer before Sleep. Alice Lucas. TrJP

Blessed. Soné, *tr. fr. Hebrew by* David Kuselewitz. TrJP

Blessed above women/ shall Jael the wife of Heber the Kenite be. Bible, *O.T. Fr.* Judges. AWP; BoWoP; PBWP; WPOW

Blessed angell not a word replies, The. Ariosto, *tr. by* Sir John Harington. *Fr.* Orlando Furioso. OBVE

Blessed are the flabby people at Walgreen's. Beatitude. Claire Bateman. CrSp

Blessed are the man and the woman. Bible, *O.T., paraphrased by* Sir Thomas Wyatt. *See* Blessed is the man that walketh not in the counsel of the ungodly [*or* wicked].

Blessed are the poor[e] in spirit for theirs is the kingdom[e] of heaven. Bible, *N.T. Fr.* St. Matthew. OBVE

Blessed Are They. Wilhelmina Stitch. PoToHe

Blessed are they of the Easter faith. Easter Beatitudes. Clarence M. Burkholder. BLRP

Blessed are they that have eyes to see. Some Blesseds. John Oxenham. WGRP

Blessed are they who are pleasant to live with — . Blessed Are They. Wilhelmina Stitch. PoToHe

Blessed are they who sow but do not reap. Blessed. Soné, *tr. fr. Hebrew by* David Kuselewitz. TrJP

Blessed Art Thou, No-One. Myra Sklarew. BTR

Blessed Art Thou, O Lord. *Unknown, tr. by* Theodor H. Gaster. *Fr.* Dead Sea Scrolls, The. TrJP

Blessed Assurance. Fanny Crosby. AH

Blessed be. (*LL*) All life is your own. Starhawk. EaPr

Blessëd be all these in you! (*LL*) An Odd Conceit. Nicholas Breton. ElL

Blessed be my brain. Robin Morgan. *Fr.* Network of the Imaginary Mother, The. CrSp

Blessed be that lady bright. A Cause for Wonder. *Unknown.* MeEL

Blessed be the Creator. Alla Renee Bozarth. EaPr

Blessed be the English and all their ways and works. Jobson's Amen. Kipling. OBTV

Blessed Be the Happy Mother. Paul Johann Ludwig Heyse, *tr. fr. German by* Philip L. Miller. RiWo

Blessed Be the Holy Will of God. *Unknown, tr. fr. Irish by* Douglas Hyde. TIRV

Blessed be the memory. *Unknown.* ISE

Blessed Be The Paps. Richard Crashaw. *See* Suppose he had been tabled at thy teats.

Blessed Be The Paps which Thou Hast Sucked. Richard Crashaw. *See* Suppose he had been tabled at thy teats.

Blessed be the works of your hands. Diann Neu. EaPr

Blessed be thou, levedy. *Unknown.* MiEL

Blessed be you, harsh matter, barren soil, stubborn rock. Pierre Teilhard de Chardin. EaPr

Blessed Bible, sacred treasure. The Best of All. Fanny Crosby. BLRP

Blessed by the day which bids my grief subside. To Mr. William Long, On His Recovery from a Dangerous Illness, 1785. William Hayley. Son

Blessed Comforter Divine. Lydia Huntley Sigourney. AH

Blessed conversion, and a strange, A. The Conversion of S. Paul. George Wither. ChIV-2

Blessed Damozel, The. Dante Gabriel Rossetti. AWP; BLPL; EBEvV, (*sts.* 1–9); EBVV; EnVR; ImPo; LiTB; NAEL-2; NOBE; NOBVV; NoP; OAEL-2; OBEV; OBNC; OxAEP-2; PoE; PoEL-5; TEP; TFi; TrGrPo

Blessed damozel leaned out, The. The Blessed Damozel. Dante Gabriel Rossetti. AWP; BLPL; EBEvV, (*sts.* 1–9); EBVV; EnVR; ImPo; LiTB; NAEL-2; NOBE; NOBVV; NoP; OAEL-2; OBEV; OBNC; OxAEP-2; PoE; PoEL-5; TEP; TFi; TrGrPo

Blessed He. Paul Johann Ludwig Heyse, *tr. fr. German by* Philip L. Miller. RiWo

Blessed He, by whom the world was created. Blessed He. Paul Johann Ludwig Heyse, *tr. fr. German by* Philip L. Miller. RiWo

Blessed Is Everyone. *Unknown.* AH

Blessed Is God. Bible, Apocrypha, *tr. fr. Greek by* D. C. Simpson. *Fr.* Tobit. TrJP

Blessed Is the Man. Marianne Moore. ChIV-1

Blessed is the man that walketh not in the counsel of the ungodly [*or* wicked]. Bible, *O.T., paraphrased by* Sir Thomas Wyatt. *Fr.* Psalms. AWP

(Blessed are the man and the woman.) EnlH
(Happy Is the Man.) TrJP
(O blessed man, that in th' advice.) SCAP
(Tree and the Chaff, The.) WGRP

Blessed is the spot, and the house. Baha 'U' Lla'h. EaPr

Blessed land of Judea! thrice hallowed of song. Palestine. Whittier. WBLP

Blessed Lord, What It Is to Be Young. David McCord. NTCP

Blessed Mary. *Unknown.* OxBSP

Blessed Mary, moder virginal. A Short Prayer to Mary. *Unknown.* MeEL

Blessed Match, The. Hannah Senesh, *tr. fr. Yiddish.* TrJP

Blessed Name, The. George Washington Bethune. *See* There Is No Name So Sweet on Earth.

Blessed offender [*or* offendour], who thyself hast [*or* haist] tried [*or* try'd]. To Saint Mary Magdalen ("Blessed Offendour: who thyself haist try'd.") Henry Constable. NoSic; PoEL-2

Blessed poster girl leaned out, The. The Poster Girl. Carolyn Wells. BXAP

Blessed sister, holy mother, spirit of the fountain. T. S. Eliot. *Fr.* Ash Wednesday. EaPr; LiTA; MoAB; MoAmPo; OxBA; VGW

Blessed the match that was burned. The Blessed Match. Hannah Senesh, *tr. fr. Yiddish.* TrJP

Blessed Trinity have pity! Childless. Giolla Brighde MacNamee, *tr. fr. Irish by* Frank O'Connor. BIrV

Blessed Virgin Compared to the Air We Breathe, The. Gerard Manley Hopkins. EaPr; MeMBP; NOBVV; PeVV

Blessed with a joy that only she. The Gift of God. E. A. Robinson. MoAB; MoAmPo; OxBA

Blessednes of Brytaine, The, *sels.* Morris Kyffin.
"Adore November's sacred seventeenth day." AngWe

Blessing, The. Paula Gunn Allen. SRLS

Blessing, The. Carolyn Kizer. CAPP; MDDM; MeEL; Poetr

Blessing, A. Mekeel McBride. SM

Blessing, A. James Wright. ArNa; CAPP; GoJo; GrPl; InPK; InPS; NAAL-2; NaP; NOAM; NOBA; NoP; PoE; Poetr; PPP; RaBo; TRP; TwCP; VCAP

Blessing a Bride and Groom; a Wedding Night Poem. Robert Peters. BXAP

Blessing for the Blessed, A, *sels.* Laurence Alma-Tadema.
"When the sun has left the hill-top." BoTP

Blessing his handiwork, his drawbridge closed. Artificer. X. J. Kennedy. TwCP

Blessing in Disguise, A. John Ashbery. PoM

Blessing Mrs. Larkin. Margery Swett Mansfield. GoYe

Blessing of galaxies, blessing of stars. *Unknown, tr. fr. Chinook Indian.* EaPr

Blessing of the Priests. Bible, *O.T. See* Lord bless thee and keep thee, The.

Blessing on Little Boys. Arthur Guiterman. TrPWD

Blessing on you, Mrs. Larkin, for planting my trees! A. Blessing Mrs. Larkin. Margery Swett Mansfield. GoYe

Blessing the Hounds. Mary Winter. GoYe

Blessing without Company. *Unknown.* BPo

Blessings as rich and fragrant crown your heads. To the Best, and Most Accomplished Couple. Henry Vaughan. PeECV

Blessings in abundance come. The Good-Night, or Blessing. Robert Herrick. CaPo

Blessings [*or* Blessing] on the hand of women! The Hand That Rocks the Cradle Is the Hand That Rules the World. William Ross Wallace. BLPL; PoLF; WBLP

Blessings on thee, little man. Whittier. *Fr.* Barefoot Boy, The. FaBoBe; FaPON; GGP; GN; LiTA; OBAL; OBCA; PoLF; WBLP, *abr*

Blessings That Remain, The. Annie Johnson Flint. BLRP

Blest are the pure in heart. Purity of Heart. John Keble. BLRP

Blest are your North parts, for all this long time. To Mr. I. L. John Donne. SeCP

Blest be the boat. Sea Prayer. *Unknown, tr. fr. Gaelic by* Alexander Carmichael. ScCV

Blest be the day, and blest the month and year. Petrarch, *tr. fr. Italian. Fr.* Sonnets to Laura. NAWM-1, *tr. by* Joseph Auslander (Father in heaven, after each lost day.) NAWM-1, *tr. by* Bernard Bergonzi

Blest be the God of love. Even-Song. George Herbert. ESCV

Blest be the man, who first the method found. To My Brother at St. John's College in Cambridge. Elizabeth Tollet. ECWP

Blest be the thing that brought the shadow hither. *(LL)* I Heard a Noise and Wishèd for a Sight. *At. to* Thomas Bateson. EBEV; HAP; InvP

Blest Be the Wondrous Grace. George Barrell Cheever. *AH*

Blest be thy rest. *(LL)* Lullaby. William Barnes. SCGP

Blest, Blest and Happy He. *Unknown.* GBL

Blest is t' bride at t' sun shines on. Wedding and Funeral. *Unknown.* GBP

Blest is the man who loves and after early play. Boys and Sport. Solon, *tr. fr. Greek by* John Addington Symonds. PeHV

Blest Is the Man Whose Tender Breast. Abijah Davis. AH

Blest leaf! whose aromatic gales dispense. Isaac Hawkins Browne. *Fr.* Pipe of Tobacco, A. BXAP; UV

Blest Order, which in power dost so excell. The Priesthood. George Herbert. ESCV

Blest pair of Sirens, pledges of Heaven's joy. Milton. *Fr.* At a Solemn Music [*or* Musick]. EPCY; GTBS; GTBS-P; HeIP; NOBE; OBEV; PoEL-3; SCGP

Blest privacy! Happy retreat, wherein. My Country Audit. Mildmay Fane, 2d Earl of Westmorland. BeJo; NOSC

Blest the infant Babe. Wordsworth. *Fr.* Prelude [or, Growth of a Poet's Mind], The. EnRP; OAEL-2; TOF

Blew out the golden light. *(LL)* Shall Then Another. Kenneth Mackenzie. NOBAu

Blight. Arna Bontemps. CDC

Blight. Emerson. NOBA; NoP

Blight from England's present-day, A. Bonis Avibus. Douglas Oliver. VaA

Blight of Love, The. Mary E. Tucker. CBWP-1

Blight rests in your face, The. To a Publisher . . . Cut-out. Amiri Baraka. NeAP

Blighted apples will not shine. Apple Blight. Paul Zimmer. VGW

Blighter, The. Fernando Pessoa, *tr. fr. Portuguese by* Charles Eglington. PeSAV

Blighter that is at the end of the sea, The. The Blighter. Fernando Pessoa, *tr. fr. Portuguese by* Charles Eglington. PeSAV

Blighters. Siegfried Sassoon. CMoP; FaBoTw; MoP; NoAM; OxBSP; PoWW

Blind. John Kendrick Bangs. PoToHe

Blind. Norman V. Pearce. PoToHe

Blind Adolphus. Angela McCabe. AmPA

Blind Bartimaeus at the gates. Jericho's Blind Beggar. Longfellow. WBLP
(Blind Bartimæus.) ChIV-2

Blind Beggar, The. *Unknown.* AmFP

Blind Boy, The. Colley Cibber. GTBS; GTBS-P; NOEC; OxBChV

Blind Boy's Pranks, The. William Thom. OBEV

Blind children are brought to the beach. On a Japanese Beach. Nina Cassian, *tr. fr. Romanian by* Daniela Gioseffi *and the author.* WoWa

Blind clouds, poisonous vapors hang over this mountain city. Overjoyed at Soviet Russia's Entry into the War. Liu Ya-tzu, *tr. fr. Chinese by* Wu-chi Liu. SuSp

Blind Date. Conrad Aiken. DL

Blind fortune, if thou wants a guide. Fortune's Legacy. *Unknown.* NOSC

Blind girl singing on the radio, A. Singing in the Dark. Irma Wassall. PoNe

Blind, I Speak to the Cigarette. Joanne de Longchamps. GoYe

Blind Leading the Blind, The. Lisel Mueller. IHMS

Blind Linnet, The. Robert Williams Buchanan. FM

Blind Man, The. Anne Batten Cristall. ECWP

Blind Man, The. Margaret E. Sangster. PoToHe

Blind Man, The, *sels.* Judith Wright.
Country Dance. CBAP

Blind Man at the Fair, The. Joseph Campbell. AWP

Blind man, blind man. Mother Goose. OxNR

Blind Man Lay beside the Way. *Unknown.* AS

Blind-Man's Buff. Blake. WiR

Blind Men and the Elephant, The. John Godfrey Saxe. BLPA; BoTP; FaBoBe; OBCA; OTCP; PoToHe; WBLP

Blind Musicians, The. *Unknown, tr. fr. Chinese by* Robert Payne. TAL

Blind Old Woman. Clarence Major. PoBA

Blind poet, fiddler, Raftery. For Raftery. Alan Alexander. NOBAu

Blind Samson. William Plomer. PeSA

Blind Saxophonist Dies. David Hilton. Jaz

Blind School/ Rasps with crying, The. Vincent Buckley. FaBoMA

Blind Sheep, The. Randall Jarrell. NYBP; OBAL

Blind Steersmen. Francis Ernest Kobina Parkes. PBA

Blind Thamyris, and blind Maeonides. Ode to the Human Heart. Edward Laman Blanchard. NOBL

Blind with love, my daughter. Pain for a Daughter. Anne Sexton. Poetr

Blinded Bird, The. Thomas Hardy. CMoP; LiTM

Blinded mole, or else a burnèd fly, A. *(LL)* Absence. Sir Philip Sidney. SiPS

Blinded they into folly run and grief for pleasure take. *(LL)* Love winged my hopes and taught me how to fly. *Unknown.*

Blindest and most frantic prayer. The Deserter. Edward Rowland Sill. AnAmPo

Blindest buzzard that I know, The. A Sketch. Christina Rossetti. GTBS-P

Blinding sun at ten o'clock, The. The Church. Edwin Ford Piper. WGRP

Blindman's Buff. Peter Viereck. LiTM; MoAmPo

Blindness. Delmira Agustini, *tr. fr. Spanish by* D. M. Pettinella. PBWP

Blindness of Samson, The. Milton. *Fr.* Samson Agonistes. FHYEP; ImPo; LiTB; OAEL-1; PoEL-3

Blindness we may forgive, but baseness we will smite. *(LL)* An Ode in Time of Hesitation. William Vaughn Moody. AnAmPo; OxBA; PAH

Blinkered Mind, The. Amy Witting. NOBAu

Blinking in crazy perspective on stories he's out of. *(LL)* Picaro. Harry Clifton. IB

Bliss. George Johnston. NOBC

Bliss for which our spirits pine, The. The True Heaven. Paul Hamilton Hayne. WGRP

Bliss of man, The (could pride that blessing find). Pope. *Fr.* Essay on Man, An. NOEC; NU

Blisses about my pilgrimage as pain. *(LL)* Hap. Thomas Hardy. AWP; CMoP; EBVV; EnVR; ImPo; MeMBP; MoBrPo; NAEL-2; NoAM; NoP; OAEL-2; Poetr; PoEP; Son; TEP

Blistered and dry was the desert I trod. The Palm. Roy Campbell. MoBrPo

Blizzard, The. Roger McDonald. NOBAu

Blizzards of paper. Unlearning to Not Speak. Marge Piercy. CrSp

Bloated/ on rotten eggs. The Skunk. Philip Dow. BXAP

Block City. Robert Louis Stevenson. FaPON; NTCP

Block the cannon; let no trumpets sound! Sunset Horn. Myron O'Higgins. PoNe

Blockhouse. Olga Kirsch, *tr. fr. Afrikaans by* Jack Cope. PeSA

Blocking the Pass. Charles Madge. FaBoMo

Blocks. Frank O'Hara. HCAP; LCAP

Blocks, The/ which are the buildings and walls. Comforted by Limestone. Edward Dorn. *Fr.* Oxford. NOBA

Blodwen,/ Her name like the hours. Her Name like the Hours. Gloria Evans Davies. OBWVE

Bloke I know came rolling home as shickered as he could be, A. Shickered As He Could Be. *Unknown.* NOBAu

Blond. Joseph de Roche. HeIP

Blond Bombshell. Lynn Emanuel. NAmP90

Blond girl is bent over a poem, A. Episode in a Library. Zbigniew Herbert, *tr. fr. Polish by* Czeslaw Milosz *and* Peter Dale Scott. AnRep

Blond in gray and black and silver. Stay Beautiful. Jeff Wright. UL

Blond stones all round-sided. Morning at Point Dume. May Swenson. DiPo

Blonde & Aussie. John Forbes. FaBoMA

Blonde hair at the edge of the pavement. Mitching. Michael Smith. CIP

Blood. Ray Bremser. NeAP

Blood, The. Nina Cassian, *tr. fr. Romanian by* Laura Schiff. WPOW

Blood. Naomi Shihab Nye. NGP

Blood. Franz Wright. LCAP

Blood Countess, The, *sels.* Robert Peters.

Blood Donor. Robert Morgan. AngWe

Blood falling in drops to the earth. Where Are the Men Seized in This Wind of Madness? Alda do Espírito Santo, *tr. fr. Portuguese by* Alan Ryder. TTY; WPOW

Blood flows in me, but what does it have to do. Living by the Red River. James Wright. NNaP

Blood from your ravaged wound. *(LL)* Another Alexandra. Mongane Wally Serote. PeSAV

Blue sky, blue noon, and the secret line if flung. The Sounding. Conrad Aiken. AnAmPo

Blue Sleep. Winifred Bryher. PoA

Blue, so blue that eye of sky. Jacques Rabémanganjara, tr. fr. French by Ellen Conroy Kennedy. NegPo

Blue Sparks in Dark Closets. Richard Snyder. Poetsp

Blue Specks. Nurunnessa Choudhury, tr. fr. Bengali by the author and Paul Joseph Thompson. AIW

Blue Springs, Georgia. Ree Young. GOYP

Blue Swallows, The. Howard Nemerov. NoP; Poetr

Blue-Tail Fly, The. Unknown. GBP

Blue Taj, The. Mei-Mei Berssenbrugge. UL

Blue Tanganyika. Lebert Bethune. PoBA

Blue Tango. Michael van Walleghen. NAmP90

Blue. The green. The river-bed, The. The Scene. Agnes Nemes Nagy, tr. fr. Hungarian by Bruce Berlind. PoSu

Blue toads are dying all over Minnesota. Walking through a Cornfield in the Middle of Winter I Stumble over a Cow Pie and Think of the Sixties Press. Barbara Harr. BXAP

Blue vein, bright on her temple, pitifully beating, The. (LL) Boy with His Hair Cut Short. Muriel Rukeyser. LiTM; MoAB; NALW; NoAM; TwCP; VGW; WPE

Blue water; upon it two possible movements. The Landfall. James Dickey. PoA

Blue West, The. Dahlia Ravikovitch, tr. fr. Hebrew by Chana Bloch. PBWP

Blue Whale, The. Robert Watson. MAT

Blue Winter. Robert Francis. LCAP

Bluebeard's Closet. Rose Terry Cooke. AmWP

Bluebells. Olive Enoch. BoTP

Bluebells. Juliana Horatia Ewing. BoTP

Bluebells. P. A. Ropes. BoTP

Bluebells for Grainne. Dermot Bolger. IB

Bluebells for Love. Patrick Kavanagh. IPY

Blueberry Man. David Bergman. GLP

Bluebird &/ honeymoon over. Spring. Reed Bye. TTTS

Bluebird, be quick now, spy me out the road. (LL) For ever hard to meet, and as hard to part. Li Shang-yin. PLT

Bluehawk. Anne Waldman. Jaz

Bluejay screeches from a pine. (LL) What Happened Here Before. Gary Snyder. NNaP; PoM

Blueprint. D. B. Steinman. GoYe

Blues. Léon Damas, tr. fr. French. NegPo, tr. by Ellen Conroy Kennedy

Blues. John Fuller. NOBL

Blues, The. Langston Hughes. TLR

Blues. Sonia Sanchez. BCF

Blues. Léopold Sédar Senghor, tr. fr. French. Jaz

Blues Ain' Nothin', De. Unknown. AS

Blues ain't culture. Liberation / Poem. Sonia Sanchez. NBV

Blues and Bitterness. Lerone Bennett, Jr.. FF; PoBA

Blues at Dawn. Langston Hughes. SAmP

Blues at Lord's, The. Siegfried Sassoon. PeLV

Blues Five Spot. Art Lange. Jaz

Blues for an Old Blue. Walker Gibson. NYBP

Blues for Bessie. Myron O'Higgins. PoNe

Blues for Franks Wooten. Tom Weatherly. NBV

Blues for Harold. Ray Bremser. Jaz

Blues for John Coltrane, Dead at 41. William Matthews. Jaz

Blues for Sister Sally. Lenore Kandel. NMM

Blues for the Nightowl. Elton Glaser. PBCAP

Blues (in Two Parts), The. Val Ferdinand. NBV

Blues is the black o' the face, The. Black Blues. Bloke Modisane. PBA

Blues lady/ with the beaded face. Grinding Vibrato. Jayne Cortez. BlSi

Blues meant Swiss-Up, The. Riding across John Lee's Finger. Stanley Crouch. PoBA

Blues/ Never climb a hill. Get Up, Blues. James A. Emanuel. PoBA

Blues Note. Bob Kaufman. PoBA

Blues Poem. Jack Micheline. Jaz

Blues, spreading their robes, stretching their waterfalls, The. Natural Being. Octavio Paz, tr. fr. Spanish by Eliot Weinberger. AnRep

Blues Today, The. Mae Jackson. PoBA

Bluff Henry the Eighth to six spouses was wedded. Henry VIII. Unknown. FaBoUs

Bluish, pale, The. Moontan. Mark Strand. NYBP

Blum. Dorothy Aldis. MoShBr

Blunt good looks cut out day. Passing Strange. Alan Bernheimer. UL

Blur of elements, a cataract, A. Mud. Alan Michael Parker. FoLa

Blurt, Master Constable, sels. Thomas Middleton.
    "Love for such a cherry lip." EiL
    Midnight. EiL
     (Noises in the Night.) Mes
    True Love Ditty, A. EiL

Blush as of roses, A. Le Marais du Cygne. Whittier. PAH

Blush is on the flower, and the bloom is on the tree, The. My Own Cáilin Donn. George Sigerson. FaBoBe

Blyth Aberdeane, throw beriall of all tounis. To Aberdein. William Dunbar. FaBoPP

Blythe Was She. Burns. ScCV

Blythsome Bridal, The. At. to Francis Sempill. GBP

Bmp Bmp. William Matthews. Jaz

Bo-peep/ Little Bo-peep. Unknown. OxNR

Bo peeper. Unknown. OxNR

Boadicea; an Ode. William Cowper. BeLS; FaBoEH; FaPoR

Boadicea often would goad. Douglas Catley. PeLi

Board floats on the river, The. Such Different Wants. Robert Bly. ArLo

Board Meets, The. John Gloag. FiBHP

Board of War has quelled the mutiny, The. To the Minister Liu. Yü Hsüan-chi, tr. fr. Chinese by Geoffrey R. Waters. BoWoP

Boarded Up. Al Masarik. NGP

Boarder, The. Louis Simpson. InPK; SM

Boarding nettings are triced for fight, The. Jack Creamer. James Jeffrey Roche. PAH

Boar's Head Carol, The. Unknown. See Caput apri refero.

Boast not proud English, of thy birth and blood. Roger Williams. GOA; SCAP

Boast of heraldry, the pomp of pow'r, The. Thomas Gray. Fr. Elegy Written in a Country Churchyard. AWP; ClHu; DL; EBEV; EBEvV; EnRP; FaBoBe; FaBoPP; FaBoPV; FaBoRV; FaPoR; FHYEP; GGP; GN; GTBS; GTBS-P; HAP; HeIP; ImPo; InPK; InPS; LiTB; NOBE; NOEC; NoP; OAEL-1; OBD; OBEV; OxAEP-1; PoEL-3; Poetr; PoLF; PPP; PrIm; SCGP; SCV; TEP; TFi; TrGrPo; UnPo; UV; WBLP; WeW

Boast of Masopha. Z. D. Mangoaela, tr. fr. Sotho. PeSA

Boastful young fellow of Neath, A. Frank Richards. PeLi

Boasting of Sir Peter Parker, The. Clinton Scollard. PAH

Boat, The. Caroline Gilman. OBCA

Boat, The. Robert Pack. CoAP; SM

Boat is chafing at our long delay, The. John Davidson. OBEV

Boat-load of emigrant Huns, A. The Wreck of the Deutschland. David Annett. BXAP; PeLi, parody

Boat of sandalwood and oars of magnolia, A. Boating Song. Li Po, tr. fr. Chinese by Robert Payne. TAL

Boat on the Serchio, The, sels. Shelley.
    "Our boat is asleep on Serchio's stream." Mes

Boat Poem. Bernard Spencer. FaBoTw; OxBTC

Boat-pullers, The. Mei Yao Ch'en, tr. fr. Chinese by Jonathan Chaves. SuSp

Boat Sails Away, The. Kate Greenaway. MoShBr

Boat Song. H. Cordelia Ray. CBWP-3

Boat Song, A. St. Columbanus, tr. fr. Latin. NOIV

Boat Song. Sir Walter Scott. See Hail to the chief who in triumph advances.

Boathouse, The. Robert Minhinnick. AngWe

Boatie Rows, The. Unknown. OxBSS, ad. by John Ewen

Boating Song. Li Po, tr. fr. Chinese by Robert Payne. TAL

Boatman, The. Jay Macpherson. MoCV

Boatman, have they crossed? "Not all." Doom Ferry. Sir Arthur Quiller-Couch. EBVV

Boatman he can dance and sing, The. Dance the Boatman. Unknown. AiP

Boatman of Ts'ang-lang is quite old, The. Fisherman. Ts'en Shen, tr. fr. Chinese by C. H. Wang. SuSp

Boatman's shout breaks the heart, The. Szechuan Boatman's Song. Ts'ai Ch'i-chiao, tr. fr. Chinese. LHF, tr. by Hualing Nieh

Boatman's Song, A. Wang Chien, tr. fr. Chinese by William H. Nienhauser. SuSp

Boats Are Afloat, The. Chu Hsi, tr. fr. Chinese by Kenneth Rexroth. NaP

Boats at Night. Edward Shanks. CH

Boats in a Fog. Robinson Jeffers. NAAL-2; NoP; OxBA

Boats sail on the rivers. The Rainbow. Christina Rossetti. Fr. Sing-Song. OxBChV

Boats sail upstream and downstream alike, The. Poem to the Sun ("The boats sail upstream and downstream alike.") Ancient Egyptian Oral Tradition, tr. by Christopher Wertz. TTTS

Boats that carry sugar. Freight Boats. James S. Tippett. FaPON

Boatswain's Call, The. Unknown. OxBSS

Bob. C. K. Williams. PWE

Bob Anderson, My Beau. *Unknown.* PAH

Bob-ing split-able heads. Solitary Visions of a Kaufmanoid. James Cunningham. JB

Bob Robin. Mother Goose. OxNR

Bob Southey! You're a poet — poet-laureate. Byron. *Fr.* Don Juan. CTC; EnRP; OAEL-2; OBSV (Southey and Wordsworth.) TrGrPo

Bobbing with the crowds. The Urban Experience; Part One. Lew Blockcolski. VoR

Bobby Blue. John Drinkwater. FaPON

Bobby Culture ("full of roots and culture.") Made in the Tropics. Vijay Seshadri. UTF

Bobby Shaftoe's [or Shafto's] gone to sea. Mother Goose. CBLP; GBP; OxNR; ReMoGo

Bobby Snooks. *Unknown.* ReMoGo

Bobby's First Poem. Norman Gale. FiBHP; MoShBr

Bobo waro fero Satodeh. Everybody Loves Saturday Night. *Unknown.* SWP

Bobolinks, The. Christopher Pearse Cranch. GN

Bobo's Metamorphosis, *sels.* Czeslaw Milosz, *tr. fr. Polish by the author.*

Bob's Lane. Edward Thomas. PoE

Bodega, Goodbye. Edwin Honig. NoAM

Bodies. Ken Smith. PWE

Bodies are resurrected. Easter Sunday 1988, the Grand Canyon, Arizona. Ray Gonzáles. FoLa

Bodies on fire. Black Hills Survival Gathering, 1980. Linda Hogan. WoWa

Bodiless, nameless God. Prayer of the Young Stoic. Stephen P. Dunn. TrPWD

Body, The. William Bronk. VGW

Body, The. Robert Herrick. CaPo

Body and Soul, *sels.* Donald Justice.
Hotel. BAP-91
Rain. BAP-91
Street Musician. BAP-91

Body Count. Leonard Nathan. PBCAP

Body cupping a body, A. Young Snail. Meena Alexander. VBLP

Body Fished from the Seine. Gregory Corso. SM

Body in fog and the tongue, The. Michael Palmer. *Fr.* Six Hermetic Songs. BAP-90

Body into a finger-ring, for a keepsake forever, A. (*LL*) Counting Small-boned Bodies. Robert Bly. CAPP; NaP

Body is like a November birch facing the full moon, The. Solitude Late at Night in the Woods. Robert Bly. VGW

Body is the soul's poor house, or home, The. The Body. Robert Herrick. CaPo

Body Is the Victory and the Defeat of Dreams, The. Katerina Anghelaki-Rooke, *tr. fr. Greek by* Philip Ram. WPOW

Body leaning slightly back, the arms held firm and straight, The. Sonata. John Fuller. DiPo

Body lies under the ground. Gavin Bantock. OxBTC

Body, long oppressed, The. This Corruptible. Elinor Wylie. MoAB; MoAmPo

Body my house. Question. May Swenson. LiTM; PrIm; SM; VGW

Body of a fourteen year old caught playing politics, The. No Man's Land. Gloria Escoffery. PBCV

Body of a Rook. David Wevill. MoCV

Body of a Woman. Pablo Neruda, *tr. fr. Spanish by* Robert Bly. RaBo

Body of God, The. D. H. Lawrence. ChIV-2

Body of John. R. A. K. Mason. PeNZ

Body of my love is a familiar country, The. Mary Stanley. PeNZ

Body perishes, the heart stays young, The. Old Age. *Zulu Oral Tradition, tr. by* H. Tracey. WTO

Body, Soul, And Godhead. "Angelus Silesius," *tr. fr. German. Fr.* Cherubical Wanderer, The. GePo, *tr. by* George C. Schoolfield

Body's Beauty. Dante Gabriel Rossetti. *Fr.* House of Life, The. OAEL-2; Son; TrGrPo

Body's products become, The. Dido. John Ashbery. *Fr.* Two Sonnets. VGW

Body's Speech, The. *Unknown, tr. fr. Irish by* Frank O'Connor. PeIV

Boer War, The. William Plomer. FaBoEH; IHNG

Boers have poked another, The. Steve Biko is Dead. Jack A. Mapanje. PeSAV

Boethius at Cavalzero. John Macoubrie. CRP

Bofors A. A. Gun, The. Gavin Ewart. PoWW

Bog and Candle. Robert David Fitzgerald. CBAP

Bog-Face. Stevie Smith. RB

Bog Queen. Seamus Heaney. AnAn; NoAM

Bogart in the Dumb Waiter. Ken Smith. PWE

Boggy wood as full of springs as trees, A. The Idea of Entropy at Maenporth Beach. Peter Redgrove. FaBoMo

Boghos Sarkissian, A Watchmaker of Karpet, Remembers the Turkish Atrocities of 1915. Leo Hamalian. BTR

Bogland. Seamus Heaney. HeIP; IPY; NoAM; NOIV; NoP; PBCIP; PNI

Bogs, purgatory, wolves and ease, by fame. Barten Holyday. FaBoEE

Bohemia. Dorothy Parker. AnAmPo; NBLV

Bohemian Hymn, The. Emerson. WGRP

Bohemians, The. Ivor Gurney. PeFWW

Boiling an Egg. Stanley Cook. OTCP

Boita and Goitie sat on de coib. Bertha and Gertie. *Unknown.* RoPo

Bolakins was a very fine mason. Lamkin. *Unknown.* AmFP

Bold Adventures of Captain Ross. *Unknown.* OxBSS

Bold Captain of the Body-Guard. Zagonyi. George Henry Boker. PAH

Bold, cautious, true, and my loving comrade. (*LL*) As Toilsome I Wander'd Virginia's Woods. Walt Whitman. NAAL-1

Bold Dragoon, A ("In the dragon's ride from out of the north.") *Unknown.* OBET

Bold Dragoon, The ("My father is a knight and a man of high renown.") *Unknown.* OBET

Bold General Wolfe. *Unknown.* OBET

Bold General Wolfe to his men did say. *Unknown.* FaBoEH

Bold Jack Donahue. *Unknown.* AmFP

Bold Lanty was in love, you see, with lively Rosie Carey. Lanty Leary. *Unknown.* ChTr

Bold outlines are drawn to encompass. Charcoal. Wilson Harris. PBCV

Bold Pedlar and Robin Hood, The. *Unknown.* AmFP; ESPB

Bold Princess Royal. *Unknown.* OxBSS

Bold Reynard the Fox. *Unknown.* OBET

Bold Robin has robed him in ghostly attire. Robin Hood and the Grey Friars. Thomas Love Peacock. *Fr.* Maid Marian. OxAEP-2

Bold Troubleshooters. Peter Veale. NOBL

Bolding Vedas! Shanks New Nisa! Place-Names of China. Alan Bennett. FaBoPa; NOBL; UV

Boldness[e] in Love. Thomas Carew. CaPo; ErPo; SeCV-1

Boll Weevil Song. *Unknown.* AS

Boll-weevil's coming, and the winter's cold. November Cotton Flower. Jean Toomer. CDC; MoP; NoAM; UnPo

Bollam's Replover, The: Farewell to Jabberwocky. Hugh Haughton. CBNP

Bolobo-eya-bolo. (*LL*) Woman. Elolongue Epanya Yondo. NegPo

Bolsum Brown. *Unknown.* AS

Bolt and bar the shutter. Mad as the Mist and Snow. W. B. Yeats. ChTr; RaBo

Bolt of silk for each clear toned song, A. Written at a Party Where My Lord Gave Away a Thousand Bolts of Silk. Ch'ien T'ao, *tr. fr. Chinese by* Kenneth Rexroth *and* Ling Chung. WPC

Bolt upright, reading her Bible for hours. Great-great-grandmother. Guy Butler. PeSAV

Bomb. Gregory Corso. PoBeRe

Bomb City, Bomb City, Bomb City drummed into us, Night and Day. The Other Side. Natalie Hardwick. IIP

Bomb Disposal, The. Ciaran Carson. CIP; IIP

Bomb-disposal/ combed the area. Peace-Time. Mervyn Morris. PBCV

Bomb Is Made, The. Keith Sinclair. PeNZ

Bomb will explode in the bar at twenty past one, The. The Terrorist, He Watches. Wislawa Szymborska, *tr. fr. Polish by* Adam Czerniawski. PoSu

Bombardment of Bristol, The. *Unknown.* PAH

Bombax Tree, The. Fily-Dabo Sissoko, *tr. fr. French by* Ellen Conroy Kennedy. NegPo

Bomber, The. "Brian Vrepont." NOBAu

Bomber roared over their dream, The. (*LL*) The Bomber. "Brian Vrepont." NOBAu

Bombers. C. Day Lewis. CMoP; MoAB

Bombing at about ninety miles an hour with the exhaust skittering. Cocktails. Ciaran Carson. BiHa; PBCIP; PWE

Bon Jour. (*LL*) Bon jour, bon jour a vous! *Unknown.* MiEL

Bon jour, bon jour a vous! *Unknown.* MiEL

Bon Mot, A. *Unknown.* ErPo

Bon soir, ma chérie. Comrades in Arms: Conversation Piece. *Unknown.* ErPo

Bona dies, Bona dies. Sir David Lindsay. *Fr.* Ane Satire [*or* Satyre] of the Three [*or* Thrie] Estaitis. SeCP

Bona nox; you're an ox. Kanonentext. Wolfgang Amadeus Mozart, *tr. fr. German by* Hugh Haughton. CBNP

Bond, The. Nuala Ni Dhomhnaill, *tr. fr. Irish by* Medbh McGuckian. PBCIP

Book of Gawain, The. Jack Spicer. *Fr.* Holy Grail, The. PoM

Book of God's Madness, The, *sels.* Ralph Chubb.
"Liveliest effigy of the human race." PeHV

Book of Hours, The, *sels.* Rainer Maria Rilke, *tr. fr. German.*
"O Lord, grant each his own, his own death indeed." OBD

Book of hours, The. The Hours. Paul Ramsey. CRP

Book of How, The. Merrill Moore. MoAmPo

Book of Hunting. Julians Barnes. WPE
Sels.
"Time of grease beginneth at Midsummer day."
"When ye hunt at the roe, then shall ye see there."
"Wheresoever ye fare by frith or by fell."

Book of Invader. Iain Sinclair. VaA

Book of Job and a Draft of a Poem to Praise the Paths of the Living, The.
George Oppen. NNaP

Book of Kells, The. Padraic Colum. BIrV; IIP

Book of Lies, The. James Tate. SM

Book of Los, The, *sels.* Blake.
Immortal, The. LiTB; MeMBP

Book of Music, A. Jack Spicer. PoM

Book of Mysteries, The. Anthony Barnett. VaA

Book of Myths, The. Joy Harjo. SRLS

Book of Persephone, The. Robert Kelly. PoM
Sels.
Dance, The.
"Earth is a woman who imagines us. She sings."
Fourth Ode to Persephone.
Glade, The.
"Persephone is the woman buried."
Second Ode to Persephone.
Third Ode to Persephone.
Versions.

Book of Roses, The, *sels.* Said Aql, *tr. fr. Arabic.*

Book of summer is the butterfly, A. The Butterfly. John Fuller. Spl

Book of Tarshish, The, *sels.* Moses ibn Ezra, *tr. fr. Hebrew by* Solomon
Solis-Cohen.
Joy of Life. TrJP

Book of the Dead., *sels. Unknown, tr. fr. Egyptian by* Robert Hillyer.
Adoration of the Disk by King Akhnaten and Princess Nefer Neferiu
Aten. AWP
"Cattle roam again across the field, The." FaPON
Dead Man Ariseth and Singeth a Hymn to the Sun, The. AWP
He Approacheth the Hall of Judgment. AWP
He Asketh Absolution of God. AWP
He Biddeth Osiris to Arise from the Dead. AWP
He Cometh Forth into the Day. AWP
He Commandeth a Fair Wind. AWP
He Defendeth His Heart against the Destroyer. AWP
He Embarketh in the Boat of Ra. AWP
He Entereth the House of the Goddess Hathor. AWP
He Establisheth His Triumph. AWP
He Holdeth Fast to the Memory of His Identity. AWP
He Is Declared True of Word. AWP
He Is like the Lotus. AWP
(Death as a Lotus Flower.) TTY, *tr. by* Ulli Beier
He Is like the Serpent Saka. AWP
He Kindleth a Fire. AWP
He Knoweth the Souls of the East. AWP
He Knoweth the Souls of the West. AWP
He Maketh Himself One with Osiris. AWP
He Maketh Himself One with the God Ra. AWP
He Maketh Himself One with the Only God, Whose Limbs Are the Many
Gods. AWP
He Overcometh the Serpent of Evil in the Name of Ra. AWP
He Prayeth for Ink and Palette That He May Write. AWP
He Singeth a Hymn to Osiris, the Lord of Eternity. AWP
He Singeth in the Underworld. AWP
He Walketh by Day. AWP
Other World, The. AWP; OBD

Book of the Duchesse, The, *sels.* Chaucer.

Book of the Law, The. John Whitworth. FaBoBl

Book of the Two Married Women and the Widow, The, *sels.* William
Dunbar.
Widow Speaks, The. PoEL-1

Book of Thel, The. *sels.* (Daughters of the Seraphim led round their sunny
flocks, The.) Blake. EnRP; MeMBP; NAEL-2; NoP; OAEL-2; OBNC;
PoE; PoEL-4; TEP
"O little cloud," the virgin said, "I charge thee tell to me." OBD
Secrets of the Earth, The. NOBE
Thel's Motto. ChTr, *4 ll.*

Book of True Love, The, *sels.* Juan Ruiz, Archpriest of Hita, *tr. fr. Spanish
by* Hubert Creekmore.
"When you're together with her, and you have a good excuse." ErPo

Book of verses underneath the bough, A. Omar Khayyám, *tr. fr. Persian by*
Edward Fitzgerald. *Fr.* Rubáiyát of Omar Khayyám of Naishápúr,
The. AWP; EBVV, *abr.;* FaBoBe; FaBoRV, *abr.;* FaPoR, *abr.;* HAP,
abr.; HoPM; LiTB; NAEL-2; NOBE; NoP; OBEV; PoEL-5; PrIm,
abr.; TrGrPo; TRP

Book of Wisdom, The. Stephen Crane. *Fr.* Black Riders, The. HoPM;
MoAmPo

Book of Wisdom, The. Robert Lowell. ChIV-1

Book of Yolek, The. Anthony Hecht. WeW

Book Our Mothers Read, The. Whittier. *Fr.* Miriam. BLRP

Book Review. Russell Davies. FaBoEE

Book unfold! (*LL*) Bedouin Song. Bayard Taylor. AnAmPo; FaBoBe;
VPP

Book was writ of late called *Tetrachordon*, A. On the Detraction Which
Followed upon My Writing Certain Treatises. Milton. PoE; Son

Book-Worms, The. Burns. ChTr; FaBoEE; FiBHP

Booker T. and W. E. B. Dudley Randall. MoP; NoAM

Booker Washington Trilogy, The, *sels.* Vachel Lindsay.
John Brown. MoAmPo
Simon Legree — a Negro Sermon. LiTA; MeMAP; TAP
(Negro Sermon, A — Simon Legree.) MoAmPo

Bookmaking. Julia Alvarez. BAP-91

Bookmark. St. Theresa of Avila. *See* Let nothing disturb thee.

Bookmoth: Moth devoured words, A. When I heard. *Unknown, formerly at.
to* Cynewulf. *See* Moth ate a word. To me it seemed, A.

Books. Wordsworth. *Fr.* Prelude [or, Growth of a Poet's Mind], The.
EnRP; OAEL-2

Books and the Man I sing, the first who brings. Pope. *Fr.* Dunciad, The.
CBNP

Books are a load of crap. (*LL*) A Study of Reading Habits. Philip
Larkin. InPK; NOBL; PPP

Books, books, books! Elizabeth Barrett Browning. *Fr.* Aurora Leigh.
WPOW

Book's Creed, The. Joseph S. Cotter, Sr. AAP

Books Fall Open. David McCord. OBCA

Books litter the bed. October. James Schuyler. ArNa

Books of Ovid's changed shapes, The. In the Praise of Music. Humphrey
Gifford. NoSic

Books of the Old Testament, The. Thomas Russell. *See* Great Jehovah
speaks to us, The.

Bookshop Idyll, A. Kingsley Amis. OxBTC; PeLV

Boola boola Pensacoola hullabaloo! (*LL*) Boston Charlie. Walt Kelly.
FiBHP; GoJo

Boom! Howard Nemerov. LiTM; NBLV; NIP

Boom above my knees lifts, and the boat, The. Sailing to an Island.
Richard Murphy. IPY; PBCIP

Boom/ The shrill whistle of the wolf. Bird of Power. Jim Tollerud. VoR

Boomerang. William Hart-Smith. NOBAu; NTP

Boomerang, The. Carrie May Nichols. PoToHe

Boon Companion, The. Oliver St. John Gogarty. *See* If medals were
ordained for drinks.

Boon nature scattered, free and wild. Flowers and Trees. Sir Walter
Scott. *Fr.* Lady of the Lake, The. OxAEP-2

Boon Nature to the woman bows. The Tribute. Coventry Patmore. *Fr.*
Angel in the House, The. EBEV; OBNC

Boosting the Booster ("Boost your city, boost your friend.") *Unknown.*
WBLP

Boosting the hula hoop, fates. Blonde & Aussie. John Forbes. FaBoMA

Boot Camp Incantation. Martín Espada. UTF

Booth Killed Lincoln. *Unknown.* AmFP

Booth led boldly with his big bass drum. General William Booth Enters into
Heaven. Vachel Lindsay. AmPP; ChIV-2; CMoP; ImPo; LiTA; LiTM;
MeMAP; MoAB; MoAmPo; NOBA; OxBA; PoA; PoE; TAP; TrGrPo;
WGRP

Booths knew nothing either. They built themselves in. The Old Sipsey
Valley Road. Thomas Rabbitt. MT

Bootie Black and the Seven Giants. Mike Cook. JB

Boots. Kipling. BLPA; FaPoR; MoBrPo

Boots and Saddles. Nicolas Saboly, *tr. fr. Provençal.* OHIP

Boots and Shoes. Lilian McCrea. BoTP

Boots are being polished. Where Will You Be? Patricia Parker. GLP

Boots,/ Shoes. *Unknown.* OxNR

Booty from the German War. Friedrich von Logau, *tr. fr. German.* GePo,
tr. by George C. Schoolfield

Booze and the blowens cop the lot. (*LL*) Villon's Straight Tip to All Cross
Coves. W. E. Henley, *after* Villon. AWP; CBNP; FaBoCo; InvP;
OxAEP-2

Booze Turns Men into Women. Bernadette Mayer. UL

Bop Lyrics. Allen Ginsberg. OBAL

Botanical Trope, A. William Meredith. Poetr

Botany Bay. John Freeth. NOEC

Both bud and fade, both blow and wither. (LL) To A. L.: Perswasions to Love. Thomas Carew. SeCP

Both gentlemen, or yoemen bould. A True Tale of Robin Hood. Unknown. ESPB

Both her mourner and her tomb. (LL) On the Countess Dowager of Pembroke. At. to William Browne. AWP; HAP; InVP; JCP; NoP; OAEL-1; PoEL-2; PoRA; TFi

Both in mirth and mourning. (LL) What If a Day [or a Month or a Year]. Thomas Campion. AAS; EBEV; ElL; EnRePo; PrIm

Both Keats and Boccaccio tell a. Joyce Johnson. PeLi

Both Less and More. Richard Watson Dixon. SCGP

Both Plutarch and Pausanius tell a story. Kleomedes. David Wright. MoP

Both robbed of air, we both lie in one ground. Hero and Leander. John Donne. NoSic; SoSe

Both shade and substance, beef and bone. (LL) The Dog in the River. Phaedrus. AWP

Both skyed. Japanese Print. Austin Clarke. IPY; NOIV

Both the year's, and the day's deep midnight is. (LL) A Nocturnal[l] upon Saint Lucy's [or S. Lucies] Day, Being the Shortest Day. John Donne. EBEV; EnRePo; ESCV; FHYEP; GBL; JCP; LiTB; MeLP; NAEL-1; NOBE; NoP; NOSC; OAEL-1; OxAEP-1; PoE; PoEL-2; PPP; SCGP; SeCP; SeCV-1; TEP; TFi

Both wash, and wing my soul. (LL) The Storm. Henry Vaughan. FaBoPP

Both were so shy. Two. Robert Canzoneri. HoPM

Both Your Mothers. Jerzy Ficowski. PoSu

Bothie of Tober-na-Vuolich, The [A Long-Vacation Pastoral]. "Therefore the Oxford party went off to adorn for the dinner." Arthur Hugh Clough. OBF
Sels.
"Ah, you have much to learn, we can't know all things at twenty." FaBoPV
"As at return of tide the total weight of ocean." FaBoPV
"But in the interval here the boiling, pent-up water." EnVR
"But on the morrow Elspie kept out of the way of Philip." EnVR
"I have been kissed before, she added, blushing slightly." FaBoVe
"I have been kissed before, she added, blushing slightly." FaBoVe
"Nodding and beckoning across, observed of Attaché and Guardsman." FaBoPV
"Somewhat more splendid in dress, in a waistcoat work of a lady." FaBoVe
"Then was the dinner served, and the Minister prayed for a blessing." PeLV
"There is a stream, I name not its name." BoNaP; FaBoVe
(Highland Glen near Loch Ericht, A.) FaBoPP
"This is the letter of Hobbes the kilted and corpulent hero." FaBoPV

Bothwell Bridge. Unknown. See O Billie, billie, bonny billie.

Botticellian Trees, The. William Carlos Williams. AmPP; LiTA

Bottle, The. Ralph Knevet. ChIV-2

Bottle, The. Al Levine. GrPl

Bottle-brush is best, it likes sweet water. Divination. Christine Churches. FaBoMA

Bottle Creek Blues. Sam Hunt. PeNZ

Bottle of perfume that Willie sent, The [or A]. Limerick. Unknown. PeLi

Bottle Should Be Plainly Labeled "Poison." Sara Henderson Hay. GoYe

Bottled. Jill Breckenridge. LoHo

Bottled [New York]. Helene Johnson. BlSi; CDC; PoBA; ShDr

Bottles, The. Alexander Craig. Fr. Sea Change. FaBoMA

Bottles are empty, the breakfast was good, The. The Morning After. Heine, tr. fr. German by Louis Untermeyer. ErPo

Bottles are for sleeping in. Bottles in the Zoological Museum. William Peskett. PNI

Bottles in the Zoological Museum. William Peskett. PNI

Bottom with your ballast fill was laded., The. (LL) Of an Heroical Answer of a Great Roman Lady to Her Husband. Sir John Harington. BoLoP; ErPo; OxBM

Bottomed by tugging combs of water. The Swan. W. R. Rodgers. PNI

Bottomlands Farmer Suffers a Sea Change, A. Jo McDougall. NGP

Bottomless pits. There's one in Castleton. National Trust. Tony Harrison. Fr. School of Eloquence, The. NAEL-2; NoAM; SCBI

Bottom's Dream. Shakespeare. Fr. Midsummer Night's Dream, A. CBNP

Bottom's Song. Shakespeare. Fr. Midsummer Night's Dream, A. CTC

Boudoir Feelings. Li Shang-yin, tr. fr. Chinese by Eugene Eoyang and Irving Y. Lo. SuSp

Boudoir Lament. Yü Hsüan-chi, tr. by Geoffrey R. Waters. BoWoP

Boudoir Thoughts., sels. Hsü Kan, tr. fr. Chinese.
"Deepening shadows bring on sorrow, The." SuSp
"Drifting clouds, distant and vast." SuSp

"Sadly, sadly the season draws to an end." SuSp
"Steep, steep the lofty mountain peak." SuSp

Bouge of Court, The, sels. John Skelton.
"Sail is up, Fortune ruleth our helm, The." NoSic

Boughs do shake and the bells do ring, The. Harvest Song. Unknown. BoTP; OxNR

Boughs, the boughs are bare enough, The. Winter with the Gulf Stream. Gerard Manley Hopkins. CMoP; NoAM

Bought at the drug store, very cheap; and later pawned. Green Light. Kenneth Fearing. PoE; VGW

Bought/ from the flower-peddler's tray. Magnolia Blossom. Li Ch'ing-chao, tr. by C. H. Kwôck and Vincent McHugh. PBWP

Bought Locks. Martial, tr. fr. Latin by Sir John Harington. AWP

Boulogne to Amiens and Paris. Dante Gabriel Rossetti. Fr. Trip to Paris and Belgium, A. PeVV

Bounce ball! Bounce ball! Song for a Ball-Game. Wilfrid Thorley. BoTP

Bounce, buckram, velvet's dear. Unknown. OxNR

Bounce to Fop; an Heroick Epistle from a Dog at Twickenham to a Dog at Court. Pope. FM

Bounce to Pope. A. D. Hope. OBF

Bound. Theodore Roethke. PoA

Bound and free. Eudaimon. Kathleen Raine. PBWP

Bound each to each by natural piety. (LL) My heart leaps up [when I behold]. Wordsworth. EBEvV; EnRP; FaBV; GTBS; GTBS-P; InPK; InPS; NAEL-2; NOBE; NoP; NTP; OAEL-2; OBNC; OxBSP; TEP; TrGrPo

Bound Feet. Cyrus Cassells. UTF

Bound for the terraced. Lost in the Philippines. David Mura. ETG

Bound in a moonlight circle. The 49 Stomp. Lew Blockcolski. VoR

Bound to my heart as Ixion to the wheel. Dirge for the New Sunrise. Edith Sitwell. Fr. Three Poems of the Atomic Bomb. CMoP; MoAB; MoBrPo

Boundaries. José Emilio Pacheco, tr. fr. Spanish by John Frederick Nims. STV

Boundary. A. L. Hendricks. PBCV

Boundary Conditions. Gwen Harwood. FaBoMA

Bounding Billow, cease thy motion. Stanzas Written between Dover and Calais, in July, 1792. Martha Robinson. ECWP

Boundless, bitter is her sorrow. "Dreaming of the South." Wen T'ing-yün, tr. fr. Chinese by William R. Schultz. SuSp

Boundless Moment, A. Robert Frost. NAAL-2

Boundless the leaves roused by spring. Willow. Li Shang-yin, tr. fr. Chinese by A. C. Graham. PLT

Boundless will to ease us, A. (LL) To Cloe. George Granville. FaBoEE; NBLV

Bounty. Josephine Miles. NoAM

Bounty of Jehovah Praise, The. George Sandys. AH

Bounty of Our Age, The. Henry Farley. FaBoCh; FaBoEE; NOSC

Bouquet in Dog Time. Hayden Carruth. GrPl

Bouquet of Belle Scavoir. Wallace Stevens. MoAB; MoAmPo

Bouquets. Robert Francis. ArNa

Bourbons. Walter Savage Landor. OBSV

Bourne, The. Christina Rossetti. ELP; OBNC

Bourtree, bourtree, crookit rung. The Elder, or Bourtree. Unknown. GBP
(Elder Tree, The.) ChTr

'Bout th' husband oak [or oke], the vine. To Castara, upon an Embrace. William Habington. Fr. Castara. BeJo

Bout with Burning. Vassar Miller. LiTM; MoAmPo; MT

Bow, daughter of Babylon, bow thee to dust! Babylon. Tennyson. ChIV-1

Bow Down, Mountain. Norma Farber. AH

Bow down my soul in worship very low. St. Isaac's Church, Petrograd. Claude McKay. PoBA
(Russian Cathedral.) CDC

Bow Down Your Head and Cry. Unknown. WTO

Bow hither out of heaven and see and save. (LL) Easter Hymn. A. E. Housman. EBEV; MoAB

Bow-legged Annie. (LL) Annie Bolanny. Unknown. ChTr

Bow-wow, says the dog. Mother Goose. OxNR

Bow, wow, wow,/ Whose dog art thou? Mother Goose. OxNR
(Caesar's Song.) ReMoGo

Bowed by the weight of centuries he leans. The Man with the Hoe. Edwin Markham. AnAmPo; BLPA; BLPL; LiTA; MoAmPo; PrIm; TFi; TrGrPo; WBLP; WGRP

Bower of Bliss, The. Spenser. Fr. Faerie Queene, The. PoEL-1

Bower of Peace, The. Robert Southey. Fr. Ode Written during the War with America, 1814. PAH

Bower of Roses, A. Louis Simpson. ArOW

Bower was a philosopher. He would double up. Introduction to Philosophy. John Drew. PWE

Bowge of Courte, The. ("In Autumpne, whan the sonne in Vyrgyne.") John Skelton. AAS

Sels.

Dreamer Meets Riot, The. OxBLMV

Bowing "New Sabbath" or "Mount Ephraim." (*LL*) A Church Romance. Thomas Hardy. FaBoTw; NOBE; OxAEP-2; OxBTC; PeECV

Bowl, The. Mimi Khalvati. NWP

Bowl, The. The Earl of Rochester. *See* Vulcan, contrive me such a cup.

Bowl is big and blue. A flash of leaf, The. The Bowl. Mimi Khalvati. NWP

Bowl of cold turkie fool. Fud at Foster's. Philip Lamantia. PoBeRe

Bowl of Roses, A. W. E. Henley. MoBrPo

Bowlegged, pinchered sand-digger. Statilius Flaccus, *tr. fr. Greek by* Barriss Mills. GrAn

Bowling-Green, The, sels. William Somervile.
"Where fair Sabrina's wand'ring currents flow." NOEC

Bows glided down, and the coast, The. Ballad of the Long-legged Bait. Dylan Thomas. MeMBP

Box Comes Home, A. John Ciardi. ArOW

Box is only temporary, The. (*LL*) The Arrival of the Bee Box. Sylvia Plath. FaBoMo; FaBoWP; HCAP; NALW; NaP

Boxcar Poem, The ("The boxcars drift by.") David Young. AmPA

Boxers, The. Paul Whitehead. *Fr.* Gymnasiad, The, or Boxing Match. ECEV

Boxes break, The/ At the corners. Christmas Ornaments. Valerie Worth. PChr

Boxing. Kipling. *Fr.* Verses on Games. OtMeF

Boxing the Fox. Pearse Hutchinson. CIP

Boy, The. David Trinidad. ETG

Boy, A. John Ashbery. NeAP

Boy Actor, The. Noël Coward. OxBTC

Boy and Girl. Mother Goose. *See* There was a little boy and a little girl.

Boy and the Deer, The. Andrew Peynetsa, *tr. by* Dennis Tedlock. STP

Boy and the Dream, The. Anna Wickham. AIW

Boy and the Flute, The. Bjøørnstjerne Bjøørnson, *tr. fr. Norwegian by* Sir Edmund Gosse. AWP

Boy and the Mantle, The. *Unknown.* ESPB; OxBB

Boy and the Parrot, The. John Hookham Frere. OxBChV

Boy and the Snake, The. Charles Lamb *and* Mary Lamb. OxBChV

Boy and the Sparrow. Mother Goose. *See* Little cock sparrow sat on a green tree, A.

Boy at Target Practice; a Contemplation. W. R. Moses. NYBP

Boy at the Paterson Falls. Toi Derricotte. PBCAP

Boy at the Window. Richard Wilbur. Mes; NoP; RaBo

Boy Breaking Glass. Gwendolyn Brooks. AiP; MoP; NAAL-2; NoAM; NoP

Boy! bring an ounce of Freeman's best. Isaac Hawkins Browne. *Fr.* Pipe of Tobacco, A.
(Boy! Bring an Ounce.) BXAP

Boy, bring me candles on a silver salver. Candles. Hélène Swarth, *tr. fr. Dutch by* Jonathan Crewe. WPOW

Boy Brittan. Forceythe Willson. PAH

Boy brought in the logs to start the fire, The. Mesón Brujo. E. A. Lacey. PeHV

Boy Died in My Alley, The. Gwendolyn Brooks. NoAM

Boy drove into the city, his wagon loaded down, A. The Little Black-eyed Rebel. Will M. Carleton. FaPON; PAH

Boy Fishing, The. E. J. Scovell. FaBoWP

Boy from his bedroom-window, The. At Ballyshannon, Co. Donegal. William Allingham. FaBoPP; NOBVV

Boy from Rome, Da. T. A. Daly. FaPON

Boy had run all the way home, The. Mending Crab Pots. Dave Jeddie Smith. MT

Boy He Had an Auger, A. *Unknown.* AS

Boy hid under the house, The. Fear. David Lehman. NAmP90

Boy, hold my wreath for me. The Serenader. *Unknown, tr. fr. Greek by* Dudley Fitts. GrAn

Boy, I detest the Persian pomp. Horace. *See* Boy, I have their empty shouts.

Boy, I have their empty shouts. I, 38. Simplicity. Horace, *tr. fr. Latin by* Austin Dobson. *Fr.* Odes. InPK; NBLV
(Ah child, no Persian — perfect art.) OBVE, *tr. by* Gerard Manley Hopkins
(Boy, I detest the Persian pomp.) InPK; NBLV
(Chicago Analogue.) NBLV, *tr. by* Keith Preston
(Davus, I detest.) NBLV, *tr. by* Austin Dobson
(Dear Lucy, you know what my wish is.) NBLV, *tr. by* Thacheray
(Fie on Eastern Luxury.) InPK, *tr. by* Hartley Coleridge
(I do not share the common craze.) NBLV, *tr. by* Keith Preston

(Myrtle for Two.) NBLV, *tr. by* George F. Whicher
(Nay, nay, my boy — 'tis not for me.) InPK, *tr. by* Hartley Coleridge
(Persian flummery.) NBLV, *tr. by* George F. Whicher
(Persian Fopperies.) AWP, *tr. by* William Cowper
(Persian pomps, boy, ever I renounce them.) OBVE, *tr. by* Christopher Smart
(Persicos Odi: Pocket Version.) NBLV, *tr. by* Austin Dobson
(Preference Declared, The.) InPK, *tr. by* Eugene Field; NBLV, *tr. by* Eugene Field
(Victorian Paraphrase, A.) NBLV, *tr. by* Thacheray

Boy in Ice. Laurie Lee. NYBP

Boy in our midst was fufering. Pain, A. Haircut. Edward Kleinschmidt. UnDi

Boy in the Barn, The. *Unknown.* ReMoGo

Boy in the Bay Window 1939. Maurice Kenny. BCF

Boy is as old as the stars, A. To My God in His Sickness. Philip Levine. NNaP

Boy just like you took me out to see them, A. What the End Is For. Jorie Graham. NAmP90

Boy Liu in Leafy Mound, visitor of the autumn wind. A Bronze Immortal Takes Leave of Han. Li Ho, *tr. fr. Chinese by* A. C. Graham. PLT

Boy looked out of eyes like Euclid's eyes, The. Form Was the World. Maurice English. NYBP

Boy loves a girl, A. Heine. RiWo

Boy-mad no longer. Leaving, the Boys Behind. Rufinus, *tr. fr. Greek by* Alan Marshfield. GrAn; PeHV

Boy-Man. Karl Shapiro. NYBP

Boy of fifteen, A. Honi Soit Qui Mal Y Pense. Ian Young. PeHV

Boy of Quebec, The. *At. to* Kipling. *See* There was a young boy [or man] of Quebec.

Boy of Seventeen, The. Juan Felipe Herrera. AfAz

Boy; or, Son of Rip-off, The. Malcolm Glass. BXAP

Boy, presuming on his intellect, A. At Woodward's Gardens. Robert Frost. PoA

Boy Reading. John Holmes. ImGa

Boy Reciter, The. David Everett. *See* You'd scarce expect one of my age.

Boy Remembers in the Field. Raymond Knister. NOBC

Boy Riding Forward Backward. Robert Francis. LCAP

Boy Serving at Table, The. John Lydgate. OxBChV

Boy Shepherds' Simile, The. David Bottoms. MT

Boy should have an open fireplace, A. A Boy's Need. Herbert Clark Johnson. PoNe

Boy sits in the classroom, The. Learning Experience. Marge Piercy. FF; NoAM

Boy stood in the supper-room, The. *Unknown.* ISE

Boy stood on the burning deck, The. Casabianca. Felicia Dorothea Hemans. BeLS; BLPA; EBEvV; FaBoBe; FaBoPa; FaPON; VPP; WBLP

Boy stood on the burning deck, The/ His feet were covered with blisters. *Unknown.* FaBoPa

Boy stood on the burning deck, The/ His fleece was white as snow. Familiar Lines. *Unknown.* FiBHP

Boy stood on the burning deck, The/ Peeling potatoes by the peck. *Unknown.* RoPo

Boy stoops, picking greens with his mother, A. Greens. David Ray. SM; VGW

Boy that is good, The [or A]. The Description of a Good Boy. Henry Dixon. OxBChV; OxNR, *st.* 1

Boy that is truthful and honest, A. The Boy We Want. *Unknown.* WBLP

Boy Thirteen, A. Jeff Irish. DL

Boy was lying upside-down from me, The. Too Dark. Mark McCloskey. PoA

Boy We Want, The. *Unknown.* WBLP

Boy Who Became Sky, The. David Wagoner. AnAn

Boy who Dreamed the Country Night, The. Christopher Koch. NOBAu

Boy who throws the ball, The. The Beadle's Testimony. Jerome Rothenberg. NNaP

Boy with a Cart, The, sels. Christopher Fry.
"In our fields, fallow and burdened, in grass and furrow." LiTB

Boy with His Hair Cut Short. Muriel Rukeyser. LiTM; MoAB; NALW; NoAM; TwCP; VGW; WPE

Boy with yellow hair, his clothes in place, A. War Memento (Somewhere in France 1915). Roger Hecht. CRP

Boyang the Wandering Recluse ("Boyang-Boyang-Boyang-Boyang-Boyang.") Al Robles. ETG

Boyhood in Tobacco Country. Robert Penn Warren. AnAn

Boyhood of Christ, The. St. Columbanus. NOIV

Boyne Water, The. *Unknown.* FaBoEH, abr.; FaPoR; IIP; NOIV

Boyo: When I came to this country, I could. Scene 6 The Boat Passage. Gabriel Gbadamosi. *Fr.* No Blacks, No Irish. NBrP

Boys, The. Oliver Wendell Holmes. WBLP

Boys. Winifred M. Letts. TIRV

Boys and girls come out to play. Mother Goose. OxNR

Boys and Sport. Solon, *tr. fr. Greek by* John Addington Symonds. PeHV

Boys, by Girls Held in Their Thighs. John Peale Bishop. ErPo

Boy's cocks, Diodore. Strato, *tr. fr. Greek by* Thomas Meyer. GrAn; PeHV

Boys flying kites haul in their white-winged birds. Words. *Unknown.* PoLF

Boys forget about women. The Excuse. Carl H. Greene. NBV

Boy's Head, A. Miroslav Holub, *tr. fr. Czech by* Ian Milner *and* George Theiner. CBNP; TSaS

Boys/ I don't promise you nothing. Admonitions. Lucille Clifton. BPo; CAPP; NALW; NMM

Boys in Bellingham like picking raspberries best, The. Maschlacki. Lora Berg. BTR

Boys in sporadic but tenacious droves. The Horse Chestnut Tree. Richard Eberhart. CMoP; LiTM; MoAB; MoAmPo

Boys Make Men. *Unknown.* PWR

Boy's Mother, A. James Whitcomb Riley. OHIP

Boy's Need, A. Herbert Clark Johnson. PoNe

Boys of Mullabaun [*or* Mullaghbawn], The. *Unknown.* BIrV; GBP

Boys of Sanpete County, The. *Unknown.* AmFP

Boys of '69, The. Michael O'Loughlin. *Fr.* Shards, The. IB

Boys of These Men Full Speed. Muriel Rukeyser. NNaP

Boys of Tyre are beautiful, The. Meleager, *tr. fr. Greek by* Peter Whigham. PeHV

Boys of Wexford, The. *Unknown.* ELP

Boys on street corners in Santa Ana. *Unknown.* BAP-90

Boys' Own. Michael Hofmann. SCBI

Boy's Place, A. Rose Burgunder. PDV

Boy's Poem, A, *sels.* Alexander Smith.
"Steamer left he black and oozy wharves, The." PeVV

Boy's Prayer, A. Henry Charles Beeching. *See* God who created me.

Boy's Song, A. James Hogg. BoTP; CH; CoGr; FaPON; FaPoR; MoShBr; OBEV; OTCP; OxAEP-2; OxBChV; PlP; WiR

Boys, that was the show that paid. (*LL*) The Clown's Baby. "Margaret Vandegrift." VPP

Boysick (by gadzooks thunderstruck), The. The Honey Lamb. Jonathan Williams. PoM

Bozzy and Piozzi, *sels.* "Peter Pindar."
Introduction and Anecdotes. PoEL-3

Br-r-r-am-m-m, rackety-am-m, om, am. What the Motorcycle Said. Mona Van Duyn. NIP

Braced in the sinewy vigour of thy breed. The Horse and His Rider. Joanna Baillie. ECWP; NOEC

Bracelet, The. John Donne. NoSic

Bracelet, The. John Peck. AnAn

Bracelet, The. Thomas Stanley. BeJo

Bracelet eat into the flesh/ the gangrene of/ applause. Piaf and Holiday Go Out. Carole Bergé. Jaz

Bracelet, The: To Julia, Robert Herrick. OBEV; TrGrPo

Bracelets. William Strode. NOSC

Bracing on air. (*LL*) Firstborn. Katherine Gallagher. VBLP

Bracken Hills in Autumn. "Hugh MacDiarmid." ScCV

Brackish reach of shoal off Madaket, A. The Quaker Graveyard in Nantucket. Robert Lowell. CMoP; HAP; LiTM; MoAB; MoP; NAAL-2; NoAM; NOBA; NoP; OxBA; PeECV; Poetr; TAP; UnPo; VCAP

Braddan Vicarage. Thomas Edward Brown. FaBoPP

Braddock's Fate, with an Incitement to Revenge. Stephen Tilden. PAH

Brady. *Unknown.* AS

Braemar. Galway Kinnell. PoA

Braes o' Ballochmyle, The. Burns. ScCV

Braes o' Menstrie, The. *Unknown.* ScCV

Braes o' Yarrow, The. *Unknown.* See Late at een, drinkin' the wine.

Braes of Yarrow, The. John Logan. GTBS; GTBS-P; SCGP

Braes of Yarrow, The. *Unknown.* ESPB; OxBB

Brag, A. *Unknown.* RoPo

Brag, sweet tenor bull. Basil Bunting. *Fr.* Briggflatts [An Autobiography]. NoAM; PoE

Brahma. Emerson. AmPP; AWP; GGP; HAP; ImPo; LiTA; MeMAP; NOBA; NoP; OBEV; OxBA; PFP; PoE; PoRA; TAP; TFi; TrGrPo; UnPo; UV; WGRP

Brahma. Andrew Lang. BXAP; FaBoCo; NOBL; PeLV; UV

Brahma, the World Idea, *Fr.* Rig Veda. *Unknown, tr. fr. Sanskrit by* Romesh Dutt. *Fr.* Vedic Hymns. WGRP

Brahms/ stabbed me in the ear. St. Julien's Eve. James Cunningham. JB

Braid Claith. Robert Fergusson. NOEC; OxBS

Braid of creatioin trembles. (*LL*) The Snakes of September. Stanley Kunitz. AnAn; FoLa

Brain Cells, The. Donald Hall. TAP

Brain Drain. "The Mighty Chalkdust." PBCV

Brain forgets, but the blood will remember, The. The Dark Chamber. Louis Untermeyer. MoAmPo

Brain is wider than the sky, The. Cause. Emily Dickinson. EnlH; MoAB; MoAmPo; MoP; NAAL-1; NAWM-2; NTP; OxBA; Poetr

Brain itself in its skull, the. Harsh Climate. Charles Simic. LCAP

Brain, within its groove, The. Emily Dickinson. NoAM; NOBA; SAmP

Brainless creatures simply fuck. Vive La Différence. Strato, *tr. fr. Greek by* Teddy Hogge. GrAn

Brainsick race that wanton youth ensues, The. *Unknown.* NoSic

Brainstorm. Howard Nemerov. HAP; SM; TRP

Brainwashing Dramatized. Don Johnson. PoNe

Brakes, like young stag's horns, come up in Spring, The. London versus Epping Forest. John Clare. *Fr.* Child Harold. FaBoPP

Bramble. Peretz Kaminsky. BTR

Bramble Jam. Irene F. Pawsey. BoTP

Bran, a chaff, a very barley [y]awn, A. Edward Taylor. *Fr.* Preparatory Meditations Before My Approach to the Lord's Supper. ChIV-2; NOSC

Branch of may, it does look gay, A. May Song. *Unknown.* OBET

Branches ripped by a storm tide. Walking the Beach. Sarah Youngblood. IHMS

Branches, you, The/ And you. (*LL*) The Mysteries Remain. Hilda Doolittle ("H. D."). NOBA; TAP; VGW; WPOW

Branchy leafy oak-tree, The. Sweeney Praises the Trees. *Unknown, tr. fr. Irish by* Seamus Heaney. RB

Brand, *sels.* Ibsen, *tr. fr. Norwegian by* C. H. Herford.
Brand Speaks. WGRP

Brand Speaks. Ibsen, *tr. fr. Norwegian by* C. H. Herford. *Fr.* Brand. WGRP

Brandish't sword of God before them blaz'd, The. Milton. *Fr.* Paradise Lost. EPCY
(Expulsion from Paradise.) ChTr

Branwell's Sestina. James Reaney. *Fr.* Suit of Nettles, A. MoCV

Branwen was buried here, so long ago. At Branwen's Grave. Dudley G. Davies. AngWe

Branwen's Starling. R. Williams Parry, *tr. fr. Welsh by* Gwyn Jones. OBWVE

Brasen tower with doors close barred, The. Horace, *tr. by* Sir Walter Ralegh. *Fr.* Odes. SiPSBD

Brasília. Sylvia Plath. CAPP

Brass and parrot feathers. Oshun, the River Goddess. *Yoruba Oral Tradition, tr. by* Ulli Beier. WTO

Brass buttons, blue coat! *Unknown.* RoPo

Brass Furnace Going Out: Song, after an Abortion. Diane Di Prima. PoBeRe

Brass Horse, The. Drummond Allison. FaBoTw

Brass Knuckles. Stuart Dybek. PBCAP

Brass Spittoons. Langston Hughes. MoAmPo; NoAM; Poetr

Brass Tacks. Denise Levertov. InPS

Brassica (oleracea) is a cabbage. Cabbage. Rosemary Norman. BrRo

Brats. X. J. Kennedy. NBLV

Bratzlav Rabbi to His Scribe, The. Jacob Glatstein, *tr. fr. Yiddish by* Jacob Sloan. TrJP

Brave, The. G. K. Chesterson. OtMeF

Brave and high-souled Pilgrims, you who knew no fears. Thanksgiving Day. Annette Wynne. OHIP

Brave and undaunted stood young Brennan on the moor. (*LL*) Brennan on the Moor. *Unknown.* AmFP; FaBoBa; GBP

Brave as a postage stamp. Sporting Goods. Philippe Soupault, *tr. fr. French by* Rosemarie Waldrop. TTTS

Brave at Home, The. Thomas Buchanan Read. AnAmPo

Brave Collier Lads. *Unknown.* OBET

Brave flowers, that I could gallant it like you. A Contemplation upon Flowers. Henry King. BoNaP; ELP; MeLP; NoP; OBEV; SCGP; SeCP; TrGrPo

Brave Grant, thou hero of the war. Gen. Grant — the Hero of the War. George Moses Horton. AAP

Brave infant of Saguntum, clear[e]. To the Immortal Memory and Friendship of That Noble Pair, Sir Lucius Cary and Sir Henry [*or* H.] Morison. Ben Jonson. NAEL-1; NOBE; NoP; NOSC; OAEL-1; PoEL-2; SeCP; SeCV-1

Brave lads in olden musical centuries. Alcaics; to H. F. B. Robert Louis Stevenson. OBEV

Brave Man, The. Wallace Stevens. PFP; SAmP; SOTW

Brave Man and Brave Woman. Mrs. Henry Linden. CBWP-4

Brave man with a sword!, The. *(LL)* He did not wear his scarlet coat. Oscar Wilde. BeLS; EBEvV; MoBrPo; NoAM; NOBE; NOBVV; OBMV; OBNC; OBNV; OtMeF; OxAEP-2; PeIV; TFi; UV

Brave New World. Archibald MacLeish. NOBA; OxBA

Brave New World. Shakespeare. *Fr.* Tempest, The. OAEL-1; TrGrPo

Brave news is come to town. *Unknown.* OxNR

Brave Old Duke of York, The. *Unknown. See* Oh [*or* O], the noble [*or* brave *or* grand old] duke of York.

Brave Old Oak, The. Henry Fothergill Chorley. FaBoBe

Brave Old Ship, the *Orient*, The. Robert Traill Spence Lowell. FaBoBe

Brave Paulding and the Spy. *Unknown.* PAH

Brave Rover. Max Beerbohm. NBLV

Brave Teuton, though thy awful name. Schemmelfennig. Bret Harte. OBAL

Brave undaunted robber bold was Brennan on the Moor, A. *(LL)* Brennan on the Moor. *Unknown.* FaBoBa; GBP

Brave weathercock, I see thou'lt set thy nose. Upon the Weathercock. Bunyan. OxBChV

Brave Wolfe. *Unknown.* PAH

Brave youth, to whom Fate in one hour. For a Picture Where a Queen Laments over the Tomb of a Slain Knight. Thomas Carew. CaPo

Bravely from Fairyland he rode, on furlough. The Broken Girth. Robert Graves. BIrV

Bravery of Their Tinkling Ornaments, The. Bible, *O.T. Fr.* Isaiah. CBCK

Bravery runs in my family. Coward. A. R. Ammons. OBAL

Bravest Battle, The. Joaquin Miller. WBLP

Braving the Wilds All Unexplored. Robert Freeman. AH

Braw, snortin', roarin', fearsome beastie. To a Bull Moose. Eugene O'Neill. UV

Brawling in the bush with himself. Ann Arbor Solitary. Lawrence Goldstein. NGP

Brawling of a sparrow in the eaves, The. The Sorrow of Love. W. B. Yeats. MeMBP; NAEL-2; OAEL-2; PeVV; TEP

Brazen Image. Anne Hartigan. CIP

Brazen Tongue. William Rose Benét. MoAmPo

Brazil. Tony Harrison. *Fr.* Sentences. OBTV

Brazil, January 1, 1502. Elizabeth Bishop. FaBoWP; NoAM; VCAP

Brazilian Fazenda. P. K. Page. FaBoWP

Brazos River, The. *Unknown.* PrIm

Breach of clear heaven opens, A. Enlightment. Ch'en Yu Yi, *tr. fr. Chinese* by Kenneth Rexroth. OHMPC

Breach of Or, The. Molly Peacock. PRA

Bread. Stanley Burnshaw. TrJP

Bread. James Dickey. LCAP

Bread. Brendan Kennelly. PBCIP

Bread. W. S. Merwin. VCAP

Bread. Gabriela Mistral, *tr. fr. Spanish* by Allan Francovich *and* Kathleen Weaver. WPOW

Bread. H. E. Wilkinson. BoTP

Bread and a Pension. Louis Johnson. PeNZ

Bread and Milk for Breakfast. Christina Rossetti. NTP

Bread and Music. Conrad Aiken. *See* Music I heard with you was more than music.

Bread and Roses. James Oppenheim. SWP

Bread and Wine, *sels.* Friedrich Hölderlin, *tr. fr. German* by Robert Bly. "Oh friend, we arrived too late." NU; RaBo

Bread crombs and the tea, The. *(LL)* Boy stood in the supper-room, The. *Unknown.* ISE

Bread Hot from the Oven, The. John Thompson. NOBC

Bread: I'm told a certain object grows. *Unknown, formerly at. to* Cynewulf, *tr. fr. Anglo-Saxon* by Kevin Crossley-Holland. *Fr.* Riddles (Exeter Book). ASW

Bread is a lovely thing to eat. Lovely Things. H. M. Sarson. BoTP

Bread Is Born. Anne Hébert, *tr. fr. French* by Maxine W. Kumin. BoWoP

Bread of Heaven, on Thee We Feed. Josiah Conder. TrCP

Bread of This World, The; Praises III. Thomas McGrath. RaBo

Bread that bringeth strength I want to give, The. I Shall Not Pass Again This Way. *Unknown.* BLRP; WBLP

Bread-Word Giver. John Wheelwright. ChIV-2

Breadth. Circle. Desert. Monarch. Month. Wisdom. John Hollander. PoA

Break, The. E. N. Sargent. NYBP

Break and trail home. The Girl I Left behind Me. *Unknown.* AmFP

Break, Break, Break. J. C. Squire. *See* Fly, Muse, thy wonted themes, nor longer seek.

Break, Break, Break. Tennyson. AWP; BLPL; CBLP; CH; ClHu; DL; EBEvV; EnVR; FaBoBe; FaBV; FaPoR; FF; FHYEP; GoJo; GTBS-P; HAP; HeIP; ImPo; LiTB; MeMBP; NAEL-2; NIP; NOBE; NOBVV;

NoP; OBNC; OHCV; PlP; PoEL-5; Poetr; PoRA; PrIm; PWR; RB; SoSe; TEP; TFi; TrGrPo; WBLP; WeW

Break not my loneliness, O Wanderer! The Dove's Loneliness. George Darley. OBNC

Break not the slumbers of the bride. An Hymeneal Song on the Nuptials of the Lady Anne Wentworth and the Lord Lovelace. Thomas Carew. CaPo

Break[e] of Day. John Donne. EnRePo; ErPo; LiTB; NAEL-1; SoSe

Break of Day. *Unknown, at. to* John Donne. ElL; TrGrPo

Break of Day in the Trenches. Isaac Rosenberg. FaBoMo; GTBS-P; MoBrPo; NAEL-2; NoAM; NOBE; NoP; NSI; OAEL-2; OBWP; OxAEP-2; PAW; PeFWW; PoA; PoWW; TFi

Break Thou the Bread of Life. Mary Artemisia Lathbury. AH

Break through and stare. *(LL)* Your love is dead, lady, your love is dead. R. S. Thomas. BoLoP; EnLoPo

Break-up, The. A. M. Klein. NOBC

Breakdown, The. Sherod Santos. SM

Breake now my heart and dye! Oh no, she may relent. Thomas Campion. AAS

Breakers' jumbled yard: valley, The. Port Talbot. John Davies. AngWe

Breakers over the Sea. *Malay Oral Tradition, tr.* by R. O. Winstedt. WTO

Breakfast. W. W. Gibson. OBMV; OxBTC

Breakfast. Harry Graham. EBNV

Breakfast. Thom Gunn. OxBC

Breakfast. Everette Maddox. MT

Breakfast. Ljubomir Simovic, *tr. fr. Serbo-Croatian* by Charles Simic. HSix

Breakfast. Robert Wells. SCBI

Breakfast. William Carlos Williams. SAmP

Breakfast for Barbarians, A. Gwendolyn MacEwen. NOBC

Breakfast in Bed (Influenza in War-time). Donald McDonald. PBCV

Breakfast over, islanded by noise. Woman in Kitchen. Eavan Boland. BiHa

Breakfast over, to Memorial Park we'd go. Quatrains for Pegasus. James Merrill. BAP-90

Breakfast Song in Time of Diet. Stoddard King. OBAL

Breakfast with Gerard Manley Hopkins. Anthony Brode. BXAP; FaBoPa; FiBHP; NOBL

Breakfasting alone in Karachi, Delhi, Calcutta. Solitary Travel. Louis MacNeice. OBTV

Breaking. Cynthia Huntington. NAmP90

Breaking, The. Edwin Muir. PlP

Breaking and Entering. Ralph Angel. NAmP90

Breaking Days. Sara Boyes. DT

Breaking from under that thy cloudy veil. Lord Herbert of Cherbury. OxAEP-1

Breaking Green. Michael Ondaatje. NOBC

Breaking Out. A. R. Ammons. CAPP

Breaking Point. Sylvia Auxier. GoYe

Breaking sea came by, The. *(LL)* After the Poem. Sydney Clouts. PeSAV

Breaking the Chain. Tony Harrison. UV

Breaking the morning ice on the well's bucket was no great hardship. On the Pilgrim's Way in Kent, as It Leads to the Coldrum Stones. "Asphodel." BrRo

Breaking the night's maidenhead. *(LL)* The Dog. Valentin Iremonger. BIrV

Breaking waves dashed high, The. The Landing of the Pilgrim Fathers [in New England]. Felicia Dorothea Hemans. BeLS; BLPA; FaBoBe; FaBV; FaPON; GN; OHIP; PAH; VPP; WBLP; WPE (Pilgrim Fathers, The.) BoTP

Breaking with honey buds, shall ever equal. *(LL)* The Express. Stephen Spender. CMoP; GoJo; HeIP; LiTM; MoAB; MoBrPo; MoP; NoAM; TwCP

Breakings. Henry Taylor. GrPl

Breaklight. Lucille Clifton. CAPP

Breaks, and in accents mellifluous, follows the thoughts of the author. *(LL)* The Metre Colombian. *Unknown.* BXAP; UV

Breaks like the Atlantic Ocean on my head. *(LL)* Man and Wife. Robert Lowell. AmPP; BoLoP; CAPP; NAAL-2; VCAP

Breaks up in obelisks on the river. Ice. Ai. FYAP

Breaks upon me now, while dark water crumbles the moon. *(LL)* Night along the Mackinac Bridge. Roberta Hill Whiteman. CDW

Breakthrough. Carolyn M. Rodgers. BPo

Breakwaters. Ted Walker. NYBP

Breast/ below ground. The Dance. Robert Kelly. *Fr.* Book of Persephone, The. PoM

Breast/ Is best. Note on Feeding. *Unknown.* FaBoUs

Breastdown fluttering in the breeze. Sparrow in Winter. Takahashi Shinkichi, tr. fr. *Japanese by* Lucien Stryk *and* Takashi Ikemoto. NU

Breastés round, and long small armés twain, The. (*LL*) Smiling mouth and laughing eyn grey, The. Charles, Duc d'Orléans. MiEL

Breasts. Maxine Chernoff. UL

Breasts. Tess Gallagher. AmPA

Breasts. Donald Hall. OBAL

Breasts. Charles Simic. NNaP; RaBo

Breasts of a barmaid of Crale, The. *Unknown.* NOBL

Breasts of Mnasidice, The. Pierre Louÿs, tr. fr. *French.* Fr. Chansons de Bilitis. PeHV

Breath, The. Robert Bly. Fr. Two Translations from Kabir. PRA

Breath. James Dickey. SM

Breath. Mark Strand. HCAP

Breath all of thee and only thee. (*LL*) O Mary sing thy songs to me. John Clare. CBLP

Breath of Air, A. James Wright. NOBA

Breath of life imbued those few dim days, The. Jessie Redmond Fauset. CDC; ShDr

Breath of my life, The — no less. Meleager, tr. fr. *Greek by* Peter Whigham. GrAn; PeHV

Breath on the Oat. Joseph Russell Taylor. PAH

Breath'd back again. (*LL*) Echo. Thomas Moore. ELP

Breathe and blow. Dragon Smoke. Lilian Moore. SiSoPo

Breathe Dust. Fred Wah. NOBC

Breathe in experience, breathe out poetry. Poem Out of Childhood. Muriel Rukeyser. NMM

Breathe my breath also through these songs. (*LL*) Chanting the Square Deific. Walt Whitman. NAAL-1

Breathe not, hid Heart: cease silently. To an Unborn Pauper Child. Thomas Hardy. FaBoRV; GTBS-P; LiTB; MeMBP; NAs

Breathe on the mirror. Reeves Timber Yard. John Hall. VaA

Breathers, The. James Reiss. AmPA

Breathes there a man with hide so tough. Samuel Hoffenstein. FiBHP

Breathes There the [*or* a] Man [with Soul So Dead]. Sir Walter Scott. Fr. Lay of the Last Minstrel, The. BLPA; EBEvV; EnRP; OxBS; PlP; SoSe; TFi
  (Innominatus.) OBEV
  (Love of Country.) VPP; WBLP
  (My Native Land.) GN
  (Native Land.) TrGrPo
  (Patriot, The.) FaPoR; OBNC
  (Patriotism.) NOBE; OxAEP-2

Breathing, The. Denise Levertov. NaP; RFM

Breathing. James Tate. LCAP

Breathing do I draw that air to me. Song of Breath. Peire Vidal, tr. fr. *French by* Ezra Pound. AWP

Breathing Exercises. Leonard Nathan. PBCAP

Breathing his last music, Mozart is supposed. Lost Letter to James Wright, with Thanks for a Map of Fano. Gibbons Ruark. MT

Breathing something German at the end. The Gift to Be Simple. Howard Moss. Poetsp; TwCP

Breathing Space July. Tomas Tranströmer, tr. fr. *Swedish by* Robert Bly. RB

Breathing, the last possession. Paris Aubade. Susan Ludvigson. VBLP

Breathing the Strong Smell. Harold Norse. PeHV

Breathless. Wilfred Noyce. OBTV

Breathless she stood, her graceful head bent low. Listening Nydia. H. Cordelia Ray. CBWP-3

Breathless, we flung us on the windy hill. The Hill. Rupert Brooke. MoBrPo; OxBTC; Son

Breaths. Birago Diop, tr. fr. *French by* Anne Atik. TTY

Brébeuf and His Brethren, sels. E. J. Pratt.
  Martyrdom of Brébeuf and Lalemant, 16 March 1649, The. NOBC

Brébeuf and His Brethren. F. R. Scott. NOBC

Brechfa Chapel. Roland Mathias. AngWe

Brecon Beacons and the Black Mountains, The. Henry Vaughan. FaBoPP

Bred up at home, full early I begun. Pope. Fr. Second Epistle of the Second Book of Horace Imitated, The. TOF

Bredon Hill. A. E. Housman. Fr. Shropshire Lad, A. EBVV; FaBoPP; FaPoB; MoAB; MoBrPo; NAEL-2; OxAEP-2; PlP; SoSe; UV

Breech, The. Michael McClure. NeAP

Breed's described, The: Now, Satire, if you can. Daniel Defoe. Fr. Trueborn Englishman, The. APAS; OBSV

Breeze has swelled the whitening sail, The. Song of the Pilgrims. Thomas Cogswell Upham. PAH

Breeze in Translation. Belle Waring. NAmP90; PBCAP

Breeze is blowing, The. *Unknown, tr. fr. Maori by* A. Armstrong *and* R. Nagata. WTO

Breeze is chasing the zephyr, The. Nobody's Chasing Me. Cole Porter. CBLP

Breeze is on the bluebells, The. Bluebells. Juliana Horatia Ewing. BoTP

Breezes at dawn have secrets to tell you, The. Jalal al-Din Rumi, tr. by John Moyne *and* Colman Barks. EaPr

Breezes went steadily thro' the tall pines, The. Nathan Hale. *Unknown.* PAH

Breezeways in the tropics winnow the air. A Letter from the Caribbean. Barbara Howes. CoAP; IMW; UnPo

Breezing Dawn of the New Day, The. Mongane Wally Serote. PeSAV

Breitmann in Politics, sels. Charles Godfrey Leland.
  "Dere's a liddle fact in hishdory vitch few hafe onnershtand." OBAL

Brennan on the Moor. *Unknown.* AmFP; FaBoBa; GBP

Brennhaum. Ezra Pound. Fr. Hugh Selwyn Mauberly. (Life and Contacts). AmPP; CMoP; InPS; LiTA; LiTM; MoAmPo; NoAM; NOBA; NoP; TAP

Brent; a Poem to Thomas Palmer Esq. William Diaper. FaBoPP
Sels.
  "Had mournful Ovid been to Brent condemned." OBSV
  "Happy are you, whom Quantock overlooks." NOEC; OBSV

Brereton Omen, The, sels. Felicia Dorothea Hemans.
  "Yes! I have seen the ancient oak." CTC

Brest Left Behind. John Farrar. PAH

Bretagne had not her peer. In the province far or near. Lady of Castlenoire. Thomas Bailey Aldrich. BeLS

Brethren, The. Seamus Deane. PNI

Breton Afternoon. Ernest Dowson. OBNC

Brevities. Siegfried Sassoon. PoLF

Brewer, A. *Unknown.* FaBoCo

Brewer's Man, The. L. A. G. Strong. FaBoCo; FiBHP; PeLV

Brewing of Soma, The. (Fagots blazed, the caldron's smoke, The.) Whittier. PoEL-4
Sels.
  "Dear Lord and Father of Mankind." AH; NOCV; TrPWD

Brian O'Linn. *Unknown.* CBNP; FaBoBa; FaBoNo; NBLV; RB

Brick, The. Paul Roche. NYBP

Brick distinguishes this country. Amsterdam Letter. Jean Garrigue. NYBP; VCAP

Brickie who had a fine tool, A. E. O. Parrott. PeLi

Bricklayer tells the busdriver, The. The Continuity. Paul Blackburn. NeAP

Bricklayer's Labours, The. Robert Tatersal. NOEC

Bricklay'r throws his trowel by, The. Religion and the Lower Classes. Evan Lloyd. Fr. Methodist, The. NOEC

Bricks of their quiet house were bright as rose, The. Transformations. Rachel Blake. NWP

Brickster, The. *Unknown.* OBET

Brid one brere, brid, brid one brere. *Unknown.* MiEL

Bridal Birth. Dante Gabriel Rossetti. Fr. House of Life, The. Son

Bridal Feet, The. Briar Wood. NWP

Bridal of Helon. Maria Gowen Brooks. Fr. Zophiël. AmWP

Bridal Piece. Louise Glück. SM

Bridal Song. George Chapman. Fr. Hero and Leander. AAS; NOBE; NoP; OBEV

Bridal Song. George Chapman. Fr. Masque of the Middle Temple and Lincoln's Inn, The. EiL; OxBSP

Bridal Song, A ("Beauty arise, show forth thy glorious shining!") Thomas Dekker *and others. See* Beauty, Arise!

Bridal Song: "Roses, their sharp spines being gone." John Fletcher *and* William Shakespeare. Fr. Two Noble Kinsmen, The. EiL; NOBE; NOSC; NoSic

Bridal Song ("Cynthia, to thy power.") Beaumont *and* John Fletcher. Fr. Maid's Tragedy, The. OBEV

Bridal Song ("Hold back thy hours.") Beaumont *and* Fletcher *and* John Fletcher. Fr. Maid's Tragedy, The. EiL; ErPo; TrGrPo

Bridal Song to Amala. Thomas Lovell Beddoes. Fr. Death's Jest Book. GBL; OBNC

Bridal Veil, The. Alice Cary. AmWP

Bridal weath. White rhododendron. Dogwood. May, Home after a Year Away. Gail Mazur. NAmP90

Bride, The. Bella Akhmadulina, tr. fr. *Russian.* AIW; BoWoP, tr. by Stephan Stepanchev

Bride, A. Harry Fainlight. BoLoP

Bride, The. D. H. Lawrence. NoAM; OxBTC

Bride, The. Sir John Suckling. Fr. Ballad [*or* Ballade] upon a Wedding, A. BeJo; CaPo; CoMu; EBEV; EBNV; FaBoBa; InvP; JCP; NoP; OxBM; SeCP; SeCV-1; TrGrPo

Bride cam' out o' the byre, The. Wooed and Married and A'. Alexander Ross. OxBS

Bright-footed Thetis did the sphere aspire. Homer, *tr. fr. Greek by* George Chapman. *Fr.* Iliad, The. NoSic

Bright, glowing Sappho! child of love and song. Ode to Sappho. Elizabeth Oakes Smith. AmWP

Bright green young grass comes up in the garden. Life Is Long. *Unknown, tr. fr. Chinese by* Kenneth Rexroth. OHMPC

Bright-haired am I, my face and body white. First Song. T. Carmi, *tr. fr. Hebrew by* Ruth Finer Mintz. *Fr.* René's Songs. MHP

Bright-haired Spirit! Golden Brow! Onward to Far Ida. George Darley. *Fr.* Nepenthe. OBNC

Bright hard day over habour where sea, A. Winter Lanscape — Halifax. Douglas Lochhead. NIP

Bright House. Fukao Sumako, *tr. fr. Japanese by* Kenneth Rexroth *and* Ikuko Atsumi. UnAS; WPJ

Bright is the moon on the deep. Tennyson. *Fr.* Princess, The. PIP

Bright is the ring of words. Robert Louis Stevenson. *Fr.* Songs of Travel. OBNC; TrGrPo

Bright miles, among crowds changingly beautiful. (*LL*) New York Sonnet. Judith Rodriguez. NOBAu

Bright mirror I braved, The: the devil in it. Cleopatra to the Asp. Ted Hughes. EBEV

Bright moon. "Ping Hsin," *tr. fr. Chinese by* Kenneth Rexroth *and* Ling Chung. *Fr.* Multitudinous Stars. WPC

Bright moon appears from the east ridge, The. Moonlit Night at Fragrant Mountain Temple. Wang Shih-chieng, *tr. fr. Chinese by* Richard John Lynn. SuSp

Bright moon illumines the night-prospect, A. *Unknown, tr. fr. Chinese by* Arthur Waley. BoWoP

Bright moon rising above T'ien Shan, A. Moon over Mountain Pass. Li Po, *tr. fr. Chinese by* Joseph J. Lee. SuSp

Bright moon shines upon the pavilion, A. Seven Poems of Lament. Ts'ao Chih, *tr. fr. Chinese by* Ronald C. Miao. SuSp

Bright moon soars over the Mountain of Heaven, The. The Moon over the Mountain Pass. Li Po, *tr. fr. Chinese by* Robert Payne. TAL

Bright moon, when will she appear?, The. "Prelude to Water Music." Su Shih, *tr. fr. Chinese by* Eugene Eoyang. SuSp

Bright moon white and silver, The. *Unknown, tr. fr. Chinese by* Charles Hartman. SuSp

Bright on the banners of lily and rose. Welcome to the Nations. Oliver Wendell Holmes. PAH

Bright over Europe fell her golden hair. (*LL*) Letty's Globe. Charles Tennyson Turner. NOBVV; OBEV; OHCV; PeVV

Bright purple teeth bopped to the music, hinting of sex. Ghazals a Go-Go. Henrietta O'Neill. UnDi

Bright Queen of Heaven, God's Virgin Spouse. The Knot. Henry Vaughan. MiEL

Bright ran thy line, O Galloway. Lord Galloway. Burns. OxBoLi

Bright shadows of true Rest! some shoots of bliss[e]. Son-Days. Henry Vaughan. CBCK; GeHe; NOSC; SeCP
(Sondayes.) AngWe

Bright she is, no daisy whiter. (*LL*) My mistress is as fair as fine. Thomas Ravenscroft. CH; OxBoLi

Bright shines the sun; play, beggars, play! In Praise of a Beggar's Life. "A. W." EIl; TrGrPo

Bright spark, shot from a brighter place. The Starre. George Herbert. ESCV; MiEL; PeECV

Bright Star! Would I Were Steadfast as Thou Art. Keats. ArLo; BLPL; CBLP; EnLoPo; GBL; GTBS; GTBS-P; HAP; ImPo; InPK; InPS; LiTB; MeMBP; NAEL-2; NAWM-2; NIP; OAEL-2; PoE; PPP; PrIm; SCV; Son; TrGrPo
(Bright Star.) TFi

Bright sun lights out over the western bank. T'ao Ch'ien, *tr. fr. Chinese by* Eugene Eoyang. SuSp

Bright town, tossed by waves of time to a hill. Ode to Swansea. Vernon Watkins. OBWVE

Bright tulips, we do know. To a Bed of Tulips. Robert Herrick. CaPo

Bright vocabularies are transient as rainbows. Precious Moments. Carl Sandburg. MoAmPo

Bright wanderer, fair coquette of heaven. Lines Written in the Bay of Lerici. Shelley. NAEL-2; OAEL-2

Bright waves scour the wound of Carthage, The. Rome Remember. Sidney Keyes. MoAB

Bright white street lights, The. Allegory in Black. Carl Clark. JB

Bright yellow flower and a new red pot, A. (*LL*) Five Little Sisters Walking in a Row. Kate Greenaway. MoShBr

Brighter sunshine of their own, A. (*LL*) To the Memory of the Brave Americans. Philip Freneau. AiP; AmPP; EAP; PoLF

Brighter than the brightness they destroy. (*LL*) Beauty and Terror. Lesbia Harford. CBAP

Brightest and Best of the Sons of the Morning. Reginald Heber. GN; WGRP

Brightest of the Bright, The. Egan O'Rahilly, *tr. fr. Irish by* James Clarence Mangan. BIrV

Brightest threads on life's pathway, The. Home and Mother. Hettye Rayburn Ramsey. PWR

Brightly colored for a new season. Merry-go-round. Oliver Jenkins. GoYe

Brightly shone the sun in my hut. Those Who Lost Everything. David Diop, *tr. fr. French by* Langston Hughes. PBA

Brightly the sun of summer shone. Memory. Anne Brontë. EBVV

Brightness. Denis Glover. PeNZ

Brightness most bright I beheld on the way, forlorn. Egan O'Rahilly, *tr. fr. Irish by* Thomas Kinsella. NOIV

Brightness of Brightness. Egan O'Rahilly, *tr. fr. Irish by* Frank O'Connor. IIP; PeIV

Brightness to Cast Shadows, A. David Constantine. PWE

Brighton Rock by Graham Greene. William Knott. UL

"Brigid is a caution, sure!" — What's that ye say? Her Sister. "Moira O'Neill." AIW; OxBTC

Brignall Banks. Sir Walter Scott. *Fr.* Rokeby. EnRP; OBEV

Brihadaranyaka Upanishad. *Unknown, tr. fr. Hindi. Fr.* Upanishads, The.

Brilliant beard of ice, A. Icicles. Robert Pinsky. SM

Brilliant-bellied newt flashes, The. Summer Matures. Helene Johnson. BISi; CDC; PoNe
(Summer matures. Brilliant Scorpion.) ShDr

Brilliant Day, A. Charles Tennyson Turner. NOBVV

Brilliant fierce eagles. The Lancet. Denis Devlin. NOIV

Brilliant kernel of the night, The. Robert Louis Stevenson. *Fr.* Light-Keeper, The. EBVV

Brilliant stills of food, the cozy, The. The Ladies' Home Journal. Sandra M. Gilbert. NIP

Bring — . (*LL*) Exile. Marta Fenyves. LoHo

Bring a leaf to me. Invitation Standing. Paul Blackburn. VGW

Bring a Torch, Jeanette, Isabella. Nicolas Saboly, *tr. fr. Provençal.* OHIP

Bring cypress, rosemary and rue. Grover Cleveland. Joel Benton. PAH

Bring Daddy home. *Unknown.* OxNR

Bring down the moon for genteel Janet. Goodbye Now, or, Pardon My Gauntlet. Ogden Nash. FiBHP

Bring dreams of Christ to dusky cane-lipped throngs. (*LL*) Georgia Dusk. Jean Toomer. BPo; CDC; NAAL-2; NoAM; NoP; PoBA; Poetr

Bring fair flowers to birth. (*LL*) God stir the soil. *Unknown.* EaPr

Bring flowers, fresh flowers, the fairest spring can yield. The Consumptive. Emma Catherine Embury. AmWP

Bring in her bill, once more, the Branch of Peace. (*LL*) Farewell Frost; or, Welcome the Spring. Robert Herrick. CaPo

Bring in the Wine. Li Ho, *tr. fr. Chinese by* A. C. Graham. PLT

Bring Kateen-beug and Maurya Jude. Beg-Innish. J. M. Synge. MoBrPo; PeIV

Bring little children unto me. Sunday Schools. Anna Sawyer. ECWP

Bring me a letter, postman! The Postman. Alice Todd. BoTP

Bring me men to match my mountains. Sam Walter Foss. *Fr.* Coming American, The. BLPA; FaBoBe

Bring me my rose-buds, drawer, come. A Frolic. Robert Herrick. FaBoEE

Bring Me the Cup. Moses ibn Ezra, *tr. fr. Hebrew by* Solomon Solis-Cohen. *Fr.* Wine-Songs. TrJP

Bring me the sunflower to plant in my garden here. The Sunflower. Eugenio Montale, *tr. fr. Italian by* Maurice English.
(Bring me the sunflower so that I can transplant it.) ArNa, *tr. by* Kate Farrell

Bring me the sunset in a cup. Emily Dickinson. MoAmPo; NOCV

Bring me to the blasted oak. Crazy Jane and the Bishop. W. B. Yeats. CMoP; LiTM

Bring me wine, but wine which never grew. Bacchus. Emerson. AmPP; AWP; LiTA; NOBA; OBEV; OxBA; PoEL-4

Bring me winne with the self God. (*LL*) A Cry to Mary. St. Godric. MeEL

Bring now the last flower in to warm this room. At My Mother's Bedside. Marcia Lee Masters. WPE

Bring, O Morn, thy music! Bring, O night, thy hushes! "Who Wert and Art and Evermore Shalt Be." William Channing Gannett. TrPWD

Bring on the Clowns. Jack Prelutsky. OTCP

Bring out the tall tales now that we told. Ghost Story. Dylan Thomas. OBCP

Bring that red mouth of yours. Madrigal de Verano. Federico García Lorca, *tr. fr. Spanish by* Paul Blackburn. ErPo

Bring the biggest bath you've seen. The Song of the Bath. Margaret E. Gibbs. BoTP

Bring the comb and play upon it! Marching Song. Robert Louis Stevenson. BoTP; FaPON

Bring the Day! Theodore Roethke. CRP

Bring the good old bugle, boys, we'll sing another song. Marching through Georgia. Henry Clay Work. FaPoR; PAH

Bring the hearse to the station. The Telegrams. Julia Ward Howe. AmWP

Bring the holy crust of bread. Charmes. Robert Herrick. BeJo

Bring the North. William Stafford. LCAP

Bring Us In Good Ale. Unknown. CH; EBEV; FaBoCo; MeEL; MiEL; OAEL-1

Bringer of sun, arrower of evening, star-begetter and moon-riser. Hymnal. Harold Vinal. TrPWD

Bringers of Beethoven, The. Reiner Kunze, tr. fr. German by Gordon Brotherston and Gisela Brotherston. PoSu

Bringing a Dead Man Back into Life. Russell Edson. TRP

Bringing Flowers. Roberta Spear. AmPA

Bringing home the Buddha. The Lesser Vehicle. John Drew. PWE

Bringing It Down. Stephen P. Dunn. BAP-91

Brings my mild father. (LL) Blue Jay [or Bluejay]. Robert Francis. LCAP

Brings to, and comes from Heaven. (LL) The Sap. Henry Vaughan and Thomas Stanley. ESCV

Brisk Chaunticleer his matins had begun. A Morning-Piece; or, An Hymn for the Hay-Makers. Christopher Smart. NOEC

Brisk methinks I am, and fine. Anacreontic Verse. Robert Herrick. PeLV

Brisk Wind, A. William Barnes. SCGP

Brisk Young Widow, A. Unknown. OBET

Brissit brawnis and broken banis. The Bewteis of the Fute-Ball. Unknown. FaBoCo; OxBS; ScCV

Bristled with cities, us the sea received. (LL) A Dream. Matthew Arnold. EnVR; GBL; GTBS-P; OBTV

Bristol. Richard Savage. FaBoPP

Bristol and Clifton. Sir John Betjeman. CMoP

Bristol Channel, The. Thomas Edward Brown. NOBVV

Bristowe Tragedie: or, The Dethe of Syr Charles Bawdin. Thomas Chatterton. EnRP; OxBB

Britain. Goldsmith. Fr. Travel[l]er, The; or, A Prospect of Society. NOEC

Britannia. James Thomson. See Heavens! What a goodly prospect spreads around.

Britannia and Raleigh. John Ayloffe. APAS

Britannia now lament for our hero that is dead. Lamentation on the Death of the Duke of Wellington. Unknown. OBET

Britannia rules the waves. On a Parisian Boulevard. James Kenneth Stephen. Fr. England and America. NOBL

Britannia to Columbia. Alfred Austin. See What is this voice I hear.

Britannia's Baby. D. H. Lawrence. NAs

Britannia's daughters, much more fair than nice. On Women ("Britannia's daughters.") Edward Young. Fr. Satires. ECEV

Britannia's daughters, much more fair than nice. Edward Young. Fr. Love of Fame, the Universal Passion. OBSV

Britannia's gallant streamers. Yankee Thunders. Unknown. PAH

Britannia's isles proclaim. To the First of August. Ann Plato. BlSi

Britannia's Pastorals., sels. William Browne.
"As that Arabian bird (whom all admire)." OAEL-1
Course of the Tavy, The. FaBoPP
Devonshire Walk, A. FaBoPP
Frolic Mariners of Devon, The. ChTr
(Hail, Thou my Native Soil.) OxAEP-1
Gentle Nymphs, Be Not Refusing. EIL
Glide Soft, Ye Silver Floods. EIL, II, Song 1
Golden Age, The. NOSC
"Muses' friend, The (grey-eyed Aurora), yet." JCP
(Morning.) NOSC
"He sung the heroic knights of Fairy Land." EPCY
"Shall I tell you whom I love?" EIL; NOSC
"So shuts the marigold her leaves." ChTr
(Memory.) OBEV

Brither-men wha eftir us live on. Ballat o the Hingit. Villon, tr. fr. French by Tom Scott. OBVE

British Army now carries two rifles, The. Identification in Belfast (I.R.A. Bombing). Robert Lowell. OxBC

British Church, The. George Herbert. AngWe; ESCV; PeECV

British Connection, The. Padraic Fiacc. PNI

British Grenadier, The. Unknown. PAH

British Grenadiers, The. Unknown. OxBoLi

British Journalist, The. Humbert Wolfe. FaBoEE; FiBHP; IHNG; OxBTC

British Leftish Poetry, 1930-40. "Hugh MacDiarmid." CMoP; FaBoTw; NoAM

British Lyon Roused, The. Stephen Tilden. PAH

British Man-of-War, A. Unknown. OBET

British Museum Reading Room, The. Louis MacNeice. LiTM; MoAB; MoBrPo; NOBE

British [or Brittish] Church, The. Henry Vaughan. ESCV; PeECV

British Prison Ship, The, sels. Philip Freneau.
Hessian Doctor, The. EAP
Hospital Prison Ship, The. AmPP

British, the Ethiopians, and the Italians are squabbling, The. Our Country Is Divided. Faarah Nuur, tr. fr. Somali by B. W. Andrzejewski and I. M. Lewis. WTO

British Valor Displayed. Francis Hopkinson. See Gallants attend, and hear a friend.

British Workman and the Government, The. D. H. Lawrence. IHNG

Britomart at Isis' Church. Spenser. Fr. Faerie Queene, The. PoE

Britons grown big with pride. A Poem Containing Some Remarks on the Present War. Unknown. PAH

Brittain's Ida., sels. Phineas Fletcher.
"Fond men! whose wretched care the life soon ending." EIL

Brittan's Remembrancer, sels. George Wither.
"I know that if thou please thou canst provide." SeCV-1

Brittle beauty [or beautie], that nature made so frail[e]. The Earl of Surrey. AAS; EnLoPo; SiPS; SiPSBD; TrGrPo
(Frailty and Hurtfulness of Beauty, The.) HoPM

Brittle streets, with midnight walking flung, The. Sonnet on a Still Night. J. V. Cunningham. PoA

Broad-acred Ascra bore me. Mnasalcas, tr. fr. Greek by Edward Lucie-Smith. GrAn

Broad and ample he warms himself. Unknown, tr. fr. Irish by Thomas Kinsella. NOIV

Broad August burns in milky skies. Day-Dreams. William Canton. NOBVV; NTP

Broad-Ax, The. Walt Whitman. Fr. Song of the Broad-Ax [or Broad-Axe]. MoAmPo

Broad-backed hippopotamus, The. The Hippopotamus. T. S. Eliot. AWP; CBNP; HoPM; ImPo; LiTB; NAEL-2; OBMV; VGW

Broad-based, broad-fronted, bounteous, multiform. Ben Jonson. Swinburne. Fr. Sonnets of English Dramatic Poets. EPCY; Son

Broad beach, The/ Sea wind and the sea's irregular rhythm. Afternoon: Amagansett Beach. John Hall Wheelock. BoNaP; PoRA

Broad Bean Sermon, The. Les A. Murray. FaBoMA

Broad Is the Road. Isaac Watts. AH; AmFP

Broad meadows in the twilight gray. Dreaming through the Twilight. Otto Julius Bierbaum, tr. fr. German by Philip L. Miller. RiWo

Broad Sea Sparkled, The. Heine, tr. fr. German by Philip L. Miller. RiWo

Broad sun, The. The Far-Farers. Robert Louis Stevenson. BoTP

Broadcast. Ivan V. Lalic, tr. fr. Serbo-Croatian by Charles Simic. HSix

Broadcast. Philip Larkin. CBLP

Broads. David R. Slavitt. BXAP

Broadway. Carl Sandburg. AiP

Broadway. Walt Whitman. NAAL-1

Broadway! Broadway! Gilbert Sorrentino. Jaz

Broagh. Seamus Heaney. FaBoVe

Brobdingnag. Adrien Stoutenburg. NYBP

Brocade curtains have just rolled back, The. Peonies. Li Shang-yin, tr. fr. Chinese by A. C. Graham. PLT

Brocadós and Damasks, and Tabbies, and Gawzes. An Excellent New Song on a Seditious Pamphlet. Swift. CoMu

Brock. Paul Muldoon. NoAM

Brocks snuffle from their holt within. The Badgers. Eden Phillpotts. BoTP

Broken, The. W. S. Merwin. LCAP

Broken altar, Lord, thy servant rears, [or reares] A. The Altar. George Herbert. AngWe; ChIV-1; ESCV; GeHe; HoPM; InPS; JCP; NAEL-1; NOSC; OAEL-1; Poetr; SeCP; SeCV-1; TrCP; TrGrPo

Broken Appointment, A. Thomas Hardy. GBL; NAEL-2; NoAM; NOBVV; NoP

Broken Back Blues. Robert Creeley. Jaz

Broken Belfast Street. Gang-Bang, Ulster Style. Linda Anderson. WoWa

Broken, bewildered by the long retreat. Retreat. W. W. Gibson. NSI

Broken Bowl, The. James Merrill. PoA

Broken by blood. (LL) Young Snail. Meena Alexander. VBLP

Broken Doll, The. Nuala Ni Dhomhnaill, tr. fr. Irish by John Montague. BiHa

Broken Dreams. Hugo Williams. CBLP

Broken-Face Gargoyles. Carl Sandburg. AmPP; MoAmPo; OxBA

Broken from the bursting bough. The Apple. Ray Smith. TrCP

Broken Gauges. David St. John. BAP-89

Broken Girth, The. Robert Graves. BIrV

Broken Heart, The. John Donne. EBEV

Broken Heart, The, *sels.* John Ford.
"Beasts onely capable of sense, enjoy." PoEL-2
Can You Paint a Thought? InvP; PoEL-2
"Oh [*or* O], no more, no more, too late." GBL; NOSC; PoEL-2
(Love's Martyrs.) NOBE
(Oh No More, No More.) ELP
(Song: "Oh no more, no more, too late.") OxBSP
Broken Heart. H. Cordelia Ray. CBWP-3
Broken Heart, Broken Machine. Richard E. Grant. PoBA
Broken-hearted Gardener, The. *Unknown.* ChTr; GBP
Broken Home, The. James Merrill. HAP; HCAP; MoP; NAAL-2; NoAM;
NOBA; NYBP; PPP
Broken Home. William Stafford. NNaP
Broken in pieces all asunder. Affliction ("Broken in pieces all asunder.")
George Herbert. ESCV; GeHe; JCP; NOSC
Broken, Incan roads. The stones laid perfect. Resurrections. Benjamin
Saenz. AfAz
Broken lines continue, you know, way past. The Breach of Or. Molly
Peacock. PRA
Broken mirror, The. X, Oh X. Mark Simpson. GOYP
Broken Off by the Music. John Yau. EOEF
Broken or sold. Or given away. Or used and forgotten. Or lost. (*LL*)
Green Light. Kenneth Fearing. PoE; VGW
Broken pillar of the wing jags from the clotted shoulder, The. Hurt Hawks.
Robinson Jeffers. AmPP; CMoP; FYAP; LiTA; LiTM; MoAB;
MoAmPo; MoP; NAAL-2; NoAM; NOBA; NoP; OxBA; PrIm; RB;
TAP; TFi; TRP; UnPo
Broken sods, a whipped flag, The. A Burial. Seamus Deane. CIP; PNI
Broken String, The. *Unknown, tr. fr. Bushman by* W. H. I. Bleek. PeSA
Broken Sword, The. Edward Rowland Sill. *See* This I beheld, or dreamed
it in a dream.
Broken the pot, there's still the jar. Loves of the Birds. *Malay Oral
Tradition, tr. by* R. J. Wilkinson *and* R. O. Winstedt. WTO
Broken Token, The. *Unknown. See* Pretty Fair Maid, A.
Broken Tower, The. Hart Crane. AmPP; CMoP; LiTM; MeMAP; MoAB;
MoAmPo; NoAM; NOBA; NoP; OxBA; Poetr; TrGrPo
Broken wagon wheel that rots away beside the river, A. Pioneers. Badger
Clark. FaBoBe
Brome, brome on hill. The Broomfield Hill. *Unknown.* CH
Broncho Dan halts midway of the stream. A Health at the Ford. Robert
Cameron Rogers. FaBoBe
Broncho That Would Not Be Broken, The. Vachel Lindsay. MeMAP
Bronx. Joseph Rodman Drake. AnAmPo
Bronxville Darby And Joan. Noël Coward. *Fr.* Sail Away.
Bronze god running, The. At Guaracara Park. Eric Roach. PBCV
Bronze Head, A. W. B. Yeats. LiTB; MeMBP
Bronze Immortal Takes Leave of Han, A. Li Ho, *tr. fr. Chinese by* A. C.
Graham. PLT
Bronze Legacy, The. Mary Effie Lee Newsome. ShDr
Bronze pillars melt away with the years, The. (*LL*) On and On for Ever.
Li Ho. PLT
Bronze soldier hitches a bronze cape, The. In Memoriam Francis
Ledwidge. Seamus Heaney. CIP; NoAM
Bronze Statuette of Kwan-yin, A. Charles Wharton Stork. GoYe
Bronze warship-beaks, old voyage-avid weapons. Philip of Thessalonica, *tr.
fr. Greek by* Edwin Morgan. GrAn
Bronzeville Man with a Belt in the Back. Gwendolyn Brooks. PoBA
Bronzeville Woman in a Red Hat. Gwendolyn Brooks. NALW
Brooch, The. Olga Drucker. BTR
Brood her high lonely mysteries. (*LL*) He Remembers Forgotten Beauty.
W. B. Yeats. CTC
Brooding and blissful halcyon days!, The. (*LL*) Halcyon Days. Walt
Whitman. OxBA
Brooding Grief. D. H. Lawrence. CMoP; IMW; PoE
Brooding on the eightieth letter of *Fors Clavigera.* Geoffrey Hill. *Fr.*
Mercian Hymns. HAP; PoE
Brooding upon its unexerted power. Gas and Hot Air. Morris Bishop.
OBAL
Brook, The. Tennyson. *Fr.* Brook, The; An Idyl. BoNaP; BoTP; EBEvV;
FaBV; FaPON; FHYEP; GN; GoJo; OxAEP-2, *complete*
Brook, The. Edward Thomas. OAEL-2
Brook, The, *sels.* William Bull Wright.
Brook, The; An Idyl. ("Here, by this brook, we parted; I to the East.")
Tennyson. OxAEP-2, *complete*
Sels.
Brook, The. BoNaP; BoTP; EBEvV; FaBV; FaPON; FHYEP; GN; GoJo
(Brook's Song, The.) FaBoBe
Brook glides on over the river, the. Reverie. H. Cordelia Ray. CBWP-3
Brook in February, The. Sir Charles G. D. Roberts. BoNaP

Brook in the City, A. Robert Frost. OxBA
Brook in Winter, The. James Russell Lowell. *Fr.* Vision of Sir Launfal,
The. GN
Brook speaks with an eloquent tongue, The. Sent to Chief Abbot of Tung-
lin Monastery. Su Shih, *tr. fr. Chinese by* Chiang Yee. SuSp
Brookfield, *sels.* William E. Marshall.
Brooklet, stop rippling! Mine! Wilhelm Müller, *tr. fr. German by* Philip L.
Miller. *Fr.* Beautiful Maid of the Mill, The. RiWo
Brooklyn at Santiago, The. Wallace Rice. PAH
Brooklyn Branding Parlors, The. James Purdy. NGP
Brooklyn Bridge, The. Edna Dean Proctor. PAH
Brooklyn Bridge. Sir Charles G. D. Roberts. PAH
Brooklyn Heights. John Wain. LiTM; OBTV; OxBTC
Brooklyn Theater Fire, The. *Unknown.* AmFP
Brook's Lullaby, The. Wilhelm Müller, *tr. fr. German by* Philip L. Miller.
Fr. Beautiful Maid of the Mill, The. RiWo
Brook's Song, The. Tennyson. *See* I come from haunts of coot and hern.
Broom, Green Broom. *Unknown.* LiTB; OxBoLi; PoRA
Broom of Cowdenknows, The. *Unknown.* ESPB
Broom out the floor now, lay the fender by. June. Francis Ledwidge.
BIrV; NOIV; PeIV
Broom Squire's Song, The. *Unknown.* OxNR
Broomfield Hill, The. *Unknown.* ESPB; OxBB
Broomfield Hill, The. *Unknown.* AmFP, A *and* B *vers.*; CH, A *and* B
vers.; ESPB, A *and* B *vers.*; OxBB
Broomfield Hill, The. *Unknown.* ESPB
Broomfield Wager, The. *Unknown.* OBET
Brooms. Charles Simic. AmPA; NNaP, *early vers.*
Broomstick Train, The, *sels.* Oliver Wendell Holmes.
"Look out! Look out, boys! Clear the track!." FaPON
Broon hens keckle and bouk, The. "Hugh MacDiarmid." *See* Ke-uk, ke-uk,
ke-uk, ki-kwaik.
Brother, The. Peter Everwine. FYAP; NNaP
Brother. Mary Ann Hoberman. SiSoPo
Brother. Jewel C. Latimore. JB
Brother, The. Semion Y. Nadson, *tr. fr. Russian by* H. Badanes. TrJP
Brother, The. Larry Rubin. ArOW
Brother Alberto, one hot summer day. Pietro Aretino, *tr. fr. Italian.* PeHV
Brother and Sister. "Lewis Carroll." ChTr; FaBoNo
Brother and Sister. "George Eliot." NALW
Sels.
"But sudden came the barge's pitch-black prow." NOBVV
I Cannot Choose but Think upon the Time. GN; Son
"Long hears have left their writing on my brow." GN
"Our brown canal was endless to my thought." NOBVV
"Our mother bade us keep the trodden ways." GN
School Parted Us. Son
"Those long days measured by my little feet." NOBVV
"We had the selfsame world enlarged for each." GN
Brother and Sisters. Judith Wright. FaBoWP
Brother Astolfo sated appetite. Pietro Aretino, *tr. fr. Italian.* PeHV
Brother Baptis' on Woman Suffrage. Rosalie Jonas. BlSi
Brother, Come! And What Shall You Say? Joseph S. Cotter, Sr. CDC;
PoBA; PoNe
Brother Fire. Louis MacNeice. MoAB; MoP; NoAM; NOBE
Brother Green. *Unknown.* AmFP
Brother, Hast Thou Wandered Far. James Freeman Clarke. AH
Brother-in-Law, The. Larry Rubin. MT
Brother John. *Unknown.* SWP
Brother Jonathan, Brother Kafka, *sels.* Vincent O'Sullivan.
"Figure who stands on the beach, A." PeNZ
"Last things/ the turning leaves slip in the wind." PeNZ
"To be in a place for spring and not have lived its winter." PeNZ
Brother Jonathan's Lament for Sister Caroline. Oliver Wendell Holmes.
PAH
Brother nightwatchman I have shared your way. Nightwatchman. Deborah
Randall. PWE
Brother Number Three comes strolling along. "Song of the Lunar Palace."
Lu Chih, *tr. fr. Chinese by* Hellmut Wilhelm. SuSp
Brother of the Mount of Olives. Paul Monette. NAmP90
Brother of the Streets. Sam Cornish. TRP
Brother soldiers — With them in battle I reached the waters of the Sava. By
the Waters of the Sava. Uri Zvi Greenberg, *tr. fr. Hebrew by* Ruth
Finer Mintz. MHP
Brother Symmes conversed with her on the ship. Ann Stanford. *Fr.*
Covenant of Grace, The. CRP
Brother, Though from Yonder Sky. James Henry Bancroft. AH
Brother to the firefly. Morning Light. Mary Effie Lee Newsome. CDC;
PoBA; PoNe; ShDr

Brotherhood. "J. J. W." PeHV

Brotherhood is not by the blood certainly, The. Speech to Those Who Say Comrade. Archibald MacLeish. OxBA

Brotherhood of Men. Richard Eberhart. PoWW
Sels.
"Rumors of liberation. We could not believe it."

Brotherless Sisters. *Unknown, tr. fr. Serbo-Croatian by* Charles Simic. HSix

Brotherly sign, come to nourish men's dreams, The. *(LL)* Listen, Comrades. David Diop. NegPo

Brothers. Robert Currie. Poetsp

Brothers, The. Edwin Muir. GTBS-P; HeIP; Mes; NoP; NTP; PrIm

Brothers. Marcia Southwick. NAmP90

Brothers. Giuseppe Ungaretti, *tr. fr. Italian by* Jonathan Griffin. PeFWW

Brothers and men that shall after us be. Ballad of the Gibbet. Villon, *tr. fr. French by* Andrew Lang. AWP

Brothers and Sisters. Michael Foley. PNI

Brothers and sisters have I none. *Unknown.* ISE

Brothers at the Bar. Naomi Long Madgett. NBV

Brothers/ brothers/ everywhere. Utopia. Jewel C. Latimore. BPo

Brothers Grief, The. Paul Mariah. PFL

Brothers in blood! They who this wrong began. To the United States of America. Robert Bridges. PAH

Brothers, my teeth hurt. Strictly for Posterity. Charles Simic. NNaP

Brothers of the sea. *Unknown, tr. by* Waray. EaPr

Brought back from the tedium of dying. Return of a Popular Statesman. Vincent Buckley. CBAP

Brought gifts/ home for me. My Daddy, Whenever He Went Some Place. David Huddle. PBCAP

Brought here in slave ships and pitched overboard. Love Your Enemy. Yusef Iman. BPo; TTY

Brought up as I was to ask of the weather. Point Grey. Daryl Hine. NOBC

Brought up never getting punched. He/She. Stephen Dunn. NAmP90

Broughty Wa's. *Unknown.* ESPB

Brow-brinker. *Unknown.* RoPo

Brow, brow, brenty. *Unknown.* OxNR

Brown Adam. *Unknown.* ESPB; OxBB

Brown Aesthete Speaks, A. Mae V. Cowdery. ShDr

Brown and furry. Christina Rossetti. *Fr.* Sing-Song. FaBoVe (Caterpillar, The.) BoTP; FaPON; GoJo; OxBChV; SiSoPo

Brown arms of the mothering plateau, The. The Lowveld. Charles Eglington. PeSA

Brown Autumn came, and at her solemn close. In the House of the Aylors. Albery Allson Whitman. *Fr.* Not a Man and Yet a Man. AAP

Brown Baby Blues. Una Marson. PBCV

Brown Baby Cobina, with his large black velvet eyes. Baby Cobina. Gladys May Casely Hayford. CDC; ShDr

Brown Bear, The. Mary Austin. FaPON

Brown book stashed, The. To Wait and Hart. Harold Norse. ETG

Brown Boy to Brown Girl. Countee Cullen. PoBA

Brown bread and delicious moon. *(LL)* August. Federico García Lorca. EaPr

Brown, brittle, wait-a-bit weeds. The Indian Cave Jerry Ramsey Found. William Stafford. NoAM

Brown bunny sits inside his burrow. The Rabbit. Edith King. BoTP

Brown Circle. Louise Glück. NAmP90

Brown-coloured Trotter! The Praises of the Canna. *Unknown,* Thomas Arbonsset; *Eng. vers. by* John Croumbie Brown. PeSAV

Brown-dappled fawn, The. The Fawn in the Snow. William Rose Benét. MoAmPo

Brown enormous odor he lived by, The. The Prodigal. Elizabeth Bishop. ChIV-2; CoAP; InvP; LCAP; LiTM; MoAB; NYBP; PPP; TwCP

Brown-faced nurse has murmured something unintelligible, The. Microcosmos. Susan Miles. OxBTC

Brown Family, The. Colleen Thibaudeau. NOBC

Brown Frog, The. Mary K. Robinson. BoTP

Brown Girl, The. *Unknown.* ELP; ESPB; (A *and* B *vers.*); OBET

Brown girl chanting Te Deums on Sunday. Ruth. Pauli Murray. NMM

Brown Girl Dead, A. Countee Cullen. TAP

Brown hawthorn berry, red dogrose. *(LL)* Stranger to Europe. Guy Butler. PeSAV

Brown in the snow, a car with a heater. Strangers. William Stafford. NNaP

Brown Is My Love. *Unknown.* ElL; GBL

Brown lived at such a lofty farm. Brown's Descent; or, The Willy-Nilly Slide. Robert Frost. MoAmPo; PoRA

Brown Lullaby. Adam Small. PeSAV

Brown not black, the color of an earthen. A Dream of Scorpions. Jean Hanff Korelitz. PWE

Brown o' San Juan. "Home, Sweet Home," with Variations ("Brown o' San Juan.") H. C. Bunner. *Fr.* Home. OBAL

Brown of her — her eyes, her hair, her hair, The. *(LL)* The Farmer's Bride. Charlotte Mew. BoLoP; CBLP; EBNV; ErPo; FaBoWP; MoAB; MoBrPo; NALW; OxBM; OxBTC; TrGrPo; WPE

Brown of Ossawatomie. Whittier. PAH

Brown owl sits in the ivy bush, The. The Great Brown Owl. Jane Euphemia Browne. OxBChV

Brown paper worn next to the skin. B. L. Howarth. BXAP

Brown Penny. W. B. Yeats. BoLoP; CBLP; CMoP; ELP; FaBoCh; IIP; LPA; PFP

Brown River, Smile. Jean Toomer. *Fr.* Blue Meridian, The. PoBA; PoNe

Brown Robin. *Unknown.* ESPB; OxBB

Brown Robyn's [*or* Robin's] Confession. *Unknown.* CH; ESPB; GBP

Brown semicolons move doggedly. The Ant Trap. Joe Rosenblatt. NOBC

Brown Skin Girl. Tommy McClennan. FaBoVe

Brown-skinned boy asleep beneath a clump, A. Mind Pictures. Beatrice Hastings. PeSAV

Brown Thrush, The. Lucy Larcom. BoTP; FaPON; OBCA

Brownies' Celebration, The. Palmer Cox. OBCA

Browning. Robert Louis Stevenson. NOBVV

Browning Finds 'The Book' in the Piazza di San Lorenzo, on a Day of Buzzing and Blaze in June 1860. Robert Browning. *Fr.* Ring and the Book, The. CBCK

Browning makes the verses. Browning. Robert Louis Stevenson. NOBVV

Browning, old fellow. In a Copy of Browning. Bliss Carman. AnAmPo

Brownout. Tony Perez. TSaS

Brown's Descent; or, The Willy-Nilly Slide. Robert Frost. MoAmPo; PoRA

Brown's wife, herself a normal type. Family Life. Allan M. Laing. FiBHP

Browny Bee. Irene F. Pawsey. BoTP

Browny Hen, The. Irene F. Pawsey. BoTP

Bruadar and Smith and Glinn. A Curse. *Unknown, tr. fr. Irish by* Douglas Hyde. BIrV

Bruce, The, *sels.* John Barbour.
Before Bannockburn. OxBS
Freedom [*or* Fredome]. FaBoCh; OBEV; OxBS; TrGrPo
"Inglis archeris schot sa fast, The." ScCV
"Storys to rede ar delitabill." OxBS

Bruce and the Spider. Bernard Barton. BeLS

Bruce Ismay's Soliloquy. Derek Mahon. PNI

Bruckner. James Camp. MAT

Brueghel in Naples. Dannie Abse. NIP

Bruised by the masseur's final whack. Health and Fitness. J. B. Morton. FaBoCo

Bruised Reed Shall He Not Break, An. Christina Rossetti. OxAEP-2

Bruised Titans, The. Keats. *Fr.* Hyperion; a Fragment. EnRP; OAEL-2; OBNC

Brummell at Calais. John Glassco. MoCV

Brunanburg. *Unknown, tr. fr. Anglo-Saxon by* Kemp Malone. PoE

Brund. Jean Hanff Korelitz. PWE

Bruno, our father, joyous, gentle, old. Epitaph for Bruno of Angers. Marbod of Rennnes, *tr. fr. Latin by* Helen Waddell. MLL

Brush Fire. Fily-Dabo Sissoko, *tr. fr. French by* Ellen Conroy Kennedy. NegPo

Brush Fire. Tchicaya U Tam'si, *tr. fr. French by* Sangodare Akanji. NegPo

Brush of evening clouds, A. To the Tune "Intoxicated with Shadows of Flowers." Yü Ch'ing-tseng, *tr. fr. Chinese by* Kenneth Rexroth *and* Ling Chung. WPC

Brush Up Your Shakespeare. Cole Porter. OBAL

Brushes and paints are all I have. Quatrains. Gwendolyn B. Bennett. CDC

Brushing back the curls from your famous brow. The Copulating Gods. Carolyn Kizer. CAPP; Poetr; Prf

Brushing my clothes, I followed the sandy dikes. Passing White Banks Pavilion. Hsieh Ling-yün, *tr. fr. Chinese by* Francis Westbrook. SuSp

Brushing out my daughter's dark. 35/10. Sharon Olds. CrSp; MDDM

Brussels and Oxford. William Hurrell Mallock. EBVV

Brussels in Winter. W. H. Auden. OBTV; OxBTC

Brut, The, *sels.* Layamon.
Passing of Arthur, The. PoE

Bruton Town. EnSB

Brutus adsum jam forte. *Unknown.* ISE

Brutus' Last Song. Christiania Whitehead. NWP

Bryan and Pereene. James Grainger. ECEV

Bryan, Bryan, Bryan, Bryan. Vachel Lindsay. CMoP; LiTA; MeMAP; OxBA; OxBoLi

Bryan O'Lynn. *Unknown. See* Bryan O'Lynn was a Dutchman born.

Bryan O'Lynn was a Dutchman born. Brian O'Linn. *Unknown.* CBNP; FaBoBa; FaBoNo; NBLV; RB
(Bryan O'Lynn.) FaBoVe; GBP

Bryan's Last Battle. *Unknown.* AmFP

Bryant. James Russell Lowell. *Fr.* Fable for Critics, A. NOBA; TAP

Brynbeidog. Jeremy Hooker. AngWe; SCBI

Brynbwrla. Kingsley Amis. *Fr.* Evans Country, The. NOBL

Bryng us all to his blisse! *(LL)* Robin Hood and the Monk. *Unknown.* ESPB; FaBoBa; OBNV, *abr.*

B's the Bus. Phyllis McGinley. *Fr.* All around the Town. FaPON

Bubble, The. Lydia Huntley Sigourney. AmWP

Bubble, The. Swift. FaBoEH

Bubble; a Song, The. Robert Herrick. CaPo

Bubbles. Bill Berkson. UL

Bubbles. George Garrett. MT

Bubbles. L. Nicholson. BoTP

Bubbles on the Water. Yang Wan-li, *tr. fr. Chinese by* Jonathan Chaves. SuSp

Bubbles soar and die in the sterile bottle, The. Notes for the Chart in 306. Ogden Nash. NYBP

Bubbling Wine. Abu Zakariya, *tr. fr. Arabic by* A. J. Arberry. TTY

Buchenwald, 1945. Ai. *Fr.* He Kept On Burning. AnAn

Buchlyvie. *Unknown.* GBP

Buck. Michael S. Harper. CAPP

Buck has a headache. Tony ate. The Garden of Earthly Delights. Charles Simic. NoP

Buck in the Snow, The. Edna St. Vincent Millay. NALW; PFP

Buckdancer's Choice. James Dickey. HeIP; NoAM; NOBA; NoP; NYBP; PoNe

Buckee Bene. *Unknown.* CH

Bucket of Sea-Serpents. Howard Ant. GoYe

Buckets of blood in which the moon verbs are washed. Piracy. Iván Argüelles. UL

Bucking Bronco. *Unknown.* AmFP

Buckingham Palace. A. A. Milne. OxBChV; PDV

Buckinghamshire. *Unknown.* GBP

Buckles glitter, billies lean, The. American Twilights, 1957. James Wright. CoAP

Buckley. Paul Monette. PFL

Bucko-Mate. Samuel Schierloh. GoYe

Buck's Elegy, The. *Unknown.* OBET

Bucolic Eclogues., *sels.* Ethel Anderson.
Waking, Child, While You Slept. WPE

Bud fantasies, dreams of an ear of corn. Paean to Eve's Apple. James Liddy. CIP

Bud Powell, Paris, 1959. William Matthews. Jaz

Bud Powell's story is never complete. Un Poco Loco. Clayton Eshleman. Jaz

Bud, The/ stands for all things. Saint Francis and the Sow. Galway Kinnell. CAPP; FYAP; InPK; RB

Budapest is like a stage-set. Déjà vu. Christine McNeill. NWP

Budded with Child. Meridel Le Sueur. ETG

Buddha. Arno Holz, *tr. fr. German by* William Ellery Leonard. AWP

Buddha at Kamakura. Francis Hastings Kipling. OBTV

Buddha entrusts herself to me. *(LL)* I entrust myself to earth. Thich Nhat Hanh. EaPr

Buddha in Glory. Rainer Maria Rilke, *tr. fr. German by* Stephen Mitchell. EnlH

Buddha is not more strange. In a Warm Bath. Carl Rakosi. TAP

Buddhist Priest, A. Ho Xuan Huong, *tr. fr. Vietnamese by* Nguyen Ngoc Bich *and* Burton Raffel. PBWP

Budding floweret blushes at the light [*or* Boddynge flourettes bloshes atte the lyghte], The. Thomas Chatterton. *Fr.* Aella; a Tragycal Enterlude.
(Mynstrelles Songe ("Boddynge flourettes bloshes atte the lyghte").)
EnRP
(Song of the Three Minstrels.) TrGrPo
(There Lackethe Somethynge Style.) OxAEP-1

Budding young playwright named Coward, A. Doris Pulsford. PeLi

Buddy Holly Watching *Rebel Without a Cause*, Lubbock, Texas, 1956. David Wojahn. *Fr.* Mystery Train: A Sequence. PBCAP

Budger of history. Bomb. Gregory Corso. PoBeRe

Budgie Finds His Voice. Wendy Cope. FaBoPa; UV

Budging the sluggard ripples of the Somme. Hospital Barge at Cérisy. Wilfred Owen. OBTV; RB

Budmouth Dears. Thomas Hardy. *Fr.* Dynasts, The. CH

Buds from winter's frost-work lift, The. The Coming of Spring. H. Cordelia Ray. CBWP-3

Buen Matina. Sir John Salusbury. ElL

Buena Vista. Albert Pike. PAH

Buenaventura Roig. La Tumba de Buenaventura Roig. Martín Espada. AfAz

Buffalo. Florence Earle Coates. PAH

Buffalo. Henry Dumas. PoBA

Buffalo. Charles Eglinton. PeSA

Buffalo, The. Marianne Moore. PoA

Buffalo. *Unknown, tr. fr. Yoruea by* Ulli Beier. *Fr.* Hunter Poems of the Yoruba. OBAP; RB

Buffalo Bill's. E. E. Cummings. AmPP; CMoP; HeIP; InPK; LiTA; NAAL-2; NOBA; OBD; OxBSP; PoE; RB; TAP; VGW

Buffalo Blood. Lance Henson. STP

Buffalo Boy. Huang T'ing-chien, *tr. fr. Chinese by* Michael E. Workman. SuSp

Buffalo Boy. *Unknown.* AmFP

Buffalo breathed quietly inside, The. The Crow-Children Walk My Circles in the Snow. Ray A. Young Bear. CDW

Buffalo, buffalo, buffalo, buffalo. Death Chant. Peter Blue Cloud. VoR

Buffalo Country. A. B. Paterson. OBAP

Buffalo Dusk. Carl Sandburg. GOA; OBAP; OBCA; PDV; RFM; SiSoPo

Buffalo — Isle of Wight Power Cable. Anselm Hollo. PoM

Buffalo Skinners, The. *Unknown.* AmFP; AS; GBP; RB; SWP

Buffalo Skinners, The. *Unknown.* AmFP; GBP; RB

Buffalo Skull, A. Ted Kooser. FoLa

Buffaloes are gone, The. Buffalo Dusk. Carl Sandburg. GOA; OBAP; OBCA; PDV; RFM; SiSoPo

Buffel's Kop. Roy Campbell. PeSA

Bufo. Pope. *Fr.* Epistle to Dr. Arbuthnot. FHYEP; InPS; NoP; OAEL-1; OBSV; OxAEP-1; PoE; PoEL-3; TFi

Bug and a flea/ Went out to sea, A. *Unknown.* ISE

Bug, flower, bird on slipware fired and fluted. Syrinx. James Merrill. HCAP

Bugle Song. Tennyson. *See* Splendor falls on castle walls, The.

Bugle Song of Peace. Thomas Curtis Clark. WBLP; WGRP

Bugler boy from barrack (it is over the hill), A. The Bugler's First Communion. Gerard Manley Hopkins. NoAM; PeHV

Bugler's First Communion, The. Gerard Manley Hopkins. NoAM; PeHV

Bugles!, The. *(LL)* The Call of the Bugles. Richard Hovey. AnAmPo

Bugles!/ And the great nation thrills and leaps to arms! The Call of the Bugles. Richard Hovey. AnAmPo

Bugle's for him, The. Burial. Momcilo Nastasijevic, *tr. fr. Serbo-Croatian by* Charles Simic. HSix

Bugs. Mary Ann Hoberman. OBCA
Sels.
Cockroach.
Combinations. OBSP

Bugs. Will Stokes. MoShBr

Bugville team was surely up against a rocky game, The. Casey — Twenty Years Later. S. P. McDonald. BLPA

Buick. Karl Shapiro. CMoP; HoPM; LPA; MoAB; Poetr; TrGrPo

Buik of Alexander, The, *sels.* John Barbour.
Prologue to the Avowis of Alexander. OxBS

Build at Kallundborg by the sea. Kallundborg Church. Whittier. BeLS

Build for yourself a strong-box. Then Laugh. Bertha Adams Backus. BLPA; PoToHe; PWR; WBLP

"Build me a nation," said the Lord. Then and Now. Frances E. W. Harper. PWR

Builder builded a temple, A. Two Temples. Hattie Vose Hall. BLPA

Builder demolishes houses, The. Dialectics. Edvard Kocbek, *tr. by* Michael Scammell *and* Veno Taufer. PoSu

Builder of Continents, The. "Ping Hsin," *tr. fr. Chinese by* Kai-yu Hsu. *Fr.* Stars, The. WPOW

Builders, The. Longfellow. AnAmPo; PFP; PWR

Builders, The, *sels.* Henry van Dyke.
"Grant us the knowledge that we need." TrPWD

Builder's Lesson, A. John Boyle O'Reilly. PoLF; PoToHe, (*St. 1 only*); PWR

Building, The. As You Come In. Anne Marriott. NOBC

Building. I. E. Dickenga. PWR

Building. Gary Snyder. BAP-89

Building a poem is like building a house. To Build a Poem. Christine E. Hemp. GOYP

Building an Outhouse. Ronald Wallace. PBCAP

Building for Eternity. N. B. Sargent. BLPA

Building in Stone. Sylvia Townsend Warner. MoBrPo

Burying Ground by the Ties. Archibald MacLeish. *Fr.* Frescoes for Mr. Rockefeller's City. GOA; MoAmPo; UnPo

Bus, The. Leonard Cohen. HeIP

Bus, The. "Peter." BoTP

Bus Driver. Linda France. NWP

Bus driver. We Thank You! L. E. Cox. BoTP

Bus goes through the mist, The. Going Home. Peter Riley. *Fr.* One Day. VaA

Bus halts its long brawl, The. At Kfar Kana. Charles Causley. TOF

Bus Ride. Kate Daniels. PBCAP

Bus Ride. Lenore Kandel. NMM

Bus Ride. Selma Robinson. *Fr.* Ferry Ride. FaPON

Bus Stop. Donald Justice. CAPP; FYAP; LCAP

Bus-Stop on the Somme, The. David Rowbotham. NOBAu

Bus talk. Simon Armitage. PWE

Bus Trip, The. Joel Oppenheimer. NeAP

Bush, The, *sels.* Bernard O'Dowd.
"To other eyes and ears you are a great." CBAP

Bush, a gathering smoke, The. Blackthorn. Euros Bowen, *tr. fr. Welsh by the author.* OBWVE

Bush Justice. Charles Harpur. CBAP

Bush land scrub land. The Country North of Belleville. Alfred W. Purdy. NOBC

Bush Navigator: The Last Morning of Hands. Peggy Shumaker. PBCAP

Bush Section, A, *sels.* B. E. Baughan.
"Logs, at the door, by the fence; broadcast over the paddock." PeNZ

Bush Speaks, The. Ernest G. Moll. NOBAu

Bush was on that dump, A. The Burnt Bush. Jack R. Clemo. FaBoTw

Bush, The. Yes. It burned like they say it did. Deuteronomy. Robert Bringhurst. NOBC

Bushed. Earle Birney. MoCV; NoAM; NOBC; NoP

Bushed. Charles Lillard. NOBC

Bushed. Barry McKinnon. NOBC

Bushel of wheat, bushel of barley. Hide and Seek. *Unknown.* RoPo

Bushes and Briars. *Unknown.* OBET

Bushranger, A. Kenneth Slessor. CBAP; NOBAu

Bushwoman lies, The. In a South African Museum. Evangeline Paterson. NBrP

Business, The. Robert Creeley. CAPP

Business Girls. Sir John Betjeman. UV

Business Is Business. Berton Braley. WBLP

Business Life, The. David Ignatow. NNaP

Business-like harlot named Draper, A. *Unknown.* PeLi

Business Man's Prayer, A. William Ludlum. BLRP

Business men with awkward hips. The City. Sir John Betjeman. TEP

Business Reverses. Edgar Lee Masters. ChIV-2

Businessman of Alicante, The. Philip Levine. NaP

Busk, Pierce. Maggie O'Sullivan. NBrP

Bussy d'Ambois., *sels.* George Chapman.
"Ile sooth his plots: and strow my hate with smiles." PoEL-2
"Now all the peacefull regents of the night." PoEL-2
"Now shall we see, that nature hath no end." PoEL-2

Bustan, The. Sadi, *tr. fr. Persian by* Sir Edwin Arnold. AWP
Sels.
Dancer, The
Great Physician, The

Bustle in a house, The. Emily Dickinson. FaBV; HAP; HeIL; HeIP; NAAL-1; NoP; OBD; OxBA; PoEL-5; PoLF; SAmP; WGRP

Busts and Bosoms Have I Known. *Unknown.* ErPo

Busy, curious, thirsty fly! On a Fly Drinking out of [*or* from] His Cup. William Oldys. ImPo; OBEV; OxAEP-1; TrGrPo
(Fly, The.) SCGP

Busy Heart, The. Rupert Brooke. MoBrPo

Busy in study be thou, child. Demeanour. *Unknown.* OxBChV

Busy is the life of the weaving woman! Song of the Weaving Woman. Yüan Chen, *tr. fr. Chinese by* Wu-chi Liu. SuSp

Busy Old Fool. Ian Kelso. BXAP

Busy [*or* Busie] old fool [*or* foole], unruly sun [*or* sunne]. The Sun [*or* Sunne] Rising. John Donne. BoLoP; CBLP; ClHu; EBEvV; EnRePo; ESCV; FF; FHYEP; GBL; HAP; HeIL; HeIP; InPS; InvP; JCP; LiTB; MeLP; NAEL-1; NIP; NOBE; NoP; NOSC; OAEL-1; PFP; PoE; PoEL-2; Poetr; PPP; SCV; SeCP; SeCV-1; TEP; TFi; TrGrPo; WeW

Busy old lady, charitable tray. Reason for Refusal. Martin Bell. PAW; PWE

Busy with love, the bumble bee. Meleager, *tr. fr. Greek by* Peter Whigham. BoLoP; GrAn

Busy with Many Jobs. Tadeusz Rózewicz, *tr. fr. Polish by* Adam Czerniawski. PoSu

Busy with very urgent jobs. Busy with Many Jobs. Tadeusz Rózewicz, *tr. fr. Polish by* Adam Czerniawski. PoSu

Busy yellow bee, after his mighty quest, A. *Unknown.* NOIV

But. Vladimir Holan, *tr. fr. Czech by* Ian Milner *and* Jarmila Milner. PoSu

But a charmer has to know. (*LL*) Ballad of Old Women & of How They Are Constrained To Simulate Youth In Order To Avoid Shocking the Young. Norman Talbot. NOBAu

But a kiss frae aff his rosy lips gies strength anew to me. (*LL*) Wee Willie Winkie rins [*or* runs] through the town. William Miller. NOBVV; OxNR; ReMoGo

But a large quantity of brandy. A Small Faculty Stag for the Visiting Poet. Earle Birney. OxBC; PeLV

But a little while ago. Winter and Spring. *Unknown.* BoTP

But a llama is numero uno. (*LL*) Argentine gaucho named Bruno, An. *Unknown.* NOBL

But a piece of it all. (*LL*) Who Am I? Felice Holman. RFM

But ae braithless note. Sydney Goodsir Smith, *after the French of* Tristan Corbiére. *Fr.* Gangrel Rymour and the Pairdon of Sanct Anne, The. OBVE

But affluent the doom. (*LL*) Birthday of but a single pang. Emily Dickinson. NAs

But after her I'll whoop and hollo. (*LL*) Birds' Lament. John Clare. PoEL-4

But after one such love, can love no more. (*LL*) The Broken Heart. John Donne. EBEV

But after the *second* you die. (*LL*) The Viper. Hilaire Belloc. FaBoNo; NoAM

But ah! he left the thorn wi' me. (*LL*) The Banks of Doon. Burns. BoLoP; GTBS; GTBS-P; NOBE; NOEC; OBEV; PrIm; TrGrPo; WBLP

But ah! more wondrous still the charming fair. (*LL*) A Compliment to the Ladies. Blake. BXAP

But, ah! ye maids, beware the gipsy's lures! A Warning against the Gypsies. John Langhorne. *Fr.* Country Justice, The. ECEV

But, alas, who less could do, that found so good occasion? (*LL*) Think'st thou to seduce me then with words that have no meaning? Thomas Campion. EiL; NAEL-1; OxAEP-1; OxBSP

But all in vain are Pray'rs, extatick Thoughts. Ardelia's Spiritual Progress. The Countess of Winchilsea. *Fr.* Fragment, A. CBCK

But always one your own both firm and stable. (*LL*) Each man me telleth I change most my devise. Sir Thomas Wyatt. SiPS

But always, without fail, THE NECK. (*LL*) The Travel[l]er's Curse after Misdirection. Robert Graves. CMoP; FiBHP; HoPM; LiTM; MeMBP; MoAB; MoBrPo; NBLV

But anxious cares the pensive nymph oppressed. Pope. *Fr.* Rape of the Lock, The. EBNV, *abr.*; FHYEP; HAP; ImPo; NoP; OAEL-1; OBNV; OxAEP-1; PeLV; PoEL-3; TEP; TrGrPo

But are not of? (*LL*) Midnight on the Great Western. Thomas Hardy. CH; NOBE; OxAEP-2

But are these landscapes to be imagined. Ronald Johnson. *Fr.* Letters to Walt Whitman. VGW

But as I said, wiped out. (*LL*) Diringer's *The Alphabet: A Key to the History of Mankind.* Stephanie Strickland. LoHo

But as long liv'd as present love. (*LL*) Of English Verse. Edmund Waller. BeJo; NAEL-1; NOSC; OAEL-1; PoE; SeCP

But as pretty a thing as may be. (*LL*) A Proper Song, Entitled: Fain Would I Have a Pretty Thing to Give unto My Lady. *Unknown.* CoMu; EiL; InvP; NoSic

But, as reward, death for to be my meed? (*LL*) Resound my voyse [*or* voice], ye wodes [*or* woods] that here [*or* hear] me plain. Sir Thomas Wyatt. AAS; SiPS; SiPSBD

But as the Devil not half so true. (*LL*) The Apostasy of One and But One Lady. Richard Lovelace. CaPo

But as they left the dark'ning heath. Battle, The ("But as they left the dark'ning heath.") Sir Walter Scott. *Fr.* Marmion. ELP

But as yet there's nae chickens appear'd at Cockpen. (*LL*) The Laird o' Cockpen. Lady Nairne, 2 *added sts. by* Susan Ferrier. BeLS; WPE

But ask now the beasts. Bible, *O.T.* *Fr.* Job. EaPr; NAWM-1, *abr.*

But at a distance, in another tree. (*LL*) No Possum, No Sop, No Taters. Wallace Stevens. HCAP; MeMAP; OxBA; TAP; VGW

But at the common table. (*LL*) Te Deum. Charles Reznikoff. ChIV-1; TrJP

But at the immolation of a race who cries? (*LL*) Death of a Whale. John Blight. CBAP; OBD

But, baby, where are you?" (*LL*) Ballad of Birmingham. Dudley Randall. BPo; HeIL; HeIP; InPK; MoP; NIP; NoAM; Poetr; SoSe

But Bacchus was not so content: he quyght forsooke their land. King Midas. Ovid, *tr. by* Arthur Golding. *Fr.* Metamorphoses. CTC

But bargains: those he will not strike. (*LL*) Age. Walter Savage Landor. FaBoEE; NOBVV; PoEL-4

But be contented: when that fell arrest. Shakespeare. *Fr.* Sonnets. NAEL-1; OxAEP-1; Son

But black is the colour of my true love's hair. Black Is The Colour. *Unknown.* GBP

But blest to fold but thee. *(LL)* Herman Melville. Conrad Aiken. AnAmPo; NoAM; NOBA; TAP

But brims the poisoned well. *(LL)* Fragments of a Lost Gnostic Poem of the Twelfth Century. Herman Melville. NOBA; NoP; OxBSP; PoEL-5

But bring us in good ale! *(LL)* Bring Us In Good Ale. *Unknown.* CH; EBEV; FaBoCo; MeEL; MiEL; OAEL-1

But brought the spring. *(LL)* Force. Edward Rowland Sill. AnAmPo

But can see better there, and laughing there. Pygmies Are Pygmies Still, Though Percht on Alps. Gwendolyn Brooks. *Fr.* Notes from the Childhood and the Girlhood. LCAP; PoNe

But cannot see our sack behind. *(LL)* Suffenus, whom so well you know [or whom you know]. Catullus. AWP, *tr.* by Walter Savage Landor; OBVE, *tr.* by Matthew Prior

But capricious about you. *(LL)* Choice. Flavien Ranaivo. NegPo

But cast it. Summertime, goodnight! *(LL)* Persephone Pauses. Carolyn Kizer. SRLS

But, clasp'd to his bosom, the infant was dead. *(LL)* The Erl-King. Goethe. AWP; OBVE

But colourless. Colourless. *(LL)* Poppies in July. Sylvia Plath. FaBoWP; LCAP; NaP; RB

But could not touch it. *(LL)* High on the upper, outermost bough. Sappho. InMo

But Custard keeps crying for a nice safe cage. *(LL)* The Tale of Custard the Dragon. Ogden Nash. FaPON; OBCA; OTCP; PoRA; PYC

But death./ I am I. *(LL)* The Tattooed Man. Robert Hayden. CAPP; NoAM

But deplorable absence of ecticut. *(LL)* Benjamin. Ogden Nash. PeLi

But did not paradise itself contain. Age of Innocence. Graham Hough. PoRA

But die a sad and scornful death down in this foreign land. *(LL)* The Flying Cloud. *Unknown.* AmFP; OBET; OxBSS

But do not let us quarrel any more. Andrea del Sarto. Robert Browning. CTC; EnVR; MeMBP; NAEL-2; NOBVV; NoP; OAEL-2; PoE; PoEL-5

But do the threat'ning clouds precipitate. A Method of Preserving Hay from Being Mow-Burnt, or Taking Fire. Robert Dodsley. *Fr.* Agriculture. FaBoUs

But does every man feel like this at forty. The Second Life. Edwin Morgan. OxBS

But doesn't heaven. England, Autumn. Wayne Brown. PBCV

But Don John of Austria rides home from the Crusade. *(LL)* Lepanto. G. K. Chesterton. CoGr; EBEvV, *(ll.* 1–35); EBNV; FaBV; FaPoR; MoBrPo; OBMV; OBNV; OtMeF; RB

But don't call Mother Damnable names. Around the Corner. Laura Riding. *Fr.* Forgotten Girlhood. RB

But don't forget . . . the drover's boy. *(LL)* The Drover's Boy. Ted Egan. NOBAu

But, down on down, the uninhabitable sorrow. *(LL)* The Kingfisher. Amy Clampitt. HCAP; SM

But dropped like Adamant. *(LL)* 'Twas warm—at first—like us. Emily Dickinson. CMoP; LiTA; NAWM-2; SoSe

But Dwell in Darkness. George Chapman. *Fr.* Coronet for His Mistress Philosophy, A. Son

But easy writing's vile hard reading. *(LL)* Clio's Protest. Sheridan. FaBoEE

But equally a want of books and men! *(LL)* Great Men Have Been among Us. Wordsworth. EnRP; FaBoPV; MeMBP; PoEL-4; Son

But ere sterne conflict mixt both strengths, faire Paris stept before. Homer, *tr.* by George Chapman. *Fr.* Iliad, The. OBVE

But failte and hospitality, inducing fresh acquaintance. *(LL)* Galway Races. *Unknown.* OxBoLi

But, fair Iëmpsar (wife of Potiphar). Joshua Sylvester. *Fr.* Maidens Blush, The. ChIV-1

But fate and gloomy night encompass thee around. *(LL)* To The Memory of Mr. Oldham. Dryden. AWP; EBEV; EPCY; HAP; InPK; InPS; NIP; NOBE; NoP; NOSC; OAEL-1; OxAEP-1; PoE; PoEL-3; Poetr; PPP; Prf; SCGP; SeCV-2; TFi; TRP

But fear, thirst, hunger, and this huddled chill. *(LL)* Montana Pastoral. J. V. Cunningham. MAT; MoAmPo; PrIm; VGW

But Fear Thou Not, O Jacob. Bible, *O.T. Fr.* Jeremiah. TrJP

But finding nothing, sullenly withdrew. *(LL)* Range-finding. Robert Frost. MoP; NIP; NoAM; NoP; OBWP; Poetr; RB

But first one must free oneself. Patrizia Cavalli, *tr. fr. Italian* by Robert McCracken *and* Patrizia Cavalli. NeIt

But for a brief/ Moment, a poised minute. A Grasshopper. Richard Wilbur. HAP; HoPM

But for an hour's sleep in a filthy bed. Recall. Reed Whittemore. NYBP

But for His bride. *(LL)* World, The (1). Henry Vaughan. AWP; ChIV-2; EBEV; ESCV; FaBV; HAP; ImPo; JCP; LiTB; NAEL-1; NOBE; NOCV;

NOSC; OAEL-1; OxAEP-1; PeECV; PoEL-2; PPP; SCGP; SeCP; SeCV-1; TEP; TFi; TrCP; TrGrPo; WGRP

But for Lust. Ruth Pitter. FaBoTw; OxBTC

But for the broken firing pin. Spider Reeves. Henry Carlile. Poetsp

But for the eight, interior rays. Comb Jelly. John Hay. FoLa

But for the steady wash of rain. No Country You Remember. Robert Mezey. FF

But for the wits of either Charles's days. Pope. *Fr.* First Epistle of the Second Book of Horace, Imitation of. EPCY

But for their powers, accept my piety. *(LL)* To William Camden. Ben Jonson. AWP; BeJo; JCP; NAEL-1; NOSC; SeCV-1

But for them the bombers answer everything. *(LL)* Second Air Force. Randall Jarrell. CMoP; LiTM; NAAL-2

But for to make it spring againe. *(LL)* The Hock-Cart, or Harvest Home. Robert Herrick. BeJo; CaPo; EBEV; FaBoPV; JCP; NAEL-1; NOSC; OxAEP-1; SeCP; SeCV-1

But for your terror. To Death. Oliver St. John Gogarty. FaBoEE; OBD; OBMV; OtMeF

But Fortune governed all their works till when. Aeschylus, *tr. fr. Greek* by Elizabeth Barrett Browning. *Fr.* Prometheus Bound. SiPSBD, *tr. by* Sir Walter Ralegh

But frankley, gayly shall we get the gods. *(LL)* Meditation at Kew. Anna Wickham. FaBoTw; MoBrPo; NALW

But gi'e her my breast-knot, white an' blue? *(LL)* White an' Blue. William Barnes. GBL; GTBS-P

But give in return the sweetness of your young heart. *(LL)* With a Violet. John Olaf Paulsen. RiWo

But give me for my soul, those beauteous maids. Those Beauteous Maids. Moses ibn Ezra, *tr. fr. Hebrew* by Solomon Solis-Cohen. TrJP

But give them me, the mouth, the eyes, the brow! Orpheus and Eurydice. Robert Browning. CTC
(Eurydice to Orpheus.) CBLP

But grant I may relapse, for want of grace. Pope. *Fr.* Second Epistle of the Second Book of Horace Imitated, The. TOF

But gratious [or gracious] God, how well dost thou provide. Dryden. *Fr.* Hind and the Panther, The. TrPWD

But, Greatest Anna! while Thy Arms pursue. Matthew Prior. *Fr.* Ode Humbly Inscrib'd to the Queen, A. FaBoEH

But hark! a sound is stealing on my ear. Charles Stuart Calverley. *Fr.* Beer. BXAP; FaBoCo; FiBHP

But hark! the cry is Astur. Horatius. Macaulay. *Fr.* Lays of Ancient Rome. OBWP

But hark! The sharp beat of the Afric drum. William Hosack. *Fr.* Isle of Streams; or, the Jamaica Hermit, The. PBCV

But has neither Money nor Cloaths. *(LL)* The Crafty Miss of London; or, The Fryar Well Fitted. *Unknown.* CoMu; OxBB

But haven't we always known? "Scientists find universe awash in tiny diamonds." Pat Mayne Ellis. CrSp

But he did for them both by his plan of attack. *(LL)* The General. Siegfried Sassoon. CMoP; CoGr; FaBoEH; FaBV; FiBHP; LiTM; NAEL-2; NoAM; OBWP; OtMeF; OxBoLi; OxBSP; OxBTC; PlP; PoE

But he didn't catch me. *(LL)* The Little Turtle. Vachel Lindsay. FaPON; GoJo; NTCP; OBAL; OBCA; OBSP; PDV; SiSoPo

But he dropped the phone on the lawn and went inside. *(LL)* Into a Cordless Phone. Robert McDowell. UTF

But he just smiled to me from beyond his life. *(LL)* Requiescat. Haim Guri. MHP

But he never would tell us of whom. *(LL)* There was an old man of Khartoum. *At. to* William Ralph Inge. NOBL; PeLi

But he rose up and knew himself a Greek. *(LL)* Keats. Lizette Woodworth Reese. AmWP

But he takes it wherever he goes. *(LL)* Elephant carries a great big trunk, The. *Unknown.* RoPo

But He Was Cool; or, He Even Stopped for Green Lights. Don L. Lee. BPo; MoP; PoBA

But hear. If you stay, and the child be born. In the Restaurant. Thomas Hardy. *Fr.* Satires of Circumstance. MoAB; MoBrPo

But her own canary. *(LL)* Little Clotilda. *Unknown.* BoTP

But here's the piece, made up to sell. The Landscape. George Daniel. NOSC

But his actual candle blazed with artifice. *(LL)* A Quiet Normal Life. Wallace Stevens. NAAL-2; NoAM

But his shoes were far too tight. *(LL)* Incidents in the Life of My Uncle Arly. Edward Lear. CBNP; FaBoNo; MoShBr; OAEL-2; OxBoLi; TrGrPo

But his Trull, but his Trull, but his Trull holds up the Kettle. *(LL)* A Ballad of All the Trades. *Unknown.* CoMu; ErPo

"But hold y . . . hold y . . ." says Robin. The Jolly Pinder of Wakefield. *Unknown.* ESPB, (B *vers.*)

But holy Death is kinder? *(LL)* Early Death. Hartley Coleridge. OBEV

But How It Came from Earth. Conrad Aiken. MoAB; MoAmPo

But how many merry monthes be in the yeere? Robin Hood and the Curtal Friar. *Unknown.* ESPB

But — "How many were sorry when he passed away?" (*LL*) The Measure of a Man. *Unknown.* BLPL; PoLF

But how much more unfortunate are those. Hilaire Belloc. UV

But how shall we this union well expresse? In What Manner the Soule Is United to the Body. Sir John Davies. *Fr. Nosce Teipsum.* LiTB; NoSic, abr.; PoEL-2; SiPS
  (Soul and the Body, The.) CTC; NOBE

But how thoroughly departmental. (*LL*) Departmental. Robert Frost. GoYe; HeIP; HoPM; MoAB; MoAmPo; NAAL-2; NOBA; NOBL; OBAL; PeLV; SoSe

But I Am Growing Old and Indolent. Robinson Jeffers. NOBA; TAP

"But I am here." "You are not," your mother said. (*LL*) A Queer Thing. Nancy Keesing. NOBAu

But I answer, "No." (*LL*) To the Tune "A Dream Song." Wu Tsao. WPC

But I dine at Clio's every night, poor lamb. (*LL*) Clio's. Mick Imlah. CBLP

But I Do Not Need Kindness. Gregory Corso. NeAP

But I don't care where the water goes if it doesn't get into the wine. (*LL*) Wine and Water. G. K. Chesterton. ChIV-1; FaBoCo; FiBHP; MoBrPo

But I fear that is almost too few. (*LL*) There Was an Old Man Who Said, "Do." *Unknown.* FaPON

But I hae dream'd a dreary dream. Fey. *Unknown. Fr.* Battle of Otterbourne, The. OtMeF, (C *vers.*)

But I haven't come to that — and I hope I never shall — and that's the Village Poor House! (*LL*) Our Village — by a Villager. Thomas Hood. FaBoVe; OBSV

But I hear the beating of dead boughs. (*LL*) Blight. Arna Bontemps. CDC

But I, I shot straight to his heart. (*LL*) The Soldier. Adelbert von Chamisso. RiWo

But I just wondered who you were and what on earth you said. (*LL*) They Told Me, Heraclitus. Guy Hanlon. UV

But I made the words. (*LL*) The Day before April. Mary Carolyn Davies. BoTP; FaPON

But I Mean Any Kind of Thief. Judy Grahn. BCF

But I offer it to you, anyway. (*LL*) The Crux. Alma Villanueva. SRLS

But I remember when the fight was hot. Staff Officer. Shakespeare. *Fr.* King Henry IV, Pt. I. NAEL-1; OtMeF

But I shall be gone. (*LL*) The Sound of Trees. Robert Frost. NoAM

But I sing of the quality of bamboo. (*LL*) Bamboo. Eric Rolls. NOBAu

But I still seemed to bid him kiss my a ———. (*LL*) Five winter days at Mannheim shall I be. James Boswell. OBTV

But I think I was somewhat to blame. (*LL*) Papa Love Baby. Stevie Smith. NALW

But I think mice/ Are nice. (*LL*) Mice. Rose Fyleman. BoTP; FaPON; NTCP; PDV; SiSoPo

But I think the king of that country comes out from his tireless host. The Gospel of Labor. Henry van Dyke. WGRP

But I, Too, Want to Be a Poet. Fanny Howe. VBLP

But I waked — and all was done. (*LL*) A Report Song [in a Dream]. Nicholas Breton. GBL; NoSic

But I was dead, an hour or more. Escape. Robert Graves. MoBrPo

But I was young and foolish, and now am full of tears. (*LL*) Down by the Salley Gardens. W. B. Yeats. CBLP; CMoP; CTC; EBEvV; EBVV; EnLoPo; MeMBP; NAEL-2; NoAM; OBEV; PoEL-5; PrIm; SoSe

But I was your officer. (*LL*) In Memoriam[, Private D. Sutherland]. E.A. Mackintosh. PoWW

But I will not say so. (*LL*) These women all. — — Heath. NoSic

But I'd drop dead again. (*LL*) If I Should Die Tonight. Ben King. BLPL; FiBHP; PoLF

But, "if a man die, shall he live again?" Albery Allson Whitman. *Fr.* Octoroon, The. AAP

But if a man should eat green figs at noon. Beware of Figs. Nicophon, *tr. fr.* Greek by Charles Duke Yonge. FaBoUs

But if ! look the ice is gone from the lake. Spring of the Thief. John Logan. CAPP; NNaP

But if I tell you how my heart swings wide. Sunflower Sonnet Number One. June Jordan. SM; Son

But if I were to have a lover, it would be someone. The Faithful Wife. Barbara L. Greenberg. SM

But if I'm right in my surmise he's gone the other way. (*LL*) Sam Bass. *Unknown.* AmFP; AS; BeLS

But if in endless Drinking you delight. A Poem Dedicated to Mrs. Blennerhasset, the Only Female Member of the Limerick Hell Fire Club. Daniel Hayes. IIP

But, if it's got so they like the flavor . . . well. (*LL*) Nightmare Number Three. Stephen Vincent Benét. MoAmPo

But if there be a power too just and strong. Dryden. *Fr.* Religio Laici. NOCV; SeCV-2

But if you break the bloody glass you won't hold up the weather. (*LL*) Bagpipe Music. Louis MacNeice. CMoP; EBEvV; GTBS-P; ImPo; LiTB; LiTM; MoP; NAEL-2; NBLV; NoAM; NOBE; NOBL; NoP; OAEL-2; OBSV; OxBTC; PeLV; PlP; RB; TFi; UV, (abr.)

But I'm the one from whom they stole a button from his trouser leg. Milorad Pavic. *Fr.* Holy Mass For Relja Krilatica. HSix

But I'm the one to whom others spit in the hand when he works. Milorad Pavic. *Fr.* Holy Mass For Relja Krilatica. HSix

But I'm the one who carries a garlic clove in the ear. Milorad Pavic. *Fr.* Holy Mass For Relja Krilatica. HSix

But in her heart a cold December. (*LL*) All Seasons in One. *Unknown.* GBL; HeIP; TrGrPo

But in it mirrored the sky. (*LL*) The Portuguese Sea. Fernando Pessoa. PeSAV

But in love I woke alone. (*LL*) Loop. Kate Ruse-Glason. VBLP

But in the crowding darkness not a word did they say. The Old-Marrieds. Gwendolyn Brooks. PoBA

But in the dome of mighty Mars the red. Chaucer. *Fr.* Canterbury Tales, The. EnVB; OBWP

But in the end one tires of the high-flown. About the Phoenix. James Merrill. NoAM

But in the interval here the boiling, pent-up water. Arthur Hugh Clough. *Fr.* Bothie of Tober-na-Vuolich, The [A Long-Vacation Pastoral]. EnVR; OBF

But in the last days it shall come to pass. Bible, *O.T. Fr.* Micah. PAW

But in the shade I will believe what in the sun I loved. (*LL*) On the Sun Coming Out in the Afternoon. Thoreau. OxBSP; PoEL-4

But in their graves. (*LL*) Daily Trials. Oliver Wendell Holmes. PoEL-5

But in Wormie's Wood she shall aye wone.' (*LL*) Kemp Owyne. Alice Cary. EnSB; ESPB; OHIP

But, inches from it, felt, and turned aside. (*LL*) At a Low Mass for Two Hot-Rodders. X. J. Kennedy. NGP; Poetsp

But is sewn on with needle and thread. (*LL*) The Bison. Hilaire Belloc. FaBoNo; NoAM

But it could knock you over with one blow. (*LL*) These Days. Mang Ke. SpMi

But it glitters with fishes of gold. (*LL*) My banks they are furnished with bees. William Shenstone. BoNaP

But it keeps them on the knife. (*LL*) I eat my peas with honey. *Unknown.* NTCP; RoPo

But it leads at last to a golden Town where golden Houses are. (*LL*) Roofs. Joyce Kilmer. BLPL; PoLF

But It May Be So. Ralph Hawkins. VaA

But it never comes again! (*LL*) There Are Gains for All Our Losses. Richard Henry Stoddard. AnAmPo

But it was right that she. His Wife. Shirley Kaufman. LCAP

But it won't be that way. Hilda Doolittle ("H. D."). *Fr.* Sigil. AnAn

But Jesus, Mary's Son. (*LL*) Hospitality in Ancient Ireland. *Unknown.* TIRV

But, John, have you seen the world, said he. Angle of Vision. Robert Rendall. OxBTC

But keep that earlier, wilder image bright. (*LL*) To Cole, the Painter, Departing for Europe. Bryant. AiP; AmPP; EAP; TAP

But know not what's resisted. (*LL*) Address to the Unco Guid, or the Rigidly Righteous. Burns. ChIV-1; EnRP; NOBE; NOCV; NoP; OxBS; TrGrPo

But, knowing now that they would have her speak. The Defense of Guenevere. William Morris. NAEL-2; TEP

But later, whitehaired genteel. (*LL*) Dandelions. Gerda Mayer. Spl

But leaf dot Yawcob Strauss. (*LL*) Yawcob Strauss. Charles Follen Adams. VPP

But leave, because I cannot as I should! (*LL*) To John Donne. Ben Jonson. BeJo; EPCY; NAEL-1; SeCV-1

But Leonard tarries long! (*LL*) Datur Hora Quieti. Sir Walter Scott. GTBS; GTBS-P

But let applause be dealt in all we may. George Crabbe. *Fr.* Borough, The. OBNC; OBSV

But let me now my lovely charge remind. Soame Jenyns. *Fr.* Art of Dancing, The. ECEV; FaBoUs

But Little John Nobody, that dare not once speak. (*LL*) Little John Nobody. *Unknown.* CBNP; OxBoLi

But lo! at length the day is lingered out. Francis Thompson. *Fr.* Sister Songs. OBMV

But, lo! from forth a copse that neighbours by. Shakespeare. *Fr.* Venus and Adonis. BeLS; FM
  (Courser and the Jennet, The.) NOBE

But lo, Polites, one of Priam's sons. Virgil, *tr. fr. Latin* by Robert Fitzgerald. *Fr.* Aeneid [*or* Eneados], The. NAWM-1; SiPSBD, *tr. by* Henry Howard, Earl of Surrey

But lo! The reaking surface of the vale. John Singleton. *Fr.* General Description of the West Indian Islands, A. PBCV

But look a trial down from some far height. Full Vision. H. Cordelia Ray. AmWP; CBWP-3

But look in your mirror for the other one, Antonio Machado Ruiz, *tr. by* Robert Bly. *Fr.* Moral Proverbs and Folk Songs. RaBo

But look/ look at him out there. What Her Friend Said. Kapilar, *tr. fr. Tamil* by A. K. Ramanujan. PLW

But look! o'er the fall see the angler stand. The Angler. Thomas Buchanan Read. AnAmPo

But love curdles to milk in this climate. Harbour. Edward Kamau Brathwaite. PBCV

But love whilst that thou mayst be loved again. Samuel Daniel. *Fr.* To Delia. ElL; ESo; NoP; NoSic

But mark what he did. Charles Morris. FaBoEH

But mark you well the words I say. Horatio Nelson Huggins. *Fr.* Hiroona. PBCV

But means to speak the rest by signs. (*LL*) To Mrs K. T. (Who Asked Him Why He Was Dumb). John Cleveland. CBLP

But meanwhile in the centre. The Fight in the Centre. Macaulay. *Fr.* Battle of the Lake Regillus, The. OtMeF

But Men Loved Darkness Rather Than Light. Richard Crashaw. ChIV-2

But Milton next, with high and haughty stalks. Joseph Addison. *Fr.* Account of the Greatest English Poets, An. EPCY

But minds me o' my Jean. (*LL*) Of A' the Airts [the Wind Can Blaw]. Burns. AWP; EnRP; NoP; OxBS

But Money gives me pleasure all the time. (*LL*) Fatigue. Hilaire Belloc. FaBoCo; NBLV; NOBL; OxBTC; UV

But most beautiful of all is the Un-found Island. The Most Beautiful. Guido Gozzano, *tr. fr. Italian* by Victoria Pesce. TTTS

But most by numbers judge a poet's song. Pope. *Fr.* Essay on Criticism. ECEV; EPCY; FaBoUs; FHYEP; HAP; NIP; PoEL-3; Poetr

But, most of all, my heart, beware thyself. (*LL*) Be Sad, My Heart. Francis Quarles. NIP

But most wretched I am, now Love awakes my desire. (*LL*) Fortune, Nature, Love. Sir Philip Sidney. PoE

But Mudville hearts are happy now – for Casey hit the ball! (*LL*) Casey's Revenge. James Wilson. BLPA

But my father brings fresh glazed donuts in a white bag. (*LL*) Love from My Father. Carole Gregory Clemmons. PoBA

But my good little man, you have made a mistake. To a Boy-Poet of the Decadence. Sir Owen Seaman. FiBHP; PeLV

But my guests will long remember them. (*LL*) Autumn Twilight in the Mountains. Wang Wei. OHMPC

But my heart is set on the life of a hermit. (*LL*) Twilight Comes. Wang Wei. OHMPC

But nane but thee for me. (*LL*) The False Lover Won Back. *Unknown*. ESPB; OxBB

But nearer than Guardian Angel. Hilda Doolittle ("H. D."). *Fr.* Tribute to the Angels. NALW

But nevermore the May! (*LL*) Youth. Georgia Douglas Johnson. PoNe

But Night determines here, Away. (*LL*) The Apparition of His Mistress[e] Calling Him to Elizium [*or* Elysium]. Robert Herrick. CaPo; SeCP; SeCV-1

But the, the reserved, the reticent, gives more than it takes. (*LL*) As One Put Drunk into the Packet-Boat. John Ashbery. HAP; HCAP; VCAP

But no good girl's lip out of Paris. (*LL*) Ballad of the Women of Paris. Villon. AWP

But no, the familiar symbol, as that the. Conrad Aiken. *Fr.* Time in the Rock [*or*, Preludes to Definition]. VGW

But not a knight asleep! (*LL*) The Virginians of the Valley. Francis Orrery Ticknor. PAH

But not from her protecting care. (*LL*) Beloved, may your sleep be sound. W. B. Yeats. BoLoP; FaBoTw; OBMV

But not in our alley! (*LL*) Sally in Our Alley. Henry Carey. AnAmPo; AWP; BLPL; BoLoP; CoMu; FaBoBe; GGP; GTBS; GTBS-P; NOBE; OBEV; OxAEP-1

But not, oh God, such peace, such ghastly peace as this. (*LL*) Te Whetu Plains. Edward Tregear. PeNZ

But not on a shell, she starts. The Paltry Nude Starts on a Spring Voyage. Wallace Stevens. HCAP

But not our English hills!' (*LL*) Where a Roman Villa Stood, above Freiburg. Mary Elizabeth Coleridge. OBNC; OBTV

But Not That One. John Ashbery. LCAP

But not to make a constant stay. (*LL*) The Familie. George Herbert. ESCV

But not upon me! (*LL*) The Rain. *Unknown*. BoTP; OxNR

But nothing answered anything. (*LL*) The Hens. Elizabeth Madox Roberts. GoJo; OBCA; PDV

But nothing happens. (*LL*) Exposure. Wilfred Owen. FaBoMo; FaPoB; InPS; MeMBP; NoAM; OBWP; PAW; PeFWW; PlP; PoWW; RB

But nothing promised that is not performed. (*LL*) To Juan at the Winter Solstice. Robert Graves. CMoP; EBEV; FaBoMo; ImPo; LiTB; LiTM; MeMBP; MoBrPo; MoP; NAEL-2; NoAM; OAEL-2; PoE; RaBo; TwCP

But now at thirty years my hair is grey. Growing old. Byron. *Fr.* Don Juan. NOBE; SCV

But now came the men of right visiting claims; Leigh Hunt. *Fr.* Feast of the Poets, The. EPCY

But now farewell. I am going a long way. Tennyson, *incorporated in* Idylls of the King *with changes, as* The Passing of Arthur. *Fr.* Morte d'Arthur. DL; EBVVPR; FaBoBe; FaBoRV; NIP; NOBVV; OAEL-2; OBNV; PoEL-5

But now hear what meat there needs eat thou must. Eating in Hall. Alexander Barclay. *Fr.* Eclogues. NoSic

But now I call him dirty louse. (*LL*) The Immortals. Isaac Rosenberg. FaBoTw; NSI; TrJP

But now I have a Deity. (*LL*) Poverty. Thomas Traherne. Prf; TEP; TrCP

But now I only know I am, – that's all. (*LL*) I Feel I Am. John Clare. OAEL-2

But now Mr. Ferritt. And Mr. Ferritt. Judith Wright. MoBrPo

But now more serious let me grow. Matthew Green. *Fr.* Spleen, The. PoEL-3

But now my Muse toyled with continuall care. Richard Barnfield. *Fr.* Sonnets. PeHV

But now, no longer deaf to honour's call. Homer, *tr. by* Pope. *Fr.* Iliad, The. OBVE

But now the gentle dew-fall sends abroad. Looking Down on Nether Stowey. Samuel Taylor Coleridge. *Fr.* Fears in Solitude. EnRP; FaBoPP; OBWP

But now the salmon-fishers moist. Carrying Their Coracles. Andrew Marvell. *Fr.* Upon Appleton House, to My Lord Fairfax. ChTr; SeCP; SeCV-1

But now the wholesome music of the wood. Vivien's Song ("But now the wholesome music of the wood.") Tennyson. *Fr.* Idylls of the King. OAEL-2

But now the wounded queen with heavy care. Virgil, *tr. fr. Latin* by Robert Fitzgerald. *Fr.* Aeneid [*or* Eneados], The. NAWM-1; SiPSBD, *tr. by* Henry Howard, Earl of Surrey

But now you come at noon. (*LL*) Dillar, a dollar, A,/ A ten o'clock scholar. Mother Goose. FaBoBe; OxNR; ReMoGo

But O! delighting me. (*LL*) Reason Has Moons. Ralph Hodgson. FaBoCh; OxBSP

But, O immortals! What had I to plead. Christopher Smart. *Fr.* Hymn to the Supreme Being on Recovery from a Dangerous Fit of Illness. NOEC

But O, my Muse, what numbers wilt thou find. Joseph Addison. *Fr.* Campaign, The. FaBoEH
(Poem to His Grace the Duke of Marlborough, A.) OBWP

But O! the freedom, pleasure and the ease. On Giving Up Smoking. Lawrence Spooner. *Fr.* Looking-Glass for Smokers, A. NOEC

But O! thy grief, thy grief doth kill. (*LL*) The Eclipse. Henry Vaughan. OxBSP

But of all the plagues, the greatest is untold. Juvenal, *tr. by* Dryden. *Fr.* Satires. OBSV

But oh! how different is each sight and sound. Forest Thoughts. Sir Roger Casement. TIRV

But oh! how much besides! (*LL*) Disillusioned. "Lewis Carroll."

But oh, no man could hold it, for twas thine. (*LL*) The Legacy [*or* Legacie]. John Donne. SeCP; TrGrPo

But on the morrow Elspie kept out of the way of Philip. Arthur Hugh Clough. *Fr.* Bothie of Tober-na-Vuolich, The [A Long-Vacation Pastoral]. EnVR; OBF

But once upon a time. Cranach. Sir Herbert Read. FaBoMo

But one and all if they would dusk the day. (*LL*) A Death Song. William Morris. NAEL-2

But one apocalyptic lion's whelp (in flesh). There Is No Opera like "Lohengrin." John Wheelwright. NYBP

But one half glaunce, most gladly dye[or die]. (*LL*) Vanity of Spirit. Henry Vaughan. SeCV; GeHe; NOSC; TOF

But one night went betwixt. (*LL*) Kind Are Her Answers. Thomas Campion. BoLoP; CBLP; ELP; TrGrPo

But only God can make a tree. (*LL*) Trees. Joyce Kilmer. BLPA; EBEvV; FaBoBe; FaPON; UV; WBLP; WGRP

But only great as I am good. (*LL*) Tall Oaks from Little Acorns Grow. David Everett.

But only how did you die. (*LL*) How Did You Die? Edmund Vance Cooke. BLPA; PWR

But only multiply in the green grass. (*LL*) Necropolis. Karl Shapiro. MoAB; PoA

But only my Corinna's eye? (*LL*) The Eye. Robert Herrick. CaPo

But only one mother the wide world over. (*LL*) Only One Mother. George Cooper. OHIP

But only that we yield. And we yield. (*LL*) Venetian Interior, 1889. Richard Howard. VCAP

But only to be memories of spiritual gate. Immortality. Samuel Greenberg. LiTA

But only to build memories of spiritual gates. (*LL*) Emblems of Conduct. Hart Crane. ImPo; LiTA; LiTM; MeMAP

But only we can sing them. (*LL*) Fish Story: How Language Carries Us into the Unknown. Brigitte Frase. LoHo

But Oothoon is not so; a virgin filled with virgin fancies. Desire and Jealousy. Blake. *Fr.* Visions of the Daughters of Albion. ECEV; OAEL-2

But our love shall endure forever! (*LL*) Of Eternal Love. Josef Wenzig. RiWo

But peaceful was the night. Milton. *Fr.* On the Morning of Christ's Nativity. FaBoCh; MeLP; NAs; NOCV; NoP; PoEL-3; SCGP; WGRP

But Perhaps. Nelly Sachs, *tr. fr.* German by Ruth Mead *and* Matthew Mead. BoWoP

But piteous things we are — when I am gone. Robert Nichols. *Fr.* Sonnets to Aurelia. OBMV

But pitie which sometimes doth Lyon's move. Barnabe Barnes. *Fr.* Parthenophil and Parthenophe. ESo

But pity for the grief they cannot feel. (*LL*) The Prisoners. Stephen Spender. FaBoMo; MoAB; MoBrPo

But please, sir, to mention *your pay.* (*LL*) Epistle to Mr. Murray. Byron. FaBoUs

"But plett a wand o bonnie birk." Sweet William's Ghost. *Unknown.* ESPB

But pray to God that he forgive us all. (*LL*) The Epitaph in Form of a Ballad. Villon. CTC

But pretty though as/ roses is. Three Sayings from Highlands, North Carolina. Jonathan Williams. OBAL

But proves at night a bed of down. (*LL*) Upon the Sudden Restraint of the Earl[e] of Somerset, Then Falling from Favor [*or* Favour]. Sir Henry Wotton. ELP; FaBoEH; JCP; NOBE; NoP; NOSC; SeCP

But Robin he walkes in the greene fforest. Robin Hood and the Butcher. *Unknown.* ESPB

But rosemary will with thee go. (*LL*) The Dying Man in His Garden. George Sewell. GTBS; GTBS-P

But scarce observ'd, the knowing and the bold. On Gold. Samuel Johnson. *Fr.* Vanity of Human Wishes, The: The Tenth Satire of Juvenal Imitated. EBEV; ECEV; IHNG; NOEC; NoP; OAEL-1; OxAEP-1; PoEL-3; PrIm; TEP; TFi

But see here comes thy reverend Sire. Milton. *Fr.* Samson Agonistes. EBEV; FHYEP; OAEL-1; PoEL-3

But see! the well-plumed hearse comes nodding on. Robert Blair. *Fr.* Grave, The. ECEV

But shall not question much. (*LL*) Twice. Christina Rossetti. GBL; NOBE; OBEV; OBNC; TOF; TrCP

But she didn't do it. And now it's too late. (*LL*) Too Many Daves. "Dr. Seuss." OBCA

But she died shortly after her son was killed. (*LL*) His Mother. Haim Guri. MHP

But — She has gone away. (*LL*) The House of the Apple-Trees. Alice Milligan. VBLP

But she is long dead. (*LL*) Remembrance. Joseph Freiherr von Eichendorff. RiWo

But she shed not any tear. (*LL*) Prince Robert. *Unknown.* AmFP

But she thought she should go back to Sweden. (*LL*) There was a young lady of Sweden. Edward Lear. CBNP; EBEV; PeVV

But shoots its cause, and is a cource of joy. (*LL*) A Choice of Weapons. Stanley Kunitz. LiTM; VGW

But should some snarling critic chance to view. Jane Brereton. *Fr.* Epistle to Mrs Anne Griffiths. ECWP

But, sires o word forgat I in my tale. Chaucer. *Fr.* Canterbury Tales, The. EBEV; EnVB; FHYEP; HAP; NAEL-1; NoP; OAEL-1; PoE; PoEL-1

But sits at amber sunset round a tomb. (*LL*) This Amber Sunstream. Mark Van Doren. GoYe; LiTA

But sleep on all the same. (*LL*) Hoping Against Hope. Christina Rossetti. CBLP

But some feathers are still floating/ In the sky. (*LL*) My Great Grand Uncle. Tarapada Ray. TSaS

But some mean what they say. (*LL*) Ends. Robert Frost. TRP

But some one will ask, "How are the dead raised?" Bible, *N.T. Fr.* First Corinthians. DL

But something went wrong with the plann: I am still on the train. (*LL*) Observation Car. A. D. Hope. MoP; NoAM

But soon th'endearments of a husband cloy. Soame Jenyns. *Fr.* Modern Fine Lady, The. ECEV; NOEC

But sorrow to look back on. (*LL*) Life Is Long. *Unknown.* OHMPC

But Still in Israel's Paths They Shine. Carter Revard. VoR

But still regard the destitute. (*LL*) Lord, Hear My Prayer. John Clare. ChIV-1; NOCV; NoP; TrCP

But still the child squealed on. (*LL*) The Tender Infant, Meek and Mild. Samuel Johnson. CBNP; OxAEP-1

But still the thunder of Los peals loud and thus the thunder's cry. Blake. *Fr.* Jerusalem. OAEL-2

But still we'll think on Table Bay and the old ship *Waterloo!* (*LL*) Verses. William Henry. PeSAV

But stop and loiter all the time to sing it in ecstatic songs. (*LL*) Beginning My Studies. Walt Whitman. NAAL-1; OxBA

But sudden came the barge's pitch-black prow. "George Eliot." *Fr.* Brother and Sister. NALW; NOBVV

But sweet sister death has gone debauched today and stalks. David Jones. *Fr.* In Parenthesis. OBWP; OxAEP-2; PeFWW

But teeming women, when desire grows strong. Cravings during Pregnancy. M. Saint-Marthe, *tr. fr. French. Fr.* Paedotrophiae; or, The Art of Bringing Up Children. FaBoUs

But tell me, child, your choice; what shall I buy You? The Handsome Heart. Gerard Manley Hopkins. FaBoVe

But that from slow dissolving pomps of dawn. Darkness. Arthur Hugh Clough. OxBSP

But That Is Another Story. Donald Justice. CoAP

But that, oh me, I both must write and love! (*LL*) I know that all beneath the moon decays. William Drummond of Hawthornden. JCP; Son

But that Thou art my wisdom, Lord. Submission. George Herbert. JCP

But that was long ago. I was only seventeen. (*LL*) Maquillage. Lynda Hull. UTF

But that was nothing to what things came out. Welsh Incident. Robert Graves. CBNP; CMoP; EBEvV; MeMBP; NOBE; OBSP; OxBTC

But that we meet, and that we love. (*LL*) Meeting. George Crabbe. OBEV

But that which from these accents flows. (*LL*) Speaking and Kissing. Thomas Stanley. BeJo

But that which most I wonder at, which most. Innocence. Thomas Traherne. ChIV-2; ESCV; MiEL; NOSC

But the blessing of earth is toil. (*LL*) The Gospel of Labor. Henry van Dyke. WBLP

But the breeze has dropped, and silence is the last word. (*LL*) Fear of Death. John Ashbery. FaBoMo; PIP; TAP

But the brief pleasures of life! but the. The Lyf So Short. Palladas, *tr. fr. Greek by* Dudley Fitts. GrAn

But the chief. The Poet the Chief of Artists. Mark Akenside. *Fr.* Pleasures of Imagination, The. EPCY

But the clover is honey and sun and the smell of sleep. (*LL*) Nebuchadnezzar. Elinor Wylie. ChIV-1; MoAmPo

But the Copperbelt night is a snake. The Leader. Dorothy Livesay. MoCV

But the dear knows who I'll marry. (*LL*) I Know Where I'm Going. *Unknown.* ELP; GBP; MoShBr; NTP; OBET; WTO

But the difference. Janet Fisher. NWP

But the Forest Department are rubbing their hands. (*LL*) Afforestation. E. A. Wodehouse. FiBHP

But the horrible *double entendre.* (*LL*) There was an old man of Boulogne. *Unknown.* PeLi

But the last black horse of all. The Last Ones. "Robin Hyde." PeNZ

But the morning does not renew, this city. We Are Green, Then Grey, Then Nothing in This World. Iain Sinclair. VaA

But the plain landscape, the bleak sea shore, or the barren plain, with the common sky & sun, — or at night the moon & stars. (*LL*) Beauty. Walt Whitman. WeW

But the programme is J. B., so Happy New Year. (*LL*) Radio Cradle-song. Eugène Marais. PeSAV

But the rose with all its thorns excels them both. (*LL*) Comparisons. Christina Rossetti. OxBChV

But the scent of the roses will hang 'round it still. (*LL*) Long, Long Be My Heart with Such Memories Filled. Thomas Moore. BLPL; FaBoBe

But the sheet was Belfast linen. (*LL*) The Ballad of William Bloat. *Unknown.* NOBL; PeLV

But the show was over. (*LL*) The Artist. William Carlos Williams. InPS; LCAP; NYBP; RB; SAmP

But the soul that courts it, it must die, a low unlovely thing. (*LL*) The Merry Jovial Beggar. Peter Casey. TIRV; WTO

But the sweet little Bees large Monument. (*LL*) A Black Patch on Lucasta's Face. Richard Lovelace. BeJo; CaPo; SeCP

But the vast pile th' amazed vulgar views. The Destruction of Troy. Virgil, *tr. by* Sir John Denham. *Fr.* Aeneid [*or* Eneados], The. NAWM-1; SeCV-1

But Thee, but Thee, O sovereign Seer of time. Sidney Lanier. *Fr.* Crystal, The. TrPWD

But their comprehensive silence stays the same. (*LL*) Learning the Trees. Howard Nemerov. VCAP

But Then and There the Sun Bore Down. N. Scott Momaday. CDW

But then, how it was sweet! (*LL*) Confessions. Robert Browning. CBLP; ELP; GTBS-P; NOBE; NOBVV

But then that is my own truth and ecstasy. (*LL*) "Advice" to a Young Poet. Mazisi Kunene. PeSAV

But there is no black jaw which cannot be broken by our word. Kenneth Patchen. *Fr.* Journal of Albion Moonlight, The. NaP

But there is no joy in Mudville — Mighty Casey has struck out. (*LL*) Casey at the Bat. Ernest Lawrence Thayer. AnAmPo; BeLS; BLPA; FaBoBe; PoRA

But there is no road through the woods. (*LL*) The Way through the Woods. Kipling. CH; CoGr; EBEvV; FaBoCh; FaPON; NoAM; NOBE; NTP; OBEV; OBNC; OxAEP-2; OxBChV; OxBTC; PFP; PlP; RFM; SCGP; WHSW

But there was/ once/ a time. Eléni Vakaló, *tr. fr. Greek by* John Stathatos. WPOW

But there will be less to say. (*LL*) Length of Moon. Arna Bontemps. CDC; LiTM; PoNe

But there's still no trace of the assailants. (*LL*) Still There's No Trace. Zim Mnotoza. PeSAV

But these lip-songs are most despicable! (*LL*) On African Writing. Jack A. Mapanje. HBAPE

But they come by tens." (*LL*) Old Lem. Sterling A. Brown. BPo; PoBA; PoNe; TTY

But thine arithmetic is quite correct. (*LL*) Fragment of a Greek Tragedy. A. E. Housman. FaBoNo; NOBL; PeLV

But this by sure experiment we know. Ovid, *tr. by* Dryden. *Fr.* Metamorphoses. FM

But this dull unlovely translation! (*LL*) Babel. Michael O'Loughlin. IB

But this fruit-dish (I suppose it is for fruit). A Good Thing. Ray Mathew. CBAP

But this security in Jove the great sea-rector spied. Neptune Goes to the Greeks. Homer, *tr. fr. Greek. Fr.* Iliad, The. NOSC, *tr. by* George Chapman

But this, so feminine? Donald Davie. *Fr.* Forests of Lithuania, The. OxBTC

But thou, Israel, My servant. Israel, My Servant. Bible, *O.T. Fr.* Isaiah. TrJP

But thou my deere sweet-sounding lute be still. Richard Lynche. *Fr.* Diella. AAS

But till that day, plase God, I'll stick to wearin' o' the Green. (*LL*) The Wearing of [*or* Wearin' o'] the Green. *Unknown.* AWP; FaPoR; GBP; IIP; OxBoLi; WTO

But to go on where we left off. Mary Evelyn. *Fr.* Voyage to Marry-Land; Or, The Ladies Dressing Room, A. CBCK

But to know, that I love thee and would be loved. (*LL*) To Mr. Rowland Woodward. John Donne. ESCV

But to live in the tragic world forever. (*LL*) A Story about Chicken Soup. Louis Simpson. BTR; NNaP; PoE; PoWW; TAP

But to the bad children, Christmas does not come. (*LL*) A Curse on Herod. Amy Witting. ChIV-2; NOBAu

But to the heavens, lo, it fled, for to receive his doom. (*LL*) In winter's just return, when Boreas gan his reign. The Earl of Surrey. AAS; SiPS; SiPSBD

But to you will say nothing, not ever. (*LL*) The Return. Matthew Sweeney.

But touch us too: we have something to redeem. (*LL*) The Visitation. Jan Owen. NOBAu

But trembling Dido eagerly now bent. Virgil, *tr. fr. Latin by* Robert Fitzgerald. *Fr.* Aeneid [*or* Eneados], The. NAWM-1; SiPSBD, *tr. by* Henry Howard, Earl of Surrey

But true expression, like th' unchanging sun. Pope. *Fr.* Essay on Criticism. FHYEP; PoEL-3

But true love is a durable fire. Sir Walter Ralegh. *Fr.* As You Came from the Holy Land. CBLP; OBD; OxAEP-1

But turning toward Ololon in terrible majesty Milton. Blake. *Fr.* Milton. OxAEP-2

But 'twas a famous victory. (*LL*) The Battle of Blenheim. Robert Southey. BeLS; CoGr; EnRP; FaBoPV; FaBV; FaPoR; GN; OBNC; OBWP; PoLF; TFi; TrGrPo; VPP; WBLP

But 'twas a time when Europe was rejoiced. Wordsworth. *Fr.* Prelude [*or*, Growth of a Poet's Mind], The. EnRP; FaBoPV; OAEL-2; PoEL-4

But twelve short years you lived, my son. His Son. Callimachus, *tr. fr. Greek by* G. B. Grundy. AWP

But unto you pertains the loss. (*LL*) For Pity, Pretty Eyes, Surcease. Thomas Lodge. ElL

But Venus first. Sister Juana Inés de la Cruz, *tr. fr. Spanish by* Samuel Beckett. *Fr.* First Dream. BoWoP

But was I the first martyr, who. Stephen to Lazarus. C. S. Lewis. ChIV-2

But was there ever dog that praised his fleas? (*LL*) To a Poet, Who Would Have Me Praise Certain Bad Poets, Imitators of His and Mine. W. B. Yeats. CTC; FaBoEE

But we are exiles from our fathers' land. (*LL*) Canadian Boat Song. *At. to* John Galt *and also to* "Christopher North." BLPA; FaBoCh; FaPoR; OBEV; OBNC

But we are leaving. (*LL*) I search/ for the straight path. Florence Dacey. LoHo

But we are set to strive to make our mark. Frederick Goddard Tuckerman. *Fr.* Sonnets. TrCP

But we don't call this cold in Quebec. (*LL*) There was a young boy [*or* man] of Quebec. *At. to* Kipling Kipling. FaBoCo

But we have only begun. Beginners. Denise Levertov. CrSp

But we left him alone with his glory. (*LL*) The Burial of Sir John Moore [*after* (*or* at) Corunna]. Charles Wolfe. ChTr; EBEvV; EnRP; FaBoEH; FaBoPa; FaBoRV; FaBoB; FaPoR; GN; GTBS; GTBS-P; NOBE; NTP; OBEV; OBWP; OxAEP-2; PeIV; PlP; PoRA; PWR; TFi; UV; VPP; WBLP

But We Shall Bloom. Haim Guri, *tr. fr. Hebrew by* David Kuselewitz. TrJP

But we, whose sands run low. Helen Waddell. MLL

But we'll leave it to be hackneyed by the fellows in the rear. (*LL*) The Men Who Come Behind. Henry Lawson. NOBAu

But were always a rose. (*LL*) The Rose Family. Robert Frost. OBAL; OBCA

But westward, look, the land is bright. (*LL*) Say Not the Struggle Nought Availeth. Arthur Hugh Clough. AWP; CoGr; EBEvV; EBVV; EnVR; FaBoRV; FaPoR; GGP; GTBS-P; LiTB; NAEL-2; NOBE; NOBVV; NTP; OAEL-2; OBEV; OBNC; OtMeF; PlP; SCGP; TEP; TFi; TrGrPo; WGRP

But What I'm Trying to Say Mother Is. Ai. MDDM

But what is strength without a double share. Milton. *Fr.* Samson Agonistes. ChIV-1; FHYEP; OAEL-1; PoEL-3

But What Is the Reader to Make of This? John Ashbery. InPS

But what the waur am I? (*LL*) Rigid Body Sings. James Clerk Maxwell. FaBoCo; FaBoPa; UV

But whaur's the Minister? (*LL*) Last Lauch. Douglas Young. FaBoCo; NBLV; OxBS

But when I waked, I saw that I saw not. A Storm at Sea. John Donne. *Fr.* Storme, The. NOBE; NoSic

But when it was my turn to wrestle with the angel. Under the Ladder to Heaven. Elizabeth Fenton. NMM

But when the Gods and Heroes heard, they brought. Matthew Arnold. *Fr.* Balder Dead. PeVV

But when the golden-thron'd Aurora made. *Unknown, formerly at. to* Homer, *tr. fr. Greek by* Congreve. *Fr.* Hymn to Venus, The. OBVE

But when the next day brake from underground. Percivale's Quest. Tennyson. *Fr.* Idylls of the King. OAEL-2

But when the water roars around us. The Ocean. Louis Dudek. *Fr.* Provincetown. MoCV

But when to mischief mortals bend their will. Pope. *Fr.* Rape of the Lock, The. FHYEP; HAP; ImPo; NoP; OAEL-1; OBNV; OxAEP-1; PeLV; PoEL-3; TEP; TrGrPo

But when you reach the Bridge of Dread. The Bridge of Dread. Edwin Muir. MeMBP

But where are snows of a bygone year? (*LL*) Tell me where, in what country, where. Villon. STV

But where are the snows of yester-year? (*LL*) Ballad[e] of Dead Ladies. Villon. AWP; CTC; HeIL; OBVE; PoRA; PrIm

But where began the change; and what's my crime? George Meredith. *Fr.* Modern Love. PoEL-5

But where has this Praxiteles been prying? (*LL*) Spoken by Venus on Seeing Her Statue Done by Praxiteles. *Unknown.* FaBoEE

But where they lie the frost does no harm. (*LL*) How Words Meet to Make a Poem. Aidan Carl Mathews. IB

But where to find the happiest spot below. The First, Best Country. Goldsmith. *Fr.* Travel[l]er; or, A Prospect of Society, The. GN

But wherefore did he take away the crown? Shakespeare. *Fr.* King Henry IV, Pt. II. OxAEP-1

But where's the bloody horse? (*LL*) On Some South African Novelists. Roy Campbell. FaBoCo; FaBoEE; GTBS-P; InPK; MoBrPo; NOBL; OxAEP-2; OxBTC; PeLV

But where's the man who counsel can bestow. Pope. *Fr.* Essay on Criticism. OxAEP-1; PoEL-3

Buy Me an Ounce and I'll Sell You a Pound. E. E. Cummings. OxBA

Buy my cherries, whiteheart, blackheart, golden girls, O buy! (LL) For Exmoor. Jean Ingelow. OBEV

Buy One Now. D. J. Enright. NOBL

Buy the paper, take it home. Coming and Going. Mitchell Goodman. VGW

Buy Us a Little Grain. Christine Lavant, tr. fr. German by Michael Hamburger. WPOW

Buy with gold the old associations! (LL) The Golden Mile-Stone. Longfellow. PoEL-5

Buying a Record. Robert Peters. BXAP

Buying Flowers. Po Chü-i, tr. fr. Chinese by Robert Payne. TAL

Buying new shoes/ takes so long. New Shoes. John Agard. OTCP

Buying Wine. Sascha Feinstein. Jaz

Buz[z], Quoth the Blue Fly. Ben Jonson. Fr. Oberon, the Fairy Prince. CBNP; TEP

Buzz. Jim Tollerud. VoR

Buzz frantic. Buzz in the Window. Ted Hughes. Fr. Orts. NoAM

Buzz in the Window. Ted Hughes. Fr. Orts. NoAM

Buzz saw snarled and rattled in the yard, The. "Out, Out." Robert Frost. DL; FF; HAP; HeIP; NAAL-2; OxBA; Poetr; RB; SoSe; TRP; UnPo; VGW

Buzzard. George Garrett. MT

Buzzards over Pondy Woods, The. Pondy Woods. Robert Penn Warren. MoAmPo

Buzzing darkly almost like thunder. Mosquitoes. P'i Jih-hsiu, tr. fr. Chinese by William H. Nienhauser. SuSp

BW. Aaron Fogel. BAP-89

Bwagamoyo. Lebert Bethune. PoBA

By a bank as I lay. Unknown. NoSic

By a Bank of Pinks and Lilies. Unknown. ErPo

By a broken bridge outside the courier station. Tune: "Song of Divination" — On the Plum Tree. Lu Yu, tr. fr. Chinese by James J. Y. Liu. SuSp

By a Chapel as I Came. Unknown. ChTr; GBP

By a clear well, within a little field. Of Three Girls and of Their Talk. Boccaccio, tr. fr. Italian by Dante Gabriel Rossetti. Fr. Sonnets. AWP

By a cloud, by rings on the moon. The Portents. Phyllis McGinley. ArOW

By a dismal cypress lying. A Song from the Italian. Dryden. Fr. Kind Keeper, The. SeCV-2

By a flat rock on the shore of the sea. The Rock. Unknown, tr. fr. Welsh by Geoffrey Grigson. ChTr; GBL

By a forest as I gan fare. Unknown. MiEL

By a loading bay that smells of millet. Whitman at a Grain Depot. James Reiss. AnAn

By a peninsula the painter sat. Conduct. Samuel Greenberg. LiTA

By a peninsula the wanderer sat and sketched. Emblems of Conduct. Hart Crane. ImPo; LiTA; LiTM; MeMAP

By a quiet little stream on an old mossy log. The Frog and the Bird. Vera Hessey. BoTP

By a route obscure and lonely. Dream-Land. Poe. AmPP; AnAmPo; LiTA; MeMAP; NAAL-1; NOBA; OxBA (Dreamland.) TAP

By a silvergreen flex of urine earthing me to the ground. (LL) The Man Who Stepped Out of Feeling. Dermot Bolger. IB

By a Stream on Mount T'ien-t'ung. Wang An-shih, tr. fr. Chinese by Jan W. Walls. SuSp

By a thousand, thousand things! (LL) The Heart's Proof. James Buckham. BLRP; WBLP

By absence, and unkind neglect. The Visit. Unknown. ECWP

By absence from the heart. (LL) To the Evening Star. Thomas Campbell. GTBS; GTBS-P

By Achmelvich Bridge. Norman MacCaig. OxBS

By all I touch on the way. (LL) Under Stars. Tess Gallagher. InPK

By all means sing of love, but if you do. The Truest Poetry Is the Most Feigning; or, Ars Poetica for Hard Times. W. H. Auden. NYBP

By all our loves conjure him not to stay. (LL) A Letter to Her Husband. Anne Bradstreet. AnAmPo; LiTA

By all the Dodos! these are thoughts of weight. Dodoism. William John Courthope. Fr. Paradise of Birds, The. OtMeF

By all the glories of the day. Before Action. William Noel Hodgson. PAW; WGRP

By all the published facts in the case. About Children. Phyllis McGinley. OBAL

By an ancient road, abundant thistle plants. Liu Tsung-yüan, tr. by Jan W. Walls. Fr. Farmers. SuSp

By an old maid. (LL) Lemonade. Unknown. GBP

By and by. Epitaph on a Waiter. David McCord. NBLV; NIP; OBAL

By and by, the seasons come and go. T'ao Ch'ien, tr. by Eugene Eoyang. Fr. Seasons Come and Go, The. SuSp

By April mist. Spring Song. Katharine O'Brien. GoYe

By archy/ the roach that scurries. Ballade of the Under Side. Don Marquis. Fr. Archys Life of Mehitabel. InvP

By art a poet is not made; For a Poet. George Wither. ChIV-2

By Arthur's Dale as late I went. Bonny Bee Hom. Unknown. ESPB

By Babel's Streams. Philip Freneau. AH

By battle or by pot. (LL) The General Elliott. Robert Graves. PeLV

By becoming a Cabinet Minister. (LL) On the Birth of His Son. Su Tung-p'o. AWP; OBVE

By being never green. (LL) Telephone Poles. John Updike. FYAP; Poetsp

By Birth I'm a Slave, yet can give you a Crown. Enigma. Matthew Prior. PeLV

By Blue Ontario's Shore, sels. Walt Whitman.
   "Are you he who would assume a place to teach or be a poet here in the States?" FaBoPV
   Poet, The. MoAmPo

By bluster, graft, and doing people down. A Tribute to the Founder. Kingsley Amis. IHNG

By, by, lully, lullay. (LL) Coventry Carol. Unknown. ELP; MeEL; PChr

By Canoe through the Fir Forest. James Dickey. NYBP

By Cavité on the bay. The Battle of Manila. Richard Hovey. PAH

By channels of coolness the echoes are calling. Bell-Birds. Henry Clarence Kendall. NOBAu

By Chickamauga's crooked stream the martial trumpets blew. The Ballad of Chickamauga. Maurice Thompson. PAH

By Clyde's bonny banks where I sadly did wander. The Blantyre Explosion. Unknown. OBET; SWP

By Cool Siloam's Shady Rill. Reginald Heber. ELP; NOCV

By Cypris, Cupid! Meleager, tr. fr. Greek by Peter Whigham. GrAn

By dark severance the apparition head. Painted Head. John Crowe Ransom. LiTA; LiTM; MeMAP; NoAM; NOBA; OxBA
   (Painting: A Head.) MoAB; MoAmPo

By Day. Paul Celan, tr. fr. German by Joachim Neugroschel. AnAn

By day and also by night and you are. Ian Wedde. Fr. Earthly: Sonnets for Carlos. PeNZ

By day Golgotha sleeps, but when night comes. Night at Gettysburg. Don C. Seitz. OHIP

By day she woos me, soft, exceeding fair. The World. Christina Rossetti. BoWoP; NALW

By day the bat is cousin to the mouse. The Bat. Theodore Roethke. GoJo; OBCA; PDV; PYC; SiSoPo; ZA

By day the fields and meadows cry. The Poet's Call. Thomas Curtis Clark. WGRP

By day the skyscraper looms in the smoke and sun and has a soul. Skyscraper. Carl Sandburg. ImGa

By day these men ask nothing, and obey. Infantry. Alun Lewis. PoWW

By day we are singular and often lonely. (LL) Bedtime. Denise Levertov. IHMS; NaP; SM; TwCP

By daybreak a north wind has shaken. After the Chinese. Tess Gallagher. NAmP90

By death, whom he'd imagined out of town? (LL) At Shagger's Funeral. Bruce Dawe. NOBAu

By dint of color. A Dab of Color. Theodore Weiss. VGW

By divination came the Dorians. In Arcadia. Lawrence Durrell. MoBrPo

By dreams, each one into a several world. (LL) Dreams. Robert Herrick. BeJo; CaPo; HAP; NAEL-1; OxBSP; Spl

By duty bound and not by custom led. To the Memory of My Dear and Ever Honored Father Thomas Dudley Esq. Anne Bradstreet. NAAL-1

By ear, he sd. I, Maximus of Gloucester, to You ("By ear, he sd.") Charles Olson. Fr. Maximus Poems, The. NeAP

By eating Miss Foggerty's cake. (LL) Miss Foggerty's Cake. Unknown. BLPA; NBLV

By-Election Idyll. Peter Dickinson. FiBHP

By every ebb of the river-side. Pisgah. Willard Austin Wattles. WGRP

By faith and hope and charity,/ America befriend! (LL) Peace Hymn of the Republic. Henry van Dyke. AH

By Faith Not Sight. Heather McHugh. PFL

By fame on earth, by glory in the skies! (LL) Epitaph. William Cowper. EPCY

By fate, not option, frugal Nature gave. Xenophanes. Emerson. NOBA

By favorable breezes fanned. Cythère. Paul Verlaine, tr. fr. French by Arthur Symons. AWP

By feathers green, across Casbeen. The Phoenix. A. C. Benson. OBEV

By Fiat of Adoration. Oscar Williams. LiTM

By Fire or by Water. Karen Brodine. ETG

By the Babylonish waters. By the Waters of Babylon. Heine, *tr. fr. German by* Charles Godfrey Leland. *Fr.* Hebrew Melodies. TrJP

By the beard of the Prophet the Bashaw swore. How We Burned the *Philadelphia.* Barrett Eastman. PAH

By the Beautiful Ohio. Joan LaBombard. SM

By the bivouac's fitful flame. (*LL*) By the Bivouac's Fitful Flame. Walt Whitman. NoAM; NoP; OxBA; PoE

By the Bivouac's Fitful Flame. Walt Whitman. NoAM; NoP; OxBA; PoE

By the blue wooden sea. Switchback. Edith Sitwell. PBWP

By the Boat House, Oxford. Anne Stevenson. FaBoWP

By the bonnie milldams o' Binnorie. (*LL*) Binnorie; or, The Two Sisters. *Unknown.* OBEV; PoE; TrGrPo

By the Bridge. Ted Walker. NYBP

By the brilliant ramp. 3 A.M. John Updike. AnAmPo

By the City Gate. Ts'ui Hao, *tr. fr. Chinese by* Kenneth Rexroth. OHMPC

By the Conemaugh. Florence Earle Coates. PAH

By the crumbling fire we talked. Witness. John Montague. CIP

By the Deep Nine. *Unknown.* ChTr

By the Deep Sea. Byron. *See* Oh! that the desert [*or* desart] were my dwelling-place.

By the dry road the fathers cough and spit. The Brief Journey West. Howard Nemerov. NoAM

By the end of the longest day of the year he could not. Summer Solstice, New York City. Sharon Olds. NAmP90; NGP

By the Exeter River. Donald Hall. MoBS

By the fierce flames of love I'm in a sad taking. Royall Tyler. TAP

By the Fire. Mother Goose. OxNR

By the Fire-Side. Robert Browning. EBVV; OAEL-2

By the first hour we knew the day's luck. Rituals along the Arkansas. William Mills. MT

By the flat cup and the splash of new vontage. I, 31. By the Flat Cup ("Quid dedicatum.") Horace, *tr. fr. Latin by* Austin Dobson. *Fr.* Odes. CTC, *tr. by* Ezra Pound

By the flow of the inland river. The Blue and the Gray. Francis Miles Finch. AnAmPo; BLPA; BLPL; FaBoBe; PAH; VPP; WBLP

By the Ford. Edward Thomas. OxBSP

By the gas-fire, kneeling. Olga Poems. Denise Levertov. LCAP; NNaP

By the gate with star and moon. Medallion. Sylvia Plath. HeIP; NoP; SM

By the Gold River, in mid-autumn, the bows of our enemy are drawn. Early Geese. Tu Mu, *tr. fr. Chinese.* SuSp

By the Great Face behind. (*LL*) The Last Chrysanthemum. Thomas Hardy. CMoP; LiTB; MeMBP

By the great stones we chose our ground. In Love, at Stonehenge. Coventry Patmore. *Fr.* Angel in the House, The. FaBoPP

By the highway the stream downslope. Runoff. A. R. Ammons. PPP

By the Hoof of the Wild Goat. Kipling. *Fr.* Plain Tales from the Hills. OBNC

By the images of things. Epoch. Vladimir Holan, *tr. fr. Czech by* Ian Milner *and* Jarmila Milner. PoSu

By the injustice of the skies for punishment? (*LL*) The Cold Heaven. W. B. Yeats. AWP; CTC; GTBS-P; HAP; NoAM; OAEL-2; OxBSP; RB; TEP

By the Isar, in the twilight. River Roses. D. H. Lawrence. CMoP; GBL; OAEL-2

By the king's tree I walked afraid. Alison Brackenbury. SCBI

By the lamplit stall I loitered, feasting my eyes. Sight. W. W. Gibson. MoBrPo

By the light of the harvest moon. Moons. Peter Fallon. BiHa

By the light of the moon. (*LL*) So, We'll Go No More a-Roving. Byron. AWP; BLPL; BoLoP; CBLP; ClHu; CoGr; EBEvV; ELP; EnRP; FaPoB; FF; FHYEP; HAP; HeIP; ImPo; LiTB; MeMBP; NAEL-2; NOBE; NoP; OAEL-2; OtMeF; OxBS; OxBSP; PlP; PoE; PoEL-4; Poetr; PoRA; PrIm; SCGP; TFi; TTTS

By the little river. The Willows. Walter Prichard Eaton. FaPON; OHIP

By the lyre I rose, fell with the flute. Thebes. Honestus, *tr. fr. Greek by* Peter Jay. GrAn

By the Margin of the Great Deep. "Æ." OBEV; OHCV

By the margin of the ocean, one morning [*or* one pleasant evening] in the month of June. The Bonny Bunch of Roses O. *Unknown.* FaBoBa; OxBoLi

By the Moon ("By the moon we sport and play.") *At. to* John Lyly *and to* Thomas Ravenscroft. *Fr.* Mayde's Metamorphosis, The. CH

By the new Boot's, a tool-chest with flagpoles. Aberdacy: The Main Square. Kingsley Amis. *Fr.* Evans Country, The. NoAM; NOBL; OxBTC

By the newly bulldozed logging road, for a hundred yards. Working against Time. David Wagoner. MAT

By the North Gate, the wind blows full of sand. Lament of the Frontier Guard. Li Po, *tr. fr. Chinese by* Ezra Pound. OBVE; OBWP; VGW

By the North Sea., *sels.* Swinburne.
"Land that is lonelier than ruin, A." PoEL-5
Suffolk. FaBoPP
Where Dunwich Used to Be. FaBoPP

By the old Moulmein Pagoda, lookin' eastward to [*or* lazy at] the sea. Mandalay. Kipling. CoGr; EBEvV; FaBV; LiTB; MoBrPo; NOBE; OBTV; OxAEP-2; TrGrPo

By the Open Window. C. P. Cavafy, *tr. fr. Greek by* Rae Dalven. ArNa

By the Pasture Bars. George Sands Johnson. PWR

By the Peonies. Czeslaw Milosz, *tr. fr. Polish by* Czeslaw Milosz. ArNa

By the Pool at the Third Rosses. Arthur Symons. *Fr.* In Ireland. FaBoPP; OBNC

By the Potomac. Thomas Bailey Aldrich. PAH; Son

By the public hook for the private eye. River Song. Weldon Kees. PPP

By the Pump Dry-eyed. Janet Fisher. NWP

By the River Ashley., *sels.* Mary Ursula Bethell.
"Hour is dark. The river comes to its end, The." PeNZ
"Sauntering home from church we lingered." PeNZ
"That bridge from the city, that was Waimakariri." PeNZ

By the River Eden. Kathleen Raine. NYBP

By the rivers of Babylon. Bible, *O.T., paraphrased by* Sir Thomas Wyatt. *Fr.* Psalms. AWP; NAWM-1; OAEL-1; OBVE; TrJP

"By the Rivers of Babylon." Mary Weston Fordham. CBWP-2

By the Rivers of Babylon We Sat Down and Wept. Byron. ChIV-1

By the Road. Geoffrey Grigson. OxBTC

By the road in spring, rain has added flowers. Tune: "Happy Events Approaching." Ch'in Kuan, *tr. fr. Chinese by* James J. Y. Liu. SuSp

By the road to the contagious hospital. Spring and All. William Carlos Williams. CMoP; HAP; InPK; InPS; LiTM; MeMAP; MoP; NAAL-2; NoAM; NOBA; OxBA; PoE; TAP; TFi; TRP
(Poem: "By the road to the contagious hospital.") MoAB; MoAmPo; UnPo

By the roots of my hair some god got hold of me. The Hanging Man. Sylvia Plath. HCAP; VCAP

By the rude bridge that arched the flood. Concord Hymn. Emerson. AiP; AmPP; AWP; BLPA; BLPL; ClHu; FaBoBe; FaBoEH; FaPON; FaPoR; GN; GOA; HAP; HeIP; LiTA; MeMAP; NOBA; NoP; OBWP; OxBA; PAH; PAW; PeECV; PlP; TAP; TFi; TrGrPo
(Hymn: 'By the rude bridge that arched the flood' .) AnAmPo
(Hymn Sung at the Completion of the Concord Monument.) EBEvV; NAAL-1

By the rushy-fringed bank. Sabrina's Song. Milton. *Fr.* Comus; a Masque Presented at Ludlow Castle. FHYEP; NOSC; OAEL-1

By the sad waters of separation. Exile. Ernest Dowson. BoLoP

By the Saltings. Ted Walker. NYBP

By the sandy water I breathe in the odor of the sea. The Wind Blows from the Sea. *Unknown, tr. fr. Papago Indian by* Frances Densmore. ArNa

By the Sea. Emily Dickinson. *See* I started early — took my dog.

By the Sea. Richard Watson Dixon. OBNC

By the Sea. Christina Rossetti. BoNaP; NOBVV

By the sea's side hear the dark-vowelled birds. (*LL*) Especially When the October Wind. Dylan Thomas. AngWe; LiTB; MeMBP; MoAB; MoBrPo; OBWVE; OxAEP-2; OxBTC

By the season and life goes finish. (*LL*) New Guinea Time. Louis Johnson. PeNZ

By the shores of Gitche [*or* Gitchee] Gumee. Longfellow. *Fr.* Song of Hiawatha, The. EBEvV; FaPON; WBLP
(At the door on summer evenings.) BoTP
(Downward through the evening twilight.) FaBV
(Hiawatha's Childhood.) FaPoB; PFP

By the side of a green stagnate pool. George Alexander Stevens. CoMu; ErPo

By the smell of the orange trees. (*LL*) Distant Children. Cole Swenson. UTF

By the Statue of King Charles [*or* I] at Charing Cross. Lionel Johnson. FaBoEH; FaBoRV; MoBrPo; NOBE; OBEV; OBMV; OBNC; PeVV; PoEL-5

By the Stream. Wilhelm Müller, *tr. fr. German by* Philip L. Miller. *Fr.* Winter's Journey, The. RiWo

By the time. Betony. Mary Mackey. SRLS

By the time the priest started into his sermon. The Divorce Referendum, Ireland, 1986. Paul Durcan. BiHa; PBCIP

By the time you read this. Letter. W. S. Merwin. HAP

By the time you swear you're his. Unfortunate Coincidence. Dorothy Parker. BXAP; FaBoUs; NoP

By the trime we reach the shore it seems as though the Fith / Month were Autumn. (*LL*) The Excursion. Tu Fu. AWP, *tr. by* Amy Lowell *and* Florence Ayscough

By the troubled ghosts who haunt it. (*LL*) Deep Night. Yuan Chi. OHMPC

By the twilight. Some Scandal That Has Floated Down from Higher Circles. Anthony Barnett. VaA

By the Waterfall. Friedrich Adler, tr. fr. German by Jethro Bithell. TrJP

By the Waters of Babylon. Heine, tr. fr. German by Charles Godfrey Leland. Fr. Hebrew Melodies. TrJP

By the Waters of Babylon. Emma Lazarus. WPE
Sels.
Currents.
Exodus (August 3, 1492), The.

By the waters of Babylon we sat down and wept. Super Flumina Babylonis. Swinburne. PoEL-5

By the Waters of the Sava. Uri Zvi Greenberg, tr. fr. Hebrew by Ruth Finer Mintz. MHP

By the wayside, three crows sat on a cross. Adam on His Way Home. Robert Pack. ErPo

By the well in front of the gate. The Linden Tree. Wilhelm Müller, tr. fr. German by Philip L. Miller. Fr. Winter's Journey, The. RiWo

By the wells. Zippora Returns to Moses at Rephidim. Rose Drachler. BCF

By the West Pavilion, on a thousand feet of cliff. Midnight. Tu Fu, tr. fr. Chinese by A. C. Graham. PLT

By the wireless I can hear. Wireless. Rodney Bennett. BoTP

By the women of Marblehead! (LL) Skipper Ireson's Ride. Whittier. AnAmPo; BeLS; NOBA; OBAL; OBCA; OxBA; PAH; PoLF

By thee, thee, only thee. (LL) Thee, Thee, Only Thee. Thomas Moore. GBL; OBNC

By Themis & the wine that made me tipsy. Phanias, tr. fr. Greek by Thomas Meyer. GrAn

By themselves in the twilight. Leonidas, tr. fr. Greek by Kenneth Rexroth. PGA

By these, by these same chains, O Rome. Alcuin, tr. fr. Latin by Helen Waddell. MLL

By these old memories and these old shadows. (LL) At Rundane. Aasmund Olavsen Vinje. RiWo

By thine own named town made famous in thy fall. Michael Drayton. Fr. Polyolbion. NOSC

By this cold shuddering fit of fear. The Glen of Silence. "Hugh MacDiarmid." CMoP

By this he knew she wept with waking eyes. George Meredith. Fr. Modern Love. EnLoPo; EnVR; NAEL-2; NOBVV; NoP; OAEL-2; OHCV; OxBM; PoE; PoEL-5; Son
(End of Love, The.) HoPM

By this, Leander, being near the land. Christopher Marlowe. Fr. Hero and Leander. AAS; EBEV; ErPo; NoP

By this mass of death; unable to follow its vast progression. (LL) The Coral Reef. John Blight. NOBAu

By this [or thys] fire [or fyre] I warm[e] my handes [or handys]. Unknown. MiEL
(Months, The.) ChTr

By this single creek. (LL) Cascadilla Falls. A. R. Ammons. NOBA

By this the Northerne wagoner had set. Spenser. Fr. Faerie Queene, The. FHYEP; NoSic

By this the sun had sucked up the vast deep. Michael Drayton. Fr. Noah's Flood. NOSC

By this, though deep the evening fell. Battle, The ("By this, though deep the evening fell.") Sir Walter Scott. Fr. Marmion. PoEL-4

By this time had they reached the Stygian pool. Ben Jonson. Fr. On the Famous Voyage. NOSC

By this time long-gowned Lumen walked abroad. William Rankins. Fr. Satyrus Peregrinans. OBSV

By those soft tods of wool[l]. A Conjuration, to Electra. Robert Herrick. GBL; PoEL-3

By those true tears y'are weeping. (LL) To a Gentlewoman Objecting to Him His Grey Hairs. Robert Herrick. BeJo; CaPo; JCP

By Timo's locks. Meleager, tr. fr. Greek by Peter Whigham. GrAn

By T'ing Yang Waterfall. Hsieh Ling-yün, tr. fr. Chinese by Kenneth Rexroth. OHMPC

By Tre, Pol and Pen. Cornishmen. Unknown. FaBoUs

By tucking her chin in toward her chest, she can look up darkly through. Love: Shyness. C. K. Williams. CBLP

By two black eyes my heart was won. Unknown. FaBoCo

By unnumbered ways of dream to death. (LL) Immortality. "Æ." AWP; OBMV; TIRV; WGRP

By Vows of Love Together Bound. Eleazar Thompson Fitch. AH

By Sir W. R. Which He Writ the Night Before His Execution. Sir Walter Ralegh. See Even such is time, that takes in trust.

By Wauchopeside. "Hugh MacDiarmid." EBEV; OxAEP-2

By way of impress, all my future moan. (LL) Affliction ("Kill me not every day.") George Herbert. NOSC; TEP

By Way of Preface. Edward Lear. See How Pleasant to Know Mr. Lear.

By way of pretext. Yakamochi, tr. by Arthur Waley. Fr. Manyo Shu, Part 1 of 4. AWP

By ways remote and distant waters sped. On the Burial of His Brother. Catullus, tr. fr. Greek by Aubrey Beardsley. AWP; IMW

By west, under a wilde wode-side. Unknown. MiEL

By what appalling dim upheaval. Simon Gerty. Elinor Wylie. OBAL

By what miracle. Judith Morley. EaPr

By what right do they call Zeus a lover? Palladas, tr. fr. Greek by Sam Hamill. InMo

By what sends. Children's Rhymes. Langston Hughes. BPo

By who knew enough to save for something. The Black Hose. Bruce Weigl. NAmP90

By World Laid Low. Unknown, tr. fr. Irish. ChTr

By Yangtse and Han, a stranger who thinks of home. Yangtse and Han. Tu Fu, tr. fr. Chinese by A. C. Graham. PLT

By Yangtse and Han the mountains pile their barriers. At the Corner of the World. Tu Fu, tr. fr. Chinese by A. C. Graham. PLT

By yellow Chame, where all the Muses reign. Cambridge and the Cam. Phineas Fletcher. Fr. Apollyonists, The. FaBoPP

By younde the Brugge on thi right hand. The Way to Jerusalem. Unknown. OBTV

By your breasts. Conversation between the Chevalier de Chamilly and Mariana Alcoforado in the Manner of a Song of Regret. Unknown, tr. fr. Portuguese by Helen R. Lane. BoWoP

By your unnumbered charities. Hospital for Defectives. Thomas Blackburn. GTBS-P; OxBTC

Bye, baby bunting. Mother Goose. OxNR; ReMoGo

Bye, bye, baby bunting/ Your daddy's gone a-hunting. Unknown. OxNR

Bye Bye Blackbird. John James. VaA

Byelorussia, sels. Moishe Kulbak, tr. fr. Yiddish by Leonard Wolf.

By'm By. Unknown. AS

B'york! but it's lovely under the leaf. Spring Song. Donald Finkel. NYBP

Byrnies, The. Thom Gunn. MoP; NoAM; OxBTC

Byron. J. Gordon Coogler. OBAL

Byron. Lucretia Davidson. AmWP

Byron, sels. Joaquin Miller.
In Men Whom Men Condemn as Ill. PoLF

Byron and Shelley and Keats. The Lives and Times of John Keats, Percy Bysshe Shelley, and George Gordon Noel, Lord Byron. Dorothy Parker. Fr. Pig's-Eye View of Literature, A. NALW

Byron, how sweetly sad thy melody. To Lord Byron. Keats. EPCY

Byron Recollected at Bologna. Samuel Rogers. Fr. Italy. OBNC

Byron's Oak at Newstead Abbey. Timothy Thomas Fortune. AAP

By's beard the Goat, by his bush-tail the Fox. Of Kate's Baldness. John Davies of Hereford. FaBoEE

Bystander, The. Rosemary Dobson. CBAP; Mes

Bytuene [or Bytwene or Betwene or Bitwene or Bitweene] Mersh [or March or Mershe] and [or ant] Averil [or April]. Alison. Unknown. CBLP; MeEL; MiEL; NAEL-1; NoP; OAEL-1; OBEV; PeLV

Byzantium. W. B. Yeats. CMoP; EBEV; FaBoMo; HAP; InPS; LiTM; MeMBP; MoAB; MoBrPo; MoP; NAEL-2; NAWM-2; NIP; NoAM; NOBE; NoP; OAEL-2; OxBTC; PoE; Poetr; PPP; TEP

C

C — — e, whom providence hath placed. To the Hon. Mrs. C — — e. Jane West. ECWP

C. & W. Michael Hofmann. SCBI

C. C. Rider. Unknown. AS

C. G. Jung's "First Years." Thomas Kinsella. IPY

C. L. M. John Masefield. LiTM; MoBrPo; OxBTC

C Major of this life, The: so, now I will try to sleep. (LL) Abt Vogler. Robert Browning. FHYEP; NAEL-2; OAEL-2; TOF; WGRP

C Stands for Civilization. Kenneth Fearing. TrJP

Ca' the Yowes. Burns. EnRP

Ca' the Yowes to the Knowes. Isobel Pagan. OBEV; OxAEP-1

Ca' the Yowes to the Knowes. Unknown. OxBS

Cabal at Nickey Nackey's, The. Aphra Behn. NOSC

Cabaret. Sterling A. Brown. Jaz

Cabbage. Rosemary Norman. BrRo

Cabin-Boy, The. George Villiers. NOSC

Cabin Creek Flood, The. Unknown. AmFP

Cabin in Minnesota, A. Marvin Bell. HoPM

Cabin North of It All, The. James McMichael. AmPA

Cabin Site, Christmas Island, N.S. Martin Edmunds. UTF

Caledonia. Anthony Powell. NOBL

Calendar. Cecil Bodker, *tr. fr. Danish* by Nadia Christensen *and* Alexander Taylor. BoWoP

Calendar of Oengus, The, *sels. Unknown.* "This sad world we inhabit." NOIV

Calendar Rhyme. Flora Willis Watson. BoTP

Calendars. Wilma Elizabeth McDaniel. ETG

Calenture. Alastair Reid. NYBP; PrIm

Calf-Path, The. Sam Walter Foss. PoLF

Caliban in the Coal Mines. Louis Untermeyer. MoAmPo; PDV; TrJP

Caliban upon Setebos; or, Natural Theology in the Island. Robert Browning. AWP; EBEV; EnVR; FHYEP; NAEL-2; NOBVV; NoP; OAEL-2; OxAEP-2; PeVV; WGRP

Calico-pale paddocks through the window, The. Song for Past Midnight. Geoffrey Lehmann. CBAP

Calico Pie. Edward Lear. FaBoCh; FaPON; NTP; PYC; TrGrPo

California. Gerald Locklin. NGP

California. Lydia Huntley Sigourney. PAH

California. *Unknown.* AS

California Crack, The. Wanda Coleman. NGP

California Dreaming. Charles Wright. CAPP

California Hills in August. Dana Gioia. DiPo; InPK

California Oaks, The. Yvor Winters. GOA

California Peninsula: El Camino Real. Al Young. NGP

California Phrasebook, The. Dennis Schmitz. AmPA

California Quail in January. Will C. Jumper. GrPl

California song, A. Song of the Redwood-Tree. Walt Whitman. AmPP

California Sonnets: Night Sequence. Robert Vasquez. AfAz

California Winter, *sels.* Karl Shapiro.

California Winter. Karl Shapiro. AiP

Californian, The. *Unknown.* AmFP

Californian, The. *Unknown.* AmFP

Californians, The. Theodore Spencer. NYBP

Caliph shot a gazelle, The. Humorous Verse. Abu Dolama, *tr. fr. Arabic* by Raoul Abdul. TTY

Calisto, *sels.* John Crowne. "Kind lovers, love on." InvP; OxBSP

Call. Sebastian Barry. IB

Call, The. John Hall. MeLP; NOSC

Call, The. Dennis Haskell. NOBAu

Call. Audre Lorde. SRLS

Call, The. Charlotte Mew. CoGr

Call, The. Thomas Osbert Mordaunt, *formerly at. to* Scott. *See* Sound, Sound the Clarion.

Call, The. *At. to* Thomas Osbert Mordaunt. *See* Sound, Sound the Clarion.

Call, The. Jules Supervielle, *tr. fr. French* by Geoffrey Gardner. NU

Call, The. *Unknown.* OBEV

Call, A. Thomas Holley Chivers. Poetr

"Call All." *Unknown.* PAH

Call all hands to man the capstan, see the cable is all clear. Rolling Home. *Unknown.* OxBSS

Call alligator long-mouth. Don't Call Alligator Long-Mouth till You Cross River. John Agard. OBAP

Call and assemble together Aotearoa. Call Together. Kohine Whakarua Ponika, *tr. fr. Maori* by Sam Karetu. PeNZ

Call — call — and bruise the air. Expression. Isaac Rosenberg. MoBrPo

Call down the hawk from the air. The Hawk. W. B. Yeats. PoA

Call dumbly on gulls, on incoming tides. *(LL)* Bad Run at King's Rest. Douglas Livingstone. PeSAV

Call for more pens, more paper, and more ink. *(LL)* Cacoëthes Scribendi. Oliver Wendell Holmes. NBLV

Call for the Robin-Redbreast and the Wren. John Webster. *Fr.* White Devil, The. ChTr; EBEV; FaBoCh; HAP; NoP; NOSC; OxAEP-1; PoEL-2; PoRA; PrIm; RB; SCGP; TFi

Call him drunken Ira Hayes, he won't answer any more. Ballad of Ira Hayes. Peter La Farge. MAT

Call Him the Lover and call me the Bride. The Song the Body Dreamed in the Spirit's Mad Behest. William Everson. ErPo

Call in the Midst of the Crowd, A, *sels.* Alfred Corn. Fire: The People. NAAL-2; VCAP

Call is for belief, The. The Fundament Is Shifted. Abbie Huston Evans. NYBP

Call It a Good Marriage. Robert Graves. BoLoP; OxBM

Call it a louse — I'm. Cid Corman. VGW

Call it neither love nor spring madness. Without Name. Pauli Murray. PoBA; PoNe

Call it not vain; they do not err. The Minstrel Responds to Flattery. Sir Walter Scott. *Fr.* Lay of the Last Minstrel, The. OBNC

(Nature's Sympathy with the Poet.) OxAEP-2

Call it our craziness even. Roots. Lucille Clifton. CAPP

Call Martha Corey. The Trial. Longfellow. *Fr.* Giles Corey of the Salem Farms. PAH

Call me bad when me start walk de streets. Eighties, De. Frederick Williams. PBCV

Call me no more. His Lachrimae or Mirth, Turn'd to Mourning. Robert Herrick. SeCV-1

Call me no more, O gentle stream. To a River in the South. Sir Henry Newbolt. CH

Call Me Not Back from the Echoless Shore. *Unknown.* BLPA

Call Me Not Dead. Richard Watson Gilder. WGRP

Call me not false, beloved. The Bridegroom. Kipling. *Fr.* Epitaphs of the War, 1914–1918. FaBoEE; NoP; OBWP

Call me Polyxena, the wife of Archelaus. Dioscorides, *tr. fr. Greek* by Barbara Hughes Fowler. *Fr.* Epigrams. HePo

Call me to the one among your moments. Rainer Maria Rilke, *tr. fr. German. Fr.* Sonnets to Orpheus. EnlH, *tr.* by Stephen Mitchell

Call me Zamboni. Nights my job is hockey. Rink Keeper's Sestina. George Draper. PrIm

Call my name. *(LL)* Disappeared Woman I. Marjorie Agosin. LoHo

Call my spirit to the fields above? *(LL)* The Song of Fionnuala. Thomas Moore. BIrV

Call not thy wanderer home as yet. Germinal. "Æ." BIrV; MoBrPo; OBEV; OBMV

Call of Aristippus, The, *sels.* John Gilbert Cooper. Elves and Fairies. ECEV

Call of Nature, The. Tony Harrison. NoAM

Call of the Air, The. Day Jeffery. NSI

Call of the Bugles, The. Richard Hovey. AnAmPo

Call of the Christian, The. Whittier. NOCV

Call of the River Nun, The. Gabriel Okara. PBA

Call out the colored girls. For the Record. Audre Lorde. LoHo

Call the cows home! Thunder. Walter de la Mare. BoNaP

Call the Horse, Marrow. *Unknown.* OBET

Call the roller of big cigars. The Emperor of Ice-Cream. Wallace Stevens. AmPP; AnAmPo; CBNP; CMoP; FaBoMo; FF; HAP; HCAP; HeIP; InPK; LiTA; MeMAP; MoP; NAAL-2; NAWM-2; NIP; NoAM; NOBA; OPOP; OxBA; PoE; Poetr; TAP; TFi; TRP; WeW

Call the seller of used cars. Sunday Service. Michael Heffernan. BXAP

Call Them Back. Chris Petrakos. GOYP

Call to Action, A. Ch'iu Chin, *tr. fr. Chinese* by Kenneth Rexroth *and* Ling Chung. PBWP; WPC

Call to Action, A. Charles Hamilton Sorley. NSI

Call to Arms. Lu Hsun, *tr. fr. Chinese* by William R. Schultz. SuSp

Call to Arms, A. Mary Raymond Shipman Andrews. PAH

Call to Pentecost, A. Inez M. Tyler. BLRP

Call to the Colors, The. Arthur Guiterman. PAH

Call to the Strong, The. William Pierson Merrill. BLRP

Call Together. Kohine Whakarua Ponika, *tr. fr. Maori* by Sam Karetu. PeNZ

Callaloo. Merle Collins. NBrP

Called across water then it is over. *(LL)* Elegy for My Sister. Howard Moss. VCAP

Called Back. Emily Dickinson. *See* Just lost, when I was saved!

Called out by the clap of the thunder. *(LL)* The Hag. Robert Herrick. BeJo; CaPo; FaBoCh; WiR

Called out on Christmas Eve for a working-party. Devil on Ice. Donald Davie. NoAM

Called Oysters. Robert Fergusson. ScCV

Called Proud. Walter Savage Landor. GBL

Called the "Hiawatha's brothers." *(LL)* Hiawatha's Brothers. Longfellow. BoTP

Caller Herrin. Lady Nairne. OxBS; ScCV; WoRP

Caller rain frae abune. Douglas Young. OBVE

Callicles' Song. Matthew Arnold. *See* Through the black, rushing smoke-burst.

Calligram, 15 May 1915. Guillaume Apollinaire, *tr. fr. French by* O. Bernard. OBWP

Calling. Alma Villanueva. SRLS

Calling all black people, come in, black people, come/ on in. *(LL)* SOS. Amiri Baraka. BPo; PoBA

Calling all butterflies of every race. From a Milkweed Pod. Robert Frost. (Pod of the Milkweed.) LiTM

Calling, and Correcting. Robert Herrick. BeJo

Calling black people. SOS. Amiri Baraka. BPo; PoBA

Calling Dreams. Georgia Douglas Johnson. ShDr

Calling Lucasta from Her Retirement. Richard Lovelace. CaPo

Calling my eyes back from the sea. The Axehandle. Robert Wells. SCBI

Calling of Jerusalem, The. Julia Vinograd. BCF

Calling on a Taoist Priest in Tai-t'ien Mountain but Failing to See Him. Li Po, *tr. fr. Chinese* by Joseph J. Lee. SuSp

Calling on all. *(LL)* A Robin. Walter de la Mare. ChTr; CMoP; FaBoRV

Calling on Peadar O'Donnell at Dungloe. John Hewitt. CIP

Calling One's Own. *Unknown, tr. fr. Ojibwa Indian* by Charles Fenno Hoffman. AnAmPo

Calling Spring VII-MMMC. Ogden Nash. FaBoCo

Calling the Doctor (1000 A.D.). Nizami Arudi, *tr. fr. Persian* by Omar S. Pound. ArPe

Calling the Roll. Nathaniel Graham Shepherd. *See* "Corporal Green!" the orderly cried.

Calling to mind[e], mine eie long went about [*or* my eyes went long about]. The Excuse. Sir Walter Ralegh. AAS; SiPS; SiPSBD

Calling to [my] mind [*or* minde] since first my love begun. Michael Drayton. *Fr.* Idea. EnRePo; ESo; NOBE; PoEL-2; SCGP

Calling to you Honey I'm home. *(LL)* This Is a Poem for the Dead. Michael Ryan. AmPA

Calling Trains. *Unknown.* AmFP

Calling Your Name in the Zoo, sels. Hugo Williams.

Calliope. *Unknown.* AS

Calliope in the Labour Ward. Elaine Feinstein. BrRo

Calliope's Nymph Brings the Poet to the Palace to Honour. Gawin Douglas. *Fr.* Palace [*or* Palice] of Honor [*or* Honour], The. OxBLMV

Callipaedia; or, The Art of Getting Beautiful Children. Claude Quillet, *tr. fr. Latin* by George Sewell. FaBoUs
Sels.
"Beneath those parts, where stretching to its bound." ECEV
Best Time for Conception, The.
How to Conceive Boys.

Calls through the valleys of Hall. *(LL)* Song of the Chattahoochee. Sidney Lanier. AnAmPo; BoNaP; FaBoBe; FaBV; LiTA

Calm, The. Langston Hughes. *See* Calm, The/ Cool face.

Calm as that second summer which precedes. Charleston. Henry Timrod. AmPP; AnAmPo; NOBA; OxBA; PAH; TAP

Calm, The/ Cool face. Suicide's Note. Langston Hughes. CDC
(Calm, The.) SAmP

Calm down, my sorrow, we must move with care. Meditation. Baudelaire, *tr. fr. French* by Robert Lowell. InPK; NAWM-2

Calm garden. French Garden. Léopold Sédar Senghor, *tr. fr. French* by Ellen Conroy Kennedy. NegPo

Calm hair, meandering in pellucid gold. *(LL)* On Seeing a Hair of Lucretia Borgia. Walter Savage Landor. HAP; WeW

Calm in the twilight. Muted. Paul Verlaine, *tr. fr. French* by Philip L. Miller. RiWo

Calm is all nature as a resting wheel. Written in Very Early Youth. Wordsworth. EnRP

Calm is the landscape when the storm has passed. Peace in the Welsh Hills. Vernon Watkins. GTBS-P; OxBTC

Calm is the morn without a sound. Tennyson. *Fr.* In Memoriam A. H. H. ChTr; EBEV; EBVV, *abr.*; ELP; EnVR; FaBoRV; FHYEP; HeIP; LiTB; NOBE; NoP; OAEL-2, *abr.*; OBNC; PeECV, *abr.*; PlP; PoEL-5; TrGrPo
(Lincolnshire Wolds and Lincolnshire Sea.) FaBoPP

Calm martyr of a noble cause. Jefferson Davis. Walker Meriwether Bell. PAH

Calm on the bosom of thy God. Felicia Dorothea Hemans. *Fr.* Siege of Valencia, The. OBEV
(Dirge, A ("Calm on the bosom of thy God").) WoRP

Calm, on the Listening Ear of Night. Edmund Hamilton Sears. AH

Calm Soul of All Things! [Make It Mine]. Matthew Arnold. *Fr.* Lines Written in Kensington Gardens. FaBoPP; FHYEP; TrPWD; WGRP

Calm thou mayst smile, when all around thee weep. *(LL)* On parent knees, a naked new-born child. Sir William Jones, *after the Sanskrit of* Kalidasa. FaBoEE; OBEV

Calm was the day, and through the trembling air. Spenser. *Fr.* Prothalamion. AAS; AWP; ChTr; EBEV; EBEvV, (*Pts.* I *and* II *only*); EIL; EnRePo; FaBoPP; GTBS; GTBS-P; HAP; ImPo; LiTB; Mes; NoP; NoSic; OBEV; PPP; SCGP; TFi
(Calme was the day, and through the trembling ayre.) OxAEP-1

Calm was the even, and clear [*or* cleer] was the sky. Dryden. *Fr.* Evening's Love, An. FF; SeCV-2

Calm was the evening and clear was the sky. Amintas and Claudia; or, The Merry Shepherdess. *Unknown.* CoMu

Calm Winter Sleep. Hilary Corke. NYBP

Calm[e], The. John Donne. NoSic

Calme was the day, and through the trembling ayre. Spenser. *See* Calm was the day, and through the trembling air.

Calmest joy she'll yield to thee. *(LL)* Fancy and Imagination. H. Cordelia Ray. CBWP-3

Calmest Thoughts, The. Keats. *See* After Dark Vapours.

Calmly beside her tropic strand. Charleston. Paul Hamilton Hayne. PAH

Calmly in the twilight made. Muted. Paul Verlaine, *tr. fr. French* by C. F. MacIntyre. UnAS

Calmly We Walk Through This April's Day. Delmore Schwartz. *Fr.* Repetitive Heart, The. LiTM; PrIm

Caltrop leaves tug on the waves, the lotus quivers in the wind. Lotus-gatherer's Song. Po Chü-i, *tr. fr. Chinese* by Irving Y. Lo. SuSp

Calvary. Padraig de Brun, *tr. fr. Irish* by Máire Mhac an tSaoi. TIRV

Calvary. E. A. Robinson. MoAmPo; Son; WGRP

Calvary. Libby Stopple. GoYe

Calvary. *Unknown.* AH

Calvary. W. B. Yeats. PeECV

Calvary and Easter. "Susan Coolidge." WBLP

Calverly's. E. A. Robinson. NoAM

Calvinist Sang. Alexander Scott. OxBS

Calv'ry's tragedy is ended. The Empty Tomb. Clara Ann Thompson. CBWP-2

Calvus to a Fly. Charles Tennyson Turner. FM; NOBVV

Calypso. W. H. Auden. CBLP; PeLV

Calypso/ Is a bit of a dipso. Forever Ambrosia. Christopher Morley. OBAL

Calypsomania. Anthony Brode. FiBHP; PeLV

Calypso's Island. Archibald MacLeish. MoAB; NoP

Calypso's Song to Ulyssess. Adrian Mitchell. GBL

Calyx of the Oboe Breaks, The. Conrad Aiken. NYBP

Cam' Ye By [the Salmon Fishers]. *Unknown.* CH; GBP

Camberwell Clerkenwell Muswell a haze. The Remembered City. Ken Smith. *Fr.* As It Happens. PWE

Cambodia. James Fenton. SCBI

Cambria, sels. John Davies of Hereford.
"Great Grandame Wales, from whom those ancestors." AngWe

Cambrian, sels. Eeva-Liisa Manner, *tr. fr. Finnish* by Jaakko A. Ahokas.
"If they wanted freedom." PBWP
"To move over shifting borders." PBWP
"Turn the page of stone and smoke." PBWP

Cambrian Swain, The. Edward Davies. *Fr.* Chepstow: A Poem. OBWVE

Cambridge. John James. NBrP

Cambridge and the Alps. Wordsworth. *Fr.* Prelude [*or*, Growth of a Poet's Mind], The. EnRP; OAEL-2; PoEL-2; PoEL-5

Cambridge and the Cam. Phineas Fletcher. *Fr.* Apollyonists, The. FaBoPP

Cambridge Elegy. Sharon Olds. IMW

Cambridge Ladies Who Live in Furnished Souls, The. E. E. Cummings. *Fr.* Sonnets — Realities. AmPP; HeIL; HeIP; MoP; NAAL-2; NoAM; NOBA; NoP; OBAL; OxBA; Poetr; TAP

Cambridge Songs, sels. *Unknown, tr. fr. Latin* by Willis Barnstone.
"Wind is thin." BoWoP

Camden, most reverend head, to whom I owe. To William Camden. Ben Jonson. AWP; BeJo; JCP; NAEL-1; NOSC; SeCV-1

Camden's Remains. *Unknown.* OtMeF

Came a stranger late among us. In Memory of James M. Rathel. Josephine D. Henderson Heard. CBWP-4

Came back untouch'd. This man hath travail'd well. *(LL)* To William Roe. Ben Jonson. NOSC; OAEL-1; SeCV-1

Came back untouched. This man hath travelled well. *(LL)* To William Roe. Ben Jonson. BeJo; OAEL-1

Came fresh transfigurings of freshest blue. *(LL)* Sea Surface Full of Clouds. Wallace Stevens. AmPP; CMoP; MoAB; MoAmPo; VGW

Came in my full youth to the midnight cave. Ajanta. Muriel Rukeyser. LiTA; LiTM; MoAB; MoAmPo; NNaP

Came of eating too freely of cake. *(LL)* A Quadrupedremian Song. Thomas Hood. FaBoNo

Came riding on a nanny goat, selling of pigstails. *(LL)* Shon a Morgan. *Unknown.* GBP; OxNR

Came the morning of that day. Sumter. Edmund Clarence Stedman. PAH

Came to lakes; came to dead water. A Field of Light. Theodore Roethke. LiTM; TwCP

Came to me. Rudaki, *tr. fr. Persian* by Basil Bunting. BoLoP; OBVE

Came to my side, and put down his head in love. *(LL)* The Dream. Louise Bogan. InPK; LiTA; LiTM; MAT; MoAB; MoAmPo; NALW; NoAM

Came You Not from Newcastle. *Unknown.* GBP

Camel. Laila Akhyaliyya, *tr. fr. Arabic* by Willis Barnstone. BoWoP

Camel, The. Carmen Bernos de Gasztold, *tr. by* Rumer Godden. OBAP

Camel, The. Ogden Nash. SiSoPo

Camel and plow. The sharp blade. Tiller of the Soil. Avraham Shlonsky, *tr. fr. Hebrew* by Ruth Finer Mintz. MHP

Camel at the close of day, The. The Kneeling Camel. Anna Temple Whitney. BLPA
(Submission and Rest.) BLRP

Camel has a single hump, The. The Camel. Ogden Nash. SiSoPo

Camel-Rider, The. *Unknown, tr. fr. Arabic by* Wilfrid Scawen Blunt. AWP

Cameleopard, The. Hilaire Belloc. FaBoNo

Camel's Complaint, The. Charles Edward Carryl. *See* Canary-birds feed on sugar and seed.

Camel's hump is an ugly lump, The. The Hump. Kipling. *Fr.* Just-So Stories. OxBChV

Camels in Persia. Dorothy Wellesley. OBTV

Camels of the Kings. Leslie Norris. *See* Camels, the Kings' Camel, The.

Camels, the Kings' Camel, The. Leslie Norris. PChr

Cameo. David Chaloner. VaA

Cameo, The. Edna St. Vincent Millay. FYAP; LiTA; MeMAP; MoAmPo; UnPo; WPE

Cameo No. II. June Jordan. BPo

Cameos. Rita Dove. NAmP90

Camera. Ted Kooser. Poetsp

Camera angles. Drear lighting. Mediatrix. David Haynes. NBrP

Camera at the crossing sees the city. Gauley Bridge. Muriel Rukeyser. NNaP

Camera Obscura, The. John Addington Symonds. NOBVV

Camerados. Bayard Taylor. AnAmPo; UnPo

Cameroon. (*LL*) My Country. Elolongue Epanya Yondo. NegPo

Camões, alone, of all the lyric race. Luis de Camões. Roy Campbell. FaBoTw; OxAEP-2; PeSA

Camoes and the Debt. Sophia de Mello Breyner Andresen, *tr. fr. Portuguese by* Willis Barnstone *and* Nelson Cerqueira. BoWoP

Camouflaged, they detach lengths of sea and sky. Destroyers in the Arctic. Alan Ross. PAW; PoWW

Camouflaged Troop-Ship. Amy Lowell. AiP

Camp in the Prussian Forest, A. Randall Jarrell. BTR; CMoP; MoAmPo; OBWP; OxBC; PoWW

Camp Notes. Mitsuye Yamada. WPOW
Sels.
In the Outhouse
On the Bus

Camp of Souls, The. Isabella Valancy Crawford. NOBC

Camp quiet again. (*LL*) Kilaben Bay Song. *Unknown.* NOBAu

Camp Site. Denis Glover. *Fr.* Arawata Bill. PeNZ

Campaign, The, *sels.* Joseph Addison.
"But O, my Muse, what numbers wilt thou find." FaBoEH
(Poem to His Grace the Duke of Marlborough, A.) OBWP

Campaign. Ciaran Carson. BiHa; CIP; PNI; PWE

Campaign, The. Josephine Miles. WPE

Campesinos bend in the 115 degree heat. The Sustenance. Ray Gonzáles. AfAz

Campesino's Lament, The. Judith Ortiz Cofer. AfAz

Campfire Extinguished. Raymond Roseliep. InPK; SM

Campground. Elliot Fried. NGP

Campi Flegrei. Barend Toerien, *tr. fr. Afrikaans by the author.* PeSA

Campidoglio. Robert Garioch, *after* Giuseppe Belli. OBVE

Camping Out. William Empson. CMoP; FaBoMo; OxBTC

Camping Out on Rainy Mountain. Jim Barnes. CDW

Camping Provencial. Notices: (1). Peter Reading. *Fr.* Travelogue. PeLV

Campion white, The. The Lamp Flower. Margaret Cecilia Furse. BoTP

Camps held their distance of brown chestnuts and grey smoke, The. Derek Walcott. *Fr.* Midsummer. BTR

Camptown Races, The. Stephen Collins Foster. AnAmPo

Campus, The. David Posner. NYBP

Campus on the Hill, The. W. D. Snodgrass. AiP; LiTM; NoAM; PRA; TAP; TwCP

Can again be written in beads. (*LL*) The Sleep of My Lions. Douglas Livingstone. PeSAV

Can America be reckoned as the country of the free? The Negro Ballot. L. A. J. Moorer. CBWP-3

Can any good thing come to God out of poor Nazareth? (*LL*) The Divine Office of the Kitchen. Cecily Hallack. PoLF

Can be brought forth by tears. (*LL*) Like Melodies. Klaus Groth. RiWo

Can be heavenly. (*LL*) The Frog Prince. Stevie Smith. HAP; Mes; NTP

Can Bourbon or Nassau claim higher? (*LL*) On Himself. Matthew Prior. FaBoEE

Can bring sight to such reason. (*LL*) Canzone: Donna Mi Priegha. Cavalcanti. CTC

Can-Can. John Fuller. *Fr.* Fox-Trot. PeLV

Can centre both the worlds of Heaven and Hell. (*LL*) Stanzas ("Often rebuked, yet always back returning.") *At. to* Emily Brontë, *also at. to* Charlotte Brontë. LiTB; MeMBP; NOBVV; OAEL-2; OBNC; OHCV; PBWP; SCGP

Can come as often as he wants. (*LL*) Doesn't he realize/ that I am not/ like the swaying kelp. Ono no Komachi. BoWoP; WPJ; WPOW

Can fail to make reality its heart. (*LL*) Spring 1943. Roy Fuller. LiTB; LiTM

Can fan into a fire. (*LL*) Youth Sings a Song of Rosebuds. Countee Cullen. PoLF; PoNe

Can get across it if I try. (*LL*) I May, I Might, I Must. Marianne Moore. FaBoWP; FF; HeIL; OBAL; OxBSP

Can have heaven on earth. (*LL*) Mother, Father, God, Universal Power. Jo Poore. EaPr

Can he be fair that withers at a blast. Francis Quarles. *Fr.* Pentelogia. PeECV

Can. Hist. Earle Birney. OxBC

Can I easily say. Sisters. Adrienne Rich. IHMS

Can I explain this to you? Your eyes. The Knife. Keith Douglas. NoAM

Can I forget the sweet days that have been. Days That Have Been. W. H. Davies. AngWe; FaBoPP

Can I forget thee? No, while mem'ry lasts. On Parting with a Friend. Mary Weston Fordham. AmWP; CBWP-2

Can I go on loving anyone at fifty. The Book of Wisdom. Robert Lowell. ChIV-1

Can I not come to Thee, my God, for these. To His Ever-loving God. Robert Herrick. TrPWD

Can I not sin, but thou wilt be. To His Conscience. Robert Herrick. BeJo; ChIV-1; NAEL-1; NoP; PoEL-3

Can I not sing but "hoy." The Jolly Shepherd. *Unknown.* NOBE

Can — I — poet. For Some Poets. Mae Jackson. PoBA

Can I Say. Dolly Bird. WPOW

Can I see another's woe. On Another's Sorrow. Blake. *Fr.* Songs of Innocence. AWP; EnRP; FaBV; FHYEP; OxAEP-2; PoEL-4

Can I Tell You This Story, Or Will You Send Me through All Kinds of Changes? Larry Neal. BCF

Can I Tempt You to a Pond Walk? James Schuyler. PoA

Can I, who have for others oft compil'd. Of My Dear Son [*or* Deare Sonne], Gervase Beaumont. Sir John Beaumont. JCP; NOBE; PIP
(Of My Dear Son Gervaise.) IMW

Can imagine to be its ears. (*LL*) In Arizona. Louis Zukofsky. TRP

Can it be growing colder when I begin. Adrienne Rich. *Fr.* Twenty-one Love Poems. GLP; NAAL-2

Can it be urged to give what I can give? Elizabeth Barrett Browning. *Fr.* Sonnets from the Portuguese. CTC; OHCV; Son

Can it be true, that we can meet. Slumbering Passion. Josephine D. Henderson Heard. CBWP-4

Can keep my own away from me. (*LL*) Waiting. John Burroughs. AnAmPo; BLPA; FaBoBe; WGRP

Can Life Be a Blessing. Dryden. *Fr.* Troilus and Cressida.

Can life's best consciousness of joy. Questioning. H. Cordelia Ray. CBWP-3

Can. Lit. Earle Birney. NOBC

Can love be controlled by advice? John Gay. *Fr.* Beggar's Opera, The. OAEL-1; OxBSP

Can make a right Rose Tres." (*LL*) The Rose Tree. W. B. Yeats. CMoP; ELP; FaBoPV; OBMV

Can make me worthy of loving. (*LL*) Love Letter. W. H. Auden. CBLP

Can man forget this story? (*LL*) A Hymn [*or* Hymne] on the Nativity [*or* Nativitie] of My Saviour. Ben Jonson. BeJo; ChIV-2; SeCV-1; TrCP

Can never break, can never break in vain. (*LL*) Constancy. The Earl of Rochester. OBEV

Can never fail cuckolding two or three spouses. (*LL*) Two or Three; a Recipe [*or* Receipt] to Make a Cuckold. Pope. BoLoP; FaBoEE

Can nothing settle my uncertain breast. Galatians 6.14. Francis Quarles. ChIV-2

Can one be jealous of one's own kin? Psyche. Corneille, *tr. fr. French by* Philip L. Miller. RiWo

Can reach us here. (*LL*) Watercourse. Ruth Padel. VBLP

Can redwhite & blue I enter. Self World. Clarence Major. NBV

Can someone make my simple wish come true? Lonely Hearts. Wendy Cope. OBF

Can stand against the sea? (*LL*) The Tides Run up the Wairau. Eileen Duggan. PeNZ

Can the German language crack and snore and rumble, thunder. The German Language. Friedrich von Logau, *tr. fr. German.* GePo, *tr. by* George C. Schoolfield

Can the lover share his soul. W. J. Turner. OBMV

Can the Mole Take. C. Day Lewis. OBMV

Captain Kid's Farewell to the Seas; or, The Famous Pirate's Lament. *Unknown.* OxBSS

Captain Mansfield's Fight with the Turks at Sea. *Unknown.* OxBSS

Captain Molly. William Collins. ImGa

Captain of a Seventy-three, The. (*LL*) Little Billee. Thackeray. FaBoCh; FaBoCo; NOBL; OHCV; OxAEP-2; PlP

Captain of a Space Ship. Dermot Bolger. IB

Captain of the *Shannon* came sailing up the bay, The. *Shannon* and the *Chesapeake*, The. Thomas Tracy Bouvé. PAH

Captain, or colonel, or knight in arms. When the Assault Was Intended to the City. Milton. GTBS; GTBS-P; NoP; DCBMS; VGW
(Sonnet: "Captain or colonel or knight in arms.") OAEL-1; OxAEP-1

Captain Quiros and Mr William Lane. Terra Australis. Douglas Stewart. NOBAu

Captain Reece. W. S. Gilbert. FiBHP; GN

Captain said, Quack! Quack!, The. (*LL*) I saw a ship a-sailing. Mother Goose. FaBoBe; MoShBr; NTCP; OxNR; ReMoGo

Captain Spud and His First Mate, Spade. John Ciardi. OBCA

Captain Stood on the Carronade, The. Frederick Marryat. *Fr.* Snarleyyow; or, The Dog Fiend.

Captain Stood on the Carronade, The. The Captain Stood on the Carronade. Frederick Marryat. *Fr.* Snarleyyow; or, The Dog Fiend. (Old Navy, The.) VPP

Captain Stratton's Fancy. John Masefield. MoBrPo; OBEV

Captain Sword. Leigh Hunt. GN

Captain Ward and the *Rainbow*. *Unknown.* ESPB; OBET; OxBSS

Captain Wattle and Miss Roe. Charles Dibdin. OxBoLi

Captain! we often heretofore. To Our House-Dog Captain. Walter Savage Landor. PoEL-4

Captain Wedderburn's Courtship ("As I walked out one evening down by the Strawberry Lane.") *Unknown.* AmFP, (A and B vers.); ESPB, (A and B vers.)

Caption Block. David Chaloner. VaA

Captive. Rose Terry Cooke. AmWP

Captive. Peretz Hirshbein, *tr. fr. Yiddish by* Joseph Leftwich. TrJP

Captive, The. Pushkin, *tr. fr. Russian by* Philip L. Miller. RiWo

Captive. Marion Strobel. ErPo

Captive Dove, The. Anne Brontë. EBVV; OHCV; PlP

Captive Escaped in the Wilds of America. Addressed to the Honorable Mrs. O'Neill, The. Charlotte Smith. Son

Captive of Love. Ovid, *tr. by* Christopher Marlowe. *Fr.* Elegies. AWP

Captive of the White City, The. Ina Coolbrith. AmWP

Captive or king, it's all a matter of chance. The Temple of Hsiang Yü. Li Shan-fu, *tr. fr. Chinese by* Irving Y. Lo. SuSp

Captive Ships at Manila, The. Dorothy Paul. PAH

Captive Stone, The. Jim Barnes. CDW

Captived Bee; or, The Little Filcher, The. Robert Herrick. CaPo

Captive's Hymn, The. Edna Dean Proctor. PAH

Captivity. Louise Erdrich. HATNAP; NoAM

Captivity, The, *sels.* Goldsmith.
O Memory, Thou Fond Deceiver'. OxBSS
(Memory.) OBEV

Captivity. Samuel Rogers. OBNC

Capture of Edwin Alonzo Boyd, The. Peter Miller. MoCV

Capture of Little York. *Unknown.* PAH

Caput apri refero. *Unknown.* MiEL
(Boar's Head Carol, The.) MeEL

Capystranus. *Unknown.* OxBLMV

Car Cemetery, The. Ciaran Carson. CIP

Car conveys us where we've been, The. Moving between Beloit and Monroe. Bink Noll. GrPl

Car dropped the pallid boy, The. The Pale Boy and the Old Woman. Rachel Blake. NWP

Car/ I give you over to. Car Wash. Myra Cohn Livingston. NTCP

Car is also, A/ a high-speed hermitage. Portrait of the Autist as a New World Driver. Les A. Murray. CBAP

Car is heavy with children, The. The Road Back. Anne Sexton. NYBP

Car je suis La Belle France. (*LL*) The Deodand. Anthony Hecht. DiPo; NoAM

Car Wash. Myra Cohn Livingston. NTCP

Caraguin, The, *sels.* Robert Dunbar.
"Angelica has gain'd the dell." PBCV

Carapace. Denise Levertov. PWE

Caravaggio Dying, Porto Ercole, July 1610, Aged 36, *sels.* Edward Lucie-Smith.
"My own head. Seen in mirrors. Cleanly axed." PeHV

Caravan. Michael Longley. CIP; PNI

Caravan, The. Gwendolyn MacEwen. MoCV

Caravan, The. Madeleine Nightingale. BoTP

Caravans. Irene Thompson. BoTP

Caravans in the marram by the 17th green. Sarsaparilla. Matthew Sweeney. IB

Caravati's Junkyard. Elizabeth Morgan. GrPl

Carcassonne. Gustave Nadaud, *tr. fr. French by* John R. Thompson. BLPA; FaBoBe

Card comes to tell you, A. Non Piangere, Liù. Peter Porter. CBLP; FaBoMA; OxBC

Card-Players, The. Philip Larkin. OxBC

Card-Players, The. David Ray. VGW

Card table in the library stands ready, A. Lost in Translation. James Merrill. *Fr.* Book of Ephraim, The. FYAP; HCAP; LCAP; NAAL-2; NoAM; VCAP

Cardiff Castle., *sels.* Taliesin Williams.
"Tourist, as he views the place, The." AngWe

Cardinal Bembo's Epitaph on Raphael. Thomas Hardy, *after* Pietro Bembo. FaBoEE

Cardinal Ideograms. May Swenson. OBCA

Cardinal Newman. Christina Rossetti. NAEL-2

Cardinal Wolsey's Farewell. John Fletcher *and* William Shakespeare. *See* Farewell! A long farewell, to all my greatness!

Cardinals. John Engels. FoLa

Cardinal's Dog, The. John Glassco. MoCV

Cardplayers, The. Peter Fallon. PeIV

Cards and Kisses. John Lyly. *See* Cupid and my Campaspe played [*or* playd].

Care. Josephine Miles. NYBP

Care. Richard Murphy. IPY

Care and heavy thought weigh me down. Estat ai en greu cossirier. Beatrice, Countess de Die, *tr. fr. Provençal by* Paul Blackburn. ErPo

Care Away. *Unknown.* OxBoLi

Care away, away, away,/ Murninge away! *Unknown.* MiEL

Care Away ("Care away, away, away,/ Care away for evermore!") *Unknown.* MiEL; OxBoLi

Care-Charmer Sleep. Bartholomew Griffin. *See* Care-charmer sleepe, sweet ease in restles miserie.

Care-charmer sleep, son[ne] of the sable night. Samuel Daniel. *Fr.* To Delia. AAS; EnRePo; ESo; GTBS; GTBS-P; InPS; NAEL-1; NOBE; NoP; NoSic; SCGP; TFi; TrGrPo
(Care-Charmer Sleep.) ImPo; LiTB; NIP; OAEL-1; OxAEP-1; Son
(Sonnet: "Care-charmer sleep[e], son[ne] of the sable night.") ElL; PoEL-2

Care-charmer sleepe, sweet ease in restles miserie. Bartholomew Griffin. *Fr.* Fidessa, More Chaste than Kind[e]. ESo
(Care-Charmer Sleep.) AAS; NoSic; SCGP

Care-charming Sleep [Thou Easer of All Woes]. John Fletcher. *Fr.* Tragedy of Valentinian, The. ELP; FaBoRV; OxBSP; SCGP; TrGrPo

Care not for the place wherever it be. (*LL*) Mosque is the Earth, and as holy it is. Alamsaeen. EaPr

Care of Bees, The. Virgil, *tr. by* Dryden. *Fr.* Georgics. FaBoUs

Care thy father once bestowed on me, The. To My Nephew, J. B. Clement Barksdale. OxBSP

Careers. Amiri Baraka. TRP

Careers. Marjorie Welish. UL

Careful man I ought to be, A. The Little Chap Who Follows Me. *Unknown.* PoToHe

Careful: my knife drills your soul. The Killer. A'yunini, *tr. fr. Cherokee Indian by* Jerome K. Rothenberg. STP

Careful suburban dead turn their backs, The. Sacrificial Wolf. Anne Rouse. NWP

Careful[l] observers may foretell the hour. A Description of a City Shower. Swift. GGP; HeIP; MAT; NAEL-1; NOEC; NoP; OAEL-1; OBSV; PoE; PPP; TEP; UnPo
(City Shower, A.) SCGP

Carefully. Jean Pedrick. ETG

Carefully circumventing. Carefully. Jean Pedrick. ETG

Carefully she opened her tunic. The Breasts of Mnasidice. Pierre Louÿs, *tr. fr. French. Fr.* Chansons de Bilitis. PeHV

Careless Content. John Byrom. NOEC

Careless explorer named Blake, A. Ogden Nash. PeLi

Careless Gallant, The. Thomas Jordan. CoMu; HAP; OxBoLi

Careless Good Fellow, The. John Oldham. APAS; SeCV-2

Careless Love. *Unknown.* UnPo

Careless Love. *Unknown.* AS; UnPo

Careless old cook of Salt Ash, An. *Unknown.* PeLi

Careless Talk. Mark Hollis. FiBHP; NBLV

Careless Willie. *Unknown.* FaPON

Carelesse Nurse Mayd, The. Thomas Hood. FaBoNo

Carentan O Carentan. Louis Simpson. ArOW; CoAP; MoBS; NOBA; OBWP; PoE; PrIm; RB

Cares of Majesty, The. Shakespeare. *Fr. King Henry IV, Pt. II.* LiTB

Cargoes. John Masefield. BLPL; CMoP; CoGr; EBEvV; FaBV; FaPON; FaPoR; GGP; InPK; LiTM; MoAB; MoBrPo; NOBE; OBEV; OBMV; OtMeF; PlP; PoRA; TEP; TFi

Cargoes of the Radanites. Harry Alan Potamkin. TrJP

Carhop floated up, The. Chicken. Dave Etter. MAT

Caria and Philistia considered. Cry Faugh! Robert Graves. MoBrPo

Caribbean Woman Prayer. Grace Nichols. NBrP

Cariboo Horses, The. Alfred W. Purdy. HeIP; NOBC

Caries. Solyman Brown. *Fr. Dentologia; a Poem on the Diseases of the Teeth and Their Proper Remedies.* FaBoUs

Caring for Animals. Jon Silkin. TSaS

Carious Exposure. Gladys Cardiff. CDW

Carissima Joannissima, ave. Letter from the Alpes-Maritimes. Marilyn Hacker. EOEF

Carl Hamblin. Edgar Lee Masters. *Fr. Spoon River Anthology.* CMoP; LiTA; LiTM; OBSV

Carle He Came o'er the Croft, The. Allan Ramsay. OxBS

Carlino! what art thou about, my boy? To My Child Carlino. Walter Savage Landor. NoP

Carlos, calm down, love. Carlos Drummond de Andrade. *See* Carlos, keep calm, love.

Carlos, keep calm, love. Don't Kill Yourself. Carlos Drummond de Andrade, *tr. fr. Portuguese by* Elizabeth Bishop.
(Carlos, calm down, love.) AnRep, *tr. by* Mark Strand

Carlyle combined the lit'ry life. Thomas Carlyle. Dorothy Parker. *Fr. Pig's-Eye View of Literature, A.* FiBHP; NALW

Carlyle on Burns. William Jeffrey. *Fr. On Glaister's Hill.* OxBS

Carmarthen hills are green and low. Carmarthenshire. Dudley G. Davies. AngWe

Carmarthenshire. Dudley G. Davies. AngWe

Carmel Point. Robinson Jeffers. NAAL-2; NoAM; NoP

Carmelite. Raymond Murray, *tr. fr. Irish by the author.* TIRV

Carmen. Victor Hernandez Cruz. PoBA

Carmen. Newman Levy. FiBHP

Carmen Bellicosum. Guy Humphreys McMaster. GN; PAH

Carmen Elegiacum. Thomas Morton. SCAP

Carmen Possum. *Unknown.* BLPA; NBLV

Carmen Saeculare. C. H. Sisson, *after the Latin of* Horace. OBVE

Carmencita loves Patrick. Little Song. Langston Hughes. TLR

Carmina, *sels.* Catullus, *tr. fr. Latin.*
"Fabullus I will treat you handsomely." OBVE, *tr. by* Richard Lovelace
"My mistress sayes she'll marry none but me." OBVE, *tr. by* Richard Lovelace
Odi et Amo. CTC, *tr. by* Ezra Pound
(I hate and love; wouldst thou the reason know?.) OBVE, *tr. by* Richard Lovelace
(I love and hate. Ah! never ask why so!.) OBVE, *tr. by* Walter Savage Landor
"Suffenus, whom so well you know [*or* whom you know]." AWP, *tr. by* Walter Savage Landor; OBVE, *tr. by* Matthew Prior
(To Varus.) AWP, *tr. by* Walter Savage Landor
"That me alone you lov'd, you once did say." FMP; OBVE
"That no fair woman will, wonder not why." OBVE, *tr. by* Richard Lovelace

Carmina Amico. Edward James. PeHV
Sels.
"He had a many-coloured glance like flowers"
"You have returned. You have returned, my joy"

Carmina Burana., *sels. Unknown, tr. fr. Latin by* Willis Barnstone.
"Come, come, my companion." GePo
"Crown of all travailing." MLL, *tr. by* Helen Waddell
"I am constantly wounded." PGA
"I loved/ secretly." BoWoP
"O Fortune." MLL, *tr. by* Helen Waddell
"O happy hour." MLL, *tr. by* Helen Waddell
"She stood in her scarlet gown." MLL, *tr. by* Helen Waddell
"They have crucified their Lord afresh." MLL, *tr. by* Helen Waddell
"What profit to Darius of his reign?." MLL, *tr. by* Helen Waddell

Carnal and the Crane, The. *Unknown.* ESPB; OBET

Carnal Knowledge. Thom Gunn. BoLoP

Carnal Knowledge. Gwen Harwood. CBAP

Carnation Milk ("Carnation milk is the best in the land.") *Unknown.* InPK

Carnations and Butterflies. Pope. *Fr. Dunciad, The.* NOEC

Carnies. Debra Allbery. PBCAP

Carnival at the River. Robert Greacen. PNI

Carnival is over, The. The high tents. Sunday Night in Santa Rosa. Dana Gioia. GoJo; GrPl

Carnival Songs., *sels.* Lorenzo de' Medici, *tr. fr. Italian by* Richard Aldington.
Triumph of Bacchus and Ariadne. CTC

Caro mio, Pulcinello, kindly hear my wail of woe. A Nocturne at Danieli's. Sir Owen Seaman. UV

Caro, that dream (after the diagnosis). Investiture at Cecconi's. James Merrill. PFL

Carol. Howard Nemerov. TrCP

Carol: "Deep in the fading leaves of night." W. R. Rodgers. OBCP

Carol: "Garden and gardener He made." Thomas Kinsella. TIRV

Carol: "Mary laid her Child among." Norman Nicholson. OBCP

Carol: "Mary, the mother, sits on the hill." Langdon Elwyn Mitchell. OHIP

Carol: "My lady went to Canterbury [*or* Caunterbury]." *Unknown.* FaBoCo; FaBoNo
(Nonsense Song, A.) OxBLMV

Carol: "There was a boy bedded in bracken." John Short. FaBoCh; FaBoTw

Carol: "When the herd[s] were watching." William Canton. OHIP
(Bethlehem.) BoTP

Carol: "While shepherds watched their flocks by night." "Saki." NSI; UV

Carol and I headed for the Blues Rock Bar — walking, or more likely. Trappings. Lynda Schramfragel. BAP-89

Carol, every violet has. Alfred Noyes. *Fr. Flower of Old Japan, The.* MoBrPo

Carol for Advent. John Heath-Stubbs. OxBC

Carol, for Candlemas Day. *Unknown.* NOSC

Carol for St. Stephen's Day, A. *Unknown. See* Seynt Stevene was a clerk.

Carol for the Last Christmas Eve. Norman Nicholson. OBCP

Carol for Twelfth Day, A. *Unknown.* OHIP

Carol in Praise of the Holly and Ivy. *Unknown.* OHIP

Carol, in the Park, Chewing on Straws. Judy Grahn. *Fr. Common Woman, The.* PeHV; WPOW

Carol: "My heart of gold as true as steel." *Unknown. See* My heart [*or* harte] of gold[e] as true as steel [*or* stele].

Carol of Agincourt, A. *Unknown. See* Our king went forth to Normandy.

Carol of Agincourt, A. *Unknown. See* Our[e] king[e] went forth to Normandy.

Carol of Death, The. Walt Whitman. *See* Come lovely and soothing death.

Carol of Patience. Robert Graves. OBCP

Carol of St. George, A. *Unknown.* MeEL

Carol of the Birds. *Unknown, tr. fr. French.* OHIP

Carol of the Brown King. Langston Hughes. PChr

Carol of the Numbers. *Unknown.* AmFP

Carol of the Poor Children, The. Richard Middleton. OBCP

Carol of the Russian Children. *Unknown, tr. fr. Russian.* OHIP

Carol of the Three Kings. W. S. Merwin. PChr

Carol Singers, The. Margaret G. Rhodes. BoTP

Carol: "Villagers all, this frosty tide." Kenneth Grahame. *See* Villagers all, this frosty tide.

Carolina. Henry Timrod. PAH

Carolina, in which he was killed. (*LL*) Robert G. Shaw. H. Cordelia Ray. AAP; BlSi; CBWP-3; Son

Carolina mourns to-day. For he, the gifted. Tribute to Capt. F. W. Dawson. Mary Weston Fordham. CBWP-2

Caroline and Her Young Sailor Bold. *Unknown.* AmFP

Caroline of Edinboro' Town. *Unknown.* AmFP

Caroline Pink, she fell down the sink. *Unknown.* ISE

Caroling softly souls of slavery. (*LL*) Song of the Son. Jean Toomer. CDC; NIP; PoBA

Carolyn's Neighbor. Deborah S. Snyder. BTR

Carousel, The. Gloria C. Oden. PoBA

Carp are secrets, The. Lifting Illegal Nets by Flashlight. William Stafford. NNaP

Carpe Diem. "Laurence Hope." *Fr. In the Early, Pearly Morning.* OtMeF

Carpe Diem. Shakespeare. *See* Oh [*or* O] mistress mine, where are you roaming?

Carpenter. George Mackay Brown. OxBC

Carpenter, The. George Macdonald. TrPWD

Carpenter, The. Mary Brent Whiteside. TrCP

Carpenter is intent on the pressure of his hand, The. El Greco: Espolio. Earle Birney. MoCV

Carpenter living in Crewe, A. E. O. Parrott. PeLi

Carpenter's Complaint, The. Edward Baugh. PBCV

Carpenter's made a hole, The. A Hole in the Floor. Richard Wilbur. NOBA

Carpenter's Son, The. John Berryman. ChIV-2

Cat was once a weaver, The. What the Gray Cat Sings. Arthur Guiterman. MoShBr

Cat Washing. Linda Molony. NOBAu

Cat went here and there, The. The Cat and the Moon. W. B. Yeats. CMoP; CRH; FaBoCh; GoJo; OBAP; OFC; SoCa; TTTS; WHSW

Cat which no one's bothered to bury, The. A Small Death. Jill Maughan. NWP

Cat! who hast pass'd thy grand climacteric. To a Cat. Keats. FaBoCh; OFC; SoCa
   (On Mrs. Reynolds's Cat.) FM

Cat, who sleeps upon the mat, The. The Stray. Barbara Euphan Todd. CRH

Cat Will Rhyme with Hat. Spike Milligan. CRH

Cataclysmic if it were so. "What You See Is Me." Barbara Gibbs. NYBP

Catalog. Rosalie Moore. *Fr.* Catalogue. NTCP; OFC

Catalogue, *sels.* Rosalie Moore.
   Catalog. NTCP; OFC

Catalogue of the Ships, The. Homer, *tr. fr. Greek by* Alexander Pope. *Fr.* Iliad, The. CBCK

Catalpa Tree. Miriam Waddington. MoCV

"Catamount Tavern" is lively to-night, The. Parson Allen's Ride. Wallace Bruce. PAH

Catapult-stones of lust. (*LL*) Negev. David Rokeah. MHP

Cataract. Margoret Smith. NYBP

Cataract of Death far thundering from the heights, The. (*LL*) Mezzo Cammin. Longfellow. NAAL-1; NoP; PoE; TAP

Cataract of Lodore, The. ("How does the water"/ Come down at Ladore?) Robert Southey. GN; NTP; OxBChV; TEP; WBLP
   Sels.

Cataract, whirling to the precipice, The. John Clare. BoNaP

Cataracts flying down a thousand fathoms roll up a raging billow. Liu Ya-tzu, *tr. by* Wu-chi Liu. *Fr.* Miscellaneous Poems on Lake Biwa. SuSp

Catch, A. Henry Aldrich. *See* If all be true that I do think.

Catch. Robert Francis. InPK; RaBo

Catch, The. Brewster Ghiselin. FoLa; HAP

Catch. Langston Hughes. NoAM

Catch, A. Ben Jonson. *See* Buz[z], Quoth the Blue Fly.

Catch. Mother Goose. OxNR; ReMoGo

Catch, The. Richard Wilbur. DiPo; WeW

Catch a Little Rhyme. Eve Merriam. OBCA; PDV

Catch a moth in the Amazon; pin it under glass. Every Where and Every When. Arthur Sze. OpBo

Catch by the Hearth, A. *Unknown.* OHIP

Catch her and hold her if you can. Defiance. Walter Savage Landor. CBLP

Catch him coming off the thing after a state of the union. Strategies. Welton Smith. PoBA

Catch him, crow! Carry him, kite! *Unknown.* OxNR

Catch, my Uncle Jack said. Elizabeth. Michael Ondaatje. NoAM

Catch not my breath, O clamorous heart. Tennyson. *Fr.* Maud[: A Monodrama]. NAEL-2

Catch: On a Wet Day. Franco Sacchetti, *tr. fr. Italian by* Dante Gabriel Rossetti. AWP

Catch the rising stars! (*LL*) Desert Days on the Reservoir. Henri Cole. UTF

Catch What You Can. Jean Garrigue. VGW

Catching One Clear Thought Alive. Paula Gunn Allen. WPOW

Catching Webs. Judith Beveridge. NOBAu

Catechism. Betsy Sholl. CrSp

Catechism, 1958. W. M. Ransom. CDW

Catechism of d Neoamerican Hoodoo Church. Ishmael Reed. NBV

Caterpillar, The. Christina Rossetti. *See* Brown and furry.

Caterpillar, The. Miller Williams. MT

Caterpillar. "I'm learning/ to crawl." (*LL*) The Tickle Rhyme. Ian Serraillier. NTCP; PYC; Spl

Caterpillars. Aileen Fisher. TLR

Caterpillar's Lullaby. Jane Yolen. Spl

Catharine of Aragon. Eloise Bibb. CBWP-4

Cathedral Builders. John Ormond. PeECV

Cathedral Close, The. Coventry Patmore. *Fr.* Angel in the House, The. EBVV

Cathedral Is, The. John Ashbery. InPK

Cathedral 1941. Johannes Bobrowski, *tr. fr. German by* Ruth Mead *and* Matthew Mead. AnRep

Cathedral still rises, The. Going Back. Marina Roscher. BTR

Catherine. Karla Kuskin. NTCP; PDV

Catherine, describing a perfect circle. Virgin Martyrs. John Heath-Stubbs. OxBC

Catherine said "I think I'll bake." Catherine. Karla Kuskin. NTCP; PDV

Cathexis. Frederick Bryant, Jr. NBV; PoBA

Cathleen. *Unknown, tr. fr. Irish by* Thomas MacIntyre. BIrV

Cathleen Sweeping. George Johnston. NOBC

Catholic Bells, The. William Carlos Williams. CMoP; NOBA; OxBA; SAmP

Catholic Boys. David Kirby. NGP

Catkins, like caterpillars slung arow. Lost Lane. Dorothy Wellesley. WPE

Catmint. Eric Clough Taylor. CRH

Catnip and Dogwood. Howard Moss. OFC; SoCa

Cato, *sels.* Joseph Addison.
   Cato's Soliloquy. WBLP

Cato. C. H. Sisson. NOCV

Cato's Soliloquy. Joseph Addison. *Fr.* Cato. WBLP

Catrine woods were yellow seen, The. The Braes o' Ballochmyle. Burns. ScCV

Cats. Baudelaire, *tr. fr. French.* OFC, *tr. by* Roy Campbell; SoCa, *tr. by* Richard Howard.

Cats, The. Samuel Exler. GOYP

Cats. Eleanor Farjeon. OTCP; PDV; WHSW

Cats, The. Weldon Kees. NaP; SoCa

Cats and Dogs. N. M. Bodecker. TLR

Cats and Dogs. Howard Moss. OBAL

Cats and kittens, kittens and cats. Country Barnyard. Elizabeth J. Coatsworth. CRH

Cat's Conscience, A. *Unknown.* OFC; PoLF

Cats Crept Up on Me Slowly. Ursula Laird. Mes

Cat's eye marble is green, The. Backyard. Alice Notley. UL

Cats have gone off to hunt, The. Last winter. The Cats. Samuel Exler. GOYP

Cats hung out with witches quite a lot. The Thing About Cats. John L'Heureux. SoCa

Cats like Angels. Marge Piercy. CAPP

Cats making love in the temple. Kawai Chigetsu-ni, *tr. fr. Japanese by* Kenneth Rexroth *and* Ikuko Atsumi. WPJ

Cat's Meat. Harold Monro. OBMV; OFC

Cat's Menu. Richard Shaw. CRH

Cats No Less Liquid Than Their Shadows. A. S. J. Tessimond. OBAP

Cats of Balthus, The. Bin Ramke. SoCa

Cats of Campagnatico, The. Peter Porter. OBTV

Cats of Kilkenny, The. *Unknown.* OFC; PeLi; ReMoGo

Cats of Saint Nicholas, The. George Seferis, *tr. fr. Greek by* Edmund Keeley. SoCa

Cats purr. I Speak, I Say, I Talk. Arnold L. Shapiro. GrPl

Cat's purr, A. At the Loom. Robert Duncan. *Fr.* Passages. VGW

Cat's quite different from a dog, A. Catnip and Dogwood. Howard Moss. OFC; SoCa

Cats sleep/ Anywhere. Cats. Eleanor Farjeon. OTCP; PDV; WHSW

Cats sleep/ Anywhere. (*LL*) Cats. Eleanor Farjeon. OTCP; PDV; WHSW

Cats sleep fat and walk thin. Catalog. Rosalie Moore. *Fr.* Catalogue. NTCP; OFC

Cat's Song, The. *Unknown.* GBP

Cattail fluff. Porous. William Carlos Williams. NYBP

Cattail Wind. Joseph Bruchac. FoLa

Cattle. Ralph Hawkins. NBrP

Cattle. Peter Skrzynecki. CBAP

Cattle browse peacefully. Akhenaton, *tr. fr. Egyptian.* *Fr.* Hymn to the Sun. EaPr, *tr. by* Jacquetta Hawkes

Cattle in the common field, The. On the Heights. Walter Savage Landor. FaBoEE

Cattle Loading. Gordon Mackay-Warna, *tr. fr. Aborigine by* Georg von Brandenstein. NOBAu

Cattle of His Hand, The. Wilbur Underwood. WGRP

Cattle roam again across the field, The. *Unknown, tr. fr. Egyptian by* Robert Hillyer. *Fr.* Book of the Dead. AWP; FaPON

Cattle Show. "Hugh MacDiarmid." FaBoMo; HAP; MoBrPo; OBMV; OxBTC

Cattle then are sick, The. (*LL*) 'Tis summer time on Bredon. Hugh Kingsmill. FaBoCo; NOBL

Cattle Thief, The. Emily Pauline Johnson. WPOW

Cattle Train to Magdeburg. John Z. Guzlowski. BTR

Cattle-trains edge along the river, bringing morning on a white vibration. Ceiling Unlimited. Muriel Rukeyser. MoAmPo

Catullus to Lesbia. James Reeves. ErPo

Caught. Rodney Jones. NAmP90

Caught and composed, motionless blue, behind. The Desire of Water. Mark Jarman. PoA

Caught at hanger's ends the limp. Goodwill, Inc. Dennis Schmitz. AmPA

Celia Singing. Thomas Stanley. BeJo; NOSC

Celia's Home-coming. Agnes Mary Frances Robinson. OBEV

Celimena, of my heart. Damon and Celimena. Dryden. *Fr.* Evening's Love, An. InvP

Cell, The. George Rostrevor Hamilton. TrPWD

Cell, The. John Thelwall. NOEC

Cell by cell the baby made herself, the cells. Sara in Her Father's Arms. George Oppen. NNaP

Cell Lay Inside Her Body, The. Murray Edmond. *Fr.* Patching Together, A. NAs

Cell of Himself, The. Arthur Freeman. TwCP

Cell Song. Etheridge Knight. NNaP; PoBA

Cellar Door, sels. Sue Standing.
   "Room to go to, A." MDDM

Cello sobs, the symphony begins, The. The Festival. Frederic Prokosch. LiTA

Cells Breathe in the Emptiness. Galway Kinnell. NaP; VGW

Cells hold mock convention in the brain, The. Lobotomy. Kenneth Pitchford. PoA

Celluloid of a photograph holds them well, The. Six Young Men. Ted Hughes. NSI; OBWP; PAW; PoWW

Celtic Cross. Norman MacCaig. OxBS

Celtic Cross, The. Thomas D'Arcy Magee. TIRV

Celtic Fringe, The. Stevie Smith. FaBoNo

Celtic Lyric, The. J. C. Squire. BXAP

Celtic tribes speak an anapestic lilt. Forked Tongue. Helen Ruggieri. LoHo

Celts, The. Thomas D'Arcy Magee. PeIV; TIRV

Celts, The. Stevie Smith. NoP

Cemeteries are places for departed souls. Lines Written at the Grave of Alexander [or Alexandre] Dumas. Gwendolyn B. Bennett. CDC; PoNe

Cemetery, A. Emily Dickinson. *See* This quiet dust was gentlemen and ladies.

Cemetery at Academy, California, The. Philip Levine. NaP; NYBP

Cemetery Nights. Stephen Dobyns. SV

Cemetery of Orange Trees in Crete, The. Gerald Stern. CAPP

Cenci, The. Shelley. EnRP

Cenotaph, The. Charlotte Mew. OxAEP-2; WPE

Cenotaph at the Isthmos. Simonides, *tr. fr. Greek by* Peter Jay. GrAn

Cenotaph of Lincoln. James Thompson McKay. OHIP

Cenotaph stands in the Park, The. Greenwood's. Michael Sharkey. NOBAu

Censorship. John Ciardi. NBLV

Censorship. Arthur Waley. OxBTC

Census man, The. Madam and the Census Man. Langston Hughes. SAmP

Centaur, The. May Swenson. FaBoWP; GrPl; NMM; NTP; TwCP

Centaur, siren [or syren], I forgo [or foregoe], The. Another ("The centaur, siren I forgo.") Richard Lovelace. CaPo; PoEL-3

Centaur Song. Hilda Doolittle ("H. D."). VGW

Centaurs, The. Paul Muldoon. BiHa

Centenarian's Story, The. Walt Whitman. CTC

Centenary's Day. Marcus Garvey. PBCV

Centennial Hymn. Bryant. PAH

Centennial Hymn. Whittier. PAH

Centennial Meditation of Columbia, The. Sidney Lanier. PAH
   Sels.
   Dear Land of All My Love. GN

Centennial Meditation of Columbia, The. Sidney Lanier. PAH

Center of all centers, core of cores. Buddha in Glory. Rainer Maria Rilke, *tr. fr. German by* Stephen Mitchell. EnlH

Center of Attention, The. Daniel Hoffman. FYAP; UnPo

Centipede, The. Ogden Nash. FaPON

Centipede, The. *Unknown. See* Centipede was happy quite, A.

Centipede adown the street, The. Archy at the Zoo. Don Marquis. *Fr.* Archy and Mehitabel. NBLV; OBAL

Centipede along the threshold crept, The. Thomas Hood. *Fr.* Haunted House, The. EBEV; WiR

Centipede was happy quite, A. A Centipede. *Unknown.*
   (Centipede, The.) OBSP
   (Puzzled Centipede, The.) FaPON

Central. Ted Kooser. Poetsp

Central. Douglas Oliver. VaA

Central Heating System. Stephen Spender. GrPl

Central Highlands, Viet Nam, 1968. Geary Hobson. ETG

Central Park. Robert Lowell. LiTM

Central Park. Julian Symons. PeLV

Central Park Some People (3 P.M.). Nancy Morejón, *tr. fr. Spanish by* Sylvia Carranza. PBWP

Central Park South. Donald Revell. UTF

Central Park West. Jack Spicer. PeHV

Central stream of what we feel indeed, The. (*LL*) Below the Surface-Stream. Matthew Arnold. NOBVV; OxBSP

Centre of equal daughters, equal sons. America. Walt Whitman. GOA

Century Piece for Poor Heine, A. John Logan. NNaP

Century Prayer, The. James Ephriam McGirt. AAP

Century since, out in the West, A. Betty Zane. Thomas Dunn English. PAH

Ceremonies for Christmas[se]. (Come, bring with a noise.) Robert Herrick. BeJo; GN; OBCP; OHIP; TEP
   Sels.
   Dear Land of All My Love. GN
   "Wassail the trees, that they may bear." PChr

Ceremony. Kattie M. Cumbo. BlSi

Ceremony. Jewel C. Latimore. BlSi

Ceremony, A, sels. Robin Morgan. SRLS
   "We will grow old, and older." CrSp

Ceremony. William Stafford. FoLa; LCAP

Ceremony. Richard Wilbur. CoAP; MoP; NAAL-2; NoAM

Ceremony, A. Robin Morgan. SRLS

Ceremony after a Fire Raid. Dylan Thomas. CMoP

Ceremony must be found, The. Speaking of Poetry. John Peale Bishop. LiTA; OxBA

Ceremony of Sending, sels. *Unknown, tr. fr. Osage Indian by* Barbara Tedlock.
   Hidden People and the Star People, The. STP

Ceremony upon Candlemas Eve. Robert Herrick. OBCP

Cernunnos. Hugh Maxton. CIP

Cerritos. Donna Hilbert. NGP

Certain Americans refuse to return. Change. Phyllis Janowitz. EOEF

Certain bear, whose dam had licked him ill, A. The Bear and the Garden Lover. Jean De la Fontaine. OBF

Certain Bend, A. William Stafford. CAPP

Certain bones are from other bones distinguished. Discoveries of Bones and Stones. Geoffrey Grigson. OBTV

Certain branches cut. October. Denise Levertov. TRP

Certain Choices. Richard Shelton. Poetsp

Certain dark underground eyes. Picture of Loot. Alan Sillitoe. OxBTC

Certain day became a presence to me, A. Variation on a Theme by Rilke. Denise Levertov. CrSp; EaPr

Certain Evening, A. G. K. Chesteron. OxAEP-2

Certain events are not unlike new snow. Hit by a Space Station. Steve Abbott. ETG

Certain great statesman, whom all of us know, A. Ballynahinch. George Canning. FaBoCo

Certain Lady, A. Dorothy Parker. NIP

Certain landscapes insist on fidelity. Leaving Sonora. Agha Shahid Ali. FoLa

Certain Maxims of Archy. Don Marquis. OBAL
   Sels.
   Archy, the Cockroach, Speaks. FaPON
   "I once heard the survivors." NBLV

Certain Maxims of Archy. Don Marquis. OBAL

Certain Maxims of Hafiz, sels. Kipling.
   Maxim. OtMeF

Certain Mercies. Robert Graves. GTBS-P

Certain moments will never change, nor stop being. Thinking about the Past. Donald Justice. MT

Certain painter, leaving in the morning, A. The Saddled Ass. La Fontaine, *tr. fr. French by* Deems Taylor. NBLV

Certain pasha, dead five thousand years, A. A Turkish Legend. Thomas Bailey Aldrich. GN

Certain People. Richard Jones. NAmP90

Certain people would not clean their buttons. The Bohemians. Ivor Gurney. PeFWW

Certain Presbyterian Pair, A. The Presbyterian Wedding. *Unknown.* CoMu; ErPo; FaBoBl

Certain presuppositions are altered. Upland. A. R. Ammons. NOBA

Certain Questions for Monsieur Renoir. John Ormond. AngWe

Certain Slant of Light, A. Emily Dickinson. *See* There's a certain slant of light.

Certain Statesman, A. Sir Osbert Sitwell. IHNG

Certain Tall Buildings. Franz Wright. NAmP90

Certain things here are quietly American. Midsummer. Derek Walcott. NAEL-2

Change, move, dead clock, that this fresh day. Small Prayer. Weldon Kees. IMW; PoA; VGW

Change of Address. Kathleen Fraser. NYBP

Change onward from ours to that of beings who walk other spheres, The. (*LL*) The World below the Brine. Walt Whitman. ArNa; BoNaP; FM; MAT; NoP; PFP

Change Should Breed Change. William Drummond of Hawthornden. OBEV

Change [Thy Mind since She Doth Change]. Earl of Essex. EIL

Change to One-Way after Repaving, The. Richard Robbins. NGP

Change-up. Don L. Lee. PoBA

Changed. Charles Stuart Calverley. FiBHP; NOBVV

Changed and not changed. Three million years. Fossil, 1975. Janet Lewis. CRP

Changed Mind (or the Day I Woke Up). Tejumola Ologboni. NBV

Changed, Yet Constant. Thomas Stanley. BeJo

Changeful Beauty. *Unknown, tr. fr. Greek by* Andrew Lang. EnLoPo

Changeless Shore. Sarah Leeds Ash. GoYe

Changeling, The. Charlotte Mew. CH; CoGr

Changeling, The. Thomas Middleton. PoEL-2
   Sels.
   "Here we are, if you have any more."
   "What makes your lip so strange?"

Changeling VIII. Kristjana Gunnars. NOBC

Changes. Sally Cline. VBLP

Changes. "Owen Meredith." PoLF

Changes. Martha Sansom. UnDi

Changes to Corinna, The. Robert Herrick. JCP

Changing, *sels.* Liv Ullmann.

Changing Diapers. Gary Snyder. RaBo

Changing guests, each in a different mood, The. Inclusiveness. Dante Gabriel Rossetti. *Fr.* House of Life, The. NAEL-2

Changing Light at Sandover, The, *Sels.* James Merrill.
   Book of Ephraim, The.
      "Backdrop: The dining room at Stockholm." NoAM
      Life like the periodical not yet. HCAP
      "Maya in the city has a dream." NAAL-2
      "Zero hour. Waiting yet again." HCAP
   Mirabell's Books of Number
      "And Maddening-it's all by someone else." NAAL-2
      "It starts in the small hours. An interlude." NoAM
      "World was everything that was the case? The." HCAP

Changing the Wheel. Bertolt Brecht, *tr. fr. German by* Michael Hamburger. PoSu

Changing water. Adding aspirin. Nitrogen, potash or. Flowers. Kathleen Fraser. CrSp

Channel Crossing. George Barker. GTBS-P

Channel Firing. Thomas Hardy. CMoP; EBEV; HAP; HeIP; ImPo; LiTB; MeMBP; MoP; NAEL-2; NIP; NoAM; NoP; OAEL-2; OxAEP-2; OxBTC; PeECV; PeFWW; PoE; PoEL-5; Poetr; PoRA; PoWW; PrIm; RB; SoSe; TFi; UnPo

Channel moon went down, as ignorance, The. The Outlanders. Andrew Glaze. NYBP

Chanson. Pernette de Guillet, *tr. fr. French by* Joan Keefe *and* Richard Terdiman. PBWP

Chanson du Décervelage, La. Alfred Jarry, *tr. fr. French by* Cyril Connolly *and* Simon Taylor. *Fr.* Ubu Cocu. CBNP

Chanson of a Lady in the Shade. Paul Celan, *tr. fr. German by* Michael Hamburger. AnRep

Chansons d'Automne. Paul Verlaine, *tr. fr. French by* Arthur Symons. AWP

Chansons de Bilitis. Pierre Louÿs, *tr. fr. French.* PeHV
   Sels.
   Agonizing Memory, The.
   Breasts of Mnasidice, The.
   Complaisant Friend, The.
   Love.
   Meeting, The.
   Penumbra.

Chansons Innocentes, *sels.* E. E. Cummings.
   "In just-/ spring when the world is mud." AmPP; FaBoVe; FaBV; FaPON; HeIL; HeIP; MoAB; MoAmPo; MoShBr; NAAL-2; NIP; NoP; Poetr; PrIm; SoSe; WeW
   (In Just-.) InPK
   "Little tree." NTCP; OBCP; PChr; PDV

Chant for All the People on Earth. Leslie Woolf Hedley. BTR

Chant for Dark Hours. Dorothy Parker. VBLP

Chant for Reapers. Wilfrid Thorley. OBEV

Chant for Young/Brothas and Sistuhs, A. Sonia Sanchez. BPo

Chant no more your old rhymes about bold Robin Hood. *Unknown. See* No more chant your old rhymes about bold Robin Hood.

Chant of Hate against England, A. Ernst Lissauer, *tr. by* Barbara Henderson. *Fr.* Hymn of Hate against England, A. OtMeF

Chant Out of Doors, A. Marguerite Wilkinson. TrPWD

Chant-Pagan. Kipling. FaBoPV

Chant Royal. Robert Morgan. SM

Chant to Io. Tiwai Paraone, *tr. fr. Maori by* A. Alpers. WTO

Chanted Calendar, A. Sydney Thompson Dobell. *Fr.* Balder. BoTP; OBEV

Chanting, peering into the distance, in anguish my white head droops. (*LL*) Autumn Meditation. Tu Fu. PLT

Chanting sun, as ever, rivals, The. The. Goethe, *tr. by* Louis MacNeice. *Fr.* Faust. NAWM-2

Chanting the Square Deific. Walt Whitman. NAAL-1

Chanting These Verses on My Way to Yodoe. Su Man-shu, *tr. fr. Chinese by* Wu-chi Liu. SuSp

Chants, The, *sels.* María Sabina, *tr. fr. Mazatec Indian by* Henry Munn. "Ah, Jesu Kri." STP

Chants Communal, *sels.* Horace L. Traubel.
   What Can I Do? TrJP

Chaos! Cosmos! Cosmos, Chaos! who can tell how all will end? Tennyson. *Fr.* Locksley Hall Sixty Years After. FaBoEH

Chap was so pose that was adi, A. Arthur Shaw. PeLi

Chapel, as the pivot of this valley, The. For the Altarpiece of the Roseau Valley Church, Saint Lucia. Derek Walcott. NoP

Chapel at the crossways bore no scar, The. The Guard's Mistake. Edmund Blunden. NSI

Chapel Snake, The. Lavinia Greenlaw. NWP

Chaperon, The. H. C. Bunner. AnAmPo

Chaplet, The. Moses Mendes. TrJP
   Sels.
   Ass, The.
   Philanderer, The.

Chaplet of Southernwood, A, *sels.* John Gambril Nicholson.
   "I love him wisely if I love him well." PeHV

Chaplinesque. Hart Crane. CMoP; HeIP; LiTM; MoP; NAAL-2; NoAM; NOBA; OxBA; SoCa; VGW

Chapman the Translator. Michael Drayton. *Fr.* To Henry Reynolds, of Poets and Poesy. EPCY

Chapmen. *Unknown. See* We ben chapmen lyght of fote.

Chapter Heading. Ernest Hemingway. PoA

Chapter of Kings, The. John Collins. FaBoUs

Character. Emerson. LiTA; OxBSP

Character, A. Blake. *See* Her Whole Life Is an Epigram.

Character, A. Clara Reeve. ECWP

Character, A. Tennyson. EBVVPR
   Sels.
   "With a half-glance upon the sky." Mes

Character, indistinct, entered, A. Thomas Kinsella. *Fr.* Songs of the Psyche. NoAM

Character of a Certain Whig, The. William Shippen. APAS

Character of a Critic. Charles Churchill. *Fr.* Rosciad, The. NOEC

Character of a Good Parson, The. Dryden. NOCV

Character of a Happy Life, The. Sir Henry Wotton. EBEvV; EIL; GTBS; GTBS-P; LiTB; NOBE; NOSC; NTP; OBEV; TrGrPo

Character of a Roundhead, The. *Unknown.* FaBoPV; NOSC

Character of a Trimmer, The. *Unknown.* APAS

Character of Holland, The. Andrew Marvell. NOBL
   Sels.
   "Holland, that scarce deserves the name of land." ChTr; OBSV; PeLV

Character of Love Seen as a Search for the Lost, The. Kenneth Patchen. NaP; VGW

Character of Sir Robert Walpole, The. Swift. FaBoEE; PoE

Character of the Happy Warrior. Wordsworth. EnRP; FaBoBe; LiTB; MeMBP

Charade. Winthrop Mackworth Praed. GN

Charade. *Unknown.* OxNR

Charcoal. Wilson Harris. PBCV

Charcoalman, The. John Townsend Trowbridge. AnAmPo

Chard Whitlow. Henry Reed. BXAP; FaBoCo; FaBoNo; FaBoPa; FiBHP; LiTM; MoBrPo; NBLV; NOBL; NoP; OxBTC; PeLV; UnPo; UV

Charge, A. Herbert Trench. OBEV

Charge at Santiago, The. William Hamilton Hayne. PAH

Charge by the Ford, The. Thomas Dunn English. PAH

Charge of the Light Brigade, The, *sels.* Tennyson.
   "Stormed at with shot and shell." Poetr

Charge of the Light Brigade, The. Tennyson. BeLS; BLPA; EBEvV; EnVR; FaBoBe; FaBoEH; FaBV; FaPON; FaPoR; FHYEP; GN; HoPM; NAEL-2; NOBVV; OBWP; OxAEP-2; PeVV; PrIm; TEP; TFi; UV; VPP; WBLP

Charge the the Bread Brigade, The. Ezra Pound *and* Noel Stock. *Fr.* Poems of Alfred Venison, the Poet of Titchfield Street, The. UV

Charge to the Poets, A, *sels.* William Whitehead.
   "If nature prompts you, or if friends persuade." OBSV
   "Life of writing, unless wondrous short, A." ECEV

Chase and the Race, The. Adam Lindsay Gordon. *Fr.* Ye Wearie Wayfarer. OtMeF

Chase Henry. Edgar Lee Masters. OBD

Chased from my calling to this hackneyed trade. James Kennedy. *Fr.* Exile's Reveries, The. NOEC

Chasing the Sun. Jiang He, *tr. fr. Chinese by* Donald Finkel *with* Li Guohua. SpMi

Chasm. A. R. Ammons. OBAL

Chaste Arabian Bird, The. The Earl of Rochester. ErPo

Chaste, biddable, out of all likelihood. *(LL)* Cover Her Face. Thomas Kinsella. CIP; IPY

Chaste Florimel. Matthew Prior. BoLoP; ErPo

Chaste Maid in Cheapside, A, *sels.* Thomas Middleton. Parting. EIL

Chaste, pious, prudent Charles the Second. The History of Insipids. John Freke. APAS

Chaste Stranger, The. James Tate. NoAM

Chaste trees, dark-clustered, The. A Leaf in Love and War. Veripatiya Kamakkanniyar, *tr. fr. Tamil by* A. K. Ramanujan. PLW

Chastity ("I Mean That Too, But Yet a Hidden Strength.") Milton. *Fr.* Comus; a Masque Presented at Ludlow Castle. FHYEP; NOSC; OAEL-1

Chateaux en Espagne. H. Cordelia Ray. CBWP-3

Chatte-Show Host came with us, yclept Wogan, A. Chaucer: The Wogan's Tale. Stanley J. Sharpless. UV

Chatter of birds two by two. Prairie Waters by Night. Carl Sandburg. NAAL-2

Chattering finch and water-fly. The Skeleton. G. K. Chesteron. FaBoTw

Chattering swallow! what shall we. The Swallow. Thomas Stanley. AWP

Chatterton. Rina Hands. Mes

Chatting on deck was Dryden too. Walter Savage Landor. *Fr.* To Wordsworth. EPCY

Chaucer. Longfellow. AWP; HeIP; InvP; MeMAP; NOBA; NoP; OBEV; OxBA; PoE; PoRA; PrIm; Son; TAP; TFi; TrGrPo

Chaucer, Langland, Douglas, Dunbar with all your. Ode to the Medieval Poets. W. H. Auden. PoA

Chaucer: The Wogan's Tale. Stanley J. Sharpless. UV

Chaucer's Wishes for his 'Troilus.' Chaucer. *See* Go, litel book, go litel myn tragedy.

Chaunt of the Brazen Head, The, *sels.* Winthrop Mackworth Praed. "I think the thing you call Renown." OBSV

Che is with-out longing. *(LL)* I Have a Young Sister. *Unknown.* CH; CoGr; FaBoVe; MeEL; MiEL; NAEL-1; NoP; OAEL-1

Cheap Replicas of the Eiffel Tower. Elton Glaser. PBCAP

Cheap Thrills. Eva Salzman. NWP

Cheat, The. Joseph Beaumont. NOSC

Cheat of Cupid; or, The Ungentle Guest, The. Robert Herrick, *after* Anacreon. AWP; OBVE

"Check it in here," he said. New Carpentry. Chris Wallace-Crabbe. FaBoMA

Check to Song. "Owen Meredith." *See* I dream'd that I walk'd in Italy.

Checking their watches, sticking to sarsaparilla. *(LL)* Sarsaparilla. Matthew Sweeney. IB

Checks the wild pigeons taking them to breast. *(LL)* Letter across Doubt and Distance. M. Carl Holman. PoNe

Chee, chee, chee. *(LL)* Robert of Lincoln. Bryant. EAP; FaBoBe; FaPON; OBCA; WBLP, *abr*

Cheer and salute for the Admiral, and here's to the Captain bold, A. The Men behind the Guns. John Jerome Rooney. BLPA; FaBoBe; PAH

Cheer for the Consumer. Nixon Waterman. OBAL

Cheer, oh, cheer up! my own Jeannette, tho' far away I go. Jeannot's Answer. Charles Jefferys. BLPA

Cheer up, cheer up, you sons of toil, and listen to my song. Striking Times. *Unknown.* OBET

Cheer Up, My Mates. Abraham Cowley. OxAEP-1

Cheer up, my mates, the wind does fairly blow. Cheer Up, My Mates. Abraham Cowley. OxAEP-1

Cheer up, my young men all; let nothing fright you. Brave Wolfe. *Unknown.* PAH

Cheered with this hope, to Paris I returned. Wordsworth. *Fr.* Prelude [or, Growth of a Poet's Mind], The. EnRP; OAEL-2; PoEL-4

Cheerfu' supper done, wi' serious face, The. The Cotter's Saturday Night. Burns. BeLS; EnRP; FaBoBe; PoLF; WGRP

Cheerful arn he blaws in the marn, The. The Cheerful Horn. *Unknown.* CH

Cheerful Chilterns, The. Frank Sidgwick. BXAP

Cheerful Girls at Smiller's Bar, The. Jack A. Mapanje. HBAPE; PeSAV

Cheerful Horn, The. *Unknown.* CH

Cheerful Welcome, A. *Unknown.* MeEL

Cheerio My Deario. Don Marquis. *Fr.* Archy and Mehitabel. FaBoCo

Cheers, Cheers for Old Cha Cha Ass ("Cheers, cheers for old Patchogue High.") Walta Borawski. GLP

Cheese for the Archdeacon, A. Thomas Hughes. AngWe

Cheese it is a peevish elf. *Unknown.* FaBoUs

Cheetah. Charles Eglington. OBAP

Cheetie-Poussie-Cattie, O. *Unknown. See* There was a wee bit mousikie.

Chefs and saints may still appear to blithe it. *(LL)* Moon Landing. W. H. Auden. OxAEP-2

Chekhov, my country is Ward 6. Ward 6. Tanure Ojaide. HBAPE

Chelmsfords Fate. Benjamin Tompson. SCAP

Chemicals ripen the citrus. In California. Donald Davie. NoAM

Chemicals rising. Lyn Lifshin. *Fr.* Love Canal. NGP

Chemin Des Dames. Crosbie Garstin. NSI

Chemistry of Character, The. Elizabeth Dorney. BLPA

Chen-chou Quatrains, *sels.* Wang Shih-chieng, *tr. fr. Chinese by* Daniel Bryant.

Chengtu. Tu Fu, *tr. fr. Chinese by* Robert Payne. TAL

Chepstow: A Poem. Edward Davies. OBWVE
Sels.
Cambrian Swain, The
Tintern Abbey
"Will no young British bard, on rhyme intent." AngWe

Chercheuses de Poux, Les. Rimbaud, *tr. by* T. Sturge Moore. *Fr.* Illuminations. AWP

Chernobyl Chernobyl Chernobyl. *(LL)* The International Meteorological Committee Reports. Suzanne Gardinier. UTF

Cherokee, The. Mary Weston Fordham. AmWP; CBWP-2

Cherrie-ripe. Robert Herrick. *See* Cherry-ripe.

Cherries, *sels.* Edward Kamau Brathwaite.
So When the Hammers of the Witnesses of Heaven Are Raised All Together. NAs

Cherries. Joe Lamb. RaBo

Cherries. Zalman Schneour, *tr. fr. Yiddish by* Joseph Leftwich. TrJP

Cherries. Lucien Stryk. CAPP

Cherries; a Parable, The. Thomas Moore. OBSV

Cherry. Gene Baro. ErPo

Cherry. Stuart Dybek. PBCAP

Cherry, A. *Unknown.* ReMoGo

Cherry and pear are white. The Crowns. John Freeman. CH

Cherry and the Slae, The, *sels. At.* to Alexander Montgomerie. "About ane bank, where birdis on bewis." ScCV

Cherry-Blossom Wand, The. Anna Wickham. MoBrPo

Cherry Blossoms. Basho, *tr. fr. Japanese by* Lucien Stryk. ArNa

Cherry blossoms, The. Spring. Princess Shikishi, *tr. fr. Japanese by* Hiroaki Sato. PBWP

Cherry Bombs. Alice Fulton. NAmP90

Cherry Boy, The. Royston Ellis. PeHV
Sels.
"All my sex life, I had been drifting"
"It was an international rage"

Cherry-lipped Adonis. Richard Barnfield. *Fr.* Cynthia. Son

Cherry-lipt Adonis in his snowie shape. Richard Barnfield. *Fr.* Sonnets. PeHV

Cherry-Ripe. Thomas Campion. *See* There Is a Garden in Her Face.

Cherry-ripe. Robert Herrick. BeJo; CaPo; CH; EBEvV; ELP; OBEV; PeLV; TEP

Cherry Robbers. D. H. Lawrence. MoAB; MoBrPo

Cherry Tree. Ivy O. Eastwick. BoTP

Cherry Tree, The. Thom Gunn. GLP; Poetsp

Cherry-Tree Carol, The. *Unknown.* AmFP

Cherry-Tree Carol, The. *Unknown.* AmFP; ChTr, A *and* B *vers.*; EBEV, A *and* B *vers.*; ELP; EnSB; ESPB; FaBoBa; GBP; HeIL; HeIP; OAEL-1; OBCP; OBET; OxBB; OxBoLi; PeECV; SCGP; TFi; TrGrPo

Cherry Tree Carol, The. *Unknown. See* As Joseph Was a-Walking [or a-Waukin'].

Cherry Trees, The. Edward Thomas. NAEL-2; OBWP; PeFWW; Spl

Cherry year, A. *Unknown.* OxNR

Cherrylog Road. James Dickey. CoAP; HAP; HCAP; InPS; MT; NAAL-2; NIP; NYBP; Poetr; PrIm; TwCP; WeW

Cherubic Pilgrim, The. "Angelus Silesius," *tr. fr. German. Fr.* Cherubical Wanderer, The. WGRP

Cherubical Wanderer, The, *sels.* "Angelus Silesius," *tr. fr. German.*
Abomination Of Evil, The. GePo, *tr. by* George C. Schoolfield
Belief. GePo, *tr. by* George C. Schoolfield
Body, Soul, And Godhead. GePo, *tr. by* George C. Schoolfield
Chance And Essence. GePo, *tr. by* George C. Schoolfield
Cherubic Pilgrim, The. WGRP

Child Is Father to the Man, The. Gerard Manley Hopkins. FaBoCo; NOBVV; NTP

Child Is Introduced to the Cosmos at Birth, The. *Unknown, tr. fr. Omaha Indian by* Alice C. Fletcher. AnAmPo; EaPr

Child is like a rare bird, A. Praise of a Child. *Yoruba Oral Tradition, tr. by* Ulli Beier *and* B. Gbadamosi. WTO

Child is like a sailor cast up by the sea, The. Lucretius, *tr. by* C. H. Sisson. *Fr.* De Rerum Natura (On the Nature of Things). NAs

Child is moaning. The candle burning low, The. Count Arsenii Arkadyevich Golenishchev-Kutuzov, *tr. fr. Russian by* Philip L. Miller. *Fr.* Songs and Dances of Death. RiWo

Child is not dead, The. The Child Who Was Shot Dead by Soldiers at Nyanga. Ingrid Jonker, *tr. fr. Afrikaans by* Jack Cope *and* Uys Krige. PeSA; PeSAV, *tr. by* Jack Cope *and* William Plomer

Child is Something Else Again, A. Yehuda Amichai, *tr. fr. Hebrew by* Chana Bloch *and* Stephen Mitchell. ArLo

Child is the only one awake, The. She decides not to kill. Not a Dream, Just Thoughts. Marion Cohen. BTR

Child, is thy father dead? Ebenezer Elliot. FaBoEH

Child-King, The. Morris Wintchevsky, *tr. fr. Yiddish by* Alter Brody. TrJP

Child Labor. Charlotte Perkins Gilman. AnAmPo

Child Life. Mary E. Tucker. CBWP-1

Child like mustard seed, The. War-Baby. D. H. Lawrence. NAs

Child listen/ I am singing. White-arm, *tr. fr. Crow Indian by* W. S. Merwin *after* Robert Lowie. STP

Child Maurice. *Unknown.* ESPB, B *vers.*

Child most infantine, A. A Child of Twelve. Shelley. *Fr.* Revolt of Islam, The. GN

Child-Musician, The. Austin Dobson. GN

Child My Choice, A. Robert Southwell. PeECV

Child Myro made this tomb, The. Anyte, *tr. fr. Greek by* Sally Purcell. GrAn

Child Next Door, The ("The child next door has a wreath on her hat.") Rose Fyleman. FaPON

Child Noryce is a clever young man. Child Maurice. *Unknown.* ESPB, B *vers.*

Child not yet is lulled to rest, The. Cradle-Song at Twilight. Alice Meynell. NOBVV

Child of bewitching night. Night's Protégé. Marjorie Marshall. ShDr

Child of death. Praises of the King of Oyo. *Yoruba Oral Tradition, tr. by* Ulli Beier. WTO

Child of distress, who meet'st the bitter scorn. To the Poor. Anna Laetitia Barbauld. ECWP

Child of Loneliness. Norman Gale. WGRP

Child of maize! Red Monkey. *Unknown, tr. fr. Yoruba by* Ulli Beier. *Fr.* Hunter Poems of the Yoruba. RB

Child of Mary Queen of Scots, The. James I. Kipling. FaBoEH

Child of my parents! Sister of my soul! Wordsworth. *Fr.* Prelude [or, Growth of a Poet's Mind], The. EnRP; OAEL-2; PoEL-4

Child of My Winter Born. W. D. Snodgrass. *Fr.* Heart's Needle. MoAmPo

Child of Our Time. Eavan Boland. CIP

Child of patient industry. Invitation to the Bee. Charlotte Smith. OxBChV

Child of silence and shadow. Yvonne Caroutch, *tr. fr. French by* David Cloutier. BoWoP

Child of the potent spell and nimble eye. Henry Headly. *Fr.* Invocation to Melancholy, An. ECEV

Child of the Romans. Carl Sandburg. NAAL-2

Child of the season of adventure, child of the heart. Child. E. N. Sargent. NYBP

Child of the sun, in whom his rays appear. La Gialletta Gallante, or the Sunburned Exotic Beauty. Lord Herbert of Cherbury. NOSC

Child of the World. Edna L. S. Barker. GoYe

Child of Twelve, A. Shelley. *Fr.* Revolt of Islam, The. GN

Child on the Judgment Seat, The. Elizabeth Rundle Charles. BLPA

Child on Top of a Greenhouse. Theodore Roethke. LCAP; VGW

Child Owlet. *Unknown.* ESPB

Child Playing with a Watch, The. Frances Sargent Osgood. AmWP

Child Reads an Almanac, The ("The child reads on; her basket of eggs stands by.") Francis Jammes, *tr. fr. French by* Ludwig Lewisohn. AWP; FaPON

Child running wild in woods of Lissadell. Remembering Con Markievicz. C. Day Lewis. IIP

Child said *What is the grass?*, A. Walt Whitman. *Fr.* Song of Myself. AmPP; LiTA; MoAmPo, *abr.*; NOBA; NoP; OxBA; SAmP; SOTW, *much abr.*

(Grass.) BLPL; ImPo

Child saw the bombers skate, The. Come to the Stone. Randall Jarrell. VGW

Child screams in his room, Rage, The. Unjustly Punished Child. Sharon Olds. PBCAP

Child should always say what's true, A. Whole Duty of Children. Robert Louis Stevenson. FaBoUs; NBLV; OxBChV

Child stood in the shed, The. The child went mad. The Carpenter's Son. John Berryman. ChIV-2

Child Taken from the Mother, The. Minnie Bruce Pratt. GLP

Child That Has a Cold, A. Thomas Dibdin. ChTr; FaBoNo

Child, the current of your breath is six days long. Unknown Girl in the Maternity Ward. Anne Sexton. MoP; NAs; NoAM

Child to His Sick Grandfather, A. Joanna Baillie. ECWP; NOEC; WoRP

Child Waters. *Unknown.* ESPB, A *and* B *vers.*; FaBoBa; OBET; OxBB

Child! we must quit these visionary scenes. Hannah More. *Fr.* Search after Happiness, The. ECWP

Child went out one day, A. I Eat Kids Yum Yum! Dennis Lee. TLR

Child Who Was Shot Dead by Soldiers at Nyanga, The. Ingrid Jonker, *tr. fr. Afrikaans by* Jack Cope *and* Uys Krige. PeSA; PeSAV, *tr. by* Jack Cope *and* William Plomer

Child, who went gathering the flowers of death. Haroun Al-Rachid for Heart's-Life. *Unknown, tr. fr. Arabic by* E. Powys Mathers. *Fr.* Thousand and One Nights, The. AWP

Child with a Cockatoo. Rosemary Dobson. CBAP

Child with Six Fingers. Carol Muske. AmPA

Child, you were conceived in my upstairs room. To a Child Born in Time of Small War. Helen Sorrells. WPE

Childbirth. Ted Hughes. NAs

Childcity, Aprilcity. Paris. Gregory Corso. VGW

Childe Harold's Pilgrimage, *sels.* Byron.
Dedication: To Ianthe. OBNC
Dying Gladiator, The. NOBE
"He who, grown aged in this world of woe." EPCY
"I stood in Venice on the Bridge of Sighs." EnRP, *abr.*; OBTV, *abr.*
(On the Bridge of Sighs.) FaBoPP, 4 *sts.*
"Is thy face like thy mother's, my fair child!" EnRP; OAEL-2, *abr.*
It Is the Hush of Night. LiTB; MeMBP
Lake Leman ("Clear, placid Leman! thy contrasted lake.") OBNC, *sl. diff. sel.*
"Lake Leman woos me with its crystal face." InPS
(Lake Leman.) PoEL-4
Ocean, The. PoEL-4
(Apostrophe to the Ocean.) WBLP
(By the Deep Sea.) OBNC
(Deep and Dark Blue Ocean.) ChTr
(Ocean, The.) FaBV; MeMBP; TFi; TrGrPo
(Roll On, Thou Deep and Dark Blue Ocean.) FaPON; UV
(Sea, The.) GGP; ImPo; BLPL; FaBoBe; LiTB
("There is a pleasure in the pathless woods.") OxAEP-2
(To the Ocean.) GN; WGRP
"Oh love! no habitant of earth thou art." CBLP
(Fatal Spell, The.) OBNC
"Oh, thou! in Hellas deemed of heavenly birth." NAEL-2, *much abr.*
"On, on the vessel flies, the land is gone." OBTV
"Once more upon the waters! yet once more!" FHYEP, *shorter sel.*
Rome by Metella's Tomb. FaBoPP
"Stop! for thy tread is on an empire's dust!" InPS
"There was a sound of revelry by night." EBEV; FaBoEH; OBWP; OxAEP-2
(Eve of Waterloo, The.) EBEvV; OtMeF; BeLS; FaBoBe; FaBoCh; 08FaBoEn; FaBV; 08HBV 1-2; NOBE; OBNC
(Night before the Battle of Waterloo, The.) WBLP
(Night before Waterloo, The.) GN
(There Was a Sound of Revelry by Night.) TFi
(Waterloo.) TrGrPo
To Eddleston. PeHV
"What from this barren being do we reap?" FHYEP, *shorter sel.*

Childe Maurice. *Unknown.* ESPB

Childe Maurice hunted the Silver Wood. *Unknown. See* Gill Morice stood in stable-door.

Childe Roland, etc. Elder Olson. OBAL

Childe Roland to the Dark Tower Came. Robert Browning. EnVR; NAEL-2; NOBVV; NoP; OAEL-2; OBNV; OtMeF; PeVV; PoE; PPP

Childe Rolandine. Stevie Smith. BrRo

Childe Watters in his stable stoode. Child Waters. *Unknown.* ESPB; FaBoBa; OxBB

Childheart, time alone is not enough. A Late Spring. James Scully. NYBP

Childhood. Jens Baggesen, *tr. fr. Danish by* Longfellow. AWP

Childhood. William Barnes. NOBVV

Childhood. Bruce Beasley. UTF

Childhood. Johannes Bobrowski, *tr. fr. German by* Ruth Mead *and* Matthew Mead. AnRep

Childhood. Anne Bradstreet. *Fr.* Four Ages of Man, The. KTR

Childhood. Frances Cornford. FaBoWP; OxBSP; OxBTC

Childhood. Chitra Divakaruni. OpBo

Childhood. Jean Joubert, *tr. fr. French*. TSaS, *tr. by* Denise Levertov

Childhood. Donald Justice. AnAn; LCAP

Childhood. Jewel C. Latimore. JB

Childhood. Sir Thomas More. *See* I am called Childhood. In Play is all my mind.

Childhood. Edwin Muir. CMoP; HeIP; NoP

Childhood. Rainer Maria Rilke, *tr. fr. German by* M. D. Herter Norton. SOTW

Childhood. Maura Stanton. SM

Childhood. Thomas Traherne. TrGrPo

Childhood. Henry Vaughan. BOEP; NOSC

Childhood. Margaret Walker. IHMS; PBWP; PoBA; Son; WPOW

Childhood. Chris Wallace-Crabbe. FaBoMA

Childhood and School-Time. Wordsworth. *Fr.* Prelude [*or*, Growth of a Poet's Mind], The. CH; EnRP; GN; HAP; NOBE; NoP; NU; OAEL-2; OBNC; OxAEP-2; PoE; SCV

Childhood Fled. Charles Lamb. EnRP

Childhood in Jacksonville, Florida. Jane Cooper. TAP

Childhood is health. (*LL*) Holy Baptisme. George Herbert. PoEL-2

Childhood is not from birth to a certain age and at a certain age. Childhood Is the Kingdom Where Nobody Dies. Edna St. Vincent Millay. FaBoWP; NALW

Childhood Is the Kingdom Where Nobody Dies. Edna St. Vincent Millay. FaBoWP; NALW

Childhood Is the Only Lasting Flower. Ramon Diaz Eterovic, *tr. fr. Spanish by* Teresa Rozo Moorhouse. TSaS

Childhood Lane. Rachel Blake. NWP

Childhood of a Spy. Dick Davis. DiPo

Childhood of a Stranger. Claire Bateman. CrSp

Childhood of an Equestrian, The. Russell Edson. AmPA

Childhood Painting Lesson. Henry Rago. WHSW

Childhood remembrances [*or* memories] are always a drag. Nikki-Rosa. Nikki Giovanni. AIW; BlSi; CrSp; HeIP; IHMS; MoP; PoBA; TAP

Childhood's glad smile was on my lip, life's sunshine on my brow. Emma Catherine Embury. AmWP

Childhood's Retreat. Robert Duncan. NoAM

Childish Game, A. Reinmar von Hagenau, *tr. fr. German by* Jethro Bithell. AWP

Childish Prank, A. Ted Hughes. OAEL-2; OxBC

Childless. Giolla Brighde MacNamee, *tr. fr. Irish by* Frank O'Connor. BIrV

Childless couple, The. Restoration. Jeffrey Skinner. PBCAP

Childless Father, The. Wordsworth. CH

Children. Russell Edson. AmPA

Children, The. William Heyen. BTR

Children, The. Susan MacDonald. IHMS

Children. Sandra McPherson. AnAn; FaBoWP

Children. Bill Manhire. PeNZ

Children, The. Robert Minhinnick. AngWe

Children. Pantiyan Arivutai Nampi, *tr. fr. Tamil by* A. K. Ramanujan. PLW

Children. Po Chü-i, *tr. fr. Chinese by* Arthur Waley. ArLo

Children. Laura Riding. *Fr.* Forgotten Girlhood. RB

Children, The. William Soutar. PAW

Children, The. Constance Urdang. CoAP; IHMS

Children, The. William Carlos Williams. SAmP

Children and Sir Nameless, The. Thomas Hardy. NoP

Children. Teaching the Children. Myra Sklarew. CRP

Children are at the door. At the Door. Lillie Fuller Merriam. PoToHe

Children are dumb to say how hot the day is. The Cool Web. Robert Graves. AWP; GTBS-P; MoP; NAEL-2; NoAM; NoP; OxBTC; PoA; Poetr; PrIm; SCV

Children aren't happy with nothing to ignore. The Parent. Ogden Nash. Spl

Children Band, The. Sir Aubrey De Vere. OBEV

Children begin at green dawn nimbly to build. The Altars in the Street. Denise Levertov. CAPP

Children, behold the chimpanzee. The Chimpanzee. Oliver Herford. FaBV; FiBHP

Children, billy goat, have put crimson reins, The. Anyte, *tr. fr. Greek by* Barbara Hughes Fowler. *Fr.* Epigrams. HePo

Children born of fairy stock. I'd Love to Be a Fairy's Child. Robert Graves. BoTP; FaPON; PDV

Children conceived when two nightgowns. The Submarine Bed. John Peale Bishop. LiTA

Children cried: "Mummy!," The. Massacre of the Innocents. Tadeusz Różewicz, *tr. fr. Polish by* Jan Darowski. OBD

Children dear, was it yesterday. Matthew Arnold. *Fr.* Forsaken Merman, The. BeLS; BoTP; CoGr; EBEV; EBVVPR; FaBoCh; FaPoR; FHYEP; GN; NAEL-2; NTP; OBNV; OBSP; OHCV

Children do not ask the proper questions. Leaping into the Gulf. Patricia Beer. OxBC

Children enter, The. Sundown at Darlington 1878. Lance Henson. VoR

Children go forward with their little satchels, The. The School Children. Louise Glück. AmPA; HCAP; Poetr; WeW

Children have put purple, The. Anyte, *tr. fr. Greek by* Kenneth Rexroth. PGA

Children have tied you, billy-goat, with bright, The. Anyte, *tr. fr. Greek by* Sally Purcell. GrAn

Children I told you I tell you our sun was a hail of gold! Summers Ago. Isabella Gardner. CAPP

Children, if you dare to think. Warning to Children. Robert Graves. CBNP; FaBoCh; MeMBP; NoP; NTP; OAEL-2

Children in the life, The. One by One. Melvin Dixon. PFL

Children in the Wood, The. *Unknown. See* Now ponder well, you parents dear.

Children March, The. Elizabeth Riddell. CBAP

Children of Adam. Walt Whitman. *See* From Pent-up Aching Rivers.

Children of dreams are in terror, The. A Text for These Distracted Times. Rodney Hall. CBAP

Children of earth. Sleep warm. (*LL*) Night Plane. Frances Frost. FaPON; PDV

Children of Greenock, The. W. S. Graham. FaBoTw

Children of Israel prayed for bread; The. Old Sam's Wife. *Unknown*. ChTr

Children of Light. Robert Lowell. CMoP; MoAB; NAAL-2; OxBA

Children of Love. Harold Monro. MoBrPo

Children of Stare, The, *sels*. Walter de la Mare. "Winter is fallen early." Mes

Children of Terezin, The. Stanley Cooperman. BTR

Children of the Epoch. Wislawa Szymborska, *tr. fr. Polish by* Austin Flint. WoWa

Children of the future Age. Blake. *See* In the Age of Gold.

Children of the Heavenly King. John Cennick. WGRP

Children of the Night, The. E. A. Robinson. OxBA

Children of the Owl and the Pussy-Cat, The. Edward Lear. FaBoNo

Children of the Poor, The. Gwendolyn Brooks. *Fr.* Womanhood, The. PoA, *complete*; WPE, 1 *and* 2

Children of the Ritz. Noël Coward. *Fr.* Words and Music. IHNG

Children of the world are on the march, The. The Children March. Elizabeth Riddell. CBAP

Children of yesterday. Song of Hope. Mary Artemisia Lathbury. BLPA

Children picking up our bones. A Postcard from the Volcano. Wallace Stevens. HAP; HCAP; LiTA; MeMAP; NoAM; SAmP; WeW

Children Playing Checkers at the Edge of the Forest. Adrienne Rich. LCAP; WeW

Children set fires in ashbarrels. Galway Kinnell. *Fr.* Avenue Bearing the Initial of Christ into the New World, The. NaP

Children sleep at night. Children. Laura Riding. *Fr.* Forgotten Girlhood. RB

Children, the Sandbar, That Summer. Muriel Rukeyser. LCAP

Children they move stand, The. Clear. Angelo Lewis. PoBA

Children/ this is the blood. Brother of the Streets. Sam Cornish. TRP

Children Waking: Indian Hill Station. Ralph Nixon Currey. PeSA

Children walk. City. Jane Stembridge. NMM

Children Walking Home from School through Good Neighborhood. Donald Justice. DiPo; NIP

Children wandered up and down, The. The Cruise of the *Mystery*. Celia Laighton Thaxter. OBCA

Children were around my feet like dogs, The. Seventh Birthday of the First Child. Sharon Olds. PBCAP

Children were frightened by crescendoes, The. A Fete. Larry Eigner. NeAP

Children were shouting together, The. Frolic. "Æ." BoTP; FaPON; MoBrPo

Children, when was. Napoleon. Miroslav Holub, *tr. fr. Czech by* Káča Poláčková. PoSu, *tr. by* Kaca Polackova; TSaS, *tr. by* Kaca Polačkova

Children who love more than they hate. Families. Thomas Blackburn. OxBSP

Children, why do you fear, why turn away? For Miriam. Marjorie Oludhe Macgoye. WPOW

Children, you are very little. Good and Bad Children. Robert Louis Stevenson. *Fr.* Child's Garden of Verses, A. EBVV; FaBoCh; OxBChV

Chorus: "Got up and dressed up." Jack Kerouac. *Fr.* Mexico City Blues. NeAP

Chorus: "Great Fortune is an hungry thing." Aeschylus, *tr. by* Gilbert Murray. *Fr.* Agamemnon. AWP; NAWM-1

Chorus: He Leadth Me. *(LL)* Joseph Henry Gilmore. AH; BLRP; WBLP; WGRP

Chorus: "If I drink water while this doth last." Thomas Love Peacock. *Fr.* Crotchet Castle. NBLV

Chorus: "In the name of the people." Matsemela Manaka. *Fr.* Pula. PeSAV

Chorus: "In the ocean there's a very sad turtle." Jack Kerouac. *Fr.* Mexico City Blues. PoM

Chorus: "Love's multitudinous boneyard." Jack Kerouac. *Fr.* Mexico City Blues. NeAP

Chorus: "Nobody knows the other side." Jack Kerouac. *Fr.* Mexico City Blues. NeAP

Chorus: "Oh, may my constant feet not fail." Sophocles, *tr. by* Robert Whitelaw. *Fr.* Oedipus the King [*or* Oedipus Rex]. NAWM-1; WGRP

Chorus: "Old Man Mose." Jack Kerouac. *Fr.* Mexico City Blues. Jaz; NeAP

Chorus: Oh, My Darling Clementine. *(LL)* *At. to* Percy Montross. AnAmPo; FaBoBe

Chorus: "Only awake to Universal Mind." Jack Kerouac. *Fr.* Mexico City Blues. NeAP

Chorus: "Praised be man, he is existing in milk." Jack Kerouac. *Fr.* Mexico City Blues. NeAP

Chorus: "Saints, I give myself up to thee." Jack Kerouac. *Fr.* Mexico City Blues. NeAP

Chorus: "Summer holds, The: upon its glittering lake." W. H. Auden. *Fr.* Dog beneath the Skin, The. OxBTC

Chorus: "Sweet are the ways of death to weary feet." Lord De Tabley. *Fr.* Medea. OBEV

Chorus: "Those mindes that wholy dote upon delight." Lady Elizabeth Carey. *Fr.* Mariam. KTR; WPE

Chorus: "To throw away the key and walk away." W. H. Auden. *See* To throw away the key and walk away.

Chorus: "Void that's highly embraceable, The." Jack Kerouac. *Fr.* Mexico City Blues. NeAP

Chorus: "We do not wish anything to happen." T. S. Eliot. *Fr.* Murder in the Cathedral. OxBTC

Chorus: "We have not been happy, my Lord, we have not been too happy." T. S. Eliot. *Fr.* Murder in the Cathedral. OxBTC

Chorus. We Three Kings of Orient Are. *(LL)* John Henry Hopkins, Jr. AH; PChr

Chorus: "What man is he that yearneth." Sophocles, *tr. by* A. E. Housman. *Fr.* Oedipus at Colonus. AWP

Chorus: "Wheel of the quivering Meat, The." Jack Kerouac. *Fr.* Mexico City Blues. NeAP; PoBeRe; PoM

Chorus: "When the hounds of spring are on winter's traces." Swinburne. *See* When the hounds of spring are on winter's traces.

Chorus: "Who hath given man speech? or what hath set therein." Swinburne. *Fr.* Atalanta in Calydon. EnVR; OAEL-2

Chorus: "World's great age begins anew, The." Shelley. *See* World's great age begins anew, The.

Chorus: "Worlds on worlds are rolling ever." Shelley. *See* Worlds on worlds are rolling ever.

Chorus: "You are the town and we are the clock." W. H. Auden. *Fr.* Dog beneath the Skin, The. OxBTC

Chorus for Survival, *sels.* Horace Gregory.
"Ask no return for love that's given." VGW
(Ask No Return.) MoAmPo

Chorus from "Hellas." Shelley. *See* World's great age begins anew, The.

Chorus from "The Rock." T. S. Eliot. *Fr.* Rock, The. LiTB

Chorus-leading, splashing out the wine. *(LL)* A Postcard from North Antrim. Seamus Heaney. IPY; PBCIP; PNI

Chorus of a Song That Might Have Been Written by Albert Chevalier. Max Beerbohm. UV

Chorus of Angels. Cardinal Newman. *See* Praise to the Holiest in the height.

Chorus of Birds. Aristophanes, *tr. fr. Greek by* Swinburne. *Fr.* Birds̓, The. AWP

Chorus of Priests. Fulke Greville. *See* Oh [*or* O] wearisome condition of humanity.

Chorus of Satyrs, Driving Their Goats. Euripides, *tr. fr. Greek by* Shelley. *Fr.* Cyclops. AWP

Chorus of Scyrian Maidens. Philip Bainbrigge. *Fr.* Achilles in Scyros. PeHV

Chorus of the Dead. Nelly Sachs, *tr. fr. German by* Ruth Mead *and* Matthew Mead. WoWa

Chorus of the Rescued. Nelly Sachs, *tr. fr. German.* PoSu; WPOW, *tr. by* Ruth Mead *and* Matthew Mead

Chorus of the Unborn. Nelly Sachs, *tr. fr. German by* Ruth Mead *and* Matthew Mead. NYBP

Chorus of the Years. Thomas Hardy. *See* Yea, the coneys are scared by the thud of hoofs.

Chorus Primus of Bashaws or Cadis. Fulke Greville. *Fr.* Mustapha. NOSC

Chorus Sacerdotum. Fulke Greville. *Fr.* Mustapha. HAP; InvP; JCP; LiTB; NAEL-1; NOBE; OAEL-1; PoEL-1; PPP

Chorus Speaks Her Words as She Dances, The. Linda Gregg. AnAn

Chorus to the Gods. Dryden. *See* All, all of a piece throughout.

Chosen. Marilyn Nelson Waniek. NAmP90

Chosen. W. B. Yeats. BoLoP; CMoP

Chosen Light, A. John Montague. *See* At night, sometimes, when I cannot sleep.

Chosen of God. Stefan Zweig, *tr. fr. German by* Eden *and* Cedar Paul. *Fr.* Jeremiah. TrJP

Chosen People, The. W. N. Ewer. FaBoEE

Chosen Three, on Mountain Height, The. David H. Ela. AH

Chou and the South, *sels.* Confucius, *tr. fr. Chinese by* Ezra Pound. "In the South be drooping trees." CTC

Chou and the South. *Unknown, tr. by* Ezra Pound. *Fr.* Shi King. CTC

Chough. Rex Warner. PoRA

Chough and crow to roost are gone, The. The Outlaw's Song. Joanna Baillie. OBEV

Christ. *Unknown, tr. fr. Greek by* Guy Davenport. GrAn

Christ./ May I die at night. Robert Lowell. OBD

Christ and Satan, *sels. Unknown, tr. fr. Anglo-Saxon by* Charles W. Kennedy.
Lamentations of the Fallen Angels. AnOE

Christ and the Little Ones. Julia Gill. BLPA

Christ and the Pagan. John Banister Tabb. TrCP

Christ, and when I sleep. Poem for Francis Harvey. Madge Herron. VBLP

Christ butterflies a bent nail to a string. *(LL)* Jonathan Lazarus Wright, 1702–1729. Martin Edmunds. UTF

Christ, by dark clouds of worldliness concealed. Prayer before Meat. Una W. Harsen. TrPWD

Christ Calls Man Home. *Unknown.* MeEL

Christ Child, The. Mary Weston Fordham. CBWP-2

Christ child lay on Mary's lap, The. G. K. Chesteron. BoTP; OBCP; OHIP

Christ Church Meadows, Oxford. Donald Hall. NYBP

Christ Climbed Down. Lawrence Ferlinghetti. VGW

Christ Complains to Sinners. *Unknown.* MeEL

Christ Crucified. Richard Crashaw. OBEV

Christ for the World! We Sing. Samuel Wolcott. AH

Christ Goodbye. Padraic Fiacc. IHNG

Christ hath a garden walled around. Isaac Watts. FaBoCh

Christ home, Christ and his mother and all his hallows. *(LL)* The Starlight Night. Gerard Manley Hopkins. EnVR; GTBS-P; InPS; LiTM; MeMBP; MoAB; MoBrPo; NAEL-2; PoE; PPP

Christ How My Circumspect Heart. Gillian Eve Hanscombe *and* Suniti Namjoshi. DT

Christ, I have read, did to His chaplains say. Salutation. Robert Herrick. ChIV-2

Christ I Wudint Know Normal if I Saw It When. Bill Bissett. NOBC

Christ in Alabama. Langston Hughes. PoBA

Christ in Flanders. Lucy Whitmell. NSI

Christ in the Clay-Pit. Jack R. Clemo. GTBS-P

Christ in the Universe. Alice Meynell. MoBrPo; NOBE; OxAEP-2

Christ-in-the-Woods. Sebastian Barry. IB

Christ Inviting Sinners to His Grace, *sels.* Henry Alline.
Amazing Sight! The Saviour Stands. AH

Christ is a nigger. Christ in Alabama. Langston Hughes. PoBA

Christ Is Arisen. Goethe, *tr. fr. German.* *Fr.* Faust. TrCP

Christ is now risen again. Of the Resurrection. Miles Coverdale. ChIV-2

Christ Is Risen! Mrs. D. H. Dugan. BLRP

Christ Is Risen. Dmitri Sergeyevich Merezhkovski, *tr. fr. Russian by* Philip L. Miller. RiWo

Christ is the Fact of facts, the Bible's Theme. The Greatest Person in the Universe. Daniel L. Marsh. BLRP

Christ keep the Hollow Land. William Morris. *Fr.* Hollow Land, The. ChTr
(Song: "Christ keep the Hollow Land.") PoEL-5

Christ made a trance on Friday view. Good Friday. *Unknown.* ChTr

Christ made [or maketh] to man a fair present. Divine Love. *Unknown.*
OAEL-1

(Love Unlike Love.) MeEL

Christ, My Beloved. William Baldwin. EiL; ELP; NOCV

Christ, my Life, my Only Treasure. During His Courtship. Charles
Wesley. NOCV

Christ of His gentleness. In the Wilderness. Robert Graves. CH; ChIV-2;
MoAB; MoBrPo

Christ of Judea, look thou in my heart! Richard Watson Gilder. *Fr.*
Credo. TrPWD

Christ of the Abyss, The. Bruce Dawe. FaBoMA

Christ of the Andes, The, *sels.* Edwin Markham.
"O Christ of Olivet, you hushed the wars." TrPWD

Christ 1. *Unknown, tr. fr. Anglo-Saxon by* Charles W. Kennedy.
Sels.
Advent Lyrics.
"O my Joseph, Jacob's son." ASW, *tr. by* Kevin Crossley-Holland.
"You govern the locks, You open life." ASW, *tr. by* Kevin Crossley-
Holland.
"Bless earth with Thine Advent, O Saviour Christ!" AnOE
"Hail, O most worthy in all the world!" AnOE
"O holy Jerusalem, Vision of peace." AnOE
"To the King./ Thou art the wall-stone rejected"
AnOE

Christ risen was rarely recognized by sight. For They Shall See God. Luci
Shaw. TrCP

Christ the Lord is risen to-day. Easter Hymn. Charles Wesley. OHIP

Christ, the Man. W. H. Davies. WGRP

Christ! These are her angels! The Unicorn and the Lady. Jean Garrigue.
NYBP

Christ 3, *sels. Unknown, tr. fr. Anglo-Saxon by* Charles W. Kennedy.
Last Judgment, The. AnOE

Christ to His Spouse [or The Beloved to the Spouse]. William Baldwin.
EiL; NOCV

Christ to Lazarus. David Constantine. PWE

Christ to seek the lost was sent. Sympathy. L. A. J. Moorer. CBWP-3

Christ Triumphant. *Unknown. See* I Have Labored Sore.

Christ 2, *sels.* Cynewulf, *tr. fr. Anglo-Saxon by* Charles W. Kennedy.
Voyage of Life, The. AnOE

Christ Walking on the Water. W. R. Rodgers. MoAB

Christ Walks in This Infernal District Too. Malcolm Lowry. MoCV;
NOBC

Christ was born on Christmas day. Thomas Helmore. OHIP

Christ was the Word that spake it. *Unknown.* NoSic

Christ washed the feet of Judas! *(LL)* The Feet of Judas. George Marion
McClellan. AAP; PoNe

Christ washed the feet of Judas! The Feet of Judas. George Marion
McClellan. AAP; PoNe

Christ, wha'd ha'e been Chief Rabbi gin he lik't. Up to Date. "Hugh
MacDiarmid." FaBoCo

Christ! What are patterns for? *(LL)* Patterns. Amy Lowell. AWP;
BoWoP; DL; LiTA; MoAmPo; OxBA; TrGrPo; WHSW

Christ, when a child, a garden made. A Legend. *At. to* Peter Ilich
Tchaikovsky, *tr. fr. Russian by* Nathan Haskell Dole. OHIP

Christ, whose glory fills the skies. Morning Hymn. Charles Wesley. TOF

Christ, you walked on the sea, In the Twentieth Century. James
McAuley. ChIV-2

Christabel. Samuel Taylor Coleridge. CH, ll. 1-65; EnRP; FHYEP;
OAEL-2
Sels.
Christabel and Geraldine. PeHV
In the Touch of This Bosom There Worketh a Spell. RB
Scars Remaining, The. OBNC
"'Tis the middle of night by the castle clock." FaBoVe; MeMBP;
NAEL-2

Christabel and Geraldine. Samuel Taylor Coleridge. *Fr.* Christabel. CH,
ll. 1-65; EnRP; FHYEP; OAEL-2; PeHV

Christchurch Bells. *Unknown.* OBET

Christchurch, N. Z. Earle Birney. OxBC

Christendom. Thomas Traherne. PoEL-2

Christening, A. Donald Davie. OxBC

Christenings. Peter Porter. NAs

Christian, Be Up. Robert Nathan. AH

Christian constellations run, The. The Circle. L. A. J. Moorer. CBWP-3

Christian Ethics, *sels.* Thomas Traherne.
"All music, sauces, feasts, delights and pleasures." OxBSP
Contentment. NOCV
(For man to act as if his soul did see.) NOCV

Christian Freedom. George Matheson. TrPWD

Christian has trousers on. *Unknown.* CBNP

Christian Life, The. Samuel Longfellow. WGRP

Christian Pilgrim's Hymn, The. William Williams. *See* Guide Me, O Thou
Great Jehovah.

Christian psalm for thee, A. *(LL)* Ruth; or, The Influences of Nature.
Wordsworth. EnRP; GTBS; GTBS-P; PoEL-4

Christian Rome. Hildebert, *tr. fr. Latin by* Helen Waddell. MLL

Christian Settlements in Africa. Lydia Huntley Sigourney. AmWP

Christiana. Peter Redgrove. OxBC

Christianite. William Stafford. NoAM

Christians awake, salute the happy morn. A Hymn for Christmas Day.
John Byrom. ECEV; NOCV; PoEL-3

Christian's "Good-Night," The. Sarah Doudney. BLPA

Christians have always been pilgriming. "Faith and Practice." John
Balaban. GOA

Christian's New-Year Prayer, The, *sels.* Ella Wheeler Wilcox.
"If my vain soul needs blows and bitter losses." TrPWD

Christian's Reply to the Philosopher, The. (Good in graves as heavenly seed
are sown, The.) Sir William Davenant. MeLP
Sels.

Christina. Louis MacNeice. BoLoP

Christine to Her Son. Christine de Pisan, *tr. fr. French by* Barbara Howes.
BoWoP

Christmas. Sir John Betjeman. OBCP; OxBTC; PIP

Christmas, The. Doll. Myra Cohn Livingston. TLR

Christmas. George Herbert. GeHe; NOSC; PeECV; SeCV-1; TOF; TrCP

Christmas. Leigh Hunt. OBCP

Christmas. Peter McDonald. PNI

Christmas. "Mary I." BoTP

Christmas. Shakespeare. *See* Some say that ever 'gainst that season comes.

Christmas. Nahum Tate. *See* While Shepherds Watched [Their Flocks by
Night].

Christmas — always, forever, a Morning and a Coming. Vlamingh and
Rottnest Island. Francis Webb. FaBoMA

Christmas and Common Birth. Anne Ridler. FaBoTw

Christmas and Death. Janet Frame. PeNZ

Christmas Antiphones, *sels.* Swinburne.
"Thou whose birth on earth." TrPWD

Christmas at Freelands. James Stephens. TIRV; TrCP

Christmas at Sea. Robert Louis Stevenson. BLPL; CH; EBVV; FaBoBe;
FaBV; Mes; OBTV; PeVV

Christmas Ballad. St. John of the Cross, *tr. fr. Spanish by* John Frederick
Nims. STV

Christmas Bells. Longfellow. AH. AnAmPo; BLRP; FaPON; OBCP; PChr,
st. 1; WBLP

Christmas bells, awake and ring. Christmas Morning. Harry Behn. PChr

Christmas Bills. Joseph Hatton. OBCP

Christmas Card. Ted Hughes. OBCP

Christmas Carol: "As Joseph was a-Walking". *Unknown. See* As Joseph
Was a-Walking [or a-Waukin'].

Christmas Carol, A: "Everywhere, everywhere, Christmas tonight!" Phillips
Brooks. *See* Everywhere, everywhere, Christmas tonight!

Christmas Carol: "Angel told Mary, An." Harry Behn. PChr

Christmas Carol: "Christ child lay on Mary's lap, The." G. K. Chesteron.
BoTP; OBCP; OHIP; UV

Christmas Carol: "Christ was born on Christmas day." Thomas Helmore.
OHIP

Christmas Carol: "Close to a quarter of a century since then." T. H. Parry-
Williams, *tr. fr. Welsh by* Joseph P. Clancy. OBWVE

Christmas Carol: "From the starry heav'ns descending." J. R. Newell.
BLRP

Christmas Carol: "God bless the master of this house." *Unknown.* BoTP;
OHIP

(Grace, A.) MoShBr

Christmas Carol, A. ("In the bleak mid-winter"). Christina Rossetti. ChTr;
InPS; NOBVV; OHIP
Sels.
My Gift. FaPON; PChr

Christmas Carol: "So now is come our joyful'st feast." George Wither.
(Our Joyful Feast.) OHIP

Christmas Carol: "Thank God, thank God, we do believe." Christina
Rossetti. PChr

Christmas Carol: "There's a song in the air!" Josiah Gilbert Holland. GN;
OHIP

Christmas Carol: "Three outas from the [High] bleak Karoo." D. J.
Opperman, *tr. fr. Afrikaans by* Anthony Delius. PeSA; PeSAV

Christmas Carol: "Thys ender nyght." *Unknown.* TrGrPo, abr.

Christmas Carol: "When Christ was born in Bethlehem." *Unknown, tr. fr.
Italian by* Longfellow. OHIP

Christmas Carol: "Villagers all, this frosty tide." Kenneth Grahame. *See* Villagers all, this frosty tide.

Christmas Caroll Sung to the King in the Presence at White-Hall, A. (What sweeter music [*or* musick] can we bring.) Robert Herrick. GoJo; PChr, *st.* 1

Sels.

"Darling of the world is come, The."

Christmas Carols. Patricia Beer. OxBC

Christmas Carols. Longfellow. BoTP

Christmas Childhood, A. Patrick Kavanagh. IIP; IPY

Sels.

"My father played the melodion." PChr; RB

Christmas come tomorrow. Christmas with the Holy Family. Susan Cavin. GLP

Christmas comes but once a year. Mother Goose. OxNR; ReMoGo

Christmas comes like this: Wise men. Christmas Comes to Moccasin Flat. James Welch. CDW; MAT; NoAM

Christmas Comes to Moccasin Flat. James Welch. CDW; MAT; NoAM

Christmas Creek. Henry Clarence Kendall. CBAP

Christmas Day. Roy Fuller. OBCP

Christmas Day. Andrew Young. OBCP

Christmas Day in the Workhouse. George R. Sims. BeLS; BLPA; EBNV

Christmas Day [Is Come]. Luke Wadding. NOSC; TIRV

Christmas day is come; let all prepare for mirth. Christmas Day [Is Come]. Luke Wadding. NOSC; TIRV

Christmas Day. 1696. Nicholas Hasluck. *Fr.* Rottnest Island. NOBAu

Christmas Day, *sts.* 6–9. Christopher Smart. *See* Where is this stupendous stranger.

Christmas Day; the Family Sitting. John Meade Falkner. ChIV-2; NOCV; OxBTC

Christmas declares the glory of the flesh. Christmas and Common Birth. Anne Ridler. FaBoTw

Christmas Dinner. Michael Rosen. OBCP

Christmas dinner was at two, The. A Summer Christmas in Australia. Douglas Sladen. OBCP

Christmas 1898, *sels.* Sir Lewis Morris.

"'Tis nigh two thousand years." TrPWD

Christmas Eve. A. R. Ammons. NAs

Christmas Eve. Patricia Beer. OBCP

Christmas Eve. Charlotte Druitt Cole. BoTP

Christmas Eve. John Davidson. *See* "Letter from my love today, A!"

Christmas Eve. Eugene Field. OHIP

Christmas Eve. L. A. J. Moorer. CBWP-3

Christmas Eve. Karl Shapiro. NYBP

Christmas Eve. Edna Kingsley Walla. BoTP

Christmas-Eve and Easter-Day, *sels.* Robert Browning. Earth Breaks Up. TrCP

Christmas Eve, and twelve of the clock. The Oxen. Thomas Hardy. BoTP; CMoP; EBEV; HAP; InPK; LiTM; MeMBP; MoAB; MoBrPo; MoP; NoAM; NOBE; NTP; OAEL-2; OBCP; OxAEP-2; OxBTC; PChr; PeECV; Poetr; PPP; RB; SoSe; TFi; TOF; TRP; WeW

Christmas Eve — Another Ceremony. Robert Herrick. OHIP

Christmas Eve at Beitzinger's Hardware. Living Room. Michael Heffernan. NGP

Christmas Eve in Nineteen-fourteen. Christmas 1914. Mike Harding. OBET

Christmas Eve in Whitneyville, 1955. Donald Hall. UnPo

Christmas Eve: My Mother Dressing. Toi Derricotte. NAmP90

Christmas Eve Service at Midnight at St. Michael's. Robert Bly. NNaP

Christmas Eve, South, 1865. Mary E. Tucker. CBWP-1

Christmas Eve under Hooker's Statue. Robert Lowell. CAPP; FF; OxBA

Christmas Everywhere. Phillips Brooks. BLRP; PWR; WBLP

Christmas Family Reunion. Peter De Vries. NBLV; NOBL

Christmas Folk-Song, A. Lizette Woodworth Reese. FaPON; OBCA; OHIP; TrCP

Christmas Ghost, A. Priscilla Jane Thompson. CBWP-2

Christmas Ghost-Story, A. Thomas Hardy. OBWP

Christmas hath made an end. Carol, for Candlemas Day. *Unknown.* NOSC

Christmas Holiday. Alun Lewis. PoWW

Christmas Hymn. *Unknown, tr. fr. Irish by* Douglas Hyde. TIRV

Christmas Hymn, A. Alfred Domett. GN; WGRP

Christmas Hymn, A. Richard Wilbur. ChIV-2; OBCP; PChr; TrCP

Christmas Hymn, A: "Once in royal David's City." Cecil Frances Alexander. *See* Once in Royal David's City.

Christmas in Africa, *sels.* Jeni Couzyn.

"One autumn afternoon when I was nine." PWE

Christmas in England. Sir Walter Scott. *Fr.* Marmion. GN, *abr.*

Christmas in Penang. John Leyden. OBTV

Christmas in the Heart. *Unknown.* OHIP

Christmas in the Midwest. Maureen Seaton. LoHo

Christmas in the Wood. Frances Frost. TrCP

Christmas is coming [*or* a-coming],/ And the geese are getting fat. *Unknown.* ISE; NTCP; OxNR; PChr; ReMoGo

Christmas Is Really for the Children. Steve Turner. OBCP

Christmas Landscape. Laurie Lee. OBCP

Christmas Legend, A. Frank Sidgwick. OHIP

Christmas Letter Home. G. S. Fraser. OxBTC

Christmas Letter, 1970, *sels.* May Sarton.

"Yes," you say, "of course at Christmas. CrSp

Christmas Lights. Valerie Worth. PChr

Christmas Mass. Elizabeth Wood. NGP

Christmas Mass for a Little Atheist Jesus. Claude Maillard, *tr. fr. French by* Maxine W. Kumin *and* Judith Kumin. BoWoP

Christmas Message, A. Gavin Ewart. FaBoMo

Christmas Morn. *Unknown. See* Shall I tell you who [*or* what] will come.

Christmas Morning. Harry Behn. PChr

Christmas Morning. Elizabeth Madox Roberts. MoAmPo; PChr

Christmas Morning I. Carol Freeman. PChr; PoBA; TTY

Christmas Mourning. Vassar Miller. ChIV-2; MoAmPo

Christmas Night. B. E. Milner. BoTP

Christmas Night. Lawrence Sail. OBCP

Christmas Night in the Quarters, *sels.* Irwin Russell. Fust Banjo, De. BLPA

Christmas night: the solstice storm. The Narrows of Birth. William Everson. PoM

Christmas 1989. Ceaucescu. The Solarium. Rachel Hadas. UnDi

Christmas 1915. Padraic Pearse. PeIV

Christmas 1959 et Cetera. Gerald William Barrax. PChr

Christmas 1914. Mike Harding. OBET

Christmas 1970. Spike Milligan. OBCP

Christmas 1962. Paul Mariah. GLP

Christmas: 1924. Thomas Hardy. FaBoEE; OBCP

Christmas Now Is Drawing Near. *Unknown.* OBET

Christmas Ornaments. Valerie Worth. PChr

Christmas Package, A, *sels.* David McCord.

"My stocking's where." PChr

"That broken star." PChr

Christmas Party. Kate Daniels. NAmP90

Christmas Party, The. Adeline White. BoTP

Christmas Prayer, A. George Macdonald. PChr

Christmas Prayer, A. Robert Louis Stevenson. TrCP

Christmas Present, The. Patricia Hubbell. PDV

Christmas Revel, A. Dafydd Bach ap Madog Wladaidd, *tr. fr. Welsh.* OBWVE

Christmas Rhyme, A. George Sands Johnson. PWR

Christmas Rhyme: North Tyrone. *Unknown.* FaBoVe

Christmas Rose, The. C. Day Lewis. TIRV

Christmas Rush, The. Clara Ann Thompson. CBWP-2

Christmas, season of streamers, coloured lights. Christmas Story (1980). Pat Arrowsmith. BrRo

Christmas Sermon, A, *sels.* Robert Louis Stevenson. To Be Honest, to Be Kind. PoLF

Christmas Shopping. Louis MacNeice. OBCP

Christmas Silence, The. Margaret Deland. OHIP

Christmas Song. At. to Eugene Field. BoTP; OHIP

Christmas Song ("Trees are all bare not a leaf to be seen, The.") *Unknown.* NTP

Christmas Song, A ("Winds through the olive trees.") *Unknown. See* Winds through [*or* thro'] the olive trees.

Christmas, South, 1866. Mary E. Tucker. CBWP-1

Christmas Spider, The. Michael Richards. Spl

Christmas Story (1980). Pat Arrowsmith. BrRo

Christmas Thank You's. Mick Gowar. OBCP

Christmas, the Year One, A.D. Sara Henderson Hay. PoRA

Christmas Thoughts, by a Modern Thinker. William Hurrell Mallock. NOBVV

Christmas Times. Maggie Pogue Johnson. CBWP-4

Christmas Tree, The. Patricia Beer. OBCP

Christmas Tree, A. William Burford. SoSe

Christmas Tree. Stanley Cook. OBCP

Christmas Tree, The. Peter Cornelius. PChr

Christmas Tree, The. Isabel de Savitzsky. BoTP

Christmas Tree. Aileen Fisher. PDV

Christmas Tree, The. L. A. J. Moorer. CBWP-3

Christmas Tree. Laurence Smith. OBCP

Christmas Tree in the Nursery, The. Richard Watson Gilder. OHIP

Christmas-Tree Song, A. Rodney Bennett. BoTP

Christmas Trees, The. Mary Frances Butts. OHIP

Christmas Trees. Geoffrey Hill. NOCV

Christmas twigs crispen and needles rattle, The. New Year's Poem. Margaret Avison. LiTM; NOBC

Christmas Verse, A. "Kay." BoTP

Christmas was in the air and all was well. Karma. E. A. Robinson. AmPP; CMoP; HeIP; MoAB; MoAmPo; TrCP

Christmas Wish, A. Rose Fyleman. BoTP

Christmas with the Holy Family. Susan Cavin. GLP

Christophe. Russell Atkins. PoNe

Christopher Columbus, sels. William Hart-Smith. PoA

Christopher Columbus! Unknown. RoPo

Christopher Marlowe. Michael Drayton. Fr. To Henry Reynolds, of Poets and Poesy. ChTr

Christopher Marlowe. Swinburne. Fr. Sonnets of English Dramatic Poets. EPCY; Son; TrGrPo

Christopher of the Shenandoah, A. Edith M. Thomas. PAH

Christopher Robin Changes Guard with Dylan Thomas. Bill Greenwell. UV

Christopher Robin goes/ Hoppity, hoppity. Hoppity. A. A. Milne. FaBV; NTCP

Christopher Smart. Stanley Shaw. UV

Christopher Street Liberation Day, June 28, 1970. Fran Winant. PeHV

Christopher White. Unknown. ESPB

Christo's. Paul Muldoon. CIP

Christ's Bounty. Unknown, tr. fr. Irish by Brendan Kennelly. TIRV

Christ's Childhood. Robert Southwell. ChIV-2

Christ's Descent into Hell. Rainer Maria Rilke, tr. fr. German by James Wright and Sarah Youngblood. Prf

Christ's Kirk on the Grene. (Was never in Scotland hard nor sene.) At. to James V, King of Scotland. OxBS
   Sels.
   "Than Robene Roy begouth to revell." ScCV

Christ's Life Our Code. Benjamin Copeland. AH

Christ's Nativity. Henry Vaughan. ESCV

Christ's Passion. Abraham Cowley. ChIV-2

Christ's Reply. Edward Taylor. Fr. God's Determinations [touching his Elect]. EAP; NAAL-1; PoEL-3

Christ's Resurrection and Ascension. Philip Doddridge. NOCV

Christs Sleeping Friends. Robert Southwell. ESCV

Christ's Tear Breaks My Heart. Unknown. MeEL

Christ's teeth ascended with him into heaven. The Linen Workers. Michael Longley. Fr. Wreaths. BiHa; CIP

Christ's Triumph after Death. Giles Fletcher the Younger. Fr. Christ's Victory and Triumph, IV.

Christ's Victory and Triumph, sels. Giles Fletcher the Younger.
   Christ's Triumph after Death.
      Celestial City, The. OBD
      (In midst of this city celestial.) NOBE
      Easter Morn. EiL; NOCV
      Halcyon's Nest, The. FaBoPP
   Christ's Victory in Heaven.
      Excellency of Christ. WGRP
      Mercy Pleads for Mankind. JCP
   Christ's Victory on Earth.
      "His haire was blacke and in small curls did twine." SeCV-1
      "Seemèd that Man had them devoured all." PeECV
      "Upon a grassie hillock He was laid." PeECV
      Wooing Song. EiL; OBEV
      (Enchantress' Song, The.) NOSC
   "Here let my Lord hang up his conquering lance." ChIV-2, sts. 30-44; NOSC

Christ's Victory in Heaven. Giles Fletcher the Younger. Fr. Christ's Victory and Triumph.

Christ's Victory on Earth. Giles Fletcher the Younger. Fr. Christ's Victory and Triumph.

Christus; a Mystery, sels. Longfellow.
   Fate of the Prophets, The. WGRP

Christus Natus Est. Countee Cullen. ChIV-2

Christus natus est! the cock. The Animals' Carol. Charles Causley. NAs

Chrome Babies Eating Chocolate Snowmen in the Moonlight. A. K. Redwing. VoR

Chronic Meanings. Bob Perelman. BAP-91

Chronicle. Mei-Mei Berssenbrugge. OpBo

Chronicle, The. Robert Glück. ETG; NGP

Chronicle. Aidan Carl Mathews. IB

Chronicle, A. Unknown. BLPL; CBNP

Chronicle; a Ballad, The. Abraham Cowley. OxAEP-1; SeCV-1

Chronicler, The. Alexander Bergman. TrJP

Chronographia Continuata. John Riley. VaA

Chronology. Turner Cassity. PoA

Chrysalides. Thomas Kinsella. BIrV

Chrysanthemums. Irene McKinney. PBCAP

Chrysanthemums last too long for these ravenous ladies. Starved Lovers. Archibald MacLeish. MeMAP

Chrystal streames, wherein my love did swimme, The. Giles Fletcher the Elder. Fr. Licia. ESo

Chuang Tzu and Hui Tzu. The Joy of Fishes. Chuang Tzu, tr. fr. Chinese by Thomas Merton. Mes

Chuck: A Reminiscence. Sarah Pelham. UnDi

Chuck it, Smith! (LL) Antichrist, or the Reunion of Christendom; an Ode. G. K. Chesteron. FaBoCo; IHNG; NOBE; NOBL; OBSV; OxAEP-2

Chuck Will's Widow Song. Unknown. BPo

"Chuff! chuff! chuff!" An' a mountain-bluff. A Song of Panama. Damon Runyon. PAH

Chug! Puff! Chug! Tugs. James S. Tippett. FaPON

Chung-i Temple, The, sels. Wen Cheng-ming, tr. fr. Chinese by Jonathan Chaves.

Chung Shin. Stephen Shu Ning Liu. ETG

Chunks of night. Shadows. Patricia Hubbell. Spl

Church, The. Edwin Ford Piper. WGRP

Church, The. Jules Romains, tr. fr. French by Jethro Bithell. WGRP

Church and clergy here, no doubt, The. Verses Written upon Windows. Swift. IHNG

Church,/ Chapel. Unknown. OxNR

Church and State. W. B. Yeats. CMoP

Church and the World walked far apart, The. The Church Walking with the World. Matilda C. Edwards. BLPA

Church at little Winwick, The. Winwick, Lancashire. Unknown. GBP

Church Bells, The. Mrs. Henry Linden. CBWP-4

Church Bells. Clara Ann Thompson. CBWP-2

Church bells ring — it is the Sabbath day, The. The Lifting of the Cloud. Thomas MacDonagh. TIRV

Church Burning: Mississippi. James A. Emanuel. PoBA; PoNe

Church Festivals. Christopher Harvey. NOSC

Church-Floor [or Floore], The. George Herbert. EBEV; ESCV; MeLP; NOSC; OAEL-1; PeECV

Church Going. Philip Larkin. CMoP; GTBS-P; HeIP; LiTM; MoBrPo; MoP; NAEL-2; NIP; NoAM; NoP; OAEL-2; Poetr; PPP; PrIm; SCV; SoSe; TFi; TwCP; UnPo

Church in the Heart, The. Morris Abel Beer. PoToHe

Church is a business, and the rich, The. After Lorca. Robert Creeley. InPS; LCAP; NaP

Church is an iceberg, The. Winter Night. Charles Simic. HCAP

Church-Lock and Key. George Herbert. ESCV; GeHe; OxBSP

Church Monuments. George Herbert. GeHe; HAP; JCP; NAEL-1; NOCV; NoP; NOSC; OAEL-1; PoE; TRP

Church Mouse commends: tapeworms and slugs grow wings. Critics and Poets. Geoffrey Grigson. FaBoEE

Church-Music[k]. George Herbert. ESCV; GeHe; OxBSP; SeCV-1

Church of a Dream, The. Lionel Johnson. OAEL-2; OBMV

Church of England's Glory, The. Unknown. APAS

Church of Heaven's triumphal Car, The. Live, Evil Veil. John Wheelwright. ChIV-1

Church of San Antonio de la Florida, The. Paul Petrie. NYBP

Church of the Revolution, The. Hezekiah Butterworth. PAH

Church on Comiaken Hill, The. Richard Hugo. Prf; SM

Church-Porch, The. George Herbert. ESCV; OBF

Church Romance, A. Thomas Hardy. FaBoTw; NOBE; OxAEP-2; OxBTC; PeECV

Church steeple fingers the sky, The. Asleep in the City. Michael Smith. PBCIP

Church the Garden of Christ, The. Isaac Watts. NOCV; PeECV

Church Today, The. Sir William Watson. WGRP

Church tower crowned the town, A. The Glass Town. Alastair Reid. NYBP

Church Universal, The. Samuel Longfellow. WGRP

Church Walking with the World, The. Matilda C. Edwards. BLPA

Churches are best for prayer, that have least light. Dark Churches. John Donne. Fr. Hymn [or Hymne] to Christ, at the Author's Last Going into Germany. EBEV; FaBoRV; JCP; LiTB; MeLP; SeCV-1

Churches, Chapels, Stores, and Houses. A General Description of Men and Things in Cape Town. Frederic Brooks. PeSAV

Churches mystical repast, The. (LL) Superliminare. George Herbert. ESCV; NOSC; SeCP

Church's One Foundation, The. Samuel John Stone. UV; WGRP

Church's publication, The. Believers' Best Buy. Roger Woddis. UV
Church's Restoration, The. Sir John Betjeman. FaBoPa
Churchyard leans to the sea with its dead, The. The Old Churchyard of Bonchurch. Philip Bourke Marston. EBVV; OBNC
Churchyard on the Sands, The. Lord De Tabley. CH, *abr.*; FaBoPP; GBL; OBNC
Churchyard under Snow. David Scott. PWE
Churl that wants another's fare, The. The Dog in the River. Phaedrus, *tr. fr. Latin* by Christopher Smart. AWP
Churlyshe Cat, The. John Skelton. *See* That vengeaunce I ask and cry [crye].
Churning (or Lovemaking): "Young man made for the corner, A." Unknown, formerly at. to Cynewulf, *tr. fr. Anglo-Saxon.* Fr. Riddles (Exeter Book). PeLV, *tr.* by Kevin Crossley-Holland
Churning the compost, dazed. To Earth. James Applewhite. PoA
Chyrsanthemums, *sels.* Yün Shou-p'ing, *tr. fr. Chinese* by Jonathan Chaves.
Ci-vi-li-za-tion. (*LL*) Sell Out. Léon Damas. NegPo
Cibber! write all thy verses upon glasses. Pope. FaBoEE
Cicada. Li Shang-yin, *tr. fr. Chinese* by Eugene Eoyang *and* Irving Y. Lo. SuSp
Cicada, The. Ou-yang Hsiu, *tr. fr. Chinese* by Arthur Waley. AWP
Cicada. Adrien Stoutenburg. NYBP; RFM
Cicada. *Unknown, tr. fr. Greek* by Willis Barnstone. EaPr
Cicadas in brambled foliage, The. The House-Builders. Kamala Das. PBWP
Cicala stoned with dew. Meleager, *tr. fr. Greek* by Peter Whigham. GrAn
Cider and Vesalius. John Peck. AmPA
Cider Song. Mildred Weston. BoNaP
Cigales. Richard Wilbur. NOBA
Cigales cannot hear. (*LL*) Cigales. Richard Wilbur. NOBA
Cigar Smoke, Sunday, after Dinner. Louise Townsend Nicholl. FYAP
Cigarette. A. *Mongol Oral Tradition, tr.* by C. R. Bawden. WTO
Cigarette my girl is smoking, A. Jealousy. *Malay Oral Tradition, tr.* by R. J. Wilkinson *and* R. O. Winstedt. WTO
Cigarette Poem, The. Faye Kicknosway. IHMS
Cigarette Salesman, The. Barbara Helfgott Hyett. ETG
Cigarette smoke floated. Milne's Bar. Norman MacCaig. FaBoTw
Cigarettes Will Spoil Yer Life. *Unknown.* AS
Cill Chais. *Unknown, tr. fr. Irish* by Thomas Kinsella. NOIV
Cimabuella. Bayard Taylor. BXAP
Cincirinella Had a Mule. *Unknown, tr.* by Maria Cimino. FaPON
Cincophrenicpoet. Bob Kaufman. PoNe
Cinderella. Olga Broumas. InPK
Cinderella. Miroslav Holub, *tr. fr. Czech* by Ian Milner *and* George Theiner. AnRep
Cinderella. Randall Jarrell. LCAP; NAAL-2; VCAP
Cinderella. Ruby C. Saunders. BlSi
Cinderella. Anne Sexton. HeIP; InPS; NAAL-2
Cinderella, dressed in yellow. *Unknown.* RoPo
Cinderella is sorting the peas. Cinderella. Miroslav Holub, *tr. fr. Czech* by Ian Milner *and* George Theiner. AnRep
Cinema is cruel, The. An Image of Leda. Frank O'Hara. HCAP; LCAP
Cinéma Vérité. Dorothy Walters. IHMS
Cinnamon Peeler, The. Michael Ondaatje. NOBC
Cino. Ezra Pound. VGW
Cinq Ans Après. Gelett Burgess. *See* Ah, Yes, I Wrote the "Purple Cow."
Cinquain: A Warning. Adelaide Crapsey. *See* Just now/ Out of the strange.
Cinque. Janet Campbell Hale. VoR
Cinque Ports, The. *Unknown.* FaBoUs
Cipriana. Ernesto Trejo. AfAz
Circe. Lord De Tabley. NOBVV
Circe. Hilda Doolittle ("H. D."). PoRA
Circe. Gavin Ewart. FaBoBl
Circe. William Gibson. PoA
Circe. A. D. Hope. PPP
Circe. Louis MacNeice. OBMV
Circe, *sels.* Augusta Webster.
  "Sun drops luridly into the west, The." PeVV
Circe/ Mud Poems, *sels.* Margaret Atwood.
  "Men with the heads of eagles." NoAM
  "People come from all over to consult me, bringing their limbs." NALW
Circa a lute she on — you say. Enchanter's Nightshade. Richard Caddel. NBrP
Circle, The. Jean Garrigue. LiTA
Circle, The. L. A. J. Moorer. CBWP-3
Circle, A. Theodore Spencer. NYBP
Circle, a Square, a Triangle and a Ripple of Water. Jane Cooper. TAP

Circle Game, The. Margaret Atwood. MoCV
  Sels.
  "Being with you."
  "Returning to the room."
  "Summer again."
Circle of Struggle. William Pitt Root. NYBP
Circle of Totems, The. Peggy Shumaker. PBCAP
Circle of Weeping, The. Amir Gilboa, *tr. fr. Hebrew* by Ruth Finer Mintz. MHP
Circle Sleeper. Jean H. Marvin. CRH
Circle to the left, Old Brass Wagon. Old Brass Wagon. *Unknown.* AS
Circles. Celia Gilbert. MDDM
Circles never fully round, but change, The. Perspective of Co-ordination. Arthur Davison Ficke. PoA
Circling shadow on the measured dial, The. Chronology. Turner Cassity. PoA
Circling the Daughter. Etheridge Knight. ETG
Circuit closes, The. House and heart. Winter Night. Louis O. Coxe. NYBP
Circuit Judge, The. Edgar Lee Masters. *Fr.* Spoon River Anthology. FaBoEE
Circuit of Apollo, The. The Countess of Winchilsea. NALW
Circulation, The. Thomas Washbourne. NOCV
Circulation of the Blood, The. Sir Richard Blackmore. *Fr.* Creation. FaBoUs
Circumambulation of Mt. Tamalpais. Andrew Hoyem. PoA
Circumstance. Tennyson. CBLP
Circus. Milton Kaplan. GoYe
Circus, The. Elizabeth Madox Roberts. FaPON
Circus Animals' Desertion, The. W. B. Yeats. CMoP; EPCY; FaBoMo; FaBoTw; HeIL; LiTB; MAT; MeMBP; MoP; NAEL-2; NAWM-2; NIP; NoAM; NOBE; NOIV; NoP; OAEL-2; OxBTC; PrIm; TEP; TFi
Circus at the Barber's Shop. Kendrick Smithyman. PeNZ
Circus Garland, A, *sels.* Rachel Field.
  Equestrienne. OBCA
  Gunga. OBCA
  "Nothing now to mark the spot." OBCA
  Parade. OBCA
  Performing Seal, The. OBCA
Circus Parade, The. Katharine Pyle. OBCA
Circus-Postered Barn, The. Elizabeth J. Coatsworth. MoAmPo
Circus runaway, tattooed from head to toe in yellow. Finding the Tattooed Lady in the Garden. Pattiann Rogers. MT
Circus was never meant for children, The. Circus. Milton Kaplan. GoYe
Cirque d'Hiver. Elizabeth Bishop. InPS; LiTA
Cirrus bow of surf is blown, The. A Fantasy of Little Waters. James Scully. NYBP
Cissbury Ring. Paul Coltman. PAW
Citation and Examination of William Shakespeare, The, *sels.* Walter Savage Landor.
  Maid's Lament, The. OBEV; OBNC
Cities, The. "Æ." OBMV
Cities and Desire, *sels.* Italo Calvino, *tr. fr. Italian.*
  "From there, after six days and seven nights, you arrive at Zobeide." AnRep, *tr.* by William Weaver
Cities and Seas. Norman Jordan. PoNe
Cities and Signs, *sels.* Italo Calvino, *tr. fr. Italian.*
  "No one, wise Kublai, knows better than you." AnRep, *tr.* by William Weaver
  "Travelers return from the city of Zirma with distinct memories." AnRep, *tr.* by William Weaver
  "You walk for days among trees and among stones." AnRep, *tr.* by William Weaver
Cities and the Dead, *sels.* Italo Calvino, *tr. fr. Italian.*
  "No city is more inclined than Eusapia to enjoy life and flee care." AnRep, *tr.* by William Weaver
Cities and the Sky, *sels.* Italo Calvino, *tr. fr. Italian.*
  "Those who arrive at Thekla can see little of the city." AnRep, *tr.* by William Weaver
Cities and Thrones and Powers. Kipling. *Fr.* Puck of Pook's Hill. CoGr; GoJo; NOBE; NTP; OBNC; OtMeF; OxBTC; PoEL-5
Cities and towns, ye haunts of wretchedness! Industrial Evils. Joseph Cottle. *Fr.* Malvern Hills. NOEC
Cities are walled. It is a cruel land. Memory. Babette Deutsch. PoA
Cities Drowned. Sir Henry Newbolt. CH
Cities Have Fallen, The. Fragano Ledgister. PBCV
Cities of dream wander under the bark of a December forest, The. A December Forest. Vesna Krmpotic, *tr. fr. Croatian* by Vasa D. Mihailovich. WPOW
Cities of the Plain, The. Whittier. ChIV-1

Clambering up the Cold Mountain path. Han-shan, *tr. fr. Chinese* by Gary Snyder. EnlH

Clamming. Reed Whittemore. NYBP; TAP

Clammy cement, The. Cold. Dennis Brutus. PeSAV

Clamor the bells falling bells. Lear Town. Anne Carson. *Fr. Life of Towns, The.* BAP-90

Clamour of the wind making music. St. Columcille, *tr. fr. Irish* by John Montague. BIrV

Clams. Ishigaki Rin, *tr. fr. Japanese* by Hiroaki Sato. PBWP

Clan is all together, eating Passover matzoh, joking, The. This Passover or the Next I Will Never Be in Jerusalem. Hilton Obenzinger. BCF

Clan Meeting: Births and Nations: A Blood Song. Michael S. Harper. NoAM

Clanking past the crest of a dune. Bad Run at King's Rest. Douglas Livingstone. PeSAV

Clap, clap handies. Clap Handies. *Unknown.* ReMoGo

Clap, clap the double nightcap on! William Gifford. Walter Savage Landor. FaBoEE; GTBS-P

Clap Handies. *Unknown.* ReMoGo

Clap hands, clap hands/ Hie, Tommy Randy. *Unknown.* OxNR

Clap hands, clap hands/ Till father comes home. *Unknown.* OxNR

Clap hands, Daddy comes/ With his pocket full of plums. *Unknown.* OxNR

Clap hands, Daddy's coming/ Up the waggon way. *Unknown.* OxNR

Clap Your Hands for Herod. Josef Hanzlik, *tr. fr. Czech* by Ian Milner. OBCP

Clapping Chant, A. *Unknown.* FaBoVe

Clara strolled in the garden with the children. Souvenir of the Ancient World. Carlos Drummond de Andrade, *tr. fr. Portuguese* by Mark Strand. AnRep; TSaS

Clare de Kitchen. *Unknown.* BLPA

Clarel, *sels.* Herman Melville.
  Of Rome. OxBA
  On Mammon. OxBA
  Prelusive. AmPP
  Sodom. AmPP
  Ungar and Rolfe. OxBA

Clarence ("Clarence Lee from Tennessee.") Shel Silverstein. OBCA

Clarence Mangan. Thomas Kinsella. CIP

Clarence Short Bull died. Sitting Bull's Will versus the Sioux Treaty of 1868 and Monty Hall. A. K. Redwing. VoR

Clarendon had law and sense. On the Young Statesmen. Charles Sackville. APAS

Clari, the Maid of Milan, *sels.* John Howard Payne.
  Home, Sweet Home. AnAmPo; BLPA; EBEvV; FaBoBe; WBLP

Clarimonde. Théophile Gautier, *tr. fr. French* by Lafcadio Hearn. *Fr. Taches Jaunes, Les.* AWP

Clarion-Call, The. *Unknown.* BLRP

Claritas. Denise Levertov. VGW

Clarity. A. R. Ammons. HCAP; TAP

Clark Colven and his gay ladie. Clerk Colvill. *Unknown.* EnSB; ESPB; FaBoBa; GBP; OxBB

Clash of salutation. As keels thrust into shingle. Geoffrey Hill. *Fr. Mercian Hymns.* NoAM; NoP

Clasp me in your infinite gaze, Lady of All Knowledge. *(LL)* Our Lady. Janine Canan. SRLS

Clasp you the God within yourself. The Last Round. Anna Wickham. MoBrPo

Clasping of Hands. George Herbert. PoEL-2

Class Incident from Graves. Alan Brownjohn. OxBTC

Class Room. Virginia A. Houston. ShDr

Class Song of '91. Eloise Bibb. CBWP-4

Classic. A. R. Ammons. NOBA

Classic Ballroom Dances. Charles Simic. LCAP; WeW

Classic Case, A. Gilbert Sorrentino. NeAP

Classic Encounter. "Christopher Caudwell." OxBTC

Classic landscapes of dreams are not, The. The Snowfall. Donald Justice. CRP; Poetr; VGW

Classic Scene. William Carlos Williams. NAAL-2; OxBA

Classic Verses. Rade Drainac, *tr. fr. Serbo-Croatian* by Charles Simic. HSix

Classic Waits for Me, A. E. B. White. BXAP; NYBP

Classical Quatrain, A. Paul Goodman. VGW

Classics can console. But not enough, The. *(LL)* Sea Grapes. Derek Walcott. TRP

Classics Society. Tony Harrison. *Fr. School of Eloquence, The.* NAEL-2; NoAM; SCBI

Classified Ad. Kate Ellen Braverman. PRA

Classroom in October. Elias Lieberman. GoYe

Claud Cockburn. Thomas McCarthy. IB; PBCIP

Claude Allen. *Unknown.* AmFP

Claude to Eustace. Arthur Hugh Clough. *Fr. Amours de Voyage.* CBLP; NOBVV

Claude to Eustace ("Ah, Let Me Look.") Arthur Hugh Clough. *Fr. Amours de Voyage.* EnVR; NOBVV

Claude to Eustace ("I am in love.") Arthur Hugh Clough. *Fr. Amours de Voyage.* EnVR; FaBoVe; NOBVV

Claude to Eustace ("No, The Christian Faith.") Arthur Hugh Clough. *Fr. Amours de Voyage.* EnVR; NOBVV

Claudio's Lament: "Pardon, goddess of the night." Shakespeare. *Fr. Much Ado about Nothing.*

Claudius Gilbert. John Wilson. SCAP

Claudy. James Simmons. BiHa; CIP; PBCIP; PWE

Claus von Stauffenberg. Thom Gunn. OBWP

Claustrophobia. Sean O Riordain, *tr. fr. Irish* by Thomas Kinsella. NOIV

Clavering. E. A. Robinson. OxBA

Claw marks deep in the wood. *(LL)* Winter. Philip Salom. NOBAu

Claws from the cinders onto the hot tracks. *(LL)* On the Death of Sylvia Plath. Judith Herzberg. WPOW, *tr.* by Manfred Wolf

Claws of the tropics will gather your pile and the dealer gets it all, The. *(LL)* Down and Out. Clarence Leonard Hay. BeLS; BLPA

Clay is the word and clay is the flesh. Patrick Kavanagh. *Fr. Great Hunger, The.* IPY; NoAM; OxBTC

Clay Jug, The. Kabir, *ad fr. Hindi* by Robert Bly. NU

Clay-Land Moods. Jack R. Clemo. PWE

Clay, sand, and rock, seem of a diff'rent birth. Barten Holyday. FaBoEE

Clay when the wire slackens, sheds its velvet light. John Wilkinson. NBrP

Clayming [*or* Claiming] a Second Kiss(e) by Desert. Ben Jonson. *Fr. Celebration of Charis in Ten Lyric[k] Peeces [or pieces], A.* BeJo; OxAEP-1; SeCP

Clean as a lady. Tulip. Humbert Wolfe. MoBrPo

Clean birds by sevens. A Charm against a Magpie. *Unknown.* ChTr (Dove, The.) GBP

Clean for her kiss? *(LL)* Tempted. Edward Rowland Sill. AnAmPo

Clean Hands. Austin Dobson. TrPWD

Clean in the light, with nothing to remember. Aspects. Norman MacCaig. OxBS

Clean is the autumn wind. Li Po, *tr. fr. Chinese* by Robert Payne. TAL

Clean slate, with your own face on, A. *(LL)* You're. Sylvia Plath. FaBoTw; FaBoWP; NAs; RB

Clean the spittoons, boy. Brass Spittoons. Langston Hughes. MoAmPo; NoAM; Poetr

Clean thin hollow of breast. Reflections. Anita Barrows. NMM

Cleaned the Crocodile's Teeth. *Unknown.* TSaS, *tr.* by Terese Svoboda

Cleaning a Fish. Dave Jeddie Smith. NoAM

Cleaning the Fish. Robert Pack. SM

Cleaning the Well. Fred Chappell. MT

Cleaning woman opened the rusty door, A. The Church of San Antonio de la Florida. Paul Petrie. NYBP

Cleanliness. Stephen Dunn. SoCa

Cleanliness. Charles Lamb *and* Mary Lamb. OxBChV

Cleanly rush of the mountain air, The. The Dead Knight. John Masefield. CH; GTBS-P

Cleanly, sir, you went to the core of the matter. A Correct Compassion. James Kirkup. FaBoTw; OxBTC

Cleanness, *sels. Unknown, tr. fr. Middle English* by Brian Stone.
  "He who would acclaim Cleanness in becoming style." NOCV

Cleansing Fires. Adelaide Anne Procter. WGRP

Clear. Angelo Lewis. PoBA

Clear Air of October, The. Robert Bly. NaP

Clear and Cool. Charles Kingsley. *Fr. Water Babies, The.* GN

Clear Ankor, on whose silver-sanded shore. Another to the River Ankor. Michael Drayton. *Fr. Idea.* ESo; NOSC

Clear are her eyes. Upon Her Eyes. Robert Herrick. BeJo

Clear as my ash tree through the glass. Housing. Denise Riley. NBrP

Clear Bright. Huang T'ing-chien, *tr. fr. Chinese* by Kenneth Rexroth. OHMPC

Clear Bright. Li Ch'ing-chao, *tr. fr. Chinese* by Kenneth Rexroth. BoWoP

Clear bright morning, with its scented air, The. The Fair Morning. Jones Very. NOBA

Clear brown eyes, kindly and alert, with 12-20 vision, The. Portrait. Kenneth Fearing. MoAmPo

Clear church bells ring in the Christmas morn, The. *(LL)* The Epic. Tennyson. EnVR; NAEL-2

Clear cool note of the cuckoo which has ousted the legitimate nest-holder, The. Sincere Flattery of W. W. (Americanus). James Kenneth Stephen. FiBHP; NOBL

Clockwork skating Wordsworth on the ice, A. Xmas for the Boys. Gavin Ewart. OBSV

Clod and the Pebble, The. Blake. *Fr.* Songs of Experience. EnLoPo; EnRP; FaBV; FHYEP; InPS; NAEL-2; NOBE; NoP; OBNC; OtMeF; OxAEP-2; OxBSP; PoE; PrIm; RB; SCGP; SCV; TEP; TFi; TrGrPo

Clodian Songbook, sels. C. K. Stead.
  "Air New Zealand." PeNZ
  "Fucking, I feel at one with the world." PeNZ

Cloe. George Granville. *See* Cloe's the wonder of her sex.

Cloe ("Bright as the day, and like the morning fair.") George Granville. FaBoCo; FaBoEE; NIP

Cloe, blooming sweet as May. To Cloe. Hildebrand Jacob. NOEC

Cloe, by your command, in verse I write. A Letter from Artemisa in the Town, to Chloe [*or* Cloe], in the Country. The Earl of Rochester. PoE; SeCV-2

Cloe to Artimesa. *Unknown.* ECWP

Cloe's the wonder of her sex. To Cloe. George Granville. FaBoEE; NBLV
  (Cloe.) OxBSP

Clogged and soft and sloppy eyes. The Parents: People Like Our Marriage Maxie and Andrew. Gwendolyn Brooks. *Fr.* Notes from the Childhood and the Girlhood. LCAP

Cloister. Conrad Aiken. *See* So, in the evening, to the simple cloister.

Clonakilty. *Unknown.* FaBoEE

Clonfeacle. Paul Muldoon. CIP

Clonmacnoise. Angus O'Gillan. *See* In a quiet water'd land, a land of roses.

Clonmel Jail. *Unknown, tr. fr. Irish by* Valentin Iremonger. BIrV

Cloudburst an' soarin' mune. Cloudburst and Soaring Moon. "Hugh MacDiarmid." NoAM

Cloosmit the herring, hosts in the night. Ko-Ishin-Mit Goes Fishing. George Clutesi. HATNAP

Clora, come view my soul and tell. The Gallery. Andrew Marvell. ESCV; MeLP; NoP; PoE

Clorinda and Damon. Andrew Marvell. ESCV; SeCP

Cloris, I cannot say your eyes. To Cloris. Sir Charles Sedley. BoLoP

Cloris, it is not thy disdaine. To the Tune of, In Fayth I Cannot Keepe My Father's Sheepe. Sidney Godolphin.
  (Song: "Chloris, it is not thy disdaine.") MeLP

Cloris misfortunes that can be exprest. Elizabeth Wilmot, Countess of Rochester. KTR

Close by the basement door-step. A Toad. Elizabeth Akers Allen. OBCA

Close by those meads, for ever crowned with flow'rs. Pope. *Fr.* Rape of the Lock, The. EBEvV; EBNV; FaBoEH; FHYEP; HAP; ImPo; NoP; OAEL-1; OBNV; OxBoLi, *sl. abr.;* PeLV; PoEL-3; TEP; TrGrPo
  (Hampton Court.) FaBoPP, *shorter sel.;* OBSV, *shorter sel.*

Close by, to the north, there were two oranges. Jean-Joseph Rabéarivelo, *tr. fr. French by* Ellen Conroy Kennedy. NegPo

Close Clan, The. Mark Van Doren. GoYe

Close his eyes; his work is done! Dirge for a Soldier. George Henry Boker. AnAmPo; PAH

Close is lust's expectation. On a Bath-House in which Both Men and Women Bathe. Paulus Silentiarius, *tr. fr. Greek by* Andrew Miller. GrAn

Close keep your lips, if that you meane. To Women, to Hide Their Teeth, if They Be Rotten or Rusty. Robert Herrick. FaBoUs

Close now the door; shut down the light. The Supremer Sacrifice. Suzanne Gardinier. CBAP

Close now thine eyes, and rest secure. A Good-Night. Francis Quarles. TrGrPo

Close of Day, The. Wesley Curtright. CDC

Close Quarters. John Banister Tabb. OBAL

Close Season for Marriage. *Unknown.* FaBoUs

Close the dim eyes, for expression hath left them. Lines on a Dead Girl. Priscilla Jane Thompson. CBWP-2

Close thine eyes, and sleep secure. On a Quiet Conscience. Charles I, King of England. CH

Close to a quarter of a century since then. T. H. Parry-Williams, *tr. fr. Welsh by* Joseph P. Clancy. OBWVE

Close to Aminta, on the Loss of Her Lover. Sarah Dixon. ECWP

Close to nature my brother, your thoughts ring softly. To an Indian Poet. Patty L. Harjo. VoR

Close to the end of my tether. (*LL*) Down on My Luck. A. R. D. Fairburn. PeNZ

Close to the fireside confined. The Invitation from a Country Cottage. Martha Sansom. ECWP

Close to the gates a spacious garden lies. The Gardens of Alcinous. Homer, *tr. by* Pope. *Fr.* Odyssey. NAWM-1; OAEL-1; OBVE

Close to the sod. The Snowdrop. Anna Bunston de Bary. BoTP

Close under here, I watched two lovers once. "Robin Hyde." *Fr.* Beaches, The. FaBoWP; PeNZ

Close-up. A. R. Ammons. PoA

Close-Up. Christine McNeill. NWP

Close-up. Heather McPherson. PeNZ

Close up the casement, draw the blind. Shut Out That Moon. Thomas Hardy. CMoP; NoAM; NOBE

Close up wolf about my mouth. Animal. Bill Griffiths. NBrP

Close-ups of Summer. Norman MacCaig. OxBC

Close Your Eyes! Arna Bontemps. CDC; PoBA; PoNe

Close your eyes; walk bravely through. (*LL*) Close Your Eyes! Arna Bontemps. CDC; PoBA; PoNe

Close your sleepy eyes, or the pale moonlight will steal you. Aqua Laluah. ShDr

Closed Door, The. Theodosia Garrison. BLPA; PoToHe

Closed Doors. Marie Thorson. PWR

Closed eyes can't see the white roses. Give Them the Flowers Now. *Unknown.* WBLP

Closed is that curious ear by Death's cold hand. Thomas Gray's View of Nature. William Mason. *Fr.* English Garden, The. EPCY; NOEC

Closed like confessionals, they thread. Ambulances. Philip Larkin. FaBoTw; NAEL-2; OxBC

Closed Mill. Maggie Anderson. PBCAP

Closed window looks down, A. Ka 'Ba. Amiri Baraka. BPo; NBV; TAP

Closed World, The. Denise Levertov. NoP

Closer First to Earth. Anne Hazlewood-Brady. IHMS

Closest to men, thou pitying Son of Man. To Jesus of Nazareth. Frederic Lawrence Knowles. TrPWD

Closing Album, The, sels. Louis MacNeice.
  Dublin. CIP; FaBoPP; IIP; OBTV; OxBTC

Closing my eyes I sink down into a darkness. In the Suburbs. Michael O'Loughlin. IB

Closing of the Rodeo, The. William Jay Smith. AiP; GOA; TwCP

Closing Prayer. Johnstone G. Patrick. TrPWD

Closing Scene, The. Thomas Buchanan Read. AnAmPo

Closing the doors of the house and the head also! (*LL*) Asmodai. Geoffrey Hill.

Closing the House. Jim Wayne Miller. MT

Closing Time. David Wagoner. NYBP

Clote (Water-Lily), The. William Barnes. ELP; FaBoVe; PoEL-4

Cloth of Gold. Francis Reginald. MoCV

Cloth-plant grew till it covered the bush, The. Widow's Lament. *Unknown, tr. fr. Chinese by* Arthur Waley. *Fr.* Shih Ching. BoWoP

Cloth was laid in the Vorkhouse hall, The. The Workhouse Boy. *Unknown.* GBP

Clothed in yellow, red and green. *Unknown.* OxNR

Clother of the lily, feeder of the sparrow. They Toil Not neither Do They Spin. Christina Rossetti. TrPWD
  (Prayer: "Clother of the lily, feeder of the sparrow.") OBD

Clothes. Edgar Bowers. ArOW

Clothes. Wislawa Szymborska, *tr. fr. Polish by* Grazyna Drabik *and* Sharon Olds. PoSu

Clothes Do but Cheat and Cozen Us. Robert Herrick. CaPo; ErPo

Clothes-Line, The. Charlotte Druitt Cole. BoTP

Clothes-line is a Rosary, The. A Thought for Washing Day. Julia Ward Howe. AmWP

Clothes make no sound when I tread ground. The Swan. Unknown, formerly at. to Cynewulf, *tr. by* Geoffrey Grigson. *Fr.* Riddles (Exeter Book). ChTr; RB

Clothes Make the Man. Jack Conway. NBLV

Clothes Maketh the Man. Theodore Weiss. NoAM

Clothes on the Washing Line. Frank Flynn. OTCP

Clothes Pit, The. Douglas Dunn. OxBTC

Clothing us in a robe of more than glory. (*LL*) The Coliseum. Poe. AmPP; NOBA

Clotho. Hilaire Kirkland. *Fr.* Clotho, Lachesis, Atropos. PeNZ

Clotho, Lachesis, Atropos. Hilaire Kirkland. PeNZ
  Sels.
  Atropos.
  Clotho.
  Lachesis.

Cloud, The. Edwin Muir. OBTV

Cloud, The. Shelley. ArNa; BLPL; EnRP; FaPON; FHYEP; GN; LiTB; MeMBP; NAEL-2; NoP; PoEL-4; PWR; TrGrPo

Cloud, The. Derek Walcott. ChIV-1

Cloud-backed heron will not move, The. The Heron. Vernon Watkins. AngWe; GTBS-P; TwCP; UnPo

Cloud capped peaks fill the eyes. On a Visit to Ch'ung Chen Taoist Temple. Yü Hsüan-chi, *tr. by* Kenneth Rexroth *and* Ling Chung. PBWP; WPC

Cloud — cloud — cloud — hurls. It. Gary Snyder. LCAP

Cloud Dissects Itself. Lin Ling, *tr. fr. Chinese by* Kenneth Rexroth *and* Ling Chung. WPC

Cloud doth gather, the green wood roar, The. Thekla's Song. Schiller, *tr. fr. German by* Samuel Taylor Coleridge. *Fr.* Piccolomini, The. AWP

Cloud-dyed lake tended to utter a lost crimson song, The. *(LL)* Dusk on the Veranda by Lake Mendota. Chung Ling. WPC

Cloud Fantasy. H. Cordelia Ray. CBWP-3

Cloud-Flower Lullaby, The. *Unknown, tr. fr. Tewa Indian by* H. J. Spinden. WTO

Cloud Hairdress. Chao Luan-luan, *tr. fr. Chinese by* Kenneth Rexroth *and* Ling Chung. WPC

Cloud in Trousers, A, *abr. Vladimir Mayakovsky, tr. fr. Russian by* Peter Bogdanoff. SOTW

Cloud is the post office between continents, The. To Modigliani to Prove to Him That I Am a Poet. Max Jacob, *tr. fr. French by* Wallace Fowlie. TrJP

Cloud-maidens that float on forever. Song of the Clouds. Aristophanes, *tr. fr. Greek by* Oscar Wilde. *Fr.* Clouds, The. AWP

Cloud moved close, A. The bulk of the wind shifted. The Visitant. Theodore Roethke. CMoP; PoE; RB; TRP; UnPo

Cloud of dust on the long white road, A. The Teams. Henry Lawson. CBAP

Cloud of esters escapes as Elena splits an orange, A. The Romance of Citrus. Christy Sheffield Sanford. UL

Cloud of witnesses, A. To whom? To what? A Fanfare for the Makers. Louis MacNeice. NOBE

Cloud Parade, The. Laura Jensen. LCAP

Cloud-piles o'er Kona's sea whet my joy, The. Fathomless Is My Love. Kalola, *tr. fr. Hawaiian by* N. B. Emerson. WTO

Cloud possessed the hollow field, A. The High Tide at Gettysburg. Will Henry Thompson. AnAmPo; BeLS; BLPA; FaBoBe; PAH; VPP

Cloud-puffball, torn tufts, tossed pillows. That Nature Is a Heraclitean Fire and of the Comfort of the Resurrection. Gerard Manley Hopkins. EnlH; EnVR; FaBoMo; FaBoVe; GTBS-P; LiTB; MeMBP; MoAB; NoP; OAEL-2; PoE; PoEL-5; TEP

Cloud reflections float on flooded paddles. On the Way to Huang-ch'ang River. Wang Shih-chieng, *tr. fr. Chinese by* Richard John Lynn. SuSp

Cloud River. Charles Wright. MT

Cloud River. H. Cordelia Ray. CBWP-3

Cloud Spots. Steven Lavoie. UL

Cloud swells. Ocean chop. Exhaustion's. An Essay on Friendship. J. D. McClatchy. BAP-91

Cloud Unfolding, The. Ernesto Trejo. AfAz

Cloud was hidden by the sun as she steeped tea, A. Floating. Michael Brownstein. UL

Cloudburst and Soaring Moon. "Hugh MacDiarmid." NoAM

Cloudburst and steady downpour now. Gifts of Rain. Seamus Heaney. IPY

Clouded Morning, The. Jones Very. NOBA

Clouded with snow. Winter. Walter de la Mare. OAEL-2; OBMV

Clouds, The, *sels.* Aristophanes, *tr. fr. Greek by* Oscar Wilde. Song of the Clouds. AWP

Clouds. Rupert Brooke. OBEV; OBMV; OxBTC

Clouds. Bruce Dawe. FaBoMA

Clouds. Denise Levertov. VCAP

Clouds. Philip Levine. LCAP

Clouds, The. Mirabai, *tr. from Medieval Hindi; English version by* Robert Bly. EnlH; NU

Clouds. *Unknown. See* White sheep, white sheep, on a blue hill.

Clouds, The. William Carlos Williams. Poetr; VGW

Clouds and mountains all tangled together up to the blue sky. Han-shan. EaPr

Clouds and the stars didn't wage this war, The. For the Record. Adrienne Rich. CAPP; NIP; VCAP

Clouds and Windows. Andrew Crozier. VaA

Clouds are flowing in the river, waves are flying in the sky. Eveline Beumkes. EaPr

Clouds as I see them, rising, The. Clouds. Denise Levertov. VCAP

Clouds behind the Forest, *sels.* H. Leivick, *tr. fr. Yiddish by* Benjamin *and* Barbara Harshav.

Clouds fill the sky. The Morning after . . . Love. Kattie M. Cumbo. BlSi

Clouds Have Left the Sky, The. Robert Bridges. CH

Clouds hover over the river's waves, the evening's in a haze. On a Painting by Hsia Kuei Entitled "Returning in Wind and Snow to a Village Home." Kao Ch'i, *tr. fr. Chinese by* Irving Y. Lo. SuSp

Clouds of Evening. Robinson Jeffers. MoAmPo

Clouds of the heavens. Ephesos. Duris, *tr. fr. Greek by* Peter Jay. GrAn

Clouds on the Sea. Ruth Dallas. *Fr.* Letter to a Chinese Poet. PeNZ; TSaS

Clouds over Islands. James Seay. MT

Clouds shouldered a path up the mountains, The. The Drought. Gary Soto. NoAM

Clouds spout upon her. Rain on a Grave. Thomas Hardy. OxAEP-2

Clouds That Are So Light, The. Edward Thomas. FaBoTw

Clouds, the source of rain, one stormy night, The. Lost in Heaven. Robert Frost. MoAmPo

Clouds were fishbone, The. Walden in July. Donald Junkins. NYBP

Clouds, which rise with thunder, slake, The. All's Well. Whittier. OxBSP

Cloudy Bay. Ellen Duggan. PeNZ

Cloudy Day. Jimmy Santiago Baca. InPS

Cloudy tempest, and a too fair day, A. *(LL)* Advice to My Best Brother, Colonel Francis Lovelace. Richard Lovelace. BeJo; CaPo

Clove, salmon knocking. For Lerida. David St. John. AmPA; AnAn

Clove-scent: the dark room where the lovers lie. An Orange of Cloves. Alison Brackenbury. SCBI

Clover, The. James Whitcomb Riley. AnAmPo

Clown, The. Dorothy Aldis. PDV

Clown, The. Margaret E. Bruner. PoToHe

Clown, The. Janet Frame. PeNZ

Clown, The. Donald Hall. NYBP

Clown and beggar. *(LL)* The Maid. Nathan Alterman. MHP

Clownlike, happiest on your hands. You're. Sylvia Plath. FaBoTw; FaBoWP; NAs; RB

Clown's Baby, The. "Margaret Vandegrift." VPP

Clown's Song, The. Shakespeare. *See* Come away, come away, death.

Clown's Song. Shakespeare. *See* When that I was and a little tiny boy.

Club, The. Mitsuye Yamada. LoHo

Clubs and Social Meetings. George Crabbe. *Fr.* Borough, The. OBF

Clubwoman. Mary Carter Smith. PoNe

Clucking Hen, The. *Unknown.* BoTP

Clumped murmuring above a sump of loam. The Woodlot. Amy Clampitt. HCAP

Clumsy clot of shadow in the fold, A. A Moth. Henry Bellyse Baildon. NOBVV

Clumsy cross burns, A. Pillar of Flame. Barbara Unger. LoHo

Clumsy in his drunken joints. Animal Pictures. Lawrence Locke. GrPl

Clustered trees filled with the sounds of autumn. Yuan Hao-wen, *tr. by* Stephen West. *Fr.* Random Verses on Mountain Life. SuSp

Clusters in Thy vineyard turn to gold, O God, The. Grape-gathering. Avraham Shlonsky, *tr. fr. Hebrew by* I. M. Lask. TrJP

Clyde's Waters. *Unknown.* ESPB, A *vers.*; OxBB

Clymène, A. Paul Verlaine, *tr. by* Arthur Symons. AWP

Cnut's Song. *Unknown. Fr.* Canute at Ely. PoE

Co-operation. J. Mason Knox. BLPA

Coach,/ Carriage. *Unknown.* OxNR

Coach is at the door at last, The. Farewell to the Farm. Robert Louis Stevenson. BoTP; FaPON

Coach waits, long, hot in the sun, The. Croeso i Gymru. Philip Owens. AngWe

Coachman, The. Mother Goose. *See* Up at Piccadilly oh!

Coal. Audre Lorde. BlSi; NALW; NBV; NoAM; NoP; PoBA; VCAP

Coal car,/ boxcar,/ CABOOSE! *(LL)* Crossing. Philip Booth. GOA

Coal Diggin' Blues. *Unknown.* AmFP

Coal Fire in Winter, A. Thomas McGrath. NU; RaBo

Coal Loadin' Blues. *Unknown.* AmFP

Coal Miner's Goodbye, A. *Unknown.* AmFP

Coal-Owner and the Pitman's Wife, The. *Unknown.* CoMu

Coal-white bird appears this spring, A. Almanac Verse. Samuel Danforth. SCAP

Coals go out, The. Galway Kinnell. *Fr.* Middle of the Way. RaBo

Coarse/ jocosity/ catches the crowd. Archy Confesses. Don Marquis. *Fr.* Archy and Mehitabel. FiBHP

Coast, The: Norfolk. Frances Cornford. OxBTC

Coast hills at Sovranes Creek, The. The Place for No Story. Robinson Jeffers. AiP

Coast View, A, *sels.* Charles Harpur.
  "Dead city walls may pen us in, but still." CBAP

Coastguard House, The. Robert Lowell, *ad. fr. the Italian of* Eugenio Montale. NaP

Coastline. Elaine Feinstein. BrRo

Coasts of Cerigo, The. A. D. Hope. FaBoMA

Coat, The. Dennis Lee. TLR

Coat, A. W. B. Yeats. CMoP; EPCY; IIP; LiTM; NAEL-2; NoAM; OxAEP-2; OxBSP; PoEL-5

Coat-of-Mail: Dank earth, wondrously cold, The. Unknown, formerly at. to Cynewulf, tr. fr. Anglo-Saxon. Fr. Riddles (Exeter Book). ASW, tr. by Kevin Crossley-Holland

Cob, thou nor soldier, thief, nor fencer art. To Pertinax Cob. Ben Jonson. BeJo; JCP

Cobalt. Tom Weatherly. UL

Cobb Would Have Caught It. Robert Fitzgerald. GrPl; HAP; InvP; TwCP

Cobbler, The. Unknown. BoTP

Cobbler, cobbler, mend my shoe. Mother Goose. OxNR

Coble o Cargill, The. Unknown. ESPB

Coblerone I'm told, A. Mutton and Leather. Unknown. CoMu

Cobra is the night image of a chinese water-print. North Express. Joyce Mansour, tr. fr. French by the author. WPOW

Cobwebs. E. L. M. King. BoTP

Cobwebs. Christina Rossetti. NAEL-2; NALW

Cocaine Lil [and Morphine Sue]. Unknown. AS; CBNP; GBP; MAT; OxBoLi; RB

Cock, A. Anyte, tr. fr. Greek by Sally Purcell. GrAn

Cock a doodle doo!/ My dame has lost her shoe. Mother Goose. BoTP; OxNR; ReMoGo

Cock-a-doodle-doo the brass-lined rooster goes [or says]. Dog. John Crowe Ransom. InPS; LiTA; OBAL

Cock-a-Hoop. Isabella Gardner. WPE

Cock and Bull Story, A. Unknown. ReMoGo

Cock and Hen: I watched a couple of curious creatures. Unknown, formerly at. to Cynewulf, tr. fr. Anglo-Saxon. Fr. Riddles (Exeter Book). ASW, tr. by Kevin Crossley-Holland

Cock and the Bull, The. Charles Stuart Calverley. BXAP; FaBoCo; FaBoNo; FaBoPa

Cock and the Fox, The. La Fontaine, tr. fr. French by Elizur Wright. AWP

Cock and the Hen, The. Chaucer. See Poore [or Povre] widwe [or widow], somdeel [or somedeal or somedel] stape in age, A.

Cock and the Hen, The. Unknown. See Cock, cock, cock, cock.

Cock before Dawn. Norman MacCaig. OxBC

Cock, cock, cock, cock. Unknown. OxNR
(Cock and the Hen, The.) ReMoGo

Cock-Crow. Ralph Nixon Currey. PeSA

Cock-Crow. Edward Thomas. GTBS-P; MoAB; MoBrPo; NTP; OxBSP; RB

Cock-Crow. Unknown. ReMoGo

Cock-crow and early-rise! Dawn. Joseph Kumbirai, tr. fr. Shona by Douglas Livingstone. PeSAV

Cock-crowing. Henry Vaughan. ESCV; GeHe; OAEL-1; SeCV-1

Cock crows, The. Depression before Spring. Wallace Stevens. OBAL; SOTW

Cock doth crow, the wind doth blow, The. Mother Goose. GBP

Cock doth crow, The/ To let you know. Mother Goose. OxNR

Cock has crow's an hour ago, The. The Morning Quatrains. Charles Cotton. NOSC; PeECV

Cock is crowing, The. Written in March. Wordsworth. BoNaP; BoTP; EnRP; FaPON; GoJo; NAEL-2; NTCP; PFP; PYC; SCGP; UnPo
(Merry Month of March, The.) MoShBr

Cock of Glory is the coq français, The. The French, 1870-1871. Unknown. FaBoEE

Cock of the Game, The. Unknown. OBET

Cock Robin. Mother Goose. See Who Killed Cock Robin.

Cock Robin got up early. Unknown. BoTP; OxNR

Cock shall crow, The. Robert Louis Stevenson. TrGrPo

Cock that crowed this dawn up, heard, The. Copernicus. Robert David Fitzgerald. NOBAu

Cock, warm roosting 'mid his feathers mates, The. A Winter's Day. Joanna Baillie. WoRP

Cock, warm roosting midst his feathered dames, The. Morning. Joanna Baillie. Fr. Winter Day, A. ECWP

Cockaigne: A Dream. L. E. Sissman. DiPo

Cockcrow. Ted Hughes. AnAn

Cocker of Snooks, A. Phyllis Gotlieb. NOBC

Cockles and Mussels. Unknown. ELP

Cocklorel would needs have the devil his guest. Dinner for the Devil. Ben Jonson. Fr. Gypsies Metamorphosed, The. NOSC

Cocklorrel. Ben Jonson. CBNP

Cockney of the North, The. Harry Graham. UV

Cockpit in the Clouds. Dick Dorrance. FaPON

Cockroach. Mary Ann Hoberman. Fr. Bugs. OBCA

Cocks and Mares. Ruth Stone. RaBo

Cocks crow in the morn. Cock-Crow. Unknown. ReMoGo

Cock's crow means profit, The. Tseng Jui, tr. by Wayne Schlepp. Fr. Tune: "Sheep on Mountain Slope" — Lamenting the Times. SuSp

Cock's on the housetop blowing his horn, The. A Cock and Bull Story. Unknown. ReMoGo

Cock's on the wood pile, The. Unknown. OxNR

Cocktail is a pleasant drink, The. R-E-M-O-R-S-E. George Ade. FiBHP; NBLV; OBAL; PeLV

Cocktail Party, The. T. S. Eliot. Fr. Battle of Blenheim, The. FaBoEH

Cocktails. Ciaran Carson. BiHa; PBCIP; PWE

Cocktails. Cyn Zarco. BCF

Cocoa coursing through their veins. (LL) In Praise of Cocoa, Cupid's Nightcap. Stanley J. Sharpless. ErPo; FiBHP; NBLV; PeLV

Cocoa Morning. Bob Kaufman. NBV

Cocoa-nut Tree, The. Frances Sargent Osgood. AmWP

Coconut, The. "Ande." FiBHP

Coconut for Katerina, A. Sandra McPherson. LCAP

Cocoon. Ishigaki Rin, tr. fr. Japanese by Ayusawa Takako. WPOW

Cocoon. David McCord. OBCA

Cocooning, The. Frédéric Mistral, tr. by Harriet Waters Preston. Fr. Mirèio. AWP

Cod-Liver Oil and the Orange Juice. Hamish Imlach. FaBoBl

Coda. Basil Bunting. Fr. Briggflatts [An Autobiography]. OAEL-2

Coda, sels. Marilyn Hacker.
"Did you love well what very soon you left?" NoAM

Coda. Louis MacNeice. CBLP

Coda. Ezra Pound. NOBA

Coda. James Tate. AmPA; NYBP

Coda. William Carlos Williams. NOBA

Coda: The Higher Keys, sels. James Merrill.
"Empty perfection, as I take you in." NoAM

Code, The. Robert Frost. OBNV; PoA; UnPo

Code Book Lost. Robert Penn Warren. Poetr

Code of Morals, A. Kipling. FaBoCo

Codex. Stephen Rodefer. UL

Codex Minor. Rachel Hadas. EOEF

Codfish lays ten thousand eggs, The. Advertisement. Unknown. FaBoUs

Codfish Shanty, The. Unknown. GBP

Codicil. Mabel MacDonald Carver. GoYe

Codicil. Ruth Stone. BoWoP

Codicil. Derek Walcott. MoP; NoAM

Coelia, sels. William Percy.
"It shall be said [or sayd] I died [or dy'de] for Coelia." EIL
"Judged by my goddess' doom to endless pain." Son
"Relent, my dear yet unkind Coelia." AAS; Son

Coffee. J. V. Cunningham. MoAmPo; PrIm; VGW

Coffee and cigarettes in a clean café. Small Comfort. Katha Pollitt. CrSp

Coffee and jasmine on a tray. Convalescence. James McAuley. CBAP

Coffee and Tea. Unknown. ReMoGo

Coffee cups cool on the Vicar's harmonium. A Game of Consequences. Paul Dehn. ErPo; FiBHP; NOBL

Coffin, The. Heine, tr. fr. German by Louis Untermeyer. AWP

Coffin-Worm, The. Ruth Pitter. MoBrPo

Cogitabo Pro Peccato Meo. William Habington. ChIV-1

Cogito Ergo. Jerzy Ficowski, tr. fr. Polish by Frank J. Corliss, Jr., and Grazyna Sandel. PoSu

Coil there and squat, and pay your fee? (LL) Interview with Doctor Drink. J. V. Cunningham. OxBSP; VGW

Coiled asp, The. My Grandfather. Joanne Hotchkiss. CrSp

Coiled like a lyncher's rope. Portrait in Georgia. Jean Toomer. NAAL-2

Coils the Robot. Floria Herrero Pinto, tr. fr. Spanish. TSaS, tr. by Barbara Chacón

Coilyear, gudlie in feir, tuke him be the hand, The. Unknown. Fr. Rauf Coilyear. OxBS

Coin in the Fist. Florence Kerr Brownell. GoYe

Coins for the ferry, The. (LL) Being Called For. Rosemary Dobson. CBAP; Mes

Coins handsome as Nero's; of good substance and weight. Geoffrey Hill. Fr. Mercian Hymns. FaBoMo; HAP; NoAM

Cokkils. Sydney Goodsir Smith. OxBS; PoA

Cold. Dennis Brutus. PeSAV

Cold. Brian Coffey. CIP

Cold. Robert Francis. LCAP; PoA

Cold, The. Lance Henson. CDW

Cold. Dorothy Roberts. NOBC

Cold, The. Charles Simic. HCAP

Cold air drains down from the peaks. In the Mountains as Autumn Begins. Wen T'ing-yün, *tr. fr. Chinese* by Kenneth Rexroth. OHMPC

Cold and clear-cut face, why come you so cruelly meek. Tennyson. *Fr.* Maud[: A Monodrama]. EBVVPR; EnVR, *sect.* I, iii

Cold and, cymbals fizz with no old animals among railroad tracks. Coming Forth by Day. John Taggart. Jaz

Cold and Heat. *Unknown, tr. fr. Hawaiian* by M. W. Beckwith. WTO

Cold and raw the north wind doth blow. Winter. Mother Goose. ReMoGo

Cold and the colors of cold: mineral, shell. Cold. Robert Francis. LCAP; PoA

Cold April, A. *Unknown.* FaBoUs

Cold Are the Crabs. Edward Lear. CBNP; FaBoNo; GoJo; NAEL-2

Cold as a tomb of an infant emperor. (*LL*) Shelley. Charles Simic. TRP

Cold as no love, and wild with all negation. Stevie Smith. FaBoEE

Cold as no plea. The Death Sentence. Stevie Smith. NoP

Cold as the breath of winds that blow. Lucasta's World. Richard Lovelace. BeJo; CaPo; SeCP

Cold as thy grace, whose hand shall comfort me? (*LL*) In whose will is our peace? Thou happiness. J. V. Cunningham. VGW

Cold-blooded Creatures. Elinor Wylie. OxBSP

Cold-blooded in warm waters, my Nurse. Among Sharks. Alfred M. Lee. AmPA

Cold blows the blast — the night's obscure. George Colman the Younger. *Fr.* Maid of the Moor, The; or, The Water-Fiends. NOEC

Cold Blows the Wind. John Hamilton. CH

Cold blows the wind to my true-love [*or* tonight, sweetheart]. The Unquiet Grave. *Unknown.* FaBoBa; OBET

Cold blows the winter wind: 'tis Love. Love at the Door. Meleager, *tr. fr. Greek* by John Addington Symonds. AWP

Cold bugle calls, and the city moves on, A. (*LL*) Armistice Day. Charles Causley. NAEL-2; OBWP

Cold Ceremony. Hannah More. *Fr.* Bas Bleu, The; or, Conversation. ECWP

Cold chain of life presseth heavily on me tonight, The. Adah Isaacs Menken. CBWP-1

Cold, clear, and blue, the morning heaven. The Morning Star. Emily Brontë. ChTr

Cold, Cold. *Unknown, tr. fr. Eskimo.* EaPr

Cold, cold!/ Cold tonight is broad Moylurg. A Song of Winter. *Unknown, tr. fr. Middle Irish* by Kuno Meyer. CH

Cold! Cold!/ Wide Lurg Plain is cold tonight. *Unknown.* NOIV

Cold, cold is the north wind and rude is the blast. The Battle of Lovell's Pond. Longfellow. PAH

Cold, cold the year draws to its end. Old Poem. *Unknown, tr. fr. Chinese* by Arthur Waley. AWP; BoWoP

Cold Colloquy. Patrick Anderson. *Fr.* Poem on Canada. NOBC

Cold comes about, The. North Dakota, North Light. N. Scott Momaday. HATNAP

"Cold coming we had of it, A." Journey of the Magi. T. S. Eliot. EBEvV; FaBoCh; FaBoMo; HAP; HeIP; ImPo; InPK; LiTA; LiTM; MoAB; MoAmPo; NAEL-2; NIP; NOCV; NoP; OBCP; OBMV; OxBTC; PChr; PoE; Poetr; TAP; TFi; TrGrPo; TRP; TwCP

Cold, deserted and silent. *Unknown. Fr.* Winter on Black Mingo. FiBHP

Cold drool on his chin, warm drool in his lap, a sigh. A Dimpled Cloud. Frederick Seidel. FYAP

Cold earth slept below, The. Shelley. EnRP

Cold evening. The saxophonist shivers, A. Street Musician. Donald Justice. *Fr.* Body and Soul. BAP-91

Cold Fear. Elizabeth Madox Roberts. WPE

Cold felt cold until our blood, The. Phantasia for Elvira Shatayev. Adrienne Rich. NALW

Cold Fire. George Starbuck. NYBP

Cold fire sings in us, A. The Rush to Ending. Kevin Jeffrey Clarke. PFL

Cold Fly, The. Yang Wan-li, *tr. fr. Chinese* by Jonathan Chaves. SuSp

Cold Front, A. William Carlos Williams. NAs

Cold front's blowing in; the fragrant air, A. The Last Dusk of August. Aleda Shirley. Jaz

Cold Green Element, The. Irving Layton. NOBC; NoP

Cold grey walls. San Francisco County Jail Cell B-6. Conyus. PoBA

Cold has put blue horses where lambs were, The. Blue Horses. Ed Roberson. PoBA

Cold Heaven, The. W. B. Yeats. AWP; CTC; GTBS-P; HAP; NoAM; OAEL-2; OxBSP; RB; TEP

Cold holds its own, inside and out. Si Monumentum Requiris. Daryl Hine. EOEF

Cold hue newly clears, a belt of haze, The. Autumn Spring. Hsüeh T'ao, *tr. fr. Chinese* by Eric W. Johnson. SuSp

Cold in the earth, and the deep snow piled above thee! Remembrance. Emily Brontë. BLPL; BoLoP; BoWoP; CH; CoGr; EBEV; EnLoPo;

GGP; HAP; IMW; LiTB; NAEL-2; NOBE; NOBVV; NoP; OBNC; OxAEP-2; PBWP; PoE; PoEL-5; Poetr; TEP; TFi; TrGrPo; WeW; WPE (R. Alcona to J. Brenzaida.) BrRo; CBLP; EBVV; EnVR; NALW; OPOP

Cold Irish Earth, The. Knute Skinner. InPK

Cold is the winter. The wind is risen. *Unknown.* NOIV

Cold it is, O my King, how cold alone on the wold. (*LL*) Marvel of Marvels. Christina Rossetti. NOBE; WGRP

Cold Kiss, The. Thomas Stanley. CBLP

Cold Lantern, The. Yang Wan-li, *tr. fr. Chinese* by Jonathan Chaves. SuSp

Cold limbs of the air, The. A Mountain Wind. "Æ." AWP

Cold meat, mutton pies. *Unknown.* ISE

Cold morning early. Two Mornings. Lawrence McGaugh. PoBA

Cold mornings, he would warm his hands. Coroner. Elton Glaser. PBCAP

Cold Mountain, The. Wang Wei, *tr. fr. Chinese* by Robert Payne. TAL

Cold mountain turns dark green. The Cold Mountain. Wang Wei, *tr. fr. Chinese* by Robert Payne. TAL

Cold night, the sidewalk we walk on icy, A. Christmas Eve Service at Midnight at St. Michael's. Robert Bly. NNaP

Cold nights outside the taverns in Wyoming. Accountability. William Stafford. LCAP; NoP

Cold of autumn's frost penetrates the curtain, The. Tune: "Immortal's Auspicious Crane, An" — On Plum Blossoms. Hsin Ch'i-chi, *tr. fr. Chinese* by Irving Y. Lo. SuSp

Cold Oxford unfamiliar now, around. Above the High. Geoffrey Grigson. EnLoPo

Cold Pastoral. Diotimus, *tr. fr. Greek* by Dudley Fitts. GrAn

Cold remote islands, The. Night. Louise Bogan. Poetr; UnPo

Cold Rendering, A. *Unknown.* BXAP

Cold, Sharp Lamentation. Douglas Hyde, *tr. fr. Irish* by Lady Augusta Gregory. OBMV

Cold shuttered loveless star, skulker in clouds. News of the World I. George Barker. LiTB; MeMBP

Cold slope is standing in darkness, The. December Night. W. S. Merwin. CAPP

Cold soft drinks. Sho Nuff. Nilene O. A. Foxworth. AIW

Cold spot on the heart repeats, A. Deep. Timothy Holmes. PeSAV

Cold Spring, A. Elizabeth Bishop. TwCP

Cold Spring. Kao Ch'i, *tr. fr. Chinese* by Irving Y. Lo. SuSp

Cold steel may penetrate the flesh. Heart Wounds. Claire Richcreek Thomas. PoToHe

Cold Term. Amiri Baraka. BPo; SOTW

Cold transparent ham is on my fork, The. Sonnet to Vauxhall. Thomas Hood. PoEL-4

Cold was the night wind, drifting fast the snows fell. The Widow. Robert Southey. NOEC; UV

Cold water falling out of the split rock. Leonidas of Tarentum, *tr. fr. Greek* by Peter Levi. GrAn

Cold, we sit in the warmth. Written on the Wall of Halfway Mountain Temple. Wang An-shih, *tr. fr. Chinese* by Jan W. Walls. SuSp

Cold-Weather Love. Ronald G. Everson. MoCV

Cold Weather Proverb. Robert Graves. PlP

Cold wind., The. (*LL*) The Hounded Lovers. William Carlos Williams. NYBP; TrGrPo

Cold wind stirs the blackthorn, A. Endure Hardness. Christina Rossetti. NOBVV

Cold wind streamed her hair, A. Girl on a Swing, 10.00pm. Tony Flynn. PWE

Cold winds swept the mountain's height, The. The Mother in the Snow-Storm. Sebald Smithon. VPP

Cold winter's in the wood. In the Wood. Eileen Mathias. BoTP

Cold world awakens, The. (*LL*) If the Owl Calls Again. John Haines. ArNa; BoNaP; CoAP; HeIP; NU

Colder Fire. Robert Penn Warren. *Fr.* To a Little Girl, One Year Old, in a Ruined Fortress. LiTM

Coldly, sadly descends. Rugby Chapel. Matthew Arnold. EBVVPR; EnVR; FaBoEH; PeECV; PoEL-5; WGRP

Cold's the wind, and wet's the rain. Drinking Song. Thomas Dekker *and others. Fr.* Shoemaker's Holiday, The. TrGrPo
(Saint Hugh.) 09OBSC
(Troll the Bowl!) EIL

Cole Porter's Son. Gerrit Henry. EOEF

Cole Younger. *Unknown.* AmFP; BeLS

Colebrook Dale, *sels.* Anna Seward.
"While neighbouring cities waste the fleeting hours." NOEC

Coleman Hawkins (d. 1969), RIP. William Matthews. Jaz

Colenso Rhymes for Orthodox Children. Bret Harte. OBAL

Coleridge. Medbh McGuckian. CIP

Coleridge. R. S. Thomas. TOF

Coleridge. Theodore Watts-Dunton. Son

Coleridge caused his wife unrest. Theme and Variation. Peter De Vries. NYBP

Coleridge received the Person from Porlock. Thoughts about the Person from Porlock. Stevie Smith. FaBoCo; NAEL-2; NoAM; NoP

Cole's Island. Charles Olson. *Fr.* Maximus Poems, The. PoM

Colin. Anthony Munday. *See* Beauty sat bathing by a spring.

Colin Clout, *sels.* John Skelton.
"And if ye stand in doubt." NAEL-1; OAEL-1
"Doctors that learned be." OBSV
Prelates, The. TrGrPo

Colin Clout's Come Home Again, *sels.* Spenser.
Her Heards Be Thousand Fishes. ChTr
"Of loves perfection perfectly to speake." OAEL-1

Colin, my dear and most entire beloved. To the Most Excellent and Learned Shepherd, Colin Clout. William Smith. *Fr.* Chloris [or the Complaint of the Passionate Despised Shepheard]. AAS; Son

Colin, my deare, when shall it please thee sing. November. Spenser. *Fr.* Shepheardes [or Shepeards or Shepherd's] Calender, The. PoEL-1

Colin, well fits thy sad cheer this sad stound. A Pastoral Eclogue upon the Death of Sir Philip Sidney Knight. Lodowick Bryskett. NoSic

Colin, you can tell my words are crippled now. James K. Baxter. *Fr.* Jerusalem Sonnets. PeNZ

Coliseum, The. Poe. AmPP; NOBA

Colkelbie Sow, *sels. Unknown.*
"Penny lost in the lak, The." OxBS

Collage for Richard Davis — Two Short Forms, A. De Leon Harrison. PoBA

Collapsible lover, the spider in iniquitousness, The. Anthology of Nouns. Parker Tyler. PoA

Collar, The. George Herbert. AWP; BLPL; ClHu; EBEV; FaBoVe; FaPoB; GeHe; HAP; HeIP; ImPo; InPS; JCP; LiTB; MeLP; NAEL-2; NIP; NOBE; NOCV; NoP; NOSC; OAEL-1; OBWVE; PoE; PoEL-2; PoRA; PPP; SCGP; SCV; SeCP; SeCV-1; TEP; TFi; TOF; TrGrPo; WeW

Collarbone [Collar-Bone] of a Hare, The. W. B. Yeats. CBNP; NTP; OxAEP-2; OxBTC; RB

Collection of Emblemes, Ancient and Moderne, A, *sels.* George Wither.
Husbandman, The. NOSC
Marigold, The. NOSC
Planting. NOSC
Spade and the Wreath, The. NOSC
Spade, The. NOSC
"Why, silly Man! so much admirest thou." SeCV-1

Collection of Hymns . . . of the Moravian Brethren, A, *sels. Unknown.*
"Chicken blessed and caressed." NOEC
"What does a bird in Cross's air." NOEC

Collections. Cole Porter. *Fr.* I've a Shooting Box In Scotland. CBCK

Collective Portrait, The. Robert Finch. MoCV

Collector, The. Desirée Flynn. BrRo

Collector, The. Raymond Souster. ErPo

Collector of lost beads, buttons, bird bones. The Pack Rat. Robert Pack. PPP

Collector of the Sun, The. Dave Jeddie Smith. SM

Collector's Marginalia, The. Peter Sirr. PBCIP

Collects her motions into shape. (*LL*) Nude Descending a Staircase. X. J. Kennedy. CoAP; HoPM; NIP; OxBSP; PoA; SM

Colleen Rue. *Unknown.* BIrV

College Colonel, The. Herman Melville. OBWP

Colley's Run-I-O. *Unknown.* AmFP

Collier, The. Vernon Watkins. FaBoTw; OBWVE

Collier Lad's Lament, The. *Unknown.* OBET

Collier Lass, The. Frankie Armstrong. BrRo

Colliers' March, The. John Freeth. OBET

Collier's Rant, The. *Unknown.* OBET

Collier's Wedding, The, *sels.* Edward Chicken.
"At last the beef appears in sight." NOEC

Collier's Wife, The. D. H. Lawrence. FaBoVe; OxBTC

Collins. Lionel Johnson. OxAEP-2

Colloque Imaginaire. "Sagittarius." IHNG

Colloquy. Weldon Kees. NaP; NYBP

Colloquy in Black Rock. Robert Lowell. CAPP; MoAB; MoAmPo; NAAL-2

Colloquy of Silences, A. Michael Heffernan. SM

Colloquy with a King-Crab. John Peale Bishop. LiTA

Collusion. Medbh McGuckian. BiHa

Colobus Monkey. *Unknown, tr. fr. Yoruba by* Ulli Beier. *Fr.* Hunter Poems of the Yoruba. RB

Cologne. Samuel Taylor Coleridge. FaBoEE; NBLV; OBTV; PFP

Colon Bay. *Unknown.* FaBoVe

Colonel, The. Carolyn Forché. InPS; OBWP; SoSe

Colonel. Kate Llewellyn. NOBAu

Colonel B. Afforestation. E. A. Wodehouse. FiBHP

Colonel Chartres. John Arbuthnot. *See* Here continueth to rot.

Colonel Cold strode up the line. Winter Warfare. Edgell Rickword. OBWP; OxBTC; PAW; PeFWW; PoWW

Colonel Ellsworth. Richard Henry Stoddard. PAH

Colonel Fantock. Edith Sitwell. MoAB; MoBrPo; OBMV

Colonel Fazackerley. Charles Causley. OTCP

Colonel from Cheltenham stopped everyone, A. W. H. Auden. *Fr.* Happy New Year, A. OBSV

Colonel in a casual voice, The. Gallantry. Keith Douglas. NAEL-2; NoAM; OBWP

Colonels here in solemn manner meet, The. Thomas Brown. FaBoEE

Colonels live here, commuters to the Pentagon. Springfield, Virginia. Anne Rouse. NWP

Colonel's Soliloquy, The. Thomas Hardy. OBWP

Colonial Nomenclature. John Dunmore Lang. NOBAu

Colonialism ("The colonialist governments.") Cabdullaahi Qarshe, *tr. fr. Somali by* J. W. Johnson. WTO

Colonist, The. Robert Wells. SCBI

Colonist in His Garden, A. William Pember Reeves. IHNG

Colonists/ unearth their wealth. Shaman Breaks. Gerald Vizenor. HATNAP

Colonization in Reverse. Louise Bennett. PBCV

Colonus' Praise. Sophocles, *tr. by* W. B. Yeats. *Fr.* Oedipus at Colonus. OBVE

Colophon. Oliver St. John Gogarty. OBMV

Colophon for Lan-t'ing Hsiu-hsi. John Peck. AmPA

Colophon to a Roll of Erinna's Poems. Asclepiades, *tr. fr. Greek by* Lee T. Pearcy. GrAn

Color — caste — denomination. Emily Dickinson. TAP

Color of silence is the oyster's color, The. Earliness at the Cape. Babette Deutsch. FYAP; NYBP

Color of the flowers, The/ has faded. Ono no Komachi, *tr. fr. Japanese by* Kenneth Rexroth. BoWoP

Color of the grave is green, The. Emily Dickinson. PoE

Colorado Blvd. Lorna Dee Cervantes. NAmP90

Colorado Sand Storm, A. Eugene Fieldson, Jr.. LiTA

Colorado Trail, The. *Unknown.* AS

Colored child at carnival: Langston Hughes. *See* Where is the Jim Crow section.

Colored Hats. Gertrude Stein. *Fr.* Tender Buttons. TTTS

Colored Heroes, Hark the Bugle. Robert Charles O'Hara Benjamin. AAP

Colored heroes stand your standard. Colored Heroes, Hark the Bugle. Robert Charles O'Hara Benjamin. AAP

Colored pictures/ of all things to eat: dirty. Charles Olson. *Fr.* Maximus Poems, The. NeAP; NoAM

Colored Soldiers, The. Paul Laurence Dunbar. AAP

Coloring high means that the strange reason is in front. An Umbrella. Gertrude Stein. *Fr.* Tender Buttons. TTTS

Colorizing: Turner Broadcasting Enterprises, Computer Graphics Division, Burbank, California, 1987. David Wojahn. *Fr.* Mystery Train: A Sequence. PBCAP

Colors for Mama. Barbara Mahone. PoBA

Colors of Desire, The. David Mura. NAmP90

Colors of spring have returned to West Lake, A. Song of Spring at West Lake, A, Sent to Circuit Officer Hsieh. Ou-yang Hsiu, *tr. fr. Chinese by* Irving Y. Lo. SuSp

Colors of the Dark One have penetrated Mira's body, The. Why Mira Can't Go Back to Her Old House. Mirabai, *tr. fr. Medieval Hindi by* Robert Bly. EnlH; NU

Colors of the flowers fade, The. Ono no Komachi, *tr. fr. Japanese by* Kenneth Rexroth *and* Ikuko Atsumi. WPJ

Colors of tulips and roses are not the same, The. Asadullah Khan Ghalib, *tr. fr. Urdu by* Jane Hirshfield. EnlH

Colors on the elephant's body, The. What She Said to Her Friend ('The colors on the elephant's body'). Kapilar, *tr. fr. Tamil by* A. K. Ramanujan. PLW

"Colors," she said, "are never so fine." The Green and the Black. Anthony Bailey. NYBP

Colors shifting. Time of Fish Dying. Gabriela Melinescu, *tr. fr. Romanian by* Stavros Deligiorgis. BoWoP

Colors we depend on are, The. The Love Bit. Joel Oppenheimer. PoM

Coloss. 3.3. George Herbert. *See* My words and thoughts do both express this notion.

Colossal:/ Like towers and pavilions from the flat plain. Hsü Wei, *tr. fr. Chinese by* Irving Y. Lo. SuSp

Colosseum. Harold Norse. TrJP

Come, all ye men of England, and listen unto me. Verses. William Henry. PeSAV

Come All Ye Mourning Pilgrims. John A. Granade. AH

Come all ye [or you] young fellows that [or who] follow the sea. Blow the Man Down. *Unknown.* AmFP; AS

Come, All Ye People. George R. Seltzer. AH

Come all ye railroad section men. Jerry, Go and Ile [or Oil] That Car. *Unknown.* SWP
(Jerry, Go an' Ile That Car.) AS

Come, all ye seamen [or you sailors] bold. The Death of Admiral Benbow. *Unknown.* CoMu; GBP
(Admiral Benbow.) EnSB

Come all ye sons of Brittany. Braddock's Fate, with an Incitement to Revenge. Stephen Tilden. PAH

Come all ye true-born Irishmen, a story I will tell. The *City of Baltimore. Unknown.* OxBSS

Come all ye [or you] true born shanty-boys, wherever you may be [or whoever that ye be]. The Jam on Gerry's Rock. *Unknown.* AmFP; AS; FaBoBa

Come all ye valiant seamen. The Man-of-War's Garland. *Unknown.* OxBSS

Come all ye wits, that with immortal rhymes. Invites Poets and Historians to Write in Cynthia's Praise. Philip Ayres. Son

Come all ye Yankee sailors, with swords and pikes advance. The *Constellation* and the *Insurgente. Unknown.* PAH

Come all ye young people and all my relations. Mr. Davis's Experience. *Unknown.* AmFP

Come all you blessed Christians dear. A Ballad from the Seven Dials Press. *Unknown.* CoMu

Come all you bold sailors that follow the lakes. Red Iron Ore, *Unknown.* AS

Come all you bonny boys. The Bullard's Song. *Unknown.* OBET

Come all you brave Americans. Brave Paulding and the Spy. *Unknown.* PAH

Come all you brave boys whose courage is bold. A Copy of Verses Composed by Captain Henry Every. *Unknown.* OxBSS

Come, all you brave gallants, and listen a while. Robin Hood and the Butcher. *Unknown.* ESPB

Come all you brave sailors, that sails on the Main. The Famous Fight at Malago; or, The Englishmen's Victory over the Spaniards. *Unknown.* CoMu; OxBSS

Come all you brave seamen that ploughs on the main. Captain Barton's Distress on Board the *Lichfield. Unknown.* OxBSS

Come all you brave soldiers, both valiant and free. On Independence. Jonathan Mitchell Sewall. PAH

Come all you brave young shanty-boys. James Whaland. *Unknown.* AS

Come all you British hearts of oak, and listen unto me. Glorious Victory of Navarino! The. *Unknown.* CoMu

Come all you cockers, far and near. The Bonny Grey. *Unknown.* GBP

Come all you fair gallants, fair gallants attend. Pretty Polly of Topsham. *Unknown.* AmFP

Come all you fine young fellows with hearts so warm and true. Flat River Girl. *Unknown.* AS

Come all you focsle lawyers that always take deli ght. The Merchant Shipping Act. *Unknown.* OxBSS

Come all you gallant heroes, I'd have you lend an ear. Major André. *Unknown.* AmFP

Come all you gallant poachers, that ramble free from [or void of] care. Van Dieman's Land. *Unknown.* CoMu; FaBoBa; NOBAu; OBET; OBTV; PeVV

Come all you girls and all you boys. Kitty Morey. *Unknown.* AmFP

Come all you good people/ From all over the World. Lula Vires. *Unknown.* AmFP

Come all you hearty roving blades, and listen to my song. The Frolicsome Parson Outwitted. *Unknown.* CoMu

Come all you heroes, where'er you be. The Dying Sergeant. *Unknown.* AmFP

Come all you jolly cowboys and listen to my song. The Buffalo Skinners. *Unknown.* GBP; RB

Come all you jolly fellows, come listen to my song. The Shanty Boys and the Pine. *Unknown.* AmFP

Come all you jolly freighters that ever hit the road. Freighting from Wilcox to Globe. *Unknown.* AmFP

Come all you jolly-hearted sailors. False Nancy. *Unknown.* AmFP

Come all you jolly highwaymen and outlaws of the land. Bold Jack Donahue. *Unknown.* AmFP

Come all you jolly lumbermen, and listen to my song. Colley's Run-I-O. *Unknown.* AmFP

Come all you jolly lumbermen, I'd have you for to know. The Banks of the Gaspereaux. *Unknown.* AmFP

Come all you jolly ploughmen. The Painful Plough. *Unknown.* OBET

Come all you jolly railroad men, and I'll sing you if I can. Way Out in Idaho. *Unknown.* AmFP

Come all you jolly seamen who plough that restless deep. Jimmy Judge. *Unknown.* AmFP

Come all you jolly shanty boys that work the shanty and go. Turner's Camp on the Chippewa. *Unknown.* AmFP

Come all you Lachlan men, and a sorrowful tale I'll tell. The Streets of Forbes. Jack McGuire. CBAP; NOBAu

Come all you lads of high renown and listen to my story. Country Statutes. *Unknown.* OBET

Come all you loyal Unionists, wherever you may be. Virginia's Bloody Soil. *Unknown.* AmFP

Come all you maids that live at a distance. I Live Not Where I Love. *Unknown.* OBET

Come all you married couples gay. The Dunmow Flitch of Bacon. *Unknown.* OBET

Come all you married seamen bold, a few lines to you I'll write. The Dockyard Gate. *Unknown.* OxBSS

Come all you men and maidens. Rufus Mitchell's Confession. *Unknown.* AmFP

Come all you noble, bold commanders. Captain James. *Unknown.* OxBSS

Come, all you painters, all you who are the best. Anacreon, *tr. fr. Greek by* Sam Hamill. InMo

Come all you people from every land. Ellen Flannery. *Unknown.* AmFP

Come all you pretty fair maids. Green Willow, Green Willow. *Unknown.* AmFP

Come all you pretty fair maids, I pray you attend. My New Garden Field. *Unknown.* AmFP

Come all you rounders [or muckers] if you want [or for I want you] to hear. Casey Jones. *Unknown.* AmFP; AS; BeLS; FaBV; OxBoLi; PeLV; TrGrPo

Come all you sailors bold. The Death of Admiral Benbow. *Unknown.* CoMu; GBP

Come all you saucy landladies, what makes you look so gay? The Royal Light Dragoon. *Unknown.* OBET

Come all you sons of Erin, attention now I crave. Morrissey and the Russian Sailor, *Unknown.* AS

Come all you sons of freedom and listen to my theme. Once More a-Lumbering Go. *Unknown.* AmFP

Come, all you sons of Liberty, that to the seas belong. The *General Armstrong. Unknown.* PAH

Come all you Sussex heroes with courage stout and bold. The Smuggler's Victory. *Unknown.* OxBSS

Come all you swaggering farmers, whoever you may be. The Times Have Altered. *Unknown.* CoMu

Come all you thoughtless young men, a warning take by me. The Murder of Maria Marten. W. Corder. CoMu; OBET

Come All You Tonguers. *Unknown.* PeNZ

Come all you valiant heroes and listen unto me. New Song on the Total Defeat of the French Fleet, A, *Unknown.* OxBSS

Come all you valiant sailors of courage stout and bold. Sailor's Lamentation, The, *Unknown.* OxBSS

Come all you very merry London girls that are disposed to travel. The Maidens of London's Brave Adventures, Or, a Boon Voyage Intended for the Sea. Laurence Price. NOSC

Come all you wild and wicked youths. Van Dieman's Land. *Unknown.* OBET

Come all you wild young men. Valiant Sailor, The, *Unknown.* OxBSS

Come all you wild young people and listen to my song. Young Edwin in the Lowlands Low. *Unknown.* OBET

Come all you young and handsome ladies. Little Sparrow. *Unknown.* AmFP

Come all you young fellows so young and so fine. Dark As a Dungeon. Merle Travis. SWP

Come all you young fellows that follow the gun. Young Molly Ban. *Unknown.* FaBoBa

Come all you young fellows who follow the sea. *Unknown. See* I'll put on my boots and I'll blow the man down.

Come All You Young Ladies and Gentlemen. *Unknown.* OBET

Come all you young ladies and make no delay. *Unknown.* OxNR

Come all you young maidens I pray you attend. Sally Munro. *Unknown.* OxBSS

Come all you young people, a story I will tell. Naomi (Omie) Wise. *Unknown.* AmFP

Come all you young people/ That live far and near. The Murder of Goins. *Unknown.* AmFP

Come all you young people who handle the gun. Shooting of His Dear. *Unknown.* OxBoLi

Come, John, sit thee down I have somewhat to say. An Amorous Dialogue between John and His Mistress. *Unknown.* CoMu

Come jolly sailors join with me. The Lucky Sailor; or, The Sailor's Invitation to Go with Admiral Anson. *Unknown.* OxBSS

Come Juju come. (*LL*) A Juju of My Own. Lebert Bethune. PoBA; PoNe

Come knock your heads against this stone. Blake. TEP

Come lads and listen to my song, a song of honest toil. The English Labourer. *Unknown.* OBET

Come, Landlord, Fill the Flowing Bowl. *Unknown.* OxBoLi

Come lasses and lads, take leave of your dads. The Rural Dance about the Maypole. *Unknown.* GBP; OxBoLi

Come Laugh with Me. *Gond Oral Tradition, tr. by* V. Elwin *and* S. Hivale. WTO

Come leave the loathed stage. Ode to Himsel[f]e. Ben Jonson. BeJo; NAEL-1; OAEL-1; SeCP
(On *The New Inn*: Ode, To Himself.) EPCY

Come, let me take thee to my breast. Burns. CBLP

Come let us be going my brothers. Come Home. *Unknown, tr. fr. Zulu by* Jack Cope. PeSA

Come, let us build a temple to oblivion. Tabernacle. D. H. Lawrence. ChIV-1

Come let us burne our severall horrid peeces. Antemasque, The: Witches the Nomber Beinge Five. Lady Jane Cavendish *and* Lady Elizabeth Brackley. *Fr.* Pastorall, A. KTR

Come, let us down. Ode: Hastening His Friend into the Country. Eldred Revett. NOSC

Come, let us drain. Wanderlust. Justinus Kerner, *tr. fr. German by* Philip L. Miller. RiWo

Come, let us go a-roaming! Travellers. Arthur St. John Adcock. BoTP

Come, let us join this festal lay. Rally Song. Mary Weston Fordham. CBWP-2

Come Let Us Mock at the Great. W. B. Yeats. *Fr.* Nineteen Hundred and Nineteen. IHNG

Come, let us now resolve at last. The Reconcilement. John Sheffield, Duke of Buckingham and Normandy. OBEV

Come let us now to each discover. The Lover. "Eliza." KTR

Come, let us pity those who are better off than we are. The Garret. Ezra Pound. AnAmPo; ArLo; SOTW

Come, let us plant the apple-tree. The Planting of the Apple-Tree. Bryant. GN; OHIP

Come let us rejoice. About Savannah. *Unknown.* PAH

Come, let us sigh a requiem over love. Robert Nichols. *Fr.* Sonnets to Aurelia. OBMV

Come, let us tell the weeds in ditches. Last Hill in a Vista. Louise Bogan. FaBoWP

Come, Let Us Tune Our Loftiest Song. Robert A. West. AH

Come, let us walk. Spring in Virginia. Ramona Wilson. VoR

Come let's begin to revel't out. *Unknown.* BoTP

Come, let's go climb on that jasmine-mantled rock. What Her Girlfriends Said to Her. Okkur Macatti, *tr. fr. Tamil by* A. K. Ramanujan. BoWoP

Come, let's to bed. Mother Goose. GBP; OxBoLi; OxNR

Come, Let's to Bed. *Unknown.* ReMoGo

Come light and listen, you gentlemen all. Robin Hood and the Beggar, I. *Unknown.* ESPB

Come, list and hark, the bell doth toll. The Passing Bell. Thomas Heywood. *Fr.* Rape of Lucrece, The. FaBoRV

Come list you gallant Englishmen who ramble at your ease. Loss of the *Amphitrite. Unknown.* OxBSS

Come listen a while and give ear to my song. Hard Times. *Unknown.* AmFP

Come listen a while, you gentlemen all. Robin Hood Newly Revived. *Unknown.* ESPB

Come, listen all unto my song. How Cyrus Laid the Cable. John Godfrey Saxe. AnAmPo; PAH

Come listen all ye feeling people while this sad story I relate. The Wreck of the *Northfleet. Unknown.* OxBSS

Come listen, and hear me tell/ the end of a tale so true. The Lass of Lynn's New Joy, for Finding a Father for Her Child. *Unknown.* CoMu

Come listen and I'll tell you. The Yankee Privateer. Arthur Hale. PAH

Come listen awhile, and I'll sing you a song. The Silly Old Man. *Unknown.* CoMu

Come listen awhile with attention. Bold Adventures of Captain Ross. *Unknown.* OxBSS

Come listen, good neighbors of every degree. The Liberty Pole. *Unknown.* PAH

Come listen, good people, to what I shall say. A Ballad Called Perkins's Figary. *Unknown.* APAS

Come listen to another song. The Old Scottish Cavalier. William Edmonstoune Aytoun. GN

Come listen to me, you gallants so free. Robin Hood and Allen [*or* Allin] -a-Dale. *Unknown.* ESPB; FaBoBe; GBP; MoShBr; OxAEP-1

Come, listen to my story, ye landsmen, one and all. Raging Canawl. *Unknown.* AS

Come, listen to my tragedy, good people, young and old. Mary Wyatt and Henry Green. *Unknown.* AmFP

Come listen to the story of brave Lathrop and his men. The Lamentable Ballad of the Bloody Brook. Edward Everett Hale. PAH

Come listen, ye Whigs, to my pitiful moan. The Salamanca Doctor's Farewell. *Unknown.* APAS

Come, little babe, come, silly soul. Nicholas Breton. NOBE; OBEV (Sweet Lullaby, A.) EIL

Come, little infant, love me now. Young Love. Andrew Marvell. OxAEP-1

Come, little John, tell me the lovely tale. Whom Jesus Loved. John Barford. PeHV

Come, Little Leaves. George Cooper. FaPON

Come Live with Me. Naomi Marks. BXAP

"Come live with me and be my love." Bacchanal. Peter De Vries. BXAP; NBLV; NOBL; OBAL

Come, live with me and be my love. C. Day Lewis. BoLoP; NoAM; OBMV
(Song: "Come, live with me and be my love.") NIP; NoP; Poetr

Come live with me[e] and be[e] my love. The Bait[e]. John Donne. CBLP; CoGr; ErPo; HoPM; InPK; InPS; LPA; NAEL-1; NOSC; OAEL-1; PoRA; RB; TEP

Come, live with me and be my love. Samuel Hoffenstein. *Fr.* Invocation. NBLV

Come live with me[e] and be my love. The Passionate Shepherd to His Love. Christopher Marlowe. AAS; ArLo; AWP; BoLoP; CBLP; ClHu; CoGr; CTC; EBEvV; EIL; ELP; FaBoBe; FF; GGP; GTBS; GTBS-P; HAP; HeIL; HeIP; HoPM; ImPo; InPK; InPS; LiTB; NAEL-1; NBLV; NIP; NOBE; NoP; NoSic; OAEL-1; OBEV; OxAEP-1; PoE; Poetr; PoLF; PoRA; PPP; RB; SCV; SiPSBD; TFi; TrGrPo; TRP; TTTS; UV; WeW
(Shepherd to His Love, The.) GN
(Shepherd's Plea, The.) SiPS

Come live with me and be my whore. The Wooing Rogue. *Unknown.* CoMu

Come live with me and be my wife. The Passionate Shepherd to His Love. Delmore Schwartz. PIP; SCGP

Come, love, for now the night and day. Song for Autumn. Andrew Young. GBL

Come, Love, Let's Walk. *Unknown.* EIL

Come lovely and soothing death. Walt Whitman. *Fr.* Memories of President Lincoln. AmPP; AWP; HAP; LiTA; MeMAP; MoAmPo; NAAL-1; NOBA; NoP; OxBA; PoEL-5; PoRA; PPP; SAmP; SCV; TAP; TFi; TrGrPo
(Carol of Death, The.) DL

Come, lovely Muse, desert for me. Samuel Hoffenstein. BXAP

Come loyal Britons all rejoice with joyful acclamations. English Courage Displayed; or, Brave News from Admiral Vernon, *Unknown.* OxBSS

Come, Madam, come, all rest my powers defie [*or* defly]. Going to Bed. John Donne. *Fr.* Elegies. EBEV; EnRePo; ESCV; LiTB; NAEL-1; PPP
(Elegie XIX: To His Mistris Going to Bed.) OxAEP-1; SeCP
(Elegie: Going to Bed.) OxBM, *sect.* XIX
(To His Mistress [*or* Mistris] Going to Bed.) BoLoP; CBLP; ErPo; FaBoBl; JCP; NoP; NoSic; OAEL-1; PoE; TEP

Come, Make an End. Alcuin, *tr. fr. Latin by* Helen Waddell. MLL

Come! Marget, come! — the team is at the gate! The Country Lovers; or, Isaac and Marget Going to Town, on a Summer's Morning. George Smith. NOEC

Come, me canny Tynesiders, an' lissen. The Strike. *Unknown.* OBET

Come, memory, let us seek them there in the shadows. (*LL*) On the Death of Friends in Childhood. Donald Justice. InPK; LCAP

Come, Muse, migrate from Greece and Ionia. The Muse in the New World. Walt Whitman. *Fr.* Song of the Exposition. MoAmPo

Come muster, my lads, your mechanical tools. The New Roof. Francis Hopkinson. PAH

Come, my brothers. The Only Tourist in Havana Turns His Thoughts Homeward. Leonard Cohen. MoCV; MoP

Come, My Celia. Ben Jonson. *See* Come, my Celia, let us prove.

Come, my Celia, let us prove. Ben Jonson. *Fr.* Volpone. BeJo; CBLP; EIL; OBVE; TEP; TFi
(Come, My Celia.) FaBV; FF; NoP; TrGrPo
(Song to Celia.) ErPo; JCP; OAEL-1; SeCP; SeCV-1
(Song: To Celia.) BeJo; EnRePo
(To Celia.) OxAEP-1; PFP

Come, my Corinna, come, let's go a-Maying. (LL) Corinna's Going a-Maying. Robert Herrick. BeJo; BoNaP; CaPo; GN; HAP; InPS; JCP; NAEL-1; NIP; NOBE; NoP; NOSC; OAEL-1; OBEV; PoE; PoEL-3; PPP; PrIm; SCGP; SeCP; SeCV-1; TEP; TFi; TrGrPo

Come (my dear) whilst youth conspires. Time Recover'd. Thomas Stanley, after the Italian of Girolamo Casone. OBVE

Come, my fine cat, against my loving heart; The Cat. Baudelaire, tr. fr. French by Roy Campbell. OFC

Come my friends and listen unto me. The Parson Grocer. Unknown. CoMu

Come, my lad, and drink some beer. (LL) Hermit Hoar. Samuel Johnson. NBLV

Come, my lad, and sit beside me; we have often talked before. The Story of a Stowaway. Clement Scott. VPP

Come, my little Robert, near. Cleanliness. Charles Lamb and Mary Lamb and Mary Lamb. OxBChV

Come, my Lucasia, since we see. Friendship's Mysterys, to my dearest Lucasia. Katherine Philips. KTR; PeHV

Come my own one, come my fond one. The Saucy Sailor. Unknown. OBET

Come, my pretty little Muse. On My Pretty Marten. Charles Cotton. FM

Come, my songs, let me express our baser passions. Ezra Pound. Fr. Lustra. PoA
(Further Instructions.) TwCP

Come, my tan-faced children. Pioneers! O Pioneers! Walt Whitman. FaBoBe

Come, mysterious night. A Hymn to Night. Max Michelson. TrJP

Come, neighbour, take a walk with me. Hannah More. Fr. Gin-Shop, The; A Peep into Prison. ECWP

Come, neighbours, no longer be patient and quiet. The Riot; or, Half a Loaf Is Better than No Bread. Hannah More. NOEC

Come night. News from Mount Amiata. Robert Lowell, tr. fr. Italian by Eugenio Montale. NaP

Come not in here, Nuncle, here's a spirit. Lear's Madness. Shakespeare. Fr. King Lear. CBNP

Come Not Near My Songs. Unknown, tr. fr. Shoshone Indian by Mary Austin. AWP; WPE

Come not the earliest petal here, but only. Quiet. Marjorie Pickthall. NOBC

Come Not the Seasons Here. E. J. Pratt. NoP

Come not, when I am dead. Tennyson. FaBoRV; GBL; PeVV
(Go By.) OBNC

Come now, and let us wake them: time. Unknown, tr. fr. German by Jethro Bithell. AWP

Come now behold. The Glory of and Grace in the Church Set Out. Edward Taylor. Fr. God's Determinations [touching his Elect]. AmPP

Come now each gen'rous feeling heart. The Framework-knitters Lamentation. Unknown. CoMu

Come now, my love, the moon is on the lake. Albery Allson Whitman. Fr. Twasinta's Seminoles; Or Rape of Florida. AAP

"Come now," said Bell, "this is choice." Frank Richards. PeLi

Come now! You supercilious detractors of America. Meredith Phyfe. Edgar Lee Masters. Fr. New Spoon River, The. GOA

Come, O come, my life's delight. My Life's Delight. Thomas Campion. ElL; InvP; TrGrPo

Come, o come soon! (LL) Each night I sleep more lightly. Herman von Lingg. RiWo

Come, O Friend, to Greet the Bride. Solomon Halevi Alkabez, tr. fr. Hebrew into German by Heine; English vers. by Louis Untermeyer. TrJP

Come, O Lord, Like Morning Sunlight. Milton S. Littlefield. TrPWD

Come, O Sabbath Day. Gustav Gottheil. AH

Come, O thou traveller unknown. Wrestling Jacob. Charles Wesley. NOBE; NOCV; NOEC; OBEV; OxAEP-1; PeECV; PoEL-3; TOF

Come o'er the hills, and pass unto the wold. A Winter Hymn — to the Snow. Ebenezer Jones. OBNC

Come o'er the stream, Charlie. McLean's Welcome. James Hogg. OxBS

Come, oh come in pious Laies. A Hymne I: Generall Invitation to Praise God. George Wither. Fr. Hallelujah; or, Britain's Second Remembrancer. SeCV-1

Come on, come on! and where you go. Ben Jonson. Fr. Pleasure Reconciled to Virtue. NAEL-1; OAEL-1

Come on! Come on! This hillock hides the spire. Sunday Afternoon Service in St. Enodoc Church, Cornwall. Sir John Betjeman. NOCV

Come on, good fellow, make an end. A Dialogue between Death and Youth. Unknown. NoSic

Come On Home. Sharon Scott. JB

Come On in, the Senility Is Fine. Ogden Nash. AiP

Come on, let's kill ourselves, I say to my friends. Friends. Martin Sorescu, tr. fr. Romanian by Michael Hamburger. PWE

Come on, my fellow pilgrims, come. At. to Sarah Lancaster. AmFP

Come On, My Lucky Lads. Edmund Blunden. PeFWW

Come on out of there with your hands up, Charlie. Patriotic Ode on the Fourteenth Anniversary of the Persecution of Charlie Chaplin. Bob Kaufman. PoBA

"Come on" sayd sche, "this ordenance to vysyte." Calliope's Nymph Brings the Poet to the Palace to Honour. Gawin Douglas. Fr. Palace [or Palice] of Honor [or Honour], The. OxBLMV

Come on, sir; here's the place. Stand still. Shakespeare. Fr. King Lear. OxAEP-1
(Dover, the Samphire Cliff.) FaBoPP

Come on, sir. Now, you set your foot on shore. Ben Jonson. Fr. Alchemist, The. PoEL-2

Come on then, ye dwellers by nature in darkness. Chorus of Birds. Aristophanes, tr. fr. Greek by Swinburne. Fr. Birds, The. AWP
(Grand Chorus of Birds.) PoEL-5

Come on, ye critics! Find one fault who dare. On Mr. Edward Howard, upon His British Princes. Charles Sackville. OBSV

Come on, you . . . Do you want to live forever? (LL) Losers. Carl Sandburg. CMoP; MoAB; MoAmPo; NoAM; TrGrPo

Come once again and love me. (LL) Lady Greensleeves. Unknown. GBL; PoEL-2

Come, Ophrah, fill my cup — but not with wine. The Splendor of Thine Eyes. Moses ibn Ezra, tr. fr. Hebrew by Solomon Solis-Cohen. TrJP

Come out and climb the garden path. Luriana, Lurilee. Charles Elton. Mes

Come out come out come out. Moon Eclipse Exorcism. Unknown, tr. fr. Alsea Indian by Armand Schwerner. STP

Come out, come out, this sunny day. Hay-Time. C. M. Lowe. BoTP

Come out from the bath. (LL) The Bath. Gary Snyder. CAPP; NNaP; PoBeRe; TAP; VCAP

Come Out into the Sun. Robert Francis. NYBP

Come out of Crete/ and find me here. Sappho, tr. fr. Greek by Guy Davenport. OBVE

Come out of the Golden Gate. Old Counsel. Herman Melville. FaBoRV

Come out of your body among us & we're all one. How to Get Grizzly Spirit. Unknown, tr. fr. Tlingit Indian by James Koller. STP

Come out, 'tis now September. The Ripe and Bearded Barley. Unknown. BoNaP; ChTr; GBP

Come over the born bessy. A Songe betwene the Quenes Majestie and Englande. William Birche. CoMu

Come Painter, you and I, you know, dare do. Old England. Nahum Tate. APAS

Come, passer-by, sit in this plane-tree's shade. Inscription on a Statue. Hermocreon, tr. fr. Greek by Alistair Elliot. GrAn

Come Peace, on snowy pinions. Ode to Peace. Mary Weston Fordham. CBWP-2

Come people; Aaron's drest. (LL) Aaron. George Herbert. ChIV-1; GeHe; MeLP; NOSC; OAEL-1; PeECV

Come, Phoenix, come, if such a bird there be. On the Phoenix. Jean Adams. ECWP

Come pity me, young maidens all. Disconsolate Judy's Lamentation. Unknown. OxBSS

Come pity us, all ye, who see. Widow's Tears, The or, Dirge of Dorcas. Robert Herrick. ChIV-2

Come play with me. To a Squirrel at Kyle-na-no. W. B. Yeats. FaPON; FM; PDV; SiSoPo

Come play with me said the sun. Play. Frank Asch. NTCP

Come praise Colonus' horses, and come praise. Colonus' Praise. Sophocles, tr. by W. B. Yeats. Fr. Oedipus at Colonus. OBVE

Come, Precious Soul. Unknown. AH

Come quick, come quick, come quick, come quick. (LL) The Watch. Frances Cornford. InPK; MoBrPo; OxBTC

Come rede me, dame, come tell me, dame. Nine Inch Will Please a Lady. Burns. ErPo

Come, rejoice, 'tis Easter Day! Christ Is Risen! Mrs. D. H. Dugan. BLRP

Come right in this house, Will Johnson! Mrs. Johnson Objects. Clara Ann Thompson. AIW; BlSi; CBWP-2

Come, rouse up, ye bold-hearted Whigs of Kentucky. Old Tippecanoe. Unknown. PAH

Come! rouse ye brothers, rouse! a peal now breaks. Spirit Voice, The; or Liberty Call to the Disfranchised (State of New York). Charles Lewis Reason. AAP

Come rouse ye, my lads, though no land we are near. The Sailor's Christmas Day. Unknown. OxBSS

Come rude Boreas, blustering railer, list ye landsmen all to me. Rude Boreas. Unknown. OBET

Come, Sable Night. John Ward. EnRePo

Come saddle me my fastest steed. Geordie. *Unknown.* AmFP; ESPB, A and B *vers.*; FaBoBa; OBET; OxBB

Come, Said My Soul. Walt Whitman. NOBA

"Come!" said Old Shellover. Old Shellover. Walter de la Mare. BoTP; OxBChV

Come, saints and sinners, hear me tell. A Parody. Frederick Douglass. *Fr. Narrative of the Life of an American Slave.* NAAL-1; NAWM-2

Come sapless blossom, creep not stil on earth. The Sap. Henry Vaughan *and* Thomas Stanley. ESCV

Come, see the Dolphin's anchor forged! — 'tis at a white heat now. The Forging of the Anchor. Sir Samuel Ferguson. PeIV

Come See the Place Where the Lord Lay. Richard Crashaw. ChIV-2

Come sheathe your swords! my gallant boys. Sergeant Champe. *Unknown.* PAH

Come, Shepherds, Come! John Fletcher. *Fr.* Faithful Shepherdess, The. EIL; ErPo

Come sing, come sing, come sing sing/ And sing. (*LL*) Yardbird's Skull. Owen Dodson. Jaz; PoBA; VGW

Come sing to me. (*LL*) What Is a Jewish Poem? Myra Sklarew. CRP

Come sing with me in chorus: it's nothing, all we know. Antonio Machado Ruiz, *tr. fr. Spanish by* John Frederick Nims. STV

Come sit beneath my pine. On a Statue of Pan. *Unknown, tr. fr. Greek by* W. G. Shepherd. GrAn

Come, sit thee down by these cool streams. Then Lose in Time Thy Maidenhead. *Unknown.* ErPo

Come, sleep. Beaumont *and* John Fletcher. *Fr.* Woman-Hater, The. EIL; ELP

Come sleepe, O sleepe, the certaine knot of peace. Sir Philip Sidney. *Fr.* Astrophel and Stella. AAS; EIL; EnRePo; ESo, *sl. abr.*; GGP; HeIL; *Sonnets,* I–CVIII *and* 11 *Songs*; NAEL-1; NoP; NoSic; OxAEP-1; PoE; Poetr; PoRA; PPP; SCGP, *Sonnets,* I–CVIII *and* 11 *Songs*; SCV; SiPS, *Sonnets,* I–CVIII *and* 11 *Songs*; SiPSBD, *Sonnets,* I–CVIII *and* 11 *Songs*; Son; TEP; TFi; TrGrPo
(Sleep.) OBEV
(To Sleep.) NOBE

Come slowly — Eden. Emily Dickinson. CMoP; FaBoVe; NALW

Come smoke a coca-cola. The Billboard Song. *Unknown.* CBNP

Come, sons of Mars, who thirst for blood. A Drinking-Song, against All Sorts of Disputes in Drinking. William Wycherley. SeCV-2

Come, sons of summer, by whose toil[e]. The Hock-Cart, or Harvest Home. Robert Herrick. BeJo; CaPo; EBEV; FaBoPV; JCP; NAEL-1; NOSC; OxAEP-1; SeCP; SeCV-1

Come soon. (*LL*) Be kind to me. Sappho. PeHV

Come soon, O Deep River, O Dark Stream. (*LL*) Deep River. Eugène Marais. PeSAV

Come soon, soon! (*LL*) To Night. Shelley. AWP; EnRP; FHYEP; MeMBP; NAEL-2; NoP; OAEL-2; OBNC; PIP; PoLF; PoRA; TEP; TFi; TrGrPo; WiR

Come, sound up your trumpets and beat up your drums. The Young Earl of Essex's Victory over the Emperor of Germany. *Unknown.* ESPB; OBET

Come sounding thro' the town. (*LL*) The Bonny Earl of Murray. *Unknown.* ESPB, A *vers.*; FaBoBa; NOSC; OBEV; OxBB; OxBS; PrIm; ScCV; SCGP, A *vers.*

Come, spread foam rubber on the floor. I Can't Have a Martini, Dear, but You Take One. Ogden Nash. PoRA

Come spur [*or* spurre] away. An Ode to Mr. [*or* Master] Anthony Stafford to Hasten Him into the Country. Thomas Randolph. BeJo; NOBE; NOSC; OBEV

Come, stack arms, men! Pile on the rails. Stonewall Jackson's Way. John Williamson Palmer. PAH

Come, stir the fire. Safe. James Walker. OBCP

Come suddenly, O Lord, or slowly come, Take Ye Heed, Watch and Pray. Jones Very. ChIV-2

Come! supper is ready. The Good Moolly Cow. Eliza Lee Follen. OBCA

Come swallow your bumpers, ye Tories, and roar. Massachusetts Song of Liberty. *At. to* Mrs. Mercy Warren. PAH

Come take up your hats, and away let us haste. The Butterfly's Ball. William Roscoe. OxBChV

Come tawny bees. Diodorus Zonas, *tr. fr. Greek by* Alistair Elliot. GrAn

Come, the wind may never again. D.G.C. to J.A. Emily Brontë. BrRo, 1 *st.*; EnLoPo, 1 *st.*

Come then, and like two doves with silv'rie [*or* silvery] wings. The Apparition of His Mistress[e] Calling Him to Elizium [*or* Elysium]. Robert Herrick. CaPo; SeCP; SeCV-1

Come then! and while the slow icicle hangs. Henry Vaughan. *Fr.* To His Retired Friend, an Invitation to Brecknock. FaBoRV

Come then, as ever, like the wind at morning! Invocation to Youth. Laurence Binyon. OBEV

Come then, my soule, approach this royall Burse. Francis Quarles. *Fr.* Emblems. ESCV

Come think with me: the Paris sky, the giant meadow-saffron. Memory of France. Paul Celan, *tr. fr. German by* Joachim Neugroschel. AnAn

Come, Thou Almighty King. Charles Wesley. WGRP

Come, thou monarch of the vine. A Drinking Song. Shakespeare. *Fr.* Antony and Cleopatra. NoSic

Come thou, who art the wine and wit. His Winding-Sheet. Robert Herrick. CaPo; OBEV

Come Thunder. Christopher Okigbo. HBAPE

Come tip a few with me. Alcaeus, *tr. fr. Greek by* Sam Hamill. InMo

Come to guard us, come to bless us. The Triple Benison. H. Cordelia Ray. CBWP-3

Come to Me. *Gond Oral Tradition, tr. by* V. Elwin *and* S. Hivale. WTO

Come To Me. Friedrich Rückert, *tr. fr. German by* Philip L. Miller. RiWo

Come to me, Beloved. Homo Factus Est. Digby Mackworth Dolben. TrPWD

Come to me broken dreams and all. The Still Voice of Harlem. Conrad Kent Rivers. PoBA

Come to me, Eros, if you needs must come. To the God of Love. E. V. Knox. NOBL

Come to me from Crete to this holy temple. Sappho, *tr. fr. Greek by* Richmond Lattimore. WPOW

Come to me, grief, for ever. A Funerall Song. *Unknown.* CH

Come to me in my dreams, and then. Longing. Matthew Arnold. PoLF; SoSe

Come to me in the night — we shall sleep closely together [*or* Let us sleep entwined]. Else Lasker-Schüler, *tr. fr. German.* BoWoP, *tr. by* Michael Gillespie; TrJP, *tr. by* Michael Gillespie

Come to me in the silence of the night. Echo. Christina Rossetti. BoLoP; CH; EBEvV; EBVV; ELP; GBL; MeMBP; NOBE; NoP; OAEL-2; OBNC; OHCV; PFP; PIP; PoE; PoEL-5; VBLP

Come to me pig, you who dress yourself as a courtier. Flirting with a Pig. Aleksandar Ristovic, *tr. fr. Serbo-Croatian by* Charles Simic. HSix

Come to me when the swelling wind assails the wood with a sealike roar. Late Light. Edmund Blunden. EnLoPo

Come to my window in the evening twilight. Sunset. Hayyim Nahman Bialik, *tr. fr. Hebrew by* Helena Frank. TrJP

Come to Noah's for wine and strong waters. *Unknown.* PeLi

Come to Sunny Prestatyn. Sunny Prestatyn. Philip Larkin. NoAM

Come to term the started child shocks. Multipara: Gravida 5. Marie Ponsot. VGW

Come to the festal board tonight. The Festal Board. *Unknown.* BLPA

Come to the judgment, golden threads. The Judgment of the May. Richard Watson Dixon. OBNC

Come to the Stone. Randall Jarrell. VGW

Come to the vintage feast! Emma Catherine Embury. AmWP

Come to weep out the night. (*LL*) To the Willow-Tree. Robert Herrick. CaPo; OBEV; SCGP

Come to your heaven, you heavenly choirs [*or* quires]. New Heaven, New War[re]. Robert Southwell. ChIV-2; ESCV; NOBE; NoP

Come townsmen all and women too. Funny Rigs of Good and Tender-hearted Masters. *Unknown.* OBET

Come trotting up. Foal. Mary Britton Miller. PDV

Come, try this exercise. In the Dark. James Merrill. LCAP

"Come, try your skill, kind gentlemen." The Gipsy Girl. Ralph Hodgson. MoBrPo

Come Turn to Mee, Thou Pretty Little One. *Unknown.* CoMu

Come under My Plaidie. Hector MacNeill. ScCV

Come unto Me, When Shadows Darkly Gather. Catharine H. Watterman. AH

Come unto me, ye heroes. Saratoga Song. *Unknown.* PAH

Come unto these yellow sands. Shakespeare. *Fr.* Tempest, The. BoTP; CH; EIL; NOSC; NoSic; OAEL-1; OBEV; SCGP; SoSe; TFi; TTTS
(Ariel's Song: "Come unto these yellow sands.") CTC; FaBoCh; GN; GoJo; NOBE; TEP
(Song: "Come unto these yellow sands.") EBEvV; PoEL-2

Come Up from the Fields Father. Walt Whitman. AnAmPo; MoAmPo; OBWP; OxBA; PPP; SAmP; UnPo

Come Up, Methuselah. C. Day Lewis. OBMV

Come up, my horse, to Budleigh Fair. *Unknown.* OxNR

Come up to me at early dawn. Invitation. Solomon ibn Gabirol, *tr. fr. Hebrew by* Israel Zangwill. TrJP

Come up unto the hills — thy strength is there. Strength from the Hills. Elizabeth Oakes Smith. AmWP

Come, virgin tapers of pure wax. Richard Crashaw. NOCV

Come visit my pancake collection. The Pancake Collector. Jack Prelutsky. OBCA

Come, walk with me. Emily Brontë. NOBVV

Come, warm your hands. Driftwood. Witter Bynner. FYAP

Come Wary One. Ruth Manning-Sanders. CH

Come, wed me, Lady Singleton. Lady "Rogue" Singleton. Stevie Smith. FaBoWP; OxBSP

Come, weele associate this jolly Pilgrimage! (*LL*) What Fair[e] Pomp[e]. Thomas Campion. GBL; NoSic; PoEL-2; Prf; SCGP

Come wench, are we almost at the well. Fair Maiden. George Peele. *Fr.* Old Wives' [*or* Wife's] Tale, The. PoEL-2

Come, when no graver cares employ. To the Rev. F. D. Maurice. Tennyson. GTBS-P; NOBVV; OBF; PeECV

Come when the leaf comes, angle with me. The Angler's Invitation. Thomas Tod Stoddart. GN

Come when you're called. Mother Goose. OxNR (Good Advice.) ReMoGo

"Come, wife," said good old Farmer Gray. The Little Dog under the Wagon. *Unknown.* PoLF

Come, "Will," let's be good friends again. Sunshine after Cloud. Josephine D. Henderson Heard. CBWP-4

Come Wisdom Sweet. Morgan Llwyd. AngWe

Come wisdom sweet, my spirit meet, for at thy feet I fall. Come Wisdome Sweet. Morgan Llwyd. AngWe

Come with clean hands. *Unknown, tr. fr. Greek by* Edward Lucie-Smith. GrAn

Come with Me. Robert Bly. NoAM; NOBA

Come with me and you may see. A Christmas Rhyme. George Sands Johnson. PWR

Come with me into those things that have felt this despair for so long. Come with Me. Robert Bly. NoAM; NOBA

Come with Me into Winter's Disheveled Grass. Karen Swenson. GrPl

Come, with our voices let us war. The Musical Strife, in a Pastoral Dialogue. Ben Jonson. BeJo

Come with rain, O loud Southwester! To the Thawing Wind. Robert Frost. OxBA

Come with the Spring-time, forth fair maid, and be. The Meddow Verse; or, Aniversary to Mistris Bridget Lowman. Robert Herrick. SeCV-1

Come, Woeful Orpheus. William Byrd. EnRePo

Come worthy Greek, Ulysses [*or* Vlisses], come. Ulysses and the Siren [*or* Syren]. Samuel Daniel. EiL; EnRePo; HAP; NAEL-1; NOBE; NoP; OBEV; OxAEP-1; PoE; PoEL-2; TEP

Come, Ye Disconsolate. Thomas Moore. WGRP

Come ye hither all, whose taste. The Invitation. George Herbert. ChIV-1; ESCV

Come, Ye Lads, Who Wish to Shine. *Unknown.* PAH

Come ye old English huntsmen that love noble sport. The Old Pack. *Unknown.* APAS

Come, ye thankful people, come. Harvest Home. Henry Alford. WGRP

Come yee my servants of my father Blessed. (*LL*) Uppon the First Sight of New England, June 29, 1638. Thomas Tillam. GOA; SCAP

Come you, cartoonists. Halsted Street Car. Carl Sandburg. NAAL-2

Come you fatall sisters three. Whipping Cheare. *Unknown.* FaBoBa

Come you gallants all, to you I do call. Robin Hood's Chase. *Unknown.* ESPB

Come you ladies and you gentlemen and listen to my song. Down on Penny's Farm. *Unknown.* SWP

Come, You Pretty False-eyed Wanton. Thomas Campion. ELP

Come, You Whose Loves Are Dead. Beaumont *and* John Fletcher. *Fr.* Knight of the Burning Pestle, The. EiL

Comeahead then comeahead. Love Song of Tommo Frogley. Roger Crawford. FaBoBl; UV

Comedian as the Letter C, The. Wallace Stevens. OxBA

Comedian, holding a chunk of flaming shale, The. Why That's Bob Hope. William Hathaway. SM

Comedy of Art: Henri de Toulouse Lautrec, The. Richard Howard. AnAn

Comely and capable one of our race. On the Portrait of a Woman about to Be Hanged. Thomas Hardy. CMoP

Comely widow named Ransom, A. *Unknown.* PeLi

Comes a brown. Corkby, Part Two. Jerome Rothenberg. NNaP

Comes a cry from Cuban water. Cuba Libre. Joaquin Miller. PAH

Comes a time. The Poet in Old Age Fishing at Evening. Desmond O'Grady. CIP

Comes after the storm and gloom. (*LL*) Life's Lessons. *Unknown.* BLRP; PoLF

Comes bleeding through the heat like a deep gangrene. (*LL*) After the Massacre. Musaemura Bonus Zimunya. PeSAV

Comes Death, and takes the table clean away. (*LL*) A Comparison of the Life of Man. Richard Barnfield. NoSic; OxBSP

Comes home dull with coal-dust deliberately. Her Husband. Ted Hughes. OxBC

Comes like an idiot, babbling and stewing flowers. (*LL*) Spring. Edna St. Vincent Millay. BoWoP; MeMAP; MoAB; MoAmPo; NoP

Comes not the springtime here. Come Not the Seasons Here. E. J. Pratt. NoP

Comes out like a ribbon lies flat on the brush. (*LL*) Poem, or Beauty Hurts Mr. Vinal. E. E. Cummings. InPS; MoAB; MoAmPo; NAAL-2; OBAL; OxBA; PeLV; TRP

Comes the day, when he must die. Muspilli. *Unknown, tr. fr. German by* Carroll Hightower. GePo

Comes the deer to my singing. Hunting-Song. *Unknown, tr. fr. Navajo Indian by* Natalie Curtis. AWP

Comes the time when it's later. A Wicker Basket. Robert Creeley. CAPP; HAP; MoP; NoAM; NoP; Poetr; SM

Comes to nothing: the bite of postmarks, ink. (*LL*) Letter to My Mother. Suzanne Gardinier. UTF

Comet, The. Maria Luisa Spaziani, *tr. fr. Italian by* Beverly Allen. NeIt

Comet at Yell'ham, The. Thomas Hardy. CMoP; GBL

Comets and Princes. Samuel Johnson. FaBoEE

Comfort. Walter de la Mare. PFP

Comfort. Maura Stanton. SoSe

Comfort. Margaret Widdemer. GoYe

Comfort for a wedded pair! (*LL*) The Ballad of Hiram Hover. Bayard Taylor. AnAmPo; BXAP; FaBoCo; OBAL

Comfort in Puirtith. Helen B. Cruickshank. OxBS

Comfort notions/ correction. Road. Kevin Magee. BAP-90

Comfort of the Trees, The. Richard Watson Gilder. PAH

Comfort that does not comprehend. (*LL*) The Return. Edna St. Vincent Millay. LiTA; MeMAP; MoAB; MoAmPo; MoP; NoAM; OxBA; Poetr

Comfort thyself, my woeful [*or* woful] heart. Sir Thomas Wyatt. SiPS; SiPSBD

Comfort to a Youth That Had Lost His Love. Robert Herrick. NOBE; OBEV

Comfort ye, comfort ye my people. Bible, *O.T. Fr.* Isaiah. OBVE, *sts.* 1–8; TrJP, (1-5)

Comfortable Strangers. Terence Winch. UL

Comfortable Words. Gillian Allnutt. NBrP

Comforted by Limestone. Edward Dorn. *Fr.* Oxford. NOBA

Comforters, The. Dora Sigerson Shorter. CH

Comic Adventures of Old Mother Hubbard and Her Dog, The. Sarah Catherine Martin. *See* Old Mother Hubbard.

Comic Miseries. John Godfrey Saxe. AnAmPo

Comical Revenge, The, *sels.* Sir George Etherege. "Ladies, though to your conquering eyes." OxBSP

Comin' fer to carry me home. (*LL*) Swing Low, Sweet Chariot. *Unknown.* FaPON; UnPo

Comin' for to carry me home. (*LL*) Swing Low, Sweet Chariot. *Unknown.* AnAmPo

Comin thro' the Rye. ("Comin' thro' the rye, poor body.") Burns. CBLP; FaBoVe; OxBS

Comin' thro' the Rye. ("Gin a body meet a body.") Burns. LiTB; UV, *abr.*; WBLP

Comin thro' the rye. (*LL*) Comin thro' the Rye. Burns. CBLP; FaBoVe; OxBS

Comin thro the rye, poor body. Comin thro' the Rye. Burns. CBLP; FaBoVe; OxBS

Comin' Throu the Rye. Burns. FaBoBl, *diff. vers.*

Coming. Philip Larkin. MoBrPo; OxBTC; PlP

Coming Across. Mehri, *tr. fr. Farsi by* Deirdre Lashgari. WPOW

Coming Again to Heng-yang, I Mourn for Liu Tsung-yüan. Liu Yu Hsi, *tr. fr. Chinese by* Daniel Bryant. SuSp

Coming American, The, *sels.* Sam Walter Foss. "Bring me men to match my mountains." BLPA; FaBoBe

Coming and Going. Robert Francis. TLR

Coming and Going. Mitchell Goodman. VGW

Coming and going these several seasons. Abiku. J. P. Clark Bekederemo. HBAPE

Coming around the corner of a dark trail . . . what was wrong with the valley? The Inquisitors. Robinson Jeffers. MoAmPo

Coming around the corner of a dream. Cockaigne: A Dream. L. E. Sissman. DiPo

Coming around the Horn. John A. Stone. AmFP

Coming at an end, the lovers. A Book of Music. Jack Spicer. PoM

Coming Back. Joseph Bruchac. CDW

Coming Back. Ellsworth McGranaham Keane. PBCV

Coming back again and again. (*LL*) Emu Shot. Tjinapirrgarri. NOBAu

Coming Back Home. Ray A. Young Bear. CDW

Coming back in the fall dark. At the Wayside. Jeff Daniel Marion. ETG

Coming back one evening through deserted fields. Through All Your Abstract Reasoning. Brian Patten. FaBoTw

Coming back over the col between. Strength through Joy. Kenneth Rexroth. FYAP; VGW

Coming Back to America. James Dickey. NYBP

Coming back to this generous island. Returning to Store Bay. Barbara Howes. Poetsp

Coming by evening through the wintry city. At a Bach Concert. Adrienne Rich. NIP; SM

Coming down into an air brown as whiskey, the plane. Autobiography, Chapter XLII: Three Days in Louisville. Jim Barnes. HATNAP

Coming Down to It. Malcolm Glass. BXAP

Coming Forth by Day. John Taggart. Jaz

Coming from Evening Church. Charles Causley. NTP

Coming from the deli. This Dark Apartment. James Schuyler. NGP

Coming from the south. Six Ten Sixty-nine. Conyus. PoBA

Coming, going, the waterbirds. On Non-dependence of Mind. Dogen. EnlH

Coming Home. Philip Levine. CAPP

Coming Home. Dorothy Coffin Sussman. ArOW

Coming Home. Brian Turner. PeNZ

Coming Home from Abroad. David Holbrook. OBTV

Coming home, I find you still in bed. Abortion. Ai. BoWoP

Coming Home in March. Harold Littlebird. VoR

Coming home late through the smoky. Coming Home. Brian Turner. PeNZ

Coming home with the last load I ride standing. Emergency Haying. Hayden Carruth. NNaP

Coming Homeward out of Spain. Barnabe Googe. EIL; NoSic

Coming in again, you know the town by boards it makes eyes touch. Autobiography: Last Chapter. Jim Barnes. CDW

Coming in off the dock after writing. Station. Sharon Olds. PBCAP

Coming into the high room again after years. Late Spring. W. S. Merwin. AnAn

Coming into the store at first angry. The Man Who Finds That His Son Has Become a Thief. Raymond Souster. NOBC

Coming into Their Own. Sheenagh Pugh. AngWe

"Coming" is an empty word, "going" leaves no trace. Li Shang-yin, tr. fr. Chinese by James J. Y. Liu. SuSp

Coming lightly, perfectly. For Me at Sunday Sermons, the Serpent. Lynn Emanuel. ETG

Coming of Age in the County Jail. Carter Revard. VoR

Coming of Arthur, The. Tennyson. Fr. Idylls of the King.

Coming of Dusk upon a Village in Haiti, The. Henry Rago. HoPM

Coming of Good Luck, The. Robert Herrick. FaBoEE; JCP; OxBSP; Spl

Coming of His Feet, The. Lyman W. Allen. BLPA

Coming of Light, The. Mark Strand. HCAP

Coming of Raka, The. N. P. van Wyk Louw, tr. fr. Afrikaans by Guy Butler. Fr. Raka. PeSAV

Coming of Spring, The. Nora Perry. PWR

Coming of Spring, The. H. Cordelia Ray. CBWP-3

Coming of Teddy Bears, The. Dennis Lee. TLR

Coming of that limpid star is twice, The. Louise Labé, tr. fr. French by Willis Barnstone. BoWoP

Coming of the Cold, The. Theodore Roethke. OBCP

Coming of the King, The. Unknown. See Yet if his majesty, our sovereign [or soveraign] Lord.

Coming of the Plague, The. Weldon Kees. ChIV-1; NaP; VGW

Coming of the White Man, The. Patrick Anderson. Fr. Poem on Canada. MoCV

Coming of War; Actaeon, The. Ezra Pound. CMoP; PoA; PoE

Coming of Wisdom with Time, The. W. B. Yeats. FaBoEE; SoSe

Coming Out. Jacqueline Lapidus. IHMS

Coming out of the house on a fresh March morning. March 1st. Kathleen Spivack. NYBP

Coming out of the mountains of a summer evening. St. Gervais. Michael Roberts. FaBoCh

Coming Poet, The. Francis Ledwidge. PeIV

Coming Suddenly to the Sea. Louis Dudek. NOBC

Coming through the Rye. Burns. FaBoVe; OxAEP-2

Coming through the rye, poor body. Coming Through the Rye. Burns. FaBoVe; OxAEP-2

Coming to light. (LL) To Light. Linda Hogan. HATNAP

Coming to the farm that winter afternoon. Burragorang. Nan McDonald. NOBAu

Coming to the Salt Lick. John Woods. FoLa

Coming to This. Mark Strand. HCAP; VCAP

Coming together. Recreation. Audre Lorde. NoP

Coming up England by a different line. I Remember, I Remember. Philip Larkin. NOBL; NTP

Coming up the green lane from the sea. Tryst. John Hewitt. BiHa

Coming was an empty promise, you have gone, and left no footprint. Li Shang-yin, tr. fr. Chinese by A. C. Graham. PLT

Coming Woman, The. Mary Weston Fordham. AmWP; CBWP-2

Command, The. Avraham Huss, tr. fr. Hebrew by Ruth Finer Mintz. MHP

Command a white birch to stand guard! (LL) Sensuous during life. Lois Wickenhauser. EaPr

Command, and I'll forsake thee then. (LL) To His Mistress. James Shirley. BeJo

Commandeered. L.G. Moberley. NSI

Commandeering the Wind. Su Shun-ch'in, tr. fr. Chinese by Irving Y. Lo. SuSp

Commander, The. Count Arsenii Arkadyevich Golenishchev-Kutuzov, tr. fr. Russian by Philip L. Miller. Fr. Songs and Dances of Death. RiWo

Commander Lowell. Robert Lowell. VGW

Commanding asker, if it be. The Fair Beggar. Richard Lovelace. BeJo

Commanding Elephants. Philip Levine. NaP

Commands of Love. Molly Peacock. PFL

Commemoration. Sir Henry Newbolt. FaBoTw

Commemoration Ode, sels. Harriet Monroe.
Washington. FaBoBe
(Two Heroes.) OHIP

Commemorative of a Naval Victory. Herman Melville. AiP; HAP; UnPo

Commencement. Constance Carrier. WPE

Commendatory Verses to Edmund Spenser's Fairy Queen, sels. Sir Walter Ralegh.
Vision upon This Conceit of the Faerie [or Fairy] Queene [or Queen], A. NAEL-1; NoSic; SCGP; SiPSBD; Son
(Of Spenser's Faery Queen.) SiPS

Comment. Dorothy Parker. Fr. Some Beautiful Letters. AnAmPo; NBLV; NIP; OBAL; VBLP

Commentary Applied to Spiritual Things. St. John of the Cross, tr. fr. Spanish by K. Kavanaugh and O. Rodrigues. TOF

Commentary Applied to Spiritual Things. St. John of the Cross, tr. fr. Spanish by K. Kavanaugh and O. Rodrigues. TOF

Comments. Peggy Susberry Kenner. JB

Commerce or contemplation. (LL) Large Bad Picture. Elizabeth Bishop. NoP; NYBP; OxBC

Commination, A. A. D. Hope. ChIV-2

Commingling sky, A. Freely Espousing. James Schuyler. NeAP; NoP

Commission. Ezra Pound. BoLoP; OPOP; TwCP

Commissioner bet me a pony, The — I won, The. Robert Lowe. Fr. Songs of the Squatters. NOBAu

Commit them not, but banish them thy land. (LL) My CLose-Committee. Mildmay Fane, 2d Earl of Westmorland. BeJo

Committee, The. C. Day Lewis. CMoP

Committee, The — now a permanent body. Dream. Marianne Moore. NYBP

Committee's fat, The. Un-American Investigators. Langston Hughes. BPo

Common a-Took In, The. William Barnes. EnVR

Common Bill. Unknown. AmFP; AS

Common Blessings. Thomas Curtis Clark. TrPWD

Common Conditions, sels. Unknown.
Lustily, Lustily. OxBSS

Common cormorant or shag, The. Birds, Bags, Bears, and Buns. Unknown. OtMeF

Common Cormorant [or Shag], The. Christopher Isherwood. ChTr; FaBoCh; FaBoCo; FaBoNo; FiBHP; NBLV; PYC

Common Dawn. Guy Butler. PeSA

Common Dust. Georgia Douglas Johnson. PoBA; ShDr; TTY

Common Form. Kipling. Fr. Epitaphs of the War, 1914–1918. FaBoEE; FaBoTw; NoP; OBWP; PeFWW

Common Gain, Reverted, The. J. H. Prynne. VaA

Common Grave, The. James Dickey. CoAP

Common Ground. John Daniel. FoLa

Common Ground, A. Denise Levertov. PoM

Common Inference, A. Charlotte Perkins Gilman. WGRP

Common Lot, The. Adelbert Sumpter Coats. TrPWD

Common Lover's Song, The. Flavien Ranaivo. See Do not love me, my friend.

Common Man, The. A. J. M. Smith. NOBC

Common miracle. Miracle Mart. Wislawa Szymborska, tr. fr. Polish by Adam Czerniawski. PoSu

Common Occurrence, A. Priscilla Jane Thompson. CBWP-2

Common Path, The. Glyn Jones. AngWe

Common People, The. Rowland Watkyns. AngWe

Common Prayer. Lynn Ungar. CrSp

Common Road, The. Silas H. Perkins. BLPA; FaBoBe

Common Sailor, The. Unknown. OxBSS

"May poverty, without offence, approach." NOEC

Complaisant Friend, The. Pierre Louÿs, *tr. fr. French. Fr.* Chansons de Bilitis. PeHV

Complaisant Swain, The. Ovid, *tr. by* F. A. Wright. *Fr.* Amores. AWP

Complaynt. Anne Waldman. UL

Compleinte of Chauser to His Empty Purs, The Chaucer's Complaint to His Empty Purse. Chaucer. *See* To you [*or* yow], my purse [*or* purs], and to non [*or* no *or* noon] other wight.

Complement, The. Thomas Carew. CBLP

Complete Birth if the Cool, The. C. D. Wright. LCAP

Complete Cynic, The. Keith Preston. NBLV

Complete Destruction. William Carlos Williams. SAmP

Complete in Thee, No Work of Mine. Aaron R. Wolfe. AH

Complete innocence, A. John James. VaA

Complete Introductory Lectures on Poetry, The. Bernadette Mayer. UL

Complete Misanthropist, The. Morris Bishop. FiBHP

Completely to your embraces. (*LL*) Spring Song. Meng Chu. WPC

Completely worn out. Train. Tuo Ssu, *tr. fr. Chinese by* Kenneth Rexroth *and* Ling Chung. WPC

Compleynt of the Comoun Weill of Scotland, The. Sir David Lindsay. *See* And thus as we were talking to and fro.

Complicity killed you. I know. I know. Closer First to Earth. Anne Hazlewood-Brady. IHMS

Compliment to the Ladies, A. Blake. BXAP

Compliment upon a crutch, A. To a Lady, with a Present of a Walking-Stick. John Hookham Frere. FaBoUs

Compline. Donald Davie. *Fr.* Horae Canonicae. CRP

Components. Roger McDonald. CBAP

Compose compose beds. Sacred. Gertrude Stein. OBAL

Compose for Red a proper verse. For Malcolm, a Year After. Etheridge Knight. BCF

Composed at Neidpath Castle, the Property of Lord Queensberry, 1803. Wordsworth. GTBS; GTBS-P

Composed at Sunset at the Dunes of Ho-yen. Ts'en Shen, *tr. fr. Chinese by* Ronald C. Miao. SuSp

Composed at thirty, my funeral oration: Here lies. A Funeral Oration. David Wright. PeSAV

Composed by the Seaside, near Calais, August, 1802. Wordsworth. EnRP; Son

Composed, generally defined. The Map. Mark Strand. NYBP

Composed in One of the Valleys of Westmoreland, on Easter Sunday. Wordsworth. ChIV-2

Composed in the Composing Room. Franklin P. Adams. NIP; OBAL

Composed in the Tower before his execution. "More Light! More Light!" Anthony Hecht. ArOW; BTR; CoAP; HAP; NoAM; NOBA; NoP; OBWP; Poetr; RB; SM; TwCP; UnPo; VCAP; VGW

Composed near Calais, on the Road Leading to Ardres, August 7, 1802. Wordsworth. FaBoPV

Composed on a Journey Homeward; the Author Having Received Intelligence of the Birth of a Son. Samuel Taylor Coleridge. Son

Composed on a Moonlit Night Outing on Ancient West, *sels.* Shu Wei, *tr. fr. Chinese by* Barry L. Gartell.

Composed on a Spring Day and Shown to Yang Tzu-sha, *sels.* Chang Hui-yen, *tr. fr. Chinese by* An-yan Tang.

Composed on Horseback, Returning from Lakeview Pavilion at Hangchow, Presented to Yü-ju and Lo-tao. Wang An-shih, *tr. fr. Chinese by* Jan W. Walls. SuSp

Composed on the Theme "Willows by the Riverside." Yü Hsüan-chi, *tr. fr. Chinese by* Jan W. Walls. SuSp; WPOW

Composed upon an Evening of Extraordinary Splendour and Beauty. Wordsworth. EnRP; OAEL-2

Composed upon Westminster Bridge, September 3, 1802. Wordsworth. AWP; BLPL; ChTr; ClHu; CoGr; EnRP; FaBoCh; FaBoPP; FaBoRV; FaBV; FF; HAP; HeIP; ImPo; InPK; InPS; InvP; NAEL-2; NAWM-2; NoP; OAEL-2; OBNC; PoE; PoEL-4; PoLF; PrIm; SCGP; Son; TEP; TFi; TrGrPo; UnPo

Composed While under Arrest. M. Y. Lermontov, *tr. fr. Russian by* Max Eastman. AWP

Composer, The. W. H. Auden. MeMAP

Composing mortals with immortal fire. (*LL*) Song for St. Cecilia's Day. W. H. Auden. FaBoTw; TwCP

Composition. Peter Blue Cloud. VoR

Composition in Black and White. Katha Pollitt. GrPl

Compositions in harmony. Big Bluejay Composition. Ron Padgett. PRA

Compost. James Grainger. *Fr.* Sugar Cane, The. NOEC

Compost Heap, The. Vernon Watkins. NYBP

Compound Eye, The. Peter Davison. SM

Compound Eye, The. Sandra McPherson. AnAn

Compound Melancholy, A. Shakespeare. *Fr.* As You Like It. CBCK

Compounded in confusion. The New Litany. Rita Mae Brown. PeHV

Comprehend its mystery!' (*LL*) The Galley of Count Arnaldos. Longfellow. OBEV

Comprehensive Death. W. H. Auden. *See* As the poets have mournfully sung.

Compromise, The. Ibn al-Rumi, *tr. fr. Arabic by* Omar S. Pound. ArPe

Compromised by sorrow. Elegy for Chief Sealth. Duane Niatum. CDW

Compulsive Qualifications. Richard Howard. PoA
Sels.
"Richard, may I ask a question? What is an episteme?"
"Richard, what will it be like when you ask the questions?"

Computation, The. John Donne. CBNP; NoSic; OxBSP; SoSe

Computer's First Christmas Card, The. Edwin Morgan. FaBoCo; PChr

Computer's First Proverbs, The. Peter Finch. NBrP

Comrade and Confidant to me. (*LL*) Autumn day its course has run — the Autumn evening falls, The. Charlotte Brontë. NOBVV

Comrade Jesus. Sarah Norcliffe Cleghorn. WGRP

Comrades. Henry R. Dorr. PAH

Comrades: an Episode. Robert Nichols. NSI

Comrades in Arms: Conversation Piece. *Unknown.* ErPo

Comrades, leave me here a little, while as yet 'tis early morn. Locksley Hall. Tennyson. BLPL; EBEV; EnVR; FaBoBe; ImPo; NAEL-2; OAEL-2

Comrades Marathon, The. Chris Mann. PeSAV

Comrades, the morning breaks, the sun is up. Hafiz, *tr. by* Richard Le Gallienne. *Fr.* Odes. AWP

Comrades, you may pass the rosy. The Lay of the Lovelorn. William Edmonstoune Aytoun *and* Sir Theodore Martin. FaBoCo

Comus; a Masque Presented at Ludlow Castle. (Before the starry threshold of Jove's court.) Milton. FHYEP; OAEL-1, *with music*
Sels.
Chastity ("I Mean That Too, But Yet a Hidden Strength"). NOSC
Comus's Praise of Nature. PoEL-3
Echo. ELP; OBEV
(Lady Sings, The.) NOBE
(Lady's Song.) TrGrPo
Mask, A. OxAEP-1
"Nay, lady, sit; if I but wave this wand"
Sabrina Fair. EBEV; ELP; FaBoCh, (*much abr.*); GN; PoEL-3
(Sabrina.) CH, (*abr.*); NOBE; OBEV
(Song.) OxAEP-1
Sabrina's Song. NOSC
"Star that bids the shepherd fold, The." FaBoCh; OBEV
(Comus' Invocation to His Readers.) TrGrPo
(Comus Speaks.) NOBE
(Comus' Summons.) NOSC
(Mask, A.) 09FiP
"To the ocean now I fly." OBEV; OxAEP-1
(Farewell of the Attendant Spirit.) TrGrPo
(Spirit Epiloguizes, The.) NOBE
(Spirit's Epilogue, The.) NOSC

Comus' Invocation to His Readers. Milton. *See* Star that bids the shepherd fold, The.

Comus Speaks. Milton. *See* Star that bids the shepherd fold, The.

Comus' Summons. Milton. *See* Star that bids the shepherd fold, The.

Comus's Praise of Nature. Milton. *Fr.* Comus; a Masque Presented at Ludlow Castle. FHYEP; OAEL-1; PoEL-3

Concealment: Ishi, the Last Wild Indian, The. William Stafford. NaP

Conceit. Mervyn Laurence Peake. Spl

Conceit Begotten by the Eyes. Sir Walter Ralegh. EnRePo; NoSic; SiPS

Conceit upon the Feet. Wislawa Zaranka. BXAP

Conceited Man. *Gond Oral Tradition, tr. by* V. Elwin *and* S. Hivale. WTO

Conceited Pedlar, The, *sels.* Thomas Randolph.
Come from Thy Palace. OxBSP

Conceits, *sels.* Arlo Bates.

Conceived on a mattress of human hair. Innocence. Wislawa Szymborska, *tr. fr. Polish by* Jan Darowski. PoSu

Concentration Camps, The. May Sarton. *Fr.* Invocation to Kali, The. BTR; SRLS

Concentred here th' united wisdom shines. The Federal Convention. *Unknown.* PAH

Concentric. Richard Kostelanetz. TAP

Concept like "I," which I am told by many, A. I Brood about Some Concepts, for Example. Alicia Ostriker. PBCAP

Conception. Josephine Miles. FaBoWP

Conception, an Archbishop said, The. L. E. J. PeLi

Conception is interesting, The: to see, as though reflected. Wet Casements. John Ashbery. NAAL-2; PoM

Concepts and Their Bodies (The Boy in the Field Alone). Pattiann Rogers. MT

Contemplations of Mary. Roy McFadden. PNI

Contemplative Sentry, The. W. S. Gilbert. *Fr.* Iolanthe. FiBHP

Contemporania, *sels.* Ezra Pound.
 Tenzone. MeMAP; PoA

Contemporaries all surpassed, see one. William Cowper. *Fr.* Table Talk.
 EPCY

Contemporary. Hortense Flexner. PoA

Contemporary Muse, The. Edgell Rickword. OBSV

Contemporary Song. Theodore Spencer. LiTA

Contempt for the World, *sels.* Bernard of Cluny.
 "Scarcely believe things shameful to utter which yet I shall speak of."
 PeHV

Contempt of the World. *Unknown. See* Were [*or* Where] beth [*or* beeth]
 they [that] biforen us weren.

Contemptuous of his home beyond. A Frog's Fate. Christina Rossetti.
 NOBVV

Contend in a sea which the land partly encloses. The Yachts. William
 Carlos Williams. AmPP; CMoP; HeIP; ImPo; LiTA; LiTM; MeMAP;
 MoAB; MoAmPo; MoP; NoAM; NOBA; NoP; OxBA; PoE; PPP;
 SAmP; TFi

Content. Dora Greenwell. PoToHe

Content. Geffrey Whitney. EIL

Content and Rich. (I dwell in Grace's court.) Robert Southwell. ChIV-2;
 NoSic
 Sels.
 "I wrastle not with rage." OBF

Content, content! within a quiet room. Content. Dora Greenwell. PoToHe

Content has been carried off since dawn. Permanent Face. Laura
 Rosenthal. UL

Content the, greedy heart. The Size. George Herbert. GeHe

Content, though blind, had I no better guide. (*LL*) To Mr. Cyriack Skinner
 upon His Blindness. Milton. NOSC; PeECV; Son

Content Thyself with Thy Estate. *Unknown.* EIL

Content with the labor of tearing down. (*LL*) Which Are You?
 Unknown. PoLF

Content within his wigwam warm. Canonicus and Roger Williams.
 Unknown. PAH

Contented with the bed of one. (*LL*) An Epitaph upon a Sober Matron.
 Robert Herrick. CaPo

Contention between Four Maids Concerning That Which Addeth Most
 Perfection to That Sex. Sir John Davies. SiPS

Contention Betwixt a Wife, a Widow, and a Maid, A, *sels.* Sir John
 Davies.
 Maidenhood. CBCK

Contention betwixt a Wife, a Widow, and a Maid, A. Sir John Davies.
 SiPS

Contention of Ajax and Ulysses, The, *sels.* James Shirley.
 "Glories of our blood and state, The." BeJo; ChTr; EBEvV; FaBoRV;
 HAP; InvP; JCP; NoP; OBD; PeECV; PoRA; PPP; SCGP; TrGrPo
 (Death the Leveller.) BLPL; FaPoR; FF; GGP; GTBS; GTBS-P; ImPo;
 LiTB; NOBE; OBEV; OtMeF; PlP; UnPo
 (Dirge: "Glories of our blood and state, The.") AWP; OAEL-1; PoEL-2

Contentment. Charles Stuart Calverley. NOBVV

Contentment. Nathaniel Cotton. OxBChV

Contentment. William Cowper. ChIV-2

Contentment. Oliver Wendell Holmes. *Fr.* Autocrat of the Breakfast Table,
 The. AmPP; AnAmPo; OxBA; PWR

Contentment. Benjamin Schlipf. BLRP

Contentment. Sir Philip Sidney. *See* Get Hence Foule Griefe.

Contentment. Thomas Traherne. *Fr.* Christian Ethics. NOCV

Contentment is a sleepy thing. Contentment. Thomas Traherne. *Fr.*
 Christian Ethics. NOCV
 (For man to act as if his soul did see.) NOCV

Contentment of Willoughby, The. Frances Alexander. GoYe

Continent's End. Robinson Jeffers. AWP; FaBV

Continual Conversation with a Silent Man. Wallace Stevens. LiTM; NoP

Continually, a bell rings in my heart. Wanting to Move. Vijaya
 Mukhopadhyay, *tr. fr. Hindi.* TSaS, *tr. by* Mukhopadhyay Vijaya

Continually they cackle thus. Sir Osbert Sitwell. *Fr.* How Shall We Rise
 to Greet the Dawn? PoWW

Continuation of a Long Poem of These States, *sels.* Allen Ginsberg.
 S.F. Southward. NAAL-2

Continuation of *The Cook's Tale*, The. William Zaranka. BXAP

Continuaunce/ of remembraunce. A Lover Left Alone. *Unknown.* MeEL

Continued. Matthew Arnold. Son

Continues ceasing and ceasing. (*LL*) The Extermination of the Jews.
 Marvin Bell. BTR; CAPP

Continuing City, The. Laurence Housman. WGRP

Continuity. "Æ." MoBrPo

Continuity, The. Paul Blackburn. NeAP

Continuous. Tony Harrison. SCBI

Continuous, a medley of old pop numbers. The Songs. Martin Bell. FF

Continuous Cities, *sels.* Italo Calvino, *tr. fr. Italian.*
 "You reproach me because each of my stories." AnRep, *tr. by* William
 Weaver

Continuous Time. Milo De Angelis, *tr. fr. Italian by* Lawrence Venuti.
 NeIt

Contours. Noël Coward. UV

Contours of Fixation, The. Weldon Kees. NaP

Contours of Indifference, The. Nick Totton. VaA

Contra Mortem. Hayden Carruth. PoA

Contra Mortem, *sels.* Hayden Carruth.
 "Wherever shadow falls wherever the drowning." PoA

Contraception, — that's the bizarre, proper slang. The Crystal Palace. John
 Davidson. PeVV

Contracts. Marilyn Kitchell. UL

Contradiction. Alice Cary. AmWP

Contradictions: Tracking Poems, *sels.* Adrienne Rich.

Contrary Theses (I). Wallace Stevens. OxBA; SAmP

Contrary to popular belief, the lowest circle of hell is not. Pan Cogito's
 Thoughts on Hell. Zbigniew Herbert, *tr. fr. Polish by* Adam
 Czerniawski. FaBoPV

Contrast; the Parrot and the Wren, The. Wordsworth. FM

Contre Jour. Elizabeth Bartlett. FaBoWP

Contretemps, The. Thomas Hardy. CMoP; LiTM

Contribution on Pornography, A. Wislawa Szymborska, *tr. fr. Polish by*
 Adam Czerniawski. PoSu

Contrition. Ralph Knevet. ChIV-2

Contrition. Henry More. *Fr.* Psychozoia, or, the Life of the Soul. NOSC

Controlled woolgathering is my work too. (*LL*) Sheepdog Trials in Hyde
 Park. C. Day Lewis. MoP; NoAM; NoP; OxBTC

Controlling the Tongue. Chaucer. *Fr.* Canterbury Tales, The. EnVB;
 OxBChV

Controls, The. Harrison Fisher. UL

Conundrum. Carl Clark. JB

Conundrum of the Workshops, The. Kipling. MoBrPo

Convalescence. Noël Coward. TTTS

Convalescence. James McAuley. CBAP

Convalescence. Lynne McMahon. NAmP90

Convent in '45, The. Maria Luisa Spaziani, *tr. fr. Italian by* Beverly
 Allen. NeIt

Convent of Pleasure, The, *sels.* Margaret Cavendish, Duchess of Newcastle.
 My Cabinets Are Oyster-Shells. ELP
 (Song: "My cabinets are oyster-shells.") WPE

Convent Threshold, The. Christina Rossetti. MeMBP; NALW; NoP; PFP

Convent Threshold, The, *sels.* Christina Rossetti.
 "I tell you what I dreamed last night." PeVV

Convention Song. *Unknown.* PAH

Convergence of the Twain (Lines on the Loss of the *Titanic*), The. Thomas
 Hardy. FaBoEH; FaBoTW; HeIP; InPK; InPS; LiTB; LiTM; MeMBP;
 MoAB; MoBrPo; MoP; NAEL-2; NIP; NoAM; NoP; OAEL-2; OHCV;
 OxBTC; PeVV; PFP; Poetr; PrIm; SCGP; TEP; TFi

Conversation. John Berryman. LiTA; LiTM

Conversation. Buson, *tr. fr. Japanese.* NTCP; SiSoPo

Conversation. Rose Fyleman. BoTP

Conversation. David McCord. GrPl

Conversation. Louis MacNeice. TEP

Conversation, A. Barbara Howes. IHMS

Conversation, A. Dylan Thomas. RFM

Conversation between the Chevalier de Chamilly and Mariana Alcoforado in
 the Manner of a Song of Regret. *Unknown, tr. fr. Portuguese by* Helen
 R. Lane. BoWoP

Conversation brings us so close! Opening. Looking into a Face. Robert
 Bly. CAPP; NOBA

Conversation by the Body's Light. Jane Cooper. VBLP

Conversation by the Body's Light. Rachel Hadas. UnDi

Conversation in Black and White. May Sarton. GoYe

Conversation in Craven Street, Strand. James Smith *and* Sir George Rose.
 FaBoCo

Conversation in Gibraltar 1943. Charles Causley. PoWW

Conversation in the Bush. A. R. D. Fairburn. *Fr.* Album Leaves. PeNZ

Conversation of Prayer, The. Dylan Thomas. EBEV; GTBS-P; NoP;
 OxAEP-2

Conversation Piece. Arthur Freeman. ErPo

Conversation Piece. Robert Graves. GrPl

Conversation with a Fireman from Brooklyn. Tess Gallagher. CrSp

Conversation with a Poet. Miroslav Holub, *tr. by* Ewald Osers. PWE

Conversation with an Angel. Wanda Barford. Mes

Conversation with Rain. Louise D. Gunn. GoYe

Conversation with Rilke about Dragons. Rose Drachler. BCF

Conversational. *Unknown.* FiBHP

Conversations among Poems. Tim Longville. VaA

Conversations are simple, The: about food. Under the Window: Ouro Preto. Elizabeth Bishop. NYBP; VCAP

Conversations from Childhood: the Victrola. Joseph Langland. SM

Conversations in Courtship, *sels. Unknown, tr. fr. Egyptian into Italian by* Boris de Rachewiltz; *tr. into English by* Ezra Pound. "Darling, you only, there is no duplicate." CTC

Conversations in Crisis. Audre Lorde. Poetr

Conversations in Mayan. Alonzo Gonzales Mó, *tr. fr. Mayan by* Allan F. Burns. STP

Conversations in the Mountains. Li Po, *tr. fr. Chinese by* Robert Payne. RaBo; TAL

Conversations with Strangers. George Buchanan. PNI

Conversion. Frances Angermayer. PoLF

Conversion. T. E. Hulme. FaBoMo; OxBSP

Conversion of S. Paul, The. George Wither. ChIV-2

Convert, The. G. K. Chesterton. ChIV-2

Convert, The. Margaret Danner. BPo

Convert Comes to the City, A. Nathan Alterman, *tr. fr. Hebrew by* Ruth Finer Mintz. *Fr. Joy of the Poor, The.* MHP

Convert's but a fly, that turns about, A. Samuel Butler. FaBoEE

Convex face of the black countries, The. The First Psalm. Bertolt Brecht, *tr. fr. German by* Robert Bly. NU

Convict. Edward Vincent Swart. PeSAV

Convict of Clonmel, The. *Unknown, tr. fr. Irish by* Jeremiah Joseph Callanan. PeIV

Convict Song, The. Alfred Cruickshank. PBCV

Convicts' Rum Song. *Unknown.* FaBoVe; NOBAu

Convict's Tour to Hell, A. Francis MacNamara. NOBAu

Convinced by Sorrow. Elizabeth Barrett Browning. *Fr. Cry of the Human, The.* BLRP; WBLP

Convulsed, foaming immortal blood: farewell. (*LL*) A Professor's Song. John Berryman. HeIP; MoP; NAAL-2; NoAM; NOBA; OxBC

Convulsions came; and, where the field. The Apparition. Herman Melville. NoP

Coo-Coo. *Unknown.* AS

Cooing pigeons, nursling swallows, all quiet without a sound. Spring Day. Su Shih, *tr. fr. Chinese by* Irving Y. Lo. SuSp

Cook, The. Ray A. Young Bear. CDW

Cook admired the native courage, made. Rex Ingamells. *Fr. Great South Land, The.* NOBAu

Cook called McMurray, A. Ogden Nash. PeLi

Cook they hadde with hem for the nones. Chaucer. *Fr. Canterbury Tales, The.* EnVB; FHYEP; NoP; OAEL-1; PPP, *abr.*

Cookers, The: A Song of the Transport. A. P. Herbert. NSI

Cooking Eggs. Dave Jeddie Smith. AnAn

Cook's Tale, The. Chaucer. *Fr. Canterbury Tales, The.* BXAP; EnVB

Cooks who'd roast a sucking-pig. Roasted Sucking Pig. *Unknown.* BXAP

Cooky-Nut Trees, The. Albert Bigelow Paine. OBCA

Cool. Beverlyjean Smith. ETG

Cool and certain, their oars will be lifted in dusk. "Robin Hyde." *Fr. Beaches, The.* PeNZ

Cool as from underground springs and pure enough to drink. (*LL*) The Man-Moth. Elizabeth Bishop. CAPP; CBNP; LiTA; LiTM; MAT; MoAB; MoAmPo; MoP; NALW; NoAM; NOBA; Poetr; PPP

Cool black night thru the redwoods. First Party at Ken Kesey's with Hell's Angels. Allen Ginsberg. PoBeRe; TRP

Cool in its dream, I kissed the stone. The Stream Sings to the Stone. Leah Goldberg, *tr. fr. Hebrew by* Ruth Finer Mintz. *Fr. Songs of the Stream.* MHP

Cool in summer's heat. The Well: Two Songs. *Gond Oral Tradition, tr. by* V. Elwin *and* S. Hivale. WTO

Cool it is, and still. Basho, *tr. fr. Japanese by* Harold G. Henderson. TAL

Cool it Mag. Margaret Are You Drug. George Starbuck. InPK; MAT

Cool perfume of bamboo pervades my room. Summer Night. Tu Fu, *tr. fr. Chinese by* Robert Payne. TAL

Cool red rose and a pink cut pink, A. Red Roses. Gertrude Stein. *Fr. Tender Buttons.* TTTS

Cool reek of the field. Reek of companions. (*LL*) Cobb Would Have Caught It. Robert Fitzgerald. GrPl; HAP; InvP; TwCP

Cool shades and dews are round my way. A Scene on the Banks of the Hudson. Bryant. AnAmPo

Cool shadows blanked dead cities, falling. Falling. Bob Kaufman. PoBA

Cool small evening shrunk to a dog bark and the clank of a bucket, A. Full Moon and Little Frieda. Ted Hughes. NTP; OxBC; OxBSP

Cool that came off sheets just off the line, The. Seamus Heaney. *Fr. Clearances.* CIP; PBCIP; PNI

Cool Tombs. Carl Sandburg. AmPP; BLPL; CMoP; HAP; HeIL; HeIP; MoAB; MoAmPo; MoP; NAAL-2; NoAM; NOBA; OxBSP; PoLF; TAP; TFi; TrGrPo

Cool Web, The. Robert Graves. AWP; GTBS-P; MoP; NAEL-2; NoAM; NoP; OxBTC; PoA; Poetr; Prlm; SCV

Coole Park and Ballylee, 1931. W. B. Yeats. CMoP; GTBS-P; NoAM; NOIV; OBMV; PPP

Coole Park, 1929. W. B. Yeats. IIP; OAEL-2; OBMV

Coolie Chinee, The. Septimus Winner. OBAL

Coolie Mother. David Dabydeen. NBrP

Coolie Odyssey. David Dabydeen. NBrP

Cools like the rain . . . (*LL*) World feels dusty, The. Emily Dickinson. MoAmPo

Coon Can (Poor Boy). *Unknown.* AS

Coon Fire. Tom Weatherly. *Fr. Cantos.* PoBA

Coon Hunt. Thomas Rabbitt. MT

Coon Song. A. R. Ammons. MoP; NOBA

Cooper. James Russell Lowell. *Fr. Fable for Critics, A.* NOBA; OxBA; TAP

Cooper & Bailey Great London Circus, The. Robert Hershon. MAT

Cooper o' Dundee, The. *Unknown.* CoMu

Cooper, whose name is with his country's woven. Red Jacket. Fitz-Greene Halleck. AnAmPo

Cooper's Hill, *sels.* Sir John Denham. "O could I flow like thee, and make thy stream." EPCY

Cooper's Hill. (Sure there are poets which did never dream.) Sir John Denham. BeJo; SeCP; SeCV-1

Sels. "Here have I seen the king, when great affairs." PoE "Here should my wonder dwell, and here my praise." NAEL-1 (Thames, The.) NOSC "My eye descending from the Hill, surveys." OAEL-1; OxAEP-1 "There Faunus and Sylvanus keep their courts." JCP

Cootchie. Elizabeth Bishop. FaBoWP

Cop holds me up like a fish, The. Fish. Larry Levis. AmPA

Cop, The/ with a cold. High-cool/2. James Cunningham. JB

Cope sent a letter frae Dunbar. Johnnie Cope. Adam Skirving. OxBS; ScCV

Copenhagen Dreaming of Leningrad. Michael O'Loughlin. IB

Copernican System, The. Thomas Chatterton. FaBoUs

Copernicus. Robert David Fitzgerald. NOBAu

Cophetua. "Hugh MacDiarmid." OxBS

Coplas about the Soul Which Suffers with Impatience to See God, *sels.* St. John of the Cross, *tr. fr. Spanish by* Roy Campbell. "I live without inhabiting/ Myself." OBVE

Copper cobra comes out of his slit, The. The Banded Cobra. C. Louis Leipoldt, *tr. fr. Afrikaans by* Uys Krige, Jack Cope, *and* Ruth Miller. PeSA

Coppersmith. Richard Murphy. IPY

Coptic Poem ("A Coptic deputation, going to Ethiopia.") Lawrence Durrell. FaBoCo

Copulate in the foam. (*LL*) News for the Delphic Oracle. W. B. Yeats. CMoP; FaBoMo; LiTB; LiTM; MeMBP; NoAM

Copulating Gods, The. Carolyn Kizer. CAPP; Poetr; Prf

Copy of an Intercepted Despatch from His Excellency Don Strepitoso Diabolo. Thomas Moore. OBSV

Copy of Non Sequitors, A. *Unknown.* FaBoNo

Copy of Verses, A. John Wilson. SCAP

Copy of Verses Composed by Captain Henry Every, A. *Unknown.* OxBSS

Copy of Verses on Jefferys the Seaman, A. *Unknown.* OxBSS

Copy out only that, and save expense. (*LL*) Jordan. George Herbert. GeHe; NAEL-1; OAEL-1; OBWVE; PPP; SeCP

Copycat. Robert Heidbreder. OTCP

Copycat, copycat/ Shadow's a copycat! Copycat. Robert Heidbreder. OTCP

Coquette, The. Aphra Behn. TrGrPo

Coquettes with doctors; hoards her breath. The Old Beauty. Phyllis McGinley. FaBoEE

Coracle, The. Lucan, *tr. fr. Latin by* Sir Walter Ralegh. ChTr

Coracle Fishers, The. Robert Bloomfield. *Fr. Banks of Wye, The.* OBNC

Coral Grove, The. James Gates Percival. GN

Coral Reef, The. John Blight. NOBAu

Coral Reef, The. Laurence Lieberman. CoAP

Corda Concordia, *sels.* Edmund Clarence Stedman.

Cordate head meanders through himself, The. Pit Viper. N. Scott Momaday. CDW; HATNAP

Cordelia. Veronica Forrest-Thomson. VaA

Cordial Advice. *Unknown.* OxBSS

'Cordin to de present perdicament. Subtlety. Bruce St. John. PBCV

Cordon Negro. Essex Hemphill. GLP

Cordova. Ibn Zaydun, *tr. fr. Arabic by* H. A. R. Gibb. AWP

Core of Masculinity, The. Jalal al-Din Rumi, *tr. fr. Persian by* Coleman Barks. RaBo

Core of masculinity does not derive from being male, The. The Core of Masculinity. Jalal al-Din Rumi, *tr. fr. Persian by* Coleman Barks. RaBo

Corfou. Richard Monckton Milnes. *Fr.* Ionian Islands, The. OBTV

Coridon and Phillis. Robert Greene. *Fr.* Perimedes [or Perimedes, the Blacksmith].

Coridon's Song. John Chalkhill. NOSC

Corinna, from Athens, to Tanagra. Walter Savage Landor. *Fr.* Pericles and Aspasia. OBEV

Corinna, Having Tried, with Her Own Hand. Ovid, *tr. by* Rolfe Humphries. *Fr.* Amores. NAs

Corinna in Vendome. Pierre de Ronsard, *tr. fr. French by* Robert Mezey. BoLoP; ErPo

Corinna, pride of Drury-Lane. A Beautiful Young Nymph Going to Bed. Swift. ECEV; NOEC; OPOP

Corinna to Tanagra. Walter Savage Landor. *See* Tanagra! think not I forget.

Corinna, to Tanagra, from Athens. Walter Savage Landor. *See* Tanagra! think not I forget.

Corinnae Concubitus. Ovid. *See* In summer's heat, and mid-time of the day.

Corinnae Concubitus, I, 5. Ovid, *tr. fr. Latin by* Christopher Marlowe. *Fr.* Amores. EBEV; GBL; OBVE

Corinna's Going a-Maying. Robert Herrick. BeJo; BoNaP; CaPo; GN; HAP; InPS; JCP; NAEL-1; NIP; NOBE; NoP; NOSC; OAEL-1; OBEV; PoE; PoEL-3; PPP; PrIm; SCGP; SeCP; SeCV-1; TEP; TFi; TrGrPo

Corinne at the Capitol. Felicia Dorothea Hemans. BrRo

Coriolan, *sels.* T. S. Eliot.
    Triumphal March. OBWP

Coriolanus, *sels.* Shakespeare.
    "All tongues speak of him, and the bleared sights." FaBoPV
    "He that will give good words to thee, will flatter." FaBoPV
    "Madam, the Lady Valeria is come to visit you." OxAEP-1
    "O world, thy slippery turns! Friends now fast sworn." OBF
    "Read it not, noble lords." OxAEP-1
    "Why dost not speak?" OxAEP-1

Cork popped off the, The. New Year's Eve. David Trinidad. BAP-91

Corkby, Part Two. Jerome Rothenberg. NNaP

Cormac Mac Airt Presiding at Tara. *Unknown, tr. fr. Irish by* Douglas Hyde. BIrV

Cormorant. Peter Preece. AngWe

Cormorant, The. Rosanna Warren. BAP-90

Cormorant has, The. Tails and Heads. Suzanne Knowles. RB

Cormorant in His Element, The. Amy Clampitt. InPK

Cormorant still screams, The. Late. Louise Bogan. PBWP; VGW

Cormorants. John Blight. CBAP; FaBoMA

Corn, The. Daniel David Moses. HATNAP

Corn-blossom maidens. Masahongva, *tr. fr. Hopi Indian by* Natalie Curtis. WTO

Corn Children. Carol Lee Sanchez. SRLS

Corn does not hurry, and the black grape swells. Second Wisdom. Henry Morton Robinson. GoYe

Corn-grinding Song. *Unknown, tr. fr. Tewa Indian by* N. Barnes. WTO

Corn-grinding Song. *Unknown, tr. fr. Laguna Indian by* Natalie Curtis. AWP

Corn Harvest, The. William Carlos Williams. *Fr.* Pictures from Brueghel. ArNa; PPP

Corn has stood ripe on the stalks for months, The. The Frost in the Corn. Robert McAlmon. AiP

Corn King beckoning to his Spring Queen, The. (*LL*) A Girl in a Library. Randall Jarrell. NAAL-2; NoAM; NOBA; NoP

Corn-Pone-y, The. Carolyn Wells. *Fr.* Baker's Dozen of Wild Beasts, A. OBCA

Corn rigs, an' barley rigs, &c. (*LL*) The Rigs o' Barley. Burns. LiTB

Corn Rigs Are Bonnie. Burns. *See* It was upon a Lammas night.

Corn-Song, The. Whittier. GN; OHIP

Corn-Stalk Fiddle, The. Paul Laurence Dunbar. AAP

Corneille's Pompey, *sels.* Katherine Philips.
    Cornelia's Defiance. NOSC

Cornelia, *sels.* Thomas Kyd.

Of Fortune. EIL

Cornelian, The. Byron. PeHV

Cornelia's Defiance. Katherine Philips. *Fr.* Corneille's Pompey. NOSC

Cornelia's Song. John Webster. *See* Call for the Robin-Redbreast and the Wren.

Cornelius Varro knows his husbandry. The Bad Shepherd. Gwyneth Lewis. NWP

Corner bank has lost a great window, The. High Wind at the Battery. Ralph Pomeroy. NYBP

Corner Knot, The. Robert Graves. NYBP

Corner me in the coral & I die. (*LL*) Poetics. Diane Di Prima. PoBeRe

Cornered and trapped, The. For Mack C. Parker. Pauli Murray. PoBA

Cornfield, The. Elizabeth Madox Roberts. GoJo

Cornfields in Accra. Christine Ama Ata Aidoo. WPOW

Cornhusk bag. Talking Designs. Liz Sohappy Bahe. CDW

Cornish Emigrant's Song, The. Robert Stephen Hawker. EBVV

Cornish Magic. Ann Durell. FaPON

Cornishmen. *Unknown.* FaBoUs

Cornwallis led a country dance. The Dance. *Unknown.* PAH

Cornwallis's Surrender. *Unknown.* PAH

Corona. Paul Celan. PoSu, *tr. fr. German by* Michael Hamburger

Corona. Sir Philip Sidney. *Fr.* Arcadia. SiPSBD

Coronach. Sir Walter Scott. *Fr.* Lady of the Lake, The. CH; EnRP; GTBS; GTBS-P; OHIP; OxAEP-2; OxBS; SCGP; TrGrPo; WiR

Coronary Thrombosis. William Price Turner. OxBS

Coronation. Helen Hunt Jackson. AmWP; BeLS; GN

Coronation. Edward Perronet. *See* All Hail the Power of Jesus' Name.

Coronemus Nos Rosis Antequam Marcescant. Thomas Jordan. *See* Let us drink and be merry, dance, joke, and rejoice [or rejoyce].

Coroner. Elton Glaser. PBCAP

Coroner's Jury. L. A. G. Strong. OxBTC

Coronet, The. Andrew Marvell. ESCV; FHYEP; GeHe; MeLP; NAEL-1; NOCV; NoP; NOSC; PoE; SCGP; SeCV-1; TOF

Coronet for His Mistress Philosophy, A, *sels.* George Chapman.
    But Dwell in Darkness. Son
    Love Flows Not from My Liver. Son
    Muses That Sing Love's Sensual Empery. EIL; SCGP; Son

"Corporal Green!" the orderly cried. Roll-Call. Nathaniel Graham Shepherd. OHIP
    (Calling the Roll.) OBCA

Corporal Pym. Walter de la Mare. FaBoEE

Corporal Who Killed Archimedes, The. Miroslav Holub, *tr. fr. Czech by* Ian Milner *and* Jarmila Milner. PoSu; PWE

Corporate Entity. Archibald MacLeish. OBAL

Corposant. Peter Redgrove. OxBTC

Corps d'Esprit. Heather McHugh. AmPA

Corpse-bearing. Thomas Ashe. EBVV; NOBVV

Corpse, clad with carefulness. Of Misery. Thomas Howell. EIL; FF

Corpse has walked across my shadow, A. Into the Known. Tess Gallagher. AnAn

Corpse-Keeper, The. *Unknown, tr. fr. Catalan by* W. S. Merwin. BoWoP

Corpses in the Wood. Ernst Toller, *tr. fr. German by* E. Ellis Roberts. TrJP

Corpses of angels, The. (*LL*) Selective Service. Carolyn Forché. Poetr

Corpus Christi. *Unknown. See* Lully, lullay, lully, lullay.

Corpus Christi Carol, The. *Unknown.* HAP; MeEL; OxBLMV

Corpus Christi Carol. *Unknown.* ChTr; EnVB; GBP; MeEL; MiEL; NAEL-1; NOBE; NoP; OAEL-1; OBD; SCV

Corpus Christi Carol, The ("Heron flew east, the heron flew west, The.") *Unknown.* GBP

Correct Compassion, A. James Kirkup. FaBoTw; OxBTC

Correction. Eric Millard. IHNG

Correggio's Cupolas at Parma. Aubrey Thomas De Vere. Son

Correlated Greatness. Francis Thompson. *See* O nothing in this corporal earth of man.

Correspondence. Henri Coulette. DiPo

Correspondence. Peter Reading. PeLV

Correspondence:/ when I have sad thoughts. Lady Ise, *tr. fr. Japanese by* Etsuko Terasaki *and* Irma Brandeis. BoWoP

Correspondence between Mr. Harrison in Newcastle and Mr. Sholto Peach Harrison in Hull. Stevie Smith. FaBoNo; NBLV; OxBC

Correspondence School Instructor Says Goodbye to His Poetry Students, The. Galway Kinnell. NoAM; NOBA; NoP; TAP

Correspondences. Baudelaire, *tr. fr. French by* Allen Tate. AWP

Correspondences. Robert Duncan. PoM

Correspondences, *sels.* Anne Stevenson.
    Love Letter, A: Ruth Arbeiter to Major Paul Maxwell. OxBM

Corridor. Federico García Lorca, *tr. fr. Spanish.* CBNP

Corridor, The. E. A. Robinson. AnAmPo

Corridors of the soul! Rebirth. Antonio Machado Ruiz, *tr. fr. Spanish by* Robert Bly. NU

Corroding Air, The. Jack Marshall. UL

Corrugated iron shack. One room, A. The Cradle. Roland Robinson. NOBAu

Corrupt Man in the French Pub, The. Brian Higgins. OxBTC

Corruption. Henry Vaughan. ESCV; GeHe; JCP; NAEL-1; NOCV; NOSC; OAEL-1; Prf; SeCP; SeCV-1

Corrymeela. "Moira O'Neill." AWP

Cors-y-Gwaed: Fenland of Blood. A. G. Prys-Jones. AngWe

Corsair, The, *sels.* Byron.
Sunset over the Aegean. OBNC

Corsica, *sels.* Anna Laetitia Barbauld.
On General Paoli and the Corsican Struggle for Liberty. ECWP

Corsons Inlet. A. R. Ammons. CoAP; FoLa; MoP; NAAL-2; NoAM; NOBA; NoP; PPP; VCAP

Cortège. Paul Verlaine, *tr. fr. French by* Arthur Symons. AWP; OBVE

Cortege for Colette. Jean Garrigue. NYBP

Corydon and Thyrsis. Virgil, *tr. by* Dryden. *Fr. Eclogues.* AWP

Corydon to His Phyllis. Sir Edward Dyer. EIL

Corydon's Farewell, on Sailing in the Late Expedition Fleet. *Unknown.* NOEC

Cosmic Eye. A. K. Redwing. VoR

Cosmic Leviathan, that monstrous fish. Cosmogony. Edgell Rickword. FaBoTw

Cosmogony. D. C. Berry. BXAP

Cosmogony. Edgell Rickword. FaBoTw

Cosmos in London. Arthur Nortje. HBAPE; PeSAV

Cosmus hath more discoursing in his head. Sir John Davies. *Fr. Epigrams.* NoSic

Cost, The. Anthony Hecht. OxBC

Cost of Seriousness, The. Peter Porter. NoAM

Costa Geriatrica. Stanley J. Sharpless. PeLV

Costumes are a kind of late-colonial, The. Totalled. Peter McDonald. PNI

Costumes of Jerusalem. Julia Vinograd. BCF

Cot, The. Grover Amen. NYBP

Côte d'Azur. Katherine Hoskins. NYBP

Cottage, The. Jones Very. OxBA

Cottage at Chigasaki, The. Edmund Blunden. OBTV

Cottage Hospital, The. Sir John Betjeman. GTBS-P; MoBrPo; NoAM; NOBE; OBD; PlP; UnPo

Cottage in the Wood, A. Russell Edson. LCAP

Cottage Song. John Drinkwater. UV

Cottage Street, 1953. Richard Wilbur. CAPP; FaBoMo; HCAP

Cottage was a thatch'd one, The. Little Jim. Edward Farmer. VPP

Cottager to Her Infant, The. Dorothy Wordsworth. CH; NTP; OxBChV; TTTS

Cottager's Complaint, on the Intended Bill for Enclosing Sutton-Coldfield, The. John Freeth. NOEC; OBET

Cotter's Saturday Night, The. Burns. BeLS; EnRP; FaBoBe; PoLF; WGRP

Cotton. Harry Edmund Martinson, *tr. fr. Swedish by* Robert Bly. RB

Cotton blouse you wear, your mother said, The. McDonogh Day in New Orleans. Marcus B. Christian. PoNe

Cotton Boll, The. Henry Timrod. AmPP

Cotton Song. Jean Toomer. BPo; CDC

Cottonmouth Country. Louise Glück. CoAP

Cottonmouth white faces survey the marshes. Okeechobee. John Allison. GrPl

Cottonwood, willow, and briar. Leaves like Fish. Gladys Cardiff. CDW

Couch Fantasy. Adrian C. Louis. NAmP90

Couch Grass. John Hall. VaA

Cou'd we stop the time that's flying. The Unequal Fetters. The Countess of Winchilsea. VBLP

Cougar. Brendan Galvin. FoLa

Coughed up those shirts and flagged the train. (*LL*) The Goat. *Unknown.* BLPL; PoLF

Coughing in a shady grove. Ipecacuanha. George Canning. ChTr; FaBoNo

Coughing up blood. Differences. Ray A. Young Bear. NU

Could build so strong in a weak heart. (*LL*) The Church-Floor [*or* Floore]. George Herbert. EBEV; ESCV; MeLP; NOSC; OAEL-1; PeECV

Could but compose man's image and his cry. (*LL*) The Sorrow of Love. W. B. Yeats. MeMBP; NAEL-2; OAEL-2; PeVV; TEP

Could every time-worn heart but see Thee once again. To the Child Jesus. Henry van Dyke. TrPWD

Could fathom to this pond's black bed. (*LL*) The Midnight Skaters. Edmund Blunden. FaBoTw; GoJo; GTBS-P; MoBrPo; NOBE; OBD; PeFWW

Could he have made Priscilla share. Llewellyn and the Tree. E. A. Robinson. BeLS

Could I but become a crimson rose. *Unknown, tr. fr. Greek by* W. G. Shepherd. GrAn

Could I but retrace. Tanka (I–VIII). Lewis Alexander. CDC

Could I but ride indefinite. Emily Dickinson. SAmP

Could i have a dollar? Southwestern Trek in Four Part Harmony. Alurista. ETG

Could I remove the stones from the river? Song of Longing. *Gond Oral Tradition, tr. by* V. Elwin *and* S. Hivale. WTO

Could I Say I Touched You. Harold Littlebird. VoR

Could I take me to some cavern from this hiding. O for the Wings of a Dove. Euripides, *tr. by* Gilbert Murray. *Fr. Hippolytus.* AWP; NAWM-1, *tr. by* Rex Warner

Could it be, Bud. For Bud. Michael S. Harper. PoE

Could it be Madness — this? (*LL*) First day's night had come, The. Emily Dickinson. ImPo; LiTA; LiTM; OxBA; PoE; TRP; WPOW

Could it be true we live on earth? Nezalhualcoyotl. EaPr

Could It Have Been a Shadow? Monica Shannon. FaPON

Could make the children of my race bleed. (*LL*) Thresholds of Identity. Lionel Abrahams. PeSAV

Could man be drunk for ever. Could Man Be Drunk for Ever. A. E. Housman. LiTM; NAEL-2; OBMV; OtMeF; PPP

Could Man Be Drunk for Ever. A. E. Housman. LiTM; NAEL-2; OBMV; OtMeF; PPP

Could mortal lip divine. Emily Dickinson. RB

Could not once blinding me, cruel, suffice? Samson to His Delilah. Richard Crashaw. ChIV-1; TrGrPo

Could our first father, at his toilsome plough. Adam Posed. The Countess of Winchilsea. ChIV-1; ECWP

Could to my sight that heavenly face restore. (*LL*) Sonnet on Catherine Wordsworth. Wordsworth. IMW; SCGP

Could we be so now! (*LL*) Even So. Dante Gabriel Rossetti. NOBE; NOBVV; OBNC

Could ye come back to me, Douglas, Douglas. Douglas, Douglas, Tender and True. Dinah Maria Mulock Craik. BLPA

Could you bid an acorn. Lover's Reply to Good Advice. Richard Hughes. MoBrPo

Could you but learn? (*LL*) If You But Knew. *Unknown.* BLPA; FaBoBe

Could you indeed come lightly. Song for a Departure. Elizabeth Jennings. GOYP

Could you register birds. Holocaust. Myra Sklarew. CRP

Could you, so arrantly of earth, so cool. Animal. Max Eastman. FYAP

Could you tell me the way to Somewhere. Somewhere. Walter de la Mare. FaPON

Couldn't put Humpty Dumpty together again. (*LL*) Humpty Dumpty sat on a wall. Mother Goose. FaBoBe; OxBoLi; OxNR; ReMoGo; RoPo; *diff. vers.*

Couldn't wish our love away. (*LL*) To Charlotte von Stein. Goethe. STV

Could'st thou (O Earth) live thus obscure, and now. George Alsop. SCAP

Councell Given to Master Bartholmew Withipoll. George Gascoigne. AAS

Council of Horses, The. John Gay. GN

Council of Satan, The. Milton. *See* So Satan spake, and him Beëlzebub.

Councils. Marge Piercy. CrSp

Counsel. Naomi Lewis. Mes

Counsel of Moderation, A. Francis Thompson. MoBrPo

Counsel to Girls. Robert Herrick. *See* Gather ye rosebuds, while ye may.

Counsel to Unreason. Léonie Adams. PoA

Counsels of Sigrdrifa. *Unknown, tr. fr. Old Norse by* William Morris *and* Eirikr Magnusson. *Fr.* Elder Edda, The. AWP

Count all the miner's hours, all his breathing. A Hymn to Liberty. Jeffrey Wainwright. *Fr.* Mad Talk of George III, The. SCBI

Count Carrots. Gerda Mayer. OBSP

Count each affliction, whether light or grave. Sorrow. Aubrey Thomas De Vere. BLPA; WGRP

Count, if you can, every leaf on every tree. Anacreon, *tr. fr. Greek by* Sam Hamill. InMo

Count me o'er earth's chosen heroes — they were souls that stood alone. James Russell Lowell. *Fr.* Present Crisis, The. WGRP

Count not his broken pledges as a crime. *Unknown.* FaBoEH (Lloyd George.) FaBoCo

Count of Senlis at His Toilet, The. Lord De Tabley. PeVV

Count on dead fingers of time the years that pass. Poem for Garcia Lorca. George Woodcock. NOBC

Count Ten. Bonaro W. Overstreet. PoToHe

Count That Day Lost. "George Eliot."

Cover Her Face. Thomas Kinsella. CIP; IPY

Cover my earth mother four times with many flowers. *Unknown, tr. fr. Zuni Indian.* EaPr

Cover my eyes with your palm. Ruth Miller. *Fr. Cycle.* PeSA

Cover the face. *(LL)* After. Robert Browning. TrGrPo

Cover us with your pools of fir. *(LL)* Oread. Hilda Doolittle ("H. D."). AWP; CMoP; GoJo; HeIP; InPS; MoAmPo; MoP; NAAL-2; NALW; NoAM; NOBA; OxBA; Poetr; TAP

Cover your heavens, Zeus. Prometheus. Goethe, *tr. fr. German by* Philip L. Miller. RiWo

Cover your teeth. *(LL)* Kalaloch. Carolyn Forché. AmPA; AnAn; NoAM

Covered Bridge. Robert Penn Warren. AiP

Covered with snow, the herd, with none to guide. Without the Herdsman. Diotimus, *tr. fr. Greek by* John William Burgon. AWP

Covered with yellow leaves. Memory Gardens. Allen Ginsberg. NNaP

Covers his eyes like memory like a sheet. *(LL)* Idiot. Allen Tate. FaBoMo; LiTA

Covers it, like a stone covered in grass. *(LL)* Of the Lady Pietra degli Scrovigni. Dante. AWP; OAEL-2; OBVE

Covert. Helen Hunt Jackson. AmWP

Covetous Nebraskaites, The. Elymas Payson Rogers. *Fr.* Repeal of the Missouri Compromise Considered, The. AAP

Covetousness. Peter Idley. OxBChV

Covey of cotton-dressed, apple-breasted girls, A. Wax. Winfield Townley Scott. ErPo

Covey struts across the chrome-green roof, The. California Quail in January. Will C. Jumper. GrPl

Cow. Janet Reed McFatter. GrPl

Cow, The. Ogden Nash. NBLV; NoP; RB

Cow, The. Theodore Roethke. FiBHP; OBAL; OBCA

Cow, The. Robert Louis Stevenson. FaPON; FM; NTCP; OxBChV; PWR; TLR; WHSW

Cow, The. Ann Taylor. OxBChV

Cow, The. *Unknown.* FaBoUs

Cow and a calf, A. *Unknown.* OxNR

Cow and the Ass, The. Ann Taylor. BoTP

Cow Ate the Piper, The. *Unknown.* GBP

Cow-Boy's Song, The. Anna Maria Wells. OBCA

Cow-Chace, The. John André. PAH

Cow eats green grass, The. Response to Rimbaud's Later Manner. T. Sturge Moore. OBMV

Cow in Apple Time, The. Robert Frost. MoAB; MoAmPo; OxBSP; PoLF

Cow is of the bovine ilk, The. The Cow. Ogden Nash. NBLV; NoP; RB

Cow-lady, or sweet lady-bird. Lines to a Lady-Bird. Lord De Tabley. FM

Cow low'd sadly o'er the distant gate, The. Rose and Cushie. Charles Tennyson Turner. Mes

Cow of morning spurted, The. The Last Vision of Eoghan Rua Ó Súilleabháin. Michael Hartnett. PBCIP

Cow of Our Time, A. Tom Disch. EOEF

Cow Slips Away, The. Ben King. AnAmPo

Cow walks away from him, The. Thomas in the Fields. Lois Moyles. NYBP

Coward. A. R. Ammons. OBAL

Coward, The. Kipling. *Fr.* Epitaphs of the War, 1914–1918. FaBoEE; FaBoTw; NoP; OBWP; PeFWW

Coward, The. Eve Merriam. TrJP

Coward, — of heroic size. Grizzly. Bret Harte. AnAmPo

Cowardice, sels. Gavin Ewart.

　"Do you remember, in the Twenties." FaBoEH

Cowards die many times before their deaths. Shakespeare. *Fr.* Julius Caesar. FF

　(That Men Should Fear.) TrGrPo

Cowards fear to die, but courage stout. On the Snuff of a Candle. Sir Walter Ralegh. FaBoEE; OBD; SiPS

　(Sir W. Ralegh, on the Snuff of a Candle the Night Before He Died.) SiPSBD

Cowardy, cowardy, custard. *Unknown.* ISE, *sl. diff. vers.;* RoPo, *sl. diff. vers.*

Cowboy, The. John Antrobus. FaBoBe; FaPON

Cowboy. *Unknown.* ChTr

Cowboy Film. Tom Matthews. PNI

Cowboy Song. Charles Causley. PoRA

Cowboy stands beneath, The. Vaquero. Edward Dorn. NeAP; PoM

Cowboys and Indians. Rafael Zepeda. NGP

Cowboys, come and hear a story of Roy Bean in all his glory. Roy Bean. *Unknown.* AnAmPo; BeLS; OBAL

Cowboy's Lament, The. *Unknown. See* As I Walked Out in the Streets of Laredo.

Cowboy's Lament, The. Smoky Mountains. *Unknown.* AmFP

Cowboy's Life Is a Very Dreary Life, The. *Unknown.* AmFP

Cowherd, The; a Song. Ch'u Kuang-hsi, *tr. fr. Chinese by* Joseph J. Lee. SuSp

Cowhorn-crowned, shockheaded, cornshuck-bearded. The Knight, Death, and the Devil. Randall Jarrell. WeW

Cowlady cowlady. Ladybird. *Unknown.* FaBoVe

Cowley's Style. Walter Savage Landor. EPCY

Cowpasture and the ragged line. Abbey Cwmhir. Harri Webb. AngWe

Cowper. John Clare. EPCY

Cowper, the poet of the fields. Cowper. John Clare. EPCY

Cowper's Grave. Elizabeth Barrett Browning. OxAEP-2

Cowper's Tame Hare. Norman Nicholson. RB

Cowper's Three Hares. Charles Tennyson Turner. FM

Cows. Lauris Edmond. PWE

Cows. Peter Kocan. NOBAu

Cows. Stanley Plumly. AnAn

Cows. James Reeves. NTCP; NTP

Cows at Night, The. Hayden Carruth. SV

Cows bring in the last light, The. The Black Plateau. W. S. Merwin. NNaP

Cows graze across the hill. Cows. Peter Kocan. NOBAu

Cows near the Graveyard, The. Howard Nelson. NU

Cows they had, many, like heavy clouds drifting in the meadow. The Wheelbarrow. Russell Edson. LCAP

Cowslips for her covering. *(LL)* An Epitaph upon a Virgin. Robert Herrick. CaPo; FaBoEE; OxBoLi; PoEL-3; SeCV-1

Coxcomb, The. Joseph Hall. OxAEP-1

Coxcomb Bird, The. Pope. *Fr.* Moral Essays. ImPo

Coxcomb bird, so talkative and grave, The. The Coxcomb Bird. Pope. *Fr.* Moral Essays. ImPo

Coy Lass Dress'd Up in Her Best, The. *Unknown.* ErPo

Coy Shepherdess; or, Phillis and Amintas, The. *Unknown.* CoMu

Coyne's. John Ennis. PBCIP

Coyote. Bret Harte. AnAmPo; OBAP

Coyote, The. Carter Revard. VoR

Coyote/ running. Sweat Song. Peter Blue Cloud. VoR

Coyote/ song/ done. *(LL)* Sweat Song. Peter Blue Cloud. VoR

Coyote and the Locust, The. *Unknown. See* What is a locust?

Coyote Fragments. Lance Henson. HATNAP

Coyote Makes the First People. Peter Blue Cloud. BCF

Coyote Man and the Young Lady. Peter Blue Cloud. BCF

COYOTE stopped to drink at a big lake and saw his reflection. Coyote Makes the First People. Peter Blue Cloud. BCF

Coyote Sun. Carlos Cumpian. AfAz

Coyotes. Robert Vasquez. AfAz

Crab Orchard Sanctuary, Late October. Thomas Kinsella. IPY

Crabbed Age and Youth. Shakespeare. *Fr.* Passionate Pilgrim, The. EBEvV; GBL; InPS; LiTB; NoSic; OBEV

Crabbed age and youth cannot live together. Crabbed Age and Youth. Shakespeare. *Fr.* Passionate Pilgrim, The. EBEvV; GBL; InPS; LiTB; NoSic; OBEV

　(Age and Youth.) EiL

　(Madrigal, A: "Crabbed age and youth.") GTBS; GTBS-P; InPS

Crabbing for Blue-claws. James Ulmer. UTF

Crabs. Marge Piercy. NBLV

Crack, The. Michael Goldman. NYBP

Crack, The. Denise Levertov. NALW

Crack, A. Gu Cheng, *tr. fr. Chinese by* Donald Finkel *with* Chang Sheng-Tai. SpMi

Crack in the Wall Holds Flowers. Adam David Miller. PoBA

Crack is moving down the wall, The. Weldon Kees. *Fr.* Five Villanelles. SM

Crack ran through our hearthstone long ago, A. The Refugees. Edwin Muir. NoAM

Crack — recall it vividly as first fabric. Light. Richard Kenney. Son

Cracked is the very foundation. Epigram: To Charinus, a Catamite. Martial, *tr. fr. Latin.* PeHV

Cracked Looking Glass. Jean Garrigue. VCAP

Cracked Portraits. Agha Shahid Ali. OpBo

Cracks, and rejoices in the flame. *(LL)* A Description of Maidenhead. The Earl of Rochester. NOBL

Cracks in eight log buildings, counting sheds. Montana Ranch Abandoned. Richard Hugo. CAPP

Cracks on the walls, The. Star Blanket. Ray A. Young Bear. CDW

Cradle, The. Roland Robinson. NOBAu

Cradle Hymn. *At.* to Martin Luther. *See* Away in a Manger.

Cradle Hymn, A. Isaac Watts. OBEV; OxBChV; PoEL-3; SCGP

Cradle Song: "Angels are bending, The." W. B. Yeats. NOBVV

Cradle Song: "Child is moaning. The candle burning low, The." Count Arsenii Arkadyevich Golenishchev-Kutuzov, tr. fr. Russian by Philip L. Miller. Fr. Songs and Dances of Death. RiWo

Cradle Song: "Clock's untiring fingers wind the wool of darkness, The." Louis MacNeice. MoAB; MoBrPo
(Cradle Song for Miriam.) NAs

Cradle Song: "Come, little babe, come, silly soul." Nicholas Breton. NOBE; OBEV
(Sweet Lullaby, A.) Ell

Cradle Song: "Curled like a hoop in sleep." Lawrence Durrell. NAs

Cradle Song: "Dream, dream, my sweet life." Richard Dehmel, tr. fr. German by Philip L. Miller. RiWo

Cradle Song: "From groves of spice." Sarojini Naidu [or Nayadu]. FaPON
(Hindu Cradle Song.) BoTP

Cradle Song, A: "Golden slumbers kiss your eyes." Thomas Dekker and others. See Golden slumbers kiss your eyes.

Cradle Song: "Lullaby, my little one." Carl Michael Bellman. FaPON

Cradle Song, A: "O man from the fields." Padraic Colum. TIRV

Cradle Song, A: ("Sleep baby sleep!/ Thy father watches the sheep.") Unknown. See Sleep, Baby, Sleep ("Sleep baby sleep!/ Thy father watches the sheep.")

Cradle Song: "Sleep, my child, my little daughter." Unknown, tr. fr. Yiddish by Joseph Leftwich. TrJP

Cradle Song: "Sleep, sleep, beauty bright." Blake. EnRP; OBEV; PoLF

Cradle Song: "Sweet dreams, form a shade." Blake. Fr. Songs of Innocence. EnRP; FHYEP; OBCP

Cradle Song: "What does little birdie say?" Tennyson. Fr. Sea Dreams. BoTP; OxBChV

Cradle Song at Bethlehem. E. J. Falconer. BoTP

Cradle-Song at Twilight. Alice Meynell. NOBVV

Cradle Song for Miriam. Louis MacNeice. See Clock's untiring fingers wind the wool of darkness, The.

Cradle Song of the Elephants. Adriano del Valle, tr. fr. Spanish by Alida Malkus. FaPON

Cradle Will Rock, The, sels. Marc Blitzstein.
Art for Art's Sake. TrJP

Cradled and warm, fur-warm, in the she-wolf's lair. Wolf-Boy. David Malouf. CBAP

Craftsman, The. Marcus B. Christian. PoNe

Craftsman, The. Kipling. CoGr

Craftsman. Luci Shaw. TrCP

Craftsmen. V. Sackville-West. OxBTC

Craftsmen of the Little Box, The. Vasco [or Vasko] Popa, tr. fr. Serbo-Croatian by Charles Simic. AnRep; HSix

Crafty Butcher, The. Susan Hampton. NOBAu

Crafty Farmer, The. Unknown. ESPB

Crafty Farmer, The. Unknown. AmFP; ESPB

Crafty Miss of London; or, The Fryar Well Fitted, The. Unknown. CoMu; OxBB

Craigbilly Fair. Unknown. ChTr; GBP

Crammed, blackening, subsiding, warped. Bunhill Fields. Andrew Waterman. SCBI

Cramming all those almonds into a bag. (LL) Edward Lear in February. Christopher Middleton. TwCP

Cramped like sardines on the Queens, and sedated. Tourists. Howard Moss. FiBHP; NYBP; PeLV

Cranach. Sir Herbert Read. FaBoMo

Cranberry Song, The. Barney Reynolds. AmFP

Crane, The, sels. Saleem Barakat, tr. fr. Arabic by Lena Jayyusi and Naomi Shihab Nye.

Crane. Joseph Langland. NYBP

Crane, The. Charles Tomlinson. MoBrPo

Crane, The. Tu Mu, tr. fr. Chinese by John M. Ortinau. SuSp

Crane-fly trembles in the windowpane, A. Playing Through Old Games of Chess. Andrew Waterman. SCBI

Crane from the shore standing at the top of the steps, The. Going Alone to Spend a Night at the Hsien-Yu Temple. Po Chü-i, tr. fr. Chinese by Arthur Waley. Mes

Crane Is My Neighbor, The. John Shaw Neilson. CBAP

Cranes, The. Po Chü-i, tr. fr. Chinese by Arthur Waley. OBVE

Cranial Nerves, The. Unknown. FaBoUs

Crankadox leaned o'er the edge of the moon, The. Craqueodoom. James Whitcomb Riley. OBAL

Cranmer. C. H. Sisson. FaBoEH; FaBoTw

Cranmer was person of this parish. Cranmer. C. H. Sisson. FaBoEH; FaBoTw

Cranmer's Prophecy of Queen Elizabeth. John Fletcher and William Shakespeare. Fr. King Henry VIII. WGRP

Cranston Near the City Line. Ted Berrigan. UL

Crapshooters. Carl Sandburg. VGW

Craqueodoom. James Whitcomb Riley. OBAL

Cras amet qui nunquam amavit, quiquam amavit cras Moriatur. Refrains. John Hollander. AnAn

Crash. Things to Do in Providence. Ted Berrigan. UL

Crashes into the orchestra, which explodes. (LL) Cadenza. Ted Hughes. CMoP; NYBP

Crass Times Redeemed by Dignity of Souls, sels. Peter Viereck.
"Tenderness of dignity of souls, The." HoPM

Craswall. Roland Mathias. OBWVE

Crateas the doctor and Damon the sexton. Unknown, tr. fr. Greek by Peter Porter. GrAn

Craven. Sir Henry Newbolt. PAH

Craven Images. John James. VaA

Craving of Samuel Rouse for clearance to create, The. The Slave and the Iron Lace. Margaret Danner. BPo

Cravings during Pregnancy. M. Saint-Marthe, tr. fr. French. Fr. Paedotrophiae; or, The Art of Bringing Up Children. FaBoUs

Crawl Blues. Vincent McHugh. ErPo

Crawled near my mind's poor birds. (LL) Dramatic Fragment. Trumbull Stickney. InPK; OxBA; OxBSP

Crawlers, The. Keaulumoku, tr. fr. Hawaiian by M. W. Beckwith. Fr. Kumulipo, The; a Creation Chant. WTO

Crawlin' aboot like a snail in the mud. The Image o' God. Joe Corrie. ChIV-1; OxBS

Crawling glaciers pierce me with the spears. Shelley. Fr. Prometheus Unbound. EnRP; FHYEP; OAEL-2

Crawls from the dry grass. (LL) Exeunt. Richard Wilbur. BoNaP; HeIP; Poetsp; PoLF

Crayons. Martha Sansom. UnDi

Crayons/ crayons/ i need to color this day. Crayons. Martha Sansom. UnDi

Crazed. Walter de la Mare. OxBSP

Crazed. Mary E. Tucker. CBWP-1

Crazed Girl, The. W. B. Yeats. InPS; Son

Crazed Man in Concentration Camp. Agnes Gergely, tr. fr. Hungarian by Edwin Morgan. BoWoP; PAW

Crazy/ to be alive in such a strange. Lawrence Ferlinghetti. FF

Crazy Arithmetic. D'Arcy Wentworth Thompson. FaBoCo

Crazy as hell and typical of us. Making Contact. John Manifold. CBAP

Crazy Bill to the Bishop. Robert Peters. BXAP

Crazy Dog Events. Jerome Rothenberg. RaBo

Crazy Gypsy. Luis Omar Salinas. AfAz

Crazy Horse Monument. Peter Blue Cloud. HATNAP

Crazy Horse: The Last Morning. Lance Henson. VoR

Crazy Jane and Jack the Journeyman. W. B. Yeats. CMoP

Crazy Jane and the Bishop. W. B. Yeats. CMoP; LiTM

Crazy Jane Grown Old Looks at the Dancers. W. B. Yeats. CMoP; EBEV

Crazy Jane on God. W. B. Yeats. CMoP; EBEV; MoAB; OxBTC

Crazy Jane on the Day of Judgment. W. B. Yeats. CMoP; SOTW

Crazy Jane on the Mountain. W. B. Yeats. CMoP

Crazy Jane Reproved. W. B. Yeats. CMoP

Crazy Jane Talks with the Bishop. W. B. Yeats. BoLoP; CMoP; EBEV; ErPo; InPK; MeMBP; MoP; NAEL-2; NoAM; NoP; OAEL-2; OxAEP-2; PoE; PPP; TOF; TRP

Crazy ladies are singing again, The. The Belly Dancer in the Nursing Home. Ronald Wallace. GOYP

Crazy Pigeon. Etheridge Knight. NBV

Crazy pigeon strutting outside my cell. Crazy Pigeon. Etheridge Knight. NBV

Crazy Quilt. Jane Wilson Joyce. CrSp

Crazy Song to the Air of "Dixie." "Andy Lee." AS

Crazy Weather. John Ashbery. AnAn; PoE

Crazy Woman, The. Gwendolyn Brooks. NALW

Crazy Woman. Anne Elder. FaBoMA

Cream of phosphorescent light, A. Jonah. Aldous Huxley. ChTr

Cream-Puffin, The. Carolyn Wells. Fr. Baker's Dozen of Wild Beasts, A. OBCA

Cream Song, The. Apirana Ngata, tr. fr. Maori by Margaret Orbell. PeNZ

Creamcheese babies square and downy as bolsters. The Peaceable Kingdom. Marge Piercy. TwCP

Creamy Breasts. Chao Luan-luan, tr. fr. Chinese by Kenneth Rexroth and Ling Chung. WPC

Creases of the shouldery mountain. Childhood. Chris Wallace-Crabbe. FaBoMA

In This Strange Labyrinth How Shall I Turn? NAEL-1

Crown of Windflowers, A. Christina Rossetti. OxBChV

Crown Prince of Dullness, The. Dryden. *See* All human[e] things are subject to decay.

Crown with Him who wipes off tears, A. (*LL*) An Epitaph Upon the Lady Elizabeth, Second Daughter to his Late Majesty. Henry Vaughan. BeJo

Crown your Bacchus with lettuce leaves, not ivy. Lucilius, *tr. fr. Greek by* Peter Porter. GrAn

Crowned Crane. *Unknown.* TSaS

Crowned, girdled, garbed and shod with light and fire. Christopher Marlowe. Swinburne. *Fr.* Sonnets of English Dramatic Poets. EPCY; Son; TrGrPo

Crowned with flowers, I saw fair Amarillis. *Unknown.* EnLoPo

Crowning a bluff where gleams the lake below. Pontoosuce. Herman Melville. NOBA

Crowns, The. John Freeman. CH

Crowns all thy mean affairs. (*LL*) Waldeinsamkeit. Emerson. NOBA; WGRP

Crown's far too weighty, The. Thomas D'Urfey. FaBoEH

Crows, The. Louise Bogan. FaBoWP; NALW

Crows, The. David McCord. MoAmPo

Crows. David McCord. MoAmPo; PDV; RFM

Crows. Marge Piercy. CAPP

Crows. Lizette Woodworth Reese. AmWP

Crows, The. Maria Valli. CBAP

Crows. Valerie Worth. ImGa

Crows are cawing, The. Coming and Going. Robert Francis. TLR

Crows are come again to pick my eyes, The. Soliloquy on Death. F. K. Fiawoo. PBA

Crows came in, The. Caw Caw the Crows Caw Caw. *Unknown, tr. fr. Seneca Indian by* Jerome K. Rothenberg *and* Richard Johnny John. STP

Crows crowd croaking overhead. Summer Evening. John Clare. BoTP

Crow's Ditty. *Unknown.* GBP

Crow's First Lesson. Ted Hughes. MoP; NoAM

Crows in Spring. John Clare. EnRP

Crows mark, The. African Day. Gloria de Sant'Ana, *tr. fr. Portuguese by* Allan Francovich *and* Kathleen Weaver. PBWP

Crow's Nest. Richard F. Armknecht. GoYe

Crows the hour through Hobart Town. (*LL*) Hobart Town, Van Diemen's Land (11th June, 1837). Hal Porter. NOBAu

Crow's Way. Duane Niatum. CDW

Crow's wings not feet — pinions. Rosario Morales. *Fr.* Old. ETG

Crucified. Francis Quarles. NOSC

Crucified Jesus on a yellow cross. Crucifixion. Ljubomir Simovic, *tr. fr. Serbo-Croatian by* Charles Simic. HSix

Crucified Lord, you swim upon your cross. Lachrimae Verae. Geoffrey Hill. *Fr.* Lachrimae. NAEL-2; NoAM; NoP

Crucifix, The. Daniel Berrigan. CRP

Crucifix Corner. Ivor Gurney. NSI

Crucifixion. "Anna Akhmatova," *tr. fr. Russian by* Richard McKane. *Fr.* Requiem 1935-1940. BoWoP; IMW

Crucifixion. Hayden Carruth. BAP-90

Crucifixion, The. Mary Weston Fordham. CBWP-2

Crucifixion. Eva Gore-Booth. WGRP

Crucifixion. "Marie Madelaine," *tr. fr. German by* Ferdinand E. Kappey. PeHV

Crucifixion. Ljubomir Simovic, *tr. fr. Serbo-Croatian by* Charles Simic. HSix

Crucifixion, The. ("At The cry of the first birds.") *Unknown, tr. fr. Irish by* Kuno Meyer. TIRV

Crucifixion, The. ("I sike when I sing.") *Unknown. See* I sike when I singe.

Crucifixion. ("They crucified my Lord.") *Unknown.* BPo; TAP; TrGrPo

Crucifixion of Our Blessed Lord, The. Christopher Smart. ChIV-2

Crucifixion to the World by the Cross of Christ. Isaac Watts. *See* When I Survey the Wondrous Cross.

Cruciform. Winifred Welles. NYBP

Crucifying. John Donne. *Fr.* La Corona. ChIV-2; ESCV; Son

Crude Foyer. Wallace Stevens. LiTM; MeMAP

Cruel arrows gone, The. Fleche. Larry Eigner. VGW

Cruel Behold my Heavy Ending. Peter Thabit Jones. FaBoEH

Cruel Brother, The. *Unknown.* AmFP; ESPB; B *vers.;* OxBB

Cruel, Clever Cat. Geoffrey Taylor. ChTr; FaBoEE

Cruel death he died, The. (*LL*) On the Lamented Death of Mrs. Throckmorton's Bullfinch. William Cowper. NOEC; PPP

Cruel fingers setting the ocean's curls. (*LL*) The Dyke-Builder. Henry Treece. LiTB

Cruel Maid, The. Robert Herrick. CaPo

Cruel Mother, The. *Unknown.* AmFP; ESPB, A, B, C, *and* P *vers.;* FaBoBa; InPK; OBET; OxBB

Cruel Sister, The. *Unknown. See* There was an old woman lived on the seashore.

Cruel Sister, The. *Unknown.* OxBB

Cruel, unkind! I say farewell! farewell! (*LL*) Heaven and earth, and all that hear me plain. Sir Thomas Wyatt. SiPSBD

Cruel You Be. George Puttenham. EIl

Cruel, you pull away too soon your lips whenas you kiss me. *Unknown.* NoSic

Cruelty and rain could be expected. The House on 15th S.W. Richard Hugo. CAPP

Cruelty has a human heart. A Divine Image. Blake. *Fr.* Songs of Experience. ChIV-1; ChTr; NAEL-2; NoP; OBNC; PAW; RB; TEP

Cruelty of ages past affects us now, The. MMDCCXIII½. Lorenzo Thomas. UL

Cruise, The, *sels.* Robert Dunbar.
 "Summit gain'd how glorious the reward, The." PBCV

Cruise of the Fair American, The. *Unknown.* PAH

Cruise of the *Monitor,* The. George Henry Boker. PAH

Cruise of the *Mystery,* The. Celia Laighton Thaxter. OBCA

Crum Appointment, The. L. A. J. Moorer. CBWP-3

Crumble Hall, *sels.* Mary Leapor.
 In the Kitchen. ECWP

Crumbled rock of London is dripping under, The. Roy Fuller. PoA

Crumbling and weathered, their features half-erased. Small Park in East Germany: 1969. Gerda Mayer. OBTV

Crumbling centuries are thrust, The. The Jewels. Austin Clarke. MoAB

Crumbling Infrastructure, The. Tom Disch. BAP-90

Crumbling is not an instant's act. Emily Dickinson. AmPP; NOBA; PPP

Crumbs for the robin; well he knew. The Robin. William Bell Scott. FM

Crumbs or the Loaf. Robinson Jeffers. CMoP

Crumpled like a carnation, mauve and dim. Paul Verlaine. *See* Dark, puckered hole: a purple carnation.

Crunch, The. Gerda Mayer. OBSP

Crunking crane heard high amongst the clouds, The. George Farewell. *Fr.* Country Man, The. NOEC

Crusader. Roger McGough. PAW

Crusaders knew the Holy Places, The. Jenny Mastoraki, *tr. fr. Modern Greek by* Nikos Germanakos. BoWoP; PBWP

Crusader's wife slipped from the garrison, A. Ogden Nash. PeLi

Cruse, The. Louise Townsend Nicholl. NYBP

Crush the manroot, swallow what you desire. Learning the Spells; a Diptych. Anita Endrezze-Danielson. CDW

Crushed by an ambulance, he survived. The Lame Waltzer. Matthew Sweeney. IB

Crushed by that just contempt his follies bring. On Poet Ninny. The Earl of Rochester. APAS

Crushed by the waves upon the crag was I. Sea Dirge. Archias of Byzantium, *tr. fr. Greek by* Andrew Lang. AWP

Crushed Flower, The. Mary E. Tucker. CBWP-1

Crushed grape/ withers on the vine, The. People of the Harvest. Naomi Quinonez. AfAz

Crushing of a thousand petals, Lord, The. The Poet Prays. Grace Noll Crowell. TrPWD

Crushing out life than waving me farewell!. (*LL*) Kashmiri Song. "Laurence Hope." BLPA; BLPL; FaBoBe

Crusoe in England. Elizabeth Bishop. FaBoVe; HCAP

Crust of bread and a corner to sleep in, A. Life. Paul Laurence Dunbar. AnAmPo; CDC

Crustaceans. Roy Fuller. NoAM

Crutches. Robert Herrick. CaPo

Crux, The. Alma Villanueva. SRLS

Cry, The. R. S. Thomas. PWE

Cry, "All flesh is grass." (*LL*) On a Clergyman's Horse Biting Him. *Unknown.* FaBoCo; FaBoEE; NBLV; OxBoLi

Cry, Baby. *Unknown.* ISE, *diff. vers.;* ReMoGo; RoPo, *diff. vers.*

Cry, crow. Hayden Carruth. NNaP; Son

Cry Faugh! Robert Graves. MoBrPo

Cry for Light, A. *Unknown.* BLRP

Cry from the Canadian Hills, A. Lilian Leveridge. BLPA

Cry from the Ghetto, A. Morris Jacob Rosenfeld, *tr. fr. Yiddish by* Charles Weber Linn. TrJP

Cry in Distress, A. Bible, *O.T., paraphrased by* Sir Thomas Wyatt. *See* My God, my God, why hast thou forsaken me?

Cry "Infidel!" Alfred Gibbs Campbell. AAP

Cry, The, is: "Back to God!" Without respite. The Homeward Journey. Leonard Aaronson. TrJP

Cry "O what fools were we!" (LL) The Future Verdict. Ada Cambridge. NOBAu

Cry of a Stone, A, sels. Anna Trapnell.
"Therefore John read how that thou wouldst." ChIV-2; KTR

Cry of South Africa, The. Olive Schreiner. PeSAV

Cry of the Age, The. Hamlin Garland. WGRP

Cry of the Child, The. William Zaranka. BXAP

Cry of the Children, The. (Do ye hear the children weeping, O my brothers.) Elizabeth Barrett Browning. CoGr; EBVV; FaBoEH; OxAEP-2
Sels.
"They look up with their pale and sunken faces." OBD

Cry of the Daughter of My People, The. Bible, O.T. Fr. Jeremiah. TrJP

Cry of the Dreamer, The. John Boyle O'Reilly. BLPA

Cry of the Human, The, sels. Elizabeth Barrett Browning. Convinced by Sorrow. BLRP; WBLP

Cry of the Peoples, The. Alter Brody. TrJP

Cry of those being eaten by America, The. Those Being Eaten by America. Robert Bly. CoAP; NaP

Cry out for Sakhr when a dove with necklaces. Elegy for Her Brother Sakhr. Al-Khansa, tr. fr. Arabic by Willis Barnstone. BoWoP

Cry to Arms, A. Henry Timrod. PAH

Cry to Mary, A. St. Godric. MeEL

Cry went through me like a stab of a knife, A. W. H. Auden. Fr. Happy New Year, A. OBSV

Cryer, The. Michael Drayton. See Good folk [or folke], for gold or hire [or hyre].

Cryin' "Jean, Jean, Jean!" (LL) Tam i' the Kirk. Violet Jacob. GBL; OtMeF

Crying. Galway Kinnell. NTCP

Crying Asia! that famous place. The Marriage of Hector and Andromache. Sappho, tr. fr. Greek by Guy Davenport. OBVE

Crying from exile, I. Marilyn Hacker. Jaz

Crying in Early Infancy, sels. John Tranter.
"Chicago 'Manuel of Style' is really neat, The." NoAM
"Giving up women is worse than animal laxatives." NoAM
"It's bad luck with a coughing baby." CBAP
Sonnet 63: "In a distant." FaBoMA
"Spy bears his bald intent like a maniac, The." CBAP
"Sweat is a style of the body." NoAM
"They burn the radio and listen to the blues." NoAM

Crying only a little bit. Crying. Galway Kinnell. NTCP

Crying out for the help of me. (LL) Holy Well, The ("As it fell out one May morning.") Unknown. FaBoCh; GBP; NOCV

Crying to us to buy their fish. (LL) At Ch'en Ch'u. Wang Shih-chieng. OHMPC

Crying unseen, birds awaken me from my sleep. Impressions. Lu Yu, tr. fr. Chinese by Irving Y. Lo. SuSp

Cryptic philosopher, Kant, The. E. F. C. PeLi

Crystal, The. George Barker. LiTM; OBMV

Crystal. Faye Kicknosway. IHMS

Crystal, The, sels. Sidney Lanier.
"But Thee, but Thee, O sovereign Seer of time." TrPWD

Crystal beads slide. Rosary. Rita Magdaleno. AfAz

Crystal Cabinet, The. Blake. CH; FaBoCh; MeMBP; OAEL-2; OBNC; PoEL-4

Crystal Gazer, The. Sara Teasdale. MoAmPo

Crystal Lithium, The. James Schuyler. PoM; VCAP

Crystal Palace, The. John Davidson. PeVV

Crystal Palace, The, sels. Thackeray.
Mr. Molony's Account of the Great Exhibition. CBCK

Crystal Palace Market. James Laughlin. ArLo

Crystal parting the meads. The River in the Meadows. Léonie Adams. MoAB; MoAmPo

Crystal tree lets fall a crystal leaf, A. (LL) Decoration. Louise Bogan. MoAB; MoAmPo

Crystals like Blood. "Hugh MacDiarmid." HAP; NoP; RB

C.S.A. Commissioners, The. Unknown. PAH

Cú Chuimne in his youth. Epitaph for Cú Chuimne. Unknown, tr. fr. Irish by Thomas Kinsella. NOIV

Cu Chuimne in youth. Unknown, tr. fr. Irish by John V. Kelleher. BIrV

Cuba. Thomas MacDermot. PBCV

Cuba. Paul Muldoon. CIP; PNI

Cuba. Harvey Rice. PAH

Cuba. Edmund Clarence Stedman. PAH

Cuba, disheveled, naked to the waist. On a Monument to Martí. Walter Adolphe Roberts. PBCV; TTY

Cuba Libre. Joaquin Miller. PAH

Cuba Night. Dave Jeddie Smith. NAmP90

Cuba, 1962. Ai. AmPA

Cuba Street. Matthew Sweeney. IB

Cuba to Columbia. Will M. Carleton. PAH

Cubana bird touched down, The. Waiting for Fidel. John Agard. PBCV

Cubist Portrait. Marjorie Allen Seiffert. PoA

Cubs of bears a living lump appear, The. The Phoenix Self-born. Ovid, tr. by Dryden. Fr. Metamorphoses. ChTr

Cuchulain Comforted. W. B. Yeats. CMoP; LiTM; OAEL-2; TOF

Cuchulainn. Michael O'Loughlin. BiHa; IB; PBCIP

Cuckold. Mary E. O'Donnell. NWP

Cuckolded husbands have no certain sign. Palladas, tr. fr. Greek by Tony Harrison. GrAn

Cuckoo, The. Gerard Manley Hopkins. MoAB; MoBrPo; OxBSP; RB; TTTS

Cuckoo, The. Edward Thomas, tr. fr. Spanish. OBD

Cuckoo, The. ("Cuckoo is a bonny bird, The.") Unknown. AmFP; ChTr; GBP; NTP; OBET, 2 vers.; OxNR; RB

Cuckoo, The. ("In April/Come he will.") BoTP; FaBoVe, diff. vers.

Cuckoo. Andrew Young. ChTr

Cuckoo and the gowk, the. Unknown. FaBoVe

Cuckoo and the Nightingale, The, sels. Sir Thomas Clanvowe.

Cuckoo, are you calling me. The Cuckoo Wood. Edmund Beale Sargant. NSI

Cuckoo Calls from the Bamboo Grove, The. Unknown, tr. fr. Chinese by Kenneth Rexroth. OHMPC

Cuckoo, cherry tree. Unknown. FaBoVe

Cuckoo comes in April, The. Unknown. OxNR

"Cuckoo! The," cried my child, the while I slept. The Oocuck. Justin Richardson. FiBHP

Cuckoo cries, The/ Go home, go home. Tune: "Song of Great Virtue" — Spring. Kuan Han-ch'ing, tr. fr. Chinese by Jerome P. Seaton. SuSp

Cuckoo!/ Cuckoo! Chiyojo, tr. fr. Japanese by Kenneth Rexroth and Ikuko Atsumi. WPJ

Cuckoo, cuckoo, cherry tree. Unknown. OxNR

Cuckoo, cuckoo!/ Is it thy double note I hear. Cuckoo. Andrew Young. ChTr

Cuckoo, cuckoo/ What do you do? Unknown. OxNR

Cuckoo, glad cuckoo, Oh! where wilt thou rest to-night? Cuckoo Song. H. Cordelia Ray. CBWP-3

Cuckoo: In former days my father and mother [or mother and father]. Unknown, formerly at. to Cynewulf, tr. fr. Anglo-Saxon. Fr. Riddles (Exeter Book). AnOE, tr. by Charles W. Kennedy; ASW, tr. by Kevin Crossley-Holland

Cuckoo is a bonny [or fine or merry] bird, The. The Cuckoo. Unknown. AmFP; ChTr; NTP; OBET, 2 vers.; OxNR

Cuckoo, noisy among the Shenbaka flowers. Andal, tr. fr. Tamil by Willis Barnstone. BoWoP

Cuckoo [or Cuccu] Song, The. Unknown. See Summer [or Sumer] is icumen [or y-comen] in.

Cuckoo Song. Kipling. NTP

Cuckoo Song. H. Cordelia Ray. CBWP-3

Cuckoo Song. Unknown. See Summer [or Sumer] is icumen [or y-comen] in.

Cuckoo-throb, the heartbeat of the Spring, The. Ardour and Memory. Dante Gabriel Rossetti. Fr. House of Life, The. OAEL-2

Cuckoo Waltz. Unknown. AS

Cuckoo Wood, The. Edmund Beale Sargant. NSI

Cuckoos. Andrew Young. ChTr

Cuckoo's double note, The. Wiltshire Downs. Andrew Young. GTBS-P; NTP; OxBTC

Cuckoo's note would be drowned by the voice of my dead, The. (LL) The Cuckoo. Edward Thomas. OBD

Cucumber, The. Nazim Hikmet, tr. fr. Turkish. TSaS, tr. by Randy Blasing and Mutlu Knouk

Cucumber. (LL) Pudden Tame. Unknown. ChTr; FaBoNo

Cuddie [or Cuddy], for shame hold up thy heavy[e] head. October. Spenser. Fr. Shepheardes [or Shepeards or Shepherd's] Calender, The. NAEL-1; OAEL-1

Cuddle Doon. Alexander Anderson. GN

Cudgeled Husband, The. Swift. See As Thomas was cudgell'd [or cudgel'd] one day by his wife.

Cuernavaca. Aline Pettersson, tr. fr. Spanish. TSaS, tr. by Judith Infante

Cui Bono? Thomas Carlyle. WGRP

Cuidado Amigo. Iván Argüelles. UL

Cuillin, The, sels. Sorley MacLean.

Cuisine Bourgeoise. Wallace Stevens. LiTA; MeMAP

Culbin Sands. Andrew Young. GTBS-P; OxBS; OxBTC

Culloden and After. Iain Crichton Smith. OxBS

Culprit Fay, The, *sels.* Joseph Rodman Drake. AnAmPo
Assembling of the Fays, The. GN
Fairy Dawn. GN
Fairy in Armor, A. FaPON
(Elfin Knight, An.) BoTP
Fay's Crime, The. GN
Fay's Departure, The. GN
Fay's Sentence, The. GN
"If the spray-bead gem be won." GN
Throne of the Lily-King, The. GN

Cult of the Celtic, The. Anthony C. Deane. BXAP; NOBL; PeLV

Cultivated Signals types. Footnote to Enright's "Apocalypse." Martin Bell. FaBoMo

Cultivation. Mrs. Henry Linden. CBWP-4

Cultural Exchange. Langston Hughes. BPo; PoBA; PoNe

Cultural Notes. Kenneth Fearing. CMoP; PoE

Culture and Anarchy. Adrienne Rich. NALW

Culture of a people, The. Anthropology. Anselm Hollo. UL

Cultured gentleman, mature, congenial, refined. Personal. Samuel Yellen. NYBP

Cultured Girl Again, The. Ben King. FiBHP; OBAL

Cum here, Mandy, what's you chewin.' When Daddy Cums from Wuk. Maggie Pogue Johnson. CBWP-4

Cumberland, The. Longfellow. PAH

Cumberland, The. Herman Melville. PAH

Cumberland and the *Merrimac* . . . The. *Unknown.* AmFP

Cumberland Station. Dave Jeddie Smith. HCAP

Cumberland's Crew, The. *Unknown.* AmFP

Cummerbund, The. Edward Lear. OBTV

Cumnor Hall. William Julius Mickle. BeLS; OxBB

Cuncta Semper. Rodolfo Di Biasio, *tr. fr. Italian by* Stephen Sartarelli. NeIt

Cunjah Man, De. James Edwin Campbell. AAP

Cunning and art he did not lack. The Allansford Pursuit. Robert Graves. RB

Cunning Clerk, The. *Unknown.* OxBB

Cunning Cobbler Done Over, The. *Unknown.* CoMu

Cunning, wise, cautious, folly is, by which. Upon the Most Useful Knowledge, Craft or Cunning, Which Is More Wisdom, as 'Tis Less Wit. William Wycherley. SeCV-2

Cup, The. John Oldham. AWP

Cup, The. Judith Wright. FaBoWP

Cup capsizes along the formica, A. In the Snack-Bar. Edwin Morgan. FF

Cup clinks out, my friend, The. Apollonides, *tr. fr. Greek by* Peter Whigham. GrAn

Cup of Happiness, The. Gilbert Thomas. TrPWD

Cup takes its sweet joy and tells how it touches, The. Meleager, *tr. fr. Greek by* Barbara Hughes Fowler. *Fr.* Epigrams. HePo

Cupbearer, O victorious Falcon, come! Qorratu'l-Ayn, *tr. fr. Farsi by* Deirdre Lashgari. *Fr.* He the Beloved. WPOW

Cupbearer Speaks, The. Goethe, *tr. fr. German by* John Weiss. *Fr.* West-Easterly Divan. PeHV

Cupboard, The. Walter de la Mare. FaPON; NTCP

Cupid. Bernard O'Dowd. NOBAu

Cupid. Sir Philip Sidney. *Fr.* Arcadia. SiPS

Cupid. *Unknown.* ElL

Cupid a Plowman. Moschus. *See* His lamp, his bow, and quiver laid aside'.

CUPID abroad was lated in the night. A Night Visitor. Robert Greene. NoSic

Cupid and Campaspe. John Lyly. *See* Cupid and my Campaspe played [*or* playd].

Cupid and Death, *sels.* James Shirley.
Victorious Men of Earth. TrGrPo
(Last Conqueror, The.) GTBS; GTBS-P
(Song.) BeJo

Cupid and My Campaspe. John Lyly. *See* Cupid and my Campaspe played [*or* playd].

Cupid and my Campaspe played [*or* playd]. John Lyly. *Fr.* Alexander and Campaspe. CBLP; GBL; NoSic

Cupid and Venus. Mark Alexander Boyd. *See* Fra banc to banc, fra wod to wod, I rin.

Cupid as he lay among. The Wounded Cupid. Robert Herrick. AWP; OBVE

Cupid at Venus' breast. Meleager, *tr. fr. Greek by* Peter Whigham. GrAn

Cupid Defends Women. Thomas Hoccleve. *Fr.* Letter of Cupid, The. OxBLMV

Cupid, Dumb Idol. Michael Drayton. *Fr.* Idea. EnRePo; ESo

Cupid, dumb idol, peevish saint of love. Cupid, Dumb Idol. Michael Drayton. *Fr.* Idea. EnRePo; ESo

Cupid Far Gone. Richard Lovelace. CaPo; OPOP

Cupid, I Hate Thee. Michael Drayton. SCGP

Cupid, I hate thee, which I'd have thee know. Cupid, I Hate Thee. Michael Drayton. SCGP

Cupid in a Bed of Roses. *Unknown.* ElL

Cupid, Love, and Fie for shame. (*LL*) Song of the Stygian Naiades. Thomas Lovell Beddoes. EnRP; OAEL-2

Cupid the Ploughboy. *Unknown.* OBET

Cupid, thou naughty boy, when thou wert loathed. Fulke Greville. *Fr.* Caelica. EnRePo; Son

Cupid Turned Plowman. Moschus, *tr. fr. Greek by* Matthew Prior. AWP

Cupid's Call. James Shirley. BeJo; ErPo; NOSC

Cupid's Indictment. John Lyly. *Fr.* Galathea. ElL

Cupid's Revenge, *sels.* Beaumont *and* Fletcher *and* John Fletcher. Lovers Rejoice! ElL

Cupio Dissolvi. William Habington. ChIV-2

Cupping her chin and lying there, the Bren. Defensive Position. John Manifold. MoBrPo

Cur foretells the knell of parting day, The. Ambrose Bierce. *Fr.* Devil's Dictionary, The. OBAL

Curate Thinks You Have No Soul, The. St. John Lucas. BLPA

Curb for stubborn steed. Earliest Christian Hymn. Clement of Alexandria, *tr. fr. Greek by* Edward H. Plumptre. WGRP

Cure-All. Edith M. Thomas. *See* Tell me, is there sovereign cure.

Cure at Porlock, A. Amy Clampitt. NoAM

Cure for Fault Finding, A. Strickland W. Gillilan. *See* Just stand aside and watch yourself go by.

Cure for Poetry, A. Annabella Blount. ECWP

Cure for Poetry, A. *Unknown, after the Latin of* George Buchanan. FaBoEE

Cure me with quietness. For Sleep, or Death. Ruth Pitter. TrPWD

Cures all again. (*LL*) Why, Soldiers, Why? *At. to* James Wolfe. OBET

Curfew. Paul Éluard, *tr. fr. French by* Quentin Stevenson. BoLoP

Curfew. Longfellow. AnAmPo; MeMAP; OxBA

Curfew Must Not Ring Tonight. Rose Hartwick Thorpe. BeLS; BLPA; BLPL; FaBoBe; FaPON; VPP; WBLP

Curfew tolls the hour of locking up, The. Elegy in Newgate. William Cobbett. UV

Curfew tolls the knell of parting day, The. Thomas Gray. *Fr.* Elegy Written in a Country Churchyard. AWP; ClHu; DL; EBEV; EBEvV; EnRP; FaBoBe; FaBoPP; FaBoPV; FaBoRV; FaPoR; FHYEP; GGP; GN; GTBS; GTBS-P; HAP; HeIP; ImPo; InPK; InPS; LiTB; NOBE; NOEC; NoP; OAEL-1; OBEV; OxAEP-1; PoEL-3; Poetr; PoLF; PPP; PrIm; SCGP; SCV; TEP; TFi; TrGrPo; UnPo; UV; WBLP; WeW

Curfew tolls the knell of parting day, The. If Gray Had Had to Write His Elegy in the Cemetery of Spoon River Instead of in That of Stoke Poges. J. C. Squire. BXAP; FaBoPa

Curfew tolls the knell of parting day, The. Diversions of the Re-Echo Club. Carolyn Wells. OBAL

Curing Homosexuality. Jim Everhard. GLP

Curio's rich sideboard seldom sees the light. On a Stingy Beau. John Winstanley. FaBoEE

Curiosity. Alastair Reid. SoSe

Curiosity, *sels.* Charles Sprague.

Curiosity-Shop, The. Peter Redgrove. OxBC

Curious child, who dwelt upon a tract, A. Wordsworth. *Fr.* Excursion, The. WGRP

Curious, compelling way in which the light, The. Winter Light. Jon Anderson. AnAn

Curious Discourse That Passed between the Twenty-five Letters at Dinner-Time, A. *Unknown.* FaBoUs

Curious is this stonework! The Fates destroyed it. The Ruin. *Unknown, tr. fr. Anglo-Saxon by* Gavin Bone. EBEV

Curious knot God made in paradise, A. Upon Wedlock and Death of Children. Edward Taylor. AmPP; EAP; NAAL-1; NoP

Curled fingers tighten in his curly hair. St. Christopher. Dick Davis. SCBI

Curled like a hoop in sleep. Lawrence Durrell. NAs

Curled like a question mark asleep. (*LL*) Christ Walking on the Water. W. R. Rodgers. MoAB

Curliest Thing, The. *Unknown.* BoTP

Curling them around. Cutting Greens. Lucille Clifton. CAPP; CrSp

Curly Locks! Curly Locks! wilt thou be mine? Mother Goose. OxNR; ReMoGo

Curly nibby has put to flight, The. Allelauder. "Hugh MacDiarmid." FaBoEH

Curr dhoo, curr dhoo. Mother Goose. OxNR

Currency During the War. Laura Rosenthal. UL

Currency Lads may fill their glasses, The. The Lass in the Female Factory. *Unknown.* NOBAu

Current, The. James Merrill. NYBP

Currents. Emma Lazarus. *Fr.* By the Waters of Babylon. WPE

Curricle and hansom, The. The Great Garret, or 100 Wheels. James McMichael. AmPA

Curriculum Vitae. Ingeborg Bachmann, *tr. fr.* German by Jerome K. Rothenberg. BoWoP

Curriculum Vitae. Robert Gray. NOBAu

Curriculum Vitae. Lawrence Joseph. PBCAP

Curs'd be the Stars which did ordain. Curse. *Unknown.* IHNG

Curs'd be those dull, unpointed, dogg'rel rhymes. Charles Sackville. *Fr.* Faithful Catalogue of Our Most Eminent Ninnies, A. FaBoEH

Curse, The. John Hollander. UnPo

Curse, The. J. M. Synge. ChTr; FaBoCo; FaBoEE; NOIV; PeIV

Curse, A. ("Bruadar and Smith and Glinn.") *Unknown, tr. fr. Irish by* Douglas Hyde. BIrV

Curse. ("Curs'd be the start.") *Unknown.* IHNG

Curse, The; a Song. Robert Herrick. CaPo

Curse for a Nation, A. Elizabeth Barrett Browning. NALW; WPE; WPOW

Curse of Cromwell, The. W. B. Yeats. BIrV; IIP

Curse of Kehama, The, *sels.* Robert Southey.
  Kehama's Curse. OBNC
  Love Indestructible. OBNC

Curse of the Cat Woman. Edward Field. WeW

Curse on Herod, A. Amy Witting. ChIV-2; NOBAu

Curse on the star, dear Harry, that betrayed. An Epistle from a Half-Pay Officer in the Country to His Friend in London. Richardson Pack. NOEC

Curse on Uruk, A. Enheduanna, *tr. fr. Sumerian by* Aliki *and* Willis Barnstone. BoWoP

Curse the tongue in my head. Good Night! Good Night! John Holmes. PoToHe

Curse upon Edward, The. Thomas Gray. OBEV

Curse upon that faithless maid, A. Aphra Behn. *Fr.* Emperor of the Moon. WPE

Cursed Be the Day. Bible, *O.T. Fr.* Jeremiah. TrJP

Cursed with a body. Hands: Abraham Kunstler. Michael D. Riley. BTR

Curses. Ljubomir Simovic, *tr. fr. Serbo-Croatian by* Charles Simic. HSix

Cursive crawl, the squared-off characters, The. Writing. Howard Nemerov. NYBP; VCAP

Curtain. Lance Henson. VoR

Curtain, The. Judith Wright. FaBoMA

Curtain falls; the play is done, The. It's Going Out. Heine, *tr. fr. German by* Alistair Elliot. OBD

Curtain rung down on his wise old age, The. *Unknown, tr. fr. Greek by* W. G. Shepherd. GrAn

Curtains. Ruth Stone. NAmP90

Curtains drawn back, the door ajar. Robinson at Home. Weldon Kees. CoAP; NYBP

Curtains in the House of the Metaphysician, The. Wallace Stevens. PoA

Curtains Now Are Drawn, The. Thomas Hardy. CMoP

Curtains of rock. Orpheus in the Underworld. David Gascoyne. FaBoTw

Curtains were half drawn, the floor was swept, The. After Death. Christina Rossetti. GBL; NAEL-2; NALW; WeW

Curvd lines toe-drawn, round cornerd squares, The. Hop, Skip, and Jump. Gary Snyder. LCAP; PRA

Curving, leaping line of light, A. Prairie Fires. Hamlin Garland. OBCA

Curzon! thou shouldst be living at this hour. Sonnet to the "Most Distinguished Chancellor" that Oxford Has Had. Max Beerbohm *and* William Rothenstein. UV

Cushendall. *Unknown.* WTO

Cushie Butterfield. George Ridley. FaBoVe; NTP

Cushy cow, bonny, let down thy milk. Mother Goose. GBP; OxNR; ReMoGo

Custer. Edmund Clarence Stedman. PAH

Custer Lives in Humbolt County. Janet Campbell Hale. VoR

Custer's Last Charge. Frederick Whittaker. PAH; PoLF

Custom, in this small article I find. On Snuff-Taking. Elizabeth Teft. ECWP

Custom Job: Hank Williams, Jr., and the Death Car, 1958. David Wojahn. *Fr.* Mystery Train: A Sequence. PBCAP

Custom of the World, The. Louis Simpson. BoLoP

Customize the Grass. Peter Finch. NBrP

Customs Change. *Unknown.* OxBChV

Cut. Sylvia Plath. CAPP; TAP

Cut branches back for a day. Trail Crew Camp at Bear Valley. 9000 Feet. Gary Snyder. HCAP

Cut Flower, A. Karl Shapiro. BoNaP; HAP; WeW

Cut Grass. Philip Larkin. NoAM; NTP; OxBC; PrIm; RB

Cut loose, without devotion, a man becomes a comic. Without Devotion. Marie Howe. NAmP90

Cut of Women's Clothes, The. Gwyneth Lewis. NWP

Cut-outs today, her mother said. Cutting Loose. Liz Cashdan. NWP

Cut the Grass. A. R. Ammons. CAPP; HAP; Poetr; PPP; TAP; WeW

Cut them on Monday, you cut them for health. *Unknown.* OxNR

Cut thistles in May. *Unknown.* FaBoUs; OxNR

Cut yer name across my backbone. Convicts' Rum Song. *Unknown.* FaBoVe; NOBAu

Cut your nails on Monday, cut for health. *Unknown.* RoPo

Cute secretary, none cuter, A. Ogden Nash. PeLi

Cutter risen from the mollusks, it is a god, A. The Memoirs. Carl Rakosi. PoA

Cutting back/ wherever the weather. The Pruning. Adam David Miller. NBV

Cutting Edge, The. Philip Levine. NYBP

Cutting Greens. Lucille Clifton. CAPP; CrSp

Cutting Loose. Liz Cashdan. NWP

Cutting Prow, The. Edward Sanders. PoBeRe

Cutting that jungle road from Lugardville. Surveyor. Guy Butler. PeSA

Cutting, they called it. Castration. Nigel Jenkins. AngWe

Cutting up an Ox. Chuang Tzu, *tr. fr. Chinese by* Thomas Merton. EnlH

Cuttings ("Sticks-in-a-drowse droop over sugary loam.") Theodore Roethke. HCAP; LCAP; MoP; NAAL-2; NoAM; NOBA; TAP; UnPo

Cuttings ("This urge, wrestle, resurrection of dry sticks.") Theodore Roethke. CAPP; HCAP; LCAP; MoP; NAAL-2; NoAM; NOBA; TAP; TRP; UnPo; VCAP

Cutty Sark. Hart Crane. *Fr.* Bridge, The. FaBoMo; LiTA; NAAL-2

Cutty Wren, The. *Unknown.* GBP; OxBoLi; SWP; UV, abr.; WiR

Cwmchwefri. T. Harri Jones. AngWe

Cwmrhydyceirw Elegiacs. Vernon Watkins. PoA

Cyanide jar seals life, as sonnets move, The. Butterfly Bones; or, Sonnet against Sonnets. Margaret Avison. LiTM

Cyclamens. "Michael Field." NOBVV

Cycle. Langston Hughes. FaPON

Cycle. Ruth Miller. PeSA
  Sels.
  "Cover my eyes with your palm."
  "Dropped leaf, The."
  "To eat pain like bread is a condition."

Cycle for Mother Cabrini, A, *sels.* John Logan.
  "Saint, who overlaps." CRP

Cycle of life is a worrisome thing, The. On Covering the Bones of Chang Chin, the Hired Man. Liu Tsung-yüan, *tr. fr. Chinese by* Jan W. Walls. SuSp

Cycle sings, A. Nature. Walter Stone. NYBP

Cycle was closed and rounded, A. Bennington. William Henry Babcock. PAH

Cycles, Cycles. Suzanne Berger Rioff. NMM

Cyclist, The. Marge Piercy. NoAM

Cyclists, The. Amy Lowell. WPE

Cyclop! if any ask thee who imposed. Ulysses Insults over the Cyclops. Homer, *tr. fr. Greek by* Robert Fitzgerald. *Fr.* Odyssey. NAWM-1; NOSC, *tr. by* George Chapman

Cyclops. Euripides, *tr. fr. Greek by* Shelley. AWP
  Sels.
  Chorus of Satyrs, Driving Their Goats.
  "One with eyes the fairest."

Cyclops. Ovid. *See* More whyght thou art than primrose leaf my Lady Galatee.

Cyclops, The ("And so an easier life.") Theocritus [*or* Theokritus]. *See* And so an easier life our Cyclops drew.

Cyder, *sels.* John Philips.
  Apple-Culture. OxAEP-1
  How to Catch Wasps. FaBoUs
  Pruning. FaBoUs

Cymbals crash, The. A Victory Dance. Alfred Noyes. NSI; PoLF

Cymbeline, *sels.* Shakespeare.
  "Fear no more the heat o' the Sun." AWP; CH; ChTr; ClHu; CoGr; EBEV; EIL; ELP; EnRePo; FaPoB; FF; GBL; HAP; ImPo; InPS; LiTB; Mes; NAEL-1; NoP; NoSic; OBD; OxAEP-1; PoRA; PrIm; RB; SCGP; SCV; SoSe; TFi; TrGrPo
  (Dirge: "Fear no more the heat o' the sun.") OAEL-1
  (Dirge for Fidele.) NOBE
  (Fidele.) GTBS; GTBS-P; OBEV
  (Fidele's Dirge.) FaBoCh

(Song: "Fear[e] no more the heat[e] o' the sun.") CTC; EBEvV; NOSC; PoE; PoEL-2

Hark! Hark! the Lark. AWP; BoTP; CH; ChTr; EnRePo; FaBoCh; FaBV; FaPON; ImPo; LiTB; NIP; NoP; NoSic; PFP; PrIm; TFi; TrGrPo; UV

(Aubade: "Hark! hark! the lark at heaven's gate sings.") OBEV

(Morning Song, A.) GN

(Song: "Hark! hark! the lark at heaven's gate sings.") NOSC; EBEvV; EIL; 09FiP

"How found you him?" OxAEP-1

"With fairest flowers,/ Whilst summer lasts." EBEV; RB

Cymbeline, Tempest, Much Ado, Verona. Memoria Technica for the Plays of Shakespeare. *Unknown.* FaBoUs

Cymon and Iphigenia. (Old as I am, for ladies' love unfit.) Dryden. EPCY; OBNV

Sels.

Militia, The. OBSV

Cymru. David Gwenallt Jones, *tr. fr. Welsh by* Gwyn Jones. OBWVE

Cynara. Ernest Dowson. *See* Last night, ah, yesternight, betwixt her lips and mine.

Cynddylan on a Tractor. R. S. Thomas. AngWe

Cynderaxa kind and good. Trim's Song: The Fair Kitchen-Maid. Sir Richard Steele. *Fr.* Funeral, The. OxBSP

Cynic, The. (Whoever to finding fault inclines.) St. George Tucker. OBAL

Sels.

"Once at a merry wedding feast." NBLV

Cynic Satire, A. John Marston. *Fr.* Satires. NoSic

Cynic says: Now that we know, A. Thomas Thorneley. PeLi

Cynical Portraits. Louis Paul. NBLV

Cynical sage with a kink, A. Hassall Pitman. PeLi

Cynotaph, The. "Thomas Ingoldsby." *Fr.* Ingoldsby Legends, The. FM

Cynthia, *sels.* Richard Barnfield.

Cherry-lipped Adonis. Son

Sighing, and Sadly Sitting by My Love. Son

Cynthia in the Snow. Gwendolyn Brooks. TLR

Cynthia Matz, with my finger in your cunt. Each Day. David Ignatow. NNaP

Cynthia on Horseback. Philip Ayres. EnLoPo

Cynthia, to thy power. Bridal Song ("Cynthia, to thy power.") Beaumont *and* Fletcher *and* John Fletcher. *Fr.* Maid's Tragedy, The. OBEV

Cynthia's Revels, *sels.* Ben Jonson.

Glove, The. EIL; GBL

Hymn to Diana. AWP; CH; ChTr; EIL; GTBS; GTBS-P; HAP; NOBE; NoP; OAEL-1; OBEV; PoRA; SeCP; TFi; TrGrPo; WiR

(Hesperus' Hymne[e] to Cynthia.) JCP; SeCV-1

(Hesperus' Song.) GN

(Hymn: "Queen and huntress, chaste, and fair.") EnRePo; InPS; PlP; PoEL-2

(Hymn to Cynthia.) NOSC; PoE; PrIm; SCGP

Slow, Slow, Fresh Fount. BeJo; ChTr; EIL; ELP; InPS; NIP; NoP; OAEL-1; PrIm; SCGP; TFi

(Echo's Lament for Narcissus.) CH; OxAEP-1

(Echo's [*or* Eccho's] Song.) JCP; NOSC; SeCV-1; TrGrPo

(Song: "Slow, slow fresh fount, keep time with my salt tears.") EnRePo; OxBSP; PoEL-2; SeCP

Cypassis, that a thousand ways trimm'st hair. Ovid, *tr. by* Christopher Marlowe. *Fr.* Amores. EBEV

Cypress Grove. Austin Clarke. IPY

Cypress stood up like a church, The. Bianca among the Nightingales. Elizabeth Barrett Browning. BrRo; GTBS-P

Cypresses. Robert Francis. LCAP

Cypresses. D. H. Lawrence. FaBoPP; NAEL-2

Cypris who puts the sea to rest. Philodemus, *tr. fr. Greek by* William Moebius. GrAn

Cyriack, this three years' day these eyes, though clear. To Mr. Cyriack Skinner upon His Blindness. Milton. NOSC; PeECV; Son

(Sonnet.) OxAEP-1

(To Cyriack Skinner ("Cyriack, this three years' day").) TrGrPo

Cyriack, whose grandsire, on the royal bench. To Cyriack Skinner ("Cyriack, whose grandsire.") Milton. GTBS; GTBS-P; NoP; OBEV; Son

(Sonnet: "Cyriack, whose grandsire, on the royal bench.") NOSC; OxAEP-1

Cyril aand Methodius, *sels.* Aleksandar Vuco, *tr. fr. Serbo-Croatian by* Charles Simic.

"Cyril and Methodius." HSix

Cyril and Methodius. Aleksandar Vuco, *tr. fr. Serbo-Croatian by* Charles Simic. *Fr.* Cyril aand Methodius. HSix

Cythera. David Ferry. DiPo

Cythera. Suniti Namjoshi. AIW

Cythère. Paul Verlaine, *tr. fr. French by* Arthur Symons. AWP

Cytherea. Mary Mackey. SRLS

Cywdd to Morvydd, The. Dafydd ap Gwilym, *tr. fr. Welsh.* NOEC

Cywydd o Fawl. Harri Webb. AngWe

Czargrad. John Riley. VaA

Czar's Last Christmas Letter: A Barn in the Urals, The. Norman Dubie. NoAM

Czestochowa, Jasna Gora, Auschwitz, Nova Huta. Lolek. John Jordan. TIRV

D

D . . . dronken. *Unknown.* MiEL

D Blues. Calvin C. Hernton. PoBA

D. C. Karl Shapiro. NYBP

D-Dawn. Margaret McGarvey. GoYe

D. G. Rossetti. Dorothy Parker. *Fr.* Pig's-Eye View of Literature, A. NALW

D. H. Lawrence and James Joyce. Humbert Wolfe. FaBoEE

D is for Dog. W. H. Davies. OxBSP

D-Y Bar. James Welch. CDW

D-Zug. Julian Croft. NOBAu

Da Silva Gives the Cue. Walter Hart Blumenthal. TrJP

Dab of Color, A. Theodore Weiss. VGW

Dabbling in the Dew. *Unknown.* CH

Daccus is all bedaub'd with golden lace. Against Gaudy-Bragging-Undoughty Daccus. John Davies of Hereford. FaBoEE

Dachau. Mary Kathryn Stillwell. BTR

Dachau Moon. Michael Waters. BTR

Dachshunds ("The dachshund leads a quiet life.") William Jay Smith. OBAL

Dactylos was silent and impersonal. Daedalus, The Maker. Thomas McCarthy. IB

Dad. Elaine Feinstein. AIW

Dad and the Cat and the Tree. Kit Wright. OTCP

Dad waited while Mum bought the ham. Coral E. Copping. PeLi

Dad would turn up the stereo. Midsummer. Claire Collett. Jaz

Dada would have liked a day like this. Lawrence Ferlinghetti. *Fr.* Pictures of a Gone World. NeAP

Daddy. Sylvia Plath. BoWoP; CAPP; CMoP; CoAP; HCAP; HeIP; InPK; InPS; LiTM; MoP; NAAL-2; NALW; NaP; NIP; NMM; NoAM; NOBA; NoP; OPOP; PoE; Poetr; PrIm; TFi; TwCP; UnPo; VCAP

Daddy and Mummy. Life Story. Tomioka Taeko, *tr. fr. Japanese by* Harry Guest, Lynn Guest, *and* Kajima Shozo. WPOW

Daddy, daddy, you bastard, I'm through. (*LL*) Daddy. Sylvia Plath. BoWoP; CAPP; CMoP; CoAP; HCAP; HeIP; InPK; InPS; LiTM; MoP; NAAL-2; NALW; NaP; NIP; NMM; NoAM; NOBA; NoP; OPOP; PoE; Poetr; PrIm; TFi; TwCP; UnPo; VCAP

Daddy eat dog shark, malingay. Dog Shark. *Unknown.* PBCV

Daddy Fell into the Pond. Alfred Noyes. FaPON; PDV

Daddy fixed breakfast [*or* the breakfast]. Mummy Slept Late and Daddy Fixed Breakfast. John Ciardi. PDV

"Daddy, how old is Groucho Marx?" A Child in the 80's. Derwent May. OBD

Daddy Long-legs and the Fly, The. Edward Lear. CBNP

Daddy Poem, A. William J. Harris. NBV

Daddy sits/ in his brown. Sunflowers and Saturdays. Melba Joyce Boyd. BlSi

Daddyboy/ trickster hero. Daring. Carol Konek. IHMS

Dae what ye wull ye canna parry. "Hugh MacDiarmid." *Fr.* Drunk Man Looks at the Thistle, A. EBEV; OxAEP-2

Daedal of my death, A. William Drummond of Hawthornden. NOSC

Daedalus. Ovid, *tr. by* Arthur Golding. *Fr.* Metamorphoses. CTC; OBVE

Daedalus. Alastair Reid. NYBP

Daedalus, The Maker. Thomas McCarthy. IB

Daemon, The. Louise Bogan. NYBP

Daemon, The, *sels.* M. Y. Lermontov, *tr. fr. Russian by* Babette Deutsch *and* Avrahm Yarmolinsky.

"On the sightless seas of ether." AWP

Daemon Lover, The. *Unknown. See* "O where [*or* whare] have you [*or* hae ye] been, my dear, dear [*or* dearest dear *or* long, long] love."

Daffodil. Waldo Williams, *tr. fr. Welsh by* Gwyn Jones. OBWVE

Daffodils. Michael Heffernan. SM

Daffodils. P. A. Ropes. BoTP

Daffodils, The. Wordsworth. BoNaP; EnRP; FaBoPP; FaPoB; InPK; InPS; NAEL-2; NoP; OAEL-2; PoRA; SoSe; TEP; TTTS; UnPo

Daffodils, The. Wordsworth. *See* I wandered lonely as a cloud.

Daffodils. Wordsworth. *See* I wandered lonely as a cloud.

Daffy-down-dilly is new come to town [*or* Daffadowndilly has come up to town]. Mother Goose. NTCP; OxNR

Daffy Duck in Hollywood, *sels.* John Ashbery. Hollywood Everything, A. CBCK

Daft Days, The. Robert Fergusson. NOEC; OxAEP-1; ScCV

Daft gowk, in macaroni dress. On Seeing a Butterfly in the Street. Robert Fergusson. ScCV

Dafydd ap Gwilym Resents the Winter. Rolfe Humphries. NYBP

Dagger. M. Y. Lermontov, *tr. fr. Russian by* Max Eastman. AWP

Dagger, The ("A dagger rests in a drawer.") Jorge Luis Borges, *tr. fr. Spanish by* Norman Thomas di Giovanni. NYBP

Dago shovelman sits by the railroad track, The. Child of the Romans. Carl Sandburg. NAAL-2

Daguerreotype Taken in Old Age. Margaret Atwood. BoWoP; NoAM

Dahlias. Padraic Colum. GoJo

Dahn the Plug'ole. *Unknown, tr. by* Robert Bly. RB

Dahomey. Audre Lorde. NAAL-2

Dai horse neighs against the bleak wind of Etsu, The. South-Folk in Cold Country. Ezra Pound, *after the Chinese.* OBVE

Dai K lives at the end of a valley. One is not quite sure. Synopsis of the Great Welsh Novel. Harri Webb. AngWe

Dai, Live. Jon Dressel. AngWe

Daily Bread. James Ulmer. UTF

Daily dirge, and rites divine, The. (*LL*) The Grave of King Arthur. Thomas Warton the Younger. EnRP

Daily going out, The. Waterpot. Grace Nichols. PBCV

DAILY HERALD/ Is unkind, The. A Certain Statesman. Sir Osbert Sitwell. IHNG

Daily I go to the carpet warehouse. Love at Cooter's Carpet, Fort Lawn, S.C. Susan Ludvigson. NGP

Daily Living, *sels.* Rosemary Dobson. Folding the Sheets. FaBoMA; NOBAu Visiting. FaBoMA

Daily Manna, The. Sara Henderson Hay. GoYe

Daily Prayer, A, *sels.* Jean Pearson. "We ate no flesh in Eden, but afterwards." EaPr

Daily the Drum. Anne Wilkinson. NOBC

Daily the neighbour's dog is withdrawn to the park. Hilaire Kirkland. *Fr.* Observations. PeNZ

Daily the Ocean between Us. Patricia Goedicke. TAP

Daily the wind-flowers age, and so do I. Weaving Love-Knots. Hsüeh T'ao, *tr. by* Carolyn Kizer. BoWoP

Daily to turn in Paul's, and help the trade. (*LL*) On English Monsieur. Ben Jonson. NBLV; NoP

Daily Trials. Oliver Wendell Holmes. PoEL-5

Daily Wages. Amrita Pritam, *tr. fr. Punjabi by the author* and Charles Brasch. PBWP

Daily walked the fair and lovely. The Azra. Heine, *tr. fr. German by* John Hay. AWP

Daily with You. Annie Johnson Flint. BLRP

Dainty fine bird, that art encaged there. Prisoners. *Unknown.* EiL

Dainty Fine King Indeed, A. *Unknown.* FaBoEH

Dainty little maiden, whither would you wander? The City Child. Tennyson. BoTP; OxBChV

Dainty Miss Apathy. Pooh! Walter de la Mare. HAP; PeLV

Dainty Sweet Bird. Thomas Vautor. EnRePo

Dainty sweet bird, thou art encagèd there. Dainty Sweet Bird. Thomas Vautor. EnRePo

Dainty white lilies, and sad flowers well prized. (*LL*) Brown Is My Love. *Unknown.* EiL; GBL

Daisies, The. Bliss Carman. AnAmPo; BoNaP

Daisies, The. James Stephens. AWP

Daisies. Andrew Young. GoJo

Daisies and Grasses. *Unknown.* BoTP

Daisies and kingcups and honeysuckle-flowers. (*LL*) The City Child. Tennyson. BoTP; OxBChV

Daisies of Florence. Kathleen Raine. NYBP

Daisies so bright. Daisies and Grasses. *Unknown.* BoTP

Daisy, The. Burns. *See* Wee, modest, crimson-tippèd flow'r.

Daisy, The, *sels.* James Montgomery. Field Flower, A. BoTP

Daisy, The. Tennyson. EnLoPo; NOBVV; OBNC; PoEL-5

Daisy. Francis Thompson. AWP; BeLS; FaBV; MoAB; MoBrPo; OBEV; OBNC

Daisy, *sels.* Francis Thompson. Tokens, The. OtMeF

Daisy. William Carlos Williams. MoAB; MoAmPo

Daisy, The. Marya Zaturenska. GrPl; MoAmPo

Daisy, dead and dry, A. (*LL*) For the Candle Light. Angelina Weld Grimké. BlSi; CDC; PoNe

Daisy Fraser. Edgar Lee Masters. *Fr.* Spoon River Anthology. CMoP; HAP; PoE

Daisy's Mistake, The. Frances Sargent Osgood. AmWP

Daisy's Song. Keats. BoNaP

Dakota: Five Times Six. Joseph Hansen. NYBP

Dakota Land. *Unknown.* AS

Dakota: October, 1822, Hunkpapa Warrior. Rod Taylor. WeW

Dakota Wheat-Field, A. Hamlin Garland. OBCA

Dalesman's Litany, The. *Unknown.* OBET

Dall in overalls, A. Something went wrong, they say. (*LL*) Abandoned Farmhouse. Ted Kooser. WeW

Dalliance of the Eagles, The. Walt Whitman. AmPP; FM; HAP; HeIL; HeIP; NAAL-1; NoP; PPP; PrIm; SAmP; TAP; TRP

Dalyaunce. *Unknown.* CH

Dam/ defended by a heavy flak, A. The Moehne Dam. Martin Stokes. PWE

Dam Neck, Virginia. Richard Eberhart. LiTA; MoAB; PoWW

Damages, Two Hundred Pounds. Thackeray. OBSV

Damastes (Also Known As Procrustes) Speaks. Zbigniew Herbert, *tr. fr. Polish by* John Carpenter *and* Bogdana Carpenter. PoSu

Dame, dame! the watch is set. The Witches' Charms. Ben Jonson. *Fr.* Masque of Queens, The. EiL

Dame, get up and bake your pies. *Unknown.* BoTP; OxNR

Dame Jane a sprightly nun and gay. The Penitent Nun. John Lockman. ErPo

Dame Liberty Reports from Travel. Dorothy Cowles Pinkney. GoYe

Dame Music. Stephen Hawes. *Fr.* Pastime of Pleasure, The. PoEL-1

Dame Nature. Spenser. *Fr.* Faerie Queene, The. PoEL-1

Dame, said the Panther, times are mended well. Dryden. *Fr.* Hind and the Panther, The. PoEL-3

Dame Trot and her cat. Mother Goose. BoTP; OxNR; ReMoGo

Dame Wiggins of Lee. *Unknown. Fr.* Dame Wiggins of Lee [and Her Seven Wonderful Cats]. FaBoBe; FaBoNo; OFC; OxBChV

Dame Wiggins of Lee [and Her Seven Wonderful Cats], *sels. Unknown.* "Dame Wiggins of Lee." FaBoBe; FaBoNo; OFC; OxBChV

Damelus' [*or* Damelias'] Song to His Diaphenia. *At. to* Henry Constable *and also to* Henry Chettle. *See* Diaphenia.

Dames of France are fond and free, The. The Girl I Left behind Me. Thomas Osborne Davis. FaBoBe

Damis set this up, to commemorate. Anyte, *tr. fr. Greek by* John Heath-Stubbs *and* Carol A. Whiteside. GrAn

Damit blackman. Domestics. Kattie M. Cumbo. BlSi

Damn it all! all this our South stinks peace. Altaforte. Ezra Pound. CMoP; FaBoTw; ImPo; LiTA; MoAB; MoAmPo; NOBA; SOTW

Damn it, honey, neither one of us. In the Twenty-Fifth Year of Marriage, It Goes On. Alicia Ostriker. PBCAP

Damn that celibate farm, that cracker-box house. Censorship. John Ciardi. NBLV

Damn the Dictatorship. Mila D. Anguilar. WoWa

Damn the snow. Elegy for Thelonious. Yusef Komunyakaa. Jaz

Damn the U.S. – Marcos dictatorship. Damn the Dictatorship. Mila D. Anguilar. WoWa

Damn Yankees, *sels.* Richard Adler *and* Jerry Ross.

Damn you, you dark poisons. Sleep. Georg Trakl, *tr. fr. German by* Joachim Neugroschel. AnAn

Damnation follows death in other men. On Poets. Pope. FaBoEE

Damnation of Vancouver, *sels.* Earle Birney.

Damn'd for thy false apostasy. (*LL*) To My Inconstant Mistress [*or* Mistris]. Thomas Carew. BeJo; EnLoPo; MeLP; NOBE; SeCV-1; TFi; TrGrPo

Damned, The. A. R. Ammons. BAP-90

Damned bird, why have you ruined my sleep. Argentarius, *tr. fr. Greek by* Fleur Adcock. GrAn

Damned his soul to water springs. (*LL*) Epitaph after Reading Ronsard's Lines from Rabelais. J. M. Synge. FaBoEE

Damned in this world, can I be damned again? (*LL*) Out scouting for sound counsels? How to prosper? Ausiàs March. STV

Damned Minoan crevices, that I clog them up! Paranoia in Crete. Gregory Corso. NeAP

Damned Women. Baudelaire, *tr. fr. French by* Roy Campbell. BoLoP

Damocles. Robert Graves. NYBP

Damoetas and Daphnis. Theocritus [*or* Theokritus], *tr. fr. Greek by* Barbara Hughes Fowler. *Fr.* Idylls. HePo

Damon and Celimena. Dryden. *Fr.* Evening's Love, An. InvP

Damon and Cupid. John Gay. EnLoPo

Damon and Phyllis squared. *Unknown.* NoSic

Damon and Pythias. Robert Creeley. LCAP

Damon come drive thy flocks this way. Clorinda and Damon. Andrew Marvell. ESCV; SeCP

Damon forbear, and don't disturb your Muse. The Court. *Unknown.* APAS

Damon the Mower. Andrew Marvell. ESCV; GeHe; JCP; NAEL-1; NOSC; OAEL-1

Damp[e], The. John Donne. NOSC; SeCP

Damsel, The. Omar b. Abi Rabi'a, *tr. fr. Arabic by* W. G. Palgrave. AWP

Damsel came in midnight rain, A. Over, Over. Thomas Love Peacock. *Fr. Maid Marian.* OxAEP-2

Damside. Margaret Atwood. LCAP

Dan Ellis's Boys. *Unknown.* AmFP

Danaë. Barbara Howes. WPE

Danc'd by the streams. *(LL)* Dew Sat on Julia's Hair. Robert Herrick. ELP

Dance, The. *At. to* Thomas Campion. EIL; FaBoCh

Dance, The. Hart Crane. *Fr.* Bridge, The. LiTA; LiTM; MoAB; MoAmPo; NAAL-2; OxBA

Dance, The. Gareth Alban Davies, *tr. fr. Welsh by* Gwyn Jones. OBWVE

Dance, The. Robert Duncan. NeAP

Dance, The. Jim Gustafson. UL

Dance, The. Robert Kelly. *Fr.* Book of Persephone, The. PoM

Dance, The. Irene McKinney. PBCAP

Dance, The. Spenser. *See* It was an hill placed in an open plain.

Dance, The. Mark Strand. LCAP

Dance, The. Maud Sulter. DT

Dance, The. *Unknown.* PAH

Dance, The. *Unknown, tr. fr. French by* John Lydgate. *Fr.* Dance of Death, The. PoEL-1

Dance. Lula Lowe Weeden. CDC

Dance, The. William Carlos Williams. AmPP; CMoP; GoJo; GrPl; HAP; HeIL; HeIP; InPK; LiTM; MeMAP; MoP; NAAL-2; NIP; NoAM; NOBA; NoP; OxBA; PoE; Poetr; PrIm; SAmP; SoSe; TAP; TFi

Dance a baby diddy. Mother Goose. OxNR

Dance and Eye Me (Wicked)ly My Breath a Fixed Sphere. Rochelle Owens. NMM

Dance begins with the sun descending, The. Marrakech. Richard Eberhart. LiTM

Dance Chant, A. *Unknown, tr. fr. Iroquois Indian by* E. S. Parker. WGRP

Dance Chant, A. *Unknown, tr. by* D. G. Brinton. WGRP

Dance, dance in this museum case. Love Song to Eohippus. Peter Viereck. MoAmPo

Dance Figure. Ezra Pound. HeIP; MoAB; MoAmPo

Dance for joy within me. *(LL)* May all things move and be moved in me. *Unknown.* EaPr

Dance for Ma Rainey, A. Al Young. Jaz; NBV

Dance for Militant Dilettantes, A. Al Young. NBV; PoBA

Dance Half Done, The. Mary Ann Larkin. IIP

Dance Hymn. Isaiah Shembe, *tr. fr. Zulu by* B. G. M. Sundkler. WTO

Dance in the township hall is nearly over, The. Country Dance. Judith Wright. *Fr.* Blind Man, The. CBAP

Dance is on the Bridge of Death, The. The Bridge of Death. *Unknown, tr. fr. French by* Andrew Lang. AWP

Dance Lessons of the Thirties. Donald Justice. BAP-89

Dance, little baby, dance up high. Dance, Little Baby. *At. to* Mother Goose. ReMoGo
(Baby's Dance, The.) OxBChV; OxNR

Dance of birds, The. *(LL)* Kopis'taya. Paula Gunn Allen. HATNAP

Dance of blue-bells in the shady places, A. Sweet Surprises. Sarah Doudney. BoTP

Dance of Death, The, *sels.* Robert Browning.

Dance of Death, The, *sels. Unknown, tr. fr. French by* John Lydgate. Dance, The. PoEL-1
"Sir Emperour, lorde of al the ground." OxBLMV

Dance of Despair, The. Hayyim Nahman Bialik, *tr. fr. Hebrew by* A. M. Klein. TrJP

Dance of Dust, The. Louis Untermeyer. BXAP

Dance of Huntsmen, Nymphs, Warriors *and* Lovers. *(LL)* The Secular Masque. Dryden. NAEL-1; PoE; PoEL-3; PrIm; SCGP; SeCV-2

Dance of Love, The. Sir John Davies. *Fr.* Orchestra; or, A Poem[e] of Da[u]ncing. EiL; NoSic, *abr.;* SiPS; SiPSBD

Dance of Saul with the Prophets, The. Saul Tchernichowsky, *tr. fr. Hebrew by* I. M. Lask. TrJP

Dance of the Abakweta. Margaret Danner. PoNe

Dance of the Elephants, The. Michael S. Harper. LCAP

Dance of the Graces, The. Spenser. *Fr.* Faerie Queene, The.

Dance of the Infidels. Al Young. NBV; PoBA

Dance of the Letters. Vince Gotera. OpBo

Dance of the Macabre Mice. Wallace Stevens. CMoP; NOBA; OxBA

Dance of the Rain, The. Eugène Marais, *tr. fr. Afrikaans by* Jack Cope *and* Uys Krige. PeSA

Dance of the Rain Gods. *Unknown, tr. fr. Cora Indian by* Anselm Hollo. STP

Dance of the Sevin Deidly Synnis, The. William Dunbar. *See* Off Februar the fyiftene nycht.

Dance of the sun!, The. *(LL)* All winter long. *Unknown.* EaPr

Dance on Pushback. James Still. GrPl

Dance Poem, *sels.* Michele Murray.
"I am giving you the dark birds of night." MDDM

Dance round their queen./ It's Hallowe'en. *(LL)* Hallowe'en. Harry Behn. FaPON; PDV

Dance Song. *Unknown, tr. fr. Chinese by* Arthur Waley. FaBoCh

Dance-Song of the Lightning. *Unknown, tr. fr. Hottentot.* PeSA

Dance the Boatman. *Unknown.* AiP

Dance there upon the shore. To a Child Dancing in the Wind. W. B. Yeats. IIP

Dance, Thumbkin, dance. Mother Goose. OxNR; ReMoGo

Dance to thee daddy, my little lamb. *(LL)* Dance to your [*or* thee] daddy. Mother Goose. FaBoVe; OBET; OxNR, 2 *vers.;* ReMoGo

Dance to your [*or* thee] daddy. Mother Goose. FaBoVe; OBET; OxNR, 2 *vers.;* ReMoGo

Dance with Banderillas. Richard Duerden. NeAP

Dance with you, my sweet brown Harlem girl. *(LL)* Juke Box Love Song. Langston Hughes. GrPl; PoBA; SAmP; TTTS

Dancehall, The. Matthew Sweeney. IB

Dancer, The. Joseph Campbell. OBMV

Dancer, The. Sadi, *tr. fr. Persian by* Sir Edwin Arnold. *Fr.* Bustan, The. AWP

Dancer. Roy Scheele. GOYP

Dancer, The. W. J. Turner. NOBAu; OBMV

Dancer, The. Edmund Waller. CBLP; TrGrPo

Dancer, The. Al Young. PoBA

Dancer!/ A one-headed drum. A Poet to a Dancer. Auvaiyar, *tr. fr. Tamil by* A. K. Ramanujan. PLW

Dancer from the Dance, The. Suzanne Juhasz. IHMS

Dancers at the Moy. Paul Muldoon. BIrV

Dancers Exercising. Amy Clampitt. NoAM

Dancers Inherit the Party, The. Ian Hamilton Finlay. FF

Dancer's Life, A. Donald Justice. LCAP

Dancers of Colbek, The. Robert Mannyng. *Fr.* Handling Sin. PoE

Dancers with cane whistles. Memory. Elizabeth Cook-Lynn. *Fr.* Journey. HATNAP

Dances like Italy, imagining red. *(LL)* Walt Whitman at Bear Mountain. Louis Simpson. CAPP; LiTM; TRP

Dances of Death, *sels.* Alexander Blok, *tr. fr. Russian by* Jon Stallworthy *and* Peter France.
"Night, street, a lamp, a chemist's window." OBVE

Dancing, The. Gerald Stern. LCAP

Dancing. Yang Kuei-fei, *tr. fr. Chinese by* Florence Ayscough *and* Amy Lowell. FaPON

Dancing at Whitsun. Austin John Marshall. OBET

Dancing Bear, The. Rachel Field. NTCP

Dancing Bear, The. Albert Bigelow Paine. OBCA

Dancing Bear, The. Robert Southey. FM

Dancing Cabman, The. J. B. Morton. MoShBr; NOBL

Dancing Dog, The. Florence Weinberger. BTR

Dancing-Girl's Song. Kshetrayya, *tr. fr. Telugu by* Tambimuttu *and* R. Appalaswamy. BoWoP

Dancing in the Dark. Lillie D. Chaffin. ETG

Dancing on the Shore. M. M. Hutchinson. BoTP

Dancing School. Jonathan Holden. Poetsp

Dancing Sea, The. Sir John Davies. *Fr.* Orchestra; or, A Poem[e] of Da[u]ncing. ChTr; NoSic, *abr.;* SiPS; SiPSBD

Dancing Songs. *Unknown.* PBCV
Sels.
"Hipsaw! my deaa! you no do like a-me!"
"Tajo, tajo, tajo! tajo, my mackey massa!"

Dancing the Shout to the True Gospel; or, The Song Movement Sisters Don't Want Me to Sing. Rita Mae Brown. CrSp; NMM; PeHV

Dancing to Ellington. Jan Selving. Jaz

Dancing with God. Stephen P. Dunn. NIP

Dancing with Poets. Ellen Bryant Voigt. CrSp

Dancing with the Dog. Susan Kennedy. NGP

Danda with a Dead Fish. Deborah Randall. PWE

Dandelion. Hilda Conkling. FaPON; PDV

Dandelion Greens. Jane Flanders. CrSp

Dandelion Puff, The. Mary K. Robinson. BoTP

Dandelion stares, The. The Little Dandelion. Lula Lowe Weeden. CDC

Dandelions. Gerda Mayer. Spl

Dandelions. Craig Raine. NoAM

Dandelions. Will D. Stanton. SoSe

Dandelions, The. *Unknown.* BoTP

Dandelions for Chains ("Dandelions meet me wherever I am.") Sarah Kirsch, *tr. fr. German by* Michael Hamburger. WPOW

Dandelions purr in their sleep. Of Dandelions & Tourists. Joe Rosenblatt. NOBC

Dandelions, wrecked on their stems, The. Late Dandelions. Ben Belitt. NYBP

Dandering home from work at mid. Christ Goodbye. Padraic Fiacc. IHNG

Dandy Horse, The. *Unknown.* OBET

Dandy O, The. *Unknown.* CoMu

Dane-Geld. Kipling. FaBoEH; OxBTC

Danebury. *Unknown.* PeHV

Danger. Helen Hunt Jackson. AmWP

Danger of Loss, The. Robert Bly. LPA

Dangerous Dreams. Stephen Knight. UnDi

Dangerous dreams can harm those who sleep with me. Dangerous Dreams. Stephen Knight. UnDi

Dangers. Robin Becker. ETG

Dangers of Sexual Excess, The. John Armstrong. *Fr.* Art of Preserving Health, The. FaBoUs

Daniel. Vachel Lindsay. ChTr

Daniel and Abigail. Miguel de Barrios, *tr. fr. Spanish.* TrJP

Daniel at Breakfast. Phyllis McGinley. OBSV; OxBM

Daniel Boone. Stephen Vincent Benét. GOA

Daniel Boone. Arthur Guiterman. FaPON; MoShBr

Daniel in the lion's den. Nebuchadnezzar's Kingdom-Come. David Rowbotham. ChIV-1; NOBAu

Daniel Jazz, The. Vachel Lindsay. *See* Darius the Mede was a king and a wonder.

Daniel Webster. Oliver Wendell Holmes. PAH

Daniel Webster's Horses. Elizabeth J. Coatsworth. MoAmPo; OBCA

Danish Cradle Song, A. *Unknown.* BoTP

Danish Wit. John Hollander. NBLV

Dank, limber verses, stuft with lakeside sedges. Some of Wordsworth. Walter Savage Landor. ChTr

Dannie Abse, Douglas Dunn. On Consulting "Contemporary Poets of the English Language." Anthony Thwaite. PeLV

Danny. Malcolm Cowley. PoA

Danny. J. M. Synge. PeVV

Danny Deever. Kipling. CoGr; EBEvV; EBVV; FaBoBa; FaPoR; GTBS-P; InPS; LiTB; MoBrPo; NAEL-2; NoAM; NOBE; NOBVV; OHCV; OxBoLi; OxBTC; PeVV; PlP; PoLF; SCGP; SCV; TEP; TFi; TrGrPo; UnPo

Danny Murphy. James Stephens. BoTP

Dans l'Allée. Paul Verlaine, *tr. fr. French by* Arthur Symons. AWP

Dan's Shoe Repair: 1959. Christine Lahey. BTR

Danse Russe. William Carlos Williams. CMoP; PPP

Dante, *sels.* Robert Duncan.
"I know a little language of my cat, tho Dante says." PoM

Dante. Michelangelo, *tr. fr. Italian by* Longfellow. AWP

Dante. H. Cordelia Ray. CBWP-3

Dante, a sigh that rose from the heart's core. To Dante Alighieri: He Reports, in a Feigned Vision, the Successful Issue of Lapo Gianni's Love. Cavalcanti, *tr. fr. Italian by* Dante Gabriel Rossetti. AWP

Dante Alighieri, a dark oracle. Inscription for a Portrait of Dante. Boccaccio, *tr. fr. Italian by* Dante Gabriel Rossetti. *Fr.* Sonnets. AWP

Dante Alighieri, Cecco, your good friend. Sonnet: To Dante Alighieri on the Last Sonnet of the Vita Nuova. Cecco Angiolieri, da Siena, *tr. fr. Italian by* Dante Gabriel Rossetti. AWP

Dante Alighieri, if I jest and lie. Sonnet: To Dante Alighieri (He Writes to Dante, Then in Exile at Verona, Defying Him as No Better Than Himself). Cecco Angiolieri, da Siena, *tr. fr. Italian by* Dante Gabriel Rossetti. AWP

Dante Alighieri in Becchina's praise. Sonnet: He Rails against Dante, Who Had Censured His Homage to Becchina. Cecco Angiolieri, da Siena, *tr. fr. Italian by* Dante Gabriel Rossetti. AWP

Dante Études, *sels.* Robert Duncan.
Work, The. CAPP

Dante Gabriel Rossetti. D. G. Rossetti. Dorothy Parker. *Fr.* Pig's-Eye View of Literature, A. NALW

Dante, if thou within the sphere of Love. To Dante in Paradise, after Fiammetta's Death. Boccaccio, *tr. fr. Italian by* Dante Gabriel Rossetti. *Fr.* Sonnets. AWP

Dante, whenever this thing happeneth. To Dante Alighieri: He Conceives of Some Compensation in Death. Cino da Pistoia, *tr. fr. Italian by* Dante Gabriel Rossetti. AWP

Danton is waiting to die. Dead Leaves. Aleksandar Ristovic, *tr. fr. Serbo-Croatian by* Charles Simic. HSix

Danube to the Severn gave, The. Tennyson. *Fr.* In Memoriam A. H. H. EBVV, *abr.*; EBVVPR; EnVR; FF; GTBS-P; NoP; OAEL-2, *abr.*; PeECV, *abr.*
(Hushing of the Wye, The.) FaBoPP

Daphnaïda, *sels.* Spenser.
"She fell away in her first ages spring." OBEV

Daphne. Thomas Samuel Jones, Jr. OHIP

Daphne. John Lyly. *See* My Daphne's hair is twisted gold.

Daphne. Selden Rodman. PoNe

Daphne. Swift. NOBL

Daphne and Apollo. Ovid, *tr. by* Matthew Prior. *Fr.* Metamorphoses. NOEC

Daphne knows, with equal ease. Daphne. Swift. NOBL

Daphne Morse. Pamela Gillilan. PWE

Daphne Stillorgan. Denis Devlin. CIP

Daphnis the fair-skinned, who plays country songs. Theocritus [*or* Theokritus], *tr. fr. Greek by* Anthony Holden. GrAn

Daphnis to Ganymede. Richard Barnfield. *Fr.* Affectionate Shepherd, The. EIL

Dapple-gray. Mother Goose. *See* I had a little pony.

Dappled sky, a world of meadows, A. Jean Ingelow. *Fr.* Divided. OBNC

Darby and Joan were dressed in black. *Unknown.* OxNR

Dardanelles 1916. Padraic Fallon. CIP

Dare a mighty *row* in Zion an' de *debbil's gittin' high.* Linin' ub De Hymns, De. Daniel Webster Davis. AAP

Dare I in such momentous points advise. Soame Jenyns. *Fr.* Art of Dancing, The. ECEV; FaBoUs

Dare to Do Right. George Lansing Taylor. PWR

Dare we despair? Through all the nights and days. He Leads Us Still. Arthur Guiterman. OHIP

Dare you see a Soul at the White Heat? Emily Dickinson. NALW

Daredevil. Kirby Congdon. PeHV

Dareios. C. P. Cavafy, *tr. fr. Greek by* Edmund Keeley *and* Philip Sherrard. AnAn

Dares trust such power with so much piety. (*LL*) To the King, on His Navy. Edmund Waller. BeJo

Darest Thou Now O Soul. Walt Whitman. TrGrPo; WGRP

Darien. Sir Edwin Arnold. PAH

Daring. Carol Konek. IHMS

Daring young lady of Guam, A. *Unknown.* PeLi

Darius Green and His Flying-Machine. John Townsend Trowbridge. AnAmPo; BeLS; BLPL; FaBoBe; MoShBr; OBAL; OBCA; OxBChV; PoLF

Darius the Mede was a king and a wonder. Daniel. Vachel Lindsay. ChTr
(Daniel Jazz, The.) TrGrPo

Dark, The. Myra Cohn Livingston. TLR

Dark, The. Richard Poole. AngWe

Dark accurate plunger down the successive knell. The Subway. Allen Tate. NOBA

Dark Actress — Somewhere, A. Blanche Taylor Dickinson. ShDr

Dark an' stormy may come de wedder. Slave Marriage Ceremony Supplement. *Unknown.* BPo; TAP

Dark and dim, the Bamboo Grove Monastery. Saying Goodby to the Monk Ling-ch'e. Liu Ch'ang-ch'ing, *tr. fr. Chinese by* Dell R. Hales. SuSp

Dark and Falling Summer, The. Delmore Schwartz. ImGa; NYBP

Dark Angel, The. Lionel Johnson. CoGr; GTBS-P; LiTB; MoBrPo; NOBE; NOBVV; OAEL-2; OBMV; OxAEP-2

Dark angel who art clear and straight. Serenade: Any Man to Any Woman. Edith Sitwell. NALW

Dark Angel, with thine aching lust. The Dark Angel. Lionel Johnson. CoGr; GTBS-P; LiTB; MoBrPo; NOBE; NOBVV; OAEL-2; OBMV; OxAEP-2

Dark as a cow. It's a downpour. Jazz Impressions in the Garden. C. D. Wright. Jaz

Dark As a Dungeon. Merle Travis. SWP

Dark as the clouds of even. The Black Regiment. George Henry Boker. AnAmPo; GN; PAH

Dark as the night's rough husk. (*LL*) When My Desire. Ono no Komachi. VBLP

Dark as the spring river, the earth. Farm Wife. Ellen Bryant Voigt. MT

Dark as wells, his eyes. Long Person. Gladys Cardiff. CDW

Dark whispers. Night Gives Old Woman the Word. Gail Tremblay. HATNAP

Dark wind blows in the forest, crows and magpies mourn. Ballad of a Ferocious Tiger. Kao Ch'i, *tr. fr. Chinese by* Irving Y. Lo. SuSp

Dark wine rolled spattering the ground. *(LL)* The Two of Them. Hugo von Hofmannsthal. STV

Dark Wings. James Stephens. PoA

Dark Wood, The. Dante, *tr. fr. Italian by* Seamus Heaney. *Fr. Divina Commedia.* BiHa; MeMAP; NAWM-1, *tr. by* John Ciardi

Darkened bedroom, the double bed, The. Driving Wheel. Sherley Anne Williams. BlSi

Darkened farmhouse is asleep, The. Saving the Harvest. Geoffrey Lehmann. CBAP

Darkened in the Soul. Napa, *tr. fr. Eskimo.* WTO

Darkened Windows. Ronald Bottrall. PoA

Darkening Garden, The. *Unknown.* BoTP

Darkening Hotel Room. Alfred Corn. VCAP

Darkening the azure roof of Nero's world. Domine Quo Vadis? Sir William Watson. WGRP

Darkening was like riches in the room, The. Rainer Maria Rilke. *See* Darkness was a richness in the room, The.

Darker by far than any coalpit stone. *(LL)* Infinity, when all things it beheld. Edward Taylor. AmPP; EAP; HAP; MeMAP; NAAL-1; NOBA; OxBA; SCAP

Darker by far than any coalpit stone. *(LL)* The Preface. Edward Taylor. NOSC

Darker darkness, A/ over the river. *(LL)* When Howitzers Began. Hayden Carruth. Poetsp

Darkling Chicken, The. Robert Peters. BXAP

Darkling I listen; and for many a time. Keats. *Fr.* Ode to a Nightingale. AWP; BLRP; ClHu; EBEV; EnRP; FaBoBe; FaPoB; GTBS; GTBS-P; HAP; HeIP; ImPo; InPS; LiTB; NAEL-2; NAWM-2; NOBE; NoP; OAEL-2; OBD; OBEV; OBNC; OPOP; PoE; PoEL-4; PoRA; PPP; PrIm; RB; SCGP; SoSe; TEP; TFi; TOF; TrGrPo; UnPo

Darkling Thrush, The. Thomas Hardy. ClHu; CMoP; EBVV; GGP; HAP; ImPo; InPS; LiTB; LiTM; MeMBP; MoAB; MoBrPo; MoP; NAEL-2; NIP; NoAM; NOBE; NOBVV; NoP; OAEL-2; OBEV; OBNC; OHCV; PoE; Poetr; PPP; RB; SoSe; TEP; TFi; TOF; TrGrPo; UnPo

Darkmotherscream. Andrei Voznesensky, *tr. fr. Russian by* Robert Bly *and* Vera Dunham. NU; RaBo

Darkness. Byron. EnRP; LiTB; MeMBP; NAEL-2; OAEL-2; OPOP; PoE; PoEL-4; TEP

Darkness. Joseph Campbell. BIrV

Darkness. Arthur Hugh Clough. OxBSP

Darkness. Desanka Maksimovic, *tr. fr. Serbo-Croatian by* Charles Simic. HSix

Darkness/ above all things/ the Sun/ makes/ rise. A Prayer to the Sun. Geoffrey Hill. PRA

Darkness and silence, the two eyes that see God. Great staring eyes. *(LL)* Black-out. Robinson Jeffers. LiTA; LiTM

Darkness and stars i' the mid-day! they invite. A Rhapsody. Henry Vaughan. BeJo; NAEL-1

Darkness begins a/ retreat. After Christmas. Michael Richards. OBCP

Darkness comes out of the earth. Twilight. D. H. Lawrence. OBMV

Darkness crumbles away, The. Break of Day in the Trenches. Isaac Rosenberg. FaBoMo; GTBS-P; MoBrPo; NAEL-2; NoAM; NOBE; NoP; NSI; OAEL-2; OBWP; OxAEP-2; PAW; PeFWW; PoA; PoWW; TFi

Darkness falls from some air inside a slow. Like an Aerolith. Peter Philpott. VaA

Darkness falls like a wet sponge. The Picture of Little J.A. in a Prospect of Flowers. John Ashbery. CAPP; PPP

Darkness has called to darkness, and disgrace. As a Plane Tree by the Water. Robert Lowell. CMoP; CoAP; LiTM; MoAB; MoAmPo; NOBA; OxBA; TrGrPo

Darkness has dawned in the east. Shelley. *Fr.* Hellas. EnRP

Darkness has feathered all night. Dawn Feeding. Leslie Ullman. NAmP90

Darkness I desire is full of you, The. *(LL)* Unborn. John Le Gay Brereton. NOBAu

Darkness in the room was like enormous riches, The. Rainer Maria Rilke. *See* Darkness was a richness in the room, The.

Darkness is closing around us, The. In Orbit. Henry Taylor. BXAP

Darkness is falling through darkness. The Hermit. Robert Bly. CAPP

Darkness is not dark, nor sunlight the light of the sun. Foal. Vernon Watkins. AngWe; OxBTC

Darkness lifts, imagine, in your lifetime, The. The Undertaking. Louise Glück. FaBoWP

Darkness like a guillotine, The. Nightfall on Sedgemoor. Andrew Young. FaBoPP

Darkness Music. Muriel Rukeyser. BoWoP

Darkness presses all around, The. Government! Tuta Nihoniho, *tr. fr. Maori by* A. Armstrong. WTO

Darkness reigned. Sacrifice. Nana Issaia, *tr. fr. Modern Greek by* Helle Tzalopoulou Barnstone. BoWoP

Darkness still shadows the mountain road. I Spend the Night in a Room by the River. Tu Fu, *tr. fr. Chinese by* Mark Perlberg. SuSp

Darkness, sunlight and a little holy spit. Potato Song. Stanley Moss. NGP

Darkness that man must dread at last. *(LL)* Tenebrae. Austin Clarke. BIrV; CIP; IPY; NOIV

Darkness: the rain sluiced down; the mire was deep. The Redeemer. Siegfried Sassoon. WGRP

Darkness was a richness in the room, The. From a Childhood. Rainer Maria Rilke, *tr. fr. German by* C. F. MacIntyre. TrJP
(Darkening was like riches in the room, The.) TTTS, *tr. by* M. D. Herter Norton
(Darkness in the room was like enormous riches, The.) RaBo, *tr. by* Robert Bly

Darkness was born in the forest. I found it there. Darkness. Desanka Maksimovic, *tr. fr. Serbo-Croatian by* Charles Simic. HSix

Darkness wears off, and, dawning into light. The Figures on the Frieze. Alastair Reid. ErPo; NYBP

Darky Sunday School. *Unknown.* OxBoLi

Darling! Because My Blood Can Sing. E. E. Cummings. InvP; OxBA

Darling Cory. *Unknown.* AmFP

Darling, each morning a bloodred rose. Corinna in Vendome. Pierre de Ronsard, *tr. fr. French by* Robert Mezey. BoLoP; ErPo

"Darling," he said, "I never meant." Forgetfulness! Josephine D. Henderson Heard. CBWP-4

Darling Henriette, if fate were symmetrical. Casanova on His Deathbed. Philip Casey. BiHa

Darling, how long before this breath will cease? Evanishings. Mary E. Tucker. CBWP-1

Darling I steal, and with hushed footsteps slow. Midnight at Baiae; a Dream Fragment of Imperial Rome. John Addington Symonds. PeHV

Darling, I won't be your hot love. Sulpicia, *tr. fr. Latin by* Aliki *and* Willis Barnstone. BoWoP

Darling, If You Only Knew. Edward Newman Horn. ErPo

Darling of God and Men. Lucretius. *See* Great Venus, Queene [*or* Queen] of Beautie [*or* Beauty] and of grace.

Darling of the world is come, The. Robert Herrick. *Fr.* Christmas Caroll Sung to the King in the Presence at White-Hall, A. GoJo; PChr, *st.* 1

Darling, on the moving stairs. And No Regrets. Lex Banning. NOBAu

Darling Shell, where hast thou been. Walter Savage Landor. CBLP

Darling, the plates have been cleared away. Beauty and the Beast. Rita Dove. NoAM

Darling, you only, there is no duplicate. *Unknown, tr. fr. Egyptian into Italian by* Boris de Rachewiltz; *tr. into English by* Ezra Pound. *Fr.* Conversations in Courtship. CTC

Darned Mounseer, The. W. S. Gilbert. *Fr.* Ruddigore. NOBL

Dar's a skool in West Virginny. To Professor Byrd Prillerman. Maggie Pogue Johnson. CBWP-4

Dar's plenty t'ings to write erbout. Dat Mule ob Brudder Wright's. Maggie Pogue Johnson. CBWP-4

Dart, The. "Eliza." KTR

Dart, The. *Unknown.* GBP

Dart, here's a man. The River Dart. *Unknown.* GBP

Dart of Izdabel prevails! 'twas dipt, The. The Dying Indian. Joseph Warton. NOEC; OxAEP-1

Dartmoor: Sunset at Chagford. Thomas Edward Brown. NOBVV

Darwin Descending. Russell Edson. LCAP

Darwin in 1881. Gjertrud Schnackenberg. NoAM; SM

Darwin on Species. *Unknown.* FaBoUs

Darwinism in the Kitchen. *Unknown.* FiBHP; NBLV

Das Kapital. Amiri Baraka. PoM

Das Liebesleben. Thom Gunn. ErPo

Dash back that ocean with a pier. Tennyson. *Fr.* Mechanophilus. FaBoCo

Dash for the Colors, The. Frederick G. Webb. BeLS

Dash him to dust, and let the world repose. *(LL)* Advice to a Raven in Russia [December, 1812]. Joel Barlow. AmPP; NAAL-1; NOBA; OBWP; OxBA

Dasius, chucker-out/ at the Turkish Baths. Martial, *tr. fr. Latin by* Peter Porter. OBVE

Dat Mule ob Brudder Wright's. Maggie Pogue Johnson. CBWP-4

Dat Sunshine Special comin' around de bend. C. C. Rider. *Unknown.* AS

Data, data, data. Transfigured Night. Ralph Gustafson. MoCV

Data in the glass jar: some ten scorpions, The. In the Laboratory. Dan Pagis, *tr. fr. Hebrew by* Robert Friend. PoSu

Date with Robbe-Grillet, A. Elaine Equi. PeVV; UTF

Dated Valmont 10 — 16. Eugene Delacroix Says. Edward Dorn. BCF

Dates. *Unknown, tr. fr. Arabic* by E. Powys Mathers. *Fr.* Thousand and One Nights, The. AWP; FaPON

Dates on bridges, The. History and Abstraction. Thomas Lux. AmPA

Datur Hora Quieti. Sir Walter Scott. GTBS; GTBS-P

Dauber, *sels.* John Masefield.
"All through the windless night the clipper rolled." CMoP
Rounding the Horn. MoAB; MoBrPo

Daufuskie. Mari Evans. BlSi

Daughter. Mary Dorcey. AIW

Daughter. Ellen Bryant Voigt. MT

Daughter, how the door is creaking. Evening Prayer. Arthur Fitger, *tr. fr. German* by Jethro Bithell. AWP

Daughter-my-mother. The Blessing. Carolyn Kizer. CAPP; MDDM; MeEL; Poetr

Daughter of Admetus, A. T. Sturge Moore. FaBoTw

Daughter of Debate, The. Elizabeth I, Queen of England. *See* Doubt of future foes exiles my present joy, The.

Daughter of earth and child of the wave be appeased. William Everson. *Fr.* Tendril in the Mesh. NoAM

Daughter of Jairus, The. Marina Tsvetayeva, *tr. fr. Russian* by Paul Schmidt. BoWoP
Sels.
"And now the riverbank. For the last time."
"And now the riverbank. I cling."
"I catch the movement of his lips." VBLP
"Our last bridge."
"Past factory workshops, empty."
"Rain. A heavy mane."
"To lose it all at once."

Daughter of Jove, relentless power. Hymn to Adversity. Thomas Gray. EnRP; GTBS; GTBS-P

Daughter of Night, chaotic Queen! Ode to the German Drama. *Unknown.* NOEC

Daughter of the Regiment, The. Clinton Scollard. PAH

Daughter of th'Italian heaven! Corinne at the Capitol. Felicia Dorothea Hemans. BrRo

Daughter, take this amulet. Mwana Kupona Msham, *tr. fr. Swahili* by J. W. T. Allen. *Fr.* Poem to Her Daughter. AIW, *ad.* by Deirdre Lashgari; WPOW, *ad.* by Deirdre Lashgari

Daughter to that good Earl, once President. To the Lady Margaret Ley. Milton. GTBS; GTBS-P; OBEV

Daughters. Astra. BrRo

Daughter's Difficulties as a Wife, A: Mrs. Reuben Chandler to Her Mother in New Orleans. Anne Stevenson. OxBM

Daughter's House, A. Norma Hope Richman. GOYP

Daughters, in the wind's boisterous roughing. Vernal Equinox. Ruth Stone. MoAmPo

Daughters of Beulah! Muses who inspire the Poets Song. Blake. *Fr.* Milton. PeECV

Daughters of Blum, The. Charles Wright. CoAP; SM

Daughters of Jove, whose voice is melody. Hymn to Selene. *Unknown, tr. fr. Greek* by Shelley. *Fr.* Homeric Hymns. AWP

Daughters of Time, the hypocritic Days. Days. Emerson. AmPP; AnAmPo; HAP; HeIL; HeIP; LiTA; MeMAP; NAAL-1; NOBA; NoP; OxBA; OxBSP; PoE; PoEL-4; TAP; TFi; TrGrPo

Daughters of War. Isaac Rosenberg. PeFWW

Daughter's Rebellion, The. Francis Hopkinson. PAH

Dauncing (bright Lady) then began to bee. Sir John Davies. *Fr.* Orchestra; or, A Poem[e] of Da[u]ncing. NoSic, *abr.*; PoEL-2; SiPS; SiPSBD (Praise of Dancing, The.) NOBE

D'Avalos' Prayer. John Masefield. TrPWD

Dave Dirt's dog is a horrible hound. Heads or Tails? Kit Wright. OTCP

Daventry Wonder, The. "Agricola." NOEC

David. Earle Birney. NOBC

David. Linda Pastan. CRP

David. Charles Reznikoff. ChIV-1

David and Bathsheba in the Public Garden. Robert Lowell. ChIV-1

David and [Fair] Bethsabe, *sels.* George Peele.
"And now the riverbank. For the last time."
"And now the riverbank. I cling."
Bethsabe's Song. ChIV-1; EnRePo; GBL; NOBE; NoP; NoSic; OxBoLi; OxBSP; PoEL-2; RB; TEP
(Bathsabe's Song.) ImPo
(Bathsheba Bathing.) ElL; TrGrPo

David and Goliath. Nathaniel Crouch. OxBChV

David and Goliath, *sels.* Michael Drayton.
"Our sacred Muse, of Israel's Singer sings." ChIV-1

David and Goliath. Priscilla Jane Thompson. CBWP-2

David and Goliath. P. Hately Waddell. ChIV-1

David and his three captains bold. David in the Cave of Adullam. Charles Lamb. ChIV-1

David and I that summer cut trails on the Survey. David. Earle Birney. NOBC

David and Jonathan. Abraham Cowley. *Fr.* Davideis. PeHV

David Drummond's destinie. The Coble o Cargill. *Unknown.* ESPB

David Garrick. Goldsmith. *Fr.* Retaliation. IHNG; NOEC; OxBoLi

David Guest. Martin Bell. OBF

David Hume ate a swinging great dinner. On the Author of the *Treatise of Human Nature.* James Hay Beattie. FaBoCo

David in the Cave of Adullam. Charles Lamb. ChIV-1

David Lowston. *Unknown.* PeNZ

David sang to his hooknosed harp. King David. Stephen Vincent Benét. ChIV-1

David the king was grieved and moved. David's Lamentation. William Billings. AmFP

David, we must have looked comic, sitting. Elegy for David Beynon. Leslie Norris. AngWe

Davideis, *sels.* Abraham Cowley.
David and Jonathan. PeHV
Gabriel's Appearance. NOSC
"Michal her modest flames sought to conceal." ChIV-1
Music and Poetry. EPCY
Power of Numbers, The.
(Number, Weight, and Measure.) NOSC
"So covetous Ballaam with fond intent." ChIV-1
Supplication, A. GTBS, III; GTBS-P, III
(Music.) OxAEP-1
"With sober pace an heav'enly Maid walks in." SeCV-1

David's Epitaph on Jonathan. Francis Quarles. ChIV-1

David's Lament. Bible, *O.T. See* Beauty of Israel is slain [*or* slaine] upon thy high places, The.

David's Lament for Jonathan. Peter Abelard, *tr. fr. Latin* by Helen Waddell. NAWM-1; PeHV

David's Lament for Saul and Jonathan. Bible, *O.T. See* Beauty of Israel is slain [*or* slaine] upon thy high places, The.

David's Lament over Saul. Bible, *O.T. See* Beauty of Israel is slain [*or* slaine] upon thy high places, The.

David's Lamentation. William Billings. AmFP

David's Peccavi. Robert Southwell. ChIV-1

Davis Matlock. Edgar Lee Masters. *Fr.* Spoon River Anthology. LiTA; LiTM

Davus, I detest. Horace. *See* Boy, I have their empty shouts.

Davy and the Goblin, *sels.* Charles Edward Carryl.
Robinson Crusoe
(Robinson Crusoe's Story.) BeLS; FiBHP; PoRA
Walloping Window-Blind, The. NBLV; OBCA
(Nautical Ballad, A.) FaPON; OBAL
(Oh, a capital ship for an ocean trip.) MoShBr

Davy Crockett. *Unknown.* FaBoVe

Davy Davy Dumpling. *Unknown.* OxNR

Dawlish Fair. Keats. NTP; PeLV

Dawn. Gordon Bottomley. BoTP; MoBrPo

Dawn. Jeni Couzyn. NBrP

Dawn. Day Jeffery. NSI

Dawn. Paul Laurence Dunbar. AnAmPo; PoLF; PoNe

Dawn. John Ford. *Fr.* Lover's Melancholy, The. OBEV, V, i

Dawn. Federico García Lorca, *tr. fr. Spanish* by William B. Logan. SOTW

Dawn. Angelina Weld Grimké. ShDr

Dawn. Joseph Kumbirai, *tr. fr. Shona* by Douglas Livingstone. PeSAV

Dawn. *Malay Oral Tradition, tr.* by R. J. Wilkinson. WTO

Dawn, *sels.* Harold Monro.
God. WGRP

Dawn. Eileen Myles. UL

Dawn. Rachel, *tr. fr. Hebrew* by A. M. Klein. TrJP

Dawn. Rimbaud, *tr.* by Enid Rhodes Peschal. *Fr.* Illuminations. SOTW; TTTS

Dawn. Rimbaud, *tr. fr. French* by Enid Rhodes Peschal. *Fr.* Season in Hell, A. TTTS

Dawn. Paul Armand Silvestre, *tr. fr. French* by Philip L. Miller. RiWo

Dawn. Edith Södergran, *tr. fr. Swedish* by Daisy Aldan *with* Leif Sjöberg

Dawn. Lucien Stryk. CAPP

Dawn, The. Tennyson. NAEL-2

Dawn, The. *Unknown.* PoToHe

Dawn. Ella Wheeler Wilcox. PWR

Dawn. William Carlos Williams. MoAB; MoAmPo

Dawn, The. W. B. Yeats. PFP

Dawn: a good wind blows from the sea. Semantic. Robert Conquest. TEP

Dawn after dawn after dawn/ then suddenly the Dark One. Ammianus, tr. fr. Greek by Tony Harrison. GrAn

Dawn after dawn comes on the wine. Ammianus, tr. fr. Greek by Kenneth Rexroth. PGA

Dawn: and foot on the cold stair treading. Aubade for Hope. Robert Penn Warren. MoAmPo

Dawn and night of fighting, lovers like actual wars. Sonnet: Kamikaze. Bernadette Mayer. UL

Dawn; and the jew's-harp's sawing seesaw song. Pilots, Man Your Planes. Randall Jarrell. MoAB; MoAmPo

Dawn at Chiao Mountain, Seeing Off K'un-lun on His Way Back to Ching-k'ou. Wang Shih-chieng, tr. fr. Chinese by Richard John Lynn. SuSp

Dawn. Birds sing in the courtyard. Spring Morning. Ch'en Yu Yi, tr. fr. Chinese by Kenneth Rexroth. OHMPC

Dawn Boy's Song. Unknown, tr. fr. Navajo Indian by Washington Matthews. FaBV

Dawn breaking as I woke. Alba. Derek Walcott. GoJo

Dawn Chill, The. Irina Ratushinskaya, tr. fr. Russian by Alan Myers. PWE

Dawn chill at the year's declension, The. The Dawn Chill. Irina Ratushinskaya, tr. fr. Russian by Alan Myers. PWE

Dawn Chorus. Mary Holtby. UV

Dawn cried out: the brutal voice of a bird. In All These Acts. William Everson. NoP

Dawn drizzle [or Dawndrizzle] ended dampness steams from. Anglo Saxon Street. Earle Birney. HeIP; NOBC

Dawn Feeding. Leslie Ullman. NAmP90

Dawn. First light tearing. Clouds. Philip Levine. LCAP

Dawn Has Yet to Ripple In. Melville Cane. MoAmPo

Dawn Hippo. Sydney Clouts. PeSA

Dawn Horse, A. William Harmon. FYAP

Dawn in a tree of birds, A. Kenneth Rexroth. InPK

Dawn in Britain, The, sels. Charles Montague Doughty.
    Bladyn's Song of Cloten. PoEL-5
    Gauls Sacrifice, The. FaBoTw
    Hymn to the Sun. FaBoTw
    Roman Officer Writes, A. FaBoTw

Dawn in January. Lance Henson. CDW

Dawn in my mind. Chicgo Scene (1952, 1969). Martin Robbins. BTR

Dawn in New York comes. Dawn. Federico García Lorca, tr. fr. Spanish by William B. Logan. SOTW

Dawn in Stone City. Li Ho, tr. fr. Chinese by A. C. Graham. PLT

Dawn in the Heart of Africa. Patrice Emery Lumumba. PBA; TTY

Dawn in the Valley. Fily-Dabo Sissoko, tr. fr. French by Ellen Conroy Kennedy. NegPo

Dawn is grey here, she went on to tell him. It was not always like this, The. Henri Michaux, tr. fr. French by Richard Ellmann. Fr. I Am Writing to You from a Far-Off Country. . AnRep

Dawn is, in essence, sinister as fire. Dew. Jennifer Maiden. CBAP

Dawn is smiling on the dew that covers, The. The Genesis of Butterflies. Victor Hugo, tr. fr. French by Andrew Lang. AWP

Dawn lightly laid her rosy hand. (LL) A Ballad of a Nun. John Davidson. BeLS; MeMBP; MoBrPo; UV, sh. vers.

Dawn near an Old Battlefield, in a Time of Peace. James Wright. AnAn

Dawn of a pleasant morning in May. Lee to the Rear. John Randolph Thompson. PAH

Dawn of Day. William Browne. Fr. Shepherd's Pipe, The. ElL

Dawn of Day, The. Keaulumoku, tr. fr. Hawaiian by M. W. Beckwith. Fr. Kumulipo, The; a Creation Chant. WTO

Dawn of Love, The. H. Cordelia Ray. BlSi; CBWP-3

Dawn of the Space Age. John Ciardi. OBAL

Dawn off the Foreland — the young flood making. Mine Sweepers 1914-18. Kipling. CoGr

Dawn on the drab North Sea! North Sea. Day Jeffery. NSI; PoWW

Dawn on the East Coast. Alun Lewis. OBWP

Dawn Patrol, The. Paul Bewsher. NSI

Dawn peered through the pines as we dashed at the ford. Riding with Kilpatrick. Clinton Scollard. PAH

Dawn Raid on an Orchard. Tom Pickard. NBrP

Dawn/ rose like a nail at the edge of dark. Crazy Horse: The Last Morning. Lance Henson. VoR

Dawn Separates the Light from the Shadow, The. Gabriele D'Annunzio, tr. fr. Italian by Philip L. Miller. RiWo

Dawn shakes the candle, shoots a flame. May It Be. Boris Pasternak, tr. fr. Russian by C. M. Bowra. TrJP

Dawn Song. Unknown, tr. fr. French by Willard R. Trask. VBLP

Dawn, streaks of rose-brown, dry. Living Together. Jean Valentine. LCAP

Dawn that cares for nobody. February. W. S. Merwin. NNaP

Dawn the child of God and Darkness. (LL) Earth our mother, breathe forth life. Unknown. EaPr

Dawn Wail for the Dead. Kath Walker. CBAP

Dawn Walkers. Jenny Joseph. PWE

Dawn was apple-green, The. Green. D. H. Lawrence. GBL; MoBrPo; PoA

Dawn Wind on the Islands. Francis Webb. FaBoMA

Dawning. Richard Watson Dixon. NOBVV

Dawning, The. George Herbert. ESCV; NOSC

Dawning, The. Henry Vaughan. GeHe; NOCV; TrPWD

Dawning Fair, Morning Wonderful. Unknown. AH

Dawning of morn, the daylight's sinking, The. Thee, Thee, Only Thee. Thomas Moore. GBL; OBNC

Dawning of the Day, The. Edward Walsh. PeIV

Dawning sun; The/ Shines down on the dunes. Siilenboor. Mongol Oral Tradition, tr. by C. R. Bawden. WTO

Dawn's Carol. H. Cordelia Ray. CBWP-3

Dawns I Have Seen. Ivor Gurney. FaBoPP

Dawn's precise pronouncement waits, The. The Edge of Day. Laurie Lee. NYBP

Dawn's Rose. Ted Hughes. Fr. Crow. FF; PoE

Day, The. Roy Fuller. OxBTC

Day, The. John Glassco. MoCV

Day. Cecil Arthur Spring-Rice. BoTP

Day, A. William Leroy Stidger. PoToHe; SoSe

Day after Chasing Porcupines. James Welch. NoAM

Day after Conference, The. Josephine D. Henderson Heard. CBWP-4

Day after Day. Li Shang-yin, tr. fr. Chinese by A. C. Graham. PLT

Day after Day. Rabindranath Tagore. Fr. Gitanjali. OBMV

Day after day as the day sets. Tirzah. Jacob Cohen, tr. fr. Hebrew by Ruth Finer Mintz. MHP

Day after day, flow without end. (LL) The Bamboo Shaded Pool. Chang Wên-chi. WPC

Day after day I sit and write. Advice to Young Ladies. Ann Plato. AAP

Day after day it goes on. How Much Longer? Robert Mezey. OBWP

Day after day I've longed for my husband. Yosami, tr. fr. Japanese by Kenneth Rexroth and Ikuko Atsumi. WPJ

Day after day my silk dresses grow more loose. The New Wife. Ng Shao, tr. fr. Chinese by Kenneth Rexroth. OHMPC

Day after day, O lord of my life, shall I stand before thee face to face? Day after Day. Rabindranath Tagore. Fr. Gitanjali. OBMV

Day after day spring's glory vies with the glorious sun. Day after Day. Li Shang-yin, tr. fr. Chinese by A. C. Graham. PLT

Day after decapitation, The. The Head. Padraic Fallon. CIP

Day after Sunday, The. Phyllis McGinley. MoAmPo; OBSV; UnPo

Day agone, as I rode sullenly, A. Dante, tr. fr. Italian by Dante Gabriel Rossetti. Fr. Vita Nuova, La. AWP

Day and Night. Lewis Alexander. CDC

Day and Night. James Stephens. BoTP

Day and night are never weary. Greek Epigram. Ezra Pound. MoAB; MoAmPo

Day and Night Handball. Stephen Dunn. AmPA

Day and night I wander widely through the wilderness of thought. God. Gamaliel Bradford. WGRP

Day arises. Unknown, tr. fr. Eskimo. EaPr

Day arrives of the autumn fair, The. A Sheep Fair. Thomas Hardy. Prf

Day at the Farm, A. "L. J." BoTP

Day Aviva Came to Paris, The. Irving Layton. MoCV

Day befo' Thanksgibin', De. Maggie Pogue Johnson. CBWP-4

Day before April, The. Mary Carolyn Davies. BoTP; FaPON

Day before Christmas. Marchette Chute. NTCP; SiSoPo

Day before my father came home from the war, The. Coming Home. Dorothy Coffin Sussman. ArOW

Day before the holidays began, The. One Christmas-Time. Wordsworth. Fr. Prelude [or, Growth of a Poet's Mind], The. EnRP; OAEL-2; RB

Day before the houses sank beneath the waves, The. The Day the Houses Sank. Constance Urdang. MAT

Day Before They Bombed Nagasaki, The. Rebecca Baggett. CrSp

Day began with dismal dougt, The. Unknown. PoToHe

Day Begins, A. Denise Levertov. NaP

Day Begins at Governor's Square Mall. Leon Stokesbury. MT

Day begins to droop, The. Winter Nightfall. Robert Bridges. MoAB; MoBrPo; OBEV; SCGP

Day-Breakers [or Daybreakers], The. Arna Bontemps. CDC; PoBA; PoNe

Day breaks, The. Morning Inscription. Miodrag Pavlović, *tr. fr. Serbo-Croatian* by Charles Simic. HSix

Day breaks — the first rays of the riising Sun, stretching her arms, The. Sunrise Sequence. *Unknown, tr. fr. Aborigine* by Ronald M. Berndt. *Fr.* Dulngulg Song Cycle, The. NOBAu

Day breaks, your mind aches, The. For No One. John Lennon *and* Paul McCartney. WTO

Day by Day. Julia Harris May. BLRP

Day by day I float my paper boats/ one by one down the running stream. Paper Boats. Rabindranath Tagore. FaPON

Day by Day the Manna Fell. Josiah Conder. TrCP

Day by day the Organ-Builder in his lonely chamber wrought. The Legend of the Organ-Builder. Julia Caroline Ripley Dorr. BeLS; BLPA; FaBoBe

Day by day the soul of things. The Soul of Things. Edith M. Thomas. AmWP

Day concludes burning, The. Desmond O'Grady. *Fr.* Dying Gaul, The. CIP

Day creeps down. The moon is creeping up. The Man on the Dump. Wallace Stevens. HAP; NAWM-2; NoAM

Day dawns with scent of must and rain, The. Mirror in February. Thomas Kinsella. CIP; GTBS-P; NoAM

Day does not come with violence. Deer in Aspens. Kay DeBard Hall. GoYe

Day-Dream. Samarendra Sengupta. TSaS, *tr.* by Lila Ray

Day Dream, A. Emily Brontë. NALW

Day-Dreams. William Canton. NOBVV; NTP

Day Dreams, or Ten Years Old. Margaret Johnson. BLPA

Day Duke Raised, The; May 24th, 1974. Quincy Troupe. Jaz

Day Flight. Jack Davis. CBAP

Day Glo Question of Identity, The. Jeffrey Miller. UL

Day goes down red darkling, The. Desolate. Gerald Massey. EBVV

Day grows old, the low-pitched lamp hath made, The. Yet a Little While Is the Light with You. Francis Quarles. ChIV-2

Day had awakened all things that be. Daybreak. Shelley. GN

Day had lapsed to twilight, The. Teatime Variations: After A. E. Housman. Peter Titheradge. FaBoPa

Day had lapsed to twilight. Peter Titheradge. *Fr.* Teatime Variations. FaBoPa

Day has her star, as well as Night. The Two Stars. W. H. Davies. MoBrPo

Day has pleasures of its own, The. I Love the Night. Matilda C. Edwards. PWR

Day has risen, The. *Unknown, tr. fr. Hopi Indian.* EaPr

Day He Died, The. Ted Hughes. OxAEP-2

Day he first spoke to me of love, The. When He Spoke to Me of Love. M. A. Mokhomo, *tr. fr. Sotho* by Dan Kunene *and* Jack Cope. PeSA

Day I Married, The. Jo Carson. ETG

Day I married, my mother, The. The Day I Married. Jo Carson. ETG

Day I Once Dreamed, The. Pat Arrowsmith. AIW

Day I put him off the sun outside, The. Long Tour: The Country Music Star Explains Why He Put off the Bus and Fired a Good Lead Guitar in West Texas. James Whitehead. MT

Day I was born my father bought me a 22, The. Sometimes . . . Injustice. Maurice Kenny. BCF

Day in an' day oot on his auld farrant loom. A Song for February. Thomas Given. FaBoVe

Day in August, A. Frank Ormsby. IIP; PBCIP; PNI

Day in Autumn, A. R. S. Thomas. BoNaP

Day in France, A. David Holbrook. OBTV

Day in June, A ("And what is so rare as a day in June?") James Russell Lowell. *Fr.* Vision of Sir Launfal, The. FaPON

Day in the City, A. L. E. Sissman. NYBP

Day in the Life, A. Stef Pixner. BrRo

Day in the Life of a Poet, A. Quincy Troupe. NBV

Day invited me to walk, The. To Mrs. ———, on the Death of Her Husband. Hannah Wallis. ECWP

Day is a Negro, The. Day and Night. Lewis Alexander. CDC

Day is again begun. Unrest. Richard Watson Dixon. OBNC

Day is broke, The! Melpomene, begone. Iter Boreale. Robert Wild. APAS

Day is chilly, birds each lean upon another, The. Returning from Kuang-ling. Ch'in Kuan, *tr. fr. Chinese* by Stephen West. SuSp

Day is cold, and dark, and dreary, The. The Rainy Day. Longfellow. AWP; PoLF

Day is colorless like Swiss characters in a novel, The. For Guillaume Apollinaire. William Meredith. CoAP

Day Is Coming, The. William Morris. WGRP

Day is curled about again, The. An Anniversary on the Hymeneals of My Noble Kinsman, Thomas Stanley, Esquire. Richard Lovelace. CaPo

Day is dark, The. Sehnsucht; or, What You Will. Korinna. FiBHP

Day is dark and dreary, The. If. Franklin P. Adams. OBAL

Day Is Done, The, *parody.* Phoebe Cary. AnAmPo; BXAP; OBAL

Day Is Done, The. Longfellow. AnAmPo; BLPA; FaBoBe; MeMAP; NOBA; OxBA; PoRA; PWR; TrGrPo

Day is done, the winter sun, The. Castle Wood. Emily Brontë. MeMBP

Day is drawing to its fall, A. First Sight of Her and After. Thomas Hardy. FaBoVe; PoEL-5

Day Is Dying in the West. *At.* to Mary Artemisia Lathbury. AH; WGRP

Day Is Gone, The. Keats. EnRP

Day is great and strong, The. World without Peculiarity. Wallace Stevens. HCAP

Day is long; the worn noon dreams, The. Noon's Dream-Song. Eugene Lee-Hamilton. NOBVV

Day is o'er and twilight's shade, The. Gerarda. Eloise Bibb. AAP; CBWP-4

Day Is Past and Gone, The. John Leland. AH

Day is past, the sun is set, The. Evening. Thomas Miller. OxBChV

Day is quenched, and the sun is fled, The. A Song of Doubt. Josiah Gilbert Holland. WGRP

Day, The/ is ready to close. Saturday Night in the Village. Giacomo Leopardi, *tr. fr. Italian* by Robert Lowell. OBVE

Day is taken by each thing and grows complete, The. Taken By Each Thing. Linda Gregg. FoLa; PRA

Day is the children's friend. The Prejudice against the Past. Wallace Stevens. LiTM

Day is turning ghost, The. A Commonplace Day. Thomas Hardy. NOBVV

Day is warm, The. June. Aileen Fisher. PDV

Day Kua-fu set out he was already old, The. Chasing the Sun. Jiang He, *tr. fr. Chinese* by Donald Finkel *with* Li Guohua. SpMi

Day Lady Died, The. Frank O'Hara. CAPP; HCAP; Jaz; LCAP; MoP; NAAL-2; NeAP; NoAM; NOBA; NoP; PoBeRe; PoE; Poetr; PoM; RaBo; SOTW; TRP; VCAP

Day lay in the glass and the blood was gone, The. (*LL*) The Last Supper. Oscar Williams. ImPo; LiTA; LiTM

Day, like our souls, is fiercely dark. Battle Song. Ebenezer Elliot. OxAEP-2

Day-long bluster of the storm was o'er, The. The Drowned Spaniel. Charles Tennyson Turner. PeVV

Day-long cold hard rain drove, The. Surviving. James Welch. CDW; HATNAP

Day my girl is lost for an hour, The. The Quest. Sharon Olds. NAmP90

Day of anger after the holy night, The. News from a Pacified Area. James K. Baxter. OxBC

Day of Atonement. Charles Reznikoff. ChIV-1

Day of Chung Yang, The. Mao Tse-tung. ArNa

Day of Denial, The. Jones Very. NOBA

Day of Doom, The. (Still was the night, serene and bright.) Michael Wigglesworth. NAAL-1, *abr.*; SCAP
Sels.
"Then to the bar, all they drew near." OBCA

Day of doom. (*LL*) The Day of Doom. Michael Wigglesworth. NAAL-1, *abr.*; SCAP

Day of glory! Welcome day! The Fourth of July. John Pierpont. PAH

Day of God! Thou Blessed Day. Hannah Flagg Gould. AH

Day of her wedding, she crouches in the kitchen, The. The Feast of St. Tortoise. Nancy Willard. LCAP

Day of hunting done. Twilight in California. Philip Dow. AmPA

Day of Inverlochy, The. Iain Lom, *tr. fr. Gaelic* by John Stuart Blackie. ScCV

Day of Judgement, The. Swift. BIrV; ChIV-1; FaBoRV; NOBE; NOEC; OAEL-1; OBSV; PPP; SCGP

Day of Judgement. Henry Vaughan. ChIV-2

Day of Judgement, The. Isaac Watts. *See* When the fierce north wind with his airy forces.

Day of Judgement [*or* Judgment]; an Ode, The. Isaac Watts. ECEV; HAP; NOBE; NOEC; NoP; OBEV

Day of Judgment, The. Thomas of Celano, *tr. fr. Latin* by Wentworth Dillon. TIRV

Day of Judgment, The. Thomas of Celano. *See* Hears't thou, my soul, what serious things.

Day of my double birth, if such the year. John Thelwall. *Fr.* Lines Written at Bridgewater, 27 July 1797. NOEC

Day of Renewal. Louis MacNeice. NAs

Day of Resurrection, The. Saint John of Damascus, *tr. fr. Greek* by John Mason Neale. TrCP

Day of sunny face and temper, A. Big Bessie Throws Her Son into the Street. Gwendolyn Brooks. VGW

Day of tender memory, A. Memorial Day. Emma A. Lent. WBLP

Day of the fête, The — and what a day for it. School Cadets. Anne Elder. CBAP

Day of the Sentry, The. David St. John. AnAn

Day of the Statue, The. Francis Webb. FaBoMA

Day of These Days. Laurie Lee. BoNaP; PAW

Day of Wrath, that dreadful day, The. The Day of Judgment. Thomas of Celano, *tr. fr. Latin by* Wentworth Dillon. TIRV

Day on Kind Continent. Robert David Cohen. NYBP

Day seemed suddenly to give to black-&-white, The. Meridian. David St. John. NAmP90

Day she visited the dissecting room, The. Two Views of a Cadaver Room. Sylvia Plath. CMoP; GoYe

Day Song. Lance Henson. HATNAP

Day that Eliot died I stood, The. Thanks in Winter. Harri Webb. AngWe

Day that ends the world will be the one, The. Like a Whisper. Ethan Ayer. GoYe

Day That I Have Loved. Rupert Brooke. PoLF

Day that I was christened, The. Godmother. Dorothy Parker. PoRA

Day that my dear came to us, The. Early Mornings. *Unknown, tr. by* Louis Untermeyer. AS

Day the birds were lifted from my shoulders, The. The Nest. Marvin Bell. CAPP

Day the fat woman, The. The Beach in August. Weldon Kees. VGW

Day the Houses Sank, The. Constance Urdang. MAT

Day the Tide, The. Philip Booth. CoAP

Day the two old women were dissecting two birds, The. Richard Brought His Flute. Nancy Morejón, *tr. fr. Spanish by* Kathleen Weaver. AIW

Day the wind was hardly, A. Letter VI. W. S. Graham. FaBoMo

Day the Winds, The. Josephine Miles. FaBoWP

Day the world was O.K, The. O.K. Ann Ziety. DT

Day They Busted the Grateful Dead, The. Richard Brautigan. MAT

Day They Came for Our House, The. Don Mattera. PeSAV

Day They Cleaned Up the Border El Salvador, February, 1981, The. Wendy Rose. HATNAP

Day they laid your grandfather away, The. Second Wind. Fred Chappell. MT

Day they strung the cable from America to Europe, The. Cotton. Harry Edmund Martinson, *tr. fr. Swedish by* Robert Bly. RB

Day Thou Gavest, Lord, Is Ended, The. John Ellerton. EBVV; FaPoR

Day time failed began as usual, The. Burial of a Fisherman in Hydra. Grace Schulman. BoWoP

Day transports fallen snows, muddied, mildewed, ruined, The. Spring over the City. Anne Hébert, *tr. fr. French by* Kathleen Weaver. PBWP

Day Trip. Evan Gwyn Williams. AngWe

Day Twenty-three. Victor Coleman. NOBC

Day very solid February 12th, 1944, A. Hayden Carruth. *Fr.* Paragraphs. Jaz

Day was close, overcast like a grey belly, The. Winter. Philip Salom. NOBAu

Day was here when it was his to know, The. The New Tenants. E. A. Robinson. NoAM

Day was like pewter, The. The Sow's Head. Robert Peters. ETG

Day was one of weariness, The. The Beggar. Margaret E. Bruner. PoToHe

Day was rainy and blustery, The. In the Churchyard. Detlev von Liliencron, *tr. fr. German by* Philip L. Miller. RiWo

Day We Buried Our Bully, The. Mbuyiseni Oswald Mtshali. PeSAV

Day we die, The. *Unknown.* EaPr

Day when Charmus ran with five, The. A Mighty Runner. E. A. Robinson. MeMAP; OBAL

Day when it will not matter, The. The Day. John Glassco. MoCV

Day Which Endures Not, A. A. G. Prys-Jones, *tr. fr. Welsh by* Anthony Conran. OBWVE

Day will come when I will, The. A Farewell to a Southern Melody. Huang O, *tr. fr. Chinese by* Kenneth Rexroth *and* Ling Chung. BoWoP; WPC

Day will come when you will cease to know, The. Warning. Robert Frost. AnAmPo

Day will come, when't shall be said, The. Swift. *Fr.* Life and Character of Dean Swift, The. NOIV

Day will dawn, when one of us shall harken, The. One of Us Two. Ella Wheeler Wilcox. PoToHe

Day will return with a fresher boon. A Song of Faith. Josiah Gilbert Holland. WGRP

Day will rise and the sun from eastward. George Campbell Hay. OxBS

Day will soon be gone, The. Fujiwara no Michinobu, *tr. fr. Japanese by* Curtis Hidden Page. *Fr.* Hyaku-Nin-Isshu. AWP

Day with the Foreign Legion, A. Reed Whittemore. CoAP; LiTM

Day writhes in an immense crater, The. John James. VaA

Day you appeared I began to speak, The. To Your Question. Duane Niatum. CDW

Day You Are Reading This, The. William Stafford. PoA

Day you came, The. Breasts. Tess Gallagher. AmPA

Day you came naked to Paris, The. The Day Aviva Came to Paris. Irving Layton. MoCV

Day you mean one more. (*LL*) The Low Road. Marge Piercy. CrSp

Day Zimmer Lost Religion, The. Paul Zimmer. InPK; PBCAP

Daybreak. Frances Cornford. FM

Daybreak. Galway Kinnell. FoLa

Daybreak. Longfellow. BoTP; PoLF; PWR

Daybreak. George Marion McClellan. AAP

Daybreak. W. S. Merwin. NAAL-2

Daybreak. Carl Sandburg. PDV

Daybreak. Shelley. GN

Daybreak. Samuel Francis Smith. *See* Morning Light Is Breaking, The.

Daybreak. Stephen Spender. BoLoP

Daybreak. *Unknown, at. to* John Donne. *See* Stay, O sweet, and do not rise!

Daybreak comes first. Daybreak. Carl Sandburg. PDV

Daybreak/ Have you already seen the dawn. Three Dawns. Jean-Joseph Rabéarivelo, *tr. fr. French by* Ellen Conroy Kennedy. NegPo

Daybreak in a Garden. Siegfried Sassoon. BoTP

Daybreak: the household slept. Father and Child. Gwen Harwood. CBAP; WPE

Daybreak upon the hills! Peace. Adeline D. T. Whitney. PAH

Daylight announces. Sunrise Comes to Second Avenue. Thylias Moss. TRP

Daylight. For everyone but me. *Nap.* Dreams by No One's Daughter. Leslie Ullman. PBCAP

Daylights. Rosanna Warren. NoAM

Daylong this tomcat lies stretched flat. Esther's Tomcat. Ted Hughes. OFC; OxBC; SoCa

Days. Joseph Campbell. PeIV

Days. Emerson. AmPP; AnAmPo; HAP; HeIL; HeIP; LiTA; MeMAP; NAAL-1; NOBA; NoP; OxBA; OxBSP; PoE; PoEL-4; TAP; TFi; TrGrPo

Days. Philip Larkin. EBEV; FaBoMo; Mes; NTP; OxAEP-2; OxBC; OxBSP; PeECV; RB; TOF

Days and Nights. Kenneth Koch. NoAM

Sels.

"I certainly have lost something."

Stones of Time, The.

Days are cold, the nights are long, The. The Cottager to Her Infant. Dorothy Wordsworth. CH; NTP; OxBChV; TTTS

Days are sad, it is the holy tide, The. The Holy Tide. Frederick Tennyson. OBEV

Days are short, The. January. John Updike. PDV

Day's Blood. Jimmy Santiago Baca. AfAz

Days can be sunny. I Got Rhythm. Ira Gershwin. CBLP

Days damp has shuffled bent of back into the. Paul Brown. *Fr. De Rebus.* NBrP

Days dawn on us that make amends for many. The Interpreters. Swinburne. PoEL-5

Days Drawing In. E. J. Scovell. *Fr.* First Year, The. FaBoWP

Days fail: night broods over afternoon, The. Days Drawing In. E. J. Scovell. *Fr.* First Year, The. FaBoWP

Days go I remain, The. (*LL*) The Mirabeau Bridge. Guillaume Apollinaire. BoLoP, *tr. by* Quentin Stevenson; LPA; OBVE, *tr. by* W. S. Merwin

Days Gone By, The. James Whitcomb Riley. OBCA

Days grow and the stars cross over, The. Darkness Music. Muriel Rukeyser. BoWoP

Days grow shorter in December. Winter Memories. Stephen Knight. UnDi

Days grow shorter, the nights grow longer, The. Ella Wheeler Wilcox. BLPA

Day's grown old, the fainting sun, The. Evening. Charles Cotton. PoEL-3; WiR

(Evening Quatrains.) ChTr; NOSC; SCGP

(Summer Evening.) TrGrPo

Day's in dread of losing her bright features, The. Ausiàs March, *tr. fr. Catalan by* John Frederick Nims. STV

Days in White. Ingeborg Bachmann, *tr. fr. German.* BoWoP, *tr. by* Daniel Huws

Days like this, off Jake's, the August fog. Jake's Wharf. Philip Booth. NYBP

Days of 1896. C. P. Cavafy, *tr. fr. Greek by* Edmund Keeley *and* Philip Sherrard. PeHV

Days of fiesta, The. Tío-Vivo, or the Merry-go-round. Federico García Lorca, *tr. fr. Spanish*. CBNP

Days of 'Forty-nine, The. *Unknown*. PAH

Days of misfortune pass and are gone. *Unknown, tr. fr. German by* Geoffrey Dunlop. OBD

Days of my life, The. Days. Joseph Campbell. PeIV

Days of 1941 and '44. James Merrill. GLP

Days of 1964. James Merrill. CoAP; HCAP; NAAL-2; PoE; VCAP

Days of 1978. Gerald Stern. CAPP

Days of Our Youth, The. *Unknown, tr. fr. Arabic by* Wilfrid Scawen Blunt. AWP

Days of spring are here, The! the eglantine. Hafiz, *tr. by* Gertrude Lowthian Bell. *Fr.* Odes. AWP

Days of the Unicorns, The. Phyllis Webb. NOBC

Days pass easy over these ancient hills. We Are a People. Lance Henson. VoR

Days Pass: Men Pass. Stephen Vincent Benét. AnAmPo

Day's sweetest moments are at dawn. Dawn. Ella Wheeler Wilcox. PWR

Days That Have Been. W. H. Davies. AngWe; FaBoPP

Days that sparkle with joys renewed. (*LL*) With You. David Diop. NegPo

Days themselves, The. Position. Léon Damas, *tr. fr. French by* Ellen Conroy Kennedy. NegPo

Days through Starch and Bluing. Alice Fulton. GOYP

Days Too Short. W. H. Davies. MoBrPo

Days went by, The. I took up the old days. Tuscan Life. Elizabeth Barrett Browning. *Fr.* Aurora Leigh. FaBoPP

Day's Work. Lucha Corpi, *tr. fr. Spanish by* Catherine Rodriguez-Nieto. AfAz

Dayseye hugging the earth, The. Daisy. William Carlos Williams. MoAB; MoAmPo

Daystar. Rita Dove. LCAP; NIP

Daytrip. Anne Rouse. NWP

Dazzle. Dorothy Roberts. NOBC

Dazzle on the sea, my darling, The. Leaving Barra. Louis MacNeice. EBEV

Dazzled blood, The. Faustus Triumphant. Thom Gunn. FaBoMo

Dazzled [*or* Dazel'd] thus with height of place. Upon the Sudden Restraint of the Earl[e] of Somerset, Then Falling from Favor [*or* Favour]. Sir Henry Wotton. ELP; FaBoEH; JCP; NOBE; NoP; NOSC; SeCP

De. Robert Alan Jamieson. FaBoVe

De Aegypto. Ezra Pound. VGW

De Ambiente. Tatiana de la Tierra. GLP

De Amore. (Shall one be sorrowful because of love.) Ernest Dowson. OBNC

Sels.
"Lord over life and all the ways of breath." TrPWD

De Civitate Hominum. Thomas MacGreevy. CIP

De Coenatione Micae. Martial, *tr. fr. Latin by* Robert Louis Stevenson. FaBoCh

De Consulatu Stilichonis, *sels.* Claudian, *tr. fr. Latin by* Osborn Bokenham. Rome Araieth Stilico in Vesture of the Consul. OxBLMV

De Contemptu Mundi, *sels.* Bernard of Cluny, *tr. fr. Latin by* John Mason Neale.
Jerusalem the Golden. WGRP
"Scarcely believe things shameful to utter which yet I shall speak of." PeHV

De Gustibus. (Your ghost will walk, you lover of trees.) Robert Browning. FHYEP; InPS; SCGP
Sels.
"Italy, my Italy?" PIP
"What I love best in all the world." OBTV
(Italy of the South.) FaBoPP
"Your ghost will walk, you lover of trees." PIP

De Imagine Mundi. John Ashbery. FaBoMo

De Morte. Sir Henry Wotton. NOSC; OxBSP

De Naevo in Facie Faustinae. Thomas Bastard. FaBoEE

De Ponto. Ovid, *tr. fr. Latin by* Henry Vaughan. OBVE
Sels.
"Shall I complain or not? Or shall I mask."
"You have consum'd my language, and my pen."

De Profundis. Bible, *O.T., paraphrased by* Sir Thomas Wyatt. *See* Out of the depths [*or* deep] have I cried [*or* called] (unto) Thee, O Lord.

De Profundis, *sels.* Elizabeth Barrett Browning.
"Whatever's lost, it first was won." TrPWD

De Profundis. Walter de la Mare. OBD

De Profundis, *sels.* George Gascoigne.
"From depth of dole wherein my soul doth dwell." ChIV-1

"Skies gan scowl, o'ercast with misty clouds, The." ChIV-1

De Profundis. David Gascoyne. PoWW

De Profundis. Dorothy Parker. ErPo; NAAL-2

De Profundis. Amos N. Wilder. TrPWD

De Puero Balbutiente. Thomas Bastard. *See* Methinks 'Tis Pretty Sport [to Hear a Child].

De Rebus, *sels.* Paul Brown.
"Almost believed in." NBrP
"Days damp has shuffled bent of back into the." NBrP
"Don't talk to me." NBrP
"Saltpetre sucked up the cigarette with." NBrP
"This morning trampled." NBrP
"Unbowel the meaning." NBrP

De Regimine Principum, *sels.* Thomas Hoccleve.
Lament for Chaucer. OBEV; OxBLMV
"Musing upon the restless bisinesse." PoEL-1
"O maister deere and fader reverent!" EBEV

De Rerum Natura. Andrei Codrescu. UL

De Rerum Natura (On the Nature of Things), *sels.* Lucretius, *tr. fr. Latin*.
Address to Venus. AWP, *tr. by* Spenser
(Darling of God and Men.) ArLo, *tr. by* Basil Bunting
(Prayer to Venus.) ElL, *tr. by* Spenser
Against the Fear of Death. DL, *abr.*
(Ah Wretch! thou cry'st, ah! miserable me.) AWP, *tr. by* Dryden; FaBoRV, *tr. by* Dryden; OAEL-1, *tr. by* Dryden; OBVE, *tr. by* Dryden
Argument of the Fourth Booke, The. KTR, *tr. by* Lucy Hutchinson
"Child is like a sailor cast up by the sea, The." NAs
Concerning the Nature of Love. ErPo
"Delight of humane kind, and gods above." OBVE
"If all this world had no original." SiPSBD, *tr. by* Sir Walter Ralegh
No Single Thing Abides. AWP
"Nor will ingenious women, free from pride." KTR, *tr. by* Lucy Hutchinson
"Now since the members of the world we view." OBVE
Suave Mari Magno. AWP
What Has This Bugbear Death. CTC; OBD
"Why only in the spring are roses borne?" KTR, *tr. by* Lucy Hutchinson

De Roberval, *sels.* John Hunter-Duvar.

De Sade. John Fuller. NBLV; PeLV

De Se. John Weever. FaBoEE

De Souza Prabhu. Eunice De Souza. FaBoVe

Dea ex Machina. John Updike. UV

Deacon Brown's Conclusion. George Sands Johnson. PWR

Deacon Jones' Grievance. Paul Laurence Dunbar. AAP

Deacon Morgan. Naomi Long Madgett. BlSi

Deacon's Masterpiece, The; or, The Wonderful "One-Hoss Shay." Oliver Wendell Holmes. *Fr.* Autocrat at the Breakfast Table, The. AmPP; LiTA; MoShBr; NOBA; OBAL; OBCA; OxBA; PoLF; PoRA; TAP; TFi; VPP; WBLP

Deacon's wife was a bit desirish, The. Pride of Ancestry. Robert Frost. OBAL

Dead, The. Rene Arcos, *tr. fr. French by* Christopher Middleton. PeFWW

Dead, The. Mathilde Blind. WGRP

Dead, The ("Blow out, you bugles, over the rich dead!") Rupert Brooke. *Fr.* 1914. WGRP

Dead, The ("These hearts were woven.") Rupert Brooke. *Fr.* 1914. CH; LiTB; OtMeF; PeFWW; PoA; SoSe

Dead, The. C. Day Lewis. TwCP

Dead, The. Louis Dudek. NOBC

Dead, The. Charles Heavysege. *See* How Great unto the Living Seem the Dead!

Dead. Lionel Johnson. OBNC; PoEL-5

Dead, The. David Morton. PAH

Dead, The. A. J. M. Smith. NOBC

Dead, The. Mark Strand. HeIP

Dead, The. Jones Very. AnAmPo; HAP; NOBA; OxBA; TAP

Dead abide with us, The! Though stark and cold. The Dead. Mathilde Blind. WGRP

Dead and divine and brother of all, and here again he lies. (*LL*) A Sight in Camp [in the Daybreak Gray and Dim]. Walt Whitman. AmPP; MoP; NAAL-1; NoAM; OxBA; PoE; PoEL-5; SAmP; TAP

Dead are a cadmium blue, The. Charles Wright. *Fr.* Homage to Paul Cézanne. HCAP; VCAP

Dead are always searched, The. The Enemy Dead. Bernard Gutteridge. PoWW

Dead are horizontal and motionless, The. Ancestor Worship. Emyr Humphreys. AngWe

Dead are not dead, The. (*LL*) Those who are dead are never gone. Birago Diop. EaPr

Though Mine Eye Sleep Not.

Dead Seal. Alfred W. Purdy. MoCV; MoP

Dead Seal near McClure's Beach, The. Robert Bly. NNaP; NU

Dead Shall Be Raised Incorruptible, The. Galway Kinnell. NOBA; PoE Sels.

Dead shall rise again, The. The Raising of Lazarus. Lucille Clifton. CrSp

Dead shalt thou lie; and nought. Achtung. Sappho, tr. fr. Greek by Thomas Hardy. CTC; OBVE

Dead Sheep, The. Andrew Young. FM

Dead sheep/ beside the highway. Preparations. Leslie Silko. VoR

Dead Sister, The. Caroline Gilman. OBCA

Dead Soldier. Nicolás Guillén, tr. fr. Spanish by Langston Hughes. TTY

Dead Soldiers. James Fenton. NoAM; OBTV; OBWP

Dead Soldiers, The. Max Plowman. PoWW

Dead soul's epitaph in every face!, A. (LL) The Street. James Russell Lowell. AnAmPo; Son

Dead Spaniard who wanted to live forever. (LL) Ponce de León: A Morning Walk. Al Young. HoPM

Dead Sparrow, The. William Cartwright. CH

Dead stare out of empty sockets, The. The Dead. A. J. M. Smith. NOBC

Dead Statesman, A. Kipling. Fr. Epitaphs of the War, 1914–1918. FaBoEE; IHNG; NBLV; NoP; OBWP; PoWW

Dead stay with you always, The. Rain in the hills. Lauris Edmond. PWE

Dead Still. Andrei Voznesensky, tr. fr. Russian by Richard Wilbur. BoLoP

Dead the fire, though we blow. (LL) Another to the Maids. Robert Herrick. OHIP

Dead, they'll burn you up with electricity. Argentarius, tr. fr. Greek by Kenneth Rexroth. PGA

"Dead," was all he answered. (LL) The Death of the Hired Man. Robert Frost. AmPP; CMoP; HeIP; HoPM; MoAB; MoAmPo; NAAL-2; NoP; OxBA; SAmP; TrGrPo

Dead Weasel, A. David Helwig. NOBC

Dead "Wessex" the Dog to the Household. Thomas Hardy. FM

Dead who die in the Lord!, The. (LL) The Four Roads. Alice Greene. PeSAV

Dead who grew up on me!, The. (LL) The Cry of South Africa. Olive Schreiner. PeSAV

Dead Wingman, The. Randall Jarrell. PoWW

Dead wood with its load of stones. The Water-Wheel. Jack R. Clemo. PWE

Dead Words, The. Vernon Watkins. LiTM

Dead, you will lie under a yard of earth. Argentarius, tr. fr. Greek by Fleur Adcock. GrAn

Deader they die here, or at least. Fall Comes in Back-Country Vermont. Robert Penn Warren. NYBP; VGW

Deadfall. Martha Keller. GoYe

Deadly Dance, The. Unknown, tr. fr. Aztec Indian by Edward Kissam. STP

Deadly James (For All the Victims of Police Brutality). James A. Emanuel. ETG

Deadly Kisses. Pierre de Ronsard, tr. fr. French by Andrew Lang. AWP

Deadly Seven, The. Sydney Bernard Smith. PeLi

Deadly Weapon. Beatrix Gates. GLP

Deadman's Dirge. George Darley. See Prayer unsaid, and mass unsung.

Dead's right grain, The. The Future and the Ancestor. Andrée Chedid, tr. fr. French by Samuel Hazo and Mirène Ghossein. WPOW

Deadsong. Don Domanski. NOBC

Deaf. Barry O. Higgs. PeSA

Deaf-and-Dumb School. Anthony Delius. PeSA

Deaf children were monkey-nimble, fish-tremulous and sudden, The. Deaf School. Ted Hughes. NoP

Deaf, giddy, helpless, left alone. On His Own Deafness. Swift. BIrV; FaBoEE

Deaf Girl Playing. James Tate. LCAP

Deaf is like. Deaf. Barry O. Higgs. PeSA

Deaf-Mute in the Pear Tree. P. K. Page. NoAM; PoE

Deaf School. Ted Hughes. NoP

Deaf Things, sels. Momcilo Nastasijevic, tr. fr. Serbo Croatian by Charles Simic.
"Beauty since." HSix
"I know by the arrow of darkness." HSix
"It has hardened." HSix, sect. 2
"Not one whisper." HSix
"Pain/ so it turned black." HSix

Deaf to God, who calls and walks. Doomsday Morning. Genevieve Taggard. MoAmPo

Deafness. Richard Ryan. BIrV; PBCIP

Dealer, bewitched by gain-promising dreams, A. Bush Justice. Charles Harpur. CBAP

Dealer in shirt-sleeves told his assistant Jenny, The. Newcombe at the Croydon Gallery. Arthur Nortje. HBAPE

Dean and prebendary, A. The Battle Royal between Dr. Sherlock, Dr. South, and Dr. Burnet. William Pittis. APAS

Dean Inge. Humbert Wolfe. FaBoEE; PIP

Dean of Paul's did search for his wife, The. Fragment of a Song on the Beautiful Wife of Dr. John Overall. Unknown. BoLoP

Dean of the University said, The. May 1968. Sharon Olds. NAmP90; NIP

Dear. Erica Hunt. VBLP

Dear/ A pinhole of light. Dear. Erica Hunt. VBLP

Dear Albert, of Saxe-Coburg-Gotha. W. F. N. Watson. PeLi

Dear Alice! you'll laugh when you know it. The Talented Man. Winthrop Mackworth Praed. EnRP; FiBHP; NOBL; PeLV

Dear and great Angel, wouldst thou only leave. The Guardian-Angel. Robert Browning. PeECV

Dear, and very dear relation. To Ann Lear. Edward Lear. CBNP

Dear Ann, wherever you are. For Ann Scott-Moncrieff. Edwin Muir. GTBS-P

Dear Antigone,/ after going over all the arguments. Letter. Leonard Nathan. PBCAP

Dear architect of fine Chateaux en l'air. To William Hayley, Esq.: In Reply to His Solicitation to Write with Him in a Literary Work. William Cowper. Son

Dear as the Moon. Gond Oral Tradition, tr. by V. Elwin and S. Hivale. WTO

Dear Auntie/ Oh, what a nice jumper. Christmas Thank You's. Mick Gowar. OBCP

Dear, back my wounded heart restore. The Divorce. Thomas Stanley. MeLP

Dear, beauteous death! the jewel of the just. Henry Vaughan. Fr. Ascension Hymn. OBD

Dear Bess,/ He'll have rings and linen things. Rime for the Christmas Baby. Anne Spencer. ShDr

Dear Bill,/ When I search the past for you. A Letter to William Carlos Williams. Kenneth Rexroth. NNaP

Dear Black Head. Unknown, tr. by Sir Samuel Ferguson. BIrV

Dear Body. Janine Canan. SRLS; UL

Dear Boy, What a superlative day for a funeral. Micheál Mac Liammóir. Paul Durcan. PBCIP

Dear boy, you will not hear me speak. Pangloss's Song [A Comic-Opera Lyric]. Richard Wilbur. IHNG; MoP; NBLV; NoAM

Dear Brethren, Are Your Harps in Tune? Eunice Smith. AH

Dear Brook, farewell! To-morrow's noon again. Wordsworth. Fr. Evening Walk, An. EnRP

Dear brother Robin, this comes from us all. Country Letter. John Clare. EnVR

Dear brother, would you know the life. A Letter. Emerson. OxBA

Dear brothers and sisters, we love one another. The Ark. Noah Calwell Cannon. AAP

Dear child, first-born, what I could give outright. Hand-Shadows. Jarold Ramsey. NIP

Dear child of nature, let them rail! To a Young Lady. Wordsworth. EnRP

Dear child, these words which briefly I declare. The Maiden's Best Adorning. Unknown. OxBChV

Dear Child Whom I Begot. J. V. Cunningham. NAs

"Dear children," they asked in every town. The Wise Men Ask the Children the Way. Heine, tr. fr. German by Geoffrey Grigson. OBCP (Kings from the East, The.) ChTr

Dear Cleo, I can't complain about your absence. To the Muse. Philip Whalen. PoM

Dear Clive, I've meant to scribble you a letter. Letter to Myself. Christopher Reid. FaBoPa

Dear Cloe [or Chloe], how blubbered is that pretty face! Answer to Cloe [or Chloe] Jealous. Matthew Prior. NOBE
(Better Answer, A.) OxAEP-1
(Better Answer to Cloe [or Chloe] Jealous, A.) AWP; ELP; NAEL-1; NOEC; PoEL-3

Dear Colonel, name the day. From a Young Woman to an Old Officer Who Courted Her. Elizabeth Frances Amherst. ECWP

Dear common flower, that grow'st beside the way. James Russell Lowell. Fr. To the Dandelion. AnAmPo; FaPON, 2 sts.; GN; NAAL-1

Dear Craoibhin Aoibhin, look into our case. At The Abbey Theatre (Imitated from Ronsard). W. B. Yeats. Son

Dear creature by the fire a-purr. The Cat. Lytton Strachey. OFC

Dear critic, who my lightness so deplores. To a Captious Critic. Paul Laurence Dunbar. BPo

Dear Czecho-Slovakia. Neville Chamberlain. FaBoEH

Dear Dave: Rain five days and I love it. Letter to Wagoner from Port Townsend. Richard Hugo. NNaP

Dear, dear, dear. The Thrush's Song. *Unknown, tr. fr. Gaelic by* William MacGillivray. CH

Dear, dear! what can the matter be? Oh, Dear! *Unknown.* ReMoGo

Dear Denise: Long way from, long time since Boulder. Letter to Levertov from Butte. Richard Hugo. NNaP

Dear Dennice: I'm this close but the pass is tough this year. Letter to Scanlon from Whitehall. Richard Hugo. NNaP

Dear/ Diana. Andy-Diana DNA Letter. Andrew Weiman. HAP

Dear Dolly, stay thy scampering joints one minute. Ode to a Country Hoyden. "Peter Pindar." NOEC

Dear Dove, that bear'st to my sole-laboring ark. Ad Amicam. Francis Thompson. Son

Dear earth, take old Amyntichus to your heart. *Unknown, tr. fr. Greek by* Alistair Elliot. GrAn

Dear Echo, do me a favour; it's somewhat . . . Some what? Gauradas, *tr. fr. Greek by* Peter Jay. GrAn

Dear Emily, my tears would burn your page. To Emily Dickinson. Yvor Winters. Son

Dear Eustatio, I write that you may write me an answer. Arthur Hugh Clough. *Fr. Amours de Voyage.* EBVV; EBVVPR; FaBoVe; NOBVV; OBTV; OxAEP-2

Dear, farewell, a little while. Anacreontic, on Parting with a Little Child. Samuel Wesley. NOEC

Dear father and dear mother: Let me crave. Erotion. Martial, *tr. fr. Latin by* Kirby Flower Smith. AWP

Dear Father Christmas. Russell Davies. FaBoPa

Dear Father/ hear and bless. Margaret Wise Brown. PDV

Dear Father, Look Up. "Orpheus C. Kerr." OBAL

Dear father, mother, sister, come listen while I tell. The Ashland Tragedy. Elijah Adams. AmFP

Dear Father, take care of Thy children, THE BOYS! *(LL)* The Boys. Oliver Wendell Holmes. WBLP

Dear Father, tell me, Why are women? Why? Walter de la Mare. FiBHP

Dear fellow-artist, why so free. To a Young Beauty. W. B. Yeats. CMoP

Dear fellow castaway, the cruise ships. Weathering the Depths. Alfred M. Lee. AmPA

Dear Female Heart. Stevie Smith. FaBoEE; NALW

Dear Fergusson — They've Ramsay's statue clean. Letter to Robert Fergusson. Alexander Scott. OxBS

Dear Folks. Patrick Kavanagh. FaBoTw

Dear Frank, Here is a poem. Josephine Miles. NALW

Dear Frank, with fancy, fire and style. Upon an Ingenious Friend, Over-Vain. Thomas Fitzgerald. OxBSP

Dear friend! Believe me, Love's not always blind. Love Has Eyes. William Forster. CBAP

Dear friend, far off, my lost desire. Tennyson. *Fr.* In Memoriam A. H. H. EBVV, *abr.;* EBVVPR; FHYEP; OAEL-2, *abr.;* PeECV, *abr.*

Dear friend, I fear my heart will break. Out of French. Sir Charles Sedley. FaBoEE

Dear Friend,/ I hear this town does so abound. An Epistolary Essay from M. G. to O. B. upon Their Mutual Poems. The Earl of Rochester. APAS

Dear friend, I heard thee say to me. The True Witness. Lucy Larcom. AmWP

Dear friend, I pray thee, if thou wouldst be proving. Friendship. Ella Wheeler Wilcox. PoToHe

Dear Friend, since you have chosen to associate. Tennyson's Poems. Josephine D. Henderson Heard. CBWP-4

Dear [or Deare] friend, sit down: the tale is long and sad. Love Unknown. George Herbert. JCP; Prf

Dear Friend:/ The day you brought me geraniums. Red August Letter. Colette Inez. ETG

Dear friend, the here-there emphasis is made. Letter. Janet Frame. PeNZ

Dear friend! whose holy, ever-living lines. The Match. Henry Vaughan *and* Thomas Stanley. ESCV

Dear Friend, Whose Presence in the House. James Freeman Clarke. AH

Dear friends, let your disease be what God will. Saffold's Cures. *At. to* Thomas Saffold. FaBoUs

Dear friends, we are gathered together. A Tribute to the Bride and Groom. Priscilla Jane Thompson. CBWP-2

Dear Fronto, famed alike in peace and war. Country Pleasures. Martial, *tr. fr. Latin by* F. A. Wright. AWP

Dear Future,/ What a tease you are, big old gassy thing. Letter Poem. Edward Kleinschmidt. UnDi

Dear galway/ it is flooding here, in missouri. A Poem to Galway Kinnell. Etheridge Knight. NNaP

Dear gentle hands have stroked my hair. Mother's Hands. W. Dayton Wedgefarth. PoToHe

Dear gentle soul, who went so soon away. Camões, *tr. fr. Portuguese by* Roy Campbell. BoLoP

Dear Gill I ne'er thought till last night. The New Married Couple; or, A Friendly Debate between the Country Farmer and His Buxome Wife. *Unknown.* CoMu

Dear girl, you're growing very thin. To a Sick Friend. Hannah Wallis. ECWP

Dear God. Barbara Brooker. SRLS

Dear God,/ give us a flood of water. The Prayer of the Little Ducks. Carmen Bernos de Gasztold, *tr. fr. French by* Rumer Godden. PDV; SiSoPo

Dear God, I didn't know that Cytherea was bathing. Rufinus Domesticus, *tr. fr. Greek by* Barbara Hughes Fowler. *Fr.* Epigrams. HePo

Dear God, I humbly pray. Prayer of a Beginning Teacher. Ouida Smith Dunnam. TrPWD

Dear God our Father, at Thy knee confessing. For Deeper Life. Katharine Lee Bates. TrPWD

Dear Grandmamma, with what we give. Grandmamma's Birthday. Hilaire Belloc. FiBHP

Dear, had the world in its caprice. Respectability. Robert Browning. CBLP; EnLoPo

Dear Happy Souls. Eunice Smith. AH

Dear Harp of My Country. Thomas Moore. EnRP; NOIV

Dear Harriet. Naked Poetry. Peter Cooley. SM

Dear heart, you lay above the ground. *(LL)* The Yew-Tree. *Unknown.* ChTr; GBL

Dear ———,/ Hi, you can be in my new poem, if you're a Yankees fan. The History of the Human Body/ Winfield's Infield Hit/ The Lassitude of the Infinite. Elinor Nauen. UL

Dear hope! Earth's dowry and heaven's debt! For Hope. Richard Crashaw. LiTB
(Answer for Hope.) MeLP
(M. [*or* Mr.] Crashaw's Answer for Hope.) NOSC; SeCV-1
(On Hope.) NOBE

Dear Horace! be melted to tears. Epistle, from Algiers, to Horace Smith. Thomas Campbell. OBTV

Dear Husband. Yamba Ouologuem, *tr. fr. French by* Ellen Conroy Kennedy. NegPo

Dear, I must be gone. Parting. W. B. Yeats. FaBoTw

Dear, if unsocial privacies obsess me. J. V. Cunningham. VGW

Dear, If You Change. *At. to* John Dowland. EIL; EnLoPo; EnRePo; InvP

Dear, if you change, I'll never choose again. Dear, If You Change. *At. to* John Dowland. EIL; EnLoPo; EnRePo; InvP
(Deare, If You Change.) PoEL-2

Dear J. D.: One should think of Chief Joseph here. Letter to Reed from Lolo. Richard Hugo. NNaP

Dear Jim: This is as far as I ever chased a girl. Letter to Welch from Browning. Richard Hugo. NNaP

Dear John. Lindsay MacRae. DT

Dear John, Dear Coltrane. Michael S. Harper. AmPA; Jaz; NIP; VCAP

Dear John: This is a Dear John Letter from booze. Letter to Logan from Milltown. Richard Hugo. NNaP

Dear John, whoever now takes pen to write. James McAuley. *Fr.* Letter to John Dryden, A. CBAP

Dear kindly Sergeant Krupke. Gee, Officer Krupke. Stephen Sondheim. OBAL

Dear Knight, how great a drudge is he. Hudibras and Milton Reconciled. William Somervile. NOEC

Dear Kong. Fay Wray to the King. Judith Rechter. NMM

Dear Lady of the Cherries, cool, serene. Sonnet for the Madonna of the Cherries. Lord Wavell. OtMeF

Dear Lamp, she swore by you. Asclepiades, *tr. fr. Greek by* Edward Lucie-Smith. GrAn

Dear Land of All My Love. Sidney Lanier. *Fr.* Centennial Meditation of Columbia, The. GN; PAH

Dear Land of Hope, thy hope is crowned. Land of Hope and Glory. A. C. Benson. FaPoR

Dear Lela is my joy and crown. Lela's Charms. L. A. J. Moorer. CBWP-3

Dear letters, fond letters. Love Letters. Josephine D. Henderson Heard. CBWP-4

Dear little bird, the Graces' favourite. Tymnes, *tr. fr. Greek by* Peter Jay. GrAn

Dear little bog-face. Bog-Face. Stevie Smith. RB

Dear little Mosca. Xenia. Eugenio Montale, *tr. fr. Italian by* G. Singh. OBD

Dear little tree that we plant to-day. An Arbor Day Tree. *Unknown.* OHIP

Dear Liza, I is bin down town. Nigger's Got to Go, De. Daniel Webster Davis. AAP

Death and the Woodman. La Fontaine, *tr. fr. French* by Edward Marsh. OBD

Death-angel smote Alexander McGlue, The. Mr. Slimmer's Funeral Verses for the *Morning Argus.* "Max Adeler." (Out of the Hurly-Burly.) OBAL

Death as a Lotus Flower. *Unknown. See* I am the pure lotus.

Death as History. Jay Wright. PoBA

Death at Winson Green, A. Francis Webb. FaBoMA

Death be nimble. Fairy Book Lines. Edward Kleinschmidt. UnDi

Death, Be Not Proud. John Donne. *See* Death, be not proud, though some have called thee.

Death be not proud, though some have called thee. John Donne. *See* Death, be not proud, though some have called thee.

Death, be not proud, though some have called thee. John Donne. *Fr.* Holy Sonnets. ChTr; DL; EBEvV; EiL; EnRePo; ESCV; FaBoRV; FaBV; FF; FHYEP; HAP; HeIL; HeIP; ImPo; InPK; InPS; InvP; JCP; LiTB; MeLP; NAEL-1; NAWM-1; NIP; NOBE; NoP; NOSC; OAEL-1; OBD; OxAEP-1; PoE; PoEL-2; Poetr; PoRA; PPP; PrIm; SCGP; SCV; SeCP; SeCV-1; SoSe; TEP; TrCP; TrGrPo; TRP; WeW (Death.) OBEV (Death be not proud, though some have called thee.) PeECV, *sect.* X (Death, Be Not Proud.) ClHu; TFi

Death be not proud, thy hand gave not this blow. Lucy Harington, Countess of Bedford. PeECV; WPE

Death, become a shewolf. Crown of Happiness. Anne Hébert, *tr. fr. French* by Willis Barnstone. BoWoP

Death Bed, The. Waring Cuney. CDC

Death-Bed, The. Thomas Hood. CoGr; EnRP; GTBS; GTBS-P; NOBE; OBD; OBEV; OBNC

Death Bed. Thomas Kinsella. CIP; PBCIP

Death-Bed, The. Siegfried Sassoon. LiTM; NSI; PeFWW

Death-bed, A. Kipling. IHNG; PoWW

Death-Bed Song. *Unknown.* AmFP

Death before forty's no bar. Lo! Obit on Parnassus. F. Scott Fitzgerald. NBLV; NYBP; PrIm

Death by Drowning. Elizabeth Brewster. NOBC

Death by Rarity. Marguerite Young. LiTA

Death by Water. T. S. Eliot. *Fr.* Waste Land, The. AmPP; CMoP; FaBoMo; HAP; LiTA; LiTM; MoAB; MoAmPo; NAWM-2; NoAM; NOBA; NOBE; NoP; OAEL-2; OBVE; OxBA; OxBTC; TAP; UnPo

Death came before Marriage, Philaenion. Perses, *tr. fr. Greek* by Peter Whigham. GrAn

Death Camp. Irena Klepfisz. GLP

Death can be so lazy at times. Death of a Lady. J. P. Clark Bekederemo. HBAPE

Death, can you too be enamored? To Death. Johann Wilhelm Ludwig Gleim, *tr. fr. German* by George C. Schoolfield. GePo

Death-cell, A? The shack of the coastguards. The Coastguard House. Robert Lowell, *tr. fr. the Italian of* Eugenio Montale. NaP

Death Certificate. Rui Knopfli, *tr. fr. Portuguese by the author.* PeSAV

Death Chant. Peter Blue Cloud. VoR

Death Circus, The. John Tranter. CBAP

Death comes in quantity from solved. The Tolerance of Crows. Charles Donnelly. CIP

Death Crown. Robert Morgan. MT

Death Described by His True Effects. George Chapman. *Fr.* Eugenia. NOSC

Death designs swirl high above faces that are of disbelief. War Walking Near. Ray A. Young Bear. CDW

Death devours all lovely things. Passer Mortuus Est. Edna St. Vincent Millay. CMoP; FaBoWP; MoAmPo; OBD; OxBA

Death did not come to my mother. Conception. Josephine Miles. FaBoWP

Death does away with sickness; Hell cures chance. Consolations. Paul Ramsey. *Fr.* Three Epigrams. CRP

Death, Don't Be Boring. Roy Kelly. BXAP

Death-Doomed. Will M. Carleton. VPP

Death feeds us up, keeps an eye on our weight. Palladas, *tr. fr. Greek* by Tony Harrison. GrAn

Death for the Dark Stranger. Thomas McGrath. VGW

Death fought; before giving in. *(LL)* The Sacrifice. Frank Bidart. GLP; VCAP

Death found strange beauty on the polished brow. Death of an Infant. Lydia Huntley Sigourney. AmWP

Death from Cancer. Robert Lowell. *Fr.* In Memory of Arthur Winslow. TwCP

Death Fugue. Paul Celan, *tr. fr. German.* AnRep, *tr. by* Clement Greenberg; PoSu, *tr. by* John Felstiner; TrJP, *tr. by* Clement Greenberg

Death gallops up the bridge of red railtie girders. Death and the Bridge. Robert Lowell. HCAP

Death has got something to be said for it. Delivery Guaranteed. Kingsley Amis. OBD

Death Has No Features of His Own. Gwen Harwood. NOBAu

Death has torn ten years from us. Philodemus, *tr. fr. Greek by* Kenneth Rexroth. PGA

Death hath deprived me of my dearest friend. A Remembrance of My Friend Mr. Thomas Morley. John Davies of Hereford. OxBSP

Death himself. LMFBR. Gary Snyder. PoM

Death I recant, and say, unsaid by me. Elegy on Mistress Boulstred. John Donne. JCP

Death, I repent. Kathleen Raine. *Fr.* Two Invocations of Death. OxBTC (Invocation of Death.) MoAB

Death, if thou be. *(LL)* A Dialogue. Swinburne. PoEL-5

Death, if thou wilt, fain would I plead with thee. A Dialogue. Swinburne. PoEL-5

Death in his thousand eyes like cataract. *(LL)* Death of a Fly. Goethe. STV

Death in January. Vincent Buckley. FaBoMA

Death in Leamington. Sir John Betjeman. NoP; OxAEP-2; RB

Death in Life. Thomas, Lord Vaux. *See* How can the tree but waste and wither away.

Death in the Aquarium. Richard Hugo. AnAn

Death in the country is an event. The Funeral. Bramwell Jones. AngWe

Death in the Desert, A. Charles Tomlinson. FF

Death in the Evening. Miroslav Holub, *tr. fr. Czech by* George Theiner. PoSu

Death in Winter, A. Jeni Couzyn. PWE

Death in Yorkville. Langston Hughes. PoBA

Death Invited. May Swenson. WPE

Death Invoked. Philip Massinger. *Fr.* Emperor of the East, The.

Death Is. Iain Sinclair. VaA

Death is a dialogue between. Emily Dickinson. WGRP

Death Is a Door. Nancy Byrd Turner. BLPA

Death Is a Matter of Mathematics. Barry Amiel. PoWW

Death is Abstract. Martha Sansom. UnDi

Death is all metaphors, shape in one history. Dylan Thomas. *Fr.* Altarwise by Owl-Light. CMoP; LiTM; MoAB; Son

Death is another milestone on their way. The Funeral. Stephen Spender. CMoP; MoAB; MoBrPo; NoAM

Death is more than. One X. E. E. Cummings. FaBoMo

Death is not death, for death is but the borning day. Birth is Death, Death is Birth. Friedrich von Logau, *tr. fr. German.* GePo, *tr. by* George C. Schoolfield

Death is not harsh: Death is our lot: but harsh. Epitaph from a Tomb in Asia Minor. *Unknown, tr. fr. Greek by* Peter Whigham. GrAn

Death/ Is nothing to us, has no relevance. Against the Fear of Death. Lucretius, *tr. by* Rolfe Humphries. *Fr.* De Rerum Natura (On the Nature of Things). DL, *abr.* (Ah Wretch! thou cry'st, ah! miserable me.) AWP, *tr. by* Dryden; FaBoRV, *tr. by* Dryden; OAEL-1, *tr. by* Dryden; OBVE, *tr. by* Dryden

Death is only a technical correction of the market. Answer Yes or No. Robert Penn Warren. *Fr.* Tale of Time. LCAP

Death is only an old door. Death Is a Door. Nancy Byrd Turner. BLPA

Death is reincarnated in every flower. Day's Work. Lucha Corpi, *tr. fr. Spanish by* Catherine Rodriguez-Nieto. AfAz

Death is stronger than all the governments. Death Snips Proud Men. Carl Sandburg. CMoP

Death is the cook of nature, and we find. Margaret Cavendish, Duchess of Newcastle. *Fr.* Nature's Cook. CBCK; PBWP

Death is the Cool Night. Heine, *tr. fr. German by* Philip L. Miller. RiWo

Death is the fuel we are using up; its smell not. Death Is. Iain Sinclair. VaA

Death is the strongest of all living things. Warning to One. Merrill Moore. MoAmPo; TrGrPo

Death is the supple Suitor. Emily Dickinson. NALW

Death Jazz: A Review. Jack Mueller. Jaz

Death killed the rich. *Yoruba Oral Tradition, tr. by* W. Abimbola. WTO

Death King, The. Anne Sexton, *tr. fr. Czech by* Jeffrey Fiskin *and* Erik Vestville. AnAn

Death knocks all night at my door. Journey to the Place of Ghosts. Jay Wright. VCAP

Death-Lace. David Ray. MAT

Death lay in ambush. Christopher Okigbo. *Fr.* Distances. TTY

Death lies dead. *(LL)* A Forsaken Garden. Swinburne. EBEV; EBEvV, *(sts. 1–2)*; FaBoPP; GTBS-P; LiTB; NOBE; NOBVV; NoP; OAEL-2; OBNC; OxAEP-2; SCGP; TEP

Death lies on her like an untimely frost. Frost on the Flower. Shakespeare. *Fr.* Romeo and Juliet. FaBoRV

Death loves rich people. Funny Poem. William Knott. PBCAP

Death Mask of John Clare, The. Edmund Blunden. EPCY

Death May Be Very Gentle. Oliver St. John Gogarty. PoRA

Death Mazurka, The. Charles Fishman. BTR

Death, my lifes Mistress, and the soveraign Queen. To His Mistress for Her True Picture. Lord Herbert of Cherbury. SeCP

Death never troubled Damocles. Damocles. Robert Graves. NYBP

Death News. Allen Ginsberg. MoP

Death, 1976. Chris Wallace-Crabbe. FaBoMA

Death of a Butcher, The. Lavinia Greenlaw. NWP

Death of a Ceiling. Medbh McGuckian. DT

Death of a Comic Opera Composer. Peter Porter. Fr. Baroque Quatrains. AnAn

Death of a Dove. Nurunnessa Choudhury, tr. fr. Bengali by the author and Paul Joseph Thompson. AIW

Death of a Fly. Goethe, tr. fr. German by John Frederick Nims. STV

Death of a Friend. Witter Bynner. IMW

Death of a Friend. Pauli Murray. PoBA

Death of a Grandparent. Mrs. Jennette Bonneau. Mary Weston Fordham. CBWP-2

Death of a Lady. J. P. Clark Bekedereme. HBAPE

Death of a man is like the fall of a mighty nation, The. The Fall. Czeslaw Milosz, tr. fr. Polish by Czeslaw Milosz and Lillian Vallee. OBD

Death of a Naturalist. Seamus Heaney. HAP; NoAM; OxBC; WeW

Death of a Negro Poet, The. Conrad Kent Rivers. BPo

Death of a Poet. Charles Causley. OxBTC

Death of a Ram. Sedulius Scottus, tr. fr. Latin. NOIV

Death of a Soldier, The. Wallace Stevens. OBWP; OxBSP; SAmP; SoSe

Death of a Son. Jon Silkin. FF; GTBS-P; MoP; OxBTC

Death of a Species. Anthony Conran. AngWe

Death of a Toad, The. Richard Wilbur. CMoP; LiTM; MoP; NAAL-2; NoAM; NoP; PoA; Poetr

Death of a Vermont Farm Woman. Barbara Howes. MoAmPo; SM

Death of a Warrior, The. Jenny Mastoraki, tr. fr. Modern Greek by Kimon Friar. BoWoP

Death of a Whale. John Blight. CBAP; OBD

Death of a Young Lady at the Retreat for the Insane. Lydia Huntley Sigourney. AmWP

Death of a Young Son by Drowning. Margaret Atwood. BoWoP; NOBC

Death of Admiral Benbow, The. Unknown. CoMu; GBP

Death of Admiral Benbow, The. Unknown. OxBSS

Death of Adonis, The. Philip Ayres, after the Greek of Theocritus. OBVE

Death of Adonis, The. Shakespeare. See Lo! here the gentle lark, weary of rest.

Death of Alexander, The. Unknown. OxBS

Death of Allegory, The. Billy Collins. WeW

Death of Altheëtor. Maria Gowen Brooks. Fr. Zophiël. AmWP

Death of an Aircraft. Charles Causley. MoBS

Death of an Angel, The. Russell Edson. LCAP

Death of an Elephant, The. Gianfranco Pagnucci. NU

Death of an Infant. Lydia Huntley Sigourney. AmWP

Death of an Irishwoman. Michael Hartnett. CIP; IIP; PBCIP

Death of Artemidora, The. Walter Savage Landor. Fr. Pericles and Aspasia. EnRP; OBNC

Death of Colman, The. Thomas Frost. PAH

Death of Cuchulain, The. W. B. Yeats. ChTr

Death of Daphnis, The. Theocritus [or Theokritus], tr. by Charles Stuart Calverley. Fr. Idylls. AWP

Death of David, The. Hayyim Nahman Bialik, tr. fr. Hebrew by Herbert Danby. TrJP, ad. by Sholom J. Kahn

Death of Dr. King. Sam Cornish. PoBA

Death of Don Pedro, The. Unknown, tr. fr. Spanish by John Gibson Lockhart. AWP

Death of Europe, The. Charles Olson. NeAP

Death of Eurydice and Orpheus' Journey to Hell, The. Ovid, tr. by George Sandys. Fr. Metamorphoses. JCP

Death of faithful Dobbin I deplore, The. An Elegy on the Death of Dobbin, the Butterwoman's Horse. Francis Fawkes. NOEC

Death of Fathers, The. Theodore Weiss. SV

Death of Friends, The. Adele Levi. GoYe

Death of Gaudentis. "Harriet Annie." WBLP

Death of General Pike, The. Laughton Osborn. PAH

Death of General Uncebunke, The; a Biography in Little, sels. Lawrence Durrell.
   "My uncle sleeps in the image of death." FaBoMo

Death of God, The. Howard Nemerov. OxBC; OxBSP

Death of Goody Nurse, The. Rose Terry Cooke. PAH

Death of Harrison, The. Nathaniel Parker Willis. PAH

Death of Hektor, The, sels. Brian Coffey.
   "Homer where born where buried of whom the son." BiHa

Death of Herminius, The. Macaulay. Fr. Battle of the Lake Regillus, The. OtMeF

Death of Hoel, The. Thomas Gray. NOEC

Death of Irish, The. Aidan Carl Mathews. PBCIP

Death of Jefferson, The. Hezekiah Butterworth. PAH

Death of Justice, The. Walter Everette Hawkins. PoBA

Death of Kin Chuen Louie, The. Michael McClure. PoBeRe

Death of King Edward I, The. Unknown. MeEL

Death of King Edward VII, The. Unknown. OxBoLi

Death of King George V. Sir John Betjeman. See Spirits of well-shot woodcock, partridge, snipe.

Death of Kings, The. Shakespeare. Fr. King Richard II. FaBoBe; TrGrPo; TRP

Death of Leander, The. Thomas Hood. Fr. Hero and Leander. EnRP

Death of Leonidas, The. George Croly. BeLS

Death of Lesbia's Bird, The. Catullus, tr. fr. Latin by Samuel Taylor Coleridge. AWP

Death of Lincoln, The. Bryant. NAAL-1; TAP

Death of Little Boys. Allen Tate. LiTA; MoAB

Death of Lord Warriston, The. Unknown. OxBB

Death of Lovers, The. Baudelaire, tr. fr. French by Roy Campbell. OBD

Death of Lyon, The. Henry Peterson. PAH

Death of Marilyn Monroe, The. Sharon Olds. HeIP

Death of Morgan, The. Unknown. FaBoBa

Death of Moses, The. "George Eliot." ChIV-1

Death of Moses, The. Frances E. W. Harper. Fr. Moses: A Story of the Nile. AAP

Death of Moses, The. Unknown, tr. fr. Hebrew by Alice Lucas. TrJP

Death of Mother Jones, The. Unknown. SWP

Death of My Aunt. Unknown. OxBoLi

Death of Myth-making, The. Sylvia Plath. PoA

Death of Nelson, The. Unknown. OxBoLi

Death of Sir Nihil, book the nth. Tywater. Richard Wilbur. ArOW; CMoP; LiTA; LiTM; MoAB; TRP

Death of Parcy Reed, The. Unknown. ESPB, A vers.

Death of Potchikoo, The. Louise Erdrich. Fr. Old Man Potchikoo. HATNAP

Death of Queen Jane, The. Unknown. AmFP, 2 vers.; ESPB, A and B vers.; OBET

Death of Robert, Earl of Huntingdon, sels. Anthony Munday.
   "Weep, weep, ye woodmen! wail." CH
   (Dirge: "Weep, weep, ye woodmen, wail.") CTC
   (Robin Hood's Funeral.) WiR
   (Song: "Weep, weep, ye woodmen, wail.") EiL

Death of Robin Hood, The. Unknown. EnSB

Death of Rufus, The. Menella Bute Smedley. FaBoEH

Death of Samson. Milton. See Come, come, no time for lamentation now.

Death of Samuel Adams, The. Unknown. AmFP

Death of Saul, The. Philip Levine. ChIV-1

Death of Sohráb, The. Firdausi, tr. fr. Persian. Fr. Shahnamah, The. TAL, tr. by James Atkinson

Death of Southwell, The, sels. John Logan.
   "Topcliffe's horses shake." CRP

Death of Tammuz, The. Saul Tchernichowsky, tr. fr. Hebrew by L. V. Snowman. TrJP

Death of the Ball Turret Gunner, The. Randall Jarrell. ArOW; CAPP; ClHu; CMoP; FF; HAP; HeIP; HoPM; InPK; LCAP; LiTM; MoAmPo; MT; NAAL-2; NAs; NIP; NoAM; NOBA; NoP; OBD; OBWP; OxBA; PoE; Poetr; PoWW; PPP; PrIm; RB; SoSe; TAP; TFi; UnPo; VCAP; VGW

Death of the Beloved, The. Rainer Maria Rilke, tr. fr. German by J. B. Leishman. OBD

Death of the Bird, The. A. D. Hope. FaBoMA

Death of the Bosun's Mate. Louis Johnson. PeNZ

Death of the Craneman, The. Alfred Hayes. LiTA

Death of the Day. Walter Savage Landor. NoP

Death of the Flowers, The. Bryant. AnAmPo; BLPL; BoNaP; EAP; GN; OBCA; PoLF; WBLP

Death of the Gods; an Ode Written in Imitation of Pindar, The. L. Ker. NOEC

Death of the Hired Man, The. Robert Frost. AmPP; CMoP; HeIP; HoPM; MoAB; MoAmPo; NAAL-2; NoP; OxBA; SAmP; TrGrPo

Death of the Kapowsin Tavern. Richard Hugo. CAPP; NAAL-2

Death of the King's Canary, The, sels. William Empson.
   "Not your winged lust but his must now change suit." UV

Death of the Lincoln Despotism. Unknown. PAH

Deathwatch. Michael S. Harper. AmPA; PoBA

Debate in the Sennit, The. James Russell Lowell. *Fr.* Biglow Papers, The. PAH

Debate: Question, Quarry, Dream. Robert Penn Warren. VGW

Debits and Credits., *sels.* Kipling.
We and They. NoAM

Deborah as Scion. James Dickey. SV

Debout, *sels.* Tchicaya U Tam'si, *tr. fr. French by* E. S. Yntema.
"Here is the stream again under the rainbow." PBA

Debridement. Michael S. Harper. NoAM

Debris of Life and Mind. Wallace Stevens. SAmP

Debt. Sunay Akin, *tr. fr. Turkish.* TSaS, *tr. by* Yusuf Eradam

Debt, The. Paul Laurence Dunbar. CDC

Debt. *Gond Oral Tradition, tr. by* V. Elwin *and* S. Hivale. WTO

Debt is paid, The. The Past. Emerson. FaBoCh; LiTA; MeMAP; PoEL-4; TAP

Debt Problem, The. S. J. Litherland. NWP

Debtor, The. Edwin Muir. MeMBP

Debutante was sitting in the parlor of her flat, A. Song: "Don't Tell Me What You Dreamt Last Night." Franklin P. Adams. FiBHP

Decade, [A]. Amy Lowell. MoAmPo; NALW

Decadent Voyeurs, The. Tom Pickard. IHNG

Decades ago. Story. Jo McDougall. NGP

Decades behind me. A Right-of-Way: 1865. William Plomer. PeLV

Decampment. Ernst Stadler, *tr. fr. German by* David McDuff. PeFWW

Decanonization, The. Sylvia Kantaris. FaBoBl

Decay. John Clare. EnVR

Decay. George Herbert. ESCV; SCGP; SeCP; SeCV-1

Decay of Piety. Wordsworth. TrCP

Decease Release. Robert Southwell. *See* Pounded spice [*or* spise] both taste [*or* tast] and scent [*or* sent] doth please, The.

Deceased. Cid Corman. VGW

Deceased, The. Keith Douglas. FaBoTw

Deceav'd and undeceav'd to be. The Self-Deceaver. Thomas Stanley. OBVE

Deceiv'd Deceiver, and Imposter cheated! Mary Pix. *Fr.* Deceiver Deceived, The. KTR

Deceive, deceive me once again! (*LL*) You Smiled, You Spoke, and I Believed. Walter Savage Landor. BoLoP; CBLP; GBL

Deceiver Deceived, The, *sels.* Mary Pix.
"Deceiv'd Deceiver, and Imposter cheated!" KTR

Deceiving World. Robert Greene. *See* Deceiving world, that with alluring toys.

Deceiving world, that with alluring toys. A Palinode. Robert Greene. *Fr.* Greene's Groatsworth of Wit.
(Deceiving World.) NoSic

December. John Clare. OBCP

December. Robert Francis. LCAP

December. Josephine D. Henderson Heard. CBWP-4

December. Maurice Kenny. HATNAP

December. Hilda Morley. ArNa

December. H. Cordelia Ray. CBWP-3

December. Gary Snyder. InPS

December And at Christmass I drink red wine. (*LL*) Januar: by this fire [*or* thys fyre] I warme my handes. *Unknown.* EBEV

December among the Vanished. W. S. Merwin. NaP

December, and the closing of the year. Christmas Eve in Whitneyville, 1955. Donald Hall. UnPo

December at Yase. Gary Snyder. *Fr.* Four Poems for Robin. MoP; NNaP; NoAM; NOBA; NoP; SOTW

December Cats. Mark Van Doren. OFC

December Day, Hoy Sound. George Mackay Brown. OxBS

December Day in Honolulu. Galway Kinnell. AnAn

December Eclipse. Margo Lockwood. Poetsp

December 15, 1811. Poem for My Family: Hazel Griffin and Victor Hernandez Cruz. June Jordan. BPo

December Forest, A. Vesna Krmpotic, *tr. fr. Croatian by* Vasa D. Mihailovich. WPOW

December Fragments. Richmond Lattimore. PChr

December Morning. Anna Seward. ECWP

December narrows our day to a thread of light. Song in the Cold Season. Samuel French Morse. PoA

December Night. W. S. Merwin. CAPP

December nights are frosts and stars. Helen Waddell. MLL

December 1974: a Lament. Abdur-Rahman Slade Hopkinson. PBCV

December pools, latent, crosshatched. Instructions for Fishing the Eel. Dennis Schmitz. AnAn

December Portrait. Kathleen Tankersley Young. ShDr

December: Prayer to St. Nicholas. John Heath-Stubbs. OBCP

December Saturday, star-clear, A. After Edgehill, 1642. Gladys Mary Coles. FaBoEH

December Stillness. Siegfried Sassoon. CMoP

December sun sits low over hedgegrows, glitter. What Shines in Winter Burns. T. R. Hummer. MT

December: the trees chafing. Mile Hill. Dennis Schmitz. LCAP

December 30th. Ivor Gurney. NAEL-2

December 21st. Jean Valentine. LCAP

December 24 and George McBride Is Dead. Richard Hugo. HoPM

December 27, 1966. L. E. Sissman. DiPo; SM

December's Husbandry. Thomas Tusser. *Fr.* Five Hundred Points of Good Husbandry. NoSic

December's Picture. Antionia Quintana Pigno. AfAz

Decent docent doesn't doze, The. History of Education. David McCord. OBAL

Deception. Alfred Corn. PoA

Deception. Josephine D. Henderson Heard. CBWP-4

Deceptions. Philip Larkin. CMoP; ErPo; GTBS-P; OxAEP-2

Deceptive Grin of the Gravel Porters, The. Gavin Ewart. FaBoMo

Deceptive Present, the Phoenix Year, The. Delmore Schwartz. BoNaP

Deceptrices, The. William Carlos Williams. NYBP

Deciduous Spring. Robert Penn Warren. ArNa

Decimation before Phraata, The. Alan Dugan. AnAn

Decision, The. Owen Dodson. PoNe

Decision, The. Theodore Roethke. CRP; VGW

Decision. *Unknown.* PoToHe

Decision, A. Edith Södergran, *tr. fr. Swedish by* Jaakko A. Ahokas. PBWP

Deck thee with flowers which fear not rage of days! (*LL*) Change Should Breed Change. William Drummond of Hawthornden. OBEV

Deck thyself, maiden. Esthonian Bridal Song. Johann Gottfried von Herder, *tr. fr. German by* W. Taylor. AWP

Deck us all with Boston Charlie. Boston Charlie. Walt Kelly. FiBHP; GoJo

Decked in October light adobe grows gold. Chimayo. Demetria Martinez. AfAz

Decked, stacked, pillaged from. The Middle Passage and After. Larry Neal. NBV

Decks awash,/ Mast-top dipping. Archilochus, *tr. fr. Latin by* Guy Davenport. OBVE

Declaimer, The. Henry Baker. NOEC

Declair, ye bankis of Helicon. *Unknown. Fr.* Bankis of Helicon, The. OxBS

Declaration, The. Nathaniel Parker Willis. AnAmPo; OBAL

Declaration of Independence. Michael Brownstein. UL

Declaration of Independence, II. Jane Oliensis. UTF

Declare, my pretty maid. The Philanderer. Moses Mendes. *Fr.* Chaplet, The. TrJP

Declare, O mind, from fond desires excluded. A Counterlove. *Unknown.* NoSic

Declasse Memory. Michael O'Loughlin. IB

Declension. Stephen Sandy. PoA

Declining of a Gallant, The. *Unknown.* FaBoUs

Deconstructions. Liz Cashdan. NWP

Decorating the Soldiers' Graves. Minot Judson Savage. OHIP

Decoration. Mary Ursula Bethell. PeNZ

Decoration. Louise Bogan. MoAB; MoAmPo

Decoration. Thomas Wentworth Higginson. OHIP

Decoration Day. George Hurlbut Barbour. OHIP

Decoration Day. Josephine D. Henderson Heard. CBWP-4

Decoration Day. Julia Ward Howe. OHIP

Decoration Day. Longfellow. OHIP

Decorations climbing up the loft on a wobbly ladder. My Christmas; Mum's Christmas. Sarah Forsyth. OBCP

Decoy. John Ashbery. PoM

Decoy Partridge, A. Simmias [*or* Simias] of Rhodes, *tr. fr. Greek by* Peter Jay. GrAn

Decoys, The. W. H. Auden. CMoP; PoE

Decoys. Leslie Norris. FoLa

Decrees of God, The. Chao Ying-tou, *tr. fr. Chinese by* William C. White. TrJP

Decrepit Old Gasman, A. *Unknown.*

Dedicated, The. Philip Larkin. OxBC

Dedicated Dancing Bull and the Water Maid, The, *sels.* Stevie Smith.
"Hop hop, thump thump." WPE

Dedicated to a Young Lady Representing the Indian Race at Howard University. Alfred Islay Walden. AAP

Deep in the shady sadness of a vale. Keats. *Fr.* Hyperion; a Fragment. EnRP; FHYEP; OAEL-2; OxAEP-2, *bk.* I – III; PoEL-4 (Saturn.) OBNC; TrGrPo

Deep in the Siberian mine. Message to Siberia. Pushkin, *tr. fr. Russian by* Max Eastman. AWP; TTY

Deep in the wave is a coral grove. The Coral Grove. James Gates Percival. GN

Deep in the winter plain, two armies. Two Armies. Stephen Spender. OBWP; OxBTC

Deep in the wood I made a house. August. Katharine Pyle. OBCA

Deep in the woods we'll go. Heart of the Woods. Wesley Curtright. PoNe

Deep in this grave her bones remain. Reflections, Written on Visiting the Grave of a Venerated Friend. Ann Plato. BlSi

Deep in Winter. Tu Fu, *tr. fr. Chinese by* A. C. Graham. PLT

Deep in your cheeks. Origins. Keorapetse Kgositsile. PoBA

Deep into autumn the acorns ripen. Lament of a Woman Acorn-gatherer. P'i Jih-hsiu, *tr. fr. Chinese by* William H. Nienhauser. SuSp

Deep into the midst of a great, dark, wood. The Snail's Lesson. Priscilla Jane Thompson. CBWP-2

Deep lane, poor families; I have few friends. At the End of Spring. Yü Hsüan-chi, *tr. fr. Chinese by* Geoffrey R. Waters. BoWoP

Deep Mining. Irene McKinney. PBCAP

Deep Night. Yuan Chi, *tr. fr. Chinese by* Kenneth Rexroth. OHMPC

Deep night. I cannot sleep. Deep Night. Yuan Chi. *tr. fr. Chinese by* Kenneth Rexroth. OHMPC

Deep on the convent-roof the snows. St. Agnes' Eve. Tennyson. LiTB; MeMBP; OBEV

Deep peace of the running wave to you. *Unknown, tr. fr. Gaelic by* Mary Rogers. EaPr

Deep peace of the Sun of Peace to you! *(LL)* Deep peace of the running wave to you. *Unknown.* EaPr

Deep peace, pure white of the moon to you. "Fiona Macleod." *Fr.* Invocation of Peace. BoTP

Deep prolonged entry with the strong pink cock. She Loves. Olga Broumas. GLP

Deep red bogs divided. Richard Murphy. *Fr.* Battle of Aughrim, The. CIP

Deep River. Eugène Marais, *tr. fr. Afrikaans by* Hugh Finn. PeSAV

Deep River ("Deep river, my home is over Jordan.") *Unknown.* BPo; TAP

Deep river, Lord; I want to cross over into camp ground. *(LL)* Deep River ("Deep river, my home is over Jordan.") *Unknown.* BPo; TAP

Deep-Sea Pearl, The. Edith M. Thomas. AmWP

Deep Sea Soundings. Sarah Williams. WGRP

Deep Sea Tug. Harry Robertson. OxBSS

Deep sorrow in the song, The. *(LL)* Melancholy. Joseph Freiherr von Eichendorff. RiWo

Deep Spring. *Unknown.* AmFP

Deep sunk in floods of grief. Bible, *O.T., paraphrased by* Sir Thomas Wyatt. *See* Out of the depths [*or* deep] have I cried [*or* called] (unto) Thee, O Lord.

Deep-sworn Vow, A. W. B. Yeats. CMoP; OAEL-2; PFP; PoE; UnPo

Deep under the willows' shade the horse treads proudly. Passing by Kamata. Su Man-shu, *tr. fr. Chinese by* Wu-chi Liu. SuSp

Deep waters silent roul, so Grief like mine. Elegy on the Earl of Rochester. Anne Wharton. KTR; NOSC

Deep Well, *sels.* Roland Robinson. "I am at Deep Well where the spirit-trees." CBAP; NOBAu

Deep well knows it certainly, The. World-Secret. Hugo von Hofmannsthal, *tr. fr. German by* Charles Wharton Stork. TrJP

Deep wooden note, A. Overheard. Denise Levertov. PoM

Deepened, like an old colour, and understood. *(LL)* Apis Mellifica. Roger McDonald. NOBAu

Deepening-Green Pavilion. Chu Yi-tsun, *tr. fr. Chinese by* Chang Yin-nan *and* Lewis C. Walmsley. SuSp

Deepening shadows bring on sorrow, The. Hsü Kan, *tr. by* Ronald C. Miao. *Fr.* Boudoir Thoughts. SuSp

Deeper than sleep but not so deep as death. Night Feeding. Muriel Rukeyser. MDDM; NMM; WPE

Deepest kiss in the world, The. *(LL)* Victims of the Latest Dance Craze. Cornelius Eady. UTF

Deeply repentant of my sinful ways. Gaspara Stampa, *tr. fr. Italian by* Lorna De' Lucchi. WPOW

Deer, The. Mary Austin. FaPON

Deer. John Drinkwater. CH

Deer. No Ch'ŏn-myŭng, *tr. fr. Korean by* Ko Won. PBWP

Deer. Kenneth Rexroth. *Fr.* Bestiary, A. HoPM; OBAL

Deer among Cattle. James Dickey. CAPP

Deer and the Snake, The. Kenneth Patchen. MoAmPo

Deer are gentle and graceful. Deer. Kenneth Rexroth. *Fr.* Bestiary, A. HoPM; OBAL

Deer are just thankful it's over, The. Thanksgiving. Liz Rosenberg. PBCAP

Deer carcass hangs from a rafter, The. Gathering the Bones Together. Gregory Orr. AmPA; Poetsp

Deer feed on. Upon Leaving the Parole Board Hearing. Conyus. PoBA

Deer gather in flocks by nature. Living in the Mountains. Tai Shu-lun, *tr. fr. Chinese by* William H. Nienhauser. SuSp

Deer Hunt. Judson Jerome. RFM

Deer Hunt, Salt Lake Valley. Helen Handley. GrPl

Deer in Aspens. Kay DeBard Hall. GoYe

Deer is humble, lovely as God made her, The. The Deer and the Snake. Kenneth Patchen. MoAmPo

Deer Isle. Philip Booth. VGW

Deer Lay Down Their Bones, The. Robinson Jeffers. NoAM

Deer-of-the-Waters: he laboured hard on his grammar. Red Indian Corpse. Peter Redgrove. OxBC

Deer on pine mountain. Yoshinobu, *tr. fr. Japanese by* Kenneth Rexroth. PoBeRe

Deer on the High Hills — a Meditation, *sels.* Iain Crichton Smith.

Deer Park. John Montague. PBCIP

Deer Sing, *sels.* Confucius, *tr. fr. Chinese by* Ezra Pound. Fraternitas. CTC; OBVE

Deer Song. Leslie Silko. VoR

Deer were bounding like blown leaves, The. Fire on the Hills. Robinson Jeffers. CMoP; RaBo

Deer which lives, The. Yoshinobu, *tr. fr. Japanese by* Arthur Waley. *Fr.* Shui Shu. AWP

Deer's Cry, The. *At. to* St. Patrick Saint Patrick, *tr. fr. Old Irish by* Whitley Stokes, John Strachan, *and* Kuno Meyer. WGRP

Deer's Cry, The. *At. to* St. Patrick Saint Patrick. *See* I arise today.

Deer's Request, The. Elizabeth Jennings. OBAP

Deevil's Waltz, The. Sydney Goodsir Smith. FaBoTw

Defeat. Witter Bynner. PoNe

Defeat, A. Denise Levertov. PBWP

Defeat and Victory. Wallace Rice. PAH

Defeat may serve as well as victory. Victory in Defeat. Edwin Markham. BLPL; PoLF

Defeat of the Norsemen, The, *sels.* Sedulius Scottus, *tr. fr. Latin.* "Heavens, ocean, and all earth, rejoice!" NOIV

Defence of Lawrence, The. Richard Realf. PAH

Defence of Lucknow, The. Tennyson. BeLS

Defence of Poetry, A. Giolla Brighde Mac Con Midhe. NOIV

Defence of Satire. Pope. *See* Ask you what provocation I have had?

Defence of the Alamo. Joaquin Miller. *See* Santa Anna *or* Ana came storming, as a storm might come.

Defend his own stand! *(LL)* The Guest in Your House. *Unknown.* OBF

Defend the bad against the worse. *(LL)* Where Are the War Poets? C. Day Lewis. FaBoMo; OBWP; OxBSP; PAW

Defend Us, Lord, from Every Ill. John Hay. AH

Defender, The. Arthur M. Sampley. GoYe

Defender — / a partner doesn't dance with prison bars. Poem for the Wife of an Imprisoned Leader *especially for Winnie Mandela.* James Berry. NBrP

Defender of his country, The — the founder of liberty. Epitaph on Washington. *Unknown.* OHIP

Defense of Guenevere, The. William Morris. NAEL-2; TEP

Defense of the Alamo, The. Joaquin Miller. BeLS; FaBoBe; PAH

Defense Rests. Vassar Miller. MoAmPo

Defensive Position. John Manifold. MoBrPo

Defiance, The. Aphra Behn. EnLoPo

Defiance. Solomon ibn Gabirol, *tr. fr. Hebrew by* Emma Lazarus. TrJP

Defiance. Walter Savage Landor. CBLP

Defied, — no past is mine, no future: look at me! *(LL)* Orpheus and Eurydice. Robert Browning. CTC

Defiled Is My Name Full Sore. *At. to* Anne Boleyn. WPE

Defined, plotted; which maps do not speak. *(LL)* Colville 1964. Kendrick Smithyman. PeNZ

Defining an Absence. John Cassidy. PWE

Definition. Grace Noll Crowell. PoToHe

Definition. Wilma Elizabeth McDaniel. ETG

Definition. Lauren Shakely. FYAP

Definition for Blk/Children. Sonia Sanchez. PoBA

Definition of a Waterfall. John Ormond. AngWe

Definition of Beauty, The. Robert Herrick. BeJo; CaPo

Definition of Blue. John Ashbery. CAPP; NAAL-2

Definition of Love, The. Andrew Marvell. BLPL; BoLoP; CBLP; EBEV; ESCV; FHYEP; GBL; GeHe; HoPM; ImPo; InPS; JCP; LiTB; MeLP; NAEL-1; NOBE; NoP; NOSC; OAEL-1; OBEV; PoEL-2; SCGP; SeCP; SeCV-1; TEP; TFi; TrGrPo; UnPo

Definition of Nature. Eugene B. Redmond. NBV; PoBA

Definition of the Soul. Boris Pasternak, tr. fr. Russian by Babette Deutsch. TrJP

Definitions. Joseph Joel Keith. PoToHe

Definitions. Susan Sherman. ETG

Definitions, sels. E. B. White.
Critic. NBLV

Deflowering. Mahmood Jamal. NBrP

Deformed Mistress, The. Sir John Suckling. BXAP; ErPo

Deft hands called Chopin's music from the keys. Modjeska. Celia Laighton Thaxter. AmWP

Deft, practised, eager. Usquebaugh. Wendy Cope. UV

Deftly, admiral, cast your fly. W. H. Auden. GTBS-P

Degas. Paul Monette. AmPA

Degenerate Age, A. Solomon ibn Gabirol, tr. fr. Hebrew by Emma Lazarus. TrJP

Degenerate Douglas! O the unworthy lord! Composed at Neidpath Castle, the Property of Lord Queensberry, 1803. Wordsworth. GTBS; GTBS-P

Degli Sposi. Rika Lesser. FYAP; UnAS

Degrees. Elizabeth Bartlett. IHNG

Degrees of Gray in Philipsburg. Richard Hugo. CAPP; CoAP; NAAL-2; NoAM; NoP; TRP; VCAP

Deh 'Pon Um Again. Michael McTurk. PBCV

Deid is now that divour and dollin in erd. The Widow Speaks. William Dunbar. Fr. Book of the Two Married Women and the Widow, The. PoEL-1

Deid is now that dyvour and dollin in erd. The Widow Has Buried Her Second Husband. William Dunbar. Fr. Tua Mariit Wemen and the Wedo, The. OxBLMV

Deid sall ye ligg, and ne'er a memorie. Douglas Young, after the Greek of Sappho. OBVE

Deign, dear, to listen once to what your lips are saying . . . (LL) Girl with Mind Wandering. Paul Valéry. STV

Deign, Laura — now again the rainy season's here. Girl with Mind Wandering. Paul Valéry, tr. fr. French by John Frederick Nims. STV

Deir El Bahari: Temple of Hatshepsut. D. J. Enright. OBTV

Deirdre. James Stephens. AWP; CMoP; OBMV; PoRA

Deirdre's [or Deidre's] Lament for the Sons of Usnach. Unknown, tr. fr. Irish by Sir Samuel Ferguson. IIP; NOIV; PeIV

Deity of Love Incorporate, A. Edward Taylor. Fr. Preparatory Meditations Before My Approach to the Lord's Supper. TAP

Déjà vu. Christine McNeill. NWP

Dejection, sels. Samuel Taylor Coleridge.
"Grief without a pang, void, dark, and drear, A." IMW

Dejection. Derek Mahon. PBCIP

Dejection. Georg Trakl, tr. fr. German by Michael Hamburger. PeFWW

Dejection; an Ode. Samuel Taylor Coleridge. EnRP; FHYEP; HeIP; LiTB; MeMBP; NAEL-2; NAWM-2; NOBE; NoP; OAEL-2; OBNC; OxAEP-2; PoE; PoEL-4; PPP; TFi; TOF

Déjeuner sur l'herbe. Anne Rouse. NWP

Dekunle, handsome man, hail! Omobayode Arowa, tr. fr. Yoruba. Fr. Dirge for Fajuyi. WTO

Del Cascar. William Stanley Braithwaite. CDC

Delacroix pentit Chopin's heid. Ye Mongers Aye Need Masks for Cheatrie. Sydney Goodsir Smith. OxBS

Delay. William Hammond. CBLP

Delay. Elizabeth Jennings. NIP; OxBTC

Delay, whose parents Phlegm and Slumber are. Delay. William Hammond. CBLP

Delayed Action. Christian Morgenstern, tr. fr. German by W. D. Snodgrass and Lore Segal. RB

Delcaration of the Death of John Lewes, A. Thomas Gilbart. NoSic

Delete "Wax Effigy, some Pins, one Witch." Correction. Eric Millard. IHNG

Delfica. Gérard de Nerval, tr. fr. French by Andrew Hoyem. NU

Delia Holmes ("Delia, Delia, why didn't you run?") At. to "Whistling Bill" Ruff. AmFP

Delia Very Angry. Unknown. NOEC

Deliberate as scrimshaw. Cat Washing. Linda Molony. NOBAu

Deliberately, long ago/ the carcasses. From an Old House in America. Adrienne Rich. NNaP; TRP

Delicate blue veins on your legs. Not Even Because You Have Pearl-White Teeth. Angela de Hoyos. AfAz

Delicate, delicate, delicate, delicate — now! (LL) The Base Stealer. Robert Francis. GoJo; NTCP

Delicate eyes that blinked blue Rockies all ash. On Neal's Ashes. Allen Ginsberg. CAPP; PoM

Delicate fabric of bird song, A. May Day. Sara Teasdale. BoNaP

Delicate foot of, The. Essay on Meter. Bernard Keith. PRA

Delicate girl was eager to air, The. Princess Elizabeth of Bohemia, as Perdita. Frank O'Hara. PoA

Delicate Mother Kangaroo. D. H. Lawrence. GrPl

Delicate mother kangaroo. D. H. Lawrence. Fr. Kangaroo. OBAP

Delicate old injuries, the spines of names and leaves. (LL) Indian Boarding School: The Runaways. Louise Erdrich. HATNAP; NoAM

Delicate, Plummeting Bodies, The. Stephen Dobyns. FYAP

Delicate sound of a moth; a page turning. The Moths. Sean O Riordain, tr. fr. Irish by Thomas Kinsella. NOIV

Delicate young Negro stands, A. Anonymous Drawing. Donald Justice. CoAP; HeIP

Delicately bordered by poplars. (LL) In the Dordogne. John Peale Bishop. OBWP; PeFWW; PoWW; VGW

Delicious beauty that doth lie. John Marston. EIL

Delicious morning! how thy gentle beams. Blank Verse Written on the Sea Shore. Hannah Cowley. ECWP

Delight in books from evening. Francis Daniel Pastorius. NOSC; SCAP

Delight in Disorder. Robert Herrick. BeJo; CaPo; ClHu; EBEV; EBEvV; EnLoPo; ErPo; FaBV; FF; GGP; GTBS; GTBS-P; HAP; HeIP; InPK; InPS; JCP; LiTB; NAEL-1; NIP; NOBE; NoP; NOSC; OAEL-1; OBEV; OxAEP-1; PeLV; PoE; Poetr; PoRA; PPP; PrIm; SCGP; SeCP; SeCV-1; TEP; TFi; TrGrPo; TRP; WeW

Delight of humane kind, and gods above. Lucretius, tr. by Dryden. Fr. De Rerum Natura (On the Nature of Things). OBVE

Delight of Melancholy. Goethe, tr. fr. German by Philip L. Miller. RiWo

Delight of Solitariness, The. Sir Philip Sidney. See O sweet woods, the delight of solitariness.

Delight Song of Tsoai-Talee, The. N. Scott Momaday. CDW; EaPr; GrPl; InPK

Delighted, incredulous bride, A. Maud Fitzgerald. Unknown. PeLi

Delighteth to forgive. (LL) A Prayer in the Prospect of Death. Burns. TrPWD; WGRP

Delightful, book, your trip. Aoibhinn, A Leabhráin, Do Thriall. Unknown, tr. fr. Irish by Flann O'Brien. BIrV

Delightful change from the town's abode. Barnyard Melodies. Fred Emerson Brooks. OBAL

Delightful mansion! blest retreat! A Thought in a Garden. John Hughes. ECEV

Delights of the Door, The. Francis Ponge, tr. fr. French by Robert Bly. NU; RaBo

Delilah. Ellen Bryant Voigt. CrSp

Delineaments of the Giants, The. William Carlos Williams. See Paterson lies in the valley under the Passaic Falls.

Delinquent Travellers, The. Samuel Taylor Coleridge. OBTV

Delirium in Vera Cruz. Malcolm Lowry. FaBoTw; OxBTC

Deliverance. Frances E. W. Harper. AmWP; WPOW

Deliverance from a Fit of Fainting. Anne Bradstreet. TAP

Deliverance is not for me in renunciation. Rabindranath Tagore. Fr. Gitanjali. WGRP

Deliverance of Jehovah, The. Bible, O.T., paraphrased by Sir Thomas Wyatt. See Lord is my light and my salvation, The; whom shall I fear?

Delivered out of raw continual pain. St. Peter and the Angel. Denise Levertov. PWE

Delivered/ Palpable/ Ours. (LL) Snapshots of a Daughter-in-Law. Adrienne Rich. FaBoWP; HCAP; NAAL-2; NALW; NIP; NMM; NoAM; NoP; Poetr; VCAP

Delivering the Times, 1952-1944. David Huddle. PBCAP

Delivery Guaranteed. Kingsley Amis. OBD

DeLiza Spend the Day in the City ("DeLiza drive the car to fetch, Alexis.") June Jordan. NoAM

Dell, The. Gavin Ewart. OxBC

Dell's hounds leap like the damned around the trunk. Coon Hunt. Thomas Rabbitt. MT

Delos. Lawrence Durrell. OxAEP-2

Delos. Bernard Spencer. NoAM

Delta, The. Michael Dennis Browne. NYBP

Delta. Adrienne Rich. NIP

Delta Traveller. Charles Wright. AmPA; LCAP

Delug'd with tears, by what you heard before. To My Honoured Patron Humphery Davie. Benjamin Tompson. SCAP

Deluge. John Clare. BoNaP

Deluge, The. Wilhelm Müller, tr. fr. German by Philip L. Miller. Fr. Winter's Journey, The. RiWo

Deluge, The, *sels. Unknown.*
  Animals in the Ark, The. ChTr; GBP
Deluge, The. *Unknown, tr. by* C. S. Rafinesque. *Fr.* Walam [*or* Wallum] Olum; or, Red Score. LiTA
Deluge 1939, The. Saunders Lewis, *tr. fr. Welsh by* Gwyn Morgan. OBWVE
Delusion. Wilhelm Müller, *tr. fr. German by* Philip L. Miller. *Fr.* Winter's Journey, The. RiWo
Delusions of the days that once have been. Longfellow. *Fr.* Giles Corey of the Salem Farms. PAH
Dem Belly Full. Legon Cogil *and* Carlton Barrett. PBCV
Dem say him born. For Don Drummond. Lorna Goodison. PBCV
Dem say/ who say? Black Bud. Michael Smith. PBCV
Demaeneta sent eight sons. Dioscorides. PAW
Demagogue, The. Phyllis McGinley. FaBoEE
Demanded to be born. (*LL*) Things Grow Up out of the Dark. Joan Dobbie. LoHo
Demands. Roger Hilton. CBCK
Demands more Praise than Tongues can give. (*LL*) The Church the Garden of Christ. Isaac Watts. NOCV; PeECV
Demands my soul, my life, my all. (*LL*) When I Survey the Wondrous Cross. Isaac Watts. AmFP; FaPoR; WGRP
Demands of the Muse. Vernon Watkins. PoA
Deme as Ye List Uppon Goode Cause. Sir Thomas Wyatt. PoEL-1
Demeanour. *Unknown.* OxBChV
Dementia Praecox. Morris Bishop. PoA
Demesne lord died in the gradual morning, The. Chronicle. Aidan Carl Mathews. IB
Demeter Grieving. Michele Roberts. NBrP
Demeter has torn off. Demeter Grieving. Michele Roberts. NBrP
Demetrius fled the fight in fear. Erycius of Cyzicus. PAW
Demiurge's Laugh, The. Robert Frost. OxBA
Democracy works (*entre nous*). W. Stewart. PeLi
Democratic Barber; or, Country Gentleman's Surprise, The. John Parrish. NOEC
Democratic wisdom underneath, like solid ground for all, The. (*LL*) The Commonplace. Walt Whitman. MoAmPo; TrGrPo
Democritus and Heraclitus. Matthew Prior. OxBSP
Democritus, dear droll, revisit Earth. Democritus and Heraclitus. Matthew Prior. OxBSP
Demolition, The. Anne Stevenson. OxBSP
Demon in Paradise. Minuchihri, *tr. fr. Persian by* Omar S. Pound. ArPe
Demon-Lover. Sylvia Paskin. DT
Demon Lover, The. Adrienne Rich. IHMS
Demon Lover, The. *Unknown.* EnSB; HAP; LiTB; MAT; SCGP; TFi; UnPo; WeW
Demon of the Mirror, The. Bayard Taylor. BeLS
Demon [*or* Daemon] Lover. *Unknown. See* "Well met, well met, my own true love."
Demon vanishes before a prayer, The. (*LL*) Full Vision. H. Cordelia Ray. AmWP; CBWP-3
Demonstration. W. S. Merwin. PRA
Demonstrators who filled the streets of Seoul, The. It's Not the Same. Fukunaka Tomoko, *tr. fr. Japanese by* Kenneth Rexroth *and* Ikuko Atsumi. WPJ
Demoted I Arrive at Lan-t'ien Pass and Show This Poem to My Brother's Grandson Han Hsiang. Han Yü, *tr. fr. Chinese by* Charles Hartman. SuSp
Demure you are over your left shoulder. Lines on a Boer War Pin-up Girl Seen in the Falcon Hotel, Bude. Christopher Hope. PeSAV
Denial. George Herbert. GeHe; JCP; NAEL-1; NOBE; NoP; OAEL-1
Denial, A. Elizabeth Barrett Browning. GBL; OBNC
Deniall. George Herbert. *See* When my devotions could not pierce.
Denise. Robert Beverly Hale. GrPl
Denmark. Humbert Wolfe. OBTV
Dennis. Dan Sicoli. NGP
Denouement. Ruth Stone. BoWoP
Dense on the stream the vapours lay. The Mowers: An Anticipation of the Cholera, 1848. Charles MacKay. EBVV; OHCV
Dense ravine, no inch, A. Portola Valley. Amy Clampitt. EOEF
Dense, the white cloud of moths whirling. Hitler Spring. Eugenio Montale, *tr. fr. Italian by* William Arrowsmith. AnAn
Dense white clouds embrace Thunder Peak. Written during My Stay at White Clouds Monastery on West Lake. Su Man-shu, *tr. fr. Chinese by* Wu-chi Liu. SuSp
Dented spider like a snowdrop white, A. In White. Robert Frost. TRP
Dentist, A. *Unknown.* FaBoCo; FaBoEE

Dentists continue to water their lawns even in the rain. The Great Society. Robert Bly. NoAM
Dentist's Window, A. James K. Baxter. OxBC
Dentologia; a Poem on the Diseases of the Teeth and Their Proper Remedies. Solyman Brown. FaBoUs
Sels.
  Artificial Teeth.
  Caries.
  Tartar.
  Value of Dentistry, The.
Denunciation, A. Mahammed Abdille Hassan, *tr. fr. Somali by* B. W. Andrzejewski. WTO
Denunciation; or, Unfrock'd Again. Philip Whalen. NeAP
Denzel Brush zipped up his periscope and treed the bartender. Errant. John Godfrey. UL
Deo Gracias! (*LL*) Adam Lay yBounden [*or* I-bounden]. *Unknown.* ChIV-2; ChTr; CTC; EnVB; HAP; InPS; MiEL; NOBE; NOCV; NoP; OAEL-1; OxBLMV; OxBoLi; PoE; PoEL-1; TFi; TOF; TRP; WeW
Deo gracias. (*LL*) The Agincourt Carol. *Unknown.* OAEL-1; OBET
Deo Gracias, Anglia. *Unknown. See* Our[e] king[e] went forth to Normandy.
Deo gracias [*or* gracias], Anglia. The Agincourt Carol. *Unknown.* EBEV; OAEL-1; OBET
Deo Optimo Maximo. Louise Imogen Guiney. TrPWD
Deodand, The. Anthony Hecht. DiPo; NoAM
Deor. *Unknown, tr. fr. Anglo-Saxon.* ASW, *tr. by* Kevin Crossley-Holland; TEP, *tr. by* Walter Kendrick
Deor. *Unknown, tr. fr. Anglo-Saxon.* EBEV, *tr. by* John Wain; TEP, *tr. by* Walter Kendrick
Deor's Lament. *Unknown, tr. fr. Anglo-Saxon by* Charles W. Kennedy. AnOE; OAEL-1
Depairt, depairt, depairt [*or* Departe, departe, departe]. Lament of the Master of Erskine. Alexander Scott. GBL
  (Depart, depart, depart.) CoGr
  (Lament, 1547, A. *abr.*) CH
  (Lament of the Maister of Erskine.) CoGr
Depart, depart, depart. Alexander Scott. *See* Depairt, depairt, depairt [*or* Departe, departe, departe].
Depart from Me. Mary Elizabeth Coleridge. TrPWD
"Departed Friend," A. Julia A. Moore. FiBHP
Departed Youth. Hannah Cowley. ECWP
Departing at dawn, carriage bells ajingle. An Early Walk on Shang Mountain. Wen T'ing-yün, *tr. fr. Chinese by* William R. Schultz. SuSp
Departing Words to a Son. Robert Pack. GOYP
Departmental. Robert Frost. GoYe; HeIP; HoPM; MoAB; MoAmPo; NAAL-2; NOBA; NOBL; OBAL; PeLV; SoSe
Departure. Edmund Blunden. OxBSP
Departure. Van K. Brock. MT
Departure. Carolyn Forché. AnAn; PAW
Departure. Edna St. Vincent Millay. MoAmPo
Departure, The. William Vaughn Moody. AnAmPo
Departure, The. Coventry Patmore. *Fr.* Unknown Eros, The. NOBE; OBEV; OBNC
Departure, The. Frank Steele. GOYP
Departure. Wang Wei, *tr. fr. Chinese by* Robert Payne. TAL
Departure, The. Reed Whittemore. TAP
Departure, The; an Elegy. Henry King. SeCP
Departure Aria. Johann Christian Günther, *tr. fr. German by* George C. Schoolfield. GePo
Departure in Middle Age. Roland Mathias. CRP; OBWVE
Departure in the Dark. C. Day Lewis. TwCP
Departure of the Good Daemon, The. Robert Herrick. CoGr; FaBoRV
Departure (Southampton Docks: October 1899). Thomas Hardy. Son
Departure's Girlfriend. Roberta Hill Whiteman. ETG
Departures of Friends in Childhood, The. Douglas Dunn. OBF
Dependencies, The. Howard Nemerov. VCAP
Deportation. "M. B.," *tr. fr. Polish by* A. Glanz-Leyeles. TrJP
Deposition, The. Thomas Stanley. CBLP
Deposition by John Wilmot, A. Vincent McHugh. ErPo
Deposition from Love, A. Thomas Carew. BeJo; CaPo; MeLP
Depot, The. Lewis Turco. GrPl
Depot Blues. *Unknown.* AmFP
Depot in Rapid City. Roberta Hill Whiteman. BoWoP
Depreciating Her Beauty. Wilfrid Scawen Blunt. *Fr.* Love Sonnets of Proteus, The. OBMV
Depressed by the Death of the Horse That He Bought from Robert Bly. Henry Taylor. BXAP
Depression. Robert Bly. NaP

Diamond Lily. *Unknown.* FaBoBl

Diamond of a morning, A. Morning Song. Sara Teasdale. AnAmPo

Diamonds are forever so I gave you quartz. The Hardness Scale. Joyce Peseroff. TRP

Dian, Isis, Artemis, whate'er thy name. W. J. Turner. *Fr.* Seven Days of the Sun, The. OBMV

Diana. (Sever'd from sweete Content, my live's sole light.) Henry Constable. ESo
Sels.
"Dear to my soul! then leave me not forsaken!" AAS; CBLP
   (Sonnet: 'Dear to my soul! then leave me not forsaken!') EIL
"Hope, like the hyaena [*or* hyena], coming to be old." EnLoPo; SCGP; Son
"If ever Sorrow spoke from soul that loves." EIL
"Miracle of the world, I never will deny." SCGP
"My lady's presence makes the roses red." EIL; NIP
"Needs must I leave and yet needs must I love." InvP
Resolved to Love. Son
"To live in hell, and heaven to behold." AAS; Son
   (If Love In These Be Founded.) CBCK
"Whilst Echo cries [*or* eccho cryes], "What shall become of me[e]?" AAS

Diana. Jorge de Montemayor, *tr. fr.* Spanish *by* Bartholomew Young. EIL
Sels.
"Shepherd, who can pass such wrong."

Diana and Actaeon. Dick Davis. SCBI

Diana Fitzpatrick Mauleverer James. Miss James. A. A. Milne. MoShBr

Diana guardeth our estate. Hymn to Diana. Catullus, *tr. fr.* Latin *by* Richard Claverhouse Jebb. AWP

Diana was a white girl. What abou' de Law? Adam Small, *tr. fr. Afrikaans by* Carrol Lasker. PeSAV

Diana's Hunting-Song. Dryden. *Fr.* Secular Masque, The. NAEL-1; NOBE; PoE; PoEL-3; PrIm; SCGP; SeCV-2

Diane de Poitiers, Josephine and Pompadour. Mother Goose Rhyme. Kenneth Rexroth. ErPo

Diapered in hospital linen. The Recovery Room: Lying-in. Helen Chasin. IHMS

Diaphenia. *At.* to Henry Constable *and also to* Henry Chettle. CH; EIL; GTBS; GTBS-P; NOBE

Diarrhea Sestina. Edward Kleinschmidt. UnDi

Diary, The. Goethe, *tr. fr. German by* John Frederick Nims. STV

Diary. David Wagoner. CoAP

Diary. Mary Wilson. Spl

Diary of a Church Mouse. Sir John Betjeman. OxBTC

Diary of a Palestinian Wound, *sels.* Mahmoud Darwish, *tr. fr. Arabic by* Lena Jayyusi *and* Christopher Middleton.

Diary of a Raccoon. Gertrude Ryder Bennett. GoYe

Diary of a Silence, The. Michael O'Loughlin. IB

Diary of a Tashkent Jew. Gloria Glickstein. BTR

Diary of a Woodcutter, *sels.* Fuad Rifka.
"Wrinkles in the lake." TSaS, *tr. by* Faud Rifka *and* Shirley Kaufman

Diary of an Old Soul. George Macdonald. TrCP
Sels.
Be With Me, Lord.
That Thou Art Nowhere to Be Found.
This Day Be with Me.

Diary of Days for Adjoa. Jackie Kay. DT

Diary of the Waning Moon, The, *sels.* Abutsu the Nun, *tr. fr. Japanese by* Edwin O. Reischauer.
"Shore wind is cold on my travel clothes, The." PBWP

Diary without Dates, A. Nakamura Chio, *tr. fr. Japanese by* Kenneth Rexroth *and* Ikuko Atsumi. WPJ

Diatribe of the Kite, The. Norman Dubie. NAmP90

Dic Siôn Dafydd. Thomas Jacob Thomas, *tr. fr. Welsh by* H. Idris Bell. OBWVE

Dicamus Bona Verba. Tibullus, *tr. fr.* Latin *by* Constance Carrier. NAs

Dick, a Maggot. Swift. NBLV

Dick and Jane. Judith Kroll. AmPA

Dick Briggs a wealthy farmer's son. Dick Briggs from Australia. Charles Robert Thatcher. NOBAu

Dick Briggs from Australia. Charles Robert Thatcher. NOBAu

Dick Hairbrain Learns the Social Graces. John Trumbull. *Fr.* Progress of Dulness, The. AmPP

Dick is the one with the weenie. Dick and Jane. Judith Kroll. AmPA

Dick o' the Cow. *Unknown.* ESPB; IBB; OxBB

Dick Turpin and Black Bess. *Unknown.* AmFP

Dick Turpin's Ride ("Dick Turpin bold! Dick, hie away.") *Unknown.* OBET

Dickens in Camp. Bret Harte. AnAmPo

Dickensian borough of Coketown, The. Martin Fagg. PeLi

Dickery Dean. Dennis Lee. TLR

Dickery, dickery, dare. (*LL*) Dickery [*or* dickory], dickery [*or* dickory], dare. Mother Goose. OxNR; ReMoGo

Dickery [*or* dickory], dickery [*or* dickory], dare. Mother Goose. OxNR; ReMoGo

Dicky-Birds. Natalie Joan. BoTP

Dicky, Dicky Dout. *Unknown.* ISE

Dictates of nature prove school-knowledge weak, The. Repentance. George Alexander Stevens. NOEC

Dictionary Is an *His*torian, The: A Found Political Poem. Judith McCombs. IHMS

Did all the lets and bars appear. The March into Virginia. Herman Melville. BLPL; HAP; ImPo; LiTA; NAAL-1; NoP; PoE; TAP; TrGrPo

Did any seer of ancient time forbode. The Steam Threshing-Machine. Charles Tennyson Turner. OBNC

Did but the law appoint us one. A Popular Functionary. Charles Dibdin. NOEC

Did he get on? (*LL*) Nancy Hanks. Rosemary *and* Stephen Vincent Benét. FaBV; FaPON; NTCP

Did he meet Lud at the Fleet Gate? did count the top. David Jones. *Fr.* Anathemata, The. EBEV

Did he say I said you said she said that? *Unknown.* RoPo

Did he strike soundings off Vecta Insula? Angle-Land. David Jones. *Fr.* Anathemata, The. NoAM

Did I evah tell you, Sonny. Uncle Jimmie's Yarn. Priscilla Jane Thompson. CBWP-2

Did I ever tell you that Mrs. McCave. Too Many Daves. "Dr. Seuss." OBCA

Did I ever think. Ono no Takamura, *tr. by* Arthur Waley. *Fr.* Kokin Shu. AWP

Did I follow Truth wherever she led. Herman Altman. Edgar Lee Masters. *Fr.* Spoon River Anthology. OxBA

Did I hear it half in a doze. Tennyson. *Fr.* Maud[: A Monodrama]. EnVR

Did I my lines intend for public[k] view. The Countess of Winchilsea. NAEL-1; NALW; WPOW

Did I not say we grow old. Rufinus, *tr. fr. Greek by* Alan Marshfield. GrAn

Did I not tell you, my soul, "By Cypris, you will be caught." Meleager, *tr. fr. Greek by* Barbara Hughes Fowler. *Fr.* Epigrams. HePo

Did I this morn devoutly pray. Self-Examination. *Unknown.* FaBoUs

Did it go wrong just about a hundred. Counter-Revolution. W. H. Oliver. PeNZ

Did ivver ye see the like o' that? Pride. Violet Jacob. OxBS

Did my father curse his father for his lust I wonder. The Young Man Thinks of Sons. R. A. K. Mason. PeNZ

Did my hand ever touch your hair? Birth. Takahashi Shinkichi, *tr. fr. Japanese by* Geoffrey Bownas *and* Anthony Thwaite. OxBM

Did Not. Thomas Moore. BoLoP; ErPo; PeLV

Did not the heavenly rhetoric of thine eye. The Heavenly Rhetoric. Shakespeare. *Fr.* Love's Labour's Lost. ImPo; LiTB; Son

Did not true love disdain to own. On the Infrequency of Celia's Letters. William Hammond. CBLP

Did one look at what one saw. Hart Crane. AnAn

Did Ophelia ask Hamlet to bed? A. Cinna. PeLi

Did our best moment last. Emily Dickinson. NOBA

Did Saints, for this, bring in their Plate. Samuel Butler. *Fr.* Hudibras. FaBoEH

Did seem to me by much the wiser creature. (*LL*) Tunbridge Wells. The Earl of Rochester. FaBoPP; OBSV

Did Shriner die or make it to New York? A Disappearance in West Cedar Street. L. E. Sissman. TwCP

Did somebody give you a pat on the back? Pass. Edmund Vance Cooke. PWR

Did Someone Say "Babies"? Ogden Nash. OxBM

Did someone say that there would be an end. All Souls. May Sarton. CrSp; IMW

Did soon draw in again [*or* agen] (*LL*) Upon Her Feet. Robert Herrick. BeJo; CaPo; CBLP; OxBSP; PoE

Did the harebell loose her girdle. Emily Dickinson. FaBoVe; FaBV

Did the people of Vietnam. What Were They Like? Denise Levertov. HeIP; NIP; OBWP; PAW; VGW; WPE

Did their Catullus walk that way? (*LL*) The Scholars. W. B. Yeats. CMoP; NoP; OAEL-2; PoA

Did they catch as it were in a Vision at shut of the day. Jezreel. Thomas Hardy. NoP

Did they dare, did they dare, to slay Owen Roe O'Neill? Lament for the Death of Eoghan Ruadh O'Neill. Thomas Osborne Davis. NOIV; PeIV

Did This Happen to Your Mother? Alice Walker. VBLP

Diringer's *The Alphabet: A Key to the History of Mankind.* Stephanie Strickland. LoHo

Dirt is under my cracked nails;, The. (*LL*) The Hill Farmer Speaks. R. S. Thomas. GTBS-P; OBWVE; PIP

Dirtiest Man in the World, The. Shel Silverstein. OBCA

Dirty Floor, The. Edward Field. *See* Floor Is Dirty, The.

Dirty grey of the day at a Flanders dawn. Repetition. Anthony Rhodes. NSI

Dirty Hand, The. Carlos Drummond de Andrade, *tr. fr. Portuguese by* Mark Strand. AnRep

Dirty Little Accuser, The. Norman Cameron. OxBS

Dirty money and the sleazy hearts, The. The Matadors. Josephine Jacobsen. TAP

Dirty Niggers. Jacques Roumain, *tr. fr. French by* Ellen Conroy Kennedy. NegPo

Dirty No Gooder Blues. Bessie Smith. VBLP

Dirty river by religious explorers, The. Mystic River. John Ciardi. NYBP

Dirty Word, The. Karl Shapiro. CoAP; InPK; PoA

Dis[h], a dis[h], a green grass, A. Green Grass. *Unknown.* BoTP; CH; GBP; OxBoLi; OxNR

Dîs Aliter Visum; or, Le Byron de Nos Jours. Robert Browning. CBLP; NAEL-2

Dis is Ned dat am er-speakin.' Ned's Psalm of Life for the Negro. Joseph S. Cotter, Sr. AAP

Dis Long Time, Gal. *Unknown.* PBCV

Dis Mornin', Dis Evenin', So Soon. *Unknown.* AS

Dis sun are hot. This Sun Is Hot. *Unknown.* BPo

Dis Time No Stan' Like befo' Time. James Martinez. PBCV

Disabled. Wilfred Owen. CMoP; FF; InPS; LiTM; MeMBP; MoP; NAEL-2; NoAM; NSI; OBWVE; OxBTC; PeFWW; SCGP

Disabled Debauchee, The. The Earl of Rochester. BoLoP; GGP; HAP; NAEL-1; NOBL; OBSV; PPP

Disabled garment worker, The. In the Age of Postcapitalism. Lawrence Joseph. PBCAP

Disagreeable Man, The. W. S. Gilbert. FiBHP

Disagreements. John Hollander. AnAn

Disappearance. Willis Barnstone. IMW

Disappearance in West Cedar Street, A. L. E. Sissman. TwCP

Disappearance of Deanna Durbin, The. Michael C. Ford. NGP

Disappeared Woman I. Marjorie Agosin, *tr. fr. Spanish by* Cola Franzen. LoHo

Disappointed Sailor, The. *Unknown.* OxBSS

Disappointed Shrimper, The. P. A. Ropes. BoTP

Disappointment, The. Aphra Behn. NALW; NOSC; VBLP

Disappointment, The. Jane Taylor. FaBoUs

Disappointment. Mary E. Tucker. CBWP-1

Disappointment, A. Joanna Baillie. NOEC; WoRP

Disappointment — His Appointment. Edith Lillian Young. BLRP; WBLP

Disarmed with so genteel an air. The Answer. The Countess of Winchilsea. NALW

Disarrayed, The. John Blight. FaBoMA

Disarticulated/ arm torn out. Last Affair: Bessie's Blues Song. Michael S. Harper. HCAP; LCAP

Disaster. Charles Stuart Calverley. FM; NBLV

Disaster, The. Mary Savage. ECWP

Disaster has struck the people. "Decorous and Pretty" — Respectfully Offered to Circuit Inspector Kao. Liu Chih, *tr. fr. Chinese by* Richard John Lynn. SuSp

Disasters numb within us, The. Life at War. Denise Levertov. NMM; VGW

Discarded in old town, bunched. Old Helen. Judy Grahn. BCF

Discerns in speechless tears, both prayer and praise. (*LL*) Bereavement. Elizabeth Barrett Browning. WPE

Disciple, The. Oscar Wilde. OAEL-2

Discipline. George Herbert. FHYEP; GeHe; LiTB; MeLP; NAEL-1; NOBE; NOCV; NoP; OBEV; OxAEP-1; PoLF; TrGrPo

Disciplined in the school of hard campaigning. Horace. *See* Let the hardened by a sharp soldier's life.

Disconnection, The. Rita Mae Brown. IHMS

Disconsolate I/ from the thinning line. Witness to Death. Richmond Lattimore. VGW

Disconsolate Judy's Lamentation. *Unknown.* OxBSS

Discontented Student, The. St. George Tucker. OBAL

Discontents in Devon. Robert Herrick. BeJo; CaPo; OxBSP; SeCV-1

Discordants, *sels.* Conrad Aiken.
    "Dead Cleopatra lies in a crystal casket." PoA
    Music I Heard. AWP; BLPL; CMoP; ImPo; LiTA; LiTM; NOBA; OxBA; PoRA
    (Bread and Music.) MoAB; MoAmPo

Discords. Fabio Doplicher, *tr. fr. Italian by* Dana Gioia. NeIt

Discourse of Melancholy, A. Margaret Cavendish, Duchess of Newcastle. NOSC

Discourse of the Wanderer, and an Evening Visit to the Lake. Wordsworth. *Fr.* Excursion, The. EnRP

Discourse on the Principle in All the Cantos, The, *sels.* Laura Terracina, *tr. fr. Italian by* Muriel Kittel.

Discovered in Mid-Ocean. Stephen Spender. *See* He will watch the hawk with an indifferent eye.

Discoverer. James Michie. DiPo

Discoverer, The. Edmund Clarence Stedman. AnAmPo

Discoveries. Vernon Watkins. ImPo; LiTM

Discoveries in Arizona. James Wright. NoP

Discoveries of Bones and Stones. Geoffrey Grigson. OBTV

Discovering. Sharon Scott. JB

Discovering God Is Waking One Morning. John L'Heureux. BoNaP

Discovering Lasseter. Conal Fitzpatrick. NOBAu

Discovering My Daughter. Dabney Stuart. SM

Discovering Your Subject. Pattiann Rogers. MT

Discovery. Hilaire Belloc. OxBSP

Discovery. Benjamin Keech. PoToHe

Discovery, The. Gwendolyn MacEwen. NOBC

Discovery of America, The. James Logie Robertson. NOBVV

Discovery of Lake Michigan, The. "Antler." NGP

Discovery of LSD a True Story, The. Anselm Hollo. PoM

Discovery of San Francisco Bay. Richard Edward White. PAH

Discovery of the New World. Carter Revard. SoSe; VoR

Discovery of the Pacific, The. Thom Gunn. HeIP

Discovery of This Time. Archibald MacLeish. LiTA

Discreet. Maria Flook. EOEF

Discreet householder exclaims on the grandsire, A. Old Man Playing with Children. John Crowe Ransom. MeMAP

Discreet Majo, The. Fernando Periquet Y Zuaznabar, *tr. fr. Spanish by* Philip L. Miller. RiWo

Discreet, not cryptic. I write to you from the garden. A Message. Fleur Adcock. DiPo

Discriminator, The. Vernon Scannell. OxBC

Discuss the Influence of Posture upon Bodily Function. Give up to Twelve Examples. John Latham. FaBoBl

Discussions in the trenches often coupled pleasant wenches. Trench Fever. Robert Swan. NSI

Disdain. Sir Thomas Wyatt. *See* If in the World There Be More Woe.

Disdain me not. (*LL*) Disdain Me Not. Sir Thomas Wyatt. EnRePo; SiPS

Disdain Me Not. Sir Thomas Wyatt. EnRePo; SiPS

Disdain Me Still. The Earl of Pembroke. CBLP; EiL

Disdain Punished. Dryden. *Fr.* Theodore and Honoria, From Boccace. EBNV; NOSC

Disdain Returned. Thomas Carew. BeJo; PFP

Disdainful Mistress, The. *Malay Oral Tradition*, *tr. by* R. J. Wilkinson *and* R. O. Winstedt. WTO

Disdainfully watching her kin go by. (*LL*) Country Barnyard. Elizabeth J. Coatsworth. CRH

Disdaining butterflies. The Woman Who Loved Worms. Colette Inez. NMM

Disdains to crop a weed, and will not come. (*LL*) My thoughts hold mortal[l] strife. William Drummond of Hawthornden. EiL; GTBS; GTBS-P; NOSC; OxBSP

Diseases of Bath; a Satire, The, *sels. Unknown.*
    "If to the Pump Room in the morn we go." NOEC

Disembarking at Quebec. Margaret Atwood. PoE

Disenchanted, The. Clive Wilmer. SCBI

Disentangling our lives. The X-Ray. Andrew Elliott. PNI

Disfigure me, Lord. Take pity on me. Antipsalm. Novica Tadic, *tr. fr. Serbo-Croatian by* Charles Simic. HSix

Disfigurement. Yannis Ritsos, *tr. fr. Greek by* Edmund Keeley. AnAn

Disgrace he'd brought on an ancient name. "Rake" Windermere. Leonard Pounds. VPP

Disguised in my mouth as a swampland. In the Morning. Jayne Cortez. BCF; BlSi

Disguises. Thomas Edward Brown. WGRP

Disgusted with crimes that are piffling and messy. Crime at Its Best. Stoddard King. NBLV

Dish for a Poet, A. *Unknown.* OBCP

Dish of Tea, The. Philip Freneau. EAP

Dishonest Miller, The. *Unknown.* AmFP

Dishonor. Edwin Denby. ErPo

Disillusion. Maureen Burge. AIW; BrRo

Disillusion. Bessie B. Decker. PoToHe

Disillusion. *Unknown, tr. fr. Tewa Indian by* H. J. Spinden. WTO

Disillusion with the French Revolution. Charlotte Smith. *Fr.* Emigrants, The; a Poem. ECWP

Disillusioned. "Lewis Carroll."

Disillusionment. Virginia Graham. NBLV

Disillusionment of Ten o'Clock. Wallace Stevens. AnAmPo; CBNP; CMoP; FF; InPS; NAAL-2; NoAM; OxBA; RB; SAmP; SoSe; SOTW; TRP; TTTS

Disinherited, The, *sels.* Mary Gilmore.

Disinherited, The. Charles Spear. PeNZ

Disintegration. Richard Kostelanetz. InPK

Disinterment. James Sherry. UL

Dismal as a toad's domed eye, a cloud. John Cassidy. PWE

Dismantled Ship, The. Walt Whitman. AmPP; NoP; OxBA

Dismiss the instruments that for your pleasure. Music in Venice. Louis Simpson. NYBP

Dismissing reports and men, he put pressure on the wax. Geoffrey Hill. *Fr.* Mercian Hymns. HAP

Dismounting, I offer you wine. Seeing Someone Off. Wang Wei, *tr. fr. Chinese by* Irving Y. Lo. SuSp

Disobedience. A. A. Milne. NTCP; OTCP; TLR; UV, (*ll.* 1–11)

Disorder and Frailty. Henry Vaughan. ChIV-1

Dispensary, The. Sir Samuel Garth. OBSV
Sels.
 "As bold Mirmillo the grey dawn descries." ECEV
 "How impotent a deity am I!"
 "Oft has this planet rolled around the sun."
 "This wight all mercenary projects tries."

Dispenser of wide-wasting woe. Cowley's Style. Walter Savage Landor. EPCY

Dispersion and Convergence. Tom Clark. UL

Displacement. Lorenzo Thomas. PRA

Display thy breasts, my Julia: there let me. Upon Julia's Breasts. Robert Herrick. CaPo; NoP

Disposal. W. D. Snodgrass. CAPP

Disposed to wed, e'en while you hasten, stay. George Crabbe. *Fr.* Parish Register, The. FaBoUs

Disposing of a Pregnant Daughter. *Unknown. Fr.* Fyftene Joyes of Maryage, The. OxBLMV

Dispossessed, The. John Berryman. VGW

Dispossessed, The. Thomas Kinsella. NOCV

Dispossessed. Evangeline Paterson. NBrP

Dispossessions. Jane Cooper. FaBoWP

Dispraise of Absalom, The. *Unknown, tr. fr. Irish by* Robin Flower. BIrV

Dispraise of Love, and Lovers' Follies. "A. W." EIL; TrGrPo

Dispute between Women, A. *Unknown, tr. fr. Eskimo by* Tom Lowenstein. STP

Dispute of the Heart and Body of François Villon, The. Villon, *tr. fr. French by* Swinburne. AWP; OBVE

Dispute over Suicide, A. *Unknown, tr. fr. Egyptian by* T. Eric Peet. TTY

Disquieting Muses, The. Sylvia Plath. NALW; NMM

Disregard. Ai. NoAM

Dissatisfaction with Metaphysics. William Empson. CMoP

Dissembler. Charles Shaw. GoYe

Dissent of trees over the space of roots, The. This Spring. Regina DeCormier-Shekejian. LoHo

Dissenters' Thanksgiving for the Late Declaration, The. *Unknown.* APAS

Dissolution, The. John Donne. SeCV-1

Distaff, The. Erinna, *tr. fr. Greek by* Marylin Arthur. WPOW

Distaff Side, The. Harry Clifton. PBCIP

Distance. Anthony Delius. PeSA

Distance. Peter Everwine. NNaP

Distance doesn't matter, Francisco. Extracts: From the Journal of Elisa Lynch. Maura Stanton. AmPA

Distance from Loved Ones. James Tate. BAP-90

Distance is deceptive. Sydney glitters invisible, The. Reading Horace outside Sydney: 1970. David Malouf. FaBoMA

Distance is swept by the smooth. Radar. Alan Ross. FF

Distance of a City. James Berry. PBCV

Distance Spills Itself, The. Yocheved Bat-Miriam, *tr. fr. Hebrew by* Ruth Finer Mintz. MHP.

Distance that the dead have gone, The. Emily Dickinson. AnAmPo; MeMAP; OBD

Distances, The. Jim Carroll. PoA

Distances. Katherine Gallagher. AIW

Distances. Richard Hugo. CAPP

Distances. Jeremy Kingston. NYBP

Distances, The. W. S. Merwin. NOBA

Distances, *sels.* Christopher Okigbo.
 "Death lay in ambush." TTY

Distances, The. Charles Olson. NAAL-2; NeAP; NoP

Distances of Longing. Fawziyya Abu Khalid, *tr. fr. Arabic by* May Jayyusi. TSaS.

Distances to the Friend, The. Jonathan Williams. NeAP

Distant and faint the Herd-Boy Star. *Unknown, tr. fr. Chinese by* Dell R. Hales. SuSp

Distant as the Duchess of Savoy. *Unknown. See* O! mestress, why.

Distant Children. Cole Swenson. UTF

Distant Drum, The. Calvin C. Hernton. FF; TTY

Distant Footsteps, The. César Vallejo, *tr. fr. Spanish by* James Wright *and* John Knoepfle. RaBo

Distant Fury of Battle, The. Geoffrey Hill. NoP

Distant Howling. Miroslav Holub, *tr. by* Ewald Osers. PWE

Distant music. Parisian Streets. Duane Big Eagle. ETG

Distant Orgasm, The. James Tate. AmPA

Distant Runners, The. Mark Van Doren. GOA; LiTA; LiTM; MoAmPo

Distant Seychelles are not so remote, The. Eireann. Osbert Lancaster. *Fr.* Afternoons with Baedeker. NOBL; PeLV

Distant soughing of pine forests caresses my ear, The. Yitzhak Lamdan, *tr. fr. Hebrew by* Ruth Finer Mintz. *Fr.* In the Khamsin. MHP

Distant View. Uys Krige, *tr. fr. Afrikaans by* Uys Krige *and* Jack Cope. PeSA

Distant View of England from the Sea. William Lisle Bowles. EnRP

Distant Winter, The. Philip Levine. VGW

Distaste. Ammianus, *tr. fr. Greek by* Peter Jay. GrAn

Distich. Shuraikh, *tr. fr. Arabic.* TrJP

Distichs. John Hay. AnAmPo

Distil not poison in mine ears. John Hall. OxBSP

Distillation. Richard Hovey. AnAmPo

Distilled Water. M. K. Joseph. PeNZ

Distinct Call of the Alligator, The. Betsy Sholl. PBCAP

Distinctions. Charles Tomlinson. CMoP; PRA

Distinguish carefully between these two. The Justice of the Peace. Hilaire Belloc. IHNG; NOBVV; OBSV

Distinguished, and familiar, and aloof. (*LL*) And what is love? Misunderstanding, pain. J. V. Cunningham. CRP; HAP; HoPM; PoA

Distinguished the belt feed lever from the belt holding pawl. (*LL*) The Fury of Aerial Bombardment. Richard Eberhart. ArOW; CMoP; FaBoMo; FF; FYAP; HeIP; HoPM; InPK; LiTA; LiTM; MoP; NIP; NoAM; NoP; OBWP; PoWW; PrIm; RB; TAP; TFi; TwCP; UnPo; VGW

Distracted Puritan, The. Richard Corbett [*or* Corbet]. BeJo; OxBoLi

Distracted the Mother Said to Her Boy. Gregory Harrison. Mes

Distracted with care. The Despairing Lover. William Walsh. ELP; FaBoCh; NBLV; NOBL; OxBoLi; PeLV

Distraction. A. R. Ammons. CAPP

Distraction. Henry Vaughan. GeHe; SeCP

Distractions and the Human Crowd. Stevie Smith. OxBC

Distress. Flavien Ranaivo, *tr. fr. French by* Ellen Conroy Kennedy. NegPo

Distressed Men of War. *Unknown.* OxBSS

Distribution of Honours for Literature. Walter Savage Landor. FaBoEE

Distrust. Robert Herrick. CaPo

Disturb me not, oh bouyant youths! *Unknown, tr. fr. Maori by* John White. WTO

Disturbance. John Cassidy. PWE

Disturbed by consciousness. Satori. Gayl Jones. BlSi

Disturbed by the chatter. Neighbour's Pear Tree. Tony Curtis. AngWe

Disturbed, the kudu are running. On Clouds. Douglas Livingstone. PeSAV

Disturbing the Sallies Forth. Clark Coolidge. UL

Disturbing to have a person. Barbara Guest. FaBoWP

Disused Shed in Co. Wexford, A. Derek Mahon. AnAn; BiHa; CIP; FaBoPV; NOIV; OxBC; PBCIP; PNI; SCBI

Disused Temple, The. Norman Cameron. OxBS; OxBTC

Ditchdigger's Tears, The, *sels.* Pier Paolo Pasolini, *tr. fr. Italian by* Lawrence R. Smith.

Ditty: "Cock shall crow, The." Robert Louis Stevenson. TrGrPo

Ditty: "I went into my garden to gather some herbs." Sister Bertken, *tr. fr. Dutch by* Jonathan Crewe. WPOW

Ditty: "If you refuse me once, and think again." Lord Herbert of Cherbury. NOSC

Ditty, A: "My true love hath my heart, and I have his." Sir Philip Sidney. *See* My true love hath my heart, and I have his.

Ditty: "O holy Love, religious saint!" Sir Robert Chester. *Fr.* Love's Martyr. EIL

Ditty, A.: "Peace, peace, peace, make no noise." John Day. *Fr.* Humour Out of Breath. EIL

Ditty, A: "See where she sits upon the grassy green." Spenser. *See* See where she sits upon the grassie [*or* grassy] green[e].

Ditty: "Where did the Jewish god go?" Harvey Shapiro. BTR

Ditty: "Why dost thou hate return instead of love." Lord Herbert of Cherbury. NOSC

Ditty in Imitation of the Spanish ["Entre Tanto Que L'Avril"], A. Lord Herbert of Cherbury. EIL

Dīvāni Shamsi Tabrīz, *sels. Unknown, tr. fr. Persian.*
 "Man of God is drunken without wine, The." TAL, *tr. by* Reynold A. Nicholson

Diva's First Song (White's Hotel, London), The. Karl Kirchwey. BAP-91

Dive could come who was its fledgling first, The. Nijinsky. Parker Tyler. PoA

Diver, The. Dick Davis. SCBI

Diver, The. Robert Hayden. AmPP; BPo

Diver, The. Ben Howard. SM

Diver, The. Edward Leslie Mayo. CoAP

Diver, The. Leonard Nathan. ErPo

Diver, The. W. W. Eustace Ross. NOBC

Diver. R. A. Simpson. CBAP

Diverne wanted to die, that August night. Chosen. Marilyn Nelson Waniek. NAmP90

Divers, The. Peter Quennell. MoBrPo

Divers Doth Use. Sir Thomas Wyatt. NAEL-1; SiPS; Son

Divers [or Diverse] thy death do diversely bemoan. The Earl of Surrey. SiPSBD
 (Death of Wyatt, The.) SiPS
 (Dyvers thy death doo dyverslye bemone.) AAS

Diverse Gifts of Pasha Bailey Ben, The. W. S. Gilbert. *Fr.* Pasha Bailey Ben. CBCK

Diversely Holy Darkness. Henry Vaughan. *See* Dear Night! this world's defeat.

Diversely passioned is the lover's heart. The Eleventh Property. Sir Thomas More. *Fr.* Twelve Weapons of Spiritual Battle, The. EnRePo

Diversions of the Re-Echo Club. Carolyn Wells. OBAL

Diverting History of John Gilpin, The. William Cowper. *See* John Gilpin.

Dives and Lazarus ("As it fell out upon a day.") *Unknown.* ELP; ESPB; FaBoBa; OBET; OxBB

Dives and Lazarus ("There was a man in olden times.") *Unknown.* AmFP

Dives and Laz'us. *Unknown.* TTY

Dives to his rest. (*LL*) The Chipmunk's Day. Randall Jarrell. OBAP; OBCA

Dives, when you and I go down to Hell. To Dives. Hilaire Belloc. ChIV-2; OBSV

Divide the land from the sea! (*LL*) The Leak in the Dike. Phoebe Cary. FaPON; VPP

Divided. Walter de la Mare. CBLP

Divided, *sels.* Jean Ingelow.
 "Dappled sky, a world of meadows, A." OBNC

Divided Heart, The. George Wither. *Fr.* Fair Virtue, the Mistress of Philarete. TrGrPo

Dividing the Sky. Jiang He, *tr. fr. Chinese by* Donald Finkel *with* Li Guohua. SpMi

Divina Commedia. ("Oft have I seen at some cathedral door.") Dante, *tr. fr. Italian.* MeMAP
Sels.
Inferno. NAWM-1, *tr. by* John Ciardi
 "And now we walked along the solid mire." OBVE
 Dark Wood, The. BiHa
 "Like fire-flies that the peasant on the hill." Prf
 "Middle of life's journey; I, The." STV, *tr. by* John Frederick Nims
 "Now the hard margin bears us on, while steam." PeHV
 Pier delle Vigne. HoPM
 "Through me you enter the city of lament."
 Ugolino. AnAn; FaBoPV
Paradiso.
 'But you who are so happy here, tell me.' EnlH, *tr. by* Stephen Mitchell
 "Glory of Him who moves all things rays forth, The."
 "Glory of the great all-mover goes, The."
 "Piercing brightness of the living ray, The." TOF, *tr. by* Dorothy L. Sayers *and* Barbara Reynolds
 Saints in Glory, The. WGRP, *tr. by* Henry F. Cary
 "That sun that breathed love's fire into my youth."
 "Then, in the form of a white rose, the host."
Purgatorio.
 "As the day stands when the Sun begins to glow."
 "At the hour when the heat of the day is overcome."
 Celestial Pilot, The. WGRP

"Earnest to explore within and all around." OBVE

"For better waters now the little bark."

"Love of God, unutterable and perfect, The." EnlH, *tr. by* Stephen Mitchell

"This mountain of release is such that the." EnlH, *tr. by* Stephen Mitchell

"When the Septentrion of the First Heaven."

Divination. Christine Churches. FaBoMA

Divination by a Cat. Anthony Hecht. OFC; SoCa

Divination by a Daffadill [*or* Daffodil]. Robert Herrick. CaPo; SeCV-1

Divine Abundance. *Unknown.* BLRP

Divine approval is thy sweetest praise. (*LL*) To My Father. H. Cordelia Ray. AAP; BISi; CBWP-3; Son

Divine Blacksmith, The. Matthew Prior. FaBoNo

Divine by the name of McWhinners, A. *Unknown.* PeLi

Divine Century of Spiritual Sonnets, A, *sels.* Barnabe Barnes.
 "Blast of wind, a momentary breath, A." EBEV
 (Life of Man, The.) CBCK
 God's Virtue. NOCV
 (Sonnet: "World's bright comforter, whose beamsome light, The.") EIL
 No More Lewd Lays. Son

Divine destroyer, pity me no more. A La Bourbon. Richard Lovelace. CaPo

Divine Fancies, The, *sels.* Francis Quarles.
 High Perfections of OUr Transitory Days, The. CBCK
 On Death. PeECV
 On God's Favour. PeECV
 On Our Saviour's Passion. PeECV
 On Sin. CBCK
 On the Life of Man. PeECV

Divine Hand, The. William Williams. *See* Guide Me, O Thou Great Jehovah.

Divine Image, A ("Cruelty has a human heart.") Blake. *Fr.* Songs of Experience. ChIV-1; ChTr; NAEL-2; NoP; OBNC; PAW; RB; TEP

Divine Image, The ("To mercy, pity, peace, and love.") Blake. *Fr.* Songs of Innocence. BoTP; CoGr; EnRP; FHYEP; MeMBP; NAEL-2; NOBE; NOEC; NoP; OAEL-2; OBNC; PeECV; PFP; PoE; PoEL-4; PPP; TEP; WGRP

Divine Insect, The. John Hall Wheelock. GoYe; NYBP

Divine Love. Michael Benedikt. AmPA; CoAP

Divine Love. *Unknown.* OAEL-1

Divine Love. Charles Wesley. *See* Love Divine, All Loves Excelling.

Divine Meditations. William Alabaster. Son
Sels.
 "Beehould a cluster to itt selfe a vine." ESCV
 "Haile gracefull morning of eternall Daye." ESCV
 "Jesu, thie love within mee is soe maine." ESCV
 "My soule a world is by Contraccion." ESCV
 Night, the Starless Night of Passion, The. ESCV
 "Now I have found thee, I will ever more." ESCV
 "Now that the midd day heate doth scorch my shame." ESCV
 "O starry Temple of unvalted space." ESCV
 "O sweete and bitter monuments of paine." ESCV
 "Sunne begins uppon my heart to shine, The." ESCV
 "Three sortes of teares doe from myne eies distraine." ESCV
 Up to Mount Olivet.
 "Way feare with thy projectes, noe false fyre, A." ESCV
 "What meaneth this, that Christ an hymne did singe." ESCV
 "When without tears I looke on Christ, I see." ESCV

Divine Mission, The. Alfred Gibbs Campbell. AAP

Divine Mistress, A. Thomas Carew. BeJo

Divine Office of the Kitchen, The. Cecily Hallack. BLRP; PoLF

Divine Rapture. Francis Quarles. *See* Ev'n [*or* E'en *or* Even] like two little bank-dividing brooks [*or* brookes].

Divine Revenge. Friedrich von Logau, *tr. fr. German by* George C. Schoolfield. GePo.

Divine Sonnet, A. William Alabaster. NoSic

Divine, to the Divinitiy. (*LL*) The Dark Angel. Lionel Johnson. CoGr; GTBS-P; LiTB; MoBrPo; NOBE; NOBVV; OAEL-2; OBMV; OxAEP-2

Divine voice sings through all creation, A. (*LL*) How wonderful, O Lord, are the works of your hands! *Unknown.* EaPr

Divine Weeks and Works, The, *sels.* Guillaume de Salluste Du Bartas.
 Fourth Day of the First Week, The
 Zodiac, The. NOSC

Divine Weeks and Works of Guillaume de Saluste Sieur Du Bartas, The, *sels.* Joshua Sylvester.
 Tower of Babel, The. NoSic

Divine Wooer, The, *sels.* Phineas Fletcher.
 "Me Lord? can'st Thou mispend." TOF; TrPWD

Divinely superfluous beauty. (*LL*) Divinely Superfluous Beauty. Robinson Jeffers. HeIP; MoAmPo

Divinely Superfluous Beauty. Robinson Jeffers. HeIP; MoAmPo

Do You Remember Me? Walter Savage Landor. *Fr.* Ianthe. EnRP

Do you remember me? or are you proud? Walter Savage Landor. *See* Do You Remember Me?

Do you remember Mr. Goodbeare, the carpenter. Elegy for Mr. Goodbeare. Sir Osbert Sitwell. MoBrPo

Do You Remember 1926? Idris Davies. AngWe; OBWVE

Do You Remember That Night? *Unknown, tr. fr. Irish by* Eugene O'Curry. BIrV; PeIV

Do you remember the lizard? The Lizard. Rona Murray. NOBC

Do you remember the peacocks. Bird of Glass. Rhyll McMaster. FaBoMA

Do you remember the ritual of candle-wax. Sliding. Sam Adams. AngWe

Do you remember, when you were first a child. Message from Home. Kathleen Raine. WPE

Do you say/ its progesterone. What Do You Say When a Man Tells You, You Have the Softest Skin. Mary Mackey. FF

Do you see this grain of sand. A Grain of Sand. Frances E. W. Harper. PWR

Do you see this ragged stocking. The Ragged Stocking. Frances E. W. Harper. AmWP

Do you see this square old yellow Book, I toss. Robert Browning. *Fr.* Ring and the Book, The. FaBoVe

Do you suppose I shall stay when I can go so easily? *(LL)* Lightly Bound. Stevie Smith. NALW

Do You Think? Josephine D. Henderson Heard. CBWP-4

Do you think of me at all. Dead "Wessex" the Dog to the Household. Thomas Hardy. FM

Do you think we skip. The Zobo Bird. Frank A. Collymore. GoJo

Do you think you will hug the shore, Captain, to-day? Hugging the Shore. Mary E. Tucker. CBWP-1

Do you want to know his name? The Porch. R. S. Thomas. NOCV

Do you wish the world were better? Better, Wiser and Happier. Ella Wheeler Wilcox. WBLP

Do your balls hang low? *Unknown.* NSI

Do Your Best. Mrs. Henry Linden. CBWP-4

Doan't You Be What You Ain't. Edwin Milton Royle. BLPA

Dobbin. George Bowering. NOBC

Docility. Jules Supervielle, *tr. fr. French by* George Bogin. ArNa

Docker. Seamus Heaney. HeIL; HeIP; IIP; MoP; NOIV; Poetr

Dockyard Gate, The. *Unknown.* OxBSS

Doctor, The. Roger Woddis. UV

Dr. Berman, my old lady listens to you. Deuce: 12:23 a.m. Barbara Anderson. NAmP90

Doctor Bill Williams. Ernest Walsh. InvP

Dr. Birch and His Young Friends, *sels.* Thackeray. End of the Play, The. GN

Dr. Booker T. Washington to the National Negro Business League. Joseph S. Cotter, Sr.. AAP

Doctor Bottom was preparing to leave. Medical Aid. Walter Hard. BXAP

Doctor, doctor, it fits real fine. Vet's Rehabilitation. Ray Durem. PoBA

Doctor Faustus. ("Not marching in the fields of Trasimene.") Christopher Marlowe. NAEL-1; OAEL-1
Sels.
"Ah, Faustus,/ Now hast thou but one bare hour [*or* hower] to live." FaBoVe; HeIP; PeECV
(End of Doctor Faustus, The.) PoEL-2
(End of Faustus, The.) TrGrPo
Was This the Face. EBEV; EBEvV; GBL; LPA; TrGrPo
(Face of Helen, The.) FaBV
(Helen of Troy.) FF
(Helen.) BLPL; ImPo; LiTB
"Where are you damn'd?" OBD

Doctor Fell. Thomas Brown, *after the Latin of* Martial. ChTr; FaBoCo; FaBoEE; ISE; MoShBr; NBLV; OBVE; OxNR

Doctor Foster is a good man. *Unknown.* OxNR

Doctor Foster went to Gloucester [*or* Glo'ster]. Mother Goose. OxBoLi; OxNR; ReMoGo

Doctor Frolic. Robert Pinsky. NoAM

Dr. Halley never eat any thing. Edmond Halley. Roy Fuller. OxBC

Doctor in a clean, starched band, The. The Reasons That Induced Dr. Swift to Write a Poem Called "The Lady's Dressing-Room." Lady Mary Wortley Montagu. FaBoBl

Dr. Invisible and Mr. Hide. Charles Webb. NGP

Doctor Johnson. Soame Jenyns. FaBoEE; OBSV

Dr. Johnson, when sober or pissed. A. Cinna. PeLi

Dr. Johnson's Ghost. Elizabeth Moody. ECWP

Dr. Joseph Goebbels. W. D. Snodgrass. *Fr.* Führer Bunker, The. CAPP

Doctor loves the patient, The. The Bed. A. D. Hope. NoAM; OxBC; OxBSP

Dr. Newman with the crooked pince-nez. Robert Graves. *Fr.* Grotesques. CMoP; PeLV

Dr. Potatohead Talks to Mothers. Judith Johnson Sherwin. MoP

Doctor punched my vein, The. Scyros. Karl Shapiro. HoPM; ImPo; LiTA; LiTM

Doctor Type. Wayne Koestenbaum. PFL

Doctor Who Sits at the Bedside of a Rat, The. Josephine Miles. VGW

Dr. Wild's Ghost. *Unknown.* APAS

Doctor, you say there are no haloes. Monet Refuses the Operation. Lisel Mueller. FYAP

Doctors attended behind each chair. W. H. Auden. *Fr.* Happy New Year, A. OBSV

Doctor's fortunate indeed, A. The Physicians' Fortune. Friedrich von Logau, *tr. fr. German, tr. by* George C. Schoolfield. GePo

Doctors' Row. Conrad Aiken. HAP

Doctor's Story, The. Will M. Carleton. BLPA

Doctors tender of their fame, The. Swift. *Fr.* Verses on the Death of Doctor Swift [D.S.P.D., Occasioned by Reading a Maxim in Rochefoucauld]. NOBL

Doctors that learned be. John Skelton. *Fr.* Colin Clout. OBSV

Doctrine of initiates completes the meditation!, The. *(LL)* The Night Is a Space of White Marble. Philip Lamantia. PoBeRe

Documentary on Airplane Glue, A. David Henderson. MAT

Doddledy, doodledy, doodledy, dan. *Unknown.* OxNR

Dodger, The. *Unknown.* AmFP; GBP

Dodger, The. *Unknown.* SWP, (*with music, sl. diff.*)

Dodo, The. Hilaire Belloc. ChTr

Dodo. Henry Carlile. Poetsp

Dodo used to walk around, The. The Dodo. Hilaire Belloc. ChTr

Dodoism. William John Courthope. *Fr.* Paradise of Birds, The. OtMeF

Do[e] not their profane orgies hear[e]. To Castara. William Habington. *Fr.* Castara. BeJo

Doe of the mountains east. Mother/ Deer/ Lady. Harold Littlebird. VoR

Doe take in greate indulgin. *(LL)* A Devonshire Song. *At. to* William Strode. PoEL-2, *sl. diff. vers.*

Doeg, though without knowing how or why. John Dryden *and* Nahum Tate. *Fr.* Absalom and Achitophel, Pt. II. FHYEP; PoEL-3

Does a lot for the famous Critic K. *(LL)* St Cecilia's Day Epigram. Peter Porter. PeLV

Does a word as a widow in the brain. Elegy for Sir Ifor Williams. Anthony Conran. AngWe

Does anybody listen to advice? Senior Poet. Robert Pinsky. *Fr.* Three on Luck. AnAn

Does Charidas lie beneath you? If you mean. Callimachus, *tr. fr. Greek by* Peter Jay. GrAn

Does he know the road to Flanders, does he know the criss-cross tracks. The Flight to Flanders. Lessel Hutcheon. NSI

Does he regard on what we dine? *(LL)* Epigram on Fasting. Swift. OBVE

Does he think of me in the merry throng. The Question. Josephine D. Henderson Heard. CBWP-4

Does it become a girl so wise. Walter Savage Landor. CBLP

Does It Matter? Siegfried Sassoon. CoGr; MoBrPo; PAW; PeFWW; PoWW

Does it wear a yarmulka. What Is a Jewish Poem? Myra Sklarew. CRP

Does man love Art? Man visits Art, but squirms. The Chicago Picasso. Gwendolyn Brooks. *Fr.* Two Dedications. BPo; LiTM

Does morning always have to come? The Second Hymn to the Night. "Novalis", *prose poem vers., tr. fr. German by* Robert Bly. *Fr.* Hymns to the Night. NU

Does mother get praised as often as she should. The Woman Back in the Kitchen. Nicholas Lloyd Ingraham. PWR

Does my voice reach you? You are. Light Years and the Love Lost in the Oleanders. Alane Rollings. WeW

Does nature bear a tyrant's breast? John Langhorne. *Fr.* Owen of Carron. FaBoCo

Does not know what sort of blossoms her roses are. *(LL)* Nothing Is Sweeter Than Eros. Nossis of Locri. VBLP

Does now like one of them appear. *(LL)* Upon Appleton House, [to My Lord Fairfax]. Andrew Marvell. FaBoPV; GeHe; SeCP; SeCV-1

Does Spring Come to a Lost Land? Sang-hua Lee, *tr. fr. Korean by* Chang-soo Koh. PAW

Does That Answer Your Question, Mr Shakespeare? Stanley J. Sharpless. PeLV

Does that bird. Princess Nukada, *tr. fr. Japanese by* Kenneth Rexroth *and* Ikuko Atsumi. WPJ

Does the Eagle know what is in the pit? Thel's Motto. Blake. *Fr.* Book of Thel, The. ChTr, 4 *ll.*; EnRP; MeMBP; NAEL-2; NoP; OAEL-2; OBNC; PoE; PoEL-4; TEP

Donibristle Moss Moran Disaster, The. *Unknown.* WTO

Donkey, The. G. K. Chesteron. ChIV-2; CoGr; EBEvV; FaBV; FaPoB; FaPoR; InPK; MoBrPo; OBEV; PoLF; RB; WGRP

Donkey, The. Rose Fyleman. BoTP

Donkey, The. Theodore Roethke. GrPl; OBCA

Donkey and the Lapdog, The. La Fontaine, *tr. fr. French by* Marianne Moore. OBVE

Donkey doctor came covered with rain, The. Big Friend of the Stones. Steve Orlen. Poetsp

Donkey, donkey, do not bray. *Unknown.* OxNR

Donkey, donkey, old and gray. *Unknown.* ReMoGo

Donkey walks on four legs. *Unknown.* ISE

Donna Julia. Byron. *Fr. Don Juan.* PoEL-4

Donna Mi Priegha. Cavalcanti. *See* Lady asks me, A.

Donne. Hartley Coleridge. EPCY

Donne, the delight of Phoebus, and each Muse. To John Donne. Ben Jonson. BeJo; EPCY; NAEL-1; SeCV-1

Donner Party, The, *sels.* George Keithley.

Donnybrook. James Stephens. TIRV

Donought would have everything. Ebenezer Elliot. NOBVV

Don's Holiday. George Rostrevor Hamilton. FaBoCo

Don't. Strato, *tr. fr. Greek by* Fergus Pickering. FaBoBl

Don't ape what must be born in one. The Donkey and the Lapdog. La Fontaine, *tr. fr. French by* Marianne Moore. OBVE

Don't ask a geologist about rocks. No More Soft Talk. Diane Wakoski. FF; IHMS

Don't ask — knowing's taboo — what's in the cards, darling, for you, for me. Horace. *See* Seek not, Leuconöe, to know how long you're going to live yet.

Don't ask me what to wear. Sappho, *tr. fr. Greek by* Mary Barnard. PBWP

Don't Ask Me Who I Am. James A. Randall, Jr.. BPo

Don't ask whose face it is when you see me. Humiliation in Its Disguises. Andrew Crozier. NBrP; VaA

Don't be afraid of dying. The glass of water. Couplets, XX. Robert Mezey. FYAP; NU

Don't Be Foolish Pray. *Unknown.* CoMu

Don't be in a hurry, Miranda. For My Daughter. Judith Kazantzis. AIW

Don't Believe in War. Bulat Okudzhava, *tr. fr. Russian by* George Reavey. PAW

Don't bite your nails, Amanda! Amanda! Robin Klein. OTCP

Don't blame me, ladies, if I've loved. No sneers. Louise Labé, *tr. fr. French.* BoWoP, *tr. by* Willis Barnstone ("Don't scold me, ladies, if I have loved.") PBWP, *tr. by* Carol Cosman

Don't bother a bit, you are only a dream you are having. A Real Question Calling for a Solution. Robert Penn Warren. PPP

Don't bother telling me about the programs. TV. John Forbes. CBAP

Don't bother with hallo. You're Julia. Douglas Oliver. VaA

Don't bow down before [to] the little box. The Enemies of the Little Box. Vasco [*or* Vasko] Popa, *tr. fr. Serbo-Croatian by* Charles Simic. AnRep; HSix

Don't Call Alligator Long-Mouth till You Cross River. John Agard. OBAP

Don't Call Me Pedant. Berta Freistadt. DT

Don't call to me father. To My Dead Father. Frank O'Hara. CAPP

Don't care didn't care. *Unknown.* GBP; NTP; OTCP

Don't-Care Negro, The. Joseph S. Cotter, Sr.. AAP

Don't care was made to care. *Unknown.* ISE

Don't care where you come from. African. Peter Tosh. PBCV

Don't cry/ over the happy dead. *Unknown, tr. fr. Greek by* Peter Porter. GrAn

Don't curse your hands. A Manifesto for the Faint-Hearted. Carole Oles. SM

Don't cut it to make a flute. The Bamboo by Li Ch'e Yun's Window. Po Chü-i, *tr. fr. Chinese by* Kenneth Rexroth. OHMPC

Don't destroy the world. Ellen Bass. EaPr

Don't. Don't destroy the world. (*LL*) Don't destroy the world. Ellen Bass. EaPr

Don't dress for it. Chiyojo, *tr. fr. Japanese by* David Ray. BoWoP

Don't drink the beer that's brewed in Pennsylvania. O Rolling. Three Mile Island. Maureen Owen. UL

Don't drive me out of my mind. Second Honeymoon. *Unknown, tr. fr. Irish by* Augustus Young. BIrV

Don't Ever Cross a Crocodile. Kaye Starbird. PDV

Don't fash yourself, man! Don't complain. Palladas, *tr. fr. Greek by* Tony Harrison. GrAn

Don't fear me! There's the grey beginning. Zooks! (*LL*) Fra Lippo Lippi. Robert Browning. CTC; EBVV; EBVVPR; EnVR; FHYEP; NoP; OAEL-2; OtMeF; OxAEP-2; TEP

Don't Fish in My Sea. Gertrude Rainey. VBLP

Don't Forget. Stephen Berg. PoA

Don't Forget. Alice Sadongei. HATNAP

Don't forget the crablike/ hands. The Hands. Denise Levertov. NeAP; PoM

Dont forget to fly. (*LL*) For Poets. Al Young. PoBA; RFM

Don't forget when the sticks are ready for picking. Don't Forget. Alice Sadongei. HATNAP

Don't give everything. David Foster. *Fr.* Fleeing Atalanta, The. NOBAu

Don't Give Up. C. C. Cameron. *Fr.* Success. PoToHe

Don't give up hoping when the ship goes down. Hang to Your Grit! Louis E. Thayer. WBLP

Don't go. Larry Eigner. PoM

Don't go anywhere without me. In the Arc of Your Mallet. Jalal al-Din Rumi, *tr. fr. Persian by* John Moyne *and* Coleman Barks. UnAS

Don't go back to sleep! (*LL*) Breezes at dawn have secrets to tell you, The. Jalal al-Din Rumi. EaPr

Don't Go Out of the Door. Li Ho, *tr. fr. Chinese by* A. C. Graham. PLT

Don't Grieve. Jalal al-Din Rumi, *tr. fr. Persian by* John Moyne *and* Colman Barks. EaPr
(Don't grieve. Anything you lose comes round.) EnlH, *tr. by* Coleman Barks *and* A. J. Arberry

Don't Grow Old, *sels.* Allen Ginsberg.
Father Death Blues. SM

Don't halt your voyage, sailor, nor drop sail. Johannes Barbucollas, *tr. fr. Greek by* Peter Jay. GrAn

Don't hand me over with a word, Toihau. Reply to a Marriage Proposal. Irihapeti Rangi Te Apakura, *tr. fr. Maori by* Roger Oppenheim *and* Allen Curnow. PBWP

Don't Hope to Gain by What Has Preceded. Joanne Kyger. PoM

Don't it make you want to cry? (*LL*) Those Boys That Ran Together. Lucille Clifton. PoBA

Don't judge men by their gravestones. Antipater of Thessalonica, *tr. fr. Greek by* Alistair Elliot. GrAn

Don't Kill Yourself. Carlos Drummond de Andrade, *tr. fr. Portuguese by* Elizabeth Bishop.

Don't kiss the mouth of Alphaeus. *Unknown, tr. fr. Greek by* Sam Hamill. InMo

Don't knock on my door, little child. Motherhood. Georgia Douglas Johnson. ShDr

Don't Knock the Rawleigh's Man. Vincent O'Sullivan. PeNZ

Don't know/ Nice, though. (*LL*) Ode on a Grecian Urn Summarized. Desmond Skirrow. NIP; NOBL

Don't know why I. Angola Question Mark. Langston Hughes. BPo; TTY

Don't leave me. Ion of Chios, *tr. fr. Greek by* Sam Hamill. InMo

Don't let freezing hands play with these pearls. Meng Chiao, *tr. by* Stephen Owen. *Fr.* Apricots Die Young. SuSp

Don't let it matter much, Philaenis. Tymnes, *tr. fr. Greek by* Alistair Elliot. GrAn

Don't let me lose you. How Tuesday Began. Kathleen Fraser. NYBP

Don't Let That Horse. Lawrence Ferlinghetti. CBNP; RB

Don't Let Them Chip Away at Our Language. Kitty Tsui. ETG

Don't let them die out. New Poem. For Us. Sonia Sanchez. PoBA

Don't lie down again. Lying Down. *Unknown, tr. fr. Bella Bella Indian by* Franz Boas. STP

Don't lock me in wedlock, I want. About Marriage. Denise Levertov. NALW; NMM

Don't Look Now but Mary Is Everybody. Peter Viereck. LiTA

Don't love me, my sweet. Song of a Common Lover. Flavien Ranaivo, *tr. fr. French by* Alan Ryder. TTY

Don't Make Fun of the Fair, *sels.* Noël Coward.
"Don't make fun of the festival." FaBoEH

Don't make fun of the festival. Noël Coward. *Fr.* Don't Make Fun of the Fair. FaBoEH

Don't mind the train or the rollin' sea. The Grey Funnel Line. Cyril Tawney. OBET

Don't neglect the quiet hour. Communion. J. L. Spicer. BLRP

Don't offend/ the fullbloods. Song of the Breed. Carroll Arnett. ETG

Don't open the little box. The Craftsmen of the Little Box. Vasco [*or* Vasko] Popa, *tr. fr. Serbo-Croatian by* Charles Simic. AnRep; HSix

Don't pay any attention. Martial, *tr. fr. Greek by* Kenneth Rexroth. PGA

Don't pull that bud, it yet may grow. To George Pulling Buds. Adelaide O'Keeffe. FaBoUs

Don't Quit. *Unknown.* BLPA

Don't read odes, boy, timetables. For a Senior College Textbook. Hans Magnus Enzensberger. PoSu

Don't remove the glasses and plates. Instructions for a Waitress. Yehuda Amichai, *tr. fr. Hebrew by* Harold Schimmel. PoSu

Doorbells. Rachel Field. FaPON

Doors. David Chaloner. VaA

Doors. Thérèse Plantier, tr. fr. French by Willis Barnstone and Elene Kolb. BoWoP

Doors Are Closed, The. Robert Bly. Fr. Two Translations from Kabir. PRA

Doors flapped open in Ulysses' house, The. Return, The. Edwin Muir. CMoP

Doors hast thou opened for us, thinker, seer! R. W. E. Lucy Larcom. AmWP

Doors open, The/ and the heat undoes itself. In the Beach House. Anne Sexton. PPP

Doors open by themselves, The. The Chicken. Vladimir Holan, tr. fr. Czech by Ian Milner and Jarmila Milner. PoSu

Doors ripped off houses. Boghos Sarkissian, A Watchmaker of Karpet, Remembers the Turkish Atrocities of 1915. Leo Hamalian. BTR

Doors, where my heart was used to beat. Tennyson. Fr. In Memoriam A. H. H. EBVV, abr.; EnVR; FHYEP; NoP; OAEL-2, abr.; OBNC; PeECV, abr.; PoEL-5; SCV

Doorstep, Lightning, Waif-Dreaming. James Dickey. CAPP

Doorway to my home is made of light, The. Surround of Rainbows. Meridel LeSueur. SRLS

Dope. Amiri Baraka. BCF

Doppelganger, The. Daryl Hine. UTF

Doppelgänger. Jason Shinder. UTF

Dora versus Rose. Austin Dobson. NOBL; PDV

Dora Williams. Edgar Lee Masters. Fr. Spoon River Anthology. HAP

Dorcas, be off! & tell her this. Meleager, tr. fr. Greek by Peter Whigham. GrAn

Dorchester Giant, The. Oliver Wendell Holmes. FaPON

Doré knew this overhang. View from the Gorge. Ben Belitt. NYBP

Doretha wore the short blue lace last night. The Reception. June Jordan. FaBoWP; NMM

Doria. Ezra Pound. MoAB; MoAmPo

Doric. Angelos Sikelianos, tr. fr. Greek by Edmund Keeley and Philip Sherrard. ErPo

Doricha. Poseidippus, tr. fr. Greek by E. A. Robinson. AWP; FaBoEE; OBVE

Doricha, your soft bones are. Poseidippus, tr. fr. Greek by Edward Lucie-Smith. GrAn

Dorinda's sparkling wit, and eyes. Charles Sackville. OBEV; SeCV-2
(On Dorinda.) OxBSP
(On the Countess of Dorchester.) APAS
(Song: "Dorinda's sparkling wit, and eyes.") NOSC

Doris. Congreve. NOEC

Doris and Philemon, sels. J. C. Squire.
"Now the declining fulgent orb of day." BXAP

Doris, I that could repell. The Snow-Ball. Thomas Stanley. CBLP

Doris lay down, all out of pity. (LL) When Doris Danced. Richard Eberhart. CMoP; ErPo

Dormant bear., The. (LL) D-Y Bar. James Welch. CDW

Dormouse, The. Charlotte Druitt Cole. BoTP

Doron's Description of Samela. Robert Greene. Fr. Menaphon. PoEL-2

Doron's Jigge. Robert Greene. Fr. Menaphon. PoEL-2

Dorothy Q. Oliver Wendell Holmes. NOBA

Dorothy Wordsworth, dying, did not want to read. My Sisters, O My Sisters. May Sarton. NALW

Dorothy's Dower. Phoebe Cary. AmWP

Dose of a mere, The. The Discovery of LSD a True Story. Anselm Hollo. PoM

Dosn't thou 'ear my 'erse's legs, as they canters awaäy. Northern Farmer. Tennyson. NAEL-2; PeVV

Dosn't thou 'ear my 'erse's legs, as they canters awaäy? Northern Farmer: New Style. Tennyson. EnVR; OxAEP-2

Dosser in Springtime, The. Douglas Stewart. ErPo

Dost know Grief well? Hast known her long? Acquainted with Grief. Helen Hunt Jackson. AmWP

Dost see how unregarded now. Sir John Suckling. BeJo; CaPo; ELP; NOSC

Dost tha hear my horse's feet, as he canters away? Lord Tennyson and Lord Melchett. D. H. Lawrence. FaBoEE

Dost therefore swell and pout with pride. A Tyrant in Sleep, Naught Differeth from a Common Man. Timothy Kendall. NoSic

Dost thou forget. Shakespeare. Fr. Tempest, The. OAEL-1; OxAEP-1

Dost thou remember ever, for my sake. Mathilde Blind. Fr. Love in Exile. OBNC

Dostoievsky's Daughters. Michael Hamburger. NAs

Dot a dot dot dot a dot dot. Weather. Eve Merriam. SiSoPo; TLR

Doth lead, Doth teach, Doth sweare. (LL) Her [or hir] face her [or hir] tongue [or tong] her [or hir] wit. At. to Sir Arthur Gorges. CBLP; GBL

Doth Not a Tenarif, or Higher Hill. John Donne. Fr. Anatomy [or Anatomie] of the World, An[: The First Anniversary]. ChTr

Doth not thou, Castara, read. A Dialogue between Araphil and Castara. William Habington. Fr. Castara. BeJo

Doth then the world go thus, doth all thus move? William Drummond of Hawthornden. GTBS; GTBS-P

Dotito is Our Brother. Charles Mungoshi. PeSAV

D'Où Venons Nous? Que Sommes Nous? Où Allons Nous. A. L. Hendricks. PBCV
Sels.
"I touch jig-saw fragments."
"Looking out toward the stars."
"Woman in the garden gathers lilacs, A."

Double, The. Irving Feldman. NYBP

Double Agent. Heather McHugh. AnAn

Double Autumn, The. James Reeves. OxBSP

Double Axe, The. Anne Hazlewood-Brady. IHMS

Double Ballad of Good Counsel, A. Villon, tr. fr. French by Swinburne. AWP

Double Bass. Sue May. NBrP

Double boiler fixed on fiery wheels, A. On Shakespeare Critics. A. D. Hope. Fr. Dunciad Minor. OxBC

Double Bubble of Infinity, The. Kate Farrell. ArLo

Double curtains hang deep in the room of Never Grieve. Li Shang-yin, tr. fr. Chinese by A. C. Graham. PLT

Double Date. Lincoln Kirstein. FaBoBl; PeLV

Double, double, toil and trouble. Mister the Blitzkit. Ruth Pitter. OFC

Double Dutch. Walter de la Mare. CRH

Double Elegy. Michael S. Harper. NoAM

Double Exposure. Ian Young. PeHV

Double Feature. Robert Hayden. NoAM

Double flesh/ Double way. Freud: Dying London, He Recalls the Smoke of His Cigar Beginning to Sing. James Schevill. TAP

Double-Goer, The. Daryl Hine. See All that I do is clumsy and ill timed.

Double-headed Snake, The. John Newlove. MoCV

Double-horned, nocturnal Moon. Philodemus, tr. fr. Greek by William Moebius. GrAn

Double in the minds of government. (LL) The Mother-in-Law of the Marquis de Sade. Jennifer Maiden. NOBAu

Double L and single T. The Spelling of Elliot. Unknown. FaBoUs

Double-lived in regions new! (LL) Bards of passion and of mirth. Keats. EnRP; OBEV

Double Looking Glass, The. A. D. Hope. CBAP

Double Mock Sonnet. Charles O. Hartman. SM

Double Ode. Muriel Rukeyser, tr. by Edmund Keeley. AnAn

Double Rock, The. Henry King. CBLP; NOSC; SeCP

Double Semi-Sestina. George Starbuck. SM

Double Sestine [or Sestina]. Sir Philip Sidney. See Ye [or you] Goat-herd Gods, [that love the grassy mountains].

Double Shame, The. Stephen Spender. LiTB; LiTM

Double Sonnet. Anthony Hecht. SM; Son

Double Sonnet for Mickey. Gerald Burns. BAP-91

Double Standard, The. Franklin P. Adams. OBAL

Double Standard, A. Frances E. W. Harper. AAP; AmWP; BlSi; PWR; VBLP

Double Take at Relais de L'Espadon. Thadious M. Davis. BlSi

Double Transformation, The. Goldsmith. OBNV

Double Vision of Manannan, The. Unknown, tr. fr. Irish by John Montague. BIrV

Doubled at their feet. (LL) King Harald's Trance. George Meredith. EBNV; PeVV

Doubly unfortunate are those who dwell in Hell — . Lucilius, tr. fr. Greek by Peter Porter. GrAn

Doubt. Mary Elizabeth Coleridge. NALW

Doubt. Margaret Deland. TrPWD

Doubt. Fernand Gregh, tr. fr. French by Ludwig Lewisohn. WGRP

Doubt. Helen Hunt Jackson. WGRP

Doubt, The. Nestor Vasilyevich Kukolnik, tr. fr. Russian by Philip L. Miller. RiWo

Doubt. Pat Nolan. UL

Doubt. Lizette Woodworth Reese. AmWP

Doubt. Tennyson. See You say, but with no touch of scorn.

Doubt. Clara Ann Thompson. CBWP-2

Doubt, cypress crowned, upon a ruined arch. Annihilation. Elizabeth Oakes Smith. Fr. Atheism. AmWP

Down in Dallas. X. J. Kennedy. FF

Down in Dumbarton there wonnd a rich merchant. Bonnie Annie. *Unknown.* ESPB, A *and* B *vers.*

Down in front of Casey's old brown wooden stoop. The Sidewalks of New York. James W. Blake. BLPA; FaBoBe

Down in green valleys a town in Yorkshire. Bonnets So Blue. *Unknown.* OBET

Down in history we find it and in grandest works of art. Negro Heroines. L. A. J. Moorer. CBWP-3

Down in London where I was raised. Barbara Allen. *Unknown.* FaBoBa

Down in my good old home? (*LL*) The Old Folks at Home. Stephen Collins Foster. AnAmPo; FaBoBe; WBLP

Down in Natchitoches there is a statue in a public square. The Sévignés. Anne Spencer. ShDr

Down in our cellar on a Monday and a Tuesday. Old Ellen Sullivan. Winifred Welles. FaPON

Down in St. Louis at 12th and Carr. Brady. *Unknown.* AS

Down in some lone valley, in some lonesome place. Pretty Saro. *Unknown.* AmFP

Down in some lonesome piney grove. Lonesome Dove. *Unknown.* AmFP

Down in the bleak December bay. The Mayflower. Erastus Wolcott Ellsworth. FaBoBe; PAH

Down in the cabin all things were gay. Thwarted. Priscilla Jane Thompson. CBWP-2

Down in the dell. Sunrise. H. Cordelia Ray. *Fr.* Idyl. BlSi; CBWP-3

Down in the depth of mine iniquity. Fulke Greville. *Fr.* Caelica. EnRePo; NoSic

(Sonnet: "Down[e] in the depth of mine iniquity.") NOSC

Down in the flood of remembrance, I weep like a child for the past. (*LL*) Piano. D. H. Lawrence. BLPL; CMoP; FaPoB; GrPl; GTBS-P; HAP; HeIL; HeIP; InPK; InvP; LiTB; MoAB; MoBrPo; MoP; NAEL-2; NoAM; NOBE; NoP; OAEL-2; OxBSP; PoE; Poetr; PPP; RB; SCGP; TFi; TRP; UnPo; WeW

Down in the Forest. *Unknown.* OBET

Down in the Frantic Mountains. A Survey. William Stafford. RB

Down in the grassy hollow. Merry Little Men. Kathleen M. Chaplin. BoTP

Down in the green wood shady. (*LL*) All, All a-Lonely. *Unknown.* ChTr; OxBoLi

Down in the henhouse on my knees. *Unknown.* RoPo

Down in the hole we go, boys. Lament while Descending a Shaft. *Unknown.* AmFP

Down in the jungle/ Living in a tent. *Unknown.* WTO

Down in the Lonesome Garden. *Unknown.* BPo

Down in the meadow. *Unknown.* CBNP

Down in the meadow, sprent with dew. Revelation. Alice Brown. *Fr.* Road to Castaly, The. WGRP

Down in the mine, in the dark, dismal drift. Only a Miner. *Unknown.* AmFP

Down in the south, by the waste without sail on it. Beyond Kerguelen. Henry Clarence Kendall. NOBAu

Down in the Valley. *Unknown.* AS; WTO

Down in yon garden sweet and gay. Willy Drowned in Yarrow. *Unknown.* GTBS; GTBS-P

Down in Yonder Meadow. *Unknown.* CH

Down [*or* Downe] lay the shepherd swain. Hye Nonny Nonny Noe. *Unknown.* FaBoCo; NOBL; PeLV

Down Loudon Lanes, with swinging reins. Mosby at Hamilton. Madison Cawein. PAH

Down mountain roads like scars across a fist. At Tripolis. Constance Carrier. WPE

Down near the end of a wandering lane. A Rhyme of the Dream-Maker Man. William Allen White. PoLF

Down on My Luck. A. R. D. Fairburn. PeNZ

Down on Penny's Farm. *Unknown.* SWP

Down she comes from her vermilion tower, her face freshly adorned. A Song of Spring Replying to a Poem by Po Chü-yi. Liu Yu Hsi, *tr. fr. Chinese by* Daniel Bryant *and* Ronald C. Miao. SuSp

Down streams of centuries grown old. Women of My Land. Frankie Armstrong. BrRo

Down stucco sidestreets. Dublinesque. Philip Larkin. NoAM; OxBC

Down swept the chill wind from the mountain peak. The Brook in Winter. James Russell Lowell. *Fr.* Vision of Sir Launfal, The. GN

Down the assembly line they roll and pass. The Brides. A. D. Hope. HAP

Down the blue night the unending columns press. Clouds. Rupert Brooke. OBEV; OBMV; OxBTC

Down the centuries, eternal. From a Venetian Sequence. Adèle Naudé. PeSA

Down the close, darkening lanes they sang their way. The Send-off. Wilfred Owen. LiTB; MoAB; MoBrPo; NSI; OBWP; OBWVE; OxBTC; PAW; PeFWW; PoWW; RB

Down the cloud ladder, but the problem has not been/ solved. (*LL*) Our Youth. John Ashbery. SOTW; VGW

Down the coast south of here. Earth. Jim Tollerud. VoR

Down the dawn-brown. The Current. James Merrill. NYBP

Down the dead streets of sun-stoned Frederiksted. The Virgins. Derek Walcott. OxBC; SoSe

Down the deep steps of stone, through iron doors. Judgment. William Rose Benét. AnAmPo

Down the dripping pathway dancing through the rain. Rainy Song. Max Eastman. FaBoBe

Down the fresh clean night. (*LL*) Wellfleet Sabbath. Marge Piercy. SRLS

Down the Glimmering Staircase. Siegfried Sassoon. *Fr.* Vigils. CMoP; PoLF

Down the goldenest of streams. Mater Amabilis. Emma Lazarus. OHIP

Down the green hill-side fro' the castle window. Lady Jane. Sir Arthur Quiller-Couch. FiBHP; PeLV

Down the imperturbable street. (*LL*) An Aspect of Love, Alive in the Ice and Fire. Gwendolyn Brooks. BPo; CAPP; TAP

Down the Little Big Horn. Francis Brooks. PAH

Down the long hall she glistens like a star. Venus of the Louvre. Emma Lazarus. AmWP

Down the M4. Dannie Abse. OxBC

Down the Mississippi. John Gould Fletcher. LiTA

Down the Mississippi. *Unknown.* RoPo

Down the Nile. Robert Lowell. HCAP

Down the North Channel Paul Jones did steer just at break of day. (*LL*) The Yankee Man-of-War. *Unknown.* FaBoBe; OxBSS; PAH; VPP

Down the picket-guarded lane. How Are You, Sanitary? Bret Harte. AnAmPo

Down the red stock route. Song for the Cattle. David Campbell. NOBAu

Down the road someone is practicing scales. Sunday Morning. Louis MacNeice. FaBoMo; LiTB; MoAB; MoBrPo; NAEL-2; NIP; OxAEP-2; Son

Down the rock chute into the tombs of the kings. This Is the Life. Louis MacNeice. NoAM

Down the track of a Philippine Island. The Enclosure. James Dickey. ArOW

Down the valley gan he track. The Palmer. Robert Greene. NoSic

Down the white steps, into the night, she came. Victory. Lionel Johnson. NOBVV

Down the wintry mountain. Dinah Maria Mulock Craik. *Fr.* Highland Cattle. GN

Down the Wolf river. Feasts of Death, Feasts of Love. Stuart Z. Perkoff. NeAP

Down their carved names the rain-drop ploughs. (*LL*) During Wind and Rain. Thomas Hardy. CMoP; ELP; GTBS-P; HAP; Mes; NAEL-2; OAEL-2; OxBTC; PeVV; PoE; PPP; TEP; TFi; TOF; TRP

Down there a poor woman. The Potter. *Unknown, tr. fr. Geez by* Halim El-Dabh. TTY

Down there, we're just another noise. (*LL*) Cockpit in the Clouds. Dick Dorrance. FaPON

Down there where I was. The Story of My Life. Carroll Arnett. VoR

Down through the earth as a last gift. Meleager, *tr. fr. Greek by* Kenneth Rexroth. PGA

Down through the spheres there came the Name of One. The Path of the Stars. Thomas Samuel Jones, Jr.. WGRP

Down through the tomb's inward arch. Ikon: The Harrowing of Hell. Denise Levertov. BAP-90

Down to Sleep. Helen Hunt Jackson. GN

Down to the man moving in the clay. (*LL*) The Well. Philip Salom. NOBAu

Down to the Puritan marrow of my bones. Elinor Wylie. *Fr.* Wild Peaches. BoWoP; FaBoWP; LiTA; LiTM; NAAL-2; NALW; OxBA; WPE

(Puritan Sonnet, IV.) MoAB; MoAmPo; TrGrPo

Down to the Sacred Wave. Samuel Francis Smith. AH

Down toward the deep-blue water, marching to throb of drum. Your Lad, and My Lad. Randall Parrish. PAH

Down valley a smoke haze. Mid-August at Sourdough Mountain Lookout. Gary Snyder. HAP; InPK; MAT; NaP; NoP; PoBeRe; TAP; VCAP

Down, Wanton, Down! Robert Graves. BoLoP; CBLP; CMoP; ErPo; FaBoBl; FaBoTw; HeIP; InPK; LiTM; MeMBP; MoP; NAEL-2; NoAM; NoP; OAEL-2; PoE; Poetr; TEP

Down where New York's a-glare at night. Exiles. Patrick O'Connor. TIRV

Down wind, down wind, a soft sweep of hours. Wind and Absence. Peter Scupham. SCBI

Down with Fanatics! Roger Woddis. IHNG

Down with the lambs. *Unknown.* OxNR

Down with the rosemary and bay[e]s. Ceremonies for Candlemas[se] Eve. Robert Herrick. BeJo; CaPo; JCP

Down with the rosemary, and so. Ceremony upon Candlemas Eve. Robert Herrick. OBCP

Down you go alone, so late, into the surge-black fissure. (*LL*) You Will Know When You Get There. Allen Curnow. PeNZ

Down, you mongrel, Death! The Poet and His Book. Edna St. Vincent Millay. MoAmPo

Downe to the king's most bright-kept baths they went. Homer, *tr. fr. Greek by* Robert Fitzgerald. *Fr.* Odyssey. CTC, *tr. by* George Chapman, IV; NAWM-1

Downfall of Charing Cross, The. *Unknown.* FaBoCo

Downfall of Heathendom, The. *Unknown, tr. fr. Irish by* Frank O'Connor. IIP

Downfall of many, The. (*LL*) I Must Sing of That. Beatrice, Countess de Die. VBLP

Downfall of Piracy, The. *At. to* Benjamin Franklin. PAH

Downfall of the Chancellor, The. *Unknown.* APAS

Downfall of the Gael, The. Fearflatha O'Gnive, *tr. fr. Late Middle Irish by* Sir Samuel Ferguson. AWP

Downfall of the Tyrant. Bible, *O.T. Fr.* Isaiah. TrGrPo

Downhill [*or* Down hill] I came, hungry, and yet not starved. The Owl. Edward Thomas. ChTr; EBEV; FaBoRV; FaBoTw; FF; GTBS-P; LiTB; MoP; NAEL-2; NIP; NoAM; NOBE; NoP; OAEL-2; OBWVE; OxAEP-2; PeFWW; PlP; PoE; Poetr; RB; SCGP; TFi; TRP; UnPo

Downland Crisis, A, *sels.* D. B. Wyndham Lewis. "Ale they drink in Giggleswick, The." UV

Downright Country-Man; or, The Faithful Dairy Maid, The. *Unknown.* CoMu

Downs and tender-tinted cliffs are lost, The. The Needles' Lighthouse from Keyhaven, Hampshire. Charles Tennyson Turner. FaBoPP

Downstairs, a door. Summer Storm. John Montague. IPY

Downstream. Thomas Kinsella. PBCIP

Downtown-Boy Uptown. David Henderson. PoNe

Downtown pigeons peck at dirty. July in Chicago. Lorri Jackson. NGP

Downward through the evening twilight. Longfellow. *See* By the shores of Gitche [*or* Gitchee] Gumee.

Downward to darkness, on extended wings. (*LL*) Sunday Morning. Wallace Stevens. AmPP; BLPL; CMoP; HAP; HCAP; HeIP; ImPo; InPS; LiTA; LiTM; MeMAP; MoAB; MoAmPo; MoP; NAAL-2; NAWM-2; NIP; NoAM; NOBA; NoP; OxBA; PoA, *early vers.*; PoE; Poetr; SAmP; SoSe; TAP; TFi; TRP

Dow's Flat. Bret Harte. AnAmPo; FaBoBe

Dowsed coals fume and hiss after your meal, The. The Book of Yolek. Anthony Hecht. WeW

Doxology. Josephine D. Henderson Heard. CBWP-4

Doxology. Bert Leston Taylor. OBAL

Doxy, oh! thy glaziers shine. The Maunder's Praise of His Strowling Mort. *Unknown.* CBNP; OxBoLi; PeLV

Doyen of walls. Apologia (Nkomati). Wole Soyinka. HBAPE

Dozen dozen in her place, A. (*LL*) Out upon it! I have loved [*or* lov'd]. Sir John Suckling. BeJo; EBEvV; NBLV; PeLV; PoE

Dozen machines, A. A Time for Building. Myra Cohn Livingston. PDV

Dozen sparrows scuttled on the front, A. France. Douglas Dunn. OxBM

Dozens of girls would storm up. Embraceable You. Ira Gershwin. CBLP

Dozens of wrangling sparrows have built their. Power Transformer. Ian Wedde. *Fr.* Earthly: Sonnets for Carlos. PeNZ

Draft Horse, The. Robert Frost. CMoP; HeIP; HoPM; PoE; SAmP; TRP

Draft of a Modern Love Poem. Tadeusz Rózewicz. *See* And yet white[ness].

Draft of a Reparations Agreement. Dan Pagis, *tr. fr. Hebrew by* Stephen Mitchell. PoSu

Draft Riot, The. Charles de Kay. PAH

Drafted. Su Wu, *tr. fr. Chinese by* Kenneth Rexroth. OHMPC

Drafts for a Quatrain. Edmund Wilson. OBAL

Drafty winds and fine rain. Spring Joy. Chu Shu-chen, *tr. fr. Chinese by* Kenneth Rexroth *and* Ling Chung. WPC

Drag Race. Dave Jeddie Smith. AnAn

Dragging a rake through layers of my sleep. Finding the Pistol. Gibbons Ruark. MAT

Dragging him up the stairs to one who lies dead. (*LL*) The Conversation of Prayer. Dylan Thomas. EBEV; GTBS-P; NoP; OxAEP-2

Dragging his hunger through the sky. The Vulture. Samuel Beckett. *Fr.* Echo's Bones. NoAM

Dragging in Winter. David McElroy. AmPA

Dragon. Ruth Bidgood. AngWe

Dragon, The. Vuyelwa Carlin. NWP

Dragon. Olive Dove. OTCP

Dragon, The. Mary Mullineaux. BoTP

Dragon Country: To Jacob Boehme. Robert Penn Warren. PPP

Dragon-Fly, The. Walter Savage Landor. OBEV

Dragon has come, A. Dragon. Olive Dove. OTCP

Dragon hatched a cockatrice, The. China. William Empson. OBTV

Dragon House, The. John James. VaA

Dragon is in the street dancing beneath windows, The. Chinese New Year. Lynda Hull. UTF

Dragon Lady Considers Dinner, The. Colleen J. McElroy. BCF

Dragon Lady's Legacy, The. Colleen J. McElroy. BCF

Dragon never rears its head before sending down torrential rain. Filled with Emotions on the Moon-ferrying Bridge at Arashiyama. Liu Ya-tzu, *tr. fr. Chinese by* Wu-chi Liu. SuSp

Dragon Night. Jane Yolen. OTCP

Dragon of the Seas, The. Thomas Nelson Page. PAH

Dragon Skate. Gladys Cardiff. CDW

Dragon Smoke. Lilian Moore. SiSoPo

Dragon that our seas did raise his crest, The. Of the Great and Famous . . . Sir Francis Drake, and of My Little-Little Selfe. Robert Hayman. CH; FaBoCh; NoP

Dragon-Tree. Robert Penn Warren. PFP

Dragonflies were here before us, friend, The. Woodniche. Aidan Carl Mathews. PeIV

Dragonfly, The. Louise Bogan. HeIP; Poetr

Dragonfly, A. Eleanor Farjeon. FaPON; PDV

Dragonfly, The. Howard Nemerov. GoJo; PoA

Dragonfly-Mother, The. Denise Levertov. InPS; SRLS

Dragons and Snakes. Liu Ya-tzu, *tr. fr. Chinese by* Wu-chi Liu. SuSp

Dragons in the Snow. Jeremy Hooker. SCBI

Drags his tail on the ground, damn thief. Thief. Novica Tadic, *tr. fr. Serbo-Croatian by* Charles Simic. HSix

Drainage, The. Peter Didsbury. PWE

Drained Cup, The. D. H. Lawrence. CBLP; FaBoVe

Drained spittle from his pipe, then scrammed. (*LL*) To William Carlos Williams. Galway Kinnell. NoAM; Poetr; SM

Drainlayer. Duncan Bush. AngWe

Drake he's in his hammock an' a thousand mile away. Drake's Drum. Sir Henry Newbolt. EBEvV; FaBoCh; FaBoEH; FaPoR; OBMV; OtMeF; PoRA; UV; VPP

Drake, who the world hast conquered like a scroll. To the Noble Sir Francis Drake. Thomas Beedome. OxBSP

Sir Drake, whom well the world's end knew. Epigram: On Sir Francis Drake. *Unknown.* OBTV

(On Francis Drake.) NOSC

Drake's Drum. Sir Henry Newbolt. EBEvV; FaBoCh; FaBoEH; FaPoR; OBMV; OtMeF; PoRA; UV; VPP

Drama. Christine McNeill. NWP

Drama's vitallest expression is the common day. Emily Dickinson. NOBA

Dramatic Fragment. Trumbull Stickney. InPK; OxBA; OxBSP

Drank lonesome water. Lonesome Water. Roy Helton. MoAmPo

Draped in khaki, Jurgis. Jurgis Petrakas, the Workers' Angel, Organizes the First Miners' Strike in Exeter, Pennsylvania. Anthony Petrosky. FYAP

Drat my hateful birthday. Sulpicia, *tr. fr. Latin by* John Dillon. PBWP

Draw a bucket of water. *Unknown.* FaBoVe

Draw a historical parallel. Entrance Exams. "Cuthbert Bede." FaBoNo

Draw a little closer, comrades! The Fisherman's Story. H. Cordelia Ray. CBWP-3

Draw a pail of water. *Unknown.* BoTP; FaBoVe; MoShBr; OxNR

Draw closer to me, God, than were I one. Prayer of an Unbeliever. Lizette Woodworth Reese. TrPWD

Draw fear in white threads back and forth through my body. (*LL*) Port Bou. Stephen Spender. OBTV; TwCP

Draw me nere [*or* near], draw me nere [*or* near]. *Unknown.* EBEV (Jolly Jugger, The.) NoP

(Magician and the Baron's Daughter, The.) MeEL

"Draw me," the cypress said. Childhood Painting Lesson. Henry Rago. WHSW

Draw near,/ And list what with our council we have done. Shakespeare. *Fr.* King Richard II. OxAEP-1

Draw near [*or* neer],/ You lovers that complain. The Exequies. Thomas Stanley. BeJo; MeLP

Draw near, young men, and learn of me. McAfee's Confession. *Unknown.* AmFP

Draw up, in a mini, at exactly eleven. (*LL*) Lissadell. Matthew Sweeney. IB

Drunkard's Wife, The. Mary E. Tucker. CBWP-1

Drunken Americans. John Ashbery. HCAP

Drunken Fisherman, The. Robert Lowell. AmPP; ChIV-2; CMoP; ImPo; LiTA; LiTM; NOBA; OxBA; VGW

Drunken night in my house with a, A. Dream Record: June 8, 1955. Allen Ginsberg. NOBA

Drunken Poem. David Helwig. NOBC

Drunken Rose, The. Amarou, *tr. fr. Sanskrit by* E. Powys Mathers. AWP

Drunken sun, The/ totters among the clouds. Orgy (That Is, Vegetable Market, at Sarno). Gina Labriola, *tr. fr. Italian by* Edgar Pauk. WPOW

Drunkenness. Friedrich von Logau, *tr. fr. German.* GePo, *tr. by* George C. Schoolfield

Dry. Samuel Hoffenstein. BXAP

Dry August and warm. *Unknown.* FaBoUs

Dry brown coughing beneath their feet, The. Beverly Hills, Chicago. Gwendolyn Brooks. Poetr; VGW

Dry earth near this salt sea, The. Laocoön. Wilson Harris. PBCV

Dry Gapa dingy general store. Western Town. David Wadsworth Cannon, Jr. PoNe

Dry leaves. Hazels. Geoffrey Fraser Dutton. PWE

Dry Loaf. Wallace Stevens. MeMAP; NOBA; OxBA; PoRA; RaBo

Dry not, dry not. Delight of Melancholy. Goethe, *tr. fr. German by* Philip L. Miller. RiWo

Dry River. *Unknown.* FaBoVe

Dry River Bed. Andrew Salkey. PBCV

Dry Rock Number. Tina Reid. AIW

Dry Root in a Wash. Simon J. Ortiz. HATNAP

Dry Salvages, The. T. S. Eliot. *Fr.* Four Quartets. AiP; LiTB; NoP; OxBA

Dry tree with an empty honeycomb, A. The Tomb of Heracles. James McAuley. *Fr.* Hero and the Hydra, The. FaBoMA

Dry up my tears, and dwell within her heart. *(LL)* Sweet Violets. *Unknown.* NoP

Dry Your Tears, Africa! Bernard Dadié, *tr. fr. French by* Donatus Ibe Nwoga. TTY

Dryad Song. Margaret Witter Fuller. WGRP

Dryden. The Earl of Rochester. FaBoBl

Dryden in vain tried this nice way of wit. Dryden. The Earl of Rochester. FaBoBl

Drying Clothes. Yang Wan-li, *tr. fr. Chinese by* Jonathan Chaves. SuSp

Drynaun Dhun, The. *Unknown.* GBP

Drysdale and Mantle Whitey Ford and to You. Steve Carey. UL

Du bist wie eine Blume. Heine, *tr. fr. German by* Kate Freiligrath Kroeker. *Fr.* Homeward Bound. AWP.

Du yuh dash that wid luv, Sta. Lureline. A Love Like War. Ruth Asher-Pettipher. VBLP

Dual, The. Richard Lovelace. CaPo

Dual Site, The. Michael Hamburger. TwCP

Dualisms. Tennyson. EnVR

Duality. Katherine Thayer Hobson. GoYe

Dub Eleven. Jeff Nuttall. NBrP

Dublin. Louis MacNeice. *Fr.* Closing Album, The. CIP; FaBoPP; IIP; OBTV; OxBTC

Dublin Girl, Mountjoy, 1984. Dermot Bolger. BiHa; IB

Dublin Made Me. Donagh MacDonagh. OxBTC

Dublinesque. Philip Larkin. NoAM; OxBC

Duc and Duchess de Guermantes loved Swann, The. Visit. Norman Dubie. *Fr.* Duchess' Red Shoes, The. AnAn

Duchess after the Burial, The. Norman Dubie. *Fr.* Duchess' Red Shoes, The. AnAn

Duchess of Malfi, The. (You are welcome to your country, dear Antonio.) John Webster. NAEL-1
Sels.
Hark, Now Everything Is Still. CoGr; EiL; HAP; NoP; OBD; SCGP (Hark.) CH
(Shrouding of the Duchess of Malfi, The.) NOBE; OBEV
"I am come to make thy tomb." ChTr
Madman's Song, The. EiL
(Song: "O, let us howl some heavy note.") InvP
"O that it were possible we might." IMW
"What death?" OBD
"What hideous noyse was that?" PoEL-2
"Yond's the Cardinall's window: This fortification." PoEL-2

Duchess of York's Ghost, The. *Unknown.* APAS

Duchess' Red Shoes, The. Norman Dubie. AnAn
Sels.
Duchess after the Burial, The

"Swann had gone to the estate that afternoon to tell his."
"Swann has visited the Duc and Duchess de Guermantes."
Visit

Duchesses. David Campbell. NOBAu

Duchess's Lullaby, The. "Lewis Carroll." *See* Speak roughly to your little boy.

Duck. John Lyle Donaghy. BIrV

Duck, The. Edith King. BoTP

Duck, The. Ogden Nash. MoShBr; RB; SiSoPo

Duck. Valerie Worth. NTCP

Duck and a drake, A. Mother Goose. OxNR
(Ducks and Drakes.) ReMoGo

Duck, and Mallard first, the falconers only sport, The. Michael Drayton. *Fr.* Polyolbion. FM
(Birds in the Fens.) ChTr

Duck and the Kangaroo, The. Edward Lear. OxBChV

Duck-chasing. Galway Kinnell. TwCP; VGW

Duck fats rot in the roasting pan, The. Throwing Out the Flowers. Gwendolyn Brooks. *Fr.* Notes from the Childhood and the Girlhood. LCAP

Duck in Central Park. Frances Higginson Savage. GoYe

Duck patrol is waddling down the odd-number side of Raglan, The. Army. Ciaran Carson. BiHa; PBCIP

Duck Pond at Mini's Pasture, a Dozen Years Later, The. Philip Dow. AmPA

Duck who had got such a habit of stuffing, A. The Notorious Glutton. Ann Taylor. OxBChV

Ducking: After Maupassant. Dave Jeddie Smith. AnAn

Ducks. Norman Ault. BoTP

Ducks. ("From troubles of the world"), *sels.* Frederick William Harvey. "Yes, ducks are valiant things." BoTP

Ducks. Katrina Porteous. NWP

Ducks and Drakes. Mother Goose. *See* Duck and a drake, A.

Ducks' Ditty. Kenneth Grahame. *Fr.* Wind in the Willows, The. BoTP; FaPON; GoJo; MoShBr; NTCP; OTCP; OxBChV; PDV; WHSW

Ducks flew up from the Morton Pond, The. The Run to Mourne End Wood. John Masefield. *Fr.* Reynard the Fox. EBNV

Duckweed. Leopold Staff, *tr. fr. Polish by* Adam Czerniawski. PoSu

Duds doomed to join the dodo: the dugong. Birds of America, The; Weeki Wachee. Tony Harrison. *Fr.* Art & Extinction. SCBI

Due but to one, and crownèd with one crest. *(LL)* Helena and Hermia. Shakespeare. GN; OBF

Due of the Dead, The. Thackeray. OBWP

Due on the tide, my father's rusted hulk. Homecoming. Matt Simpson. PWE

Duel, The. Eugene Field. BeLS; FaBoBe; FaPON; MoShBr; OBAL; OBCA; PoLF; PoRA; TFi

Duel in the Park. Lisa Grenelle. GoYe

Duel with Verses over a Great Man. *Unknown, tr. fr. Hebrew.* TrJP
Sels.
"Against the guide of Truth."
"Forgive us, son of Amram, be not wroth."
"Here lies a man, and still no man."
"Thou fool profane, be silent!"
"Thou Guide to doubt, be silent evermore."
"What thought ye to burn, when ye kindled the pyre."

Duellist, The, *sels.* Charles Churchill.
"First (entitled to the place), The." OBSV

Duende. Nina Zivančević, *tr. fr. Serbo-Croatian by* Charles Simic. HSix

Duenna, The, *sels.* Sheridan.
"Give Isaac the nymph who no beauty can boast." NOIV
"I ne'er could any lustre see." NOEC
"Oh, the days when I was young." OxAEP-1

Duet. Kathleen Jamie. PWE

Duet, A. T. Sturge Moore. OBEV

Duet. Tennyson. *Fr.* Becket. GBL

Duet, The. Ella Wheeler Wilcox. AnAmPo

Dug-out, The. Siegfried Sassoon. CH; MoBrPo; NSI; OHIP

Dugall Quin, (A *and* B *vers.*). *Unknown.* ESPB

Duino Elegies, *sels.* Rainer Maria Rilke, *tr. fr. German by* Stephen Mitchell.
"Not wooing, no longer shall wooing, voice that has outgrown it." EnlH, *tr. by* Stephen Mitchell
"Who, if I cried out, would hear me among the angels?." NAWM-2
"Why, if this interval of being can be spent serenely." EnlH; NAWM-2

Duke Ellington Dream, The. Paul Zimmer. Jaz; PBCAP

Duke let the sacred music begin. *(LL)* The Day Duke Raised; May 24th, 1974. Quincy Troupe. Jaz

Duke o' Athole's Nurse, The. *Unknown.* OxBB

Duke of Atholl's Nurse, The. *Unknown.* ESPB

Duke of Buccleuch, The. J. A. Phelp. NOBAu

Duke of Buckingham, The. Pope. *Fr.* Moral Essays. NOBE

Duke of Gordon's Daughter, The ("The Duke of Gordon has three daughters.") *Unknown.* ESPB

Duke of Grafton, The. *Unknown.* ChTr; GBP

Duke of Marlborough, The. *Unknown.* OBET

Duke of Plaza-Toro, The. W. S. Gilbert. *Fr.* Gondoliers, The. FaPON; FiBHP

Duke of York's Statue, The. Walter Savage Landor. FaBoEE

Duke was in his hammock and a thousand miles away, The. The Great Poll-Tax Victory of '88. Noel Petty. UV

Duke William. *Unknown.* OxBSS

Duke William was a wench's son. Song of Duke William. Hilaire Belloc. FaBoNo

Duke's Song, The. Mary Sidney Wroth, Countess of Montgomery. *Fr.* Urania. WPE

Dulce et Decorum Est. Wilfred Owen. CMoP; DL; FaBoEH; FaBoPV; FaBoTw; FaBV; FaPoB; FF; HeIL; HeIP; HoPM; InPK; InvP; LiTB; LiTM; MeMBP; MoAB; MoBrPo; NAEL-2; NIP; NoAM; NoP; OAEL-2; OBWP; PAW; PeFWW; PoE; Poetr; PoWW; PPP; PrIm; RaBo; TFi; TRP; UnPo

Dulce it is, and decorum, no doubt, for the country to fall. Arthur Hugh Clough. *Fr.* Amours de Voyage. EBVV; EnVR; FaBoPV; NOBVV; OxAEP-2

Dull as a bat, said my mother. Cousin Sidney. Dannie Abse. AngWe

Dull as I was, to think that a court fly. A Black Patch on Lucasta's Face. Richard Lovelace. BeJo; CaPo; SeCP

Dull. Dull indeed! What shall it e'er be thus? Edward Taylor. *Fr.* Preparatory Meditations Before My Approach to the Lord's Supper. ChIV-1

Dull heap, that thus thy head above the rest dost rear. Stonehenge. Michael Drayton. *Fr.* Polyolbion. FaBoPP

Dull Is My Verse. Walter Savage Landor. PoEL-4

Dull masses of dense green. Down the Mississippi. John Gould Fletcher. LiTA

Dull people, A. From Colony to Nation. Irving Layton. NOBC

Dull soul aspire. To the Soul. John Collop. TrGrPo

Dull, Sullen Prisoners. Pope. *See* Most souls, 'tis true, but peep out once an age.

Dull to myself and almost dead to these. The Bad Season Makes the Poet Sad. Robert Herrick. BeJo; CaPo; LiTB; NAEL-1; PrIm; SCGP

Dull unwashed windows of eyes. A Poem Some People Will Have to Understand. Amiri Baraka. BPo; NOBA; RaBo

Dulled by the slow glare of the yellow bulb. A Wartime Dawn. David Gascoyne. LiTM

Dullest people I knew, The. When I Was Dying. William Hathaway. UL

Dulnesse. George Herbert. ESCV; MiEL

Dulngulg Song Cycle, The, *sels.* *Unknown.* Sunrise Sequence. NOBAu

Dumb are the trumpets, cymbals. Solomon. Heine, *tr. fr. German by* Emma Lazarus. TrJP

Dumb,/ Bloodied, the severed. A Grafted Tongue. John Montague. BIrV; CIP; PBCIP

Dumb Dick. Leslie A. Fiedler. ErPo

Dumb Friend, A. Christina Rossetti. OBF

Dumb genius blows. From Another Room. Gregory Corso. NeAP

Dumb man came to shout hurray, A. (*LL*) One fine day in the middle of the night. *Unknown.* ISE

Dumb Oxen. Sister Mary Madeleva. *Fr.* Of Mary. CRP

Dumb Soldier, The. Robert Louis Stevenson. OxBChV

Dumb thing near a drunken man., A. (*LL*) The Dumb World. W. H. Davies. OBWVE; OxBTC

Dumb World, The. W. H. Davies. OBWVE; OxBTC

Dumbfounding, The. Margaret Avison. NOBC

Dummer the shepherd sacrific'd. Cotton Mather. SCAP

Dump, The. Greg Kuzma. PoA

Dumping (left over from the autumn). Enemy Encounter. Padraic Fiacc. IIP; PNI

Dumps, The. Nigel Wells. PWE

Dumpy Ducky. Lucy Larcom. OBCA

Dun brown tomorrow. The unicorn. The Unicorn Is a Symbol of Virginity. Christiania Whitehead. NWP

Dun-Colour [*or* Dun-Color]. Ruth Pitter. FM; PoRA

Dunbar. Anne Spencer. CDC

Duncan. Thom Gunn. BAP-90

Duncan and his brother was playing pool. Brady. *Unknown.* AS

Duncan Gray. Burns. CoMu; ErPo; FaBoBl

Duncan Gray ("Duncan Gray cam here to woo.") Burns. GTBS; GTBS-P

Dunce, The. *Unknown.* OxNR

Dunciad, The, *sels.* Pope.

"Books and the Man I sing, the first who brings." CBNP

Carnations and Butterflies. NOEC

Certain Type of Scientist Speaks, A. ECEV

"Here she beholds the chaos dark and deep." FHYEP (Bad Poetry.) EPCY

Idle Pursuits. ECEV; OBSV

"Mighty mother, and her son who brings, The." OBSV; PoE (To Dr. Jonathan Swift.) OxAEP-1

"More she had spoke, but yawn'd — All nature nods." FHYEP

"Oh (cry'd the Goddess) for some pedant Reign!" FaBoEH

"She somes! she comes! the sable throne behold." ECEV

"This labour passed, by Bridewell all descend." OxAEP-1

"Three college sophs, and three pert templars came." FHYEP

Triumph of Dullness [*or* Dulness], The. EBEV; FaBoPV; NOBE; NOEC; NoP; SCV

"Yet, yet a moment, one dim ray of light." NAEL-1; OAEL-1; PoEL-3

Young Traveller Is Presented to the Goddess Dulness, A. NOEC

Dunciad Minor, *sels.* A. D. Hope.

"Now Muse assist me, aptly to describe." BXAP

On Shakespeare Critics. OxBC

Dunes. A. R. Ammons. FoLa

Dunes are graying that were blackest. Aubade: The Desert. Frederick Bock. PoA

Dunes lean back on the permanence, The. Sand. Angela Greene. NWP

Dungeon horrible, on all sides round, A. Milton. *Fr.* Paradise Lost. EPCY; OBD

Dunlavin Green. *Unknown.* FaBoBa

Dunmow Flitch of Bacon, The. *Unknown.* OBET

Dunna thee tell me it's his'n, mother. Whether or Not. D. H. Lawrence. MoBrPo

Dunno a heap about the what an' why. Vagabond. John Masefield. OtMeF

Duns Scotus's Oxford. Gerard Manley Hopkins. EBEV; FaBoPP; GTBS-P; MeMBP; NAEL-2; NoAM; OBMV; OxAEP-2; PeECV; PoEL-5

Dunt Dunt Dunt Pittie Pattie. *Unknown.* FaBoVe

Duomo, The. Maria Luisa Spaziani, *tr. fr. Italian by* Beverly Allen. NeIt

Duplicity of Women, The. John Lydgate. MeEL

Durand of Blonden. Ludwig Uhland, *tr. fr. German by* James Clarence Mangan. AWP

Durban, Birmingham. Question and Answer. Langston Hughes. BPo

Dürer; Innsbruck, 1495. "Ern Malley." CBAP

Dürer would have seen a reason for living. The Steeple-Jack. Marianne Moore. *Fr.* Part of a Novel, Part of a Poem, Part of a Play. BoWoP; CMoP; FaBoMo; FaBoWP; HAP; InPS; NoAM; NOBA; NoP; OxBA; PBWP; Poetr; WPE

Durham. Tony Harrison. NoAM

Durham. *Unknown, tr. fr. Anglo-Saxon by* Kevin Crossley-Holland. ASW

"Durham," "Devonia," "Allendale," — their houses, those. A Summer Cloud. Waldo Williams, *tr. fr. Welsh by* Joseph P. Clancy. OBWVE

Durham Field. *Unknown.* ESPB

Durham Lock-out, The. *Unknown.* CoMu

Durham Old Women. *Unknown.* GBP

Duriesdyke. Swinburne. OxBB

During a Bombardmant by V-Weapons. Roy Fuller. OxBSP

During a Fit of Positive Thinking even as Snow Threatens Our February Spring. Jim Mitsui. ETG

During December's Death. Delmore Schwartz. NYBP

During His Courtship. Charles Wesley. NOCV

During Long Walks. Janet Sutherland. NBrP

During March while hoeing long rows. Hoeing. Gary Soto. PBCAP

During Music. Arthur Symons. NOBVV

During my glorious. Distraction. A. R. Ammons. CAPP

During one period I remember. Eveningsong 2. Ramona Wilson. VoR

During spring break Debbie Schwartz and I would bike. Northern Idylls. Beth Bentley. BAP-89

During the Depression my grandmother. One Foot in the Door. Anne Elder. CBAP

During the early winter. Poem for Shane on Her Brother's Birthday. Donald T. Sanders. TTTS

During the Eichmann Trial, *sels.* Denise Levertov.

"From blacked-out streets." BTR

"He had not looked." BTR

During the final minutes of the raid. Mushroom Clouds. John Engman. NAmP90

During the holidays. Holidays. Eva Mylonas, *tr. fr. Modern Greek by* Kimon Friar. BoWoP

During the Holocaust. God's Death. Florence W. Freed. BTR

During the late and long continuing cold. Eikon Basilike. Peter Didsbury. PWE

During the Pageant at Medicine Lodge. Charles G. Ballard. VoR

During the plague I came into my own. Tarantula or the Dance of Death. Anthony Hecht. CoAP; OBD

During the season of cut organs we. Initiation. Jayne Cortez. PoBA

During the very rich times of the Duke. The Substitute Bassist. C. D. Wright. Jaz

During the War. Marvin Bell. CAPP

During the winter she began. Division. John Ratti. NYBP

During this season of the long rains. (LL) Wet Thursday. Weldon Kees. NaP; NYBP

During War, the Timeless Air. John Seed. VaA

During Wind and Rain. Thomas Hardy. CMoP; ELP; GTBS-P; HAP; Mes; NAEL-2; OAEL-2; OxBTC; PeVV; PoE; PPP; TEP; TFi; TOF; TRP

Durst ye not stoop to play the fools for him? (LL) On Those That Deserve It. Francis Quarles. NOCV; NOSC

Dusk. Frank Mkalawile Chipasula. Fr. Nightsong. HBAPE

Dusk. Mae V. Cowdery. ShDr

Dusk. Angelina Weld Grimké. CDC; ShDr

Dusk. Abraham Z. Lopez-Penha, tr. fr. Spanish by Thomas Walsh. TrJP

Dusk. Gabriela Mistral, tr. fr. Spanish by David Garrison. BoWoP

Dusk. Yannis Ritsos, tr. fr. Greek by Paul Merchant. AnRep

Dusk. Helen Welshimer. PoToHe

Dusk./ Above the/ water hang the. Swan and Shadow. John Hollander. InPK; NoP; PoA; VCAP

Dusk-haired and gold-robed o'er the golden wine. For "The Wine of Circe" by Edward Burne-Jones. Dante Gabriel Rossetti. UV

Dusk in Creason's Park comes on slow. Late Afternoon, Late in the Twentieth Century. Jeffrey Skinner. PBCAP

Dusk in the Country. Harry Edmund Martinson, tr. fr. Swedish by Robert Bly. ArNa; RB

Dusk in Winter. W. S. Merwin. NaP

Dusk/ no dawns, and silver linings. No Dawns. Julianne Perry. PoBA

Dusk of Horses, The. James Dickey. LiTM; NYBP

Dusk on the Veranda by Lake Mendota. Chung Ling, tr. fr. Chinese by Kenneth Rexroth and Ling Chung. WPC

Dusk over the lake. Virgil Hutton. InPK

Dusk so dark woodsmoke, A. One for the Road. Martin Edmunds. UTF

Dusky night rides down the sky, The. Hunting Song. Henry Fielding. Fr. Don Quixote in England. OxBoLi; PeLV

Dust. "Æ." WGRP

Dust. Rupert Brooke. MoBrPo; OxBTC

Dust. Waring Cuney. CDC

Dust. P. A. Ropes. BoTP

Dust. André Spire, tr. fr. French by Jethro Bithell. TrJP

Dust. Kathleen Spivack. BoWoP

Dust. Randolph Stow. CBAP; FaBoMA

Dust. (LL) The Day They Came for Our House. Don Mattera. PeSAV

Dust . . . in the cool tombs, The. (LL) Cool Tombs. Carl Sandburg. AmPP; BLPL; CMoP; HAP; HeIL; HeIP; MoAB; MoAmPo; MoP; NAAL-2; NoBA; NOBA; PoLF; TAP; TFi; TrGrPo

Dust always blowing about the town. A Peck of Gold. Robert Frost. PDV

Dust and clay. Ascension Hymn ("Dust and clay.") Henry Vaughan. ESCV; GeHe; NOSC; SeCV-1; TrCP

Dust as we are, the immortal spirit grows. Wordsworth. Fr. Prelude [or, Growth of a Poet's Mind], The. CH; EnRP; GN; HAP; NOBE; NoP; NU; OAEL-2; OBNC; OxAEP-2; PoE; SCV

Dust Bowl. Langston Hughes. PoA

Dust cools easily. South Texas Summer Rain. Rebecca Gonzales. AiP

Dust now is the old-fashioned house. Hart Crane. AnAn

Dust of all the saints of the ages, The. Cymru. David Gwenallt Jones, tr. fr. Welsh by Gwyn Jones. OBWVE

Dust of pine pollen covers the path. (LL) The Rustic Temple Is Hidden. Chu Chen Po. OHMPC

Dust of Snow. Robert Frost. CMoP; MoShBr; OxBA; OxBSP; PDV; PrIm; SAmP; SoSe; TAP; UnPo; WeW

Dust of Timas, The. Sappho, tr. fr. Greek by E. A. Robinson. AWP

Dust on Spring Street. Louis Grudin. NoP

Dust swirls behind you. Drawing to an Inside Straight. Kirk Robertson. NGP

Dust thou art, but dust carefully. Ralph Hodgson. Fr. Flying Scrolls. FaBoTw

Dust,/ Through which. Dust. Waring Cuney. CDC

Dust to Dust. Walter de la Mare. TrPWD

Dust to Dust. Gwen Harwood. FaBoMA

Dust to Dust. Thomas Hood. NBLV

Duster, dust away, my friend. Dust. André Spire, tr. fr. French by Jethro Bithell. TrJP

Dusters beside their beds. (LL) Dust. Randolph Stow. CBAP; FaBoMA

Dusting. Rita Dove. HCAP; HeIP; LCAP; Poetr

Dusting of the Books, The. Dorothy Hughes. GoYe

Dustman, The. Clive Sansom. BoTP

Dustman, The. Unknown. BoTP

Dusty Miller, The. Unknown. ReMoGo

Dusty road is mine to tread, A. Pedlar Jim. Florence Hoare. BoTP

Dutch, The. George Canning. See In matters of commerce the fault of the Dutch.

Dutch April. Daniel Halpern. GrPl

Dutch Cleanser. John Updike. PRA

Dutch in the Medway, The. Andrew Marvell. Fr. Last Instructions to a Painter, The. APAS; FaBoEH

Dutch Interior. May Sarton. SM

Dutch Lover, The, sels. Aphra Behn.
  "Ah false Amyntas, can that hour." WPE
  Amyntas Led Me to a Grove. ErPo
  (Willing Mistress, The.) NALW

Dutch Lullaby, A. Eugene Field. See Wynken, Blynken, and Nod one night.

Dutch Picture, A. Longfellow. MoShBr

Dutch Proverb, A. Matthew Prior. FaBoEE; NOEC

Dutch straps mr universe jock caps 1001 nights genuine rechy. Soho. Edwin Morgan. FaBoBl

Dutchess of Monmouth's Lamentation for the Loss of Her Duke, The. Unknown. CoMu; FaBoBa

Dutty Tough. Louise Bennett. PBCV

Duty. Arthur Hugh Clough. EBVV; EnVR

Duty. Emerson. Fr. Voluntaries. GN

Duty. Ellen S. Hooper. BLPA

Duty, or Truth at Work. L. A. J. Moorer. CBWP-3

Duty? — who really needs it? Trust your Love. (LL) The Diary. Goethe. STV

Dvonya. Louis Simpson. NNaP; NOBA

Dwarf, The. Wallace Stevens. MeMAP

Dwarf barefooted, chanting, The. The Peasants. Alun Lewis. LiTM; PoWW

Dwarf of Disintegration. Oscar Williams. ImPo; LiTM

Dwarf pines; the wild plum on the wind-grassed shore. Colloquy with a King-Crab. John Peale Bishop. LiTA

Dwell, awful Silence, on the shady hills. Pan Piping. Plato, tr. fr. Greek by Thomas Stanley. FaBoEE

Dweller and a joy, A. (LL) To the Snipe. John Clare. FaBoPV; OBNC

Dwelling-Place, The. Henry Vaughan. GeHe; MeLP; NOSC; PeECV; TrPWD; WGRP

Dwindling Forest of Arden, The. Michael Drayton. Fr. Polyolbion. FaBoPP

Dyddgu Replies to Dafydd. Gillian Clarke. SCBI

D'ye ken John Peel with his coat so gay [or gray]? John Peel. John Woodcock Graves. CH; OxBoLi

D'ye ken the big village of Balmaquhapple. The Village of Balmaquhapple. James Hogg. FaBoCo; FaBoPP

Dyer, The. Unknown. ChTr; OxNR

Dying. Adah Isaacs Menken. CBWP-1

Dying. Robert Pinsky. HCAP; VCAP

Dying. John Stigall. CRP

Dying Airman, The. Unknown. AS; FaBoNo; OxBoLi; PeLV; RB

Dying: An Introduction. L. E. Sissman. NYBP

Dying Animals, The. Gavin Ewart. OBD

Dying Away. William Meredith. NoAM

Dying Californian, The. Unknown. AmFP

Dying Chair, The. Randolph Stow. FaBoMA

Dying Child, The. John Clare. EnRP; TrGrPo

Dying Child's Request, The. Hannah Flagg Gould. OBCA

Dying Christian to His Soul, The. Pope, par. fr. the Latin of Emperor Hadrian. See Vital spark of heavenly flame!

Dying Cowboy, The. Unknown. FaBoBa

Dying Cowboy, The. Unknown. See "O [or Oh] bury me not on the lone prairie."

Dying Father's Farewell, The, diff. vers. Berryman Hicks. See Time Is Swiftly Rolling On, The.

Dying firelight slides along the quirt, A. The End of the Weekend. Anthony Hecht. FaBoMo; HAP; LiTM; SM; WeW

Dying Garden, The. Howard Nemerov. Poetsp

Dying Gaul, The, sels. Desmond O'Grady. BIrV; PBCIP
  "Day concludes burning, The." CIP

Dying Girl, The. Mary Weston Fordham. CBWP-2

Dying Gladiator, The. Byron. Fr. Childe Harold's Pilgrimage. NOBE

Dying Hobo, The. *Unknown.* AmFP

Dying Hogger, The. *Unknown.* AS

Dying in Your Garden of Death to Go Back into My Garden. *Unknown.* BAP-90

Dying Indian, The. Joseph Warton. NOEC; OxAEP-1

Dying Lover, The. Richard Henry Stoddard. AnAmPo

Dying Man in His Garden, The. George Sewell. GTBS; GTBS-P

Dying Mine Brakeman, The. Orville Jenks. AmFP

Dying Prostitute, The; an Elegy. Thomas Holcroft. NOEC

Dying Race, A. Andrew Motion. SCBI

Dying Sergeant, The. *Unknown.* AmFP

Dying Song. Anton Ulrich, *tr. fr. German by* George C. Schoolfield. GePo

Dying Speech of an Old Philosopher. Walter Savage Landor. *See* I strove with none, for none was worth my strife.

Dying sun, shine warm a little longer! Lament for Pasiphae. Robert Graves. FaBoTw

Dying Swan, The. T. Sturge Moore. OBMV

Dying Swan, The. Tennyson. WiR

Dying Swan, The. *Unknown.* ChTr

Dying Synagogue at South Terrace, The. Thomas McCarthy. BiHa; IB

Dying tiger — moaned for drink, A. Emily Dickinson. InPK

Dying Viper, A. "Michael Field." FM

Dying Wife to Her Husband, A. Moses ibn Ezra, *tr. fr. Hebrew.* TrJP

Dying with Amish Uncles. Julia Kasdorf. PBCAP

Dying Words of Stonewall Jackson, The. Sidney Lanier. PAH

Dying Year, The. Clara Ann Thompson. CBWP-2

Dyke-Builder, The. Henry Treece. LiTB

Dykes, The. Kipling. CoGr; OBWP

Dykes in the Garden. Sharon Barba. PeHV

Dylan, Who Is Dead. Samuel Allen. PoBA

Dynamite Song. *Unknown.* AmFP

Dynasts, The, *sels.* Thomas Hardy.
   Budmouth Dears. CH
   Eve of Waterloo, The. OAEL-2; OBWP
      (Before Waterloo.) MoAB
   Field of Talavera, The. CMoP
   Men Who March Away. CH; OBWP; PoWW
   Night of Trafalgar, The. ChTr; FaBoCh; MoBrPo; OBMV
      (Trafalgar.) CH
   "Yea, the coneys are scared by the thud of hoofs." FaBoEH
      (Chorus of the Years.) CMoP
      (Field of Waterloo, The.) FaBoCh; 08LoBV

Dyvers dothe use as I have heard and kno. Sir Thomas Wyatt. *See* Divers Doth Use.

Dyvers thy death doo dyverslye bemone. The Earl of Surrey. *See* Divers [or Diverse] thy death do diversely bemoan.

Dzogbese Lisa has treated me thus. Songs of Sorrow. Kofi Awoonor. HBAPE

E

E hó hì ura bhì. Waulking Song: Two. Minnie Bruce Pratt. GLP

E. Jarvis-Thribb (17) and Keith's Mum. On the Tercentenary of Milton's Death. Gavin Ewart. OxBC

E. P. Ode Pour l'Election de Son Sepulchre. Ezra Pound. *See* For three years, out of key with his time.

E Questo il Nido in Che la Mia Fenice? A. D. Hope. OxBC

E-ri-e, The. *Unknown.* AS

E stands for egg. Hilaire Belloc. *Fr.* Moral Alphabet, A. NoAM

E Tenebris. Oscar Wilde. ChIV-2; MoBrPo; NAEL-2; OxAEP-2; Son; TIRV; TrPWD

È, the Feasting Florentines. Daniel Hoffman. VGW

E u w/ i a o. Heights. Aleksei Kruchenykh. CBNP

E Uni Que A The Hi A Tho, Father. Roberta Hill Whiteman. VoR

'E was sittin' on a door-step. The Road to Vagabondia. Dana Burnet. PoLF

'E was the greatest man on earth. The Greatest Man on Earth. *Unknown.* RoPo

'E was warned agin 'er. The Sergeant's Weddin.' Kipling. OxBTC

Each a glimpse and gone for ever! (*LL*) From a Railway Carriage. Robert Louis Stevenson. BoTP; FaPON; OTCP; OxBChV; PDV; PYC

Each a Part of All. Augustus Wright Bamberger. WBLP

Each and All. Emerson. AmPP; AnAmPo; AWP; BLPL; MeMAP; NAAL-1; NOBA; OxBA; TAP; WGRP

Each beast can choose his fere according to his mind. The Earl of Surrey. SiPSBD
   (Of a Lady That Refused to Dance with Him.) SiPS

Each bird is hushed that stretched its pinions to the day. (*LL*) Sleep Upon the World. Alcman. ChTr

Each Bird Walking. Tess Gallagher. CrSp; FaBoWP; NAmP90; SV

Each blest drop, on each blest limb. On the Water of Our Lord's Baptism. Richard Crashaw. GeHe

Each body has its art, its precious prescribed. Still Do I Keep My Look, My Identity . . . . Gwendolyn Brooks. PoA

Each burning deed and thought! (*LL*) The Village Blacksmith. Longfellow. AiP; AnAmPo; BLPL; EBEvV; FaBoBe; FaPON; FaPoR; OBAL; OBCA; PWR; UV, sh. vers.; VPP; WBLP

Each care decays, and yet my sorrow springs. (*LL*) The Soote Season. The Earl of Surrey, *after* Petrarch. AAS; EnRePo; InPS; NAEL-1; NoP; NoSic; SiPSBD; Son

Each care-worn face is but a book. The Strangers. Jones Very. AnAmPo; OxBA

Each colour sits beside. Thomas A. Clark. *Fr.* Sixteen Sonnets. NBrP

Each dawn is clear. Gary Snyder. *Fr.* Myths and Texts. NaP

Each Day. David Ignatow. NNaP

Each Day. Sister Maura. CRP

Each day brings its toad, each night its dragon. Jerome. Randall Jarrell. PPP

Each day gropes colder. What we see. Brund. Jean Hanff Korelitz. PWE

Each day I live, each day the sea of light. Poem against the Rich. Robert Bly. NOBA

Each day I long so much to see. The One Who Is at Home. Franciso Albanez, *tr. fr. Spanish by* Robert Bly. RaBo

Each day I sink in sleep, as into death. Of the Resurrection of the Body. Marbod of Rennnes, *tr. fr. Latin by* Helen Waddell. MLL

Each day, I take the lift from the sublet down. The Beds. Elizabeth Spires. NAmP90

Each day I walk with wonder. Clinton Scollard. TrPWD

Each day into the upper air. Election Reflection. M. Keel Jones. NBLV

Each day is a full. After My Grandmother's Death. Michele Roberts. AIW

Each day is an iceberg. Nightdream. Charles Wright. CAPP

Each day of thine, sweete month of May. To the Month of May. Sir John Davies. *Fr.* Hymns of Astræa [in Acrostic Verse]. SiPSBD

Each day some further light each day some farther dark. Peter Riley. *Fr.* Eight Preludes. VaA

Each day the tide withdraws; chills us; pastes. Wreaths. Geoffrey Hill. PoA

Each day was like another. Ballad of the Hidden Dragon. *Unknown, tr. fr. Chinese.* WTO

Each day's morning tastes of thinking of you. Every Day that I Love You. Teresita Fernández, *tr. fr. Spanish by* Margaret Randall. AIW

Each face in the street is a slice of bread. Bread. W. S. Merwin. VCAP

Each face its own phantom. Cartagena de Indias. Earle Birney. MoCV

Each feels the amazing, murderous legends move. (*LL*) The Figures on the Frieze. Alastair Reid. ErPo; NYBP

Each for himself is still the rule. In the Great Metropolis. Arthur Hugh Clough. EnVR; OHCV

Each Found Himself at the End Of . . . . Ebbe Borregaard. NeAP

Each gesture. A Reason. Robert Creeley. NaP

Each grain of sand has an architecture, but. Proposition II. Keith Waldrop. InPK

Each hour has some glory all its own. The Hour's Glory. H. Cordelia Ray. CBWP-3

Each house had its ghost. Sigmund Freud. Howard Nemerov. PoA

Each In His Own. "Angelus Silesius," *tr. fr. German. Fr.* Cherubical Wanderer, The. GePo, *tr. by* George C. Schoolfield

Each in His Own Tongue. William Herbert Carruth. BLPA; WBLP; WGRP

Each in the end when each is overthrown. (*LL*) Beyond Religion. Lucretius. AWP

Each instinctively knowing his terminus. (*LL*) The Lit Stations. Kathy Fagan. UTF

Each is beautiful. Tell Our Daughters. Besmilr Brigham. CrSp; IHMS

Each known mile comes late. The Train Runs Late to Harlem. Conrad Kent Rivers. PoBA

Each Lon was a notable man. L. G. Udall. PeLi

Each lover's longing leads him naturally. To Dante Alighieri: He Interprets Dante's Dream. Cino da Pistoia, *tr. fr. Italian by* Dante Gabriel Rossetti. AWP

Each man has/ his own way. The End Bit. Jim Burns. FF

Each man is limited by inborn traits. Love Is Kind. Benjamin Keech. PoToHe

Each man me telleth I change most my devise. Sir Thomas Wyatt. SiPS

Each man to his forced march; this is mine. Hitchhiker. Jack Marshall. NYBP

Each moment of the long-liv'd day. Catullus, *tr. fr. Latin by* Tom Brown. OBVE

Each month hath praise in some degree; The Month of September. Sir John Davies. *Fr.* Hymns of Astræa [in Acrostic Verse]. SiPSBD

Each More Melodious Note I Hear. Thoreau. OxBSP

Each Morning. Amiri Baraka. *Fr.* Hymn for Lanie Poo. PoBA

Each morning and each noon. Moving. Jeanne Foster. CrSp

Each morning she is wheeled into the picture. Living in the La Brea Tar Pits. Nancy Vieira Couto. PBCAP

Each morning the birds awake me. Morning Vigil. Phillip William George. VoR

Each morning they bring me the condemned man's brekker. Analogy. Brian Higgins. FaBoTw

Each morning they pass over. The Starling Migration. Jeffrey Skinner. PBCAP

Each new daybreak we are born again. Palladas, *tr. fr. Greek by* Tony Harrison. GrAn

Each new passenger, on the tramcar. The Sentence. Martin Sorescu, *tr. fr. Romanian by* Paul Muldoon *and* Ioana Russell-Gebbett. PWE

Each night a star to guide thy feet to Heaven. (*LL*) Opportunity. Walter Malone. BLPA; BLPL; FaBoBe; PWR; WBLP

Each night father fills me with dread. Edward Gorey. PeLi

Each night for seven nights beyond the gulf. The Oleaster. Robert Graves. OBTV

Each night I sleep more lightly. Herman von Lingg, *tr. fr. German by* Philip L. Miller. RiWo

Each night with moist leaves. Bamboo Elegy: Two. Edmond Yi-Teh Chang. OpBo

Each object by a few short years how changed! A Visit to the Author's Paternal Seat. Richard Polwhele. *Fr.* Influence of Local Attachment, The. NOEC

Each of them must have terrified. In Memory of the Utah Stars. William Matthews. Poetsp

Each of us, each with a tale to tell. The Botanic Garden Oath. Ken Smith. PWE

Each of us holds a locked razor. (*LL*) Waking in the Blue. Robert Lowell. CoAP; HCAP; MoAmPo; UnPo

Each of us like you. Adonis. Hilda Doolittle ("H. D."). AWP; LiTA

Each of us pursues his trade. The Scholar and the Cat. Frank O'Connor. OBF

Each one, by nature, loves to be a king. (*LL*) Ambition. Robert Herrick. CaPo

Each one swimming its own way. (*LL*) After the Night. Mang Ke. SpMi

Each other satire humbler arts has known. Mock-Epic Satire. Walter Harte. EPCY

Each other? Why are the beautiful sick and divided/ like myself? (*LL*) Cold Term. Amiri Baraka. BPo; SOTW

Each photographed face. Valerio Magrelli, *tr. fr. Italian by* Dana Gioia. NeIt

Each poem has its own pattern of tones. An Old Poem to Yän ChÅF/. Hsüeh T'ao, *tr. fr. Chinese by* Kenneth Rexroth *and* Ling Chung. WPC

Each poet with a different talent writes. Earl of Roscommon. *Fr.* Essay on Translated Verse, An. EPCY; FaBoUs

Each prisoner is so sad in the glare. The Line-up. Joan Swift. SM

Each second I'm new-born from some new grave. (*LL*) Struggle. Sidney Lanier. LiTA; OxBA

Each shining light above us. The Light of Love. John Hay. AnAmPo

Each silently, but not alone. (*LL*) You Are the Brave. Raymond R. Patterson. NIP; PoBA

Each single wing-. The Memory of Cock Robin Dwarfs W. D. W. D. Snodgrass. BAP-89

Each storm-soaked flower has a beautiful eye. Rain. Vachel Lindsay. CMoP; RaBo

Each subtlety hard for the pedant to solve. Coming Across. Mehri, *tr. fr. Farsi by* Deirdre Lashgari. WPOW

Each Sunday I climb the mountain to picnic. Picnic. Nellie Wong. OpBo

Each time, greenbones, you pressed the neat trigger. Boy at Target Practice; a Contemplation. W. R. Moses. NYBP

Each time his will abdicated. Possession. Lynne Lawner. ErPo

Each time I order her to go. Forgiveness. Alice Walker. MDDM

Each time I return to this place. The Marsh. Marcia Southwick. FoLa

Each to Each. Melville Cane. GoYe

Each traveller prays, "Let me be far from any." Journey to Iceland. W. H. Auden. OBTV; PoA

Each tugs in a different way, And the greatest of all is John Bull. (*LL*) The World Is a Bundle of Hay. Byron. EnRP; FF

Each unblinking eyelet linked now. The Self. Robin Morgan. *Fr.* Network of the Imaginary Mother, The. SRLS

Each way the turn. The Turn. Robert Creeley. LCAP

Each week or so, by the post. The Losses. Reed Whittemore. OBF

Each week they meet to rehearse. The Voyagers. Askold Melnyczuk. UTF

Each with each has borne in patience. To Edom. Heine, *tr. fr. German.* TrJP

Each writes long letters. Absent Friends. Anne Bloch. *Fr.* Separation. Mes

Each year for a short season. Folk Wisdom. Thomas Kinsella. TwCP

Each year I have a birthday. A Giant's Cake. Evelina San Garde. BoTP

Each year, the court expands. The Old Pro's Lament. Paul Petrie. TAP

Eachie, peachie, pearie, plum. *Unknown.* GBP

Eadwacer. *Unknown, tr. fr. Anglo-Saxon.* PBWP, *tr. by* Kemp Malone; WPE

Eager he look'd. Another train of years. Joel Barlow. *Fr.* Columbiad, The. AmPP

Eager note on my door said 'Call me,' The. Frank O'Hara. CAPP; NoAM; NOBA; Poetr

Eager Spring. Gordon Bottomley. MoBrPo

Eager Street. Kendra Kopelke. AiP

Eager to breathe out. Mocking Song against Qaqortingneq. Piuvkaq, *tr. fr. Eskimo.* WTO

Eagerly/ Like a woman hurrying to her lover. Four Glimpses of Night. Frank Marshall Davis. NoP; PoBA; PoNe

Eagerness of objects to, The. Interior (With Jane). Frank O'Hara. LCAP

Eagle, The. "Fiona Macleod." *Fr.* Transcripts from Nature. FM

Eagle. Robin Skelton. NOBC

Eagle, The. Tennyson. BoTP; CH; ClHu; CoGr; FaBoCh; FaPON; FF; FHYEP; FM; GN; GoJo; GTBS-P; HeIL; HeIP; InPK; MeMBP; NAEL-2; NOBVV; NoP; NTCP; NTP; OAEL-2; OxBSP; PDV; Poetr; PrIm; SCGP; TFi; TrGrPo; TRP; UnPo; WiR

Eagle above Us, The. Santiago Altamirano, Willard R. Trask (OBAP). OBAP; STP

Eagle and the Beetle, The. La Fontaine, *tr. fr. French by* Elizur Wright. OBVE

Eagle and the Mole, The. Elinor Wylie. AWP; BoWoP; LiTA; LiTM; MoAB; MoAmPo; NALW; UnPo

Eagle and Vulture, The. Thomas Buchanan Read. PAH

Eagle Bar, The. John Wieners. BCF

Eagle-eyed Wisdom, life's lodestar. Of Her Wisdom. Sir John Davies. *Fr.* Hymns of Astræa [in Acrostic Verse]. SiPSBD

Eagle-Feather Fan, The. N. Scott Momaday. CDW

Eagle for an Emperor. Falconry. Anne Wilkinson. MoCV

Eagle glides above the plain, An. Central Highlands, Viet Nam, 1968. Geary Hobson. ETG

Eagle in New Mexico, *sels.* D. H. Lawrence. "Towards the sun, towards the south-west." RB

Eagle is my power, The. The Eagle-Feather Fan. N. Scott Momaday. CDW

Eagle looked at this changing world, The. Mount Eagle. John Montague. BiHa; IIP

Eagle of Corinth, The. Henry Howard Brownell. PAH

Eagle of Pengwern. *Unknown, tr. fr. Welsh by* Gwyn Williams. PBWP

Eagle of the tomb, whose tomb is this? Why. *Unknown, tr. fr. Greek by* Peter Whigham. GrAn

Eagle Poem. Joy Harjo. CrSp; HATNAP; WeW

Eagle soars in the summit of heaven, The. T. S. Eliot. *Fr.* Rock, The. OBMV

Eagle Song. Gordon Bottomley. *Fr.* Suilven and the Eagle. MoBrPo

Eagle, stooping from yon snow-blown peaks, The. Whittier. GOA

Eagle That Is Forgotten, The. Vachel Lindsay. AWP; CMoP; LiTA; MeMAP; MoAB; MoAmPo; NOBA; OxBA

Eagle Valor, Chicken Mind. Robinson Jeffers. LiTA; OxBA; OxBSP

Eagle! why soarest thou above that tomb? Spirit of Plato. *Unknown, tr. fr. Greek by* Shelley. AWP; OBVE (Plato's Tomb.) FaBoCh

Eagles, The. Jones Very. TAP

Eagles have practically left America, The. Inability to Depict an Eagle. Richard Eberhart. GOA

Eagle's nest on the head of an old redwood, An. The Beaks of Eagles. Robinson Jeffers. NOBA

Eagle's shadow runs across the plain, The. Zebra. "Isak Dinesen." GoJo; RFM

Eagle's Song, The. Mary Austin. GOA

Eagle's Song, The. Richard Mansfield. PAH

Eagles, that wheel above our crests. The Cedars of Lebanon. Alphonse Marie Louis de Lamartine, *tr. fr. French by* Toru Dutt. AWP

Eaper Weaper, chimney sweeper. *Unknown.* FaBoNo; ISE; OxBoLi

Ear, The. Louis MacNeice. OxBSP

Ear Ear. Concrete Cat. Dorthi Charles. InPK

Ear Is Not Deaf. Irene Dayton. GoYe

Ear-string, An. William Strode. NOSC

Earl Bothwell. *Unknown.* ESPB

Earl Brand. *Unknown.* AmFP; ESPB

Earl Brand. *Unknown.* OxBB

Earl Brand (The Douglas Tragedy). *Unknown.* FaBoBa

Earl Crawford. *Unknown.* ESPB

Earl March look'd on his dying child. The Maid of Neidpath. Thomas Campbell. GTBS; GTBS-P

Earl Mar's Daughter. *Unknown.* GN

Earl Mertoun's Song. Robert Browning. *Fr.* Blot in the 'Scutcheon, A. OBEV

Earl o' Quarterdeck, The. George Macdonald. BeLS

Earl of Aboyne, The. *Unknown.* ESPB

Earl of Cassillis' ladie, The. (*LL*) The Gypsy Laddie. *Unknown.* ESPB, B *vers.*; FaBoBa

Earl of Errol, The. *Unknown.* ESPB

Earl of Mar's Daughter, The. *Unknown. See* It was intill a pleasant time.

Earl of Westmoreland, The. *Unknown.* ESPB

Earl of Wigton had three daughters, The. Richie Story. *Unknown.* ESPB

Earl Percie of Northumberland. Chevy Chase. *Unknown.* EnSB

Earl Rothes. *Unknown.* ESPB

Earlier in the evening the moon. The Moon. Robert Creeley. VGW

Earliest Christian Hymn. Clement of Alexandria, *tr. fr. Greek by* Edward H. Plumptre. WGRP

Earliest Spring. William Dean Howells. OBEV

Earliest Spring. Denise Levertov. LCAP

Earliness at the Cape. Babette Deutsch. FYAP; NYBP

Early Affection. George Moses Horton. AAP

Early April on Broadway, south of Union Square. Seeing Off a Friend. Stephen Dobyns. AnAn

Early Arrival: Sydney. Vivian Smith. NOBAu

Early, at cockcrow. The Forsaken Girl. Eduard Friedrich Mörike, *tr. fr. German by* Philip L. Miller. RiWo

Early autumn enters my rickety house. Thoughts in Early Autumn: Thirty Rhymes Sent to Lu-wang. P'i Jih-hsiu, *tr. fr. Chinese by* Irving Y. Lo. SuSp

Early Autumn in the Mountains. Wen T'ing-yün, *tr. fr. Chinese by* William R. Schultz. SuSp

Early autumn, white rabbits. Wang Chien, *tr. by* William H. Nienhauser. *Fr.* Palace Poems. SuSp

Early before the day doth spring. Of Astræa. Sir John Davies. *Fr.* Hymns of Astræa [in Acrostic Verse]. SiPSBD

Early bird got up and whet his beak, The. A Birthday Ode to Mr. Alfred Austin. Sir Owen Seaman. NOBL

Early bird may catch the worm, The. Samuel Hoffenstein. *Fr.* As the Crow Flies, Let Him Fly. NBLV

Early blossoms — could a single. Permanence in Change. Goethe, *tr. by* John Frederick Nims. HoPM; STV

Early, cheerful, mounting Lark. To the Lark. Sir John Davies. *Fr.* Hymns of Astræa [in Acrostic Verse]. SiPSBD

Early Copper. Carl Sandburg. HeIP

Early Death. Hartley Coleridge. OBEV

Early dew woos the half-opened flowers, An. Haroun's Favorite Song. *Unknown, tr. fr. Arabic by* E. Powys Mathers. *Fr.* Thousand and One Nights, The. AWP

Early Discoveries. David Malouf. CBAP

Early Dutch. Jennie M. Palen. GoYe

Early, each morning, Martha Blake. Martha Blake at Fifty-one. Austin Clarke. CIP; IPY; NOIV

Early early early. Mississippi Mornings. Tom Dent. UL

Early, Early in the Spring. *Unknown.* OBET

Early Electric! With what radiant hope. The Metropolitan Railway. Sir John Betjeman. EBEV; OxAEP-2; OxBTC

Early Evening Quarrel. Langston Hughes. SAmP; UnPo

Early Frost. Leslie Norris. AngWe

Early Geese. Tu Mu, *tr. fr. Chinese.* SuSp

Early Graves, The. Friedrich Gottlieb Klopstock, *tr. fr. German by* J. W. Thomas. GePo

Early have a miser's insinuating rub, The. Timers. Flora J. Arnstein. GoYe

Early I rose. *Unknown, tr. fr. Papago Indian by* Mary Austin. AWP; LiTA

Early in March we pitched our scar. Winterward. William Stafford. SM

Early in the first century, sometime during. The Voice from Paxos. Jonathan Aaron. BAP-91

Early in the morning. A Watering Rhyme. P. A. Ropes. BoTP

Early in the Morning. Louis Simpson. TRP

Early in the morning I hear monkeys call from the mouth of the gorge. West Cliff. Chu Yi-tsun, *tr. fr. Chinese by* Chang Yin-nan *and* Lewis C. Walmsley. SuSp

Early in the morning, let's go to the country. *Unknown.* RoPo

Early in the spring when the snow is all gone. A Trip to the Grand Banks. Amos Hanson. AmFP

Early in the Springtime. *Unknown.* OBET

Early January. W. S. Merwin. VGW

Early Losses; a Requiem. Alice Walker. BlSi

Early Love. Samuel Daniel. *Fr.* Hymen's Triumph. ErPo

Early Lynching. Carl Sandburg. ChIV-2; MoAmPo

Early March. Norman Nicholson. PAW

Early may fly the Babylonian woe. (*LL*) On the Late Massacre [*or* Massacher] in Piedmont [*or* Piemont]. Milton. AWP; GTBS; GTBS-P; HAP; HeIP; LiTB; NAEL-1; NOBE; NoP; OBWP; PAW; PoEL-3; Poetr; PPP; SCGP; Son; TFi; TRP; UnPo; WeW

Early Morn. W. H. Davies. CH

Early Morning, The. Hilaire Belloc. ArNa; BoNaP; BoTP; OxBSP; Spl; TLR

Early Morning. Eduard Friedrich Mörike, *tr. fr. German by* Philip L. Miller. RiWo

Early morning, a woman sits up in bed. Sherod Santos. BAP-91

Early Morning Meadow Song. Charles Dalmon. CH

Early morning over Rouen, hopeful. Rouen. May Wedderburn Cannan. NAEL-2; OBWP; OxBTC

Early Morning Test Light over Nevada, 1955. Robert Vasquez. AfAz

Early Morning Woman. Joy Harjo. CrSp

Early Mornings. *Unknown, tr. by* Louis Untermeyer. AS

Early, my God, without delay. Isaac Watts. AmFP

Early on a Monday morning. Kevin Barry. *Unknown.* AS; SWP

Early on the morning of Monday. Omens. *Unknown, tr. fr. Gaelic by* Alexander Carmichael. RB

(I heard the cuckoo with no food in my stomach.) ScCV

Early One Morning. *Unknown.* ChTr

Early one morning. Voodoo on the Un-Assing of Janis Joplin. Carolyn M. Rodgers. JB

Early one morning in the spring. The Disappointed Sailor. *Unknown.* OxBSS

Early Ones, The. William Stafford. CAPP

Early Pregnancy. Penelope Shuttle. BrRo

Early Rebels, The. Mervyn Morris. PBCV

Early Rising. John Godfrey Saxe. AnAmPo; BLPL; PoLF

Early Song. Carroll Arnett. ETG

Early Spring. Eloise Bibb. CBWP-4

Early Spring. Sidney Keyes. MoBrPo

Early Summer Sea-Tryst. Frederick Macartney. CBAP

Early Summer Waking from a Nap. Yang Wan-li, *tr. fr. Chinese by* Sherwin S. S. Fu. SuSp

Early sun on Beaulieu water. Youth and Age on Beaulieu River, Hants. Sir John Betjeman. FaBoTw; TwCP

Early Sunday Morning. John Stone. MT

Early Supper. Barbara Howes. GoJo; GrPl; SM

Early that afternoon, as we keep. The "Portland" Going Out. W. S. Merwin. NYBP

Early thou goest forth, to put to rout. To a "Tenting" Boy. Charles Tennyson Turner. OBNC

Early Thoughts of Marriage. Nathaniel Cotton. OxBChV

Early to bed and early to rise. New Proverb. Shirley Brooks. FaBoNo

Early to bed and early to rise. *Unknown.* FaBoBe; FaBoUs

Early Unfinished Sketch. Austin Clarke. ErPo

Early, up without breakfast. Moving. Janet Reed McFatter. GrPl

Early Views of Manchester and Paris: First View. John Ash. SCBI

Early wagons left no sign, The. The Trail into Kansas. W. S. Merwin. GOA

Early Waking. Léonie Adams. LiTM

Early Walk on Shang Mountain, An. Wen T'ing-yün, *tr. fr. Chinese by* William R. Schultz. SuSp

Early Winter. Weldon Kees. NaP

Earlye, Earlye, in the Spring. *Unknown.* AmFP

Earnest, earthless, equal, attuneable. Spelt from Sibyl's Leaves. Gerard Manley Hopkins. CMoP; EnVR; FaBoMo; LiTM; MeMBP; NOBVV; OAEL-2; PrIm; TOF

Earnest elements of nature. (*LL*) Boats in a Fog. Robinson Jeffers. NAAL-2; NoP; OxBA

Earnest Liberal's Lament, The. Ernest Hemingway. OBAL; OBSV

Earnest to explore within and all around. Dante, *tr. by* Shelley. *Fr.* Divina Commedia. MeMAP; OBVE

Earnest young leftie named Tariq. Bernard Levin. PeLi

Earnestly on me — *She had been asleep!* (*LL*) The Declaration. Nathaniel Parker Willis. AnAmPo; OBAL

Earning a Dinner. Matthew Prior. NBLV

Earrings. Annette Bialik Harchik. BTR

Ears. Sonja Åkesson, *tr. fr. Swedish by* Joanna Bankier. WPOW

Ears afire, I knock at Kent House door. Westminster Synagogue. Aaron Kramer. BTR

Ear's Delight, The. George Chapman. *Fr.* Ovid's Banquet of Sense. NoSic

Ears in the Turrets Hear. Dylan Thomas. FaBoTw

Ears on the floor were pressed to the ground. (*LL*) The Colonel. Carolyn Forché. InPS; OBWP; SoSe

Earth. Margaret Atwood. PoE

Earth. "Lynn Doyle." UTF

Earth, The. David Gwenallt Jones, *tr. fr. Welsh by* Dyfnallt Morgan. OBWVE

Earth. Jim Tollerud. VoR

Earth, The. Jones Very. AnAmPo; OxBA

Earth ("Planet doesn't explode, A.") John Hall Wheelock. LiTM; OBD; SoSe

Earth a flower. For Nothing. Gary Snyder. NNaP

Earth Abideth Forever, The. Bible, *O.T. Fr.* Ecclesiastes. FaPON

Earth, The/ adorned with heights and gentle slopes and plains. *Unknown, tr. fr. Sanskrit by* Romesh Dutt. *Fr.* Vedic Hymns. EaPr

Earth and Fire. Wendell Berry. FF

Earth and Fire. Vernon Watkins. NYBP

Earth and Goddess of Birth. Macedonius, *tr. fr. Greek by* Alistair Elliot. GrAn

Earth and I Gave You Turquoise. N. Scott Momaday. CDW; HATNAP; UnPo

Earth and sky black. Camp Site. Denis Glover. *Fr.* Arawata Bill. PeNZ

Earth and water, air and stars. Immortality. "Nicolai Maksimovich Minsky," *tr. fr. Russian by* Babette Deutsch. TrJP

Earth Angel. Jeffrey Skinner. PBCAP

Earth Asks and Receives Rain, The. Phyllis Haring. PeSA

Earth beneath, and stars above. (*LL*) Alpine Spirit's Song. Thomas Lovell Beddoes. OBNC; OBTV

Earth bleeds/ as a breast bleeds, The. Kassak. Birago Diop, *tr. fr. French by* Ellen Conroy Kennedy. NegPo

Earth Breaks Up. Robert Browning. *Fr.* Christmas-Eve and Easter-Day. TrCP

Earth brings us into life. Thich Nhat Hanh. EaPr

Earth Buried. Kenneth Mackenzie. CBAP

Earth Chorus. Juan Felipe Herrera. AfAz

Earth did tremble; and heaven's closed eye, The. On Our Saviour's Passion. Francis Quarles. *Fr.* Divine Fancies. PeECV

Earth does not ever grow fat, The. Ngoni Burial Song. *Unknown, tr. fr. Zulu.* PeSA

Earth does not understand her child. The Return. Edna St. Vincent Millay. LiTA; MeMAP; MoAB; MoAmPo; MoP; NoAM; OxBA; Poetr

Earth dries up and withers, The. Bible, *O.T. Fr.* Isaiah. EaPr

Earth exhales, The. (*LL*) Slough. Sir John Betjeman. MoBrPo; NoAM; OxAEP-2

Earth Felicities, Heavens Allowances. Richard Steere. SCAP

Earth for the sun her lover. Spring Song. Milton, *tr. fr. Latin by* Helen Waddell. MLL

Earth from her winter slumber breaks. Decoration Day. Julia Ward Howe. OHIP

Earth goes on the earth glittering in gold, The. Inscribed in Melrose Abbey. *Unknown.* FaBoEE; FaBoRV

Earth ("Grasshopper, your fairy song.") John Hall Wheelock. EaPr; LiTA; MoAmPo

Earth grown old. (*LL*) Advent. Christina Rossetti. TrCP

Earth grown old, yet still so green. Advent. Christina Rossetti. TrCP

Earth has borne a little son. The Aconite. A. M. Graham. BoTP

Earth has no sorrow that God cannot heal. (*LL*) Come, Ye Disconsolate. Thomas Moore. WGRP

Earth has not anything to show more fair. Composed upon Westminster Bridge, September 3, 1802. Wordsworth. AWP; BLPL; ChTr; ClHu; CoGr; EnRP; FaBoCh; FaBoPP; FaBoRV; FaBV; FF; HAP; HeIP; ImPo; InPK; InPS; InvP; NAEL-2; NAWM-2; NoP; OAEL-2; OBNC; PoE; PoEL-4; PoLF; PrIm; SCGP; Son; TEP; TFi; TrGrPo; UnPo (Upon Westminster Bridge.) FaPoB

Earth has not anything to show more fair. On Mrs. W — — . Nicolas Bentley. FiBHP

Earth Has Shrunk in the Wash. William Empson. CMoP

Earth holds the sunlit. For Spring. Douglas G. Jones. NOBC

Earth in its course and farther beyond the cycle of the Sun. (*LL*) Bless Thee, O Lord, for the living arc of the sky over me this morning. Carl Sandburg. EaPr

Earth in Spring, The. Judah Halevi, *tr. fr. Hebrew by* Edward G. King. TrJP

Earth is a beautiful place, The. The Third Sermon on the Warpland. Gwendolyn Brooks. BPo

Earth is a place on which England is found, The. Geography. G. K. Chesterton. *Fr.* Songs of Education. OBSV (Empire Day.) CoGr

Earth is a woman who imagines us. She sings. Robert Kelly. *Fr.* Book of Persephone, The. PoM

Earth, The/ is a wonderful. Poem for Friends. Quincy Troupe. PoBA

Earth is at the same time, The. Hildegard von Bingen, *tr. fr. Latin.* EaPr

Earth is green and heaven is blue. To the Spring. Sir John Davies. *Fr.* Hymns of Astræa [in Acrostic Verse]. SiPSBD

Earth is perishing, The. (*LL*) Spirit of Love. Barbara Deming. EaPr

Earth is raw with this one note. Crows. Lizette Woodworth Reese. AmWP

Earth is sweet with roses, The. Easter Eve. Prudentius, *tr. fr. Latin by* Helen Waddell. MLL

Earth is taken: this is not your home., The. (*LL*) Travelogue for Exiles. Karl Shapiro. MoAmPo; TrJP

Earth is the Lord's, and the fullness thereof, The. Bible, *O.T., paraphrased by* Sir Thomas Wyatt. *Fr.* Psalms. AWP; FaPON, *sts.* 1–4; TrJP (Lift Up Your Heads.) TrGrPo

Earth is weary of our foolish wars, The. Let Us Have Peace. Nancy Byrd Turner. PoToHe

Earth keeps some vibration going, The. Edgar Lee Masters. *Fr.* Spoon River Anthology. CMoP; LiTA; NoAM; OxBA; TAP; TrGrPo

Earth, Late Choked with Showers, The. Thomas Lodge. *Fr.* Scilla's Metamorphosis. EiL

Earth mother, star mother. Starhawk. EaPr

Earth, My Likeness. Walt Whitman. MeMAP; OxBA

Earth now adieu: my ravished thought. Of Her Mind. Sir John Davies. *Fr.* Hymns of Astræa [in Acrostic Verse]. SiPSBD

Earth, ocean, air, belovèd brotherhood! Shelley. *Fr.* Alastor; or, The Spirit of Solitude. EnRP; NAEL-2; OAEL-2

Earth our mother, breathe forth life. *Unknown, tr. fr. Pawnee Indian.* EaPr

Earth out of Earth. *Unknown.* MeEL

Earth Outside, The. Muzahim al-Ugaili, *tr. fr. Arabic by* Omar S. Pound. ArPe

Earth Poems, *sels.* Javier Heraud, *tr. fr. Spanish by* Maureen Ahern.

Earth Psalm. Denise Levertov. PPP

Earth puts her colours by. P. H. B. Lyon. BoTP

Earth rais'd up her head. Earth's Answer. Blake. *Fr.* Songs of Experience. ChIV-1; EnRP; FHYEP; InPS; NAEL-2; NAWM-2; NOEC; OAEL-2; PoE

Earth rebelled, The./ The good and patient earth. And the Earth Rebelled. Yuri Suhl, *tr. fr. Yiddish by* Max Rosenfeld. BTR; TrJP

Earth, receive an honoured guest. W. H. Auden. *Fr.* In Memory of W. B. Yeats. ChTr; CMoP; EPCY; FaBoRV; FaBoTw, (4 *sts.*); HAP; HeIP; HoPM; IIP; ImPo; LiTB; LiTM; MeMAP; Mes; MoAB; MoBrPo; NoAM; NOBE; OAEL-2; OxAEP-2; OxBTC; Poetr; PPP; PrIm; TFi; TrGrPo; TRP; UnPo; WeW

Earth Said to Death. Helen Waddell. MLL

Earth says have a place, be what that place, The. In Response to a Question. William Stafford. FoLa

Earth says to the earth, All this is ours, The. (*LL*) Inscribed in Melrose Abbey. *Unknown.* FaBoEE; FaBoRV

Earth sees in thee. To Sultan Murad II. James Clarence Mangan, *tr. fr. Turkish.* NOIV

Earth shows her face to the moon, The. Eclipse II. Linda Hogan. HATNAP

Earth, Sky. Sydney Clouts. PeSA

Earth Song. Thomas Love Peacock. VoR

Earth spins to my finger-tips and, The. The Globe in North Carolina. Derek Mahon. BiHa; PBCIP

Earth stopped. The Holy City hit a mountin. Joshua. X. J. Kennedy. ChIV-1

Earth teach me stillness. *Unknown, tr. fr. Ute Indian.* EaPr

Earth that lightly covers her, The. (*LL*) Upon a Child That Died. Robert Herrick. BeJo; CaPo; CH; CoGr; InPK; NoP; OBEV; Poetr; SeCV-1

Earth to earth, and dust to dust. Death and Resurrection. George Croly. WGRP

Earth to Tell of the Beasts. David Rivard. NAmP90

Earth Took of Earth. *Unknown.* HAP

Earth Trembles Waiting. Blanche Shoemaker Wagstaff. PoLF

Earth Tremor in Lugano. James Kirkup. NYBP

Earth turns, The/ like a rainbow. When You Read This Poem. Pinkie Gordon Lane. BlSi

Earth Walk. William Meredith. MAT

Earth was green, the sky was blue, The. A Green Cornfield. Christina Rossetti. BoTP

Earth was young, the world was fair, The. The Saxon Legend of Language. Mary Weston Fordham. AAP; AmWP; CBWP-2

Earth, water, air, and fire combined to make this food. *Unknown*. EaPr

Earth will be going on a long time, The. Lute Music. Kenneth Rexroth. TAP

Earth, with all its fullness, is the Lord's, The. Poor for Our Sakes. Mary Brainerd Smith. BLRP

Earth, with her thousand voices, praises God. (*LL*) Hymn before Sunrise, in the Vale of Chamouni. Samuel Taylor Coleridge. EnRP; WGRP

Earth with thunder torn[e], with fire blasted, The. Fulke Greville. *Fr.* Caelica. AAS; EnRePo; NoSic
(Sonnet: "Earth with thunder torn, with fire blasted, The.") JCP

Earth Worm, The. Denise Levertov. NOBA

Earth wraps your body, Kallisto, in its lap. Epitaph from Piraeus. *Unknown, tr. fr. Greek by* Peter Jay. GrAn

Eartha my mother's name, now earth. Crinagoras, *tr. fr. Greek by* Alistair Elliot. GrAn

Earthblue eye of the boatpond smiled at the sky, The. "X." Jean Valentine. PFL

Earthen bowl churned into foam. (*LL*) A Sound from the Earth. William Stafford. NNaP; RFM

Earthly Illusion. Louise Leighton. GoYe

Earthly Paradise, The, *sels.* William Morris.
Apology, An. AWP; EBVV; EnVR; LiTB; NAEL-2; NoP; OAEL-2; OBNC; OPOP
(Prologue.) OtMeF
March. OtMeF
November. EnVR
October. EnVR; OBNC
Outlanders, The. EBVV
(Minstrels and Maids.) GN
Prologue: The Wanderers. EBVV
(Introduction.) EnVR
Road of Life, The. OBNC
"Under a bent when the night was deep." PChr

Earthly roses at God's call have made, The. On the Death of a Pious Lady. Olof Wexionius, *tr. fr. Swedish by* Sir Edmund Gosse. AWP

Earthly: Sonnets for Carlos, *sels.* Ian Wedde.
"By day and also by night and you are." PeNZ
"Diesel trucks past the Scrovegni chapel." PeNZ
"If thy wife is small bend down to her and." PeNZ
Power Transformer. PeNZ

Earthmoving Malediction. Heather McHugh. NAmP90

Earthquake. R. A. D. Ford. NOBC

Earthquake, The. *Unknown, tr. fr. Zuni Indian by* K. Kennedy. WTO

Earthquake of 1886, The. Josephine D. Henderson Heard. CBWP-4

Earthquaked, my house collapsed. Antiphilus, *tr. fr. Greek by* Lee T. Pearcy. GrAn

Earth's Answer. Blake. *Fr.* Songs of Experience. ChIV-1; EnRP; FHYEP; InPS; NAEL-2; NAWM-2; NOEC; OAEL-2; PoE

Earth's blueish animals are few. (*LL*) Variation on a Sentence. Louise Bogan. FM

Earth's Bondman. Betty Page Dabney. GoYe

Earth's Bounty. Auvaiyar, *tr. fr. Tamil by* A. K. Ramanujan. PLW

Earth's Children Cleave to Earth. Bryant. AnAmPo

Earth's first Adam, he lay in the grass. Adam and Eve. Itsik Manger, *tr. fr. Yiddish by* Jacob Sonntag. TrJP

Earth's Lyric. Bliss Carman. AnAmPo

Earth's sea white with waves. (*LL*) Adore we the Lord. *Unknown*. NOIV

Earth's Song. W. E. R. La Farge. EaPr

Earth's victor-captain be. (*LL*) Cupid. Bernard O'Dowd. NOBAu

Earthworm, The. Harry Edmund Martinson, *tr. fr. Swedish by* Robert Bly. ArNa; RaBo; RB

Earthworms. Parody. Martha Paley Francescato, *tr. fr. Spanish by* Willis Barnstone. BoWoP

Earthy Anecdote. Wallace Stevens. CMoP; GoJo; RB; RFM; SAmP

Early [or Earthly] nourris [or nouris or nourrice] sits and sings, An. The Great Silkie of Sule Skerry. *Unknown*. ChTr; ESPB; FaBoBa; FaBoCh; GBP; MAT
(Grey Selchie of Sule Skerry, The.) OxBB
(Grey Selchie, The.) ScCV

Ease. William Cowper. *Fr.* Task, The. TEP

Ease. Po Chü-i, *tr. fr. Chinese by* Arthur Waley. Spl

Ease is the pray'r of him who, in a whaleboat. Sapphics: At the Mohawk-Castle, Canada. Thomas Morris. NOEC

Ease your weary limbs, stranger, under this elm — . Anyte, *tr. fr. Greek by* John Heath-Stubbs *and* Carol A. Whiteside. GrAn

Easie earth that covers her, Th.' (*LL*) Here a pretty baby lies. Robert Herrick. OBEV

Easier to encapsulate your lives. Granddaughter. Adrienne Rich. *Fr.* Grandmothers. HCAP; NAAL-2; NoAM

Easiest Room in Hell, The. Peter Porter. FaBoMA

Easing My Heart. Tu Mu, *tr. fr. Chinese by* A. C. Graham. PLT

East, The. Matthew Arnold. *Fr.* Obermann Once More. OtMeF

East 116th/ and a long red car. Tiburón. Martín Espada. UTF

East A-Callin', The. Oscar Wilde. *Fr.* Ave Imperatrix. OtMeF

East Anglian Bathe. Sir John Betjeman. NoP

East Anglian Fen. George Crabbe. *Fr.* Tales of the Hall. FaBoPP

East bow'd low before the blast, The. The East. Matthew Arnold. *Fr.* Obermann Once More. OtMeF

East Coast Journey. James K. Baxter. NoP; PeNZ

East Coker. T. S. Eliot. *Fr.* Four Quartets. HAP; PPP; VGW

East is a clear violet mass, The. A Street Scene. Lizette Woodworth Reese. OBCA

East is merely a myth no longer!, The. (*LL*) Capital "I." Gu Cheng. SpMi

East London. Matthew Arnold. SCGP; WGRP

East Moors. Gillian Clarke. SCBI

East of the river there's a foul bird. A Parable. Ch'en Tzu-lung, *tr. fr. Chinese by* Irving Y. Lo. SuSp

East of the sun's slant, in the vineyard that never failed. Harvest. Gary Soto. PBCAP

East 116th. Tiburón. Martín Espada. ETG

East St. Louis Blues. *Unknown*. AmFP

East Texas. Leon Stokesbury. SM

East Watch House, The. Jim Mitsui. ETG

East, West, North, South. *Unknown*. RoPo

East Wind asperges Boston with Lynn's sulphurous brine, An. Father. John Wheelwright. UnPo

East wind sighs, the fine rains come, The. Li Shang-yin, *tr. fr. Chinese by* A. C. Graham. PLT

East wind whirling, light clouds in strands, The. "Beautiful Lady Yü, The" — Spring Sorrow. Ch'en Liang, *tr. fr. Chinese by* Hellmut Wilhelm. SuSp

East wind's whistlin' cauld an' shrill, The. A Schule Laddie's Lament on the Lateness o' the Season. James Logie Robertson. NOBVV

Easter. Mary Carolyn Davies. OHIP

Easter ("I got me flowers to straw Thy Way.") George Herbert. BoTP; CH; FaBoCh; FHYEP; NAEL-1; NOBE; OBEV; OHIP; TrGrPo

Easter ("Rise, heart, thy Lord is risen.") George Herbert. ESCV; GeHe; NAEL-1; NOSC; PeECV; SeCV-1; TrCP

Easter. Joyce Kilmer. PDV

Easter. Howard Nemerov. NoP

Easter. Edwin L. Sabin. OHIP

Easter. Benjamin Saenz. AfAz

Easter. C. H. Sisson. OxBSP

Easter. Spenser. *See* Most glorious lord of life that on this day.

Easter again, and a small rain falls. The Other Side of the River. Charles Wright. MT; VCAP

Easter Beatitudes. Clarence M. Burkholder. BLRP

Easter Bonnet, The. Clara Ann Thompson. CBWP-2

Easter Bunny Blues or All I Want for Xmas Is the Loop, The. Ebon Dooley. PoBA

Easter Canticle, An. Charles Hanson Towne. OHIP; TrPWD

Easter Carol. George Newell Lovejoy. OHIP

Easter Carol. H. Cordelia Ray. CBWP-3

Easter Carol, An. Christina Rossetti. OHIP

Easter Chick, An. Thirza Wakley. BoTP

Easter Chorus. Goethe. *See* Christ Is Arisen.

Easter dawn! Morning, Noon, And. Hawley Truax. NYBP

Easter-Day. Henry Vaughan. ESCV; PeECV

Easter Day. Oscar Wilde. OxAEP-2

Easter Day, Naples, 1849. Arthur Hugh Clough. EBVVPR

Easter Eve. Prudentius, *tr. fr. Latin by* Helen Waddell. MLL

Easter Eve. Muriel Rukeyser. VGW

Easter Garland, An. Carol Rumens. FaBoWP

Easter has come around. W. D. Snodgrass. *Fr.* Heart's Needle. CAPP; VCAP

Easter Hymn. A. D. Hope. ChIV-2; FaBoMA

Easter Hymn. A. E. Housman. EBEV; MoAB

Easter Hymn. Henry Vaughan. ChIV-2; ESCV

Easter Hymn. Charles Wesley. OHIP

Easter Hymn, An. Richard Le Gallienne. OHIP

Easter in Christmas. Alun Lewis. PoWW

Easter Light, The. Clara Ann Thompson. CBWP-2

Easter lilies! Can you hear. On Easter Day. Celia Laighton Thaxter. FaPON

Easter Monday. Eleanor Farjeon. PAW

Easter Monday. Ralph Hawkins. VaA

Easter Monday. Christina Rossetti. NOCV

Easter Morn. Giles Fletcher the Younger. *Fr.* Christ's Victory and Triumph. EiL; NOCV

Easter Morn. Josephine D. Henderson Heard. CBWP-4

Easter Morning. A. R. Ammons. HCAP; NAAL-2; NoAM; NoP

Easter Morning. Amy Clampitt. ChIV-2

Easter Morning. Spenser. *See* Most glorious lord of life that on this day.

Easter Night. Alice Meynell. BrRo; ChIV-2; OHIP

Easter 1984. Les A. Murray. ChIV-2

Easter, 1916. W. B. Yeats. CMoP; FaBoMo; FaBoPV; FaPoR; HAP; HeIP; IIP; InPS; LiTM; MoAB; MoP; NAEL-2; NAWM-2; NIP; NoAM; NOBE; NOIV; NoP; OAEL-2; OBWP; OxAEP-2; OxBTC; PoE; PPP; TFi

Easter, 1968. May Sarton. CrSp

Easter, 1923. John G. Neihardt. OHIP

Easter; or, Spring-Time. L. A. J. Moorer. CBWP-3

Easter Poem. Kathleen Raine. LiTB

Easter Praise. Rodney Bennett. BoTP

Easter Song, An. "Susan Coolidge." *See* Song of sunshine through the rain, A.

Easter Song. Mary Artemisia Lathbury. OHIP

Easter Song, An. *Unknown.*

Easter Sunday 1988, the Grand Canyon, Arizona. Ray Gonzáles. FoLa

Easter: Wahiawa, 1959. Cathy Song. OpBo

Easter Week. Charles Kingsley. OHIP

Easter Wings. George Herbert. AngWe; ChIV-1; ESCV; FHYEP; GeHe; HAP; HeIP; InPK; InPS; LiTB; MeLP; NAEL-1; NIP; NoP; NOSC; OAEL-1; PoE; PoEL-2; Poetr; PPP; SeCP; TEP; TFi; TOF; TrCP; TRP; WeW

Easter with Horses. Nigel Wells. PWE

Eastern guard tower. Etheridge Knight. BPo; MoP; SM; TAP

Eastern Slope, sels. Su Tung-p'o, *tr. fr. Chinese by* Burton Watson.

Eastern spices I bring with me. Venio ex Oriente. Nuala Ni Dhomhnaill. BiHa

Eastern Tempest. Edmund Blunden. MoBrPo

Eastmuir king, and Wastmuir king. Fause Foodrage. *Unknown.* ESPB

Eastward, etched in purple by a sun. Appalachian Convalescence. Robert Conquest. OxBC

Eastward spurs tip backward from the sun, The. Nigger's Leap, New England. Judith Wright. NOBAu

Eastward, the faint glimmer of the early dawn. Starting Early from Yü-p'u Deep. Meng Hao Jan, *tr. fr. Chinese by* Daniel Bryant. SuSp

Eastward the sea and sky, and a lengthening evening. Evening View at River Pavilion, Inviting Guest. Po Chü-i, *tr. fr. Chinese by* Irving Y. Lo. SuSp

Easy as a Bat. *Gond Oral Tradition, tr. by* V. Elwin *and* S. Hivale. WTO

Easy as cove-water rustles its pebbles and shells. Part of a Letter. Richard Wilbur. CMoP

Easy in the presence of her lover. *(LL)* Laboratory Poem. James Merrill. CAPP; InPK; MAT; TwCP

Easy Morning's Rid —, A. *(LL)* A Hummingbird. Emily Dickinson. HeIP; NAAL-1; NoP; PoEL-5

Easy thing, O Power Divine, An. The Things I Miss. Thomas Wentworth Higginson. TrPWD

Easy tub returned, The. *(LL)* The River Now. Richard Hugo. VCAP

Easy way out. Nayo-Barbara Watkins. NBV

Eat/ 300 feet. The Anthropophagites See a Sign on NC Highway 177 That Looks like Heaven. Jonathan Williams. OBAL

Eat and Walk. James Norman Hall. BLPA

Eat, eat me, Soul, and thou shalt never die. *(LL)* Meditation Eight. Edward Taylor. ChIV-2

Eat-It-All Elaine. Kaye Starbird. PDV

Eat, let's eat, now we have corn meal! A Mayan Prophecy. Sharon Spencer. WoWa

Eat me to the root. Vine v. Goat. Euenos, *tr. fr. Greek by* Alistair Elliot. GrAn

"Eat my cake, eat," cried the young. To the Last Wedding Guest. Horace Gregory. NYBP

Eat thou and drink; tomorrow thou shalt die. The Choice. Dante Gabriel Rossetti. ChIV-2

Eat what you wish; I'll teach ye all to die. Death Described by His True Effects. George Chapman. *Fr.* Eugenia. NOSC

Eat with Care. *Unknown.* FaBoUs

Eat your banana, Annie dear. Sales Talk for Annie. Morris Bishop. NBLV

Eat Your Heart Out, Edward Lear! Roger Woddis. UV

Eaten away by light. *(LL)* Daguerreotype Taken in Old Age. Margaret Atwood. BoWoP; NoAM

Eaten Heart, The. *Unknown, tr. fr. Middle English by* Pearl London. *Fr.* Knight of Curtesy, The. TrGrPo

Eaters saddened every heart in Tenejapa, The. A Story of the Eaters. Santiago Mendes Zapata, *tr. fr. Tzeltal Indian by* W. S. Merwin. STP

'Eathen, The. Kipling. OxBTC

Eating Alone. Li-Young Lee. TRP; WeW

Eating Bamboo-Shoots. Po Chü-i, *tr. fr. Chinese by* Arthur Waley. OBVE

Eating Ice-Cream with a Girl. George MacBeth. PRA

Eating in Hall. Alexander Barclay. *Fr.* Eclogues. NoSic

Eating our way down. *(LL)* Millions of Strawberries. Genevieve Taggard. FaPON; MoShBr

Eating Poetry. Mark Strand. CAPP; GrPl; MAT; MoP; NoAM; PPP; TAP

Eating Shepherd's-purse. Mei Yao Ch'en, *tr. fr. Chinese by* Jonathan Chaves. SuSp

Eating the living germs of grasses. Song of the Taste. Gary Snyder. CAPP; EaPr; LCAP

Eau-Forte. F. S. Flint. OxBTC

Eaves. Ellis Jones, *tr. fr. Welsh by* Anthony Conran. OBWVE

Eavesdropper. Breyten Breytenbach, *tr. fr. Afrikaans by* Ernst van Heerden. PeSAV

Eavesdropper, The. Bliss Carman. AnAmPo

Eavesdropping on their conversation. I'm Walking behind the Spanish. Luis Omar Salinas. AfAz

Ebb. Edna St. Vincent Millay. AnAmPo

Ebb and Flow, The. Edward Taylor. AmPP; SCAP

Ebb on, tide, moving swiftly outwards! Invalid's Song. Harata Tangikuku, *tr. fr. Maori by* Margaret Orbell. PeNZ

Ebb slips from the rock, the sunken, The. Night. Robinson Jeffers. AWP; LiTA; MoAmPo; NOBA; OxBA

Ebb Tide, The. Robert Southey. OBNC

Ebb-tide to me as to the sea; old age brings me reproach [*or* Ebb tide has come for me:/My life drifts downward]. The Hag of Beare. *Unknown, tr. fr. Irish.* BIrV, *tr. by* John Montague; NOIV, *tr. by* Thomas Kinsella; OBVE, *tr. by* Lady August Gregory; PBWP, *tr. by* John Montague

Ebb/ with the flow. Daufuskie. Mari Evans. BlSi

Ebba Dawson: Mardel Rest Home, Haskell, New Jersey. Maria Gillan. CrSp

Ebba sits at the window. Ebba Dawson: Mardel Rest Home, Haskell, New Jersey. Maria Gillan. CrSp

Ebbed and flowed the muddy Pei-ho by the gulf of Pechili. Blood Is Thicker than Water. Wallace Rice. PAH

Ebony Wood, sels. Jacques Roumain, *tr. fr. French by* Ellen Conroy Kennedy.
"Negro peddler of revolt." NegPo

Ecce Homo. Witter Bynner. WGRP

Ecce Homo. David Gascoyne. *Fr.* Miserere. ChIV-2; LiTM; OBWP; PeECV

Ecce Homunculus. R. A. K. Mason. PeNZ

Ecce Puer. James Joyce. BIrV; ChIV-2; EBEV; IMW; MoP; NAs; NoAM; OPOP; TrCP

Eccentric propositions of its fate, The. *(LL)* Men Made out of Words. Wallace Stevens. MeMAP; MoAB; NOBA; OxBSP; TAP; VGW

Eccho, An. *Unknown.* AngWe

Eccles Street, Bloomsday, 1982. Harry Clifton. PBCIP

Ecclesiastes, sels. Bible, *O.T.*
"Cast thy bread upon the waters." AWP, *sts.* 1–6; OBVE, (1-8)
Earth Abideth Forever, The. FaPON
"I returned, and saw under the sun." Prf
"It Is Better . . . ." TrJP
Light Is Sweet, The. FaPON
Remember Now Thy Creator. AWP; ChTr; OBVE
(Remember Then Thy Creator.) TrJP
(Youth and Age.) TrGrPo
To Everything There Is a Season. EaPr; FF; NAWM-1; OBVE
(For everything there is a season.) DL
(Time for Everything, A.) TrGrPo
"Two are better than one; because they have a good reward for their labour." OBF
"Vanity of vanities, saith the Preacher, vanity of vanities; all is vanity." FaBoPV; NAWM-1; TrJP, *sect.* I, *ll.* 2–9

Ecclesiastes. G. K. Chesteron. ChIV-1; MoBrPo; OxBSP

Ecclesiastes. Derek Mahon. BIrV; ChIV-1; CIP; PNI

Ecclesiastical Chronicle, An, sels. John Heath-Stubbs.
"Year of Our Lord two thousand one hundred and seven, The." NOBL

Ecclesiastical Sonnets, *sels.* Wordsworth.
  Edward VI. EPCY
  Inside of King's College Chapel, Cambridge. EnRP; OBNC
  (Within King's College Chapel, Cambridge.) GTBS; GTBS-P
  Mutability. EBEV; EnRP; HeIP; InPK; LiTB; MeMBP; NOBE; NoP;
    OAEL-2; OBEV; PoEL-4; PrIm
  Trepidation of the Druids. Son.
Ecclesiasticus, *sels.* Bible, Apocrypha.
  "All flesh waxeth old as a garment." OBVE
  "By his commandment hee maketh the snow to fall apace." OBVE
  "Forsake not an old friend." OBF
  "He that toucheth pitch shall be defiled therewith; and he that hath." OBF
  "Instead of a friend become not an enemy; for thereby thou shalt inherit
    an." OBF
  "Let us now praise famous men." ChTr; FaBoEH; OBVE
  (Our Fathers.) TrJP
  Music. TrJP
  O Death. TrJP
  Test of Men, The. TrJP
  "Whoso casteth a stone at the birds frayeth them away." OBF
  "Whoso discovereth secrets loseth his credit." OBF
Ech, Sic a Pairish. *Unknown.* FaBoCo; FiBHP
Eche man me telleth I chaunge moost my devise. Sir Thomas Wyatt. AAS
Eche time and season hath his delite and joyes. Alexander Barclay.
  FaBoEH
Echo, The. William Barnes. SCGP
Echo. Leonard Clark. Mes
Echo. Walter de la Mare. OBMV
Echo. Viscountess Grey of Fallodon. CH
Echo. Elizabeth Stanton Hardy. GoYe
Echo. Milton. *Fr.* Comus; a Masque Presented at Ludlow Castle. ELP;
  FHYEP; OAEL-1; OBEV
Echo. Thomas Moore. ELP
Echo. Vasco [*or* Vasko] Popa, *tr. fr. Serbo-Croatian. Fr.* Besieged
  Serenity. PoSu
Echo. Christina Rossetti. BoLoP; CH; EBEvV; EBVV; ELP; GBL;
  MeMBP; NOBE; NoP; OAEL-2; OBNC; OHCV; PFP; PIP; PoE;
  PoEL-5; VBLP
Echo. John Godfrey Saxe. AnAmPo
Echo. Sir Philip Sidney. *Fr.* Arcadia. SiPS
Echo. Mildred Weston. BoNaP
Echo always mocks the sound, The. Rabindranath Tagore. *Fr.* Epigrams.
  PoA
Echo, An. William Alexander, Earl of Stirling. NOSC
Echo and Narcissus. Gerda Mayer. PeLV
Echo and the Ferry. Jean Ingelow. EBVV
Echo Canyon. *Unknown.* AmFP
Echo-Elf Answers, The. Thomas Hardy. CBLP
Echo, I ween, will in the wood reply. A Gentle Echo on Woman. Swift.
  FaBoCo; FiBHP; NBLV; NU
Echo:/ mimic,/ last sip. Euodos, *tr. fr. Greek by* Robin Skelton. GrAn
Echo Poem. M. Allan. FiBHP
Echo Reverie. H. Cordelia Ray. CBWP-3
Echo Song. Sir Philip Sidney. *See* Fair rocks, goodly rivers, sweet woods,
  when shall I see peace?
Echo, the beating of the tide. Prophecy on Lethe. Stanley Kunitz. PoA
Echo to a Rock. Lord Herbert of Cherbury. PoEL-2
Echo, tongueless, sings her sweet. Satyrus, *tr. fr. Greek by* Robin Skelton.
  GrAn
Echo Turned to Stone. Vasco [*or* Vasko] Popa, *tr. fr. Serbo-Croatian by*
  Charles Simic. AnRep
Echo Well. (*LL*) Echo to a Rock. Lord Herbert of Cherbury. PoEL-2
Echo your thought in ours? "Destroy! Destroy!" (*LL*) Brother Fire. Louis
  MacNeice. MoAB; MoP; NoAM; NOBE
Echoes, *sels.* W. E. Henley.
  Blackbird, The. MoBrPo; TrGrPo
  (To A. D.) HoPM
  "I am the reaper." OBNC
  Invictus. BLPA; CoGr; EBEvV; FaBoBe; FaBV; FaPoR; GGP; HoPM;
    ImPo; LiTB; MoBrPo; NOBE; OBEV; OBMV; OBNC; OHCV; OtMeF;
    TEP; TrGrPo
  Margaritæ Sorori, [I. M.]. MoBrPo; NOBE; OBEV; OBNC; PIP; TrGrPo;
    WGRP
  (Late Lark, A.) PoRA
  On the Way to Kew. MoBrPo; TrGrPo
  We'll Go No More a-Roving. MoBrPo
Echoes. Emma Lazarus. AmWP
Echoes. Thomas Moore. *See* How sweet the answer Echo makes.
Echoes. R. S. Thomas. OxAEP-2
Echoes between the darkening trees. (*LL*) Visit to the Monastery of Good
  Omen. Lu Chi. OHMPC

Echoes from Theocritus, *sels.* Edward Cracroft Lefroy, *after the Greek of*
  Theocritus.
  Cleonicos. AWP
  Epitaph of Eusthenes, The. AWP
  Flute of Daphnis, The. AWP
  Grave of Hipponax, The. AWP
  Monument of Cleita, The. AWP
  Sacred Grove, A. AWP
  Sylvan Revel, A. AWP
  Thyrsis. AWP
Echoes of Childhood. Alice Corbin. PoNe
Echoes of the hymns return. Grandfather's Sermon and Michael Smith. E.
  A. Markham. PBCV
Echoes of Wheels. "Furnley Maurice." NOBAu
Echoes of wheels and singing lashes. Echoes of Wheels. "Furnley
  Maurice." NOBAu
Echoing [*or* Ecchoing] Green, The. Blake. *Fr.* Songs of Innocence.
  BoTP; CH; FHYEP; NAEL-2; NTP; OxAEP-2; PoE; UnPo; WiR
Echo's Bones. Samuel Beckett. NoAM
  Sels.
  "Asylum under my tread all this day."
  Vulture, The.
Echo's Complaint. H. Cordelia Ray. CBWP-3
Echo's Lament for Narcissus. Ben Jonson. *See* Slow, slow, fresh fount,
  keep time with my salt tears.
Echo's [*or* Eccho's] Song. Ben Jonson. *See* Slow, slow, fresh fount, keep
  time with my salt tears.
Eclipse. Anita Endrezze-Danielson. CDW
Eclipse. Ed Roberson. PoNe
Eclipse, The. Henry Vaughan. OxBSP
Eclipse and glory of her kind?, The. (*LL*) On [*or* To] His Mistress, the
  Queen of Bohemia. Sir Henry Wotton. CBLP; EIL; ELP; EnLoPo;
  GBL; HAP; JCP; MeLP; NoP; NOSC; PIP; SCGP; SeCP; TFi; TrGrPo
Eclipse of the Moon, The. Lu T'ung, *tr. fr. Chinese by* A. C. Graham.
  PLT
Eclipse II. Linda Hogan. HATNAP
Eclipse while he lived, and decease at his dying. (*LL*) Cardinal Bembo's
  Epitaph on Raphael. Thomas Hardy, *after* Pietro Bembo. FaBoEE
Eclipsed she is, and her bright rays. Of the Organs of Her Mind. Sir John
  Davies. *Fr.* Hymns of Astræa [in Acrostic Verse]. SiPSBD
Eclipses. Nancy Sullivan. TAP
Eclogue: "Industry undressing in front of Agriculture." Michael Hofmann.
  SCBI
Eclogue: "What makes you look so black, so glum, so cross?" Edward
  Lear. FaBoNo
Eclogue IV: The Poet. Charles Jenner. AWP
  Sels.
  Soliloquy in the Suburbs, A. NOEC
Eclogue for Christmas, An. Louis MacNeice. FaBoMo; NoAM; OBMV
Eclogue of the Shepherd and the Townie. Anthony Hecht. BAP-90
Eclogue to Mr. Johnson, An, *sels.* Thomas Randolph.
Eclogues, *sels.* Alexander Barclay.
  "Miseries of Courtiers." by Æneas Sylvius Ricolomini, The
    Eating in Hall. NoSic
    Winter. OxBLMV
Eclogues, *sels.* Virgil, *tr. fr. Latin.*
  Corydon and Thyrsis. AWP
  For Thee, Little Boy. ArLo, *tr. by* James Laughlin
  Lycidas and Moeris. AWP
  Messiah, The. AWP, *tr. by* Dryden
  (Sicilian Muse, I Would Try Now a Somewhat Grander Theme.) NAs,
    tr. by C. Day Lewis
  (Sicilian Muses, sing we greater things.) OBVE, *tr. by* Sir John
    Beaumont
  Shepherd's Gratitude, The. AWP
Ecologue. Michael Hofmann. SCBI
Economics. Alvin Aubert. MT
Economics. Mona Van Duyn. SM
Economy of Vegetation, The. Erasmus Darwin. *Fr.* Botanic Garden, The.
Economy of Vegetation, The. Erasmus Darwin. FaBoUs
  Sels.
  Action of Electricity, The.
  Action of Invisible Ink, The.
  Protection of Plants, The.
Ecstacy, An. Richard Crashaw. *See* Lord, when the sense of Thy sweet
  grace.
Ecstasy, The. John Donne. BoLoP; EnRePo; FHYEP; HAP; ImPo; InPS;
  JCP; LiTB; NAEL-1; NOBE; NoP; OAEL-1; OBEV; PoE; PrIm; TEP;
  TFi; TOF; TrGrPo
Ecstasy. Virginia A. Houston. ShDr
Ecstasy. Hélène Swarth, *tr. fr. Dutch by* Jonathan Crewe. WPOW

Ecstasy. W. J. Turner. CH

Ecstasy, 1 st., at. to John Leland. *Unknown. See* Oh, When Shall I See Jesus?

Ecstasy of the moon. (*LL*) Mandoline. Paul Verlaine. AWP; OBMV

Ecstatic bird songs pound. Dawn. William Carlos Williams. MoAB; MoAmPo

Ecstatic Longing. Goethe, *tr. fr. German by* John Frederick Nims. STV

Ecstatic thought's the thing. Poetry. Mary Elizabeth Fullerton. NOBAu

Ed ascoltando al leggier mormorio. Ezra Pound. *Fr.* Cantos. PoE

Ed Dying. Paul Monette. PFL

Eddi, priest of St. Wilfrid. Eddi's Service. Kipling. CoGr; OBCP

Eddie the sphaghetti nut. The Spaghetti Nut. Jack Prelutsky. SiSoPo

Eddi's Service. Kipling. CoGr; OBCP

Eden. James Simmons. PNI

Eden. Thomas Traherne. ChIV-1; ESCV; GeHe; PoEL-2; SeCV-2; TrGrPo

Eden. David Woo. OpBo

Eden Is a Zoo. Margaret Atwood. WPE

Eden is that old-fashioned House. Emily Dickinson. ChIV-1; NALW

Eden Rock. Charles Causley. NTP

Eden Says No. Robert Johnstone. PNI

Edenhall. "Susan Coolidge." OBCA

Edenlike as your name. Edge. John Montague. IPY

Edgar A. Guest Considers "The Good Old Woman Who Lived in a Shoe." and the Good Old Truths Simultaneously. Louis Untermeyer. *Fr.* Mother Goose Up-to-Date.

Edgar A. Guest Considers "The Old Woman Who Lived in a Shoe." and the Good Old Verities at the Same Time. Louis Untermeyer. *See* It takes a heap o' children to make a home that's true.

Edgar A. Guest Syndicates the Old Woman Who Lived in a Shoe. Louis Untermeyer. *See* It takes a heap o' children to make a home that's true.

Edgar Allan Poe. Timothy Thomas Fortune. AAP

Edgar's Story, *sels.* X. J. Kennedy.

Edge, The. Rosemary Dobson. NOBAu

Edge. Robert David Fitzgerald. CBAP

Edge. John Montague. IPY

Edge. Sylvia Plath. FaBoWP; HCAP; NAAL-2; NALW; PoE; TAP; VCAP

Edge, The. Sandra Price. LoHo

Edge-Hill; or, The Rural Prospect Delineated and Moralised, *sels.* Richard Jago.
    Iron Industry in Birmingham, The. NOEC
    Sage Philosophy. ECEV

Edge of America. Jo McDougall. NGP

Edge of Autumn, The. Michael Anania. NoAM

Edge of Day, The. Laurie Lee. NYBP

Edge of our bed was a wide grid, The. Sisters in Arms. Audre Lorde. VBLP

Edge of the cancer, The. Front Lines. Gary Snyder. PoE

Edge their love of freedom with contempt of luxury. (*LL*) Shine, Republic. Robinson Jeffers. FaBoPV

Edges of the gorges hack up sun and moon, The. Meng Chiao, *tr. by* Stephen Owen. *Fr.* Laments of the Gorges. SuSp

Edgy. Fred Voss. NGP

Edi be thu, Hevene Quene. In Praise of Mary. *Unknown.* MeEL

Edinburgh after Flodden, *sels.* William Edmonstoune Aytoun.
    "Then the Provost he uprose." OBWP

Edinburgh from the Pentland Hills. Sir Walter Scott. *Fr.* Marmion. FaBoPP

Editor Whedon. Edgar Lee Masters. *Fr.* Spoon River Anthology. CMoP; FaBoEE; NOBA; OBSV; OxBA; PoE

Editor's Wooing, The. "Orpheus C. Kerr." OBAL

Edmond Halley. Roy Fuller. OxBC

Edmonton, thy cemetery. Stevie Smith. OxBTC

Edmund Burke. Goldsmith. *See* Here lies our good Edmund, whose genius was such.

Edmund Davie 1682; Annagram. Benjamin Tompson. SCAP

Edmund Pollard. Edgar Lee Masters. *Fr.* Spoon River Anthology. ErPo

Edmund's Song. Sir Walter Scott. *See* O [*or* Oh], Brignal[l] banks are wild and fair.

Edna St. Vincent Millay Exhorts Little Boy Blue. Louis Untermeyer. *Fr.* Mother Goose Up-to-Date. MoAmPo

Edna's Hymn. Barry Humphries. NOBAu

Edom. Isaac Watts. AmFP

Edom o' Gordon. *Unknown.* OxBB

Educated Love Bird, The. Peter Newell. FiBHP

Education in Wales. Goronva Camlan. AngWe

Education of Nature, The. Wordsworth. *See* Three Years She Grew in Sun and Shower.

Education regarding chills is not well handled in this country, The. Henri Michaux, *tr. fr. French by* Richard Ellmann. *Fr.* I Am Writing to You from a Far-Off Country. AnRep

Edvard Munch. Charles Wright. HCAP

Edward [*or* Edward, Edward]. *Unknown.* AmFP; CH; ClHu; EBEV; EBEvV; ELP; EnRP; ESPB; FaBoBa; FaPoR; GGP; HAP; HoPM; InPK; InPS; LiTB; Mes; NAEL-1; NOBE; NoP; OBEV; OxBB; OxBS; PoEL-1; PoRA; PrIm; SCGP; SoSe; TFi; TrGrPo; TRP

Edward VI. Wordsworth. *Fr.* Ecclesiastical Sonnets. EPCY

"Edward back from the Indian Sea." Neglectful Edward. Robert Graves. MoBrPo

Edward Hopper's Nighthawks, 1942. Joyce Carol Oates. BAP-91

Edward Lear. W. H. Auden. InvP; OxAEP-2

Edward Lear in February. Christopher Middleton. TwCP

Edward/ Paterson has grown older. William Carlos Williams. *Fr.* Paterson. NoAM

Edward the Dyke and Other Poems, *sels.* Judy Grahn.
    "In the place where." NALW; PeHV

Edward the Second., *sels.* Christopher Marlowe.
    "Now, lusty lords now, not by chance of war." FaBoEH

Edward the Third had seven sons. The Ballad of Banners (1944). John Lehmann. MoBS

Edwardus Comes Clarendoniae. Bibliotheca Bodleiana. Geoffrey Grigson. GBL

Edwin in the Lowlands Low. *Unknown.* AmFP

Edwin, The Minstrel. James Beattie. OxAEP-1

Ee calazi. Hammer-Song. *Unknown.* FaBoVe

"EEK/ a nigger." At the National Black Assembly. Amiri Baraka. BCF

Eek!/ Her legs are caught in something. The Orlando Commercial. George MacBeth. NOBL; PeLV

Eel, The. Eugenio Montale, *tr. fr. Italian by* John Frederick Nims. STV; WeW

Eel, The. Ogden Nash. FaBV; FaPON; NTCP

Eeling. Rhyll McMaster. FaBoMA

Eels and Tortoises. William Diaper, *after the Greek of* Oppian. *See* Strange the formation of the eely race.

Eemis-Stane, The. "Hugh MacDiarmid." NAEL-2

E'en as a lovely flower. Du bist wie eine Blume. Heine, *tr. fr. German. Fr.* Homeward Bound. AWP, *tr. by* Kate Freiligrath Kroeker
    (Thou Seemest Like a flower.) TrJP, *tr. by* Emma Lazarus

E'en as the sculptor chisels patiently. The Tireles Sculptor. H. Cordelia Ray. CBWP-3

E'en from my heart the strings do break. (*LL*) When to Her Lute Corinna [*or* Corrina] Sings. Thomas Campion. AAS; NAEL-1; NoP; NoSic; OAEL-1; PoE

E'en like two little bank-dividing brooks. The Best-Beloved. Francis Quarles. OxBM

E'en this, Lord, didst thou bless. Insomnia. John Banister Tabb. TrPWD

Eenie, meenie, mackeracka. *Unknown.* OxNR

Eenie, meenie, minie, mo. (*LL*) Eenie, meenie, minie, mo/ Catch a thief by the toe. *Unknown.* FaPON; ImGa; OxNR; RoPo

Eenie, meenie, minie, mo/ Catch a thief by the toe. *Unknown. Fr.* Counting-out Rhymes. FaPON; ImGa; OxNR; RoPo

Eenity, feenity, fickety, feg. *Unknown.* OxNR

Eeny meeny figgety fig. Tig. *Unknown.* FaBoVe

Eeny, weeny, winey, wo. *Unknown.* OxNR

E'er she can raise the member she enjoys. (*LL*) Epitaph on Charles II. The Earl of Rochester. FaBoEH

Eerie, ourie, you're out. (*LL*) Counting-out Rhyme. *Unknown.* ChTr; GBP

Ef I had wings like Noah's dove. Dink's Song. *Unknown.* ErPo; OxBoLi

Ef you/ Don't/ Watch/ Out! (*LL*) Little Orphant Annie. James Whitcomb Riley. AnAmPo; FaPON; MoShBr; NBLV; OBAL; OBCA; OxBChV; VPP

Effacements. Peter Scupham. SCBI

Effeminate Englishmen. William Cowper. *Fr.* Task, The. EBEvV; ECEV

Effendi. Michael S. Harper. PoBA

Effervescence and Evanescence. Keith Preston. OBAL

Efficiency Apartment. Gerald William Barrax. PoBA

Efficient Wife's Complaint, The. Confucius, *tr. fr. Chinese by* Ezra Pound. *Fr.* Airs of Pei. CTC

Effingham, Grenville, Raleigh, Drake. Admirals All. Sir Henry Newbolt. FaPoR

Effort at Speech. William Meredith. Prf; SM

Effort at Speech between Two People. Muriel Rukeyser. FYAP; MoAB; MoAmPo; Poetr; TrGrPo; TrJP; TwCP

Effortlessly,/ Love flows from God into man. Mechthild von Magdeburg, *tr. fr. German by* Jane Hirshfield. EnlH

Eftsoones they heard a most melodious sound. Spenser. *Fr.* Faerie Queene, The. EBEvV; NOBE; PoEL-1; SCV

Eftsoons they saw an hideous host array'd. Sea Monsters. Spenser. *Fr.* Faerie Queene, The. ChTr

Egan O Rahilly. *Unknown, tr. fr. Irish by* James Stephens. EBEV; OBMV

Egg, The. Clarence Day. NBLV

Egg, The. Jean Follain, *tr. fr. French by* W. S. Merwin. AnRep

Egg, An. *(LL)* In marble walls [or halls] as white as milk. Mother Goose. ChTr; GBP; OxNR

Egg and the Machine, The. Robert Frost. MoAmPo

Egg Boiler, The. Gwendolyn Brooks. PoBA

Egg for Easter, An. Irene F. Pawsey. BoTP

Egg I have chosen is sandy brown, The. Boiling an Egg. Stanley Cook. OTCP

Egg is a grand thing for a journey, An. How the Hen Sold Her Eggs to the Stingy Priest. Nancy Willard. LCAP

Egg of the universe fell open, The. The Egg of the Universe Hatches All Things. Erica Helm. *Fr.* Creation Songs of Eurynome, The. SRLS

Egg of the Universe Hatches All Things, The. Erica Helm. *Fr.* Creation Songs of Eurynome, The. SRLS

Egg Thoughts. Russell Hoban. NTCP, *St.* 1 *only, sl. diff.*; OTCP

Egg won't roll well, An. An Airline Breakfast. William Matthews. AnAn

Eggleston was a taxi-driver. Cynical Portraits. Louis Paul. NBLV

Sir Eggnogg. Bayard Taylor. BXAP

Eggomania. Felicia Lamport. NBLV

Eggplants Have Pins and Needles, The. Novella Matveyeva, *tr. fr. Russian by* Daniel Weissbort. WPOW

Eggs. Sharon Olds. CrSp

Eggs, The. Peter Redgrove. NAs

Eggs. Susan Wood. SoSe

Eggs, butter, cheese, bread. *Unknown.* ISE

Eggs for Breakfast. Irene F. Pawsey. BoTP

Eggs from a chain store grocery. One No. 7. John Frederick Frank. GoYe

Sir Eglamour. Samuel Rowlands. *Fr.* Melancholy Knight, The. EIL; FaBoCh; FaBoNo; InvP

Eglwys Newydd. John Tripp. AngWe

Egnatius has fine teeth, and those. Catullus, *tr. fr. Latin by* Walter Savage Landor. OBVE

Ego. Philip Booth. TwCP

Ego. Norman MacCaig. GTBS-P

Ego. Robert Siegel. PoA

Ego Dominus Tuus. W. B. Yeats. *Fr.* Wild Swans at Coole, The. EPCY, abr.

Ego Dominus Tuus. W. B. Yeats. CMoP

Ego-perverted love. *(LL)* The Mess of Love. D. H. Lawrence. ArLo; CBLP; OAEL-2

Ego sum, I am. *Unknown.* ISE

Ego Tripping [(There May Be a Reason Why)]. Nikki Giovanni. CrSp; MoP; Poetsp; RaBo

Egocentric. Stevie Smith. FaBoNo

Egoism. W. Craddle. FiBHP

Egoisme à Deux. Louisa S. Guggenberger. NOBVV

Egoist is not / good for himself. *(LL)* The Immoral Proposition. Robert Creeley. LiTM; NeAP; PoM

Sir Egrabell had sonnes three. Sir Lionel. *Unknown.* AmFP; ESPB

Egrets. Tu Mu, *tr. fr. Chinese by* A. C. Graham. PLT

Egrets. Tu Mu, *tr. fr. Chinese by* Irving Y. Lo. SuSp

Egrets. Judith Wright. GoJo; OBAP

Egypt. Martin Edmunds. UTF

Egypt. Wendy Mulford. NBrP

Egypt, divided by the river Nile. Milton. *Fr.* Paradise Lost. EPCY; FaBoPV

Egypt, Tobago. Derek Walcott. AnAn

Egyptian Dancer. Terence Tiller. OBTV

Egyptian Dancer at Shubra. Bernard Spencer. NoAM

Egyptian Passage, An. Theodore Weiss. TAP

Egyptian Pulled Glass Bottle in the Shape of a Fish, An. Marianne Moore. NALW; PBWP

Egyptian Tomb, The. William Lisle Bowles. OBTV

Egyptians think it sin to root up, or to bite. Juvenal, *tr. by* Sir Walter Ralegh. *Fr.* Satires. SiPSBD

Egypt's Favorite, *sels.* Sir Francis Hubert. Joseph in Carcere. ChIV-1

Egypt's Might Is Tumbled Down. Mary Elizabeth Coleridge. CH; CoGr

"Eheu, eheu," doves follow to the close of March. The Doves. Peter Scupham. SCBI

Eheu Fugaces. "Thomas Ingoldsby." FaBoEE; OxBoLi

Eia, with handbells, jews' harps, risible. Geoffrey Hill. *Fr.* Hymns to Our Lady of Chartres. DiPo

8 A.M. Shadows. *Unknown.* SiSoPo

Eight and eight are sixteen. *Unknown.* RoPo

Eight Aspects of Melissa, *sels.* Lawrence Durrell.
Adepts, The. ErPo
Visitations. MoBrPo

Eight hands across, form a ring. Mississippi Sawyer. *Unknown.* AmFP

Eight Hour Day, The. *Unknown.* SWP

Eight little whores, with no hope of Heaven. *Unknown.* FaBoEH

VIII. More than most fair [or fayre], full of the living fire [or fyre]. Spenser. *Fr.* Amoretti. AAS; ESo, lacking epigrams I–IV; HeIL; NoP; PoE; Son; TEP; TrGrPo

Eight o'Clock. A. E. Housman. CMoP; InPK; MoAB; MoBrPo; MoP; NoAM; NoP; OxBSP; PoE; Poetr; SoSe; TrGrPo

8:00 O'Clock Movie, The. Tino Villanueva. ETG

Eight Preludes, *sels.* Peter Riley.
"Each day some further light each day some farther dark." VaA
"If you want messages you must provide an orifice." VaA
"Night outside is the theatre of our patience." VaA
"Willing also to be remembered, lost." VaA

Eight Sandbars on the Takano River. Gary Snyder. NOBA; NoP; VGW

Eight-toes, teetering. Magpie. Peter Davison. GrPl

Eight years ago this May. A Spring Night in Shokoku-ji. Gary Snyder. *Fr.* Four Poems for Robin. ArLo; MoP; NNaP; NoAM; NOBA; NoP; SOTW; VGW

Eight years' difference in age seems now, The. Terminal. Thom Gunn. PFL

Eight years of age and time enough to dream. Process. Aidan Carl Mathews. IB

Eighteen. Maria Banus, *tr. fr. Romanian by* Willis Barnstone *and* Matei Calinescu. BoWoP

1808 Wordsworth dies from fall while hiking in Scotland. Other Lives of the Romantics. Jane Flanders. PBCAP

1887. A. E. Housman. *Fr.* Shropshire Lad, A. FaPoB; FaPoR; NIP; NOBVV; PlP; PrIm; SCGP; UnPo

1805. Robert Graves. FaBoCh; FaBoEH; OBSV; PeLV; PlP

Eighteen-Forty-Three. *Unknown.* FaBoCo

1892-1941. Louis Zukofsky. PoA

Eighteen-Seventy, *sels.* Rimbaud, *tr. fr. French.*
Evil. OBWP
Napoleon after Sedan. FaBoPV; OBWP
Poster of Our Dazzling Victory at Saarbrucken, A. FaBoPV; OBWP
Sleeper in the Valley, The. OBWP
(There's a green hollow where a river sings.) AWP, *tr. by* Ludwig Lewisohn
To the French of the Second Empire. FaBoPV; OBWP

Eighteen sixty nine being the date of the year [or and the year]. A Ballad of Master McGrath. *Unknown.* FaBoBa

(Master McGrath.) OBET

18,000 Feet. Ed Roberson. PoNe

Eighteen Verses Sung to a Tatar Reed Whistle, *sels.* Ts'ai Yen, *tr. fr. Chinese by* Kenneth Rexroth *and* Ling Chung.
"I have no desire to live, but I am afraid of death." WPC; WPOW
"I never believed that in my broken life." BoWoP; WPC; WPOW
"I was born in a time of peace." BoWoP; WPC; WPOW
"Seventeenth stanza, The. My heart aches, my tears fall." WPC; WPOW
"Sun sets, The. The wind moans." BoWoP; WPC; WPOW
"Tatar chief forced me to become his wife, A." WPC; WPOW

Eighteenth of October, The. The Fire of Frendraught. *Unknown.* ESPB; OxBB

Eighth Air Force. Randall Jarrell. ArOW; CAPP; FF; MoP; NoAM; NOBA; NoP; OBWP; PoWW; SM; TRP; VCAP

Eighth child of an eighth child, your wilful advent. Birth of a Great Man. Robert Graves. NYBP

Eighth Elegy, *sels.* Muriel Rukeyser.
Children's Elegy. LCAP

Eighties Becoming, The. Bob Rosenthal. UL

Eighties, De. Frederick Williams. PBCV

80's Miracle Diet, The. Melvin Dixon. PFL

Eighty and nine with their captain. The Charge by the Ford. Thomas Dunn English. PAH

Eighty-four Tanka., *sels.* Fujiwara no Teika, *tr. fr. Japanese by* Hiroaki Sato.

LXXXIX. "Like as the culver on the bared bough." Spenser. *Fr.* Amoretti. AAS; ESo, lacking epigrams I–IV; FF; GBL; HeIL; PoE

'Eighty-nine was bad. Graves at Elkhorn. Richard Hugo. UnPo; VCAP

LXXXI. "Fair [or Fayre] is my love, when her fair [or fayre] golden heares." Spenser. *Fr.* Amoretti. AAS; EIL; ESo, lacking epigrams I–IV; HeIL; NoP; Son

80 papers/ was all there was. Delivering the Times, 1952-1944. David Huddle. PBCAP

Eighty-seven Hokku., *sels.* Buson, *tr. fr. Japanese by* Hiroaki Sato.
LXXXIII. "Let not one sparke of filthy lustfull fyre." Spenser. *Fr.* Amoretti. AAS; ESo, lacking epigrams I–IV; HeIL; TEP
LXXXII. "Joy of my life, full oft for loving you." Spenser. *Fr.* Amoretti. AAS; ESo, lacking epigrams I–IV; HeIL; HeIP
Eighty years ago a woman passed. Tomorrow Is a Birthday. Gwendolen Haste. GoYe
Eikon Basilike. Peter Didsbury. PWE
Eileann Chanaidh, *sels.* Kathleen Raine.
Eileen Aroon, *sels.* Gerald Griffin.
  "When like the rising day." OBEV
Eileithyia, brought safe. Leonidas, *tr. fr. Greek by* Kenneth Rexroth. PGA
Eileithyia, once more. Callimachus, *tr. fr. Greek by* Peter Jay. GrAn
Ein feste Burg ist unser Gott. Martin Luther, *tr. by* M. Woolsey Stryker. CTC
Ein Fichtenbaum steht einsam. Heine, *tr. fr. German by* James Thomson. AWP
Eine Kleine Snailmusik. May Sarton. NBLV
Einem alten Architekten in Rom. Joseph Brodsky, *tr. fr. Russian by* George L. Kline. AnAn
Einstein, *sels.* Archibald MacLeish.
Einstein's Bathrobe. Howard Moss. VCAP
Eire. David O'Bruadair, *tr. fr. Irish by* Austin Clarke. BIrV
Eireann. Osbert Lancaster. *Fr.* Afternoons with Baedeker. NOBL; PeLV
Eisenhower Years, The. Paul Zimmer. NGP; PBCAP
Eisenhower's Visit to Franco, 1959. James Wright. NaP
Either get out of my house or conform to my tastes, woman. Martial, *tr. fr. Latin by* James Michie. FaBoEE
Either in or out of. The Finger. Robert Creeley. PRA
Either nude & pulled behind as well as. A Bull Called Remorse. Iain Sinclair. NBrP
Either She was Foul. Ovid. *See* Either she was foule, or her attire was bad.
Either she was foule, or her attire was bad. Ovid, *tr. by* Christopher Marlowe. *Fr.* Amores. OBVE
  (Either She was Foul.) FaBoBl
  (Shameful Impotence.) ErPo
Either to keep the thinking in. Country Ways. Marcia Lee Masters. *Fr.* Impressions of My Father. GoYe
Either you will. Prospective Immigrants Please Note. Adrienne Rich. AiP; GOA; VGW
Ejaculating into their vaginas — young girls of the western tribes. *Unknown, tr. fr. Aborigine by* Ronald M. Berndt. *Fr.* Goulburn Island Song Cycle. NOBAu
Ejected Wife, The. *Unknown, tr. fr. Chinese by* Arthur Waley. OBVE
El-a-noy. *Unknown.* AS
El Abandonado. *Unknown, tr. by* Frank J. Dobie. AS
El Aghir. Norman Cameron. *See* Sprawled on the crates [*or* bags] and sacks [*or* crates] in the rear of the truck.
El Alamein. Steve Crow. HATNAP
El Alamein Revisited. Roy Macnab. PeSA
El Beso. Angelina Weld Grimké. ShDr; VBLP
El Dorado. Richard Ryan. BIrV
El Greco. Edward Leslie Mayo. HoPM
El Greco: Espolio. Earle Birney. MoCV
El-Hajj Malik El-Shabazz. Robert Hayden. PoBA
El Hombre. William Carlos Williams. CMoP; LiTA; SAmP
El; in the top of his head: to tell/ him. (*LL*) Plato Told Him. E. E. Cummings. AmPP; CTC; MoP; NoAM; NOBA; OxBA; PoE
El Pablo was a bad dude. Jimmy Santiago Baca. BCF
El Paso Sex. Belinda Subraman. NGP
El Ropero. Antonio di Montorio. TrJP
El Sueño de la Razón. Jane Cooper. FaBoWP
Elaine, pretending it was salt. E. Aitken. UV
Elate of heart and confidence of fame. Samuel Taylor Coleridge. *Fr.* Monody on the Death of Chatterton. EPCY
Elbow to elbow, they prop one another. Mer-men, First-form. Mary E. O'Donnell. NWP
Elder Brother, The, *sels.* John Fletcher.
  "Beauty clear and fair." NOSC; OBEV
Elder Edda, The, *sels. Unknown, tr. fr. Old Norse by* William Morris *and* Eirikr Magnusson.
  Counsels of Sigrdrifa. AWP
  (Part of the Lay of Sigrdrifa.) OBVE
  First Lay of Gudrun, The. AWP
  Gudrun Laments over Sigurd. OBVE
  Lay [*or* Short Lay] of Sigurd, The. AWP
  "And now one prayer" OBVE
  Voluspo. AWP

"Elder Father, though thine eyes." The Holy of Holies. G. K. Chesteron. WGRP
Elder, or Bourtree, The. *Unknown.* GBP
Elder Sister, The. Sharon Olds. NIP
Elder Stonegate treats the body like a dream. Written in Jest on Elder Stonegate's Eastern Balcony. Liu Tsung-yüan, *tr. fr. Chinese by* Jan W. Walls. SuSp
Elder Tree, The. *Unknown. See* Bourtree, bourtree, crookit rung.
Elderly bride of Port Jervis, An. Ogden Nash. PeLi
Elderly Discontented Women. D. H. Lawrence. IHNG
Elderly discontented women ask for intimate. Elderly Discontented Women. D. H. Lawrence. IHNG
Elder's Reproof to his Wife, An. 'Abdillaahi Muuse, *tr. fr. Somali by* B. W. Andrzejewski *and* I. M. Lewis. TTY; WTO
Elders/ we have been here so short a time. W. S. Merwin. EaPr
Eldest is calling, The. Tip-of-the-Single-Feather. Velema, *tr. fr. Fijian by* B. H. Quain. WTO
Eldest son bestrides him, The. The Undertaker's Horse. Kipling. FaBoNo; FM
Eldon Hole. David Constantine. PWE
Eldorado. Poe. AmPP; AnAmPo; AWP; FaBoBe; FaBoCh; MeMAP; NOBA; NoP; NTP; OxBA; TAP; WiR
Eleanor ———. Hayden Carruth. AnAn
Eleanor Rigby. John Lennon *and* Paul McCartney. PrIm; WTO
Eleanor (she spoiled in a British climate). Ezra Pound. *Fr.* Cantos. NoAM; NOBA
Eleanora Duse, *sels.* Amy Lowell.
  Seeing You Stand Once More before My Eyes. Son
Eleazar Wheelock. Richard Hovey. OBAL
Elect. Mary Ursula Bethell. PeNZ
Elected Knight, The. *Unknown, tr. fr. Danish by* Longfellow. AWP
Elected Silence. Siegfried Sassoon. MoBrPo
Elected Silence, sing to me. The Habit of Perfection. Gerard Manley Hopkins. ChIV-2; ImPo; LiTB; MeMBP; MoAB; MoBrPo; MoP; NoAM; NoP; OBEV; OBMV; OxAEP-2; Poetr; PoRA; RB; TFi; TrGrPo
Election, The. Leonard Nathan. PBCAP
Election Reflection. M. Keel Jones. NBLV
Election Songs. *Yoruba Oral Tradition, tr. by* Ulli Beier. WTO
Election Time. *Unknown.* FaBoPa; UV
Electric Cop, The. Victor Hernandez Cruz. PoBA
Electric Eel, The. Ron Padgett. *Fr.* Three Animals. PoBA
Electric Telegraph, The. Thomas Baker. *Fr.* Steam Engine; or, The Power of the Flame, The. FaBoUs
Electricity Is Funny! John Currier. GrPI
Electrocution. Lola Ridge. WPE
Electrodes attached to a flautist's cheeks. First Night. Michael Hofman. CBLP
Electroplating the Baby. Jo Shapcott. PWE
Elegance. Christopher Smart. *Fr.* Hymns for the Amusement of Children. NOCV
Elegant Things. Sei Shonagon, *tr. fr. Japanese by* Ivan Morris. CBCK
Elegant use of foliage and grace, An. More. Gertrude Stein. *Fr.* Tender Buttons. PBWP
Elegant Women, The. Tu Fu, *tr. fr. Chinese by* Mark Perlberg. SuSp
Elegantly destroy. (*LL*) Water. Emerson. AmPP; OxBSP; PoEL-4
Elegiac Ballad, An. Hannah Cowley. ECWP
Elegiac Stanzas Suggested by a Picture of Peele Castle, in a Storm [Painted by Sir George Beaumont]. Wordsworth. EnRP; FaBoPP; GTBS; GTBS-P; NAEL-2; NoP; OAEL-2; OBNC; PoE
Elegiac Verse, *sels.* Longfellow.
  "Like a French poem is life; being only perfect in structure." OBF
Elegiack Verse on Mr. Elijah Corlet, An. Nehemiah Walter. SCAP
Elegie: "Let me be what I am, as Virgil cold." Ben Jonson. PoEL-2; SeCP
Elegie, An: "Though beautie be the marke of praise." Ben Jonson. *See* Though beauty be the mark of praise.
Elegie: Going to Bed. John Donne. *See* Come, Madam, come, all rest my powers defie [*or* defy].
Elegie: "Nature's lay ideot, I taught thee to love." John Donne. *See* Nature's lay idiot [*or* Ideot], I taught thee to love.
Elegie V: His Picture. John Donne. *See* Here take my picture; though I bid farewell.
Elegie XVI: On His Mistress. John Donne. *See* By our first strange and fatal [*or* fatall] interview.
Elegie XIX: To His Mistris Going to Bed. John Donne. *See* Come, Madam, come, all rest my powers defie [*or* defy].
Elegie Made by Mr. Aurelian Townshend in Remembrance of the Ladie Venetia Digby, An. Aurelian Townshend. SeCP
Elegie on the Deploreable Departure of the Honored and Truely Religious Chieftain John Hull, An. John Saffin. SCAP

Elegy does not raise its wistful tone in downpour of southern shine, An. To Tarshish. Shimon Halkin, *tr. fr. Hebrew by* Ruth Finer Mintz. MHP

Elegy for a Cove Full of Bones. John Ciardi. ArOW

Elegy for a Dead Soldier. (White sheet on the tail-gate of a truck, A.) Karl Shapiro. ArOW; HAP; LiTM; OBWP; OxBA
Sels.

Elegy for a Diver. Peter Meinke. Poetsp

Elegy for a Five Year Old. Aidan Carl Mathews. IB

Elegy for a Forest Clear-Cut by the Weyerhaeuser Company. David Wagoner. NoAM

Elegy for a Nature Poet. Howard Nemerov. BoNaP; HoPM

Elegy for a Puritan Conscience. Alan Dugan. CAPP; SM

Elegy for a School-Friend. Augustus Young. BIrV

Elegy for a Schoolmate. Vincent O'Sullivan. PeNZ

Elegy for a White Cock. Mei Yao Ch'en, *tr. fr. Chinese by* Jonathan Chaves. SuSp

Elegy for Alto. Christopher Okigbo. HBAPE

Elegy for an 88 Gunner. Keith Douglas. *See* Three weeks gone and the combatants gone.

Elegy for Bella, Sarah, Rosie, and All the Others. Sonya Dorman. GOA

Elegy for Chief Sealth. Duane Niatum. CDW

Elegy for David Beynon. Leslie Norris. AngWe

Elegy for Delina. Albert Rowe. CRH

Elegy for Dr. Donne, *sels.* Lord Herbert of Cherbury.
"Having delivered now what praises are." EPCY

Elegy for Drowned Children. Bruce Dawe. NOBAu

Elegy for Dylan Thomas. Edith Sitwell. PoA

Elegy for Frank Stanford. Thomas Lux. AnAn

Elegy for Her Brother Sakhr. Al-Khansa, *tr. fr. Arabic.* BoWoP, *tr. by* Willis Barnstone; WPOW, *tr. by* Bridget Connelly

Elegy for Her Brother Sakhr. Al-Khansa, *tr. fr. Arabic by* Willis Barnstone. BoWoP

Elegy (for Himself). Moses Rimos of Majorca, *tr. fr. Hebrew by* Israel Abrahams. TrJP

Elegy for Himself. Chidiock Tichborne. *See* My prime of youth is but a frost of cares.

Elegy for His Daughter Ellen. Goronwy Owen, *tr. fr. Welsh by* George Borrow. OBWVE

Elegy for Sir Ifor Williams. Anthony Conran. AngWe

Elegy for Integral Domains, The. Norman Dubie. NAmP90

Elegy for Jack Bowman. Joseph Bruchac. CDW

Elegy for Jack Moffat. Charlotte Painter. IMW

Elegy for Jane. Theodore Roethke. AmPP; CAPP; CoAP; FF; HAP; HCAP; IMW; InPK; InPS; LiTM; MoAB; MoAmPo; NoP; PoE; Poetr; TAP; TFi; TRP; TwCP; WeW

Elegy for John, My Student Dead of AIDS. Robert Cording. PFL

Elegy for Kenny Dorham. Joel Wolk. Jaz

Elegy for Llwelyn Humphries. Meic Stephens. AngWe

Elegy for Lyn James. Leslie Norris. OBWVE

Elegy for Minor Poets. Louis MacNeice. PNI

Elegy for Mr. Goodbeare. Sir Osbert Sitwell. MoBrPo

Elegy for Mr. Lewis (Welsh). Meic Stephens. AngWe

Elegy for My Father. Howard Moss. CoAP; LiTM

Elegy for My Father. Mark Strand. HCAP; LCAP
Sels.
Empty Body, The. UnPo
New Year, The. UnPo
Your Shadow. Prf

Elegy for My Father, *sels.* Irving Wexler.

Elegy for My Mother. Richard Katrovas. SM

Elegy for My Sister. Howard Moss. VCAP

Elegy for N. N. Czeslaw Milosz, *tr. fr. Polish by* Larence Davis. AnRep; SV

Elegy for Professor Longhair. Elton Glaser. Jaz

Elegy for Slit-Drum. Christopher Okigbo. HBAPE

Elegy for the Dead of Soweto. Thembinkosi Ndlovu, *tr. fr. Zulu by* Chris Mann. PeSAV

Elegy for the Giant Tortoises. Margaret Atwood. BoWoP; EaPr; FoLa

Elegy for the Lost Parish. Douglas Dunn. DiPo

Elegy for the Monastery Barn. Thomas Merton. VGW

Elegy for the Nightbound. Anthony Cronin. PBCIP

Elegy for the Other. Cleopatra Mathis. MT

Elegy for the Silent Voices and the Joiners of Everything. Kenneth Patchen. NaP

Elegy for the Unknown Soldier. Michael O'Loughlin. PBCIP

Elegy for the Wife of a Friend. Yü Hsüan-chi, *tr. fr. Chinese by* Geoffrey R. Waters. BoWoP

Elegy for Thelonious. Yusef Komunyakaa. Jaz

Elegy for Two Banjos. Karl Shapiro. LiTA; TrJP

Elegy for W. C. W, the Lovely Man, An. John Berryman. *Fr.* Dream Songs. NoP

Elegy for William Soutar. William Montgomerie. OxBS

Elegy for Wright & Hugo. Norman Dubie. NoAM

Elegy for Yards, Pounds, and Gallons. David Wagoner. PoA

Elegy in a Country Churchyard. G. K. Chesterton. CoGr; FaBoEH; FaPoR; MoBrPo; NSI; OBWP; OxBSP; TrGrPo

Elegy in a Presbyterian Burying-Ground. Robert Noble Denison Wilson. BIrV

Elegy in a Theatrical Warehouse. Kenneth Fearing. NYBP

Elegy in an Abandoned Boatyard. Dave Jeddie Smith. VCAP

Elegy in Memory of the Worshipful Major Thomas Leonard Esq, An. Samuel Danforth, Jr.. SCAP

Elegy in Newgate. William Cobbett. UV

Elegy Is Preparing Itself, An. Donald Justice. CRP; HoPM

Elegy Just in Case. John Ciardi. ArOW; TwCP

Elegy of Fortinbras. Zbigniew Herbert, *tr. fr. Polish by* Czeslaw Milosz. FaBoPV; PoSu

Elegy on a Favorite Cat, An, *sels.* Anne Francis.
"When cats like him submit to fate." ECWP

Elegy on a Lady, Whom Grief for the Death of Her Betrothed Killed. Robert Bridges. OBEV

Elegy on a Maiden Name, An. Jane Cave. ECWP

Elegy on a Nordic White Protestant. John Gould Fletcher. PoNe

Elegy on a Young Thrush Which Escaped from the Writer's Hand. Helen Maria Williams. ECWP

Elegy on Albert Edward the Peacemaker. *Unknown.* CoMu

Elegy on an Australian Schoolboy, *sels.* Zora Cross.

Elegy on Any Lady by George Moore. Max Beerbohm. FaBoEE

Elegy on Ben Jonson, An. John Cleveland. MeLP

Elegy on Captain Matthew Henderson, *sels.* Burns.

Elegy on Cynddylan, The, *sels. Unknown, tr. fr. Welsh by* Kenneth Hurlstone Jackson.
"Stand out, maids, and look on the land of Cynddylan." OBWVE

Elegy on D. D. Sidney Godolphin. BeJo

Elegy on Gordon Barber. Gene Derwood.

Elegy on His Mistress. John Donne. *See* By our first strange and fatal [*or* fatall] interview.

Elegy on John Donne, *sels.* Sidney Godolphin.
"Passion's excess for thee we need no fear." EPCY

Elegy on Lucky Wood in the Canongate, May 1717. Allan Ramsay. ScCV

Elegy on Mistress Boulstred. John Donne. JCP

Elegy on Shakespeare. William Basse. EIL; FaBoRV

Elegy on That [*or* the] Glory of Her Sex, Mrs. Mary Blaize, An. Goldsmith. FaBoNo; PIP

Elegy on the Archpoet William Butler Yeats Lately Dead, *sels.* Oliver St. John Gogarty.
On Dublin. IHNG

Elegy on the Death of a Mad Dog, An. Goldsmith. *Fr.* Vicar of Wakefield, The. BeLS; BLPA; CoGr; FaBoBe; FaBoCh; FaBoCo; GN; NBLV; NOEC; NOIV; OBNV; OxAEP-1; TEP; TFi

Elegy on the Death of Bingo Our Trench Dog. Sir Edward de Stein. NSI

Elegy on the Death of Dobbin, the Butterwoman's Horse, An. Francis Fawkes. NOEC

Elegy on the Death of Furuhi, An. Okura. DL

Elegy on the Death of Her Husband. Anne Howard, Duchess of Arundel. *See* In sad and ashy weeds.

Elegy on the Death of John Keats, An. Shelley. *See* Peace, peace! he is not dead, he doth not sleep.

Elegy on the Death of Scots Music. Robert Fergusson. ScCV

Elegy on the Dust. Thom Gunn. NoAM

Elegy on the Earl of Rochester. Anne Wharton. KTR; NOSC

Elegy on the Lady Jane Paulet, An, *sels.* Ben Jonson.
"How did she leave the world? with what contempt?" OBD

Elegy on Thomas Hood. Martin Fagg. FaBoPa; NOBL; UV

Elegy on Thyrza. Byron. *See* And thou art dead, as young and fair.

Elegy, or Friend's Passion for His Astrophil [*or* Astrophel], An, *sels.* Matthew Royden.
On Sir Philip Sidney. EIL

Elegy over a Tomb. Lord Herbert of Cherbury. EIl; GGP; MeLP; NOBE; OBEV; OBWVE; PoEL-2

Elegy, to an Old Beauty, An. Thomas Parnell. ECEV; NOEC

Elegy: To Spring, *sels.* Michael Bruce.
"Farewell, ye blooming fields! ye cheerful plains!" NOEC

Elegy to the Memory of an Unfortunate Lady. (What beckoning ghost, along the moonlight shade.) Pope. ECEV; NOBE; NOEC; OAEL-1; OBD; OBEV; SCGP; TEP

Sels.
"Most souls, 'tis true, but peep out once an age." CH
  (Dull, Sullen Prisoners.) FaBoRV
Elegy to the Sioux. Norman Dubie. FoLa
Elegy upon His Tomb in Herndon-Hill Church, Erected by His Wife, Who
  Speaks, An. James Howell. OBWVE
Elegy upon Old Freeman, An, *sels.* Matthew Stevenson.
  "Here in this homely cabinet." NOSC
Elegy upon S W[alter] R[aleigh], An. Henry King. *See* I will not weep,
  for 'twere as great a sin.
Elegy Upon the Death of His Own Father, An. Richard Corbett [*or*
  Corbet]. BeJo; NOSC
Elegy upon the Death of Mrs. A. Behn, the Incomparable Astrea, An.
  Unknown. KTR
Elegy upon the Death of That Holy Man of God Mr. John Allen, An.
  Edward Taylor. PoEL-3
Elegy upon the Death of the Dean of [St.] Paul's, Dr. John Donne, An.
  (Can we not force from widowed poetry.) Thomas Carew. CaPo; JCP;
  NoP
Sels.
"Most souls, 'tis true, but peep out once an age." CH
  (Dull, Sullen Prisoners.) FaBoRV
On the Death of Donne. NOBE
Elegy upon the Most Incomparable King Charles the First, An, *sels.* Henry
  King.
Elegy Variations., *sels.* Rachel Hadas.
  Parting. UnDi
  Tears. UnDi
  Voice, The. UnDi
Elegy Written at the Sea-Side, and Addressed to Miss Honoria Sneyd. Anna
  Seward. PeHV
Elegy Written in a Country Churchyard. (Curfew tolls the knell of parting
  day, The.) Thomas Gray. AWP; ClHu; DL; EBEV; EBEvV; EnRP;
  FaBoBe; FaBoPP; FaBoPV; FaBoRV; FaPoR; FHYEP; GGP; GN;
  GTBS; GTBS-P; HAP; HeIP; ImPo; InPK; InPS; LiTB; NOBE; NOEC;
  NoP; OAEL-1; OBEV; OxAEP-1; PoEL-3; Poetr; PoLF; PPP; PrIm;
  SCGP; SCV; TEP; TFi; TrGrPo; UnPo; UV; WBLP; WeW
Sels.
"Most souls, 'tis true, but peep out once an age." CH
"Boast of heraldry, the pomp of pow'r, The." OBD
"Curfew tolls the knell of parting day, The."
"Here rests his head upon the lap of earth."
  (Epitaph, The.) FHYEP; SCGP
Elegy Written in a Country Coal-Bin. Christopher Morley. OBAL
Elegy, Written with His Own Hand in the Tower before His Execution.
  Chidiock Tichborne. *See* My prime of youth is but a frost of cares.
Elegy Wrote in the Tower, 1554, *shorter vers.* John Harington. EIL
Elegye: "Constant to none, but ever false to me." Thomas Campion. AAS
Element. P. K. Page. MoCV
Element. Peter Steele. FaBoMA
Element Fire Boasts of the Constellations, The. Anne Bradstreet. *Fr.* Four
  Elements, The. CBCK
Element that utters doves, angels and cleft flames. Air. Kathleen Raine.
  MoAB; MoBrPo
Elemental. D. H. Lawrence. NoP
Elemental. Heather McHugh. FoLa
Elemental Journey: Anniversary Gift. Alicia Gaspar De Alba. AfAz
Elementary. Linda France. NWP
Elementary. Jim Tollerud. VoR
Elementary Cosmogony. Charles Simic. NNaP
Elementary Scene, The. Randall Jarrell. CMoP; PoE
Elementary School Classroom in a Slum, An. Stephen Spender. FaBoMo;
  FF; LiTB; MoAB; MoBrPo; TrGrPo; TwCP; UnPo
Elementary Thoughts, *sels.* Nelo Risi, *tr. fr. Italian by* Gavin Ewart.
Elements, The. W. H. Davies. MoBrPo
Elements, The. Tom Lehrer. FaBoUs; UV
Elements. Carolyn Wilson Link. GoYe
Elements have merged into solicitude, The. The Racer's Widow. Louise
  Glück. AmPA; NYBP; SM
Elements of San Joaquin, The. (Wind sprays pale dirt into my mouth,
  The.) Gary Soto. PBCAP
Sels.
  Rain. NoAM
  Wind. NoAM
Elena's Song. Sir Henry Taylor. *Fr.* Philip van Artevelde. OBEV
Elene. Cynewulf, *tr. fr. Anglo-Saxon by* Charles W. Kennedy. AnOE
Sels.
  Constantine's Vision of the Cross.
  Helena Embarks for Palestine.
Eleonora: A Panegyrical Poem, Dedicated to the Memory of the Late
  Countless of Abingdon, *sels.* John Dryden *and* Nahum Tate.

"Then wonder not to see this Soul extend." OBF
Elephant, The. Herbert Asquith. BoTP
Elephant, The. Hilaire Belloc. BoTP
Elephant. Alan Brownjohn. OBAP
Elephant, The. Carlos Drummond de Andrade, *tr. fr. Portuguese by* Mark
  Strand. AnRep
Elephant, The. E. J. Falconer. BoTP
Elephant, The. A. E. Housman. *See* Tail behind, a trunk in front, A.
Elephant, *sels.* Pablo Neruda, *tr. fr. Spanish.*
  "Gross innocent." TTTS
Elephant, The. Louis Phillips. ZA
Elephant. *Unknown, tr. fr. Yoruba by* Ulli Beier. *Fr.* Hunter Poems of the
  Yoruba. RB
Elephant always carries his trunk, The. The Elephant's Trunk. Alice
  Wilkins. ImGa
Elephant beaten with candy and little pops and chews. A Sound. Gertrude
  Stein. *Fr.* Tender Buttons. TTTS
Elephant carries a great big trunk, The. *Unknown.* RoPo
Elephant is like a wall, The. The Elephant. E. J. Falconer. BoTP
Elephant Is Slow to Mate, The. D. H. Lawrence. ArNa; LiTB; LiTM;
  MeMBP; PPP; TEP
Elephant Languor. April Bernard. UTF
Elephant of long service to a circus, An. The Retirement of the Elephant.
  Russell Edson. AmPA
Elephant of Moissel, hear my pious prayer. Léopold Sédar Senghor, *tr. fr.*
  French by Ellen Conroy Kennedy. *Fr.* Return of the Prodigal Son.
  GrPl; NegPo
Elephant [I], The ("Elephant who brings death."). *Unknown, tr. fr. Yoruba*
  by Gbadamosi *and* Ulli Beier. TTTS; TTY
Elephant, or the Force of Habit, The. A. E. Housman. NOBL
Elephant Rock. Primus St. John. PoBA
Elephant ("Tall-topped acacia.") *Unknown.* PeSA
Elephant, the huge old beast, The. The Elephant Is Slow to Mate. D. H.
  Lawrence. ArNa; LiTB; LiTM; MeMBP; PPP; TEP
Elephant [II], The ("Elephant hunter, take your bow!") *Unknown, tr. fr.*
  Gabon Pigmy by C. M. Bowra. TTY
Elephant who brings death. Elephant [I], The ("Elephant who brings
  death.") *Unknown, tr. fr. Yoruba by* Gbadamosi *and* Ulli Beier.
  TTTS; TTY
Elephants Are Different to Different People. Carl Sandburg. MoAmPo
Elephants Are in the Yard, The. Indran Amirthanayagam. OpBo
Elephants Dying, The. Michael C. Blumenthal. NoAM
"Elephants in bed," my daughter says. Vision. Louis Johnson. PeNZ
Elephants May Parade before Your House. Gond Oral Tradition, *tr. by* V.
  Elwin *and* S. Hivale. WTO
Elephant's Trunk, The. Alice Wilkins. ImGa
Elephants walking. Holding Hands. Lenore M. Link. FaPON; MoShBr;
  NTCP
Eletelephony. Laura E. Richards. FaPON; GoJo; ImGa; MoShBr; NBLV;
  NTCP; OBCA; OxBChV; PDV; PYC; SiSoPo
Élévation. Baudelaire, *tr. fr. French by* Arthur Symons. AWP
Elevator Landscapes., *sels.* Stephen Vincent.
Elevator Man Adheres to Form, The. Margaret Danner. PoBA; PoNe
Elevator Man, 1949. Rita Dove. NAmP90
Elevator operator. Mr. 'Gator. N. M. Bodecker. NTCP
Elevator rises, Negro men, The. Poem to Negro and Whites. Maxwell
  Bodenheim. PoNe
Eleven. Archibald MacLeish. HAP; MeMAP; WeW
Eleven Addresses to the Lord. John Berryman. OxBC
Sels.
"Master of beauty, craftsman of the snowflake." UnPo
Prayer for the Self, A. PPP
"Sole watchman of the flying stars, guard me." UnPo
Eleven A.M. on My Day Off, My Sister Phones Desperate for a Babysitter.
  Sharon Hashimoto. OpBo
Eleven Cent Cotton. Emma Dermer *and* Bob Miller. SWP
Eleven Compositions: Roadside, *sels.* Robert David Fitzgerald.
"Below the paved road." FaBoMA
"Having said that all the gums have not been cut." FaBoMA
"Thick dust on Paddy's lucerne, burr." FaBoMA
"Wash your hands clean of guilt, and scour." FaBoMA
"1100 Exposition." Newletter from My Mother. Michael S. Harper. PoBA
Eleven men of England. The Red Thread of Honour. Sir Francis Hastings
  Doyle. OtMeF
Eleven o'clock and the bar is empty. The Hat Factory. Paul Durcan.
  BiHa
Eleven o'clock, and the curtain falls. End of the Comedy. Louis
  Untermeyer. BiHa
"A 11" ("River that must turn full after I stop dying.") Louis Zukofsky.
  Fr. "A" (1–12). VGW

11 rue Daguerre. John Montague.

Eleven-thirty and hot. The Cyclist. Marge Piercy. NoAM

Eleven years ago I left for good. Elegy for My Mother. Richard Katrovas. SM

Eleventh of April has come about, The. A Dainty Fine King Indeed. *Unknown.* FaBoEH

Eleventh Property, The. Sir Thomas More. *Fr.* Twelve Weapons of Spiritual Battle, The. EnRePo

Eleventh Song. Sir Philip Sidney. *See* Who Is It That This Dark Night.

Elf and the Dormouse, The. Oliver Herford. FaBoBe; FaPON

Elfer Hill. *Unknown, tr. fr. Danish by* Robert Jamieson. AWP

Elfin Knight, The. *Unknown.* ESPB

Elfin Knight, The. *Unknown.* AmFP

Elfin Knight, An. Joseph Rodman Drake. *See* He put his acorn helmet on.

Elfin Pedlar, The. George Darley. BoTP

Elfin People Fill the Tubes, The. Winifred M. Letts. BoTP

Eli, Eli. Miriam Kessler. CrSp

Eli, Eli. Judith Wright. CBAP

Eli 1943. R. M. Cooper. BTR

Eli the Thatcher. Max Beerbohm *and* William Rothenstein. FaBoNo

Elihu. Alice Cary. VPP

Elijah Speaking. Doug Fetherling. NOBC

Elijah this/ The Children of Israel that. The Nile. Albert Goldbarth. NAmP90

Elijah's mantle fell upon. A Little Song of Work. Sarah Elizabeth Sprouse. BLRP

Elijah's Wagon knew no thill. Emily Dickinson. ChIV-1

Elinda's [or Ellinda's] Glove. Richard Lovelace. CaPo; CBLP; NOSC

Elinor Frost's Marble-Topped Kneading Table. Pattiann Rogers. LoHo

Elinor Wylie fell in love with Shelley. A Thought in Time. Robert Silliman Hillyer. NYBP

Elinour Rumming, *sels.* John Skelton.
    "Instead of coin and money." NoSic

Eli's Poem. Ken Smith. PWE

Elisa ("Ye dainty nymphs, that in this blessed brook.") Spenser. *Fr.* Shepheardes [or Shepeards or Shepherd's] Calender, The. NAEL-1; PoEL-1

Elixir, The. George Herbert. BoTP; EnlH; FaBoCh; GeHe; GN; NoP; NOSC; OHIP; SeCV-1; TrGrPo; WGRP

Elixir. Richard Murphy. BiHa

Eliza. Erasmus Darwin. VPP

Eliza and Anne were extremely distress'd. The Bird's Nest. Elizabeth Turner. OHIP

Eliza Harris. Frances E. W. Harper. AAP

Eliza in Uncle Tom's Cabin. Eloise Bibb. CBWP-4

Eliza Telefair. Jocelyn Macy Sloan. GoYe

Elizabeth. Caroline Griffin. DT

Elizabeth. Michael Ondaatje. NoAM

Elizabeth. Sylvia Townsend Warner. MoAB; MoBrPo

Elizabeth, Elspeth, Betsy, and Bess. Mother Goose. OxNR; ReMoGo

Elizabeth, frigidly stretched. This Houre Her Vigill. Valentin Iremonger. CIP; NOIV; OxBTC

Elizabeth in Italy. Richard Weber. BoLoP

Elizabeth of Bohemia. Sir Henry Wotton. *See* You meaner beauties of the night.

Elizabeth Reflects on Hearing of Mary's Execution. John Loveridge. FaBoEH

"Elizabeth the Beloved." Elizabeth. Sylvia Townsend Warner. MoAB; MoBrPo

Elizabeth Walters is my name. Elizabeth Walters. FaBoVe

"Elizabethans Called It Dying, The." James Schuyler. NeAP; PoM

Elizabeth's War with the Christmas Bear. Norman Dubie. LCAP; NoAM

Elk on Mutability, The. John Bensko. MT

Elk Song. Linda Hogan. FoLa

Elk Uncovers the Heavens, The. John Bensko. MT

Elk, The Whelk, The. Robert Williams Wood. NBLV

Ella, fell a/ Maple tree. Picnic. Hugh Lofting. GoJo; OTCP

Ella, in a Square Apron, along Highway 80. Judy Grahn. *Fr.* Common Woman, The. NALW; NMM

Ella Mi Fu Rapita! Gavin Ewart. NoAM

Ella Speed. *Unknown.* AmFP

Ellas and the Statues. Gülten Akin, *tr. fr. Turkish by* Nermin Menemencioglu. PBWP

Ellen Flannery. *Unknown.* AmFP

Ellen Learning to Walk. Frances Sargent Osgood. AmWP

Ellen Taylor. *Unknown.* OBET

Ellen West. Frank Bidart. NAAL-2

Ellie Mae Leaves in a Hurry. Peter Klappert. SM

Ellington Indigos. Aleda Shirley. Jaz

Elliott Hawkins. Edgar Lee Masters. *Fr.* Spoon River Anthology. OxBA

Ellsworth. *Unknown.* PAH

Elm. Sylvia Plath. NoAM; NOBA; NoP; Poetr

Elm is turned to crystal, The. Weather. William Meredith. NYBP; Poetr

Elm lets fall its leaves before the frost, The. The Pine. Augusta Webster. OHIP

Elm Speaks, The. Sylvia Plath. *See* I know the bottom, she says. I know it with my great tap root.

Elms. Louise Glück. NoAM

Elms are bad, sinister trees. Breakwaters. Ted Walker. NYBP

Elms have to fight, The. Home Movies. Carter Revard. VoR

Eloisa to Abelard. (In these deep solitudes and awful cells.) Pope. NAEL-1; PoEL-3; TEP
    Sels.
    Vestal, The.
    (Life of a Nun.) ECEV

Elopement and civil wedding . . . the sham squire. The Distaff Side. Harry Clifton. PBCIP

Eloquent between the formal hedges. Affair of Honour. George Whalley. MoCV

Elphin knight sits on yon hill, The. The Elfin Knight. *Unknown.* ESPB

Elsa Wertman. Edgar Lee Masters. *Fr.* Spoon River Anthology. MoP; NoAM; OxBA

Elsdon. Freda Downie. FaBoPP

"Else a Great Prince in Prison Lies." Denise Levertov. NaP; PPP; VGW

Else tears heap all within one clay-cold hill. *(LL)* To Emily Dickinson. Hart Crane. CMoP; NIP; NoAM; NOBA; NoP; Son; TAP

Elsewhere and not far from here. *(LL)* Solstice. Kathy Fagan. UTF

Elsie Marley is grown so fine. *Unknown.* OxNR

Elusive Maid, The. Abraham ibn Chasdai, *tr. fr. Hebrew by* J. Chotzner. TrJP

Elustrious Dame whose vertues rare doe shine. An Acrostick on Mrs. Elizabeth Hull. John Saffin. SCAP

Elver Fishers. Ivor Gurney. FaBoPP

Elves and Fairies. John Gilbert Cooper. *Fr.* Call of Aristippus, The. ECEV

Elves' Dance, The. *At. to* John Lyly *and to* Thomas Ravenscroft. *Fr.* Mayde's Metamorphosis, The. CH; FaPON

Elvin's Blues. Michael S. Harper. BPo; Jaz

Elwha River, The. Gary Snyder. NoAM

Elysee. Larry Eigner. VGW

Elysium is as far as to. Emily Dickinson. GrPl; MoAB; MoAmPo; OxBA; WPE
    (Suspense.) AWP

em'-er-*gen*'-cy. *(LL)* Learning My Father's Language. Lorraine Duggin. LoHo

Em pom pee para me. A Clapping Chant. *Unknown.* FaBoVe

Emancipation. Maltbie D. Babcock. BLRP; WBLP

Emancipation. Priscilla Jane Thompson. CBWP-2

Emancipation. *Unknown.* BLPA

Emancipation Day. L. A. J. Moorer. CBWP-3

Emancipation from British Dependence. Philip Freneau. PAH

Emancipators, The. Randall Jarrell. PoA

Emanglons, The, *sels.* Henri Michaux, *tr. fr. French.*
    "At the theater they reveal their taste for the remote." AnRep, *tr. by* Richard Ellmann
    "If, while an Emanglon is home entertaining somebody." AnRep, *tr. by* Richard Ellmann
    "Music is discrete there. The musicians even more so." AnRep, *tr. by* Richard Ellmann
    "Sick person who does not suffer from chaotic respiration is taken care of, The." AnRep, *tr. by* Richard Ellmann
    "Without any apparent cause an Emanglon will suddenly start to weep." AnRep, *tr. by* Richard Ellmann

Emaricdulfe. "E. C." EiL

Emaricdulfe. "E. C." Son
    Sels.
    My Heart Is like a Ship.
    Within Her Hair.

Embalm, O Muse, in an appropriate lay. The Holiday. Thomas Frank Bignold. OBTV

Embalmer. Rossana Ombres, *tr. fr. Italian by* Ruth Feldman. NeIt

Embankment [or Fantasia of a Fallen Gentleman], The. T. E. Hulme. EBEV; FaBoMo; GTBS-P; OxBSP; OxBTC

Embarcation. Thomas Hardy. OBWP

Embarkation, The. Longfellow. *Fr.* Evangeline. BeLS; PAH

Embarkation, 1942. John Jarmain. PoWW

Embarrassing Episode of Little Miss Muffet, The. Guy Wetmore Carryl. FaPON; OBCA

Engine Driver, The. "G. S. O." BoTP

Engine Driver's Story, The. William Wilkins. BeLS

Engine of the excavator rumbles, The. The Excavator. Emily Borenstein. BTR

Engine on the bank, The. Geoffrey Fraser Dutton. PWE

Engineer's Story, The. Eugene J. Hall. VPP

Engineer's Story, The. *Unknown.* BeLS

England. Kipling. *Fr.* Return, The. OtMeF

England. Marianne Moore. LiTA; MeMAP; MoAB; MoAmPo

England. Mary Jo Salter. DiPo

England. A. S. J. Tessimond. IHNG

England. *Unknown.* FaBoEE; OxBSP

England, 1802, I. Wordsworth. *See* O Friend! I know not which way I must look.

England, 1802, II. Wordsworth. *See* Milton! thou should'st be living at this hour.

England, 1802, III. Wordsworth. *See* Great men have been among us; hands that penned.

England, 1802, V. Wordsworth. *See* When I have borne in memory what has tamed.

England, 1802 ("It is not to be thought of"). Wordsworth. *See* It Is Not to Be Thought Of [That the Flood].

England and America, *sels.* James Kenneth Stephen.
  On a Parisian Boulevard. NOBL

England and America, 1863. Richard Monckton Milnes. EBVV; OHCV

England and America in 1782. Tennyson. PAH

England and Switzerland 1802. Wordsworth. *See* Two voices are there; one is of the Sea.

England and Yesterday. (*LL*) In the States. Robert Louis Stevenson. AiP; OHCV

England, Autumn. Wayne Brown. PBCV

England, Autumn 1938. A. S. J. Tessimond. *See* Plush bees above a bed of dahlias.

England! awake! awake! awake! Blake. *Fr.* Jerusalem. EnRP; FHYEP; NoP
  (Prelude: "England! awake! awake! awake!"). OBNC

England be your sepulchre. (*LL*) Song to the Men of England. Shelley. EnRP; InPS; TrGrPo

England Expects. Ogden Nash. PeLV

England Expects? Sir Owen Seaman. NOBL

England, I stand on thy imperial ground. At Gibraltar. George Edward Woodberry. GN

England in 1819. Shelley. EnRP; FaBoEH; FaBoPV; FF; MAT; NAEL-2; NAWM-2; NOBE; NoP; OAEL-2; OxAEP-2; Poetr; Son; TFi; TrGrPo; UnPo

England, My England. W. E. Henley. BLPL; MoBrPo; OBEV; PoLF

England, my England — you have been my tutrix. W. H. Auden. *Fr.* Letter to Lord Byron. OBSV

England Nil. Anne Rouse. NWP

England that was the glory of the earth. On the Death of Henry the Lion. Hildebert, *tr. fr. Latin by* Helen Waddell. MLL

England! the time is come when thou shouldst wean. Wordsworth. Son

England, unlike junior nations. Remember Suez? Adrian Mitchell. OxBTC

England, we love thee better than we know. Gibralter. Richard Chenevix Trench. OBTV

England! with all thy faults I love thee still. Byron. *Fr.* Beppo; a Venetian Story. NOBL, *abr;* OBNV, *abr;* OBSV; PIP; UnPo

England, with all thy faults, I love thee still. Effeminate Englishmen. William Cowper. *Fr.* Task, The. BeEvV; ECEV

England's Alfred Abroad. Sir Owen Seaman. UV

England's coast a shadow. Lindisfarne: Dole. John Seed. VaA

England's Darling; or, Great Britain's Joy and Hope on That Noble Prince James, Duke of Monmouth. *Unknown.* CoMu

England's Great Loss by a Storm of Wind. *Unknown.* OxBSS

England's Heart. Martin Farquhar Tupper. VPP

England's heart! Oh never fear. England's Heart. Martin Farquhar Tupper. VPP

England's Heroical Epistles, *sels.* Michael Drayton.
  Owen Tudor to Queen Katherine. NoSic
  Queen Katherine to Owen Tudor. NoSic

England's ingratitude still blots. What Jenner Said on Hearing in Elysium That Complaints Had Been Made of His Having a Statue [in Trafalgar Square]. Shirley Brooks. FaBoEE

England's lads are miniature men. Boy-Man. Karl Shapiro. NYBP

England's on the anvil — hear the hammers ring. The Anvil. Kipling. FaBoEH

England's Sovereigns in Verse. *Unknown.* BLPA

England's Standard. Macaulay. *Fr.* Armada, The. BeLS; CoGr; FaBoCh; FaBoEH; FaPoR; GN; OtMeF; WBLP

England's sun was slowly setting. Curfew Must Not Ring Tonight. Rose Hartwick Thorpe. BeLS; BLPA; BLPL; FaBoBe; FaPON; WBLP

England's Triumph. *Unknown.* CoMu

English. Osbert Lancaster. *Fr.* Afternoons with Baedeker. FaBoCo; NOBL; PeLV

English, The. Stevie Smith. IHNG

English, The. *Unknown.* GBP

English Alphabet, An. *Unknown.* CBNP

English Are Frosty, The. Alice Duer Miller. *Fr.* White Cliffs, The. PoLF

English Are So Nice!, The. D. H. Lawrence. RaBo

English Ballad, on the Taking of Namur by the King of Great Britain, 1695, An. Matthew Prior. PoEL-3

English Bards and Scotch Reviewers, *sels.* Byron.
  "As Sisyphus against the infernal steep." OBSV
  "Behold! in various throngs the scribbling crew." EnRP; OAEL-2
  "Illustrious Holland! hard would be his lot." OBSV
  "Next comes the dull disciple of thy school." EPCY
  "There be who say, in these enlightened days." EPCY
  "Thus Lays of Minstrels — may they be the last! –" EPCY
  "Time has been, when yet the muse was young, The." FHYEP
  "Time was, ere yet in these degenerate days." EPCY; FHYEP
  "When Vice triumphant holds her sov'reign sway." FHYEP

William Lisle Bowles. OBNC

English Beach Memory: Mr. Thuddock. Sir Osbert Sitwell. NYBP

English Courage Displayed; or, Brave News from Admiral Vernon. *Unknown.* OxBSS

English Earthquake, The. Eva Salzman. NWP

English Fog, The. John Dyer. *Fr.* Fleece, The. TrGrPo

English Garden, The, *sels.* William Mason.
  How to Build a Ha-ha. FaBoUs
  "Nor, Shenstone, thou/ Shalt pass withou thy meed, thou son of peace!" EPCY
  Thomas Gray's View of Nature. EPCY; NOEC

English Girl. *Unknown, tr. fr. Chinese by* E. Powys Mathers. OBMV

English Graves, The. G. K. Chesteron. NSI

English History in Rhyme, or a Rhyming Epitome of the History of England, from B.C. 55 to A.D. 1872, *sels.* Edward B. Goodwin.
  "Growth of Heptarchy we trace, The." FaBoUs

English Labourer, The. *Unknown.* OBET

English lad, who, reading in a book, An. Keats. Lizette Woodworth Reese. AmWP

English Language, The. William Wetmore Story. GN

English Lesson. John Pook. AngWe

English Liberal. Geoffrey Taylor. FaBoEE

English man fell in love, An. On the State of Englishness (A Fairy Tale). Deborah Levy. DT

English professor named Brooks, An. D. H. Cudmore. PeLi

English Queen, The. Henry Lawson. NOBAu

English Succession, The. *Unknown.* OxBChV

English Thornton. Edgar Lee Masters. *Fr.* Spoon River Anthology. OxBA

English War, The. Dorothy L. Sayers. OtMeF

English Was Only a Second Language. Walta Borawski. GLP

English Wood, An. Robert Graves. PIP

Englishman, The. Eliza Cook. VPP

Englishman, The. W. S. Gilbert. *Fr.* H. M. S. Pinafore. NOBL

Englishman at the Table, The. James Cawthorn. *See* Time was, a [wealthy] Englishman would join.

Englishman from Holland, An. *Unknown, tr. fr. French.* CBNP

Englishman in Italy, The. (Fortù, fortù, my beloved one.) Robert Browning. PoEL-5
Sels.
  Piano di Sorrento. FaBoPP

Englishman in the old days, An. Carl Sandburg. *Fr.* People, Yes, The. FYAP

Englishman on the French Stage, The. Sir Owen Seaman. OBTV

Englishman with an Atlas; or, America the Unpronounceable, An. Morris Bishop. GOA

Englishman's Home, The. Harry Graham. *Fr* Some Ruthless Rhymes. CBNP; PeLV

Engraved on the case. Gold Watch. Patrick Kavanagh. InPS

Engraved on the Collar of a Dog, Which I Gave to His Royal Highness. Pope. *See* I am his Highness' dog at Kew.

Enhancement of life. Blood's to defeat its preordination or. Quasi Quasi . . . as If Repeated. Glenda George. NBrP

Enhances nature now. (*LL*) Further in summer than the birds. Emily Dickinson. AmPP; NOBA; NoP; PoE

Enid's Song. Tennyson. *Fr.* Idylls of the King. FaBoRV

Enigma, *sels.* Anne-Marie Albiach, *tr. fr. French by* Keith Waldrop.

Enigma. Jessie Redmond Fauset. PoNe

Enigma. Matthew Prior. PeLV

Enigma, An. Poe. Son

Enigma Variations. David Lehman. NAmP90

Enigma Variations, The. Paul Petrie. NYBP

Enigma was plagued with vertigo, The. Romance. Richard Stull. EOEF

Enigmas. Pablo Neruda, *tr. fr. Spanish by* Robert Bly. NU

Enigmatical, tremulous. The Barrel-Organ. Arthur Symons. NOBVV

Enion Replies from the Caverns of the Grave. Blake. *Fr.* Vala; or The Four Zoas. OBNC

Enitharmon Revives with Los. Blake. *Fr.* Vala; or The Four Zoas. OBNC

Enitharmon's Song. Blake. *See* I sieze the sphery harp. I strike the strings.

Enjoy him without stint or break! *(LL)* Expecting the Lord. Ann Griffiths. VBLP

Enjoy his lust, eat well and play the flute? *(LL)* Soliloquy at Potsdam. Peter Porter. NOBAu

Enjoy it a', ye've nae mair for't. *(LL)* Ode to Mr. F — [*or* Mr. Forbes]. Allan Ramsay, *after* Horace. NOEC; OBVE

Enjoy such liberty. *(LL)* To Althea, from Prison. Richard Lovelace. AWP; BeJo; BLPA; CaPo; EBEvV; FaBoBe; GBL; GGP; GTBS; GTBS-P; HAP; ImPo; InPS; JCP; LiTB; MeLP; NAEL-1; NOBE; NoP; NOSC; OBEV; PoE; PoRA; SCGP; SeCP; SeCV-1; TEP; TFi; TrGrPo

Enjoy Thy April Now. Samuel Daniel, *after the Italian of* Giambattista Marini. *Fr.* Description of Beauty, A. EIL; ELP

Enjoy your fortune as if you were about to die. Lucianus, *tr. fr. Greek by* Edwin Morgan. GrAn

Enjoy your time, my soul! another race. Enjoyment. Theognis, *tr. fr. Greek by* John Hookham Frere. AWP

Enjoy'd the lady. *(LL)* I asked a thief to steal me a peach. Blake. NAEL-2; NoP; OBNC; PoE

Enjoying Coolness. Wang Wei, *tr. fr. Chinese by* Hugh M. Stimson. SuSp

Enjoying of myself I lie. *(LL)* Love Made in the First Age: To Chloris. Richard Lovelace. BeJo; CaPo; JCP; NAEL-1; OAEL-1; SeCP

Enjoyment. Theognis, *tr. fr. Greek by* John Hookham Frere. AWP

Enjoyment, The. *Unknown.* ErPo

Enjoyment of sex, although great, The. *Unknown.* PeLi

Enjoys his Wish, and well imploys his time. *(LL)* The Advice. Charles Sackville. FaBoUS

Enkindled Spring, The. D. H. Lawrence. NoAM

Enlarge your fortifications, Zeus. Philip of Macedon. Alcaeus, *tr. fr. Greek by* Alistair Elliot. GrAn

Enlightment. Ch'en Yu Yi, *tr. fr. Chinese by* Kenneth Rexroth. OHMPC

Enlisted Man, The. Robert Graves. IHNG

Enlisted on the other front. *(LL)* Beach Burial. Kenneth Slessor. CBAP; FaBoMA; PAW

Enmeshed in steel stands a stone. The Captive Stone. Jim Barnes. CDW

Ennui. Langston Hughes. OBAL; OBCA

Ennui. Peter Viereck. NYBP

Enobarbus, Antony. Shakespeare. *Fr.* Antony and Cleopatra. OxAEP-1

Enoch. Bible, Pseudepigrapha. TrJP
  Sels.
  Seven Metal Mountains.
  Wisdom's Plight.

Enoch. Jones Very. ChIV-1; HAP

Enoch Arden. Tennyson. BeLS
  Sels.
  November in the Isle of Wight. FaBoPP

Enoch Arden. Tennyson. BeLS

Enoch Made Them — Enoch Shall Break Them. *Unknown.* FaBoEH

Enormous cloud-mountains that form over Point Lobos and into the sunset. Clouds of Evening. Robinson Jeffers. MoAmPo

Enormous meal of eel on the spit. Pace all'anima sua. *(LL)* Fish Speaking Veneto Dialect. Judith Baumel. UTF

Enough! Bunyan. *See* He that is down, needs fear no fall.

Enough. Digby Mackworth Dolben. EBVV

Enough. Arthur Gregor. TAP

Enough. Tom Masson. OBAL

Enough. Marianne Moore. NOBA

Enough; and leave the rest to fame. Andrew Marvell. OBEV

Enough complaining. An Arab Chieftain to His Young Wife. Abid ibn al-Abras, *tr. fr. Arabic by* Omar S. Pound. ArPe

Enough for him? *(LL)* Another Time Track. Ilze Mueller. LoHo

Enough kind Heaven! to purpose I have liv'd. To Mrs. W. on Her Excellent Verses. Aphra Behn. KTR

Enough! Let this season end. Enough. Arthur Gregor. TAP

Enough, my Muse, of earthly things. Christ's Passion. Abraham Cowley. ChIV-2

Enough of Grongar and the shady dales. John Dyer. AngWe

Enough of those who study the oblique. A Good Resolution. Roy Campbell. OBSV

Enough of Thought, Philosopher, *sels.* Emily Brontë. "O for the time when I shall sleep." OBD

"Enough," she said. But the dust still rained around [*or* about] her. Dust. Randolph Stow. CBAP; FaBoMA

Enough! Why should a man bemoan. Per Iter Tenebricosum. Oliver St. John Gogarty. OBMV

Enquiry after Peace. A Fragment. The Countess of Winchilsea. ECWP; PoE

Enrica, 1865. Christina Rossetti. NALW; TEP

Enrich My Resignation. Hart Crane. PoA

Ensamples of Our Savior. Robert Southwell. PoEL-2

Enslav'd, the daughters of Albion weep: a trembling lamentation. Visions of the Daughters of Albion. Blake. OAEL-2

Enslaved. Claude McKay. BPo

Enslaved by passions, swelled with pride. The Execration. Elizabeth Thomas. ECWP

Ensnaring Flower of Psalms. Rossana Ombres, *tr. fr. Italian by* Ruth Feldman. NeIt

Ensuing Copy the Late Printer Hath Been Pleased to Honour, by Mistaking It Among Those of the Most Ingenious and Too Early Lost Sir John Suckling, The. *At. to* Sir John Suckling *and to* Owen Felltham. *See* When, dearest, I but think on [*or* of] thee.

Entailed Farm, The. John Glassco. MoCV; NOBC

Entanglement. Francis Sparshott. MoCV

Enter and learn the story of the rulers. Inscriptions at the City of Brass. *Unknown, tr. fr. Arabic by* E. Powys Mathers. *Fr.* Thousand and One Nights, The. AWP

Enter and see this tomb, sirs, do not fear. Epitaph on Some Bottles of Sack and Claret Laid in Sand. Robert Wild. NOSC

Enter Harlem. Walk with de Mayor of Harlem. David Henderson. PoBA

Enter in the circle. Edouard J. Maunick, *tr. fr. French by* Ellen Conroy Kennedy. *Fr.* As Far as Yoruba Land. NegPo

Enter our thoughts! *(LL)* You are singing, little dove. *Unknown.* EaPr

Enter said the blush of wine. Digging Potatoes. Linda France. NWP

Enter the dream-house, brothers and sisters, leaving. Newsreel. C. Day Lewis. MoAB; MoBrPo

Entered in the Minutes. Louis MacNeice. LiTB

Entering Moscow. Pushkin, *tr. fr. Russian by* Thomas de Waal. *Fr.* Evgeny Onegin. CBCK

Entering the Body, *sels.* Stephen Berg. Survivor, The. NaP

Entering the hall, she meets the new wife. The Ejected Wife. *Unknown, tr. fr. Chinese by* Arthur Waley. OBVE
  (Rejected Wife, The.) ArLo

Entering the Kingdom of the Moray Eel. James Wright. PRA

Entering the midnight. Talking Late with the Governor about the Budget. Gary Snyder. BCF

Entering the Mouth of P'eng-li Lake. Hsieh Ling-yün, *tr. fr. Chinese by* Francis Westbrook. SuSp

Entering the publisher's warehouse, a foreign young lady. Anecdote from William IV Street. D. J. Enright. OxBC

Entering/ You will find yourself in a climate of nut castanets. A Climate of Nut Castanets. James Fenton. *Fr.* Pitt-Rivers Museum, Oxford, The. CBCK

Enterprise and *Boxer. Unknown.* PAH

Entertainer, The. Bruce Beaver. NOBAu

Entertainment Industry, The, *mod. by* Donald Attwater. William Langland. *Fr.* Vision of Piers Plowman, The. NOCV

Entertainment of War, The. Roy Fisher. FaBoMo

Entertainment, or Porch-Verse, at the Marriage of Master Henry Northleigh and the Most Witty Mistress Lettice Yard, The. Robert Herrick. CaPo

Entertainment to James, *sels.* Thomas Sheare *and others.* Troynovant ("Troynovant is now no more a city"). ChTr

Entgegenwärtigung Town. Anne Carson. *Fr.* Life of Towns, The. BAP-90

Enthroned above the world although he sit. Immanence. Richard Hovey. WGRP

Enthusiast, The. Herman Melville. ChIV-1; NAAL-1

Enthusiast: or, The Lover of Nature, The. Joseph Warton. EnRP; NOEC

Enthusiast; The; or, The Lover of Nature. Joseph Warton. EnRP; PoEL-3
  Sels.
  "Ye green-robed Dryads, oft at dusky eve." ECEV, *ll.* 1 – 15; NOEC

Enthusiastically hurting a clouded yellow bud and. A New Cup and Saucer. Gertrude Stein. *Fr.* Tender Buttons. TTTS

Enticing Lane, The. Christopher Hewitt. PFL

Entire country is overrun with private property, The. Gypsy. Josephine Miles. MoP; NoAM

Epigram: "Kissing Hippomenes, I crave." Paulus Silentiarius, *tr. fr. Greek* by Andrew Miller. GrAn; PeHV

Epigram: "Labienus, each hair on your bosom that grows." Martial, *tr. fr. Latin.* PeHV

Epigram: "Lady gave me a gift she had not, A." Sir Thomas Wyatt. SiPSBD

Epigram: "Lasses, like nuts at bottom brown." Allan Ramsay. FaBoEE

Epigram: "Life flows to death as rivers to the sea." J. V. Cunningham. VGW

Epigram: "Like when the burning sun doth rise." Strato, *tr. fr. Greek by* Sydney Oswald. PeHV

Epigram: Likeness, The. Martial, *tr. fr. Latin* by Brian Hill. PeHV

Epigram: "Listen, you know the pains of love." Meleager, *tr. fr. Greek by* Peter Whigham. PeHV

Epigram: "Lo! Beauty flashed forth sweetly; from his eyes." Meleager, *tr. fr. Greek by* Sydney Oswald. PeHV

Epigram: "Long hair, endless curls trained by the devoted." Strato, *tr. fr. Greek by* Teddy Hogge. GrAn; PeHV

Epigram: "Look how yon lecher's legs are worn away." John Taylor. NOSC

Epigram: "Loss of our learning brought darkness, weakness and woe." *Unknown, tr. fr. Greek by* Thomas Kinsella. NOIV

Epigram: "Love brought me quietly in the dreaming night." Meleager, *tr. fr. Greek by* Sydney Oswald. PeHV

Epigram: "Love signed the contract blithe and leal." John Swanwick Drennan. BIrV

Epigram: "Lusty wench as nimble as an eel, A." John Taylor. NOSC

Epigram: "Lutheran, Popish, Calvinistic, all of these confessions three." Friedrich von Logau, *tr. fr. German.* GePo, *tr.* by George C. Schoolfield

Epigram: "Lux my fair falcon, and your fellows all." Sir Thomas Wyatt. AAS; OBF; SiPS
(Epigram: "Lux my fair falcon, and your fellows all.") SiPSBD
(Luckes, my faire falcon, and your fellowes all.) AAS
(Lux, My Faire Falcon.) OxBSP

Epigram: "Lying with unstable pego 'twixt a brace of vigorous boys." Martial, *tr. fr. Latin.* PeHV

Epigram: "Me Polytimus vexes and provokes." Martial, *tr. fr. Latin.* PeHV

Epigram: "Member of the modern great, A." John Cunningham. FaBoEE

Epigram: "Midas, they say, possesed the art of old." "Peter Pindar." NIP

Epigram: "Milo's from home; and, Milo being gone." Martial, *tr. fr. Latin* by Elijah Fenton. OBVE

Epigram: "Most inexplicable the wiles of boys I deem." Rhianus, *tr. fr. Greek by* Sydney Oswald. PeHV

Epigram: "My better half, why turn a peevish scold." Martial, *tr. fr. Latin.* PeHV

Epigram: "My heart still hovering round about you." Robert, Earl Nugent. NOEC

Epigram: "My soul, sit thou a patient looker-on." Francis Quarles. NOBE; PoToHe
(Epigram: Respice Finem.) OBEV
(My Soul, Sit Thou a Patient Looker-on.) NIP

Epigram: "My soul, thy love is dear: 'twas thought a good." Francis Quarles. *Fr. Emblems.* OAEL-1

Epigram: "Naked I came, naked I leave the scene." J. V. Cunningham. *See* Naked I came, naked I leave the scene.

Epigram: "Need from exce ss — excess from folly growing." Samuel Bishop. NOEC

Epigram: "Nicander, ooh, your leg's got hairs!" Alcaeus, *tr. fr. Greek by* Tony Harrison. GrAn; PeHV

Epigram: "Now art thou fair, Diodorus." Strato, *tr. fr. Greek by* Sydney Oswald. PeHV

Epigram: "Now, *Priam*'s Son, thou may'st be mute." Allan Ramsay. ScCV

Epigram: "O Diodorus, in a storm of spring." *Unknown, tr. fr. Greek by* Sydney Oswald. PeHV

Epigram: "Of purpose Love chose first for to be blind." Sir Thomas Wyatt. SiPSBD

Epigram IV.v: Of Treason. Sir John Harington. *See* Treason doth never prosper [*or* Treason never prospers]; what's the reason?

Epigram: "Oft mighty elephants by little Moors are led." Friedrich von Logau, *tr. fr. German.* GePo, *tr.* by George C. Schoolfield

Epigram: On a Slanderer. Martial, *tr. fr. Latin.* PeHV

Epigram: On Hedylus. Martial, *tr. fr. Latin.* PeHV

Epigram: On Inclosures. *Unknown. See* 'Tis bad enough in man or woman.

Epigram: "On parent knees, a naked new-born child." Sir William Jones, *after the Sanskrit of* Kalidasa. FaBoEE; OBEV
(Moral Tetrastich, A.) OxBSP

Epigram: On Sir Francis Drake. *Unknown.* OBTV

Epigram: On Sir Roger Phillimore. *Unknown.* FaBoCo; NBLV

Epigram: "Once noble custom was: by blood on battleground." Friedrich von Logau, *tr. fr. German.* GePo, *tr.* by George C. Schoolfield

Epigram: "Passing the flower-stalls there did I perceive." Strato, *tr. fr. Greek by* Sydney Oswald. PeHV

Epigram: "Perchance some coming after." Strato, *tr. fr. Greek by* Sydney Oswald. PeHV

Epigram: Political Reflection. Howard Nemerov. *See* No bars are set too close, no mesh too fine.

Epigram: "Poverty? wealth? seek neither." Kassia, *tr. fr. Greek by* Patrick Diehl. WPOW

Epigram: "Prepare to meet the King of Terrors," cried." Ebenezer Elliot. NOBVV

Epigram: "Quoth Satan to Arnold: 'My worthy good fellow.'" *Unknown.* PAH

Epigram: "Reincarnating Pythagoras, say." Ausonius, *tr. fr. Latin.* PeHV

Epigram: Respice Finem. Francis Quarles. *See* My soul, sit thou a patient looker-on.

Epigram: Riddle, A. Martial, *tr. fr. Latin* by Brian Hill. PeHV

Epigram: "Rudely forced to drink tea, Massachusetts, in anger." *Unknown.* PAH

Epigram: "She sat and sewed that hath done me the wrong." Sir Thomas Wyatt. SiPSBD

Epigram: "Sighs are my food, drink are my tears." Sir Thomas Wyatt. SiPS
(Sighs Are My Food.) NoSic; OxBSP

Epigram: "Since first you knew my am'rous smart." Robert, Earl Nugent. NOEC

Epigram: "Since I'm completely drunk." *Unknown, tr. fr. Greek by* Peter Jay. PeHV

Epigram: "Sir, I admit your general [*or* gen'ral] rule," *At.* to Pope Pope, *also at.* to Matthew Prior *and to* Samuel Taylor Coleridge. FaBoEE; FiBHP; LiTB
(Fool and the Poet, The.) NBLV

Epigram: "Sometime I fled the fire that me brent." Sir Thomas Wyatt. NoSic; SiPSBD

Epigram: "Soul is a prisoner, and body is its jail." Friedrich von Logau, *tr. fr. German.* GePo, *tr.* by George C. Schoolfield

Epigram: "Stand whoso list upon the slipper top." Sir Thomas Wyatt. SiPSBD

Epigram: "Stolen kisses, wary eyes." Strato, *tr. fr. Greek by* Sydney Oswald. PeHV

Epigram: "There chanced to meet together in an inn." John Taylor. NOSC

Epigram: "There was this gym-teacher." Strato, *tr. fr. Greek by* Teddy Hogge. GrAn; PeHV

Epigram: "This *Humanist* Whom No Beliefs Constrained." J. V.

Epigram: "This is my curse, Pompous, I pray." J. V. Cunningham. HAP

Epigram: "Those snooty boys in all their purple drag!" Strato, *tr. fr. Greek by* Tony Harrison. GrAn; PeHV

Epigram II: "Thou fool profane, be silent!" *Unknown, tr. fr. Hebrew. Fr.* Duel with Verses over a Great Man. TrJP

Epigram I: "Thou Guide to doubt, be silent evermore." *Unknown, tr. fr. Hebrew. Fr.* Duel with Verses over a Great Man. TrJP

Epigram: "Thy eyes are sparks, Lycines, god-like made." Strato, *tr. fr. Greek by* Sydney Oswald. PeHV

Epigram: "Thy nags (the leanest things alive)." Matthew Prior. FaBoEE

Epigram: "Time heals not: it extends a sorrow's scope." J. V. Cunningham. IMW; VGW

Epigram LXVII: Time, the Interpreter. Hugh Crompton. NOSC

Epigram: "Time was when once upon a time, such toys." Glaukos, *tr. fr. Greek by* Peter Jay. GrAn; PeHV

Epigram: To Charinus, a Catamite. Martial, *tr. fr. Latin.* PeHV

Epigram: To Dindymus. Martial, *tr. fr. Latin* by Brian Hill. PeHV

Epigram: "To John I ow'd great obligation." Matthew Prior. FaBoCo; FaBoEE; OBVE
(Quits.) AWP

Epigram: To Lygdus. Martial, *tr. fr. Latin.* PeHV

Epigram: To Papilus. Martial, *tr. fr. Latin.* PeHV

Epigram: To Philaenis. Martial, *tr. fr. Latin.* PeHV

Epigram: To Polycharmus. Martial, *tr. fr. Latin.* PeHV

Epigram: To the Small-Pox, An. Ben Jonson. NOSC

Epigram: "Tom's sickness did his morals mend." Matthew Prior. FaBoEE

Epigram: "Treason doth never prosper [*or* Treason never prospers]; what's the reason?" Sir John Harington. FaBoEE; FF; InPK; NoSic; OxBoLi; SoSe
(Epigram IV.v: Of Treason.) NOSC
(Epigram.) OtMeF
(On Treason.) FiBHP
(Treason.) FaBoCo
(Treason never prospers; what's the reason?.) InvP

"Get out of my hut, you stealthy vermin! Leonidas'". HePo
"Gloomy minister of Hades who sail this stream." HePo
"His ball, beautiful leaved, and his noisy boxwood rattle." HePo
"If the tombstone placed over me is small to see and close." HePo
"Old Platthis often thrust away her morning's sleep." HePo
Spinning Woman, The. AWP
"Theris, thrice-old, who got his living from." HePo
"Thundering sea, why in savage storm did you plunge." HePo
"To Gluttony and Guzzling, that fastidious gourmet." HePo
"To Pallas, Theris, cunning of hand, dedicated." HePo
"Wallet, the hide of a goat, tough and untanned, a stick, A." HePo
"Whoever then are you? Whose wretched bones are these." HePo
Epigrams, *sels.* Meleager, *tr. fr. Greek by* Barbara Hughes Fowler.
Fisherman, The. AWP
"Cup takes its sweet joy and tells how it touches, The." HePo
"Did I not tell you, my soul, "By Cypris, you will be caught." HePo
"Flower-feasting bee, why do you touch upon." HePo
"I foster a Love fond of playing ball. It throws." HePo
"I say that my sweetly prattling Heliodora will someday." HePo
"I was a quick-footed, long-eared hare, just snatched from my mother's."
HePo
"If you burn my scorched soul too often, Love, she'll fly." HePo
"I'll weave in the white violet. I'll weave in." HePo
"I'm down. Step on my neck, you savage god, with your heel." HePo
"Love fed Heliodora's fingernail and made." HePo
"Love-prone Asclepias with eyes like a summer's day." HePo
"Mosquito, may you fly, a swift courier for me." HePo
"Mosquitoes, shameless and shrill of voice, sucking the blood." HePo
"Now the white violet blooms and narcissus that loves." HePo
"Pour and say again and again and yet again." HePo
"Pour for Heliodora Persuasion and pour for Cypris." HePo
"Sell it, though it sleeps still at its mother's breast!." HePo
"Shrilling cicada, drunk on drops of dew, you sing." HePo
"Still in his mother's lap the baby Love played." HePo
"Tears beneath the earth, Heliodora, I give." HePo
"Within my heart Love himself made Heliodora." HePo
"Yes, I'd rather hear Heliodora's voice." HePo
"You're sleeping, Zenophila, my tender bloom. I wish." HePo
Epigrams, *sels.* Mnasalcas, *tr. fr. Greek by* Barbara Hughes Fowler.
"Say, stranger, that this is the tomb of the mare Aethyia." HePo
Epigrams, *sels.* Philodemus, *tr. fr. Greek by* Barbara Hughes Fowler.
"I fell in love with Demo of Paphos. No big surprise." HePo
"In the middle of the night I slipped away from my husband." HePo
"I've been in love. Who hasn't? I went out and got drunk." HePo
"O foot, O leg, O thighs for which I rightly died." HePo
"O two-horned moon, you love the parties that last all night." HePo
"Philaenion is small and swart, but her hair curls more." HePo
"Xanthippe's strumming, her chatter, her speaking eye, her song." HePo
Epigrams, *sels.* Rufinus Domesticus, *tr. fr. Greek by* Barbara Hughes
Fowler.
"Dear God, I didn't know that Cytherea was bathing." HePo
"Lamplighter, if you can't set two equally." HePo
"Melissias denies her love, but her body screams." HePo
"Rhodoclea, I send you this wreath which I wove with my own hands."
HePo
"Silver-footed girl was bathing, letting the water, The." HePo
"Time has not quenched your beauty. Much of your bygone prime." HePo
"When Pallas and golden-sandaled Hera saw Maeonis." HePo
Epigrams, *sels.* Rabindranath Tagore.
"Echo always mocks the sound, The." PoA
Epigrams, *sels.* Tymnes, *tr. fr. Greek by* Barbara Hughes Fowler.
Maltese Dog, A. FaBoCh; FaBoEE; OBD; Spl
(Dog from Malta, The.) GrAn
"Stone says that it covers here the white dog, The." HePo
Epigrams, I-IX. Howard Nemerov. OBAL
Epigrams and Epitaphs., *sels.* C. S. Lewis.
"Save yourself. Run and leave me. I must go back." EBEV
Epigrams for My Father, *sels.* Eugene B. Redmond.
"45 – degree hat, Bulldurham butt hailing from lips." ETG
"Fatherlore: papa-rites, daddyhood." ETG
"Stone-story. The story of stone, brokenbricks." ETG
"Sun-son. Stonebone. Blackblitz." ETG
"Wanderer across waters." ETG
Epigrams must be curt, nor seem. Walter Savage Landor. FaBoEE
Epigrams on Priapus. *Unknown.* ErPo
Epigrams to Ernesto Cardenal in Defense of Claudia, *sels.* Dionne Brand.
"Give up the bitterness." PBCV
Epigraph. Blake. *See* I give you the end of a golden string.
Epil y Filiast. Harri Webb. AngWe
Epilog: "Like the ears of wheat in a wheat-field growing." Heine. *See* Like
the stalks of wheat in the fields.
Epilogue: "After our Epilogue this crowd dismisses." Congreve. *Fr.* Way
of the World, The. NAEL-1

Epilogue: "At the midnight in the silence of the sleep-time." Robert
Browning. *Fr.* Asolando. EnVR; FaBV; NOBE; OBNC; TEP; TrGrPo
(Epilogue: "At the midnight in the silence of the sleep-time.") NAEL-1
(Epilogue to Asolando.) PFP
Epilogue: "Away, for we are ready to a man!" James Elroy Flecker. *Fr.*
Golden Journey to Samarkand, The. FaBoRV; NOBE
Epilogue: "Carol, every violet has." Alfred Noyes. *Fr.* Flower of Old
Japan, The. MoBrPo
Epilogue: "Child! we must quit these visionary scenes." Hannah More. *Fr.*
Search after Happiness, The. ECWP
Epilogue: "Giver of bliss and pain, of song and prayer." William A. Percy.
TrPWD
Epilogue: "He is not dead nor liveth." Dorothy Wellesley. *Fr.* Deserted
House. OBMV
Epilogue: "Heaven, which man's generations draws." Francis Thompson.
Fr. Judgment in Heaven, A. MoAB; MoBrPo
Epilogue: "I have seen flowers come in stony places." John Masefield.
FaBoEE; OxBTC
Epilogue: Is there one desires to hear." William Larminie. *Fr.* Fand. PeIV
Epilogue: "Like the stalks of wheat in the fields." Heine, *tr. fr. German.*
Fr. North Sea, The. TrJP, *tr.* by Emma Lazarus
(Epilog: "Like the ears of wheat in a wheat-field growing.") AWP, *tr.* by
Louis Untermeyer
Epilogue: "Nothing now to mark the spot." Rachel Field. *Fr.* Circus
Garland, A. OBCA
Epilogue: "Now my charms are all o'erthrown." Shakespeare. *Fr.* Tempest,
The. CTC; OAEL-1
Epilogue: "O chansons foregoing." Ezra Pound. OxBA
Epilogue: "On the first of the Feast of Feasts." Robert Browning. ChIV-2
Epilogue: "Our Poet tells me I am very pretty." Delariviere Manley. *Fr.*
Royal Mischeif, The. KTR
Epilogue: "Our revels now are ended. *See* Our revels now are ended.
Epilogue: "Painted autumn overwhelms, The." John Meade Falkner.
FaBoPP
Epilogue: "Phoenix on the hot sirocco's breath." Herbert B. Mallalieu. PoA
Epilogue: "That death might not be casual." Burns Singer. FaBoTw
Epilogue: "There I learned how faces fall apart." "Anna Akhmatova," *tr.* by
D. M. Thomas. *Fr.* Requiem 1935-1940. AIW; BoWoP
Epilogue: "They who have best succeeded on the stage." Dryden. *Fr.*
Conquest of Granada, The. SeCV-2
Epilogue: "Those blessed structures, plot and rhyme." Robert Lowell.
CAPP; HCAP; NAAL-2; VCAP
(Those blessèd structures, plot and rhyme.) NoAM; NoP
Epilogue: "Thus far, with rough and all-unable pen." Shakespeare. *Fr.*
King Henry V. CTC
Epilogue: "Time is a thing." Stephen Spender. MoBrPo
Epilogue: "Truly my Satan thou art but a dunce." Blake. *Fr.* For the
Sexes; the Gates of Paradise. LiTB; PoE; PoEL-4
(Epilogue.) PeECV
(To the Accuser Who is the God of This World.) FHYEP; SCGP
Epilogue: "Truly, my Satan, thou art but a dunce." Blake. *Fr.* For the
sexes; the Gates of Paradise. HAP; ImPo; OAEL-2; OBNC; PoE; WeW
(To the Accuser Who Is the God of This World.) NoP; OxBSP; TrGrPo
Epilogue: "Well, when all is said and done." "Æ." MoBrPo
Epilogue: "What Epilogues are made, for who can tell." Catherine Trotter.
Fr. Queen Catharine; or, The Ruines of Love. KTR
Epilogue: "What shall we do for Love these days?" Lascelles Abercrombie.
Fr. Emblems of Love. CH; MoBrPo
Epilogue: "With heart at rest I climbed the citadel's." Baudelaire, *tr. fr.*
French by Arthur Symons. AWP
Epilogue: "At the midnight in the silence of the sleep-time." Robert
Browning. *See* At the midnight in the silence of the sleep-time.
Epilogue for a Masque of Purcell. Adrienne Rich. NYBP
Epilogue: " 'O where are you going?' said reader to rider." W. H. Auden.
See O where are you going? said reader to rider.
Epilogue: " 'O where are you going?' said reader to rider.") (Five Songs.
Alan Ross. *See* Orange air grows fetid with smoke, The. The uneasy
dark.
Epilogue of the Man of Law's Tale, The. Chaucer. *Fr.* Canterbury Tales,
The. EnVB
Epilogue Spoken by Mrs. Boutell. Dryden. SeCV-2
Epilogue: "Terence, this is stupid stuff." A. E. Housman. *See* Terence,
This Is Stupid Stuff.
Epilogue to a Human Drama. Stephen Spender. CMoP
Epilogue to a Poetry Reading. M. K. Joseph. PeNZ
Epilogue to Alun Mabon. John Ceiriog Hughes, *tr. fr. Welsh by* H. Idris
Bell. OBWVE
Epilogue to an Empire 1600-1900. Jon Stallworthy. FaBoEH

(Epitaph, An.) OBEV

(Other, An.) SeCV-2

Epitaph: "Time and the World, whose magnitude and weight." Robert Southey. OBNC

Epitaph: "Time that brings [or bringes] all things to light." Thomas Morton. NOSC; SCAP

Epitaph: "To the chimney a bull's horns." Ljubomir Simovic, tr. fr. Serbo-Croatian by Charles Simic. HSix

Epitaph: "Tread softly; bid a solemn music sound." J.B. Morton. FaBoEE

Epitaph: "When I am gone." Josephine D. Henderson Heard. AAP; CBWP-4

Epitaph: "Underneath this marble stone." Abraham Cowley. See

Epitaph: "Write on my grave when I am dead." Katharine Tynan. WGRP

Epitaph: "Young then,/ we were bored already." Eleanor Wilner. ChIV-1

Epitaph after Reading Ronsard's Lines from Rabelais. J. M. Synge. FaBoEE

Epitaph, An. Thomas Carew. See This little vault, this narrow room.

Epitaph, An. Julius Chingono. PeSAV

Epitaph, An. Stephen Hawes. See O mortal folk you may behold and see.

Epitaph, An. Sir William Watson. See His friends he loved. His direst earthly foes.

Epitaph, An: On a Man for Doing Nothing. John Hoskyns. NOSC

Epitaph. Caecil. Boulstr. Lord Herbert of Cherbury. SeCP

Epitaph Ending in And, The. William Stafford. LCAP; NaP

Epitaph: "Even Such Is Time, Which Takes in Trust." Sir Walter Ralegh. See Even such is time, that takes in trust.

Epitaph I: "Here lies a man, and still no man." Unknown, tr. fr. Hebrew. Fr. Duel with Verses over a Great Man. TrJP

Epitaph for a Beatnik Poet. Guy Owen. CRP

Epitaph for a Bigot. Dorothy Vena Johnson. PoNe

Epitaph for a Cat. Margaret E. Bruner. PoLF

Epitaph for a Dog. Samuel Twardowski, tr. fr. Polish by Jerzy Peterkiewicz and Burns Singer. OBD

Epitaph for a Godly Man's Tomb, An. Robert Wild. ChTr; FaBoEE

Epitaph for a Good Mouser. Anne Stevenson. Spl

Epitaph for a Judge. Benedict Jeitteles, tr. fr. Hebrew by Joseph Chotzner. TrJP

Epitaph for a Meat-Packer. Guy Owen. CRP

Epitaph for a Negro Woman. Owen Dodson. PoNe

Epitaph for a Persian Kitten. Miriam Vedder. CRH

Epitaph for a Poet. Homero Aridjis, tr. fr. Spanish by John Frederick Nims. STV

Epitaph for a Postal Clerk. X. J. Kennedy. NIP

Epitaph for a Reviewer. Frances Cornford. OBD

Epitaph for a Scientist. Lex Banning. NOBAu

Epitaph for a Sportsman. Leonard Barras. IHNG

Epitaph for Bruno of Angers. Marbod of Rennnes, tr. fr. Latin by Helen Waddell. MLL

Epitaph for Castlereagh, An. Byron.

Epitaph for Cleonicus. Alexander of Pleuron, tr. fr. Greek by W. S. Merwin. GrAn

Epitaph for Cú Chuimne. Unknown, tr. fr. Irish by Thomas Kinsella. NOIV

Epitaph for Erotion. Martial, tr. fr. Latin by James Michie. FaBoEE

Epitaph for G. B. Shaw. Max Beerbohm. FaBoEE

Epitaph for George Moore. Thomas Hardy. FaBoEE

Epitaph for Sir Henry Lee. Unknown. FaBoEE

Epitaph for His Niece, Sophia. Paul the Deacon, tr. fr. Latin by Helen Waddell. MLL

Epitaph for James Smith. Burns. See Lament him, Mauchline husbands a.

Epitaph for Jean Maillard. Unknown, tr. fr. French. PeHV

Epitaph for Sir Lawrence Tanfield. Lady Elizabeth Tanfield. See Here shadow[e] lie.

Epitaph for Mael Mhuru. Unknown. NOIV

Epitaph for Maria Wentworth. Thomas Carew. See And here the precious dust is laid [or layd].

Epitaph for Mr. Moses Levy. Unknown. TrJP

Epitaph for My Cat. Jean Garrigue. TAP

Epitaph for One Killed at Roncesvalles. Unknown, tr. fr. Latin by Helen Waddell. MLL

Epitaph for One Who Would Not Be Buried in Westminster Abbey. Pope. FaBoEE; OBD

Epitaph for [or on] Thomas Clere. The Earl of Surrey. NoSic; SiPSBD

Epitaph for Paulinus of Aquileia and Arno of Salzburg. Alcuin, tr. fr. Latin by Helen Waddell. MLL

Epitaph for Peter Stuyvesant. Henricus Selyns. SCAP

Epitaph for St. Amand, Bishop of Utrecht. Alcuin, tr. fr. Latin by Helen Waddell. MLL

Epitaph for Someone or Other. J. V. Cunningham. Fr. Five Epigrams. OBAL; SM; TRP

Epitaph for the Poet. George Barker. OxBSP

Epitaph for the Race of Man, sels. Edna St. Vincent Millay. "See where Capella with her golden kids." CMoP; MoAB; MoAmPo

Epitaph for the Unknown Soldier. W. H. Auden. FaBoCo

Epitaph for the Western Intelligentsia. Richard Allen. NOBAu

Epitaph for William Pitt. Byron. FaBoEE

Epitaph from a Tomb in Asia Minor. Unknown, tr. fr. Greek by Peter Whigham. GrAn

Epitaph from Athens. Unknown, tr. fr. Greek by Richmond Lattimore. GrAn

Epitaph from Athens. Unknown, tr. fr. Greek by Peter Jay. GrAn

Epitaph from Piraeus. Unknown, tr. fr. Greek by Peter Jay. GrAn

Epitaph from The Great Gatsby. F. Scott Fitzgerald. Fr. Great Gatsby, The. OxBM

Epitaph in a Churchyard at Thetford, in Norfolk. Unknown. FaBoUs

Epitaph in Christ Church, Bristol, on Thomas Turner, Twice Master of the Company of Bakers. Francis Jeffrey. See Like to a baker's oven is the grave.

Epitaph in Dialogue on the Sceptic Philosopher Pyrrho. Julianus of Egypt, tr. fr. Greek by Lee T. Pearcy. GrAn

Epitaph: In Obitum M.S., X° Maij [or Maii], 1614. William Browne. EIL; FaBoEE; JCP; NOBE; OBEV

Epitaph in St. Olave's, Southwark, on Mr. Munday. Unknown. FaBoCo; OxBoLi

Epitaph in Sirmio. David Morton. PoLF

Epitaph in the Bermuda Tongue, Which Must Be Pronounced With the Accent of the Grunting of a Hog. John Taylor. CBNP

Epitaph in the Borghese Gardens. Unknown, tr. fr. Greek by Peter Whigham. GrAn

Epitaph in the Utopian Tongue. John Taylor. CBNP

Epitaph, Intended for Himself. James Beattie. ScCV

Epitaph Intended for Sir Isaac Newton, [or in Westminster Abbey]. Pope. See Nature and Nature's laws lay hid in Night.

Epitaph of a Dog. Unknown, tr. fr. Greek by Dudley Fitts. GrAn

Epitaph of a Girl. Unknown, tr. fr. Greek by Dudley Fitts. GrAn

Epitaph of a Nicene Actor. Unknown, tr. fr. Greek by Dudley Fitts. GrAn

Epitaph of a Sailor. Antiphilus, tr. fr. Greek by Dudley Fitts. GrAn

Epitaph of a Sailor. Damagetus, tr. fr. Greek by Dudley Fitts. GrAn

Epitaph of Cleonicus. Theocritus [or Theokritus], tr. fr. Greek by Charles Stuart Calverley. FaBoEE

Epitaph of Dionysia. Unknown. OBEV

Epitaph of Eusthenes, The. Edward Cracroft Lefroy, after the Greek of Theocritus. Fr. Echoes from Theocritus. AWP

Epitaph of Graunde [or La Graunde] Amoure, The. Stephen Hawes. Fr. Pastime of Pleasure, The. ChTr; CoGr; EBEV; FaBoRV; NoSic; OBEV; TrGrPo

Epitaph of Sir Griffith ap Rhys, The. Unknown. AngWe

Epitaph of Hipponax. Theocritus [or Theokritus], tr. fr. Greek by Charles Stuart Calverley. FaBoEE

Epitaph of Maister Win Drowned in the Sea, An. George Turberville. FaBoEE

Epitaph of Nearchos. Ammianus, tr. fr. Greek by Dudley Fitts. WeW

Epitaph of Our Late Queen Mary, An. George Cavendish. NoSic

Epitaph of Pyramus and Thisbe. Abraham Cowley. EnLoPo; FaBoEE

Epitaph of Sardanapalos, The. Unknown, tr. fr. Greek by Kenneth Rexroth. PGA

Epitaph of the Death of Nicholas Grimald, An. Barnabe Googe. EnRePo; SCGP

Epitaph of Sir Thomas Gravener [Knight], An. Sir Thomas Wyatt. SiPS

Epitaph on a Betrothed Girl. Erinna, tr. fr. Greek by Lenore Mayhew. GrAn

Epitaph on a Child Killed by Procured Abortion. Unknown. NOEC

Epitaph on a Dentist. Unknown. See Stranger! Approach this spot with gravity!

Epitaph on a Diamond Digger. Albert Brodrick. PeSAV

Epitaph on a Dormouse. Unknown. OxBChV

Epitaph on a Dwarf. Emmanuel ben David Frances, tr. fr. Hebrew by Hyam Maccoby. OBD

Epitaph on a Fir-Tree. Richard Murphy. FaBoTw

Epitaph on a Great Sleeper. Sir Aston Cokayne. FaBoEE

Epitaph on a Hare. William Cowper. CoGr; FM; HAP; NOEC; NoP; PoEL-3

Epitaph on a Jacobite. Macaulay. See To my true king I offered free from stain.

Epitaph on a New Army. Michael Thwaites. PAW

Epitaph on a Party Girl. Richard Usborne. FaBoEE

Epitaph on a Pessimist. Thomas Hardy. FaBoEE; FF; TRP

Epitaph on a Robin Redbreast, An. Samuel Rogers. FaBoEE; FM

Epitaph on a Schoolmaster. Burns. FaBoCo; FaBoEE

Epitaph on a Soldier. Cyril Tourneur. *Fr.* Atheist's Tragedy, The. ElL

Epitaph on a Tomb near Rome. *Unknown, tr. fr. Greek by* Frank Kuenstler. GrAn

Epitaph on a Tyrant. W. H. Auden. HeIP; MeMAP; NoAM; OxBSP; PAW; RB

Epitaph on a Waiter. David McCord. NBLV; NIP; OBAL

Epitaph on a Willing Girl. *At. to* Thomas Rowlandson. FaBoEE

Epitaph on a Young Child. Ivor Gurney. FaBoEE

Epitaph on a Young Poet Who Died before Having Achieved Success. Amy Lowell. OBAL

Epitaph on Achilles. *Unknown, tr. fr. Greek by* William M. Hardinge. AWP

Epitaph on an Army of Mercenaries. A. E. Housman. *Fr.* Last Poems. CoGr; EBEvV; NSI; OtMeF; PAW; SCGP; SoSe

Epitaph on an Infant. Crinagoras, *tr. fr. Greek by* John William Burgon. AWP

Epitaph on an Irish Priest. *Unknown.* FaBoEE

Epitaph on an Unfortunate Artist. Robert Graves. FaBoEE; NOBL

Epitaph on Charles I. James Graham, Marquess of Montrose. *See* Great, good and just, could I but rate.

Epitaph on Charles II. The Earl of Rochester. FaBoEH

Epitaph on Charles II. The Earl of Rochester. FaBoCo; FiBHP; SCGP; TrGrPo

Epitaph on Claudy Phillips, a Musician, An. Samuel Johnson. *See* Phillips! whose touch harmonious could remove.

Epitaph on Colonel Francis Chartres. John Arbuthnot. FaBoEE

Epitaph on Dr. Donne, Dean of Paul's, An. Richard Corbett [*or* Corbet]. BeJo; EPCY

Epitaph on Dr. Keene. Thomas Gray. FaBoEE

Epitaph on Dr. Keene's Wife. Thomas Gray. FaBoEE

Epitaph on Dr Samuel Johnson. Soame Jenyns. ECEV

Epitaph on Elizabeth, L. H. Ben Jonson. BeJo; EIL; ELP; EnRePo; FaBoEE; HAP; NAEL-1; NIP; NoP; NOSC; OBEV; PoE; Poetr; SCGP; SeCP; SeCV-1

Epitaph on Fop. William Cowper. OBD

Epitaph on G — —. Pope. OBD

Epitaph on Henry Prince of Wales. Hugh Holland. *See* Lo now he shineth yonder.

Epitaph on her Son *H. P.* at St. Syth's Church. Katherine Philips. KTR

Epitaph on Her Son H. P. at St. Syth's Church, where Her Body also Lies Interred. Katherine Philips. *See* What on Earth deserves our Trust?

Epitaph on Herself, An. Mehetabel Wright. ECWP

Epitaph on Himself. Samuel Taylor Coleridge. FaBoEE

Epitaph on Himself. Pope. FaBoEE

Epitaph on His Wife. Dryden. TrGrPo

Epitaph on Hogarth. Samuel Johnson. *See* Hand of art here torpid lies, The.

Epitaph on James Moore Smythe. Pope. FaBoEE

Epitaph on John Dove. Burns. FaBoCo

Epitaph on John Knott. *Unknown.* ChTr; FaBoEE; SeCV-1

Epitaph on Lady Ossory's Bullfinch. Horace Walpole. *Fr.* Epitaphs [*or* Epitaph] on Two Piping-Bullfinches of Lady Ossory's, Buried under a Rose-Bush in Her Garden. ChTr; FaBoEE; NOEC

Epitaph on Laurence Sterne. David Garrick. FaBoEE

Epitaph on M. H., An. Charles Cotton. EBEV; FaBoEE; OPOP

Epitaph on Maria Wentworth. Thomas Carew. PoEL-3

Epitaph on Master Philip Gray, An. Ben Jonson. FaBoEE

Epitaph on Master Vincent Corbett, An. Ben Jonson. BeJo; JCP

Epitaph on Pegasus, a Limping Gay. "Panormitanus", *tr. fr. Latin.* FaBoBl; PeHV

Epitaph on Peter Robinson. Francis Jeffrey. *See* Here lies the preacher, judge, and poet, Peter.

Epitaph on Sir Philip Sidney. *At. to* Fulke Greville *and to* Sir Edward Dyer. EnRePo; LiTB; Prf; SCGP

Epitaph on Sir Philip Sidney. *At. to* Sir Walter Ralegh. SiPS

Epitaph on Sir Philip Sidney, An. James I, King of England. Son

Epitaph on Prince Frederick. *Unknown. See* Here lies Fred.

Epitaph on Prince Henry. Hugh Holland. FaBoEE

Epitaph on Robert Southey. Thomas Moore. FaBoCo; FaBoEE

Epitaph on S. P. Ben Jonson. *See* Weep [*or* Weepe] with me, all you that read.

Epitaph on S. P. [Salomon *or* Salathiel Pavy], a Child of Q[ueen] El[izabeth's] Chapel. Ben Jonson. BeJo; EIL; EnRePo; HoPM; JCP; Mes; NAEL-1; NoP; NOSC; OAEL-1; OBD; OBEV; PoEL-2; PPP; SCGP; SeCP; SeCV-1; TrGrPo; UnPo

Epitaph on Some Bottles of Sack and Claret Laid in Sand. Robert Wild. NOSC

Epitaph on the Admirable Dramatic Poet, W. Shakespeare, An. Milton. *See* What needs my Shakespear[e] for his honoured [*or* honour'd *or* honored] bones.

Epitaph on the Countess[e] Dowager of Pembroke. *At. to* William Browne. *See* Underneath this sable hearse [*or* herse].

Epitaph on the Duke of Grafton. Sir Fleetwood Shepherd. FaBoEE

Epitaph on the Earl of Leicester. Sir Walter Ralegh. EnRePo; RB; SiPS

Epitaph on the Earl of Strafford. John Cleveland. FaBoEE; FaBoEH; FaBoPV; JCP; NOBE; NOSC; OtMeF; PeECV; TrGrPo

Epitaph on the Fart in the Parliament House. John Hoskyns. FaBoEE

Epitaph on the Favourite Dog of a Politician. Hilaire Belloc. OBSV

Epitaph on the Lady Mary Villiers. Thomas Carew. BeJo; CaPo; FaBoEE; NOBE; OBEV; SeCV-1

Epitaph on the Lady Mary Villiers, An. Thomas Carew. SeCP

Epitaph on the Late King of the Sandwich Isles. Winthrop Mackworth Praed. FiBHP

Epitaph on the Monument of Sir William Dyer at Colmworth, 1641. Lady Catherine Dyer. *Fr.* Sir William Dyer, Knight. BoLoP; EnLoPo; OxBM

Epitaph on the Monument of Sir William Strode. William Strode. NOSC

Epitaph on the Politician Himself. Hilaire Belloc. FaBoEE; IHNG; MoBrPo; NBLV; OBSV

Epitaph on the Secretary to the Muses. Jane Barker. FaBoCo

Epitaph on the Stanton-Harcourt Lovers. Pope. *Fr.* Three Epitaphs on John Hewet and Sarah Drew. FaBoEE; NIP; OBD

Epitaph on the Tombstone of a Child, the Last of Seven That Died Before. Aphra Behn. KTR; NOSC

Epitaph — on the Wife of Dr. Greenwood. Dr. ———— Greenwood. FaBoUs

Epitaph on the World. Thoreau. FF

Epitaph on Thomas Clere. The Earl of Surrey. *See* Norfolk sprang [*or* sprung] thee, Lambeth holds thee dead.

Epitaph on Sir Thomas Wyatt. The Earl of Surrey. *See* Wyatt Resteth Here.

Epitaph on True, Her Majesty's Dog, An. Matthew Prior. FM

Epitaph on Tuft-Hunter. Thomas Moore. FaBoCo; FaBoEE

Epitaph on Sir Walter Pye. John Hoskyns. FaBoEE

Epitaph: On Sir Walter Rawleigh at His Execution. *Unknown.*

Epitaph on Washington. *Unknown.* OHIP

Epitaph on William Hogarth. Samuel Johnson. EBEV

Epitaph on William Jones. *Unknown.* FaBoEE

Epitaph on William Whitehead. *Unknown.* FaBoEE

Epitaph Placed on His Daughter's Tomb. "Mark Twain." PoLF, *ad. by* Robert Richardson
Underneath this marble stone/ Lie two beauties join'd in one.

Epitaph to a Dog. Byron. BLPA

Epitaph upon a Child, An. Robert Herrick. FaBoEE; SeCV-1

Epitaph Upon a Child that Died. Robert Herrick. *See* Here she lies, a pretty bud.

Epitaph upon a Sober Matron, An. Robert Herrick. CaPo

Epitaph upon a Virgin, An. Robert Herrick. CaPo; FaBoEE; OxBoLi; PoEL-3; SeCV-1

Epitaph upon a Young Married Couple Dead and Buried Together, An. Richard Crashaw. *See* To these, whom death again did wed.

Epitaph upon Husband and Wife Who Died and Were Buried Together, An. Richard Crashaw. EBEV; NOBE; OBEV; OxAEP-1; OxBM; TrGrPo

Epitaph upon My Dear Brother, Francis Beaumont, An. Sir John Beaumont. JCP

Epitaph upon That Profound and Learned Casuist, the Late Ordinary of Newgate, An. Thomas Brown. OBSV

Epitaph Upon the Celebrated Claudy Phillips, Musician, Who Died Very Poor, An. Samuel Johnson. NOEC

Epitaph Upon the Lady Elizabeth, Second Daughter to his Late Majesty, An. Henry Vaughan. BeJo

Epitaph Upon the Right Honorable Sir Philip Sidney. *At. to* Fulke Greville *and to* Sir Edward Dyer. *See* Silence augmenteth grief, writing increaseth rage.

Epitaph upon the Right Honorable Sir Philip Sidney, sels. *Unknown.* "He was (woe worth that word!) to each well thinking mind." EPCY

Epitaph upon the right Honourable Sir Philip Sidney Knight, Lord Governor of Flushing, An. *At. to* Sir Walter Ralegh. *See* To praise thy life or wail thy worthy death.

Epitaph upon Thomas, Lord Fairfax, An. George Villiers. NOSC

Epitaphium Citharistriae. Victor Plarr. EnLoPo; NBLV

Epitaphium Meum. William Bradford. SCAP

Epitaphs, sels. Robert Francis. "Everyman/ Preacher or lecher, saint or sot." CRP

Epitaphs, *sels.* Gloria A. Maxson.

Epitaphs from Karansko Cemetery. Ljubomir Simovic, *tr. fr. Serbo-Croatian by* Charles Simic. HSix

Epitaphs of the War, 1914–1918. (A. "I was a Have." B. "I was a Have Not.".) Kipling. NoP; OBWP
Sels.
Beginner, The. FaBoTw
Bridegroom, The. FaBoEE
Common Form. FaBoEE; FaBoTw; PeFWW
Coward, The. FaBoEE; FaBoTw; PeFWW
Dead Statesman, A. FaBoEE; IHNG; NBLV; PoWW
Drifter off Tarentum, A. FaBoEE; NSI; PeFWW; PoWW
Equality of Sacrifice. FaBoTw
Pelicans in the Wilderness (A Grave near Halfa). PeFWW
Refined Man, The. FaBoEE; FaBoTw; PeFWW
Servant, A. PeFWW
Son, A. FaBoEE; PeFWW

Epitaphs [*or* Epitaph] on Two Piping-Bullfinches of Lady Ossory's, Buried under a Rose-Bush in Her Garden. (All flesh is grass, and so are feathers too.) Horace Walpole. FaBoEE; NOEC
Sels.
Epitaph on Lady Ossory's Bullfinch. ChTr

Epitaphy of la Graunde Amoure. Stephen Hawes. *See* O mortal folk you may behold and see.

Epithalamia. Thomas Lovell Beddoes. *See* We have bathed, where none have seen us.

Epithalamion: "Singing, today I married my white girl." Dannie Abse. OBWVE

Epithalamion: "These are the small hours when." Michael Longley. CIP

Epithalamion. (Ye learned sisters which have oftentimes.) Spenser. AAS; BoLoP; EiL; EnRePo; FHYEP; InPS; NOBE; NoP; NoSic; OAEL-1; OBEV; OxAEP-1; PoEL-1; TEP
Sels.
"Wake, now my love, awake; for it is time." GBL
Who Is the Same, Which at My Window Peepes? NAs

Epithalamion Made at Lincolnes Inne. John Donne. SeCP

Epithalamion on the Lady Elizabeth and Count Palantine Being Married on St. Valentine's Day, An, *sels.* John Donne.
"Hail, Bishop Valentine, whose day this is." ChTr

Epithalamion, or a Song Celebrating the Nuptials of That Noble Gentleman, Mr. Jerome Weston. Ben Jonson. BeJo

Epithalamion Teratos. George Chapman. *Fr.* Hero and Leander. AAS; EiL; NoP; NoSic

Epithalamium: "Can the lover share his soul." W. J. Turner. OBMV

Epithalamium: "Come, virgin tapers of pure wax." Richard Crashaw. NOCV

Epithalamium: "Hymen, god of marriage bed." Joseph Rutter. NOSC

Epithalamium: "Hymen hath together tied." R. Hatton. NOSC

Epithalamium: "Let mother Earth now deck herself in flowers." Sir Philip Sidney. *Fr.* Arcadia. OxAEP-1; SiPS
(Epithalamium: "Let mother Earth.") SiPSBD

Epithalamium: "Lo! Hymen passes through th' admiring crowds." *Unknown.* ECWP

Epithalamium: "So you are married, girl. It makes me sad." Roy McFadden. PNI

Epithalamium: "This girl all in white is my crystal of light." Francis Warner. OxBM

Epithalamium: "Voice that breathed o'er Eden, The." John Keble. NOCV

Epithalamium: "Let mother Earth." Sir Philip Sidney. *See* Let mother Earth now deck herself in flowers.

Epithalamium: To Mistress M. A. Martin Lluellyn [*or* Lluelyn]. NOSC

Epithalamium upon the Marriage of Captain William Bedloe, An. Richard Duke. APAS

Epithalamy. Alexander Brome. NOSC

Epithalamy to Sir Thomas Southwell and His Lady, An. Robert Herrick. CaPo

Epitome. Ruth G. Dixon. ShDr

Epoch. Vladimir Holan, *tr. fr. Czech by* Ian Milner *and* Jarmila Milner. PoSu

Epoch ends, the world is still, The. Matthew Arnold. *Fr.* Bacchanalia; or, The New Age. OAEL-2

Epode. Ben Jonson. BeJo; SeCP; SeCV-1

Epodes, *sels.* Horace, *tr. fr. Latin.*
Counterblast against Garlic, A. NBLV
Country Life. AWP

Epos. Harold Rosenberg. PoA

Eppie Morrie. *Unknown.* ESPB; OxBB

Eppur Si Muove? Robert Silliman Hillyer. GoYe

Equal, An. *Unknown.* ReMoGo

Equal, equipped at last (O joy! O fruit of all!) them to fulfill, O Soul! (*LL*) Darest Thou Now O Soul. Walt Whitman. TrGrPo; WGRP

Equality of Sacrifice. Kipling. *Fr.* Epitaphs of the War, 1914–1918. FaBoTw; NoP; OBWP

Equanimity. Les A. Murray. NOBAu

Equation. Charles Wright. CAPP

Equestrian fell from his horse, An. The Childhood of an Equestrian. Russell Edson. AmPA

Equestrienne. Rachel Field. *Fr.* Circus Garland, A. OBCA

Equilibrists, The. John Crowe Ransom. CMoP; HAP; LiTM; MeMAP; MoAB; MoP; NAAL-2; NoAM; NOBA; OxBA; PPP; TAP

Equinox, The. DuBose Heyward. PoA

Equipment. Paul Laurence Dunbar. TrPWD

Equipment. Edgar A. Guest. PoToHe

Er-Heb beyond the Hills of Ao-Safai. The Sacrifice of Er-Heb. Kipling. PeVV

Erase the lines under your titles. That's right. Service Includes Free Lifetime Updating. Jendi Reiter. BAP-90

Erasers. *Unknown.* PoToHe

Erasers are the nicest things! Erasers. *Unknown.* PoToHe

Erce, Erce, Erce, mother of earth. Charms for Unfruitful Land. *Unknown, tr. fr. Anglo-Saxon by* Charles W. Kennedy. AnOE

Erd sould trymbill, the firmament sould schaik, The. Quod Dunbar to Kennedy. William Dunbar. OxBoLi

Ere famous Winthrops bones are laid to rest. Chelmsfords Fate. Benjamin Tompson. SCAP

Ere five score years have run their tedious rounds. A Prophecy. Arthur Lee. PAH

Ere freedom out of man. (*LL*) O tenderly the haughty day. Emerson. GN

Ere God had built the mountains. Wisdom. William Cowper. ChIV-1

E're I forget the zenith of your love. To My Cosen Mrs. Ellinor Evins. George Alsop. SCAP

Ere I freeze, to sing bravely. Poem of the Frost and Snow. Lewis Morris, *tr. fr. Welsh by* Anthony Conran. OBWVE

Ere I had told/ Ten birthdays when among the mountain-slopes. Skating. Wordsworth. *Fr.* Prelude [or, Growth of a Poet's Mind], The. CH; EnRP; GN; HAP; NOBE; NoP; NU; OAEL-2; OBNC; OxAEP-2; PoE; SCV; TOF

Ere I know it — next moment I dance at the King's! (*LL*) The Laboratory; Ancien Régime. Robert Browning. EnVR; NAEL-2; OBEV

Ere I prove false to faith, or strange to you. (*LL*) Dear, If You Change. At. to John Dowland. EiL; EnLoPo; EnRePo; InvP

Ere lang the waves war foamin'. (*LL*) The Mermaid. *Unknown.* CH; ESPB

Ere long they come, where that same wicked wight. Spenser. *Fr.* Faerie Queene, The. NOBE; OAEL-1; OBNV

Ere Murfreesboro's thunders rent the air. The Battle of Murfreesboro. Kinahan Cornwallis. PAH

Ere my heart beats too coldly and faintly. The Truants. Walter de la Mare. MoBrPo

Ere on my bed my limbs I lay. The Pains of Sleep. Samuel Taylor Coleridge. EnRP; FHYEP; NAEL-2; OBNC; TEP
(Child's Evening Prayer, A.) OxBChV; TrPWD

E're since hath in her Sun-shine liv'd. (*LL*) Lucasta's World. Richard Lovelace. BeJo; CaPo; SeCP

Ere Sleep Comes Down to Soothe the Weary Eyes. Paul Laurence Dunbar. CDC; PoNe

Ere space exists, or earth, or sky. The Lord Is King. *Unknown, tr. fr. Hebrew by* Solomon Solis-Cohen. TrJP

Ere the beard of thistle sails. The Seasons. Thomas Holcroft. NOEC

Ere their story die. (*LL*) In Time of "The Breaking of Nations." Thomas Hardy. BoLoP; ChIV-1; CMoP; CoGr; EBEV; EBEvV; HAP; LiTB; LiTM; MeMBP; MoAB; MoBrPo; MoP; NAEL-2; NoAM; NOBE; NoP; OAEL-2; OBEV; OBWP; OxAEP-2; PAW; Poetr; PoWW; PPP; RB; TFi; WeW

Ere thou proceed in this sweet pains. Of the Innumerable Virtues of Her Mind. Sir John Davies. *Fr.* Hymns of Astræa [in Acrostic Verse]. SiPSBD

Ere we can call it ours. (*LL*) 'Tis true our life is but a long dis-ease. Katherine Philips. OxBSP

Ere yet your footsteps quit the place. Verses Addressed to a Friend, Just Leaving a Favourite Retirement. Samuel Henley. NOEC

Ere You Were Queen of Sheba. Sir Arthur Shipley. FaBoCo

Eremites, The. Robert Graves. LiTB

Eric. John Barford. PeHV

Eric Dolphy. Anne Waldman. Jaz

Erica. Mary Ursula Bethell. PeNZ

Eride, *sels.* Trumbull Stickney.
Now in the Palace Gardens. LiTA

Erie Canal, The. William S. Allen. AS

Erie-Lackawanna trains are the ghost, The. Note in a Bottle. Gerald McCarthy. NGP

Erige Cor Tuum ad Me in Caelum. Hilda Doolittle ("H. D."). CMoP

Erinna. Antipater of Sidon, *tr. fr. Greek* by A. J. Butler. AWP

Erinna's Distaff. Antipater of Sidon, *tr. fr. Greek* by Peter Jay. GrAn

Erith, on the Thames. *Unknown.* ChTr; FaBoPP; GBP

Erl-King, The. Goethe, *tr. fr. German* by Sir Walter Scott. AWP; OBVE

Erlinton. *Unknown.* ESPB

Erlinton. *Unknown.* ESPB, A *and* B *vers.*

Erlking, The. Goethe, *tr. fr. German* by Philip L. Miller. RiWo

Erminia's steed this while his mistress bore. Tasso, *tr. fr. Italian* by Edward Fairfax. *Fr.* Godfrey of Bulloigne; or, The Recoverie of Jerusalem. NoSic

Ernie Morgan found him, a small. Barn Owl. Leslie Norris. AngWe

Ernst was an elephant, a great big fellow. The Four Friends. A. A. Milne. PYC

Eros. Otto Benzon, *tr. fr. Norwegian* by Philip L. Miller. RiWo

Eros. Robert Bridges. CMoP; LiTB; NOBE; PoEL-5

Eros. Emerson. FaBoBe

Eros. Louise Glück. *Fr.* Dedication to Hunger. AnAn

Eros at Temple Stream. Denise Levertov. NALW

Eros cast in wax, molded into a candle, An. Anacreon, *tr. fr. Greek* by Sam Hamill. InMo

Eros D'Aute. Theodore Wratislaw. GBL

Eros has changed his quiver. Paulus Silentiarius, *tr. fr. Greek* by Kenneth Rexroth. PGA

Eros Out of the Sea. Dilys Bennett Laing. PoA

Eros, playing among the roses. Anacreon, *tr. fr. Greek* by Sam Hamill. InMo

Eros seizes and shakes my very soul. Sappho, *tr. fr. Greek* by Sam Hamill. InMo

Eros taught Pratalidas his adolescent beauty. Leonidas of Tarentum, *tr. fr. Greek* by Peter Levi. GrAn

Eros, that bane of men, molded soft as marrow. Dioscorides, *tr. fr. Greek* by Barbara Hughes Fowler. *Fr.* Epigrams. HePo

Eros, thou yet behold'st me? Shakespeare. *Fr.* Antony and Cleopatra. EBEV; OxAEP-1

Eros Turannos. E. A. Robinson. CMoP; GBL; HAP; HeIP; LiTA; LiTM; MeMAP; MoAB; MoAmPo; MoP; NAAL-2; NoAM; NOBA; NoP; OxBA; PoA; PoE; Poetr; TAP; TFi; TRP

Erosion. Linda Pastan. NIP

Erotic Suite, *sels.* José Luis Vega, *tr. fr. Spanish* by Julio Marzán.

Erotion. Martial, *tr. fr. Latin* by Kirby Flower Smith. AWP

Erotion. Swinburne. PoEL-5

Erotion rests here, in the. Martial, *tr. fr. Greek* by Kenneth Rexroth. PGA

Erotopaegnia, *sels.* Edoardo Sanguineti, *tr. fr. Italian* by Lawrence R. Smith.

Errant. John Godfrey. UL

Errantry. Robert Fitzgerald. NYBP

Errata. Charles Simic. NNaP

Erratum. E. J. Thribb. PeLV

Errore. Pier Giorgio di Cicco. NOBC

Erskineville. The sun came round a corner. Pioneer Lane. Michael Dransfield. FaBoMA; NOBAu

Erté obelisk, a spire, the solitary, An. The Swordfish Tooth. Cynthia Zarin. UTF

Erthe oute of erthe is wonderly wroghte. Earth out of Earth. *Unknown.* MeEL

Erthe Toc of Erthe. *Unknown.* HAP

Erthe tok of erthe erthe with woh. *Unknown.* MiEL

Erudite, solemn/ The pious bird. Rev Owl. A. M. Klein. TrJP

'E's crowdin' us out! — 'er majesty's poet — soldier an' sailor too! (*LL*) As I was walkin' the jungle round, a-killin' of tigers an' time. Guy Wetmore Carryl. BXAP; NBLV

Es fällt ein Stern herunter. Heine, *tr. fr. German* by Richard Garnett. AWP

Es Lebe Der König. J. H. Prynne. VaA

Es Stehen Unbeweglich. Heine, *tr. fr. German* by James Thomson. AWP; TrJP

Es war einmal . . . No, it's too heavy. Märchenbilder. John Ashbery. LCAP; NOBA

Esanzo. Antoine-Roger Bolamba, *tr. fr. French* by Ellen Conroy Kennedy. NegPo

Escalator, The. Alex Glasgow. OBET

Escape. Edmund Blunden. NSI

Escape. Lillie D. Chaffin. ETG

Escape. Robert Graves. MoBrPo

Escape, The. Ivor Gurney. OxBSP

Escape. Georgia Douglas Johnson. PoBA; ShDr

Escape, The. William Stafford. NNaP

Escape, The. Mark Van Doren. MoAmPo

Escape. Elinor Wylie. LiTA; MoAmPo

Escape, An. Abu Nuwas, *tr. fr. Arabic* by E. Powys Mathers. ErPo

Escape at Bedtime. Robert Louis Stevenson. OTCP; TrGrPo

Escape from the weekday time. Which deadens and endures. (*LL*) Sunday Morning. Louis MacNeice. FaBoMo; LiTB; MoAB; MoBrPo; NAEL-2; NIP; OxAEP-2; Son

Escape into You, The, *sels.* Marvin Bell.
   Homage to the Runner. CAPP
   Obsessive. SM

Escape me?/ Never. Life in a Love. Robert Browning. FHYEP; OBNC; TrGrPo

Escape to Love, *sels.* Patrick MacDonogh.
   "Alone and Godless, stopped by the sudden edge." BIrV

Escape with the children but. Kristallnacht. Iain Sinclair. VaA

Escaped the gloom of mortal life, a soul. Epitaph, Intended for Himself. James Beattie. ScCV

Escorted by obstinate memories, I take giant steps up the stairway of music. Old Poem. Octavio Paz, *tr. fr. Spanish* by Eliot Weinberger. AnRep

Ese Chicano. Jimmy Santiago Baca. ETG

Eshu, the God of Fate ("Eshu turns right into wrong"). *Yoruba Oral Tradition*, *tr. by* Ulli Beier. WTO

Eskimo Baby, An. Lucy Diamond. BoTP

Eskimo Chant. *Unknown, tr. fr. Eskimo* by Knud Rasmussen. RFM

Eskimo, explorers state, The. The Immoral Arctic. Morris Bishop. FiBHP

Eskimo Nell. *Unknown.* FaBoBl

Eskimo Occasion. Judith Rodriguez. CBAP; FaBoWP; NOBAu

Eskimos in Manitoba. Recital. John Updike. OBAL

Esmeralda! Now we rest. Lines Written in Oregon. Vladimir Nabokov. NYBP

ESP. Carter Revard. VoR

España, Aparta de me Este Caliz, *sels.* César Vallejo, *tr. fr. Spanish.* Masses. RB

Especially he loves. God Poem. Stanley Moss. VGW

Especially in weeping. Valerio Magrelli, *tr. fr. Italian* by Dana Gioia. NeIt

Especially on hot summer Sumdays. Hot Summer Sunday. A. L. Hendricks. PBCV

Especially When the October Wind. Dylan Thomas. AngWe; LiTB; MeMBP; MoAB; MoBrPo; OBWVE; OxAEP-2; OxBTC

Essay. Hayden Carruth. FoLa

Essay. Bernadette Mayer. UL

Essay on Criticism. Pope. PoEL-3
   Sels.
   Art of Poetry, The. ECEV
   "Avoid extremes; and shun the fault of such." FHYEP
   "But most by numbers judge a poet's song." ECEV; EPCY; FaBoUs; FHYEP; HAP; NIP; Poetr
   "But true expression, like th' unchanging sun." FHYEP
   "But where's the man who counsel can bestow." OxAEP-1
   "First follow Nature, and your judgment frame." EPCY; FHYEP; HAP
   "Hear how Timotheous varied lays surprise." EPCY
   "In wit, as nature, what affects our hearts." HAP
   "Little learning is a dangerous thing, A." EBEvV; HAP; HoPM; PoLF; TrGrPo
      (Little Learning, A.) ChTr; ImPo; LiTB; NOBE
   "Pride, Malice, Folly, against Dryden rose." EPCY
   "Some are bewildered in the maze of schools." OBSV
   "Some beauties yet no precepts can declare." HAP
   "Some ne'er advance a judgment of their own." OBSV
   "Some to conceit alone their tast confine." EPCY
   "Some to Conceit alone their taste confine." OxAEP-1
   "Still green with bays each ancient altar stands." EPCY
   "Such shameless bards we have; and yet 'tis true." OBSV
   "'Tis hard to say, if greater want of skill." HAP; NAEL-1; OAEL-1; OxAEP-1; TFi
   "True ease in writing comes from art, not chance." HAP; InPK; PrIm; TrGrPo
      (Sound and Sense.) SoSe; UnPo
   "Unhappy wit, like most mistaken things." EPCY

Essay on Epic Poetry, An, *sels.* William Hayley.
   "Apart, and on the sacred hill retired." EPCY

Essay on Friendship, An. J. D. McClatchy. BAP-91

Essay on Lunch. Walker Gibson. NYBP

Essay on Man. *Unknown.* PoToHe

Essay on Man, An, *sels.* Pope.
   "All are but parts of one stupendous whole." FHYEP; WGRP
   "All Nature is but art, unknown to thee." ECEV
   "Awake, my St. John! leave all meaner things." NAEL-1; NoP; PoEL-3
      (Wild Garden, The.) PrIm, *ll.* 1–16
   "Behold the child, by Nature's kindly law." ECEV; FaBoRV
   "Bliss of man, The (could pride that blessing find)." NOEC; NU

Faith. WGRP
"Far as creation's ample range extends." ECEV; FM
"For forms of government let fools contest." ECEV
"Honor and shame from no condition rise." TrGrPo
"Hope humbly then; with trembling pinions trust." EBEvV; TrGrPo
"Know then thyself, presume not God to scan." BLPL, *ll.* 1–18; EBEvV;
  ECEV, *ll.* 1–18; FHYEP; LiTB, (*fr.* II *and* IV); NAEL-1; NOEC, *ll.*
  1–18; NoP; OAEL-1, *ll.* 1–18; PoEL-3; TFi, *ll.* 1–42; TrGrPo,
  ll. 1–18
  (Know Then Thyself). ImPo, *ll.* 1–66
  (Know Thyself). NOBE, *ll.* 1–18
  (Man). PrIm, *ll.* 1–18
  (Proper Study of Mankind, The). 09FiP, *ll.* 1–30
"Lo, the poor Indian! whose untutor'd mind." NU
"Look round our world; behold the chain of love." FHYEP; OBD
"Nor think, in nature's state they blindly trod." OAEL-1
"Placed on this isthmus of a middle state." WeW
Soul's Calm Sunshine, The. FaBoRV
"What if the foot, ordain'd the dust to tread." FaBoPV
"What would this Man? Now upward will he soar." HeIP
"Whate'er the passion — knowledge, fame, or pelf." TrGrPo
"What's fame? A fancied life in others' breath." FHYEP
Essay on Marriage., *sels.* Anne Finch.
"O, love, in your sweet name enough." FaBoTw
Essay on Memory., *sels.* Robert David Fitzgerald.
"Rain in my ears: impatiently there raps." CBAP
Essay on Meter. Bernard Keith. PRA
Essay on Poetry, *sels.* John Sheffield, Duke of Buckingham and Normandy.
  On Writing for the Stage. FaBoUs
Essay on Psychiatrists, *sels.* Robert Pinsky.
Dionysus as Psychiatrist. HCAP
Invocation. NoAM
Mad, The. NoAM
Peroration, Concerning Genius. NoAM
Proposition. HCAP; NoAM
Some Terms. HCAP
Their Patients. NoAM
Their Philistinism Considered. NoAM
Their Seriousness, with Further Comparisons. NoAM
Their Speech, Compared with Wisdom and Poetry. NoAM; PoA
Essay on Satire, Particularly on The Dunciad, An, *sels.* Walter Harte.
"Above all flattery, all thirst of gain." EPCY
"In Albion then, with equal lustre bright." EPCY
Essay on the Different Styles of Poetry, The, *sels.* Thomas Parnell.
Essay on the Fleet Riding in the Downes, An. "J. D." CoMu
Essay on Translated Verse, An, *sels.* Earl of Roscommon.
"Each poet with a different talent writes." EPCY; FaBoUs
"Have we forgot how Raphael's numerous prose." EPCY
Essay on Woman, An. Mary Leapor. ECWP; NOEC
Essay upon Satire, An. *At. to* John Sheffield, Duke of Buckingham and
  Normandy John Sheffield. APAS
Esse. Czeslaw Milosz. TOF
Essence Is Not in the Living, The. Mairtin O Direain, *tr. by* Douglas Sealy
  and Tomás MacSiomóin. BiHa
Essence of Existence, The. Jack Kerouac. *Fr.* Mexico City Blues. NeAP
Essence of orchids in her tumbled hair, a goddess of spring. A Song of
  Chang Ching-yüan Picking Lotus Flowers. Wen T'ing-yün, *tr. fr.*
  Chinese by William R. Schultz. SuSp
Essential oils — are wrung. Emily Dickinson. AmPP
Essential poem at the center of things, The. A Primitive like an Orb.
  Wallace Stevens. NOBA
Essentials. Samuel Greenberg. LiTA
Essex Regiment March. George Edward Woodberry. PAH
Essie Parrish in New York. Essie Parrish, *tr. fr. Kashia Pomo Indian by*
  George Quasha. STP
Está Muy Caliente. George Bowering. MoCV
"Established" is a good word, much used in garden books. Time. Mary
  Ursula Bethell. FaBoWP
Establishment has taken to the hills. First Letter to an Irish Novelist. Roy
  McFadden. PNI
Establishment of peace in our hearts and on earth. Amen. (*LL*) As we are
  together, praying for peace, let us be truly with each other. Thich Nhat
  Hanh. EaPr
Estat ai en greu cossirier. Beatrice, Countess de Die, *tr. fr. Provençal by*
  Paul Blackburn. ErPo
Estate, The, *sels.* Charles Brasch.
"What have you seen on the summits, the peaks that plunge their." PeNZ
Estate and an earldom at seventy-four, An! Horace Walpole. FaBoEE
Estelí/ this mountain town means something. Resurrection. Joy Harjo.
  HATNAP
Estella, Estella, they're cooking up paella. Song in Praise of Paella. C. W.
  V. Wordsworth. FiBHP

Esteville fire begins to burn. On Summer. George Moses Horton. AAP
Esther [a Young Man's Tragedy], *sels.* Wilfrid Scawen Blunt.
"He who has once been happy is for aye." OBMV; OBNC; TrGrPo
  (With Esther.) OBEV
I Will Not Tell the Secrets. Son
"When I hear laughter from a tavern door." OBMV; TrGrPo
Esther. Helen Hunt Jackson. AmWP
Esther K. Comes to America: 1931. Jerome Rothenberg. NNaP
Esther's Tomcat. Ted Hughes. OFC; OxBC; SoCa
Esthete in Harlem. Langston Hughes. BPo
Esthétique du Mal. Wallace Stevens. LiTM
Sels.
"He was at Naples writing letters home." CMoP; MeMAP; NOBA
"How red the rose that is the soldier's wound." CMoP; NOBA
"Life is a bitter aspic. We are not." CMoP
"Sun, in clownish yellow, but not a clown, The." NOBA
Esthonian Bridal Song. Johann Gottfried von Herder, *tr. fr. German by* W.
  Taylor. AWP
Estrich, thou feathered fool and easy prey. Lucasta's Fan, with a Looking-
  Glass in It. Richard Lovelace. CaPo
Estuarial Republic, The. Douglas Dunn. FaBoMo
Estuary. Ted Walker. NYBP
Esyllt. Glyn Jones. AngWe; OBWVE
Et Cetera. Léon Damas, *tr. fr. French by* Ellen Conroy Kennedy. NegPo
Et cetera. (*LL*) The Cheerful Girls at Smiller's Bar. Jack A. Mapanje.
  HBAPE; PeSAV
Et Cetera. Dee Lawrence Walker. GoYe
Et cætera, et cætera, et cætera. (*LL*) An Austrian Army. *At. to* Alaric
  Alexander Watts. FaBoCo; FiBHP; NOBL; PeLV
Et in Arcadia Ego. W. H. Auden. CMoP
Et Incarnatus Est. William Langland. *Fr.* Vision of Piers Plowman, The.
  NOBE, Passus II (C *text*)
Et Quid Amabo Nisi Quod Aenigma Est. Stephen Sandy. NYBP
État, *sels.* Anne-Marie Albiach, *tr. fr. French by* Paul Auster.
"Of the unended in the speed of." PBWP
Etc. (*LL*) Frog Went a-Courtin.' *Unknown.* BLPA
Etcetera. (*LL*) Position. Léon Damas. NegPo
Etched Away From. Paul Celan, *tr. fr. German by* Michael Hamburger.
  OBVE
Etchings. James William Chichetto. BTR
Eternal City, The. A. R. Ammons. CAPP; HCAP
Eternal City stands, The. (*LL*) City of God. Samuel Johnson. WGRP
Eternal Contour. Florida Watts Smyth. GoYe
Eternal Father, Strong to Save. William Whiting. FaPoR; NOCV
Eternal Female groan'd, The! it was heard over all the earth. A Song of
  Liberty. Blake. EnRP
Eternal gates' terrific porter lifted the northern bar. The Secrets of the
  Earth. Blake. *Fr.* Book of Thel, The. EnRP; MeMBP; NAEL-2;
  NOBE; NoP; OAEL-2; OBNC; PoE; PoEL-4; TEP
Eternal God (for whom whoever dare). Upon the Translation of the Psalms
  by Sir Philip Sidney, and the countess of Pembroke His Sister. John
  Donne. EPCY
Eternal God, How They're Increased. Cotton Mather. AH
Eternal God! maker of all. The Book. Henry Vaughan. AngWe; GeHe;
  JCP; SeCV-1
Eternal God, our life is but. "Yehoash," *tr. fr. Yiddish by* Isidore
  Goldstick. TrJP
Eternal God, Whose Power Upholds. Henry Hallam Tweedy. AH
Eternal God Whose Searching Eye Doth Scan. Edwin McNeill Poteat.
  TrPWD
Eternal Goodness, The. (O friends! with whom my feet have trod.)
  Whittier. PFP; WGRP
Sels.
"And Thou, O Lord! by whom are seen." TrPWD
"I know not what the future hath." BLRP, *abr.*; NOCV
Eternal Image, The. Ruth Pitter. MoBrPo; OxBTC
Eternal Jew, The. Jacob Cohen, *tr. fr. Hebrew by* I. M. Lask. TrJP
Eternal King, grant me true quietness. Angilbert's Prayer. Angilbert, *tr. fr.*
  Latin by Helen Waddell. MLL
Eternal Kinship, The. Maurice E. Peloubet. GoYe
Eternal Light! Thomas Binney. NOCV; WGRP
Eternal lightning of Lenin's bones, The. (*LL*) The Skeleton of the Future.
  "Hugh MacDiarmid." MoBrPo; OBMV; OBTV
Eternal Lord! Eased of a Cumbrous Load. Michelangelo, *tr. fr. Italian by*
  Wordsworth. TrPWD
Eternal Love, Maintain thy life in me. (*LL*) Leave me, O love which
  reachest but to dust. Sir Philip Sidney. ESo
Eternal Love, maintain thy life in me. (*LL*) Love Me, O Love. Sir Philip
  Sidney. HeIP
Eternal Masculine. William Rose Benét. AWP; MoAmPo

Even the bad news came slowly and was afraid. Washington Heights, 1959. Michael C. Blumenthal. HCAP

Even the barnacle has certain rights. This Octopus Exploits Women. James Fenton. CBNP; NoAM

Even the dirt kept breathing a small breath. (LL) Root Cellar. Theodore Roethke. AmPP; AnAmPo; BoNaP; HelP; InPK; NoP; PPP; VCAP

Even the dissident ones speak. America. John Newlove. NOBC

Even the liveliest of us had. Another and Another and. Theodore Weiss. DiPo

Even the lone man. Brazil. Tony Harrison. Fr. Sentences. OBTV

Even the long-dead are willing to move. Gentle Communion. Pat Mora. AfAz; NIP

Even the night will blossom as the rose. (LL) On Growing Old. John Masefield. CMoP; ImPo; LiTB; LiTM; MoAB; MoBrPo; PoLF; PoRA

Even the rainbow has a body. The Rainbow. D. H. Lawrence. NTP

Even the sky here in Connecticut has it. A Winter without Snow. J. D. McClatchy. FYAP

Even the spring water. The Cutting Edge. Philip Levine. NYBP

Even the sun-clouds this morning cannot manage such skirts. Poppies in October. Sylvia Plath. FaBoWP; HCAP; LCAP; NoAM

Even the sun, still warm. August/Fresno 1973. Roberta Spear. AmPA

Even the train is taller than those shacks. Homecoming. John Thompson. MAT

Even the walls are flowing, even the ceiling. Variation on Heraclitus. Louis MacNeice. MoP; NoAM

Even the Whales. Tom Matthews. PNI

Even the whales now. Even the Whales. Tom Matthews. PNI

Even the worst intelligence must needs ride. Sir Gelli to R.S. Roland Mathias. AngWe

Even then I said. Antiphilus, tr. fr. Greek by Alan Marshfield. GrAn

Even There. Lyn Lifshin. IHMS

Even this late it happens. The Coming of Light. Mark Strand. HCAP

Even this love's heat must be its curb and rein. (LL) Cantica: Our Lord Christ: Of Order. At. to St. Francis of Assisi Saint Francis of Assisi, also at. to Jacopone da Todi. AWP; OBVE

"Even this shall pass away." (LL) Even This Shall Pass Away. Theodore Tilton. BLPA; WGRP

Even This Shall Pass Away. Theodore Tilton. BLPA; WGRP

Even this suburb has overcome Death. Easter. Howard Nemerov. NoP

Even though he lies underground. Erucius, tr. fr. Greek by Peter Levi. GrAn

Even though home was set behind me. (LL) Ropley District. Sebastian Barry. IB

Even though my hands/ are rough from much rice-pounding. Unknown, tr. fr. Japanese by Kenneth Yasuda. BoWoP

Even time, An. What I Do. Denise Riley. NBrP

Even to each other. Merely to be mere, ly to be. (LL) Song Form. Amiri Baraka. SOTW; TTTS

Even to say good-bye. Come Back Safely. Meena Alexander, tr. fr. Armenian by Diana Der Hovanessian. VBLP

Even to the children/ on the disenchanted shore. The Blade of Grass Sings to the River. Leah Goldberg, tr. by Robert Friend. Fr. Songs of the Stream. TrJP

Even tonight and I need to take a walk and clear. Poem about My Rights. June Jordan. GLP; NoAM

Even when a man has earned much. Children. Pantiyan Arivutai Nampi, tr. fr. Tamil by A. K. Ramanujan. PLW

Even when black Saturn. Pari's Green Land, Remembered. Kapilar, tr. fr. Tamil by A. K. Ramanujan. PLW

Even when I cross those places. Six on the Desert Ways. Otalantaiyar, tr. fr. Tamil by A. K. Ramanujan. PLW

Even when I fall asleep early. Insomnia. Lu Yu, tr. fr. Chinese by Kenneth Rexroth. OHMPC

Even while he sung Sir Proteus rose. Thomas Love Peacock. Fr. Sir Proteus, a Satirical Ballad. CBNP

Even while the blue light darts into his room. The Blue Light. Tom Dent. UL

Even whilst I watch him I am remembering. To T. A. R. H. Stephen Spender. PeHV

Even with its own ax[e] to grind, sometimes. The Mind, Intractable Thing. Marianne Moore. LiTM; NYBP

Even with the good knight Charlemain. (LL) Ballad of the Lords of Old Time. Villon. AWP; PeVV

Evenen in the Village. William Barnes. EBVV

Evening. Richard Aldington. MoBrPo

Evening. Joanna Baillie. Fr. Summer Day, A. ECWP

Evening, after Sappho. Byron. Fr. Don Juan. TrGrPo

Evening. John Clare. NOBVV

Evening. Charles Cotton. PoEL-3; WiR

Evening. Emily Dickinson. See She sweeps with many-colored brooms.

Evening. Hilda Doolittle ("H. D."). CMoP; FaBoMo; VGW; WPE

Evening. Andreas Gryphius, tr. fr. German by George C. Schoolfield. GePo

Evening. Frances Horovitz. PWE

Evening. John Keble. TrPWD

Evening. King D. Kuka. VoR

Evening. W. S. Merwin. NAAL-2

Evening. Thomas Miller. OxBChV

Evening. Edith Sitwell. MoBS

Evening. James Stephens. MoBrPo

Evening. Unknown. BoTP

Evening. Victor van Vriesland, tr. fr. Dutch by Adriaan J. Barnouw. TrJP

Evening. James Wright. NOBA; NYBP; PrIm

Evening — another evening — and the lights flare. Thomas McGrath. Fr. Letter to an Imaginary Friend, Part Two. NNaP

Evening! A flight of pigeons in clear sky! The Flute; a Pastoral. José-Maria de Heredia, tr. fr. French by H. J. C. Grierson. AWP

Evening Alone at Bunyah, sels. Les A. Murray. "There is a glow in the kitchen window now." FaBoMA

Evening, An. William Allingham. EnLoPo; NOBVV

Evening, An. Robert Mezey. NaP

Evening; an Elegy. Horace Smith. BXAP

Evening, and Maidens. William Barnes. OBEV

Evening and morning old Platthis kept. Leonidas, tr. fr. Greek by Kenneth Rexroth. PGA

Evening, as slow thy placid shades descend. William Lisle Bowles. NOEC

Evening at [or on] the Farm. John Townsend Trowbridge. FaPON; GN

Evening before Rain. L. A. G. Strong. OxBTC

Evening by the Sea. Swinburne. FaBoPP

Evening calm envelops the cold city. Listening to the Washblock in the Moonlight. Liu Ch'ang-ch'ing, tr. fr. Chinese by Dell R. Hales. SuSp

Evening came, a child was missing. Little Bell. Mary E. Tucker. CBWP-1

Evening came, a paw, to the gray hut by the river. Fall Journey. William Stafford. NaP

Evening clouds dispersed. Tune: "Joy All Under Heaven" — Sunset on the Western Hill. Hsu Tsai-ssu, tr. fr. Chinese by Sherwin S. S. Fu. SuSp

Evening Comes. Li Shang-yin, tr. fr. Chinese by Kenneth Rexroth. OHMPC

Evening comes and sorrow crowds my mind. Kasa no Iratsume, tr. fr. Japanese by Kenneth Rexroth and Ikuko Atsumi. WPJ

Evening comes. My mind is troubled. Evening Comes. Li Shang-yin, tr. fr. Chinese by Kenneth Rexroth. OHMPC

Evening comes, the fields are still, The. The First-born Star. Matthew Arnold. Fr. Bacchanalia; or, The New Age. FaBoRV

Evening Contemplation. George Washington Doane. AH; BLPA; BLPL; FaBoBe

Evening Dance of the Grey Flies. P. K. Page. NOBC

Evening Darkens Over, The. Robert Bridges. CMoP; HAP; NOBVV; PoEL-5; SCGP

Evening Ebb. Robinson Jeffers. NoAM

Evening falls on the smoky walls. Ballad of the Londoner. James Elroy Flecker. EnLoPo

Evening: for Chang Chi and Chou K'uang. Han Yü, tr. fr. Chinese by A. C. Graham. PLT

Evening, Gertrude. Anne Batten Cristall. ECWP

Evening. Grandmother scolding the white chickens. Childhood. Jean Joubert, tr. fr. French. TSaS, tr. by Denise Levertov

Evening Harbour. Tom Paulin.

Evening has brought its. Witnesses. W. S. Merwin. LCAP

Evening Hawk. Robert Penn Warren. NAAL-2; VCAP

Evening Hour. Robert Penn Warren. MT

Evening Hymn. William Henry Furness. FaBoBe

Evening Hymn, sels. George Macdonald. "O God, whose daylight leadeth down." TrPWD

Evening Hymn, An. Thomas Ken. OxBChV

Evening Hymn in the Hovels. Francis Lauderdale Adams. OxBS

Evening in Paradise. Milton. See Now came still evening on, and twilight gray.

Evening in the Garden Clear after Rain. Ch'u Ch'uang I, tr. fr. Chinese. OHMPC

Evening in the Sanitarium. Louise Bogan. FaBoWP; FYAP; IHMS; NALW; TwCP

Evening in the yard. Peyanar, tr. fr. Tamil by A. K. Ramanujan. Fr. Seven Said by the Foster-Mother. PLW

Evening is clogged with gnats as the light fails. Alceste in the Wilderness. Anthony Hecht. PoA

Evening is coming, The. Bed-time. Thomas Hood. BoTP

Evening is coming, the red sun pours. From Monte Pincio. Bjørnstjerne Bjørnson, *tr. fr. Norwegian by* Philip L. Miller. RiWo

Evening is tawny on the old. Gold. Martin Armstrong. BoTP

Evening Knell, The. John Fletcher. *See* Shepherds all, and maidens fair.

Evening lapses. No pity or pain, the badgered. From Government Buildings. Denis Devlin. IPY

Evening Lights on the River. Chiang Shih-ch'üan, *tr. fr. Chinese by* Kenneth Rexroth. OHMPC

Evening Lull, An. Walt Whitman. NAAL-1

Evening Meal in the Twentieth Century. John Holmes. AiP

Evening Musicale. Phyllis McGinley. OBAL; Son

Evening of Russian Poetry, An. Vladimir Nabokov. NYBP

Evening of the Mind, The. Donald Justice. VCAP

Evening of the Whirlwind. Amir Gilboa, *tr. fr. Hebrew by* Ruth Finer Mintz. MHP

Evening on Calais Beach. Wordsworth. *See* It Is a Beauteous Evening, [Calm and Free].

Evening on the Broads. Swinburne. TEP

Evening on the Farm. John Townsend Trowbridge. *See* Over the hill the farm-boy goes.

Evening on the Potomac. Richard Hovey. AnAmPo

Evening Out, The. Ogden Nash. MoAmPo

Evening outdoors is only a larger lobby. One-Night Expensive Hotel. Ronald G. Everson. NOBC

Evening Prayer. Arthur Fitger, *tr. fr. German by* Jethro Bithell. AWP

Evening Prayer. Thomas Ken. *See* Glory to Thee, My God, This Night.

Evening Prayer. Thomas Merton. ChIV-1

Evening Prayer. H. Cordelia Ray. CBWP-3

Evening Prayer. *Unknown, tr. fr. Hebrew by* Solomon Solis-Cohen. TrJP

Evening Prayer, An. Laura E. Kendall. BLRP

Evening Primrose. John Clare. CH; TrGrPo

Evening Quatrains. Charles Cotton. *See* Day's grown old, the fainting sun, The.

Evening Quiet. Jovan Hristic, *tr. fr. Serbo-Croatian by* Charles Simic. HSix

Evening red and morning gray. *Unknown.* FaBoBe; FaBoUs; FaBoVe; OxNR

Evening Rendezvous. Cheng Min, *tr. fr. Chinese by* Kenneth Rexroth *and* Ling Chung. WPC

Evening Revery, An, *sels.* Bryant.

Evening river carries no sound, The. Black River — Summer 1981. Maurice Kenny. BCF; ETG

Evening Schoolboys. John Clare. OBF

Evening Shade. John Leland. *See* Day Is Past and Gone, The.

Evening Song. Cecil Frances Alexander. OHIP

Evening Song. John Fletcher. *See* Shepherds all, and maidens fair.

Evening Song. Edith King. BoTP

Evening Song. Sidney Lanier. AnAmPo; UnPo

Evening Song. Jean Toomer. BPo; CDC

Evening Song. Philipp von Zesen, *tr. fr. German by* George C. Schoolfield. GePo

Evening Star, The. *Aborigine Oral Tradition, tr. by* R. M. Berndt. *Fr.* Moon-Bone Song [*or* Cycle]. CBAP; WTO

Evening Star. George Barker. ErPo

Evening Star, The. John Clare. *See* Hesperus! the day is gone.

Evening Star, The. Rainer Maria Rilke, *tr. fr. German by* Randall Jarrell. ArNa

Evening Star, enemy of lovers, why. Evening Star. George Barker. ErPo

Evening star sparks, The. Friday Evenings. George Charlton. PWE

Evening star that in the vaulted skies, The. Verse Written in the Album of Mademoiselle. Pierre Dalcour, *tr. fr. French by* Langston Hughes. PoNe; TTY

Evening star that softly sheds, The. Refracted Lights. Celia Parker Wooley. WGRP

Evening Sun, The. Emily Brontë. CH

Evening sun-beams threw their golden light, The. The Suttee. Thomas Skinner. OBTV

Evening sun sets beyond the western ranges, The. Spending the Night at the Hillside Lodge of Master Yeh and Waiting for My Friend Ting. Meng Hao Jan, *tr. fr. Chinese by* Daniel Bryant. SuSp

Evening swallows keep twittering by my curtain. Late Spring. Yüan Chen, *tr. fr. Chinese by* Dell R. Hales. SuSp

Evening, the heather, The. Invasion Summer. Laurie Lee. OxBSP

Evening Thought, An. Jupiter Hammon. PoNe

Evening traffic homeward burns. Before Disaster. Yvor Winters. HoPM

Evening Twilight. Heine, *tr. by* John Todhunter. *Fr.* North Sea, The. AWP

Evening View as the Snow Clears. Chia Tao, *tr. fr. Chinese by* Stephen Owen. SuSp

Evening View at River Pavilion, Inviting Guest. Po Chü-i, *tr. fr. Chinese by* Irving Y. Lo. SuSp

Evening View at the Western Palace. Liu Sha-ho, *tr. fr. Chinese. Fr.* Two Poems of Peking. LHF, *tr. by* Hualing Nieh

Evening Walk. Sonja Åkesson, *tr. fr. Swedish by* Joanna Bankier. WPOW

Evening Walk, An, *sels.* Wordsworth. "Dear Brook, farewell! To-morrow's noon again." EnRP

Evening Walk in Bengal, An. Reginald Heber. OBTV

Evening was in the wood, louring with storm. Haunted. Siegfried Sassoon. CMoP

Evening-Watch, The. Henry Vaughan *and* Thomas Stanley. ESCV

Evening Waterfall. Carl Sandburg. ImPo

Evening When the Full Moon Rose as the Sun Set, An. Robert Bly. ArNa

Evening without Angels. Wallace Stevens. VGW

Evenings ever more willing lapse into my world's evening. Denis Devlin. *Fr.* Memoirs of a Turcoman Diplomat. IPY; NOIV

Evenings I hear. A Plague of Starlings. Robert Hayden. NoAM

Evening's late November, clouds hump and streak, The. Wild Night at Treweithan. Gwyn Williams. AngWe

Evening's Love, An, *sels.* Dryden.
    After the Pangs of a Desperate Lover. ELP; PeLV
    (Love's Fancy.) ErPo
    "Calm was the even, and clear [*or* cleer] was the sky." FF; SeCV-2
    Damon and Celimena. InvP
    "You charm'd me not with that fair face." SeCV-2

Evenings/ When the house is quiet. Setting the Table. Dorothy Aldis. FaPON

Eveningsong. Ramona Wilson. VoR

Eveningsong 2. Ramona Wilson. VoR

Evenlode, The. Hilaire Belloc. OxAEP-2

Evensong. Carleton Drewry. GoYe

Evensong. Paul Gerhardt, *tr. fr. German by* Ingrid Waløe-Engel. GePo

Evensong. C. S. Lewis. TIRV; TrCP

Evensong. Robert Louis Stevenson. TrPWD

Event, The. Rita Dove. NoAM

Event, The. T. Sturge Moore. OBMV

Event. Sylvia Plath. NOBA

Event, An. Edward Field. CoAP

Event Which Makes No News, An. Shinkawa Kazue, *tr. fr. Japanese by* Kenneth Rexroth *and* Ikuko Atsumi. WPJ

Event worse than the omen, Th'; as his bride. The Death of Eurydice and Orpheus' Journey to Hell. Ovid, *tr. by* George Sandys. *Fr.* Metamorphoses. JCP

Eventful, should supply her with a theme. (*LL*) Yardley Oak. William Cowper. NOEC

Eventual Proteus. Margaret Atwood. MoCV; VBLP

Ever. (*LL*) A Life's Parallels. Christina Rossetti. MeMBP; NAEL-2; PoEL-5

Ever been kidnapped. Kidnap Poem. Nikki Giovanni. BPo; GOYP; Poetr; TAP

Ever, ever come? (*LL*) Beyond the Hunting Woods. Donald Justice. NYBP

Ever, ever in unanimous voice we drift. The Highest Wind That Ever Blew: Homage to Louis. Fred Chappell. Jaz

Ever faithful, ever sure. (*LL*) Let Us with a Gladsome Mind. Milton. WGRP

Ever-Fixed Mark, An. Kingsley Amis. ErPo; MoP; NoAM; PeHV

Ever let the Fancy roam. The Realm of Fancy. Keats. *Fr.* Fancy. EnRP; GTBS; GTBS-P; OBEV

Ever moulded by the lips of man. (*LL*) To Virgil [*or* Vergil]. Tennyson. AWP; ChTr; EBVVPR; GTBS-P; MeMBP; NoP; OAEL-2; PoEL-5

Ever myn happe is slack and slo in commyng. Petrarch, *tr. fr. Italian by* Sir Thomas Wyatt. OBVE

Ever Notice How It Is with Women? Margaret Randall. AIW

Ever or never. (*LL*) The Arraignment of a Lover. George Gascoigne. AAS

Ever Present. Philip Ayres. OxBSP

Ever since boyhood it has been my joy. The Everlasting Mercy. J. C. Squire. BXAP

Ever since I realized there was someone callt. No More Love Poems #1. Ntozake Shange. *Fr.* For Colored Girls Who Have Considered Suicide When the Rainbow Is Enuf. BlSi

Ever since my daughters started to walk. The Green Tree. James Reiss. AmPA

Every October millions of little fish come along the shore. Birds and Fishes. Robinson Jeffers. NAAL-2; NoP

Every old man I see. Memory of my Father. Patrick Kavanagh. InPS; RB

Every one of these, stood, separate, upright, above ground. David Jones. *Fr.* In Parenthesis. PeECV

Every one of us saw it. Silence. Alvin Aubert. MT

Every path a green lady. Four Songs from the Book of Samuel. Eli W. Mandel. MoCV

Every peak is a crater. This is the law of volcanoes. Adrienne Rich. *Fr.* Twenty-one Love Poems. GLP; NAAL-2; NALW; NoAM

Every planet is a small plane. The Plane: Earth. Sun-Ra. PoBA

Every rose on the little tree. The Little Rose Tree. Rachel Field. FaPON

Every Second Thought., *sels.* Theodore Weiss. "Grey and dankish thing, A." DiPo

Every Shuiler Is Christ. Joseph Campbell. TIRV

Every Single Night. J. P. Ward. AngWe

Every stance seemed crooked. He had. Saint Ras. Anthony McNeill. PBCV

Every summer. Lemonade Stand. Myra Cohn Livingston. TLR

Every Sunday she prepared the brown oak table. The Poet of the Mountains. Thomas McCarthy. CIP

Every Thing. Harold Monro. MoBrPo

Every thread of summer is at last unwoven. Puella Parvula. Wallace Stevens. HCAP; LCAP

Every Thursday morning. The Dustman. Clive Sansom. BoTP

Every Time I Climb a Tree. David McCord. NTCP; PDV

Every time I come to town. *Unknown.* RoPo

Every time I smell Lava soap it is 1948. The Story of Lava. David Allan Evans. Poetsp

Every time I write a letter. Writing Letters. Rodney Bennett. BoTP

Every time Lady Lowbodice swoons. Lady Lowbodice. *Unknown.* FaBoBl; PeLi; PeLV

Every time the bucks went clattering. Earthy Anecdote. Wallace Stevens. CMoP; GoJo; RB; RFM; SAmP

Every time you hear me sing this song. The Railroad Blues. *Unknown.* AmFP

Every towered city, every street. Exodus from a Renaissance Gallery. Ellen M. V. Acton. GoYe

Every Town a Home Town. Kaniyan Punkunran, *tr. fr. Tamil by* A. K. Ramanujan. PLW

Every town with black Catholics has a St. Peter Claver's. St. Peter Claver. Toi Derricotte. PBCAP

Every valley drinks. Winter Rain. Christina Rossetti. BoNaP; WiR

Every Where and Every When. Arthur Sze. OpBo

Every wild she-bird has nest and mate in the warm April weather. The Virgin Martyr. Ada Cambridge. NOBAu

Every year in June — up here, that's the month for lilacs. What the Light Was Like. Amy Clampitt. FaBoWP

Every year men harvest grapes, not seeing. Macedonius, *tr. fr. Greek by* Adrian Wright. GrAn

Every year they try to rob us. Berlin Metro. Desmond O'Grady. BiHa

Every year without knowing it I have passed the day. For the Anniversary of My Death. W. S. Merwin. CoAP; HCAP; InPK; NAAL-2; NaP; NOBA; Poetr; VCAP

Everybody but Me. Margaret Goss Burroughs. BlSi

Everybody dancin'. Cakewalkman. Sam Abrams. UL

Everybody else, then, going. Exeunt Omnes. Thomas Hardy. FaBoVe; UV

Everybody knew Clifton Cockerell was not half bright. The Beating. T. R. Hummer. MT

Everybody knows her, for they see her every day. Pay Your Debts. Mrs. Henry Linden. CBWP-4

Everybody loved Chick Lorimer in our town. Gone. Carl Sandburg. NOBA

Everybody Loves Saturday Night. *Unknown.* SWP

Everybody Says. Dorothy Aldis. FaPON

Everybody stop and listen to my ditty. Prince of Wales' Marriage. *Unknown.* CoMu

Everybody wants to know why I sing the blues. Why I Sing the Blues. B. B. King. MAT

Everybody who has a baby thinks everybody who hasn't a baby. Did Someone Say "Babies"? Ogden Nash. OxBM

Everybody who's anybody longs to be a tree. Horse and Tree. Rita Dove. TRP

"Everybody Works but Father" as W. S. Gilbert Would Have Written It. Arthur G. Burgoyne. FiBHP

Everybody's mad about ya. *Unknown.* FaBoEH

Everyday, Dietrich teaches a mambo class of hillbilly patients. At the Treatment Center. Jerome Sala. UL

Everyday mind is Buddha's mind. (*LL*) Looking at Your Empty Plate. Thich Nhat Hanh. EaPr

Everyday Things. Jean Ayer. BoTP

Everymaid. John Oxenham. TrCP

Everyman. (I pray you all give [*or* gyve] your audience [*or* audyence].) *Unknown.* NAEL-1; NAWM-1; OAEL-1; OxBLMV; PoEL-1

Sels. "On thee thou must take a long journey." OBD

Everyman. Siegfried Sassoon. MoBrPo

Everyman/ Preacher or lecher, saint or sot. Robert Francis. *Fr.* Epitaphs. CRP

Everyman's Library. John Ashbery. NoP

Everyone at Lake Kearney had a nickname. Sway. Louis Simpson. NoAM

Everyone else slept and we. Heat. Jim Powell. PRA

Everyone, everyone went away today. Presences. Donald Justice. CAPP

Everyone gets junk mail, a bill, a notice. Another Letter to Lord Byron. David R. Slavitt. SM

Everyone grows younger; my thinning hair. Figures of Authority. Edward Watkins. NYBP

Everyone grumbled. The sky was grey [*or* gray]. Daddy Fell into the Pond. Alfred Noyes. FaPON; PDV

Everyone had turned off their televisions. Petroglyph. Joy Harjo. NAmP90

Everyone has only one leg. Great Infirmities. Charles Simic. AnAn

Everyone in me is a bird. In Celebration of My Uterus. Anne Sexton. CAPP; CrSp; NALW

Everyone in the World. Joel Dailey. UL

Everyone is asleep. Enomoto Seifu-Jo, *tr. fr. Japanese by* Kenneth Rexroth *and* Ikuko Atsumi. WPJ

Everyone is gone. Everyone. Blue. Christopher Gilbert. *Fr.* Beginning by Example. FYAP

Everyone Knows the World Is Ending. Alice Fulton. EOEF

Everyone Knows Whom the Saved Envy. James Galvin. FoLa

Everyone makes love to their bereft & go. Bernadette Mayer. VBLP

Everyone Sang. Siegfried Sassoon. EBEvV; FaBV; GGP; GTBS-P; InvP; MoBrPo; NAEL-2; NoAM; NOBE; NSI; OBEV; OBWP; OxBSP; OxBTC; PAW; TrJP

Everyone silent, moving. . . . Take my hand. Speak to me. (*LL*) Effort at Speech between Two People. Muriel Rukeyser. FYAP; MoAB; MoAmPo; Poetr; TrGrPo; TrJP; TwCP

Everyone speaks of the sad autumn with a heavy heart. Sounds of Autumn. Lu Yu, *tr. fr. Chinese by* Irving Y. Lo. SuSp

Everyone suddenly burst out singing. Everyone Sang. Siegfried Sassoon. EBEvV; FaBV; GGP; GTBS-P; InvP; MoBrPo; NAEL-2; NoAM; NOBE; NSI; OBEV; OBWP; OxBSP; OxBTC; PAW; TrJP

Everyone thinks I am poisonous. I am not. The Tarantula. Reed Whittemore. CoAP

Everyone Will Write Poetry. Branko Miljkovic, *tr. fr. Serbo-Croatian by* Charles Simic. HSix

Everyone's buys with something. My Share. Salih Bolat, *tr. fr. Turkish.* TSaS, *tr. by* Yusuf Eradam

Everyone's going to ride tomorrow. Gabriel's Blues. Calvin Forbes. PoA

Everyone's on about Walter's willy. Underneath the Archers *or* What's All This about Walter's Willy? Kit Wright. FaBoBl

Everyone's shadow is taller than really. 8 A.M. Shadows. *Unknown.* SiSoPo

Everything. Ana Blandiana. CBCK

Everything/ can be retouched. The Need for Censorship. Reiner Kunze, *tr. fr. German by* Michael Hamburger. PoSu

Everything! Counter and scales. Business Reverses. Edgar Lee Masters. ChIV-2

Everything: Eloy, Arizona, 1956. Ai. AmPA; FF

Everything fades away beyond oneself. Looking in a Mirror the Day before the Advent of Autumn. Li Yi, *tr. fr. Chinese by* William H. Nienhauser. SuSp

Everything flows. Denise Levertov. *Fr.* Olga Poems. NAAL-2

Everything has its limit, including sorrow. To Urania. Joseph Brodsky. PRA

Everything has lasted till today. The Unknown Soldier. Alun Lewis. MoBrPo

Everything I do I do for you. Julian of Norwich. Kathleen Jamie. VBLP

Everything I do is against meaning. Against Meaning. Andrei Codrescu. UL

Everything I do is stitched with its color. (*LL*) Separation. W. S. Merwin. HAP; NoP

Everything I love is near at hand. (*LL*) My Car Slides Off the Road. Sarah Gorham. VBLP

Everything in Its Place. Arthur Guiterman. NBLV; OBAL

Everything in the room was too clean. Horsechestnuts. Brendan Kennelly. PWE

Everything is Going to be All Right. Derek Mahon. PBCIP

Everything is holy. (LL) My paw is holy. James Koller. EaPr

Everything is laughing, singing. It Is a Pleasant Day. Unknown. BoTP

Everything is, once was not. Life after Death. Richard W. Thomas. PoBA

Everything Is Plundered. "Anna Akhmatova," tr. fr. Russian by Stanley Kunitz. WPOW

Everything Is Possible. Robert Pack. PPP

Everything is pure, is pure! (LL) Song of the Snow. Zalman Schneour. MHP

Everything Is Round. Gabriela Mistral, tr. fr. Spanish. PBWP, tr. by D. M. Pettinella

Everything is sexual at the beach. Concerning Unnatural Nature: An Inverted Form. Hollis Spurgeon Summers. ErPo

Everything Is Swimming. Stevie Smith. FaBoNo

Everything Is Wonderful. Jayne Cortez. AIW

Everything Juts Up in Europe. Wallace Stevens. Fr. Greenest Continent, The. CBCK

Everything lives and nothing is dead. The Fugs. Edward Sanders. PoM

Everything makes love with silence. Signs. Alejandra Pizarnik, tr. by Susan Bassnett. VBLP

Everything passes and vanishes. William Allingham. NOBVV

Everything passes away before my eyes. (LL) From the Most Distant Time. Emperor Wu of Han. OHMPC

Everything Promised Him to Me. "Anna Akhmatova," tr. fr. Russian by Jane Kenyon and Vera Dunham. ArLo

Everything shall be erased. Villa Sciarra: Rome. Christine Turner Curtis. GoYe

Everything That Acts Is Actual. Denise Levertov. NoAM

Everything that has been said for several centuries. Atlantis. John Engman. NAmP90

Everything that lives has its own proper pride. Proper Pride. D. H. Lawrence. FaBoEE

Everything they tie down with ropes. (LL) Mission Work-Boat. Unknown. NOBAu

Everything this generation has told me. (LL) Isaiah by Kerosene Lantern Light. Robert Harris. ChIV-1; NOBAu

Everything was put to use. The Seven Words. Jerzy Ficowski, tr. fr. Polish by Keith Bosley and Krystyna Wandycz. PoSu

Everything was wrong; the local slaves wore smiles. Harpers Ferry. Selden Rodman. PoNe

Everything was yellow. The Painters. Judith Hemschemeyer. Poetsp

Everything We Do. Peter Meinke. GOYP

Everything we look upon is blest. (LL) A Dialogue of Self and Soul. W. B. Yeats. CMoP; FaBoMo; LiTB; LiTM; MeMBP; MoBrPo; NAEL-2; NoAM; PoE

Everything we say. (LL) Neither war, nor cyclones, nor earthquakes. Antipater of Thessalonica. GrAn; PGA

Everything we stand up in. Spectrum. Aidan Carl Mathews. IB; PBCIP

Everything will be forsaken then. Apocrypha. János Pilinszky, tr. fr. Hungarian by Ted Hughes. PoSu

Everything's been different. The Birthday Child. Rose Fyleman. FaPON

Everything's laughter/ everything dust. Glycon, tr. fr. Greek by Peter Jay. GrAn

Everything's normal in Soweto today. Quote from the Bureau of Information, from the Argus, August 27, 1986: "The Situation in Soweto Is Not Abnormal." Mavis Smallberg. WoWa

Everything's still on down the rows of cells of beds with men/ asleep. The Great Escape. Ralph Adamo. MT

Everythng's just as it was: fine hard snow. The Guest. "Anna Akhmatova," tr. fr. Russian by Jane Kenyon and Vera Dunham. RaBo

Everywhere. Plantings. Catalina Cariaga. LoHo

Everywhere about is landscape as far as foot can feel. Homage to Paul Delvaux. Ramon Guthrie. PoE

Everywhere, everywhere. (LL) Camerados. Bayard Taylor. AnAmPo; UnPo

Everywhere, everywhere, Christmas tonight! Christmas Everywhere. Phillips Brooks. BLRP; PWR; WBLP
(Christmas Carol, A: "Everywhere, everywhere, Christmas tonight!.") OHIP

Everywhere, everywhere, following me. Camerados. Bayard Taylor. AnAmPo; UnPo

Everywhere fish wheeled and fled. Noah. Wayne Brown. PBCV

Everywhere is the green of new growth. Unknown, tr. fr. Chinook Indian. EaPr

Everywhere it is red. (LL) Celebration: Birth of a Colt. Linda Hogan. HATNAP

Everywhere on Earth, wet beginnings. Common Ground. John Daniel. FoLa

Everywhere Pregnant Women Appear. Eric Nelson. NGP

Everywhere things have been taking place. Summer. Douglas Crase. NoP

Everywoman Her Own Theology. Alicia Ostriker. CrSp

Eves Apologie. Emilia Lanier. Fr. Salve Deus Rex Judaeorum. BoWoP

Eve's Commentary. Michelene Wandor. NBrP

Eve's Daughter. Edward Rowland Sill. AnAmPo

Eve's tinted shadows slowly fill the fane. Sir Walter Scott at the Tomb of the Stuarts in St. Peter's. Richard Monckton Milnes. EBVV; OBTV

Evesong. Maureen Duffy. PeHV

Evgeny Onegin, sels. Pushkin, tr. fr. Russian by Thomas de Waal. Entering Moscow. CBCK

Eviction, The. William Allingham. Fr. Laurence Bloomfield in Ireland. BIrV; NOIV

Eviction. Lucille Clifton. NTCP

Evidence. Robert Polito. BAP-91

Evidence at the Witch Trials. James K. Baxter. OxBC

Evidence: from a Reporter's Notebook. Jonathan Aaron. BAP-91

Evidence Read at the Trial of the Knave of Hearts. "Lewis Carroll." Fr. Alice's Adventures in Wonderland. FaBoNo; GTBS-P; NOBVV; OxBoLi; PeLV

Evidently Chicken Town. John Cooper Clarke. FaBoPV

Evil. Rimbaud, tr. by Robert Lowell. Fr. Eighteen-Seventy. OBWP

Evil Color, The. Wilhelm Müller, tr. fr. German by Philip L. Miller. Fr. Beautiful Maid of the Mill, The. RiWo

Evil does not go always. Lines for a Hard Time. Gena Ford. IHMS

Evil Eye, The. John Ciardi. MoBS; NAs

Evil, if rightly understood. On the Origin of Evil. John Byrom. NOEC

Evil Is No Black Thing. Sarah Webster Fabio. PoBA

Evil Man, An! Richard Beer-Hofmann, tr. fr. German by Ludwig Lewisohn. Fr. Graf von Charolais, Der. TrJP

Evil Nigger Waits for Lightnin.' Amiri Baraka. NOBA

Evil [or Evill] spirit, your beauty, haunts me still, An. Michael Drayton. Fr. Idea. AAS; EiL; ESo; GBL; NOBE; NoSic

Evil word it is,/ This Love, An. (LL) In Memory of Radio. Amiri Baraka. NAAL-2; NeAP; NoP; PoBeRe; Poetr; PoM

Ev'n for your sake. (LL) Address to the Deil. Burns. EnRP; NOEC; OAEL-1; OxBS; PoEL-4

Ev'n God himself being pressed for my sake. (LL) The Bunch of Grapes. George Herbert. ChIV-1; ESCV; GeHe; NAEL-1; NOSC; TOF

Ev'n [or E'en or Even] like two little bank-dividing brooks [or brookes]. My Beloved Is Mine, and I Am His; He Feedeth among the Lillies. Francis Quarles. Fr. Emblems. MeLP; NOBE; OBEV; TrGrPo, abr. (Divine Rapture.) OBEV

Ev'n's sated with variety. (LL) The Scrutiny [or Scrutinie]. Richard Lovelace. BeJo; BoLoP; CaPo; ELP; EnLoPo; GBL; MeLP; NoP; SeCP; TrGrPo

Ev'n so thou, Siddons! meltest my sad heart! (LL) As When a Child. Charles Lamb. Son

Evoe!. Edith M. Thomas. AmWP

Evolution. John Blight. CBAP

Evolution. Ben King. AnAmPo

Evolution. Peter Porter. OBD

Evolution. Langdon Smith. BeLS; BLPA; FaBoBe

Evolution. May Swenson. TrGrPo

Evolution. Israel Zangwill. TrJP

Evolution from the Fish. Robert Bly. MoP; NoAM; NOBA

Evolution of the Flightless Bird, The. Richard Kenney. FoLa

Evolutionary Hymn. C. S. Lewis. NOBL

Ev'ry morning at half-past four. Hard Times in the Mill. Unknown. SWP

Ev'ry morning at seven o'clock. Drill, Ye Tarriers, Drill. Thomas F. Casey. SWP

Ev'rybody's building the big ships and the boats. Quinn the Eskimo. Bob Dylan. RaBo

Ewes and lambs, loving the far hillplaces, The. Ad Limina. Joseph Campbell. BIrV

Ex and Squarey. Unknown. ChTr; GBP, (1 st.)

Ex-Basketball Player. John Updike. InPK; NYBP; SM; TRP

Ex-Deputy Sheriff Remembers the Eastern Oklahoma Murderers, An, sels. Jim Barnes.
Red Oak. NGP, sect. ii
Summerfield. HATNAP, sect. i; NGP, sect. i

Ex Nihilo. David Gascoyne. Fr. Miserere. GTBS-P

Ex nihilo nihil fit. (LL) Epitaph on James Moore Smythe. Pope. FaBoEE

Ex Ore Infantium. Francis Thompson. BoTP; FaBV; OHIP; OxBChV

Ex-Poet, The. Bill Zavatsky. UL

Ex-Queen among the Astronomers, The. Fleur Adcock. FaBoWP; NALW

Ex-soldier remembered that this had been the evening, An. Armistice Day. William Plomer. IHNG

Exact beat from, The. Hayden Carruth. *Fr.* Paragraphs. Jaz

Exaggerated lives, phony body postures, overblown gestures. Triplets. Michael Brownstein. UL

Exaltatio Humanae Naturae. William Alabaster. NoSic

Exaltation. Franz Werfel, *tr. fr. German by* Edith Abercrombie Snow. TrJP

Examination, The. Priscilla Jane Thompson. CBWP-2

Examination at the Womb-Door. Ted Hughes. NAEL-2; NAs; OxBC

Examination of Conscience before Going to Sleep. T. Carmi, *tr. fr. Hebrew by* Stephen Mitchell. OBD

Examine not the inscrutable Heart. Of the Passions of Her Heart. Sir John Davies. *Fr.* Hymns of Astræa [in Acrostic Verse]. SiPSBD

Example, The. W. H. Davies. MoBrPo; TrGrPo

Example, An. Brendan Kennelly. PWE

Example of Kant's sterling wit, An. Victor Gray. PeLi

Example, pattern: lead them to thy light. (*LL*) St. Simeon Stylites. Tennyson. NOBVV; OAEL-2

Exasperated, worn, you conjure a mansion. Desires of Men and Women. John Berryman. LiTM

Excavator, The. Emily Borenstein. BTR

Excavator, explore rock from the great Ice Age. The Cave-Drawing. Vernon Watkins. LiTB

Exceeding glorious is this star: Of the Sunbeams of Her Mind. Sir John Davies. *Fr.* Hymns of Astræa [in Acrostic Verse]. SiPSBD

Exceeding sorrow/ Consumeth my sad heart! O Mors! Quam Amara Est Memoria Tua Homini Pacem Habenti in Substantiis Suis. Ernest Dowson. OBMV

Exceeds a thousand days of mirth. (*LL*) Great God, attend while Zion sings. Isaac Watts. AmFP

Excelente Balade of Charitie, An. Thomas Chatterton. EBEV; EnRP; NOEC; OxAEP-1

Excellency of Christ. Giles Fletcher the Younger. *Fr.* Christ's Victory and Triumph. WGRP

Excellency of stars, precious stone of the night. (*LL*) Welcome to the Moon. *Unknown.* BoNaP; ChTr

Excellent Epitaph of Sir Thomas Wyatt, An. The Earl of Surrey. *See* Wyatt Resteth Here.

Excellent jewels would you see. Of Her Memory. Sir John Davies. *Fr.* Hymns of Astræa [in Acrostic Verse]. SiPSBD

Excellent New Ballad, Called the Brawny Bishop's Complaint, An. Arthur Mainwaring. APAS

Excellent New Ballad Called the Prince of Darkness, An. *Unknown.* APAS

Excellent New Ballad Giving a True Account of the Birth and Conception of a Late Famous Poem Called the Female Nine, An. Charles Sackville. APAS

Excellent New Song, An. *Unknown.* OxBSS

Excellent New Song, Being the Intended Speech of a Famous Orator against Peace, An. Swift. APAS

Excellent New Song Called "Mat's Peace," An. Arthur Mainwaring. APAS

Excellent New Song on a Seditious Pamphlet, An. Swift. CoMu

Excellent New Song upon His Grace Our Good Lord Archbishop of Dublin, An. Swift. CoMu

Excellent ritual of oils, of anointing. Sarcophagi. Bernard Spencer. OBD

Excellente Balade of Charity. Thomas Chatterton. *See* In Virgyne the sweltrie sun gan sheene.

Excelsior! (*LL*) Excelsior. Longfellow. EBEvV; FaPON; FaPoR; NAAL-1; OBCA; OBSP; PrIm; UV, sh. vers.; VPP; WBLP

Excelsior. Longfellow. EBEvV; FaPON; FaPoR; NAAL-1; OBCA; OBSP; PrIm; UV, sh. vers.; VPP; WBLP

Excelsior. *Unknown.* BXAP

Excelsior. Walt Whitman. SAmP

Except for the fat. Return. John Robert Lee. PBCV

Except I Love. Robert Parry. *Fr.* Mirror of Knighthood, The. EIL

Except ourselves, we have no other prayer. Without Ceremony. Vassar Miller. MoAmPo; SM

Except the Heaven had come so near. Emily Dickinson. SAmP

Except the Lord build the house. Bible, *O.T., paraphrased by* Sir Thomas Wyatt. *Fr.* Psalms. TrJP

Except the Lord, That He for Us Had Been. Henry Ainsworth. AH

Except the mill-wheel's sound. (*LL*) Charles the First. Shelley.

Except thou mind to put thy friend to pain. (*LL*) Accused though I be without desert. Sir Thomas Wyatt. SiPS

Except through death, a refuge and a crown. (*LL*) To Vittoria Colonna. Michelangelo. AWP

Except to be left, in the last resort, alone, quite alone. (*LL*) Desire. D. H. Lawrence. CBLP

Except to prove the sweetness of a shower. (*LL*) Tall Nettles. Edward Thomas. BoTP; ChTr; FaBoTw; FaBoVe; MoAB; MoBrPo; OxBSP

Excepting the diner. Poem to Be Read at 3 A.M. Donald Justice. HoPM

Excerpt from a Report to the Galactic Council. Robert Conquest. OxBC

Exchange, The. Samuel Taylor Coleridge. FiBHP

Exchange. George Rostrevor Hamilton, *after the Greek of* Plato. FaBoEE

Exchange. Dabney Stuart. HoPM

Exchange between the Poet and St. Augustine, An. Petrarch, *tr. fr. Latin by* W. H. Draper. *Fr.* Secretum. OxBLMV

Exchange in greed the ungraceful signs. Thrust. The Violent Space. Etheridge Knight. BPo

Exchange of Poems by Tung-yang Stream, An, *sels.* Hsieh Ling-yün, *tr. fr. Chinese by* Burton Watson.

Exchanges. Ernest Dowson. OBMV

Excited woodwinds, staccato strings in noisy clamor. Tune: "Squabbling Quails." Kuan Yun-shih, *tr. by* Richard John Lynn. *Fr.* Medley of Southern and Northern Tunes — Scenic Tour of West Lake. SuSp

Excitement. Louise Bennett. PBCV

Excitement of too much, An. German Bite. Iain Sinclair. NBrP

Exclusive Blue. Robert Francis. CRP

Excrement Poem, The. Maxine W. Kumin. CAPP; FaBoWP

Excursion. Niyi Osundare. HBAPE

Excursion, The. Tu Fu, *tr. fr. Chinese.* AWP, *tr. by* Amy Lowell *and* Florence Ayscough

Excursion, The, *sels.* Wordsworth.
"Curious child, who dwelt upon a tract, A." WGRP
Despondency Corrected. EnRP
Discourse of the Wanderer, and an Evening Visit to the Lake. EnRP
Prospectus. EnRP; NoP; OAEL-2
(Prospectus [*incl. in* The Excursion].) FHYEP
Solitary, The. EnRP
Wanderer Recalls the Past, The. OBNC
Wanderer, The. EnRP, *abr.*
(Ruined Cottage, The, *diff. vers.*) NoP; OAEL-2

Excursion of the Speech and Hearing Class, The. David Wagoner. VCAP

Excursion to Ravenna of a Young Girl with Her Parents, *sels.* Rossana Ombres, *tr. fr. Italian by* Robert McCracken *and* Pietro Pedace.
Afternoon Hours. PeFWW
Morning Hours. NeIt

Excursion to the Dragon Pool Temple on Chung-nan, An. Meng Chiao, *tr. fr. Chinese by* A. C. Graham. PLT

Excursion to the Suburbs, An, *sels.* Tsung Ch'en, *tr. fr. Chinese by* Jonathan Chaves.

Excuse, The. Carl H. Greene. NBV

Excuse, The. Morgan Llwyd. *Fr.* 1648. AngWe

Excuse, The. Sir Walter Ralegh. AAS; SiPS; SiPSBD

Excuse for So Much Writ upon My Verses, An. Margaret Cavendish, Duchess of Newcastle. KTR

Excuse me. Half-caste. John Agard. NBrP

Excuse of Absence, An. Thomas Carew. CaPo; SeCP

Exeat. Stevie Smith. NAEL-2; NoAM

Execration, The. Elizabeth Thomas. ECWP

Execration upon Vulcan, An. Ben Jonson. BeJo; SeCP

Execution. James A. Randall, Jr.. BPo

Execution of Alice Holt. *Unknown.* OxBoLi

Execution of Five Pirates for Murder. *Unknown.* OxBSS

Execution of King Charles, The. Andrew Marvell. PoRA

Execution of Luke Hutton, The. *Unknown.* OBET

Execution of Madame du Barry, The. J. J. Bray. NOBAu

Executive. Sir John Betjeman. NOBL; PIP

Executive's Death, The. Robert Bly. CoAP; NaP

Exeo in a spasm. Enueg I. Samuel Beckett. CIP

Exequies, The. Thomas Stanley. BeJo; MeLP

Exequy, The. (Accept, thou shrine of my dead saint.) Henry King. CoGr; GBL; HAP; InvP; JCP; MeLP; NoP; OxBM; PoEL-2; PrIm; SCGP; SeCP; TEP

Sels.
"Curious child, who dwelt upon a tract, A." WGRP
Despondency Corrected. EnRP
"Sleep on, my love, in thy cold bed." CH; OBD; TrGrPo

Exequy, An. Peter Porter. NoAM; OxBC

Exercise. W. S. Merwin. NOBA

Exercise ("Get loaded."). Pat Nolan. UL

Exercise in a Meadow. Jane Elliot. GoYe

Exercise ("Just as I stood up."). Pat Nolan. UL

Exercise No. 2. William Carlos Williams. SAmP

Exercise of Affection, The. Sir Robert Ayton.

Exercises in Scriptural Writing, *sels.* Carl Rakosi.
"Sandlewood comes to my mind." ChIV-1

Exercration Upon Vulcan, An, *sels.* Ben Jonson.
Better Books to Burn. CBCK

Exert thy voice, sweet harbinger of Spring! To the Nightingale. The Countess of Winchilsea. ECWP; NALW; WPE

Exeter Riddle, An. Gavin Ewart. OxBC

Exeunt. Richard Wilbur. BoNaP; HeIP; Poetsp; PoLF

Exeunt Omnes. Thomas Hardy. FaBoVe; UV

Exhausted now her sighs, and dry her tears. Walter Savage Landor. CBLP; FaBoEE

Exhortation of a Father to His Children, The. Robert Smith. OxBChV

Exhortation: Summer, 1919. Claude McKay. CDC

Exhortation to His Grace the King, An. Sir David Lyndsay. ScCV

Exhortation to Learn of Others' Trouble. The Earl of Surrey. *See* My Ratclif [*or* Ratcliffe], when the retchlesse [*or* retchless *or* rechless] youth offendes.

Exhortation to Prayer. William Cowper. NOCV

Exhortation to Prince Henry, An, *sels.* Sir William Alexander. "I, Henry, hope with this mine eyes to feed." ScCV

Exhorting Myself. Ssu-k'ung Shu, *tr. fr. Chinese by* Hellmut Wilhelm. SuSp

Exhumation. Zoé Karélli, *tr. fr. Greek by* Rae Dalven. WoWa

Exile. Ingeborg Bachmann, *tr. fr. German by* Daniel Huws. PoSu

Exile, The. Vuyelwa Carlin. NWP

Exile. Ernest Dowson. BoLoP

Exile. Marta Fenyves. LoHo

Exile. George Rostrevor Hamilton, *after the Greek of* Isidoros of Aigai. FaBoEE

Exile. Li Shang-yin, *tr. fr. Chinese by* A. C. Graham. PLT

Exile. Milton. *See* So spake our Mother Eve, and Adam heard.

Exile, *sels.* "St.-John Perse," *tr. fr. French by* Denis Devlin.

Exile, The. Larry Rubin. GoYe

Exile. Karl Shapiro. *Fr.* Adam and Eve. CRP

Exile. Jennette Yeatman. GoYe

Exile from God. John Hall Wheelock. WGRP

Exile in Nigeria. Ezekiel Mphahlele. PBA

Exile lingering here, An. (*LL*) Infelix. Adah Isaacs Menken. AAP; AmWP; CBWP-1

Exile of Erin, The. *Unknown.* NOBAu

Exile of the Sons of Uisliu. *Unknown, tr. fr. Irish by* Thomas Kinsella. NOIV

Sels.
"Conchobor, what are you thinking, you."
"Sweet in your sight the fiery stride."

Exile: Welsh Service from Daventry. Llewelyn Wyn Griffith. AngWe

Exiled. Edna St. Vincent Millay. PoRA

Exiled Asraea is come again. Of Her Justice. Sir John Davies. *Fr.* Hymns of Astræa [in Acrostic Verse]. SiPSBD

Exiled Heart, The. Maurice Lindsay. OxBS

Exiled under silver birch and conifers. Lure of the Cascadura. John C. M. Lyons. NBrP

Exiles. "Æ." BIrV; MoBrPo

Exiles, The. W. H. Auden. OxBTC

Exiles. Judy F. Ham. LoHo

Exiles. Patrick O'Connor. TIRV

Exiles, The. Paul Ramsey. *Fr.* Three Epigrams. CRP

Exile's Lament, The. Frances Sargent Osgood. AmWP

Exile's Letter. Li Po, *tr. fr. Chinese by* Ezra Pound. CTC; FaBoMo; OxBA

Exile's Letter: After the Failed Revolution. Marilyn Chin. LoHo

Exile's Letter (Or: An Essay on Assimilation). Marilyn Chin. OpBo

Exile's Return, The. Robert Lowell. AmPP; OxBA

Exile's Return, The. Slavko Mihalic, *tr. by* Peter Kastmiler *and* Charles Simic. PoSu

Exile's Reverie, The. Mary Weston Fordham. CBWP-2

Exile's Reveries, The, *sels.* James Kennedy. "Chased from my calling to this hackneyed trade." NOEC

Exist, without a man cook. (*LL*) The Coming Woman. Mary Weston Fordham. AmWP; CBWP-2

Existentialism. Lloyd Frankenberg. FiBHP

Existentialist. Janet Fisher. NWP

Exit. E. A. Robinson. MoAmPo; OxBSP

Exit from Eden, The. Milton. *See* So spake our Mother Eve, and Adam heard.

Exit Line. John Ciardi. WeW

Exit on Feedback. Gavin Selerie. NBrP

Exit, Pursued by a Bear. Ogden Nash. NYBP

(Exit the hors d'oeuvres). (*LL*) Item. E. E. Cummings. MoAB; MoAmPo

Exits and Entrances. Naomi Long Madgett. BlSi

Exmatriate. Jacqueline Lapidus. LoHo

Exodus, *sels.* Bible, *O.T.*

Exodus. PAW
(Triumphal Chant.) TrGrPo
"Let us synge unto the Lorde, for he is become glorious." OBVE
Ten Commandments, The. WBLP
Then Sang Moses. OBWP

Exodus. Bible, *O.T. Fr.* Exodus. PAW

Exodus. Anita Endrezze-Danielson. CDW

Exodus. Carolyn Kizer. AnAn

Exodus. Mary Effie Lee Newsome. ShDr

Exodus. George Oppen. ChIV-1

Exodus. Charles Reznikoff. ChIV-1

Exodus, *sels. Unknown, tr. fr. Anglo-Saxon by* Charles W. Kennedy. Parting of the Red Sea, The. AnOE

Exodus (August 3, 1492), The. Emma Lazarus. *Fr.* By the Waters of Babylon. WPE

Exodus from a Renaissance Gallery. Ellen M. V. Acton. GoYe

Exodus from Egypt, The. Ezekielos of Alexandria, *tr. fr. Greek by* E. H. Gifford. TrJP

Exodus to Connacht. Fear Dorcha O'Meallain, *tr. fr. Irish by* Thomas Kinsella. FaBoPV; TIRV

Exorcism of the Straight/ Man/ Demon. Aaron Shurin. GLP

Expanded waters gather on the plain, The. The Flood. Ovid, *tr. fr. Latin. Fr.* Metamorphoses. ChTr; OBVE, *tr. by* Dryden

Expanding in the chill. Cold-Weather Love. Ronald G. Everson. MoCV

Expanding with the starr'd nocturnal flowers. (*LL*) From My Diary, July 1914. Wilfred Owen. FaBoMo; LiTM; MeMBP; MoAB; MoBrPo

Expands to admit its adversary. (*LL*) For Jane Myers. Louise Glück. FaBoWP

Expansive puppets percolate self-unction. The Canadian Authors Meet. F. R. Scott. NOBC

Expatriates. R. S. Thomas. AngWe

Expatriates. David Woo. OpBo

Expect No Turbulence. Barbara Ferland. PBCV

Expect Nothing. Alice Walker. AmPA; FF

Expectans Expectavi. Charles Hamilton Sorley. FaBoCh; WGRP

Expectant faces brimmed the waiting square. Rome Sunday June 1960. John Hewitt. TIRV

Expectant Mother. Penelope Shuttle. BrRo

Expectation. Thomas Stanley. BeJo

Expected Guest, The. Sidney Keyes. PoWW

Expected Ship, The. John Godfrey Saxe. AnAmPo

Expecting the Lord. Ann Griffiths, *tr. fr. Welsh by* Tony Conran. VBLP

Expecting the main things from you. (*LL*) Poets to Come. Walt Whitman. FF; LiTA; TrGrPo

Expedition to Wessagusset, The. Longfellow. *Fr.* Courtship of Miles Standish, The. AiP, (*st.* 1); BeLS; PAH

Expense of spirit in a waste of shame, The [*or* Th']. Shakespeare. *Fr.* Sonnets. AWP; EBEV; EnRePo; ErPo; GBL; HAP; HeIP; ImPo; InPS; LiTB; NAEL-1; NIP; NOBE; NoP; NoSic; OAEL-1; OBEV; OtMeF; OxAEP-1; PoE; PoEL-2; Poetr; PPP; SCGP; SCV; Son; TEP; TFi; TrGrPo; UnPo
(Lust in Action.) PlP
(Sonnet 129.) CoGr

Expense of spirit in a waste of shame, Th.' The Garden of Proserpine. Veronica Forrest-Thomson. VaA

Expense of spirits is a crying shame, The. Wendy Cope. *Fr.* Strugnell's Sonnets. FaBoBl

Expensive Wife, The. Judah ibn Sabbatai. *Fr.* Gift of Judah the Woman-Hater, The. TrJP

Experience, The. Bruce Bennett. PeECV

Experience. Emerson. LiTA; MeMAP; PoEL-4; TAP

Experience. Lesbia Harford. CBAP

Experience. Dorothy Parker. NAAL-2

Experience. James Simmons. BIrV; PWE

Experience, The. Edward Taylor. *See* Oh! that I always breath'd in such an aire.

Experience that eludes you intrigues you more, The. Season Ticket. Gloria Frym. UL

Experience, though noon auctoritee. The Wife of Bath's Prologue. Chaucer. *Fr.* Canterbury Tales, The. EnVB; FHYEP; NAEL-1; OAEL-1; OxBoLi, (*abr.*); PeLV, (*shorter vers.*)
(If there were no authority on earth.) CoGr
(Prologue to the Wife of Bath's Tale, The.) OxBM; PoEL-1

Experienced men, inured to city ways. John Gay. *Fr.* Trivia; or, The Art of Walking the Streets of London. OAEL-1

Experienced wife, An. A Midwife's Story; Two. Anne Szumigalski. NOBC

Experiment. Wislawa Szymborska, *tr. fr. Polish by* Magnus J. Krynski. PoSu

Eyeballs on her behind are like fire, The. The Leopard. Lorenzo Thomas. UL

Eyeful Glances. Niyi Osundare. HBAPE

Eyeing the Eyes of One's Mistress. Ebenezer Jones. NOBVV

Eyelashes did their job. The Stillborn (Domesticity # three). William Knott.
(Fear of Domesticity: After Reading Plath and Sexton.) UL

Eyeless labourer in the night, The. Woman to Man. Judith Wright. CBAP; FaBoMA; WPE

Eyelids glowing, some chill morning, The. Monet: "Les Nymphéas." W. D. Snodgrass. CoAP

Eyelids meet, The. He'll catch a little nap. In the Smoking-Car. Richard Wilbur. LiTM; MoAmPo

Eyelids of eve fall together at last, The. The Eve of Waterloo. Thomas Hardy. Fr. Dynasts, The. OAEL-2; OBWP
(Before Waterloo.) MoAB

Eyes. W. H. Davies. FM

Eyes and Tears. Andrew Marvell. GeHe; PFP

Eyes bright, as it dipped and soared away — his treasure. (LL) Winter Noon. Umberto Saba. STV

Eyes, Calm beside Thee (Lady, Could'st Thou Know!). Robert Browning. Son

Eyes do not lie. Remainder. Frederika Blankner. GoYe

Eyes Fastened with Pins. Charles Simic. VCAP

Eyes filled with speaking fire. Irenaius, tr. fr. Greek by Andrew Miller. GrAn

Eyes/ flatterers of Soul. Meleager, tr. fr. Greek by Peter Whigham. GrAn

Eyes Hide My Love. Samuel Daniel. Fr. Hymen's Triumph. ElL

Eyes in the Air. Gilbert Frankau. NSI

Eyes knees and of your Etcetera. (LL) My Sweet Old Etcetera. E. E. Cummings. AmPP; AnAmPo; CMoP; FF; HeIP; InPS; OBAL; OBWP; OxBA; PeFWW; PPP; SOTW

Eyes like the morning star. The Colorado Trail. Unknown. AS

Eyes look front in humans, The. Teleology. May Swenson. VCAP

Eyes of Flesh, The. Sandra Hochman. NMM

Eyes of grey — a sodden quay. The Lovers' Litany. Kipling. CBLP

Eyes of men running, falling, screaming. Unknown. OBWP

Eyes of My Regret, The. Angelina Weld Grimké. CDC

Eyes of Night-Time. Muriel Rukeyser. BoWoP

Eyes of slain stag. In Some Seer's Cloud Car. Christopher Middleton. TwCP

Eyes of twenty centuries, The. Judas Iscariot. Stephen Spender. MoAB; MoBrPo; NIP

Eyes on the plate — the scoop of mashed potato. Hostel. Evan Jones (b. 1927). FaBoMA

Eyes open to a cry of pulleys, The. Love Calls Us to the Things of This World. Richard Wilbur. AmPP; CAPP; CMoP; HAP; HeIL; HeIP; InPS; MoAmPo; NIP; PoE; Poetr; PoRA; PPP; TAP; TFi; TrGrPo; UnPo; VCAP; VGW

Eyes red, the lips blue, The. The Three Seamstresses. Isaac Leibush Peretz, tr. fr. Yiddish by Joseph Leftwich. TrJP

Eyes shining without mystery. Pantoum. John Ashbery. SM

Eyes shut tight. Madness. Yoshihara Sachiko, tr. fr. Japanese by James Kirkup and Shozo Tokunaga. BoWoP

Eyes So Tristful. Diego de Saldaña, tr. fr. Spanish by Longfellow. AWP

Eyes that drew from me such fervent praise, The. Petrarch, tr. by Edwin Morgan. Fr. Sonnets to Laura. NAWM-1

Eyes that glass fear, though fear on furtive foot. A Hare. Walter de la Mare. EBEV

Eyes That Last I Saw in Tears. T. S. Eliot. NOBE

Eyes that weep for pity of the heart, The. Dante, tr. fr. Italian by Dante Gabriel Rossetti. Fr. Vita Nuova, La. AWP; WGRP, sl. diff. vers.

Eyes, the Blood, The. David Meltzer. PoM

Eyes: . . . . . . .Medium. All There Is to Know about Adolph Eichmann. Leonard Cohen. InPK

Ezek'el saw de wheel. Ezekiel, You and Me. Unknown. AS

Ezekiel, sels. Bible, O.T.
Lamentation. TrJP
Riches of Tyrus, The. CBCK
Thy Mother Was like a Vine. TrJP

Ezekiel. Whittier. ChIV-1

Ezekiel, You and Me. Unknown. AS

Ezra Pound. Robert Lowell. MoP; NAAL-2; NoAM; NOBA

Ezra, whom not with eye nor with ear have I ever. Epistle to the Rapalloan. Archibald MacLeish. PoA

Ezry. Archibald MacLeish. NOBA

F

F. Jack Marshall. UL

F. de Samara to A. G. A. Emily Brontë. NALW; VBLP

F for finny. Unknown. ISE

F is the fighting Firetruck. Phyllis McGinley. Fr. All around the Town. FaPON

Fa La La. John Hilton. See My mistress frowns when she should play.

Fa la la! (LL) Now is the month of maying. Unknown. EBEV; NoSic

Fa la la! (LL) Sing We and Chant It. At. to Thomas Morley. EBEV; EnRePo; NoSic

Fa la la la. (LL) The Whale. Unknown. ChTr

Fa, Mi, Fa, Re, La, Mi. Unknown. InPK

Fa saw the Forty-second. The Forty-second. Unknown. GBP

Fab Four Tour Deutschland: Hamburg, 1961. David Wojahn. Fr. Mystery Train: A Sequence. PBCAP

Fabius Lind's Diary, sels. A. Leyeles, tr. fr. Yiddish by Benjamin and Barbara Harshav.

Fable. James Facos. NBLV

Fable, A. John Hookham Frere. See Dingy donkey, formal and unchanged, A.

Fable: "In Aesop's tales an honest wretch we find." Matthew Prior. NoP

Fable: "Mountain and the squirrel, The." Emerson. AmPP; AnAmPo; BeLS; BLPL; BoTP; FaBoBe; FaBV; FaPON; GoJo; ImPo; LiTA; MeMAP; NBLV; OBAL; OBCA; TFi

Fable: "Once upon a time/ there was a lonely wolf." János Pilinszky, tr. fr. Hungarian by Ted Hughes and János Csokits. OBVE; PoSu; RB

Fable: "Some cawing Crows, a hooting Owl." Ella Wheeler Wilcox. AmWP

Fable: "There is an inevitability." Norman Harris. NYBP

Fable: "Under a dung-cake." D. J. Opperman, tr. fr. Afrikaans by Jack Cope. PeSA; PeSAV

Fable for Critics, A, sels. James Russell Lowell.
Bryant. NOBA; TAP
Cooper. NOBA; OxBA; TAP
Hawthorne. AmPP; NOBA; OxBA; TAP
Holmes. NOBA
Irving. TAP
Lowell. AmPP; NOBA; OxBA; TAP
Poe and Longfellow. AmPP; NOBA; OxBA; TAP
(Poe.) TAP
"There are truths you Americans need to be told." OBSV
"There comes Emerson first, whose rich words, every one." NAAL-1
(Emerson.) AmPP; NOBA; OxBA; TAP
Whittier. AmPP; NOBA; OxBA

Fable in Two Languages, A, sels. Charles W. Pratt.

Fable of Midas, The. Swift. APAS

Fable of the Magnet and the Churn, The. W. S. Gilbert. Fr. Patience. FaPON

Fable of the Piece of Glass and the Piece of Ice, The. John Hookham Frere. OxBChV

Fable of the Speckled Cow. D. J. Opperman, tr. fr. Afrikaans by Jack Cope, Uys Krige, and Ruth Miller. PeSA

Fable of the War, A. Howard Nemerov. ArOW; OBWP

Fable of the Widow and Her Cat, A. Swift. OFC; SoCa

Fable of the Young Man and His Cat, The. Christopher Pitt. ECEV

Fable XXI: The Rat-catcher and Cats. John Gay. OxAEP-1

Fabled queen of love, The. (LL) When Phoebe formed a wanton smile. William Collins. EnLoPo; OxBSP

Fables, sels. John Gay.
Butterfly and the Snail, The. FM
Lion and the Cub, The. GN
Mother, the Nurse, and the Fairy, The. PeLV
Poet and the Rose, The. PeLV; TEP
Wild Boar and the Ram, The. FM; NOEC

Fabrication of Ancestors. Alan Dugan. CAPP; NoAM

Fabrique of Things Spent. Edith M. Thomas. AmWP

Fabulary Satire IV. Daryl Hine. NOBC

Fabullus I will treat you handsomely. Catullus, tr. fr. Latin. Fr. Carmina. OBVE, tr. by Richard Lovelace

Fabullus that they'd make thee nose all ore. (LL) Fabullus I will treat you handsomely. Catullus. OBVE, tr. by Richard Lovelace

Fabulous Wizard of Oz, The. Unknown. PeLi

Façade, sels. Edith Sitwell.
Hornpipe. FaBoMo; GTBS-P; OAEL-2
Sir Beelzebub. BoWoP; FaBoWP; HoPM; MoAB; MoBrPo; NALW; OxBTC; PrIm
(When Sir Beelzebub.) FaBoMo
Trio for Two Cats and a Trombone. NAEL-2; PBWP

Face, The. Anthony Euwer. See As a Beauty I Am Not a Star.

Face, The. Susan Mitchell. NAmP90

Face, The. Edwin Muir. GTBS-P

Face, The. Lucien Stryk. ArOW

Face. Jean Toomer. CDC; NoP

May. GN
Mermaids, The. ChTr
Mutability. PoEL-1
Mutability Claims to Rule the World. NoSic
Nature's Reply to Mutability. NOBE
Nought is on earth more sacred or divine. OAEL-1
"Nought is there under heav'ns wide hollownesse." FHYEP
"Nought vnder heauen so strongly doth allure." NoSic
"Now, at the time that was before agreed." OAEL-1
"O goodly golden chaine, wherewith yfere." FHYEP
"Redoubted knights, and honorable Dames." NoP
"First was Fancy, like a lovely boy, The."
"Noble Mayde, still standing, all this vewd, The." PoEL-1
"Right well I wote [or wrote] most mighty Soueraine [or soveraine]."
NoSic; OAEL-1
Rivers Come to the Hall of Proteus for the Marriage of the Thames and
the Medway, The. FaBoPP
Rivers of Ireland, The. CBCK
"Rugged forhead that with grave foresight, The." OAEL-1
Scudamor in the Temple of Venus. PoE
Sea Monsters. ChTr
Sea Nymphs, The. CBCK
"So as they travelled, the drouping night." OAEL-1
"So forth she comes, and to her coche does clyme." NAEL-1; OAEL-1
"So oft as I with state of present time." OAEL-1
"Sudden upriseth from her stately palace." PPP
Summer. GN
Temple of Venus, The. EiL
"Then said that royall Pere in sober wise." OAEL-1
"Thence forward by that painfull way they pas." OAEL-1
"There the most daintie Paradise on ground." EBEV
"They sate to meat, and Satyrane his chaunce." OAEL-1
"Tho when as chearelesse night ycovered had." OAEL-1
"Thus being entered, they behold around." OAEL-1
Vision of the Graces, The. NoSic
"Well may I weene, faire ladies, all this while." OAEL-1
What If Some Little Paine the Passage Have. CH
"What man is he, that boasts of fleshly might." FHYEP
"What man so wise, what earthly wit so ware." FHYEP
"When I bethinke me on that speech whyleare." NoSic; OAEL-1
"Whiles someone did chant this lovely lay, The." OBVE
(Gather the Rose.) EiL
(Song of Bliss.) FF
"Whilom, as antique stories tellen us." EPCY
"Who now does follow the foule Blatant Beast." OAEL-1
"Who travels [or trauels] by the weary [or wearie] wandring way." OBD;
OxAEP-1
Winter. GN
"Young knight, what ever that dost armes professe." FHYEP
Faeries' Song, The. Ben Jonson. See Faery Beam upon You, The.
Faery Beam upon You, The. Ben Jonson. Fr. Gypsies Metamorphosed,
The. BeJo; EBEV; OxBSP; TEP
Faery Song. Keats. See Shed no tear! O, shed no tear!
Fafnir and the Knights. Stevie Smith. Mes
Faggots and their friends now live in Ramrod, The. Larry Mitchell. GLP
Faggots created a rite of cleansing, The. The faggots sit in a circle. Sons
and Fathers. Larry Mitchell. GLP
Faggots in Ancient Rome. Juvenal, tr. fr. Latin. Fr. Satires. PeHV
Faht's in there? What's in There? Unknown. CH
Failing the Examination. Meng Chiao, tr. fr. Chinese by Stephen Owen.
SuSp
Fails on her breast. (LL) Statue and Birds. Louise Bogan. MoAB;
MoAmPo
Failure. Kate Tucker Goode. PWR
Failure. H. Cordelia Ray. CBWP-3
Failure, A. C. Day Lewis. NOBE
Failure and Success. Richard Watson Gilder. PWR
Failure, the longed-for valley, takes him in. (LL) In the Smoking-Car.
Richard Wilbur. LiTM; MoAmPo
Failures. Arthur W. Upson. WGRP
Fain I Would. Unknown. EiL
Fain would I be sleeping, dreaming. The Plaint of the Wife. Unknown, tr.
fr. Russian by W. R. S. Ralston. AWP
Fain Would I Change That Note. At. to Tobias Hume. EiL; ELP; PoEL-2
Fain would I die to end this stress./ Remédiless. (LL) Of Misery. Thomas
Howell. EiL; FF
Fain would I have a pretty thing. A Proper Song, Entitled: Fain Would I
Have a Pretty Thing to Give unto My Lady. Unknown. CoMu; EiL;
InvP; NoSic
Fain would I kiss my Julia's dainty leg. Her Legs. Robert Herrick. NOSC
Fain would I rival thee. To the Eagle. Mary Weston Fordham. CBWP-2
Fain Would I Wed. Thomas Campion. NAEL-1

Faint Falls the Gentle Voice. Henry Timrod. AH
Faint flush spread all over her cheeks, still sleepy-eyed, A. Tune: "Sand of
Silk-washing Stream." Wu Wei-yeh, tr. fr. Chinese by Irving Y. Lo.
SuSp
Faint-flushed buds awake within the cup, The. Awakening. H. Cordelia
Ray. CBWP-3
Faint Heart. Rufinus, tr. by F. A. Wright. ErPo
Faint Music. Walter de la Mare. FaBoCh
Faint not — fight on! To-morrow comes the song. (LL) Be Strong. Maltbie
D. Babcock. AH; BLPA; FaBoBe; PWR; SoSe; WBLP
Faint now in the evening pallor. Silver Jubilee. Llewelyn Wyn Griffith.
OBWVE
Faint shines the far moon. The Road. Nikolay P. Ogarev, tr. fr. Russian
by P. E. Matheson. AWP
Faint stars wake and wonder, The. On the River. William Vaughn
Moody. AnAmPo
Faintheart in a Railway Train. Thomas Hardy. CBLP; CTC; EnLoPo
Faintly answering still the notes that once were so dear. (LL) At the Mid
Hour of Night. Thomas Moore. GTBS; GTBS-P; NOBE; OBEV;
OBNC; PeIV; PoEL-4
Fair am I, mortals, as a stone-carved dream. Beauté, La. Baudelaire, tr. fr.
French by Lord Alfred Douglas. AWP
Fair Amazon of Heaven who tookst in hand. To Saint Margaret. Henry
Constable. NoSic
Fair Amoret is gone astray. A Hue and Cry after Fair Amoret. Congreve.
NOEC; OBEV
Fair and bright assembly, A: never strode. Thomas Lovell Beddoes. Fr.
Death's Jest Book. CTC
Fair and Fair. George Peele. Fr. Arraignment of Paris, The. EiL; OBEV
Fair and free soul of poesy, O Keats! Keats. Walter Savage Landor.
EPCY
Fair and Unfair. Robert Francis. VGW
Fair Annie. Unknown. CH; ESPB, (A, B, and E vers.); FaBoBa; OxBB
Fair Annie an Sweet Willie. Lord Thomas and Fair Annet. Unknown.
ESPB
Fair Annie had a costly bower. The Holy Nunnery. Unknown. ESPB
Fair Annie of Lochyran. Unknown. AS
Fair at Windgap, The. Austin Clarke. OxBTC
Fair Beatrice tucks her coat up somewhat high. John Taylor. NOSC
Fair Beauty Bride, The. Unknown. AmFP
Fair Beggar, The. Richard Lovelace. BeJo
Fair below Helvellyn, The. Wordsworth. Fr. Prelude [or, Growth of a
Poet's Mind], The. EnRP; FaBoPP; HAP, (short sel.); OAEL-2;
PoEL-4, (sl. shorter)
"Fair bosom! fraught with virtue's richest treasure." Spenser. Fr. Amoretti.
AAS; ESo, lacking epigrams I–IV; HeIL; NIP
Fair boy, alas, why fliest thou me. The Black Maid to the Fair Boy.
Henry Reynolds. NOSC
Fair Candia now no more beneath her lee. William Falconer. Fr.
Shipwreck, The. ScCV
Fair Caroline, I wonder what. To C. F. H. on Her Christening-Day.
Thomas Hardy. NAs
Fair Cassidy. Unknown, tr. fr. Irish by Donagh MacDonagh. BIrV
Fair cheek under a merry blue eye, two brows, A. The Beloved. David
Roberts, tr. fr. Welsh by H. Idris Bell. OBWVE
Fair Cloris in a pig-stye lay. A Song to Cloris. The Earl of Rochester.
ErPo
(Song: "Fair Chloris in a pigsty lay.") NOSC
Fair copy of my Celia's face. To T. H., a Lady Resembling My Mistress.
Thomas Carew. NOSC
Fair Cynthia, all the Homage that I may. Thoughts on the Sight of the
Moon. Sarah Kemble Knight. SCAP
Fair Cynthia mounted on her sprightly pad. Cynthia on Horseback. Philip
Ayres. EnLoPo
Fair daffodils [or Faire daffadills], we weep to see. To Daffodils [or
Daffadils]. Robert Herrick. AWP; BeJo; BoNaP; CaPo; EBEvV; ELP;
FaBoCh; GN; GoJo; GTBS; GTBS-P; InPS; JCP; LiTB; NOBE; NoP;
NOSC; NTP; OBEV; OxAEP-1; PlP; PoEL-3; PoRA; PPP; SCGP; SeCP;
SeCV-1; TFi; TrGrPo; TTTS; UnPo
Fair Damsel from London, The. Unknown. AmFP
Fair Danubie is praised for being wide. Rivers. Thomas Storer. EiL;
FaBoCh
Fair Days; or, Dawns Deceitful. Robert Herrick. CaPo
Fair Eve knelt close by the guarded gate. The Rose of Eden. Susan K.
Phillips. BeLS
Fair Excellence! such strange Commands you lay. To the Honoured
Eugenia, Commanding Me to Write to Her. "Ephelia." KTR
Fair fa' your honest, sonsie face. To a Haggis. Burns. FaBoVe; ScCV
Fair famous flood, which sometimes did divide. Sonnet: On the River
Tweed. Sir Robert Ayton. NOSC
Fair flower of fifteen springs, that still. To His Young Mistress. Pierre de
Ronsard, tr. fr. French by Andrew Lang. AWP

Fair Flower of Northumberland, The. *Unknown.* ESPB; OxBB

Fair flower, that dost so comely grow. The Wild Honeysuckle. Philip Freneau. AmPP; AnAmPo; BLPL; EAP; LiTA; NAAL-1; NOBA; OxBA; PoEL-4; PoLF; TAP; TrGrPo

Fair, fragile Una, golden-haired. The Enchanted Shell. H. Cordelia Ray. CBWP-3

Fair friend, 'tis true your beauties move. Sidney Godolphin. NOSC

Fair girl tripping out to meet her love, A. The Power of Interval. Lord De Tabley. NOBVV; OxBSP

Fair Golden Age! When milk was th' on[e]ly food. Sir Richard Fanshawe, *after the Italian of* Giovanni Battista Guarini. *Fr.* Il Pastor Fido. OBVE
   (Golden Age, The.) NOSC; OAEL-1

Fair, great, and good, since seeing you, we see. To the Countess of Salisbury. John Donne. PeECV

Fair gull on the water's bank. The Seagull. Siôn Phylip, *tr. fr. Welsh by* Joseph P. Clancy. OBWVE

Fair Helen. *Unknown. See* I wish I were where Helen lies.

Fair Hills of Ireland, The. *Unknown, tr. fr. Modern Irish by* Sir Samuel Ferguson. FaBoPP; OBEV; PeIV

Fair Hope with lucent light in her glad eyes. The Quest of the Ideal. H. Cordelia Ray. AmWP; CBWP-3

Fair in the Woods, The. Thom Gunn. AnAn

Fair Ines. Thomas Hood. EnRP; OBEV

Fair insect! that, with threadlike legs spread out, To a Mosquito. Bryant. EAP

Fair Iris I love, and hourly I die. Dryden. *Fr.* Amphitryon. AWP
   (Mercury's Song [to Phaedra].) NOSC; OxBSP; PoEL-3; SeCV-2

"Fair is Alexis," I no sooner said. On Alexis. Plato, *tr. fr. Greek by* Thomas Stanley. AWP

Fair is her body, bright her eye. *Unknown, tr. fr. French by* John Addington Symonds. *Fr.* Medieval Norman Song. AWP

Fair is my dove, my loved one. Marriage Song. Judah Halevi, *tr. fr. Hebrew by* Alice Lucas. TrJP

Fair Is My Love. Samuel Daniel. *See* Fair is my love, and cruel as she's fair.

Fair Is My Love. Robert Greene. *Fr.* Perimedes [*or* Perimedes, the Blacksmith]. EIL

Fair Is My Love. *At. to* Shakespeare Shakespeare. *Fr.* Passionate Pilgrim, The. EIL

Fair is my love, and cruel as she's fair. Samuel Daniel. *Fr.* To Delia. AAS; ESo; NOBE; NoP; TEP; TrGrPo
   (Beauty, Time and Love.) OBEV
   (Fair Is My Love.) EnRePo; LiTB
   (Sonnet: "Fair is my love, and cruel as she's fair.") EIL; HoPM

Fair is not my face. A Woman Grows Soon Old. Larin Paraske, *tr. fr. Finnish by* Jaakko A. Ahokas. PBWP

Fair is Our Lord's Own City. *Unknown, tr. fr. Irish by* Coslett Quin. TIRV

Fair Is the Rose. *Unknown.* EIL

Fair Is the World. William Morris. FaBoRV

Fair Is Too Foul an Epithet. Christopher Marlowe. *See* Ah, fair Zenocrate, divine Zenocrate.

Fair Isabel, poor simple Isabel! Isabella; or, The Pot of Basil. Keats. EnRP

Fair Isabel sat in her bower door. Hind Etin. *Unknown.* OxBB

Fair Isabell of Rochroyall. *Unknown.* OxBB

Fair Isle at Sea — thy lovely name. Robert Louis Stevenson. NOBVV

Fair Janet. *Unknown.* ESPB; OxBB

Fair lady Isabel sits in her bower sewing. Lady Isabel and the Elf-Knight. *Unknown.* ESPB; FaBoBa

Fair lady, what's your face to me? Love for Enjoying. James Shirley. BeJo

Fair lady, will you travel. The Wooing of Etain. *Unknown, tr. fr. Irish by* John Montague. BIrV

Fair Lass of Islington, The. *Unknown. See* There was a Lass of Islington.

Fair little girl sat under a tree, A. Good Night and Good Morning. Richard Monckton Milnes. BoTP; OxBChV

Fair lovely maid, or if that title be. To the Fair Clarinda, Who Made Love to Me, Imagin'd More than Woman. Aphra Behn. NALW; VBLP

Fair Lucy was sitting in her own cabin door. Lizie Wan. *Unknown.* AmFP
   (Lizie Wan sits at her father's bower door.) FaBoVe

Fair Lunacy! I see thee, with a crown. Mirthful Lunacy. Thomas Tod Stoddart. *Fr.* Death-Wake, The; or, Lunacy. OBNC

Fair Maid and the Sun, The. Arthur O'Shaughnessy. BeLS

Fair Maid by the Shore, The. *Unknown.* AmFP

Fair maid, had I not heard thy baby cries. To a Lofty Beauty, from Her Poor Kinsman. Hartley Coleridge. OxAEP-2

Fair Maid of Amsterdam, The. *Unknown.* OxBoLi; PeLV; RB

Fair Maid of the Exchange, The, *sels. At. to* Thomas Heywood. Ye Little Birds That Sit and Sing. EIL

Fair Maid of the West, The. *Unknown.* CoMu

Fair maid sat in her bower-door, A. The False Lover Won Back. *Unknown.* ESPB

Fair maid who, the first of May. The First of May. *Unknown.* ReMoGo

Fair maid, you need not take the hint. To a Lady. Burns. ScCV

Fair Maiden. George Peele. *Fr.* Old Wives' [*or* Wife's] Tale, The. PoEL-2

Fair Maiden. George Peele. *See* Gently dip: but not too deepe.

Fair maiden, fair maiden. Invocation to the Muse. Richard Hughes. MoBrPo

Fair maiden, white and red. A Voice [Speaks] from the Well. George Peele. *Fr.* Old Wives' [*or* Wife's] Tale, The. CBNP; FaBoCh; NOBE; OxBoLi

Fair Margaret and Sweet William. *Unknown.* ESPB, (B *vers.*); OBET

Fair Margaret and Sweet William ("As it fell out in a long summer's day.") *Unknown.* ESPB, A *vers.*; OxBB

Fair Margaret and Sweet William ("Little Marg'et sitting in her high hall door.") *Unknown.* AmFP

Fair Margaret and Sweet William ("Sweet William he would a-wooing ride.") *Unknown.* OBET

Fair Margret was a young ladye. Proud Margret. *Unknown.* OxBB
   (Proud Lady Margaret.) ESPB, (B *vers.*)

Fair Marjorie sat i her bower-door. Young Benjie. *Unknown.* ESPB

Fair Mary of Wallington. *Unknown.* ESPB

Fair Mary sat at her father's castle gate. Willie of Winsbury. *Unknown.* AmFP

Fair Melody: To Be Sung by Good Christians, A. Hans Sachs, *tr. fr. German by* Catherine Winkworth. GePo

Fair Mildred wide her lattice threw. Mildred's Doves. H. Cordelia Ray. CBWP-3

Fair morn unbars her gates of gold. Dawn's Carol. H. Cordelia Ray. CBWP-3

Fair Morning, The. Jones Very. NOBA

Fair Mother Earth lay on her back last night. Ode to the Spirit of Earth in Autumn. George Meredith. TEP

Fair mouth's broken tooth, A. (*LL*) August 1914. Isaac Rosenberg. EBEV; NOBE; OBWP; OPOP; OxBTC; PAW; PeFWW

Fair Musidora starry-eyed. Musidora's Vision. H. Cordelia Ray. CBWP-3

Fair nights beneath the mellow moon. The Maid of Ehrenthal. H. Cordelia Ray. CBWP-3

Fair now is the springtide, now earth lies beholding. The Message of the March Wind. William Morris. OBNC; WiR

Fair one! if thus kind you be. To the Tune — "Once I Lov'd a Maiden Fair." Patrick Carey. CBLP

Fair one, to you this monitor I send. Mira to Octavia. Mary Leapor. ECWP

Fair, order'd lights (whose motion without noise). The Constellation. Henry Vaughan. SeCV-1

Fair Phoebe and Her Dark-eyed Sailor. *Unknown.* AmFP

Fair Phyllis I saw sitting all alone. *Unknown.* GBL

Fair [*or* Faire] pledges of a fruitful tree. To Blossoms. Robert Herrick. BeJo; BoNaP; CaPo; GTBS; GTBS-P; JCP; NAEL-1; NOSC; OBEV; SCGP; SeCP; SeCV-1

Fair princess of the spacious air. The Falcon. Richard Lovelace. CaPo

Fair Protarchus doesn't want to. Alcaeus, *tr. fr. Greek by* Thomas Meyer. GrAn

Fair rebel to thyself and time. The Revenge. Pierre de Ronsard, *tr. fr. French by* Thomas Stanley. AWP

Fair, Rich, and Young. Sir John Harington, *after the Latin of* Martial. EIL; NIP

Fair rocks, goodly rivers, sweet woods, when shall I see peace? Echo. Sir Philip Sidney. *Fr.* Arcadia. SiPS
   (Echo Song.) SiPSBD

Fair rosa. *Unknown.* FaBoVe

Fair Rosa was a lovely child. Fair rosa. *Unknown.* FaBoVe

Fair Salamis, the billow's roar. Sophocles, *tr. fr. Greek by* Winthrop Mackworth Praed. *Fr.* Ajax. AWP

Fair seed-time had my soul, and I grew up. Childhood and School-Time. Wordsworth. *Fr.* Prelude [*or*, Growth of a Poet's Mind], The. CH; EnRP; GN; HAP; NOBE; NoP; NU; OAEL-2; OBNC; OxAEP-2; PoE; SCV
   (Introduction — Childhood and School-Time.) PoEL-4
   (On the Solitary Fells around Hawkshead.) FaBoPP

Fair Sex Avenged by the Fair Sex, or a New Satire on Husbands, The, *sels.* Mlle de ——— , *tr. fr. French by* Dorothy Backer. ECWP

Fair shadow, faithless as my sun! The Dream. Sir Edward Sherburne. OxBSP

Fair, shining mountains of my pilgrimage. The Brecon Beacons and the Black Mountains. Henry Vaughan. FaBoPP

Fair ship, that from the Italian shore. Tennyson. *Fr.* In Memoriam A. H. H. EBVV, *abr.*; EBVVPR; EnVR; OAEL-2, *abr.*; PeECV, *abr.*; PeHV

Fair Singer, The. Andrew Marvell. EnLoPo; MeLP; NOBE; NoP; PoEL-2; SCGP

Fair stands the wind again. Henley, July 4: 1914-1964. L. E. Sissman. PrIm

Fair star of evening, splendor of the west. Composed by the Seaside, near Calais, August, 1802. Wordsworth. EnRP; Son

Fair [or Faire] stood the wind for France. Michael Drayton. EBEvV; EBNV

  (Agincourt.) BeLS; EiL; FaBoBe; FaBoCh; OBEV; OxAEP-1
  (Ballad of Agincourt, The.) EnRePo; NTP
  (Battle of Agincourt, The.) FaBoEH

Fair Summer Droops. Thomas Nashe. *See* Fair summer droops, droop men and beasts therefore.

Fair summer droops, droop men and beasts therefore. Thomas Nashe. *Fr.* Summer's Last Will and Testament. NoSic; PlP

  (Baning Summer.) OxBSP; SCGP
  (Fair Summer Droops.) EiL

Fair, that you may truly know. To Amoret. Edmund Waller. SeCV-1

Fair, the young acacia, thick with leaves. The Young Acacia. Hayyim Nahman Bialik, *tr. fr. Hebrew* by Helena Frank. TrJP

Fair these broad reeds — these hoary woods are grand. Canadian Boat Song. At. to John Galt *and also to* "Christopher North." BLPA; FaBoCh; FaPoR; OBEV; OBNC; OxBS

Fair Thou Art. Mordecai ben Isaac, *tr. fr. Hebrew* by Herbert Loewe. TrJP

Fair-tinted cheeks, clear eyelids drawn. Cimabuella. Bayard Taylor. BXAP

Fair Ursly, in a merry mood. Annibal Cruceius, *tr. fr. Latin.* FaBoEE

Fair Verna! loveliest village of the mead. The Flourishing Village. Timothy Dwight. *Fr.* Greenfield Hill. EAP

Fair Virtue, the Mistress of Philarete. (I wandered out awhile agone). *sels.* George Wither.

  Divided Heart, The. TrGrPo
  Hence, Away, You Sirens. EiL
  "I wandered out a while agone." NOSC
  Shall I, Wasting in Despair. EiL; LiTB; OxAEP-1; SCGP
    (Author's Resolution, The.) AWP; OBEV
    (Lover's Resolution, A.) BoLoP; NOBE
    (Manly Heart, The.) FaBV; GTBS; GTBS-P
    (Sonnet: "Shall I, wasting in despair.") SeCV-1
    (What Care I.) TrGrPo

Fair was the dawn, and but e'en now the skies. Fair Days; or, Dawns Deceitful. Robert Herrick. CaPo

Fair was this yonge wyf, and therwithal. Chaucer. *Fr.* Canterbury Tales, The. EBEV; EnVB; FaBoBl; NAEL-1; OAEL-1; OxBoLi; PeLV

Fair were our visions! Oh, they were as grand. In the Land Where We Were Dreaming. Daniel B. Lucas. PAH

Fair witch crept to a young man's side, A. The Witch-Bride. William Allingham. NOBVV

Fair Would I Have a Prettie Thing to Give unto My Ladie. *Unknown. See* Fair would I have a pretty thing.

Fair Would I Have a Pretty Thing. *Unknown. See* Fair would I have a pretty thing.

Fair would I have a pretty thing. *Unknown.* EiL
  (Fair Would I Have a Prettie Thing to Give unto My Ladie.) CoMu
  (Fair Would I Have a Pretty Thing.) InvP

Fair young wanton lady, A. (*LL*) The Gypsy Laddie. *Unknown.* ESPB, A *vers.*; HAP

Faire art thou Phillis, I, so faire (sweet mayd). Thomas Lodge. *Fr.* Phyllis. ESo

Fair[e] as unshaded light; or as the day. To the Queen[e], Entertain[e]d at Night by the Countess[e] of Anglesey. Sir William Davenant. MeLP; NOSC

Faire Is My Love. Bartholomew Griffin. *Fr.* Fidessa, More Chaste than Kind[e]. GBL; PoEL-2

Faire knight (quoth he) Hierusalem that is. Spenser. *Fr.* Faerie Queene, The. FaBoPV

Faire soule, how long shall veyles thy graces shroud? At Home in Heaven. Robert Southwell. EnVR; ESCV

Fairest action of our human life, The. Lady Elizabeth Carey. *Fr.* Mariam. WPE

Fairest day that ever yet has shone, The. The Lost. Jones Very. NOBA

Fairest flower, all flowers excelling. To a Child [of] Five Years Old. Nathaniel Cotton. ECEV; OxBChV

Fairest isle, all isles excelling. Song of Venus. Dryden. *Fr.* King Arthur. OxBoLi; PoEL-3

Fairest Lord Jesus. *Unknown, tr. fr. German.* WGRP

Fairest Nymph that ever bless'd our Shore. Mary Pix. *Fr.* Spanish Wives, The. KTR

Fairest of Freedom's Daughters. Jeremiah Eames Rankin. PAH

Fairest of Her Days, The. *Unknown.* EiL

Fairest of stars, that with your persant light. Balade Simple. John Lydgate. GBL

Fairest of trees under heaven and on earth. Hymn to the Orange. Shih Ching, *tr. fr. Chinese* by Wu-chi Liu. SuSp

Fairest thing that shines below. Clad All in White. Abraham Cowley. *Fr.* Mistress, The. SeCV-1

Fairfax, whose name in armes through Europe rings. On the Lord Gen[eral] Fairfax at the Siege of Colchester. Milton. FaBoEH; NOSC

Fairground. W. H. Auden. NYBP

Fairies, The. William Allingham. CH; ChTr; CoGr; FaBoCh; FaBoPP; FaBV; FaPON; Mes; NOBE; NOBVV; OBEV; OTCP; OxBChV; PDV; TFi

Fairies. Rose Fyleman. FaPON; OxBChV

Fairies, The. Robert Herrick. FaPON

Fairies, The. *Unknown.* BoTP

Fairies Are Dancing All Over the World, The. Michael Rumaker. GLP; PeHV

Fairies are taken into the world, The. Scenes of Childhood. Carl Morse. GLP

Fairies Break Their Dances, The. A. E. Housman. OxBSP; PeVV

Fairies' Farewell, The, *sels.* Richard Corbett [or Corbet].
  "Farewell rewards and fairies." OtMeF

Fairies' Farewell, The. Richard Corbett [or Corbet]. *Fr.* Her Boreale. BeJo; CoGr; NOSC; OxAEP-1

Fairies Feast, The. Charles Montague Doughty. CH

Fairies Have Never a Penny to Spend, The. Rose Fyleman. FaPON

Fairies hold a fair, they say, The. The Faerie Fair. Florence Harrison. BoTP

Fairies' Lullaby, The. Shakespeare. *See* You spotted snakes [with double tongue].

Fairies of the Caldon-Low, The. Mary Howitt. BeLS

Fairies' Siege, The. Kipling. OtMeF

Fairweill. *Unknown.* OxBS

Fairweill. I say no moir. (*LL*) Gife Langour. Lord Darnley. OxBS

Fairy and the soul proceeded, The. The Magic Car Moved On. Shelley. *Fr.* Queen Mab. GN

Fairy Blessing, The. Shakespeare. *See* Now the Hungry Lion Roars.

Fairy Book, The. Norman Gale. OHIP

Fairy Book Lines. Edward Kleinschmidt. UnDi

Fairy Cobbler, The. A. Neil Lyons. BoTP

Fairy Dances. At. to John Lyly *and to* Thomas Ravenscroft. *See* By the Moon ("By the moon we sport and play.")

Fairy Dawn. Joseph Rodman Drake. *Fr.* Culprit Fay, The. GN

Fairy Dream, A. Dorothy Graddon. BoTP

Fairy! Fairy! list and mark. The Fay's Crime. Joseph Rodman Drake. *Fr.* Culprit Fay, The. GN

Fairy Feet. Phyllis L. Garlick. BoTP

Fairy Flute, The. Rose Fyleman. BoTP

Fairy Folk, The. William Allingham. *See* Up the airy mountain.

Fairy in Armor, A. Joseph Rodman Drake. *Fr.* Culprit Fay, The. FaPON

Fairy Land, 1. Shakespeare. *See* Over Hill, over Dale.

Fairy Land, 2. Shakespeare. *See* You spotted snakes [with double tongue].

Fairy Lullaby. Shakespeare. *See* You spotted snakes [with double tongue].

Fairy Music. Enid Blyton. BoTP

Fairy Palace, The, *sels.* Michael Drayton.
  This Palace Standeth in the Air. Mes

Fairy Ring, The. *Unknown.* BoTP

Fairy Ring, The. Andrew Young. ChTr; Spl

Fairy Shoemaker, The. Phyllis L. Garlick. BoTP

Fairy Sleep and Little Bo-Peep, The. *Unknown.* BoTP

Fairy Song. Keats. FaPON

Fairy Song ("Over hill, over dale.") Shakespeare. *See* Over Hill, over Dale.

Fairy Song. W. B. Yeats. *See* Wind Blows out of the Gates of the Day, The.

Fairy Songs ("Now the hungry lion roars.") Shakespeare. *See* Now the Hungry Lion Roars.

Fairy Songs ("Now, until the break of day.") Shakespeare. *See* Now, Until the Break of Day.

Fairy Songs ("You spotted snakes with double tongue.") Shakespeare. *See* You spotted snakes [with double tongue].

Fairy Story. Stevie Smith. OBSP

Fairy Story. Robert Penn Warren. *See* Hunt, hunt again. If you do not find it, you.

Fame is a fickle food. Emily Dickinson. SAmP; TAP

Fame is a food that dead men eat. Fame and Friendship. Austin Dobson. OBEV

Fame let thy trumpet sound. Joel Barlow. AmPP

Fame, like a wayward girl, will still be coy. Keats. *Fr.* Two Sonnets on Fame. EnRP

Fame Makes Us Forward. Robert Herrick. CaPo

Fame, wisdom, love, and power were mine. All Is Vanity, Saith the Preacher. Byron. ChIV-1; TrCP

Famed big-hitter in cricket, A. Douglas Catley. PeLi

Famed ship *California*, a ship of high renown, The. The Girls around Cape Horn. *Unknown.* AmFP

Fame's pillar here, at last, we set. The Pillar of Fame. Robert Herrick. BeJo; CaPo; JCP; NIP; SeCP

Familial. Jacques Prévert, *tr. fr. French by* D. J. Enright. OBD

Familiar Epistle, A. Ann Murry. WPE

Familiar Epistle to J. B. Esq., A, *sels.* Robert Lloyd. "Mark yon round parson, fat and sleek." ECEV, *ll.* 1–60; OBSV Public Schools. NOEC

Familiar Faces, Long Departed. Robert Silliman Hillyer. NYBP

Familiar Friends. James S. Tippett. BoTP

Familiar Letter to Several Correspondents, A. Oliver Wendell Holmes. FaBoUs

Familiar Lines. *Unknown.* FiBHP

Familiar Music. Bill Berkson. UL

Familiar Poem from Nisa to Fulvia of the Vale. Ann Yearsley. ECWP

Familiar pull of the slow train, The. Homecoming. Desmond O'Grady. IIP

Familiar Story. Alan Shapiro. DiPo; NIP

Familiarity Dangerous. William Cowper, *tr. fr. Latin by* Vincent Bourne. OFC

Familie, The. George Herbert. ESCV

Families. Thomas Blackburn. OxBSP

Families, when a child is born. On the Birth of His Son. Su Tung-p'o, *tr. fr. Chinese by* Arthur Waley. AWP; OBVE

Family, The. Donna R. Lydston. PoToHe

Family. Norman MacCaig. FF

Family. Josephine Miles. FaBoWP; FYAP; GrPl

Family, A. W. S. Merwin. CAPP

Family Album, The. Lisa Ress. BTR

Family at Christmas, The. John Norton. BCF

Family Cat, The. Roy Fuller. OxBC; TEP

Family Court. Ogden Nash. CoGr; FiBHP; PeLV

Family Evening. Daniel Huws. NYBP

Family Fool, The. W. S. Gilbert. *Fr.* Yeoman of the Guard. NBLV

Family Fortunes. C. H. Sisson. OxBC

Family Goldschmitt, The. Henri Coulette. CoAP; FF

Family Golschmitt., The. (*LL*) The Family Goldschmitt. Henri Coulette. CoAP; FF

Family Group. Ken Smith. PWE

Family Grove. Albert Goldbarth. HCAP

Family History. Irving Feldman. VCAP

Family Is All There Is, The. Pattiann Rogers. NIP

Family Jewels. Essex Hemphill. GLP

Family Life. Allan M. Laing. FiBHP

Family Life. *Unknown.* FaBoBl

Family Man, A. Maxine W. Kumin. IHMS; TAP

Family Matter, A. Allen Curnow. *Fr.* Trees, Effigies, Moving Objects. PeNZ

Family Name, The. Charles Lamb. Son

Family of Love, The, *sels.* James McAuley. Song of Shem. ChIV-1

Family of Plants, A, *sels.* Liu Sha-ho.
Cactus. LHF, *tr. by* Hualing Nieh
Goldfish, The. LHF, *tr. by* Hualing Nieh
Ivy. LHF, *tr. by* Hualing Nieh
Plum. LHF, *tr. by* Hualing Nieh
Poisonous Mushroom. LHF, *tr. by* Hualing Nieh
Poplar. LHF, *tr. by* Hualing Nieh
Wish, The. LHF, *tr. by* Hualing Nieh

Family Outing — a Celebration. Nicki Jackowska. BrRo

Family Photograph. Gerald Vizenor. VoR

Family Photograph 1939, A. James K. Baxter. OxBC

Family Pictures. Mervyn Morris. PBCV

Family Plot, October. Gail Mazur. NAmP90

Family Portrait. Eka Budianta, *tr. fr. Japanese.* TSaS, *tr. by* E.U. Kratz

Family portrait not too stale to record, A. Father and Son: 1939. William Plomer. PeSA

Family Portraits. Mary E. Tucker. CBWP-1

Family Prime. Mark Van Doren. VGW

Family Procession, A. J. P. Clark Bekedereme. HBAPE

Family Reunion. Louise Erdrich. HATNAP; NoAM

Family Reunion. Maxine W. Kumin. CAPP

Family Reunion. Hollis Spurgeon Summers. GoYe

Family story tells, and it was told true, The. Funnel. Anne Sexton. MoAmPo

Family Trees. Douglas Malloch. OHIP

Family Turn, A. William Stafford. CAPP

Family were gathered, The. Kisimiso. Musaemura Bonus Zimunya. HBAPE

Famine. Tran Thi Nga *and* Wendy Wilder Larsen, *and* Wendy Wilder Larsen. WoWa

Famine once we had. New England's Growth. William Bradford. PAH

Famine Road, The. Eavan Boland. FaBoWP

Famine Song. *Unknown. See* Oh, the praties they grow small.

Famine Year, The. Lady Wilde. IIP; TIRV

Famish me, nor over-fill. (*LL*) What Kind of Mistress He Would Have. Robert Herrick. CaPo; TrGrPo

Famished arrow sang before., The. (*LL*) All in Green Went My Love Riding. E. E. Cummings. CMoP; FaBV; GoJo; HeIL; HeIP; LiTA; LiTM; MoP; NoAM; NoP; OxBA; PoRA

Famished end to my tale this night, A. Maghnas O Domhnaill. NOIV

Famous Fight at Malago; or, The Englishmen's Victory over the Spaniards, The. *Unknown.* CoMu; OBET; OxBB

Famous Flower of Serving-Men; or, The Lady Turn'd Serving-Man, The. *Unknown.* ESPB; OBET; OxBB

Famous kingdom of the birds, The. Somewhere Is Such a Kingdom. John Crowe Ransom. CMoP; LiTA

Famous philosopher, Kant, The. C. S. Cook. PeLi

Famous Poet. Ted Hughes. LiTM

Famous poet Everette, The. The Great Man's Death: An Anecdote. Everette Maddox. MT

Famous Sea-Fight, A. John Looke. CoMu

Famous Tay Whale, The. William McGonagall. PeVV

Famous theatrical actress, A. *Unknown.* PeLi

Famously she descended, her red hair. A Recollection. John Peale Bishop. LiTA; Son

Fan-Piece, for Her Imperial Lord. Ezra Pound. MoAB

Fan, the Filly. Wilfrid Thorley. BoTP

Fanaticism? No. Writing is exciting. Baseball and Writing. Marianne Moore. BoWoP

Fanatics have their dreams, wherewith they weave. Keats. *Fr.* Fall of Hyperion, The. EnRP; OAEL-2; TOF

Fancy. Robert Creeley. NOBA

Fancy. Keats. EnRP; OBEV
Sels.
Realm of Fancy, The. GTBS; GTBS-P

Fancy. Shakespeare. *See* Tell Me Where Is Fancy [*or* Fancie] Bred.

Fancy. Jonathan Smedley. OxBSP

Fancy, A. Thomas Carew. BeJo; NOSC

Fancy, A. Thomas Lodge. *See* When I admire the rose.

Fancy, A. Thomas Lodge. *Fr.* Rosalynde; or Euphues' Golden Legacy. ElL

Fancy, A. *Unknown.* FaBoNo

Fancy, and I, last Evening walkt. To Amoret Gone from Him. Henry Vaughan. BeJo; EnLoPo; MeLP; SeCP

Fancy and Imagination. H. Cordelia Ray. CBWP-3

Fancy Dress. Dorothea MacKellar. NOBAu

Fancy, Farewell. Sir Edward Dyer. EnRePo

Fancy, farewell, that fed my fond delight. Fancy, Farewell. Sir Edward Dyer. EnRePo

Fancy Frigate, The. *Unknown.* OxBSS

Fancy halts my feet at the way-side well, A. The Way-Side Well. Joseph S. Cotter, Sr.. CDC; PoNe

Fancy (quoth he) farewell, whose badge I long did bear. The Green Knight's Farewell to Fancy. George Gascoigne. EnRePo; NoSic; OPOP

Fancy the sunrise left the door ajar! (*LL*) I know some lonely houses off the road. Emily Dickinson. MoAB; MoAmPo; OxBA; PoRA

Fancy, which that I have served long, The. The Earl of Surrey. SiPSBD (Restless Heart, The.) SiPS

Fancy's Knell. A. E. Housman. FaBoCh; PlP; PoRA

Fand, *sels.* William Larminie.
Consolation. PeIV
Epilogue. PeIV
Speech of Emer, The. PeIV

Fane Wald I Luve. *At. to* Sir John Clerk. OxBS

Fanfare for the Makers, A. Louis MacNeice. NOBE

Fanfare of drums, wooden bells: iron chapter. Thunder Can Break. Christopher Okigbo. HBAPE

Fanfare of glory. . . . And which of us dares to deny him?, A. *(LL)* Tetélestai. Conrad Aiken. LiTA; LiTM; MoAB; MoAmPo; PrIm

Fannie ("Fannie has the sweetest foot"). Thomas Bailey Aldrich. AnAmPo; OBAL

Fannie Lou Hamer. Sam Cornish. ETG

Fanny, *sels.* Fitz-Greene Halleck.
  "Fanny was younger once than she is now." CTC
  "We owe the ancients something. You have read." OBAL

Fanny Foo-Foo was a Japanese girl. The Japanese Lovers. *Unknown.* BeLS; BLPA

Fanny! If in your arms my soul could slip. Keats to Fanny Brawne. Edgar Lee Masters. PoA

Fanny was younger once than she is now. Fitz-Greene Halleck. *Fr.* Fanny. CTC

Fanny's Removal in 1714. John Winstanley. NOEC

Fantasia. Rose Terry Cooke. AmWP

Fantasia. Dorothy Livesay. MoCV

Fantasies of old age. Merced. Adrienne Rich. NOBA

Fantastic Simile, A. Thomas Lovell Beddoes. Son

Fantasy. Gwendolyn B. Bennett. BlSi; CDC; ShDr

Fantasy in Purple. Langston Hughes. CDC

Fantasy of an African Boy. James Berry. NTP; PBCV

Fantasy of Little Waters, A. James Scully. NYBP

Fantasy spaceman, The. Star Trek III. Richard Harteis. GLP

Fantasy under the Moon. Emmanuel Boundzekei-Dongala, *tr. fr. French by* Gerald Moore *and* Ulli Beier. TTY

Fantoches. Paul Verlaine, *tr. by* Arthur Symons. AWP; OBMV

Far. Anthony Barnett. VaA

Far and Close. Gu Cheng, *tr. fr. Chinese.* TSaS, *tr. by* Edward Morin

Far and near, and now, from never. Beauty. Isaac Rosenberg. TrJP

Far and wide as the eye can wander. The Peatbog Soldiers. *Unknown.* SWP

Far and wide/ outside St. Vincent. Soufrière. Andrew Salkey. PBCV

Far as creation's ample range extends. Pope. *Fr.* Essay on Man, An. ECEV; FM

Far as man can see,/ Comes the rain. Song of the Rain Chant. *Unknown, tr. fr. Navajo Indian by* Natalie Curtis. AWP

Far as the shades of Arabia. Arabia. Walter de la Mare. CoGr

Far away and blue. *(LL)* Chillingham. Mary Elizabeth Coleridge. BoTP

Far away from my heart. *(LL)* Nobody Riding the Roads Today. June Jordan. BPo; NoAM

Far away in the depth of the mountains. Shih T'ao. EaPr

Far away the spring comes down among clustered peaks. Cold Spring. Kao Ch'i, *tr. fr. Chinese by* Irving Y. Lo. SuSp

Far away, we saw three chimneys in the trees. Chimneys. Ruth Bidgood. AngWe

Far back, in the time of ice. The Ghost Hunter. John Haines. AnAn

Far back up country does enormous things. *(LL)* The Scales. William Empson. CBLP; CMoP; FaBoMo; LiTM

Far back when I went zig-zagging. Orion. Adrienne Rich. MoP; NAAL-2; NIP; NoAM; NoP; Poetr; WPE

Far beyond all the girls of Pirelli. I. D. M. Morley. PeLi

Far brighter than this gaudy melon-flower! *(LL)* Home Thoughts from Abroad. Robert Browning. ArNa; AWP; BoNaP; BoTP; ClHu; CoGr; EBEvV; EBVV; FaBoBe; FaBV; FaPoB; FaPON; FaPoR; FHYEP; GN; HeIL; HeIP; ImPo; LiTB; MeMBP; NAEL-2; NOBE; NOBVV; NoP; OBEV; OBNC; OBTV; OHCV; OtMeF; PlP; PoLF; PoRA; PrIm; TEP; TFi; TrGrPo; UV

Far court opens for us all July, The. Prothalamion. Maxine W. Kumin. NYBP

Far Cry after a Close Call, A. Richard Howard. NYBP; UnPo

Far Cry from Africa, A. Derek Walcott. HeIP; MoP; NAEL-2; NoAM; PBCV; TTY; UnPo

Far Cry to Heaven, A. Edith M. Thomas. WGRP

Far different dejection once was mine. Wordsworth. *Fr.* Prelude [or, Growth of a Poet's Mind], The. EnRP; OAEL-2; OBTV; PoEL-4 (Crossing the Alps.) RB, *sl. shorter*

Far down, down through the city's great gaunt gut. Subway Wind. Claude McKay. PBCV

Far down the purple wood. The Constant Bridegrooms. Kenneth Patchen. LiTM; NaP

"Far enough down is China," somebody said. Digging for China. Richard Wilbur. GoJo; GoEP; ImGa; TwCP

Far far from gusty waves the children's faces. An Elementary School Classroom in a Slum. Stephen Spender. FaBoMo; FF; LiTB; MoAB; MoBrPo; TrGrPo; TwCP; UnPo

Far far from here. Matthew Arnold. *Fr.* Empedocles on Etna. GTBS-P

Far, far from home they rode on their excursions. Two Englishmen. Douglas Stewart. CBAP

Far, far out lie the white sails all at rest. An Ocean Musing. H. Cordelia Ray. CBWP-3

Far far the least of all, in want. The Prisoners. Stephen Spender. FaBoMo; MoAB; MoBrPo

Far, faraway, steep mountain paths. Shih Te, *tr. fr. Chinese by* James M. Hargett. SuSp

Far-Farers, The. Robert Louis Stevenson. BoTP

Far-fetched with tales of other worlds and ways. Home from Abroad. Laurie Lee. OBTV

Far Field, The. Theodore Roethke. NAAL-2; NoAM; NoP; PrIm

Far footfalls died away till none were left. *(LL)* Ball's Bluff. Herman Melville. OBWP

Far from a cultural centre he was used. W. H. Auden. *Fr.* Sonnets from China. CMoP; NoAM

Far from Africa: Four Poems. Margaret Danner. PoBA
  Sels.
  Garnishing the Aviary. BPo

Far from cruel men. *(LL)* Cactus. Jean-Joseph Rabéarivelo. NegPo

Far from hence the evill Sp'rite. *(LL)* The Spell. Robert Herrick. CaPo

Far from his father's house, in alien Canaan. *(LL)* Abraham. Edwin Muir. ChIV-1

Far from Home. Joseph Freiherr von Eichendorff, *tr. fr. German by* Philip L. Miller. RiWo

Far from Italy, far from my native Tarentum. Leonidas of Tarentum, *tr. fr. Greek by* Fleur Adcock. GrAn

Far from kingdoms. Patrizia Cavalli, *tr. fr. Italian by* Judith Baumel. NeIt

Far from Our Friends. Jeremy Belknap. AH

Far from our garden at the edge of a gulf. The Gulf. Denise Levertov. NNaP

Far from the deep roar of the Aegean main. Plato, *tr. fr. Greek by* Charles Whibley. AWP

Far from the happy homeland I adore. *(LL)* On a Shipmate, Pero Moniz, Dying at Sea. Camões. PeSAV

Far from the loud sea beaches. A Visit from the Sea. Robert Louis Stevenson. FM; GN

Far from the Madding Crowd. Nixon Waterman. BLPA; FaBoBe

Far from the parlour have your kitchen placed. William King. *Fr.* Art of Cookery, The. ECEV; FaBoUs

Far from the Rapahannock, the silent. Into the Duck-Charged Air. John Ashbery. CBCK

Far from the scent of the crocus. That's Life? Alan Bold. FF

Far from the sea far from the sea. The Canticle of Jack Kerouac. Lawrence Ferlinghetti. PoBeRe

Far from the sun and summer gale. Thomas Gray. *Fr.* Progress of Poesy, The. EPCY

Far from the tender tribe of boys remove. Tibullus, *tr. fr. Latin by* John Dart. *Fr.* Odes. PeHV

Far from the thronged luxurious town. On Honour. Bernard Mandeville. NOEC

Far from the trouble and toil of town. Old Man Platypus. Andrew Barton Paterson. OBAP; ZA

Far from the vulgar haunts of men. On the Same. Roy Campbell. OxBTC

Far from their homes they lie, the men who fell. On a War-worker, 1916. Arundell James Kennedy Esdaile. NSI

Far from thy dearest self, the scope. To His Mistress in Absence. Tasso, *tr. fr. Italian by* Thomas Stanley. AWP

Far from your crumpled mountains, plains that vultures ponder. Jamaica. Louis Simpson. PBCV

Far greater numbers have been lost by hopes. Samuel Butler. FaBoEE

Far hence amid an isle of wondrous beauty. Old Ireland. Walt Whitman. IIP

Far In a Western Brookland. A. E. Housman. *Fr.* Shropshire Lad, A. AWP; FaPoB; PoEL-5

Far in the east, far below. House Song to the East. *Unknown, tr. fr. Navajo Indian.* TTTS

Far in the Heavens my God retires. The Incomprehensible. Isaac Watts. WGRP

Far in the land of sunny South. A Southern Scene. Priscilla Jane Thompson. CBWP-2

Far in the woods my stealthy flute. The Magic Flute. W. D. Snodgrass. NYBP

Far inland/ go my sad thoughts. *Unknown, tr. fr. Eskimo by* Knud Rasmussen. BoWoP, *ad. by* Willis Barnstone

Far Land, The. John Hall Wheelock. WGRP

Far moon maketh lovers wise, The. Moonlight. Walter de la Mare. EnLoPo

Far more than night bewearièd. (*LL*) His Age, Dedicated to His Peculiar Friend, Master John Wickes, under the Name of Posthumus. Robert Herrick. CaPo; SeCP

Far off a lonely hound. The Hounds. John Freeman. OBMV; OxBSP

Far off, above the plain the summer dries. Second Air Force. Randall Jarrell. CMoP; LiTM; NAAL-2

Far-off/ at the core of space. Swan. D. H. Lawrence. CMoP; PoE

Far off brough, A. *Unknown*. FaBoVe

Far off, demimordial, I hear an epitaph of ears, someone. Poem. William Knott. UL

Far-off, most secret, and inviolate Rose. The Secret Rose. W. B. Yeats. MeMBP; NAEL-2

Far-off mountains hide you from me, The. Absent Lover. *Unknown, tr. fr. Xhosa by* A. C. Jordan. PBA

Far off the sea is grey and still as the sky. Week-End by the Sea. Edgar Lee Masters. MoAmPo

Far, oh, far is the Mango island. The Constant Cannibal Maiden. Wallace Irwin. AnAmPo; OBAL

Far on its rocky knoll descried. Scenes from Carnac. Matthew Arnold. FaBoPP; OBTV

Far out at sea. White Horses. Irene F. Pawsey. BoTP

Far out beyond the city's lights, away from din and roar. The Country Store. *Unknown*. BLPA

Far out in the estuary all night. Nightshift. John Seed. VaA

Far out of sight forever stands the sea. The Slow Pacific Swell. Yvor Winters. NOBA

Far over the hills, a good way off. *Unknown*. RoPo

Far Side of Introspection, The. Alfred M. Lee. CoAP

Far spread, below. The Story of Vinland. Sidney Lanier. *Fr. Psalm of the West.* PAH

Far spread the moory ground, a level scene. The Moors. John Clare. EnVR

Far Sweeter than Honey. Abraham ibn Ezra, *tr. fr. Hebrew by* Israel Abrahams. TrJP

Far to the left he saw the huts of men. East Anglian Fen. George Crabbe. *Fr.* Tales of the Hall. FaBoPP

Far up among the forest-belted mountains. The Desolate Valley. Thomas Pringle. OBTV

Far up the cold mountain the stony path slopes. Travelling in the Mountains. Tu Mu, *tr. fr. Chinese by* A. C. Graham. PLT

Far up the dim twilight fluttered. The Unknown God. "Æ." MoBrPo; WGRP

Far up the River — hark! 'tis the loud shock. A Flight of Wild Ducks. Charles Harpur. NOBAu

Far Within Us, *sels.* Vasco [*or* Vasko] Popa, *tr. fr. Serbo-Croatian*.
"Look that is that uninvited." PoSu, *tr. by* Anne Pennington
"Streets of your glances, The." PoSu, *tr. by* Anne Pennington
"These are your lips." PoSu, *tr. by* Anne Pennington

Fara Diddle Dyno. *At. to* Thomas Weelkes. CBNP; EiL; FaBoCh; FaBoCo; FaBoNo

Faraway hands are folded and folded. The Starry Night. George Starbuck. NYBP

Fare Thee Well. Byron. BLPA; CBLP; EnRP; MeMBP; OBNC; PoEL-4

Fare Thee Well. Eli Siegel. GOA

Fare thee well! and if for ever. Fare Thee Well. Byron. BLPA; CBLP; EnRP; MeMBP; OBNC; PoEL-4

Fare thee well, my lovely Dinah, a thousand times adieu. The Holy Ground. *Unknown*. OxBSS

Fare thee well, O Honey, fare thee well. (*LL*) Dink's Song. *Unknown*. ErPo; OxBoLi

Fare thee well to Prince's Landing Stage, River Mersey fare thee well. The Leaving of Liverpool. *Unknown*. OxBSS

Fare Well. Walter de la Mare. EBEvV; GTBS-P; NOBE; OBEV

Fare well fare well, kind poetry my friend. She Begining to Study Phisick, Takes Her Leave of Poetry. Jane Barker. KTR

Fare Ye Well, Lovely Nancy. *Unknown*. OxBSS

Fare you well, my blue-eyed girl. Blue-eyed Girl. *Unknown*. AmFP

Fare You Well, My Darling. *Unknown*. AmFP

Fare you well, my own true love, for growing. (*LL*) The Trees They Do Grow High. *Unknown*. OBET

Fareswell, thou humid main. (*LL*) O Billows Bounding Far. A. E. Housman. BoNaP

Fareweel to a' our Scottish fame. Such a Parcel of Rogues in a Nation. Burns. OxBS

Fareweill, with patience perforce till day. (*LL*) The Solsequium. Alexander Montgomerie. NoP

Fareweill, with patience perforce till day. (*LL*) The Solsequium. Alexander Montgomerie. NoP; OxBS

Farewel, dear daughter Sara; now Thou'rt gone. In Saram. John Cotton. SCAP

Farewel to Love, A. Elizabeth Singer. KTR

Farewel to Worldly Joyes, A ("Farewel to unsubstantial joyes.") Anne Killigrew. BoWoP

Farewel ye guilded follies, pleasing troubles. *Unknown*. MeLP

Farewele Advent; Cristemas [*or* Christemas] is cum [*or* come]. James Ryman. MiEL
(Farewell Advent.) MeEL

Farewell. Byron. *See* Farewell! If Ever Fondest Prayer.

Farewell. Federico García Lorca, *tr. fr. Spanish by* W. S. Merwin. OBD

Farewell. (*LL*) Upon His Departure Hence. Robert Herrick. FaBoRV; Poetr

Farewell — farewell to thee, Araby's daughter! The Peri's Lament for Hinda. Thomas Moore. *Fr.* Lalla Rookh. OBNC

Farewell, A. Matthew Arnold. *Fr.* Switzerland. EnVR; MeMBP

Farewell, A. George Gascoigne. *See* And if I did, what then?

Farewell, A: "It was a' for our rightfu' king." Burns. *See* It Was A' for Our Rightfu' King.

Farewell! A long farewell, to all my greatness! Wolsey's Farewell to His Greatness. John Fletcher *and* William Shakespeare. *Fr.* King Henry VIII.
(Cardinal Wolsey's Farewell.) LiTB
(Farewell to Greatness.) TrGrPo

Farewell, A: "Venus, take my votive glass." Matthew Prior, *after the Greek of* Plato. *See* Venus, take my votive glass.

Farewell: "Far from the deep roar of the Aegean main." Plato, *tr. fr. Greek by* Charles Whibley. AWP

Farewell: "Farewell to the bushy clump close to the river." John Clare. NoP

Farewell: "Flow down, cold rivulet, to the sea." Tennyson. FaBoRV; PFP

Farewell: "Gone, gone — sold and gone." Whittier. AWP; PoNe

Farewell: "Good-bye! — no [*or* nay] do not grieve that it is over." Harriet Monroe. PoA

Farewell: "I search/ for the straight path." Florence Dacey. LoHo

Farewell: "Juliet, farewell. I would not be forgiven." Wilfrid Scawen Blunt. *Fr.* Love Sonnets of Proteus, The. TrGrPo

Farewell: "Linden blossomed, the nightingale sang, The." Heine, *tr. fr. German by* John Todhunter. AWP

Farewell: "My boat goes west, yours east." Ch'ao Li-houa, *tr. fr. Chinese by* J. P. Seaton. BoWoP

Farewell: "My fairest child, I have no song to give you." Charles Kingsley. BLPA; EBVV; GN; OxBChV

Farewell: "No more/ The feel of your hand." Mae V. Cowdery. ShDr

Farewell: "Not soon shall I forget — a sheet." Katharine Tynan. CH

Farewell: "Oft have I mused, but now at length I find." Sir Philip Sidney. EiL; EnRePo; GBL; NOBE; SiPS

Farewell: "Shores of my native land." Isaac Toussaint L'Ouverture, *tr. fr. French by* Edna Worthley Underwood. TTY

Farewell: "Smell of death was in the air, The." John Press. PoRA

Farewell: "Well, you have gone now, comrades." E.A. Mackintosh. NSI

Farewell: "What is there left to be said?" A. R. D. Fairburn. PeNZ

Farewell: "With all my will, but much against my heart." Coventry Patmore. *Fr.* Unknown Eros, The. BoLoP; EnLoPo; GTBS-P; NOBE; OBEV; OBNC; PoEL-5; PoNe

Farewell: "You sang round-dance songs." Liz Sohappy Bahe. CDW

Farewell! Adieu! Good-bye! So long! (*LL*) To a Thesaurus. Franklin P. Adams. BLPL; NBLV

Farewell, adieu, that courtly life. Haltersick's Song. John Pickering. *Fr.* Horestes. NoSic
(Song: "Farewell, adieu, that court-like life!") EiL

Farewell Advent. James Ryman. *See* Farewele Advent; Cristemas [*or* Christemas] is cum [*or* come].

Farewell! Advent. James Ryman. MeEL

Farewell, all my welfare. Sir Thomas Wyatt. GBL; SiPS; SiPSBD

Farewell all pleasure! welcome pain and smart! (*LL*) Absence absenting causeth me to complain. Sir Thomas Wyatt. SiPS; SiPSBD

Farewell and adieu to you, Spanish ladies. Spanish Ladies. *Unknown*. FaBoCh; OxBSS

Farewell and Good. Denis Devlin. IPY

Farewell, Bristola's dingy piles of brick. Last Verses. Thomas Chatterton. TrGrPo

Farewell! — but whenever you welcome the hour. Long, Long Be My Heart with Such Memories Filled. Thomas Moore. BLPL; FaBoBe

Farewell content. Shakespeare. *Fr.* Othello. TrGrPo

Farewell dear babe, my heart's too much content. In Memory of My Dear Grandchild Elizabeth Bradstreet Who Deceased August, 1665, Being a Year and a Half Old. Anne Bradstreet. EAP; NAAL-1; NOCV; SCAP; WPE

Farewell, dear love! Since thou wilt needs be gone. *Unknown*. EiL; NoSic

Farewell, dear scenes, for ever closed to me. Lines Written upon a Window-Shutter at Weston. William Cowper. NOEC

Farewell false friends, farewell ill wine. Farewell to England. *Unknown.* APAS

Farewell, false love, the oracle of lies. A Farewell to False Love. Sir Walter Ralegh. BoLoP; ElL; LPA; NAEL-1; NoSic; SiPSBD (False Love.) SiPS

Farewell, farewell! Before our prow. Dover to Munich. Charles Stuart Calverley. NOBL, *abr.*; OBTV

Farewell, farewell! but this I tell. Samuel Taylor Coleridge. *Fr.* Rime of the Ancient Mariner, The. BeLS; CH; EBEV; EBNV; EnRP; FaBoBe; FaBoCh; FaBV; FaPoB; FHYEP; HAP; HeIP; HoPM; ImPo; InPS; LiTB; MeMBP; NOBE; NoP; OAEL-2; OBEV; OBNC; OBNV; OtMeF; OxAEP-2; PeECV; PFP; PoE; PoEL-4; PrIm; SCGP; TEP; TFi; TOF, *abr.*; TrGrPo

Farewell, farewell, my pretty maid. The True Lover's Farewell. *Unknown.* AS

Farewell, farewell, Your Royal Highness. *(LL)* A Luncheon. Max Beerbohm. FaBoCo; NOBL; OBSV; OxBTC; PeLV

Farewell! for now a stormy morn and dark. Outward Bound. Edward Sydney Tylee. PAH

Farewell Frost; or, Welcome the Spring. Robert Herrick. CaPo

Farewell has long been said; I have forgone thee. After a Parting. Alice Meynell. NOBVV

Farewell! I goe to sleep; but when. The Evening-Watch. Henry Vaughan *and* Thomas Stanley. ESCV

Farewell! If Ever Fondest Prayer. Byron. EnRP

Farewell in a Dream. Stephen Spender. MoAB; MoBrPo

Farewell, incomparable element. Hymn to Earth. Elinor Wylie. LiTM; MoAB; MoAmPo

Farewell, Life. Thomas Hood. EnRP

Farewell, little girl, until tomorrow. *(LL)* Jota. Manuel de Falla. RiWo

Farewell, love, and all thy laws [*or* lawes] for ever. Sir Thomas Wyatt. AAS; CBLP; LiTB; NAEL-1; NoSic; OAEL-1; SCGP; SiPS; SiPSBD (Lover Renounceth Love, The.) TrGrPo (Renancing of Love, A.) GBL; Son

Farewell Mercy, farewell thy piteous grace. John Lydgate. *Fr.* Court of Sapience. PoEL-1

Farewell my Betty, and farewell my Annie. Christian Carstairs. ECWP

Farewell, my dearer half, joy of my heart. First Farewell to J. G. "Ephelia." NOSC

Farewell, my dearest dear, now I must leave thee. The Seamen and Soldiers' Last Farewell to Their Dearest Jewels. *Unknown.* OxBSS

Farewell, my Youth! for now we needs must part. Ave atque Vale. Rosamund Marriott Watson. NOBE; OAEL-2; OBEV; OBNC

Farewell now, poesy's secret cell, thy ordered grace. Farewell to Hendre Fechan. William Phylip, *tr. fr. Welsh by* H. Idris Bell. OBWVE

Farewell, O Prince, farewell, O sorely tried! Theodor Herzl. Israel Zangwill. TrJP

Farewell, O Sun, Arcadia's clearest light. Sestina: "Farewell, O Sun." Sir Philip Sidney. *Fr.* Arcadia. SiPSBD

Farewell of an Old Man. Tu Fu, *tr. fr. Chinese by* Michael E. Workman. SuSp

Farewell of the Attendant Spirit. Milton. *See* To the ocean now I fly.

Farewell, old friend, we part at last. My Old Straw Hat. Eliza Cook. BrRo

Farewell, Old Year! Old and New. *Unknown.* BLRP

Farewell old year, for Thou canst ne're return. A Farewell to the Year. *Unknown.* FaBoEH

Farewell, Peace. *Unknown.* PAH

Farewell Performance. James Merrill. PFL

Farewell, Petrovsky Castle, witness. Entering Moscow. Pushkin, *tr. fr. Russian by* Thomas de Waal. *Fr.* Evgeny Onegin. CBCK

Farewell Poem, *sels.* Tu Mu, *tr. fr. Chinese by* A. C. Graham. "Passion too deep seems like none." PLT

Farewell, politics, utterly! What can I do? I can not. Arthur Hugh Clough. *Fr.* Amours of Voyage. FaBoPV; NOBVV

Farewell poor Turkeys I must say. *(LL)* A Melancholy Lay. Marjory Fleming. FaBoCh; FiBHP; NBLV

Farewell rewards and Fairies. A Proper New Ballad, Intitled The Fairies' Farewell. Richard Corbett [*or* Corbet]. PeLV; SCGP

Farewell rewards and fairies. Richard Corbett [*or* Corbet]. *Fr.* Fairies' Farewell, The. OtMeF

Farewell, rewards and fairies. The Fairies' Farewell. Richard Corbett [*or* Corbet]. *Fr.* Her Boreale. BeJo; CoGr; NOSC; OxAEP-1

Farewell, sweet boy; complain not of my truth. Fulke Greville. *Fr.* Caelica. EnRePo; FaBoRV; GBL; Son

Farewell (sweet Cooke-ham) where I first obtain'd. The Description of Cooke-ham. Emilia Lanier. KTR

Farewell, Sweet Dust. Elinor Wylie. LiTA

Farewell, sweet Jane, for I must go across the flowing sea. Sweet Jane. *Unknown.* AmFP

Farewell, Sweet Mary. *Unknown.* AmFP

Farewell, the bell upon a ram's neck hung. Corydon's Farewell, on Sailing in the Late Expedition Fleet. *Unknown.* NOEC

Farewell the reign of cruelty. Sir Thomas Wyatt. SiPS

Farewell the rest, the soil will be disdain'd. *(LL)* The Advice. Sir Walter Ralegh. AAS; SiPS; SiPSBD

Farewell, This World. (Farewell, this world! I take my leve for ever.) *Unknown.* EnVB; MeEL, *abr.*; MiEL

Sels.
Garnishing the Aviary. BPo
"This lyfe, I see, is but a cheyre feyre." ChTr

Farewell This World. *Unknown.* OxBLMV

Farewell! Thou art too dear [*or* deare] for my possessing. Shakespeare. *Fr.* Sonnets. CBLP; EBEV; EBEvV; EiL; GTBS; GTBS-P; ImPo; InPS; InvP; LiTB; NAEL-1; NOBE; NoSic; OAEL-1; OBEV; OxAEP-1; PeHV; PoEL-2; Son; TFi; TrGrPo

Farewell; thou busy world, and may. The Retirement. Charles Cotton. *Fr.* To Mr. Izaak Walton. FaBoPP

Farewell, thou child of my right hand, and joy. On My First Son [*or* Sonne]. Ben Jonson. AWP; BeJo; CiHu; CoGr; EBEV; EiL; EnRePo; FaBoEE; FF; HAP; HoPM; IMW; InPK; InPS; JCP; LiTB; NAEL-1; NIP; NoP; NOSC; OAEL-1; OBD; OxBSP; PFP; PoE; PoEL-2; Poetr; RaBo; RB; SCGP; SeCP; SeCV-1; TEP; TFi; TRP; WeW (On My Son.) NOBE

Farewell Thou Minstrel Harp. Sir Walter Scott. *See* Harp of the North, Farewell! The Hills Grow Dark.

Farewell, thou thing, time-past so known, so dear. His Farewell to Sack. Robert Herrick. BeJo; CaPo; NAEL-1; SeCP; SeCV-1

Farewell to a Fondling, A. Thomas Churchyard. EiL

Farewell to a Friend. Hsüeh T'ao, *tr. fr. Chinese by* Eric Johnson. SuSp

Farewell to a Jovial Friend. Gloria Escoffery. PBCV

Farewell to a Southern Melody, A. Huang O, *tr. fr. Chinese by* Kenneth Rexroth *and* Ling Chung. BoWoP; WPC

Farewell to a Trappist. Lucy Boston. VBLP

Farewell to Allen University. Josephine D. Henderson Heard. CBWP-4

Farewell to an idea . . . A cabin stands. Wallace Stevens. *Fr.* Auroras of Autumn, The. CMoP; HCAP

Farewell to an idea . . . The mother's face. Wallace Stevens. *Fr.* Auroras of Autumn, The. CMoP; HCAP

Farewell to Anactoria. Sappho, *tr. fr. Greek by* Allen Tate. AWP

Farewell to Arms, A. George Peele. *See* His golden locks time hath to siluer turn'd.

Farewell to Barn and Stack and Tree. A. E. Housman. *Fr.* Shropshire Lad, A. CMoP; FaPoB; MoAB; MoBrPo; UnPo

Farewell to Bath. Lady Mary Wortley Montagu. WPE

Farewell, To C. E. G, A. Charles Kingsley. BoTP

Farewell to Democracy. William Plomer. IHNG

Farewell to Dostoevski. "Hugh MacDiarmid." *Fr.* Drunk Man Looks at the Thistle, A. NAEL-2

Farewell to England. *Unknown.* APAS

Farewell to English, A, *sels.* Michael Hartnett.
"Gaelic is the conscience of our leaders." CIP
"Half afraid to break a promise." NOIV

Farewell to Europe. William Pillen. BTR

Farewell to False Love, A. Sir Walter Ralegh. BoLoP; ElL; LPA; NAEL-1; NoSic; SiPSBD

Farewell to Fan Yun at An Ch'eng. Shen Yüeh, *tr. fr. Chinese by* Kenneth Rexroth. OHMPC

Farewell to Florida. Wallace Stevens. NoAM

Farewell to Folly, *sels.* Robert Greene.
Maesia's Song. CTC; UnPo
(Mind Content, A.) CBCK; EiL
(Poor Estate, The.) TrGrPo
(Song: "Sweet are the thoughts that savour of content.") PoEL-2

Farewell to Greatness. John Fletcher *and* William Shakespeare. *See* Farewell! A long farewell, to all my greatness!

Farewell to Hendre Fechan. William Phylip, *tr. fr. Welsh by* H. Idris Bell. OBWVE

Farewell to Hiruharama. Haere Ra. James K. Baxter. PeNZ

Farewell to Ireland. At. *to* St. Columcille Saint Columcille, *tr. by* Douglas Hyde. AWP

Farewell to Juliet. Wilfrid Scawen Blunt. *Fr.* Love Sonnets of Proteus, The.

Farewell to Juliet ("I see you, Juliet, still, with your straw hat.") Wilfrid Scawen Blunt. *Fr.* Love Sonnets of Proteus, The. BoLoP; EnLoPo; OxBTC

Farewell to Kingsbridge. *Unknown.* ECEV

Farewell to Kurdistan. Rosemary Tonks. OxBTC

Farrell O'Reilly. Oliver St. John Gogarty. OxBTC

Farrier's Dog. Paul Hyland. PWE

Farther he went the farther home grew, The. For the Grave of Daniel Boone. William Stafford. NoP

Farther in the summer than the birds. Emily Dickinson. *See* Further in summer than the birds.

Farther than I have been. The Summit. Kathleen Raine. *Fr.* Beinn Naomh. OxBS

Farthest from any war, unique in time. Hollywood. Karl Shapiro. LiTM; OxBA

Farthest thunder that I heard, The. Emily Dickinson. NAAL-1

Farthing, A. *Unknown.* OxNR

Fascinated by rains of empty joy. Waiting Out Rain, Sheltered by Overhang. Reg Saner. FoLa

Fascination of What's Difficult, The. W. B. Yeats. BIrV; NAEL-2; OxAEP-2; PoEL-5

Fascist, erect and irate, A. Thomas Thorneley. PeLi

Fa'se Footrage. *Unknown. See* King Easter has courted her for her gowd.

Fashion. Ada Cambridge. NOBAu

Fashion. Horace Twiss. BXAP

Fashion changes! Maidens do not wear, The. Andrew Lang. *Fr.* To Lord Byron. EPCY

Fashionable blood. Drip Drip or Not Bloody Likely. Gerda Mayer. PeLV

Fashioned After the Manner of Master Geoffrey Chaucer in His Assembly of Fowls. Thomas, the Elder Warton. ChIV-1

Fashions in Dogs. E. B. White. FiBHP

Fast Ball. Jonathan Williams. NeAP

Fast Break. Edward Hirsch. DiPo; EOEF; VCAP

Fast falls the snow, O lady mine. To F. C. Mortimer Collins. NOBVV

Fast hearts, skies deep-descended intervene. (*LL*) Twilit Revelation. Léonie Adams. MoAB; MoAmPo

Fast-locked the land for weeks. Of ice we dream. Silver Lake. Brigit Pegeen Kelly. NAmP90

Fast rode the knight. Stephen Crane. *Fr.* War Is Kind. MeMAP; NAAL-2

Fasten the chamber! Bluebeard's Closet. Rose Terry Cooke. AmWP

Fastened her down forever! (*LL*) Ginevra. Samuel Rogers. BeLS; OxAEP-2; PoLF

Faster than fairies, faster than witches. From a Railway Carriage. Robert Louis Stevenson. BoTP; FaPON; OTCP; OxBChV; PDV; PYC

Fat and Skinny had a race. *Unknown.* RoPo

Fat black bucks in a wine-barrel room. The Congo. Vachel Lindsay. CMoP; LiTA; MeMAP; MoAB; MoAmPo; NOBA; OxBA; PoNe; PoRA; TAP

Fat Blues. Charmaine Crowell. AIW

Fat Boy's Dream, The. Richard McCann. GrPl

Fat Budgie, The. John Lennon. NBLV

Fat cat on the mat, The. Cat. J. R. R. Tolkien. CRH

Fat friar stroking golf balls, The. Walking along the Hudson. Donald Petersen. CoAP

Fat girls have more fun in the woods. Bernadette Murphy, 1943-1955. Thomas Rabbitt. NAmP90

Fat-kneed god! Feeder of mangy leopards! You Also, Gaius Valerius Catullus. Archibald MacLeish. NoAM; TAP

Fat Man in the Mirror, The. Robert Lowell. PoA

Fat men. After Hilary, Age 5. Faye Kicknosway. UL

Fat Men, The. Cyril Dabydeen. PBCV

Fat men go about the streets, The. Ballade of the Poetic Life. J. C. Squire. OBMV

Fat red barns lean east along Highway 109. Leaving Mendota, 1956. Lawrence Locke. GrPl

Fat sixty-year-old man woke me, A. "Hello." Birthday. John Ciardi. NAs

Fat-tailed Dwarf Lemur, in bed, A. Gerry Hamill. PeLi

Fat White Woman Speaks, The. G. K. Chesteron. UV

Fatal Dream; or, The Unhappy Favourite, The. Emanuel Collins. NOEC

Fatal Interview, *sels.* Edna St. Vincent Millay.
   Love Is Not All. Son

Fatal Love. Matthew Prior. FaBoCo; NBLV

Fatal Sisters, The. Thomas Gray, *after the Icelandic.* EnRP

Fatal Spell, The. Byron. *See* Oh love! no habitant of earth thou art.

Fatal, to put the end before the means. Begging the Question. Daryl Hine. PFL

Fatales Poetae. Henry Parrot. FaBoEE

Fatality. D. H. Lawrence. PeECV

Fate. Susan Marr Spalding. BLPA; PoToHe

Fate and the Younger Generation. D. H. Lawrence. OxBoLi

Fate brought three men to birth. Petronius Arbiter, *tr. fr. Latin. Fr.* Satyricon. MLL, *tr. by* Helen Waddell

Fate cannot touch me: I have dined to-day. (*LL*) Beer. Charles Stuart Calverley. BXAP; FaBoCo

Fate didn't hustle Gessius to his death. Palladas, *tr. fr. Greek by* Tony Harrison. GrAn

Fate gave the word, the arrow sped. A Mother's Lament for the Death of Her Son. Burns. HoPM

Fate in Incognito. Michael Benedikt. OBAL

Fate of John Burgoyne, The. *Unknown.* PAH

Fate of the Cabbage Rose, The. Wallace Irwin. FiBHP

Fate of the Oak, The. "Barry Cornwall." OHIP

Fate of the Prophets, The. Longfellow. *Fr.* Christus; a Mystery. WGRP

Fate of the Sons of Usna, The. John Todhunter. *Fr.* First Duan: The Coming of Deidre, The. PeIV

Fate on the left hand, and Death on the right. And Again. Humphrey Evans. BXAP

Fate struck the hour! Lincoln. Jane L. Hardy. OHIP

Fate to beauty still must give. Claudian, *tr. fr. Latin by* Howard Mumford Jones. AWP

Fateful slumber floats and flows, The. For the Briar Rose. William Morris. NOBVV

Fates of Men (Exeter Book). *Unknown, tr. fr. Old English by* Charles W. Kennedy. AnOE

Fates of the Apostles, *sels.* Cynewulf, *tr. fr. Anglo-Saxon by* Charles W. Kennedy.
   "Now I pray the man who may love this lay." AnOE

Father. Paul Carroll. NeAP

Father, The. John Donne. *Fr.* Litanie, The. NOCV; PoEL-2

Father. Arthur Davison Ficke. TrPWD

Father. Frances Frost. FaPON

Father. Margit Kaffka, *tr. fr. Hungarian by* Laura Schiff. PBWP

Father. Jean Lipkin. AIW; PeSA

Father. Myra Cohn Livingston. NTCP

Father. John Wheelwright. UnPo

Father . . . — Say the confiteor. — I said it. The Confessor. Giuseppe Gioacchino Belli, *tr. fr. Italian by* Harold Norse. ErPo

Father, and bard revered! to whom I owe. Dedicatory Sonnet to S. T. Colerige. Hartley Coleridge. OAEL-2; Son

Father and Child. Gwen Harwood. CBAP; WPE

Father and Daughter. Jean Follain, *tr. fr. French by* W. S. Merwin. AnRep

Father and Daughter. Cathy Song. OpBo

Father and His Children, The. *Unknown.* OxBChV

Father and Mother. X. J. Kennedy. GrPl

Father and Son. Robert Greacen. PNI

Father and Son. F. R. Higgins. BIrV; OBMV

Father and Son. Tomasz Jastrun, *tr. fr. Polish.* TSaS, *tr. by* Daniel Bourne

Father and Son. Stanley Kunitz. CAPP; MoP; Poetr; TwCP

Father and Son. Delmore Schwartz. LiTA

Father and Son: 1939. William Plomer. PeSA

Father, between Thy strong hands Thou has bent. Prayer of a Teacher. Dorothy Littlewort. TrPWD

Father calls me William, sister calls me Will. Jest 'fore Christmas. Eugene Field. FaBV; FaPON; PoLF

Father dead and mother dead. The Female Principle. A. D. Hope. OxBC

Father, dear father, come home with me now! Come Home, Father. Henry Clay Work. VPP

Father Death Blues. Allen Ginsberg. *Fr.* Don't Grow Old. SM

Father Father Son and Son. Jon Swan. NYBP

Father, father, where are you going? Little Boy Lost, The ("Father, father, where are you going?") Blake. *Fr.* Songs of Innocence. EnRP; FHYEP; NoP

Father grew up here. Red Hills of Home. Chenjerai Hove. HBAPE

Father Grumble. *Unknown.* AmFP

Father Guru. Allen Ginsberg. BCF

Father Guru unforlorn. Father Guru. Allen Ginsberg. BCF

Father, Hear the Prayer We Offer. Love Maria Willis. AH

Father heard his children scream. The Stern parent. Harry Graham. *Fr.* Some Ruthless Rhymes. CBNP; ChTr; PeLV

Father, hello and goodbye. (*LL*) Elegy. Alan Dugan. CAPP; NIP

Father, here a temple in Thy name we build. Hymn of Dedication. Elizabeth E. Scantlebury. BLRP

Father, How Wide Thy Glories Shine. Charles Wesley. TrPWD

Father Hunger and Son. Roger Weingarten. NAmP90

Father! I bless thy name that I do live. In Him We Live. Jones Very. OxBA

Father, I expect your eyes. Before the Mountain. Elizabeth Libbey. AmPA

Feather Plucked from the Tail of the Fiery Hen, A. Novica Tadic, *tr. fr.* *Serbo-Croatian by* Charles Simic. HSix

Feather that all, The. Abukbo. Jim Barnes. *Fr.* Four Things Choctaw. HATNAP

Featherd fowl's in your orchard, father, A. Brown Robin. *Unknown.* ESPB

Featherd songster chaunticleer, The. Bristowe Tragedie: or, The Dethe of Syr Charles Bawdin. Thomas Chatterton. EnRP; OxBB

Feathered Friends. Robert Peters. BXAP

Feathers blacken against the sun. Manifest Destiny. Anita Endrezze-Danielson. CDW

Feathers in a fan, The. Man. Humbert Wolfe. MoBrPo

Feather[s] lopped off, spur[r]s everywhere did lie. *(LL)* Ad Johannuelem Leporem, Lepidissimum, Carmen Heroicum. *Unknown.* CBNP; FaBoNo

Feathers of Snow. *Unknown.* GBP

Feathers of the willow, The. Richard Watson Dixon. BoNaP; CH; FaBoCh; GTBS-P; NOBE; OBNC
   (Willow.) OBEV

Feathers or Lead? James Richard Broughton. NeAP

Feathers up fast, and steeples; then in clods. The Fountain. Donald Davie. GTBS-P; OxBTC

Feather's Weight, A. George Parsons Lathrop. FaBoUs

Featherstone's Doom. Robert Stephen Hawker. OBNC

Feathery forests are blown back, frost rends, The. Winter. John Lyle Donaghy. BIrV

Featureless ghost under the wall cannot jerk out at us, The. Elegy for the Silent Voices and the Joiners of Everything. Kenneth Patchen. NaP

Featureless pain at the back of the head, The. Cuidado Amigo. Iván Argüelles. UL

February. John Clare. *Fr.* Shepherd's *[or* Shepheards] Calendar, The. NOBE; OBNC

February. John Heath-Stubbs. OBCP

February. W. S. Merwin. NNaP

February. Lolly Quinones. IMW

February. Dorothy Una Ratcliffe. BoTP

February. H. Cordelia Ray. CBWP-3

February. Folgore da San Geminiano, *tr. fr. Italian by* Dante Gabriel Rossetti. *Fr.* Sonnets of the Months. AWP

February. James Schuyler. NeAP

February Afternoon. Edward Thomas. NoAM; PeFWW; PoWW

February 11, 1977. Frederick Morgan. DiPo

February Evening in New York. Denise Levertov. NoAM

February Evenings. Andrew Crozier. VaA

February 14th — Valentine's Day. *Unknown.* ISE

February in Sydney. Yusef Komunyakaa. Jaz

February Morning. King D. Kuka. VoR

February Park. Gerald Vizenor. VoR

February; the Boy Breughel. Norman Dubie. LCAP

February 13, 1980, *sels.* Lucille Clifton.
   "Twenty-one years of my life you have been." CrSp; MDDM

February Town, The. Sebastian Barry. IB

February 22. John Updike. GOA

February Twilight. Sara Teasdale. FaPON; OBCA; PDV

February's Forgotten Mitts. Raymond Knister. NOBC

Feckless Dinner Party, The. Walter de la Mare. FaBoTw

Fedele and Fortunio, *sels.* Anthony Munday.
   I Serve a Mistress. EiL
      (Fedele's Song.) CBCK
      (I serve a mistress whiter than snow.) HAP; SCGP

Fedele's Song. Anthony Munday. *See* I Serve a Mistress.

Federal Constitution, The. William Milns. PAH

Federal Convention, The. *Unknown.* PAH

Federation. W. T. Goodge. NOBAu

Federico's Ghost. Martín Espada. AfAz

Fee, faw, fum! bubble and squeak! Holy-Cross Day. Robert Browning. OtMeF

Fee, fi, fo, fum. *Unknown.* OxNR

Feeble race of man!, The. *(LL)* Express. William Allingham. NOBVV

Feed, silly sheep, although your keeper pineth. William Smith. *Fr.* Chloris [or the Complaint of the Passionate Despised Shepheard]. Son

Feed still thy self, thou fondling, with belief. *Unknown.* NoSic

Feed the Mexican Back into Her. Cherríe Moraga. GLP

Feed Thou my feeble shoots. *(LL)* Long Barren. Christina Rossetti. PBWP; TrCP

Feed/ Upon anticipation as you sow the seed. Harvest Time. Star Powers. GoYe

Feede on my flocks securely. To His Flocks. *At. to* Henry Constable *and also to* Henry Chettle. FM

Feeding, The. Joel Oppenheimer. NeAP

Feeding a Child. Nuala Ni Dhomhnaill, *tr. fr. Irish by* Michael Hartnett. CIP

Feeding Ducks. Norman MacCaig. OxBS

Feeding Ground. Thomas McCarthy. CIP

Feeding the Dog. Russell Edson. RaBo

Feeding the ducks at the Howard Johnson Motel. Susan Mitchell. NAmP90

Feeding the Lions. Norman Jordan. PoBA

Feeding the Sun. William Knott. PBCAP

Feel for your bad fall how could I fail. A Sympathy, a Welcome. John Berryman. GrPl; NYBP

Feel free. To Bobby Seale. Lucille Clifton. PoBA

Feel like a Bird. May Swenson. TrGrPo

Feel my eye breaking. *(LL)* The Window. Robert Creeley. CAPP; NoAM; NOBA; TAP; VGW

Feel of it was hairy and coarse, The. Pulling a Pig's Tail. Dave Jeddie Smith. NAmP90

Feel the sharpness. The Meeting. Ramona Wilson. VoR

Feeling, The. William Bronk. VGW

Feeling a pain in his breast, when he speaks. Ellas and the Statues. Gülten Akin, *tr. fr. Turkish by* Nermin Menemencioglu. PBWP

Feeling and Form. Marilyn Hacker. NoAM

Feeling Fucked Up. Etheridge Knight. NNaP; PBCAP; RaBo

Feeling it with me. Walking on Water. James Dickey. ChIV-2

Feeling my face has the terrible shine of fish. Element. P. K. Page. MoCV

Feeling Old Age. Liu Tsung-yüan, *tr. fr. Chinese by* Jan W. Walls. SuSp

Feeling the icy kick, the endless waves. The Swimming Lesson. Mary Oliver. CAPP

Feeling the urge my mother. Birth. Edith Bruck, *tr. fr. Italian by* Ruth Feldman *and* Brian Swann. BoWoP

Feelings I don't have I don't have, The. To Women, as Far as I'm Concerned. D. H. Lawrence. InPS; OxBSP; RaBo

Feelings of a Republican on the Fall of Bonaparte. Shelley. Son

Fees, The! The fees! The mighty fees! God or Mammon. Alfred Cruickshank. PBCV

Feet. Mary Carolyn Davies. WGRP

Feet. Irene Thompson. BoTP

Feet at their loveliest are like two hands. Conceit upon the Feet. William Zaranka. BXAP

Feet Man, The. Philip Dacey. NGP

Feet of Judas, The. George Marion McClellan. AAP; PoNe

Feet of morning the feet of noon and the feet of evening, The. The Domestic Stones (fragment). Hans Arp, *tr. fr. French by* David Gascoyne. CBNP

Feet of the Young Men, The. Kipling. OtMeF

Feet skirr the membrane. Walking the Water. Pauline Stainer. PWE

Feigned Courage. Charles Lamb *and* Mary Lamb *and* Mary Lamb. GN; OxBChV

Feld, groes or goers, hus, doeg, dung. Returning to Roots of First Feeling. Robert Duncan. PoA

Felicia Ropps. Gelett Burgess. FaPON

Felicitous Life, A. Czeslaw Milosz, *tr. fr. Polish by* Czeslaw Milosz *and* Lillian Vallee. PoSu

Felicitous phenomenon. *(LL)* O to Be a Dragon. Marianne Moore. ChIV-1; CTC; GoYe; NALW; PFP

Felicity the healer isn't young. Doctor Frolic. Robert Pinsky. NoAM

Feliks Skrzynecki. Peter Skrzynecki. CBAP

Félire Oengus, *sels.* John Montague.

Felis Infelix! Cat unfortunate. Ode to a Bob-Tailed Cat. *Unknown.* OFC

Félise. Swinburne. BeLS

Felix Randal. Gerard Manley Hopkins. EBEV; EBVV; EnVR; FaBoMo; FaBoVe; FaPoB; GTBS-P; HAP; HeIL; ImPo; InPS; LiTB; LiTM; MeMBP; MoAB; MoBrPo; MoP; NAEL-2; NoAM; NOBE; NoP; OBD; OBEV; OBNC; OxAEP-2; PeECV; PoE; Poetr; PoRA; PrIm; SCGP; Son; SOTW; TFi; WeW

Felix Randal the farrier, O is he dead then? my duty all ended. Felix Randal. Gerard Manley Hopkins. EBEV; EBVV; EnVR; FaBoMo; FaBoVe; FaPoB; GTBS-P; HAP; HeIL; ImPo; InPS; LiTB; LiTM; MeMBP; MoAB; MoBrPo; MoP; NAEL-2; NoAM; NOBE; NoP; OBD; OBEV; OBNC; OxAEP-2; PeECV; PoE; Poetr; PoRA; PrIm; SCGP; Son; SOTW; TFi; WeW

Felix rapina. The flap. The Feast of the Assumption of the Virgin. Ellen Bryant Voigt. CrSp

Felixstowe; or, The Last of Her Order. Sir John Betjeman. OxBTC

Fell. Anthony Barnett. VaA

Fell fast I loitered still. *(LL)* An Apple Gathering. Christina Rossetti. NAEL-2; OBNC

Fell the edge of the knife. Shoriken. Charles Brasch. PeNZ

Felled Plane Tree, The. Anna Hajnal, *tr. fr. Hungarian by* William Jay Smith. BoWoP

Feller I Know, A. Mary Austin. FaPON

Feller isn't thinkin' mean, A. Out Fishin.' Edgar A. Guest. BLPL; PoLF

Feller's always mostly man,/ Out fishin', A. (*LL*) Out Fishin.' Edgar A. Guest. BLPL; PoLF

Felling a Tree. Ivor Gurney. FaBoVe

Fellow countrymen. He Was a Man of Jokes outside Office. Oswald Basize Dube. PeSAV

Fellow from far Erewhon, A. W. F. N. Watson. PeLi

Fellow Mortal, A. John Masefield. OxAEP-2

Fellow who fucked but as few can, A. *Unknown*. PeLi

Fellow, you have no flair for art, I fear. The Sitting Bard. Sir Owen Seaman. NOBL

Fellows up in Personnel, The. The Perforated Spirit. Morris Bishop. FiBHP

Fellowship. *Unknown*. BLPA

Felo de Se. Thomas Blackburn. OxBTC

Felo de Se. Richard Hughes. OBMV

Felo de Se. Vernon Scannell. OBD

Felt for thee as a lover or a child! (*LL*) When I Have Borne in Memory. Wordsworth. EnRP; GTBS; GTBS-P; MeMBP

Felucca and Pinnace. The Waterfront Girls. Rufinus, *tr. fr. Greek by* Alan Marshfield. GrAn

Female Cabin Boy, The. *Unknown*. OxBSS

Female Dancer. James Camp. Son

Female Education. Lydia Huntley Sigourney. AmWP

Female Frailty, *sels*. Philip Freneau.
    Song of Thyrsis. LiTA

Female Friend, The. Cornelius Whur. FaBoCo; OBF

Female genital, like the blank page anticipating the poem, The. Sentience. Sandra McPherson. PoA

Female giants, fauna of women. The Women of Rubens. Wislawa Szymborska, *tr. fr. Polish by* Celina Wieniewska. WPOW

Female God, The. Isaac Rosenberg. FaBoTw

Female Husband, Who Had Been Married to Another Female for Twenty-one Years, The. *Unknown*. CoMu

Female is fertile, and discipline, The. Praise for Sick Women. Gary Snyder. NeAP; PoBeRe

Female mind like a rude fallow lies, A. Anne, Viscountess Irwin Ingram. *Fr*. Epistle to Mr. Pope Occasioned by His Characters of Women, An. ECWP

Female of the Species, The. Kipling. BLPA; FaBoEH, Abr.; OtMeF

Female Parricide, The. *Unknown*. APAS

Female Principle, The. A. D. Hope. OxBC

Female Sailor, The. *Unknown*. OBET

Female spider/ swept her legends into her palms. Roots of Blue Bells. Nia Francisco. HATNAP

Female Transport, The. *Unknown*. NOBAu

Female Wits, The: A Song by a Lady of Quality. *Unknown*. NOSC

Female's Lamentations, The; or, The Village in Mourning. Hannah Wallis. ECWP

Femina. Daphne Marlatt. NOBC

Femina Contra Mundum. G. K. Chesteron. OxAEP-2

Feminine mouth in Utopia, The. W. F. N. Watson. PeLi

Feminism, baby, feminism. Male Rage Poem. Pier Giorgio di Cicco. NOBC

Femme et Chatte. Paul Verlaine, *tr. fr. French by* Arthur Symons. AWP; OBVE

Fen-Men of Lincolnshire's Holland, The. Michael Drayton. *Fr*. Polyolbion. FaBoPP

Fence beyond fence from breakfast. The Names of the Humble. Les A. Murray. CBAP

Fence or an Ambulance, A. Joseph Malins. BLPA

Fence walker, balancer, your devil-may-care. Divination by a Cat. Anthony Hecht. OFC; SoCa

Fence Wire. James Dickey. NYBP; VGW

Fenceposts wear marshmallow hats, The. On a Snowy Day. Dorothy Aldis. PDV

Fencing. Anthony Lawrence. NOBAu

Fencing instructor named Fisk, A. *Unknown*. PeLi

Fencing School. John Manifold. CBAP; FaBoMA

Fenyeit Freir of Tungland, The. William Dunbar. OxBLMV

Feodosia. Osip Mandelstam, *tr. fr. Russian by* W. S. Merwin *and* Clarence Brown. AnAn

Feral Pioneers, The. Ishmael Reed. PoBA; PoNe; UnPo

Ferdinand De Soto lies. The Distant Runners. Mark Van Doren. GOA; LiTA; LiTM; MoAmPo

Ferdinando and Elvira; or, The Gentle Pieman. W. S. Gilbert. FaBoCo; FaBoNo; FiBHP

Ferguson's Conquistadores 77. Joy Walsh. Jaz

Ferishtah's Fancies, *sels*. Robert Browning.
    When I Vexed You. OxBSP

Fern. Ted Hughes. NYBP

Fern Hill. Dylan Thomas. AngWe; ClHu; CMoP; FaBoPP; FaBV; FaPoB; GoJo; GTBS-P; HAP; HeIL; HeIP; ImPo; InPK; InPS; LiTB; LiTM; MeMBP; MoAB; MoBrPo; MoP; NAEL-2; NIP; NoAM; NOBE; NoP; NTP; OAEL-2; OBWVE; OxBTC; PoE; Poetr; PoLF; PoRA; PPP; SoSe; TFi; TrGrPo; TRP; TwCP

Fern-life. Lucy Larcom. AmWP

Fernando, el mixteco. Every Breath a Prayer. Luis J. Rodriguez. AfAz

Fernando ("Fernando has a basketball.") Marci Ridlon. NTCP

Ferniehirst Castle. Richard Hugo. NoAM

Ferns and the Night. John Ash. SCBI

Ferret. Stewart Conn. PWE

Ferry Me across the Water. Christina Rossetti. *Fr*. Sing-Song. ChTr; GoJo; NTP; OxBChV; PDV; TLR

Ferry Pirate, The. Douglas Oliver. NBrP

Ferry Ride, *sels*. Selma Robinson.
    Bus Ride. FaPON

Ferrying toward Nanaimo. We Go as American Tourists. Nellie Wong. ETG

Ferryman, The. Christina Rossetti. *See* Ferry Me across the Water.

Fertile and rank and rich the coastal rains. Advent. William Everson. NeAP; TrCP

Fertile Muck, The. Irving Layton. NoAM; NOBC

Fertile Valley of the Nile, The. Eve Merriam. IHMS

Fervid breath of our flushed Southern May, The. Evening on the Potomac. Richard Hovey. AnAmPo

Festal Board, The. *Unknown*. BLPA

Festal Song. William Pierson Merrill. *See* Rise Up, O Men of God.

Feste Burg Ist Unser Gott, Ein. Martin Luther. *See* Mighty Fortress Is Our God, A.

Feste's Song ("When that I was and a little tiny boy.") Shakespeare. *See* When that I was and a little tiny boy.

Festival, The. Frederic Prokosch. LiTA

Festival of the Nativity, The. Richard de Ledrede, *tr. fr. Latin by* Robert Wyse Jackson. TIRV

Festivals have I seen that were not names. Calais, August 15, 1802. Wordsworth. NAs

Festive draperies override the claims of. A Naming Day. Odia Ofeimun. HBAPE

Fetch in the holly from the tree. Holly and Mistletoe. Eleanor Farjeon. PChr

Fetch me a red flower from that meadow. Speech Warts. Myra Sklarew. CRP

Fetchin Water. Claude McKay. PBCV

Fetching Cows. Norman MacCaig. OxBC

Fete, A. Larry Eigner. NeAP

Fete confused me, The. Guests played the part of gods. Sigismundo. Linda Gregg. AmPA

Fêtes, Fates. John Malcolm Brinnin. LiTA

Feuerzauber. Louis Untermeyer. TrJP

Feuilles d'Automne, *sels*. Victor Hugo, *tr. fr. French by* Francis Thompson.
    Heard on the Mountain. AWP
    Sunset, A. AWP

Fever. Judith Ortiz Cofer. AfAz

Fever, The. Rosemary Dobson. FaBoWP

Fever. Thom Gunn. PeHV

Fever, A. John Donne. OAEL-1

Fever 103°. Sylvia Plath. CMoP; FaBoWP; NoAM; NOBA; VCAP; VGW

Fever Toy, The. Charles Wright. AmPA

Feverish room and that white bed, The. White Heliotrope. Arthur Symons. BoLoP; EBEV; PeVV

Fevers of winter have flown away, The. Turning. Linda Hogan. BCF

Few beds are stonier than one shared by a sleeper. Bed Time. Peter Davison. UnPo

Few Blue Words to the Wise, A. Ted Joans. PoBeRe

Few days ago, A. A Wife Talks to Herself. Stephen Berg. NaP

Few days before you died, death, A. To a Pope. Pier Paolo Pasolini, *tr. fr. Italian by* James Kirkup. PeHV

Few ever came to help you speak or sell. Peter Dale. *Fr*. Fragments, The. NOCV

Few hairs, made fewer by the comb. Master Liu Painted a Portrait of Me in My Old Age and Asked Me to Write a Poem About the Picture. Yang Wan-li, *tr. fr. Chinese by* Jonathan Chaves. SuSp

Few Happy Matches. Isaac Watts. NOEC

Fields are white, The. Nothing to Do. James Ephriam McGirt. AAP

Fields are wrapped in silver snow, The. The Christmas Present. Patricia Hubbell. PDV

Fields behind the house ascend in a shell, The. Mine. Tim Longville. VaA

Fields flame with it, endless, blue, The. Indigo. Chitra Divakaruni. OpBo

Fields from Islington to Marybone, The. Blake. *Fr.* Jerusalem. ChTr, 4 *sts.*; FaBoPV; OBNV

Fields of Learning. Josephine Miles. NoAM

Fields, Teruko-san, are threshed, The. A good. The Hibakusha's Letter (1955). David Mura. OpBo

Fields Where We Slept. Muriel Rukeyser. NNaP

Fiend, The. Ted Berrigan. PRA

Fiend, The. James Dickey. PPP

Fiend/ Saw undelighted all delight, all kind, The. Milton. *Fr.* Paradise Lost. EPCY; FaBoPV

Fierce and brooding holocaust of faith, The. Edgar Bowers. *Fr.* Two Poems on the Catholic Bavarians. CRP

Fierce and stupid all dogs are. Dog Poem. Philip Levine. BAP-89

Fierce Dream, The. Jeffrey Wainwright. DiPo

Fierce is the wind tonight. The Viking Terror. *Unknown, tr. fr. Old Irish by* Fred Norris Robinson.
(Since tonight the wind is high.) IIP, *tr. by* Frank O'Connor
(There's a wicked wind tonight.) PeIV, *tr. by* Brendan Kennelly

Fierce musical cries of a couple of sparrowhawks hunting on the headland, The. Birds. Robinson Jeffers. InPS; VGW

Fierce passions discompose the mind, Contentment. William Cowper. ChIV-2

Fierce they drove on, impatient to destroy. Homer, *tr. by* Pope. *Fr.* Iliad, The. OBVE

Fierce west wind. Tune: "Remembering the Lady of Ch'in" — Loushan Pass. Mao Tse-tung, *tr. fr. Chinese by* Eugene Eoyang. SuSp

Fierce wind urges me to change into my quilted cotton gown. Strolling in the Countryside. Chao Yi, *tr. fr. Chinese by* Chang Yin-nan *and* Lewis C. Walmsley. SuSp

Fierce with moustaches of gold. *(LL)* Bomb. Gregory Corso. PoBeRe

Fierce wrath of Solomon. The Burning of the Temple. Isaac Rosenberg. FaBoMo; PeFWW; TrJP

Fiercely the battle raged, and, sad to tell. Ambrose Bierce. *Fr.* Devil's Dictionary, The. OBAL

Fiery and the snuffy are raring to go, The. *(LL)* I Ride an Old Paint. *Unknown.* AmFP; AS

Fiery songs, their five long toes trembling in the soaked earth, The. *(LL)* Johnson's Cabinet Watched by Ants. Robert Bly. MoP; NOBA

Fiery wheel without beginning. Sunflower. Tuvia Rivner, *tr. fr. Hebrew by* Ruth Finer Mintz. MHP

Fiery young fellow called Bryant, A. Barney Blackley. PeLi

Fiesolan Idyl, A. Walter Savage Landor. EnRP

Fife and Drum. Dryden. *Fr.* Song for St. Cecilia's Day, 1687, A. AWP; FaBoTw; FHYEP; GGP; GN, 8 *ll.*; GTBS; GTBS-P; HAP; InPS; LiTB; NOSC; OAEL-1; OBEV; OPOP; PoEL-3; PPP; SCGP; SeCV-2; TEP; TFi; TrGrPo

Fife Tune. John Manifold. CBAP; FaBoMA; GoJo; ImPo; InPS; LiTB; LiTM; Mes; NBLV; NOBAu

Fifine at the Fair, *sels.* Robert Browning.

Fifteen Acres, The. James Stephens. BoTP

Fifteen Boys, or Perhaps Even More. Bella Akhmadulina, *tr. fr. Russian by* Daniel Weissbort. WPOW

Fifteen churches lie here. At Dunwich. Anthony Thwaite. MoBS

Fifteen day of July, The. Lord Willoughby. *Unknown.* CoMu

Fifteen Days of Judgment, The. Sebastian Evans. NOBVV

Fifteen foresters in the Braid alow. Johnie Cock. *Unknown.* ESPB

Fifteen Haiku, *sels.* Masaoka Shiki, *tr. fr. Japanese by* Burton Watson.

Fifteen Hokku, *sels.* Naito Joso, *tr. fr. Japanese by* Hiroaki Sato.

Fifteen Hokku, *sels.* Shiba Sonome, *tr. fr. Japanese by* Hiroaki Sato.

Fifteen men on the dead man's chest. Derelict. Young Ewing Allison. BLPA; FaBoBe

Fifteen men on the Dead Man's Chest. Pirate Ditty. Robert Louis Stevenson. *Fr.* Treasure Island. NOBVV

Fifteen Million Plastic Bags. Adrian Mitchell. OBSV; OxBTC

Fifteen Ships on Georges Banks. *Unknown.* AmFP

Fifteen to Eighteen. Marilyn Hacker. GLP

XV. "Ye tradeful merchants that, with weary toil." Spenser. *Fr.* Amoretti. AAS; ESo, lacking epigrams I–IV; HeIL; HeIP; LiTB; NIP; OAEL-1; Son; TrGrPo

Fifteen years in the coal mine. Coal Diggin' Blues. *Unknown.* AmFP

15th Kühl-Psalm, The. Quirinus Kuhlmann, *tr. fr. German by* George C. Schoolfield. GePo

15th March 1939. Gerda Mayer. PAW

15th Raga: For Bela Lugosi. David Meltzer. *Fr.* Ragas. NeAP

Fifth Choir of Angelicals. Cardinal Newman. *See* Praise to the Holiest in the height.

Fifth Column, The. Duncan Forbes. FaBoBl

Fifth-Floor Window, The. Lola Ridge. WPE

Fifth Grade Autobiography. Rita Dove. NIP

Fifth Hell, The. Jerome Rothenberg. *Fr.* Seven Hells of Jigoku Zoshi, The. NNaP

Fifth month, golden plums are ripe. Evening in the Garden Clear after Rain. Ch'u Ch'uang I, *tr. fr. Chinese.* OHMPC

Fifth Ode of Horace, The. Horace. *See* What slender youth bedewed with liquid odours.

Fifth Season, The. Reg Saner. FYAP

Fifth Sense, The. Patricia Beer. MoBS

Fifth Variation. Andrew Crozier. VaA

Fifth year of the new Son of Heaven, The. The Eclipse of the Moon. Lu T'ung, *tr. fr. Chinese by* A. C. Graham. PLT

Fifties, The. Marvin Bell. Jaz

Fifties, The. Robert McDowell. *Fr.* Home in America. BAP-89

Fifties, The. Wendy Rose. WoWa

Fifties, The. Ira Sadoff. AmPA

Fifty. Kenneth Rexroth. TAP

Fifty Faggots. Edward Thomas. MoAB; MoBrPo; PeFWW; PoWW

50 – 50. Langston Hughes. NoAM; NOBA; PoE

LV. "So oft as I her beauty do behold." Spenser. *Fr.* Amoretti. AAS; ESo, lacking epigrams I–IV; HeIL; Son; TrGrPo

LIV. "Of this world's theatre in which we stay." Spenser. *Fr.* Amoretti. AAS; ESo, lacking epigrams I–IV; HeIL; NAEL-1; NoP; OAEL-1

Fifty, not having expected to arrive here. Journey toward Evening. Phyllis McGinley. GoYe; NYBP

Fifty-one Tanka, *sels.* Lady Izumi Shikibu, *tr. fr. Japanese by* Hiroaki Sato.

LVI. "Fair ye be sure, but cruel and unkind." Spenser. *Fr.* Amoretti. AAS; ESo, lacking epigrams I–IV; HeIL; Son

Fifty stories more to fall. Rhyme of Rain. John Holmes. GrPl

Fifty thousand people uprooted by mfecane. The Mantatee Horde. Mtutuzeli Matshoba. PeSAV

Fifty times the rose has flower'd and faded. On the Jubilee of Queen Victoria. Tennyson. UnPo

Fifty today, old lad? Ode to Me. Kingsley Amis. NAs

Fifty wizards working in the wind. A Poem to Explain Everything about a Certain Day in Vermont. Genevieve Taggard. NYBP

Fifty Years On. Janet Fisher. NWP

Fig, an Olive, and a Bay, A. *(LL)* Detail. Mary Ursula Bethell. PeNZ

Fig for the Lower House, A. Patrick Carey. *See* And now a fig for the lower house.

Fig for Thee, Oh! Death, A. Edward Taylor. NAAL-1

Fig for those by law protected, A! Drinking Song. Burns. *Fr.* Jolly Beggars, The. EnRP, *sl. diff. vers.*; NBLV; PoEL-4; TrGrPo

Fig-tree, a falling woolshed, a filled-in well, A. Mullabinda. David Rowbotham. CBAP

Fig-trees, weird fig-trees. Bare Fig-trees. D. H. Lawrence. FaBoVe

Figgie Hobbin. Charles Causley. NTP

Fight at Dajo, The. Alfred E. Wood. PAH

Fight at Sumter, The. *Unknown.* PAH

Fight at [the] San Jacinto, The. John Williamson Palmer. PAH

Fight in the Centre, The. Macaulay. *Fr.* Battle of the Lake Regillus, The. OtMeF

Fight of Paso del Mar, The. Bayard Taylor. BeLS

Fight of the Armstrong Privateer, The. James Jeffrey Roche. PAH

Fight of the Red Cross Knight and the Heathen Sansjoy, The. Spenser. *Fr.* Faerie Queene, The. FHYEP; NoSic

Fight of the Year, The. Robert McGough. OBCP

Fight over the Body of Keitt, The. *Unknown.* PAH

Fight thou with shafts of silver, and o'ercome. Money Gets the Mastery. Robert Herrick. CaPo

Fight was at its hottest, The. Rev. Andrew Brown, over the Hill to Rest. Josephine D. Henderson Heard. CBWP-4

Fight was over, and the battle won, The. An Allegory. Barcroft Henry Boake. CBAP

Fight With An Angel. Tadeusz Rózewicz, *tr. fr. Polish by* Victor Contoski. PoSu

Fight your little fight, my boy. Don'ts. D. H. Lawrence. LiTB; LiTM; MeMBP; OxBoLi; PeLV

Fighter, The. Samuel Ellsworth Kiser. BLPA

Fighting nature of the intellect, The. Vast Light. Richard Eberhart. CMoP

Fighting on the South Frontier. Li Po, *tr. fr. Chinese by* Robert Payne. TAL

Fighting Race, The. Joseph I. C. Clarke. AnAmPo; BLPA; BLPL; PAH

Finding You. Virginia Gilbert. IHMS

Finds names for them all. (*LL*) The Naming of the Beasts. Francis Sparshott. NOBC

Finds ways enough to ease thine heaviness. (*LL*) Of Money. Barnabe Googe. EiL; FF; NBLV; NoP; NoSic; SoSe

Fine Day, A. Michael Drayton. *See* Clear [*or* Cleere] had the day been [*or* bin] from the dawn [*or* dawne].

Fine Day for Straw Hats, A. Louis Simpson. PBCV

Fine delight that fathers thought; the strong, The. To R. B. Gerard Manley Hopkins. CMoP; EnVR; EPCY; GTBS-P; InvP; OAEL-2; OxAEP-2

Fine evening may I have. Courtship. Rita Dove. LCAP

Fine feelings under blockade! Cargoes just in from Kamschatka! Winter Coming On. Martin Bell, *after the French of* Jules Laforgue. FaBoMo; OBVE; OxBTC

Fine! Fine! Isaac Rosenberg. *Fr.* Moses. PeFWW

Fine fish to net. Ezra Pound, *after the Chinese.* OBVE

Fine flash Yankee barman, and once more cut a shine, A. (*LL*) The Flash Colonial Barman. *At. to* William W. Coxon. NOBAu

Fine Flowers in the Valley. Burns. ScCV

Fine game is grab-bag, a fine game to see, A! Grab-Bag. Helen Hunt Jackson. OBCA

Fine, green pajama cotton, The. Size and Sheer Will. Sharon Olds. Poetr

Fine Knacks for Ladies. *Unknown.* CH; EBEV; EiL; EnRePo; HAP; LiTB; NoP; NoSic

Fine knacks for ladies, cheap, choice, brave and new! Fine Knacks for Ladies. *Unknown.* CH; EBEV; EiL; EnRePo; HAP; LiTB; NoP; NoSic (Peddler's Song, A.) OAEL-1

Fine Madam Would-Be, wherefore should you fear. To Fine Lady Would-Be. Ben Jonson. FaBoEE; JCP; NoP; NOSC; OxBSP

Fine merry franions. Going or Gone. Charles Lamb. BXAP

Fine Old English Gentleman, The. *Unknown.* CH

Fine Old English Gentleman; New Version, The. Charles Dickens. CoMu; FaBoBa; NOBVV; OBSV

Fine rain falls, greening their garden, A. The Visitor. Michael Dennis Browne. OBTV

Fine rain, gentle thunder. Tune: "Full River Red" — A Four-season Song on the Hardships and Joys of Farming Life. Cheng Hsieh, *tr. fr. Chinese by* Irving Y. Lo. SuSp

Fine strong gentle cat is prowling, A. The Cat. Baudelaire, *tr. fr. French by* Roy Campbell. OFC

Fine view, but I'm still getting thinner. Tune: "Pleasure of Returning to the Fields: A Prelude." Huang T'ing-chien, *tr. fr. Chinese by* James J. Y. Liu. SuSp

Fine weather since yesterday. Han Yü, *tr. fr. Chinese by* A. C. Graham. *Fr.* South Mountains, The. PLT

Fine Work with Pitch and Copper. William Carlos Williams. OxBA

Fine Young Folly. William Habington. *Fr.* Queen of Aragon, The.

Fine youth Ciprius is more terse and neat, The. Sir John Davies. *Fr.* Epigrams. NoSic

Fineness of midnight. Midnight. Gabriela Mistral, *tr. fr. Spanish by* David Garrison. BoWoP

Finer flesh, air's odour, A. Airs and Distance. Tim Longville. VaA

Finesse be first, whose elegance deplores. Six Poets in Search of a Lawyer. Donald Hall. NYBP

"Finest summer I remember" Old George says. Andrew Greig. *Fr.* Len's Poems. PWE

Fingal's Weeping. Neil Munro. NSI

Finger, The. Robert Creeley. PRA

Finger, The, *sels.* Felix Pollak.

Finger Folk. H. M. Tharp. BoTP

Finger of death touched me, The. He Is Gone. Anna Swirszczynska, *tr. fr. Polish by* Czeslaw Milosz *and* Leonard Nathan. PoSu

Finger Play. *Unknown.* BoTP

Finger Play for a Snowy Day, A. *Unknown.* BoTP

Fingernail Sunrise. Vernon Watkins. NYBP

Fingers lie in the lap, The. Year's End. Ellen Bryant Voigt. NoAM

Finglas Lilies. Dermot Bolger. IB

Finigan's Wake. *Unknown. See* Tim Finnegan [*or* Finnigin *or* Finigan] liv'd in Walkin [*or* lived in Walker] Street.

Finis. Walter Savage Landor. *See* I strove with none, for none was worth my strife.

Finished. Kate Llewellyn. NOBAu

Finished at last, he escaped from that hideous. Christ's Descent into Hell. Rainer Maria Rilke, *tr. fr. German by* James Wright *and* Sarah Youngblood. Prf

Finished Course, The. St. Joseph of the Studium, *tr. fr. Latin by* John Mason Neale. WGRP

Finished Gentleman, A. Geoffrey Dutton. NOBAu

Finistére. Thomas Kinsella. IPY

Finite Intuition. Milo De Angelis, *tr. fr. Italian by* Lawrence Venuti.

Finnegans Wake, *sels.* James Joyce.
  Ballad of Persse O'Reilly, The. CBNP; FaBoBa; LiTB; PeLV
  Ondt and the Gracehoper, The. BIrV

Finnegan's Wake, *Unknown.* CBNP; FaBoBa; NBLV

Finnesburh Fragment, The. *Unknown, tr. fr. Anglo-Saxon by* Kevin Crossley-Holland. ASW; OBWP

Finney's Bar. Deborah Randall. PWE

Finnigin to Flannigan. Strickland W. Gillilan. FaBoBe

Finnish Champion. Gabriela Mistral, *tr. fr. Spanish by* Doris Dana. WoWa

Finnish Champion, you are stretched out. Finnish Champion. Gabriela Mistral, *tr. fr. Spanish by* Doris Dana. WoWa

Finn's Wishes. Desmond O'Grady, *tr. fr. Irish by the author.* CIP

Fir-Tree, The. Edith M. Thomas. OHIP

Fir-Tree of Bosnia, The. Dante Gabriel Rossetti. FaBoNo

Fir trees taper into twigs and wear, The. Firwood. John Clare. TrGrPo

Fire. William Carpenter. Poetsp

Fire, The. Robert Creeley. NOBA

Fire. Fazil Hüsnü Daglarca. CRP

Fire, The. Robert Duncan. *Fr.* Passages. VGW

Fire. Langston Hughes. NOBA

Fire. Mark O'Connor. NOBAu

Fire, The. Sir Walter Scott. OBCP

Fire. Dorothy Wellesley. OBMV

Fire and Brimstone; or, The Destruction of Sodom, *sels.* George Lestey.
  Lament of the Sodomites. PeHV

Fire and honey oozes from cracks in the earth. Es Lebe Der König. J. H. Prynne. VaA

Fire and Ice. Robert Frost. AmPP; CMoP; EBEvV; FaBoEE; FF; HeIP; HoPM; InPK; LiTA; LiTM; MoAB; MoAmPo; MoP; NAAL-2; NoAM; NOBA; OxBA; Poetr; PPP; PrIm; RaBo; SoSe; TAP; TFi; TrGrPo

Fire and sword with ease subdues. (*LL*) Beauty. Thomas Stanley, *after the Greek of* Anacreon. AWP; OBVE

Fire at Alexandria, The. Theodore Weiss. NoAM; PoA; SAmP; TAP

Fire-Bringer, The, *sels.* William Vaughn Moody.
  I Stood within the Heart of God. AH
  (Pandora Speaks.) WGRP

Fire burns bright on my hearth to-night, The. The Fire Guest. George Alfred Townsend. PWR

Fire Burns Low, The. John Leax. TrCP

Fire can burn what's in it. (*LL*) Joy! a heart so overflowing. Bernard de Ventadour. STV

Fire crackles in the kitchen range, and big, The. In the Kitchen. Bible, Apocrypha, *tr. fr. French.* TSaS, *tr. by* Denise Levertov

Fire darkens, the wood turns black, The. Song for the Sun That Disappeared behind the Rainclouds. *Hottentot Oral Tradition, tr. by* Ulli Beier. TTTS; TTY

Fire-Dragon and the Treasure, The. *Unknown, tr. by* Charles W. Kennedy. *Fr.* Beowulf. AnOE; ASW, *tr. by* Kevin Crossley-Holland

Fire falls, the night, The. Summer Is a Poem by Ovid. Douglas G. Jones. NIP

Fire, fire. Henry Bold. GBL

Fire, fire! *Unknown.* RoPo

Fire! Fire! said [*or* says] the town crier. *Unknown.* GBP; OxNR

Fire Guest, The. George Alfred Townsend. PWR

Fire, Hair, Meat and Bone. Fred Johnson. PoBA

Fire high up in air, The. A Bird's Song. Edith Sitwell. NALW

Fire I praise was once perduring flame, The. Allen Tate. *Fr.* Sonnets of the Blood. PoA

Fire in leaf and grass, The. The Living. Denise Levertov. PWE; VGW; WPE

Fire in My Meditation Burned. Henry Ainsworth. AH; ChIV-1

Fire in the Heavens. Christopher John Brennan. *Fr.* Quest of Silence, The. CBAP; NOBAu

Fire in the heavens, and fire along the hills. Fire in the Heavens. Christopher John Brennan. *Fr.* Quest of Silence, The. CBAP; NOBAu

Fire in the Hole. Gary Snyder. NAAL-2

Fire in the olive groves throughout the night. Vineta. Charles Spear. PeNZ

Fire in the Snow, The. Vernon Watkins. LiTM

Fire in the Stone, The. Tuvia Rivner, *tr. fr. Hebrew by* Ruth Finer Mintz. MHP

Fire is out, and spent the warmth thereof, The. Dregs. Ernest Dowson. OBMV

Fire is out, the house dark, The. (*LL*) The Nurse's Lament. Mary Elizabeth Coleridge. NOBVV; OxBSP

Fire is passing up through the soles of my feet!, A. (*LL*) Evolution from the Fish. Robert Bly. MoP; NoAM; NOBA

Fire Island. Rita Mae Brown. IHMS

Fire Island. May Swenson. PoA; TAP

Fire Island pixie called "Mary," A. *Unknown.* PeHV

Fire-kindled satellite. Napkin and Stone. Vernon Watkins. NYBP

Fire left to itself might smoulder weeks, The. The Morning After. Tony Harrison. FaBoEH

Fire-Logs. Carl Sandburg. AnAmPo

Fire, mean time, walks in a broader gross, The. Dryden. *Fr. Annus Mirabilis.* FaBoEH

Fire-mist and a planet, A. Each in His Own Tongue. William Herbert Carruth. BLPA; WBLP; WGRP

Fire more priceless than diamonds rare. The Father's Love. Mary E. Tucker. CBWP-1

Fire of Drift-wood, The. Longfellow. AmPP; BLPL; MeMAP; NAAL-1; NOBA; NoP; OxBA; TAP

Fire of Frendraught, The. *Unknown.* ESPB; OxBB

Fire of Frendraught, The. *Unknown.* ESPB

Fire of London, The. Dryden. *Fr. Annus Mirabilis.* ChTr

Fire of Meditation burns, The. A Præfatory Poem to the Little Book, Entituled, Christianus per Ignem. Nicholas Noyes. SCAP

Fire of our victims, The. The Knell. Muhammad al-Faituri, *tr. fr. Arabic by* Samir M. Zoghby. TTY

Fire off the bells, ring out wild guns. Another Prince Is Born. Adrian Mitchell. NAs

Fire: On earth there's a warrior of curious origin. Unknown, formerly at. to Cynewulf, *tr. fr. Anglo-Saxon. Fr.* Riddles (Exeter Book). ASW, *tr. by* Kevin Crossley-Holland

Fire on the Hills. Robinson Jeffers. CMoP; RaBo

Fire Poem, The. Theodore Enslin. CRP

Fire-Queen. Ruth Fainlight. PoA

Fire rides calmly in the air. At War. Charles Madge. FaBoMo

Fire Roses. Cynthia Fuller. VBLP

Fire Screen. Rhyll McMaster. FaBoMA

Fire Seven Times Tried This, The. Shakespeare. *Fr. Merchant of Venice, The.* CTC

Fire shimmied & reached up. Temples of Smoke. Yusef Komunyakaa. NAmP90

Fire Ship, The. *Unknown.* OxBSS

Fire Side, The; a Pastoral Soliloquy. Isaac Hawkins Browne. *Fr.* Foundling Hospital for Wit, The. NOEC

Fire Station's Delight, The. Susan Hampton. NOBAu

Fire Story, A. Joseph Bruchac. ETG

Fire that cancels all that is. Burning Love Letters. Howard Moss. HoPM

Fire the heather. Joseph Gordon MacLeod. *Fr.* Men of the Rocks. OxBS

Fire: The People. Alfred Corn. *Fr.* Call in the Midst of the Crowd, A. NAAL-2; VCAP

Fire the river that is to say, the. Brush Fire. Tchicaya U Tam'si, *tr. fr. French by* Sangodare Akanji. NegPo

Fire threatens, the. The Hyena Addressing Her Young Ones. *Unknown, tr. fr. Hottentot by* W. H. I. Bleek. PeSAV
(Hyena's Song to her Children.) PeSA

Fire to see my wrongs for anger burneth, Title. Sir Philip Sidney. *Fr.* Arcadia. SiPSBD
(Wronged Lover, The.) SiPS

Fire-Truck, A. Richard Wilbur. AiP

Fire was furry as a bear, The. Dark Song. Edith Sitwell. CMoP; FaBoTw; PBWP

Fire, water, woman, are man's ruin! A Dutch Proverb. Matthew Prior. FaBoEE; NOEC

Fire will not ask me to make its bed, The. Asseverations. Arthur Nortje. HBAPE

Fire, with well-dried logs supplied, The. The Fire. Sir Walter Scott. OBCP

Firebell for Peace. Joyce Lee. NOBAu

Fireblade/ Flame scimitar's cutting edge. Suncoming. Oliver La Grone. NBV

Firebombing, The. James Dickey. ArOW; OBWP

Firebowl. Sydney Clouts. PeSAV

Firebreathers at the Café Deux Magots, The. Miller Williams. MT

Fired Pot, The. Anna Wickham. FaBoTw; FaBoWP; OxBTC

Fireflies. Faustin Charles. PBCV

Fireflies. Edgar Fawcett. AnAmPo

Fireflies. Carolyn Hall. FaPON

Fireflies. Mary Ann Hoberman. SiSoPo

Fireflies. "Fiona Macleod." *Fr.* Transcripts from Nature. FM

Fireflies, The, *sels.* Charles Mair.

Fireflies at twilight. Fireflies. Mary Ann Hoberman. SiSoPo

Fireflies in the Garden. Robert Frost. OxBSP; SAmP

Fireflies' light, The. Chine-Jo, *tr. fr. Japanese by* Kenneth Rexroth *and* Ikuko Atsumi. WPJ

Firefly. Li Po. SiSoPo
Sels.
"I think."

Firefly, The. Sandra McPherson. AnAn

Firefly. Elizabeth Madox Roberts. GoJo; NTCP; PDV; SiSoPo

Firefly, airplane, satellite, star. Back Yard, July Night. William Cole. BoNaP

Firefly light. Summer. Ramona Wilson. VoR

Firelight. E. A. Robinson. NoAM

Firelight flickered on the age-old beams, The. At the Ship. R. P. Lister. FiBHP

Firelight in sunlight, silver-pale. The Marriage of Heaven and Earth. Howard Nemerov. NYBP

Fireman Save My Child. *Unknown. See* There was a little man and he had a little can.

Fires. Elizabeth Fleming. BoTP

Fires in the fall! (*LL*) Autumn Fires. Robert Louis Stevenson. NTP

Fires overtaking the city and the sky shine, The. Old Ash Tree on Ching Hill. Ai Ch'ing, *tr. fr. Chinese.* LHF, *tr. by* Hualing Nieh

Firestone. David Rivard. PBCAP

Firetail's Nest, The. John Clare. EnRP

Firewood, iron-ware, and cheap tin trays. (*LL*) Cargoes. John Masefield. BLPL; CMoP; CoGr; EBEvV; FaBV; FaPON; FaPoR; GGP; InPK; LiTM; MoAB; MoBrPo; NOBE; OBEV; OBMV; OtMeF; PlP; PoRA; TEP; TFi

Fireworks. Babette Deutsch. NYBP; Poetr

Fireworks. Valerie Worth. NTCP

Fireworks explode like thunderclaps all over Chungking. On Hearing the News of the Japanese Surrender. Liu Ya-tzu, *tr. fr. Chinese by* Wu-chi Liu. SuSp

Firm and well-fixed foundation. (*LL*) The Pillar of Fame. Robert Herrick. BeJo; CaPo; JCP; NIP; SeCP

Firm as young bones, fine as blown spume, still. Paradigm. Babette Deutsch. TrJP

Firm Belief. *Unknown.* PoToHe

Firm of Happiness, Limited, The. Norman Cameron. FaBoTw

Firmament Displays on High, The. Barend Toerien, *tr. fr. Afrikaans by the author.* PeSA

Firmament Doth Shake, The. Ken Edwards. NBrP

Firmly, sweetly,/ refusing. Portrait of a Woman (and a Man). John Figueroa. PBCV

Firmness. Anthony Hecht. OBAL

Firs/ born Xmas day. Christopher Reid. *Fr.* Memres of Alfred Stoker. FaBoVe

First/ A far thud. Fireworks. Valerie Worth. NTCP

First a flicker of telepathy. Word of Art. Alan Bernheimer. UL

First a monkey, then a man. Dawn of the Space Age. John Ciardi. OBAL

First a sea: soft sand, muds, and marls. What Happened Here Before. Gary Snyder. NNaP; PoM

First a terror of choice, but that was done. I Had a Terror — Since September. Gerald William Barrax. MT

First act of love in a new house, The. Moving In. Frank Ormsby. PeIV

First Actor to Hamlet. Ivan V. Lalic, *tr. fr. Serbo-Croatian by* Charles Simic. HSix

First Adventurer for her fame I stand, The. Delariviere Manley. *Fr.* Lost Lover, The. KTR

First Aid at 4 A.M. Christopher Bursk. InPK

First AIDS Case in Selingsgrove, The. Gary Fincke. PFL

First American Congress, The. Joel Barlow. PAH

First American Sailors, The. Wallace Rice. PAH

First and Last Man. Ralph McTell. OBET

First and Second Law. Michael Flanders. FaBoUs

First Anniversary, The. John Donne. *Fr.* Anatomy [*or* Anatomie] of the World, An[: The First Anniversary]. NAEL-1; SeCV-1

First, April, she with mellow showers. The Four Sweet Months. Robert Herrick. BoTP; WiR
(July: The Succession of the Four Sweet Months.) FaPON

First, are you our sort of a person? The Applicant. Sylvia Plath. MAT; NAAL-2; NaP; NMM; NOBA; TwCP

First Aspen, *sels.* Lynn Strongin.
"Sensuous Latin poet, now I will go off with a thermos, A." IHMS

First Autumn Night. Katie Donovan. BiHa

First Beginning, The. *Unknown.* CBNP

First beginning was Sellinger's Round, The. The First Beginning. *Unknown.* CBNP

First, Best Country, The. Goldsmith. *Fr.* Travel[l]er; or, A Prospect of Society, The. GN

First Birth, The. Rodney Jones. MT

First blossom was the best blossom, The. Apple Blossom. Louis MacNeice. NTP; PeECV; RB

First blow caught me sideways, my jaw, The. The Beating. Ann Stanford. SoSe; WPE

First born of Chaos, who so fair didst come. Hymn: To Light. Abraham Cowley. MeLP; OxAEP-1; SeCV-1

First-born Star, The. Matthew Arnold. *Fr.* Bacchanalia; or, The New Age. FaBoRV

First calls of the migrant geese, no more cicadas. Li Shang-yin, *tr. fr. Chinese* by A. C. Graham. *Fr.* Lady in the Moon, The. PLT

First came the primrose. A Chanted Calendar. Sydney Thompson Dobell. *Fr.* Balder. BoTP; OBEV
(Procession of the Flowers, The.) GN

First Canzone of the Convito, The. Dante, *tr. fr. Italian* by Shelley. OBVE

First Carolina Said-Song. A. R. Ammons. OBAL

First cat that was ever killed by Care, The. (*LL*) New England. E. A. Robinson. GOA; HeIP; MeMAP; MoAB; MoAmPo; NAAL-2; NOBA; NoP; OxBA; PFP; TAP

First chap to fuck little Sophie, The. Victor Gray. PeLi

First Child, Born Out of Breach in Mid-May. Sherod Santos. *Fr.* Sheltering Ground, The. Son

First — Chill — then Stupor — then the letting go. (*LL*) After great pain, a formal feeling comes. Emily Dickinson. AmPP; BoWoP; GGP; HAP; HeIP; IMW; InPS; LiTA; MoAB; MoAmPo; NAAL-1; NALW; NAWM-2; NIP; NoAM; NOBA; NoP; PoE; Poetr; PrIm; SAmP; TAP; TFi; TRP; UnPo

First Christmas, The. Emilie Poulsson. OHIP

First Chronicles, *sels.* Bible, *O.T.*
Begats, The. CBCK

First Circle, The. Kofi Awoonor. HBAPE

First Claims Poem. Victor Hernandez Cruz. NBV

First clan of autumn, thistleball on a stem. Thistledown. James Merrill. UnPo

First cocks begin clearing the throat of morning, The. A Valley Where I Don't Belong. Marge Piercy. IHMS

First Coffin Poem. David Ignatow. CAPP

First cold front came in, The. Winter's Onset from an Alienated Point of View. Alan Dugan. FF

First cold rain. Basho, *tr. fr. Japanese* by Kenneth Koch *and* Harold Henderson. TTTS

First colour? Just like a captive, The. Three-Coloured Banner. János Pilinszky, *tr. fr. Hungarian* by Peter Jay. PoSu

First come I. My name is Jowett. Henry Charles Beeching. *Fr.* Balliol Rhymes. FaBoCo; FaBoEE; ISE; NOBL; PeLV

First comes love and then comes marriage. Autograph Book/ Prophecy. Anne Halley. NMM

First Confession. X. J. Kennedy. PPP

First Corinthians, *sels.* Bible, *N.T.*
"But some one will ask, "How are the dead raised?" DL
"Now I would remind you, brethren." DL
Though I Speak with the Tongues of Men and Angels. OAEL-1
(Greatest of These, The, *abr.*) TrGrPo

First Corinthians at the Crossroads. Bruce Dawe. NoAM

First country to die was normal in the evening, The. The Last War. Kingsley Amis. OBSV; OxBC

First cousin to Ragged-and-Tough. (*LL*) Not Ragged-and-Tough. *Unknown.* ChTr; FaBoNo

First cries were, The. Mother Poem. Joel Oppenheimer. PoM

First cut the gourds in slices, and then run. Recipe: Gourds. Nicander, *tr. fr. Greek.* FaBoUs

First Cycle of Love Poems, *sels.* George Barker.
My Joy, My Jockey, My Gabriel. ErPo; MoBrPo

First Day, The. Christina Rossetti. *See* I wish I could remember the first day.

First Day at Boarding School. Prunella Power. Mes

First day he had gone, The. A Space in the Air. Jon Silkin. TrJP

First day he was travelling in Asia, The. The Shape-Changer. Chris Wallace-Crabbe. NOBAu

First day, The/ I came to in the dark cold trembling. The Creation of the World. Éva Tóth, *tr. fr. Hungarian* by Laura Schiff. AIW

First day I shot dope, The. Summer Words of [*or* for] a Sistuh [*or* Sister] Addict. Sonia Sanchez. BlSi; BPo; UnPo

First day in your house, The. The Guest in Your House. *Unknown*, *tr. by* Charlotte *and* Wolf Leslau. OBF

First day of Christmas, The. The Twelve Days of Christmas. *Unknown.* AmFP; OxBoLi; OxNR; PChr

First day of false spring, I hit the street, The. Green Market, New York. Julia Kasdorf. LoHo

First day of May Jack. Tony Baker. NBrP

First Day of Teaching. Bonaro W. Overstreet. TrPWD

First Day of the Hunting Moon, The. Patricia Low. VGW

First day of the week he spoke to them, The. Eutychus. Rosemary Dobson. ChIV-2

First day of this month I saw. Snowdrops. George MacBeth. OBCP

First day of Yole have we in mind, The. Sing We Yule. *Unknown.* MeEL

First day she passed up and down through the Heavens, The. Petrarch, *tr. fr. Italian*. *Fr.* Sonnets to Laura. OBMV

First-Day Thoughts. Whittier. AmPP; NoP; TrCP

First Days, The. James Wright. *See* First thing I saw in the morning, The.

First day's night had come, The. Emily Dickinson. ImPo; LiTA; LiTM; OxBA; PoE; TRP; WPOW

First Days of Spring. Ryokan, *tr. fr. Japanese* by Stephen Mitchell. ArNa; EnlH

First days of spring — the sky. First Days of Spring. Ryokan, *tr. fr. Japanese* by Stephen Mitchell. ArNa; EnlH

First Death. Donald Justice. IMW; MT; SM

First Death in Nova Scotia. Elizabeth Bishop. CoAP; FaBoWP; LCAP; NOBA; NYBP

First Did I Fear. Giles Fletcher the Elder. *Fr.* Licia. Son

First Dimension of Skunk, The. Ray A. Young Bear. HATNAP

First draw the sea, that portion which between. Instructions to a Painter. Edmund Waller. APAS

First Dream, *sels.* Sister Juana Inés de la Cruz, *tr. fr. Spanish* by Samuel Beckett.
"But Venus first." BoWoP

First Duan: The Coming of Deidre, The, *sels.* John Todhunter.
Fate of the Sons of Usna, The. PeIV

First Elegy for the Dead in Cyrenaica. Hamish Henderson. OxBS

First enters wearing the neon armour, The. Ten Types of Hospital Visitor. Charles Causley. OxBC

First (entitled to the place), The. Charles Churchill. *Fr.* Duellist, The. OBSV

First Epistle of the First Book of Horace Imitated, The, *sels.* Pope.
"Well, if a King's a lion, at the least." OBSV
(Profiteers.) ECEV

First Epistle of the Second Book of Horace, Imitation of, *sels.* Pope.
"But for the wits of either Charles's days." EPCY
"Milton's strong pinion now not heaven can bound." EPCY
"Of little use the man you may suppose." EBEV
"Shakespeare (whom you and every playhouse bill)." EPCY
"We conquered France, but felt our captive's charms." (?) EPCY
"Who now reads Cowley? if he pleases yet." EPCY

First Families Move Over! Ogden Nash. FaBoCo

First Farewell to J. G. "Ephelia." NOSC

First, feel, then feel, then. Young Soul. Amiri Baraka. BPo

First few wounds are nearly invisible, The. Shooting a Farmhouse. Ted Kooser. PBCAP

First Fig. Edna St. Vincent Millay. *Fr.* Figs from Thistles. AiP; CoGr; FaBoWP; FaBV; FF; NoAM; NoP; PoA; PoLF; TAP

First Fight. Then Fiddle. Gwendolyn Brooks. InPK; NIP; Poetr; PoNe

First Flight. Daniel Hoffman. GrPl

First Flight. Dorothy Wellesley. OBTV

First follow Nature, and your judgment frame. Pope. *Fr.* Essay on Criticism. EPCY; FHYEP; HAP; PoEL-3

First, for effusions due unto the dead. Upon His Sister-in-Law, Mistress Elizabeth Herrick. Robert Herrick. CaPo

First forget what time it is. Exercise. W. S. Merwin. NOBA

First form your artful looks with studious care. Charlotte Lennox. *Fr.* Art of Coquetry. ECWP

First fruits from her fruitful bed, The. Dioscorides, *tr. fr. Greek* by Peter Whigham. GrAn

First full moon of overgrown buffalo. America's Wounded Knee. Phillip William George. VoR

First girl I ever kissed was Sally Adams, The. First Kiss. Jonathan Holden. GOYP

First girl I wanted to marry, The. My First Proper Girlfriend. Robert Adamson. FaBoMA

First, Goodbye. John Smith. GOYP

First Grade. Phillip William George. VoR

First Grey Hair, The. Mary E. Tucker. CBWP-1

First Grief, The. Felicia Dorothea Hemans. *See* Oh, call my brother back to me.

First of Autumn, The. Meng Hao Jan, *tr. fr. Chinese by* Paul W. Kroll. SuSp

First of God by whom all grace is spread. Sources of Good Counsel. Peter Idley. OxBChV

First of May, The. Anne Porter. ArNa

First of May, The. *Unknown.* ReMoGo

First of My Lovers, The. Sydney Carter. OBET

First of summer, lovely sight. *Unknown.* NOIV

First of that train which cursed the wave. To the First Slave Ship. Lydia Huntley Sigourney. AmWP

First of the Emigrants, The. *Unknown.* OxBSS

First of the first,/ Such I pronounce Pompilia, then as snow. Robert Browning. *Fr.* Ring and the Book, The. EBVVPR

First of the gods I honor in my prayer is Mother Earth. The Eumenides. Aeschylus, *tr. fr. Greek by* Robert Fagles. NAWM-1

First of the Month, The. Adrian C. Louis. NAmP90

First of the undecoded messages read: "Popeye sits in thunder," The. Farm Implements and Rutabagas in a Landscape. John Ashbery. CBNP; CoAP; SM

First on TV, A. David Ignatow. RaBo

First one shoe, then the other. (*LL*) Handbook for Revolutionaries. Aidan Carl Mathews. IB

First one was the gunner's wife and she was dressed in green, The. The Sailors' Wives. *Unknown.* OxBSS

First or Last. Thomas Hardy. CMoP

First paint a cage. Jacques Prévert. *See* First [of all] paint a cage.

First paint a cage. To Make the Portrait of a Bird. Jacques Prévert, *tr. fr. French by* Harriet Zinnes. ArNa

First pale shoots, The. On a Picture of Your House. Douglas G. Jones. NOBC

First Party at Ken Kesey's with Hell's Angels. Allen Ginsberg. PoBeRe; TRP

First Pearle, The: Religion. Lady Diana Primrose. *Fr.* Chain of Pearl, A. KTR

First period, The: the epoch of thought. Six Periods of Creation. *Maori Oral Tradition*, tr. by Richard Taylor. WTO

First person I loved, The. Coming Out. Jacqueline Lapidus. IHMS

First person to set foot on land was Noah's daughter, The. Ballad of Noah's Daughter. Rossana Ombres, *tr. fr. Italian by* Ruth Feldman. NeIt

First Philosopher's Song. Aldous Huxley. AWP

First Photos of Flu Virus. Harold Witt. SM

First, pick up chicken, rock back. To Pose a Chicken. Judith C. Root. PRA

First point is to love but one alone, The. The First Property. Sir Thomas More. *Fr.* Twelve Weapons of Spiritual Battle, The. EnRePo

First Practice. Gary Gildner. AmPA; PBCAP

First Praise. William Carlos Williams. VGW

First Pregnancy. Alta. NMM

First Prelude. Francis J. Smith. CRP

First Problem. Aimé Césaire, *tr. fr. French by* Ellen Conroy Kennedy. NegPo

First Proclamation of Miles Standish, The. Margaret Junkin Preston. PAH

First Property, The. Sir Thomas More. *Fr.* Twelve Weapons of Spiritual Battle, The. EnRePo

First Psalm, The. Bertolt Brecht, *tr. fr. German by* Robert Bly. NU

First purple wisteria, The. Wisteria. Philip Levine. ArNa

First Rain. Robert Creeley. CAPP

First rape a people. Pan Recipe. John Agard. PBCV

First Reader, The. Winfield Townley Scott. PoA

First restless flaws of morning, The. David Chaloner. VaA

First retainer, The. A Marriage. Robert Creeley. LiTM; NeAP; RaBo

First Rondeau: After a French Poet of the Fourteenth Century. Johann Nikolaus Götz, *tr. fr. German by* George C. Schoolfield. GePo

First rose a low shore pastures green to the water. The Waving of a Hand. W. S. Merwin. CAPP

First Rule. Maurice Kenny. HATNAP

First rule is to pacify the wives, The. Advice on Adultery. Gwyneth Lewis. *Fr.* Welsh Espionage. NWP

First Samuel, *sels.* Bible, *O.T.*
  "And David fled from Naioth in Ramah." OBF
  "And it came to pass, when he had made." OBF
  "And Saul said unto his servants." OBF
  Hannah's Song of Thanksgiving. AWP
  (Song of Hannah, The.) TrCP, *ad. by* Michael Drayton
  Hannah's Thanksgiving. BoWoP
  "Now the Philistines fought against Israel." OBF

First Satans Assault Against Those That First Came up to Mercys Terms. Edward Taylor. *Fr.* God's Determinations [touching his Elect]. EAP

First Satire of the Second Book of Horace, The. (There are (I scarce can think it, but I am told).) Pope. OAEL-1; PPP
Sels.
  "Alas, young man! your days can ne'er be long." EPCY
  Question of Libel, A. PrIm, *abr*
  "With all a woman's virtues but the pox." OBSV

First see those ample melons – brindled o'er. A Basket Of Summer Fruit. Charles Harpur. NOBAu

First shall the heavens want starry light. A Fancy. Thomas Lodge. *Fr.* Rosalynde; or Euphues' Golden Legacy. EIL

First Shaman Song. Gary Snyder. *Fr.* Myths and Texts. NOBA

First she heard a sound. The Sound. Robert Kelly. PoM

First Shoe, The. Máire Mhac an tSaoi, *tr. fr. Gaelic by* Brendan O Hehir. TSaS, *tr. by* Brendan O Hehir

First shot out of that sling, The. After Goliath. Kingsley Amis. NOBL; OxBTC

First Sight. Philip Larkin. BoNaP; NTCP

First Sight of Her and After. Thomas Hardy. FaBoVe; PoEL-5

First sign was your hair, The. I'm Just a Stranger Here, Heaven Is My Home. Carole Gregory Clemmons. PoBA

First Six Verses of the Ninetieth Psalm, The. Burns. ChIV-1

First Snow. Marie Louise Allen. SiSoPo

First Snow. Ted Kooser. GrPl

First Snow in Alsace. Richard Wilbur. ArOW; NoP; OBWP

First Snow on an Airfield. John Ciardi. PoA

First snow was sleet, The. It swished heavily. Sleet. Norman MacCaig. OBCP

First snow wet against the windshield. In the Third Month. David Ray. RaBo

First Snowfall, The. James Russell Lowell. BLPA; BLPL; FaBoBe; TAP; WBLP
Sels.
  "Snow had begun in the gloaming, The." AnAmPo; FaPON

First Snowfall [*or* Snow-Fall], The. James Russell Lowell. AnAmPo; BLPA; BLPL; FaBoBe; FaPON; TAP; WBLP

First Snowflake. N. M. Bodecker. TLR

First Solitude, The. Luis de Góngora y Argote, *tr. fr. Spanish by* Edward Meryon Wilson. OBVE
Sels.
  River Compared to an Oratorical Sentence, The.
  Wedding Feast, The.
  Young Pilgrim Finds Refuge with the Goatherds, The.

First Song. T. Carmi, *tr. fr. Hebrew by* Ruth Finer Mintz. *Fr.* René's Songs. MHP

First Song. Galway Kinnell. CAPP; GoJo; GOYP; GrPl; LiTM; NoP; Poetr; TwCP

First Song. Sir Philip Sidney. *See* Doubt you to whom my Muse these notes intendeth [*or* entendeth].

First Song/ Bankei/ 1653. Stephen Berg. BAP-90

First Song of Moses, The. George Wither. ChIV-1

First Sorrow, Last Jest. Wilhelm Müller, *tr. fr. German by* Philip L. Miller. *Fr.* Beautiful Maid of the Mill, The. RiWo

First sorrow of autumn, The. The Seven Sorrows. Ted Hughes. NAEL-2

First Spring. Duane Niatum. BCF; HATNAP

First Spring Day, The. Christina Rossetti. FaBoVe; WiR

First Spring Morning. Robert Bridges. BoNaP; BoTP

First stands the lofty Washington. Our Presidents. *Unknown.* BLPA

First Step, The. C. P. Cavafy, *tr. fr. Greek by* Edmund Keeley *and* Philip Sherrard. Mes

First Steps Up Parnassus. Michael Drayton. *See* My dearly loved friend how oft have we.

First Stone of the New Castle, The. *Unknown, tr. fr. Dutch by* H. C. V. Leibbrandt. PeSAV

First strawberry, The. Original Strawberry. Nancy Willard. LCAP

First, suicide notes should be. Suicide. Alice Walker. FF

First Sun Day of the year. Tonight. Galway Kinnell. *Fr.* Avenue Bearing the Initial of Christ into the New World, The. NaP

First Sunday I missed Mass on purpose, The. The Day Zimmer Lost Religion. Paul Zimmer. InPK; PBCAP

First, The/ tale of Gotham City, the Beggar. The Beggar at the Gate. Ian Wedde. PeNZ

First Test, The. Susan Fromberg Schaeffer. IHMS

First Thanksgiving, The. Jack Prelutsky. NTCP

First Thanksgiving, The. Clinton Scollard. PAH

First Thanksgiving Day, The. Alice Williams Brotherton. OHIP

First Thanksgiving Day. Margaret Junkin Preston. PAH

First Thanksgiving of All. Nancy Byrd Turner. FaPON

First that broke silence was good old Ben, The. David Mallet. *Fr.* Of Verbal Criticism. EPCY

First the falls, then the cave. Behind the Falls. William Stafford. RFM

First, the irretrievable arrow of the military road. On Hearing Michael Hartnett Read His Poetry in Irish. Michael O'Loughlin. IB

First the melody, clean and hard. How High the Moon. Lance Jeffers. PoBA

First the pleasures fire the heart. From Belfast to Suffolk. William Peskett. PNI

First, the scene endlessly diminishes. Travelling Backward. Gene Baro. NYBP

First the soul of our house left, up the chimney. Tornado. William Stafford. NaP

First, the two men stand pondering. Verona. James Wright. NNaP

First, then, soliloquies had need be few. On Writing for the Stage. John Sheffield, Duke of Buckingham and Normandy. *Fr.* Essay on Poetry. FaBoUs

First there was a dream not wholly mine. Clouds over Islands. James Seay. MT

First there was a god of night and tempest. From Mythology. Zbigniew Herbert, *tr. fr. Polish by* Czeslaw Milosz. FaBoPV

First there was putting hot-water bottles to it. Inevitable. Sir John Betjeman. MoBrPo

First there was the island. The Sea and Other Stories. Jennifer Rankin. NOBAu

First there was the lamb on knocking knees. Dylan Thomas. *Fr.* Altarwise by Owl-Light. CMoP; LiTM

First there were two of us, then there were three of us. The Storm. Walter de la Mare. NTP

First Thesis. Tom Weatherly. *Fr.* Cantos. PoBA

First they were stiff and gaudy. The Magi. George Garrett. MT

First thing I ever knew was funny, The. Laughing Backwards. Jim Hall. GOYP

First thing I saw in the morning, The. Mantova. James Wright. NNaP (First Days, The.) TRP

First thing in the morning. Josephine's Garden. Steve Kowit. NGP; PFL

First thing that happened, The. The Cat. Galway Kinnell. SoCa

First thing that I remember was Carlo tugging away, The. Asleep at the Switch. George Hoey. BeLS; VPP

First Thing to Do in a House, The. Anna Wickham. Mes

First Things. Lucienne Desnoues, *tr. fr. French by* Miller Williams. WPOW

First Things First. W. H. Auden. CBLP; NYBP

First Three, The. Clinton Scollard. PAH

First Time, The. Karl Shapiro. ErPo; SM; VGW

First Time: 1950. Honor Moore. GLP

First Time Ever I Saw Your Face, The. Ewan MacColl. UnAS

First time he kissed me, he but only kissed. Elizabeth Barrett Browning. *Fr.* Sonnets from the Portuguese. BLPA; BLPL; CTC; FaBoBe

First time I flew over Florida I was amazed, The. The Distinct Call of the Alligator. Betsy Sholl. PBCAP

First time I heard Ornette, The. One of Three Musicians. Steve Jonas. Jaz

First time I lied to my baby, I told him that it was his face, The. How Lies Grow. Maxine Chernoff. UL

First time I looked seaward, westward. Lone Kauri Road ("First time I looked seaward, westward.") Allen Curnow. *Fr.* Trees, Effigies, Moving Objects. PeNZ

First time I meet Oliver Cromwell, The. Manager, Perhaps? Brendan Kennelly. PWE

First time I met him, The. Moon Mullins. Carlos Reyes. NGP

First time I saw her between her embroidered curtains, The. Tune: "Joy in Spring's Coming" — Seven Songs. *Unknown, tr. fr. Chinese by* Wayne Schlepp. SuSp

First time I visited your parents' house, The. The Old Girl. Gary Lenhart. UL

First time I walked, The. Oranges. Gary Soto. NoAM; WeW

First time I was sweet sixteen. Nayo-Barbara Watkins. NBV

First Time In. Ivor Gurney. FaBoVe

First time out. Lives. Derek Mahon. PBCIP

First time that the sun rose on thine oath, The. Elizabeth Barrett Browning. *Fr.* Sonnets from the Portuguese. EnVR; NAEL-2; WPE

First timepieces were encased in delicate silver skulls, The. Steve Abbott. ETG

First to climb the parapet, The. The Cricketers of Flanders. *Unknown.* NSI

First to God and then to you. *(LL)* My Ghostly Father, I me confess. Charles, Duc d'Orléans. BoLoP

First, to the feet, as they bear what you have grown to live in. Praise. William Matthews. AmPA

First Tooth, The. Charles Lamb *and* Mary Lamb. OxBChV; WoRP

First travelers to the coves of the Blue Ridge. The Hollow. Robert Morgan. MT

First Travels of Max. John Crowe Ransom. MoAmPo

First Tuesday in the next October. An Auctioneer's Handbill. William Hall. FaBoUs

First Voyage of John Cabot, The. Hezekiah Butterworth. PAH

First Walk on the Moon. May Swenson. AnAn

First was Fancy, like a lovely boy, The. Spenser. *Fr.* Faerie Queene, The. NOBE; NoP

First we hear the bone-on-bone of skeletons dancing. The Island of the Living. Aleida Rodríguez. ETG

First we locked our fingers, wove them. My Blood Brother. Frank Mkalawile Chipasula. HBAPE

First week the soil was clean, The. Digging for Indians. Gary Gildner. AmPA; PBCAP

First were invented. *(LL)* The Elf and the Dormouse. Oliver Herford. FaBoBe; FaPON

First when Maggie was my care. Whistle o'er the Lave o't. Burns. OxBS

First William the Norman. *Unknown.* OxNR

First Winter: Joy. Peggy Shumaker. PBCAP

First Winter Storm. William Everson. NU

First World War Poets. Edward Bond. IHNG

First Year, The, *sels.* E. J. Scovell.
Days Drawing In. FaBoWP

First you bite your fingernails. American Rhapsody. Kenneth Fearing. MoAmPo

First you must blow a bottle round your sleep. Directions for Dreamfishing. Martin Johnston. CBAP

First you must love your body, in games. Lew Welch. EaPr

First, you think they are dead. Lobsters in the Window. W. D. Snodgrass. NYBP; TAP; TRP

First, you will say goodbye. You will turn. First, Goodbye. John Smith. GOYP

Firstborn. Katherine Gallagher. VBLP

Firstborn Land, The. Ingeborg Bachmann, *tr. fr. German by* Daniel Huws. BoWoP

Firste stok, fader of gentilesse, The. Chaucer. MiEL
(Gentilesse.) AWP; NAEL-1; OAEL-1

Firstfruits in 1812. Wallace Rice. PAH

Firwood. John Clare. TrGrPo

Fisbo, *sels.* Robert Nichols.
"Talking of Ezra Pound and long-dead pantos." OBSV

Fish, The. Elizabeth Bishop. CAPP; FaBoWP; GoJo; HAP; HeIP; HoPM; InPK; LiTM; MoAB; MoAmPo; MoP; NAAL-2; NALW; NoAM; NOBA; NoP; NTP; NU; OPOP; PoE; Poetr; RB; TFi; TrGrPo; TRP

Fish, The. Rupert Brooke. FM

Fish. Daniel Halpern. AmPA

Fish. Larry Levis. AmPA

Fish, The. Marianne Moore. AmPP; FaBoWP; MeMAP; MoAB; MoAmPo; MoP; NAAL-2; NoAM; OxBA; Poetr

Fish, The. Ogden Nash. AnAmPo

Fish, The. Mary Oliver. CAPP

Fish. Joe Rosenblatt. NOBC

Fish. W. W. Eustace Ross. MoCV; NTP

Fish. Takahashi Shinkichi, *tr. fr. Japanese by* Lucien Stryk. NU

Fish. Emily Townsend. NYBP

Fish/ always accurately know where to move and when. Brief Reflection on Accuracy. Miroslav Holub, *tr. by* Ewald Osers. PWE

Fish and Bird. Rosemary Brinckman. BoTP

Fish and Chips on the Merry-Go-Round. K. O. Arvidson. PeNZ

Fish Answers, A. Leigh Hunt. *Fr.* Fish, the Man, and the Spirit, The. ChTr; EnRP; FiBHP; FM; GGP; HAP; NBLV; NOBL; NTP; OBEV; PoEL-4; SCGP

Fish at Mass, The. *Unknown, tr. fr. Latin by* J. F. Webb. BIrV

Fish bones walked the waves off Hatteras. Cottonmouth Country. Louise Glück. CoAP

Fish cannot drown in water, A. Mechthild von Magdeburg, *tr. fr. German by* Jane Hirshfield. EnlH

Fish Crier. Carl Sandburg. OxBA

Fish dripping, A. Fish. W. W. Eustace Ross. MoCV; NTP

Fish factory wriggles free of the Baltic, The. Anchorage. Lavinia Greenlaw. NWP

Fish (fly-replete, in depth of June). Heaven. Rupert Brooke. EBEV; HoPM; LiTB; LiTM; MoBrPo; NOBE; NSI; PFP; PoRA; WGRP

Fish Food. John Wheelwright. LiTA

Fish gnaw the Flushing capons, hauled from fleeced. The Nuptial Torches. Tony Harrison. SCBI

Fish has laid her succulent eggs. Vicissitudes of the Creator. Archibald MacLeish. MeMAP

Fish in River: "My house is not quiet, I am not loud." Unknown, formerly at. to Cynewulf, *tr.* by Charles W. Kennedy. *Fr.* Riddles (Exeter Book). AnOE

Fish in the Stone, The. Rita Dove. HCAP; Poetr

Fish in the unruffled lakes. W. H. Auden. BoLoP; CBLP; CMoP; MoAB; MoBrPo; MoP

Fish leaping. Where the Lilies Were in Flower. Kumattur Kannanar, *tr. fr. Tamil* by A. K. Ramanujan. PLW

Fish of the sea couldn't come. How They Brought the Good News by Sea. Norma Farber. PChr

Fish Peddler and Cobbler. Kenneth Rexroth. NNaP

Fish Replies, A. Leigh Hunt. *See* Amazing monster! that, for aught I know.

Fish shall not swim. Embrace the Flood. Pien Chih-lin, *tr. fr. Chinese. Fr.* Poems Written at the Construction Site of the Ming Tombs Dam. LHF, *tr.* by Hualing Nieh

Fish Shop Windows. Geoffrey Dutton. NOBAu

Fish Speaking Veneto Dialect. Judith Baumel. UTF

Fish Story: How Language Carries Us into the Unknown. Brigitte Frase. LoHo

Fish-teeming sea. Amergin. *Fr.* Amergin's Songs. NOIV

Fish, the Man, and the Spirit, The. (You strange, astonished-looking, angle-faced.) Leigh Hunt. ChTr; EnRP; FM; HAP; NOBL; NTP; OBEV; PoEL-4

Sels.

  Fish Answers, A. FiBHP; GGP; NBLV; SCGP

  (Fish Replies, A.) PeLV

  (Fish to Man.) MoShBr

  Fish Turns Into a Man, and Then Into a Spirit, and Again Speaks, The. GGP

  To a Fish. GGP; NBLV; PeLV; SCGP

Fish to Man. Leigh Hunt. *See* Amazing monster! that, for aught I know.

Fish took a notion, A. Tip-Toe Tail. Dixie Willson. NTCP

Fish Turns Into a Man, and Then Into a Spirit, and Again Speaks, The. Leigh Hunt. *Fr.* Fish, the Man, and the Spirit, The. ChTr; EnRP; FM; GGP; HAP; NOBL; NTP; OBEV; PoEL-4

Fish wade, The/ through black jade. The Fish. Marianne Moore. AmPP; FaBoWP; MoAB; MoAmPo; MoP; NoAM; OxBA

Fish Weeps, The. *Unknown, tr. fr. Chinese* by Kenneth Rexroth. OHMPC

Fish weeps in the, The. The Fish Weeps. *Unknown, tr. fr. Chinese* by Kenneth Rexroth. OHMPC

Fish, when he's exposed to air, The. The Fish. Ogden Nash. AnAmPo

Fish with the Deep Smile, The. Margaret Wise Brown. PDV

Fisher, The. Roderic Quinn. CBAP

Fisher Cat, The. Richard Eberhart. GrPl

Fisher, in your bright bark rowing. The Fisherman. *Unknown, tr. fr. Portuguese* by Anne Higginson Spicer. FaPON

Fisher-lad, A (no higher dares he look). Phineas Fletcher. *Fr.* Piscatorie Eclogues. SeCV-1

Fisher Lad of Whitby, The. *Unknown.* OxBSS

Fisherman, The. Abbie Farwell Brown. FaPON

Fisherman, The. Goethe, *tr. fr. German* by John Frederick Nims. STV

Fisherman, The. Leonidas of Tarentum, *tr.* by Andrew Lang. *Fr.* Epigrams. AWP

Fisherman, The. David McCord. PDV

Fisherman, The. Jay Macpherson. Mes; NOBC

Fisherman, The. Janice Mirikitani. OpBo

Fisherman, The, *sels.* Su Shih, *tr. fr. Chinese.*

  "Fisherman drinks, The." SuSp

  "Fisherman, laughing, The." SuSp

  "Fisherman wakes, The." SuSp

  "Fisherman's drunk, The." SuSp

Fisherman. Ts'en Shen, *tr. fr. Chinese* by C. H. Wang. SuSp

Fisherman, The. *Unknown, tr. fr. Portuguese* by Anne Higginson Spicer. FaPON

Fisherman, The. W. B. Yeats. CMoP; HAP; NoAM

Fisherman drinks, The. Su Shih, *tr.* by Irving Y. Lo. *Fr.* Fisherman, The. SuSp

Fisherman goes out at dawn, The. The Fisherman. Abbie Farwell Brown. FaPON

Fisherman, laughing, The. Su Shih, *tr.* by Irving Y. Lo. *Fr.* Fisherman, The. SuSp

Fisherman on a Southern Stream. Lu Kuei Meng, *tr. fr. Chinese* by Robin D. S. Yates. SuSp

Fisherman wakes, The. Su Shih, *tr.* by Irving Y. Lo. *Fr.* Fisherman, The. SuSp

Fisherman's drunk, The. Su Shih, *tr.* by Irving Y. Lo. *Fr.* Fisherman, The. SuSp

Fisherman's Hands, The. Nanine Valen. CRH

Fisherman's Rhyme. *Unknown.* FaBoVe

Fisherman's Song, The. Thomas D'Urfey. NOSC

Fisherman's Songs, *sels.* Chang Chih-ho, *tr. fr. Chinese.*

  "Before dusk on the lake, the moon just full." SuSp

  "Near the rim of Hsi-sai Mountain, white egrets fly." SuSp

  "Oh, about the joy of owning a crab hut at Sung-chiang!" SuSp

Fisherman's Story, The. H. Cordelia Ray. CBWP-3

Fisherman's swapping a yarn for a yarn, The. The Flower-Boat. Robert Frost. PoA

Fisherman's Wife, The. Amy Lowell. BoWoP

Fishermen. Basil Bunting. PoA

Fishermen, The. Theocritus [*or* Theokritus], *tr.* by Charles Stuart Calverley. *Fr.* Idylls. AWP; OBVE

Fishermen among the fireweed, The. By Rail through the Earthly Paradise, Perhaps Bedfordshire. Denise Levertov. NNaP

Fishermen at Ballyshannon. Limbo. Seamus Heaney. CIP; NoAM; OxBC

Fishermen, Drowned beyond the West Coast. Vivian Smith. CBAP

Fishermen say, when your catch is done, The. The Sea Wolf. Violet McDougal. FaPON

Fishermen who go, The. What She Said ("The fishermen who go.") Ammuvanar, *tr. fr. Tamil* by A. K. Ramanujan. PLW

Fishermen will relate that in the South. The Lord of the Isle. Stefan George, *tr. fr. German* by Ludwig Lewisohn. AWP

Fishermen's Song. *Unknown, tr. fr. Maori* by Margaret Orbell. PeNZ

Fisher's Boy, The. Thoreau. ChTr

Fisher's Life, The. *Unknown.* ChTr; GBP

Fishes, The. *Unknown.* GBP

Fishes and the Poet's Hands, The. Frank Yerby. PoNe

Fishes' Lamentation, The. *Unknown.* OxBSS

Fishes swim in water clear. *Unknown.* OxNR

Fishing. William Hart-Smith. FaBoMA

Fishing. Dorothy Wellesley. OBMV

Fishing alone in a frail boat. Walking Out. Betty Adcock. MT

Fishing at dawn, trap them east of town. A Fishing Trapping Song. Wen T'ing-yün, *tr. fr. Chinese* by William R. Schultz. SuSp

Fishing boats have returned, The! "Ping Hsin," *tr. fr. Chinese* by Julia C. Lin. *Fr.* Three Poems. PBWP

Fishing Boats in Martigues. Roy Campbell. FaBoEE; FaBoPP; OxBSP

Fishing cove and long lines of fishermen's huts, A. Ch'ien Ch'ien-i, *tr.* by Irving Y. Lo. *Fr.* Poems Written in Prison. SuSp

Fishing Lass of Hakin, The. Lewis Morris. AngWe

Fishing on a wide river from a boat. Supreme Death. Douglas Dunn. FaBoMo

Fishing, one morning early in July. Lines in Memory of My Father. Basil Payne. IIP; PeIV

Fishing Pole, The ("A fishing pole's a curious thing.") Mary Carolyn Davies. FaPON

Fishing Rod, The. Shen Yüeh, *tr. fr. Chinese* by Richard B. Mather. SuSp

Fishing skiff in the light. Robert Adamson. *Fr.* Growing Up Alone. FaBoMA

Fishing Song. *Maori Oral Tradition, tr.* by A. Armstrong *and* R. Ngata. WTO

Fishing-Tackle, The. Bertolt Brecht, *tr. fr. German* by Lee Baxendall. PoSu

Fishing: the Late Wish. Greg Glazner. FoLa

Fishing Trapping Song, A. Wen T'ing-yün, *tr. fr. Chinese* by William R. Schultz. SuSp

Fishing Village. Louis Dudek. *Fr.* Provincetown. MoCV

Fishmarket closed, the fishes gone into flesh, The. Galway Kinnell. *Fr.* Avenue Bearing the Initial of Christ into the New World, The. NaP

Fishnet. Robert Lowell. HCAP; VCAP

Fish's Nightsong. Christian Morgenstern. WeW

Fisk is/ a/ negroid/ institution. Sharon Scott. JB

Fist Fight. Doug Cockrell. Poetsp

Fist-shut Left, so dextrous with the dirk, The. On the Left. Roy Campbell. IHNG

Fit for the soul to wear those clothes again. (*LL*) The Soul's Garment. Margaret Cavendish, Duchess of Newcastle. WPE

Fit of Rhyme against Rhyme, A. Ben Jonson. *See* Rime, the rack of finest wits.

Fit of Rime against Rime, A. Ben Jonson. BeJo; InvP; MAT; OAEL-1; PoEL-2; SeCP; SeCV-1

Fit Only for Apollo. Francis Beaumont. *See* Shake off your heavy trance!

Fit only for barbarians. (*LL*) Translation. Roy Fuller. NOBE; OxBTC

Fit place to observe the transit of Venus, A. Tahiti. Louis Johnson. PeNZ

Fit to be worshipped. (*LL*) Adonis. Hilda Doolittle ("H. D."). AWP; LiTA

Fit to grace the solar year. (*LL*) Alphonso of Castile. Emerson. NOBA

Fits a head. (*LL*) A Girl's Head. Katherine Gallagher. NOBAu

Fits the dress I wore as a bride. *(LL)* Running. Leslie Ullman. PBCAP

Fitter said: *"Madame, vous avez maigri"*, The. The Fitting. Edna St. Vincent Millay. NALW

Fitting, The. Edna St. Vincent Millay. NALW

Fitz Adam's Story. James Russell Lowell. AmPP

Five a.m., and I've been. Dawn. Lucien Stryk. CAPP

Five Arabic Verses in Praise of Wine. *Unknown, tr. fr. Arabic by* Hartwig Hirschfeld. TrJP

Five barrels of flour seventy sticks. Making Old Bones. Alberta Turner. LCAP

Five Bells. Kenneth Slessor. CBAP; FaBoMA; NOBAu; PoRA

Five bells. Five bells coldly ringing out./ Five bells. *(LL)* Five Bells. Kenneth Slessor. CBAP; FaBoMA; NOBAu; PoRA

Five Best Doctors, The. O. S. Hoffman. PoToHe

Five best doctors anywhere, The. The Five Best Doctors. O. S. Hoffman. PoToHe

Five Birds Rise. William Hayward. NYBP

Five buds were on the parent tree. Family Portraits. Mary E. Tucker. CBWP-1

Five cents a glass! Does anyone think. Price of a Drink. Josephine Pollard. VPP

Five Dawn Skies in November. David Wagoner. VCAP

Five-Day Rain, The. Denise Levertov. NeAP

Five Domestic Interiors. Vernon Scannell. OxBC

Five Epigrams, *sels.* J. V. Cunningham.
And Now You're Ready Who While She Was Here. OBVE
(Epigram: "And now you're ready who while she was here.") ErPo
"Bride loved old words, and found her pleasure marred." OBAL
Epitaph for Someone or Other. OBAL; SM; TRP
(Epigram: "Naked I came, naked I leave the scene.") VGW
"Lip was a man who used his head." OBAL
(Lip.) ErPo

Five Eyes. Walter de la Mare. CRH; OFC

Five fearless knights of the first renown. The First American Sailors. Wallace Rice. PAH

Five Feet, The. Edward Sanders. UL

515 Madison Avenue. Rhapsody. Frank O'Hara. NoAM

Five-Fingered Maple, The. Kate Louise Brown. BoTP

Five Flower World Variations. *Unknown, tr. fr. Yaqui Indian by* Jerome K. Rothenberg. STP

Five for the Grace of Man. Winfield Townley Scott. VGW

5.40. The Bay View. After the office. Aberdarcy: The Chaucer Road. Kingsley Amis. *Fr.* Evans Country, The. FaBoBl; NOBL

Five Ghost Songs. *Ambo Oral Tradition.* TTTS
Sels.
"Ah! the roofs."
"Dove stays in the garden, The."
"Ghost is gone in rags, The."
"I have no rattles."
"See how it circles."

Five gleaming crows. In Air. Peter Clarke. PBA

Five Groups of Verse, *sels.* Charles Reznikoff.
After I Had Worked All Day. PrIm; VGW

Five Hens, The. *Unknown.* GBP

Five hours (and who can do it less in?). The Lady's Dressing Room. Swift. ErPo; FaBoBl; IHNG; NoP; TEP

Five Hundred Points of Good Husbandry, *sels.* Thomas Tusser.
Advice of Housewives. NoSic
December's Husbandry. NoSic

Five inches from/ such eyes. Desire. Paul Hoover. BAP-91

Five Joys of Mary, The. *Unknown.* MeEL

Five Kernels of Corn. Hezekiah Butterworth. PAH

Five Little Brothers. Ella Wheeler Wilcox. BoTP

Five Little Chickens. *Unknown.* PDV

Five little monkeys/ Swinging from a tree. The Monkeys and the Crocodile. Laura E. Richards. FaPON

Five Little Sisters Walking in a Row. Kate Greenaway. MoShBr

Five Little Squirrels. *Unknown.* SiSoPo

Five little squirrels sat up in a tree. *Unknown.* RoPo

Five Lovesick Poems, *sels.* Gillian Eve Hanscombe.
"From her grave." AIW

Five Men. Zbigniew Herbert, *tr. fr. Polish by* Czeslaw Milosz *and* Peter Dale Scott. AnRep; PoSu

Five-Minute Orlando Macbeth, The. George MacBeth. NOBL; PeLV

Five Minutes after the Air Raid. Miroslav Holub, *tr. fr. Czech by* Ian Milner *and* George Theiner. OBD

Five minutes, five minutes more, please! Bedtime. Eleanor Farjeon. OTCP

Five minutes with his paintings and I remember. Fauviste. Donald Revell. UTF

Five months after your death, I come like the others. Elegy for a Forest Clear-Cut by the Weyerhaeuser Company. David Wagoner. NoAM

Five nights a week I work as a factory girl. Factory Girl. Katrina Porteous. NWP

Five on the Crabs. Orampokiyar, *tr. fr. Tamil by* A. K. Ramanujan. PLW
Sels.
What Her Girl Friend Said to the Foster-Mother ("If you think, mother.")
What Her Girl Friend Said to the Foster-Mother ("In his fields, mother.")
What She Said ("In his fields.")
What She Said ("In his place, mother,/ field-crabs cut into the pink.")
What She Said ("In his place, mother,/ mud-spattered spotted crabs.")

Five on the Riverside Cane. Orampokiyar, *tr. fr. Tamil by* A. K. Ramanujan. PLW
Sels.
What She Said ("Bees, six tiny legs and wings all lovely.")
What She Said ("Green creepers planted inside the house.")
What She Said ("Hovering like the heron.")
What She Said ("In the full river.")
What She Said ("Like the high fanning tufts on swift horses").

Five oxen, grazing in a flowery mead. On a Seal. Plato, *tr. fr. Greek by* Thomas Stanley. AWP; FaBoEE

5 Poems. Robert Gray. CBAP

Five Poems about Poetry. George Oppen. NNaP
Sels.
From Virgil.
Gesture, The.

Five Poems for Grandmothers, *sels.* Margaret Atwood.
"How little I know." CrSp

Five Poems on Returning to Hangchou, *sels.* Yüan Mei, *tr. fr. Chinese by* Jonathan Chaves.

Five Reasons, The. Henry Aldrich. *See* If all be true that I do think.

V. "Rudely thou wrongst my dear heart's desire." Spenser. *Fr.* Amoretti. AAS; ElL; ESo, *lacking epigrams I–IV;* HeIL

Five Sestinas, *sels.* James K. Baxter.
Dark Welcome, The. PeNZ

Five Sisters. Kate Greenaway. *See* Five Little Sisters Walking in a Row.

Five soldiers fixed by Mathew Brady's eye. Looking into History. Richard Wilbur. VCAP; VGW

Five Songs. W. H. Auden. *See* O where are you going? said reader to rider.

Five Souls. W. N. Ewer. NSI

Five Stages of Grief, The. Linda Pastan. IMW

Five Students, The. Thomas Hardy. CMoP; GTBS-P; PoEL-5

Five summer days, five summer nights. The Blue-Fly. Robert Graves. CMoP; NAEL-2; NoAM; NYBP

Five Things Sought For — — In the Manner of Han Wo, *sels.* Hsü Pen, *tr. fr. Chinese by* Jonathan Chaves.

Five Things White. Edward May. FaBoEE

5:30 A.M. Adrienne Rich. NMM; NOBA

5:32, The. Phyllis McGinley. *Fr.* I Know a Village. NMM; OxBM; WPE

Five thousand million years ago, this earth. Driving to Midnight Mass: Dublin, Christmas Eve. John F. Deane. PeIV

Five times since July my father. Stopping by Home. David Huddle. GOYP

529 1983. Gerda Mayer. Spl

Five Unmistakable Marks, The. David Jones. *Fr.* In Parenthesis. NAEL-2

Five Villanelles, *sels.* Weldon Kees.
"Crack is moving down the wall, The." SM

Five Visions of Captain Cook, *sels.* Kenneth Slessor.

Five Ways to Kill a Man. Edwin Brock. DL

Five Were Foolish. Arthur J. Hodge. AH

Five winter days at Mannheim shall I be. James Boswell. OBTV

Five Words for Joe Dunn on His 22nd Birthday. Jack Spicer. PoM

Five years ago I gouged it after dark. Your Name in Arezzo. James Wright. SM

Five years ago we knew such ecstasies. Interim. Frank Ormsby. CIP

Five years of toil and blood and tears and sweat. Mr. Churchill. A. P. Herbert. FaBoEH

Five years since you died and I am. Letter to a Dead Father. Richard Shelton. PBCAP

Fivesucked the features of my girl by glory. Nicholas Moore. PoA

Fix. Michael Dransfield. NOBAu

Fix thy corporeal, and internal eye. Matthew Prior. *Fr.* Solomon on the Vanity of the World. FM

Fixer of Midnight. Reuel Denney. OBAL

Fixture, A. Bill Berkson. UL

Fixture, A. May Swenson. NYBP

Flaccus gave me, the silver lamp. Statilius Flaccus, *tr. fr. Greek by* W. G. Shepherd. GrAn

Flag, The. James Jeffrey Roche. PAH

Flag Goes By, The. Henry Holcomb Bennett. FaBoBe; FaPON; GN; PWR; WBLP

Flag is passing by!, The. (*LL*) The Flag Goes By. Henry Holcomb Bennett. FaBoBe; FaPON; GN; PWR; WBLP

Flag of the heroes who left us their glory. Union and Liberty. Oliver Wendell Holmes. OHIP

Flagpole Sitter, The. Donald Finkel. CoAP

Flagrant Mala Puta, The. Alma Villanueva. ETG

Flags of all sorts. Things We Dreamt We Died For. Marvin Bell. CoAP

Flags of war like storm-birds fly, The. The Battle Autumn of 1862. Whittier. PAH

Flags Vex a Dying Face. Emily Dickinson. *See* World feels dusty, The.

Flake diamond of/ the sea. Larry Eigner. PoM

Flake on flake, snow. Sightings. Frances Horovitz. PWE

Flame. Frederick Seidel. PRA

Flame burns in the morning, A. Le Chariot. John Wieners. VGW

Flame-flower, day-torch, Mauna Loa. Lines to a Nasturtium. Anne Spencer. CDC; PoNe; ShDr; VBLP

Flame-Heart. Claude McKay. CDC; PoNe

Flame out, you glorious skies. The Dead Heroes. Isaac Rosenberg. MoBrPo; NSI

Flame rather than firelight. Local Colour. Andrew Crozier. VaA

Flame Tree, The, *sels.* K. O. Arvidson.

Flames. Jill Maughan. NWP

Flames and Dangling Wire. Robert Gray. NOBAu

Flames are shooting. Song of the Fire-Charm. *Unknown*, *tr. fr. Chippewa Indian by* Frances Densmore; *English vers. by* Jerome Rothenberg. STP

Flames, the arrows, all lie here, The. (*LL*) An Epitaph on the Lady Mary Villiers. Thomas Carew. SeCP

Flamiing in the sun. (*LL*) For Malcolm Who Walks in the Eyes of Our Children. Quincy Troupe. PoBA

Flaming Heart, The. (Well meaning readers! you that come as friends.) Richard Crashaw. LiTB; NAEL-1; OAEL-1, *abr*; PoEL-2; SeCV-1; TEP

Sels.
    "Crack is moving down the wall, The." SM
    "Live in these conquering leaves; live all the same." OxAEP-1
    "O Heart! the equal poise of love's both parts." GeHe; TrGrPo
    "O thou undaunted daughter of desires!" HAP
        (Upon the Book and Picture of the Seraphical Saint Teresa.) NOBE; OBEV

Flaming Terrapin, The, *sels.* Roy Campbell.
    "Maternal Earth stirs redly from beneath." MoBrPo

Flamingo. Eleanor Farjeon. OBAP

Flammonde. E. A. Robinson. AmPP; CMoP; LiTA; LiTM; MeMAP; NoAM

Flanagan got up on a Saturday morning. Lament for Barney Flanagan. James K. Baxter. NoP

Flanged, all bright colors — red, yellow, blue — the discs. Frisbee. Rolfe Humphries. GrPl

Flanking Sheep in Mosedale. David Scott. PWE

Flannan Isle. W. W. Gibson. CH; PoRA

Flannery O'Connor. Dorothy Walters. IHMS; PoRA

Flap, flap, the captive bird in the cage. The Scholar in the Narrow Street. Tso Ssu, *tr. fr. Chinese by* Arthur Waley. AWP

Flap, flap, the sounds of autumn. Spending the Night in an Inn at Swatow and Writing about My Feelings, Sent to Liang Shih-wu. Huang Tsun-hsien, *tr. fr. Chinese by* An-yan Tang. SuSp

Flap my sole, bim bam! Bim Bam. Dorothy Rosenberg. PoNe

Flap we our lips, praise Big Man. Cywydd o Fawl. Harri Webb. AngWe

Flapper, The. Charles Larcom Graves. NSI

Flash Colonial Barman, The. *At. to* William W. Coxon. NOBAu

Flash Crimson. Carl Sandburg. MoAmPo

Flash of blue, A. The Kingfisher. Dyneley Hussey. NSI

Flash of light across the night, A. Ulric Dahlgren. Kate Brownlee Sherwood. PAH

Flash of lightning does not satisfy thirst, A. Modern Love Songs. *Unknown, tr. fr. Somali by* B. W. Andrzejewski *and* I. M. Lewis. TTY

Flashed out between the middle and extreme. (*LL*) The Definition of Beauty. Robert Herrick. BeJo; CaPo

Flashing and glimmering at the edge of the horizon. (*LL*) East Coast Journey. James K. Baxter. NoP; PeNZ

Flat as to an eagle's eye. George Meredith. *Fr.* Nuptials of Attila, The. PeVV

Flat calm. The ships have gone. The Drowned. David Constantine. SCBI

Flat end of sorrow here, The. The First Circle. Kofi Awoonor. HBAPE

Flat, eventless afternoon. To a Fish Head Found on the Beach Near Malaga. Philip Levine. FoLa

Flat on the bank I parted. The Trout. John Montague. IIP; IPY; PBCIP; PeIV; PNI; PoE

Flat One, A. W. D. Snodgrass. CAPP; LiTM; SM

Flat River Girl. *Unknown*. AS

Flat underbellied fish-shaped scar on his forehead, The. Orcio and Fiasco. Judith Baumel. UTF

Flattened your words against your speaking mouth. (*LL*) Hearing your words, and not a word among them. Edna St. Vincent Millay. CMoP; MoP; NoAM; Poetr; VGW

Flattered Flying Fish, The. Emile Victor Rieu. PDV

Flaubert in Egypt. Robert Penn Warren. NoAM

Flaubert wanted to write a novel. Style. Howard Nemerov. NoAM

Flaunt of the sunshine I need not your bask. Walt Whitman. *Fr.* Song of Myself. AmPP; LiTA; MoAmPo, *abr*.; NOBA; OxBA; SOTW, *much abr*.; TrGrPo

Flavia's a name a deal too free. *Unknown*. FaBoEE

Flavius, If Your Girl Friend. Catullus, *tr. fr. Latin by* Horace Gregory. ErPo

Flavor of vanilla drifts, A. Dark Romance. Lucha Corpi, *tr. fr. Spanish by* Catherine Rodriguez-Nieto. WPOW

Flavor the speaking of this one. Not to Forget Miss Dickinson. Marshall Schacht. LiTM

Flavour in mild times, there are no great men, The. Climbing to Lo-yu Plateau, before Leaving for Wu-hsing. Tu Mu, *tr. fr. Chinese by* A. C. Graham. PLT

Flaw in Paganism, The. Dorothy Parker. NBLV

Flawless His Heart. James Russell Lowell. PAH

Flax. Ivan Bunin, *tr. fr. Russian by* Babette Deutsch *and* Avrahm Yarmolinsky. AWP

Flaxen-headed cow-boy, as simple as may be, A. John O'Keefe. NOEC

Flea, The. John Donne. BLPL; BoLoP; EBEV; ESCV; FF; FM; HoPM; ImPo; InPK; InPS; JCP; LiTB; MAT; NAEL-1; NBLV; NIP; NoSic; OAEL-1; OxAEP-1; PoE; Poetr; SCV; SeCP; SeCV-1; TEP; TFi; TrGrPo

Flea and the Fly, The. *Unknown*. *See* Fly and a flea [flew up] in a flue, A.

Flea flew by a bee, A. The bee. Combinations. Mary Ann Hoberman. *Fr.* Bugs. OBCA; OBSP

Flea said, "Whoops, there's a horse on me," The. (*LL*) Horse and a flea and three blind mice, A. *Unknown*. RoPo

Fleadh Cheoil. Pearse Hutchinson. PBCIP

Fleance. Michael Longley. CIP; PNI

Flears, The. John Hollander. AnAn

Fleas, The. Augustus de Morgan. *See* Great Fleas.

Fleas. Valerie Worth. OBAP

Fleche. Larry Eigner. VGW

Fled are the frosts, and now the fields appear. Farewell Frost; or, Welcome the Spring. Robert Herrick. CaPo

Fled are those times, when, in harmonious strains. Truth in Poetry. George Crabbe. *Fr.* Village, The. EPCY; FHYEP

Fled gasping from the House. (*LL*) I years had been from home. Emily Dickinson. BLPL; NOBA; OxBA; PoRA; SAmP

Fled is the swiftness of all the white-footed ones. Joseph Auslander. TrJP

Fledgling. Anthony Conran. AngWe

Flee always from the snare. (*LL*) A Rondel of Luve [*or* Love]. Alexander Scott. BoLoP; OBEV; OxBS

Flee from [*or* Fle fro] the press [*or* prees *or* pres] and dwelle with soothfastnesse [*or* sothefastnesse *or* sothfastnesse]. Balade de Bon Conseill. Chaucer. EnVB; MiEL; SCGP; TrGrPo
    (Ballade of Good Counsel.) TrGrPo, *mod. vers. by* Henry van Dyke
    (Truth Shall Set You Free.) MeEL
    (Truth.) AWP; NAEL-1; NoP; OAEL-1

Flee on Your Donkey. Anne Sexton. NYBP; Poetr

Flee, stately Juno, Samos fro. Ludovic Lloyd. *Fr.* Sidanen. AngWe

Fleece, The, *sels.* John Dyer.
    "Ah gentle shepherd, thine the lot to tend." PoEL-3
    Bedford Level. FaBoPP
    English Fog, The. TrGrPo
    Happy Workhouse and the Good Effects of Industry, The. NOEC
    How to Shear Sheep. FaBoUs
    Treating Sheep Ailments. ECEV
    Wool Trade, The.
        (Urban Progress.) ECEV, *ll.* 1–20

Fleeing across the roofs. (*LL*) The Roofwalker. Adrienne Rich. CoAP; NAAL-2; PPP

Fleeing Atalanta, The, *sels.* David Foster.
    "Alchemists say the Stone turns lead to gold." NOBAu
    "Don't give everything." NOBAu
    "Seeking heat men become cold, and look for meaning." NOBAu

Fleeing from threatened flood, they sailed. The First Invasion of Ireland. *Unknown, tr. fr. Irish by* John Montague. BIrV

Fleeing partridge finds the forbidden frain., The. (*LL*) The White and the Black. N. M. Khaketla. PeSA

Fleeing the short-haired mad executives. The Climbers. W. H. Auden. MeMAP

Fleet and fair. Gazelles and Unicorn. John Gray. *Fr.* Long Road, The. ChTr

Fleet astronomer can bore, The. Vanity [*or* Vanitie]. George Herbert. GeHe; NoP; NOSC; SeCV-1

Fleet at Santiago, The. Charles E. Russell. PAH

Fleet,/ light,/ my heart stifled. The Gazelle. Carmen Bernos de Gasztold, *tr. by* Rumer Godden. OBAP

Fleet ships encountering on the high seas. Good Ships. John Crowe Ransom. MeMAP; WeW

Fleet with flags arrayed, A. A Ballad of the French Fleet. Longfellow. PAH

Fleeting birds may soon in ocean swim, The. To Miss Laetitia Van Lewen. Constantia Grierson. ECWP; WPE

Fleeting glory or decay — are wind and lightning. A Monk of Auspicious Fortune Monastery Asking Me to Name a Pavilion. Su Shih, *tr. fr. Chinese by* Chiang Yee. SuSp

Fleeting Passion, A. W. H. Davies. NSI

Fleeting pomps of the world are like the green willow trees, The. Song of Nezahualcoyotl. *Unknown.* DL

Fleggit Bride, The. "Hugh MacDiarmid." OxBS

Fleming Helphenstine. E. A. Robinson. MeMAP

Flemington Racecourse. Kevin Hart. NOBAu

Flesh. Deborah Levy. AIW

Flesh, a spirit for the stone, The. (*LL*) Post Mortem. Robinson Jeffers. MoAmPo; TrGrPo

Flesh and Blood. Rebecca Gonzales. AfAz

Flesh and the Spirit, The. Anne Bradstreet. AmPP; AnAmPo; ChIV-2; LiTA; NAAL-1; NOBA; OxBA; SCAP; TAP

Flesh chase night, weather booming and dark. Major Bowes' Diary. Amiri Baraka. NAAL-2

Flesh Coupon. Jeff Wright. UL

Flesh Eggs. Iain Sinclair. VaA

Flesh-Fly and the Bee, The. Coventry Patmore. FaBoEE

Flesh, I Have Knocked at Many a Dusty Door. John Masefield. *Fr.* Sonnets. LiTM

Flesh I recognize too easily, A. (*LL*) Beat It Night Dog. Aimé Césaire. NegPo

Flesh is sad, alas, The! and all the books are read. Sea-Wind. Stéphane Mallarmé, *tr. fr. French by* Arthur Symons. AWP

Flesh on their hands was green, The. (*LL*) La Luna Verde. Cyrus Cassells. UTF

Flesh will heal and pain will fade. Claire Richcreek Thomas. PoToHe

Fleshing his dream of the beautiful, needful thing. (*LL*) Frederick Douglass. Robert Hayden. CAPP; GOA; HCAP; NIP; PoBA; PoNe; Son; TTY; VCAP

Flew away towards the moon. (*LL*) The Birds from the Mountains. Chang Chi. OHMPC

Flexed suddenly the muscles of the stomach. Rolling in Money. John Forbes. FaBoMA

Flicker, The. Lew Blockcolski. VoR

Flicker flies by. Bend in the River. Simon J. Ortiz. HATNAP

Flicker in falling, like waifs and flakes of flame. (*LL*) Leaves. Frederic Manning. NOBAu

Flicker with a broken neck, A. On Addy Road. May Swenson. GOYP

Flickering of incessant rain. John Gould Fletcher. *Fr.* Irradiations. MoAmPo

Flickknife's steel wings unfurl in the man's palm, The. Frankenstein in the Markets. Dermot Bolger. IB

Flie hand in hand to heav'n. (*LL*) Sunday. George Herbert. GeHe; PeECV; SeCV-1; TrCP

Flies. Valerie Worth. OBAP

Flies, flies are on the plane tree, on the streets. (*LL*) As a Plane Tree by the Water. Robert Lowell. CMoP; CoAP; LiTM; MoAB; MoAmPo; NOBA; OxBA; TrGrPo

Flies wear/ Their bones. Flies. Valerie Worth. OBAP

Flight. Barbara Howes. NYBP

Flight, The. Theodore Roethke. *Fr.* Lost Son, The. HAP; HCAP; LiTM; NAAL-2; RB; TrGrPo; TRP; VGW

Flight. Harold Vinal. FaPON

Flight from Bootle, The. Sir John Betjeman. PeLV

Flight in the Desert, The. William Everson. ChIV-2; VGW

Flight into Egypt, The. W. H. Auden. *Fr.* For the Time Being; a Christmas Oratorio. OxBA

Flight into Egypt, The. W. H. Auden. *See* Well so that is that. Now we must dismantle the tree.

Flight into Egypt, The. Peter Quennell. ImPo; LiTB; LiTM

Flight into Midian. Frances E. W. Harper. *Fr.* Moses: A Story of the Nile. AAP

Flight is deeper than your father, boy., The. (*LL*) A Presentation of Two Birds to My Son. James Wright. PPP

Flight is past: and man forgot, The. (*LL*) Sic Vita. *At.* to Henry King. CBCK; CoGr; ELP; FF; NOBE; NOSC; OxBSP; SCGP; SeCP

Flight is the bird's value. Aesthetic. Norman Rosten. PoA

Flight of Fancy, A. Frances Sargent Osgood. AmWP

Flight of Leeona. Albery Allson Whitman. *Fr.* Not a Man and Yet a Man. AAP

Flight of the Birds, The. Edmund Clarence Stedman. GN

Flight of the Bucket, The. Kipling. BXAP

Flight of the Earls, The, 1607, *sels.* Fearghal Og MacWard, *tr. fr. Irish.* "All Ireland's now one vessel's company." BIrV

Flight of the Roller Coaster. Raymond Souster. NOBC

Flight of the Spirit. Felicia Dorothea Hemans. Son

Flight of the White South Africans, The. Christopher Hope. PeSAV

Flight of Wild Ducks, A. Charles Harpur. NOBAu

Flight to Flanders, The. Lessel Hutcheon. NSI

Flight to Italy, *sels.* C. Day Lewis. "Winged bull trundles to the wired perimeter, The." OxBTC

Flights. Roger McDonald. CBAP

Flighty young lady from Loddon, A. Ida Thurtle. PeLi

Fling Out the Banner! George Washington Doane. AH

Fling this useless book away. Written in a Lady's Prayer Book. The Earl of Rochester. BoLoP

(Verses Put into a Lady's Prayer-Book.) NOSC

Fling weh de wash pan, drop de cloes! Excitement. Louise Bennett. PBCV

Fling/ yourself/ upon the sky. To a Red Kite. Lilian Moore. SiSoPo

Flint. Christina Rossetti. *Fr.* Sing-Song. OxBChV

Flint Hills, The. Lew Blockcolski. VoR

Flintlike, her feet struck. Hardcastle Crags. Sylvia Plath. GoYe (Night Walk.) NYBP

Flip, clack! The windscreen wipers clear. Seven Rainy Months. William Plomer. OxBTC

Flipochinos. Cyn Zarco. UL

Flippantly,/ In the cinemas past sleep. Before Dawn. Horace Hamilton. NYBP

Flirt, The. W. H. Davies. EnLoPo

Flirting with a Pig. Aleksandar Ristovic, *tr. fr. Serbo-Croatian by* Charles Simic. HSix

Flitting, The. John Clare. FaBoPV; OxAEP-2

Flitting, The. Medbh McGuckian. PBCIP; PNI

Flitting the sea-bed, wide and flat. Skate. Alan Brownjohn. OBAP

Float free for a hundred feet with the gossamer? (*LL*) Day after Day. Li Shang-yin. PLT

Float less than April fog below our hermitage. (*LL*) Sanctuary. Louise Imogen Guiney. AmWP

Float over us, Florence, your banners. History as Decoration. Rosanna Warren. DiPo

Floated, then slowly sank. (*LL*) The Submerged Door. Matthew Sweeney. IB

Floating. Michael Brownstein. UL

Floating, a floating, A. A Myth. Charles Kingsley. GN

Floating across the lake. Not Thinking of America. Judith Kroll. AmPA

Floating Candles, The. Sydney Lea. SM

Floating down and cleaving to their shapes. (*LL*) Owls. Louise Erdrich. TRP

Floating, face up, on the open. Queer's Song. Richard Howard. *Fr.* Gaiety. ErPo

Floating Houses. David Wojahn. SM

Floating, like a vapor, on the soft summer air. (*LL*) Jeanie with the Light Brown Hair. Stephen Collins Foster. AnAmPo

Floating Old Man, The. Edward Lear. *See* There was an old man in a boat.

Floating perfectly through the net. (*LL*) Fast Break. Edward Hirsch. DiPo; EOEF; VCAP

Floating scent encircles the curved shore. Lotuses on the Crooked Pond. Lu Chao-lin, *tr. fr. Chinese by* Paul W. Kroll. SuSp

Floats the white moon. (*LL*) Winter. Walter de la Mare. OAEL-2; OBMV

Flock. Lance Henson. VoR

Flock of birds, soaring, twisting, turning, A. Love Is. Ann Darr. GrPl

Flock of bright red lanterns/ Has settle, A. (*LL*) About an Excavation. Charles Reznikoff. NTCP; PrIm; VGW

Flock of crows high from the Northland flies, A. Autumn. Detlev von Liliencron, *tr. fr. German by* Ludwig Lewisohn. AWP

Flock of Guinea Hens Seen from a Car, A. Eudora Welty. GrPl; NYBP; PrIm

Flock of sheep that leisurely pass by, A. To Sleep. Wordsworth. EnRP; GTBS; GTBS-P; TrGrPo

Flock of winds came winging [*or* flying] from the North, A. The Roaring Frost. Alice Meynell. EBVV; WPE

Flocks of birds fly high and vanish. Sitting Alone in Ching-t'ing Mountain. Li Po, *tr. fr. Chinese by* Irving Y. Lo. SuSp

Flocks of chicken clucking from every corner. Tu Fu, *tr. by* Irving Y. Lo. *Fr.* Ch'iang Village. SuSp

Flodden Field. *Unknown.* ESPB

Flood, The. Charles G. Bell. GrPl

Flood. Mary Grant Charles. GoYe

Flood, The. John Clare. RB

Flood. James Joyce. MoBrPo

Flood. Roger McGough. FF

Flood, The. Milton. *Fr.* Paradise Lost. EPCY; NOSC

Flood, The. Ovid, *tr. fr. Latin. Fr.* Metamorphoses. ChTr; OBVE, *tr. by* Dryden

Flood, The. Dara Wier. NAmP90

Flood Viewed by the Tourist from Iowa, The. James Whitehead. SM

Flood Water. *Unknown, tr. fr. Aborigine by* Mungayana Nundhirribala. NOBAu

Flood water, flood water. (*LL*) Flood Water. *Unknown.* NOBAu

Flood Year. Judith Wright. NoAM

Flooded Mind. Norman MacCaig. OxBC

Flooded Valley, The. Roland Mathias. AngWe

Flooding with a brilliant mist. To the Moon. Goethe, *tr. fr. German by* John Frederick Nims. STV

Floods all the soul with its melodious seas. (*LL*) Milton. Longfellow. AmPP; AWP; NoP; TAP; TrGrPo

Floods and gales. Et Cetera. Dee Lawrence Walker. GoYe

Floods, by nature enemies to land, The. Ovid, *tr. fr. Latin. Fr.* Metamorphoses. OBVE, *tr. by* Dryden

Floods Clap Their Hands, The. Bible, *O.T., paraphrased by* Sir Thomas Wyatt. *See* O [*or* Oh] sing unto the Lord [*or* Jehovah] a new song.

Floods of men. All the Spirit Powers Went to Their Dancing Place. Gary Snyder. UnPo

Floods of tears well from my deepest heart, The. Immanuel di Roma, *tr. fr. Italian by* J. Chotzner. TrJP

Floods Swell around Me, Angry, Appalling. Zachary Eddy. AH

Floodtide. Askia Muhammad Touré. PoBA; PoNe

Flooer o the Gean. George Campbell Hay. OxBS

Floor and the Ceiling, The. William Jay Smith. GoJo; GrPl; OBCA

Floor boards have a sour breath, The. Dust on Spring Street. Louis Grudin. NoP

Floor Is Dirty, The. Edward Field. NeAP

Floor lay paved with broken hearts, The. (*LL*) Gratiana Dancing [*or* Dauncing] and Singing. Richard Lovelace. BeJo; CaPo; JCP; MeLP; OBEV, 2 *sts.*; SeCV-1, 2 *sts.*

Floor of the path in autumn, The. At Licenza. Robert Wells. SCBI

Floor Plans. Maxine Scates. PBCAP

Floorboards creak, The. The New Apartment, Minneapolis. Linda Hogan. HATNAP

Flora's Lamentable Passion ("Flora's in her grove.") *Unknown.* CoMu

Florella; or, The Jealous Lover. *Unknown.* AmFP

Florence. Nina Zivančević, *tr. fr. Serbo-Croatian by* Charles Simic. HSix

Florence Nightingale. Michael Longley. FaBoEH

Florence Vane. Philip Pendleton Cooke. AnAmPo

Florida. Dannie Abse. OxBC

Florida. Elizabeth Bishop. TwCP

Florida. Karen Murai. UTF

Florida. Carl Rakosi. TAP

Florida Road Workers. Langston Hughes. MoAmPo

Florin to the willing guard, A. The Rosy Bosom'd Hours. Coventry Patmore. EnLoPo; NOBVV

Florio, one ev'ning, brisk, and gay. Epigram on Florio. John Winstanley. FaBoEE

Florist was told, cyclamen or azalea, The. Lines to Accompany Flowers for Eve. Carolyn Kizer. BoWoP

Florus, canst thou define that innate spark. To Mr. ———, an Unlettered Poet, on Genius Unimproved. Ann Yearsley. NOEC

Flos Lunae. Ernest Dowson. OBMV; PeVV

Floss of the reed flowers, The. Waterlilies. Ma Hsiang-lan, *tr. fr. Chinese by* Kenneth Rexroth *and* Ling Chung. WPC

Floss won't save you from an abyss. Emily Dickinson. LiTA

Flounders in mud. O Jesus, make it stop! (*LL*) Attack. Siegfried Sassoon. MoBrPo; NOBE; OxBTC; PIP

Flour is exhaustion. Kitchen. Laura Jensen. LCAP

Flour of England, fruit of Spain. Mother Goose. OxNR (Plum Pudding, A.) ReMoGo

Floure and the Leafe, The, *sels.* Chaucer. Courtly Scene and a Sudden Storm, A. OxBLMV

Flourish of silver, A. Deer Park. John Montague. PBCIP

Flourish of sunlight in the room where, A. Claud Cockburn. Thomas McCarthy. IB; PBCIP

Flourishing Village, The. Timothy Dwight. *Fr.* Greenfield Hill. EAP

Flow down, cold rivulet, to the sea. Tennyson. FaBoRV; PFP

Flow Forth, Abundant Tears. William Barley. EnRePo

Flow Gently, Sweet Afton. Burns. AWP; BLPL; FaBoBe; ImPo

Flow gently, sweet Afton, disturb not her dream. (*LL*) Flow Gently, Sweet Afton. Burns. AWP; BLPL; FaBoBe; ImPo

Flow Not So Fast. John Dowland. EnRePo

Flow not so fast, ye fountains. Flow Not So Fast. John Dowland. EnRePo

Flow, O My Tears! *Unknown.* EIL

Flow of people looking, A. At the National Gallery. Judith Kazantzis. AIW

Flow swiftly into thee, and in thee ever end. (*LL*) Upon Nothing. The Earl of Rochester. NOSC; OBSV; OxAEP-1; PoEL-3; TrGrPo

Flower, The. Robert Creeley. CAPP

Flower, The. George Herbert. AngWe; AWP; ELP; ESCV; FaBoRV; FaPoB; GeHe; JCP; NAEL-1; NOBE; NOCV; NoP; PFP; PoEL-2; SeCP; SeCV-1

Flower, A. Po Chü-i, *tr. fr. Chinese by* Robert Payne. TAL

Flower and not a flower; of mist yet not of mist, A. P'u — Hua Fei Hua. Po Chü-i, *tr. fr. Chinese by* Duncan Mackintosh. IMW

Flower and the Leaf, The, *sels.* Lady of the Arbour. "And at the last I cast my mine eye aside." WPE

Flower, and yet not a flower, A. Tune: "Flower unlike Flower." Po Chü-i, *tr. fr. Chinese by* Eugene Eoyang. SuSp

Flower-Boat, The. Robert Frost. PoA

Flower Chorus. Emerson. BoTP

Flower Ensnarer of Psalms. Rossana Ombres, *tr. fr. Italian by* I. L. Salomon. BoWoP

Flower-feasting bee, why do you touch upon. Meleager, *tr. fr. Greek by* Barbara Hughes Fowler. *Fr.* Epigrams. HePo

Flower-fed Buffaloes, The. Vachel Lindsay. ChTr; CMoP; FaPON; GoJo; MoAmPo; NOBA; OBAP; OBCA; PoE; RB; RFM; TRP; VGW

Flower-fed buffaloes of the spring, The. The Flower-fed Buffaloes. Vachel Lindsay. ChTr; CMoP; FaPON; GoJo; MoAmPo; NOBA; OBAP; OBCA; PoE; RB; RFM; TRP; VGW

Flower, flower, flower. (*LL*) Dear God. Barbara Brooker. SRLS

Flower for the New Year, A. Robert Kelly. BAP-91

Flower from Robert Kennedy's Grave, A. Edward Sanders. BCF

Flower Given to My Daughter, A. James Joyce. OBMV; RaBo; RB

Flower Herding on Mount Monadnock. Galway Kinnell. HeIP; LCAP; NaP; NoAM; NOBA

Flower in the Crannied Wall. Tennyson. BoNaP; FaBV; FaPON; ImPo; InPK; LiTB; MeMBP; NAEL-2; TEP; TFi; TrGrPo; WGRP

Flower in the leaves, only as heaven pleases. Deep in Winter. Tu Fu, *tr. fr. Chinese by* A. C. Graham. PLT

Flower Is Looking, A. Harold Monro. *Fr.* Strange Meetings. MoBrPo

Flower is withered on the stem, The. The Nurse's Lament. Mary Elizabeth Coleridge. NOBVV; OxBSP

Flower Master, The. Medbh McGuckian. PNI

Flower, The/ my heart. Poem to Be Recited Every 8 Years While Eating Unleavened Tamales. *Unknown, tr. fr. Aztec Indian by* Anselm Hollo. STP

Flower of Flame, The, *sels.* Robert Nichols. "Before I woke I knew her gone." OBMV

Flower of Mullein, A. Lizette Woodworth Reese. MoAmPo

Flower of Old Japan, The, *sels.* Alfred Noyes. "Carol, every violet has." MoBrPo

FLOWER of roses, angels' joy. Hymn to the Virgin. *Unknown.* NoSic

Flower of the flock. On Sweet Killen Hill. Tom MacIntyre. CIP (Sweet Killen Hill.) PBCIP

Flower of the foam of the waves. The Captive of the White City. Ina Coolbrith. AmWP

Flower of the pear-tree gathers and turns to fruit, The. At the End of Spring. Po Chü-i, *tr. fr. Chinese by* Arthur Waley. ArLo

Flower of the race, The. Gentlemen. Geoffrey Taylor. FaBoEE

Flower of This Purple Dye. Shakespeare. *Fr.* Midsummer Night's Dream, A. CTC

Flower of Virtue is the heart's content, The. Sonnet: Of Virtue. Folgore da San Geminiano, *tr. fr. Italian by* Dante Gabriel Rossetti. AWP

Flower of waves, A. Lady Ise, *tr. fr. Japanese by* Etsuko Terasaki *and* Irma Brandeis. BoWoP

Flower Pot, The. David Shimoni, *tr. fr. Hebrew by* Ruth Finer Mintz. MHP

Flower-Press, The. Penelope Shuttle. AIW

Flower-Seller, The ("The flower-seller's fat.") Eleanor Farjeon. BoTP

Flower that smiles to-day, The. Mutability. Shelley. EnRP; NAEL-2; NoP; OBNC; PFP

Flower-tinted cheek, the flowery close, A. Hafiz, *tr. by* Gertrude Lowthian Bell. *Fr.* Odes. AWP; TAL

Flower unblown; a book unread; A. The Year Ahead. Horatio Nelson Powers. WBLP
(New Year, The.) PoToHe

Flower was offered to me, A. My Pretty Rose Tree. Blake. *Fr.* Songs of Experience. BoLoP; FHYEP; NAEL-2

Flowering Absence, A. John Montague. BiHa; CIP; PBCIP

Flowering Bars, The. Charles Donnelly. CIP

Flowering Cherry, The. Janet Frame. PeNZ

Flowering Currant. Patrick MacDonogh. ErPo

Flowering Light of the Godhead, The, *sels.* Mechthild von Magdeburg, *tr. fr. German.*

Flowering of the Rod, The, *sels.* Hilda Doolittle ("H. D.").
"Blue-geese, white-geese, you may say." NOBA
"It is no madness to say." FaBoMo

Flowering Urn, The. Laura Riding. LiTA

Flowering War, The. *Unknown, tr. fr. Aztec Indian by* Jerome K. Rothenberg. STP

Flowering Without End. Stefan Zweig, *tr. fr. German by* Eden *and* Cedar Paul. *Fr.* Jeremiah. TrJP

Flowers. Harry Behn. FaPON

Flowers. Roo Borson. NOBC

Flowers. Kathleen Fraser. CrSp

Flowers. *Gond Oral Tradition, tr. by* V. Elwin *and* S. Hivale. WTO

Flowers. Frances Horovitz. PWE

Flowers, The. Robert Louis Stevenson. FaPON

Flowers,/ a dozen or more. Flowers. Frances Horovitz. PWE

Flowers and Men ("Flowers achieve their own floweriness and its's a miracle.") D. H. Lawrence. FaBoEE

Flowers and Trees. Sir Walter Scott. *Fr.* Lady of the Lake, The. OxAEP-2

Flowers are blooming still, those hypocrites, The. Summer. Duo Duo, *tr. fr. Chinese by* Donald Finkel *with* Li Guohua. SpMi

Flowers are dead, The. Scenery. Ted Joans. PoBA

Flowers aren't choosy. Are Flowers Whores? Elizabeth Smart. VBLP

Flowers — at ease and tall. The king is dead. (*LL*) No Swan So Fine. Marianne Moore. AnAmPo; MeMAP; NALW; NoP; OxBA; PFP; PoA; PrIm; UnPo

Flowers' Ball, The. Ben King. AnAmPo

Flowers bloom, flowers fall. To Send Away Melancholy. Huang Tsun-hsien, *tr. fr. Chinese by* An-yan Tang. SuSp

Flowers by the Sea. William Carlos Williams. CMoP; GoJo; MoAB; MoAmPo; NoAM; RB; TAP

Flowers can be cousins of the stars. There Are Different Gardens. Carl Sandburg. ImGa

Flowers did not seem to unfurl from slow bulbs, The. An Easter Garland. Carol Rumens. FaBoWP

Flowers do not regret that they fall. Poems of the Hundred Flowers Blooming. Ch'en Hsiao-keng, *tr. fr. Chinese.* LHF, *tr. by* Hualing Nieh

Flowers, Flowers. *Unknown.* CBNP

Flowers, flowers, high-no! Flowers, Flowers. *Unknown.* CBNP

Flowers for Luis Bunuel. Stuart Z. Perkoff. NeAP

Flowers for the Brave. Celia Laighton Thaxter. OHIP

Flowers from the earth have arisen, The. Nature's Easter Music. Lucy Larcom. OHIP

Flowers get a darkening brilliance now, The. The Dying Garden. Howard Nemerov. Poetsp

Flowers hang their heavy heads, The. (*LL*) Spring Rain. Tu Fu. OHMPC

Flowers hast thou in thyself, and foliage. Sonnet: To His Lady Joan, of Florence. Cavalcanti, *tr. fr. Italian by* Dante Gabriel Rossetti. AWP

Flowers have come! Nezahualcoyotl. EaPr

Flowers have come out in our garden. The Canadian Diplomat, 1942. Thomas McCarthy. IB

Flowers have fenced-in. The Clearing. Peter Everwine, *after the Nahuatl Indian.* NNaP

Flowers have lost their withered red, The. Spring Scene. Su Tung-p'o, *tr. fr. Chinese by* Robert Payne. TAL

Flowers heavy on the City of Brocade. (*LL*) Spring Night, A — Rejoicing in Rain. Tu Fu. SuSp

Flowers, I said, will come of it. (*LL*) April 5, 1974. Richard Wilbur. HCAP

Flowers in bud on the trees, The. On the Death of a New Born Child. Mei Yao Ch'en, *tr. fr. Chinese by* Kenneth Rexroth. NaP

Flowers in legions bloomed around in forest, scrub, and marsh. Tasmanian Scenes. Louisa Meredith. NOBAu

Flowers in the Valley. *Unknown.* OxBoLi

Flowers in the Ward. John Shaw Neilson. CBAP

Flowers left thick at nightfall in the wood, The. In Memoriam (Easter, 1915). Edward Thomas. GTBS-P; NOBE; OBWP; OBWVE; OxBTC; PeFWW; Spl

Flowers like a gangster's funeral. Viewing the Body. W. D. Snodgrass. CAPP

Flower's Name, The. Robert Browning. *Fr.* Garden Fancies. CTC

Flowers nodding gaily, scent in air. A Duet. T. Sturge Moore. OBEV

Flowers of Darkness. Frank Marshall Davis. NoP; PoBA; PoNe

Flowers of fire. (*LL*) To the Tune "Soaring Clouds." Huang O. BoWoP; PBWP; WPC; WPOW

Flowers of Politics, I, The. Michael McClure. NeAP

Flowers of Politics, II, The. Michael McClure. NeAP

Flowers of red silk and purple velvet grew. The Garden. Judith Wright. FaBoMA

Flowers of the flags, The. By Loch Etive. Bryan Guinness. PeIV

Flowers of the Foothills and Mountain Valleys. Alice Notley. UL

Flowers of the Forest, The. Alison Rutherford Cockburn. ECWP

Flowers of the Forest, The. Jane (*or* Jean) Elliot. CH; CoGr; ECWP; FaBoCh; FaBoRV; OxBS; ScCV; SCGP; WPE

Flowers of the willow, light, fluffy by the second moon. Willow Catkins. Hsüeh T'ao, *tr. fr. Chinese by* Eric W. Johnson. SuSp

Flowers shall hang upon the palls. Death. John Clare. GTBS-P

Flowers that in thy garden rise, The. Sir Henry Newbolt. FaBoTw

Flowers through the window. Nantucket. William Carlos Williams. AnAmPo; HAP; InPS; OxBA; SOTW; TAP; TRP; WeW

Flowers upon the rosemary spray, The. The Rosemary Spray. Luis de Góngora y Argote, *tr. fr. Spanish by* E. Churton. AWP

Flowers will do us no good on our tombstones. *Unknown, tr. fr. Greek by* Kenneth Rexroth. PGA

Flowing into the Ohio. (*LL*) Ohio Is the Iroquois Word for Beautiful. Helen Ruggieri. LoHo

Flowing robe of words you weave, The. The Lethal Thought. Mary Boyd Wagner. GoYe

Flowing Summer, The, *sels.* Charles Bruce.

Flowrets — wreaths — thy banks along. To a Gentleman, Who Desired Proper Materials for a Monody. *Unknown.* NOEC

Fluent with a friend. *Unknown.* OBF

Flukum couldn't stand the strain. 2 Poems for Black Relocation Centers. Etheridge Knight. NNaP

Flung on the sands of a sunless eternity. (*LL*) Dead Embryos. Judit Tóth. WPOW

Flunked out and laid-off. The Eisenhower Years. Paul Zimmer. NGP; PBCAP

Flush or Faunus. Elizabeth Barrett Browning. FM

Flush with the pond the lurid furnace burned. The Steam Threshing-Machine. Charles Tennyson Turner. OBNC

Flushed by the spirit of the genial year. James Thomson. *Fr.* Seasons, The. OxAEP-1

Flushed with the hope of high desire. My Hero. Benjamin Brawley. PoNe

Flute, The. Pierre Louÿs, *tr. fr. French by* Philip L. Miller. RiWo

Flute; a Pastoral, The. José-Maria de Heredia, *tr. fr. French by* H. J. C. Grierson. AWP

Flute Notes from a Reedy Pond. Sylvia Plath. FaBoMo

Flute of Daphnis, The. Edward Cracroft Lefroy, *after the Greek of* Theocritus. *Fr.* Echoes from Theocritus. AWP

Flute of May, The. Harry Woodbourne. GoYe

Flute Player. *Gond Oral Tradition, tr. by* V. Elwin *and* S. Hivale. WTO

Flute-Priest Song for Rain, *sels.* Amy Lowell.

Flute Song. Hilda Doolittle ("H. D."). AnAmPo

Flute Song. *Unknown, tr. fr. Hopi Indian by* Natalie Curtis. WTO

Flutes, and the harp on the plain. Home on the Range, February, 1962. Edward Dorn. BCF

Fluttering Leaves. Rodney Bennett. BoTP

Flux. Richard Eberhart. Poetsp; VGW

Fly, The. Philip Ayres, *after the Spanish of* Quevedo. OBVE

Fly, The. Blake. *See* Little Fly,/ Thy summers [*or* summer's] play.

Fly, The. Walter de la Mare. OTCP

Fly, The. Barnabe Googe. *See* Once Musing as I Sat.

For human-kind, weak slaves of cumbrous pride! (*LL*) The Wild Duck's Nest. Wordsworth. FM

For human nature Hope remains alone. Hope. Theognis, *tr. fr. Greek by* John Hookham Frere. AWP

For I am fallen down. (*LL*) Madboy's Song. Muriel Rukeyser. MoAmPo; TrJP

For I am not without authority in my jeopardy. God Hath Sent Me to Sea for Pearls. Christopher Smart. *Fr.* Jubilate Agno. CBCK; FaBoVe

For I am now at liberty. (*LL*) The Lover Rejoiceth. Sir Thomas Wyatt. SiPS; TrGrPo

For I bless the Prince of Peace and pray that all the guns may be nail'd up. Christopher Smart. *Fr.* Jubilate Agno. FaBoVe; InPS

For I can snore like a bullhorn. After Making Love We Hear Footsteps. Galway Kinnell. InPS; NIP; NoAM; RaBo; VCAP

For I Dipped [*or* Dipt] into the Future. Tennyson. *Fr.* Locksley Hall. BLPL; EBEV; EBVVPR; EnVR; FaBoBe; ImPo; NAEL-2; OAEL-2; PoLF

For I Have Done a Good and Kindly Deed. Franz Werfel, *tr. fr. German by* Edith Abercrombie Snow. TrJP

For I have learned. Wordsworth. *Fr.* Lines Composed a Few Miles above Tintern Abbey [on Revisiting the Banks of the Wye during a Tour, July 13, 1798]. BLPL; EBEvV; EnRP; FaBoPP; FF; FHYEP; HeIP; InPS; LiTB; MeMBP; NoP; NU; OAEL-2; OBNC; OxAEP-2; PoEL-4; Poetr; PPP; PrIm; SCGP; TEP; TFi; TrGrPo

For I have loved long, I crave rewarde. Bartholomew Griffin. *Fr.* Fidessa, More Chaste than Kind[e]. ESo

For I have loved [*or* lov'd] the rural walk through lanes. The Sofa. William Cowper. *Fr.* Task, The. EnRP
(Rural Sights and Sounds.) NOEC

For I have seen the false mermaid. (*LL*) Clerk Colvill. *Unknown.* EnSB; ESPB; FaBoBa; GBP; OxBB

For I inhabit a wood. Marban, a Hermit Speaks. *Unknown, tr. fr. Irish by* Michael Hartnett. BIrV; CIP

For I know where she bought it. (*LL*) Bought Locks. Martial. AWP

For I learn as the years roll onward. Lessons of the Year. *Unknown.* BLRP

For I must ne'er love him whom thou dost hate. (*LL*) Say that thou didst forsake me for some fault. Shakespeare. OxAEP-1

For I not whider I shall ne how longe here dwelle. (*LL*) Winter [*or* Wynter] Wakeneth All [*or* Al] My Care. *Unknown.* HAP; MiEL

For I prophesy that they will understand the blessing and virtue of the rain. Christopher Smart. *Fr.* Jubilate Agno. ECEV; FaBoVe

For I prophesy that we shall have our horns again. Christopher Smart. *Fr.* Jubilate Agno. ChIV-1; FaBoVe

For I rejoice in my cat Matty. Jubilate Matteo. Gavin Ewart. UV

For I shall know Olivia by her voice. (*LL*) Endimion Porter and Olivia. Sir William Davenant. MeLP; NOBE

For I shall love the very scorne which for my sake you do put on. (*LL*) Or love me [*or* mee] less [*or* lesse], or love me [*or* mee] more. Sidney Godolphin. BeJo; JCP

For I Will Consider My Cat Jeoffry. Christopher Smart. *Fr.* Jubilate Agno. FaBoVe; NTP; OBF; OFC; OxAEP-1; UV, sh. vers.

For I will consider my dog Poochkin. Jubilate Canis. Erica Jong. PRA

For I will dare none Good Lord, walk dead still. (*LL*) On Something, That Walks [*or* Walkes] Somewhere. Ben Jonson. BeJo; NAEL-1; OxBSP; PoE; SCGP; SeCP; SeCV-1

For ice cream. (*LL*) I scream/ You scream. *Unknown.* FaBoNo; ISE; RoPo

For if alone thou thinke to waft my love. Giles Fletcher the Elder. *Fr.* Licia. ESo

For if he gapes, by Josh, you're dead. (*LL*) Andrew Gear of Sunderland. *Unknown.* FaBoCo

For if it prosper, none dare call it treason. (*LL*) Of Treason. Sir John Harington. FaBoEE; FF; InPK; NoSic; OxBoLi; SoSe

For if you knew our hardships you'd never poach again. (*LL*) Van Dieman's Land. *Unknown.* CoMu; FaBoBa; NOBAu; OBET; OBTV; PeVV

For if you sport with pretty maids you are sure to have your change. (*LL*) The Leicester Chambermaid. *Unknown.* CoMu; OBET

For if your boone be askeable. Thomas Cromwell. *Unknown.* ESPB

For I'm old and ill and terrified and tight. (*LL*) Sun and Fun. Sir John Betjeman. PIP

For I'm wearied with hunting and fain would lie down. (*LL*) Lord Randal[l]. *Unknown.* AmFP; AWP; EBEV; EBEvV; EBNV; EnRP; ESPB, *A, B, and J vers.*; FaBoBa; FF; GGP; HAP; HeIL; HeIP; HoPM; ImPo; LiTB; NoP, *A vers.*; NTP; OAEL-1; OxBB; OxBS; Poetr; SCGP; TFi; TrGrPo; TRP; WeW

For Imelda. James Simmons. PNI

For in the body's health the soul's forgot. (*LL*) The Grave-Yard. Jones Very. NOBA

For incense. (*LL*) Obsession. Léon Damas. NegPo

For Innocents' Day. Luke Wadding. NOIV; TIRV

For Inspiration. Michelangelo, *tr. by* Wordsworth. WGRP

For Instance. Robert McAlmon. PoA

For instance/ if the sea should break. If Something Should Happen. Lucille Clifton. MAT

For it is the day of the Lord's vengeance. God's Vengeance. Bible, *O.T. Fr.* Isaiah. FM

For its people's hopes are fled! (*LL*) The Conquered Banner. Abram Joseph Ryan. AnAmPo; PAH

For Jaime Sabines. Ernesto Trejo. AfAz

For James Baldwin. Kay Boyle. NMM

For James Dean. Frank O'Hara. NeAP; NNaP

For Jan, in Bar Maria. Carolyn Kizer. VGW

For Jane. Charles Bukowski. HoPM

For Jane Myers. Louise Glück. FaBoWP

For Jean Vincent d'Abbadie, Baron St.-Castin. Alden Nowlan. NOBC

For Jed. X. J. Kennedy. PFL

For Jillian of Berry she dwells on a hill. Jillian of Berry. Beaumont *and* John Fletcher. *Fr.* Knight of the Burning Pestle, The. EIL

For Jim, Easter Eve. Anne Spencer. PoNe

For Joan of Arc goes riding by. (*LL*) The Good Joan. Lizette Woodworth Reese. FaPON; MoShBr

For John Berryman. Robert Lowell. NOBA

For John Chappell. Gary Snyder. NNaP

For John Clare. John Ashbery. FYAP

For John Keats, Apostle of Beauty. Countee Cullen. *Fr.* Four Epitaphs. CDC; PoBA

For Johnny. John Pudney. CoGr; FaBoEH; OBWP

For joy. (*LL*) Upon a Spider Catching a Fly. Edward Taylor. AmPP; EAP; MeMAP; NOBA; NoP; OxBA; PeECV; PoEL-3; SCAP; TAP

For July, in Sierra, by the willow-tree. July. Folgore da San Geminiano, *tr. fr. Italian by* Dante Gabriel Rossetti. *Fr.* Sonnets of the Months. AWP

For just a brief while every day. Rendezvous. Mary Scott Fitzgerald. PoToHe

For Just Men Light Is Sown. Michael Wigglesworth. AH

For K. R. on Her Sixtieth Birthday. Richard Wilbur. NoP

For Kai Snyder. Philip Whalen. PoM

For kissing of my dame. (*LL*) Kissing of My Dame. *Unknown.* GBP

For knighthood is not in the feats of war. The True Knight [*or* True Knighthood]. Stephen Hawes. *Fr.* Pastime of Pleasure, The. OBEV; TrGrPo

For Kuo Hsiang. Yü Hsüan-chi, *tr. fr. Chinese by* Geoffrey R. Waters. BoWoP

For lack of knowledge do my people die! My People Are Destroyed for Lack of Knowledge. Jones Very. ChIV-1

For Langston Hughes. Etheridge Knight. NBV

For Lerida. David St. John. AmPA; AnAn

For Li Po. Tu Fu, *tr. fr. Chinese by* Eugene Eoyang. SuSp

For Life I Had Never Cared Greatly. Thomas Hardy. CMoP; LiTM; NoAM

For life will not be given us again. (*LL*) Of Those Who Go, Not to Return. Benyamin Galai. MHP

For lighter, whiter skin in just ten days. Brainwashing Dramatized. Don Johnson. PoNe

For Lil Louis. Tom Dent. Jaz

For little dreams to go. (*LL*) Hold Fast Your Dreams. Louise Driscoll. BLPA; FaBoBe; FaPON

For "Little Giffen," of Tennessee. (*LL*) Little Giffen. Francis Orrery Ticknor. GOA; PAH

For Lo! My Jonah How He Slumped. John Wilson. AH

For lo! the board with cups and spoons is crown'd. Pope. *Fr.* Rape of the Lock, The. FHYEP; HAP; ImPo; NoP; OAEL-1; OBNV; PeLV; PoEL-3; TEP; TrGrPo; UV

For lo! the sea that fleets about the land. The Dancing Sea. Sir John Davies. *Fr.* Orchestra; or, A Poem[e] of Da[u]ncing. ChTr; NoSic, *abr.*; SiPS; SiPSBD

For, lo, the winter is past. Bible, *O.T. Fr.* Song of Solomon, The. PDV (Lo, the Winter Is Past.) FaPON; SiSoPo

For lofty sense. Wild Shakespeare. James Thomson. *Fr.* Seasons, The. EPCY

For long days, brush fire has overcome the steppe. (*LL*) Brush Fire. Fily-Dabo Sissoko. NegPo

For, Lord, the Crowded Cities Be. Rainer Maria Rilke, *tr. fr. German by* Ludwig Lewisohn. AWP; TrJP

For lost honour among thieves. (*LL*) The Thieves. Robert Graves. BoLoP; CMoP; GTBS-P; LiTM; OAEL-2

For Lotus Flower. Li Shang-yin, *tr. fr. Chinese by* Eugene Eoyang *and* Irving Y. Lo. SuSp

For Love. Robert Creeley. NOBA; VCAP

For love he offered me his perfect world. Gift to a Jade. Anna Wickham. OxBSP

For love — I would. The Warning. Robert Creeley. NeAP; TAP; VGW

For love no time has she, or inclination. Soame Jenyns. Fr. Modern Fine Lady, The. NOEC; OBSV

For love there is no other drug, Nicias. Theocritus [or Theokritus]. See And so an easier life our Cyclops drew.

For Love's-sake, kiss(e) me once again(e). Begging Another, on Colour of Mending the Former. Ben Jonson. Fr. Celebration of Charis in Ten Lyric[k] Peeces [or pieces], A. BeJo; CBLP; OxAEP-1; PoEL-2; SeCP

For Love's Sake Only. Elizabeth Barrett Browning. See If thou must love me, let it be for nought.

For Mack C. Parker. Pauli Murray. PoBA

For Malcolm X. Nanina Alba. PoBA

For Malcolm X. Margaret Walker. BPo; PoBA; Son

For Malcolm, a Year After. Etheridge Knight. BCF

For Malcolm: After Mecca. Gerald William Barrax. PoBA

For Malcolm Who Walks in the Eyes of Our Children. Quincy Troupe. PoBA

For Malcolm's eyes, when they broke. A Poem for Black Hearts. Amiri Baraka. PoBA; PoM; SOTW

For Malka Who Lived Three Days Dying. Laura Kasischke. BTR

For man is between the pinchers while his soul is shaping and purifying. Christopher Smart. Fr. Jubilate Agno. ChIV-1; FaBoVe

For man to act as if his soul did see. Thomas Traherne. See Contentment is a sleepy thing.

For man to tell how human life began. Milton. Fr. Paradise Lost. ChIV-1; EPCY

For many a year I've watched the ships a-sailing to and fro. The Ships. J. J. Bell. BoTP

For many distant travelers. Acoma. William Oandasan. HATNAP

For many lang year I ha'e heard frae my grannie. The Hazlewood Witch. Richard Gall. ScCV

For many, many days together. Riding Together. William Morris. EnVR; NOBE; OAEL-2

For many thousand ages. Es Stehen Unbeweglich. Heine, tr. fr. German by James Thomson. AWP; TrJP

For many unsuccessful years. Advice to a Lover. Thomas Yalden. ECEV

For many unsuccessful years. Against Modesty in Love. Matthew Prior. ErPo

For many years. (LL) Many Years. Bei Dao. SpMi

For Mao Tse-tung; a Meditation on Flies and Kings. Irving Layton. NOBC

For Margaret. Stanley Moss. IMW

For Maria Magdalenes. Desanka Maksimovic, tr. fr. Serbo-Croatian by Charles Simic. HSix

For Marianne Moore's Birthday. Kay Boyle. NMM

For Mary McLeod Bethune. Margaret Walker. PoNe

For Masturbation. Alan Dugan. CAPP

For Me at Sunday Sermons, the Serpent. Lynn Emanuel. ETG

For me, for me, two horses wait. The Wizard's Funeral. Richard Watson Dixon. ELP; NOBVV; PeVV

For Me from You. Rita Anyiam – St. John. VBLP

For me, me, me. (LL) The Cupboard. Walter de la Mare. FaPON; NTCP

For me no other girls exist. (LL) 'S Wonderful. Ira Gershwin. CBLP

For me O dear! on Zero Street. (LL) Wichita Vortex Sutra. Allen Ginsberg. PoBeRe

"For me," says Jane. (LL) Bunches of Grapes. Walter de la Mare. GoJo; GrPl; MoShBr; NTP; OxBChV

For me, the naked and the nude. The Naked and the Nude. Robert Graves. MeMBP; NYBP; SoSe

For me who go. Parting. Buson, tr. fr. Japanese by Harold G. Henderson. ArLo

For mercy, courage, kindness, mirth. Laurence Binyon. BoTP; MoBrPo

For Miklos Radnóti: 1909-1944. Kate Daniels. NAmP90

For Miles. Gregory Corso. Jaz

For mine, I ween, is free. (LL) Johnie Cock. Unknown. ESPB

For Miriam. Marjorie Oludhe Macgoye. WPOW

For "Mr. Dudley," a Black Spy. James A. Emanuel. BPo; NBV

For modes of faith let graceless Zealots fight. Faith. Pope. Fr. Essay on Man, An. WGRP

For months and years in a forgotten war. Human Nature. Karl Shapiro. ArOW

For months, coming home late at night. Shards, the. Michael O'Loughlin. Fr. Shards, The. IB

For months/ my books were stacked. February Park. Gerald Vizenor. VoR

For more than sixty years he has been blind. War Blinded. Douglas Dunn. DiPo; OBWP

For morn, my dome of blue. A Child's Prayer. Siegfried Sassoon. BoTP

For mortal love, that might not die of it. (LL) Oh, sleep forever in the Latmian cave. Edna St. Vincent Millay. CMoP; LiTM; MoAmPo; NALW; NoAM; NoP; Poetr

For mortals, mortal things. And all things leave us. Lucianus, tr. fr. Greek by Edwin Morgan. GrAn

For mother-love and father-care. We Thank Thee. Unknown. FaPON

For M.S. Singing Fruhlingsglaube in 1945. Frances Cornford. BrRo

For Munday hath hang'd himselfe. (LL) Epitaph in St. Olave's, Southwark, on Mr. Munday. Unknown. FaBoCo; OxBoLi

For Musia's Grandchildren. Irving Layton. NOBC

For My Ancestors. Rolfe Humphries. PoRA

For my answer is a rose. (LL) The Rose. George Herbert. LiTB; PoEL-2

For My Brother Jesus. Irving Layton. NoP

For My Brother Who Died before I Was Born. Baron Wormser. GOYP

For My Contemporaries. J. V. Cunningham. CoAP; SM; VCAP

For My Daughter. Judith Kazantzis. AIW

For My Daughter. Weldon Kees. CoAP; SM

For My Daughter. John Logan. CRP

For My Daughter's Twenty-First Birthday. Jeanne Murray Walker. MDDM

For My Father. Paul Potts. FaBoTw

For my first poem there are specific images. Mr. Nabokov's Memory. Thomas McCarthy. IB

For My Funeral. A. E. Housman. CMoP; TrPWD

For My Grandfather. Francis Webb. FaBoMA

For My Grandmother. Countee Cullen. Fr. Four Epitaphs. CDC; MoAmPo; PoBA; VGW

For My Grandmother, Bridget Halpin. Michael Hartnett. BIrV; IIP; PBCIP

For My Husband. Ellen Bryant Voigt. NoP

For my innocent days will come back no more. (LL) The Girl's Lamentation. William Allingham. TIRV

For My Lover, Returning to His Wife. Anne Sexton. CBLP; HCAP; IHMS; LPA; NMM; Poetr; UnPo; WPE

For My Mother. Doris Brett. NOBAu

For My Mother. David Diop, tr. fr. French by Ellen Conroy Kennedy. NegPo

For My Mother. Louise Glück. UnPo

For My Mother. June Jordan. BoWoP; NMM

For My Mother. Philip Schultz. NAmP90

For My Mother. Iain Crichton Smith. OxBS

For My Mother. Ellen Bryant Voigt. NIP

For My Mother: Genevieve Jules Creeley. Robert Creeley. PoM; TRP

For My Mother, Who Lives. Lorraine Duggin. LoHo

For My Own Monument. Matthew Prior. GGP; OBEV

For my part, I never care. Tips Tongueless. Robert Herrick. CaPo

For my part, I'le not meddle with the cause. Homer, tr. by George Chapman. Fr. Odyssey. CTC; NAWM-1

For My People. Wendy Rose. CDW

For My People. Margaret Walker. PoBA; PoNe

For my poor passage to the stall of Night? (LL) On an Anniversary. J. M. Synge. FaBoEE; NOIV; OBMV; PeIV

For my sins I live in the city of New York. Whitman in Black. Ted Berrigan. UL

For my sister's sake. Hitomaro, tr. by Arthur Waley. Fr. Manyo Shu, Part 1 of 4. AWP

For My Son, Noah, Ten Years Old. Robert Bly. CAPP; InPS; RaBo

For My Son on the Highways of His Mind. Maxine W. Kumin. MAT

For My Torturer, Lieutenant D — — . Leila Djabali, tr. fr. French by Anita Barrows. WPOW

For My Unborn and Wretched Children. Alfred B. Spellman. PoBA

For My Wife 1936 – 1974. James Lewisohn. ETG

For myself more than anyone. (LL) From a Republican Grave: Daniel Henry Deniehy, 1828 – 1865. Philip Mead. NOBAu

For nations vague as weed. Nothing to Be Said. Philip Larkin. OxBTC

For nearly fifty years I've been a cocky. Now I'm Easy. Eric Bogle. OBET

For Nelly Sachs. Kinereth Gensler. BTR

For New Year, Postumus, ten years ago. A Roman Thank-You Letter. Martial, tr. fr. Latin by James Michie. OBCP

For Nicholas, Born in September. Tod Perry. NYBP

For nine months. The Rite. Peter Dale. NAs

For No Clear Reason. Robert Creeley. VGW

For No Good Reason. Peter Redgrove. PoE

For No One. John Lennon and Paul McCartney. WTO

For no watchman is waiting for you and for me. (LL) The Butterfly's Ball. William Roscoe. OxBChV

For noble minds, the worst of miseries. Poverty. Theognis, tr. fr. Greek by John Hookham Frere. AWP

For Stephen Procter. Frances Horovitz. PWE

For still 'tis only dawning Day. (*LL*) The Burial of King Cormac. Sir Samuel Ferguson. NOIV; PeIV; TIRV

For strife comes with manhood, and waking with day. (*LL*) Lullaby of an Infant Chief. Sir Walter Scott. EnRP; FaPON; OxBChV

For Stuart Porter, Who Asked for a Poem That Would Not Depress Him Further. Jeffrey Skinner. PBCAP

For such as you, I do believe. The Mother in the House. Hermann Hagedorn. OHIP
(Mother.) PoToHe

For Summer's bloom and Autumn's blight. Josiah Gilbert Holland. *Fr.* Bitter-sweet. TrPWD

For Sunday's play he never makes excuse. The Lout. John Clare. EnVR

For sunlight on the garden. (*LL*) The Sunlight on the Garden. Louis MacNeice. CMoP; EBEV; GTBS-P; HAP; InPS; LiTB; NAEL-2; NOBE; NOIV; NoP; OxAEP-2; OxBTC; PFP; PNI; PrIm; TRP; TwCP

For sunlit hours and visions clear. Gratitude. Clyde McGee. BLRP

For surfeits sooner kill than fasts. (*LL*) Against Absence. Sir John Suckling. CaPo

For sweet things dying. (*LL*) A Dirge. Christina Rossetti. ChTr; EBVV; NOBVV; SCGP

For Talbot's de dog, and James is de ass. (*LL*) Lilli Burlero [or Lilliburlero]. Thomas, Lord Wharton. APAS; FaBoEH; NOIV; OxBoLi

For ten-and-sixpence sterling. (*LL*) Alnwick Castle. Fitz-Greene Halleck. AnAmPo

For ten years Boss was always on a trip. The Fifties. Robert McDowell. *Fr.* Home in America. BAP-89

For ten years the sycamores. Brynbeidog. Jeremy Hooker. AngWe; SCBI

For that free Grace bringing us past terrible risks. Minnesota Thanksgiving. John Berryman. GOA

For that goatfucker, goatfooted. Leonidas, *tr. fr. Greek* by Kenneth Rexroth. GrAn; PGA

For That He Looked Not upon Her. George Gascoigne. ElL; NoP

For that I never knew you, I only learned to dread you. St. Roach. Muriel Rukeyser. GLP

For that rare, random descent. (*LL*) Black Rook in Rainy Weather. Sylvia Plath. LiTM; NAAL-2; Poetr; SM

For that the sonnet no doubt was my own true. Late Sonnet. Hayden Carruth. SM; Son

For that they housed Him from the cold! (*LL*) A Christmas Folk-Song. Lizette Woodworth Reese. FaPON; OBCA; OHIP; TrCP

For that's the best cure for a little pussy cat. (*LL*) Who's that ringing at my door bell? *Unknown*. FaBoCh; OxNR

For the air is purified by prayer which is made aloud. Christopher Smart. *Fr.* Jubilate Agno. FaBoVe; Prf

For the Altarpiece of the Roseau Valley Church, Saint Lucia. Derek Walcott. NoP

For the Anniversary of My Death. W. S. Merwin. CoAP; HCAP; InPK; NAAL-2; NaP; NOBA; Poetr; VCAP

For the Athenian Dead at Plataia. Simonides, *tr. fr. Greek* by Peter Jay. GrAn

For the Baptist. William Drummond of Hawthornden. *See* Last and greatest herald of Heaven's King, The.

For the Bed at Kelmscott. William Morris. *See* Wind's on the wold, The.

For the black plunge-line nightdress. (*LL*) The Skunk. Seamus Heaney. NAEL-2; OxBC; PoE

For the Bones of Josef Mengele, Disinterred June 1985. Robert Bringhurst. NIP

For the Book of Love. Jules Laforgue, *tr. fr. French* by Jethro Bithell. AWP; ErPo

For the Briar Rose. William Morris. NOBVV

For the bumps bangs and scratches of. Auto Mobile. A. R. Ammons. FF; OBAL

For the Candle Light. Angelina Weld Grimké. BlSi; CDC; PoNe

For the Cenotaph of a Lost Soldier. Theon, *tr. fr. Greek* by Dudley Fitts. GrAn

For the cherub's listening ear. (*LL*) Tirzah. Jacob Cohen. MHP

For the child of her love is no longer a slave. (*LL*) She's Free! Frances E. W. Harper. AIW; BlSi; Son

For the Children. David McKain. BTR

For the Children. Thomas Love Peacock. VoR

For the Children. Gary Snyder. NoP

For the Children or the Grown-ups? *Unknown*. OBCP

For the Company Underground. Francis MacNamara. NOBAu

For the country will bring us no peace. (*LL*) Raleigh Was Right. William Carlos Williams. NIP; NoAM; Poetr; RB

For the Courtesan Ch'ing Lin. Wu Tsao, *tr. fr. Chinese* by Kenneth Rexroth *and* Ling Chung. BoWoP; VBLP; WPC; WPOW

For the Crèche. G. K. Chesteron. *Fr.* Songs of Education. FaBoCo

For the Cultural Campaign. Chimedin Jigmed, *tr. fr. Mongol Oral Tradition* by C. R. Bawden. WTO

For the Dancer of the King of Wu. Li Po, *tr. fr. Chinese* by Robert Payne. TAL

For the days when nothing happens. Thanksgiving. Margaret E. M. Sangster. BLRP

For the Dead. Adrienne Rich. AnAn; NAAL-2

For the Death of 100 Whales. Michael McClure. PoBeRe

For the different sexes of sparrow. (*LL*) An Old Lady of Harrow. *Unknown*. PeLi

For the dim regions whence my fathers came. Outcast. Claude McKay. PoBA

For the doubling of flowers is the improvement of the gardners talent. Christopher Smart. *Fr.* Jubilate Agno. ChIV-2; FaBoVe; NOEC

For the dreams of your image that bolssoms a rose in the deeps of my heart. (*LL*) The Lover Tells of the Rose in His Heart. W. B. Yeats. CMoP

For the El Paso Weather Bureau. Peter Wild. MAT

For the Examination at Ho-nan-fu: Songs of the Twelve Months, *sels*. Li Ho, *tr. fr. Chinese* by Burton Watson.

For the expectant is the glory. Zealots of Yearning. David Rokeah, *tr. fr. Hebrew* by Ruth Finer Mintz. MHP

For the Fallen. Laurence Binyon. CoGr; EBEvV; FaBoEH; NOBE; OBEV; OBWP; OxBTC; PlP

For the Family of Cuchonnacht O Dalaigh. David O'Bruadair, *tr. fr. Irish* by Thomas Kinsella. NOIV

For the First Manned Moon Orbit, *sels*. James Dickey. "So long." AiP

For the first time. A Poem for Positive Thinkers. Barbara Mahone. PoBA

For the first time since anyone remembers. Rhapsody on Main Street. Patrick Williams. PNI

For the first twenty years/ [or yeares] since yesterday. The Computation. John Donne. CBNP; NoSic; OxBSP; SoSe

For the floating world? (*LL*) I, who cut off my sorrows. Akazome Emon. BoWoP; WPJ; WPOW

For the flowers anyhow. (*LL*) What's the balm. Alan Dugan. CAPP; SM

For the flowers of the Forest are a' wade away. (*LL*) The Flowers of the Forest. Alison Rutherford Cockburn. ECWP

For the Fly-Leaf of a School-Book. Norman Cameron. OxBS

For the forced-fire/ of roses. (*LL*) The Porcupine. Galway Kinnell. FoLa; NaP; NOBA

For the fount of life undying. Paradise. Peter Damian, *tr. fr. Latin* by Helen Waddell. MLL

For the Fourth Birthday of My Daughter. George Barker. NAs

For the friendships of youth are more instant. Daryl Hine. OBF

For the future to grow upon. *Unknown*. Ice mountain melted. EaPr

For the Gifts of the Spirit. Edward Rowland Sill. TrPWD

For the girl, it was a growing up. Moon of the First Communion. Kathleen Norris. CrSp

For the Girls 'cause They Know. Harold Littlebird. VoR

For the God of Peyote. *Unknown*, *tr. fr. Huichol Indian* by Jerome K. Rothenberg. STP

For the Goddess Too Well Known. Elsa Gidlow. PeHV

For the Good of the Pythian Order. Mrs. Henry Linden. CBWP-4

For the Grave of Daniel Boone. William Stafford. NoP

For the great flint to come singing into his heart. (*LL*) Bushed. Earle Birney. MoCV; NoAM; NOBC; NoP

For the Green! (*LL*) After Aughrim. Arthur G. Geoghegan. PeIV

For the house that is mine. (*LL*) The Tenancy. Mary Gilmore. CBAP

For the Hyacinthine festival he has given me. The Flute. Pierre Louÿs, *tr. fr. French* by Philip L. Miller. RiWo

For the Jellicle Moon and the Jellicle Ball. (*LL*) The Song of the Jellicles. T. S. Eliot. EBEvV; FaBoCh; FaBoNo; ImGa; OFC; OxBChV

For the Kindling of the Light on Easter Eve. Prudentius, *tr. fr. Latin* by Helen Waddell. MLL

For the King's Birthday, 1790, *sels*. Thomas Warton the Younger. "And lo, amid the watery roar." FaBoEH

For the Lady Olivia Porter; a Present upon a New Year's Day. Sir William Davenant. JCP; MeLP; NOSC

For the Lame. Lucille Clifton. CAPP

For the last time. (*LL*) The Thumb. Dennis Saleh. MAT

For the last time Beowulf uttered his boast. Beowulf and Wiglaf Slay the Dragon. *Unknown*, *tr. fr. Beowulf.* AnOE; ASW, *tr. by* Kevin Crossley-Holland.

For the Last Time, Fire. Dennis Scott. PBCV

For the Last Wolverine. James Dickey. FoLa

For the lifting up of mountains. Mountains. Lucy Larcom. WBLP

For the Lord your God. Bible, *O.T. Fr.* Deuteronomy. EaPr

For the Lordes parte is his folke. Bible, *O.T.*, *tr. by* William Tyndale. *Fr.* Deuteronomy. OBVE

For the Lord's Day Evening. Isaac Watts. OxBChV

For the love of God is broader. There's a Wideness. Frederick William Faber. WBLP

For the Magdalene. William Drummond of Hawthornden. ChIV-2; PoEL-2

For the Market. Jane Mayhall. TAP

For the Marriage of Faustus and Helen. (Mind has shown itself at times, The.) Hart Crane. InPS; NoAM; NOBA
Sels.
"Capped arbiter of beauty in this street." FaBoMo; ImPo; LiTM

For the Marsh's Birthday. James Wright. NYBP

For the marvelous grace of Your Creation. *Unknown.* EaPr

For the Master's Use. *Unknown.* BLPA

For the mighty wind arises, roaring seaward, and I go. (*LL*) Locksley Hall. Tennyson. BLPL; EBEV; EnVR; FaBoBe; ImPo; NAEL-2; OAEL-2

For the Moment. Pierre Reverdy, *tr. fr. French by* Ron Padgett. ArLo; TTTS

For the murderous gallows, black and grim, is cheated of its dead! (*LL*) Death-Doomed. Will M. Carleton. VPP

For the Mute. Lucille Clifton. CAPP

For the New Union Dead in Alabama. Edward Dorn. PoM

For the New Year. Robert Creeley. NaP

For the New Year. Eduard Friedrich Mörike, *tr. fr. German by* Philip L. Miller. RiWo

For the New Year 1981. Denise Levertov. ArNa

For the nightemare. *Unknown.* MiEL

For the Nightly Ascent of the Hunter Orion over a Forest Clearing. James Dickey. TwCP

For the old Kentucky home, far away. (*LL*) My Old Kentucky Home, [Good Night]. Stephen Collins Foster. AnAmPo; FaBoBe; FaBV; PoLF; TrGrPo

For the one more cast-off shell. (*LL*) Sand Dunes. Robert Frost. MoAB; MoAmPo; RFM

For the One Who Would Take Man's Life in His Hands. Delmore Schwartz. LiTA; LiTM; MoAB; MoAmPo; VGW

For the Opening of the William Dinsmore Briggs Room. Yvor Winters. CRP

For the Palace that lies desolate. We Sit Solitary. *Unknown.* TrJP

For the Passing of Groucho's Pursuer. John Hollander. *See* Now that high, oft-affronted bosom heaves.

For the Poet Who Said Poets Are Struck by Lightning Only Two or Three Times. Peter Klappert. NBLV

For the Poets. Jayne Cortez. BCF

For the power of some animal is predominant in every language. Reflections on Sounds and Language. Christopher Smart. *Fr.* Jubilate Agno. FaBoVe

For the Queen Mother. Sir John Betjeman. NAs

For the Rain It Raineth Every Day. Robert Graves. GoJo; NYBP

For the raindrop, joy is in entering the river. Asadullah Khan Ghalib, *tr. fr. Urdu by* Jane Hirshfield. EnlH

For the Record. Roy Blount, Jr. OBAL

For the Record. George Jonas. MoCV

For the Record. Audre Lorde. LoHo

For the Record. Roy McFadden. PNI

For the Record. "Ping Hsin," *tr. fr. Chinese by* Kenneth Rexroth *and* Ling Chung. WPC

For the Record. Adrienne Rich. CAPP; NIP; VCAP

For the right to be free. (*LL*) Giovanni Azania. Don Mattera. PeSAV

For the rosebud's break of beauty. Lucy Larcom. *Fr.* Thanksgiving, A. OHIP; TrPWD

For the Safety of Lovers. John James. NBrP

For the sake of a night of a little sleep. Daughter of Minamoto no Toshitaka, *tr. fr. Japanese by* Kenneth Rexroth *and* Ikuko Atsumi. WPJ

For the Sake of Retrieval. Linda Bierds. NAmP90

For the sea is his truest home! (*LL*) The Sea-Gull. Mary Howitt. BoTP; OxBChV

For the Sexes; the Gates of Paradise. Blake. LiTB; MeMBP; PoEL-4
Epilogue: "To the Accuser Who Is The God of This World." HAP; ImPo; OAEL-2; OBNC; PeECV; PoE; WeW
(To the Accuser Who Is the God of This World.) FHYEP; NoP; OxBSP; SCGP; TrGrPo
"Truly my Satan thou art but a dunce." PoE

For the Sin. *Unknown, tr. fr. Hebrew.* TrJP

For the Sleepwalkers. Edward Hirsch. FYAP

For the Slender Beech and the Sapling Oak. Thomas Love Peacock. *Fr.* Maid Marian. EnRP

For the Snark *was* a Boojum, you see. (*LL*) The Hunting of the Snark. "Lewis Carroll." CBNP; EBEvV, *Pt.* 1 *only*; FaBoNo; FiBHP, *much abr.*; OBNC; OBNV; PoEL-5

For the snow. John James. VaA

For the Spartan Dead at Plataia. Simonides, *tr. fr. Greek by* Peter Jay. GrAn

For the Spartan Dead at Thermopylai (480 B.C.). Simonides. *See* Go tell at Sparta, traveler passing by.

For the spiritual musick is as follows. Christopher Smart. *Fr.* Jubilate Agno. FaBoVe; NOEC

For the steeplechase on Father Riley's horse! (*LL*) Father Riley's Horse. Andrew Barton Paterson. NOBAu

For the Student Strikers. Richard Wilbur. OxBC

For the Sun Declined, sels. Yitzhak Lamdan, *tr. fr. Hebrew by* Simon Halkin.
"Where am I, O awesome friend?" TrJP

"For the tenth time, dull Daphnis," said Chloe. *Unknown.* PeLi

For the Theft of Cattle. *Unknown, tr. fr. Anglo-Saxon by* Kevin Crossley-Holland. ASW

For the third time in ten years. Tunes for Bears to Dance To. Ronald Wallace. GOYP

For the tie is unbroken on the Plains of Emu. (*LL*) The Exile of Erin. *Unknown.* NOBAu

For the Time Being; a Christmas Oratorio, sels. W. H. Auden.
Flight into Egypt, The. OxBA
Fugal-Chorus. LiTM
If on Account of the Political Situation. LiTA
"Led by the light of an unusual star." PChr
"Our Father, whose creative Will." TrPWD
Well, So That Is That. LiTA; OAEL-2; OBCP
(After Christmas.) MoAB; MoBrPo
(Flight into Egypt, The.) OxBA
(Narrator.) MeMAP

For the times they are a-changin.' (*LL*) The Times they Are A-Changin.' Bob Dylan. PoBeRe

For the treason of all clerks. (*LL*) At the Grave of Henry James. W. H. Auden. LiTA; NoP

For the tropic traveler! (*LL*) Morning Light. Mary Effie Lee Newsome. CDC; PoBA; PoNe; ShDr

For the Union Dead. Robert Lowell. AmPP; CoAP; FaBoPV; FYAP; HAP; HCAP; HeIP; InPS; LCAP; LiTM; MoP; NAAL-2; NaP; NoAM; NOBA; NoP; OBWP; PoE; Poetr; SCV; TFi; TRP; TwCP; UnPo; VCAP; WeW

For the voyage of oblivion awaits you. (*LL*) The Ship of Death. D. H. Lawrence. CMoP; FaBoRV; FaBoTw; GTBS-P; LiTB; MeMBP; MoAB; MoBrPo; MoP; NAEL-2; NoAM; NoP; OAEL-2; OxAEP-2; PrIm

For the West. Gary Snyder. NaP

For "The Wine of Circe" by Edward Burne-Jones. Dante Gabriel Rossetti. UV

For the woman/ African in ancestry. A Freedom Song for the Black Woman. Carole C. Gregory. BlSi

For the Word Is Flesh. Stanley Kunitz. VGW

For the world we have. (*LL*) How strange and wonderful is our home, our earth. Edward Abbey. EaPr

For the Yonghy-Bonghy-Bo. (*LL*) The Courtship of the Yonghy-Bonghy-Bo. Edward Lear. EnLoPo; FaBoNo; OAEL-2; OxBM; WiR

For the Young Who Want To. Marge Piercy. Poetsp

For thee I shall not die. I Shall Not Die for Thee. *Unknown, tr. fr. Irish by* Douglas Hyde. IIP
(O Woman, Shapely as the Swan.) BIrV, *tr. by* Padraic Colum; CTC

For Thee, Little Boy. Virgil, *tr. fr. Latin.* *Fr.* Eclogues. ArLo, *tr. by* James Laughlin.

For thee, little boy, will the earth pour forth gifts. For Thee, Little Boy. Virgil, *tr. fr. Latin.* *Fr.* Eclogues. ArLo, *tr. by* James Laughlin.

For thee, O dear dear country! Jerusalem the Golden. Bernard of Cluny, *tr. fr. Latin by* John Mason Neale. *Fr.* De Contemptu Mundi. WGRP

For Thee to live; in Thee to die. (*LL*) Feast of the Most Holy Trinity. Aubrey Thomas De Vere. TIRV

For thee to wear, but this of thine own Blood. (*LL*) Upon the Body of Our Blessed Lord, Naked and Bloody. Richard Crashaw. InvP; NOSC; SeCP

For Them. Michael Brownstein. UL

For them, the Arctic is the image, a touch of eternity. For Them. Michael Brownstein. UL

For there are two heavens, sweet. Two Heavens. Leigh Hunt. GN

For there is an African virtue of the tree. Edouard J. Maunick, *tr. fr. French by* Ellen Conroy Kennedy. *Fr.* As Far as Yoruba Land. NegPo

For there is hope for a tree. Bible, *O.T.* *Fr.* Job. ChTr; DL; NAWM-1, *abr.*; OBVE

For there is my father. Work Rules. John Norton. BCF

For there is no friend like a sister. Christina Rossetti. *Fr.* Goblin Market. EBEV; NAEL-2; NOBVV; OBF; OBNV

For there is no God found stronger than death; and death is a sleep. *(LL)* Hymn to Proserpine. Swinburne. EBVV; EnVR; NAEL-2; OAEL-2; OBNC; PoEL-5; TEP

For there is yet song for them within you. *(LL)* Song Yet Song. Amir Gilboa. MHP

For there's nae, &c. *(LL)* The Sailor's Wife. *At. to* William Julius Mickle, *also at. to* Jean Adam. BeLS; GN; GTBS; GTBS-P

For these brothers. *(LL)* Brother of the Streets. Sam Cornish. TRP

For these dead Birds, sigh a prayer. *(LL)* The Phoenix and the Turtle. Shakespeare. EnRePo; ImPo; LiTB; NOBE; NoP; NoSic; OAEL-1; OBEV; OxAEP-1; PeECV; PoEL-2; SCGP; TEP

For these old alcoholics? *(LL)* Drinking with Friends amongst the Blooming Peonies. Liu Yu Hsi. OHMPC

For these water-sizzlers, no man at night has his rest! *(LL)* Blacksmiths. *Unknown.* WiR

For they are dead. Respect for the Dead. Laura Riding. LiTA

For they are frank and free. *(LL)* The Rantin Laddie. *Unknown.* AmFP; ESPB; HAP; OxBA; TAP

For they are made in my image. *(LL)* Ghetto. Guy Tirolien. NegPo

For they never came back again. *(LL)* What Became of Them? *Unknown.* BoTP; OBCA; OxBChV

For They Shall See God. Luci Shaw. TrCP

For they were deep in the earth and what is possible swiftly took hold. *(LL)* Orpheus and Eurydice. Jorie Graham. VCAP

For they were sent to do judgement on him! *(LL)* God's Judgment on a Wicked Bishop. Robert Southey. ChTr; EnRP; OBNV

For thine is the kingdom. Lord's Prayer. D. H. Lawrence. PeECV

For thinking on my dearie. *(LL)* Simmer's a Pleasant Time. Burns. PoEL-4

For thinking that thou art not ill. *(LL)* England. *Unknown.* FaBoEE; OxBSP

For this additional declaration. The Dissenters' Thanksgiving for the Late Declaration. *Unknown.* APAS

For this and for all enclosures like it the archetype. The Cave of Making. W. H. Auden. FaBoVe; OxAEP-2

For this fresh air and fragrant wine. *(LL)* Garden at Heidelberg. Walter Savage Landor. OBTV

For this is my true language. *(LL)* To the Banquet of the Earth. Martial Sinda. NegPo

For this is not the road against which stand enemy lines. Piyyut for Rosh Hashana. Haim Guri, *tr. fr. Hebrew by* Ruth Finer Mintz. MHP

For This Is Wisdom. "Laurence Hope." *Fr.* Teak Forest, The. PoLF

For this monk is to blame. *(LL)* The Weak Monk. Stevie Smith. BoWoP; FaBoTw

For this particular silence. *(LL)* The Memory of Elena. Carolyn Forché. NoAM

For this peculiar tint that paints my house. My House. Claude McKay. CDC

For this poor wreath, give Thee a crown of praise. *(LL)* A Wreath. George Herbert. GeHe; JCP; NOSC; OAEL-1; OxBSP; Poetr; SeCP

For this same night art [Bucklesfeildberry]. Little Musgrave and Lady Barnard. *Unknown.* ESPB

For this she starred her eyes with salt. Elinor Wylie. MoAmPo

For this the ancient stars were hurled. Evolution. Israel Zangwill. TrJP

For this your mother sweated in the cold. To Jesus on His Birthday. Edna St. Vincent Millay. ChIV-2; HeIP; TrCP; TrGrPo

For Thomas Moore. James Simmons. BiHa; PBCIP

For Thomas Stearns Eliot on the Occasion of His One Hundredth Birthday. Thomas Rabbitt. NAmP90

For those my unbaptized rhymes. His Prayer for Absolution. Robert Herrick. BeJo; SeCV-1; TrPWD

For those that never know the light. The Children of the Night. E. A. Robinson. OxBA

For those we tore to pieces. *(LL)* Van Diemen's Land. Allen Afterman. NOBAu

For Those Who Always Fear the Worst. *Unknown.* NBLV

For Those Who Fail. Joaquin Miller. PoToHe

For those who place their blooms on new-made graves. Time's Hand Is Kind. Margaret E. Bruner. PoToHe

For those who worship Thee there is no death. The Trees of Life. Jones Very. NOBA

For thou art with me here upon the banks. Wordsworth. *Fr.* Lines Composed a Few Miles above Tintern Abbey [on Revisiting the Banks of the Wye during a Tour, July 13, 1798]. BLPL; EBEvV; EnRP; FaBoPP; FF; FHYEP; HeIP; InPS; LiTB; MeMBP; NoP; OAEL-2; OBNC; OxAEP-2; PoEL-4; Poetr; PPP; Prf; PrIm; SCGP; TEP; TFi; TrGrPo

For thou shalt reign unrivaled there. *(LL)* By Babel's Streams Philip Freneau. AH

For Though the Eaves [*or* Caves] Were Rabbeted [*or* Rabbited]. Thoreau. OxBSP; PoEL-4

For though, with men of high degree. Sir Walter Scott. *Fr.* Marmion. OtMeF

For though ye be true of your tongue and honestly earn. Good Works. William Langland. *Fr.* Vision of Piers Plowman, The. NOCV

For thoughts that curve like winging birds. I Yield Thee Praise. Philip Jerome Cleveland. TrPWD

For thousands of years, the wide. The Han River Ballad. Ts'ai Ch'i-chiao, *tr. fr. Chinese.* *Fr.* Han River, The. LHF, *tr. by* Hualing Nieh

For three swift days. Gennady Trifonov, *tr. fr. Russian by* Simon Karlinsky. PeHV

For three years, out of key with his time. Ezra Pound. *Fr.* Hugh Selwyn Mauberly. (Life and Contacts). AmPP; CMoP; HAP; InPS; LiTA; LiTM; MoAmPo; NAAL-2; NoAM; NOBA; NoP; OxBA; TAP; UnPo; VGW

    (E. P. Ode Pour l'Election de Son Sepulchre.) HAP; MoAmPo; MoP; NAAL-2; NoAM; VGW

    (Hugh Selwyn Mauberley.) MeMAP

    (Pour l'Election de Son Sepulchre, I-V.) FaBoMo

For Thus saith The Lord to the men of Judah and Jerusalem. Bible, *O.T.* *Fr.* Jeremiah. OBVE

For thus the royal *Mandate* ran. Burns. *Fr.* Second Epistle to John Lapraik. OBF

For to [ ] yow guid name. *(LL)* To the Merchantis of Edinburgh. William Dunbar. FaBoPP; OxBS

For to Admire. Kipling. MoBrPo

For to adore the new-born Prince. *(LL)* For Twelfth Day. Luke Wadding. TIRV

For to Aske the Waye. *Unknown.* *Fr.* Lytell Treatyse for to Lerne Englysshe and Frens, A. OxBLMV

For to keep it clean. *(LL)* Keep It Clean. Charlie Jordan. CBNP

For to sit upon a serpent's knee. *(LL)* Dives and Lazarus ("As it fell out upon a day.") *Unknown.* ELP; ESPB; FaBoBa; OBET; OxBB

For Tom Numkena, Hopi/Spokane. Harold Littlebird. VoR

For t'other kiss will cure the dead. *(LL)* Love for Enjoying. James Shirley. BeJo

For Travelers Going Sidereal. Robert Frost. OBAL

For treuthe [*or* trewthe] telleth that love [*or* loue] is triacle to abate sinne [*or* of hevene]. The Incarnation. William Langland. *Fr.* Vision of Piers Plowman, The. OBEV

    (Incarnation, The.) PoEL-1

For truth, and like the Preacher found it not. *(LL)* Lift not the painted veil which those who live. Shelley. EnRP; OBNC, *sl. diff. vers.*; Son

For Twelfth Day. Luke Wadding. TIRV

For twenty years and more surviving after. Widows. Edgar Lee Masters. MoAmPo

For two who. For Two Who Slipped Away Almost Entirely. Alice Walker. CrSp

For Two Who Slipped Away Almost Entirely. Alice Walker. CrSp

For two years I looked forward. Breakfast. Thom Gunn. OxBC

For Uncle Jim's deep-fried, all-fat, real gone / whale steaks. *(LL)* Naughty Boy. Robert Creeley. HeIP; NoAM; NOBA

For Under the Volcano. Malcolm Lowry. NOBC

For upon the field I will make a bran-mash of his brains, mixed with the maille of his armor. *(LL)* A Perigord pres del muralh. Bertrans de Born. CTC

For us, born into a still. C. Day Lewis. *Fr.* Overtures to Death. CMoP

For us like any other fugitive. Another Time. W. H. Auden. MeMAP; OxBA

For Us No Night Can Be Happier. Nikolaus Ludwig, Graf von Zinzendorf, *tr. fr. German.* AH

For us, the dead, though young. The Unreturning. Clinton Scollard. PAH

For us their life, their death, are bread. Tristan und Isolt. Gottfried von Strassburg, *tr. fr. German.* OBD

For vacant hours of man's destructive leisure. To a Gentleman Who Invited Me to Go A-Fishing. Elizabeth Moody. ECWP

For vacant song behold a shining theme! On Some Humming-Birds in a Glass Cage. Charles Tennyson Turner. FM

For vanished Hellas and Hebraic pain. *(LL)* Venus of the Louvre. EmmaLazarus. AmWP

For Venus' ceston every line you make. *(LL)* A Sonnet to the Noble Lady, the Lady Mary Wroth. Ben Jonson. BeJo

For Victims. David Shapiro. BTR

For Victor Jara. Miller Williams. SM

For Virginia Chavez. Lorna Dee Cervantes. BCF

For Virgins, away to the City, *to be.* *(LL)* The Merry Hay-Makers; or, Pleasant Pastime between the Young-Men and Maids, in the Pleasant Meadows. *Unknown.* CoMu; ErPo

For vulgar praise, doth it too dearely buy. (*LL*) To My Book. Ben Jonson. BeJo; FaBoVe; NAEL-1; SeCV-1

For Walter Lowenfels. Wendy Rose. CDW

For Walter Washington. Tom Dent. NBV

For want I will in woe I plain. Sir Thomas Wyatt. SiPS

For want of a nail. Mother Goose. FaBoBe; OxNR; ReMoGo

For want of will in woe I plain. Sir Thomas Wyatt. SiPSBD

For wars his life and half a world away. Randall Jarrell. HCAP; OxBC

For W.C.W. Robert Creeley. LCAP

For we are all one. (*LL*) Long ago. Harriet Kofalk. EaPr

For We Are Thy People. *Unknown.* TrJP

For we have thought the longer thoughts. Chapter Heading. Ernest Hemingway. PoA

For weariness of life, not love of Thee. (*LL*) To Heaven. Ben Jonson. BeJo; ChIV-2; EnRePo; HAP; JCP; LiTB; NAEL-1; NOCV; NOSC; SCGP; SeCP; TRP; TrPWD; UnPo

For weeks and weeks the autumn world stood still. How One Winter Came in the Lake Region. Wilfred Campbell. NOBC

For weeks before it comes I feel excited, yet when it. Afterthought. Elizabeth Jennings. OBCP

For weeks, now months, the year in burden goes. Ninth Month. Robert Lowell. *Fr.* Marriage. NAs

For weeks the poem of your body. The Poem Unwritten. Denise Levertov. CAPP

For wha ere had a lealer luve. Brown Adam. *Unknown.* ESPB

For What as Easy. W. H. Auden. NoP

For what as easy. For What as Easy. W. H. Auden. NoP (Love Song.) PeLV

For what flower, plucked,/ Lingers long? (*LL*) Flowers of Darkness. Frank Marshall Davis. NoP; PoBA; PoNe

For what has neither blood nor banes. (*LL*) The House o' the Mirror. Helen Adam. MAT; NMM

For what is Freedom, but the unfettered use. Samuel Taylor Coleridge. *Fr.* Destiny of Nations, The. EnRP

For what mad lover ever died. Samuel Butler. *Fr.* Hudibras. OBD

For what the world admires I'll wish no more. The Resolve. Mary Lee, Lady Chudleigh. ECWP; WPE

For what to-morrow shall disclose. Quid Sit Futurum Cras Fuge Quaerere. Matthew Prior. FaBoEE

For what we owe to other days. Exit. E. A. Robinson. MoAmPo; OxBSP

For whatever did it — the cider. A Cure at Porlock. Amy Clampitt. NoAM

For when he kicked Miss Roe, she kicked him again. (*LL*) Captain Wattle and Miss Roe. Charles Dibdin. OxBoLi

For when they meet, the tensile air. The Paradigm. Allen Tate. NOBA

For "Where there's a will there's a way." (*LL*) Where There's a Will There's a Way. Eliza Cook. BLPA

For which all long has never yet been built. (*LL*) Peace in the Welsh Hills. Vernon Watkins. GTBS-P; OxBTC

For Whigs admit no force but argument. (*LL*) King to Oxford sent a troop of horse, The. Sir William Browne. FaBoCo; FaBoEE

For Whitsuntide. Hildebert, *tr. fr. Latin by* Helen Waddell. MLL

For Who? Mary Weston Fordham. CBWP-2

For who can bear to feel himself forgotten? (*LL*) The Night Mail. W. H. Auden. ChTr; GrPl; OxBTC

For who can longer hold? when every Press. John Oldham. *Fr.* Satires [*or* Satyrs] upon the Jesuits. SeCV-2

For whoever pays the taxes old Mus' Hobden owns the land. (*LL*) The Land. Kipling. CoGr; MoBrPo

For whom are you intended, wine in the corked bottle. Old Motif. Aleksandar Ristovic, *tr. fr. Serbo-Croatian by* Charles Simic. HSix

For Whom I must decline? (*LL*) He Put the Belt Around My Life. Emily Dickinson. TRP

For whom it may concern. (*LL*) To Whom It May Concern. Jon Stallworthy. CBLP

For whom now will you comb your hair in lover's fashion? Paulus Silentiarius, *tr. fr. Greek by* Andrew Miller. GrAn

For whom the possessed sea littered, on both shores. Requiem for the Plantagenet Kings. Geoffrey Hill. FaBoEH; NAEL-2; NoAM

For whore and rogue; and dog and bitch. (*LL*) Epigram on Scolding. Swift. FaBoEE; FaBoVe

For why should we mourn for the blest? (*LL*) Bright Be the Place of Thy Soul! Byron. HoPM

For why? the gaines doth seeldome quitte the charge. (*LL*) All were to little for the merchauntes hande. George Gascoigne. AAS

For why? the gaines doth seldome quitte the charge. George Gascoigne. AAS

For why? The gains doth seldom quit the change. George Gascoigne. *Fr.* Gascoigne's Memories. EnRePo; Son

For Widower — wanted, house-keeper. *Unknown.* PeLi

For William Edward Burghardt Du Bois on His Eightieth Birthday. Bette Darcie Latimer. PoBA; PoNe

For William Edward Burghardt Dubois on His Eightieth Birthday. Bette Darcie Latimer. PoNe

For Wilma. Don Johnson. GOYP

For Windows. Robert Grenier. UL

For Witches. Susan Sutheim. NMM

For X. Louis MacNeice. *See* When clerks and navvies fondle.

For years I dreamt you. Firstborn. Katherine Gallagher. VBLP

For years I had not seen such a town. Reunion. Judith Herzberg, *tr. fr. Dutch by* Shirley Kaufman. BoWoP

For years I have been a coal miner. A Coal Miner's Goodbye. *Unknown.* AmFP

For years I thought I knew, at the bottom of the dream. The Meeting. Louise Bogan. NoAM; NYBP

For years I was doomed to worship a contemptible woman. The Viper. Nicanor Parra, *tr. fr. Spanish by* W. S. Merwin. AnRep

For years I've heard. Robin Blaser. NeAP

For years I've suffered from extreme poverty. Writing Poetry in the Back Garden. Chao Yi, *tr. fr. Chinese by* Chang Yin-nan *and* Lewis C. Walmsley. SuSp

For Years Now. David Constantine. SCBI

For years now I have heard the cracking of. Studying Physics with My Daughter. Jeanne Murray Walker. WeW

For years now through your face the skull has shown. For Years Now. David Constantine. SCBI

For years she smiled. The Metamorphosis of Aunt Jemima. William Childress. MAT

For years the old Italians have been dying. Lawrence Ferlinghetti. *Fr.* Old Italians Dying, The. NGP

For years we endured his insolence. Mask-Maker. Michael Jackson. PeNZ

For You. Carl Sandburg. MoAmPo

For You. James Harvey Spencer. PWR

For you! (*LL*) The Strange Visitor. *Unknown.* ChTr; FaBoCh; GBP

For you and that big dark blue. (*LL*) Down at the Docks. Kenneth Koch. PrIm; VGW

For you, for you I am trilling these songs. (*LL*) For You, O Democracy. Walt Whitman. TrGrPo; UV

For you have tied my hands. (*LL*) Johnny Sands ("A man whose name was Johnny Sands.") *Unknown.* CoMu; OBET

For you I have emptied the meaning. Louis Zukofsky. NoAM

For you I have stored up an ocean of thought. Thinking of Someone. Hsiung-hung, *tr. fr. Chinese by* Kenneth Rexroth *and* Ling Chung. WPC

For you/ I will be a ghetto jew. The Genius. Leonard Cohen. MoCV

For you I would have built a herb-garden. The Rarest Thyme. Thomas McCarthy. IB

For You, Mamá. Cherríe Moraga. GLP

For You, My Son. Horace Gregory. MoAmPo

For You, O Democracy. Walt Whitman. TrGrPo; UV

For you only can say, "Wee! wee!" (*LL*) The Three Little Pigs. Sir Alfred Scott Gatty. BoTP; OxBChV

For you Time past could not forget. Hymn to Proust. Gavin Ewart. NYBP

For you, tormentors, (*LL*) Where Are the Men Seized in This Wind of Madness? Alda do Espírito Santo. TTY; WPOW

For your next lover. (*LL*) Girl. Hugo Williams. CBLP

For your silken girls to sing? (*LL*) Her Husband Asks Her to Buy a Bolt of Silk. Ch'en Tao. OHMPC

For Zbigniew Herbert, Summer, 1971, Los Angeles. Larry Levis. FYAP

For Zion's Sake. Bible, *O.T. Fr.* Isaiah. TrJP

Foraging for wood in a forest recently burned. After a Summer Fire. Lance Henson. ETG

Foray of Queen Meave, The, *sels.* Aubrey Thomas De Vere. Combat at the Ford, The. PeIV

Forbear, bold youth, all's heaven here. An Answer to Another Persuading a Lady to Marriage. Katherine Philips. HAP; VBLP; WeW (To One Persuading a Lady to Marriage.) OBEV

Forbear, fond taper: what thou seek'st, is fire. Francis Quarles. *Fr.* Hieroglyphics of the Life of Man. OBD

Forbear this liquid fire, fly. A Fly about a Glass of Burnt Claret. Richard Lovelace. CaPo

Forbear, thou great good husband, little ant. The Ant. Richard Lovelace. CaPo

Forbearance. Samuel Taylor Coleridge. ChIV-2

Forbearance. Emerson. AnAmPo; GN; LiTA; MeMAP; TAP; TrGrPo; WGRP

Forbearance of kinsmen's wrongs. The Tiger. Kuramakal Ilaveyini, *tr. fr. Tamil by* A. K. Ramanujan. PLW

Forbidden, The. Phyllis Haring. PeSA

Forbidden gate, palace trees, a moon's flitting trace. Presented to a Lady within the Palace. Chang Yü, *tr. fr. Chinese by* Ronald C. Miao. SuSp

Forc'd from home, and all its pleasures. The Negro's Complaint. William Cowper. FaBoEH

Force. Edward Rowland Sill. AnAmPo

Force. *Unknown.* FaBoUs

Force. Derek Walcott. OxBC

Force-feeding swans — let me tell. Farmers. Thomas Lux. LCAP

Force of habit is so strong, The. (*LL*) The Elephant, or the Force of Habit. A. E. Housman. NOBL

Force of Love, The. Samuel Jones. NOEC

Force That through the Green Fuse Drives the Flower, The. Dylan Thomas. BLPL; CMoP; EaPr; EBEV; FaBoMo; InPS; LiTB; LiTM; MeMBP; MoAB; MoBrPo; MoP; NAEL-2; NoAM; NOBE; NoP; OBWVE; OxAEP-2; OxBTC; PoE; Poetr; PPP; PrIm; RB; SCV; TEP; TFi; UnPo

Force you to turn away your eyes. (*LL*) If you had lusted after something noble or decent. Sappho. InMo

Forced Bridal, The. *Unknown.* VPP

Forced by soft violence of prayer. Matthew Green. *Fr.* Spleen, The. ECEV

Forced Feelings, *sels.* Wang Chiu-ssu, *tr. fr. Chinese by* Jonathan Chaves.

Forced Music, A. Robert Graves. MoBrPo

Forced to express my excess love on cloth. (*LL*) Ironing Their Clothes. Julia Alvarez. CrSp; VBLP

Forcing House. Theodore Roethke. CAPP

Ford Madox Ford. Robert Lowell. OxBC

Ford Madox Ford. Robert Lowell. OxBC; TwCP

Ford Manor. Derek Mahon. PBCIP

Ford o' Kabul River. Kipling. FaBoTw; PeVV

Fording the River. Seamus Deane. PBCIP; PNI

'Fore I'll return again. (*LL*) Son David. *Unknown.* OxBB; OxBS

Forebears. Elizabeth Riddell. FaBoMA

Foreboding, The. Robert Graves. ELP; GBL; PoA

Foreboding sudden of untoward change. By the Conemaugh. Florence Earle Coates. PAH

Forecast. Howard Fergus. PBCV

Forecast. Josephine Miles. NoAM

Foreclosure. Sterling A. Brown. PoBA; PoNe

Forefathers. Edmund Blunden. NOBE; OBEV; OBMV; OxBTC

Forehead, Eyes, Cheeks, Nose, Mouth, and Chin. Mother Goose. *See* Here sits the Lord Mayor.

Forehead without scalp, dry shell without yolk of eye. Crinagoras, *tr. fr. Greek by* Alistair Elliot. GrAn

Foreign. Carol Ann Duffy. NBrP

Foreign Affairs. Stanley Kunitz. LiTM; NYBP

Foreign Aid. Lionel Kearns. NOBC

Foreign Children. Robert Louis Stevenson. BoTP

Foreign Element, The. Greg Johnson. PFL

Foreign Gate, The, *sels.* Sidney Keyes.
"Moon is a poor woman, The." OBWP

Foreign Inhabitant. Juan Felipe Herrera. ETG

Foreign Lands. Robert Louis Stevenson. BoTP; PFP

Foreign Literature. Thackeray. FaBoNo

Foreign room, slab faces, dusty panes, A. The Rebel General. Chris Wallace-Crabbe. CBAP

Foreign Ruler, A. Walter Savage Landor. OBSV

Foreign thing desertless in origin, A. (*LL*) Apologia pro Vita Sua. A. R. Ammons. CAPP; HCAP; NOBA

Foreign Woman. Rosario Castellanos, *tr. fr. Spanish by* J. M. Cohen. WPOW

Foreigners. Meredith Stricker. LoHo

Foreigners at the Fair. Fred Emerson Brooks. OBAL

Foreland, the ever-returning roses of dawn. (*LL*) Apology for Bad Dreams. Robinson Jeffers. AmPP; LiTA; MoAB; MoAmPo; NOBA; OxBA

Foremost of the r. . . . brood, The. On George IV. *Unknown.* IHNG

Forenoon and afternoon and night. Life. Edward Rowland Sill. BLRP

Forensic Jocularities. Sir George Rose. OxBoLi

Foreplay of the Alphabet. Darrell Gray. UL

Forerunners. Emerson. OBEV; OxBA

Forerunners, The. George Herbert. AngWe; ESCV; GeHe; JCP; NAEL-1; NoP; TOF

Foreseen for so many years: these evils, this monstrous violence. May-June, 1940. Robinson Jeffers. LiTA; MoAB; MoAmPo (Battle.) LiTM

Foresight. Lincoln Kirstein. ArOW; OBWP; PoWW

Forest. Harriet Gray Blackwell. GoYe

Forest. Jean Garrigue. LiTM; NOBA

Forest, The. Miroslav Holub, *tr. fr. Czech by* George Theiner. PoSu

Forest and fields are deserted. Trepak. Count Arsenii Arkadyevich Golenishchev-Kutuzov, *tr. fr. Russian by* Philip L. Miller. *Fr.* Songs and Dances of Death. RiWo

Forest animals walk there. What She Said ('Forest animals walk there'). Kapilar, *tr. fr. Tamil by* A. K. Ramanujan. PLW

Forest Birds (A Woman Speaks), *sels.* Chu Yün-ming, *tr. fr. Chinese by* Jonathan Chaves.

Forest Hymn, A. (Groves were God's first temples, The. Ere man learned.) Bryant. EAP; TAP
Sels.
"Father, thy hand/ Hath reared." TrPWD

Forest Leaves in Autumn, *sels.* John Keble.
November. OBEV
(Red o'er the forest glows the setting sun.) OBNC

Forest nuns, who sheltered us and healed, The. The Krankenhaus of Leutkirch. Richmond Lattimore. NYBP

Forest of background noises, A. Latitude 5°N. Harry Clifton. IB

Forest of Europe. Derek Walcott. PBCV

Forest of the Dead, The. J. Griffyth Fairfax. NSI; PoWW

Forest says, "I'm always the one who's sacrificed," The. Docility. Jules Supervielle, *tr. fr. French by* George Bogin. ArNa

Forest Song. Shane Leslie. TIRV

Forest Thoughts. Sir Roger Casement. TIRV

Forest was fair and wide, The. Tristrem and the Hunters. *At. to* Thomas of Erceldoune. *Fr.* Sir Tristrem. OxBS

Forester's Song. A. E. Coppard. FaPON

Forests are branches of a tree lying down. Flying Home from Utah. May Swenson. WPE

Forests of Lithuania, The, *sels.* Donald Davie.
"But this, so feminine?" OxBTC

Forests were on fire, The. Two Drops. Zbigniew Herbert, *tr. fr. Polish by* Czeslaw Milosz. RB

Foresworn now the love-vows! Meleager, *tr. fr. Greek by* Peter Whigham. GrAn

Forever. Charles Stuart Calverley. NOBL; NOBVV

Forever. (*LL*) Earth mother, star mother. Starhawk. EaPr

Forever. Charles-Jean Grandmougin, *tr. fr. French by* Philip L. Miller. *Fr.* Poem of a Day. RiWo

Forever. (*LL*) O Lord. Ishpriya. EaPr

Forever. John Boyle O'Reilly. WGRP

Forever. (*LL*) Song for Baby-O, Unborn. Diane Di Prima. PoBeRe

Forever. (*LL*) The Club. Mitsuye Yamada. LoHo

Forever a lagging wound. (*LL*) The Window. Dino Campana. STV

Forever Ambrosia. Christopher Morley. OBAL

Forever brigands and pirates, the Cretans are never just. Leonidas of Tarentum, *tr. fr. Greek by* Barbara Hughes Fowler. *Fr.* Epigrams. HePo

Forever, chum, just see it may way, & I do. (*LL*) American Landscape with Clouds & a Zoo. Jon Anderson. AnAn

Forever Dead. Sappho, *tr. fr. Greek by* William Ellery Leonard. AWP

Forever, from our shore. (*LL*) Song of Marion's Men. Bryant. AnAmPo; PAH

Forever in her small, pathetic pail. (*LL*) Greens. David Ray. SM; VGW

Forever in My Dream and in My Morning Thought. Thoreau. PoEL-4

Forever, it comes from the head. Venom. James Dickey. PoA

Forever over now, forever, forever gone. The Cameo. Edna St. Vincent Millay. FYAP; LiTA; MeMAP; MoAmPo; UnPo; WPE

Forever the little thud of names, falling. Empty Dwelling Places. Kenneth Patchen. PoA

Forever; 'tis a single word! Forever. Charles Stuart Calverley. NOBL; NOBVV

Forever you're within me. (*LL*) Love. Elolongue Epanya Yondo.

Forevermore shall reign. (*LL*) Lord Descended from Above, The. Thomas Sternhold. AH

Foreword to New Numbers. Christopher Logue. OxBTC

Forfeit their Paradise by their pride. (*LL*) The Flower. George Herbert. AngWe; AWP; ELP; ESCV; FaBoRV; FaPoB; GeHe; JCP; NAEL-1; NOBE; NOCV; NoP; PFP; PoEL-2; SeCP; SeCV-1

Forfeiture, The. Henry King. NOSC

Forge, The. Seamus Heaney. NAEL-2; OxAEP-2

Forge me a tool, my Seamus. His Request. Owen Roe O'Sullivan, *tr. fr. Irish by* Joan Keefe. BIrV

Forger, The. Derek Mahon. SCBI

Forget each kindness that you do. A Memory System. *Unknown.* PWR

Forget him and forget her. *(LL)* To the Tune of the Coventry Carol. Stevie Smith. FaBoTw; OPOP

Forget It. *Unknown.* PoLF; WBLP

Forget-Me Flower, The. Wilhelm Müller, *tr. fr. German by* Philip L. Miller. *Fr.* Beautiful Maid of the Mill, The. RiWo

Forget Me Not. Austin Clarke. CIP

Forget-Me-Not, The. *Unknown.* BoTP

Forget not this! *(LL)* Forget [*or* Fforget] Not Yet. Sir Thomas Wyatt. AAS; EiL; EnRePo; FaBoVe; HAP; NAEL-1; NoP; NoSic; OBEV; SCGP; SiPS; SiPSBD

Forget [*or* Fforget] Not Yet. Sir Thomas Wyatt. AAS; EiL; EnRePo; FaBoVe; HAP; NAEL-1; NoP; NoSic; OBEV; SCGP; SiPS; SiPSBD

Forget [*or* Fforget] not yet the tried intent. Forget [*or* Fforget] Not Yet. Sir Thomas Wyatt. AAS; EiL; EnRePo; FaBoVe; HAP; NAEL-1; NoP; NoSic; OBEV; SCGP; SiPS; SiPSBD
(Steadfastness.) NOBE
(Supplication, A.) GTBS; GTBS-P

Forget our pride, our faces, our common love. *(LL)* Do Others Speak of Me Mockingly, Maliciously? Delmore Schwartz. LiTA

Forget roadside crossings. How to See Deer. Philip Booth. FoLa; Poetsp

Forget six counties overhung with smoke. Prologue: The Wanderers. William Morris. *Fr.* Earthly Paradise, The. EBVV
(Introduction.) EnVR

Forget the great blue heron flying low. Bones — A City Poem. Cheryl Savageau. ETG

Forget the past and live the present hour. Now. Sarah Knowles Bolton. PWR

Forget the slander you have heard. Just Forget. Myrtle May Dryden. WBLP

Forget Thee? John Moultrie. BLPA; FaBoBe; PoToHe

Forget thine anguish. Meditations. Solomon ibn Gabirol, *tr. fr. Hebrew by* Emma Lazarus. TrJP

Forget to mail my letter to my friend Death. Overdue Balance Sheet. Thérèse Plantier, *tr. fr. French by* Maxine W. Kumin *and* Judith Kumin. BoWoP

Forget What Did. Philip Larkin. NoAM

Forget what I said. Snow Line. Bei Dao, *tr. fr. Chinese by* Donald Finkel *with* Chen Xueliang. SpMi

Forget your life. Say God is Great. Get up. Say Yes Quickly. Jalal al-Din Rumi, *tr. fr. Persian.* EnIH, *tr. by* Coleman Barks *and* A. J. Arberry; RaBo, *tr. by* Coleman Barks *and* John Moyne

Forgetful Number. Vasco [*or* Vasko] Popa, *tr. fr. Serbo-Croatian.* *Fr.* Yawn of Yawns, The. AnRep, *tr. by* Charles Simic; HSix, *tr. by* Charles Simic

Forgetfulness! Josephine D. Henderson Heard. CBWP-4

Forgetfulness. James Russell Lowell. AnAmPo

Forgetting God. Forgetting God. Sir Thomas Seymour. NoSic

Forgetting God. Sir Thomas Seymour. NoSic

Forgetting how to observe, what. The Disarrayed. John Blight. FaBoMA

Forgetting the way back. *(LL)* Lord, the air smells good today, straight from the mysteries. Jalal al-Din Rumi. EaPr

Forging of the Anchor, The. Sir Samuel Ferguson. PeIV

Forgive and Forget. Frances Sargent Osgood. AmWP

Forgive and Forget. Totius, *tr. fr. Afrikaans by* Anthony Delius. PeSA

Forgive — forget! I own the wrong! Forgive and Forget. Frances Sargent Osgood. AmWP

Forgive me if I speak possessively of him. To a New Daughter-in-Law. *Unknown.* PoToHe

Forgive me, if I wound your ear. In a Letter to A.R.C. on Her Wishing to Be Called Anna. Matilda Betham-Edwards. ECWP; WoRP

Forgive me, my God, and overlook my sins. His Illness. Solomon ibn Gabirol, *tr. fr. Hebrew by* David Goldstein. TOF

Forgive Me, Sire. Norman Cameron. FaBoEE; GTBS-P; OxBS; OxBSP

Forgive me that I pitch your praise too low. Apology for Understatement. John Wain. OxBTC

Forgive me, you whom they cast in a name. Avraham Shlonsky, *tr. fr. Hebrew by* Francis Landy. MHP, *tr. by* Ruth Finer Mintz

Forgive, O Lord, forgive our Trespasses. *(LL)* And Forgive Us Our Trespasses. Aphra Behn. EBEV

Forgive, O Lord, My Little Jokes on Thee. Robert Frost. LiTM; Poetr; SAmP

Forgive, O Lord, this worldly one. A Prayer for Forgiveness. Aengus the Culdee, *tr. fr. Irish by* Eoin Neeson. TIRV

Forgive the hours spent listening to radios. Looking at a Dead Wren in My Hand. Robert Bly. NNaP

Forgive them Father for they know not what they do. *(LL)* Grey Wolf. O. Fred Donaldson. EaPr

Forgive them, for they know not what they do! Abraham Lincoln. Edmund Clarence Stedman. PAH

Forgive these nigguhs that know not what they do. *(LL)* Riot. Gwendolyn Brooks. BPo; NALW; NBV; PoBA; TAP

Forgive us, son of Amram, be not wroth. *Unknown, tr. fr. Hebrew.* *Fr.* Duel with Verses over a Great Man. TrJP

Forgive your son! *(LL)* Ecce Puer. James Joyce. BIrV; ChIV-2; EBEV; IMW; MoP; NAs; NoAM; OPOP; TrCP

Forgiven. Margaret E. M. Sangster. PoToHe

Forgiven, for Jesus' sake. Amen. *(LL)* A Christmas Prayer. Robert Louis Stevenson. TrCP

Forgiven Past, The. Laura Riding. PBWP

Forgiveness. Alice Walker. MDDM

Forgiveness. Whittier. TrCP

Forgiveness Dream; Man from the Warsaw Ghetto, The. Jean Valentine. LCAP

Forgiving My Father. Lucille Clifton. CAPP

Forgotten City, The. William Carlos Williams. LiTA

Forgotten Dreams. Edward S. Silvera. PoNe

Forgotten Girlhood. Laura Riding. RB
Sels.
All the Way Back.
Around the Corner.
Children.
In Laddery Street Herself.
Into Laddery Street.

Forgotten Island., *sels.* Radclyffe Hall.
"As a lamp of fine crystal, wonderfully wrought." PeHV

Forgotten Majo, The. Fernando Periquet Y Zuaznabar, *tr. fr. Spanish by* Philip L. Miller. RiWo

Forgotten Man, The. Edwin Markham. BLPL; PoLF

Forgotten One (A Ballad), The. Count Arsenii Arkadyevich Golenishchev-Kutuzov, *tr. fr. Russian by* Philip L. Miller. *Fr.* Songs and Dances of Death. RiWo

Fork. Charles Simic. AmPA; HCAP; LCAP; TRP; WeW

Fork in the path, The. The Two Roads. Andrew Waterman. SCBI

Fork of the Road, The. William Renton. NOBVV

Forked Radish, A. Jonathan Price. CBLP

Forked Tongue. Helen Ruggieri. LoHo

Forked Tree, The. Marion Lomax. PWE

Forlorn and glum the couples go. The Houses. Eden Phillpotts. OxBTC

Forlorn and lonely, my time will never come. Parting from Wang Wei. Meng Hao Jan, *tr. fr. Chinese by* Daniel Bryant. SuSp

Forlorn Saphira, with reclining head. Against Homosexuality. Thomas Gilbert. *Fr.* View of the Town, A. In an Epistle to a Friend. NOEC

Form decreed of tree and flower, The. Dominica Pentecostes. Aubrey Thomas De Vere. TIRV

Form is the woods: the beast. James Harrison. FoLa; VGW

Form of Epitaph, A. Laurence Whistler. GTBS-P; Mes

Form of life. *(LL)* Consider the life of trees. Cedric Wright. EaPr

Form of Passion, A. David McFadden. NOBC

Form of this "sport" is pain, The. Homage to the Runner. Marvin Bell. *Fr.* Escape into You, The. CAPP

Form of Women, A. Robert Creeley. CAPP; NaP

Form of youth without blemish, is not such the form divine, The? Song of My Soul. Ralph Chubb. PeHV

Form Rejection Letter. Philip Dacey. AmPA

Form Was the World. Maurice English. NYBP

Formal Application. Donald W. Baker. FF

Formal as a minuet or sonnet. Mystery Story. Howard Nemerov. NBLV

Formal exercise for withered fingers, A. Old Fisherman with Guitar. George Mackay Brown. OxBC

Formalized/ by middle age. The Song of Bullets. Jessica Hagedorn. ETG

Formation of a Separatist. Susan Howe. BCF
Sels.
"S/ Rebuke boyne."

Formed long ago, yet made today. Mother Goose. OxNR

Former Barn Lot. Mark Van Doren. FaBV; MoAmPo; PDV

Former Beauties. Thomas Hardy. *Fr.* At Casterbridge Fair. CBLP; NoAM; OBMV; OBNC

Former Life, The. Robert de Bonnières, *tr. fr. French by* Philip L. Miller. RiWo

Formerly a Slave. Herman Melville. PoNe; TAP

Formerly I thought of you twice. Four Notions of Love and Marriage. N. Scott Momaday. HATNAP

Forming Child Poems. Simon J. Ortiz. CDW

Forms of Love, The. George Oppen. NNaP

Forms of the Earth at Abiquiu. N. Scott Momaday. CDW

Fornication is a filthy business. Petronius Arbiter, *tr. fr. Greek by* Kenneth Rexroth. PGA

Forsake not an old friend. Bible, Apocrypha. *Fr.* Ecclesiasticus. OBF

Forsaken. Zalman Schneour, *tr. fr. Yiddish by* Joseph Leftwich. TrJP

Forsaken, The. Duncan Campbell Scott. NOBC

Forsaken. *Unknown.* AmFP

Forsaken Bride, The. *Unknown. See* Oh [*or* O] waly, waly, up the [*or* yon] bank.

Forsaken Garden, A. Swinburne. EBEV; EBEvV, *sts.* 1–2; FaBoPP; GTBS-P; LiTB; NOBE; NOBVV; NoP; OAEL-2; OBNC; OxAEP-2; SCGP; TEP

Forsaken Girl, The. Eduard Friedrich Mörike, *tr. fr. German by* Philip L. Miller. RiWo

Forsaken Merman, The. (Come, dear children, let us away.) Matthew Arnold. BeLS; CoGr; EBEV; EBVVPR; FaBoCh; FaPoR; FHYEP; GN; NAEL-2; NTP; OBNV; OBSP; OHCV
Sels.
"Children dear, was it yesterday." BoTP

Forsaken of all comforts but these two. Upone Tabacco. Sir Robert Ayton. OxBS

Forsaken Wife, The. Elizabeth Thomas. ECWP

Forsaken woods, trees with sharp storms opressed. Robert Sidney. NoSic

"Forsaking all" — You mean. The Word. Margaret Avison. MoCV

Forsee or more control than robin or wren. (*LL*) Fifty Faggots. Edward Thomas. MoAB; MoBrPo; PeFWW; PoWW

Forsoke thine eme's lore. (*LL*) Against the Baron's Enemies. *Unknown.* MeEL

Forsythia. Andrew Crozier. VaA

Forsythia. Mary Ellen Solt. BoWoP

Fort Bowyer. Charles L. S. Jones. PAH

Fort by the oak trees there, The. The Fort of Rathangan. *At. to* Berchan, *tr. fr. Old Irish by* Kuno Meyer. CH; ChTr; FaBoCh

Fort Duquesne. Florus B. Plimpton. PAH

Fort McHenry. *Unknown.* PAH

Fort of Ard Ruide, The. *Unknown.* NOIV

Fort of Rathangan, The. *At. to* Berchan, *tr. fr. Old Irish by* Kuno Meyer. CH; ChTr; FaBoCh

Fort to perish all at the heart. (*LL*) The Bitter Withy. *Unknown.* OBET

Fort Wayne. Jack Spicer. CBNP

Forth Feasting., *sels.* William Drummond of Hawthornden.
"What blust'ring noise now interrupts my sleep." NOSC

Forth from his breast, and read it through. (*LL*) Peace. Charles Stuart Calverley. EBVV

Forth from the east, up the ascent of Heaven. Matthew Arnold. *Fr.* Balder Dead. PeVV

Forth from the purple battlements he fared. Sir Eggnogg. Bayard Taylor. BXAP

Forth goes the weeding dame; her daily task. Peasants at Work. James Hurdis. *Fr.* Favourite Village, The. ECEV

Forth into the warm darkness faring wide. Wings in the Dark. John Gray. NOBVV

Forth rushed from Envy sprung and Self-conceit. Protest against the Ballot. Wordsworth. FaBoEH

Forth, to the alien gravity. The Launch. Alice Meynell. PeVV; WPE

Forth went the candid man. The Candid Man. Stephen Crane. *Fr.* War Is Kind. MoAmPo

Forthwith the sounds and seas, each creek and bay. Milton. *Fr.* Paradise Lost. ChIV-1; EPCY

Forties Flick. John Ashbery. NoAM

Fortification of New Ross, The, *sels. Unknown, tr. fr. Norman French.*
"I have a whim to speak in verse." NOIV

Fortitude. Christopher Smart. ChIV-2

Fortitude. *Somali Oral Tradition, tr. by* B. W. Andrzejewski *and* I. M. Lewis. WTO

Fortnight before Christmas gypsies were everywhere, A. The Gypsy. Edward Thomas. NoAM; NoP

Fortress, The. Anne Sexton. LiTM

Fortress of Static, A. Static. Judith Kazantzis. DT

Fortunate,/ Being articulate. Nocturne of the Self-evident Presence. Thomas MacGreevy. BIrV; CIP

Fortunate Isles, The. Joaquin Miller. WGRP

Fortunate Traveller, The. Derek Walcott. NoAM

Fortunatus Nimium. Robert Bridges.

Fortune. Charles Madge. FaBoMo

Fortune. *Unknown.* HeIP

Fortune. Sir Thomas Wyatt. *See* Marvel [*or* Marvaill] no more although [*or* all tho].

Fortune always boosts the dumb. The Weighing-In. Ibn al-Rumi, *tr. fr. Arabic by* Omar S. Pound. ArPe

Fortune and Virtue. Thomas Dekker *and others. Fr.* Old Fortunatus. NoSic

Fortune did not mean to give you promotion. On a Worthless Politician. *Unknown, tr. fr. Greek by* Peter Jay. GrAn

Fortune doth frown. Sir Thomas Wyatt. NoSic

Fortune favours the brave, old proverbs say. Mr. Cromek to Mr. Stothard. Blake. FaBoEE

Fortune has brought me down — her wonted way. His Children. Hittan of Tayyi, *tr. fr. Arabic by* Sir Charles Lyall. *Fr.* Hamasah. AWP

Fortune Hath Taken Away. Sir Walter Ralegh. NoSic; SiPSBD

Fortune hath taken away my love. Fortune Hath Taken Away. Sir Walter Ralegh. NoSic; SiPSBD

Fortune, in power imperious. Of Fortune. Thomas Kyd. *Fr.* Cornelia. EIL

Fortune, Nature, Love. Sir Philip Sidney. PoE

Fortune smiles, cry holy day! [*or* holiday]. Fortune and Virtue. Thomas Dekker *and others. Fr.* Old Fortunatus. NoSic

Fortune-Teller, The. Adelbert von Chamisso, *tr. fr. German by* Philip L. Miller. RiWo

Fortune-tellers say I won't last long. Antipater, *tr. fr. Greek by* Kenneth Rexroth. PGA

Fortune's Legacy. *Unknown.* NOSC

Fortunes locked in the Hua-kai stars, why seek anything. Self-mockery. Lu Hsun, *tr. fr. Chinese by* William R. Schultz. SuSp

Fortunes of Men, The. *Unknown, tr. fr. Anglo-Saxon by* Kevin Crossley-Holland. ASW
Sels.

Fortunes of War. Kit Wright. PeLV

Fortunes of War, I Tell You Plain, The. *Unknown.* InPK

Fortune's Treachery. Judah Halevi, *tr. fr. Hebrew by* Solomon Solis-Cohen. TrJP

40. Paul Monette. PFL

40 Acres and a Mule. Dick Gallup. UL

Forty Days, *sels.* John Wheelwright.
Second Ascension of Christ, The. NOCV

48 Words for a Woman's Dance Song. Jerome Rothenberg. PoM

45–degree hat, Bulldurham butt bailing from lips. Eugene B. Redmond. *Fr.* Epigrams for My Father. ETG

Forty-five Years Since the Fall of the Ch'ing Dynasty. Philip Whalen. *See* Summer Palace burnt, the Winter Palace, wherever it was, The.

Forty-four Hokku, *sels.* Issa, *tr. fr. Japanese by* Hiroaki Sato.

Forty-four Tanka, *sels.* Wakayama Bokusui, *tr. fr. Japanese by* Hiroaki Sato.

XLIV. "When those renowned noble peers of Greece." Spenser. *Fr.* Amoretti. AAS; ESo, lacking epigrams I–IV; HeIL; PoE

40 ——— Love. Roger McGough. Poetr

'49 dawn set me high on a roaring yellow tractor, The. In Kansas. Carter Revard. HATNAP

"49" Songs. *Unknown, tr. fr. Kiowa Indian.* STP
Sels.
"I don't care if you're married, I'll still get you."
"If you really love me honey, hey- yah."
"She said she don't love me anymore because I drink whiskey."
"You know that I love you, sweetheart, but every time I come around."

49 Stomp, The. Lew Blockcolski. VoR

Forty-second, The. *Unknown.* GBP

Forty-seven Tanka in Three Lines, *sels.* Ishikawa Takuboku, *tr. fr. Japanese by* Hiroaki Sato.

Forty-three years ago today. The Story I Can't Tell. P. H. Liotta. ArOW

Forty-two years ago (to me if to no one else). Star-Gazer. Louis MacNeice. NAEL-2; NoP

Forty years back, when much had place. George Meredityih (1828-1909). Thomas Hardy. EPCY

Forty years, every working day he drove. Visiting My Father in Florida. David Citino. NGP

Forward abrupt. Night and a Distant Church. Russell Atkins. PoBA

Forward-like, but however, and like favourable heaven heard these. (*LL*) The Bugler's First Communion. Gerard Manley Hopkins. NoAM; PeHV

Forward rush by the lamp in the gloom, A. The Contretemps. Thomas Hardy. CMoP; LiTM

Forward, sons of the tribe! Tambourine song for Soldiers Going into Battle. Hind bint Utba, *tr. fr. Arabic by* Bridget Connelly *and* Deirdre Lashgari. WPOW

Forward violet thus did I chide, The. Shakespeare. *Fr.* Sonnets. OxAEP-1

Forward young woman, Miss Chaos, A. The Trumpeter. *Unknown.* CoMu

Fosses where Caractcsus fought Rome, The. Loving Memory. Tony Harrison. *Fr.* Art & Extinction. SCBI

Fossil. E. D. Blodgett. NOBC

Fossil, The. Boynton Merrill, Jr.. CRP

Fossil, 1975. Janet Lewis. CRP

Fossil Raindrops, The. Harriet Prescott Spofford. OBCA

Fossils, The. Galway Kinnell. NYBP

Fo'ty acres jes' fo' me! Freedom in Mah Soul. David Wadsworth Cannon, Jr. PoNe

Foul canker of fair virtuous action. To Detraction I Present My Poesie. John Marston. *Fr.* Scourge of Villainy [*or* Villanie], The. NoSic

Foul fa' the breast first treason bred in. Hobie [*or* Hobbie] Noble. *Unknown.* ESPB; IBB; OxBB

Foul hyena's prey, The. (*LL*) The African Chief. Bryant. BLPA; VPP

Foul sod covers a bad one here. Crinagoras, *tr. fr. Greek by* Alistair Elliot. GrAn

Foules Rondel. Chaucer. *See* Now Welcom[e], Somer [*or* Summer].

Found. Goethe, *tr. fr. German by* John Frederick Nims. STV

Found. Carol Muske. AmPA

Found a family, build a state. Fragments of a Lost Gnostic Poem of the Twelfth Century. Herman Melville. NOBA; NoP; OxBSP; PoEL-5

Found a hole with a light in it, and saying. The Little Random Creatures. *Unknown, tr. fr. Fox Indian by* Armand Schwerner. STP

Found and Lost. Robert Long. NAmP90

Found dead a rat — no case could sure be harder. *Unknown.* FaBoEE

Found for me. (*LL*) A Chill. Christina Rossetti. BoTP

Found Frozen. Helen Hunt Jackson. AmWP

Found in a Storm. William Stafford. RFM

Found in the garden — dead in his beauty. The Burial of the Linnet. Juliana Horatia Ewing. OxBChV

Found in the Woods. Irene F. Pawsey. BoTP

Found Poem. Howard Nemerov. NGP

Found — Who Lost? Mary E. Tucker. CBWP-1

Foundation of American Industry, The. Donald Hall. GOA

Foundations. Leopold Staff, *tr. fr. Polish by* Adam Czerniawski. PoSu

Founder, The. Gerald Stern. NAmP90

Founder thou; these are thy race! The. (*LL*) Experience. Emerson. LiTA; MeMAP; PoEL-4; TAP

Founders of Ohio, The. William Henry Venable. PAH

Founding Fathers, Nineteenth-Century Style. Robert Penn Warren. *Fr.* Promises. NoAM

Founding of New Hampshire, The. Carl Rakosi. PRA

Foundling Hospital for Wit, The, *sels.* Isaac Hawkins Browne. Fire Side, The; a Pastoral Soliloquy. NOEC

Foundry's stench, A; the rolling mill's clamor. The Blast Furnace. Luis J. Rodriguez. AfAz

Fount there is, doth overfling, A. At the Fountain. Marcabrun, *tr. fr. French by* Harriet Waters Preston. AWP

Fountain. The. William Cowper. *See* There is a fountain filled with blood.

Fountain, The. Donald Davie. GTBS-P; OxBTC

Fountain. Elizabeth Jennings. WPE

Fountain, The. Don Johnson, *tr. fr. Arabic by* Dulcie L. Smith. AWP

Fountain, The. Denise Levertov. CrSp

Fountain, The. James Russell Lowell. AnAmPo; BoTP; OBCA

Fountain, The. Wordsworth. EnRP; GTBS; GTBS-P; OxAEP-2

Fountain, a Bottle, a Donkey's Ears and Some Books, A. Robert Frost. VGW

Fountain at the Tomb, The. Nicias, *tr. fr. Greek by* Charles Merivale. AWP

Fountain at Tzarskoye Selo, The. Pushkin, *tr. fr. Russian by* Philip L. Miller. RiWo

Fountain, coolest fountain. Ballad of the Cool Fountain. *Unknown, tr. fr. Spanish by* Edwin Honig. BoWoP

Fountain of Fire whom all divide. I Seek Thee in the Heart Alone. Herbert Trench. WGRP

Fountain of light, Light, Source of light. Prayer at Night. Alcuin, *tr. fr. Latin by* Helen Waddell. MLL

Fountain of tears, river of grief. Christine de Pisan, *tr. fr. French by* Joanna Bankier. WPOW

Fountain of Youth, The. Hezekiah Butterworth. PAH

Fountain unbroken, The. (*LL*) Truth. "Æ." MoBrPo

Fountains are dry and the roses over, The. The Manor Garden. Sylvia Plath. FaBoWP; LCAP

Fountains, gushing silver light. *Unknown.* FaBoEH

Fountains mingle with the river, The. Love's Philosophy. Shelley. ArLo; BLPA; BLPL; BoLoP; EnRP; FaBoBe; FaBV; FHYEP; GTBS; GTBS-P; HoPM; MeMBP; OxAEP-2; PoToHe; SCGP; TrGrPo

Fountains ("Proud fountains, wave your plumes.") Sir Osbert Sitwell. MoBrPo

Fountains that frisk and sprinkle. Ballade Made in the Hot Weather. W. E. Henley. MoBrPo
(Made in the Hot Weather.) GN

Fountains ("This night is pure and clear as thrice refinèd silver.") Sacheverell Sitwell. MoBrPo

Founts of Song, The. "Fiona Macleod." WGRP

Four Ages of Man, The, *sels.* Anne Bradstreet. Childhood. KTR

Four Ages of Man, The. W. B. Yeats. TrCP

4 A.M. and still snowing. Elegy for the Other. Cleopatra Mathis. MT

Four and Eight. Ffrida Wolfe. BoTP

Four-and-eighty years are o'er me. The Battle of Monmouth. Thomas Dunn English. PAH

Four, and More; for Miles Davis. Quincy Troupe. Jaz

Four and twentieth day of May, The. The Swimming Lady; or, A Wanton Discovery. *Unknown.* ErPo

Four and twenty bonny boys. Sir Hugh; or, The Jew's Daughter. *Unknown.* CH; ESPB, A *and* C *vers.*; FaBoBa (Hugh of Lincoln.) EnSB; OxBB

Four-and-twenty Highland men. Eppie Morrie. *Unknown.* ESPB; OxBB

Four-and-twenty ladies fair. Bonny Baby Livingston. *Unknown.* ESPB

Four and Twenty Merulae. J. Moyr Smith. FaBoNo

Four and twenty noblemen they rode thro Banchory fair. Glenlogie; or, Jean o Bethelnie. *Unknown.* ESPB

Four and twenty nobles sits in the king's ha. Glenlogie; or, Jean o Bethelnie. *Unknown.* ESPB

Four and twenty tailors. Mother Goose. OxNR (Snail, The.) ReMoGo

Four and twenty virgins. *Unknown. Fr.* Ball of Kirriemuir, The. FaBoBl

Four and twenty white bulls. *Unknown.* GBP

Four arms, two necks, one wreathing. *Unknown.* CBLP; EIL

Four be the things I am wiser to know. Inventory. Dorothy Parker. CBCK; NBLV

Four, Being a Prayer to the Western Wind. Ken Smith. *Fr.* Tristan Crazy. PWE

Four Best Things, The. Robert Herrick. *See* Health is the first good lent to men.

Four Bird Songs. Simon J. Ortiz. HATNAP

Four birds. *Unknown. See* Robin and the wren, The.

Four blue stones in this thrush's nest. The Nest. Andrew Young. Spl

Four boards of the coffin lid, The. After Death. Swinburne. NOBVV; PeVV

Four by four, in column of route. Marching. Isaac Rosenberg. NSI

Four Chinatown Figures. Garrett Kaoru Hongo. NAmP90

Four Christmas Carols, *sels. Unknown, tr. fr. Spanish by* Cheli Durán. "How cold the snow." PChr

Four days long the guns had thundered. Salonika Campaign. Owen Rutter. *Fr.* Song of Tiadatha, The. NSI

Four days with you, my father three months dead. The Stream. Mona Van Duyn. VCAP

Four decades, I've aroused the southeast with flute and sword. To a Friend, Using the Same Rhymes of a Peom He Sent Me. Liu Ya-tzu, *tr. fr. Chinese by* Wu-chi Liu. SuSp

Four Deer, The. Mary Hoxie Jones. GoYe

Four Ducks on a Pond. William Allingham. EBEvV; NOBVV; NOIV; OxAEP-2

Four Elements, The, *sels.* Anne Bradstreet. Element Fire Boasts of the Constellations, The. CBCK

Four Elements in Newfound-land, The. Robert Hayman. *See* Air in Newfound-land [*or* Aire in Newfoundland-land] is wholesome, good, The.

Four Epigrams on the Naturalization Bill. John Byrom. NOBL *Sels.*
"Come all ye foreign strolling gentry."
"Now upon sale, a bankrupt island."
"This act reminds me, ge'men, under favour."

Four Epitaphs. Countee Cullen. CDC; PoBA *Sels.*
For a Lady I Know. HeIL; HeIP; InPK; NIP; OBAL; PoNe; TAP; TRP (Lady I Know, A.) MoAmPo
For John Keats, Apostle of Beauty
For My Grandmother. MoAmPo; VGW
For Paul Laurence Dunbar.

Four feet up, under the bruise-blue. Small Woman on Swallow Street. W. S. Merwin. CoAP

4:50 and dark. Ron Padgett. *Fr.* 3 Little Poems. ArLo

Four fingers o' his right han.' (*LL*) Brown Adam. *Unknown.* ESPB; OxBB

Four foot box, a foot for every year., A. (*LL*) Mid-Term Break. Seamus Heaney. InPS; NoP

Four-footed friar in orders of gray! A. (*LL*) Coyote. Bret Harte. AnAmPo; OBAP

Four for Sir John Davies. Theodore Roethke. MoAmPo; NoAM; NOBA

Four Friends, The. A. A. Milne. PYC

Four Furry Seals, Four Funny Fat Seals. Jack Prelutsky. ZA

Four gallant ships from England came. The Battle of Stonington on the Seaboard of Connecticut. Philip Freneau. PAH

Four gents up and swing Sally Goodin. Sally Goodin. *Unknown.* AmFP

Four Glimpses of Night. Frank Marshall Davis. NoP; PoBA; PoNe

Four Glosses. *Unknown.* NOIV
Sels.
"Bird is calling from the willow, A."
"How lovely it is today!"
"Little bird, The."
"Wall of woodland overlooks me, A."

Four great walls have hemmed me in. Four Walls. Blanche Taylor Dickinson. CDC; ShDr

Four Heads & How to Do Them. John Forbes. CBAP

Four hooves rang out and now are still. Early Waking. Léonie Adams. LiTM

Four Horsemen, The. Bible, *N.T. Fr.* Revelation. PAW; TrGrPo

Four Horses, The. James Reeves. TLR

4 in 2 goes twice as fast. Crazy Arithmetic. D'Arcy Wentworth Thompson. FaBoCo

Four Irish scholars went. The Little Cat. *Unknown, tr. fr. Medieval Latin by Helen Waddell.* CRH

Four Japanese Paintings, *sels.* Arthur Davison Ficke.
Wave Symphony, The. PoA

Four Last Songs of Richard Strauss at Takahe Creek above the Kaipara, The, *sels.* K. O. Arvidson.

Four-Leaf Clover. Ella Higginson. FaPON

Four-legg'd Elder; or, A Horrible Relation of a Dog and an Elder's Maid, The. Sir John Birkenhead. CoMu

Four-legg'd Quaker, The. *Unknown.* CoMu

Four Lines of a Black Love Letter Between Teachers. Ed Roberson. NBV

Four little children. The Lost Angel. Philip Levine. NOBA

Four Little Foxes. Lew Sarett. FaPON; PDV; RFM

Four little girls. Birmingham Sunday. Langston Hughes. PoNe

Four Lyrics for Sibilla Aleramo, *sels.* Dino Campana, *tr. fr. Italian by L. R. Lind.*

Four May Poems. *Unknown. See* When Flora Had Ourfret the Firth.

Four May Poems. *Unknown. See* O Lusty May, with Flora queen!

Four May Poems, II. *Unknown.* OxBS

Four May Poems: "Be glaid, al ye that luvaris bene." *Unknown.* OxBS

Four men stood by the grave of a man. Alexander the Great. *Unknown.* CH

Four more days and we are free. *Unknown.* RoPo

Four Mountain Wolves. Leslie Silko. VoR

Four Nights' Drunk, The. *Unknown. See* First night when I came home, The.

Four Notions of Love and Marriage. N. Scott Momaday. HATNAP

Four o'Clock Flower Blues ("Four o'clock flowers bloom out in the mornin' .") *Unknown.* AmFP

IV, 1. To Venus ("Intermissa, Venus.") Horace, *tr. fr. Latin by Austin Dobson. Fr. Odes.* AWP, *tr. by Ben Jonson;* OBVE, *tr. by Ben Jonson*

Four-Paws. Helen Parry Eden. BoTP

Four pelicans went over the house. Pelicans. Robinson Jeffers. FM; MoAmPo

Four Poems for Robin. Gary Snyder. MoP; NNaP; NoAM; NOBA; NoP; SOTW
Sels.
Autumn Morning in Shokoku-ji, An. HAP; VGW; WeW
December at Yase.
Siwashing It Out Once in Siuslaw Forest.
Spring Night in Shokoku-ji, A. ArLo; VGW

Four Poems for the New Year. Charles Wright. AnAn
Sels.
"All day at the window seat."
"How strange it is to awake."
"I have nothing to say about the way the sky tilts." CAPP
"I'll tell you I never asked for it."

Four Poems for The St. Louis Sporting News. Jack Spicer. PoM

Four Poems from the Sequence "Singing of the Moon," *sels.* Yang Shen, *tr. fr. Chinese by Jonathan Chaves.*

Four Poems from the Strontium Age, *sels.* Louis Johnson.

Four Poems On the Ch'ung-wu Festival, *sels.* Chang Yü, *tr. fr. Chinese by Jonathan Chaves.*

Four Poems to the Tune "Ch'ing-chiang yin," *sels.* Ma Chih-yüan, *tr. fr. Chinese by Jonathan Chaves.*

Four pointes, my will, or I hence departe. A Last Will and Testament. *Unknown.* MeEL

Four Preludes on Playthings of the Wind. Carl Sandburg. CMoP; MoAB; MoAmPo; NOBA

Four Quartets, *sels.* T. S. Eliot.
Burnt Norton. CMoP; LiTM; MoAB; MoAmPo; NAAL-2; PoE
Dry Salvages, The. AiP; LiTB; NoP; OxBA
East Coker. HAP; PPP; VGW
Little Gidding. FaBoMo; FaBoPV; FaBoTw; GTBS-P; MoP; NAEL-2; NAWM-2; NoAM; NOBA; NOBE; OAEL-2; OxAEP-2; OxBTC; PeECV; PrIm; TAP; TFi
"Ash on an old man's sleeve."

Four Quartz Crystal Clocks. Marianne Moore. AmPP; TwCP

Four Quatrains., *sels.* Jalal al-Din Rumi, *tr. fr. Persian by Coleman Barks and John Moyne.*
"In the shambles of love, they kill only the best." RaBo
"Tonight with wine being poured." RaBo
"Two strong impulses: One." RaBo
"Where is a foot worthy to walk a garden." RaBo

Four Recollections. Shen Yüeh, *tr. fr. Chinese by Richard B. Mather.* SuSp

Four Roads, The. Alice Greene. PeSAV

Four roads lead out of the town. The Four Roads. Alice Greene. PeSAV

Four sails of the mill, The. Lubber Breeze. T. Sturge Moore. CH

Four Saints in Three Acts, *sels.* Gertrude Stein.
"Pigeons on the grass alas." TAP

Four Scarlet Berries. Mary Vivian. BoTP

Four-score and seven, so the papers say. The Old Boatman of Death's River. R. Williams Parry, *tr. fr. Welsh by Joseph P. Clancy.* OBWVE

Four Seasons. *Unknown. See* Spring is showery, flowery, bowery.

Four seasons fill the measure of the year. The Human Seasons. Keats. EnRP; GTBS; GTBS-P; WiR

Four Seasons in the Mountains, The, *sels.* Chang Yü, *tr. fr. Chinese by Jonathan Chaves.*

Four Seasons of His Discontent. Roger Weingarten. NAmP90

Four Seasons of the Year, The. Anne Bradstreet. SCAP

IV, 7. "The snow dissolv'd no more is seen" ("Diffugere nives.") Horace, *tr. fr. Latin by Austin Dobson. Fr. Odes.* NAEL-1, *tr. by Samuel Johnson;* OBVE, *tr. by Samuel Johnson*

Four Sheets to the Wind and a One-Way Ticket to France. Conrad Kent Rivers. BPo; PoBA; PoNe

Four Songs, *sels.* Nikos Gatsos, *tr. fr. Greek by Edmund Keeley and Philip Sherrard.*

Four Songs from the Book of Samuel. Eli W. Mandel. MoCV

Four Songs in Imitation of Wang Chien, *sels.* Fan Ch'eng-ta, *tr. fr. Chinese.*
Farming Family Invites the Guest to Stay Overnight, A. SuSp
Pressing for Tax Payment. SuSp
Reeling Silk. SuSp
Rejoicing the Spirits. SuSp

4 squirrels/ are as busy as monks. Maine Vastly Covered with Much Snow. John Tagliabue. InPK

Four Stanzas Written in Anxiety. George Jonas. MoCV

Four stiff-standers. *Unknown.* ChTr; GBP; OxNR, *diff. vers.*

Four Sweet Months, The. Robert Herrick. BoTP; WiR

Four Tao philosophers as cedar waxwings. Waxwings. Robert Francis. LCAP; NU; RaBo

IV, 10. "O Ligurinus" ("O crudelis adhuc.") Horace, *tr. fr. Latin by Austin Dobson. Fr. Odes.* PeHV

Four Things. Henry van Dyke. PoLF; PoToHe

Four things are white, the fifth exceeds the rest. Five Things White. Edward May. FaBoEE

Four Things Choctaw. Jim Barnes. HATNAP
Sels.
Abukbo.
Baii.
Isuba.
Nashoba.

Four Things Make Us Happy Here. Robert Herrick, *tr. fr. Greek by Robert Herrick.* CaPo

Four Things to Do. Henry van Dyke. *See* Four Things.

IV, 13. Revenge ("Audivere, Lyce.") Horace, *tr. fr. Latin by Austin Dobson. Fr. Odes.* AWP, *tr. by Louis Untermeyer*

Four III. E. E. Cummings. FaBoMo; TTTS

Four times the sun had risen and set; and now on the fifth day. The Embarkation. Longfellow. *Fr.* Evangeline. BeLS; PAH

Four trees upon a solitary acre. Emily Dickinson. PoEL-5

IV, 2. Praise of Pindar, The ("Pindarum quisquis studet aemulari.") Horace, *tr. fr. Latin by Austin Dobson. Fr. Odes.* OAEL-1, *tr. by Abraham Cowley*

Four *Tz'u* from Tun-huang, *sels. Unknown, tr. fr. Chinese* by Burton Watson.

Four Voices Ending on Some Lines from Old Jazz Records, *sels.* Rod Jellema.
Any Little Woman. Jaz
Get the Hell off My Note. Jaz
I Wouldn't Be a Methodist. Jaz
Riffin'. Jaz

Four Walls. Blanche Taylor Dickinson. CDC; ShDr

Four-way winds of the world have blown, The. Strike the Blow. *Unknown.* PAH

Four Ways of Dying. Steve Chimombo. HBAPE

Four Ways of Silence. Ron Schreiber. ETG

Four wet winters and now the dry. Runoff. William Everson. NoAM

Four white heifers with sprawling hooves. The Orotava Road. Basil Bunting. NoAM

Four Winds. Hal Porter. NOBAu

Four winds and seven seas have called me friend. From Life to Love. Countee Cullen. ChIV-1

Four winds contend on the sea's face. A Vision of Beasts. John Heath-Stubbs. ChIV-1

Four Winds dry their wooden shoes, The. *(LL)* Fishing Boats in Martigues. Roy Campbell. FaBoEE; FaBoPP; OxBSP

Four Women. Nina Simone. MAT

Four-Word Lines. May Swenson. GLP; WPE

Four Years. Pamela Gillilan. PWE

Four years ago I met your death here. Letter from Chicago. May Sarton. NALW

Four years ago,/ in this knot of a village north of the university. The Madwoman of Papine. Abdur-Rahman Slade Hopkinson. PBCV

Four years! — and didst thou stay above. Geist's Grave. Matthew Arnold. FM; NOBVV; TEP

Four young men, of a Monday morn. Prize of the *Margaretta*, The. Will M. Carleton. PAH

Foure Monarchies, The, *sels.* Anne Bradstreet.
Semiramis. KTR

Fourfooted, tiptoe. *(LL)* The Fallow Deer at the Lonely House. Thomas Hardy. AWP; CH; CMoP; OBAP; OxBSP; RB; TTTS

Fourpence a Day. *At.* to Thomas Raine. OBET; SWP

Fourteen, a sonneteer thy praises sings. A Sonnet upon Sonnets. Burns. Son

14 de Julio. Sandra Cisneros. ETG

14 July 1956. Laurence David Lerner. PeSA

Fourteen Men. Mary Gilmore. CBAP

1492. Emma Lazarus. WPE

Fourteen small broidered berries on the hem. What the Sonnet Is. Eugene Lee-Hamilton. HoPM; Son

Fourteen Ways of Touching Peter. George MacBeth. CRH

Fourteen-year-old boy is out rambling alone, A. Backside to the Wind. Paul Durcan. PBCIP

14-Year-Old Convalescent Cat in the Winter, A. Gavin Ewart. OBD; OxBSP

Fourteen-Year-Old Samuel Palmer's Watercolor Notations for the Sketch "A Lane at Thanet," The. Jonathan Williams. ETG

Fourteen years old, learning the alphabet. The Reading Lesson. Richard Murphy. IPY; PBCIP

Fourteenth of July had come, The. La Tricoteuse. George Walter Thornbury. BeLS

Fourth Act. Robinson Jeffers. LiTA

Fourth and fifth months are when the tea is best in mountain groves, The. On Hearing that Holders of the *Chin-shih* Degree Are Dealing in Tea. Mei Yao Ch'en, *tr. fr. Chinese* by Jonathan Chaves. SuSp

Fourth Book of Sibylline Oracles, The, *sels.* "The Jewish Sibyl," *tr. fr. Greek* by Bohn.
There Is a City. TrJP

Fourth Dance Poem. Gerald William Barrax. PoBA

Fourth Day of the First Week, The. Guillaume de Salluste Du Bartas. *Fr.* Divine Weeks and Works, The.

Fourth Eclogue, The. George Wither. *Fr.* Shephe[a]rd's Hunting, The. SeCV-1, *abr.*

Fourth, eleventh, ninth, and sixth. The Months of the Year. *Unknown.* FaBoUs

Fourth Floor, Dawn, Up All Night Writing Letters. Allen Ginsberg. CAPP; PoBeRe

Fourth Month, The. Shih Ching, *tr. fr. Chinese* by C. H. Wang. SuSp

Fourth month: summer already, The. The Fourth Month. Shih Ching, *tr. fr. Chinese* by C. H. Wang. SuSp

Fourth Napoleon., *sels.* J. A. R. McKellar.

Fourth Ode to Persephone. Robert Kelly. *Fr.* Book of Persephone, The. PoM

Fourth of July, The. John Pierpont. PAH

4th of July. William Carlos Williams. PoA

Fourth Pearl, The: Temperance. Lady Diana Primrose. *Fr.* Chain of Pearl, A. WPE

4th Sheppard Speakes This, The. Lady Jane Cavendish *and* Lady Elizabeth Brackley. *Fr.* Pastorall, A. KTR

Fourth Song, The. Francis Beaumont. *See* Ye [*or* You] should stay longer if we durst.

Fourth Song the Night Nurse Sang. Robert Duncan. VGW

Fourth Street, San Rafael. Bill Berkson. UL

Fourth Wish. Alberta Turner. LCAP

Fower-an-twenty Heilandmen. *Unknown.* FaBoNo

Fowler, The. W. W. Gibson. NTP

Fowls [*or* Foweles] in the Frith. *Unknown.* FaBoVe; HAP; MiEL; NAEL-1; OxBSP

Fowre muckle angels wi their trumpets, stalkin. Judgment Day. Robert Garioch, *after the Italian of* Giuseppe Belli. OBVE

Fox. David Campbell. CBAP

Fox. Clifford Dyment. OxBSP

Fox, The. Philip Levine. SoSe

Fox, The. R. Williams Parry, *tr. fr. Welsh* by Gwyn Williams. OBWVE

Fox. Kenneth Rexroth. *Fr.* Bestiary, A. NNaP; OBAL

Fox, The. Marjorie Somers Scheuer. GoYe

Fox, The, *diff. versions. Unknown.* OxNR

Fox and crow, their dirty business finished, The. Fabulary Satire IV. Daryl Hine. NOBC

Fox and the Ape Go to Court, The. Spenser. *Fr.* Mother Hubbard's Tale. NoSic

Fox and the Crow, The. La Fontaine, *tr. fr. French* by Marianne Moore. NAWM-2; OBVE; PPP

Fox and the Flood, The. Lucile Adler. FoLa

Fox and the Goose, The. *Unknown.* OxBLMV

Fox and the Grapes, The. La Fontaine, *tr. fr. French* by Marianne Moore. FM

Fox and the Hare, The. *Unknown.* OBET

Fox at your neck and snakeskin on your feet, A. Leaving Something Behind. David Wagoner. CoAP; GoJo

Fox Came into my Garden, A. Charles Causley. OTCP

Fox came lolloping, lolloping, The. Hunting Song. Donald Finkel.
(Fox he came lolloping, lolloping, The.) CoAP; MoBS

Fox Dancing. Suzanne Knowles. RB

Fox don't make a fauz pas! A. Polka. John Fuller. *Fr.* Fox-Trot. PeLV

Fox flees the farm in a red rogue dazzle. For Hani, Aged Five, That She Be Better Able to Distinguish a Villain. Gene Baro. NYBP

Fox Glove Song. Christina Beer. PeNZ

Fox he came lolloping, lolloping, The. Donald Finkel. *See* Fox came lolloping, lolloping, The.

Fox he was strong, he was full of running, The. John Masefield. *Fr.* Reynard the Fox. CoGr

Fox Hole. Karl Shapiro. ArOW

Fox is after dinner, too, The. *(LL)* The Sycophantic Fox and the Gullible Raven. Guy Wetmore Carryl. BLPA; FiBHP; NBLV; OBCA

Fox is very clever, The. Fox. Kenneth Rexroth. *Fr.* Bestiary, A. NNaP; OBAL

Fox jumped up one winter's night, A. The Fox. *Unknown.* OxNR
(Fox Went Out One Frosty Night, The.) BLPA

Fox knew well, that before they tore him, The. John Masefield. *Fr.* Reynard the Fox. OBNV; OtMeF

Fox/ like a tawny rope, The. The Fox. Marjorie Somers Scheuer. GoYe

Fox may steal your hens, sir, A. John Gay. *Fr.* Beggar's Opera, The. NOEC; OAEL-1
(Lawyer, The.) IHNG
(Soldier and a Sailor, A.) TEP

Fox of Gascon, though some say of Norman descent, A. The Fox and the Grapes. La Fontaine, *tr. fr. French* by Marianne Moore. FM

Fox Running, *sels.* Ken Smith.
"Beginning again and again." PWE

Fox-Trot, *sels.* John Fuller.
Can-Can. PeLV
Polka. PeLV

Fox Went Out One Frosty Night, The. *Unknown. See* Fox jumped up one winter's night, A.

Fox Who Watched for the Midnight Sun, The. Norman Dubie. LCAP

Fox woman/ dances, string of blue beads. Second Skins — a Peyote Song. Joseph Bruchac. CDW

Foxes, The. Janet Frame. WPE

Foxes. Mary Ann Hoberman. SiSoPo

Foxfire. Nancy Willard. IHMS

Foxglove bells, with lolling tongue, The. Foxgloves. Mary Webb. BoTP

Foxglove by the cottage door, The. Four and Eight. Ffrida Wolfe. BoTP

Foxgloves. Mary Webb. BoTP

Fox's Counsel, The. Huw Llwyd, *tr. fr. Welsh by* Joseph P. Clancy. OBWVE

Fox's Song. Barbara Angell. ImGa

Foxtail Pine. Gary Snyder. NaP; NU

Fra banc to banc, fra wod to wod, I rin. Fra Bank to Bank, Fra Wood to Wood I Rin. Mark Alexander Boyd. NoP; Son
　(Cupid and Venus.) InPK
　(Sonet: "Fra bank [*or* banc] to bank [*or* banc], fra wood [*or* wod] to wood [*or* wod] I rin.") EBEV; ESo; OBEV
　(Venus and Cupid.) HAP; Prf

Fra Bank to Bank, Fra Wood to Wood I Rin. Mark Alexander Boyd. NoP; Son

Fra Lippo Lippi. (I am poor brother Lippo, by your leave!) Robert Browning. CTC; EBVV; EBVVPR; EnVR; FHYEP; NoP; OAEL-2; OtMeF; OxAEP-2; TEP
　Sels.
　"I shall paint/ God in the midst." Prf

Fra Pandolf, have you tried to reproduce. Technique. Burnham Eaton. GoYe

Fractal Lanes, The. Alice Fulton. BAP-91

Fractured Fairy Tale. David Trinidad. BAP-91

Fradel Schtok. Irena Klepfisz. ETG

Frae fields where Spring her sweets has blawn. Ode to the Gowdspink. Robert Fergusson. ScCV

Frae great Apollo, poet say. The Poet's Wish; an Ode. Allan Ramsay, *after* Horace. OBVE

Frae nirly, nippin', Eas'lan' breeze. Ille Terrarum. Robert Louis Stevenson. OxBS

Fragile, *sels.* Tchicaya U Tam'si, *tr. fr. French by* Ellen Conroy Kennedy.
　"I am no longer master of my tears." NegPo

Fragile blades of grass. The Builder of Continents. "Ping Hsin," *tr. fr. Chinese by* Kai-yu Hsu. Fr. Stars, The. WPOW

Fragment: "As for him who/ finds fault." William Carlos Williams. Spl

Fragment: "At her step the water-hen." Dante Gabriel Rossetti. FM

Fragment: "Boy stood on the burning deck, The/ His feet were covered with blisters." *Unknown.* FaBoPa

Fragment: "Breath of life imbued those few dim days, The." Jessie Redmond Fauset. CDC; ShDr

Fragment: "Cataract, whirling to the precipice, The." John Clare. BoNaP

Fragment: "Cold chain of life presseth heavily on me tonight, The." Adah Isaacs Menken. CBWP-1

Fragment: "Encinctured with a twine of leaves." Samuel Taylor Coleridge. *See* Encinctured with a twine of leaves.

Fragment: "Flower in the crannied wall." Tennyson. *See* Flower in the Crannied Wall.

Fragment: "He is an inharmonious note." Sir Roger Casement. TIRV

Fragment: "I am as brisk." Keats. CBNP

Fragment: "I cannot find my way to Nazareth." Yvor Winters. OBSV

Fragment 68: "I envy you your chance of death." Hilda Doolittle ("H. D."). NoAM

Fragment 36: "I know not what to do." Hilda Doolittle ("H. D."). CMoP; NALW; OxBA; VBLP; VGW

Fragment: "I saw his round mouth's crimson deepen as it fell." Wilfred Owen. OAEL-2

Fragment: "I saw the Sibly at Cumæ." Dante Gabriel Rossetti. PeVV

Fragment: "I walked [*or* walk'd] along a stream for pureness rare." At. to Gervase Markham. CTC

Fragment: "I would to heaven that I were so much clay." Byron. *Fr.* Don Juan. CTC; NAEL-2; NOBL; NoP; OAEL-2; OxBSP; PrIm

Fragment: "I'm happiest when most away." Emily Brontë. *See* I'm happiest when most away.

Fragment: "In Cloe's chamber, she and I." John Bancks. NOEC

Fragment: "Isn't ligature — or is it ligament? — a lovely word?" Rupert Brooke. NSI

Fragment: "Language has not the power to speak what love indites." John Clare. FaBoEE; OAEL-2; OBNC; OxBSP; PoEL-4

Fragment: "Locke sank into a swoon." W. B. Yeats. NoAM; PrIm

Fragment: "Love's memories haunt my footsteps still." John Clare. NOBVV

Fragment: "Mark you how the peacock's eye." Gerard Manley Hopkins. FM

Fragment: "Mountain summits sleep, glens, cliffs, and caves, The." Alcman. *See* Mountain summits sleep, The: glens, cliffs, and caves.

Fragment: "My lips (the inconstancy of man!)" Rupert Brooke. NSI

Fragment 113: "Not honey!/ not the plunder of the bee." Hilda Doolittle ("H. D."). NAAL-2

Fragment: "O grant that like to Peter I." Keats. CBNP
　(O Grant.) ChIV-2

Fragment: "Our fancies are but joys all unexprest." H. Cordelia Ray. CBWP-3

Fragment: "Pity, Religion has so seldom found." William Cowper. WGRP

Fragment: "Say, reverend man, why midst this stormy night." Anne Batten Cristall. ECWP

Fragment: "Spruce and limber yellow-hammer, The." Samuel Taylor Coleridge. FM

Fragment: "There pipes the wood-lark, and the song thrush there." Thomas Gray. FM

Fragment: "Thou strainest through the mountain fern." Robert Louis Stevenson. NOBVV

Fragment: "Walk with thy fellow-creatures: note the hush." Henry Vaughan. WGRP

Fragment: "What is poetry? Is it a mosaic." Amy Lowell. WGRP

Fragment, A, *sels.* The Countess of Winchilsea.
　Ardelia's Spiritual Progress. CBCK

Fragment Descriptive of the Miseries of War. Charlotte Smith. ECWP

Fragment for the Dark. Elizabeth Jennings. FaBoWP

Fragment from "Clemo Uti — the Water Lilies." Ring Lardner. FiBHP

Fragment from the Elizabethans. W. Bridges-Adams. FaBoCo

Fragment from "The Maladjusted: A Tragedy." Morris Bishop. NBLV

Fragment in Imitation of Wordsworth. Catherine Fanshawe. FaBoNo; FaBoPa

Fragment of a Character. Thomas Moore. FaBoCo

Fragment of a Greek Tragedy. A. E. Housman. FaBoNo; NOBL; PeLV

Fragment of a Poem on Hunting, A, *sels.* Thomas Tickell.
　"Such be the dog, I charge, thou mean'st to train." ECEV

Fragment of a Song. "Lewis Carroll." FaBoNo

Fragment of a Song on the Beautiful Wife of Dr. John Overall. *Unknown.* BoLoP

Fragment of a Sonnet. Pierre de Ronsard, *tr. fr. French by* Keats. AWP; OBVE

Fragment of an Agon. T. S. Eliot. LiTB

Fragment of an Anti-Papist Ballad. *Unknown.* CoMu

Fragment of an Ode to Maia Written on May Day, 1818. Keats. EnRP; OAEL-2; OBEV; PoEL-4

Fragment of Death. Villon. *See* And Paris be it or Helen dying.

Fragment of Petronius, A. Petronius Arbiter. *See* Doing, a Filthy Pleasure Is, and Short.

Fragment on Death, A. Villon, *tr. fr. French by* Swinburne. CTC; PeVV

Fragment Reflection I. Doris Turner. JB

Fragment, The ("Repeat that, repeat.") Gerard Manley Hopkins. *See* Repeat that, repeat.

Fragment: To the Moon. Shelley. *See* Art thou pale for weariness.

Fragment: Wake the Serpent Not. Shelley. SCGP

Fragmenti. Ezra Pound. PoA

Fragments, The, *sels.* Peter Dale.
　"Few ever came to help you speak or sell." NOCV

Fragments. Catherine Fanshawe. *See* There is a river clear and fair.

Fragments, *sels.* Michael Jackson.

Fragments Intended for the Dramas, *sels.* Thomas Lovell Beddoes.

Fragments of a Lost Gnostic Poem of the Twelfth Century. Herman Melville. NOBA; NoP; OxBSP; PoEL-5

Fragments of Ancient Poetry, Collected in the Highlands of Scotland, *sels.* James Macpherson.
　"I sit by the mossy fountain; on the top of the hill of winds." NOEC

Fragments of the Green Island, *sels.* Errol Francis.
　"If only/ Under the canopy of stars." NBrP

Fragments on Nature and Life, *sels.* Emerson.

Fragments up of every word. The Hots. Michael Sharkey. NOBAu

Fragrance of her life, The. (*LL*) My Mother's Garden. Alice E. Allen. BLPA; BLPL; FaBoBe

Fragrance of the red lotus fades, The. Poem to the Tune of "Yi chian mei." Li Ch'ing-chao, *tr. fr. Chinese.* WPOW, *tr. by* Marsha Wagner

Fragrance would call me out of the house, A. Catching Webs. Judith Beveridge. NOBAu

Fragrances that like a wind disturb. The Islands Where I Was Born. Gloria Rawlinson. PeNZ

Fragrant grass in front of the courtyard. Spoken to Pines and Bamboos. Wei Chuang, *tr. fr. Chinese by* Robin D. S. Yates. SuSp

Fragrant prayer upon the air, A. A Poem to Be Said on Hearing the Birds Sing. Biddy Crummy, *tr. fr. Irish by* Douglas Hyde. AWP; WTO

Fragrant roundness. Pitcher. Renee Ferrer De Arrellaga, *tr. fr. Spanish.* TSaS, *tr. by* Raquel Chaves *with* Naomi Shihab Nye

Fragrant the grasses of high Kane-hoa. Anklet Song. *Unknown, tr. fr. Hawaiian by* N. B. Emerson. WTO

Fragrant the Prayer. *Unknown, tr. fr. Irish by* Alice Furlong. TIRV

Fragrant Thy Memories. "Judah," *tr. fr. Hebrew by* Herbert Loewe. TrJP

Fragrant Tree, The. Shen Yüeh, *tr. fr. Chinese by* Richard B. Mather. SuSp

Fragrant with powder, moist with perspiration. Creamy Breasts. Chao Luan-luan, *tr. fr. Chinese by* Kenneth Rexroth *and* Ling Chung. WPC

Frail and tenuous mist lingers on baffled and intricate branches, A. Leaves. Frederic Manning. NOBAu

Frail as our flesh crumble to dust. (*LL*) Epitaph on Maria Wentworth. Thomas Carew. PoEL-3

Frail as the leaves that quiver on the sprays. Homer, *tr. by* Samuel Johnson. *Fr.* Iliad, The. OBVE

Frail children of sorrow, dethroned by a hue. Hope. Georgia Douglas Johnson. CDC

Frail duration of a flower, The. (*LL*) The Wild Honeysuckle. Philip Freneau. AmPP; AnAmPo; BLPL; EAP; LiTA; NAAL-1; NOBA; OxBA; PoEL-4; PoLF; TAP; TrGrPo

Frail scorched grasses are ripped now, The. Drought. Oumar Ba, *tr. fr. French by* Kathleen Weaver. PBWP

Frail sound of a tunic trailing, A. Antonio Machado Ruiz, *tr. fr. Spanish by* John Dos Passos. AWP

Frail the white rose and frail are. A Flower Given to My Daughter. James Joyce. OBMV; RaBo; RB

Fraile as our flesh, crumble to dust. (*LL*) Maria Wentworth. Thomas Carew. CaPo; JCP; MeLP; OBD; PeECV; SeCV-1

Frailty. George Herbert. NOCV

Frailty and Hurtfulness of Beauty, The. The Earl of Surrey. *See* Brittle beauty [*or* beautie], that nature made so frail[e].

Frailty of Beauty, The. "J. C." *Fr.* Alcilia. EIL

Frailty, Thy Name is Woman. Shakespeare. *See* O! that this too too solid flesh would melt.

Frame for the Angels, A, *sels.* Paul Smyth.
  "Spring that I was six I found in the woods, The." CRP

Frame within frame, the evolving conversation. Dancers Exercising. Amy Clampitt. NoAM

Framed. Claire Harris. PBCV

Framed by the open window, a lone Stearman. Randolph Field, 1938. R. S. Gwynn. ArOW

Framed in her phoenix fire-screen, Edna Ward. Cottage Street, 1953. Richard Wilbur. CAPP; FaBoMo; HCAP

Fragment of Bion, A. Philip Freneau. *Fr.* Fredonian, The. EAP

Framer of the earth and sky. Saint Ambrose, *tr. fr. Latin.* TrCP

Framework-knitters Lamentation, The. *Unknown.* CoMu

Framework-Knitters Petition, The. C. Briggs. CoMu

Fran, you lay belly up in a bed. Good Timing. Carol Ebbecke. PFL

France. Douglas Dunn. OxBM

France. Wordsworth. *Fr.* Prelude [*or, Growth of a Poet's Mind*], The. EnRP; OAEL-2

France; an Ode. Samuel Taylor Coleridge. EnRP

France! It is I answering. Republic to Republic. Witter Bynner. PAH

France leered me forth; the realm that I had crossed. Wordsworth. *See* O pleasant exercise of hope and joy!

Francesco García y Gabaldon. (*LL*) A Feller I Know. Mary Austin. FaPON

Francesco's Fortunes, *sels.* Robert Greene.

Francie-the-Possessed. Oswald Durand, *tr. fr. French by* Ellen Conroy Kennedy. NegPo

Francine's Room. Louise Erdrich. NoAM

Francis Beaumont's Letter from the Country to Jonson. Francis Beaumont. *See* Sun which doth the greatest comfort bring[e], The.

Sir Francis Drake, *sels.* Charles Fitz-Geffry.
  Bee, The. EIL

Sir Francis Drake; or, Eighty-eight. *Unknown.* GBP; OxBSS

Sir Francis, Sir Francis, Sir Francis is come. Upon Sir Francis Drake's Return from His Voyage about the World, and the Queen's Meeting Him. *Unknown.* CoMu; EIL; FaBoCh; OxBSS

Francisco Coronado rode forth with all his train. Quivíra. Arthur Guiterman. PAH

François am I, heavy my lot. Villon. OBD

Frank Albert and Viola Benzena Owens. Ntozake Shange. BISi

Frank Baker's my name, and a bachelor I am. Starving to Death on a Government Claim. *Unknown.* AmFP; OBAL
  (Lane County Bachelor, The.) AS

Frank, Frank,/ Turned the crank. *Unknown.* RoPo

Frank James, the Roving Gambler. *Unknown.* AmFP

Frank O'Hara. Ted Berrigan. UL

Frank Plume, a spark about the town. The Inquisitive Bridegroom. William Somervile. ECEV

Frank Ryan Dead in Dresden. Michael O'Loughlin. *Fr.* Shards, The. IB

Frank, wilt live handsomely? Trust not too far. Advice to My Best Brother, Colonel Francis Lovelace. Richard Lovelace. BeJo; CaPo

Frankeleyn was in his companye. Chaucer. *Fr.* Canterbury Tales, The. EnVB; FHYEP; NoP; OAEL-1; PPP, *abr.*

Frankenstein. Edward Field. FF

Frankenstein in the Markets. Dermot Bolger. IB

Frankfurt. János Pilinszky, *tr. fr. Hungarian by* János Csokits *and* Ted Hughes. PoSu

Frankie and Johnny [*or* Johnnie *or* Albert]. *Unknown.* AmFP; AS; BeLS; EBEvV; EBNV; FF; NIP; NOBA; NTP; OxBoLi; RB; TrGrPo; UnPo

Frankie Blues. *Unknown.* AS

Frankie Silvers. Frances Silvers. AmFP

Frankie was a good woman. Frankie Blues. *Unknown.* AS

Franklin Hyde. Hilaire Belloc. FaBoUs; NBLV

Franklin James. Edgar Lee Masters. *Fr.* Spoon River Anthology. OBD

Franklin sailed a key-hung kite. Fable. James Facos. NBLV

Franklin's Prologue, The. Chaucer. *Fr.* Canterbury Tales, The. EnVB; NAEL-1; OAEL-1

Franklin's Tale, The. Chaucer. *Fr.* Canterbury Tales, The. EnVB; NAEL-1; OAEL-1

Frankly, I prefer the blue. Sentimental Lines to a Young Man Who Favors Pink Wallpaper While I Personally Lean to the Blue. Margaret Fishback. FiBHP

Frantic as a prentice poet. Niyi Osundare. *Fr.* Moonsongs. HBAPE, *sect.* V

"Frater Ave atque Vale." Tennyson. ChTr; EBVV; FaBoPP; GTBS-P; HAP; InPS; NAEL-2; NoP; OBTV; OxBSP

Fraternitas. Confucius, *tr. fr. Chinese by* Ezra Pound. *Fr.* Deer Sing. CTC; OBVE

Fratri Dilectissimo. John Buchan. OtMeF

Frau Bauman, Frau Schmidt, and Frau Schwartze. Theodore Roethke. CoAP; MoAB; MoP; NAAL-2; NoAM; NOBA; NYBP; TAP

Fraudulent Days. Michael Benedikt. PoA

Fraudulent perhaps in that they gave. Swans. Lawrence Durrell. MoBrPo

Fräulein Reads Instructive Rhymes. Maxine W. Kumin. NYBP; Poetsp

Fray of Suport, The. *Unknown.* IBB

Frayed cables bear perilously the antiquated lift. Hospice. Lynda Hull. PFL

Freak is the other, The. Celebrating the Freak. Cynthia MacDonald. Poetsp

Freaks at Spurgin Road Field, The. Richard Hugo. LCAP; NoAM; SM; SoSe

Freaks of Fashion. Christina Rossetti. FM

Freckled and frivolous cake there was, A. The Frivolous Cake. Mervyn Laurence Peake. CBNP; PeLV

Freckles numberless as stars on my forehead. My Portrait. Moyshe-Leyb Halpern, *tr. fr. Yiddish by* Joseph Leftwich. TrJP

Fred Apollus at Fava's. Nicholas Moore. ErPo

Fred, where is north? West-running Brook. Robert Frost. BLPL; MoAB; MoAmPo; NOBA; NoP

Fredensborg. Friedrich Gottlieb Klopstock, *tr. fr. German by* George C. Schoolfield. GePo

Frederick Douglass. Sam Cornish. PoBA

Frederick Douglass. Joseph S. Cotter, Sr.. AAP

Frederick Douglass. Paul Laurence Dunbar. PoBA

Frederick Douglass. Robert Hayden. CAPP; GOA; HCAP; NIP; PoBA; PoNe; Son; TTY; VCAP

Frederick Douglass: 1817-1895. Langston Hughes. BPo

Fredericksburg. Thomas Bailey Aldrich. AnAmPo; PAH

Frederiksted, Dusk. Derek Walcott. NoAM

Fredonian, The, *sels.* Philip Freneau.
  Frament of Bion, A. EAP

Fred's Breakfast. David Trinidad. BAP-91

Free America. Joseph Warren. PAH

Free are the Muses, and where freedom is. Breath on the Oat. Joseph Russell Taylor. PAH

Free as las', free at las.' I Thank God I'm Free at Las.' *Unknown.* BPo; TAP

Free bird leaps, A. Caged Bird. Maya Angelou. WeW

Free evening fades, outside the windows fastened with decorative iron grilles, The. Evening in the Sanitarium. Louise Bogan. FaBoWP; FYAP; IHMS; NALW; TwCP

Free Fantasia on Japanese Themes. Amy Lowell. MoAmPo

Free Grace. Charles Wesley. NOCV

Free hands. Hands. Bernard Dadié, *tr. fr. French by* Ellen Conroy Kennedy. NegPo

Free I have my own self-reliance. I Drift in the Wind. Ingrid Jonker, *tr. fr. Afrikaans by* Jack Cope. PeSA; WPOW

Free Intelligence, The. Anna Wickham. OBD

Free Kirk, The. Eighteen-Forty-Three. *Unknown.* FaBoCo

Free Little Bird. *Unknown.* AmFP

Free of excoriating pain, free of this disease. (*LL*) Ward 6. Tanure Ojaide. HBAPE

Free One, A. W. H. Auden. *See* Watch any day his nonchalant pauses, see.

Free Parliament Litany, A. *Unknown.* OxBoLi

Free Silver. *Unknown.* AmFP

Free things are magnets to the moving eye. Birds on a Blighted Tree. Grace Schulman. AnAn

Free thinker! Do you think you are the only thinker. Golden Lines. Gérard de Nerval, *tr. fr. French by* Robert Bly. NU

Free Thoughts on Several Eminent Composers. Charles Lamb. FaBoCo; OxBoLi; PeLV

Free to look at fact. To the New Women. John Davidson. OHCV

Free Union. André Breton, *tr. fr. French by* David Antin. TTTS

Free Up de Lan, White Man. Mutabaruka. PBCV

Free woman, A. At last free! The mother of Sumangala, *tr. fr. Pali by* Willis Barnstone. AIW; BoWoP

Free Women Blooming like Fields of Flowers. Ch'iu Chin. *See* How many wise men and heroes.

Freeborn Man. Ewan MacColl. OBET

Freeborn Pindaric never does refuse. A Pindaric on the Grunting of a Hog. Samuel Wesley. NOBL

Freed dove flew to the Rajah's tower, The. The Dove of Dacca. Kipling. GN

Freedom. Joan Agnew. BoTP

Freedom [*or* Fredome]. John Barbour. *Fr.* Bruce, The. FaBoCh; OBEV; OxBS; TrGrPo

Freedom. Wimal Dissanayake. TSaS

Freedom. Carolina Hospital. LoHo

Freedom. Langston Hughes. PoBA

Freedom. Abraham ibn Ezra, *tr. fr. Hebrew by* Solomon Solis-Cohen. TrJP

Freedom. Friedrich von Logau, *tr. fr. German.* GePo, *tr. by* George C. Schoolfield

Freedom. Sean O Riordain, *tr. fr. Irish by* Coslett Quin. TIRV

Freedom, *sels.* Charles Lewis Reason.
   "O Freedom! Freedom! O! how oft." AAP

Freedom a Come Oh! *Unknown.* FaBoVe; PBCV

Freedom; a Poem, Written in Time of Recess from the Rapacious Claws of Bailiffs, *sels.* Andrew Brice.
   Poet's Terror at the Bailiffs of Exeter, The. NOEC

Freedom and dignity have reached us. Independence. *Somali Oral Tradition, tr. by* B. W. Andrzejewski *and* I. M. Lewis. WTO

Freedom and Love. Thomas Campbell. GTBS; GTBS-P

Freedom at McNealy's. Priscilla Jane Thompson. CBWP-2

Freedom called them — up they rose. The Gallant Fifty-one. Henry Lynden Flash. PAH

Freedom for the Mind. William Lloyd Garrison. FaBoBe

Freedom! Freedom! Freedom! (*LL*) Isle!/ Island of the syllables of flame! Jacques Rabémanganjara. NegPo

Freedom Hair. Raymond Washington. NBV

Freedom in Mah Soul. David Wadsworth Cannon, Jr.. PoNe

Freedom in Peril. Sagittarius. UV

Freedom is a dream. Dark Testament. Pauli Murray. BlSi

Freedom is a hard-bought thing. Song of the Settlers. Jessamyn West. FaPON

Freedom is more than a word, more than the base coinage. The *Nabara.* C. Day Lewis. EBNV; OBNV

Freedom, New Hampshire. Galway Kinnell. LCAP; NaP

Freedom of the wholly mad, The. The Phenomenology of Anger. Adrienne Rich. PoE

Freedom Song for the Black Woman, A. Carole C. Gregory. BlSi

Freedom to worship God. (*LL*) The Landing of the Pilgrim Fathers [in New England]. Felicia Dorothea Hemans. BeLS; BLPA; FaBoBe; FaBV; FaPON; GN; OHIP; PAH; VPP; WBLP; WPE

Freedom will not come. Freedom. Langston Hughes. PoBA

Freely. Awake! before it is too late. (*LL*) Awake! W. R. Rodgers. LiTM

Freely Espousing. James Schuyler. NeAP; NoP

Freely the dead bracken breaks to your stride. Argenteuil County. Peter Dale Scott. MoCV

Freeman, I treat tonight, and treat your friends. The Invitation. Leonard Welsted. NOEC

Freethinker's Baptism, A. Linda Saunders. NWP

Freeway 280. Lorna Dee Cervantes. ETG; NoAM; WeW

Freeze-frame. Alison Fell. NBrP

Freeze, freeze, thou bitter sky. Shakespeare. *Fr.* As You Like It. AWP; CH; ChTr; EIL; ELP; EnRePo; GBL; GTBS; GTBS-P; ImPo; InPS; LiTB; NAEL-1; NOBE; NoP; NoSic; OAEL-1; OBEV; OBF; PrIm; SCGP; TrGrPo; WiR

Freezing Night. T'ao Hung Ching, *tr. fr. Chinese by* Kenneth Rexroth. OHMPC

Freight Boats. James S. Tippett. FaPON

Freight Train, The. Rowena Bastin Bennett. PDV

Freighter, gay with rust, The. Jews at Haifa. Randall Jarrell. MoAmPo

Freighting from Wilcox to Globe. *Unknown.* AmFP

Freind! for your epitaphs I'm griev'd. Epigram on One Who Made Long Epitaphs. Pope. FaBoEE

Freindship and Single Life against Love and Marriage, *sels.* Sir John Denham.
   "Love! in what poyson is thy Dart." OBF

French. Osbert Lancaster. *Fr.* Afternoons with Baedeker. FaBoCo; NOBL; PeLV

French, 1870-1871, The. *Unknown.* FaBoEE

French and Russian they matter not. A Chant of Hate against England. Ernst Lissauer, *tr. by* Barbara Henderson. *Fr.* Hymn of Hate against England, A. OtMeF

French are a race among races, The. *Unknown.* PeLi

French clocks struck two-thirty, and above, The. Under the Arc de Triomphe: October 17. Marilyn Hacker. PoA

French cognac 1944 is death. In Remembrance of the Children of Izieu. Arlene Maass. BTR

French Desire. Keith Abbott. UL

French Dress. Friedrich von Logau, *tr. fr. German.* GePo, *tr. by* George C. Schoolfield

French Fops. John Gay *and* Alexander Pope. *Fr.* Epistle to the Right Honourable William Pulteney, Esq. ECEV

French Garden. Léopold Sédar Senghor, *tr. fr. French by* Ellen Conroy Kennedy. NegPo

French government, The — or maybe it was the English — placed. Birds in the Night. Luis Cernuda, *tr. fr. Spanish by* Erskine Lane. PeHV

French homework due in Tuesday scribbled. Jonathan. Janet Fisher. NWP

French Lisette; a Ballad of Maida Vale. William Plomer. ErPo

French Peasants. Monk Gibbon. TIRV

French poodle espied in the hall, A. *Unknown.* PeLi

French Prisoner, The. János Pilinszky, *tr. fr. Hungarian by* János Csokits *and* Ted Hughes. PoSu

French Revolution, The, *sels.* Blake.

French spoken. Sheep Meadow. Samuel Menashe. Mes

Frende, god save you. For to Aske the Waye. *Unknown. Fr.* Lytell Treatyse for to Lerne Englysshe and Frens, A. OxBLMV

Frenzy. George Crabbe. *Fr.* Sir Eustace Grey. NOBE

Frenzy softens the air. Radiant Silhouette IV. John Yau. OpBo

Frere ther was, a wantown and a merye. Chaucer. *Fr.* Canterbury Tales, The. EnVB; FHYEP; NoP; OAEL-1; PPP, *abr.*

Fresco-Sonnets to Christian Sethe. Heine, *tr. fr. German by* John Todhunter. AWP

Frescoes for Mr. Rockefeller's City. Archibald MacLeish. UnPo
Sels.
   Burying Ground by the Ties. GOA; MoAmPo
   Landscape as a Nude. AmPP; CMoP

Fresh Air. Kenneth Koch. NeAP; NNaP

Fresh Air, The. Harold Monro. CH

Fresh and fair the morn awaketh. Morn. Josephine D. Henderson Heard. CBWP-4

Fresh bread and the smile, The. Twice. David Chaloner. VaA

Fresh breezes waft across march orchid fragrance as. Tune: "Moth Fluttering Against Lamp." Kuan Yun-shih, *tr. by* Richard John Lynn. *Fr.* Medley of Southern and Northern Tunes — Scenic Tour of West Lake. SuSp

Fresh, changeful, constant, upward, like thee! (*LL*) The Fountain. James Russell Lowell. AnAmPo; BoTP; OBCA

Fresh Cheese and Cream. Robert Herrick. CBLP

Fresh day cracks, goat's milkspurt. Six-forty-two Farm Commune Struggle Poem. Jay Leifer. MAT

Fresh fields and woods! the Earth's fair face. Retirement. Henry Vaughan. ChIV-1

Fresh from the dewy hill, the merry year. Blake. EnRP; PeECV

Fresh From the Void. Masaoka Shiki, *tr. fr. Japanese by* Kenneth Rexroth. ArNa

Fresh-hearted May on hearing what he said. The Merchant's Tale. Chaucer. *Fr.* Canterbury Tales, The. EnVB; OxBM

Fresh I'm cum fra Sandgate Street. Do Li A. *Unknown.* GBP

Fresh morning gusts have blown away all fear. Sonnet: To a Young Lady Who Sent Me a Laurel Crown. Keats. EnRP

Fresh Paint. Boris Pasternak, *tr. fr. Russian by* Babette Deutsch. TrJP

Fresh palms for the Old Dominion! The Battle of Charlestown. Henry Howard Brownell. PAH

Fresh roost for the Holy Ghost., A. *(LL)* First Confession. X. J. Kennedy. PPP

Fresh savannas of the Sangamon, The. The Painted Cup. Bryant. EAP

Fresh strewings allow. The Peter-Penny. Robert Herrick. CaPo

Fresh water goddess, Lake Erie, The. In My Black Book. Frank Polite. NGP

Fresh were the breathings of the nightborn gale. Wild Nature. Charles Newton. *Fr.* Stanzas. NOEC

Freshmen. Barry Spacks. NYBP

Fret not thyself because of evildoers. Bible, *O.T.*, *paraphrased by* Sir Thomas Wyatt. *Fr.* Psalms.
(Trust in the Lord, *paraphrased by* Charles Frederic Sheldon.) BLRP, 1–7

Freud: Dying London, He Recalls the Smoke of His Cigar Beginning to Sing. James Schevill. TAP

Freud Town. Anne Carson. *Fr.* Life of Towns, The. BAP-90

Friar and the Nun, The. *Unknown.* OxBLMV

Friar and the Nun, The. *Unknown.* GBP

Friar Complains, A. *Unknown.* MeEL

Friar had said his paternosters duly, The. Necrological. John Crowe Ransom. MeMAP

Friar in the Well, B *vers.* *Unknown.* ESPB

Friar in the Well, The, A *vers.* *Unknown. See* As I Lay Musing ("As I lay musing all alone.")

Friar Lubin. Clément Marot. *tr. fr. French by* Longfellow. AWP

Friar of Orders Gray, The. *Unknown.* NOEC

Friars' Enormities. *Unknown.* MeEL

Friar's Prologue, The. Chaucer. *Fr.* Canterbury Tales, The. EnVB; PoE

Friar's Tale, The. Chaucer. *Fr.* Canterbury Tales, The. EnVB; PoE

Friday. Sir Walter Scott. BoTP

Friday before your funeral I taught, The. A Dream of Nightingales. David Bergman. PFL

Friday came and the circus was there. The Circus. Elizabeth Madox Roberts. FaPON

Friday Evening. Sean Lucy. CIP

Friday Evenings. George Charlton. PWE

Friday night's dream, on Saturday told. Dreams. *Unknown.* ReMoGo

Friday takes a step in the right direction. Today Backwards. David Chaloner. VaA

Friday the Thirteenth. Allen Ginsberg. NNaP

Friday. Wet Dusk. Christopher Logue. OxBTC

Friday's all-staff meeting dissolves. Indian College Blues. Adrian C. Louis. NAmP90

Fridays, when I draw my pension. Betjeman at the Post Office. Stanley J. Sharpless. FaBoPa

Fried, lionized, lbiled, or mashed? *(LL)* The Cultured Girl Again. Ben King. FiBHP; OBAL

Friend!. *(LL)* Hands. Bernard Dadié. NegPo

Friend, The. Marge Piercy. CAPP; CrSp; NALW; NMM; Poetr

Friend. Hone Tuwhare, *tr. fr. Maori by* Kumeroa Ngoingoi Pewhairangi. PeNZ

Friend, A. Santob de Carrion. *Fr.* Proverbios Morales. TrJP

Friend, A. Marguerite Power. FaBoCo

Friend, A. W. D. Snodgrass. MAT

Friend, A. Sir Thomas N. Talfourd. PoToHe

Friend, A. *Unknown.* PoToHe

Friend, a poet, wrote me near the end, A. The Drouth. Jon Dressel. AngWe

Friend Advises Me to Stop Drinking, A. Mei Yao Ch'en, *tr. fr. Chinese by* Kenneth Rexroth. HoPM

Friend, Ah You Have Changed! Frank Mkalawile Chipasula. HBAPE

Friend and brother, and yet more than brother. To Joseph Brenan. James Clarence Mangan. PeIV

Friend and Foe. Karen Alkalay-Gut. WoWa

Friend by enemy I call you out. To Others Than You. Dylan Thomas. MeMBP

Friend calls us, A. Six Years. Alice Bloch. PeHV

Friend Cato. Anna Wickham. MoBrPo

Friend Col and I, both full of whim. David Garrick. FaBoEE

Friend, coming in a friendly wise. If Any Be Pleased to Walk into My Poor Garden. Francis Daniel Pastorius. SCAP

Friend, don't be angry. Mirabai, *tr. fr. Hindi by* Willis Barnstone *and* Usha Nilsson. BoWoP

Friend Hedylus' cloak is a sight to behold. Epigram: On Hedylus. Martial, *tr. fr. Latin.* PeHV

Friend, his seas swell and roar. What She Said. Ammuvanar, *tr. fr. Tamil by* A. K. Ramanujan. PLW

Friend, hope for the Guest while you are alive. To Be a Slave of Intensity. Kabir, *tr. fr. Hindi by* Robert Bly. RaBo

Friend, how can I meet my lord? Mirabai, *tr. fr. Hindi by* Willis Barnstone *and* Usha Nilsson. BoWoP

Friend, if the mute and shrouded dead. Love and Death. Catullus, *tr. fr. Latin by* H. W. Garrod. AWP

Friend in a tipi in the, A. Two Fawns That Didn't See the Light This Spring. Gary Snyder. HCAP

Friend in Need Will Be Around in Five Minutes, A. Ogden Nash. OBF

Friend in the Garden, A. Juliana Horatia Ewing. BoTP; FaPON; OxBChV

Friend/ like someone who gets drunk secretly. What She Said to Her Girl Friend, and What Her Girl Friend Said in Reply. Uruttiran, *tr. fr. Tamil by* A. K. Ramanujan. PLW

Friend, listen. What She Said Ammuvanar, *tr. fr. Tamil by* A. K. Ramanujan. PLW

Friend, now for ever gone. To One Who Died in a Garret in Cardiff. Huw Menai. AngWe

Friend of Humanity and the Knife Grinder, The. George Canning *and* John Hookham Frere. BXAP; FaBoCo; UV

Friend of man desires, The. *(LL)* Progress. Matthew Arnold. ChIV-2

Friend of Ronsard, Nashe and Beaumont. On a Birthday. J. M. Synge. ChTr; GBL; OBMV; PeIV

Friend of that poor queen, The. *(LL)* Deirdre. James Stephens. AWP; CMoP; OBMV; PoRA

Friend of the Family, A. Louis Simpson. NNaP

Friend of the Fourth Decade, The. James Merrill. NYBP

Friend of the wise! and teacher of the good! To William Wordsworth. Samuel Taylor Coleridge. EnRP; EPCY; FHYEP; NAEL-2; OAEL-2

Friend of Two, A. Wilbur D. Nesbit. PoLF

Friend, on This Scaffold Thomas More Lies Dead. J. V. Cunningham. InPK

Friend, on this sunny day, snow sparkling. Letter to Jean-Paul Baudot, at Christmas. Lucien Stryk. ArOW; CAPP

Friend, Ortho of Syracuse gives thee this charge. Ortho's Epitaph. Theocritus [*or* Theokritus], *tr. fr. Greek by* Charles Stuart Calverley. FaBoEE

Friend!/ Poor, foolish blossom! Beauty. Peter Hille, *tr. fr. German by* Jethro Bithell. AWP

Friend sparrow, do not eat, I pray. Basho, *tr. fr. Japanese by* Curtis Hidden Page. AWP

Friend — the face I wallow toward. What I Like. Alice Fulton. WeW

Friend, there be they on whom mishap. Contentment. Charles Stuart Calverley. NOBVV

Friend thinks he knows best, A. The Late Victorian Girl. Bill Manhire. PeNZ

Friend, when I think of your delicate feminine face. On the Death of an Acquaintance. Oscar Williams. *Fr.* Variations on a Theme. LiTA

Friend Who Just Stands By, The. B.Y. Williams. PoLF; PoToHe

Friend Who Never Came. William Stafford. SM

Friend, whose unnatural early death. David Gascoyne. FaBoTw; TwCP

Friend, with regard to this same hare. To the Rev. Mr. Powell. Christopher Smart. OBWVE

Friend writes, We're not talking about any port, A. Report from Another Country. Charlene Langfur. LoHo

Friend, yes, the winter following. A Diagnosis. David Craig Austin. PFL

Friend, you are grieved that I should go. Creeds. Karle Wilson Baker. WGRP

Friend, you seem thoughtful. I not wonder much. A Sea Dialogue. Oliver Wendell Holmes. OBAL

Friendless and faint, with martyred steps and slow. Calvary. E. A. Robinson. MoAmPo; Son; WGRP

Friendly Address, A. Thomas Hood. PoEL-4

Friendly Beasts, The. *Unknown.* FaPON; PChr

Friendly Cinnamon Bun, The. Russell Hoban. OTCP

Friendly cow all red and white, The. The Cow. Robert Louis Stevenson. FaPON; FM; NTCP; OxBChV; PWR; TLR; WHSW

Friendly Game of Football, A. Edward Dyson. CBAP

Friends. John Ashbery. LCAP

Friends, The. Bertolt Brecht, *tr. fr. German by* Michael Hamburger. OBF; PoSu

Friends. Thomas Curtis Clark. PoToHe

Friends. Ray Durem. PoBA

Friends, The. Kipling. OBF

Friends. Richard Moore. SM

Friends. Martin Sorescu, *tr. fr. Romanian by* Michael Hamburger. PWE

Friends. W. B. Yeats. IIP; MoP; NoAM

Friends and loves we have none, nor wealth, nor blest abode. The Seekers. John Masefield. WGRP

From a lonesome old house, near Holbeach Wash-way. From the Country, to Mr. Rowe in Town. Susanna Centlivre. ECWP

From a Marriage Broker's Card, 1776. *Unknown.* FaBoUs

From a Milkweed Pod. Robert Frost.

From a Museum Man's Album. John Hewitt. OxBTC

From a new peony. Sonnet for Minimalists. Mona Van Duyn. WeW

From a Pill-Box on the Solent. Jeremy Hooker. SCBI

From a place I came. Kathleen Raine. *Fr.* Two Invocations of Death. OxBTC

From a precipitous cliff, a withered pine hangs upside down. Tune: "Intoxication in the East Wind" Autumn Scenery. Lu Chih, *tr. fr. Chinese* by Sherwin S. S. Fu. SuSp

From a Printed Bill, Fixed in the Beak of One in a Group of Five Stuffed Owls in the Shop Window of a Bird Stuffer, at Richmond, Yorkshire. *Unknown.* FaBoUs

From a Railway Carriage. Robert Louis Stevenson. BoTP; FaPON; OTCP; OxBChV; PDV; PYC

From a Republican Grave: Daniel Henry Deniehy, 1828–1865. Philip Mead. NOBAu

From a rived tree, that stands beside the grave. Anna Seward. ECWP

From a ruler that's a curse. Charles Cotton. OBSV

From a Saxon Monk to His Love. Christiania Whitehead. NWP

From a Spanish Cloister. G. K. Chesteron. UV

From a Survivor. Adrienne Rich. AnAn; NALW

From a thousand Chinese dinners, one cookie: Robert Mezey. *Fr.* Thousand Chinese Dinners, A. RaBo

From a Tobacco Wrapper. *Unknown.* FaBoUs

From a Venetian Sequence. Adèle Naudé. PeSA

From a Very Little Sphinx. Edna St. Vincent Millay. OBAL; SiSoPo

From a village up the Hudson. The Dark Girl Dressed in Blue. *Unknown.* BeLS

From a Walking Song. Charles Williams. BoTP

From a Window in Princes Street. W. E. Henley. EBVV

From a woman, the gods turned me into stone. Niobe. *Unknown, tr. fr. Greek* by Peter Jay. GrAn

From a Woman to a Greedy Lover. Norman Cameron. *Fr.* Three Love Poems. FaBoEE; FaBoTw; GTBS-P

From a world more full of weeping than he can/ Understand. (*LL*) The Stolen Child. W. B. Yeats. CMoP; NAEL-2; NoP; OHCV

From a Young Woman to an Old Officer Who Courted Her. Elizabeth Frances Amherst. ECWP

From Abertillery and Aberdare. The Angry Summer. Idris Davies. AngWe

From across the stream, on the side of the opposite hill. Not Seeing Is Believing. Paul Petrie. TAP

From Age to Age They Gather. Frederick L. Hosmer. AH

From Albert to Bapaume. Alec Waugh. NSI

From all my lame defeats and oh! much more. The Apologist's Evening Prayer. C. S. Lewis. TrCP

From All Peoples, *sels.* Nathan Alterman, *tr. fr. Hebrew* by Simon Halkin. "When our children cried in the shadow of the gallows." TrJP

From All Sides Laughter Shall Strike Them. Amir Gilboa, *tr. fr. Hebrew* by Ruth Finer Mintz. MHP

From all that dwells below the skies. *Unknown.* EaPr

From all that terror teaches. Litany. G. K. Chesteron. *Fr.* O God of Earth And Altar. OtMeF

From all the other countries in the world. (*LL*) Australia. Gary Catalano. NOBAu

From All These Events. Stephen Spender. LiTB

From Alpine heights where clad in snow. Ode to the Lake of Geneva. William Parsons. OBTV

From America. James M. Whitfield. BPo

From among ten thousand trees autumn wind rises. Sent in Lieu of a Letter to Shih-wu, Lan-ku, and Other Friends. Huang Tsun-hsien, *tr. fr. Chinese* by An-yan Tang. SuSp

From an Afternoon Caller. Sister Mary Madeleva. CRP

From an Asylum; Kathy Chattle to Her Mother, Ruth Arbeiter. Anne Stevenson. BrRo

From an English Sensibility. Roy Fisher. VaA

From an Island You Cannot Name. Martín Espada. UTF

From an Old House in America. Adrienne Rich. NNaP; TRP

From an old house shaded with macrocarpas. James K. Baxter. *Fr.* Pig Island Letters. PeNZ

From Ancient Fangs. Peter Viereck. LiTA

From ancient woods arise. (*LL*) The Abbot of Inisfalen. William Allingham. GN; TIRV

From anger into the pit of sleep. Wife to Husband. Fleur Adcock. PeNZ

From Another Room. Gregory Corso. NeAP

From Arranmore the weary miles I've come. Mavrone. Arthur Guiterman. BXAP; FiBHP

From Battle Clamour. Samuele Romanelli, *tr. fr. Hebrew* by Nina Davis Salaman. TrJP

From battlement to keep. The Wings. Debora Greger. *Fr.* Afterlife, The. BAP-91

From beauty to the other beauty, peace, the night splendor. (*LL*) Gale in April. Robinson Jeffers. MoAB; MoAmPo

From behind the Bars, *sels.* Fadwa Tuqan, *tr. fr. Arabic* by Hatem Hossaini.
From the Diary of ——. WPOW

From Belfast to Suffolk. William Peskett. PNI

From below, the waist-thick pine. Yggdrasill. Paul Muldoon. PBCIP

From Belsen a crate of gold teeth. William Heyen. BTR; SM; SoSe

From beneath a stone. Planting a Cedar. Linda Hogan. BCF

From bill to breast a snake. Swan. Edward Lowbury. GTBS-P

From blacked-out streets. Denise Levertov. *Fr.* During the Eichmann Trial. BTR

From Blenheim's clocktower a cheerful bell bangs out. Distilled Water. M. K. Joseph. PeNZ

From Blossoms. Li-Young Lee. ArNa; TRP

From blossoms comes. From Blossoms. Li-Young Lee. ArNa; TRP

From Braddon's penniless subornation. A New Litany in the Year 1684. *Unknown.* APAS

From breakfast on through all the day. The Land of Nod. Robert Louis Stevenson. PWR

From breezeway or through front porch screen. The Sheets. Timothy Steele. DiPo

From Brooklyn heights a Hessian doctor came. The Hessian Doctor. Philip Freneau. *Fr.* British Prison Ship, The. EAP

From Brooklyn, over the Brooklyn Bridge, on this fine morning. Invitation to Miss Marianne Moore. Elizabeth Bishop. NALW

From Calpe's rock, with loss of leg. The Soldier That Has Seen Service. *Unknown.* NOEC

From camp to camp, through the fool womb of time. Shakespeare. *Fr.* King Henry V. FaBoRV; OxAEP-1; RB

From Canaan Joseph shall return, whose face. Hafiz, *tr. fr. Persian* by Gertrude Lowthian Bell. *Fr.* Odes. AWP; TAL

From Cavan and from Leitrim and from Mayo. Lough Derg. Patrick Kavanagh. PeIV

From cavities of bones. From the Cavities of Bones. Patricia Parker. BlSi

From Childhood's Hour. Poe. MeMAP; PoEL-4

From childhood's hour I have not been. From Childhood's Hour. Poe. MeMAP; PoEL-4
(Alone.) NAAL-1; NTP

From Clee to heaven the beacon burns. 1887. A. E. Housman. *Fr.* Shropshire Lad, A. FaPoB; FaPoR; NIP; NOBVV; PlP; PrIm; SCGP; UnPo

From coast to coast. Alpha November Golf Sierra Tango. Tom Clark. UL

From Colony to Nation. Irving Layton. NOBC

From continent to continent. (*LL*) The Orphan. Muhammad al-Maghut. TSaS, *tr.* by May Jayyusi *and* Naomi Shihab Nye

From Countless Hearts. Gail Brook Burket. AH

From Craig y Foelallt I can see it all. Gwyneth Lewis. *Fr.* Welsh Espionage. NWP

From Creature to Ghost. Pauline Hanson. TAP

From darkness/ I go onto the road/ of darkness. Lady Izumi Shikibu, *tr. fr. Japanese.* BoWoP, *tr.* by Willis Barnstone
(From darkness/ Into the path of darkness.) PBWP, *tr.* by Edwin A. Cranston

From darkness/ Into the path of darkness. Lady Izumi Shikibu. *See* From darkness/ I go onto the road/ of darkness.

From dawn till now that it is growing dusk. Robert Browning. *Fr.* Ring and the Book, The. EBVVPR

From dawn to dark, and back from dark to dawn. Hedylos, *tr. fr. Greek* by William Moebius. GrAn

From dawn to dark they stood. "Our Left." Francis Orrery Ticknor. PAH

From death to life thou might'st him yet recover. (*LL*) Since There's No Help, Come Let Us Kiss and Part. Michael Drayton. AAS; AWP; BoLoP; ClHu; ElL; EnLoPo; ESo; GBL; HAP; HelP; InPS; JCP; NAEL-1; NOBE; NoP; OAEL-1; PoEL-2; PrIm; SCGP; Son; SoSe; TEP; TFi; TrGrPo

From Death's Point of View. Duo Duo, *tr. fr. Chinese* by Donald Finkel *with* Li Guohua. SpMi

From deep sleep. Nightmare. James A. Emanuel. BPo

From Deepest Need. Quirinus Kuhlmann, *tr. fr. German* by George C. Schoolfield. GePo

From deepest need cry out, oh hungered heart! From Deepest Need. Quirinus Kuhlmann, *tr. fr. German* by George C. Schoolfield. GePo

From depth of dole wherein my soul doth dwell. George Gascoigne. *Fr.* De Profundis. ChIV-1

From depths of green unknown. *(LL)* The Creek. W. W. Eustace Ross. MoCV

From Depths of Woe I Cry to You. Martin Luther, *tr. fr. German by* F. Samuel Janow. GePo

From distant grove I hear the occasional knell of a monastery bell. Inscribed on the Painting of "Garden for Retirement": Pavilion of Sincerity, on Rocky Mountain. Chu Yi-tsun, *tr. fr. Chinese by* Chang Yin-nan *and* Lewis C. Walmsley. SuSp

From Drogheda all along the coast, the Irish sea. Back to Dublin. R. A. D. Ford. MoCV

From dusk till dawn the livelong night. Betsy's Battle Flag. Minna Irving. PAH

From dusk to dawn I sit under the canopy of a pine. In the Country. Ssu-k'ung Shu, *tr. fr. Chinese by* Hellmut Wilhelm. SuSp

From Eastertide to Eastertide. A Ballad of a Nun. John Davidson. BeLS; MeMBP; MoBrPo; UV, *sh. vers.*

From Emily Dickinson in Southern California. X. J. Kennedy. NBLV

From End to End. J. H. Prynne. VaA

From every cabin. *(LL)* Ark. Gu Cheng. SpMi

From Exile. Dafydd Benfras, *tr. fr. Welsh by* Anthony Conran. OBWVE

From fair Jamaica's fertile plains. Ada. BlSi

From Fairest Creatures. Shakespeare. *Fr.* Sonnets. CTC; HeIP; ImPo; LiTB; TrGrPo

From fairest creatures we desire increase. From Fairest Creatures. Shakespeare. *Fr.* Sonnets. CTC; HeIP; ImPo; LiTB; TrGrPo

From famous Banbury fair. *(LL)* As I was going to Banbury. *Unknown.* OxNR

From Far Away. Delmira Agustini, *tr. fr. Spanish by* D. M. Pettinella. PBWP

From Far Away. William Morris. OHIP

From far away we come to you. From Far Away. William Morris. OHIP

From Far, from Eve and Morning. A. E. Housman. *Fr.* Shropshire Lad, A. CMoP; FaPoB; HAP; MoBrPo; PoEL-5; PrIm

From Father to Son. Emyr Humphreys. AngWe; OBWVE

From fealty to light. *(LL)* The Enthusiast. Herman Melville. ChIV-1; NAAL-1

From fear to fear, successively betrayed. Reflection from Rochester. William Empson. PoA

From Feathers to Iron, *sels.* C. Day Lewis.
  Now She Is like the White Tree-Rose. CMoP; FaBoTw; MoBrPo
  Though Bodies Are Apart. NAs

From first light we fear falling. Hotel Fire: New Orleans. Paul Ruffin. InPK

From Florrie Abraham Witness, December 1972. Jack A. Mapanje. HBAPE

From forth th' Elisian Fields. Mad Maudlin is Come. *Unknown.* CBNP

From France, desponding and betray'd. On the British Invasion. Philip Freneau. PAH

From frozen climes, and endless tracks [*or* tracts] of snow. A Winter-Piece. Ambrose Philips. NOEC; OBTV

From garden to garden, ridge to ridge. John Muir. RFM

From Generation to Generation. Sir Henry Newbolt. FaBoTw

From German lips into my English ear. *(LL)* Dreams in German. "David Martin." NOBAu

From ghoulies and ghosties. *Unknown.* (Things That Go Bump in the Night.) NTCP

From Gloucester Out. Edward Dorn. NOBA; PoM

From Gloucester out. *(LL)* From Gloucester Out. Edward Dorn. NOBA; PoM

From gorge to gorge. Elena Clementelli, *tr. fr. Italian by* Ruth Feldman *and* Brian Swann. *Fr.* Etruscan Notebook. PBWP

From Government Buildings. Denis Devlin. IPY

From grass-stained eggs we bred eight. Six Filled the Woodshed with Soft Cries. Maura Dooley. PWE

From green and blue things and arguments that cannot be proven. *(LL)* Canal Bank Walk. Patrick Kavanagh. CIP; CMoP; FaBoTw; IPY; MoBrPo; NoAM

From Greenland's Icy Mountains. Reginald Heber. AnAmPo; FaPoR; PlP; WGRP

From Grenoble. James Elroy Flecker. OBTV

From grief and groan, to a golden throne, beside the King of Heaven. *(LL)* Lenore. Poe. AmPP; AnAmPo; LiTA

From groves of spice. Sarojini Naidu [*or* Nayadu]. FaPON (Hindu Cradle Song.) BoTP

From Halifax station a bully there came. Halifax Station. *Unknown.* PAH

From Harvest to January. Charles Tennyson Turner. NOBVV

From having done nothing up to now. Reality. Léon Damas, *tr. fr. French by* Ellen Conroy Kennedy. NegPo

From heart through mind into image. The Past. William Oandasan. BCF (Words of Tayko-mol.) HATNAP

From Heart to Heart. William Channing Gannett. AH

From Heaven Above to Earth I Come. Martin Luther, *tr. fr. German.* GePo

From Heaven High I Come to You. *At. to* Martin Luther, *tr. fr. German.* PChr

From Heaven's Gate to Hampstead Heath. The Ballad of Hampstead Heath. James Elroy Flecker. MoBrPo

From heavy dreams fair Helen rose. William and Helen. Sir Walter Scott. EnRP

From hence began that Plot, the nation's curse. Dryden. *Fr.* Absalom and Achitophel, Pt. I. FaBoEH; NoP; OAEL-1; SeCV-2

From her bed's high and odoriferous roome. Homer, *tr. by* George Chapman. *Fr.* Odyssey. CTC; NAWM-1

From her grave. Gillian Eve Hanscombe. *Fr.* Five Lovesick Poems. AIW

From her leafy balcony my sweetheart. On the Leafy Balcony. Paul Johann Ludwig Heyse, *tr. fr. German by* Philip L. Miller. RiWo

From her lustral face. *(LL)* Lightly stepped a yellow star. Emily Dickinson. MoAmPo; MoShBr; OxBA; SAmP

From Heraclitus. Alan Dugan. PoA

From here, the quay, one looks above to mark. The Harbour Bridge. Thomas Hardy. NoAM

From here through tunnelled gloom the track. The Railway Junction. Walter de la Mare. OxBTC

From here to the frontiers of this world. The Panther. *Unknown, tr. fr. Anglo-Saxon by* Kevin Crossley-Holland. ASW

From here to there/ To Washington Square. *Unknown.* OxNR

From his brimstone bed at break of day. The Devil's Thoughts. Robert Southey *and* Samuel Taylor Coleridge. CBNP; CoGr, *abr.*; FaBoCo, *abr.*; IHNG, *abr.*; OBSV; OxBoLi, *abr.*; PeLV, *abr.*

From his cradle in the glamourie. Peak and Puke. Walter de la Mare. Mes

From his garden bed our Lord. The Harvesting of the Roses. Menahem ben Jacob, *tr. fr. Hebrew.* TrJP

From his heavenly Father, our Fortress and Strength. *(LL)* The Wanderer. *Unknown.* AnOE; NAWM-1; OAEL-1

From his library in Surrey. Nothing Sacred. Roger Woddis. NOBL

From his mouth he takes out. The Night Game of the Maker of Faces. Novica Tadic, *tr. fr. Serbo-Croatian by* Charles Simic. HSix

From his own solitude to the world unheeding. Llewelyn Wyn Griffith. *Fr.* Barren Tree, The. OBWVE

From his shoulder Hiawatha. Hiawatha's Photographing. "Lewis Carroll." BXAP; FaBoCo; FaBoPa; FiBHP; NOBL; NoLV

From his small city Columbus. Voyage. Josephine Miles. LiTM

From his wanderings far to eastward. Longfellow. *Fr.* Song of Hiawatha, The. GOA

From hollows of a tree. Fable of the Speckled Cow. D. J. Opperman, *tr. fr. Afrikaans by* Jack Cope, Uys Krige, *and* Ruth Miller. PeSA

From holy flower to holy flower. The Study of a Spider. Lord De Tabley. NOBVV

From Holy, Holy, Holy ones. The Lancashire Puritane. *Unknown.* CoMu

From honey-dew of milking. Feeding a Child. Nuala Ni Dhomhnaill, *tr. fr. Irish by* Michael Hartnett. CIP

From horizon to horizon: Abel and flocks. *(LL)* Shepherd. Avraham Shlonsky. MHP

From house to house he goes. *Unknown.* BoTP

From inland ledges I had dreamed this bay. At the Battery Sea-Wall. Clifford James Laube. GoYe

From inside the bird a dream hums itself out and turns. These Horses Came. Ray A. Young Bear. CDW

From its dancers circulates among the other/dancers. The Dance. Robert Duncan. NeAP

From its fair face, shall bid our spirits fly. *(LL)* To My Brothers. Keats. NAs; Son; TEP

From its mouth. *(LL)* Dream Garden. Gu Cheng. SpMi

From itself never turning. *(LL)* As You Came from the Holy Land [of Walsingham]. *Unknown, sometimes at. to* Sir Walter Ralegh. AAS; ChTr; EIL; EnLoPo; GBL; HAP; InPS; NoP; NoSic; NTP; OBEV; PoEL-2; PrIm; RB; SiPSBD; TFi; TrGrPo

From joy I part still living in annoy. *(LL)* To Mary: It Is the Evening Hour. John Clare. BoLoP; ChTr; GBL; Mes

From keel to fighting top, I love. Manila Bay. Arthur Hale. PAH

From left to right, she leads the eye. Myth on Mediterranean Beach: Aphrodite as Logos. Robert Penn Warren. HAP

From Lewis, Monsieur Gérard came. Yankee Doodle's Expedition to Rhode Island. *Unknown.* PAH

From Life to Love. Countee Cullen. ChIV-1

From life's grim nightmare he is now released. Jacob Epstein. *Unknown.* FaBoCo

From Lois in London. Angela McCabe. AmPA

From low to high doth dissolution climb. Mutability. Wordsworth. *Fr.* Ecclesiastical Sonnets. EBEV; EnRP; HeIP; InPK; LiTB; MeMBP; NOBE; NoP; OAEL-2; OBEV; PoEL-4; PrIm

From Lucy: Holiday Reflections. James Berry. PBCV

From Malay. David Shapiro. UL

From Manhattan, a glittering shambles. My Cousin Muriel. Amy Clampitt. BAP-90

From many a field with patriot blood imbrued. Decoration Day. George Hurlbut Barbour. OHIP

From Many a Mangled Truth a War is Won. Clifford Dyment. PAW

From March 1979. Tomas Tranströmer, *tr. fr. Swedish by* Robin Fulton. PWE

From marrying in haste, and repenting at leisure. A New Litany, Occasioned by an Invitation to a Wedding. Elizabeth Thomas. ECWP

From masons laying up brick. Mason's Trick. James Hayford. InPK

From Matlock Bath's half-timbered station. Matlock Bath. Sir John Betjeman. NYBP

From me, who whilom sung the town. A Ballad to Mrs. Catherine Fleming in London from Malshanger Farm in Hampshire. The Countess of Winchilsea. ECWP

From mental mists to purge a nation's eyes. George Canning *and* John Hookham Frere. *Fr.* New Morality. NOEC

From millions whose hands can turn this rock into children. *(LL)* Laurentian Shield. F. R. Scott. NOBC

From Minneapolis and Rio, from Sidney and Hendon South. Evolution. Peter Porter. OBD

From Miss Biddy Fudge to Miss Dorothy ———. Thomas Moore. *Fr.* Fudge Family in Paris, The. PeLV

From Mobberley on a bright morning, on a snow-white pure-bred mare. The Wizard of Alderley Edge. Peter Coe. OBET

From moccasins to shoes. First Grade. Phillip William George. VoR

From Molepolole and Morogoro. Reflexions on the Seizure of the Suez, and on a Proposal to Line the Banks of That Canal with Bill. Howard Nemerov. NBLV

From Montauk Point. Walt Whitman. RFM

From Monte Pincio. Bjøornstjerne Bjøornson, *tr. fr. Norwegian by* Philip L. Miller. RiWo

From moonwater, from mirror mist, a slender porcelain. Gift Hour. Maria Banus, *tr. fr. Romanian by* Willis Barnstone *and* Matei Calinescu. BoWoP

From morn to [*or* till] midnight, all day through. Expectans Expectavi. Charles Hamilton Sorley. FaBoCh; WGRP

From mortal gratitude, decide, my Pope. Andrew Lang. *Fr.* Epistle to Mr. Alexander Pope. EPCY

From Mt. Arima/ over the bamboo plains of Ina. Daini no Sanmi, *tr. fr. Japanese by* Kenneth Rexroth *and* Ikuko Atsumi. WPJ

From My Arm-Chair. Longfellow. BLPA

From My Diary, July 1914. Wilfred Owen. FaBoMo; LiTM; MeMBP; MoAB; MoBrPo

From my disease's danger, and from thee. *(LL)* To Doctor Empiric[k]. Ben Jonson. FaBoEE; NoP; SeCP

From my favorite place in the Chung-nan Mountains. Oxhead Temple. Ssu-k'ung Shu, *tr. fr. Chinese by* Hellmut Wilhelm. SuSp

From my front wheels the scared rabbits. Iowa, June. Michael Dennis Browne. AmPA

From my heart. *(LL)* My help is in the mountain. Nancy Wood. EaPr

From My High Love. Kenneth Patchen. MoAmPo

From my high window I can watch. Winter in Minneapolis. Richard Ryan. PBCIP

From my mind beyond the lightning's flash. Far from Home. Joseph Freiherr von Eichendorff, *tr. fr. German by* Philip L. Miller. RiWo

From My Lai the Thunder Went West. Richard Ryan. CIP

From my lyre within the sky. *(LL)* Israfel. Poe. AmPP; AWP; BLPL; ImPo; LiTA; MeMAP; NAAL-1; NOBA; PoE; PoEL-4; TAP

From my mother's sleep I fell into the State. The Death of the Ball Turret Gunner. Randall Jarrell. ArOW; CAPP; ClHu; CMoP; FF; HAP; HeIP; HoPM; InPK; LCAP; LiTM; MoAmPo; MT; NAAL-2; NAs; NIP; NoAM; NOBA; NoP; OBD; OBWP; OxBA; PoE; PoWW; PPP; PrIm; RB; SoSe; TAP; TFi; UnPO; VCAP; VGW

From my personal album. For Malcolm X. Nanina Alba. PoBA

From My Rural Pen. T. S. Watt. FiBHP

From my tears spring up. Heine. RiWo

From My Thought. Daniel Smythe. GoYe

From My Window. Mary Elizabeth Coleridge. OBNC

From My Window. C. K. Williams. CAPP; PRA; SV

From my years young in dayes of youth. Epitaphium Meum. William Bradford. SCAP

From my youth up I never liked the city. I Return to the Place I Was Born. T'ao Ch'ien, *tr. fr. Chinese by* Kenneth Rexroth. OHMPC

From Mythology. Zbigniew Herbert, *tr. fr. Polish by* Czeslaw Milosz. FaBoPV

From narrow provinces. The Moose. Elizabeth Bishop. DiPo; FaBoWP; NAAL-2; NALW

From near the sea, like Whitman my great predecessor, I call. Ode: Salute to the French Negro Poets. Frank O'Hara. GLP; NeAP; NNaP; PoM; PoNe

From newspapers and clocks and stuffy trains. Voyage. Suzanne Gardinier. BAP-89

From noise of scare-fires rest ye free. The Bellman. Robert Herrick. CaPo; CH

From non-being into being: the cloud peaks gather. Sent to a Ch'an Master. Han Wo, *tr. fr. Chinese by* Irving Y. Lo. SuSp

From now on kill America out of your mind. James Agee. GOA

From Number Nine, Penwiper Mews. Edward Gorey. PeLi

From Oberon, in fairy land. Robin Goodfellow. *Unknown.* FaBoCh

From One of Case's Pill-Boxes. John Case. FaBoUs

From one of the cages on the periphery. The London Zoo. C. H. Sisson. IHNG

From one of the white throats which it hid among? *(LL)* Vision by Sweetwater. John Crowe Ransom. CMoP; FaBoMo; MeMAP; MoAB; NOBA; OxBA; RB

From one shaft at Cleator Moor. Cleator Moor. Norman Nicholson. FaBoTw

From One Who Stays. Amy Lowell. BoWoP; IMW

From opening some more tomorrow. *(LL)* Country House. Ch'u Ch'uang I. OHMPC

From Orford Ness to Shingle Street. Dawn on the East Coast. Alun Lewis. OBWP

From Our Album. Lawson Fusao Inada. AmPA

From our loves, heat and light are taught to twine. Mutual Love. William Hammond. JCP

From our low seat beside the fire. The Call. Charlotte Mew. CoGr

From Our Master. Whittier. *See* Immortal Love, Forever Full.

From out a book into my lap. A Withered Rose. "Yehoash," *tr. fr. Yiddish by* Isidore Goldstick. TrJP

From out Cologne there came three kings. The Three Kings. Eugene Field. GN

From out my deep, wide-bosomed West. Rejoice. Joaquin Miller. PAH

From out of a wood did a cuckoo fly. The Birds. *Unknown.* PChr

From out of the North-land his leaguer he led. Saint Leger. Clinton Scollard. PAH

From out of the waters it came with a moan. The Beast in Man. George Clutesi. HATNAP

From out the crowd of vanity and noise. A New Cantata. Clara Reeve. ECWP

From out the heart of Summer's joy. *(LL)* Pomona. William Morris. NOBVV; WiR

From out the lips of any tree. *(LL)* Be Different [*or* Deferent] to Trees. Mary Carolyn Davies. FaPON; OHIP

From out the South the genial breezes sigh. The Mother. *Unknown, tr. fr. Chinese by* George Barrow. OHIP

From out the stormy sea unto the shore. Azariah di Rossi, *tr. fr. Hebrew by* A. B. Rhine. TrJP

From Paumanok Starting I Fly like a Bird. Walt Whitman. GOA

From peace with the French and war with the Dutch. Lines Written in a Lincoln's Inn Boghouse. *Unknown.* FaBoEH

From Pent-up Aching Rivers. Walt Whitman. BoLoP; NAAL-1; NOBA

From Phylace, and from the flow'ry fields. Homer, *tr. fr. Greek by* William Cowper. *Fr.* Iliad, The. CBCK

From pitch and catch. Fungo. Stanley Plumly. AmPA

From plains that reel to southward, dim. Heat. Archibald Lampman. NOBC; NTP

From plane of light to plane, wings dipping through. Evening Hawk. Robert Penn Warren. NAAL-2; VCAP

From Plane to Plane. Robert Frost. MoAmPo

From pleasure of the bed. The Chambermaid's Second Song. W. B. Yeats. ErPo

From plum-tree and cherry. Flowering Currant. Patrick MacDonogh. ErPo

From Potomac to Merrimac. Edward Everett Hale. PAH

From prehistoric distance, beyond clocks. Street Fight. Harold Monro. FaBoTw

From Prison. Todros Ben Judah Abulafia, *tr. fr. Hebrew by* David Goldstein. TOF

From Prison. Osip Mandelstam. Spl

From public noise and factious strife. To a Young Gentlemen in Love; a Tale. Matthew Prior. TEP

Fugue. Constance Carrier. GoYe

Fugue. Howard Nemerov. TAP

Fugue of Death. Paul Celan. *See* Black milk of dawn [*or* daybreak] we drink it at dusk [*or* nightfall].

Führer Bunker, The, *sels.* W. D. Snodgrass.
Dr. Joseph Goebbels. CAPP
Eva Braun. CAPP

Führer wears a black mask, The. (*LL*) The New Dawn. Mafika Pascal Gwala. PeSAV

Fuimus Fumus. Joshua Sylvester. FaBoEE

Fulfill, O gracious God, to-day. Pentecost. Adelbert Sumpter Coats. TrPWD

Fulfillment. Helene Johnson. CDC; PoNe; ShDr

Fulfillment. William Augustus Mühlenberg. WGRP

Fulgurous Flash, A. Allen Grossman. *Fr.* Ether Dome (an Entertainment), The. BAP-91

Fulguruos flash! Le remède dans le mal, A. A Fulgurous Flash. Allen Grossman. *Fr.* Ether Dome (an Entertainment), The. BAP-91

Full, and filled-full, than when full-filled before. (*LL*) God's Mercy. Robert Herrick. BeJo

Full and True Account of a Horrid and Barbarous Robbery, A, *sels.* John Byrom.
"Dear Martin Folkes, dear scholar, brother, friend." NOBL

Full be the year, abundant be the grain. Ezra Pound, after the Chinese. OBVE

Full Circle. Maud Sulter. DT

Full Consciousness. Juan Ramón Jiménez, *tr. fr. Spanish by* Robert Bly. NU

Full Cycle. John White Chadwick. PAH

Full days come striding with measured, The. Concerning the Awakening of My Soul. Henriëtte Roland-Holst, *tr. fr. Dutch by* Jonathan Crewe. WPOW

Full early in the morning. *Unknown.* BoTP

Full Fathom Five. A. R. D. Fairburn. PeNZ

Full Fathom Five. Shakespeare. *Fr.* Tempest, The. AWP; ChTr; ClHu; EBEV; EIL; ELP; FaBoCh; HAP; HoPM; ImPo; InPK; InPS; LiTB; NAEL-1; NoP; NoSic; OAEL-1; OBEV; OxBSP; PoE; PoRA; TEP; TFi

Full fathom five thy father lies. June Mercer Langfield. FaBoPa; SCGP

Full fathom [*or* fadom] five thy father lies. Full Fathom Five. Shakespeare. *Fr.* Tempest, The. AWP; ChTr; ClHu; EBEV; EIL; ELP; FaBoCh; HAP; HoPM; ImPo; InPK; InPS; LiTB; NAEL-1; NoP; NoSic; OAEL-1; OBEV; OxBSP; PoE; PoRA; TEP; TFi
(Ariel's Dirge.) GoJo
(Ariel's Song: "Full fathom five thy father lies.") EBEvV; GN; NOBE; NOSC; NTP
(Sea Dirge, A.) GTBS; GTBS-P; TrGrPo
(Song: "Full fathom [*or* fadom] five thy father lies.") PoEL-2

Full hardly earneth Mat. his dinner. (*LL*) Earning a Dinner. Matthew Prior. NBLV

Full Heart, The. Robert Nichols. BoNaP

Full in her glory, she as Tirzah fair. The Prophet Jeremiah and the Personification of Israel. *At. to* Eleazar ben Kalir, *tr. fr. Hebrew by* Nina Davis Salaman. TrJP

Full in the hand, heavy. September Afternoon at Four O'Clock. Marge Piercy. NIP

Full many a dreary hour have I past. To My Brother George. Keats. EnRP

Full many a gem of purest ray serene. A "Prize" Poem. Shirley Brooks. FaBoCo; FaBoNo

Full many a glorious morning have I seen[e]. Shakespeare. *Fr.* Sonnets. AWP; EBEV; EBEvV; EIL; HAP; ImPo; InPS; NIP; NoP; NoSic; OAEL-1; OtMeF; OxAEP-1; PoRA; PPP; SCGP; Son; TEP; TFi; TrGrPo; WeW

Full many sing to me and thee. The Barren Shore. Coventry Patmore. GBL

Full Moon. Walter de la Mare. BoNaP

Full Moon. Robert Graves. NOBE

Full Moon. Robert Hayden. BPo

Full Moon. V. Sackville-West. MoShBr; NTP

Full Moon. Sappho, *tr. fr. Greek by* William Ellery Leonard. AWP

Full Moon. Elinor Wylie. MoAB; NALW

Full Moon and Little Frieda. Ted Hughes. NTP; OxBC; OxBSP

Full Moon at Tierz; before the Storming of Huesca. John Cornford. OBWP

Full moon drains me, The. These Nights. James Ulmer. UTF

Full moon easterly rising, furious, The. A Love Story. Robert Graves. CMoP; FaBoTw; LiTB; NAEL-2

Full Moon in Malta. "Asphodel." BrRo

Full moon is partly hidden by cloud, The. A Fable of the War. Howard Nemerov. ArOW; OBWP

Full moon is so fierce that I can count the, The. Europa. Derek Walcott. AnAn; NoP

Full moon on the Colosseum, The. Colosseum. Harold Norse. TrJP

Full moon. Our Narragansett gales subside. John Berryman. *Fr.* Dream Songs. CoAP

Full Moon, Rising. Jonathan Holden. GOYP

Full moon rising on the waters of my heart. Evening Song. Jean Toomer. BPo; CDC

Full Moon; Santa Barbara. Sara Teasdale. OBCA

Full moon shines across the lawn, The. Translation from a Lost Source. Richard Caddel. NBrP

Full moonlit night people. The Net of Moon. *Unknown, tr. fr. Pawnee Indian by* Jerome K. Rothenberg. STP

Full-nelsoned in earth's arms the Crusher sleeps. Last Lines on a Wrestler. X. J. Kennedy. CRP

Full night. The moon has yet to rise. Sodom. Herman Melville. *Fr.* Clarel. AmPP

Full nineteen centuries have passed since then. A Call to Pentecost. Inez M. Tyler. BLRP

Full of beauty, awaits our coming. (*LL*) Pleasant Reverie. Otto Julius Bierbaum. RiWo

Full of concrete caves. The Fifties. Wendy Rose. WoWa

Full of courage and promise like the geese gone away. The Prince Enters the Forest. Henri Cole. DiPo

Full of her long white arms and milky skin. The Equilibrists. John Crowe Ransom. CMoP; HAP; LiTM; MeMAP; MoAB; MoP; NAAL-2; NoAM; NOBA; OxBA; PPP; TAP

Full of old stories that still go walking in my sleep. (*LL*) South of My Days. Judith Wright. NoAM

Full of red marines. (*LL*) Here's the Tender Coming. *Unknown.* GBP

Full of sentiment, clever at mechanics, and we love our luxuries. (*LL*) Ave Caesar. Robinson Jeffers. FaBoPV; MoP; NoAM; NOBA; OxBA; OxBSP

Full of superstition. The New Notebook. Maria Banus, *tr. fr. Romanian by* Laura Schiff *and* Dana Beldiman. AIW; PBWP

Full of the Moon. Karla Kuskin. PDV

Full of years and seasoned like a salt timber. Islandman. Brenda Chamberlain. AngWe; OBWVE

Full oft doth Mat. with Topaz dine. Earning a Dinner. Matthew Prior. NBLV

Full oft of old the islands changed their name. Epitaph on an Infant. Crinagoras, *tr. fr. Greek by* John William Burgon. AWP

Full often as I rove by path or stile. Wind on the Corn. Charles Tennyson Turner. EBVV

Full, ripe apple, a pear and banana. Rainer Maria Rilke, *tr. by* Christopher Hawthorne. *Fr.* Sonnets to Orpheus. SOTW

Full September moon sheds floods of light, The. A September Night. George Marion McClellan. AAP

Full summer and at noon; from a waste bed. Noon. "Michael Field." NOBVV

Full Tide. Paraire Henare Tomoana, *tr. fr. Maori by* Margaret Orbell. PeNZ

Full Vision. H. Cordelia Ray. AmWP; CBWP-3

Full Well I Know. Hartley Coleridge. Son

Full well I know that she is there. Gertrude Stein. *Fr.* Stanzas in Meditation. PoA

Full well it may be seen. Sir Thomas Wyatt. SiPS

Full well, my gentle sir, I know. To an Artful Theatre Manager. Lorenzo da Ponte, *tr. fr. Italian by* John Mazzinghi. *Fr.* Capriccio Dramatico, Il. TrJP

Full year since, I took this eager city, A. An Irishman in Coventry. John Hewitt. BIrV; CIP; IIP; PNI

Fuller and Warren. *At. to* Moses Whitecotton. AmFP; BeLS

Fullfillment. Eunice Tietjens. *See* Lo, I have opened unto you the wide gates of my being.

Fullness of the Deity, The. (*LL*) The Night. Henry Vaughan. ChIV-2; EBEV; ESCV; GeHe; LiTB; MeLP; NAEL-1; NOBE; NOCV; NoP; OAEL-1; OBEV; OBWVE; OxAEP-1; PoEL-2; SCGP; SeCV-1; TFi; TOF

Fulvia, our Consul bids me thank thee: why. Familiar Poem from Nisa to Fulvia of the Vale. Ann Yearsley. ECWP

Fum and Hum, the Two Birds of Royalty. Thomas Moore. OBSV

Fumble the ropes of her long swinging beads. (*LL*) Nuns at Eve. John Malcolm Brinnin. MoAB; TwCP

Fumetti. Robert Long. NAmP90

Fun with Fishing. Eunice Tietjens. FaPON

Function of Blizzard. Robert Penn Warren. AnAn

Function Room, The. Patrice Phillips. MAT

Fundament Is Shifted, The. Abbie Huston Evans. NYBP

Future Verdict, The. Ada Cambridge. NOBAu

Future weighs down on me, The. The Blue Anchor. Jane Cooper. WoWa

Future Work. Fleur Adcock. DiPo

Fuzzy fellow without feet, A. Emily Dickinson. TAP

Fuzzy-Wuzzy. Kipling. MoBrPo; TrGrPo

Fuzzy Wuzzy. *Unknown.* PYC

Fuzzy Wuzzy was a bear. *Unknown.* NTCP; RoPo

Fy let us a to the bridal. The Blythsome Bridal. *At. to* Francis Sempill. GBP

Fyftene Joyes of Maryage, The, *sels. Unknown.* Disposing of a Pregnant Daughter. OxBLMV

Fyllr. Gavin Selerie. NBrP

G

G. Hilaire Belloc. FiBHP

G/ as/ tro/ nom/ ists/ remark. Fish Speaking Veneto Dialect. Judith Baumel. UTF

G. B. Shaw wrote to Yeats: "P'raps it's mad of me." W. A. Rathkey. PeLi

G. I. Graves in Tuscany. Richard Hugo. CAPP

G. K. Chesterton. Humbert Wolfe. TrJP

G. K. Chesterton on His Birth. A. E. Housman. FaBoNo; NBLV

G. M. B. Donald Davie. OxBC

G stands for Gnu, whose weapons of defence. Hilaire Belloc. FaBoNo

G. Wilson humbly as before. From the *Caledonian Mercury. Gavin Wilson.* FaBoUs

Gaa-a-Muna, a Mountain Flower. Harold Littlebird. VoR

Gaberlunzie Man, The. *Unknown.* EnSB; OxBB; OxBS

Gables are not burning, The. The Finnesburh Fragment. *Unknown, tr. fr. Anglo-Saxon by* Kevin Crossley-Holland. ASW; OBWP

Gabriel. Adrienne Rich. VGW

Gabriel, from Hevene-King. The Annunciation. *Unknown.* MeEL

Gabrielle, the terrapin, whose tiny eyes. The Terrapin. Elizabeth Smither. PeNZ

Gabriel's Appearance. Abraham Cowley. *Fr. Davideis.* NOSC

Gabriel's Blues. Calvin Forbes. PoA

Gaby at the U.N. Observation Post. Susan Tichy. BTR

Gadflies swarm on the weary horse. On Mount Ching. Meng Chiao, *tr. fr. Chinese by* A. C. Graham. PLT

Gaelic is the conscience of our leaders. Michael Hartnett. *Fr.* Farewell to English, A. CIP

Gaeltacht. Pearse Hutchinson. BIrV; PBCIP

Gaeta from wool and weaving first began. In Gaetam. Thomas Bastard. FaBoEE

Gaffer Gray. Thomas Holcroft. NOEC; OxAEP-1

Gaia's Alchemy: Ruin and Renewal of the Elements. Ralph Metzner. EaPr

Gaiety, *sels.* Richard Howard. Queer's Song. ErPo

Gaily bedight,/ A gallant knight. Eldorado. Poe. AmPP; AnAmPo; AWP; FaBoBe; FaBoCh; MeMAP; NOBA; NoP; NTP; OxBA; TAP; WiR

Gaily into Ruislip Gardens. Middlesex. Sir John Betjeman. OxBTC

Gaily they grow, the quiet throng. Heather Flowers. Eliseus Williams, *tr. fr. Welsh by* Kenneth Hurlstone Jackson. OBWVE

Gain without gladness. Liadain. *Unknown, tr. by* Frank O'Connor. PeIV; WPOW

Gal, I'm tellin you, I'm tired fo true. The Lament of the Banana Man. Evan Jones (b. 1927). PBCV

Sir Galahad [*or* The Purple Heart]. Tennyson. OHCV

Galahs. William Hart-Smith. OBAP

Galang dada/ galang gwaan yaw sah. Reggae fi Dada. Linton Kwesi Johnson. NBrP; PBCV

Galante Garden: I. Juan Ramón Jiménez, *tr. fr. Spanish by* H. R. Hays. ArLo

Galataea, *sels.* Callimachus, *tr. fr. Greek by* Barbara Hughes Fowler. "Or rather the sacred fish with the golden faces." HePo

Galathea, *sels.* John Lyly. Cupid's Indictment. EIL

Galatians 6.14. Francis Quarles. ChIV-2

Galaxies. Alan Gould. NOBAu

Gale in April. Robinson Jeffers. MoAB; MoAmPo

Gales. Anne Stevenson. Spl

Galicia Gypsy tongue sucks salt water. Geography of the Trinity Corona. Víctor Hernández Cruz. AfAz

Galilee Shore. Allen Ginsberg. ChIV-2

Gallant Château. Wallace Stevens. MoAB; MoAmPo

Gallant Fifty-one, The. Henry Lynden Flash. PAH

Gallant Fighting "Joe," The. James Stevenson. PAH

Gallant foeman in the fight, A. Robert E. Lee. Julia Ward Howe. PAH

Gallant frigate, *Amphitrite*, she lay in Plymouth Sound, The. Rounding the Horn. *Unknown.* OxBSS

Gallant Irish Yeoman, The. Oliver St. John Gogarty. FaBoBl

Gallant laird of Lamington, The. Katharine Jaffray. *Unknown.* ESPB, A, B, *and* C *vers.*

Gallant Ship, The. Sir Walter Scott. BoTP

Gallant Youth, who may have gained, The. Yarrow Revisited. Wordsworth. EnRP

Gallantry. Keith Douglas. NAEL-2; NoAM; OBWP

Gallants attend, and hear a friend. The Battle of the Kegs. Francis Hopkinson. AnAmPo; OBAL

(British Valor Displayed.) PAH

Gallants,/ If, as you say, you Love Varietie, "Ephelia." *Fr.* Pair-Royal of Coxcombs, The. KTR

Gallery. Duo Duo, *tr. fr. Chinese by* Donald Finkel *with* Li Guohua. SpMi

Gallery, The. Andrew Marvell. ESCV; MeLP; NoP; PoE

Gallery, The. Tomas Tranströmer, *tr. fr. Swedish by* Samuel Charters. AnAn

Gallery of My Heart. King D. Kuka. VoR

Gallery Shepherds. Patricia Beer. OxBC

Galley of Count Arnaldos, The. Longfellow. OBEV

Galley-Slave, The. Kipling. PeVV

Galliass, The. Walter de la Mare. FaBoTw

Gallio's Song. Kipling. ChIV-2

Gallipoli, *sels. Unknown.* Song of Blood, A. NSI

Gallipoli. Mary Morison Webster. NSI

Gallon of gin and a flitch of pork, A. Obsequy for Dylan Thomas. James K. Baxter. PeLV

Gallop a dreary dun. (*LL*) Master and Man. Mother Goose. OxNR; ReMoGo

Gallop apace, you fiery-footed steeds[*or* fierie footed steades]. Shakespeare. *Fr.* Romeo and Juliet. CBLP; EBEvV; GBL

Galloping Cat, The. Stevie Smith. BrRo; CoGr; OFC

Galloping collection of boards, The. Somewhere. Robert Creeley. NoAM

Gallops about doing good. (*LL*) The Galloping Cat. Stevie Smith. BrRo; CoGr; OFC

Gallow Hill. William J. Tait. OxBS

Gallows, The. Edward Thomas. FM; InPS; LiTB; MoAB; MoBrPo; MoP; NoAM; SCGP; UnPo

Gallows in my garden, people say, The. A Ballade of Suicide. G. K. Chesterton. CoGr; FiBHP; NBLV

Galoshes. Rhoda Warner Bacmeister. NTCP; SiSoPo

Galveston with a seawall. Wasn't That a Mighty Storm? *Unknown.* AmFP

Galway is a blackguard place. Clonakilty. *Unknown.* FaBoEE

Galway Races. *Unknown.* OxBoLi

Gamarra is a dainty steed. "Blood Horse," The. "Barry Cornwall." GN

Gambit. Tony Curtis. AngWe

Gamble. Linda Hogan. HATNAP

Gambler, The. *Unknown.* AmFP

Gamblers, The. Ai Ch'ing, *tr. fr. Chinese.* LHF, *tr. by* Hualing Nieh

Gamblers, The. Anthony Delius. PeSA

Gambler's life I do admire, du-da, du-da. The Gambler. *Unknown.* AmFP

Gamblers lose it/ I could use it. (*LL*) Money. Richard Armour. NBLV

Gambling. Vince Gotera. OpBo

Gambling. Royall Tyler. TAP

Gamboling Man, The. *Unknown.* AS

Game, The. Edvard Kocbek, *tr. fr. Slovene by* Michael Scammell *and* Veno Taufer. PoSu

Game after Supper. Margaret Atwood. FaBoWP; LCAP

Game at Salzburg, A. Randall Jarrell. NoAM

Game called kick the can, which used to last about a month, A. We Used to Play. Don Welch. Poetsp

Game of Chance, A. Howard Moss. PoA

Game of Chess, A. T. S. Eliot. *Fr.* Waste Land, The. AmPP; CMoP; FaBoMo; HAP; LiTA; LiTM; MoAB; MoAmPo; NAWM-2; NoAM; NOBA; NOBE; NoP; OAEL-2; OxBA; OxBTC; SCV; TAP; UnPo

Game of Consequences, A. Paul Dehn. ErPo; FiBHP; NOBL

Game of Cricket, The. Hilaire Belloc. FiBHP

Game of Life, The. John Godfrey Saxe. BLPA; BLPL

Game on the Fingers, A. *Unknown.* CBNP

Game out of Hand. Allison Ross. GoYe

Game Resumed. Richmond Lattimore. NYBP

Gamecock. James Dickey. HoPM; UnPo

Gamekeeper of Lady Chatterley, The. Gerry Hamill. PeLi

Games. Sandra McPherson. LCAP

Games. Vasco [*or* Vasko] Popa, *tr. fr. Serbo-Croatian by* Anne
Pennington. RB
Sels.
Ashes.
(Some are nights the others ashes.) HSix, *tr. by* Charles Simic
Before Play.
He. CBNP; PoSu
Hide-and-Seek. HSix
Hunter. HSix, *tr. by* Charles Simic
Nail, The. PoSu
Rose Thieves, The.
(Someone is a rose bush.) HSix
Seed, The. PoSu

Gammer Gurton's Needle, *sels. At. to* William Stevenson *and also to* John
Still.
Back and Side Go Bare, Go Bare. HeIP; InvP; LiTB; NAEL-1
(Drinking Song.) WiR, *tr. by* John Still
(In Praise of Ale.) TrGrPo, *at. to* John Still
(Of Jolly Good Ale and Old.) EIL
(Song of Ale, A.) SCGP
Jolly Good Ale and Old. GGP

Gampta, my little grey sister. The Desert Lark. Eugène Marias, *tr. fr.*
Afrikaans by Uys Krige *and* Jack Cope. PeSA

Gane were but the winter cauld. Gone Were but the Winter Cold. Allan
Cunningham. CH

Gang-Bang, Ulster Style. Linda Anderson. WoWa

Gang doun wi a sang, gang doun. (*LL*) Whaur yon broken brig hings
owre. William Soutar. OxBS

Gang of labourers on the piled wet timber, A. Morning Work. D. H.
Lawrence. MoAB; MoBrPo

Gang wanted to give Oedipus Rex a going away present, The. Oedipus.
Josephine Miles. SoSe; WPE

Ganga. Thomas Blackburn. MoBS

Ganges, The. Norman Dubie. LCAP

Gangrel Rymour and the Pairdon of Sanct Anne, The, *sels.* Sydney Goodsir
Smith, *after the French of* Tristan Corbiére.
"But ae braithless note." OBVE

Gangrene. Philip Levine. VGW

Gangster's Death, The. Ishmael Reed. PoBA

Gangue. Edward Kleinschmidt. BAP-90

Ganymede. Goethe, *tr. fr. German by* Philip L. Miller. RiWo

Ganymede. William Plomer. PeHV

Ganymede and Helen. Unknown, *tr. fr. Latin.* PeHV

Gaol Song, The. Unknown. GBP

Gap between the Sunday papers and lunch, The. (*LL*) Against Coupling.
Fleur Adcock. CBLP; FaBoBl; NALW

Gap in the Cedar, The. Roy Scheele. Poetsp; SM

Gape on, as they do to be paid, gape on! (*LL*) A Parley with His Empty
Purse. Thomas Randolph. JCP

Garage in Co. Cork, A. Derek Mahon. DiPo; PBCIP

Garage Sale. Karl Shapiro. Poetsp

García Lorca. Louis Dudek. MoCV; NOBC

García Lorca: A Photograph of the Granada Cemetery, 1966. Larry Levis.
AnAn

Garcia Lorca Murdered in Granada. John Manifold. CBAP

Garden, The. Joseph Beaumont. JCP; NOSC

Garden, The, *sels.* Abraham Cowley.
Great Diocletian. ChTr

Garden, The. William Cowper. *Fr.* Task, The. EnRP; FaBoRV; NAEL-1;
PoE

Garden. Hilda Doolittle ("H. D."). LiTA; NoAM

Garden, The. Emma Catherine Embury. AmWP

Garden, The. Louise Glück. AmPA; HCAP; NAAL-2; VCAP

Garden, The. Nicholas Grimald. OAEL-1

Garden. Brooks Haxton. BAP-91

Garden, The, *sels.* Andrew Marvell.
What Wondrous Life Is This I Lead! ArNa

Garden, The. Andrew Marvell. AWP; BLPL; ClHu; ESCV; GeHe; HAP;
ImPo; InPS; InvP; JCP; LiTB; MeLP; NAEL-1; NIP; NOBE; NoP;
NOSC; OAEL-1; PoE; PoEL-2; Poetr; PoLF; PoRA; PPP; SCGP; SeCP;
SeCV-1; TEP; TFi; TOF; TrGrPo; TRP

Garden, The. Rose Parkwood. WGRP

Garden, The. Ezra Pound. AWP; HeIP; LiTA; MoAB; MoAmPo; NIP;
NoP; OxBSP; PPP; SOTW; TwCP

Garden, The. Jacques Prévert, *tr. fr. French by* Harriet Zinnes. ArLo

Garden, The. James Shirley. BeJo; NOSC

Garden, The. Mark Strand. CAPP; NoAM

Garden, The. Jones Very. OxBA; TAP

Garden, The. Robert Penn Warren. PoA

Garden, The. Oscar Wilde. *See* Lily's withered chalice falls, The.

Garden, The, *sels.* William Carlos Williams.
Mental Hospital Garden, The. CRP; FYAP

Garden, The. Judith Wright. FaBoMA

Garden, The. (You are clear,/ O rose, cut in rock.) Hilda Doolittle ("H.
D."). LiTA; NoAM
Sels.
Heat. ArNa; CMoP; HeIL; HeIP; InPK; MoAmPo; OxBA; PrIm; TAP;
TRP; UnPo

Garden, A. Andrew Marvell. *See* See how the flowers, as at parade.

Garden Abstract. Hart Crane. MeMAP

Garden and gardener He made. Thomas Kinsella. TIRV

Garden at Heidelberg. Walter Savage Landor. OBTV

Garden by the Sea, A. William Morris. *Fr.* Life and Death of Jason,
The. CH; EBEvV; NOBE; OAEL-2; OBNC; PlP; PoEL-5

Garden Calendar. N. M. Bodecker. TLR

Garden called Gethsemane, The. Gethsemane. Kipling. FaBoTw; PeFWW

Garden clenched like a root, bare branches, The. The Veil Poem. Andrew
Crozier. VaA

Garden Fancies, *sels.* Robert Browning.
Flower's Name, The. CTC
Sibrandus Schafnaburgensis. CTC; EBVV; TEP

Garden flew round with the angel, The. The Pleasures of Merely
Circulating. Wallace Stevens. LiTA; MAT; OBAL

Garden Hose, The. Beatrice Janosco. NTCP

Garden, The ("How vainly men themselves amaze.") Andrew Marvell.
AWP; BLPL; HAP; InPS; InvP; JCP; LiTB; MeLP; NIP; NOBE; NoP;
OAEL-1; PoEL-2; PoLF; PoRA; PPP; SeCP; SeCV-1; TEP; TrGrPo
Sels.
"What wondrous life is this I lead!" BoNaP; CH; ChTr

Garden in a garden; a green spot, A. On Keats, 18 January, 1948 (Eve of
St Agnes). Christina Rossetti. EPCY

Garden in the middle of a hundred acres is half-covered with moss, The.
Tune: "Sand of Silk-washing Stream." Wang An-shih, *tr. fr. Chinese*
by James J. Y. Liu. SuSp

Garden is a loathsome thing, God wot, A. My Garden. P. R. Hines. UV

Garden is a lovesome thing, God wot!, A. My Garden. Thomas Edward
Brown. BLPL; EBEvV; FaBV; InPK; OBEV; PoLF; UV; WBLP;
WGRP

Garden is a lovesome thing? What rot!, A. My Garden. J. A. Lindon.
InPK

Garden is rich with diversity, The. Unknown, *tr. fr. Chinook Indian.* EaPr

Garden-Lion. Mary Ursula Bethell. ArNa; ChTr

Garden Lore. Juliana Horatia Ewing. OxBChV

Garden of a Child, The. Nirendranath Chakravarti, *tr. fr. Hindi.* TSaS, *tr.*
by Chakravarti Nirendranath

Garden of Adonis, The. Spenser. *Fr.* Faerie Queene, The. NOBE; PoEL-1

Garden of Amour, The. Guillaume de Lorris *and* Jean de Meun, *tr. by*
Chaucer. *Fr.* Romance [*or* Romaunt] of the Rose, The. PoEL-1

Garden of Appleton House, The ("When in the east the morning ray.")
Andrew Marvell. *Fr.* Upon Appleton House, to My Lord Fairfax.
NOBE; SeCP; SeCV-1

Garden of Cymodoce, The, *sels.* Swinburne.
Sark. FaBoPP

Garden of Earthly Delights, The. Charles Simic. NoP

Garden of God, The. "Æ." WGRP

Garden of Love, The. Blake. *Fr.* Songs of Experience. AWP; EnLoPo;
EnRP; FaBV; FHYEP; GBL; HAP; LiTB; MAT; NAEL-2; NoP;
OxAEP-2; PoE; RB; SCGP; TEP; TFi; TOF; TRP

Garden of mouthings, A. Purple, scarlet-speckled, black. The Beekeeper's
Daughter. Sylvia Plath. IHMS

Garden of my grandfather, The. (*LL*) Call. Sebastian Barry. IB

Garden of my soul grows duller, The. The Unfading. "Marie Madelaine,"
tr. fr. German by Ferdinand E. Kappey. PeHV

Garden of Proserpina, The. Spenser. *Fr.* Faerie Queene, The. ChTr

Garden of Proserpine, The. Veronica Forrest-Thomson. VaA

Garden of Proserpine, The. Swinburne. AWP; BLPA; BLPL; FaBoRV;
FaBV; FaPoR; HAP; LiTB; NAEL-2; NOBE; NOBVV; NoP; OBNC;
PoE; PoEL-5; PoRA; SCV; TrGrPo
Sels.
"From too much love of living." IMW; OBD
Garden of Proserpine, The. PeVV; PlP; TFi
Proserpine. ChTr
Swan Song. OtMeF

Garden of Proserpine, The. Swinburne. *Fr.* Garden of Proserpine, The.
AWP; BLPA; BLPL; FaBoRV; FaBV; FaPoR; HAP; LiTB; NAEL-2;
NOBE; NOBVV; NoP; OBNC; PeVV; PlP; PoE; PoEL-5; PoRA; SCV;
TFi; TrGrPo

Garden of Self-Delight, The. Tom Paulin. SCBI

Garden of Shadow, The. Ernest Dowson. OBNC

Gate Lodge. Richard Murphy. PBCIP

Gate of Horn. William Rose Benét. AnAmPo

Gate, red lights revolving in the leaves. (LL) First Party at Ken Kesey's with Hell's Angels. Allen Ginsberg. PoBeRe; TRP

Gate Tower of Ch'i-an City, The. Tu Mu, tr. fr. Chinese by A. C. Graham. PLT

Gate was open, The; the fence under the aspens, fallen. Mountain Corral. Helen Sorrells. WPE

Gateposts. Medbh McGuckian. BiHa; PBCIP

Gates are open on the road, The. The Seekers. Charles Hamilton Sorley. WGRP

Gates clanged and they walked you into jail, The. The Conscientious Objector. Karl Shapiro. OxBA

Gates fly open with a pretty sound, The. Under the Hill. Daryl Hine. MoCV

Gates of Paradise, The, sels. Blake. see For the Sexes: the Gates of Paradise, sels.

Gate's Open, The. John Blight. CBAP

Gates to England, The. Marjorie Wilson. BoTP

Gateshead Grammar. George Charlton. PWE

Gateway, The. A. D. Hope. BoLoP; ErPo; FaBoMA

Gather for festival. Hilda Doolittle ("H. D."). Fr. Songs from Cyprus. MoAmPo

Gather into the mind. First of August. A. J. Seymour. PBCV

Gather or take fierce degree. A Short Poem for Armistice Day. Sir Herbert Read. PeFWW

Gather Paradise, To. (LL) I dwell in possibility. Emily Dickinson. EnlH; HeIP; NALW; NAWM-2; NoAM; NOBA; OxBA; Poetr

Gather the Rose. Spenser. See Whiles someone did chant this lovely lay, The.

Gather while you may. Rose. Kathleen Raine. WPE

Gather ye bank-notes while ye may. Election Time. Unknown. FaBoPa; UV

Gather, ye brave sons of Ukadi Awaka! Moon Song. Chuba Nweke. PBA

Gather Ye Rosebuds. Laurence Fowler. BXAP

Gather ye rosebuds, while ye may. To [the] Virgins, to Make Much of Time. Robert Herrick. AWP; BeJo; BLPA; BoLoP; CaPo; ChTr; ClHu; CoGr; EBEvV; ELP; EnLoPo; ErPo; FaBV; FF; GBL; HAP; HeIP; ImPo; InPK; InPS; JCP; LiTB; NAEL-1; NBLV; NIP; NOBE; NoP; NOSC; OAEL-1; OBEV; OxAEP-1; PoE; PoEL-3; Poetr; PrIm; SCGP; SCV; SeCP; SeCV-1; SoSe; TEP; TFi; TrGrPo; UV (Counsel to Girls.) GTBS; GTBS-P

Gathered and howling in the heat of the sun. (LL) This Place Rumord to Have Been Sodom. Robert Duncan. NeAP; NOBA; PoM; PPP

Gathered at the River. Denise Levertov. CrSp; SV

Gathered in inter-admiration. When the Five Prominent Poets. Josephine Jacobsen. TAP

Gathered on Oaxaca's. Coyote Sun. Carlos Cumpian. AfAz

Gatherer, The. Ali Al-Mak, tr. fr. Arabic by Al-Fatih Mahjoub and Constance E. Berkeley. TSaS

Gathering, The. E. J. Pratt. Fr. Towards the Last Spike. MoCV

Gathering, The. Sir Walter Scott. Fr. Lady of the Lake, The. OBNC

Gathering, The. Herbert B. Swett. PAH

Gathering fruit while the rain holds off? (LL) To a Child. Aidan Carl Mathews. IB

Gathering Leaves. Robert Frost. RB; VGW

Gathering Lotus. Chu Ch'ing-yu, tr. fr. Chinese by Irving Y. Lo. SuSp

Gathering Mushrooms. Paul Muldoon. BiHa; CIP; PBCIP; PNI

Gathering of the Grand Army, The. Charlotte L. Forten Grimke. AAP

Gathering of Waves, The. Thomas McCarthy. IB

Gathering Place, The. Alan Alexander. NOBAu

Gathering Song of Donald the Black. Sir Walter Scott. See Pibroch of Donuil Dhu.

Gathering Song of Donuil Dhu. Sir Walter Scott. See Pibroch of Donuil Dhu.

Gathering the bloom of all the fairest boys that be. Strato, tr. fr. Greek by Sydney Oswald. PeHV

Gathering the Bones Together. Gregory Orr. AmPA; Poetsp

Gauguin. Derek Walcott. NoAM

Gauley Bridge. Muriel Rukeyser. NNaP

Gauley Bridge is a good town for Negroes. George Robinson: Blues. Muriel Rukeyser. NNaP

Gauls Sacrifice, The. Charles Montague Doughty. Fr. Dawn in Britain, The. FaBoTw

Gaunt in gloom. Nightpiece. James Joyce. PoA

Gaunt in the midst of the prairie. Chicago. John Boyle O'Reilly. PAH

Gaunt kept house with her child for the old man. Montana Fifty Years Ago. J. V. Cunningham. Prf

Gaunt thing, The. Babylon Revisited. Amiri Baraka. BPo; MoP; NoAM

Gaunt wild man whose lovely sons were dead, The. (LL) Ancient History. Siegfried Sassoon. ChIV-1; Mes

Gautama in the Deer Park at Benares. Kenneth Patchen. NaP

Gauze flutterings of vegetation. (LL) For My Mother. Louise Glück. UnPo

Gave me things I. Swallow the Lake. Clarence Major. PoBA

Gave proof through the night. Poem to My Sister, Ethel Ennis, Who Sang "The Star-spangled Banner" at the Second Inauguration of Richard Milhous Nixon. June Jordan. TAP

Gave up his teeth. (LL) The Voyagers. Askold Melnyczuk. UTF

Sir Gawain and the Green Knight. (Siege and the assault being ceased at Troy, The.) Unknown, tr. fr. Middle English by Brian Stone. OAEL-1 Sels.

Gawain and the Lady of the Castle. EBEV

"Mony klyf he overclambe in contrayes straunge." FaBoVe

"Now neghes the New Yere and the night passes." EnVB

Passage of a Year, The. PoEL-1

Sir Gawayn Goes to Receive His Return Blow from the Green Knight. FaBoPP

"This kyng lay at Camylot upon Krystmasse." PoE

Gawain and the Lady of the Castle. Unknown, tr. fr. Middle English by Brian Stone. Fr. Sir Gawain and the Green Knight. EBEV; OAEL-1

Sir Gawain Encounters Sir Priamus. Tennyson, incorporated in Idylls of the King with changes, as The Passing of Arthur. Fr. Morte d'Arthur. DL; EBVVPR; FaBoBe; FaBoRV; NIP; NOBVV; OAEL-2; OBNV; PoEL-1; PoEL-5

Sir Gawaine and the Green Knight. Yvor Winters. MoP; NoAM; PoRA; VGW

Sir Gawayn Goes to Receive His Return Blow from the Green Knight. Unknown, tr. fr. Middle English by Brian Stone. Fr. Sir Gawain and the Green Knight. FaBoPP; OAEL-1

Gawayn spurred on, and he picked out a path. Sir Gawayn Goes to Receive His Return Blow from the Green Knight. Unknown, tr. fr. Middle English by Brian Stone. Fr. Sir Gawain and the Green Knight. FaBoPP; OAEL-1

Gay, The. "Æ." OBMV

Gay belles of fashion may boast of excelling, The. The Needle. Samuel Woodworth. GN

Gay blade on the gentle hedgerow. Daffodil. Waldo Williams, tr. fr. Welsh by Gwyn Jones. OBWVE

Gay Boys. James Kirkup. PeHV

Gay citizen, myself, and thoughtful friend. Allen Tate. Fr. More Sonnets at Christmas. LiTA; LiTM

Gay colors flow. Goto Miyoko, tr. fr. Japanese by Kenneth Rexroth and Ikuko Atsumi. WPJ

Gay Epiphany. James Mitchell. PeHV

Gay, gay, gay, gay. Remember the Day of Judgement. Unknown. MeEL

Gay go up and gay go down. The Bells of London. Unknown. BoTP; OxNR; PoRA
(London Bells.) CBNP; ChTr; LiTB; OxBoLi; PeLV

Gay Goshawk [or Goss-Hawk], The. At. to Anna Gordon Brown. ESPB, A and E vers.; GN; OxBB; WPE

Gay little Girl-of-the-Diving-Tank. At the Carnival. Anne Spencer. BlSi; CDC; PoNe; ShDr

Gay Old Hag, The. Unknown. BIrV

Gay Psalm from Fort Valley, A. Louie Crew. GLP

Gay Robin Is Seen No More. Robert Bridges. BoTP

Gay soccer spectator from Wix, A. Cyril Mountjoy. PeLi

Gay Summer's Bliss, Good-bye. Dietmar von Aist, tr. fr. German by J. W. Thomas. GePo

Gaze North-east. Unknown, tr. fr. Irish by John Montague. BIrV

Gaze not on Swans, in whose soft breast. Beauty Extoll'd. At. to Henry Noel and to William Strode. ChTr; ELP
(On His Mistress.) PoEL-2

Gaze not on thy beauties pride. Good Counsel [or Counsell] to a Young Maid. Thomas Carew.
(Song: Good Counsel to a Young Maid.) CaPo

Gaze not upon my outside, friend. Apple Dumplings. Mary E. Tucker. AmWP; CBWP-1

Gaze on! I thrill beneath thy gaze. The Statue to Pygmalion. Frances Sargent Osgood. AmWP

Gazelle, The. Carmen Bernos de Gasztold, tr. by Rumer Godden. OBAP

Gazelle Calf, The. D. H. Lawrence. OxBTC; RB

Gazelle-girl/gazelle. King Solomon Vistas. Ian Wedde. PeNZ

Gazelles, The. T. Sturge Moore. OBMV

Gazelles and Unicorn. John Gray. Fr. Long Road, The. ChTr

Gazing as I climbed a high peak. Han Yü, tr. fr. Chinese by A. C. Graham. Fr. South Mountains, The. PLT

Gazing quietly at your image. (LL) Put a Woman into the Memory Box. Brigitte Frase. LoHo

Genteel in personage,/ Conduct and equipage. The Maid's Husband. Henry Carey. ECEV

Gentian weaves her fringes, The. Emily Dickinson. PoRA

Gentil mauneiple was ther of a Temple, A. Chaucer. *Fr.* Canterbury Tales, The. EnVB; FHYEP; NoP; OAEL-1; PPP, *abr.*

Gentile or Hebrew or simply one. Luke 23. Jorge Luis Borges, *tr. fr. Spanish by* Irving Feldman. OBF

Gentilesse. Chaucer. *See* Firste stok, fader of gentilesse, The.

Gentill butler, bell ami. Fill the Bowl, Butler! *Unknown.* MeEL

Gentle Alice Brown. W. S. Gilbert. FaBoCo; FiBHP

Gentle Anarchist, The. Brunton Stephens. NOBAu

Gentle and generous, brave-hearted, kind. The Comfort of the Trees. Richard Watson Gilder. PAH

Gentle and smiling as before. The Wheel. Robert Hayden. BPo

Gentle Annie, willow wind, the West, A. Four Winds. Hal Porter. NOBAu

Gentle as a maiden's dream. The Snow Storm. Mary Weston Fordham. CBWP-2

Gentle at last, and as clean as ever. Grandfather in the Old Men's Home. W. S. Merwin. LiTM; SM

Gentle breeze has died down, The. To the Tune "Spring at Wu Ling." Li Ch'ing-chao, *tr. fr. Chinese by* Kenneth Rexroth. OHMPC

Gentle breeze, morning dew. I Wake Up Alone. Li Shang-yin, *tr. fr. Chinese by* Kenneth Rexroth. OHMPC

Gentle breeze rustles through reeds and rushes, A. In a boat, Getting Up at Night. Su Shih, *tr. fr. Chinese by* Irving Y. Lo. SuSp

Gentle Check, The. Joseph Beaumont. NOSC

Gentle, cheerful ticking of a clock, The. Quiet Days. Mildred T. Mey. PoToHe

Gentle Christ? (*LL*) Marban, a Hermit Speaks. *Unknown.* BIrV; CIP

Gentle Communion. Pat Mora. AfAz; NIP

Gentle Craft, The, *sels.* Thomas Deloney.
Would God That It Were Holiday! EIL

Gentle Echo on Woman, A. Swift. FaBoCo; FiBHP; NU

Gentle Echo on Woman, A. Swift. FaBoCo; FiBHP; NBLV; NU

Gentle footsteps on the sand. The Crows. Maria Valli. CBAP

Gentle Goddess. Lew Welch. EaPr

Gentle hands that never weary. Lines to Mother. Rose M. Stein. PWR

Gentle Heart, A: Two. Judith Johnson Sherwin. BoWoP

Gentle hunter. Leopard. *Unknown, tr. fr. Yoruba by* Ulli Beier. *Fr.* Hunter Poems of the Yoruba. RB; WTO

Gentle Jesus Meek and Mild. Charles Wesley. OxBChV

Gentle knight was pricking on the plaine, A. Spenser. *Fr.* Faerie Queene, The. EBEV; FHYEP; NAEL-1; OAEL-1; Poetr

Gentle Lamb. Arthur Gregor. NGP

Gentle Locke sits down to write his famous treatise. At Work. Artur Miedzyrzecki, *tr. fr. Polish by* Artur Miedzyrzecki *and* John Batki. PoSu

Gentle Mary, noble maiden, give us help! Prayer to the Virgin. St. Columcille, *tr. fr. Irish by* Kuno Meyer *and* John Strachan. TIRV

Gentle Name. Selma Robinson. MoShBr

Gentle Nymphs, Be Not Refusing. William Browne. *Fr.* Britannia's Pastorals. EIL

Gentle of hand, the Dean of St. Patrick's guided. A Sermon on Swift. Austin Clarke. BIrV; IPY

Gentle Owen was a man well set, The. Owen Tudor. Hugh Holland. AngWe

Gentle Park, A. Moss Herbert. GoYe

Gentle River, Gentle River. *Unknown, tr. fr. Spanish by* Thomas Percy. AWP

Gentle Shepherd, The, *sels.* Allan Ramsay.
"My Peggy is a young thing." GN; OxBS; ScCV
(Peggy.) OBEV
(Wawking of the Fauld, The.) SCGP

Gentle slopes are green to remind you, The. The Five Unmistakable Marks. David Jones. *Fr.* In Parenthesis. NAEL-2

Gentle Spenser. Wordsworth. *Fr.* Prelude [or, Growth of a Poet's Mind], The. EnRP; EPCY; FaBoPP; HAP; OAEL-2; OxAEP-2, *abr.*

Gentle squire would gladly entertain, A. Joseph Hall. *Fr.* Virgidemiarum. NoSic

Gentle thought there is will often start, A. Dante, *tr. fr. Italian by* Dante Gabriel Rossetti. *Fr.* Vita Nuova, La. AWP

Gentle Wind, A. Fu Hsüan, *tr. fr. Chinese by* Arthur Waley. AWP

Gentle wind that waves, The. Kitty and I. W. H. Davies. CBLP

Gentle Word, A. *Unknown.* PoToHe

Gentle youth, forbear. Hero Feels the Shaft of Love. Christopher Marlowe. *Fr.* Hero and Leander. AAS; GBL; NoP

Gentleman, The. Menahem ben Judah Lonzano, *tr. fr. Hebrew by* A. B. Rhine. TrJP

Gentleman cam oure the sea, A. The Cruel Brother. *Unknown.* ESPB

Gentleman in hunting rode astray, A. The Beggar Woman. William King. ECEV; NOEC

Gentleman, most wretched in his lot, A. Reformation. The Countess of Winchilsea. ECWP

Gentleman's Study, in Answer to The Lady's Dressing-Room, The. Miss W——. ECWP

Gentlemen. (*LL*) An Ancient to Ancients. Thomas Hardy. CMoP; GTBS-P; LiTM; OxBTC; SCGP

Gentlemen. W. N. Ewer. IHNG

Gentlemen. Geoffrey Taylor. FaBoEE

Gentlemen, as we take our seats. The Rehearsal. Horace Gregory. VGW

Gentlemen, look on this wonder. The Adhesive Autopsy of Walt Whitman. Jonathan Williams. PoM

Gentlemen-Rankers. Kipling. CoGr; NOBVV

Gentlemen,/ the situation is tragic. State of the Union. Aimé Césaire, *tr. fr. French by* Denis Kelly. NegPo

Gentlemen, which of these three vegetables: tomatoes, pumpkins, or squash. A Paragraph Made Up of Seven Sentences Which Have Entered My Memory. Chuck Wachtel. UL

Gentlest air, thou breath of lovers. A Sigh. The Countess of Winchilsea. ECWP

Gentlest of women, put your weapons by. Lay Your Arms Aside. Pierce Ferriter, *tr. fr. Irish by* Eilean Ni Chuilleanain. BIrV

Gentlewoman of the dealing trade, A. Epigarm XXIX. Samuel Rowlands. NOSC

Gently about this tomb wind gently O Ivy. At the Tomb of Sophokles. Simmias [*or* Simias] of Rhodes, *tr. fr. Greek by* Dudley Fitts. GrAn

Gently Dip. George Peele. *Fr.* Old Wives' [*or* Wife's] Tale, The. ELP; InPS

Gently dip: but not too deepe. Gently Dip. George Peele. *Fr.* Old Wives' [*or* Wife's] Tale, The. ELP; InPS
(Fair Maiden.) PoEL-2
(Song for the Head.) RB
(Voice from the Well [of Life Speaks to the Maiden], The.) ChTr; GGP; NOBE; NoSic

Gently! Gently! Gently! The Ocean Is like a Wreath. Kuapakaa, *tr. fr. Hawaiian.* WTO

Gently, gently prithee, time. *Unknown.* NOSC

Gently I stir a white feather fan. In the Mountains on a Summer Day. Li Po, *tr. fr. Chinese by* Arthur Waley. AWP

Gently I took that which ungently came, Forbearance. Samuel Taylor Coleridge. ChIV-2

Gently I wave the visible world away. The Absinthe-Drinker. Arthur Symons. FaBoTw; NOBVV

Gently, Johnny My Jingalo. *Unknown.* OBET

Gently Lucrezia, do not bite. (*LL*) Pope Alexander VI. Geoffrey Lehmann. NOBAu

Gently, so as not to rouse/ His skinny girl. Lucilius, *tr. fr. Greek by* Alistair Elliot. GrAn

Genty Tibby and Sonsy Nelly. Allan Ramsay. ScCV

Genuine, you are interested in poetry. (*LL*) Poetry. Marianne Moore. AmPP; BLPL; BoWoP; CMoP; FaBoWP; FF; HAP; HeIL; HeIP; ImGa; ImPo; LiTA; LiTM; MoAB; MoAmPo; MoP; NAAL-2; NALW; NIP; NoAM; NOBA; NoP; OxBA; PoE; Poetr; TAP; TFi; UnPo

Geocentric. Pattiann Rogers. NAmP90

Geode, the troll's melon. James Merrill. *Fr.* In Nine Sleep Valley. HCAP

Sir Geoffrey Chaucer. Robert Greene. *See* His stature was not very tall.

Geographers, The. Karl Shapiro. OxBA

Geography. G. K. Chesteron. *Fr.* Songs of Education. OBSV

Geography, *sels.* Michael Dransfield.
"In the forest, in unexplored." CBAP
"Sky ceases. There is only." CBAP

Geography. Eleanor Farjeon. FaPON

Geography. Kenneth Koch. NoAM

Geography Lesson. Christine McNeill. NWP

Geography Lesson. Deborah Pease. PRA

Geography Lesson. Carol Rumens. FaBoWP

Geography of Music. Kenneth Patchen. UnAS

Geography of the Trinity Corona. Víctor Hernández Cruz. AfAz

Geometry. Rita Dove. HCAP; HeIP; Poetr

Geordie. *Unknown.* ESPB; FaBoBa; OxBB

Geordie. *Unknown.* AmPP; ESPB, A *and* B *vers.*; FaBoBa; OBET; OxBB

Geordie. *Unknown.* OBET

George. Hilaire Belloc. FiBHP

George. Dudley Randall. BPo; NoAM

George I — Star of Brunswick. Thackeray. *Fr.* Georges, The. FaBoEE; FaBoEH

George III. E. C. Bentley. *See* George the Third.

George III. Robert Lowell. FaBoPV

George III. Thackeray. *Fr.* Georges, The. FaBoEE

George III and the Sailor. "Peter Pindar." *Fr.* Royal Tour, and Weymouth Amusements, The. NOEC; OxBoLi

George III Visits Whitbread's Brewery. "Peter Pindar." *Fr.* Instructions to a Celebrated Laureat. NOEC

George IV. Thackeray. *Fr.* Georges, The. FaBoEE

George Allen. *Unknown.* AmFP

George Aloe and the Sweepstake, The ("George Alow came from the South.") *Unknown.* ESPB

George-Aloe and the Sweepstake too, The. The Sailor's Only Delight. *Unknown.* OxBSS

George and Genevieve. George Hugnet. Gertrude Stein. NoAM

George Burns likes to insist that he always. Of Time and the Line. Charles Bernstein. UL

George Collins came home last Saturday night. Lady Alice ("George Collins came home last Saturday night.") *Unknown.* AmFP

George Collins come home last Friday night. Lady Alice ("George Collins come home last Friday night.") *Unknown.* AmFP

George Crabbe. E. A. Robinson. BLPL; CMoP; LiTA; LiTM; MeMAP; MoAB; MoAmPo; NAAL-2; NOBA; NoP; OxBA; PoEL-5; TAP

George Hugnet. Gertrude Stein. NoAM

George! I dunno how you do it George. Toronto Board of Trade Goes Abroad. Earle Birney. PeLV

George Jones. *Unknown.* OxBSS

George Mereditiyh (1828-1909). Thomas Hardy. EPCY

George Moses Horton, Myself. George Moses Horton. AAP

George Ridler's Oven. *Unknown.* OBET

George Robinson: Blues. Muriel Rukeyser. NNaP

George Sand. Dorothy Parker. *Fr.* Pig's-Eye View of Literature, A. FiBHP; NALW

"George," she said, "come out of the rain!" The Man in the Rain. Van K. Brock. MT

George Stephenson said: "These repairs." Frank Richards. PeLi

George tells the story. The Controls. Harrison Fisher. UL

George the First was always reckoned. The Georges. Walter Savage Landor. ChTr; FaBoCo; FaBoEE; FaBoEH; FiBHP; NIP; OBSV (On the Four Georges.) FaBoCo

George the Fourth, the son of Third, the grandson of the Second. Lines on the Succession of the Kings of England (Reversed). *Unknown.* FaBoUs

George the Third. E. C. Bentley. *Fr.* Clerihews. CBNP; FaBoCo; FiBHP; NOBL; OxBoLi (George III.) PeLV

George III said with a smile. *Unknown.* FaBoUs

George the Third's Soliloquy. Philip Freneau. EAP; NOBA

George Washington. Rosemary *and* Stephen Vincent Benét *and* Stephen Vincent Benét. FaPON

George Washington. John Hall Ingham. OHIP; PAH

George Washington. *Unknown.* OHIP

George Washington said to his dad. Frank Richards. PeLi

George Washington, your name is on my lips. Patriotic Poem. Diane Wakoski. VGW

Georges, The. Walter Savage Landor. ChTr; FaBoCo; FaBoEE; FaBoEH; FiBHP; NIP; OBSV

Georges, The. H. J. Daniels. FaBoEE
Sels.
George I — Star of Brunswick. FaBoEH
George III.
George IV.
"In most things I did as my father had done." FaBoEH

Georgia. Bin Ramke. MT

Georgia Dusk. Jean Toomer. BPo; CDC; NAAL-2; NoAM; NoP; PoBA; Poetr

Georgiad, The, *sels.* Roy Campbell.
"Hail, mediocrity, beneath whose spell." MoBrPo
"Next him Jack Squire through his own tear-drops sploshes." OxBTC

Georgian Spring. Roy Campbell. OBSV

Georgics, *sels.* Virgil, *tr. fr. Latin.*
Care of Bees, The. FaBoUs
Gravid Mares, The. ArNa, *tr. by* David R. Slavitt
"Observe the daily circle of the sun." FaBoUs
"What makes a plenteous harvest." AWP

Georgics of Heisod, The, *sels.* Hesiod.
Winter. NOSC

Georgie Porgie, pudding and pie. Mother Goose. OxNR; ReMoGo

Georgie Wedlock. *Unknown.* AmFP

Geraint and Enid. Tennyson. *Fr.* Idylls of the King.

Gerald the Bitter, with your polished smile. The Widow's Curse. *Unknown, tr. fr. Irish by* Thomas Kinsella. NOIV

"Gerald's here!" my mother called. A Voice in the Garden. Selima Hill. FaBoWP

Geranium, The. Theodore Roethke. CoAP; UnPo; WeW

Geranium, The. Sheridan. BoLoP; ErPo

Geranium, houseleek, laid in oblong beds. John Gray. NOBVV

Geraniums. W. W. Gibson. NSI

Geraniums, The. Genevieve Taggard. VGW

Geraniums lip blossom. Geraniums, South London. Ken Edwards. NBrP

Geraniums, South London. Ken Edwards. NBrP

Gerarda. Eloise Bibb. AAP; CBWP-4

Gereint ab Erbin. *Unknown, tr. fr. Welsh by* Joseph P. Clancy. OBWVE

Germ, The. Ogden Nash. MoShBr; RB

Germ of new life, whose powers expanding slow. To a Little Invisible Being Who Is Expected Soon to Become Visible. Anna Laetitia Barbauld. ECWP; WoRP

German Bite. Iain Sinclair. NBrP

German Graves, The. A. P. Herbert. NSI

German Language, The. Friedrich von Logau, *tr. fr. German.* GePo, *tr. by* George C. Schoolfield

German Prisoners. Joseph Lee. NSI

German Requiem, A. James Fenton. NAEL-2; NoAM; SCBI

German Shepherd. Myra Cohn Livingston. RFM

Germanic. Crossing. Anthony Barnett. VaA

Germans in Greek, The. Porson on German Scholarship. Richard Porson. FaBoCo; FaBoEE

Germans live in Germany, The. Home. J. H. Goring. MoShBr

Germany of three confessions now shall keep a single one. One Faith and No Faith. Friedrich von Logau, *tr. fr. German.* GePo, *tr. by* George C. Schoolfield

Germinal. "Æ." BIrV; MoBrPo; OBEV; OBMV

Geron and Histor. Sir Philip Sidney. *Fr.* Arcadia. SiPS

Geronimo. Ernest McGaffey. PAH

Gerontion, *sels.* T. S. Eliot.
"Vacant shuttles/ Weave the wind. I have no ghosts." UV

Gerontion. T. S. Eliot. AmPP; CMoP; EBEV; GTBS-P; HAP; ImPo; InPS; LiTA; LiTM; MoP; NAAL-2; NoAM; NOBA; OAEL-2; OxAEP-2; OxBA; PPP; TAP; TFi

Gertie Green made eyes at me. Serve Her Right. John Barford. PeHV

Gertrude and Gulielma, sister-twins. Frederick Goddard Tuckerman. *Fr.* Sonnets. HAP

Gertrude Stein at Snails Bay. Peter Porter. OxBC

Gest of Robyn Hode. (Lythe and listin, gentilmen.) *Unknown.* ESPB; OxBB, *complete*
Sels.
"They toke togyder theyr counsell." PeECV

Gest of Robyn Hode, A. *Unknown.* OxBLMV

Gestalt at Sixty., *sels.* May Sarton.
"I am not ready to die." CrSp

Gesture. Donald Finkel. InPK

Gesture, The. George Oppen. *Fr.* Five Poems about Poetry. NNaP

Gesture by a Lady with an Assumed Name, A. James Wright. LiTM

Gesture the gesture the gesture the gesture, The. Michael McClure. *Fr.* Hymn to St. Geryon. NeAP

Get a transfer. (*LL*) Get a Transfer. *Unknown.* BLPA; WBLP

Get a Transfer. *Unknown.* BLPA; WBLP

Get Angry, Compass. Inoue Michiko, *tr. fr. Japanese by* Kenneth Rexroth *and* Ikuko Atsumi. WPJ

Get away from Eros! Archias, *tr. fr. Greek by* Peter Jay. GrAn

"Get down, get down, lovin' Henry," she cried. Loving Henry. *Unknown.* AmFP

Get drunk, my boy, don't weep, you're. Asclepiades, *tr. fr. Greek by* Kenneth Rexroth. PGA

Get Hence Foule Griefe. Sir Philip Sidney. *Fr.* Arcadia. PoEL-1

Get into the Boosting Business. *Unknown.* WBLP

Get It & Feel Good. Ntozake Shange. VBLP

Get it right or let it alone. Morals. James Thurber. *Fr.* Further Fables for Our Time. FaBV

Get loaded. Exercise ("Get loaded.") Pat Nolan. UL

Get out of my hut, you stealthy vermin! Leonidas. Leonidas of Tarentum, *tr. fr. Greek by* Barbara Hughes Fowler. *Fr.* Epigrams. HePo

Get out of this, dainty blood in. J. H. Prynne. VaA

Get ready your money and come to me. *Unknown.* OxNR

Get Somebody Else. Paul Laurence Dunbar. BLRP

Get the Gasworks. David Ignatow. InPK

Get the Hell off My Note. Rod Jellema. *Fr.* Four Voices Ending on Some Lines from Old Jazz Records. Jaz

Ghosts in the Ark, The. Dermot Bolger. IB

Ghosts man the phantom ships that ply between. Gallipoli. Mary Morison Webster. NSI

Ghosts of a Lunatic Asylum. Stephen Vincent Benét. AnAmPo

Ghosts of hedgers and ditchers. Ash Keys. Michael Longley. PBCIP

Ghosts of the Buffaloes, The. Vachel Lindsay. MeMAP; MoAmPo

Ghosts, Places, Stories, Questions. Vincent Buckley. NOBAu

Ghost's Song, The. *Unknown. See* Wae's me, wae's me.

Ghosts there must be with me in this old house. Solitude. Walter de la Mare. CMoP

Ghoul, The. Jack Prelutsky. OBCA

Ghoul Care. Ralph Hodgson. MoBrPo

G.I. Joe from Kokomo. William Trowbridge. ArOW

Giant Decorative Dahlias. Molly Holden. OxBTC

Giant Has Swallowed the Earth, A. Pattiann Rogers. MT

Giant Killer. George Garrett. CRP

Giant moths like sparrows! So many drowned, The. The Night of the Moths. Douglas Stewart. FaBoMA

Giant-Power from earth's remotest caves, The. Steam Power. Erasmus Darwin. *Fr.* Botanic Garden, The. NOBEV

Giant Puffball, The. Edmund Blunden. FaBoTw

Giant sparkler,/ Lights of the river. "A 4" ("Giant sparkler,/ Lights of the river.") Louis Zukofsky. *Fr.* "A" (1–12). VGW

Giant Thunder. James Reeves. BoNaP; OTCP

Giant whispering and coughing from. Broadcast. Philip Larkin. CBLP

Giantess. Baudelaire, *tr. fr. French.* ErPo, *tr.* by Karl Shapiro; OBVE, *tr.* by Roy Campbell

Giantess, The. Baudelaire, *tr. fr. French by* Roy Campbell. OBVE

Giantesses, female fauna. The Women of Rubens. Wislawa Szymborska, *tr. fr. Polish by* Magnus F. Krynski. PoSu

Giant's Cake, A. Evelina San Garde. BoTP

Giaour, The, *sels.* Byron.

Gibber, The. Theodore Roethke. *Fr.* Lost Son, The. HAP; HCAP; LiTM; NAAL-2; VGW

Gibbs, *sels.* Muriel Rukeyser.

Gibraltar. Wilfrid Scawen Blunt. OBEV

Gibralter. Richard Chenevix Trench. OBTV

Gidget and Larue. Gossip. David Trinidad. BAP-91

Gie corn to my horse, mither. The Mother's Malison; or, Clyde's Water. *Unknown.* ESPB

Gi'e me a lass with a lump of land. Lass with a Lump of Land. Allan Ramsay. NOEC

Gie the Lass her Fairin.' Burns. CoMu; ErPo

Gife Langour. Lord Darnley. OxBS

Gift. Gerald William Barrax. MT

Gift, The. Margaret E. Bruner. PoToHe

Gift, The. John Ciardi. BTR; LiTM

Gift, The. Robert Creeley. NOBA

Gift, The. Greg Delanty. BiHa

Gift. Carol Freeman. *See* Christmas Morning I.

Gift, The. Louise Glück. FaBoWP

Gift, The. Li-Young Lee. OpBo; RaBo

Gift, The. Ed Ochester. Poetsp

Gift, The. Luada Sandler. BTR

Gift, The. Dara Wier. FoLa

Gift, The. William Carlos Williams. ChIV-2

Gift, The. Francis Brett Young. NSI

Gift, A. Amy Lowell. AnAmPo

Gift, A. *Unknown, tr. fr. Greek by* Guy Davenport. GrAn

Gift for the Queen. *Unknown.* OxNR

Gift for you should not be vulgar, A. Inscribed on a Painting of Windy Bamboo, to Be Presented to Tzu-kan. Hsü Wei, *tr. fr. Chinese by* Chiang Yee. SuSp

Gift from Kenya. May Miller. BlSi

Gift from the cold and silent past! The Norsemen. Whittier. PAH

Gift he gave to Immanuel, The. (*LL*) The Friendly Beasts. *Unknown.* FaPON; PChr

Gift Hour. Maria Banus, *tr. fr. Romanian by* Willis Barnstone *and* Matei Calinescu. BoWoP

Gift of Faith, the crown of Song!, The. (*LL*) Our Country. Julia Ward Howe. PAH

Gift of God, The. E. A. Robinson. MoAB; MoAmPo; OxBA

Gift of Great Value, A. Robert Creeley. LCAP; NaP

Gift of Judah the Woman-Hater, The, *sels.* Judah ibn Sabbatai. Expensive Wife, The. TrJP

Gift of Life, The. Lavinia Greenlaw. NWP

Gift of Song, The. Anthony Hecht. NYBP

Gift of Speech, The. Sadi, *tr.* by L. Cranmer-Byng. *Fr.* Gulistan, The. AWP

Gift of Tongues, The. Robert Morgan. MT

Gift Outright, The. Robert Frost. AiP; AmPP; CMoP; GOA; LiTM; MeMAP; MoAB; MoAmPo; MoP; NAAL-2; NoAM; NOBA; NoP; OxBA; Poetr; PPP; TFi; TRP

Gift to a Jade. Anna Wickham. OxBSP

Gift to Be Simple, The. Howard Moss. Poetsp; TwCP

Gift was delivered to Laura, A. Edward Gorey. *Fr.* Listing Attic, The. CBNP

Gifts, The. David Craig Austin. PFL

Gifts. Mary Elizabeth Coleridge. PBWP

Gifts, The. John Heath-Stubbs. OxBC

Gifts. Emma Lazarus. TrJP; WGRP

Gifts. Shu Ting, *tr. fr. Chinese by* Carolyn Kizer *with* Y.H. Zhao. SpMi

Gifts. Karen Snow. FYAP

Gifts. James Thomson ("B.V."). *Fr.* Sunday up the River. OBEV

Gifts her kinship and our loves reveal, The. (*LL*) Chicago. Bret Harte. AiP; PAH

Gifts of God, The. George Herbert. *See* When God at first made Man.

Gifts of Rain. Seamus Heaney. IPY

Gifts that come through grace, which has no bounds. (*LL*) The Edge. Sandra Price. LoHo

Gifts to a Lady. Antiphilus, *tr. fr. Greek by* W. S. Merwin. GrAn

Gigantic Beauty of a Stallion, A. Walt Whitman. *Fr.* Song of Myself. AmPP; ImGa; LiTA; MoAmPo, *abr.*; NOBA; OxBA; PDV; SOTW, *much abr.*

Gigantic beauty of a stallion, fresh and responsive to my caresses, A. A Gigantic Beauty of a Stallion. Walt Whitman. *Fr.* Song of Myself. AmPP; ImGa; LiTA; MoAmPo, *abr.*; NOBA; OxBA; PDV; SOTW, *much abr.*

Gigantic Grandfather. Karl Heinrich Marx. Hans Magnus Enzensberger, *tr. fr. German by* Michael Hamburger. FaBoPV

Gil Brenton. *Unknown.* ESPB; OxBB

Gil Brenton is my father's name. (*LL*) Gil Brenton. *Unknown.* ESPB; OxBB

Gil Morrice. *Unknown.* OxBB

Gilbertus Glanvil, whose heart was a hard as an anvil. *Unknown, tr. fr. Latin by* Matthew Prior. FaBoEE

Gildas a Latin "History of Britain's Conquest" wrote. Principal British Writers. Edward B. Goodwin. FaBoUs

Gilded Boys, The. Felice Picano. PeHV

Gilded Man, The. Ai. AnAn
Sels.
Barquisimeto, Venezuela, October 27, 1561.
Orinoco, 1561, The.

Gilderoy. *Unknown.* OBET

Giles Collin he said to his mother one day. Lady Alice ("Giles Collin he said to his mother one day.") *Unknown.* ESPB, C *vers.*

Giles Collins he said to his old mother. Lady Alice ("Giles Collins he said to his old mother.") *Unknown.* ESPB, B *vers.*

Giles Corey. Lucy Larcom. PAH

Giles Corey of the Salem Farms. Longfellow. PAH
Sels.
"Delusions of the days that once have been."
Trial, The.

Giles Corey was a wizzard strong. Giles Corey. Lucy Larcom. PAH

Giles Johnson, Ph.D. Frank Marshall Davis. BPo; PoBA

Gilgamesh, *sels.* Herbert Mason.
"I asked unanswerable questions a child asks." IMW

Gilgamesh washed his grimy hair, polished his weapons. *Unknown, tr. by* E. A. Speiser. *Fr.* Epic of Gilgamesh, The. Prf

Gill Morice stood in stable-door. Childe Maurice. *Unknown.* ESPB (Childe Maurice hunted the Silver Wood.) OBSP

Gillespie. Sir Henry Newbolt. PeVV

Gilliflower of Gold, The. William Morris. HeIL

Gilly Silly Jarter. *Unknown.* OxNR

Gimboling. Isabella Gardner. ErPo

Gin a body meet a body. Comin' thro' the Rye. Burns. LiTB; UV, *abr.*; WBLP

Gin a body meet a body. Rigid Body Sings. James Clerk Maxwell. FaBoCo; FaBoPa; UV
(In Memory of Edward Wilson.) BXAP

Gin by Pailfuls. Sir Walter Scott. ChTr

Gin I Were a Doo. *Unknown.* GBP

Gin I were on my milkwhite steed. The Bents and Broom. *Unknown.* OxBB

Gin is better than the water in Lethe. (*LL*) The Scarlet Woman. Fenton Johnson. PoBA; PoNe

Gin on the bun-shops and copy-book stalls. (*LL*) G. K. Chesterton on His Birth. A. E. Housman. FaBoNo; NBLV

Gin she this sight did see! (*LL*) Rose the Red and White Lil[l]y. *Unknown*. ESPB; OxBB

Gin-Shop, The; A Peep into Prison, *sels*. Hannah More. "Come, neighbour, take a walk with me." ECWP

Gin the Goodwife Stint. Basil Bunting. CTC

Gin ye hae'd corneich airth an' time. To His Coy Mistress. Gerry Hamill. BXAP

Ginevra. Samuel Rogers. BeLS; OxAEP-2; PoLF

Ginevra, *sels*. Shelley.

Ginger Bread Mama. Doughtry Long, Jr.. BPo; PoBA

Ginger mog, my angular black Anubis. (*LL*) Dark Mothers. Anne Cluysenaar. VBLP

Gingerbread Heart. Aleksandar Ristovic, *tr. fr. Serbo-Croatian by* Charles Simic. HSix

Gingerbread Man, The. Rowena Bastin Bennett. SiSoPo

Gingerbread man gave a gingery shout, The. The Gingerbread Man. Rowena Bastin Bennett. SiSoPo

Gingham dog and the calico cat, The. The Duel. Eugene Field. BeLS; FaBoBe; FaPON; MoShBr; OBAL; OBCA; PoLF; PoRA; TFi

Ginkgoes in Fall. Howard Nemerov. HCAP

Ginny at a table of young men belly dancing. Soup Kitchen. Betsy Sholl. PBCAP

Giorno dei Morti. D. H. Lawrence. FaBoRV; NOBE

Giotto's Campanile. Guy Butler. PeSA

Giovanni Azania. Don Mattera. PeSAV

Giovanni da Fiesole on the Sublime; or, Fra Angelico's "Last Judgment." Richard Howard. Prf

Giovinette, Che Fate All'Amore. Lorenzo da Ponte, *tr. fr. Italian by* Natalie MacFarren. *Fr*. Don Giovanni. TrJP

Gipsies. John Clare. ChTr; FHYEP

Gipsies came to Lord Cassilis' gate, The. Johnny Faa, the Lord of Little Egypt. *Unknown*. EnSB

Gipsies lit their fire by the chalk-pit anew, The. The Idlers. Edmund Blunden. BoTP; CH

Gipsies seek wide sheltering woods again, The. Gipsies. John Clare. ChTr; FHYEP

Gipsies tell me my life-line's a short one, The. Antipater of Thessalonica, *tr. fr. Greek by* Tony Harrison. GrAn

Gipsies ("The snow falls deep.") John Clare. CH; PoEL-4

Gipsy Camp, The. John Clare. *See* Snow falls deep, The; the forest lies alone.

Gipsy Girl, The. Ralph Hodgson. MoBrPo

Gipsy Jane. William Brighty Rands. BoTP; FaPON

Gipsy Laddie, The. *Unknown*. FaBoCh; OxBoLi

Gipsy Man. Dorothy King. BoTP

Gipsy-Night. Richard Hughes. OBWVE

Gipsy of the sea. Stormpetrel. Richard Murphy. IPY

Gipsy Queen. John Alexander Chapman. OBEV

Gipsy Song. Ben Jonson. *See* Faery Beam upon You, The.

Gipsy Trail, The. Kipling. PoRA

Gipsy Vans. Kipling. OtMeF

Gipsy's Warning, The. *Unknown*. BeLS

Giraffe, The. Geoffrey Dearmer. ZA

Giraffe, The, *sels*. Nikolai Gumilev, *tr. fr. Russian by* C. M. Bowra. "Listen:/ There roams, far away, by the waters of Clead." FaPON

Giraffe, The. Ron Padgett. *Fr*. Three Animals. TTTS

Giraffe. Stanley Plumly. AmPA

Giraffe. *Unknown, tr. fr. Hottentot*. PeSA

Giraffe and the Woman, The. Laura E. Richards. PDV

Giraffe and Tree. W. J. Turner. CH; GrPl

Giraffes, The. Roy Fuller. OBAP

Giraffes, yes, even the strongest. Frank Davies. PeLi

Girandole. Dorothy Donnelly. NYBP

Gird up thy loins now like a man. Out of the Whirlwind. Bible, *O.T.* *Fr*. Job. AWP; NAWM-1, *abr*.; OBVE

Gird your beard three times with a belt and light a stove. Flying Temple. Milorad Pavic, *tr. fr. Serbo-Croatian by* Charles Simic. HSix

Girdle, A. William Strode. NOSC

Girdle round the Earth, A. Anthony Thwaite. PeLV

Girl. Octavio Paz, *tr. fr. Spanish by* John Frederick Nims. STV

Girl. *Unknown, tr. fr. Serbian by* Anne Pennington. RB

Girl. Hugo Williams. CBLP

Girl, A. Ezra Pound. MoAB; MoAmPo

Girl and Her Fawn, The. Andrew Marvell. *See* With sweetest milk and sugar first.

Girl at the Seaside. Richard Murphy. BIrV

Girl attacked me once with a number 2 Eagle pencil, A. A Blasphemy. Rodney Jones. WeW

Girl, Boy, Flower, Bicycle. M. K. Joseph. PeNZ

Girl brought me into the house of love, A. A Secret Kept. Judah al-Harizi, *tr. fr. Hebrew by* Robert Mezey. UnAS

Girl by Green River, The. *Unknown, tr. fr. Chinese by* Kenneth Rexroth. OHMPC

Girl by the Han River. Ts'ai Ch'i-chiao, *tr. fr. Chinese*. *Fr*. Han River, The. LHF, *tr. by* Hualing Nieh

Girl by the River. Federico García Lorca, *tr. fr. Spanish*. CBNP

Girl-child and amazon. The Crux. Alma Villanueva. SRLS

Girl Combs Her Hair, A. Li Ho, *tr. fr. Chinese by* A. C. Graham. PLT

Girl comes out of a doorway in the morning, A. Back Street. A. R. D. Fairburn. *Fr*. Album Leaves. PeNZ

Girl Friday. Elaine Equi. UL

Girl Friend Describes the Bull Fight, The. Uruttiran, *tr. fr. Tamil by* A. K. Ramanujan. PLW

Girl from Flower Mountain, The. Han Yü, *tr. fr. Chinese by* Charles Hartman. SuSp

Girl gathering lotus upon a brook, A. Upon a Brook. Ku K'uang, *tr. fr. Chinese by* Irving Y. Lo. SuSp

Girl grows up hidden in innermost rooms, A. In a Boat on a Summer Evening, I Heard the Cry of a Water Bird. Lu Yu, *tr. fr. Chinese by* Burton Watson. SuSp

Girl Held without Bail. Margaret Walker. BPo; PoBA

Girl Help. Janet Lewis. HeIP; InPK

Girl I Call Alma, The. Linda Gregg. AmPA; AnAn

Girl I Left behind Me, The. Thomas Osborne Davis. FaBoBe

Girl I Left behind Me, The. *Unknown*. AmFP; OBET

Girl I Took to the Cocktail Party, The. Trevor Williams. FiBHP

Girl in a grey frock. A Grey Frock. Zinaida Hippius, *tr. fr. Russian by* Temira Pachmuss. PBWP

Girl in a Library, A. Randall Jarrell. NAAL-2; NoAM; NOBA; NoP

Girl in a Nightgown. Wallace Stevens. OxBA

Girl in a torn chemise, A. State and 32nd, Cold Morning Blues. Kenneth Rexroth. *Fr*. Written to Music. Jaz

Girl in a Window, A. James Wright. ErPo

Girl in the Hall, The. John Stone. MT

Girl in the lane, The. Mother Goose. OxNR; ReMoGo

Girl in the picture is seventeen, The. From a Box of Old Photographs. James Ulmer. UTF

Girl in the sand, The. Nude Kneeling in Sand. John Logan. ErPo

Girl in the tea shop, The. The Tea Shop. Ezra Pound. HeIP

Girl in the Willow Tree, The. Carolyn Maisel. IHMS

Girl in trousers wheeling a red baby, The. Metamorphoses. Roy Fuller. OxBTC

Girl in yellow slacks kept watching me, A. Between You and Me. Samuel Hazo. GOYP

Girl lying in the grass, A. Finglas Lilies. Dermot Bolger. IB

Girl My Age, A. Lizbeth Parker. NGP

Girl Named Spring, A. Betsy Sholl. PBCAP

Girl of All Periods: An Idyll, The. Coventry Patmore. EnVR

Girl of the Future, feared of all. A Dresscessional. Carolyn Wells. WBLP

Girl of water/ and lips of fruit. Water Girl. Juan Felipe Herrera. AfAz

Girl of Yueh, The. Li Po, *tr. fr. Chinese by* Robert Payne. TAL

Girl on a Swing, 10.00pm. Tony Flynn. PWE

Girl on the stairs listens to her father, A. Tours. Charles David Wright. MT

Girl, Prince, Lizard. Heather Ross Miller. MT

Girl Sings to the Stream, The. Leah Goldberg, *tr. fr. Hebrew by* Ruth Finer Mintz. *Fr*. Songs of the Stream. MHP

Girl threw an apple to a cloud, A. *Unknown, tr. fr. Serbo-Croatian by* Charles Simic. HSix

Girl to Soldier on Leave. Isaac Rosenberg. PeFWW

Girl today, dreaming, A. Auf dem Wasser zu Singen. Stephen Spender. EnLoPo

Girl Walking. Charles G. Bell. ErPo

Girl Warrior. Mary E. O'Donnell. NWP

Girl, when rejecting me you never guessed. To a Jilt. Martin Armstrong. FaBoEE

Girl who, in 1971, when I was living by myself, painfully lonely, A. Shame. C. K. Williams. PWE

Girl who is bespectacled, A. Lines Written to Console Those Ladies Distressed by the Lines "Men Never Make Passes, etc." Ogden Nash. PeLV

Girl Who Loved the Sky, The. Anita Endrezze-Danielson. HATNAP

Girl who was touring Zambesi, A. *Unknown*. PeLi

Girl with all that raising, A. Ballad of the Girl Whose Name is Mud. Langston Hughes. SAmP

Girl with Doves. Stephen Gray. PeSA

Girl with Long Dark Hair. Stephen Gray. PeSA

Girl with Mind Wandering. Paul Valéry, *tr. fr. French by* John Frederick Nims. STV

Girl with Pitcher. Ruth Dallas. PeNZ

Girl with the beautiful legs, The. The Tides. Paul Blackburn. PoM

Girl with the Green Skirt. Dana Naone. CDW

Girl with the Jersey, The. Ben King. AnAmPo

Girl working the xerox in the stationery store, The. For Emily (Dickinson). Maureen Owen. UL

Girl Writing Her English Paper, The. Robert Wallace. Poetsp

Girl wrote that once, A. The Sky Is Full of Blue and Full of the Mind of God. Kathleen Norris. CrSp

Girlfriend. Tomioka Taeko, *tr. fr. Japanese by* Kenneth Rexroth *and* Ikuko Atsumi. WPJ

Girls. Kenneth Rosen. AmPA

Girls and boys come out to play. *Unknown*. BoTP; PYC; ReMoGo

Girls are dandy. *Unknown*. RoPo

Girls are simply the prettiest things. My Cat and I. Roger McGough. OFC; OxBTC; SoCa

Girls around Cape Horn, The. *Unknown*. AmFP

Girls Bathing, Galway 1965. Seamus Heaney. InPS

Girls, brighter than wine, are clothed and naked, The. Night Club. F. R. Scott. NOBC

Girls' Chorus. Christopher Logue. IHNG

Girl's far treble, muted to the heat, The. Milkmaid. Laurie Lee. BoLoP; FaBoTw

Girl's Hair, A. Dafydd ab Edmwnd, *tr. fr. Welsh by* Gwyn Williams. OBWVE

Girl's Head, A. Katherine Gallagher. NOBAu

Girls in the Plural. Medbh McGuckian. DT

Girls in Their Seasons. Derek Mahon. BoLoP

Girl's Lamentation, The. William Allingham. TIRV

Girls of Llanbadarn, The. Dafydd ap Gwilym, *tr. fr. Welsh by* Leslie Norris. DiPo

Girls of Llanbadarn, The. Dafydd ap Gwilym, *tr. fr. Welsh by* Rolfe Humphries. OBWVE

Girls of the riverside, Nereids, did you see. Pan Asks about Daphnis. Diodorus Zonas, *tr. fr. Greek by* Alistair Elliot. GrAn

Girls of Yueh, The. Li Po, *tr. fr. Chinese by* Robert Payne. TAL

Girls on mopeds rode to Fécamp parties. The Musical Orchard. Douglas Dunn. FaBoMo

Girls on the Yueh River. Li Po, *tr. fr. Chinese*. ChTr

Girls' School. Alan Moore. BiHa

Girls scream. School's Out. W. H. Davies. OBMV

Girls today in society, The. Brush Up Your Shakespeare. Cole Porter. OBAL

Girls wake, stretch, and pad up to the door, The. Apartment Cats. Thom Gunn. GrPl

Girls Working in Banks. Karl Shapiro. WeW

Girod Street Cemetery: New Orleans. Harry Morris. GoYe

Girt in my guiltless gown, as I sit here and sew. At. to The Earl of Surrey Henry Howard, Earl of Surrey. SiPSBD

(Woman's Answer, A.) SiPS

Girtonian Funeral, A. *Unknown*. FaBoCo

Gislebertus' Eve. John Berryman. LCAP

Gisli, the Chieftain, *sels*. Isabella Valancy Crawford.

Git Along Down to Town. *Unknown*. AmFP

Git Along, Little Dogies. *Unknown*. *See* As I was a-walking [*or* walked out] one morning for pleasure.

Git ma my aäle I tell tha, an' if I mun doy I mun doy. (*LL*) Northern Farmer: Old Style. Tennyson. EnVR

Gita Govinda, The, *sels*. Jayadeva, *tr. fr. Sanskrit*.

Hymn to Vishnu. AWP

"Sandal and garment of yellow and lotus garlands upon his body of blue." ErPo; TAL

Gitanjali, *sels*. Rabindranath Tagore.

Day after Day. OBMV

"Deliverance is not for me in renunciation." WGRP

"Have you not heard his silent steps?" WGRP

"He it is, the innermost one, who awakens my being with his deep hidden touches." WGRP

"Here is thy footstool and there rest thy feet." WGRP

I Have Got My Leave. OBMV

"I know not from what distant time thou art ever coming nearer to meet me." WGRP

If It Is Not My Portion. OBMV

"Leave this chanting and singing and telling of beads." WGRP

On the Slope of the Desolate River. OBMV

Thou Art the Sky. OBMV

Giuseppe, da barber, ees greata for "mash." Mia Carlotta. T. A. Daly. NBLV

Giv but to things their tru esteem. Right Apprehension. Thomas Traherne. PoEL-2

Give a man a horse he can ride. Gifts. James Thomson ("B.V."). *Fr.* Sunday up the River. OBEV

Give a man his. Wait for Me. Robert Creeley. NOBA; PPP

Give a single penny that we may not sing in vain. (*LL*) The Children's Carol. Eleanor Farjeon. PChr

Give a thing, take it back. *Unknown*. ISE

Give All to Love. Emerson. AmPP; AnAmPo; ArLo; AWP; LiTA; MeMAP; NOBA; OBEV; OxBA; PoEL-4; PoLF; TAP; TrGrPo

Give all you have been, or could be. (*LL*) Barter. Sara Teasdale. FaBV; FaPON; SoSe

Give, and take the cash. Strato, *tr. fr. Greek by* W. G. Shepherd. GrAn

Give as you would if an angel. How to Give. *Unknown*. BLRP

Give attention to my ditty and I'll not keep you long. My Grandfather's Days. *Unknown*. OBET

Give back my dead! The Cry of South Africa. Olive Schreiner. PeSAV

Give beauty all her right. Thomas Campion. AAS

(Beauty Is Not Bound.) TrGrPo

Give Crabbe, dear Helen, on your shelf, To Helen, with Crabbe's Poems: a Birthday Present. Winthrop Mackworth Praed. EPCY

Give ear my children to my words. John Rogers' Exhortation to His Children. *Unknown*. *Fr.* New England Primer, The. OBCA

Give Ear, O God, to My Loud Cry. Thomas Prince. AH

Give Ear, O Heavens, to That Which I Declare. Henry Ainsworth. AH; ChIV-1

Give ear, O my people, to my law. Bible, *O.T., paraphrased by* Sir Thomas Wyatt. *Fr.* Psalms.

(Psalm LXXVIII: "There where the deepe did show his sandy flore," *paraphrased by* the Countess of Pembroke.) OBVE

Give ear to my prayer, O God. Bible, *O.T., paraphrased by* Sir Thomas Wyatt. *Fr.* Psalms. AWP

(Psalm LV: Exaudi, Deus: "My God most glad to look, most prone to hear," *paraphrased by* the Countess of Pembroke.) OBVE, *sts.* 1–4; WPE

Give Ear, Ye Heavens. Bible, *O.T.* *Fr.* Deuteronomy. TrJP

Give ear you lusty gallants. A Famous Sea-Fight. John Looke. CoMu

Give God thy heart. Motto for a Sundial. *Unknown*. FaBoEE

Give greatly of your grunts, O pig. Hymn to Joy. Julia Cunningham. PChr

Give her a tune and she'll break it they said. Lotte Lenya. Michael O'Loughlin. *Fr.* Two Women. IB

Give him the darkest inch your shelf allows. George Crabbe. E. A. Robinson. BLPL; CMoP; LiTA; LiTM; MeMAP; MoAB; MoAmPo; NAAL-2; NOBA; NoP; OxBA; PoEL-5; TAP

Give Isaac the nymph who no beauty can boast. Sheridan. *Fr.* Duenna, The. NOIV

Give Lucinda pearl nor stone. To the New Year. Thomas Carew. CaPo

Give me a boy whose tender skin. Martial, *tr. fr. Latin by* Brian Hill. PeHV

Give me a chair. Song of the Poor Man. *Unknown, tr. by* Anselm Hollo. TTY

Give me a color. America. Wendy Rose. CDW

Give me a death like Buddha's. Let me fall. Stanley Moss. SM

Give me a girl (if one I needs must meet). Women. William Cartwright. BeJo; ErPo

Give me a good digestion, Lord,/ And also something to digest. An Ancient Prayer. Thomas H. B. Webb. BLPA; FaBoBe

(Prayer Found in Chester Cathedral, A.) PoToHe

Give me a happy heart and suasive tongue. A Happy Heart. Josephine D. Henderson Heard. CBWP-4

Give me a harsh land to wring music from. This Land. Ian Mudie. NOBAu

Give me a heart where no impure. To Castara ("Give me a heart where no impure.") William Habington. *Fr.* Castara. BeJo

Give Me a Kiss from Those Sweet Lips of Thine. *Unknown*. InvP

Give me a man that is not dull. His Desire. Robert Herrick. OxBSP

Give me a mattress on the ship's poop some day. Antiphilus, *tr. fr. Greek by* Peter Jay. GrAn

Give me a pen. Testament of a Rebel. Breyten Breytenbach, *tr. fr. Afrikaans by* André P. Brink. PeSAV

Give me a royal niche — it is my due. George III. Thackeray. *Fr.* Georges, The. FaBoEE

Give me a son. The blessing sent. The Mother, the Nurse, and the Fairy. John Gay. *Fr.* Fables. PeLV

Give me a spoon of oleo, Ma. Domestic Science. *Unknown.* WBLP

Give me a thrill, says the reader. Fiction and the Reading Public. Philip Larkin. NOBL; OBSV

Give me back my stones! (*LL*) The Testing-Tree. Stanley Kunitz. FYAP; MAT; UnPo

"Give me but two brigades," said Hooker. The Battle of Lookout Mountain. George Henry Boker. PAH

Give me death. (*LL*) The Maja's Glance. Fernando Periquet Y Zuaznabar. RiWo

Give me, give me Buriano. Bacchus's Opinion of Wine, and Other Beverages. Francesco Redi, *tr. fr. Italian by* Leigh Hunt. *Fr.* Bacchus in Tuscany. AWP; OBVE

Give me, great God! said I, a little farm. Verses Written in the Chiosk [of the British Palace], at Pera, Overlooking [the City of] Constantinople. Lady Mary Wortley Montagu. ECEV; ECWP; OBTV

Give me hunger. At a Window. Carl Sandburg. FaBoBe; PoToHe; TrPWD

Give me, in this inconstant ebb and flow. Seaward Bound. Alice Brown. TrPWD

Give Me Jesus. *Unknown.* BPo

Give Me Leave. "A. W." TrGrPo

Give me leave to rail at you. The Earl of Rochester. NOSC

Give me more love, or more disdain. Mediocrity in Love Rejected. Thomas Carew. BeJo; PFP

Give me my captive soul, or take. Church Lock-and-Key. George Herbert. GeHe

Give Me My Infant Now. Te-whaka-io-roa, *tr. fr. Maori by* John White. NAs; WTO

Give me, my love, that billing kiss. The Kiss. Thomas Moore. EnLoPo

Give me my robe, put on my crown; I have. Shakespeare. *Fr.* Antony and Cleopatra. OxAEP-1
(Cleopatra's Death.) TrGrPo
(Immortal Longings.) FaBoRV

Give me my scallop-shell of quiet. The Passionate Man's Pilgrimage. Sir Walter Ralegh. AAS; ChIV-2, *st. 1 only*; ChTr; EBEvV, (*st. 1 only*); EIL; EnRePo; LiTB; NOBE; NoP; NoSic; PeECV; PoE; PoEL-2; PoRA; RB; SCGP, (*st. 1 only*); SiPSBD; TFi, (*st. 1 only*); TrGrPo
(Give mee my Escallope shell of Quiett.) OxAEP-1
(His Pilgrimage.) GGP; OBEV
(My Pilgrimage.) WGRP
(Pilgrimage, The.) SiPS
(Verses made by Sir Walter Raleigh the Night before he was Beheaded.) OxAEP-1

Give Me My Work. George Whetstone. EIL

Give me new Phoenix wings to fly at my desire. (*LL*) On Sitting Down to Read "King Lear" Once Again. Keats. EBEV; EnRP; EPCY; NAEL-2; NoP

Give me, O indulgent fate! The Countess of Winchilsea. *Fr.* Petition for an Absolute Retreat, The. ECWP; NOSC; PoEL-3; TrGrPo; WPE, *abr.*

Give me of every language, first my vigorous English. The English Language. William Wetmore Story. GN

Give me of your bark, O Birch-tree! Longfellow. *Fr.* Song of Hiawatha, The. Mes
(Hiawatha's Canoe.) OHIP

Give me one kiss. To Dianeme. Robert Herrick. CaPo; FaBoBe

Give me one small smothering of earth. Leonidas of Tarentum, *tr. fr. Greek by* Peter Levi. GrAn

Give me something to eat. Poor Crow! Mary Mapes Dodge. OBCA

Give me sweet nectar in a kiss. *Unknown.* FaBoEE

Give me that man that dares bestride. His Cavalier. Robert Herrick. CaPo; GoJo

Give me the avowed, erect and manly foe. George Canning *and* John Hookham Frere. *Fr.* New Morality. OBF

Give me the bracelets that your warriors wear. Tarpeia. Anne Lynch Botta. AmWP

Give me the broom. The leftovers sweep the leavings away. (*LL*) The Floor Is Dirty. Edward Field. NeAP

Give me the dance of your boughs, O Tree. Song to a Tree. Edwin Markham. FaPON

Give me the Daulian bird and Locrian Arsinoë. From V. C. (a Gentleman of Verona). Gavin Ewart. OxBC

Give me the lowest place: not that I dare. The Lowest Place. Christina Rossetti. NOBVV; TrPWD

Give me the merchants of the Indian mines. Mine Argosy from Alexandria. Christopher Marlowe. *Fr.* Jew of Malta, The. ChTr

Give me the Muse whose generous force. Isaac Watts. *Fr.* Adventurous Muse, The. EPCY

Give me the right of way. Irish. Paul Celan, *tr. fr. German by* Michael Hamburger. OBVE

Give Me the Splendid Silent Sun. Walt Whitman. BoNaP; FaPON; HAP; MoAmPo; NOBA

Give me the wretched refuse of your teams: pitchers with sore elbows. Amurrika! Philip Appleman. BXAP

Give me those flowers there, Dorcas. Reverend sirs. Shakespeare. *Fr.* Winter's Tale, The. OxAEP-1

Give me three grains of corn. (*LL*) Give Me Three Grains of Corn, Mother. Amelia Blandford Edwards. AS; BLPA

Give Me Three Grains of Corn, Mother. Amelia Blandford Edwards. AS; BLPA

Give me truths. Blight. Emerson. NOBA; NoP

Give me white paper! Columbus. Edward Everett Hale. PAH

Give me wide walls to build my house of Life. Wide Walls. *Unknown.* PoToHe

Give me your hand old Revolutionary. The Centenarian's Story. Walt Whitman. CTC

Give me your pardon, sir. I have done you wrong. Shakespeare. *Fr.* Hamlet. DL; NAWM-1

Give me your tired, your poor. The Tragic Condition of the Statue of Liberty. Bernadette Mayer. UL

Give mee my Escallope shell of Quiett. Sir Walter Ralegh. *See* Give me my scallop-shell of quiet.

Give money me, take friendship whoso list. Of Money. Barnabe Googe. EIL; FF; NBLV; NoP; NoSic; SoSe

Give my heart. (*LL*) A Christmas Carol. Christina Rossetti. ChTr; InPS; NOBVV; OHIP

Give Not Our Blankets, Tax-Fed Squire. Ebenezer Elliot. *Fr.* Year of Seeds, The. Son

Give oftener what is heard of than received. (*LL*) For the Lady Olivia Porter; a Present upon a New Year's Day. Sir William Davenant. JCP; MeLP; NOSC

Give [*or* Geve] Place, Ye Lovers. The Earl of Surrey. *See* Give place, ye lovers (here before).

Give Our Conscience Light. Aline Badger Carter. TrPWD

Give over, now, red roses. Warning of Winter. Mary Ursula Bethell. FaBoWP; PeNZ

Give over to high things the fervent thought. To Lovers of Earth: Fair Warning. Countee Cullen. CDC

Give pardon, blessèd soul, to my bold cries. On the Death of Sir Philip Sidney. Henry Constable. EIL; OBEV
(To Sir Philip Sidney's Soul.) EIL; NoSic

Give patient eare to something I man saye. Admonition to Montgomerie. James I, King of England. GTBS; GTBS-P; OxBS

Give Peace in These Our Days, O Lord. Edmund Grindal. AH

Give Peace, O God, the Nations Cry. John W. Norris. AH

Give place all ye that doth rejoice. Sir Thomas Wyatt. SiPS

Give place, ye lovers (here before). The Earl of Surrey. EnRePo; GGP; SiPSBD
(Give [*or* Geve] Place, Ye Lovers.) AAS; SiPS
(Praise of His Love, Wherein He Reproveth Them That Compare Their Ladies with His, A.) EIL

Give place, you ladies, and be gone! A Praise of His Lady. *At. to* John Heywood. EIL; OBEV

Give sorrow words; the grief that does. Shakespeare. *Fr.* Macbeth. IMW

Give store of days, good Jove, give length of years. Juvenal, *tr. by* Henry Vaughan. *Fr.* Satires. OBSV

Give Thanks. Helen Isabella Tupper. BLRP

Give thanks for this turn for the better. A Change in Style. Eochadh O'Hussey. NOIV

Give the barber a pinch of snuff. (*LL*) Barber, barber, shave a pig. Mother Goose. OxNR; ReMoGo

Give the king thy judgments, O God. Bible, *O.T., paraphrased by* Sir Thomas Wyatt. *Fr.* Psalms.
(Psalm LXXII: "Looke how the woods, where enterlaced trees," *paraphrased by* the Countess of Pembroke.) OBVE

Give the sounds of the curved mated phonographs. Three Found Poems. George Hitchcock. OBAL

Give them back/ to me. Blues. Léon Damas, *tr. fr. French.* NegPo, *tr. by* Ellen Conroy Kennedy

Give them my regards when you go to the school reunion. More of a Corpse than a Woman. Muriel Rukeyser. NALW; NMM

Give Them the Flowers Now. *Unknown.* WBLP

Give them to my sister Kate. (*LL*) Now I lay me down to sleep,/ A bag of peanuts at my feet. *Unknown.* RoPo

Give thou my sacred relics burial. (*LL*) His Return to London. Robert Herrick. BeJo; CaPo; FaBoPP; FF; NAEL-1

Give to me the life I love. The Vagabond. Robert Louis Stevenson. OxAEP-2

Give to the Living. Ida Goldsmith Morris. WBLP

Give to the winds thy fears. Courage. Paul Gerhardt, *tr. fr. German by* John Wesley. WGRP

Give unto the Lord, O ye mighty. Bible, *O.T., paraphrased by* Sir Thomas Wyatt. *Fr.* Psalms. AWP

Give up the bitterness. Dionne Brand. *Fr.* Epigrams to Ernesto Cardenal in Defense of Claudia. PBCV

Give us a kiss and off we go. *(LL)* Children's Ball-Bouncing Song. *Unknown.* NOBAu

"Give us a song!" the soldiers cried. The Song of the Camp. Bayard Taylor. AnAmPo; BeLS; GN; WBLP

Give us a virile Christ for these rough days! A Virile Christ. Rex Boundy. WGRP

Give us a watchword for the hour. Evangelize! Henry Crocker. BLRP

Give us another poem, he said. Patrick Kavanagh. IPY; PeIV

Give Way! Charlotte Perkins Gilman. WGRP

Give way, an ye be ravished by the sun. To Marygolds. Robert Herrick. NAEL-1

Give Way, Ye Gates. Theodore Roethke. CMoP

Giveaway, The. Phyllis McGinley. PoRA

Given away in poems, only their solitude kept. *(LL)* The Correspondence School Instructor Says Goodbye to His Poetry Students. Galway Kinnell. NoAM; NOBA; NoP; TAP

"Given faith," sighed the vicar of Deneham. *Unknown.* PeLi

Given Flesh Returns Nothing but Bread, The. Kelly Aileen. ChIV-2

Given to a Lady Who Asked Me to Write a Poem. Janet Little. ECWP

Given to death and life, no choice. Material Soul. Peter Riley. VaA

Given to love. *(LL)* Agony, An. As Now. Amiri Baraka. AmPP; BPo; LiTM; NAAL-2; PoE; PPP

Givenchy Field. H. d'A. B. NSI

Giver of bliss and pain, of song and prayer. William A. Percy. TrPWD

Gives it a wipe, — and all is gone. *(LL)* The Poet's Fate. Thomas Hood. FaBoEE; FiBHP

Gives to each dead his ressurection day. *(LL)* The Yew-Tree. Vernon Watkins. LiTB

Giving. *Unknown.* PoToHe

Giving and Forgiving. Thomas Grant Springer. PoToHe

Giving her mother's/ zealous eye. Paulus Silentiarius, *tr. fr. Greek by* Andrew Miller. GrAn

Giving oneself to the dentist or doctor who is a good one. The Kind of Act Of. Robert Creeley. NeAP

Giving Potatoes. Adrian Mitchell. NBLV; RB

Giving Rabbit to My Cat Bonnie. Anne Stevenson. FaBoWP

Giving Thanks, 4. Bible, *O.T., paraphrased by* Sir Thomas Wyatt. *See* Make a joyful noise unto the Lord, all ye lands.

Giving Up Butterflies. Geraldine Kudaka. ETG

Giving up women is worse than animal laxatives. John Tranter. *Fr.* Crying in Early Infancy. NoAM

Giving, while the rain lasts, soft noises. Eaves. Ellis Jones, *tr. fr. Welsh by* Anthony Conran. OBWVE

Gizzard and some ruby inner parts, A. Margaret Avison. HAP

Glacier. Norman Nicholson. OBTV

Glad and blithe mote ye be. A Hymn of the Incarnation. *Unknown.* MeEL

Glad at the Cold (1955). Alan Dugan. NoAM

Glad, but not flush'd with gladness. Swinburne. *Fr.* Before the Mirror. OBEV

Glad Christmas comes, and every hearth. December. John Clare. OBCP

Glad Day. Louis Untermeyer. TrJP

Glad Eye, The. Paul Muldoon. NoAM

Glad harvest greets us, The; brave toiler for bread. Song of the Harvest. Henry Stevenson Washburn. OHIP

Glad hymns of praise from land and sea. *(LL)* Eternal Father, Strong to Save. William Whiting. FaPoR; NOCV

Glad that I live am I. A Little Song of Life. Lizette Woodworth Reese. FaPON; OBCA

Glad youth had come thy sixteenth year to crown. Ausonius, *tr. fr. Latin.* PeHV

Glade, The. Robert Kelly. *Fr.* Book of Persephone, The. PoM

Gladstone was still respected. Yeux Glauques. Ezra Pound. *Fr.* Hugh Selwyn Mauberly. (Life and Contacts). AmPP; CMoP; InPS; LiTA; LiTM; MoAmPo; NoAM; NOBA; NoP; TAP

Glamis thou art, and Cawdor; and shalt be. Shakespeare. *Fr.* Macbeth. OxAEP-1

Glamors the landscape. *(LL)* Stars around the luminous moon — how soon they. Sappho. STV

Glamour of the end attic, the smell of old, The. Perdita. Louis MacNeice. PoA

Glance, The. George Herbert. ESCV

Glance. Peter Schmitt. NGP

Glance, A. *Unknown, tr. fr. Irish by* Thomas Kinsella. NOIV

Glanced down at Shannon from the sky-way. Irish-American Dignitary. Austin Clarke. BIrV

Glances. William Stafford. SM

Glanmore Sonnets, *sels.* Seamus Heaney.
    "I dreamt we slept in a moss in Donegal." NoP
    "This evening the cuckoo and the corncrake." IPY
    "Thunderlight on the split logs: big raindrops." IPY
    "Vowels plowed into other: opened ground." NoP

Glaring sunshine never knew! The. *(LL)* All's Well. Whittier. OxBSP

Glasgerion, B *vers. Unknown.* ESPB

Glasgow 1956. Gerald Mangan. PWE

Glasgow Peggie. *Unknown.* ESPB

Glasgow Schoolboys, Running Backwards. Douglas Dunn. OxBC

Glasgow Street. William Montgomerie. OxBS

Glasnevin Cemetery. Michael O'Loughlin. PBCIP

Glass. Vickie Karp. UTF

Glass, The. Sharon Olds. NIP

Glass. Takako Uchino Lento, *tr. fr. Japanese by the author.* BoWoP

Glass Blower, The. James Scully. NYBP; TwCP

Glass Bubbles, The. Samuel Greenberg. LiTA

Glass falls lower, The. Sad Green. Sylvia Townsend Warner. MoBrPo

Glass goblet, A. Bring in the Wine. Li Ho, *tr. fr. Chinese by* A. C. Graham. PLT

Glass has been falling all the afternoon, The. Storm Warnings. Adrienne Rich. AiP; GOYP; NAAL-2; NIP

Glass I've wanted to live. Through You. Edwin Honig. TAP

Glass King, The. Eavan Boland. CIP

Glass man, without external reference, The. *(LL)* Asides on the Oboe. Wallace Stevens. FaBoMo; MoAB; MoAmPo

Glass of Beer, A. James Stephens. CMoP; FaBoCo; FiBHP; InPK; MoP; NBLV; OBMV; OxBS; OxBTC; PeIV; RB

Glass of Water, The. Wallace Stevens. MeMAP; MoAB; MoAmPo; OxBA; TAP

Glass on the picture from the Bible, The. Darkening Hotel Room. Alfred Corn. VCAP

Glass, out of deep and out of desperate want. Upon Glass: Epigram. Robert Herrick. JCP

Glass Town, The. Alastair Reid. NYBP

Glass was the street. Emily Dickinson. OxBA

Glassblower lies here at rest, A. J. B. Morton. FaBoEE

Glassed with cold sleep and dazzled by the moon. Train Journey. Judith Wright. FaBoMA; PBWP

Glasses are raised, the voices drift into laughter, The. Pub. Julian Symons. LiTB

Glassily strand tthe sea. *(LL)* The Undead. Richard Wilbur. CoAP; OxBC

Glaucopis. Richard Hughes. OBMV

Glaucus, pilot of the Nessus strait, born. On the Death of the Ferryman, Glaucus. Antiphilus, *tr. fr. Greek by* W. S. Merwin. GrAn

Glaukon and Korydon, mountain herdsmen. Erucius, *tr. fr. Greek by* Peter Levi. GrAn

Glazed day crumbles to its fall, The. Provincetown, Mass. Harvey Shapiro. PoA

Glazier, The. Stéphane Mallarmé, *tr. fr. French.* OBVE, *tr. by* Keith Bosley

Glazing the pale hair, the duplicate gray standard faces. *(LL)* Dolor. Theodore Roethke. AmPP; CMoP; HCAP; HeIP; HoPM; LiTM; MoP; NoAM; OxBSP; PoA; TRP

Glazunoviana. John Ashbery. LCAP; VCAP

Gleamed a resplendent star. At Christmas-Tide. H. Cordelia Ray. CBWP-3

Gleaming with agitated torches. *(LL)* Opal. Amy Lowell. NALW

Gleaner, The. Jane Taylor. OxBChV

Gleaners of grain they did not sow. Rooks: December. Huw Menai. AngWe

Gleaning. David Shimoni, *tr. fr. Hebrew by* Ruth Finer Mintz. MHP

Glee-fulfiller, fruit-producer, cook who glad the year can feed. Concerning the Fruit-bringing Autumn Season. Catharina Regina von Greiffenberg, *tr. fr. German by* George C. Schoolfield. GePo

Glen Canyon on the Colorado. Richard Shelton. FoLa

Glen Lough. Geoffrey Grigson, *tr. fr. Irish by* James Clarence Mangan. FaBoPP; OBTV

Glen of Silence, The. "Hugh MacDiarmid." CMoP

Glenaradale. Walter Chalmers Smith. OBEV; PeVV

Glenarm. John Lyle Donaghy.

Glenaveril, *sels.* "Owen Meredith."
    Tears. EBVV

Glencoe, *sels.* Douglas Stewart.

"Sigh, wind in the pine." CBAP; FaBoMA

Glengormley. Derek Mahon. CIP; IIP

Glenkindie was ance a harper gude. Glasgerion. *Unknown.* ESPB

Glenlogie. *Unknown.* GN

Glenlogie; or, Jean o Bethelnie, A *vers. Unknown.* ESPB

Glenlogie; or, Jean o Bethelnie, B *vers. Unknown.* ESPB

Glenn Miller and I were heroes. Jack Kerouac. *Fr.* Mexico City Blues. NeAP

Glens, The. John Hewitt. IIP; PeIV

Glib little beer-buff from Troon, A. Bill Greenwell. PeLi

Glide gently, thus for ever glide. Remembrance of Collins, Composed upon the Thames near Richmond. Wordsworth. EPCY

Glide Soft, Ye Silver Floods. William Browne. *Fr.* Britannia's Pastorals. EIL, II, Song 1

Glides white through the phosphorus sea. *(LL)* Commemorative of a Naval Victory. Herman Melville. AiP; HAP; UnPo

Glimpse. Pearl Cleage Lomax. PoBA

Glimpse, A. Frances Cornford. OBMV

Glimpse, A. Walt Whitman. AmPP; AnAmPo; OxBA; PeHV; PPP; RaBo

Glimpse of a once-loved face, The. What Do They Say. Gary Snyder. NNaP

Glimpse of Shere Khan, A. Chris Wallace-Crabbe. OBAP

Glimpse of Starlings, A. Brendan Kennelly. PWE

Glimpse of the Body Shop, A. Stephen Berg. NaP

Glimpse through an interstice caught, A. A Glimpse. Walt Whitman. AmPP; AnAmPo; OxBA; PeHV; PPP; RaBo

Glimpsed. Vladimir Holan, *tr. fr. Czech* by Ian Milner *and* Jarmila Milner. PoSu

Glimpsed from the train, which takes shadow for truth. Glimpsed. Vladimir Holan, *tr. fr. Czech* by Ian Milner *and* Jarmila Milner. PoSu

Glimpsed world, halfway through the film, A. The Malice of Innocence. Denise Levertov. NNaP

Glimpses of Infancy. Priscilla Jane Thompson. CBWP-2

Glinting in their tresses. *(LL)* Here lies the dust of Timas. Sappho. InMo

Glion? — Ah, twenty years, it cuts. Obermann Once More. Matthew Arnold. PoEL-5

Glistening at my core. *(LL)* Four-Word Lines. May Swenson. GLP; WPE

Glistening bone, faeces. *(LL)* Cave Painter. Aidan Carl Mathews. IB

Glitter green, over such a spell of kisses. *(LL)* So let's live — really live! — for love and loving. Catullus. STV

Glittering, adroit, the Sicilian wonder. Death and Empedocles 444 B.C. Horace Gregory. PoA

Glittering high in the midnight sky the starry rockets soar. Dewey and His Men. Wallace Rice. PAH

Glittering leaves of the rhododendrons, The. Green Symphony. John Gould Fletcher. MoAmPo

Glittering rises in flocks, The. The Approaches. W. S. Merwin. NOBA; Prf

Glittering topaz in your glass, The. At a Danse Macabre. Charles Spear. PeNZ

Gloat, glittering talmudist. Talmudist. Stanley Burnshaw. DiPo

Globe, a paper of the Tories, The. A Suggestion Made by the Posters of the *Globe.* J. E. Thorold Rogers. FaBoEE

Globe in North Carolina, The. Derek Mahon. BiHa; PBCIP

Globe of th'earth on which we dwell, The. On the Tack. Thomas Hearne. ECEV

Glog-Hole, The. "Hugh MacDiarmid." NTP

Gloire de Dijon. D. H. Lawrence. CMoP; ELP; EnLoPo; ErPo; GBL; NoAM

Glompse of that fierce green land of mink and henna. *(LL)* To the Lady Portrayed by Margaret Dumont. John Hollander. OBAL; PoA

Gloom of death is on the raven's wing, The. The Raven. E. A. Robinson, *after* Nicarchus. AWP; FaBoEE; OBAL

Gloom of night had overspread the land, The. The Nativity. Mary Weston Fordham. CBWP-2

Glooms of the live-oaks, beautiful-braided and woven. The Marshes of Glynn. Sidney Lanier. AmPP; AnAmPo; ImPo; LiTA; NOBA; OxBA; PrIm; WGRP

Gloomy am I, oppressed and sad. The Poet's Arbour in the Birchwood. Edward Williams, *tr. fr. Welsh* by Kenneth Hurlstone Jackson. OBWVE

Gloomy and dark art thou, O chief of the mighty Omahas. To the Driving Cloud. Longfellow. ChTr; FaBoRV; PoEL-5

Gloomy Cathedral, A. Paris. Gertrud Kolmar, *tr. fr. German* by David Kipp. PBWP

Gloomy Day Is Ended, The. Pushkin, *tr. fr. Russian* by Philip L. Miller. RiWo

Gloomy day is ended; the darkness of the gloomy night, The. The Gloomy Day Is Ended. Pushkin, *tr. fr. Russian* by Philip L. Miller. RiWo

Gloomy grammarians in golden gowns. Of the Manner of Addressing Clouds. Wallace Stevens. PoA

Gloomy lowering of the sky, The. Written on a Gloomy Day, in Sickness. Susanna Blamire. ECWP

Gloomy minister of Hades who sail this stream. Leonidas of Tarentum, *tr. fr. Greek* by Barbara Hughes Fowler. *Fr.* Epigrams. HePo

Gloomy night before us flies, The. Jefferson and Liberty. *Unknown.* SWP

Gloomy night embraced the place. The Shepherds' Hymn. Richard Crashaw. *Fr.* In the Holy Nativity of Our Lord God. GeHe; NOBE; PoEL-2; SeCV-1

Gloomy Night of Sadness, The. *Unknown.* AH

Gloomy thought, Ben Bulben, A. The Deserted Mountain. *Unknown, tr. fr. Irish* by John Montague. BIrV

Gloria in Excelsis. *Unknown.* WGRP

Gloriana Dying. Sylvia Townsend Warner. FaBoEH; FaBoWP

Glories of our blood and state, The. James Shirley. *Fr.* Contention of Ajax and Ulysses, The. BeJo; ChTr; EBEvV; FaBoRV; HAP; InvP; JCP; NoP; OBD; PeECV; PoRA; PPP; SCGP; TrGrPo

(Death the Leveller.) BLPL; FaPoR; FF; GGP; GTBS; GTBS-P; ImPo; LiTB; NOBE; OBEV; OtMeF; PlP; UnPo

(Dirge: "Glories of our blood and state, The.") AWP; OAEL-1; PoEL-2

Glories of the world struck me, made me aria, once, The. John Berryman. *Fr.* Dream Songs. HCAP

Glorious dead, walking, The. Shadow Songs. J. H. Prynne. VaA

Glorious it is/ to see long-haired winter caribou. *Unknown, tr. fr. Eskimo. Fr.* Song of Caribou, Musk Oxen, Women, and Men Who Would Be Manly. RFM; WTO

Glorious Maid, whose soule to Heaven is gone, The. The Arguement. Anna Hume. *Fr.* Triumphs of Death. KTR

Glorious Strike of the Builders, The. *Unknown.* FaBoVe

Glorious the day when in arms at Assunpink. Assunpink and Princeton. Thomas Dunn English. PAH

Glorious the sun in mid career. Christopher Smart. *Fr.* Song to David, A. ChTr; EBEV; FaBoCh; NAEL-1; NOBE, *abr.*; OAEL-1; PoEL-3; TrGrPo, *abr.*

Glorious Things of Thee Are Spoken. John Newton. NOCV; WGRP

Glorious Victory of Navarino! The. *Unknown.* CoMu

Glorious Virgin, heavenly vision. O Virgin. *Unknown, tr. fr. Gaelic by* Douglas Hyde. WTO

Glorious Wonders of the DEITY, The. *(LL)* Eden. Thomas Traherne. ChIV-1; ESCV; GeHe; PoEL-2; SeCV-2; TrGrPo

Glory. D. H. Lawrence. OxBSP

Glory. Marianne Moore. NYBP

Glory, The. Edward Thomas. OxBTC; PAW; TOF

Glory. Joseph Wise. AH

Glory and Enduring Fame. William Gilmore Simms. Son

Glory and loveliness have passed away. To Leigh Hunt, Esq. Keats. EnRP; Son

(Dedication: To Leigh Hunt, Esq.) OBNC

Glory be! I'm sixty! *(LL)* Emancipation. *Unknown.* BLPA

Glory Be to Chingwe's Hole. Jack A. Mapanje. HBAPE

Glory be to God for dappled things. Pied Beauty. Gerard Manley Hopkins. ArNa; AWP; CBCK; ClHu; CMoP; EaPr; EBEvV; EBVV; EnlH; EnVR; FaBoMo; FaPoB; GGP; GoJo; GTBS-P; HAP; HeIP; HoPM; ImPo; InPK; InPS; InvP; LiTB; LiTM; LPA; MeMBP; MoAB; MoBrPo; MoP; NAEL-2; NoAM; NOBE; NOBVV; NoP; NTP; OAEL-2; OBEV; OBMV; OBNC; OxAEP-2; OxBSP; PFP; PoE; Poetr; PoRA; PPP; PrIm; RaBo; RB; SCGP; SCV; SoSe; SOTW; TEP; TFi; TrGrPo; TTTS; UV; WeW

Glory be to God for Hopkins' verse. Pied Beauty. Stanley J. Sharpless. UV

Glory be to God on high. The Incarnation. Charles Wesley. NOCV

Glory be to God on high, and on earth peace, good-will towards men. Gloria in Excelsis. *Unknown.* WGRP

Glory Dead. *Unknown.* PBCV

Glory Hallelujah! or, John Brown's Body. *At. to* Charles Sprague Hall *and to* Thomas Brigham Bishop. *See* John Brown's Prayer.

Glory is of the sun, too, and the sun of suns. Glory. D. H. Lawrence. OxBSP

Glory of and Grace in the Church Set Out, The. Edward Taylor. *Fr.* God's Determinations [touching his Elect]. AmPP

Glory of God, The. Bible, *O.T., paraphrased by* Sir Thomas Wyatt. *See* Law of Jehovah is perfect, restoring the soul, The.

Glory of God in Creation, The. Thomas Moore. OHIP

Glory of Hanalei is its heavy rain, The. Alfred Alohikea, *tr. fr. Hawaiian by* S. H. Elbert *and* N. Mahoe. WTO

Glory of Him who moves all things rays forth, The. Dante, *tr. fr. Italian. Fr.* Divina Commedia. MeMAP; NAWM-1, *tr. by* John Ciardi

Glory of Love is brightest when the glory of self is dim, The. The True Apostolate. Ruby Weyburn Tobias. BLRP

Glory of my Work, and Me, The. (*LL*) His Prayer for Absolution. Robert Herrick. BeJo; SeCV-1; TrPWD

Glory of Nature, The. Frederick Tennyson. OBNC

Glory of the beauty of the morning, The. The Glory. Edward Thomas. OxBTC; PAW; TOF

Glory of the Day Was in Her Face, The. James Weldon Johnson. CDC; PoBA

Glory of the Garden, The. Kipling. ArNa

Glory of the great all-mover goes, The. Dante, *tr. fr. Italian. Fr.* Divina Commedia. MeMAP; OBD, *tr. by* T. W. Ramsey

Glory of Women. Siegfried Sassoon. NAEL-2; OBWP; OxAEP-2; PAW; PeFWW

Glory to God and to God's Mother chaste. To Dante Alighieri (He Commends the Work of Dante's Life). Giovanni Quirino, *tr. fr. Italian by* Dante Gabriel Rossetti. AWP

Glory to Osiris, the Prince of Everlastingness. He Singeth a Hymn to Osiris, the Lord of Eternity. *Unknown, tr. fr. Egyptian by* Robert Hillyer. *Fr.* Book of the Dead. AWP

Glory to Thee, My God, This Night. Thomas Ken. NOCV

GLory to you O God, from age to age. (*LL*) O Lord, how lovely it is to be your guest. Gregory Petrov. EaPr

Glory to you, oh pain, sorrow unending! The Grey-eyed King. "Anna Akhmatova," *tr. fr. Russian by* Robert Tracy. PBWV

Glory Trumpeter, The. Derek Walcott. NAEL-2

Glose. Michael Malinowitz. EOEF

Gloss. Padraic Fiacc. CIP; PNI

Gloss. David McCord. OBAL

Gloucester Moors. (Mile behind is Gloucester town, A.) William Vaughn Moody. AnAmPo; NOBA; OxBA

Sels.

"This earth is not the steadfast place." WGRP

Gloucestershire Wassail. *Unknown.* OBET

Glove, The. Harold Bond. NYBP

Glove, The. Ben Jonson. *Fr.* Cynthia's Revels. EiL; GBL

Glove and the Lions, The. Leigh Hunt. BeLS; FaPON; GN; WBLP

Gloves waiting for hands. (*LL*) The Daughters of Blum. Charles Wright. CoAP; SM

Glow and beauty of the stars, The. Sappho, *tr. fr. Greek by* Willis Barnstone. BoWoP

Glow, little glow-worm, fly of fire. The Glow-Worm. Johnny Mercer. OBAL

Glow-Worm, The. Johnny Mercer. OBAL

Glow-Worm, The. Charlotte Smith. FM

Glow-worm-like the daisies peer. Summer. John Davidson. BoNaP

Glow-Worms. P. A. Ropes. BoTP

Glowworm. David McCord. NTCP

Glowworm, The. Thomas Stanley. BeJo; NOSC

Glowworm in a garden prayed, A. A Very Minor Poet Speaks. Isabel Valle. BLPA

Gloze upon This Text, Dominus iis opus habet, A. George Gascoigne. ChIV-2

Glunk!/ I toss my heels up to my head. Oiseaurie. Margaret Widdemer. BXAP

Glutted, half asleep, browsing in. The Grace of Geldings in Ripe Pastures. Maxine W. Kumin. CAPP

Glutton, The. Robert Graves. CMoP

Glutton [*or* Glutton in the Tavern], The. William Langland. *Fr.* Vision of Piers Plowman, The. PoE

Glutton, The. John Oakman. OxBChV

Glycine's Song. Samuel Taylor Coleridge. *Fr.* Zapolya. CH; OBEV

Glykon, glory of Asia/ born in Pergamum. Antipater of Thessalonica, *tr. fr. Greek by* Alistair Elliot. GrAn

Glyn Cynon Wood. *Unknown, tr. fr. Welsh by* Gwyn Williams. OBWVE

Glyndwr, see thy comet flaming. Glyndwr's War Song. John Jones. AngWe

Glyndwr's War Song. John Jones. AngWe

Glyph. *Unknown, tr. fr. Washoe-Paiute Indian by* Mary Austin. LiTA

Gnarly and bent and deaf's a pos.' Zeke. L. A. G. Strong. MoBrPo

Gnat, The. Joseph Beaumont. FM; NOSC

Gnawed by a beetle. (*LL*) My lover capable of terrible lies. Kaccipettu Nannakaiyar. BoWoP; PBWP; WPOW

Gnawing the Breast. Sandra McPherson. LCAP

Gnome. Samuel Beckett. BIrV; OxBSP

Gnome, The. Harry Behn. FaPON; PDV

Gnomic Verses, *sels.* Blake.

Abstinence Sows Sand All Over. EBEV; FaBoEE; FF; GBL; MeMBP; OxBM; TrGrPo

Angel That Presided o'er My Birth, The. InPK; NAs; OxBSP; RB; TrGrPo

Great Things [Are Done]. ArNa; OxBSP

"He has observed the golden rule." TrGrPo

"Sword sang on the barren heath, The." FaBoEE; TrGrPo

(Sword and the Sickle, The.) ChTr

"They said this mystery shall never cease." TrGrPo

Gnu up at the zoo, The. John Hall Wheelock. NYBP

Go and ask Robin to bring the girls over. Vision by Sweetwater. John Crowe Ransom. CMoP; FaBoMo; MeMAP; MoAB; NOBA; OxBA; RB

Go and catch a falling star. Song. John Donne. AWP; ClHu; CoGr; EBEV; EIL; ELP; EnRePo; FaBV; FHYEP; HAP; HeIP; ImPo; InPK; InPS; JCP; LiTB; NAEL-1; NAWM-1; NIP; NOBE; NoP; NoSic; OBEV; OxAEP-1; SoSe; TFi; TrGrPo

(Goe and catche a falling starre.) CBNP; ESCV; FaPoB; HoPM; MeLP; NBLV; PoEL-2; SeCP; SeCV-1

(Song: Go and Catch a Falling Star.) ArLo; EBEvV; GGP; NOSC; PoE

Go and tell Aunt Nancy. The Old Grey Goose. *Unknown.* ChTr

Go and tell Aunt Nancy. *Unknown. See* Go tell Aunt Rhody [*or* Nancy].

Go back now; pause to mark. Horizon Thong. George Abbe. GoYe

Go back when you're rich, behung with lice. (*LL*) A Terrestrial Cuckoo. Frank O'Hara. CBNP; SOTW

Go, bar the door, you fool, she cries. (*LL*) Epigram on Florio. John Winstanley. FaBoEE

Go bet, penny, go bet, go! *Unknown.* MiEL

Go boy, and thy good mistress tell. Macbeth. Horace Smith *and* James Smith. BXAP

Go break to the needy charity's bread. How Long Shall I Give? *Unknown.* BLRP

Go Bring Me Back My Blue-eyed Boy. *Unknown.* AS

"Go Bring Me," Said the Dying Fair. William Hunter. AH

Go bring the captive, he shall die. Ortiz. Hezekiah Butterworth. PAH

Go, burning sighs, unto the frozen heart. Sir Thomas Wyatt. SiPSBD

Go By. Tennyson. *See* Come not, when I am dead.

Go by, go by. (*LL*) Come not, when I am dead. Tennyson. FaBoRV; GBL; PeVV

Go by, its clear depths never change. (*LL*) A Mountain Spring. Ch'u Ch'uang I. OHMPC

Go by train from here in any direction. Views of Where One Is. John Riley. VaA

Go call a careful painter, let him show. Of the French Kings Nativity. Benjamin Harris. SCAP

Go charge Agrippa. Shakespeare. *Fr.* Antony and Cleopatra. OBF

Go child, who is my sin and nothing more. (*LL*) Unknown Girl in the Maternity Ward. Anne Sexton. MoP; NAs; NoAM

Go! cotton lords and corn lords, go! A Chartist Chorus. Ernest Charles Jones. CoGr

Go, daughters of Zion. The Death of Tammuz. Saul Tchernichovsky, *tr. fr. Hebrew by* L. V. Snowman. TrJP

Go Down Death. James Weldon Johnson. DL; PoBA

Go Down, Moses. *Unknown.* AnAmPo; BPo; PeECV; SWP

Go Down, O Sun, Out from the Motu River. Te Aomuhurangi Te Maaka, *tr. fr. Maori by the author.* PeNZ

Go Down, Old Hannah, *diff. versions. Unknown.* AmFP

Go down to Kew in lilac-time, in lilac-time, in lilac-time. The Barrel-Organ. Alfred Noyes. BLPL; BoTP; FaBV; MoBrPo; PoRA

Go, draw aside the curtain, and discover. Shakespeare. *Fr.* Merchant of Venice, The. OxAEP-1

Go, dumb-born book. Envoi (1919). Ezra Pound. *Fr.* Hugh Selwyn Mauberly. (Life and Contacts). AmPP; CMoP; HAP; InPS; LiTA; LiTM; MoP; NoAM; NOBA; NoP; TAP; UnPo; VGW

(Envoi: "Go, dumb-born book.") MoAB; MoAmPo; OxBA

Go fetch to me a pint o'wine. The Silver Tassie. Burns. GTBS; GTBS-P; NOBE; OBEV; ScCV

(My Bonnie Mary.) GGP

Go find Avicenna. Calling the Doctor (1000 A.D.). Nizami Arudi, *tr. fr. Persian by* Omar S. Pound. ArPe

Go, flaunting Rose! The Aesthete to the Rose. *Unknown.* BXAP

"Go, Flee?" — A man like me does not flee! Prophet, Go, Flee! Hayyim Nahman Bialik, *tr. fr. Hebrew by* Ruth Finer Mintz. MHP

Go Fly a Saucer, *sels.* David McCord.

"I've seen one flying saucer. Only when." FaPON

Go, for they call you, shepherd, from the hill. The Scholar Gipsy. Matthew Arnold. *Fr.* Scholar-Gipsy, The. ChTr; EBEV; EBVV; EBVVPR; EnVR; FaBoPP; FHYEP; HAP; MeMBP; NAEL-2; NOBE; NOBVV; NoP; OAEL-2; OBEV; OBNC; OxAEP-2; PoE; PoEL-5; SCGP; TEP; TFi

(Scholar-Gypsy, The.) ImPo

Go; — for 'tis Memorial morning. Memorial Day. Clara Ann Thompson. CBWP-2

Go forth from life in guise of mendicants. (*LL*) For, Lord, the Crowded Cities Be. Rainer Maria Rilke. AWP; TrJP

Go forth my little volume. God Speed. George Clinton Rowe. AAP

Go Forward. "A. R. G." BLRP

Go from me: I am one of those who fall. Mystic and Cavalier. Lionel Johnson. MoBrPo

Go from me. Yet I feel that I shall stand. Elizabeth Barrett Browning. *Fr.* Sonnets from the Portuguese. BLPL; CBLP; OBEV; OxAEP-2; TrGrPo

Go get me some of your father's gold. Pretty Polly. *Unknown.* AS

Go Get the Axe. *Unknown.* AS

Go, go, queint folies, sugred sin. Idle Verse. Henry Vaughan. MiEL

Go, grieving rimes of mine, to that hard stone. Petrarch, *tr. fr. Italian.* *Fr.* Sonnets to Laura. NAWM-1

Go hand-in-hand with modern days. (*LL*) Other Fabrics, Other Mores! Anna Maria Lenngren. AIW; PBWP

Go, Happy Rose. Martial, *tr. fr. Latin by* Brian Hill. PeHV

Go, happy rose, and wreathe my dear friend's brow. Go, Happy Rose. Martial, *tr. fr. Latin by* Brian Hill. PeHV

Go, Hart. *Unknown. See* Go, Heart, unto the Lamp of Licht.

Go, hart, unto thy Saviour. (*LL*) Go, Heart, unto the Lamp of Licht. *Unknown.*

Go Heart, Hurt with Adversity. *Unknown. See* Go hert, hurt with adversité.

Go, Heart, unto the Lamp of Licht. *Unknown.*

Go hert, hurt with adversité. *Unknown.* (Go Heart, Hurt with Adversity.) MeEL; OxBLMV

Go Home. Janet Reed McFatter. GrPl

Go home and look after your wives. (*LL*) An Encomium upon a Parliament. Daniel Defoe. APAS

Go home, you see, well I wouldn't run a risk like that. (*LL*) My Hat. Stevie Smith. BrRo; CBNP

Go! hunt the whiter ermine, and present. For the Lady Olivia Porter; a Present upon a New Year's Day. Sir William Davenant. JCP; MeLP; NOSC

Go I must. (*LL*) Cuckoo, cuckoo/ What do you do? *Unknown.* OxNR

Go I must; when I am gone. To His Tomb-Maker. Robert Herrick. SeCV-1

Go Idle Lines. Thomas Watson. *Fr.* Tears of Fancy, The. Son

Go, ill-sped book, and whisper to her ear. John Berryman. BoLoP

Go inside a stone. Stone. Charles Simic. InPS; NU

Go, let the fatted calf be killed. The Welcome. Abraham Cowley. *Fr.* Mistress, The. BoLoP; SeCV-1

Go, let us go my friends, go home. Home. *Unknown, tr. by* H. Tracey. WTO

Go, litel book, go litel myn tragedy. Go, Little Book ("Go, litel book, go litel myn tragedy.") Chaucer. *Fr.* Troilus and Criseyde [*or* Criseide]. EnVB; OAEL-1

(Chaucer's Wishes for his 'Troilus'.) EPCY

Go! little bill, and command me hertely. She Saw Me in Church. *Unknown.* MeEL

(Go, litull bill, and command me hertely.) MiEL

Go! little bill, and do me recommende. A Love Letter. *Unknown.* MeEL

Go Little Book. Robert Louis Stevenson. *See* Wishes.

Go, Little Book ("Go, litel book, go litel myn tragedy.") Chaucer. *Fr.* Troilus and Criseyde [*or* Criseide]. EnVB; OAEL-1

Go litle book, par avion. Richard Tillinghast. MT

Go, little quair. L'Envoy: To His Book. John Skelton. EnRePo

Go, litull bill, and command me hertely. *Unknown. See* Go! little bill, and command me hertely.

Go, Lovely Rose. Edmund Waller. AWP; BeJo; BoLoP; ClHu; CTC; EBEvV; EnLoPo; FF; GGP; GTBS; GTBS-P; HAP; HeIP; InPK; NAEL-1; NOBE; OBEV; OPOP; PoE; PoRA; TEP; TFi; TrGrPo; UnPo; WeW

Go, loving woodbine, clip with lovely grace. On a Pair of Garters. Sir John Davies. OPOP; SiPS

Go measure the distance from Cape Town to Pretoria. Measure for Measure. Sipho Sepamla. PeSAV

Go, my flock, go get you hence. Ninth Song. Sir Philip Sidney. *Fr.* Astrophel and Stella. AAS; ESo, sl. abr.; GGP; HeIL, Sonnets, I–CVIII and 11 Songs; NoSic; Poetr; SCGP, Sonnets, I–CVIII and 11 Songs; SiPS, Sonnets, I–CVIII and 11 Songs; SiPSBD, Sonnets, I–CVIII and 11 Songs

Go, my songs, seek your praise from the young and from the intolerant. Ité. Ezra Pound. HAP; MoAB; MoAmPo

Go, my songs, to the lonely and the unsatisfied. Commission. Ezra Pound. BoLoP; OPOP; TwCP

Go, My Thought. Ingeborg Bachmann, *tr. fr. Hebrew by* Mark Anderson. PoSu

Go, my thought, as long as a word clear enough for flight. Go, My Thought. Ingeborg Bachmann, *tr. fr. Hebrew by* Mark Anderson. PoSu

Go, Nightly Cares. John Dowland. EnRePo

Go, nightly cares, the enemy to rest. Go, Nightly Cares. John Dowland. EnRePo

Go north any way and sadness clings to the ground. Belfast. Donald Revell. SM

Go not, happy day. Tennyson. *Fr.* Maud [: A Monodrama]. EBVV; EnVR

Go not to the hills of Erinn. The Wind on the Hills. Dora Sigerson Shorter. NOBVV

Go not too frequently thy friends to see. Advice to Bores. Abraham ibn Chasdai, *tr. fr. Hebrew by* J. Chotzner. TrJP

Go not too near a house of rose. Emily Dickinson. MoAB; MoAmPo; NIP

Go Now, My Song. Andrew Young. ChTr

Go on, brave heros, you whose merits claim. An Ironical Encomium. *Unknown.* APAS

Go on! Go on! A Sermon at Clevedon. Thomas Edward Brown. NOBVV

Go on! go on! and love away! The Perfidious. Walter Savage Landor. CBLP

Go on, high ship, since now, upon the shore. Farewell to Florida. Wallace Stevens. NoAM

Go on, thou noisy one! Praise of a Train. *Zulu Oral Tradition, tr. by* B. W. Vilakazi. WTO

Go [*or* goe], lovely rose. Go, Lovely Rose. Edmund Waller. AWP; BeJo; BoLoP; ClHu; CTC; EBEvV; EnLoPo; FF; GGP; GTBS; GTBS-P; HAP; HeIP; InPK; NAEL-1; NOBE; OBEV; OPOP; PoE; PoRA; TEP; TFi; TrGrPo; UnPo; WeW

(Song: "Go [*or* Goe] lovely rose.") ArLo; ELP; GBL; GoJo; JCP; NoP; NOSC; OAEL-1; OxAEP-1; PoEL-3; Poetr; PrIm; SeCP; SeCV-1; SoSe

Go Out. Eileen Mathias. BoTP

Go out and camp somewhere. You're lying down. Mapooram. *Aborigine Oral Tradition, tr. by* Fred Biggs. NOBAu

Go out in the midday sun. (*LL*) Mad Dogs and Englishmen. Noël Coward. FiBHP; NBLV; NOBL; OBTV; PeLV

Go out in this dear summertide. Paul Gerhardt, *tr. fr. German by* George C. Schoolfield. GePo

Go out to play, she said! Boy in the Bay Window 1939. Maurice Kenny. BCF

Go patter to lubbers and swabs, do ye see. Poor Jack. Charles Dibdin. BeLS

Go, perjured man, and if thou e'er return. Curse, The; a Song. Robert Herrick. CaPo

Go, perjured youth, and court what nymph you please. To Philaster. Sarah Fyge Egerton. ECWP

Go! piteous hart, rased with dedly wo. Unfriendly Fortune. John Skelton. MeEL

Go pretty [*or* prettie] child and bear[e] this flower. To His Saviour, a Child; a Present, by a Child. Robert Herrick. BeJo; ChIV-2; OHIP; PeECV; SeCP; TrCP

(Child's Present, A.) OxBChV

Go Right along the Seashore. *Unknown.* PeNZ

Go, rose, my Chloe's bosom grace. Love's Emblem. John Clare. NIP

Go, Sad Complaint. Charles, Duc d'Orléans. EnVB; MeEL

Go sad or sweet or riotous with beer. The Old Women. George Mackay Brown. OxBS

Go, said old Lyce, senseless lover, go. Lyce. William Walsh. BoLoP

Go shorn and come woolly. The Clipping Blessing. *Unknown, tr. fr. Gaelic by* Alexander Carmichael. ScCV

Go, Silly Worm. Joshua Sylvester. *See* Go, silly worm, drudge, trudge, and travell.

Go, silly worm, drudge, trudge, and travell. Omnia Somnia. Joshua Sylvester. FaBoEE

(Go, Silly Worm.) EIL

Go Slow. Langston Hughes. LiTM

Go slowly, go slowly, oh moon, upon your way. (*LL*) They That Sow at Night. Shin Shalom. MHP

Go slowly, go slowly, oh moon, upon your way. We are sowing by your light. They That Sow at Night. Shin Shalom, *tr. fr. Hebrew by* Ruth Finer Mintz. MHP

Go [*or* Goe], smiling souls [*or* soules], your new-built cages break. To the Infant Martyrs. Richard Crashaw. ChIV-2; GeHe; NAEL-1; NoP; OxBSP; SeCV-1

Go softly past the graveyard where. Leonidas of Tarentum, *tr. fr. Greek by* Fleur Adcock. GrAn

Go, solitary wood, and henceforth be. On the Death of a Nightingale. Thomas Randolph. BeJo

Go Songs. Francis Thompson. *See* Go, songs, for ended is our brief, sweet play.

Go, songs, for ended is our brief, sweet play. Francis Thompson. MoBrPo

(Go Songs.) FaBV

Go, Soul [*or* Goe soule], the body's guest. The Lie. Sir Walter Ralegh. AAS; ChTr; CTC; EBEV; EnRePo; FaBoPV; HAP; ImPo; InvP; LiTB; NAEL-1; NOBE; NoP; NoSic; OPOP; PoEL-2; RB; SCGP; SCV; SiPS; SiPSBD; TEP; TFi; TrGrPo; WGRP
(Soul's Errand, The.) WGRP

Go soule, go sweetest soule for ever blest. Ariosto, *tr. by* Sir John Harington. *Fr.* Orlando Furioso. OBVE

Go, swallow, and tell, now that the summer is dying. Cwmrhydyceirw Elegiacs. Vernon Watkins. PoA

Go Take the World. Jay Macpherson. MoCV

Go talk with those who are rumored to be unlike you. For the Student Strikers. Richard Wilbur. OxBC

Go tell at Sparta, traveler passing by. On the Spartan Dead at Thermopylae. Simonides. WeW
(For the Spartan Dead at Thermopylai 480 B.C.) GrAn
(Inform the Lakedaimonians, friend — we rest.) GrAn
(Take this news to the Lakedaimonians, friend.) GrAn

Go tell Aunt Rhody [*or* Nancy]. The Old Gray Goose. *Unknown.* AmFP; GBP
(Go and tell Aunt Nancy.) ChTr, *sl. diff. vers*

Go tell him to clear me one acre of ground. The Elfin Knight. *Unknown.* AmFP

Go tell the king — the carven hall is felled. *Unknown, tr. fr. Greek by* Peter Jay. GrAn

Go tell the king: the daedal. The Last Utterance of the Delphic Oracle. *Unknown, tr. fr. Greek by* Kenneth Rexroth. OBVE

Go tell the Spartans, thou that passest by. Thermopylae. Simonides, *tr. fr. Greek by* William Lisle Bowles. AWP; OBVE; OBWP

Go, the rich chariot instantly prepare. The Muse. Abraham Cowley. EPCY

Go, then, and join the murmuring city's throng! To a Friend. William Lisle Bowles. Son

Go then, my dove, but now no longer mine. Cotton Mather. AiP; SCAP

Go thou forth, my book, though late. To His Book. Robert Herrick. CaPo

Go, thou gentle whispering wind. A Prayer to the Wind. Thomas Carew. BeJo

Go, thou that vainly dost mine eyes invite. Henry King. OxBSP

Go thou thy way, and I go mine. Mizpah. Julia Aldrich Baker. BLPA; FaBoBe

Go Thou to Rome. Shelley. *Fr.* Adonais; an Elegy on the Death of John Keats. ChTr; EBEV; EnRP; FHYEP; HoPM; ImPo; MeMBP; NoP; OAEL-2; PoEL-4; TrGrPo

Go through the gates with closed eyes. Close Your Eyes! Arna Bontemps. CDC; PoBA; PoNe

Go through the pockets of the enemy wounded. Love Letters of the Dead. Douglas Street. PAW

Go to Bed. *Unknown.* ChTr; GBP; OxNR

Go to bed early wake up with joy. *Unknown.* BoTP

Go to bed first. Go to Bed. *Unknown.* ChTr; GBP; OxNR

Go to bed late. *Unknown.* OxNR

Go to bed, Tom. *Unknown.* OxNR

Go to my son, by whom my medicine's sold. (*LL*) Advertising Epitaph: On a Quack. *Unknown.* FaBoUs

Go to Old Ireland. *Unknown.* AmFP

Go to sleep, go to sleepy. All the Pretty Little Horses. *Unknown.* AmFP

Go to sleep — though of course you will not. A Goodnight. William Carlos Williams. MoAB; MoAmPo

Go to Sleepy. *Unknown.* AS

Go to sleepy, little baby. (*LL*) All the Pretty Little Horses. *Unknown.* AmFP; OxBoLi; TTTS

Go to the Ant. Stanley J. Sharpless. NOBL

Go to the Ant [Thou Sluggard]. Bible, *O.T. Fr.* Proverbs. FaPON; TrJP

Go to the ant, you sluggard. Proverbs 6:6. David Curzon. ChIV-1

Go to the meadow behind Braim's pond. Cattail Wind. Joseph Bruchac. FoLa

Go to the moon/white folks going to the moon/going to. Moon Bound. Raymond Washington. NBV

Go to the patch some afternoon. How to make Rhubarb Wine. Ted Kooser. PBCAP

Go to the western gate, Luke Havergal. Luke Havergal. E. A. Robinson. AmPP; AWP; GBL; LiTA; LiTM; MeMAP; MoAB; MoAmPo; NAAL-2; NoAM; NOBA; PoEL-5; TFi; UnPo

Go to thy nest and lay. (*LL*) The Five Hens. *Unknown.* GBP

Go, Valentine. Robert Southey. Son

Go, wash thyself in Jordan — go, wash thee and be clean! Naaman's Song. Kipling. ChIV-1; OtMeF

Go 'way, fiddle! folks is tired o' hearin' you a-squawkin. Fust Banjo, De. Irwin Russell. *Fr.* Christmas Night in the Quarters. BLPA

Go 'Way f'om Mah Window. *Unknown.* AS

Go 'way from dat window, "My Honey, My Love." Song to the Runaway Slave. *Unknown.* BPo

Go Where Glory Waits Thee. Thomas Moore. OBNC; PlP

Go where my mind will. Tune: "Four Pieces of Jade" — Idle Leisure. Kuan Han-ch'ing, *tr. fr. Chinese by* Jerome Seaton. SuSp

Go where we will, at ev'ry time and place. Charles Churchill. *Fr.* Times, The. PeHV
(Against Sodomy.) ECEV

Go with a bending stature. (*LL*) Great Friend. Thoreau. PoEL-4

Go with a perm or a duck tail. How to Dress Like a Femmy Dyke. Jane Barnes. GLP

Go with the winds and crack the rotted oak. (*LL*) Gipsies. John Clare. ChTr; FHYEP

Go Work in My Vineyard. Frances E. W. Harper. PWR

Go ye afar. Go teach all nations. Missionary Hymm. James Burke. TIRV

Go ye into the highways. Compel Them to Come In. Leonard Dodd. BLRP

Go you, O winds that blow from north to south. Alexander Craig. EIL
(To Pandora.) Son

"Go, your lover lives!" said Cromwell; "Curfew shall not ring tonight!" (*LL*) Curfew Must Not Ring Tonight. Rose Hartwick Thorpe. BeLS; BLPA; BLPL; FaBoBe; FaPON; VPP

Goanna. *Unknown, tr. fr. Aborigine by* Mungayana Nundhirribala. NOBAu

Goanna chases grasshopper. Goanna. *Unknown, tr. fr. Aborigine by* Mungayana Nundhirribala. NOBAu

Goat, The. *Unknown.* BLPL; PoLF

Goat-foot Pan has quit his flocks. Meleager, *tr. fr. Greek by* Peter Whigham. GrAn

Goat God, The. Cesare Pavese, *tr. fr. Italian by* William Arrowsmith. AnAn

Goat Paths, The. James Stephens. AWP; CH; GoJo; LiTB; SCGP; UnPo

Goat was nibbling on a vine, A. The Vine and the Goat. Aesop, *tr. fr. Greek by* William Ellery Leonard. AWP

Goat's blood blossoms on the river banks. The Ballad of Deceived Flowers. Vesna Parun, *tr. fr. Yugoslavian by* Ivana Spalatin *and* Daniela Gioseffi. WoWa

Goats eat ivy. (*LL*) Infir Taris. *Unknown.* ChTr; ISE; OxNR

Goat's-Leaf. Marie de France, *tr. by* Aline Allard. PBWP

Gobbolino, the Witch's Cat. G. C. Westcott. CRH

Goblin, The. Rose Fyleman. BoTP; NTCP

Goblin, The. Jack Prelutsky. TLR

Goblin Feet. J. R. R. Tolkien. FaPON

Goblin Goose, The. *Unknown.* FaBoPa

Goblin has a wider mouth, The. How to Tell Goblins from Elves. Monica Shannon. FaPON

Goblin lives in our house, in our house, in our house, A. The Goblin. Rose Fyleman. BoTP; NTCP

Goblin marked his monarch well, The. The Fay's Departure. Joseph Rodman Drake. *Fr.* Culprit Fay, The. GN

Goblin Market. Christina Rossetti. EBEV; NAEL-2; NOBVV; OBNV
Sels.
"For there is no friend like a sister." OBF
"Good folk," said Lizzie. FaBoVe
"Laughed every goblin." BrRo
Laura and Lizzie Asleep. PeHV
"Morning and evening." BoTP; EBEvV, *ll.* 1 – 31; NALW; OxAEP-2
(Worrying Fruit.) CBCK

Goblins came, on mischief bent. The Temptation of St. Anthony. *Unknown, tr. fr. French by* R. L. Gales. OBF

Goblin's Song, The. James Telfer. ChTr

God. Gamaliel Bradford. WGRP

God. (*LL*) Flowers have come! Nezalhualcoyotl. EaPr

God, *sels.* Alexander McLachlan. EaPr

God. Harold Monro. *Fr.* Dawn. WGRP

God? Cristoir O'Flynn. TIRV

God. James Cowden Wallace. *See* There is an Eye that never sleeps.

God, a man at Yale, adopted a monkey. Monkey. Josephine Miles. LiTM

God, A Poem. James Fenton. DiPo; NoAM

God above, for man's delight, The. A New Ballade of the Marigolde. William Forrest. CoMu

God almighty's colly cow. The Ladybird. *Unknown.* GBP

God aloft in majesty. God Supreme. Abraham ibn Ezra, *tr. fr. Hebrew by* David Goldstein. TOF

God alone is God! Mohammed rassoul Allah!. Desert. Birago Diop, *tr. fr. French by* Ellen Conroy Kennedy. NegPo

God, although this life is but a wraith. Prayer. Louis Untermeyer. WGRP

God and I in space alone. Illusion. Ella Wheeler Wilcox. WGRP

God and Saint [*or* Sanct] Peter was gangand be the way. How the First Hielandman of God Was Made. *Unknown.* FaBoCo; GBP; OBSV

God and the devil in these letters. The Postman's Bell Is Answered Everywhere. Horace Gregory. MoAmPo; NYBP

God and the devil still are wrangling. For a Mouthy Woman. Countee Cullen. ChIV-1; OBAL; PoBA

God and the Soul., *sels.* John Lancaster Spalding.

God and Yet a Man, A? *Unknown.* HAP; MiEL

God! ask me not to record your wonders. Scholfield Huxley. Edgar Lee Masters. *Fr.* Spoon River Anthology. LiTA; TrPWD

God banish from your house. Benediction. Stanley Kunitz. VGW

God be here, God be there. *Unknown.* OxNR

God be in my head. The Knight's Prayer. *Unknown.* BoTP

God Be in My Head. *Unknown. Fr.* Sarum Primer.

God be merciful unto us, and bless us. Bible, *O.T., paraphrased by* Sir Thomas Wyatt. *Fr.* Psalms.
(Let the Nations Be Glad.) FaPON

(God be praised!) the Georges ended. *(LL)* The Georges. Walter Savage Landor. ChTr; FaBoCo; FaBoEE; FaBoEH; FiBHP; NIP; OBSV

God be thanked, I carry a knife. *(LL)* Arms and the Woman. Dorothea MacKellar. NOBAu

God Be with You. *Unknown.* PoToHe

God be with you in the Springtime. Through the Year. Julian S. Cutler. BLPA

God Be with You till We Meet Again. Jeremiah Eames Rankin. AH

God being with thee when we know it not. *(LL)* It Is a Beauteous Evening[, Calm and Free]. Wordsworth. AWP; BLPL; ChTr; EnRP; FaBoPP; FaBoRV; FHYEP; HeIP; ImPo; LiTB; LPA; MeMBP; NAEL-2; NIP; NoP; OAEL-2; OBTV; OxAEP-2; PoEL-4; PoLF; PPP; SCGP; Son; TEP; TFi

God, bless all little boys who look like Puck. Blessing on Little Boys. Arthur Guiterman. TrPWD

God bless all policemen. Goodbat Nightman. Roger McGough. MoP

God Bless America. John Fuller. OBSV; PeLV

God Bless Henry. He lived like a rat. John Berryman. *Fr.* Dream Songs. CAPP

God bless me, what a deal you've seen! *(LL)* Nonsense. Thomas Moore. FaBoEE

God bless our country's emblem. Our Country's Emblem. *Unknown.* WBLP

God bless our good and gracious King. Impromptu on Charles II. The Earl of Rochester. ChTr; FaBoEE; NBLV; NOBL; NTP; OBSV; OxAEP-1; PeLV
(We have a pritty witty king.) FaBoEH

God bless our meat. *Unknown.* OxNR

God Bless Our Native Land. Frances E. W. Harper. PWR

God bless the field and bless the furrow. The Robin's Song. C. Lovat Fraser. BoTP; MoShBr

God bless the King! — I mean the Faith's Defender. Jacobite Toast. John Byrom. FaBoCo; FaBoEE; OtMeF
(Extempore [Verses] Intended to Allay the Violence of Party-Spirit.) NOBL; PeLV

God bless the man who first invented sleep! Early Rising. John Godfrey Saxe. AnAmPo; BLPL; PoLF

God bless the master of this house. *Unknown.* BoTP; OHIP
(Grace, A.) MoShBr

God bless the master of this house, and all that are therein. The Singers in the Snow. *Unknown.* OHIP

God bless thee and keep thee thro' the coming days. A New Year's Wish. "J. H. S." BLRP

God bless this food, and bless us all. *Unknown.* BLRP

God bless this house from thatch to floor. *Unknown.* OxNR

God bless us all! That's quite another thing. *(LL)* Jacobite Toast. John Byrom. FaBoCo; FaBoEE; OtMeF

God bless you! *(LL)* Christmas is coming [or a-coming],/ And the geese are getting fat. *Unknown.* ISE; NTCP; OxNR; PChr; ReMoGo

God Bless You. *Unknown.* PoToHe

God bless you, and God bless me! *(LL)* The Robin's Song. C. Lovat Fraser. BoTP; MoShBr

God bless you. Guilt is magical. *(LL)* Adultery. James Dickey. CAPP; MT; TAP

God braced me with His firm hand. The Tool of Fate. "Yehoash," *tr. fr. Yiddish by* Isidore Goldstick. TrJP

God breathed. Creation. Robin Gurr. NOBAu

God bring you safe from the death sleep of night. A Donegal Hush Song. Cathal O'Byrne. TIRV

God broke into my house last night. Scapegoat. W. R. Rodgers. CIP

God broke the years to hours and days. As Thy Days So Shall Thy Strength Be. "George Klingle." BLRP

God broke upon this upturned field; trees. Body of a Rook. David Wevill. MoCV

God brought perfect man to fruition. Douglas Catley. PeLi

God! but the interest! *(LL)* The Debt. Paul Laurence Dunbar. CDC

God Cares. Helen Annis Casterline. BLRP

God Cares. "Marianne Farningham." BLRP; WBLP

God certainly wasn't. Blasphemy. Yoshihara Sachiko, *tr. fr. Japanese by* Kenneth Rexroth *and* Ikuko Atsumi. WPJ

God, consider the soul's need. Death Song for Owain ab Urien. Taliesin, *tr. fr. Welsh by* Anthony Conran. OBWVE

God created Cat and asked. *Unknown.* CRH

God created His image. Fill and Illumined. Joseph Ceravolo. ChIV-1

God decided he was tired. Budgie Finds His Voice. Wendy Cope. FaBoPa; UV

God did forbid the Israelites, to bring. The Ass. Robert Herrick. ChIV-1

God does for virtue goal and urge and crown afford. Virtue's Goal Is God. "Angelus Silesius," *tr. fr. German. Fr.* Cherubical Wanderer, The. GePo, *tr. by* George C. Schoolfield

God does not live to expalin. *(LL)* New Hampshire, February. Richard Eberhart. LiTM; TwCP

God Everywhere. Abraham ibn Ezra, *tr. fr. Hebrew by* D. E. de L. TrJP

God exists, though he doesn't exist. Phallus. Shiraishi Kazuko, *tr. by* Ikuko Atsumi. BoWoP

God from His Throne with Piercing Eye. Joseph Steward. AH

God gave His children memory. Roses in December. G. A. Studdert-Kennedy. BLPA

God gave my son in trust to me. My Son. James D. Hughes. BLPA

God, give me back the simple faith that I so long have clung to. A Prayer for Faith. Margaret E. Sangster. PoToHe

God, give me speech, in mercy touch my lips. The Unutterable Beauty. G. A. Studdert-Kennedy. TrPWD

God Give to Men ("God give the yellow man.") Arna Bontemps. BPo; CDC; PoNe

God, Give Us Men! Josiah Gilbert Holland. BLPA; WBLP

God gives them sleep on ground, on straw. Roger Williams. SCAP

God gives us joy taht we may give. Giving. *Unknown.* PoToHe

God!/ glad I'm black. Blue Black. Bloke Modisane. PBA

God, God, be lenient her first night there. Prayer for a Very New Angel. Violet Alleyn Storey. BLPA

God, God it is whom ye praise! *(LL)* To the Infinite. Friedrich Gottlieb Klopstock. RiWo

God grant that I may never be. Prayer in April. Sara Henderson Hay. TrPWD

God grant thee thine own wish, and grant thee mine. John Donne. OBVE

God grant thee thine own wish, and grant thee mine. *(LL)* God grant thee thine own wish, and grant thee mine. John Donne. OBVE

God guard me from those thoughts men think. A Prayer for Old Age. W. B. Yeats. IIP

God Hasn't Made Room. Mririda n'Ait Attik, *tr. by* Daniel Halpern *and* Paula Paley. PBWP

God hath not promised. What God Hath [or Has] Promised! Annie Johnson Flint. BLRP; WBLP

God Hath Sent Me to Sea for Pearls. Christopher Smart. *Fr.* Jubilate Agno. CBCK; FaBoVe

God hath two wings, which He doth ever move. Mercy and Love. Robert Herrick. SeCV-1

God He rejects all prayers that are sleight. Prayers Must Have Poise. Robert Herrick. LiTB

God heard the embattled nations sing and shout. 1914. J. C. Squire. FaBoEH

God help who follows his father's craft! The Passing of the Poets. Fearflatha O'Gnive. NOIV

God help who looks upon Enniskillen. A Visit to Enniskillen. Tadhg Dall O'Huiginn. NOIV

God help you on that fatal day. *(LL)* Be Frugal. Richard Church. OxBSP; OxBTC

God, how I envy you these great oak roots. A Jew Walks in Westminster Abbey. Aubrey Hodes. TrJP

God! How I Long for You. Kenneth Mackenzie. CBAP

God, how my mouth swam. Sparrow Hills. Robley Wilson, Jr.. PBCAP

God! how they plague his life, the three damned sisters. The Little Brother. James Reeves. OxBTC

God, I am travelling out to death's sea. Valley of the Shadow. John Galsworthy. OHIP; TrPWD

God I love thee in Thy robe of roses. Zebaoth. Else Lasker-Schüler, *tr. fr. German by* Jethro Bithell. TrJP

God, I need a job because I need money. Alan Dugan. CAPP; NoAM

God if he exists. The Man Root. Shiraishi Kazuko, *tr. fr. Japanese by* Kenneth Rexroth *and* Ikuko Atsumi. WPJ

God if he isn't is. Phallic Root. Shiraishi Kazuko. WPOW

God, if this were enough. If This Were Faith. Robert Louis Stevenson. *Fr.* Songs of Travel. OBNC; TrPWD; WGRP

God in the Nation's Life. *Unknown.* BLRP; WBLP

God in Three Persons, Blessed Trinity. *(LL)* Holy, Holy, Holy. Reginald Heber. OHIP

God in Wrath, A. Stephen Crane. *Fr.* Black Riders, The. MeMAP; OxBSP; TAP

God Is. Roland Mathias. CRP

God is a flasher. The Wisdom of the Streets. Gavin Ewart. FaBoBl

God is a pure no-thing. "Angelus Silesius," *tr. fr. German by* Stephen Mitchell. EnlH

God is above the sphere of our esteem. What God Is. Robert Herrick. BeJo; NOSC

God Is at the Anvil. Lew Sarett. WGRP

God Is Faithful. Frances Ridley Havergal. BLRP

God is Good. It Is a Beautiful Night. Wallace Stevens. SAmP

God is great and God is good. *Unknown.* BLRP

God Is in Every Tomorrow. Laura A. Barter Snow. BLRP

God is in Heaven. Yes. *(LL)* I have nothing to say about the war. Yehuda Amichai. PoSu, *tr. by* Yehuda Amichai *and* Ted Hughes

God is indeed a jealous God. Emily Dickinson. NOBA

God, is it sinful if I feel. Mary Dixon Thayer. TrPWD

God Is Kind. Mae V. Cowdery. ShDr

God Is Love. Sir John Bowring. FaBoBe

God is love. Then by inversion. History of Ideas. J. V. Cunningham. NIP; VCAP

God is my staff, my path, my goal, my game, my fire. God Is To Me What I Desire. "Angelus Silesius," *tr. fr. German. Fr.* Cherubical Wanderer, The. GePo, *tr. by* George C. Schoolfield

God, The, is near, and/ difficult to grasp. Patmos. David Gascoyne. OBVE

God is never sure He has found. Walking the Wilderness. William Stafford. NaP

God is no botcher, but when God wrought you two. On Botching. John Heywood. FaBoCo; FaBoEE

God Is Not Dumb. James Russell Lowell. *Fr.* Bibliolaters. ChIV-1; WGRP

God is not dumb, that he should speak no more. God Is Not Dumb. James Russell Lowell. *Fr.* Bibliolaters. ChIV-1; WGRP

God is not only merciful, to call. Calling, and Correcting. Robert Herrick. BeJo

God Is Nothing Physical. "Angelus Silesius," *tr. fr. German. Fr.* Cherubical Wanderer, The. GePo, *tr. by* George C. Schoolfield

God is older than the sun and moon. Maximus. D. H. Lawrence. TOF

God is our guide! from field, from wave. George Loveless. FaBoEH

God is our refuge and strength, a very present help in trouble. Bible, *O.T., paraphrased by* Sir Thomas Wyatt. *Fr.* Psalms. AWP

(Though the Earth Be Removed.) TrGrPo

God is our strength and our refuge: therefore will we not tremble. Hexameters. Samuel Taylor Coleridge. ChIV-1

God is praise and glory. Psalm of Battle. *Unknown, tr. fr. Arabic by* E. Powys Mathers. *Fr.* Thousand and One Nights, The. AWP

God is shaping the great future of the islands of the sea. The Islands of the Sea. George Edward Woodberry. PAH

God is still glorified. Building in Stone. Sylvia Townsend Warner. MoBrPo

God is the great urge that has not yet found a body. The Body of God. D. H. Lawrence. ChIV-2

God is the Most High. Muhammedan Call to Prayer. Bilal, *tr. fr. Arabic by* Raoul Abdul. TTY

God Is To Me What I Desire. "Angelus Silesius," *tr. fr. German. Fr.* Cherubical Wanderer, The. GePo, *tr. by* George C. Schoolfield

God IS Working His Purpose Out. A. C. Ainger. BLRP; FaPoR

God, keep all claw-denned alligators. Prayer for Reptiles. Patricia Hubbell. PDV

God, keep me still unsatisfied. *(LL)* God, though [*or* although] this life is but a wraith. Louis Untermeyer. MoAmPo; TrJP; WGRP

God keep us struggling shapes. *(LL)* Unit. Mary Elizabeth Fullerton. NOBAu,

God Knoweth Best. *Unknown.* WBLP

God knoweth why! *(LL)* There Is No Unbelief. Elizabeth York Case. WBLP; WGRP

God knows it, I am with you. To a Republican Friend, 1848. Matthew Arnold. EBVVPR

God knows/ We have our troubles too. High to Low. Langston Hughes. HCAP

God knows what beat him down into that deadland. At the Entrance. Douglas Stewart. CBAP

God knows what was done to you. Bruce Beaver. *Fr.* Letters to Live Poets. CBAP; FaBoMA

God knows why. *(LL)* The Ballad of Don and Dave and Di. John Heath-Stubbs. EBNV

God lay dead in heaven. Stephen Crane. *Fr.* Black Riders, The. AmPP

God, let me be a giver, and not one. Let Me Be a Giver. Mary Carolyn Davies. PoToHe

God let me find the lonely ones. Prayer for a Day's Walk. Grace Noll Crowell. PoToHe

God let never soe old a man. Old Robin of Portingale. *Unknown.* ESPB

God, listen through my words to the beating of my heart. Margueritte Harmon Bro. TrPWD

God love you. A Poem for the Old Man. John Wieners. BCF; NeAP

God love you now, if no one else will ever. Ode for the American Dead in Korea. Thomas McGrath. VGW

(Ode for the American Dead in Asia.) AiP; RaBo

God loves us all, I'm pleased to say. God's Love. Vikram Seth. TRP

God Lyaeus, Ever Young. John Fletcher. *Fr.* Tragedy of Valentinian, The. OBEV

God made a little gentian. Emily Dickinson. FaBV

God Made a Trance. *Unknown.* OBET

God made a wonderful mother. A Wonderful Mother. Pat O'Reilly. BLPA

God made Him birds in a pleasant humour. The Making of Birds. Katharine Tynan. TIRV

God made my mother on an April day. My Mother. Francis Ledwidge. OHIP; TIRV

God made the bees. Mother Goose. Spl

God Made the Country. William Cowper. *Fr.* Task, The. PoEL-3

God made the sex-shop keeper. Fiona Pitt-Kethley. UV

God made the sugar cane grow where it's hot. Bundaberg Rum. W. N. Scott. NOBAu

God made the wicked grocer. The Song against Grocers. G. K. Chesteron. FaBoCo; IHNG; UV, *sts. 1–2 only*

God-Maker, Man, The. Don Marquis. WGRP

God Makes a Path. Roger Williams. PAH; WGRP

God makes all things for good; 'tis man. Man Leavens the Batch. Mildmay Fane, 2d Earl of Westmorland. BeJo

God makes not good men wantons, but doth bring. Good Men Afflicted Most. Robert Herrick. LiTB

God makes sech nights all white an' still. The Courtin.' James Russell Lowell. *Fr.* Biglow Papers, The. AmPP; AnAmPo; BeLS; NOBA; OBAL

"God, mercy"; and so die. *(LL)* To Death. Robert Herrick. BeJo

God moves in a mysterious way. William Cowper. EBEvV; ELP

(Light Shining Out of Darkness.) EBEV; ECEV; EnRP; FaBoCh; FHYEP; ImPo; LiTB; NOBE; NOCV; NOEC; NoP; PoEL-3; PWR; SCGP; TFi; TOF; TrGrPo; WGRP

God never planted a garden. Anne Spencer. ShDr

God, O God, whom I have begged. A Poem in Praise of Colum Cille. *At. to* Dallán Forgaill. NOIV

God of Abraham, of Isaac, and of Jacob. *Unknown, tr. fr. Yiddish by* Olga Marx. TrJP

God of all power and might. Cecil Arthur Spring-Rice. *Fr.* In Memoriam, A. C. M. L. TrPWD

God of Bethel Heard Her Cries, The. Richard Allen. AH

God of Fair Beginnings, The. The Song of Diego Valdez. Kipling. OtMeF

God of grave nights. A Chant Out of Doors. Marguerite Wilkinson. TrPWD

God of his goodnes, praysed that he be. *Unknown. Fr.* Praise of Waterford, The. NOIV

God of irony. They would crush it under their heels and add it to their dishes. *(LL)* From Mythology. Zbigniew Herbert. FaBoPV

God of light and blossom. James P. Mousley. GoYe

God of love among the silent flowers, A. The Moment of the Rose. Dunstan Thompson. LiTA

God of Mercy. Kadya Molodovsky, *tr. fr. Yiddish by* Irving Howe. WPOW

God of Might, God of Right. *Unknown.* TrJP

God of My Life! Benjamin Colman. AH

God of Our Fathers. Melanchthon W. Stryker. AH

God of Our Fathers, Bless This Our Land. John Henry Hopkins, Jr. AH

God of our fathers, known of old. Recessional. Kipling. AWP; BLPA; BLPL; BLRP; CoGr; EBEvV; FaBoPV; FaBV; GN; LiTB; MoBrPo; NoAM; NOBE; NOBVV; NoP; OBEV; OBNC; OxAEP-2; PiP; PWR; SCGP; TFi; TrGrPo; UnPo; UV; WBLP; WGRP

God of Our Fathers, Whose Almighty Hand. Daniel C. Roberts. AH

God of peace! before thee. Hymn of Freedom. Michael J. Barry. TIRV

God of Peace, in Peace Preserve Us. Ernst W. Olson. AH

God of Sheep, The. John Fletcher. *Fr.* Faithful Shepherdess, The. EIL; FaBoCh

God of song and laughter long ago, The. But. Vladimir Holan, *tr. fr. Czech by* Ian Milner *and* Jarmila Milner. PoSu

God of Summer — I have seen. Touring. David Morton. TrPWD

God of the Granite and the Rose! Elizabeth Doten. *Fr.* Reconciliation. TrPWD

God of the Living, The. John Ellerton. WGRP

God of the Nations. Walter Russell Bowie. AH; TrPWD

God of the Nations, Near and Far. John Haynes Holmes. AH

God of the Prophets! Bless the Prophets' Sons. Denis Wortman. AH

God of the strong, God of the weak. Richard Watson Gilder. TrPWD (God of the Strong, God of the Weak *abr.*) AH

God of the World. Israel Najara, *tr. fr.* Hebrew by Israel Abrahams. TrJP

God of the World, Thy Glories Shine. Sewall Sylvester Cutting. AH

God of Thy people, hear us cry to Thee! (*LL*) God of the Nations. Walter Russell Bowie. AH; TrPWD

God of us who kill our kind! Percy MacKaye. *Fr.* Prayer of the Peoples, A. TrPWD, 3 *sts.*; WGRP

God of Visions. Emily Brontë. *See* O [*or* Oh] thy bright eyes must answer now.

God of War, The. Bertolt Brecht. FaBoPV

God of your fathers, known of old. Post-Recessional. G. K. Chesterton. UV

God or Mammon. Alfred Cruickshank. PBCV

God ordered motion, but ordained no rest. (*LL*) Man. Henry Vaughan. ESCV; GeHe; MeLP; NOBE; NOCV; OBEV; PoEL-2; SCGP; SeCV-1

God ought surely to shut up soon,/ As I go. (*LL*) To the Moon. Thomas Hardy. BoNaP; ChTr

God ought to bow profoundly for the favour. (*LL*) Exhausted now her sighs, and dry her tears. Walter Savage Landor. CBLP; FaBoEE

God Our Father. Frederick William Faber. WGRP

God our fathers formerly knew. Headlined in Heaven. Paul Grano. NOBAu

God, Our Lady, *sels.* Concha Michel, *tr. fr.* Spanish by Kate Flores.

God, patient of beginnings. A Prayer for the New Year. Violet Alleyn Storey. TrPWD

God pity all the brave who go. God's Pity. Louise Driscoll. WGRP

God, pity broken little families. A Prayer for Broken Little Families. Violet Alleyn Storey. PoToHe

God pity the wretched prisoners. In Prison. Michael Smith. PWR

God placed the Russian peasant. Gentlemen. W. N. Ewer. IHNG

God Poem. Stanley Moss. VGW

God Prays. Angela Morgan. WGRP

God prosper long our Gracious King. An Ode for the New Year. *At. to* John Gay. OxBoLi

God prosper long our noble king. Chevy Chase. *Unknown.* FaBoBa; GN; OBET

God Provides. Bible, *N.T. Fr.* St. Matthew. BLRP

God provideth for the morrow. (*LL*) Providence. Reginald Heber. GN; OHIP

God reigns; — let the earth be glad. (*LL*) This Is My Father's World. Maltbie D. Babcock. AH; BLRP

God Replies, XXXVIII: 2–41. Bible, *O.T. Fr.* Job. AWP; NAWM-1, *abr.*

God rest that Jewy woman. Song for the Clatter-Bones. F. R. Higgins. ChIV-1; ImPo; LiTB; OBMV

God rest the soul of Ireland. After the Flight of the Earls. Fearflatha O'Gnive. NOIV

God Rest You Merry. Dinah Maria Mulock Craik. *See* God Rest You [*or* ye] Merry, Gentlemen.

God rest you merry gentlemen. A Christmas Carol. G. K. Chesterton. UV

God Rest You [*or* ye] Merry, Gentlemen. Dinah Maria Mulock Craik. GN, *sl. diff. vers.*; LiTB

God rot the guts and the guts' indulgences. Palladas, *tr. fr.* Greek by Tony Harrison. GrAn

God said, Let Newton be! and all was light. (*LL*) Nature and Nature's laws lay hid in Night. Pope. FaBoCo; FaBoEE

God said, "Let there be light, and there was light." Mysteries of Life. Mary E. Tucker. CBWP-1

God save great George our King. God Save the King. *Unknown.* EBEvV

God Save Great Thomas Paine. Joseph Mather. FaBoEH, *abr.*; NOEC

God save me from the Porkers. County. Sir John Betjeman. IHNG

God save our gracious King. God Save the King. James Elroy Flecker. NSI

God save our gracious King. God Save the King. *At. to* Henry Carey. WBLP

God Save Our President. Francis DeHaes Janvier. PAH

God Save the King. *At. to* Henry Carey. WBLP

God Save the King. James Elroy Flecker. NSI

God save the King! (*LL*) God Save the King. James Elroy Flecker. NSI

God Save the King. *Unknown.* EBEvV

God save the King, that King that sav'd the land. Benjamin Harris. SCAP

God Save the People. Ebenezer Elliot. BLPA; WBLP

God save the people! (*LL*) God Save the People. Ebenezer Elliot. BLPA; WBLP

God save the plough! (*LL*) God Save the Plough. Lydia Huntley Sigourney. AnAmPo; OBAL

God Save the Plough. Lydia Huntley Sigourney. AnAmPo; OBAL

God save the Rights of Man! Philip Freneau. GOA

God Scatters Beauty. Walter Savage Landor. EnRP

God scatters beauty as he scatters flowers. Walter Savage Landor. *See* God Scatters Beauty.

God-seeking. Sir William Watson. WGRP

God Send Easter. Lucille Clifton. CrSp

God send her well to speede! (*LL*) The Boy and the Mantle. *Unknown.* ESPB; OxBB

God send the Devil is a gentleman. The Knight Fallen on Evil Days. Elinor Wylie. MoAmPo

God send the land deliverance. *Unknown. See* Liddesdale Crosiers hae ridden a race, The.

God send us a little home. A Prayer for a Little Home. Florence Bone. BLPA; FaBoBe

God send us peace, and keep red strife away. At Fredericksburg. John Boyle O'Reilly. PAH

God send vs alle good endyng! (*LL*) Chevy Chase. *Unknown.* EnSB, *sl. diff. vers.*; OxBB, *sl. diff. vers.*

God sent us here to make mistakes. Mistakes. Ella Wheeler Wilcox. PoToHe

God sent us wit to banish far. Peace in the World. John Galsworthy. PoLF

God Set Us Here. Nicasius de Sillè, *tr. fr.* Dutch. AH

God signs to us. Inventing Sin. George Ella Lyon. CrSp

God sits on the firmament arch. The Creation of Light. Sister Maura. CRP

God Sour the Milk of the Knacking Wench. Alden Nowlan. MoCV

God Speed. George Clinton Rowe. AAP

God Speed the Plough! *Unknown.* EnVB

God spoke once that made your girdle fall, The. Daphne. Selden Rodman. PoNe

God stir the soil. *Unknown.* EaPr

God stopped and the car. Not Singing. Kate Daniels. PBCAP

God strengthen me to bear myself. The Battle Within [*or* Who Shall Deliver Me?] Christina Rossetti. (Who Shall Deliver Me?) TOF

God Supreme. Abraham ibn Ezra, *tr. fr.* Hebrew by David Goldstein. TOF

God Supreme! To Thee We Pray. Penina Moise *and* Edward N. Calisch. AH

God takes a text, and preacheth patience. (*LL*) Judge Not the Preacher; for He is Thy Judge. George Herbert. OxAEP-1

God Teaches Us How to Forgive, but We Forget. Louis Phillips. BTR

God, that all this mightes may. *Unknown.* MiEL

God That Doest Wondrously. Moses ibn Ezra, *tr. fr.* Hebrew by Solomon Solis-Cohen. TrJP

God, that mad'st her well regard her. Dieu Qu'il la Fait. Charles, Duc d'Orléans, *tr. fr.* French by Ezra Pound. AWP

God the Architect. Harry Hibbard Kemp. WGRP

God the Artist. Angela Morgan. BLPA; PoToHe

God the Father. Richard Ryan. PeIV

God the Omniscient. James Cowden Wallace. BLRP

God then. Denise Levertov. *Fr.* Mass for the Day of St. Thomas Didymus. CrSp

God — / they fear you, they hold you so. Testimony. Carolyn M. Rodgers. BPo

God, thou great symmetry. Anna Wickham. MoBrPo

God, though (or although) this life is but a wraith. Louis Untermeyer. MoAmPo; TrJP; WGRP

God to Be First Served. Robert Herrick. OxBChV

God to bestow a second benefit. (*LL*) Thanksgiving. Robert Herrick. LiTB

God to Man. *Unknown, tr. fr. Hebrew. Fr.* Talmud, The. TrJP

God to Thee We Humbly Bow. George Henry Boker. AH

God, to whom we look up blindly. Bayard Taylor. *Fr.* Poet's Journal, The. TrPWD

God told Noah about the rainbow sign. Lining Track. *Unknown.* AmFP

God tried to teach Crow how to talk. Crow's First Lesson. Ted Hughes. MoP; NoAM

God Wants a Man. *Unknown.* BLRP

God wants our best. He in the far-off ages. What Shall We Render. *Unknown.* BLRP

God wants the souls of the faithful. The Marrano. Barry Goldensohn. NAmP90

God wants to be thought of. Julian of Norwich. CrSp

God was made man once more. *(LL)* Night and Morning. Austin Clarke. CIP; IPY; MoAB

God, we don't like to complain. Caliban in the Coal Mines. Louis Untermeyer. MoAmPo; PDV; TrJP

God, what a day it is to be abroad! Out-of-Doors. Robert Whitaker. TrPWD

God, what a world, if men in street and mart. True Brotherhood. Ella Wheeler Wilcox. WBLP

God, when he walked on earth. *(LL)* Shine, Perishing Republic. Robinson Jeffers. CMoP; FF; LiTA; LiTM; MAT; MoAB; MoP; NAAL-2; NoAM; NOBA; NoP; OxBA; PrIm; TAP; TFi; UnPo; VGW

God, when you thought of a pine tree. God the Artist. Angela Morgan. BLPA; PoToHe

God who created me. Prayers. Henry Charles Beeching. BoTP; OBEV (Boy's Prayer, A.) GN

God, who devisedst man who then devised. Prayer for the Age. Myron H. Broomell. TrPWD

God who fled down with a standard yard, The. William Empson. *Fr.* Bacchus. NoAM; PoA

God who formed the mountains great. All Nature Has a Voice to Tell. James Gilchrist Lawson. BLRP

God, Who Hath Made the Daisies. E. P. Hood. OHIP

God, who made man out of dust. The Continuing City. Laurence Housman. WGRP

God who mounts the winged winds, The. Homer, *tr. by* Pope. *Fr.* Odyssey. NAWM-1; OBVE

God, who touchest earth with beauty. A Prayer-Poem. Mary S. Edgar. BLRP

God, Whom Shall I Compare to Thee? Judah Halevi, *tr. fr. Hebrew by* Alice Lucas. TrJP

God whose goodness filleth every clime, The. Jean Racine, *tr. fr. French by* Charles Randolph. *Fr.* Athalie. WGRP

God, whose kindly hand doth sow. Francis Ledwidge. *Fr.* Dream of Artemis, A. TrPWD

God, whose love and joy. "Angelus Silesius," *tr. fr. German by* Stephen Mitchell. EnlH

God will have all, or none; serve Him, or fall. Neutrality Loathsome. Robert Herrick. ChIV-1; LiTB; NoP

God will never fail us. God Is Faithful. Frances Ridley Havergal. BLRP

God will not let my field lie fallow. The Ploughman. Karle Wilson Baker. WGRP

God will sentence me to repeating it endlessly and forever. *(LL)* When I Hear Your Name. Gloria Fuertes. VBLP

God wills no man a slave. The man most meek. Washington. James Jeffrey Roche. PAH

God wrought as like a botcher, as God might do. *(LL)* On Botching. John Heywood. FaBoCo; FaBoEE

God/ you aint. I Wonta Thank Ya. Tejumola Ologboni. NBV

God, you could grow to love it, [God-fearing, God-chosen purist little puritan that]. Ecclesiastes. Derek Mahon. BlrV; ChIV-1; CIP; PNI

God/ You do not mind if I an unbaptized. Prayer of a Pagan Woman. Cothrai Gogan. TIRV

God, You Have Been Too Good to Me. Charles Wharton Stork. TrPWD; WGRP

Goddès mother be. *(LL)* I Sing of a Maiden. *Unknown.* CH; ChIV-2; EBEV; ELP; FaBoCh; FF; ImPo; InPK; InPS; LiTB; MeEL; MiEL; NAEL-1; NOBE; NOCV; NoP; OAEL-1; OxBLMV; PoE; PoEL-1; SCGP; SCV; TFi; TOF; TrGrPo

Goddess, The. Denise Levertov. LiTM; NALW; NeAP; NOBA; PoM; SRLS

Goddess. Judith Johnson Sherwin. BoWoP

Goddess adored! who gained my early love. The Housewife's Prayer on the Morning Preceding a Fete. Elizabeth Moody. ECWP

Goddess by god, with Antony. *(LL)* Cleopatra. Swinburne. BeLS

Goddess capricious is Fame, A. Langford Reed. PeLi

Goddess Fortune be praised (on her toothed wheel), The. The Unpredicted. John Heath-Stubbs. BoLoP; OxBC

Goddess of rhyme, that didst inspire. An Epithalamium upon the Marriage of Captain William Bedloe. Richard Duke. APAS

Goddess of threads gladly. *Unknown, tr. fr. Icelandic by* George Johnston. *Fr.* Saga of Gisli, The. OBVE

Goddesse bade the nymphs remove, The. *Unknown, tr. by* Thomas Stanley. *Fr.* Vigil of Venus, The. AWP, *tr. by* Thomas Stanley; GBL, *tr. by* Allen Tate; OBVE

Goddesse, excellently bright. Prolegomenon. Edward Dorn. BCF

Goddesses Three, *sels. Unknown.* Judgment of Paris, The. OtMeF

Goddis sonne is borne. A Cause for Wonder. *Unknown.* MeEL

Goddwyn, *sels.* Thomas Chatterton. Ode to Liberty. TrGrPo

Gode sire, pray ich thee. I Am from Ireland. *Unknown.* MeEL

Godfrey Gordon Gustavus Gore. William Brighty Rands. FaPON

Godfrey of Bulloigne; or, The Recoverie of Jerusalem, *sels.* Tasso, *tr. fr. Italian by* Edward Fairfax.
"Erminia's steed this while his mistress bore." NoSic
"Joyous birds, hid under greenewood shade, The." OBVE
"Palace great is builded rich and round." NoSic
"Sweet Armida tooke this charge on hand, The." OBVE

Godhorse. Kojo Laing. HBAPE

Godiva. D. C. Berry. BXAP

Godiva. Tennyson. BeLS; EBVVPR

Godiva. Tennyson. BeLS; FaBoEH

Godly Dream, A. Elizabeth Melvill, Lady Culross. WPE
Sels.
"I looked down and saw a pit most black."
"Into that pit when I did enter in."
"Then up I rose, and made no more delay."
"This pit is Hell where through thou now must go."
"Weary I was, and thought to sit at rest."

Godly Girzie. Burns. CoMu; ErPo; FaBoBl

Godmother. Dorothy Parker. PoRA

Gododdin, The, *sels.* Aneirin, *tr. fr. Welsh*
"Men went to Catraeth, keen their war-band." OBWVE
"Men went to Gododdin, laughter-loving." OBWP
"To Cattraeth's vale in glitt'ring row." OBVE

Godolphin Horne. Hilaire Belloc. FaBoCo

Gods, The. Dennis Lee. NOBC

Gods, The. W. S. Merwin. NaP

Gods are happy, The. The Strayed Reveller to Ulysses. Matthew Arnold. *Fr.* Strayed Reveller, The. EBVVPR; OAEL-2; OBEV

Gods Are Mighty, The. N. P. van Wyk Louw. *tr. fr. Afrikaans by* Jack Cope. PeSA

God's armies of Heaven, with pinions extended. Pro Patria. Adah Isaacs Menken. CBWP-1

Gods arrive, The. *(LL)* Give All to Love. Emerson. AmPP; AnAmPo; ArLo; AWP; LiTA; MeMAP; NOBA; OBEV; OxBA; PoEL-4; PoLF; TAP; TrGrPo

God's blessing on the monarch who rules on Lombard Street in Philadelphia. *(LL)* Rulers: Philadelphia. Fenton Johnson. PoNe

God's blessings all are uniform. They Are the Same. Priscilla Jane Thompson. CBWP-2

God's boundless mercy is, to sinful man. God's Mercy. Robert Herrick. BeJo

Gods chase/ Round vase. Ode on a Grecian Urn Summarized. Desmond Skirrow. NIP; NOBL

God's child in Christ adopted — Christ my all. My Baptismal Birthday. Samuel Taylor Coleridge. ChIV-2; NOCV

God's Controversy with New-England. Michael Wigglesworth. EAP; SCAP

God's Dark. John Martin. PoLF

God's Death. Florence W. Freed. BTR

God's defrocked, and Troy a rubbish heap, The. *(LL)* In a Bed-Sitter. Hal Porter. NOBAu

God's Determinations [touching his Elect], *sels.* Edward Taylor.
Christ's Reply. EAP; NAAL-1; PoEL-3
(Christ's Reply ("I am a Captain to Your Will").) EAP
Extasy of Joy Let in by This Reply Returned In Admiration. EAP
First Satans Assault Against Those That First Came up to Mercys Terms. EAP
Frowardness of the Elect in the Work of Conversion, The. EAP; SCAP
Glory of and Grace in the Church Set Out, The. AmPP
God's Selecting Love in the Decree. PoEL-3, *sl. shorter vers.*
(Man in this Lapst Estate at very best.) EAP
"Infinity, when all things it beheld." AmPP; EAP; HAP; MeMAP; NAAL-1; NOBA; OxBA; SCAP
Joy of Church Fellowship Rightly Attended, The. AmPP; EAP; MeMAP; NAAL-1; OxBA; SCAP
(In Heaven Soaring Up.) AH
Soul's Groan to Christ for Succo[u]r, The. NAAL-1; PoEL-3

Golden gilliflower to-day, A. The Gilliflower of Gold. William Morris. HeIL

Golden globe incontinent, The. Midsummer Day in France. Alexander Hume. *Fr.* Of the Day Estivall. FaBoPP; NOCV; OxBS; ScCV

Golden Glove, The. *Unknown.* AmFP

Golden God, the Self, the immortal Swan, The. *Unknown, tr. fr. Hindi. Fr.* Upanishads, The. EnIH; *vers.* by Stephen Mitchell

Golden Grove, The. Sergei Essenin, *tr. fr. Russian* by R.A.D. Ford. ArNa

Golden Grove, Carmarthen. Rowland Watkyns. AngWe

Golden hair that Gulla wears, The. Bought Locks. Martial, *tr. fr. Latin by* Sir John Harington. AWP

Golden head by golden head. Laura and Lizzie Asleep. Christina Rossetti. *Fr.* Goblin Market. EBEV; NAEL-2; NOBVV; OBNV; PeHV

Golden Hour, The. Thomas Moore. *Fr.* Lalla Rookh. OBNC

Golden Island; or, the Darian Song, The. *Unknown.* KTR

Golden Journey to Samarkand, The. James Elroy Flecker. FaBoRV
Sels.
"Blood! This is no farfetched analogy." OFC
"And how beguile you? Death has no repose." CoGr; OxBTC
"Away, for we are ready to a man!" NOBE
"We who with songs beguile your pilgrimage." FaPoR; GoJo; OBMV; OxBTC; PlP; UV
(Prologue: "We Who with Songs Beguile Your Pilgrimage.) CoGr

Golden Jubilee of Wilberforce. Mrs. Henry Linden. CBWP-4

Golden light has presently, The. Evening Song. Philipp von Zesen, *tr. fr. German by* George C. Schoolfield. GePo

Golden Lines. Gérard de Nerval, *tr. fr. French by* Robert Bly. NU

Golden Mean, The. The Earl of Surrey, *after* Horace. OBVE; SiPS

Golden Mile-Stone, The. Longfellow. PoEL-5

Golden mists o'er Cloudland wreathing. Fancy and Imagination. H. Cordelia Ray. CBWP-3

Golden Moonrise. William Stanley Braithwaite. PoBA

Golden one is gone from the banquets, The. Hilda Doolittle ("H. D."). PoA

Golden pallor of voluptuous light, A. The Mocking Bird. Paul Hamilton Hayne. AnAmPo

Golden Pheasant. William Hart-Smith. NOBAu

Golden Pheasant. Mating Pair. Golden Pheasant. William Hart-Smith. NOBAu

Golden prince of pictorial war, A. (*LL*) Uccello. Gregory Corso. FF; NeAP; PoM

Golden Road, The. James Elroy Flecker. *Fr.* Hassan. OtMeF

Golden Road to Barcelona: 1992, The. Martin Fagg. UV

Golden Rod, The. Frank Dempster Sherman. FaPON

Golden Sea-Otter, The. Wakarpa, *tr. by* Arthur Waley. *Fr.* Kutune Shirka (The Ainu Epic). WTO

Golden Shower, The, *sels.* Roy Campbell.
"Here, where relumed by changing seasons, burn." OxBTC

Golden Slumbers. Thomas Dekker *and others. Fr.* Pleasant Comedy of Patient Grissell [*or* Grissel *or* Grissill], The. ELP; NoSic; OxAEP-1; SCGP

Golden slumbers kiss your eyes. Golden Slumbers. Thomas Dekker *and others. Fr.* Pleasant Comedy of Patient Grissell [*or* Grissel *or* Grissill], The. ELP; NoSic; OxAEP-1; SCGP
(Cradle Song, A: "Golden slumbers kiss your eyes.") OxBChV, IV, ii; SCGP, IV, ii; TrGrPo, IV, ii
(Lullaby: "Golden slumbers kiss your eyes.") EIL

Golden spider of the sky, The. Solar Myth. Genevieve Taggard. MoAmPo

Golden State. Frank Bidart. NoAM

Golden sun that brings the day, The. In Praise of the Sun. "A. W." CTC

Golden sun upon his fiery wheels, The. Michael Drayton. *Fr.* Idea's Mirrour. NoSic

Golden [*or* Goldyn] Targe, The. William Dunbar. OxBS
Sels.
Poet's Dream, The. PoEL-1
(Ryght as the stern of day begouth to schyne.) OxBLMV

Golden through the golden morning. The Return. Eleanor Rogers Cox. PAH

Golden trees of England, The. The Jungle Trees. Marjorie Wilson. BoTP

Golden Vanitie, The. *Unknown.* EnSB

Golden Vanity, The. *Unknown.* FaBoCh

Golden Vanity, The. *Unknown.* CH; ELP; FaBoCh; OBET; WiR

Golden Vanity, The. *Unknown.* WiR

Golden Vanity, The. *Unknown.* CH; ELP; FaBoCh; OBET; WiR

Golden Vanity, The. *Unknown.* ELP

Golden Voyage; or, The Prosperous Arrival of the *James and Mary*, The. *Unknown.* OxBSS

Golden Wedding, The. David Gray. FaBoBe

Golden Wings. William Morris. OBNC

Sels.
"Midways of a walled garden." ChTr
Song of Jehane du Castel Beau, The. ChTr

Golden wings of time, The. The Transition — S.M. Alfred Islay Walden. AAP

Golden, within this golden hive. Danaë. Barbara Howes. WPE

Goldenrod [*or* Golden-rod] is yellow, The. September [Days Are Here]. Helen Hunt Jackson. FaPON; GoJo; OBCA; PoLF

Goldfinches. Keats. *See* Sometimes goldfinches one by one will drop.

Goldfish, The. Liu Sha-ho, *tr. fr. Chinese. Fr.* Family of Plants, A. LHF, *tr. by* Hualing Nieh

Goldfish. Barrie Wade. OTCP

Goldfish on the Writing Desk. Max Brod, *tr. fr. German by* Babette Deutsch *and* Avrahm Yarmolinsky. TrJP

Goldfish waves/ its large feathery tail. The Goldfish. Liu Sha-ho, *tr. fr. Chinese. Fr.* Family of Plants, A. LHF, *tr. by* Hualing Nieh

Goldfish Wife, The. Sandra Hochman. NYBP; UnPo

Golf. Matthew Sweeney. IB

Golf Links, The. Sarah Norcliffe Cleghorn. ImPo; InPK; PoLF

Golfer's Rubaiyat, The. H. W. Boynton. BXAP

Golgotha. X. J. Kennedy. NYBP

Golgotha. Andrew Lansdown. ChIV-2

Golgotha Is a Mountain. Arna Bontemps. CDC; PoNe

Goliath and David. Louis Untermeyer. TrJP

Goliath was known for ferocity. Frank Richards. PeLi

Goliathus goliathus, the one banana. The Zoo. Gilbert Sorrentino. NeAP

Goll Mac Morna Parts from His Wife. *Unknown.* NOIV

Gollihar/ Burned the winter grass from his fields. Rahab. Diane Glancy. CRP

Golly, How Truth Will Out. Ogden Nash. LiTA; MoAmPo

Gombeen, The. Joseph Campbell. BIrV

Gondibert, *sels.* Sir William Davenant.
City Morning, The. NOSC
"Of all the Lombards, by their Trophies knowne." SeCV-1
Praise and Prayer. OBEV

Gondoliers, The, *sels.* W. S. Gilbert.
Duke of Plaza-Toro, The. FaPON; FiBHP
There Lived a King. FiBHP

Gondwanaland. Gavin Ewart. OBAP

Gone. Mary Elizabeth Coleridge. OBEV; OBNC

Gone. Walter de la Mare. GoJo

Gone. Carl Sandburg. NOBA

Gone. Mary E. Tucker. CBWP-1

Gone, A. Larry Eigner. NeAP

Gone are the coloured princes, gone echo, gone laughter. The Ruin. Richard Hughes. OBMV

Gone Are the Days. Norman MacCaig. OxBC

Gone are the drab monosyllabic days. Tilth. Robert Graves. FaBoEE; OBSV

Gone are the games we played all night. Mahsati, *tr. fr. Farsi by* Deirdre Lashgari. WPOW

Gone as his mouth's last sighs. (*LL*) The Burning of the Temple. Isaac Rosenberg. FaBoMo; PeFWW; TrJP

Gone bad. (*LL*) Cytherea. Mary Mackey. SRLS

Gone down in the flood, and gone out in the flame! The Sinking of the *Merrimac.* Lucy Larcom. PAH

Gone Gone. For Langston Hughes. Etheridge Knight. NBV

Gone, Gone Again. Edward Thomas. OxAEP-2; PeFWW; PoWW

Gone, gone — sold and gone. Whittier. AWP; PoNe

Gone, I say, and walk from church. The Truth the Dead Know. Anne Sexton. IMW; LCAP; MoAmPo; NoAM; PBWP; TAP; VCAP

Gone in the Wind. James Clarence Mangan, *after the German of* Friedrich Rückert. PeIV; TIRV

Gone is another summer's day. (*LL*) Summer Evening. Walter de la Mare. FM; MoAB; MoBrPo; MoShBr

Gone is she, scorning my bought! (*LL*) The Tree and the Lady. Thomas Hardy. MoAB; MoBrPo

Gone is the city, gone the day. The Right Kind of People. Edwin Markham. BLPA; PoToHe

Gone Is the Sleepgiver. Penelope Shuttle. BrRo

Gone Is Youth. Salamah, son of Jandal, *tr. fr. Arabic by* Sir Charles Lyall. *Fr.* Mufaddaliyat, The. AWP

Gone now the baby's nurse. Home after Three Months Away. Robert Lowell. HCAP; NoP

Gone she is a long, long way. Upon a Maid. Robert Herrick. CaPo

Gone the three ancient ladies. Frau Bauman, Frau Schmidt, and Frau Schwartze. Theodore Roethke. CoAP; MoAB; MoP; NAAL-2; NoAM; NOBA; NYBP; TAP

Gone to sleep I wake up. The Wrong Way Round. Peter Handke, *tr. fr. German by* Michael Hamburger. CBNP

Gone were but the winter. Spring Quiet. Christina Rossetti. ArNa; BoNaP; BoTP; CH; GTBS-P; InPS; MeMBP; PoE; PoEL-5; WPE

Gone Were but the Winter Cold. Allan Cunningham. CH

Gone, with all her sparkling beauty. Gone. Mary E. Tucker. CBWP-1

Goneys an' gullies an' all o' the birds o' the sea. Sea Change. John Masefield. FaBoTw; OBMV; RB

Gonna be great in south africa. (*LL*) In Memoriam Ben Zwane. Wopko Jensma. PeSAV

Gonna dig my grave both long and narrow. Dig My Grave. *Unknown.* AmFP

Gonna Lay My Head Down on Some Railroad Line. *Unknown.* AmFP

Good. R. S. Thomas. PAW

Good Advice. Mother Goose. *See* Come when you're called.

Good aged Bale, that with thy hoary hairs. To Doctor Bale. Barnabe Googe. NoSic

Good and Bad. James Stephens. MoBrPo

Good and bad and right and wrong. Good and Bad. James Stephens. MoBrPo

Good and bad are in my heart. The Twins. James Stephens. RaBo

Good and Bad Children. Robert Louis Stevenson. *Fr.* Child's Garden of Verses, A. EBVV; FaBoCh; OxBChV

Good and Bad Luck. John Milton Hay, *after the German of* Heine. *See* Good Luck and Bad ("Good luck is the gayest of all gay girls.")

Good and Bad Wives. *Unknown.* CoMu

Good and Clever. Elizabeth Wordsworth. OxBTC

Good, and great God, can I not think[e] of thee. To Heaven. Ben Jonson. BeJo; ChIV-2; EnRePo; HAP; JCP; LiTB; NAEL-1; NOCV; NOSC; SCGP; SeCP; TRP; TrPWD; UnPo

Good and great God! How should I fear. No Coming to God without Christ. Robert Herrick. OxBSP

Good Appetite. Mark Van Doren. OxBSP; Spl

Good bailiff of my farm, that snug domain. Horace, *tr. fr. Latin by* John Conington. OBVE

Good, better, best. *Unknown.* OxNR

Good Bishop, A. *Unknown, tr. fr. German by* William Taylor. WGRP

Good Boy, The. *Unknown.* AS

Good Boy, A. Robert Louis Stevenson. PWR

Good-By. Margaret E. Bruner. PoToHe

Good-By. Grace Denio Litchfield. PoToHe

Good-by and Keep Cold. Robert Frost. CMoP

Good-by can be a happy word. Good-By. Margaret E. Bruner. PoToHe

Good-by er Howdy-do. James Whitcomb Riley. CTC

Good-by *or* Goodbye, good-by to summer! Robin Redbreast. William Allingham. FaBoBe; MoShBr; OxBChV

Good-By Liza Jane. *Unknown.* AS

Good-by, my son, good-by. The Wayward Son. Mrs. Henry Linden. CBWP-4

Good-by, sweetheart, our days of bliss. The Parting Lovers. Mrs. Henry Linden. CBWP-4

Good-by, the tears are in my eyes. Villon, *tr. fr. French by* Andrew Lang. AWP

Good-bye. Walter de la Mare. NoP

Good-bye. Emerson. AnAmPo; LiTA; MeMAP; PFP; PoToHe; PWR; TAP; WGRP

Good-bye — and hail! my Fancy. (*LL*) Good-Bye, My Fancy! Walt Whitman. ImPo; LiTA; MeMAP; NAAL-1; PrIm; SAmP; TAP

Good-bye for a Long Time. Roy Fuller. CBLP

Good-bye, good-bye, to everything! (*LL*) Farewell to the Farm. Robert Louis Stevenson. BoTP; FaPON

"Good-bye," I said to my conscience. Conscience and Remorse. Paul Laurence Dunbar. AnAmPo

Good-bye, little desk at school, good-bye. Vacation Time. Frank Hutt. BoTP

Good-bye 'Liza Jane. *Unknown.* AS

Good-Bye, My Fancy! Walt Whitman. ImPo; LiTA; MeMAP; NAAL-1; PrIm; SAmP; TAP

Good-bye Nellie. *Unknown.* NSI

Good-bye! — no [*or* nay] do not grieve that it is over. Harriet Monroe. PoA

Good-bye now, and good luck! Enjoy your liberty! Finale. W. H. Auden. *Fr.* Man of La Mancha. AnAn

Good-bye! Off for Kansas. John Willis Menard. AAP

Good-bye, proud world! I'm going home. Good-bye. Emerson. AnAmPo; LiTA; MeMAP; PFP; PoToHe; PWR; TAP; WGRP

"Good-bye," said the river, "I'm going downstream." Howard Nemerov. WeW

Good-bye to the Mezzogiorno. W. H. Auden. OxBTC

Good-bye ye bloody scenes of long ago! Good-bye! Off for Kansas. John Willis Menard. AAP

"Good-bye," you said, and your voice was an echo. Tak for Sidst. Babette Deutsch. PoA

Good Captain, Maker of the light. For the Kindling of the Light on Easter Eve. Prudentius, *tr. fr. Latin by* Helen Waddell. MLL

Good care of them. (*LL*) My Father's Hands. Jeni Couzyn. PeSAV

Good Catholic girl, she didn't mind the cleaning. Snow White and the Seven Deadly Sins. R. S. Gwynn. SoSe

Good children, refuse not these lessons to learn. A Schoolmaster's Admonition. *Unknown.* OxBChV

Good christian Reader judge me not. God's Controversy with New-England. Michael Wigglesworth. EAP; SCAP

Good Christians. Robert Herrick. LiTB

Good Christians all attend unto my ditty. A Ballad of the Strange and Wonderful Storm of Hail. *Unknown.* CoMu

Good Christians all, both great and small. The Avondale Mine Disaster. *Unknown.* AmFP

Good cigar bought at a Betting Shop, A. London Impossibilities. *Unknown.* CBCK

Good come out/ prison. (*LL*) Cell Song. Etheridge Knight. NNaP; PoBA

Good Company. Karle Wilson Baker. FaPON; WGRP

Good Company. Henry VIII, King of England. *See* Pastime with good company.

Good Company. *Unknown.* OBET

Good Counsel. *Unknown, tr. fr. Turkish by* James Clarence Mangan. NOIV

Good Counsel. *Unknown, tr. fr. Welsh by* Glyn Jones. OBWVE

Good Counsel [*or* Counsell] to a Young Maid. Thomas Carew.

Good Counsel to a Young Maid ("When you the sunburnt pilgrim see.") Thomas Carew. ErPo

Good creatures, do you love your lives. A. E. Housman. PeVV

Good Creed, A. *Unknown. See* If any little word of mine.

Good dame looked from her cottage, The. The Leak in the Dike. Phoebe Cary. FaPON; VPP

Good dame Mercy with dame Charite, The. The Seven Deadly Sins. Stephen Hawes. *Fr.* Pastime of Pleasure, The. PoEL-1

Good day, good day. In Honour of Christmas. *Unknown.* MeEL

Good day's work, two contracts made, A. Between a Contractor and His Wife. *Unknown.* NOEC

Good Day/you're in tune to If You're Going To Do It. Inaugural Address. John James. VaA

Good Dr. Arthur Shadwell, who lends lustre to a name. The Flapper. Charles Larcom Graves. NSI

Good Doctor gnashed his way through, The. On to the Source. James Tate. AnAn

Good Dream, The. Denise Levertov. NNaP

Good end! (*LL*) Grandmother. Fily-Dabo Sissoko. NegPo

Good English Hospitality. Blake. *Fr.* Island in the Moon, An. CoMu

Good evening, my dear. A Serenade in Vain. Anton Wilhelm Florentin von Zuccalmaglio, *tr. fr. German by* Philip L. Miller. RiWo

Good Fairies have trooped off one by one, The. Christenings. Peter Porter. NAs

Good faith, Mr. Parson, excuse me from that! (*LL*) On Marriage. Thomas Flatman. FaBoUs; FiBHP; NOBL; PeLV

Good father, I have sent for you because. The Merry Little Maid and Wicked Little Monk. *Unknown.* ErPo

Good flat earth . . . and not so very high, The. Two Mountains Men Have Climbed. Pauline Starkweather. GoYe

Good folk [*or* folke], for gold or hire [*or* hyre]. The Crier. Michael Drayton. ElL; InvP; NOSC (Cryer, The. PoEL-2; SCGP

Good folk, go gain. God's Gifts. Albrecht von Johannsdorf, *tr. fr. German by* F. C. Nicholson. GePo

"Good folk," said Lizzie. Christina Rossetti. *Fr.* Goblin Market. EBEV; FaBoVe; NAEL-2; NOBVV; OBNV

Good folks ever will have their way. The Doctor's Story. Will M. Carleton. BLPA

Good for good is only fair. Good Counsel. *Unknown, tr. fr. Welsh by* Glyn Jones. OBWVE

Good for Nothing Man, *sels.* Kenneth Pitchford. Pickup in Tony's Hashhouse. ErPo

Good Fortune, when I hailed her recently. Epigram. J. V. Cunningham. VCAP

Good Frend, *sels.* Hilda Doolittle ("H. D."). "Time has an end, they say." NOBA; VGW

Good Friday. Christy Brown. TIRV

Good Friday. George Herbert. GeHe

Good Friday. Christina Rossetti. ChIV-2; MeMBP; PoEL-5

Good Night. Wilhelm Müller, *tr. fr. German by* Philip L. Miller. *Fr.* Winter's Journey, The. RiWo

Good-night. James Shirley. BeJo

Good-Night. Edward Thomas. NoP

Good Night. William Carlos Williams. SAmP

Good-Night, A. Francis Quarles. TrGrPo

Good Night and Good Morning. Richard Monckton Milnes. BoTP; OxBChV

Good night and sweet repose. *Unknown.* ISE

Good Night, at last. Robert Duncan. *Fr.* Passages. VGW

Good night, big world. Back to the Ghetto. Jacob Glatstein, *tr. fr. Yiddish by* Joseph Leftwich. TrJP

Good-night; ensured release. Parta Quies. A. E. Housman. NOBE; TEP

Good-night, God bless you. *Unknown.* OxNR

Good-night, good-bye. *(LL)* Félise. Swinburne. BeLS

Good night! Good night! *(LL)* Good Night. Victor Hugo. BoTP; FaPON

Good Night! Good night! John Holmes. PoToHe

Good night! Good night!/ Far flies the light. Good Night. Victor Hugo, *tr. fr. French.* BoTP; FaPON

Good night, my boy! *(LL)* A Serenade in Vain. Anton Wilhelm Florentin von Zuccalmaglio. RiWo

Good night, my table & chairs. Good Night. Joel Dailey. UL

Good night, my two little cloud ladies. For the Girls 'cause They Know. Harold Littlebird. VoR

Good Night Near Christmas. Robert Francis. ArNa

Good-Night, or Blessing, The. Robert Herrick. CaPo

"Good Night," Says the Owl. Lady Erskine Crum. BoTP

Good night/ Sleep tight. *Unknown.* ISE; RoPo

Good night, sweet repose. *Unknown.* ISE; OxNR

Good-night to the Season, Good-night! *(LL)* Goodnight to the Season! Winthrop Mackworth Praed. InvP; NOBE; NOBL; OBNC; OxBoLi; PeLV; PoEL-4

Good night to the Season! 'Tis over! Goodnight to the Season! Winthrop Mackworth Praed. InvP; NOBE; NOBL; OBNC; OxBoLi; PeLV; PoEL-4

Good night to the Year Academic. A Grouchy Good Night to the Academic Year. Ted Pauker. NOBL; PeLV

Good night to thee, Fair Goddess. Sunset Song. *Unknown, tr. fr. Pueblo Indian by* N. Barnes. WTO

Good Night, Willie Lee, I'll See You in the Morning. Alice Walker. CrSp; IMW; WeW

Good of the chaplain to enter Lone Bay. Billy in the Darbies. Herman Melville. *Fr.* Billy Budd, Foretopman. HAP; NAAL-1; NAWM-2; NOBA; OxBoLi; PoEL-5

Good Old Body. C.M. Donald. AIW

Good Old Days, The. Barbara Fried. NBLV

Good Old Dog, The. Toi Derricotte. InPS

Good Old Harry. John James. VaA

Good old, honest Deacon Brown. Deacon Brown's Conclusion. George Sands Johnson. PWR

Good old Mother Fairie. To Mother Fairie. Alice Cary. OBCA

Good Parson, The, *mod. vers. by* H. C. Leonard. Chaucer. *See* Good man was there [*or* ther] of religion [*or* religioun], A.

Good pastry is vended/ In Cité Fadette; Loulou and Her Cat. Frederick Locker-Lampson. OFC

Good People. Maura Stanton. SM

Good people all attend I pray. The Wreck of the *Royal Charter.* *Unknown.* OxBSS

Good people all come listen to my melancholy tale. George Jones. *Unknown.* OxBSS

Good people all, I pray attend. The New-fashioned Farmer. *Unknown.* OBET

Good people all, of every sort. An Elegy on the Death of a Mad Dog. Goldsmith. *Fr.* Vicar of Wakefield, The. BeLS; BLPA; CoGr; FaBoBe; FaBoCh; FaBoCo; GN; NBLV; NOEC; NOIV; OBNV; OxAEP-1; TEP; TFi

(On the Death of a Mad Dog.) NTP

Good people all, with one accord. An Elegy on That [*or* the] Glory of Her Sex, Mrs. Mary Blaize. Goldsmith. FaBoNo; PlP

Good people attend now, and I will declare. Man's Amazement. *Unknown.* CoMu

Good people come buy. A New Song of an Orange. *Unknown.* CoMu; FaBoEH

Good people do but lend an ear. The Sea Martyrs. *Unknown.* OxBSS

Good people draw near as you pass along. Alphabetical Song on the Corn Law Bill. *Unknown.* OxBoLi

Good people, give attention, a story you shall hear. Lord Delamere. *Unknown.* ESPB

Good people give attention, and listen for a while. The Queen's Dream. *Unknown.* PeVV

Good people give attention and listen unto me. The Carpet-Weavers' Lament. *Unknown.* OBET

Good people give attention who now around me stand. The Female Sailor. *Unknown.* OBET

Good people I pray. The Orange. Matthew Prior. PeLV

Good people, I pray now attend to my muse. The Lord Chancellours Villanies Discovered; or, His Rise and Fall in the Four Last Years. *Unknown.* CoMu

Good people of old England, come listen unto me. On the Late Engagement in Carles Town River. *Unknown.* OxBSS

Good people pay attention and listen to my song. A Great Favourite Song, Entitled The Sailor's Hornpipe. *Unknown.* OxBSS

Good people, what, will you of all be bereft. A Ballad on the Taxes. *At. to* Edward Ward. OxBoLi

(Ballad on the Times, A.) APAS

Good Play, A. Robert Louis Stevenson. FaPON; MoShBr; OTCP; PWR

Good prince, what? The dog that keeps, A. Of a Good Prince and an Evil. Timothy Kendall. NoSic

Good rain knows its season, A. Spring Night, A — Rejoicing in Rain. Tu Fu, *tr. fr. Chinese by* William H. Nienhauser. SuSp

Good rain knows its season, A. Spring Rain. Tu Fu, *tr. fr. Chinese by* Kenneth Rexroth. OHMPC

Good reader! if you e'er have seen. Nonsense. Thomas Moore. FaBoEE

Good Reason for Our Forgetting, The. Marie Howe. BAP-89

Good repute is water carried in a sieve. Lalleswari, *tr. fr. Kashmiri by* George Grierson. WPOW, *ad. by* Deirdre Lashgari

Good Resolution, A. Roy Campbell. OBSV

Good Samaritan, The. Cardinal Newman. OBTV

Good Shepherd's Sorrow for the Death of His Beloved Son, The. Anne Howard, Duchess of Arundel. NOSC

Good Ship, The. Michael Stephens. UL

Good Ships. John Crowe Ransom. MeMAP; WeW

Good sign, The. *(LL)* Meta-A and the A of Absolutes. Jay Wright. TRP

Good sir, if you will shew the best of your skill. How to Choose a Wife. *Unknown.* FaBoUs

Good sirs, be civil, can one man, d'ye think. The Answer of Mr. Waller's Painter to His Many New Advisers. *Unknown.* APAS

Good Susan, Be as Secret as You Can. *Unknown.* ErPo

Good sword and a trusty hand, A! The Song of the Western Men. Robert Stephen Hawker. EBEvV; EnRP; FaBoEH; FaPoR; OBNC; PlP; VPP (And Shall Trelawny Die?) OxAEP-2

Good Taste. Christopher Logue. OBSP

Good Thanksgiving, A. "Marian Douglas." PoLF

Good Thing, A. Ray Mathew. CBAP

Good thing about an immaculate conception, The. The Immaculate Conception. Lindsay MacRae. DT

Good Thoughts. Katherine Maurine Haaff. PoToHe

Good thoughts are the threads. Good Thoughts. Katherine Maurine Haaff. PoToHe

Good Time Coming, The. Charles Mackey. VPP

Good time of the year, The. Bernard de Ventadour, *tr. fr. French by* John Frederick Nims. STV

Good Times. Lucille Clifton. AmPA; BPo; FF; GoJo; GrPl; InPS; PoBA; SoSe; TAP; TRP; TwCP

Good Timing. Carol Ebbecke. PFL

Good Town, The. Edwin Muir. CMoP

Good traveler has no fixed plans, A. Lao Tzu, *tr. fr. Chinese.* *Fr.* Tao Te Ching. EnlH, *vers. by* Stephen Mitchell

Good Trembling. Baron Wormser. PRA

"Good trembling," CJ said as we. Good Trembling. Baron Wormser. PRA

Good Wif [*or* Wyf] was ther of biside [*or* bisyde] Bathe, A. Chaucer. *Fr.* Canterbury Tales, The. EBEV; EnVB; FHYEP; InPS; NoP; OAEL-1; PPP, *abr.*

(Good Wyf was Ther of Bisyde Bathe, A.) TrGrPo

(There was a Wife from Bath, a well-appearing, *mod. vers. by* Louis Untermeyer.) TrGrPo

Good Wife, The. Bible, O.T. *See* Who can find a virtuous woman? for her price is far above rubies.

Good Will to Men — Christmas Greetings in Six Languages. Dorothy Brown Thompson. OBCP

Good wine maketh good blood. Logic. *Unknown.* FaBoUs

Good Wish. *Unknown, tr. fr. Gaelic by* Alexander Carmichael. FaBoCh

Good wood. Food for Fire, Food for Thought. Robert Duncan. NeAP

Good Works, *mod. by* Donald Attwater. William Langland. *Fr.* Vision of Piers Plowman, The. NOCV

Good Wyf was Ther of Bisyde Bathe, A. Chaucer. *See* Good Wif [*or* Wyf] was ther of biside [*or* bisyde] Bathe, A.

Good, your worship, cast your eyes. The Maunding Soldier; or, The Fruits of Warre Is Beggery. Martin Parker. CoMu

Goodbat Nightman. Roger McGough. MoP

Goodby Betty, Don't Remember Me. E. E. Cummings. CMoP; PoE

Goodbye. Bella Akhmadulina, *tr. fr. Russian by* Barbara Einzig. BoWoP

Goodbye. Vickie Karp. UTF

Goodbye. Alun Lewis. AngWe; BoLoP; NAEL-2; OBWP; OxBM; OxBTC; PoWW

Goodbye, The. Myra Sklarew. GOYP

Goodbye, bright creature. In the Cloud of Unknowing. Carol Rumens. DiPo

Goodbye David Tamunoemi West. Margaret Danner. BPo

Goodbye: I bite the word back. Paulus Silentiarius, *tr. fr. Greek by* Andrew Miller. GrAn

"Goodbye" is not quite true; we'll meet tonight. Letter to My Mother. Suzanne Gardinier. UTF

Goodbye, lady in Bangor, who sent me. The Correspondence School Instructor Says Goodbye to His Poetry Students. Galway Kinnell. NoAM; NOBA; NoP; TAP

Goodbye, Little Bonny Blue Eyes. *Unknown.* AmFP

Goodbye Nkrumah. Diane Di Prima. PoM

Goodbye Now, or, Pardon My Gauntlet. Ogden Nash. FiBHP

"Goodbye, O sun," said Cleombrotus of Ambracia. Callimachus, *tr. fr. Greek. Fr. Epigrams.* HePo

Goodbye red moon. Moonset, Gloucester, December 1, 1957, 1:58 A.M. Charles Olson. CAPP

Goodbye, Sally. James Simmons. BIrV

"Goodbye Sun!" said the Ambracian. Callimachus, *tr. fr. Greek by* Peter Jay. GrAn

Goodbye the day. Good luck to me. (*LL*) A Ballad of a Mine. Robin Skelton. MoBS

Goodbye to Brigid/ An Agnus Dei. Padraic Fiacc. CIP

Goodbye to London. Louis MacNeice. PeECV

Goodbye to Regal. Daniel Huws. NYBP

Goodbye to Serpents. James Dickey. NYBP

Goodbye to the Bay of Naples. Wendy Mulford. NBrP

Goodbye to the Poetry of Calcium. James Wright. CAPP

Goodbye to Tolerance. Denise Levertov. NoAM

Goodbye/ Until such time as bobolinks do dine. To Janet. Ralph Pomeroy. NYBP

Goodbye, Winter. Prognosis. Louis MacNeice. CMoP; Mes; NOBE

Goodbyes, The. John Ash. SCBI

Goodliest Pearle in faire *Eliza's* Chaine, The. First Pearle, The: Religion. Lady Diana Primrose. *Fr.* Chain of Pearl, A. KTR

Goodly Child, A. *Unknown.* OxBChV

Goodly host one day was mine, A. Mine Host of "The Golden Apple." Thomas Westwood. GN; OHIP

Goodman's Sauce. *Unknown.* FaBoUs

Goodness. Benny Andersen, *tr. fr. Danish.* TSaS, *tr. by* Alexander Taylor

Goodness gracious, save my soul!/ Hang me on a hickory pole. *Unknown.* RoPo

Goodness gracious, save my soul!/ Lead me to the sugar bowl. *Unknown.* RoPo

Goodnight. John Ciardi. OBAL

Goodnight. James Shirley. *See* Bid me no more good-night; because.

Goodnight. Stevie Smith. FaBoWP

Goodnight, A. William Carlos Williams. MoAB; MoAmPo

Goodnight God. Danu Baxter. EaPr

Goodnight is Queen Mary's death. Cruel Behold my Heavy Ending. Peter Thabit Jones. FaBoEH

Goodnight to the Season! Winthrop Mackworth Praed. InvP; NOBE; NOBL; OBNC; OxBoLi; PeLV; PoEL-4

Goods Train at Night. Kenneth H. Ashley. PlP

Goodtime Jesus. James Tate. LCAP

Goodwill, Inc. Dennis Schmitz. AmPA

Goody Blake and Harry Gill, *sels.* Wordsworth.

Goody Bull and her daughter together fell out. The World Turned Upside Down. *Unknown.* PAH

Goody O'Grumpity. Carol Ryrie Brink. FaPON

Goodyere, I'm glad and grateful to report. To Sir Henry Goodyere. Ben Jonson. NOSC

Goofy Moose, the walking house-frame, The. Mooses. Ted Hughes. OBAP

Goops they lick their fingers, The. Table Manners. Gelett Burgess. OBCA

Goose. Richard Emil Braun. NoAM

Goose and the Gander, The. *Unknown.* GBP; RB

Goose and the Swans, The, *sels.* Edward Moore.

Goose Fish, The. Howard Nemerov. CMoP; HeIP; LiTM; NIP; NoAM; NoP; PoE; Poetr; SM

Goose girl ganders. The Bridal Feet. Briar Wood. NWP

Goose Pond. Stanley Kunitz. PoA

Goose that laid the golden egg, The. Ars Poetica. X. J. Kennedy. ErPo

Goose that on our Ock's green shore, The. Goodman's Sauce. *Unknown.* FaBoUs

Gooseberries. Stephen Berg. NaP

Gooseberry Fool ("The gooseberry's no doubt an oddity."). Amy Clampitt. NoAM

Goosey, goosey, gander, where shall I wander? Mother Goose. OxNR; ReMoGo

Goosey, goosey gander,/ Who stands yonder? Betsy Baker. *Unknown.* OxNR

Gorbo, as thou cam'st this way. The Shepheard's Daffodil. Michael Drayton. *Fr.* Shepherd's Garland, The. EIL

Gordion Knot, The. Thomas Tomkis. *Fr.* Lingua. EIL

Goree. Niyi Osundare. HBAPE

Gorg, a Detective Story. B. P. Nichol. NOBC

Gorges of Wu are hoary and im in the season of mist and rain, The. Liu Yu Hsi, *tr. by* Daniel Bryant. *Fr.* Bamboo Branch Song. SuSp

Gorgo, a Cretan bitch, on a deer's track. Antipater of Thessalonica, *tr. fr. Greek by* Alistair Elliot. GrAn

Gorgo and Praxinoa. Theocritus [*or* Theokritus], *tr. fr. Greek by* Barbara Hughes Fowler. *Fr.* Idylls. HePo

Gorilla Gorilla. Bruce Dawe. NoAM

Gorilla lay on his back, The. Au Jardin des Plantes. John Wain. OxBTC

Goring, The. Sylvia Plath. OBTV

Gormley's Laments, *sels.* Gormley, Queen of Ireland, *tr. fr. Irish by* Joan Keefe.
"I have loved thirty by three." PBWP

Gospel. Kevyn Arthur. PBCV

Gospel According to You, The. *Unknown.* BLRP

Gospel of Labor, The. Henry van Dyke. WBLP; WGRP

Gospel of Mr. Pepys, The. Christopher Morley. NBLV

Gospel of Peace, The. James Jeffrey Roche. PAH

Gosport Tragedy, The. *Unknown.* AmFP

Gossip. Penelope Gilliatt. PRA

Gossip. Mrs. Henry Linden. CBWP-4

Gossip. David Trinidad. BAP-91

Gossip is most of it, a barrier of thorns and small berries. Talking with Poets. Dick Allen. BAP-91

Got a cornstalk fiddle. *Unknown.* RoPo

Got a peek/ at the moon. Last Night. Oku Onuora. PBCV

Got Dem Blues. *Unknown.* AS

Got up and dressed up. Jack Kerouac. *Fr.* Mexico City Blues. NeAP

Got up, went to school. Diary. Mary Wilson. Spl

Gotham. Charles Churchill. NOEC
Sels.
European Crimes
Poet as King of Gotham, The

Gothic columns of petrified motion. M. G. Mainwaring. TOF

Gothic Dusk, The. Frederic Prokosch. PoA

Gothic Gesture, A. Steve Levine. UL

Gothic Landscape. Irving Layton. TrJP

Gothic looks solemn, The. On Oxford. Keats. SCGP
(Lines Rhymed in a Letter Received by J. H. R. from Oxford.) PeLV
(On Oxford. A Parody.) OxAEP-2

Goulburn Island Song Cycle, *sels. Unknown, tr. fr. Aborigine by* Ronald M. Berndt.
"Bird saw the young Burara girls, twisting their strings, making string figures, The." NOBAu
"Ejaculating into their vaginas — young girls of the western tribes." NOBAu
"They saw the young girls twisting their strings, Goulburn Island." NOBAu
"They seize the young girls of the western tribes, with their swaying." NOBAu

Gourd Dancer, The. N. Scott Momaday. CDW

Gourd has still its bitter leaves, The. I Wait My Lord. *Unknown, tr. by* Helen Waddell. *Fr.* Shi King. AWP

Gourmand, The. Harry Graham. FaBoPa; UV

Gourmet's Love-Song, The. P. G. Wodehouse. NOBL

Gout and Wings. Charles Tennyson Turner. NOBVV

Gouty Merchant and the Stranger, The. Horace Smith. BeLS

Gouzeaucourt: The Deceitful Calm. Edmund Blunden. PeFWW

Govern a life. *(LL)* Words. Sylvia Plath. HCAP; LCAP; NAAL-2; NALW; PoE; Poetr; VCAP

Government! Tuta Nihoniho, *tr. fr. Maori by* A. Armstrong. WTO

Government had just been overthrown, The. Mimosas. Louis Aragon, *tr. fr. French.* CBNP

Government in Exile. Dick Davis. SCBI

Government Injunction. Josephine Miles. PoNe

Government Quarters. Harry Clifton. IB

Governor and the seer are talking at night in a room, The. Lachlan MacQuarie's First Language. Les A. Murray. FaBoMA

Governor came to visit in the mountains, The. He Shot Arrows, but Not at Birds Perching. Gary Snyder. BCF

Governor loves to go mapping — round and round, The. Sydney Cove, 1788. Peter Porter. NoAM

Governor your husband lived so long, The. John Berryman. *Fr.* Homage to Mistress Bradstreet. NOBA

Gowa! Gowa! Crow's Ditty. *Unknown.* GBP

Gowan glitters on the sward, The. The Trysting Bush. Joanna Baillie. WPE

Gr-r-r — there go, my heart's abhorrence! Soliloquy of the Spanish Cloister. Robert Browning. FaBoCo; FaBoVe; FHYEP; ImPo; InPK; LiTB; MeMBP; NAEL-2; NIP; NOBL; NOBVV; NoP; OAEL-2; OtMeF; PeVV; TEP; TOF; TrGrPo; UV, *sh. vers.*

Grab-Bag. Helen Hunt Jackson. OBCA

Grace. Emerson. AmPP; NoP; PFP; TrPWD

Grace. Joy Harjo. ETG; NAmP90

Grace. George Herbert. ChIV-1; GeHe; JCP; SeCV-1

Grace. Robert Herrick. *See* Here a little child I stand.

Grace. Johnstone G. Patrick. TrPWD

Grace. Richard Wilbur. LiTA

Grace, A. Thomas Tiplady. TrPWD

Grace, A. *Unknown. See* God bless the master of this house.

Grace Abounding. A. R. Ammons. HCAP

Grace after Dinner. Burns. FaBoEE

Grace after Meals. *Unknown, tr. fr. Hebrew by* Alice Lucas. TrJP

Grace and Thanksgiving. Elizabeth Gould. BoTP

Grace and wonder. *(LL)* Hail Mother, who art the earth. Bill Faherty. EaPr

Grace at Evening. Edgar A. Guest. TrPWD

Grace at Evening. Edwin McNeill Poteat. TrPWD

Grace at Kirkudbright. Burns. NTP; OxBSP

Grace before Meat. Robert David Fitzgerald. NOBAu

Grace before Meat. Robert Herrick. *See* Here a little child I stand.

Grace before Sleep. Sara Teasdale. TrPWD

Grace by his priest. The feast is ended. *(LL)* Oberon's Feast. Robert Herrick. BeJo; CaPo; NOSC; SeCV-1; TrGrPo

Grace Darling. Michael Longley. FaBoEH

Grace Darling. *Unknown.* OBET; OxBSS

Grace for a Child. Robert Herrick. AWP; FaPON; InPS; MoShBr; NAEL-1; PoE; TFi; TrGrPo

Grace for Children, A. Robert Herrick. OxBChV

Grace for Gardens. Louise Driscoll. TrPWD

Grace for Light. "Moira O'Neill." TIRV

Grace for the sleepers, by your leave, and this their slumber song! *(LL)* A Slumber Song of the Gardens. John Runcie. PeSAV

Grace, Grace, dressed in lace. *Unknown.* RoPo

Grace is the focal point. Bar Giamaica, 1959-60. Charles Wright. EOEF

Grace more then thine, that Gods, the world hath none. *(LL)* At Home in Heaven. Robert Southwell. EnVR; ESCV

Grace of Animals, The. Richard Harteis. GLP

Grace of Cynthia's Maidenhood, The. Vinnie-Marie D'Ambrosio. IHMS

Grace of Geldings in Ripe Pastures, The. Maxine W. Kumin. CAPP

Grace of the Way, *sels.* Francis Thompson.
"Now of that vision I, bereaven." MoAB; MoBrPo

Grace of Tullies eloquence doth excell, The. Classics Society. Tony Harrison. *Fr.* School of Eloquence, The. NAEL-2; NoAM; SCBI

Grace that is the health of creatures can only be held in common, The. Healing. Wendell Berry. AnAn

Grace that never can be told. All Needs Met. J. H. Sammis. BLRP

Grace, thou source of each perfection. Epiphany. Christopher Smart. *Fr.* Hymns and Spiritual Songs. NOCV

Grace to Be Said at the Supermarket. Howard Nemerov. SoSe

Graceful Acacia. Walter Savage Landor. PoEL-4

Graceful as acorus or lotus flower. Aliter. Confucius, *tr. fr. Chinese by* Ezra Pound. *Fr.* Songs of Ch'en. CTC

Graceful Bastion, The. William Carlos Williams. NYBP

Graceful error may correct the cave, A. *(LL)* Mind. Richard Wilbur. CMoP; HCAP; HoPM; OxBSP; PPP; SoSe; VCAP

Gracefullest leaper, the dappled fox-cub. Young Reynard. George Meredith. HoPM

Graceless girl. *(LL)* I longed to. Sappho. InMo

Graces, if the beautiful Dionysios. *Unknown, tr. fr. Greek by* Peter Jay. GrAn

Graces of the Holy Ghost, The. *Unknown, tr. fr. Irish by* Douglas Hyde. TIRV

Gracie. Faye Kicknosway. NMM

Graciela. Gary Soto. NoAM

Graciela wouldn't fuck me. De Ambiente. Tatiana de la Tierra. GLP

Gracing the tide-warmth, this seagull. The Seagull. Dafydd ap Gwilym, *tr. fr. Welsh by* Glyn Jones. OBWVE

Gracious dreams, come back again! *(LL)* In Praise of Night. Matthaus Von Collin. RiWo

Gracious Goodness. Marge Piercy. Poetsp

Gracious Saviour let me make. Thou Lovest Me. Josephine D. Henderson Heard. CBWP-4

Gracious Saviour, We Adore Thee. Sewall Sylvester Cutting. AH

Gracious Time, The. Shakespeare. *See* Some say that ever 'gainst that season comes.

Gracius and gay. *Unknown.* MiEL

Grackle, The. Ogden Nash. CBNP; NBLV

Grackle's voice is less than mellow. The Grackle. Ogden Nash. CBNP; NBLV

Gradatim. Josiah Gilbert Holland. WGRP

Gradual bud and bloom and seedfall speeded up. July 4th. May Swenson. PoA

Gradual self-effacement of the death, The. *(LL)* First month of his absence, The. Alun Lewis. LiTM; NAEL-2; OBWP

Graduated row of children, the biggest, A. A Dim View of Berkeley in the Spring. Philip Whalen. PoBeRe

Graecinus (well I wot) thou told'st me once. Ovid, *tr. by* Christopher Marlowe. *Fr.* Amores. EBEV

Graeme and Bewick. *Unknown.* EnSB

Graf von Charolais, Der, *sels.* Richard Beer-Hofmann, *tr. fr. German by* Ludwig Lewisohn.
"Evil Man, An!" TrJP

Graffiti. Julian Croft. NOBAu

Graffiti. "James." NBLV

Graft anneal upon perennial trees. *(LL)* Invitation to Juno. William Empson. CBLP; CMoP; FaBoMo

Grafted Bud, The. Mary Weston Fordham. CBWP-2

Grafted Tongue, A. John Montague. BIrV; CIP; PBCIP

Grail, The. Sidney Keyes. FaBoTw

Grain of Sand, The. Maria Luisa Spaziani, *tr. fr. Italian by* Beverly Allen. NeIt

Grain of Sand, A. Frances E. W. Harper. PWR

Grain of sand, the beginning of the desert, The. The Grain of Sand. Maria Luisa Spaziani, *tr. fr. Italian by* Beverly Allen. NeIt

Grains of corn were planted, The. Story of the Corn. K. Fisher. BoTP

Grains of snow ride down here as bits. Letter from a Black Soldier. Bill Anderson. VGW

Gramercy, Death, as you've my love to win. Sonnet: He Argues His Case with Death. Cecco Angiolieri, da Siena, *tr. fr. Italian by* Dante Gabriel Rossetti. AWP

Grammar commences with a 5-line curse. Palladas, *tr. fr. Greek by* Tony Harrison. OBVE

Grammar itself at. Transparent Itineraries: 1984. Gustaf Subin. BAP-90

Grammar Lesson. Linda Pastan. Poetsp

Grammar-Rules. Sir Philip Sidney. *See* LXIII. "O grammar-rules, O now your virtues show."

Grammarian's daughter, The. Palladas, *tr. fr. Greek by* Peter Jay. GrAn

Grammarian's Funeral, A. Robert Browning. NAEL-2; NOBVV; PeECV; WGRP

Grammer's Shoes. William Barnes. EBVV; EnVR

Grampa. Dennis Scott. NTP; PBCV

Gran Sasso. Robert Wells. SCBI

Granada (1000 A.D.). Abu Ishaq al-Ilbin, *tr. fr. Arabic by* Omar S. Pound. ArPe

Grand Abacus. John Ashbery. PoA

Grand attempt some Amazonian dames, A. On a Fortification at Boston Begun by Women. Benjamin Tompson. GOA; NOSC; PAH; SCAP

Grand Canyon, The. James Merrill. TAP

Grand Central Hotel, The. Roy McFadden. PNI

Grand Chorus of Birds. Aristophanes. *See* Come on then, ye dwellers by nature in darkness.

Grand Commander, 1916, The. Vinnie-Marie D'Ambrosio. WoWa

Grand Conversation on Brave Nelson. *Unknown.* OBET

Grand-dad, they say you're old and frail. A Child to His Sick Grandfather. Joanna Baillie. ECWP; NOEC; WoRP

Grand Entry, The. Gary Snyder. NoAM

Grand Finale. Irving Layton. NOBC

Grand Guignols of Love, The. Michael Benedikt. AmPA

Grand Night, A. D. J. Enright. NSI

Grand-Père. Robert W. Service. NSI

Grand Rapids. Julia A. Moore. OBAL

Grand rough old Martin Luther. The Twins. Robert Browning. FaBoVe; Mes

Grand Tradition of Western Culture, The. Julia Stein. LoHo

Grandad, I didn't burn it, I. Legacy. Gena Ford. IHMS

Granddaddy longlegs did twilight, The. Ohio Valley Swains. James Wright. NNaP

Granddaughter. Adrienne Rich. Fr. Grandmothers. HCAP; NAAL-2; NoAM

Grande Jetée. Mary Mackey. Fr. Arabesque: Five Poems for Women without Children. AIW

Grandest ship-of-war which e'er to sea was known, The. She Is the Greatest Wealth. Georg Rudolph Weckherlin, tr. fr. German by George C. Schoolfield. GePo

Grandest writer of late ages, The. Distribution of Honours for Literature. Walter Savage Landor. FaBoEE

Grandeur of Ghosts. Siegfried Sassoon. MoBrPo; OBMV

Grandeza Mexicana, sels. Bernardo de Balbuena, tr. fr. Spanish by Samuel Beckett.

Grandfa' Grig/ Had a pig. Unknown. OxNR

Grandfather. George Bowering. NOBC

Grandfather, The. Michael Dransfield. FaBoMA

Grandfather. Michael S. Harper. CAPP; LCAP; TAP; VCAP

Grandfather. Lance Henson, tr. fr. Cheyenne Indian by Lance Henson. CDW; HATNAP

Grandfather. Derek Mahon. OxBC

Grandfather and Grandmother in Love. David Mura. ETG; TRP

Grandfather at the Indian Health Clinic. Elizabeth Cook-Lynn. HATNAP

Grandfather Great Spirit. Unknown, tr. fr. Sioux Indian. EaPr

Grandfather in the Old Men's Home. W. S. Merwin. LiTM; SM

"Grandfather" in Winter. Frederick Feirstein. BTR

Grandfather,/ Look at our brokenness. Unknown, tr. fr. Ojibwa Indian. EaPr

Grandfather Never Wrote a Will. Leroy V. Quintana. AfAz

Grandfather Poem, A. William J. Harris. PoBA

Grandfather puts down his tea-glass. A Night in Odessa. Louis Simpson. NNaP

Grandfather, sleepless in a room upstairs. John Berryman. Fr. Black Book, The. VGW

Grandfather's Clock. Henry Clay Work. BLPA

Grandfather's Rockery. David Woo. OpBo

Grandfather's Sermon and Michael Smith. E. A. Markham. PBCV

Grandiloquent Goat, The. Carolyn Wells. MoShBr

Grandma and the children left at night. My Polish Grandma. Edward Field. Prf

Grandma Bruchac lies with closed eyes. Plums. Joseph Bruchac. ETG

Grandma Chooses Her Plot at the County Cemetery. Paul Ruffin. GOYP

Grandma Fire. Charles G. Ballard. VoR

Grandma Harriet/ pushes her white tub machine. Wash Days. Beverlyjean Smith. ETG

Grandma lit the stove. History. Gary Soto. PBCAP

Grandma sleeps with. Medicine. Alice Walker. CrSp; NMM

Grandma stuffed her fur coat into the icebox. Ode. Philip Schultz. NAmP90

Grandmamma's Birthday. Hilaire Belloc. FiBHP

Grandma's Advice. Unknown. OBET

Grandma's Advice, sl. diff. vers. Unknown. See My grandmother lived on yonder green.

Grandma's Bureau. Robert Morgan. EOEF; WeW

Grandma's Lost Balance. Sydney Dayre. OBCA

Grandma's Man. James Welch. NoAM

Grandmither, Think Not I Forget. Willa Cather. WPE

Grandmother. Paula Gunn Allen. MDDM; SRLS

Grandmother, The. Wendell Berry. MT

Grandmother. Siv Cedering. PBCAP

Grandmother. Fily-Dabo Sissoko, tr. fr. French by Ellen Conroy Kennedy. NegPo

Grandmother. Louise Glück. Fr. Dedication to Hunger. AnAn

Grandmother. Marilyn Krysl. CrSp

Grandmother, The. Gérard de Nerval, tr. fr. French by Barbara Howes. IMW

Grandmother. Sameeneh Shirazie, tr. fr. Arabic. TSaS

Grandmother, The. Tennyson. PFP

Grandmother Came Down to Visit Us, The. Joseph Bruchac. CDW

Grandmother Grace. Ronald Wallace. GOYP; Poetr; SM

Grandmother, I dreamed of you again. The Visit. Phillip William George. IMW; VoR

Grandmother Jackson. David Jackson. OBCP

Grandmother, Rocking. Eve Merriam. GrPl

Grandmother Sleeps. Liz Sohappy Bahe. CDW

Grandmother spoke of you. To Ioan Madog, Poet, Ancestor. John Idris Jones. AngWe

Grandmother Watching at Her Window. W. S. Merwin. PrIm; VGW

Grandmother,/ your face is dangerous. Letter to Vienna from Paris, 1942. Maurya Simon. BTR

Grandmothers, The. Mary Oliver. WPE

Grandmothers. Adrienne Rich. HCAP; NAAL-2; NoAM
    Sels.
    Granddaughter.
    Hattie Rice Rich.
    Mary Gravely Jones. MDDM

Grandmother's Father Was Killed by Some Tejanos. Leroy V. Quintana. AfAz

Grandmothers Land. William Oandasan. HATNAP

Grandmother's mother: her age, I guess. Dorothy Q. Oliver Wendell Holmes. NOBA

Grandmother's Ninetieth Birthday. Christine Churches. FaBoMA

Grandmother's Old Armchair. Unknown. BLPA

Grandmother's Story of Bunker-Hill Battle. Oliver Wendell Holmes. PAH

Grandmothers who wring the necks. Classic Ballroom Dances. Charles Simic. LCAP; WeW

Grandpa Bear's Lullaby. Jane Yolen. SiSoPo

Grandpa, I saw you die in the Indian hospital at Pawnee. Hartico. Anna Walters. VoR

Grandparents. Sheila Bramfit. OxBM

Grandparents. Robert Lowell. LiTM

Grandpa's .45. W. M. Ransom. CDW

Grandson, The. James Scully. NYBP

Grandson Is a Hoticeberg, A. Margaret Danner. BlSi

Granite and Cypress. Robinson Jeffers. AmPP

Granite and Grass. Donald Hall. DiPo

Granite and Steel. Marianne Moore. NYBP

Granite cliff on either shore, A. The Brooklyn Bridge. Edna Dean Proctor. PAH

Granite ridges, sweeps of sky, sweat. The Lake. Alma Villanueva. SRLS

Granizo. Leroy V. Quintana. AfAz

Granny and I with dear Dadu. A Very Odd Fish. D'Arcy Wentworth Thompson. OxBChV

Granny Crack. James Reaney. NOBC

Granny Maxwell sits alone on her porch. Tornado Touch Down at Worth, Mo. Stephen Knight. UnDi

Grant a canoe that shall be swift as a fish! Prayer on Making a Canoe. Unknown, tr. fr. Hawaiian by N. B. Emerson. WTO

Grant at Appomattox. Gertrude Claytor. GoYe

Grant Heaven could once have given us liberty. Predestination and Free Will. Dryden. Fr. State of Innocence, The. NOCV

Grant it, Father. Petition. Eleanor Slater. TrPWD

Grant me, indulgent Heaven, a rural seat. The Choice. Nahum Tate. OxBSP

Grant me sweet Christ the grace to find. The Hermitage. Unknown, tr. fr. Irish by Frank O'Connor. IIP

Grant me the ability to be alone. Nachman of Bratslav. EaPr

Grant me the great and solemn breath withdrawn. Invocation and Prelude. Stefan George, tr. fr. German by Ludwig Lewisohn. AWP

Grant me to share the common, human lot. The Common Lot. Adelbert Sumpter Coats. TrPWD

Grant that no Hobgoblins fright me. John Day. Spl

Grant us the knowledge that we need. Henry van Dyke. Fr. Builders, The. TrPWD

Grant Wood's American Landscape. Winfield Townley Scott. GOA

Granted it came as something of a shock. Adam's Commentary After the Fall. Aidan Carl Mathews. IB

Granted that what we summon is absurd. T. R. Donald Hall. PoA

Granted, we die for good. Table Talk. Wallace Stevens. NoP

Grape-gathering. Avraham Shlonsky, tr. fr. Hebrew by I. M. Lask. TrJP

Grapes. Unknown, tr. fr. Greek by Alma Strettell. AWP

Grapes Making. Léonie Adams. FYAP; UnPo

Great Brown Owl, The. Jane Euphemia Browne. OxBChV

Great buck-wagon, our "desert ship," The. A Song of the Wagon-whip. Samuel Cron Cronwright. PeSAV

Great bumble. Sleek. In the Pinewoods, Crows and Owl. Mary Oliver. Poetr

Great captain if you will! great Duke! great Slave! Wellington. Charles Harpur. NOBAu

Great Central Railway, Sheffield Victoria to Banbury. Sir John Betjeman. NYBP

Great Citadels whereon the Gold Sun Falls. John Berryman. Fr. Sonnets. Son

Great Cowley then, a mighty genius, wrote. Joseph Addison. Fr. Account of the Greatest English Poets, An. EPCY

Great cry, A, went up from the stockyards and slaughterhouses. The Delicate, Plummeting Bodies. Stephen Dobyns. FYAP

Great cup tumbled, ringing like a bell, The. The Grail. Sidney Keyes. FaBoTw

Great Dark, The. Martin Carter. PBCV

Great Day. Unknown. SWP

Great Day, The. W. B. Yeats. BIrV; CMoP; FF; IHNG; OxBSP

Great Despair of the London Whigs, The. Unknown. APAS

Great Diocletian. Abraham Cowley. Fr. Garden, The. ChTr

Great dream stinks like a whale gone aground, The. Why the Soup Tastes like the Daily News. Marge Piercy. MAT

Great-enough both accepts and subdues. Phenomena. Robinson Jeffers. NOBA; OxBA

Great Escape, The. Ralph Adamo. MT

Great Expectations, sels. Charles Dickens. Joe Gargery's Epitaph on His Father. FaBoVe

Great Farewells, The. Amanda Benjamin Hall. GoYe

Great Farter, The. Nakasuk, tr. fr. Eskimo by Jerome K. Rothenberg. STP

Great father Alighier, if from the skies. To Dante. Vittorio Alfieri, tr. fr. Italian by Lorna De' Lucchi. AWP

Great Father Eating His Children, The. Hesiod, tr. by Richmond Lattimore. Fr. Theogony. RaBo

Great Favorit Beheaded, A. Sir Richard Fanshawe, after the Italian of Giovanni Battista Guarini. See Bloody trunk [or Bloudy trunck] of him who did possess[e], The.

Great Favourite Song, Entitled The Sailor's Hornpipe, A. Unknown. OxBSS

Great feathered fist clenched on its haft, A. (LL) Bateleur. Douglas Livingstone. PeSAV

Great Figure, The. William Carlos Williams. AiP; HeIP; InPK; MoP; NoAM; SAmP; TTTS

Great fish's eyes never shut, The. Rosario Castellanos, tr. fr. Spanish by Willis Barnstone. BoWoP

Great Fleas. Augustus de Morgan. BXAP

Great folks are of a finer mould. Epigram on Scolding. Swift. FaBoEE; FaBoVe

Great fool, The. Work Song. Raymond Mazisi Kunene, tr. fr. Zulu by D. K. Rycroft. WTO

Great Fortune is an hungry thing. Aeschylus, tr. by Gilbert Murray. Fr. Agamemnon. AWP; NAWM-1

Great Fountains, The. Anne Hébert, tr. fr. French by Willis Barnstone. BoWoP

Great Freight, The. Ingeborg Bachmann, tr. fr. German by Bill Crisman. PBWP

Great Friend. Thoreau. PoEL-4

Great friend and servant of the good. Ben Jonson. Fr. Pleasure Reconciled to Virtue. NAEL-1; OAEL-1

Great Garret, or 100 Wheels, The. James McMichael. AmPA

Great Gatsby, The, sels. F. Scott Fitzgerald. Epitaph from The Great Gatsby. OxBM

Great Gawd, I'm Feelin' Bad. Unknown. AS

Great Giver has ended His disposing, The. Day of Atonement. Charles Reznikoff. ChIV-1

Great God accept our gratitude. Doxology. Josephine D. Henderson Heard. CBWP-4

Great God, attend while Zion sings. Isaac Watts. AmFP

Great God, How Frail a Thing Is Man. Mather Byles. AH

Great God, how short's mans time; each minute speaks. Meditations for July 19, 1666. Philip Pain. SCAP

Great God I ask thee for no meaner pelf. Great God, I Ask Thee for No Meaner Pelf. Thoreau. NOBA; PFP; TrPWD

Great God, I Ask Thee for No Meaner Pelf. Thoreau. NOBA; PFP; TrPWD

Great God, let all my tuneful pow'rs. Ottiwell Heginbothom. AmFP

Great God of Nations, now to Thee. Hymn of Gratitude. Unknown. BLRP

Great God, our King! (LL) America. Samuel Francis Smith. AiP; AnAmPo; EBEvV; FaBoBe; FaPON; PoLF; WBLP

Great God Pan, The. Elizabeth Barrett Browning. See What was he doing, the great god Pan.

Great God Paused among Men. Daniel Berrigan. MAT

Great God, Preserver of All Things. Francis Daniel Pastorius. AH

Great God, the Followers of Thy Son. Henry Ware, Jr. AH

Great God, Thou giver of all good. Unknown. BLRP

Great God, Thy Works. Mather Byles. AH

Great Goddesse to whose throne in Cynthian fires. The Shadow of Night. George Chapman. PoEL-2

Great, good and just, could I but rate. His Metrical Vow. James Graham, Marquess of Montrose. OxBS
(Epitaph on Charles I.) NOBE
(Lines on the Execution of King Charles I.) ScCV

Great Grandame Wales, from whom those ancestors. John Davies of Hereford. Fr. Cambria. AngWe

Great-Grandfather. Freda Downie. FaBoWP

Great-grandfather at Waterloo. Frank Richards. PeLi

Great-Grandfathers, blessed by great-grandmothers. Geneology. Bob Kaufman. NBV

Great-great Grandma, Don't Sleep in Your Treehouse Tonight. X. J. Kennedy. GrPl

Great-great-grandmother. Guy Butler. PeSAV

Great grief came over me. Aleqaajik, tr. fr. Eskimo. WTO

Great grieved heart, an iron will, A. The Rough Sketch. Julia Ward Howe. AmWP

Great Guest Comes In, The. Edwin Markham. WBLP

Great heart, who taught thee so to dye? Epitaph: On Sir Walter Rawleigh at His Execution. Unknown.
(On Sir Walter Rawleigh at His Execution.) NOSC

Great-hearted Christ, importunate and mild. Chad Walsh. Fr. Psalm of Christ, The. TrCP

Great Helmsman, The. David Woo. OpBo

Great Hogarth's honour'd Dust is here. (LL) Epitaph on William Hogarth. Samuel Johnson. EBEV

Great Horse Fair, The. Desmond O'Grady. PBCIP

Great Hunger, The, sels. Patrick Kavanagh.
"April, and no one able to calculate." IPY
"Clay is the word and clay is the flesh." IPY; NoAM; OxBTC
"He gave himself another year." BIrV
"Health and wealth and love he too dreamed of in May." MoAB
"Maguire is not afraid of death, the Church will light him a candle." CIP
"Poor Paddy Maguire, a fourteen-hour day." IPY

Great Hymm. Ntsikana Gaba, tr. fr. Xhosa by John Knox Bokwe. PeSAV

Great Hymn. Ntsikana Gaba, tr. fr. Xhosa by Thomas Pringle. PeSAV

Great-in-counsels made her this reply, The. Ulysses Leaves the Nymph Calypso. Homer, tr. by George Chapman. Fr. Odyssey. JCP; NAWM-1

Great Infirmities. Charles Simic. AnAn

Great Insohreckshan, Di. Linton Kwesi Johnson. FaBoPV

Great is a drink of snow. Asclepiades, tr. fr. Greek by Alan Marshfield. GrAn

Great is Caesar: He has conquered Seven Kingdoms. Fugal-Chorus. W. H. Auden. Fr. For the Time Being; a Christmas Oratorio. LiTM

Great is Jehovah, the Lord, for heaven and earth proclaim. Omnipotence. Johann Ladislaus von Felsö-Eör Pyrker, tr. fr. German by Philip L. Miller. RiWo

Great is my envy of you, earth, in your greed. Petrarch, tr. fr. Italian. Fr. Sonnets to Laura. NAWM-1, tr. by Edwin Morgan

Great is the folly of a feeble brain. Joseph Hall. Fr. Virgidemiarum. EBEV

Great is the sun, and wide [or wise] he goes. Summer Sun. Robert Louis Stevenson. MoBrPo; PWR

Great is thy worke in Wildernesse, Oh man. Mr. Eliot Pastor of the Church of Christ at Roxbury. Edward Johnson. SCAP

Great Jack of Lent, clad in a robe of air. A Copy of Non Sequitors. Unknown. FaBoNo

Great Jehovah speaks to us, The. The Names and Order of the Books of the Old Testament. Thomas Russell. BLPA
(Books of the Old Testament, The.) ChIV-1

Great king. Harvest of War. Kappiyarrukkappiyanar, tr. fr. Tamil by A. K. Ramanujan. PLW

Great King. Tuini Ngawai, tr. fr. Maori by Margaret Orbell. PeNZ

Great king, the sovereign [or sov'raigne] ruler of this land. To His Late Majesty Concerning the True Form of English Poetry. Sir John Beaumont. JCP

Great Lakes of Canada, The. Gordon Perry. FaBoUs

Great Lalula, The. Christian Morgenstern. CBNP

Great learned lady, whom I long have known. To the Lady Arabella. Emilia Lanier. NOSC

Great light was born in Athens when, A. Simonides, *tr. fr. Greek by* Kenneth Rexroth. PGA

Great Lord of All, Whose Work of Love. Jacob Duché. AH

Great love goes mad to be spoken: you went out. Preserves. Jack Butler. MT

Great Lover, The, *sels.* Rupert Brooke.

Great Lover, The. Rupert Brooke. HoPM; ImPo; LiTB; LiTM; MoBrPo; PAW; PoRA; TrGrPo

Great [*or* Greate] Macedon, that out of Persia chased, The. The Earl of Surrey. SiPSBD

(Greate Macedon that out of Persy chased, The.) AAS

(In Praise of Wyatt's Psalms.) AAS; SiPS

Great Man, The. Eunice Tietjens. WGRP

Great Man's Death: An Anecdote, The. Everette Maddox. MT

Great many gentlemen take great delight, A. Bold Reynard the Fox. *Unknown.* OBET

Great master! Boyish, sympathetic man! To John Keats. Amy Lowell. Son

Great master of the poet's art! John Greenleaf Whittier. Phoebe Cary. AmWP

Great Men Have Been among Us. Wordsworth. EnRP; FaBoPV; MeMBP; PoEL-4; Son

Great men have been among us; hands that penned. Great Men Have Been among Us. Wordsworth. EnRP; FaBoPV; MeMBP; PoEL-4; Son

(England, 1802, III.) OBEV

Great Merchant, Dives Pragmaticus, Cries His Wares, The, *sels.* Thomas Newbery.

"What lack you, sir? What seek you? What will you buy?" OxBChV

Great moment in *Blade Runner* where Roy. Final Farewell. Tom Clark. UL

Great Monarch, whose feared hands the thunder fling. A Paraphrase Upon Part of the CXXXIX Psalm. Thomas Stanley. ChIV-1

Great Moth, The. Robert Gittings. OxBTC

Great Mother, The. Susan Griffin. SRLS

Great Mourning. Bible, Apocrypha. *Fr.* First Maccabees. TrJP

Great mystery of sleep. *Unknown.* EaPr

Great Nature clothes the soul, which is but thin. The Soul's Garment. Margaret Cavendish, Duchess of Newcastle. WPE

Great nature she doth clothe the soul within. Soul and Body. Margaret Cavendish, Duchess of Newcastle. OxBSP

Great Nebula in Andromeda, The. Hugh Seidman. AmPA

Great odes have had no revival, The. Ancient Airs. Li Po, *tr. fr. Chinese by* Joseph J. Lee. SuSp

Great or small, you furnish your parts toward the soul. (*LL*) Crossing Brooklyn Ferry. Walt Whitman. AmPP; InPS; LiTA; MoP; NAAL-1; NoAM; NOBA; NoP; TAP

Great Overdog, The,/ That heavenly beast. Canis Major. Robert Frost. *Fr.* Sky Pair, A. MoAB; MoAmPo

Great Pacific railway, The. The Railroad Cars Are Coming. *Unknown.* AS; FaPON

Great Painter! to thy soul aglow with thought. Raphael. H. Cordelia Ray. CBWP-3

Great Palaces of Versailles, The. Rita Dove. NoAM

Great Panjandrum [Himself], The. Samuel Foote. CBNP; FaBoCh; FaBoCo; MoShBr; PoLF

Great Pelides, stretch'd along the shore. The Ghost of Patroclus. Homer, *tr. by* Pope. *Fr.* Iliad, The. PeHV

Great philosopher did choke, A. Samuel Butler. FaBoEE

Great Physician, The. Sadi, *tr. fr. Persian by* Sir Edwin Arnold. *Fr.* Bustan, The. AWP

Great Poll-Tax Victory of '88, The. Noel Petty. UV

Great Pretenderer, The. Pat Nolan. UL

Great River, The. Henry van Dyke. TrPWD

Great River wraps an arm, The. On the River. Yü Hsüan-chi, *tr. fr. Chinese by* Jan W. Walls. SuSp

Great St. Bernard, The. Samuel Rogers. OBTV

Great Santa Barbara Oil Disaster OR, The. Conyus. AmPA; NBV

Great Sassacus fled from the eastern shores. Death Song. Alonzo Lewis. PAH

Great Scarf of Birds, The. John Updike. NYBP

Great Sea, The. Uvavnuk. *Unknown, tr. fr. Eskimo by* Knud Rasmussen. NU

(Song of Joy.) WTO

Great sea has set me in motion, The. Uvavnuk, *tr. fr. Eskimo.* EaPr; EnlH, *tr. by* Stephen Mitchell

Great sea-roads to England, The. The Gates to England. Marjorie Wilson. BoTP

Great Serbian Migration 1690. Milorad Pavic, *tr. fr. Serbo-Croatian by* Charles Simic. HSix

Great Silkie of Sule Skerry, The. *Unknown.* ChTr; ESPB; FaBoBa; FaBoCh; GBP; MAT

Great Sir, having just had the good luck to catch. Copy of an Intercepted Despatch from His Excellency Don Strepitoso Diabolo. Thomas Moore. OBSV

Great sir, our poor hearts were ready to burst. The Humble Address [*or* of the Loyal Professors of Divinity and Law that Want Preferment and Practice]. *Unknown.* APAS; FaBoEH

Great Society, The. Robert Bly. NoAM

Great Soul of Friendship whither art thou fled. On Rosania's Apostasy, and Lucasia's Friendship. Katherine Philips. KTR

Great soul, thou sittest with me in my room. To the Spirit of Keats. James Russell Lowell. Son

Great soul, to all brave souls akin. The Star. Marion Couthouy Smith. PAH

Great South Land, The, *sels.* Rex Ingamells.

"Cook admired the native courage, made." NOBAu

"They made impudent inspection of our coast." CBAP

Great Spaces. Howard Moss. TwCP

Great Spirit. *Unknown. Fr.* U.N. Environmental Sabbath Program. FHYEP

Great Spirit of the speeding spheres. John Haynes Holmes. TrPWD

Great Spirit takes care of me, The. (*LL*) I'm an Indian. John Lame Deer. EaPr

Great Spirit, whose dry lands thirst, help us to find. *Unknown. Fr.* U.N. Environmental Sabbath Program. FHYEP

Great Spirits Now on Earth. Keats. Son

Great star has fallen into my lap, A. Reconciliation. Else Lasker-Schüler, *tr. fr. German by* Robert Alter. PBWP

Great Statue of the General Du Puy, The. Wallace Stevens. *Fr.* Notes toward a Supreme Fiction. LiTA

Great Stone Face. George Bradley. BAP-91

Great stone hearth has gone, The. Fire. Dorothy Wellesley. OBMV

Great streets of silence led away. Emily Dickinson. NOCV

Great Stubbs' picture of the great Eclipse, The. Derby Day: An Exhibition. Alison Brackenbury. SCBI

Great success need not be proud. Tseng Jui, *tr. by* Wayne Schlepp. *Fr.* Tune: "Sheep on Mountain Slope" — Lamenting the Times. SuSp

Great Summons, The. Ch'u Yüan, *tr. fr. Chinese by* Arthur Waley. AWP

Great Swamp Fight, The. Caroline Hazard. PAH

Great tempest on the Plain of Ler, A. *Unknown.* NOIV

Great Things. Thomas Hardy. GTBS-P; NOBE

Great Things [Are Done]. Blake. *Fr.* Gnomic Verses. ArNa; OxBSP

Great things are done when men and mountains meet. Great Things [Are Done]. Blake. *Fr.* Gnomic Verses. ArNa; OxBSP

Great Things Have Happened. Alden Nowlan. GOYP

Great thoughts, grave thoughts, thoughts lasting to the end. (*LL*) Sorrow. Aubrey Thomas De Vere. BLPA; WGRP

Great thrushes have not appeared this year, The. The Unremarkable Year. Roy Fuller. OxBC

Great Time, A. W. H. Davies. AngWe; ImPo; LiTB; MoBrPo

Great *Titanic. Unknown.* AmFP

Great Tom. Richard Corbett [*or* Corbet]. OxBoLi

Great Unaffected Vampires and the Moon. Stevie Smith. NoAM

Great Uncle Joe. Apology. Duane Niatum. HATNAP

Great unequal conflict past, The. Occasioned by General Washington's Arrival in Philadelphia, on His Way to His Residence in Virginia. Philip Freneau. PAH

Great Venus, Queene [*or* Queen] of Beautie [*or* Beauty] and of grace. Address to Venus. Lucretius, *tr. fr. Latin. Fr.* De Rerum Natura (On the Nature of Things). AWP, *tr. by* Spenser

(Darling of God and Men.) ArLo, *tr. by* Basil Bunting

(Prayer to Venus.) EiL, *tr. by* Spenser

Great Victory, The. R. V. Gilbert. BLRP

Great Wager, The. G. A. Studdert-Kennedy. TrCP

Great Wagon, The. Tontaiman Ilantiraiyan, *tr. fr. Tamil by* A. K. Ramanujan. PLW

Great Wall, The. Chu Ch'ing-yu, *tr. fr. Chinese by* Irving Y. Lo. SuSp

Great War, The. Vernon Scannell. NSI; OBWP

Great Way has no age, The. Wu-Men, *tr. fr. Chinese by* Stephen Mitchell. EnlH

Great Way isn't difficult, The. The Mind of Absolute Trust. Seng-ts'an, *tr. fr. Chinese by* Stephen Mitchell. EnlH

Great Wheel, The. "Hugh MacDiarmid." OxBS

Great white lilies in the grass, The. Pallor. Agnes Mary Frances Robinson. NOBVV

Great, wide, beautiful, wonderful World. The Wonderful World. William Brighty Rands. FaPON
(Child's World, The.) OHIP
(World, The.) BoTP; OxBChV

Great Wind, The. Chang Hsien-liang, *tr. fr. Chinese.* LHF, *tr.* by Hualing Nieh

Great wind rises, A. Song of the Great Wind. Liu Pang, *tr. fr. Chinese* by Ronald C. Miao. SuSp

Great without pomp, without ambition brave. Tribute to Washington. *Unknown.* OHIP

Great woe, fire & war come on me. Skythinos, *tr. fr. Greek* by Thomas Meyer. GrAn; PeHV

Great you call Demosthenes. Self-Portrait. Moses Mendelssohn, *tr. fr. German.* TrJP

Greate Macedon that out of Persy chased, The. The Earl of Surrey. *See* Great [*or* Greate] Macedon, that out of Persia chased, The.

Greater Cats, The. V. Sackville-West. CoGr; OBMV; OTCP; Spl

Greater cats with golden eyes, The. The Greater Cats. V. Sackville-West. CoGr; OBMV; OTCP; Spl

Greater Courage. Natan Zach, *tr. fr. Hebrew* by Peter Everwine *and* Shulamit Yasny-Starkman. PoSu

Greater Friendship Baptist Church, The. Carole C. Gregory. BlSi

Greater Gift, The. Margaret E. Bruner. PoToHe

Greater, he called them, than Homer or Chaucer. The Men of Sudbury. Carlos Baker. GOA

Greater Love. Wilfred Owen. CMoP; EnLoPo; FaBoMo; FaBoRV; GTBS-P; ImPo; LiTB; LiTM; MeMBP; MoAB; MoBrPo; MoP; NoAM; TFi

Greater than memory of Achilles or Ulysses. The Wallabout Martyrs. Walt Whitman. GOA

Greater Trial, The. The Countess of Winchilsea. TrGrPo

Greatest in many things, in some the least. On a Distinguished Politician. J. E. Thorold Rogers. FaBoEE

Greatest Love, The. Anna Swirszczynska, *tr. fr. Polish* by Czeslaw Milosz *and* Leonard Nathan. PoSu

Greatest Man on Earth, The. *Unknown.* RoPo

Greatest of These, The, *abr.* Bible, *N.T. See* Though I Speak with the Tongues of Men and Angels.

Greatest Person in the Universe, The. Daniel L. Marsh. BLRP

Greatest saints and sinners have been made, The. Samuel Butler. FaBoEE

Greatest self-made man in the world today, The. Our Noble Booker T. Washington. Mrs. Henry Linden. CBWP-4

Greatest things to me! (*LL*) Great Things. Thomas Hardy. GTBS-P; NOBE

Greatly shining,/ The autumn moon floats in the thin sky. Wind and Silver. Amy Lowell. BoWoP; HeIP; MoAmPo; Spl

Greatness. Thomas Love Peacock. *Fr.* Crochet Castle. OtMeF

Greatness in Little. Richard Leigh. NOSC

Greatness of Music, The. The Great. Clark Coolidge. Jaz

Greatrakes, The Healer. Thomas McCarthy. IB

Grecian Kindness. The Earl of Rochester. OxBSP

Greece. Robert Browning. *Fr.* Cleon. OAEL-2; OtMeF

Greece. William Haygarth. OBTV
Sels.
"Genius of Greece! thou livest, though thy domes."
"Mournful is the remembrance which awakes."

Greece. Derek Walcott. AnAn

Greece was; Greece is no more. The "White City." Richard Watson Gilder. PAH

Greed. (*LL*) Stone Gullets. May Swenson. VCAP

Greed. *Unknown.* OxNR

Greed and Aggression. Sharon Olds. RaBo

Greedy-in-love, leave go! Leave go! (*LL*) Her Mouth and Mine. W. H. Davies. CBLP

Greedy Jane. *Unknown.* OxBChV

Greedy Little Pig, The. Irene F. Pawsey. BoTP

Greedy Man, The. *Unknown.* ReMoGo

Greedy Richard. Jane Taylor. OxBChV

Greedy Seasons. Eileen Myles. UL

Greedy snowslide. *Unknown.* TSaS, *tr.* by Lawrence Millman

Greedy the People, The. E. E. Cummings. SoSe

Greedy Tom. *Unknown.* OxNR

Greedyguts. Kit Wright. OTCP

Greek Alphabet. *Unknown.* ISE

Greek Archipelagoes. Patrick Leigh-Fermor. OBTV

Greek Architecture. Herman Melville. NoP

Greek Epigram. Ezra Pound. MoAB; MoAmPo

Greek Room, The. James W. Thompson. BPo

Greek ship, A/ Sails on the sea. The Couple. Sandra Hochman. NYBP

"Greek Tragedy" of course is the sort of thing. Their Philistinism Considered. Robert Pinsky. *Fr.* Essay on Psychiatrists. NoAM

Greeks, The. Tom Clark. PoA

Greeks' chieftains, all irked with the war, The. Virgil, *tr.* by the Earl of Surrey. *Fr.* Aeneid [*or* Eneados], The. NAWM-1; OAEL-1

Green. Walter de la Mare. FaBoNo

Green. D. H. Lawrence. GBL; MoBrPo; PoA

Green. Paul Verlaine, *tr. fr. French* by Philip L. Miller. RiWo

Green & white valley and the river. Pure Dread. Peter Riley. VaA

Green Acres. David Trinidad. BAP-91

Green Afternoon, The. Henry Rago. VGW

Green and blue the reedy shallows. At Yuen Yang Lake. Wu Wei-yeh, *tr. fr. Chinese* by Kenneth Rexroth. OHMPC

Green and growing thorn-tree, A. Forgive and Forget. "Totius," *tr. fr. Afrikaans* by Anthony Delius. PeSA

Green and silent spot, amid the hills, A. Fears in Solitude. Samuel Taylor Coleridge. EnRP; FHYEP; OBWP

Green and the Black, The. Anthony Bailey. NYBP

Green and Yellow. *Unknown.* OBET

Green Apples. Ruth Stone. InPS

Green are the tussocks of the marsh-grass springing. Yellow. Kenton Kilmer. GoYe

Green arsenic smeared on an egg-white cloth. L'Art, 1910. Ezra Pound. HeIL; HeIP; OxBA

Green as a seedling the one lane shines. City Traffic. Eve Merriam. PDV

Green as that summer fly. Silk Robe. Jeffrey Skinner. PBCAP

Green Autumn Stubble, The. *Unknown, tr. fr. Irish* by Patrick Browne. WTO

Green be the turf above thee. On the Death of Joseph Rodman Drake. Fitz-Greene Halleck. AnAmPo; BLPA; PAH; PoEL-4

Green Bed, The. *Unknown.* AmFP

Green-blue ground, The. On Gay Wallpaper. William Carlos Williams. MeMAP; MoAB; MoAmPo; TAP

Green, blue, yellow, and red. The One. Patrick Kavanagh. MoBrPo; TIRV

Green Breeks. Douglas Dunn. FaBoPV

Green Briar Shore, The. *Unknown.* AmFP

Green Broom. *Unknown. See* There was an old man and he lived [out] in a wood.

Green Buddhas/ On the fruit stand. Watermelons. Charles Simic. OBAL; VCAP

Green, but a very mock turtle!, The. (*LL*) The Song of the Turtle and the Flamingo. James Thomas Fields. GN

Green Candles. Humbert Wolfe. MoBrPo

Green catalpa tree has turned, The. April Inventory. W. D. Snodgrass. CAPP; CoAP; HAP; LiTM; NoAM; NoP; Poetr; TAP; TRP; TwCP; VCAP

Green Chateau, The. Wendy Mulford. NBrP

Green cheese, yellow laces. *Unknown.* OxNR

Green Chile. Jimmy Santiago Baca. NAmP90

Green Coconuts: Rio. Lawrence Durrell. OBTV

Green Cornfield, A. Christina Rossetti. BoTP

Green creepers planted inside the house. What She Said ("Green creepers planted inside the house.") Orampokiyar, *tr. fr. Tamil* by A. K. Ramanujan. *Fr.* Five on the Riverside Cane. PLW

Green Dryad's Plea, The. Thomas Hood. *Fr.* Plea of the Midsummer Fairies, The. OBNC

Green elm with the one great bough of gold, The. October. Edward Thomas. NoAM

Green Enravishment of Human Life. Sister Juana Inés de la Cruz, *tr. fr. Spanish.* WPOW, *tr.* by Samuel Beckett *and* Octavio Paz

Green Eye, The. James Merrill. PoA

Green eye — and a red — in the dark, A. The Train. Mary Elizabeth Coleridge. BoTP

Green Eye of the Yellow God, The. J. Milton Hayes. BLPA; EBEvV; EBNV; VPP

Green-eyed Care. Old Cat Care. Richard Hughes. OBMV

Green Family, The. Colleen Thibaudeau. NOBC

Green field stretches out like a mind at ease, The. Saying Good-bye. Duo Duo, *tr. fr. Chinese* by Donald Finkel *with* Li Guohua. SpMi

Green Frog at Roadstead, Wisconsin. James Schevill. TAP

Green garden of growing weeds, A. Playing with Fire. James Simmons. CIP

Green-Gown, The. *Unknown.* CoMu

Green grape, and you refused me. Brief Autumnal. *Unknown, tr. fr. Greek* by Dudley Fitts. GrAn; WeW

Green Grass. *Unknown.* BoTP; CH; FaBoVe; GBP; OxBoLi; OxNR

Green Grass Growing All Around, The. *Unknown.* MoShBr

Green Grass Grows All Around, The. *Unknown.* RoPo

Green grass is bowing, The. The Wind in the Grass. Siegfried Emerson. BoTP

Green grass tendrils like silk. The Wandering Gentleman. *Unknown, tr. fr. Chinese by* Ronald C. Miao. SuSp

Green Gravel. *Unknown.* FaBoVe

Green gravel green gravel. Green Gravel. *Unknown.* FaBoVe

Green, Green, and Green Again. Conrad Aiken. *Fr.* And in the Human Heart. Son

Green, Green Is El Aghir. Norman Cameron. MoBS; OBWP; OxBTC

Green grow, etc. (LL) Green Grow the Rashes, O. Burns. CoMu, *diff. vers.*; CTC; EnRP; ErPo, *diff. vers.*; LiTB; NAEL-2, *diff. vers.*; NoP; OAEL-1; PFP; PPP; SCGP, *diff. vers.*

Green Grow the Rashes, O. Burns. CoMu, *diff. vers.*; CTC; EnRP; ErPo, *diff. vers.*; LiTB; NAEL-2, *diff. vers.*; NoP; OAEL-1; PFP; PPP; SCGP, *diff. vers.*

Green Grow the Rushes O. *Unknown. See* I'll sing you [a] one-O [or twelve O].

Green Groweth the Holly. *Unknown.* NoSic; OxBLMV

Green Grows the Rashes. Burns. *See* Green Grow the Rashes, O.

Green Hammock, White Magnolia Tree. Ruth Gilbert. PeNZ

Green Hills of Africa, The. Roy Fuller. NoP; OBTV

Green hills on both banks — mounds of rice kernels. Insscribed on a Painting. Cheng Hsieh, *tr. fr. Chinese by* Irving Y. Lo. SuSp

Green, humped, wrinkled hills: with such a look, The. The Green Hills of Africa. Roy Fuller. NoP; OBTV

Green I love you green. Sleepwalkers' Ballad. Federico García Lorca, *tr. fr. Spanish by* John Frederick Nims. WeW

Green Ice. Vivienne Finch. BrRo

Green is the grass on riverbanks. *Unknown, tr. fr. Chinese by* Dell R. Hales. SuSp

Green is the night, green kindled and apparelled. The Candle, a Saint. Wallace Stevens. PoRA

Green it's your green I love. Sleepwalkers' Ballad. Federico García Lorca, *tr. fr. Spanish by* John Frederick Nims. STV

Green Jade Plum Trees in Spring. Ou-yang Hsiu, *tr. fr. Chinese by* Kenneth Rexroth. NaP

Green Knight's Farewell to Fancy, The. George Gascoigne. EnRePo; NoSic; OPOP

Green Lady, The. Charlotte Druitt Cole. BoTP

Green lady, green lady, come doon for thy tea. *Unknown.* GBP

Green lamp flares on the table, The. This Life. Rita Dove. AmPA; VBLP

Green lawn/ a picket fence. Alice Walker. *Fr.* Once. BlSi; PoBA

Green Leaf that will outlast the winter. Louis Zukofsky. VGW

Green leaves. Change. Hsiao Kang, *tr. fr. Chinese by* Henry H. Hart. EaPr

Green leaves, what are you doing. The Five-Fingered Maple. Kate Louise Brown. BoTP

Green Light. Kenneth Fearing. PoE; VGW

Green light floods the city square, The. Sunken Evening [in Trafalgar Square]. Laurie Lee. LiTM; NYBP

Green light — go. At the Corner of Muck and Myer. Paul Violi. UL

Green Linnet, The. Wordsworth. EnRP; GTBS; GTBS-P

Green little vaulter in the sunny grass. To the Grasshopper and the Cricket. Leigh Hunt. EnRP; GN; OBNC; Son
(Grasshopper and the Cricket, The.) OxAEP-2

Green lotus leaves, a canopy on the pond. *Unknown, tr. by* Michael E. Workman. *Fr.* Tzu-yeh Songs of the Four Seasons. SuSp

Green Lowland of Pianos, A. Jerzy Harasymowicz, *tr. fr. Polish by* Czeslaw Milosz. CBNP

Green Market, New York. Julia Kasdorf. LoHo

Green Martyrs. Richard Murphy. *Fr.* Battle of Aughrim, The. NOIV

Green mistletoe! Winter. Walter de la Mare. ChTr; OAEL-2; OBMV

Green Mossy Banks of the Lee, The. *Unknown.* OBET

Green mothering of moss knits shadow and light, The. Rain Forest. Dave Jeddie Smith. HCAP; MT

Green Mountain Boy. Florida Watts Smyth. GoYe

Green Mountain Boys, The. Bryant. PAH

Green mountain lies beyond the north wall of the city, The. Saying Farewell to a Friend. Li Po, *tr. fr. Chinese by* Robert Payne. TAL

Green mountains on three sides, a bamboo fence all around. Sitting on a Rock by Mountain Stream. Ch'en Yu Yi, *tr. fr. Chinese by* Irving Y. Lo. SuSp

Green mwold on zummer bars do show. Tokens. William Barnes. PoEL-4

Green nut tree, The. The Fruited Month. Zalman Schneour, *tr. fr. Hebrew by* Ruth Finer Mintz. MHP

Green of Jesus, The. Spring Song. Lucille Clifton. CrSp

Green pine grows in eastern garden, A. T'ao Ch'ien, *tr. by* Wu-chi Liu. *Fr.* Drinking Wine. SuSp

Green Place, A. William Jay Smith. GrPl

Green Plumes of Royal Palms. LeRoy V. Brant. AH

Green Rain. Dorothy Livesay. NALW; NIP; NOBC

Green Rain. Mary Webb. BoNaP; CH; FaPON

Green Red Brown and White. May Swenson. VGW

Green Refrain, The. Avraham Huss, *tr. fr. Hebrew by* Ruth Finer Mintz. MHP

Green Revolutions. Barbara Guest. FaBoWP

Green River. Bryant. AnAmPo; NOBA; OxBA

Green River, The. Lord Alfred Bruce Douglas. OBEV

Green Roads, The. Edward Thomas. FaBoPP; NoAM

Green rushes with red shoots. Plucking the Rushes. *Unknown, tr. fr. Chinese.* BoLoP; Mes; OBVE

Green rustlings, more-than-regal charities. Royal Palm. Hart Crane. CMoP; MoAB; MoAmPo; MoP; NoAM; NoP; TrGrPo

Green scapulars to wear over your shroud. (LL) The Strand at Lough Beg. Seamus Heaney. AnAn; CIP; NoAM; NoP; OBWP

Green-shadowed people sit, or walk in rings. Spring. Philip Larkin. MoBrPo

Green Shepherd, The. Louis Simpson. NYBP

Green shutters, shut your shutters! Windyridge. Sir John Betjeman. *Fr.* Beside the Seaside. OxBTC

Green Slates. Thomas Hardy. FaBoPP

Green Sleeves [and Tartan Ties]. *Unknown.* FaBoVe; GBP

Green Snake, when I hung you round my neck. To the Snake. Denise Levertov. AmPP; LiTM; NMM; PoA

Green soaks into the dark trees. Twilight in West Virginia: Six O'Clock Mine Report. Irene McKinney. PBCAP

Green Song. Philip Booth. BoNaP

Green Spring receiveth. The Great Summons. Ch'u Yüan, *tr. fr. Chinese by* Arthur Waley. AWP

Green Sussex. Tennyson. *Fr.* Prologue to General Hamley. FaBoPP

Green sweater a little rubbed. The Ceiling. Alexander Craig. FaBoMA

Green Symphony. John Gould Fletcher. MoAmPo

Green Things Growing. Dinah Maria Mulock Craik. GN; OHIP

Green Tree, The. James Reiss. AmPA

Green trees that in the forest grew. (LL) A Dialogue between the Soul and [the] Body. Andrew Marvell. ESCV; GeHe; HAP; InPS; JCP; MeLP; NAEL-1; NoP; OAEL-1; OxAEP-1; PoEL-2; PPP; SeCP; SeCV-1; SoSe; TEP; TFi

Green Valley. Dorothy Vena Johnson. PoNe

Green Valley, The. Sylvia Townsend Warner. MoBrPo

Green Wall, The. Rachel Hadas. UnDi

Green Willow, The. *Unknown.* EBEvV; SCGP

Green Willow, Green Willow. *Unknown.* AmFP

Green willows, fragrant grass, the many-stationed road. Tune: "Spring in Jade Pavilion." Yen Shu, *tr. fr. Chinese by* An-yan Tang. SuSp

Green Windows. Carol Rumens. PWE

Green woodpecker flying up and down, The. The Green Woodpecker's Nest. John Clare. FaBoVe

Green Woodpecker's Nest, The. John Clare. FaBoVe

Greenback Dollar, The. *Unknown.* AmFP

Greener Grass. Frank Steele. Poetsp

Greene's Farewell to Folly, *sels.* Robert Greene.
  "Sweet are the thoughts that savour of content." PoEL-2; PoToHe

Greene's Groatsworth of Wit, *sels.* Robert Greene.
  Fie, Fie on Blind Fancy! EIL
  Palinode, A
  (Deceiving World.) NoSic

Greene's Mourning Garment, *sels.* Robert Greene.
  Hexametra Alexis in Laudem Rosamundi. EIL; GBL; PoEL-2
  Shepherd's Wife's Song, The. EIL; HAP; NoSic

Greene's Vision, *sels.* Robert Greene.
  Description of Sir Geoffrey Chaucer, The. CTC; NoSic; SCGP
  (Sir Geoffrey Chaucer.) FaBoCh

Greenest Continent, The, *sels.* Wallace Stevens.
  Everything Juts Up in Europe. CBCK

Greenest of grass in the long meadow grows, The. June. Jane G. Stewart. BoTP

Greenfield Hill, *sels.* Timothy Dwight.
  Destruction of the Pequods, The. EAP
  Flourishing Village, The. EAP
  Prospect, The. EAP

Greengrocer, The. Michael Longley. *Fr.* Wreaths. BiHa

Greenhalgh's Pub. Julian Croft. NOBAu

Greenham Women. Wendy Poussard. AIW

Greenhouse [or Green-house] is my summer seat, The. The Faithful Friend. William Cowper. FM; OBF

Greenhouse Vanity, The. Les A. Murray. FaBoVe

Greenland Men, The. *Unknown.* OxBSS

Greenland Voyage; or, The Whale Fisher's Delight, The. *Unknown.* OxBSS

Greenland Whale, The. *Unknown. See* 'Twas in the year of forty-nine.

Greenland Whale Fishery, The. *Unknown.* AmFP; OBET; OxBSS

Greenland Winter, A. Lucy Diamond. BoTP

Greenland's History. Sven Holm, *tr. fr. Danish.* TSaS, *tr. by* Paula Hostrup-Jessen

Greenness. Angelina Weld Grimké. CDC

Greens. David Ray. SM; VGW

Greens. *Unknown.* AS

Greensleeves. *Unknown. See* Alas! my love, you [*or* ye] do me wrong.

Greensleeves. *Unknown.* TTTS

Greenwich Observatory. Sidney Keyes. MoAB; MoBrPo

Greenwood fawn at the hidden brook, The. Song for the Greenwood Fawn. I. L. Salomon. GoYe

Greenwood's. Michael Sharkey. NOBAu

Greeting. H. Cordelia Ray. CBWP-3

Greeting, A. W. H. Davies. MoBrPo

Greeting from England. *Unknown.* PAH

Greeting to Lu Hung-Chien, A. Li Yeh, *tr. fr. Chinese by* Kenneth Rexroth *and* Ling Chung. WPC

Greeting to Queen Elizabeth, the Rare White Heron of Single Flight, A. Wiremu Kingi Kerekere, *tr. fr. Maori by* Wiremu Kingi Kerekere. PeNZ

Greetings, great evangelist! Lines on the Return to Britain of Billy Graham. E. J. Thribb. PeLV

Greetings! you seven students of Professor Aristides. *Unknown, tr. fr. Greek by* Peter Jay. GrAn

Gregory Griggs, Gregory Griggs. *Unknown.* OxNR

Sir Gregory Nonsense's News from No Place, *sels.* John Taylor. "It was in June the eight and thirtieth day." CBNP; NOSC

Gregory's House. David Huddle. PBCAP

Greg's Got Custody of Sally. Julia Alvarez. CrSp

Greg's got custody of Sally and wants. Greg's Got Custody of Sally. Julia Alvarez. CrSp

Grenadier. A. E. Housman. OBMV; OBWP

Grenadier, The. *Unknown.* GBP; OxNR

Grenadiers, The. Heine, *tr. fr. German by* Philip L. Miller. RiWo

Grendel. *Unknown, tr. by* Burton Raffel. *Fr. Beowulf.* ASW, *tr. by* Kevin Crossley-Holland; NU

Grene groweth the holy. Love Ever Green. Henry VIII, King of England. MeEL

Gresford Disaster, The. *Unknown.* GBP; OBET

Gretel in Darkness. Louise Glück. AmPA; NoAM

Grevus is my sorow. Unkindness Has Killed Me. *Unknown.* MeEL

Grew in Hades. Creation. *Maori Oral Tradition, tr. by* Richard Taylor. WTO

Grey already the hair at my temples. Strato, *tr. fr. Greek by* Teddy Hogge. GrAn

Grey and dankish thing, A. Theodore Weiss. *Fr. Every Second Thought.* DiPo

Grey and Green. Arthur Symons. *Fr. At Dieppe.* FaBoPP; NOBVV; PeVV

Grey as a guinea-fowl is the rain. Two Kitchen Songs. Edith Sitwell. CMoP

Grey beards wag, the bald heads nod, The. Miniature. Eden Phillpotts. OxBSP

Grey brick upon brick. Dublin. Louis MacNeice. *Fr. Closing Album, The.* CIP; FaBoPP; IIP; OBTV; OxBTC

Grey Brother. U. M. Montgomery. BoTP

Grey Cock, The. *Unknown.* ELP; FaBoBa; OBET

Grey Cock, or, Saw You My Father?, The. *Unknown.* ELP; ESPB; FaBoBa; OBET

Grey courtyards where the imprisoned. Via Margutta. Maria Luisa Spaziani, *tr. fr. Italian by* Beverly Allen. NeIt

Grey dust runs on the ground like a mouse, The. Dust. P. A. Ropes. BoTP

Grey earth. Sorrows. Mang Ke, *tr. fr. Chinese by* Donald Finkel *with* Chang Sheng-Tai. SpMi

Grey Eye Weeping, A. Egan O'Rahilly, *tr. fr. Irish by* Frank O'Connor. FaBoPV; OBMV; PeIV

Grey-eyed King, The. "Anna Akhmatova," *tr. fr. Russian by* Robert Tracy. PBWP

Grey flies, fragile, slender-winged and slender-legged. Evening Dance of the Grey Flies. P. K. Page. NOBC

Grey flowers in thier pleated urns. Jeremy Taylor: The Rule and Exercise of Holy Dying, 1663. Peter Scupham. *Fr. Marginalia.* SCBI

Grey Frock, A. Zinaida Hippius, *tr. fr. Russian by* Temira Pachmuss. PBWP

Grey Funnel Line, The. Cyril Tawney. OBET

Grey girl who had not been singing stopped, The. New Year's Eve. John Berryman. LiTM

Grey goat grazed on the hill, The. Grey Brother. U. M. Montgomery. BoTP

Grey-green stretch of sandy grass, The. Grey and Green. Arthur Symons. *Fr. At Dieppe.* FaBoPP; NOBVV; PeVV

Grey Hair, The. Judah Halevi, *tr. fr. Hebrew by* J. Chotzner. TrJP

Grey hills of that country fall away, The. Cadaver Politic. Tom Paulin. PNI

"Grey Horse Troop," The. Robert W. Chambers. PAH

Grey, low ceiling, sough of sea wind along forest. The Lairdless Place. Kate Rennie Archer. GoYe

Grey Monk, The. Blake. PeECV

Grey October. "The Critics." OBET

Grey Ones, The. Louis MacNeice. CMoP

Grey [*or* Gray] sea and the long black land, The. Meeting at Night. Robert Browning. AWP; BoLoP; CBLP; EBEvV; ELP; EnVR; FaBoVe; FaBV; FF; FHYEP; GBL; HeIP; InPS; InvP; LPA; NAEL-2; NOBE; NOBVV; OBEV; OBNC; OHCV; OPOP; OxBSP; PeVV; PoRA; SCGP; SCV; SoSe; TFi; TrGrPo; UnPo

Grey psychopath in her season, The. Cat. Joe Rosenblatt. NOBC

Grey pussy-willows. Slumber in Spring. Elizabeth Gould. BoTP

Grey Selchie, The. *Unknown. See* Eartly [*or* Earthly] nourris [*or* nouris *or* nourrice*] sits and sings, An.

Grey Selchie of Sule Skerry, The. *Unknown.* OxBB

Grey Selchie of Sule Skerry, The. *Unknown. See* Eartly [*or* Earthly] nourris [*or* nouris *or* nourrice*] sits and sings, An.

Grey sky, grey city-smoke. 9th July, 1932. Mary Ursula Bethell. PeNZ

Grey sky/ mottled with blue &. The Fourteen-Year-Old Samuel Palmer's Watercolor Notations for the Sketch "A Lane at Thanet." Jonathan Williams. ETG

Grey the sky, and growing dimmer. Twilight. Louisa S. Guggenberger. NOBVV

Grey Time moves silently, and creeping on. *Unknown, tr. fr. Greek by* Peter Jay. GrAn

Grey trees, grey skies, and not a star. Dawn. Angelina Weld Grimké. ShDr

Grey was the morn, all things were grey. A Bit of Colour. Horace Smith. BoTP

Grey water tanks in grey mist. Bayonne Turnpike to Tuscarora. Allen Ginsberg. NNaP

Grey were the geese and green was the grazing. (*LL*) Three grey geese in a green field grazing. *Unknown.* OxNR

Grey Wolf. O. Fred Donaldson. EaPr

Grey Wolf, The. Arthur Symons. FaBoTw

Grey Woman. Gladys Cardiff. CDW

Greyer than the tide below, the tower. Homage to Jack Yeats. Thomas MacGreevy. OBMV

Greyhound should be headed like a snake, A. The Properties of a Good Greyhound. Dame Juliana Berners. RB

Greying, becoming equal. Sketches from Berlin. Harry Clifton. IB

Greyport Legend, A. Bret Harte. AnAmPo; GN

Grief. Wendell Berry. MT

Grief. Elizabeth Barrett Browning. EBEvV; HeIP; IMW; InPK; NALW; NOBVV; OBEV; OBNC; PoLF; TrGrPo; WPE

Grief. Catullus, *tr. fr. Latin by* Jacob Rabinowitz. RaBo

Grief. Maureen Seaton. LoHo

Grief. *Unknown, tr. fr. Welsh by* Aneirin Talfan Davies. OBWVE

Grief and God. Stephen Phillips. WGRP

Grief and Joy, *sels.* Frederic Lawrence Knowles. "Joy is a partnership." IMW

Grief fills the room up of my absent child. Shakespeare. *Fr. King John.* OBD

Grief for her absent master in her wrought. The Dog. Frederick William Faber. FM

Grief hath been known to turn the young head gray. The Young Gray Head. Caroline Southey. BeLS

Grief: I've grieved as a solitary phoenix grieves. Kuan Han-ch'ing, *tr. by* Jerome P. Seaton. *Fr. Tune:* "Intoxication in the East Wind." SuSp

Grief/ o grief. Alarum. Urszula Koziol, *tr. fr. Polish by* Czeslaw Milosz. WPOW

Grief of a Girl's Heart, The. *Unknown. See* It is late last night the dog was speaking of you.

Grief of Love, The. *Unknown, tr. fr. Arabic by* Wilfrid Scawen Blunt. AWP

Grief Plucked Me Out of Sleep. Jill King. PeSA

Grief reached across the world to get me. Grief. Catullus, *tr. fr. Latin by* Jacob Rabinowitz. RaBo

Grief Streams Down My Chest. Lance Jeffers. PoBA

Grief without a pang, void, dark, and drear, A. Samuel Taylor Coleridge. *Fr.* Dejection. IMW

Griefe, interrupted speach with teares supplyes. (*LL*) A Pastorall Dialogue. Thomas Carew. CaPo; GBL; SeCP

Griefe, killing griefe: have nott my torments binn. Mary Sidney Wroth, Countess of Montgomery. *Fr.* Urania. KTR; WPE

Griefs of Women, The. David R. Slavitt. BXAP

Grief's prodigals, where are you? Unthrifts, where? Upon Mr. Hopton's Death. Henry Halswell. NOSC

Griesly Wife, The. John Manifold. MoBrPo; MoBS

Grievance, A. James Kenneth Stephen. BXAP; FaBoPa

Grieve Not, Dear Love. John Digby. *See* Grieve not, dear love, although we often part.

Grieve not, dear love, although we often part. John Digby. NOSC (Grieve Not, Dear Love.) OxBSP

Grieve Not for Beauty ("Grieve not for the invisible, transported brow.") Witter Bynner. PoA

Grieve Not the Holy Spirit, &c. George Herbert. ESCV

Grieving the sapless limbs, the shorn and shaken. (*LL*) Dead Boy. John Crowe Ransom. CMoP; FaBoMo; LiTA; MeMAP; Mes; NoAM; NoP; OBD; OxBA; PoE; TwCP

Grievous folly shames my sixtieth year, A. Hafiz, *tr.* by Richard Le Gallienne. *Fr.* Odes. AWP

"Grill me some bones," said the Cobbler. At the Keyhole. Walter de la Mare. MoAB; MoBrPo

Grim monarch! see, deprived of vital breath. To a Lady on the Death of Her Husband. Phillis Wheatley. TAP

Grime on a tenement is as beautiful as the sunrise, The. (*LL*) How I Wrote It. David Dooley. TRP

Grimsby Fisherman, The. *Unknown.* OxBSS

Grimsby Lads, The. John Conolly *and* Bill Meek. OxBSS

Grinder, who serenely grindest. Lines on Hearing the Organ. Charles Stuart Calverley. FaBoCo; FiBHP; NOBL

Grinders; or, The Saddle on the Right Horse, The. *Unknown.* GBP

Grinding Vibrato. Jayne Cortez. BlSi

Grinding yoke from Israel's neck he tore, The. Eulogy for Hasdai ibn Shaprut. *Unknown, tr. fr. Hebrew by* Israel Abrahams. TrJP

Grinning, the foreman asked them for a vote. In the Jury Room. Hodding Carter. MAT

Grip down and begin to awaken. (*LL*) Spring and All. William Carlos Williams. CMoP; HAP; InPK; InPS; LiTM; MeMAP; MoP; NAAL-2; NoAM; NOBA; OxBA; PoE; TAP; TFi; TRP

Gripe. Lincoln Kirstein. PoWW

Griselda's dead, and so's her patience. Patient Griselda. Chaucer. *Fr.* Canterbury Tales, The. EnVB; PoRA

Grit. Geoff Page. NOBAu

Grit and Snow. Tracey Herd. NWP

Grizzel Grimme. *Unknown.* FaBoEE

Grizzly. Bret Harte. AnAmPo

Grizzly Bear. Mary Austin. FaPON; GoJo; PDV

Grizzly Bear, The. Ted Hughes. *See* I See a Bear.

Grizzly bear is huge and wild, The. Infant Innocence. A. E. Housman. ChTr; FaBoCh; FaBoCo; FaBoNo; ImPo; LiTB; NOBL; OxBoLi; PeLV; Spl

Groans of nature in this nether world, The. William Cowper. *Fr.* Task, The. NoP

"Grob! Grob," goes the raven peering from his rift. Cypress Grove. Austin Clarke. IPY

Grocery had provided him with, The. Dialog outside the Lakeside Grocery. Ishmael Reed. UL

Grocery Store, The. Maura Stanton. NAmP90

Grodek. Georg Trakl, *tr. fr. German by* Michael Hamburger. PeFWW

Groin, come of age, his 'state sold out of hand. On Groin. Ben Jonson. NOSC

Groined by deep glens and walled along the west. The Glens. John Hewitt. IIP; PeIV

Groins, for his fleshly burglary of late. Upon Groins: Epigram. Robert Herrick. CaPo

Grongar Hill. (Silent nymph, with curious eye!) John Dyer. AngWe; ChTr; EnRP; FaBoPP; NOEC; NoP; OxAEP-1; PoEL-3
Sels.
  "O may I with myself agree." TrGrPo

Groom of the Chamber's Religion in King Henry the Eighth's Time, A. John Harington. NoSic

Groping along the tunnel, step by step. The Rear-Guard. Siegfried Sassoon. MoBrPo; NAEL-2; NoAM; OBWP; PoWW

Groping back to bed after a piss. Sad Steps. Philip Larkin. NoAM; NoP

"Gross, Coarse, Hideous" (Police Description of My Pictures). D. H. Lawrence. FaBoEE

Gross innocent. Pablo Neruda, *tr. fr. Spanish. Fr.* Elephant. TTTS

Grotesque. Amy Lowell. BoWoP

Grotesque. Frederic Manning. PeFWW

Grotesque and queerly huddled. The Troop ship. Isaac Rosenberg. NSI; PoWW

Grotesque Love-Letter, A. *Unknown.* MeEL

Grotesque, the line of trees, pronged. Outside. Phyllis Beauvais. IHMS

Grotesques. Robert Graves. CMoP
Sels.
  "Dr. Newman with the crooked pince-nez." PeLV
  "Sir John addressed the Snake-god in his temple." PeLV

Grotesques, *sels.* Don Marquis.
  "Was it fancy, sweet nurse." FiBHP

Grotto, The. Francis Scarfe. PoA

Grouchy Good Night to the Academic Year, A. Ted Pauker. NOBL; PeLV

Ground beneath my feet is cracked, The. Day Twenty-three. Victor Coleman. NOBC

Ground drops back, The. Aeroplane. Pudjipangu, *tr. fr. Aborigine by* Georg von Brandenstein. NOBAu

Ground for the Floor. *Unknown.* OBET

Ground Hog Day. Marnie Pomeroy. ZA

Ground Hog Lock. Gerald Stern. AnAn

Ground-Mist, The. Denise Levertov. FoLa

Ground-Squirrel Song. *Navajo Indian Oral Tradition.* TTTS

Ground was frozen so hard, The. Dying with Amish Uncles. Julia Kasdorf. PBCAP

Groundhog, The. Richard Eberhart. CMoP; FaBoMo; ImPo; LiTA; LiTM; MoAB; MoAmPo; MoP; NoAM; NoP; NU; RaBo; TAP; TFi; TRP; UnPo

Groundhog, The. Luci Shaw. TrCP

Groundhog is, at best, a simple soul, The. The Groundhog. Luci Shaw. TrCP

Groundhog we dumped in the woods, The. Middle Age. Paula Rankin. MT

Group in Tartarus. Schiller, *tr. fr. German by* Philip L. Miller. RiWo

Group of jolly cowboys, discussing plans at ease, A. When the Work's All Done This Fall. *Unknown.* AS

Group of Musings, A. H. Cordelia Ray. CBWP-3
Sels.
  Noonday Thought.
  Starlight Thought.
  Sunrise Thought.
  Sunset Thought.

Group of Officials, A, *sels.* Yang Shih-ch'i, *tr. fr. Chinese by* Jonathan Chaves.

Group of professional, A. The Physics of Ochun. Victor Hernandez Cruz. UL

Group Photo from Pretoria Local on the Occasion of a Fourth Anniversary (Never Taken). Jeremy Cronin. PeSAV

Grove, The. Edwin Muir. LiTM

Grove beyond the Barley, The. Alden Nowlan. MoCV

Grover Cleveland. Joel Benton. PAH

Groves are down, The. Gary Snyder. *Fr.* Myths and Texts. NaP

Groves of Blarney, The. Richard Alfred Millikin. FaBoPP; OxBoLi; PeIV

Groves of Eden, vanished now so long, The. Pope. *Fr.* Windsor Forest. OAEL-1

Grow dim, or cease to be! (*LL*) I Want to Die While You Love Me. Georgia Douglas Johnson. BlSi; CDC; ShDr

Grow lovely, growing old? (*LL*) Let Me Grow Lovely. Karle Wilson Baker. BLPA; FaBoBe; TrPWD

Grow Old Along With Me! Robert Browning. *See* Grow old along with me!

Grow old along with me. Grow Old with Me. John Lennon. LPA

Grow old along with me! Rabbi Ben Ezra. Robert Browning. *Fr.* Rabbi Ben Ezra. BLPL; FaBV; MeMBP; NAEL-2; OBNC; PoToHe; TEP; WGRP
  (Grow Old Along With Me!) ImPo; LPA

Grow Old with Me. John Lennon. LPA

Grow weary if you will, let me be sad. Lesbia. Richard Aldington. PoLF

Growing. (*LL*) The More It Snows. A. A. Milne. NTCP; PYC; SiSoPo

Growing Dark. James Schuyler. GLP

Growing, he saw his friends increase. Tony White. Richard Murphy. BiHa

Growing in Grace. Jack R. Clemo. NOCV

Growing Old. Matthew Arnold. EnVR; FHYEP; MeMBP; NAEL-2; NOBVV; OAEL-2; PoEL-5

Growing old. Byron. *Fr.* Don Juan. NOBE; SCV

Growing Old. *Unknown, tr. fr. Irish by* Frank O'Connor. ErPo

Growing Old [*or* Growing Older]. Rollin J. Wells. BLPA; WBLP

Growing Rhyme, A. J. M. Westrup. BoTP

Growing Rich. Alice Cary. AmWP

Growing River, The. Rodney Bennett. BoTP

Growing Smiles. *Unknown.* PoLF

Growing Together. Joyce Carol Oates. CrSp; IHMS

Growing Up. Harry Behn. PDV

Growing Up. C. J. Dennis. ZA

Growing Up. U. A. Fanthorpe. AIW

Growing Up Alone, *sels.* Robert Adamson.
"Fishing skiff in the light." FaBoMA

Growltiger's Last Stand. T. S. Eliot. FaBoCh; OBCA

Grown and Flown. Christina Rossetti. NOBVV

Grown old are these strong elements of tragedy. One Hundred Lines for the Coast. Kojo Laing. HBAPE

Grown old in love from seven till seven times seven. Blake. FaBoEE; OAEL-2

Grown sick of war, and war's alarms. On the British King's Speech. Philip Freneau. PAH

Grown-up. Edna St. Vincent Millay. NoAM

Grown-ups. Geoffrey Holloway. OTCP

Grown-ups say things like. Chivvy. Michael Rosen. OTCP

Grows deathless by the sacrifise. (*LL*) Friendship's Mysterys, to my dearest Lucasia. Katherine Philips. KTR; PeHV

Growth of Heptarchy we trace, The. Edward B. Goodwin. *Fr.* English History in Rhyme, or a Rhyming Epitome of the History of England, from B.C. 55 to A.D. 1872. FaBoUs

Growth of Love, The, *sels.* Robert Bridges.
"Man that sees by chance his picture made, A." NoAM
My Lady Pleases Me. Son
O Weary Pilgrims. MoAB; MoBrPo
"They that in play can do the thing they would." NoAM
Whole World Now, The. Son

Grr — what's that? A dog? A poet? From a Spanish Cloister. G. K. Chesteron. UV

Grudge, The. Dimitris Tsaloumas. FaBoMA

Grudges mend and wear and turn in winter. Household. Laura Jensen. LCAP

Gruesome ghoul, the grisly ghoul, The. The Ghoul. Jack Prelutsky. OBCA

Grumble Family, The. *Unknown.* PWR; WBLP

Grunion. Myra Cohn Livingston. RFM

Grunion. Wendy Rose. CDW

Gryll Grange, *sels.* Thomas Love Peacock.
Love and Age. NOBVV; OBEV; OBNC

Gryll/ Had his fill. Gryll's State. Roy Blount, Jr.. OBAL

Gryll's State. Roy Blount, Jr.. OBAL

Guadalupe, W.I. Nicolás Guillén, *tr. fr. Spanish by* Anselm Hollo. TTY

Guard at the Binh Thuy Bridge, The. John Balaban. FYAP

Guard-Duty. August Stramm, *tr. fr. German by* Patrick Bridgwater. PeFWW

Guard her well. (*LL*) A Gentle Echo on Woman. Swift. FaBoCo; FiBHP; NBLV; NU

Guard Me, Oh God. Shin Shalom, *tr. fr. Hebrew by* Ruth Finer Mintz. MHP

Guard me, Oh God, from hating man my brother. Guard Me, Oh God. Shin Shalom, *tr. fr. Hebrew by* Ruth Finer Mintz. MHP

Guard me, oh God, from the cold winds that blow. A Woman's Prayer. Yehuda Karni, *tr. fr. Hebrew by* Ruth Finer Mintz. MHP

Guard of the Sepulcher, A. Edwin Markham. WGRP

Guard picks dead leaves from plants, The. In an Urban School. Toi Derricotte. PBCAP

Guarded Wound, The. Adelaide Crapsey. WPE

Guardian-Angel, The. Robert Browning. PeECV

Guardian Angel. Rolf Jacobsen, *tr. fr. Norwegian by* Robert Bly. RaBo

Guardian of Helicon, Urania's son. Catullus, *tr. by* Frederic Raphael *and* Kenneth McLeish. OxBM

Guardian Prince of Albion burns in his nightly tent, The. A Prophecy. Blake. *Fr.* America. FaBoEH

Guardians, The. Geoffrey Hill. NoP

Guarding the doors of the Hispanic Society. The Spanish Lions. Phyllis McGinley. NYBP

Guard's Mistake, The. Edmund Blunden. NSI

Guards of the Heart, *sels.* Joe Ross.

Guatemala, Your Blood. Alenka Bermudez, *tr. fr. Spanish by* Sara Miles. WoWa

Gubbinal. Wallace Stevens. NAAL-2; SOTW

Gud Ber. *Unknown.* FaBoVe

Gude and Godlie Ballatis, The, *sels. Unknown.*
Till Christ ("Till Christ, quhome I am haldin for to lufe"). OxBS

Gude Lord Graeme is to Carlisle gane. The Bewick and the Graeme. *Unknown.* OxBB

Gude Lord Scroop's to the huntin[g] gane. Hughie [the] Gra[e]me. *Unknown.* ESPB, *C vers.*; IBB, *diff. vers.*

Gude Wallace. *Unknown.* ESPB

Gude Wallace, A *vers. Unknown.* ESPB

Gudrun Laments over Sigurd. *Unknown, tr. by* William Morris *and* Eirikr Magnusson. *Fr.* Elder Edda, The. AWP; OBVE

Gudrun of old days. The First Lay of Gudrun. *Unknown, tr. by* William Morris *and* Eirikr Magnusson. *Fr.* Elder Edda, The. AWP

Gudveig. Francis Berry. OBTV

Guerillas. Seamus Deane. BiHa

Guerrilla-Cong, The. Michael S. Harper. NBV

Guerrilla Handbook, A. Amiri Baraka. PoBA

Guerrillas. Roger McTair. PBCV

Guess Who. Fred Chappell. NBLV

Guess who is this creature. A Song to the Wind. Taliesin, *tr. fr. Welsh by* A. P. Graves. FaBoCh

Guessed you but how I loved you, watched your smile. To W. J. M. "G. G." PeHV

Guessing. *Unknown, tr. fr. Burmese by* U Win Pe. PBWP

Guest, The. "Anna Akhmatova," *tr. fr. Russian by* Jane Kenyon *and* Vera Dunham. RaBo

Guest. D. J. Enright. Mes; OxBC

Guest. E. A. Lacey. PeHV

Guest, The. *Unknown. See* Yet if his majesty, our sovereign [*or* soveraign] Lord.

Guest, A. May Sarton. ArNa

Guest Ellen at the Supper for Street People, The. David Ferry. NIP

Guest in Your House, The. *Unknown, tr. by* Charlotte *and* Wolf Leslau. OBF

Guest Is Inside, The. Kabir, *tr. fr. Hindi by* Robert Bly. RaBo

Guest is inside you, and also inside me, The. The Guest Is Inside. Kabir, *tr. fr. Hindi by* Robert Bly. RaBo

G'uggery G'uggery Nunc. Sir John Betjeman. PeLi

Guid[-]Jday now, bonnie Robin. Robin Redbreast's Testament. *Unknown.* GBP; NTP

Guid-Mornin to Your Majesty! Burns. *Fr.* Dream, A. NAs

Guide and Friend. *Unknown.* BLRP

Guide Me, O Thou Great Jehovah. William Williams. OBWVE

Guide to Dungeness Spit, A. David Wagoner. FoLa

Guide to Familiar American Incest, A, *sels.* Dennis Saleh.

Guide to Holland. A. Peter Sirr. PBCIP

Guide to Patrons, A. Alattur Killar, *tr. fr. Tamil by* A. K. Ramanujan. PLW

Guide to the Perplexed. David Malouf. NOBAu

Guide to the Symphony. Weldon Kees. VGW

Guide where our Infant Redeemer is laid! (*LL*) Brightest and Best of the Sons of the Morning. Reginald Heber. GN; WGRP

Guided Missiles Experimental Range. Robert Conquest. OxBC

Guidepost, The. Wilhelm Müller, *tr. fr. German by* Philip L. Miller. *Fr.* Winter's Journey, The. RiWo

Guides urged us, praised us up to the Lion Gate, its. Remembering Mykenai. Alfred Corn. SM

Guido, I wish that you and Lapo and I. Dante, *tr. fr. Italian by* Kenneth Koch. ArLo; RB; TTTS

Guido, I would that Lapo, thou, and I. Sonnet: To Guido Cavalcanti. Dante, *tr. fr. Italian by* Shelley. AWP
(Sonnet: Dante Alighieri to Guido Cavalcanti.) OBVE

Guidon flags flutter gaily in the wind, The. (*LL*) Cavalry Crossing a Ford. Walt Whitman. AiP; AmPP; ChTr; HeIP; InPK; InPS; MoP; NAAL-1; NoAM; NoP; OxBA; PPP; SAmP; TAP; TFi; TRP; UnPo

Guild, The. Sharon Olds. RaBo

Guild lay under his engine dead. (*LL*) Guild's Signal. Bret Harte. VPP

Guild's Signal. Bret Harte. VPP

Guile and softness of the Saxon race, The. On the Welch. *Unknown.* AngWe

Guilielmus Rex. Thomas Bailey Aldrich. AnAmPo

Guilt. Lorenzo Thomas. UL

Guilt and Sorrow, *sels.* Wordsworth.
Salisbury Plain and Stonehenge. FaBoPP

Guilt, Desire and Love. James Baldwin. GLP

Guilty, my Lord, what can I more declare? Edward Taylor. *Fr.* Preparatory Meditations Before My Approach to the Lord's Supper. ChIV-1, Division II, *sect.* XXV

Gypsy Countess, The. *Unknown.* OBET

Gypsy Countess, The. *Unknown.* OBET

Gypsy Davy. *Unknown.* AS

Gypsy Davy, The. *Unknown.* AmFP

Gypsy, gypsy, please tell me. *Unknown.* RoPo

Gypsy Laddie, The. *Unknown.* ESPB, A *vers.*; HAP

Gypsy Laddie, The. *Unknown.* ESPB, B *vers.*; FaBoBa

Gypsy Music in Krakow. Tom Pickard. NBrP

Gypsy-race my pity rarely move, The. Gypsies. John Langhorne. *Fr.* Country Justice, The. NOEC

Gyres, The. W. B. Yeats. GTBS-P; HAP; NoAM

Gyre's Galax. Norman Henry, II Pritchard. PoBA

Gyroscope. Howard Nemerov. NoAM

H

H——y P——tt. *Unknown.* CoMu

H. Baptism. George Herbert. GeHe

H. Baptism II. George Herbert. *See* Since, Lord, to thee/ A narrow way and little gate.

H. Baptisme. George Herbert. *See* Since, Lord, to thee/ A narrow way and little gate.

H. Communion, The. George Herbert. ChIV-1; ESCV; MiEL

H. M. S. *Glory* at Sydney. Charles Causley. OBTV

H. M. S. *Hero.* Michael Roberts. OxBTC

H. M. S. *Pinafore,* sels. W. S. Gilbert.
    Englishman, The. NOBL
    Sir Josephs's Song. LiTB
    (First Lord's Song, The.) PeLV

H-óran ó a vee-ó. A Complaint about Exile. Mairi MacLeod, *tr. fr. Gaelic by* Joan Keefe. PBWP

H. Scriptures. Henry Vaughan. ChIV-2; ESCV

H. Scriptures II. George Herbert. *See* Oh that I knew how all thy lights combine.

H. Scriptures, The ("Oh Book! infinite sweetness!") George Herbert. ChIV-1; ESCV; MiEL

H. Scriptures, The ("Oh that I knew how all thy lights combine.") George Herbert. GeHe

H$_2$O. Belinda Subraman. NGP

H, U, uckle. *Unknown.* RoPo

Ha, ha, give me ale. *(LL)* In Praise of Ale. *At. to* Thomas Bonham.

Ha ha ha ha ha ha ha ha ha ha ha ha ha ha ha. *(LL)* Funny Lotus Blues . . . Ray Bremser. PoBeRe

Ha ha! ha ha! This world doth pass. Fara Diddle Dyno. *At. to* Thomas Weelkes. CBNP; EiL; FaBoCh; FaBoCo; FaBoNo
    (Madrigal: "Ha ha! ha ha! This world doth pass.") OxBoLi
    (Madrigal.) PeLV

Ha, ha, the wooing o't. *(LL)* Duncan Gray ("Duncan Gray cam here to woo.") Burns. GTBS-P; GTBS-P

Ha' not you seen, Camillo? Shakespeare. *Fr.* Winter's Tale, The. OxBM

Ha! Original Sin. Ogden Nash. FaBoCo; NBLV

Ha! sir, I have seen you sniffing and snoozling. The Faun. Ezra Pound. FaBoCh; FaBoTw

Ha! tott'ring Johnny strut and boast. The Creditor to His Proud Debtor. George Moses Horton. AAP

Ha' we lost the goodliest fere o' all. Ballad of the Goodly Fere. Ezra Pound. ChIV-2; CMoP; ImPo; LiTA; LiTM; MeMAP; MoAB; MoAmPo; MoBS; PoRA; TrCP; TrGrPo

Ha! whare ye gaun, ye crowlin' ferlie! To a Louse [on Seeing One on a Lady's Bonnet at Church]. Burns. BLPA; EnRP; FaBoVe; InvP; LiTB; NAEL-2; NOEC; OxBS; PrIm

Haa-low, okay. Don't Let Them Chip Away at Our Language. Kitty Tsui. ETG

Haanetjie's Morning Dialogue. Essop Patel. PeSAV

Haarlem Heights. Arthur Guiterman. PAH

Habeas Corpus. Anthony Barnett. VaA

Habeas Corpus. Helen Hunt Jackson. WGRP

Habeas Corpus Blues, The. Conrad Aiken. NYBP

Haberdasshere and a carpenter. Chaucer. *Fr.* Canterbury Tales, The. EnVB; FHYEP; NoP; OAEL-1; PPP, *abr.*

Habit. David Woo. OpBo

Habit of Perfection, The. Gerard Manley Hopkins. ChIV-2; ImPo; LiTB; MeMBP; MoAB; MoBrPo; MoP; NoAM; NoP; OBEV; OBMV; OxAEP-2; Poetr; PoRA; RB; TFi; TrGrPo

Habit of staring, The. Habit. David Woo. OpBo

Habitable planets are unknown or too. Native's Letter. Arthur Nortje. HBAPE; PeSAV

Habitat. Judith Wright. CBAP

Sels.
    "Charity lotteries for dream houses, The"
    "Furniture: humble, dependent"

Habitation. Margaret Atwood. BoWoP; FaBoWP; WeW

Habitation, The. Ralph Knevet. NOSC

Habits of the Hippopotamus. Arthur Guiterman. FaBV; FiBHP; OBCA

Habitué. Helen Frith Stickney. GoYe

Habla Usted Español? James Reiss. AmPA

Hackeysack Players, The. Cynthia Huntington. NAmP90

Hackney Coachman, The; Or, The Way to Get a Good Fare. Hannah More. WoRP

Had a quiet talk. *(LL)* Spring. Tanikawa Shuntaro. EaPr

Had anything been wrong, we should certainly have heard. *(LL)* The Unknown Citizen. W. H. Auden. FF; HeIL; HeIP; InPK; LiTA; LiTM; MeMAP; MoAB; NBLV; NIP; NOBL; NYBP; OBSV; Poetr; PoRA; SoSe; TRP; UnPo

Had broken and thrown away! *(LL)* The Slave's Dream. Longfellow. FaPoR; NAAL-1; PoNe

Had Cowley ne'er spoke, Killigrew ne'er writ. Sir John Denham. FaBoEE

Had cut grooves too deeply across our backs. *(LL)* Hard Rock Returns to Prison from the Hospital for the Criminal Insane. Etheridge Knight. InPS; MoP; NIP; NNaP; PBCAP; TAP; TRP; UnPo

Had damned him to the hell of impotence. *(LL)* The Disappointment. Aphra Behn. NALW; NOSC; VBLP

Had everyone Suum. To the Archbishop of Tuam. *Unknown.* FaBoEE

Had foolishly denied. *(LL)* Against Modesty in Love. Matthew Prior. ErPo

Had Gadyaa Kid, a Kid. *Unknown, tr. fr. Hebrew.* TrJP

Had he and I but met. The Man He Killed. Thomas Hardy. CMoP; DL; FF; HAP; HeIP; LiTB; LiTM; MeMBP; MoAB; MoBrPo; NIP; OBWP; PAW; Poetr; RB; TFi; WeW

Had I a man's fair form, then might my sighs. To ******. Keats. OxAEP-2

Had I an inn at Bethlehem. Lineage. Robert Farren. TIRV

Had I been an ox or horse. Wang An-shih, *tr. by* Jan W. Walls. *Fr.* In the Style of Han Shan and Shih Te. SuSp

Had I been mindful of my high descent. Hadewijch, *tr. fr. Dutch by* Frans van Rosevelt. PBWP

Had I but plenty of money, money enough and to spare. Up at a Villa — Down in the City. Robert Browning. CoGr; FaBoPP; FHYEP; GTBS-P; InPS; NOBE; OBTV; PoRA; PPP

Had I but strength enough, and time. Charles Robinson. BXAP

Had I but the torrent's might. The Death of Hoel. Thomas Gray. NOEC

Had I concealed my love. Elinor Wylie. BLPL

Had I fore-knowne of this thy least desire. Better Books to Burn. Ben Jonson. *Fr.* Exercration Upon Vulcan, An. CBCK

Had I heard my father mention. Never in My Life. Walter McDonald. MT

Had I lived till now. Poem for the Year Twenty Twenty. Alfred M. Lee. AmPA

Had I my wish I would distend my guts. The Extravagant Drunkard's Wish. Edward Ward. CBNP; NOEC

Had I not perceived so much of worth in her. The Legacy. Heinrich von Morungen, *tr. fr. German by* F. C. Nicholson. GePo

Had I not seen him by a swerve of eye. Heron in Swamp. Frances Minturn Howard. GoYe

Had I, Pygmalion like, the power. The Choice. Soame Jenyns. ECEV

Had I the Choice. Walt Whitman. Poetr; SoSe

Had I the heavens' embroidered cloths. He Wishes for the Cloths of Heaven. W. B. Yeats. ArLo; FaPoB; MoBrPo; NoAM; OBEV

Had I the tenth part of your great descriptive. Infernal Regions and the Invisible Girl. Alfred Corn. BAP-91

Had I the wings of a bird. Thoughts. Maggie Pogue Johnson. CBWP-4

Had it been for food, I would have long gone. *(LL)* The Slighted Wife. Aaron Hodza. PeSAV

Had lasted a minute more. *(LL)* A Thunderstorm in Town. Thomas Hardy. BoLoP; CBLP; EnLoPo; GBL; OxBSP

Had Life remained one whole. Unit. Mary Elizabeth Fullerton. NOBAu,

Had Lucan hid the truth to please the time. To the Translator of Lucan [or Lucan's Pharsalia, 1614]. Sir Walter Ralegh. SiPS; SiPSBD

Had me a cat, the cat pleased me. Fiddle-I-Fee. *Unknown.* AmFP

Had mournful Ovid been to Brent condemned. William Diaper. *Fr.* Brent; a Poem to Thomas Palmer Esq. FaBoPP; OBSV

Had my soul tottered off to sleep. Wondrous the Merge. James Richard Broughton. GLP

Had not these me against myself defended. *(LL)* Grace. Emerson. AmPP; NoP; PFP; TrPWD

Had reason good against my rime. *(LL)* Almanac Verse. Samuel Danforth. SCAP

Had Sacharissa liv'd when Mortals made. At Penshurst [Another]. Edmund Waller. BeJo; OAEL-1; SeCV-1

Had seldom seen a costlier funeral. (LL) Enoch Arden. Tennyson. BeLS

Had she come all the way for this. The Haystack in the Floods. William Morris. BeLS; EBEV; EBNV; EBVV; EnVR; HAP; NAEL-2; NoP; OAEL-2; OBNC; OBNV; OxAEP-2; PeVV; PoEL-5; PoRA

Had somewhere to get to and sailed calmly on. (LL) Musée des Beaux Arts. W. H. Auden. ClHu; CMoP; FF; GTBS-P; HAP; HeIL; HeIP; ImPo; InPK; InPS; LiTB; MeMAP; MoAB; MoP; NAEL-2; NoAM; NOBE; NoP; OxAEP-2; PoE; Poetr; PoRA; PPP; PrIm; RaBo; SCV; SoSe; TEP; TFi; TrCP; TrGrPo; TRP; TwCP

Had Sorrow Ever Fitter Place. Samuel Daniel. Fr. Hymen's Triumph. EIl

Had sowed these fruits, and got the harvest in. (LL) To the Immortal Memory and Friendship of That Noble Pair, Sir Lucius Cary and Sir Henry [or H.] Morison. Ben Jonson. NAEL-1; NOBE; NoP; NOSC; OAEL-1; PoEL-2; SeCP; SeCV-1

Had stayed at home behind me and was fast asleep in bed. (LL) My Shadow. Robert Louis Stevenson. FaBoBe; FaBV; FaPON; OTCP; OxBChV; PDV; PFP; PWR; TEP; UV

Had there been falsehood in my breast. Emily Brontë. NOBVV

Had there been peace there never had been riven. Drummond Allison. FaBoTw

Had this effulgence disappeared. Composed upon an Evening of Extraordinary Splendour and Beauty. Wordsworth. EnRP; OAEL-2

"Had we a king," said Wallace then. Gude Wallace. Unknown. ESPB

Had We But Met. Frances Sargent Osgood. AmWP

Had we but met in life's delicious spring. Had We But Met. Frances Sargent Osgood. AmWP

Had we but World enough, and Time. To His Coy Mistress. Andrew Marvell. ArLo; AWP; BoLoP; CBLP; ClHu; CoGr; EBEV; EBEvV; ELP; EnLoPo; ErPo; ESCV; FaBV; FaPoB; FF; FHYEP; GBL; GeHe; HAP; HeIL; HeIP; HoPM; ImPo; InPK; InPS; InvP; JCP; LiTB; MAT; MeLP; NAEL-1; NIP; NOBE; NoP; NOSC; OAEL-1; OBD; OBEV; OPOP; OtMeF; OxAEP-1; PlP; PoE; PoEL-2; Poetr; PoLF; PoRA; PPP; PrIm; SCGP; SCV; SeCP; TFi; TRP; UV

Had we but world enough, and time. To His Coy Mistress. Stanley J. Sharpless. BXAP

Had we but world enough, and time. To His Importunate Mistress. Peter De Vries. NBLV; NIP

Had We Two Met. Walter Savage Landor. FaBoEE; OxBSP

Had you been born. Ten Years Ago. Eileen Moeller. CrSp

Hadad, sels. James Abraham Hillhouse.

Hadn't heard of the atom bomb. The Seals in Penobscot Bay. Daniel Hoffman. TwCP

Hadrian's Address to His Soul When Dying. Emperor Hadrian, tr. fr. Latin by Byron. OBVE
Sels.
"Ah! gentle, fleeting, wav'ring sprite." OBD

Hae ye ivver been at Elsdon? At Elsdon. George Chatt. FaBoPP

Haemorrhage. Padraic Fiacc. CIP

Haere Ra. James K. Baxter. PeNZ

Hag, The. Robert Herrick. BeJo

Hag, The. Robert Herrick. BeJo; CaPo; FaBoCh; WiR

Hag and the Slavies, The. La Fontaine, tr. fr. French by Edward Marsh. AWP; OBVE

Hag is astride, The. The Hag. Robert Herrick. BeJo; CaPo; FaBoCh; WiR

Hag of Béara, The. Unknown. NOIV

Hag of Beare, The. Unknown, tr. fr. Irish. BIrV, tr. by John Montague; NOIV, tr. by Thomas Kinsella; OBVE, tr. by Lady August Gregory; PBWP, tr. by John Montague

Hag-ridden. Robert Graves. BIrV

Hagar. Francis Lauderdale Adams. OxBS

Hagar. Elisabeth Eybers, tr. fr. Afrikaans by the author. PeSA

Hagar and Ishmael. Else Lasker-Schüler, tr. fr. German. BoWoP, tr. by Rosemarie Waldrop

Haggadah. A. M. Klein. TrJP

Haggai. John Chagy. ChIV-1

Haggard daylight steer, The. (LL) The Death of a Toad. Richard Wilbur. CMoP; LiTM; MoP; NAAL-2; NoAM; NoP; PoA; Poetr

Hai! daughter of the Thundercloud. Dance-Song of the Lightning. Unknown, tr. fr. Hottentot. PeSA

Haidée and Don Juan. Byron. Fr. Don Juan. OBNC

Haikat. Myrna Davis. OFC

Haiku: "August heat." Gerald Vizenor. VoR

Haiku: "Autumn's bright moon." Kaga no Chiyo, tr. fr. Japanese by R. H. Blyth. PBWP

Haiku: "Dew of the rouge-flower, The." Kaga no Chiyo, tr. fr. Japanese by R. H. Blyth. PBWP

Haiku: "Eastern guard tower." Etheridge Knight. BPo; MoP; SM; TAP

Haiku: "Fallen flowers rise." Arakida Moritake, tr. fr. Japanese by Harold G. Henderson. SoSe

Haiku: "Falling flower, The." Arakida Moritake, tr. fr. Japanese by Babette Deutsch. SoSe

Haiku: "Fluent with a friend." Unknown. OBF

Haiku: "God is a flasher." Gavin Ewart. FaBoBl

Haiku: "I feel a sudden chill — ." Buson. IMW

Haiku: "Lightning flashes, The!" Basho, tr. fr. Japanese by Earl Miner. SoSe

Haiku: "Lightning gleam, A." Basho, tr. fr. Japanese by Harold G. Henderson. SoSe

Haiku: "Mountain snow." Gerald Vizenor. HATNAP

Haiku: "On the verandah." Mimi Khalvati. NWP

Haiku: "Spring rain." Kaga no Chiyo, tr. fr. Japanese by R. H. Blyth. PBWP

Haiku Ambulance. Richard Brautigan. InPK

Haiku for Margaretta D'Arcy on Her Rubbishing of My Play. Howard Brenton. IHNG

Haiku Master, The. Elizabeth Spires. BAP-91

Haiku (Slightly Overlength). James Laughlin. ArNa

Hail, aged God who lookest on thy Father. He Prayeth for Ink and Palette That He May Write. Unknown, tr. fr. Egyptian by Robert Hillyer. Fr. Book of the Dead. AWP

Hail and beware the dead who will talk life until you are blue. A Newly Discovered "Homeric" Hymn. Charles Olson. MoP; NeAP; NoAM; PoM

Hail, beauteous Dian, queen of shades. Hymn to Diana. Thomas Heywood. Fr. Golden Age, The. EIl

Hail, beauteous stranger of the grove [or wood]! To the Cuckoo. Michael Bruce, rev. by John Logan. OBEV
(Ode: To the Cuckoo.) NOEC

Hail, Bishop Valentine, whose day this is. John Donne. Fr. Epithalamion on the Lady Elizabeth and Count Palantine Being Married on St. Valentine's Day, An. ChTr

Hail, Columbia. Joseph Hopkinson. AnAmPo; FaBoBe; PAH

Hail, Comly and Clene. Unknown. Fr. Second Shepherd's Play, The. NAEL-1; NAs; PoEL-1

Hail, curious wights! to whom so fair. To the Virtuosos. William Shenstone. ECEV

Hail! Dawn is shining glory doing. Kilaben Bay Song. Unknown, tr. fr. Aborigine by Perce Haslam. NOBAu

Hail dawning Peace! Speed on thy glorious rise! The End of the Whole Matter. Albery Allson Whitman. Fr. Not a Man and Yet a Man. AAP

Hail, Dionysos. Dudley Randall. BPo

Hail, ever-pleasing Solitude! Hymn on Solitude. James Thomson. NOEC

Hail, fathers, hail! Flute Song. Unknown, tr. fr. Hopi Indian by Natalie Curtis. WTO

Hail Flag of the Union! Hail Flag of the free! Stars and Stripes. Mary Weston Fordham. CBWP-2

Hail, forest nymphs, daughters of the river. Moiro, tr. fr. Greek by Fleur Adcock. GrAn

Hail, Freedom! thy bright crest. New National Hymn. Francis Marion Crawford. PAH

Hail, Garcia, hammer of pigeons. Paul Evans. Fr. Sofa Book, The. NBrP

Hail, glorious day; mayst thou be writ in gold. Simon Ford. Fr. London's Resurrection. NOSC

Hail, glorious day which miracles adorn. On Christmas Day. the Earl of Orrery. TIRV

HAIL graceful morning of eternal day. To the Blessed Virgin. William Alabaster. NoSic

Hail, great Apollo! guide my feeble pen. The British Lyon Roused. Stephen Tilden. PAH

Hail[e] great Redeemer, man, and God, all hail[e]. A Hymn[e] to Our Saviour on the Cross[e]. George Chapman. PeECV; PoEL-2

Hail, guest! We ask not what thou art. America Greets an Alien. Unknown.
(Welcome over the Door of an Old Inn.) PoToHe

Hail! Hail! Hail! A Dance Chant. Unknown, tr. fr. Iroquois Indian by E. S. Parker. WGRP

Hail, happy bride, for thou art truly blest! On the Death of Mrs. Bowes. Lady Mary Wortley Montagu. BoWoP

Hail, happy Britain, Freedom's blest retreat. "Prophecy." Gulian Verplanck. PAH

Hail, happy day, when, smiling like the morn. To the Right Honourable William, Earl of Dartmouth. Phillis Wheatley. AmPP; NALW

Hail, happy lot of the laborious man. Poverty, in Imitation of Milton. Samuel Jones. NOEC

Hail, happy Pope, whose generous mind. Swift. Fr. Libel on the Reverend Dr. Delany, A. EPCY

Hail, happy saint, on thine immortal throne. On the Death of the Rev. Mr. George Whitefield. Phillis Wheatley. NAAL-1

Hail, happy virgin! of celestial race. To Almystrea, on her Divine Works. Elizabeth Thomas. ECWP

Hail happy William, thou art strangely great. A Panegyric. *Unknown.* APAS

Hail! Ho!/ Sail! Ho! A Sea-Song from the Shore. James Whitcomb Riley. BoTP

Hail, Holy Land. Thomas Tillam. *See* Hayle holy-land wherein our holy lord.

Hail, holy Lead! — of human feuds the great. Ambrose Bierce. *Fr. Devil's Dictionary, The.* OBAL

Hail, holy light, offspring [*or* offspring] of Heav'n [*or* heaven] first born. Milton. *Fr. Paradise Lost.* EPCY; OAEL-1; PeECV, *ll.* 1–69; SCV; TOF
(Hail, Holy Light.) ImPo; PIP, *ll.* 1–26
(Holy Light.) NOBE
(Invocation to Light.) NOSC, *bk.* III, *ll.* 1–55
(Light.) LiTB; OBEV

Hail! home of exiles and of Seminoles! Albery Allson Whitman. *Fr. Twasinta's Seminoles; Or Rape of Florida.* AAP

Hail! King I thee call. A Lyric from a Play. *Unknown.* MeEL

Hail Matrimony, made of Love! Blake. *Fr. Island in the Moon, An.* CBLP

Hail, mediocrity, beneath whose spell. Roy Campbell. *Fr. Georgiad, The.* MoBrPo

Hail, meek-eyed maiden, clad in sober grey. Ode to Evening. Joseph Warton. OxAEP-1

Hail mer-/ry, tricky, and clandestine. Ode to Pornography. Jack Anderson. PoA

Hail Mother, who art the earth. Bill Faherty. EaPr

Hail, Muse! et caetera. — We left Juan sleeping. Byron. *Fr. Don Juan.* OAEL-2

Hail native language, that by sinews weak. Milton. *Fr. At a Vacation Exercise [in the College].* JCP

Hail, O most worthy in all the world! *Unknown, tr. fr. Anglo-Saxon by* Charles W. Kennedy. *Fr. Christ 1.* AnOE

Hail, Oh Hail to the King. Beatrice Quickenden. AH

Hail, old patrician trees, so great and good! Of Solitude. Abraham Cowley.
(On Solitude.) OxAEP-1
(Solitude.) NOSC

Hail Our Incarnate God! William Duke. AH

Hail! Oure patron and lady of erthe. Salve Regina. *Unknown.* MiEL

Hail peaceful Shade, whose sacred verdant side. To the University. Alicia D'Anvers. *Fr. Academia; or The Humours of the University of Oxford.* KTR; NOSC

Hail, pious days! thou most propitious time. On the Sentence Passed by the House of Lords on Dr. Sacheverell. *Unknown.* APAS

Hail, Queen of Heaven. *Unknown.* OxBSP

Hail, sacred shades! cool, leafy house! Upon the Priory Grove, His Usual Retirement. Henry Vaughan. BeJo

Hail sacred shades! cool, leavy house! Upon the Priory Grove, His Usual Retirement. Henry Vaughan. FaBoPP

Hail, Silimela! The Pleiades. S. E. K. Mqhayi, *tr. fr. Xhosa by* Jeff Opland. PeSAV

Hail[e], sister springs! Saint Mary Magdalene. Richard Crashaw. GeHe; MeLP; SeCV-1
(And now where're he strayes.) FaBoCo
(Weeper, The.) ESCV; OAEL-1, *abr.*; OBEV; SeCP

Hail sons of generous valor. To the Defenders of New Orleans. Joseph Rodman Drake. PAH

Hail South Australia! *Unknown.* NOBAu

Hail Sovereign Queen of secrets, who hast power. John Fletcher *and* William Shakespeare. *Fr. Two Noble Kinsmen, The.* PoEL-2

Hail, Sympathy! thy soft idea brings. William Lisle Bowles. Byron. *Fr. English Bards and Scotch Reviewers.* OBNC

Hail! the Glorious Golden City. Felix Adler. AH; WGRP

Hail then ye daring few! who proudly soar. The Air Balloon. Henry James Pye. *Fr. Aerophorion.* NOEC

Hail, thou Great God in thy Boat. He Embarketh in the Boat of Ra. *Unknown, tr. fr. Egyptian by* Robert Hillyer. *Fr. Book of the Dead.* AWP

Hail, Thou my Native Soil. William Browne. *See* Hail, thou my native soil! thou blessed plot.

Hail, thou my native soil! thou blessed plot. The Frolic Mariners of Devon. William Browne. *Fr. Britannia's Pastorals.* ChTr
(Hail, Thou my Native Soil.) OxAEP-1

Hail, thou sole Empress of the Land of wit. A Pindarick To Mrs. Behn on her Poem on the Coronation. *Unknown.* KTR

Hail thou sweet and welcome day. The First of August in Jamaica. Joshua McCarter Simpson. AAP

Hail, thou who shinest from the moon. He Establisheth His Triumph. *Unknown, tr. fr. Egyptian by* Robert Hillyer. *Fr. Book of the Dead.* AWP

Hail to Hobson! Hail to Hobson! hail to all the valiant set! The Men of the Merrimac. Clinton Scollard. PAH

Hail to the Brightness of Zion's Glad Morning. Thomas Hastings. AH

Hail to the chief who in triumph advances. Hail to the Chief Who in Triumph Advances. Sir Walter Scott. *Fr. Lady of the Lake, The.* EnRP; PoEL-4
(Boat Song.) OxAEP-2

Hail to the Chief Who in Triumph Advances. Sir Walter Scott. *Fr. Lady of the Lake, The.* EnRP; PoEL-4

Hail to the coming time! (*LL*) The Fine Old English Gentleman; New Version. Charles Dickens. CoMu; FaBoBa; NOBVV; OBSV

Hail to the Joyous Day. Royall Tyler. AH

Hail to the Queen. *Unknown.* AH

Hail to the Sabbath Day. Stephen Greenleaf Bulfinch. AH

Hail to the sage divine of Milan's plains! On Hearing That Torture Was Suppressed throughout the Austrian Dominions. John Codrington Bampfylde. Son

Hail to Thee, Blithe Owl. Ring Lardner. OBAL

Hail to thee, blithe roadster! To a Bicycle. *Unknown.* BXAP

Hail to thee, blithe Spirit! To a Skylark. Shelley. EBEvV, *sts.* 1–3 *only*; EnRP; FaBoBe; FaBV; FaPON; FHYEP; GN; GTBS; GTBS-P; HAP; ImPo; InPS; InvP; LiTB; MeMBP; NAEL-2; NoP; OAEL-2; OBEV; OBNC; OxAEP-2; PoLF; SCGP, (*sts.* 1–3 *only*); TEP; TFi, (*sts.* 1–3 *only*); TrGrPo
(Ode to a Skylark.) NOBE

Hail to thee, gallant foe. Cervera. Bertrand Shadwell. PAH

Hail to thee thou holy Babe. Christmas Hymn. *Unknown, tr. fr. Irish by* Douglas Hyde. TIRV

Hail, Tranquil Hour of Closing Day. Leonard Bacon. AH

Hail Wedded Love! Jay Macpherson. MoCV

Hail wedded love, mysterious law, true source. Milton. *Fr. Paradise Lost.* EPCY
(Unfallen Love.) NOSC, *bk.* IV, *ll.* 750–75

Haile from the dead, or from eternity. Lines on a Purple Cap Received as a Present from My Brother. George Alsop. SCAP

Haile gracefull morning of eternall Daye. William Alabaster. *Fr. Divine Meditations.* ESCV; Son

Haill! Quene of Heven and steren of blis. A Little Hymn to Mary. *Unknown.* MeEL

Haill warld waited, The. Problems. Alexander Scott. FF

Hailstone, The. Peter Didsbury. PWE

Hailstones falling like sharp blue sky chips. Crazy Horse Monument. Peter Blue Cloud. HATNAP

Hailstorm in May. Gerard Manley Hopkins. Spl

Hain't no use to weep, hain't no use to moan. Down in the Lonesome Garden. *Unknown.* BPo

Hair. Remy de Gourmont, *tr. fr. French by* Jethro Bithell. AWP; ErPo

Hair, The. Pierre Louÿs, *tr. fr. French by* Philip L. Miller. RiWo

Hair, The. May Swenson. *Fr. Poet to Tiger.* GLP

Hair — / silver-gray. Face. Jean Toomer. CDC; NoP

Hair, a small light, touching each leaf. (*LL*) A Small Light. Cathy Song. TRP

Hair-bowed Rose, deep in lush grass of the river. Profile of Rose. Glyn Jones. OBWVE

Hair — braided chestnut. Portrait in Georgia. Jean Toomer. NoP

Hair ornament of the sun, The. Mitsuhashi Takajo, *tr. fr. Japanese by* Kenneth Rexroth and Ikuko Atsumi. BoWoP; WPJ

Hair — shiny black geisha hair. Portrait. Beverly Acuff Momoi. LoHo

Hair-Tonic Bottle, The. Ben King. OBAL

Hair which boldly speaks in Bernice's despite, A. Description of Perfect Beauty. Christian Hofmann von Hofmannswaldau, *tr. fr. German by* George C. Schoolfield. GePo

Hairband, homespun, opera-hat, afghan. Motley. Peter Davison. NBLV

Haircut. Edward Kleinschmidt. UnDi

Haircut. Sue May. DT

Haircut. Karl Shapiro. TwCP

Hairline Fracture, A. Amy Clampitt. NoAM

Hairy Dog, The. Herbert Asquith. FaPON; PDV

Hairy Toe, The. *Unknown.* OBSP; PYC

Hairy was here. News from the Cabin. May Swenson. NYBP

Haka: Hinemotu. Te Aomuhurangi Te Maaka. PeNZ

Haka: The Blossoming. Pita Sharples, *tr. fr. Maori by* Pita Sharples. PeNZ

Haka: The Feathered Albatross. Muru Walters, *tr. fr. Maori by the author.* PeNZ

Halcyon, *sels.* Hilda Doolittle ("H. D.").
"I'm not here." MoAmPo

Halcyon Days. Jim Barnes. CDW; VCAP

Halcyon Days. Walt Whitman. OxBA

Halcyon's Nest, The. Giles Fletcher the Younger. *Fr.* Christ's Victory and Triumph. FaBoPP

Half. Hawley Truax. NYBP

Half a bar, half a bar. The Village Choir. *Unknown.* FaBoPa; UV

Half a Hedgehog. Miroslav Holub, *tr. by* Ewald Osers. PWE

Half a league, half a league. The Charge of the Light Brigade. Tennyson. BeLS; BLPA; EBEvV; EnVR; FaBoBe; FaBoEH; FaBV; FaPON; FaPoR; FHYEP; GN; HoPM; NAEL-2; NOBVV; OBWP; OxAEP-2; PeVV; PrIm; TEP; TFi; UV; VPP; WBLP

Half a lifetime now, I've played my art on the stage. Tune: "Slow Chant." Ma Chih-yüan, *tr. fr. Chinese by* Sherwin S. S. Fu. SuSp

Half a loaf, half a loaf. The Charge the Bread Brigade. Ezra Pound *and* Noel Stock. *Fr.* Poems of Alfred Venison, the Poet of Titchfield Street, The. UV

Half a mile into the Pacific. Sea Lions off Monterey. John Cassidy. OBAP

Half a pint of porter. *Unknown.* ISE

Half afraid to break a promise. Michael Hartnett. *Fr.* Farewell to English, A. NOIV

Half an hour after our heads were cut off. (*LL*) She and I. Norman Cameron. OxBSP; RB

Half Asleep. Gareth Owen. OTCP

Half-asleep in the house of the holy ghost. (*LL*) Sleeping in Santo Spirito. Bruce Beasley. UTF

Half awake in my Sunday nap. Three Green Windows. Anne Sexton. NYBP

Half-Ballad of Waterval. Kipling. PeSAV

Half-bent Man. Richard Eberhart. NYBP

Half Black, Half Blacker. Sterling Plumpp. PoBA

Half-bridge over nothingness. Northhanger Ridge. Charles Wright. HCAP

Half-caste. John Agard. NBrP

Half-Caste Girl. Judith Wright. NALW

Half close your eyelids, loosen your hair. Aedh Thinks of Those Who Have Spoken Evil of His Beloved. W. B. Yeats. NoAM

"Half-cracked" to Higginson, living. "I Am in Danger — Sir — ." Adrienne Rich. HCAP; NALW; NOBA

Half-door, hall door. Purgatory. W. B. Yeats. CMoP

Half-hanging is the rage in Kildare. Rebecca Hill. Brendan Kennelly. PWE

Half-hidden by trees, the sheer roof of the barn. The Barn. Stephen Spender. CMoP

Half-hidden in a graveyard. The Stranger. Walter de la Mare. OxBTC

Half Holiday. Olive Enoch. BoTP

Half-holiday for the burial, A. Of course, they punish. Black Spring. Robert Lowell, *ad. fr. Russian of* Innokenti Annensky. NaP

Half in Love. Rachel Hadas. UnDi

Half in the dim light from the hall. To ———. William Stanley Braithwaite. PoBA

Half into the mountains — a mountain monastery. Climbing to a Mountain Monastery. Tu Hsün-ho, *tr. fr. Chinese by* Edward H. Schafer. SuSp

Half-Life, A. Henri Cole. PFL

Half loving-kindliness, and half disdain. To My Cat. Rosamund Marriott Watson. OFC

Half-Mast. Lloyd Mifflin. PAH

Half Moon. Federico García Lorca, *tr. fr. Spanish by* W. S. Merwin. RFM

Half-moon hangs on sparse *wu-t'ung* tree. Tune: "Song of Divination." Su Shih, *tr. fr. Chinese by* Eugene Eoyang. SuSp

Half-moon westers low, my love, The. A. E. Housman. CBLP

Half-moons of her calves eclipse, The. Notes on a Girl. Peter Kane Dufault. ErPo

Half my friends are dead. Sea Canes. Derek Walcott. HeIP

Half of a clasping of the hands. Half. Hawley Truax. NYBP

Half of his/ body hung in. Spirits. Victor Hernandez Cruz. PoBA

Half of Life. Friedrich Hölderlin, *tr. fr. German by* James Blair Leishman. ChTr; OBVE

Half of my life is gone, and I have let. Mezzo Cammin. Longfellow. NAAL-1; NoP; PoE; TAP

Half of our borders, rivers and mountains were gone. In the Home of the Scholar Wu Su-chiang. Wu Tsao, *tr. fr. Chinese by* Kenneth Rexroth *and* Ling Chung. BoWoP; WPC; WPOW

Half of the land, conscious of love and grief. The Coasts of Cerigo. A. D. Hope. FaBoMA

Half Past Four, October. Anna Hajnal, *tr. fr. Hungarian by* Daniel Hoffman. BoWoP

Half past nine — high time for supper. In Praise of Cocoa, Cupid's Nightcap. Stanley J. Sharpless. ErPo; FiBHP; NBLV; PeLV

Half-past three in the morning! Louise on the Door-Step. Charles MacKay. EBVV

Half-shut doors through which we heard that music, The. Multitudes Turn in Darkness. Conrad Aiken. PoA

Half Sigh. *Unknown, tr. by* Miriam Koshland. PBA

Half spirit, the older. The Jest. Austin Clarke. BIrV

Half squatter, half tenant (no rent). Manuelzinho. Elizabeth Bishop. FaBoWP; NYBP

Halfe the bed and all the clothes. (*LL*) Good night, sweet repose. *Unknown.* ISE; OxNR

Half the lamp is lit tonight. For Malka Who Lived Three Days Dying. Laura Kasischke. BTR

Half the spring has gone by since our parting. Tune: "Pure Serene Music." Li Yü, *tr. fr. Chinese by* Daniel Bryant. SuSp

Half the time they munched the grass, and all the time they lay. Cows. James Reeves. NTCP; NTP

Half the year has hot nights, like this. Elegies for the Hot Season. Sandra McPherson. AmPA

Half-way across the racing river. Midstream. D. J. Enright. OxBC

Half-way, for One Commandment Broken. A. E. Housman. OxBSP; PeHV

Half-Way Pause, A. Dante Gabriel Rossetti. NOBVV

Half yet remains unsung, but narrower bound. Milton. *Fr.* Paradise Lost. EPCY; FaBoPV

Halfe Dead: and rotten at the Coare: my Lord! Edward Taylor. *Fr.* Preparatory Meditations Before My Approach to the Lord's Supper. EAP

Halfway. Maxine W. Kumin. GoYe

Halfway across a bridge one night. The Swerve. William Stafford. SM

Halfway Down. A. A. Milne. FaPON

Halfway Street, Sidcup. Fleur Adcock. Spl

Halfway to Avalon. Andrew Taylor. FaBoMA

Halibut Cove Harvest. Kenneth Leslie. NOBC

Halieutica, *sels.* William Diaper, *after the Greek of* Oppian.
  "Lamprey, glowing with uncommon fires, The." ECEV; OBVE
  "Shelly crawlers each returning year, The." FM
  "Strange the formation of the eely race." OBVE
    (Eels and Tortoises.) NOEC
    (Sex-life of Fish, The.) ECEV
  "When pleasing heat, and fragrant blooms inspire." BXAP
  "When they in throngs a safe retirement seek." OBVE

Halifax Station. *Unknown.* PAH

Hall by the water where flowers grow dense, A. An Occasional Poem. Ssu-k'ung Shu, *tr. fr. Chinese by* Irving Y. Lo. SuSp

Hall of Ifor Hael, The. Evan Evans, *tr. fr. Welsh by* Gwyn Williams. OBWVE

Hall of Ocean Life. John Hollander. PoA

Hallaj's corpse was burnt and when the flame. Farid-uddin Attar, *tr. fr. Persian by* Afkham Darbandi *and* Dick Davis. *Fr.* Conference of the Birds, The. TOF

Hallali, L'. Frederick Seidel. *Fr.* AIDS Days. BAP-90

Hallelujah! A. E. Housman. CBNP; FaBoNo; FiBHP; PeLV

Hallelujah./ Praise the Lord, O my soul. Bible, *O.T., paraphrased by* Sir Thomas Wyatt. *Fr.* Psalms. TrJP

Hallelujah/ Praise ye the Lord . . . . Bible, *O.T., paraphrased by* Sir Thomas Wyatt. *See* Praise ye the Lord!/ For it is good to sing praises unto our God.

Hallelujah, Bum Again. *Unknown. See* Oh, why don't you [*or* I] work like other men do?

Hallelujah, I'm a Bum. *Unknown.* AS; SWP

Hallelujah; or, Britain's Second Remembrancer, *sels.* George Wither.
  Hymn L: Rocking Hymn, A. SeCV-1
    (Rocking Hymn, A.) OxBChV
  Hymne I: Generall Invitation to Praise God, A. SeCV-1

Hallelujah! Praise the Lord. Edwin Francis Hatfield. AH

"Hallelujah!" was the only observation. Hallelujah! A. E. Housman. CBNP; FaBoNo; FiBHP; PeLV
  (On the Death of a Female Officer of the Salvation Army.) FaBoNo

Hallelujee! (*LL*) At Leeds. *Unknown.* FaBoCo

Hallo My Fancy. William Cleland. CH; OxBoLi

Hallow days o Yule are come, The. The Wife of Usher's Well. *Unknown.* ESPB

Hallow-Fair. Robert Fergusson. OxBS

Hallow the threshold, crown the posts anew! On the Queen's Return from the Low Countries. William Cartwright. OBEV

Hallowed be the Ordainer of/ the world! A Little Prayer. Paul Goodman. LiTA

Hallowed be the Sabbaoth. Epitaph in St. Olave's, Southwark, on Mr. Munday. *Unknown.* FaBoCo; OxBoLi

Hallowed bed according to Thy Word. Amen. (*LL*) They Toil Not neither Do They Spin. Christina Rossetti. TrPWD

Hand that rocks the cradle, The — but there is no such hand. The Modern Baby. William Croswell Doane. BLPA

Hand That Rocks the Cradle Is the Hand That Rules the World, The. William Ross Wallace. BLPL; PoLF; WBLP

Hand That Signed the Paper [Felled a City], The. Dylan Thomas. MeMBP; MoAB; MoBrPo; MoP; NoAM; NOBE; NoP; OBWP; PAW; RB; TrGrPo

Hand that swept the sounding lyre, The. On a Dead Poet. Frances Sargent Osgood.
(Hand That Swept The Sounding Lyre, The.) AmWP

Hand That Swept The Sounding Lyre, The. Frances Sargent Osgood. See Hand that swept the sounding lyre, The.

Hand trembling towards hand; the amazing lights. Sonnet Reversed. Rupert Brooke. NOBL; PeLV

Handbell Choir, The. Jane Flanders. PBCAP

Handbook for Revolutionaries. Aidan Carl Mathews. IB

Handbook of Versification. Gilbert Sorrentino. PoA

Handcart Song, The. Unknown. AmFP

Handful came to Seicheprey, A. Seicheprey. Unknown. PAH

Handful of Dust, A. James Oppenheim. TrJP

Handful of old men walking down the village street, A. Memorial Day. Theodosia Garrison. OHIP

Handful of Pebbles, Mouthful of Stones. . Pegatha Hughes. LoHo

Handfuls of Wind. Yekhi'el [or Yehiel] Mar, tr. fr. Hebrew by Ruth Finer Mintz. MHP

Handicaps. Bob Henry Baber. ETG

Handle a large kingdom with as gentle a touch. Lao Tzu, tr. by Witter Bynner. Fr. Tao Te Ching. OBD

Handle for the Flutist, A. Odia Ofeimun. HBAPE

Handling Sin, sels. Robert Mannyng.
Dancers of Colbek, The. PoE

Handloom, The. Judith Rodriguez. FaBoWP

Handmaid of Religion, The. Edgell Rickword. OBSV

Hands. Bernard Dadié, tr. fr. French by Ellen Conroy Kennedy. NegPo

Hands. Donald Finkel. CoAP; MAT

Hands. Alex Glasgow. OBET

Hands, The. Tony Harrison. FaBoTw

Hands. Robinson Jeffers. GOA

Hands. Edvard Kocbek, tr. fr. Slovene by Michael Scammell and Veno Taufer. PoSu

Hands, The. Denise Levertov. NeAP; PoM

Hands: Abraham Kunstler. Michael D. Riley. BTR

Hands are being plated, The; they'll be brass. Clock without Hands. John Frederick Nims. PoA

Hands clenched under my shawl. "Anna Akhmatova," tr. fr. Russian by Robert Tracy. PBWP

Hands Full of Sun. David Rokeah, tr. fr. Hebrew by Ruth Finer Mintz. MHP

Hands full of sun are in spring's longing for you. Hands Full of Sun. David Rokeah, tr. fr. Hebrew by Ruth Finer Mintz. MHP

Hands gripped hard on the desert, The. (LL) At the Bomb Testing Site. William Stafford. CAPP; CoAP; LiTM; NIP; NoAM; NoP; OBWP; PAW; Poetr; RB

Hands have no tears to flow. (LL) The Hand That Signed the Paper [Felled a City]. Dylan Thomas. MeMBP; MoAB; MoBrPo; MoP; NoAM; NOBE; NoP; OBWP; PAW; RB; TrGrPo

Hands must touch and handle many things, The. The New Man. Jones Very. NOBA

Hands of God, The. D. H. Lawrence. ChIV-2

Hands that eased my mother's labor drew, The. Rhyme for the Child as a Wet Dog. Judith Johnson Sherwin. TAP

Hands were yours, the arms were yours, The. The Empty Body. Mark Strand. Fr. Elegy for My Father. HCAP; LCAP; UnPo

Hands, wings, found. (LL) Icarus. Stephen Spender. MoP; PrIm

Handsome friend, charming and kind. Beatrice, Countess de Die, tr. fr. Provençal by Meg Bogin. WPOW

Handsome Heart, The. Gerard Manley Hopkins. FaBoVe

Handsome one, white-black checkered son of the water. The Muscovy Drake. E. A. S. Lesoro, tr. fr. Sotho by Dan Kunene and Jack Cope. PeSA

Handsome young airman lay dying, A. The Dying Airman. Unknown. AS; FaBoNo; OxBoLi; PeLV; RB

Handsome young monk in a wood, A. Unknown. PeLi

Handsome youth with a golden whip, A. Tune: "Mountain Hawthorns." Yen Chi-tao, tr. fr. Chinese by James J. Y. Liu. SuSp

Handsworth Liberties, sels. Roy Fisher.
"At the end of the familiar." VaA
"Shines coldly away." VaA

Handwriting on the Wall, The. Knowles Shaw. BLPA

Handwriting on the Wall. Unknown. AmFP

Handy dandy. Unknown. OxNR

Handy Pandy, Jack-a-Dandy. Mother Goose. See Handy Spandy, Jack-a-dandy.

Handy Spandy, Jack-a-dandy. Mother Goose.
(Handy Pandy, Jack-a-Dandy.) ReMoGo

Hang a small bugle cap on, as big as a crown. The Beau's Receipt for a Lady's Dress. Unknown. CoMu

Hang at my hand as I write now. Verses for a First Birthday. George Barker. MoAB; MoBrPo

Hang by threads above. Batman and Robin. David Trinidad. BAP-91

Hang flags in the airs of July. John Heath-Stubbs. Fr. Two Wedding Songs. NTP

HANG him, base gull; I'll stab him, by the Lord. Boreas. Samuel Rowlands. NoSic

Hang it all, Robert Browning. Ezra Pound. Fr. Cantos. AmPP; HAP; MeMAP; MoAB; MoAmPo; NoAM; NOBA; OxBA; PoA

Hang Me, O Hang Me, and I'll Be Dead and Gone. Unknown. AmFP

Hang out our banners on the outward walls. Shakespeare. See To-morrow, and to-morrow, and to-morrow.

Hang out your cloth, and let the trumpet sound. The Character of a Trimmer. Unknown. APAS

Hang sorrow, cast away care. Unknown. NOSC

Hang that day with black, that night, sinister, moonless. Hegesippus, tr. fr. Greek by Edwin Morgan. GrAn

"Hang that," said Suction; "let us have a song." Blake. Fr. Island in the Moon, An. CBNP

Hang the miller up by his neck. (LL) Millery, millery, dustipole. Unknown. ISE; OxNR

Hang to Your Grit! Louis E. Thayer. WBLP

Hang up hooks and shears to scare. Another Charm for Stables. Robert Herrick. BeJo

Hang Up the Baby's Stocking! Unknown. OBCP

Hang up those dull and envious fools. In the Person of Womankind (In Defense of Their Inconstancy). Ben Jonson. BeJo; NAEL-1
(Another. In Defence of Their Inconstancie. SeCP

Hang your serious songs. Sipsop's Song. Blake. Fr. Island in the Moon, An. FaBoNo

Hanged man, please grow wild and luminous. To Her Dead Mate: Montana, 1966. Elizabeth Libbey. AmPA

Hanging, A. Frank Mkalawile Chipasula.

Hanging/ out under the bridge. Getting Across. Carter Revard. VoR

Hanging Burley. Jim Wayne Miller. MT

Hanging Fire. Audre Lorde. NIP; NoAM; NoP; Poetr; TRP

Hanging from a tree — I see a body! (LL) I Know I'm Not Sufficiently Obscure. Ray Durem. BPo; PoBA

Hanging from the beam. The Portent. Herman Melville. AmPP; AnAmPo; InPK; NAAL-1; NOBA; NoP; OBWP; OxBA; PoE; PoEL-5; PrIm; TAP; WiR

Hanging from the branches of a green/ willow tree. Lady Ise, tr. fr. Japanese by Willis Barnstone. BoWoP

Hanging Johnny. Unknown. GBP

Hanging Man, The. Sylvia Plath. HCAP; VCAP

Hanging of Sam Archer, The. Unknown. AmFP

Hanging of the Crane, The, sels. Longfellow.
New Household, A. GN

Hanging on the daylight black. Bride Town. Anne Carson. Fr. Life of Towns, The. BAP-90

Hanging on the wall, an iron face watches me. The Mask. Irma McClaurin. BlSi

Hanging on the walls. Gallery of My Heart. King D. Kuka. VoR

Hanging Out the Linen Clothes. Unknown. AS

Hanging, Zomba Central Prison, A. Frank Mkalawile Chipasula. See His pendulous body tolled.

Hangman. Ai. AmPA

Hangman's Love Song, The. Stanley Moss. VGW

Hangman's Room, The. János Pilinszky, tr. fr. Hungarian by Peter Jay. PoSu

Hangover Cure. "Alexis," tr. fr. Greek. FaBoUs

Hangover Cure. Amphis, tr. fr. Greek. FaBoUs

Hangover Cure. Nicochares, tr. fr. Greek. FaBoUs

Hangover Mass. X. J. Kennedy. DiPo

Hangs./ whipped/ blood. Biography. Amiri Baraka. TAP

Hangs and cannot wake itself. (LL) Laser. A. R. Ammons. CAPP; NAAL-2; NoAM; NOBA

Hangs heavy/ down into trees. Haze. James Schuyler. BAP-90

Hangy Bangy cut my throat. Unknown. ISE

Hank never loved nuthin'. The Untold Truth about Hank. Charles Ghigna. NGP

Happy people die whole, they are all dissolved in a moment. Post Mortem. Robinson Jeffers. MoAmPo; TrGrPo

Happy rural seat of various view, A. Milton. *Fr.* Paradise Lost. EPCY; PeECV, *bk.* IV, *ll.* 246–275

Happy, Saviour, Would I Be. Edwin H. Nevin. AH

Happy Sheep, The. Wilfrid Thorley. ZA

Happy Swain, The. Ambrose Philips. EnLoPo

Happy that first white age! when wee. Boethius, *tr.* by Henry Vaughan. *Fr.* Consolation of Philosophy, The. NOSC; OBVE

Happy the dead! Consolation in War. Lewis Mumford. NYBP

Happy the Man. Horace. *See* Descended of an ancient line.

Happy the man, who free as air. The Widower. Royall Tyler. OBAL

Happy the man, who his whole time doth bound. The Old Man of Verona. Claudian, *tr. fr. Latin* by Abraham Cowley. AWP; OBVE

Happy the man who in his pot contains. The Suet Dumpling. *Unknown.* BXAP

Happy the man who, safe on shore. The Hurricane. Philip Freneau. EAP; TAP

Happy the man, who, void of cares and strife. John Phillips. *Fr.* Splendid Shilling, The. BXAP; NOEC; OAEL-1, *abr.*

Happy the man whose wish and care. Ode on [*or* to] Solitude. Pope. AWP; EBEvV; FHYEP; GGP; HeIL; HeIP; InVP; NAEL-1; NOSC; PoRA; Prf; SCGP; TEP

  (Quiet Life, The. GTBS; GTBS-P; PoToHe

  (Solitude.) ArNa; ImPo; TrGrPo

Happy the nations of the moral North! Donna Julia. Byron. *Fr.* Don Juan. PoEL-4

Happy the savage of those early times. European Crimes. Charles Churchill. *Fr.* Gotham. NOEC

Happy the wild birds that can soar. Unfair to Men. *Unknown, tr. fr. Welsh* by Gwyn Jones. OBWVE

Happy the year, the month, that finds alive. To William Wordsworth on His Seventy-Fifth Birthday. Hartley Coleridge. EPCY

Happy those early days [*or* dayes]! when I. The Retreat[e]. Henry Vaughan. AWP; BLPL; CIHu; ESCV; FF; GeHe; GTBS; GTBS-P; HAP; ImPo; InPK; InPS; InvP; JCP; LiTB; MeLP; NAEL-1; NIP; NOBE; NOCV; NoP; NOSC; OAEL-1; OBEV; OBWVE; PeECV; PoE; PoEL-2; PoRA; PPP; SCGP; SeCP; SeCV-1; TFi; TOF; TrGrPo

Happy Thought. Robert Louis Stevenson. BoTP; FaBoBe; OxBChV; PWR; Spl

Happy, too happy was the world. Boethius, *tr. fr. Latin.* *Fr.* Consolation of Philosophy, The. MLL, *tr.* by Helen Waddell

Happy Too Much. Boethius, *tr.* by Elizabeth I, Queen of England. *Fr.* Consolation of Philosophy, The. CTC

Happy Tree, The. Gerald Gould. WGRP

Happy trifles, can ye bear. Sent to Miss Bell H — — , with a Pair of Buckles. John Cunningham. FaBoUs

Happy View, A. C. Day Lewis. CMoP

Happy Warrior, The. Sir Herbert Read. NSI; PeFWW

Happy Were He. Earl of Essex. EIL; NoSic; OxBSP

Happy were he could finish forth his fare. Happy Were He. Earl of Essex. EIL; NoSic; OxBSP

Happy who like Ulysses, or that lord. Heureux Qui, comme Ulysse, A Fait un Beau Voyage. Joachim du Bellay, *tr. fr. French* by G. K. Chesterton. AWP

Happy Workhouse and the Good Effects of Industry, The. John Dyer. *Fr.* Fleece, The. NOEC

Happy Youth, that shalt possesse. To My Cousin (C.R.) Marrying My Lady (A.). Thomas Carew. SeCP

"Happy ye leaves whenas those lily [*or* lilly] hands." Spenser. *Fr.* Amoretti. AAS; EBEV; ESo, lacking epigrams I–IV; HeIL; NAEL-1; OAEL-1; PoE; Son

Happy ys he that may obtaine her love. (*LL*) From Tuscan came my lady's worthy race. The Earl of Surrey. AAS; SiPS; SiPSBD

Happy's the man whose pleasant labours with the lark. The Ploughman, in Imitation of Milton. Samuel Jones. NOEC

Harangue on the Death of Hayyim Nahman Bialik. César Tiempo, *tr. fr. Spanish* by Donald Devenish Walsh. TrJP

Harbach 1944. János Pilinszky, *tr. fr. Hungarian* by János Csokits *and* Ted Hughes. PoSu

Harbinger, *sels.* Nellie Wong.

Harbingers are come, The. See, see their mark. The Forerunners. George Herbert. AngWe; ESCV; GeHe; JCP; NAEL-1; NoP; TOF

Harbor. Nancy Price. IHMS

Harbor, The. Carl Sandburg. TAP

Harbor at Seattle, The. Robert Hass. SV

Harbor Dawn, The. Hart Crane. *Fr.* Bridge, The. AmPP; CMoP; FaBV; GOA; LiTA; LiTM; MoAB; MoAmPo; NAAL-2; NoAM; NOBA; OxBA; PrIm; TrGrPo

Harbor of Illusion, The. Charles Bernstein. UL

Harbour. Edward Kamau Brathwaite. PBCV

Harbour, The. Winifred M. Letts. TIRV

Harbour Bridge, The. Thomas Hardy. NoAM

Harbour in the Evening, The. Tom Paulin. *See* Bereaved years, they've settled to this, The.

Harbour roars out, The. Creide's Lament for Cael. *Unknown.* NOIV

Hard aport! Now close to shore sail! Adrian Block's Song. Edward Everett Hale. PAH

Hard as hurdle arms, with a broth of goldish flue. Harry Ploughman. Gerard Manley Hopkins. EnVR; FaBoMo; MeMBP

Hard brown bug, maybe a beetle, A. He Faces the Second Winter. Philip Levine. *Fr.* Sierra Kid. PoA

Hard, but you can polish it. Stone. Donald Justice. *Fr.* Things. CRP

Hard by Pall Mall lives a wench call'd Nell. Nell Gwynne. *Unknown.* FaBoEH

Hard by the lilied Nile I saw. A Crocodile. Thomas Lovell Beddoes. *Fr.* Last Man, The. FM; NOBVV; OBTV; RB

Hard by the tall elms and a wooded hill. The Old Rustic Mill. George Sands Johnson. PWR

Hard captains of industry, The. Still Century. Tom Paulin. BiHa

Hard cold fire of the northerner, The. Belfast. Louis MacNeice. PeECV

Hard Country. Philip Booth. CoAP

Hard energy, like the stars. (*LL*) My Sad Captains. Thom Gunn. CMoP; FaBoMo; LiTM; NAEL-2; NoAM

Hard Frost. Andrew Young. BoNaP

Hard ground, The. (*LL*) Prayer to the Masks. Léopold Sédar Senghor. NegPo

Hard heart of a child, The. (*LL*) Beauty. Elinor Wylie. NAAL-2; OxBA

Hard Heart of Mine. Henry Alline. AH

Hard helmets and high boots. Daredevil. Kirby Congdon. PeHV

Hard is my fate, thus to want bread. Between an Unemployed Artist and His Wife. *Unknown.* NOEC

Hard is the doubt, and difficult to deeme. Spenser. *Fr.* Faerie Queene, The. OAEL-1

Hard is the stone, but harder still. The Image-Maker. Oliver St. John Gogarty. OBEV; OBMV; PoRA

Hard it is, very hard. The Choice of the Cross. Dorothy L. Sayers. *Fr.* Devil to Pay, The. TrCP

Hard Journey, A. Yes. Hayden Carruth. VGW

Hard knowledge to come by. The Music of the Spheres. Marvin Bell. PoA

Hard Listener, The. William Carlos Williams. OxBSP

Hard Lovers, The. George Dillon. PoA

Hard Questions. Margaret Tsuda. RFM

Hard Rain's A-Gonna Fall, A. Bob Dylan. PoBeRe

Hard Road Blues. *Unknown.* FaBoVe

Hard Rock Returns to Prison from the Hospital for the Criminal Insane. Etheridge Knight. InPS; MoP; NIP; NNaP; PBCAP; TAP; TRP; UnPo

Hard Rock was "known not to take no shit." Hard Rock Returns to Prison from the Hospital for the Criminal Insane. Etheridge Knight. InPS; MoP; NIP; NNaP; PBCAP; TAP; TRP; UnPo

Hard sand breaks, The. Hermes of the Ways. Hilda Doolittle ("H. D."). LiTA; WPE

Hard stones! Hard stones! The Convict Song. Alfred Cruickshank. PBCV

Hard Structure of the World, The. Richard Eberhart. NoAM

Hard Times. John Ashbery. NoAM

Hard Times. *Unknown.* AmFP

Hard times, bad year, and a family dispossessed. On a Moonlit Night, Sent to my Brothers and Sisters. Po Chü-i, *tr. fr. Chinese* by Irving Lo. SuSp

Hard Times in the Mill. *Unknown.* SWP

Hard to Bear. Tudor Jenks. OBCA

Hard to pronounce and play, the OBOE. Oboe. Laurence McKinney. NBLV

Hard Traveling. Woody Guthrie. SWP

Hard was thy fate in all the scenes of life. William Roscoe. OBD

Hard-working Miner, The ("The hard-working miners.") *Unknown.* AmFP, 2 *vers.*

Hardcastle Crags. Sylvia Plath. GoYe

Harden now thy tyred hart with more then flinty rage. Thomas Campion. AAS; OBVE

Hardened in a leaf? (*LL*) Sea Rose. Hilda Doolittle ("H. D."). FaBoMo; HeIP; NoAM; NoP; TRP

Harder Task, The. *Unknown.* BLRP

Harder time is coming, A. The Respite. Ingeborg Bachmann, *tr. fr. German* by Michael Hamburger. WPOW

Hardest, The. Ron Schreiber. PFL

Hardest thing in the world, The. To the Tune "A Watered Silk Dress." Ho Shuang-ch'ing, *tr. fr. Chinese* by Kenneth Rexroth *and* Ling Chung. WPC

Hardest work I ever did, The. Bile Them Cabbage Down. *Unknown.* AmFP

Hardly a ghost left to talk with. The slavs moved on. The River Now. Richard Hugo. VCAP

Hardly a Man Is Now Alive. Ring Lardner. OBAL

Hardly a shot from the gate we stormed. Badminton. Sir Alfred Comyn Lyall. *Fr.* Studies at Delhi, 1876. OBTV; PeVV

Hardly believing it, we left each other. Human Geography. Andrew Motion. SCBI

Hardly can disagree. (*LL*) You Would Have Understood Me. Paul Verlaine. BoLoP; MoBrPo; NOBVV

Hardly spring, with ice. Chiyojo, *tr. fr. Japanese by* David Ray. BoWoP

Hardnes[s] of her h[e]art[e] and truth of mine [*or* myne]. Sir John Davies. *Fr.* Gulling[e] Sonnets, The. ESo; Son

Hardness Scale, The. Joyce Peseroff. TRP

Hardon ("Get One Today.") Ian Wedde. PeNZ

Hardship of Accounting, The. Robert Frost. FaBoCh; FaBoCo; OBAL

Hardweed Path Going. A. R. Ammons. HCAP; UnPo; VGW

Hardy Perennial. Richard Eberhart. GOYP

Hardy's Plymouth. Geoffrey Grigson. FaBoPP

Hare, A. Walter de la Mare. EBEV

Hare. Molly Holden. TEP

Hare-hunting. William Somervile. *Fr.* Chase, The. NOEC

Hare-skin sky. A distinct. By Day. Paul Celan, *tr. fr. German by* Joachim Neugroschel. AnAn

Hare we had run over, The. Interruption to a Journey. Norman MacCaig. RB

Hares at Play. John Clare. NTP; RB

Hares on the Mountain. *Unknown.* ErPo; OBET; PeLV

Hares on their forms at dusk were not so still. "Robin Hyde." *Fr.* Houses, The. PeNZ

Hari helps his people. Mirabai, *tr. fr. Hindi by* Willis Barnstone *and* Usha Nilsson. BoWoP

Hari, look at me a while. Mirabai, *tr. fr. Hindi by* Willis Barnstone *and* Usha Nilsson. BoWoP

Hark! A Sacrifice. Robert Davenport. NOSC

Hark. John Webster. *See* Hark, Now Everything Is Still.

Hark! ah, the nightingale. Philomela. Matthew Arnold. EBVVPR; FHYEP; OAEL-2; OBEV; PPP; UnPo

Hark, All Ye Lovely Saints. *Unknown.* OAEL-1

Hark, All You Ladies. Thomas Campion. EIL ("Hark[e], al[l] you ladies that do sleep.") AAS; EBEV; PoEL-2

Hark, and Hear My Trumpet Sounding. *Unknown.* AH

Hark! do I hear again the roar. Columbus Dying. Edna Dean Proctor. PAH

Hark! from the tombs a doleful sound. Plenary. *Unknown.* AmFP

Hark! from yon covert, where those tow'ring oaks. Hare-hunting. William Somervile. *Fr.* Chase, The. NOEC

Hark! from yon high grey Downs the tremulous musical sheep-bells. Above the Medway. A. J. Munby. *Fr.* Vales of the Medway, The. FaBoPP

Hark, happy lovers, hark! A Kiss. William Drummond of Hawthornden. EIl

Hark! Hark! Hibiscus and Salvia Flowers. D. H. Lawrence. FaBoPV

Hark! hark! down the century's long reaching slope. Yorktown Centennial Lyric. Paul Hamilton Hayne. PAH

Hark! hark! that pig — that pig! the hideous note. Ode to a Pig while His Nose Was Being Bored. Robert Southey. NOBL

Hark, hark, the bark as Fido springs. Dawn Chorus. Mary Holtby. UV

Hark, Hark, the Dogs Do Bark. Mother Goose. CoGr; OxNR; ReMoGo

Hark! Hark! the Lark. Shakespeare. *Fr.* Cymbeline. AWP; BoTP; CH; ChTr; EnRePo; FaBoCh; FaBV; FaPON; ImPo; LiTB; NIP; NoP; NoSic; PFP; PrIm; TFi; TrGrPo; UV

Hark! hark! the lark at heaven's gate sings. Hark! Hark! the Lark. Shakespeare. *Fr.* Cymbeline. AWP; BoTP; CH; ChTr; EnRePo; FaBoCh; FaBV; FaPON; ImPo; LiTB; NIP; NoP; NoSic; PFP; PrIm; TFi; TrGrPo; UV
(Aubade: "Hark! hark! the lark at heaven's gate sings.") OBEV
(Morning Song, A.) GN
(Song: "Hark! hark! the lark at heaven's gate sings.") NOSC; EBEvV; EIl; 09FiP

Hark! Hark! with Harps of Gold. Edwin Hubbell Chapin. AH

Hark! — heard ye the signals of triumph afar? The Caffer Commando. Thomas Pringle. PeSAV

Hark how the mower Damon sung. Damon the Mower. Andrew Marvell. ESCV; GeHe; JCP; NAEL-1; NOSC; OAEL-1

Hark, how the Passing Bell. Upon a Passing Bell. Thomas Washbourne. FaBoRV

Hark, I hear the bells of Westgate. Westgate-on-Sea. Sir John Betjeman. OxBoLi

Hark I hear the cannons roar. A Carrouse to the Emperor, the Royal Pole, and the Much-wronged Duke of Lorrain. *Unknown.* CoMu

Hark! I hear the tramp of thousands. The Reveille. Bret Harte. GN; OHIP; OtMeF; PAH

Hark — like the murmur of the swelling sea. Group in Tartarus. Schiller, *tr. fr. German by* Philip L. Miller. RiWo

Hark! My Beloved! Bible, O.T. *Fr.* Song of Solomon, The. TrJP

Hark, my Flora! Love doth call us. A Song of Dalliance. William Cartwright. ErPo; JCP; NOSC

Hark, my soul! it is the Lord. Lovest Thou Me? William Cowper. ChIV-2

Hark, Now Everything Is Still. John Webster. *Fr.* Duchess of Malfi, The. CoGr; EIL; HAP; NAEL-1; NoP; OBD; SCGP

Hark! O hark, you guilty trees. Orpheus to Woods. Richard Lovelace. CaPo

Hark! one saith: "Proclaim!" All Flesh Is Grass. Bible, O.T. *Fr.* Isaiah. TrJP

Hark, reader! wilt be learn'd i' th' wars? To My Truly Valiant, Learned Friend, Who in His Book Resolved the Art Gladiatory into the Mathematics. Richard Lovelace. CaPo; PoEL-3

Hark! she is call'd, the parting houre is come. On the Glorious Assumption of Our Blessed Lady. Richard Crashaw.
(On the Assumption.) ESCV

Hark! — the black squadrons wheeling down to death! (*LL*) Fredericksburg. Thomas Bailey Aldrich. AnAmPo; PAH

Hark, the bonny Christchurch bells! Christchurch Bells. *Unknown.* OBET

Hark! the Dogs Howl! Tennyson. EnVR

Hark! the dogs howl! the sleetwinds blow. Hark! the Dogs Howl! Tennyson. EnVR

Hark! the flow of the four rivers. Farewells from Paradise. Elizabeth Barrett Browning. OBEV

Hark! the herald angels sing/ timidly. Dean Inge. Humbert Wolfe. FaBoEE; PlP
(On Dean Inge.) ChTr

Hark! the Mavis. Burns. *See* Ca' the Yowes.

Hark! the tiny cowslip bell. Spring Has Come. *Unknown.* BoTP

Hark! the Vesper Hymn Is Stealing. Thomas Moore. EnRP

Hark! They cry! I hear by that. Yolp, Yolp, Yolp, Yolp. *Unknown.* EIL

Hark! 'tis freedom that calls, come, patriots, awake! *Unknown.* PAH

Hark! 'Tis the Saviour of Mankind. John Murray. AH

Hark! 'tis the twanging horn o'er yonder bridge. The Winter Evening. William Cowper. *Fr.* Task, The.
(Arrival of the Mail.) ECEV

Hark! 'tis the voice of the mountain. The Battle of Eutaw. William Gilmore Simms. PAH

Hark to the blackbird's pleasing note. The Bullfinch in Town. Henrietta Knight, Lady Luxborough. ECWP

Hark to the rumble of the earthquake god! Ruaumoko — the Earthquake God. Mohi Turei, *tr. fr. Maori by* A. Armstrong. WTO

Hark to the story of Willie the Weeper. Willy the Weeper. *Unknown.* GBP

Hark to the thrush gurgling in yonder tree! The Thrush. Alfred Austin. TEP

Hark to the whimper of the sea-gull. The Sea-Gull. Ogden Nash. ImPo

Hark, ye sighing sons of sorrow. The Mouldering Vine. *Unknown.* AmFP

Harken that happy shout — the schoolhouse door. Evening Schoolboys. John Clare. OBF

Harlackenden, among these men of note Christ hath thee seated. Among These Troopes of Christs Souldiers, Came . . . Mr. Roger Harlackenden. Edward Johnson. SCAP

Harlech Castle. John Corben. Spl

Harlem. Jean Brierre, *tr. fr. French by* John F. Matheus. TTY

Harlem. Langston Hughes. *Fr.* Lenox Avenue Mural. AiP; AmPP; GLP; HCAP; HeIL; HeIP; HoPM; InPS; NoP; Poetr; PoNe; RaBo; SAmP

Harlem. Maureen Seaton. LoHo

Harlem (A Dream Deferred). Langston Hughes. *See* What happens to a dream deferred.

Harlem Dancer, The. Claude McKay. BPo; FF; NIP; NoAM; Son; TAP

Harlem dud. For "Mr. Dudley," a Black Spy. James A. Emanuel. BPo; NBV

Harlem Freeze Frame. Lebert Bethune. PoBA

Harlem Gallery., sels. Melvin B. Tolson.
Birth of John Henry, The. BPo; TTY
Sea-Turtle and the Shark, The. PoBA

Harlem Gallery: From the Inside. Larry Neal. BPo; NBV

Harlem is vicious. Return of the Native. Amiri Baraka. BPo

Harlem, Montana; Just Off the Reservation. James Welch. CDW; HATNAP

Harlem Riot, 1943. Pauli Murray. PoBA

Harlem Shadows. Claude McKay. AmPP; PoNe

Harlem Sweeties. Langston Hughes. LiTM; NoP; PoNe; TTY

Harlot's Catch. Robert Nichols. ErPo; FaBoTw

Harlot's House, The. Oscar Wilde. EBVV; GGP; MoBrPo; NAEL-2; NoAM; OHCV

Harmonics. William Vaughn Moody. AnAmPo

Harmonie du Soir. Baudelaire, *tr. fr. French* by Lord Alfred Douglas. AWP

Harmony. Thomas Grant Springer. PoToHe

Harmony. *Unknown, tr. fr. Greek* by William J. Philbin. GrAn

Harnet and the Bittle, a Wiltshire Tale, The ("A harnet zet in a hollur tree.") John Yonge Akerman. ChTr

Harold the Dauntless., *sels.* Sir Walter Scott. Tis Merry in Greenwood. FaPON; OHIP

Harold Wilson's Selected Poems, *sels.* Mary Wilson. "I went out of the conf'rence to get a pint of beer." UV

Harold's Song: Rosabelle. Sir Walter Scott. *See* O [*or* Oh] listen, listen, ladies gay!

Haroun Al-Rachid for Heart's-Life. *Unknown, tr. fr. Arabic* by E. Powys Mathers. *Fr.* Thousand and One Nights, The. AWP

Haroun's Favorite Song. *Unknown, tr. fr. Arabic* by E. Powys Mathers. *Fr.* Thousand and One Nights, The. AWP

Harp, The. Ralph Knevet. ChIV-2

Harp, The. Po Chü-i, *tr. fr. Chinese* by Robert Payne. TAL

Harp of David, The. Jacob Cohen, *tr. fr. Hebrew* by Sholom J. Kahn. TrJP

Harp of David, The. "Yehoash," *tr. fr. Yiddish* by Alter Brody. TrJP

Harp of Sorrow, The. Ethel Clifford. WGRP

Harp of the North, Farewell! Sir Walter Scott. *See* Harp of the North, Farewell! The Hills Grow Dark.

Harp of the North, Farewell! The Hills Grow Dark. Sir Walter Scott. *Fr.* Lady of the Lake, The. PFP

Harp of the North! that mouldering long hast hung. The Chase. Sir Walter Scott. *Fr.* Lady of the Lake, The. EnRP

Harp of Wild and Dream-like Strain. Emily Brontë. Mes

Harp Song of the Dane Women. Kipling. *Fr.* Puck of Pook's Hill. HAP; OBNC; OtMeF; PAW; PoRA

Harp That Once through Tara's Halls, The. Thomas Moore. BLPL; EnRP; FaPoR; GN; NAEL-2; OBNC; PoLF

Harp the Monarch Minstrel Swept, The. Byron. ChIV-1

Harpers Ferry. Selden Rodman. PoNe

Harpkin. *Unknown.* FaBoVe; GBP

Harpkin gaed up t'the hill. Harpkin. *Unknown.* FaBoVe; GBP

Harps Hung Up in Babylon. Arthur Willis Colton. AnAmPo; WGRP

Harried/ earth is swept, The. The Wind Increases. William Carlos Williams. NAAL-2

Harriet. Audre Lorde. BlSi

Harriet. Robert Lowell. NoP

Harriet Beecher Stowe. Paul Laurence Dunbar. AAP; BPo

Harriet Beecher Stowe. Dorothy Parker. *Fr.* Pig's-Eye View of Literature, A. NALW

Harriet Beecher Stowe's Works. Frank Barbour Coffin. AAP

Harriet in the Promised Land. Sam Cornish. ETG

Harriet Simper Has Her Day. John Trumbull. *Fr.* Progress of Dulness, The. AmPP

Harriet there was always somebody calling us crazy. Harriet. Audre Lorde. BlSi

Harriet Tubman. Margaret Walker. PoNe

Harrow and Flanders. Marquess of Crewe. NSI

Harry Fat and Uncle Sam. James K. Baxter. PeLV

Harry Lenga. Julie N. Heifetz. BTR

Harry Parry. *Unknown.* GBP; OxNR

Harry Ploughman. Gerard Manley Hopkins. EnVR; FaBoMo; MeMBP

Harry the Black. Alun Rees. AngWe

Harry Vaughan, *sels.* John L. Thomas. "His father did intend that Harry should." AngWe

Harry, whose tuneful and well-measured song. To Mr. H. Lawes on His Airs. Milton. AWP; NoP

(Sonnet: To Mr. H. Lawes, on His Air[e]s.) NOSC

Harsh bray and hollow, The. Two Kitchen Songs. Edith Sitwell. CMoP

Harsh Climate. Charles Simic. LCAP

Harsh cry the crows. The Solitary. Friedrich Wilhelm Nietzsche, *tr. fr. German* by Ludwig Lewisohn. AWP

Harsh with salt of the sea. (*LL*) A Drover. Padraic Colum. AWP; MoBrPo; OBMV; RB

Hart Crane. Julian Symons. PoA

Hart he loves the high wood, The. Mother Goose. FaBoCh; GBP; OxNR; ReMoGo

Hart-Leap Well. Wordsworth. BeLS

Hart Loves the High Wood, The. *Unknown.* RB

Hartico. Anna Walters. VoR

Hartnett, the poet, might as well be dead. Michael Hartnett, *tr. fr. Irish* by Gabriel Fitzmaurice. *Fr.* Purge, The. BiHa

Hart's Castle. Gawin Douglas. *Fr.* King Hart. PoEL-1

Haruko, I give up my mind to you. Her Husband Speaks to Her of Dragons. Marion Lomax. PWE

Harum Scarum. Roger McGough. OTCP

Harvard. Julian Symons. PeLV

Harvard, Cambridge, Mass. Harvard. Julian Symons. PeLV

Harvest, The. Alice Corbin. BoTP

Harvest. M. M. Hutchinson. BoTP

Harvest. Philip Levine. AnAn

Harvest, The. Morgan Llwyd. *Fr.* 1648. AngWe

Harvest. Gene Shuford. GoYe

Harvest. Gary Soto. PBCAP

Harvest, The. Alma Villanueva. ETG

Harvest approaches with its bustling day. August. John Clare. *Fr.* Shepherd's [*or* Shepheards] Calendar, The. EnVR

Harvest Bow, The. Seamus Heaney. BiHa; NoAM; PBCIP; PNI

Harvest Dawn Is Near, The. George Burgess. AH

Harvest: delicate, serene . . . (*LL*) Gleaning. David Shimoni. MHP

Harvest Home. Henry Alford. WGRP

Harvest Home. Dryden. *Fr.* King Arthur. PrIm

Harvest-Home. Theocritus [*or* Theokritus], *tr.* by Charles Stuart Calverley. *Fr.* Idylls. AWP

Harvest Hymn. Whittier. *Fr.* For an Autumn Festival. OHIP

Harvest Moon, The. Longfellow. GN

Harvest Mouse. Clive Sansom. OBAP

Harvest-mouse with caution smites, The. Rustler. William Stroud. Spl

Harvest, 1925. Eleanor Ross Taylor. BAP-89

Harvest of Sorrow, The. A. K. Tolstoy, *tr. fr. Russian* by Philip L. Miller. RiWo

Harvest of the Sea. Máire Mhac an tSaoi. PBWW

Harvest of War. Kappiyarrukkappiyanar, *tr. fr. Tamil* by A. K. Ramanujan. PLW

Harvest ripe, the farmers rejoice, The. Hastily Composed on the Mo-ling Road. Wang An-shih, *tr. fr. Chinese* by Jan W. Walls. SuSp

Harvest Song. Richard Dehmel, *tr. fr. German* by Ludwig Lewisohn. AWP

Harvest Song. Ludwig Heinrich Christoph Hölty, *tr. fr. German* by Charles T. Brooks. AWP

Harvest Song. Jean Toomer. NoP

Harvest Song. *Unknown.* BoTP; OxNR

Harvest Time. Star Powers. GoYe

Harvest Time. G. A. Watermeyer, *tr. fr. Afrikaans* by Guy Butler, Uys Krige, *and* Jack Cope. PeSA

Harvest to Seduce, A. Melville Cane. NYBP

Harvester, harbinger, harrow my heaven. (*LL*) A Blason. A. D. Hope. NOBAu

Harvesters, The. Mary Gilmore. NOBAu

Harvester's Song. George Peele. *Fr.* Old Wives' [*or* Wife's] Tale, The. TrGrPo

Harvesting. David Campbell. *Fr.* Works and Days. FaBoMA

Harvesting of the Roses, The. Menahem ben Jacob, *tr. fr. Hebrew.* TrJP

Harvesting Wheat for the Public Share. Li Chü, *tr. fr. Chinese* by Kenneth Rexroth *and* Ling Chung. BoWoP; PBWP; WPC

Harvey Always Wins. Jack Prelutsky. NTCP

Harvey, the happy above happiest men. To the Right Worshipful My Singular Good Friend, Mater Gabriel Harvey, Doctor of the Laws. Spenser. NoSic

Has a gold tooth, sits long hours. Black Bourgeoisie. Amiri Baraka. BPo

Has a kiss of desire on the lips. (*LL*) A White Rose. John Boyle O'Reilly. OBEV; PeIV

Has Any One Supposed It Lucky to Be Born? Walt Whitman. *Fr.* Song of Myself. AmPP; LiTA; MoAmPo, *abr.*; NAs; NOBA; OxBA; SOTW, (*much abr.*)

Has anybody seen my mouse? Missing. A. A. Milne. MoShBr; PDV

Has Anyone Seen the Boy? Jalal-Din Rumi, *tr. fr. Sanskrit* by Coleman Barks and John Moyne. RaBo

Has anyone seen the boy who used to come here? Has Anyone Seen the Boy? Jalal al-Din Rumi, *tr. fr. Sanskrit* by Coleman Barks and John Moyne. RaBo

Has auld Kilmarnock seen the dell? Tam Samson's Elegy. Burns. PoEL-4

Has bitten off your head. (*LL*) O Have You Caught the Tiger? A. E. Housman. BXAP; FaBoNo

Has broken many more! (*LL*) Fair Ines. Thomas Hood. EnRP; OBEV

Has but the wisdom of a hare? (*LL*) The Horn. Léonie Adams. MoAB; MoAmPo

Has done the lover mortal hurt. (*LL*) Vergissmeinnicht. Keith Douglas. FaBoEH; FaBoMo; GTBS-P; InPS; NAEL-2; NoAM; OBD; OBWP; OxBTC; PoWW; RB; SoSe

Has faded away for ten years now. (*LL*) Mourning. Kuan P'an-p'an. WPC

Has gone far away but is still inaudibly near. (*LL*) A Melody. Lan Ling. WPC

Has gone to the city Ispahan. (*LL*) When the Sultan Goes to Ispahan. Thomas Bailey Aldrich. BeLS; FaBoBe

Has he no friend, no loving mother near? (*LL*) The Fruit Plucker. Samuel Taylor Coleridge. CH

Has he tempered the viol's wood. Ezra Pound. *Fr.* Cantos. HAP

Has left a note saying GONE AWAY. (*LL*) Ending. Gavin Ewart. NBLV; OxBSP; SoSe

Has metamorphosed me into an ass! (*LL*) The Metamorphosis. Sir John Suckling. CaPo; FaBoEE

Has mother finally gone to sleep. The Fortune-Teller. Adelbert von Chamisso, *tr. fr. German by* Philip L. Miller. RiWo

Has not altered. Spenser's Ireland. Marianne Moore. FaBoWP; IIP; LiTA; LiTM; MeMAP; NoAM; NOBA; OxBA; TAP

Has not changed since Thou wast young! (*LL*) Ex Ore Infantium. Francis Thompson. BoTP; FaBV; OHIP; OxBChV

Has not come back. (*LL*) To the Tune "The Bodhisattva's Barbaric Headdress." Lady Wei. WPC

Has not his flying-crooked gift. (*LL*) Flying Crooked. Robert Graves. FaBoMo; LiTM; OxBSP; PeLV; PlP; RB; TwCP

Has not the night been as a drunken rose. The Drunken Rose. Amarou, *tr. fr. Sanskrit by* E. Powys Mathers. AWP

Has quite escaped my mind! (*LL*) A Chronicle. *Unknown.* BLPL; CBNP

Has rather a classical sound. (*LL*) The Pleasures of Merely Circulating. Wallace Stevens. LiTA; MAT; OBAL

Has set me softly down beside you. The poem is you. (*LL*) Paradoxes and Oxymorons. John Ashbery. CAPP; HeIP; NoAM; NoP; Poetr

"Has the Marquis La Fayette." A New Song. Joseph Stansbury. PAH

Has there any old fellow got mixed with the boys? The Boys. Oliver Wendell Holmes. WBLP

Has thrust his nose under every board. Ego. Robert Siegel. PoA

Hasbrouck and the Rose. H. Phelps Putnam. OxBA

Haschish, The. Whittier. AnAmPo; OBAL

Hassan, *sels.* James Elroy Flecker.
  Golden Road, The. OtMeF
  Hassan's Serenade. OBEV
  (Yasmin.) CoGr
  "Thy dawn, O Master of the world, thy dawn." OtMeF
  War Song of the Saracens. CoGr; FaBV; MoBrPo; OtMeF
  (We are they who come faster than fate: we are they who ride.) EBEvV

Hassan's Serenade. James Elroy Flecker. *Fr.* Hassan. OBEV

Hast Never Come to Thee an Hour. Walt Whitman. SAmP

Hast then sweet Love our wished flight. (*LL*) Come Away, Come, Sweet Love. *At. to* John Dowland. NAEL-1; NoSic; PoEL-2

Hast thou a charm to stay the morning-star. Hymn before Sunrise, in the Vale of Chamouni. Samuel Taylor Coleridge. EnRP; WGRP

Hast thou a cunning instrument of play. Preparation. Thomas Edward Brown. OBEV

Hast Thou Given the Horse Strength. Bible, *O.T. Fr.* Job. AWP; ChTr; NAWM-1, *abr.*

Hast Thou Heard It, O My Brother. Theodore Chickering Williams. AH

Hast thou named all the birds without a gun? Forbearance. Emerson. AnAmPo; GN; LiTA; MeMAP; TAP; TrGrPo; WGRP

Hast thou no mercy, wind, that thou should'st tear from me. The Mother's Lament. Mary E. Tucker. CBWP-1

Hast Thou Not Seen an Aged Rifted Tower. Hartley Coleridge. EnRP

Hast thou seen reversed the prophet's miracle. Frederick Goddard Tuckerman. *Fr.* Sonnets. NOBA

"Hast thou seen that lordly castle." The Castle by the Sea. Ludwig Uhland, *tr. fr. German by* Longfellow. AWP

Hast thou seen the down i' th' air. A Song to a Lute. Sir John Suckling. BeJo; CaPo; TrGrPo
  (Song: "Hast thou seen the down i' th' air.") EnLoPo

Hast thou, spirit. Shakespeare. *Fr.* Tempest, The. OAEL-1; OxAEP-1

Haste, haste my verses with your sharpened teeth. Unto the Breach. A. Poliziano, *tr. fr. Latin by* John Addington Symonds. PeHV

Haste thee, nymph, and bring with thee. Milton. *Fr.* L'Allegro. AWP; FaPoB; FHYEP; GN; GTBS; GTBS-P; HAP; HoPM; ImPo; JCP; LiTB; NoP; NOSC; OAEL-1; OBEV; PPP; TEP; TFi; TrGrPo
  (Mirth, with Thee I Mean to Live.) FaBV

Haste to the mighty ocean. August. H. Cordelia Ray. CBWP-3

Haste to the Wedding. Alex Comfort. ErPo

Hasten (great prince) unto thy British Isles. On the Numerous Accesse of the English to Waite upon the King in Holland. Katherine Philips. KTR
  (On the Numerous Access of the English to Wait upon the King in Flanders.) NOSC

Hasten hither, little book. Company in Loneliness. *Unknown.* NOIV

Hastening on, the wanderer strode. The Wanderer. "Yehoash," *tr. fr. Yiddish by* Isidore Goldstick. TrJP

Hastily Composed on the Mo-ling Road. Wang An-shih, *tr. fr. Chinese by* Jan W. Walls. SuSp

Hasty Pudding, The. Joel Barlow. AmPP; EAP; NOBA; OBAL, *abr.*; OxBA; TAP

Hat Bar. Mildred Weston. FiBHP

Hat Factory, The. Paul Durcan. BiHa

Hat Lady, The. Linda Pastan. SoSe

Hat Thrown in the Air, a Leg That's Lost, A. Iain Sinclair. VaA

Hat-Tomb. Guillaume Apollinaire, *tr. fr. French.* CBNP

Hatched in a rasping darkness of dry sand. Letter IV. William Empson. LiTB

Hate!. P. G. Antokolsky, *tr. fr. Russian by* Babette Deutsch. TrJP

Hate. James Stephens. MoAB; MoBrPo

Hate and the Love of the World, The. Max Ehrmann. PoToHe

Hate, be a faithful prop, and find. Hate! P. G. Antokolsky, *tr. fr. Russian by* Babette Deutsch. TrJP

Hate Hitler? No, I spared him hardly a thought. IFF. Howard Nemerov. ArOW

Hate is an old man fucking, arduous. Ed Dying. Paul Monette. PFL

Hate is only one of many responses. Frank O'Hara. NeAP; SOTW

Hate Mail. Steve Kowit. UL

Hate me or love, I care not, as I pass. The Unicorn. Ruth Pitter. MoBrPo

Hate-Song, A. Shelley. EnLoPo

Hate the Idle Pleasures. Shakespeare. *See* Now is the winter of our discontent.

Hate Whom Ye List. Sir Thomas Wyatt. EnRePo; SiPSBD

Hated by the Muses! B kw rm. Euenos, *tr. fr. Greek by* Alistair Elliot. GrAn

Hateful Old Age., *sels. Unknown, tr. fr. Welsh by* Gwyn Jones.
  "Before my back was bent I was eloquent." OBWVE

Hater he came and sat by a ditch, A. A Hate-Song. Shelley. EnLoPo

Hath any loved you well, down there. Marie de France, *tr. fr. French by* Arthur O'Shaughnessy. *Fr.* Chartivel. EnLoPo; WPOW
  (Song from "Chartivel.") AWP

Hath baffled justice and humanity! (*LL*) The Dancing Bear. Robert Southey. FM

Hath brought thee to be loved by none. (*LL*) To His Forsaken Mistress. Sir Robert Ayton. EiL; ErPo; OBEV

Hath cared to look upon thy face. (*LL*) Eros. Robert Bridges. CMoP; LiTB; NOBE; PoEL-5

Hath God, who freely gave you his own Son. To the Rev'd Mr. Jno. Sparhawk on the Birth of his Son. Samuel Sewall. SCAP

Hath got the Prize. (*LL*) The Resolve. Henry Vaughan *and* Thomas Stanley. ESCV

Hath melted like snow in the glance of the Lord! (*LL*) The Destruction of Sennacherib. Byron. BeLS; BLPA; BLPL; ChIV-1; CoGr; EBEvV; EnRP; FaBoBe; FaBoCh; FaPON; FaPoR; FF; FHYEP; GN; HAP; HeIP; InPS; NoP; OBWP; OxAEP-2; PoLF; RB; SCGP; TFi; TrCP; WBLP; WeW; WGRP

Hath not the morning dawned with added light? Ethnogenesis. Henry Timrod. AmPP; AnAmPo; NOBA; OxBA

Hath oftener left me mourning. (*LL*) Simon Lee. Wordsworth. EnRP; NAEL-2

Hath only anger an omnipotence. Upon the Ass That Bore Our Saviour. Richard Crashaw. ChIV-2; GeHe

Hath slipped thy hold and thou art dead and gone. (*LL*) In mourning wise since daily I increase. Sir Thomas Wyatt. NoSic; PeECV

Hath the Rain a Father? Jones Very. ChIV-1

Hatikvah — a Song of Hope. Naphtali Herz Imber, *tr. fr. Hebrew by* Henry Snowman. TrJP

Hatred. Gwendolyn B. Bennett. BlSi; CDC; PoBA; RaBo; ShDr

Hatred. Máire Mhac an tSaoi. WoWa

Hatred and greed and pride shall die. He Shall Speak Peace. Thomas Curtis Clark. WBLP

Hatred and vengeance, my eternal portion. Lines Written During a Period of Insanity. William Cowper. *Fr.* Task, The. EBEV; FaBoRV; HAP; NOEC; NoP; OAEL-1; OPOP; PPP; Prf
  (Lines Written Under the Influence of Delerium.) ChIV-1

Hatred of Men with Black Hair. Robert Bly. NaP

Hatred Surely Does Not Kiss. Kaspar Stieler, *tr. fr. German by* George C. Schoolfield. GePo

Hatred's swift repulsions play. (*LL*) The Visit. Emerson. AnAmPo; NOBA

Hats. F. S. Flint. NSI

Hats Around the World. Maxine Chernoff. PRA

Hats off!/ Along the street there comes. The Flag Goes By. Henry Holcomb Bennett. FaBoBe; FaPON; GN; PWR; WBLP

Hatshepsut, old girl, old friend. Sister Pharaoh. Ruth Whitman. MAT

Hattage. A. P. Herbert. FiBHP

Hatteras Calling. Conrad Aiken. BoNaP; NOBA; TAP

Hatters, The. Nan McDonald. NOBAu

Hattie Rice Rich. Adrienne Rich. *Fr.* Grandmothers. HCAP; NAAL-2; NoAM

Haud ictus sapio. (*LL*) Councell Given to Master Bartholmew Withipoll. George Gascoigne. AAS

Haud ictus sapio. (*LL*) Divorce of a Lover, The ("Divorce me nowe good death.") George Gascoigne. AAS

Haud ictus sapio. (*LL*) Gascoigne's Good-Morrow. George Gascoigne. AAS; EnRePo; NOCV; NoSic

Haud ictus sapio. (*LL*) Gascoigne's [*or* Gascoygnes] Good-Night. George Gascoigne. AAS; NOCV; NoSic

Haughty lion, from his burning sand, A. The Lion and the Wave. William Allingham. FM

Haugtussa, sels. Arne Garborg, tr. fr. *Norwegian by* Philip L. Miller.

Haul Away, My Rosy. *Unknown.* AmFP

Haul up the flag, you mourners. Elegy for Two Banjos. Karl Shapiro. LiTA; TrJP

Hauled up from the field by obscure. The Victors. Anthony McNeill. PBCV

Hauling over Wolf Creek Pass in Winter. Walter McDonald. MT

Haunched like a faun, he hooed. Metamorphosis. Sylvia Plath. PoA

Haunt him in his massive hour/ child, I call. (*LL*) The Brother-in-Law. Larry Rubin. MT

Haunt him, Mona! Haunt him, demon sister! The Brother-in-Law. Larry Rubin. MT

Haunted. Martha Sansom. UnDi

Haunted. Siegfried Sassoon. CMoP

Haunted Beach, The. Mary Robinson. ECWP

Haunted Country. Robinson Jeffers. OxBA

Haunted House. E. A. Robinson. MeMAP

Haunted House, The. (Some dreams we have are nothing else but dreams.) Thomas Hood. EBEV

Sels.

"Centipede along the threshold crept, The." WiR

Haunted Houses. Longfellow. PWR

Haunted Oak, The. Paul Laurence Dunbar. AAP; UnPo

Haunted Palace, The. Poe. *Fr.* Fall of the House of Usher, The. AnAmPo; BeLS; CH; ChTr; LiTA; MeMAP; NOBA; OxBA; PoEL-4; PrIm; TAP; TFi; TrGrPo; WiR

Haunter, The. Thomas Hardy. NOBE

Haunting the Western Moor. (*LL*) A Trampwoman's Tragedy. Thomas Hardy. BeLS; NAEL-2; OBNC; OBNV

Haunts me the lugubrious shape. Half-bent Man. Richard Eberhart. NYBP

Havana Birth. Susan Mitchell. BAP-90; NAmP90

Havana Blues. Henry Carlile. SM

Havana Dreams. Langston Hughes. PoNe

Have a being less durable even than he. (*LL*) The Poplar Field. William Cowper. CH; ChTr; ELP; FaBoPP; FaBoRV; FHYEP; GTBS; GTBS-P; HAP; NOBE; NOEC; PoEL-3; TrGrPo; WiR

Have a Nice Day. Robert Long. NAmP90

Have a Nice Day. Jack Myers. NAmP90

Have all built their nests in my beard! (*LL*) There Was an Old Man with a Beard. Edward Lear. CBNP; ChTr; FaBoCo; FaBoNo; NOBL; OHCV; OxBChV; PDV; PeLi; PeLV; PFP; Poetr; PYC; TEP; TLR

Have almost all migrated. The Birds of Sorrow. Ron Schreiber. PFL

Have an almost human grin. (*LL*) Planting Trout in the Chicago River. Dennis Schmitz. AnAn

Have-at a Venture. *Unknown.* CoMu; ErPo

Have broken more treaties. The United States of America We. Sam Abrams. UL

Have caged a broken heart. (*LL*) The Fowler. W. W. Gibson. NTP

Have certain periods set, and hidden fates. (*LL*) Dost see how unregarded now. Sir John Suckling. BeJo; ELP; NOSC

Have changed. (*LL*) Careers. Amiri Baraka. TRP

Have Courage, My Boy, to Say No! L. M. Hilton. WTO

Have developed from a flea! (*LL*) Darwinism in the Kitchen. *Unknown.* FiBHP; NBLV

Have done, you men and women all! The Animals in the Ark. *Unknown.* *Fr.* Deluge, The. ChTr; GBP

Have ending. (*LL*) White Island; or, [The] Place of the Blest. Robert Herrick. BeJo; ChTr; JCP; NoP; NOSC; OAEL-1; PFP; TOF; WiR

Have fair fallen, O fair, fair have fallen, so dear. Henry Purcell. Gerard Manley Hopkins. MeMBP; TEP

Have Faith. Edward Carpenter. WGRP

Have gathered them and will do never again. (*LL*) In Memoriam (Easter, 1915). Edward Thomas. GTBS-P; NOBE; OBWP; OBWVE; OxBTC; PeFWW; Spl

Have Gentlemen perhaps forgotten this? A Poet Speaks from the Visitors' Gallery. Archibald MacLeish. NYBP

Have good day, now, Mergerete. *Unknown.* MiEL

Have, have ye no regard, all ye. His Saviour's Words, Going to the Cross. Robert Herrick. ChIV-2; NOCV

Have heard a kitten in the wilderness. (*LL*) Chaplinesque. Hart Crane. CMoP; HeIP; LiTM; MoP; NAAL-2; NoAM; NOBA; OxBA; SoCa; VGW

Have heard her massive sandal set on stone. (*LL*) Euclid Alone Has Looked on Beauty Bare. Edna St. Vincent Millay. CMoP; HeIP; MeMAP; MoAB; MoAmPo; NAAL-2; NoP; Son; TAP

Have I a hundred years since or. John Landless Leads the Caravan. Iwan Goll, *tr. fr. French by* William Carlos Williams. TrJP

Have I a wife? Bedam I have! The Brewer's Man. L. A. G. Strong. FaBoCo; FiBHP; PeLV

Have I caught my heavely Jewel. Second Song. Sir Philip Sidney. *Fr.* Astrophel and Stella. AAS; ESo, *sl. abr.*; GGP; HeIL, (*Sonnets, I–CVIII and 11 Songs*); NoSic; Poetr; SCGP, (*Sonnets, I–CVIII and 11 Songs*); SiPS, (*Sonnets, I–CVIII and 11 Songs*); SiPSBD, (*Sonnets, I–CVIII and 11 Songs*)

Have I Found Her? At. to Francis Pilkington. EiL; EnRePo

Have I found her (O rich finding!). Have I Found Her? At. to Francis Pilkington. EiL; EnRePo

Have I found you? Small Animal. Alberta Turner. FoLa

Have I no weapon-word for thee — some message brief and fierce? To the Pending Year. Walt Whitman. OxBSP

Have I not blessed thee? Then go forth; nor fear. To His Book. Robert Herrick. CaPo

Have I spent all my life turning. Simon and the Tarantula. James Wright. AnAn; NNaP

Have I the heart to wander on the earth. George Santayana. *Fr.* Sonnets. AnAmPo

Have I the power to bid the frost not melt. To Barba. Edward May. FaBoEE

Have I, this moment, led thee from the beach. Walter Savage Landor. GBL

Have I told you the name of a lady? Have You Seen the Lady? John Philip Sousa. OBAL

Have killed for you today. (*LL*) A Flat One. W. D. Snodgrass. CAPP; LiTM; SM

Have mercy, Lord, on me. Lord, Have Mercy. Nahum Tate. TIRV

Have once a thought to turne. (*LL*) Though I regarded not. The Earl of Surrey. AAS; SiPS

Have patience; it is fit that in this wise. Sorrow. George Santayana. WGRP

Have pity, pity, friends, have pity on me. Epistle in Form of a Ballad to His Friends. Villon, *tr. fr. French by* Swinburne. AWP

Have power for aye in wonted gulf to glide. (*LL*) The Lover to the Thames of London, to Favour [*or* Favor] His Lady Passing Thereon. George Turberville. ChTr; EiL; NoP

Have proved by every line you write. (*LL*) A Critic. Walter Savage Landor. ChTr; FaBoEE

Have saved them from the gas. (*LL*) "It Out-Herods Herod. Pray You, Avoid It." Anthony Hecht. CoAP; NIP; NoAM; NOBA; OxBC

Have sheltered for the night. (*LL*) After the Winter. Claude McKay. PoBA; PoNe

Have sifted out the substance of thy feet. (*LL*) The Lion's Skeleton. Charles Tennyson Turner. FM; NOBVV

Have stood aside and watched yourself go by. (*LL*) Watch Yourself Go By. Strickland W. Gillilan. BLPA; PoToHe

Have the poets left a single spot for a patch to be sewn? Antar, *tr. by* A. J. Arberry. *Fr.* Mu'allaqat, The. TTY

Have thou no other gods but me. The Ten Commandments. *Unknown.* FaBoUs; OxBChV

Have waked marooned upon the coasts of morning. (*LL*) Bout with Burning. Vassar Miller. LiTM; MoAmPo; MT

Have we forgot how Raphael's numerous prose. Earl of Roscommon. *Fr.* Essay on Translated Verse, An. EPCY

Have we managed to fade them out like God? The Concentration Camps. May Sarton. *Fr.* Invocation to Kali, The. BTR; SRLS

Have ye beheld (with much delight). Upon the Nipples of Julia's Breast. Robert Herrick. CaPo; ErPo; NAEL-1; NOSC; PeLV

Have ye heard of our hunting, o'er mountain and glen. The Hunters of Men. Whittier. AnAmPo

Have ye seen the morning sky. The Happy Swain. Ambrose Philips. EnLoPo

Have ye seen the would-be-not-humble dandy. The Road to Zoagli. Max Beerbohm. FaBoNo

Have you a gold cup. The Question. Robert Duncan. NeAP

Have you any gooseberry wine. Mazilla and Mazura. *Unknown.* ChTr

Have You Anything to Say in Your Defense? César Vallejo. RaBo

Have You Been at Carrick? *Unknown, tr. fr. Irish by* Edward Walsh. BIrV

Have you been at sea on a windy day. A Windy Day. Winifred Howard. FaPON

Have you been in our wild west country? then. The West Country. Alice Cary. AmWP

Have you been to that country where the gold. Mignon. Goethe, *tr. by* Robert Bly. *Fr. Wilhelm Meister's Apprenticeship.* NU
(Knowest thou the land where bloom the lemon trees.) AWP, *tr. by* James Elroy Flecker
(You know that land, her lemon groves in bloom?) STV, *tr. by* John Frederick Nims

Have you come to the Red Sea place in your life. At the Place of the Sea. Annie Johnson Flint. BLPA
(Red Sea Place in Your Life, The.) BLRP

Have you dug the spill. Harlem Sweeties. Langston Hughes. LiTM; NoP; PoNe; TTY

Have you ever been ordered to strip. Solitary Confinement. Robert Walker. NOBAu

Have you ever heard of lynching in the great United States? Lynching. L. A. J. Moorer. CBWP-3

Have you ever heard of the Sugar-Plum Tree? The Sugar-Plum Tree. Eugene Field. NBLV; OTCP; OxBChV

Have you ever heard that a tailor was ill? The Tailor. Joseph Leftwich. TrJP

Have you ever heard the wind go "Yooooo?" The Night Wind. Eugene Field. FaPON

Have you ever sat by the railroad track. Empties Coming Back. Angelo de Ponciano. BLPA

Have you ever sat in crystal space, enjoying the sensations. The Call of the Air. Day Jeffery. NSI

Have you ever seen the moon. Have You Seen It. Lula Lowe Weeden. CDC

Have you ever smelled summer? That Was Summer. Marci Ridlon. NTCP

Have you ever watched your old mother. Mother. Vladimir Holan, *tr. fr. Czech by* Ian Milner *and* Jarmila Milner. PoSu

Have you forgotten yet? Aftermath. Siegfried Sassoon. MoBrPo; NSI; PoWW; TrJP

Have you gone forever, my friend. Funeral Ode. Mu Tan, *tr. fr. Chinese. LHF, tr. by* Hualing Nieh

Have you got a brook in your little heart. Emily Dickinson. FaBV

Have you got a sister? *Unknown.* ISE

Have you got your tickets? There's No First Class to Heaven. Pennethorne Hughes. IHNG

Have you had a kindness shown? Pass It On. Henry Burton. BLRP; PWR

Have you heard, my friend, the slander that the Negro has to face? Immortality. L. A. J. Moorer. CBWP-3

Have you heard of a collier of honest renown. Patient Joe; or, The Newcastle Collier. Hannah More. ECWP; WoRP

Have You Heard of Artemisia? Heather McPherson. PeNZ

Have you heard of one Humpty Dumpty. The Ballad of Persse O'Reilly. James Joyce. *Fr. Finnegans Wake.* CBNP; FaBoBa; LiTB; PeLV

Have you heard of our fighting Twenty-first. The Dash for the Colors. Frederick G. Webb. BeLS

Have you heard of the dreadful fate. The Ashtabula Disaster. Julia A. Moore. OBAL

Have you heard of the terrible family They. They Say. Ella Wheeler Wilcox. WBLP

Have you heard of the wonderful one-hoss shay. Deacon's Masterpiece, The; or, The Wonderful "One-Hoss Shay." Oliver Wendell Holmes. *Fr. Autocrat of the Breakfast Table, The.* AmPP; LiTA; MoShBr; NOBA; OBAL; OBCA; OxBA; PoLF; PoRA; TAP; TFi; VPP; WBLP
(Wonderful "One-Hoss Shay," The.) BeLS; FaBoBe

Have you heard the blinking toad. The Song of the Toad. John Burroughs. FaPON

Have you heard the latest miser story. Nicarchus of Alexandria, *tr. fr. Greek by* Peter Porter. GrAn

Have you heard the story that gossips tell. John Burns of Gettysburg. Bret Harte. AnAmPo; OHIP; PAH

Have you heard the tale of the aloe plant. The Aloe Plant. Henry Harbaugh. BLPA

Have you heard? The troubles. Sulpicia, *tr. fr. Latin by* Aliki *and* Willis Barnstone. BoWoP

Have you listened for the things I have left out? Unsaid. A. R. Ammons. NOBA

Have you lived long, sir, in these parts? An Interview. K. W. Grandsen. OxBTC

Have You Lost Faith? *Unknown.* WBLP

Have you made your life worth? (*LL*) After Experience Taught Me. W. D. Snodgrass. ArOW; CAPP; CoAP; OBWP; PPP; TAP

Have you news of my boy Jack? My Boy Jack. Kipling. OtMeF

Have you no thought O dreamer that it may be all maya, illusion? (*LL*) Are You the New Person Drawn toward Me? Walt Whitman. OxBSP; PPP

Have you not fallen asleep to strong men's rowing. The Rowers. Laura Benét. GoYe

Have you not heard his silent steps? Rabindranath Tagore. *Fr. Gitanjali.* WGRP

Have you not heard the poets tell. The Ballad of Baby Bell. Thomas Bailey Aldrich. AnAmPo

Have you not heard the song. The Song That Sounds Like This. James Fenton. SCBI

Have you not in a chimney seen. A Description of Maidenhead. The Earl of Rochester. NOBL

Have you not noted, in some family. The Birth-Bond. Dante Gabriel Rossetti. *Fr. House of Life, The.* OHCV; Son

Have you not seen the grasses on the riverbank? Pao Chao, *tr. by* Irving Y. Lo. *Fr. Weary Road, The.* SuSp

Have you noticed. Angels. Anne Szumigalski. Mes; NOBC

Have you noticed? Ghosts. Mary Oliver. Poetr

Have you noticed the docile appeal. Letter from a State Hospital. Frank Mundorf. GoYe

Have you preserved time. Peace Project (5). Eric Mottram. NBrP

Have you provided for her grace's servants? Ben Jonson. *Fr. Alchemist, The.* FaBoEH

Have you really come home? (*LL*) The Father of My Country. Diane Wakoski. NoAM; TAP

Have you seen a little dog anywhere about? My Dog. Emily Lewis. OTCP

Have you seen an apple orchard in the spring? An Apple Orchard in the Spring. William Martin. GN; PWR

Have you seen but a bright lily grow. Ben Jonson. *Fr. Devil is an Ass, The.* FaBoCh
(So Sweet Is She.) GN
(So White, So Soft, So Sweet.) TrGrPo

Have you seen Hugh. The King of Connacht. *Unknown, tr. fr. Early Irish by* Frank O'Connor. IIP; PeIV

Have You Seen It. Lula Lowe Weeden. CDC

Have you seen my cousin? Shakespeare. *Fr. Troilus and Cressida.* OxAEP-1

Have You Seen our Little Sister? To Little Sister from No. 16. *Unknown.* NSI

Have You Seen the Lady? John Philip Sousa. OBAL

Have you seen the listening snake? The Vines. John Gray. NOBVV

Have you seen walking through the village. Ollie McGee. Edgar Lee Masters. OBD

Have you sometimes, calm, silent let your tread aspirant rise. Heard on the Mountain. Victor Hugo, *tr. fr. French by* Francis Thompson. *Fr. Feuilles d'Automne.* AWP

Have you the Giesbach seen? a fall. Arthur Hugh Clough. *Fr. Mari Magno.* OBTV

Have you time for a story. Charity Overcoming Envy. Marianne Moore. NYBP

Haven. Donald Jeffrey Hayes. PoNe

Haven and last refuge of my pain, The. Michelangelo, *tr. fr. Italian by* George Santayana. *Fr. Three Poems.* AWP

Haven't seen my friend Li Po for some time. No Word. Tu Fu, *tr. fr. Chinese by* Eugene Eoyang. SuSp

Having a Coke with You. Frank O'Hara. GLP; VCAP

Having a crush was how I existed. A Suburban Childhood. Liz Rosenberg. PBCAP

Having a fine new suit. Apologue. Tony Connor. BoLoP

Having a Wonderful Time. D. B. Wyndham Lewis. FiBHP

Having attained success in business. Robert Whitmore. Frank Marshall Davis. BPo; NoP; PoBA; PoNe

Having avantbiographed the world. En Passant. Andrei Codrescu. UL

Having avoided fatal accidents. The Requirement. William Pillen. BTR

Having been tenant long to a rich Lord. Redemption. George Herbert. *Fr. Temple, The.* ESCV; FF; GeHe; HAP; InPK; InPS; JCP; LiTB; MeLP; NAEL-1; NOBE; NOCV; NoP; NOSC; PeECV; PoE; Poetr; SCGP; SCV; SeCP; SeCV-1; Son; SoSe; TEP; TFi; TrCP; WeW

Having Built the Coop. Ed Ochester. ETG
Having come to this place. This Place in the Ways. Muriel Rukeyser. AiP
Having commanded Adam to bestow. Naming the Animals. Anthony Hecht. ChIV-1
Having confused me. A Voice from the Roses. Maxine W. Kumin. NMM
Having crowded once onto the threshold of mortality. Divinities. W. S. Merwin. PoA
Having delivered now what praises are. Lord Herbert of Cherbury. *Fr.* Elegy for Dr. Donne. EPCY
Having dined yesterday on a goat's foot. Automedon, *tr. fr. Greek by* Peter Jay. GrAn
Having Eaten Breakfast. D. C. Berry. BXAP
Having fallen down the manhole. Rick De Travaille. Lewis Turco. *Fr.* Bordello. SM
Having gone out through the west city wall in the chilly dawn. Arriving after Rain at the Temple of Heavenly Peace. Wang Shih-chieng, *tr. fr. Chinese by* Richard John Lynn. SuSp
Having Had You. Mae V. Cowdery. ShDr
Having had you once. Having Had You. Mae V. Cowdery. ShDr
Having heard the instruction. One Modern Poet. Carl Sandburg. OBAL
Having held me in their thrall for years now. The Sound of Drums. Karen Randlev. NGP
Having hooded my face with hair. The Sibyl's Song. Michele Roberts. BrRo
Having inherited a vigorous mind. My Descendants. W. B. Yeats. *Fr.* Meditations in Time of Civil War. LiTB
Having interred [*or* interr'd] her infant-birth. Ode, upon a Question Moved, Whether Love Should Continue Forever? An. Lord Herbert of Cherbury. JCP; MeLP; NOBE; OxAEP-1; SeCP
Having invented a new Holocaust. U. S. 1946 King's X. Robert Frost. NIP
Having known war and peace. Turning Fifty. Judith Wright. NAs
Having left hard [*or* solid] ground behind. The Insular Celts. Ciaran Carson. BIrV; CIP; IIP
Having left the great mean city, I make. Goodbye to London. Louis MacNeice. PeECV
Having lost my leather purse. My Son. Ruth Stone. WPE
Having Lost My Sons, I Confront the Wreckage of the Moon: Christmas, 1960. James Wright. CoAP; HCAP; NAAL-2
Having mortified myself with a hangover. Devotions. Douglas Houston. PWE
Having myself been scared silly when I was young. The Thief. Alden Nowlan. RaBo
Having no father anymore, having got up. The Homecoming of Emma Lazarus. Galway Kinnell. NaP
Having power is nothing to be concerned about. Wang Fun-chih, *tr. fr. Chinese by* Eugene Eoyang. SuSp
Having put yourself on the way. Spirits, Dancing. Arthur Gregor. NYBP; VGW
Having Replaced Love with Food and Drink. Diane Wakoski. NAs
Having rid Hamelin town of its vermin. Ted Thompson. PeLi
Having said that all the gums have not been cut. Robert David Fitzgerald. *Fr.* Eleven Compositions: Roadside. FaBoMA
Having seen thy salvation. (*LL*) A Song for Simeon. T. S. Eliot. ChIV-2; LiTB; NAs; NOCV
Having so rich a treasury, so fine a hoard. The Daisy. Marya Zaturenska. GrPl; MoAmPo
Having split up the chaparral. The Wide Land. A. R. Ammons. TwCP
Having taken her slowly by surprise. A Pause for Breath. Ted Hughes. NYBP
Having this day my horse, my hand, my lance. Sir Philip Sidney. *Fr.* Astrophel and Stella. AAS; EnRePo; ESo; GGP; HAP; NAEL-1; PoE; Poetr; SiPS; SiPSBD; Son
Having to Love Something Else, The. Russell Edson. AnAn
Having traveled ten *li* from the high city walls. Traveling at Break of Day. Huang Ching-jen, *tr. fr. Chinese by* Chang Yin-nan *and* Lewis C. Walmsley. SuSp
Having used every subterfuge. A Renewal. James Merrill. OxBSP; SM; VCAP
Having worked from 12 midnight to 6:58 A.M. Edgy. Fred Voss. NGP
Having written several poems which I will not publish. Baedeker for Metaphysicians. Brian Higgins. FaBoTw
Haw Lantern, The. Seamus Heaney. NoAM; PNI
Hawaii Dantesca. Charles Wright. HCAP; LCAP
Hawk, The. George Mackay Brown. RB
Hawk, The. W. B. Yeats. PoA
Hawk and Snake. Leslie Silko. VoR
Hawk eye of the sun slowly shuts, The. Wellfleet Sabbath. Marge Piercy. SRLS

Hawk Is a Woman. Hildegarde Flanner. WPE
Hawk Nailed to a Barn Door. Peter Blue Cloud. VoR
Hawk Roosting. Ted Hughes. CMoP; GTBS-P; HAP; HeIP; LiTM; OBAP; OxBTC; PPP; TwCP; UnPo
Hawke. Sir Henry Newbolt. FaBoEH
Hawking for the Partridge. Thomas Ravenscroft. OxBoLi
Hawk's Eyes. Yvor Winters. PoA
Hawk's Way. Ted Olson. HoPM
Hawktree. Dave Jeddie Smith. HCAP
Haworth Churchyard., *sels.* Matthew Arnold.
  "Where, behind Keighley, the road." FaBoPP
Hawthorn, The. *Unknown.* ChTr; EnVB; GBP; MiEL
Hawthorn Hedge, The. Judith Wright. FaBoMA; WPE
Hawthorn morning moving, The. Renewal by Her Element. Denis Devlin. CIP; IIP
Hawthorne. Longfellow. PoEL-5
Hawthorne. James Russell Lowell. *Fr.* Fable for Critics, A. AmPP; NOBA; OxBA; TAP
Hawthorne Garland, A. Richard Harter Fogle. OBAL
Hay Appeareth, The. Bible, *O.T. Fr.* Proverbs. FaPON
Hay, ay, hay, ay. *Unknown.* MiEL
Hay Fever. A. D. Hope. NoAM
Hay for the Horses. Gary Snyder. CAPP; GrPl; NaP; TRP
Hay Harvest. Patrick R. Chalmers. BoTP
Hay has long been built into the stack, The. From Harvest to January. Charles Tennyson Turner. NOBVV
Hay, hay, by this day. The Scholar Complains. *Unknown.* MeEL
Hay, Hey, Hey, Hey! I Will Have the Whetstone and I May. *Unknown.* CBNP
Hay Hotel, The. Oliver St. John Gogarty. BIrV
Hay is for horses. *Unknown.* OxNR
Hay making. Joanna Baillie. OxAEP-2
Hay-Making. Gillian Clarke. AngWe
Hay-Time. C. M. Lowe. BoTP
Hay-Time; or, The Constant Lovers. A Pastoral. Josiah Relph. NOEC
Hayeswater. Matthew Arnold. *Fr.* Hayeswater Boat, The. FaBoPP
Hayeswater Boat, The, *sels.* Matthew Arnold.
  Hayeswater. FaBoPP
Hayle holy-land wherein our holy lord. Upon the First Sight of New England, June 29, 1638. Thomas Tillam. GOA; SCAP
  (Hail, Holy Land.) AH
Haylle, Comly and Clene. *Unknown. See* Hail, Comly and Clene.
Haymakers, Rakers. Thomas Dekker *and others. Fr.* Sun's Darling, The. ELP
Haymaking. E. M. Adams. BoTP
Haymaking. A. P. Graves. BoTP
Haymaking. Edward Thomas. MoAB; MoBrPo
Haymaking, *sels.* Edward Thomas.
  "In the field sloping down." FaBoEH
Haymaking. William Carlos Williams. *Fr.* Pictures from Brueghel. NoAM
Hayseed. *Unknown.* AS
Haystack in the Floods, The. William Morris. BeLS; EBEV; EBNV; EBVV; EnVR; HAP; NAEL-2; NoP; OAEL-2; OBNC; OBNV; OxAEP-2; PeVV; PoEL-5; PoRA
Haytime. Irene F. Pawsey. BoTP
Hazard's friend Elliot is homosexual. Wholesome. William Meredith. TAP
Haze. James Schuyler. BAP-90
Haze. Thoreau. *See* Woof of the sun, ethereal gauze.
Haze, char, and the weather of All Souls.' In the Elegy Season. Richard Wilbur. InPK; MoAB; NYBP
Hazel Stick for Catherine Ann, A. Seamus Heaney. NoAM
Hazels. Geoffrey Fraser Dutton. PWE
Hazlewood Witch, The. Richard Gall. ScCV
Hazlitt Sups. Katharine Day Little. GoYe
He. John Ashbery. CBNP; SOTW
He. Lawrence Ferlinghetti. NeAP; PoM
He. Stanley Kunitz. VGW
He. Vasco [*or* Vasko] Popa, *tr. fr. Serbo-Croatian by* Anne Pennington. *Fr.* Games. CBNP; PoSu; RB
He Abjures Love. Thomas Hardy. CBLP; OBNC
He accepts the circle, speech and so. Anne-Marie Albiach, *tr. fr. French by* Keith Waldrop. BoWoP
He adored the desk, its brown-oak inlaid with ebony. Geoffrey Hill. *Fr.* Mercian Hymns. HAP; NoAM; NoP
He: Age Doesn't Matter When You're Both in Love. Julia Alvarez. *Fr.* 33. Son
He all that time among the sewers of Troy. Troy. Edwin Muir. CMoP

He also was a stormy day: a squat mountain man. Family Group. Ken Smith. PWE

He always bathed afterwards. Bathing. Kate Daniels. NAmP90

He always comes on market days. The Balloon Man. Rose Fyleman. BoTP

He always has something to grumble about. A Chip on His Shoulder. *Unknown.* BLPA; WBLP

He always loved the sea. Fado. Briar Wood. NWP

He ambles along like a walking pin cushion. Hedgehog. Chu Chen Po, *tr. fr. Chinese* by Kenneth Rexroth. OHMPC

He and his, unwashed all winter. The Native. W. S. Merwin. PoRA

He and I. End of a Course. I. A. Richards. CRP

He and She. Sir Edwin Arnold. BLPA

He and She. Eugene Fitch Ware. PoLF

He/ and she, A. A Pair. May Swenson. RFM

He Approacheth the Hall of Judgment. *Unknown, tr. fr. Egyptian* by Robert Hillyer. *Fr.* Book of the Dead. AWP

He arises on that portion. Poisonous Mushroom. Liu Sha-ho, *tr. fr. Chinese. Fr.* Family of Plants, A. LHF, *tr.* by Hualing Nieh

He as O, A. E. E. Cummings. InPS

He ascended from a lonely crag in winter. On the Death of Karl Barth. Jack R. Clemo. NOCV

He ask'd, and hoped, through Christ, Do thou the same! (*LL*) Stop, Christian passer-by! — Stop, child of God. Samuel Taylor Coleridge. EnRP; NAEL-2; NOCV; NoP; OAEL-2

He Asked about the Quality. C. P. Cavafy, *tr. fr. Greek* by Edmund Keeley *and* Philip Sherrard. PeHV

He asked for bread, and he received a stone. (*LL*) On the Setting Up of Mr. Butler's Monument in Westminster Abbey. Samuel Wesley. InvP; NBLV; NOEC; OBD; OxBSP

He Asked Them What Did They Know & They Told Him. *Unknown, tr. fr. Seneca Indian* by Jerome K. Rothenberg *and* Richard Johnny John. STP

He Asketh Absolution of God. *Unknown, tr. fr. Egyptian* by Robert Hillyer. *Fr.* Book of the Dead. AWP

He avoids the momentous rhythm. The Last Man. Thom Gunn. OxAEP-2

He awoke this morning from a strange dream. Chief Leschi of the Nisqually. Duane Niatum. CDW

He Bade Me Be Happy. Frances Sargent Osgood. AmWP

He bare him [*or* hym] up, he bare him [*or* hym] down. The Corpus Christi Carol. *Unknown.* HAP; MeEL; OxBLMV

He bathes his soul in women's wrath. The Irish Patriarch. Ruth Pitter. NALW

He beat me with the hem of a kimono. The Club. Mitsuye Yamada. LoHo

He behind the straight plough stands. Ploughman at the Plough. Louis Golding. OHIP

He Biddeth Osiris to Arise from the Dead. *Unknown, tr. fr. Egyptian* by Robert Hillyer. *Fr.* Book of the Dead. AWP

He blinks upon the hearth-rug. On a Cat Aging. Sir Alexander Gray. OFC

He bought an old ship's lifeboat. A Fine Day for Straw Hats. Louis Simpson. PBCV

He breathes in the air, breathes in the early grass. Man. Bulat Okudzhava, *tr. fr. Russian* by George Reavey. PAW

He brings me ghost money. (*LL*) Chinese New Year. Lynda Hull. UTF

He brought a Grecian queen, whose youth and freshness. Portrait of Helen. Shakespeare. *Fr.* Troilus and Cressida. TrGrPo

He brought a light so she could see. Strains of Sight. Robert Duncan. CMoP; PoE

He brought our saviour to the western side. Rome. Milton. *Fr.* Paradise Regained [*or* Regain'd]. NOSC

He built a house, time laid it in the dust. His Monument. Sarah Knowles Bolton. PWR

He built himself a house. Fairy Tale. Miroslav Holub, *tr. fr. Czech* by George Theiner. PAW; RB

He buy she dem expensive ring. Love Story (Part 2). Marsha Prescod. VBLP

He by no means flies straight at petunia. The Bee and the Petunia. Katherine Hoskins. ErPo

He called a conquered land his own. Wolfe Tone. Austin Clarke. CIP

He called her: golden dawn. Paris and Helen. Judy Grahn. CrSp

He calleth to me out of Seir, Watchman, what of the night? Watchman, What of the Night? Bible, *O.T. Fr.* Isaiah. AWP

He calls it their stage which echoes our first misrecognition of unity. Instances. The Swan. Mei-Mei Berssenbrugge. OpBo

He calls you in his wedding coat. The Wedding Coat. Harriet Rose. BrRo

He came, a youth, singing in the dawn. Paul Laurence Dunbar. James David Corrothers. PoNe

He came all so still. Ancient Christmas Carol. *Unknown.* OHIP; PChr

He came and took me by the hand. The Mystery. Ralph Hodgson. CH; MoAB; MoBrPo; WGRP

He came apart in the open. Martin's Blues. Michael S. Harper. HCAP; PoBA

He came back. Dry River Bed. Andrew Salkey. PBCV

He came back and shot. He shot him. When he came. Incident. Amiri Baraka. NoAM

He came from hills to comfortable plains. The Mountaineer. Robert Nathan. TrJP

He came from Malta; and Eumelus says. A Maltese Dog. Tymnes, *tr. by* Edmund Blunden. *Fr.* Epigrams. FaBoCh; FaBoEE; OBD; Spl (Dog from Malta, The.) GrAn

He came from where he started. The Tramp. Ben King. AnAmPo

He came in she said he had come in. Adelaide's Dream. Christopher Middleton. FaBoBl; PeLV

He came in silvern armor, trimmed with black. Gwendolyn B. Bennett. CDC; PoBA; PoNe

He came over to London and straight away strode. Dinky Di. *Unknown.* NOBAu

He came,/ striding. Paul Bunyan. Arthur S. Bourinot. *Fr.* Legend of Paul Bunyan, A. FaPON

He came to his love's window at the dead of the night. The Little Drummer. *Unknown.* AmFP

He came to my desk with a quivering lip. New Leaf, A [*or* The]. *At. to* Helen Field Fischer, *at. to* Kathleen Wheeler. BLRP; PoToHe; WBLP

He came to the desert of London town. William Blake. James Thomson ("B.V."). EPCY

He Came to Visit Me. Martin Seymour-Smith. FaBoTw

He came upon her strangely. The Figurehead. Pauline Stainer. PWE

He can curse the God that made him for the colour of his hair. (*LL*) Oh Who Is That Young Sinner with the Handcuffs on His Wrists? A. E. Housman. FaBoTw; NOBVV; PeHV; SoSe

He can only drink tea now, screwed and filed. Pink Slip at Tool & Dye. Dave Jeddie Smith. NoAM

He can only hurt me a piece at a time. (*LL*) Everything: Eloy, Arizona, 1956. Ai. AmPA; FF

He can snuggle back in the telephone pole. (*LL*) The Woodpecker. Elizabeth Madox Roberts. FaPON; OBCA; TLR

He can touch me with a look. November. Kathleen Jamie. PWE

He cannot forget the third signal. (*LL*) Unforgettable. Mark Pawlak. BTR

He can't remain forever underwater. The Diver. Ben Howard. SM

He cares not — yet, prithee, be kind to his fame. (*LL*) For My Own Monument. Matthew Prior. GGP; OBEV

He Careth. "Marianne Farningham." *See* What can it mean? Is it aught to Him.

He carries shadows in his face like caves. On the Apparition of Oneself. William Burford. PoA

He cast his net at morn where fishers toiled. Failure. Kate Tucker Goode. PWR

He catch'd at love, and fill'd his arm with bayes. (*LL*) The Story of Phoebus and Daphne Applied, [etc.]. Edmund Waller. InvP; NAEL-1; NOSC

He chants a boy-chant. The Grace of Cynthia's Maidenhood. Vinnie-Marie D'Ambrosio. IHMS

"He chases shadows," sneered the British tars. The First Voyage of John Cabot. Hezekiah Butterworth. PAH

He chirped for joy to see himself deceived. (*LL*) Upon Mistress Elizabeth Wheeler under the Name of Amarillis. Robert Herrick. CaPo

He circles slowly and the walls of the room. Baba Mostafa. Mimi Khalvati. NWP

He claims he can translate palés matos.' Tito Madera Smith. Tato Laviera. BCF

He clasps the crag with crooked hands. The Eagle. Tennyson. BoTP; CH; ClHu; CoGr; FaBoCh; FaPON; FF; FHYEP; FM; GN; GoJo; GTBS-P; HeIL; HeIP; InPK; MeMBP; NAEL-2; NOBVV; NoP; NTCP; NTP; OAEL-2; OxBSP; PDV; Poetr; PrIm; SCGP; TFi; TrGrPo; TRP; UnPo; WiR

He climbed, devoured. In her mouth. Cat in the Dovecote. Avner Trainin, *tr. fr. Hebrew* by Ruth Finer Mintz. MHP

He climbs the stair. Waterchew! Gregory Corso. VGW

He Comes Among. George Barker. OBMV

He comes down to the shadow. Heron. Ted Walker. NYBP

He comes from the house as lightning flickers in the sky. Love and Music. *Gond Oral Tradition, tr. by* V. Elwin *and* S. Hivale. WTO

He comes from the north. *Unknown, tr. fr. Sioux Indian* by James Koller. *Fr.* Sioux Metamorphoses. STP

He comes gusting out of the house. Spring Storm. Jim Wayne Miller. GOYP

He comes in the night! He comes in the night! Santa Claus. *Unknown.* BoTP

He comes Not To-night. Josephine D. Henderson Heard. CBWP-4

He comes running. A Poem about a Wolf Maybe Two Wolves. *Unknown, tr. fr. Seneca Indian by* Jerome K. Rothenberg *and* Richard Johnny John. STP

He comes, the old one, his shabby cap askew. Old Man with a Mowing Machine. May Carleton Lord. GoYe

He comes through the door. The Assassin's Fatal Error. Lawrence Raab. AmPA

He comes to brood and sit. *(LL)* Peace. Gerard Manley Hopkins. ELP; GTBS-P; OxBSP; TrCP

He comes to near that comes to be denied. *(LL)* The Lady's Resolve. Lady Mary Wortley Montagu. BoWoP; OxBSP

He comes with autumn, when the leaves flake. Shoni Onions. Sheenagh Pugh. AngWe

He comes with western winds, with evening's wandering airs. Emily Brontë. *Fr.* Prisoner, The. ELP; NOBE; NoP; OBEV

He Cometh. Judah Halevi, *tr. fr. Hebrew by* Emma Lazarus. TrJP

He Cometh Forth into the Day. *Unknown, tr. fr. Egyptian by* Robert Hillyer. *Fr.* Book of the Dead. AWP

He cometh, O bliss! He Cometh. Judah Halevi, *tr. fr. Hebrew by* Emma Lazarus. TrJP

He Commandeth a Fair Wind. *Unknown, tr. fr. Egyptian by* Robert Hillyer. *Fr.* Book of the Dead. AWP

He confessed to me that at night he shuts the cat in the lift. Passion. Jena Lengold, *tr. by* Richard Burns. VBLP

He could have come to tell us. Never Give a Bum an Even Break. James Welch. NoAM

He could hit a blade of grass with his spear. Skilful Spearman! A. *Unknown, tr. fr. Hawaiian.* WTO

He could not die when trees were green. The Dying Child. John Clare. EnRP; TrGrPo

He could see the little lake. The Lake. James Stephens. MoBrPo

He could see things. Another Kind of Country. Charles Sullivan. IIP

He could sing sweetly on a string. Orpheus. Elizabeth Madox Roberts. MoAmPo

He could trimble. Oui Papa. Delano Abdul Malik de Coteau. PBCV

He couldn't carve a duck. *(LL)* When Father Carves the Duck. Ernest Vincent Wright. BLPL; FaBV; NTCP; PoLF

He courts her up there on the roof. The Muse Is Always the Other Woman. Constance Urdang. PBCAP

He crawls to the edge of the foaming creek. Meeting the Mountains. Gary Snyder. NoAM; TAP

He created beauty and your face. *(LL)* Blessed He. Paul Johann Ludwig Heyse. RiWo

He cried aloud to God: "The men below." Genius. Edward Lucas White. WGRP

He crouches, and buries his face on his knees,/ And hides in the dark of his hair. The Last of His Tribe. Henry Clarence Kendall. CBAP

He, cursed with an ugly wife. Palladas, *tr. fr. Greek by* Sam Hamill. InMo

He cut a sappy sucker from the muckle rodden-tree. The Whistle. Charles Murray. OxBS

He cuts down the lakes so they appear straight. He. John Ashbery. CBNP; SOTW

He dances to that music in the wood. The Andean Flute. Derek Mahon. SCBI

He debated whether. Arthur Ridgewood, M.D. Frank Marshall Davis. BPo

He: Deep in the cockerel's golden heart. A Samurai Who Tried to Kill All the Roosters in Japan. George Steiner. PRA

He Defendeth His Heart against the Destroyer. *Unknown, tr. fr. Egyptian by* Robert Hillyer. *Fr.* Book of the Dead. AWP

He delivered meat to the secret police, slabs. The Death of a Butcher. Lavinia Greenlaw. NWP

He did his duty both by peers and peasants. King George V. Charles W. Hayward. NOBAu

He did not come/ A gnostic. Incarnation Poem. John Leax. TrCP

He did not come of a long line of stone-cutters. The Man Who Went Absent from the Native Literature. Anthony Cronin. CIP

He did not come to woo U Nu. Just Dropped In. William Cole. FiBHP; GoJo

He Did Not Know. Harry Hibbard Kemp. WGRP

He did not think me strange or older, Nor I, him. *(LL)* All Souls' Night. Frances Cornford. EnLoPo; OBD; OxBSP; OxBTC

He did not wear his scarlet coat. Oscar Wilde. *Fr.* Ballad of Reading Gaol, The. BeLS; EBEvV; MoBrPo; NoAM; NOBE; NOBVV; OBMV; OBNC; OBNV; OtMeF; OxAEP-2; PeIV; TFi; UV

(Condemned Man, The.) EBNV

He did not wear his swallow tail. The Gourmand. Harry Graham. FaBoPa; UV

He Didn't Oughter. A. P. Herbert. FiBHP

He died privately. Ram. Gillian Clarke. AngWe

He Died Smiling. Wilfred Owen. PAW

He died so quietly. *(LL)* The Dying Child. John Clare. EnRP; TrGrPo

He "Digesteth Harde Yron." Marianne Moore. CMoP; NoAM

He dines alone surrounded by reflections. Witch Doctor. Robert Hayden. MAT; NoAM

He disagrees with Simone de Beauvoir. His Plans for Old Age. William Meredith. TAP

He discovers himself on an old airfield. The Old Pilot. Donald Hall. LCAP

He does not come. Ono no Komachi, *tr. fr. Japanese by* Kenneth Rexroth *and* Ikuko Atsumi. WPJ

He does not lounge with the old men. For William Edward Burghardt Dubois on His Eightieth Birthday. Bette Darcie Latimer. PoNe

He does not think that I haunt here nightly. The Haunter. Thomas Hardy. NOBE

He doesn't like it, of course. His Body. Sandra McPherson. AmPA

He doeth well who doeth good. Best of All. *Unknown.* WBLP

He Done His Level Best. "Mark Twain." AiP

He draws a line, the oval of a head. An Ending. Sebastian Barry. IB

He dreamed first. Adam's Dying. Ridgely Torrence. FYAP

He dreamed not that the ocean would bear ships. A. J. Seymour. *Fr.* For Christopher Columbus. PBCV

He dreamed of/ an open window. The Dream. Felix Pollak. RaBo

He dreamed of lovely women as he slept. Undergraduate. Merrill Moore. ErPo

He dreamt that he saw the buffalant. A Quadrupedremian Song. Thomas Hood. FaBoNo

(Song.) CBNP

He drew a circle that shut me out. Outwitted. Edwin Markham. BLPA; MoAmPo; PoToHe

He drew hundreds of women. Beauty and Sadness. Cathy Song. NoAM

He drives onto the grassy shoulder and unfastens. Earth Walk. William Meredith. MAT

He dropped, more sullenly, than wearily. The Dead-Beat. Wilfred Owen. PeFWW

He drove her to wander over sand. Departure's Girlfriend. Roberta Hill Whiteman. ETG

He drowsed and was aware of silence heaped. The Death-Bed. Siegfried Sassoon. LiTM; NSI; PeFWW

He dumped her in the wheelbarrow. Wheelbarrow. Eleanor Farjeon. FiBHP

He dwelt among "Apartments let." Jacob. Phoebe Cary. OBAL

He dyes/ his white hair black. The Compromise. Ibn al-Rumi, *tr. fr. Arabic by* Omar S. Pound. ArPe

He either fears his fate too much. The Touch. James Graham, Marquess of Montrose. *Fr.* My Dear and Only Love. BeJo; JCP; OtMeF

He Embarketh in the Boat of Ra. *Unknown, tr. fr. Egyptian by* Robert Hillyer. *Fr.* Book of the Dead. AWP

He ended, and they both descend the hill. Milton. *Fr.* Paradise Lost. EPCY; NAWM-1

(Adam Fallen.) NOCV

He ended; and thus Adam last replied. Milton. *Fr.* Paradise Lost. EPCY; HeIP

(Retreat from Paradise, The.) PoEL-3

He ended, nor the Argicide refus'd. Homer, *tr. by* William Cowper. *Fr.* Odyssey. NAWM-1; OBVE

He entered with the authority of politeness. The Southerner. Karl Shapiro. NYBP; PoNe

He Entereth the House of the Goddess Hathor. *Unknown, tr. fr. Egyptian by* Robert Hillyer. *Fr.* Book of the Dead. AWP

He escape the lynch days. He survives. Wole Soyinka. HBAPE

He Establisheth His Triumph. *Unknown, tr. fr. Egyptian by* Robert Hillyer. *Fr.* Book of the Dead. AWP

He Faces the Second Winter. Philip Levine. *Fr.* Sierra Kid. PoA

He fails who climbs to power and place. Failure and Success. Richard Watson Gilder. PWR

He feared angina from his thirtieth year. Angina. David Campbell. *Fr.* Starting from Central Station. FaBoMA

He feared money so much he was known. The Usual Immigrant Uncle Poem. Askold Melnyczuk. UTF

He fears, and flies from Marion's men. *(LL)* The Swamp Fox. William Gilmore Simms. BeLS; FaBoBe; PAH

He fed them generously who were his flocks. W. D. Snodgrass. Son

He feels small as he awakens. The Awakening. Robert Creeley. NeAP

He Fell among Thieves. Sir Henry Newbolt. EBVV; FaPoR; OBEV; OBWP; OxBTC

He fell for a beautiful. The Love of the Quartz Pebble. Vasco [*or Vasko*] Popa, *tr. fr. Serbo-Croatian. Fr.* Quartz Pebble, The. PoSu, *tr. by Anne Pennington*

He fell from the roof. News. Louis Dudek. *Fr. Provincetown.* MoCV

He fell in victory's fierce pursuit. The General Elliott. Robert Graves. PeLV

He felt the wild beast in him betweenwhiles. George Meredith. *Fr.* Modern Love. EnVR; NOBVV

He finds night day. (*LL*) The Two Spirits [an Allegory]. Shelley. CH; OAEL-2; Prf; WiR

He first deceased; she for a little tried. Upon the Death of Sir Albert [*or us*] Morton's Wife. Sir Henry Wotton. BoLoP; CoGr; EnLoPo; FaBoEE; GGP; NoP; OBD; OBEV; OxBM; SeCP; TrGrPo; WeW

He flew awa in a blazing flame. (*LL*) Riddles Wisely Expounded. *Unknown.* ESPB, 3 *vers.*; FaBoBa; GBP

He flies so easy, when he sings. (*LL*) Driving in Oklahoma. Carter Revard. HATNAP; VoR

He floated upwards, and regain'd the steep. (*LL*) The White Horse of Westbury. Charles Tennyson Turner. EBEV; PeVV

He floats down the Seine. Body Fished from the Seine. Gregory Corso. SM

He followed his own mind. *Unknown, tr. fr. Tlingit Indian by* James Koller. STP

He followed me up and he followed me down. Lady Isabel and the Elf Knight (Pretty Polly). *Unknown.* AmFP

He followed their lilting stanzas. A Local Poet. John Hewitt. PNI

He forgot why his lips moved, his body swayed. (*LL*) Tales of Shatz. Dannie Abse. OxBC

He found a formula for drawing comic rabbits. Epitaph on an Unfortunate Artist. Robert Graves. FaBoEE; NOBL

He found her by the ocean's moaning verge. George Meredith. *Fr.* Modern Love. EnVR; NoP; OAEL-2

He from the wind-bitten North with ship and companions descended. A Drifter off Tarentum. Kipling. *Fr.* Epitaphs of the War, 1914–1918. FaBoEE; NoP; NSI; OBWP; PeFWW; PoWW

He fumbles at your soul. Emily Dickinson. NAAL-1; NOCV; TRP (He fumbles at your spirit.) CBLP

He fumbles at your spirit. Emily Dickinson. *See* He fumbles at your soul.

He gave answers to questions they didn't ask. Dorothee Sölle. CrSp

He gave himself another year. Patrick Kavanagh. *Fr.* Great Hunger, The. BIrV

He gave his strength and his loveliness for his country. On a Soldier Killed in the Great War. R. Williams Parry, *tr. fr. Welsh by* H. Idris Bell. OBWVE

He gave joy to men & more joy. Krantor. Theaitetos, *tr. fr. Greek by* Dennis Schmitz. GrAn

He gave silver shoes to the rabbit. Blake Leads a Walk on the Milky Way. Nancy Willard. OBCA

He gave the solid rail a hateful kick. The Egg and the Machine. Robert Frost. MoAmPo

He gave us all a good-bye cheerily. Messmates. Sir Henry Newbolt. CH; EBVV; OHCV; PeVV

He gave us eyes to see them, And lips that we might tell, How great is God Almighty, Who has made all things well. (*LL*) All Things Bright and Beautiful. Cecil Frances Alexander. FaPoR; OHIP; OxBChV; PlP; TIRV; UV

He gives her a kick. (*LL*) Golden Pheasant. William Hart-Smith. NOBAu

He giveth his beloved-sleep. (*LL*) The Sleep. Elizabeth Barrett Browning. ChIV-1; OxAEP-2; WGRP

He Giveth More. Annie Johnson Flint. BLRP; WBLP

He goes regularly to the taverna. The Twenty-fifth Year of His Life. C. P. Cavafy, *tr. fr. Greek by* Edmund Keeley *and* Philip Sherrard. PeHV

He gossips like my grandmother, this man. The Cleaving. Li-Young Lee. NAmP90; OpBo

He got a rhythm in his wrist so quick. For Stephane Grappelli. Roger Mitchell. Jaz

He got his friends to agree to shoot him standing against a stone wall. David Ignatow. *Fr.* Leaving the Door Open. CAPP

He grappled with the lilac. Ivy. Liu Sha-ho, *tr. fr. Chinese. Fr.* Family of Plants, A. LHF, *tr. by* Hualing Nieh

He grew bored, my Ophion. Eurynome Banishes Ophion and Completes Creation. Erica Helm. *Fr.* Creation Songs of Eurynome, The. SRLS

He grew where waves ride nine feet high. In Memoriam: Roy Campbell. Ralph Nixon Currey. PeSA

He had a many-coloured glance like flowers. Edward James. *Fr.* Carmina Amico. PeHV

He had been coming a very long time. For Malcolm Who Walks in the Eyes of Our Children. Quincy Troupe. PoBA

He had been long t'wards Mathematicks. Portrait of Sidrophel. Samuel Butler. *Fr.* Hudibras. PoEL-3

He had done with fleets and squadrons, with the restless roaming seas. Admiral Dugout. Cicely Fox Smith. NSI

He had driven half the night. Hay for the Horses. Gary Snyder. CAPP; GrPl; NaP; TRP

He had drunk from founts of pleasure. Drawing Water. Phoebe Cary. AmWP

He had got, finally. A Poem for Speculative Hipsters. Amiri Baraka. NoAM; NOBA

He had just surrendered the secret of the sun. A Mat to Weave. Tchicaya U Tam'si, *tr. fr. French by* Ellen Conroy Kennedy. NegPo

He had need of a way. Being Somebody. Edwin Honig. TAP

He had no friend. About to Die. *Gond Oral Tradition, tr. by* V. Elwin *and* S. Hivale. WTO

He had no royal palace. A Christmas Verse. "Kay." BoTP

He had not looked. Denise Levertov. *Fr.* During the Eichmann Trial. BTR

He had not reckoned on a visitor. Death Was a Woman. Sydney King Russell. GoYe

He "Had Not Where to Lay His Head." Frances E. W. Harper. PWR

He had nothing to say. (*LL*) To Hell with Your Fertility Cult. Gary Snyder. NAs

He had only one tune. Yesterday Vivaldi Visited Me. Alison Brackenbury. SCBI

He had played for his lordship's levee. The Child-Musician. Austin Dobson. GN

He had red hair. A Boy Thirteen. Jeff Irish. DL

He had smiled at us. Maximus, to Gloucester, Letter 19. Charles Olson. *Fr.* Maximus Poems, The. CMoP

He had studied in private years ago. Artichoke. Henry Taylor. MT

He had the plowman's strength. Lost in France Jo's Requiem. Ernest Rhys. PAW

He had this idea about the hill. Jill, Afterwards. Philip Dacey. SM

He had to be four times cuckold. (*LL*) The Temperaments. Ezra Pound. BoLoP; ErPo; FaBoBl; MeMAP; NoAM; NOBA

He had worked out at Gold's Gym. The Stud. Fred Voss. NGP

He hadn't been right. Whitley at Three O'Clock. Jeff Worley. GOYP

He halted in the wind, and — what was that. A Boundless Moment. Robert Frost. NAAL-2

He hands/ down the gift. The Gift. Robert Creeley. NOBA

He hands them back when he sees they are done. (*LL*) The Toaster. William Jay Smith. GrPl; OTCP

He has an eye for cities. Among his rows. Lewis Mumford. George Buchanan. PNI

He has annihilated the enemies! War Song. *Zulu Oral Tradition, tr. by* D. K. Rycroft. WTO

He has built himself a cottage in the wood. A Cottage in the Wood. Russell Edson. LCAP

He has come back at last, the boy with the inky fingers. Self-Congratulatory Ode on Mr. Auden's Election to the Professorship of Poetry at Oxford. Ronald Mason. FaBoPa

He has come to report himself. The Missing Person. Donald Justice. CAPP; NYBP; Poetr

He has gone into the forest. Journey to the Interior. William Jay Smith. DiPo; PFL

He has hanged himself — the Sun. November. Frederick William Harvey. OxBTC

He has held. Perevin Muruvalar, *tr. fr. Tamil by* A. K. Ramanujan. PLW

He has lain here for a terrible, motionless. Woody Gurthie Visited by Bob Dylan: Brooklyn State Hospital, New York, 1961. David Wojahn. *Fr.* Mystery Train: A Sequence. PBCAP

He has never heard of tides. German Shepherd. Myra Cohn Livingston. RFM

He has not woo'd, but he has lost his heart. A Country Dance. Charles Tennyson Turner. NOBVV

He has observed the golden rule. Blake. *Fr.* Gnomic Verses. TrGrPo

He has only to pass by a tree moodily walking head down. The Fiend. James Dickey. PPP

He has opened all his parcels. The Hippopotamus's Birthday. Emile Victor Rieu. Mes

He has solved it — Life's wonderful problem. Laurels and Immortelles. *Unknown.* BLPA

He has some crack for everyone. Bus Driver. Linda France. NWP

He has the sign. Portrait of Malcolm X. Etheridge Knight. PoBA

He has three singles on the charts and in. Tattoo, Corazon: Ritchie Valens, 1959. David Wojahn. *Fr.* Mystery Train: A Sequence. PBCAP

He hasn't gone to work. The Poem Circling Hamtramck, Michigan All Night in Search of You. Philip Levine. NNaP

He hasn't got a ticket. A Ticket. Bei Dao, tr. fr. Chinese by Donald Finkel with Chen Xueliang. SpMi

He Hath Need of Rest. Josephine D. Henderson Heard. CBWP-4

He Hath No Parallel. Sadi, tr. by L. Cranmer-Byng. Fr. Gulistan, The. AWP

He hath no place to rest his head. Judaeus Errans. Louis Golding. TrJP

He hears it not now, but used to notice such things? (LL) Afterwards. Thomas Hardy. BoNaP; CH; ChTr; CMoP; CoGr; EBEV; FaBoRV; GTBS-P; InPS; LiTB; LiTM; MeMBP; MoAB; MoBrPo; NoBE; NoP; OAEL-2; OBNC; OtMeF; OxAEP-2; PoEL-5; TFi; TOF; TrGrPo

He Hears the Bugle at Killarney. Tennyson. See Splendor falls on castle walls, The.

He Hears the Cry of the Sedge. W. B. Yeats. OxBTC; RB

He hears the summer at a distance. Vanishing Point. Peter Cooley. AmPA

He Held Radical Light. A. R. Ammons. CAPP; PoE; VCAP

He Hides within the Lily. William Channing Gannett. AH

He hie fie finger. The Man. Robert Creeley. OBAL

He Hola. Keri Hulme. PeNZ

He Holdeth Fast to the Memory of His Identity. Unknown, tr. fr. Egyptian by Robert Hillyer. Fr. Book of the Dead. AWP

He hones his knife. Slap in the Face. Tien Ch'ien, tr. fr. Chinese. LHF, tr. by Hualing Nieh

He hoped to write one good line; died believing in God. (LL) A Funeral Oration. David Wright. PeSAV

He imagines her. Hugh Seidman. Fr. Modes of Vallejo Street, San Diego, Los Angeles, The. UnPo

He in Christ's doctrine deals by way of trade. Portrait of a Bishop. Evan Lloyd. AngWe

He Intercedes with Charlemagne for His Brother in Exile. Paul the Deacon, tr. fr. Latin by Helen Waddell. MLL

He invented a rainbow but lightning struck it. Bushed. Earle Birney. MoCV; NoAM; NOBC; NoP

He is 25, it is the last day. Kathleen Jamie. Fr. Katie's Poems. PWE

He is a bad sleeper and it is a joy to me. A Bad Sleeper. Paul Verlaine, tr. fr. French by François Pirou. PeHV

He is a friendly TOAD. (LL) A Friend in the Garden. Juliana Horatia Ewing. BoTP; FaPON; OxBChV

He is a leopard — he bought himself in a shop. (LL) Leopard Skin. Douglas Stewart. NOBAu

He is a parricide to his mother's name. In Praise of Women in General. Thomas Randolph. NOSC

He is a path, if any be misled. Excellency of Christ. Giles Fletcher the Younger. Fr. Christ's Victory and Triumph. WGRP

He is a tower unleaning. But how will he not break. Vaunting Oak. John Crowe Ransom. OxBA; VGW

He is a young knight from the south of Han-tan. Youth of Han-tan, The; a Song. Kao Shih, tr. fr. Chinese by Joseph J. Lee. SuSp

He is almost a god, a man beside you. Sappho, tr. fr. Greek by Sam Hamill. InMo

He is always right. The Interrogator. Elizabeth Jennings. WPE

He is an Englishman! The Englishman. W. S. Gilbert. Fr. H. M. S. Pinafore. NOBL

He is an inharmonious note. Sir Roger Casement. TIRV

He is an utter failure as a devil. A Devil. Zbigniew Herbert, tr. fr. Polish by Czeslaw Milosz. RB

He is beautiful and still. He May Be a Photograph of Himself. Tina Reid. AIW

He is coming, Adzed-Head. Unknown. NOIV

He is coming, my long-desired lord. The River of Heaven. Unknown, tr. by Lafcadio Hearn. Fr. Manyo Shu, Part 3 of 4. AWP

He is daily with us, loving, loving, loving. "Daily with You." Annie Johnson Flint. BLRP

He is dangerous even though asleep and unarmed. (LL) He. John Ashbery. CBNP; SOTW

He is dead, the beautiful youth. Killed at the Ford. Longfellow. OHIP

He is Declared True of Word. Unknown, tr. fr. Egyptian by Robert Hillyer. Fr. Book of the Dead. AWP

He is destined at last to meet. (LL) White Gloves. William Plomer. PeSAV

He Is Far. Unknown. See Were it undo that is ido [or y-do].

He is firm and strong. Oriki Erinle. Unknown, tr. fr. Yoruba by Ulli Beier. PBA; TTY

He is from those mountains. What She Said ("He is from those mountains.") Kapilar, tr. fr. Tamil by A. K. Ramanujan. PLW

He Is Gone. Anna Swirszczynska, tr. fr. Polish by Czeslaw Milosz and Leonard Nathan. PoSu

He is gone on the mountain. Coronach. Sir Walter Scott. Fr. Lady of the Lake, The. CH; EnRP; GTBS; GTBS-P; OHIP; OxAEP-2; SCGP; TrGrPo; WiR

He is having his hair cut. Towels are tucked. Alex at the Barber's. John Fuller. PeLV

He is knit with his doom. (LL) Exiles. "Æ." BIrV; MoBrPo

He is knit with his doom. (LL) Germinal. "Æ." BIrV; MoBrPo; OBEV; OBMV

He is less than Lu who married Never Grieve. (LL) Ma-wei. Li Shang-yin. PLT

He is like a cloud that for an instant. Jacqueline Osherow. UTF

He Is like the Lotus. Unknown, tr. fr. Egyptian by Robert Hillyer. Fr. Book of the Dead. AWP

He Is like the Serpent Saka. Unknown, tr. fr. Egyptian by Robert Hillyer. Fr. Book of the Dead. AWP

He is made one with Nature; there is heard. Shelley. Fr. Adonais; an Elegy on the Death of John Keats. EBEV; EnRP; EPCY; FHYEP; HoPM; ImPo; MeMBP; NoP; OAEL-2; PoEL-4; TrGrPo; WGRP

He is making love with his wife on the roof. The Roof of the World. Michael Dennis Browne. AmPA

He is more than a hero. Sappho, tr. fr. Greek by Mary Barnard. PBWP; VBLP

He is murdered upright in the day. Vaticide. Myron O'Higgins. PoBA

He Is My Countryman. Antoni Slonimski, tr. fr. Polish by Frances Notley. TrJP

He is my love/ my sweet nutgrove. Unknown, tr. fr. Irish by Michael Hartnett. BIrV

He is no friend who in thine hour of pride. Friendship. Sadi, tr. by L. Cranmer-Byng. Fr. Gulistan, The. AWP

He is no one I really know. Piccola Commedia. Richard Wilbur. PRA

He is not a brother to me. The Brother. Semion Y. Nadson, tr. fr. Russian by H. Badanes. TrJP

He Is Not Dead. James Whitcomb Riley. See I cannot say, and I will not say.

He is not dead — he is just away. (LL) Away. James Whitcomb Riley. BLRP; WGRP

He is not dead nor liveth. Dorothy Wellesley. Fr. Deserted House. OBMV

He is not ded that somtyme hath a fall. Sir Thomas Wyatt. AAS; OBVE

He is not here, the old sun. No Possum, No Sop, No Taters. Wallace Stevens. HCAP; MeMAP; OxBA; TAP; VGW

He is not John, the gardener. A Friend in the Garden. Juliana Horatia Ewing. BoTP; FaPON; OxBChV

He is now at rest. Samuel Rogers. Fr. Italy. EPCY; OBNC

He is old, two weeks to eighty. Blue Sparks in Dark Closets. Richard Snyder. Poetsp

He is older than the naval side of British history. Chief Petty Officer. Charles Causley. OxBTC

He is one of the prophets come back. He. Lawrence Ferlinghetti. NeAP; PoM

He is only beautiful. Aborigine. Hugo Williams. OBTV

He Is Out of Heart with His Time. Guerzo di Montecanti, tr. fr. Italian by Dante Gabriel Rossetti. AWP

He is patient. Obatala, the Creator. Yoruba Oral Tradition, tr. by Ulli Beier. WTO

He is quick, thinking in clear images. In Broken Images. Robert Graves. TRP

He is repulsed indeed — but you are [you're] undone. (LL) To the Noblest and Best of Ladies, the Countess of Denbigh. Richard Crashaw. GeHe; JCP; MeLP

He is risen now that was so long asleep. War. Georg Heym, tr. fr. German by Patrick Bridgwater. PeFWW

He is rust/ in moonlight. Coyote Fragments. Lance Henson. HATNAP

He is sherrier. The Thinnest Shadow. John Ashbery. TTTS

He is sleeping, soundly sleeping. A "Departed Friend." Julia A. Moore. FiBHP

He is stark mad, who ever says. The Broken Heart. John Donne. EBEV

He, is the Great God, Who is in heaven. Great Hymm. Ntsikana Gaba, tr. fr. Xhosa by John Knox Bokwe. PeSAV

He is the King amang us three! (LL) Willie Brew'd [or Brewed] a Peck o' Maut. Burns. AWP; EnRP; OxBS

He Is the Lonely Greatness. Madeleine Caron Rock. CH

He is the oldest grandfather. The Memory Sire. Barney Bush. HATNAP

He is the one who waves. (LL) Salt Water Story. Richard Hugo. NAAL-2; NoAM; NoP

He is the pond's old father, its brain. The Snapper. William Heyen. AmPA

He is to weet a melancholy carle. A Portrait. Keats. BXAP (Stanzas on Charles Armitage Brown.) UV

He is trying to write down a book he wrote years ago in his head. South America. Tom Raworth. NBrP

He is up on a roof with the sun. Man on a Roof. George Charlton. PWE

He is very busy with his looking. Young Heroes. Gwendolyn Brooks. BPo

He is walking in the road. Conceited Man. *Gond Oral Tradition*, tr. by V. Elwin *and* S. Hivale. WTO

He is wasted now. Dylan, Who Is Dead. Samuel Allen. PoBA

He isn't a religious man. The People Next Door. Louis Simpson. BAP-89

He isn't all Indian. Our Hired Man (And His Daughter, Too). Monica Shannon. FaPON

He it is, the innermost one, who awakens my being with his deep hidden touches. Rabindranath Tagore. *Fr.* Gitanjali. WGRP

He jangles his keys in the rain. The Ram. Selima Hill. FaBoBl; NBrP; VBLP

He jests at scars [that never felt a wound]. Shakespeare. *Fr.* Romeo and Juliet. EBEvV; ImPo; LiTB

(Living Juliet, The.) TrGrPo, II, i

He journeys over the dark land. St Sava's Journey. Vasco [*or* Vasko] Popa, *tr. fr. Serbo-Croatian. Fr.* St Sava's Spring. PoSu, *tr. by* Anne Pennington

He jumped me while I was asleep. Assailant. John Raven. BPo

He jumped, seeing an island like a hand. Hart Crane. Julian Symons. PoA

He keeps the photos in his briefcase. Touching Up. Janet Fisher. NWP

He Kept On Burning. Ai. AnAn

Sels.
Buchenwald, 1945.
Peru, 1955.
Spain, 1929.

He [*or* When he] killed the noble Mudjokivis. The Modern Hiawatha. George A. Strong. *Fr.* Song of Milkanwatha, The. FaBoCo; FaBoPa; FaPON; FiBHP; MoShBr; PeLV; UV

(Hiawatha Revisited.) BXAP

(When he killed the Mudjokivis.) EBEvV

He Kindleth a Fire. *Unknown, tr. fr. Egyptian by* Robert Hillyer. *Fr.* Book of the Dead. AWP

He kindly trains us to endure. (*LL*) The Angel of Patience. Whittier. WGRP

He knelt, the Savior knelt and prayed. The Agony in the Garden. Felicia Dorothea Hemans. TrCP

He knew how death hunts/ at distance. Epitaph: Atticus. Paulus Silentiarius, *tr. fr. Greek by* Andrew Miller. GrAn

He knew it was waiting for him somewhere. My Father's Death. Constance Urdang. PBCAP

He knew nothing about death. Nani Worries about Her Father's Happiness in the Afterlife. Ana Castillo. AfAz

He knew what I wanted. O Dirty Bird Yr Gizzard's Too Big & Full of Sand. James Koller. PoM

He Knoweth Not That the Dead Are Thine. Mary Elizabeth Coleridge. OBNC

He Knoweth the Souls of the East. *Unknown, tr. fr. Egyptian by* Robert Hillyer. *Fr.* Book of the Dead. AWP

He Knoweth the Souls of the West. *Unknown, tr. fr. Egyptian by* Robert Hillyer. *Fr.* Book of the Dead. AWP

He knows he must explain this. Hugh Seidman. *Fr.* Modes of Vallejo Street, San Diego, Los Angeles, The. UnPo

He knows the depths of smokestacks. Survivor. Florence Weinberger. BTR

He larved ond he larved on he merd such a nauses. The Ondt and the Gracehoper. James Joyce. *Fr.* Finnegans Wake. BIrV

He lay, and those who watched him were amazed. The Sprig of Lime. Robert Nichols. GTBS-P

He lay in the middle of the world, and twitcht. John Berryman. *Fr.* Dream Songs. HCAP; NoP; PoE

He lay on the couch night after night. Saturn. Sharon Olds. RaBo

He lay on the floor covered in shit. 999 Call. Elizabeth Bartlett. FaBoWP

He lay with quiet heart in the stern asleep. Prayer at Night. Alcuin, *tr. fr. Latin by* Helen Waddell. MLL

He Leadeth Me. Joseph Henry Gilmore. AH; BLRP; WBLP; WGRP

He Leadeth Me. *Unknown*. BLRP

He leads us on. Through the Maze. *Unknown*. BLRP

He Leads Us Still. Arthur Guiterman. OHIP

He leans over his beer, elbows on knees. Kathleen Jamie. *Fr.* Katie's Poems. PWE

He left his pants upon a chair. The Mistake. Theodore Roethke. *Fr.* Three Epigrams. NBLV

He left the office where he'd been given. He Asked about the Quality. C. P. Cavafy, *tr. fr. Greek by* Edmund Keeley *and* Philip Sherrard. PeHV

He lies/ Beside me. On Death and Love. Janet Campbell Hale. VoR

He lies low in the levelled sand. At the Grave of Walker. Joaquin Miller. AnAmPo

He lifted a drop of ambrosia. Ambrosia. William Hart-Smith. FaBoMA

He lifted up, among the actuaries. So Long? Stevens. John Berryman. *Fr.* Dream Songs. HAP; HCAP; NOBA

He lifts his small hands. Mantis. Ruth Miller. PeSAV

He lifts the heavy tube. The Elk Uncovers the Heavens. John Bensko. MT

He lighted with his golden lamp on high. Walter Savage Landor. *Fr.* Shakespeare. EPCY

He Liked the Dead. Malcolm Lowry. OxBTC

He liked to watch the big cats. Letting the Puma Go. Stephen Dunn. BAP-89

He listened at the porch that day. A Year's Spinning. Elizabeth Barrett Browning. NAEL-2

He Lived a Life., *sels.* H. N. Fifer.
"What was his creed?" PoToHe

He Lived amidst th' Untrodden Ways. Hartley Coleridge. FaBoCo; UV

He lived at Dingle Bank — he did. Dingle Bank. Edward Lear. FaBoNo

He lived in a small farmhouse. A Refusal to Mourn. Derek Mahon. PNI

He lives—he then unties the string. (*LL*) Warning to Children. Robert Graves. CBNP; FaBoCh; MeMBP; NoP; NTP; OAEL-2

He lives in my garden. The Dragon. Vuyelwa Carlin. NWP

He lives in the outer land. Blood Marksman and Kureldei the Marksman. *Tatar (Turkic) Oral Tradition*. WTO

He lives in the sky. The Eagle above Us. Santiago Altamirano, Willard R. Trask (OBAP). OBAP; STP

He Lives Long Who Lives Well. Thomas Randolph. WBLP

He lives on edge throughout his days. Hare. Molly Holden. TEP

He lives, who last night flopped from a log. Burning. Galway Kinnell. CoAP

He liveth long who liveth well. Length of Days. Horatius Bonar. PWR

He loathed the fraud, yet would not be alone. (*LL*) Ulysses. Robert Graves. CBLP; CMoP; FaBoTw; MoP; NoAM; PrIm

He lolls in the supermarket. Portrait of a House Detective. Hans Magnus Enzensberger. PoSu

He looked about six or seven, only much too thin. The Forgiveness Dream; Man from the Warsaw Ghetto. Jean Valentine. LCAP

He looked at my face but he was looking at my skull. (*LL*) Portrait: The Freedom Fighter. George Jonas. NOBC

He looked out the window when he asked. Geography Lesson. Christine McNeill. NWP

He looks back at me. The Guerrilla-Cong. Michael S. Harper. NBV

He looks back over the last metaphor. The Great Artist Reconsiders the Homeric Simile. John Tranter. NoAM; NOBAu

He looks down to watch the river twist. Gargoyle. Thomas Rabbitt. MT

He looks like a fat little old man. Dead Seal. Alfred W. Purdy. MoCV; MoP

He look't [*or* looked] and saw what numbers numberless. The Parthians. Milton. *Fr.* Paradise Regained [*or* Regain'd].
(Parthian Powers.) NOSC, *Bk.* III, *ll.* 310–43

He loved America all his life! (*LL*) Washington. Nancy Byrd Turner. FaPON

He loved her and she loved him. Ted Hughes. LPA

He loved his cabin: there. Salt Water Story. Richard Hugo. NAAL-2; NoAM; NoP

He loved the brook's soft sound. The Peasant Poet. John Clare. FHYEP; OAEL-2; OBNC; WGRP

He loved three things in life. "Anna Akhmatova," *tr. fr. Russian by* Barbara Einzig. BoWoP
(He Loved Three Things.) RaBo, *tr. by* Jerome Bullitt
(He loved three things.) RaBo, *tr. by* Jerome Bullitt

He Loves. David Schirmer, *tr. fr. German by* George C. Schoolfield. GePo

He Loves and He Rides Away. Sydney Thompson Dobell. OBNC

He Loves in Vain. Christian Hofmann von Hofmannswaldau, *tr. fr. German by* George C. Schoolfield. GePo

He loves it when the lawyer shouts. Watching TV, the Elk Bones Up on Metaphysics. John Bensko. MT

He loves me. *Unknown*. OxNR

He lying spilt like water from a bowl. Alison Boodson. ErPo

He made peace with eternity. Second-Class Citizen. Slavko Mihalic, *tr. by* Charles Simic. PoSu

He makes me feel bright by comparison. (*LL*) Limericks and Puns. *Unknown*. PeLi

He Maketh Himself One with Osiris. *Unknown, tr. fr. Egyptian by* Robert Hillyer. *Fr.* Book of the Dead. AWP

He Maketh Himself One with the God Ra. *Unknown, tr. by* Robert Hillyer. *Fr.* Book of the Dead. AWP

He Maketh Himself One with the Only God, Whose Limbs Are the Many Gods. *Unknown, tr. fr. Egyptian by Robert Hillyer. Fr.* Book of the Dead. AWP

He making speedy way through spersed ayre. Spenser. *Fr.* Faerie Queene, The. NoSic

He-man, the sea-man, The. Pickup in Tony's Hashhouse. Kenneth Pitchford. *Fr.* Good for Nothing Man. ErPo

He May Be a Photograph of Himself. Tina Reid. AIW

He may be six kinds of a liar. Loyalty. Berton Braley. BLPA

He may express Whose badge he wears. *(LL)* A Dedication of My First Son. Mildmay Fane, 2d Earl of Westmorland. BeJo

He Measured Out His Spirit Tower. Shih Ching, *tr. fr. Chinese by* Heng Kuan. SuSp

He Meditates on the Life of a Rich Man. Douglas Hyde, *tr. fr. Irish by* Lady Augusta Gregory. OBMV

He meets, by heavenly chance express. The Lover. Coventry Patmore. *Fr.* Angel in the House, The. OxAEP-2

He met a lady. From the Hazel Bough. Earle Birney. HeIP

He met his death in a foreign land. The Forgotten One (A Ballad). Count Arsenii Arkadyevich Golenishchev-Kutuzov, *tr. fr. Russian by* Philip L. Miller. *Fr.* Songs and Dances of Death. RiWo

He might happen to take thee for one, my dear. *(LL)* The Young May Moon. Thomas Moore. ELP; EnRP; OBEV; PeLV

He motions me over with a question. Kidnaper. Tess Gallagher. AmPA (Kidnapper.) AnAn

He must be dead first! Let it alone, for me. *(LL)* An Epitaph on Dr. Donne, Dean of Paul's. Richard Corbett [*or* Corbet]. BeJo; EPCY

He must be hardly twenty-two. And yet. The Next Table. C. P. Cavafy, *tr. fr. Greek by* John Mavrogordato. PeHV

He must himself a weeder turn. *(LL)* Man Leaves the Batch. Mildmay Fane, 2d Earl of Westmorland. BeJo

He Na Tye Woman. Paula Gunn Allen. SRLS

He needs no foil, but shines by his own proper light. *(LL)* The Character of a Good Parson. Dryden. NOCV

He needs you. Dorothee Sölle. *Fr.* When He Came. CrSp

He never acted well by man or woman. George IV. Thackeray. *Fr.* Georges, The. FaBoEE

He never brings them once to th' push of pikes. *(LL)* Good Men Afflicted Most. Robert Herrick. LiTB

He Never Did That to Me. Noël Coward. NBLV

He Never Expected Much. Thomas Hardy. NAEL-2; NAs; NoAM; OxBTC; SCV

He never felt twice the same about the flecked river. This Solitude of Cataracts. Wallace Stevens. LCAP

He never has been living since! *(LL)* The Guinea-Pig. *Unknown.*

He never lives to tell. Calenture. Alastair Reid. NYBP; PrIm

He never made the dive — not while I watched. The Springboard. Louis MacNeice. PoA

He never spoke a word to me. Simon the Cyrenian Speaks. Countee Cullen. BPo; ChIV-2; HAP; MoAmPo; TrCP; TTY

He nice frum far, but far frum nice. Vicious Circle. Marsha Prescod. VBLP

He no longer wears a plait. Changes. Sally Cline. VBLP

He nothing common did or mean. King Charles on [*or* upon] the Scaffold. Andrew Marvell. *Fr.* Horatian Ode upon Cromwell's [*or* Cromwel's] Return from Ireland, An. ChTr; EBEV; ESCV; FaBoRV; GeHe; GTBS; GTBS-P; HAP; IIP; InPS; JCP; NOBE; NoP; NOSC; OAEL-1; OBEV; OBWP; OxAEP-1; PoEL-2; SCGP; SeCP; SeCV-1; TFi

He, of his gentleness. In the Wilderness. Robert Graves. CH; MoAB; MoBrPo; PeECV

He offers, between planes. Conversation with a Fireman from Brooklyn. Tess Gallagher. CrSp

He often came and stood outside my door. The Lonely Dog. Margaret E. Bruner. PoToHe

He often would ask us. The Choirmaster's Burial. Thomas Hardy. PeECV

He once did love with fond affection. Forsaken. *Unknown.* AmFP

He only happy is, and wise. How to Ride Out a Storm. Mildmay Fane, 2d Earl of Westmorland. NOSC

He only knew of death what all men may. The Death of the Beloved. Rainer Maria Rilke, *tr. fr. German by* J. B. Leishman. OBD

He opened the car door. There was a low rumble. The Meeting. Nicki Jackowska. BrRo

He opens his eyes with a cry of delight. A Child's Christmas Day. *Unknown.* OBCP

He ordered the poor to build castles. *Unknown.* FaBoEH

He Overcometh the Serpent of Evil in the Name of Ra. *Unknown, tr. fr. Egyptian by* Robert Hillyer. *Fr.* Book of the Dead. AWP

He Paid Me Seven. *Unknown.* BPo

He paints the sand when a tide has gone. Sketch from the Great Bull Wall. Sebastian Barry. IB

He paused on the sill of a door ajar. The Newcomer's Wife. Thomas Hardy. BoLoP; OxBTC

He Perceives His Rashness in Love, but Has No Choice. Guido Guinicelli, *tr. fr. Italian by* Dante Gabriel Rossetti. AWP

He perishes toward Hercules. *(LL)* This Dim and Ptolemaic Man. John Peale Bishop. LiTA; LiTM

He picked up. The Bee Dice Game. Paule Barton, *tr. fr. Creole by* Howard Norman. PRA

He picks up in his hands things that don't match — a stone. Approximately. Yannis Ritsos, *tr. fr. Greek by* Nikos Stangos. CBCK

He picks up what he thinks is/ a road map. My Father; October 1942. William Stafford. CAPP; NaP

He planked down sixpence and he took his drink. Henry Turnbull. W. W. Gibson. FaBoTw

He played by the river when he was young. Washington. Nancy Byrd Turner. FaPON

He Praises the Trees. *Unknown, tr. fr. Irish by* Robin Skelton. BIrV

He prayed for patience; Care and Sorrow came. His Answer. Clara Ann Thompson. BlSi; CBWP-2

He Prayeth Best. Samuel Taylor Coleridge. *Fr.* Rime of the Ancient Mariner, The. BeLS; CH; EBEV; EBNV; EnRP; FaBoBe; FaBoCh; FaBV; FaPoB; FaPON; FHYEP; HAP; HeIP; HoPM; ImPo; InPS; LiTB; MeMBP; NOBE; NoP; OAEL-2; OBEV; OBNC; OBNV; OtMeF; OxAEP-2; PeECV; PoE; PoEL-4; PrIm; SCGP; TEP; TFi; TOF, *abr.*; TrGrPo

He Prayeth for Ink and Palette That He May Write. *Unknown, tr. fr. Egyptian by* Robert Hillyer. *Fr.* Book of the Dead. AWP

He Prayeth Well. Samuel Taylor Coleridge. *See* He Prayeth Best.

He preached upon "Breadth" till it argued him narrow. Emily Dickinson. AmPP; NAWM-2; NOCV

He preaches to the crowd that power is lent. Vox Populi. Dryden. *Fr.* Medal [*or* Medall], The. NOBE

He preferr'd Hanover to England. George I — Star of Brunswick. Thackeray. *Fr.* Georges, The. FaBoEE; FaBoEH

He prefers the dawn audience to her scented bed. *(LL)* Her Beauty Is Hidden. Li Shang-yin. OHMPC

He pried from the insect jaws the bright crumb of steel. *(LL)* Metropolitan Nightmare. Stephen Vincent Benét. NYBP

He prophesies across my years. *(LL)* Firebell for Peace. Joyce Lee. NOBAu

He pumps her up, po-faced, his right leg rising. Making Love to Marilyn Monroe. Paul Groves. FaBoBl

He pushes behind the words. Waiting. Robert Creeley. VGW

He put away his tiny pipe. Spring Cricket. Frances Rodman. FaPON

He put down his pen. Lamento. Tomas Tranströmer, *tr. fr. Swedish.* TSaS, *tr. by* May Swenson *with* Leif Sjoberg

He put his acorn helmet on. A Fairy in Armor. Joseph Rodman Drake. *Fr.* Culprit Fay, The. FaPON (Elfin Knight, An.) BoTP

He put the belt around my life. Emily Dickinson. TRP

He puts four dimes into the slot. Vending Machine. Hans Magnus Enzensberger. PoSu

He Puts Me to Rest. David Ignatow. VGW

He quickly arms him for the field. Pigwiggin Arms Himself. Michael Drayton. *Fr.* Nymphidia. MoShBr (Arming of Pigwiggen, The.) GN

He quotes the Scripture and eats hares.' *(LL)* A Case at Sessions. Walter Savage Landor. OBSV

He rais'd no Money, for he paid in land. Daniel Defoe. *Fr.* True-born Englishman, The. APAS; FaBoEH

He Raise a Poor Lazarus. *Unknown.* AH

He raised his sword. Happily Ever After, from the Story of the Same Name. Janet Dubé. DT

He ran a good shop, and he died. The Greengrocer. Michael Longley. *Fr.* Wreaths. BiHa

He ran the course and as he ran he grew. Innocence. Thom Gunn. LiTM

He rattled like a drum. *(LL)* I had a little brother. *Unknown.* RoPo

He reaches Weymouthtreads the Esplanade. The Royal Tour. "Peter Pindar." OxBoLi; PeLV

He Remembers Forgotten Beauty. W. B. Yeats. CTC

He Remembers How He Didn't Understand What Lieutenant Dawson Meant. James Whitehead. MT

He Remembers Something from the War. James Whitehead. ArOW

He Resigns. John Berryman. OxBSP; SM; WeW

He Resolves to Say No More. Thomas Hardy. TEP

He rested in the cool, that traveller. The African Tramp. Geoffrey Haresnape. PeSA

He Revisits Cambridge. Tennyson. *See* I past [*or* passed] beside the reverend walls.

He rides about the ranks, and strives t'inspire. Richard III's Speech. Sir John Beaumont. *Fr.* Bosworth Field. JCP

He rides at their head. The College Colonel. Herman Melville. OBWP

He rises and begins to round. The Lark Ascending. George Meredith. WiR

He riseth up early in the morning. The Mighty Hunter. J. B. Worley. PoLF

He roars in the swamp. The Alligator. Beatrice Ravenel. WPE

He rode a white horse. Colonel. Kate Llewellyn. NOBAu

He rode forth armed: breast-plate and crest. A Romance. Chester Kallman. PoA

He rode into town upon a wild-eyed mountain horse. Yellowjacket. Peter Blue Cloud. HATNAP

He rose at dawn and, fired with hope. The Sailor Boy. Tennyson. SCGP

He rose the morrow morn. *(LL)* The Rime of the Ancient Mariner. Samuel Taylor Coleridge. BeLS; CH; EBEV; EBNV; EnRP; FaBoBe; FaBoCh; FaPoB; FHYEP; HAP; HeIP; HoPM; ImPo; InPS; LiTB; MeMBP; NOBE; NoP; OAEL-2; OBEV; OBNC; OBNV; OtMeF; OxAEP-2; PeECV; PoE; PoEL-4; PrIm; SCGP; TEP; TFi; TOF, *abr.*; TrGrPo

He rose up on his dying bed. Hope. Langston Hughes. OBAL

He rubbed his eyes and wound the silver horn. Little Boy Blue. John Crowe Ransom. LiTM

He runs before the wise men: He. He. Stanley Kunitz. VGW

He runs into an Old Acquaintance. Alden Nowlan. GOYP

He runs like the rough satyr Sun. *(LL)* Country Dance. Edith Sitwell. MoP; NoAM

He Said. Jean Valentine. TAP

He said:/ "Let's stay here." Party Piece. Brian Patten. BoLoP

He said: "Darling, I pay through the nose." *(LL)* There was a young man of Montrose. Arnold Bennett. FaBoNo; OxBoLi; PeLi

He said, "Good-night, my heart is light." Premonition. Richard Hovey. AnAmPo

He said. He said, *Now. (LL)* First Practice. Gary Gildner. AmPA; PBCAP

He said he would be back and we'd drink wine together. Waiting for Icarus. Muriel Rukeyser. LCAP; NNaP

He said — (I only give the heads) — he said. Byron. *Fr.* Vision of Judgment, The. EnRP; EPCY; OAEL-2; TEP

He Said: "If in His Image I Was Made." Trumbull Stickney. LiTA

He said: "Last night I dreamed." The Hair. Pierre Louÿs, *tr. fr. French by* Philip L. Miller. RiWo

He said, then calmly died. *(LL)* The Cherokee. Mary Weston Fordham. AmWP; CBWP-2

He said to them, Look at this: you see. The Tall Wind. K. O. Arvidson. PeNZ

He said, unreal the buffalo is standing. Unreal the Buffalo Is Standing. *Unknown.* GOA

He sang in another room. Montecastelli Poem. Sophie Behrens. NBrP

He sang of joy; whate'er he knew of sadness. A Hero. Florence Earle Coates. OHIP

He sang of life, serenely sweet. The Poet. Paul Laurence Dunbar. AAP; BPo

He sat alone upon an ash-heap by. Love. Nicholas Moore. ErPo

He sat at the Algonquin, smoking a cigar. At the Algonquin. Howard Moss. Poetsp

He sat at the dinner table. Just like a Man. *Unknown.* BoTP

He sat by a fire of seven-fold heat. The Refiner's Fire. *Unknown.* BLRP

He sat in a wheeled chair, waiting for dark. Disabled. Wilfred Owen. CMoP; FF; InPS; LiTM; MeMBP; MoP; NAEL-2; NoAM; NSI; OBWVE; OxBTC; PeFWW; SCGP

He sat in his cell staring. The Baboon. Rhydwen Williams, *tr. fr. Welsh by* R. Gerallt Jones. OBWVE

He sat up slowly, and around his left side. Lazarus. Agnes Nemes Nagy, *tr. fr. Hungarian by* Frederic Will. PoSu

He sat upon the rolling deck. Sailor. Langston Hughes. PoA

He saw a face swollen beyond ugliness. What the Intern Saw. Phillis Levin. PFL

He saw, abandoned to the sand. The Trail beside the River Platte. William Heyen. GOA

He saw in every palm-leaf something new. On the Flesh of Christ. John William Corrington. MT

He saw it clearly and clairvoyant bright. Blueprint. D. B. Steinman. GoYe

He saw the rope, the moving mob. The Lynching. Dorothea Matthews. ShDr

He saw the skull within the looping. Epitaph for a Scientist. Lex Banning. NOBAu

He saw the sun, the Light-giver, step down behind the oak. The Ballad of the Homing Man. Ernest Rhys. AngWe

He saw thee Lord of all his creatures stand. *(LL)* The Created. Jones Very. NOCV

He saw again, "Good fences make good neighbors." *(LL)* Mending Wall. Robert Frost. AmPP; AnAmPo; ClHu; CMoP; CoGr; EBEvV; FaBoPV; FaBV; HAP; HeIP; HoPM; ImGa; InPS; LiTA; LiTM; MeMAP; MoAB; MoAmPo; MoP; NAAL-2; NoAM; NOBA; NoP; OtMeF; OxBA; PoE; Poetr; PrIm; SAmP; SCV; SoSe; TAP; TFi; VGW; WeW

He says he doesn't feel like working today. My Erotic Double. John Ashbery. LCAP; PoE; VCAP

He says, "How do you do?" *(LL)* Manners. Mariana Griswold van Rensselaer. FaPON

He says it to the young couple. No More Kissing — AIDS Everywhere. Michael C. Blumenthal. PFL

He says *my reign is in peace,* so slays. A Foreign Ruler. Walter Savage Landor. OBSV

He says the waves in the ship's wake. Leaving Forever. Denise Levertov. InPK

He says when he comes in a bar. Meeting My Best Friend from the Eighth Grade. Gary Gildner. SM

He scanned it, staggered, dropped the loop. Emily Dickinson. OBD; PoEL-5

He scans the world with calm and fearless eyes. The New Negro. James Edward McCall. CDC

He scarce had ceas't [or ceased] when the superior fiend. Milton. *Fr.* Paradise Lost. EPCY
(Satan and the Fallen Angels.) LiTB; 09OBS
(Satan's Summons.) NOSC, *bk.* I, *ll.* 283–313

He scattered tarantulas over the roads. The Devil in Texas. *Unknown.* NBLV; RB

He scorned his land, his tongue denied. Dic Siôn Dayfydd. Thomas Jacob Thomas, *tr. fr. Welsh by* H. Idris Bell. OBWVE

He scribbles some in prose and verse. Dilettante, The: A Modern Type. Paul Laurence Dunbar. AnAmPo

He seeks a manner cleanly lean and spare. The Colonist. Robert Wells. SCBI

He seemed to know the harbour. The Shark. E. J. Pratt. NOBC; OBAP

He Sees His Beloved. James I, King of Scotland. *Fr.* Kingis Quair, The. PoEL-1

He sees them pass. Once. Eric N. Batterham. CH

He sees through stone. *(LL)* Etheridge Knight. MT; NNaP; PBCAP; PoBA

He Sees through Stone. Etheridge Knight. MT; NNaP; PBCAP; PoBA

He seized me round the waist and kissed my throat. Charleston in the 1860s. Adrienne Rich. CoAP; NAAL-2

He sends us, stripped and naked, to the grave. *(LL)* Ambition. Nathaniel Parker Willis. OBCA

He served his God so faithfully and well. On a Puritan. Hilaire Belloc. FaBoEE

He served his master well from youth to age. Old Stephen. Charles Tennyson Turner. EBVV

He set out and kept hunting. The Hunter. Frank O'Hara. NNaP

He set out snares. Poultry. Diana Der Hovanessian. GrPl

He shall not hear the bittern cry. Lament for Thomas MacDonagh. Francis Ledwidge. BIrV
(Thomas MacDonagh.) NOIV
(Thomas McDonagh.) PeIV

He Shall Speak Peace. Thomas Curtis Clark. WBLP

He Shall Speak Peace unto the Nations. Lila V. Walters. WBLP

He shifts on the bed carefully, so as. The Man on the Hotel Room Bed. Galway Kinnell. VCAP

He Shook off the Beast. Charles Wesley. ChIV-2

He Shot Arrows, but Not at Birds Perching. Gary Snyder. BCF

He should, he could, he would, he did the best. *(LL)* Look [or Looke] Home. Robert Southwell. ESCV; NOCV; NoSic

He showed me hights I never saw. Emily Dickinson. PoE

He shows me tonight. Nobody. Novica Tadic, *tr. fr. Serbo-Croatian by* Charles Simic. HSix

He shuddered briefly and stared down the long valley. The Return of Robinson Jeffers. Robert Hass. AmPA; AnAn

He shudders . . . feeling on the shaven spot. Electrocution. Lola Ridge. WPE

He shuffled my file. Lilith and the Doctor. Kathleen Norris. CrSp

He silence loves, or gentle sounds. *(LL)* A New Year's Gift. William Cartwright. BeJo

He Singeth a Hymn to Osiris, the Lord of Eternity. *Unknown, tr. fr. Egyptian by* Robert Hillyer. *Fr.* Book of the Dead. AWP

He Singeth in the Underworld. *Unknown, tr. fr. Egyptian by* Robert Hillyer. *Fr.* Book of the Dead. AWP

He sipped at a weak hock and seltzer. The Arrest of Oscar Wilde at the Cadogan Hotel. Sir John Betjeman. CMoP; EBEV; FaBoEH; InvP; MoBrPo; MoP; NoAM; NoP; OxBTC

He sits above the clang and dust of Time. The Sovereign Poet. Sir William Watson. WGRP

He sits at a table in artificial light. Lili Marlene. Matthew Sweeney. IB

He sits at the bar in the Alhambra. Simple. Naomi Long Madgett. PoBA

He Sits Down on the Floor of a School for the Retarded. Alden Nowlan. GOYP

He sits in front of the bright, blazing grate. The Old Freedman. Priscilla Jane Thompson. CBWP-2

He sleeps fast-pinned to his dream. The Lepidopterist's Dream. Linda Saunders. NWP

He sleeps on the top of a mast. The Unbeliever. Elizabeth Bishop. LiTA; NAAL-2; NoAM

He slept like a rock or a man that's dead. (LL) The Weary Blues. Langston Hughes. FaBV; Jaz; MoP; NoAM; NOBA; NoP; PoNe; SAmP

He slept through the night. Still Alive. Ron Schreiber. PFL

He slew the noble Mudjekeewis. What Hiawatha Probably Did. Unknown. NBLV

He slid out of the skin, leaving it. Summer. Diane Wakoski. VGW

He slumbers well and has a right to slumber. The Poet to the Sleeping Saki. Goethe, tr. fr. German by John Weiss. PeHV

He smears. John Wilkinson. NBrP

He smelled bad and was red-eyed with the miseries. Portrait from the Infantry. Alan Dugan. ArOW

He smiles and looks gay. (LL) The Description of a Good Boy. Henry Dixon. OxBChV; OxNR, st. 1

He smorit thame with smuke. (LL) Off Februar the fyiftene nycht. William Dunbar. MiEL

He snores in his sleep and rubs his nose. (LL) The Jolly Woodchuck. Marion Edey and Dorothy Grider. FaPON; PDV

He snuggles his fingers. After Winter. Sterling A. Brown. PoBA; PoNe

He sought the mountain and the loneliest height, Jesus Praying. Hartley Coleridge. ChIV-2

He spake no dream, for as his words had end. The Banquet. Milton. Fr. Paradise Regained [or Regain'd]. NOSC

He spake, to whom I, answ'ring, thus replied. Homer, tr. by William Cowper. Fr. Odyssey. NAWM-1; OBD

He speaks not well who doth his time deplore. The Heroic Age. Richard Watson Gilder. OHIP

He speaks of voyages. Tour Guide: La Maison des Esclaves. Melvin Dixon. ETG

He speaks to me of other things. Differences. Kath McKay. DT

He spends longer and longer on his knees. (LL) Temptations of St. Antony by His Housekeeper. Elizabeth Smither. PeNZ

He spoke. And drank rapidly a glass of water. (LL) Next to of course god america i. E. E. Cummings. AmPP; FaBoPV; HeIL; InPK; LiTM; MeMAP; NAAL-2; NBLV; NoP; OBWP; OPOP; OxBA; PAW; PoWW; TAP; VGW

He spoke, and what he spoke was soon obeyed. London Subverted by the Furies. Abraham Cowley. NOSC

He spoke of undying love. The Talker. Benjamin Appel. TrJP

He Sports by Himself. Susan Miles. BXAP

He spreads his wings over them. (LL) The Eagle above Us. Santiago Altamirano. OBAP; STP

He springs, that bends until they touch the ground. (LL) Grasshoppers. John Clare. EnVR; TTTS

He stalks in his vivid stripes. A Tiger in the Zoo. Leslie Norris. OTCP

He stalls above me like an elephant. (LL) "To Speak of Woe That Is in Marriage." Robert Lowell. CAPP; MoP; NAAL-2; NoAM

He stands, cold in the morning wind. Roll-Call In the Concentration Camp. Dan Pagis, tr. fr. Hebrew by Robert Friend. PoSu

He stands, feet spread apart, without a pole —. The Vietnamese Fisherman on Tampa Bay. Peter Meinke. NGP

He stands in the door. Dried Fruit. Philip Dow. BXAP

He stands with his forefeet on the drum. Two Performing Elephants. D. H. Lawrence. RB

He stared at ruin. Ruin stared straight back. John Berryman. Fr. Dream Songs. CAPP; HCAP

He stares through shades at the earth rolling to one side. (LL) Amsterdam. Dermot Bolger. IB

He stares upward at a monstrous face. Pieta, The, Rhenish, 14th C., The Cloisters. Mona Van Duyn. Prf

He startles awake. His eyes are full of white light. The Hermit Wakes to Bird Sounds. Maxine W. Kumin. GrPl; Poetsp

He stayed, and was imprisoned in possession. W. H. Auden. Fr. Sonnets from China. CMoP

He steps down from the dark train, blinking; stares. Ten Days Leave. W. D. Snodgrass. ArOW; MoAmPo; Poetsp; UnPo

He steps out from the others. Passion of Ravensbrück. János Pilinszky, tr. fr. Hungarian by Ted Hughes and Janos Csokits. PoSu

He still believes by middle-age. The Traveler. Duane Niatum. HATNAP

He still may leave thy garland green. (LL) Love and Friendship. Emily Brontë. EBVV; ELP; InPK; MeMBP; OBF; VBLP

He stirs, beginning to awake. A Field Hospital. Randall Jarrell. ArOW

He stole us out of our lives. The Poacher. Gregory Orfalea. BTR

He stood, a worn-out City clerk. Peace. Charles Stuart Calverley. EBVV (Peace: A Study.) NOBVV

He stood alone within the spacious square. James Thomson ("B.V."). Fr. City of Dreadful Night, The. NOBVV; OBNC; WiR

He stood among a crowd at Drumahair [or Dromahair]. The Man Who Dreamed of Faeryland. W. B. Yeats. CMoP; NAEL-2; NoAM; NoP

He stood and call'd/ His legions, angel forms, who lay intranced. Milton. Fr. Paradise Lost. EPCY (Satan's Legions and the Beech Leaves of the Casentino.) FaBoPP

He stood, and heard the steeple. Eight o'Clock. A. E. Housman. CMoP; InPK; MoAB; MoBrPo; MoP; NoAM; NoP; OxBSP; PoE; Poetr; SoSe; TrGrPo

He stood before his finished work. The Artist. Frances E. W. Harper. AmWP

He stood before my heart's closed door. The Refiner's Gold. Frances E. W. Harper. PWR

He stood before the Sanhedrim. Religion and Doctrine. John Milton Hay. WGRP

He stood in his shoes/ And he wondered. (LL) There Was a Naughty Boy. Keats. BoTP, sts. 1 and 2; CBNP; FaBoCh; FaBoCo, (st. 4); FHYEP, (sts. 1 and 4); LiTB; MoShBr; OxBChV, (sts. 1 and 4)

He stood on his head by the wild seashore. His Mother-in-Law. Walter Parke. FiBHP

He stood upon the coast of County Clare. St. Enda. Laurence David Lerner. PeSA

He stoops down eating sunflowers. Healing Song. Michael S. Harper. CAPP

He stopped on the irreproachable sidewalk. Elysee. Larry Eigner. VGW

He strays from sun to shade. Diana and Actaeon. Dick Davis. SCBI

He strides across the grassy corn. The Scarecrow. Andrew Young. FaBoTw

He struts about. Sir Thomas More, tr. fr. Latin. FaBoEH

He strutted into the house. The Visitor. Brendan Kennelly. PWE

He sucks with greed the treacherous attraction. Death of a Fly. Goethe, tr. fr. German by John Frederick Nims. STV

He sung the heroic knights of Fairy Land. William Browne. Fr. Britannia's Pastorals. EPCY; JCP

He swings down like the flourish of a pen. Skier. Robert Francis. RFM

He switched on the electric light and laughed. Intimate Supper. Peter Redgrove. FaBoMo; OxBC

He takes his love much as he takes his wine. Nordic. Lillian Byrnes. ShDr

He takes the long review of things. To a Certain Most Certainly Certain Critic. David McCord. OBAL

He talked of Africa. Companion – North-East Dug-out. Ivor Gurney. OBF

He talked of Delhi brothels half the night. Long Tom. W. W. Gibson. OxBTC

He talks and talks. Like Ripples on the Water. Gond Oral Tradition, tr. by V. Elwin and S. Hivale. WTO

He tells many bad things. Young Training. Lawrence McGaugh. PoBA

He tells me about the time. Learning My Father's Language. Lorraine Duggin. LoHo

He tells me in Bangkok he's robbed. Baby Villon. Philip Levine. CoAP; NaP

He tells you when you've got on too much lipstick. The Perfect Husband. Ogden Nash. FaBoUS; Poetr

He that but once too nearly hears. The Music of Forefended Spheres. Coventry Patmore. Fr. Victories of Love, The. FaBoRV

He that can trace a ship making her way. The Heart Is Deep. Roger Wolcott. ChIV-1; SCAP

He that dwelleth in the secret place of the most High. Bible, O.T., paraphrased by Sir Thomas Wyatt. Fr. Psalms. AWP (Everlasting Arms, The, Moulton, Modern Reader's Bible. WGRP (Mighty Fortress, A.) TrGrPo

He that for fear his Master did deny. To St. Peter and St. Paul. Henry Constable. NoSic; Son

He that had come that morning. Ballad of John Cable and Three Gentlemen. W. S. Merwin. CoAP; NOBA

He that has grown to wisdom hurries not. Sonnet: Of Moderation and Tolerance. Guido Guinicelli, tr. fr. Italian by Dante Gabriel Rossetti. AWP

He that has seen a great oak dry and dead. Joachim du Bellay, tr. fr. French by Spenser. Fr. Ruins of Rome. FaBoPP

He That Hath No Mistress. Unknown. GBL; OxBSP

He that hath set his headlong heart. Boethius, *tr. fr. Latin. Fr.* Consolation of Philosophy, The. MLL, *tr.* by Helen Waddell

He that holds fast the golden mean. Moderation. Horace, *tr. fr. Latin by* William Cowper. *Fr.* Odes. PoToHe

He that in youthe no vertu will yowes. *Unknown.* MiEL

He that intends to take a wife. The Wife-Hater. *Unknown.* CoMu

He that is by Mooni now. Mooni. Henry Clarence Kendall. OBEV

He that is down, needs fear no fall. Bunyan. *Fr.* Pilgrim's Progress, The. EBEV; EBEvV
(Enough!) BLRP
(Shepherd Boy Sings [in the Valley of Humiliation], The.) GN; NOBE; OBEV; WGRP
(Shepherd Boy's Song, The.) BoTP; NTP
(Song of the Shepherd Boy.) OxBSP

He That Is Slow to Anger. Bible, *O.T. Fr.* Proverbs. FaPON

He that is weary, let him sit. Employment ("He that is weary, let him sit.") George Herbert. FaBoVe; GeHe; JCP; SeCP; TEP

He that lies at the stock. *Unknown.* OxNR
(Rock, Ball, Fiddle.) CBNP; CH; OxBoLi

He That Loves. Sir Philip Sidney. ErPo

He that loves a rosy cheek. Disdain Returned. Thomas Carew. BeJo; PFP

He That Loves a Rosy Cheek. Heinrich von Rugge, *tr. fr. German by* Jethro Bithell. AWP

He that loves and fears to try. He That Loves. Sir Philip Sidney. ErPo

He that loves Glass without G. *Unknown.* ISE

He That Ne'er Learns His ABC. *Unknown.* GBP

He that of such a height hath built his mind. To the Lady Margaret, Countess [*or* Countesse] of Cumberland. Samuel Daniel. NOSC

He that owns wealth, in mountain, wold, or waste. Wealth. Sadi, *tr.* by Sir Edwin Arnold. *Fr.* Gulistan, The. AWP

He That Regards the Precious Things of Earth. Moses ibn Ezra, *tr. fr. Hebrew by* Solomon Solis-Cohen. *Fr.* World's Illusion, The. TrJP

He that spendes muche and getes nothing. *Unknown.* MiEL

He that to God's law doth cling. Freedom. Abraham ibn Ezra, *tr. fr. Hebrew by* Solomon Solis-Cohen. TrJP

He that to number all the stars would seek. The Zodiac. Guillaume de Salluste Du Bartas, *tr.* by Sylvester, Joshua. *Fr.* Divine Weeks and Works, The. NOSC

He that toucheth pitch shall be defiled therewith; and he that hath. Bible, Apocrypha. *Fr.* Ecclesiasticus. OBF

He that will be a lover in every wise. Three Things Jeame Lacks. *Unknown.* MeEL

He that will court a wench that is coy. *Unknown.* ErPo

He that will give good words to thee, will flatter. Shakespeare. *Fr.* Coriolanus. FaBoPV

He that will not love must be. Not to Love. Robert Herrick. CaPo

He that would live for aye. *Unknown.* FaBoUs

He that would the daughter win. *Unknown.* FaBoUs

He that would thrive must rise at five. *Unknown.* FaBoUs; OxNR

He that would write an epitaph for thee. An Epitaph on Dr. Donne, Dean of Paul's. Richard Corbett [*or* Corbet]. BeJo; EPCY

He the Beloved., *sels.* Qorratu'l-Ayn, *tr. fr. Farsi by* Deirdre Lashgari. "Cupbearer, O victorious Falcon, come!" WPOW

He there now does enjoy eternal rest. Spenser. *Fr.* Faerie Queene, The. (Sleep after Toil.) ChTr

He thinks it is Scandanavian. (*LL*) The Shoplifter. Matthew Sweeney. IB

He Thinks of His Past Greatness When a Part of the Constellations of Heaven. W. B. Yeats. MeMBP; PoEL-5

He thinks when we die we'll go to China. Heaven. Cathy Song. NoAM

He thought he kept the universe alone. The Most of It. Robert Frost. EaPr; HAP; NAAL-2; NoP; NU; TOF; TRP; WeW

He thought he saw a buffalo [*or* a banker's clerk *or* an elephant]. The Mad Gardener's Song. "Lewis Carroll." *Fr.* Sylvie and Bruno. BLPL; CBNP; FaBoCo; FaBoNo; FiBHP, 6 *sts.*; OxBChV; WiR

He thought he saw a long way off the ocean. Victim of Himself. Marvin Bell. BAP-90

He thought to quell the stubborn hearts of oak. Buonaparte. Tennyson. Son

He threw them out and slammed the gate shut. Eden. James Simmons. PNI

He thrust his joy against the weight of the sea. The Surfer. Judith Wright. WPE

He tipped the Oly up to the blue. I'm a Yurok Indian & I'm Proud & You Can Take Your Goddam White Man's Religion Back Over the Ocean Where It Came from & Shove It. Hilton Obenzinger. BCF

He tips his boy baby's hand in an icy. Three Sonnets for Iva. Marilyn Hacker. GLP

He told her. The Alley. Lorna Dee Cervantes. *Fr.* Lots. ETG

He Told His Life Story to Mrs Courtly. Stevie Smith. NBLV

He told me he had spent. Shortening the Road. Michael Davitt, *tr. fr. Irish by* Philip Casey. PBCIP

He told the crowd "The devils." John Logan. *Fr.* Short Life of the Hermit, A. CRP

He too has an eternal part to play. The Historical Judas. Howard Nemerov. NoP; Poetr

He too must with we wash his body, though. An Anniversary of Death. John Wieners. PoM

He took a thousand islands and he didn't lose a man. Dewey in Manila Bay. R. V. Risley. PAH

He took castle and towns; he cut short limbs and lives. Greatness. Thomas Love Peacock. *Fr.* Crocket Castle. OtMeF

He Took Her. Tom Masson. OBAL

He took her fancy when he came. What He Took. *Unknown.* CoMu

He took her with a sigh. (*LL*) Never Seek to Tell Thy Love. Blake. CBLP; ELP; EnLoPo; EnRP; FaBV; InPS; NOBE; OBNC; PoEL-4; SCGP

He took three big gulps. Big Man. Mason Jordan Mason. PoNe

He touches, and the wheel of time goes round. Hurdy-Gurdy Man in Winter. Vernon Watkins. NYBP

He touches her breasts, a sunburned neck, a back bent. The Pillow. Cyrus Cassells. UTF

He travels after a winter sun. Tilly. James Joyce. RB

He Tries out the Concords Gently. "Eduard Bagritzky ," *tr. fr. Russian by* C. M. Bowra. TrJP

He trudges the street of Blantyre. Tramp. Frank Mkalawile Chipasula. HBAPE; PeSAV

He turned his field into a meeting-place. W. H. Auden. *Fr.* In Time of War. SCV

He turns to you, measly immortal page. Page. Sandra McPherson. PoA

He Understands the Great Cruelty of Death. Petrarch. *See* My flowery and green age was passing away.

He unto whom thou art so partial. Post-Obits and the Poets. Martial, *tr. fr. Latin by* Byron. AWP; FaBoEE; OBVE

He used me today. The Gardener. Evelyn Eaton. GoYe

He used to dream of things he'd do. The Dreamer. Thomas Nunan. WBLP

He usually managed to be there when. Because He Liked to Be at Home. Kenneth Patchen. NaP

He wakens from the clover rick. The Sun-Witch to the Sun. George Howe. NYBP

He wakes; speak to him. Shakespeare. *Fr.* King Lear. SCV

He walked up and down the street 'till the shoes fell off his feet. Tramp, Tramp, Tramp, Keep on a-Tramping. *Unknown.* AS

He Walketh by Day. *Unknown, tr. fr. Egyptian by* Robert Hillyer. *Fr.* Book of the Dead. AWP

He walks still upright from the root. The Hewel, or Woodpecker. Andrew Marvell. *Fr.* Upon Appleton House, to My Lord Fairfax. ChTr; SeCP; SeCV-1

He waltzes into the lane. Makin' Jump Shots. Michael S. Harper. PoE

He wanders with his country, too. (*LL*) Another ("The centaur, siren I forgo.") Richard Lovelace. CaPo; PoEL-3

He Wanted Someone to Cook Chicken. Lavinia Greenlaw. NWP

He wanted to rise up to the moment. The Poet Lied. Odia Ofeimun. HBAPE

He wants it back with interest. (*LL*) The Lady's-Maid's Song. John Hollander. ErPo; LiTM; TwCP

He wants to be. Self-Portrait. Robert Creeley. NoAM

He warranted no better, I don't know. (*LL*) Mr. Bleaney. Philip Larkin. HoPM; InPS; OxBC; PoE; TRP; UV

He was a big man, says the size of his shoes. Abandoned Farmhouse. Ted Kooser. WeW

He was a big two-fisted brute. Bucko-Mate. Samuel Schierloh. GoYe

He was a blessing one never prays for — . Obituary. Steve Chimombo. HBAPE

He was a farmer, he didn't think much of towns. Stephen Vincent Benét. *Fr.* John Brown's Body. AiP

He was a G.I. and she was huddled with the others. A Couple of Survivors. David Ray. BTR

He was a good boy. Uncle's First Rabbit. Lorna Dee Cervantes. ETG; NoAM

He Was a Man of Jokes outside Office. Oswald Basize Dube. PeSAV

He was a might poet — and. Shelley. *Fr.* Peter Bell the Third. EPCY

He was a mighty hunter in his youth. The White Cat of Trenarren. A. L. Rowse. OFC; OxBTC

He was a poet he was. Poem for a Dead Poet. Roger McGough. NTP

He was a rat, and she was a rat. What Became of Them? *Unknown.* BoTP; OBCA; OxBChV

He was a real nice man! He liked me too! (*LL*) Seumas Beg. James Stephens. FaPON; GrPl; OxBTC

He was a reprobate I grant. The Deceased. Keith Douglas. FaBoTw

He was a selfish shellfish. Idyll: "He was a selfish shellfish." Stoddard King. NBLV

He was a singer caroling in dark. Countee Cullen. Eugene T. Maleska. PoNe

He was a stranger; we had never met. Something to Remember Me By. Inge Auerbacher. BTR

He was a young god. Genesis. Evan Jones (b. 1927). PBCV

He was always the same. Portrait. Leopold Staff, *tr. fr. Polish by* Adam Czerniawski. PoSu

He was an old wolf, no teeth, his tail all but bare. *Unknown, tr. fr. Sioux Indian by* James Koller. *Fr.* Sioux Metamorphoses. STP

He was as loyal as them all — and more. Peeping Tom. Francis Hope. ErPo

He was as old as old could be. Danny Murphy. James Stephens. BoTP

He was at Naples writing letters home. Wallace Stevens. *Fr.* Esthétique du Mal. CMoP; LiTM; MeMAP; NOBA

He was back. Said nothing. Homecoming. Wislawa Szymborska, *tr. fr. Polish by* Adam Czerniawski. PoSu

He was beautiful, the monster. Monsters. Vuyelwa Carlin. NWP

He was beautifully arrayed. To the Memory of Bernard Berenson. James Liddy. PeIV

He was born in Alabama. Of De Witt Williams on His Way to Lincoln Cemetery. Gwendolyn Brooks. *Fr.* Street in Bronzeville, A. BlSi; BPo; CAPP; FaBoWP; NMM; NoAM; NOBA

He was born in Deutschland, as you would suspect. The Progress of Faust. Karl Shapiro. MoAB; NYBP

He was caught in the whirlpool of dismay. The Whirlpool. *Unknown.* PoToHe

He was found by the Bureau of Statistics to be. The Unknown Citizen. W. H. Auden. FF; HeIL; HeIP; InPK; LiTA; LiTM; MeMAP; MoAB; NBLV; NIP; NOBL; NYBP; OBSV; Poetr; PoRA; SoSe; TRP; UnPo

He was Haitian too. Voodoo Cucumbers. Martín Espada. UTF

He was impoverished, possessing a full island. Castaway. John Nerber. PoA

He was in logic a great critic. The Metaphysical Sectarian. Samuel Butler. *Fr.* Hudibras. MeLP; PeLV

(Hudibras, the Presbyterian Knight, *abr.*) OxBoLi

(Portrait of Hudibras.) PoEL-3

(Sir Hudibras, His Passing Worth.) FaBoCo

He was just a young aviator. Lindbergh. *Unknown.* AmFP

He was just back. Vietnam. Clarence Major. PoBA

He was like the Lord drunk. Alcoholic. F. D. Reeve. NYBP

He was lost. Conqueror of a Forbidden Landscape. Amryl Johnson. NBrP

He Was Lucky. Anna Swirszczynska, *tr. by* Magnus J. Krynski *and* Robert A. Maguire. PoSu

He was my Friend, the truest Friend. Abraham Cowley. *Fr.* On the Death of Mr. William Hervey [*or* Harvey]. EBEV; FaBoRV; OBEV; OBF; SeCP; SeCV-1

He was my man, but he done me wrong. (*LL*) Frankie and Johnny [*or* Johnnie *or* Albert]. *Unknown.* AmFP; AS; BeLS; EBEvV; EBNV; FF; NIP; NOBA; NTP; OxBoLi; RB; TrGrPo; UnPo

He was my sovereign, my heart's delight, my charming young Gilderoy. (*LL*) Gilderoy. *Unknown.* OBET

He was no good. Somewhere. Black Jess. Peter Kane Dufault. NYBP

He was no longer my father. The Mirror. Michael Davitt, *tr. fr. Irish by* Paul Muldoon. BiHa; CIP; PBCIP

He was not able to read or write. The Gardener. Louis MacNeice. *Fr.* Novelettes. IIP

He was not bad, as emperors go, not really. Two Pieces for Suetonius. Robert Penn Warren. NOBA

He was not the Godric who fled from the fight. . . (*LL*) The Battle of Maldon. *Unknown.* AnOE, *tr. by* Kevin Crossley-Holland; OAEL-1, *tr. by* Kevin Crossley-Holland; OBWP, *tr. by* Kevin Crossley-Holland

He was/ oald as the fells. A.L.B. (1917–1978). Jonathan Williams. ETG

He was older and. Passage. John M. Roderick. GOYP

He was once a tiny, helpless thing. Aaron Nicholas, Almost Ten. Janet Campbell Hale. VoR

He was praying before the lamp. Vistasp. Gieve Patel, *tr. fr. Hindi.* TSaS

He was preparing an Ulster fry for breakfast. The Civil Servant. Michael Longley. *Fr.* Wreaths. BiHa

He was quiet again. Manuel Is Quiet Sometimes. Martín Espada. ETG

He was reading late, at Richard's, down in Maine. Henry's Understanding. John Berryman. CAPP; MoP; NoAM; NOBA

He was really her favorite. In Spite of His Dangling Pronoun. Lyn Lifshin. IHMS

He was short and sturdy, one of dim Picton's Silurians. In Memory of Idris Davies. John Tripp. AngWe

He was standing on the edge of us. We Never Know. Yusef Komunyakaa. MT

He was standing on the hotel balcony. Revenge. Chase Twichell. BAP-91

He was still Uncle. The Empress Brand Trim: Ruby Reminisces. Sherley Anne Williams. BlSi

He was such a curious lover of shells. Full Fathom Five. A. R. D. Fairburn. PeNZ

He was the best postilion. The Postilion Has Been Struck by Lightning. Patricia Beer. OxBC

He was the doctor up to Combe. Coroner's Jury. L. A. G. Strong. OxBTC

He was the first always: Fortune. Envy. Adelaide Anne Procter. NOBVV

He was the first to see the snow. (*LL*) First Snow in Alsace. Richard Wilbur. ArOW; NoP; OBWP

He was the slave of Ambition. The Mills of the Gods. *Unknown.* BLPA

He was the uncle who when he was young. I Would Visit Him in the Corner. Alberto A. Ríos. AfAz

He was their servant (some say he was blind). W. H. Auden. *Fr.* Sonnets from China. CMoP

He was there./ He was! (*LL*) The Lamb Was Bleating Softly. Juan Ramón Jiménez. NU; PChr

He was there/ Old Man Coyote. Medicine-Tail, *tr. fr. Crow Indian by* W. S. Merwin. STP

He was, through boyhood's storm and shower. G. K. Chesteron. FiBHP

He was to weet a man of full ripe years. Spenser. *Fr.* Faerie Queene, The. UV, *sect.* VI, *canto* III

He was warned aginst the *womern.* On a Splendud Match. James Whitcomb Riley. AnAmPo

He was wearing a pink T-shirt, ballerina pink, with a bright. Cocktails. Cyn Zarco. BCF

He was wilder than a wolf when he brought. With Bill Pickett at the 101 Ranch. Colleen J. McElroy. NGP

He was wise. (*LL*) Hunting Song. Donald Finkel.

He was (woe worth that word!) to each well thinking mind. *Unknown. Fr.* Epitaph Upon the Right Honorable Sir Philip Sidney. EPCY

He was, you might say, killed by implication. (*LL*) Epitaph for a Scientist. Lex Banning. NOBAu

He wasn't handsome or young or even clever, but oh. On Don Juan del Norte, Not Don Juan Tenorio del Sur. Alan Dugan. ErPo

He watch her like a coonhound watch a tree. Balance. Marilyn Nelson Waniek. NAmP90

He watched each TV game for all he was worth, while. My Father's Football Game. David Wagoner. NGP

He watched the stars and noted birds in flight. W. H. Auden. *Fr.* Sonnets from China. CMoP

He watched them as they walked towards the tree. The Tree. Dorothy Auchterlonie. NOBAu

He watched with all his organs of concern. W. H. Auden. PoA

He wears a beard to let us see that he is pure within. Sanctimony. *Malay Oral Tradition, tr. by* R. J. Wilkinson. WTO

He wears striped jim-jam pyjamas. Jim-jam Pyjamas. Gina Wilson. BAP-91

He welcomes us still. His Welcome. Auvaiyar, *tr. fr. Tamil by* A. K. Ramanujan. PLW

He went down to the woodshed. No One Heard Him Call. Dorothy Aldis. TLR

He went inside the café where they used to sit together. Lovely White Flowers. C. P. Cavafy, *tr. fr. Greek by* Edmund Keeley *and* Philip Sherrard. OBD

He went into his harvest barn. The Farmer. Mary Elizabeth Fullerton. CBAP

He went out of the room in which he was praying. He spent there. Or. Ali Darwish, *tr. fr. Arabic.* TSaS, *tr. by* Darwish Ali

He went out to their glorious. The Summons. James Laughlin. LiTA

He went there. Poem of the Conscripted Warrior. "Rui Nogar," *tr. fr. Portuguese by* Dorothy Guedes *and* Philippa Rumsey. TTY

He went to fix the awning. Fixer of Midnight. Reuel Denney. OBAL

He went to the wood and caught it. *Unknown.* GBP; OxNR

He went with another. Gabriela Mistral, *tr. fr. Spanish by* Muriel Kittel. AIW

He whittled scallops for a hardy thatch. The Thatcher. Brendan Kennelly. CIP

He who ascends to mountain-tops shall find. The Isolation of Genius. Byron. WBLP

He who began from brick and lime. In Obitum Ben. Jons. Mildmay Fane, 2d Earl of Westmorland. OxBSP

(In Obitum Ben Johnson Poetae Eximii.) NOSC

(On Ben Jonson.) BeJo

He who binds to himself a joy. Eternity. Blake. *Fr.* Several Questions Answered. ArNa; AWP; EBEV; EnlH; FaBoEE; ImPo; MeMBP;

Headless limbless/ it appears. The Quartz Pebble. Vasco [or Vasko] Popa, tr. fr. Serbo-Croatian. Fr. Quartz Pebble, The. PoSu, tr. by Anne Pennington

Headless squirrel, some blood, A. A Day Begins. Denise Levertov. NaP

Headless torsos, faceless lovers, friends of mine. (LL) The Onion, Memory. Craig Raine. NAEL-2; NoAM; NoP

Headless young Beau, A. Unknown, tr. fr. French. CBNP

Headline History. William Plomer. FaBoCo

Headline to Summarize a Passion. Tchicaya U Tam'si, tr. fr. French by Ellen Conroy Kennedy. NegPo

Headlined in Heaven. Paul Grano. NOBAu

Headlong Hall, sels. Thomas Love Peacock.
In His Last Binn Sir Peter Lies. EnRP

Headmaster. John Tripp. AngWe

Headquarters. Gilbert Frankau. NSI

Headrock. Brian Coffey. CIP

Heads, impenetrable, The. Oxen: Ploughing at Fiesole. Charles Tomlinson. OxBTC

Heads in the Women's Ward. Philip Larkin. OBD

Heads moved in a wide, slow semi-circle. Fishing. William Hart-Smith. FaBoMA

Heads of strong old age are beautiful, The. Promise of Peace. Robinson Jeffers. LiTA; LiTM; MoAB; MoAmPo

Heads or Tails? Kit Wright. OTCP

Headstones are thin, The; the trees are thick. The Cows near the Graveyard. Howard Nelson. NU

Headstrong Boy, A. Gu Cheng, tr. fr. Chinese by Donald Finkel with Yi Jinsheng. SpMi; TSaS

Headstrong young lady of Ealing, A. Edward Gorey. PeLi

Heal Me, My God. Judah Halevi, tr. fr. Hebrew by David Goldstein. TOF

Heal my body, heart, and soul. Amen. (LL) Beloved Lord, Almighty God! Hazrat Inayat Khan. EaPr

Healed of My Hurt. Herman Melville. AmPP

Healer, The. Charles Simic. AnAn

Healer of broken bones. (LL) Elegy for Her Brother Sakhr. Al-Khansa. BoWoP, tr. by Willis Barnstone; WPOW, tr. by Bridget Connelly

Healing. Wendell Berry. AnAn

Healing. D. H. Lawrence. RaBo

Healing. Abraham Reisen, tr. fr. Yiddish by Joseph Leftwich. TrJP

Healing. Yannis Ritsos, tr. fr. Greek. TSaS, tr. by Edmund Keeley

Healing Animal. Joy Harjo. ETG

Healing of the Leper, The. Vernon Watkins. FaBoTw

Healing seem a neutral, pathetic act. (LL) Greatrakes, The Healer. Thomas McCarthy. IB

Healing Song. Michael S. Harper. CAPP

Healing Song. Unknown, tr. by Frances Densmore. OBVE

Health, A. Edward Coote Pinkney. AnAmPo

Health and Fitness. J. B. Morton. FaBoCo

Health and wealth and love he too dreamed of in May. Patrick Kavanagh. Fr. Great Hunger, The. MoAB

Health at the Ford, A. Robert Cameron Rogers. FaBoBe

Health Counsel. Sir John Harington. FaBoUs

Health Food. Unknown. FaBoUs

Health from the lover of the country, me. To Fuscus Arustus. Horace, tr. fr. Latin by Abraham Cowley. Fr. Epistles. AWP

Health! I seek thee; dost thou love. Robert Bloomfield. Fr. Shooter's Hill. OBNC

Health is the first good lent to men. Four Things Make Us Happy Here. Robert Herrick, tr. fr. Greek by Robert Herrick. CaPo
(Four Best Things, The.) Spl

Health of Body Dependent on Soul. Jones Very. WGRP

Health to great Gloucester — from a man unknown. Charles Churchill. OBSV

Health to my fair Odelia! Some that know. To Odelia. James Shirley. BeJo

Health to the Maxwels' veteran Chief! To Terraughty, on His Birth-Day. Burns. NAs

Health to the Tackers, A. Unknown. APAS

Health unto His Majesty, A. Jeremy Savile. ChTr

Healthy Spot, A. W. H. Auden. AiP

Heap cassia, sandal-buds and stripes. Robert Browning. Fr. Paracelsus. OBEV

Heap earth upon it. (LL) Requiescat. Oscar Wilde. EBVV; InvP; MoBrPo; OBNC; OHCV; PeVV; TrGrPo

Heap high the farmer's wintry hoard. The Corn-Song. Whittier. GN; OHIP

Heap of Rags, The. W. H. Davies. NSI

Heap on more wood! — the wind is chill. Sir Walter Scott. Fr. Marmion. OBCP

Heaped on the balance her beauty breeds. (LL) And let me never. William Everson. EaPr

Hear. Susan Howe. BCF
Sels.
"Antimony one."

Hear all men speak, but credit few or none. (LL) Distrust. Robert Herrick. CaPo

Hear father yet thou Long-Armed Lord! these latest words I say. Unknown, tr. by Sir Edward Arnold. Fr. Bhagavad-Gita, The. TAL

Hear! hear! Lilian's Song. George Darley. OBNC

Hear, Hear, O Ye Nations. Frederick L. Hosmer. AH

Hear how selection was the efficient cause. Darwin on Species. Unknown. FaBoUs

Hear how the fiddles play! (LL) While I Wait. Vilhelm Andreas Wexels Krag. RiWo

Hear how Timotheous varied lays surprise. Pope. Fr. Essay on Criticism. EPCY; PoEL-3

Hear in the sea, Thetis, Memnon's alive. Asclepiodotus, tr. fr. Greek by Alistair Elliot. GrAn

Hear, Lord, hear. The Leper Cleansed. John Collop. TrGrPo

Hear me/ don't you hear me. Tambourine. James Cunningham. JB

Hear me,/ helper of mankind. The Homeric Hymn to Ares. Unknown, tr. fr. Greek by Shelley. Fr. Homeric Hymns. RaBo, tr. by Charles Boer

Hear me, my God, and hear me soon. The Petition. Thomas Beedome. NOSC

Hear me [or Heare mee], O God! A Hymn to God the Father. Ben Jonson. BeJo; EnRePo; NoP; NOSC; OxAEP-1; Poetr; SeCP; SeCV-1; TrCP; TrPWD
(Hymne to God the Father, A.) PFP

Hear me, whom I betrayed. J. V. Cunningham. VGW

Hear me, ye cold hearts in the North. Eros. Otto Benzon, tr. fr. Norwegian by Philip L. Miller. RiWo

Hear me, ye smokeless skies and grass-green earth. Charles Mair. Fr. Last Bison, The. NOBC

Hear Me Yet. Unknown. ElL

Hear my call. (LL) To You. Elolongue Epanya Yondo. NegPo

Hear my voice, birds of war! Ojibwa War Songs. Unknown, tr. fr. Ojibwa Indian by H. H. Schoolcraft. AWP

Hear now a curious dream I dreamed last night. My Dream. Christina Rossetti. BrRo

Hear now, O Soul, the last command of all. The Final Mystery. Sir Henry Newbolt. WGRP

Hear, O Humankind, the prayer of my heart. Manitongquat. EaPr

Hear, O Israel! Adah Isaacs Menken. AAP; CBWP-1

Hear, O Israel! André Spire, tr. fr. French by Stanley Burnshaw. TrJP

Hear, O Israel:/ To arms! (LL) Hear, O Israel! André Spire. TrJP

Hear, O Israel!/ Will you never tire of repeating in your prayers. Hear, O Israel! André Spire, tr. fr. French by Stanley Burnshaw. TrJP

Hear, O Israel. Shema Yisrael. Unknown. TrJP

Hear, O Israel! and plead my cause against the ungodly nation. Hear, O Israel! Adah Isaacs Menken. AAP; CBWP-1

Hear, O Israel, Jehovah, the Lord our God is one. Israel. Israel Zangwill. TrJP

Hear, O Israel, the commandments of life. The Path of Wisdom. Bible, Apocrypha. Fr. Baruch. TrJP

Hear, O Lord, my loud cry. The Serenity of Faith. Bible, O.T., paraphrased by Sir Thomas Wyatt, tr. by McFayden. Fr. Psalms. BLRP

Hear, sweet spirit, hear the spell. A Voice Sings. Samuel Taylor Coleridge. Fr. Remorse. CH
(Invocation, An.) PeECV

Hear the Bird of Day. David Campbell. NOBAu

Hear the dreary, dreary rain. Voices of the Rain. H. Cordelia Ray. CBWP-3

Hear the fluter with his flute. The Amateur Flute. Unknown. BXAP

Hear the legend of the Admen. The Legend of the Admen. Everett W. Lord. BLPA

Hear the music, the thunder of the wings. Love the wild swan. (LL) Love the Wild Swan. Robinson Jeffers. HeIL; MoAB; MoAmPo; NoAM; Son

Hear the sledges with the bells. The Bells. Poe. AnAmPo; FaPON, st. 1; GN; LiTA; MeMAP; OBAL; OBCA; PoLF; TAP; TFi; WBLP
(Hear the sledges with the bells, (st. 1).) FaPON

Hear the voice of the Bard! Blake. Fr. Songs of Experience. ChIV-1; EBEV; ELP; NAEL-2; NAWM-2; NOBE; NU; PoE; RB; TFi
(Bard, The.) WGRP
(Hear the Voice.) OBEV

(Introduction: "Hear the voice of the bard!") EnRP; FHYEP; HAP; InPS; NOEC; NoP; OAEL-2; PoEL-4; TEP
(Poet's Voice, The.) ChTr

Hear the Word of the Lord. Bible, *O.T. Fr.* Isaiah. TrJP

Hear the word that Jesus spake. A Lost Word of Jesus. Henry van Dyke. TrCP; WGRP

Hear this and tremble, all. Upon My Lord Chief Justice's Election of My Lady Anne Wentworth for His Mistress. Thomas Carew. CaPo

Hear through the morning drums and trumpets sounding. Jackson at New Orleans. Wallace Rice. PAH

Hear what Claudius suffered: When his wife knew he was asleep. Juvenal, *tr. by* Hubert Creekmore. *Fr.* Satires. ErPo

Hear what God the Lord hath spoken. Hymn 10. William Cowper. ChIV-1

Hear what the Lord has done for me! *(LL)* Exhortation to Prayer. William Cowper. NOCV

Hear, ye children, the instruction of a father. The Legacy. Bible, *O.T. Fr.* Proverbs. TrJP

Hear, Ye Ladies [That Despise]. John Fletcher. *Fr.* Tragedy of Valentinian, The. CBLP; EIL; ELP; NOBE; OBEV

Hear, ye virgins, and I'll teach. To Virgins. Robert Herrick. CaPo

Heard all the crickets singing, and was glad. *(LL)* A Prayer in Darkness. G. K. Chesteron. MoBrPo; PoLF; TrGrPo

Heard him gladly. *(LL)* Waldere 1. *Unknown, tr. fr.* Anglo-Saxon by Charles W. Kennedy. AnOE

Heard in a Violent Ward. Theodore Roethke. HCAP

Heard in the Cougate. Robert Garioch. OxBTC

Heard on a Boat. T'an Yuan-ch'un, *tr. fr.* Chinese by Irving Y. Lo. SuSp

Heard on the Mountain. Victor Hugo, *tr. fr.* French by Francis Thompson. *Fr.* Feuilles d'Automne. AWP

Heard the one about the guy from Heaton Mersey? Snow Joke. Simon Armitage. PWE

Heard ye eer of the silly blind harper. The Lochmaben Harper. *Unknown.* ESPB; OxBB

Heard ye how the bold McClellan. How McClellan Took Manassas. *Unknown.* PAH

Heard ye o' the tree o' France. The Tree of Liberty. Burns. FaBoPV

Heard ye that thrilling word. Dirge for Ashby. Margaret Junkin Preston. PAH

Heard ye the thunder of battle. Trafalgar. Francis Turner Palgrave. BeLS; FaBoBe

Hearing. W. S. Merwin. NoAM

Hearing a low growl in your throat, you'll know that it's started. Death, the Last Visit. Marie Howe. NAmP90

Hearing a sound that may be thy return. Hildegarde Flanner. *Fr.* Sonnets in Quaker Language. WPE

Hearing Aid, The. Richard Jones. NAmP90

Hearing: Hearing. Spring Poem. Colleen Thibaudeau. TSaS

Hearing how tourists, dazed with reverence. Aldport (Mystery Tour). Kingsley Amis. *Fr.* Evans Country, The. NOBL
(Terrible Beauty.) ErPo

Hearing I ask from the holy races. Voluspo. *Unknown, tr. by* Henry Adams Bellows. *Fr.* Elder Edda, The. AWP

Hearing Men Shout at Night on MacDougal Street. Robert Bly. InPS

Hearing of Harvests Rotting in the Valleys. W. H. Auden. MoAB; MoBrPo

Hearing of you, I never lost a brother. Stepping Outside. Tess Gallagher. AmPA

Hearing one saga, we enact the next. Remembering the 'Thirties. Donald Davie. FaBoPV; OxBTC

Hearing Russian Spoken. Donald Davie. GTBS-P

Hearing Steps. Charles Simic. HCAP

Hearing That His Friend Was Coming Back from the War. Wang Chien, *tr. fr.* Chinese by Arthur Waley. ArLo

Hearing that on Sunday I would leave. The Emerald. James Merrill. *Fr.* Up and Down. CAPP

Hearing the stones cry out under the horizons. *(LL)* Wind. Ted Hughes. NAEL-2; Poetr

Hearing the Wind at Night. May Swenson. BoNaP

Hearing, this June day, the thin thunder. Home Thoughts from Abroad. W. R. Rodgers. PeIV

Hearing your words, and not a word among them. Edna St. Vincent Millay. CMoP; MoP; NoAM; Poetr; VGW

Heark how she laughs aloud. Lucasta Laughing. Richard Lovelace. PoEL-3

Hearken all ye, 'tis the feast o' Saint Stephen. The Feast o' Saint [*or* St.] Stephen. Ruth Sawyer. OBCP; OHIP

Hearken, Lady Betty, hearken. Christopher Anstey. *Fr.* New Bath Guide, The. NOEC

Hearken the stirring story. The Fall of Maubila. Thomas Dunn English. PAH

Hearken, thou craggy ocean pyramid! To Ailsa Rock. Keats. EnRP; OBNC

Hearken to me, gentlemen. King Estmere. *Unknown.* ESPB; OBNV; OxBB

Hears not my Phillis how the birds. Sir Charles Sedley. EnLoPo; SeCV-2

Hears now this song of mine. *(LL)* Evoe! Edith M. Thomas. AmWP

Hears the sound of laughter as green flames start up inside its nest. *(LL)* A Piece for Magic Strings. Li Ho. PLT

Hears thy voice right, now he is gone. *(LL)* Memorial Verses. Matthew Arnold. EBVVPR; NAEL-2; OAEL-2

Hearse comes up the road, The. Twelve Minutes. J. C. Hall. OBD

Hearse/ you carry/ within. Death. Anthony Barnett. VaA

Hearse Song, The. *Unknown.* AS, *A and* B vers., OxBoLi; RB

Hearse was the oven of the crematory, The. The Funeral. "M. J.," *tr. fr. Polish by* A. Glanz-Leyeles. TrJP

Hears't thou, my soul, what serious things. Dies Irae. Thomas of Celano, *tr. fr. Latin by* Richard Crashaw. AWP; TIRV
(Day of Judgment, The.) OBVE

Heart. Guillaume Apollinaire, *tr. fr.* French by Roger Shattuck. *Fr.* Heart, Crown, and Mirror. TTTS

Heart, The. Stephen Crane. *See* In the Desert.

Heart, The. Michael Drayton. NOSC

Heart. Donald Justice. MT

Heart, The. Harvey Shapiro. HoPM

Heart, The. Jakov Steinberg, *tr. fr.* Hebrew by Harry H. Fein. TrJP

Heart, The, *sels.* Francis Thompson.
"Heart you hold too small and local thing, The." OBMV
"O nothing in this corporal earth of man." OBMV
(All's Vast.) MoAB; MoBrPo; Son
(Correlated Greatness.) GTBS-P

Heart aches. Breathless. Wilfred Noyce. OBTV

Heart all hunger, A. *(LL)* Cabin Site, Christmas Island, N.S. Martin Edmunds. UTF

Heart and Mind. Edith Sitwell. OxBTC; TwCP

Heart and service to you proffer'd, The. Sir Thomas Wyatt. SiPS

Heart asks pleasure — first, The. Emily Dickinson. AmPP; CMoP; MeMAP; MoAB; MoAmPo; NAAL-1; NOBA; NoP; OxBA; PPP; PrIm; TrGrPo; WPE

Heart Attack in the Country, A. Terry Hummer. NAmP90

Heart be content, though she be gone. Ostella forth of Town: To My Heart. John Tatham. NOSC

Heart Beats the Rent Collector. John Ceely. NGP

Heart cold in the breast with terror, grieving. Lament for Llywelyn ap Gruffudd. Gruffudd ab yr Ynad Coch, *tr. fr.* Welsh by Joseph P. Clancy. OBWVE

Heart, Crown, and Mirror, *sels.* Guillaume Apollinaire, *tr. fr.* French by Roger Shattuck.
Heart. TTTS
"In this mirror I am enclosed." TTTS
"Kings who have died." TTTS

Heart does hurt, The. It Really Is the Heart. Denise Riley. NBrP

Heart Exchange. Sir Philip Sidney. *See* My true love hath my heart, and I have his.

Heart Flies Up, Erratic as a Kite, The. Delmore Schwartz. PoA

Heart Has Its Reasons, The. Felice Picano. PeHV

Heart has need of some deceit, The. Only the Polished Skeleton. Countee Cullen. PrIm; VGW

Heart-Hungry. Josephine D. Henderson Heard. CBWP-4

Heart Is Deep, The. Roger Wolcott. ChIV-1; SCAP

Heart is sensual, though five eyes break, The. *(LL)* When All My Five and Country Senses See. Dylan Thomas. MoAB; MoBrPo; NoAM; PoA; Son

Heart, knowing, The. What He Said. Allur Nanmullai, *tr. fr.* Tamil by A. K. Ramanujan. PLW

Heart leaps with the pride of their story, The. The Fleet at Santiago. Charles E. Russell. PAH

Heart, let us this once reason together. Heart. Donald Justice. MT

Heart made full of thought, A. Maghnas O Domhnaill. NOIV

Heart of a Girl Is a Wonderful Thing, The. *Unknown.* BLPA

Heart of a Woman, The. Georgia Douglas Johnson. BlSi; CDC; PoLF; PoNe; ShDr; VBLP

Heart of Autumn. Robert Penn Warren. MT; Poetr

Heart of Herakles, The. Kenneth Rexroth. *Fr.* Lights in the Sky are Stars, The. NU

Heart of London beating warm, The. *(LL)* London. John Davidson. MeMBP; NOBE; OBNC

Heart of Midlothian, The, *sels.* Sir Walter Scott.
Proud Maisie ("Proud Maisie is in the wood"). CH; ChTr; EnRP;
FaBoCh; FF; Mes; NAEL-2; OAEL-2; OBEV; OxBS; PoEL-4; SCGP;
TEP; TFi; TrGrPo; UnPo
(Madge Wildfire Sings.) OBNC
(Madge Wildfire's Death Song.) HAP
(Madge Wildfire's Song.) NOBE
(Pride of Youth, The.) GTBS; GTBS-P

Heart of my heart, the world is young. Unity. Alfred Noyes. PFP

Heart of Oak. David Garrick. FaBoEH; NOEC; OxBoLi

Heart of oak etc. (*LL*) Heart of Oak. David Garrick. FaBoEH; NOEC; OxBoLi

Heart of O'Leary, S.J., The. David Phillips. PeLi

Heart of standing is we cannot fly, The. (*LL*) Hours before dawn we were woken by the quake. William Empson. FaBoMo; FaBoTW; LiTB; OxAEP-2; OxBTC

Heart of the Backlog. Robert Penn Warren. MT

Heart-of-the-Daybreak. Eugène Marais, *tr. fr. Afrikaans by* Uys Krige *and* Jack Cope. PeSA

Heart of the heartless world. Huesca. John Cornford. BoLoP
(To Margot Heinemann.) OBWP; OxBTC

Heart of the matter is where we know, The. No Head for Heights. Ralph Hawkins. VaA

Heart of the Quartz Pebble, The. Vasco [*or* Vasko] Popa, *tr. fr. Serbo-Croatian. Fr.* Quartz Pebble, The. PoSu, *tr. by* Anne Pennington

Heart of the Tree, The. H. C. Bunner. OHIP

Heart of the Woods. Wesley Curtright. PoNe

Heart of the World, The. Rabbi Nahman of Bratzlav, *tr. fr. Yiddish by* Joseph Leftwich. TrJP

Heart on the Hill, The. Petrarch, *tr. fr. Italian. Fr.* Sonnets to Laura. AWP

Heart oppress'd with desperate thought. Sir Thomas Wyatt. SiPS

Heart-summoned. Jesse Stuart. GoYe

Heart that beats so. (*LL*) I See, I See the Crescent Moon. "Anna Akhmatova." VBLP

Heart to heart! In a Silence. Richard Hovey. AnAmPo

Heart, we will forget him! Emily Dickinson. SAmP

Heart whose love is innocent!, A. (*LL*) She Walks in Beauty. Byron.
ArLo; AWP; BLPA; BoLoP; CBLP; EBEvV; ELP; EnRP; FaBoBe; FF;
FHYEP; GTBS; GTBS-P; HeIP; ImPo; InPS; LiTB; MeMBP; NAEL-2;
NOBE; NoP; OBEV; OBNC; OxAEP-2; PlP; PoE; PoEL-4; PrIm; SCGP;
TFi; TrGrPo

Heart Wounds. Claire Richcreek Thomas. PoToHe

Heart you hold too small and local thing, The. Francis Thompson. *Fr.* Heart, The. OBMV

Heartbeat. (*LL*) Black Hills Survival Gathering, 1980. Linda Hogan. WoWa

Heartbeat. Jack Skelley. UTF

Heartbeat of the glacier. (*LL*) Conversation by the Body's Light. Rachel Hadas. UnDi

Heartbeats. Melvin Dixon. PFL

Heartbreak Camp. Roy Campbell. OxBTC

Hearth. Peggy Bacon. FaPON

H ear t h. Janet Sutherland. NBrP

Hearth and Home. Stoddard King. OBAL

Hearth of Urien, The. Llywarch the Aged, *tr. fr. Welsh by* William Barnes. ChTr

Hearth Song. John Montague. PNI

Hearthstone. Harold Monro. OBMV

Heartland. Jim Barnes. HATNAP

Hearts, The. Robert Pinsky. VCAP

Heart's Abysses, The. Walter Savage Landor. FaBoEE; OBSV

Heart's Anchor, The. William Winter. PoToHe

Heart's Content. *Unknown.* PoLF

Hearts-Ease. Walter Savage Landor. EnRP

Heart's Ease. Mary E. Tucker. CBWP-1

Heart's Haven. Dante Gabriel Rossetti. *Fr.* House of Life, The. Son

Hearts, like doors, will ope with ease. *Unknown.* OxNR

Heart's Location, The. Peter Meinke. GOYP

Heart's Music. *At. to* Thomas Campion. AAS; OBEV

Heart's Needle, *sels.* W. D. Snodgrass.
Child of My Winter Born. MoAmPo
"Easter has come around." CAPP; VCAP
"I thumped on you the best I could." NoAM
"Late April and you are three; today." VCAP
"Vicious winter finally yields, The." SM

Heart's Proof, The. James Buckham. BLRP; WBLP

Hearts that are great beat never loud. A Thought. Abram Joseph Ryan. PWR

Heartthrobs. Joan Jobe Smith. NGP

Heat. Hilda Doolittle ("H. D."). *Fr.* Garden, The. ArNa; CMoP; HeIL;
HeIP; InPK; LiTA; MoAmPo; NoAM; OxBA; PrIm; TAP; TRP; UnPo

Heat. Archibald Lampman. NOBC; NTP

Heat. Kenneth Mackenzie. CBAP

Heat. Jim Powell. PRA

Heat goes deep as cold. *Unknown, tr. fr. Irish by* Thomas Kinsella. NOIV

Heat is past that did me fret, The. A Farewell to a Fondling. Thomas Churchyard. EIL

Heat Lightning. Robert Penn Warren. MT

Heat Lightning in a Time of Drought. Andrew Hudgins. BAP-89

Heat-lightning streak. Basho, *tr. fr. Japanese.* InPK

Heat the furnace hot. To the New Men. John Davidson. OHCV

Heathen Are Come into Thine Inheritance, The. Bible, *O.T., paraphrased by* Sir Thomas Wyatt. *See* O God, the heathen are come into Thine inheritance.

Heathen Chinee, The. Bret Harte. *See* Which I wish to remark.

Heathen Hymn, A, *sels.* Sir Lewis Morris.
"I praise Thee not, with impious pride." TrPWD

Heathen Pass-ee, The. Arthur Clement Hilton. FaBoCo; NOBL; UV

Heather Flowers. Eliseus Williams, *tr. fr. Welsh by* Kenneth Hurlstone Jackson. OBWVE

Heat's on the hooker, The. Translations from the English. George Starbuck. VGW

Heave at the windlass! — Heave O, cheerly, men! Windlass Song. William Allingham. GN

Heave Away ("Heave away, heave away! I'd rather court a yellow gal,"). *Unknown.* AS

Heave Away, My Johnny. *Unknown.* OxBSS

Heaven. Rupert Brooke. EBEV; HoPM; LiTB; LiTM; MoBrPo; NOBE;
NSI; PFP; PoRA; WGRP

Heaven. Mark Doty. NAmP90

Heaven. George Herbert. ESCV; GeHe; SeCP; TrCP; TrGrPo; TTTS

Heaven. Langston Hughes. *See* Heaven, Heaven, Heaven Is the Place.

Heaven. Philip Levine. LCAP; NaP

Heaven. Cathy Song. NoAM

Heaven. A. S. J. Tessimond. OxBM

Heaven. *Unknown.* PoLF

Heaven. Isaac Watts. *See* There is a land of pure delight.

Heaven above is softer blue. Possession. *Unknown.* BLRP

Heaven and Earth. James I, King of England. *See* Azured [*or* Azur'd] vault, the crystal circles bright, The.

Heaven and earth a rotating ball. Tune: "Wild Geese Have Come Down;
Song of Victory" — Idle Leisure. Teng Yu-ein, *tr. fr. Chinese by* Hellmut Wilhelm. SuSp

Heaven and earth, and all that hear me plain. Sir Thomas Wyatt. SiPSBD (Protest, A.) SiPS

Heaven and Hell. Nalungiaq, *tr. fr. Eskimo by* Edward Field. DL; STP

Heaven and Hell. Willie Nelson. InPK

Heaven and Hell. Francis Thompson. OxBSP

Heaven: Behind Closed Doors. Michael Foley. FaBoBl

Heaven for Railroad Men. David Wojahn. NGP

Heaven, from thy endless goodness, send prosperous life. This Royal Infant. John Fletcher *and* William Shakespeare. *Fr.* King Henry VIII. NAs

Heaven had not won, nor earth so timely lost. (*LL*) Epitaph for [*or* on] Thomas Clere. The Earl of Surrey. NoSic; SiPSBD

Heaven-Haven. Gerard Manley Hopkins, *tr. fr. Hebrew.* EBEvV; HeIL;
HeIP; MoAB; MoBrPo; MoP; NoAM; NOBE; NOCV; OBEV; OBNC;
OxAEP-2; OxBSP; PeECV; RB; SoSe; SOTW; TFi; TOF; TrGrPo

Heaven, Heaven, Heaven Is the Place. Langston Hughes. AH

Heaven in Ordinarie. Daniel Wolff. SM

Heaven in the South, earth Northward. Kuan Han-ch'ing, *tr. by* Jerome P. Seaton. *Fr.* Tune: "Intoxication in the East Wind". SuSp

Heaven Is Here. John G. Adams. AH

Heaven is inscrutable. Don't Go Out of the Door. Li Ho, *tr. fr. Chinese by* A. C. Graham. PLT

Heaven is not reached [*or* gained] at [*or* by] a single bound. Gradatim. Josiah Gilbert Holland. WGRP

Heaven is what I cannot reach. Emily Dickinson. NOCV

Heaven itself would stoop to her. (*LL*) Comus; a Masque Presented at Ludlow Castle. Milton. FHYEP; OAEL-1

Heaven of Animals, The. James Dickey. CAPP; CoAP; EaPr; FoLa; HeIP;
LiTM; MT; NAAL-2; NoAM; NOBA; PoE; TAP; TRP; VCAP

Heaven ope to Indians wild, but shut to thee. (*LL*) Boast not proud English, of thy birth and blood. Roger Williams. GOA; SCAP

Heaven opened wide. Milton. *Fr.* Paradise Lost. ChIV-1; EPCY

Heaven-reflecting, usual moon, The. Coming from Evening Church. Charles Causley. NTP

Heaven shall forgive you bridge at dawn. Ballade d'une Grande Dame. G. K. Chesteron. OxBoLi

Heaven, the earth, and all the liquid main [or mayne], The. Virgil, tr. by Sir Walter Ralegh. Fr. Aeneid [or Eneados], The. NAWM-1; OBVE; SiPSBD

Heaven vows to keep him. (LL) Epitaph on S. P. [Salomon or Salathiel Pavy], a Child of Q[ueen] El[izabeth's] Chapel. Ben Jonson. BeJo; EIL; EnRePo; HoPM; JCP; Mes; NAEL-1; NoP; NOSC; OAEL-1; OBD; OBEV; PoEL-2; PPP; SCGP; SeCP; SeCV-1; TrGrPo; UnPo

Heaven which art in Heaven Our Father in Heaven. Kay Smith. Fr. Footnote to the Lord's Prayer. TrCP

Heaven, which man's generations draws. Francis Thompson. Fr. Judgment in Heaven, A. MoAB; MoBrPo

Heaven Will Protect the Working-Girl, sels. Edgar Smith. "You may tempt the upper classes." FiBHP

Heavenly Aeroplane, The. Unknown. NOCV

Heavenly Archer, bend thy bow. Dust to Dust. Walter de la Mare. TrPWD

Heavenly City, The. Stevie Smith. FaBoTw

Heavenly Eloquence. Samuel Daniel. See Power above powers, O heavenly Eloquence.

Heavenly Evil, holy One. Hymn to Evil. Louis Ginsberg. PoA

Heavenly Father, bless this food. Unknown. BLRP

"Heavenly Father," take to thee. Emily Dickinson. PoEL-5

Heavenly fields of Paradise, The. Heine, tr. fr. German by Alistair Elliot. Fr. Zum Lazarus. OBD

Heavenly Foreigner, The, sels. Denis Devlin. "Spires, firm on their monster feet rose light and thin, The." CIP

Heavenly Rhetoric, The. Shakespeare. Fr. Love's Labour's Lost. ImPo; LiTB; Son

Heavenly Stranger, The. Ada Blenkhorn. BLRP

Heavenly Vision. William Billings. AmFP

Heavens, The. Bible, O.T., paraphrased by Sir Thomas Wyatt. See Law of Jehovah is perfect, restoring the soul, The.

Heavens, The, sels. Caterina Bon Brenzoni, tr. fr. Italian by Muriel Kittel.

Heavens Above and the Law Within, The. Bible, O.T., paraphrased by Sir Thomas Wyatt. See Law of Jehovah is perfect, restoring the soul, The.

Heavens are wrath — the thunder's rattling peal, The. Written in a Thunder Storm July 15th, 1841. John Clare. EnVR

Heavens bespeak the glory of God, The. Daniel Berrigan. EaPr

Heavens bright lamp, shine forth some of thy light. George Alsop. SCAP

Heavens declare the glory of God, The. Bible, O.T., paraphrased by Sir Thomas Wyatt. Fr. Psalms. AWP; FaPON, sts. 1–4; NAWM-1; OBVE, tr. by Miles Coverdale; WBLP
(Heavens declare God's glory, The.) EnlH

Heavens Do Declare, The. Unknown. BLRP

Heavens doe declare, The. Bible, O.T., paraphrased by Sir Thomas Wyatt. See Law of Jehovah is perfect, restoring the soul, The.

Heavens doe declare/ The majesty of God, The. Unknown. Fr. Bay Psalm Book, The. SCAP

Heavens join with the clouds, The. To the Tune "Honor of a Fisherman." Li Ch'ing-chao, tr. fr. Chinese by Kenneth Rexroth and Ling Chung. WPC

Heaven's Last Best Work. Pope. Fr. Of the Characters of Women. PIP

Heaven's lights and you to me will shine. (LL) Dear, when I did from you remove. Lord Herbert of Cherbury. EIL

Heaven's mercy shines, wonders and glorys meet. The Mercies of the Year. John Danforth. SCAP

Heaven's mills are grinding slowly, but they grind exceeding small. Divine Revenge. Friedrich von Logau, tr. fr. German. GePo, tr. by George C. Schoolfield

Heavens, ocean, and all earth, rejoice! Sedulius Scottus, tr. fr. Latin. Fr. Defeat of the Norsemen, The. NOIV

Heaven's power is infinite; earth, air, and sea. Ovid, tr. by Arthur Golding. Fr. Metamorphoses. CTC; OAEL-1, tr. by Dryden

Heavens proclaim the glory of the Infinite, The. Nature's Praise of God. Christian Fürchtegott Gellert, tr. fr. German by Philip L. Miller. RiWo

Heaven's River. Issa, tr. fr. Japanese by Harold G. Henderson. ArNa

Heavens' sun perfected in your eyes, The. (LL) Woman. Randall Jarrell. CBLP; NOBA

Heavens themselves, the planets and this center, The. Shakespeare. Fr. Troilus and Cressida. FaBoEH

Heavens! What a goodly prospect spreads around. Happy Britannica. James Thomson. Fr. Seasons, The.
(Britannia.) FaBoPP, ll. 1–19

Heavily Flapping Are the Bustards' Plumes. Shih Ching, tr. fr. Chinese by C. H. Wang. SuSp

Heaviness of twilight at noon, The. Monsoon. Beckian Fritz Goldberg. NAmP90

Heaving mountain in the sea. The Song of the Whale. Kit Wright. OBAP

Heaving Roses of the Hedge Are Stirred, The. Richard Watson Dixon. CH

Heaving the Lead Line. Unknown. AmFP

Heav'n, Heav'n will make amends for all! (LL) A Consolatory Poem Dedicated unto Mr. Cotton Mather. Nicholas Noyes. SCAP

Heavy As Ever. Tim Longville. VaA

Heavy Bear, The. Delmore Schwartz. See Heavy bear who goes with me, The.

Heavy bear who goes with me, The. Delmore Schwartz. Fr. Repetitive Heart, The. LiTA; LiTM; NoAM; NOBA; Poetr; TAP; TrJP; TwCP; UnPo
(Heavy Bear, The.) ImPo

Heavy dew. Thick mist. Dense grass. Passing a Ruined Palace. Wen T'ing-yün, tr. fr. Chinese by Kenneth Rexroth. OHMPC

Heavy glacier and the terrifying Alps, The. Long Lines. Paul Goodman. VGW
(Long Lines: Youth and Age.) PeHV

Heavy hangs the raindrop. The Two Children. Emily Brontë. MeMBP; PoEL-5

Heavy-hearted. Judah al-Harizi, tr. fr. Hebrew. TrJP

Heavy Heavy Heavy. John Malcolm Brinnin. NYBP

Heavy, heavy, heavy, hand and heart. Tenebrae. Denise Levertov. NoP

Heavy heavy lies over our head. Game out of Hand. Allison Ross. GoYe

Heavy mist, A. A muffled sea. Atheling Grange; or, The Apotheosis of Lotte Nussbaum. William Plomer. OBNV

Heavy smells of Spring, The. Jack. Louis Golding. TrJP

Heavy sobs which rise up and choke me, The. Unknown, tr. fr. Japanese by Kenneth Rexroth and Ikuko Atsumi. WPJ

Heavy sounds are over-sweet, The. City-Storm. Harold Monro. MoBrPo

Heavy, to hurt those sacred seeds of thee. (LL) To His Dying Brother, Master William Herrick. Robert Herrick. CaPo; NOSC; SeCV-1

Heavy umbrellas, The. Crocus Night. James Schuyler. PoM

Heavy Water Blues. Bob Kaufman. NBV

Heavy with child. In My Name. Grace Nichols. AIW

Heavy with salt, and warm. The Equinox. DuBose Heyward. PoA

Heavyweight champ of Seattle, The. Unknown. OBAL

Hebrew Melodies., sels. Heine, tr. fr. German by Charles Godfrey Leland. By the Waters of Babylon. TrJP

Hebrew nation did not write it, The. Blake. OAEL-2

Hebrew of Your Poets, Zion, The. Charles Reznikoff. ChIV-1; VGW

Hebrews. James Oppenheim. TrJP

Hebrides, The. Michael Longley. PBCIP

Hecale, sels. Callimachus, tr. fr. Greek by Barbara Hughes Fowler. "As long as it was still noon and the earth." HePo
"South wind does not shed so great a cast, The." HePo
"They fell asleep but not for long, for soon." HePo

Hecatompathia; or, Passionate Century of Love, sels. Thomas Watson. Come, Gentle Death! EIL
Here Lieth Love. EIL
"Some that reporte great Alexanders life." AAS
"Speake gentle heart, where is thy dwelling place?" AAS
Time. CBCK; FaBoRV

Hector. Valentin Iremonger. CIP

Hector Arms. Homer, tr. fr. Greek. Fr. Iliad, The. NOSC, tr. by George Chapman

Hector Protector was dressed all in green. Mother Goose. MoShBr; OxNR; ReMoGo

Hector, the captain bronzed, from simple fight. Geoffrey Scott. Fr. Skaian Gate, The. OBMV

Hector's Defiance. Homer, tr. fr. Greek. Fr. Iliad, The. NOSC, tr. by George Chapman

Hecuba's Testament. Rosario Castellanos, tr. fr. Spanish by John Frederick Nims. STV

He'd become completely degraded. His erotic tendencies. Days of 1896. C. P. Cavafy, tr. fr. Greek by Edmund Keeley and Philip Sherrard. PeHV

He'd been sitting in the café since ten-thirty. Two Young Men, 23 to 24 Years Old. C. P. Cavafy, tr. fr. Greek by Edmund Keeley and Philip Sherrard. FaBoBL; PeHV

He'd had enough of lying in the furze. The Ghostly Father. Peter Redgrove. MoBS

He'd laugh and build a world with snow. (LL) My Father Moved through Dooms of Love. E. E. Cummings. CMoP; FYAP; HAP; LiTA; MeMAP; MoAB; MoP; NAAL-2; NoAM; NOBA; NoP; OxBA; TAP; UnPo

He'd take the piss. Barbus Vulgaris. Matt Simpson. PWE

Hedge before me, one humble, A. Unknown, tr. fr. Irish by Flann O'Brien. BIrV

Hedge Life. James Dickey. LCAP

Her father lov'd me; oft invited me. Shakespeare. *Fr.* Othello. EBEV; OxAEP-1; SCV

Her features unfold as she lowers her head. Sex, Politics, and Religion. Lavinia Greenlaw. NWP

Her feet beneath her petticoat. The Bride. Sir John Suckling. *Fr.* Ballad [*or* Ballade] upon a Wedding, A. BeJo; CaPo; CoMu; EBEV; EBNV; FaBoBa; InvP; JCP; NoP; OxBM; SeCP; SeCV-1; TrGrPo

Her fingers. Frigga with Hela. Judy Grahn. UL

Her fingers bore the winecup in. The Two of Them. Hugo von Hofmannsthal, *tr. fr.* German by John Frederick Nims. STV

Her fingers on the girl's bare neck, light. Timarista and Krito. Rosanna Warren. *Fr.* Funerary Portraits. NoAM

Her fingers shame the ivory keys. Amy Wentworth. Whittier. AnAmPo; BeLS

Her flowers were exclusive blue. Exclusive Blue. Robert Francis. CRP

Her fond creation true. (*LL*) A Day Dream. Emily Brontë. NALW

Her foot sparkled like silver. Rufinus Domesticus, *tr. fr.* Greek by Sam Hamill. InMo

Her for a mistress would I fain enjoy. How to Choose a Mistress. *Unknown.* NOSC

Her fork clinks. Widow's Supper. Mary Jane Moffat. IMW

Her Friend Flo. Gerda Mayer. OBF

Her Garden. Freda Downie. FaBoWP

Her gentle limbs did she undress. Christabel and Geraldine. Samuel Taylor Coleridge. *Fr.* Christabel. CH, ll. 1-65; EnRP; FHYEP; OAEL-2; PeHV

Her God began to pulse through me. Ruth. Diane Q. Lewis. CrSp

Her grandmother called her from the playground. Legacies. Nikki Giovanni. CrSp

Her grieving parents cradled here. Sylvia Townsend Warner. MoBrPo

Her Hair. Sir Robert Chester. *Fr.* Love's Martyr. EIL

Her hair the net of golden wire. So Fast Entangled. *Unknown.* TrGrPo

Her hair upgathered thus behind the neck. Doric. Angelos Sikelianos, *tr. fr.* Greek by Edmund Keeley and Philip Sherrard. ErPo

Her hair was tawny with gold, her eyes with purple were dark. A Court Lady. Elizabeth Barrett Browning. BeLS

Her hand a goblet bore for him. The Two. Hugo von Hofmannsthal, *tr. fr.* German by Ludwig Lewisohn. AWP

Her hand seemed milk in milk, it was so white. (*LL*) Of Phyllis. William Drummond of Hawthornden. CBLP; EIL; GN

Her head covered with black feathers. (*LL*) Descending Figure. Louise Glück. AnAn; FaBoWP

Her health is good. She owns to forty-one. Occupation: Housewife. Phyllis McGinley. *Fr.* I Know a Village. WPE

Her Heards Be Thousand Fishes. Spenser. *Fr.* Colin Clout's Come Home Again. ChTr

Her Heart. Bartholomew Griffin. *See* Fly [*or* Flye] to her heart; hover about her heart.

Her heart had a sonnet. (*LL*) Auf meiner Herzliebsten Äugelein. Heine. AWP

Her heart is like her garden. My Mother's Garden. Alice E. Allen. BLPA; BLPL; FaBoBe

Her heart it brak in twa O. (*LL*) Willie and Lady Margerie [*or* Maisry]. *Unknown.* ESPB; OxBB

Her heart so stricken, Helen. Alcaeus, *tr. fr.* Greek by Sam Hamill. InMo

Her hearts of oak! (*LL*) God save the Rights of Man! Philip Freneau. GOA

Her heavy lot to bear. (*LL*) The Little Shroud. Letitia Elizabeth Landon. VPP

Her heels worn raw. Autistic Poses. Iain Sinclair. VaA

Her house is become like a man dishonored. Dirge. Bible, Apocrypha. *Fr.* First Maccabees. TrJP

Her house is wide open, a shack house. On Maricopa Road. Rita Magdaleno. AfAz

Her Husband. Ted Hughes. OxBC

Her Husband Asks Her to Buy a Bolt of Silk. Ch'en Tao, *tr. fr.* Chinese by Kenneth Rexroth. OHMPC

Her Husband Speaks to Her of Dragons. Marion Lomax. PWE

Her husband was *hors de combat*. C. Vita-Finzi. PeLi

Her I was and her I drank. Gud Ber. *Unknown.* FaBoVe

Her imaginary playmate was a grown-up. Cinderella. Randall Jarrell. LCAP; NAAL-2; VCAP

Her Irish maids could never spoon out mush. Mary Winslow. Robert Lowell. PPP

Her iron beats. Domestic Scene. Michael Hartnett. BIrV

Her Justice next appears, which did support. Sixth Pearle, The: Justice. Lady Diana Primrose. *Fr.* Chain of Pearl, A. KTR

Her Kind. Anne Sexton. CAPP; CoAP; FF; HCAP; HeIP; LiTM; NALW; Poetr; PPP; TAP; TwCP; VCAP; WPOW

Her knees and elbows are only glued together. (*LL*) When a Man Has Married a Wife. Blake. ErPo; FaBoEE; FF; OAEL-2

Her — "last Poems." Emily Dickinson. NALW

Her last words wandered across the ceiling. Death in the Evening. Miroslav Holub, *tr. fr.* Czech by George Theiner. PoSu

Her Left Toe, and her Right Toe. (*LL*) Of all the girls that e'er were seen. John Gay. CoMu; ErPo

Her leggings could burn. Of Three Friendly Warnings This Is the Third. *Unknown, tr. fr.* Seneca Indian by Jerome K. Rothenberg *and* Richard Johnny John. STP

Her Legs. Robert Herrick. NOSC

Her legs go upwards into eternity & well. Big Meal. Iain Sinclair. VaA

Her Letter. Bret Harte. AnAmPo; PoLF

Her life is in the marble! yet a fall. Her, a Statue. Thomas Tod Stoddart. OBNC

Her limp lover Maud couldn't pardon. Kit Wright. PeLi

Her Lips Are Copper Wire. Jean Toomer. NoAM

Her lips they are redder than coral. *Unknown.* FaBoCo

Her long with ardent look his eye pursu'd. Milton. *Fr.* Paradise Lost. EPCY; UnPo

Her Longing. Theodore Roethke. NAAL-2; NU

Her Losses make our Gains ashamed. Emily Dickinson. NALW

Her love hath end; my woe must ever last. (*LL*) Sufficeth it to you [*or* yow] my joys [*or* joyes] interred. Sir Walter Ralegh. SiPS, *sl. abr.*

Her love is true I know. True Love. Waring Cuney. CDC

Her Man Described by Her Own(e) Dictamen. Ben Jonson. *Fr.* Celebration of Charis in Ten Lyric[k] Peeces [*or* pieces], A. BeJo; OxAEP-1; SeCP

Her Merriment. W. H. Davies. EnLoPo

Her morning adornment finished now. Tune: "Casket of Pearls, A." Li Yü, *tr. fr.* Chinese by Daniel Bryant. SuSp

Her Mother. Alice Cary. OHIP

Her mother died when she was young. Kemp Owyne. Alice Cary. EnSB; ESPB; OHIP

Her mouth an O. The Poetess Kō Ōgimi. Helen Chasin. NMM

Her Mouth and Mine. W. H. Davies. CBLP

Her mouth is as fragrant as a vine. Cleopatra. Swinburne. BeLS

Her name, before she was a queen, boots not. Memoir of a Queen. Helen Hunt Jackson. AmWP

Her name is at my tongue whene'er I speak. Ever Present. Philip Ayres. OxBSP

Her name is Dragon Fly. (*LL*) Lalai (Dreamtime). Sam Woolagoodjah. NOBAu

Her Name Is Helen. Beth Brant. GLP

Her Name like the Hours. Gloria Evans Davies. OBWVE

Her name was Marian Claribel Lee. The Ballad of Sir Brian and the Three Wishes. Newman Levy. FiBHP

Her new-born child she holdeth, but feels within her heart. The Slave-mother. Maria White Lowell. AmWP

Her old age/ is waiting for her. Night Prayers. Dinah Livingstone. DT

Her own self-will made void her own self's will. (*LL*) The End of It. Francis Thompson. NOBVV; OxBSP

Her parents and her dolls destroyed. Belsen, Day of Liberation. Robert Hayden. ArOW

Her Passing. William Drummond of Hawthornden. *See* Beauty [*or* Beautie], and the life, The.

Her perfect naked breast. Argentarius, *tr. fr.* Greek by Sam Hamill. InMo

Her perfect peace. (*LL*) Dream Land. Christina Rossetti. BrRo

Her pinched grey body. Supper ("Her pinched grey body.") Walter de la Mare. OFC

Her power is to fall like razors. Her Power Is to Open What Is Shut/ Shut What Is Open. Diane Di Prima. *Fr.* Loba. SRLS

Her Power Is to Open What Is Shut/ Shut What Is Open. Diane Di Prima. *Fr.* Loba. SRLS

Her Praises. Anthony Scoloker. EIL

Her Precious Leg. Thomas Hood. *Fr.* Miss Kilmansegg and Her Precious Leg. NOBVV

Her pretty feet. Upon Her Feet. Robert Herrick. BeJo; CaPo; CBLP; OxBSP; PoE

Her red cloth is like the lightning. Red Beauty. *Unknown, tr. fr.* Gond Oral Tradition by V. Elwin *and* S. Hivale. WTO

Her refusal to accept a room of solitude. Pieces. Duane Niatum. HATNAP

Her Reply. Sir Walter Ralegh. *See* If all the world and love were young.

Her Retirement. Anne Rouse. NWP

Her ringlets glistened like the gold of morn. A Picture. H. Cordelia Ray. CBWP-3

Her rising anger snapped taut. She Passed the Test. He Would Not Let Her Drive. Martin Stokes. PWE

Her Rival for Aziza. *Unknown, tr. fr. Arabic* by E. Powys Mathers. *Fr.* Thousand and One Nights, The. AWP

Her saffron gown. *Unknown, tr. fr. Greek* by Peter Jay. GrAn

Her sails are spread and colours flying. The Emigrant Ship. Henry Dalton. PBCV

Her scarf *à la* Bardot. Twice Shy. Seamus Heaney. TwCP

Her Second Husband Hears Her Story. Thomas Hardy. OBD

Her sense of humor has no gold stop. Telephonist. Janet Frame. WPE

Her Seventeenth Winter. John Leax. CRP

Her shoes could burn. Of Three Friendly Warnings This Is the Second. *Unknown, tr. fr. Seneca Indian* by Jerome K. Rothenberg *and* Richard Johnny John. STP

Her sight is short, she comes quite near. Jenny Wren. W. H. Davies. MoBrPo

Her silken gown rustles. Wang Chien, *tr.* by William H. Nienhauser. *Fr.* Palace Poems. SuSp

Her sins to her Saviour! (*LL*) The Bridge of Sighs. Thomas Hood. BeLS; CoGr; EBEV; EnRP; FaPoR; GTBS; GTBS-P; OBEV; OxAEP-2; WBLP

Her Sister. "Moira O'Neill." AIW; OxBTC

Her sleeping head with its great gelid mass. Perseus. Robert Hayden. NoAM

Her soft plump shoulders. What Her Girl Friend Said to Him. Ammuvanar, *tr. fr. Tamil* by A. K. Ramanujan. PLW

Her Son. Ebba M. Leaf. PWR

Her songs died on the air. (*LL*) She sat and sang alway. Christina Rossetti. GBL; NAEL-2

Her son's back is leather; wet. Bloodline. Dan Masterson. NGP

Her soul, and strikes her contemplation dumb. (*LL*) The Lark. *Unknown.* GBP

Her soul is a select district. Paysage Choisi. Francis Sparshott. MoCV

Her spirit hiding among skin and bones. Beside a Deathbed. Vassar Miller. MT

Her stiffening captor lies in wait. Mercedes, Her Aloneness. Colette Inez. IHMS

Her Story. Naomi Long Madgett. IHMS; PoBA

Her strong enchantments failing. A. E. Housman. FaBoTw; MAT; NOBE; NOBVV; NTP; OAEL-2; OPOP; PeVV

Her/ strong/ white/ legs. Romp. Dave Etter. WeW

Her sweet converts to gall. (*LL*) Judah in Exile Wanders. George Sandys. AH; ChIV-1

Her sweet weight on my heart a night. Emily Dickinson. PeHV

Her that I love, I hate! "How's that, do you know?" they wonder. Catullus, *tr. fr. Latin* by John Frederick Nims. STV

Her thin puny little body. Clinic Day. Jo Barnes. BrRo

Her Time. Theodore Roethke. NAAL-2

Her Triumph. Ben Jonson. *See* See the chariot at hand here of Love.

Her udder shrivels and the milk goes dry. (*LL*) The Cow in Apple Time. Robert Frost. MoAB; MoAmPo; OxBSP; PoLF

Her veil blows across my face. Love-Life. Hugo Williams. CBLP

Her veil was artificial flowers and leaves. Christopher Marlowe. *Fr.* Hero and Leander. AAS; HoPM; NoP

Her Voice. Barney Bush. HATNAP

Her Voice Could Not Be Softer. Austin Clarke. NOIV

Her voice did quiver as we parted. On Fanny Godwin. Shelley. OBNC

Her voice forever match to dry wood. Dirge in Jazz Time. Vassar Miller. Jaz

Her voice is like some angel picking at the door. Alan Brunton. PeNZ

Her voice shifts as if it were light. January Afternoon, with Billie Holiday. Lisel Mueller. Jaz

Her walleyed girls who never would come home. (*LL*) Mina Bell's Cows. Wesley McNair. TRP

Her Whole Life Is an Epigram. Blake. FaBoEE; InPK; OAEL-2

Her wraithful turnings and her soft answers head me off. Soft Answers. Robert Bagg. FF

Her young employers, having got in late. A Summer Morning. Richard Wilbur. FaBoMo; NBLV

Her-zie. Stevie Smith. Mes

Hera, Hung from the Sky. Carolyn Kizer. NMM; SRLS; WPE

Heraclitus. William Johnson Cory, *par. from the Greek of* Callimachus. AWP; EBEvV; EBVV; FaBoEE; FaPoR; InPK; NOBE; OBEV; OBNC; OtMeF; OxAEP-2; OxBSP; PeHV; PoRA; SCGP; UV

Herakles. Parrhasios, *tr. fr. Greek* by Peter Jay. GrAn

Herakles' rebuttal was too much. Philodemus, *tr. fr. Greek* by Kenneth Rexroth. PGA

Heralds of Christ. Laura S. Copenhaver. AH

Herbert Street Revisited. John Montague. CIP; IIP; IPY; PBCIP; PNI

Herbert White. Frank Bidart. AmPA

Herbertson telephoned. For the Record. Roy McFadden. PNI

Hercules Furens., *sels.* Seneca, *tr. fr. Latin* by Jasper Heywood. "Let oken club now strike, and poast of might." OBVE

Hercules Oetaeus., *sels.* Seneca, *tr. fr. Latin* by John Studley. "Let other mount aloft, let other sore." OBVE

Herd, The. Frances Cornford. FM

Herd, The. Peter Fallon. PBCIP

Herd Boy, The. Lu Yu, *tr. fr. Chinese* by Arthur Waley. ChTr

Herd of Impala. Colin Style. OBAP

Herder who hailed from Terre Haute, A. *Unknown.* PeLi

Herdmen, The. *At. to* William Byrd. *See* What pleasure have great princes.

Herds, The. W. S. Merwin. NaP; NYBP

Herdsmen, The. Theocritus [*or* Theokritus], *tr.* by Charles Stuart Calverley. *Fr.* Idylls. AWP

Here. A Zorro Man. Maya Angelou. VBLP

Here. Marvin Bell. AmPA

Here. Robert Creeley. NOBA

Here. Philip Larkin. CMoP; PoE

Here. Bob Orr. PeNZ

Here. Octavio Paz, *tr. fr. Spanish* by John Frederick Nims. STV

Here. Octavio Paz, *tr. fr. Spanish* by Charles Tomlinson. ArNa

Here. R. S. Thomas. GTBS-P; RB

Here/ With my beer/ I sit. Beer. George Arnold. OBAL

Here/ High on the hill. Song of the Hill. Edith Lodge. GoYe

Here. Hat Bar. Mildred Weston. FiBHP

Here, a dark sea speaks with white hands. (*LL*) Bone Thoughts on a Dry Day: Chicago. George Starbuck. GoYe; NYBP; TwCP

Here a little child I stand. Grace for a Child. Robert Herrick. AWP; FaPON; InPS; MoShBr; NAEL-1; PoE; TFi; TrGrPo
(Another Grace for a Child.) BeJo; CoGr; GoJo; InvP; NOSC; NTP; OxBChV; SCGP; SeCV-1
(Child's Grace, A.) BoTP; FaBoCh; OBEV; OxAEP-1
(Grace before Meat.) ChTr
(Grace.) OtMeF

Here a pretty baby lies. Robert Herrick. OBEV
(Upon a Child.) SeCV-1; TrGrPo

Here, a sheer hulk, lies poor Tom Bowling. Poor Tom. Charles Dibdin. NOEC; OxBoLi
(Tom Bowling.) OxAEP-1; PlP

Here a solemn fast we keep[e]. An Epitaph upon a Virgin. Robert Herrick. CaPo; FaBoEE; OxBoLi; PoEL-3; SeCV-1

Here, above/ cracks in the buildings are filled with battered moonlight. The Man-Moth. Elizabeth Bishop. CAPP; CBNP; LiTA; LiTM; MAT; MoAB; MoAmPo; MoP; NALW; NoAM; NOBA; Poetr; PPP

Here again (she said) is March the third. March the 3rd. Edward Thomas. NAs

Here, all star-paven at our Lady's well. A Heretic's Pilgrimage. Eva Gore-Booth. TIRV

Here all the passions, for their greater sway. Thomas Parnell. *Fr.* Essay on the Different Styles of Poetry, The. EPCY

Here, almost everything does. (*LL*) Few things that grow here poison us. Lew Welch. EaPr

Here am I. Please to Remember. Walter de la Mare. NTP

Here am I, little jumping Joan. Mother Goose. NTCP; OxNR
(Little Jumping Joan.) ReMoGo

Here am I now cast down. Ex Nihilo. David Gascoyne. *Fr.* Miserere. GTBS-P

Here am I, sitting in a German inn. James Boswell. OBTV

Here among long-discarded cassocks. Diary of a Church Mouse. Sir John Betjeman. OxBTC

Here, and here only in an age of iron. Terra Australis. Chris Wallace-Crabbe. PAW

Here and hereafter, touch a Paradise. (*LL*) To Ned. Herman Melville. NAAL-1; NOBA; PoEL-5

Here and in hell. (*LL*) The Nameless One. James Clarence Mangan. BIrV; EnRP; GGP; IIP; NOIV; OBEV; PeIV

Here and Now. Catherine Cater. PoNe

Here and Now. Philip Levine. PoA

Here and now is clear so we. 20-200 on 737. Heather McHugh. NIP

Here and There. Ralph Meredith. Mes

Here and there in the searing beam. Deer among Cattle. James Dickey. CAPP

Here and there upon the trees. Last Hope. Wilhelm Müller, *tr. fr. German* by Philip L. Miller. *Fr.* Winter's Journey, The. RiWo

Here are/ blue teapot. Components. Roger McDonald. CBAP

Here are cakes for thy body. The Other World. *Unknown, tr. fr. Egyptian* by Robert Hillyer. *Fr.* Book of the Dead. AWP; OBD

Here are fine gifts, children. Sappho, *tr. fr. Greek* by Willis Barnstone. BoWoP

Here are fruits, flowers, leaves, and branches. Green. Paul Verlaine, *tr. fr. French by* Philip L. Miller. RiWo

Here are grapes ready to turn to wine. Crinagoras, *tr. fr. Greek by* Alistair Elliot. GrAn

Here are no signs of festival. African Christmas. John Press. OBCP

Here are old trees, tall oaks, and gnarled pines. The Antiquity of Freedom. Bryant. EAP

Here are six men, their tools, a cart. Photograph: Sheepshearing. Jo Shapcott. PWE

Here are sweet peas, on tiptoe for a flight. Sweet Peas. Keats. *Fr.* I Stood Tiptoe [upon a Little Hill]. EnRP; FaPON; FHYEP; GN

Here are the fireworks. The men who conspired and labored. Pearl Harbor. Robinson Jeffers. ArOW

Here are the lady's knives and forks. *Unknown.* OxNR

Here are the path, the field. He takes this way. The Attributes. Robert Wells. SCBI

Here are the Schubert Lieder. Now begin. For M.S. Singing *Fruhlingsglaube* in 1945. Frances Cornford. BrRo

Here are two pictures from my father's head. Wounds. Michael Longley. FaBoPV; OBD; PBCIP; PNI

Here are weeds about his mouth. Wide Empty Landscape with a Death in the Foreground. N. Scott Momaday. CDW

Here as I sit by the Jumna bank. Studies at Delhi, 1876. Sir Alfred Comyn Lyall. OBTV

Here, as in a painting, yellow noon burns [*or* noon burns yellow]. Natalya Gorbanevskaya, *tr. fr. Russian by* Daniel Weissbort. BoWoP; PBWP

Here at my right hand. (*LL*) Shimmer. James Schuyler. VCAP

Here at right of the entrance this bronze head. A Bronze Head. W. B. Yeats. LiTB; MeMBP

Here, at the airport, waiting. At the Airport. John Malcolm Brinnin. MoAB

Here at the center of the turning year. New Year. Stephen Spender. AWP

Here at the seashore they use the clouds over & over. Rhode Island. William Meredith. NGP; NoP

Here at the Vespasian-Carlton, it's just one. Boom! Howard Nemerov. LiTM; NBLV; NIP

Here at the wayside station, as many a morning. The Wayside Station. Edwin Muir. FaBoTw; MeMBP

Here at this sudden age of mine. An Autumn Walk. Witter Bynner. GoYe

Here at Woodlands, Moriah. Salmon Courage. Marlene Philip. PBCV

Here, because of the shock, the sudden. Desmond O'Grady. *Fr.* Hellas. PBCIP

Here beside dwelleth. The Magician and the Baron's Daughter. *Unknown.* MeEL

  (Juggler and the baron's daughter, The.) NoSic

Here beside the threshing floor, O hardworking ant. Antipater of Sidon, *tr. fr. Greek by* Barbara Hughes Fowler. *Fr.* Epigrams. HePo

Here blooms the legend, fed by Time and Chance. Rouen, Place de la Pucelle. Maria White Lowell. AmWP

Here bounds the gaudy, gilded chair. The Birth-Day. Mary Robinson. ECWP; WoRP

Here bring your purple and gold. Flowers for the Brave. Celia Laighton Thaxter. OHIP

Here busy and yet innocent lyes dead. On the Death of a Monkey. Thomas Heyrick. FM

Here, but Unable to Answer. Richard Hugo. CAPP

Here by a snowbound river. To Robert Nichols. Robert Graves. PeFWW

Here by the grey north sea. A Northern Vigil. Bliss Carman. OBEV

Here by the moorway you returned. Your Last Drive. Thomas Hardy. OBNC

Here, by the seashore, there lies/ Archilochus. Gaetulicus, *tr. fr. Greek by* Edward Lucie-Smith. GrAn

Here, Caelia [*or* Celia], for thy sake I part. To the Mutable Fair. Edmund Waller. BeJo; SeCP

Here Cleita sleeps. You ask her life and race? The Monument of Cleita. Edward Cracroft Lefroy, *after the Greek of* Theocritus. *Fr.* Echoes from Theocritus. AWP

Here come a cropper'. That's what I said. (*LL*) American Lights, Seen from Off Abroad. John Berryman. LCAP; OBAL

Here come I to my own again. The Prodigal Son. Kipling. *Fr.* Kim. NoAM

Here come real stars to fill the upper skies. Fireflies in the Garden. Robert Frost. OxBSP; SAmP

Here come the capybaras on their bikes. Wild ones. James Fenton. *Fr.* Wild Life Studies. PeLV; SCBI

Here come the line-gang pioneering by. The Line-Gang. Robert Frost. OxBSP

Here comes a girl so damned shapely. Girl Walking. Charles G. Bell. ErPo

Here Comes a Lusty Wooer. *Unknown.* CH; NTP; OxNR

Here comes another, bumping over the sage. Tumbleweed. David Wagoner. BoNaP

Here comes Kate Summers who, for gold. The Bird of Paradise. W. H. Davies. NSI

Here comes my husband from his whist. (*LL*) Dîs Aliter Visum; or, Le Byron de Nos Jours. Robert Browning. CBLP; NAEL-2

Here comes my lady with her little baby. *Unknown.* OxNR

Here comes Old Man Adkins with a battle-ax. Coal Loadin' Blues. *Unknown.* AmFP

Here Comes the Band. William Cole. SiSoPo

Here comes the bride. *Unknown.* RoPo

Here comes the elephant. The Elephant. Herbert Asquith. BoTP

Here comes the Marshal. The Proclamation. Longfellow. *Fr.* John Endicott. PAH

Here comes the powdered milk I drank. Spring Snow. William Matthews. AnAn

Here comes the shadow not looking where it is going. Sire. W. S. Merwin. CoAP; NaP; VGW

Here comes the smoking Bouillabaisse! (*LL*) The Ballad of Bouillabaisse. Thackeray. OBEV; OBTV; OHCV; OxAEP-2

Here continueth to rot. Epitaph on Colonel Francis Chartres. John Arbuthnot. FaBoEE

  (Colonel Chartres.) OBSV

Here costive many minutes did I strain. Privy-Love for My Landlady. George Farewell. NOEC

Here cursing swearing Burton lies. Burns. FaBoEE

Here Dead Lie We. A. E. Housman. CoGr; FaBoEE; NoP; OAEL-2; OtMeF; PoLF; Spl

Here dead lie we because we did not choose. Here Dead Lie We. A. E. Housman. CoGr; FaBoEE; NoP; OAEL-2; OtMeF; PoLF; Spl

  (Epitaph.) NOBVV

Here deare Iöas lies. Iöas' Epitaph. William Drummond of Hawthornden. PoEL-2

Here, decayed, an old. Harlech Castle. John Corben. Spl

Here Delia's buried at fourscore. Hildebrand Jacob. FaBoEE

Here did his fathers live and pass. The Ploughman: In Welsh Uplands. A. G. Prys-Jones. AngWe

Here did sway the eltrot flow'rs. Times o' Year. William Barnes. BoNaP

Here died St. Amand, shepherd of his sheep. Epitaph for St. Amand, Bishop of Utrecht. Alcuin, *tr. fr. Latin by* Helen Waddell. MLL

Here do I put my name for to betraye. *Unknown.* FaBoUs

Here dock and tare. In the Grave No Flower. Edna St. Vincent Millay. NAAL-2

Here doth Dionysia lie. Epitaph of Dionysia. *Unknown.* OBEV

Here down my wearied limbs I'll lay. Robert Herrick. *Fr.* On Himself[e]. CaPo

Here, dying for the world, the world's life hung. On the Cross. Alcuin, *tr. fr. Latin by* Helen Waddell. MLL

Here enter not vile bigots, hypocrites. Inscription above the Entrance to the Abbey of Theleme. Rabelais, *tr. fr. French by* Sir Thomas Urquhart. *Fr.* Gargantua and Pantagruel. FaBoRV

Here erect I guard the land/ and Phrikon's crops and hut. Priapus the Scarecrow. Antistius Vetus, *tr. fr. Greek by* Alistair Elliot. GrAn

Here even experts can. Ragoût Fin de Siècle (with Reference to Certain Cafés). Erich Kästner, *tr. fr. German by* Walter Kaufmann. ErPo; PeHV

Here, ever since you went abroad. What News. Walter Savage Landor. BoLoP

Here, far from all the pomp ambition seeks. Sonnet upon a Swedish Cottage. Sir John Carr. OBTV

Here, five feet deep, lies on his back. On the Astrologer and Almanac Maker, John Partridge. Swift. FaBoEE

Here Follows Some Verses upon the Burning of Our House [July 10th, 1966. Copied Out of a Loose Paper]. Anne Bradstreet. *See* In silent night, when rest I took.

Here Followeth the Songe of the Death of Mr. Thewlis. *Unknown.* CoMu

Here for a little we pause. Benicasim. Sylvia Townsend Warner. OBWP

Here, from laborious art, proud towns, ye rose! On Catania and Syracuse Swallowed Up by an Earthquake, from the Italian of Filicaja. Anna Seward. Son

Here from the start, from our first of days, look. The Tally Stick. Jarold Ramsey. NIP

Here goes a poor old chimney sweeper. The Chimney Sweeper. *Unknown.* AmFP

Here Goes My Lord. *Unknown.* ReMoGo

Here has my salient faith annealed me. Key West. Hart Crane. CMoP

Here Have I Been These One and Twenty Years. Arthur Hugh Clough. NAs

Here have I seen the king, when great affairs. Sir John Denham. *Fr.* Cooper's Hill. BeJo; PoE; SeCP; SeCV-1

Here is a cup left empty in their. Broken Home. William Stafford. NNaP

Here is a family so little famous. Photograph in a Stockholm Newspaper for March 13, 1910. Don Coles. NOBC

Here is a famous world. There Is No Place to Hide. Gwendolyn MacEwen. *Fr.* T. E. Lawrence Poems, The. NOBC

Here is a fountain of Christ's blood. Our Saviour's Love. *Unknown.* OBET

Here is a green Jew. Soap. Gerald Stern. BTR

Here is a heart-shaped leaf. Maple Leaf. Shu Ting, *tr. fr. Chinese by* Carolyn Kizer *with* Y.H. Zhao. SpMi

Here is a house with a pointed door. A Little Finger Game. E. J. Falconer. BoTP

Here is a merry song; if that you please to buy it. A Net for a Night Raven. *Unknown.* OxBSS

Here is a place that is no place. Madhouse. Calvin C. Hernton. ETG; PoNe

(Patient: Rockland County Sanitarium, The.) PoBA

Here is a poem for the two of us to play. The Newly Pressed Suit. Roger McGough. MoP

Here is a rarity. Know Thyself. Kenneth Burke. OBAL

Here Is a Song. John Peck. AH

Here is a symbol in which. Rock and Hawk. Robinson Jeffers. NoAM; NOBA; OxBA; Poetr

Here Is a Toast That I Want to Drink. Walter Lathrop. PoLF

Here is another poem in a picture. Daryl Hine. NoAM

Here is daddy's hayrake. *Unknown.* RoPo

Here is Danda with a dead fish. Danda with a Dead Fish. Deborah Randall. PWE

Here is fresh matter, poet. Church and State. W. B. Yeats. CMoP

Here is Israel. Pictures at an Exhibition. Nathan Rosenbaum. GoYe

Here is Joe Blow the poet. On Being Asked for a Peace Poem. Howard Nemerov. OxBC

Here is Klito's little shack. Kenneth Rexroth, *after the Greek of* Leonidas, *tr. fr. Greek by* Kenneth Rexroth. GrAn; NNaP; PGA

Here Is Much Burning Anger. Shimon Halkin, *tr. fr. Hebrew by* Ruth Finer Mintz. MHP

Here is much burning anger, mighty hate. Here Is Much Burning Anger. Shimon Halkin, *tr. fr. Hebrew by* Ruth Finer Mintz. MHP

Here is no peace, although the air has fainted. Innocent Landscape. Elinor Wylie. OxBA

Here is no shadow but cloudshadow and nightshadow. Hide in the Heart. Lloyd Frankenberg. LiTA

Here is not good enough. Father and Son. Tomasz Jastrun, *tr. fr. Polish.* TSaS, *tr. by* Daniel Bourne

Here is stillness, there is still more. Still. Andrew Greig. PWE

Here is the ancient floor. The Self-Unseeing. Thomas Hardy. EBEV; HAP; MoBrPo; NOBE; NOBVV; OBNC; OxAEP-2; PrIm; RB; WeW

Here is the beehive. Where are the bees? *Unknown.* RoPo

Here is the church, and here is the steeple. *Unknown.* OxNR

Here is the Dog. Since time began. The Dog. Oliver Herford. FaBV

Here is the elm that casts. Infidelity. Théophile Gautier, *tr. fr. French by* Philip L. Miller. RiWo

Here is the fern's frond, unfurling a gesture. Fern. Ted Hughes. NYBP

Here is the foreign cliff and the fabled sea. On a Picture by Michele Da Verona, of Arion as a Boy Riding upon a Dolphin. Anne Ridler. PoA

Here is the guillotine. Lullaby. Christopher Logue. IHNG

Here is the haven: pain touched with soft magic. Hospital. Wilfred J. Funk. PoToHe

Here is the house, in readiness for you. To the New Owner. Lucile Hargrove Reynolds. PoToHe

Here is the long-bided hour: the labor of years is accomplished. Work. Pushkin, *tr. fr. Russian by* Babette Deutsch *and* Avrahm Yarmolinsky. AWP

Here is the News. Michael Rosen. OBSP

Here is the perfect vision: in the dawn. First Flight. Dorothy Wellesley. OBTV

Here is the place, my lord; good my lord, enter. Shakespeare. *Fr.* King Lear. OxAEP-1

Here is the place; right over the hill. Telling the Bees. Whittier. AnAmPo; AWP; BLPL; NOBA; TAP

Here is the river Eurotas. Antiphilos, *tr. fr. Greek by* Sam Hamill. InMo

Here is the shadow of truth for only the shadow is true. A Way to Love God. Robert Penn Warren. NAAL-2

Here is the soundless cypress on the lawn. The Nightingale near the House. Harold Monro. MoBrPo

Here is the stream again under the rainbow. Tchicaya U Tam'si, *tr. fr. French by* E. S. Yntema. *Fr.* Debout. PBA

Here is the tale and you must make the most of it! Jack and Jill — as Kipling Might Have Written It. Anthony C. Deane. FaBoPa

Here is the tale of Carrousel. The Ballad of a Barber. Aubrey Beardsley. NOBVV

Here is the train! The Holiday Train. Irene Thompson. BoTP

Here is the way the white man's heaven felt. On a Picture by Pippin, Called "The Den." Selden Rodman. PoNe

Here is the world's bitter end. Wind. Tribal Homeland. Evangeline Paterson. NBrP

Here is the yoke, with arrow and share near by. The Laborer. José-Maria de Heredia, *tr. fr. French by* Wilfrid Thorley. AWP

Here is this horse from a bad family, hating his burden and snaffle, not patient. Mule. Rodney Jones. NAmP90

Here is thy footstool and there rest thy feet. Rabindranath Tagore. *Fr.* Gitanjali. WGRP

Here it is night: I stay at the Summit Temple. The Summit Temple. Li Po, *tr. fr. Chinese by* Robert Payne. TAL

Here it is spring again. The Late Singer. William Carlos Williams. SAmP

Here it is three years since my grandmother died. The Grandmother. Gérard de Nerval, *tr. fr. French by* Barbara Howes. IMW

Here its like that. Blue Tanganyika. Lebert Bethune. PoBA

Here it's rose-time again, chick-peas in season. Philodemus, *tr. fr. Greek by* William Moebius. GrAn

Here Jack and Tom are paired with Moll and Meg. George Meredith. *Fr.* Modern Love. EnVR; InvP; PoEL-5

Here Johnson lies — a sage by all allow'd. Epitaph. William Cowper. EPCY

Here Keats and Shelley heard. Piazza di Spagna. Willard M. Grimes. GoYe

Here Klito spent eighty years. (*LL*) Here is Klito's little shack. Kenneth Rexroth, *after the Greek of* Leonidas. GrAn; NNaP; PGA

Here lapped in hallowed slumber Saon lies. Saon of Acanthus. Callimachus, *tr. fr. Greek by* John Addington Symonds. AWP

Here lay a fair fat land. Culbin Sands. Andrew Young. GTBS-P; OxBS; OxBTC

Here let me rest me feet! Reverie of a Mum. Nancy Keesing. CBAP; NOBAu

Here let my Lord hang up his conquering lance. Giles Fletcher the Younger. *Fr.* Christ's Victory and Triumph. ChIV-2, *sts.* 30–44; NOSC

Here let the brows be bared. At the Tomb of Washington. Clinton Scollard. OHIP

Here let the Muse perform the painter's art. *Unknown. Fr.* Clio's Picture. ECWP

Here let's jump rope together. Picnic to the Earth. Tanikawa Shuntaro, *tr. fr. Japanese.* TSaS, *tr. by* Harold Wright

Here lie a grasshopper and a/ Cicada. Argentarius, *tr. fr. Greek by* Fleur Adcock. GrAn

Here lie Ciardi's pearly bones. Elegy Just in Case. John Ciardi. ArOW; TwCP

Here lie I, Martin Elginbrodde. *At. to* George Macdonald. FaBoEE; OtMeF; WGRP

(At Aberdeen.) FaBoCo

Here lie I, once a witty fair. Samuel Wesley. NOEC

Here lie I, Timon. Timon's Epitaph. Shakespeare. *Fr.* Timon of Athens. AWP

Here lie John Hughes and Sarah Drew. Lady Mary Wortley Montagu. ECWP

Here lie my old bones: my vexation now ends. Messenger Mounsey. FaBoEE

Here lie the banes o' Tammy Messer. Tammy Messer. *Unknown.* FaBoEE

Here lie the bones of Elizabeth Charlotte. *Unknown. See* Here lies the body of Elizabeth Charlotte.

Here lie the relics of a martyred knight. On Sir John Fenwick. Henry Hall. APAS

Here lie two poor lovers, who had the mishap. Epitaph on the Stanton-Harcourt Lovers. Pope. *Fr.* Three Epitaphs on John Hewet and Sarah Drew. FaBoEE; NIP; OBD

Here lie Willie Michie's [*or* M — hie's] banes. Epitaph on a Schoolmaster. Burns. FaBoCo; FaBoEE

(On a Schoolmaster in Cleish Parish, Fifeshire.) OBD

Here Lies. Stevie Smith. PoA

Here lies a bard, Hipponax — honored name! The Grave of Hipponax. Edward Cracroft Lefroy, *after the Greek of* Theocritus. *Fr.* Echoes from Theocritus. AWP

Here lies a bard, let epitaphs be true. My Epitaph. H. J. Daniel. FaBoEE

Here lies a Bond under this tomb. On Bond the Usurer. *Unknown.* NOSC

Here lies a clerk who half his life had spent. The Volunteer. Herbert Asquith. OBWP; OtMeF; OxBTC; PAW

Here lies a digger, all his chips departed. Epitaph on a Diamond Digger. Albert Brodrick. PeSAV

Here lies a Doctor of Divinity. Richard Porson. FaBoEE

Here lies the man who in life. On a Contentious Companion. John Hoskyns. FaBoEE

Here lies the man who stripp'd Sin bare. Ebenezer Elliot. FaBoEE

Here lies the noble flesh of Spartacus the knave. Sonnet. Daniel Casper von Lohenstein. *Fr. Arminius.* GePo

Here lies the noble warrior that never blunted sword. Epitaph on the Earl of Leicester. Sir Walter Ralegh. EnRePo; RB; SiPS

Here lies the preacher, judge, and poet, Peter. On Peter Robinson. Francis Jeffrey. FaBoCo; FaBoEE; NBLV
(Epitaph on Peter Robinson.) OxBoLi

Here lies the Reverend Jonathan Doe. On the Reverend Jonathan Doe. *Unknown.* ChTr; FaBoEE

Here lies the street of the three balls. To an Avenue Sport. Helen Johnson Collins. PoNe

Here lies Thomas Logge — a Rascally Dogge. Thomas Logge. Walter de la Mare. FaBoEE

Here lies to each her parents' ruth. On My First Daughter. Ben Jonson. BeJo; EBEV; EnRePo; FaBoEE; HoPM; InPS; JCP; NAEL-1; NOBE; NoP; NOSC; PoE; SeCP; SeCV-1; TEP
(Here lyes to each her parents ruth.) PFP

Here lies what had not birth, nor shape, nor frame. Epitaph on James Moore Smythe. Pope. FaBoEE

Here lies, whom hound did ne'er pursue. Epitaph on a Hare. William Cowper. CoGr; FM; HAP; NOEC; NoP; PoEL-3

Here lies Will Smith — and, what's something rarish. On Will Smith. *Unknown.* FaBoCo

Here lies wise and valiant dust. Epitaph on the Earl of Strafford. John Cleveland. FaBoEE; FaBoEH; FaBoPV; JCP; NOBE; NOSC; OtMeF; PeECV; TrGrPo

Here lies with Death auld Grizzel Grimme. Grizzel Grimme. *Unknown.* FaBoEE

Here lies, within his tomb, so calm. On the Clerk of a Country Parish. William Shenstone. FaBoEE

Here lies wrapped up tight in sod. Epitaph for a Postal Clerk. X. J. Kennedy. NIP

Here lieth John Cruker, a maker of bellows. The Bellows Maker of Oxford. John Hoskyns. FaBoEE

Here Lieth Love. Thomas Watson. *Fr. Hecatompathia; or, Passionate Century of Love.* EIl

Here lieth One whose name was writ on water! On Keats. Shelley. FaBoEE

Here lieth the worthy warrior/ Who never bloodied sword. *Unknown.* FaBoEH
(On the Earl of Leicester.) FaBoEE

Here lieth Thom Nick's body. Upon a Fool. John Hoskyns. FaBoEE

Here lieth under this marble ston. *Unknown.* MeEL; MiEL

Here lith the fresshe flowr of Plantagenet. On the Death of Elizabeth, Queen of Henry VII–, and Mother of Henry VIII. *Unknown.* FaBoRV

Here Live Your Life Out! Robert Graves. FaPoB

Here Lives the Jewish People, *sels.* H. Leivick, *tr. fr. Yiddish by Benjamin and Barbara Harshav.*

Here Lockyer lyes interred, enough his Name. Advertising Epitaph: On One Lockyer, Inventor of a Patent Medicine. *Unknown.* FaBoUs

Here, Lord, Retired, I Bow in Prayer. Matthew Bolles. AH

Here luxury's common lot. The light. Grasse: The Olive Trees. Richard Wilbur. NAAL-2; NoAM; NOBA; NYBP

Here lyes a Boy y finest child from me. On My Boy Henry. Lady Elizabeth Brackley. KTR

Here lyes to each her parents ruth. Ben Jonson. *See* Here lies to each her parents' ruth.

Here lyeth he, who was born and cried. On One That Lived Ingloriously. John Hoskyns, *after the Greek of* Simonides. FaBoEE

Here Lysis set an empty tomb. Phanias, *tr. fr. Greek by* Peter Porter. GrAn

Here make an end of singing? (*LL*) If all the world were [*or* was] paper. *Unknown.* CBNP; EBEvV; FaBoCo; FaBoNo; GBP; NOSC; NTCP; OxNR; PYC; TTTS

Here may Paulinus rest, for ever rest. Epitaph for Paulinus of Aquileia and Arno of Salzburg. Alcuin, *tr. fr. Latin by* Helen Waddell. MLL

Here men walk alone. The City. Ogden Nash. CBNP

Here morning in the ploughman's songs is met. Ploughman Singing. John Clare. EnVR

Here, mower, take my shiners bright. The Recruiting Sergeant. *Unknown.* OBET

Here must I tell the praise. *Unknown.* FaBoEH

Here must wee rest; and where else should wee rest? A Serious and a Curious Night-Meditation. Thomas Traherne. SeCP

Here my chamelion [*or* or camelion] muse her self[e] doth cha[u]nge. To His Good Friend [*or* Freinde] Sir Anthony Cooke. Sir John Davies. *Fr. Gulling[e] Sonnets, The.* ESo; Son

Here, my child with fever sleeps. Caesura. Patricia Cumming. MDDM

Here my meat is, clean and dressed. Epitaph for a Meat-Packer. Guy Owen. CRP

Here, newness is all. Or almost all. And like. Day Begins at Governor's Square Mall. Leon Stokesbury. MT

Here, next the mountain, the cold comes early. Early Autumn in the Mountains. Wen T'ing-yün, *tr. fr. Chinese by* William R. Schultz. SuSp

Here not the flags, the rhythmic. Neutrality. Sidney Keyes. MoAB; MoBrPo

Here now once more I lie. Tenth Reunion. Edward Steese. GoYe

Here, O my Lord, I see Thee face to face. Horatius Bonar. *Fr. This Do in Remembrance of Me.* TrPWD

Here often, when a child, I lay reclined. Tennyson. FaBoPP

Here on Earth. Rachel, *tr. fr. Hebrew by* Ruth Finer Mintz. MHP

Here on the earth — not in high clouds. Here on Earth. Rachel, *tr. fr. Hebrew by* Ruth Finer Mintz. MHP

Here, on the farthest point of the peninsula. Of Politics, & Art. Norman Dubie. BAP-90

Here on the mellow hill. Autumn Scene. Basil Dowling. BoNaP

Here on the ridge where the shrill north-easter trails. Ridge, The: 1919. W. W. Gibson. PAW

Here on this open, ancient book. Diary of a Raccoon. Gertrude Ryder Bennett. GoYe

Here once did sound sweet words, a-spoke. The Vield Path. William Barnes. NOBVV

Here once the evenings sobbed. The Pear-Tree. Iwan Goll, *tr. fr. German by* Babette Deutsch *and* Avrahm Yarmolinsky. TrJP

Here, or not many feet from hence. Certain True Woords Spoken Concerning One Benet Corbett after Her Death. Richard Corbett [*or* Corbet]. SeCP

Here Pause: The Poet Claims at Least This Praise. Wordsworth. EnRP

Here penned within the human fold. The Human Fold. Edwin Muir. LiTM

Here Philip the father buried. Callimachus, *tr. fr. Greek. Fr. Epigrams.* HePo

Here, reader, turn your weeping eyes. The Orator's Epitaph. Lord Brougham. NBLV

Here redbuds like momentary trees. Locus. Robert Hayden. FYAP

Here rests his head upon the lap of earth. Thomas Gray. *Fr. Elegy Written in a Country Churchyard.* AWP; ClHu; DL; EBEV; EBEvV; EnRP; FaBoBe; FaBoPP; FaBoPV; FaBoRV; FaPoR; FHYEP; GGP; GN; GTBS; GTBS-P; HAP; HeIP; ImPo; InPK; InPS; LiTB; NOBE; NOEC; NoP; OAEL-1; OBEV; OxAEP-1; PoEL-3; Poetr; PoLF; PPP; PrIm; SCGP; SCV; TEP; TFi; TrGrPo; UnPo; UV; WBLP; WeW
(Epitaph, The.) FHYEP; SCGP

Here rests poor Stella's restless part. Stella's Epitaph. Mary Jones. ECWP

Here rests Tiosav. Epitaphs from Karansko Cemetery. Ljubomir Simovic, *tr. fr. Serbo-Croatian by* Charles Simic. HSix

Here Reynolds is laid, and to tell you my mind. Sir Joshua Reynolds. Goldsmith. *Fr. Retaliation.* FaBoEE; FaBoEH; NOEC; OBD; OxBoLi

Here Rhodoklea/ is a garland. Rufinus, *tr. fr. Greek by* Alan Marshfield. GrAn

Here [*or* How] richly, with ridiculous display. Epitaph on the Politician Himself. Hilaire Belloc. FaBoEE; IHNG; MoBrPo; NBLV; OBSV

Here Saon of Akanthos, Dikon's son. Callimachus, *tr. fr. Greek by* Peter Jay. GrAn

Here shadow lie. Lady Elizabeth Tanfield. TOF
(Epitaph for Sir Lawrence Tanfield.) NOSC

Here she beholds the chaos dark and deep. Pope. *Fr. Dunciad, The.* FHYEP
(Bad Poetry.) EPCY

Here she lies, a pretty bud. Upon a Child That Died. Robert Herrick. BeJo; CaPo; CH; CoGr; InPK; NoP; OBEV; Poetr; SeCV-1
(Epitaph Upon a Child that Died.) OBD; OBEV

Here she lies (in bed of spice). Upon a Maid. Robert Herrick. CaPo; ChTr; FaBoCh; FaBoEE; OxBoLi

Here She Stands. Jean-Joseph Rabéarivelo, *tr. fr. French by* Miriam Koshland. PBA

Here She Was Wont to Go. Ben Jonson. *Fr. Sad Shepherd, The.* BeJo; OxBSP

Here shift the scene, to represent. Swift. *Fr. Verses on the Death of Doctor Swift [D.S.P.D., Occasioned by Reading a Maxim in Rochefoucauld].* OBD

Here should my wonder dwell, and here my praise. Sir John Denham. *Fr. Cooper's Hill.* BeJo; NAEL-1; SeCP; SeCV-1
(Thames, The.) NOSC

Here silken twines, there locks you see. An Ear-string. William Strode. NOSC

Here sit a shepherd and a shepherdess. The Green Shepherd. Louis Simpson. NYBP

Here where I live it is Sunday. A Poem for Nelson Mandela. Elizabeth Alexander. NGP

Here, where men's eyes were empty and as bright. Ghosts of a Lunatic Asylum. Stephen Vincent Benét. AnAmPo

Here where no increase is. Supplication. Josephine Johnson. TrPWD

Here where our Lord once laid his head. Upon the Holy Sepulchre. Richard Crashaw. FaBoEE

Here, where [or when] precipitate Spring with one light bound. A Fiesolan Idyl. Walter Savage Landor. EnRP

Here, where relumed by changing seasons, burn. Roy Campbell. Fr. Golden Shower, The. OxBTC

Here, where summer slips. The Red and the Green. Anne Wilkinson. MoCV

Here, where the baby paddles in the gutter. Lean Street. G. S. Fraser. OxBS

Here, where the breath of the scented-gorse floats through the sun-stained air. Breton Afternoon. Ernest Dowson. OBNC

Here where the fields lie lonely and untended. A Deserted Home. Sidney Royse Lysaght. CH

Here where the meadows gave ease to tired feet. On One Dying in a Convent. Stephen Lucius Gwynn. TIRV

Here, where the noises of the busy town. In the Jewish Synagogue at Newport. Emma Lazarus. AmWP

Here where the parrots come down. Thomas and Charlie. Peter Wild. AmPA

Here, where the red man swept the leaves away. Frederick Goddard Tuckerman. Fr. Sonnets. NOBA; TAP

Here where the roses bloom, where vine and laurel intertwine. Anacreon's Grave. Goethe, tr. fr. German by Philip L. Miller. RiWo

Here, where the taut wave hangs. Life's Circumnavigators. W. R. Rodgers. GTBS-P

Here where the wind is always north-north-east. New England. E. A. Robinson. GOA; HeIP; MeMAP; MoAB; MoAmPo; NAAL-2; NOBA; NoP; OxBA; PFP; TAP

Here, where the world is quiet. The Garden of Proserpine. Swinburne. Fr. Garden of Proserpine, The. AWP; BLPA; BLPL; FaBoRV; FaBV; FaPoR; HAP; LiTB; NAEL-2; NOBE; NOBVV; NoP; OBNC; PeVV; PlP; PoE; PoEL-5; PoRA; SCV; TFi; TrGrPo

Here, where Vespasian's legions struck the sands. Embarcation. Thomas Hardy. OBWP

Here where you left me alone. Letter from Slough Pond. Isabella Gardner. CAPP

Here! Whoever dares check these Balamanja dreamers? (LL) Baobab Fruit Picking; or, Development in Monkey Bay. Jack A. Mapanje. PeSAV

Here with a Loaf of Bread beneath the Bough. Omar Khayyám, tr. fr. Persian by Edward Fitzgerald. Fr. Rubáiyát of Omar Khayyám of Naishápúr, The. AWP; EBVV, abr.; FaBoBe; FaBoRV, abr.; FaPoR, abr.; HAP, abr.; LiTB; NAEL-2; NoP; PoEL-5; PrIm, abr.; TrGrPo; UV

Here with roses in bloom, with woodbine twining the laurel. Anacreon's Grave. Goethe, tr. fr. German by John Frederick Nims. STV

Here with the desert so austere that only. Burial Flags. Ralph Nixon Currey. PoWW

Here X. lies dead, but God's forgiving. J. E. Thorold Rogers. FaBoEE

Here you are beside me again. Shadow. Guillaume Apollinaire, tr. fr. French by Christopher Middleton. PeFWW

Here you can find joy in cloudy weather or bright, day or night. Tune: "Coda." Kuan Yun-shih, tr. by Richard John Lynn. Fr. Medley of Southern and Northern Tunes — Scenic Tour of West Lake. SuSp

Here you find no counted seeds. Right of Way. Eugene McCarthy. IIP

Here! You sons of the men. English Thornton. Edgar Lee Masters. Fr. Spoon River Anthology. OxBA

Here you've got time to think. In Line at the Supermarket. Greg Pape. PBCAP

Hereabouts the signs are good. Midsummer. Thomas Kinsella. IPY

Hereafter fame, here martyrdom. (LL) The Prophet. Abraham Cowley. JCP; TrGrPo

Hereafter shall smell of the lamp, not thee. (LL) His Farewell to Sack. Robert Herrick. BeJo; CaPo; NAEL-1; SeCP; SeCV-1

Heredity. Arthur Guiterman. OBAL; PeLi

Heredity. Thomas Hardy. CTC; EBEV; RB

Heredity. Tony Harrison. Fr. School of Eloquence, The. NAEL-2; NoAM

Heredity. William Dean Howells. AnAmPo

Here's A, B, and C. A Learned Song. Unknown. Fr. Mother Goose's Melody. FaBoUs

Here's a body — there's a bed! Good Night. Thomas Hood. OTCP; Spl

Here's a cosy warm house of Edward and me. (LL) Address to a Child during a Boisterous Winter Evening. Dorothy Wordsworth. NTP; OxBChV; WoRP

Here's a fine bag of meat. Bags of Meat. Thomas Hardy. FM; RB

Here's a good piece of cheese (I perhaps might have kept it). A Cheese for the Archdeacon. Thomas Hughes. AngWe

Here's a good rule of thumb. Reflection on Ingenuity. Ogden Nash. RB

Here's a guessing story. What Is It? H. E. Wilkinson. BoTP

Here's a hand to the boy who has courage. Our Heroes. Phoebe Cary. BLPA

Here's a health to the blacksmith, the best of all fellows. The Blacksmith's Song. Unknown. GBP

Here's a health to the Tackers, my boys. A Health to the Tackers. Unknown. APAS

Here's a health unto His Majesty. A Health unto His Majesty. Jeremy Savile. ChTr

Here's a hotel where even the stairs. Hot Springs. Earle Birney. OxBC

Here's a jolly couple! Oh the jolly jolly couple! Unknown. NOSC

Here's a large one for the lady. The Broom Squire's Song. Unknown. OxNR

Here's a little mouse and. Four III. E. E. Cummings. FaBoMo; TTTS

Here's a man who falls hard asleep. Man Asleep in a Child's Bed. Thomas Lux. AnAn

Here's a poor widow from Babylon. Unknown. OxNR

Here's a song. Season Song. Unknown, tr. fr. Irish by Flann O'Brien. RB
(Scel Lem Duib.) BIrV

Here's a song of praise for a beautiful world. The Beautiful World. W. Lomax Childress. OHIP

Here's a subject made to your hand! (LL) A Light Woman. Robert Browning. OBF

Here's a world of pomp and state. At. to Beaumont, Francis and William Basse Francis Beaumont and to William Basse. Fr. On the Tombs in Westminster Abbey. PlP

Here's an example from/ A butterfly. The Example. W. H. Davies. MoBrPo; TrGrPo

Here's an old lady, almost ninety-one. Two Old Ladies. Siegfried Sassoon. OxBTC

Here's another Spaniard! Welcome! Antonio Machado Ruiz, tr. fr. Spanish by John Frederick Nims. STV

Here's Cooper, who's written six volumes to show. Cooper. James Russell Lowell. Fr. Fable for Critics, A. NOBA; OxBA; TAP

Here's Dog Diogenes, you ferryman. Unknown, tr. fr. Greek by Edward Lucie-Smith. GrAn

Here's Finiky Hawkes. Unknown. OxNR

Here's flowers for you. Shakespeare. Fr. Winter's Tale, The. GBL

Here's fourteen. Care to count them? And that's that. (LL) Sonnet Right off the Bat. Lope de Vega. STV

Here's fourteen pills for thirteen pence. From One of Case's Pill-Boxes. John Case. FaBoUs

Here's my story; the stag cries. My Story. Unknown, tr. fr. Irish by Brendan Kennelly. PeIV

Here's no more news, than virtue, I may as well. To Sir Henry Wotton. John Donne. OxAEP-1

Here's one dog won't get under horse's hoofs. Farrier's Dog. Paul Hyland. PWE

Here's one in whom Nature feared — faint at such vying. Cardinal Bembo's Epitaph on Raphael. Thomas Hardy, after Pietro Bembo. FaBoEE

Here's praise to the nape of the neck. Nape. Jane Epton Seale. CrSp

Here's proof — as if one needed any. Dedicatory Epistle, with a Book of 1949. Roy Fuller. PeLV

Here's scraps enough to serve to-day. (LL) In Praise of a Beggar's Life. "A. W." ElL; TrGrPo

Here's something folk tales tell. Remember Haiti, Cuba, Vietnam. Andrew Salkey. PBCV

Here's Sulky Sue. Mother Goose. OxNR
(Sulky Sue.) ReMoGo

Here's the garden she walked across. The Flower's Name. Robert Browning. Fr. Garden Fancies. CTC

Here's the spot. Look around you. Above on the height. Caldwell of Springfield. Bret Harte. PAH

Here's the Tender Coming. Unknown. GBP

Here's to Lysidice: pour in ten ladles, boy. Argentarius, tr. fr. Greek by Fleur Adcock. GrAn

Here's to that bedraggled sparrow. Sparrow of Espanola. Michael Pettit. NAmP90

Here's to the baby of five or fifteen. In the Same Boat. H. Crawford. FaBoEH

Here's to the blood, in his mettle and pride. The Cock of the Game. Unknown. OBET

Here's to the Grimsby lads out at the trawling. The Grimsby Lads. John Conolly and Bill Meek. OxBSS

Here's to the Maiden. Sheridan. See Here's to the maiden of bashful fifteen.

Herois do Mar. Manuel Igrejas. NGP

Heroism. Lizette Woodworth Reese. AmWP

Heron. Philip Booth. Poetsp

Heron, The. Phoebe Hesketh. OBAP

Heron. Stanley Plumly. AmPA

Heron, The. Theodore Roethke. OBAP; PDV; RFM

Heron, The. Unknown. See Heron [or Hern] flew east, the heron [or hern] flew west, The.

Heron. Ted Walker. NYBP

Heron, The. Vernon Watkins. AngWe; GTBS-P; TwCP; UnPo

Heron [or Hern] flew east, the heron [or hern] flew west, The. Corpus Christi Carol, The ("Heron flew east, the heron flew west, The.") Unknown. GBP
(Heron, The.) EnSB
(Knight in the Bower, The.) ChTr

Heron in Swamp. Frances Minturn Howard. GoYe

Heron stalks, The. Sunset at Twin Lake. Anita Endrezze-Danielson. HATNAP

Heron stands in water where the swamp, The. The Heron. Theodore Roethke. OBAP; PDV; RFM

Heron Weather. Douglas Crase. NoP

Herons. Robin Blaser. NeAP

Herons, The. Francis Ledwidge.

Hero's Portion. John Montague. NOIV

Herr Bruckner often wandered into church. Lives of the Great Composers. Dana Gioia. EOEF

Herrick, thou art too coarse to love. (LL) The Vision. Robert Herrick. CaPo; ErPo; JCP; SCGP; SeCP

Herrick's Julia. Helen Smith Bevington. BXAP

Herring. Kenneth Rexroth. Fr. Bestiary, A. HoPM; OBAL

Herring and ling! The Red Herring. Unknown. FaBoNo

Herring is prolific, The. Herring. Kenneth Rexroth. Fr. Bestiary, A. HoPM; OBAL

Herring loves the merry moonlight, The. The Oyster. Sir Walter Scott. Fr. Antiquary, The. FaBoCh, 1 st.; NTP

Herring Weir, The. Sir Charles G. D. Roberts. Fr. Songs of the Common Day. NOBC

Hers could not stay for sympathy. (LL) It Is Not Beauty I Demand. George Darley. GGP; OAEL-2

Herself. Lorna Dee Cervantes. Fr. Lots. ETG

Herself. John Holmes. HoPM

Herself, as long as she survives and floats. (LL) The Yacht. Catullus. AWP; OBVE

Herself listening to herself, having no name. Herself. John Holmes. HoPM

Hersilia. William Johnson Cory. NOBVV

Hertha. Swinburne. OAEL-2

Hervé Riel. Robert Browning. BeLS; FaBoBe; GN; OtMeF

Hervenis, harping on the hackneyed text. Sunday: A Fragment Transcribed from a Ms. in Chatterton's Handwriting. Thomas Chatterton. ECEV

Hervordshir, shild and spere. The Shires. Unknown. CBCK

He's a dragon, see. Strato, tr. fr. Greek by Tony Harrison. GrAn

He's a fool that marries at Yule. A Scottish Proverb. Unknown. FaBoUs

He's a high clear forehead. Robert Johnstone. Fr. Every Cache. PNI

He's a little dog, with a stubby tail, and a moth-eaten coat of tan. Bum. W. Dayton Wedgefarth. BLPA

He's after me. (LL) If you don't like my apples. Unknown. GBP; OxBoLi

He's an old grey horse, with his head bowed sadly. The Old Whim Horse. Edward Dyson. CBAP

He's Christian enough that repents, and that stitches. (LL) The Candidate. Thomas Gray. PPP

He's Coming. Mark Van Doren. FaBV

He's dead/ the dog won't have to. Death. William Carlos Williams. NAAL-2; OxBA; VGW

He's Doing Natural Life. Conyus. PoBA

He's filled himself with himself. The Secret of the Quartz Pebble. Vasco [or Vasko] Popa, tr. fr. Serbo-Croatian. Fr. Quartz Pebble, The. PoSu, tr. by Anne Pennington

He's from another time track. Another Time Track. Ilze Mueller. LoHo

He's gone, and all our plans. To His Love. Ivor Gurney. NAEL-2; NTP; OBWP; PeFWW; PoWW

He's gone, and Fate admits of no return. Epitaph on the Secretary to the Muses. Jane Barker. FaBoCo

He's Gone Away. Unknown. AS

He's gone, I am now sad and lonely. My Johnny. Unknown. OBET

He's gone to bed at last, that flaring, glaring. My Stearine Candles. James Henry. NOBVV

He's got a radio on his shoulder. Street Music. Greg Pape. PBCAP

He's had enough of the circle. The Adventure of the Quartz Pebble. Vasco [or Vasko] Popa, tr. fr. Serbo-Croatian. Fr. Quartz Pebble, The. PoSu, tr. by Anne Pennington

He's helping me now — this moment. This Moment. Annie Johnson Flint. BLRP

He's laying her dust, for fear of its rising. (LL) Dust to Dust. Thomas Hood. NBLV

He's lean/ He's clean. Dry Rock Number. Tina Reid. AIW

He's learning to shoot. Shirley Kaufman. Fr. Watts. CrSp

He's lost him completely. And he now tries to find. In Despair. C. P. Cavafy, tr. fr. Greek by Edmund Keeley and Philip Sherrard. PeHV

He's man who won't fit in. (LL) The Men That Don't Fit In. Robert W. Service. BLPA; BLPL

He's neither Chinese. A Buddhist Priest. Ho Xuan Huong, tr. fr. Vietnamese by Nguyen Ngoc Bich and Burton Raffel. PBWP

He's not from some country. What She Said about Her Unfaithful, Estranged Husband. Netumpalliyattan, tr. fr. Tamil by A. K. Ramanujan. PLW

He's nothing much but fur. A Kitten. Eleanor Farjeon. CRH; OFC

He's now the ruler of the country which once exiled him. The Exile's Return. Slavko Mihalic, tr. by Peter Kastmiler and Charles Simic. PoSu

He's on my front porch rapping. The Businessman of Alicante. Philip Levine. NaP

He's only a talented man! (LL) The Talented Man. Winthrop Mackworth Praed. EnRP; FiBHP; NOBL; PeLV

He's only rich that cannot tell his store. (LL) Against Fruition ("Stay here, fond youth, and ask no more, be wise.") Sir John Suckling. BeJo; CaPo; NOSC

He's out stuck in a bird's craw. Gary Snyder. Fr. Myths and Texts. NaP; NeAP; PoM

He's played hookey to see the flick again. Buddy Holly Watching Rebel Without a Cause, Lubbock, Texas, 1956. David Wojahn. Fr. Mystery Train: A Sequence. PBCAP

He's ready for his dinner. (LL) If you should meet a crocodile. Unknown. PDV

He's still young — ; thirty, but looks younger. Self-Portrait. Frank Bidart. HCAP

He's sure to cry. (LL) Little Boy Blue, come blow [up] your horn! Mother Goose. BoTP; FaBoBe; OxNR

He's the man who climbs his barn. Man in the Moon. Linda Hogan. HATNAP

He's weary o' the girdin' o't. (LL) Duncan Gray. Burns. CoMu; ErPo; FaBoBl

Hesh! my baby; stop yer fuss. Aunt Chloe's Lullaby. Daniel Webster Davis. AAP

He/She. Stephen Dunn. NAmP90

Hesiod's is the theme and his the style. Callimachus, tr. fr. Greek. Fr. Epigrams. HePo

Hesiod's style and themes: the poet from Soloi. Callimachus, tr. fr. Greek by Peter Jay. GrAn

Hesitant door chain, The. Into Blackness Softly. Mari Evans. PoBA

Hesitation. Lu Hsun, tr. fr. Chinese by William R. Schultz. SuSp

Hesitations. Naomi Quinonez. AfAz

Hesperia. Swinburne. OBNC

Hesperia the Grecians call the place. Virgil, tr. fr. Latin by Robert Fitzgerald. Fr. Aeneid [or Eneados], The. NAWM-1; SiPSBD, tr. by Sir Walter Ralegh

Hesperides, The. Tennyson. OAEL-2

Hesperos, you bring home all the bright dawn disperses. Sappho, tr. fr. Greek by Willis Barnstone. BoWoP

Hesperus. John Clare. EBVV; FaBoRV; GTBS-P; NOBVV; OAEL-2

Hesperus' Hymne to Cynthia. Ben Jonson. See Queen and huntress, chaste and fair.

Hesperus' Song. Ben Jonson. See Queen and huntress, chaste and fair.

Hesperus the Bringer. Byron. See O Hesperus! thou bringest all good things.

Hesperus! the day is gone. Hesperus. John Clare. EBVV; FaBoRV; GTBS-P; NOBVV; OAEL-2
(Evening Star, The. ChTr

Hessian Doctor, The. Philip Freneau. Fr. British Prison Ship, The. EAP

Hester. Charles Lamb. EnRP; GTBS; GTBS-P; OBEV

Hester MacDonagh. Jeannette Slocomb Edwards. GoYe

Hetero-sex is best for the man of a serious turn of mind. Argentarius, tr. fr. Greek by Fleur Adcock. FaBoBl; GrAn; PeHV

Heterosexual Poem. Strato, tr. fr. Greek by Teddy Hogge. GrAn

Heterosexuals can get AIDS too. An Alarming New Development. Ron Schreiber. GLP

"Heu Quam Praecipih Mersa Profundo." Boethius. See Alas, his mind is sunk.

Heu quam precipiti. Boethius, tr. by John Walton. *Fr.* Consolation of Philosophy, The. OBMV

Heureux Qui, comme Ulysse, A Fait un Beau Voyage. Joachim du Bellay, *tr. fr.* French by G. K. Chesterton. AWP

Hev ye seen owt o' maw bonnie lad. Maw Bonnie Lad. *Unknown.* GBP

Heve hes Cock Robin. Mother Goose. *See* Who Killed Cock Robin.

Heven, it es a riche ture. *Unknown.* MiEL

Hewel, or Woodpecker, The. Andrew Marvell. *Fr.* Upon Appleton House, to My Lord Fairfax. ChTr; SeCP; SeCV-1

Hex on the Mexican X, A. David McCord. FiBHP

Hexameter and Pentameter. *Unknown.* ChTr; FaBoNo

Hexameters. Samuel Taylor Coleridge. ChIV-1

Hexametra Alexis in Laudem Rosamundi. Robert Greene. *Fr.* Greene's Mourning Garment. ElL; GBL; PoEL-2

Hey Betty Martin. *Unknown.* AS

Hey, boy! Bring me a napkin and a drink! *(LL)* The Time of Martyrdom. David Diop. NegPo

Hey, boys, joint ahead. Track-lining Song. *Unknown.* AmFP

Hey, Boys! Up Go We! *Unknown.* NOBAu

Hey diddle diddle/ And hey diddle dan! *Unknown.* OxNR

Hey diddle diddle/ The physicists fiddle. Paul Dehn. *Fr.* Rhymes for a Modern Nursery. FiBHP

Hey [*or* Sing hey], diddle, diddle,/ The cat and the fiddle. Mother Goose. FaBoBe; HoPM; OxBoLi; OxNR
(High Diddle Diddle. CBNP; ReMoGo

Hey diddle dinkety, poppety, pet. Mother Goose. OxNR
(Merchants of London, The. GBP; ReMoGo

Hey diddle, dinkety, poppety pet. *Unknown.* BoTP

Hey diddle dout,/ My candle's out. *Unknown.* OxNR

Hey ding a ding. *Unknown.* OxNR

Hey, dorolot, dorolot! *Unknown.* OxNR

"Hey, down a down!" did Dian sing. A Nymph's Disdain of Love. *Unknown.* ElL

Hey Father Death, I'm flying home. Father Death Blues. Allen Ginsberg. *Fr.* Don't Grow Old. SM

Hey, for cattle cook'd and cut! *(LL)* Donought would have everything. Ebenezer Elliot. NOBVV

Hey girl, how long you been here? Motown/ Smokey Robinson. Jessica Hagedorn. UL

Hey! hey! by this day! The Unhappy Schoolboy. *Unknown.* OxBChV

Hey, hey, hey, hey! *Unknown.* MiEL

Hey, hey, hey, hey/ I will have the whetstone. I Will Have the Whetstone. *Unknown.* FaBoNo; GBP

Hey ho! chill love no more. *(LL)* Though Amaryllis Dance in Green. *Unknown.* ElL; NAEL-1

Hey-ho-day! me no care a dammee! Negro Song at Cornwall. *Unknown.* PBCV

Hey-ho Knave; a Catch. *Unknown.* GBP

Hey, Ho, Nobody Home. Hey, Ho, Nobody Home. *Unknown.* SWP

Hey, Ho, Nobody Home. *Unknown.* SWP

Hey ho, what shall I say? Thomas Ravenscroft. CBLP

Hey-How for Hallowe'en. *Unknown.* FaBoCh
(Witches, The.) ChTr

Hey! Lean to hear my feeble voice. Black Elk. EaPr

Hey let's fight that shaman, let's fight that ghost first & then that shaman. Ghost & Shaman. *Unknown, tr. fr. Bella Bella Indian by* Franz Boas. STP

Hey Mama, what's revolution? Bedtime Story. Nayo-Barbara Watkins. NBV

Hey, my kitten, my kitten. Mother Goose. OxNR
(My Kitten.) ReMoGo

Hey! My Pony! Eleanor Farjeon. FaPON

Hey Nellie,/ how long you been here? did you. Smokey's Getting Old. Jessica Hagedorn. OpBo

Hey nonny no! *(LL)* Hey Nonny No! *Unknown.* CH; ChTr; EBEV; ElL; OBEV; TrGrPo

Hey Nonny No! *Unknown.* CH; ChTr; EBEV; ElL; OBEV; TrGrPo

Hey! now, now, now. Welcome! Our Messiah. *Unknown.* MeEL

Hey! [*or* Hay!] now [*or* nou] the day dawis [*or* daunss]. The Night Is Near [*or* Neir] Gone. Alexander Montgomerie. OBEV; OxBS
(Hey! Now the Day Dawns.) CH

Hey! Now the Day Dawns. Alexander Montgomerie. *See* Hey! [*or* Hay!] now [*or* nou] the day dawis [*or* daunss].

Hey noyney! I will love our Sir John and I love eny. *Unknown.* MiEL

Hey, pop!/ Re-bop!/ Mop!/ Y-e-a-h! *(LL)* Dream Boogie. Langston Hughes. AmPP; HCAP; Jaz

Hey Robin. Joseph Skipsey. EBVV

Hey there poleece. Poem to a Nigger Cop. Bobb Hamilton. TTY

Hey, Wully Wine. *Unknown.* CH

Hey, young bride! Teasing Song. Princess Magogo, *tr. fr. Zulu by* D. K. Rycroft. WTO

Heye Louerd, thou here my bone. *Unknown.* MiEL

Heyhow for Hallow e'en. *(LL)* Hey-How for Hallowe'en. *Unknown.* FaBoCh

Heyl, Levedy, see-sterre bright. William Herebert. MiEL

Hezekiah, *sels.* Thomas Parnell.
"From the black beach and broad expanse of sea." ChIV-1

Hezekiah's Display. John Keble. ChIV-1

H'had *Shows* of Reason, and few *Men* have more. *(LL)* On the Death of a Monkey. Thomas Heyrick. FM

Hi!. Walter de la Mare. IHNG; OBD; PeLV

Hi De Buckras Hi! Grace Nichols. AIW

Hi-Fashion Girl. Elaine Equi. UL

Hi, Jimmis, nagah, matty man, you deh 'pon um again. Deh 'Pon Um Again. Michael McTurk. PBCV

Hi, mawning Susie, how yuh is? yuh get de small-pox yet? Lizzie Discourses on the Small-Pox. Edward Cordle. PBCV

Hi! Miss Liza's got er banjer. Miss Liza's Banjer. Daniel Webster Davis. AAP

Hi-oo, hi-oo, oo-oo. *(LL)* Night-herding Song. Harry Stephens. NTP

Hi Roy. Hope all is well. Blue Lonely Dreams. Marc Cohen. BAP-91

Hi! shoo aller birds. Bird Starver's Cry. *Unknown.* FaBoVe

Hi there. My name is George. Notes on the Peanut. June Jordan. NoAM

Hi-tiddley-i-ti, brown bread! *Unknown.* ISE

Hi! we shout with voice ecstatic. Roundel in the Rain. *Unknown.* FiBHP

Hialmar Speaks to the Raven. Charles Marie René Leconte de Lisle, *tr. fr.* French by James Elroy Flecker. AWP

Hiatus. Margaret Avison. HAP

Hiawatha Revisited. George A. Strong. *See* He [*or* When he] killed the noble Mudjokivis.

Hiawatha's Brothers. Longfellow. *Fr.* Song of Hiawatha, The. BoTP

Hiawatha's Canoe. Longfellow. *See* Give me of your bark, O Birch-tree!

Hiawatha's Childhood. Longfellow. *See* By the shores of Gitche [*or* Gitchee] Gumee.

Hiawatha's Photographing. "Lewis Carroll." BXAP; FaBoCo; FaBoPa; FiBHP; NOBL; PeLV

Hiawatha's Wooing. Longfellow. *Fr.* Song of Hiawatha, The. BeLS; EBNV

Hibakusha's Letter (1955), The. David Mura. OpBo

Hibernia. Stuart Howard-Jones. NOBL

Hibernia's Helicon is dry. William Dunkin. *Fr.* Epistle to Robert Nugent, Esq. with a Picture of Doctor Swift in Old Age, An. NOEC

Hibiscus. Su Shih, *tr. by* Irving Y. Lo. *Fr.* On Chao Ch'ang's Flower Paintings in Wang Po-yang's Collection. SuSp

Hibiscus and Salvia Flowers. D. H. Lawrence. FaBoPV

Hibiscus Flowers. Li Shang-yin, *tr. fr. Chinese by* Eugene Eoyang *and* Irving Y. Lo. SuSp

Hibiscus is flaming and frillier. Ruth Silcock. PeLi

Hibiscus on the Sleeping Shores. Wallace Stevens. InPS

Hibou et Minou allèrent à la mer. Le Hibou et la Poussiquette. Francis Steegmuller. NYBP

Hic hoc horum genitivo. *(LL)* Amo, Amas. John O'Keefe. ChTr; GBL

Hic, Hoc, the Carrion Crow. *Unknown.* OxBoLi

Hic Jacet Arthurus Rex Quondam Rexque Futurus. Francis Brett Young. OtMeF

Hic jacet Tom Shorthose. *Unknown.* FaBoEE

Hic liber ad me pertinet. Robert Barclay. FaBoUs

Hic liber est meus. To the Borrower of This Book. Samuel Showell, Jr.. FaBoUs

Hic Vir, Hic Est. Charles Stuart Calverley. OxBoLi; PeLV

Hicche-Hykeres Tale, The. W. F. N. Watson. BXAP

Hiccup, snick up. *Unknown.* RoPo

Hiccups. Léon Damas, *tr. fr.* French by Ellen Conroy Kennedy. NegPo

Hick-a-more, Hack-a-more. Mother Goose. OxNR
(Sunshine.) ReMoGo

Hickamore hackamore. *Unknown.* FaBoVe

Hickery, dickery, 6 and 7. A Counting-out Rhyme. *Unknown.* ReMoGo

Hickery, pickety. Mother Goose. BoTP
(Black Hen, The. ReMoGo

Hickety pickety i sillickety [*or* i-silicity]. *Unknown.* GBP; OxNR

Hickety, pickety, my black hen. Mother Goose. *See* Higgledy, piggledy, my black hen.

Hickory, dickory, dock. *(LL)* Mother Goose. FaBoBe; OxNR; ReMoGo, *diff. vers.*; RoPo, (*diff. vers.*)

Hickup, hickup, go away. Charm: Hiccups. *Unknown.* FaBoUs

Hid by the august foliage and fruit. To a Chameleon. Marianne Moore. GoYe

High in the woodland, on the mountain-side. The Ant-Heap. A. C. Benson. EBVV

High Island. Richard Murphy. CIP; NOIV

High June. Catherine A. Morin. BoTP

High King of Glory permit her to get the mange, The. *(LL)* A Glass of Beer. James Stephens. CMoP; FaBoCo; FiBHP; InPK; MoP; NBLV; OBMV; OxBS; OxBTC; PeIV; RB

High King, wilt hear me plead? He Intercedes with Charlemagne for His Brother in Exile. Paul the Deacon, *tr. fr. Latin by* Helen Waddell. MLL

High-loping Cowboy, The. Curley W. Fletcher. AiP

High Midnight was garlanding her head, The. Moonlight. Jacques Tahureau, *tr. fr. French by* Andrew Lang. AWP

High Modes: Vision as Ritual: Confirmation. Michael S. Harper. NBV

High o'er his moldering castle walls. A Voice from the Invisible World. Goethe, *tr. fr. German by* James Clarence Mangan. AWP

High o'er the Hills. William Walker. AH

High on a rock, coeval with the skies. The Temple of Chastity. Mary Robinson. Poetr

High on a slope in New Guinea. The Man in the Dead Machine. Donald Hall. ArOW; CAPP

High on a throne of royal state, which far. Milton. *Fr.* Paradise Lost. EPCY; FHYEP; NIP; OAEL-1, *ll.* 1–309; OxAEP-1

High on his figured couch beyond the waves. Theseus and Ariadne. Robert Graves. HAP

High on his stockroom ladder like a dunce. Playboy. Richard Wilbur. FF; MoP; NoAM; NOBA; NoP

High on some cliff, to heaven up-piled. William Collins. *Fr.* Ode on the Poetical Character. EPCY

High on the dove-cot. Doves. E. J. Falconer. BoTP

High on the mountain of sunrise where standeth the Temple of Sebek. He Knoweth the Souls of the West. *Unknown, tr. fr. Egyptian by* Robert Hillyer. *Fr.* Book of the Dead. AWP

High on the upper, outermost bough. Sappho, *tr. fr. Greek by* Sam Hamill. InMo

High on the wall that holds Jerusalem. G. K. Chesteron. OBTV

High over Mecca Allah's prophet's corpse. Dissatisfaction with Metaphysics. William Empson. CMoP

High overhead. Thomas Edward Brown. NOBVV

High Perfections of Our Transitory Days, The. Francis Quarles. *Fr.* Divine Fancies, The. CBCK

High perfections, wherewith heav'n do's please, The. The High Perfections of OUr Transitory Days. Francis Quarles. *Fr.* Divine Fancies, The. CBCK

High-piled ambiguous cargo, The. *(LL)* Sailor's Harbor. Henry Reed. MoAB; MoBrPo

High piled cumulus. Thomas A. Clark. *Fr.* Twenty Poems. NBrP

High pink wall; plaster in map shapes peeling, A. Blue Arm. Bernard Spencer. NoAM

High-placed above me the branches quiver. The Lost. *Malay Oral Tradition, tr. by* R. J. Wilkinson *and* R. O. Winstedt. WTO

High plane for whom the winds incline. Airman's Virtue. William Meredith. ArOW

High poetry and low. Wallace Stevens. PoA

High poets are gone, The. For the Family of Cuchonnacht O Dalaigh. David O'Bruadair, *tr. fr. Irish by* Thomas Kinsella. NOIV

High Priest, The. *Unknown, tr. fr. Hebrew by* Arthur Davis. TrJP

High Priests of telescopes and cyclotrons, The. Ode to Terminus. W. H. Auden. HAP

High Renaissance. George Starbuck. NBLV; OBAL

High Resolve. *Unknown.* PoToHe

High-speed metal snake switches its tail, A. The Chief of the West, Darkling. David Knight. MoCV

High-spirited friend. The Noble Balm. Ben Jonson. OBEV (High-spirited friend.) BeJo

High stretched upon the swinging yard. Disguises. Thomas Edward Brown. WGRP

High Summer. Ebenezer Jones. NOBVV

High Summer on the Mountains. Idris Davies. OxBTC; PlP

High summer's sheen upon all things. The Web. Theodore Weiss. CoAP

High Talk. W. B. Yeats. CBNP; FaBoVe; RaBo

High tensile wire, when strained. Fencing. Anthony Lawrence. NOBAu

High, The/ the low. Hildegard von Bingen, *tr. fr. Latin.* EaPr

High the vanes of Shrewsbury gleam. The Welsh Marches. A. E. Housman. FaBoTw; SCGP

High Tide. Jean Starr Untermeyer. MoAmPo

High Tide at Gettysburg, The. Will Henry Thompson. AnAmPo; BeLS; BLPA; FaBoBe; PAH; VPP

High Tide on the Coast of Lincolnshire (1571), The. Jean Ingelow. BeLS; EBVV; FaBoPP; GN; Mes, *abr.*; OtMeF; OxAEP-2; VPP

High time now gan it wex for Una faire. Spenser. *Fr.* Faerie Queene, The. FHYEP

High to Low. Langston Hughes. HCAP

High-toned Old Christian Woman, A. Wallace Stevens. CMoP; MoP; NAAL-2; NoAM; NOBA; Poetr; PPP; TAP

High-toned Old Fascist Gentleman, A. William Zaranka. BXAP

High towers the grass where once we'd meet and wander. Parting. *Malay Oral Tradition, tr. by* R. J. Wilkinson *and* R. O. Winstedt. WTO

High up among the mountains, through a lovely grove of cedars. Bears. Arthur Guiterman. PoRA

High up in the courts of heaven today. A Little Dog-Angel. Norah M. Holland. PoLF

High upon the hillside where the shadows play. Skippets, the Bad One. Christine E. Bradley. BoTP

High walls and huge the body may confine. Freedom for the Mind. William Lloyd Garrison. FaBoBe

High Way to the Spital House, The, *sels.* Robert Copland. "To write of Sol in his exaltation." NoSic

High Wind, The. *Unknown. See* Arthur O'Bower has broken his bands [*or* band].

High Wind at the Battery. Ralph Pomeroy. NYBP

High Windows. Philip Larkin. FaBoMo; NAEL-2; NoAM

High wind . . . They turn their backs to it, and push. Glasgow Schoolboys, Running Backwards. Douglas Dunn. OxBC

High Wonders. Naomi Marks. BXAP

High Wood. Philip Johnstone. NSI; PAW

High-yellow of my heart, with breasts like tangerines. The Peasant Declares His Love. Emile Roumer, *tr. fr. French by* John Peale Bishop. ErPo; NegPo; TTY

High Zero, *sels.* Andrew Crozier.
"All of your ideas." NBrP
"All that it should be." NBrP
"In the time it takes." NBrP
"Then in the smoke." NBrP

Higher. *Unknown.* FiBHP

Higher Argument. Milton. *See* No more of talk where God or Angel Guest.

Higher Catechism, The. Sam Walter Foss. WGRP

Higher Empiricism, The. Francis C. Golffing. PoA

Higher Good, The. Theodore Parker. FaBoBe

Higher Love. Jeff Wright. UL

Higher Pantheism, The. Tennyson. EnVR; OHCV; WGRP

Higher Pantheism in a Nutshell, The. Swinburne. *Fr.* Heptalogia, The. BXAP; CBNP; EnVR; FaBoNo; OHCV; PeVV

Higher than a house,/ Higher than a tree. Mother Goose. OxNR; ReMoGo

Higher than gull's nests, higher than children go. Rock Climbing. Jane Cooper. NMM

Higher than heaven they sit. The Hope of the World. Sir William Watson. WGRP

Highest Divinity. *Unknown, tr. fr. Hebrew by* Israel Zangwill. TrJP

Highest of Immortals bright. Indra, the Supreme God. *Unknown, tr. fr. Sanskrit by* Romesh Dutt. *Fr.* Vedic Hymns. AWP

Highest spires were ablaze with the movement of feet, The. *(LL)* Victoria Market. Francis Brabazon. NOBAu

Highest Wind That Ever Blew: Homage to Louis, The. Fred Chappell. Jaz

Highland Cattle., *sels.* Dinah Maria Mulock Craik. "Down the wintry mountain." GN

Highland Glen near Loch Ericht, A. Arthur Hugh Clough. *See* There is a stream, I name not its name.

Highland Harry Back Again. *At. to* Burns Burns. EBEV

Highland Mary. Burns. AWP; EnRP; GTBS; GTBS-P; OBEV; TrGrPo; WBLP

Highland Mary. Mary Weston Fordham. CBWP-2

Highland Tinker, The. *Unknown.* CoMu

Highlandmen hae a' come down, The. The Lady of Arngosk. *Unknown.* ESPB

Highlands of Hudson! ye saw them pass. The Storming of Stony Point. Arthur Guiterman. PAH

Highly bored damsel called Brown, A. *Unknown.* PeLi

Highty, tighty, paradighty, clothed [all] in green. *Unknown.* ChTr; OxNR

Highway, The. William Channing Gannett. WGRP

Highway, The. W. S. Merwin. PoA

Highway, The. Sir Philip Sidney. *See* Highway, since you my chief Parnassus be.

Highway ended, The. 7 Years from Somewhere. Philip Levine. AnAn

Highway is full of big cars, The. Come, And Me My Baby. Maya Angelou. ArLo

Highway, since you my chief Parnassus be. Sir Philip Sidney. *Fr.* Astrophel and Stella. AAS; EIL; EnRePo; ESo; GGP; Poetr; SiPS; SiPSBD
(Highway, The.) LiTB; OBEV; OxAEP-1
Highway to Glory Song. W. H. Auden. *Fr.* Man of La Mancha. AnAn
Highwayman, The. Alfred Noyes. BeLS; EBEvV; EBNV; FaBV; FaPON, *abr.;* NTP; OBNV; OBSP; PoLF
Highwayman, The. *Unknown.* ECEV
Highwaymen, The. John Gay. *Fr.* Beggar's Opera, The. OAEL-1; WiR
Hijack. Lincoln Kirstein. ArOW
Hiking. Joseph Bruchac. CDW
Hilaire Belloc. Humbert Wolfe. FaBoEE
Hilarious, leap from bough to bough. *(LL)* 'Tis Midnight. *Unknown.* NTCP
Hilas, o Hilas, why sit we mute. Chloris and Hilas. Made to a Saraban. Edmund Waller. SeCV-1
Hilbert's Program. Milo De Angelis, *tr. fr. Italian by* Lawrence Venuti. NeIt
Hildegund eagerly urged him. Waldere 1. *Unknown, tr. fr. Anglo-Saxon by* Kevin Crossley-Holland. ASW
Hill, The. Rupert Brooke. MoBrPo; OxBTC; Son
Hill, The. Robert Creeley. CRP; RaBo; TRP
Hill, A. Anthony Hecht. CoAP; FoLa; NYBP; VCAP
Hill, The. Horace Holley. WGRP
Hill, The. Edgar Lee Masters. *Fr.* Spoon River Anthology. CMoP; FYAP; LiTA; LiTM; NoAM; NOBA; OxBA; TAP
Hill-billy, hill-billy come to buy. Pedlar. Confucius, *tr. fr. Chinese by* Ezra Pound. *Fr.* Wei Wind. CTC; OBVE
Hill Farmer Speaks, The. R. S. Thomas. GTBS-P; OBWVE; PlP
Hill flank overlooking the Axe valley, A. Watching Post. C. Day Lewis. PAW
Hill Fort, Caerleon. Sam Adams. AngWe
Hill full, a hole full, A. The Mist. *Unknown.* ReMoGo
"Hill of Jews," says one. Montjuich. Philip Levine. AnAn
Hill of the Graces, The. Spenser. *Fr.* Faerie Queene, The. NOBE
Hill of Zion yields, The. Mount Zion. *Unknown.* AmFP
Hill Summit, The. Dante Gabriel Rossetti. *Fr.* House of Life, The. NoP; PFP
Hill Wife, The. (One ought not to have to care.) Robert Frost. CMoP; HAP; InPS; LiTM; NoP
Sels.
House Fear. NTP; VGW
Impulse, The. ArLo; HoPM; RaBo
Loneliness. VGW
Oft-Repeated Dream, The. Poetr
Hillcrest. E. A. Robinson. MeMAP; MoAB; OxBA
Hills, The. Frances Cornford. MoBrPo
Hills, The. D. H. Lawrence. ChIV-1
Hills afloat across the water are. Lamentation on Ninety-Mile Beach. Barry Mitcalfe. PeNZ
Hills and rivers of the lowland country, The. A Protest in the Sixth Year of Ch'ien Fu. Ts'ao Sung, *tr. fr. Chinese by* Arthur Waley. FaBV
Hills are calling me from care and reason, The. Bright Abandon. Tessa Sweazy Webb. GoYe
Hills are white, but not with snow, The. An Orchard at Avignon. Agnes Mary Frances Robinson. NOBVV; OBTV
Hills are wroth, The; the stones have scored you bitterly. To a Young Girl Leaving the Hill Country. Arna Bontemps. CDC
Hills fled from our sight; but left his golden load. *(LL)* To Autumn. Blake. BoNaP; NAEL-2; WiR
Hills haven the last cloud. However white. From. First Moment of Autumn Recognized. Robert Penn Warren. ArNa
Hills, I told them; and water, and the clear air, The. Instead of an Interview. Fleur Adcock. OBTV
Hills in emerald robes of richest dye, The. Among the Berkshire Hills. H. Cordelia Ray. CBWP-3
Hills moved. I watched their shadows. Beetle on the Shasta Daylight. Shirley Kaufman. NYBP; WPE
Hills of God, Break Forth in Singing. John Wright Buckham. AH
Hills of Rest, The. Albert Bigelow Paine. WGRP
Hills o Salt. Dahlia Ravikovitch, *tr. fr. Hebrew by* Chana Bloch. WPOW
Hills picking up the/ moonlight like. Nina Cassian, *tr. fr. Romanian by* Stavros Deligiorgis. BoWoP
Hills sleep on in their eternity, The. *(LL)* To a Friend. Hartley Coleridge. PoLF
Hills step off into whiteness, The. Sheep in Fog. Sylvia Plath. FaBoWP; HCAP; LCAP; NaP
Hills stirring under their woven, The. Goethe's Blues. Denise Levertov. FaBoWP

Hills Surround Me. Mok-wol Park, *tr. fr. Korean by* Chang-soo Koh. PAW
Hills surround me, and, The. Hills Surround Me. Mok-wol Park, *tr. fr. Korean by* Chang-soo Koh. PAW
Hills turn hugely in their sleep, The. Robert Silliman Hillyer. *Fr.* Prothalamion. MoAmPo
Hills yet hills, and still the yellow town, The. Naples Again. Arthur Freeman. NYBP
Hillside Pause. Catharine Morris Wright. GoYe
Hillside Thaw, A. Robert Frost. CMoP
Hilltop, The. Richard Hugo. CAPP; Poetr
Hilo, Hanakahi, rain rustling lehua. *Unknown, tr. fr. Hawaiian by* S. H. Elbert *and* N. Mahoe. WTO
Him and his affections ever. *(LL)* A Charme, or an Allay for Love. Robert Herrick. FaBoCh; FaBoUs
Him, as He is, is labour without end. *(LL)* 'Tis Hard to Find God. Robert Herrick. LiTB
Him that doth love me! *(LL)* Blue and White. Mary Elizabeth Coleridge. OBEV
Him that I love I wish to be. Even. Anne Morrow Lindbergh. AiP
Himalayan Balsam. Anne Stevenson. FaBoWP; OxAEP-2; VBLP
Himself, *sels.* Edwin John Ellis.
"At Golgotha I stood alone." OBMV
Himself. Peter Fallon. PBCIP
Himself. *(LL)* The Sunday before Easter. Askold Melnyczuk. UTF
Himself, his Maker, and the angel Death. *(LL)* The Good Great Man. Samuel Taylor Coleridge. PWR
"Himself on the Wood there," says one. Cross Talk. Cyril Cusack. TIRV
Himself, the "guilty" child! *(LL)* "Guilty or Not Guilty?" *Unknown.* BeLS; BLPA
Himself-to Him-a Fortune /Exterior-to Time. *(LL)* This was a poet — It is that. Emily Dickinson. AmPP; NAAL-1; NOBA
Hind and the Panther, The, *sels.* Dryden.
"But gratious [*or* gracious] God, how well dost thou provide." TrPWD
"Dame, said the Panther, times are mended well." PoEL-3
"Milk white Hind, immortal and unchang'd, A." SeCV-2; UV
"One evening, while the cooler shade she sought." PoEL-3
"Portly prince, and goodly to the sight, A." OBSV
Presbyterians, The. NOSC
Private Judgement Condemned
(Confessio Fidei.) NOBE
"To this the Panther, with a scornful smile." SeCV-2
Hind Etin. *Unknown.* OxBB
Hind Etin. *Unknown.* ESPB, A *and* B *vers.;* OxBB
Hind Horn. *Unknown.* AmFP; ESPB, A *and* B *vers.*
Hindenburg, The. Van K. Brock. BTR
Hindoo: He Doesn't Hurt a Fly or a Spider Either, The. A. K. Ramanujan. OxBC
Hinds of Kerry, The. William S. Wabnitz. GoYe
Hindu Cradle Song. Sarojini Naidu [*or* Nayadu]. *See* From groves of spice.
Hinky Dinky, Parlee-Voo. *Unknown.* AS
Hinky Dinky Parlez Vous. *Unknown.* SWP
Hint for the Incomplete Angler. Kendrick Smithyman. PeNZ
Hint from Voiture. William Shenstone. EnLoPo
Hint of gold where the moon will be, A. The Want of You. Angelina Weld Grimké. ShDr
Hinted Wish, A. Martial, *tr. fr. Latin by* Francis Lewis. AWP
Hints from Horace, *sels.* Byron.
"Peace to Swift's faults! his wit hath made them pass." EPCY
Hints on Pronunciation for Foreigners. *Unknown.* FaBoUs
Hinty, minty, cuty, corn. *Unknown.* Fr. Counting-out Rhymes. FaPON; ImGa
Hinx! minx!/ The old witch winks! *Unknown.* MAT; OxNR
(Hinx, minx, the old witch winks.) ISE
Hinx, minx, the old witch winks. *Unknown. See* Hinx! minx!/ The old witch winks!
Hip, hip, hip, harvest home! *(LL)* Harvest Song. *Unknown.* BoTP; OxNR
Hippity hop to the barber shop. *Unknown.* RoPo
Hippo, The. Theodore Roethke. VGW
Hippo. Margaret Toms. OBAP
Hippo is a visual joke, A. Hippo. Margaret Toms. OBAP
Hippodromania; or, Whiffs from the Pipe, *sels.* Adam Lindsay Gordon.
"Rest, and be thankful! On the verge." CBAP
Hippolytus. Euripides, *tr. fr. Greek.* NAWM-1, *tr. by* Rex Warner.
Sels.
No More, O My Spirit. AWP
O for the Wings of a Dove. AWP
Hippolytus, *sels.* Seneca.

"Light griefs can speak." IMW

Hipponax. Alcaeus, *tr. fr. Greek* by Alistair Elliot. GrAn

Hippopotamothalamion. John Hall Wheelock. FiBHP; FYAP

Hippopotamus, The. Hilaire Belloc. FaBoNo; FiBHP; InPK

Hippopotamus. Joanna Cole. NTCP

Hippopotamus, The. T. S. Eliot. AWP; CBNP; HoPM; ImPo; LiTB; NAEL-2; OBMV; VGW

Hippopotamus, The. Ogden Nash. FaBV

Hippopotamus had a bride, A. Hippopotamothalamion. John Hall Wheelock. FiBHP; FYAP

Hippopotamus is strong, The. Habits of the Hippopotamus. Arthur Guiterman. FaBV; FiBHP; OBCA

Hippopotamus's Birthday, The. Emile Victor Rieu. Mes

Hipsaw! my deaa! you no do like a-me! *Unknown*. *Fr*. Dancing Songs. PBCV

Hir bowgy cheekes been as softe as clay. A Description of His Ugly Lady. Thomas Hoccleve. MeEL

Hiraeth. *Unknown, tr. fr. Welsh* by Aneirin Talfan Davies. OBWVE

Hiraeth in N.W.3. Wynford Vaughan-Thomas. NOBL

Hiram, I think the sump is backing up. Mending Sump. Kenneth Koch. BXAP; InPK; MoP; NeAP; NoAM

Hiram Powers' "Greek Slave." Elizabeth Barrett Browning. NALW

Hired Man's Way, The. John Kendrick Bangs. OBCA

Hireling. R. S. Thomas. PWE

Hireling's wages to the priest are paid, A. Poet vs. Parson. Ebenezer Elliot. Son

Hiroona. Horatio Nelson Huggins. PBCV

Sels.
"But mark you well the words I say."
"Clear transparent sea with light, The."

Hiroshige. Mark Perlberg. NYBP

His Age, Dedicated to His Peculiar Friend, Master John Wickes, under the Name of Posthumus. Robert Herrick. CaPo; SeCP

His All-Mind bids us keep this sacred place! *(LL)* Substitution. Anne Spencer. BlSi; CDC; ShDr

His alto leaks steam, a radiator of sound. Buying Wine. Sascha Feinstein. Jaz

His Ancestry. George Clinton Rowe. *Fr*. Toussaint L'Overture. AAP

His anchor, seaweed-probing, boat-securing. Philip of Thessalonica, *tr. fr. Greek* by Edwin Morgan. GrAn

His Answer. Clara Ann Thompson. BlSi; CBWP-2

His Answer to "Her Letter." Bret Harte. AnAmPo

His Are the Thousand Sparkling Rills. Cecil Frances Alexander. TIRV

His armies love massacre. A King's Double Nature. Kakkai Patiniyar Naccellaiyar, *tr. fr. Tamil* by A. K. Ramanujan. PLW

His art is eccentricity, his aim. Pitcher. Robert Francis. OxBSP; RaBo; WeW

His artificial feet calumped in holy rhythm. Deacon Morgan. Naomi Long Madgett. BlSi

His ass, and the Ratcatcher's daughter! *(LL)* The Ratcatcher's Daughter. *Unknown*. ChTr; GBP; OxBoLi

His ball, beautiful leaved, and his noisy boxwood rattle. Leonidas of Tarentum, *tr. fr. Greek* by Barbara Hughes Fowler. *Fr*. Epigrams. HePo

His balls: it sure was pleasant to spend 2 day in the country. *(LL)* Farm Implements and Rutabagas in a Landscape. John Ashbery. CBNP; CoAP; SM

His Banner over Me. Gerald Massey. WGRP

His Banquets Cure Most Ills. Al-Lajjam al-Harrani, *tr. fr. Arabic* by Omar S. Pound. ArPe

His bare feet warmed by the thick black dust. Shelly Beach. Christopher Koch. NOBAu

His bark/ The daring mariner shall urge far o'er. Prophecy. Luigi Pulci, *tr. fr. Italian*. *Fr*. Morgante Maggiore, Il. PAH

His being gone is a gift to my people. Wulf and Eadwacer. *Unknown, tr. by* Willis Barnstone *and* Elene Kolb. BoWoP

His Being Was in Her alone. Sir Philip Sidney. ELP

His best/ were the two. My Father's Fights. Stuart Dybek. PBCAP

His bicycle stood at the window-sill. A Constable Calls. Seamus Heaney. *Fr*. Singing School. FaBoPV; IPY; NOIV

His blood's sweet current much more loud to be. *(LL)* Church-Lock and Key. George Herbert. ESCV; GeHe; OxBSP

His Body. Sandra McPherson. AmPA

His body: a perfect shock absorber. *(LL)* Passage. Billy Marshall-Stoneking. NOBAu

His body be arched when he play — like Miles. 1 Poem 2 Voices A Song. Sherley Anne Williams. Jaz

His body doubled. On the Swag. R. A. K. Mason. PeNZ

His body is in my hands. *(LL)* The Call. Dennis Haskell. NOBAu

His body lies interred within this mould. Epitaph on a Soldier. Cyril Tourneur. *Fr*. Atheist's Tragedy, The. ElL

His Books. Robert Southey. *See* My days among the dead are past.

His Boyhood. George Clinton Rowe. *Fr*. Toussaint L'Overture. AAP

His brother after dinner. Uncle Bull-Boy. June Jordan. PoBA

His Camel. Alqamah, *tr. fr. Arabic* by Sir Charles Lyall. *Fr*. Mufaddaliyat, The. AWP

His card shows nothing sinister. He stands. The Poulterer. Mimi Khalvati. NWP

His care-free swagger was a fine invention. W. H. Auden. *Fr*. Sonnets from China. CMoP

His case inspires interest. A Man of Words. John Ashbery. PoA

His Cavalier. Robert Herrick. CaPo; GoJo

His changing eyes. *(LL)* The Cat and the Moon. W. B. Yeats. CMoP; CRH; FaBoCh; GoJo; OBAP; OFC; SoCa; TTTS; WHSW

His Charge to Julia at His Death. Robert Herrick. SeCV-1

His Children. Hittan of Tayyi, *tr. fr. Arabic* by Sir Charles Lyall. *Fr*. Hamasah. AWP

His chosen comrades thought at school. What Then? W. B. Yeats. CMoP

His clumsy body is a golden fruit. Deaf-Mute in the Pear Tree. P. K. Page. NoAM; PoE

His coat threadbare like a wolf pack. Gogol. Tomas Tranströmer, *tr. fr. Swedish* by Samuel Charters. AnAn

His cock is big and red when I am there. Paul Goodman. PeHV

His collar is frayed, and his trousers unpressed. Shabby Old Dad. Anne Campbell. PoToHe

His compassionate face, slightly wan. On the Street. C. P. Cavafy, *tr. fr. Greek* by Rae Dalven. BoLoP

His Content in the Country. Robert Herrick. CaPo; SeCV-1; TEP

His corpse below. *(LL)* Spirit of Plato. *Unknown*. AWP; OBVE

His corpse owre a' the city lies. The Dead Liebknecht. "Hugh MacDiarmid", *after the German of* Rudolf Leonhard. FaBoPV; OBVE

His country seared its conscience through its gain. William Lloyd Garrison. Joseph S. Cotter, Sr.. AAP

His Creed. Robert Herrick. BeJo

His crisp combs, and that comes those ways we know. *(LL)* Patience, hard thing! the hard thing but to pray. Gerard Manley Hopkins. NOBVV; OBNC

His cross is every tree. *(LL)* I See His Blood upon the Rose. Joseph Mary Plunkett. PeIV; PoLF; TIRV; WGRP

His cycle kerbed, the peeler found. Bigamy. Roy McFadden. *Fr*. Memories of Chinatown. PNI

His daughter Charlotte said to Mr. Brontë. Sampler from Haworth. Frances Minturn Howard. WPE

His day was not really complete until. Letters from Baron Von Hügel to a Niece. David Scott. PWE

His death into the sweater. *(LL)* The Sweater. Gregory Orr. TRP

His Defence Against the Idle Critic. Michael Drayton. NOSC

His Desire. Robert Herrick. OxBSP

His desires, growing. Black Man's Feast. Sarah Webster Fabio. PoBA; PoNe

His dinner on the stove, Grandpa smirked at our jar. Leftover Blessings. Julia Kasdorf. PBCAP

His Discourse with Cupid. Ben Jonson. *Fr*. Celebration of Charis in Ten Lyric[k] Peeces [*or* pieces], A. BeJo; OxAEP-1; SeCP

His dogs would follow him. They are pure. Hunter. Rosanna Warren. *Fr*. Funerary Portraits. NoAM

His Dream of the Sky-Land: A Farewell Poem, *sels*. Li Po, *tr. fr. Chinese* by Shigeyoshi Obata.

His "Ecclesiastical Sonnets." *(LL)* Other Lives of the Romantics. Jane Flanders. PBCAP

His echoing axe the settler swung. The Settler. Alfred Billings Street. FaBoBe; PAH

His Ejaculation to God. Robert Herrick. SeCV-1

His eldest son, Arradas' heir. His Boyhood. George Clinton Rowe. *Fr*. Toussaint L'Overture. AAP

His endless look. *(LL)* This Lunar Beauty. W. H. Auden. ArNa; MoAB; MoBrPo; OBMV; OxBTC; RB; SOTW

His English stream so pure did flow. Sir John Denham. *Fr*. On Mr. Abraham Cowley, His Death and Burial amongst the Ancient Poets. EPCY

His Epitaph. Sir Walter Ralegh. *See* Even such is time, that takes in trust.

His Excellency General Washington. Phillis Wheatley. *See* Celestial choir, enthron'd in realms of light.

His Excuse for Loving. Ben Jonson. *Fr*. Celebration of Charis in Ten Lyric[k] Peeces [*or* pieces], A. BeJo; EnRePo; JCP; NOSC; OxAEP-1; PoEL-2; SeCP; SeCV-1

His eyes are green and his nose is brown. The King of the Hobbledygoblins. Laura E. Richards. OBCA

His eyes are quickened so with grief. Lost Love. Robert Graves. AWP; CBLP; CH; CoGr; FaBoCh; Mes; MoAB; MoBrPo; NoP

His eyes he opened, shut, again unclosed. Juan and Haiidée. Byron. Fr. Don Juan. EBNV

His Face. Florence Earle Coates. OHIP

His face grew stern and sad. (LL) Poeta Fit, Non Nascitur. "Lewis Carroll." FaBoNo; OBSV

His face is streaked with prepared tears. The Clown. Janet Frame. PeNZ

His face is trodden deeper in the mud. (LL) Glory of Women. Siegfried Sassoon. NAEL-2; OBWP; OxAEP-2; PAW; PeFWW

His face was glad as dawn to me. Shule, Shule, Shule, Agrah! "Fiona Macleod." OHCV

His face was the oddest that ever was seen. The Strange Man. Unknown. FaPON

His fair large front and eye sublime declared. Paradise. Milton. Fr. Paradise Lost. EPCY; PIP

His fame endures; we shall not quite forget. Kensall Green. FaBoEH

His farces are physic; his physic a farce is. (LL) On Sir John Hill, M. D., Playwright. David Garrick. FaBoCo; FaBoEE; NBLV

His Farewell to His Unkind and Unconstant Mistress. Francis Davison. EIL

His Farewell to Sack. Robert Herrick. BeJo; CaPo; NAEL-1; SeCP; SeCV-1

His father and grandfather before him were coachmen. Birth of a Coachman. Paul Durcan. PBCIP

His father did intend that Harry should. John L. Thomas. Fr. Harry Vaughan. AngWe

His father gave him a box of truisms. The Truisms. Louis MacNeice. IIP; NOBE; OBSV; PNI

His Father's Hands. Thomas Kinsella. PoE

His faults were great, his virtues less. Byron. Lucretia Davidson. AmWP

His Feet are shod with Gauze. Emily Dickinson. SAmP

His fellow traveller. (LL) Epigram: On Sir Francis Drake. Unknown. OBTV

His fingers tell water like prayer. The Water-Diviner. Gillian Clarke. SCBI

His fingers wake, and flutter; up the bed. Conscious. Wilfred Owen. NSI; PoWW

His first bullet is a present, a mark of intelligence that will. The Knee. Ciaran Carson. PNI

His first day they asked. Arbeit Macht Frei. Dennis Schmitz. AnAn

His flaming Rome, and as it burn'd, he play'd. (LL) Of My Lady Isabella Playing on the Lute. Edmund Waller. HAP

His friend the watchman was still awake. A Leave-Taking. Arno Holz, tr. fr. German by Jethro Bithell. AWP

His friends he loved. His direst earthly foes. Sir William Watson. NOBVV (Epitaph, An.) OBF

His Friend's Last Battle. Theodore Nicholl. AngWe

His friends went off and left Him dead. The Resurrection. Jonathan Henderson Brooks. CDC; PoNe

His fur resembles waves. Lynx. Ben Howard. GrPl

His Gift and Mine. Unknown. BLRP

His gimpy leg was testimony to/ some other surgeon's art. Old Doc. Mark Vinz. Poetsp

His glory and his monuments are gone. (LL) Meru. W. B. Yeats. NoAM; OAEL-2; PoA

His Golden Locks [Time Hath to Silver Turned]. George Peele. Fr. Polyhymnia. EIL; EnRePo; FaBoRV; NIP; NoP; SCGP; TFi

His golden locks time hath to siluer turn'd. His Golden Lock[e]s [Time Hath to Silver Turned]. George Peele. Fr. Polyhymnia. EIL; EnRePo; FaBoRV; NIP; NoP; SCGP; TFi
(Farewell to Arms, A.) NOBE; OBEV; OBWP; OxAEP-1; PoRA
(Farewell to the Court.) NoSic
(Old Knight, The.) ChTr; TrGrPo
(Sonnet, A: "His golden locks time hath to silver turned.") ELP; InPS; PoEL-2

His Grace! impossible! what dead! A Satirical Elegy on the Death of a Late Famous General. Swift. FaBoEH; FF; HoPM; NBLV; NoP; OBSV; PoE; PoEL-3; Poetr

His Grange, or Private Wealth. Robert Herrick. BeJo; CaPo; FM; GoJo; SeCV-1

His Grateful Opponents Set Up This Statue Of Apis The Boxer. Lucilius, tr. fr. Greek by Peter Porter. GrAn

His green eyes on the homestead of another man. The Snake. Andrew Suknaski. NOBC

His green garden's twytined digging fork. To Priapos. Unknown, tr. fr. Greek by Guy Davenport. GrAn

His haire was blacke and in small curls did twine. Giles Fletcher the Younger. Fr. Christ's Victory and Triumph. SeCV-1

His hand came out of the east. Homer, tr. by Christopher Logue. Fr. Iliad, The. OBVE

His Hand Shall Cover Us. Isaac ben Samuel of Dampière, tr. fr. Hebrew by Nina Davis Salaman. TrJP

His hands old edging out of time. Geraldine Monk. NBrP

His hands. Why do people lie to one another? (LL) Mummy of a Lady Named Jemutesonekh XXI Dynasty. Thomas James. AmPA; SM

His hat is rammed on. Near the School for Handicapped Children. Thomas W. Shapcott. CBAP

His head is so white it shines. Cleaned the Crocodile's Teeth. Unknown. TSaS, tr. by Terese Svoboda

His head split in four parts. Promenade. David Ignatow. TrJP

His headstone said. The Funeral of Martin Luther King, Jr. Nikki Giovanni. BPo; LPA

His heart swells. Peyanar, tr. fr. Tamil by A. K. Ramanujan. Fr. Seven Said by the Foster-Mother. PLW

His heart, to me, was a place of palaces and pinnacles and shining towers. I Have Been through the Gates. Charlotte Mew. MoAB; MoBrPo; TrGrPo

His heart to the darkness and into the sadness of joy. (LL) First Song. Galway Kinnell. CAPP; GoJo; GOYP; GrPl; LiTM; NoP; Poetr; TwCP

His Helplessness. John Berryman. Fr. Dream Songs. NoP

His hide is sure to flatten 'em. (LL) The Hippopotamus. Hilaire Belloc. FaBoNo; FiBHP; InPK

His Hill. Kapilar, tr. fr. Tamil by A. K. Ramanujan. PLW

His home is on the heights; to him. The Poet. Edwin Markham. WGRP

His hooves have rest. (LL) The Mount. Léonie Adams. MoAB; MoAmPo

His Hope or Sheet-Anchor. Robert Herrick. CaPo

His hottest love and most delight. The Happy Hen. James Agee. ErPo

His Illness. Solomon ibn Gabirol, tr. fr. Hebrew by David Goldstein. TOF

His Immortality. Thomas Hardy. CMoP

His Importance. The Diverse Gifts of Pasha Bailey Ben. W. S. Gilbert. Fr. Pasha Bailey Ben. CBCK

His in-trays are everywhere, like the mouths of Avernus. The Jar. Peter Didsbury. PWE

His iron-frame, long deem'd so ably plann'd. Watt's Improvements to the Steam Engine. Thomas Baker. Fr. Steam Engine; or, The Power of the Flame, The. FaBoUS

His is a world-wide fatherland! (LL) The Fatherland. James Russell Lowell. GN

His jacket, boots kept outside the holding cell. After Stroke. Bill Griffiths. NBrP

His kind velvet bonnet. The Cat. Edith Sitwell. NTP

His kingdom is forever. (LL) A Mighty Fortress Is Our God. Martin Luther. AWP; GePo; PWR, tr. by Frederick Henry Hedge

His Lachrimae or Mirth, Turn'd to Mourning. Robert Herrick. SeCV-1

His Lady's Cruelty. Sir Philip Sidney. See With how sad steps, O Moone, thou climb'st the skies!

His Lady's Death. Pierre de Ronsard, tr. fr. French by Andrew Lang. AWP

His Lady's Tomb. Pierre de Ronsard, tr. fr. French by Andrew Lang. AWP

His lamp, his bow, and quiver laid aside. Cupid Turned Plowman. Moschus, tr. fr. Greek by Matthew Prior. AWP
(Cupid a Plowman.) OBVE

His landlocked dreams were rainbow-tides that ran. Old Voyager. Walter Blackstock. GoYe

His languid tail above us, lit with myriad spots of light. (LL) Indian upon God, The [or An]. W. B. Yeats. MoBrPo; WGRP

His large ears hear. My Father at 85. Robert Bly. BAP-89

His last days linger in that low attic. The Old Jockey. F. R. Higgins. OBMV; OxBTC

His last glimpse of the former wife. After Eden. James Simmons. PNI

His last scrum done, Joe's ready for his God. Epitaph for a Sportsman. Leonard Barras. IHNG

His last white eärms, an' they stood still. (LL) The Turnstile. William Barnes. CH; NOBVV

His Late Wife's Wedding-Ring. George Crabbe. See Ring, so worn as you behold, The.

His Letanie, to the Holy Spirit. Robert Herrick. See In the hour [or houre] of my distress [or distresse].

His life is in the body of the living. The Soul and Body of John Brown. Muriel Rukeyser. MoAmPo

His lips move ceaselessly. The Humped Ox. Flavien Ranaivo, tr. fr. French by Ellen Conroy Kennedy. NegPo

His Litany to the Holy Spirit. Robert Herrick. BeJo; BLPL; ELP; JCP; NOSC; PeECV; PoLF; TEP

His little heart to cheer. (LL) Robin Redbreast. William Allingham. FaBoBe; MoShBr; OxBChV

His little one and his wife. (LL) The Carpenter's Wife. Unknown. OAEL-1, diff.vers.; OBET; OxBB

His living name. (*LL*) Those blessed structures, plot and rhyme. Robert Lowell. CAPP; HCAP; NAAL-2; VCAP

His logic unperturbed, exacting new. Metaphysician. Robert Fitzgerald. PoA

His look will flow like oil over us. (*LL*) Ank'hor Vat. Denis Devlin. BIrV; CIP; IPY; NOIV

His lordship's steed. Riding. William Allingham. OxBChV

His Lunch Bucket. Doug Cockrell. Poetsp

His lungs heaving all day in a sulphur mist. Black Money. Tess Gallagher. NGP

His Majesty, Heaven guide His Grace. Leith Races. Allan Ramsay. ScCV

His Manhood. George Clinton Rowe. *Fr.* Toussaint L'Overture. AAP

His mansion in the pool. Emily Dickinson. OBAL

His marriagebed. (*LL*) Wedding at Aughrim, Galway 1900. Catherine Byron. VBLP

His master coming through the door. (*LL*) My Dog. John Kendrick Bangs. BLPA; BLPL; FaBoBe

His Metrical Prayer. James Graham, Marquess of Montrose. *See* Let them bestow on every airt[h] a limb.

His Metrical Vow. James Graham, Marquess of Montrose. OxBS

His mind moves upon silence. (*LL*) Long-legged Fly. W. B. Yeats. CMoP; FaBoMo; FaBoTw; InPS; LiTM; MoP; NAEL-2; NoAM; NOBE; NoP; OPOP; PoE; TEP

His Monument. Sarah Knowles Bolton. PWR

His Mother. Haim Guri, *tr. fr. Hebrew by* Ruth Finer Mintz. MHP

His Mother in Her Hood of Blue. Lizette Woodworth Reese. OHIP

His Mother-in-Law. Walter Parke. FiBHP

His Mother's Service to Our Lady. Villon, *tr. fr. French by* Dante Gabriel Rossetti. AWP; CTC

His Mother's Wedding Ring. George Crabbe. *See* Ring, so worn as you behold, The.

His mouth to my mouth. (*LL*) My Grief on the Sea. Biddy Cussrooee. OBEV; WTO

His moving likeness on the page. (*LL*) Lens. Anne Wilkinson. MoCV; NOBC

His naked skin clothed in the torrid mist. The Serf. Roy Campbell. GTBS-P; LiTB; MoBrPo; OBMV

His Name, and when they do't be most my Joys. (*LL*) Hosanna. Thomas Traherne. ChIV-2; PoEL-2; SeCV-2

His name/ filled my scream. Come Away. Pamela Gillilan. PWE

His name is Jason, he's. Stud. Michael Lassell. *Fr.* Times Square Poems. GLP

His name is/ Rubin. Rubin. Charles Cooper. PoBA

His name it is Pedro-Pablo-Ignacio-Juan-/ Francesco García y Gabaldon. A Feller I Know. Mary Austin. FaPON

His name was Chance, Jack Chance, he said. Ballad of a Strange Thing. H. Phelps Putnam. OxBA

His Necessary Darkness. Nancy Sullivan. TAP

His nights in the aunts' house, their talk and tea. A Provincial Adolescence. Michael Foley. PNI

His nobler task is — to forget. (*LL*) The Crowing of the Red Cock. Emma Lazarus. AmWP

His nose is short and scrubby. My Dog. Marchette Chute. FaPON; ImGa; PDV; WHSW

His Offering, With the Rest, At the Sepulcher. Robert Herrick. ChIV-2

His old age fell on years of abundant harvest. A Felicitous Life. Czeslaw Milosz, *tr. fr. Polish by* Czeslaw Milosz *and* Lillian Vallee. PoSu

His one Desired, whose own room splendour enters. (*LL*) The Resolute Desire That Enters. Arnaut Daniel. STV

His [*or* Memory] he had like a Scarf. [*or* Inward Parts of Mr] Shrovetide. Rabelais, *tr. fr. French by* Peter LeMotteux. *Fr.* Gargantua and Pantagruel. CBCK

His overalls hung on the hook by his hat, and I noticed. Treasures. Claire Richcreek Thomas. PoToHe

His own drum beats, the silkworm lays her death. (*LL*) Convict. Edward Vincent Swart. PeSAV

His Own Epitaph. Robert Herrick. CaPo

His Own Epitaph, When He Was Sick. John Hoskyns. FaBoEE

His Own True Wife. Wolfram von Eschenbach, *tr. fr. German by* Jethro Bithell. AWP

His pads furring the scarp's rime. The Snow-Leopard. Randall Jarrell. CAPP; LiTM; TwCP

His paintings grew darker every year. The Artist. Stanley Kunitz. CAPP

His palms spotless. What She Said to Him, after Meeting His Concubine. Cakalacanar, *tr. fr. Tamil by* A. K. Ramanujan. PLW

His paper propped against the electric toaster. Daniel at Breakfast. Phyllis McGinley. OBSV; OxBM

His Parting from Her. John Donne. *Fr.* Elegies. EBEV

His pendulous body tolled. A Hanging. Frank Mkalawile Chipasula.

(Hanging, Zomba Central Prison, A.) PeSAV

His pendulous stomach hangs a-shaking. (*LL*) Wagner. Rupert Brooke. FaBoTw; NOBL; PeLV

His Petition to Mr. Speaker. James Carkesse. CBNP

His Petition to Queen Anne of Denmark (1618). Sir Walter Ralegh. SiPS

His Picture. John Donne. *Fr.* Elegies. EnRePo

His Pilgrimage. Sir Walter Ralegh. *See* Give me my scallop-shell of quiet.

His place, as he sat and as he thought, was not. A Quiet Normal Life. Wallace Stevens. NAAL-2; NoAM

His place is before, not in, the National Gallery. London Pavement Artist. James Schevill. TAP

His Plans for Old Age. William Meredith. TAP

His plumage is dun. Jailbird. Vernon Scannell. OxBC

His poems, yellow, torn and fading. Langston Hughes. Lew Blockcolski. VoR

His Poetrie His Pillar. Robert Herrick. *See* Only [*or* Onely] a little more.

"His policy," do you say? Mr. Johnson's Policy of Reconstruction. Charles Graham Halpine. PAH

His poor mother gives Mikythos. Leonidas, *tr. fr. Greek by* Kenneth Rexroth. PGA

His power to maintain. (*LL*) Lion and the unicorn, The. Mother Goose. BoTP; OxBoLi; OxNR; ReMoGo

His Praises. Swidi-Nonkamfela Mhlongo, *tr. fr. Zulu by* Elizabeth Gunner. PeSAV

His Prayer for Absolution. Robert Herrick. BeJo; SeCV-1; TrPWD

His Prayer to Ben Jonson [*or* Johnson]. Robert Herrick. BeJo; CaPo; JCP; NAEL-1; NoP; NOSC; OxBoLi; OxBSP; PeLV; SeCV-1; TrGrPo

His Prayer to Ben Jonson [*or* Johnson]. Robert Herrick. CaPo; JCP; NoP; OxBoLi; SeCV-1; TrGrPo

His Presence Came Like Sunrise. Ralph Spaulding Cushman. BLRP

His pride/ Had cast him out from Heaven, with all his host. Milton. *Fr.* Paradise Lost. EPCY

(Satan "His pride/ Had cast him out from Heaven, with all his host".) TrGrPo

His Prime. George Clinton Rowe. *Fr.* Toussaint L'Overture. AAP

His Remedie for Love. Michael Drayton. *Fr.* Idea. AAS; ESo

His Request. Owen Roe O'Sullivan, *tr. fr. Irish by* Joan Keefe. BIrV

His Request to Julia. Robert Herrick. BeJo; CaPo; NOSC

His rest, and his lips their honey made. (*LL*) Love Sleeping. Plato. AWP; FaBoEE

His Return to London. Robert Herrick. BeJo; CaPo; FaBoPP; FF; NAEL-1

His right hand holds his slingshot. For the Record. "Ping Hsin", *tr. fr. Chinese by* Kenneth Rexroth *and* Ling Chung. WPC

His role is to invert the fairy tale. Psychiatrist. Peter De Vries. OBAL

His Rule of Behaviour: If You Are Civil, I Am Sober. James Carkesse. NOSC

His sad and usual heart, dry as a winter leaf. (*LL*) Aspects of Robinson. Weldon Kees. CoAP; NaP; NYBP

His Sailing from Julia. Robert Herrick. PoEL-3

His Saviour's Words, Going to the Cross. Robert Herrick. ChIV-2; NOCV

His shadow monstrous on the palace wall. Oedipus. Thomas Blackburn. FaBoTw

His shared cigarette still alive in your lips. (*LL*) No Man Knows War. Edwin Rolfe. TrJP

His Shield. Marianne Moore. LiTM; NALW

His shoulder did I hold. Any Saint. Francis Thompson. MoBrPo

His sins were scarlet, but his books were read. (*LL*) On His Books. Hilaire Belloc. FaBoCo; FaBoEE; MoBrPo; NBLV; OxBoLi; WeW

His sister named [*or* called] Lucy O'Finner. "Lewis Carroll." FaBoNo; PeLi

His Slightly Longer Story Song. James Whitehead. NGP

His Son. Callimachus, *tr. fr. Greek by* G. B. Grundy. AWP

His soul is gone aloft. (*LL*) Poor Tom. Charles Dibdin. NOEC; OxBoLi

His soul is with the saints, I trust. (*LL*) The Knight's Tomb. Samuel Taylor Coleridge. EnRP; FaBoCh; GN; MeMBP; RB

His soul stretched tight across the skies. T. S. Eliot. *Fr.* Preludes (I–IV). HeIP; LiTA; NoP; OBMV; PPP; SOTW; TwCP; UnPo; VGW; WeW

His soul to God! on a battle-psalm! Albert Sidney Johnston. Francis Orrery Ticknor. PAH

His Sovereignty. Kalonymos ben Moses of Lucca, *tr. by* Nina Davis Salaman. TrJP

His sovereignty is o'er my gathered throng. His Sovereignty. Kalonymos ben Moses of Lucca, *tr. by* Nina Davis Salaman. TrJP

His speculation he regretted. I Want a Tenant; a Satire. John O'Keefe. NOEC

His spirit in smoke ascended to high heaven. The Lynching. Claude McKay. PoBA

His stars eternally. (*LL*) Drummer Hodge. Thomas Hardy. AWP; EBEV; GTBS-P; HAP; InPS; MoP; NAAL-2; NoAM; NOBVV; NoP; OBWP; OxAEP-2; PAW; PeFWW; Poetr; WeW

His stature was not very tall. The Description of Sir Geoffrey Chaucer. Robert Greene. *Fr.* Greene's Vision. CTC; NoSic; SCGP (Sir Geoffrey Chaucer. FaBoCh

His Story. Sandra Cisneros. ETG

His sullen kinsmen, by the winter sea. Santa Claus. Dom Moraes. NoAM

His sun went down in the morning. Our Ernest. "Elmo." PWR

His sun's arms and grappling. Isaac: a Poise. Peter Cole. ChIV-1

His Swans. Geoffrey Grigson. FaBoRV

His teare-wet Feet still drying with her Haire. (*LL*) For the Magdalene. William Drummond of Hawthornden. ChIV-2; PoEL-2

His Tears to Thamesis. Robert Herrick. FaBoPP; NOSC

His teeth are white as curds. The Arrow of Desire. *Gond Oral Tradition*, *tr. by* V. Elwin *and* S. Hivale. WTO

His Temple she, and He her Soul. (*LL*) Dominica Pentecostes. Aubrey Thomas De Vere. TIRV

His theme/ over and over. Williams: An Essay. Denise Levertov. InPS

His Thirst. Robert Wells. SCBI

His Throne Is with the Outcast. James Russell Lowell. TrCP

His thumb had a rainbow. (*LL*) Where Knock Is Open Wide. Theodore Roethke. HAP; VGW

His tongue out with its fork. (*LL*) Eve. Christina Rossetti. CH; ChIV-1; FM; GTBS-P; MeMBP; NALW; NIP; PoEL-5; Poetr

His Tool was Large. Martial, *tr. fr. Latin by* Fiona Pitt-Kethley. FaBoBl

His tool was large and so was his nose. His Tool was Large. Martial, *tr. fr. Latin by* Fiona Pitt-Kethley. FaBoBl

His triumphs of a moment done. On the Departure of the British from Charleston. Philip Freneau. PAH

His trousers are wind. Song to a Lover. *Unknown, tr. fr. Amharic by* Willis Barnstone. BoWoP

His tummy a/ source of. Vindictiveness of Religion. William Dickey. PFL

His twelve-year-old/ son. Callimachus, *tr. fr. Greek by* Peter Jay. GrAn

His Uncle came on Franklin Hyde. Franklin Hyde. Hilaire Belloc. FaBoUs; NBLV

His vast frame splayed on an uneasy chair. Confrontation with an Artist. Elisabeth Eybers. PeSAV

His waiting becomes a time to hear thoughts, the sound. Picture of a Japanese Farmer, Woodland, California, May 20, 1942. Jim Mitsui. OpBo

His was a landscape of wounds and disease. Greatrakes, The Healer. Thomas McCarthy. IB

His was the first corpse I had ever seen. My Wicked Uncle. Derek Mahon. OxBC

His was the mastery of life. Conscientious Objector. Edward Davison. NSI

His was the treasure of two thousand years. James Thomson. *Fr.* Seasons, The. EPCY

His way home to the mark. (*LL*) Boston Hymn. Emerson. PAH; WGRP

His weight in lead he was. Her Bed. Linda Saunders. NWP

His Welcome. Auvaiyar, *tr. fr. Tamil by* A. K. Ramanujan. PLW

His well shaped ears were chestnut brown and they. The Huckster's Horse. Julia Hurd Strong. GoYe

His wheel of logic whirled and spun all day. The Philosopher. Edward Rowland Sill. AnAmPo

His whiskers didn't come, his mustache was gone. A Mustacheless Bard. J. Gordon Coogler. OBAL

His Wife. Shirley Kaufman. LCAP

His Wife. Rachel, *tr. fr. Hebrew by* Sholom J. Kahn. WPOW

His wife, that he may live. (*LL*) A Reasonable Affliction. Matthew Prior. NOEC; NoP; TrGrPo

His wild heart beats with painful sobs. The Happy Warrior. Sir Herbert Read. NSI; PeFWW

His Will Be Done. Annie Johnson Flint. BLRP

His Winding-Sheet. Robert Herrick. CaPo; OBEV

His window is over the factory flume. Widow Brown's Christmas. John Townsend Trowbridge. BeLS

His words of beuty bloom / forevermore! (*LL*) On a Dead Poet. Frances Sargent Osgood.

His words were left after him. The Stargazer's Legacy. Vasco [*or* Vasko] Popa, *tr. fr. Serbo-Croatian by* Charles Simic. AnRep

His words were magic and his heart was true. Uncle Ananias. E. A. Robinson. MoAmPo; NIP

His work is done, his toil is o'er. Faithful unto Death. Richard Handfield Titherington. PAH

His work was done; his blessing lay. The Death of Moses. Frances E. W. Harper. *Fr.* Moses: A Story of the Nile. AAP

His works we reverence, while we pity thine. (*LL*) Shakespeare. Lucretia Davidson. AmWP

His wound was lighter than the pain of spring. (*LL*) Crooked River. Li Shang-yin. PLT

Hisperica Famina. Jack Spicer. CBNP

Hiss and flashing lights of a jet, The. Strategic Air Command. Gary Snyder. BCF

Hiss of flame before earth, The. H ear t h. Janet Sutherland. NBrP

Hist, but a word, fair and soft! Master Hugues of Saxe-Gotha. Robert Browning. OAEL-2

Histoire. Harry Mathews. NIP

Historic, sidelong, implicating eyes. La Gioconda, by Leonardo Da Vinci, in the Louvre. "Michael Field." PeVV

Historical Judas, The. Howard Nemerov. NoP; Poetr

Historical Museum, Manitoulin Island. Lisel Mueller. PoA

Historical Poem, An. *Unknown. See* Of a tall stature and of sable hue.

Historical Reflections. John Hollander. OBAL

Historie of Squyer William Meldrum, The, *sels.* Sir David Lindsay. Squire Meldrum at Carrickfergus. OxBS

Histories. Mary E. O'Donnell. NWP

Historiography. Lorenzo Thomas. UL

History. G. K. Chesteron. *Fr.* Songs of Education. OBSV

History. Robert Fitzgerald. FYAP

History. Jorie Graham. BTR

History. Arthur Gregor. TAP

History. Donald Hall. BAP-89

History. Art Lange. UL

History. D. H. Lawrence. RaBo

History. James Liddy, *tr. fr. Irish.* CIP

History. Robert Lowell. CAPP; HCAP; TAP; VCAP

History. Thomas McGrath. FoLa

History. Gary Soto. PBCAP

History among the Rocks. Robert Penn Warren. *Fr.* Kentucky Mountain Farm. GOA; MoAmPo

History and Abstraction. Thomas Lux. AmPA

History as Decoration. Rosanna Warren. DiPo

History Classes. Tony Harrison. *Fr.* School of Eloquence, The. NAEL-2; NoAM

History during Nocturnal Snowfall. Robert Penn Warren. DiPo

History has to live with what was here. History. Robert Lowell. CAPP; HCAP; TAP; VCAP

History hibernates here. Maridunum. Douglas Phillips. AngWe

History is not a sentence. Movie. Bob Perelman. BAP-89

History Lesson. Mark Van Doren. NYBP

History Lesson, A. Miroslav Holub, *tr. fr. Czech by* George Theiner. PAW; PoSu; RB

History Lessons. Seamus Deane. BiHa; PBCIP; PNI

History Makers. George Campbell. PBCV

History of a Literary Movement. Howard Nemerov. PoE

History of blacklife is put down in the motions, The. The Sound of Afroamerican History Chapt I. S. E. Anderson. PoBA

History of Civilization, A. Albert Goldbarth. HCAP

History of Education. David McCord. OBAL

History of Ideas. J. V. Cunningham. NIP; VCAP

History of Insipids, The. John Freke. APAS

History of Jazz, The. Kenneth Koch. Jaz

History of Lesbianism, A. Judy Grahn. GLP; PeHV

History of Love, A. William Carlos Williams. VGW

History of My Feeling, The. Kathleen Fraser. CrSp

History of my feeling (or is it the way you change), The. The History of My Feeling. Kathleen Fraser. CrSp

History of My Heart. Robert Pinsky. Jaz

History of Poetry, The. Peter Cooley. NAmP90

History of the Flood, The. John Heath-Stubbs. MoBS; NTP; OxBTC

History of the Human Body/ Winfield's Infield Hit/ The Lassitude of the Infinite, The. Elinor Nauen. UL

History of the Word. Robert Graves. MeMBP

History of Truth, The. W. H. Auden. FaBoMo

History of World Languages. D. J. Enright. OxBC

History she (Zelda) said stops here. Inside History. Angela McCabe. AmPA

History Teacher in the Warsaw Ghetto Rising. Evangeline Paterson. PAW

History Teaches, But It Has No Pupils. John Seed. VaA

History, the angel, was stirred. Northern Ireland: Two Comments. Seamus Deane. CIP

History theirs whose language is the sun, The. (*LL*) An Elementary School Classroom in a Slum. Stephen Spender. FaBoMo; FF; LiTB; MoAB; MoBrPo; TrGrPo; TwCP; UnPo

Hit betidde somtime in the termes of Judé. *Unknown. Fr.* Patience. EnVB

Hit by a Space Station. Steve Abbott. ETG

Hit in the Head. Charles B. Stetler. NGP

Hold back the hand that works the mill. A Water-mill. Antipater of Thessalonica, *tr. fr. Greek by* Alistair Elliot. GrAn

Hold back thy hours. Bridal Song ("Hold back thy hours.") Beaumont *and* John Fletcher. *Fr.* Maid's Tragedy, The. EiL; ErPo; TrGrPo
(Song: "Hold back thy hours, dark night, till we have done.") OxBSP

Hold Fast Your Dreams. Louise Driscoll. BLPA; FaBoBe; FaPON

Hold, furious youth — better thy heat assuage. The Best Time for Conception. Claude Quillet, *tr. fr. Latin by* George Sewell. *Fr.* Callipaedia; or, The Art of Getting Beautiful Children. FaBoUs

Hold hard, Ned! Lift me down once more, and lay me in the shade. The Sick Stockrider. Adam Lindsay Gordon. CBAP

Hold her softly, not for long. At a Child's Baptism. Vassar Miller. GoJo

Hold, hold it tight. Song for a Girl on Her First Menstruation. *Unknown, tr. fr. Boikin by* Joe Prentuo. BoWoP

Hold, hold your hand, hold; mercy, mercy, spare. A Sonnet on Sir William Alexander's Harsh Verses after the English Fashion. James I, King of England. Son

Hold it up sternly — see this it sends back, (who is it? is it you?). A Hand-Mirror. Walt Whitman. NAAL-1; OxBA

Hold my hand, Auntie, Auntie. The British Workman and the Government. D. H. Lawrence. IHNG

Hold my Rooster. *Unknown.* FaBoVe

Hold my rooster, hold my hen. Hold my Rooster. *Unknown.* FaBoVe (Precious Things.) TTY

Hold not your lips so close; dispense. Kiss, The 1656. To Mrs. C. Thomas Shipman. NOSC

Hold! pale death, at the poor man's shack and the pasha's palace. I, 4. Ode: "Hold! pale death, at the poor man's shack and the pasha's palace." Horace, *tr. fr. Latin by* Austin Dobson. *Fr.* Odes. OBD, *tr. by* James Michie

Hold the Fort. *Unknown.* SWP

"Hold the horse's head" the farmer said. The Horse's Head. Brendan Kennelly. CIP

Hold the pen close to your ear. The Thin Prison. Leslie Norris. OTCP

Hold the Wind. *Unknown.* GBP; OBD

Hold the Wind. Villon. OBD

Hold them now, Earth, now hand of man cannot. The Last Survivor's Speech. *Unknown, tr. by* Alfred David. *Fr.* Beowulf. ASW, *tr. by* Kevin Crossley-Holland; NAEL-1

Hold up your head. *Unknown.* OxNR

Hold with both hands. With Only One Life. Martin Sorescu, *tr. fr. Romanian by* D. J. Enright *and* Ioana Russell-Gebbett. PWE

"Hold your hand, Lord Judge," she says. The Maid Freed from the Gallows. *Unknown.* ESPB

Hölderlin Town. Anne Carson. *Fr.* Life of Towns, The. BAP-90

Holding a jug of wine among the flowers. Drinking Alone under Moonlight. Li Po, *tr. fr. Chinese by* Robert Payne. TAL

Holding a picture up to the wall. Sketch. Robert Farnsworth. GOYP

Holding black whips. Thoughts of Chairman Mao. David Young. AmPA

Holding Hands. Lenore M. Link. FaPON; MoShBr; NTCP

Holding its huge life open to the sky. To My Friends. Stephen Berg. NaP; NYBP

Holding on to health and youth. Bar Light. Ammon Wrigley. UnDi

Holding the arm of his helper, the blind. The Visitor. Gibbons Ruark. MT

Holding the feathered dancing string. Koel (Rainbird) and Effigy. *Unknown, tr. fr. Aborigine by* Mungayana Nundhirribala. NOBAu

Holding the Mirror Up to Nature. Howard Nemerov. PoA

Holding the Sky. William Stafford. RFM

Hole. Leonard Nathan. PBCAP

Hole in the Floor, A. Richard Wilbur. NOBA

Hole in the Sea, The. Marvin Bell. NYBP

Hole, Where Once in Passion We Swam. Dave Jeddie Smith. NoAM

Holes, The. Stephen Berg. NaP; NYBP

Holes Commence Falling. David Huddle. PBCAP

Holes in my arms. For Real. Jayne Cortez. PoBA

Holes, spaces — not just in the small of the back. Widower. Bible, Apocrypha. OxBM

Holiday, The. Thomas Frank Bignold. OBTV

Holiday, A. Ella Wheeler Wilcox. OxBM

Holiday at Hampton Court. John Davidson. EBVV; MeMBP

Holiday Gown. John Cunningham. ECEV

Holiday in Reality. Wallace Stevens. OxBA

Holiday Train, The. Irene Thompson. BoTP

Holidays. Eva Mylonas, *tr. fr. Modern Greek by* Kimon Friar. BoWoP

Holidays. Dara Wier. NAmP90

Holiest of all holidays are those, The. Longfellow. PoToHe

Holiness[e] on the head. Aaron. George Herbert. ChIV-1; GeHe; MeLP; NOSC; OAEL-1; PeECV

Holla, boys, holla, hip hip hurrah!. *(LL)* Apple Wassail. *Unknown.* OBET

Holland, that scarce deserves the name of land. Andrew Marvell. *Fr.* Character of Holland, The. ChTr; NOBL; OBSV; PeLV

Hollin, Green Hollin. *Unknown.* GBP

Hollis laughed. Johnna at the Windmill. Diane Glancy. CRP

Hollo! keep it up, boys — and push around the glass. Drinking Song. Robert Fergusson. OxAEP-1

Holloe Menn, The. Harrison Everard. BXAP

Hollow, The. Robert Morgan. MT

Hollow Cost. Joan Jobe Smith. BTR

Hollow Echo. Fazil Hüsnü Daglarca. CRP

Hollow eyes of shock remain, The. Two Years Later. John Wieners. PoM; RaBo

Hollow Land, The, *sels.* William Morris.
"Christ keep the Hollow Land." ChTr
(Song: "Christ keep the Hollow Land.") PoEL-5

Hollow Men, The. T. S. Eliot. FaPoB; ImPo; InPS; LiTA; LiTM; MoAB; MoAmPo; NAAL-2; OAEL-2; OBMV

Hollow sound of your hard felt hat, The. Hats. F. S. Flint. NSI

Hollow Thesaurus, The. Roger McDonald. CBAP

Hollow Tree, A. Robert Bly. NNaP

Hollow winds begin to blow, The. Signs of Rain. Edward Jenner. BLPA; BoNaP; FaBoUs

Holly, The. Walter de la Mare. CMoP

Holly against Ivy. *Unknown.* MeEL

Holly against Ivy: "Holy bereth beries." *Unknown. See* Holly Beareth Berries.

Holly and Ivy. *Unknown.* MeEL

Holly and Ivy a great party. Carol in Praise of the Holly and Ivy. *Unknown.* OHIP
(Holly and the Ivy, The.) PeECV

Holly and Ivy ("Holy stand in the hall.") *Unknown.* MeEL

Holly and Mistletoe. Eleanor Farjeon. PChr

Holly and the Ivy, The ("The holly and the ivy,/ When they are both full grown.") *Unknown.* CH; ChTr; ELP; GBP; OBET; PChr

Holly Beareth Berries, *abr. Unknown.*

Holly Gone. Gloria Evans Davies. AngWe

Holly gone I discover. Holly Gone. Gloria Evans Davies. AngWe

Holly Tree, The. Robert Southey. EnRP

Holly tree, A. *(LL)* Highty, tighty, paradighty, clothed [all] in green. *Unknown.* ChTr; OxNR

Hollyhocks are ten feet tall, The. Wet Summer. May Williams Ward. GoYe

Holly's up, the house is all bright, The. The Christmas Tree. Peter Cornelius. PChr

Hollywood. Karl Shapiro. LiTM; OxBA

Hollywood Boulevard Cemetery. Robert Peters. NGP

Hollywood Everything, A. John Ashbery. *Fr.* Daffy Duck in Hollywood. CBCK

Hollywood Jazz. Lynda Hull. Jaz

Holmes. James Russell Lowell. *Fr.* Fable for Critics, A. NOBA

Holocaust. Myra Sklarew. CRP

Holocaust, pentecost: what heaped heartbreak. My Grandfather's Church Goes Up. Fred Chappell. SM

Holofernes's Letter. Shakespeare. *Fr.* Love's Labour's Lost. CBNP

Holstenwall. Sidney Keyes. FaBoTw

Holver and Hivy made a gret party. *Unknown.* MiEL

Holy. George Campbell. PBCV

Holy and incurable. *(LL)* Physics. Chase Twichell. VBLP

Holy and mighty poet of the spirit. Shelley. Thomas Wade. EPCY

Holy angels, in envy I cast no sigh. Gaspara Stampa, *tr. fr. Italian by* J. Vitiello. BoWoP

Holy Baptisme. George Herbert. PoEL-2

Holy be the white head of a Negro. Holy. George Campbell. PBCV

Holy bereth beris. Holly against Ivy. *Unknown.* MeEL

Holy Bible, Book Divine. John Burton. BLRP; WBLP

Holy boy, The. Children of Love. Harold Monro. MoBrPo

Holy City, The. Frederic E. Weatherly. BLRP; WBLP

Holy Communion, The. Henry Vaughan *and* Thomas Stanley. ESCV

Holy Cross. Shane Leslie. TIRV

Holy-Cross Day. Robert Browning. OtMeF

Holy Fair, The. Burns. EnRP; OBSV

Holy Family. Peter Cooley. NAmP90

Holy Family. Muriel Rukeyser. ChIV-2; MoAmPo

Holy Family. Katharine Tynan. TIRV

Holy Father, Great Creator. Alexander V. Griswold. AH

Holy flame of fire, The. (LL) Remember, remember the circle of the sky. *Unknown.* EaPr

Holy Ghost, The. John Donne. *Fr.* Litanie, The. NOCV; PoEL-2

Holy Ghost Hospital. Allen Grossman. PRA

Holy ghost woman. Call. Audre Lorde. SRLS

Holy God, We Praise Thy Name. Clarence A. Walworth. AH

Holy Grail, The, *sels.* Jack Spicer.
Book of Gawain, The. PoM

Holy Grail, The. Tennyson. *Fr.* Idylls of the King.

Holy Ground, The. *Unknown.* OxBSS

Holy Hill, A. "Æ." AWP

Holy, Holy, Holy. Reginald Heber. OHIP

"Holy, holy, holy!" the choir chants sweet and low. An Opening Service. Clara Ann Thompson. CBWP-2

Holy Innocents, The. Robert Lowell. InvP; MoAB; MoAmPo; OBCP; OxBC

Holy is the moon and our own Selene. *Unknown, tr. fr. Greek by* Peter Porter. GrAn

Holy Jesus, Thou art born. Victoria Saffelle Johnson. TrPWD

Holy Land of Walsingham, The. *Unknown, sometimes at. to* Sir Walter Ralegh. *See* As You Came from the Holy Land [of Walsingham].

Holy Light. Milton. *See* Hail, holy light, offspring [*or* offspring] of Heav'n [*or* heaven] first born.

Holy light of loneliness, The. Breaking. Cynthia Huntington. NAmP90

Holy Longing, The. Goethe, *tr. fr. German by* Robert Bly. NU; RaBo

Holy man, ungird your gabardeen. Rest. Roots. Seymour Mayne. NOBC

Holy Mass For Relja Krilatica, *sels.* Milorad Pavic.
"But I'm the one from whom they stole a button from his trouser leg." HSix
"But I'm the one to whom others spit in the hand when he works." HSix
"But I'm the one who carries a garlic clove in the ear." HSix
"Rejoice bather between two waters." HSix
"Rejoice eleventh finger reckoner of stars." HSix
"Rejoice mason of years." HSix
"Rejoice singer of songs for the deaf." HSix
"Rejoice you who sleep with a finger in your ear." HSix

Holy melodies of love arise, The. (LL) The Arsenal at Springfield. Longfellow. AmPP

Holy moder, that bere Crist. William Herebert. MiEL

Holy Night. Lucille Clifton. CrSp; NALW

Holy Nunnery, The. *Unknown.* ESPB

Holy of Holies, The. G. K. Chesteron. WGRP

Holy of holies — a hill-top chapel. Bridestones. Ted Hughes. AnAn

Holy Office, The. James Joyce. FaBoTw; NoAM; OxBTC

Holy Ones, the Young Ones, The. Chayyim Zeldis. TrJP

Holy Order. J. B. Boothroyd. FiBHP

Holy persons draw to themselves all that is earthly. Hildegard von Bingen. EaPr

Holy Poet, I have heard. John Hall Wheelock. *Fr.* Thanks from Earth to Heaven. TrPWD

Holy Rood, The, *sels.* John Davies of Hereford.
Although We Do Not All the Good We Love. Son

Holy-Rood come forth and shield. The Old Wives Prayer. Robert Herrick. SeCV-1

Holy Rose, The. Vyacheslav Ivanov, *tr. fr. Russian by* Babette Deutsch *and* Avrahm Yarmolinsky. AWP

Holy Satyr. Hilda Doolittle ("H. D."). MoAmPo

Holy Scripture, Writ Divine. From a London Bookshop. *Unknown.* FaBoUs; NBLV

Holy Sonnets, *sels.* John Donne.
"As due by many titles I resign[e]." ESCV; JCP
"At the round earth's imagined corners, blow." BLPL; ChIV-2; ClHu; EBEV; EnRePo; ESCV; FaBoRV; FHYEP; HAP; HeIL; HeIP; ImPo; InPS; JCP; LiTB; MeLP; NAEL-1; NAWM-1; NOBE; NoP; NOSC; OAEL-1; OBD; OxAEP-1; PFP; PoE; PoEL-2; PPP; SCGP; SeCP; SeCV-1; Son; TEP; TFi; TOF
(Blow Your Trumpets.) ChTr
"Batter my heart, three person'd [personed] God; for you." BLPL; ClHu; EBEV; EBEvV; EnRePo; ESCV; FF; FHYEP; HAP; HeIP; HoPM; ImPo; InPK; InPS; JCP; LiTB; MeLP; NAEL-1; NIP; NOBE; NoP; NOSC; OAEL-1; OxAEP-1; PeECV; PoE; PoEL-2; Poetr; PPP; PrIm; SeCP; SeCV-1; Son; SoSe; TEP; TFi; TOF; TrCP; TrGrPo; TrPWD
"Death, be not proud, though some have called thee." ChTr; DL; EBEvV; ElL; EnRePo; ESCV; FaBoRV; FaBV; FF; FHYEP; HAP; HeIL; HeIP; ImPo; InPK; InPS; InvP; JCP; LiTB; MeLP; NAEL-1; NAWM-1; NIP; NOBE; NoP; NOSC; OAEL-1; OBD; OxAEP-1; PoE; PoEL-2; Poetr; PoRA; PPP; PrIm; SCGP; SCV; SeCP; SeCV-1; SoSe; TEP; TrCP; TrGrPo; TRP; WeW
(Death.) OBEV
(Death be not proud, though some have called thee.) PeECV, *sect.* X
(Death, Be Not Proud.) ClHu; TFi

"Father, part of his double interest." ESCV; JCP; Son
"I am a little world made cunningly." ChIV-1; EnRePo; ESCV; NAEL-1; NIP; NoP; PoE; SeCP; Son; TEP
"If faithful soules be alike glorifi'd." ESCV
"If poisonous [*or* poysonous] mineral[l]s, and if that tree." EBEV; EnRePo; ESCV; FaBoVe; ImPo; JCP; LiTB; NAEL-1; NoP; OAEL-1; OxAEP-1; PFP; PoEL-2; PPP; SCGP; SeCP; Son; UnPo
"O might those sighes and teares returne againe." ESCV
"Oh my black[e] soul[e]! now thou art summoned." EBEV; ESCV; JCP; OAEL-1; OxAEP-1; Son; TEP; TOF
(Oh My Black Soul.) Poetr
"Oh, to vex me, contraries [*or* contraryes] meet in one." ESCV; NOSC; OAEL-1; PoEL-2; Son
(Oh, to vex me, two contraries meet in one.) ChIV-2
"Show me dear[e] Christ, thy spouse, so bright and clear." ESCV; MeLP; NAEL-1; NoP; NOSC; PoE; Son
(Show me, dear Christ, Thy Spouse, so bright and clear.) PeECV, *sect.* XVIII
"Since she whom I lov'd hath paid [*or* payd] her last debt." ESCV; JCP; NAEL-1; NOSC; Son
"Spit in my face you Jew[e]s, and pierce my side." ESCV; JCP; Son; TOF
"This is my play's [*or* playes] last scene, here heavens appoint." EBEV; ESCV; FaBoVe; JCP; MeLP; SeCP; Son; TEP
"Thou hast made me, and shall thy work[e] decay?" EBEV; EnRePo; ESCV; MeLP; NAEL-1; NOBE; NOCV; NoP; NOSC; OxAEP-1; PoEL-2; SCGP; SeCP; Son; TEP
"What if this present were the world's last night?" EBEV; ESCV; HeIP; ImPo; InPS; JCP; LiTB; MeLP; NAEL-1; NOCV; NOSC; OxAEP-1; PeECV; PoE; Son; TEP
"Why are we[e] by all creatures waited on?" ESCV; JCP; NOCV; PoE; PoEL-2; TrCP
"Wilt thou love God, as he thee! then digest." ESCV; JCP; TrCP

Holy Spirit, Faithful Guide. Marcus Morris Wells. AH

Holy Spirit,/ giving life to all life. Hildegard von Bingen, *tr. fr. German by* Stephen Mitchell. EnlH

Holy Spirit, Lord of light. Hymn to the Holy Spirit. Stephen Langton. TrCP

Holy Spirit, Truth Divine. Samuel Longfellow. AH

Holy stond in the hall [*or* halle]. Holly and Ivy. *Unknown.* MeEL
(Nay, Ivy, Nay.) CH

Holy the silence of your calm retreat. (LL) Sonnet: Leaves. William Barnes. BoNaP; ChTr; FaBoRV; OBNC

Holy Thursday. Charles Wright. AnAn

Holy Thursday ("Is this a holy thing to see.") Blake. *Fr.* Songs of Experience. EnRP; FF; FHYEP; InPS; NAEL-2; NOEC; NoP; OAEL-2; TEP

Holy Thursday (" 'Twas on a Holy Thursday, their innocent faces clean.") Blake. *Fr.* Songs of Innocence. CH; EnRP; FHYEP; InPS; MeMBP; NAEL-2; NAWM-2; NOBE; NOEC; NoP; OAEL-2; PeECV; PoE; SCV; TEP; TFi; TrCP

Holy Tide, The. Frederick Tennyson. OBEV

Holy Transportations, *sels.* Charles Fitz-Geffry.
Take Frankincense, O God. ChTr

Holy Was Demeter Walking th' Corn Furrow. Edward Sanders. PoM

Holy water come and bring. The Spell. Robert Herrick. CaPo

Holy Well, The ("As it fell out on a holiday.") *Unknown.* OBET

Holy Well, The ("As it fell out one May morning.") *Unknown.* FaBoCh; GBP; NOCV

Holy Willie's Prayer. Burns. EBEV; FaBoBl; NOEC; OBSV; OxBS; PoE; PoEL-4; PPP; TFi

Holy Wroughte of sterres bright. William Herebert. MiEL

Holyhead, Sept. 25th, 1727. Swift. BIrV

Holywell, *sels.* John Jones.
"Now slowly winding from the mountain's head." AngWe

Homage. Gilbert Highet. *See* And so depart into dark.

Homage. Gustave Kahn, *tr. fr. French by* Jethro Bithell. TrJP

Homage. R. J. Schoeck. GoYe

Homage and Lament for Ezra Pound in Captivity. Robert Duncan. NOBA

Homage: Light from the Hall. David Wojahn. *Fr.* Mystery Train: A Sequence. PBCAP

Homage to a Government. Philip Larkin. EBEV; FaBoPV; NoAM

Homage to Arthur Waley. Weldon Kees. NaP

Homage to Chagall. Duane Niatum. CDW

Homage to Coleman Hawkins. Ken Irby. Jaz

Homage to Diana. Sir Walter Ralegh. *See* Praised be Diana's fair and harmless light.

Homage to Ezra Pound. Gilbert Highet.

Homage to Faiz Ahmed Faiz. Agha Shahid Ali. OpBo

Homage to Ferd. Holthausen. Gwen Harwood. NOBAu

Homage to Hieronymus Bosch. Thomas MacGreevy. BIrV

Honey, the humming of a million bees, The. Flame. Frederick Seidel. PRA

Honey, trus' der Lawd a bit, an' doan fohgit to smile! Trus' an' Smile. B.Y. Williams. BLRP

Honey/ When de man. Sister Lou. Sterling A. Brown. PoBA; PoNe

Honeycomb, The. Pauline Stainer. PWE

Honeyed by time. The Wooden Chamber. Anne Hébert, *tr. fr. French by* Birgit Swenson. WPOW

Honeymoon. Samuel L. Albert. GoYe

Honeymoon. Barry Goldensohn. NAmP90

Honeymoon, The. James Simmons. PNI

Honeymoon, South Coast. Evan Jones (b. 1927). FaBoMA

Honeystain/ the rhetoricians of blackness. The Anti-Semanticist. Everett Hoagland. BPo; NBV

Honeysuckle (Chevrefoil). Marie de France, *tr. by* Patricia Terry. BoWoP

Honeysuckle, nightshade. Poem for L. C. Peter Klappert. AmPA

Honeysuckle Was the Saddest Odor of All, I Think. Thadious M. Davis. BlSi

Honeysuckle's siege at the nerve-ends. Infamous Doctrine. Paul Evans. NBrP

Honi Soit Qui Mal Y Pense. Ian Young. PeHV

Honor a going thing, goldfinch, corporation, tree. Mechanism. A. R. Ammons. HAP

Honor and shame from no condition rise. Pope. *Fr.* Essay on Man, An. TrGrPo

Honor and truth and manhood. Things That Endure. Ted Olson. WBLP

Honor hereafter to be layde by thee. (*LL*) Elegy on Shakespeare. William Basse. EiL; FaBoRV

"Honor," said the man. Definitions. Joseph Joel Keith. PoToHe

Honora, should that cruel time arrive. To Honora Sneyd. Anna Seward. ECWP

Honour. Abraham Cowley. BoLoP

"Honour be to Mudjekeewis!" Longfellow. *Fr.* Song of Hiawatha, The. UV

Honour Dishonoured. Wilfrid Scawen Blunt. OBMV

Honour him for their memory, whose bones he goes among! (*LL*) The Forging of the Anchor. Sir Samuel Ferguson. PeIV

Honour is flashed off exploit, so we say. In Honour of St. Alphonsus Rodriguez. Gerard Manley Hopkins. EBEV; OxAEP-2

Honour is so sublime perfection. To the Countesse of Bedford. John Donne. MeLP

Honour of Bristol, The. *At. to* Laurence Price. OxBSS

Honour plays a bubble's part. John Gay. *Fr.* Polly; an Opera. PeLV

Honour thy parents; but good manners call. God to Be First Served. Robert Herrick. OxBChV

Honour us all. (*LL*) Epitaph on a Schoolmaster. Burns. FaBoCo; FaBoEE

Honour with age. Walter Kennedy. OxBS

Honourable Entertainment Given to the Queen's Majesty in Progress at Elvetham, 1591, The, *sels.* Nicholas Breton *and others.*
  "In the merry month of May." EBEvV; NoSic
    (Pastoral, A.) TrGrPo
  (Phillida and Coridon.) OBEV; TTTS
  (Phyllida and Corydon.) EiL
  (Ploughman's Song, The.) NOBE
  With Fragrant Flowers We Strew the Way. EiL

Honourable Winifred Wemyss, The. *Unknown.* PeLi

Honoured I lived e'erwhile with honoured men. Honour Dishonoured. Wilfrid Scawen Blunt. OBMV

Honours that the people give always, The. The Thespians at Thermopylae. Norman Cameron. GTBS-P

Honure, joy, helthe, and plesaunce. Charles, Duc d'Orléans. MiEL

Hoo, Suffolk. *Unknown.* GBP

Hooded in angry mist, the sun goes down. Herbert Asquith. *Fr.* Nightfall. OBD

Hoofer, The. A. K. Redwing. VoR

Hoogh, quoth he. (*LL*) There Was a Lady Loved a Swine. *Unknown.* GBP; OxNR

Hook shot kisses the rim and, A. Fast Break. Edward Hirsch. DiPo; EOEF; VCAP

Hooked for two years now on wrinkle creams. Aging. Erica Jong. CrSp

Hooker's Across! George Henry Boker. PAH

Hooly and Fairly. Joanna Baillie. WoRP

Hoop, a rolling O, oh those have power, A. Ode on Zero. Phoebe Pettingell. PoA

Hoopoe. George Darley. *See* Solitary wayfarer!

"Hooray, hooray, hooray!" (*LL*) The Three Badgers. "Lewis Carroll." CBNP; FaBoNo

Hoosen Johnny. *Unknown.* AS; FaPON

Hooter wakes me up to face the day again, The. Unaccompanied. Harvey Andrews. OBET

Hooters. Meic Stephens. AngWe

Hoover, in grim silence, sat, The. David Woodsford. PeLi

Hop-Garden, The, *sels.* Christopher Smart.
  Hops along the Medway. FaBoPP
  How to Cure Hops and Prepare Them for Sale. FaBoUs

Hop hop, thump thump. Stevie Smith. *Fr.* Dedicated Dancing Bull and the Water Maid, The. WPE

Hop-poles stand in cones, The. The Midnight Skaters. Edmund Blunden. FaBoTw; GoJo; GTBS-P; MoBrPo; NOBE; OBD; PeFWW

Hop, Skip, and Jump. Gary Snyder. LCAP; PRA

Hope. William Lisle Bowles. EnRP

Hope. Emily Brontë. NoP

Hope, *sels.* William Cowper.
  "Though clasp'd and cradled in his nurse's arms." PoEL-3

Hope. Josephine D. Henderson Heard. CBWP-4

Hope. George Herbert. ChIV-2; PoEL-2; WeW

Hope. Langston Hughes. OBAL; OBCA; TRP

Hope. Randall Jarrell. MoAB; MoAmPo

Hope. Georgia Douglas Johnson. CDC

Hope. F. D. Reeve. PoA

Hope. Christopher Smart. ChIV-1

Hope. Edith Södergran, *tr. by* Jaakko A. Ahokas. PBWP

Hope. Theognis, *tr. fr. Greek by* John Hookham Frere. AWP

Hope. Clara Ann Thompson. CBWP-2

Hope. Mary E. Tucker. CBWP-1

Hope. *Unknown, tr. fr. Irish by* Brendan Kennelly. PeIV

Hope. *Unknown, tr. fr. Irish by* Frank O'Connor. CIP; IIP

Hope and Despair. Lascelles Abercrombie. OBMV

Hope and Faith. Isaac Leibush Peretz, *tr. fr. Yiddish by* Henry Goodman. TrJP

Hope and Fear. Swinburne. FaBoBe

Hope and Joy. Christina Rossetti. OxBChV

Hope Chest. Elaine Equi. VBLP

Hope Deferred. Clara Ann Thompson. CBWP-2

Hope Evermore and Believe. Arthur Hugh Clough. WGRP

Hope! Fortune! Je m'en fous! Palladas, *tr. fr. Greek by* Tony Harrison. GrAn

Hope humbly then; with trembling pinions soar. Pope. *Fr.* Essay on Man, An. EBEvV; TrGrPo

Hope I dreamed of was a dream, The. Mirage. Christina Rossetti. BoLoP; CoGr; PoRA

Hope is like a harebell trembling from its birth. Comparisons. Christina Rossetti. OxBChV

Hope is the thing with feathers. Emily Dickinson. AmPP; BLPL; MeMAP; MoAB; MoAmPo; MoShBr; NOBA; OxBA; SAmP; TAP

Hope is what skims time always from our lives. Julius Polyaenus, *tr. fr. Greek by* Peter Jay. GrAn

Hope, like the hyaena [*or* hyena], coming to be old. Henry Constable. *Fr.* Diana. EnLoPo; ESo; SCGP; Son

Hope! Not distant is the Springtime. Hope and Faith. Isaac Leibush Peretz, *tr. fr. Yiddish by* Henry Goodman. TrJP

Hope, of all ills that men endure. In Praise of Hope. Abraham Cowley. OxAEP-1

Hope of burning off at least the top crust of the time's uncleanness, from the acid bottles. (*LL*) Prescription of Painful Ends. Robinson Jeffers. LiTA; MoAB; MoAmPo; OxBA

Hope of the World, The. Sir William Watson. WGRP

Hope Thou in God. Josephine D. Henderson Heard. CBWP-4

Hope! Thou vain, delusive maiden. Hope. Josephine D. Henderson Heard. CBWP-4

Hope was but a timid friend. Hope. Emily Brontë. NoP

Hope we not in this life only. Not in Vain. *Unknown.* BLRP

Hope, whose weak being ruined is. Against Hope. Abraham Cowley. *Fr.* Mistress, The. LiTB; MeLP; NOSC; SeCV-1
  (On Hope.) NOBE

Hope ye, my verses, that posterity. Joachim du Bellay, *tr. fr. French by* Spenser. *Fr.* Ruins of Rome. PoE

Hopeful old fellow called Rousseau, A. John Fay. PeLi

Hopeful Spiritual Athlete, The. Kabir, *tr. fr. Hindi by* Robert Bly. RaBo

Hopeless Desire Soon Withers and Dies. "A. W." NoSic

Hopeless longing of the day, The. (*LL*) Longing. Matthew Arnold. PoLF; SoSe

Hopeless steady cursing in Dutch. (*LL*) Vanderdecken. Douglas Livingstone. PeSAV

Hopelessly handcuffed to a mysterious butterfly. A Lost Mohican Visits Hell's Kitchen. A. K. Redwing. VoR

Hopelessly I answer, "Yes." (*LL*) Night Without End. *Unknown.*
  OHMPC
Hope's Okay. A. R. Ammons. HCAP
Hoping Against Hope. Christina Rossetti. CBLP
Hoping all the time. *Unknown, tr. by* Arthur Waley. *Fr.* Kokin Shu.
  AWP
Hoping it might be so. (*LL*) The Oxen. Thomas Hardy. BoTP; CMoP;
  EBEV; HAP; InPK; LiTM; MeMBP; MoAB; MoBrPo; MoP; NoAM;
  NOBE; NTP; OAEL-2; OBCP; OxAEP-2; OxBTC; PChr; PeECV; Poetr;
  PPP; RB; SoSe; TFi; TOF; TRP; WeW
Hoping this night my true love to see. *Unknown.* FaBoUs
Hopkins Enters the Roman Catholic Church. David Scott. PWE
Hopper o'ditches, A. *Unknown.* FaBoVe
Hoppity. A. A. Milne. FaBV; NTCP
Hoppy. Reginald Gibbons. DiPo; SoCa
Hops. Boris Pasternak, *tr. fr. Russian by* Jon Stallworthy *and* Peter France.
  BoLoP; TTTS
Hops along the Medway. Christopher Smart. *Fr.* Hop-Garden, The.
  FaBoPP
Hop't She. *Unknown.* GBP
Hora Christi. Alice Brown. TrPWD; WGRP
Horae Canonicae, *sels.* W. H. Auden.
  Lauds. TrCP
  Prime. CMoP; PoE
  Vespers. FaBoMo
Horae Canonicae. Donald Davie. CRP
Sels.
  Compline.
  Prime.
Horat. Ode 29. Book 3. Horace. *See* Descended of an ancient line.
Horatian Epode to the Duchess of Malfi. Allen Tate. FaBoMo
Horatian Ode. Joseph Warren Beach. PoA
Horatian Ode upon Cromwell's [*or* Cromwel's] Return from Ireland, An.
  (Forward youth that would appear, The.) Andrew Marvell. EBEV;
  ESCV; GeHe; GTBS; GTBS-P; HAP; IIP; InPS; JCP; NOBE; NoP;
  NOSC; OAEL-1; OBEV; OBWP; OxAEP-1; PoEL-2; SCGP; SeCP;
  SeCV-1; TFi
Sels.
  King Charles on [*or* upon] the Scaffold. ChTr; FaBoRV
  "What field of all the civil wars." FaBoEH
  "Where, twining subtile fears with hope." OBD
Horatian Variation. Leonard Bacon. NYBP
Horatians, The. W. H. Auden. NYBP
Horatio, of ideal courage vain. Feigned Courage. Charles Lamb *and* Mary
  Lamb. GN; OxBChV
Horatius. Macaulay. *Fr.* Lays of Ancient Rome. OBWP
Horatius. Macaulay. *See* Lars Porsena of Clusium.
Horatius at the Bridge. Macaulay. *Fr.* Lays of Ancient Rome. BeLS;
  FaBoCh; FaPoR; OBNV, *abr.;* OBWP; PoLF
Horch, horch, die Bell am Backdoor ringt! Morning Song. Kurt M. Stein.
  FiBHP
Horeb's mountain top of old. Mountain Tops. L. A. J. Moorer. CBWP-3
Horestes, *sels.* John Pickering.
  Haltersick's Song. NoSic
    (Song: "Farewell, adieu, that court-like life!") EiL
  Song Sung by Egistus and Clytemnestra. NoSic
  Vice's Song, The. NoSic
Horizon, The. Kevin Hart. NOBAu
Horizon Thong. George Abbe. GoYe
Horizons for the man Flammonde. (*LL*) Flammonde. E. A. Robinson.
  AmPP; CMoP; LiTA; LiTM; MeMAP; NoAM
Horizontal Cosmology, *sels.* Christopher Gilbert.
  Backyard, The. Jaz
  Saxophone. Jaz
Horizontal in a deckchair on the bleak ward [*or* Horizontal on a deckchair in
  the Ward]. Ezra Pound. Robert Lowell. MoP; NAAL-2; NoAM;
  NOBA
Horizontal on rough grass. Lines in Wasdale Head. John Seed. VaA
Horn, The. Léonie Adams. MoAB; MoAmPo
Horn, The. James Reeves. OTCP
Horn for weapon, and wool for shield. The Zodiac Song. John Ruskin.
  NOBVV
Horn: I'm loved by my lord, and his shoulder. Unknown, formerly at. to
  Cynewulf, *tr. fr. Anglo-Saxon. Fr.* Riddles (Exeter Book). ASW, *tr.*
  by Kevin Crossley-Holland.
Horn: "Time was when I was weapon and warrior." Unknown, formerly at.
  to Cynewulf, *tr. by* Charles W. Kennedy. *Fr.* Riddles (Exeter Book).
  AnOE
Horned Lizard. Charles Molesworth. GrPl
Horned Snake, The. Louis Oliver. HATNAP

Hornet. Anne Sexton. AnAn
Hornets occasionally build their nests near roads. Homer, *tr. by* Christopher
  Logue. *Fr.* Iliad, The. OBVE
Hornless hart carries off the harem, The. The Royal Stag. "Hugh
  MacDiarmid." FaBoMo
Hornpipe. Edith Sitwell. *Fr.* Façade. FaBoMo; GTBS-P; OAEL-2
Horns protruded from the. The Rising. Jayne Cortez. NBV
Horn's sweet note and the tooth of the hound, The. (*LL*) Two Songs of a
  Fool. W. B. Yeats. CMoP; RB
Horns [*or* Hornes] to bulls wise Nature lends. Beauty. Thomas Stanley,
  after the Greek of Anacreon. AWP; OBVE
Horny-Goloch, The. *Unknown.* FaBoCh
Horoscope. Rasa Livada, *tr. fr. Serbo-Croatian by* Charles Simic. HSix
Horoscope. Eva Salzman. NWP
Horrible crime was committed, A. Pearl Bryan. *Unknown.* AmFP
Horrible Decree, The, *sels.* Charles Wesley.
  "Sinners, abhor the Fiend." NOCV
Horrible of hue, hideous to behold. Sir Thomas Wyatt. SiPSBD
Horrible Tangents. Victoria Kohn. UTF
Horrid Voice of Science, The. Vachel Lindsay. PoA
Horror. Peter Baum, *tr. fr. German by* Jethro Bithell. AWP
Horror Comic. Robert Conquest. OxBTC
Horror Story Written for the Cover of a Matchbook, A. Chuck Wachtel.
  UL
Hors de Combat. Anvari, *tr. fr. Persian by* Omar S. Pound. ArPe
Horse, The. Bible, *O.T. See* Hast Thou Given the Horse Strength.
Horse. Louise Glück. AnAn; NALW
Horse, The. Philip Levine. CoAP; VCAP
Horse, The. Francis Ponge, *tr. fr. French by* Beth Archer. AnRep; NU
Horse. Kenneth Rexroth. *Fr.* Bestiary, A. NNaP; OBAL
Horse, The. Naomi Royde-Smith. FaBoCo; FiBHP
Horse & Rider. Wey Robinson. BXAP
Horse above on the mountain, The. (*LL*) Sleepwalkers' Ballad. Federico
  García Lorca. STV
Horse and a flea and three blind mice, A. *Unknown.* RoPo
  (Whoops!) NTCP
Horse and hattock. The Witch's Broomstick Spell. *Unknown.* ChTr; GBP
Horse and His Rider, The. Joanna Baillie. ECWP; NOEC
Horse and pelatis, ho, ho! (*LL*) The Witch's Broomstick Spell.
  Unknown. ChTr; GBP
Horse and the Mule, The. John Huddlestone Wynne. OxBChV
Horse and Tree. Rita Dove. TRP
Horse Boyle was called Horse Boyle because of his brother Mule.
  Dresden. Ciaran Carson. CIP; PBCIP; PNI
Horse by Moonlight. Alberto Blanco, *tr. fr. Spanish.* TSaS, *tr. by* Jennifer
  Clement
Horse can't pull while kicking, A. Horse Sense. *Unknown.* BLPA; PWR;
  WBLP
Horse Chestnut. Gary Miranda. SM
Horse-Chestnut Time. Kaye Starbird. PDV
Horse Chestnut Tree, The. Richard Eberhart. CMoP; LiTM; MoAB;
  MoAmPo
Horse Cursed by the Sun, The. *Unknown, tr. fr. Hottentot by* W. H. I.
  Bleek. PeSAV
Horse Did Not Come Back, The. Erumai Veliyanar, *tr. fr. Tamil by* A. K.
  Ramanujan. PLW
Horse Escaped from the circus, A. Horse by Moonlight. Alberto Blanco,
  tr. fr. Spanish. TSaS, *tr. by* Jennifer Clement
Horse, huge. Inviolable. Daniel Hoffman. GrPl
Horse in the Drugstore, The. Tess Gallagher. AmPA; AnAn
Horse/ Is more so, The. (*LL*) Horse & Rider. Wey Robinson. BXAP
Horse Landscape, The. Helen Dunmore. PWE
Horse Latitudes. Frankie Paino. NAmP90
Horse Named Bill, The. *Unknown.* AS
Horse: not one less than twenty. Isuba. Jim Barnes. *Fr.* Four Things
  Choctaw. HATNAP
Horse on the Wall. Marcia Southwick. NAmP90
Horse Power. Tom Raworth. NBrP
Horse Sense. *Unknown.* BLPA; PWR; WBLP
Horse Show, The. William Carlos Williams. CMoP; NOBA; TAP; VGW
Horse that carried Miss Kilmansegg, The. Her Accident. Thomas Hood.
  Fr. Miss Kilmansegg and Her Precious Leg. EBVV
Horse Thief, The. William Rose Benét. MoAmPo
Horse Trader's Song, The. *Unknown.* AmFP
Horse weather hangs. Easter with Horses. Nigel Wells. PWE
Horse Weebles. Edward Kamau Brathwaite. PBCV

Horse with a chestnut mane reflected in the green waves of the spring river. Tune: "Echoing Heaven's Everlastingness." Wang Kuo-wei, *tr. fr. Chinese by* Ching-i Tu. SuSp

Horse with birds on its mane, doubt on its tail, The. Godhorse. Kojo Laing. HBAPE

Horseback on Sunday morning. The Wild Geese. Wendell Berry. TRP

Horsechestnuts. Brendan Kennelly. PWE

Horseman, The. Walter de la Mare. GoJo

Horseman on the Skyline, The. Henry Lawson. CBAP

Horsemeat, *sels.* Charles Bukowski.
"20 minutes later." NGP
"My women of the past keep trying to locate me." NGP

Horses, The. Ted Hughes. NoAM

Horses. Edwin Muir. CMoP; FaBoCh; OAEL-2

Horses. Gwyn Thomas, *tr. fr. Welsh by* Joseph P. Clancy. OBWVE

Horses. Dorothy Wellesley. OBMV; OxBTC

Horses Aboard. Thomas Hardy. FM

Horses and Men in the Rain. Carl Sandburg. PoLF

Horses are standing in rain. Great Aso. Miyoshi Tatsuji, *tr. fr. Japanese.* TSaS, *tr. by* Edith Marcombe Shiffert *and* Yuki Sawa

Horses at Valley Store. Leslie Silko. VoR

Horses, The ("Barely a twelvemonth after.") Edwin Muir. CMoP; GGP; HAP; HeIP; MoBrPo; MoP; NoAM; NOBE; NoP; OAEL-2; OxBTC; PAW; PoE; Poetr; RB; TEP; TRP; WeW

Horses Chawin' Hay. Hamlin Garland. OBAL

Horse's Head, The. Brendan Kennelly. CIP

Horses in horsecloths stand in a row. Horses Aboard. Thomas Hardy. FM

Horses in Snow. Roberta Hill Whiteman. NoAM

Horse's mind, The. Unity. Fazil Hüsnü Daglarca, *tr. fr. Turkish by* Tâlat S. Halman. RaBo

Horses of Achilles, The. C. P. Cavafy, *tr. fr. Greek by* Edmund Keeley *and* Philip Sherrard. OBD

Horses of Marini, The. Tania van Zyl. PeSA

Horses of the sea, The. Christina Rossetti. *Fr.* Sing-Song. FaPON; GoJo; NTCP

Horses on the Camargue. Roy Campbell. GTBS-P; OBAP; OBTV; PeSA

Horses out of their brains bored all, The. Flying Noises. Thomas Lux. LCAP

Horses, the pigs, The. Familiar Friends. James S. Tippett. BoTP

Horsewoman of charm at Uttoxeter, A. R. D. Condon. PeLi

Horsey Gap. *Unknown.* FaBoPP; GBP

Horst Wessel on Alcatraz. Douglas Houston. PWE

Hortatory Address to the Greeks, *sels.* Saint Justin Martyr.
"Then marking this my sacred speech, but truly lend." SiPSBD, *tr. by* Sir Walter Ralegh

Hos Ego Versiculos. Francis Quarles. *Fr.* Argalus and Parthenia. NOSC

Hosanna. Thomas Traherne. ChIV-2; PoEL-2; SeCV-2

Hosanna — musick is divine. Psalm CXLVII: "Praise ye the Lord." Christopher Smart. NOCV

Hosanna to Christ. Isaac Watts. NOCV

Hosannah the home run! (*LL*) Dream of a Baseball Star. Gregory Corso. VGW

Hose and Iron. Greg Kuzma. MAT

Hospice. Lynda Hull. PFL

Hospital. Wilfred J. Funk. PoToHe

Hospital, The. Patrick Kavanagh. BIrV; CIP

Hospital. Geoffrey C. Millard. PeSA

Hospital. Karl Shapiro. VGW

Hospital Barge at Cérisy. Wilfred Owen. OBTV; RB

Hospital Evening. Gwen Harwood. FaBoWP

Hospital for Defectives. Thomas Blackburn. GTBS-P; OxBTC

Hospital for sick and needy Jews, A. The New Jewish Hospital at Hamburg. Heine, *tr. fr. German by* Charles Godfrey Leland. TrJP

Hospital Prison Ship, The. Philip Freneau. *Fr.* British Prison Ship, The. AmPP

Hospital — Retrospections, The. Kenneth Mackenzie. CBAP

Hospital Songs, *sels.* Jack Dann.

Hospital State, The. Betsy Sholl. PBCAP

Hospital Window, The. James Dickey. CAPP; HCAP; MT; NoAM; VCAP

Hospitality in Ancient Ireland. *Unknown, tr. fr. Irish by* Kuno Meyer. TIRV

Hospital/Poem. Sonia Sanchez. BPo; PoBA

Hospitals. Rachel Hadas. UnDi

Hoss, The. James Whitcomb Riley. AnAmPo

Host, The. William Heyen. FoLa

Host is riding from Knocknarea, The. The Hosting of the Sidhe. W. B. Yeats. NoAM

Host of peaks rear up into the color of cold, A. Spending the Night at a Mountain Temple. Chia Tao, *tr. fr. Chinese by* Stephen Owen. SuSp

Host of the Air, The. W. B. Yeats. CH

Hostel. Evan Jones (b. 1927). FaBoMA

Hostess' Daughter, The. Ludwig Uhland, *tr. fr. German by* Margarete Münsterberg. AWP

Hostess of the Ferry Inn, The. Gwerfyl Mechain, *tr. fr. Welsh by* H. Idris Bell. OBWVE

Hosting of the Sidhe, The. W. B. Yeats. NoAM

Hot Afternoons Have Been in West 15th Street. Paul Blackburn. VGW

Hot Bath in an Old Hotel. Paula Rankin. MT

Hot Boiled Beans. *Unknown.* ReMoGo

Hot breath among the pale crystal, A. Arte Popular. Pat Mora. AfAz

Hot Club de France Reprise on MTV. Vince Gotera. Jaz

Hot Codlins. *Unknown.* ReMoGo

Hot cross buns! Hot-cross buns!/ One a penny, two a penny. Mother Goose. BoTP; OxNR; ReMoGo

Hot Day In Sydney, A. *Unknown.* NOBAu

Hot Dog Poem, The. Jane Barnes. GLP

Hot Flame of My Grief, The. Moses ibn Ezra, *tr. fr. Hebrew by* Solomon Solis-Cohen. TrJP

Hot horn hand in my face is all. My Mother Shoots the Breeze. Fred Chappell. MT

Hot, humid, the smell of sewage. Greenhalgh's Pub. Julian Croft. NOBAu

Hot in June a narrow winged. A Nameless One. Margaret Avison. HeIP; NOBC

Hot Line. Carmen Tafolla. AfAz

Hot midsummer night on Water Street, A. Hot Night on Water Street. Louis Simpson. CAPP; TwCP

Hot — my lungs on fire, my hands, knees. Sweat-lodge. Hilton Obenzinger. BCF

Hot night makes us keep our bedroom window open, The. "To Speak of Woe That Is in Marriage." Robert Lowell. CAPP; MoP; NAAL-2; NoAM

Hot night of the ramparts. Embrace the Blade. Joyce Mansour, *tr. fr. French by* Carol Cosman. PBWP

Hot Night on Water Street. Louis Simpson. CAPP; TwCP

Hot Pease Man, The. Mother Goose. OxNR; ReMoGo

Hot red rocks of Aden, The. Home Thoughts. *Unknown.* NSI

Hot Springs. Earle Birney. OxBC

Hot Stuff. Edward Botwood. PAH

Hot summer day, A. Lapel Button. Edward Kleinschmidt. UnDi

Hot Summer Sunday. A. L. Hendricks. PBCV

Hot sun [*or* sunne], cool[e] fire, tempered with sweet air[e]. Bethsabe's Song. George Peele. *Fr.* David and [Fair] Bethsabe. ChIV-1; EnRePo; GBL; NOBE; NoP; NoSic; OxBoLi; OxBSP; PoEL-2; RB; TEP (Bathsheba's Song.) ImPo (Bethsabe Bathing.) ElL; TrGrPo

Hot the tears Del Cascar wept. (*LL*) Del Cascar. William Stanley Braithwaite. CDC

Hotel. Donald Justice. *Fr.* Body and Soul. BAP-91

Hotel Ameridemocratogrando. Black Man, 13th Floor. James A. Emanuel. NBV

Hotel bar, A; One more compartment. The Language of Delight. Tim Longville. VaA

Hotel de l'Univers et Portugal. James Merrill. MoAB; PoA

Hotel doorman's frantic whistle, The. Theatre Hour. Ogden Nash. ImGa

Hotel Fire: New Orleans. Paul Ruffin. InPK

Hotel in Paris. Dennis Trudell. PoA

Hotel Paradiso e Commerciale. John Malcolm Brinnin. NYBP; TwCP

Hôtel Transylvanie. Frank O'Hara. NeAP; PoM

Hotel Tropicana. Michael Burkard. BAP-89

Hotel Zingo. David Chaloner. VaA

Hots, The. Michael Sharkey. NOBAu

Hottentot, The. Thomas Pringle. OBTV

Hottentot Venus. Stephen Gray. PeSAV

Houdini. Eli W. Mandel. NIP; NOBC

Hough gruntough wough Thomough. Epitaph in the Bermuda Tongue, Which Must Be Pronounced With the Accent of the Grunting of a Hog. John Taylor. CBNP

Hound, The. Robert Francis. SoSe

Hound, The/ Could never be called refined. The Angry Poet. Frank O'Connor, *tr. fr. Irish.* CIP

Hound Dog, *sels.* Leiber *and* Stoller.
You Ain't Nothin' But a Hound Dog. LPA

Hound of Heaven, The. Francis Thompson. BLPL; ChIV-2; EBEvV, *ll.* 1–15; EnVR; FaBV; GGP, *ll.* 1–15; ImPo; LiTB; LiTM; MoAB; MoBrPo; NAEL-2; OBMV; OtMeF; PoEL-5; TFi; TrGrPo; WGRP

Hounded Lovers, The. William Carlos Williams. NYBP; TrGrPo

Hounded slave that flags in the race, leans by the fence, The. The Wounded Person. Walt Whitman. *Fr.* Song of Myself. AmPP; LiTA; MoAmPo, *abr.*; NOBA; OxBA; PoNe; SOTW, *much abr.*

Hounds, The. John Freeman. OBMV; OxBSP

Hounds are breathing at my trail, The. Can-Can. John Fuller. *Fr.* Fox-Trot. PeLV

Hounds of Spring, The. Swinburne. *Fr.* Atalanta in Calydon. AWP; CTC; EBVV; EnVR; FaBoBe; FaBV; GTBS-P; HAP; LiTB; NAEL-2; NOBE; NoP; OAEL-2; OBEV; PoE; PrIm; SCGP; TEP; TFi; TrGrPo; WeW

Hounds of the Soul, The. Louis Ginsberg. TrJP

Hounds sleep well, The. It is not they who stir the fox. With Hands like Leaves. James Still. GrPl

Hounds that heralded the rich, The. Against Paradise. Jonathan Holden. NAmP90

Hour, The. Vivian Virtue. PBCV

Hour after hour the cards were fairly shuffled. Whist. Eugene Fitch Ware. PoLF

Hour at last come round, The. The Dying Gaul. Desmond O'Grady. BIrV; PBCIP

Hour for truth and her, The. (LL) Sloe was lost in flower, The. A. E. Housman. CBLP

Hour gets later, the times get worse, The. Preliminary Poem. John Heath-Stubbs. OxBC

Hour-Glass, The. Robert Herrick. BeJo; CaPo

Hour Glass, The ("Consider this small dust, here in the glass.") Ben Jonson. BLPL; ImPo; LiTB

Hour-glass whispers to the lion's roar, The. Our Bias. W. H. Auden. MoP; NoP; Poetr

(Hour-glass whispers to the lion's paw, The.) OxAEP-2

Hour-hand and the minute-hand upon a polished dial, The. The Speed Track. "Peter." BoTP

Hour is dark. The river comes to its end, The. Mary Ursula Bethell. *Fr.* By the River Ashley. PeNZ

Hour is held deep, in the underneath of time, An. Naming Souls. Uri Zvi Greenberg, *tr. fr. Hebrew by* Jon Silkin *and* Ezra Spicehandler. PeFWW

"Hour is late, The," the shepherds said. The Shepherd Left Behind. Mildred Plew Meigs. TrCP

Hour of dawn remote. (LL) Ballad of Black Grief. Federico García Lorca. STV

Hour of Death, The. Felicia Dorothea Hemans. OBNC

Hour of Magic, The. W. H. Davies. MoBrPo

Hour of Peaceful Rest, The. William Bingham Tappan.

Hour of Sleep, The. Robert Ellis, *tr. fr. Welsh by* H. Idris Bell. OBWVE

Hour ten he rose, ten-sworded, every finger. Timoshenko. Sidney Keyes. OBWP

Hour, the spot, are here at last, The. At Harper's Ferry Just Before the Attack. Edward W. Williams. AAP

Hour was on us, The; where the man? Lincoln. John Vance Cheney. OHIP

Hour with Thee, An. Sir Walter Scott. BoLoP

Hourglass, The. Joseph Beaumont. NOSC

Hourglass, The. Russell Edson. AnAn

Hourglass [or The Houre-Glasse], The ("Do but consider this small dust.") Ben Jonson. BeJo; EnLoPo; EnRePo; NIP; OAEL-1; SeCP

Hours, The. John Peale Bishop. OxBA

Hours, The. Christopher Pearse Cranch. PWR

Hours, The. David Diop, *tr. fr. French by* Ellen Conroy Kennedy. NegPo

Hours, The. Paul Ramsey. CRP

Hours Ago, 1973. Thomas McCarthy. IB

Hours and hours go by, traffic flows. The Them Decade. Terence Winch. UL

Hours are viewless angels, The. The Hours. Christopher Pearse Cranch. PWR

Hours before dawn we were woken by the quake. William Empson. FaBoMo; FaBoTw; LiTB; OxAEP-2; OxBTC

Hours before my death. Epitaph. Julio Marzán. ETG

Hours from the ceremony, laying out her dress. Sitting This One Out. Steven Sher. BTR

Hour's Glory, The. H. Cordelia Ray. CBWP-3

Hours I spent with thee, dear heart, The. The Rosary. Robert Cameron Rogers. FaBoBe; WBLP

Hours of rest are over, The. To-Day. Lessie M. Drown. PWR

Hours of Sleep. *Unknown.* NBLV

Hours of Sleepy Night, The. Thomas Campion. *Fr.* Mountebank's Mask, The. EiL

Hours of the Day, The, *sels.* Richard Kenney.
In Retrospect. Son

Hours of the Passion., *sels.* Eleanor Hamilton King.

Hours of the Passion, The. *Unknown. See* At the time of Matines, Lord, thu were itake.

Hours of the Passion., *sels.* William of Shoreham.

Hours pass/ slowly as a snail. Clockface. Judith Thurman. Spl

Hours Rise Up, The. E. E. Cummings. OxBA

House, The. George Bowering. NOBC

House, The. Alison Brackenbury. SCBI

House. Robert Browning. NAEL-2

House. Murray Edmond. PeNZ

House, The. Philip Levine. CAPP

House. Sue May. NBrP

House, The. Robert Minhinnick. AngWe

House, The. Paula Nelson. GoYe

House, The. Tania van Zyl. PeSA

House, The. William Carlos Williams. VGW

House, A. Libby Houston. NBrP

House across the Way, The. Ralph Hodgson. FaBoTw

House and hollow; village and valley-side. Winter Encounters. Charles Tomlinson. LiTM

House and Land. Allen Curnow. PeNZ

House Beautiful, The. Robert Louis Stevenson. NOBE

House Blessing. Arthur Guiterman. TrPWD

House Blessing, A. William Cartwright. *See* Saint Francis and Saint Benedight.

House-Builders, The. Kamala Das. PBWP

House by the Side of the Road, The. Sam Walter Foss. AnAmPo; BLPA; BLPL; FaBoBe; WBLP; WGRP

House Carpenter, The. *Unknown. See* "Well met, well met, my own true love."

House Carpenter, The. *Unknown.* AS

House Carpenter, The. *Unknown. See* "O where [or whare] have you [or hae ye] been, my dear, dear [or dearest dear or long, long] love."

House Divided, A. Michael Ondaatje. MoCV

House Fear. Robert Frost. *Fr.* Hill Wife, The. CMoP; HAP; InPS; LiTM; NoP; NTP; VGW

House fell head-first, quietly crushing all but a child, The. Bianor, *tr. fr. Greek by* Richard Evans. GrAn

House full, a hole full, A. *Unknown.* OxNR

House full, yard full. *Unknown.* NTCP
(Riddle.) RoPo

House Guest. Elizabeth Bishop. NYBP; TAP

House had gone to bring again, The. The Need of Being Versed in Country Things. Robert Frost. NoAM; NOBA; OxBA; PFP; SAmP; TRP; UnPo

House I knew not, newly cloth'd with skin. (LL) The Preparative. Thomas Traherne. ESCV; GeHe; PoEL-2

House in Broad Street, red brick, with nine rooms, The. The Things. Conrad Aiken. HAP; WeW

House in Byzantium, A. Agathias, *tr. fr. Greek by* Fleur Adcock. GrAn

House in Taos, A. Langston Hughes. CDC

House in the Green Well, The. John Hall Wheelock. MoAmPo

House in the Wood, The. Randall Jarrell. LCAP

House inside still looks like a house, The. Moving. Frank Steele. GOYP

House Is an Enigma. Laura Jensen. LCAP

House is cold. It's raining, The. Joseph Come Back as the Dusk. Franz Wright. LCAP

House is crammed: tier beyond tier they grin, The. Blighters. Siegfried Sassoon. CMoP; FaBoTw; MoP; NoAM; OxBSP; PoWW

House is filled, The. The last heartthrob. Near the Ocean. Robert Lowell. NOBA

House is like a garden, The. A Holiday. Ella Wheeler Wilcox. OxBM

House Is Old, The. Ron Schreiber. GLP

House is one bare room, The. Desert Stop at Noon. Dick Davis. SCBI

House is so quiet now, The. The Vacuum. Howard Nemerov. NIP; RB

House is yours, The. The House. William Carlos Williams. VGW

House leaks and leans, The. The Ancestors. John Peale Bishop. PoA

House made of dawn. *Unknown, tr. fr. Navajo Indian.* EaPr

House Made of Rain, The. Naomi Shihab Nye. NAmP90

House Martins: This wind wafts little creatures. Unknown, formerly at. to Cynewulf, *tr. fr. Anglo-Saxon. Fr.* Riddles (Exeter Book). ASW, *tr. by* Kevin Crossley-Holland

House-Mates. Leon Gellert. CBAP; NOBAu

House my earthly parent left, The. The Cottage. Jones Very. OxBA

House Next Door, The. Douglas Dunn. OxBC

House o' the Mirror, The. Helen Adam. MAT; NMM

House of Broughton Street, The. Mary Ann Larkin. AiP

House of Busyrane, The. Spenser. *Fr.* Faerie Queene, The. NoSic

House of Christmas, The. G. K. Chesteron. MoBrPo

House of Desire, The. Sherley Anne Williams. AIW; BlSi

House of Falling Leaves, The. William Stanley Braithwaite. PoLF; PoNe

House of five fires, you never raised me. In the Longhouse, Oneida Museum. Roberta Hill Whiteman. NoAM

House of God, The. A. D. Hope. OxBC

House of God is due to be converted, The. Development. D. J. Enright. OxBSP

House of Hospitalities, The. Thomas Hardy. RB

House of Life, The, *sels.* Dante Gabriel Rossetti.
　Ardour and Memory. OAEL-2
　Autumn Idleness. GBL; OAEL-2
　Barren Spring. EBVV; IMW; NoP; OAEL-2; OBNC; PoEL-5
　Birth-Bond, The. OHCV; Son
　Body's Beauty. OAEL-2; Son; TrGrPo
　(Lilith.) PoEL-5
　Bridal Birth. Son
　Choice, The. GGP; GTBS-P; OBEV
　Heart's Haven. Son
　Hill Summit, The. NoP; PFP
　Inclusiveness. NAEL-2
　Kiss, The. NOBVV; Son
　Life-in-Love. HAP
　Lost Days. EnVR
　Lost on Both Sides. EnVR; NoP
　Love Enthroned. OBNC
　Lovesight. EBVV; GTBS-P; NAEL-2; OBNC; TrGrPo
　Mid-Rapture. BLPL; FaBoBe
　Nuptial Sleep. EBVV; EnVR; NAEL-2; NOBVV
　One Hope, The. NAEL-2; OAEL-2; PFP
　Pride of Youth. OBNC
　Severed Selves. BoLoP
　Silent Noon. EnVR; HAP; NAEL-2; NoP; OBNC; PFP; PoEL-5; TrGrPo; UnAS
　Sonnet, A [*or* The: "Sonnet is a moment's monument"]. EnVR; NAEL-2; NoP; Son
　Soul's Beauty. OBEV
　(Sibylla Palmifera.) OxAEP-2
　Superscription, A. EBVV; GTBS-P; NAEL-2; NoP; OAEL-2; OBNC; PoEL-5
　Willowwood ("And now love sang: but his was such a song"). NAEL-2; OAEL-2
　Willowwood ("I sat with love upon a woodside well"). NAEL-2; OAEL-2; PoEL-5
　Willowwood ("O ye, all ye that walk in Willowwood"). NAEL-2; OAEL-2
　Willowwood ("So sang he: and as meeting rose and rose"). NAEL-2; OAEL-2
　Without Her. GBL; OBNC; PoEL-5; Son
　Woodspurge, The. EBEV; ELP; EnVR; GTBS-P; HAP; HeIP; NOBE; NoP; OAEL-2; OBEV; OBNC; PFP; PoEL-5; PrIm; SCGP; TFi; UnPo

House of Life, The, *sels.* Dante Gabriel Rossetti.
　Sea-Limits, The. EnVR; NAEL-2; OAEL-2; OHCV

House of Lords, The. W. S. Gilbert. *Fr.* Iolanthe. NAEL-2; TrGrPo

House of Madam Juju, The. Kanai Mieko, *tr. fr. Japanese by* Christopher Drake. BoWoP

House of Mercy, A. Stevie Smith. FaBoWP

House of Mourning written by Mr Scott, The. Vile Things. Keats. CBCK

House of Night, The, *sels.* Philip Freneau.
　"By some sad means, when reason holds no sway." PoEL-4
　"Trembling I write my dream, and recollect." NAAL-1, *much abr.*

House of Prayer, The. William Cowper. ChIV-2

House of Pride, The. William James Dawson. PoToHe

House of Rest. Sir John Betjeman. OxAEP-2

House of Richesse, The. Spenser. *Fr.* Faerie Queene, The. CH

House of sleepers, A – I, alone unblest. Insomnia. Edith M. Thomas. AmWP

House of the Apple-Trees, The. Alice Milligan. VBLP

House of the Mouse, The. Lucy Sprague Mitchell. NTCP; ZA

House of Wisdom, The. Bible, *O.T. Fr.* Proverbs. TrGrPo

House on a Cliff. Louis MacNeice. NOIV

House on Bentalou Street, The. Beginnings. Michael S. Weaver. PBCAP

House on Buder Street, The. Gary Gildner. TAP

House on 15th S.W., The. Richard Hugo. CAPP

House on fire, A! We stumbled over the snow. Houses Burning; Quebec. Patrick Anderson. NOBC

House on the Hill, The. E. A. Robinson. FaPON; GoJo; MoAmPo; NAEL-2; PrIm; TrGrPo

House persists, the permanent, The. The House Remembered. Eiléan Ní Chuilleanáin. PWE

House Plants. David McFadden. NOBC

House Remembered, The. Eiléan Ní Chuilleanáin. PWE

House ringed round with trees and in the trees, A. Asylum. John Freeman. OBMV

House-Rules I: Reading. Alistair Elliot. CBLP

House Slave, The. Rita Dove. NoAM

House-Slave, The. Mervyn Morris. PBCV

House-snake dwells here still, The. The Closed World. Denise Levertov. NoP

House Song to the East. *Unknown, tr. fr. Navajo Indian.* TTTS

House That Fear Built: Warsaw, 1943, The. Jane Flanders. CrSp; PBCAP

House That Isn't Mine, The. Victoria Kohn. UTF

House That Jack Built, The. Samuel Taylor Coleridge. *See* And this rest house is that the which he built.

House That Jack Built, The. Mother Goose. BoTP; FaBoBe; OxBoLi; OxNR; ReMoGo

House That Jack Built, The. *Unknown.* FaBoBe; NBLV; OxBoLi

House That Was, The. Laurence Binyon. MoBrPo

House to let. *Unknown.* RoPo

House to let, enquire within. *Unknown.* ISE

House-Top, The. Herman Melville. LiTA; NAAL-1; NOBA; Prf

House, Tree, Sky. Martha Collins. FoLa

House, village, city, land, and empire harvest hurt. Women's Rule. Friedrich von Logau, *tr. fr. German.* GePo, *tr. by* George C. Schoolfield

House Was Quiet and the World Was Calm, The. Wallace Stevens. AiP; HAP; NoP; PFP; SAmP; VGW

House was shaken by a rising wind, The. Brainstorm. Howard Nemerov. HAP; SM; TRP

House was still — the room was still, The. Charlotte Brontë. NOBVV

House where I was born, The. The Doves. Katharine Tynan. AWP

House, with blind unhappy face, The. The Gray Folk. E. Nesbit. NOBVV

House with coarse stuccoed, The. The House. Tania van Zyl. PeSA

House with Nobody in It, The. Joyce Kilmer. BLPA; BLPL

Houseboat Mouse. Charles Sullivan. ImGa

Household. Laura Jensen. LCAP

Household Dilemma. Angie Gilligan. NBrP

Household of Ruth, The. Mrs. Henry Linden. CBWP-4

Household Remedies. *Unknown.* OBET

Household words, no more depart. (*LL*) Seaweed. Longfellow. OxBA; TAP

Housekeeper, The. Vincent Bourne, *tr. fr. Latin by* Charles Lamb. GN; PoLF

Houseless Downs, The. George Ferebe. *Fr.* Shepherds' Song, Sung before Queen Anne, on the Wiltshire Downs, 11 June 1613, The. FaBoPP

Houseplant. Felicity Napier. BrRo

Houses. Agha Shahid Ali. NIP

Houses. Aileen Fisher. NTCP

Houses, The, *sels.* "Robin Hyde."
　"Adolicus; that's a creeper rug, its small." PeNZ
　"Hares on their forms at dusk were not so still." PeNZ
　"None of it true; for Christ's sake, spill the ink." PeNZ

Houses. Donald Justice.

Houses. Mary Britton Miller. SiSoPo

Houses, The. Eden Phillpotts. OxBTC

Houses, an embassy, the hospital. Days of 1964. James Merrill. CoAP; HCAP; NAAL-2; PoE; VCAP

Houses and rooms are full of perfumes. Walt Whitman. *Fr.* Song of Myself. AmPP; EBEvV; LiTA; MoAmPo, *abr.*; NOBA; OxBA; SOTW, *much abr.*; TrGrPo; UnPo

Houses are faces. Houses. Aileen Fisher. NTCP

Houses are haunted, The. Disillusionment of Ten o'Clock. Wallace Stevens. AnAmPo; CBNP; CMoP; FF; InPS; NAAL-2; NoAM; OxBA; RB; SAmP; SoSe; SOTW; TRP; TTTS

Houses are wedged between the tall stacks. Among Elms and Maples, Morgantown, West Virginia, August 1935. Maggie Anderson. ETG

Houses Burning; Quebec. Patrick Anderson. NOBC

Houses, churches, mixed together. A Description of London. John Bancks. NOEC

Houses die, and will not die, The. Heartland. Jim Barnes. HATNAP

Houses jammed one on top of the other, The. Insignificant Needs. Yannis Ritsos, *tr. fr. Greek by* Minas Sarras. AnRep

Houses of Corr an Chait are cold, The. Seamas Dall Mac Cuarta, *tr. fr. Irish by* Thomas Kinsella. NOIV

Houses of Emily Dickinson, The. Larry Rubin. NIP

Houses sway at the slightest/ tremor. (*LL*) The California Phrasebook. Dennis Schmitz. AmPA

Housewife, The. Catherine Cate Coblentz. BLRP; TrPWD

Housewife. Susan Fromberg Schaeffer. CrSp; IHMS

Housewife. Anne Sexton. NALW; NMM

Housewife Hooker. Paul Groves. FaBoBl

Housewifery. Edward Taylor. *See* Make me, O Lord, thy spinning [*or* spining] wheel[e] complete [*or compleat or* compleate] [*or* of use for thee].

Housewife's Lament, The. *Unknown.* MAT

Housewife's Letter: To Mary. Anne Halley. NMM

Housewife's Prayer on the Morning Preceding a Fete, The. Elizabeth Moody. ECWP

Housewives. Jean Follain, *tr. fr. French by* W. S. Merwin. AnRep

Housewives as the nights came in. Housewives. Jean Follain, *tr. fr. French by* W. S. Merwin. AnRep

Housework. Amanda Berenguer, *tr. fr. Spanish by* Priscilla Joslin. WPOW

Housework. David Trinidad. BAP-91

Housing. Denise Riley. NBrP

Housing Shortage. Naomi Replansky. CrSp; NMM

Hovering clouds scatter over the islet. Arriving at North Pond by Stupid Brook on a Morning Walk after the Rain. Liu Tsung-yüan, *tr. fr. Chinese by* Jan W. Walls. SuSp

Hovering like the heron. What She Said ("Hovering like the heron.") Orampokiyar, *tr. fr. Tamil by* A. K. Ramanujan. *Fr.* Five on the Riverside Cane. PLW

How? Vladimir Holan, *tr. fr. Czech by* Ian Milner *and* Jarmila Milner. PoSu

How. S. J. Marks. NYBP

How a Girl Got Her Chinese Name. Nellie Wong. WPOW

How a Girl Was Too Reckless of Grammar [by Far]. Guy Wetmore Carryl. AnAmPo; FiBHP; OBAL

How a tear makes a perfect meniscus. (*LL*) Lili Marlene. Matthew Sweeney. IB

How about that! (*LL*) To Satch. Samuel Allen. PoBA; PoNe; TTY

How all occasions do inform against me. Shakespeare. *Fr.* Hamlet. HoPM; NAWM-1

How all things shatter, fall away, and break. Holy Ghost Hospital. Allen Grossman. PRA

How am I hitched. Suffering. Albert Ehrenstein, *tr. fr. German by* Babette Deutsch. TrJP

How Amiable Are Thy Tabernacles! Bryant. *See* Thou, whose unmeasured temple stands.

How amiable are thy tabernacles, O Lord of hosts! Bible, *O.T.*, *paraphrased by* Sir Thomas Wyatt. *Fr.* Psalms. FaPON; TrJP (Psalm LXXXIV: "How lovely are thy dwellings fair!," *paraphrased by* Milton.) TrPWD

How and when to drop her dress! (*LL*) Must be some girl from the villages. Sappho. InMo

How and Where. Alice Cary. AmWP

How Annandale Went Out. E. A. Robinson. MoAB; MoAmPo; NoAM; NOBA; SoSe

How any shoelaces will they make of that! (*LL*) The Mad Yak. Gregory Corso. PoBeRe

How Apollo's laurel sapling shakes. Hymn to Apollo. Callimachus, *tr. fr. Greek by* Barbara Hughes Fowler. *Fr.* Hymns. HePo

How are our Spirituall Gamesters slipt away? An Elegy upon the Death of That Holy Man of God Mr. John Allen. Edward Taylor. PoEL-3

How are thy servants blest, O Lord! Joseph Addison. TrPWD (Hymn.) OxAEP-1

How are we living? How and Where. Alice Cary. AmWP

How Are You, Dear World, This Morning? Horace L. Traubel. TrJP

How Are You, Sanitary? Bret Harte. AnAmPo

How are you so smooth-faced. Girl. *Unknown, tr. fr. Serbian by* Anne Pennington. RB

How art thou Nothing when th'art most of all! (*LL*) On an Hour[e]-Glass[e]. John Hall. MeLP; OPOP

How at my sheet goes the same crooked worm. (*LL*) The Force That through the Green Fuse Drives the Flower. Dylan Thomas. BLPL; CMoP; EaPr; EBEV; FaBoMo; InPS; LiTB; LiTM; MeMBP; MoAB; MoBrPo; MoP; NAEL-2; NoAM; NOBE; NoP; OBWVE; OxAEP-2; OxBTC; PoE; Poetr; PPP; PrIm; RB; SCV; TEP; TFi; UnPo

How bare! How all the lion-desert lies. Macrinus against Trees. "Michael Field." WPE

How Beastly the Bourgeois Is. D. H. Lawrence. ChTr; LiTM; MeMBP; NAEL-2; OBSV

How beautiful and calm how crimson pale. The Spirit Craft. Charles G. Ballard. VoR

How beautiful is genius when combined. Sacred Poetry. "Christopher North." WBLP

How beautiful is night! Night. Robert Southey. GN

How beautiful is the rain! Rain in Summer. Longfellow. BoTP; GN

How beautiful it was, that one bright day. Hawthorne. Longfellow. PoEL-5

How beautiful it was to sleep under the snow! (*LL*) The Bear Trees. Kate Barnes. EaPr

How beautiful the Buddhist statues. Imaizumi Sogetsu-Ni, *tr. fr. Japanese by* Kenneth Rexroth *and* Ikuko Atsumi. WPJ

How beautiful the Earth is still. Anticipation. Emily Brontë. OBNC

How beautiful their feet. Martin Farquhar Tupper. *Fr.* Train of Religion, The. FaBoCo

How beautiful this hill of fern swells on! Stanzas from "Child Harold." John Clare. *Fr.* Child Harold. OBNC (In Epping Forest.) FaBoPP

How Beautiful upon the Mountains. Bible, *O.T.* *Fr.* Isaiah. TrJP

How Beautiful You Are: 3. Elaine Edelman. IHMS

How beautifully they sing. Certain Type of Bird. Tien Ch'ien, *tr. fr. Chinese.* LHF, *tr. by* Hualing Nieh

How big cherries. (*LL*) I Am a Horse. Hans Arp. FaBoNo, *tr. by* Harriet Watts.

How Big Was Alexander? Elijah Jones. BLPA

How blessed [*or* blest] was the created state. The Fall. The Earl of Rochester. ChIV-1; EnLoPo

How blest are lovers in disguise! A Song. George Farquhar. NOSC

How blest art thou, canst love the countrey, Wroth. To Sir Robert Wroth. Ben Jonson. BeJo; SeCV-1

How blest is he, who for his country dies. To the Earl of Oxford, Late Lord Treasurer. Swift, *after the Latin of* Horace. OBVE

How blest would be Ïerne's isle. Written in Ireland. Mary Alcock. ECWP; NOEC; OBTV

How blind men are! We surely cannot know. Understanding. H. W. Bliss. PoToHe

How bowed the woods beneath their sturdy storke! (*LL*) Curfew tolls the knell of parting day, The. Thomas Gray. AWP; ClHu; DL; EBEV; EBEvV; EnRP; FaBoBe; FaBoPP; FaBoRV; FaBoRV; FaPoR; FHYEP; GGP; GN; GTBS; GTBS-P; HAP; HeIP; ImPo; InPK; InPS; LiTB; NOBE; NOEC; NoP; OAEL-1; OBEV; OxAEP-1; PoEL-3; Poetr; PoLF; PPP; PrIm; SCGP; SCV; TEP; TFi; TrGrPo; UnPo; UV; WBLP; WeW

How brent is your brow, my Lady Elspat! Lady Elspat. *Unknown.* ESPB

How bright on the blue. The Kite. Harry Behn. FaPON

How busie are the sonnes of men? Roger Williams. GOA; SCAP

How busied's man. My Close-Committee. Mildmay Fane, 2d Earl of Westmorland. BeJo

How, butler, how! bevis a tout! *Unknown.* MiEL

How calm, how beautiful, comes on. The Golden Hour. Thomas Moore. *Fr.* Lalla Rookh. OBNC

How Calm the Wild Water. Geoffrey Fraser Dutton. PWE

How calmly cows move to the milking sheds. The Herd. Frances Cornford. FM

How came that blood on thy coat-lap? The Dead Brother. *Unknown.* EnSB

How can a girl with such a big belly be so desirable? Mrs. Loewinsohn &c. Ron Loewinsohn. NeAP

How can any man throw out. Rufinus Domesticus, *tr. fr. Greek by* Sam Hamill. InMo

How *can* he be? The words are wild. (*LL*) The Child Is Father to the Man. Gerard Manley Hopkins. FaBoCo; NOBVV; NTP

How can I begin to thank. Life of T. S. Eliot. Michael Frayn. FaBoPa

How can I blame the cherry blossoms. Daughter of Shunzei, *tr. fr. Japanese by* Kenneth Rexroth *and* Ikuko Atsumi. WPJ

How can I call out? How can I shout? At Night. Bella Akhmadulina, *tr. fr. Russian by* Daniel Halpern *and* Albert Todd. BoWoP

How can I care whether you sigh for me. Song: How Can I Care? Robert Graves. GBL

How can I climb the Mount of Purgatory? Cato. C. H. Sisson. NOCV

How can I complain/ that you have shaved your hair? Yokobue, *tr. fr. Japanese by* Kenneth Rexroth *and* Ikuko Atsumi. WPJ

How can I give thee up, my child, my dearest, earliest born. Wail of the Divorced. Mary E. Tucker. AmWP; CBWP-1

How can I go on under the beating storm of my thoughts? (*LL*) Freezing Night. T'ao Hung Ching. OHMPC

How can I hope a wise heart to attain. Dietmar von Aist, *tr. fr. German by* Carroll Hightower. GePo

How Can I Keep My Maidenhead. Burns. ErPo

How can I regret my life. The Signal. David Ignatow. NNaP

How can I say this? I Learned To Sew. Mitsuye Yamada. LoHo

How Can I Sing. Odia Ofeimun. HBAPE

How can I sing light-souled and fancy-free. Lorenzo de' Medici, *tr. fr. Italian by* John Addington Symonds. *Fr.* Two Lyrics. AWP

How Can I Smile? Florence B. Hodgdon. BLRP

BoLoP; CTC; EBEvV; EBVV; EnVR; FaBoBe; FaBV; FaPoB; FF; HeIP; HoPM; InPK; LitB; LPA; NAEL-2; NALW; NIP; NoP; OHCV; OxAEP-2; OxBM; PoE; Poetr; PoLF; PoRA; Son; TEP; TFi; TrGrPo; UnPo; UV; WPE

How do I love you, beech-trees, in the autumn. Beechwoods at Knole. V. Sackville-West. NTP

How do I pity that proud wealthy clown. My Estate. John Norris. NOSC

How do I spin my time away. On the Spirit Adulterated by the Flesh. Thomas, the Elder Warton. ChIV-1

How do I thank thee, death, and bless thy power. On the Lady Arabella. Richard Corbett [or Corbet]. NOSC

How do robins build their nests? What Robin Told. George Cooper. FaPON

How do they do it, the ones who make love. Sex without Love. Sharon Olds. HeIP; NIP; Poetr; TRP

How do we know, by the bank-high river. The Last Lap. Kipling. OxBTC

How Do You Do? H. Bedford Jones. WBLP

How Do You Do? Unknown. See Misty-Moisty Was the Morn.

How do you do, delicate Roumanians! Medium. Marc Kaminsky. BTR

How do you know? (LL) The Year's Awakening. Thomas Hardy. CMoP; OxBTC

How do you know it is time to bloom. Creative Force. Maude Miner Hadden. GoYe

How do you know that the pilgrim track. The Year's Awakening. Thomas Hardy. CMoP; OxBTC

How do you like to go up in a swing. The Swing. Robert Louis Stevenson. FaBoBe; GoJo; NTCP; PDV; SiSoPo; TEP; TLR

How do you like what you have. Gertrude Stein. Fr. Portraits and Repetition. AiP

How do you like your blueeyed boy/ Mister Death. (LL) Buffalo Bill's. E. E. Cummings. AmPP; CMoP; HeIP; InPK; LiTA; NAAL-2; NOBA; OBD; OxBSP; PoE; RB; TAP; VGW

How do you make bread talk, this old treasure all wrapped. Bread Is Born. Anne Hébert, tr. fr. French by Maxine W. Kumin. BoWoP

How do you recognize death? Minor Elegy. Henriqueta Lisboa, tr. fr. Portuguese by Willis Barnstone and Nelson Cerqueira. BoWoP

How Do You Shape an Axe Handle? Gary Snyder. NoAM

How do you spell change brother like frayed slogan underwear. New York City 1970. Audre Lorde. NBV

How does a person get to be a capable liar? Golly, How Truth Will Out. Ogden Nash. LiTA; MoAmPo

How does it happen, tell me. Judge Somers. Edgar Lee Masters. Fr. Spoon River Anthology. FaBoEE; OBSV

How does it help me if, with flawless art. Louise Labé, tr. fr. French by Raymond Oliver. WPOW

How does my royal lord? How fares your Majesty? Shakespeare. Fr. King Lear. Prf; SCV

How does one get outside. Dear Miss. Herman Gladwin. PeNZ

How doth the city sit solitary, that was full of people! The Misery of Jerusalem. Bible, O.T. Fr. Lamentations. AWP

How doth the little busy bee. How Doth the Little Busy Bee. Isaac Watts. FaPON; HoPM
 (Against Idleness and Mischief.) EBEvV; OxAEP-1; UV; VPP

How Doth the Little Busy Bee. Isaac Watts. FaPON; HoPM

How doth the little crocodile. "Lewis Carroll." Fr. Alice's Adventures in Wonderland. CBNP; FaBoCh; FaBoCo; FaBoEE; FaBoNo; FaPON; MoShBr; NBLV; NOBL; NOBVV; RB; TFi; TTTS; UV
 (Crocodile, The. HoPM; TrGrPo.

How drunk I got tonight. Drinking Spree Beneath the Open Sky. Slavko Mihalic, tr. by Peter Kastmiler. PoSu

How dull and how insensible a beast. An Essay upon Satire. At. to John Sheffield, Duke of Buckingham and Normandy John Sheffield. APAS

How dumb before the poleaxe they sink down. Marriages. Anthony Thwaite. OxBM

How Each Thing Save the Lover in Spring Reviveth to Pleasure. The Earl of Surrey. See When Windsor walls sustained [or sustain'd] my wearied arm.

How Early Fall Came This Year. John Z. Guzlowski. BTR

How easily my heart falls back into habits. It's All in Your Head. Marilyn Nelson Waniek. Jaz

How easily the ripe grain. The Widow. W. S. Merwin. NYBP; UnPo; VGW

How easy 'tis to sail with wind and tide! The Medal Reversed. Elkanah Settle. APAS

How empty seems the town now you are gone! From One Who Stays. Amy Lowell. BoWoP; IMW

How entrancing are the 124 ways. Larousse Gastronomique. Anne Stevenson. PeLV

How erring oft the judgment in its hate. The English Fog. John Dyer. Fr. Fleece, The. TrGrPo

How even he did not get to keep that lovely body. (LL) The Racer's Widow. Louise Glück. AmPA; NYBP; SM

How everything gets tamed. Mountain, Fire, Thornbush. Harvey Shapiro. VGW

How Everything Happens. May Swenson. HAP; RFM

How fair a flower is sown. Coventry Patmore. FaBoEE

How fair is youth that flies so fast! Then be happy, ye who may. Triumph of Bacchus and Ariadne. Lorenzo de' Medici, tr. fr. Italian by Richard Aldington. Fr. Carnival Songs. CTC

How far are they deceived who hope in vain. Ephelia to Bajazet. Sir George Etherege. APAS

How Far Is It Called to the Grave? Unknown. BLPA

How Far Is It to Bethlehem? Frances Chesterton. BoTP; PChr

How far is it to Bethlehem Town? How Far to Bethlehem? Madeleine Sweeny Miller. BLPA

How far is St. Helena from a little child at play? A St. Helena Lullaby. Kipling. CoGr; EBEV; FaBoCh; OBMV; OtMeF; PoEL-5

How Far to Bethlehem? Madeleine Sweeny Miller. BLPA

How fared you when you mortal were? After. Ralph Hodgson. MoBrPo

How fashionably sad my early poems are! About My Poems. Donald Justice. PoA

How fast. (LL) For an Album. Adrienne Rich. VCAP

How fast this water flows away! A Poem Written on a Floating Red Leaf. Han Ts'ui-p'in, tr. fr. Chinese by Kenneth Rexroth and Ling Chung. WPC

How fast thou fliest, O time, on love's swift wings. Mary Sidney Wroth, Countess of Montgomery. Fr. Urania. NOSC; WPE

How feels the guiltless dreamer, who. Memory. Edward Coote Pinkney. AnAmPo

How fell sage Helen? through a swain like thee. A Countryman's Wooing. Theocritus [or Theokritus], tr. fr. Latin by Charles Stuart Calverley. ErPo

How felt the land in every part. Washington's Vow. Whittier. OHIP

How fever'd is the man who cannot look. Keats. Fr. Two Sonnets on Fame. EnRP

How few of us are left, how few! Unknown, tr. fr. Chinese by Arthur Waley. PAW

"How few," the Muse in plaintive accents cries. Erasmus Darwin. Fr. Temple of Nature; or, The Origin of Society, The. FM

How fickle's health! when sickness thus. Upon a Friend's Pet Cat, Being Sick. John Winstanley. OFC

How fierce in its loyalties the beat of the heart. Coronary Thrombosis. William Price Turner. OxBS

How fierce was I when I did see. Upon Julia Washing Herself in the River. Robert Herrick. CaPo

How fine a light on. May Song. Goethe, tr. fr. German by John Frederick Nims. STV

How Firm a Foundation. At. to "K.", perhaps Robert Keene, sometimes at. to George Keith. WGRP

How first we met do you still remember? Brussels and Oxford. William Hurrell Mallock. EBVV

How Five and Twenty Shillings Were Expended in a Week. Unknown. OBET

How flame the glories of Belinda's hair. Thomas Parnell. Fr. To Mr. Pope. EPCY

How fleet is air! how many things have breath. William King. Fr. Mully of Mountown. FM

How fleeting is our youth. The Day of Chung Yang. Mao Tse-tung. ArNa

How fond are men of rule and place. The Lion and the Cub. John Gay. Fr. Fables. GN

How foolish men on expeditions go! On Riding to See Dean Swift in the Mist of the Morning. Pope and Thomas Parnell. FaBoEE

How forlorn and lost. Into the Open. Susan Prospere. BAP-91

How found you him? Shakespeare. Fr. Cymbeline. OxAEP-1

How frail is human life! How fleet our breath. On the Death of an Infant of Five Days Old. Elizabeth Boyd. ECWP

How fresh, O Lord, how sweet and clean. The Flower. George Herbert. AngWe; AWP; ELP; ESCV; FaBoRV; FaPoB; GeHe; JCP; NAEL-1; NOBE; NOCV; NoP; PFP; PoEL-2; SeCP; SeCV-1

How funny you are today New York. Steps. Frank O'Hara. CAPP

How gaily is at first begun. Life's Progress. The Countess of Winchilsea. ECWP

How Gentle. Joyce Carol Oates. VBLP

How gentle we are rising. How Gentle. Joyce Carol Oates. VBLP

How glad I am that I was bound apprentice. For Patrick, Aetat: LXX. Sir John Betjeman. NAs

How Glorious Are the Morning Stars. Benjamin Keach. AH

How Glorious Is Thy Name. Bible, *O.T.*, *paraphrased by* Sir Thomas Wyatt. *See* O Lord our Lord, how excellent is thy name.

How glows each patriot bosom that boasts a Yankee heart. The *United States* and *Macedonian. Unknown.* PAH

How God speeds the tax-bribed plough. Drone v. Worker. Ebenezer Elliot. FaBoPV; OBSV

How Goes the Night? *Unknown, tr. by* Helen Waddell. *Fr.* Shi King. AWP

How good to hear your voice again. The Priest Rediscovers His Psalm-Book. *Unknown, tr. fr. Irish by* Frank O'Connor. PeIV

How goodly are the tentes of Jacob and thine habitacions Israel. Bible, *O.T. See* Balaam's Blessing.

How goodly are your tents, O Jezrael! (*LL*) Jezrael. Avraham Shlonsky. MHP

How Goodly Is Thy House. Henry S. Jacobs. AH

How goot dere Athol Boetry must be! (*LL*) Athol Brose. Thomas Hood. FaBoCo

How Grand and How Bright. *Unknown.* GBP

How happened it this one time being sound. O. Laura Rosenthal. UL

How happy a thing were a wedding. On Marriage. Thomas Flatman. FaBoUs; FiBHP; NOBL; PeLV
(Bachelor's Song, The.) EnLoPo

How happy for us, that it is not at home! (*LL*) The Place of the Damn'd [*or* Damned]. Swift. CBCK; ChIV-2; FaBoEE; OBSV

How happy I can be with my love away! The Absence. Sylvia Townsend Warner. MoBrPo

How happy in his low degree. Country Life. Horace, *tr. by* Dryden. *Fr.* Epodes. AWP

How happy is he born and taught. The Character of a Happy Life. Sir Henry Wotton. EBEvV; EiL; GTBS; GTBS-P; LiTB; NOBE; NOSC; NTP; OBEV; TrGrPo
(Happy Life, The.) WGRP

How happy is the blameless vestal's lot! The Vestal. Pope. *Fr.* Eloisa to Abelard. NAEL-1; PoEL-3; TEP
(Life of a Nun.) ECEV

How happy is the little stone. Emily Dickinson. RB

How Happy the Man. *Unknown.* OBET

How happy to be a fish. Fish and Bird. Rosemary Brinckman. BoTP

How happy uncle us'd to be. Uncle an' Aunt. William Barnes. NOBVV

How happy you who varied joys pursue. Lady Mary Wortley Montagu. ECWP

How hard a fate enthrals the wretched maid. Virgil, *tr. fr. Latin by* Robert Fitzgerald. *Fr.* Aeneid [*or* Eneados], The. ECWP, *tr. by* Elizabeth Tollet; NAWM-1

How hard for unaccustomed feet. In the Time of Trouble. Leslie Savage Clark. TrPWD

How hard is my fortune. The Convict of Clonmel. *Unknown, tr. fr. Irish by* Jeremiah Joseph Callanan. PeIV

How hard it is for the river here to re-enter. Wanting a Child. Jorie Graham. FoLa

How hard it is, we say. Clothes Maketh the Man. Theodore Weiss. NoAM

How hard the years dies: no frost yet. Intercession in Late October. Robert Graves. MoAB

How hath the oppressor ceased! Downfall of the Tyrant. Bible, *O.T. Fr.* Isaiah. TrGrPo

How have I laboured? Ortus. Ezra Pound. LiTA

How have I served you? I have let you waste. John Hewitt. *Fr.* Sonnets for Roberta. PNI

How have you won? (*LL*) The Victory. Anne Stevenson. VBLP

How he advanced, with a white fillet twisted. The Lyre Player. Stefan George, *tr. by* Carol North Valhope *and* Ernst Morowitz. PeHV

How he found his life long ago. How Just One Poor Man Lives. Alonzo Gonzales Mó, *tr. fr. Mayan by* Allan F. Burns. STP

How He Saved St. Michael's. Mary A. P. Stansbury. BLPA

How He Saw Her. Ben Jonson. Celebration of Charis in Ten Lyric[k] Peeces [*or* pieces], A. BeJo; EnRePo; OxAEP-1; SeCP; SeCV-1

How He Should Like to Be Kissed. Paul Fleming, *tr. fr. German by* Harold B. Segel. GePo

How he survived then they could never understand. The Jew Wrecked in the German Cell. W. H. Auden.
(Pora, The.) LiTA; MeMAP

How he thought. Drop the Wires. Hugh Seidman. AmPA

How Heathen shrubs kisse Jesus for their King. (*LL*) Awake yee westerne nymphs, arise and sing. Samuel Danforth. SCAP

How heavy do I journey on the way. Shakespeare. *Fr.* Sonnets. OxAEP-1

How Her Teeth Were Pulled. *Unknown, tr. fr. Paiute Indian by* Jarold Ramsey. STP

How! hey! it is non les. *Unknown.* MiEL

How, hey! It is none les. A Henpecked Husband. *Unknown.* PeLV

How High the Moon. Lance Jeffers. PoBA

How high Thou art! our songs can own. The Mediator. Elizabeth Barrett Browning. TrPWD

How his own members bloat and shrink again. (*LL*) Ogres and Pygmies. Robert Graves. CMoP; FaBoMo; LiTB; LiTM; MeMBP; MoP; NoAM

How history repeats itself. Can't. Harriet Prescott Spofford. PAH

"How, how," he said. "Friend Chang," I said. The Chinese Nightingale. Vachel Lindsay. MoAmPo

How I Brought the Good News from Aix to Ghent (or Vice Versa). R. J. Yeatman *and* W. C. Sellar. BXAP; FaBoPa; FiBHP; UV

How I Came to Have a Man's Name. Emma Lee Warrior. HATNAP

How I doe love thee, Beaumont, and thy Muse. To Francis Beaumont. Ben Jonson. BeJo

How I forsook/ Elias and Pisa after, and betook. Sir Richard Fanshawe, *after the Italian of* Giovanni Battista Guarini. *Fr.* Il Pastor Fido. AWP

How I go courting a charming beauty bright. Charming Beauty Bright. *Unknown.* AmFP

How I Had to Act. Molly Peacock. NAmP90

How I hate you tonight! I and Thou. Chana Bloch. CrSp

How I long for the man who climbed Mt. Yoshino. Shizuka, *tr. fr. Japanese by* Kenneth Rexroth *and* Ikuko Atsumi. WPJ

How I love country you have heard. Samuel Alfred Beadle. AAP

How I loved those old movies. Old Movies. John Cotton. FF

How I miss my father. Poem at Thirty-nine. Alice Walker. CrSp

How I regret being late to see the flowers blossom. Sighing over Flowers. Tu Mu, *tr. fr. Chinese by* Eddie Tsang. SuSp

How I See It. Kit Wright. OTCP

How I succeed, you kindly ask. Mary Barber. *Fr.* To a Lady, Who Commanded Me to Send Her an Account in Verse. ECWP

How I wish I. The Value of pi. *Unknown.* FaBoUs

How I wish I had known/ beforehand of this journey. *Unknown, tr. fr. Japanese by* Kenneth Yasuda. BoWoP

How I wish I were able to say what I think. Gertrude Stein. *Fr.* Stanzas in Meditation. PBWP

How I Wrote It. David Dooley. TRP

How ill doth he deserve a lovers [*or* lover's] name. Eternity of Love Protested. Thomas Carew. BeJo; MeLP
(Song: Eternity of Love Protested.) NOSC

How impotent a deity am I! Sir Samuel Garth. *Fr.* Dispensary, The. OBSV

How Infinite Are Thy Ways. William Force Stead. *See* I thought the night without a sound was falling.

How innocent their lives look. Photos of a Salt Mine. P. K. Page. NIP; NoAM; NOBC

How intelligent he looks! Changing Diapers. Gary Snyder. RaBo

How intimate was the earth in days gone by. The Earth. David Gwenallt Jones, *tr. fr. Welsh by* Dyfnallt Morgan. OBWVE

How Is He Coming Then. Lucille Clifton. CrSp; NALW

How is it all gonna turn out. "Haida Charlie," *tr. fr. Tlingit Indian by* James Koller *after* John Swanton. STP

How is it I can eat bread here and cut meat. Evening Meal in the Twentieth Century. John Holmes. AiP

How is it now? Questions [2]. Donald Hall. FF

How is it proved? The Great Wager. G. A. Studdert-Kennedy. TrCP

How is it that. Tune: "Chilly East Wind." Kuan Yun-shih, *tr. by* Richard John Lynn. *Fr.* Medley of Southern and Northern Tunes — Scenic Tour of West Lake. SuSp

How is it that I am so careless here. Meditation 62. Philip Pain. NOBA

How is it with another woman? An Attempt at Jealousy. Marina Tsvetayeva, *tr. fr. Russian by* Robert Perelman *and* Aleksandar Petrov. WPOW

How is man parcell'd out? how ev'ry hour. The Tempest. Henry Vaughan *and* Thomas Stanley. ESCV

How Is My Sun. Sir Philip Sidney. *Fr.* Arcadia. SiPSBD

How is my sun, whose beams are shining bright. How Is My Sun. Sir Philip Sidney. *Fr.* Arcadia. SiPSBD

How is she going to find time to get married. (*LL*) In Spring We Gather Mulberry Leaves. *Unknown.* OHMPC

How Is the Gold Become Dim. Bible, *O.T. Fr.* Lamentations. ChTr

How it feels to be touching. We Become New. Marge Piercy. TAP

How It Goes On. Maxine W. Kumin. FoLa

How It Is. Maxine W. Kumin. CAPP; IMW; NALW; NoAM; Poetr

How It Strikes a Contemporary. Robert Browning. CTC; EnVR; FaBoPV; GTBS-P; OAEL-2

How it was in that place, how light hung in a bright pool. Wolfpen Creek. James Still. MT

How It Will Always Seem. David Rivard. PBCAP

How It's Done. Alvin Aubert. MT

How Jack Found That Beans May Go Back on a Chap. Guy Wetmore Carryl. HoPM

How joyous his neigh! Song of the Horse. *Unknown, tr. fr. Navajo Indian* by Natalie Curtis. AWP

How Just One Poor Man Lives. Alonzo Gonzales Mó, *tr. fr. Mayan by* Allan F. Burns. STP

How kind, how secretly, the sun. The Garden. Robert Penn Warren. PoA

How large unto the tiny fly. The Fly. Walter de la Mare. OTCP

How! Liberty of Conscience! that's a change. Dr. Wild's Ghost. *Unknown.* APAS

How Lies Grow. Maxine Chernoff. UL

How life and death in Thee. To Our Blessed Lord upon the Choice of His Sepulchre. Richard Crashaw. GeHe; NOSC
(Upon Our Saviour's Tomb Wherein Never Man Was Laid.) ChIV-2; OAEL-1

How like a bolt of white silk is this water. Li Po, *tr. by Irving Lo. Fr.* Songs of Ch'iu-p'u. SuSp

How like a fire doth love increase in me. Mary Sidney Wroth, Countess of Montgomery. *Fr. Urania.* NOSC; WPE

How like a rich and gorgeous picture hung. A November Landscape. Sarah Helen Whitman. AmWP

How like a winter hath my absence been[e]. Shakespeare. *Fr. Sonnets.* AWP; EIL; EnLoPo; EnRePo; GTBS; GTBS-P; HeIP; NAEL-1; NOBE; NoSic; OAEL-1; OBEV; OxAEP-1; PoRA; SCGP; Son; TEP; TFi; TrGrPo

How like an angel came I down. Wonder. Thomas Traherne. CH; ESCV; GeHe; HAP; ImPo; LiTB; NAEL-1; NoP; PoE; SeCP; SeCV-2; TOF; TrGrPo

How like the leper, with his own sad cry. The Buoy-Bell. Charles Tennyson Turner. PeVV; Son

How like to threads of flax. Psalm 119.37. Francis Quarles. ChIV-1

How Lillies Came White. Robert Herrick. BeJo; CaPo

How little I have really cared about nature: I always. Neighbors. A. R. Ammons. CAPP

How little I know. Margaret Atwood. *Fr. Five Poems for Grandmothers.* CrSp

How little of God's grace caresses you, Massadah. Yitzhak Lamdan, *tr. fr. Hebrew by* Ruth Finer Mintz. *Fr. In the Khamsin.* MHP

How little of mischief it had done. (*LL*) The Wind in a Frolic. William Howitt. MoShBr; OxBChV

How lonely is vast Freedom! I may go. Lone Freedom. Edith M. Thomas. AmWP

How Long. James M. Whitfield. AAP

How long ago Hector took off his plume. Parting in Wartime. Frances Cornford. CoGr; FaBoWP; NIP

How long ago she planted the hawthorn hedge. The Hawthorn Hedge. Judith Wright. FaBoMA; WPE

How long ago we dreamed. Carol of the Three Kings. W. S. Merwin. PChr

How long, dear Savior, O how long. Isaac Watts. AmFP

How long has this got to go on? (*LL*) We Have Been Here Before. Morris Bishop. FiBHP; NYBP

How long have you suffered from this tick? Interview with Herr Limerick. Andreas Okopenko, *tr. fr. German.* CBNP

How long, how long must I regret? The Lost Tribe. Ruth Pitter. WPOW

How Long I Sailed. Hartley Coleridge. Son

How long in these empty thermals near the cold. Crinagoras, *tr. fr. Greek* by Alistair Elliot. GrAn

How Long, Jehovah! Henry Ainsworth. AH

How long must we two hide the burning gaze. United. Paulus Silentiarius, *tr. fr. Greek by* W. H. D. Rouse. AWP

How long, O God! how long must I remain. The Negro's Lament. John Willis Menard. AAP

How long, O lion, hast thou fleshless lain? The Lion's Skeleton. Charles Tennyson Turner. FM; NOBVV

How long, O lord, shall I forgotten be? Bible, *O.T., paraphrased by* Sir Thomas Wyatt. *See* How long wilt thou forget me O Lord.

How long, O sister, how long. The Bells at Midnight. Thomas Bailey Aldrich. PAH

How long, oh gracious God! how long. How Long. James M. Whitfield. AAP

How long shall fortune faile me now. The Earl of Westmoreland. *Unknown.* ESPB

How long shall I endure without reply. The Medal of John Bays; a Satire against Folly and Knavery. Thomas Shadwell. APAS

How Long Shall I Give? *Unknown.* BLRP

How long shall this like dying life endure. Spenser. *Fr. Amoretti.* AAS; EnRePo; ESo, *lacking epigrams* I–IV; HeIL

How long shall you and I be bound. Water Whirligigs. D. J. Opperman, *tr. fr. Afrikaans by* Jack Cope *and* Uys Krige. PeSA

How long she waited for her executioner! Head of Medusa. Marya Zaturenska. MoAmPo

How long since I've spent a whole night. Love Song to a Stranger. Joan Baez. UnAS

How long this giant hugged and spanned. Windmill on the Cape. William Vincent Sieller. GoYe

How Long This Night Is, *medieval vers. Unknown. See* Merry It Is.

How long this way: that everywhere. Red Sea. James Agee. *Fr. Two Songs on the Economy of Abundance.* MoAmPo

How long we sit in front of them. Careers. Marjorie Welish. UL

How long will it last? Lady Horikawa, *tr. fr. Japanese by* Kenneth Rexroth *and* Ikuko Atsumi. WPJ; WPOW

How long wilt thou forget me O Lord. Bible, *O.T., paraphrased by* Sir Thomas Wyatt. *Fr.* Psalms.
(How long, O lord, shall I forgotten be?) NoSic, *sect.* XIII
(Psalm XIII: "How long, O Lord, shall I forgotten be?," *paraphrased by* Sir Philip Sidney.) OBVE

How Looks the Night? Gerard Manley Hopkins. OxBSP

How lost is the little fox at the borders of night. Night of Wind. Frances Frost. FaPON

How lovely are the tombs of the dead nymphs. Panope. Edith Sitwell. MoAB; MoBrPo

How lovely are thy dwellings fair! Psalm LXXXIV. Milton. TrPWD

How lovely are thy holy groves. *Unknown, tr. fr. Chinook Indian.* EaPr

How Lovely Are Thy Tabernacles. Bible, *O.T., paraphrased by* Sir Thomas Wyatt. *Fr.* Psalms. FaPON; TrJP

How lovely is the sound of oars at night. Boats at Night. Edward Shanks. CH

How lovely it is today! *Unknown. Fr.* Four Glosses. NOIV

How lovely it was, after the official fright. The Phenomenon. Karl Shapiro. CMoP; NYBP

How lovely the Imperial Mound, but when can I visit it? On the Road to Western Hill. Ch'ien Ch'ien-i, *tr. fr. Chinese by* Irving Y. Lo. SuSp

How Low Is the Lowing Herd. Walt Kelly. FiBHP

How lush, how loose, the uninhibited squash is. Squash in Blossom. Robert Francis. FYAP

How McClellan Took Manassas. *Unknown.* PAH

How many a father have I seen. Tennyson. *Fr.* In Memoriam A. H. H. EBVV, *abr.;* EBVVPR; EnVR; OAEL-2, *abr.;* PeECV, *abr.*

How many a time have I. Swimming. Byron. *Fr.* Two Foscari, The. GN

How many bards gild the lapses of time! Keats. EnRP; OxAEP-2

How many blessed groups this hour are bending. Sabbath Sonnet. Felicia Dorothea Hemans. Son

How many bullets does it take. Death in Yorkville. Langston Hughes. PoBA

How many buttons are missing today! Nobody Knows but Mother. Mary Morrison. BLPA

How many can you find? (*LL*) Step out onto the Planet. Lew Welch. EaPr

How many dawns, chill from his rippling rest. To Brooklyn Bridge. Hart Crane. *Fr.* Bridge, The. AiP; AmPP; BLPL; ChIV-1; ClHu; CMoP; HAP; HeIP; ImPo; InPS; LiTA; LiTM; MeMAP; MoAB; MoAmPo; NAAL-2; NoAM; NOBA; NoP; OxBA; PoE; PrIm; TAP; TFi; TRP; WeW
(Proem: To Brooklyn Bridge. AmFP; AmPP; CMoP; HAP; HeIP; NoAM; NoP; TAP; WeW

How many days has my baby to play? Mother Goose. OxNR; ReMoGo

How Many Days Has My Baby to Play? *Unknown.* BoTP

How Many Devils Can Dance on the Point. D. J. Enright. AnAn

How many doors will this man open. Death. Roy Fuller. NoAM

How many evenings in the arbor by the river. Tune: "As in a Dream; a Song," Li Ch'ing-chao, *tr. fr. Chinese by* Eugene Eoyang. BoWoP; SuSp

How many faults you might accuse me of. Elinor Wylie. NAAL-2

How Many Heavens. Edith Sitwell. TrCP

How many humble hearts have dipped. To a Post-Office Inkwell. Christopher Morley. PoLF

How many inert molecules are ready to break into life? (*LL*) Cells Breathe in the Emptiness. Galway Kinnell. NaP; VGW

How many men are killed by power, by power. Sejanus ("How many men are killed by power, by power.") Juvenal, *tr. by* Robert Lowell. *Fr.* Satires. OBVE

How Many Miles to Babylon? Mother Goose. BoTP; CoGr; FaBoCh; GBP; MoShBr; NTP; OxBoLi; OxBSP; OxNR

How many moments must (amazing each). E. E. Cummings. PoA

How many names. Some trouble. Hedgerows. Stanley Plumly. NAmP90

How Many New Years Have Grown Old. *Unknown.* EIL

How Many Nights. Galway Kinnell. CAPP; MAT; NaP

How many pallid Christs, with painted blood. All Around Us. Constance Urdang. PBCAP

How Many Paltry, Foolish, Painted Things. Michael Drayton. *Fr.* Idea. AAS; EnLoPo; EnRePo; ESo; GBL; HAP; HeIP; NAEL-1; NIP; NoP; NOSC; OAEL-1; PrIm; SCGP; TEP

How many pounds does the baby weigh. Weighing the Baby. Ethel Lynn Beers. PoToHe

How many prompters! what a chorus! (*LL*) Plays. Walter Savage Landor. EnRP; NBLV; NoP; OxBoLi; OxBSP; PeLV

How many roads must a man walk down. Blowin' in the Wind. Bob Dylan. PoBeRe

How many scenes, O sun. Ode to the Sun. Eloise Bibb. CBWP-4

How many stolen glances can we trade. Paulus Silentiarius, *tr. fr. Greek by* Sam Hamill. InMo

How many thousand of my poorest subjects. The Cares of Majesty. Shakespeare. *Fr.* King Henry IV, *Pt.* II. LiTB
(O Gentle Sleep.) FaBoRV

How many threads have I broken with my teeth. How many. Scratch Music. C. D. Wright. NAmP90

How Many Times? Thomas Lovell Beddoes. *See* How many times do I love thee, dear?

How many times, Death. O All Down within the Pretty Meadow. Kenneth Patchen. HAP; WeW

How many times do I love thee, dear? Thomas Lovell Beddoes. *Fr.* Torrismond. LiTB; PoEL-4; TrGrPo
(How Many Times?) ELP
(How Many Times Do I Love Thee, Dear?) EnRP; NAEL-2
(Song.) ImPo

How many times our hands will enter. Holidays. Dara Wier. NAmP90

How many times these low feet staggered. Emily Dickinson. AmPP; HAP; NAAL-1; PoEL-5; WeW

How many towers and terraces loom in the misty rain? (*LL*) Spring in Chiang-nan. Tu Mu. PLT

How many ways can you bring me ten? Making Tens. M. M. Hutchinson. BoTP

How Many Ways ("How many ways, how many times.") John Masefield. *Fr.* Sonnets. LiTB; WGRP

How many will her coldness kill! (*LL*) See, see, she wakes, Sabina wakes! Congreve. NOEC; OxBSP

How many wise men and heroes. To the Tune "The River Is Red." Ch'iu Chin, *tr. fr. Chinese by* Kenneth Rexroth *and* Ling Chung. AiP; BoWoP; PBWP; WPC
(Free Women Blooming like Fields of Flowers. WoWa

How Marigolds Came Yellow. Robert Herrick. ChTr; TTTS

How massively, with what a fine stiff rise. Erucius, *tr. fr. Greek by* Peter Jay. GrAn

How may one be spared the sorrow and regret of human life? Tune: "Song of Tzu-yeh." Li Yü, *tr. fr. Chinese by* Daniel Bryant. SuSp

How memory cuts away the years. Autumn. Jean Starr Untermeyer. MoAmPo

How Metaphor Can Save Your Life. Myra Sklarew. CRP

How mobile is the bed on these. Rain. Vladimir Nabokov. GrPl

How monarchs die is easily explained. On a Royal Demise. Thomas Hood. FiBHP

How mournful seems, in broken dreams. Not Lost, but Gone Before. Caroline E. Norton. BLRP; VPP; WBLP

How much alike they seem! (*LL*) The Ballad of Mulan. *Unknown.* SuSp

How much? — and — do you love me, kid? (*LL*) Threes. Carl Sandburg. AnAmPo; CMoP; OxBA; PoLF

How much are they deceived who vainly strive. Love and Jealousy. William Walsh. BoLoP

How much better it seems now. The Next Poem. Dana Gioia. DiPo

How much death works. Eyes Fastened with Pins. Charles Simic. VCAP

How Much Earth. Philip Levine. NNaP

How much fewer volumes of verse there'd be! (*LL*) Lovers, and a Reflection. Charles Stuart Calverley. FaBoCo; FaBoPa

How much I should like to begin. At the Edge. Denise Levertov. NAAL-2

How Much Is Not True. Kabir. RaBo

How much like a laager! (*LL*) The Mantatee Horde. Mtutuzeli Matshoba. PeSAV

How Much Longer? Robert Mezey. OBWP

How Much Longer Will I Be Able to Inhabit the Divine Sepulcher. John Ashbery. NeAP; PoM

How much more/ Of wind and rain? Tune: "Groping for Fish." Hsin Ch'i-chi, *tr. fr. Chinese by* Irving Y. Lo. SuSp

How much of me is sandwiches radio beer? Lonesome in the Country. Al Young. MAT

How much of paper's soiled! what floods of ink! An Epistle to Lady Bowyer. Mary Jones. ECWP

How much of the great poetry. Civilization and Its Discontents. William Matthews. FoLa

How much, preventing God, how much I owe. Grace. Emerson. AmPP; NoP; PFP; TrPWD

How much regret in my dream last night? Tune: "Butterflies Lingering over Flowers." Wang Kuo-wei, *tr. fr. Chinese by* Ching-i Tu. SuSp

How much shall I love her? The Echo-Elf Answers. Thomas Hardy. CBLP

"How much," sighed the gentle Narcissus. Stephen Sylvester. PeLi

How much that loyal body wanted learning. (*LL*) King George, observing with judicious eyes. Joseph Trapp. FaBoCo

How much the heart may bear and yet not break! Endurance. Elizabeth Akers Allen. PoToHe

How much wood would a woodchuck chuck? *Unknown.* ISE; RoPo; TLR
(If a Woodchuck Would Chuck.) FaPON
(Wood-chuck.) ImGa

How mutable is every thing that here. Meditation 29. Philip Pain. *Fr.* Meditations for July 26, 1666. NOBA; SCAP

How my heart leaps when it thinks. To the Infinite. Friedrich Gottlieb Klopstock, *tr. fr. German by* Philip L. Miller. RiWo

How my thoughts betray me! A Prayer for Recollection. *Unknown, tr. fr. Irish by* Frank O'Connor. PeIV

How near me came the hand of Death. A Widow's Hymn. George Wither. OBEV

How nice it is to eat! Beautiful Meals. T. Sturge Moore. BoTP

How nice mud feels/ Between the toes. (*LL*) Mud ("Mud is very nice to feel.") Polly Chase Boyden. FaBV; NTCP

How nice to be a local swan. Sitting Pretty. Margaret Fishback. PoLF

How nice to know Mr. MacBeth. With a Presentation Copy of Verses. Martin Bell. PeLV

How No Age Is Content. The Earl of Surrey. *See* Laid in my quiet bed, in study as I were.

How No Age Is Content with His Own Estate, *shorter vers.* The Earl of Surrey. *See* Laid in my quiet bed, in study as I were.

How noteless men, and Pleiads, stand. Emily Dickinson. PoE

How now! is he dead? Shakespeare. *Fr.* Antony and Cleopatra. OxAEP-1

How now, spirit! whither wander you? Shakespeare. *Fr.* Midsummer Night's Dream, A. GN

How odd/ Of God. The Chosen People. W. N. Ewer. FaBoEE
(Epigram.) OtMeF

How oft, ere morning lit the eastern steep. Richard Hall. *Fr.* Venni-Vach Revisited. AngWe

How Oft Has the Banshee Cried. Thomas Moore. AWP

How Oft Have I My Dere and Cruell Foo. Petrarch, *tr. fr. Italian by* Sir Thomas Wyatt. AAS; SiPSBD

How oft have I with publike voyce runne on? Lady Elizabeth Carey. *Fr.* Mariam. KTR, *act* I, *sc.* 1; WPE

How oft I dream of childhood days, of tricks we used to play. Rosie Nell. *Unknown.* AS

How oft I prayed to hold her in my arms. Faint Heart. Rufinus, *tr. by* F. A. Wright. ErPo

How oft in Schoolboy Days. Frederick Goddard Tuckerman. Son

How oft 'tis said, "this is a songless Land." The Songless Land. Francis Carey Slater. PeSAV

How oft we see the female sex. The School for Satire. Lady Sophia Burrell. ECWP

How oft when men are at the point of death. Shakespeare. *Fr.* Romeo and Juliet. DL; LPA

How oft, when thou, my music, music play'st. Shakespeare. *Fr.* Sonnets. EIl; NAEL-1; OxAEP-1; PoE

How often and often I wish. Frances Cornford. PeLi

How often does a man need to see a woman? The Word Made Flesh. W. J. Turner. OBMV

How often, for some trivial wrong. Retaliation. Margaret E. Bruner. PoToHe

How often hath my pen, mine heart's solicitour. *Unknown. Fr.* Zepheria. ESo

How often have I carried our family word. Quoof. Paul Muldoon. CBNP; FaBoVe; PBCIP; PNI

How often have I started out. Inspiration. Robert W. Service. WeW

How often have my tears. In Allusion to the French Song. Richard Lovelace. CaPo

How often have we known a dog to be. Beyond the Grave. Margaret E. Bruner. PoToHe

How often in the years that close. A Meditation. Herman Melville. GOA

How often my grandparents allude to death, now. Behind the Veil. Andrew Lansdown. NOBAu

How often should we think of this, that we. Meditations for August 1, 1666. Philip Pain. SCAP

How often we neglect a friend. Atonement. Margaret E. Bruner. PoToHe

How often we overslept. Adhesive: For Earlene. Robert Hass. NGP

How often, when life's summer day. Walter Savage Landor. FaBoEE

How often you forget about us! We are. The Sparrows' Chorus. Elizabeth Jennings. PIP

How Old Are You? H. S. Fritsch. PoLF; PoToHe

How Old Brown Took Harper's Ferry. Edmund Clarence Stedman. PAH; PoNe

How old may Phillis *or* Phyllis be, you ask. Phillis's *or* Phyllis's Age. Matthew Prior. EnLoPo; FaBoEE
(Phyllis's Age.) FaBoEE

How old was Mary out of whom you cast. Charlotte Mew. *Fr.* Madeleine in Church. MoAB; MoBrPo

How on Solemn Fields of Space. Elizabeth Daryush. NOCV

How One Winter Came in the Lake Region. Wilfred Campbell. NOBC

How our good king does Papists hate. Satire on Old Rowley. *Unknown.* APAS

How Paddy Stole the Rope. *Unknown.* BLPA

How pitiful is her sleep. In Memory of Kathleen. Kenneth Patchen. IMW; MoAmPo

How placid, how divinely sweet. Meandering Wye. Robert Bloomfield. *Fr.* Banks of Wye, The. OBNC

How placidly shine/ The river, the spring, and the sun. Rosalía de Castro, *tr. fr. Galician* by Benjamin M. Woodbridge, Jr. PBWP

How pleasant it is that always. Florence Smith. BLPA

How Pleasant It Is to Have Money. Arthur Hugh Clough. *See* As I sat at the café, I said to myself.

How pleasant to know Mr. Lear! (*LL*) How Pleasant to Know Mr. Lear. Edward Lear. CBNP; ChTr; EBEV; FaBoCo; FiBHP; HAP; NOBE; NOBL; NOBVV; NoP; NTP; OxAEP-2; PFP; UV, *sts.* I–V *only*

How poecile and endearing is the Porch. Frank O'Hara. CBNP

How poor, how rich, how abject, how august. Edward Young. *Fr.* Night Thoughts. OAEL-1

How poor was Jacob's motion, and how strange. On Jacob's Purchase. Francis Quarles. ChIV-1

How Potchikoo Got Old. Louise Erdrich. *Fr.* Old Man Potchikoo. HATNAP

How prone we are to sin, how sweet were made. And Forgive Us Our Trespasses. Aphra Behn. EBEV

How? "Providence," and yet a Scottish crew? John Cleveland. *Fr.* Rebel [*or* Rebell] Scot, The. NOSC

How pure at heart and sound in head. Tennyson. *Fr.* In Memoriam A. H. H. EBVV, *abr.*; MeMBP; OAEL-2, *abr.*; PeECV, *abr.*

How quickly we age. Not so the heavens. Tune: "Song of Picking Mulberry" Double-Ninth Festival. Mao Tse-tung, *tr. fr. Chinese* by Eugene Eoyang. SuSp

How quiet and how still to-day old Bethel's corners 'round. The Day after Conference. Josephine D. Henderson Heard. CBWP-4

How quiet is the morning in the hills! Morning in the Hills. Bliss Carman. NOBC

How quietly they push the flat sea from them. Assault Convoy. Norman Hampson. PIP

How rare to be born a human being! Gary Snyder. *Fr.* Myths and Texts. NaP

How red the rose that is the soldier's wound. Wallace Stevens. *Fr.* Esthétique du Mal. CMoP; LiTM; NOBA

How restless they are. David Chaloner. VaA

How rewarding to know Mr. Smith. Mr. Smith. William Jay Smith. FiBHP

How rich and pleasing thou, my Julia, art. To Julia. Robert Herrick. CaPo

How rich, O Lord! how fresh thy visits are. Unprofitablenes. Henry Vaughan. ESCV; GeHe; NOSC; SeCV-1

How rich we were, to know them, exiles. Priest Lake. William Stafford. PoA

How Roses Came Red. Robert Herrick. BeJo; CaPo; ChTr; SoSe

How rough a sea. Basho, *tr. fr. Japanese* by Harold G. Henderson. TAL

How sad it must be. A Poem for My Father. Sonia Sanchez. BPo; IHMS

How sad the note of that funereal drum. On the Death of Commodore Oliver H. Perry. John G. C. Brainard. PAH

How safe, methinks, and strong, behind. After Floods on the Wharfe. Andrew Marvell. *Fr.* Upon Appleton House, to My Lord Fairfax. FaBoPP; SeCP; SeCV-1

How say that by law we may torture and chase. She's Free! Frances E. W. Harper. AIW; BlSi; Son

How see you Echo? When she calls I see. Echo. Viscountess Grey of Fallodon. CH

How seldom, friend, a good, great man inherits. The Good Great Man. Samuel Taylor Coleridge. PWR

How shall he mighty river. Transmutation. Antoinette Adam. EaPr

How shall I a habit break? A Builder's Lesson. John Boyle O'Reilly. PoLF; PoToHe, *St.* 1 *only*; PWR

How shall I address Thee, O God? how shall I praise Thee? *Unknown, tr. fr. Hindustani.* Fr. Nanak and the Sikhs. WGRP

How shall I be a poet? Poeta Fit, Non Nascitur. "Lewis Carroll." FaBoNo; OBSV

How shall I begin my song. Songs for the Four Parts of the Night. Owl Woman, *tr. fr. Papago Indian* by Frances Densmore. PBWP

How shall I behold the face. Milton. *Fr.* Paradise Lost. EPCY; TOF

How shall I deck my love in love's habiliment. *Unknown.* Fr. Zepheria. ESo

How shall I forsake wisdom? In Praise of Wisdom. Solomon ibn Gabirol, *tr. fr. Hebrew* by Solomon Solis-Cohen. TrJP

How shall I guard my soul so that it be. The Song of Love. Rainer Maria Rilke, *tr. fr. German* by Ludwig Lewisohn. AWP

How shall I know if my love lose his youth. Strato, *tr. fr. Greek* by Sydney Oswald. PeHV

How shall I name you, immortal, mild, proud shadows? W. B. Yeats. NU

How shall I speak of doom, and ours in special. Tales from a Family Album. Donald Justice. Poetr

How shall I still mankind's good will retrieve. August, Graf von Platen. *Fr.* Sonnets to Karl Theodore German. PeHV

How shall I tell the torments of that hour. The Author Consults a Critic and Sells His Manuscript. Francis Hawling. *Fr.* Signal; or, A Satire against Modesty, The. NOEC

How Shall I Tell You? Carmen Tafolla. ETG

How shall I work that she may not forget. Owen Barfield. ArLo

How shall my tongue expresse that hallow'd fire. Francis Quarles. *Fr.* Emblems. ESCV

How shall the dead taste the deep treasure they have? (*LL*) Promise of Peace. Robinson Jeffers. LiTA; LiTM; MoAB; MoAmPo

How shall the river learn. Max Schmitt in a Single Scull. Richmond Lattimore. AiP

How shall the wine be drunk, or the woman known? A Voice from under the Table. Richard Wilbur. AmPP; HAP; NOBA

How shall we adorn. Angle of Geese. N. Scott Momaday. CDW; HATNAP

How shall we bring our dying heart up. Leah Goldberg, *tr. fr. Hebrew* by Ruth Finer Mintz. *Fr.* On Blossoming. MHP

How shall we please this age? If in a song. To Nysus. Sir Charles Sedley. FaBoEE; OBSV

How shall we praise the magnificence of the dead. Tetélestai. Conrad Aiken. LiTA; LiTM; MoAB; MoAmPo; PrIm

How Shall We Rise to Greet the Dawn? *sels.* Sir Osbert Sitwell. "Continually they cackle thus." PoWW

How Shall We Rise to Greet the Dawn? Sir Osbert Sitwell. WGRP

How shall we speak of Canada. W. L. M. K. F. R. Scott. NOBC

How shall we walk naked when. Julia Randall. *Fr.* Adam Says See. CrSp

How shall your name go down in history. To Youth. Josephine D. Henderson Heard. CBWP-4

How shalt thou bear the Cross that now. The Eternal Years. Frederick William Faber. PWR

How she lay against my side! (*LL*) She has left me, my pretty. Sylvia Townsend Warner. MoAB; MoBrPo

How She Operates. Grace Caroline Bridges. LoHo

How She Resolved to Act. Merrill Moore. MoAmPo

How Should I Be So Pleasant. Sir Thomas Wyatt. SiPS

How should I describe you — eternal. Koala. Alan Ross. OBTV

How should I, even if I could. To Catulinus That He Cannot Write Him an Epithalamium Because of the Enemy Hosts. Sidonius Apollinaris, *tr. fr. Latin* by Helen Waddell. MLL

How should I love my best? Lord Herbert of Cherbury. PoEL-2; SeCP

How should I not be glad to contemplate. Everything is Going to be All Right. Derek Mahon. PBCIP

How should I praise thee, Lord! how should my rymes. The Temper, ("How should I praise Thee, Lord.") George Herbert. ESCV; GeHe; NOCV; NoP; PFP; PoEL-2

How should I your true love know. An Old Song Ended. Dante Gabriel Rossetti. BoLoP; EBVV

How should I your true love know. Ophelia's Song. Shakespeare. *Fr.* Hamlet. EBEV; EBEvV; EnLoPo; LiTB; Mes; NAWM-1; NoSic; PoRA; SCGP
(O's Song: "How should I your true love know".) ChTr; GBL; TrGrPo
(Song: "How should I your true love know.") CH

How should the world be luckier if this house. Upon a House Shaken by the Land Agitation. W. B. Yeats. CMoP

How shril are silent tears? when sin got head. Admission. Henry Vaughan *and* Thomas Stanley. ESCV

How sick I get. Father. Paul Carroll. NeAP

How silent comes the water round that bend. Minnows. Keats. *Fr.* I Stood Tiptoe [upon a Little Hill]. EnRP; FaPON; GN

How silent it is, grandmother remarks. Viennese Remembrance. Christine McNeill. NWP

How silently the years have sped away. To My Dead Brother. Clara Ann Thompson. CBWP-2

How silly that soldier is pointing his gun at the wood. Russians. Keith Douglas. OxBTC

How silly were those sages heretofore. Samuel Butler. *Fr.* Satire upon the Licentious Age of Charles II. NOBL

How simply & how strangely. Boschlog: Being a Cartulary from The Ship of Fools. B. Catling. NBrP

How Singular. Tom Hood. FaBoNo

How singular some old words are! Singular Singulars, Peculiar Plurals. Willard R. Espy. FaBoUs

How sits this city, late most populous. The Lamentations of Jeremy, For the Most Part According to Tremelius. John Donne. ChIV-1

How sleep the brave who sink to rest. How Sleep the Brave. William Collins. GN; NOBE; OBEV; OtMeF; OxAEP-1; TFi
(Ode: "How sleep the brave, who sink to rest.") ELP; SCGP
(Ode Written in 1746.) GTBS; GTBS-P; TrGrPo
(Ode Written in the Beginning of the Year 1746.) AWP; EnRP; HAP; NAEL-1; NOEC; NoP; OxBSP; PoE; PoEL-3

How slow they are awakening, these trees. Plain Fare. Daryl Hine. CoAP

How slowly dark comes down on what we do. *(LL)* In Evening Air. Theodore Roethke. CAPP; NYBP; TAP

How slowly glide the hours by, the minutes hours seem. The Drunkard's Wife. Mary E. Tucker. CBWP-1

How slowly learns the child at school. Citizenship; Form 8889512, Sub-Section Q. G. K. Chesteron. OxBoLi

How smooth that lake expands its ample breast! Ann Radcliffe. WPE

How Socratic is Somerset Maugham! R. B. S. Instone. PeLi

How soft a caterpillar steps. Emily Dickinson. SAmP

How soon doth man decay! Mortification. George Herbert. ESCV; GeHe; NOSC; SeCP

How Soon Hath Time [the Subtle Thief of Youth]. Milton. CoGr; FF; HeIP; InPS; LiTB; NAEL-1; NAs; PFP; PoE; SCGP; Son

How soon will some self-turning. Vincent Buckley. *Fr.* Golden Builders. FaBoMA

How splendid in the morning glows. Hassan's Serenade. James Elroy Flecker. *Fr.* Hassan. OBEV
(Yasmin.) CoGr

How spoke the king, in his crucial hour victorious? King of the Belgians. Marion Couthouy Smith. PAH

How stands the glass around? Why, Soldiers, Why? *At. to* James Wolfe. OBET
(How Stands the Glass Around?) PAH

How startling to find the portraits of the gods. Roy Fuller. *Fr.* Mythological Sonnets. ErPo; Son

How stately stand yon pines upon the hill. Spring to Winter. George Crabbe. *Fr.* Ancient Mansion, The. ChTr
(In Suffolk.) FaBoPP

How still he stands as mists begin to move. The Guard at the Binh Thuy Bridge. John Balaban. FYAP

How still, how happy! These [*or* Those] are words. Emily Brontë. NOBVV; OBNC; SCGP

How still it is here in the woods. Solitude. Archibald Lampman. BoNaP

How Still the Hawk. Charles Tomlinson. LiTM

How straight it flew, how long it flew. Seaside Golf. Sir John Betjeman. PIP

How strange a thing a lover seems. Love's Perversity. Coventry Patmore. *Fr.* Angel in the House, The. EnVR

How strange and wonderful is our home, our earth. Edward Abbey. EaPr

How strange at night [*or* it is] to wake. Night and Sleep. Coventry Patmore. EBVV
(Shadow of Night, The.) CH

How strange is Love; I am not one. The Gourmet's Love-Song. P. G. Wodehouse. NOBL

How strange it is to awake. Charles Wright. *Fr.* Four Poems for the New Year. AnAn

How strange it seems! These Hebrews in their graves. The Jewish Cemetery at Newport. Longfellow. AmPP; ChIV-1; HAP; HeIP; HoPM; MeMAP; NOBA; NoP; OxBA; TAP

How strange that grass should sing. Gwendolyn B. Bennett. ShDr

How strange the pride of many Irishmen! The New Style. David O'Bruadair, *tr. fr. Irish* by John Montague. BIrV

How strange to awake in a city. Hearing Men Shout at Night on MacDougal Street. Robert Bly. InPS

How strange to think of giving up all ambition! Watering the Horse. Robert Bly. CAPP; NaP

How strange will be my death, of which I've been thinking since childhood. About Death and Other Things. Aleksandar Ristovic, *tr. fr. Serbo-Croatian* by Charles Simic. HSix

How strangely blind is prejudice, the Negro's greatest foe! Prejudice. L. A. J. Moorer. CBWP-3

How strangely this sun reminds me of my love! Stephen Spender. PeHV

How strong does my passion flow. On Her Loving Two Equally. Aphra Behn. NALW; NIP

How strongly does my passion flow. Aphra Behn. OxAEP-1

How struts my love my cavalier. Cock-a-Hoop. Isabella Gardner. WPE

How subtle-secret is your smile! Did you love none then? Nay, I know. Oscar Wilde. *Fr.* Sphinx, The. MoBrPo

How sweet and innocent are country sports. James Thomson. *Fr.* Of a Country Life. UV

How Sweet and Lovely Dost Thou Make the Shame. Shakespeare. *Fr.* Sonnets. HeIP, *sect.* XCV; SCGP, *sect.* XCV; TrGrPo, *sect.* XCV

How sweet and silent is the place. A Communion Hymn. Alice Freeman Palmer. TrPWD

How sweet, how passing sweet, is solitude! William Cowper. *Fr.* Retirement. OBF

How sweet, how sweet will be the night. How Sweet the Night. Rachael Bates. PAW

How sweet I roamed from field to field. How Sweet I Roamed from Field to Field. Blake. BoTP; EnLoPo; EnRP; LiTB; MeMBP; NAEL-2; NOEC; NoP; OAEL-2; OBNC; PoEL-4; TFi; TrGrPo
(Prince of Love, The.) NOBE
(Song.) ImPo; Poetr

How sweet is harmless solitude! Solitude. Mary Mollineux. NOSC

How sweet is mortal Sovranty! — think some. Omar Khayyám, *tr. fr. Persian* by Edward Fitzgerald. *Fr.* Rubáiyát of Omar Khayyám of Naishápúr, The. AWP; EBVV, *abr.;* FaBoBe; FaBoRV, *abr.;* FaPoR, *abr.;* HAP, *abr.;* LiTB; NAEL-2; NoP; PoEL-5; PrIm, *abr.;* TrGrPo; UV

How Sweet Is the Language of Love. Oliver Holden. AH

How sweet is the shepherd's sweet lot! The Shepherd. Blake. *Fr.* Songs of Innocence. BoTP; EnRP; FHYEP; PFP

How sweet the answer Echo makes. Echo. Thomas Moore. ELP
(Echoes.) GTBS; GTBS-P; OxAEP-2

How sweet the chime of the Sabbath bells! Creeds of the Bells. George W. Bungay. PWR

How sweet the harmonies of afternoon. The Blackbird. Tennyson. FM

How sweet the moonlight sleeps upon this bank! Shakespeare. *Fr.* Merchant of Venice, The. FaBoRV; OxAEP-1; TrGrPo

How Sweet the Night. Rachael Bates. PAW

How sweet the tuneful bells' responsive peal! William Lisle Bowles. OBTV
(Bells of Ostend, The.) EnRP
(Sonnet: At Ostend.) NOEC

How Sweet Thy Precious Gift of Rest. Menahem ben Makhir of Ratisbon, *tr. fr. Hebrew* by Herbert Loewe. TrJP

How sweet, to see the dells so shady. An Englishman with an Atlas; or, America the Unpronounceable. Morris Bishop. GOA

How sweet to wear a shape of snow. Duck in Central Park. Frances Higginson Savage. GoYe

How sweet, when weary, dropping on a bank. Summer. John Clare. BoNaP

How sweetly did the moments glide. The Cottager's Complaint, on the Intended Bill for Enclosing Sutton-Coldfield. John Freeth. NOEC; OBET

How sweetly doth My Master sound! My Master! The Odour. George Herbert.
(Odour. 2. Cor. 2, The.) ChIV-2; ESCV

How sweetly on the wood-girt town. Pentucket. Whittier. PAH

How swift along the winding way. Upon Boys Diverting Themselves in the River. Thomas Foxton. OxBChV

How that vast heaven intitled First is rolled. William Drummond of Hawthornden. EIL

How the Abbey of Saint Werewulf Juxta Slingsby Came by Brother Fabian's Manuscript. Sebastian Evans. PeVV

How the arm moved. For Robert Duncan. Tom Clark. BAP-89

How the blithe lark runs up the golden stair. The Skylark. Frederick Tennyson. GN

How the Bulls Were Begotten, *sels. Unknown, tr. fr. Irish* by Thomas Kinsella.
Two Bulls, The. NOIV

How the *Cumberland* Went Down. Silas Weir Mitchell. PAH

How the days went. Now That I Am Forever with Child. Audre Lorde. CrSp; NALW; PoBA; Poetr; VBLP

How the Death of a City Is Never More than the Sum of the Deaths of Those Who Inhabit Its Spaces. Victor Coleman. NOBC

How vainly men themselves amaze. The Garden. Andrew Marvell. AWP; BLPL; ClHu; ESCV; GeHe; HAP; ImPo; InPS; InvP; JCP; LiTB; MeLP; NAEL-1; NIP; NOBE; NoP; NOSC; OAEL-1; PoE; PoEL-2; Poetr; PoLF; PoRA; PPP; SCGP; SeCP; SeCV-1; TEP; TFi; TOF; TrGrPo; TRP
(Thoughts in a Garden.) GGP; GTBS; GTBS-P; OBEV

How varied the family Sen! Roy Fuller. PeLi

How vastly we improve our style! (*LL*) A Word of Encouragement. J. R. Pope. FiBHP; NBLV; NOBL

How Violets Came Blue. Robert Herrick. BeJo; CaPo; TTTS

How/ Walls are built why. Town of the Wrong Questions. Anne Carson. *Fr.* Life of Towns, The. BAP-90

How warm this woodland wild recess! Recollections of Love. Samuel Taylor Coleridge. NAEL-2

How was I born? Where from? Why did I come. *Unknown, tr. fr. Greek by* Peter Jay. GrAn

How was it?/ Sweet. (*LL*) Came to me. Rudaki. BoLoP; OBVE

How was thy mother a lioness. Lamentation. Bible, *O.T. Fr.* Ezekiel. TrJP

How We Beat the Favourite. Adam Lindsay Gordon. CBAP; OtMeF; PeVV

How We Became a Nation. Harriet Prescott Spofford. PAH

How We Burned the *Philadelphia*. Barrett Eastman. PAH

How we desire desire! Joy of surcease. J. V. Cunningham. VGW

How We Drove the Trotter. W. T. Goodge. NOBAu

How we envy their not caring. The Card-Players. David Ray. VGW

How we go on. (*LL*) Axe Handles. Gary Snyder. CAPP; NoAM; PoBeRe; VCAP

How We Heard the Name. Alan Dugan. CoAP; NoAM

How well (dear Brother) art thou called Stone? To My Reverend Dear Brother, M. Samuel Stone. John Cotton. SCAP

How well for the birds that can rise in their flight. *Unknown, tr. fr. Gaelic by* Frank O'Connor. WTO

How well her name an army doth present. Ana(Mary-Army)gram. George Herbert. ChIV-2; GeHe; OAEL-1

How well I have repressed the dream of death I had after the war. The Dream. C. K. Williams. PWE

How well I know him, old soldier in blue. The Ancestor. Dave Jeddie Smith. SM

How well I know that fountain. Song of the Soul That Knows God by Faith. St. John of the Cross, *tr. fr. Spanish by* Seamus Heaney. TIRV

How well I know that fountain's rushing flow. St. John of the Cross: Song of the Soul That Is Glad to Know God by Faith. Roy Campbell. PeECV

How well I know what I mean to do. By the Fire-Side. Robert Browning. EBVV; OAEL-2

How well I remember those days of danger. The Road to Pengya. Tu Fu, *tr. fr. Chinese by* Rewi Alley *and* Edward Field. Prf

How well the brittle boat doth personate. On the Same [Death of My Dear Brother, Mr. H.S., Drowned]: The Boat. William Hammond. NOSC

How well you served me above ground. Spirit's Song. Louise Bogan. NYBP

How when one entered a cottage. The Answer. John Montague. CIP; TIRV

How white. Bacchylides, *tr. fr. Greek by* Sam Hamill. InMo

How will he hear the bell at school. Mutterings over the Crib of a Deaf Child. James Wright. LCAP

How will I hide? (*LL*) Question. May Swenson. LiTM; PrIm; SM; VGW

How will I think of you. December 21st. Jean Valentine. LCAP

How will it go, crumbling earthquake, towering inferno, juggernaut, volcano, smashup. A New Reality Is Better Than a New Movie! Amiri Baraka. NoAM

How will our unborn children scoff at us. The Future Verdict. Ada Cambridge. NOBAu

How Will You Call Me, Brother. Mari Evans. BlSi

How will you cross the autumn mountain alone? Princess Oku, *tr. fr. Japanese by* Willis Barnstone. BoWoP

How will you manage. Princess Daihaku, *tr. by* Arthur Waley. *Fr.* Manyo Shu, Part 2 of 4. AWP

How will you your Christmas keep? Keeping Christmas. Eleanor Farjeon. OBCP

How wisely Nature did decree. Eyes and Tears. Andrew Marvell. GeHe; PFP

How wisely wanton is this epicene! (*LL*) Four Winds. Hal Porter. NOBAu

How — with this pounding pulse — I'd quake to go. (*LL*) When — presto — turf and trees are green. Bernard de Ventadour. STV

How wonderful, O Lord, are the works of your hands! *Unknown.* EaPr

How Words Meet to Make a Poem. Aidan Carl Mathews. IB

How wretched is a woman's fate. Woman's Hard Fate. *Unknown.* ECWP

How you became a poet's a mystery! Heredity. Tony Harrison. *Fr.* School of Eloquence, The. NAEL-2; NoAM

How You Get Born. Erica Jong. UnPo

How you go along all day. Strange. Kirby Doyle. NeAP

How young I was. Old Age. *Gond Oral Tradition, tr. by* V. Elwin *and* S. Hivale. WTO

How your eyes dazzle down into my soul! James Thomson ("B.V."). *Fr.* Sunday at Hampstead. EnVR

How'd I solve de Negro Problum? Uncle Rube on the Race Problem. Clara Ann Thompson. CBWP-2

Howdy, Honey, Howdy! Paul Laurence Dunbar. PoLF

However dry and windless. Bamboo. William Plomer. PeSA

However far down. Storm. Geoffrey Fraser Dutton. PWE

However heavy the walls of love, or well shored, they. Janet Gray. VBLP

However the battle is ended. An Inspiration. Ella Wheeler Wilcox. AnAmPo; WGRP
(Only One Way.) PWR

However the image enters. Afterimages. Audre Lorde. VCAP

However we wrangled with Britain awhile. Literary Importation. Philip Freneau. TAP

However you look at it. The Secular. Chris Wallace-Crabbe. NOBAu

Howie gave sentence of slaughter. The Desertion of the Women and Seals. George Mackay Brown. OxBC

Howl. Allen Ginsberg. AmPP; LCAP; PoM
Sels.
"I saw the best minds of my generation destroyed by madness." CAPP; GLP; InPS; MoP; NaP; NeAP; NIP; NoAM; NoP; PoBeRe; SOTW, *abr., ll.* 1–30; TEP; VCAP
"What sphinx of cement and aluminum bashed open their skulls." NeAP; SOTW, *abr.*; TAP

Howl, howl, howl! O! you are men of stones. Shakespeare. *Fr.* King Lear. OBD; OxAEP-1

Howling of Wolves, The. Ted Hughes. OxBTC; PlP

Howling storm is brewing, A. The Storm. Heine, *tr. fr. German by* Louis Untermeyer. AWP

Howling Wolf (1850–1927) Cheyenne. Duane Niatum. *Fr.* Warrior Artists of the Southern Plains. NGP, *sect.* III

Howres for the Hours of Matines, The. Richard Crashaw. PeECV

How's My Boy? Sydney Thompson Dobell. CH; GN; OHIP

How's my boy — my boy? (*LL*) "How's My Boy?" Sydney Thompson Dobell. CH; GN; OHIP

"How's your father?" came the whisper. Conversational. *Unknown.* FiBHP

Hsi-li Echoed My Poems, and I Respond to Him, *sels.* Yang Shih-ch'i, *tr. fr. Chinese by* Jonathan Chaves.

Hsi-shih dreams at dawn, in the cool of silk curtains. A Girl Combs Her Hair. Li Ho, *tr. fr. Chinese by* A. C. Graham. PLT

Huang-p'u River, I learned of you. To the Huang-pu River. Kung Liu, *tr. fr. Chinese. Fr.* Shanghai Lyrics. LHF, *tr. by* Hualing Nieh

Hub of the Universe, The. Walt Whitman. *See* I have said that the soul is not more than the body.

Hubcaps, horsedroppings rubble the sand. Returning to Kilcoole. Aidan Carl Mathews. IB

Hubert's Museum. Louis Simpson. OxBC

Hubris, off the White Cliffs. Martin Stokes. PWE

Huc omnes pariter. Boethius, *tr. by* John Walton. *Fr.* Consolation of Philosophy, The. OBMV

Huck Finn at Ninety, Dying in a Chicago Boarding House Room. James Schevill. TAP

Hucksters haggle in the mart, The. For a War Memorial. G. K. Chesterton. PoWW

Huckster's Horse, The. Julia Hurd Strong. GoYe

Hudibras, *sels.* Samuel Butler.
Argument, The. EBEV; NAEL-1; OAEL-1; SeCV-2
Arms and the Man. NOSC
"Did Saints, for this, bring in their Plate." FaBoEH
"For his religion it was fit." OBSV
"For what mad lover ever died." OBD
"In mathematic[k]s he was greater." NOBL
Independent Squire. NOBE
Metaphysical Sectarian, The. MeLP; PeLV
(Hudibras, the Presbyterian Knight, *abr.*) OxBoLi
(Portrait of Hudibras.) PoEL-3
(Sir Hudibras, His Passing Worth.) FaBoCo
Portrait of Sidrophel. PoEL-3
"Question then, to state it first, The." NOBL
"Quoth he, My faith as adamantine." OBSV
"Quoth he, to bid me not to love." NOBL
Sidrophel, the Rosicrucian Conjurer. OxBoLi
"Some were for setting up a king." EBEV
"There is a tall long-sided dame." OBSV

Hunnish horse,/ Hunnish horse. Tune: "Song of Flirtatious Laughter." Wei Ying-wu, *tr. fr. Chinese by* Hellmut Wilhelm. SuSp

Hunt, The. *Unknown.* CoMu

Hunt ceases, The. St. Eustace. Derek Mahon. BiHa

Hunt, hunt again. If you do not find it, you. Treasure Hunt. Robert Penn Warren. NoP
(Fairy Story.) NYBP

Hunt in the Black Forest, A. Randall Jarrell. CoAP; LCAP

Hunt Is Up, The. *Unknown.* CH; FaBoEH; GBP

Hunt is up, the hunt is up, The. The Hunt Is Up. *Unknown.* CH; FaBoEH; GBP

Hunt not, fish not, shoot not. Bishop Blomfield's First Charge to His Clergy. *At. to* Sydney Goodsir Smith. FaBoEE

Hunt was up, the hunt was up, The. The Capture of Edwin Alonzo Boyd. Peter Miller. MoCV

Hunted City, The, *sels.* Kenneth Patchen.
  "Little hill climbs up to the village and puts its green hands, The." NaP

Hunter, The. Wilhelm Müller, *tr. fr. German by* Philip L. Miller. *Fr.* Beautiful Maid of the Mill, The. RiWo

Hunter, The. Frank O'Hara. NNaP

Hunter. Vasco [*or* Vasko] Popa, *tr. fr. Serbo-Croatian by* Anne Pennington. *Fr.* Games. HSix, *tr. by* Charles Simic; RB

Hunter, The. Raymond Souster. NOBC

Hunter. Rosanna Warren. *Fr.* Funerary Portraits. NoAM

Hunter Once, Now an Ascetic, A. Marippittiyar, *tr. fr. Tamil by* A. K. Ramanujan. PLW

Hunter Poems of the Yoruba. *Unknown, tr. fr. Yoruba by* Ulli Beier. RB *Sels.*
  Baboon.
  Blue Cuckoo.
  Buffalo. OBAP
  Chicken.
  Colobus Monkey.
  Elephant.
  Hyena. OBAP
  Kob Antelope. OBAP
  Leopard. WTO
  Red Monkey.

Hunter Trials. Sir John Betjeman. EBEvV; FiBHP

Hunters are back from beating the winter's face, The. The Woman Thing. Audre Lorde. BlSi; NMM

Hunters in the Snow, The. William Carlos Williams. *Fr.* Pictures from Brueghel. LCAP

Hunters in the Snow: Brueghel. Joseph Langland. LiTM

Hunter's Moon. Stephen Sandy. NYBP

Hunters mount menacing as they go, The. Saville in Trouble. Albery Allson Whitman. *Fr.* Not a Man and Yet a Man. AAP

Hunters of Kentucky; or, Half Horse and Half Alligator, The. Samuel Woodworth. AS; PAH

Hunters of Men, The. Whittier. AnAmPo

Hunters of the Deer, The. Dale Zieroth. NOBC

Hunter's Prayer. *Unknown, tr. fr. Hottentot.* PeSA

Hunter's Song, The. "Barry Cornwall." GN

Hunter's Song at Nightfall, The. Goethe, *tr. fr. German by* John Frederick Nims. STV

Hunting. Tymoteusz Karpowicz, *tr. fr. Polish by* Jan Darowski. PoSu

Hunting. Gary Snyder. *Fr.* Myths and Texts.

Hunting. "Yehoash," *tr. fr. Yiddish by* Isidore Goldstick. TrJP

Hunting and Fishing. Pope. *See* See! from the brake the whirring Pheasant springs.

Hunting Civil War Relics at Nimblewill Creek. James Dickey. GOA

Hunting for Blueberries. Thomas James. AmPA

Hunting for butterflies. (*LL*) A Headstrong Boy. Gu Cheng. SpMi; TSaS

Hunting of Cupid, The, *sels.* George Peele.
  What Thing Is Love. CBLP; ELP; EnRePo; NOBE
  (Love.) EiL; ELP; NOBE

Hunting of the Cheviot, The. *Unknown. See* Perse owt of[f] Northombarlande, The.

Hunting of the Gods, The. *Unknown.* OxBoLi

Hunting of the Hare, The. Margaret Lucas, Duchess of Newcastle. FaBoVe; FM; KTR; NOSC

Hunting of the Snark, The. "Lewis Carroll." CBNP; EBEvV, *Pt.* 1 *only*; FaBoNo; FiBHP, *much abr.*; OBNC; OBNV; PoEL-5 *Sels.*
  Baker's Tale, The. EBEV; NAEL-2; OxAEP-2
  "Just the place for a Snark!" the Bellman cried. FaPoB
  Vanishing, The. OxAEP-2
  (Barrister's Dream, The.) EBNV

Hunting Pheasants in a Cornfield. Robert Bly. TRP

Hunting season. Long Hair. Gary Snyder. NOBA

Hunting Song. Henry Fielding. *Fr.* Don Quixote in England. OxBoLi; PeLV

Hunting Song. Donald Finkel.

Hunting Song. Sir Walter Scott. *Fr.* Lay of the Last Minstrel, The. EnRP; GN; GTBS; GTBS-P; SCGP; TrGrPo; WiR

Hunting Song. *Unknown, tr. fr. Chippewa Indian by* Jerome K. Rothenberg. STP

Hunting-Song. *Unknown, tr. fr. Navajo Indian by* Natalie Curtis. AWP

Hunting Song. Paul Whitehead. *Fr.* Apollo and Daphne. OxBoLi

Hunting Song ("There's my war club.") *Unknown, tr. fr. Chippewa Indian by* Jerome K. Rothenberg. STP

Hunting the Dugong. Gladys Cardiff. HATNAP

Hunting the Wren. *Unknown.* FaBoVe

Hunting tribes of air and earth, The. Man the Enemy of Man. Sir Walter Scott. *Fr.* Rokeby. WBLP

Huntington sleeps in a house six feet long. Southern Pacific. Carl Sandburg. AnAmPo

Huntsman, The. Edward Lowbury. OBSP

Hurdy-Gurdy Man, The. Elizabeth Fleming. BoTP

Hurdy-Gurdy Man, The. Wilhelm Müller, *tr. fr. German by* Philip L. Miller. *Fr.* Winter's Journey, The. RiWo

Hurdy-Gurdy Man in Winter. Vernon Watkins. NYBP

Hurl down the nerve-gnarled body hurtling head. The Final Hunger. Vassar Miller. LiTM

Hurly, hurly, roon the table. *Unknown. Fr.* Two Graces. FaBoCh

Hurlygush. Maurice Lindsay. OxBS

Huron, The. Ruth Herschberger. WPE

Huron Carol, The. Jesse Edgar Middleton. *See* 'Twas in the moon of winter time when all the birds had fled.

Hurrah! (*LL*) Desert Conflict. Calvin Makabo. PeSAV

Hurrah! etc. (*LL*) Marching through Georgia. Henry Clay Work. FaPoR; PAH

Hurrah! for a day with the farmer. A Day at the Farm. "L. J." BoTP

Hurrah for revolution and more cannon-shot! The Great Day. W. B. Yeats. BlrV; CMoP; FF; IHNG; OxBSP

Hurrah for the choice of the nation! Lincoln and Liberty. *Unknown.* AS

Hurrah for the pumpkin pie! (*LL*) Thanksgiving Day. Lydia Maria Child. FaPON; ImGa; NTCP; OHIP; WHSW

Hurrah for Thunder. Christopher Okigbo. HBAPE

Hurrahing in Harvest. Gerard Manley Hopkins. BoNaP; ChTr; CMoP; FaBoPP; InvP; MeMBP; MoAB; MoBrPo; NAEL-2; PeECV; PoE; TOF

Hurricane, The. Bryant. EAP

Hurricane, The. Hart Crane. CMoP; MoAB; MoAmPo; OxBA; TrCP

Hurricane, The. Philip Freneau. EAP; TAP

Hurricane. Archibald MacLeish. ArNa

Hurricane, The. Luis Palés Matos, *tr. fr. Spanish by* Alida Malkus. FaPON

Hurricane Drummers! Self-Aid in Haggerston. Iain Sinclair. NBrP

Hurrier, The. Harold Monro. MoBrPo

Hurry. Octavio Paz, *tr. fr. Spanish by* Eliot Weinberger. AnRep

Hurry, Chronos! To the Postilion Chronos. Goethe, *tr. fr. German by* Philip L. Miller. RiWo

Hurry, Hurry, Mary Dear! N. M. Bodecker. TLR

Hurry, hurry to the field. (*LL*) The Fatal Sisters. Thomas Gray, *after the Icelandic.* EnRP

Hurry of the Spirits, in a Fever and Nervous Disorders, The. Isaac Watts. NOEC

Hurry On, My Weary Soul. *Unknown.* AH

"Hurry!" said the leaves. A Summer Shower. *Unknown.* BoTP

Hurry the baby as fast as you can. Making a Man. Nixon Waterman. BLPA

Hurry, worry, unwary. Old Amusement Park. Marianne Moore. NYBP

Hurrying Away from the Earth. Robert Bly. NaP; PoA

Hurrying Brook, The. Edmund Blunden. BoNaP

Hurrying Eastward day and night while no one notices. (*LL*) Pien River Blocked by Ice. Tu Mu. PLT

Hurrying through the underworld, soundless. (*LL*) Second Glance at a Jaguar. Ted Hughes. NoAM; NYBP; PrIm

Hurrying to catch my Comet. Naturally the Foundation Will Bear Your Expenses. Philip Larkin. FaBoPV; PeLV

Hurt beyond hurting, never to forget. (*LL*) Good-bye for a Long Time. Roy Fuller. CBLP

Hurt, can I laugh? and honest, need I cry? (*LL*) Democritus and Heraclitus. Matthew Prior. OxBSP

Hurt Hawks. Robinson Jeffers. AmPP; CMoP; FYAP; LiTA; LiTM; MoAB; MoAmPo; MoP; NAAL-2; NoAM; NOBA; NoP; OxBA; PrIm; RB; TAP; TFi; TRP; UnPo

Hurt No Living Thing. Christina Rossetti. *Fr.* Sing-Song. FaPON; FM; OTCP; PDV; SiSoPo

Hurt not the trees. (LL) The Trees Are Down. Charlotte Mew. BoNaP; BrRo; ChIV-2; MoAB; MoBrPo; NTP; OxAEP-2; TrCP; WPE; WPOW

Hurt of Love, The. George Macdonald. TrCP

Hurt people crawl as if they. These Days. William Stafford. NNaP

Hurt./ U worried abt a. To All Sisters. Sonia Sanchez. PoBA

Hurting Small Animals. Lavinia Greenlaw. NWP

Hurtling between hedges now, I see. The Limerick Train. Brendan Kennelly. PBCIP

Husband and Heathen. Sam Walter Foss. OBAL

Husband and Wife. Bruce Dawe. FaBoMA

Husband and Wife. Arthur Guiterman. PoToHe

Husband and wife we loved each other then. The Old Man's Song, about His Wife. Unknown, tr. fr. Eskimo by Armand Schwerner. STP

Husband, if you will be my dear. Wife to Husband. John Harington. NoSic

Husband of Poverty, The, sels. Henry Neville Maughan. "There was a Knight of Bethlehem." BoTP

Husband, put down Spinoza, Pericles. Put Off Constricting Day. Mary Stanley. PeNZ

Husband! thou dull unpitied miscreant. Directed to That Inconsiderable Animal Called Husband. Unknown. IHNG

Husband to Wife. John Harington. NoSic

Husband who lived in Tiberias, A. Unknown. PeLi

Husbandman, The. George Wither. Fr. Collection of Emblemes, Ancient and Moderne, A. NOSC

Husbandman and Serving-Man, The. Unknown. OBET

Husbandry, sels. Sir Anthony Fitzherbert. Memorial Verses for Travellers. FaBoUs

Husbandry. William Hammond. JCP

Husbands and Wives. Miriam Hershenson. NTCP

Husband's Lament, The. Brian Merriman, tr. by Frank O'Connor. Fr. Midnight Court, The. NOIV, tr. by Thomas Kinsella; OBVE

Husband's Message, The. Unknown, tr. fr. Anglo-Saxon by Charles W. Kennedy. AnOE

Husband's Return, The. Priscilla Jane Thompson. CBWP-2

Hush. David St. John. LCAP

Hush-a-ba birdie [or burdie], croon, croon. Unknown. GBP; OxNR

Hush-a-baa, baby/ Dinna mak' a din. Unknown. OxNR

Hush-a-by, baby/ Your name is so lovely. Italian Lullaby. Unknown. FaPON

Hush-a-Bye. Unknown. ReMoGo

Hush-a-bye a baa lamb. Unknown. OxNR

Hush-a-bye, baby, on the tree-top. Mother Goose. OxNR; ReMoGo

Hush-a-bye, baby/ The beggar shan't have 'ee. Unknown. OxNR

Hush-a-bye, baby, they're gone to milk. Unknown. OxNR

Hush and Baloo. Unknown. GBP

Hush, baby, my dolly, I pray you don't cry. Baby Dolly. Unknown. ReMoGo

'Hush!' cried a voice at his shoulder. (LL) The Court Historian. George Walter Thornbury. CoGr; PeVV

Hush Honey. Ruby C. Saunders. BlSi

Hush, Hush. Mani Leib, tr. fr. Yiddish by Joseph Leftwich. TrJP

Hush, Hush. J. B. Morton. See Hush, hush,/ Nobody cares!

Hush, hush. Now We Are Sick. J. B. Morton. Fr. When We Were Very Silly. FaBoPa

Hush, hush, do not speak. Hush, Hush. Mani Leib, tr. fr. Yiddish by Joseph Leftwich. TrJP

Hush, hush, little baby. Evening. Unknown. BoTP

Hush, hush,/ Nobody cares! J. B. Morton. Fr. When We Were Very Silly. FaBoPa (Hush, Hush.) UV

Hush! Hush! Whisper who dares! A. A. Milne. Fr. Vespers. UV

Hush is over all the teeming lists, A. Frederick Douglass. Paul Laurence Dunbar. PoBA

Hush, little baby, don't say a word. Unknown. OxNR; TLR

Hush! lullaby, my baby, nor mix thy tears with mine. The Mother's Lullaby. John Clare. NAs

Hush, lullay. Léonie Adams. MoAB; MoAmPo

Hush, my baby, do not cry. Unknown. OxNR

Hush! my dear, lie still and slumber. A Cradle Hymn. Isaac Watts. OBEV; OxBChV; PoEL-3; SCGP

Hush, My Little Grandmother. Meridel LeSueur. SRLS

Hush! not a whisper! Oars, be still! The Coracle Fishers. Robert Bloomfield. Fr. Banks of Wye, The. OBNC

Hush of the river, The. The Canoer. Diane Wakoski. HeIP

Hush! oh ye billows. Joseph Sheridan Le Fanu. Fr. Beatrice. TIRV

Hush, Suzanne! The Mouse in the Wainscot. Ian Serraillier. OTCP; PDV

Hush thee, my babby. Unknown. OxNR

Hush Thee, Princeling. Anna Elizabeth Bennett. AH

Hush up, baby,/ Don't say a word. The Mocking Bird. Unknown. AmFP

Hush ye, hush ye! honey, darlin.' Clara Ann Thompson. CBWP-2

Hush! Yo' mouth. Hush Honey. Ruby C. Saunders. BlSi

Hushaby,/ Don't you cry. All the Pretty Little Horses. Unknown. AmFP; OxBoLi; TTTS

Hush'd Be the Camps To-Day. Walt Whitman. OHIP; SAmP

Hushed are the pigeons cooing low. The Christmas Silence. Margaret Deland. OHIP

Hushed by the Hands of Sleep. Angelina Weld Grimké. CDC

Hushed, cruel, amber-eyed. Pumas. George Sterling. OBAP

Hushed plane, the pond. Ice-fishers' lights. Still little city. Prayer for the Little City. Sydney Lea. NAmP90

Hushie ba, burdie beeton. Unknown. OxNR

Hushing of the Wye, The. Tennyson. See Danube to the Severn gave, The.

Husk of a person beyond summer's pale. The Sleeping Beauty. Rachel Hadas. UnDi

Hustle and Grin. Unknown. WBLP

Hustlers. Dennis Cooper. ETG; UL

Huswifery. Edward Taylor. EAP; FaBV; LiTA; MeMAP; NAAL-1; NIP; NOBA; NOBE; NoP; OxBA; SCAP; TAP; TFi

Hut in the bush of bark or rusty tin, The. The Hatters. Nan McDonald. NOBAu

Huts that stand like plaited baskets. Village and Factory. A. I. Bezymensky, tr. fr. Russian by Babette Deutsch. TrJP

Huxley Hall. Sir John Betjeman. OBSV

Huzza for our liberty, boys. Terrapin War. Unknown. PAH

Huzza! Hodgson, we are going. The Lisbon Packet. Byron. NBLV

Huzza, my Jo Bunkers! no taxes we'll pay. A Radical Song of 1786. St. John Honeywood. PAH

Hwaet! A dream came to me. The Dream of the Rood. Unknown, tr. by Michael Alexander. NOCV

Hy-Brasail — the Isle of the Blest. Gerald Griffin. See On the ocean that hollows the rocks where ye dwell.

Hyacinth. Louise Glück. NoAM

Hyacinth I wished me in her hand, A. (LL) Like the Idalian Queen[e]. William Drummond of Hawthornden. CBLP; NOSC; OAEL-1; SCGP

Hyacinths to Feed Thy Soul. Sadi, tr. fr. Persian. Fr. Gulistan, The. BLPA; BLPL; FaBoBe

Hyaenas [or Hyenas], The. Kipling. NAEL-2; OBSV

Hyaku-Nin-Isshu. Unknown, tr. fr. Japanese by Curtis Hidden Page. AWP Sels.
"Day will soon be gone, The."
"How can one e'er be sure."
"I would that even now."
"Like a great rock, far out at sea."

Hyder Iddle. Unknown. OxNR

Hydrographer's Imaginings, The. Ts'ai Ch'i-chiao, tr. fr. Chinese. LHF, tr. by Hualing Nieh

Hydromel and Rue. George Marion McClellan. AAP

Hye Nonny Nonny Noe. Unknown. FaBoCo; NOBL; PeLV

Hyena. Edwin Morgan. OBAP

Hyena. Carol Muske. AmPA

Hyena, The. Mike Thaler. ZA

Hyena. Unknown, tr. fr. Hottentot. PeSA

Hyena. Unknown, tr. fr. Yoruba by Ulli Beier. Fr. Hunter Poems of the Yoruba. OBAP; RB

Hyena. Unknown, tr. fr. Hurutsche by George Economou. TTY

Hyena Addressing Her Young Ones, The. Unknown, tr. fr. Hottentot by W. H. I. Bleek. PeSAV

Hyena is/ A funny bloke, The. The Hyena. Mike Thaler. ZA

Hyena-patrolled terrain. (LL) A Piece of Earth. Douglas Livingstone. PeSAV

Hyena's Song to her Children. Unknown. See Fire threatens, The.

Hygienist, in your dental chair. Ode to a Dental Hygienist. Earnest Albert Hooton. FiBHP

Hyla Brook. Robert Frost. BoNaP

Hylas. Sextus Propertius, tr. by F. A. Wright. Fr. Elegies. AWP

Hylas. Theocritus [or Theokritus], tr. fr. Greek by Barbara Hughes Fowler. Fr. Idylls. HePo

Hymen, sels. Hilda Doolittle ("H. D."). "Never more will the wind." CTC; TrGrPo

Hymen, god of marriage bed. Joseph Rutter. NOSC

Hymen hath together tied. Epithalamium. R. Hatton. NOSC

Hymenaei, sels. Ben Jonson.

Hymeneal, sels. Catullus, tr. fr. Latin by James Michie. "Unmuzzle the broad joke." PeHV

Hymeneal Song on the Nuptials of the Lady Anne Wentworth and the Lord Lovelace, An. Thomas Carew. CaPo

Hymeneall Dialogue, An. Thomas Carew. SeCP

Hymen's Triumph., *sels.* Samuel Daniel.
Early Love. ErPo
Eyes Hide My Love. EiL
Had Sorrow Ever Fitter Place. EiL
Love Is a Sickness. ELP; NOBE; OBEV; PoEL-2
(Love.) CBLP; EiL

Hymm to the Cross, A. Venantius Fortunatus. *See* Stedefast [*or* Steddefast *or* Steadfast] cross[e], inmong [*or* among] alle [*or* all] other.

Hymmnn. Allen Ginsberg. NOBA

Hymn: "And many voices marshalled in one hymn." Thomas Lovell Beddoes. NOBVV

Hymn: "By the rude bridge that arched the flood." Emerson.

Hymn: "Church's Restoration, The." Sir John Betjeman. FaBoPa

Hymn: "Dear Lord, Whose serving-maiden." Josephine Preston Peabody. TrPWD

Hymn: "Drop, drop, slow tears." Phineas Fletcher. EiL; OxBSP
(Hymn, A.) PeECV

Hymn: "Eternal Ruler of the ceaseless round." John White Chadwick. TrPWD

Hymn: "Father, we come not as of old." John White Chadwick. TrPWD

Hymn: "For Summer's bloom and Autumn's blight." Josiah Gilbert Holland. *Fr.* Bitter-sweet. TrPWD

Hymn: "Framer of the earth and sky." Saint Ambrose, *tr. fr. Latin.* TrCP

Hymn: "God of the strong, God of the weak." Richard Watson Gilder. TrPWD
(God of the Strong, God of the Weak *abr.*) AH

Hymn: "Great Spirit of the speeding spheres." John Haynes Holmes. TrPWD

Hymn: "How are thy servants blest, O Lord!" Joseph Addison. TrPWD
(Hymn.) OxAEP-1

Hymn: "Hush! oh ye billows." Joseph Sheridan Le Fanu. *Fr.* Beatrice. TIRV

Hymn: "Hymn of glory let us sing, A." The Venerable Bede, *tr. fr. Latin by* Elizabeth Charles. WGRP

Hymn: "In vain the dusky night retires." Elizabeth Rowe. ECWP

Hymn: "Lead gently, Lord, and slow." Paul Laurence Dunbar. TrPWD

Hymn: "Lord, when the wise men came from far[r]." Sidney Godolphin. BeJo; HAP; JCP; MeLP; NOCV; PeECV
(Maditation on the Nativity.) NOSC
(Wise Men and Shepherds.) BLPL; NOBE

Hymn: "Lord, with glowing heart I'd praise thee." Francis Scott Key. TrPWD

Hymn: "Lord, within thy fold I be." Priscilla Jane Thompson. CBWP-2

Hymn: "My God, I love thee, not because." St. Francis Xavier, *tr. fr. Latin.* WGRP

Hymn: "Now the day is over." Sabine Baring-Gould. OxBChV; WHSW

Hymn: "Now the shadow flee and vanish." William Williams. AngWe

Hymn: "O thou who camest from above." Charles Wesley. TrPWD
(Inextinguishable Blaze.) NOEC

Hymn: "Queen and huntress, chaste, and fair." Ben Jonson. *See* Queen and huntress, chaste and fair.

Hymn: "Room! room! make room for the bouncing belly." Ben Jonson. *See* Room! room! make room for the bouncing belly.

Hymn: "Since without Thee we do no good." Elizabeth Barrett Browning. TrPWD

Hymn: "Sing, my tongue, the Saviour's glory." St. Thomas Aquinas, *tr. fr. Latin.* WGRP

Hymn: "Thou art my God, sole object of my love." Pope. *See* Thou art my God, sole object of my love.

Hymn: "Thou God of all, whose presence dwells." John Haynes Holmes. TrPWD

Hymn: "Thou hidden love of God, whose height." John Wesley. NOEC
(Hymn.) ECEV

Hymn, The: "To the Almighty on his radiant throne." The Countess of Winchilsea. *Fr.* Pindaric Poem, A. ChIV-1

Hymn: "What is the world, and what is life." William Williams. AngWe

Hymn: "When I Survey the Wondrous Cross." Isaac Watts.

Hymn: "When storms arise." Paul Laurence Dunbar. TrPWD

Hymn: "When Winds Are Raging." Harriet Beecher Stowe.

Hymn: "Where is this stupendous stranger." Christopher Smart.

Hymn: "Wilt thou forgive that sin where I begun." John Donne. AWP; EBEV; EnRePo; HAP; InPK; JCP; LiTB; MeLP; NAEL-1; NOBE; NOSC; OAEL-1; PeECV; PoEL-2; PoRA; SCGP; SCV; SeCP; SeCV-1; SoSe; TFi; TOF; TrGrPo; TrPWD
(For Forgiveness.) WGRP

Hymn: "Ye golden lamps of heaven, farewell." Philip Doddridge *and* John Logan. ECEV

Hymn, a snare, and an exceeding sun, A. (*LL*) Boy Breaking Glass. Gwendolyn Brooks. AiP; MoP; NAAL-2; NoAM; NoP

Hymn, An: "Wake, O my soul; awake, and raise." Phineas Fletcher. NOSC

Hymn before Sunrise, in the Vale of Chamouni. Samuel Taylor Coleridge. EnRP; WGRP

Hymn: "By the rude bridge that arched the flood." Emerson. *See* By the rude bridge that arched the flood.

Hymn L: Rocking Hymn, A. George Wither. *Fr.* Hallelujah; or, Britain's Second Remembrancer. SeCV-1

Hymn for Airmen. M. C. D. H. NSI

Hymn for Atonement Day. Judah Halevi, *tr. fr. Hebrew by* Solomon Solis-Cohen. TrJP

Hymn for Christmas. Felicia Dorothea Hemans. GN

Hymn for Christmas Day, A. John Byrom. ECEV; NOCV; PoEL-3

Hymn for Easter Morn. John Mason Neale. TrCP

Hymn for Lanie Poo, *sels.* Amiri Baraka.
Each Morning. PoBA

Hymn for Morning. Prudentius, *tr. fr. Latin by* Helen Waddell. MLL

Hymn for Pentecost. James Clarence Mangan. TIRV

Hymn for St. John's Eve. *Unknown, tr. fr. Latin by* Dryden. AWP

Hymn for Saturday. Christopher Smart. *See* Now's the time for mirth and play.

Hymn for the Close of the Week. Peter Abelard, *tr. fr. Latin.* TrCP

Hymn for the Eve of the New Year. Abraham Gerondi, *tr. fr. Hebrew by* Solomon Solis-Cohen. TrJP

Hymn from the French of Lamartine, *sels.* Whittier.
"O Thou who bidst the torrent flow." TrPWD

Hymn in Adoration of the Blessed Sacrament. Richard Crashaw. *See* With all the powres my poor heart hath.

Hymn in Columbus Circle. Stephen Vincent Benét. OBAL

Hymn: "Mighty fortress is our God, A." Martin Luther. *See* Mighty Fortress Is Our God, A.

Hymn of Apollo. Shelley. EnRP; OAEL-2

Hymn of Dedication. Elizabeth E. Scantlebury. BLRP

Hymn of Freedom. Michael J. Barry. TIRV

Hymn of glory let us sing, A. The Venerable Bede, *tr. fr. Latin by* Elizabeth Charles. WGRP

Hymn of Gratitude. *Unknown.* BLRP

Hymn of Hate against England, A, *sels.* Ernst Lissauer.
Chant of Hate against England, A. OtMeF

Hymn of Pan. Shelley. EnRP; FaBoCh; MeMBP; OBEV; PoEL-4

Hymn of Saint Thomas in Adoration of the Blessed Sacrament, The. Richard Crashaw.

Hymn of Sivaite Puritans. *Unknown.* WGRP

Hymn of Thanksgiving, A. Wilbur D. Nesbit. OHIP

Hymn of the City. Bryant. EAP

Hymn of the Fairest Fair, The, *sels.* William Drummond of Hawthornden.
"In those vast fields of light, ethereal plains." NOSC

Hymn of the Incarnation, A. *Unknown.* MeEL

Hymn of the Magdalen. Marbod of Rennnes, *tr. fr. Latin by* Helen Waddell. MLL

Hymn of the Moravian Nuns of Bethlehem. Longfellow. PAH

Hymn of the West. Edmund Clarence Stedman. PAH

Hymn of the World Without. Bible, *O.T., paraphrased by* Sir Thomas Wyatt. *See* Bless the Lord, O my soul/ O Lord my God.

Hymn of Trust. Oliver Wendell Holmes. *See* O Love Divine, That Stooped to Share.

Hymn of Trust, A. Nettie M. Sargent. BLRP

Hymn of Unity. *Unknown, tr. fr. Hebrew by* H. M. Adler. TrJP

Hymn of Weeping. Amittai ben Shefatiah, *tr. fr. Hebrew by* Nina Davis Salaman. TrJP

Hymn on Froude and Kingsley, A. William Stubbs. FaBoEE

Hymn on Solitude. James Thomson. NOEC

Hymn on the Morning of Christ's Nativity [*or* On the Morning of Christ's Nativity]. Milton. *Fr.* On the Morning of Christ's Nativity. MeLP; NAEL-1; NAs; NOBE; NOCV; NoP; OBEV; OtMeF; PoEL-3; SCGP; WGRP

Hymn [*or* Hymne] on the Nativity [*or* Nativitie] of My Saviour, A. Ben Jonson. BeJo; ChIV-2; SeCV-1; TrCP

Hymn on the Omnipresence, An. John Byrom. TrPWD

Hymn on the Seasons, A. James Thomson. *Fr.* Seasons, The. EnRP

Hymn Sung at the Completion of the Concord Monument. Emerson. *See* By the rude bridge that arched the flood.

Hymn 10: "Hear What God the Lord Hath Spoken." William Cowper.

Hymn To a Woman Under Interrogation. Reiner Kunze, *tr. fr. German by* Ewald Osers. PoSu

Hymn to Adversity. Thomas Gray. EnRP; GTBS; GTBS-P

Hymn to Amen Ra, the Sun God. *Unknown, tr. fr. Egyptian by* Frank Lloyd Griffith. WGRP

Hymn to Apollo. Callimachus, *tr. fr. Greek* by Barbara Hughes Fowler. *Fr.* Hymns. HePo

Hymn to Archilochus. Edward Sanders. PoBeRe

Hymn to Artemis. Callimachus, *tr. fr. Greek* by Barbara Hughes Fowler. *Fr.* Hymns. HePo

Hymn to Athena. *Unknown, tr. fr. Greek* by Shelley. *Fr.* Homeric Hymns. AWP

Hymn to Bacchus, A. Robert Herrick. JCP

Hymn to Castor and Pollux. *Unknown, tr. fr. Greek* by Shelley. *Fr.* Homeric Hymns. AWP

Hymn [*or* Hymne] to Christ, at the Author's Last Going into Germany, A. John Donne. EBEV; JCP; LiTB; MeLP; SeCV-1
Sels.
   Dark Churches. FaBoRV

Hymn to Colour. George Meredith. OBNC

Hymn to Comus. Ben Jonson. *Fr.* Pleasure Reconciled to Virtue. EIL; NOSC; OAEL-1, *complete*; SCGP

Hymn to Contentment, A. Thomas Parnell. NOEC

Hymn to Cynthia. Ben Jonson. *See* Queen and huntress, chaste and fair.

Hymn to Death. Bryant. EAP

Hymn to Demeter. Callimachus, *tr. fr. Greek* by Barbara Hughes Fowler. *Fr.* Hymns. HePo

Hymn to Diana. Catullus, *tr. fr. Latin* by Richard Claverhouse Jebb. AWP

Hymn to Diana. Thomas Heywood. *Fr.* Golden Age, The. EIL

Hymn to Diana. Ben Jonson. *Fr.* Cynthia's Revels. AWP; CH; ChTr; EIL; GTBS; GTBS-P; HAP; NOBE; NoP; OAEL-1; OBEV; PoRA; SeCP; TFi; TrGrPo; WiR

Hymn to Earth. Elinor Wylie. LiTM; MoAB; MoAmPo

Hymn to Earth the Mother of All. *Unknown, tr. fr. Greek* by Shelley. *Fr.* Homeric Hymns. AWP

Hymn to Evil. Louis Ginsberg. PoA

Hymn to God in Time of Stress, A. Max Eastman. TrPWD

Hymn to God the Father, A. John Donne. AWP; EBEV; EnRePo; HAP; InPK; JCP; LiTB; MeLP; NAEL-1; NOBE; NOSC; OAEL-1; PeECV; PoEL-2; PoRA; SCGP; SCV; SeCP; SeCV-1; SoSe; TFi; TOF; TrGrPo; TrPWD

Hymn to God the Father, A. Ben Jonson. BeJo; EnRePo; NoP; NOSC; OxAEP-1; Poetr; SeCP; SeCV-1; TrCP; TrPWD

Hymn to Her Unknown. W. J. Turner. OBMV

Hymn to Intellectual Beauty. Shelley. BLPL; EnRP; FHYEP; HAP; HeIP; ImPo; MeMBP; NAEL-2; NoP; OAEL-2; OBNC; PoE; TOF

Hymn to Jesus, A. Richard of Caistre. MeEL

Hymn to Joy. Julia Cunningham. PChr

Hymn to Liberty, A. Jeffrey Wainwright. *Fr.* Mad Talk of George III, The. SCBI

Hymn: To Light. Abraham Cowley. MeLP; OxAEP-1; SeCV-1

Hymn to Love. Lascelles Abercrombie. *Fr.* Emblems of Love. OBEV

Hymn to Love, An. Robert Herrick. NOSC

Hymn to Marduk. *Unknown, tr. fr. Assyrian.* WGRP
Sels.
   "O Marduk, lord of countries, terrible one"
   "O Mighty, powerful, strong one of Ashur"

Hymn to Mary, A. *Unknown.* MeEL

Hymn to Mercury, *abr. Unknown, tr. fr. Greek* by Shelley. *Fr.* Homeric Hymns. OBVE

Hymn to Moloch. Ralph Hodgson. OxBTC

Hymn to My God in a Night of My Late Sickness[e], A. Sir Henry Wotton. MeLP; NOSC

Hymn to Night. Melville Cane. MoAmPo

Hymn to Night, A. Max Michelson. TrJP

Hymn to Pan. John Fletcher. *See* Sing his praises that doth keep.

Hymn to Pan. Keats. *Fr.* Endymion [a Poetic Romance]. MeMBP; PoEL-4

Hymn to Priapus. D. H. Lawrence. CMoP; MoAB; OBMV; PoE; SCGP

Hymn to Proserpine. Swinburne. EBVV; EnVR; NAEL-2; OAEL-2; OBNC; PoEL-5; TEP

Hymn to Proust. Gavin Ewart. NYBP

Hymn to St. Geryon, *sels.* Michael McClure.
   "Gesture the gesture the gesture, The." NeAP

Hymn to Saint Teresa. Richard Crashaw. *See* Love, thou are absolute sole lord.

Hymn to Science. Mark Akenside. ECEV; PoEL-3

Hymn to Selene. *Unknown, tr. fr. Greek* by Shelley. *Fr.* Homeric Hymns. AWP

Hymn to the Air Spirit. *Unknown, tr. fr. Eskimo.* WTO

Hymn to the Creator. John Clare. NOBVV

Hymn to the Evening, An. Phillis Wheatley. WPE

Hymn to the Fallen. *Unknown, tr. fr. Chinese* by Arthur Waley. OBWP

Hymn to the Graces, A. Robert Herrick. NOSC

Hymn to the Holy Spirit. Stephen Langton. TrCP

Hymn to the Moon. Lady Mary Wortley Montagu. ECWP

Hymn to the Morning, An. Phillis Wheatley. TAP

Hymn to the Name and Honour [*or* Honor] of the Admirable Saint[e] T[h]eresa, A. Richard Crashaw. JCP; NOBE; NoP; OBEV; PoEL-2; SeCV-1, *abr.*
Sels.
   "Love, thou are absolute sole lord." HAP; NOSC
      (Hymn to Saint Teresa.) EBEV; ESCV; GeHe; MeLP; WGRP
   "Thou art love's victim; and must die." OBD

Hymn to the Night. Longfellow. BLPL; MeMAP; NOBA; OxBA; PWR; TAP; TrGrPo

Hymn to the Orange. Shih Ching, *tr. fr. Chinese* by Wu-chi Liu. SuSp

Hymn to the Saints, and to Marquis Hamilton. John Donne. NOSC

Hymn to the Spirit of Nature. Shelley. *See* Life of life! thy lips enkindle.

Hymn to the Sun, The. Akhenaton, *tr. fr. Egyptian* by J. E. Manchip White. ArNa, *sh. vers.*; TTY

Hymn to the Sun, *sels.* Akhenaton. *tr. fr. Egyptian.*
   "Cattle browse peacefully." EaPr, *tr.* by Jacquetta Hawkes

Hymn to the Sun. Charles Montague Doughty. *Fr.* Dawn in Britain, The. FaBoTw

Hymn to the Sun. William A. Percy. TrPWD

Hymn to the Sun. Michael Roberts. FaBoCh; OxBTC

Hymn to the Sun. *Unknown.* TTTS

Hymn to the Supreme Being. Christopher Smart. ChIV-1

Hymn to the Supreme Being on Recovery from a Dangerous Fit of Illness, *sels.* Christopher Smart.
   "But, O immortals! What had I to plead." NOEC

Hymn to the Thousand Islands. H. Cordelia Ray. CBWP-3

Hymn to the Virgin, The, *sels.* Ieuan ap Hywel Swrdwal.
   "O mighty lady, our leading / to have." AngWe
   "O trusty Christ that wearest a crown." AngWe

Hymn to the Virgin. Sir Walter Scott. *Fr.* Lady of the Lake, The. EnRP

Hymn to the Virgin. *Unknown.* NoSic

Hymn to the Virgin Mary. Conor O'Riordan, *tr. fr. Irish* by Eleanor Hull. TIRV

Hymn to the West. Edmund Clarence Stedman. *See* O Thou, whose glorious orbs on high.

Hymn to the Winds. Joachim du Bellay, *tr. fr. French* by Andrew Lang. AWP

Hymn to Tirumal (Visnu). Kirantaiyar, *tr. fr. Tamil* by A. K. Ramanujan. PLW

Hymn to Tsui-Xgoa. *Unknown, tr. fr. Hottentot.* PeSA

Hymn to Venus, The, *sels. Unknown, formerly at.* to Homer, *tr. fr. Greek* by Congreve.
   "Among the springs which flow from Ida's head." OBVE
   "But when the golden-thron'd Aurora made." OBVE

Hymn to Vishnu. Jayadeva, *tr.* by Sir Edwin Arnold. *Fr.* Gita Govinda, The. AWP

Hymn to Zeus. Aeschylus, *tr.* by Gilbert Murray. *Fr.* Agamemnon. NAWM-1; WGRP

Hymn to Zeus. Cleanthes, *tr. fr. Greek* by Edward H. Plumptre. WGRP

Hymn Tunes, The. Edward Lucie-Smith. PBCV

Hymn Written for the Two Hundredth Anniversary of the Old South Church, Beverly, Massachusetts. Lucy Larcom. OHIP

Hymn Written in Windsor Forest, A. Pope. *See* All hail, once pleasing, once inspiring shade.

Hymnal. Harold Vinal. TrPWD

Hymne I: Generall Invitation to Praise God, A. George Wither. *Fr.* Hallelujah; or, Britain's Second Remembrancer. SeCV-1

Hymne for the Epiphanie, A; Sung as by the three Kings. Richard Crashaw. *See* Bright Babe! whose awfull beautyes [*or* beauties] make.

Hymne in Honour of Beautie, An, *sels.* Spenser.

Hymn[e] in Praise [*or* Prayse] of Neptune, A. Thomas Campion. BoNaP; NOBE; OBEV; WiR

Hymn[e] of Heavenly Beauty [*or* Beautie], An. (Rapt with the rage of mine own ravisht thoguht.) Spenser. PeECV
Sels.
   "But whoso may, thrice happy man him hold." WGRP

Hymne to Christ, at the Author's Last Going into Germany, A. John Donne. EBEV; EnRePo; ESCV; LiTB; MeLP; NAEL-1; NOSC; OxAEP-1; PeECV; SeCV-1

Hymn[e] to God My God, In My Sickness[e]. John Donne. ChTr; EBEV; EnRePo; ESCV; HeIL; HeIP; ImPo; InPS; MeLP; NAEL-1; NoP; NOSC; OAEL-1; OBD; OxAEP-1; PoE; PoEL-2; PPP; SeCP; SeCV-1; SoSe; TFi; TOF; TrPWD

Hymne to God the Father, A. Ben Jonson. *See* Hear me [*or* Heare mee], O God!

Hymn[e] to Our Saviour on the Cross[e], A. George Chapman. PeECV; PoEL-2

Hymns, *sels.* Callimachus, *tr. fr. Greek by* Barbara Hughes Fowler.
  Hymn to Apollo. HePo
  Hymn to Artemis. HePo
  Hymn to Demeter. HePo
  On the Bath of Pallas. HePo
Hymns and Spiritual Songs, *sels.* Christopher Smart.
  Ascension of Our Lord Jesus Christ. NOCV
  Epiphany. NOCV
  Nativity of Our Lord and Saviour Jesus Christ, The. EBEV; HAP; NOBE; NOCV; PoEL-3; SCGP
    (Christmas Day, *sts.* 6–9.) ChTr; OBCP
    (Hymn.) NAs; NOEC
  St. Philip and St. James. NOCV; NOEC
Hymns for the Amusement of Children, *sels.* Christopher Smart.
  Elegance. NOCV
  For Saturday. FaBoCh; NOEC; OxBChV
    (Hymn for Saturday.) OxBChV
    (Lark's Nest, A.) FaBoCh
  Gratitude. NOEC
  Long-Suffering of God. NOCV
  Loveliness. NOCV
  Mirth. OxBChV
  Moderation. NOCV
  Mutual Subjection. NOCV
    (Consideration for Others.) OxBChV
  Taste. ChIV-1; NOCV
Hymns of Astræa [in Acrostic Verse], *sels.* Sir John Davies.
  Month of September, The. SiPSBD
  Of Astræa. SiPSBD
  Of Her Justice. SiPSBD
  Of Her Magnanimity. SiPSBD
  Of Her Memory. SiPSBD
  Of Her Mind. SiPSBD
  Of Her Moderation. SiPSBD
  Of Her Will. SiPSBD
  Of Her Wisdom. SiPSBD
  Of Her Wit. SiPSBD
  Of the Innumerable Virtues of Her Mind. SiPSBD
  Of the Organs of Her Mind. SiPSBD
  Of the Passions of Her Heart. SiPSBD
  Of the Sunbeams of Her Mind. SiPSBD
  On Her Phantasy. SiPSBD
  To All the Princes of Europe. SiPSBD
  To Astræa. SiPSBD
  To Envy. SiPSBD
  To Flora. SiPSBD
  To Her Picture. SiPSBD
  To the Lark. SiPSBD
  To the Month of May. SiPSBD
  To The Nightingale. SiPSBD
  To the Rose. SiPSBD
  To the Spring. SiPSBD
  To the Sun. SiPSBD
Hymns of the Marshes, *sels.* Sidney Lanier.
  Sunrise. PoEL-5
Hymns to Our Lady of Chartres, *sels.* Geoffrey Hill.
  "Eia, with handbells, jews' harps, risible." DiPo
Hymns to the Night, *sels.* "Novalis", *prose poem vers.*, *tr. fr. German by* Robert Bly.
  Second Hymn to the Night, The. NU
Hymnus: "God be in my hede." *Unknown. See* God Be in My Head.
Hymnus in Noctem. George Chapman. *Fr.* Shadow of Night, The. PoEL-2
Hynde Horn. *Unknown.* GN
Hypatia, *sels.* Elizabeth Tollet.
  "What cruel laws depress the female kind." ECWP; NOEC
Hyperbole! Can't you arise. Prose for Des Esseintes. Donald Davie, *after the French of* Stéphane Mallarmé. OBVE
Hyperion; a Fragment. Keats. EnRP; OAEL-2
  Sels.
  Bruised Titans, The. OBNC
  "Deep in the shady sadness of a vale." FHYEP; OxAEP-2, bk. I–III; PoEL-4
    (Saturn.) OBNC; TrGrPo
  Recollection of the Stone Circle near Keswick, A. FaBoPP
  "So ended Saturn; and the God of the Sea." FHYEP
  "Thus in alternate uproar and sad peace." FHYEP
Hypnos, seeing how. Licymnios, *tr. fr. Greek by* Sam Hamill. InMo
Hypochondriacs/ Spend the winter at the bottom of Florida and the summer on top of the Adirondriacs. Oh to Be Odd! Ogden Nash. CBNP
Hypochondriacus. Charles Lamb. BXAP
Hypocrisy will serve as well. Samuel Butler. FaBoEE
Hypocrite, The. John Caryll. APAS

Hypocrite, The. Kalonymos ben Kalonymos, *tr. fr. Hebrew by* J. Chotzner. *Fr.* Touchstone, The. TrJP
Hypocrite Auteur. Archibald MacLeish. AmPP
Hypocrite is strange of race, A. The Hypocrite. Kalonymos ben Kalonymos, *tr. fr. Hebrew by* J. Chotzner. *Fr.* Touchstone, The. TrJP
Hypocrite Swift. Louise Bogan. PoA
Hypocrite Women. Denise Levertov. CAPP; MAT; NALW; NMM; PoM
Hypocrites shed tears. On Watching Politicians Perform at Martin Luther King's Funeral. Etheridge Knight. NNaP
Hypsithilla, ask me over. An Invitation to an Invitation. Catullus, *tr. fr. Latin by* Gardner E. Lewis. ErPo
Hysteria. Chu Shu-chen, *tr. fr. Chinese by* Kenneth Rexroth. NaP
Hywel and Blodwen. Idris Davies. AngWe

I

I. E. E. Cummings. NYBP
"I". Louis Golding. TrJP
I/ never/ guessed any. I. E. E. Cummings. NYBP
I/ never liked/ white folks. Alice Walker. *Fr.* Once. BlSi; PoBA
I/ want you/ to listen. Kenneth Patchen. *Fr.* Journal of Albion Moonlight, The. NaP
I, a blue wolf. The "Word" of a Wolf Encircled by the Hunt. Sandag, *tr. fr. Mongolian by* C. R. Bawden. WTO
I, a boat with a bony keel. A Dentist's Window. James K. Baxter. OxBC
I a/ cat who/ coated. Kitty and Bug. John Hollander. SoCa
  (?) SoCa
I, a Most Wretched Atlas. Heine, *tr. by* Emma Lazarus. *Fr.* Homeward Bound. TrJP
I, a princess, king-descended, decked with jewels, gilded, drest. A Royal Princess. Christina Rossetti. BrRo
I, a ship, built on the profits/ from my master's amorous trade. Philip of Thessalonica, *tr. fr. Greek by* Robin Skelton. GrAn
I, a slave, chained to an oar of poem. Stoic. Lawrence Durrell. NYBP
I a tender young maid have been courted by many. My Thing Is My Own. *Unknown.* CoMu
I, a traveler, came from south of the river. A Traveler's Moon. Po Chü-i, *tr. fr. Chinese by* Chiang Yee. SuSp
I abdicate my daily self that bled. Vita Nuova. Stanley Kunitz. VGW
I abhor the slimy [or slimie] kiss [or kisse]. Kisses Loathesome. Robert Herrick. CaPo; CBLP; FaBoBl; OxBSP
I abide and abide and better abide. Sir Thomas Wyatt. BoLoP; EnLoPo; SiPS; SiPSBD
I add my *miss you* scrawl. (*LL*) Entries in a Diary. Matthew Sweeney. IB
I add my silence. Bramble. Peretz Kaminsky. BTR
I add one further word to you, a question rather. Henri Michaux, *tr. fr. French by* Richard Ellmann. *Fr.* I Am Writing to You from a Far-Off Country. AnRep
I admire your felicitous phrasing. A. M. Sayers. PeLi
I adore you, O Beauty, with my monochordal eye! (*LL*) Negro Mask. Léopold Sédar Senghor. NegPo
I advance for as long as forever is. (*LL*) Twenty-four Years. Dylan Thomas. CMoP; MAT; MoAB; NAs; OxBSP
I advise rest; the farmhouse. To a Print of Queen Victoria. James K. Baxter. OxBC
I advocate a semi-revolution. A Semi-Revolution. Robert Frost. LiTM
I ain't gonna tell no body. 34 Blues. Charlie Patton. FaBoPV
I ain't got long to stay here. (*LL*) Steal Away to Jesus. *Unknown.* BPo
I aint, ner don't p'tend to be. My Philosofy. James Whitcomb Riley. AnAmPo
I ain't never been to heaven but Ah been told. Swing Low, Sweet Chariot. *Unknown.* GBP
I ain't superstitious. Superstitions. Maggie Pogue Johnson. CBWP-4
I almost ruined the stew and where. The Pigs for Circe in May. Joanne Kyger. PoM
I, Alphonso, live and learn. Alphonso of Castile. Emerson. NOBA
I already knew the principles of a perennial garden. What You're Teaching Me. Ron Schreiber. ETG
I always choose the plainest food. In Praise of Water-Gruel. Matthew Green. *Fr.* Spleen, The. FaBoUs
I always fall in love with tired. At Last. Eileen Myles. PFL
I always felt like a bird blown through the world. Stripping and Putting on. May Swenson. WeW
I always had a thing for Natassja Kinski. Seduced by Natassja Kinski. Ana Castillo. AfAz
I always knew/ you were singing! Throat Song: The Whirling Earth. Wendy Rose. HATNAP

I always like summer. Knoxville, Tennessee. Nikki Giovanni. BlSi; BPo; PoBA; SiSoPo

I always loved this solitary hill. Infinito, L'. Giacomo Leopardi, tr. fr. Italian by Lorna De' Lucchi. AWP

I always loved to call my lady Rose. Unknown. EIL

I always remember West Lake. Tune: "Song of the Wine Spring." P'an Lang, tr. fr. Chinese by James J. Y. Liu. SuSp

I always say I won't go back to the mountains. Sourdough Mountain Lookout. Philip Whalen. NeAP; PoBeRe; PoM

I always see, I don't know why. The Knowledgeable Child. L. A. G. Strong. OBMV

I always shout when Grandma comes. Afternoon with Grandmother. Barbara A. Huff. FaPON

I always take one you don't expect. Photograph. Sue May. DT

I always think of a coffin's quiet. A Poem for a Poet. Audre Lorde. NMM

I always thought if I could just. Place Where Things Got. Heather McHugh. NAmP90

I always wanted a red balloon. Tragedy. Jill Spargur. BLPA

I always wanted to give birth. The Mother Poem (two). Jackie Kay. NBrP

I always was afraid of Somes's Pond. Atavism. Elinor Wylie. NALW; PoA

I always wondered why. The Answer. Chuck Wachtel. UL

I Am. John Clare. CoGr; EBEV; EBVV; EnRP; ErPo; EnVR; FHYEP; GTBS-P; HAP; InvP; LiTB; NAEL-2; NOBE; NOBVV; NoP; OAEL-2; OBNC; PeECV; PlP; PoEL-4; Prf; PrIm; TFi; TOF; TrGrPo; TRP

I Am. Hilda Conkling. FaPON

I Am. Bill Kushner. UL

I am a babe of royalty. Royal Education. Winthrop Mackworth Praed. OBSV

I am a bairn. De. Robert Alan Jamieson. FaBoVe

I am a bard of no regard. Burns. Fr. Jolly Beggars, The. EnRP, sl. diff. vers.; NBLV; PoE; PoEL-4

I Am a Black Woman. Mari Evans. NMM

I am a bold Coachman, and drive a good hack. Hackney Coachman, The; Or, The Way to Get a Good Fare. Hannah More. WoRP

I am a bonded highwayman, Cole Younger is my name. Cole Younger. Unknown. AmFP; BeLS

I Am a Book I neither Wrote nor Read. Delmore Schwartz. TAP

I am a boy. A Young David: Birmingham. Helen Morgan Brooks. PoNe

I am a broken-hearted milkman, in grief I'm arrayed. Polly Perkins. Unknown. ELP; OxBoLi; PeLV; PlP

I am a bunch of red roses. Love Song ("I am a bunch of red roses.") Unknown, tr. fr. Turkish by Reza Baraheni and Zahra-Soltan Shokoohtaezeh. BoWoP

I Am a Cowboy in the Boat of Ra. Ishmael Reed. NIP; NoP; PoBA; PrIm

I Am a Creature. Giuseppe Ungaretti, tr. fr. Italian by David McDuff and Jon Silkin. PeFWW

I am a dispossessed Ontario wood. Silverthorn Bush. Robert Finch. NOBC

I am a downright Country-man, both faithful (aye) and true. The Downright Country-Man; or, The Faithful Dairy Maid. Unknown. CoMu

I am a faire maide, if my glasse doe not flatter. The Wooing Maid. Martin Parker. CoMu

I am a feather on the bright sky. The Delight Song of Tsoai-Talee. N. Scott Momaday. CDW; EaPr; GrPl; InPK

I Am A Finn, sels. James Tate.
  I Am a Finn. BAP-91
  I Am Still a Finn. BAP-91

I Am a Finn. James Tate. Fr. I Am A Finn. BAP-91

I am a frog. The Frog Prince. Stevie Smith. HAP; Mes; NTP

I am a gentle Anarchist. The Gentle Anarchist. Brunton Stephens. NOBAu

I am a gentleman in a dustcoat trying. Piazza Piece. John Crowe Ransom. AnAmPo; BoLoP; CoGr; ErPo; HeIP; MeMAP; MoAB; MoAmPo; MoP; NAAL-2; NoAM; NOBA; NoP; OPOP; OxBA; Poetr; Son; TAP; TFi; TrGrPo

I am a German just arrived. Unknown. FaBoEH

I am a gold lock. Lock and Key. Unknown. ReMoGo

I am a hand weaver to my trade. The Weaver and the Factory Maid. Unknown. OBET

I Am a Horse. Hans Arp, tr. fr. French. FaBoNo, tr. by Harriet Watts.

I Am a Hunchback. Robert Louis Stevenson. OxBSP

I am a jolly soldier. Bunker's Hill, or the Soldier's Lamentation. John Freeth. NOEC

I am a jolly young fellow. The Jolly Driver. Unknown. CoMu

I am a jovial collier lad, as blithe as blithe can be. Down in a Coal Mine. J. B. Geoghegan. AmFP; SWP

I am a jovial marriner, our calling is well known. The Jovial Marriner; or, The Sea-Man's Renown. John Playford. CoMu

I am a jovial miner. The Miner's Ballad. Lewis Morris. AngWe

I am a king's daughter, you a king's wife. A Letter to Her Mother. Eristi-Aya, tr. fr. Akkadian by Willis Barnstone. BoWoP

I am a lady. Small Sad Song. Alastair Reid. NYBP

I am a lady young in beauty waiting. (LL) Piazza Piece. John Crowe Ransom. AnAmPo; BoLoP; CoGr; ErPo; HeIP; MeMAP; MoAB; MoAmPo; MoP; NAAL-2; NoAM; NOBA; NoP; OPOP; OxBA; Poetr; Son; TAP; TFi; TrGrPo

I am a lamp, a lamp that is out. She Warns Him. Frances Cornford. EnLoPo

I am a lioness. 'Aisha bint Ahmad al-Qurtubiyya, tr. fr. Arabic by Elene Margot Kolb. WPOW

I Am a Little Church (No Great Cathedral). E. E. Cummings. MeMAP

I am a little girl with my pants pulled down around my ankles. Pants. Lisa Vice. GLP

I am a little orphan girl. An Orphan Girl. Mrs. Henry Linden. CBWP-4

I am a little world made cunningly. John Donne. Fr. Holy Sonnets. ChIV-1; EnRePo; ESCV; NAEL-1; NIP; NoP; PoE; SeCP; Son; TEP

I am a lone, unfathered chick. Orphan Born. Robert J. Burdette. OBAL

I am a man before the mast, I plough the trackless sea. The Common Sailor. Unknown. OxBSS

I am a man defeated in his loins. Beggar to Burgher. A. R. D. Fairburn. PeNZ

I am a man now. Here. R. S. Thomas. GTBS-P; RB

I am a man of war and might. A Soldier. Sir John Suckling. PoE; SeCV-1

I am a man with no ambitions. The Advantages of Learning. Martial, tr. fr. Latin by Kenneth Rexroth. ErPo

I am a miner. The light burns blue. Nick and the Candlestick. Sylvia Plath. CAPP; CoAP; LCAP; NALW; PBWP; Poetr

I am a name clanging. I Hear the Shuffle of the People's Feet. Sterling Plumpp. Jaz

I Am a Negro. Muhammad al-Faituri, tr. fr. Arabic by Halim El-Dabh. TTY

I Am a Parcel of Vain Strivings Tied. Thoreau. GGP; NoP; PFP; PoEL-4; TAP

I am a plane-tree. I was sound and strong when the blasts. Philip of Thessalonica, tr. fr. Greek by Edwin Morgan. GrAn

I am a poet, a unanimous. Italy. Giuseppe Ungaretti, tr. fr. Italian by David McDuff and Jon Silkin. PeFWW

I am a poor lad and my fortune is bad. Limbo. Unknown. OBET

I am a poor old man, come listen to my song. When This Old Hat Was New. Unknown. OBET

I am a poor prisoner condemned to die. The Execution of Luke Hutton. Unknown. OBET

I am a poor wayfaring stranger. Poor Wayfaring Stranger. Unknown. AmFP

I am a pretty wench. Unknown. OxNR

I am a puppet. Paul Hyland. Fr. Poems of Z. PWE

I am a reaper whose muscles set at sundown. All my oats are cradled. Harvest Song. Jean Toomer. NoP

I am a rebel soldier and far from my home. (LL) One Morning in May [or The Nightingale]. Unknown. AS

I am a rich widow, I live all alone. The Rich Widow. Unknown. AmFP

I am a river. No More. Carl Clark. JB

I am a roving gambler, I've gambled all around. The Roving Gambler. Unknown. AS

I am a roving shanty boy, love to sing and dance. The Roving Shanty Boy. Unknown. AmFP

I am a roving traveler and go from town to town. The Gamboling Man. Unknown. AS

I am a sailor stout and bold. The Rambling Sailor. Unknown. OxBSS

I am a sea-shell flung. Frutta di Mare. Geoffrey Scott. ChTr; Mes; OBMV

I am a senseless thing, with a hey, with a hey. A New Ballad, to an Old Tune, Called, I Am the Duke of Norfolk. Unknown. APAS

I am a shade. A Shade of Night. Amos Neufeld. BTR

I am a Sheep, and not an Ass. (LL) The Blind Sheep. Randall Jarrell. NYBP; OBAL

I am a sincere man. José Martí, tr. fr. Spanish by Seymour Resnick. Fr. Simple Verses. TTY

I am a sinful man of men. The Joyce's Repentance. Unknown, tr. fr. Irish by Douglas Hyde. TIRV

I am a skinny girl. The Skinny Girl. Anne Hébert, tr. fr. French by Willis Barnstone. BoWoP

I am a sleeping body. Ark Apprehensive. Jay Macpherson. Fr. Ark, The. NOBC

I am a soldier blithe and gay. The Rambling Soldier. *Unknown.* OBET

I am a solitary man, not a democracy. Yehuda Amichai, *tr. fr. Hebrew. Fr.* Travels of a Latter-Day Benjamin of Tudela. PoSu, *tr. by* Ruth Nevo

I am a soul in the world: in. The Invention of Comics. Amiri Baraka. CRP; LiTM; PoBA

I am a spring. The Well. Thomas Edward Brown. NOBVV

I am a stag: of seven tines. The Alphabet Calendar of Amergin. *Unknown, tr. fr. Irish by* Robert Graves. BIrV

I am a Star. Inge Auerbacher. BTR

I am a stranger in the land. Death. *Unknown.* BLPA

I am a sundial, and I make a botch. On a Sundial. Hilaire Belloc. FaBoEE

I am a sundial. Ordinary words. Hilaire Belloc. FaBoEE

I am a sundial, turned the wrong way round. Hilaire Belloc. FaBoEE

I am a thief. Listen. Jessica Hagedorn. WPOW

I am a very mature person. A Decision. Edith Södergran, *tr. fr. Swedish by* Jaakko A. Ahokas. PBWP

I am a very old pussy. An Old Cat's Confessions. Christopher Pearse Cranch. OBCA

I Am a Victim of Telephone. Allen Ginsberg. NBLV

I am a wandering, bitter shade. What's in a Name? Helen F. More. PAH

I am a weaver by my trade. Wil the Merry Weaver, and Charity the Chamber-Maid; or, A Brisk Encounter between a Youngman and His Love. *Unknown.* CoMu

I am a widow, robed in black, alone. Christine de Pisan, *tr. fr. French by* Willis Barnstone. BoWoP

I am a wild and wicked youth. The Rambling Boy. *Unknown.* OBET

I am a wise fellow; and, which is more, an officer. A Man of Qualities. Shakespeare. *Fr.* Much Ado about Nothing. CBCK

I Am a Woman, *sels.* Akhtar Amiri, *tr. fr. Farsi by* Fereshte Mahamadi. "My home is the mountain." WPOW

I am a woman and my poems. The Practice of Magical Evocation. Diane Di Prima. PoBeRe; PoM

I am a woman controlled. The Scream. May Miller. Poetr

I am a woman of Heng-t'ang. High Dike. Li Ho, *tr. fr. Chinese by* A. C. Graham. PLT

I am a woman with paper. Poem for a Chorus. Marie Cartier. CrSp

I am a young dairy maid, buxom and tight. The Buxom Young Dairy Maid. *Unknown.* OBET

I am a young executive. No cuffs than mine are cleaner. Executive. Sir John Betjeman. NOBL; PlP

I am a young girl. *Unknown, tr. fr. French by* Carol Cosman. PBWP

I am a young girl, gay. *Unknown, tr. fr. French by* Willis Barnstone. BoWoP

I am a young jolly brisk sailor. Tarpauling Jacket. *Unknown.* OxBoLi; PeVV

I am a youthful lady, my troubles they are great. A New Song Called the *Victory. Unknown.* OxBSS
(Victory.) CoMu

I am abstract. Anthony Barnett. VaA

I am adrift in a desert where too much sun. Desert Shipwreck. Barbara Leslie Jordan. GoYe

I am afraid. Wedding Day. Seamus Heaney. LPA; OxAEP-2

I am afraid it may be Ilia. Fear. Anna Hajnal, *tr. fr. Hungarian by* Daniel Hoffman. BoWoP

I am afraid of being crushed in the pincers. Sometimes. Greg Kuzma. Poetsp

I am afraid to own a body. Emily Dickinson. LiTA

I am afraid to think about my death. No Coward's Song. James Elroy Flecker. OxBSP

I am after, but not before. After. Anthony Barnett. VaA

I am alert to these letters in extraordinary numbers. Bordering Manuscript. James Applewhite. PoA

I am Alice of Daphne, and my heart clogs for John Pounden. Alice of Daphne, 1799. John Ennis. PBCIP

I am alive at night. Moon Song, Woman Song. Anne Sexton. PPP

I am alive — I guess. Emily Dickinson. NOBA

I am all bent to glean the golden ore. To His Lady Selvaggia Vergiolesi; Likening His Love to a Search for Gold. Cino da Pistoia, *tr. fr. Italian by* Dante Gabriel Rossetti. AWP

I am all things. Some Magic. James Koller. PoM

I am almost afraid, to tell the truth. Paul Verlaine, *tr. fr. French by* Philip L. Miller. RiWo

I Am Almost Asleep. Eldon Grier. MoCV

I am alone; / It is winter y. *(LL)* Alone. Walter de la Mare. CBLP; ChTr; EnLoPo

I am already a singing flower. The Singing Flower. Shu Ting, *tr. fr. Chinese by* Carolyn Kizer *with* Y.H. Zhao. SpMi

I am already quite scarce. For years [*or* now]. Dan Pagis, *tr. fr. Hebrew by* Stephen Mitchell.
(Last Ones, The.) PoSu, *tr. by* Robert Friend.

I am always aware of my mother. Mother. Nagase Kiyoko, *tr. fr. Japanese by* Kenneth Rexroth *and* Iuko Atsumi. AIW; BoWoP; WPJ

I am always here leaning against the fog. Clouds. Bruce Dawe. FaBoMA

I am Ambassador of Otherwhere. From the Embassy. Robert Graves. PoA

I Am America. Luis Omar Salinas. AfAz

I Am an American. Elias Lieberman. FaPON; PoLF

I Am an Ancient Mariner. *Unknown.* OxBSS

I am an ancient reluctant conscript. Old Timers. Carl Sandburg. NoAM

I am an apple, tossed. Sokrates to Xanthippé. Plato, *tr. fr. Greek by* Peter Jay. GrAn

I am an old woman. It Must Be. Linda Hogan. SRLS

I am an owl of orders gray. The Song of the Owl. Richard Kendall Munkittrick. OBCA

I am anxious after praise. Egoism. W. Craddle. FiBHP

I am approaching. Past dry. Loot. Thom Gunn. ErPo

I am as brisk. Keats. CBNP

I am as brown as brown can be. The Brown Girl. *Unknown.* ELP; ESPB, *A and B vers.*; OBET
(Bonny Brown Girl, The.) OxBB

I Am As God And God As I. "Angelus Silesius," *tr. fr. German. Fr.* Cherubical Wanderer, The. GePo, *tr. by* George C. Schoolfield.

I Am as Happy as a Queen on Her Throne. Mrs. Henry Linden. CBWP-4

I am as I am and so will I be. Sir Thomas Wyatt. NoSic; SiPS; SiPSBD

I am as large as God, and God as small as I. I Am As God And God As I. "Angelus Silesius," *tr. fr. German. Fr.* Cherubical Wanderer, The. GePo, *tr. by* George C. Schoolfield

I am as light as any roe. *Unknown.* MiEL

I am ashamed before the earth. Therefore I Must Tell the Truth. Torlino, *tr. fr. Navajo Indian by* Washington Matthews. STP

I am asking about the way ahead. Lenrie Peters. HBAPE

I am asking toward the light! *(LL)* I arise, facing East. Mary Austin. EaPr

I Am Asking You to Come Back Home. Jo Carson. ETG; RaBo

I am asleep, dreaming a terrible dream, so I awake. Light. Frank Bidart. *Fr.* Elegy. HCAP

I am at Deep Well where the spirit-trees. Roland Robinson. *Fr.* Deep Well. CBAP; NOBAu

I am at ease. *(LL)* Free woman, A. At last free! The mother of Sumangala. AIW; BoWoP

I am Athenian, that was my city. Erucius, *tr. fr. Greek by* Peter Levi. GrAn

I am Attibon Legba. Attibon Legba. René Depestre, *tr. fr. French by* Ellen Conroy Kennedy. *Fr.* Epiphanies of the Voodoo Gods. NegPo

I Am Babi Yar. Ginger Porter. BTR

I am back from up the country — very sorry that I went. Up the Country. Henry Lawson. CBAP

I am Baukis the bride's. Epitaph on a Betrothed Girl. Erinna, *tr. fr. Greek by* Lenore Mayhew. GrAn

I am become a frightful bloody murtherer. Fragment from the Elizabethans. W. Bridges-Adams. FaBoCo

I am become a shell of delicate alleys. Airliner. Francis Webb. CBAP; NOBAu

I am becoming a god! Everything Is Possible. Robert Pack. PPP

I am becoming one. A Poem of Towers. James Wright. CAPP

I am Bei-shung, they call me the white bear. Bei-shung. Gerard Benson. OBAP

I am beset by spirits, layer on layer. The Fathers. Ann Stanford. IMW

I am black and I have seen black hands. I Have Seen Black Hands. Richard Wright. PoBA

I am bleeding. The Song of the Woman with Her Parts Coming Out. Susan Griffin. GLP

I am blessed with my location. The Lost Pictures. Hollis Spurgeon Summers. HoPM

I am blessing two, not one. The Time of Creation Has Come. *Yoruba Oral Tradition, tr. by* Ulli Beier. WTO

I am both Watutsi and Pygmy. Old Man in New Country. James Berry. NBrP

I am Branson; Nature's laws. Henry Charles Beeching *and* John Bowyer Nichols. *Fr.* Balliol Rhymes. FaBoEE

I am bright with the wonder of you. Brightness. Denis Glover. PeNZ

"I am busy," said the sea. Day. Cecil Arthur Spring-Rice. BoTP

I am but a little woman. Kivkarjuk, *tr. fr. Eskimo.* WTO

I am but finite, yet thine infinitely. *(LL)* Artillerie [*or* Artillery]. George Herbert. GeHe; InPS; NoP; PoEL-2; SeCV-1

I am, by fate, slave to your will. To My More Than Meritorious Wife. The Earl of Rochester. OxBSP

I am called by name of man. *Unknown*. GBP

I am called Childhood. In Play is all my mind. Sir Thomas More. *Fr. Pageant Verses.* (Childhood.) EnRePo

I am called Chyldhod [*or* Childhoud], in play is all my mynde [*or* mind]. Pageant Verses. Sir Thomas More. AAS; Mes

I am carrying your grin. Diary of Days for Adjoa. Jackie Kay. DT

I Am Cassander Come Down From the Sky. Samuel Johnson. CBNP

I am caught up in her. Woman. Jane Chambers. IHMS

I am Charlotte. I don't say hello. Charlotte, Her Book. Elizabeth Bartlett. FaBoWP

I Am Cherry Alive. Delmore Schwartz. NTP; TTTS

I am climbing. *Unknown, tr. fr. Crow Indian by* W. S. Merwin. STP

I am cold and alone. The Boy Fishing. E. J. Scovell. FaBoWP

I am come into my garden, my sister, my spouse. Bible, *O.T. Fr.* Song of Solomon, The. OBVE; TOF

I am come of the seed of the people, the people that sorrow. The Rebel. Padraic Pearse. PeIV

I am come to make thy tomb. John Webster. *Fr.* Duchess of Malfi, The. ChTr; NAEL-1

I am concerned because my mind. Ballade to My Psychoanalyst. Kenneth Lillington. FiBHP

I am constantly wounded. *Unknown, tr. fr. Latin by* Willis Barnstone. *Fr.* Carmina Burana. PGA

I am content. The Fossil. Boynton Merrill, Jr. CRP

I am content, I do not care. Careless Content. John Byrom. NOEC

I am cut down. (*LL*) To the Sphinx. Silvia Dobson. VBLP

I am dangerous. Scissor-Man. George MacBeth. FaBoMo

I am dead. The Larva. Tadeusz Rózewicz, *tr. fr. Polish by* Magnus F. Krynski. PoSu

I am dead, Horatio. Wretched queen, adieu! Shakespeare. *Fr.* Hamlet. FaBoRV; NAWM-1

I am dead, to be sure. A Small Fig Tree. Donald Hall. ChIV-2

I am debtor to all, to all am I bounden. The Debtor. Edwin Muir. MeMBP

I Am Disquieted When I See Many Hills. Hyam Plutzik. VGW

I am dissatisfied with my poetry. Song for Bird and Myself. Jack Spicer. Jaz

I am dressed in my old grey running suit. The Work-out. Geoffrey Movius. MAT

I am Drink, carved by a skilled hand. On a Ring. Asclepiades, *tr. fr. Greek by* Alan Marshfield. GrAn

I am driving; it is dusk; Minnesota. Driving toward the Lac Qui Parle River. Robert Bly. LCAP; NaP; NoP

I am drunk of the pot. I, Lessimus, of Salt Lake City. Robert Peters. BXAP

I am dying, Egypt, dying. Antony to Cleopatra. William Haines Lytle. BeLS (Antony and Cleopatra. BLPA

I am ebbing — but not like the sea. The Hag of Béara. *Unknown.* NOIV

I am enamored, and yet not so much. Sonnet: He Will Not Be Too Deeply in Love. Cecco Angiolieri, da Siena, *tr. fr. Italian by* Dante Gabriel Rossetti. AWP

I am entrenched. Winter. Samuel Menashe. GrPl

I am essence of Rose Solitude. Rose Solitude. Jayne Cortez. Jaz; VBLP

I am Eve, great Adam's wife. Eve. *Unknown, tr. fr. Irish by* Thomas MacDonagh. BIrV

I am expatriate. Retired Lion by the Clothesline in the Cold Attic. Laura Jensen. AnAn

I am extensible like any honest heart. (*LL*) Headline to Summarize a Passion. Tchicaya U Tam'si. NegPo

I am far away from you. After a Death. Sandra M. Gilbert. IMW

I Am Fashion's Toy. Mary E. Tucker. CBWP-1

I am featly-tripping Lee. Henry Charles Beeching. *Fr.* Balliol Rhymes. FaBoEE

I am fevered with the sunset. The Sea Gypsy. Richard Hovey. AnAmPo; FaPON; PDV

I am filled with joy. Dead Man's Song, Dreamed by One Who Is Alive. Paulinaoq, *tr. fr. Eskimo.* WTO

I am fish. Fish. Emily Townsend. NYBP

I am five. Venus's-flytraps. Yusef Komunyakaa. NAmP90

I am fixed in waiting. Sagimusume: The White Heron Maiden. Jonny Kyoko Sullivan. WPOW

I am forgotten now. Lady Ukon, *tr. fr. Japanese by* Kenneth Rexroth *and* Ikuko Atsumi. WPJ

I am fourteen. Hanging Fire. Audre Lorde. NIP; NoAM; NoP; Poetr; TRP

I am from everywhere. Edouard J. Maunick, *tr. fr. French by* Ellen Conroy Kennedy. *Fr.* As Far as Yoruba Land. NegPo

I Am from Ireland. *Unknown.* MeEL

I am from language and will return to language. Peter Riley. VaA

I am from Rasainen. On the Jewish Dealer A.S. Johannes Bobrowski, *tr. fr. German by* Ruth Mead *and* Matthew Mead. AnRep

I am full of grief, and the tear runs from my eye. Five Arabic Verses in Praise of Wine. *Unknown, tr. fr. Arabic by* Hartwig Hirschfeld. TrJP

I am furious with myself. Elsa Tió, *tr. fr. Spanish by* Willis Barnstone. BoWoP

I am Gabriel. (*LL*) Kingdom of Heaven. Léonie Adams. MoAB; MoAmPo

I am Gaspar. I have brought frankincense. The Three Kings. Rubén Darío, *tr. fr. Spanish by* Lysander Kemp. PChr

I am giving you the dark birds of night. Michele Murray. *Fr.* Dance Poem. MDDM

I am going blind. Perhaps. Lucille Clifton. CAPP

I am going home be sea. Derek Mahon. *Fr.* Afterlives. IIP

I am going to bring back Solomon. Get to Hell Outa Here. "The Mighty Sparrow." PBCV

I am going to keep things like this. (*LL*) Hawk Roosting. Ted Hughes. CMoP; GTBS-P; HAP; HeIP; LiTM; OBAP; OxBTC; PPP; TwCP; UnPo

I am going to market. Marketing. E. J. Falconer. BoTP

I/ am going to rise. Vive Noir! Mari Evans. IHMS; PoBA; NBV

I Am Going to Sleep (Suicide Poem). Alfonsina Storni, *tr. fr. Spanish by* Aliki *and* Willis Barnstone. BoWoP

I Am Goya. Andrei Voznesensky, *tr. fr. Russian by* Stanley Kunrtz. OBWP

I am greeting you, Mayor of Lagos. Mayor of Lagos. *Yoruba Oral Tradition, tr. by* Ulli Beier. WTO

I am growing mine. Carapace. Denise Levertov. PWE

I Am Growing Old. George Sands Johnson. PWR

I Am Ham Melanite. William Millett. GoYe

I am hands. In Laddery Street Herself. Laura Riding. *Fr.* Forgotten Girlhood. RB

I am harum. Harum Scarum. Roger McGough. OTCP

I Am He That Walks with the Tender and Growing Night. Walt Whitman. *Fr.* Song of Myself. AmPP; ChTr; LiTA; MoAmPo, *abr.*; NOBA; OxBA; SOTW, *much abr.*; WeW

I am he who bursts the guarded gate. Boast of Masopha. Z. D. Mangoaela, *tr. fr. Sotho.* PeSA

I am hearing the shape of the rain. In the Mountain Tent. James Dickey. CAPP; MT

I Am Here. Jimmy Santiago Baca. NAmP90

I am here, I have traversed the Tomb. He Cometh Forth into the Day. *Unknown, tr. fr. Egyptian by* Robert Hillyer. *Fr.* Book of the Dead. AWP

I am here only. Ayohu Kanogisdi. Carroll Arnett. (Death Song.) ETG

I am here to worship the blue. Wild Asters. Ruth Stone. IMW

I am here with my beautiful bountiful downy womanful child. At a Summer Hotel. Isabella Gardner. GrPl

I am Hermes. I stand in the crossroads by a windy. Anyte, *tr. fr. Greek by* Willis Barnstone. BoWoP

I am hiding an "ay." Polo. Manuel de Falla, *tr. fr. Spanish by* Philip L. Miller. RiWo

I am his Highness' dog at Kew. Epigram Engraved on the Collar of a Dog Given [*or* Which I Gave] to His Royal Highness. Pope. CoGr; FaBoCo; FaBoEE; FM; InPK; NOEC; NTCP; OxBSP (Engraved on the Collar of a Dog, Which I Gave to His Royal Highness. ChTr; ImPo; LiTB; OxBoLi; SoSe; TTTS

I am holding this turquoise. The Serenity in Stones. Simon J. Ortiz. CDW

"I Am Home," Said the Turtle. John Ciardi. ZA

"I am home," said the turtle, as it pulled in its head. "I Am Home," Said the Turtle. John Ciardi. ZA

I am./ I am from and of The Mother. A Creed for Free Women. Elsa Gidlow. SRLS

I am immortal! I know it! I feel it! Dryad Song. Margaret Witter Fuller. WGRP

I am in a desert. Bushed. Barry McKinnon. NOBC

"I Am in Danger — Sir — ." Adrienne Rich. HCAP; NALW; NOBA

I am in great misery tonight. Suibne Geilt. NOIV

I am in love, meantime, you think; no doubt you would think so. Claude to Eustace ("I am in love.") Arthur Hugh Clough. *Fr.* Amours de Voyage. EnVR; FaBoVe; NOBVV

I am in love with the laughing sickness. Zizi's Lament. Gregory Corso. NeAP; VGW

I am in my Eskimo-hunting-song mood. Eskimo Occasion. Judith Rodriguez. CBAP; FaBoWP; NOBAu

I am in need of music that would flow. Elizabeth Bishop. LPA

I am in the old room across from the synagogue. The Old Room. W. S. Merwin. NYBP

I am in the tub with my body. To My Body. Nancy Sullivan. TAP

I am inside someone. Agony, An. As Now. Amiri Baraka. AmPP; BPo; LiTM; NAAL-2; PoE; PPP

I am invited to enter these gardens. A Welshman at St. James' Park. R. S. Thomas. AngWe

I Am Ireland. Padraic Pearse, tr. fr. Irish by Lady Augusta Gregory. IIP; OBMV; PeIV

I am Jesu that cum to fight. Unknown. MiEL
(Undo Your Heart.) MeEL

I am just going outside and may be some time. Antarctica. Derek Mahon. PBCIP

I am leading a quiet life. Autobiography. Sonja Åkesson, tr. fr. Swedish by Ingrid Claréus. BoWoP

I am letting go. (LL) Even as I Hold You. Alice Walker. MT; WeW

I am like a flag unfurled in space. Presaging. Rainer Maria Rilke, tr. fr. German by Jessie Lemont. AWP; TrJP

I am like a jackfruit on the tree. The Jackfruit. Ho Xuan Huong, tr. fr. Vietnamese by Nguyen Ngoc Bich. PBWP; VBLP

I Am like a Rose. D. H. Lawrence. OxBSP

I am like Jojon, the farmhand from Tegal. Family Portrait. Eka Budianta, tr. fr. Japanese. TSaS, tr. by E.U. Kratz

I am living. (LL) The Postcards: A Triptych. Denise Levertov. SRLS

I am living more alone now than I did. The Last Chapter. Walter de la Mare. CMoP; MoBrPo

I am locked in a little cedar box. Satan Says. Sharon Olds. PBCAP

I Am Lonely. "George Eliot." Fr. Spanish Gypsy, The. GN

I am lonely. Poem for Some Black Women. Carolyn M. Rodgers. BISi

I am/ look/ ing at. You Too? Me Too — Why Not? Soda Pop. Robert Hollander. NIP

I am looking for a past. The Journey. David Ignatow. Poetsp

I am lost in hot fits. Air. Amiri Baraka. SOTW

I am Lot's pillar, caught in turning. Columns and Caryatids. Carolyn Kizer. WPE

I am luminous with age. Rites of Ancient Ripening. Meridel LeSueur. SRLS

I am made all things to all men. At His Execution. Kipling. ChIV-2

I am made to sow the thistle for wheat, the nettle for a nourishing dainty. The Price of Experience. Blake. Fr. Vala; or The Four Zoas. EnRP; Prf
(Night II Enion's Lament.) PoE

I am making/ a wind come here. Unknown, tr. fr. Crow Indian by W. S. Merwin. STP

I am making soup. Recipe: Sausage. Axionicus, tr. fr. Greek. FaBoUs

I am making the sacred smoke. Make the Earth Bright and Thanks. Meridel LeSueur. SRLS

I am man. (LL) Sizeline. Felix Mnthali. PeSAV

"I am master of the chivalric idiom" Spenser said. Master. Brendan Kennelly. BiHa

I am mighty melancholy. Vandunk's Four Humours, in Quality and Quantity. Richard Brathwaite [or Brathwait]. NOSC

I am Miss Stein. Gertrude Stein at Snails Bay. Peter Porter. OxBC

I am monarch of all I survey. Verses Supposed to Be Written by Alexander Selkirk during His Solitary Abode on the Island of Juan Fernandez. William Cowper. EBEvV; NOEC; PoEL-3; PoLF
(Solitude of Alexander Selkirk, The. GTBS; GTBS-P; LiTB

I am my ancient self. The Pilgrim. Richard Wightman. WGRP

I Am My Beloved's. Bible, O.T., tr. fr. Hebrew. Fr. Song of Solomon, The. TrJP

I Am My Beloved's, and His Desire Is towards Me. Francis Quarles. See Like to the arctic needle, that doth guide.

I am my lover's and he desires me. Bible, O.T. See I Am My Beloved's.

I am my mother's daughter. Marge Piercy. Fr. My Mother's Novel. MDDM

I am my prison. Conundrum. Carl Clark. JB

I am myself at last; now I achieve. I Am like a Rose. D. H. Lawrence. OxBSP

I am nailing them up to the cathedral door. Everywoman Her Own Theology. Alicia Ostriker. CrSp

I Am New York City. Jayne Cortez. BoWoP

I am no brazen face to mute the Lord. Rabbi Yom-Tob of Mayence Petitions His God. A. M. Klein. TrJP

I Am No Good at Love. Noël Coward. ArLo

I am no longer master of my tears. Tchicaya U Tam'si, tr. fr. French by Ellen Conroy Kennedy. Fr. Fragile. NegPo

I am no more. (LL) Tlanusi' Yi, the Leech Place. Gladys Cardiff. CDW

I am no shepherd of a child's surmises. Montana Pastoral. J. V. Cunningham. MAT; MoAmPo; PrIm; VGW

I am Not a Conspiracy Everything Is Not Paranoid. Susan Musgrave. NoAM

I am not a handsome man. Eclipse. Ed Roberson. PoNe

I am not a mechanism, an assembly of various sections. Healing. D. H. Lawrence. RaBo

I am not a metaphor or symbol. The Distant Drum. Calvin C. Hernton. FF; TTY

I am not a painter, I am a poet. Why I Am Not a Painter. Frank O'Hara. CAPP; HCAP; NeAP; NoAM; NOBA; PoE; Poetr; PoM; VCAP

I am not a sparrow or a rat. On the Thirteenth Day of the Eleventh Month I Went to the Granary for the First Time since My Illness. Mei Yao Ch'en, tr. fr. Chinese by Jonathan Chaves. SuSp

I am not afraid. (LL) Poet of the Streets. Jack Micheline. PoBeRe

I am not/ alone. Getting Wise. Marg Yeo. DT

I am not better than my brother over the way. The Bird in the Cage. Mary Effie Lee Newsome. ShDr

I am not blind. For Steph. Wendy Rose. CDW

I am not bred and born New Englander. Late Comer. Fanny de Groot Hastings. GoYe

I am not gay by your definition. Explanation. William Barber. PeHV

I am not going to invite you. Blond. Joseph de Roche. HeIP

I am not going to turn into gold. Bassos, tr. fr. Greek by Kenneth Rexroth. PGA

I am not happy here, mother! The Exile's Lament. Frances Sargent Osgood. AmWP

I Am Not I. Juan Ramón Jiménez, tr. fr. Spanish by Robert Bly. RaBo

I am not looking for your jugular. The Threat. Andrei Codrescu. UL

I Am Not Made of Fragile Elm. Martial, tr. fr. Latin by Peter Porter. FaBoBl

I am not Mahomet. E. C. Bentley. Fr. Clerihews. NOBL

I Am Not One of Those Who Left the Land. "Anna Akhmatova," tr. fr. Russian by Stanley Kunitz with Max Hayward. AnAn

I am not one who much or oft delight. Personal Talk. Wordsworth. EnRP; NOBE

I am not poor, but I am proud. Thought. Emerson. AmPP

I am not ready to die. May Sarton. Fr. Gestalt at Sixty. CrSp

I am not resigned to the shutting away of loving hearts. Dirge without Music. Edna St. Vincent Millay. CMoP; CoGr; DL; IMW; LiTA; MeMAP; TrGrPo

I am not suited for service in a country town. Planting Bamboos. Po Chü-i, tr. fr. Chinese by Arthur Waley. ArNa

I am not sure I would always fight for my life. What Would You Fight For? D. H. Lawrence. OxBSP

I am not sure if I knew the truth. Youth. "Laurence Hope." WeW

I am not there. I do not sleep. (LL) Do not stand at my grave and weep. Unknown. EaPr

I am not treacherous, callous, jealous, superstitious. A Face. Marianne Moore. OxBSP

I am not with you, sisters, in your talk. The Tea-party. Julia Ward Howe. AmWP

I am not yet born; O hear me. Prayer before Birth. Louis MacNeice. EBEvV; FaBoVe; GTBS-P; LiTB; NAs; PAW; PNI; TIRV; TwCP

I am not yet twenty-two and I am tired of living. Asclepiades, tr. fr. Greek by Barbara Hughes Fowler. Fr. Epigrams. HePo

I am not you. Africa's Plea. Roland Tombekai Dempster. TTY

I am not your God. African Easter. Abioseh Nicol. PBA

I Am Not Yours. Sara Teasdale. VGW

I am now so weary with waiting. Gaspara Stampa, tr. fr. Italian by Harold M. Priest. WPOW

I am/ ocean voyager. Whalesong. Judith Nicholls. OBAP

I am of Ireland. The Irish Dancer. Unknown. FaBoCh; GBP; NOBE; OBEV
(I Am from Ireland.) HAP; MeEL
(Ich Am of Irlaunde.) EnVB; PoEL-1
(Icham of Irlaunde.) HAP

I Am of Ireland. Unknown. IIP

I Am of Ireland. W. B. Yeats. CMoP; IIP; LiTB

I am of little worth and poor, apart. Song of Loneliness. Judah Halevi, tr. fr. Hebrew by Nina Davis Salaman. TrJP

I Am of Old and Young. Walt Whitman. Fr. Song of Myself. AmPP; ImGa, XVI, sl. shorter; LiTA; MoAmPo, abr.; NOBA; OxBA; SOTW, much abr.

I am of old and young, of the foolish as much as the wise. I Am of Old and Young. Walt Whitman. Fr. Song of Myself. AmPP; ImGa, XVI, sl. shorter; LiTA; MoAmPo, abr.; NOBA; OxBA; SOTW, much abr.

I am of Shropshire, my shins are sharp. A Shropshire Lad. Unknown. ChTr

I Am of the Earth. Anna Walters. VoR

I am of this world. Unknown, tr. fr. Japanese by Geoffrey Bownas and Anthony Thwaite. Fr. Manyo Shu, Part 2 of 4. BoWoP; IMW

I am off down the road. Goblin Feet. J. R. R. Tolkien. FaPON

I am Ojistoh, I am she, the wife. Ojistoh. Emily Pauline Johnson. NOBC

I am old. Christopher Logue. OxBTC

I am old and blind! Milton's Prayer for [or of] Patience. Elizabeth Lloyd Howell. WGRP

I am old, sick and lonely. Su Tung-p'o, tr. fr. Chinese by Robert Payne. TAL

I am olde whan age doth apele. Unknown. MiEL

I am Omar. Crazy Gypsy. Luis Omar Salinas. AfAz

I am one of a band of outlaws, Cole Younger is my name. Cole Younger. Unknown. BeLS

I am one of passion's asses. The Girls of Llanbadarn. Dafydd ap Gwilym, tr. fr. Welsh by Rolfe Humphries. OBWVE

I am one of those troubled hearts. Human Soul. René Maran, tr. fr. French by Mercer Cook. TTY

I am only nineteen. That Distance Apart. Jackie Kay. NBrP

I am, outside. Incredible panic rules. John Berryman. Fr. Dream Songs. CAPP; VCAP

I am part of this. Jonathan's Song. Owen Dodson. BTR

I am peopled by women. A Folding and Unfolding. Welton Smith. PoNe

I am picking wild grapes last year. The Winemaker's Beat-étude. Alfred W. Purdy. MoCV

I am pleased to be here. To my left is Philippa, who will be signing for me. (LL) Pretext. Stephen Rodefer. UL

I am plural. My intents are manifold. The Nondescript. Peter Scupham. SCBI

I am poor and old and blind. Belisarius. Longfellow. PoEL-5; WiR

I am poor once more! (LL) I never lost as much but twice. Emily Dickinson. BLPL; HeIP; MoAB; MoAmPo; NAAL-1; NoAM; NOBA; NoP; TAP

I am Priapus. I was put here according to custom. Lucianus, tr. fr. Greek by Edwin Morgan. GrAn

I am proud of your soft, brown eyes. David Ignatow. Fr. Sunlight: A Sequence for My Daughter. CAPP

I am provoked. Strato, tr. fr. Greek by W. G. Shepherd. GrAn; PeHV

I am Prytherch. Forgive me. I don't know. Invasion on the Farm. R. S. Thomas. PWE

I am putting makeup on empty space. Makeup on Empty Space. Anne Waldman. SRLS

I am putting you in a painting. Summer Freezes Here. Hsiung-hung, tr. fr. Chinese by Kenneth Rexroth and Ling Chung. WPC

I am Queen Anne, of whom 'tis said. Queen Anne. Unknown. ChTr

I am quite sure he thinks that I am God. Bishop Doane on His Dog. George Washington Doane. BLPA; FaBoBe

I Am Raftery ("I am Raftery, hesitant and confused.") Derek Mahon. OxBC

I Am Raftery [or Raferty]. Anthony Raftery, tr. fr. Modern Irish. AWP, tr. by Douglas Hyde

I am Raifteiri, the poet, full of courage and love. Anthony Raftery, tr. fr. Irish by Thomas Kinsella. NOIV

I am rather tall and stately. Unknown. Fr. Balliol Rhymes. FaBoEE; NOBL

I am reading. The Distant Orgasm. James Tate. AmPA

I am reading a diary at night. Discovering Lasseter. Conal Fitzpatrick. NOBAu

I am reminded, by the tan man who wings. The Elevator Man Adheres to Form. Margaret Danner. PoBA; PoNe

I am reminded of the vestment. I'm Not Here/ Never Was. Constanta Buzea, tr. fr. Romanian by Stavros Deligiorgis. BoWoP

I am resolved, this charming day. John Dyer. Fr. Country Walk, The. ECEV

I am riding on a limited express, one of the crack trains of the nation. Limited. Carl Sandburg. HAP; MoAB; MoAmPo; OxBA

I Am Rose. Gertrude Stein. OBCA; TrJP

I am Rose like anything. (LL) I Am Rose. Gertrude Stein. OBCA; TrJP

I am rubber if you want to call me that. Song of Rubber. Shao Yen-hsiang, tr. fr. Chinese. LHF, tr. by Hualing Nieh

I Am Running into a New Year. Lucille Clifton. CrSp

I am saying goodbye to the trees. The Return. Derek Mahon. SCBI

I am Scheherazade. Scheherazade. Barbara Burford. DT

I am scorned by patterns which hold. Moon at Three A.M. Lance Henson. CDW

I am searching everywhere! (LL) The Snare. James Stephens. BoTP; CH; CMoP; CoGr; PDV; SCGP

I am seeing this: two men are sitting on a pole. The Mitchells. Les A. Murray. FaBoMA

I am sending you this letter. A Line from St. David's. R. S. Thomas. AngWe

I am serious, Mrs Acorn, are you deaf? (LL) Song (October 1969). Kath Fraser. AIW; PeHV

I am sick today. Labour Pains. Yosano Akiko, tr. fr. Japanese by Kenneth Rexroth and Ikuko Atsumi. AIW; WPJ

I am silver and exact. I have no preconceptions. Mirror. Sylvia Plath. FaBoWP; HAP; HeIL; NIP; NYBP

I Am Singing the Cold Rain. Lance Henson, tr. fr. Cheyenne Indian by the author. HATNAP; STP

I am sitting across the table. Sunday at the State Hospital. David Ignatow. CAPP; RaBo

I am sitting here. The Poor Girl's Meditation. Unknown, tr. fr. Irish by Padraic Colum. BIrV; OBMV

I am sitting in a strange room listening. Baby-Sitting. Gillian Clarke. FaBoWP; NTP

I am sitting in Mike's Place trying to figure out. One Thousand Fearful Words for Fidel Castro. Lawrence Ferlinghetti. PoBeRe; VGW

I am sitting sad and lonely. Lines to Florence. Mary Weston Fordham. CBWP-2

I am slowly dying, water evaporating. George Bowering. Fr. Summer Solstice. NOBC

I Am So Glad and Very. E. E. Cummings. CMoP

I am so little and grey. The Prayer of the Mouse. Carmen Bernos de Gasztold. PDV

I am so out of love through poverty. Sonnet: Of Why He Would Be a Sculiion. Cecco Angiolieri, da Siena, tr. fr. Italian by Dante Gabriel Rossetti. AWP

I am so passing rich in poverty. Sonnet: He Jests Concerning His Poverty. Bartolomeo di Sant' Angelo, tr. fr. Italian by Dante Gabriel Rossetti. AWP

I am so tired and weary. Supplication. Joseph S. Cotter, Sr.. CDC; PoNe

I am sorry to speak of death again. Poetics against the Angel of Death. Phyllis Webb. MoCV; NOBC

I am standing for peace and non-violence. The Patriot. Nissim Ezekiel. FaBoVe

I am standing in the post office, about. I Am A Finn. James Tate. Fr. I Am A Finn. BAP-91

I am standing on the threshold of eternity at last. On the Threshold. Unknown. BLPA

I am standing upon the seashore. The Ship. Unknown. PoLF

I am staying here. (LL) I Learned To Sew. Mitsuye Yamada. LoHo

I Am Still a Finn. James Tate. Fr. I Am A Finn. BAP-91

I am still a young boy. (LL) Moses. Amir Gilboa. MHP

I am still bitter about the last place we stayed. Codicil. Ruth Stone. BoWoP

I am still hurt, Plin. A Letter for Allhallows. Peter Kane Dufault. NYBP

I Am Still Rich. Thomas Curtis Clark. PoToHe

I am strange here and often I am still trying. Evening. W. S. Merwin. NAAL-2

I am Suibne the wanderer. Suibne Geilt. NOIV

I am summoned from my bed. White Shroud. Allen Ginsberg. PoBeRe

I am surprised to find today. The Professor Waking. James Tate. FF

I am surprised to see. Letter Written on a Ferry while Crossing Long Island Sound. Anne Sexton. CoAP; NAAL-2; NYBP; TwCP

I am taking part in a great experiment. Sacred Objects. Louis Simpson. CAPP

I Am Taliesin. I Sing Perfect Metre. Unknown, tr. fr. Welsh by Ifor Williams. OBWVE

I am Te-ngau-reka-a-tu. Taiaha Haka Poem. Apirana Taylor. PeNZ

I am telling you a number of half-conditioned ideas. Sunday Evening. Barbara Guest. NeAP

I am telling you this. Blue Ruth: America. Michael S. Harper. PoBA

I am ten. Allowance. Jim Mitsui. ETG

I am that Dido which thou here do'st see. Ausonius, tr. fr. Latin by Sir Walter Ralegh. NoSic; OBVE; SiPSBD

I am That I am. (LL) A Creed for Free Women. Elsa Gidlow. SRLS

I am that man who with a luminous look. Brevities. Siegfried Sassoon. PoLF

I am that man with helmet made of thorn. For an Ex-Far East Prisoner of War. Charles Causley. OxBC

I am that Savior that vouchsafed to die. On the Inscription Over the Head of Christ on the Cross. Henry Colman. ChIV-2

I am that serpent-haunted cave. The Pythoness. Kathleen Raine. MoBrPo

I am that which began. Hertha. Swinburne. OAEL-2

I am that woman whose works are good. Sovereign Queen. Padeshah Khatun, tr. fr. Farsi by Deirdre Lashgari. WPOW

I am the acorn. Journey. Judith Nicholls. OBSP

I am the American heartbreak. American Heartbreak. Langston Hughes. AmPP; BPo; LiTM

I am the ancient Apple-Queen. Pomona. William Morris. NOBVV; WiR

I am the Ape and I can climb. Ape. George Barker. OBAP

I Am the Autumn. Itsik Manger, tr. fr. Yiddish by Joseph Leftwich. TrJP

I Am the Beginning. Isaiah Shembe, tr. fr. Zulu by G. C. Oosthuizen. WTO

I am the biggest bird there ever was. The Condor. David Liptrot. OBAP

I am the bird of the wayside. Christine Ama Ata Aidoo. PBWP

I am the bird that flutters against your window in the. Guardian Angel. Rolf Jacobsen, tr. fr. Norwegian by Robert Bly. RaBo

I am the black centipede, the rusher with a black nose. Praises of the Train. Demetrius Segooa, tr. fr. Sotho. PeSA

I Am the Blood. Isaac Rosenberg. MoBrPo

I am the blossom pressed in a book. Briefly It Enters, and Briefly Speaks. Jane Kenyon. CrSp

I am the blue! I come from the lower world. Helen. Paul Valéry, tr. fr. French by Robert Lowell. OBVE

I am the boy with his hands raised over his head. The House That Fear Built: Warsaw, 1943. Jane Flanders. CrSp; PBCAP

I am the breath of Tethra, voice of Tethra. The Sword of Tethra. William Larminie. Fr. Moytura. PeIV

I am the captain of my soul. Probably. Keith Preston. NBLV

I Am the Cat. Leila Usher. BLPA

I am the cat of cats. I am. The Cat of Cats. William Brighty Rands. OFC; OxBChV

I am the cat that walks by himself. Kipling. CRH

I am the chaunt-rann of a Singer. The Poet. Padraic Fiacc. CIP

I am the child of the Yangtse running. Child of the World. Edna L. S. Barker. GoYe

I am the dancer of the wood. The Spirit of the Birch. Arthur Ketchum. OHIP

I am the darker brother. I, Too, Sing America. Langston Hughes. PoLF

I am the Dean, and this is Mrs. Liddell. Unknown. Fr. Balliol Rhymes. FaBoEE

I am the Dean of Christ Church, Sir. Cecil Arthur Spring-Rice. Fr. Balliol Rhymes. FaBoCo; FaBoEE; NOBL

I am the disappeared woman. Disappeared Woman I. Marjorie Agosin, tr. fr. Spanish by Cola Franzen. LoHo

I Am the Door. Richard Crashaw. GeHe; NAEL-1

I Am the Duke of Norfolk. Unknown. GBP

I am the family face. Heredity. Thomas Hardy. CTC; EBEV; RB

I am the farmer, stripped of love. The Hill Farmer Speaks. R. S. Thomas. GTBS-P; OBWVE; PIP

I am the first one home. (LL) The Dancehall. Matthew Sweeney. IB

I am the flute of Daphnis. On this wall. The Flute of Daphnis. Edward Cracroft Lefroy, after the Greek of Theocritus. Fr. Echoes from Theocritus. AWP

I am the Freshly Dead Husband. Kojo Laing. HBAPE

I am the ghost of Shadwell Stair. Shadwell Stair. Wilfred Owen. FaBoTw

I Am the Gilly of Christ. Joseph Campbell. TIRV

I am the grave of Baucis the bride. Passing by. Erinna, tr. fr. Greek by Barbara Hughes Fowler. Fr. Epigrams. HePo

I am the Great Bassist. The Great Bassist. Lawson Fusao Inada. OpBo

I am the great Professor Jowett. Unknown. FiBHP

I Am the Great Sun. Charles Causley. NTP; TOF

I am the guest, the one to be indulged. (LL) Guest. D. J. Enright. Mes; OxBC

'I am the King of Terrors,' Want replied. (LL) "Prepare to meet the King of Terrors," cried. Ebenezer Elliot. NOBVV

I am the least. The Mite. Boynton Merrill, Jr. CRP

I Am the Little Irish Boy. Thoreau. NAs

I am the little New Year, ho, ho! The New Year. Unknown. BoTP

I Am the Lord. Alexander Mack, tr. fr. German by Sheema Z. Buehne. AH

I am the Lord of Light, the self-begotten Youth. He Maketh Himself One with the God Ra. Unknown, tr. by Robert Hillyer. Fr. Book of the Dead. AWP

I Am the Loveless. Martha Sansom. UnDi

I am the maid who slept with you. Alison Brackenbury. SCBI

I am the maiden in bronze set over the tomb of Midas. Cleoboulos, tr. fr. Greek by Richmond Lattimore. GrAn

I am the man that hath seen affliction. Affliction. Bible, O.T. Fr. Lamentations. TrJP

I am the man who looked for peace and found. War Poet. Sidney Keyes. PAW; PoWW

I am the mighty He-she-it. Opus Nil. Hans Arp, tr. fr. German by Michael Hamburger. CBNP

I am the mist, the impalpable mist. The Mist. Carl Sandburg. ArNa

I am the month when roses. June. Mary Weston Fordham. CBWP-2

I am the mother of sorrows. The Paradox. Paul Laurence Dunbar. AAP; PoBA

I Am the Mountainy Singer. Joseph Campbell. MoBrPo

I am the Muse who sung alway. Solution. Emerson. OBAL

I am the music of the string duet. Duet. Kathleen Jamie. PWE

I am the North Pole. Tzu Yeh, tr. fr. Chinese by Kenneth Rexroth and Ling Chung. WPC

I Am the One. Thomas Hardy. OxBTC

I am the one in your dreams. The Dark Lord of Savaiki. Alistair Campbell. PeNZ

I am the one who bathes the dust from your feet. (LL) There are flowers of Zait in the garden. Unknown. BoWoP; PBWP

I am the one who looks the other way. The Bystander. Rosemary Dobson. CBAP; Mes

I am the one whom ringdoves see. I Am the One. Thomas Hardy. OxBTC

I am the one whose praise. Hildegard von Bingen, tr. fr. Latin. CrSp

I am the one whose praise echoes on high. Hildegard von Bingen, tr. fr. Latin. CrSp; EaPr

I am the one whose thought. Death. William Bell Scott. NOBVV

I am the only being whose doom. Emily Brontë. MAT; MeMBP; NALW

I Am the People, the Mob. Carl Sandburg. AmPP; OxBA; TAP

I am the placid animal. The Dancing Dog. Florence Weinberger. BTR

I Am the Poet Davies, William. W. H. Davies. OxBSP

I am the poet of the Body and I am the poet of the Soul. Walt Whitman. Fr. Song of Myself. AmPP; LiTA; MoAmPo, abr.; NOBA; OxBA; SOTW, much abr.; WeW

I am the poet who waits. Foreplay of the Alphabet. Darrell Gray. UL

I am the Prince. Charles Causley. FF

I am the Prince in the Field. He Maketh Himself One with Osiris. Unknown, tr. fr. Egyptian by Robert Hillyer. Fr. Book of the Dead. AWP

I am the pure lotus. He Is like the Lotus. Unknown, tr. fr. Egyptian by Robert Hillyer. Fr. Book of the Dead. AWP

(Death as a Lotus Flower.) TTY, tr. by Ulli Beier

I am the pure, the true of word, triumphant. He Defendeth His Heart against the Destroyer. Unknown, tr. fr. Egyptian by Robert Hillyer. Fr. Book of the Dead. AWP

I am the pure traveler. He Entereth the House of the Goddess Hathor. Unknown, tr. fr. Egyptian by Robert Hillyer. Fr. Book of the Dead. AWP

I am the reality of things that seem. Poetry. Ella Heath. WGRP

I am the reaper. W. E. Henley. Fr. Echoes. OBNC

I am the rooftree and the keel. Tapestry Trees. William Morris. BoNaP; FaPON; OHIP

I Am the Rose of Sharon. Bible, O.T. See I am the rose of Sharon, and the lily of the valleys.

I am the rose of Sharon, and the lily of the valleys. Bible, O.T. Fr. Song of Solomon, The. BoLoP; FF; GBL; OBVE

(I Am the Rose of Sharon.) ChTr

I am the ruined queen. Dido: Swarming. Kathleen Spivack. PoA

I am the self-appointed guardian of English literature. Souvenir de Monsieur Poop. Stevie Smith. NALW

I am the serpent, fat with years. He Is like the Serpent Saka. Unknown, tr. fr. Egyptian by Robert Hillyer. Fr. Book of the Dead. AWP

I am the seventh son of the son. Malcolm X — an Autobiography. Larry Neal. BPo

I am the shadow in the shadow of the wicker. Home Revisited: Midnight. John Ciardi. NYBP

I am the shell that awaits the word. Nursery Rhyme. Leo Hamalian. PAW

I am the sister of him. Little. Dorothy Aldis. FaPON; NTCP; WHSW

I am the small million. The Seed. Hal Summers. PAW

I am the smoke king. The Song of the Smoke. W. E. B. DuBois. PoBA; UnPo

I am the sorrow in the wheat fields. Ellen Bass. NMM

I am the stage, impassive, mute and cold. Nature. Alfred de Vigny, tr. fr. French by Margaret Jourdain. AWP

I am the stone the Persians put to bear. The Statue of Nemesis at Rhamnus. Parmenion of Macedon, tr. fr. Greek by Alistair Elliot. GrAn

I am the straw. There is solace in that thought. (LL) Beauty Is the Straw. Amy Witting. NOBAu

I am the terrour of the sea. On the Crocodile. Thomas Heyrick. FM

I am the tomb of a shipwrecked man. Sail on. Theodoridas, tr. fr. Greek by Peter Jay. GrAn

I am the tomb of Crethon; here you read. The Tomb of Crethon. Leonidas of Tarentum, tr. fr. Greek by John Hermann Merivale. AWP

I am the tomb of Tellen, I contain. Leonidas of Tarentum, tr. fr. Greek by Peter Levi. GrAn

I am the true vine, and my Father is the husbandman. Bible, N.T. Fr. St. John. OBVE

I am the trumpet blown by time. The Trumpet. Ilya Ehrenburg, tr. fr. Russian by Y. Hornstein. TrJP

I am the Turquoise Woman's son. The War God's Horse Song. *Unknown, tr. fr. Navajo Indian.* LiTA, *tr. by* Dane Coolidge *and* Mary Roberts Coolidge; RB, *tr. by* Louis Watchman; TTTS

I Am the Very Model [*or* Pattern] of a Modern Major-General. W. S. Gilbert. *Fr.* Pirates of Penzance, The. NBLV; NOBL; NoP

I am the very pattern of a modern major-gineral. W. S. Gilbert. *Fr.* Pirates of Penzance, The. UV

I am the voice that often speaks. Voice. Albie Ollivierre. NBrP

I Am the Way. Alice Meynell. NOBVV; OBMV; OxBSP

I am the wee falorie man. The Wee Falorie Man. *Unknown.* FaBoVe

I am the wind which breathes upon the sea. The Mystery. *At. to* Amergin, *tr. fr. Irish by* Douglas Hyde. TIRV

I am the woman of the principal fountain. Shaman. María Sabina, *tr. fr. Spanish by* Henry Munn. WPOW

I am the woman who sits by the river. Let Us Gather at the River. Marge Piercy. SRLS

I am the yearning for good. (*LL*) I am the one whose praise echoes on high. Hildegard von Bingen. CrSp; EaPr

I am thinking of tents and tentage, tents through the ages. Thinking of Tents. Reed Whittemore. TAP

I am thinking of that boy who bragged about the day he threw. Boy at the Paterson Falls. Toi Derricotte. PBCAP

I am thinking tonight about war. Love & War & the Future & the Martians. Libby Scheier. WoWa

I am 32 years old. Writ on the Eve of My 32nd Birthday. Gregory Corso. NAs

I am this fountain's god. The River God. John Fletcher. *Fr.* Faithful Shepherdess, The. TrGrPo

I am thy father's spirit. Shakespeare. *Fr.* Hamlet. NAWM-1; OBD

I am thy fugitive, thy votary. To the Lord Love. "Michael Field." OBMV

I Am Tired. Fernando Pessoa, *tr. fr. Portuguese by* Jonathan Griffin. AnRep

I am tired of chalk-dust. Chalk-Dust. Lillian Byrnes. ShDr

I am tired of civilization. (*LL*) Tired. Fenton Johnson. PoBA; PoLF; PoNe; TTY

I am tired of cursing the Bishop. Crazy Jane on the Mountain. W. B. Yeats. CMoP

I am tired of planning and toiling. The Cry of the Dreamer. John Boyle O'Reilly. BLPA

I am tired of the tundra of the mind. The Technology of Inspiration. Lynn Emanuel. ETG
(Inspiration. NAmP90

"I am tired of this barn!" said the colt. The Barn. Elizabeth J. Coatsworth. OBCP

I am tired of work; I am tired of building up somebody else's civilization. Tired. Fenton Johnson. PoBA; PoLF; PoNe; TTY

I am tired, that is clear. I Am Tired. Fernando Pessoa, *tr. fr. Portuguese by* Jonathan Griffin. AnRep

I am tissue paper thin. Homily. Christiania Whitehead. NWP

I am to follow her. There is much grace. George Meredith. *Fr.* Modern Love. NAEL-2; NOBVV

I am to my honey what marijuana is. Skirt Dance. Ishmael Reed. FF; UL

I am to tell you, you say, what I think of our last new acquaintance. Arthur Hugh Clough. *Fr.* Amours de Voyage. FaBoVe; NOBVV

I am told that the best people have begun saying. War Has Been Given a Bad Name. Bertolt Brecht, *tr. fr. German by* John Willett. PoSu

I Am Too Near. Wislawa Szymborska, *tr. fr. Polish by* Czeslaw Milosz. BoWoP; PBWP

I am too near, too clear a thing for you. A Flower of Mullein. Lizette Woodworth Reese. MoAmPo

I am too young to grow a beard. Street Song. Thom Gunn. HeIP; NoP; OxBC

I am troubled, I'm dissatisfied, I'm Irish. (*LL*) Spenser's Ireland. Marianne Moore. FaBoWP; IIP; LiTA; LiTM; MeMAP; NoAM; NOBA; OxBA; TAP

I am troubled to-night with a curious pain. Misalliance. Ella Wheeler Wilcox. AmWP

I am trying to decide to go swimming. The Wind Is Blowing West. Joseph Ceravolo. TTTS

I am trying to describe to you a river at first light. Ideogram. William Meredith. Poetr

I am trying to imagine. Re-forming the Crystal. Adrienne Rich. TAP

I am trying/ to learn to walk again. Walk. Frank Horne. BPo

I am trying to tell you something. (*LL*) Endurance. Carolyn Forché. SV

I Am 25. Gregory Corso. PoBeRe

I am 25 years old. My Poem. Nikki Giovanni. BPo; NBV; PoBA

I am twenty-four. The Survivor. Tadeusz Rózewicz, *tr. fr. Polish by* Adam Czerniawski. PoSu

I am two fools, I know. The Triple Fool. John Donne. GBL; NOSC; SoSe

"I am unable," yonder beggar cries. A Lame Beggar. John Donne. FF; NoSic; PeLV

I am unhappy that I am not God. He Puts Me to Rest. David Ignatow. VGW

I am unity on high. The Moon Sings to the Stream. Leah Goldberg, *tr. fr. Hebrew by* Ruth Finer Mintz. *Fr.* Songs of the Stream. MHP

I am unjust, but I can strive for justice. Why I Voted the Socialist Ticket. Vachel Lindsay. MoAmPo

I am valued by men, fetched from afar. Honey-Mead: "I am valued by men, fetched from afar." Unknown, formerly at. to Cynewulf, *tr. by* Charles W. Kennedy. *Fr.* Riddles (Exeter Book). AnOE

I am very fond of the little ribs of women. Vincent McHugh. *Fr.* Talking to Myself. ErPo

I am waiting for my case to come up. Lawrence Ferlinghetti. *Fr.* Oral Messages. AiP; CAPP; GOA

I am waiting for news, let it come. Snow Poem. Rodolfo Di Biasio, *tr. fr. Italian by* Stephen Sartarelli. NeIt

I am waiting for the dawning. Waiting for the Dawning. *Unknown.* BLRP

I am waiting for you. Hyena. Edwin Morgan. OBAP

I am walking a trail. Intimidations of an Autobiography. James Tate. NoAM

I am walking and I. Ray A. Young Bear. STP

I am walking rapidly through striations of light and dark. I Dream I'm the Death of Orpheus. Adrienne Rich. NALW; NMM

I am warm. The Promise. Johari M. Kunjufu. BlSi

I am watching them churn the last milk. The Mad Yak. Gregory Corso. PoBeRe

I am weaving absent-minded red. Spots of Blood. Phyllis Webb. NOBC

I am Weary, Mother. Mary E. Tucker. CBWP-1

I am weary of lying within the chase. Ballade de Marguerite. *Unknown, tr. fr. French by* Oscar Wilde. AWP

I Am Weary of Straying. Sarah E. York. AH

I am weary of the Garden. Said the Rose. George Henry Miles. BLPA

I am weary of the working. To Solitude. Alice Cary. AmWP

I am weary of these times and their dull burden. Quid Restat. Lucius Beebe. RFM

I am weaving a song of waters. Gwendolyn B. Bennett. BlSi; ShDr

I am who the trail took. Exploration. Daniel Hoffman. CoAP

I am willowy boughs. I Am. Hilda Conkling. FaPON

I am wind on sea. Amergin. *Fr.* Amergin's Songs. NOIV

I Am with Thee. Ernest Bourner Allen. BLRP

I Am with Those. Ingrid Jonker, *tr. fr. Afrikaans by* Jack Cope *and* William Plomer. BoWoP

I am within as white as snow. *Unknown.* ChTr; GBP

I am wondering how I could have changed her blood. Marlow and Nancy. Sandra McPherson. AmPA

I am wondering what became of all those tall abstractions. The Death of Allegory. Billy Collins. WeW

I Am Writing to You from a Far-Off Country, *sels.* Henri Michaux, *tr. fr. French by* Richard Ellmann.
"Dawn is grey here, she went on to tell him. It was not always like this, The." AnRep
"Education regarding chills is not well handled in this country, The." AnRep
"For a long, long time, she confided to him, we have been in combat with the sea." AnRep
"I add one further word to you, a question rather." AnRep
"I am writing to you from the end of the world." AnRep
"I cannot have you with a doubt, she continues, with a lack of confidence." AnRep
"She writes to him again." AnRep
"There are constantly, she told him further, lions in the village." AnRep
"We are more than ever surrounded by ants, says her letter." AnRep
"We have here, she said, only one sun in the month, and for only a little while." AnRep
"We women here all live with tightened throats." AnRep
"When you walk in the country, she further confided to him." AnRep

I am writing to you from the end of the world. Henri Michaux, *tr. fr. French by* Richard Ellmann. *Fr.* I Am Writing to You from a Far-Off Country. AnRep

I am writing to you in answer to your letter. The Connection. Daniil Kharms, *tr. fr. Russian by* George Gibian. FaBoNo

I am yesterday, to-day and to-morrow. He Walketh by Day. *Unknown, tr. fr. Egyptian by* Robert Hillyer. *Fr.* Book of the Dead. AWP

I am: yet what I am none cares or knows. I Am. John Clare. CoGr; EBEV; EBVV; EnRP; EnVR; FHYEP; GTBS-P; HAP; InvP; LiTB; NAEL-2; NOBE; NOBVV; NoP; OAEL-2; OBNC; PeECV; PlP; PoEL-4; Prf; PrIm; TFi; TOF; TrGrPo; TRP
(Written in Northampton County Asylum.) GGP; OBEV; OxAEP-2

I am your ancestor. You know next-to-nothing. Our Dust. C. D. Wright. NAmP90

I Am Your Loaf, Lord. David Ross. GoYe

I am your mother, your mother's mother. Jalal al-Din Rumi, *tr. fr. Persian by* Elizabeth Daryush. OBVE

I am your noble savage. First and Last Man. Ralph McTell. OBET

I am your son, white man! Mulatto. Langston Hughes. NAAL-2

I Am Your Wife. *Unknown.* PoToHe

I am yours, you are mine. Frau Ava, *tr. fr. German by* Willis Barnstone. BoWoP

I amna' fou' sae muckle as tired — deid dune. Sic Transit Gloria Scotia. "Hugh MacDiarmid." CMoP

I an I Alone; or Goliath. Michael Smith. PBCV

I, an unwedded wandering dame. Sylvia Townsend Warner. MoBrPo

I! and a world of Pikes passe through. (*LL*) His Cavalier. Robert Herrick. CaPo; GoJo

I and my sisters three. Victorian Song. John Farrar. GoYe

I and my white Pangur. The Monk and His Pet Cat. *Unknown, tr. fr. Old Irish.* CH

I and myself swore enmity. Alack. Interior. J. C. Squire. OxBSP

I and Pangur Bán, my cat. Pangur Bán. *Unknown, tr. fr. Gaelic by* Robin Flower. CRH; FaBoCh; OFC; RB

I and the other intruders. Of Objects Considered as Fortresses in a Baleful Place. Hyam Plutzik. VGW

I and Thou. Chana Bloch. CrSp

I, Angelo, obese, black-garmented. Angelo Orders His Dinner. Bayard Taylor. AnAmPo; BXAP

I answer not, and I return no more. (*LL*) Opportunity. John James Ingalls. AnAmPo; PoLF; WBLP

I appear like a bird from nowhere. Below Hekla. Selima Hill. FaBoWP

I approach gianthood warily. Up. Nigel Wells. AngWe

I approach with such. Something. Robert Creeley. NaP

I approached Moses and said to him. Moses. Amir Gilboa, *tr. fr. Hebrew by* Ruth Finer Mintz. MHP

I argue/ that where the body is concerned. Saddle and Cell. The Three Marias, *tr. fr. Portuguese by* Helen R. Lane. BoWoP

I arise above the clouds. The Airman's Breastplate. Oliver St. John Gogarty. TIRV

I arise and unbuild it again. (*LL*) The Cloud. Shelley. ArNa; BLPL; EnRP; FaPON; FHYEP; GN; LiTB; MeMBP; NAEL-2; NoP; PoEL-4; PWR; TrGrPo

I arise, facing East. Mary Austin. EaPr

I arise from dreams of thee. The Indian Serenade. Shelley. AWP; BLPL; CBLP; EnRP; HoPM; ImPo; LiTB; MeMBP; OBEV; PlP; RaBo; TrGrPo; TTTS
(Indian Girl's Song, The.) NAEL-2
(Lines to an Indian Air.) FaBoBe; GTBS; GTBS-P

I arise from rest with movements swift. *Unknown, tr. fr. Eskimo.* EaPr

I arise today. Saint Patrick's Breastplate; or, The Deer's Cry. At. to St. Patrick Saint Patrick, *tr. fr. Irish.* TIRV, *tr. by* Kuno Meyer; WGRP
(Deer's Cry, The.) PeIV, *tr. by* Kuno Meyer

I arise today. The Deer's Cry. At. to St. Patrick Saint Patrick, *tr. fr. Old Irish by* Whitley Stokes, John Strachan, *and* Kuno Meyer. WGRP

I arose early and stepped outside. February Morning. King D. Kuka. VoR

I arose swiftly that night, for I heard a knock at my door. The Future. James Oppenheim. TrJP

I arrive/ Langston. Do Nothing till You Hear from Me. David Henderson. PoBA

I arrive where an unknown earth is under my feet. Landfall. *Maori Oral Tradition, tr. by* A. S. Thomson. WTO

I as in love with the word "aloha." Poem for George Helm: Aloha Week 1980. Eric Chock. OpBo

I, as the night invites me, fall asleep. (*LL*) To a Lady Who Sent Me a Copy of Verses at My Going to Bed. Henry King. CBLP

I Ask. Novica Tadic, *tr. fr. Serbo-Croatian by* Charles Simic. HSix

I ask a man in the smoker where he is going and he/ answers: "Omaha." (*LL*) Limited. Carl Sandburg. HAP; MoAB; MoAmPo; OxBA

I ask all blessings. *Unknown, tr. fr. Navajo Indian by* Stephen Mitchell. EnlH

I ask but one thing of you, only one. To a Friend. Amy Lowell. PoLF

I ask but right: let her that caught me late. Ovid, *tr. by* Christopher Marlowe. *Fr.* Amores. EBEV

I ask for a moment's indulgence to sit by Thy side. Rabindranath Tagore. EaPr

I ask for the strength to follow through my life. Time of Day. Selden Rodman. PoA

I ask good things that I detest. Robert Louis Stevenson. TrPWD

I Ask My Mother to Sing. Li-Young Lee. OpBo

I ask my son what he knows of earth. Elementary. Linda France. NWP

I Ask My Teachers. Sister Mary Madeleva. *Fr.* Concerning Death. CRP

I ask no kind return of love. Fanny (Frances) Macartney Greville. *Fr.* Prayer for Indifference, A. ECWP; NOEC; OBEV

I ask not why Astrea fled away. Wit's Abuse. Anne Wharton. KTR

I ask not wit, nor beauty do I crave. The Humble Wish. B—ll M—rt—n. ECWP

I ask sometimes why these small animals. Caring for Animals. Jon Silkin. TSaS

I ask the muse about this drifting. The Muse's Answer. Gibbons Ruark. MT

I ask thee whence those ashes were. A Question. *Unknown.* NOSC

I ask thy aid, O potent rum! Resentments Composed because of the Clamor of Town Topers Outside My Apartment. Sarah Kemble Knight. AiP; SCAP

I ask, who will buy a poem? Mahon O'Heffernan, *tr. fr. Early Modern Irish by* Thomas Kinsella. NOIV

I ask You not for victory. The Prizefighter's Prayer. Menotti Vincent Caprani. TIRV

I ask you this. Langston Hughes. CDC

I ask'd a young Youth what it mean'd. Alicia D'Anvers. *Fr.* Academia; or The Humours of the University of Oxford. KTR

I asked a thief to steal me a peach. Blake. NAEL-2; NoP; OBNC; PoE (Angel, The.) ImPo; LiTB; MeMBP

I asked an aged man, a man of cares. What Is Time? James Marsden. PWR

I asked for just a crumb of bread. More than We Ask. Faith Wells. BLRP

I asked for peace. Requests. Digby Mackworth Dolben. TrPWD

I asked her, "Is Aladdin's lamp." Sorceress, The! Vachel Lindsay. PDV

I asked her why she didn't. Girl with Long Dark Hair. Stephen Gray. PeSA

I asked if I got sick and died, would you. A Question. J. M. Synge. MoBrPo; NOIV; OBMV; OxBTC; PeIV

I asked if I should pray. Mohini Chatterjee. W. B. Yeats. NoAM

I asked my dear friend, Orator Prigg. Orator Prigg. Blake. OBSV

I asked my mother for fifty cents. *Unknown.* ISE; MoShBr; OxBoLi; RoPo

I asked no other thing. Emily Dickinson. NOBA; OxBA

I asked of Echo, t'other day. Echo. John Godfrey Saxe. AnAmPo

I asked professors who teach the meaning of life to tell me what is happiness. Happiness. Carl Sandburg. AnAmPo; OxBA

I asked the heaven of stars. Night Song at Amalfi. Sara Teasdale. MoAmPo

I asked the holly, "What is your life if . . . ?" Trees. Ted Hughes. NYBP

I asked the Lord: "Sire, is this true." A Dream Question. Thomas Hardy. ChIV-1

I asked the Master for a motto sweet. God's Will. Charles E. Guthrie. BLRP

I asked thee oft what poets thou hast read. Upon the Same (Detractor). Robert Herrick. CaPo

I asked unanswerable questions a child asks. Herbert Mason. *Fr.* Gilgamesh. IMW

I at my window sit, and see. Autumn ("I at my window sit, and see.") *Unknown.* NOEC

I,/ at one time. The Self-Hatred of Don L. Lee. Don L. Lee. BPo

I ate, and can't digest. (*LL*) The Confession. "Thomas Ingoldsby." FiBHP

I ate pancakes one night in a Pancake House. The Player Piano. Randall Jarrell. MT; NAAL-2

I ate with my father. The Good Lunch of Oceans. Alberto A. Ríos. AfAz

I attended the burial of all my rosy feelings. Transaction. A. R. Ammons. HCAP; PoA

I await his coming. Guessing. *Unknown, tr. fr. Burmese by* U Win Pe. PBWP

I awake, three in the morning, sweating. Thirteen Ways of Being Looked at by a Possum. Everette Maddox. PRA

I awakened to dryness and the ferns were dead. The Tragedy of Leaves. Charles Bukowski. HoPM

I awoke happy, the house. The Revelation. William Carlos Williams. SAmP

I awoke in profuse sweat, arms aching. Hag-ridden. Robert Graves. BIrV

I awoke in the Midsummer not-to-call night, in the white and the walk of the morning. Moonrise. Gerard Manley Hopkins. EnVR; FaBoPP; MoAB; MoBrPo; NOBVV; RB

I awoke only to hear the dull clobbing of the wind. Night Shore. Barry O. Higgs. PeSA

I balance. Doing Nothing. Margaret Gibson. FoLa

I bargained with life for a penny. My Wage. Jessie Belle Rittenhouse. BLPA; PoToHe

I bear no grudge, even though my heart may break. Heine. RiWo

I become part of it. (*LL*) Mountains, I become part of it, The. *Unknown.* EaPr

I become them, sometimes. Pure fight. Pure fantasy. Lean. (*LL*) The Turncoat. Amiri Baraka. NeAP; PoE

I been 'buked an' I been scorned. Hell and Heaven. *Unknown.* OxBoLi

I been havin' some hard travelin', I thought you knowed. Hard Traveling. Woody Guthrie. SWP

I been ridin' fer cattle the most of my life. The High-loping Cowboy. Curley W. Fletcher. AiP

I been scarred and battered. Still Here. Langston Hughes. BPo
(I've been scarred and battered.) SAmP

I been t'inkin' 'bout de preachah; whut he said de othah night. Philosophy. Paul Laurence Dunbar. BPo

I before E. *Unknown.* FaBoUs

I beg death's pardon now. And mourn the dead. (*LL*) The Pardon. Richard Wilbur. MoP; NoAM; NOBA; NoP; OBD; Poetr

I beg God's grace, guardian of the parish. In Praise of Tenby. *Unknown*, *tr. fr. Welsh* by Joseph P. Clancy. OBWVE; OxBSS

I beg your pardon. *Unknown.* ISE

I began in Ohio. Stages on a Journey Westward. James Wright. LCAP; NaP

I began this fall by watching a thin red squirrel. Pick and Poke. Gerald Stern. AnAn

I began to think. The Wheel. Julie N. Heifetz. BTR

I began with everything. Speaking of Loss. Lucille Clifton. CAPP

I begin as tradition advises. Catechism. Betsy Sholl. CrSp

I begin through the grass once again to be bound to the Lord. Reconciliation. "Æ." OBMV; TrCP

I begin with a name. It isn't you. February Evenings. Andrew Crozier. VaA

I begin with the hills. This House. Ray A. Young Bear. CDW

I beheld, and lo a great multitude, which no man could number. Heavenly Vision. William Billings. AmFP

I beheld her, on a Day. How He Saw Her. Ben Jonson. *Fr.* Celebration of Charis in Ten Lyric[k] Peeces [*or* pieces], A. BeJo; EnRePo; OxAEP-1; SeCP; SeCV-1

I, being born a woman and distressed. Edna St. Vincent Millay. BoLoP; NALW; NIP; NoP; OPOP
(Sonnet: "I, being born a woman and distressed.") ErPo

I Believe. J. B. Lawrence. BLRP

I Believe. Saul Tchernichowsky, *tr. fr. Hebrew* by Reginald V. Feldman. TrJP

I believe a leaf of grass is no less than the journey-work of the stars. Walt Whitman. *Fr.* Song of Myself. AmPP; EaPr; LiTA; MoAmPo, *abr.*; NOBA; OxBA; PDV; SAmP; SOTW, *much abr.*

I believe if I should die. Creed. Mary Ashley Townsend. BLPA; FaBoBe

I believe in human kindness. A Creed. Norman Macleod. WGRP

I believe in the brook as it wanders. Nature's Creed. *Unknown.* OHIP

I believe in the English sentence not in cries. Graph. Tim Longville. VaA

I believe in the flesh and the appetites. Walt Whitman. *Fr.* Song of Myself. AmPP; LiTA; MoAmPo, *abr.*; NOBA; OxBA; Prf; SOTW, *much abr.*

I believe in the increasing of life: whatever. The Escape. Ivor Gurney. OxBSP

I believe in the ultimate justice of Fate. Credo. Georgia Douglas Johnson. PoBA

I believe in you my soul. Walt Whitman. *Fr.* Song of Myself. AmPP; LiTA; MoAmPo, *abr.*; NOBA; OxBA; Prf; SOTW, *much abr.*

I believe the dose will do. (*LL*) A Receipt to Cure [*or* for] the Vapours. Lady Mary Wortley Montagu. ECWP; NOEC; PBWP

I believe the earth/ exists. Credo. Denise Levertov. *Fr.* Mass for the Day of St. Thomas Didymus. AIW; EaPr

I believe the grief of Tantalus in Hell. Paulus Silentiarius, *tr. fr. Greek* by Sam Hamill. InMo

I believe the yellow flowers think with me. Alice Notley. UL

I believe there is no one alive who weeps for my sorrow. Heinrich von Morungen, *tr. fr. German* by Frederick Goldin. GePo

I Believe You. Anthony Barnett. VaA

I believed:/ a tree when kissed. Love. Tymoteusz Karpowicz, *tr. fr. Polish* by Czeslaw Milosz. TSaS

I bend over an old hollow cottonwood stump. A Hollow Tree. Robert Bly. NNaP

I Bended unto Me. Thomas Edward Brown. NOBVV; NTCP; OHCV

I Bent to Touch a Damp Cloth to Your Mouth. Sherod Santos. *Fr.* Sheltering Ground, The. Son

I bent unto the ground. The Voice of God. James Stephens. WGRP

I, Bertold Brecht, came out of the black forests. Of Poor B.B. Bertolt Brecht, *tr. fr. German* by Michael Hamburger. RB

I beseech God's favour, faultless your gift. Petition for Reconciliation. Cynddelw Brydydd Mawr, *tr. fr. Welsh* by Joseph P. Clancy. OBWVE

I bespeak words. Clere Parsons. FaBoTw

I bet I can hold my breath. One-Upmanship. Miriam Chaikin. NTCP

I bind unto myself to-day. St. Patrick's Breastplate. *At. to* St. Patrick Saint Patrick, *tr. fr. Irish* by Frances Alexander. FaBoCh

I blame Myrtis. Korinna, *tr. fr. Greek* by John Dillon. PBWP

I blame old women for buying paper roses. Look, No Hands. Pearse Hutchinson. PBCIP

I bleed by the black stream. Haemorrhage. Padraic Fiacc. CIP

I Bless Thee, Lord, for Sorrows Sent. Samuel Johnson. AH

I bless Thee, Lord, because I grow. Paradise. George Herbert. AngWe; GeHe; ImPo; NOSC; OAEL-1; SeCP; TrGrPo

I bobbed with a hook through the palm of my hand. (*LL*) Under the Boathouse. David Bottoms. MT

I born/ from/ a force. Motto Vision 1971. Delano Abdul Malik de Coteau. PBCV

I bought a red-brick villa. Song for Straphangers. George Buchanan. PNI

I bought a wooden whistle. *Unknown.* RoPo

I Break the Sky. Owen Dodson. PoBA

I breathe, sweet Gib [*or* Ghib], the temperate air of Wrest. To my Friend G.N. from Wrest. Thomas Carew. BeJo; CaPo

I breathe the air of another country. Australia. Gary Catalano. NOBAu

I breathed upon the aluminum microphone-stand a body's length away. Thus Crosslegged on Round Pillow Sat in Space. Allen Ginsberg. NNaP

I bring fresh showers for the thirsting flowers. The Cloud. Shelley. ArNa; BLPL; EnRP; FaPON; FHYEP; GN; LiTB; MeMBP; NAEL-2; NoP; PoEL-4; PWR; TrGrPo

I bring myself back from the streets that open like long. Home for Thanksgiving. W. S. Merwin. NoAM

I bring the mare a green apple, then ride. Near the Bravo 20 Bombing Range. Gary Short. NGP

I bring ye love. Question [*or* Quest]. What will love do? Upon Love, by Way of Question and Answer. Robert Herrick. CaPo; CBLP

I bring you. Big Dog. Anselm Hollo. UL

I bring you a goat. Hroswitha, *tr. fr. Latin* by Patrick Diehl. *Fr.* Paphnutius. WPOW

I bring you as offering. (*LL*) Orchard. Hilda Doolittle ("H. D."). CMoP; LiTA; LiTM; MoAmPo; OxBA

I bring you news. *Unknown.* NOIV

I brocht my love a cherry. Auld Sang. William Soutar. OxBS

I Brood about Some Concepts, for Example. Alicia Ostriker. PBCAP

I Brotachos of Gortyn lie here. This. Simonides, *tr. fr. Greek* by Peter Jay. GrAn

I brought a lover home. Christmas in the Midwest. Maureen Seaton. LoHo

I brought my love. Beloved. Iyamide Hazeley. VBLP

I brush the spider webs from the dismantled sky. Housework. Amanda Berenguer, *tr. fr. Spanish* by Priscilla Joslin. WPOW

I built a hut in a little wood. My Hut. Eileen Mathias. BoTP

I built my house, I built my walls. *Unknown.* ISE

I built my house upon the solid rock. Here We have No Firm Dwelling-Place. Eugène Marais, *tr. fr. Afrikaans* by Hugh Finn. PeSAV

I Built My Hut. José Juan Tablada. *See* I built my hut near where people live.

I built my hut near where people live. José Juan Tablada. *Fr.* Two Drinking Songs. NU
(I Built My Hut. AWP, *tr.* by Arthur Waley)

I built my soul a lordly pleasure-house. Tennyson. EnVR

I buried you deeper last night. (*LL*) To a Persistent Phantom. Frank Horne. CDC

I burn no incense, hang no wreath. Votive Song. Edward Coote Pinkney. AnAmPo

I burne, and cruell you, in vaine. To My Mistris, I Burning in Love. Thomas Carew. SeCP

I Burned My Candle at Both Ends. Samuel Hoffenstein. FiBHP

I burned my life that I might find. The Alchemist. Louise Bogan. AWP; MoAmPo

I, Caesar, when I learned of the fame. *Unknown.* PeLi

I Call and I Call ("I call, I call. Who do ye call?") Robert Herrick. ChTr

I call on those that call me son. Are you Content? W. B. Yeats. IIP

I call the land of Ireland. Amergin. *Fr.* Amergin's Songs. NOIV

I call up words that he may write them down. Demands of the Muse. Vernon Watkins. PoA

I call you on. Ron Padgett. *Fr.* 3 Little Poems. ArLo

I call you with honest words. Bláthmac Mac Con Brettan. *Fr.* Poem to Mary, A. NOIV

I called at your. From an Afternoon Caller. Sister Mary Madeleva. CRP

I called him to come in. Evening. James Wright. NOBA; NYBP; PrIm

I called one day — on Eden's strand. From Emily Dickinson in Southern California. X. J. Kennedy. NBLV

I called out of mine affliction. Jonah's Prayer. Bible, *O.T. Fr.* Jonah. TrJP

I called today, Peter, and you were away. The Thermal Stair. W. S. Graham. FaBoMo

I called you by sweet names by wood and linn. Ireland. Francis Ledwidge. PeIV

I Came a-Riding. Reinmar von Zweter, *tr. fr. German by* Jethro Bithell. AWP

I came as a shadow. Nocturne Varial. Lewis Alexander. PoBA; PoNe

I came back at last to my own house. The Substitute for Time. John Koethe. EOEF

I came back late and tired last night. Home. Rupert Brooke. PFP

I came before the water. Mussel Hunter at Rock Harbor. Sylvia Plath. NYBP

I came first through the warm grass. The Bee's Last Journey to the Rose. Brian Patten. OTCP

I came from England into France. The Journey into France. *Unknown.* CoMu; FaBoBa; OBTV

I came from somewhere. Poem of the Future Citizen. José Craveirinha, *tr. fr. Portuguese by* Dorothy Guedes *and* Philippa Rumsey. TTY

I came/ heavy with child in the fierce sun. Waiheke 1972 — Rocky Bay. Christina Beer. PeNZ

I came here with a young girl. The Cemetery at Academy, California. Philip Levine. NaP; NYBP

I came home and found a lion in my living room. The Lion for Real. Allen Ginsberg. GLP; HCAP; RB

I came, I saw, and was undone. The Thraldome. Abraham Cowley. *Fr.* Mistress, The. SeCV-1

I came in from the garden. Scales. Libby Houston. NBrP

I came/ in the blinding sweep. To Mother. Frank Horne. *Fr.* Letters [*or* Notes] Found near a Suicide. BPo; CDC; PoBA; PoNe

I came into the City and none knew me. An Upper Chamber. Frances Bannerman. OBEV

I came into the pasture-ground. Settlement. Ingeborg Bachmann, *tr. fr. German by* Daniel Huws. PoSu

I came out a winner. O Realm Bejewelled. Forugh Farrokhzad, *tr. fr. Farsi by* Jascha Kessler *and* Amin Banani. WPOW

I came then to the city of my brethren. The Shore of Life. Robert Fitzgerald. VGW

I came to a field. Charles Simic. NNaP

I came to a shore. And you were there. The Inlet. Jean Pedrick. ETG

I came to love, I came into my own. (*LL*) The Dream. Theodore Roethke. NoP; NYBP; UnPo

I came to the crowded Inn of Earth. The Inn of Earth. Sara Teasdale. LiTA

I came to visit my friend. Birds of Detroit. Greg Pape. PBCAP

I came to you. Africa and the Caribbean. Jennifer Brown, *tr. fr. Romanian by* Laura Schiff. AIW

I came to you with a greeting. Morning Song. A. A. Fet, *tr. fr. Russian by* Max Eastman. AWP

I came too late to the hills: they were swept bare. The Wilderness. Kathleen Raine. BoWoP; WPE

I came, yes, dear, dear. Kore in Hades. Kathleen Raine. NALW

I can & do lie down with you amidst the venomous. For the Safety of Lovers. John James. NBrP

I can afford to discriminate. The Discriminator. Vernon Scannell. OxBC

I can almost see. On the Rouge. Raymond Souster. NOBC

I can break your heart. (*LL*) The Kid. Ai. NoAM

I can build towers of my own. The Ascetic Trove of Responsive Fact. Wallace Stevens. *Fr.* Montrachet — le — Jardin. CBCK

I can close my eyes one heartbeat. My Father's Country. Joyce Lee. NOBAu

I can feel my cheek still burning. (*LL*) The Portrait. Stanley Kunitz. CAPP; IMW; Poetsp; RaBo

I can feel the tug. Punishment. Seamus Heaney. FaBoPV; InPS; NAEL-2; NoAM; NoP; OxAEP-2; PBCIP

I Can Fly. Felice Holman. NTCP

I can give myself to her. Yosano Akiko, *tr. fr. Japanese by* Kenneth Rexroth *and* Ikuko Atsumi. WPJ; WPOW

I can hear the clatter of the cattle cars. I Did Not Know, but I Remember. Tamara Fishman. BTR

I can hear the evening bell. Returning by Night to Lu-Men. Meng Hao Jan, *tr. fr. Chinese by* Kenneth Rexroth. OHMPC

I can hear the wind whistling. 40 Acres and a Mule. Dick Gallup. UL

I can imagine, in some otherworld. Humming-Bird. D. H. Lawrence. CMoP; InPS; LiTB; LiTM; MeMBP; NoAM; RB

I can imagine someone who found. California Hills in August. Dana Gioia. DiPo; InPK

I can light cheroots and gaspers with my tail. (*LL*) I Wish I Were ("I wish I were a/ Elephantiaphus.") *Unknown.* FaBoNo; OxBoLi

I can love both fair[e] and brown[e]. The Indifferent. John Donne. BoLoP; CBCK; CBLP; ESCV; NAEL-1; NAWM-1; NOSC; SeCV-1; SoSe; TEP

I can make out the rigging of a schooner. North Haven. Elizabeth Bishop. CAPP; HCAP

I can manage so few of you. Persons Unknown. Aidan Carl Mathews. BiHa

"I" Can Never Be a Great Man, An. Stephen Spender. OBMV

I can never return with my poor dog Tray. (*LL*) The Irish Harper and His Dog. Thomas Campbell. CH; CoGr

I can no longer ask how it feels. The Making of a Servant. J. J. R. Jolobe. PeSAV

I can no longer hold, my body grows. A Lover that Durst Not Speak to His M[istress]. James Shirley. NOSC

I can no longer tell dream from reality. Akazome Emon, *tr. fr. Japanese by* Kenneth Rexroth *and* Ikuko Atsumi. WPJ

I Can No Longer Untangle My Hair. *Unknown, tr. fr. Chinese by* Kenneth Rexroth. OHMPC

I can not do it alone. Jesus and I. Dan Crawford. BLRP

I can not invent it, Hilda Doolittle ("H. D."). *Fr.* Tribute to the Angels. NALW

I can not see why trials come. I Can Trust. Daniel Webster Davis. AAP

I can only say I have waited for you. Time of Waiting in Amsterdam. Ingrid Jonker, *tr. fr. Afrikaans by* Jack Cope *and* William Plomer. BoWoP

I can promise you we shall not get first in a rage. (*LL*) My Master and I. *Unknown.* CoMu; OBET

I can remember. I can remember. The Boy Actor. Noël Coward. OxBTC

I can remember looking up at him. King Billy on the Walls. Sheenagh Pugh. AngWe

I can remember our sorrow, I can remember our laughter. Memory. Helen Hoyt. PoLF

I can remember when he was a pup. (*LL*) The Span of Life. Robert Frost. HoPM; LiTM; SoSe

I can remember when there were trees. When There Were Trees. Nancy Willard. FoLa

I can see a picture. Pictures. F. Ann Elliott. BoTP

I can see its skeleton on the ground. (*LL*) A Fallen Tree. Mang Ke. SpMi

I can see my self years back at Sunion. Adrienne Rich. *Fr.* Twenty-one Love Poems. GLP

I can see outside the gold wings without birds. The Clear Air of October. Robert Bly. NaP

I can see the coast coming near. On the Ledge. Louis Simpson. ArOW

I can set the sky behind it. (*LL*) Pillar of Flame. Barbara Unger. LoHo

I can shake the wild hay, and wet seed sticks to my hand. Stalks of Wild Hay. H.L. Davis. PoA

I can sing a true song about myself. *Unknown. See* I can sing of myself a true song.

I can sing of myself a true song. *Unknown, tr. by* L. Iddings. *Fr.* Seafarer, The. CTC; FaBoTw; HeIL; HeIP; LiTA; NoP; OxBA; PoRA (I can sing a true song about myself.) ASW, *tr. by* Kevin Crossley-Holland

I can sometimes sing. Melancholy. Joseph Freiherr von Eichendorff, *tr. fr. German by* Philip L. Miller. RiWo

I can stay awake all night, if need be. Zoo Keeper's Wife. Sylvia Plath. VBLP

I can still smell the spray of the sea they forced me to cross. Black Woman. Nancy Morejón, *tr. fr. Spanish by* Lisa E. Davis, Daniela Gioseffi *with* Enildo Garcia. WoWa

I can support it no longer. Flower Herding on Mount Monadnock. Galway Kinnell. HeIP; LCAP; NaP; NoAM; NOBA

I can tell by the way the trees beat, after. The Man Watching. Rainer Maria Rilke, *tr. fr. German by* Robert Bly. NU; RaBo

I can tell you about this because I have held in my hand. Drawn by Stones, by Earth, by Things That Have Been in the Fire. Marvin Bell. CAPP; VCAP

I can think of William of Orange. The Centaurs. Paul Muldoon. BiHa

I Can Trust. Daniel Webster Davis. AAP

I can understand the war with you. The Disappearance of Deanna Durbin. Michael C. Ford. NGP

I can use it. Song of the Crab Medicine-Bag. *Unknown, tr. fr. Chippewa Indian by* Jerome K. Rothenberg. STP

I can wade grief. Emily Dickinson. HeIP; NOBA

I canna tell what has come ower me. Ich Weiss Nicht Was Soll es Bedeuten. Heine, *tr. fr. German by* Alexander Macmillan. AWP

I care not what the sailors say. Crazy Jane Reproved. W. B. Yeats. CMoP

I Carried Statues. Agnes Nemes Nagy, tr. fr. Hungarian. BoWoP, tr. by Bruce Berlind; PoSu, tr. by Bruce Berlind

I carry it on my keychain, which itself. The Ring. Diane Wakoski. PoA

I Carry My Black Sheep Back to Her Herd. Ljiljana Djurdjic, tr. fr. Serbo-Croatian by Charles Simic. HSix

I carry the ground-hog along by the tail. The Hunter. Raymond Souster. NOBC

I carry you in a glass jar. The Doll. Gregory Orr. AmPA

I carry your heart (i carry in my heart. (LL) I carry your heart with me (I carry it in). E. E. Cummings. MeMAP; TAP; UnAS

I carry your heart with me (I carry it in). E. E. Cummings. MeMAP; TAP; UnAS

I carve my first head. Then I carve another. Hallowe'en 1971. Michael Dennis Browne. AmPA

I cast from me the medications. Loneliness. Franz Werfel, tr. fr. German by Edith Abercrombie Snow. TrJP

I catch myself drifting. Harbor. Nancy Price. IHMS

I catch the movement of his lips. Marina Tsvetayeva, tr. fr. Russian by Elaine Feinstein. Fr. Daughter of Jairus, The. BoWoP; VBLP

I Catcha da Plenty of Feesh. Unknown. AS

I caught a little ladybird. Christina Rossetti. FaBoVe

I caught a tremendous fish. The Fish. Elizabeth Bishop. CAPP; FaBoWP; GoJo; HAP; HeIP; HoPM; InPK; LiTM; MoAB; MoAmPo; MoP; NAAL-2; NALW; NoAM; NOBA; NoP; NTP; NU; OPOP; PoE; Poetr; RB; TFi; TrGrPo; TRP

I caught the American bull. Buffalo. Henry Dumas. PoBA

I caught the boat just once. Night Crossing. Sylvia Kantaris. PWE

I caught this morning morning's minion. The Windhover. Gerard Manley Hopkins. ClHu; CMoP; EBEvV; EBVV; EnVR; FaPoB; GTBS-P; HAP; InPK; InPS; InvP; LiTB; LiTM; MeMBP; MoAB; MoBrPo; MoP; NAEL-2; NoAM; NOBE; NOBVV; NoP; OAEL-2; OBNC; OxAEP-2; PeECV; PFP; PoE; PoEL-5; Poetr; PoRA; PPP; PrIm; RB; SCGP; SCV; TEP; TFi; TOT; TRP; UnPo

I caught you grazing on my knee. To a Flea in a Glass of Water. Desmond A. Greig. PeSA

I cease not from desire till my desire. Hafiz, tr. by Gertrude Lowthian Bell. Fr. Odes. AWP; TAL

I celebrate myself, and sing myself. Walt Whitman. Fr. Song of Myself. AmPP; FaBoVe; LiTA; MeMAP; MoAmPo, abr.; NAWM-2; NoAM; NOBA; NoP; NTP; OxBA; PoE; RaBo; SAmP; SOTW, much abr. (I celebrate myself,/ And what I assume you shall assume.) HeIP, earlier vers. (Myself.) BLPL; FaBoBe

I celebrate myself,/ And what I assume you shall assume. Walt Whitman. See I celebrate myself, and sing myself.

I celebrate Rhegion, Italy's tip. The Tomb of Ibykos. Unknown, tr. fr. Greek by Peter Jay. GrAn

I celebrate Rhegion, Italy's tip, licked by. Unknown, tr. fr. Greek by Peter Jay. PeHV

I celebrate the personality of Jack! Jack and Jill. Charles Battell Loomis. BXAP

I certainly have lost something. Kenneth Koch. Fr. Days and Nights. NoAM

I chanced upon a new book yesterday. To Edward Fitzgerald. Robert Browning. NAEL-2; OxBSP

I chanced upon an early walk to spy. The Orchard and the Heath. George Meredith. OBNC

I-ch'ang. Ts'ai Ch'i-chiao, tr. fr. Chinese. LHF, tr. by Hualing Nieh

I, Chang P'ing-tzu, had traversed the Nine Wilds and seen their wonders. The Bones of Chuang Tzu. Chang Heng, tr. fr. Chinese by Arthur Waley. AWP

I change, and so do women too. Written on a Looking-Glass. Unknown. FaBoEE

I change bot sees, bot can not chainge my love. (LL) In Orknay. William Fowler. OxBS; ScCV

I changed a grown man's clothes on a stripped ward. In a Building Named for a Governor. Christopher L. Dornin. CRP

I charge you, O winds of the West, O. Mathilde Blind. Fr. Love in Exile. TrJP

I charm thy life. Kehama's Curse. Robert Southey. Fr. Curse of Kehama, The. OBNC

I Check My Parents' House. Julia Alvarez. CrSp

I choose not to walk among ghosts. Antigone VI. Herbert Martin. PoBA

I chopped down the house that you had been saving to live in next summer. Variations on a Theme by William Carlos Williams. Kenneth Koch. BXAP; CAPP; FF; NBLV; NIP; NoAM; NoP; PoM

I chose the blonde from the chemist's, thirty-six. Happening at Sordid Creek. Peter Porter. NoAM

I clasp in the hot pit and bed. Memorial Couplets for the Dying Ego. George Barker. EBEV

I clasp them, is because they die. (LL) Mimnermus in Church. William Johnson Cory. CoGr; NOBE; OBEV

I climb that wooded hill. Unknown, tr. fr. Chinese by Arthur Waley. PAW

I climb the black rock mountain. Where Mountain Lion Lay [or Laid] Down with Deer. Leslie Silko. ImGa; Poetr; TRP; VoR; WPOW

I climb the cold mountain by. View from the Cliffs. Tu Mu, tr. fr. Chinese by Kenneth Rexroth. OHMPC

I climb the hill: from end to end. Tennyson. Fr. In Memoriam A. H. H. EBVV, abr.; FHYEP; OAEL-2, abr.; PeECV, abr.; PoEL-5

I climb to the tower-top and lean upon broken stone. I See Phantoms of Hatred and of the Heart's Fullness and of the Coming Emptiness. W. B. Yeats. Fr. Meditations in Time of Civil War. LiTB

I climb'd a hill, whose Summit crown'd with wood. An Essay on the Fleet Riding in the Downes. "J. D." CoMu

I climb'd [or climbed] the dark brow of the mighty Hellvellyn. Hellvellyn. Sir Walter Scott. FM; TEP

I climbed a hill as light fell short. The Song of Honor [or Honour]. Ralph Hodgson. LiTB; MoBrPo; OtMeF

I climbed out, tired of waiting. Drinking from a Helmet. James Dickey. ArOW

I climbed the stair in Antwerp church. Antwerp and Bruges. Dante Gabriel Rossetti. OBTV

I climbed through woods in the hour-before-dawn dark. The Horses. Ted Hughes. NoAM

I climbed towards you on a ray of moonlight. Fantasy under the Moon. Emmanuel Boundzeki-Dongala, tr. fr. French by Gerald Moore and Ulli Beier. TTY

I cling and swing. The Fifteen Acres. James Stephens. BoTP

I cling to innocence. (LL) Silent on the subject of vengeance. Sappho. InMo

I closed my book to listen. Church Bells. Clara Ann Thompson. CBWP-2

I closed my ears with stinging bugs. Elegy for a Puritan Conscience. Alan Dugan. CAPP; SM

I closed my eyes as I sat in the jet. Day Flight. Jack Davis. CBAP

I Closed My Eyes To-Day and Saw. William Force Stead. OBMV

I Closed My Shutters Fast Last Night. Georgia Douglas Johnson. PoNe

I clothe your body nearer than the dust. The Hero. Robert Wells. SCBI

I collide with sun and foam, a fierce. L'Agulhas, A Walk. Wilma Stockenström, tr. fr. Afrikaans by Rosa Keet. PeSAV

I come alone. To surprise you. Visit. James Welch. AmPA

I come among the peoples like a shadow. Hunger. Laurence Binyon. NTP; OxBTC

I come back. (LL) Bride: Maidenhood, Maidenhood. Sappho. VBLP

I come back to the cottage in. Only Years. Kenneth Rexroth. TAP

I come back to the geography of it. Maximus, to Gloucester, Letter 27. Charles Olson. Fr. Maximus Poems, The. NOBA; PoE

I come back to try to remember the faces she saw every day. The Mad Druggest. Robert Penn Warren. Fr. Tale of Time. LCAP

I come from Alabama. Oh! [or O] Susanna. Stephen Collins Foster. AnAmPo; OBAL

I come from alcohol. Genealogy. Joan Larkin. LoHo

I come from Bohem, yet no news I bring. John Taylor. Fr. Taylor's Travels from London to Prague. OBVV

I come from Castlepatrick, and me heart is on me sleeve. Me Heart. G. K. Chesteron. OtMeF

I come from far away. I have forgotten my country. Foreign Woman. Rosario Castellanos, tr. fr. Spanish by J. M. Cohen. WPOW

I come from haunts of coot and hern. The Brook. Tennyson. Fr. Brook; An Idyl, The. BoNaP; BoTP; EBEvV; FaBV; FaPON; FHYEP; GN; GoJo; OxAEP-2, complete (Brook's Song, The.) FaBoBe

I come from heuin to tell. A Song of the Birth of Christ. Unknown. ScCV

I come from nothing, but from where. A Song of Derivations. Alice Meynell. OHCV; WGRP

I come from Salem County. Cowboy Song. Charles Causley. PoRA

I come from the city of Boston. Boston. John Collins Bossidy, also at. to Samuel C. Bushnell. FaBoCo; FaBoEE; NBLV; OBAL; OxBoLi; PeLV

I Come from the Nigger Yard, sels. Martin Carter. "I come from the nigger yard of yesterday." PBCV

I come home from you through the early light of spring. Adrienne Rich. Fr. Twenty-one Love Poems. BoWoP; GLP

I come more softly than a bird. Snow. Mary Austin. Fr. Rhyming Riddles. BoNaP; GrPl

I come, my bonnie Annie! (LL) The Trumpeter of Fyvie. Unknown. OxBB

I come of a mighty race. Hebrews. James Oppenheim. TrJP

I come out of a California orange grove. Smudging. Diane Wakoski. AmPA; PrIm

I Come to Bury Caesar. Sydney Justin Harris. PoA

I Come to Supplicate. Simeon ben Isaac ben Abun of Mainz, *tr. fr. Hebrew by* Nina Davis Salaman. TrJP

I come/ to the White Painted Woman. Puberty Rite Dance Song (Traditional). *Unknown, tr. fr. Apache Indian by* Willis Barnstone. BoWoP

I come to thee, O God long since forgot. Before the Statue of Apollo. Saul Tchernichowsky, *tr. fr. Hebrew by* L. V. Snowman. TrJP

I come to you with the vertigoes of the source. Yvonne Caroutch, *tr. fr. French by* David Cloutier. BoWoP

I come tonight to sing you songs. Korinna, *tr. fr. Greek by* Sam Hamill. InMo

I come with my pen. Island Muse. John C. M. Lyons. NBrP

I come with my word alive. (*LL*) The Question. Muriel Rukeyser. IHMS; WPOW

I conjure hem in the name of the Fader, and Sone. *Unknown*. MiEL

I, Conscience, know this Mother-Wit me it taught. The Age of Reason. William Langland. *Fr.* Vision of Piers Plowman, The. NOCV

I consecrate to thee. (*LL*) Rose Aylmer. Walter Savage Landor. AWP; BoLoP; CH; ELP; EnLoPo; EnRP; GBL; GGP; HAP; HoPM; LiTB; NAEL-2; NOBE; NoP; OAEL-2; OBEV; OBNC; OxAEP-2; PoEL-4; Poetr; SCGP; TEP; TFi; TrGrPo; UnPo; WeW

I consider I really am through. Elizabeth H. Lister. PeLi

I could always rely on the continuity. The Servant in Literature. Marjorie Welish. UL

I could bring you jewels — had I a mind to. Emily Dickinson. TAP

I could digest the white slick watery mash. Cafeteria in Boston. Thom Gunn. BAP-89

I could divide a leaf. Propositions. Phyllis Webb. MoCV

I could do nothing: nothing. Do you. The Child Taken from the Mother. Minnie Bruce Pratt. GLP

I could draw its map by heart. Amor Loci. W. H. Auden. NOCV

I could eat it! Snow. Issa. SiSoPo

I could find it only by change. (*LL*) White chrysanthemum, The. Mitsune. PoBeRe

I could go on writing like this forever. (*LL*) Squeal. Louis Simpson. BXAP; FiBHP; UnPo

I could have a job, but am too lazy to choose it. Lazy Man's Song. Po Chü-i, *tr. fr. Chinese by* Arthur Waley. OBVE

I could have been Lord Dacre or a balalaika-maker. Peter Norman. UV

I could have painted pictures like that youth's. Pictor Ignotus. Robert Browning. CTC; TEP

I could have wept and howled. Song of the Unloved. *Unknown, tr. fr. Sotho by* Jack Cope *and* Dan Kunene. PeSA

I could kill you right now. Lobo. Charles Lillard. NOBC

I could look at. Joy. Robert Creeley. PPP

I could love thee till I die. The Platonic Lady. The Earl of Rochester. NOSC

I could never dance until I met Rose at a party where. The Truth Made Breakfast. Jeffrey Miller. UL

I could no deeper love. (*LL*) Love Still Has Something of the Sea. Sir Charles Sedley. GBL; NOBE; OxAEP-1; SeCV-2

I could not dig: I dared not rob. A Dead Statesman. Kipling. *Fr.* Epitaphs of the War, 1914 – 1918. FaBoEE; IHNG; NBLV; NoP; OBWP; PoWW

I could not, ever and anon, forbear. The Solitary. Wordsworth. *Fr.* Excursion, The. EnRP

I could not hope/ to touch the sky. Sappho, *tr. fr. Greek by* Willis Barnstone. BoWoP

I could not look on Death, which being known. The Coward. Kipling. *Fr.* Epitaphs of the War, 1914 – 1918. FaBoEE; FaBoTw; NoP; OBWP; PeFWW

I could not name a single blessing. Neither Shadow of Turning. Jack R. Clemo. NOCV

I could not see to see. (*LL*) I Heard a Fly Buzz. Emily Dickinson. AmPP; AnAmPo; BoWoP; ClHu; CMoP; DL; FF; HAP; HeIP; HoPM; ImPo; InPK; LiTA; LiTM; MeMAP; MoAB; MoAmPo; MoP; NAAL-1; NALW; NAWM-2; NoAM; NOBA; NoP; OBD; OxBA; PoE; Poetr; PoRA; PPP; SAmP; SCV; SoSe; SOTW; TAP; TFi; TOF; TRP; WeW

I could not see You with my eyes. Sight and Insight. Eleanor Slater. TrPWD

I could not sleep/ For the sea was so smooth. Walrus Hunting. Aua, *tr. fr. Eskimo.* WTO

I could not sleep for thinking of the sky. John Masefield. *Fr.* Lollingdon Downs. LiTB, I – XV; LiTM

I Could Not though I Would. George Gascoigne. PoEL-1

I could replace. Earth Psalm. Denise Levertov. PPP

I could resign that eye of blue. To Cloe. Martial, *tr. fr. Latin by* Thomas Moore. AWP; NBLV

I could say. Hilda Doolittle ("H. D."). *Fr.* Sigil. AnAn

I could say it's the happiest period of my life. The Ongoing Story. John Ashbery. HCAP

I could take the Harlem night. Juke Box Love Song. Langston Hughes. GrPl; PoBA; SAmP; TTTS

I could tell he were gone. Shepherd. Jonathan Williams. ETG

I could wish to be dead! The Tragic Mary Queen of Scots, II. "Michael Field." OBMV

I couldn't bend the bow or pay the price. (*LL*) Graffiti. Julian Croft. NOBAu

I couldn't touch a stop and turn a screw. Thirty Bob a Week. John Davidson. EBEV; EBVV; FaBoPV; FaBoTw; ImPo; LiTB; MeMBP; NOBE; NOBVV; OAEL-2; OBNC; OxBS; OxBTC

I couldn't wait. My childhood angered me. The Wise Child. Edward Lucie-Smith. PBCV

I count black-lipped. Come Back Blues. Michael S. Harper. PoBA

I count my blessings. Sheep. Rochelle Kraut. UL

I, Crank Cuffin, swear to be. The Oath of the Canting Crew. *Unknown.* CBNP

I crave an ampler, worthier sphere. Anno 1829. Heine, *tr. fr. German by* Charles Stuart Calverley. AWP; OBVE

I craved for flash of eye and sword. Dreams. Israel Zangwill. TrJP

I crawl up the couch leg feeling. Whose Scene? Ruth Stone. BoWoP

I cremated Sam McGee! The Cremation of Sam McGee. Robert W. Service. BLPL; NOBC; OBNV; PoLF

I cried in my dream. Heine. RiWo

I cried unto God with my voice, even unto God with my voice. Bible, *O.T., paraphrased by* Sir Thomas Wyatt. *Fr.* Psalms. AWP

I crisscross my feelings with a view. Anne Waldman. UL

I cross the river to pluck hibiscus. *Unknown, tr. fr. Chinese by* Dell R. Hales. SuSp

I cross'd pynot [*or* crossed the pynot], an't' pynot cross'd me. Against the Magpie. *Unknown.* GBP

I crossed over the county line. Crossing the County Line. Elizabeth Randall-Mills. GoYe

I crouch over my radio. Speech. Henry Taylor. MAT; NBLV

I crowd all earth into a traveller's eye. Shillong. Bernard Gutteridge. PoWW

I cry:/ but you want comforting. Jalal al-Din Rumi, *tr. fr. Persian by* Omar S. Pound. ArPe

I cry I cry. No Categories! Stevie Smith. NoP

I cry to you beyond upon this bitter air. (*LL*) Immortal Autumn. Archibald MacLeish. CMoP; LiTA; MoAB; MoAmPo; NAAL-2; TrGrPo

I cry your mercy — pity — love! — aye, love! To Fanny. Keats. BoLoP; EBEV; EnRP; PPP; Son; TrGrPo

I cupboard these pickled peaches in Time's despite. (*LL*) Homework. Mona Van Duyn. VCAP

I curse my bearing, childhood, youth. J. M. Synge. FaBoEE

I curse the optimistic views of Haig. Scribbled at a Cabinet Meeting. Sir Edward Carson. FaBoVe

I cut in two/ A long November night. Hwang Chin-i, *tr. fr. Korean by* Peter H. Lee. ArNa; PBWP; VBLP

I cut the deck. A Valentine for Ben Franklin Who Drives a Truck in California. Diane Wakoski. NoAM

I damn such fools! — "Go, go, you're bit." (*LL*) The Day of Judgement. Swift. BIrV; ChIV-1; FaBoRV; NOBE; NOEC; OAEL-1; OBSV; PPP; SCGP

I dance and dance without any feet — . Spells. James Reeves. NTP

I dance on all the mountains. This Poem is for Deer. Gary Snyder. *Fr.* Myths and Texts. NaP; NoBA

I dance on your paper. Jack o' the Inkpot. Algernon Blackwood. BoTP

I danced along the sea. Eurynome Creates Her Consort Ophion. Erica Helm. *Fr.* Creation Songs of Eurynome, The. SRLS

I danced in the morning. Lord of the Dance. Sydney Carter. OBET

I Danced to the Rumble of the Drum. Elevena Burbank. AiP

I dare not ask a kiss. To Electra. Robert Herrick. BLPL; CaPo; HoPM; OBEV; SeCV-1

I Dare Not Pray to Thee. Maurice Baring. TrPWD

I dare not seyn when she seith "Pes!" (*LL*) A Henpecked Husband. *Unknown.* PeLV

I dare not tell it in words, not even in these songs. (*LL*) Earth, My Likeness. Walt Whitman. MeMAP; OxBA

I, dark in light, exposed. Milton. *Fr.* Samson Agonistes. FHYEP; ImPo; LiTB; OAEL-1; PoEL-3; TrGrPo, 5 *ll.*

I dedicate this poem. Daughters. Astra. BrRo

I delight in the prime of a boy of twelve. Strato, *tr. fr. Greek* by Thomas Meyer. GrAn; PeHV

I demand a thatched house. The Poet's Request. *Unknown, tr. fr. Irish* by John Montague. BIrV

I desire that my body be. When I Am Dead. George MacBeth. OxBTC

I despise love. What weighty God. Alcaeus, *tr. fr. Greek* by Sam Hamill. InMo

I despise my friends more than you. To an Enemy. Maxwell Bodenheim. TrJP

I despise neo-epic verse sagas. Callimachus, *tr. fr. Greek* by Peter Jay. GrAn

I did but look and love awhile. The Enchantment. Thomas Otway. OBEV

I did but prompt the age to quit their clogs. On the Detraction Which Followed upon My Writing Certain Treatises. Milton. FaBoPV; NoP (On the same.) Son

I did expect a ring. *(LL)* Hope. George Herbert. ChIV-2; PoEL-2; WeW

I did, I did, I did. *(LL)* Question Time. Jack Lindsay. NOBAu

I did my best;/ Farewell. *(LL)* The Sparrow. William Carlos Williams. InPS; LCAP; Poetr; PrIm; VGW

I did not cry, my good mother, the song in my hand burst in tears. The Silent Words. Haim Guri, *tr. fr. Hebrew* by Ruth Finer Mintz. MHP

I did not fall from the sky. The Women of Dan Dance with Swords in Their Hands to Mark the Time When They Were Warriors. Audre Lorde. NAAL-2; NALW; NoAM

I did not grow up among paintings. Nostalgia. Bin Ramke. MT

I Did Not Know, but I Remember. Tamara Fishman. BTR

I did not know she'd take it so. Under the Mistletoe. Countee Cullen. PChr

I Did Not Know the Truth of Growing Trees. Delmore Schwartz. LiTM

I did not know where you kept your heart. A "Case of Assault." Lydia Stephanou, *tr. fr. Modern Greek* by Kimon Friar. BoWoP

I did not live until this time. To My Excellent Lucasia, on Our Friendship. Katherine Philips. MeLP; NALW; NOSC; PeHV; VBLP; WPE; WPOW

I Did Not Lose My Heart in Summer's Even. A. E. Housman. LiTM; MeMBP

I Did Not Manage to Save. Jerzy Ficowski, *tr. fr. Polish* by Keith Bosley *and* Krystyna Wandycz. PoSu

I Did Not Notice. Franz Wright. LCAP

I did not see the frigate Constitution. Resurrection. R. P. Blackmur. PoA

I did not take the road to the capital. Tune: "Partridge Sky" — Written at the Po-shan Monastery. Hsin Ch'i-chi, *tr. fr. Chinese* by Irving Y. Lo. SuSp

I did not think that I should find them there. The Clerks. E. A. Robinson. AnAmPo; MoAB; MoAmPo; NAAL-2; PoEL-5

I did not want to be old Mr. Uncle Dog; the Poet at 9. Robert Sward. CoAP; PrIm; VGW

I did not weep my father. May Sarton. *Fr.* Of Grief. MDDM

I didn't get much sleep last night. Underwear. Lawrence Ferlinghetti. OBAL

I didn't give her a goodbye kiss. Grandmother Grace. Ronald Wallace. GOYP; Poetr; SM

I didn't know him. Suicide on Pentwyn Bridge. Gillian Clarke. AngWe

I didn't make you know how glad I was. A Servant to Servants. Robert Frost. CMoP; NAAL-2

I didnt thing I'd. I Was Surprised to Find Myself Out Here & Acting like a Crow. *Unknown, tr. fr. Seneca Indian* by Jerome K. Rothenberg *and* Johnny John. STP

I didn't want it, you wanted it. Married Blues. Kenneth Rexroth. *Fr.* Written to Music. Jaz

I didn't want this, not. Marina Tsvetayeva, *tr. fr. Russian* by Elaine Feinstein *and* Angela Livingstone. *Fr.* Poem of the End. OBVE

I die, and yet not dies in me. Dhu 'L-nun, *tr. fr. Persian* by A. J. Arberry. TOF

I Die because I Do Not Die. St. Theresa of Avila, *tr. fr. Spanish* by E. Allison Peers. TOF

I die; but when the grave shall press. Emily Brontë. TEP

I die for Your holy word without regret. Antonio Enriquez Gomez, *tr. fr. Spanish*. TrJP

I die I die the Mother said. The Grey Monk. Blake. PeECV

I die/ If I but spy. Upon Julia. Ernest Radford. BXAP

I died as mineral and became a plant. Jalal al-Din Rumi, *tr. fr. Persian* by R. A. Nicholson. TOF

I died for beauty — but was scarce. Emily Dickinson. AnAmPo; AWP; BLPL; BoWoP; ImPo; LiTA; LiTM; LPA; MeMAP; MoAB; MoAmPo; NAAL-2; NAWM-2; NOBA; NoP; SAmP

I died last night of my physician. *(LL)* The Remedy Worse than the Disease. Matthew Prior. FaBoEE; TrGrPo

I Died True. Beaumont *and* Fletcher. *See* Lay a garland on my hearse.

I died with [or at] the first blow and was buried. Autobiography. Dan Pagis, *tr. fr. Hebrew*. PoSu, *tr.* by Stephen Mitchell

I dined with Demetrius last night. Automedon, *tr. fr. Greek.* PeHV

I dinna care to tell. *(LL)* Comin' thro' the Rye. Burns. LiTB; UV, *abr.*; WBLP

I disappear! *(LL)* The Pleiades. S. E. K. Mqhayi. PeSAV

I disapprove even of eloquent/ Myrtis. Korinna, *tr. fr. Greek* by Richmond Lattimore. WPOW

I discover, remaindered from yesterday. The Strand. Michael Longley. IIP

I discovered the sweet lovely lady. Albrecht von Johannsdorf, *tr. fr. German* by Sylvia Stevens. GePo

I Discuss the Past and Not the Present, *sels.* Chin Nung, *tr. fr. Chinese* by Jonathan Chaves.

I dislike what I fancy I feel. *(LL)* There was a faith-healer of Deal. *Unknown.* PeLi

I do be thinking God must laugh. Boys. Winifred M. Letts. TIRV

I do believe. *(LL)* Dingty diddlety. Mother Goose. FaBoVe; OxNR

I do believe that die I must. His Creed. Robert Herrick. BeJo

I Do But Ask That You Be Always Fair. Edna St. Vincent Millay. Son

I do confess, in many a sigh. Lying. Thomas Moore. FiBHP

I do confess thou'rt smooth and fair. To His Forsaken Mistress. Sir Robert Ayton. EIL; ErPo; OBEV (Inconstancy Reproved.) GBL

I Do Love My Charlie So. Zelda Sayre Fitzgerald. AiP

I do not ask a flower. The Question. Wilhelm Müller, *tr. fr. German* by Philip L. Miller. *Fr.* Beautiful Maid of the Mill, The. RiWo

I do not ask for love, ah! no. Lethe. Georgia Douglas Johnson. CDC

I do not ask — for you are fair. The Complaisant Swain. Ovid, *tr.* by F. A. Wright. *Fr.* Amores. AWP

I do not ask, Oh Lord, that life may be. Per Pacem ad Lucem. Adelaide Anne Procter. TrPWD

I do not ask that God will keep all storms away. The All-sufficient Christ. Bernice W. Lubke. BLRP

I Do Not Ask Thee, Lord. *Unknown.* BLRP

I do not ask Thee, Lord, for outward sign. Jesus Himself. Henry Burton. BLRP

I do not ask Thee straightway to appear. Supplication. Edith Lovejoy Pierce. TrPWD

I Do Not Believe That David Killed Goliath. Charles Reznikoff. ChIV-1

I do not believe that Heaven and Hell are in different places. No Discharge. Arthur Waley. OBD

I do not consider myself worth counting. Kujo Takeko, *tr. fr. Japanese* by Kenneth Rexroth *and* Ikuko Atsumi. WPJ

I do not count the hours I spend. Waldeinsamkeit. Emerson. NOBA; WGRP

I do not dream of Sussex downs. Home Thoughts. Denis Glover. PeNZ

I do not enjoy. Rufinus, *tr. fr. Greek* by Alan Marshfield. GrAn

I do not envy the Duke of Sung. *(LL)* A Song of Magpies. Lady Ho. WPC

I do not fear to lay my body down. Exile from God. John Hall Wheelock. WGRP

I do not fear to tread the path that those I love long since have trod. My Creed. Jeanette Leonard Gilder. WGRP

I do not feel the peace of the saints. A Bird in the Hand. Vassar Miller. CRP

I do not grudge them: Lord, I do not grudge. The Mother. Padraic Pearse. PeIV; TIRV

I do not know, I cannot see. Confidence. *Unknown.* BLRP

I do not know much about gods; but I think that the river. The Dry Salvages. T. S. Eliot. *Fr.* Four Quartets. AiP; LiTB; NoP; OxBA

I do not know much about innocence. Lament, with Flesh and Blood. Sandra McPherson. SM

I do know/ One of my sex; no woman's face remember. Shakespeare. *Fr.* Tempest, The. OAEL-1; OxBM

I Do Not Know the Power of My Hand. Lance Jeffers. NBV

I do not know what it means. The Lorelei. Heine, *tr. fr. German* by Philip L. Miller. RiWo

I do not know what they are catching. Men Fishing in the Arno. Elizabeth Jennings. OBTV

I do not like the other sort. An Ulsterman. "Lynn Doyle." TIRV

I do not like the way you slide. Egg Thoughts. Russell Hoban. NTCP, *St.* 1 *only, sl. diff.*; OTCP

I do not listen much. Paul Hyland. *Fr.* Poems of Z. PWE

I do not live in the depthless cool. The Turning of the Year. Delaina Thomas. OpBo

I Do Not Look for Love That Is a Dream. Christina Rossetti. ArLo; GBL

I Do Not Love Thee. Caroline E. Norton. OBEV

I do not love thee, Doctor Fell. *(LL)* Doctor Fell. Thomas Brown, *after the Latin of* Martial. ChTr; FaBoCo; FaBoEE; ISE; MoShBr; NBLV; OBVE; OxNR (Non Amo Te.) AWP

I do not love thee! — no! I do not love thee! I Do Not Love Thee.
Caroline E. Norton. OBEV

I do not love to wed. The Poet Loves a Mistress, but Not to Marry.
Robert Herrick. CaPo; ErPo

I do not mean the symbol. The Woman Who Could Not Live With Her
Faulty Heart. Margaret Atwood. LCAP

I do not own an inch of land. A Strip of Blue. Lucy Larcom. WGRP

I do not praise the beauty of that voice. Nightingale Poem. John Drew.
PWE

I do not pray for peace nor ease. Prayer for Pain. John G. Neihardt.
TrPWD; WGRP

I do not share the common craze. Horace. See Boy, I have their empty
shouts.

I do not sleep at night. Night-Piece. Raymond R. Patterson. PoBA

I do not thank Thee, Lord. Thanks Be to God. Janie Alford. PoToHe

I do not think Grandmother or Grandfather. Favorite Grandson Braid.
Phillip William George. VoR

I do not think of you lying in the wet clay. In Memory of My Mother.
Patrick Kavanagh. BIrV; CIP; MoP; NoAM; RaBo

I do not think that skies and meadows are. Reciprocity. John Drinkwater.
PoA

I do not think the ending can be right. But That Is Another Story. Donald
Justice. CoAP

I do not think we can save them. The Children. William Heyen. BTR

I do not understand. The Unknown. Elmer Osborn Laughlin. BLPA

I do not understand this child. Father to Son. Elizabeth Jennings. GOYP

I do not visit his grave. He is not there. Peachstone. Dannie Abse.
AngWe; OxBC; WeW

I do not want a gaping crowd. When I Am Dead. James Edward Wilson.
PoLF

I do not want a plain box, I want a sarcophagus. Last Words. Sylvia
Plath. FYAP

I do not want only. Colleen Thibaudeau. NOBC

I do not want to be reflective any more. Wolves. Louis MacNeice.
NoAM; OxBTC

I do not want to pour out my heart any more. Marcus Aurelius. C. H.
Sisson. OxBC

I do not want to stand. My Own Hallelujahs. Zack Gilbert. PoBA

I do not want your praises later on. May 1506 (Christopher Columbus
Speaking). Winfield Townley Scott. GOA

I do not waste my breath. (LL) What the Bones Know. Carolyn Kizer.
VBLP

I do not waste what is wild. Empty Kettle. Louis Oliver. HATNAP

I do not wish to know. After the Persian. Louise Bogan. NYBP; PoA

I do not wish to speak about the bulldozer and the red dirt. Moving towards
Home. June Jordan. WoWa

I do not wish you joy without a sorrow. A Birthday Wish. Dorothy Nell
McDonald. PoToHe

I do seem to zee Grammer as she did use. Grammer's Shoes. William
Barnes. EBVV; EnVR

I doe but name thee Pembroke, and I find. To William Earle of Pembroke.
Ben Jonson. SeCP

I Done Got So Thirsty That My Mouth Waters at the Thought of Rain.
Patricia Jones. BlSi

I done try go to church, I done go for court. One Wife for One Man.
Frank Aig-Imoukhuede. PBA

I don't appwove this hawid waw. Swell's Soliloquy. Unknown. FiBHP

I don't as they put it believe in god. Dorothee Sölle. CrSp

I don't believe in a sun. Sailor's Memoirs. Muhammad al-Fayiz, tr. fr.
Arabic. TSaS, tr. by Issa Boullata and Naomi Shihab Nye

I Don't Believe in Human-tales. Brian Patten. OTCP

I don't believe there's such a thing. I Don't Believe in Human-tales. Brian
Patten. OTCP

I don't belong this far north. Washington. Lorna Dee Cervantes. Fr.
Visions of Mexico While at a Writing Symposium in Port Townsend,
Washington. NoAM

I don't care for women. Unknown, tr. fr. Greek. PeHV

I don't care if you're married, I'll still get you. Unknown, tr. fr. Kiowa
Indian. Fr. "49" Songs. STP

I don't care to speak of things past. Nan-Chin Gorge. Ts'ai Ch'i-chiao, tr.
fr. Chinese. LHF, tr. by Hualing Nieh

I don't care what you do for a living. To a Poet Who Says He's Stopped
Writing (Temporarily). Wing Tek Lum. BCF

I don't complain that time passes too soon. Tune: "Green Jade Cup." Kung
Tzu-chen, tr. fr. Chinese by An-yan Tang. SuSp

I don't dare start thinking in the morning. Blues at Dawn. Langston
Hughes. SAmP

I don't even know these roads I walk on. Shack Poem. Robert Bly.
CAPP

I don't feel like reading another book. Yang Wan-li, tr. by Jonathan
Chaves. Fr. Songs of Depression. SuSp

I don't give a ². A Radical Creed. Gelett Burgess. FaBoNo

I don't give a damn if some Thracian ape strut. Archilochus, tr. fr. Greek
by Stuart Silverman. GrAn

I don't give a duck. (LL) Poem in Time of Winter. Ray Mathew.
NOBAu

I don't go much on religion. Little Breeches. John Milton Hay. AnAmPo;
BeLS; FaBoBe; VPP

I don't go to the pub much any more. At the Criterion. John Tranter.
FaBoMA

I don't have any place to come up through. Shaman Song. Luswat, tr. fr.
Tlingit Indian by James Koller. STP

I Don't Have the Energy. Artie Gold. NOBC

I don't just want. Lover. Isobel Thrilling. DT

I don't know. A Poem against Rats. Fred Levinson. AmPA

I don't know. After Seeing Paintings in a Small Book by T. C. Cannon
(1946-1978). Alice Sadongei. HATNAP

I don't know about anything sometimes. Between Me and Anyone Who Can
Understand. Sharon Scott. JB

I don't know about you,/ but I'm sick of good poems. A. R. Ammons.
Fr. Sphere. HCAP

I don't know any greatest treat. The Parterre. E. Harriet Palmer. FaBoCo;
NOBL; PeLV

I don't know anyone at the table except. Strange Thanksgiving. Tess
Gallagher. NAmP90

I don't know as I get what D.H. Lawarence is driving at. Frank O'Hara.
LCAP

I don't know, but my folks say. Titanic, a Toast. Unknown. CBNP

I don't know how he came. Ossawatomie. Carl Sandburg. CMoP; OxBA

I don't know how it was. Mystery. "Yehoash," tr. fr. Yiddish by Marie
Syrkin. TrJP

I don't know if he is rare on these northern lakes. The Pelican. Greg
Kuzma. AmPA

I don't know man trust is a precious thing. Man in a Window. Ralph
Angel. NAmP90

I don't know much about sheep, don't know. Janet Holmes. FoLa

I don't know politics but I know the names. Kamala Das. NALW; WPOW

I don't know somehow it seems sufficient. Gravelly Run. A. R.
Ammons. CoAP; NAAL-2; NoAM; PoA; Prf; VCAP

I don't know the language. Homesick. Else Lasker-Schüler, tr. fr. German
by Michael Hamburger. PBWP

I don't know we didn't go. The Boys of '69. Michael O'Loughlin. Fr.
Shards, The. IB

I don't know who it is. The Lovely Étan. Unknown. NOIV

I don't know who they are. The Pointed People. Rachel Field. FaPON

I don't know why you tell me I'm drunk. Toxaoci, tr. fr. Tlingit Indian by
James Koller. STP

I Don't Let the Girls Worry My Mind. Unknown. AmFP

I Don't Like Beetles. Rose Fyleman. OxBChV

I Don't Like No Railroad Man. Unknown. AS

I don't like the look of little Fan, mother. Little Fan. James Reeves. Mes

I don't like weddings. The Wedding in the Courthouse. Kathleen Norris.
CrSp

I don't look back: God knows the fruitless efforts. We See Jesus. Annie
Johnson Flint. BLRP

I don't mind eels. The Eel. Ogden Nash. FaBV; FaPON; NTCP

I don't operate often. When I do. John Berryman. Fr. Dream Songs. NaP

I don't/ pity this man, I love him. Vanzetti. Charles Buckmaster. CBAP

I don't plow my southern acre. Thinking of the Way Home, a Song. Lo
Yin, tr. fr. Chinese by Geoffrey R. Waters. SuSp

I don't pretend to drink. A Welcome for Etheridge. James Cunningham.
JB

I don't refuse that kiss. Ammianus, tr. fr. Greek by Sam Hamill. InMo

I Don't Remember Anything of Then. Frank O'Hara. Fr. Ode to Michael
Goldberg's Birth and Other Births. NAs; NeAP

I don't remember exactly when Budberg died. A Magic Mountain. Czeslaw
Milosz, tr. fr. Polish by Lillian Vallee. AnAn

I don't say: that was before. Our pockets stuffed. Autumn Maneuver.
Ingeborg Bachmann, tr. by Mark Anderson. PRA

I don't sell for nothing less. (LL) The Lady in the Pink Mustang. Louise
Erdrich. HATNAP

I don't sleep. All night. Mirabai, tr. fr. Hindi by Willis Barnstone and Usha
Nilsson. BoWoP

I don't think it important. The Beast Section. Welton Smith. PoBA

I don't think that I believe in "gay life." Sonnet No. 22. Mark Ameen.
GLP

I don't travel much in these parts. Passing Ch'ien-hsi as Military Adviser in
the Third Month of the Year Yi-ssu. T'ao Ch'ien, tr. fr. Chinese by
Eugene Eoyang. SuSp

I don't understand economics. Rhymes for the Times. "Hugh MacDiarmid." IHNG

"I don't want a new dress," I said. A New Dress. Ruth Dallas. TSaS

I Don't Want Any More Visitors. Ingrid Jonker, tr. fr. Afrikaans by Ingrid Jonker. PeSA

I Don't Want to Be a Gambler. Unknown. AS

I don't want to be a nun. Unknown, tr. fr. Spanish by Willis Barnstone. BoWoP

I Don't Want to Be a Soldier. Unknown. NSI; PoWW

I don't want to boast. Vindication. Daniil Kharms, tr. fr. Russian by George Gibian. FaBoNo

I don't want to go. Reforger. Miriam Offenberg. BTR

I don't want to hear you beg. Isn't It Funny? Essex Hemphill. GLP

I don't want to pay down the last penny of my soul. Osip Mandelstam, tr. fr. Russian by W. S. Merwin and Clarence Brown. AnAn

I Don't Want to Startle You but They Are Going to Kill Most of Us. Kenneth Patchen. ArOW

I don't want your greenback dollar. The Greenback Dollar. Unknown. AmFP

I Don't Want Your Millions, Mister. Jim Garland. SWP

I doubt if ten men in all Tilbury Town. E. A. Robinson. Fr. Captain Craig. PoEL-5

I doubt if the wind in your boots. Stiles. John Pudney. NYBP

I doubt if you knew. The Rescue. John Logan. CoAP; NYBP

I doubt not God is good, well meaning, kind. Yet Do I Marvel. Countee Cullen. BPo; CDC; FF; NAAL-2; NoAM; PoBA; PoNe; Son; TAP; TTY

I doubt would serve to paint your destiny. (LL) The Answer of Mr. Waller's Painter to His Many New Advisers. Unknown. APAS

I drag a boat over the ocean. Lal Ded, tr. fr. Kashmiri by Willis Barnstone. BoWoP

I drag my shirt across the floor. Eager Street. Kendra Kopelke. AiP

I dragged my feet through desert gloom. The Prophet. Pushkin, tr. fr. Russian by Babette Deutsch. WGRP

I drank at every vine. Feast. Edna St. Vincent Millay. AnAmPo

I drank cool water from the fountain. The Raisin. James Wright. TAP

I drank firmly. His Father's Hands. Thomas Kinsella. PoE

I dranke onys; I wold drinke yette. (LL) Is tell you my mind, Annes Tayliur: Dame. Unknown. MiEL

I draw a deep breath. Remembering. Akjartoq, tr. fr. Eskimo. WTO

I draw hats on rabbits, sew women back to-. The Prestidigitator [2]. Al Young. NBV

I draw the breath of Old Japan. The Professor in Nirvana. Osman Edwards. Fr. Residential Rhymes. OBTV

I Dreaded That First Robin So. Emily Dickinson. AmPP; HAP; MeMAP; MoAmPo; NAAL-1

I dream I am flying above the city. The Question. David Ignatow. CAPP

I dream, I dream, I dream. (LL) Old War-Dreams. Walt Whitman. AnAmPo; OxBSP

I dream I stand once more. Dust to Dust. Gwen Harwood. FaBoMA

I Dream I'm the Death of Orpheus. Adrienne Rich. NALW; NMM

I dream my love goes riding out. Song for a Dancer. Kenneth Rexroth. TAP

I dream of. Memory of a Dream From the Year 1963. Tadeusz Rózewicz. PoSu

I dream of a headless man. Green Martyrs. Richard Murphy. Fr. Battle of Aughrim, The. NOIV

I dream of a red-rose tree. Women and Roses. Robert Browning. NAEL-2

I dream of Jeanie with the light brown hair. Jeanie with the Light Brown Hair. Stephen Collins Foster. AnAmPo

I dream of journeys repeatedly. The Far Field. Theodore Roethke. NAAL-2; NoAM; NoP; PrIm

I dream of Serenity. I'm a Dreamer. Kattie M. Cumbo. BlSi

I dream of the loves that are dead. (LL) Starry Night. Theodore Faullain de Banville. RiWo

I dream red dreams, an oasis of fire and light. Nellie Wong. Fr. Red Journeys. MDDM

I dream the dream. Oak Chrome. Iain Sinclair. VaA

I dream'd I walk'd in raptures high. Thomas Baker. Fr. Steam Engine; or, The Power of the Flame, The. BXAP

I dream'd that I walk'd in Italy. Going Back Again. "Owen Meredith." FiBHP

(Check to Song.) FaBoCo

I dreamed a dream: I dreamt that I espied. Arthur Hugh Clough. NOBVV

I dreamed a dream in the midst of my slumbers. Auction Extraordinary. Lucretia Davidson. AmWP

I dreamed a dream last night, when all was still. Reality. Angela Morgan. WGRP

I dreamed [or dreamt] a dream the other night. Lowlands. Unknown. ChTr; OxBoLi

I dreamed a dream the other night, when everything was still. Prospecting Dream. Unknown. AmFP

I dreamed a dreary dream this night. The Braes of Yarrow. Unknown. ESPB; OxBB

I dreamed all my fortitude screamed. Letter across Doubt and Distance. M. Carl Holman. PoNe

I dreamed I called you on the telephone. For the Dead. Adrienne Rich. AnAn; NAAL-2

I dreamed I held/ A sword against my flesh. Kasa no Iratsume, tr. fr. Japanese by Kenneth Rexroth. BoWoP; WPOW

I dreamed I lay in a little gray boat. Waking. Katharine Pyle. OBCA

I Dreamed I Moved among the Elysian Fields. Edna St. Vincent Millay. NoP

I dreamed I saw a little brook. A Vision of Children. Thomas Ashe. EBVV

I dreamed I saw Joe Hill last night. Joe Hill. Alfred Hayes. SWP; UnPo

I dreamed I stood upon a little hill. Two Loves. Lord Alfred Bruce Douglas. PeHV

I dreamed I was a barber; and there went. The Barber. John Gray. NOBVV

I dreamed I was a cave-boy. The Cave-Boy. Laura E. Richards. FaPON

I dreamed I was in a desert and because I was sick of myself. The Tablets. Nicanor Parra, tr. fr. Spanish by W. S. Merwin. AnRep

I dreamed it. (LL) On the Dark Side of the Moon. Mary Mackey. SRLS

I dreamed it rose. Black Buoy. Robert H. Davis. HATNAP

I Dreamed Last Night of My True Love. Unknown. AS

I dreamed last night, that I myself did lay. The Dream. Elizabeth Oakes Smith. AmWP

I dreamed of an island where I was the governor. Sancho Panza's Dream. W. H. Auden. Fr. Man of La Mancha. AnAn

I dreamed of colorful flowers. A Dream of Spring. Wilhelm Müller, tr. fr. German by Philip L. Miller. Fr. Winter's Journey, The. RiWo

I dreamed of him last night, I saw his face. The Dead Poet. Lord Alfred Bruce Douglas. PeHV

I dreamed of Ted Williams. Dream of a Baseball Star. Gregory Corso. VGW

I dreamed of war-heroes, of wounded war-heroes. The Heroes. Louis Simpson. OBWP

I dreamed [or dream'd] we both were in bed. The Vision to Electra. Robert Herrick. SeCP

I dreamed [or dream'd] that, as I wandered by the way. The Question. Shelley. CH; CoGr; EnRP; OBEV

(Dream of the Unknown, The. GTBS; GTBS-P

I dreamed that, buried in my fellow clay. Dream, The ("I dreamed that buried in my fellow clay.") Unknown. NOEC

I dreamed that I had died. The Mill Was Made of Marble. Joseph Glazer. SWP

I Dreamed That I Was Old. Stanley Kunitz. GOYP

I Dreamed That in a City Dark as Paris. Louis Simpson. CoAP

I dreamed that one had died in a strange place. A Dream of Death. W. B. Yeats. GBL

I dreamed that overhead. The Army of the Dead. Barry Pain. NSI

I dreamed that someone's coming. Someone like No One Else. Forugh Farrokhzad, tr. fr. Farsi by Deirdre Lashgari. WPOW

I dreamed the nymph that o'er my fancy reigns. William Alexander, Earl of Stirling. Fr. Aurora. NOSC

I dreamed the setting sun would rise no more. Parting. To ———. Robert Frost. AnAmPo

I dreamed there was an Emperor Antony. Cleopatra's Lament. Shakespeare. Fr. Antony and Cleopatra. UnPo

I dreamed there would be spring no more. Tennyson. Fr. In Memoriam A. H. H. EBVV, abr.; NOBE; OAEL-2, abr.; PeECV, abr.

I dreamed [or dream'd] this mortal part of mine. The Vine. Robert Herrick. BeJo; CaPo; ErPo; FaBoBl; NAAL-2; NoP

I dreamed you were my child, and I had come. The Dream. Paul Petrie. TAP

I dreamed you were stolen from my left side. Adam Confesses an Infidelity to Eve. David Constantine. PWE

I Dreamt a Dream. Arthur Hugh Clough. Fr. Dipsychus. NAEL-2

I dreamt a dream the other night. Lowlands. Unknown. ChTr; OxBoLi

I dreamt a dream! what can it mean? The Angel. Blake. Fr. Songs of Experience. CH; EnRP; FHYEP; LiTB

I dreamt about you last night. Dream. Unknown, tr. fr. Eskimo by Armand Schwerner. STP

I dreamt her sensual proportions. The Death of Venus. Robert Creeley. NOBA

I dreamt I came to a kind inn. A Kind Inn. George Dillon. GoYe

I dreamt I climbed to a high, high plain. The Pitcher. Yüan Chen, *tr. fr. Chinese* by Arthur Waley. AWP

I dreamt I dwelt in marble halls. The Palace of humbug. "Lewis Carroll." CBNP; FaBoNo

I dreamt I held the laughter-loving girl. Macedonius, *tr. fr. Greek* by Adrian Wright. GrAn

I dreamt I saw great Venus by me stand. A Dream of Venus. Bion, *tr. fr. Greek* by Leigh Hunt. AWP

I dreamt. I saw three ladies in a tree. The Three Ladies. Robert Creeley. NeAP

I dreamt it all, from end to end, the carriageway. Dublin Girl, Mountjoy, 1984. Dermot Bolger. BiHa; IB

I dreamt last night. For No Clear Reason. Robert Creeley. VGW

I dreamt last night. The Fierce Dream. Jeffrey Wainwright. DiPo

I dreamt last night of you, John-John. John-John. Thomas MacDonagh. AWP; PeIV

I dreamt my love was lost, uncomforted. The Consolation of Boethius. Melissa Green. BAP-91

I dreamt (no "dream" awake — a dream indeed). In Sleep. Alice Meynell. BrRo

I dreamt of the old house. To My Sister. Olga Berggolts, *tr. fr. Russian.* BoWoP, *tr.* by Daniel Weissbort

I dreamt of walking on icy waves. On the Melting Lake. Chung Ling, *tr. fr. Chinese* by Kenneth Rexroth and Ling Chung. WPC

I dreamt one night — it was a horrid dream. Out of the Frying Pan into the Fire. James Henry. NOBVV

I dreamt that I was God Himself. Ezra Pound, *after the German of* Heine. FaBoEE

I dreamt we slept in a moss in Donegal. Seamus Heaney. *Fr.* Glanmore Sonnets. NoP

I Dreamt You Went. Berta Freistadt. DT

I dressed my father in his little clothes. The Boat. Robert Pack. CoAP; SM

I Drift in the Wind. Ingrid Jonker, *tr. fr. Afrikaans* by Jack Cope. PeSA; WPOW

I drift off in a panel van waiting for Isolda. Spread Rhythm. C. D. Wright. LCAP

I drink champagne early in the morning. Cordon Negro. Essex Hemphill. GLP

I drink to your glory, God. Felix TchiKaya U'Tamsi. *See* I drink to your glory my god.

I drink to your glory my god. The Scorner. Felix TchiKaya U'Tamsi, *tr. fr. French* by Gerald Moore *and* Ulli Beier. TTY
(I drink to your glory, God.) NegPo, *tr.* by Ellen Conroy Kennedy

I drive home with the books that I will read. Edgar Bowers. *Fr.* Autumn Shade. VCAP

I drive my chariot up to the Eastern Gate. Years Vanish Like the Morning Dew. Mei Sheng *and* Fu I, *tr. fr. Chinese* by Arthur Waley. IMW

I dropped my sail and dried my dropping seines. Mass at Dawn. Roy Campbell. OxAEP-2; PeSA

I drops in to see young Ben. Chorus of a Song That Might Have Been Written by Albert Chevalier. Max Beerbohm. UV

I droun twa. (*LL*) Tweed and Till. *Unknown.* BoNaP; ChTr; FaBoCh; FaBoPP; GBP; OBEV; OxBSP

I drove to Little Hunger promontory. Little Hunger. Richard Murphy. BIrV

I drove up to the graveyard, which. The Soul Longs to Return Whence It Came. Richard Eberhart. CMoP

I dug a grave under an oak-tree. Amy Lowell. *Fr.* Dreams in War Time. BoWoP

I dug and dug amongst the snow. Christina Rossetti. FaBoEE

I dug, beneath the cypress shade. The Grave of Love. Thomas Love Peacock. CH; OxAEP-2; OxBSP
(Beneath the Cypress Shade. EnRP)

I dug in with all the spirit of spring. Knowing. Mary Coghill. BrRo

I dun already seen. (*LL*) U Name This One. Carolyn M. Rodgers. BlSi; NMM; PoBA

I dwell alone — I dwell alone, alone. Autumn. Christina Rossetti. BrRo

I dwell among the people. (*LL*) The Voice of God. Louis I. Newman. PoToHe

I dwell apart. The Hermit. Hsü Pen, *tr. fr. Chinese* by Henry H. Hart. RFM

I dwell in possibility. Emily Dickinson. EnIH; HeIP; NALW; NAWM-2; NoAM; NOBA; OxBA; Poetr

I dwell in this leaky Western castle. Dowager. John Montague. AnAn; IIP; IPY

I dwell on the misty steppe. The "Word" of an Antelope Caught in a Trap. Sandag, *tr. fr. Mongolian* by C. R. Bawden. WTO

I Eat Kids Yum Yum! Dennis Lee. TLR

I eat my peas with honey. *Unknown.* NTCP; RoPo

(Peas.) FaBoUs; FaPON

I eat what I wish. Cat's Menu. Richard Shaw. CRH

I edged back against the night. High Tide. Jean Starr Untermeyer. MoAmPo

I Edvard Grieg moved like a free man among men. An Artist in the North. Tomas Tranströmer, *tr. fr. Swedish* by Robin Fulton. PWE

I embraced the summer dawn. Dawn. Rimbaud, *tr.* by Enid Rhodes Peschal. *Fr.* Illuminations. SOTW; TTTS

I embraced the summer dawn. Dawn. Rimbaud, *tr. fr. French* by Enid Rhodes Peschal. *Fr.* Season in Hell, A. TTTS

I employ the blind mandolin player. A Music. Wendell Berry. VGW

I empty myself of the names of others. I empty my pockets. The Remains. Mark Strand. NYBP; PPP

I enact my being here. The Work. Robert Duncan. *Fr.* Dante Études. CAPP

I encountered the crowd returning from amusements. Resolution of Dependence. George Barker. FaBoTw; LiTB; LiTM; MeMBP

I Enter by the Darkened Door. Jenny King. BXAP

I enter, jingling hindu temple bells, deodorant ears. Blessing a Bride and Groom; a Wedding Night Poem. Robert Peters. BXAP

I entered into unknowning. Stanzas Concerning an Ecstasy Experienced in High Contemplation. St. John of the Cross, *tr. fr. Spanish* by K. Kavanaugh *and* O. Rodrigues. TOF

I entered it before I understood it. Spring at Nant Dywelan. Bobi Jones, *tr. fr. Welsh* by Joseph P. Clancy. OBWVE

I entered my parlor one bright summer morn. The Humming-Bird. Mary E. Tucker. CBWP-1

I entered the garden of my childhood days after. The Garden of a Child. Nirendranath Chakravarti, *tr. fr. Hindi.* TSaS, *tr.* by Chakravarti Nirendranath

I entered with a torch before me. Fleance. Michael Longley. CIP; PNI

I entrust my all to you, Aurelius. Catullus, *tr. fr. Latin.* PeHV

I entrust myself to earth. Thich Nhat Hanh. EaPr

I envy e'en the fly its gleams of joy. Written in Prison. John Clare. EnVR; OAEL-2

I Envy Not Endymion. William Alexander, Earl of Stirling. *Fr.* Aurora. Son

I Envy Not in Any Moods. Tennyson. *Fr.* In Memoriam A. H. H. EBEvV; EBVV, *abr.;* FHYEP; ImPo; LiTB; MeMBP; OAEL-2, *abr.;* OBNC; PeECV, *abr.;* PeHV

I envy the sleep. All Things Insensible. Kathleen Tankersley Young. ShDr

I envy you your chance of death. Hilda Doolittle ("H. D."). NoAM

I Epiktetos was born a slave, deformed. On Epiktetos the Stoic. *Unknown, tr. fr. Greek* by Peter Jay. GrAn

I, even I, am he who knoweth the roads. De Aegypto. Ezra Pound. VGW

I even I know the Eastern Gate of Heaven. He Knoweth the Souls of the East. *Unknown, tr. fr. Egyptian* by Robert Hillyer. *Fr.* Book of the Dead. AWP

I expect him any minute now although. A Glimpse of Starlings. Brendan Kennelly. PWE

I Expect You Think This Huge Dark Coat. C.M. Donald. GLP

I Expected My Skin and My Blood to Ripen. Wendy Rose. WPOW

I expected the lettering to carry. Victorian Guitar. Seamus Heaney. FaBoBl

I expected this face but did not predict it. Elijah Speaking. Doug Fetherling. NOBC

I fade like the waning moon. (*LL*) Since You Left. Chang Chiu-ling. OHMPC

I fail to see the ancients before my time. A Song on Climbing the Gate Tower at Yu-chou. Ch'en Tzu-ang, *tr. fr. Chinese* by Wu-chi Liu. SuSp

I failed my exam, which is difficult. I Am Still a Finn. James Tate. *Fr.* I Am A Finn. BAP-91

I, Fan-chih, wear my socks inside out. Wang Fun-chih, *tr. fr. Chinese* by Eugene Eoyang. SuSp

I fasted for some forty days on bread and buttermilk. The Pilgrim. W. B. Yeats. RB

I fasted three canonical hours. The Maiden's Plight. Brian Merriman, *tr.* by Frank O'Connor. *Fr.* Midnight Court, The. BIrV; NOIV, *tr.* by Thomas Kinsella

I fear, I fear the rarity. Death by Rarity. Marguerite Young. LiTA

I fear me much, shall hardly reach so high. (*LL*) In Commendation of George Gascoigne's Steel Glass. Sir Walter Ralegh. SiPS

I fear, Mr. Lear, you're a clot. Eric Swainson. PeLi

I fear no earthly powers. Robert Herrick. *Fr.* On Himself[e]. CaPo

I fear that appearances be worshipped throughout France. The Rat and the Elephant. La Fontaine, *tr. fr. French* by Marianne Moore. OBVE

I fear that I shall never make. Poet-Tree. Earle Birney. OxBC

I fear thy kisses, gentle maiden. Shelley. GTBS; GTBS-P

I float/ On the wind. Tamaki of a Hundred Lovers. Hirini Melbourne. PeNZ

I floated on a cloud one day. Cloud Fantasy. H. Cordelia Ray. CBWP-3

I flung my soul to the air like a falcon flying. The Falconer of God. William Rose Benét. WGRP

I follow from my window down. From the Window Down. Louis O. Coxe. NYBP

I follow my mother in from the car. In Chapel. John Pook. AngWe

I follow the army to campaign on distant roads. Joining the Army: A Song. Wang Ts'an, tr. fr. Chinese by Ronald C. Miao. SuSp

I follow the deer through shadows. Deer Hunt, Salt Lake Valley. Helen Handley. GrPl

I follow the moon into the mountains. In the Mountains. Wang An-shih, tr. fr. Chinese by Jan W. Walls. SuSp

I follow the scent of a woman. Dancing the Shout to the True Gospel; or, The Song Movement Sisters Don't Want Me to Sing. Rita Mae Brown. CrSp; NMM; PeHV

I Followed a Path. Patricia Parker. BlSi

I followed her to the station, with her suitcase in my hand. Love in Vain. Robert Johnson. UnPo

I followed my Duke ere I was a lover. Sir Richard's Song. Kipling. OtMeF

I followed, o splendid season. A Poem to Show the Trouble That Befell Him When He Was at Sea. Thomas Prys, tr. fr. Welsh by Gwyn Williams. OBTV; OBWVE

I followed the by-pass road behind Woodville. Cows. Lauris Edmond. PWE

I followed the narrow cliffside trail half way up the mountain. The Deer Lay Down Their Bones. Robinson Jeffers. NoAM

I followed where they led. His Throne Is with the Outcast. James Russell Lowell. TrCP

I ford a river to play with autumn water. In Imitation of Ancient Songs. Li Po, tr. fr. Chinese by Joseph J. Lee. SuSp

I forged I.D.'s to rescue Jews. The Hungarian Mission. Ruth Lisa Schechter. BTR

I Forget. Yoshihara Sachiko, tr. fr. Japanese by Kenneth Rexroth and Ikuko Atsumi. WPJ

I forget everything. I forget faces. The Keeper. William Carpenter. Poetsp

I forgot that my lips. Chiyojo, tr. fr. Japanese by Kenneth Rexroth and Ikuko Atsumi. WPJ

I forgotten who. Bumi. Amiri Baraka. PoBA

I foster a Love found of playing ball. It throws. Meleager, tr. fr. Greek by Barbara Hughes Fowler. Fr. Epigrams. HePo

I found a ball of grass among the hay. Mouse's Nest. John Clare. ChTr; InPK; LiTB; NAEL-2; RB

I found a dimpled spider, fat and white. Design. Robert Frost. BLPL; CMoP; HeIL; HeIP; InPK; InPS; MoP; NAAL-2; NoAM; NOBA; NoP; Poetr; PPP; PrIm; RaBo; SAmP; Son; SoSe; TAP; TFi; TRP

I found a fox, caught by the leg. A Fellow Mortal. John Masefield. OxAEP-2

I Found a Horseshoe. Unknown. AS

I found a/ hummingbird. The Container. Cid Corman. VGW

I found a little brown purse. Found in the Woods. Irene F. Pawsey. BoTP

I found a little fairy flute. Fairy Music. Enid Blyton. BoTP

I found a pigeon's skull on the machair. Perfect. "Hugh MacDiarmid." RB

I found a/ weed. Reflective. A. R. Ammons. HCAP; VCAP

I found again in the heart of a friend. (LL) The Arrow and the Song. Longfellow. AnAmPo; MeMAP; PFP; PoToHe; PWR; UV

I found at daybreak yester morn. Unknown, tr. fr. French by John Addington Symonds. Fr. Medieval Norman Song. AWP

I found her in the shade of spring. The Rose Wreaths. Friedrich Gottlieb Klopstock, tr. fr. German by J. W. Thomas. GePo

I Found Her Out There. Thomas Hardy. CH; CMoP; NoAM; NOBE; OAEL-2; OxAEP-2; PoE; PoEL-5

I found him downstairs. Dancing to Ellington. Jan Selving. Jaz

I found him in the guard-room at the Base. Lamentations. Siegfried Sassoon. OBSV; OxAEP-2; PeFWW

I found him lying near the tree. For a Bird. Myra Cohn Livingston. SiSoPo

I found him sleepy in the heat. Rattlesnake. Brewster Ghiselin. FoLa

I found his wool face, I went away. Reading Walt Whitman. Calvin Forbes. NBV; PoBA

I found in Innisfail the fair. Alfrid's Itinerary through Ireland. Unknown, tr. fr. Irish by James Clarence Mangan. OBTV; TIRV

I found in Munster, unfettered of any. Unknown, tr. fr. Middle Irish by James Clarence Mangan. Fr. Prince Alfrid's Itinerary. BIrV

I found it in a legendary land. On Discovering a Butterfly. Vladimir Nabokov. NYBP

I found it in the bottom drawer. The Manual. Larry Rubin. MT

I found myself alone, and I went there. Interiors. Aidan Carl Mathews. IB

I found myself one day all, all alone. A. Poliziano, tr. fr. Italian by John Addington Symonds. Fr. Three Ballate. AWP

I found that ivory image there. Crazy Jane Grown Old Looks at the Dancers. W. B. Yeats. CMoP; EBEV

I found the colour of your. At Castor Bay. Sam Hunt. PeNZ

I found the packets of seed in a cobwebbed drawer. Lost Seed. Patrick Williams. PNI

I found the phrase [or words] to every thought. Emily Dickinson. AmPP

I found the task that I had dreaded so. The Dreaded Task. Margaret E. Bruner. PoToHe

I found Thee in my heart, O Lord. Edward Dowden. Fr. New Hymns for Solitude. TrPWD

I found them all — I have written sooth. (LL) Alfrid's Itinerary through Ireland. Unknown. OBTV; TIRV

I found them here when I came. We Call Them Greasers. Gloria Anzaldúa. GLP

I found this jawbone at the sea's edge. Relic. Ted Hughes. NAEL-2

I found this photograph. Returning to the Town Where We Used to Live. Susan Musgrave. NOBC

I found you in a newspaper. Idea of a Swimmer. Jean-Richard Bloch, tr. fr. French by "S. P." TrJP

I found your Horace with the writing in it. On First Looking into Loeb's Horace. Lawrence Durrell. FaBoMo; LiTM

I, François Villon, ta'en at last. Would I Be Shrived? John D. Swain. BLPA

I frightened a little mouse under the chair. (LL) Pussy-Cat, Pussy-Cat,/ where have you been? Mother Goose. BoTP; FaBoBe; OxNR; ReMoGo; SoCa

I, from my chamber window, mark. Autumn Thoughts. Mary E. Tucker. CBWP-1

I from my window looked at early dawning. Bereft. Josephine D. Henderson Heard. CBWP-4

I gaed a waefu' gate yestreen. The Blue-Eyed Lassie. Burns. ScCV

I gaed to spend a week in Fife. The Annuity. George Outram. PeVV

I gat your letter, winsome Willie. To William Simpson, Ochiltree. Burns. OxBS

I gather thyme upon the sunny hills. Immalee. Christina Rossetti. BoNaP

I gave it a bang and in she dove. (LL) Mother's Nerves. X. J. Kennedy. GrPl

I gave my life to learning how to live. Postscript. Sandra Hochman. NMM

I gave myself to him. Emily Dickinson. FaBV

I gave myself to Love Divine. St. Theresa of Avila, tr. fr. Spanish by E. Allison Peers. TOF

I gave the jewel away to its owner. Lady Otomo no Sakanoe, tr. fr. Japanese by Kenneth Rexroth and Ikuko Atsumi. WPJ

I gave to Hope a watch of mine: but he. Hope. George Herbert. ChIV-2; PoEL-2; WeW

I Gaze across the Distant Hills. William Williams, tr. fr. Welsh by H. Idris Bell. OBWVE

I gaze at you. The Tattooed Man. Robert Hayden. CAPP; NoAM

I gaze upon a city. Thomas Hood. OBTV

I gaze upon the beauty of the stars. The Beauty of the Stars. Moses ibn Ezra, tr. fr. Hebrew by Solomon Solis-Cohen. TrJP

I gaze, where August's sunbeam falls. Newark Abbey. Thomas Love Peacock. NOBE; OBNC; PIP

I gaze with grief upon our generation. A Thought. M. Y. Lermontov, tr. fr. Russian by Max Eastman. AWP

I gazed, and lo! Afar and near. Battle of Somerset. Cornelius C. Cullen. PAH

I gazed through the darkness, one very dark night. The Light in the Window. C. L. Erickson. PWR

I gently touched her hand: she gave. I Pressed Her Rebel Lips. Unknown. BoLoP; ErPo

I get in between the covers as quietly as I can. The Word. Mark Cox. NAmP90

I get into bed. Every Single Night. J. P. Ward. AngWe

I get my degree. Lawd, Dese Colored Chillum. Ruby C. Saunders. BlSi

I get on. The Sleep Bus. Paule Barton, tr. fr. Creole by Howard Norman. PRA

I get up. I am sick of/ Rouging my cheeks. Morning. Chu Shu-chen, tr. fr. Chinese by Kenneth Rexroth. BoWoP

I give and bequeath. Extraordinary Will. Will Jackett. FaBoUs

I give my word on it. There is no way. Still and All. Burns Singer. OxBS

I give thanks. (LL) Awakening/ in a moment of peace. Harriet Kofalk. EaPr

I give thee all, I can no more. A Sum. "Lewis Carroll." Spl

I give thee thanks, Adonai! My Soul in the Bundle of Life. *Unknown, tr. by* E. Margaret Rowley. *Fr.* Dead Sea Scrolls, The. TrJP

I give Thee thanks, my King. Mael Isu O Brolchain. NOIV

I give you a house of snow. The Dove of New Snow. Vachel Lindsay. MoAmPo

I Give You Back. Joy Harjo. HATNAP

I Give You No Greeting. Marbod of Rennnes, *tr. fr. Latin by* Helen Waddell. MLL

I give you no greeting, Geoffrey. I Give You No Greeting. Marbod of Rennnes, *tr. fr. Latin by* Helen Waddell. MLL

I give you now Professor Twist. The Purist. Ogden Nash. FiBHP; GoJo; MoAmPo; MoShBr; NBLV; OBCA

I Give You Thanks My God. Bernard Dadié, *tr. fr. French by* Donatus Ibe Nwoga. TTY

I Give You the End of a Golden String. Blake. *Fr.* Jerusalem. NTP; Spl

I give you this Bible and more to take. Inscription on the Flyleaf of a Bible. Dannie Abse. TrJP

I go back again. Hawk and Snake. Leslie Silko. VoR

I go back ways to hurl rooftops. In My Mind. Norman MacCaig. OxBC

I Go before, my darling. *Unknown.* NoSic

I Go by Road. Catulle Mendès, *tr. fr. French by* Alice Meynell. AWP; TrJP

I go digging for clams once every two or three years. Clamming. Reed Whittemore. NYBP; TAP

I Go Dreaming Roads in My Youth. Luis Omar Salinas. AiP

I go in. It's A. Kit Robinson. UL

I go one step forward. Student. Cheng Min, *tr. by* Kenneth Rexroth *and* Ling Chung. PBWP; WPC

I go out of darkness/ Onto a road of darkness. Lady Izumi Shikibu, *tr. fr. Japanese by* Kenneth Rexroth. WPOW

I go out to totem street. Knock on Wood. Henry Dumas. PoBA

I go separately. Santa Fe Trail. Barbara Guest. NeAP; PoM

I go through hollyhocks. Las Trampas U.S.A. Charles Tomlinson. TwCP

I go to concert, party, ball. My Rival. Kipling. OxBTC

I Go to Meet Him. Grace Nichols. VBLP

I go to put a letter. Stone Age. Pat Nolan. UL

I go to say goodbye to the Cailleach. The Wild Dog Rose. John Montague. BlrV; CIP; IPY; PBCIP; PoE

I go to school in the morning. Embroidery. Catherine Nomura Crystal. AiP

I go to the Turkish shop, buy a bun. The Turkish Bakery. *Unknown, tr. fr. Korean by* Peter H. Lee. PBWP; VBLP

I go to work. Workday. Linda Hogan. HATNAP

I go, with your good grace, lords and kinsmen. Hartmann von Aue, *tr. fr. German by* Frederick Goldin. GePo

I got a brown baby. Brown Baby Blues. Una Marson. PBCV

I got a gal and she loves me. Cripple Creek. *Unknown.* AmFP

I Got a Gal at the Head of the Holler. *Unknown.* AS

I Got a Home in Dat Rock. *Unknown.* BPo

I got a letter from an old acquaintance in New York. Hate Mail. Steve Kowit. UL

I Got a Letter from Jesus. *Unknown.* AS

I got a one-eyed wife, a headless child. Guess Who. Fred Chappell. NBLV

I got down on my knees with the little. Staff. John Engman. NAmP90

I got his name and phone. On Finding Out that the One You Slept with the Night Before Was Murdered the Next Day. Chuck Ortleb. GLP

I got me flowers to straw [*or* strew *or* strow] Thy [*or the*] way. Easter ("I got me flowers to straw Thy Way.") George Herbert. BoTP; CH; FaBoCh; FHYEP; NAEL-1; NOBE; OBEV; OHIP; TrGrPo

I got no smile cause I'm down. Blues Poem. Jack Micheline. Jaz

I got one good look. Coon Song. A. R. Ammons. MoP; NOBA

I Got Rhythm. Ira Gershwin. CBLP

I got so I could take his name. Emily Dickinson. CMoP

I Got the Blues. *Unknown.* TTY

I got this job. For Hollis Sigler. Elaine Equi. UL

I got those little white schoolhouse blues. Little White Schoolhouse Blues. Florence Becker Lennon. PoNe

I got to Kansas City on a Frid'y. Kansas City. Oscar Hammerstein II. OBAL

I got up and opened the shoji. *Unknown, tr. fr. Japanese by* Kenneth Rexroth *and* Ikuko Atsumi. WPJ

I got up in the night. The Riverman. Elizabeth Bishop. NYBP

I gotta/ buy me a new. Après le Bain. William Carlos Williams. OBAL

I grant indeed that fields and flocks have charms. Rural Life. George Crabbe. *Fr.* Village, The. NOBE

I grapple dumbly with that prow-nosed face. (*LL*) Confrontation with an Artist. Elisabeth Eybers. PeSAV

I greet my love with wine and gladsome lay. Sabbath, My Love. Judah Halevi, *tr. fr. Hebrew by* Solomon Solis-Cohen. TrJP

I greet thee, my Redeemer sure. Salutation to Jesus Christ. John Calvin. WGRP

I greet you, son, with joy and winter rue. Muse in Late November. Jonathan Henderson Brooks. ChIV-1; PoNe

I grew/ for you. The Strong Bond. Juana de Ibarbourou, *tr. fr. Spanish by* Linda Scheer. PBWP

I grew from the earth. *Unknown, tr. fr. Greek by* Kenneth Rexroth. PGA

I grew great with the generation of our seed. Eurynome Births the Egg of the Universe. Erica Helm. *Fr.* Creation Songs of Eurynome, The. SRLS

I grew up bent over. Prodigy. Charles Simic. VCAP

I grew up in a village: now. Paradise. Louise Glück. NAmP90

I grieve and dare not show my discontent. On Monsieur's Departure. Elizabeth I, Queen of England. NAEL-1; NALW; VBLP; WPE

I grieve because I love you. Why. M. Y. Lermontov, *tr. fr. Russian by* Philip L. Miller. RiWo

I grieve for my second daughter. Written on Seeing the Flowers, and Remembering My Daughter. Kao Ch'i. DL

I grieve to think of you alone. Prescience. Donald Jeffrey Hayes. PoNe

I grieved for Buonaparté, with a vain. Wordsworth. EnRP (1801. Son

I grow a white rose. José Martí, *tr. fr. Spanish by* Seymour Resnick. *Fr.* Simple Verses. TTY

I grow accustomed to a new disguise. Journal. John Ciardi. PoA

I grow old under an intensity. Mirror. James Merrill. CoAP; SM

I guess an' fear! (*LL*) To a Mouse[, on Turning Her Up in Her Nest with the Plough]. Burns. EBEvV; EnRP; FaBoVe; FF; FM; HAP; HeIP; InPS; NAEL-2; NOEC; NoP; OAEL-1; OxAEP-2; OxBS; PoE; PoLF; PPP; PrIm; ScCV; SCGP; TEP; TFi; TrGrPo; UV

I guess because it was Key West. Meeting the Reincarnation Analyst. Gary Gildner. AmPA

I guess it is ever green. Evergreen Cemetery. Alfred W. Purdy. MoCV

I guess it was the summer of nineteen. Six Families of Puerto Ricans. Terence Winch. BCF

I guess it's too late to live on the farm. Essay. Bernadette Mayer. UL

I guess my mother spoiled me. A Headstrong Boy. Gu Cheng, *tr. fr. Chinese by* Donald Finkel *with* Yi Jinsheng. SpMi; TSaS

I guess there is a garden named. The Mirror Perilous. Alan Dugan. LiTM; TwCP

I Guess Work the Time Up, *sels.* Bruce Andrews.

I guess you love me now. Songs of Divorce. Jane Green, *tr. fr. Ojibwa Indian by* Frances Densmore. WPOW

I guide my boat to mooring by a misty islet. Passing the Night on a River in Chien-te. Meng Hao Jan, *tr. fr. Chinese by* Paul W. Kroll. SuSp

I gulp down seven drinks of water. Hiccups. Léon Damas, *tr. fr. French by* Ellen Conroy Kennedy. NegPo

I had a bicycle called "Splendid." Arthur Waley. Mes

I Had a Black Man. *Unknown.* OxBoLi

I had a cat. I Have a Lion. Karla Kuskin. SiSoPo

I had a cat and the cat pleased me. *Unknown.* OxNR

I had a chair at every hearth. The Lamentation of the Old Pensioner. W. B. Yeats. HAP; InPK; NoAM; TRP; WeW

I had a cow that gave such milk. *Unknown.* RoPo

I had a dog like a love. Penny Trumpet. Raphael Rudnik. MAT; NYBP

I had a dog/ Whose name was Buff. *Unknown.* OxNR

I had a donkey, that was all right. The Donkey. Theodore Roethke. GrPl; OBCA

I Had a Dove [and the Sweet Dove Died]. Keats. CH; FM
Sels.
  Song: "I had a dove, and the sweet dove died." FaPON

I Had a Dove and the Sweet Dove Died. Keats. CH; CoGr; FaPON; FM

I had a dream. Death Survey. Mongane Wally Serote. PeSAV

I Had a Dream. Irina Ratushinskaya, *tr. fr. Russian by* David McDuff. PWE

I had/ a dream of women, dark. A Dream of Women. Carolyn Maisel. IHMS

I had a dream one winter's night. A Dream. Maggie Pogue Johnson. CBWP-4

I had a dream: steeds and horse-cloths. I Had a Dream. Irina Ratushinskaya, *tr. fr. Russian by* David McDuff. PWE

I had a dream three walls stood up wherein a raven bird. Anger's Freeing Power. Stevie Smith. NTP; OxBC

I had a dream, which was not all a dream. Darkness. Byron. EnRP; LiTB; MeMBP; NAEL-2; OAEL-2; OPOP; PoE; PoEL-4; TEP

I had a duck and the young duck died. Archibald Stodart-Walker. FM

I Had a Duck-billed Platypus. Patrick Barrington. FiBHP; PeLV

I had a feeling in my neck. Mumps. Elizabeth Madox Roberts. FaPON

I Had a Future. Patrick Kavanagh. BIrV; NoAM

I had a little bird. The Orphan's Song. Sydney Thompson Dobell. CH; ELP; OBNC

I had a little boy. Blue Bell Boy. *Unknown.* ReMoGo

I had a little brother. Brother. Mary Ann Hoberman. SiSoPo

I had a little brother. *Unknown.* RoPo

I had a little chamber in the house. Elizabeth Barrett Browning. *Fr.* Aurora Leigh. FaBoPP

I had a little colt. *Unknown.* RoPo

I had a little cow. *Unknown.* OxNR

I had a little dog and his name was Blue Bell. *Unknown.* OxNR

I had a little dog, his name was Ball. *Unknown.* RoPo

I had a little hen, the prettiest ever seen. *Unknown.* BoTP; ReMoGo

I had a little hobby-horse. *Unknown.* BoTP; ReMoGo

I had a little hobby horse, it was well shod. Mother Goose. OxNR

I had a little horse, his name was Dappled Grey. *Unknown.* OxNR

I had a little husband. *Unknown.* BoTP; OxNR; ReMoGo

I had a little moppet. Mother Goose. OxNR
   (Little Moppet, The.) ReMoGo

I had a little mule and his name was Jack. *Unknown.* RoPo

I had a little nag. *Unknown.* OxNR

I had a little nut tree. A Nut Tree. *Unknown.* TTTS

I had a little nut-tree,/ nothing would it bear. Mother Goose. BoTP; CH; GBP; MoShBr; NTP; OxBoLi; OxNR

I had a little pony. Mother Goose. BoTP; OxNR
   (Dapple-gray.) ReMoGo

I had a little sorrow. The Penitent. Edna St. Vincent Millay. AnAmPo

I had a love in soft south land. Love From The North. Christina Rossetti. CBLP

I had a man in my sights. Blood Trail. Jon Forrest Glade. NGP

I had a Mother who read to me. The Reading Mother. Strickland W. Gillilan. BLPA

I had a nickel and I walked around the block. *Unknown.* RoPo

I had a silver penny. Nursery Rhyme of Innocence and Experience. Charles Causley. GoJo; NTP

I had a son and his name was John. Rundown Church (Ballad of the First World War). Federico García Lorca. RaBo

I Had a Strange Dream. Irina Ratushinskaya, *tr. fr. Russian by* David McDuff. PWE

I had a strange dream last night. I Had a Strange Dream. Irina Ratushinskaya, *tr. fr. Russian by* David McDuff. PWE

I Had a Terror — Since September. Gerald William Barrax. MT

"I had a true love but she left me." The Quaker's Wooing. *Unknown.* AS

I had ambition, by which sin. Ambition. W. H. Davies. MoBrPo; TrGrPo

I had an uncle named Sol. Nobody Loses All the Time. E. E. Cummings. CMoP; DL; FaBoCo; FF; LiTM; NAAL-2; NBLV; NOBA; RB; TwCP

I had an uncle once who kept a rock in his pocket. I've Got a Home in That Rock. Raymond R. Patterson. FF; PoBA; PoNe

I had as lief be embraced by the porter at the hotel. Two Figures in Dense Violet Light. Wallace Stevens. MoAB; MoAmPo

I had auchteen months o' the year. On Leave. John Buchan. NSI

I had awakened early. Second Ode to Persephone. Robert Kelly. *Fr.* Book of Persephone, The. PoM

I had become callous like most. On the Death of Lisa Lyman. Della Burt. BlSi

I Had Been Chained and Padlocked. William Kloefkorn. NGP

I had been happy, if the general camp. Shakespeare. *Fr.* Othello. OxBM

I had been hungry all the years. Emily Dickinson. ImPo; LiTA; LiTM; MeMAP; MoAmPo; NALW; SAmP

I had been sitting for days. Long Distance. Dana Naone. CDW

I had been thinking of Gabriel, Hilda Doolittle ("H. D."). *Fr.* Tribute to the Angels. NALW

I had been thinking of Marcel Duchamp. The Gift. Dara Wier. FoLa

I Had But Fifty Cents. *Unknown.* BeLS; BLPA; NBLV; WHSW

I had come to the edge of the water. Seamus Heaney. *Fr.* Station Island. PBCIP

I had come to the house, in a cave of trees. Medusa. Louise Bogan. AWP; BoWoP; HoPM; MoAB; MoAmPo; NALW; NoP; Poetr; WPE

I had eight birds hatcht in one nest. In Reference to Her Children, 23 June, 1656 [*or* 1659]. Anne Bradstreet. BoWoP; EAP; TAP

I had envisioned you. Poem to Lee Forest. Brenda Frazer. PoBeRe

I had for my winter evening walk. Good Hours. Robert Frost. AnAmPo

I had forgotten how to pray. When I Had Need of Him. Samuel Ellsworth Kiser. BLRP

I had four brothers over the sea. The Tokens of Love. *Unknown.* GBP

I had gone broke, and got set to come back. J. V. Cunningham. MoAmPo; OxBSP; VCAP

I had gone out to check on new lambs. Rebecca Newth. CrSp

I had heard/ before, of an. Mr. Brodsky. Charles Tomlinson. MoP; NoAM; OxBC

I had heard the bird's name, and searched with intent. The Oyster-Eaters. John Blight. NOBAu

I had just gone to bed. Petronius Arbiter, *tr. fr. Greek by* Kenneth Rexroth. PGA

I had made a mistake. Town of Finding Out about the Love of God. Anne Carson. *Fr.* Life of Towns, The. BAP-90

I had my birth where stars were born. My Birth. Minot Judson Savage. WGRP

I had my good and my. *Unknown.* MiEL

I had never heard of the whiteness. David Schloss. PoA

I had no God but these. Christ and the Pagan. John Banister Tabb. TrCP

I had no thought of violets of late. Alice Dunbar Nelson. BlSi; CDC; PoBA; PoNe; Son

I had no thought to find. Dabney Stuart. *Fr.* Opposite Field, The. NGP

I had no time to hate, because. Emily Dickinson. PoLF

I had no voice. Lilith's Child. Edward Francisco. DL

I had not an evil end in view. A True Dream. Elizabeth Barrett Browning. NALW

I had not been there before where the vagina opens. The First Birth. Rodney Jones. MT

I had not fastened my sash over my gown. Tzu Yeh, *tr. fr. Chinese by* Kenneth Rexroth *and* Ling Chung. WPC; WPOW

I had not known, in friendly life attached. Death of a Friend. Witter Bynner. IMW

I had not minded walls. Emily Dickinson. AWP

I had often, cowled in the slumberous heavy air. Dürer; Innsbruck, 1495. "Ern Malley." CBAP

I had over-prepared the event. Villanelle: The Psychological Hour. Ezra Pound. CTC; NAAL-2

I had seen, as dawn was breaking. La Nuit Blanche. Kipling. MoBrPo; UV, *abr.*

I had soaked the old house. Zimmer and His Turtle Sink the House. Paul Zimmer. Poetsp

I had some cards printed. Madam's Calling Cards. Langston Hughes. SAmP

I had some friends — but I dreamed that they were dead. The Friends. Kipling. OBF

I had the invitation of the king. This Our Life. Harold Monro. Mes

I had the lab science, the ecology of texts. The Other Syllabus. Chenjerai Hove. HBAPE

"I had this dream." My Dream. Lew Blockcolski. VoR

I had thought of putting an/ altar. Isabella Maria Brown. PoNe

I had thought of the bear in his lair as fiercely free. Part of the Darkness. Isabella Gardner. CAPP

I had three friends. Three Friends. *Unknown, tr. fr. Yoruba by* Ulli Beier. BoWoP; PBA

I had to kick their law into their teeth in order to save them. Negro Hero. Gwendolyn Brooks. CAPP

I had two pigeons bright and gay. *Unknown.* OxNR
   (Two Pigeons.) ReMoGo

I had walked life's way with an easy tread. I Met the Master. *Unknown.* BLRP; PoLF

I had walked since dawn and lay down to rest on a bare hillside. Vulture. Robinson Jeffers. NAAL-2; NoAM; NOBA; NoP

I had wanted a daughter. Mothers of Sons. Lesley Saunders. BrRo

I had watched the ascension and decline of the moon. W. J. Turner. *Fr.* Seven Days of the Sun, The. OBMV

I had written to Aunt Maud. Harry Graham. UV
   (Aunt Maud.) MoShBr

I hadn't asked her much. Grandmother. Sameeneh Shirazie, *tr. fr. Arabic.* TSaS

I hae seen great anes and sat in great ha's. My Ain Fireside. Elizabeth Hamilton. FaBoBe

I haf von funny leedle poy. Yawcob Strauss. Charles Follen Adams. VPP

I hailed me a woman from the street. My Madonna. Robert W. Service. BLPA

I hailed the bus and I went for a ride. Bus Ride. Selma Robinson. *Fr.* Ferry Ride. FaPON

I handed her my silver. The Lady and the Gypsy. Vernon Scannell. Mes

I hang by my heels from the sky. Hera, Hung from the Sky. Carolyn Kizer. NMM; SRLS; WPE

I happened once upon a time. James Hatley. *Unknown.* ESPB

I happy am, if well with you. (*LL*) In Reference to Her Children, 23 June, 1656 [*or* 1659]. Anne Bradstreet. BoWoP; EAP; TAP

'I hardly ever ope my lips,' one cries. Richard Garnett. OtMeF

I hardly ever tire of love or rhyme. *Variation on Belloc's "Fatigue".* Wendy Cope. UV

I hardly hear a Woman's Clack. (*LL*) On His Own Deafness. Swift. BIrV; FaBoEE

I hardly know how to speak to you now. Cambridge Elegy. Sharon Olds. IMW

I hardly suppose I know anybody who wouldn't rather be a success than a failure. Kindly Unhitch That Star, Buddy. Ogden Nash. LiTA

I hate an easy woman. Rufinus, *tr. fr. Greek* by Alan Marshfield. GrAn

I hate and love. Why? You may ask but. Odi et Amo. Catullus, *tr. fr. Latin. Fr.* Carmina. CTC, *tr.* by Ezra Pound
　(I hate and love; wouldst thou the reason know?) OBVE, *tr.* by Richard Lovelace
　(I love and hate. Ah! never ask why so!) OBVE, *tr.* by Walter Savage Landor

I hate and love; wouldst thou the reason know? Catullus. *See* I hate and love. Why? You may ask but.

I hate Eros. He is loathsome and will not. Alcaeus, *tr. fr. Greek* by Peter Jay. GrAn

I hate it when grown-ups say. The Frogologist. Brian Patten. OTCP

"I hate my verses, every line, every word." Love the Wild Swan. Robinson Jeffers. HeIL; MoAB; MoAmPo; NoAM; Son

I Hate Poetry. Julia Vinograd. AIW

I hate that drum's discordant sound. John Scott of Amwell. NIP; NOEC; OxAEP-1
　(Drum, The.) PAW; PeFWW
　(Ode: Against War.) ECEV

I hate the cyclic poem, nor do I rejoice. Callimachus, *tr. fr. Greek. Fr.* Epigrams. HePo

I hate the dreadful hollow behind the little wood. Tennyson. *Fr.* Maud[: A Monodrama]. EBVVPR; EnVR; FaBoPV

I hate the man who builds his name. The Poet and the Rose. John Gay. *Fr.* Fables. PeLV; TEP

I hate the Spring in parti-coloured vest. Mary Locke. ECWP

I hate these phrases: Of power absolute. Joshua Sylvester, *after the French* of Guy du Faur de Pibrac. FaBoEE

I hate to hear those crazy cocks crowing around a thatched inn. Rising Early in the Morning. Chao Yi, *tr. fr. Chinese* by Chang Yin-nan *and* Lewis C. Walmsley. SuSp

I hate to spend the night. Thanks Just the Same. *Unknown.* PoLF

"I hate your laces." The Teasing Toads. Michael Rosen. OTCP

I hated thee, fallen tyrant! I did groan. Feelings of a Republican on the Fall of Bonaparte. Shelley. Son

"I hates to think of dyin'," says the skipper to the mate. The Worried Skipper. Wallace Irwin. BLPA

I Haue [*or* Have] a Yong Suster. *Unknown. See* I have a yong suster.

I Have a Blue Piano. Else Lasker-Schüler, *tr. fr. German* by Ralph Manheim. TrJP

I have a bookcase, which is what. Shake, Mulleary, and Go-ethe. H. C. Bunner. FiBHP

I have a bottle and a pen. Thoughts from a Bottle. Carl Clark. JB

I have a bowl of paper whites. Window Ledge in the Atom Age. E. B. White. NBLV; OBAL

I have a boy of five years old. Anecdote for Fathers. Wordsworth. EnRP

I have a dog. My Doggie. C. Nurton. BoTP

I have a dog of Blenheim birth. My Dog Dash. John Ruskin. FM

I have a dream — a dreadful dream. The Mother's Son. Kipling. CoGr

I have a fairy by my side. My Fairy. "Lewis Carroll." CBNP; FaBoNo

I have a feeling that my boat. Oceans. Juan Ramón Jiménez, *tr.* by Robert Bly. NU

I have a fifth of therapy. Interview with Doctor Drink. J. V. Cunningham. OxBSP; VGW

I Have a Friend. Anne Spencer. CDC

I have a friend, she says. The Cross-eyed Lover. Donald Finkel. Prf

I have a friend who stil believes in heaven. Celestial Music. Louise Glück. BAP-91

I have a friend who would give a price for those long fingers all of one length. Snakes, Mongooses, Snake-Charmers and the Like. Marianne Moore. CMoP

I have a friend whose hair is like time. Time. Thomas Lux. BAP-90

I Have a Garden. Hayyim Nahman Bialik, *tr. fr. Hebrew* by Ruth Finer Mintz. MHP

I have a garden and I have a well. I Have a Garden. Hayyim Nahman Bialik, *tr. fr. Hebrew* by Ruth Finer Mintz. MHP

I have a garden here, shaped. Letter from an Institution: III. Michael Ryan. AmPA

I have a garden of my own. A Garden Song. Thomas Moore. BoNaP

I Have a Gentle Cock [*or* Gentil Cok]. *Unknown.* MeEL; MiEL; NOBE; NoP; PeLV

I have a golden ball. A Rune of Riches. Florence Converse. BoTP

I have a grief. Agitato ma Non Troppo. John Crowe Ransom. OxBA

I have a Gumbie Cat in mind, her name is Jennyanydots. The Old Gumbie Cat. T. S. Eliot. PFP

I have a heavenly home. The Spiritual Body. Phoebe Cary. AmWP

I have a jolly shilling, a lovely jolly shilling. The Jolly Shilling. *Unknown.* OBET

I have a kindly neighbor, one who stands. The Kindly Neighbor. Edgar A. Guest. PoToHe

I have a life that did not become. Easter Morning. A. R. Ammons. HCAP; NAAL-2; NoAM; NoP

I Have a Lion. Karla Kuskin. SiSoPo

I have a lion, a furry faced lion. The Animal House. Sandy Brechin. Mes

I have a little budgie. The Fat Budgie. John Lennon. NBLV

I have a little home amidst the city's din. The Complacent Cliff-Dweller. Margaret Fishback. PoLF

I have a little house. My Little House. J. M. Westrup. BoTP

I have a little inward light, which still. The Inward Light. Henry Septimus Sutton. WGRP

I have a little kinsman. The Discoverer. Edmund Clarence Stedman. AnAmPo

I have a little shadow that goes in and out with me. My Shadow. Robert Louis Stevenson. FaBoBe; FaBV; FaPON; OTCP; OxBChV; PDV; PFP; PWR; TEP; UV

I have a little shadow that goes out sometimes with me. My Shadow. W. Hodgson Burnett. UV

I have a little sister, they call her Peep-Peep. Mother Goose. BoTP; OxNR

I have a mackintosh shiny brown. Chestnut Buds. Evelyn M. Williams. BoTP

I have a mistress, for perfections rare. A Devout Lover. Thomas Randolph. HoPM; OBEV

I Have a New Garden. *Unknown. See* I have a new gardin.

I have a new home. A roaring Sparring Partner like a sunspot. The Newark Public Library Reading Room. Sotère Torregian. NBV

I have a new umbrella. My New Umbrella. M. M. Hutchinson. BoTP

I have a newe gardin. *Unknown.* MiEL
　(I Have a New Garden.) MeEL
　(Pear-Tree, The.) GBP

I have a place to come to. My Place. David Ignatow. CAPP

I have a pretty little flow'r. Francis Daniel Pastorius. SCAP

I have a proved, unerring Guide. The Unerring Guide. Anna Shipton. BLRP

I Have a Rendezvous with Death. Alan Seeger. AiP; BLPA; DL; FaBV

I Have a Rendezvous with Life. Countee Cullen. CDC

I have a river in my mind. Six o'Clock. Owen Dodson. PoNe

I Have a Roof. Ada Jackson. TrPWD

I have a room whereinto no one enters. Memory. Christina Rossetti. OBNC

I have a seamstress, making a shirt for me. The Seamstress. Harry Clifton. BiHa; IB

"I have a ship in the North Countrie." The Sweet Trinity; or, The Golden Vanity. *Unknown.* OBET

I have a small grain of hope. For the New Year 1981. Denise Levertov. ArNa

I have a smiling face, she said. The Mask. Elizabeth Barrett Browning. OBNC

I have a story fit to tell. The Strong Swimmer. William Rose Benét. PoNe

I have a stove. And Even, Even If They Take Away the Stove. Miron Bialoszewski, *tr. fr. Polish* by Czeslaw Milosz.
　("Oh! Oh! Should They Take Away My Stove . . ." My Inexhaustible Ode to Joy.) TSaS, *tr.* by Andrzej Busza *and* Bogdan Czaykowski

I have a theory about motion. Jazz Dancer. Cornelius Eady. UTF

I have a tree, a graft of love. Arbor Amoris. Villon, *tr. fr. French* by Andrew Lang. AWP

I have a vision. High Heels. Ron Padgett. UL

I have a whim to speak in verse. *Unknown, tr. fr. Norman French. Fr.* Fortification of New Ross, The. NOIV

I have a white cat whose name is Moon. Moon. William Jay Smith. CRH; PDV

I have a white dog. My Dog, Spot. Rodney Bennett. BoTP

I have a yong suster. I Have a Young Sister. *Unknown.* CH; CoGr; FaBoVe; MeEL; MiEL; NAEL-1; NoP; OAEL-1
　(I Haue [*or* Have] a Yong Suster.) EnVB; InPS; PoEL-1
　(I have a young suster.) EBEV
　(Love without Longing.) PeLV

I have a young love. The Sailor. Sylvia Townsend Warner. OBMV

I Have a Young Sister. *Unknown.* CH; CoGr; FaBoVe; MeEL; MiEL; NAEL-1; NoP; OAEL-1

I have a young suster. *Unknown. See* I have a yong suster.
I have achieved. That which the lonely man. The Seeker. Lascelles Abercrombie. *Fr.* Fools' Adventure, The. WGRP
I have all/ my mother's habits. Mother's Habits. Nikki Giovanni. BlSi
I Have All the Passion of Life. Lohta Lebron, *tr. fr. Spanish by* Gloria Waldman. WoWa
I have allowed myself. For Masturbation. Alan Dugan. CAPP
I have already come to the verge of. An Unborn Child. Derek Mahon. PNI
I have always aspired to a more spacious form. Ars Poetica? Czeslaw Milosz, *tr. fr. Polish by* Lillian Vallee. AnAn
I have always been sorry. To the Tune "Glittering Sword Hilts." Liu Yu Hsi, *tr. fr. Chinese by* Kenneth Rexroth. OHMPC; UnAS
I Have Always Found It So. Birdie Bell. BLRP
I Have Always Heard of These Old Men. *Unknown.* AmFP
I have always known. The Way It Is. Gloria C. Oden. IHMS
I have always laughed. Voice. Ron Padgett. UL
I have always regretted the shallowness of words. Looking at My Knife-hilt Ring, a Song. Liu Yu Hsi, *tr. fr. Chinese by* Daniel Bryant. SuSp
I have an earache. AIDS - Related Complex. Chester Weinerman. PFL
I Have an Orchard. Christopher Marlowe. *Fr.* Tragedy of Dido, The. ChTr
I have an uncle I don't like. Manners. Mariana Griswold van Rensselaer. FaPON
I have ane wallidrag, ane worm, ane auld wobat carl. William Dunbar. *Fr.* Tretis of the Twa Mariit Wemen and the Wedow, The. FaBoBl
I have answers to all of your questions. Michael Palmer. UL
I Have Approached. Alan Paton. PeSA
I have armoured my feelings. Rufinus, *tr. fr. Greek by* Alan Marshfield. GrAn
I have awakened at Missoula, Montana, utterly happy. *(LL)* In a Train. Robert Bly. CAPP; NaP; TTTS
I have awakened from the unknowing to the knowing. For William Edward Burghardt Du Bois on His Eightieth Birthday. Bette Darcie Latimer. PoBA; PoNe
I have baptized thee Withy, because of thy slender limbs. To ———? Richard Dehmel, *tr. fr. German by* Jethro Bithell. AWP
I have beaten him often, head and heel. Poète Manqué. Ernest Sandeen. CRP
I have been a censor for fifteen months. Censorship. Arthur Waley. OxBTC
I Have Been a Foster. *Unknown.* EBEV; FaBoRV; GBP; OxBSP
I have been a movie fan. He Never Did That to Me. Noël Coward. NBLV
I have been a/ way so long. Homecoming. Sonia Sanchez. PoBA
I have been abus'd of late. The Scolding Wives Vindication; or, An Answer to the Cuckold's Complaint. *Unknown.* CoMu
I have been away too long. The Rabbit's Advice. Elizabeth Jennings. PlP
I have been bent no less. Time's Mirror. Peyton Houston. *Fr.* Sonnet Variations. Son
I have been cherish'd and forgiven. Hartley Coleridge. PoEL-4
I have been cruel to a fat pigeon. Fly. W. S. Merwin. NNaP
I have been expecting it so much. Woman Wall. Lin Ling, *tr. fr. Chinese by* Kenneth Rexroth *and* Ling Chung. WPC
I have been faithful to thee, Cynara! in my fashion. *(LL)* Non Sum Qualis Eram Bonae sub Regno Cynarae [*or* Cynara]. Ernest Dowson. AWP; BeLS; BLPA; BoLoP; CBLP; ClHu; EBVV; EnLoPo; FaBoBe; FaPoB; GBL; GTBS-P; HAP; HeIP; ImPo; LiTB; MoBrPo; NOBE; NoP; OAEL-2; OBEV; OBMV; OBNC; PeVV; PlP; PoRA; PrIm; TEP; TFi; TrGrPo; UnPo
I have been figuring that in a way. The Time Is Today. John Farrar. GoYe
I have been given my charge to keep. The Fairies' Siege. Kipling. OtMeF
I have been gone for ten years. *(LL)* At Yuen Yang Lake. Wu Wei-yeh. OHMPC
I have been her kind. *(LL)* Her Kind. Anne Sexton. CAPP; CoAP; FF; HCAP; HeIP; LiTM; NALW; Poetr; PPP; TAP; TwCP; VCAP; WPOW
I have been here a year. *(LL)* Loneliness in the Tropics. Harry Clifton. IB
I have been here before. Sudden Light. Dante Gabriel Rossetti. BoLoP; CTC; EBEvV; ELP; NOBE; NOBVV; NoP; OAEL-2; OBNC; OHCV; OPOP; PlP; PoLF; TrGrPo
(Song IV: Sudden Light. CTC
I have been here. Dispersed in meditation. Agnosco Veteris Vestigia Flammae. J. V. Cunningham. VGW
I have been here for a half hour. The Library. Aidan Carl Mathews. CIP
I have been hungry all my days. The Etherial Hunger. Edith M. Thomas. AmWP
I have been in a marine aquarium and I have seen. The Marine Aquarium. Louis Dudek. *Fr.* Atlantis. MoCV

I have been in love, and in debt, and in drink. Love, Drink, and Debt. Alexander Brome. OtMeF
I have been in this bar. The Man Who Married Magdalene. Anthony Hecht. ChIV-2; PeLV
I have been kissed before, she added, blushing slightly, Arthur Hugh Clough. *Fr.* Bothie of Tober-na-Vuolich, The [A Long-Vacation Pastoral]. FaBoVe; OBF
I have been my arm. Margo Taft. NMM
I have been one acquainted with the night. *(LL)* Acquainted with the Night. Robert Frost. ChTr; CMoP; HAP; LiTM; MeMAP; MoAmPo; MoP; NoAM; NOBA; PDV; PoE; Poetr; PoLF; PPP; SAmP; Son; TAP; TFi; TRP; TwCP; VGW; WeW
I have been playing around. An End To It. Asa Benveniste. NBrP
I have been profligate of happiness. To Olive. Lord Alfred Bruce Douglas. OBEV
I have been seeing his face everywhere, the face of a former lover. The Lover. Robert Duncan. PeHV
I have been so great a lover. The Great Lover. Rupert Brooke. HoPM; ImPo; LiTB; LiTM; MoBrPo; PAW; PoRA; TrGrPo
I have been studying how I may compare. Shakespeare. *Fr.* King Richard III. OxAEP-1
I have been there again, and seen the backs. Again. Jon Stallworthy. OxBC
I have been thinking. Lynn. Jeanne Foster. CrSp
I have been thinking of the difference between water. Kabir, *tr. fr. Hindi by* Robert Bly. EnlH
I have been this way before. Pool. Cynthia Fuller. NWP
I Have Been through the Gates. MoAB; MoBrPo; TrGrPo
I have been to my God like the iris and the anemone. Saul Tchernichowsky, *tr. fr. Hebrew by* Ruth Finer Mintz. *Fr.* To the Sun. MHP
I have been to Paris since we parted. *(LL)* As Children Together. Carolyn Forché. NoAM
I have been treading on leaves all day until I am autumn-tired. A Leaf-Treader. Robert Frost. MoAmPo
I have been up and down the town. Hunger. Ruth Stone. InPS
I have been walking above Cwmchwefri. Cwmchwefri. T. Harri Jones. AngWe
I have been warned. It is more than thirty years since I wrote. But I Am Growing Old and Indolent. Robinson Jeffers. NOBA; TAP
I have been watching the war map slammed up for. Buttons. Carl Sandburg. PAW
I have been wondering. A Letter. Anthony Hecht. NYBP; OxBC
I have been young, and now am not too old. Report on Experience. Edmund Blunden. CoGr; FaBoTw; GTBS-P; NOBE; OBMV; OBWP; PeFWW; PlP
I have beene all day looking after. The Witches' Song. Ben Jonson. CH
I have begun to die. The Sentry. Alun Lewis. AngWe; PoWW
I have believed too long in one thing. March Weather. Jon Swan. NYBP
I have borne the anguish of love, which ask me not to describe. Hafiz, *tr. by* John Hindley. *Fr.* Odes. AWP
I Have Bowed before the Sun. Anna Walters. WPOW
I have broken step and faith. The Identikit. Amryl Johnson. NBrP
I have brought berries on a grape-leaf. Keepsake from Quinault. Dorothy Alyea. GoYe
I have brought it to my heart to be a still point. John Riley. VaA
I have built a world for myself. Spoiled Son, the. John Wieners. PRA
I have but one chance left, — and that is going to Florence. Arthur Hugh Clough. *Fr.* Amours de Voyage. FaBoVe; NOBVV
I have carried it with me each day: that morning I took. A Morning. Mark Strand. HCAP
I have carried my pillow to the windowsill. Summer near the River. Carolyn Kizer. CoAP; VGW
I have chatter'd like a pye. *(LL)* Anacreon's Dove. Samuel Johnson. AWP
I have climbed all the way to the summit. An Auditor Thinks about Female Nature. Jamie Grant. NOBAu
I have closed the double doors. To the Tune "Flowers Along the Path through the Field." Wu Tsao, *tr. fr. Chinese by* Kenneth Rexroth *and* Ling Chung. WPC
I have come down. Odia Ofeimun. HBAPE
I have come far enough. A Form of Women. Robert Creeley. CAPP; NaP
I have come far to have found nothing. Cid Corman. *Fr.* Three Tiny Songs. VGW
I have come to catch birds. The Bird Catcher. *Unknown, tr. fr. Egyptian by* Ulli Beier. TTY
I have come to terms with the future. M. J. Slim Hooey. EaPr
I have come to the borders of sleep. Lights Out. Edward Thomas. Mes; NOBE; OBD; OxAEP-2; PoWW
I Have Come to the Conclusion. Nelle Fertig. FF

I have come to where the world drops off. Visit to a Hospital. Jean Valentine Chace. GoYe

I have come upon the visage again. Wood Floor Dreams. Lance Henson. VoR

I have consider'd it; and find. The Resolve. Henry Vaughan *and* Thomas Stanley. ESCV

I have considered [*or* consider'd] it, and find[e]. The Reprisal[l]. George Herbert. ESCV; GeHe

I have continued to seek her. The Constant Lover. Louis Simpson. NYBP

I have courage and hardihood. Besieged. Zalman Schneour, *tr. fr. Yiddish by* Joseph Leftwich. TrJP

I Have Cut an Eagle. James Koller. PoM

I have cut the plaintain grove. The Witch. Santal. RaBo

I have deserted my post, I cdnt hold it. Poetics. Diane Di Prima. PoBeRe

I have desired to go. Heaven-Haven. Gerard Manley Hopkins, *tr. fr. Hebrew.* EBEvV; HeIL; HeIP; MoAB; MoBrPo; MoP; NoAM; NOBE; NOCV; OBEV; OBNC; OxAEP-2; OxBSP; PeECV; RB; SoSe; SOTW; TFi; TOF; TrGrPo

I have discovered a country. Connais-Tu le Pays? Richard Shelton. NYBP

I have discovered that most of. January Morning. William Carlos Williams. InPS; SOTW

I have done all I could. The Tree and the Lady. Thomas Hardy. MoAB; MoBrPo

I have done it again. Lady Lazarus. Sylvia Plath. CAPP; ChIV-2; FaBoWP; HCAP; MAT; MoP; NAAL-2; NALW; NaP; NIP; NoAM; NOBA; NoP; Poetr; PrIm; TAP; TRP; VCAP; VGW

I have done one braver thing. The Undertaking. John Donne. NAEL-1; NOBE

I have done the deed. Didst thou not hear a noise? Shakespeare. *Fr.* Macbeth. EBEV; OxAEP-1

I have dreamt it again: standing suddenly still. Wormwood. Thomas Kinsella. CIP; PBCIP

I have drifted in silence. Imitations Based on the American. Frank Polite. BXAP

I have drunk ale from the Country of the Young. He Thinks of His Past Greatness When a Part of the Constellations of Heaven. W. B. Yeats. MeMBP; PoEL-5

I have eaten/ the plums. This Is Just to Say. William Carlos Williams. FF; GoJo; HeIP; HoPM; InPK; InPS; NAAL-2; NIP; NoAM; NOBA; NoP; NTP; PFP; Poetr; SOTW; TAP; TRP

I have examin'd and do find. To Mrs. M. A. at Parting. Katherine Philips. OBF

I have fallen in love with American names. American Names. Stephen Vincent Benét. GOA; OBAL; OxBA

I have fastened everything within a black cloak. The Assignation. Juana de Ibarbourou, *tr. fr. Spanish by* Brian Swann. PBWP

I have fathered. Father Poem. Joel Oppenheimer. PoM

I have felt it as they've said. Larry Eigner. PoM

I have finally learned. Valerio Magrelli, *tr. fr. Italian by* Dana Gioia. NeIt

"I have finished another year," said God. New Year's Eve. Thomas Hardy. MoBrPo; NoAM

I Have Folded My Sorrows. Bob Kaufman. PoBA

I have followed you model. Ode to a Model. Vladimir Nabokov. OBAL

I have forgotten you as one forgets at dawning. Words. Helen Morgan Brooks. PoNe

I have forsworn it whil[e] I live [*or* life]. *Unknown.* MiEL (Wake at the Well, The.) GBP

I Have Fought the Good Fight. Jared B. Waterbury. AH

I have found out a gift for my Erin. A Pastoral Ballad by John Bull. Thomas Moore. BlrV; OBSV

I Have Found Such Joy. Grace Noll Crowell. PoToHe

I have found such joy in simple things. I Have Found Such Joy. Grace Noll Crowell. PoToHe

I have found violets. April hath come on. April. Nathaniel Parker Willis. AnAmPo

I have from you this red. Valerio Magrelli, *tr. fr. Italian by* Dana Gioia. NeIt

I Have Given Fair Warning. Philip Lamantia. PoBeRe

I have gone back in boyish wonderment. Return. Sterling A. Brown. CDC

I have gone far from my beloved ones. Jerusalem the Dismembered. Uri Zvi Greenberg, *tr. fr. Hebrew by* Charles A. Cowen. *Fr.* Jerusalem. TrJP

I have gone out, a possessed witch. Her Kind. Anne Sexton. CAPP; CoAP; FF; HCAP; HeIP; LiTM; NALW; Poetr; PPP; TAP; TwCP; VCAP; WPOW

I have gone past all those times when the poets. In Memory of Leopardi. James Wright. NaP

I have got a new-born sister. Choosing a Name. Charles Lamb *and* Mary Lamb *and* Mary Lamb. OxBChV

I Have Got My Leave. Rabindranath Tagore. *Fr.* Gitanjali. OBMV

I have great need that the Saint grant help. Cynewulf, *tr. fr. Anglo-Saxon by* Charles W. Kennedy. *Fr.* Juliana. AnOE

I have grown past hate and bitterness. Nationality. Mary Gilmore, *tr. fr. Eskimo.* CBAP; PAW; WTO

I have grown used to the retreat of seasons. Lady Anne Bathing. Anthony Delius. PeSA

I have had a most rare vision. Bottom's Dream. Shakespeare. *Fr.* Midsummer Night's Dream, A. CBNP

I have had all: over and in that all. An End. Rose Terry Cooke. AmWP

I have had not one word from her. Sappho, *tr. fr. Greek by* Mary Barnard. PeHV

I have had playmates, I have had companions. The Old Familiar Faces. Charles Lamb. AWP; BLPA; CoGr; EnRP; FaBoBe; FaBoRV; FaPoR; GTBS; GTBS-P; NOBE; OBEV; OBF; OxAEP-2; PlP; RB

I have had to learn the simplest things. Maximus, to Himself. Charles Olson. *Fr. Maximus Poems, The.* CAPP; CMoP; NeAP; NOBA; PoE; PoM; VGW

I Have Heard. *Unknown.* FiBHP

I have heard a mother bird. Welcome to Spring. Irene Thompson. BoTP

I have heard ingenuous Indians say. Roger Williams. SCAP

I have heard of fish. The Sun. Anne Sexton. NYBP; PBWP

"I have heard," said a maid from Montclair. Morris Bishop. PeLi

I have heard some jealous women say. Romantic. George Garrett. HoPM

I have heard talk of bold Robin Hood. Robin Hood's Golden Prize. *Unknown.* ESPB

I have heard tell somewhere. The Old Dog in the Ruins of the Graves at Arles. James Wright. NNaP

I have heard that far from here. *Unknown, tr. fr. Anglo-Saxon. Fr.* Phoenix, The. ASW, *tr. by* Kevin Crossley-Holland

I have heard that hysterical women say. Lapis Lazuli. W. B. Yeats. CMoP; EnlH; FaBoMo; FaBoTw; FF; HeIP; InPS; LiTB; LiTM; MAT; MeMBP; MoP; NAEL-2; NAWM-2; NoAM; NOBE; NoP; OAEL-2; TEP; TFi

I have heard the affairs in Ch'ang-an are like a game of chess. Tu Fu, *tr. by* Wu-chi Liu. *Fr.* Autumn Thoughts. SuSp

I have heard the curlew crying. Wild Geese. Katharine Tynan. IIP

I have heard the pigeons of the Seven Woods. In the Seven Woods. W. B. Yeats. CMoP; NoAM

I have heard the stirring chorus. I Have Heard. *Unknown.* FiBHP

I Have Heard Them Knock. Michael Hartnett. NOIV

I have heard your voice floating, royal and real. To Dinah Washington. Etheridge Knight. PoBA

I have hoped, I have planned, I have striven. Unsubdued. Samuel Ellsworth Kiser. PoToHe

I have hopped, when properly wound up. The Tin Frog. Russell Hoban. (I have hopped, when properly wound up, the whole length.) Spl

I have hung my lute on the wall. Pause. Wilhelm Müller, *tr. fr. German by* Philip L. Miller. *Fr.* Beautiful Maid of the Mill, The. RiWo

I have imagined all this. The Sleeping. Lynn Emanuel. AiP

I have in my hand here a brown bottle. The Bottle. Al Levine. GrPl

I have it in my heart to serve God so. Of His Lady in Heaven. Jacopo da Lentino, *tr. fr. Italian by* Dante Gabriel Rossetti. AWP

I have it now. The Stone. Henry Vaughan. ChIV-1

I have it underfoot; I have found it. For a Swarm of Bees. *Unknown, tr. fr. Anglo-Saxon by* Kevin Crossley-Holland. ASW

I have just come down from my father. (*LL*) The Hospital Window. James Dickey. CAPP; HCAP; MT; NoAM; VCAP

I have just come down from my father. The Hospital Window. James Dickey. CAPP; HCAP; MT; NoAM; VCAP

"I have just come from the salt, salt sea." The House Carpenter. *Unknown.* AS

I have just flown 1100 miles from Australia. Christchurch, N. Z. Earle Birney. OxBC

I have just returned for to marry thee. (*LL*) A Pretty Fair Maid. *Unknown.* AS

I have just seen a most beautiful thing. The Black Finger. Angelina Weld Grimké. PoBA; ShDr

I have just seen you go down the mountain. Departure. Wang Wei, *tr. fr. Chinese by* Robert Payne. TAL

I have killed the moth flying around. Moth-Terror. Benjamin de Casseres. TrJP

I have known it from the beginning. Aristophanes' Symposium. Rita Mae Brown. IHMS

I have known one bound to a bed by wrist and ankle. The Choice. Hilary Corke. NYBP

I have known the inexorable sadness of pencils. Dolor. Theodore Roethke. AmPP; CMoP; HCAP; HeIP; HoPM; LiTM; MoP; NoAM; OxBSP; PoA; TRP

I have known the silence of the stars and of the sea. Silence. Edgar Lee Masters. MoAmPo; PoToHe

I have known the strange nurses of Kindness. But I Do Not Need Kindness. Gregory Corso. NeAP

I Have Labored Sore. *Unknown*. MiEL; WeW

I have lain in the sun. Fortunatus Nimium. Robert Bridges. (Nimium Fortunatus.) MoAB; MoBrPo

I have learn'd. Shakespeare. *Fr.* King Henry IV, Pt. I. NAEL-1; OxAEP-1

I have learned not to worry about love. New Face. Alice Walker. AIW

I have led a good life, full of peace and quiet. The Good Boy. *Unknown*. AS

I Have Led Her Home, My Love, My Only Friend. Tennyson. *Fr.* Maud [: A Monodrama]. CBLP; EBVV; ELP; EnVR; MeMBP; NAEL-2; NOBVV; PoEL-5

I have left you at last. *(LL)* Ireland. Dora Sigerson Shorter. IIP; OBEV; TIRV

I have left you four flies. To the Spider in the Crevice behind the Toilet Door. Janet Sutherland. DT; VBLP

I have let all my balloons aloose. Breaking Out. A. R. Ammons. CAPP

I Have Lighted the Candles, Mary. Kenneth Patchen. TrCP

I Have Lived and I Have Loved. *Unknown*. TTTS

I have lived between my two hands. Hands. Edvard Kocbek, *tr. fr. Slovene by* Michael Scammell *and* Veno Taufer. PoSu

I have lived here, in exile, for seven years. Foreign Inhabitant. Juan Felipe Herrera. ETG

I have lived in important places, times. Epic. Patrick Kavanagh. BIrV; CIP; IPY; NOIV

I Have Lived Long Enough. Shakespeare. *Fr.* Macbeth. TrGrPo

I have lived long enough, having seen one thing, that love hath an end. Hymn to Proserpine. Swinburne. EBVV; EnVR; NAEL-2; OAEL-2; OBNC; PoEL-5; TEP

I have lived on the lip. Jalal al-Din Rumi, *tr. fr. Persian by* Coleman Barks *and* A. J. Arberry. EnlH

I Have Lived This Way for Years and Do Not Wish to Change. Michael C. Blumenthal. HCAP

I have looked at this photograph. Rescue. Dabney Stuart. NYBP

I have lost, and lately, these. Upon the Loss[e] of His Mistresses. Robert Herrick. BeJo; CaPo; NAEL-1; NOSC; PoE; SeCV-1

I have lost my melch Cow. 2 Antemasque, The: Two Countrye Wives, the Songe. Lady Jane Cavendish *and* Lady Elizabeth Brackley. *Fr.* Pastorall, A. KTR

I Have Lost My Shoes. Constantino Suasnavar, *tr. fr. Spanish by* Muna Lee. FaPON

I Have Loved England. Alice Duer Miller. *Fr.* White Cliffs, The. BLPL; PoLF

I Have Loved Flowers. Robert Bridges. GoJo; MoAB; MoBrPo

I Have Loved Hours at Sea. Sara Teasdale. ArLo

I have loved large cities, capitals of the world. The Master City. Rose J. Orente. GoYe

I have loved thirty by three. Gormley, Queen of Ireland, *tr. fr. Irish by* Joan Keefe. *Fr.* Gormley's Laments. PBWP

I have made a sirventes against the city of Toulouse. Sirventes. Paul Blackburn. NeAP; PoM

I have made tales in verse, but this man made. The Waggon-Maker. John Masefield. EBEV

I have marked, as on the heather now I strayed. As on the Heather. Reinmar von Hagenau, *tr. fr. German by* Jethro Bithell. AWP

I have mentioned it by name. Edouard J. Maunick, *tr. fr. French by* Ellen Conroy Kennedy. *Fr.* As Far as Yoruba Land. NegPo

I have met them at close of day. Easter, 1916. W. B. Yeats. CMoP; FaBoMo; FaBoPV; FaPoR; HAP; HeIP; IIP; InPS; LiTM; MoAB; MoP; NAEL-2; NAWM-2; NoAM; NOBE; NOIV; NoP; OAEL-2; OBWP; OxAEP-2; OxBTC; PoE; PPP; TFi

I have mislaid the torment and the fear. Success. William Empson. OxBTC

I have moved to Dublin to have it out with you. John Berryman. *Fr.* Dream Songs. MoP; NoAM; TRP

I have moved to this home of Immortals. Living in the Summer Mountains. Yü Hsüan-chi, *tr. fr. Chinese by* Kenneth Rexroth *and* Ling Chung. WPC

I have my heart on my fist. The Tomb of the Kings. Anne Hébert, *tr. by* Kathleen Weaver. PBWP

I have my piety too, which could. An Epitaph on Master Vincent Corbett. Ben Jonson. BeJo; JCP

I have my roots inside me. Old Mountains Want to Turn to Sand. Tommy Olofsson, *tr. fr. Swedish by* Jean Pearson. TSaS

I have neither the scholar's melancholy. A Compound Melancholy. Shakespeare. *Fr.* As You Like It. CBCK

I have never been rich before. To My Friend. Anne Campbell. PoToHe

I have never been to Woolland, downhill from. Ordnance Survey Map 178. Douglas Oliver. VaA

I have never cut my hair. Window That Watched the Pru. Anne Sexton. Poetr

I have never felt so Rococó. Velvet Baroque/Act. Juan Felipe Herrera. ETG

I have never returned. Alien. Gillian Allnutt. NBrP

I have never seen him, this invisible member of the panel, this thirteenth juror. The People vs. the People. Kenneth Fearing. MoAmPo

I have never seen the place where I was born. Birthplace. Tahereh Saffarzadeh, *tr. fr. Farsi by* Deirdre Lashgari. AIW; WPOW

I have never seen volcanoes. Emily Dickinson. PoEL-5

I have no desire to live, but I am afraid of death. Ts'ai Yen, *tr. fr. Chinese by* Kenneth Rexroth *and* Ling Chung. *Fr.* Eighteen Verses Sung to a Tatar Reed Whistle. WPC; WPOW

I have no dog, but it must be. My Dog. John Kendrick Bangs. BLPA; BLPL; FaBoBe

I have no embroidered headband. Sappho, *tr. fr. Greek by* Willis Barnstone. BoWoP

I have no friend save God! *(LL)* Death. *Unknown*. BLPA

I have no illusions. Visibility. Maura Stanton. VBLP

I have no Life but this. Emily Dickinson. FaBoVe

I have no more a golden store. The Merry Jovial Beggar. Peter Casey, *tr. fr. Irish by* Douglas Hyde. TIRV; WTO

I have no name. Infant Joy. Blake. *Fr.* Songs of Innocence. FaPON; FHYEP; GoJo; NAEL-2; NAs; NTP; OxAEP-2; OxBSP; PoLF; TEP

I have no numbers on my forearm. I Wake from a Dream of Killing Hitler. Mark Nepo. BTR

I have no other earthly friend! *(LL)* The Affliction of Margaret. Wordsworth. EnRP; GTBS; GTBS-P; PoEL-4

I Have No Pain. *Unknown*. FaBoCo

I have no rattles. Ambo Oral Tradition. *Fr.* Five Ghost Songs. TTTS

I have no seed to spread over the world. Patrizia Cavalli, *tr. fr. Italian by* Robert McCracken. NeIt

I Have No Strength for Mine. Joanne Kyger. PoM

I have no wit, no words, no tears. A Better Resurrection. Christina Rossetti. NOBVV; TrPWD

I have not ever seen my father's grave. Father Son and Holy Ghost. Audre Lorde. NoAM; PoBA

I Have Not Lingered in European Monasteries. Leonard Cohen. NOBC

I have not met thee in this outward world. To Elizabeth Barrett Browning. Anne Lynch Botta. AmWP

I have not seen your writing. The Letter. Patricia Beer. OxBC

I have not so much emulated the birds that musically sing. To Soar in Freedom and in Fullness of Power. Walt Whitman. RFM

I have not spent the April of my time. Bartholomew Griffin. *Fr.* Fidessa, More Chaste than Kind[e]. AAS (Sonnet: "I have not spent the April of my time.") EIL

I have not told my garden yet. Emily Dickinson. AnAmPo

I have not used my darkness well. Squall. Stanley Moss. CoAP

I have not written my poem. The Experiment That Failed. John Logan. NU

I have nothing new to ask of you. Another Year Come. W. S. Merwin. NYBP

I have nothing to give you, but my anger. A Love Poem for My Country. Frank Mkalawile Chipasula. HBAPE

I have nothing to say about the war. Yehuda Amichai, *tr. fr. Hebrew. Fr.* Patriotic Songs. PoSu, *tr. by* Yehuda Amichai *and* Ted Hughes

I have nothing to say about the way the sky tilts. Charles Wright. *Fr.* Four Poems for the New Year. AnAn; CAPP

I have often imagined that glances. Valerio Magrelli, *tr. fr. Italian by* Dana Gioia. NeIt

I have perceiv'd that to be with those I like is enough. Walt Whitman. *Fr.* I Sing the Body Electric. CTC; SAmP, *Pt.* I *only*

I have pined for the sight of the sea for years. The Beautiful Sea. Mary E. Tucker. CBWP-1

I have poured my dreams in the pot's dim womb. Peter Titheradge. *Fr.* Teatime Variations. FaBoPa

I have praised many loved ones in my song. Mother. Theresa Helburn. FaPON; OHIP

I have prepared the hibachi. *Unknown, tr. fr. Japanese by* Kenneth Rexroth *and* Ikuko Atsumi. WPJ

I have read, in some old marvellous tale. The Beleaguered City. Longfellow. AnAmPo

I Have Recently Edited My Unworthy Poems, *sels.* Chin Nung, *tr. fr. Chinese by* Jonathan Chaves. NOBC

I have risen from your body. The Onion. John Thompson. NOBC

I have robbed the garrulous streets. For the Goddess Too Well Known. Elsa Gidlow. PeHV

I have said/ She 's adulteress; I have said with whom. Shakespeare. *Fr.* Winter's Tale, The. OxAEP-1

I have said that the soul is not more than the body. Walt Whitman. *Fr.* Song of Myself. AmPP; EnlH, longer sel; LiTA; MoAmPo, *abr.*; NOBA; OxBA; SOTW, *much abr.* (Hub of the Universe, The.) ImPo

I have seen a court, and a dozen courts. A Christmas Revel. Dafydd Bach ap Madog Wladaidd, *tr. fr. Welsh.* OBWVE

I have seen a lovely thing. Blight. Arna Bontemps. CDC

I Have Seen Black Hands. Richard Wright. PoBA

I have seen bus depots. Reflecting on the Aging-Process. Robert Peters. BXAP

I have seen come on. Death. John Stone. MT

I have seen enough: ugliness. Knowing All Ways, Including the Transposition of Continents. Charles Olson. BCF

I have seen flowers come in stony places. John Masefield. FaBoEE; OxBTC

I have seen her, wonderful! This Version of Love. Dorothy Hewett. CBAP

I have seen mannequins. W. J. Turner. *Fr.* Seven Days of the Sun, The. OBMV

I have seen men binding their brothers in chains, and crafty. The Hate and the Love of the World. Max Ehrmann. PoToHe

I have seen much to hate here — much to forgive. Alice Duer Miller. *Fr.* White Cliffs, The. OtMeF

I have seen my ghost broken. To Conquer Variety. Hart Crane. AnAn

I have seen, O desolate one, the voice has its tower. Bell Tower. Léonie Adams. MoAB; MoAmPo

I have seen old ships sail like swans asleep. The Old Ships. James Elroy Flecker. CH; CoGr; FaBoRV; MoBrPo; OBMV; OtMeF; PoRA

I have seen rare sunshine held in the first birch leaves. Annunciation. Ken Etheridge. AngWe

I have seen the Birds of Paradise. The Birds of Paradise. John Peale Bishop. GoJo

I have seen the light coming up over the town, like ash. Overture to Strangers. Phyllis Haring. PeSA

I have seen the robins. Memory. Mary Effie Lee Newsome. ShDr

I have seen the rosebud blow. On Viewing Her Sleeping Infant. Maria Frances Cecelia Cowper. ECWP

I have seen the smallest minds of my generation. Problem in Social Geometry — the Inverted Square! Ray Durem. PoBA

I have seen the soft light flicker. Message from Ohanapecosh Glacier. W. M. Ransom. CDW

I have seen the sun break through. The Bright Field. R. S. Thomas. AngWe

I have seen the young Negroes and Puerto Ricans. A Documentary on Airplane Glue. David Henderson. MAT

I Have Seen Them. Norman Jordan. NBV

I have seen them at many hours. Moths. Julia Fields. *Fr.* Poems: Birmingham 1962 – 1964. PoBA; PoNe

I have seen them trying. I Have Seen Them. Norman Jordan. NBV

I have seen you, little mouse. The Little Mouse. *Unknown.* ReMoGo

I have seen you, my erect morning, bare chested with tree-top tousled head. Morning in My City. Avraham Shlonsky, *tr. fr. Hebrew by* Ruth Finer Mintz. MHP

I have seen you suffer in the midst of winters. Harlem. Jean Brierre, *tr. fr. French by* John F. Matheus. TTY

I have seen your feet gilded by morning. Metamorphoses of M. John Peale Bishop. ErPo

I have seen your hands asleep. I Have Told You Your Hands Are Salt. James Purdy. PFL

I Have Set My Heart So High. *Unknown.* OAEL-1

I have slept upon my couch. The Student's Serenade. Anne Brontë. OHCV

I have snapped off my burning. Maui. Meg Campbell. PeNZ

I have so much faith in you. I believe. To Trust. Antonia Pozzi, *tr. fr. Italian by* Lynne Lawner. PBWP

I Have Some Friends before Me Gone. *Unknown.* AH

I have something for you to laugh at, Cato. Catullus, *tr. fr. Latin by* James Michie. PeHV

I have sought long with steadfastness. Sir Thomas Wyatt. EnRePo; SiPS; SiPSBD

I have sought the elusive aroma. Barbecue Service. James Applewhite. MT

I have sown beside all waters in my day. A Black Man Talks of Reaping. Arna Bontemps. BPo; CDC; PoBA; PoNe

I have sown upon the fields. The Idle Flowers. Robert Bridges. BoNaP; ChTr

I have spent my life. "Stephany." NBV

I have spot-resistant trousers. Summer Song. W. W. Watt. FiBHP

I have spread wet linen. Today. Ethel Romig Fuller. PoToHe

I have stopped speaking. (*LL*) The Mother Tongue. Carolina Hospital. LoHo

I have struggled all day with a thought like a wild noble horse. Wild Horse. Elder Olson. GrPl

I have studied the tight curls on the back of your neck. Movement Song. Audre Lorde. VCAP

I have sucked them. I shall never die! (*LL*) Egypt. Martin Edmunds. UTF

I have sworn ten thousand times. Kenneth Rexroth, *after the Greek of* Palladas. NNaP; PGA

I have taken that vow. The Red-haired Man's Wife. James Stephens. MoBrPo

I have taken the woman of beauty. The Bear's Song. *Unknown, tr. by* Constance Lindsay Skinner. *Fr.* Three Songs from the Haida. AWP

I Have Ten Legs. Anna Swirszczynska, *tr. fr. Polish.* TSaS, *tr. by* Czeslaw Milosz *and* Leonard Nathan

I have that sure enclitic to my act. Hart Crane. AnAn

I have the delusion/ that you are with me. Yosano Akiko, *tr. fr. Japanese by* Kenneth Rexroth *and* Ikuko Atsumi. WPJ

I have the eyes of a real sea calf. The Seal. Guillaume Apollinaire, *tr. fr. French.* CBNP

I have the greatest fun at night. The Quilt. Mary Effie Lee Newsome. CDC

I have the obit of my lady dere. The Whole Treasure of All Wordly Bliss. Charles, Duc d'Orléans. OxBLMV

I have thee, thou hast me. *Unknown, tr. fr. German by* Alexander Gode. GePo

I have thee wonnen in fight. (*LL*) Love me broughte. *Unknown.* MiEL

I have this deal of death about my hands. Blood. Ray Bremser. NeAP

I have this large tattoo on my chest. It is like a dream I have. Confessional Poem. Louis Jenkins. RaBo

I have this nightmare someone dresses me. Florida. Karen Murai. UTF

I have this to say, if I can say it. Before Sentence Is Passed. R. P. Blackmur. LiTA

I have thought long this wild wet night that brought no rest. A Sleepless Night. Egan O'Rahilly, *tr. fr. Modern Irish by* Frank O'Connor. PeIV

I have thought of beaches, fields. Bundles. Carl Sandburg. MoAmPo

I have thought/ Of thee, thy learning, gorgeous eloquence. Wordsworth. *Fr.* Prelude [or, Growth of a Poet's Mind], The. EnRP; EPCY; OAEL-2

I Have Three Daughters. Ruth Stone. InPS; NMM

I have thrown wide my window. Midnight. Michael Roberts. OBMV

I have to get in. Maine. Elinor Nauen. UL

I have to live with myself, and so. Myself. Edgar A. Guest. BLPA; BLPL; PWR

I have to thank God I'm a woman. The Affinity. Anna Wickham. NALW

I have told you. Tenth Symphony. John Ashbery. NOBA

I Have Told You Your Hands Are Salt. James Purdy. PFL

I have tossed hours upon the tides of fever. Bout with Burning. Vassar Miller. LiTM; MoAmPo; MT

I have traveled, I have traveled. The Consumptive. Priscilla Jane Thompson. CBWP-2

I have tried to shift the stars. The Juniper Moon Pulls at My Bones. Earle Thompson. HATNAP

I have trod this path a hundred times. The Miracle. Emerson. FM

I have turned to the landscape because men disappoint me. The Ram's Horn. John Hewitt. BIrV; PNI

I Have Twelve Oxen. *Unknown.* ChTr; GBP

I have twelve oxen that be faire and brown. *Unknown.* MiEL

I have two sicknesses, Love. *Unknown, tr. fr. Greek by* Kenneth Rexroth. PGA

"I have two wives." Mohammed Ibrahim Speaks. Martha Beidler. FF

I have understood nothing. Edouard J. Maunick, *tr. fr. French by* Ellen Conroy Kennedy. *Fr.* As Far as Yoruba Land. NegPo

I have used your buses for eighteen years. To the Management. Douglas Houston. PWE

I have ventur'd. John Fletcher *and* William Shakespeare. *Fr.* King Henry VIII. FaBoEH

I have walked a great while over the snow. The Witch. Mary Elizabeth Coleridge. BrRo; NALW; OHCV; WPE

I have wanted excellence in the knife-throw. The Language of the Brag. Sharon Olds. PBCAP

I have wanted other things more than lovers. Monody to the Sound of Zithers. Kay Boyle. PoA

I have wasted my life. (*LL*) Lying in a Hammock at William Duffy's Farm in Pine Island, Minnesota. James Wright. CAPP; HAP; HCAP; HoPM; NaP; NOBA; OPOP; Poetr; TRP; VCAP

I have watched you. Saying Goodbye. Suzanne Juhasz. IHMS

I have watched your fingers drum. The Hand. Howard Moss. TAP

I have wept with the spring storm. After the Persian. Louise Bogan. PoA

I have wished a bird would fly away. A Minor Bird. Robert Frost. CMoP; SAmP

I have with fishing-rod and line. The Wounded Hawk. Herbert Edward Palmer. FaBoTw

I have wrapped my dreams in a silken cloth. For a Poet. Countee Cullen. PoNe; TTY

I have wrought these words together out of a wryed existence. The Wife's Complaint. Unknown, tr. fr. Anglo-Saxon by Michael Alexander. BoLoP

I haven't a clue where I've been. Sydney Bernard Smith. PeLi

I haven't got a key! (LL) Lock the dairy door. Unknown. OxNR

I haven't sung your praise. To My Country. Rachel, tr. fr. Hebrew by Diane Mintz. PBWP

I haven't the slightest thing to fear. (LL) The Bird. Moyshe-Leyb Halpern. PPP

I hear a sudden cry of pain! The Snare. James Stephens. BoTP; CH; CMoP; CoGr; PDV; SCGP

I hear a voice. W. S. Rendra. EaPr

I hear a whistling. Emmett Till. James A. Emanuel. NIP; PoBA

I hear again the tread of war go thundering through the land. Albert Sidney Johnston. Kate Brownlee Sherwood. PAH

I hear along our street. Christmas Carols. Longfellow. BoTP

I Hear America Singing. Walt Whitman. AiP, ll. 1–9; AnAmPo; AWP; FaBoBe; FaBV; FaPON; FF; HAP; LiTA; MoAmPo; PDV; SAmP; TFi; TrGrPo; WeW

I hear and behold God in every object, yet understand God not in the least. Walt Whitman. Fr. Song of Myself. AmPP; LiTA; MoAmPo, abr.; NOBA; OxBA; SOTW, much abr.; WGRP

I hear and is my heart not badly shaken? (LL) Shancoduff. Patrick Kavanagh. BIrV; CIP; FaBoTw; IIP; IPY; NoP; PeIV

I hear eating. Night Fun. Judith Viorst. TLR

I hear/ he won't give horses for poems. An Insult. Unknown. NOIV

I hear her voice like. Her Voice. Barney Bush. HATNAP

I hear in my heart, I hear in its ominous pulses. The Wild Ride. Louise Imogen Guiney. AmWP

I hear it in the deep heart's core. (LL) The Lake Isle of Innisfree. W. B. Yeats. ArNa; CIHu; CMoP; CoGr; EBEvV; FaBoPP; FaBV; FaPoB; FaPON; FaPoR; HeIP; IIP; InPK; InPS; LiTM; MeMBP; MoAB; MoBrPo; MoP; NAEL-2; NoAM; NOBE; NoP; NTP; OBEV; OHCV; OxAEP-2; OxBTC; PlP; PoE; Poetr; PrIm; TEP; TFi; TrGrPo; UV

I Hear It Said. Barbara Young. BLPA

I Hear It Was Charged against Me. Walt Whitman. LiTA; MoAmPo; OBF; PPP

I hear leaves drinking rain. The Rain. W. H. Davies. BoTP; OxBTC

I hear many voices. To Adhiambo. Gabriel Okara. PBA

I hear my lover. The Blacksmith. Ludwig Uhland, tr. fr. German by Philip L. Miller. RiWo

I hear [or heare] the whistling ploughman [or plough-man] all day long. On the Ploughman [or Plough-Man]. Francis Quarles. NOSC

I hear people waiting for the riot to begin in their hearts. Ray Charles at Mississippi State. Tom Dent. NBV

I hear some say, this man is not in love. Michael Drayton. Fr. Idea. ESo; TrGrPo

I hear something coming. Breathing. James Tate. LCAP

I hear that Andromeda. Sappho, tr. fr. Greek by Mary Barnard. PBWP; VBLP

I hear that the axe has flowered. Paul Celan, tr. fr. German by Michael Hamburger. PoSu

I hear the beat. The Talking Drums. Kojo Gyinaye Kyei. PBA

I hear the brooks gushing. Remembrance. Joseph Freiherr von Eichendorff, tr. fr. German by Philip L. Miller. RiWo

I hear the doctor's loud success. Waiting for the Doctor. Colette Inez. IHMS

I hear the halting footsteps of a lass. Harlem Shadows. Claude McKay. AmPP; PoNe

I hear the man downstairs slapping the hell out of his stupid wife again. .38, The. Ted Joans. WeW

I hear the noise about thy keel. Tennyson. Fr. In Memoriam A. H. H. EBVV, abr.; EnVR; OAEL-2, abr.; PeECV, abr.

I hear the robins singing in the rain. On a Gloomy Easter. Alice Freeman Palmer. OHIP

I hear the shadowy horses, their long manes a-shake. Michael Robartes Bids His Beloved Be at Peace. W. B. Yeats. MoP; NoAM

I Hear the Shuffle of the People's Feet. Sterling Plumpp. Jaz

I hear the voice. Israel. Carl Rakosi. ChIV-1

I hear voices praising Tshombe, and the Portuguese. Hatred of Men with Black Hair. Robert Bly. NaP

I Hear You. Shirley Kaufman. MDDM

I hear you call. The Call of the River Nun. Gabriel Okara. PBA

I hear you have gone to live among the village mounds. Visiting the Hermit Cheng. Po Chü-i, tr. fr. Chinese by Robert Payne. TAL

I hear you, little bird. Joy of the Morning. Edwin Markham. FaPON

I hear you say I say I say after every word I say I say. Unknown. RoPo

I hear your voice saying Hello in that guarded way. Telephoning Home. Carol Ann Duffy. NBrP

I Hear You've Let Go. Rosario Ferré, tr. fr. Spanish by Willis Barnstone. BoWoP

I heard a bird at dawn. The Rivals. James Stephens. BoTP; FaPON; InvP; OBEV; OBMV

I Heard a Bird Sing. Oliver Herford. NTCP; PDV; PoLF; SiSoPo

I heard a brooklet gushing. Whither? Wilhelm Müller, tr. fr. German by Philip L. Miller. Fr. Beautiful Maid of the Mill, The. AWP, tr. by Longfellow; RiWo

I heard a/ couple of fleas. Archy, the Cockroach, Speaks. Don Marquis. Fr. Certain Maxims of Archy. FaPON; OBAL

I heard a cow low, a bonnie cow low. Unknown. Fr. Queen of Elfan's [or Elfland's] Nourice [or Nourrice], The. ESPB; FaBoCh

I heard a fly buzz. Emily Dickinson. AmPP; AnAmPo; BoWoP; ClHu; CMoP; DL; FF; HAP; HeIP; HoPM; ImPo; InPK; LiTA; LiTM; MeMAP; MoAB; MoAmPo; MoP; NAAL-1; NALW; NAWM-2; NoAM; NOBA; NoP; OBD; OxBA; PoE; Poetr; PoRA; PPP; SAmP; SCV; SoSe; SOTW; TAP; TFi; TOF; TRP; WeW

I heard a horseman. The Horseman. Walter de la Mare. GoJo

I Heard a Linnet Courting. Robert Bridges. LiTB; LiTM; OBMV

I heard a mouse. The Mouse. Elizabeth J. Coatsworth. BoTP; FaPON; MoShBr; OBCA

I Heard a Noise. At. to Thomas Bateson. See I Heard a Noise and Wishèd for a Sight.

I Heard a Noise and Wishèd for a Sight. At. to Thomas Bateson. EBEV; HAP; InvP

I heard a small sad sound. The To-Be-Forgotten. Thomas Hardy. MeMBP

I Heard a Soldier. Herbert Trench. CH

I heard a thousand blended notes. Lines Written in Early Spring. Wordsworth. EnRP; FHYEP; GTBS; GTBS-P; NAEL-2; OAEL-2; PoLF
(Written in Early Spring.) GTBS; GTBS-P

I heard a voice at evening softly say. Day by Day. Julia Harris May. BLRP

I heard a voice that cried, "Make way for those who died!" The March. J. C. Squire. OHIP

I heard a winter tree in song. Conceit. Mervyn Laurence Peake. Spl

I heard a woman's voice that wailed. In Ruin Reconciled. Aubrey Thomas De Vere. BIrV

I heard a wood thrush in the dusk. Wood Song. Sara Teasdale. AnAmPo

I heard an ancient sound: a cock that crew. Daybreak. Frances Cornford. FM

I heard an angel speak last night. A Curse for a Nation. Elizabeth Barrett Browning. NALW; WPE; WPOW

I heard an ignorant crow call, "Life is now." Old Snapshot. Ronald G. Everson. MoCV

I heard an old farm-wife. The Son. Ridgely Torrence. InvP

I heard an owl at midday. Como lo Siento. Lorna Dee Cervantes. NoAM

I heard and slowly understood but then I saw. Central. Douglas Oliver. VaA

I Heard Christ Sing. "Hugh MacDiarmid." ChIV-2

I heard from a decent man the other day. On Hearing It Has Been Ordered in the Chapterhouse of Ireland That the Friars Make No More Songs or Verses. Padraigin Haicead, tr. fr. Irish by Thomas Kinsella. NOIV

I heard him in the autumn winds. Life in Death. Ellice Hopkins. OHCV; PeVV

I heard how, to the beat of some quick tune. The Dancer. Sadi, tr. fr. Persian by Sir Edwin Arnold. Fr. Bustan, The. AWP

I Heard Immanuel Singing. Vachel Lindsay. HAP

I heard in the night the pigeons. No Child. Padraic Colum. OBMV

I heard men saying, Leave hope and praying. The Voice of Toil. William Morris. OHCV

I heard my love was going to Yang-chou. Unknown, tr. by Arthur Waley. Fr. Tzu Yeh Songs. BoWoP

I heard my love was gone on garrison at Chin-wei Mountain. Tune: "Immortal at the River." Wang Kuo-wei, tr. fr. Chinese by Ching-i Tu. SuSp

I heard my loved published in church. The False Bride. Unknown. OBET

I heard no sound where I stood. The Sleeping House. Tennyson. Fr. Maud[: A Monodrama]. OBNC
(Maud has a garden of roses.) EnVR

I heard of a tribe where the men. Those Upright Men. Judith Kazantzis. FaBoBl

I heard of gold at Sutter's Mill. When I Went Off to Prospect. *Unknown.* AmFP

I heard on the meadow. Heinrich von Morungen, *tr. fr. German by* Frederick Goldin. GePo

I heard one who said: "Verily." Cassandra. E. A. Robinson. CMoP; ImPo; LiTA; LiTM; MeMAP; NoAM; OxBA

I heard, or seemed to hear, the chiding Sea. Sea-Shore. Emerson. LiTA; OxBA

I heard that south of the capital city. Southern Mountains. Han Yü, *tr. fr. Chinese by* Charles Hartman. SuSp

I heard the bells on Christmas Day. Christmas Bells. Longfellow. AH; AnAmPo; BLRP; FaPON; OBCP; PChr, *st.* 1; WBLP

I heard the carping [*or* herde a carpyng] of a clerk. Robyn and Gandeleyn. *Unknown.* EnSB; ESPB; OxBB
(Robin and Gandelyn.) EnSB

I heard the cuckoo with no food in my stomach. *Unknown. See* Early on the morning of Monday.

I heard the dogs howl in the moonlight night. Dream, A [*or* The]. William Allingham. BIrV; NOBVV

I heard the farm cocks crowing loud, and faint, and thin. Daybreak in a Garden. Siegfried Sassoon. BoTP

I heard the front door. After a Death. Gregory Orr. AnAn

I heard the happy lark exult. Inst., Ult., and Prox. A. P. Herbert. FaBoUs

I heard the Indian Agent say. The Old Man's Lazy. Peter Blue Cloud. HATNAP

I heard the old, old men say. The Old Men Admiring Themselves in the Water. W. B. Yeats. CMoP; LiTM; MeMBP; MoBrPo; TrGrPo; UnPo; WeW

I Heard the Old Song. B. W. Vilakazi, *tr. fr. Zulu.* PeSA

I heard the Poor Old Woman say. Lament for the Poets: 1916. Francis Ledwidge. AWP
(Blackbirds, The.) PeIV

I heard the pulse of the besieging sea. To S. C. Robert Louis Stevenson. PeVV

I heard the sighing of the reeds. In Ireland: By the Pool at the Third Rosses. Arthur Symons. FaBoPP; OBNC

I heard the snowflakes whisper in the still dark night. Snowflakes. Ruth M. Arthur. BoTP

I heard the songs. The Songs. *Unknown, tr. fr. Zuni Indian by* K. Kennedy. WTO

I heard the trailing garments of the Night. Hymn to the Night. Longfellow. BLPL; MeMAP; NOBA; OxBA; PWR; TAP; TrGrPo

I heard the weeping of the newly born in its mother's bosom. The Circle of Weeping. Amir Gilboa, *tr. fr. Hebrew by* Ruth Finer Mintz. MHP

I heard the wild geese flying. Wild Geese. Elinor Chipp. FaPON

I heard the wind coming. Hearing the Wind at Night. May Swenson. BoNaP

I heard their voice. (*LL*) Koel (Rainbird) and Effigy. *Unknown.* NOBAu

I heard them in their sadness say. Dust. "Æ." WGRP

I heard this "fucking beautiful." Poetry Reading. Eileen Myles. UL

I heard this morning. Summer nineteen seventy. Lindiwe Mabuza. WPOW

I heard two workers say, "This chaos/ Will soon be ended." Idiom of the Hero. Wallace Stevens. OxBA

I heard you coming after me. Entgegenwärtigung Town. Anne Carson. *Fr.* Life of Towns, The. BAP-90

I Heard You Solemn-sweet Pipes of the Organ. Walt Whitman. OxBA; SAmP

I heard you solemn-sweet pipes of the organ as last Sunday. I Heard You Solemn-sweet Pipes of the Organ. Walt Whitman. OxBA; SAmP

I Held a Shelley Manuscript. Gregory Corso. VGW

I held Europe in my hand. Yonder. Richard Eberhart. GOA

I Held His Name. Alberto A. Ríos. NoAM

I held it truth, with him who sings. I Held It Truth (with Him Who Sings). Tennyson. *Fr.* In Memoriam A. H. H. EBVV, *abr.*; EBVVPR; EnVR; HeIP; LiTB; MeMBP; NoP; OAEL-2, *abr.*; OBNC; PeECV, *abr.*

I Held It Truth (with Him Who Sings). Tennyson. *Fr.* In Memoriam A. H. H. EBVV, *abr.*; EBVVPR; EnVR; HeIP; LiTB; MeMBP; NoP; OAEL-2, *abr.*; OBNC; PeECV, *abr.*

I held you. Eventual Proteus. Margaret Atwood. MoCV; VBLP

I helped a little lame dog. My Little Dog. Pearl Forbes MacEwen. BoTP

I, Henry, hope with this mine eyes to feed. Sir William Alexander. *Fr.* Exhortation to Prince Henry, An. ScCV

I herde the lover sighing wondir sore. The Lady Resists the Lover's Pleas. *At. to* Alain Chartier, *tr. fr. French by* Sir Richard Ros. *Fr.* La Belle Dame sans Mercy. OxBLMV

I here, thou there, yet both but one. (*LL*) A Letter to Her Husband, Absent upon Public[k] Employment. Anne Bradstreet. EAP; HAP; HeIP; KTR; NAAL-1; NALW; NoP; PFP; SCAP

I Hereby Swear. Elinor Wylie. *See* I hereby swear that to uphold your house.

I hereby swear that to uphold your house. Elinor Wylie. *Fr.* One Person. LiTA; MoAB; NAAL-2; OxBA; Son
(I Hereby Swear). ImPo
(Sonnet from "One Person"). LiTA; MoAmPo

I, Hermes, guard Cyllene's wooded slopes. Nicias, *tr. fr. Greek by* Anthony Holden. GrAn

I, Hermes, have been set up. Anyte, *tr. fr. Greek by* Kenneth Rexroth. GrAn; OBVE; PGA

I hid my love when young while I. Secret Love. John Clare. FaBV; OBNC; PoE; PoEL-4; SCGP; TrGrPo
(I hid my love when young till I.) ArLo; FHYEP
(I Hid My Love.) ArLo
(Song: "I hid my love when young while I.") NOBVV; NTP; OAEL-2; RB

I Hid You. Miklós Radnóti, *tr. fr. Hungarian by* Steven Polgar, Stephen Berg, *and* S. J. Marks. UnAS

I hide behind simple things so you'll find me. The Meaning of Simplicity. Yannis Ritsos, *tr. fr. Greek by* Edmund Keeley. TSaS

I hired a carpenter. The Death King. Anne Sexton. *tr. fr. Czech by* Jeffrey Fiskin *and* Erik Vestville. AnAn

I hoard a little spring of secret tears. On Shooting a Swallow in Early Youth. Charles Tennyson Turner. FM; NOBVV

I Hoed and Trenched and Weeded. A. E. Housman. *Fr.* Shropshire Lad, A. FaPoB; LiTM; MeMBP; MoBrPo; TrGrPo; UnPo; WeW

I hold a chipped bowl in my hands. The Game. Edvard Kocbek, *tr. fr. Slovene by* Michael Scammell *and* Veno Taufer. PoSu

I hold a letter in my hand. A Poem for the Meeting of the American Medical Association. Oliver Wendell Holmes. PoEL-5

I hold a newspaper, reading. Fish. Takahashi Shinkichi, *tr. fr. Japanese by* Lucien Stryk. NU

I hold a rattlesnake in my hand, gently. Victory Drive, near Fort Benning, Georgia. Bin Ramke. MT

I hold him, verily, of mean emprise. He Perceives His Rashness in Love, but Has No Choice. Guido Guinicelli, *tr. fr. Italian by* Dante Gabriel Rossetti. AWP

I hold in my hands. Look Closely. Morton Marcus. FF

I hold it good — as who shall hold it bad? Columbia's Agony. "Orpheus C. Kerr." OBAL

I hold it towards you. (*LL*) This Living Hand, Now Warm and Capable. Keats. BoLoP; InPK; InPS; NoP; OAEL-2; TRP

I hold it true that thoughts are things. Secret Thoughts. Ella Wheeler Wilcox. PWR

I hold it true, whate're befall. Tennyson. *Fr.* In Memoriam A. H. H. EBVV, *abr.*; OAEL-2, *abr.*; PeECV, *abr.*; UV

I hold my honey and I store my bread. My Dreams, My Works, Must Wait Till after Hell. Gwendolyn Brooks. NoP

I hold that Christian grace abounds. My Creed. Alice Cary. AmWP; WGRP

I hold that when a person dies. A Creed. John Masefield. WGRP

I hold you in those arms. (*LL*) I Hid You. Miklós Radnóti. UnAS

I hold you tight in my jade white arms. *Unknown, tr. fr. Chinese by* Kenneth Rexroth *and* Ling Chung. *Fr.* Courtesan's Songs. WPC

I honor shit for saying: we go on. (*LL*) The Excrement Poem. Maxine W. Kumin. CAPP; FaBoWP

I hope he doesn't see me walking past his bed. Letter. Alexander Bergman. TrJP

I Hope I Don't Have You Next Semester, But. Edwin S. Godsey. HoPM

I Hope, I Fear. William Alexander, Earl of Stirling. *Fr.* Aurora. Son

I hope my good old asshole holds out. Sphincter. Allen Ginsberg. PFL

I hope the old Romans. Ancient History. Arthur Guiterman. OBCA

I hope when I am dead that I shall lie. Oblivion. Jessie Redmond Fauset, *fr. the French of* Massillon Coicou. NegPo; PoNe

I hope when you're yourself and twice my age. Metaphor for My Son. John Holmes. ImGa

I hope you'll forgive the black paint. I Have Lived This Way for Years and Do Not Wish to Change. Michael C. Blumenthal. HCAP

I huddle, hoard, hold out, hold on, hold on. (*LL*) Cold. Robert Francis. LCAP; PoA

I hung his coat and trousers to roast before a fire. (*LL*) Taffy was a Welshman, Taffy was a thief. Mother Goose. GBP; OxNR; RB; ReMoGo

I hung my verses in the wind. The Test. Emerson. OBAL

I hunt among stones. (*LL*) The Kingfishers. Charles Olson. CMoP; InPS; NAAL-2; NeAP; NOBA; PoM; VCAP

I identify, tonight, with certain insects. The Powder of Sympathy. James Tate. AnAn

I idly cut a parsley stalk. On a Midsummer Eve. Thomas Hardy. FaBoVe

I imagine a day when the children. Company. Michael Longley. IIP

I know a dog called Isaac. Three Dogs. E. C. Brereton. BoTP

I know a flower of beauty rare. The Lay of the Captive Count. Goethe, *tr. fr. German* by James Clarence Mangan. AWP

I Know a Flower So Fair and Fine. Nicolai F. S. Grundtvig, *tr. fr. Norwegian* by Olav Lee. AH

I know a forest and in that forest. The Pool. Hayyim Nahman Bialik, *tr. fr. Hebrew* by Ruth Finer Mintz. MHP

I know a funny litle man. Mr. Nobody. *Unknown.* BoTP; FaPON

I know a garden with three strange gates. The Last Gate. Stella Mead. BoTP

I know a girl. The Canal Bank. James Stephens. GrPl

I know a green grass path that leaves the field. The Green River. Lord Alfred Bruce Douglas. OBEV

I know a Jew fish crier down on Maxwell Street. Fish Crier. Carl Sandburg. OxBA

I know a little. Certain Tall Buildings. Franz Wright. NAmP90

I know a little butterfly with tiny golden wings. The Butterfly. Margaret Rose. BoTP

I know a little cupboard. The Cupboard. Walter de la Mare. FaPON; NTCP

I know a little garden-close. A Garden by the Sea. William Morris. *Fr. Life and Death of Jason, The.* CH; EBEvV; NOBE; OAEL-2; OBNC; PIP; PoEL-5
(Nymph's Song to Hylas, The.) OBEV

I know a little language of my cat, tho Dante says. Robert Duncan. *Fr. Dante.* PoM

I know a little man both ept and ert. Gloss. David McCord. OBAL

I know a little what it is like, once here at high tide. Seaweeds. Sandra McPherson. AmPA; PoA

I Know a Man. Robert Creeley. CAPP; InPS; MAT; NIP; NOBA; OxBSP; PoM; PPP; VCAP

I know a man. Illiterate. Shadab Vadji, *tr. fr. Persian* by Loftali Khaji. VBLP

I know a man — his name is Mister. *Unknown.* RoPo

I know a man named Michael Finnegan. *Unknown.* RoPo

I know a Mount, the gracious Sun perceives. Rudel to the Lady of Tripoli. Robert Browning. OtMeF

I Know a Name! *Unknown.* BLRP

I know a place all fennel-green and fine. A Green Place. William Jay Smith. GrPl

I know a place, in the ivy on a tree. The Bird's Nest. John Drinkwater. PDV

I know a place that holds the Sky. The Upside-Down World. Hamish Hendry. BoTP

I know a place/ that's oh, so green. A Boy's Place. Rose Burgunder. PDV

I know a place where the sun is like gold. Four-Leaf Clover. Ella Higginson. FaPON

I know a place whereon the wild thyme blows. Shakespeare. *See* I know a bank where the wild thyme blows.

I know a pool where nightshade preens. Crazed. Walter de la Mare. OxBSP

I know a retired dentist who only paints mountains. Mountains. W. H. Auden. FaBoPV

I know a solemn secret to keep between ourselves. The Elfin People Fill the Tubes. Winifred M. Letts. BoTP

I know a soul that is steeped in sin. I Know a Name! *Unknown.* BLRP

I know a spot where Love delights to dream. A Sacred Grove. Edward Cracroft Lefroy, *after the Greek of* Theocritus. *Fr. Echoes from Theocritus.* AWP

I Know a Village, *sels.* Phyllis McGinley.
5:32, The. NMM; OxBM; WPE
Occupation: Housewife. WPE

I know a washerwoman, she knows me. *Unknown.* ISE

I know a wasted place high in the Alps. Edgar Bowers. *Fr. Two Poems on the Catholic Bavarians.* CRP

I know a young lady's high-piled ashen hair. His Helplessness. John Berryman. *Fr. Dream Songs.* NoP

I know all. He Asked Them What Did They Know & They Told Him. *Unknown, tr. fr. Seneca Indian* by Jerome K. Rothenberg *and* Richard Johnny John. STP

"I know all," you say; of incompleteness, you have enough. Palladas, *tr. fr. Greek* by Sam Bradley. GrAn

I know, although when looks meet. Crazy Jane and Jack the Journeyman. W. B. Yeats. CMoP

I know an ice handler who wears a flannel shirt. Ice Handler. Carl Sandburg. OxBA

I know — and yet I cannot share, as once. August the First; Court Martial. The Mother Speaks. Marjorie Oludhe Macgoye. HBAPE

I know, as my life grows older. Whatever Is — Is Best. Ella Wheeler Wilcox. BLPA; PWR
(We know as we grow older.) PoToHe

I know, blue modest violets. Violets. *Unknown.* BoTP

I know. But I do not approve. And I am not resigned. (*LL*) Dirge without Music. Edna St. Vincent Millay. CMoP; CoGr; DL; IMW; LiTA; MeMAP; TrGrPo

I know but will not tell. Elegy. Alan Dugan. CAPP; NIP

I know by the arrow of darkness. Momcilo Nastasijevic, *tr. fr. Serbo Croatian* by Charles Simic. *Fr.* Deaf Things. HSix

I Know de Moonlight. *Unknown.* BPo

"I know, fair lady, how to love the lover well." Philodemus, *tr. fr. Greek* by William Moebius. GrAn

I know him, February's thrush. The Thrush in February. George Meredith. OBNC

I know him;/ He'll give no horse for a poem. *Unknown, tr. fr. Irish* by Vivian Mercier. BIrV

I know him only as a man of Sunday afternoon. Neighbour. Christine Churches. FaBoMA

I know how people get treated when they die. Andeyek, *tr. fr. Tlingit Indian* by James Koller. STP

I know I am but summer to your heart. Sonnet. Edna St. Vincent Millay. HeIP

I know I am poor. *Unknown, tr. fr. Greek* by Kenneth Rexroth. PGA

I know I am/ The Negro Problem. Dinner Guest: Me. Langston Hughes. BPo

I know I change. Daguerreotype Taken in Old Age. Margaret Atwood. BoWoP; NoAM

I know I have the best of time and space. Walt Whitman. Walt Whitman. *Fr.* Song of Myself. AmPP; LiTA; MoAmPo, *abr.*; NoAM; NOBA; OxBA; SOTW, *much abr.*

I know I look the kind of dolt. To a Junior Waiter. A. P. Herbert. FiBHP

I know/ I saw/ a spooky witch. October Magic. Myra Cohn Livingston. PDV

I know I saw those things. And Nothing Moved. Richard C. Raymond. BTR

I Know I'm Not Sufficiently Obscure. Ray Durem. BPo; PoBA

I know it is my sin [*or* sinne] which locks thine ears [*or* eares]. Church-Lock and Key. George Herbert. ESCV; GeHe; OxBSP

I know lots of men who are in love. I Never Even Suggested It. Ogden Nash. FiBHP; LiTA; PoLF

I know monks masturbate at night. The Earnest Liberal's Lament. Ernest Hemingway. OBAL; OBSV

I Know Moonlight. *Unknown.* AS

I Know Moonrise. *Unknown.* UnPo

I know: My beloved Jonathan Swift. Unfulfilled Love. Ljiljana Djurdjic, *tr. fr. Serbo-Croatian* by Charles Simic. HSix

I know my body's of so frail a kind. Man. Sir John Davies. *Fr.* Nosce Teipsum. EiL; NoSic, *abr.*; SiPS
(I Know Myself a Man.) ChTr

I Know My Soul. Claude McKay. BPo

I know my soul hath power to know all things. Sir John Davies. *Fr.* Nosce Teipsum. EiL; NoSic, *abr.*; OBEV; SiPS

I Know Myself a Man. Sir John Davies. *See* I know my body's of so frail a kind.

I know myself linked by chains of fire. Elsa Gidlow. *Fr.* Chains of Fire. CrSp

I know no couple better can agree! (*LL*) On Giles and Joan. Ben Jonson. NAEL-1; NOBL; TEP

I know no more than this. (*LL*) At Brill on the hill. *Unknown.* GBP; OxNR

I know no paint of poetry. On Fairford Windows. William Strode. NOSC

I know not by what methods rare. Eliza M. Hickock. BLRP

I know not from what distant time thou art ever coming nearer to meet me. Rabindranath Tagore. *Fr.* Gitanjali. WGRP

I know not how it falls on me. His Helplessness. Emily Brontë. NOBVV

I know not how it may be with others. Old Furniture. Thomas Hardy. OxBTC

I know not if from uncreated spheres. Michelangelo, *tr. fr. Italian* by George Santayana. *Fr.* Three Poems. AWP

I know not of what we ponder'd. Companions. Charles Stuart Calverley. FaBoCo; NOBL
(Companions, a Tale of a Grandfather.) PeLV

I know not that the men of old. The Men of Old. Richard Monckton Milnes. OBEV

I know not what I am, and what I know, I'm not. One Knows Not What One Is. "Angelus Silesius," *tr. fr. German.* *Fr.* Cherubical Wanderer, The. GePo, *tr.* by George C. Schoolfield

I know not what spell is o'er me. Lorelei. Heine, *tr. fr. German.* TrJP, *tr. by* Emma Lazarus
(Loreley, The.) NAWM-2, *tr. by* Aaron Kramer

I know not what the future hath. Whittier. *Fr.* Eternal Goodness, The. BLRP, *abr.*; NOCV; PFP; WGRP

I know not what to do. Hilda Doolittle ("H. D."). CMoP; NALW; OxBA; VBLP; VGW

I Know Not When It Was. Léopold Sédar Senghor, *tr. fr. French by* Ellen Conroy Kennedy. NegPo

I know not when it was, I still confuse childhood and Eden. I Know Not When It Was. Léopold Sédar Senghor, *tr. fr. French by* Ellen Conroy Kennedy. NegPo

I know not when this tiresome man. The Sundowner. John Shaw Neilson. CBAP

I know not where my heavy sighs to hide. Sir Thomas Wyatt. SiPSBD

I Know Not Where the Road Will Lead. Evelyn Atwater Cummins. AH

I Know Not Whether I Am Proud. Walter Savage Landor. EnRP

I know not who thou art, oh lovely one! To the Lady in the Chemisette with Black Buttons. Nathaniel Parker Willis. OBAL

I know not why, but it is true — it may. Edgar Allan Poe. Timothy Thomas Fortune. AAP

I know not why my soul is rack'd [*or* racked]. Changed. Charles Stuart Calverley. FiBHP; NOBVV

I know not why or whence he came. The Deserter. Joseph S. Cotter, Sr.. CDC

I know nothing about "love." Sonja Åkesson, *tr. fr. Swedish by* Anselm Hollo. *Fr.* What Does Your Color Red Look Like? VBLP

I know nothing but this scene. II. James Liddy. BiHa

I know now. I Thought It Was Tangiers I Wanted. Langston Hughes. PoNe

I know now when I walk over subway grates. The Lit Stations. Kathy Fagan. UTF

I know of course: it's simply luck. I, the Survivor. Bertolt Brecht, *tr. fr. German by* John Willett. PoSu

I know some lonely houses off the road. Emily Dickinson. MoAB; MoAmPo; OxBA; PoRA

I Know Something Good about You. Louis C. Shimon. BLPA; PoToHe

I know something I won't tell. *Unknown.* RoPo

I know that all beneath the moon decays. William Drummond of Hawthornden. JCP; Son

I know that any weed can tell. Louis Ginsberg. TrJP

I know that He exists. Emily Dickinson. AmPP

I know that his eyes look into mine. Assurance. Josephine D. Henderson Heard. CBWP-4

I Know That I Am a Great Sinner. Swami Purohit. OBMV

I know that I am beautiful. Terrorist. Paul Hyland. PWE

I Know That I Must Die Soon. Else Lasker-Schüler, *tr. fr. German by* Ralph Manheim. TrJP

I know that I shall meet my fate. An Irish Airman Foresees His Death. W. B. Yeats. EBEvV; FaBoCh; FaBoMo; GoJo; GTBS-P; HeIL; HeIP; HoPM; LiTM; MoAB; MoBrPo; MoP; NoAM; NOBE; NoP; OBD; OBMV; OBWP; OtMeF; Poetr; PoWW; PPP; SCV; TFi; TrGrPo; WeW

I know that if thou please thou canst provide. George Wither. *Fr.* Brittan's Remembrancer. SeCV-1

I know that life is Jason. The Golden Fleece. Oscar Williams. PoA

I know that mind. ESP. Carter Revard. VoR

I know that my Redeemer liveth — but out of the depths of time. The Redeemer. "Fiona Macleod." WGRP

I know that someone will turn over the hourglass. (*LL*) This Strange Calculation of Roots. Edouard J. Maunick. NegPo

I know that the sun rising. Pindar's Revenge. Edward Sanders. PoM

I know that this my crying, like the crying. Night. Hayyim Nahman Bialik, *tr. fr. Hebrew by* Maurice Samuel. AWP

I know that voice, tiny. Fell. Anthony Barnett. VaA

I know that what our neighbours call *longueurs.* Byron. *Fr.* Don Juan. OBSV

I know/ that when a grumbling old woman. Superstition. Minji Karibo. WPOW

I know the barn where they got you. For a Woodscolt Miscarried. John William Corrington. MT

I know the bottom, she says. I know it with my great tap root. Elm. Sylvia Plath. NoAM; NOBA; NoP; Poetr
(Elm Speaks, The. NYBP

I know the colour rose, and it is lovely. Pathology of Colours. Dannie Abse. NIP; NoAM

I know the hedge in Briar Lane. I Must Away. May Sarson. BoTP

I know the injured pride of sleep. Night and Morning. Austin Clarke. CIP; IPY; MoAB

I know the limitations of my body. The Realist. Carl H. Greene. NBV

I know the moon is troubling. I Know. David St. John. NAmP90

I know the night is near at hand. Vespers. Silas Weir Mitchell. WGRP

I know the [*or* a] thing that's most uncommon. On a Certain Lady at Court. Pope. NOBE; NOEC; OBEV; OBF; OxBSP; TrGrPo

I know the reputation. Lady Kii, *tr. fr. Japanese by* Kenneth Rexroth *and* Ikuko Atsumi. WPJ

I know the reputation/ of the idle ways. Lady Kii, *tr. fr. Japanese by* Kenneth Rexroth *and* Ikuko Atsumi. WPJ; WPOW

I know the reward of the secret tear as it humbly falls. Reward. Shimon Halkin, *tr. fr. Hebrew by* Ruth Finer Mintz. MHP

I know the ships that pass by day. The Lights. J. J. Bell. BoTP

I know the sky will fall one day. Child's Song. Gerald Gould. BoTP

I know the truth — — give up all other truths! Marina Tsvetaeva, *tr. fr. Russian by* Elaine Feinstein *and* Angela Livingstone. OBD

I know the ways [*or* wayes] of learning; both the head. The Pearl. George Herbert. EBEV; FHYEP; GeHe; HAP; JCP; NOCV; OAEL-1; PoEL-2; SeCP
(Pearl, Matt. 13:45, The.) NOSC
(Pearl, The. Matth. 13.) ChIV-2; ESCV; SeCV-1

I know thee. My name is Tom. Archaic Song of Dr. Tom the Shaman. *Unknown, tr. fr. Nootka Indian by* Jerome K. Rothenberg. STP

I know Thee not. Abide with me! (*LL*) Depart from Me. Mary Elizabeth Coleridge. TrPWD

I know there are some fools that care. The Deformed Mistress. Sir John Suckling. BXAP; ErPo

I know there is a worm in the human heart. John Clare. Jon Anderson. AmPA

I Know Things. Adèle Davide. Mes

I know this body but a sink of folly. The Tragedy of Charles Duke of Byron. George Chapman. OBD

I know thou art a senseless thing. The Old Crib. Mary E. Tucker. CBWP-1

I know to whom I write. Here, I am sure. An Epistle to Master John Selden. Ben Jonson. BeJo

I know to whom i write. Here, I am sure. Ben Jonson. *Fr.* Epistle to Master John Selden, An. OBF

I know two things about the horse. The Horse. Naomi Royde-Smith. FaBoCo; FiBHP

I know two women. The Wife. Robert Creeley. VGW

I know very well, goddess, she is not beautiful. Calypso's Island. Archibald MacLeish. MoAB; NoP

I know very well I could not. (*LL*) I Saw in Louisiana a Live-Oak Growing. Walt Whitman. AiP; AWP; ImPo; InPK; InPS; LiTA; MAT; NAAL-1; NIP; NoAM; NOBA; NoP; OxBA; Poetr; PrIm; SAmP

I know very well what I'd rather be. Rathers. Mary Austin. FaPON

I know what my heart is like. Ebb. Edna St. Vincent Millay. AnAmPo

I know what the caged bird feels, alas! Sympathy. Paul Laurence Dunbar. AAP; CDC; PoBA; PoNe

I know where I belong. Wonders. Lorenzo Thomas. UL

I Know Where I'm Going. *Unknown.* ELP; GBP; MoShBr; NTP; OBET; WTO

I know why, getting up in the cold dawn. To a Daughter with Artistic Talent. Peter Meinke. Poetsp

I know why the caged bird sings! (*LL*) Sympathy. Paul Laurence Dunbar. AAP; CDC; PoBA; PoNe

I know, within my mouth, for bashful fear. Love's Despair. Richard Lynche. *Fr.* Diella. EIL

I know You are there. The sweat is, I am here. (*LL*) Certainty before Lunch. John Berryman. LCAP; OxBC

I know you little, I love you lots. My Love For You. *Unknown.* Spl

I know you: solitary griefs. The Precept of Silence. Lionel Johnson. MoBrPo

I know you think that things. Dear Superman. Ron Koertge. NGP

I know you/ You are light as dreams. Words. Edward Thomas. PAW

I know your root. Branko Miljkovic, *tr. fr. Serbo-Croatian.* *Fr.* In Praise of Plants. HSix, *tr. by* Charles Simic

I know your ways, older brother. New Year Party. Matthew Sweeney. IB

I knowed a man, which he lived in Jones. Thar's More in the Man than Thar Is in the Land. Sidney Lanier. NOBA

I Korinna am here to sing the courage. Korinna, *tr. fr. Greek by* Willis Barnstone. BoWoP

I lack the braver mind. Confession of Faith. Elinor Wylie. MoAmPo

I laid me down upon a bank. Blake. EnLoPo; GBL

I laid my haffet on Elfer Hill. Elfer Hill. *Unknown, tr. fr. Danish by* Robert Jamieson. AWP

I Lais, once an arrow. Kenneth Rexroth, *after the Greek of* Sekundos. NNaP; PGA

I, Lais, who laughed disdainfully at Greece. Lais' Mirror. *Unknown, tr. fr. Greek by* Peter Jay. GrAn

I like being in your apartment, and not disturbing anything. Staying at Ed's Place. May Swenson. VCAP

I like being tired. After Working. Roy Fisher. VaA

I like blowing bubbles, and swinging on a swing. Things I Like. Marjorie H. Greenfield. BoTP

I like coffee, I like tea. *Unknown.* RoPo

I like fun — and I like jokes. Thoughts on a Pore Joke. James Whitcomb Riley. AnAmPo

I Like Housecleaning. Dorothy Brown Thompson. FaPON

I like it. *(LL)* Tobacco ("Tobacco is a dirty weed.") Graham Lee Hemminger. PoLF

I like it back here. Ars Poetica. Charles Wright. AnAn; FoLa

I like it here just fine. Girl Held without Bail. Margaret Walker. BPo; PoBA

I Like It When It's Mizzly. Aileen Fisher. PDV

I Like Little Pussy. Jane Taylor. FaBoBe

I like movies because. Why I Like Movies. Patricia Jones. BlSi

I Like My Body When It Is With Your Body. E. E. Cummings. *Fr.* Sonnets – Actualities. BoLoP; ErPo; Son; VGW

I like myself, I think I'm grand. *Unknown.* RoPo

I like not lady-slippers. Tiger-Lilies. Thomas Bailey Aldrich. GN

I like not tears in tune, nor will [*or* do] I prize. On the Memory of Mr. Edward King, Drowned in the Irish Seas. John Cleveland. OAEL-1; SeCP
(Upon the Death of Mr. King Drowned in the Irish Seas.) HAP

I like old houses, with steps that sag. Old Houses. Jennie Romano. PoToHe

I like people. Trombone Solo. Stoddard King. NBLV

I like rust on a nail. And the Same Words. David Ignatow. NNaP

I like sitting alone when the moon is shining. Song of the pines. Po Chü-i, *tr. fr. Chinese by* Robert Payne. TAL

I like the fall. The Mist and All. Dixie Willson. FaPON

I like the hunting of the hare. The Old Squire. Wilfrid Scawen Blunt. FaPoR; OBEV; SCGP

I like the man who faces what he must. The Inevitable. Sarah Knowles Bolton. WGRP

I like/ the quiet breathing. Night Creature. Lilian Moore. SiSoPo

I like the story of the circus waif. The Road. Herbert Morris. DiPo

I like the town on rainy nights. Rainy Nights. Irene Thompson. BoTP

I like the way, in winter, cars. The Short Days. John Updike. AnAmPo

I like the way my little harp makes trees. Weeping and Wailing. Gerald Stern. CAPP

I like the wind. Wind Secrets. Diane Wakoski. AmPA

I Like Them Fluffy. A. P. Herbert. NBLV

I like them pale, fair or honey-skinned. Strato, *tr. fr. Greek.* PeHV

I like this quiet place. Interlude. Mae V. Cowdery. ShDr

I like to crawl around the house after my brother's wife. *Unknown, tr. fr. Tlingit Indian by* James Koller. STP

I like to dance so much & a kind of mania. Craven Images. John James. VaA

I like to find. Pleasures. Denise Levertov. CAPP; NeAP; NoAM; NOBA; PoE; Poetr

I like to play close by my father's den. "Are You There?" Strickland W. Gillilan. PoToHe

I like to ride in a tramcar. Travelling. Dorothy Graddon. BoTP

I like to ride in my uncle's plane. Flying. Kaye Starbird. PDV

I like to see a thing I know. New Sights. *Unknown.* BoTP

I like to see it lap the miles. Emily Dickinson. BoWoP; FaBV; FaPON; HeIL; InPK; LiTA; LiTM; MoAB; MoAmPo; MoShBr; NAAL-1; NAWM-2; NoAM; NOBA; OBAL; OBCA; OxBA; PDV; PrIm; SoSe; TFi
(Railway Train, The.) AnAmPo

I like to see/ The spotted clown. The Clown. Dorothy Aldis. PDV

I like to see you lean back in your chair. To Don at Salaam. Gwendolyn Brooks. CAPP

I Like to Sing Also. John Updike. FiBHP

I like to think. Snowdrops. Mary Vivian. BoTP

I like to think (and/ the sooner the better!). All Watched Over by Machines of Loving Grace. Richard Brautigan. MAT

I like to think of a day for all those. Coming into Their Own. Sheenagh Pugh. AngWe

I Like to Think of Harriet Tubman. Susan Griffin. NALW; NMM

I like to think that ours will be more than just another story. Wishful Thinking. Michael C. Blumenthal. HCAP

I like to toss him up and down. My Cats. Stevie Smith. CBNP; FaBoNo

I like to walk/ And hear the black crows talk. Crows. David McCord. MoAmPo; PDV; RFM

I like to watch. The Bath. Robin Becker. PBCAP

I like working near a door. I like to have my work-bench close by. Monologue. Hone Tuwhare. PeNZ

I like you, Mrs. Fry! I like your name! A Friendly Address. Thomas Hood. PoEL-4

I like your muse because she's gay and witty. W. H. Auden. *Fr.* Letter to Lord Byron. NOBL

I like your spirit full of loving. Nine Reasons Why. Deborah Levy. DT

I liked that poem. To Li Po. Wing Tek Lum. BCF

I liked to walk in the river meadows. The Midnight Court. Brian Merriman, *tr. fr. Irish by* Frank O'Connor. PeIV

I liked your poems "Michael," We Are Seven. Dear Wordsworth. William Hathaway. UL

I likes a woman. Preference. Langston Hughes. HCAP; NOBA

I 'listed at home for a lancer. Lancer. A. E. Housman. MoBrPo; OBWP

I listen, and the mountain lakes. Maybe Alone on My Bike. William Stafford. NYBP

I listen each week to the discs. Singers of Renown. Anne Elder. FaBoMA

I listen for him through the rain. At Daybreak. Siegfried Sassoon. PeHV

I listen for the sounds of cannon, cries. On Lookout Mountain. Robert Hayden. PoE

I listen to the frantic philosophy. This Is about the Way It Should Be. Luis Omar Salinas. AfAz

I listen to the pulse of a life/ different from mine. Goto Miyoko, *tr. fr. Japanese by* Kenneth Rexroth *and* Ikuko Atsumi. WPJ

I listened, there was not a sound to hear. Full Moon; Santa Barbara. Sara Teasdale. OBCA

I listened to the Phantom by Ontario's shore. The Poet. Walt Whitman. *Fr.* By Blue Ontario's Shore. MoAmPo

I live among the grasses. The Field-Mouse. Enid Blyton. BoTP

I live among the Pigmies and the Cranes. Pigmies and Cranes. Walter Savage Landor. NOBVV

I live because of their help on the way. *(LL)* Growing Old [*or* Growing Older]. Rollin J. Wells. BLPA; WBLP

I live between heaven and earth. A Lone Wild Goose. Lu Kuei-meng, *tr. fr. Chinese by* Robin D. S. Yates. SuSp

I live but in the present, — where art thou? Today. Jones Very. TAP

I live, but not in myself. Stanzas of the Soul that Suffers with Longing to See God. St. John of the Cross, *tr. fr. Spanish by* K. Kavanaugh *and* O. Rodrigues. TOF

I live for those who love me. What I Live For. George Linnaeus Banks. BLPA; FaBoBe; WBLP
(My Aim.) WBLP
(Why Do I Live?) PoToHe, *St.* 1, *sl. diff. at. to* Thomas Guthrie; PWR

I live here: 'Wessex' is my name. A Popular Personage at Home. Thomas Hardy. ArNa; FM

I Live, I Die, I Burn, I Drown. Louise Labé, *tr. fr. French by* Helen R. Lane. VBLP

I live, I die, I burn myself and drown. Louise Labé, *tr. fr. French by* Willis Barnstone. BoWoP

I live in a doorway. Sonrisas. Pat Mora. NIP

I live in a room named East. Suddenly. Robin Blaser. PoM

I live in a town. Family Jewels. Essex Hemphill. GLP

I live in an orchard. Confetti of bruised petals. Postcard from the Garden. Marge Piercy. NoAM

I Live in Cuba. Lourdes Casal, *tr. fr. Spanish by* Margaret Randall. AIW

I Live in Great Sorrow. *Unknown. See* Fowls [*or* Foweles] in the Frith.

I live in the town. The Town Child. Irene Thompson. BoTP

I live in the twilight of my vices. A Prayer for Rivers. Keith Wilson. GOYP

I live in this house, walls being plastered. Keep Me Still, for I Do Not Want to Dream. Larry Eigner. NeAP

I live invisible (in my whole sky). Too Bright a Day. Norman MacCaig. GTBS-P

I live my life in growing orbits. Rainer Maria Rilke, *tr. fr. German by* Robert Bly. NU; RaBo

I Live Not Where I Love. *Unknown.* OBET

I live on my farm in a beautiful vale. Edward Williams. *Fr.* Happy Farmer, The. AngWe

I live on the water. Winding Up. Derek Walcott. NoAM

I live on this depraved and lonely cliff. Vittoria da Colonna, *tr. fr. Italian by* Willis Barnstone. BoWoP

I live (sweete love) whereas the gentle winde. Giles Fletcher the Elder. *Fr.* Licia. ESo

I live where darkness/ is not. Mukta Bai, *tr. fr. Marathi by* Willis Barnstone. BoWoP

I live with a lady and four cats. Wearing the Collar. Charles Bukowski. ArLo

I live without inhabiting/ Myself. St. John of the Cross, *tr. fr. Spanish by* Roy Campbell. *Fr.* Coplas about the Soul Which Suffers with Impatience to See God. OBVE

I live, yet no true life I know. I Die because I Do Not Die. St. Theresa of Avila, *tr. fr. Spanish by* E. Allison Peers. TOF

I live; yet 'tis not I. He lives in me. Devotion. Paul Fleming, *tr. fr. German by* F. Warnke. GePo

I lived a life without love, and saw the being. The Mirage. Oscar Williams. LiTM

I lived alone as happy as Larry. The Husband's Lament. Brian Merriman, *tr. by* Frank O'Connor. Fr. Midnight Court, The. NOIV, *tr. by* Thomas Kinsella; OBVE

I lived among great houses. The Statesman's Holiday. W. B. Yeats. CMoP; OxBTC

I lived for many years in the bush — far out — and I starved for lack of rain. The Gravy Train. R. R. Davidson. NOBAu

I lived here nearly 5 years before I could. Chicago Poem. Lew Welch. NeAP; PoBeRe; PoM

I lived in a wood for a number of years. Ground for the Floor. *Unknown.* OBET

I lived in an L-shaped room, my chair was. 1967–1971. Michael Hofmann. SCBI

I lived in the first century of world wars. Muriel Rukeyser. UnPo

I lived inside a machine. On Being a Householder. Alan Dugan. NoAM

I lived my days apart. A Mystic as Soldier. Siegfried Sassoon. WGRP

I lived with Mr. Punch, they said my name was Judy. Variations. Randall Jarrell. VGW

I lived with Pride; the house was hung. The House of Pride. William James Dawson. PoToHe

I loathe, abhor, detest, despise. Dried Apple Pies. *Unknown.* BLPA

I loathe [*or* lothe] that I did love. The Aged Lover Renounceth Love. Thomas, Lord Vaux. EiL; EnRePo; NoSic; OAEL-1; PoEL-1; SCGP

I loed you for yir kindness. The Deean Tractorman, Clear. Edith Anne Robertson. OxBS

I long dwelt among vast porticos. The Former Life. Robert de Bonnières, *tr. fr. French by* Philip L. Miller. RiWo

I long for the call to council. Alcaeus, *tr. fr. Greek by* Sam Hamill. InMo

I long not now, a little while at least. Protest. Countee Cullen. CDC

I long to kisse the *Image of my Death.* (*LL*) Sleep, Silence' Child. William Drummond of Hawthornden. Son

I long to spread my tiny wings. A Wreath of Holly. Joseph Cephas Holly. AAP

I long to talke with some old lover's ghost. Love's Deity [*or* Deitie]. John Donne. AWP; EiL; EnRePo; ESCV; GBL; ImPo; LiTB; SeCP; SeCV-1; SoSe

I longed to. Sappho, *tr. fr. Greek by* Sam Hamill. InMo

I look across the table and think. Incident. Norman MacCaig. FF

I look after you as you go. The Weingarten Travel Blessing. *Unknown, tr. fr. German by* Carroll Hightower. GePo

I look along the valley of my gun. The Possibility That Has Been Overlooked Is the Future. Michael Hartnett. NOIV

I look at my face in the glass and see/ a halfborn woman. (*LL*) Upper Broadway. Adrienne Rich. HCAP; InPS

I look at my hands, Momma. Laura Davis. *Fr.* Things You Gave Me. MDDM

I look at my shadow over and over in the lake. Looking in the Lake. Po Chü-i, *tr. fr. Chinese by* Robert Payne. TAL

I look at the crisp golden-threaded hair. Canzone: His Portrait of His Lady, Angiola of Verona. Fazio degli Uberti, *tr. fr. Italian by* Dante Gabriel Rossetti. AWP

I look at the swaling sunset. In Trouble and Shame. D. H. Lawrence. OBMV

I look at you, and I sigh. (*LL*) A Drinking Song. W. B. Yeats. ArLo; BoLoP; OAEL-2; PFP

I look down the mountainside. Just below my window. In a Mountain Cabin in Norway. Robert Bly. RFM

I look for a way of writing. Valerio Magrelli, *tr. fr. Italian by* Dana Gioia. NeIt

I look for an explanation. Complaint. Alistair Paterson. *Fr.* Incantations for Warriors. PeNZ

I look for the way. Poetics. A. R. Ammons. NoP

I look from afar. We stand in darkness. The Advent Carols. Clive Wilmer. SCBI

I look in vain in the snow. Numbness. Wilhelm Müller, *tr. fr. German by* Philip L. Miller. *Fr.* Winter's Journey, The. RiWo

I Look into My Glass. Thomas Hardy. EBEV; FaBoTw; HAP; NAEL-2; NOBE; NOBVV; NoP; OxAEP-2; OxBSP; PrIm; SCV; WeW

I look into the henyard. The Darkling Chicken. Robert Peters. BXAP

I look on kingship in high pines. Exile. Jennette Yeatman. GoYe

I look out at the white sleet covering the still streets. Sleet Storm on the Merritt Parkway. Robert Bly. NOBA

I look to Thee in ev'ry need. The Christian Life. Samuel Longfellow. WGRP

I look up at the night's broad back. California Sonnets: Night Sequence. Robert Vasquez. AfAz

I Look Up to the Sky. Samuel Ha-Nagid, *tr. fr. Hebrew by* David Goldstein. TOF

I look upon the world — and she resembles a garden. The End of Man Is Death. Moses ibn Ezra, *tr. fr. Hebrew by* Solomon Solis-Cohen. TrJP

I look. You look. Over. R. S. Thomas. FF

I looked and I saw. Who but the Lord? Langston Hughes. BPo

I looked at my days and saw that. Purpose. Desmond O'Grady. PBCIP

I looked at that face, dumbfounded. Esse. Czeslaw Milosz. TOF

I looked down and saw a pit most black. Elizabeth Melvill, Lady Culross. *Fr.* Godly Dream, A. WPE

I looked far back into other years, and lo, in bright array. Mary, Queen of Scots. Henry Glassford Bell. BeLS; BLPA; FaBoBe

I Looked for a Sounding-Board. Henriëtte Roland-Holst, *tr. fr. Dutch by* Jonathan Crewe. WPON

I looked for that which is not, nor can be. A Pause of Thought. Christina Rossetti. CoGr; NOBE; OBNC

I looked in my heart while the wild swans went over. Wild Swans. Edna St. Vincent Millay. CMoP; MoAmPo; PBWP; UnPo

I looked in the first glass. The Three Mirrors. Edwin Muir. NoAM

I Looked in the Mirror. Beatrice Schenk de Regniers. PDV

I looked into a lake and saw a forest. Playmates. Lillian Everts. GoYe

I looked like Abraham Lincoln. Elliott Hawkins. Edgar Lee Masters. *Fr.* Spoon River Anthology. OxBA

I looked on that prophetic land. Presences Perfected. Siegfried Sassoon. MoBrPo

I looked over Jordan and [*or* an'] what did I see. Swing Low, Sweet Chariot. *Unknown.* FaPON; UnPo

I looked to find a man who walked with God. Enoch. Jones Very. ChIV-1; HAP

I looked to find Spring's early flowers. The Lament of the Flowers. Jones Very. AnAmPo; NOBA; OxBA

I Looked Up from My Writing. Thomas Hardy. NoAM; PAW

I, Lord, of All Mortals! *Unknown, tr. by* R. O. Winstedt. WTO

I lost it — what did I lose. What Did I Lose? Sun Yü-tang. Mes

I lost my mare in Lincoln Lane. *Unknown.* OxNR

I lost my pardner, what'll I do? Skip to My Lou. *Unknown.* AmFP

I lost my soul in a fit of temper. Lost, One Soul. Sandy McIntosh. AIW

I Lost the Love of Heaven. John Clare. *See* I lost the love, of heaven above.

I lost the love, of heaven above. A Vision. John Clare. ChTr; EBVV; FaBoRV; GTBS-P; NAEL-2; NOBVV; NTP; OAEL-2; OBNC; OPOP; PoE; PPP

(I Lost the Love of Heaven.) ELP

I loue the rose both red & white. *Unknown.* FaBoEH

I lounge on the jetty in the fragrance of catalpa. Tu Fu, *tr. fr. Chinese by* Jerome Seaton. SuSp

I lov'd my selfe, bicause my selfe lov'd you. (*LL*) The Excuse. Sir Walter Ralegh. AAS; SiPS; SiPSBD

I lov'd thee from the earliest dawn. Early Affection. George Moses Horton. AAP

I Love. Stevie Smith. FaBoCo

I Love a Flower. *At. to* Thomas Philipps. MeEL

I love a man who is not worth my love. Did This Happen to Your Mother? Alice Walker. VBLP

I love a twenty yr old weekends. Blues. Sonia Sanchez. BCF

I love a wandering line. The Musician. Joseph Freiherr von Eichendorff, *tr. fr. German by* Philip L. Miller. RiWo

I Love All Beauteous Things. Robert Bridges. BoTP; CMoP; EBEV; OxAEP-2; TrCP

I love all beauteous things. I Love All Beauteous Things. Robert Bridges. BoTP; CMoP; EBEV; OxAEP-2; TrCP

I love all shining things. Shining Things. Elizabeth Gould. BoTP

I love and fear him. Kasa no Iratsume, *tr. fr. Japanese by* Kenneth Rexroth. BoWoP

I love and hate. Ah! never ask why so! Catullus. *See* I hate and love. Why? You may ask but.

I love and hate. Ah! never ask why so! Catullus, *tr. fr. Latin by* Walter Savage Landor. OBVE

I love, and he loves me again. A Nymph's Secret. Ben Jonson. BeJo; OBEV

I love and worship thee in that thy ways. Madonna Natura. "Fiona Macleod." WGRP

I love at early morn from new-mown swath. Summer Images. John Clare. ChTr; OBNC

I love bars and taverns. Bars. Nicolás Guillén, *tr. fr. Spanish by* Perry Higman. ArLo

I love beautiful things. The Proletariat Speaks. Alice Dunbar Nelson. ShDr

I love black faces. Black Faces. Anita Scott Coleman. ShDr

I love breasts, hard. Breasts. Charles Simic. NNaP; RaBo

I Love But Thee. Heine, *tr. fr. German by* Louis Untermeyer. AWP

I love contemplating — apart. Napoleon and the British Sailor. Thomas Campbell. BeLS

I love him not; but shew no reason can. Antipathy. Rowland Watkyns, *after the Latin of* Martial. FaBoEE

I love him wisely if I love him well. John Gambril Nicholson. *Fr.* Chaplet of Southernwood, A. PeHV

"I love, I love and whom love ye?" I Love a Flower. *At. to* Thomas Philipps. MeEL

I love it, I love it! and who shall dare. The Old Arm-Chair. Eliza Cook. AnAmPo; BrRo; InPK; Poetr, *St.* 1 *only;* VPP; WBLP

I Love Little Pussy. Jane Taylor. *See* I Like Little Pussy.

I love, loved, and so doth she. Sir Thomas Wyatt. SiPS

I love/ love's delicacy. Sappho, *tr. fr. Greek by* Sam Hamill. InMo

I love my dear friends. (*LL*) Goodnight God. Danu Baxter. EaPr

I love my God, but with no love of mine. Adoration. Mme Guyon. WGRP

I Love My Jean. Burns. *See* Of A' the Airts [the Wind Can Blaw].

I Love My Jesus Quite Alone. *At. to* Johannes Kelpius, *tr. fr. German by* Christopher Witt. AH

I love my little son, and yet when he was ill. The Two Parents. "Hugh MacDiarmid." FaBoTw; OxBTC

I Love My Love. Helen Adam. NeAP; NMM; WPOW

'I love my Love, and my Love loves me!' (*LL*) Answer to a Child's Question. Samuel Taylor Coleridge. ArLo; EnRP; FaBoBe; NTP; OxBChV

I love my love with a v. Gertrude Stein. *Fr.* Before the Flowers of Friendship Faded Faded. PeHV

I Love My Master. Nancy Morejón, *tr. fr. Spanish by* Kathleen Weaver. AIW

I love my neighbour. Love Thy Neighbour. D. H. Lawrence. ChIV-2

I love my prairies, they are mine. My Prairies. Hamlin Garland. FaPON

I love my wife and I love my baby. *Unknown.* RoPo

I love my work and my children. God. Ovid in the Third Reich. Geoffrey Hill. FaBoMo; NoAM

I love myself when I want. Sassy. Alma Villanueva. SRLS

I love not thy perfections. When I hear. Depreciating Her Beauty. Wilfrid Scawen Blunt. *Fr.* Love Sonnets of Proteus, The. OBMV

I love Octopussy, his arms are so long. The Octopussycat. Kenyon Cox. FaPON

I love old gardens best. A Charleston Garden. Henry Bellamann. PoLF

I love old mothers — mothers with white hair. Old Mothers. Charles Sarsfield Ross. PoToHe

I love roads. Roads. Edward Thomas. PeFWW

I love sixpence, jolly little sixpence. Mother Goose. OxNR; ReMoGo

I Love Somebody. *Unknown.* AmFP

I love sweets. Ellen West. Frank Bidart. NAAL-2

I love the ballet. Connoisseur. Joan Van Poznak. FaBoBl

I love the dark race of poets. Luminous Night. Louis Simpson. CAPP

I love the days of long ago. My Africa. Michael Dei-Anang. PBA

I love the deep quiet — all buried in leaves. Contradiction. Alice Cary. AmWP

I love the English country scene. I Love. Stevie Smith. FaBoCo

I love the evenings, passionless and fair, I love the evens. A Sunset. Victor Hugo, *tr. fr. French by* Francis Thompson. *Fr.* Feuilles d'Automne. AWP

I love the fitful gust that shakes. Autumn ("I love the fitful gust.") John Clare. BoTP

I love the lazy Southern spring. The First Julep. Bliss Carman. AnAmPo

I love the lit corners of your kerosine smile. Senior Lady Sells Garden Eggs. Kojo Laing. HBAPE

I love the little winding lanes. Lanes in Summer. Malcolm Hemphrey. BoTP

I Love the Lord. *Unknown.* AH

I Love the Night. Matilda C. Edwards. PWR

I love the old melodious lays. Whittier. AnAmPo; NoP; OxBA; TAP

I love the sea. The Sea at Evening. Christopher Laird. PBCV

I love the sex, and sometimes would reverse. Byron. *Fr.* Don Juan. CBLP

I love the small hours of the night. The Pleasant Joys of Brotherhood. James Simmons. PBCIP

I love the sound of the horn in the deep, dim woodland. The Sound of the Horn. Alfred de Vigny, *tr. fr. French by* Wilfred Thorley. AWP

I love the stillness of the wood. Solitude. "Lewis Carroll." PFP

I love the stream flowing endlessly. Robert Bly Finds Something in New Jersey. Carol Poster. BXAP

I love the way the cows go down to the water. A Knowledge of Water. Judson Mitcham. Poetr

I love the wind. Jimmy Santiago Baca. BCF

I love the word. Yes. Brendan Kennelly. CIP

I Love Thee. Josephine D. Henderson Heard. CBWP-4

I love thee, Betty. *Unknown.* OxNR

I love thee for thy fickleness. *Unknown.* NOSC

I love thee more, but I esteem thee less. (*LL*) Thou saidst that I alone thy heart cou'd move. Catullus. OBVE

I love thee when thy swelling buds appear. The Tree. Jones Very. GN; OHIP

I love these gardens, all their show. The Gardeners. Christopher Reid. DiPo

I love this boy, not for his beauty only. F. W. Soodley. PeHV

I love this byre. Shadows are kindly here. The Innkeeper's Wife. Clive Sansom. OBCP

I Love Thy Kingdom, Lord. Timothy Dwight. AH

I love to go out in late September. Blackberry Eating. Galway Kinnell. FoLa; InPK; NIP; SoSe

I love to hear the little bird. The Bird. Samuel Hoffenstein. FiBHP

I love to hear thine earnest voice. To an Insect. Oliver Wendell Holmes. AnAmPo

I love to rise ere gleams the tardy light. December Morning. Anna Seward. ECWP

I love to rise in a summer morn. The School Boy. Blake. *Fr.* Songs of Experience. BoNaP; CH; FaBoCh; FHYEP; OxAEP-2

I love to see boards lying on the ground in early spring. Old Boards. Robert Bly. NaP

I love to see the little stars. The Oneness of the Philosopher with Nature. G. K. Chesteron. CBNP; FaBoNo

I love to see the old heath's withered brake. Emmonsail's Heath in Winter. John Clare. PoEL-4

I love to see those loving and beloved. Lonely Love. Edmund Blunden. OxBTC

I love to see, when leaves depart. Autumn. Roy Campbell. GTBS-P; MoBrPo; OBMV; OxBTC

I Love to Steal Awhile Away. Phoebe Hinsdale Brown. AH

I love to think of things I hate. The Complete Misanthropist. Morris Bishop. FiBHP

I love to wander through the woodlands hoary. October. S. W. Whitman. BoTP

I love uncertain gestures. Valerio Magrelli, *tr. fr. Italian by* Jonathan Galassi. NeIt

I love watching the water. Trinket. Marvin Bell. AnAn

I love you. Hilda Doolittle ("H. D."). *Fr.* Sigil. AnAn

I Love You. Ella Wheeler Wilcox. BLPA; FaBoBe

I love you and the rosebush. Armando Uribe, *tr. fr. Spanish by* Miller Williams. HoPM

I love you as a sheriff searches for a walnut. To You. Kenneth Koch. ArLo

I love you better than I love my race. Charles Mair. *Fr.* Tecumseh. NOBC

I love you first because your face is fair. V-Letter. Karl Shapiro. NoAM; TrJP

(Love Letter.) NYBP

I love you first: but afterwards your love. Christina Rossetti. *Fr.* Monna Innominata. VBLP

I love you for all time and eternity. (*LL*) Thought of My thoughts. Hans Christian Andersen. RiWo

I love you for your brownness. To a Dark Girl. Gwendolyn B. Bennett. BlSi; CDC; PoBA; ShDr; VBLP

I love you ginger bread mama. Ginger Bread Mama. Doughtry Long, Jr.. BPo; PoBA

I love you, great new Titan! Soldier: Twentieth Century. Isaac Rosenberg. PoWW

I love you, I love you. *Unknown.* RoPo

I love you little. *Unknown.* RoPo

I love you, Mrs. Acorn. Would your husband mind. Song (October 1969). Kath Fraser. AIW; PeHV

"I love you, Mother," said little John. Which Loved Best? "Joy Allison." WBLP

(Which Loved Her Best?) OHIP

I love you, my plain pine box. First Coffin Poem. David Ignatow. CAPP

I love you,/ Not only for what you are. Love. *At. to* Roy Croft. BLPA; FaBoBe

(Why Do I Love You?) PoToHe

I love you, rotten. Medlars and Sorb-Apples. D. H. Lawrence. FaBoVe; NoAM; OAEL-2

I love you — Titan lover. Girl to Soldier on Leave. Isaac Rosenberg. PeFWW

I love you well, my steel-white dagger. Dagger. M. Y. Lermontov, tr. fr. Russian by Max Eastman. AWP

I love you. You! (LL) Bottled. Jill Breckenridge. LoHo

"I love you," you said between two mouthfuls of pudding. A Considered Reply to a Child. Jonathan Price. BoLoP

I love your eyebrows, said one. You Must Have Been a Sensational Baby. Harold Norse. GLP

I love your hands. Your Hands. Angelina Weld Grimké. CDC; PoBA

I love your lips when they're wet with wine. I Love You. Ella Wheeler Wilcox. BLPA; FaBoBe

I loved a child of this countrie. Unknown. GBL; PBWP

I Loved a Lass. George Wither. CH; NOBE; OBEV

I loved a lass, a fair one. I Loved a Lass. George Wither. CH; NOBE; OBEV
(Love Sonnet, A.) EiL; FaBoPP; GBL; NOSC

I loved booze. Clifton. Joan Larkin. GLP

I loved her softness, her warm human smell. The Lion's Bride. Gwen Harwood. BoWoP

I loved him not; and yet, now he is gone. The Maid's Lament. Walter Savage Landor. Fr. Citation and Examination of William Shakespeare, The. OBEV; OBNC

I loved him three storms ere he loved me again. Love's Flight. Else Lasker-Schüler, tr. fr. German by Jethro Bithell. TrJP

I loved my friend. (LL) I loved my friend. Langston Hughes. NTCP; SiSoPo

I loved my lord, my black-haired lord, my young love. The Magnet. Ruth Stone. MoAmPo

I loved my love from green of spring. Grown and Flown. Christina Rossetti. NOBVV

I loved/ secretly. Unknown, tr. fr. Latin by Willis Barnstone. Fr. Carmina Burana. BoWoP

I Loved Thee. Robert, Earl Nugent. NOEC; FiBHP

I loved thee long and dearly. Florence Vane. Philip Pendleton Cooke. AnAmPo

I loved thee once, I'll love no more. On A Woman's Inconstancy. Sir Robert Ayton. EiL
(To an Inconstant One.) OBEV

I loved thee, though I told thee not. The Secret. John Clare. GBL

I loved to talk of home. Pacific Epitaphs. Dudley Randall. MoP

I loved were strong enough to make me stop. (LL) My Father's Leaving. Ira Sadoff. AmPA

I Loved You, Even Now I May Confess. Pushkin, tr. fr. Russian by Reginald Mainwaring Hewitt. LPA

I loved you; even now I may confess. Pushkin. See I Loved You Once.

I Loved You Once. Pushkin, tr. fr. Russian.

I loved you, so I drew these tides of men into my hands. To S. A. Thomas Edward Lawrence. PeHV

I lower sail at river mouth. At the Chiang-ning River Mouth. Wang An-shih, tr. fr. Chinese by Jan W. Walls. SuSp

I lurk on the floor of silence. Hunting. Tymoteusz Karpowicz, tr. fr. Polish by Jan Darowski. PoSu

I made a pilgrimage to find the God. Revelation. Edwin Markham. WGRP

I made a posy [or posie], while the day ran by. Life. George Herbert. ESCV; FaBoRV; GeHe; JCP; LiTM; MeLP; NoP; NOSC; SeCP; SeCV-1

I made another garden, yea. Arthur O'Shaughnessy. OBEV

I made god upon god. Hilda Doolittle ("H. D."). Fr. Pygmalion. WGRP

I made my song a coat. A Coat. W. B. Yeats. CMoP; EPCY; IIP; LiTM; NAEL-2; NoAM; OxAEP-2; OxBSP; PoEL-5

I made myself as a tree. March Hares. Andrew Young. SAmP

I made the motions of the sacred place. Edouard J. Maunick, tr. fr. French by Ellen Conroy Kennedy. Fr. As Far as Yoruba Land. NegPo

I made the Muses sick. The Death of the Gods; an Ode Written in Imitation of Pindar. L. Ker. NOEC

I made the pilgrimage again. Derailment: A Delirium. Steve Chimombo. HBAPE

I made these mountains. Drainlayer. Duncan Bush. AngWe

I made up my mind for to change my way. The Trail to Mexico. Unknown. AmFP

I made you look, I made you look. Unknown. RoPo

I, Maister Andro Kennedy. The Testament of Mr. Andro Kennedy. William Dunbar. OxBS

I make a pact with you, Walt Whitman. A Pact. Ezra Pound. AmPP; AnAmPo; LiTA; MeMAP; MoP; NAAL-2; NoAM; NOBA; OxBA; TAP

I make a simple assertion. Working with Tools. A. R. Ammons. CAPP; TRP

I make a trip to each clock in the apartment. Two Mornings and Two Evenings. Elizabeth Bishop. PoA

I make all the poetic pauses. Dana Naone. CDW

I make an elephant/ from the little/ I have. The Elephant. Carlos Drummond de Andrade, tr. fr. Portuguese by Mark Strand. AnRep

I make fast my white barge. Visiting. Chung Ling, tr. fr. Chinese by Kenneth Rexroth and Ling Chung. WPC

I make free with old albums. At the Wailing Wall. Aidan Carl Mathews. BiHa; CIP; IB

I make my children promises in wintery afternoons. Teacher. Audre Lorde. MDDM

I make myself wake early. Waking, the Love Poem Sighs. Jim Hall. GOYP

I make this dirge for you Miss Mary Binning I miss you. Unknown, tr. fr. Hawaiian by Armand Schwerner. BoWoP

I make this song about me full sadly. The Wife's Lament. Unknown, tr. fr. Anglo-Saxon. WPE
(I make this song sadly about myself.) BoWoP, tr. by Willis Barnstone and Elene Kolb
(I sing of myself, a sorrowful woman.) PBWP, tr. by Kemp Malone
(Song I sing of sorrow unceasing, A.) AnOE, tr. by Charles W. Kennedy

I make this song sadly about myself. Unknown. See I make this song about me full sadly.

I many times thought Peace had come. Emily Dickinson. SAmP

I marched [or march'd] three miles through scorching sand. On a Curate's Complaint of Hard Duty. Swift. SCGP; TIRV

I marked all kindred powers the heart finds fair. Love Enthroned. Dante Gabriel Rossetti. Fr. House of Life, The. OBNC

I marked where lovely Venus and her court. Venus's Looking-Glass. Christina Rossetti. NALW

I married a man of the Croydon class. Nervous Prostration. Anna Wickham. AIW; FaBoWP; VBLP

I married a second time the other day. Second Marriage. Mei Yao Ch'en, tr. fr. Chinese by Jonathan Chaves. SuSp

I married in my youth a wife. J. V. Cunningham. MoAmPo

I marry the wind. (LL) The Parachutist's Wife. Sandra M. Gilbert. LoHo; WoWa

I marry'd a wife of late. Keep a Good Tongue in Your Head. Martin Parker. CoMu

I marvell'd why a simple child. Only Seven. Henry S. Leigh. BXAP

I, Maximus of Gloucester, to You ("By ear, she sd"). Charles Olson. Fr. Maximus Poems, The. NeAP

I, Maximus of Gloucester, to You ("Off-shore, by islands hidden in the blood"). Charles Olson. Fr. Maximus Poems, The. LiTM; NoAM; NOBA; PoM

I may be dead to-morrow, uncaressed. For the Book of Love. Jules Laforgue, tr. fr. French by Jethro Bithell. AWP; ErPo

I may be following you! (LL) Award. Ray Durem. BPo; PoBA; TTY

I may be smelly and I may be old. The River God. Stevie Smith. BrRo; FaBoNo; FaBoTw; FaBoWP; PBWP

I may even be. Power and Light. James Dickey. NAAL-2

I May, I Might, I Must. Marianne Moore. FaBoWP; FF; HeIL; OBAL; OxBSP

I may lie down, and wake with God. (LL) For the Lord's Day Evening. Isaac Watts. OxBChV

I may not ope again. (LL) Get Up! Joseph Skipsey. InPK; NOBVV

I may not touch the hand I saw. A Separation. William Johnson Cory. OBNC

I may picture her there. (LL) Thoughts of Phena [at News of Her Death]. Thomas Hardy. EBVV; NOBVV; NoP; OxBTC

I May Reap. Patrick Kavanagh. TIRV

I mean/ if I didn't know. Discovering. Sharon Scott. JB

I mean, I'm a no shoes hillbilly an' home. Gracie. Faye Kicknosway. NMM

I mean that too, but yet a hidden strength. Chastity ("I Mean That Too, But Yet a Hidden Strength.") Milton. Fr. Comus; a Masque Presented at Ludlow Castle. FHYEP; NOSC; OAEL-1

I mean/ the fiddleheads have forced their babies. May 10th. Maxine W. Kumin. BoNaP; NYBP; RFM

I mean to mark the Midway Day. Mezzo Cammin. Judith Moffett. SM

I mean to penetrate the particular. The Medium IV: Sights. Carl Rakosi. InPS

I measure every grief I meet. Emily Dickinson. MoAB; MoAmPo

I measure time by how a body sways. (LL) I Knew a Woman [Lovely in Her Bones]. Theodore Roethke. AmPP; BoLoP; CAPP; ErPo; HAP; HeIL; HeIP; HoPM; InPK; LiTM; LPA; MAT; MoAmPo; MoP; NAAL-2; NoAM; NOBA; NoP; PFP; PoE; Poetr; PrIm; RaBo; SM; SoSe; TAP; TFi; TRP; TwCP; UnPo; VCAP

I measured myself by the wall in the garden. Day Dreams, or Ten Years Old. Margaret Johnson. BLPA

I meditate upon a swallow's flight. Coole Park, 1929. W. B. Yeats. IIP; OAEL-2; OBMV

I meet two soldiers sometimes here in Hell. That Exploit of Yours. Ford Madox Ford. PeFWW; PoWW

I meet you as a lover. (LL) Night Sowing. David Campbell. CBAP

I meet you in an evil time. An Eclogue for Christmas. Louis MacNeice. FaBoMo; NoAM; OBMV

I member we went to the hospital that day. The Killing of the Birds. Shirley Williams. BoWoP

I mend the fyre and beikit me about. Robert Henryson. Fr. Testament of Cresseid, The. EBEV; OxBLMV; OxBS; PoE

I met a cracksman coming down the Strand. Theodore Martin. Fr. Thieves' Anthology, The. FaBoPa

I met a girl from Derrygarve. A New Song. Seamus Heaney. CIP; FaBoTw

I met a guy I used to know, who said. Ozymandias II. Howard Nemerov. Son

I met a lady/ on a lazy street. From the Hazel Bough. Earle Birney. NIP

I met a little cottage Girl. Wordsworth. Fr. We Are Seven. BLPA; BLPL; EnRP; GN; OxBChV; TEP; UV; WBLP

I met a little cottage-girl. Wordsworth on Lloyd George. Mary Visick. UV

I met a little elf man, once. The Little Elf. John Kendrick Bangs. FaBoBe; NTCP; OBCA
(Little Elfman, The.) PDV

I met a little Pacifist. The Rime of the Gentle Pacifist. "Pontiff." NSI

I met a man as I went walking. Puppy and I. A. A. Milne. BoTP; FaPON; PDV; PYC

I met a man in South Street, tall. Cutty Sark. Hart Crane. Fr. Bridge, The. FaBoMo; LiTA; NAAL-2

I met a man mowing. Hay Harvest. Patrick R. Chalmers. BoTP

I met a man with a triple-chin. The Man Who Sang the Sillies. John Ciardi. OBCA

I met a seer. The Book of Wisdom. Stephen Crane. Fr. Black Riders, The. HoPM; MoAmPo

I met a toad. Warty Bliggens, the Toad. Don Marquis. Fr. Archy and Mehitabel. FiBHP

I met a traveler [or traveller] from an antique land. Ozymandias [or Ozymandias of Egypt or Sonnet: Ozymandias]. Shelley. AWP; BeLS; CH; ClHu; DL; EnRP; FaBoBe; FaBoCh; FaBoRV; FaPoB; FaPoR; FF; GTBS; GTBS-P; HAP; HeIP; HoPM; ImPo; InPK; InPS; NAEL-2; NIP; NOBE; NoP; OAEL-2; OBNC; PlP; PoE; PoLF; PoRA; PrIm; RB; SCGP; SCV; Son; SoSe; TEP; TFi; TrGrPo; UV

I met a traveller from an antique land. Ozymandias Revisited. Morris Bishop. BXAP; CoGr; NBLV; UV

I met a woman from the sea coast. Eli's Poem. Ken Smith. PWE

I met an elf-man in the woods. How to Treat Elves. Morris Bishop. FiBHP; OBAL; OBCA

I met an honest man today. Alien. William Price Turner. OxBS

I met ayont the cairney. Empty Vessel. "Hugh MacDiarmid." FaBoTw; NoP; OxBS

I Met by Chance. Heine, tr. fr. German by John Todhunter. AWP

I met Death — he was a sportsman on Cole's Island. Cole's Island. Charles Olson. Fr. Maximus Poems, The. PoM

I met four guinea hens today. Life. Alfred Kreymborg. ZA

I met God in the morning. His Presence Came Like Sunrise. Ralph Spaulding Cushman. BLRP

I met her as a blossom on a stem. The Dream. Theodore Roethke. NoP; NYBP; UnPo

I Met Her in the Garden Where the Praties Grow. Unknown. AS

I met her in the leafy woods. A Dream. W. H. Davies. CBLP

I met him again, he was trudging along. I Fights Mit Sigel! Grant P. Robinson. BLPA

I met Louisa in the shade. Louisa. Wordsworth. EnRP; GBL

I met Musette/ In the water-closet. Vague Lyric by G. M. Max Beerbohm. FaBoEE

I Met My Solitude. Naomi Replansky. BrRo

I met Poetry, an old prostitute walking. Moral Story II. David Wright. PeSA

I met the Bishop on the road. Crazy Jane Talks with the Bishop. W. B. Yeats. BoLoP; CMoP; EBEV; ErPo; InPK; MeMBP; MoP; NAEL-2; NoAM; NoP; OAEL-2; OxAEP-2; PoE; PPP; TOF; TRP

I met the Love-Talker one eve in the glen. The Love-Talker. "Ethna Carbery." CH; WPE

I Met the Master. Unknown. BLRP; PoLF

I met the Master face to face. (LL) I Met the Master. Unknown. BLRP; PoLF

I Met This Guy Who Died. Gregory Corso. NAs; Poetsp

I met with a country lass. Thankful Country Lass, The; or, The Jolly Batchelor Kindly Entertained. Unknown. CoMu

I met with a jovial girl. Roaring Lad and the Ranting Lass, The; or, A Merry Couple Madly Met. Unknown. CoMu

I met with the girls coming from afar off. Love-Song of the Water Carriers. Unknown, tr. fr. Zulu. PeSA

I met wizened wood-woman. The Old Woman and the Sandwiches. Libby Houston. OBSP

I met you as a child. Numbers. Norah Reap. BTR

I met you by chance. At the Ball. A. K. Tolstoy, tr. fr. Russian by Philip L. Miller. RiWo

I might have been born in Beirut. Curriculum Vitae. Lawrence Joseph. PBCAP

I mind as 'ow the night afore that show. The Chances. Wilfred Owen. OxBTC

I mind me of a morning while the mountains yet were grey. Mooimeisjes. Perceval Gibbon. PeSAV

I Minded God. Henry Ainsworth. AH

I mingle with the young and gay. I Smile, but Oh! My Heart Is Breaking. Mary E. Tucker. CBWP-1

I mingle with your bones. The One Lost. Isaac Rosenberg. MoBrPo

I miss not eating fish on Friday. Pink Hands. Gary Soto. AfAz

I miss our lizards. The one who watched us. Lizards in Sardinia. Eamon Grennan. BiHa

I miss the peace and quiet of Chicago. Poem after Apollinaire. Ira Sadoff. AmPA

I miss the toad. Empty Water. W. S. Merwin. ArNa

I miss you in the morning, dear. Miss You. Unknown. PoToHe

I missed him when the sun began to bend. Lost and Found. George Macdonald. WGRP

I Missed His Book, I Read His Name. John Updike. OBAL

I missed/ the last transport. The Abandoned. Zbigniew Herbert, tr. fr. Polish by Michael March and Jaroslaw Anders. PoSu

I mix my men and booze. Sally: Twelfth Street. Naomi Long Madgett. NBV

I mock thee not, though I by thee am mocked. To Flaxman. Blake. FaBoEE; OxBoLi

I mourn for Antibia the virgin. Anyte, tr. fr. Greek by Sally Purcell. GrAn

I move among my pots and pans. Trimming the Sails. Vassar Miller. NMM

I move back by shortcut. The World. Vern Rutsala. Poetsp

I move on feeling and have learned to distrust those who don't. Poem of Angela Yvonne Davis. Nikki Giovanni. PoBA

I move the curtain back. After I Have Voted. Laura Jensen. AmPA

I Move the Meeting Be Adjourned. Nicanor Parra, tr. fr. Spanish by Miller Williams. Fr. Manifesto. HoPM

I Move to Random Consolations. William Heyen. AmPA

I move to the window. Threading the Miles. Alfred Encarnacion. OpBo

I Moved in My House. Gillian Eve Hanscombe and Suniti Namjoshi. DT

I moved, to keep the moon. On Aesthetics, More or Less. Peter Kane Dufault. NYBP

I moved with the morning. (LL) A Field of Light. Theodore Roethke. LiTM; TwCP

I much prefer fucking to feeling. (LL) There was a young lady of Ealing/ And her lover before her was kneeling. Isaac Asimov. PeLi

I Mun Be Married a Sunday. Nicholas Udall. Fr. Ralph Roister Doister. CBLP; EIL

I Muriel stood at the altar-table. Don Baty, the Draft Register. Muriel Rukeyser. NNaP

I muse, alone, an Ararat. (LL) Lakeshore. F. R. Scott. MoCV; NOBC

I mused/ Up and down, up and down, the terraced streets. Elizabeth Barrett Browning. Fr. Aurora Leigh. OBTV

I Must Away. May Sarson. BoTP

I must be. (LL) All but Blind. Walter de la Mare. FaPON; MoAB; MoBrPo; PDV; WeW

I must be dreaming through the days. Experience. Lesbia Harford. CBAP

I must be going, no longer staying. The Grey Cock. Unknown. ELP; OBET

I must be mad, or very tired. Meeting-House Hill. Amy Lowell. MoAmPo; OxBA; PoRA

I must become a child again. (LL) Innocence. Thomas Traherne. ChIV-2; ESCV; MiEL; NOSC

I must complain, yet doe enjoy my love. Thomas Campion. AAS

I must confess that often I'm. Time like an Ever-rolling Stream. P. G. Wodehouse. FiBHP

I must depart, but like to his last breath. Parted Souls. Lord Herbert of Cherbury. SeCP

I must explain why it is that at night, in my own house. Still Life. Reed Whittemore. CoAP

I must feel this soil again. Digging Soil. Peter Gruffydd. AngWe

I must go back to winter. Two Decisions. Vernon Watkins. OxBTC

I must go down to the sea again. Sea Poem. John Robinson. FaBoBl

I must go down to the seas again, to the lonely sea and the sky.
Sea-Fever. John Masefield. CoGr; EBEvV; FaBoBe; FaBV; FaPON;
FaPoR; MoAB; MoBrPo; NTP; OBTV; OtMeF; OxAEP-2; OxBTC;
PDV; PoLF; TrGrPo; UV

I must go down to the seas again, where the billows romp and reel.
Sea-Chill. Arthur Guiterman. BXAP; FaBoPa; UV

I Must Go Walk the Woods So Wild. *At.* to Sir Thomas Wyatt. MeEL;
MiEL; SiPSBD
(Wood So Wild, The.) WiR

I must have been dozing in the tub. The Soap-Pig. Paul Muldoon. PBCIP

I must have passed the crest a while ago. The Long Hill. Sara Teasdale.
LiTA; MoAmPo

I must have you! *(LL)* Epitaph from *The Great Gatsby.* F. Scott
Fitzgerald. OxBM

I must, I will have gin! — that skillet take. Strip Me Naked, or Royal Gin
for Ever; a Picture. *Unknown.* NOEC

"I must leave here," said Lady De Vere. *Unknown.* PeLi

I must lie down with them all soon and sleep. Thomas Kinsella. *Fr.*
Nightwalker. BIrV; IPY

I must not grieve my love, whose eyes would read. Samuel Daniel. *Fr.* To
Delia. ESo; OBEV
(Sonnet: "I must not grieve my love, whose eyes would read.") EIL

I must not think of thee; and, tired yet strong. Renouncement. Alice
Meynell. BoLoP; MoBrPo; NOBE; OBEV; OBMV; OBNC; PIP; Son;
WPE

I must/ Not trust. Anacreontic. Robert Herrick. CaPo

I must possess you utterly. Possession. Richard Aldington. MoBrPo

I must remember. Spreading Wings on Wind. Simon J. Ortiz. HATNAP

I must remember to dismiss. Nature Study, after Dufy. Helen Smith
Bevington. NYBP

I Must Sing of That. Beatrice, Countess de Die, *tr. fr. Provençal by*
Stephen Haynes. VBLP

I must sing of that which I would rather not. I Must Sing of That.
Beatrice, Countess de Die, *tr. fr. Provençal by* Stephen Haynes. VBLP

I must stay here with my hurt. *(LL)* Here. R. S. Thomas. GTBS-P; RB

I must tell my story. Listen. The Debt Problem. S. J. Litherland. NWP

I Must Tell the Story. Emily Borenstein. BTR

I must tell you. The Grass. George Bowering. MoCV

I must tell you. Young Sycamore. William Carlos Williams. TAP

I must wait for a stranger to knock on my door. David Ignatow. NNaP

I, my dear, was born to-day. On My Birthday, July 21. Matthew Prior.
OBEV

(I my (self)-per-por-trait-(or). Spring Bank. Geraldine Monk. NBrP

I myself and Pangur Bán. Pangur Bán. *Unknown.* NOIV

I myself have rolled the pearl screens up to their jade hooks. Tune: "Sand
of Silk-washing Stream." Li Ching, *tr. fr. Chinese by* Daniel Bryant.
SuSp

I myself saw furious with blood. Aeneas at Washington. Allen Tate.
FYAP; LiTA; NoAM; NOBA; OxBA

I nail Picasso's girl with a mirror. Notes from an Analyst's Couch. Anita
Endrezze-Danielson. CDW

I ne have joy, plesauns, nor comfort. *Unknown.* MiEL

I need a job again. I'm caught in a steel cycle. *(LL)* God, I need a job
because I need money. Alan Dugan. CAPP; NoAM

I need kai kai ah. For the Poets. Jayne Cortez. BCF

I Need No Gravestone. Bertolt Brecht, *tr. fr. German by* Michael
Hamburger. OBD

I Need Not Go. Thomas Hardy. NOBE; OBEV; OxBTC

I need not shout my faith. Thrice eloquent. Silence. Charles Hanson
Towne. WGRP

I need not your needles. *Unknown.* OxNR

I need only fall asleep/ to return. Ana Blandiana, *tr. fr. Romanian by*
Stavros Deligiorgis. BoWoP

I need so much the quiet of your love. At Nightfall. Charles Hanson
Towne. BLPA; FaBoBe
(Nightfall.) PoToHe

I need something easy. Honey Moon. Kathleen Leland Baker. NBLV

I ne'er could any lustre see. Sheridan. *Fr.* Duenna, The. NOEC

I ne'er was dress'd in forms; nor can I bend. Henry King. *Fr.* Letter, A.
OBF

I ne'er was struck before that hour. First Love. John Clare. BoLoP; ChTr;
ELP; EnLoPo; GBL; HAP; NOBVV; NoP

I ne're will owe my health to a disease. *(LL)* Against Jealousie. Ben
Jonson. CBLP

I never asked for more than thou hast given. Goldsworthy Lowes
Dickinson. PeHV

I never barked when out of season. On a Dog of Lord Eglinton's. Burns.
OxBSP

I never believed that in my broken life. Ts'ai Yen, *tr. fr. Chinese by*
Kenneth Rexroth *and* Ling Chung. *Fr.* Eighteen Verses Sung to a Tatar
Reed Whistle. BoWoP; WPC; WPOW

I never bought a young gazelle. 'Twas Ever Thus. *Unknown.* BXAP

I never cared for Life: Life cared for me. Thomas Hardy. FaBoEE;
FaBoRV

I never cast a flower away. Partings. Maria Jane Jewsbury. OxBChV

I never crossed your threshold with a grief. The Closed Door. Theodosia
Garrison. BLPA; PoToHe

I never did on cleft Parnassus dream. Prologue to the First Satire. Persius,
tr. fr. Latin by Dryden. *Fr.* Satires. AWP

I never drank of Aganippe well. Sir Philip Sidney. *Fr.* Astrophel and
Stella. AAS; EnRePo; ESo, GGP; NAEL-1; NoSic; Poetr; SCGP; SiPS;
SiPSBD; Son

I Never Even Suggested It. Ogden Nash. FiBHP; LiTA; PoLF

I never feared the darkness as a child. The Black-out. Mary Désirée
Anderson. PAW

I never felt so much. A Birthday. Edwin Muir. NAs

I never gave a lock of hair away. Elizabeth Barrett Browning. *Fr.* Sonnets
from the Portuguese. EBVV; HAP

I never go to the plains beneath the hills. Song of the Old Man of the
Hills. Meng Chiao, *tr. fr. Chinese by* A. C. Graham. PLT

I Never Had a Piece of Toast. James Payn. FaBoPa

I never have got the bearings quite. The Flag. James Jeffrey Roche. PAH

I never have to go through again. *(LL)* Cumberland Station. Dave Jeddie
Smith. HCAP

I never hear it ring without. The Door-Bell. Charlotte Becker. PoToHe

I never hear the word "escape." Emily Dickinson. CMoP; NOBA; SAmP

I never knew. *(LL)* Willy Lyons. James Wright. HCAP; NNaP; PoE

I Never Knew a Night So Black. John Kendrick Bangs. PoToHe

I never knew but one — and here he lies. *(LL)* Epitaph to a Dog. Byron.
BLPA

I never knew the earth had so much gold. Feuerzauber. Louis
Untermeyer. TrJP

I never knew you but my mother made me. Pigeons. Tim Longville. VaA

I never look upon the sea. Aunt Zillah Speaks. Herbert Edward Palmer.
FaBoTw

I never lost as much but twice. Emily Dickinson. BLPL; HeIP; MoAB;
MoAmPo; NAAL-1; NoAM; NOBA; NoP; TAP

I never loved a dear gazelle. Tèma con Variazióni. "Lewis Carroll."
FaBoNo

I never minded having such old parents. Late Child. Robert Pinsky. *Fr.*
Three on Luck. AnAn

I never need to see myself as I am in the mirror. All Is Well. Victor
Martinez. AfAz

I never quite saw fairy-folk. Very Nearly. Queenie Scott-Hopper. FaPON

I never read of any enforceable regulation. Because Sometimes You Can't
Always Be So. Kenneth Patchen. NaP

I never reared a young gazelle. 'Twas Ever Thus. Henry S. Leigh.
FaBoCo; FaBoPa; UV

I Never rested on the Muses bed. To William Drummond of Hawthornden.
Mary, of Morpeth Oxlie. KTR

I never said I loved you, John. "No, Thank You, John." Christina
Rossetti. NAEL-2; TEP

I never saw a moor. Emily Dickinson. FaPON; GN; HeIP; ImGa; ImPo;
LiTA; LiTM; MeMAP; MoAB; MoAmPo; PoLF; SAmP; TAP; TFi;
TrGrPo; WGRP

I never saw a purple cow. The Purple Cow. Gelett Burgess. CBNP;
FaBoCo; FaBoNo; FaPON; FiBHP; GrPl; NBLV; NTCP; OBAL; OBCA;
PDV; PoLF; TFi; TLR

I never saw a wild thing. Self-Pity. D. H. Lawrence. OxBTC; RB

I never saw my father old. A Celebration. May Sarton. ArLo
(Celebration for George Sarton, A.) ArLo

I never saw you madam, lay [*or* sawe my Ladye] laye apart. The Earl of
Surrey. AAS; SiPS; SiPSBD
(Complaint That His Ladie After She Knew of His Love Kept Her Face
Alway Hidden from Him, *sl. diff.*) PoEL-1

I never see the colored boats of night. The Age of Sheen. Dorothy
Hughes. NYBP

I never see the red rose crown the year. John Masefield. *Fr.* Sonnets.
GoYe

I never set my two eyes on a head was so fine as your head. A Translation
from Walter von der Vogelweide. Walther von der Vogelweide, *tr. by*
J. M. Synge. MoBrPo

I Never Shall Love the Snow Again. Robert Bridges. CH; CMoP; FaBV

I never tasted the Pierian spring. On Her Blindness. Priscilla Pointon. *Fr.*
To the Critics. ECWP

I never thought for a moment. Emily Dickinson, Bismarck and the Roadrunner's Inquiry. Ray A. Young Bear. HATNAP

I never thought that my love would leave me. Love Is Teasing. *Unknown.* OBET

I never thought to hear you speak again. Shakespeare. *Fr.* King Henry IV, Pt. II. FaBoEH

I never thought to see us. Sherley Anne Williams. *Fr.* Peacock Poems, The. MDDM

I never tire in my search of solitude. In Search of Solitude. Chao Yi, *tr. fr. Chinese by* Chang Yin-nan *and* Lewis C. Walmsley. SuSp

I never told you. What They Do to You in Distant Places. Marvin Bell. Poetsp

I never wanted to be a star. On Earth. Forugh Farrokhzad, *tr. fr. Persian by* Girdhard Tikku. BoWoP

I never was a slave — a robber took. Albery Allson Whitman. *Fr.* Twasinta's Seminoles; Or Rape of Florida. AAP

I never was attached to that great sect. The Longest Journey. Shelley. *Fr.* Epipsychidion. EnRP; OtMeF; OxBM

I never wholly feel that summer is high. High Summer. Ebenezer Jones. NOBVV

I never will complain of my dear husband, Mrs. Henn. "He Didn't Oughter." A. P. Herbert. FiBHP

I never would cry, Old chairs to mend. (*LL*) If I had [*or* I'd] as much money as I could spend. Mother Goose. OxNR

I never writ, nor no man ever loved. (*LL*) Let Me Not to the Marriage of True Minds. Shakespeare. ArLo; AWP; ClHu; EBEvV; EIL; EnLoPo; EnRePo; FaBV; FaPoB; GBL; GGP; HAP; HeIL; HeIP; InPS; InvP; LiTB; NAEL-1; NIP; NOBE; NoP; NoSic; OAEL-1; OBEV; OxAEP-1; OxBM; PeHV; PoE; PoEL-2; Poetr; PoRA; PPP; PrIm; SCGP; SCV; Son; SoSe; TEP; TFi; TrGrPo; TRP; UnPo; WeW

I never yet arraigned the will of heaven. Edward Thompson. *Fr.* Humble Wish; off Porto-Sancto, March 29, 1779, An. OBTV

I no longer believe in Arthur. Marchlyn. Ian Hughes. AngWe

I no longer care, keeping close my silence. The Chain. Christine Craig. AIW

I no longer fear the firestorm despair. No Longer. Roberta Hill Whiteman. ETG

I, no sense of being alive. A Diary without Dates. Nakamura Chio, *tr. fr. Japanese by* Kenneth Rexroth *and* Ikuko Atsumi. WPJ

I notice she didn't rebucre. (*LL*) Limerick. *Unknown.* PeLi

I, now at Carthage. He, shot dead at Rome. *Vale* from Carthage. Peter Viereck. ArOW; LiTM; MoAmPo

I now had only to retrace. Charlotte Brontë. NOBVV

I now mean to be serious; — it is time. Lady Adeline Amundeville. Byron. *Fr.* Don Juan. MeMBP; PoEL-4

I now solicit not the Muses nine. William Woty. *Fr.* Mock Invocation to Genius, A. NOEC

I now think Love is rather deaf[e] than blind. My Picture Left in Scotland. Ben Jonson. BeJo; CBLP; EnRePo; NAEL-1; PoEL-2; SeCP; SeCV-1

I now will throw myself down. A Dialogue. David Ignatow. NNaP

I nursed it in my bosom while it lived. Memory. Christina Rossetti. OBNC

I objurgate the centipede. The Centipede. Ogden Nash. FaPON

I, Oedipus, the club-foot, made to stumble. Oedipus. Edwin Muir. CMoP

I of my Spenser quite bereft. Book-Lender's Lament. *Unknown.* FaBoUs

I offer my back to the silken net. An Allegory. David Ignatow. VGW

I oft have wished for Hell for Ease from Heaven. (*LL*) Grown old in love from seven till seven times seven. Blake. FaBoEE; OAEL-2

I oft stand in the snow at dawn. Don Marquis. *Fr.* To a Lost Sweetheart. FiBHP

I often have been told. The *Constitution* and the *Guerrière*. *Unknown.* PAH

I Often Meet a Monster. Max Fatchen. OTCP

I often wonder as the fairy-story. The Lucky Marriage. Thomas Blackburn. GTBS-P

I often wonder how it is. My Playmate. Mary I. Osborn. BoTP; OTCP

I once believed a single line. For E. J. P. Leonard Cohen. NoP

I once conjectur'd that those tygers hard. Seaconk or Rehoboths Fate. Benjamin Tompson. SCAP

I once did court a damsel most beautiful and bright. A Lover's Lament. *Unknown.* AmFP

I once had a cat called Maria. Paul Griffin. PeLi

I once had a dog. *Unknown.* RoPo

I once had a sweet little doll, dears. The Lost Doll. Charles Kingsley. *Fr.* Water Babies, The. FaPON; MoShBr
(Little Doll, The.) OxBChV
(Song.) VPP

I once had money and a friend. Money and a Friend. *Unknown.* BLPA

I once heard the survivors. Don Marquis. *Fr.* Certain Maxims of Archy. NBLV; OBAL

I once knew a fellow named Arthur McBride. Arthur McBride. GBP; OBET

I once knew a lass and I oft heard her tell. So I Let Her Go. *Unknown.* AmFP

I once knew a little girl, a charming beauty bright. The Rejected Lover. *Unknown.* AmFP

I Once Knew a Man. Lucille Clifton. CAPP; Poetr

I once knew a spinster of Staines. Plaiwon. PeLi

I once knew a woman named Benedicta, who infused everything. Which One Is Genuine? Baudelaire, *tr. fr. French by* Robert Bly. RaBo

I once knowed an ole Sexion Boss but he done been laid low. The Old Section Boss. *Unknown.* BPo

I once lov'd a boy, and a bonny, bonny boy. *Unknown.* WTO

I Once Loved a Young Man. *Unknown.* AmFP

I once loved a young man as dear as my life. I'm Going to Georgia. *Unknown.* AmFP

I once may see when yeares shall wreck my wrong. Samuel Daniel. *Fr.* To Delia. AAS; ESo

I once spent an evening in a village. The Man Upright. Thomas MacDonagh. BIrV

I once thought that snowflakes were feathers. Snowflakes. Marchette Chute. PDV

I once took my girl to Southend. Veronica Nicolson. PeLi

I once wanted a white man's eyes upon. Lunchcounter Freedom. Thylias Moss. BAP-91

I once was a bold fellow and went with a team. The Carter. *Unknown.* OBET

I Once Was a Maid. Burns. *Fr.* Jolly Beggars, The. EnRP; *sl. diff. vers.*; NBLV; OxBoLi; PoEL-4

I once was a Pirate what sailed the 'igh seas. Cat Morgan Introduces Himself. T. S. Eliot. NOBL; PeLV

I once was a seaman stout and bold. Jolly Soldier. *Unknown.* AmFP

I once was happy, when, while yet a child. Charlotte Smith. *Fr.* Beachy Head. WPE

I once was in service. Rosemary Lane. *Unknown.* OBET

I once wrote a letter as follows. The Invoice. Robert Creeley. VGW

I one my mother. *Unknown.* ISE

I Only Am Escaped Alone to Tell Thee. Howard Nemerov. CoAP; HeIP; NoAM

I only feel — Farewell! — Farewell! (*LL*) Farewell! If Ever Fondest Prayer. Byron. EnRP

I only knew one poet in my life. How It Strikes a Contemporary. Robert Browning. CTC; EnVR; FaBoPV; GTBS-P; OAEL-2

I only know it shall be great. (*LL*) Unmanifest Destiny. Richard Hovey. WGRP

I only know that I was there. Ante-natal Dream. Patrick Kavanagh. NAs

I only read about you. Yom HaShoah. Estelle Gershgoren Novak. BTR

I only saw my father's face in butchery. The Bull-roarer. Gerald Stern. NAmP90

I open the phone book, and look for my adolescence. Equation. Charles Wright. CAPP

I opened my door to this nutty witch. I've been suicidal. After Reading Sylvia Plath. Alta. IHMS

I Opened the Window. Grand Duke of Russia Constantine, *tr. fr. Russian by* Philip L. Miller. RiWo

I opened the window — sadness overwhelmed me. I Opened the Window. Grand Duke of Russia Constantine, *tr. fr. Russian by* Philip L. Miller. RiWo

I opened the window wide and leaned. John Masefield. *Fr.* Everlasting Mercy, The. WGRP

I order the carriage to stop for a while. (*LL*) On the Road through Chang-te. Sun Yün-feng. BoWoP; WPC; WPOW

I ordered this, this clean wood box. The Arrival of the Bee Box. Sylvia Plath. FaBoMo; FaBoWP; HCAP; NALW; NaP

I ought to feel ashamed. Eva Braun. W. D. Snodgrass. *Fr.* Führer Bunker, The. CAPP

I Ought to Weep. *Unknown.* MeEL

I Ovid poet of my wantonnesse. Ovid, *tr. by* Christopher Marlowe. *Fr.* Amores. OBVE

I owe him for pictures. Buck. Michael S. Harper. CAPP

I owe nothing to winter. My Winter Past. Eldon Grier. NOBC

I owe you an apology. A Question of Form and Content. Jon Stallworthy. OxBC

I pace the sounding sea-beach and behold. Milton. Longfellow. AmPP; AWP; NoP; TAP; TrGrPo

I paced alone on the road across the field. The Home. Rabindranath Tagore. GoJo

I Paint What I See. E. B. White. NBLV; NYBP

I painted her a gushing thing. Disillusioned. "Lewis Carroll."

(My Fancy.) FaBoCo

I painted my eyes with black antimony. Love Song. *Unknown, tr. fr. Bagirmi by* H. Gaden. BoWoP

I painted on the roof of a skyscraper. People Who Must. Carl Sandburg. PDV

I painted the mailbox. That was fun. Painting the Gate. May Swenson. TLR; WeW

I park the car half in the ditch and switch off and sit. Stealing Trout. Ted Hughes. NYBP

I part the out thrusting branches. Wendell Berry. EaPr

I parted from my life last night. On the Death of His Wife. Muireadach Albanach O'Dalaigh, *tr. fr. Irish by* Frank O'Connor. BIrV; CIP

I Pass La Iglesia. Jimmy Santiago Baca. ETG

I pass la iglesia, then back up. I Pass La Iglesia. Jimmy Santiago Baca. ETG

I passed a tomb among green shades. Her Rival for Aziza. *Unknown, tr. fr. Arabic by* E. Powys Mathers. *Fr.* Thousand and One Nights, The. AWP

I passed along the water's edge below the humid trees. Indian upon God, The [*or* An]. W. B. Yeats. MoBrPo; WGRP

I passed by the beach. Akahito, *tr. fr. Japanese by* Kenneth Rexroth. HoPM

I passed by the house of the young man who loves me. *Unknown, tr. fr. Egyptian by* J. E. Manchip White. TTY

I past [*or* passed] beside the reverend walls. Tennyson. *Fr.* In Memoriam A. H. H. EBVV, *abr.*; OAEL-2, *abr.*; PeECV, *abr.* (He Revisits Cambridge.) FaBoPP

I patched my coat with sunlight. The Coat. Dennis Lee. TLR

I pause not now to speak of Raleigh's dreams. John Smith's Approach to Jamestown. James Barron Hope. PAH

I paused in a garden alley of cypress and rose, resembling Paradise. Last Things. Kathleen Raine. NYBP

I paused last eve beside of a blacksmith's door. At. to John Clifford. *See* Last eve I passed beside of a blacksmith's door.

I peeled bits of straw and I got switches too. John Clare. NAEL-2 (Bits of Straw. WiR

I peeped through the window. *Unknown.* OxNR

I peer adown a shining group. Tribute. Eloise Bibb. CBWP-4

I perch upon a humbler promontory. Byron. *Fr.* Don Juan. EPCY

I persist in a little fabric between me and the world. J. Michael Yates. *Fr.* Great Bear Lake Meditations, The. NOBC

I picked fresh mint. My Garden. Norah E. Hussey. BoTP

I picked myself up ignoring. Herself. Lorna Dee Cervantes. *Fr.* Lots. ETG

I picked up a leaf. Les Etiquettes Jaunes. Frank O'Hara. ArNa

I picture a wide unshowy river. The Young. Sebastian Barry. IB

I pitched my day's leazings in Crimmercrock Lane. The Dark-eyed Gentleman. Thomas Hardy. MoAB; MoBrPo; NBLV; UnPo

I pitied him for his small strategy. (*LL*) The Compassionate Fool. Norman Cameron. GTBS-P; OxBSP; OxBTC; RB

I place myself at the edge of thy Grace. *Unknown, tr. fr. Gaelic by* Douglas Hyde. WTO

I place these numbed wrists to the pane. Nightmare Begins Responsibility. Michael S. Harper. CAPP; HCAP; LCAP; TAP; VCAP

I placed a jar in Tennessee. Anecdote of the Jar. Wallace Stevens. AmPP; CMoP; HCAP; HeIP; HoPM; InPK; LiTA; MeMAP; MoAB; MoAmPo; MoP; NAAL-2; NAWM-2; NoAM; NOBA; NoP; OxBA; OxBSP; PoA; Poetr; PPP; PrIm; SAmP; SOTW; TAP; TFi; UnPo

I placed my dream in a boat. Cecília Meireles, *tr. fr. Portuguese by* Eloah F. Giacomelli. TSaS; WPOW

I planned to have a border of lavender. Paul Goodman. GLP; VGW

I plant beans at the foot of the southern hill. T'ao Ch'ien, *tr. by* Wu-chi Liu. *Fr.* On Returning to My Garden and Field. SuSp

I planted a hundred mulberry trees. Country House. Ch'u Ch'uang I, *tr. fr. Chinese by* Kenneth Rexroth. OHMPC

I planted a young tree when I was young. A Dumb Friend. Christina Rossetti. OBF

"I play a spade. — Such strange new faces." Arrivals at a Watering-Place. Winthrop Mackworth Praed. NOBL; PeLV

I play for seasons, not eternities. George Meredith. *Fr.* Modern Love. OBNC; SCGP

I play Haydn after a black day. Allegro. Tomas Tranströmer, *tr. fr. Swedish by* Robin Fulton. PWE

I play it cool. Motto. Langston Hughes. PoBA; PoNe

I play pool. I aim toward the faces. Games. Sandra McPherson. LCAP

I play the Masonic Funeral March. Julia Fields. *Fr.* Poems: Birmingham 1962 – 1964. PoBA; PoNe

I play your furies back to me at night. High Fidelity. Thom Gunn. PoA

I played I was two polar bears. The Bear Hunt. Margaret Widdemer. FaPON

I Played on the Grass with Mary. Ernest Walsh. ErPo

I played with you 'mid cowslips blowing. Love and Age. Thomas Love Peacock. *Fr.* Gryll Grange. NOBVV; OBEV; OBNC

I pledge allegiance to the old. Double Agent. Heather McHugh. AnAn

I pledge myself through thick and thin. Tory Pledges. Thomas Moore. FaBoCo; OBSV

I pluck the clustering flowers from the wall. Tune: "Sprig of Flowers, A" — Not Bowing to Old Age. Kuan Han-ch'ing, *tr. fr. Chinese by* Jerome P. Seaton. SuSp

I plucked my soul out of its secret place. I Know My Soul. Claude McKay. BPo

I plucked pink blossoms from mine apple-tree. An Apple Gathering. Christina Rossetti. NAEL-2; OBNC

I ply with all the cunning of my art. The Craftsman. Marcus B. Christian. PoNe

I poet. (*LL*) Sisters. Lucille Clifton. VBLP

I poked my finger in the dirt and put the seed. Garden. Brooks Haxton. BAP-91

I polish your skin. It is that of a woman. A Song in Praise of a Favourite Humming-Top. Hone Tuwhare. PeNZ

I Ponder on Life. Max Ehrmann. PoToHe

I pour the cream. (*LL*) Vacation. William Stafford. Poetsp

I praise a patron high-hearted in strife. In Praise of Owain Gwynedd. Cynddelw Brydydd Mawr, *tr. fr. Welsh by* Joseph P. Clancy. OBWVE

I praise God's mankind in an old woman. Lines: I Praise God's Mankind in an Old Woman. Wilfred Watson. NOBC

I praise him not. James Russell Lowell. *Fr.* Ode Recited at the Harvard Commemoration. AiP; NOBA; OBWP; PAH

I praise Saint Everyman, his house and home. Here Together Met. Louis Johnson. PeNZ

I praise sky. Praise. Dinah Livingstone. AIW

I praise the country women. Grit. Geoff Page. NOBAu

I praise the disk of the rising sun. Vidya, *tr. fr. Sanskrit by* Daniel H. H. Ingalls. *Fr.* Sun, The. PBWP; WPOW

I praise the Frenchman, his remark was shrewd. William Cowper. *Fr.* Retirement. BLPA

I praise the speech, but cannot now abide it. Of the Wars in Ireland. John Harington. NoSic

I praise Thee, Christ, that on Thy breast. Muireadhach Albannach, *tr. fr. Gaelic by* Nigel MacNeill. ScCV

I praise Thee not, with impious pride. Sir Lewis Morris. *Fr.* Heathen Hymn, A. TrPWD

I pray attend unto this Jest. The Fair Maid of the West. *Unknown.* CoMu

I pray! My little body and whole span. Supplication of the Black Aberdeen. Kipling. BLPA

I pray not for the joy that knows. Marion Franklin Ham. TrPWD

"I pray," said Rolfe, "a word." Ungar and Rolfe. Herman Melville. *Fr.* Clarel. OxBA

I pray that the great world's flowering stay as it is. The Gardener to His God. Mona Van Duyn. TrCP; UnPo; WPE

I pray the Lord my soul to take. Ogden Nash. *Fr.* One from One Leaves Two. NBLV

I pray the Lord my soul to take. (*LL*) Now I Lay me Down to Sleep. *Unknown.* CoGr; OBD

I pray the Lord my soul to take. (*LL*) Now I Lay Me Down to Take My Sleep. *Unknown.* BLRP; GBP; OxNR

I pray the prayer the Easterners do. Salaam Alaikum. *Unknown.* PoLF

I pray thee, Dante, shouldst thou meet with Love. To Dante Alighieri: He Mistrusts the Love of Lapo Gianni. Cavalcanti, *tr. fr. Italian by* Dante Gabriel Rossetti. AWP

I pray thee leave, love me no more. To His Coy Love, A Canzonet. Michael Drayton. NOSC

I pray thee Nymph Penaeis stay, I chase not as a fo. Ovid, *tr. by* Arthur Golding. *Fr.* Metamorphoses. OBVE

I pray Thee O Lord. Julian Tuwim, *tr. fr. Polish by* Wanda Dynowska. TrJP

I pray thee spare me, gentle Boy. Loves Feast. Sir John Suckling. CBLP

I pray to God another love you so. (*LL*) I Loved You Once. Pushkin.

I pray you are always above me. Artemis. Anne Waldman. SRLS

I pray you, be not wroth. *Unknown. Fr.* Vox Populi, Vox Dei. FaBoPV

I pray you, Christ, to change my heart. Christ's Bounty. *Unknown, tr. fr. Irish by* Brendan Kennelly. TIRV

I pray you, cum kiss me. *Unknown.* MiEL

I pray you, let us roam no more. Thomas Moore. *Fr.* Odes to Nea. OBNC

I prayed each twilight with the crickets. The Sunday before Easter. Askold Melnyczuk. UTF

I prayed for riches, and achieved success. Answered Prayers. Ella Wheeler Wilcox. PWR

I prefer red chile over my eggs. Green Chile. Jimmy Santiago Baca. NAmP90

I prefer to sit all day. The One Song. Mark Strand. CAPP

I press my face to the pane of death to witness. I Must Tell the Story. Emily Borenstein. BTR

I press [or presse] not to the quire, nor dare I greet. To My Worthy Friend Master George Sands [or Sandys], on His Translation of the Psalms. Thomas Carew. BeJo; CaPo; EPCY; JCP; MeLP; SeCV-1

I Pressed Her Rebel Lips. Unknown. BoLoP; ErPo

I pretend to wait for you to enlarge the minutes. Patrizia Cavalli, tr. fr. Italian by Judith Baumel. NeIt

I prithee, daughter, do not make me mad. Shakespeare. Fr. King Lear. OxAEP-1

I prithee let my heart alone. Thomas Stanley. BeJo

I prithee send me back my heart. At. to Henry Hughes Suckling and also to Sir John Suckling. JCP

I prithee spare me, gentle boy. Sir John Suckling. BeJo

I Promise Nothing. A. E. Housman. PPP

I promise to make you more alive than you've ever been. Ordeal. Nina Cassian, tr. fr. Romanian by Michael Impey and Brian Swann. PBWP

I promise you these days and an understanding. Tourist Death. Archibald MacLeish. NAAL-2

I promised once if I got hold of. Written in a Copy of Swift's Poems, for Wayne Burns. James Wright. NOBA

I propose to you. The Statue. Robert Creeley. LCAP

I protest my isolation. Waiting Inside. David Ignatow. CAPP

I prove a theorem and the house expands. Geometry. Rita Dove. HCAP; HeIP; Poetr

I puff my breast out, my neck swells. Weathercock, The: "I puff my breast out, my neck swells." Unknown, formerly at. to Cynewulf, tr. by Geoffrey Grigson. Fr. Riddles (Exeter Book). RB
(Weathercock: My breast is puffed up and my neck is swollen.) ASW, tr. by Kevin Crossley — Holland

I pump him full of lost watches. (LL) Birthplace Revisited. Gregory Corso. NeAP; PoM; VGW

I pumped the iron handle and watched the water. My Father Washes His Hands. Fred Chappell. MT

I put down my oar to lodge in what man's house? (LL) Deep in Winter. Tu Fu. PLT

I put my hand upon her toe. Gently, Johnny My Jingalo. Unknown. OBET

I put my hat upon my head. A Second Stanza for Dr. Johnson. Donald Hall. FiBHP

I put my hat upon my head. Samuel Johnson. CBNP; NOBL; OxAEP-1; UV

I put my hat upon my head, parody. F. A. V. Madden. BXAP

I put my hat upon my head. Ian Sainsbury. BXAP

I put my hat upon my head. Zan Stirling. BXAP

I put my hat upon my head. Peter Veale. BXAP; NBLV

I put on a pair of overshoes. Around My Room. William Jay Smith. TLR

I put out the light and listen to the rain. Second Fragment. John Riley. VaA

I put the chickens in and they swivel. Having Built the Coop. Ed Ochester. ETG

I put your leaves aside. The Weather-Cock Points South. Amy Lowell. NALW

I quail, lean to beginnings, sheath-wet. (LL) Cuttings ("This urge, wrestle, resurrection of dry sticks.") Theodore Roethke. CAPP; HCAP; LCAP; MoP; NAAL-2; NoAM; NOBA; TAP; TRP; UnPo; VCAP

I quarreled with kings till the Sabbath. Song of the Sabbath. Kadya Molodovsky, tr. fr. Yiddish by Jean Valentine. PBWP; WPOW

I quarreled with my brother. The Quarrel. Eleanor Farjeon. FaPON

I Quite Like Men. Fran Landesman. DT

"I quite realized," said Columbus. E. C. Bentley. Fr. Clerihews. FiBHP

I quitted, and betook myself to France. Wordsworth. Fr. Prelude [or, Growth of a Poet's Mind], The. EnRP; OAEL-2; OxAEP-2

I raced west away from the dawn. Thaba Bosio. S. D. R. Sutu, tr. fr. Sotho by Dan Kunene and Jack Cope. PeSA

I rage, I melt, I burn. John Gay. Fr. Acis and Galatea. NAEL-1

I raise my cup and invite. Moon, Flowers, Man. Su Tung-p'o, tr. fr. Chinese by Kenneth Rexroth. NaP

I raise the curtains and go out. Alone. Chu Shu-chen, tr. by Kenneth Rexroth. BoWoP

I Raised a Great Hullabaloo. Unknown. PDV

I ran from the prison house but they captured me. The Prison House. Alan Paton. PeSA

I ran onto Mehitabel again. The Old Trouper. Don Marquis. Fr. Archy and Mehitabel. FaBoCo

I ran out in the morning, when the air was clean and new. Autumn Morning at Cambridge. Frances Cornford. PoRA

I ran to the church. Journey Back to Christmas. Gwen Dunn. OBCP

I ran up and grabbed your arm, the way a man. At the Washing of My Son. David Ray. RaBo

I ran up six flights of stairs. The Whole Mess . . . Almost. Gregory Corso. PoBeRe

I ran upon life unknowing, without or science or art. Tennyson. FaBoEE

I rattle my handful of bones and the dead arise. (LL) Hottentot Venus. Stephen Gray. PeSAV

I reach from pain. Reuben, Reuben. Michael S. Harper. PoE

I reach the marble-streeted town. The Marble-streeted Town. Thomas Hardy. FaBoPP

I reached that waterhole, its mud designed. Roland Robinson. Fr. Wanderer, The. CBAP

I reached the highest place in Spoon River. Henry C. Calhoun. Edgar Lee Masters. Fr. Spoon River Anthology. LiTA; LiTM

I Read a Tight-fisted Poem Once. Nancy Woods. RFM

I read about the Blaskets and Dunquin. J. M. Synge. FaBoEE

I read how Quixote in his random ride. Parable. Richard Wilbur. OxBSP

I read in the New York Times. Not the Arms Race. Sam Abrams. UL

I read last night of the Grand Review. A Second Review of the Grand Army. Bret Harte. PAH

I read of a thousand killed. A Thousand Killed. Bernard Spencer. OBWP

I read once of a valley. After Babel. Peter Goldsworthy. NOBAu

I read or write, I teach or wonder what is truth. Apologia pro Vita Sua. Sedulius Scottus, tr. fr. Latin by Helen Waddell. BIrV

I read the class the old legend. English Lesson. John Pook. AngWe

I read your testimony and I thought. John Beecher. Fr. To Alexander Meiklejohn. GOA

I reade in ancient times of yore. The Map of Mock-Begger Hall. Unknown. CoMu

I realised today we were going to lose the war. Letter from Barcelona, A 1937. Michael O'Loughlin. IB

I really can't imagine why. Young England's Lament. Unknown. FaBoEH

I really hate to say it but I need a lady's room. (LL) The Motorcyclists. James Tate. NoAM

I really take it very kind. Domestic Asides; or, Truth in Parentheses. Thomas Hood. EnRP; PeLV

I really thought that drinking here would. Knocking Around. John Ashbery. NoAM

I reason, earth is short. Emily Dickinson. TAP

I recall a drinking party on the bridge, the Meridian Bridge. Tune: "Immortal at the River" — Ascending a Little Tower at Night. Ch'en Yu Yi, tr. fr. Chinese by James J. Y. Liu. SuSp

I recall, before the banks. By the Bridge. Ted Walker. NYBP

I recall everything, but more than all. Double Sonnet. Anthony Hecht. SM; Son

I recall/ that when I held the Leghorn. Terribilis Est Locus Iste. John Engels. AnAn

I recall the times she came. Four Recollections. Shen Yüeh, tr. fr. Chinese by Richard B. Mather. SuSp

I recall Ty Power's beauty. Hollywood Boulevard Cemetery. Robert Peters. NGP

I reckon — when I count at All. At. to Emily Dickinson. MoAmPo; NIP

I recognize the quiet and the charm. Dutch Interior. May Sarton. SM

I recognized him by his skips and hops. Pan and the Cherries. Paul Fort, tr. fr. French by Jethro Bithell. AWP

I recollect a nurse call'd Ann. A Terrible Infant. Frederick Locker-Lampson. FiBHP

I recollect in early life. My First Love. Harry Graham. FiBHP

I recover now the time I drove. Art McCooey. Patrick Kavanagh. CIP

I recreated, even by thy creature, live. (LL) To Mr. R.W. John Donne. ESCV

I rede that maid beware. (LL) Blow the Winds, I-Ho. Unknown. GBP; OxBoLi

I refuse to turn into gold. Bassus, tr. fr. Greek by Peter Jay. GrAn

I regretted the arrival of my death. What Profit? Immanuel di Roma, tr. fr. Hebrew by J. Chotzner. TrJP

I release you, my beautiful and terrible. I Give You Back. Joy Harjo. HATNAP

I Remember. Eavan Boland. PBCIP

I Remember. Thomas Hood. See I Remember, I Remember.

I Remember. Stevie Smith. BoLoP; BoWoP; FaBoWP; InPK; OxBC

I remember. William Carlos Williams. Fr. Paterson. MeMAP

I remember a far tall island. The Child's Return. Phyllis Shand Allfrey. PBCV

I remember a former day when I and a friend. Coming Again to Heng-yang, I Mourn for Liu Tsung-yüan. Liu Yu Hsi, tr. fr. Chinese by Daniel Bryant. SuSp

I romp with joy in the bookish dark. (*LL*) Eating Poetry. Mark Strand. CAPP; GrPl; MAT; MoP; NoAM; PPP; TAP

I rose at night, and visited. The Unborn. Thomas Hardy. CMoP

I rose betimes to go I knew not where. The Poor Man's Province. John Wright. NOEC

I rose from daylong desk at last. Vision. James Devaney. NOBAu

I rose the morrow morn. (*LL*) The Ancient Mariner: The Wedding Guest's Version of the Affair from His Point of View. *Unknown*. FaBoPa

I rose to catch the early morning. Slanted World. Rhyll McMaster. FaBoMA

I rub my head and find a turtle shell. The Neo-Classical Urn. Robert Lowell. NAAL-2

I run, I run, I am gathered to thy heart. (*LL*) Renouncement. Alice Meynell. BoLoP; MoBrPo; NOBE; OBEV; OBMV; OBNC; PlP; Son; WPE

I run my hand along those old grooves in the rock. (*LL*) Report to Crazy Horse. William Stafford. AnAn; NoAM

I Run With a Pair of Compasses Stuck in the Back of My Head. Novica Tadic, *tr. fr. Serbo-Croatian by* Charles Simic. HSix

I rush to your dwelling. Pursuit. Julian Tuwim, *tr. fr. Polish by* Watson Kirkconnell. TrJP

I said, Ah! what shall I write? A, a, a, Domine Deus. David Jones. FaBoTw; NOCV

I said: "God, what is al this?" (*LL*) My Purse. *Unknown*. EBEV

I said Hey Babe. The Black Back-Ups. Kate Rushin. ETG

I said, "I will find God," and forth, I went. Seeking God. Edward Dowden. WGRP

I said: "I will take heed to my ways." Bible, *O.T., paraphrased by* Sir Thomas Wyatt. *Fr.* Psalms. (Lord, Make Me to Know Mine End.) TrJP

I said, I won't read. Companion. Manjush Dasgupta, *tr. fr. Hindi*. TSaS, *tr. by* Dasgupta Manjush

I said I would always live for her. Hartmann von Aue, *tr. fr. German by* Frederick Goldin. GePo

I said I would have my fling. The Price He Paid. Ella Wheeler Wilcox. WBLP

I said I'd get her a towel and ran. Girls. Kenneth Rosen. AmPA

I said, in drunken pride of youth and you. Challenge. Sterling A. Brown. CDC

I said, lest we should die alone. (*LL*) Shadow and Shade. Allen Tate. LiTA; VGW

I said, "Let me walk in the fields." Obedience. George Macdonald. BLRP; WGRP

I said: Now will the poets sing. Scottsboro, Too, Is Worth Its Song. Countee Cullen. PoBA

I said petals from an appletree. (*LL*) Portrait of a Lady. William Carlos Williams. AmPP; ArLo; CMoP; MoP; NAAL-2; NoAM; NOBA; OxBA

I said, "That's good, that's enough." (*LL*) Each Bird Walking. Tess Gallagher. CrSp; FaBoWP; NAmP90; SV

"I," said the duck, "I call it fun." Who Likes the Rain? Clara Doty Bates. BoTP

I, said the gray fox,/ All alone. (*LL*) The Secret Song. Margaret Wise Brown. OBCA; PDV

I said: "The moon is obviously a boat." Nocturnal Landscape. Malcolm Cowley. PoA

I said the word "spatial," and in it. Space Fiction. Norman MacCaig. TEP

I said — Then, dearest, since 'tis so. The Last Ride Together. Robert Browning. BoLoP; FHYEP; LiTB; NAEL-2; OBEV; PoEL-5; UnPo

I said to Heart, "How goes it?" Heart replied. The False Heart. Hilaire Belloc. FaBoCh; FaBoEE; OxBSP (For False Heart.) MoBrPo

I said to heaven that glowed above. Hafiz, *tr. by* Emerson. *Fr.* Odes. AWP

I said to her tears: "I am fallible and hungry." Plea. John Ciardi. OxBSP

I Said to Love. Thomas Hardy. GBL

I said to Mehitabel. No Social Stuff for Mehitabel. Don Marquis. *Fr.* Archy and Mehitabel. OFC

I said to my baby. Same in Blues. Langston Hughes. *Fr.* Lenox Avenue Mural. HoPM; InPS

I said to my companion, this is walking. Victoria Market. Francis Brabazon. NOBAu

I Said to My Heart. Charles Mordaunt, Earl of Peterborough. NOEC

I Said to Poetry. Alice Walker. AIW

I said to the stream, Be still, and it was still. Miracles. Julia Randall. CRP

I said 12 Hankis, were they? Demands. Roger Hilton. CBCK

I said, "Vernon Lee?" (*LL*) Inapprehensiveness. Robert Browning. CBLP; NOBVV

I said: You find the largest. (*LL*) A Fiesolan Idyl. Walter Savage Landor. EnRP

I sail over the ocean blue. I Catcha da Plenty of Feesh. *Unknown*. AS

I sailed in my dreams to the Land of Night. Fantasy. Gwendolyn B. Bennett. BlSi; CDC; ShDr

I salute God, asylum's gift. Poem on His Death-Bed. Cynddelw Brydydd Mawr, *tr. fr. Welsh by* Joseph P. Clancy. OBWVE

I salute the most high lord. The Poet's Loves. Hywel ab Owain Gwynedd, *tr. fr. Welsh by* Gwyn Williams. OBWVE

I sang as one. The Conflict. C. Day Lewis. LiTB; LiTM; MoAB; MoBrPo; NoP

I sang the songs of red revenge. Homer. Albert Ehrenstein, *tr. fr. German by* Babette Deutsch *and* Avrahm Yarmolinsky. TrJP

I sang the songs of red ripped-up vengeance. The Poet and War. Albert Ehrenstein, *tr. fr. German by* Christopher Middleton. PeFWW

I sat all morning in the college sick bay. Mid-Term Break. Seamus Heaney. InPS; NoP

I sat alone at my window. Retrospect. Josephine D. Henderson Heard. CBWP-4

I sat alone with my conscience. Conscience. C. W. Stubbs. BLPA

I sat at my loom in silence. Weaver, The ("I sat at my loom in silence.") *Unknown*. BLRP

I sat before my glass one day. The Other Side of a Mirror. Mary Elizabeth Coleridge. BoWoP; NALW

I sat behind the glowing grate, fresh heaped. A Meditation on Rhode Island Coal. Bryant. TAP

I sat beside the glassy evening sea. The Departure. William Vaughn Moody. AnAmPo

I sat by a stream in a. Classic. A. R. Ammons. NOBA

I sat by the granite pillar, and sunlight fell. Commemoration. Sir Henry Newbolt. FaBoTw

I sat down on a rock. Walther von der Vogelweide, *tr. fr. German by* Frederick Goldin. GePo

I sat in the café and sipped at a Coke. Greedyguts. Kit Wright. OTCP

I sat in the cold limbs of a tree. The Man in the Tree. Mark Strand. CBNP

I sat in the door of our cottage. An Autumn Day. Clara Ann Thompson. CBWP-2

I sat in the school of sorrow. The School of Sorrow. Harold Hamilton. BLRP

I sat me down upon a green bank-side. Bronx. Joseph Rodman Drake. AnAmPo

I sat next to the Duchess at tea. *Unknown*. SoSe

I sat on chushioned otter-skin. The Madness of King Goll. W. B. Yeats. NAEL-2

I sat on the Dogana's steps. Ezra Pound. *Fr.* Cantos. MeMAP; TAP

I Sat Through a Distant Autumn. Martha Sansom. UnDi

I Sat Up One Night. Ntozake Shange. *Fr.* For Colored Girls Who Have Considered Suicide When the Rainbow Is Enuf. CrSp; SRLS

I sat up one nite walkin a boardin house. I Sat Up One Night. Ntozake Shange. *Fr.* For Colored Girls Who Have Considered Suicide When the Rainbow Is Enuf. CrSp; SRLS

I sat wi' my love, and I drank wi' my love. *Unknown*. GBP

I sat with John Brown. That night moonlight framed. Narrative. Russell Atkins. PoBA

I sat with love upon a woodside well. Willowwood ("I sat with love upon a woodside well.") Dante Gabriel Rossetti. *Fr.* House of Life, The. NAEL-2; OAEL-2; PoEL-5

I saw you/ on my walk last. Glimpse. Pearl Cleage Lomax. PoBA

I saw a band of warriors coming on. War Dance. Miidhu, *tr. fr. Aborigine by* Georg von Brandenstein. NOBAu

I saw a bee, I saw a flower. The Bee-Orchis. Andrew Young. ChTr

I saw a boy with eager eye. The Two Boys. Mary Lamb. WoRP

I Saw a Broken Town. Mabel Esther Allan. PAW

I saw a brown squirrel to-day in the wood. Mr. Squirrel. V. M. Julian. BoTP

I Saw a Chapel All of Gold. Blake. EnRP; ImPo; LiTB; MeMBP

I saw a cottage in the sky. Friends. John Ashbery. LCAP

I saw a dark boy. A Prayer. Mae V. Cowdery. ShDr

I saw a dead man's frear part. His Immortality. Thomas Hardy. CMoP

I saw a dog sethying sows. Hay, Hey, Hey, Hey! I Will Have the Whetstone and I May. *Unknown*. CBNP

I saw a doo flee our the dam. *Unknown*. GBP

I saw a fair maiden. A Lullaby of the Nativity. *Unknown*. MeEL (Lullay My Liking.) ELP

I saw a famous man eating soup. Soup. Carl Sandburg. NOBA; NOBE; OBCA

I Saw a Film One Sunday. John Kitching. PAW

I Saw a Fish-Pond All on Fire. *Unknown*. ChTr; GBP; NOBL; OxNR

I saw a fly within a bead. The Amber Bead. Robert Herrick. BeJo; CaPo; ChTr

I saw a frieze on whitest marble drawn. Ecstasy. W. J. Turner. CH

I saw a garden with a thousand rills. Education in Wales. Goronva Camlan. AngWe

I saw a gardener with a watering can. The Progress of Poetry. "Christopher Caudwell." OxBTC

I saw a gnome. The Gnome. Harry Behn. FaPON; PDV

I saw a gold pillar from earth to heaven. The Message of King Sakis and the Legend of the Twelve Dreams He Had in One Night. *Unknown, tr. fr. Serbo-Croatian by* Charles Simic. HSix

I saw a hawk devour a screaming bird. Hawk Is a Woman. Hildegarde Flanner. WPE

I saw a holly sprig brought from a hurst. A Vision of the World's Instability. Richard Verstegan. EIL

I saw a hunchback climb over a hill. The Hunchback. John Peale Bishop. PoA

I Saw a Jolly Hunter. Charles Causley. EBNV; PYC

I saw a little snail. Little Snail. Hilda Conkling. FaPON; SiSoPo

I saw a little tailor sitting stitch, stitch, stitching. Tailor. Eleanor Farjeon. OTCP; OxBChV

I saw a maiden, fairest of the fair. Charity. H. Cordelia Ray. AmWP; CBWP-3

I saw a man pursuing the horizon. Stephen Crane. *Fr.* Black Riders, The. AmPP; FF; HoPM; LiTA; LiTM; MAT; MeMAP; MoAMPo; NOBA

I saw a man standing. Gate of Horn. William Rose Benét. AnAmPo

I saw a mesa. Leaving Port Authority for the St. Regis Rezz. Wendy Rose. HATNAP

I saw a Monk of Charlemaine. The Monk. Blake. *Fr.* Jerusalem. EnRP

I saw a mouth jeering. Gargoyle. Carl Sandburg. MoP; NoAM; NOBA

I saw a pale tree, the leafless boughs — but two. Ecstasy. Hélène Swarth, *tr. fr. Dutch by* Jonathan Crewe. WPOW

I Saw a Peacock [with a Fiery Tail]. *Unknown.* CH; ChTr; CoGr; FaBoCh; GBP; NTP; OTCP; OxBoLi; OxBSP; OxNR; RB

I saw a people rise before the sun. Yom Kippur. Israel Zangwill. TrJP

I saw a Phoenix in the Wood Alone. Petrarch, *tr. fr. Italian. Fr.* Sonnets to Laura. AWP, *tr. by* Spenser; ChTr, *tr. by* Helen Lee Peabody

I saw a polar bear. Polar Bear. *Unknown. tr. fr. Eskimo by* T. Lowenstein. OBAP

I saw a proud, mysterious cat. The Mysterious Cat. Vachel Lindsay. ChTr; FaPON; GoJo; OBCA; OFC; SiSoPo; SoCa

I saw a shadow on the ground. The Sky. Elizabeth Madox Roberts. MoAmPo

I saw a ship a-sailing. Mother Goose. FaBoBe; MoShBr; NTCP; OxNR; ReMoGo

I saw a ship a-sailing. Romance. "Gabriel Setoun." BoTP

I Saw a Ship A-Sailing. *Unknown.* BoTP

I saw a ship a-sailing, a-sailing, a-sailing. An Old Song Re-sung. John Masefield. LiTB

I saw a ship of martial build. The Berg. Herman Melville. AmPP; LiTA; NOBA; NoP; PoEL-5; TAP

I saw a silvery creature scurrying. Riddle 29: The Moon and the Sun. *Unknown, tr. fr. Anglo-Saxon by* Burton Raffel. GoJo

I saw a slowly stepping train. God's Funeral. Thomas Hardy. WGRP

I saw/ a specialist a cook. To the Heart. Tadeusz Rózewicz, *tr. fr. Polish by* Victor Contoski. PoSu

I Saw a Stable. Mary Elizabeth Coleridge. ChIV-2; OBCP; OxBSP; PChr

I saw a stable low and very bare. I Saw a Stable. Mary Elizabeth Coleridge. ChIV-2; OBCP; OxBSP; PChr

I saw a star slide down the sky. The Falling Star. Sara Teasdale. MoShBr; OBCA; PDV

I saw a staring virgin stand. Two Songs from a Play. W. B. Yeats. *Fr.* Resurrection, The. CMoP; FaBoTw; HAP; ImPo; LiTB; MeMBP; NOBE; NoP; OAEL-2; PoE; PPP; PrIm

I saw a stately lady. The Stately Lady. Flora Sandstrom. BoTP

I saw a stranger yestreen. Rune of Hospitality. *Unknown, tr. fr. Gaelic by* Kenneth MacLeod. ScCV

I saw a swete semly syght. The Virgin's Lullaby. *Unknown.* OxBLMV

I saw a tiny pebble fall. What Price. Lulu Minerva Schultz. GoYe

I saw a trash-pit, filled and topped with earth. Where Lie All the Slain. Harry Morris. CRP

I saw a tree that was greater than all the others. Edith Södergran, *tr. fr. Swedish by* Jaakko A. Ahokas. PBWP

I saw a vision yesternight. To the State of Love; or, The Senses' Festival. John Cleveland. CBLP

I saw a vulture in the sky. Life and Death. W. J. Turner. FaBoTw

I saw a woman sitting on a beast. Spenser. ChIV-2

I saw a young snake glide. Snake. Theodore Roethke. NOBA; NYBP; RFM

I saw about her spotless wrist. Upon a Black Twist, Rounding the Arm of the Countess of Carlisle. Robert Herrick. CaPo

I saw an aged beggar in my walk. The Old Cumberland Beggar. Wordsworth. EnRP

I saw an ugly beast come from the sea. Spenser. ChIV-2

I saw, and trembled for the day. A Warning. Coventry Patmore. EnLoPo

I saw another man die. Wang Fun-chih, *tr. fr. Chinese by* Eugene Eoyang. SuSp

I saw between a shadow and a bough. The Ungathered Apples. James Wright. ErPo

I saw bleak Arrogance, with brows of brass. Arrogance. Walter de la Mare. OxBSP

I saw cold thunder in the grass. Herons. Robin Blaser. NeAP

I saw dawn creep across the sky. A Summer Morning. Rachel Field. PDV

I saw each soul as light, each single body. Night of Souls. Ann Stanford. WPE

I saw Esau kissing Kate. *Unknown.* ISE

I saw Esau sawing wood. *Unknown.* FaBoNo; Spl

I Saw Eternity. Louise Bogan. LiTA

I saw Eternity the other night. The Experience. Bruce Bennett. PeECV

I saw eternity the other night. World, The (1). Henry Vaughan. AWP; ChIV-2; EBEV; ESCV; FaBV; HAP; ImPo; JCP; LiTB; NAEL-1; NOBE; NOCV; NOSC; OAEL-1; OxAEP-1; PeECV; PoEL-2; PPP; SCGP; SeCP; SeCV-1; TEP; TFi; TrCP; TrGrPo; WGRP
(Eternity, The). OBEV

I saw fair Chloris [*or* Cloris] walk alone. On Chloris Walking in the Snow. William Strode. ELP; JCP; OAEL-1
(Chloris in the Snow). NOBE; OBEV
(On a Gentlewoman Walking in the Snow). NOSC; OxBSP

I saw five birds all in a cage. *Unknown.* GBP

I Saw French Once. Ivor Gurney. NSI

I saw French once — he was South Africa cavalry — . I Saw French Once. Ivor Gurney. NSI

I Saw from the Beach. Thomas Moore. OBNC; PeIV

I saw God! Do you doubt it? What Thomas an Buile Said in a Pub. James Stephens. MoAB; MoBrPo; MoP; PoRA; TrGrPo; WGRP
(What Tomas Said in a Pub). CMoP; NoAM

I Saw God Wash the World. William Leroy Stidger. BLPA

I saw great Satan like a Sexton stand. Lines Written during the Time of the Spy System. Charles Lamb. FaBoEH

I saw her amid the dunghill debris. Tinker's Wife. Patrick Kavanagh. CIP; InPS; MoP; NoAM

I Saw Her Dancing. Marge Piercy. SRLS

I saw her first abreast the Boston Light. The *William P. Frye.* Jeanne Robert Foster. PAH

I saw her first in gleams. The Spirit's Odyssey. M. Krishnamurti. InPK

I saw her on the bridal night. The Forced Bridal. *Unknown.* VPP

I saw her once, briefly. It Was Your Song. Steve Kowit. UL

I saw her once, one little while, and then no more. And Then No More. Friedrich Rückert, *tr. fr. German by* James Clarence Mangan. BIrV; BLPA; PeIV

I saw her plucking cowslips. The Witch. Percy H. Ilott. BoTP

I saw him a squat man with red hair. Off Brighton Pier. Alan Ross. OBWP

I saw him brought into Emergency. Empty Holds a Question. Pat Folk. GOYP

I saw him dead, a leaden slumber lyes [*or* lies]. Andrew Marvell. *Fr.* Poem upon the Death of Oliver Cromwell, A. FaBoEH; JCP
(Cromwell Dead). ChTr

I saw him forging link by link his chain. The Slave. Jones Very. TAP

I saw him in the Airstrip Gardens. Betjeman, 1984. Charles Causley. FaBoCo; NOBL; OxBTC; PeLV; UV

I saw him in the Café Royal. On Seeing an Old Poet in the Café Royal. Sir John Betjeman. UV

I saw him lying there — my father — with eyes. The Addict. Larry Rubin. GoYe

I saw him once before. The Last Leaf. Oliver Wendell Holmes. AmPP; AnAmPo; FaBoBe; FaPON; NAAL-1; PoLF; PWR; WBLP

I saw him sitting in his door. The Philosopher. Sara Teasdale. PoToHe

I saw him to the last, the grey. Painting of My Father. Padraic Fallon. NOIV

I saw him yesterday. The Quarrel. Josephine D. Henderson Heard. CBWP-4

I saw his round mouth's crimson deepen as it fell. Wilfred Owen. OAEL-2

I saw in dream a dapper mannikin. Im Traum sah ich ein Männchen klein und putzig. Heine, *tr. fr. German by* Sir Theodore Martin. AWP

I Saw in Louisiana a Live-Oak Growing. Walt Whitman. AiP; AWP; ImPo; InPK; InPS; LiTA; MAT; NAAL-1; NIP; NoAM; NOBA; NoP; OxBA; Poetr; PrIm; SAmP

I saw it all, Polly, how when you had call'd for sop. Poor Poll. Robert Bridges. EBEV; OxBoLi; OxBTC

I saw its periscope in the tide. Mangrove. John Blight. FaBoMA; NOBAu

I saw magic on a green country road. Michael Hartnett. BIrV; PBCIP

I Saw My Darling. Frederick Morgan. UnPo

I saw my grandmother grow weak. First Death. Donald Justice. IMW; MT; SM

I Saw My Lady Weep. *Unknown.* EIL; ELP; EnLoPo; LiTB; NoSic; TrGrPo

I saw my love, younger than primroses. In a Wood. E. J. Scovell. GBL

I Saw Myself. Lew Welch. PoBeRe

I saw myself leaving. Reflections. Carl Gardner. PoBA

I saw new Earth, new Heaven, said Saint John. Spenser. ChIV-2

I saw new worlds beneath the water lie. On Leaping over the Moon. Thomas Traherne. GeHe; ImPo; LiTB; Mes; NAEL-1; SeCV-2

I saw no way — the heavens were stitched. Emily Dickinson. BoWoP

I saw nothing but waves and wind. The Crooked Glen. Frances Horovitz. PWE

I saw old Autumn in the misty morn. Autumn. Thomas Hood. BLPL; ImPo; LiTB; OBEV; OxAEP-2
(Ode: Autumn.) OAEL-2; OBNC; PoEL-4; UnPo

I saw old Duchesses with their young loves. Vanity. Anna Wickham. FaBoTw

I saw on earth another light. The Light from Within. Jones Very. WGRP

I saw on the slant hill a putrid lamb. For a Lamb. Richard Eberhart. CMoP; LiTM; OxBSP; RB; SoSe

I saw, one sultry night above a swamp. Fireflies. Edgar Fawcett. AnAmPo

I saw pale Dian sitting by the brink. Sonnet Written in Keats's *Endymion.* Thomas Hood. EPCY

I saw red evening through the rain. Robert Louis Stevenson. NOBVV

I saw Shandon steeple a needle for a tailor to sew. *Unknown.* CBNP

I saw the best minds of my generation. Squeal. Louis Simpson. BXAP; FiBHP; UnPo

I saw the best minds of my generation destroyed by madness. Allen Ginsberg. *Fr.* Howl. AmPP; CAPP; GLP; InPS; LCAP; MoP; NaP; NeAP; NIP; NoAM; NoP; PoBeRe; PoM; SOTW, *abr., ll.* 1–30; TAP; VCAP

I saw the bird that can the sun endure. Joachim du Bellay, *tr. fr. French by* Spenser. *Fr.* Visions. Son

I Saw the Bird That Dares Behold the Sun. Joachim du Bellay, *tr. fr. French by* Spenser. Son

I saw the black trees leaning. Trees and Evening Sky. N. Scott Momaday. CDW

I saw the bodies of earth's men. The Navigators. W. J. Turner. OBMV

I saw the cardinal. Cardinals. John Engels. FoLa

I saw the curl of his waving lash. Reflections of a Proud Pedestrian. Oliver Wendell Holmes. AnAmPo

I saw the day lean o'er the world's sharp edge. Sunset. Ella Wheeler Wilcox. AnAmPo

I saw the early morning mist. The Dead Horse. Cecília Meireles, *tr. fr. Portuguese by* James Merrill. PBWP

I saw the farmer plough the field. Harvest. M. M. Hutchinson. BoTP

I saw the first pear. Orchard. Hilda Doolittle ("H. D."). CMoP; LiTA; LiTM; MoAmPo; OxBA

I saw the garden where my aunt had died. The Entertainment of War. Roy Fisher. FaBoMo

I saw the ghostesses. Ghostesses. *Unknown.* ChTr

I saw the islands in a ring all round me. Letter to Pearse Hutchinson. Eiléan Ní Chuilleanáin. FaBoWP

I saw the lovely arch. The Rainbow. Walter de la Mare. NTP

I saw the man that saw this wondrous sight. *(LL)* I Saw a Peacock [with a Fiery Tail]. *Unknown.* CH; ChTr; CoGr; FaBoCh; GBP; NTP; OTCP; OxBoLi; OxBSP; OxNR; RB

I saw the Master of the Sun. He stood. The Sun God. Aubrey Thomas De Vere. OHCV

I saw the midlands. Kisses in the Train. D. H. Lawrence. MoAB; MoBrPo

I saw the moon/ One windy night. Flying. J. M. Westrup. BoTP

I saw the moon over Plaza Espana. They Name Heaven. Bruce Weigl. NAmP90

I saw the moon, so broad and bright. Donnybrook. James Stephens. TIRV

I Saw the Object. Thomas Watson. *Fr.* Tears of Fancy, The. Son

I saw the old god of war stand in a bog between chasm and rockface. The God of War. Bertolt Brecht. FaBoPV

I saw the ramparts of my native land. Sonnet: Death Warnings. Francisco de Quevedo y Villegas, *tr. fr. Spanish by* John Masefield. AWP

I saw the reflection in the mirror. Drunken Americans. John Ashbery. HCAP

I saw the rosy sun's calm light. The Storm and the Calm. Juan De Arguijo, *tr. fr. Spanish by* Kate Farrell. ArNa

I saw the ruins of poetry. Seasons, THe. David Shapiro. BAP-91

I saw the salt. Ode to Salt. Pablo Neruda, *tr. fr. Spanish by* Robert Bly. NU

I saw the shapes that stood upon the clouds. London Nightfall. John Gould Fletcher. MoAmPo

I saw the shepherd fold the sheep. The Folded Flock. Wilfrid Meynell. TrPWD

I saw the Sibly at Cumæ. Dante Gabriel Rossetti. PeVV

I saw the silver morning mist. The Dead Horse. Cecília Meireles, *tr. fr. Portuguese by* James Merrill. PBWP

I saw the sky descending, black and white. Where the Rainbow Ends. Robert Lowell. HCAP; MoAB; MoAmPo; TrGrPo

I saw the spiders marching through the air. Mr. Edwards and the Spider. Robert Lowell. CAPP; CMoP; CoAP; FaBoMo; HeIP; InPS; LiTM; MoAB; NAAL-2; NOBA; NoP; SM; TFi; TwCP

I saw the spires of Oxford. The Spires of Oxford. Winifred M. Letts. PoLF; PoRA; WGRP

I saw the spot where our first parents dwelt. The Garden. Jones Very. OxBA; TAP

I Saw the Sun at Midnight, Rising Red. Joseph Mary Plunkett. TIRV

I saw the throng, so deeply separate. A General Communion. Alice Meynell. NOCV; WPE

I saw the tracks of angels in the earth. Petrarch, *tr. fr. Italian. Fr.* Sonnets to Laura. ArLo, *tr. by* Nicholas Kilmer

I saw the virtues sitting hand in hand. Humility. George Herbert. NOSC

I Saw the Wind Today. Padraic Colum. GoJo

I Saw Thee Weep. Byron. CBLP

I saw thee weep — the big bright tear. I Saw Thee Weep. Byron. CBLP

I saw their emu feather tails sticking out behind them. *(LL)* War Dance. Miidhu. NOBAu

I saw them, caught them in the act. Paulus Silentiarius, *tr. fr. Greek by* Andrew Miller. GrAn

I Saw Them Lynch. Carol Freeman. NMM; PoBA

I saw these dreamers of dreams go by. The Gold-Seekers. Hamlin Garland. FaBoBe

I saw this much from the window. The Gap in the Cedar. Roy Scheele. Poetsp; SM

I Saw Three Ships. Kevyn Arthur. PBCV

I saw three ships come sailing by. Mother Goose. OxNR

I Saw Three Ships Come Sailing In. *Unknown.* BLPA

I saw three ships go sailing by. The North Ship. Philip Larkin. RB

I saw three suns in the sky. The Mock-Suns. Wilhelm Müller, *tr. fr. German by* Philip L. Miller. *Fr.* Winter's Journey, The. RiWo

I saw three withered women limp across. The Private Meeting Place. James Wright. NYBP

I saw trees walking upside down across. Jonathan Lazarus Wright, 1702–1729. Martin Edmunds. UTF

I saw twa items on. Nuts in May. "Hugh MacDiarmid." IHNG

I Saw Two Bears. Spenser. OBAP

I Saw Two Clouds at Morning. John G. C. Brainard. PoToHe

I saw two hares in the corn. The Dance. Gareth Alban Davies, *tr. fr. Welsh by* Gwyn Jones. OBWVE

I saw two trees embracing. All That Time. May Swenson. FF

I saw/ wet clothes hanging from a clothes line dripping with. Vision from the Ghetto. Raymond Washington. NBV

I saw where in the shroud did lurk. On an Infant Dying as Soon as Born. Charles Lamb. GTBS; GTBS-P; IMW; OBEV

I saw,/ With a catch of the breath and the heart's uplifting. A War Film. Teresa Hooley. PAW

I saw with open eyes. Stupidity Street. Ralph Hodgson. CH; IHNG; LiTM; MoAB; MoBrPo; OBD; OxBTC; PDV

I saw you die. Murdered Little Bird. *Unknown.* FiBHP

I saw you on the street last night. In This New Year. Mary Jane Moffat. IMW

I saw you once, Medusa; we were alone. The Muse as Medusa. May Sarton. NALW

"I saw you take his kiss!" " 'Tis true." The Kiss. Coventry Patmore. *Fr.* Angel in the House, The. ArLo; BoLoP; EnLoPo; FiBHP; NOBVV

I saw you toss the kites on high. The Wind. Robert Louis Stevenson. BoTP; GN; OHCV

I saw you with Septimus on the parterre. A Very Shocking Poem Found among the Papers of an Eminent Victorian Divine. Gavin Ewart. FaBoBl

I saw your eyes like bumps of flint. Ogun's Friend. Jayne Cortez. BCF

I saw your manager fight. He was. Elegy for Lyn James. Leslie Norris. OBWVE

I sawe a mayd sitte on a bank. The Carelesse Nurse Mayd. Thomas Hood. FaBoNo

I say God send me better speed, and Fancy now farewell. (*LL*) The Green Knight's Farewell to Fancy. George Gascoigne. EnRePo; NoSic; OPOP

I Say Goodby to Fan An-ch'eng. Shen Yüeh, *tr. fr. Chinese by* Lenore Mayhew *and* William McNaughton. SuSp

I say hello to the sunshine. Alan Brunton. PeNZ

I Say I'll Seek Her. Thomas Hardy. CBLP

I say no moir. (*LL*) Lament of the Master of Erskine. Alexander Scott. GBL

I say no more for Clavering. Clavering. E. A. Robinson. OxBA

I say no more. — I care not though thou cease. (*LL*) The Dispute of the Heart and Body of François Villon. Villon. AWP; OBVE

I say now, Fernando, that on that day. Hibiscus on the Sleeping Shores. Wallace Stevens. InPS

I say that my sweetly prattling Heliodora will someday. Meleager, *tr. fr. Greek by* Barbara Hughes Fowler. *Fr.* Epigrams. HePo

I say that words are men and when we spell. Anna Hempstead Branch. *Fr.* Sonnets from a Lock Box. NALW

I say things to myself. Phraseology. Jayne Cortez. BlSi

I say this evening we'll all get drunk. Suction's Anthem. Blake. *Fr.* Island in the Moon, An. CBNP; FaBoNo

I say to the lead. Poem without a Title. Charles Simic. NNaP

I say to thee, do thou repeat. The Kingdom of God. Richard Chenevix Trench. WBLP

I, says the buzzard. From Virgil. George Oppen. *Fr.* Five Poems about Poetry. NNaP

I says, you says. *Unknown.* RoPo

I scalped a lie. John Hartley Williams. *Fr.* Ephraim Destiny's Perfectly Utter Darkness. PWE

I scarce believe [*or* beleeve] my love to be so pure. Love's Growth. John Donne. ESCV; JCP; NoP; NOSC; SeCV-1

I scarce should be unclasp'd at night. (*LL*) The Miller's Daughter. Tennyson. OBEV; TrGrPo

I scarcely think. The Zoo. Humbert Wolfe. MoShBr

I schal yow tel wyth hert and mode. The Philosopher's Stone. *Unknown.* OxBLMV

I scissor the stem of the red carnation. Salome. Ai. BCF; NoAM

I scorn the doubts and cares that hurt. A Garden Song. George R. Sims. NOBVV

I scraped off your smile with nails. Capital Punishment. Nina Cassian, *tr. fr. Romanian by* Nine Cassian. PoSu

I Scream You Scream. Don McKay. NOBC

I scream/ You scream. *Unknown.* FaBoNo; ISE; RoPo

I search among the plain and lovely words. Definition. Grace Noll Crowell. PoToHe

I search/ for the straight path. Florence Dacey. LoHo

I search the chemistry of specific emotions. At the Electronic Frontier. Miguel Algarin. BCF

I See a Bear. Ted Hughes. NTP

I see a beautiful gigantic swimmer swimming naked through the eddies of the sea. The Beautiful Swimmer. Walt Whitman. PeHV

I see a blind man every day. The Blind Man. Margaret E. Sangster. PoToHe

I see a chance for peace! What about water? (*LL*) Cry, crow. Hayden Carruth. NNaP; Son

I see a dirt road inside myself and on it I am walking. Appalachian Song. Sharon Doubiago. ETG

I see a girl climbing the mountain. The Pilgrim. Brendan Kennelly. TIRV

I see a man who is dull. An Ancient Song of a Woman of Fez. *Unknown, tr. fr. Arabic by* Willis Barnstone. AIW; BoWoP

I see a mill showing. Halt! Wilhelm Müller, *tr. fr. German by* Philip L. Miller. *Fr.* Beautiful Maid of the Mill, The. RiWo

I see a mystery on my hands, the young man said: A Mystery. Christine McNeill. NWP

I see around me here. The Wanderer Recalls the Past. Wordsworth. *Fr.* Excursion, The. OBNC

I see as through a skylight in my brain. Persephone. Michael Longley. PBCIP

I see before me now a traveling army halting. Bivouac on a Mountain Side. Walt Whitman. AiP; ChTr; OxBA; PoLF

I see before me the gladiator lie. The Dying Gladiator. Byron. *Fr.* Childe Harold's Pilgrimage. NOBE

I see black dragons mount the sky. Shapes and Signs. James Clarence Mangan. PeIV

I see bodies in the morning kneel. Shirley Kaufman. BoWoP

I See Chano Pozo. Jayne Cortez. ETG

I See Cleopatra. Nurunnessa Choudhury, *tr. fr. Bengali by the author* and Paul Joseph Thompson. AIW

I see forests of bullock-horns waving. (*LL*) Cattle Loading. Gordon Mackay-Warna. NOBAu

I see her against the pearl sky of Dublin. My Mother's Sister. C. Day Lewis. OxBTC

I see her close beside me with silent lips sad and tremulous. (*LL*) Once I Pass'd through a Populous City. Walt Whitman. AmPP; AnAmPo; NAAL-1; OxBA; RaBo; SAmP

I see her on a beach. Penelope. Janet Dubé. DT

I see her on a lonely forest track. The Maroon Girl. Walter Adolphe Roberts. PBCV

I see her seventeen. Arizona Highways. James Welch. CDW; NoAM

I see her stand with arms a-kimbo. Hersilia. William Johnson Cory. NOBVV

I see her still, unsteadily riding the edge. My Grandmother Washes Her Feet. Fred Chappell. MT

I see her yet, that dark-eyed one. A Memory. Adah Isaacs Menken. CBWP-1

"I see herrin'." — I hear the glad cry. With the Herring Fishers. "Hugh MacDiarmid." LiTM

I see him old, trapped in a burly house. A Pauper. Allen Tate. LiTM

I See His Blood upon the Rose. Joseph Mary Plunkett. PeIV; PoLF; TIRV; WGRP

I See, I See the Crescent Moon. "Anna Akhmatova," *tr. fr. Russian by* Richard McKane. VBLP

I see in his last preached and printed booke. On John Donne's Book of Poems. John Marriot. CH

I see in you the estuary that enlarges and spreads itself. To Old Age. Walt Whitman. Spl

I see it. Song for the Dead, III. *Unknown, tr. by* Frances S. Herskovits. TTY

I see it prophesy the path winds take. (*LL*) In the Beginning Was the Bird. Henry Treece. LiTB

I see I've come a pilgrimage. I didn't. The *Weepers Tower* in Amsterdam. Paul Goodman. VGW

I See Madmen. Tadeusz Rózewicz, *tr. fr. Polish by* Adam Czerniawski. PoSu

I see madmen who. I See Madmen. Tadeusz Rózewicz, *tr. fr. Polish by* Adam Czerniawski. PoSu

I see Mike's painting, called "sardines." (*LL*) Why I Am Not a Painter. Frank O'Hara. CAPP; HCAP; MoP; NeAP; NoAM; NOBA; PoE; Poetr; PoM; VCAP

I see my hospital bed at. Devise Your Own Form and Stick to It. Ammon Wrigley. UnDi

I see my mother waving — her unfussed, smiling. Distances. Katherine Gallagher. AIW

I See My Plaint. *At.* to John Harington. EIL

I see no bird arise. My Sun-killed Tree. Marguerite Harris. GoYe

I see no equivalents. The Poet at Night-Fall. Glenway Wescott. PoA

I see now I see. Resurrection. Margaret Atwood. CrSp

I See Phantoms of Hatred and of the Heart's Fullness and of the Coming Emptiness. W. B. Yeats. *Fr.* Meditations in Time of Civil War. LiTB

I see that chance hath chosen me. Sir Thomas Wyatt. SiPS; SiPSBD

I see that there it is on the beach. Memorial Service for the Invasion Beach Where the Vacation in the Flesh Is Over. Alan Dugan. TwCP

I see that wreath which doth the wearer arm. To My Dead Friend Ben: Johnson. Henry King. SeCP

I See the Boys of Summer. Dylan Thomas. LiTB

I see the children running out of school. The Poet Laments the Coming of Old Age. Edith Sitwell. NAEL-2; NoAM

I see the dawn e'en now begin to peer. *Unknown, tr. fr. Italian by* John Addington Symonds. *Fr.* Popular Songs of Tuscany. AWP

I see the elephants in the yard. The Elephants Are in the Yard. Indran Amirthanayagam. OpBo

"I see the good in others," answered she. (*LL*) Charity. H. Cordelia Ray. AmWP; CBWP-3

I see the horses and the sad streets. The Eye. Allen Tate. LiTA

I see the local satyr stand. Nocturne. Gerda Mayer. FaBoBl

I see the map of summer, lying still. Movies for the Home. Howard Moss. NYBP

I See the Moon. *Unknown.* GBP, *diff. vers.*; NTCP; OxNR; PYC

I see the moon, the moon sees me. *Unknown.* RoPo

I see the mosquito kneeling on the soft underside of my arm, kneeling. The Mosquito. Rodney Jones. MT

I see the temple in thy pillar reared. Jacob's Pillow, and Pillar. Henry Vaughan. ChIV-1

I see the thin bell-ringer standing at corners. The Jew at Christmas Eve. Karl Shapiro. VGW

I see the Usk, and know my blood. The Storm. Henry Vaughan. FaBoPP (I see the usk [*or* use]: and know my blood [*or* bloud].) ESCV

I see the usk [*or* use]: and know my blood [*or* bloud]. Henry Vaughan. *See* I see the Usk, and know my blood.

I see the young bride move among. George Barker. *Fr.* True Confession of George Barker, The. ErPo; MeMBP

I see thee better — in the Dark. Emily Dickinson. VBLP

I see thee ever in my dreams. The Karamanian Exile. James Clarence Mangan. PeVV

I see thee pine like her in golden story. Coleridge. Theodore Watts-Dunton. Son

I see them/ Puerto Ricans. You're Nothing but a Spanish Colored Kid. Felipe Luciano. PoBA

I see them coming up the road. A Happy Pair. Priscilla Jane Thompson. CBWP-2

I see them, crowd on crowd they walk the earth. The Dead. Jones Very. AnAmPo; HAP; NOBA; OxBA; TAP

I see them working in old rectories. The Country Clergy. R. S. Thomas. GTBS-P; OxBTC; PeECV

I see these ancestors of ours. Triptych. Frank A. Collymore. PBCV

I see they worked you over. What you in for? Coming of Age in the County Jail. Carter Revard. VoR

I see why the touched needle scents about. Mysteries Revealed after Death. John Reynolds. *Fr.* Death's Vision. NOEC

I see You. Maya Angelou. *Fr.* Thank You, Lord. CrSp

I see you, a child. The Album. C. Day Lewis. EnLoPo; OxBTC

I see you displaced, condensed, within my dream. Dream. Josephine Miles. BCF; PoA

I see you in the silver. Arctic Tern in a Museum. Mary Effie Lee Newsome. PoNe

I see you, Juliet, still, with your straw hat. Farewell to Juliet ("I see you, Juliet, still, with your straw hat.") Wilfrid Scawen Blunt. *Fr.* Love Sonnets of Proteus, The. BoLoP; EnLoPo; OxBTC

I see you now. Mountain Drive. Cothrai Gogan. TIRV

I see you sitting. Matmiya. Mary TallMountain. CrSp; HATNAP

I see you what you are: you are too proud. Shakespeare. *Fr.* Twelfth Night. OxAEP-1

I see'd her in de springtime. She Hugged Me and Kissed Me. *Unknown.* BPo

I seek in prayerful words, dear friend. God Bless You. *Unknown.* PoToHe

I seek mercy/ for the women stoned. For All Mary Magdalenes. Desanka Maksimovic, *tr. fr. Croatian by* Vasa D. Mihailovich. AIW; WPOW

I Seek Thee in the Heart Alone. Herbert Trench. WGRP

I seem to have loved you in numberless forms, numberless times. Unending Love. Rabindranath Tagore, *tr. fr. Bengali by* Rabindranath Tagore. ArLo

I seem to have travelled this landscape for years. From A Diary. Michael O'Loughlin. *Fr.* Shards, The. IB

I seem to know all about you. Poem for My Son. Bibhu Padhi, *tr. fr. Hindi.* TSaS

I seem to love the little ghost I made. (*LL*) On Shooting a Swallow in Early Youth. Charles Tennyson Turner. FM; NOBVV

I seemed at home here, at one with the cock. This Dark Longing. Sylvia Kantaris. PWE

I seen a dunce of a poet once, a-writin' a little book. Gelett Burgess. *Fr.* Protest of the Illiterate, The. FiBHP

I sell myths not poems. With each poem goes a little myth. De Rerum Natura. Andrei Codrescu. UL

I send a garland to my love. The Lover's Posy. Rufinus Domesticus, *tr. fr. Greek by* W. H. D. Rouse. AWP

I send a message, my worthy chief. A Message to a Loved One Dead. Josephine D. Henderson Heard. CBWP-4

I send a rose with a card for myself. My Regrets. Michael Andre. UL

I send, I send here my supremest kiss. His Tears to Thamesis[*or* Thamasis]. Robert Herrick. FaBoPP; NOSC

I send my poisoned candies through the mail. End of the Affair. Geoffrey Grigson. GBL

I send my voice of sorrow. Let the Bird of Earth, Fly! Meridel LeSueur. SRLS

I send thee myrrh, not that thou mayest be. Not of Itself but Thee. *Unknown, tr. fr. Greek by* Richard Garnett. AWP

I send you a lock of hair. Martial, *tr. fr. Greek by* Kenneth Rexroth. PGA

I send you here a sort of allegory. The Palace of Art. Tennyson. EnVR

I send you here a wreath of blossoms blown. Roses. Pierre de Ronsard, *tr. fr. French by* Andrew Lang. AWP

I Send You My Verses. Minuchihri, *tr. fr. Persian by* Omar S. Pound. ArPe

I sent a letter to my love. George Barker. *Fr.* True Confession of George Barker, The. FaBoTw; MeMBP

I sent for Radcliffe; was so ill. The Remedy Worse than the Disease. Matthew Prior. FaBoEE; TrGrPo

I sent my love two roses, — one. The White Flag. John Milton Hay. AnAmPo

I sent my mother copies of my poems in print. Poems. Gary Gildner. Poetsp

I sent you this bluebird of the name of Joe. Happiness. William Dickey. Poetsp

I Serve a Mistress. Anthony Munday. *Fr.* Fedele and Fortunio. ElL

I Set Aside. Mary Morison Webster. PeSA

I set forth hopeful — cotton-blossom Lal. Lalleswari, *tr. fr. Kashmiri by* George Grierson. WPOW, *ad. by* Deirdre Lashgari

I set my heart to sing of leaves. Anticipation. Lord De Tabley. ELP

I set the shorelines of the world by perpetual decrees, so. The Edge. Sandra Price. LoHo

I shake from head to foot. (*LL*) Friends. W. B. Yeats. IIP; MoP; NoAM

I shake my hair in the wind of morning. Triumph of Love. John Hall Wheelock. MoAmPo

"I shall arise." For centuries. Resurgam. *Unknown.* WGRP

I shall be able to touch you then! (*LL*) The Wicked Clamor. Tuvia Rivner. MHP

I shall be capricious, I shall have a whim. A Man's Woman. Mary Carolyn Davies. PoLF

'I shall be careful to say nothing at all.' How She Resolved to Act. Merrill Moore. MoAmPo

I shall be glad to be silent, Mother, and hear you speak. The White Thought. Stevie Smith. Spl

I shall be mad if you get smashed about. The Soldier Addresses his Body. Edgell Rickword. PeFWW; PoWW

I Shall Be Married on Monday Morning. *Unknown.* ErPo

I shall begin by learning to throw. Formal Application. Donald W. Baker. FF

I shall come back to die. In This Dark House. Edward Davison. OBMV

I shall come this way again. Auf Wiedersehen. Donald Jeffrey Hayes. CDC

I shall cry God to give me a broken foot. Flash Crimson. Carl Sandburg. MoAmPo

I shall dance, I shall have hope. Dance Hymn. Isaiah Shembe, *tr. fr. Zulu by* B. G. M. Sundkler. WTO

I shall die, but that is all that I shall do for Death. Conscientious Objector. Edna St. Vincent Millay. PAW; WPOW

I shall do nothing but look at the sky. (*LL*) Roman Wall Blues. W. H. Auden. FaBoEH; NTP

I shall find in paradise that emaciated rose shoot. Maria Luisa Spaziani, *tr. fr. Italian by* Beverly Allen. *Fr.* Star of Free Will, The. NeIt

I Shall Forget You Presently, My Dear. Edna St. Vincent Millay. HeIP; MeMAP; TAP

I shall gather myself into myself again. The Crystal Gazer. Sara Teasdale. MoAmPo

I shall give them all to my elder daughter. (*LL*) If I Should Ever by Chance. Edward Thomas. FaBoCh; GoJo; MoAB; MoBrPo; MoShBr; OBMV; OBWVE; OxBChV

I shall give you five words for your birthday. Five Words for Joe Dunn on His 22nd Birthday. Jack Spicer. PoM

I shall go among red faces and virile voices. Cattle Show. "Hugh MacDiarmid." FaBoMo; HAP; MoBrPo; OBMV; OxBTC

I shall go as my father went. The Tenancy. Mary Gilmore. CBAP

I Shall Go Back. Edna St. Vincent Millay. MeMAP; MoAmPo; UnPo

I shall go back again to the bleak shore. I Shall Go Back. Edna St. Vincent Millay. MeMAP; MoAmPo; UnPo

I shall go forth from here. Nostalgia. Marjorie Marshall. ShDr

I shall go haunting in search of a friend, a friend. (*LL*) The Ghost at Anlaby. Randolph Stow. NOBAu

I shall hate you. Hatred. Gwendolyn B. Bennett. BlSi; CDC; PoBA; RaBo; ShDr

I Shall Have a Sweetheart. Vilhelm Andreas Wexels Krag, *tr. fr. Norwegian by* Philip L. Miller. RiWo

I shall hear that grand Amen. (*LL*) The Lost Chord. Adelaide Anne Procter. EBEvV; UV, *sts.* I *and* II *only*; VPP; WGRP

I shall hide myself/ within the moon of the spring night. Chino Masako, *tr. fr. Japanese by* Kenneth Rexroth *and* Ikuko Atsumi. WPJ

I shall know why — when time is over. Emily Dickinson. NOCV; SAmP

I Shall Laugh Purely. Robinson Jeffers. LiTA; LiTM

I shall lie hidden in a hut. Prophecy. Elinor Wylie. BLPL; BoWoP; FaBoWP; NTP; PrIm; VGW

I shall look for loving crops from the birth, life, death, immortality, I plant so lovingly now. (*LL*) A Woman Waits for Me. Walt Whitman. ErPo; HeIP; NOBA

I shall make a song like your hair. Secret. Gwendolyn B. Bennett. BlSi; CDC; ShDr

I shall make it simple so you understand. Simple Poem. Anthony Thwaite. DiPo

I shall never come back again. (*LL*) The Changeling. Charlotte Mew. CH; CoGr

I shall never forget his blue eye. Dylan Thomas. *Fr.* Parachutist. UV

I shall never forget the wind. North Wind: Portrush. Derek Mahon. SCBI

I shall never forget you, Broadway. Broadway. Carl Sandburg. AiP

I shall never get you put together entirely. The Colossus. Sylvia Plath. CAPP; FaBoWP; HCAP; LiTM; NALW; NoAM; NOBA; NoP; Poetr; TAP; VCAP

I shall never, in the years remaining. Robert Browning. *Fr.* One Word More. EnVR; EPCY; MeMBP; OtMeF; PoEL-5

I shall not call for help until they coffin me. Last Lines. Egan O'Rahilly, *tr. fr. Irish by* Frank O'Connor. IIP; PeIV

I Shall Not Care. Sara Teasdale. MoAMPo; TrGrPo; UnPo

I Shall Not Die. *Unknown, tr. fr. Irish by* Frank O'Connor. PeIV

I shall not die because of you. I Shall Not Die. *Unknown, tr. fr. Irish by* Frank O'Connor. PeIV

I shall not die for thee. (*LL*) I Shall Not Die for Thee. *Unknown.* IIP

I Shall Not Die for Thee. *Unknown, tr. fr. Irish by* Douglas Hyde. IIP

I shall not fail that rendezvous. (*LL*) I Have a Rendezvous with Death. Alan Seeger. AiP; BLPA; DL; FaBV

I Shall Not Go to Heaven When I Die. Helen Waddell. MLL

I shall not linger in that draughty square. French. Osbert Lancaster. *Fr.* Afternoons with Baedeker. FaBoCo; NOBL; PeLV

I shall not live in vain. (*LL*) If I Can Stop One Heart from Breaking. Emily Dickinson. AH; PoLF; PoToHe; PWR

I Shall Not Pass Again This Way. *Unknown.* BLRP; WBLP

I shall not pass this way again. (*LL*) I Shall Not Pass This Way Again. *Unknown.* BLPA

I shall not pass this way again. (*LL*) I Shall Not Pass This Way Again. Eva Rose York. WBLP

I Shall Not Pass This Way Again. *Unknown.* BLPA

I Shall Not Pass This Way Again. Eva Rose York. WBLP

I shall not regard my swelled head as a sign of real glory. Aimé Césaire, *tr. fr. French by* Emile Snyders. *Fr.* Return to My Native Land. NegPo; TTY

I shall not repeat others' comments about me. (*LL*) Wet Casements. John Ashbery. NAAL-2; PoM

I shall not sing a May song. The Crazy Woman. Gwendolyn Brooks. NALW

I shall not soon forget. Still Life. Thom Gunn. PFL

I Shall Not Want: In Deserts Wild. Charles F. Deems. AH

I shall not weary you with poems. John Riley. VaA

I shall note first/ the ones I loved. The Chronicler. Alexander Bergman. TrJP

I shall paint/ God in the midst. Robert Browning. *Fr.* Fra Lippo Lippi. CTC; EBVV; EBVVPR; EnVR; FHYEP; NoP; OAEL-2; OtMeF; OxAEP-2; Prf; TEP

I shall rot here, with those whom in their day. In Death Divided. Thomas Hardy. SCGP

I shall save my poems. You Are There. Nikki Giovanni. HeIL

I shall say, Lord, "Is it music, is it morning." Resurgam. Marjorie Pickthall. TrCP

I Shall Say What Inordinate Love Is. Robert Frost. OxBSP

I shall say what inordinat[e] love is. *Unknown.* MiEL (Inordinate Love.) EBEV; MeEL; OxBSP

I shall see justice done. Witch. Patricia Beer. OxBC

I shall slough my self as a snake its skin. "I." Louis Golding. TrJP

I Shall Take You in Rough Weather. Frank Prewett. HATNAP

I shall tell those who pass that Midas lies here buried. (*LL*) I am the maiden in bronze set over the tomb of Midas. Cleoboulos. GrAn

I shall tune my lute to sing your litanies as the quiet hours pass. Ode to Africa. Bernard Dadié, *tr. fr. French by* Ellen Conroy Kennedy. NegPo

I Shall Vote Centre. Roger Woddis. UV

I shall vote Centre because. I Shall Vote Centre. Roger Woddis. UV

I Shall Vote Labour. Christopher Logue. UV

I shall vote Labour because. I Shall Vote Labour. Christopher Logue. UV

I shall walk down the road. Death. Maxwell Bodenheim. TrJP

I shall weave you a wreath. A Wreath for Africa. Bernard Dadié, *tr. fr. French by* Ellen Conroy Kennedy. NegPo

I Shall Weep. Peretz Hirshbein, *tr. fr. Yiddish by* Joseph Leftwich. TrJP

I shall write of the old men I knew. In These Dissenting Times. Alice Walker. InPS; PoBA

I sha'n't be gone long. — You come too. (*LL*) The Pasture. Robert Frost. BLPL; CMoP; FaPoB; FaPON; GoJo; MoAB; MoAmPo;

MoShBr; NAAL-2; NOBA; OxBA; PDV; PoE; SAmP; TLR; TRP; TTTS; WHSW

I shelter a song for you/ Secretly. (*LL*) Secret. Gwendolyn B. Bennett. BlSi; CDC; ShDr

I shipped, d'ye see, in a Revenue sloop. The Darned Mounseer. W. S. Gilbert. *Fr.* Ruddigore. NOBL

I shipped on board of a Liverpool liner. Sally Brown. *Unknown.* AmFP

I shiver, Spirit fierce and bold. At the Grave of Burns. Wordsworth. EnRP

I shoot the hippopotamus. The Hippopotamus. Hilaire Belloc. FaBoNo; FiBHP; InPK

I shop in the streets of my hometown with/ my family. Bruce Beaver. *Fr.* Letters to Live Poets. CBAP

I shot a rocket in the air. Enough. Tom Masson. OBAL

I shot an arrow into the air. A Shot at Random. D. B. Wyndham Lewis. FaBoCo; FiBHP; UV

I shot an arrow into the air. The Arrow and the Song. Longfellow. AnAmPo; MeMAP; PFP; PoToHe; PWR; UV

I Should Be Ashamed. Uvlunuaq, *tr. fr. Eskimo.* WTO

I should be glad. (*LL*) Parting Roundel. Jemal Sharah. NOBAu

I should be glad I didn't get the clap. Parting Roundel. Jemal Sharah. NOBAu

I should be glad of another death. (*LL*) Journey of the Magi. T. S. Eliot. EBEvV; FaBoCh; FaBoMo; HAP; HeIP; ImPo; InPK; LiTA; LiTM; MoAB; MoAmPo; NAEL-2; NIP; NOCV; NoP; OBCP; OBMV; OxBTC; PChr; PoE; Poetr; TAP; TFi; TrGrPo; TRP; TwCP

I should have been too glad, I see. Emily Dickinson. MeMAP; NOCV

I should have kept right on going. A Small Fat Boy Walking Backwards. Gerry Murphy. BiHa

I should have seen the sign: "Fresh paint." Fresh Paint. Boris Pasternak, *tr. fr. Russian by* Babette Deutsch. TrJP

I should have thought. At Baia. Hilda Doolittle ("H. D."). LiTA; LPA; NAAL-2; NOBA

I should know what God and man is. (*LL*) Flower in the Crannied Wall. Tennyson. BoNaP; FaBV; FaPON; ImPo; InPK; LiTB; MeMBP; NAEL-2; TEP; TFi; TrGrPo; WGRP

"I should like," said the vase from the china-store. The Toys Talk of the World. Katharine Pyle. OBCA

I should like to creep. A Mona Lisa. Angelina Weld Grimké. BlSi; CDC; ShDr

I should like to rise and go. Travel. Robert Louis Stevenson. FaBoCh; FaPON; MoShBr; OHCV; OTCP

I should like to see that country's tiled bedrooms. Keeping Their World Large. Marianne Moore. RaBo

I should live for good and all. (*LL*) The Flowers. Robert Louis Stevenson. FaPON

I should long to be fifteen. (*LL*) Song for a Girl. Dryden. ELP; ErPo

I Should Not Dare to Leave My Friend. Emily Dickinson. MeMAP

I should not presume to express any view. Triangular Legs. A. P. Herbert. NBLV

I should worry, I should care. *Unknown.* RoPo

I shouldered a kind of manhood. Funeral Rites. Seamus Heaney. BiHa; PBCIP

I shouted day and night. Let Zulu Be Heard. Isaiah Shembe, *tr. fr. Zulu by* G. C. Oosthuizen. WTO

I shouted for blood as I ran, brother. Janet Begbie. NSI

I shudder thinking. The Cold Irish Earth. Knute Skinner. InPK

I shuffled the musty floorboards. The Real Thing. Michael O'Loughlin. IB

I shut the door on the racket. Shoe Shop. Barton Sutter. SM; SoSe

I sicken of myself, my members all are shaking. To Himself. Andreas Gryphius, *tr. fr. German by* George C. Schoolfield. GePo

I sieze the sphery harp. I strike the strings. Enitharmon Revives with Los. Blake. *Fr.* Vala; or The Four Zoas. OBNC (Enitharmon's Song.) ChTr

I sigh for the heavenly country. The Heavenly City. Stevie Smith. FaBoTw

I sigh to myself I am traveling far. Recalling When I Was Drunk. Yüan Chen, *tr. fr. Chinese by* Dell R. Hales. SuSp

I sike when I singe. *Unknown.* MiEL (Crucifixion.) MeEL

I sing a song of sixpence, and of rye. Anthony C. Deane. NOBL

I sing a song of sorrow. J. L. Kubiček. BTR

I sing a song reluctantly. Beatrice, Countess de Die, *tr. fr. Provençal by* Carol Cosman *and* Howard Bloch. PBWP

I sing a theme deserving praise. The Manchester Ship Canal. *Unknown.* OBET

I sing a woeful ditty. A Ballad Called the Haymarket Hectors. *Unknown.* APAS

I Sing an Old Song. Oscar Williams. ImPo; LiTM

I sing divine Astræa's praise. Dialogue between two shepherds, Thenot and Piers, in praise of ASTRÆA. The Countess of Pembroke. SiPSBD

I Sing for the Animals. *Teton Sioux Oral Tradition*, *tr. fr. Teton Sioux Indian*. EaPr; TTTS

I sing her worth and praises hy [*or* high]. A Description. Lord Herbert of Cherbury. OPOP; SeCP

I Sing No New Songs. Frank Marshall Davis. PoBA; PoNe

I sing no song. I spin instead. Spider. Norma Farber. PChr

I sing not of the draper's praise, nor yet of William Wood. An Excellent New Song upon His Grace Our Good Lord Archbishop of Dublin. Swift. CoMu

I sing of a hero, unsung, unrecorded. Crispus Attucks McCoy. Sterling A. Brown. BPo

I Sing of a Maiden. *Unknown*. CH; ChIV-2; EBEV; ELP; FaBoCh; FF; ImPo; InPK; InPS; LiTB; MeEL; MiEL; NAEL-1; NOBE; NOCV; NoP; OAEL-1; OxBLMV; PoE; PoEL-1; SCGP; SCV; TFi; TOF; TrGrPo

I sing of a woman and summer. Canto Cantare Cantavi Cantatum. Rita Mae Brown. PeHV

I sing of brooks, of blossom[e]s, birds, and bowers. The Argument of His Book. Robert Herrick. AWP; BeJo; CaPo; EBEV; HAP; ImPo; InvP; JCP; NAEL-1; NoP; NOSC; OAEL-1; OxAEP-1; PeECV; PoE; PoEL-3; PoRA; SeCP; SeCV-1; TEP; TFi; TrGrPo; TTTS

I sing of great hotels and a man. In the foyer. The Strand Hotel, Rosslare. James Liddy. CIP

I sing of myself, a sorrowful woman. *Unknown*. *See* I make this song about me full sadly.

I sing of myself, a sorrowful woman. Wife's Lament. *Unknown*, *tr. fr. Anglo-Saxon by* Kemp Malone. PBWP; PoE

I Sing of Olaf Glad and Big. E. E. Cummings. HeIP; LiTM; MeMAP; MoP; NAAL-2; NoAM; NOBA; NoP; OBSV; OBWP; PoWW; VGW

I sing of sweepers, frequent in thy streets. The Sweepers. William Whitehead. ECEV, *ll.* 1–38, *sl. diff. vers.*; NOEC

I sing of the Good Samaritan. The Song of the Good Samaritan. Vernon Watkins. LiTM

I sing th' adventures of mine worthy wights. Thomas Morton. SCAP

I sing the birth was born [*or* borne] tonight. A Hymn [*or* Hymne] on the Nativity [*or* Nativitie] of My Saviour. Ben Jonson. BeJo; ChIV-2; SeCV-1; TrCP

I Sing the Body Electric. Walt Whitman. CTC; SAmP, *Pt.* I *only Sels.*
    "I have perceiv'd that to be with those I like is enough"
    "Man's body at auction, A"
    "O my body! I dare not desert the likes of you in other men and women, nor the likes of the parts of you." ErPo
    "This is the female form." ErPo

I sing the furious battles [*or* battails] of the spheres [*or* Sphæres]. Ad Johannuelem Leporem, Lepidissimum, Carmen Heroicum. *Unknown*. CBNP; FaBoNo

I sing the glorious Power with azure eyes. Hymn to Athena. *Unknown*, *tr. fr. Greek by* Shelley. *Fr.* Homeric Hymns. AWP

I sing the hymn of the conquered, who fell in the battle of life. Io Victis! William Wetmore Story. WGRP

I sing the Man, by Heav'ns peculiar grace. A Poem on Elijahs Translation. Benjamin Colman. SCAP

I sing the Name which none can say. To the Name above Every Name, the Name of Jesus, a Hymn. Richard Crashaw. SeCV-1
    (On the Name of Jesus.) ESCV

I sing the praise of honored wars. Soldier's Song. *Unknown*. WiR

I sing the quality of bamboo. Bamboo. Eric Rolls. NOBAu

I sing the simplest flower. Karl Shapiro. *Fr.* Six Religious Lyrics. CMoP

I sing the tree is a heron. Merce of Egypt. Charles Olson. NoP

I sing the uplift and the up-welling. Jehovah. Israel Zangwill. WGRP

I Sing This Song for Our Mothers: Ruise. Sherley Anne Williams. MDDM

I sing to the Mother Gaia. *Unknown*. EaPr

I sing *tree*, making green. Last Night's Dream. Denise Levertov. NoAM

I sing "Wild Thing" out loud — it never sounded better. (*LL*) You Make Everything Move Me. Jack Skelley. UTF

I sing you the song of the yellow star. The Song of the Yellow Star. Richard Burns. Jaz

I sink in the falling snow. Monstrance. János Pilinszky, *tr. fr. Hungarian by* Peter Jay. PoSu

I sink into a rare luminous blindness. Blindness. Delmira Agustini, *tr. fr. Spanish by* D. M. Pettinella. PBWP

I Sit and Look Out. Walt Whitman. AnAmPo; MeMAP; NAAL-1; OxBA; SAmP; TAP

I Sit and Sew. Alice Dunbar Nelson. BlSi; CDC; NALW; ShDr; WPOW

I Sit and Wait for Beauty. Mae V. Cowdery. BlSi

I sit at a gold table with my girl. At the Altar. Robert Lowell. *Fr.* Between the Porch and the Altar. InPK

I sit at the top of the tree. Crow Resting. Edward Pygge. BXAP; FaBoPa

I sit behind the bars of my dungeon. The Captive. Pushkin, *tr. fr. Russian by* Philip L. Miller. RiWo

I sit beneath the throne of Allah! I, Lord, of All Mortals! *Unknown*, *tr. by* R. O. Winstedt. WTO

I sit beside my old ship, the timbers rotting. The Old Jason, the Argonaut. Denis Glover. PeNZ

I sit beside my peaceful hearth. The Due of the Dead. Thackeray. OBWP

I sit beside old retired Italians. Park. David Ignatow. Poetsp

I sit by the mossy fountain; on the top of the hill of winds. James Macpherson. *Fr.* Fragments of Ancient Poetry, Collected in the Highlands of Scotland. NOEC

I sit by the roadside. Changing the Wheel. Bertolt Brecht, *tr. fr. German by* Michael Hamburger. PoSu

I sit by the shed. Winter Billet. Peter Huchel, *tr. fr. German by* Michael Hamburger. PoSu

I sit clumsy in my flesh, my legs. The Cigarette Poem. Faye Kicknosway. IHMS

I sit down at a table and open a book of poems. Library. Louis Jenkins. NU; RaBo

I sit down beside my brass lamp. Peeling Pippins. Mary TallMountain. HATNAP

I sit down on the floor of a school for the retarded. He Sits Down on the Floor of a School for the Retarded. Alden Nowlan. GOYP

I sit for my portrait on the veranda. Portrait. Brenda Marie Osbey. MT

I Sit Here. Kumeroa Ngoingoi Pewhairangi, *tr. fr. Maori by the author.* PeNZ

I sit here at your edge, in your embankment's screen. Shepherd-Song. Sigmund von Birken, *tr. fr. German by* George C. Schoolfield. GePo

I sit here with the wind is in my hair. To Helen of Troy (N.Y.). Peter Viereck. WeW

I sit high on this bridge in Laventille. The Spoiler's Return. Derek Walcott. PBCV

I sit in an office at 244 Madison Avenue. Spring Comes to Murray Hill. Ogden Nash. FiBHP

I sit in another house whose character is. The House Is Old. Ron Schreiber. GLP

I sit in Lees. At 11:40 PM with. A Poem for Tea Heads. John Wieners. PoBeRe

I sit in one of the dives. September 1, 1939. W. H. Auden. ArOW; CMoP; CoGr; FaBoEH, *abr.*; ImPo; LiTA; MoAB; MoBrPo; OxAEP-2; OxBA; PoE; PrIm

I sit in the dusk. I am all alone. Tableau at Twilight. Ogden Nash. FiBHP

I sit in the front parlor. Memory. Brenda Marie Osbey. *Fr.* Desperate Circumstance, Dangerous Woman. UTF

I sit in the top of the wood, my eyes closed. Hawk Roosting. Ted Hughes. CMoP; GTBS-P; HAP; HeIP; LiTM; OBAP; OxBTC; PPP; TwCP; UnPo

I sit, in treatment, at the movies, devoted. Valerio Magrelli, *tr. fr. Italian by* Dana Gioia. NeIt

I sit musing, ten minutes from the Jap. A Letter for Marian. Thomas McGrath. VGW

I sit on a hard bench in the park. Spot-Check at Fifty. Vernon Scannell. NAs

I sit on the back platform of the train. The Train Butcher. Thomas Hornsby Ferril. GoYe

I sit on the edge. The Piano. Frank Daley. NOBC

I sit on the surge called ten stories tall. The Seesaw. Oscar Williams. LiTA

I sit thinking of a rowing-boat I saw. The Waiting-Room. Robin Fulton. PoA

I sit with Joseph Conrad in Monet's garden. Zimmer Imagines Heaven. Paul Zimmer. PBCAP

I Sit with My Dolls. *Unknown*, *tr. fr. Yiddish by* Joseph Leftwich. TrJP

I sit with my toes in the brook. *Unknown*. FaBoNo

I sit within my room and joy to find. The Presence. Jones Very. HAP

I sleep but my heart is awake. Bible, *O.T. See* I Sleep, but My Heart Waketh.

I Sleep, but My Heart Waketh. Bible, *O.T. Fr.* Song of Solomon, The. TrJP

I sleep, I don't, she listed. Young Americans. Andrew Greig. PWE

I sleep, I sleep. Sleeping Beauty. Olga Broumas. VBLP

I sleep with thee, and wake with thee. To Mary: I Sleep with Thee, and Wake with Thee. John Clare. GBL
    (To Mary.) EnLoPo

I slept and dreamed that life was Beauty. Duty. Ellen S. Hooper. BLPA

I slept in the past/ that will never come back. Princess Shikishi, *tr. fr. Japanese by* Kenneth Rexroth *and* Ikuko Atsumi. WPJ

I slept under rhododendron. Siwashing It Out Once in Siuslaw Forest. Gary Snyder. *Fr.* Four Poems for Robin. MoP; NNaP; NoAM; NOBA; NoP; SOTW

I stare out of the long windowed house. Returned American. Kathleen Cain. LoHo

I stared at the printed words. Printed Words. Liz Sohappy Bahe. CDW

I start awake at night afraid of death. Sonnet 21. Paul Goodman. VGW

I start out for a walk at last after weeks at the desk. After Long Busyness. Robert Bly. CAPP; PoA

I started early — took my dog. Emily Dickinson. AmPP; HAP; InPK; LiTM; MeMAP; NAAL-1; PoEL-5; WeW
(By the Sea.) LiTA

I started on the trail of June twenty-third. The Lone Star Trail. *Unknown.* AS

I started out towards evening. Burning Ship. Jaroslav Seifert, *tr. fr. Czech by* Jeffrey Fiskin *and* Erik Vestville. AnAn

I started picking up the stones. Apologia pro Vita Sua. A. R. Ammons. CAPP; HCAP; NOBA

I starve your body, you my mind. (*LL*) The Fair Beggar. Richard Lovelace. BeJo

I stay;/ But it isn't as if. An Empty Threat. Robert Frost. RFM

I stay clear. I Have No Strength for Mine. Joanne Kyger. PoM

I stayed [*or* staid] the night for shelter at a farm. The Witch of Coös. Robert Frost. *Fr.* Two Witches. CMoP; InPS; LiTM; MeMAP; MoAB; MoP; NoAM; NOBA; PoE

I step from the wardrobe unblinking. Ryan's Rebirth. Sean O'Brien. PWE

I stepped from black to black. Black Power. Raymond R. Patterson. NBV

I stepped from plank to plank. Emily Dickinson. CMoP; NOBA; NOCV; OxBSP; SAmP

I stifled in that room. We Were Sisters Weren't We. Katie Donovan. BiHa

I still am where I was. A fig for thee. (*LL*) A Fig for Thee, Oh! Death. Edward Taylor. NAAL-1

I still do not know your name. Letter to Two Strangers. Octavio Paz, *tr. fr. Spanish by* Eliot Weinberger. AnRep

I still don't. (*LL*) The Irish Lesson. Michael O'Loughlin. IB

I still get the urge. Girl Friday. Elaine Equi. UL

I still got hope Tang says. Frank Stanford. BCF

I still remember my child playing. Only Child. Barbara Soretsky. NGP

I still remember the almost first kiss. Heavy As Ever. Tim Longville. VaA

I Still Would Plant My Apple Tree. John Greening. PWE

I stirred wet sand and gathered myself. Seamus Heaney. *Fr.* Sweeney Redivivus. NoAM

I Stole Brass. *Unknown.* ChTr

I stole through the dungeons, while everyone slept. Alternative Endings to an Unwritten Ballad. Paul Dehn. FiBHP

I stood among the wanting many. Just Making It. Richard W. Thomas. PoNe

I stood and leant upon the mast. The Voyage. Heine, *tr. fr. German by* John Todhunter. AWP

I stood and watched him dig one hole all day. Robert Frost's Left-leaning *Trespassers Will Be Shot* Sign. William Zaranka. BXAP

I stood aside to let the cows. Man and Cows. Andrew Young. EBEV

I stood at eve, as the sun went down, by a grave where a woman lies. 'Ostler Joe. George R. Sims. BeLS; BLPA

I stood at the back of the shop, my dear. At the Draper's. Thomas Hardy. *Fr.* Satires of Circumstance. MoAB; MoBrPo; OBD; OxBM

I stood before it for hours in wintertime. (*LL*) A Hill. Anthony Hecht. CoAP; FoLa; NYBP; VCAP

I stood beside a hill. February Twilight. Sara Teasdale. FaPON; OBCA; PDV

I stood by Honor and the Dean. Sahara. Coventry Patmore. *Fr.* Angel in the House, The. EBVV

I stood by the bars at evening. By the Pasture Bars. George Sands Johnson. PWR

I stood in a meadow. Green Valley. Dorothy Vena Johnson. PoNe

I stood in the gloom of a spacious room. Awake, My Lute! C. S. Lewis. FaBoNo

I stood in the gypsy camp. September 1944. Charles Fishman. BTR

I Stood in the Maytime Meadows. *Unknown.* TTTS

I stood in the ruins of Dowlais. Idris Davies. AngWe

I stood in Venice on the Bridge of Sighs. Byron. *Fr.* Childe Harold's Pilgrimage. EnRP, *abr.*; OBTV, *abr.*
(On the Bridge of Sighs.) FaBoPP, 4 *sts*

I stood nailed to a prison wall. Unfinished Poem. Jiang He, *tr. fr. Chinese by* Donald Finkel *with* Yi Jinsheng. SpMi

I stood naked in the corner as my mother. The Confusion of Planes We Must Wander in Sleep. Bruce Weigl. NAmP90

I Stood on a Tower in the Wet. Tennyson. OxBSP

I stood on Brocken's sovereign height, and saw. Lines Written in the Album at Elbingerode, in the Hartz Forest. Samuel Taylor Coleridge. OBTV

I stood on the bridge at midnight. *Unknown.* RoPo

I stood one warm night. Treachery. Karl von Lemcke, *tr. fr. German by* Philip L. Miller. RiWo

I stood still and was a tree amid the wood. The Tree. Ezra Pound. CMoP

I Stood Tiptoe [upon a Little Hill]. Keats. EnRP; FaPON
Sels.
Minnows. GN
"Sometimes goldfinches one by one will drop"
(Goldfinches. GN
Sweet Peas. FHYEP; GN

I stood today on a mound of clay. Created Clay. Maimee Lee Brown. PWR

I Stood upon a High Place. Stephen Crane. *Fr.* Black Riders, The. LiTA; MeMAP

I stood with three comrades in Parliament Square. Armistice Day. Charles Causley. NAEL-2; OBWP

I stood within the City disinterred. At Pompeii. Shelley. *Fr.* Ode to Naples. FaBoPP

I stood within the empty House of Youth. Helen Waddell. MLL

I Stood within the Heart of God. William Vaughn Moody. *Fr.* Fire-Bringer, The. AH

I stood within the little cove. The Minute-Guns. Celia Laighton Thaxter. AmWP

I stoop to gather a seabird's feather. The Feather. Vernon Watkins. FaBoTw

I stooped to the silent Earth and lifted a handful of her dust. A Handful of Dust. James Oppenheim. TrJP

I stop. I go again. Tram Driver's Song. R. A. Simpson. FaBoMA

I stop to consult my diary and think how queer. Rogation Day: Portrush. James Simmons. PBCIP

I stopped at her door for a drink of water. The Girl by Green River. *Unknown, tr. fr. Chinese by* Kenneth Rexroth. OHMPC

I stopped deep. African in Louisiana. Kojo Gyinaye Kyei. PBA

I stopped in a sidestreet surplus shop, just south of Yorkville. The Cot. Grover Amen. NYBP

I stopped in the barn's wide entrance. The Barn. Peter Didsbury. PWE

I stopped my car on Gibson Avenue. I Am Here. Jimmy Santiago Baca. NAmP90

I stopped over at a motel on E3. The Gallery. Tomas Tranströmer, *tr. fr. Swedish by* Samuel Charters. AnAn

I stopped to pick up the bagel. The Bagel. David Ignatow. CAPP; FF; TwCP

I store the sun for winter mirth. (*LL*) Tapestry Trees. William Morris. BoNaP; FaPON; OHIP

I strayed, all alone, where the Autumn. A Rose in October. James Whitcomb Riley. OBAL

I strayed along the strand with mussels strewn. Along the Strand. Alfred Mombert, *tr. fr. German by* Jethro Bithell. TrJP

I stretch out flat to the horizon. Before They Made Things Be Alive They Spoke. Lucario Cuevish, *tr. fr. Luiseño Indian by* Jerome K. Rothenberg. STP

I stretched my hand out in front of me, into the darkness. In Darkness. Amir Gilboa, *tr. fr. Hebrew by* Ruth Finer Mintz. MHP

I stroked her sheek with my finger. For My Daughter's Twenty-First Birthday. Jeanne Murray Walker. MDDM

I strolled across/ An open field. The Waking ("I strolled across/ An open field.") Theodore Roethke. RFM; TTTS

I strove with all, for all were worth my strife. Epitaph for G. B. Shaw. Max Beerbohm. FaBoEE

I Strove with None. E. M. Forster. UV

I Strove With None. Walter Savage Landor. *Fr.* Last Fruit Off an Old Tree, The. ChTr; EBEvV; EnRP; FaPoR; NOBE; OBNC; TFi; TRP; UV
(Dying Speech of an Old Philosopher.) FaBoEE; GTBS-P; NOBVV; NoP
(Finis.) 08GLGT; OBEV; 08OBVV
(On His Seventy-fifth Birthday.) AWP; BLPL; EBEV; LiTB; NTP; OAEL-2; OxAEP-2; SCGP; TrGrPo

I struck for what I deemed the right. After the Battle. George Sylvester Viereck. GoYe

I struck the board, and cried [*or* cry'd]. The Collar. George Herbert. AWP; BLPL; ClHu; EBEV; FaBoVe; FaPoB; GeHe; HAP; HeIP; ImPo; InPS; JCP; LiTB; MeLP; NAEL-2; NIP; NOBE; NOCV; NoP; NOSC; OAEL-1; OBWVE; PoE; PoRA; PPP; SCGP; SCV; SeCP; SeCV-1; TEP; TFi; TOF; TrGrPo; WeW

I struck tomorrow square in the face. Hidesong. Aig Higo. TTY

I studied in the hedge school. The Herd. Peter Fallon. PBCIP

I study out a dark similitude. The Swan. Theodore Roethke. VGW

I study the lives on a leaf: the little. The Minimal. Theodore Roethke. HCAP; MoP; NoAM; NOBA; RB

I Substitute for the Dead Lecturer. Amiri Baraka. PoE

I too but seem! *(LL)* In Utrumque Paratus. Matthew Arnold. MeMBP; OBNC; PoEL-5

I too, dislike it: there are things that are important beyond all this fiddle. Poetry. Marianne Moore. AmPP; BLPL; BoWoP; CMoP; FaBoWP; FF; HAP; HeIL; HeIP; ImGa; ImPo; LiTA; LiTM; MoAB; MoAmPo; MoP; NAAL-2; NALW; NIP; NoAM; NOBA; NoP; OxBA; PoE; Poetr; TAP; TFi; UnPo

I, too, have been a Wanderer; but, alas! Wordsworth. *Fr.* Prelude [or, Growth of a Poet's Mind], The. EnRP; OAEL-2; OxAEP-2; PoEL-4

I, too, have plucked a stalk of grass. Ronald Johnson. *Fr.* Letters to Walt Whitman. VGW

I too, saw God through mud. Apologia pro Poemate Meo. Wilfred Owen. FaBoRV; LiTM; MeMBP; MoAB; MoBrPo; NAEL-2; NSI; PeFWW

I, too, sing America. I, Too. Langston Hughes. CDC; FF; HCAP; HeIP (I, Too, Sing America.) NTP; PoBA; PoLF; PoNe

I too was born out of a lion's mouth. Let Heroes Account to Love. Alan Dugan. NoAM

I took a day to search for God. Vestigia. Bliss Carman. WGRP

I took a piece of plastic clay. Sculpture. *Unknown.* BLPL; PoLF (Sculptor, The.) PoToHe

I took a piece of the fine cloth of Ch'i. A Song of Grief. Pan Chieh-yû, *tr. fr. Chinese by* Kenneth Rexroth *and* Ling Chung. WPC

I took a piece of the rare cloth of Ch'i. A Present from the Emperor's New Concubine. Lady Pan, *tr. fr. Chinese by* Kenneth Rexroth. BoWoP; OHMPC

I took away three pictures. Sandhill People. Carl Sandburg. CMoP

I took for emblem the upland moors and the rocky. Llanafan Unrevisited. T. Harri Jones. AngWe

I took him by the arm and said. F. Mullen. UV

I took leave of my beloved one evening: how I wish. At Taliq, *tr. fr. Arabic by* A. R. Nykel. PeHV

I took money and bought flowering trees. Planting Flowers on the Eastern Embankment. Po Chü-i, *tr. by* Arthur Waley. BoNaP

I took my girl to a fancy ball. I Had But Fifty Cents. *Unknown.* BeLS; BLPA; NBLV; WHSW

I took my girlfriend to your last poetry reading. Short Order. Charles Bukowski. HoPM

I took my heart in my hand. Twice. Christina Rossetti. GBL; NOBE; OBEV; OBNC; TOF; TrCP

I took my life and threw it on the skip. The Skip. James Fenton. SCBI

I took my oath I would inquire. The Inquest. W. H. Davies. AngWe; GTBS-P; NOBE; OxBTC; RB

I took my Power in my Hand. Emily Dickinson. ChIV-1; SAmP

I took off down the town's disaster route. Soliloquy in a Motel. Walker Gibson. GrPl

I took one Draught of Life. Emily Dickinson. NTP

I took up the burden of life anew. To My Mother. Mary Weston Fordham. CBWP-2

I toss yesterday's tortillas. Day's Blood. Jimmy Santiago Baca. AfAz

I tossed my friend a wreath of roses, wet. Gifts. Mary Elizabeth Coleridge. PBWP

I touch jig-saw fragments. A. L. Hendricks. *Fr.* D'Où Venons Nous? Que Sommes Nous? Où Allons Nous. PBCV

I touch the hand there on the pillow. *(LL)* Fall Comes in Back-Country Vermont. Robert Penn Warren. NYBP; VGW

I touch you in the night, whose gift was you. The Science of the Night. Stanley Kunitz. MoAmPo; TwCP

I touch you like the waves admire the weirs. The Oasis Motel. William Olsen. NAmP90

I touch your face. Poems of Night. Galway Kinnell. NaP

I touched at isles of Paradise. *(LL)* Fair Isle at Sea — thy lovely name. Robert Louis Stevenson. NOBVV

I touched the flesh with my eyes. Fish. Joe Rosenblatt. NOBC

I touched the nothingness of air once. I Read a Tight-fisted Poem Once. Nancy Woods. RFM

I touched up sexy Hermione. Asclepiades, *tr. fr. Greek by* Alan Marshfield. GrAn

I traced the Circus whose grey stones incline. In the Old Theatre, Fiesole. Thomas Hardy. OBTV

I trained me a falcon, for more than a year. *Unknown, tr. fr. German by* Frederick Goldin. GePo

I tramp my streets into recognition. Charles Brasch. *Fr.* Home Ground. PeNZ

I travel in a train. I Am a Horse. Hans Arp, *tr. by* Harriet Watts. FaBoNo

I traveld [*or* travelled] thro' a land of men. The Mental Traveller. Blake. ChIV-2; EnRP; MeMBP; NAEL-2; OAEL-2; OPOP; PoE; PoEL-4

I Traveled [*or* travell'd] among Unknown Men. Wordsworth. *Fr.* Lucy. AWP; EBEV; EnRP; FaBV; FHYEP; GBL; GTBS; GTBS-P; NOBE; OAEL-2; OBEV; OBNC; SCGP; TFi; TrGrPo

I traveled [*or* travell'd] on, seeing the hill, where lay. The Pilgrimage. George Herbert. ChTr; ESCV; FaBoRV; GeHe; NAEL-1; NOSC; PoE

I traveled to the ocean. Prayer to the Pacific. Leslie Silko. CDW; NoP; VoR; WeW

I Traveled with Them. Don Johnson, *tr. fr. Arabic by* J. B. Trend. AWP

I travelled the land from Leap to Corbally. The Volatile Kerryman. Owen Roe O'Sullivan, *tr. fr. Irish by* Sean O'Riada. BIrV

I traversed a dominion. Mute Opinion. Thomas Hardy. CMoP

I tried each thing, only some were immortal and free. As One Put Drunk into the Packet-Boat. John Ashbery. HAP; HCAP; VCAP

I tried to explain why his manuscript had been rejected. The Rejected. Louis Simpson. PRA

I tried to live by bread alone. Satisfied. Edgar Cooper Mason. BLRP

I tried to live small. Housing Shortage. Naomi Replansky. CrSp; NMM

I tried to tell her. Offspring. Naomi Long Madgett. CrSp; SoSe

I trim my lamp, and weeping write this letter. A Letter. Shao Fei-fei, *tr. fr. Chinese by* Kenneth Rexroth *and* Ling Chung. WPC

I tripped up his heels and he fell on his nose. *(LL)* As I was going to sell my eggs. Mother Goose. OxNR

I trundle the bodies, on the iron bars. John Berryman. *Fr.* Homage to Mistress Bradstreet. NOBA

I trust I have not wasted breath. Tennyson. *Fr.* In Memoriam A. H. H. EBVV, *abr.*; EnVR; FHYEP; OAEL-2, *abr.*; PeECV, *abr.*

I try to forget, but it is in vain. To the Distant One. Po Chü-i, *tr. fr. Chinese by* Robert Payne. TAL

I try to hold your face in my mind's million eyes. A Bride's Hours. Jean Valentine. FaBoWP

I Try to Keep. Erica Jong. LPA

I try to stare at it without blinking. *(LL)* When I Blink. Gu Cheng. SpMi

I turn and the world turns on the other side. *(LL)* In the Night. Elizabeth Jennings. NYBP

I turn away from you. Phrasal. Anthony Barnett. VaA

I turn my steps where the lonely road. In Dark Hour. Seumas MacManus. WGRP

I turn out the light. I Believe You. Anthony Barnett. VaA

I turn the lea-green down. Ploughman. Patrick Kavanagh. TIRV

I turn the page and read. At the British Museum. Richard Aldington. MoBrPo

I turn to you high priests. Tadeusz Rózewicz, *tr. fr. Polish by* Magnus J. Krynski. PoSu

I turn you out of doors. Alain Chartier, *tr. fr. French by* Edward Lucie-Smith. BoLoP

I turn'd from the monitor, smiled at the warning. I Turned From the Monitor. Frances Sargent Osgood. AmWP

I turned and gave my strength to woman. Two Generations. L. A. G. Strong. OBMV

I turned, and saw them whispering about it. *(LL)* I Bended unto Me. Thomas Edward Brown. NOBVV; NTCP; OHCV

I turned aside and bowed my head and wept. *(LL)* The Tropics in New York. Claude McKay. ArNa; NoAM; PoBA; PoNe; TTY

I Turned From the Monitor. Frances Sargent Osgood. AmWP

I turned on the TV. Tube Time. Eve Merriam. TLR

I turned to speak to God. Not All There. Robert Frost. FaBoCo

I undersign'd Lord Kitchener of Karthoum. The Proclamation, or Paper Bomb. F. W. Reitz, *tr. fr. Afrikaans by* F. W. Reitz. PeSAV

I understand the large hearts of heroes. Walt Whitman. *Fr.* Song of Myself. AmPP; LiTA; MoAmPo, *abr.*; NOBA; OxBA; SAmP; SOTW, (*much abr.*)

I understand you well enough, John Donne. A Letter to John Donne. C. H. Sisson. NOCV

I understood that. Julian of Norwich. CrSp

I understood the rest too well. Understanding. Sara Teasdale. AnAmPo

I upon earth, you in heaven. The Wanderer to the Moon. Johann Gabriel Seidl, *tr. fr. German by* Philip L. Miller. RiWo

I upon the first creation. Gratitude. Christopher Smart. *Fr.* Hymns for the Amusement of Children. NOEC

I urgency, I begged. *Give me your dish,* I said, icy. Hélène Cixous, *tr. by* Anne Liddle *and* Sarah Cornell. *Fr.* Vivre L'Orange. VCAP

I used the table as a reference and just did things from there. Texas. Mei-Mei Berssenbrugge. UL

I used to be a big girl. Love Poem: Growing Down. Christian McEwen. VBLP

I used to be a drill man. Drill Man Blues. George Sizemore. AmFP; WTO

I used to believe that story. A Man Never Cries. José Craveirinha, *tr. fr. Bantu.* TSaS, *tr. by* Donald Burness

I used to drop my pocket money. Debt. Sunay Akin, *tr. fr. Turkish.* TSaS, *tr. by* Yusuf Eradam

I used to fall. My Heart Belongs to Daddy. Cole Porter. OBAL

I used to fall in love with pop stars. True Life Romance. Lindsay MacRae. DT

I used to have an old grey horse. Goin' Down to Town. *Unknown.* AS

I used to lie on my back, imagining. Childhood. Maura Stanton. SM

I Used to Love My Garden. C. P Sawyer. FaBoCo

I used to love to lie awake past bedtime. Rechargeable Dry Cell Poem. Jim Wayne Miller. GOYP

I used to make fun of you when you were a little girl & poor. Song for the Richest Woman in Wrangell. Guxnawu, *tr. fr. Tlingit Indian by* James Koller. STP

I used to prefer them and now I'm one of them. Older Men. Alfred Corn. GLP

I used to scratch medals, when I was a lad. Ambition. Joachim Ringelnatz, *tr. fr. German by* C. Middleton. OBD

I used to tell you, "Frances, we grow old." I used to tell you, "Frances, we grow old." Kenneth Rexroth, *after the Latin of* Ausonius. NNaP; PGA

I used to tell you, "Frances, we grow old." Kenneth Rexroth, *after the Latin of* Ausonius. NNaP; PGA

I Used to Think. Chirlane McCray. AIW

I used to think that grown-up people chose. Childhood. Frances Cornford. FaBoWP; OxBSP; OxBTC

I used to walk on solid gr'und. To a Sea Eagle. "Hugh MacDiarmid." MoBrPo

I used to walk the morning stream. Walk. Brian Merriman, *tr. by* Brendan Behan. *Fr.* Midnight Court, The. BIrV; NOIV, *tr. by* Thomas Kinsella

I Used to Watch You, Sleeping. Kathleen Raine. *Fr.* My Mother's Birthday. NAs

I usta wonder who i'd be. Adulthood. Nikki Giovanni. CrSp; NMM

I verse a settler's tale of olden times. Charles Harpur. *Fr.* Creek of the Four Graves, The. CBAP

I Vision God. *Unknown.* TTY

I visited my distant relatives/ by Lake Suwa in Shinshū. Walking-with-a-Cane-Pass. Ishigaki Rin, *tr. fr. Japanese by* Kenneth Rexroth *and* Ikuko Atsumi. WPJ

I vow to live always at trash point: to. More Best Jokes of the Delphic Oracle. William Knott. UL

I Vow to Thee, My Country. Cecil Arthur Spring-Rice. BoTP; CoGr; NSI

I vow to thee, my country, all earthly things above. I Vow to Thee, My Country. Cecil Arthur Spring-Rice. BoTP; CoGr; NSI

I vow'd unvarying faith; and she. Coventry Patmore. *Fr.* Angel in the House, The. NOBVV

(Constancy Rewarded.) OxBSP

I wage not any feud with death. Tennyson. *Fr.* In Memoriam A. H. H. EBVV, *abr.;* ImPo; LiTB; OAEL-2, *abr.;* OBF; PeECV, *abr.*

I wait and watch: before my eyes. The Waiting. Whittier. WGRP

I wait, dear child, for you to come. You'll Never Know. Ruby Marion Wray. PWR

I wait for his foot fall. Earth Trembles Waiting. Blanche Shoemaker Wagstaff. PoLF

I Wait My Lord. *Unknown, tr. by* Helen Waddell. *Fr.* Shi King. AWP

I wait to tangle fear around my hand. Night along the Mackinac Bridge. Roberta Hill Whiteman. CDW

I wait, with those that rest. Ark to Noah. Jay Macpherson. *Fr.* Ark, The. NOBC; PoA

I waited and worked/ To win myself leisure. Koheleth. Louis Untermeyer. ChIV-1; TrJP

I waited for the train at Coventry. Godiva. Tennyson. BeLS; EBVVPR

I waited full two hours, or more. The Tryst. Mary E. Tucker. CBWP-1

I waited in a map of dreams. In the Town With Cat-/ Shaped Maze. Kanai Mieko, *tr. fr. Japanese by* Kenneth Rexroth *and* Ikuko Atsumi. WPJ

I waited in the little sunny room. Eve's Daughter. Edward Rowland Sill. AnAmPo

I waited this long I might as well stay, I said. The Ledger. Victor Martinez. AfAz

I wake and feel the city trembling. Lines Written Near San Francisco. Louis Simpson. PRA

I Wake and Feel the Fell of Dark Not Day. Gerard Manley Hopkins. EnVR; FaBoVe; MeMBP; OxAEP-2; PeVV; TRP

I wake at midnight. Shellfish. Ishigaki Rin, *tr. fr. Japanese by* Kenneth Rexroth *and* Ikuko Atsumi. WPJ

I wake, but before I know it is done. Aging. Randall Jarrell. PoA

I wake despondent. Morning. Tove Ditlevsen, *tr. fr. Danish by* Nadia Christensen. PBWP

I Wake from a Dream of Killing Hitler. Mark Nepo. BTR

I wake in a dark flat. Afterlives. Derek Mahon. CIP

I wake in the night. Middle of the Way. Galway Kinnell. NU

I Wake, My Friend, I. Faye Kicknosway. IHMS

I Wake Thinking of Myself as a Man. Susan Griffin. GLP

I wake to find myself lying in an open field. Robert Bly Says Something Too. Henry Taylor. BXAP

I wake to sleep, and take my waking slow. The Waking. Theodore Roethke. AmPP; CAPP; CoAP; CRP; HAP; HCAP; HeIP; InPK; InPS; LiTM; MoAmPo; MoP; NAAL-2; NIP; NoAM; NOBA; NoP; OPOP; PFP; Poetr; PPP; PrIm; RaBo; SM; TAP; TFi; TwCP; VCAP; WeW

I wake to strangled voices. Stepping in the Same River. Karen Chamberlain. FoLa

I Wake Up Alone. Li Shang-yin, *tr. fr. Chinese by* Kenneth Rexroth. OHMPC

I wake up and say: I'm through. Morning Exercises. Nina Cassian, *tr. fr. Romanian by* Andrea Deletant *and* Brenda Walker. PoSu

I wake up cold, I who. The Man With Night Sweats. Thom Gunn. PFL

I wake up in the bed my grandmother died in. Stove. Philip Booth. FYAP

I wake up in your bed. I know I have been dreaming. Adrienne Rich. *Fr.* Twenty-one Love Poems. GLP; NAAL-2; NoAM; TRP; UnAS; VBLP

I wake up my car. Morning Bird Songs. Tomas Tranströmer, *tr. fr. Swedish by* Robert Bly. InPS

I waked, she fled, and day brought back my night. *(LL)* On His Deceased Wife. Milton. BLPL; CBLP; ImPo; LiTB; OBEV; OxBM; PoE; SCV; TEP; TFi

I wakened my thoughts from slumber. The Sources of My Being. Moses ibn Ezra, *tr. fr. Hebrew by* David Goldstein. TOF

I wakened on my hot, hard bed. The Watch. Frances Cornford. InPK; MoBrPo; OxBSP

I wakened, still a child. The Life Ahead. Philip Levine. NoAM

I walk a road — an ancient, trodden way. Another While. Morris Jacob Rosenfeld, *tr. fr. Yiddish.* TrJP

I walk among men with tall bones. Clouds on the Sea. Ruth Dallas. *Fr.* Letter to a Chinese Poet. PeNZ; TSaS

I walk and I wonder. Spring. Isaac Rosenberg. TrJP

I walk back. Getting the Mail. Galway Kinnell. UnPo

I walk before no man, a hawk in his fist. I Walk Before no Man (Composed While Asleep). Swift. CBNP

I walk [or walked] beside the prisoners to the road. A Camp in the Prussian Forest. Randall Jarrell. BTR; CMoP; MoAmPo; OBWP; OxBC; PoWW

I walk down a long. A Poem for Museum Goers. John Wieners. NeAP; PoBeRe

I walk down the garden paths. Patterns. Amy Lowell. AWP; BoWoP; DL; LiTA; MoAmPo; OxBA; TrGrPo; WHSW

I walk down the narrow. The Man in the Mirror. Mark Strand. NYBP

I walk east of Bleecker. Poet of the Streets. Jack Micheline. PoBeRe

I walk in loneliness through the greenwood. *Unknown, tr. fr. French by* Willis Barnstone. BoWoP

I walk in nature still alone. Great Friend. Thoreau. PoEL-4

I walk in the old street. Louis Zukofsky. VGW

I walk in your world. A Mercy, a Healing, Psalm 64. Daniel Berrigan. EaPr

I walk into your house, a friend. A Friend. W. D. Snodgrass. MAT

I Walk of Grey Noons by the Old Canal. Thomas Caulfield Irwin. PeIV

I walk on the sea-shore. Voice. Zbigniew Herbert, *tr. fr. Polish by* Czeslaw Milosz. PoSu

I walk on the waste-ground for no good reason. For No Good Reason. Peter Redgrove. PoE

I walk on up the hill, in the warm. Thoughts on the Esterházy Court Uniform. J. H. Prynne. VaA

I walk the dusty ways of life. The Troubadour of God. Charles Wharton Stork. WGRP

I walk the purple carpet into your eye. Inside Out. Diane Wakoski. CoAP; NYBP

I walk through sunlit gardens. Recollections of the Sun. A. L. Hendricks. NBrP

I walk through the long schoolroom questioning. Among School Children. W. B. Yeats. BLPL; CMoP; GTBS-P; HAP; ImPo; InPS; LiTM; MeMBP; MoAB; MoBrPo; MoP; NAEL-2; NAWM-2; NIP; NoAM; NOBE; NoP; OAEL-2; OxBTC; PoE; Poetr; PPP; PrIm; SCGP; TFi; TrGrPo; TRP

I walk treacherous mid-March. Escape. Lillie D. Chaffin. ETG

I walk upon the rocky shore. My Mother. Josephine Rice Creelman. OHIP

I walk'd in the lonesome evening. William Allingham. EnLoPo

I walked a mile with Pleasure. Along the Road. Robert Browning Hamilton. BLPA; BLPL

I walked abroad in [or on] a snowy day. Soft Snow. Blake. FF; SoSe; TEP

I walked all the way from East St. Louis. East St. Louis Blues. *Unknown.* AmFP

I was broke and out of a job in the city of London. Paddy, Get Back. *Unknown.* AmFP

I was brought up in a small town in the Mohave Desert. After Tsang Chih. Alice Notley. UL

I was brought up in Sheffield, all of a high degree. The Sheffield 'Prentice. *Unknown.* AmFP

I was brought up on old Aristotle. C. S. Cook. PeLi

I was buried near this dyke. Blake. FaBoEE

I was but [*or* bat] seven year auld [*or* alld]. The Laily Worm and the Machrel of the Sea. *Unknown.* ChTr; ESPB; InvP; OxBB; PoEL-1; SCGP

I was calling airspeed. Where We Crashed. Richard Hugo. ArOW

I was combing some long hair coming out of a tree. In the Forest. Russell Edson. LCAP

I was conceding to that. (*LL*) Welsh Incident. Robert Graves. CBNP; CMoP; EBEvV; MeMBP; NOBE; OBSP; OxBTC

I was conceived in the summer of Nineteen Eighteen. True Confessional. Lawrence Ferlinghetti. NAs

I was descending from the mountains of sleep. Afternoon Sleep. Robert Bly. NaP

I was eighteen when I came in these gates. Words from Hell. David Helwig. NOBC

I Was Fair Beat. Robert Garioch. OxBTC

I was far forward on the plain, the burning swamp. The Little Girl with Bands on Her Teeth. Genevieve Taggard. VGW

I was fishing in the abandoned reservoir. Quinnapoxet. Stanley Kunitz. AnAn

I was 5 years old. New York City — 1935. Gregory Corso. Poetsp

I was foretold that on a certain day. Sonnet XX. Louise Labé, *tr. fr. French.* BoWoP, *tr. by* Willis Barnstone
(Sonnet: "Seer foretold that I would love one day, A.") PBWP, *tr. by* Joan Keefe *and* Richard Terdiman.

I was foretold, your rebell [*or* rebel] sex. A Deposition from Love. Thomas Carew. BeJo; CaPo; MeLP

I was four in this photograph fishing. Fifth Grade Autobiography. Rita Dove. NIP

I was going along a dusty highroad. Mountain Talk. A. R. Ammons. HCAP

I was going thru the big earth. A Song about a Dead Person — or Was It a Mole? *Unknown, tr. fr. Seneca Indian by* Jerome K. Rothenberg *and* Richard Johnny John. STP

I was going thru the big smoke. Another Song about That Same Dead Person or Mole — Whichever It Was. *Unknown, tr. fr. Seneca Indian by* Jerome K. Rothenberg *and* Richard Johnny John. STP

I was going to say something. Ancestor. Thomas Kinsella. BIrV; NOIV; PBCIP; PoE

I was grown up and ready for Him now. (*LL*) The Day Zimmer Lost Religion. Paul Zimmer. InPK; PBCAP

I was Hermocrateia: twenty-nine/ children I bore. Antipater of Thessalonica, *tr. fr. Greek by* Alistair Elliot. GrAn

I was, I am not; smiled; that since did weep. Thomas Heywood. OxBSP

I was ill, lying on my bed of old papers. The Secret Garden. Rita Dove. NoAM

I was in the garden. *Unknown.* ISE

I was in the lane and saw the car pass. A and B. C. H. Sisson. OxBC

I was invested in mother-earth, the crypt of roots. Geoffrey Hill. *Fr.* Mercian Hymns. NoAM

I was just beginning to feel in the mood. An Old Husband Suspects Adultery. Gavin Ewart. NoAM

I was Kallimachos, age five. Lucianus, *tr. fr. Greek by* Peter Jay. GrAn

I was kneeling with my daughter into a chaos. Jungle Gliders. Roger Weingarten. NAmP90

I was led into captivity by the bitch business. Money. C. H. Sisson. IHNG; OxBSP

I was looking for the powerful spring grass, how powerful. Sixty-Six Poems for a Blackfoot Bundle. *Unknown, tr. fr. Blackfoot Indian by* Jerome K. Rothenberg. STP

I Was Made Erect and Lone. Thoreau. PoEL-4

I was making my way home late one night. Aisling. Paul Muldoon. PNI

I was myself blown. For My People. Wendy Rose. CDW

I was never the light lad. The Spawn of Slums. James W. Thompson. BPo

I was never the one to spot him walking. Blueberry Man. David Bergman. GLP

I was not born to Helicon, nor dare. A Gratulatory to Mr. Ben Johnson for His Adopting of Him to Be His Son. Thomas Randolph. BeJo; JCP

I was not chosen to head the dragon list. Tune: "Overtures" — On Myself. Ch'iao Chi, *tr. fr. Chinese by* Sherwin S. S. Fu. SuSp

I was not sorrowful, I could not weep. Spleen. Ernest Dowson. CoGr; MoBrPo; NOBVV

I was not supposed to go places. Why I Like to Go Places: Flagstaff, Arizona — June 1978. Kate Rushin. ETG

I was not train'd in Academic bowers. Written at Cambridge. Charles Lamb. EnRP

I was not — was born — was. Inscribed on a Statue of Hermes. *Unknown, tr. fr. Greek by* Peter Jay. GrAn

I was of delicate mind. I stepped aside for my needs. The Refined Man. Kipling. *Fr.* Epitaphs of the War, 1914–1918. FaBoEE; FaBoTw; NoP; OBWP; PeFWW

I was on a white coast once. Canticle. David Shapiro. TTTS

I was one of those who sees something cross the moon. During the War. Marvin Bell. CAPP

I was out in my kayak. Spring Fiord. *Unknown, tr. fr. Eskimo by* Armand Schwerner. STP

I was out in the country one beautiful night. The Widow's Old Broom. *Unknown.* AmFP

I was out walking an' a-ramblin' one day. The Wild Rippling Water. *Unknown.* FaBoBa

I was parading the côte d'Azur. My Father's Geography. Michael S. Weaver. PBCAP

I was patient at the start. A Touch of Impatience. Fleur Adcock. PWE

I was playing golf that day. *Unknown.* FiBHP

I was playing golf the day. The Englishman's Home. Harry Graham. *Fr.* Some Ruthless Rhymes. CBNP; PeLV

I was promised a horse but what I got instead. Palladas, *tr. fr. Greek by* Tony Harrison. GrAn

I was pulling Veronica out of the lawn when this hornet came. A. R. Ammons. *Fr.* Sphere. NoAM

I was raised up in Louisville, a town you all knew well. Frank James, the Roving Gambler. *Unknown.* AmFP

I was reading about rationalism. The Bat. Jane Kenyon. CrSp

I was round and small like a pearl. *Unknown.* GBP

I was run over by the truth one day. To Whom It May Concern. Adrian Mitchell. IHNG; OBWP

I was running back when I heard him call. Ballad for the Unknown Soldier. Allan Taylor. OBET

I was sad and thoughtful when I met you. Meeting. Charles-Jean Grandmougin, *tr. fr. French by* Philip L. Miller. *Fr.* Poem of a Day. RiWo

I was scared shitless. The Psychiatrist's Office Was Filled with Crazy People. Terence Winch. BCF

I was securing the pin in the diaper. A Visit. George Ella Lyon. CrSp

I was sent in to see her. Tear. Thomas Kinsella. IPY; NOIV

I was setting out from my house. The Dragonfly-Mother. Denise Levertov. InPS; SRLS

I was seventy-seven, come August. The Little Old Lady in Lavender Silk. Dorothy Parker. NBLV

I was sick. Jesus Was Crucified or: It Must Be Deep. Carolyn M. Rodgers. BlSi; PoBA

I Was Sick and in Prison. Jones Very. NOBA

I was sitting behind a somewhat neat old person. Concert. Josephine Miles. NALW

I Was Sitting in McSorley's. E. E. Cummings. NoAM

I was sitting in my study. Papa's Letter. *Unknown.* WeW

I was sitting in my taxi. No Admittance. Chris Daly. NGP

I was sitting there, taking my ease. Cyril Ray. PeLi

I was sixteen years of age. Song Ballet. *Unknown.* AmFP

I was sleeping. A Translation From. Fred Levinson. AmPA

I Was Sleeping Where the Black Oaks Move. Louise Erdrich. FoLa; HATNAP

I was sleepless, I was awake all night. Sleepless. Al-Khansa, *tr. fr. Arabic by* Willis Barnstone. BoWoP

I was smoking a cigarette. The Duet. Ella Wheeler Wilcox. AnAmPo

I was so chill, and overworn, and sad. Anna Wickham. MoBrPo

I was so sick last night I. Morning After. Langston Hughes. Jaz; MoP; NAAL-2; NBLV; NoAM

I was standing in a crap game doing no harm, Baby! You've Been a Good Old Wagon, but You've Done Broke Down. Ben Harney. OBAL

I was standing round a defense town one day. U. A. W.-C. I. O. Bess *and* Baldwin Hawes *and* Baldwin Hawes. SWP

I was standing there. The Oral Tradition. Eavan Boland. NBrP; PBCIP

I was stung by a man-of-war. The Lesson. Larry Rubin. GoYe

I was summoned. I am here. The House of the Apple-Trees. Alice Milligan. VBLP

I was sure I would never get lost/ in the tangled roads of love. Kenrei Mon-in Ukyo no Daibu, *tr. fr. Japanese by* Kenneth Rexroth *and* Ikuko Atsumi. WPJ

I Was Surprised to Find Myself Out Here & Acting like a Crow. *Unknown, tr. fr. Seneca Indian by* Jerome K. Rothenberg *and* Johnny John. STP

I went across the pasture lot. The Cornfield. Elizabeth Madox Roberts. GoJo

I went away. Rafael Alberti, *tr. fr. Spanish by* Mark Strand. *Fr. Metamorphosis of the Carnation.* AnAn

I went away last August. Eat-It-All Elaine. Kaye Starbird. PDV

I went back in the alley. Homecoming. Langston Hughes. SAmP; TRP

I went by footpath and by stile. Paying calls. Thomas Hardy. OBF

I went by on tiptoe. My Grandfather's Death. Vicente Aleixandre, *tr. fr. Spanish by* Stephen Kessler. IMW

I went don the tree-lined street of false gods. The Marvels of the City. Charles Simic. LCAP

I went down by Cascadilla. Cascadilla Falls. A. R. Ammons. NOBA

I went down dock the other day. Looking for a Ship. Harry Aisthorpe. OxBSS

I went down, down, down to the factory. Automation. Joseph Glazer. SWP

I Went Down into the Desert to Meet Elijah. Vachel Lindsay. WGRP

I went down to JOHNNY'S house. *Unknown.* RoPo

I went down to malcolmland. Half Black, Half Blacker. Sterling Plumpp. PoBA

I went down to my garden patch. *Unknown.* RoPo; TLR

I went down to Saint James this morning. St. James Infirmary. *Unknown.* AmFP

I Went Down to the Depot. *Unknown.* AS

I went down to the lily pond. *Unknown.* RoPo

I went down to the river. Life Is Fine. Langston Hughes. NBLV; SAmP

I went down to the river. *Unknown.* RoPo

I went down to the river, poor boy. Bow Down Your Head and Cry. *Unknown.* WTO

I Went Downtown. *Unknown.* ISE; RoPo; TLR

I went for a walk over the dunes again this morning. Corsons Inlet. A. R. Ammons. CoAP; FoLa; MoP; NAAL-2; NoAM; NOBA; NoP; PoE; PPP; VCAP

I went into a public-'ouse to get a pint o' beer. Tommy. Kipling. EBEV; FaBoEH; FaBV; FaPoR; MoBrPo; NoP; OBWP; OHCV; OxAEP-2; OxBTC; PAW; PeVV; PFP; PlP; UV, *ll.* 1–18

I went into my garden to gather some herbs. Sister Bertken, *tr. fr. Dutch by* Jonathan Crewe. WPOW

I went into my grandmother's garden/ And there I found a farden. Swinging. *Unknown.* OxNR

I went into my grandmother's garden,/ And there I found a farthing. A Farthing. *Unknown.* OxNR

I went into my mother as. To the Unborn and Waiting Children. Lucille Clifton. InPK

I Went into the Maverick Bar. Gary Snyder. CAPP; HCAP; MAT; NAAL-2; PoBeRe; PoE; VCAP

I went into the stable, to see what I could see. Old Wichet. *Unknown.* GBP

I went into the wood one day. Fairy Story. Stevie Smith. OBSP

I went my Sunday mornings round. John Clare. NOBVV

I went on Friday afternoons. Au Tombeau de Mon Père. Ronald McCuaig. NOBAu

I went out at daybreak and stood on Primrose Hill. Birds Waking. W. S. Merwin. NOBA

I Went Out into the Garden. Moses ibn Ezra, *tr. fr. Hebrew by* Solomon Solis-Cohen. TrJP

I went out of the conf'rence to get a pint of beer. Mary Wilson. *Fr. Harold Wilson's Selected Poems.* UV

I went out on a frosty morning. Ice Cold. Sean O Riordain, *tr. fr. Irish by* Thomas Kinsella. NOIV

I went out seeking love. More Stanzas Applied to Spiritual Things. St. John of the Cross, *tr. fr. Spanish by* K. Kavanaugh *and* O. Rodrigues. TOF

I went out to the city streets. The Hero. Roger Woddis. FaBoPa

I went out to the hazel wood. The Song of Wandering Aengus. W. B. Yeats. CH; CMoP; CoGr; FaBoCh; FaPoB; GoJo; MAT; MeMBP; MoAB; MoBrPo; NTP; OTCP; PFP; PoEL-5; PoRA; RaBo; SOTW; TFi; TTTS; UnAS

I went to a foreign land to work for money. Sure a Poor Man. *Unknown, tr. fr. Hawaiian by* M. K. Pukui *and* A. L. Korn. WTO

I went to a mausoleum today, and found. Lineage. Frank Bidart. *Fr. Elegy.* HCAP

I went to a party. The Rose on My Cake. Karla Kuskin. TLR

I went to bat for the Lady Chatte. A Lass in Wonderland. Francis Reginald. MoCV

I went to ch'ch, 'tother night. Sister Johnson's Speech. Maggie Pogue Johnson. CBWP-4

I went to court last night. Puck Goes to Court. Fenton Johnson. CDC

I Went to Death. *Unknown.* FaBoRV

I went to Frankfort, and got drunk. Porson's Visit to the Continent. Richard Porson. FaBoCo; FaBoEE (Epigram on an Academic Visit to the Continent.) OxBoLi; PeLV

I went to heaven. Emily Dickinson. FaBV

I went to her who loveth me no more. Arthur O'Shaughnessy. OBNC

I went to London both blithe and gay. The Highwayman. *Unknown.* ECEV

I went to market and bought me a cat. An Old Rhyme. *Unknown.* BoTP

I went to my father's garden. *Unknown.* ISE

I went to Noke. *Unknown.* GBP; OxNR

I went to play with Billy. He. What Johnny Told Me. John Ciardi. TLR

I went to see. Main Character. Jimmy Santiago Baca. NAmP90

I Went to See Irving Babbitt. Richard Eberhart. OBAL

I went to Strasbourg, where I got drunk. On a German Tour. Richard Porson. FiBHP

I went to the animal fair. Animal Fair. *Unknown.* AS; BLPA; FaBoBe; MoShBr; NTCP; RoPo

I went to the dances at Chandlerville. Lucinda Matlock. Edgar Lee Masters. *Fr.* Spoon River Anthology. CMoP; FaBV; FF; HAP; LiTA; LiTM; MoAmPo; MoP; NoAM; NOBA; OxBA

I went to the fields with the leisure I got. The Frightened Ploughman. John Clare. EnVR; PoEL-4

I went to the Garden of Love. The Garden of Love. Blake. *Fr.* Songs of Experience. AWP; EnLoPo; EnRP; FaBV; FHYEP; GBL; HAP; LiTB; MAT; NAEL-2; NoP; OxAEP-2; PoE; RB; SCGP; TEP; TFi; TOF; TRP

I went to the Hotel Broog. A Difference of Zoos. Gregory Corso. VGW

I went to the park. The Balloon. Karla Kuskin. PDV

I went to the river: couldn't get across. Keep It Clean. Charlie Jordan. CBNP

I went to the toad that lies under the wall. *Unknown.* OxNR

I went to the wood and got it. A Thorn. *Unknown.* ReMoGo

I went to the wood of flowers. The Wood of Flowers. James Stephens. BoTP; PDV

I went to turn the grass once after one. The Tuft of Flowers. Robert Frost. AWP; GoYe; LiTA; MoAB; MoAmPo; NAAL-2; OxBA; PAW; PWE

I went to visit Tim last night. He's a. Andrew Greig. *Fr.* Len's Poems. PWE

I went to worship in a house of God. Prayer in a Country Church. Ruth B. Van Dusen. TrPWD

I went up one pair of stairs/ Just like me. Just Like Me. *Unknown.* BoTP; ISE; ReMoGo

I went up to the light of truth as if into a chariot. To Truth. *Unknown, tr. fr. Greek by* J. Rendel Harris. *Fr.* Solomon. WGRP

I went uptown last Saturday night. Blue Monday. *Unknown.* AmFP

I went visiting Miss Melinda. Strawberry Jam. May Justus. FaPON

I went with the Duchess to tea. *At. to* Woodrow Wilson. PeLi

I Wept as I Lay Dreaming. Heine, *tr. fr. German by* John Todhunter. AWP

I were unkind unless that I did shed. Lines on His Companions Who Died in the Northern Seas. Thomas James. NOSC

I what I always imagined. The Face. Susan Mitchell. NAmP90

I whispered, "I am too young." Brown Penny. W. B. Yeats. BoLoP; CBLP; CMoP; ELP; FaBoCh; IIP; LPA; PFP

I, who a decade past had lived recluse. A Lawn-Tennisonian Idyll. *Unknown.* FaBoPa

I who am dead a thousand years/ And wrote this crabbed post-classic screed. To a Poet a Thousand Years Hence. John Heath-Stubbs. OxBC

I who am dead a thousand years/ And wrote this sweet archaic song. To a Poet a Thousand Years Hence. James Elroy Flecker. ChTr; FaBoRV; MoBrPo; PoRA

I, who am known as London, have faced stern times before. London under Bombardment. Greta Briggs. OtMeF; PlP

I who am nothing, and this tissue. Hoc Est Corpus. Alex Comfort. LiTB; LiTM

I who by day am function of the light. J. V. Cunningham. VGW

I, who cut off my sorrows. Akazome Emon, *tr. fr. Japanese by* Kenneth Rexroth *and* Ikuko Atsumi. BoWoP; WPJ; WPOW

I who erewhile the happy Garden sung. Milton. *Fr.* Paradise Regained [*or* Regain'd]. PeECV, *ll.* 1–7

I, who have been so many angels. The Photo That Watches. Carlota Caulfield, *tr. fr. Spanish by* Carol Maier. LoHo

I who have bred only daughters. Woman into Man. Susan Wallbank. AIW

I who have favour'd many, come to be. To the Most Learned, Wise, and Arch-Antiquary, M. John Selden. Robert Herrick. SeCV-1

I who have not sown. I May Reap. Patrick Kavanagh. TIRV

I, who used to score five, even nine times. Philodemus, *tr. fr. Greek by* William Moebius. GrAn

I, who used to ward off the starlings and that snatcher. Antipater of Sidon, *tr. fr. Greek by* Barbara Hughes Fowler. *Fr.* Epigrams. HePo

I whom thou seest with horyloge in hand. Time. Sir Thomas More. *Fr.* Pageant Verses. EnRePo

I whom you touched am other things beside. Atropos. Hilaire Kirkland. *Fr.* Clotho, Lachesis, Atropos. PeNZ

I will accept thy will to do and be. An Bruised Reed Shall He Not Break. Christina Rossetti. OxAEP-2

I will admit freely that it hurt. Small Talk in a Garden. O. B. Hardison, Jr. CRP

I will always be me, I will always be new! (*LL*) I Am Cherry Alive. Delmore Schwartz. NTP; TTTS

I will arise and go now, and go to Innisfree. The Lake Isle of Innisfree. W. B. Yeats. ArNa; ClHu; CMoP; CoGr; EBEvV; FaBoPP; FaBV; FaPoB; FaPON; FaPoR; HeIP; IIP; InPK; InPS; LiTM; MeMBP; MoAB; MoBrPo; MoP; NAEL-2; NoAM; NOBE; NoP; NTP; OBEV; OHCV; OxAEP-2; OxBTC; PlP; PoE; Poetr; PoRA; PrIm; TEP; TFi; TrGrPo; UV

I will arise and go now, and go to Inverness. The Cockney of the North. Harry Graham. UV

I Will Be. E. E. Cummings. VGW

I will be home in two months and look you in the eyes. (*LL*) Message. Allen Ginsberg. NeAP; VGW

I will be more to you than to any of the rest. (*LL*) Native Moments. Walt Whitman. MeMAP; OPOP; OxBA

I will be patient while my Lord. Cinderella. Ruby C. Saunders. BlSi

I will be the gladdest thing. Afternoon on a Hill. Edna St. Vincent Millay. AnAmPo; BoTP; FaPON; GrPl; ImGa; NTCP; OBCA; OxBA; PDV; TTTS

I will be your lover. The Bush Speaks. Ernest G. Moll. NOBAu

I will be your mouth now, to do your singing. A Funeral Plainsong from a Younger Woman to an Older Woman. Judy Grahn. GLP

I will begin to delineate the green family. The Green Family. Colleen Thibaudeau. NOBC

I Will Believe. William H. Roberts. BLRP

I will build my fire today. A Charm for Lighting the Fire. *Unknown, tr. fr. Irish by* Thomas Kinsella. NOIV

I will call you. My Friend the Wind. King D. Kuka. VoR

I will carry my coat and not put on my belt. *Unknown, tr. by* Arthur Waley. *Fr.* Tzu Yeh Songs. BoWoP

I will confess. An Hymn to Love. Robert Herrick. NOSC

I will consider the outnumbering dead. Merlin. Geoffrey Hill. InPK; TRP

I will die in Miami in the sun. Variations on a Text by Vallejo. Donald Justice. CAPP; NoAM; VCAP

I will dip my soul. Heine. RiWo

I will dream it again. (*LL*) Wormwood. Thomas Kinsella. CIP; PBCIP

I will dress myself in green. The Favorite Color. Wilhelm Müller, *tr. fr. German by* Philip L. Miller. *Fr.* Beautiful Maid of the Mill, The. RiWo

I will drink to your health, sweet Amy. To Amy. J. Gordon. OBAL

I will duly pass the day O my mother, and duly return to you. (*LL*) The Sleepers. Walt Whitman. AmPP; NAAL-1

I will enjoy thee now, my Celia, come. A Rapture. Thomas Carew. BeJo; CaPo; ErPo; JCP; NAEL-1; OAEL-1; OxAEP-1; SeCP

I will exchange a city for a sunset. Barter. Marie Blake. PoToHe

I will find that it's still there. (*LL*) Mementos, I. W. D. Snodgrass. FF; MoAmPo; UnPo; VCAP

I will follow. (*LL*) Grandfather. Lance Henson. CDW; HATNAP

I Will Give My Love an Apple without E'er a Core. *Unknown.* RB

I Will Go Back to the Great Sweet Mother. Swinburne. *Fr.* Triumph of Time, The. NAEL-2

I Will Go into the Ghetto. Charles Reznikoff. VGW

I Will Go with My Father a-Ploughing. Joseph Campbell. FaPON

I will go with the first air of morning. Fishing. Dorothy Wellesley. OBMV

I will grieve alone. In Response to a Rumor That the Oldest Whorehouse in Wheeling, West Virginia, Has Been Condemned. James Wright. CAPP; CoAP; NNaP; NoAM; VCAP

I will haunt these States. A Vow. Allen Ginsberg. OBWP

I will have all my beds blown up, not stuft. Ben Jonson. *Fr.* Alchemist, The. EBEV; FaBoBl

I Will Have the Whetstone. *Unknown.* FaBoNo; GBP

I will have the whetstone and I may. (*LL*) I Will Have the Whetstone. *Unknown.* FaBoNo; GBP

I will have to accept women. This Form of Life Needs Sex. Allen Ginsberg. NNaP

I will have to ask for my slum location again. When I Lost Slum Life. Sipho Sepamla. PeSAV

I will have to tell you what it is like. What It Is Like. Gerald Stern. NAmP90

I will have you. (*LL*) Lilies are white. *Unknown.* BoTP; OxNR

I will hold beauty as a shield against despair. Beauty as a Shield. Elsie Robinson. BLPA; PoToHe

I will in Cassio's lodging lose this napkin. Shakespeare. *Fr.* Othello. OxAEP-1

I will invest in a gun. (*LL*) A Round House. Matthew Sweeney. IB

I Will Keep Christmas. P. A. Ropes. BoTP

I will keep the fire of hope ever burning on the altar of my soul. Realization. Ananda Acharya. WGRP

I will lament, and love. (*LL*) Bitter-sweet. George Herbert. FHYEP; GeHe; NOBE; NoP; OxBSP; TrPWD

I will lay down my silk robe. The Good Old Dog. Toi Derricotte. InPS

I will leave papa to name her. (*LL*) Choosing a Name. Charles Lamb *and* Mary Lamb. OxBChV

I will lift up mine eyes unto the hills. Bible, *O.T., tr. fr. German by* Paul Gerhardt. *Fr.* Psalms. AWP; FaPON
   (I to the hills lift up mine eyes.) OBCA
   (121st Psalm of David, The.) GePo
   (Pilgrim's Song, The.) WGRP
   (Song of Trust, A.) TrGrPo

I Will Live and Survive. Irina Ratushinskaya, *tr. fr. Russian by* David McDuff. AIW; PWE

I will live in Ringsend. Ringsend. Oliver St. John Gogarty. OBMV; OxBTC; PeIV

I Will Look Up. Josephine D. Henderson Heard. CBWP-4

I will look with detachment. On Being Head of the English Department. Pinkie Gordon Lane. BlSi

I will lose you. It is written. The Sweater. Gregory Orr. TRP

I will make love. *Unknown, tr. fr. Spanish by* Willis Barnstone. BoWoP

I will make you brooches and toys for your delight. Romance. Robert Louis Stevenson. BLPL; EBVV; MoBrPo; OBEV; OtMeF; TrGrPo
   (My Valentine, *abr. vers.*) FaPON; GrPl
   (Song of a Traveller, The.) BoTP

I will never come back to you. (*LL*) You Thought I Was That Type. "Anna Akhmatova." LPA, *tr. by* Richard McKane; VBLP

"I will never eate nor drinke," Robin Hood said. Robin Hood's Death. *Unknown.* ESPB

I will never forget my only beating. The Beating. Richard Katrovas. NAmP90

I will no longer kiss. Robert Herrick. *Fr.* On Himself[e]. CaPo

I will not be inhabited. The Turtle's Belly. Ellen Pearce. IHMS

I will not, cannot go. (*LL*) Night Is Darkening round Me. Emily Brontë. MeMBP; NOBVV; OBNC; PoEL-5

I will not climb these heights again. Saint Colm-Cille and the Cairn of Farewell. John Irvine. TIRV

I will not die for you. *Unknown, tr. fr. Irish by* Thomas Kinsella. NOIV

I will not doubt, though all my ships at sea. Faith. Ella Wheeler Wilcox. BLRP; PoToHe

I will not endow you with a false glow. Miserere. William Pillen. BTR

I will not have you think me less. A Jewish Poet Counsels a King. Santob de Carrion, *tr. fr. Spanish.* *Fr.* Consejos y Documentos al Rey Dom Pedro. TrJP

I Will Not Let Thee Go. Robert Bridges. BeLS; BLPL; CMoP; EnLoPo; FaBoBe; OBNC

I will not live without him. (*LL*) Liadan Laments Cuirithir. *Unknown.* BIrV; PBWP

I will not perturbate. To the Dead Cardinal of Westminster. Francis Thompson. PeVV

I will not play at tug o' war. Hug o' War. Shel Silverstein. NTCP

I will not say to you, "This is the Way; walk in it." To My Son. *Unknown.* PoLF

I will not shut me from my kind. Tennyson. *Fr.* In Memoriam A. H. H. EBVV, *abr.*; EnVR; FHYEP; OAEL-2, *abr.*; PeECV, *abr.*

I Will Not Tell the Secrets. Wilfrid Scawen Blunt. *Fr.* Esther [a Young Man's Tragedy]. Son

I will not toy with it nor bend an inch. The White City. Claude McKay. BPo; NoAM; RaBo; TAP

I will not travel tonight. God the Father. Richard Ryan. PeIV

I will not try to reach again. The Evenlode. Hilaire Belloc. OxAEP-2

I will not weep, for 'twere as great a sin. An Elegy. Henry King. (Elegy upon S[ir] W[alter] R[aleigh], An.) NOSC

I will now only believe that he has died. Now I Will Only Believe. B. W. Vilakazi. PeSAV

I will obey you to my utmost power. To a Lady, Who Desired Me Not To Be in Love with Her. Lord Cutts. NOSC

I will outlive oppressors. (*LL*) Determination. John Henrik Clarke. PoBA

I will palm no more puns upon you. (*LL*) Epistle, from Algiers, to Horace Smith. Thomas Campbell. OBTV

I will pluck from my tree a cherry-blossom wand. The Cherry-Blossom Wand. Anna Wickham. MoBrPo

I will praise thee, O Lord, with my whole heart. Bible, *O.T., paraphrased by Sir Thomas Wyatt. Fr. Psalms.*
(I Will Sing Praise.) FaPON

I will pursue him relentlessly through all Spain. (*LL*) A Walk. Fernando Periquet Y Zuaznabar. RiWo

I Will Put Chaos into Fourteen Lines. Edna St. Vincent Millay. Son

"I will put upon you the Telephone Curse," said the witch. The Witch of East Seventy-second Street. Morris Bishop. NYBP

I will reach into the grab-bag of unconscious things. Private Pantomime. Ruth Stone. PoA

I will remember well. To the Dead Owner of a Gym. Thom Gunn. PFL

I will remember you on Bloom Street. Bloom Street. Angela McCabe. AmPA

I will rise. Wine Bowl. Hilda Doolittle ("H. D."). NoP

I will roar and squander. Folly's Song. Thomas Dekker *and others. NOSC*

I will sing a song,/ A song that is strong. My Breath. Orpingalik, *tr. fr. Eskimo by K. Rasmussen.* WTO

I will sing a song of battle. The Song of Chess. *At. to* Abraham ibn Ezra Abraham Ibn Ezra, *tr. fr. Hebrew by Nina Davis Salaman.* TrJP

I will sing, if ye will hearken. The Laird o' Logie. *Unknown.* CH; ESPB

I will sing no more songs! O'Bruadair. David O'Bruadair, *tr. fr. Irish by* James Stephens. BIrV

I will sing of the sons of Atreus. To His Lyre. Franz von Bruchmann, *tr. fr. German by* Philip L. Miller. RiWo

I will sing of the well-founded Earth. *Unknown.* EaPr, *ad. by* Elizabeth Roberts

I Will Sing Praise. Bible, *O.T., paraphrased by* Sir Thomas Wyatt. *See* I will praise thee, O Lord, with my whole heart.

I will sing unto the Lord, for he hath triumphed gloriously. Exodus. Bible, *O.T. Fr. Exodus.* PAW
(Triumphal Chant.) TrGrPo

I will sing you a song of that beautiful land. Home of the Soul. Ellen M. Huntington Gates. BLRP

I will speak about women of letters, for I'm in the racket. Carolyn Kizer. *Fr. Pro Femina.* CAPP; MAT; NALW; NMM

I will teach you my townspeople. Tract. William Carlos Williams. BLPL; DL; FF; LiTA; LiTM; MeMAP; MoAB; MoAmPo; MoP; NoAM; NOBA; SAmP; TAP; TrGrPo; TwCP; VGW

I will teach you to become American, my students. Notes for a Lecture. David Ignatow. NNaP

I will tell a true tale of myself. Seafarer. *Unknown, tr. by* Kemp Malone. PoE

I will tell you of a fellow. Common Bill. *Unknown.* AS

I will tell you of a gallant soldier. The Soldier's Wooing. *Unknown.* AmFP

I will track you down the years. Quest. Naomi Long Madgett. BPo

I will visit/ Unknown woman. Spirit Song. *Unknown, tr. fr. Eskimo.* WTO

I will walk with a lover of wisdom. Little Elegy. Denis Devlin. NOIV

I will write a poem about nothing. William of Aquitaine, *tr. fr. French.* CBNP

I Will Write Songs against You. Charles Reznikoff. VGW

I will write you a letter. I Think. James Schuyler. TTTS

I, Willie Wastle. *Unknown.* OxNR

I wish a cricket in a wicker boat. A Japanese Birthday Wish. Thomas Burnett Swann. GoYe

I wish all the/ mandragona. Blue Funk. Joel Oppenheimer. NeAP

I wish, God, for some end I do not will. Elizabeth Jennings. *Fr. Sonnets of Michelangelo, The.* PeECV; TOF

I wish, how I wish that I had a little house. The Shiny Little House. Nancy M. Hayes. BoTP

I wish I could be. Theophanes, *tr. fr. Greek by* Peter Jay. GrAn

I wish I could lend a coat. Akahito, *tr. by* Arthur Waley. *Fr. Manyo Shu,* Part 2 of 4. AWP

I Wish I Could Remember. Christina Rossetti. *Fr. Monna Innominata.* Son

I wish I could remember the first day. I Wish I Could Remember. Christina Rossetti. *Fr. Monna Innominata.* Son
(First Day, The.) BLPL; BoLoP; FaBoBe; GBL; LPA

I wish I could rest my mind. Be Still Heart. Nilene O. A. Foxworth. AIW

I wish I had a man any man. Chiaroscuro. Carole Bergé. ErPo

I wish I had an aeroplane. A Penny Wish. Irene Thompson. BoTP

I wish I had been born beside a river. The Upper Canadian. James Reaney. NOBC

I wish I had the voice of Homer. Cancer's a Funny Thing. J. B. S. Haldane. OxBTC

I wish I lived in a caravan. The Pedlar's Caravan. William Brighty Rands. BoTP; OxBChV

I wish I loved the human race. Wishes of an Elderly Man. Sir Walter Alexander Raleigh. FaBoCh; FaBoCo; FaBoEE; FiBHP; NBLV; NOBL; NTP; PeLV

I wish I owned a Dior dress. Reflections at Dawn. Phyllis McGinley. FiBHP; NBLV; NOBL

I wish I thought What Jolly Fun! (*LL*) Wishes of an Elderly Man. Sir Walter Alexander Raleigh. FaBoCh; FaBoCo; FaBoEE; FiBHP; NBLV; NOBL; NTP; PeLV

I Wish I Was a Grown Up Man. Maggie Pogue Johnson. CBWP-4

I Wish I Was a Little Bird. *Unknown.* AS

I Wish I Was a Mole in the Ground. *Unknown.* AmFP

I Wish I Was by That Dim Lake. Thomas Moore. PoEL-4

I wish I was in de land ob cotton. Dixie. Daniel Decatur Emmett. AnAmPo; FaPON; TrGrPo

I Wish I Was Single Again. *Unknown.* AmFP, *diff. vers.;* AS

I wish I was where I would be. John Clare. NOBVV

I wish I were a fish. The Lover in all Shapes. Goethe, *tr. fr. German by* Philip L. Miller. RiWo

I wish I were an Emperor. Wishes. F. Rogers. BoTP

I wish I were close. Akahito, *tr. fr. Japanese by* Kenneth Rexroth. HoPM; PoBeRe; UnAS

I Wish I Were ("I wish I were a/ Elephantiaphus.") *Unknown.* FaBoNo; OxBoLi

I Wish I Were [*or* Was] Single Again. *Unknown.* AmFP, 2 *vers.;* AS

I wish I were the wind, and you. *Unknown, tr. fr. Greek by* Barriss Mills. GrAn

I wish I were where Helen lies. Helen of Kirconnell. *Unknown.* AWP; CH; ELP; ImPo; LiTB; OBEV; SCGP
(Fair Helen.) GTBS; GTBS-P

I Wish, I Wish. *Unknown.* OBET

I wish, I *wish* he'd stay away! (*LL*) The Little Man Who Wasn't There. Hughes Mearns. FaPON

I wish it soon may have a Better. (*LL*) Verses on the Death of Dr. Swift, D.S.P.D., Occasioned by Reading a Maxim in Rochefoucauld. Swift. NOEC; OBF, *abr.;* PoEL-3; TEP

I wish not Thasos rich in mines. Mimnermus Incert. Walter Savage Landor. PoEL-4

I wish not to lie here. Iona; the Graves of the Kings. Robinson Jeffers. PrIm

I wish, O son of the Living God. The Wish of Manchin of Liath. *Unknown, tr. fr. Irish by* Kenneth Jackson.
(Hermit's Song, The.) TIRV, *tr. by* Kuno Meyer

I wish sometimes, although a worthlesse thing. Giles Fletcher the Elder. *Fr. Licia.* AAS

I wish that I could get in line. They Don't Speak English in Paris. Ogden Nash. OBAL

I wish that I could talk with her again. Mother. Bea Liu. LoHo

I wish that I were dead. (*LL*) La Vie C'est la Vie. Jessie Redmond Fauset. CDC; PoNe

I wish that my room had a floor. Gelett Burgess. FiBHP; InvP; OBCA; PeLi

I wish that there were some wonderful place. The Land of Beginning Again. Louisa Fletcher. BLPA

I wish that when you died last May. May and Death. Robert Browning. FaBoRV; IMW; NOBE

I wish the earth was turned over. The Wish. Liu Sha-ho, *tr. fr. Chinese. Fr. Family of Plants, A.* LHF, *tr. by* Hualing Nieh

I wish the rent. Little Lyric (of Great Importance). Langston Hughes. NBLV; OBAL

I wish there were a touch of these boats about my life. Boat Poem. Bernard Spencer. FaBoTw; OxBTC

I wish they were/ Grass. (*LL*) Late November in a Field. James Wright. CAPP; NAAL-2; NNaP

I wish they would hurry up their trip to Mars. A Projection. Reed Whittemore. AiP

I wish to be given beautiful things this Christmas. Six Things for Christmas. John May. Mes

"I wish to buy a dog," she said. On Buying a Dog. Edgar Klauber. NTCP

I wish to God I'd been cremated. (*LL*) The Author's Epitaph. *Unknown.* FiBHP

I wish to God my child was born. *Unknown.* AmFP

I wish to make my sermon brief. Praise of Little Women. Juan Ruiz, Archpriest of Hita, *tr. fr. Spanish by* Longfellow. AWP

I wish to paint my eyes. *Unknown, tr. fr. Egyptian hieroglyphics by* Willis Barnstone. BoWoP; UnAS

I wish we'd gone back. Hedgeapple. Marvin Bell. FoLa

I wish you for your birthday as you are. Moving In. Karl Shapiro. NAs

I wish you triumphs that are yours already. For Marianne Moore's Birthday. Kay Boyle. NMM

I wott what I doo meane. (*LL*) Me list no more to sing. Sir Thomas Wyatt. AAS; SiPS

I would ask of you, my darling. Will You Love Me When I'm Old? *Unknown.* BLPA; BLPL; FaBoBe

I Would Be a Fool To Want More Children. Alta. MDDM

I would be a soft pink rose. *Unknown, tr. fr. Greek by* Sam Hamill. InMo

I Would Be Clad in Christ's Skin. *Unknown.* EnVB; MeEL; MiEL

I would be ignorant as the dawn. The Dawn. W. B. Yeats. PFP

I would be married, but I'd have no wife. On Marriage. Richard Crashaw. FaBoEE

I would be one with the morning. Desire. Marjorie Marshall. ShDr

I would be ready, Lord. Ready. Margaret Junkin Preston. PWR

I Would Be True. Howard Arnold Walter. *See* I would be true, for there are those who trust me.

I would be true, for there are those who trust me. My Creed. Howard Arnold Walter. PoLF; WBLP
    (I Would Be True.) PoToHe

I would be wandering in distant fields. In Bondage. Claude McKay. PoBA

I would be-war. (*LL*) I loved a child of this countrie. *Unknown.* GBL; PBWP

I would but I can't. *Unknown, tr. fr. Greek by* Thomas Meyer. GrAn

I would carve it on the bark of every tree. Impatience. Wilhelm Müller, *tr. fr. German by* Philip L. Miller. *Fr.* Beautiful Maid of the Mill, The. RiWo

I would die. (*LL*) I want to lie down in dappled leaf-shade. "Antler." EaPr

"I would doubt," said the Bishop of Balham. Terence Rattigan. PeLi

I would enquire of you. The Poet Lets His Tongue Hang Down. Edward Dorn. PRA

I would fain know what she hath deserved. (*LL*) They Flee [*or* Fle] from Me That Sometime Did Me Seek [*or* Seke]. Sir Thomas Wyatt. BLPL; CBLP; ClHu; EnLoPo; EnRePo; FaBoPV; FF; GGP; HAP; HeIL; HeIP; ImPo; InPK; LiTB; LPA; NAEL-1; NoP; NoSic; OAEL-1; OPOP; OxBC; PoE; PPP; PrIm; SCV; SiPS; SiPSBD; TEP; TFi; TRP

I would follow it, I think. (*LL*) So lonely am I. Ono no Komachi. BoWoP; PBWP

I would forget how to sing. (*LL*) The Musician. Joseph Freiherr von Eichendorff. RiWo

I would give you. Poem . . . For a Lover. Mae V. Cowdery. ShDr

I would have been surprised, but I had seen him. The Messenger. Grace Schulman. AnAn

I would have gone; God bade me stay. Weary in Well-doing. Christina Rossetti. TrPWD

I would he were a young gazelle. (*LL*) 'Twas Ever Thus. Henry S. Leigh. FaBoCo; FaBoPa

I would I had thrust my hands of flesh. Edmund Pollard. Edgar Lee Masters. *Fr.* Spoon River Anthology. ErPo

I Would I Might Forget That I Am I. George Santayana. AWP

I would I were a bird so free. *Unknown, tr. fr. Italian by* John Addington Symonds. *Fr.* Popular Songs of Tuscany. AWP

I Would I Were Actaeon. At. to ———— Bewe. EIL; NoSic

I would, if I could. Mother Goose. OxNR

I would immortalize these nymphs: so bright. L'Après-Midi d'un Faune. Stéphane Mallarmé, *tr. fr. French by* Aldous Huxley. AWP

I would in rich and golden coloured raine. Thomas Lodge. *Fr.* Phyllis. AAS; ESo

I Would It Were Not As It Is. Sir Edward Dyer. SCGP

I would lie low — the ground on which men tread. The Earth. Jones Very. AnAmPo; OxBA

I would like all things to be free of me. Proof. Brendan Kennelly. CIP; PBCIP

I Would Like My Love to Die. Samuel Beckett, *tr. fr. French.* BIrV; CIP; IIP; NOIV

I would like to be as mobile as my mind. Evaporation Poems. Kathleen Norris. IHMS

I would like to be that elderly Chinese gentleman. Dreaming in the Shanghai Restaurant. D. J. Enright. OBTV

I Would Like To Describe. Zbigniew Herbert, *tr. fr. Polish by* Czeslaw Milosz. PoSu

I would like to describe the simplest emotion. I Would Like To Describe. Zbigniew Herbert, *tr. fr. Polish by* Czeslaw Milosz. PoSu

I would like to dispense with certain sorrows. Black Cross. Reed Whittemore. ArOW

I would like to dive. The Diver. W. W. Eustace Ross. NOBC

I would like to give you. Unposted Birthday Card. Norman MacCaig. NAs

I would like to go out into the world. The Evil Color. Wilhelm Müller, *tr. fr. German by* Philip L. Miller. *Fr.* Beautiful Maid of the Mill, The. RiWo

I would like to let things be. Facts of Life, Ballymoney. Eamon Grennan. PBCIP

I would like/ to make. Oh — Yeah! Sharon Scott. JB

I would like to remind/ the management. The Music Crept by Us. Leonard Cohen. FF

I would like to scream but there is no one to hear. Setting/ Slow Drag. Carolyn M. Rodgers. JB

I would like to sleep with deer. A Moral Poem Freely Accepted from Sappho. James Wright. CAPP

I would like to walk over. Frozen. Anthony Barnett. VaA

I would like to watch you sleeping. Variation on the Word *Sleep*. Margaret Atwood. NOBC

I Would Like You for a Comrade. Edward Abbott Parry. OxBChV

I would listen even again to that labouring breath. (*LL*) Remorse. Sir John Betjeman. MoBrPo; OxBSP

I would live all my life in nonchalance and insouiance. Introspective Reflection. Ogden Nash. NBLV

I would live for a day and a night. The Song-Maker. Anna Wickham. MoBrPo

I would look up-and-laugh-and love-and lift. (*LL*) My Creed. Howard Arnold Walter. PoLF; WBLP

I would make a vessel, ship, a boat. Calvary. Padraig de Brun, *tr. fr. Irish by* Máire Mhac an tSaoi. TIRV

I would make it shine. (*LL*) The Groves of Blarney. Richard Alfred Millikin. FaBoPP; OxBoLi; PeIV

I would my guests should praise it, not the cooks. (*LL*) Critics. Martial. AWP

I would need a distance of a hundred years. Classic Verses. Rade Drainac, *tr. fr. Serbo-Croatian by* Charles Simic. HSix

I would never marry a young girl or an old woman. Honestus, *tr. fr. Greek by* Edwin Morgan. GrAn

I would not alter thy cold eyes. Flos Lunae. Ernest Dowson. OBMV; PeVV

I would not ask Thee that my days. A Humble Heart. Alfred Norris. PWR
    (Prayer for Faith.) BLRP

I would not be the moon, the sickly thing. In Dispraise of the Moon. Mary Elizabeth Coleridge. BoNaP; CH

I would not feign a single sigh. John Clare. GBL

I would not have a god come in. Mastery. Sara Teasdale. WGRP

I Would Not Live Alway. William Augustus Mühlenberg. AH

I would not marry a blacksmith. Soldier Boy for Me. *Unknown.* AmFP

I would not paint — a picture. Emily Dickinson. NAAL-1; NOBA; TRP

I would not tell them why I had smashed the window. "In This House, There Shall Be No Idols." Carolyn M. Rodgers. JB

I would not write a lament for you. Salt. Anne Hartigan. CIP

I would prefer. The Counterfeiter. Michael Davitt, *tr. fr. Irish by* Philip Casey. PBCIP

I would prefer to live quietly in silks. Running through Sleep. Kathleen Norris. IHMS

I would rid myself of an old way of life. Diogenes. A. R. D. Fairburn. PeNZ

I would set all things whatsoever front to back. Wyndham Lewis. *Fr.* One-Way Song. CTC

I would speak of that grief. Torch Songs. Robert Wrigley. Jaz

I would tell a marvelous vision. The Dream of the Cross. *Unknown, tr. fr. Anglo-Saxon by* Sally Purcell. EBEV

I would that all men my hard case would know. Behold the Deeds! H. C. Bunner. NBLV

I would that even now. Princess Shoku, *tr. fr. Japanese by* Curtis Hidden Page. *Fr.* Hyaku-Nin-Isshu. AWP

I would that folk forgot me quite. Tess's Lament. Thomas Hardy. FaBoTw; FaBoVe; TEP

I would that we were, my beloved, white birds on the foam of the sea. The White Birds. W. B. Yeats. UnAS

I would the gift I offer here. Whittier. *Fr.* Songs of Labor. OxBA

I would the God of Love would die. To His Mistress. James Shirley. BeJo

I would thou wert not fair, or I were wise. Nicholas Breton. *Fr.* Strange Fortunes of Two Excellent Princes, The. EIL; InvP

I would to heaven that I were so much clay. Byron. *Fr.* Don Juan. CTC; NAEL-2; NOBL; NoP; OAEL-2; OxBSP; PrIm

I Would Visit Him in the Corner. Alberto A. Ríos. AfAz

I would wear one by my side. (*LL*) If wishes were horses. Mother Goose. FaBoBe; OxNR; ReMoGo

I would worship if I could. Great Spaces. Howard Moss. TwCP

I Wouldn't. John Ciardi. TLR

I Wouldn't Be a Methodist. Rod Jellema. *Fr.* Four Voices Ending on Some Lines from Old Jazz Records. Jaz

Ich Weiss Nicht Was Soll es Bedeuten. Heine, *tr. fr. German by* Alexander Macmillan. AWP

Ich wünscht', ich wäre ein Vöglein. The Bird. Louis Simpson. ArOW; BTR

Ichabod. Whittier. AnAmPo; LiTA; NAAL-1; NOBA; OxBA; PAH; PoEL-4; TAP

Ichabod! The Glory Has Departed. Ludwig Uhland, *tr. fr. German by* James Clarence Mangan. AWP

Icham of Irlaunde. *Unknown. See* Ich am of Irlaunde/ Ant of the holy londe of irlonde.

Icham of Irlaunde. *Unknown. See* I am of Ireland.

Ichot a burde in a bour ase beryl so bright. *Unknown.* MiEL

Ichot a burde in boure bryht. Blow, Northern Wind. *Unknown.* GBL; OBEV

(Love for a Beautiful Lady.) MeEL

Ichthycide. Joe Rosenblatt. NOBC

Ichthyos, the sign of Jesus. (*LL*) Fish Shop Windows. Geoffrey Dutton. NOBAu

Icicles. Robert Pinsky. SM

Icicles, An. *Unknown. See* Lives in winter.

Icicles upon the pane, The. February. H. Cordelia Ray. CBWP-3

Ickle ockle, blue bockle. *Unknown.* OxNR

Icon. Ephim G. Fogel. BTR

Iconoclast, The. Rose Terry Cooke. AmWP

Icons. Miriam Waddington. NOBC

Icos. Charles Tomlinson. GTBS-P

Icy, empty dawn cracks in the fields, The. Pacifists. George Woodcock. NOBC

Icy evil that struck his father down, The. El-Hajj Malik El-Shabazz. Robert Hayden. PoBA

Id. Harry Clifton. PBCIP

I'd a dream to-night. Mater Dolorosa. William Barnes. CH; NOBE; OBEV

I'd almost know, the nights I snuck in late. Fifteen to Eighteen. Marilyn Hacker. GLP

I'd already lost my hair. Now my sun. The Corn. Daniel David Moses. HATNAP

I'd been looking out for a loop of swallows. Neighbors. Maura Dooley. PWE

I'd been on duty from two till four. Stand-to: Good Friday Morning. Siegfried Sassoon. FaBoTw

I'd build a house with windows. Skycoast. Samuel Hazo. GrPl

I'd Choose to Be a Daisy. *Unknown.* BoTP

I'd do it all over again. (*LL*) The Unknown Soldier. Billy Rose. BLPA

I'd draw all this into a fine element, — a color. The Rug. Michael McClure. NeAP

I'd gie them a' to King Charlie.' (*LL*) The Bonnie House o' Airlie. *Unknown.* ESPB; OBEV; OxBB; OxBS

I'd give it five stars. Revelation: The Movie. Elton Glaser. PBCAP

I'd Have You, Quoth He. *Unknown.* ErPo; FF

I'd lay me doune and dee. (*LL*) Annie Laurie. William Douglas, *rev. by* Lady Jane Scott. FaBoBe; FaBV; GN; ImPo; ScCV; WBLP

I'd Leave. Andrew Lang. FaPON

I'd like a different dog. Dogs and Weather. Winifred Welles. FaPON

I'd Like to Be a Lighthouse. Rachel Field. PDV

I'd like to be the sort of friend that you have been to me. A Friend's Greeting. Edgar A. Guest. BLPA; BLPL

I'd like to have a word. The Book of Lies. James Tate. SM

I'd like to hear a sermon done. S.P.C.A. Sermon. Stuart Hemsley. FiBHP

I'd like to live with you. Marina Tsvetayeva, *tr. fr. Russian by* Paul Schmidt. BoWoP

I'd like to peddle toy balloons. The Balloon Seller. Elizabeth Fleming. BoTP

I'd like to/ pull. The Intelligent Sheepman and the New Cars. William Carlos Williams. OBAL

I'd like to run like a rabbit in hops. Rabbit. Tom Robinson. FaPON

I'd Love to Be a Fairy's Child. Robert Graves. BoTP; FaPON; PDV

I'd love to be a fairy's child. (*LL*) I'd Love to Be a Fairy's Child. Robert Graves. BoTP; FaPON; PDV

I'd love to give a party. A Wish. Elizabeth Gould. BoTP

I'd make a bed for you. Labasheedy (the Silken Bed). Nuala Ni Dhomhnaill, *tr. fr. Irish by the Author.* CIP; VBLP

I'd meet the wise men going in. (*LL*) Christmas Morning. Elizabeth Madox Roberts. MoAmPo; PChr

I'd never seen pain so bland. Bud Powell, Paris, 1959. William Matthews. Jaz

I'd not thought of her for twenty years. Daphne Morse. Pamela Gillilan. PWE

I'd oft heard tell of this Sledburn fair. Sledburn Fair. *Unknown.* CH

I'd often seen before. The Sheaf. Andrew Young. ChTr

I'd rather be loved, and love, than be Shakespeare. Portrait: My Wife. John Holmes. LPA; UnAS

I'd rather be the ship that sails. The Ship That Sails. *Unknown.* PoToHe

I'd rather gather. (*LL*) Than mind a child/ That yelps like this/ I'd all day work. *Unknown.* Mes

I'd rather have fingers than toes. On Digital Extremities. Gelett Burgess. FaPON; PeLi

I'd rather have the thought of you. Choice. Angela Morgan. PoLF

I'd rather listen to a flute. Samuel Hoffenstein. FiBHP

I'd *rather* you'd not go unless you must. (*LL*) A Servant to Servants. Robert Frost. CMoP; NAAL-2

I'd rock my own sweet childie to rest in a cradle of gold on a bough of the willow. Irish Lullaby. A. P. Graves. IIP

I'd run about/ on the desert. Her Elegy. *Unknown, tr. fr. Papago Indian.* BoWoP, *tr. by* Ruth Underhill; STP, *tr. by* Armand Schwerner

I'd sit inside the abandoned shack all morning. About a Year After He Got Married He Would Sit Alone in an Abandoned Shack in a Cotton Field Enjoying Himself. James Whitehead. MT

I'd sleep all the winter in a big fur bed. (*LL*) Furry Bear. A. A. Milne. SiSoPo

I'd sooner eat the plate! (*LL*) Mummy Slept Late and Daddy Fixed Breakfast. John Ciardi. PDV

I'd stop off at kenny's. After Work. Todd Moore. NGP

I'd thwack you well to cure your pride, my Woman of Three Cows! (*LL*) The Woman of Three Cows. *Unknown.* EnRP; NOIV; PeIV

I'd toddle safely home and die — in bed. (*LL*) Base Details. Siegfried Sassoon. FF; MoBrPo; OxBSP; PeFWW; PlP

I'd wake up starved on the day of the match. Reflections on Hillsborough in Memoriam. T. H. Naisby. NOBAu

I'd watched the sorrow of the evening sky. Pine-Trees and the Sky: Evening. Rupert Brooke. PFP

I'd wave the gnats away and try. Crew Practice on Lake Bled, in Jugoslavia. James Scully. NYBP

I'd weave a wreath for those who fought. Through Fire in Mobile Bay. *Unknown.* PAH

I'd wed you without herds, without money, or rich array. Cashel of Munster. *At. to* William English, *tr. fr. Irish by* Sir Samuel Ferguson. BIrV; GBL; OBEV; PeIV

Idaho. *Unknown.* GBP

Idbury bells are ringing. Country Thought. Sylvia Townsend Warner. MoBrPo

Idea. Michael Drayton. ESo

Sels.

Another to the River Ankor. NOSC

"As Love and I, late harboured in one inn." NoSic

"As other men, so I myself do muse." JCP; NOSC; NoSic; Son

Calling to [my] mind [or minde] since first my love begun. EnRePo; NOBE; PoEL-2; SCGP

Cupid, Dumb Idol. EnRePo

"Deare [*or* Dear], why should you command [*or* commaund] me to my rest." AAS; NOBE; PoEL-2; Son

(Night and Day.) LiTB

(Sonnet: "Dear [*or* Deere], why should you command me to my rest.") EIL

"Evil [*or* Evill] spirit, your beauty, haunts me still, An." AAS; EIL; GBL; NOBE; NoSic

His Remedie for Love. AAS

How Many Paltry, Foolish, Painted Things. AAS; EnLoPo; EnRePo; GBL; HAP; HeIP; NAEL-1; NIP; NoP; NOSC; OAEL-1; PrIm; SCGP; TEP

(Sonnet: "How many paltry . . . .") EIL

"I hear some say, this man is not in love." TrGrPo

"If he, from heaven that filched the living fire." AAS; NoP; TEP

"Into these loves, who but for passion look[e]s." NoP

(To the Reader of These Sonnets.) AAS; EnRePo; NAEL-1; NOSC; Son

Like an Adventurous Seafarer Am I. NOSC; Son

"Love, in a humour, played the prodigal." NoSic

Methinks I See Some Crooked Mimic Jeer. Son

(To the Critic.) NOSC, *sect.* XXXI

"Nothing but no and I, and I and no." GBL; PoEL-2

Since There's No Help, Come Let Us Kiss and Part. AAS; AWP; BoLoP; ClHu; EIL; EnLoPo; GBL; HAP; HeIP; InPS; JCP; NAEL-1; NOBE; NoP; OAEL-1; PoEL-2; PrIm; SCGP; Son; SoSe; TEP; TFi; TrGrPo

(Farewell to Love.) BLPL; ImPo; NOSC

(Love's Farewell.) GTBS; GTBS-P

(Parting, The.) CoGr; LiTB; OBEV; SCV

(Since There's No Help.) EnRePo

Stay, Speedy Time. EnRePo

"There's nothing grieves me, but that age should haste." AAS; NOSC; OAEL-1

Three Sorts of Serpents Do Resemble Thee. EnRePo
"To nothing fitter can I thee compare." EiL; SCGP; Son; TrGrPo
"Truce, gentle love, a parley now I crave." NoP; NoSic
"When first I ended, then I first began." TrGrPo
"Whilst thus my pen strives to eternize thee." AAS; Son
"Why should your fair eyes with such sovereign grace." SCGP
"Witlesse gallant, a young wench that woo'd, A." AAS
"You are [or You're] not alone when you are still alone." PoEL-2; TrGrPo
Idea armed, like Ernie O'Malley, The. Frank Ryan Dead in Dresden. Michael O'Loughlin. Fr. Shards, The. IB
Idea of a Swimmer. Jean-Richard Bloch, tr. fr. French by "S. P." TrJP
Idea of Ancestry, The. Etheridge Knight. BPo; NIP; NNaP; PBCAP; PoBA; RaBo; SV
Idea of Detroit, The. Jim Gustafson. NGP; UL
Idea of Entropy at Maenporth Beach, The. Peter Redgrove. FaBoMo
Idea of justice may be precious, An. Frank O'Hara. NeAP
Idea of Order at Key West, The. Wallace Stevens. CMoP; FF; HAP; HCAP; HeIP; MeMAP; MoAB; MoAmPo; MoP; NAAL-2; NAWM-2; NIP; NoAM; NOBA; NoP; OxBA; PoE; Poetr; PPP; PrIm; SAmP; TAP; TFi
Idea of San Francisco, The. Jim Gustafson. UL
Idea of Trust, The. Thom Gunn. Poetsp
Idea of trust, The. The Idea of Trust. Thom Gunn. Poetsp
Ideal, The. Anne Lynch Botta. AmWP
Ideal. Padraic Pearse, tr. fr. Modern Irish by Thomas MacDonagh. AWP
Ideal, An. H. Cordelia Ray. CBWP-3
Ideal and Reality. Joseph Campbell. BIrV
Ideal Angels. John Robert Colombo. MoCV
Ideal Found, The. Anne Lynch Botta. AmWP
Ideal Husband to His Wife, The. Sam Walter Foss. AnAmPo
Ideal Star-Fighter, The. J. H. Prynne. VaA
Idealism. Ronald Arbuthnott Knox. FaBoCo; NBLV
Ideals. Robert Greene. PoToHe
Idea's Mirrour, sels. Michael Drayton.
"Golden sun upon his fiery wheels, The." NoSic
"When first I ended, then I first begun." TrGrPo
Identification in Belfast (I.R.A. Bombing). Robert Lowell. OxBC
Identifications. Peretz Kaminsky. BTR
Identifying Things. Wendy Barker. PFL
Identikit, The. Amryl Johnson. NBrP
Ideogram. William Meredith. Poetr
Idiom of the Hero. Wallace Stevens. OxBA
Idiot, The. John Ashbery. Fr. Two Sonnets. VGW
Idiot, The. Adèle Naudé. PeSA
Idiot, The. Dudley Randall. BPo
Idiot. Allen Tate. FaBoMo; LiTA
Idiot, The. Keith Wilson. Poetsp
Idiot Boy, The. Wordsworth. OBNV
Idiot greens the meadows with his eyes, The. Idiot. Allen Tate. FaBoMo; LiTA
Idiot me has ended one more day's official grind! Climbing K'uai Pavilion. Huang T'ing-chien, tr. fr. Chinese by Michael E. Workman. SuSp
Idle as trout in light Colonel Jones. The Famine Road. Eavan Boland. FaBoWP
Idle Charon. Eugene Lee-Hamilton. NOBVV
Idle cuckoo, having made a feast, The. On the Cuckoo. Francis Quarles. NTP
Idle dayseye, the laborious wheel, The. O. Richard Wilbur. LiTA
Idle Flowers, The. Robert Bridges. BoNaP; ChTr
Idle Fyno. Unknown. ChTr; PoEL-2
Idle, I enjoy only tranquillity. Replying to Hsi-mei's "Thoughts in Early Autumn." Lu Kuei-meng, tr. fr. Chinese by Robin D. S. Yates. SuSp
Idle Life I Lead, The. Robert Bridges. LiTM
Idle poet, here and there, An. The Revelation. Coventry Patmore. Fr. Angel in the House, The. EnLoPo; GBL; GTBS-P; HAP; OBNC; OxBSP
Idle Pursuits. Pope. Fr. Dunciad, The. ECEV; OBSV
Idle Verse. Henry Vaughan. MiEL
Idle Visitation, An. Edward Dorn. Fr. Gunslinger. NOBA
Idle Words. Walter Savage Landor. OBSV
Idleness. Lu Yu, tr. fr. Chinese by Kenneth Rexroth. OxBM
Idler with a wand for a walking stick, An. Batyushkov. Osip Mandelstam, tr. fr. Russian by W. S. Merwin and Clarence Brown. OBVE
Idlers, The. Edmund Blunden. BoTP; CH
Idleset: "Ill's the airt o the Word the day." Thurso Berwick. OxBS
Idling pivot of the frigate bird, The. Man o' War Bird. Derek Walcott. TTY

Idly gossiping of the days of the dead emperor. (LL) The Old Harem. Li Shang-yin. OHMPC
Idly she yawned, and threw her heavy hair. George Moore. ErPo
Idolatry. Arna Bontemps. PoNe
Idols. Richard Burton. TrPWD
Idyl: "And my young sweetheart sat at board with me." Alfred Mombert, tr. fr. German by Ludwig Lewisohn. AWP
Idyll: "Engine on the bank, The." Geoffrey Fraser Dutton. PWE
Idyll: "Hermit hoar, in solemn cell." Samuel Johnson. NBLV
(Idyll: "Hermit hoar, in solemn cell." NOBL; PeLV
Idyll: "He was a selfish shellfish." Stoddard King. NBLV
Idyll: "Hermit hoar, in solemn cell." Samuel Johnson. See Hermit hoar, in solemn cell.
Idyl. H. Cordelia Ray. CBWP-3
Sels.
Midnight.
Noontide.
Sunrise. BlSi
Sunset. BlSi
Idyl, An. Tennyson. See Come down, O maid, from yonder mountain height.
Idyl of Spring, An. H. Cordelia Ray. CBWP-3
Idyll. Theocritus [or Theokritus]. See Shepherd Paris bore the Spartan bride, The.
Idyll for Ellie and Ruth. John Ash. SCBI
Idyll of the Rose. Ausonius, tr. fr. Latin by John Addington Symonds. AWP
Idylls, sels. Theocritus [or Theokritus], tr. fr. Greek.
"Amorous shepherd lov'd a charming boy, An." PeHV
"And so an easier life our Cyclops drew." OBVE, tr. by Elizabeth Barrett Browning
(Cyclops, The ("And so an easier life").) AWP
(For love there is no other drug, Nicias.) HePo, tr. by Barbara Hughes Fowler
Damoetas and Daphnis. HePo
Death of Daphnis, The. AWP
(Sweet is the whispering of that pine tree, goatherd.) HePo, tr. by Barbara Hughes Fowler
Enchantment, The. CTC; OBVE
(Where is my bay? Bring it, Thestylis. Where are my charms?) HePo, tr. by Barbara Hughes Fowler
"Eunica scorned [or skornde] me, when her I would have sweetly kissed [or kist]." NoSic; OBVE
Fishermen, The. AWP; OBVE
Gorgo and Praxinoa. HePo
Harvest-Home. AWP
(There was a time when Eucritus and I were going.) HePo, tr. by Barbara Hughes Fowler
Herdsmen, The. AWP
Hylas. HePo
Incantations, The. AWP
Little Heracles. HePo
"Shepherd Paris bore the Spartan bride, The." OBVE
(Idyll.) FaBoBl
"Wine, friend, and truth, the proverb says, agree." PeHV
Idylls of the King. Geoffrey Hill. Fr. Apology for the Revival of Christian Architecture in England, An. FaBoRV; NoAM; PoE
Idylls of the King, sels. Tennyson.
"And slowly answered Arthur from the barge." FaBoEH
Balin and Balan.
Vivien's Song ("But now the wholesome music of the wood"). OAEL-2
Coming of Arthur, The.
Merlin's Riddling. FaBoRV
Geraint and Enid.
Enid's Song. FaBoRV
Holy Grail, The.
Percivale's Quest. OAEL-2
"When the hermit made an end" PeVV
Lancelot and Elaine.
Song of Love and Death, The. OBNC
Last Tournament, The.
Lincolnshire Shores. FaBoPP
Tristram's Song. FaBoRV
Merlin and Vivien.
In Love, If Love Be Love. PoEL-5; TrGrPo
(All in All.) ImPo; LiTB
(Vivien's Song.) OBNC
"There lay she all her length and kiss'd his feet." EBVVPR
Passing of Arthur, The. FHYEP; NAEL-2; OBNC
(Morte d'Arthur.) DL; OAEL-2
"And answer made King Arthur, breathing hard." EBEV; PeECV
"But now farewell. I am going a long way." FaBoRV
Prayer: "Pray for my soul. More things are wrought by prayer." WGRP
"Then rose the King and moved his host by night." PeVV

If Marilyn Monroe. Leo Romero. AfAz

If Mary came would Mary. A Penitent Considers Another Coming of Mary. Gwendolyn Brooks. NoAM; PChr

If Mary goes far out to sea. Stately Verse. *Unknown.* FaPON

If me want for go in a Ebo. *Unknown. Fr.* Work-Songs. PBCV

If meat the gods give, I the steam. Steam in Sacrifice. Robert Herrick. CaPo

If medals were ordained for drinks. To a Boon Companion. Oliver St. John Gogarty. OBMV
(Boon Companion, The.) OtMeF

If men be judged wise. Joseph Solomon del Medigo, *tr. fr. Hebrew.* TrJP

If mine eyes can speak to do hearty errand. Sapphics. Sir Philip Sidney. *Fr.* Arcadia. SiPS

If music [*or* musique] and sweet poetry [*or* poetrie] agree. To His Friend Master R. L., In Praise of Music and Poetry. Richard Barnfield. AAS; EIL; EPCY; Son

If Music be the food of love, play on. Shakespeare. *Fr.* Twelfth Night. EBEvV
(Food of Love, The.) TrGrPo

If, My Darling. Philip Larkin. EBEV; LiTM

If my dear love were but the child of state. Shakespeare. *Fr.* Sonnets. NoSic

If my fat/ was too much for me. Invitation. Grace Nichols. AIW

If my garden oak spares one bare ledge. Creed. Anne Spencer. CDC; ShDr

If my imprisonment has no end. From Prison. Todros Ben Judah Abulafia, *tr. fr. Hebrew by* David Goldstein. TOF

If my kisses wrong you, then tit for tat. Strato, *tr. fr. Greek by* W. G. Shepherd. GrAn

If My Life Could Be Simple. Caroline Griffin. DT

If my love were meat and bread. Insatiate. Mae V. Cowdery. ShDr

If my name you wish to see. *Unknown.* ISE

If my nipples were to drip milk. Sappho, *tr. fr. Greek by* Willis Barnstone. BoWoP

If, my religion safe, I durst embrace. To Sir Henrie Savile upon His Translation of Tacitus. Ben Jonson. SeCV-1

If my torch goes out it will be dark. Search. Claribel Alegría, *tr. fr. Spanish by* Aliki *and* Willis Barnstone. BoWoP

If My Train Will Come. Katrina Porteous. NWP

If my vain soul needs blows and bitter losses. Ella Wheeler Wilcox. *Fr.* Christian's New-Year Prayer, The. TrPWD

If My Verses Had Wings. Victor Hugo, *tr. fr. French by* Philip L. Miller. RiWo

If Nancy Hanks/ Came back as a ghost. Nancy Hanks. Rosemary *and* Stephen Vincent Benét *and* Stephen Vincent Benét. FaBV; FaPON; NTCP

If nature prompts you, or if friends persuade. William Whitehead. *Fr.* Charge to the Poets, A. OBSV

If neither brass, nor marble, can withstand. The Power of Time. Swift. FaBoEE
(Shall I Repine.) OxBSP

If night takes the form of a whale and. Isabel Fraire, *tr. fr. Spanish by* Thomas Hoeksema. BoWoP

If nine times you your bridegroom kiss. The Tithe: To The Bride. Robert Herrick. CaPo

If no love is, O God, what fele I so. Chaucer. *Fr.* Troilus and Criseyde [*or* Criseide]. EnVB; FF; OAEL-1
(Song of Troylus, The.) AWP

If No One Ever Marries Me. Laurence Alma-Tadema. OxBChV

If no Pain were, how judge we of Pleasure? William Bliss. PeLi

If no such beast were, no such bird? (*LL*) Somewhere Is Such a Kingdom. John Crowe Ransom. CMoP; LiTA

If none but you in the world today. The Gospel According to You. *Unknown.* BLRP

If Not. H. A. C. Evans. FaBoPa

If not a so-called Negro bought a bottle. Racist Psychotherapy. Isaac J. Black. NBV

If not passage out of this life? (*LL*) Horse. Louise Glück. AnAn; NALW

If not, she's rich because she is content. (*LL*) Contention between Four Maids Concerning That Which Addeth Most Perfection to That Sex. Sir John Davies. SiPS

If not you? (*LL*) The Speed of Darkness. Muriel Rukeyser. GLP; LCAP

If now thou seest me a wreck, worn out and minished of sight. Old Age. Al-Aswad, Son of Ya'fur, *tr. fr. Arabic by* Sir Charles Lyall. *Fr.* Mufaddaliyat, The. AWP

If, O Maecenas, versed in lore antique. Horace, *tr. fr. Latin by* Sir Theodore Martin. OBVE

If of a beetle you'd make game. Oh That My Love Were in My Arms. *Malay Oral Tradition, tr. by* R. J. Wilkinson *and* R. O. Winstedt. WTO

If of the dead save good nought should be said. William Drummond of Hawthornden. NOSC

If of thy mortal goods thou art bereft. Hyacinths to Feed Thy Soul. Sadi, *tr. fr. Persian. Fr.* Gulistan, The. BLPA; BLPL; FaBoBe

If on a Spring night I went by. Courage. John Galsworthy. OtMeF
(Prayer, The.) UV

If on Account of the Political Situation. W. H. Auden. *Fr.* For the Time Being; a Christmas Oratorio. LiTA

If one could have that little head of hers. A Face. Robert Browning. CTC

If one revolves a vine-enamored thumb. Images for the Gospel of Christ. Paul Ramsey. CRP

If one should bring me this report. Tennyson. *Fr.* In Memoriam A. H. H. EBVV, *abr.*; EnVR; FHYEP; MeMBP; OAEL-2, *abr.*; PeECV, *abr.* (Of One Dead.) ImPo

If one should tell them what's clearly seen. Crumbs or the Loaf. Robinson Jeffers. CMoP

If Only. Christina Rossetti. TrCP

If only I could forget that Frenchman. The French Prisoner. János Pilinszky, *tr. fr. Hungarian by* János Csokits *and* Ted Hughes. PoSu

If only I could send you one small slice. Letter from the Vieux Carre. Ethel Green Russell. GoYe

If Only I Knew the Truth, I Swear I Would Act on It. Paul Goodman. ArLo

If only Life-and-Death. Lady Eguchi, *tr. fr. Japanese by* Arthur Waley. TAL

If only once the chariot of the Morn. The Glory of Nature. Frederick Tennyson. OBNC

If only that so many dead lie round. (*LL*) Church Going. Philip Larkin. CMoP; GTBS-P; HeIP; LiTM; MoBrPo; MoP; NAEL-2; NIP; NoAM; NoP; OAEL-2; Poetr; PPP; PrIm; SCV; SoSe; TFi; TwCP; UnPo

If only the phantom would stop reappearing! Faust. John Ashbery. NoP; TwCP

If only they hadn't shown that cruel mercy. A Skull Changed to Glass. Stephen Spender, *tr. by* Jeffrey Fiskin *and* Erik Vestville. AnAn

If only those scraps from Aleppo, from Qumran. I Saw Three Ships. Kevyn Arthur. PBCV

If only/ Under the canopy of stars. Errol Francis. *Fr.* Fragments of the Green Island. NBrP

If only, when one heard. *Unknown, tr. by* Arthur Waley. *Fr.* Kokin Shu. AWP

If orange chiffon sadness. Orange Chiffon. Jayne Cortez. BlSi

If Orpheus voyce had force to breathe such musickes love. Third Song. Sir Philip Sidney. *Fr.* Astrophel and Stella. AAS; ESo; GGP; PoEL-1; Poetr; SiPS; SiPSBD

If out of a dire suspicion. Wet Hair: If Now His Mother Should Come. Robert Penn Warren. *Fr.* Penological Study: Southern Exposure. NoAM

If parting be decreed for the two of us. Parting. Judah Halevi, *tr. fr. Hebrew by* Nina Davis Salaman. AWP; TrJP

If people ask me, Politeness. A. A. Milne. SiSoPo

If Pigs Could Fly. James Reeves. OTCP

If Pliny, Lord High Treasurer of all. Painture. Richard Lovelace. CaPo

If poisonous [*or* poysonous] mineral[l]s, and if that tree. John Donne. *Fr.* Holy Sonnets. EBEV; EnRePo; ESCV; FaBoVe; ImPo; JCP; LiTB; NAEL-1; NoP; OAEL-1; OxAEP-1; PFP; PoEL-2; PPP; SCGP; SeCP; Son; UnPo

If poor (you say) she drains her husband's purse. Chaucer. *Fr.* Canterbury Tales, The. EnVB; FHYEP; NAEL-1; OAEL-1; OBSV; OxBoLi, *abr.*; PeLV, *shorter vers.*

If Pope Had Written "Break, Break, Break." J. C. Squire. FaBoPa

If Profit offered immortality for gold. Anacreon, *tr. fr. Greek by* Sam Hamill. InMo

If Pythias has a customer. Poseidippus, *tr. fr. Greek by* Kenneth Rexroth. PGA

If questioning could make us wise. Because She Would Ask Me Why I Loved Her. Christopher John Brennan. CBAP

If recollecting were forgetting. Emily Dickinson. PFP

If rightly tuneful bards decide. Amoret. Mark Akenside. OBEV

If Rome so great, and in her wisest age. To Edward Allen (Alleyne). Ben Jonson.
(To Edward Alleyn.) NOSC

If sadly thinking, with spirits sinking. The Deserter's Lamentation. John Philpot Curran. FaBoRV
(Deserter, The.) OxAEP-1
(Deseter's Meditation, The.) PeIV

If St. Paul be fair and clear. *Unknown.* FaBoUs

If Sanct Paules day be fair and cleir. *Unknown.* MiEL

If satire charms, strike faults, but spare the man; Edward Young. *Fr.* Epistle II: To Mr. Pope, From Oxford. EPCY

If there exists a hell — the case is clear. To Sir Toby. Philip Freneau. NAAL-1; NoP; TAP

If There Had Anywhere Appeared. Richard Chenevix Trench. TrPWD

If there is a man white as marble. Metaphor as Degeneration. Wallace Stevens. LCAP

If There Is a Stationmaster at Stamford S.D. Hardly Sp. J. H. Prynne. VaA

If there is an outside out there. On Finding the Tree of Life. Alan Dugan. CAPP

If there is no change in the ocean. No Change in Me. *Unknown.* AmFP

If there is someone above. Double-face, *tr. fr. Crow Indian by* W. S. Merwin *after* Robert Lowie. STP

If there is the statue of a saint. In the Badlands of Desire. Beckian Fritz Goldberg. NAmP90

If there must be a god in the house, must be. Less and Less Human, O Savage Spirit. Wallace Stevens. VGW

If there was a broken whispering by night. Parting at Dawn. John Crowe Ransom. AnAmPo

If there was a house with three girls in it. Céilí. Ciaran Carson. PBCIP (It Used to Be.) CIP

If there was only a road there. The Blue West. Dahlia Ravikovitch, *tr. fr. Hebrew by* Chana Bloch. PBWP

If there was something one of them held back. Hotel. Donald Justice. *Fr.* Body and Soul. BAP-91

If there were a blessing. December. Hilda Morley. ArNa

If there were dreams to sell. Dream-Pedlary. Thomas Lovell Beddoes. BoTP; CH; EnRP; FaBoBe; HAP; LiTB; NOBE; OBEV; OBNC; OtMeF; OxAEP-2; PoEL-4; TrGrPo; WiR

If there were no authority on earth. Chaucer. *See* Experience, though noon auctoritee.

If there were no past, but specious present only. Speculative Evening. Marguerite Young. LiTA

If there were not an utter and absolute dark. The End, The Beginning. D. H. Lawrence. MeMBP

If there were, oh! an Hellespont of cream. The Author Loving These Homely Meats. John Davies of Hereford. *Fr.* Scourge of Folly, The. CBLP; CBNP; EiL; FaBoNo; Son
(Buttered Pippin-Pies.) ChTr
(Homely Meats.) FaBoCh

If there's a wind, we get it. Lobster Cove Shindig. Lillian Morrison. BoNaP

If there's no Sun, I still can have the Moon. Philosophy. John Kendrick Bangs. PoToHe

If there's no wick within the lamp. And Tomorrow Wend Our Ways. *Malay Oral Tradition, tr. by* R. J. Wilkinson *and* R. O. Winstedt. WTO

If they are mine or no. *(LL)* Tell Me Not Here [It Needs Not Saying]. A. E. Housman. CoGr; ELP; GTBS-P; LiTM; NoAM; NOBE; OAEL-2; OBNC; OxBTC; PlP; SCV

If they ask, who here doth lie. Epitaph on Sir Walter Pye. John Hoskyns. FaBoEE

If they had cursed the man. A Part-Sequence for Change. Robert Duncan. VGW

If They Honoured Me, Giving Me Their Gifts. "Michael Field." OBMV

If they made any noise in forming. Sinkholes. Janet Reed McFatter. GrPl

If they massacre me. Flesh. Deborah Levy. AIW

If they say my furred cloak. Chanson. Pernette de Guillet, *tr. fr. French by* Joan Keefe *and* Richard Terdiman. PBWP

If They Show Me a Stone and I Say Stone. Amir Gilboa, *tr. fr. Hebrew by* Ruth Finer Mintz. MHP

If they show me a stone and I say stone they will say stone. If They Show Me a Stone and I Say Stone. Amir Gilboa, *tr. fr. Hebrew by* Ruth Finer Mintz. MHP

If they show me blood and I say blood they will say color. *(LL)* If They Show Me a Stone and I Say Stone. Amir Gilboa. MHP

If they true bailiffs be, who for the law maintaining. On Mercenary and Unjust Bailiffs. Henricus Selyns. SCAP

If They Want Me To Be a Mystic, Fine. So I'm a Mystic. Fernando Pessoa, *tr. fr. Portuguese by* Edwin Honig. AnRep

If they wanted freedom. Eeva-Liisa Manner, *tr. fr. Finnish by* Jaakko A. Ahokas. *Fr.* Cambrian. PBWP

If This Be All. Anne Brontë. TrPWD

If this be love, to draw [or drawe] a weary [or wearie] breath. Samuel Daniel. *Fr.* To Delia. AAS; ESo; GBL; TrGrPo

If this book should chance to roam — . *Unknown.* ISE; RoPo

If this brain's over-tempered. I've Tasted My Blood. Milton Acorn. MoCV; NOBC

If this bright lily. A Song at Easter. Charles Hanson Towne. BLRP

If this country were a sea (that is solid rock). Pennines in April. Ted Hughes. PPP

If this don't please, old Nick is in you. *(LL)* Advice to the Ladies of London in the Choice of Their Husbands. *Unknown.* CoMu

If this is peace, this dead and leaden thing. Dead Fires. Jessie Redmond Fauset. PoNe

If this our little life is but a day. A Sonnet to Heavenly Beauty. Joachim du Bellay, *tr. fr. French by* Andrew Lang. AWP; CTC

If this uncertain age in which we dwell. The Lesson for Today. Robert Frost. LiTA; LiTM

If this was our battle, if these were our ends. To a President. Witter Bynner. OBAL

If This Were Faith. Robert Louis Stevenson. *Fr.* Songs of Travel. OBNC; TrPWD; WGRP

If this world's friends might see but once. The Seed Growing Secretly. Henry Vaughan. ChIV-2; ESCV; GeHe; SeCV-1

If thou a reason dost desire to know. To Cynthia, on Her Embraces. Sir Francis Kynaston. GBL

If thou art sleeping, maiden. Gil Vicente, *tr. fr. Spanish by* Longfellow. AWP; CTC

If thou beest he; but O how fall'n! how chang'd. Milton. *Fr.* Paradise Lost. EPCY; SCV

If thou be'st ice, I do admire. The Miracle. Sir John Suckling. CaPo

If thou canst wake with me, forget to eate. John Ford. *Fr.* Lover's Melancholy, The. PoEL-2

If thou didst feed on western plains of yore. To a Goose [or Gosse]. Robert Southey. BXAP; FM; NOBL; PeLV; Son

If thou dislik'st the piece thou light'st on first. To the Sour[e] Reader. Robert Herrick. NBLV; NoP; SeCP

If thou dost bid thy friend farewell. Parting. Coventry Patmore. PoToHe

If thou hadst lived, and lived to love me! *(LL)* To a Lock of Hair. Sir Walter Scott. GTBS; GTBS-P

If thou hast squander'd years to grave a gem. A Charge. Herbert Trench. OBEV

If thou in surety safe wilt sit. Look or You Leap. Jasper Heywood. EiL

If Thou Indeed Derive Thy Light from Heaven. Wordsworth. EnRP; TrCP

If thou kiss not me? *(LL)* Love's Philosophy. Shelley. ArLo; BLPA; BLPL; BoLoP; EnRP; FaBoBe; FaBV; FHYEP; GTBS; GTBS-P; HoPM; MeMBP; OxAEP-2; PoToHe; SCGP; TrGrPo

If thou must love me, let it be for nought. Elizabeth Barrett Browning. *Fr.* Sonnets from the Portuguese. CTC; HeIP; InPS; LiTB; OBEV; OBNC; OHCV; OxAEP-2; PFP; SoSe; TrGrPo
(For Love's Sake Only.) PoToHe

If thou of fortune be bereft. Not by Bread Alone. *Unknown, tr. fr. Greek by* James Terry White. PoLF

If thou piss free. Farmer Beresford, on Nobility in Langstrothdale Chase. Jonathan Williams. ETG

If thou serve a lord of prise. A Warning to Those Who Serve Lords. *Unknown.* MeEL

If thou shouldst ever come by choice or chance. Ginevra. Samuel Rogers. BeLS; OxAEP-2; PoLF

If Thou Shouldst Return. Clara Ann Thompson. CBWP-2

If Thou Survive My Well-contented Day. Shakespeare. *Fr.* Sonnets. EiL, *sect.* XXXII

If thou turn back and my loud crying still. *(LL)* Lo, as a careful housewife runs to catch. Shakespeare. SCGP

If thou wilt come and dwell with me at home. Daphnis to Ganymede. Richard Barnfield. *Fr.* Affectionate Shepherd, The. EiL

If thou wilt ease thine heart. Thomas Lovell Beddoes. *Fr.* Death's Jest Book. EnRP
(Dirge: "If Thou wilt ease Thine heart.") LiTB; OBNC; PoEL-4
(Wolfram's Dirge.) NOBE; OBEV; OxAEP-2

If Thou Wilt Hear. John Grave. AH

If thou wilt let down thy milk to me. *(LL)* Cushy cow, bonny, let down thy milk. Mother Goose. GBP; OxNR; ReMoGo

If Thou Wilt Mighty Be. Sir Thomas Wyatt. EnRePo; SiPS; SiPSBD

If thou wilt mighty be, flee from the rage. If Thou Wilt Mighty Be. Sir Thomas Wyatt. EnRePo; SiPS; SiPSBD

If thou wouldest roses scent. Francis Daniel Pastorius. SCAP

If Thou Wouldst Know. Hayyim Nahman Bialik, *tr. fr. Hebrew by* Harry H. Fein. TrJP

If thou would'st view fair Melrose aright. Melrose Abbey. Sir Walter Scott. *Fr.* Lay of the Last Minstrel, The. FaBoPP; OxAEP-2
(Sir William of Deloraine at the Wizard's Tomb.) OBNC

If thought can reach to Heaven. The Rabbi's Song. Kipling. ChIV-1

If through my perjured lips Thy voice may speak. A Prayer for a Preacher. Edward Shillito. TrPWD

If thus we needs must go. The Heart. Michael Drayton. NOSC

If thy wife is small bend down to her and. Ian Wedde. *Fr.* Earthly: Sonnets for Carlos. PeNZ

If tired of trees I seek again mankind. The Vantage Point. Robert Frost. MeMAP; OxBA

If you cannot on the ocean. Your Mission. Ellen M. Huntington Gates. BLPA; BLRP

If you can't be a pine on the top of the hill. Be the Best of Whatever You Are. Douglas Malloch. BLPA

If You Can't Eat You Got To. E. E. Cummings. CMoP; PrIm

If you can't trim your sails to suit the weather. If Not. H. A. C. Evans. FaBoPa

If you come as softly. Memorial I. Audre Lorde. AIW

If you come at all. Yourself and Myself. *Unknown, tr. fr. Irish by* Thomas Kinsella. NOIV

If You Come Back. Jack Cope. PeSA

If you come my way that is. Poem from Llanybri. Lynette Roberts. AngWe

If you complain your flames are hot. To Her Lover's Complaint. Jane Barker. OxBSP

If you could crowd them into forty lines! Limitations. Siegfried Sassoon. MoBrPo

If you could only keep quiet still and wait. *(LL)* Myxomatosis. Philip Larkin. CMoP; MoP; NoAM; NoP

If you could see, fair brother, how dead beat. Prolonged Sonnet: When the Troops Were Returning from Milan [or When The Troops Were Returning from Milan]. Niccolò degli Albizzi, *tr. fr. Italian by* Dante Gabriel Rossetti. AWP; OBVE

If you desire to paralyze. The Better Way. Walter Leaf. FaBoCo

If you didn't see the six-legged dog. Country Fair. Charles Simic. BAP-91

If you die you lose with rambling. Beneath the Radar — for the RAF and All Low Flying Aircraft. Geraldine Monk. NBrP

If you do love, as well as I. The Thought. Lord Herbert of Cherbury. AngWe; InvP

If you do love me weel, Willie. Fair Janet. *Unknown.* ESPB

If you do not shake the bottle. On Tomato Ketchup. *Unknown.* FaBoUs; NBLV

(Tomato Ketchup.) Spl

If you don't know German. Rough. John James. VaA

If you don't know how, why pretend? To the Tune "Red Embroidered Shoes." Huang O, *tr. fr. Chinese by* Kenneth Rexroth *and* Ling Chung. PBWP; VBLP; WPC; WPOW

If you don't know the kind of person I am. A Ritual to Read to Each Other. William Stafford. RaBo

If you don't like my apples. *Unknown.* GBP; OxBoLi

If you don't put your shoes on before I count fifteen then. One, Two, Three. Michael Rosen. OTCP

If you draw a bow, draw the strongest. Tu Fu, *tr. by* Ronald C. Miao. *Fr.* Frontier Songs, First Series. SuSp

"If you dream," said the eminent Freud. Russell Miller. PeLi

If you evah go to Houston. Midnight Special. *Unknown.* AS

If you ever, ever, ever meet a grizzly bear. Grizzly Bear. Mary Austin. FaPON; GoJo; PDV

If you fall in a river thats full of Piranha. Strippers. Dick King-Smith. OBAP

If you feel that you're right on your beam ends. Leslie Johnson. PeLi

If you find a man who does not receive. Cry "Infidel!" Alfred Gibbs Campbell. AAP

If you find a paddling pool. The Paddling Pool. E. M. Adams. BoTP

If you find for your verse there's no call. *Unknown.* PeLi

If you give me your attention, I will tell you what I am. The Disagreeable Man. W. S. Gilbert. FiBHP

If you go a-picnicking and throw your scraps about. Picnics. *Unknown.* BoTP

If you go away,/ why should I adorn myself? *Unknown, tr. fr. Japanese by* Kenneth Yasuda. BoWoP

If You Go Softly. Jenifer Kelly. OBAP

If You Had a Friend. Robert Lewis. PoToHe

If you had a friend strong, simple, true. If You Had a Friend. Robert Lewis. PoToHe

If You Had Known. Thomas Hardy. FaBoRV; GBL

If you had lusted after something noble or decent. Sappho, *tr. fr. Greek by* Sam Hamill. InMo

If You Happy Would Be. Abraham Fernández. AH

If You Have a Friend. *Unknown.*

If you have a friend worth loving. If You Have a Friend. *Unknown.*
(Say It Now.) BLPA; WBLP
(Seeds of Kindness.) PoToHe
(Speak Out.) PWR, *abr.*

If you have a tender message. Before It Is Too Late. Frank Herbert Sweet. PoToHe

If you have a thing to do. Do It Right. Samuel O. Buckner. WBLP

If you have a word of cheer. Tell Her So. Mrs. Henry Linden. CBWP-4

If you have a word of cheer. Tell Him So. J. A. Egerton. PWR

If you have ever, like me. Please Excuse Typing. J. B. Boothroyd. FiBHP

If you have forgotten water-lilies floating. Water-Lilies. Sara Teasdale. MoAmPo

If you have formed a circle to go into. To God. Blake. OAEL-2

If you have lost the radio beam, then guide yourself by the sun or the stars. Any Man's Advice to His Son. Kenneth Fearing. CMoP

If you have no time. Lady Izumi Shikibu, *tr. fr. Japanese by* Willis Barnstone. BoWoP

If you have not read the Slavic poets. To Robinson Jeffers. Czeslaw Milosz, *tr. fr. Polish by the author* and Richard Lourie. AnRep

If you have revisited the town, thin Shade. To a Shade. W. B. Yeats. LiTB; NAEL-2; PoEL-5

If you have seen the tan-shell beetles. Drawing the Blinds. Gerald Musinsky. BTR

If you have spoken something beautiful. If You Made Gentler the Churlish World. Max Ehrmann. PoToHe

If you have taken this rubble for my past. Delta. Adrienne Rich. NIP

If you have tears, prepare to shed them now. Shakespeare. *Fr.* Julius Caesar. OxAEP-1

If you haven't made noise enough to warn him, singing, shouting. Meeting a Bear. David Wagoner. FoLa; HAP; WeW

If you hear a kind word spoken. Tell Him So. *Unknown.* BLPA; BLPL; WBLP

If you hear rustling in the straw. David Philips. BXAP

If you insult me in my absence. Apollinarius, *tr. fr. Greek by* Peter Jay. GrAn

If you iron tonic need. Dietary Advice. *Unknown.* FaBoUs

If you knew that little force. Kathleen Jamie. *Fr.* Katie's Poems. PWE

If you know about the Babylonian Jews. Straus Park. Gerald Stern. PRA

If you live along with all the other people. Worm Either Way. D. H. Lawrence. NoAM

If you look at the sky. Mission to Linz. Richard Hugo. ArOW

If you look for the truth outside yourself. Tung-shan, *tr. fr. Japanese by* Stephen Mitchell. EnlH

If you look out from some high, high window. Sweet Loving Friendship. Peter Bellamy. OBET

If you love God, take your mirror between your hands and look. Mahmud Djellaladin Pasha, *tr. fr. Turkish by* E. Powys Mathers. ErPo

If you love it not, of night. *(LL)* Out in the Dark. Edward Thomas. ArNa; CH; GTBS-P; LiTM; MoAB; MoBrPo; NOBE; OBWVE; RB

If you love me. Lady Izumi Shikibu, *tr. fr. Japanese by* Willis Barnstone. BoWoP

If you love me, as I love you. Samuel Hoffenstein. FiBHP

If you love me as I love you. *Unknown.* RoPo

If you loved me ever so little. Satia Te Sanguine. Swinburne. PeVV

If You Made Gentler the Churlish World. Max Ehrmann. PoToHe

If you mean to keep this appointment. Instructions for Elijah. Myra Sklarew. CRP

If you melt some lead. Valerio Magrelli, *tr. fr. Italian by* Dana Gioia. NeIt

If you mice are looking for *food.* Ariston, *tr. fr. Greek by* W. G. Shepherd. GrAn

If you my dear mother, had e'er been at sea. Sir George Dallas. *Fr.* India Guide, The; or, Journal of a Voyage to the East Indies in 1780. OBTV

If you never do anything for anyone else. The Immoral Proposition. Robert Creeley. LiTM; NeAP; PoM

If you, O Aynabo, my fleet and fiery horse. Battle Pledge. *Somali Oral Tradition, tr. by* M. Laurence. WTO

If you pack no meat, no perfume. A Night on Goat Haunt. Sandra Alcosser. FoLa

If you put in enough hours in bars, sooner or later you get to hear. Bob. C. K. Williams. PWE

"If you raise canary birds," my grandfather said to me. Summer Nights. James Tate. AnAn

If you rattle along like your mistress's tongue. Extempore Pinned to a Lady's Coach. Burns. IHNG

If you really care for me. *Unknown, tr. fr. Spanish by* Willis Barnstone. BoWoP

If you really exist — show up. Nina Cassian, *tr. fr. Romanian by* Brenda Walker *and* Andrea Deletant. VBLP

If you really imagine wisdom grows with a beard. Lucianus, *tr. fr. Greek by* Edwin Morgan. GrAn

If you really love me honey, hey- yah. *Unknown, tr. fr. Kiowa Indian. Fr.* "49" Songs. STP

If you refuse me once, and think again. Lord Herbert of Cherbury. NOSC

If you ride in it, you mus' be holy, this train. *(LL)* This Train ("This train is bound for glory, this train.") *Unknown.* OxBoLi

If You Saw a Negro Lady. June Jordan. IHMS; NMM

If You See a Fairy Ring. *Unknown.* BoTP

If you see a tall fellow ahead of a [*or* the] crowd. Forget It. *Unknown.* PoLF; WBLP

If you see my mother, partner, tell her pray for me. Mack Maze. WTO

If You See Someone. Adaios of Macedon. *See* If you see someone beautiful.

If you see someone beautiful. Adaios of Macedon, *tr. fr. Greek by* Alistair Elliot. PeHV

(If You See Someone.) FaBoBl

If you see someone beautiful/ hammer it out right then. Adaios of Macedon, *tr. fr. Greek by* Alistair Elliot. GrAn

If You See This Man. Thomas Lux. AmPA

If you seek for Eldorado! (*LL*) Eldorado. Poe. AmPP; AnAmPo; AWP; FaBoBe; FaBoCh; MeMAP; NOBA; NoP; NTP; OxBA; TAP; WiR

If you set out in this world. The Seventh. Attila József, *tr. fr. Hungarian by* John Batki. RB

If you should bid me make a choice. The Windmill. E. V. Lucas. BoTP

If you should go before me, dear, walk slowly. Walk Slowly. Adelaide Love. BLPA

If you should meet a crocodile. *Unknown.* PDV

If you should see a man. The Truth. Ted Joans. TTY

(Voice in the Crowd.) AmFP

If you sit down at set of sun. Count That Day Lost. "George Eliot." (At Set of Sun.) PoToHe

If you smoke a cigarette. A Cigarette. *Mongol Oral Tradition, tr. by* C. R. Bawden. WTO

If you sneeze on Monday, you sneeze for danger. Sneezing. *Unknown.* ReMoGo

If you stay in comfort too long. You Will Forget. Chenjerai Hove. HBAPE

If you stay to school dinners. *Unknown.* WTO

If you still have bacon and eggs for breakfast. If. Sipho Sepamla. PeSAV

If you strike a thorn or rose. Keep a-Goin'. Frank Lebby Stanton. PWR; WBLP

If you stub your toe. *Unknown.* RoPo

If you take the moon in your hands. Hilda Doolittle ("H. D."). *Fr.* Sigil. AnAn; FaBoWP

(Moon in Your Hands, The.) BoWoP; NYBP

If you, that have grown old, were the first dead. The New Faces. W. B. Yeats. GTBS-P

If you think it crude to be rough and rude. Robert Swan. NSI

If you think, mother. What Her Girl Friend Said to the Foster-Mother ("If you think, mother.") Orampokiyar, *tr. fr. Tamil by* A. K. Ramanujan. *Fr.* Five on the Crabs. PLW

If You Think With Fire. Hsiung-hung, *tr. fr. Chinese by* Kenneth Rexroth *and* Ling Chung. WPC

If you think you are beaten, you are. The Victor. C. W. Longenecker. PWR

If you think you are beaten, you are. Thinking. Walter D. Wintle. WBLP

(Man Who Thinks He Can, The.) PoLF

If you think you are in love. *Unknown.* RoPo

If you touch blue. *Unknown.* RoPo

If you wake at midnight, and hear a horse's feet. A Smuggler's Song. Kipling. *Fr.* Puck of Pook's Hill. FaBoEH; NTP; OxBChV

If you wake up too early listen for it. Town of the Dragon Vein. Anne Carson. *Fr.* Life of Towns, The. BAP-90

If you wander far enough. Oh No. Robert Creeley. HeIP; InPK; NaP; SM

If you want a game to tame you and to take your measure in. The Trucker. Will Dyson. NOBAu

If you want a thing bad enough. Success. Berton Braley. PoToHe

If you want higher wages, let me tell you what to do. Talking Union. *Unknown.* SWP

If You Want Me to Stay with You. Natalie Clifford Barney, *tr. fr. French by* Patrice Titterington. VBLP

If you want messages you must provide an orifice. Peter Riley. *Fr.* Eight Preludes. VaA

If you want my apartment, sleep in it. Rent. Jane Cooper. FYAP; TAP

If you want to find the sergeant. The Old Battalion. *Unknown.* OBET

If You Want to Find the Sergeant. *Unknown.* NSI

If you want to get to the heaven. Litany of the Little Bourgeois. Nicanor Parra, *tr. fr. Spanish by* James Laughlin. AnRep

If you want to go to heaven. The Blood-stained Banders. *Unknown.* AmFP

If You Want to Go to Heben. *Unknown.* GBP

If you want to have the kind of a church. It Isn't the Church — It's You. *Unknown.* BLPA; WBLP

If You Want to Know Me. Noémia da Sousa, *tr. fr. Portuguese by* Margaret Dickinson. AIW

If you want to know where the privates were. Where They Were. *Unknown.* AS

If you want to live in the country. The Power of Maples. Gerald Stern. NU

If you want to live in the kind of a town. It Isn't the Town, It's You. R. W. Glover. BLPA

If you want to see an alligator. Alligator. Grace Nichols. OBAP

If you were an Eskimo baby. An Eskimo Baby. Lucy Diamond. BoTP

If you were an owl. That's What We'd Do. Mary Mapes Dodge. OBCA

If you were busy being kind. If. Rebecca Foresman. WBLP

(How to Forget.) PoToHe

If You Were Coming in the Fall. Emily Dickinson. AmPP; ArLo; CBLP; NOBA; OxBA; PoRA; SoSe

If you were exchanged in the cradle and/ your real mother died. A Story That Could Be True. William Stafford. GOYP; NTCP; RaBo

If you were going to get a pet. If You. Robert Creeley. MoP; NeAP; NoAM; NOBA; Poetr; SM

If you were here you'd photograph this shrine. The Measure of Light at the Altar on the Day of the Dead. Rosemary Catacalos. AfAz

If you were just in keeping our pact of love. Wallāda, *tr. fr. Arabic by* A. R. Nykel. PBWP

If you were only one inch tall, you'd ride a worm to school. One Inch Tall. Shel Silverstein. OBCA

If you were to ask me why I dwell among green mountains. Conversations in the Mountains. Li Po, *tr. fr. Chinese by* Robert Payne. RaBo; TAL

If you were twenty-seven. Heaven. Philip Levine. LCAP; NaP

If you will come on such a day. The Gardener. Sidney Keyes. MoAB; MoBrPo

If you will tell me why the fen. I May, I Might, I Must. Marianne Moore. FaBoWP; FF; HeIL; OBAL; OxBSP

If you wish to live for ever. *Unknown.* FaBoUs

If you wish to pull a cork. Lilliputian's Beer Song. Septimus Winner. OBAL

If you would know the love which I you bear. Sir John Davies. *Fr.* Sonnets to Philomel. SiPS

If you would learn. The Antiquary. Joseph Campbell. OxBTC

If you would only stop to count your blessings. Count Your Blessings. Mrs. Henry Linden. CBWP-4

If you would seek us. Shakespeare. *Fr.* Winter's Tale, The. OxAEP-1

If you your lips would keep from slips. Our Lips and Ears. *Unknown.* BLPA; WBLP

If you'd died I would've cut off my hair. *Unknown, tr. fr. Tlingit Indian by* James Koller *after* John Swanton. STP

If you'd have me go on loving you. Ezra Pound. *Fr.* Impressions of François-Marie Arouet (de Voltaire). MoAB

If you'll believe me when I tell you I have tried. The Bridge of Sighs. Steve Orlen. BAP-89

If you'll listen a while, I'll sing you a song. Jim Fisk. *Unknown.* AS

If you'll listen for a moment, I will tell you now, my friends. What We Teach at Claflin. L. A. J. Moorer. CBWP-3

If your child tastes salty. If. Anselm Hollo. UL

If your first memory was the arms of your father. Reprieve on the Stoop. Belle Waring. PBCAP

If your mother is a Jew, you are a Jew. A Meditation in Seven Days. Alicia Ostriker. PBCAP

If You're Anxious for to Shine in the High Aesthetic Line. W. S. Gilbert. *Fr.* Patience. NAEL-2; NBLV

If you're anxious for to shine in the high aesthetic line as a man of culture rare. Bunthorne's Song. W. S. Gilbert. *Fr.* Patience. EBVV; FiBHP; LiTB; OAEL-2

(Aesthete, The.) EBVV; OHCV

"If you're aristocratic," said Nietzsche. Gerry Hamill. PeLi

If You're Ever Going to Love Me. *Unknown.* BLPA

If you're ever in a jam. Friendship. Cole Porter. OBF

If you're not home, where. Numbers, Letters. Amiri Baraka. BPo; NOBA

If you're off to Philadelphia in the morning. Philadelphia. Kipling. OBTV

If you're so out of love with happiness. John Oldham. *Fr.* Satyr Address'd to a Friend That Is About to Leave the University, and Come Abroad in the World, A. OBSV

If you've ever been in a car. Stun. James Schuyler. MAT

If you've got a job to do. Do It Now! *Unknown.* BLPA; WBLP

If you've got but fifty cents! (*LL*) I Had But Fifty Cents. *Unknown.* BeLS; BLPA; NBLV; WHSW

Ifa divination was performed for Tiger. Tiger. *Yoruba Oral Tradition, tr. by* B. King. WTO

Ifa speaks in parables. *Yoruba Oral Tradition, tr. by* J. A. Adediji. WTO

Ifé: A Bronze Lament. Askia Muhammad Touré. BCF

IFF. Howard Nemerov. ArOW

I'll descend mid other men. Freedom. Sean O Riordain, *tr. fr. Irish by* Coslett Quin. TIRV

I'll die for him tomorrow. (*LL*) Bonny Barbara Allan ("In Scarlet Town where I was born.") *Unknown.* AWP; BoLoP; CH; ESPB; GGP; HeIP; InPK; LiTB; NAEL-1; NoP; OxBB; TrGrPo

I'll die thy valour's sacrifice. (*LL*) For a Picture Where a Queen Laments over the Tomb of a Slain Knight. Thomas Carew. CaPo

I'll dig with it. (*LL*) Digging. Seamus Heaney. BIrV; CIP; IIP; InPS; IPY; NAEL-2; TwCP

I'll do what the raids suggest. A Boy. John Ashbery. NeAP

I'll drink it down right smilingly. (*LL*) The Stirrup-Cup. Sidney Lanier. AmPP; AnAmPo

I'll drink thy Muse's health, thou shalt quaff mine. (*LL*) A Letter to Ben Jonson. Beaumont *and* Fletcher *and* John Fletcher. BeJo

I'll drink thy Muses health, thou shalt quaff mine. (*LL*) Mr. Francis Beaumont's Letter to Ben Johnson. Francis Beaumont.

I'll eat when I'm hungry, I'll drink when I'm dry. Rye Whisky. *Unknown.* OxBoLi

I'll faint no more beneath the burden. Submission. Clara Ann Thompson. CBWP-2

Ill fares the land, to hastening ills a prey. Goldsmith. *Fr.* Deserted Village, The. BeLS; EnRP; NOEC; NoP; OAEL-1; OBSV; PIP; PoEL-3; TEP; UV

Ill fates pursue me, may I never find. Lady Mary Wortley Montagu. *Fr.* Town Eclogues. ECEV

I'll find me a spruce. Christmas Tree. Aileen Fisher. PDV

I'll Find My Self-Belief. Jacob Glatstein, *tr. fr. Yiddish by* Ruth Whitman. BTR

I'll find the stable and pull out the bolt. (*LL*) The Fascination of What's Difficult. W. B. Yeats. BIrV; NAEL-2; OxAEP-2; PoEL-5

I'll Follow Thee. Clara Ann Thompson. CBWP-2

I'll frame, my Heliodora! a garland for thy hair. A Garland for Heliodora. Meleager, *tr. fr. Greek by* "Christopher North." AWP

I'll get up soon, and leave my bed unmade. The Widower in the Country. Les A. Murray. DiPo

I'll give her ten thousand pounds. (*LL*) Willie of Winsbury. *Unknown.* AmFP

I'll give to you a paper of pins. Paper of Pins. *Unknown.* AmFP
(O miss, I'll give you a paper of pins.) TLR, *diff. vers.*

I'll go among the dead to see my friend. An Afternoon at the Beach. Edgar Bowers. MT; VCAP

I'll go into the bedroom silently and lie down between the bridegroom and the bride. Love Poem on Theme by Whitman. Allen Ginsberg. CAPP; NaP

I'll go, said I, to the woods and hills. The Apostate. A. E. Coppard. OBMV

I'll go to A. *Unknown.* ISE

I'll go up on the mountain top. Liza Jane. *Unknown.* AS

I'll greet the sun once more. Once More. Forugh Farrokhzad, *tr. by* Jascha Kessler *and* Amin Banani. BoWoP

I'll Have a Collier for My Sweetheart. William Oliver. WTO

I'll have my girl I love the best, in spite of her darned old mammy. (*LL*) As I Walked Out One Morning. *Unknown.* AmFP

I'll Have the window Southward. Sang-yong Kim, *tr. fr. Korean by* Chang-soo Koh. PAW

I'll have you by the short and curly hair. Catullus, *tr. fr. Latin by* James Michie. PeHV

Ill he cannot cure a name, The. (*LL*) A Wish. Matthew Arnold. IHNG

I'll hold my candle high, and then. High Resolve. *Unknown.* PoToHe

Ill Humor. Goethe, *tr. fr. German by* John Frederick Nims. STV

I'll keep your shirt white. Death Song ("I'll keep your shirt white.") *Unknown, tr. fr. Turkish by* Reza Baraheni *and* Zahra-Soltan Shokoohtaezeh. BoWoP

I'll Kill you if you Quote it. (*LL*) Ah, Yes, I Wrote the "Purple Cow." Gelett Burgess. FiBHP

I'll kill you if you quote it! (*LL*) The Purple Cow. Gelett Burgess. CBNP; FaBoCo; FaBoNo; FaPON; FiBHP; GrPl; NBLV; NTCP; OBAL; OBCA; PDV; PoLF; TFi; TLR

Ill lay he long, upon this last return. John Berryman. *Fr.* Dream Songs. TAP

I'll lay this halfway me, which we the body name. Martin Opitz, *tr. fr. German by* George C. Schoolfield. GePo

I'll lay you five hundred pounds. The Broomfield Hill. *Unknown.* AmFP, A *and* B vers.; CH, A *and* B vers.; ESPB, A *and* B vers.; OxBB

I'll leave thy heart a-dying. (*LL*) The Cheat of Cupid; or, The Ungentle Guest. Robert Herrick, *after* Anacreon. AWP; OBVE

I'll Marry Not at All. *Unknown.* AmFP

I'll meet them in the country when I can. (*LL*) Anxiety about Dying. Alicia Ostriker. CrSp

Ill Met by Zenith. Ogden Nash. NYBP

I'll never have a river of gold. Bassos, *tr. fr. Greek by* Sam Hamill. InMo

"I'll never reach forty," my mother would say. She'd Say. Frank Davey. NOBC

I'll never see a tree at all. (*LL*) Song of the Open Road. Ogden Nash. AnAmPo; FaBoCo; OBAL

I'll Never Use Tobacco. *Unknown.* FaBoUs

I'll not forget/ I swear. The Cliffs at Manzanilla. Jan Carew. PBCV

I'll not forget the warm blue night when my bold girl. A Thing Remembered. *Unknown, tr. fr. Arabic by* E. Powys Mathers. ErPo

I'll not touch wood nor, fingers crossed. Favour. Robert David Fitzgerald. CBAP

I'll not weep that thou art going to leave me. Emily Brontë. WPE

Ill Omens. Thomas Moore. PoEL-4

I'll only show your lines, and say, *'Tis this.* (*LL*) Ode: Of Wit. Abraham Cowley. BeJo; MeLP; NAEL-1; NOSC; OAEL-1; SeCP; SeCV-1

I'll pass 'im the time o' day! (*LL*) Bill 'Awkins. Kipling. CBLP

I'll prop her, I swear, ankle, butt and chin. The Nude on the Bathroom Wall. Gena Ford. PeHV

I'll put a trinket on. (*LL*) Morns are meeker than they were, The. Emily Dickinson. BoNaP; FaPON; ImGa; OBCA; SAmP

I'll put on my boots and I'll blow the man down. Blow the Man Down. *Unknown.* OxBSS, vers. II
(Come all you young fellows who follow the sea.) OxBSS, vers. I

I'll quit punchin' cows in the sweet by an' by. (*LL*) The Old Chisholm Trail. *Unknown.* BeLS; FaBoBe; SWP

I'll rest me in this sheltered bower. The Arbour. Anne Brontë. EBVV

I'll Sail upon the Dog-Star. Thomas D'Urfey. *Fr.* Fool's Preferment, A. FaBoCh; OxBoLi

Ill sat to be with the calm, The. Essentials. Samuel Greenberg. LiTA

I'll scratch them out. (*LL*) Diodorus is nice, isn't he, Philocles? Meleager. PeHV

I'll shoot a little bird for little brother. *Unknown, tr. fr. Tlingit Indian by* James Koller *after* John Swanton. STP

I'll shout, Bugger the diet/ I'm absolutely starving. (*LL*) The Diet. Maureen Burge. AIW; BrRo

I'll sing of heroes, and of kings. Love. Abraham Cowley, *after the Greek of* Anacreon. AWP; BeJo; OBVE

I'll sing you a good old song. The Fine Old English Gentleman. *Unknown.* CH

I'll sing you a new ballad, and I'll warrant it first-rate. The Fine Old English Gentleman; New Version. Charles Dickens. CoMu; FaBoBa; NOBVV; OBSV

I'll sing you a song. A Bar on the Piccola Marina. Noël Coward. NBLV

I'll sing you a song about two true lovers. William Taylor. *Unknown.* OBET

I'll sing you a song/ and it'll be a sad one. Sioux Indians. *Unknown.* AmFP

I'll sing you a song/ Nine verses long. *Unknown.* OxNR

I'll sing you a song of Peace and Love. Whack Fol the Diddle. Peadar Kearney. FiBHP

I'll sing you a song of the world and its ways. Six Feet of Earth. *Unknown.* BLPA

I'll sing you a song/ The days are long. *Unknown.* OxNR

I'll sing you a true song of Billy the Kid. Billy the Kid. *Unknown.* FaBoBe

I'll sing you [a] one-O [or twelve O]. Carol of the Numbers. *Unknown.* AmFP
(Dilly Song, The.) GBP; OBET
(Green Grow the Rushes O.) OxBoLi

I'll stare at something less prepoceros. (*LL*) The Rhinoceros. Ogden Nash. FiBHP; MoAmPo; OBAL

I'll teach my sons. My Sons. Ron Loewinsohn. NeAP

I'll teach you, dreamer, to be up and doing. (*LL*) Time To Be Up, Marie, Young Sleepyhead. Pierre de Ronsard. STV

I'll tell my own daddy. *Unknown.* OxNR

I'll tell thee everything I can. "Lewis Carroll." *Fr.* Through the Looking-Glass. InVP; TFi; UV
(A-Sitting on a Gate.) PoRA
(Aged, Aged Man, The.) BXAP; FaBoPa; OxBChV
(Ways and Means.) FiBHP
(White Knight's Ballad, The.) FaBoNo; HAP
(White Knight's Song, The.) CBNP; FaBoCh; FaBoCo; InPS; NAEL-2; NoAM; NOBE; NOBL; NoP; OAEL-2; PeLV

I'll tell you a story, a story anon. King John and the Bishop. *Unknown.* ESPB, A *and* B vers.

I'll tell you a story/ About Jack a Nory. Mother Goose. OxNR; ReMoGo

I'll tell you a story/ concerning John and Joan. Peter Reading. PeLV

I'll tell you how the sun rose. Emily Dickinson. AmPP; FaBV; MoShBr; PDV; PoEL-5; TAP

I'm jilted, forsaken, outwitted. The Jilted Nymph. Thomas Campbell. EnLoPo

I'm Just a Stranger Here, Heaven Is My Home. Carole Gregory Clemmons. PoBA

I'm King of the cabbages green. Old King Cabbage. Richard Kendall Munkittrick. OBCA

I'm leaning out the cottage window, latch. Ending up in Kent. Eva Salzman. NWP

I'm learning how to read the rocks. Indian Ruins along Rio de Flag. Greg Pape. PBCAP

I'm like a skiff on the ocean tost. John Gay. EnLoPo

I'm like a vine supported on a stick. Leonidas of Tarentum, tr. fr. Greek by Alistair Elliot. GrAn

I'm like all lovers, wanting love to be. Lesbia Harford. NOBAu

I'm living in a cave. Unknown, tr. fr. Chippewa Indian by Jerome K. Rothenberg. STP

I'm living in the tombs. (LL) Memory. Abraham Lincoln. BLPA; FaBoBe; WBLP

I'm loath to be alive again. (LL) In mine own [or one] monument I lie [or lye]. Richard Lovelace. CBLP; OxBSP

I'm lonesome since I crossed the hill. The Girl I Left behind Me. Unknown. OBET

I'm looking for the three. Boogie Board. William Talcott. NGP

I'm looking mighty seedy while holding down my claim. Little Old Sod Shanty. Unknown. AmFP; AS

I'm/ lost/ among a/ maze of cans. Supermarket. Felice Holman. OTCP

I'm made in sport by Nature. On an Indian Tomineois, the Least of Birds. Thomas Heyrick. FM; NOSC

I'm makin' a road. Florida Road Workers. Langston Hughes. MoAmPo

"I'm Mark's alone!" you swore. Given cause to doubt you. Contemplation. John Frederick Nims. InPK

I'm melted down into a black ooze. In a Remote Cloister Bordering the Empyrean. Joel Sloman. VGW

I'm middle-aged. Political Activist Living Alone. Pat Arrowsmith. AIW; BrRo

I'm mighty glad to see you, Mrs. Curtis. The Transparent Man. Anthony Hecht. FYAP

I'm naturally lazy, carefree. Fisherman on a Southern Stream. Lu Kuei Meng, tr. fr. Chinese by Robin D. S. Yates. SuSp

I'm no Alice. Pool. Wanda Barford. Mes

I'm no He-man you know, I'm not a He. D. B. Wyndham Lewis. Fr. If So the Man You Are. OBSV

I'm no longer the bitter girl. Love Which Frees. Gloria Fuertes, tr. fr. Spanish by Philip Levine. WPOW

I'm no reformer; for I see more light. Optimism. Ella Wheeler Wilcox. PWR

I'm Nobody! Who are you? Emily Dickinson. AmPP; AnAmPo; BoWoP; CBNP; HeIP; MeMAP; NALW; NBLV; NOBA; NTP; OBCA; OTCP; OxBSP; PDV; PFP; SAmP; TAP; WPE

I'm not a butcher. Unknown. FaBoEH

I'm not a judge, I own; in short. Arthur Hugh Clough. Fr. Dipsychus. EnVR

I'm not a lover now! (LL) Palinodia. Winthrop Mackworth Praed. CBLP

I'm Not a Man. Harold Norse. GLP

I'm not at all scared of the Pleiades setting. Antipater of Thessalonica, tr. fr. Greek by Tony Harrison. GrAn

I'm not at home if people call. (LL) Arrivals at a Watering-Place. Winthrop Mackworth Praed. NOBL; PeLV

I'm Not Complaining. Philip Schultz. SoSe

I'm not even a 'bus I'm a tram. (LL) There once was a man [or There was a young man] who said, "Damn!" Maurice Evan Hare. NOBL; OxBoLi; PeLi

I'm not going to tell you everything. Closed Mill. Maggie Anderson. PBCAP

I'm not here. Hilda Doolittle ("H. D."). Fr. Halcyon. MoAmPo

I'm Not Here/ Never Was. Constanta Buzea, tr. fr. Romanian by Stavros Deligiorgis. BoWoP

I'm not interested in the poverty. I Go Dreaming Roads in My Youth. Luis Omar Salinas. AiP

I'm not planning to turn into gold. Somebody else. Bassus, tr. fr. Greek by Barbara Hughes Fowler. Fr. Epigrams. HePo

I'm not really nervous since John warned me about Toxic Shock. Nerves. Mark Rudman. PFL

"I'm not," said the Lord. (LL) Anger. Julia Vinograd. SRLS

I'm not so sure a body's there! (LL) The Cat. W. H. Davies. CRH; NOBE

I'm not the first that Love hath led astray. (LL) Love. Thomas Hood. CBLP

I'm not without you. The Place of O. Ray A. Young Bear. VoR

I'm nothing./ I'll always be nothing. Tobacco Shop. Fernando Pessoa, tr. fr. Portuguese by Edwin Honig. AnRep

I'm now arriv'd the soul desired port. Edmund Davie 1682; Annagram. Benjamin Tompson. SCAP

"I'm of no use," said a little brown seed. The Little Brown Seed. Harriett Mulford Lothrop. PWR

I'm offering for sale today. A Bargain Sale. Samuel Ellsworth Kiser. PoToHe

I'm Older than You, Please Listen. A. R. D. Fairburn. PeNZ

I'm on a straight path with the sun gone down. Luigi Fontanella, tr. fr. Italian by Michael Palma. NeIt

I'm on My Way to Canaan. Unknown. AH

I'm on my way to Canada. Away to Canada. Joshua McCarter Simpson. AAP

I'm on my way to the doctor to get the result of chest X-rays because. Philadelphia: 1978. C. K. Williams. PWE

I'm Only a Broken-down Miner. Unknown. AmFP

I'm only a cavalry charger. An Appeal. Unknown. NSI

I'm only a consumer, and it really doesn't matter. Cheer for the Consumer. Nixon Waterman. OBAL

I'm only a poor little mouse, ma'am. The Mouse. Laura E. Richards. OBCA

I'm ordered out in a heap of stones. The Outpost. Tomas Tranströmer, tr. fr. Swedish by Robin Fulton. PWE

I'm persistent as the pink locust. The Pink Locust. William Carlos Williams. SAmP

I'm Placing in Your Hands My Lover and Myself. Catullus, tr. fr. Latin by Rodney Pybus. FaBoBl

"I'm pregnant," I wrote to her in delight. 1974. Marilyn Hacker. GLP

I'm quiet as an old leather belt lapped snakewise. Quiet. Brian Swann. AmPA

I'm quite the opposite of my clever master. Faust's Servant. Roy Fuller. OxBTC

I'm reading the poems of the dead. The Blood of Others. Giaconda Belli, tr. fr. Spanish by Elinor Randall. WoWa

I'm red pepper in a shaker. Sugar in the Cane. Tennessee Williams. OBAL

"I'm rich,"/ said/ Irish. Eternities. Norman Mailer. NYBP

I'm riding in a train. I Am a Horse. Hans Arp, tr. fr. French. FaBoNo, tr. by Harriet Watts

I'm round at Heliodorus' place — . Lucilius, tr. fr. Greek by Peter Porter. GrAn

I'm rubber and you're glue. Unknown. RoPo

I'm Sad. Forugh Farrokhzad, tr. fr. Persian by Reza Baraheni. BoWoP

I'm Sad and I'm Lonely. Unknown. AS

I'm sad and serious. A Poem with a Tilde in the Title. Nina Zivančević, tr. fr. Serbo-Croatian by Charles Simic. HSix

I'm shouting/ I'm singing. Spring. Karla Kuskin. PDV

I'm sick of love; O let me lie. To Sycamores. Robert Herrick. CaPo

I'm sick of you hypocrites babbling about gods! The Sanctimonious Poets. Friedrich Hölderlin, tr. fr. German by Robert Bly. NU

I'm sitting alone by the fire. Her Letter. Bret Harte. AnAmPo; PoLF

I'm sitting by the hearthstone now. Twilight Musings. Mary Weston Fordham. CBWP-2

I'm sitting on my couch saying my rosary. I haven't. Mama Rosanna's Last Bead-Clack. Laurel Speer. CrSp; PFL

I'm sitting on the stile, Mary. The Countess of Dufferin. the Countess of Dufferin. OxAEP-2

I'm Smith of Stoke, aged sixty-odd. Epitaph on a Pessimist. Thomas Hardy. FaBoEE; FF; TRP

I'm so sorry for old Adam. Old Adam. Unknown. AS

I'm sorry but we can't go to the immersions tonight. The Ganges. Norman Dubie. LCAP

I'm sorry for the Dead — Today. Emily Dickinson. SAmP

"I'm sorry," said he, "to trouble you." (LL) W. W. James Reeves. ChTr; NTCP; SiSoPo

I'm sorry to say my dear wife is a dreamer. Be Off! Stevie Smith. OxBC

I'm speaking again. Speaking. Michael Ryan. AmPA; SoSe

I'm spending my nights in the doss house. Soup Kitchen Song. Unknown. NOBAu

I'm standing at the bus stop at the shopping centre. Venus in Concrete. Michael O'Loughlin. IB

I'm straddling the top tier, my wet shirt clinging. Hanging Burley. Jim Wayne Miller. MT

I'm sure every word that you say is absurd. A Woman's Reason. Gelett Burgess. FaBoNo

I'm sure if I were a woman I should hate. Sonnet: Equality of the Sexes. Gavin Ewart. Son

I'm sure we should all be as happy as kings. *(LL)* Happy Thought. Robert Louis Stevenson. BoTP; FaBoBe; OxBChV; PWR; Spl

I'm swinging through a department store of the future. Hi-Fashion Girl. Elaine Equi. UL

I'm taught P-l-o-u-g-h. O-U-G-H. Charles Battell Loomis. NBLV

I'm Thankful That My Life Doth Not Deceive. Thoreau. PoEL-4

I'm thankful that the sun and moon. Gasbags. *Unknown*. NOBL

I'm the Beautiful Basking Shark. The Ballad of the Basking Shark. Tom Hood. CBNP

I'm the bloke that's trained to sit behind the public stamp machines. A Song of the GPO. Gerry Hamill. NOBL; PIP

I'm the great Sir William Anson. *Unknown. Fr.* Balliol Rhymes. FaBoEE

I'm the Kilfenora teaboy. The Kilfenora Teaboy. Paul Durcan. PBCIP

I'm the king of the castle. King of the Castle. *Unknown*. OxNR

I'm the lidded voice from limbo. New Speaker. James Berry. NBrP

I'm the mad cosmic. Canto I. Vincente Huidobro, *tr*. by Eliot Weinberger. EaPr

I'm the man, the very fat man. The Man That Waters the Worker's Beer. Paddy Ryan. SWP

I'm the man who gets off the bus. Scouting. Philip Levine. BAP-90

I'm the pert little pimpernel. Pimpernel. Charlotte Druitt Cole. BoTP

I'm the queerest young fellow that you ever heard. The Ballad of Joking Jesus. James Joyce. ChIV-2

I'm the snow on mountains. Death Songs ("I'm the snow on mountains.") *Unknown, tr. fr. Turkish by* Reza Baraheni *and* Zahra-Soltan Shokoohtaezeh. BoWoP

I'm the sort of girl. Nausicäa. Irving Layton. ErPo

I'm the sub-average male *Time* reader. The Sub-average *Time* Reader. Ernest Wittenberg. FiBHP

I'm the Way I Am. Jacques Prévert, *tr. fr. French by* John Frederick Nims. STV

I'm thine for ever. *(LL)* A General Description of Men and Things in Cape Town. Frederic Brooks. PeSAV

I'm thinking about how ordinary this day is. Eva Salzman. NWP

I'm thinking about you. What else can I say? Postcard. Margaret Atwood. NoAM

I'm through with acid and with praise. Recantation. Minuchihri, *tr. fr. Persian by* Omar S. Pound. ArPe

I'm Through with You. *Unknown*. WTO

I'm tired of Love: I'm still more tired of Rhyme. Fatigue. Hilaire Belloc. FaBoCo; NBLV; NOBL; OxBTC; UV

I'm tired of murdering children. Two Vietnam Poems: (1966). William Knott. PBCAP

I'm tired of pacing the petty round of the ring of the thing I know. Wishes. Georgia Douglas Johnson. ShDr

I'm tired of seeing sights south of the river. Climbing a Solitary Islet in the River. Hsieh Ling-yün, *tr. fr. Chinese by* Francis Westbrook. SuSp

I'm tired of symbols, of laws divine. To My Generation. Benyamin Galai, *tr. fr. Hebrew by* Jacob Sonntag. TrJP

I'm tired of town and suburb life. Tristan da Cunha. Ian D. Colvin. PeSAV

I'm tired of trying to think. Existentialism. Lloyd Frankenberg. FiBHP

I'm told you raised your hand against yourself. On the Suicide of the Refugee W. B. Bertolt Brecht, *tr. fr. German by* John Willett. OBD

Im Traum sah ich ein Männchen klein und putzig. Heine, *tr. fr. German by* Sir Theodore Martin. AWP

I'm trav'ling to my grave. The Traveler. *Unknown*. AmFP

I'm up against the wall. The Wall. William Hawkins. MoCV

I'm upward boun'. *(LL)* Northboun'. Lucy Ariel Williams Holloway. BlSi; CDC; PoNe; ShDr

"I'm very drowsy," said the Bear. Hard to Bear. Tudor Jenks. OBCA

I'm Walking behind the Spanish. Luis Omar Salinas. AfAz

I'm wanton — no I've stopped that. Complaynt. Anne Waldman. UL

I'm war. Remember me? Achtung! Achtung! Mary Hacker. PAW

I'm wearin' [*or* wearing] awa', John [*or* Jean]. The Land o' the Leal. Lady Nairne. GTBS; GTBS-P; OBEV; OxBS; ScCV; WBLP; WGRP

I'm weary o' the rose as o' my brain. The Great Wheel. "Hugh MacDiarmid." OxBS

I'm weary of towns, it seems a'most a pity. Tired of Towns. Andrew Lang. EBVV; OHCV

I'm wife; I've finished that. Emily Dickinson. CMoP

I'm wild and woolly. Cowboy. *Unknown*. ChTr

I'm woken up. Central Heating System. Stephen Spender. GrPl

I'm working like a dog, testing my memory. The Expulsion. Gerald Stern. LCAP

I'm worried about Bill Manzana, he said. Epiphany. Aleida Rodríguez. ETG

I'm writing just after an encounter. Whatever You Say Say Nothing. Seamus Heaney. OBWP; OxBC

I'm wrong and know I'm wrong but can't help think. Red Suspenders, Boxes of Cigars. Joseph Hansen. PFL

I'm your new partner, Bed. Room 3366, Bed 1. Stephen Knight. UnDi

I'm yours, dearest, as are the winter towns. Marceline, to Her Husband. Elizabeth Libbey. AmPA

Image, The. Roy Fuller. GTBS-P; OxBTC

Image. Gu Cheng, *tr. fr. Chinese by* Donald Finkel *with* Yi Jinsheng. SpMi

Image, The. Richard Hughes. OBMV

Image. T. E. Hulme. InPK; OxBTC

Image. Anna de Noailles, *tr. fr. French by* Carol Cosman. PBWP

Image, As In a Hexagram, The. Lew Welch. PoBeRe

Image comes, An. Laser. A. R. Ammons. CAPP; NAAL-2; NoAM; NOBA

Image comes down to live as fact, and turns. The Shadowgraphs. Richmond Lattimore. NYBP

Image dance of change, An. Siegfried Sassoon. MoBrPo

Image flickers, a firefly, The. Broadcast. Ivan V. Lalic, *tr. fr. Serbo-Croatian by* Charles Simic. HSix

Image from Beckett, An. Derek Mahon. SCBI

Image in a Mirror. Mae Winkler Goodman. GoYe

Image in the bulb-ringed mirror. Mask. Elizabeth Cox. GoYe

Image in the Mirror. Peggy Susberry Kenner. JB

Image-Maker, The. Oliver St. John Gogarty. OBEV; OBMV; PoRA

Image-Nation (the Poësis). Robin Blaser. PoM

Image-Nation 13 (the Telephone). Robin Blaser. PoM

Image-Nation 3. Robin Blaser. PoM

Image o' God, The. Joe Corrie. ChIV-1; OxBS

Image of City. Lance Henson. VoR

Image of God, The. Francesco de Aldana, *tr. fr. Spanish by* Longfellow. WGRP

Image of Irelande, The, *sels*. John Derricke. "No table there is spread." OBTV

Image of Leda, An. Frank O'Hara. HCAP; LCAP

Image of Lethe, An. The Coming of War; Actaeon. Ezra Pound. CMoP; PoA; PoE

Image of the Engineer's model, An. Birdland. Allen Fisher. NBrP

Image of the frozen lake, The. Luigi Fontanella, *tr. fr. Italian by* Michael Palma. NeIt

Image the images the great games therefore the locked. The Book of Job and a Draft of a Poem to Praise the Paths of the Living. George Oppen. NNaP

Image, The/ the pawnees. The Pride. John Newlove. MoCV; NOBC

Imageries of dreams reveal a gracious age. The Age of a Dream. Lionel Johnson. OBMV

Images. Richard Aldington. MoBrPo; PoA

Images, *sels*. Anna Hajnal, *tr. fr. Hungarian by* Jascha Kessler.

Images. Naomi Long Madgett. ETG

Images. Kathleen Raine. NYBP

Images. Richard Schaukal, *tr. fr. German by* Ludwig Lewisohn. AWP

Images drip down my back like sweat. On the Morning of the Third Night above Nisqually. W. M. Ransom. CDW; NU

Images for the Gospel of Christ. Paul Ramsey. CRP

Images of a faded world possessed me, I cannot flee! Saul Tchernichowsky, *tr. fr. Hebrew by* Ruth Finer Mintz. *Fr.* To the Sun. MHP

Images of Angels. P. K. Page. MoCV; NoAM

Images of J — — assail him. The Bus Trip. Joel Oppenheimer. NeAP

Images! Venerable as Druidical trees. George Barker. *Fr.* In Memory of David Archer. FaBoMo

Imaginary Dialogue. Antiphilus, *tr. fr. Greek by* Dudley Fitts. GrAn

Imaginary Elegies, I-IV. Jack Spicer. NeAP

Imaginary Iceberg, The. Elizabeth Bishop. FaBoWP; ImPo; LiTM; MoAB; MoAmPo

Imaginary man, go. Here is your passport. Instructions for Crossing the Border. Dan Pagis, *tr. fr. Hebrew by* Stephen Mitchell. PoSu

Imaginary Sonnets, *sels*. Eugene Lee-Hamilton. Luther to a Bluebottle Fly. Son

Imaginary Translation. Marilyn Hacker. DiPo

Imaginary tremolo. Jean-Joseph Rabéarivelo, *tr. fr. French by* Ellen Conroy Kennedy. NegPo

Imagination. John Davidson. *Fr.* New Year's Eve. ArNa; MeMBP; MoBrPo

Imagination. Li Pai-feng, *tr. fr. Chinese. Fr.* Pearls and Earth. LHF, *tr. by* Hualing Nieh

Imagination. Margaret Cavendish, Duchess of Newcastle. *See* I language want, to dress[e] my fancies in.

Imagination. Shakespeare. *See* Lovers and madmen have such seething brains.

Imagination. Dina Uahupirapi. LoHo

Imagination and Taste, How Impaired and Restored. Wordsworth. *Fr.* Prelude [or, Growth of a Poet's Mind], The. EnRP; OAEL-2; PoE; PoEL-4, XII, *abr.*; TOF

Imagination as Nihilo frothed like salt foam, like waves breaking. Mom's Homecooked Trees. Michael Stephens. UL

Imagination, How Impaired and Restored. Wordsworth. *Fr.* Prelude [or, Growth of a Poet's Mind], The. EnRP; OAEL-2; OBNC; PoE; PoEL-4, XII, *abr.*; TOF

Imagination that we spurned and crave, The. *(LL)* To the One of Fictive Music. Wallace Stevens. MeMAP; MoAB; MoAmPo; NoP

Imaginative Life, The. Geoffrey Hill. NoAM

Imagine a place without a pipeline. Antarctica. Carole Forman. EaPr

Imagine a poem that starts with a couple. Reading in Place. Mark Strand. BAP-89

Imagine: A Town. Daphne Marlatt. *Fr.* Steveston. NOBC

Imagine being the first to say: *surveillance.* Inventors. Michael C. Blumenthal. DiPo; NoAM

Imagine bouncing bumping humping over a cliff. Drift. Alberta Turner. LCAP

Imagine father that you had a brother were. Landscape with Next of Kin. Olga Broumas. BoWoP

Imagine Grass. Knute Skinner. SM

Imagine it, a Sophocles complete. The Fire at Alexandria. Theodore Weiss. NoAM; PoA; SAmP; TAP

Imagine living in a strange, dark city for twenty years. Foreign. Carol Ann Duffy. NBrP

Imagine observing ones fear. Lyn Hejinian. UL

Imagine that any mind ever *thought* a red geranium! Red Geranium and Godly Mignonette. D. H. Lawrence. GTBS-P; NoAM

Imagine that July morning: Cape Henry and Virginia. The Tempest. William Jay Smith. MoAmPo

Imagine that motion, the turning and pressing. Elinor Frost's Marble-Topped Kneading Table. Pattiann Rogers. LoHo

Imagine the desert the cast of light. Jerusalem Shadow. Melanie Kaye/Kantrowitz. LoHo

Imagine the princess' surprise! The Frog Prince. Robert Pack. Poetr

Imagine the South. George Woodcock. MoCV; NOBC

Imagine them as they were first conceived. Images of Angels. P. K. Page. MoCV; NoAM

Imagine there being no exacting word for time. Time Out. Eva Salzman. NWP

Imagine what Mrs. Haessler would say. Dance of the Abakweta. Margaret Danner. PoNe

Imagined Arrival. Matthew Sweeney. IB

Imagining How It Would Be to Be Dead. Richard Eberhart. LiTA

Imago. Amy Clampitt. VCAP

(Im)C-A-T(mo). E. E. Cummings. HAP

Imitate the tapestry. *(LL)* The End of a Dynasty. Zbigniew Herbert. FaBoPV

Imitated from the Persian. Robert Southey. *See* Lord! Who Art Merciful as Well as Just.

Imitation of Chaucer. Pope. FaBoPa

Imitation of Julia A. Moore. "Mark Twain." OBAL

Imitation of Martial, Book II Ep, An 105. "Captain H——." NOEC

Imitation of Spenser. Keats. EnRP

Imitation of Walt Whitman. James Kenneth Stephen. *See* Clear cool note of the cuckoo which has ousted the legitimate nest-holder, The.

Imitation warrior. Warrior. Frank Mkalawile Chipasula. PeSAV

Imitations Based on the American. Frank Polite. BXAP

Immaculate Conception, The. Lindsay MacRae. DT

Immaculate stream, heavy, and swinging home again, The. *(LL)* The River That Is East. Galway Kinnell. Poetr

Immaculate Sir Walter Raleigh, The. T. L. McCarthy. PeLi

Immaculate white bed. *(LL)* Nantucket. William Carlos Williams. AnAmPo; HAP; InPS; OxBA; SOTW; TAP; TRP; WeW

Immalee. Christina Rossetti. BoNaP

Immanence. Richard Hovey. WGRP

Immanent. Walter de la Mare. PoA

Immeasurable haze. To the Holy Spirit. Yvor Winters. MoAmPo; VGW

Immeasurable height/ Of woods decaying, never to be decayed, The. Types and Symbols of Eternity. Wordsworth. *Fr.* Prelude [or, Growth of a Poet's Mind], The. CBCK; EnRP; OAEL-3; PoEL-4

Immeasurable sadness! Sadness. Tennyson. FaBoEE

Immense architecture/ building in air. Nathaniel Tarn. *Fr.* Journal of the Laguna de San Ignacio. UL

Immense coldness from the Longobards, An. The Longobards. Zbigniew Herbert, *tr. fr. Polish* by Czeslaw Milosz. PoSu

Immense hope, and forbearance, The. Spring Day. John Ashbery. NOBA

Immense pale houses! The sunshine and the snow. American Scenes (1904). Donald Justice. MT

Immensity [or Immensitie] cloistered [or cloysterd] in thy dear [or deare] womb [or wombe]. Nativity [or Nativitie]. John Donne. *Fr.* La Corona. ChIV-2; ESCV; Son

Immigrant. Arthur Nortje. PeSAV

Immigrant Daughter's Song. Mary Ann Larkin. IIP

Immigrants. Robert Frost. GOA

Immigration, women in industry, aged. Picture Collection. Marjorie Welish. UL

Immoderate Death that wouldst not once confer. On the Death of the Lord Treasurer. *Unknown.* FaBoEE

Immolation. Robert Farren. TIRV

Immoral Arctic, The. Morris Bishop. FiBHP

Immoral Proposition, The. Robert Creeley. LiTM; NeAP; PoM

Immorality, An. Ezra Pound. CMoP; GoJo; GrPl; ImPo; LiTM; MoAB; MoAmPo; NOBA; OBAL

Immortal, The. Blake. *Fr.* Book of Los, The. LiTB; MeMBP

Immortal. Sara Teasdale. WGRP

Immortal. Mark Van Doren. MoAmPo

Immortal Aphrodite, on your patterned throne. Sappho, *tr. fr. Greek by* Josephine Balmer. AIW

Immortal as our soul. *(LL)* To My Excellent Lucasia, on Our Friendship. Katherine Philips. MeLP; NALW; NOSC; PeHV; VBLP; WPE; WPOW

Immortal Autumn. Archibald MacLeish. CMoP; LiTA; MoAB; MoAmPo; NAAL-2; TrGrPo

Immortal clothing I put on. The Transfiguration. Robert Herrick. CaPo

Immortal glories in my mind revive. Joseph Addison. *Fr.* Letter from Italy [to the Right Honourable Charles Lord Halifax], A. NOEC; OBTV

Immortal Hate. Milton. *See* There the companions of his fall, o'erwhelmed.

Immortal heat, O let thy greater flame. Love ("Immortal heat, O let thy greater flame.") George Herbert. *Fr.* Temple, The. GeHe; Son

Immortal Imogen, crowned queen above. The Two Swans. Thomas Hood. CH

Immortal in a picture of an old grange. *(LL)* Haymaking. Edward Thomas. MoAB; MoBrPo

Immortal is an ample word. Emily Dickinson. NOCV

Immortal Israel. Judah Halevi, *tr. fr. Hebrew by* Solomon Solis-Cohen. TrJP

Immortal Longings. Shakespeare. *See* Give me my robe, put on my crown; I have.

Immortal[l] love, autho[u]r of this great flame [or frame]. Love. George Herbert. *Fr.* Temple, The. GeHe; HoPM; SeCV-1; Son

Immortal Love, Forever Full. Whittier. AH

Immortal Mind, The. Byron. WGRP

Immortal Newton never spoke. On Mr. Nash's Present of His Own Picture at Full Length. Earl of Chesterfield. NOEC

Immortal Part, The. A. E. Housman. *Fr.* Shropshire Lad, A. FaPoB; MeMBP; MoBrPo; SCGP; SoSe; UnPo

Immortal praise with one accord. *(LL)* London, hast thou [or thow] accused me. The Earl of Surrey. SiPSBD

Immortal stood frozen amidst, The. The Immortal. Blake. *Fr.* Book of Los, The. LiTB; MeMBP

Immortality. "Æ." AWP; OBMV; TIRV; WGRP

Immortality. Richard Henry Dana. WGRP

Immortality. Samuel Greenberg. LiTA

Immortality. Joseph Jefferson. BLPA

Immortality. "Nicolai Maksimovich Minsky," *tr. fr. Russian by* Babette Deutsch. TrJP

Immortality. Susan Langstaff Mitchell. TIRV

Immortality. L. A. J. Moorer. CBWP-3

Immortality, XIV: 1–12. Bible, O.T. *See* Man, that is borne of a woman is of a few dayes, and full of trouble.

Immortality of Verse the. Pope. *See* Lest you should think that verse shall die.

Immortall love, authour of this great frame. Love. George Herbert. HoPM; SeCV-1; Son

(Love "Immortall Love, authour of this great frame.") ESCV

Immortals, The. Isaac Rosenberg. FaBoTw; NSI; TrJP

Immortals don't stay long in the world of men. Replying to a Poem by a New Graduate Lamenting the Loss of His Wife. Yü Hsüan-chi, *tr. fr. Chinese by* Geoffrey R. Waters. SuSp

Immutable as my regret. *(LL)* The Grave of Love. Thomas Love Peacock. CH; OxAEP-2; OxBSP

Imogene. Eloise Bibb. CBWP-4

Impact of a Dollar, The. Stephen Crane. MeMAP

In a Blind Garden. David Shapiro. ChIV-1

In a boat, Getting Up at Night. Su Shih, *tr. fr. Chinese* by Irving Y. Lo. SuSp

In a Boat on a Summer Evening, I Heard the Cry of a Water Bird. Lu Yu, *tr. fr. Chinese* by Burton Watson. SuSp

In a book. (*LL*) We Shall Overcome. Breyten Breytenbach. PeSAV

In a bowl to sea went wise men three. The Wise Men of Gotham. Thomas Love Peacock. *Fr.* Nightmare Abbey. BXAP; CBNP; FaBoNo

(Men of Gotham, The.) CH

(Seamen Three.) WiR

(Three Men of Gotham.) FaBoCh; OBEV; OxAEP-2

In a branch of a willow hid. To a Caty-did. Philip Freneau. EAP; TAP

In a Building Named for a Governor. Christopher L. Dornin. CRP

In a Café. Rosemary Dobson. CBAP

In a cafe under a lazy fan. Country Nun. Geoff Page. CBAP

In a Cathedral City. Thomas Hardy. EnLoPo; FaBoPP

In a cavern [*or* cabin], in a canyon. Oh, My Darling Clementine. *At.* to Percy Montross. AnAmPo; FaBoBe

(Clementine.) AmFP; OBAL

In a certain sense, they are not serious. Their Seriousness, with Further Comparisons. Robert Pinsky. *Fr.* Essay on Psychiatrists. NoAM

In a chain reaction. Atomic Pantoum. Peter Meinke. SM; WeW

In a Chain-Store Cafeteria. Paul Grano. NOBAu

In a chair, in an empty room, in a house. (*LL*) Desperate Message #1 (History). Mark Svenvold. UTF

In a chariot of light from the regions of day. Liberty Tree. Thomas Paine. PAH

In a childhood of hats. The Hat Lady. Linda Pastan. SoSe

In a Child's Album. Wordsworth. *See* Small service is true service while it lasts.

In a Christian Churchyard. James Thomson ("B. V."). NOBVV

In a Churchyard. Richard Wilbur. HeIP

In a clear brooklet. The Trout. Christian David Schubart, *tr. fr. German* by Philip L. Miller. RiWo

In a climate where. Intuition. Anthony Delius. PeSA

In a coign of the cliff between lowland and highland. A Forsaken Garden. Swinburne. EBEV; EBEvV, *sts.* 1–2; FaBoPP; GTBS-P; LiTB; NOBE; NOBVV; NoP; OAEL-2; OBNC; OxAEP-2; SCGP; TEP

In a constant, dreamy fluttering of wings. (*LL*) Looking for Angels in New York. Jacqueline Osherow. UTF

In a cool curving world he lies. The Fish. Rupert Brooke. FM

In a Copy of Browning. Bliss Carman. AnAmPo

In a corner. Dissembler. Charles Shaw. GoYe

In a corner of blue sky. Daily Wages. Amrita Pritam, *tr. fr. Punjabi* by *the author* and Charles Brasch. PBWP

In a cottage embosom'd within a deep shade. Blue Ey'd Mary. *Unknown.* CoMu

In a cottage in Fife. Two Comical Folk. Mother Goose. OxNR; ReMoGo

In a Country Church. R. S. Thomas. FaBoMo; TOF

In a Country Museum. Patricia Beer. FaBoWP

In/ a/ cove. The Signs. Norman Henry, II Pritchard. NBV

In a dark, dark wood, there was a dark, dark house. The Dark House. *Unknown.* NTCP

In a Dark Hour. Jovan Hristic, *tr. fr. Serbo-Croatian* by Charles Simic. HSix

In a dark hour (there are more and more of them now). In a Dark Hour. Jovan Hristic, *tr. fr. Serbo-Croatian* by Charles Simic. HSix

In a Dark Time, *sels.* Theodore Roethke.

"In a dark time, the eye begins to see." CAPP; HAP; HeIP; MAT; MoAmPo; MoP; NAAL-2; NoAM; NOBA; NoP; NYBP; PeECV; PoE; Poetr; PPP; RaBo, *2 sts. only*; TAP; TFi; VCAP

In a dark time, the eye begins to see. Theodore Roethke. *Fr.* In a Dark Time. CAPP; HAP; HeIP; MAT; MoAmPo; NAAL-2; NoAM; NOBA; NoP; NYBP; PeECV; PoE; Poetr; PPP; RaBo, *2 sts. only*; TAP; TFi; VCAP

In a Day. Li Shang-yin, *tr. fr. Chinese* by Eugene Eoyang *and* Irving Y. Lo. SuSp

In a day or two the chairs will fall to pieces. Little House, Big House. Medbh McGuckian. PNI

In a dear little home of tarpaulin and boards. No Thoroughfare. Ruth Holmes. BoTP

In a dingy kitchen/ Facing a Ghetto backyard. Lamentations. Alter Brody. TrJP

In a dismal air; a light of breaking summer. G. S. Fraser. PoWW

In a distant field, small animals prepare. Sonnet 63: "In a distant." John Tranter. *Fr.* Crying in Early Infancy. FaBoMA

In a dogwood winter of grief he always turned. Bird in the House. Jim Wayne Miller. ETG

In a Double Rainbow. Harold Littlebird. VoR

In a Dream. Eleni Fourtouni, *tr. fr. Greek* by Eleni Fourtouni. VBLP

In a Dream. David Ignatow. PoA

In a Dream. Lu Yu, *tr. fr. Chinese* by Irving Y. Lo. SuSp

In a dream he fled the house. Coleridge. Medbh McGuckian. CIP

In a dream I never exactly dreamed. Another Life. Frank Bidart. HCAP; VCAP

In a dream I open the door. The Fat Boy's Dream. Richard McCann. GrPl

In a dream I returned to the river of bees. The River of Bees. W. S. Merwin. HeIP; LCAP; VCAP

In a Dream I Traveled among Ten Thousand Acres of Lotuses. Lu Yu, *tr. fr. Chinese* by Irving Y. Lo. SuSp

In a dreamlike fall, the long. Apis Mellifica. Roger McDonald. NOBAu

In a Drear-nighted December. Keats. CH; ELP; EnRP; NOBE; TEP

In a drugstore north of Ft. Lauderdale. The Story I Like to Tell. Robin Becker. PBCAP

In a Eweleaze Near Weatherbury. Thomas Hardy. EnVR

In a factory building there are wheels and gearings. Our Father's Hand. Annie Johnson Flint. BLRP

In a far-away northern county in the placid pastoral region. The Ox-Tamer. Walt Whitman. RB

In a far off hamlet near the sea. Uranne. Mary Weston Fordham. CBWP-2

In a fashionable suburb of Santa Barbara. In Montecito. Randall Jarrell. CoAP; MAT; NoP; NYBP; VGW

In a few moments. The Death of a Negro Poet. Conrad Kent Rivers. BPo

In a field. Keeping Things Whole. Mark Strand. CoAP; HCAP; HeIP; LCAP; PPP; TAP; VCAP

In a Field. Robert Pack. MAT

In a field of swaying grain. Death Seed. Ricarda Huch, *tr. fr. German* by Susan C. Strong. PBWP

In a fit, Philaenion bit me. Asclepiades, *tr. fr. Greek* by Sam Hamill. InMo

In a flowering universe. (*LL*) All are nothing but flowers. Nakagawa Soen-Roshi. EaPr

In a forest of frost, in a dawn of cornflowers. (*LL*) Poppies in October. Sylvia Plath. FaBoWP; HCAP; LCAP; NoAM

In a frith as I con fare fremede. *Unknown.* MiEL

In a frosty sunset. Winter: East Anglia. Edmund Blunden. OxBTC

In a Garden. Elizabeth Jennings. NOCV

In a garden planted. Encounter. Angela Greene. NWP

In a garden shady this holy lady. Song for St. Cecilia's Day. W. H. Auden. FaBoTw; TwCP

In a garden where the whitethorn spreads her leaves. Alba Innominata. *Unknown, tr. fr. French* by Ezra Pound. AWP

In a Garret. Herman Melville. AnAmPo; OBAL

In a gay jar upon his shoulder. The Amphora. Fyodor Sologub, *tr. fr. Russian* by Babette Deutsch *and* Avrahm Yarmolinsky. AWP

In a ghost town. Little Picture Catalogue. Novica Tadic, *tr. fr. Serbo-Croatian* by Charles Simic. HSix

In a Glass-Window for Inconstancy. Lord Herbert of Cherbury. OxBSP; SeCP

In a gleam of sunshine a gentian stood. A Story. Rose Terry Cooke. AmWP

In a glorius garden grene. The Lily-White Rose. *Unknown.* MeEL

In a glove shop. The Rose. Novica Tadic, *tr. fr. Serbo-Croatian* by Charles Simic. HSix

In a golden coach. Donald Jamieson. FaBoEH

In a Gondola, *sels.* Robert Browning.

"Moth's kiss, first, The!" BoLoP; GBL; OBEV

(Song: "Moth's kiss, first, The!") TrGrPo

In a goodly night, as in my bede I laye. Waking Alone. *Unknown.* MeEL

In a gorge titanic. Ula Masondo's Dream. William Plomer. MoBS

In a Grave-Yard. William Stanley Braithwaite. PoBA

In a green landscape, summer flowers. On An Old Painting. Eduard Friedrich Mörike, *tr. fr. German* by Philip L. Miller. RiWo

In a green place lanced through. The Blue Heron. Theodore Goodridge Roberts. NOBC

In a grove most rich of shade. Sir Philip Sidney. *Fr.* Astrophel and Stella. AAS; ESo; GGP; HeIL; NoSic; Poetr; SCGP; SiPS; SiPSBD

In a Hard Intellectual Light. Richard Eberhart. CMoP; LiTM

In a heavy light like yellow onions. (*LL*) Yellow Light. Garrett Kaoru Hongo. InPS; OpBo

In a herber [*or* a harbour *or* an arbour] green [*or* grene], asleep [*or* aslepe] whereas [*or* where as *or* where] I lay. Robert Wever. *Fr.* Lusty Juventus.

(In an Arbour Green.) ELP

(In Youth Is Pleasure.) ChTr; NOBE; OBEV

(Of Youth He Singeth.) CBLP; ElL

In a high-fashion journal for queers. *Unknown.* PeHV

In a hole of the heel of an old brown stocking. Stocking Fairy. Winifred Welles. FaPON

In a hollow of the forest. The Bomber. "Brian Vrepont." NOBAu

In a hollow where late-mown pasture lapses to straw. Looking Towards Bruny. Gwen Harwood. FaBoMA

In a home for incurables. A Visit. Anna Swirszczynska, *tr. fr. Polish by Czeslaw Milosz and Leonard Nathan.* PoSu

In a Hot Country. Wendy Mulford. NBrP

In a hotel in Tashkent. Political Relations. Audre Lorde. GLP

In a Hotel Writing-Room. John Cowper Powys. OxBTC

In a Hundred Years. *At. to* Elizabeth Doten. BLPA

In a hut of mud and fire. Gautama in the Deer Park at Benares. Kenneth Patchen. NaP

In a Letter to A.R.C. on Her Wishing to Be Called Anna. Matilda Betham-Edwards. ECWP; WoRP

In a light fantastick round. (*LL*) The Star That Bids the Shepherd Fold. Milton. FaBoCh; OBEV

In a little house keep I pictures suspended, it is not a fix'd house. My Picture-Gallery. Walt Whitman. NAAL-1

In a Lonely Place. Stephen Crane. AnAmPo

In a long forgotten snow. (*LL*) Let it be forgotten, as a flower is forgotten. Sara Teasdale. AnAmPo; MoAmPo; PoA; TrGrPo

In a loose robe of tinsel forth [*or* tynsell foorth] she came. George Chapman. *Fr.* Ovid's Banquet of Sense. OxAEP-1

In a lovely garden, filled with fair and blooming flowers. The Mission of the Flowers. Frances E. W. Harper. BlSi

In a Lovely Garden Walking. Ludwig Uhland, *tr. fr. German by* George MacDonald. AWP

In a maiden-time professed. Thomas Middleton. *Fr.* Witch, The. OxBSP

In a Meadow. John Swinnerton Phillimore. OBEV

In a meadow/ Beside the chapel three boys were playing football. Patrick Kavanagh. *Fr.* Father Mat. CIP; CMoP; MoAB; PoE

In a mean abode in [*or* on] the Shankill Road. The Ballad of William Bloat. *Unknown.* NOBL; PeLV

(Belfast Linen.) WTO

In a Mirror. Marcia Stubbs. MAT

In a Moonlight Wilderness. Samuel Taylor Coleridge. *See* Encinctured with a twine of leaves.

In a more hostile view, the psychiatrists. Dionysus as Psychiatrist. Robert Pinsky. *Fr.* Essay on Psychiatrists. HCAP

In a Motel on Lake Erie. James Tate. LCAP

In a Mountain Cabin in Norway. Robert Bly. RFM

In a Mucker fog. (*LL*) Kerr's Ass. Patrick Kavanagh. NOIV; RB

In a museum, I ask. Tutankhamen. William Dickey. Poetsp

In a Museum in the Capital. William Stafford. LCAP

In a Music-Hall. John Davidson. EBVV

In a Myrtle Shade. Blake. ChIV-1

In a nation of one hundred fine, mob-hearted, lynching, relenting, repenting millions. Bryan, Bryan, Bryan, Bryan. Vachel Lindsay. CMoP; LiTA; MeMAP; OxBA; OxBoLi

In a Neighborhood in Los Angeles. Francisco Alarcon. AfAz

In a net of mist the moon depends on the wood. Spring Song. George Brandon Saul. GoYe

In a new and different form? (*LL*) You built yourself a tower in the wind. Jean-Joseph Rabéarivelo. NegPo

In a New (bloody) Army he couldn't understand. (*LL*) Sergeant-Major Money. Robert Graves. OBWP

In a nook. In May. J. M. Synge. MoBrPo

In a Notebook. James Fenton *and* John Fuller. PlP; SCBI

In a package of minutes there is this We. An Aspect of Love, Alive in the Ice and Fire. Gwendolyn Brooks. BPo; CAPP; TAP

In a package the unpoetic may not understand. (*LL*) Zeugma. Christopher Reid. CBLP

In a painting by Brueghel. For the Children. David McKain. BTR

In a pan of stars. (*LL*) Campfire Extinguished. Raymond Roseliep. InPK; SM

In a Parlor Containing a Table. Galway Kinnell. NBLV; OxBSP

In a place that His hand hath made. (*LL*) At the Place of the Sea. Annie Johnson Flint. BLPA

In a plain pleasant cottage, conveniently neat. The Miller. John Cunningham. ECEV

In a post-coach and four, with postillions as fine. Priscilla Pointon. *Fr.* Letter to a Sister, Giving an Account of the Author's Wedding-Day. ECWP

In a Prominent Bar in Secaucus [One Day]. X. J. Kennedy. AiP; FYAP; HoPM; NBLV; NIP; OBAL; PPP; PRA; TRP

·In a pumpkin-shell coach, with two rats for her team! (*LL*) The Pumpkin. Whittier. ImGa

In a quiet dusty corner. Higashi Hongwanji. Gary Snyder. PoBeRe

In a quiet water'd land, a land of roses. The Dead at Clonmacnois [*or* Clonmacnoise]. Angus O'Gillan, *tr. fr. Irish by* Thomas William Rolleston. FaBoPP; OBEV; OBMV; PeIV

(Clonmacnoise.) IIP

In a race-course box behind the Stand. Right Royal. John Masefield. OtMeF

In a real city, from a real house. The Noodle-Vendor's Flute. D. J. Enright. NoP

In a red dress. Harriet in the Promised Land. Sam Cornish. ETG

In a red winter hat blue. Self-Portrait. William Carlos Williams. *Fr.* Pictures from Brueghel. LCAP

In a Remote Cloister Bordering the Empyrean. Joel Sloman. VGW

In a Roman tram, where the famous Roman mob. The Thief. Stanley Kunitz. MoAmPo; VGW

In a room on a shelf away from everything else. I Held His Name. Alberto A. Ríos. NoAM

In a Rose Garden. John Bennett. BLPA; FaBoBe

In a rundown tenement. The Healer. Charles Simic. AnAn

In a saffron dress, turning and returning. (*LL*) The Other Side. Meredith Stricker. LoHo

In a salt ring of moonlight. Moorings. Norman MacCaig. OxBTC

In a scented wood. The Night. Helen Leuty. BoTP

In a Season of Unemployment. Margaret Avison. MoCV; NOBC

In a sense. Life. Artie Gold. NOBC

In a shoe box stuffed in an old nylon stocking. The Meadow Mouse. Theodore Roethke. HeIP; NaP; RB; TRP

In a shuttered room I roast. Dylan Thomas. OBTV

In a sick shade of spruce, moss-webbed, rock-fed. As It Looked Then. E. A. Robinson. CMoP; MeMAP

In a Silence. Richard Hovey. AnAmPo

In a single day I have seen all the flowers of Ch'ang-an. (*LL*) After Passing the Examination. Meng Chiao. SuSp

In a single straight line. Yet none is far, none is near. (*LL*) A Song of Blue and Red. Amir Gilboa. MHP

In a small town in Scotland they sell books with one blank page hidden someplace in the volume. Instructions on *or rather* Examples of How to Be Afraid. Julio Cortázar, *tr. by* Paul Blackburn. AnRep

In a snug little cot lived a fat little mouse. The Country Mouse and the City Mouse. Richard Scrafton Sharpe *and* Mrs. Pearson. OxBChV

In a snug little court as I stood t'other day. The Pleasing Constraint. Aristaenetus, *tr. fr. Latin by* Richard Brinsley Sheridan *and* Nathaniel Brassey Halhed. ErPo

In a solitude of the sea. The Convergence of the Twain (Lines on the Loss of the *Titanic*, The). Thomas Hardy. FaBoEH; FaBoTw; HeIP; InPK; InPS; LiTB; LiTM; MeMBP; MoAB; MoBrPo; MoP; NAEL-2; NIP; NoAM; NoP; OAEL-2; OHCV; OxBTC; PeVV; PFP; Poetr; PrIm; SCGP; TEP; TFi

In a South African Museum. Evangeline Paterson. NBrP

In a Southern garden Lucinda sits. The Bones of Incontention. Robert David Cohen. NYBP

In a spathe of silence. The Messenger. Frances Horovitz. BrRo

In a spring dress with bluebells spilling from your breast. (*LL*) Bluebells for Grainne. Dermot Bolger. IB

In a Spring Still Not Written Of. Robert Wallace. BoNaP

In a stable of boats I lie still. The Lifeguard. James Dickey. NoP; NYBP; SoSe

In a stately hall at Brentford, when the English June was green. The Last Meeting of Pocahontas and the Great Captain. Margaret Junkin Preston. PAH

In a Station of the Metro. Ezra Pound. AmPP; HAP; HeIL; HeIP; InPK; MeMAP; MoAB; MoAmPo; MoP; NAAL-2; NIP; NoAM; NOBA; NoP; OxBA; PoE; Poetr; TAP; TFi; UnPo; VGW; WeW

In a still room at hush of dawn. The Eavesdropper. Bliss Carman. AnAmPo

In a Storm. Antoine-Roger Bolamba, *tr. fr. French by* Ellen Conroy Kennedy. NegPo

In a story called. Brothers. Marcia Southwick. NAmP90

In a summer [*or* somer] season, when soft[e] was the sun [*or* sunne *or* sonne]. William Langland. *Fr.* Vision of Piers Plowman, The.

(Field Full of Folk, The.) PoE

(Field of Folk, The.) PoEL-1

(In a summer season when the sun was mild.) NAEL-1

(On Malverne Hilles, the Place of Piers Plowman's Vision.) FaBoPP

(Prologue: "In a summer season, when soft was the sun," *mod. by* J. B. Trapp (B *text*).) EBVV; OAEL-1

(Prologue, The: "In a summer season when the sun was mild," *mod. by* E. T. Donaldson.) NAEL-1

In a summer season when the sun was mild. William Langland. *See* In a summer [*or* somer] season, when soft[e] was the sun [*or* sunne *or* sonne].

In a swaying boat drifting along with the stream. Seeking Hsin E in the Western Hills. Meng Hao Jan, *tr. fr. Chinese* by Daniel Bryant. SuSp

In a tabernacle of a toure [*or* tower]. *Unknown*. MeEL (Quia Amore Langueo.) MeEL

In a Tavern. Louis Jenkins. RaBo

In a temple at Kioto in far-away Japan. The Three Wise Monkeys. Florence Boyce Davis. WBLP

In a terrible fog I once lost my way. Lost. James Godden. OBSP

In a thousandth of a second. Asymmetry of the Universe. Fabio Doplicher, *tr. fr. Italian* by Stephen Sartarelli. NeIt

In a throng,/ A festival company. Wordsworth. *Fr.* Prelude [or, Growth of a Poet's Mind], The. EBEV; EnRP; OAEL-2; PoEL-4

In a Time of Pestilence. Thomas Nashe. *See* Adieu, Farewell, Earth's Bliss[e].

In a Time of Sickness. Orpingalik, *tr. fr. Eskimo* by Edward Field. STP

In a Town Garden. Donald Mattam. FiBHP; SCGP

In a town with a name as beautiful. Dogknotting in Quezaltenango. Vincent O'Sullivan. PeNZ

In a Train. Robert Bly. CAPP; NaP; TTTS

In a trance from the beginning, then as now. (*LL*) The Patterned Lute. Li Shang-yin. PLT

In a U-Haul North of Damascus. David Bottoms. FYAP; MT

In a valley in Switzerland a brass band marches. Switzerland. Anthony Thwaite. OBTV

In a valley [*or* the vale *or* the vaile] of this restless [*or* restles] mind. Quia Amore Langueo. *Unknown*, *tr.* by Helen Gardner. ImPo; NOBE; NOCV; OBEV; PoEL-1

In a Warm Bath. Carl Rakosi. TAP

In a wee cot hoose far across the muir. Kate Dalrymple. *Unknown*. GBP

In a wee, twee cul-de-sac. The Fruit of Knowledge. Robert Johnstone. PNI

In a weird, forlorn voice. The President Slumming. James Tate. OBAL

In a while they rose and went out aimlessly riding. Merlin Enthralled. Richard Wilbur. CMoP; NYBP

In a white gully among fungus red. Native Born. Eve Langley. WPE

In a white room. A Winter Story. Matthew Sweeney. IB

In a Wife I Would Desire. Blake. MeMBP

In a wind o'er the [stone] plain[s] at [of] Athenry. (*LL*) The Little Black Rose. Aubrey Thomas De Vere. BIrV

In a Wood. Thomas Hardy. OBNC

In a Wood. E. J. Scovell. GBL

In a wood they call the Rouge Bouquet. Rouge Bouquet. Joyce Kilmer. PAH

In a wooden room, surrounded by lights and/ Faces. The Killing. George MacBeth. FaBoMo

In a world of orange serenity. The Lacemaker (Vermeer). Anne Marx. GoYe

In a Xanthic Xebec went sailing the main. (*LL*) The Zealless Xylographer. Mary Mapes Dodge. AnAmPo; OBAL

In a Year. Robert Browning. CBLP

In a year the nightingales were said to be so loud. The Kingfisher. Amy Clampitt. HCAP; SM

In about a week, they say. To a Friend under Sentence of Death. Anne Elder. FaBoMA

In Adam's fall/ We sinned all. *Unknown*. *Fr.* New England Primer, The. OBCA (ABC, An.) GBP

In Aesop's tales an honest wretch we find. Matthew Prior. NoP

In Aeternum. Sir Thomas Wyatt. NoSic

In aeternum I was once determed. In Aeternum. Sir Thomas Wyatt. NoSic

In Africa. Roy Fuller. PoWW

In After Days. Austin Dobson. OBEV

In after times when strength or courage fail. Buffel's Kop. Roy Campbell. PeSA

In Age. William Lisle Bowles. *Fr.* Milton: On the Busts of Milton, in Youth and Age. Son

In Agrigentum, earlier in Olympia. Empedocles on Etna. Herbert B. Mallalieu. PoA

In Agypt's land contaygious to the Nile. Pharao's Daughter. Michael Moran. BIrV; ChIV-1

In Air. Peter Clarke. PBA

In Aku Aku is there double. Oh, Noa, Noa! William Cole. NBLV

In Alabama/ Stars hang down so low. Stars in Alabama. Jessie Redmond Fauset. ShDr

In Albion then, with equal lustre bright. Walter Harte. *Fr.* Essay on Satire, Particularly on The Dunciad, An. EPCY

In Alice's reversed world. More Lessons from a Mirror. Thylias Moss. ETG

In all great Shushan's palaces was there. Vashti. Helen Hunt Jackson. AmWP

In all humanity, we crave. The Commons' Petition to Charles II. The Earl of Rochester. FaBoCo

In all my Emma's beauties blest. Translation of a South American Ode. Goldsmith. NOIV

In all ten directions of the universe. Ryokan, *tr. fr. Japanese* by Stephen Mitchell. EnlH

In All the Days of My Childhood. Russell Edson. AmPA

In all the Eastern hemisphere. The Fall of J. W. Beane. Oliver Herford. OBAL

In all the good Greek of Plato. Survey of Literature. John Crowe Ransom. FaBoCh; LiTA; MeMAP; NBLV; OBAL; TAP; TwCP; VGW

In all the land no women found so fair. (*LL*) The Beauty of Job's Daughters. Jay Macpherson. ChIV-1; MoCV; NOBC

In All the Magic of Christmas-Tide. John Jacob Niles. AH

In all the old paintings. Annunciation. Kay Smith. NIP

In all the windows/ of stone. (*LL*) The Path among the Stones. Galway Kinnell. NNaP; NOBA; Prf

In All These Acts. William Everson. NoP

In all these rotten shops, in all this broken furniture. The Dancing. Gerald Stern. LCAP

In all those stories the hero. Heroes. Robert Creeley. NOBA; NoP; PPP

IN) all those who got. E. E. Cummings. FaBoEE

In all those years at work I must have seen. Prostate Operation. Robert Pinsky. *Fr.* Three on Luck. AnAn

In all thy humors, whether grave or mellow. Temperament. Martial, *tr. fr. Latin* by Joseph Addison. AWP; OBF

In Allusion to the French Song. Richard Lovelace. CaPo

In Alsace. Distant Howling. Miroslav Holub, *tr.* by Ewald Osers. PWE

"In America," began. The Student. Marianne Moore. NAAL-2; TwCP

In Amsterdam there dwelt a maid. The Fair Maid of Amsterdam. *Unknown*. OxBoLi; PeLV; RB

In an African folk tale, the rain. The Rain's Marriage. Marcia Southwick. NAmP90

In an Age of Fops and Toys. Emerson. *Fr.* Voluntaries. LiTA; PoLF

In an Album. James Russell Lowell. AnAmPo; OBAL

In an ancient overgrown park. Duckweed. Leopold Staff, *tr. fr. Polish* by Adam Czerniawski. PoSu

In an Arbour Green. Robert Wever. *See* In a herber [*or* a harbour *or* an arbour] green [*or* grene], asleep [*or* aslepe] whereas [*or* where as *or* where] I lay.

In an Artist's Studio. Christina Rossetti. NAEL-2; NALW; NoP; Poetr

In an Emergency. (*LL*) Faith is a fine invention. Emily Dickinson. AmPP; CoGr; FaBV; MeMAP; NAAL-1; NOBA; OxBA; TAP

In an envelope marked. Personal. Langston Hughes. NOBA; NTP; PoNe

In an eternal night. (*LL*) The Garden of Proserpine. Swinburne. AWP; BLPA; BLPL; FaBoRV; FaBV; FaPoR; HAP; LiTB; NAEL-2; NOBE; NOBVV; NoP; OBNC; PeVV; PlP; PoE; PoEL-5; PoRA; SCV; TFi; TrGrPo

In an exciting world of love-bites, nipple-nipping. The Lovesleep. Gavin Ewart. OxBC

In an Indian ditch lies. The World's Last Unnamed Poem. A. K. Redwing. VoR

In an instant, by instinct, I apprehended. An Act. Kenneth Rosen. AmPA

In an Iridescent Time. Ruth Stone. MoAmPo; NALW

In an oak there liv'd an owl. The Owl in the Oak. *Unknown*. FaBoNo (There was an owl lived in an oak, *sl. diff. vers.*) OxNR

In an old, dark house. Fly in December. Robert Wallace. NYBP

In an Old House. Spencer Brown. NYBP

In an Old Orchard. Peter Kane Dufault. NYBP

In an old worn-out basin. Ugly Things. Teresita Fernández, *tr. fr. Spanish* by Margaret Randall. AIW

In an orchard a little fountain flows. Song of the Ill-Married. *Unknown*, *tr. fr. French* by Patricia Terry. BoWoP

In an uncumbered clime / Minute inductons wake. (*LL*) Coffee. J. V. Cunningham. MoAmPo; PrIm; VGW

In an upper room at midnight. The Love Feast. W. H. Auden. ErPo

In an Urban School. Toi Derricotte. PBCAP

In ancient days there lived a Turk. Kafoozalum. *Unknown*. BeLS; BLPA

In Ancient December. Alice Notley. UL

In ancient Egypt. The Fertile Valley of the Nile. Eve Merriam. IHMS

In ancient times, as story tells. Baucis and Philemon; Imitated from the Eighth Book of Ovid. Swift. GN; NOEC; OAEL-1

In ancient times e'er peace with lenient smile. Danebury. *Unknown*. PeHV

In ancient times, no matter where. Little Britain. *Unknown*. NOEC

In ancient times — 'twas no great loss. On a Nomination to the Legion of Honour. *Unknown*. FaBoEE

In Defense of Satire. Sir Carr Scroope. APAS

In Defense of Superficiality. Elder Olson. NYBP

In deference to the cloud parade. The Cloud Parade. Laura Jensen. LCAP

In Defiance to the Dutch. *Unknown.* APAS

In depth of silence, heard and seen of none. *(LL)* On Himself. Robert Herrick. BeJo

In Derision of a Country Life. Edward Ravenscroft. NOSC

In dese hard times. *(LL)* Negro Soldier's Civil War Chant. *Unknown.* BPo

In Despair. C. P. Cavafy, *tr. fr. Greek by* Edmund Keeley *and* Philip Sherrard. PeHV

In despair at not being able to rival the creations of God. Hymn to Her Unknown. W. J. Turner. OBMV

In Dessexshire as It Befel. *Unknown.* GBP

In dim green depths rot ingot-laden ships. Sunken Gold. Eugene Lee-Hamilton. NOBVV

In Dispraise of the Moon. Mary Elizabeth Coleridge. BoNaP; CH

In Distrust of Merits. Marianne Moore. ArOW; LiTA; LiTM; MeMAP; MoAB; MoAmPo; NAAL-2; OBWP; OxBA; TrGrPo

In Dives' Dive. Robert Frost. VGW

In doleful tunes of autumn winds. We Seek You, One and Only God. Luba Krugman Gurdus. BTR

In doors and out, — summer and winter — Mirth. *(LL)* To the Grasshopper and the Cricket. Leigh Hunt. EnRP; GN; OBNC; Son

In doubtful breast whilst motherly Pity. Sir Thomas Wyatt. SiPSBD

In drab derelict marsh near the madhouse. Charles Brasch. *Fr.* Home Ground. PeNZ

In dread, all that the clergy teach the young. *(LL)* The Straying Student. Austin Clarke. BIrV; CIP; IPY; MoAB; NOIV; PeIV

In dream at your throat like a razor blade. *(LL)* Nocturnal, my panther, has eyes that spark, The. Tuvia Rivner. MHP

In dream I saw two Jews that met by chance. Moses and Jesus. Israel Zangwill. TrJP

In Dream: The Privacy of Sequence. Ray A. Young Bear. CDW

In dreams my life came toward me. American Dreams. Louis Simpson. CAPP

In Dreamy Swoon. George Darley. *Fr.* Nepenthe. OBNC; PeIV

In Dublin's fair city, where the girls are so pretty. Cockles and Mussels. *Unknown.* ELP

In due course of course you will [all] be issued with. Unarmed Combat. Henry Reed. *Fr.* Lessons of the War. HeIP; LiTB; OBWP

In Due Season. W. H. Auden. Prf

In due season the amphibious crocodile. Amphibious Crocodile. John Crowe Ransom. OBAL

In Duffryn Woods. John Stuart Williams. AngWe

In Dulci Jubilo. *Unknown, tr. fr. German by* John Wedderburn. ChTr; ScCV

In each line move the comma to follow the preceding noun, and read it again. *(LL)* I Saw a Fish-Pond All on Fire. *Unknown.* ChTr; GBP; NOBL; OxNR

In each mans heart that doth begin. Loves World. Sir John Suckling. SeCV-1

In each one of you I paint. Memory Town. Anne Carson. *Fr.* Life of Towns, The. BAP-90

In each world they may put us. Do Not Die. W. S. Merwin. CAPP

In Earliest Spring. William Dean Howells. *See* Tossing his mane of snows in wildest eddies and tangles.

In early days/ If kings were made by men. Human Debasement; a Fragment. Edward Rushton. NOEC

In early ear oats glaze; wheat is hard green. Harvesting. David Campbell. *Fr.* Works and Days. FaBoMA

In early morning. First Light. Linda Hogan. SRLS

In early morning twilight, raw and chill. The Eviction. William Allingham. *Fr.* Laurence Bloomfield in Ireland. BIrV; NOIV

In early youth's unclouded scene. Thirty-eight. Charlotte Smith. ECWP; NALW; WPOW

In Earthen Vessels. Whittier. BLRP

In eaves sole sparrow sits not more alone. David's Peccavi. Robert Southwell. ChIV-1

In Ecclesiastes I Read. J. P. White. ChIV-1

In Ecclesiastes I read, "That which is far off and exceeding deep." In Ecclesiastes I Read. J. P. White. ChIV-1

In Egypt they worshiped me. I Am the Cat. Leila Usher. BLPA

In Egypt we had the best time. World War II. Jeni Couzyn. PeSAV

In Egypt's sandy silence, all alone. On a Stupendous Leg of Granite, Discovered Standing by Itself in the Deserts of Egypt, with the Inscription Inserted Below. Horace Smith. PrIm

In 8 is alle my love. *Unknown.* MiEL

In eighteen hundred and eighty nine. Obituary. Conrad Aiken. OBAL

In eighteen hundred and forty one, I put my corduroy breeches on. Pat Works on the Railway. *Unknown.* SWP

In 1876/ The Cooper & Bailey Great London Circus. The Cooper & Bailey Great London Circus. Robert Hershon. MAT

In 1861, George Hew sailed in a rowboat. The Network. Arthur Sze. AiP; OpBo

In eighty-eight, ere I was born. Sir Francis Drake; or, Eighty-eight. *Unknown.* GBP; OxBSS

In elderis dayis, as Esope can declair. The Taill of the Foxe, That Begylit the Wolf, in the Schadow of the Mone. Robert Henryson. OxBS

In Emulation of Mr Cowleys Poem Call'd The Motto. Mary Astell. KTR; NOSC

In encampments. What the Servants Said to Him, as He Returned Home. Maturaittamilkkuttan Katuvan Mallanar, *tr. fr. Tamil by* A. K. Ramanujan. PLW

In England from the train you see. From the Train. Marjorie Wilson. BoTP

In England now I hear the window shake. At Home the Green Remains. John Figueroa. PBCV

In England rivers all are males. On the American Rivers. James Smith. FaBoUs

In England's green and pleasant bowers. *(LL)* I give you the end of a golden string. Blake. Spl

In English the poetics became meubles — furniture. A Later Note on Letter 15. Charles Olson. *Fr.* Maximus Poems, The. CAPP

In enterprise of martial kind. The Duke of Plaza-Toro. W. S. Gilbert. *Fr.* Gondoliers, The. FaPON; FiBHP

In Epping Forest. John Clare. *See* How beautiful this hill of fern swells on!

In eternum. *(LL)* In eternum I was once determed. Sir Thomas Wyatt. SiPSBD

In eternum I was once determed. Sir Thomas Wyatt. SiPSBD

(In Eternum "In eternum I was ons determined".) AAS; NOBE; SiPS

In Eternum ("In eternum I was ons determined.") Sir Thomas Wyatt. *See* In eternum I was once determed.

In ethics class so many years ago. Ethics. Linda Pastan. InPK

In Europe, you can't move without going down into history. In the Yukon. Ralph Gustafson. MoCV

In Evening Air. Theodore Roethke. CAPP; NYBP; TAP

In every clear stream. *(LL)* Whither? Wilhelm Müller. AWP, *tr. by* Longfellow; RiWo

In every dream thy lovely features rise. William Barnes. BoLoP

In every drop of water. The Hydrographer's Imaginings. Ts'ai Ch'i-chiao, *tr. fr. Chinese.* LHF, *tr. by* Hualing Nieh

In every leaf that crowns the plain. Faith. John Richard Moreland. OHIP

In every meanest face I see. Sons of Promise. Thomas Curtis Clark. PoToHe

In every old lady I chance to meet. Old Ladies. Will Allen Dromgoole. WeW

In every part of every living thing. Lake Superior. Lorine Niedecker. FaBoWP

In every place ye may well see. What Women Are Not. *Unknown.* MeEL

In every seed to breathe the flower. Faith. John Banister Tabb. WGRP

In every trembling bud and bloom. An Easter Canticle. Charles Hanson Towne. OHIP; TrPWD

In evrich mart that stands on British ground. The School-Mistress. William Shenstone. NOEC

In ev'ry race, in ev'ry clime. Lines to a Graduate. L. A. J. Moorer. CBWP-3

In ev'ry town where Thamis rolls his tide. The Alley; an Imitation of Spenser. Pope. NOEC

In Extremis. Margaret Fishback. FiBHP

In fact, he's the one and only! *(LL)* Old Man Platypus. Andrew Barton Paterson. OBAP; ZA

In fact, the slop-bucket — that hung in the well. *(LL)* The Old Oaken Bucket. *Unknown.* BLPA; WBLP

In fact, what change? The chimney of the spine. In Retrospect. Richard Kenney. *Fr.* Hours of the Day, The. Son

In Faguell, a fayre countré. The Knight of Curtesy. *Unknown.* OxBLMV

In fair Worcester City and in Worcestershire. The Gosport Tragedy. *Unknown.* AmFP

In faith, good Histor, long is your delay. Geron and Histor. Sir Philip Sidney. *Fr.* Arcadia. SiPS

In faith, I do[e] not love thee with mine eyes. Shakespeare. *Fr.* Sonnets. HeIP; OxAEP-1; PoEL-2; TrGrPo

In faith I wot not [well] what to say. Sir Thomas Wyatt. SiPS; SiPSBD

In faith, Squier, thou hast thee wel yquit. The Introduction to the Franklin's Prologue. Chaucer. *Fr.* Canterbury Tales, The. EnVB; NAEL-1

In faith thou shalt haue mine. Robin Hood Rescuing Three Squires. *Unknown.* ESPB, A *and* B vers.

In Hans' old mill his three black cats. Five Eyes. Walter de la Mare. CRH; OFC

In Harbor. Paul Hamilton Hayne. AnAmPo

In Harbor. Lizette Woodworth Reese. TrPWD

In hard/ country. Hard Country. Philip Booth. CoAP

In hardened innocence. *(LL)* The Roadmap. Thom Gunn. CBLP

In Hardwood Groves. Robert Frost. HAP

In harmony would you excel. A Cantata. *Unknown.* CBNP

In Hässelby. Evening Walk. Sonja Åkesson, *tr. fr. Swedish by* Joanna Bankier. WPOW

In haste poste haste, when first my wandering [*or* wandring] mind[e]. George Gascoigne. *Fr.* Gascoigne's Memories. AAS; EnRePo; Son (No Hast But Good.) NoSic

In he 50s, we drove each month to my uncle's house. Gambling. Vince Gotera. OpBo

In health, they do abuse. *Unknown.* FaBoUs

In hearts like thine ne'er may I hold a place. Answer to ——— 's Professions of Affection. Byron. OxBSP

In heart's space hath Eros. Meleager, *tr. fr. Greek by* Peter Whigham. GrAn

In Heaven. Ssu-k'ung Shu, *tr. fr. Chinese by* Irving Y. Lo. SuSp

In Heaven a spirit doth dwell. Israfel. Poe. AmPP; AWP; BLPL; ImPo; LiTA; MeMAP; NAAL-1; NOBA; OxBA; PoE; PoEL-4; TAP

In heaven-high musings and many. The Strength of Fate. Euripides, *tr. fr. Greek by* A. E. Housman. *Fr.* Alcestis. AWP

In Heaven Soaring Up. Edward Taylor. *See* In heaven soaring up, I dropped [*or* dropt] an ear [*or* Eare].

In heaven soaring up, I dropped [*or* dropt] an ear [*or* Eare]. The Joy of Church Fellowship Rightly Attended. Edward Taylor. *Fr.* God's Determinations [touching his Elect]. AmPP; EAP; MeMAP; NAAL-1; OxBA; SCAP

(In Heaven Soaring Up.) AH

In Heaven/ Some little blades of grass. The Blades of Grass. Stephen Crane. *Fr.* Black Riders, The. MoAmPo

In heaven, their earthly bodies left behind. *(LL)* To Lucasta, [on] Going beyond the Seas. Richard Lovelace. BeJo, *sts* 1–3; CaPo, *sts* 1–3; CBLP, *sts* 1–3; GTBS, *sts* 1–3; GTBS-P, *sts* 1–3; LiTB, *sts* 1–3; MeLP, *sts* 1–3; OBEV, *sts* 1–3; OxAEP-1, *sts* 1–3; SeCP, *sts* 1–3; SeCV-1, *sts* 1–3

In heaven, too. Heard in a Violent Ward. Theodore Roethke. HCAP

In Heavenly Realms of Hellas Dwelt. E. E. Cummings. NOBA; OBSV

In heav'n above. *(LL)* The Glance. George Herbert. ESCV

In heavy drink and in love. Atlantis. Slavko Mihalic, *tr. by* Charles Simic. PoSu

In Heavy Mind. James Agee. MoAmPo

In her body's perfect sweet. Isabel. Richard Hovey. AnAmPo

In her boudoir, the young lady — unacquainted with grief. *Unknown, tr. fr. Chinese by* Arthur Waley. OBVE

In her cold, unlighted piece. Interpreter. Lincoln Kirstein. ArOW

In her dream. Rape of Lucrece Retold. G. S. Sharat Chandra. PRA

In her dream she woke as usual. Ghosts. Marion Lomax. PWE

In her first passion woman loves her lover. Byron. *Fr.* Don Juan. ErPo

In her fled time, and in my time too. *(LL)* A Seasonal Aunt. Sebastian Barry. IB

In her gnarled sleep it/ begins. The Cherry Tree. Thom Gunn. GLP; Poetsp

In her hand the knife, brisk, brilliant as moon-claw. Cleaning a Fish. Dave Jeddie Smith. NoAM

In Her Only Way. Robert Graves. OxBSP

In Her Own Image. Eavan Boland. PBCIP

In her own isle's remotest grove. The Temple of Venus. Soame Jenyns. NOEC

In Her Praise. Robert Graves. BIrV

In her room at the prow of the house. The Writer. Richard Wilbur. CAPP; HCAP; ImGa; NoAM; OxBC; Poetr; SoSe

In her satin gown so fine. The Wedding. Julia Ward Howe. AmWP

In Her Song She Is Alone. Jon Swan. NYBP

In her tomb by the side of the sea. *(LL)* Annabel Lee. Poe. AiP; AmPP; AnAmPo; AWP; BeLS; BLPA; CH; DL; EBEvV; FaPON; HeIL; HeIP; ImPo; LiTA; MeMAP; NAAL-1; NOBA; NoP; OBCA; OBSP; OPOP; OtMeF; OxBA; PrIm; TAP; TFi; TrGrPo; WBLP

In her true love's arms she fell fast asleep. *(LL)* A Sailor's Life. *Unknown.* OxBSS

In her yard they feed. Birds in This Woman. Elizabeth Woody. BCF

In here it's seven o'clock. Seven in the Morning. Rhyll McMaster. FaBoMA

In hermetic enclosure. Jacques Rabémanganjara, *tr. fr. French by* Ellen Conroy Kennedy. *Fr.* Lamba. NegPo

In Hiding. Helen Degan Cohen. BTR

In High Places. Harriet Monroe. PoA

In hill fire Fall. Seadog and Seal. Philip Booth. PRA

In Him. James Vila Blake. WGRP

In Him. Annie Johnson Flint. BLRP

In him inexplicably mixed appeared. Byron. *Fr.* Lara. OAEL-2

In Him We Live. Jones Very. OxBA

In his blue suit, an Oxford Standard Authors. Study in Blue. Evan Jones (b. 1927). NOBAu

In his chamber, weak and dying. A Strike among the Poets. *Unknown.* FaBoCo; FiBHP

In his country. What She Said to Her Girl Friend. Kapilar, *tr. fr. Tamil by* A. K. Ramanujan. PLW

In his country of cool seas, they say. What She Said. Ceyti Valluvan Peruncattan, *tr. fr. Tamil by* A. K. Ramanujan. PLW

In His face they spit their icy scorn. New Negro Sermon. Jacques Roumain, *tr. fr. French by* Ellen Conroy Kennedy. NegPo

In his father's face flying. Icarus. Ronald Bottrall. GTBS-P

In his fields. What She Said ("In his fields.") Orampokiyar, *tr. fr. Tamil by* A. K. Ramanujan. *Fr.* Five on the Crabs. PLW

In his fields, mother. What Her Girl Friend Said to the Foster-Mother ("In his fields, mother.") Orampokiyar, *tr. fr. Tamil by* A. K. Ramanujan. *Fr.* Five on the Crabs. PLW

In His Last Binn Sir Peter Lies. Thomas Love Peacock. *Fr.* Headlong Hall. EnRP

In his low-ceilinged oaken room. The Silent Room. Kingsley Amis. OxBC

In his own image the Creator made. On Man. Walter Savage Landor. OBNC

In his place, mother,/ field-crabs cut into the pink. What She Said ("In his place, mother,/ field-crabs cut into the pink.") Orampokiyar, *tr. fr. Tamil by* A. K. Ramanujan. *Fr.* Five on the Crabs. PLW

In his place, mother,/ mud-spattered spotted crabs. What She Said ("In his place, mother,/ mud-spattered spotted crabs.") Orampokiyar, *tr. fr. Tamil by* A. K. Ramanujan. *Fr.* Five on the Crabs. PLW

In his portrait of Carlyle, Whistler builds. After Whistler. Stanley Plumly. AnAn; LCAP

In his room the man watches. Homero Aridjis, *tr. fr. Spanish. TSaS, tr. by* Eliot Weinberger

In his tall senatorial. The Drum; the Narrative of the Demon of Tedworth. Edith Sitwell. FaBoTw

In His Utter Wretchedness. John Audelay [*or* Awdelay]. MeEL

In his vast miscellaneous works we find. *Unknown.* EPCY

In history's mysteries vast. *Unknown.* PeLi

In holiday gown, and my new-fangled hat. Holiday Gown. John Cunningham. ECEV

In hollows of the land. The Ground-Mist. Denise Levertov. FoLa

In holly hedges starving birds. Christmas Eve. John Davidson. OHIP

In honnour of this heghe fest, of custume yere by yere. A Lover's New Year's Gift. John Lydgate. PoEL-1

In Honour of Christmas. *Unknown.* MeEL

In Honour of St. Alphonsus Rodriguez. Gerard Manley Hopkins. EBEV; OxAEP-2

In Honour of St. David's Day. *Unknown.* OBWVE

In Honour of Taffy Topaz. Christopher Morley. CRH; WHSW

In Honour of That High and Mighty Princess Queen Elizabeth of Happy Memory. Anne Bradstreet. NALW

In Honour of the Holy Spirit. Hildebert, *tr. fr. Latin by* Helen Waddell. MLL

In horse latitudes sailors once lashed. Horse Latitudes. Frankie Paino. NAmP90

In Hospital. James Elroy Flecker. OxBTC

In Hospital, *sels.* W. E. Henley.
    Apparition. TrGrPo
    Before. MoBrPo
    Romance. PAH
    Waiting. NAEL-2; NOBVV

In Hospital. Frank O'Hara. LCAP

In Hospital: Poona, I. Alun Lewis. AngWe; OBWVE

In hospital where windows meet. A Lady of Quality. Thomas Kinsella. PBCIP

In Hung-fu Monastery we brush off the dust from purple window gauze. Passing Hung-fu Monastery with Yüan-ming: Inscribed in Jest. Huang T'ing-chien, *tr. fr. Chinese by* Michael E. Workman. SuSp

In Illyria, the love-sick Orsino. Stanley J. Sharpless. PeLi

In imagination a building, moving with the seasons. The Poem as Light. John Riley. VaA

In Imitation of Anacreon. Matthew Prior. FaBoEE

In Imitation of Ancient Songs. Li Po, *tr. fr. Chinese by* Joseph J. Lee. SuSp

In Imitation of Ancient-style Poetry. Pao Chao, *tr. fr. Chinese* by Daniel Bryant. SuSp

In Imitation of Ancient-Style Poetry, *sels.* Singde, *tr. fr. Chinese* by William Schultz.

In Imitation of Horace. Aphra Behn. KTR; NOSC

In Imitation of Hsü Kan ("Since You Went Away.") Liu Chun, *tr. fr. Chinese* by Jan W. Walls. SuSp

In Imitation of T'ao P'eng-tse. Wei Ying-wu, *tr. fr. Chinese* by Irving Y. Lo. SuSp

In India. Karl Shapiro. NYBP

In India lives a bird that is unique. Farid-uddin Attar, *tr. fr. Persian* by Afkham Darbandi *and* Dick Davis. *Fr.* Conference of the Birds, The. TOF

In Innocence. J. V. Cunningham. OxBSP

In innocence I said. In Innocence. J. V. Cunningham. OxBSP

In Iona of my heart, Iona of my love. It Is Time for Me to Go Up into the House of Paradise. *Unknown, tr. fr. Gaelic.* ScCV

In Ionia, whence sprang old poets' fame. Endymion and Phoebe. Michael Drayton. SiPSBD

In Ireland, *sels.* Arthur Symons.
By the Pool at the Third Rosses. FaBoPP; OBNC

In Ireland. (*LL*) The Irish Dancer. *Unknown.* FaBoCh; GBP; NOBE; OBEV

In Ireland: By the Pool at the Third Rosses. Arthur Symons. FaBoPP; OBNC

In Ireland, we're all of us just. The Deadly Seven. Sydney Bernard Smith. PeLi

In it there is a dream. A Girl's Head. Katherine Gallagher. NOBAu

In it there is a space-ship. A Boy's Head. Miroslav Holub, *tr. fr. Czech* by Ian Milner *and* George Theiner. CBNP; TSaS

In Italy, where this sort of thing can occur. A Hill. Anthony Hecht. CoAP; FoLa; NYBP; VCAP

In its absence it has become beautiful. The Glove. Harold Bond. NYBP

In its antiquity. (*LL*) Elders/ we have been here so short a time. W. S. Merwin. EaPr

In its going down, the moon. Robert Hoggra. MoCV

In its seat 'twixt bowel and bladder. Guts. Lincoln Kirstein. ArOW

In its tranquillity. (*LL*) For a Black Child. David Diop. NegPo

In January. Lance Henson. ETG

In January, 1962. Ted Kooser. Poetsp

In jealously of cause and pride of plan. Autonomous. Mark Van Doren. LiTA

In Jersey City where I did dwell. The Butcher Boy. *Unknown.* AmFP

In John the Pisan's statue at Siena. Likeness. Clive Wilmer. SCBI

In jolly "hans around." (*LL*) October's Party. George Cooper. BoTP; PoLF

In joye that is so light. (*LL*) As I lay upon a night. *Unknown.* MiEL

In Judgment of the Leaf. Kenneth Patchen. UnAS; VGW

In judgment's scales, we make't a benefit. (*LL*) To Kiss God's Rod; Occasioned upon a Child's Sickness. Mildmay Fane, 2d Earl of Westmorland. BeJo

In July month, ae bonny morn. My Winsome Dear. Robert Fergusson. *Fr.* Leith Races. VGW

In july of 19 somethin. With All Deliberate Speed. Don L. Lee. JB

In jumping and tumbling. Tumbling. *Unknown.* OxBChV

In June, amid the golden fields. The Groundhog. Richard Eberhart. CMoP; FaBoMo; ImPo; LiTA; LiTM; MoAB; MoAmPo; MoP; NoAM; NoP; NU; RaBo; TAP; TFi; TRP; UnPo

In June and Gentle Oven. Anne Wilkinson. MoCV; NOBC

In June, examiners. The Grand Central Hotel. Roy McFadden. PNI

In June I give you a close-wooded fell. June. Folgore da San Geminiano, *tr. fr. Italian* by Dante Gabriel Rossetti. *Fr.* Sonnets of the Months. AWP

In June, in the Kyborg Castle, in the canton. Wake Up. Raymond Carver. BAP-90

In June the bush we call. The Victors. Denise Levertov. NoP

In June the sun is a bonnet of light. Sun. Gary Soto. TRP

In Just-. E. E. Cummings. *See* In just-/ spring when the world is mud.

In just-/ spring when the world is mud. E. E. Cummings. *Fr.* Chansons Innocentes. AmPP; FaBoVe; FaBV; FaPON; HeIL; HeIP; MoAB; MoAmPo; MoShBr; NAAL-2; NIP; NoP; Poetr; PrIm; SoSe; WeW
(In Just-.) InPK

In Kansas. Carter Revard. HATNAP

In Kansas City, I'm shopping. Edge of America. Jo McDougall. NGP

In Kansas during the war. He Remembers Something from the War. James Whitehead. ArOW

In Kensington Gardens. Arthur Symons. EnLoPo

In Kerry. J. M. Synge. FaBoPP; GBL; MoBrPo; PeIV

In *Kiss Me Deadly* Cloris Leachman asks Mike Hammer in the car. Double Sonnet for Mickey. Gerald Burns. BAP-91

In Köln [Köhln], a town of monks and bones. Cologne. Samuel Taylor Coleridge. FaBoEE; NBLV; OBTV; PFP

In kraals of slanting shade the herd. Buffalo. Charles Eglington. PeSA

In Laddery Street Herself. Laura Riding. *Fr.* Forgotten Girlhood. RB

In Lady Lusher's drawing-room, where float the strains of Brahms. The Martyred Democrat. C. J. Dennis. CBAP

In Lamplight, Watching My Wife Preparing a Flower, *sels.* Ch'ien Ch'ien-i, *tr. fr. Chinese* by Jonathan Chaves.

In Language. Eugene Gloria. OpBo

In Lantana Street's mid-morning. At the Nature-Strip. Judith Rodriguez. CBAP

In Larch Wood. Larch Wood Secrets. Ivy O. Eastwick. BoTP

In late afternoon, when the snow began. Terra Nova. Sean O'Brien. PWE

In Late Spring of the Year *Keng-hsü*, *sels.* Yüan Mei, *tr. fr. Chinese* by Jonathan Chaves.

In late winter/ I sometimes glimpse bits of steam. The Bear. Galway Kinnell. CAPP; CoAP; InPS; NNaP; RFM; TAP; TRP; VCAP; VGW

In late years, I love only the stillness. To Subprefect Chang. Wang Wei, *tr. fr. Chinese* by Irving Y. Lo. SuSp

In length and ease are alike every where. (*LL*) To Sir H. W. at His Going Ambassador to Venice. John Donne. MeLP

In Librum. Sir John Davies. FaBoEE

In Lieu. Louis MacNeice. CMoP

In life and death, O Lord, abide with me! (*LL*) Abide with Me. Henry Francis Lyte. BLRP; EBVV; FaBoBe; FaPoR; NOCV; PIP; PWR; TIRV; WBLP; WGRP

In life I was the town drunkard. Chase Henry. Edgar Lee Masters. OBD

In Life's fair morn, a FIDDLE, was his choice. On the Death of a Fiddler. Philip Freneau. EAP

In light, and nothing else, awake. (*LL*) At the San Francisco Airport. Yvor Winters. AiP; HeIP; InPK; NIP; NOBA

In light, and then the fancy sings. (*LL*) The Lark Ascending. George Meredith. WiR

In lily ponds, the plump colorful buds. What the Concubine Said When She Heard the Wife Complain about the Concubine's Wiles. Villakaviralinar, *tr. fr. Tamil* by A. K. Ramanujan. PLW

In Limerick, the besieged Irish were all plague and famine. An Example. Brendan Kennelly. PWE

In Line at the Supermarket. Greg Pape. PBCAP

In literature and song. Ron Padgett. *Fr.* 3 Little Poems. ArLo

In little O's at the spectacle of gulls. (*LL*) V-Winged and Hoary. Henri Cole. UTF

In Little Rock the people bear. The Chicago "Defender" Sends a Man to Little Rock. Gwendolyn Brooks. PoBA; Poetr

In little time I stake my claim. Ann Griffiths. Sally Roberts Jones. AngWe

In Lombardy. Donald Revell. SM

In Londes wher we go. (*LL*) Holver and Hivy made a gret party. *Unknown.* MiEL

In London city was Bicham born. Young Beichan. *Unknown.* ESPB; FaBoBa

In London City where I once did dwell, there's where I got my learning. Barbara Allen ("In London City where once I did dwell.") *Unknown.* BeLS
(Barbra Allen.) AS

In London here the streets are grey, an' grey the sky above. Irish Skies. Winifred M. Letts. TIRV

In London I never know what to be at. Country and Town. Charles Morris. NOEC

In London, September, 1802. Wordsworth. *See* O Friend! I know not which way I must look.

In London there I was bent. London Lickpenny. *Unknown.* CoMu; FaBoPP; OBSV
(London Lackpenny.) ChTr

In lonely watches night by night. Requiescant. Frederick George Scott. OHIP

In Long Valley the Finns. Washrags. Vern Rutsala. ETG

In looking o'er the prospects. The Prospect of the Future. Mrs. Henry Linden. CBWP-4

In Lord Carpenter's Country. Barry O. Higgs. PeSA

In Los Angeles/ while the mountains cleared of smog. Tongue-tied in Black and White. Michael S. Harper. HCAP

In Love. David Wevill. MoCV

In love and the enamelled flowers of song? (*LL*) Death Sweet. Thomas Lovell Beddoes. NOBVV

In Love, at Stonehenge. Coventry Patmore. *Fr.* Angel in the House, The. FaBoPP

In Love for Long. Edwin Muir. ArLo; BoLoP; LiTM; MeMBP; MoBrPo

In Love, If Love Be Love. Tennyson. *Fr.* Idylls of the King. PoEL-5; TrGrPo

In Love, if Love be Love, if Love be ours. In Love, If Love Be Love. Tennyson. *Fr.* Idylls of the King. PoEL-5; TrGrPo
(All in All.) ImPo; LiTB
(Vivien's Song.) OBNC

In love longing/ I listen to the monk's bell. At the Sutra Chanting of Her Dead Daughter. Lady Izumi Shikibu, *tr. fr. Japanese by* Kenneth Rexroth *and* Ikuko Atsumi. WPJ

In love to be sure what disasters we meet. The Lover's Arithmetic. *Unknown.* CBNP; OxBoLi; PeLV

In love with none but me. *(LL)* A Conjuration, to Electra. Robert Herrick. GBL; PoEL-3

In Love with the Bears. Greg Kuzma. NYBP

In Love with Wholes. Alberta Turner. LCAP

In Love's name you are charged: oh, fly. Love's Hue and Cry. James Shirley. BeJo

In love's rubber armor I come to you. Love Sonnet. John Updike. Son

In loving, each one hath free choice. Isabella Whitney. *Fr.* Sweet Nosegay, A, or Pleasant Posy. WPE

In loving thou know'st I am forsworn. Shakespeare. *Fr.* Sonnets. HeIP

In lowly dale, fast by a river's side. James Thomson. *Fr.* Castle of Indolence, The. EnRP; NOEC

In lungs fresh like honeycomb. Indian. Laura Jensen. AmPA

In Macon, the paper mill. Childhood. Bruce Beasley. UTF

In Magic Words. Merrill Moore. Son

In magnanimity? *(LL)* Apropos of the Falling Sleet. Harry Clifton. IB

In Maidstone Gaol, I am lamenting. Farewell to the World of Richard Bishop. *Unknown.* CoMu

In man, ambition is the common'st thing. Ambition. Robert Herrick. CaPo

In Manchester there are a thousand puddles. Watch Your Step — I'm Drenched. Adrian Mitchell. RB

In Manchester today a man was seen. Here is the News. Michael Rosen. OBSP

In man's cannot be right. *(LL)* A Double Standard. Frances E. W. Harper. AAP; AmWP; BlSi; PWR; VBLP

In Mantua-territory half is slough. Robert Browning. *Fr.* Sordello. EBVVPR

In many forms we try. The Bohemian Hymn. Emerson. WGRP

In marble walls [*or* halls] as white as milk. Mother Goose. ChTr; GBP; OxNR

In March and April, thereabout. Alison ("In March and April thereabout.") *Unknown.* HAP

In March birds couple, a new birth. *At. to* Henry Vaughan *and* Thomas Stanley, *fr. the Welsh of* Aneirin. FaBoEE; FaBoRV
(Leaves Come Again, The.) FaBoEE

In March I give you plenteous fisheries. March. Folgore da San Geminiano, *tr. fr. Italian by* Dante Gabriel Rossetti. *Fr.* Sonnets of the Months. AWP

In March I inseminated the wife. The Gift of Life. Lavinia Greenlaw. NWP

In March the seed. Mater Dei. Padraic Fallon. NOCV

In Marion, the honey locust trees are falling. Two Poems about President Harding. James Wright. CoAP; MoP

In martial sports I had my cunning tried. Sir Philip Sidney. *Fr.* Astrophel and Stella. AAS; ESo; GGP; HeIL; NAEL-1; NoSic; Poetr; SCGP; SiPS; SiPSBD

In mathematics he was greater. Samuel Butler. *Fr.* Hudibras. NOBL

In matters of commerce the fault of the Dutch. A Political Despatch. George Canning. FaBoCo
(Dutch, The.) OBTV; PeLV
(Epigram: Dutch, The.) OxBoLi

In May. J. M. Synge. MoBrPo

In May. *Unknown.* BoTP

In May, approaching the city, I. The Ritualists. William Carlos Williams. NYBP

In May I go a-walking. In May. *Unknown.* BoTP

In May it muryeth when it dawes. *Unknown.* MiEL

In May, that moder is of monthes glade. Chaucer. *Fr.* Troilus and Criseyde [*or* Criseide]. EnVB

In May, when sea-winds pierced our solitudes. The Rhodora [On Being Asked Whence Is the Flower]. Emerson. AmPP; AnAmPo; AWP; BoNaP; FaBV; GN; LiTA; MeMAP; NAAL-1; NOBA; NoP; OxBA; PFP; PoE; PWR; TAP; TFi; TrGrPo

In Mazatlán. Luis Omar Salinas. AfAz

In me, Eve, of my primavera, personified. *(LL)* The Creek. Roland Robinson. NOBAu

In me is death, in you my life. Michelangelo, *tr. fr. Italian.* OBD

In Me, Past, Present, Future Meet. Siegfried Sassoon. OBEV; OxBSP

In me something glimpsed its occasion. Passing Through. Patrick Williams. PNI

In me there is a vast and lonely place. Zora Cross. *Fr.* Love Sonnets. CBAP

In melancholic fancy. Hallo My Fancy. William Cleland. CH; OxBoLi

In Memorial. J. Gordon Coogler. OBAL

In Memoriam. "Max Adeler." FaBoCo

In Memoriam. Bernard Dadié, *tr. fr. French by* Ellen Conroy Kennedy. NegPo

In Memoriam. Padraig de Brun. WTO

In Memoriam. W. J. Gruffydd, *tr. fr. Welsh by* R. Gerallt Jones. OBWVE

In Memoriam. A. B. L. Hodgson. NSI

In Memoriam. Martin Johnston. NOBAu

In Memoriam. Michael Longley. PNI

In Memoriam. H. Cordelia Ray. *See* Muse of Poetry came down one day, The.

In Memoriam. Adrienne Rich. PFL

In Memoriam, II. Richard Weber. *See* "Suddenly she slapped me, hard across the face."

In Memoriam, A. C. M. L., *sels.* Cecil Arthur Spring-Rice.
"God of all power and might." TrPWD

In Memoriam: A. C., R.J.O., K.S. Sir John Betjeman. NYBP

In Memoriam A. H. H. Tennyson. EBVV, *abr.*; OAEL-2, *abr.*; PeECV, *abr.*
Sels.
"Again at Christmas did we weave." IMW; PChr
"And all is well, tho' faith and form." EBVVPR, *sect.* CXXXVII
As Sometimes in a Dead Man's Face, The. ImPo; LiTB
Baby New to Earth and Sky, The. MeMBP
Be Near Me When My Light Is Low. EBVVPR; ELP; EnVR; HAP; HeIP; LiTB; MeMBP; NOCV; NoP; PoEL-5; SCGP; SCV
"By night we linger'd [*or* lingered] on the lawn." EnVR; FHYEP; HAP; NoP; OBNC; PoEL-5; TOF
"Calm is the morn without a sound." ChTr; EBEV; ELP; EnVR; FaBoRV; FHYEP; HeIP; LiTB; NOBE; NoP; OBNC; PIP; PoEL-5; TrGrPo
(Lincolnshire Wolds and Lincolnshire Sea.) FaBoPP
"Contemplate all this work of Time." EnVR; FF
"Danube to the Severn gave, The." EBVVPR; EnVR; FF; GTBS-P; NoP
(Hushing of the Wye, The.) FaBoPP
Dark House, by Which Once More I Stand. EBEV; EBVVPR; EnVR; FHYEP; GTBS-P; HAP; HeIP; MeMBP; NOBE; NoP; OBD; OBNC; PeHV; PoEL-5; SCV; SoSe; UnPo
(Dark House.) ImPo; LiTB; SCGP
"Dear friend, far off, my lost desire." EBVVPR; FHYEP
"Do we indeed desire the dead." EBVVPR; EnVR; OBD
"Doors, where my heart was used to beat." EnVR; FHYEP; NoP; OBNC; PoEL-5; SCV
"Fair ship, that from the Italian shore." EBVVPR; EnVR; PeHV
"Happy lover who has come, A." EBVVPR; EnVR
"How many a father have I seen." EBVVPR; EnVR
How pure at heart and sound in head. MeMBP
"I cannot love thee as I ought." EBVVPR, *sect.* LII; EnVR, *sect.* LII
I Cannot See the Features Right. ImPo; LiTB; MeMBP; PoEL-5
"I climb the hill: from end to end." FHYEP; PoEL-5
"I dreamed there would be spring no more." NOBE
I Envy Not in Any Moods. EBEvV; FHYEP; ImPo; LiTB; MeMBP; OBNC; PeHV
"I hear the noise about thy keel." EnVR
I Held It Truth (with Him Who Sings). EBVVPR; EnVR; HeIP; LiTB; MeMBP; NoP; OBNC
"I hold it true, whate're befall." UV
"I past [*or* passed] beside the reverend walls."
(He Revisits Cambridge.) FaBoPP
"I sometimes hold it half a sin." EnVR; EPCY; IMW; TOF
"I trust I have not wasted breath." EnVR; FHYEP
"I wage not any feud with death." ImPo; LiTB; OBF
"I will not shut me from my kind." EnVR; FHYEP
"If one should bring me this report." EnVR; FHYEP; MeMBP
(Of One Dead.) ImPo
If Sleep and Death Be Truly One. MeMBP; OBNC
"In those sad words I took farewell." EnVR
"Is it, then, regret for buried time." FHYEP
"It is the day when he was born." FHYEP
"Love is and was my lord and king." EBVVPR; NOBE; NOCV; OBEV; OBNC
(My Lord and King.) ChTr
"Love that rose on stronger wings, The." EBVVPR
"My own dim life should teach me this." EnVR; FHYEP
"Now fades the last long streak of snow." FaBoRV; FHYEP; GTBS-P; NOBE; OBNC
"O days and hours, your work is this"
"O happy hour, and happier hours." EnVR
"O living will that shalt endure." EBVVPR; FaBoBe; MeMBP

(Prayer, The: "O living will that shalt endure.") WGRP
"O sorrow, cruel fellowship." EBVVPR; EnVR; HAP
"O thou that after toil and storm"
O, Wast Thou with Me, Dearest, Then. MeMBP
Oh Yet We Trust. EBVVPR; ImPo; LiTB; NoP; OBNC; TrGrPo
 (Larger Hope, The.) WGRP
 (O [or Oh], yet we trust that somehow good.) EnVR; FHYEP; MeMBP
"Old warder of these buried bones." PoEL-5
"Old yew, which graspest at the stones." EBVVPR; ELP; EnVR; GTBS-P; NOBE; NoP; OBNC; PoEL-5; UnPo
"On that last night before we went." PoEL-5
"One writes, that "other friends remain." EnVR; OBF, first two sts.; PoEL-5
"Path by which we twain did go, The." SCV
"Peace; come away: the song of woe." EBVVPR; EnVR; FHYEP; IMW
Ring out, Wild Bells (To the Wild Sky). BLPL; EBEvV; FaPON, 2 sts.; FaPoR; FHYEP; LiTB; MeMBP; OxAEP-2; PlP, 7 sts.; TrGrPo; WiR, 7 sts., incl. 2 sts. fr. CV
 (Ring Out the Old, Ring In the New.) WBLP
 (Ring Out, Wild Bells.) ImPo
"Risest thou thus, dim dawn, again." OBNC; PoEL-5
"Sad Hesper o'er the buried sun." EnVR; NoP
"So careful of the type?" but no. EBVVPR; EnVR; FF; FHYEP; HAP; NoP; OBNC; TOF
Strong Son of God (Immortal Love). EBVVPR; EnVR; HAP; LiTB; MeMBP; NAWM-2; TrCP; TrGrPo; TrPWD; WGRP
"Sweet after showers, ambrosial air."
"Tears of the widower, when he sees." PeHV
"That which we dare invoke to bless." FHYEP; NOCV; TOF; WGRP
There Rolls the Deep. FaBoRV; HAP; NOBE
"Thou comest, much wept for: such a breeze."
"Thy voice is on the rolling air." EBVVPR; FHYEP; HeIP; NoP; PeHV
"Till now the doubtful dusk reveal'd." GTBS-P
"Time draws near the birth of Christ, The." EBVVPR, sect. XXVIII; FaBoRV, sect. XXVIII; FHYEP, sect. XXVIII; NOCV, sect. XXVIII; PChr, sect. XXVIII; SoSe, sect. XXVIII
"'Tis well, 'tis something; we may stand."
To-night the Winds Begin. GTBS-P; ImPo; LiTB; NOBE; OBNC; PoEL-5
 (Tonight the winds begin to rise.) PeECV, sect. XV
"To sleep I give my powers away." EnVR
"Tonight ungathered let us leave." FHYEP
"Unwatch'd [or unwatched], the garden bough shall sway." ELP; FHYEP; GTBS-P; OBNC; PoEL-5; SCV
 (Somersby, Lincolnshire; after Leaving the Refectory.) FaBoPP
 (Unwatched, the garden bough shall sway.) PeECV, sect. CI
"We leave the well-beloved place." FHYEP; PoEL-5
What Hope Is Here for Modern Rhyme. EnVR; MeMBP
"What words are these have fallen from me." EBEV
"When Lazarus left his charnel-cave." FHYEP; TOF
When on My Bed the Moonlight Falls. MeMBP; NoP; SCGP
"When rosy plumelets tuft the larch." FHYEP; OBNC
"Wild bird, whose warble, liquid sweet." NoP
"Wish, that of the living whole, The." EBVVPR; EnVR; FHYEP; HAP; NoP; OBNC; TOF
"Witch-elms that counterchange the floor." OBNC
"With such compelling cause to grieve."
"With trembling fingers did we weave." FHYEP
"You say, but with no touch of scorn." NOCV
 (Doubt.) WGRP
In Memoriam Akbar Babool. Wopko Jensma. PeSAV
In Memoriam. Alphonse Campbell Fordham. Mary Weston Fordham. AAP; CBWP-2
In Memoriam Ben Zwane. Wopko Jensma. PeSAV
In Memoriam (Easter, 1915). Edward Thomas. GTBS-P; NOBE; OBWP; OBWVE; OxBTC; PeFWW; Spl
In Memoriam: Ernst Toller. W. H. Auden. NYBP
In Memoriam Francis Ledwidge. Seamus Heaney. CIP; NoAM
In Memoriam Frederick Douglass. Eloise Bibb. CBWP-4
In Memoriam Frederick Douglass. H. Cordelia Ray. CBWP-3
In Memoriam I, Elizabeth at Twenty. Richard Weber. ErPo
In Memoriam James Joyce, sels. "Hugh MacDiarmid."
 In the Fall. FaBoMo; InPS
 "It was Landor who first said." FaBoPV
 We Must Look at the Harebell. NAEL-2
In Memoriam, J.A.R., Drowned, East London. Guy Butler. PeSAV
In Memoriam J.H.H. C. J. Ronald. NSI
In Memoriam John Coltrane. Michael Stillman. InPK; Jaz
In Memoriam — Leo: A Yellow Cat. Margaret Sherwood. BLPA
In Memoriam: Martin Luther King, Jr. June Jordan. PoBA
In Memoriam of E. B. Clark. L. A. J. Moorer. CBWP-3
In Memoriam Paul Laurence Dunbar. H. Cordelia Ray. CBWP-3
In Memoriame D. Sutherland]. E.A. Mackintosh. PoWW
In Memoriam R. M. Stalker, Missing, September 1916. E.A. Mackintosh. OBF

In Memoriam: Roy Campbell. Ralph Nixon Currey. PeSA
In Memoriam S. L. Akintola. David Knight. MoCV
In Memoriam. Susan Eugenia Bennett. Mary Weston Fordham. CBWP-2
In Memoriam the Master — Noel Coward (1900-1973). E. J. Thribb. PeLV
In Memory, sels. Lionel Johnson.
 "Ah! fair face gone from sight." OBNC; PoEL-5
In Memory, 1978. Judith Kazantzis. AIW; BrRo
In Memory of a Friend. George Barker. OxBTC
In Memory of Ann Jones. Dylan Thomas. See After the funeral, mule praises, brays.
In Memory of Arthur Clement Williams. Eloise Bibb. CBWP-4
In Memory of Arthur Winslow, sels. Robert Lowell.
 Death from Cancer. TwCP
In Memory of Basil, Marquess of Dufferin and Ava. Sir John Betjeman. OBWP
In Memory of Bryan Lathrop. Edgar Lee Masters. PoA
In Memory of Captain Underwood Who Was Drowned. Unknown. FaBoEE
In Memory of Crossing the Columbia. Elizabeth Woody. BCF
In Memory of David Archer, sels. George Barker.
 "Images! Venerable as Druidical trees." FaBoMo
In Memory of Edward Wilson. James Clerk Maxwell. See Gin a body meet a body.
In Memory of Elizabeth Kearney, Blasket-Islander. Michael Davitt, tr. fr. Irish by the author. BiHa
In Memory of Eva Gore-Booth and Con Markiewicz. W. B. Yeats. FaBoPV; FaPoB; MoAB; NoAM; OAEL-2; OBMV; OxBTC
In Memory of Forgetting. Cyn Zarco. BCF
In Memory of Gerard Dillon. Michael Longley. PBCIP
In Memory of Gerard Dillon. Michael Longley. BiHa
In Memory of Idris Davies. John Tripp. AngWe
In Memory of James M. Rathel. Josephine D. Henderson Heard. CBWP-4
In Memory of Jane Fraser [or Frazer]. Geoffrey Hill. MoP; NAEL-2; NoAM; OxBTC
In Memory of Kathleen. Kenneth Patchen. IMW; MoAmPo
In Memory of Leopardi. James Wright. NaP
In Memory of Major Robert Gregory. W. B. Yeats. EBEV; OAEL-2; OBF; SCGP
In Memory of My Arab Grandmother. Evelyn Arcad Zerbe. WPOW
In Memory of My Country. Douglas Crase. FoLa
In Memory of My Dear Grandchild [Anne Bradstreet]. Anne Bradstreet. BoWoP; NAAL-1; TrCP
In Memory of My Dear Grandchild Elizabeth Bradstreet Who Deceased August, 1665, Being a Year and a Half Old. Anne Bradstreet. EAP; NAAL-1; NOCV; SCAP; WPE
In Memory of My Father: Australia. Joseph Brodsky. BAP-91
In Memory of My Feelings. Frank O'Hara. NAAL-2; NeAP; PoM
In Memory of My First Chapatis. Diane Di Prima. PoM
In Memory of My Mother. Patrick Kavanagh. ArLo; BIrV; CIP; MoP; NoAM; RaBo
In Memory of Radio. Amiri Baraka. NAAL-2; NeAP; NoP; PoBeRe; Poetr; PoM
In Memory of Sigmund Freud. W. H. Auden. HAP; LiTB; NoAM; OAEL-2; OxBA
In Memory of the Circus Ship Euzkera. Walker Gibson. FiBHP
In Memory of the Unknown Poet, Robert Boardman Vaughn. Donald Justice. CAPP; DiPo; NoAM
In Memory of the Utah Stars. William Matthews. Poetsp
In Memory of V. R. Lang. Mac Hammond. PoA
In Memory of W. B. Yeats. (He disappeared in the dead of winter.) W. H. Auden. CMoP; EPCY; HAP; HeIP; HoPM; IIP; ImPo; LiTB; LiTM; MeMAP; MoAB; MoBrPo; NoAM; NOBE; OAEL-2; OxAEP-2; OxBTC; Poetr; PPP; PrIm; TFi; TrGrPo; TRP; UnPo; WeW
 Sels.
 "Earth, receive an honoured guest." ChTr; FaBoRV; FaBoTw, 4 sts.; Mes
In Memory of W. H. Auden. David R. Slavitt. SM
In Memory of Walter Savage Landor. Swinburne. PoEL-5
In Mem'ry's fairest court a shrine is set. To Laura. H. Cordelia Ray. CBWP-3
In Men Whom Men Condemn as Ill. Joaquin Miller. Fr. Byron. PoLF
In Merche, after the first C. Unknown. MiEL
In Mercy, Lord, Incline Thine Ear. Isaac M. Wise. AH
In Merioneth, over the sad moor. Dead. Lionel Johnson. OBNC; PoEL-5
In merry old England, it once was a rule. On the New Laureate. Unknown. FaBoCo
In merry Scotland, in merry Scotland. Henry Martyn. Unknown. ESPB
In mery May, quhen medis springis. Prologue to the Avowis of Alexander. John Barbour. Fr. Buik of Alexander, The. OxBS
In mid-river we join the ancient force. Baptism. Dale Zieroth. NOBC
In middle life when the skin slackens. Ambulando. Charles Brasch. PeNZ

In narrow room nature's whole wealth, yea more. Paradise. Milton. *Fr.* Paradise Lost. EPCY; NOSC

In Nature There Is neither Right nor Left nor Wrong. Randall Jarrell. CBLP; OxBC

In "nature" there's no choice. Beyond the End. Denise Levertov. NeAP; VGW

In Nature's pieces still I see. A Divine Mistress. Thomas Carew. BeJo

In Neglect. Robert Frost. OxBSP; VGW

In Nets of Golden Wires. Thomas Morley. EnRePo

In New Orleans dwelt a young Creole. Alben Barkley. PeLi

In New South Wales, as I plainly see. William Forster. *Fr.* Devil and the Governor, The. CBAP

In Nick Ray's "Bigger Than Life." 1956. Maxine Scates. PBCAP

In night, when colors [*or* colours] all to black[e] are cast. Fulke Greville. *Fr.* Caelica. AAS; EnRePo; OAEL-1; Son

In Nine Sleep Valley, *sels.* James Merrill. "Geode, the troll's melon." HCAP

In 1915 my grandfather's. Grandfather. Michael S. Harper. CAPP; LCAP; TAP; VCAP

In 1945, when the keepers cried kaput. The Gift. John Ciardi. BTR; LiTM

In 1943 Althea was a welder. Of Althea and Flaxie. Cheryl Clarke. GLP (Of Flaxie and Althea.) ETG

In 1943/ my father. Post-War. Libby Houston. PAW

In nineteen hundred and twenty-two. Mr. Vachel Lindsay Discovers Radio. Samuel Hoffenstein. BXAP

In nineteen hundred they preferred. Upper Family. Maxwell Bodenheim. OBAL

In 1910 a royal princess. English. Osbert Lancaster. *Fr.* Afternoons with Baedeker. FaBoCo; NOBL; PeLV

In 1939 the skylark had nothing to say to me. The Ninth of July. John Hollander. CoAP

In 1933 my parents won in a raffle. A Man of Action. Charles B. Stetler. GOYP

In 1923. Martha Graham. Elaine Equi. UTF

In no congenial gulf for ever lost! (*LL*) On the Ice Islands Seen Floating in the German Ocean. William Cowper. OAEL-1; PrIm

In no country. No Offence. D. J. Enright. OxBTC

In No Strange Land. Francis Thompson. *See* O world invisible, we view thee.

In North Great George's Street. "Seumas O'Sullivan." BIrV

In northern climes where furious tempests blow. Daniel Defoe. *Fr.* Diet of Poland, The; a Satire. OBTV

In Norway land there lived a maid. The Grey Selchie of Sule Skerry. *Unknown.* OxBB

In Nottamun Town not a soul would look up. Nottamun Town. *Unknown.* CBNP; FaBoNo; OxBoLi

In Nottingham there lives a jolly tanner. Robin Hood and the Tanner. *Unknown.* ESPB

In November. Archibald Lampman. NOBC

In November, in the days to remember the dead. St. Malachy. Thomas Merton. VGW

In No. 64 Von Tempsky has his picture up. Von Tempsky's Dance. Murray Edmond. PeNZ

In number, weight, and measure, needs not rhyme. (*LL*) On Mr. Milton's Paradise Lost. Andrew Marvell. EPCY; JCP; NOSC

In numbers, and but these few. An Ode on the Birth of Our Saviour. Robert Herrick. GN

In Nunhead Cemetery. Charlotte Mew. FaBoWP

In obedience to the excellent spirit of Thy ways. (*LL*) I reverently speak in the presence of the. *Unknown.* EaPr

In Obitum Ben Johnson Poetae Eximii. Mildmay Fane, 2d Earl of Westmorland. *See* He who began from brick and lime.

In Obitum Ben. Jons. Mildmay Fane, 2d Earl of Westmorland. OxBSP

In Obitum Promi. Henry Parrot. FaBoCo

In Obtuse Angle's Study. Blake. *Fr.* Island in the Moon, An. FaBoNo

In Ocean's wide domains. The Witnesses. Longfellow. GOA

In October marching, taking the sweet air. Towards Lillers. Ivor Gurney. NAEL-2

In October of the year. Ox Cart Man. Donald Hall. CAPP; FYAP; InPS; LCAP

In Ohio. James Wright. NNaP

In Ohio, where these things happen. The Breathers. James Reiss. AmPA

In Oklahoma. Life Is Motion. Wallace Stevens. SAmP

In old age/ I'm back. The Pond in a Bowl. Han Yü, *tr. fr. Chinese by* Kenneth O. Hanson. SuSp

In old days those who went to fight. Hearing That His Friend Was Coming Back from the War. Wang Chien, *tr. fr. Chinese by* Arthur Waley. ArLo

In old Kentuck in de arternoon. Clare de Kitchen. *Unknown.* BLPA

In old stories the jungle was busy. The Sun-Hunters. Mark O'Connor. NOBAu

In olden days, a child, I trod thy sands. San Francisco. Ina Coolbrith. AmWP

In olden times — in forever. Words Spoken by Pasternak during a Bombing. Bella Akhmadulina, *tr. fr. Russian by* Daniela Gioseffi *with* Sophia Buzevska. WoWa

In olden times we oft have heard. The Natal Hunters. Allen F. Gardiner. PeSAV

In Olinda, if you go out with a magnifying glass and hunt carefully. Italo Calvino, *tr. fr. Italian. Fr.* Hidden Cities. AnRep, *tr. by* William Weaver

In One Battle. Amiri Baraka. BPo

In 100% surefire arsenic. Shake'nbake Ballad. Peter van Toorn. NOBC

In one of its three angles. (*LL*) A Wise Triangle. Vasco [*or* Vasko] Popa. CBNP, *tr. by* Anne Pennington *and* Charles Simic; CoGr, *tr. by* Anne Pennington *and* Charles Simic; PoSu, *tr. by* Anne Pennington

In one of these excursions, travelling then/ Through Wales on foot. Wordsworth. *Fr.* Prelude [*or*, Growth of a Poet's Mind], The. EnRP; OAEL-2; OxAEP-2; PeECV; PoEL-4
  (Climb to Snowdon, The.) FaBoRV
  (Snowdon Sunrise, The.) FaBoPP

In One of Those Excursions. Wordsworth. *Fr.* Prelude [*or*, Growth of a Poet's Mind], The. EnRP; MeMBP; OAEL-2

In one of those excursions (may they ne'er. In One of Those Excursions. Wordsworth. *Fr.* Prelude [*or*, Growth of a Poet's Mind], The. EnRP; MeMBP; OAEL-2

In One Place. Robert Wallace. Poetsp

In one weak, washy, everlasting flood! (*LL*) What's My Thought Like? Thomas Moore. FaBoEE

In only thee, my timid, fleet gazelle. The Timid Gazelle. Kasmuneh, *tr. fr. Arabic.* TrJP

In Orangeburg My Brothers Did. Alfred B. Spellman. BPo; PoBA

In Orbit. Henry Taylor. BXAP

In orchard under the hawthorne. Vergier. *Unknown, tr. fr. Provençal by* Ezra Pound. GBL

In Order To. Kenneth Patchen. NaP

In order to blow what it's like being born. (*LL*) Lester Leaps In. Al Young. SM

In order to perfect all readers. Wall, Cave, and Pillar Statements, after Asôka. Alan Dugan. CoAP

In Orknay. William Fowler. OxBS; ScCV

In other choice. (*LL*) Sun is set, and masked night, The. Robert Sidney. NoSic

In our content, before the autumn came. Elinor Wylie. *Fr.* One Person. NAAL-2; NALW

In our Country, in our Country. The Merry Hay-Makers; or, Pleasant Pastime between the Young-Men and Maids, in the Pleasant Meadows. *Unknown.* CoMu; ErPo

In our Durham County I am sorry for to say. The Durham Lock-out. *Unknown.* CoMu

In our fields, fallow and burdened, in grass and furrow. Christopher Fry. *Fr.* Boy with a Cart, The. LiTB

In our house every floor was a wailing wall. My Guardian Angel Stein. Philip Schultz. InPS

In our house we will have. Open Shelves. Marilyn Kitchell. UL

In our monotonous sublime. (*LL*) Waking Early Sunday Morning. Robert Lowell. FaBoMo; HCAP; NOBA; OxBC; VCAP

In our old shipwrecked days there was an hour. George Meredith. *Fr.* Modern Love. BoLoP; EnVR; NOBVV

In our place. Relief. Charles Vildrac, *tr. fr. French by* Christopher Middleton. PeFWW

In our souls everything. Antonio Machado Ruiz, *tr. fr. Spanish by* Robert Bly. EnlH

In our store that day. To My Father. Wing Tek Lum. BCF

In our town, people live in rows. The Fired Pot. Anna Wickham. FaBoTw; FaBoWP; OxBTC

In our world there lived a soldier. A Paper Soldier. Bulat Okudzhava, *tr. fr. Russian by* George Reavey. PAW

In Outer Space. David Trinidad. BAP-91

In Oxford City. *Unknown.* OBET

In Oxford there lived a merchant by trade. The Crafty Farmer. *Unknown.* AmFP; ESPB

In Paco town and in Paco tower. The Ballad of Paco Town. Clinton Scollard. PAH

In pain she bore the son who her embrace. Moses ibn Ezra, *tr. fr. Hebrew by* Solomon Solis-Cohen. TrJP

In Painswick Churchyard. Frances Horovitz. NBrP

In Pandora's Box, a silence of almost. The Time Machine. Jon Anderson. AnAn

In Panelled Rooms. Ruth Herschberger. LiTA

In paper case. Epitaph on a Dormouse. *Unknown.* OxBChV

In Paradise, lighted by the fires of heaven. *(LL)* When You, My Love, Ascend To Heaven. Paul Johann Ludwig Heyse. RiWo

In paradise the work week is fixed at thirty hours. Report from Paradise. Zbigniew Herbert, *tr. fr. Polish by* Czeslaw Milosz. OBD

In Parenthesis, *sels.* David Jones.
"And the place of their waiting a long burrow." FaBoMo
"And to Private Ball it came." OBWVE
"But sweet sister death has gone debauched today and stalks." OBWP; OxAEP-2; PeFWW
"But why is Father Larkin talking to the dead?" PoE
"Every one of these, stood, separate, upright, above ground." PeECV
Five Unmistakable Marks, The. NAEL-2
"Across upon this undulated board of verdure chequered bright." King Pellam's Launde. OAEL-2
"So thus he sorrowed till it was day."
"This Dai adjusts his slipping shoulder-straps." AngWe
"You can hear the silence of it." FaBoMo

In Paris, at the Opera. Temptation. Arthur Hugh Clough. *Fr.* Dipsychus. PeLV

In Parliament Square. The Statue. Edith Roseveare. Mes

In Parnell Square it's always raining. The Diary of a Silence. Michael O'Loughlin. IB

In part these nightly terrors to dispel. Moonlight . . . Scattered Clouds. Robert Bloomfield. *Fr.* Farmer's Boy, The. OBNC

In parts, through prospects scattered far and near. Birmingham and Wolverhampton. James Woodhouse. *Fr.* Life and Lucubrations of Crispinus Scriblerus, The. NOEC

In paschall feast, the end of ancient rite. Of the Blessed Sacrament of the Altar. Robert Southwell. OBEV

In Passing. Gerald Jonas. GrPl

In pasture where the leaf and wood. The Quest. James Wright. NYBP

In "pastures green"? Not always; sometimes He. He Leadeth Me. *Unknown.* BLRP

In Paths Untrodden. Walt Whitman. NOBA; OxBA

In Patterdale. Wordsworth. *Fr.* Prelude [or, Growth of a Poet's Mind], The. CH; EnRP; FaBoRV; GN; HAP; NOBE; NoP; NU; OAEL-2; OBNC; OxAEP-2; PoE; SCV

In payne, sorow, and wofull aventure. *(LL)* Alas, Death. Charles, Duc d'Orléans. OxBLMV

In peace and harmony with Mother Earth. *(LL)* Let there be peace, welfare and righteousness. Hagen Hasselbalch. EaPr

In peace, and reck'ns thee her eldest son. *(LL)* To Sir Henry Vane the Younger. Milton. Son

In peace, and yet at strife. *(LL)* Dispraise of Love, and Lovers' Follies. "A. W." ElL; TrGrPo

In Peblis town sum tyme, as I heard tell. *At. to* John Reid of Stobo. *Fr.* Thre Prestis of Peblis, The. OxBS

In Pennsylvania; it's sort of like losing. Another Night on the Porch Swing. Cathleen Quirk. NMM

In perfect, in poetic state she lies. *(LL)* First Flight. Dorothy Wellesley. OBTV

In Perfect Time. Dinah Livingstone. DT

In Perspective. Robert Graves. OxBSP

In Peterborough Churchyard. Paulus Silentiarius, *tr. fr. Greek.* FaBoEE; NOBL

In petticoat of green. Of Phyllis. William Drummond of Hawthornden. CBLP; ElL; GN
(Phyllis.) GN

In Piam Memoriam. Geoffrey Hill. OxBC

In Pilgrim Life Our Rest. Edwin Sandys. AH; ChIV-1

In Pilsen. Five Minutes after the Air Raid. Miroslav Holub, *tr. fr. Czech by* Ian Milner *and* George Theiner. OBD

In Pin-up Ruffles now she flaunts. Mary Evelyn. *Fr.* Mundus Muliebris. KTR

In Pinter's new play that's now running. Frank Richards. PeLi

In pinup ruffles now she flaunts. Mundus Muliebris. Mary Evelyn. NOSC

In pious times ere [or e'r] priest-craft did begin. Dryden. *Fr.* Absalom and Achitophel, Pt. I. EBEvV; FaBoPV; FHYEP; HAP; NoP; NOSC; OAEL-1; PoE; SeCV-2

In Piranezi's rarer prints. Prelusive. Herman Melville. *Fr.* Clarel. AmPP

In pity for man's darkening thought. Two Songs from a Play. W. B. Yeats. *Fr.* Resurrection, The. CMoP; FaBoTw; HAP; LiTB; NOBE; NoP; OAEL-2; PPP; PrIm

In place of Mammy's bibini, asleep on his wee bed. *(LL)* Close your sleepy eyes, or the pale moonlight will steal you. Aqua Laluah. ShDr

In placid hours well-pleased we dream. Art. Herman Melville. AmPP; NAAL-1; NOBA

In Plague Time. Thomas Nashe. *See* Adieu, Farewell, Earth's Bliss[e].

In plazas calcined pure white, bulls charge. Interludes. Fabio Doplicher, *tr. fr. Italian by* Stephen Sartarelli. NeIt

In Pleasant Lands Have Fallen the Lines. James Flint. AH

In poesy's spells some all their raptures find. John Clare. *Fr.* Shadows of Taste. EPCY

In Polar noons when the moonshine glimmers. The Weaver of Snow. "Fiona Macleod." OHCV

In Pompano Beach, Florida. Robin Becker. PBCAP

In Portugal, 1912. Alice Meynell. NOCV

In Prague, a rabbi, name of Pelf. The Rabbi. Christian Morgenstern, *tr. fr. German by* W. D. Snodgrass *and* Lore Segal. OBD

In praise for all his wondrous love. *(LL)* Table Rules for Little Folk[s]. *Unknown.* FaBoUs; OxBChV

In Praise of a Beggar's Life. "A. W." ElL; TrGrPo

In Praise of a Contented Mind. *Unknown, wr. at. to* Sir Edward Dyer. *See* My mind [or minde or mynde] to me a kingdom [or kyngdome] is.

In Praise of a Cremation Ground. Kataiyan Kannanar, *tr. fr. Tamil by* A. K. Ramanujan. PLW

In Praise of a Girl. Huw Morus, *tr. fr. Welsh by* Gwyn Williams. OBWVE

In Praise of Ale. *At. to* William Stevenson *and also to* John Still. *See* Back and Side Go Bare, Go Bare.

In Praise of Antonioni. Stephen Holden. NYBP

In Praise of Carnations. Wang Chi, *tr. fr. Chinese by* Hellmut Wilhelm. SuSp

In Praise of Cocoa, Cupid's Nightcap. Stanley J. Sharpless. ErPo; FiBHP; NBLV; PeLV

In Praise of Drainage. Anne Wilson. *Fr.* Teisa, a Descriptive Poem of the River Tees, Its Towns and Antiquities. ECWP

In Praise of Eliza, Queen of the Shepherds. Spenser. *Fr.* Shepheardes [or Shepeards or Shepherd's] Calender, The. NAEL-1; OBEV; PoEL-1

In Praise of Fidelia. Mildmay Fane, 2d Earl of Westmorland. BeJo; NOSC; OxBSP

In Praise of His Daphnis. Sir John Wotton. EIL

In Praise of His Lady. Matthew Grove. *Fr.* Pelops and Hippodamia. EIL

In Praise of His Love. Sir John Wotton. EIL

In Praise of His Loving and Best-beloved Fawnia. Robert Greene. *See* Ah Were She Pitiful.

In Praise of Hope. Abraham Cowley. OxAEP-1

In Praise of Isabel Pennell. John Skelton. *See* By Saint [or Saynt] Mary, my lady.

In Praise of Ivy. *Unknown. See* Ivy, chefe of trees it is.

In Praise of Ivy. *Unknown.* MeEL

In Praise of Laudanum. William Harrison. NOEC

In Praise of Limestone. W. H. Auden. CMoP; FaBoPV; FYAP; HAP; MoAB; MoP; NAEL-2; NoAM; NoP; OAEL-2; PPP

In Praise of Llamas. Arthur Guiterman. FiBHP; ZA

In Praise of Marriage. Christine de Pisan, *tr. fr. French.* OxBM

In Praise of Mary. *Unknown.* MeEL

In Praise of My Sister. Wislawa Szymborska, *tr. fr. Polish by* Adam Czerniawski. PoSu

In Praise of Night. Matthaus Von Collin, *tr. fr. German by* Philip L. Miller. RiWo

In Praise of Old Women. Marya Fiamengo. WPOW

In Praise of Owain Gwynedd. Cynddelw Brydydd Mawr, *tr. fr. Welsh by* Joseph P. Clancy. OBWVE

In Praise of Plants., *sels.* Branko Miljkovic, *tr. fr. Serbo-Croatian.* "I know your root." HSix, *tr. by* Charles Simic.

In Praise of Poor Scholars. T'ao Ch'ien, *tr. fr. Chinese by* Eugene Eoyang. SuSp

In Praise of Seafaring Men, in Hopes [or hope] of Good Fortune. Sir Richard Grenville. OBTV; OxBSS

In Praise of Tenby. *Unknown, tr. fr. Welsh by* Joseph P. Clancy. OBWVE; OxBSS

In Praise of the Sun. "A. W." CTC

In Praise of Three Young Men. Lochlann Og O Dalaigh. NOIV

In Praise of Virginity. Hroswitha, *tr. fr. Latin by* John Dillon. PBWP; VBLP

In Praise of Water-Gruel. Matthew Green. *Fr.* Spleen, The. FaBoUs

In Praise of Wine. *Unknown, tr. fr. Latin by* Helen Waddell. MLL

In Praise of Wisdom. Solomon ibn Gabirol, *tr. fr. Hebrew by* Solomon Solis-Cohen. TrJP

In Praise of Women in General. Thomas Randolph. NOSC

In Praise of Wyatt's Psalms. The Earl of Surrey. *See* Great [or Greate] Macedon, that out of Persia chased, The.

In Praise of Young Girls. Herbert Asquith. OtMeF

In Prison. William Morris. OHCV; PeVV

In Prison. Michael Smith. PWR

In prison joys, fetter'd with chains of gold. (*LL*) In court to serve, decked with fresh array. Sir Thomas Wyatt. NoSic; SiPSBD

In Procession. Robert Graves. TwCP

In Progress. Christina Rossetti. BoWoP; NAEL-2; WPE

In Prospect Street, outside the Splendid Bar. Sweeney to Mrs. Porter in the Spring. L. E. Sissman. NYBP

In protecting the earth, we found good pine needles and harsh. C. T. Mukpo. EaPr

In Protest. Li Ho, *tr. fr. Chinese by* Maureen Robertson. SuSp

In proving that one has had the experience/ Of carrying a stick? (*LL*) Critics and Connoisseurs. Marianne Moore. AmPP; CMoP; FaBoWP; MeMAP; NoAM; NOBA; OxBA; Poetr

In Puna's fragrant glades. Puna's Fragrant Glades. Princess Lili'u-o-ka-lani, *tr. fr. Hawaiian by* S. H. Elbert *and* N. Mahoe. WTO

In purest song one plays the constant fool. Infirmity. Theodore Roethke. CoAP; NAAL-2; NYBP

In Puritan New England a year had passed away. The First Thanksgiving Day. Alice Williams Brotherton. OHIP

In Pusseyville, where pussies live. Cats and Dogs. Howard Moss. OBAL

In Queen Victoria's early days. The New Vicar of Bray. Colin Ellis. NOBL

In quest of these, that them applause have wonne. (*LL*) To My Most Dearly-loved Friend, Henry Reynolds, Esquire, of Poets and Poesy. Michael Drayton. SuSp

In quietness and confidence. A Hymn of Trust. Nettie M. Sargent. BLRP

In raging winds the crows' cries continue without end. Following the Rhymes of Wang An-shih's Poem "Inscribed on the Wall of the Temple of Western Great Unity." Huang T'ing-chien, *tr. fr. Chinese by* Michael E. Workman. SuSp

In Railway Halls. Stephen Spender. FaBoMo

In Rainy September. Robert Bly. CAPP; LPA

In rainy September, when leaves grow down to the dark. In Rainy September. Robert Bly. CAPP; LPA

In re Solomon Warshawer. A. M. Klein. MoCV

In Reading Gaol by Reading Town. Oscar Wilde. *Fr.* Ballad of Reading Gaol, The. BeLS; LiTB; OBNV; OHCV; OxAEP-2

In real life it takes only one to make a quarrel. (*LL*) I Never Even Suggested It. Ogden Nash. FiBHP; LiTA; PoLF

In reality, sheep are brave, enlightened. Lies. Jo Shapcott. PWE

In reality the barn wasn't clean, ninety men. Trakl. Norman Dubie. NAmP90

In rectangular vertigo the balepress. Making Hay. Philip Hodgins. NOBAu

In red weather. (*LL*) Disillusionment of Ten o'Clock. Wallace Stevens. AnAmPo; CBNP; CMoP; FF; InPS; NAAL-2; NoAM; OxBA; RB; SAmP; SoSe; SOTW; TRP; TTTS

In red wool jacket and earflaps. The Week-End Indian. Anita Endrezze-Danielson. VoR

In Reference to Her Children, 23 June, 1656 [*or* 1659]. Anne Bradstreet. BoWoP; EAP; TAP

In Remembrance of the Children of Izieu. Arlene Maass. BTR

In Remembrance of the Forgotten. Lu Hsun, *tr. fr. Chinese by* William R. Schultz. SuSp

In Respect of the Elderly. Thomas Love Peacock. VoR

In Respectful Memory of Mr. Yarker, *sels*. John Close. "And have we lost another friend?" FaBoCo

In Response to a Question. William Stafford. FoLa

In Response to a Rumor That the Oldest Whorehouse in Wheeling, West Virginia, Has Been Condemned. James Wright. CAPP; CoAP; NNaP; NoAM; VCAP

In restaurants we argue. They Eat Out. Margaret Atwood. NoAM; NoP

In Retrospect. Maya Angelou. UnAS

In Retrospect. Richard Kenney. *Fr.* Hours of the Day, The. Son

In revel and carousing. Theodosia Burr: The Wrecker's Story. John Williamson Palmer. PAH

In rice fields of Ch'ang-ku, by the fifth month. Ch'ang-ku. Li Ho, *tr. fr. Chinese by* Maureen Robertson. SuSp

In right I have no power to live. The Soul's Bitter Cry. *Unknown, tr. fr. Tamil.* WGRP

In roaring he shall rise and on the surface die. (*LL*) The Kraken. Tennyson. EnVR; NAEL-2; NoP; OAEL-2; OBNC; PeECV; PoEL-5; TOF; WiR

In Romney Marsh. John Davidson. EBVV; FaBoPP; MeMBP; OxBTC

In, Rose, and in, Provence and La Palie. (*LL*) Les Vaches. Arthur Hugh Clough. CBLP

In rosy-fingered dawn they go. Jersey Cattle. Ralph Nixon Currey. OxBTC

In rosy morn I saw Aurora red. Shortness of Life. Thomas Fairfax, Baron Fairfax. NOSC

In royal Anna's golden days. Given to a Lady Who Asked Me to Write a Poem. Janet Little. ECWP

In Ruin Reconciled. Aubrey Thomas De Vere. BIrV

In ruling well what guerdon? Life runs low. The Two Old Kings. Lord De Tabley. OBEV

In sable clad, Urania come. Ode on the Passion. Thomas, the Elder Warton. ChIV-2

In sable weeds the beaux and belles appear. The Mourners. Bevil Higgons. APAS

In sad and ashy weeds. The Good Shepherd's Sorrow for the Death of His Beloved Son. Anne Howard, Duchess of Arundel. NOSC (Elegy on the Death of Her Husband.) WPE

In safety and in Bliss. *Unknown. Fr.* Sutta Nipata. EaPr

In Saginaw, in Saginaw. The Saginaw Song. Theodore Roethke. NBLV; RB

In Salem. Lucille Clifton. AmPA

In Salem Dwelt a Glorious King. Thomas Traherne. ChIV-1

In Salem seasick spindrift drifts or skips. Salem. Robert Lowell. AiP; Son

In San Francisco, spring was not a season. Letter from Vermont. Ellen Bryant Voigt. AnAn

In San Juan I wonder how my home is. I Wonder How My Home Is. *Unknown, tr. fr. Tewa Indian by* H. J. Spinden. WTO

In San Pedro. (*LL*) Spain, 1809. Frank Lawrence Lucas. EBNV

In sands, in fens, they died — no mother near! (*LL*) The Children Band. Sir Aubrey De Vere. OBEV

In Santa Maria del Popolo. Thom Gunn. CMoP; FaBoMo; GTBS-P; OxBC; PoE

In Saram. John Cotton. SCAP

In Saturday Market, there's eggs a-plenty. Saturday Market ("In Saturday Market, there's eggs a-plenty.") Charlotte Mew. *Fr.* Saturday Market. FaPON; WPE

In Saturn's reign, at Nature's early birth. Juvenal, *tr. by* Dryden. *Fr.* Satires. OAEL-1; OBSV; OBVE

In Saxony. Philip Levine. BTR

In Scarlet town, where I was born [*or* bound]. Barbara Allen. *Unknown.* EBEvV; EBNV (Barbara Allen's Cruelty.) OBEV (Bonny Barbara Allan.) TrGrPo

In scenes like these, which, daring to depart. William Collins. *Fr.* Ode on the Popular Superstitions of the Highlands of Scotland, An. EnRP; EPCY; NOEC; OAEL-1; OxAEP-1

In scenes of distant death bold Hezron stands. Timothy Dwight. *Fr.* Conquest of Canaan, The. EAP

In scenes paternal, not beheld through years. Anna Seward. *Fr.* Eyam. NOEC

In schomer, when the leves spryng. Robin Hood and the Potter. *Unknown.* ESPB

In School-Days. Whittier. AnAmPo; BLPA; FaBoBe; FaPON; OBCA; OxBChV

In school I was taught the names. Columbus Day. Jimmie Durham. HATNAP

In school with their white hands. (*LL*) Mending Crab Pots. Dave Jeddie Smith. MT

In Scotia so fair, 'tis a custom they say. To Lydia, with a Coloured Egg, on Easter Monday. John Jones. FaBoUs

In Scotland there was a babie born. Hind Horn. *Unknown.* ESPB

In Scotland town where I was borned. Hind Horn. *Unknown.* AmFP; ESPB, A *and* B *vers.*

In sea-cold Lyonesse. Sunk Lyonesse. Walter de la Mare. FaBoCh; LiTM

In Search of Solitude. Chao Yi, *tr. fr. Chinese by* Chang Yin-nan *and* Lewis C. Walmsley. SuSp

In search of wisdom, far from wit I fly. Wit and Wisdom. Ambrose Philips. OxAEP-1

In secreit place, this hyndir [*or* hindir] nycht [*or* nicht]. William Dunbar. MiEL (Man of Valour to His Fair Lady, The.) MeEL

In secret molecules. Snow Trivia. Ruth Stone. FoLa

In secret place where once I stood. The Flesh and the Spirit. Anne Bradstreet. AmPP; AnAmPo; ChIV-2; LiTA; NAAL-1; NOBA; OxBA; SCAP; TAP

In seed time learn, in harvest teach, in winter enjoy. Blake. *Fr.* Marriage of Heaven and Hell, The. EnRP; FF; OAEL-2 (Proverbs of Hell.) MeMBP; NAEL-2

In sensuous coil. Kings. *Unknown, tr. fr. Sanskrit by* Arthur Ryder. *Fr.* Panchatantra, The. AWP

In separateness they turn, and to the cook-house go. (*LL*) The Harvesters. Mary Gilmore. NOBAu

In Sepia. Jon Anderson. NoP

In September 1939. Bernard Gutteridge. PoWW

In seventeen hundred and fifty nine. Hawke. Sir Henry Newbolt. FaBoEH

In seventeen hundred and forty-four. The Kilruddery Hunt. Thomas Mozeen. BIrV

In seventeen hundred and seventy-five. The Bombardment of Bristol. *Unknown*. PAH

In "76" I moved to California. Running Horse. Kathleen Iddings. NGP

In shade, on cardboard squares, the sleeping obaasan. Typhoon. Cyrus Cassells. UTF

In Shadow. Hart Crane. NOBA

In Shaka's days we lived well. Those Were the Days. *Zulu Oral Tradition*, tr. by H. Tracey. WTO

In shantung suits we whites are cool. The Devil-Dancers. William Plomer. PeSA; PeSAV

In shaping the snow into blossoms. "Ping Hsin," tr. fr. *Chinese by Kai-yu Hsu. Fr. Spring Waters.* BoWoP; WPOW

In shards the sylvan vases lie. The Ravaged Villa. Herman Melville. CTC; NOBA; PoEL-5

In short, my deary, kiss me, and be quiet. (*LL*) Be plain in dress and sober in your diet. Lady Mary Wortley Montagu. FaBoEE

In Siberia's wastes. Siberia. James Clarence Mangan. BIrV; NOBVV; NOIV; PeIV

In Sickness Written Soon after the Author's Coming to Live in Ireland, upon the Queen's Death, October 1714. Swift. NOEC

In signe of favor stedfast still. To His Darrest Freind. John Steward of Baldynnis. OxBS

In silence I must take my seat. Table Rules for Little Folk[s]. *Unknown*. FaBoUs; OxBChV

In silent gaze the tuneful choir among. Stanzas to Mr. Bentley. Thomas Gray. NoP

In silent night, when rest I took. Some Verses upon the Burning of Our House, July 10th, 1666. Anne Bradstreet. NOBA; PFP; TAP
(Here Follow[e]s Some Verses upon the Burning of Our House [July 10th, 1966. Copied Out of a Loose Paper].) AiP; BoWoP; EAP; NAAL-1; NALW; NoP; Poetr; SCAP
(Upon the Burning of Our House, July 10th, 1666.) AnAmPo; NOSC; OxBA; WPE

In silks and satins the ladies went. Chemin Des Dames. Crosbie Garstin. NSI

In Silvertown, Chasing the Dragon. Ken Smith. PWE

In silvery light. (*LL*) Sea Lullaby. Elinor Wylie. BoNaP

In simmer, whan aa sorts foregether. Embro to the Ploy. Robert Garioch. OxBS

In sixteen hundred and sixty-six. *Unknown*. FaBoUs

In sixth grade Mrs. Walker. Persimmons. Li-Young Lee. NIP

In Sleep. Alice Meynell. BrRo

In sleep charmed by your image. After a Dream. Romain Bussine, tr. fr. *French by Philip L. Miller.* RiWo

In sleep the other night I met you, seventeen. Marge Piercy. *Fr.* My Mother's Body. MDDM

In sleep when an old man's body is no longer aware of its boundaries. A Journey through the Moonlight. Russell Edson. LCAP

In Sligo the country was soft; there were turkeys. Sligo and Mayo. Louis MacNeice. FaBoPP

In slipper green. (*LL*) Depression before Spring. Wallace Stevens. OBAL; SOTW

In slow procession, one by one, silently. From Far Away. Delmira Agustini, tr. fr. *Spanish by D. M. Pettinella.* PBWP

In slumbers of midnight the sailor-boy lay. The Mariner's Dream. William Dimond. BeLS

In small backyards old men's long underwear. The Patricians. Douglas Dunn. OxBC

In small green cup an acorn grew. The Acorn. *Unknown*. BoTP

In snow veined with his blood and the white bruise. Snow Owl. Dave Jeddie Smith. AnAn

In so morose a world. (*LL*) Good time of the year, The. Bernard de Ventadour. STV

In sober mornings, doe [or do] not thou reherse [or rehearse]. When He Would Have His Verses Read. Robert Herrick. BeJo; CaPo; NOBE; NOSC; SCGP; SeCV-1

In soft hanging coils, she embroiders her hair. Tune: "Southern Song, A." Wen T'ing-yün, tr. fr. *Chinese by William R. Schultz.* SuSp

In Solitary Confinement, Sea Point Police Cells. C. J. Driver. PeSA

In Some of the Bunks. Barbara Helfgott Hyett. BTR

In some of the bunks, the men. In Some of the Bunks. Barbara Helfgott Hyett. BTR

In Some Seer's Cloud Car. Christopher Middleton. TwCP

In some small town, one indifferent summer. (*LL*) Syringa. John Ashbery. HCAP; NoAM; VCAP

In some unused lagoon, some nameless bay. The Dismantled Ship. Walt Whitman. AmPP; NoP; OxBA

In some versions of the universe the stars. Stars. Howard Moss. AnAn

In Some Way or Other the Lord Will Provide. Mrs. M. A. W Cook. AH

In someone's book of fables I've read. The Cat and an Old Rat. Jean de la Fontaine. OFC

In somer when the shawes be sheyne. May in the Green-Wood. *Unknown*. OBEV

In somer, when the shawes be sheyne. Robin Hood and the Monk. *Unknown*. ESPB; FaBoBa; OBNV; *abr*.
(Robin Hode and the Munkee.) EBNV

In sooth, I know not why I am so sad. Shakespeare. *Fr.* Merchant of Venice, The. OxAEP-1

In Soto's bosom you may find. Soto, a Character. Mary Leapor. ECWP

In South Oregon the Klamath play. The Woyi. Lew Blockcolski. VoR

In Spain, where the courtly Castilian hidalgo twangs lightly. Carmen. Newman Levy. FiBHP

In Spanish he whispers there is no time left. The Visitor. Carolyn Forché. FYAP

In Spanishburg there are boys in tight jeans. Spitting in the Leaves. Maggie Anderson. ETG; PBCAP

In Sparkhill buried lies that man of mark. Local Note. Arthur Guiterman. NBLV

In Spight of his Deanship and Journeyman *Waters*. (*LL*) An Excellent New Song on a Seditious Pamphlet. Swift. CoMu

In Spite. Rufinus, tr. fr. *Greek by Alan Marshfield.* GrAn

In spite of all the learned have said. The Indian Burying Ground. Philip Freneau. AmPP; AnAmPo; EAP; HAP; LiTA; NAAL-1; NOBA; NoP; OBD, *abr*.; OxBA; PoEL-4; PoLF; TAP; TFi

In spite of all the solemn-hearted fools. The Joy of Love. Allan Dowling. ErPo

In Spite of All This Much Needed Thunder. Zack Gilbert. PoNe

In Spite of His Dangling Pronoun. Lyn Lifshin. IHMS

In spite of ice, in spite of snow. On Observing a Large Red-Streak Apple. Philip Freneau. NAAL-1

In spite of love. Family Pictures. Mervyn Morris. PBCV

In spite of my torpor, my squinting eyes, my paunch. Hurry. Octavio Paz, tr. fr. *Spanish by Eliot Weinberger.* AnRep

In spite of Rice, in spite of Wheat. Epigram on the Poor of Boston Being Employed in Paving the Streets, 1774. *Unknown*. PAH

In spite of what the quarrymen said. Clearsightedness. Andrew Salkey. PBCV

In spotted globes, that have resembled all. Greatness in Little. Richard Leigh. NOSC

In Spring. Ernst Konrad Friedrich Schulze, tr. fr. *German by Philip L. Miller.* RiWo

In Spring I look gay. *Unknown*. BoTP; OxNR

In spring if there are dogs they will bark. Ballade of Sayings. W. S. Merwin. NNaP

In Spring We Gather Mulberry Leaves. *Unknown*, tr. fr. *Chinese by Kenneth Rexroth.* OHMPC

In Springtime. Samuel Taylor Coleridge. *See* All nature seems at work. Slugs leave their lair.

In springtime the violets. Springtime. Nikki Giovanni. TLR

In Staffordshire I was born. The Posy of Thyme. *Unknown*. OBET

In stature, the Manlet was dwarfish. The Manlet. "Lewis Carroll." BXAP
(Little Man That Had a Little Gun, The.) CBNP; FaBoNo

In steaming tubs,/ Huge, unblushing. (*LL*) Dreams of Water. Donald Justice. LCAP; NYBP

In stone settlements when the moon is stone. Peter Levi. EBEV; TOF

In subsequent waves. Sleeplessness. Luigi Fontanella, tr. fr. *Italian by W. S. Di Piero.* NeIt

In such a fix to be so fertile. (*LL*) The Turtle. Ogden Nash. FiBHP; ImPo; NoP; OBAL; SoSe; TAP

In Such a Night. Shakespeare. *See* Moon shines bright, The. In such a night as this.

In such a night, when every louder wind. A Nocturnal Reverie. The Countess of Winchilsea. EBEV; ECEV; ECWP; NAEL-1; NALW; NOEC; NoP; OxAEP-1; PBWP; PoE; PoEL-3; Poetr; WPE

In such an armor he cannot be slain. (*LL*) Bronzeville Man with a Belt in the Back. Gwendolyn Brooks. PoBA

In such an armor he may rise and raid. Bronzeville Man with a Belt in the Back. Gwendolyn Brooks. PoBA

In such luxurious plentie of all pleasure. Spenser. *Fr.* Faerie Queene, The. OAEL-1

In Suffolk. George Crabbe. *See* How stately stand yon pines upon the hill.

In sullen Humour one Day Jove. Mercury and Cupid. Matthew Prior. PeLV

In summer elms are made for me. Dilemma of the Elm. Genevieve Taggard. MoAmPo

In summer I am very glad. Playgrounds. Laurence Alma-Tadema. BoTP

In Summer, in the open air. Summer Sabbath. Jessie E. Sampter. TrJP

In summer, like the theaters, I close up. Valerio Magrelli, *tr. fr. Italian by* Dana Gioia. NeIt

In summer she arrives in cotton splendour. A Seasonal Aunt. Sebastian Barry. IB

In summer this town is full of rebels. The Cannery. Lucien Stryk. CAPP

In summer time, when leaves grew green and birds were singing. King Edward the Fourth and a Tanner of Tamworth. *Unknown.* ESPB

In summer time when leaves grow green/ And birds sit on the tree. Under the Greenwood Tree. *Unknown.* GBP

In summer time, when leaves grow green and flowers are fresh and gay. Robin Hood and the Curtal Friar. *Unknown.* ESPB

In summer time, when leaves grow green/ Down a down a down. Robin Hood and the Tinker. *Unknown.* ESPB

In summer time, when leaves grow green, when they doe grow both green and long. The Noble Fisherman; or, Robin Hood's Preferment. *Unknown.* ESPB

In summer, when the days were long. Summer Days. Wathen Mark Wilks Call. EBVV

In summer, when the grass is thick, if mother has the time. The Fairy Book. Norman Gale. OHIP

In summer when the woods are green. In the Fair Forest. *Unknown.* BoTP

In Summer's Heat. Ovid. *See* In summer's heat, and mid-time of the day.

In summer's heat, and mid-time of the day. Corinnae Concubitus, I, 5. Ovid, *tr. fr. Latin by* Christopher Marlowe. *Fr.* Amores. EBEV; GBL; OBVE
(Corinnae Concubitus.) NoSic; OxAEP-1
(Elegy: "In summer's heat and mid-time of the day.") BoLoP
(In Summer's Heat.) FaBoBl

In summer's mellow midnight. The Night Wind. Emily Brontë. ChTr; EBVV; NAEL-2; NALW; OHCV; TEP

In summertime it was a paradise. The Seaside: In and Out of the Season. Charles Tennyson Turner. Son

In summertime on Bredon. Bredon Hill. A. E. Housman. *Fr.* Shropshire Lad, A. EBVV; FaBoPP; FaPoB; MoAB; MoBrPo; NAEL-2; OxAEP-2; PlP; SoSe; UV

In sunburnt parks where Sundays lie. Cobb Would Have Caught It. Robert Fitzgerald. GrPl; HAP; InvP; TwCP

In sunlight on the Avenue. Galway Kinnell. *Fr.* Avenue Bearing the Initial of Christ into the New World, The. LiTM

In sunlight raindrops look like dew. Battle of Similes. *Malay Oral Tradition,* tr. by R. J. Wilkinson *and* R. O. Winstedt. WTO

In suspicious silence. *(LL)* Gods in Vietnam. Eugene B. Redmond. PoBA

In swaying mildly in the breeze. *(LL)* One Leaf. David Ignatow. EaPr

In Sylvia Plath Country. Erica Jong. IHMS

In t' other hundred, o'er yon swarthy moor. The Country Curate. Henry Taylor. NOEC

In "taking charge of your possessions when you saw them." To the Peacock of France. Maurice Moore. MeMAP

In taking of my lonely walk on a cold and wintry day. The Collier Lad's Lament. *Unknown.* OBET

In talking. To a Lady Holding the Floor. Mildred Weston. FiBHP

In Tall Grass. Carl Sandburg. PoA

In tattered old slippers that toast at the bars. The Cane-bottomed [*or* Cane-bottom'd] Chair. Thackeray. VPP

In Taurus was the sun and flowery Spring. Ganymede and Helen. *Unknown, tr. fr. Latin.* PeHV

In tears to her mother poor Harriet came. The Disappointment. Jane Taylor. FaBoUs

In Teesdale. Andrew Young. FaBoPP; OxBSP

In temporary pain. The New God. Witter Bynner. *Fr.* New World, The. WGRP

In Temptation. Charles Wesley. *See* Jesus, Lover of My Soul.

In tender May when the sweet laugh of Christ. The Puritan. Karl Shapiro. MoAMPo

In Tenebris. (Wintertime nighs.) Thomas Hardy. LiTB; MeMBP; NOBE; NoP; PrIm
Sels.
"There have been times when I well might have passed and the ending have come." OAEL-2
"When the clouds' swoln bosoms echo back the shouts of the many and strong." ChIV-1; CMoP; LiTM; NoAM; OxBTC
"Wintertime nighs." NoAM; OAEL-2; SCGP

In Tennessee once the [heart of the] campfire glowed. Youthful Picnic Long Ago: Sad Ballad on Box. Robert Penn Warren.
(Recollection Long Ago: Sad Music.) SV

In Teos and in Samos. Anacreon. Friedrich von Hagedorn, *tr. fr. German by* George C. Schoolfield. GePo

In Texas Grass. Quincy Troupe. PoBA

In Thankfull Remembrance for My Dear Husband's Safe Arrivall Sept. 3, 1662. Anne Bradstreet. TrPWD

In that ago when being was believing. The History of Truth. W. H. Auden. FaBoMo

In that ancient time — in eternity. Words Spoken by Pasternak during a Bombing. Bella Akhmadulina, *tr. fr. Russian by* Jean Valentine *and* Olga Carlisle. BoWoP

In that awful hour when I'm on my deathbed. Repentance. Brendan Behan, *tr. fr. Irish by* Ulick O'Conner. TIRV

In that bad year and city of your birth. To the New World. Randall Jarrell. CAPP
(For an Emigrant.) OxBA

In that building, long and low. The Ropewalk. Longfellow. MeMAP

In that country of thresholds we move like vandals. Papermill Graveyard. Ben Belitt. NYBP

In that country the animals. The Animals in That Country. Margaret Atwood. NALW; NoAM; NoP

In that day I had hoped for a pair of boots to guard my feet on the terrible trek. My Head on My Shoulders. Jeremy Ingalls. GoYe

In that desolate land and lone. The Revenge of Rain-in-the-Face. Longfellow. PAH

In that fair land where slope and plain. The Maiden of the Smile. Alfred Austin. TEP

In that garden to the south. The Garden of Self-Delight. Tom Paulin. SCBI

In that great day, The Judgment Day. James Weldon Johnson. ChIV-2

In that hotel my life. The Illumination. Stanley Kunitz. TAP

In that I have so greatly failed thee, Lord. So Little and So Much. John Oxenham. BLRP

In that icy heart one voice; My Lady weeps. Table of Contents. Henry Lawes, *tr. fr. Italian by* Peggy Forsyth. CBNP

In that instant. An Image from Beckett. Derek Mahon. SCBI

In that it falls her sacrifice. *(LL)* Tell me[e] no more how fair[e] she[e] is. Henry King. EnLoPo; MeLP; SeCP

In that land all is and nothing's ought. Neither Here nor There. W. R. Rodgers. ImPo; LiTB; LiTM; MoAB; MoBrPo

In that lost Caucasian garden. The Naming of the Beasts. Francis Sparshott. NOBC

In *that* Ned — trust — had his finger. *(LL)* Fragment of a Character. Thomas Moore. FaBoCo

In that November off Tehuantepec. Sea Surface Full of Clouds. Wallace Stevens. AmPP; CMoP; MoAB; MoAmPo; VGW

In that, O Queen of queens, thy birth was free. To Our Blessed Lady. Henry Constable. NoSic

In that oblivious, concentrated, fiercely fetal decontraction peculiar. The Park. C. K. Williams. PWE

In that old house of many generations. John Crowe Ransom. *See* As hath been, lo, these many generations.

In that rapacious littoral now slaked by sea. Shore Birds. Vi Gale. GoYe

In that same beginning winter. Poem For Buddy. June Jordan. PFL

In that same gardin all the goodly flowres. Spenser. *Fr.* Faerie Queene, The. NOBE; PoEL-1

In that so sudden summer storm they tried. Summer Storm. Louis Simpson. ErPo; OxBC

In that soft mid-land where the breezes bear. Rodney's Ride. *Unknown.* PAH

In that state I came, return. *(LL)* The Retreat[e]. Henry Vaughan. AWP; BLPL; ClHu; ESCV; FF; GeHe; GTBS; GTBS-P; HAP; ImPo; InPK; InPS; InvP; JCP; LiTB; MeLP; NAEL-1; NIP; NOBE; NOCV; NoP; NOSC; OAEL-1; OBEV; OBWVE; PeECV; PoE; PoEL-2; PoRA; PPP; SCGP; SeCP; SeCV-1; TFi; TOF; TrGrPo

In that town in October. Sky of Clouds. Susan Mitchell. BAP-91

In that town were hard spaces. Town I Left. Helen Sorrells. CrSp; IHMS

In the Abbey Ruins. Victor Hugo, *tr. fr. French by* Philip L. Miller. RiWo

In the Absence of Bliss. Maxine W. Kumin. NoAM

In the absence of light. The Seed Is the Light of the Earth. Christina Pacosz. LoHo

In the Absence of Yellow. Reva Sharon. BTR

In the afternoon sun. Beams. Audre Lorde. NoAM

In the Age of Gold. A Little Girl Lost. Blake. *Fr.* Songs of Experience. FHYEP
(Children of the future Age.) FHYEP

In the Age of Postcapitalism. Lawrence Joseph. PBCAP

In the air. *(LL)* Why climb a mountain? Nanao Sakaki. EaPr

In the air over the great sea. The Precipice. Ts'ai Ch'i-chiao, *tr. fr. Chinese.* LHF, *tr. by* Hualing Nieh

In the air the clouds slide over like. Chia Kuei-hsiang. Shao Yen-hsiang, *tr. fr. Chinese.* LHF, *tr. by* Hualing Nieh

In the air to aggravate the truly menacing. *(LL)* Chez Jane. Frank O'Hara. CoAP; NeAP; NoAM; NOBA; PoA; PoE

In the airconditioned drone. Monsoon Girl. Harry Clifton. BiHa; IB; PBCIP

In the almond — what dwells in the almond? Mandorla. Paul Celan, *tr. fr. German by* Michael Hamburger. PoSu

In the Altha diner on the Florida panhandle. Mourning the Dying American Female Names. Hunt Hawkins. NGP

In the America of the dream. The Lonesome Dream. Lisel Mueller. CoAP

In the American schoolyard. The Air Base at Châteauroux, France. Sherod Santos. NAmP90

In the Antarctical Zonio. *(LL)* Antonio. Laura E. Richards. MoShBr; OBCA; PDV

In the antique forest dreary. Rhyme of the Antique Forest. H. Cordelia Ray. CBWP-3

In the April Rain. Mary Anderson. BoTP

In the Arc of Your Mallet. Jalal al-Din Rumi, *tr. fr. Persian by* John Moyne *and* Coleman Barks. UnAS

In the arms of Hellvellyn and Catchedicam. *(LL)* Hellvellyn. Sir Walter Scott. FM; TEP

In the attention it pays to each detail. Love. Kelly Cherry. CRP

In the Attic. Donald Justice. SM

In the autumn when words sound. Baba Akiko, *tr. fr. Japanese by* Kenneth Rexroth *and* Ikuko Atsumi. WPJ

In the Aztec design God crowds. Ultimate Problems. William Stafford. NU

In the back bedroom, laughing when you pull. First Time: 1950. Honor Moore. GLP

In the back of the nunnery. Monastic Outhouse. Aleksandar Ristovic, *tr. fr. Serbo-Croatian by* Charles Simic. HSix

In the Backs. Frances Cornford. BrRo

In the Backs. James Kenneth Stephen. NOBVV

In the backyard of our house on Norwood. The Minks. Toi Derricotte. NAmP90

In the bad old days a bewigged old Squire. Wigs and Beards. Robert Graves. NOBL

In the Badlands. David Wagoner. UnPo

In the Badlands of Desire. Beckian Fritz Goldberg. NAmP90

In the Baggage Room at Greyhound. Allen Ginsberg. NaP; NoP

In the barn the tenant cock. Morning. John Cunningham. NOEC

In the baroque style of coral, India. The Coral Reef. John Blight. NOBAu

In the Basement of the Goodwill Store. Ted Kooser. GOYP

In the bath I look up and see the brown moth. Now That I Am Never Alone. Tess Gallagher. NAmP90

In the Bavarian steeple, on the hour. The Spire. Ellen Bryant Voigt. NoAM

In the Bay. Arthur Symons. *Fr.* Amoris Exsul. OBNC

In the Bazaars of Hyderabad. Sarojini Naidu [*or* Nayadu]. FaPON

In the Beach House. Anne Sexton. PPP

In the beautiful Midsummernight! *(LL)* I Shall Have a Sweetheart. Vilhelm Andreas Wexels Krag. RiWo

In the beds of deer. *(LL)* The Cat. Sister Mary Norbert Körte. SRLS

In the beginnin to aa things the Wurd wis there ense. Bible, *N.T. Fr.* St. John. FaBoVe

In the Beginning. Jenny Lind Porter. GoYe

In the Beginning. Valerie Sinason. BrRo

In The Beginning. Dylan Thomas. ChIV-2

In the beginning, at every step, he turned. The Sickness of Adam. Karl Shapiro. *Fr.* Adam and Eve. CRP; MoAB

In the beginning God created the heaven and the earth. Bible, *O.T. Fr.* Genesis. NAWM-1, I–IV

In the beginning God made thee. Aholibah. Swinburne. ChIV-1

In the beginning, God, the great schoolmaster. The Autograph on the Soul. Adah Isaacs Menken. CBWP-1

In the beginning he merely marked. West Coast Indian. George Clutesi. HATNAP

In the beginning I stood by the window. Windows in Providence. Aliki Barnstone. BoWoP

In the beginning, in the wet. War Memoir: Jazz, Don't Listen to It at Your Own Risk. Bob Kaufman. Jaz

In the beginning of my love wild hearts and trees. Greenness. The waves. Tele/vision. Amiri Baraka. PRA

In the beginning, the word. You Bet Your Life. Nancy Vieira Couto. PBCAP

In the beginning there was only. Eurynome Divides Chaos. Erica Helm. *Fr.* Creation Songs of Eurynome, The. SRLS

In the beginning there were transports. Genesis. Jules Alan Wein. TrJP

In the Beginning Was a Word. Robert Graves. PoA

In the Beginning Was the Bird. Henry Treece. LiTB

In the beginning was the three-pointed star, In The Beginning. Dylan Thomas. ChIV-2

In the beginning was the Word. The Word. Bible, *N.T. Fr.* St. John. TrGrPo

In the beginning, when green came on the pasture. In the Beginning. Jenny Lind Porter. GoYe

In the bell toll of a clang. Salt. Ruth Stone. NMM

In the bend of your mouth soft murder. Lion. May Swenson. LiTM

In the Big Library. Jovan Hristic, *tr. fr. Serbo-Croatian by* Charles Simic. HSix

In the big library scholars sit and read books. In the Big Library. Jovan Hristic, *tr. fr. Serbo-Croatian by* Charles Simic. HSix

In the Big Rock Candy Mountains. *(LL)* The Big Rock Candy Mountains. *Unknown.* AmFP; ChTr; GBP; OBAL; TTTS, *shorter vers.*

In the big room my father stands. Petrified Minute. Zoltán Zelk, *tr. fr. Hungarian by* Barbara Howes. TSaS

In the Birks of Aberfeldy. *(LL)* The Birks of Aberfeldy. Burns. CTC

In the Bistro. Gwen Harwood. FaBoWP

In the black winter morning. Bereft. Thomas Hardy. BoLoP; NoAM

In the blind-drawn dark dining-room of School. Dylan Thomas. *Fr.* Under Milk Wood. FaPoB

In the blind gap between dreaming, my bed. Douglas Oliver. VaA

In the blizzard. From the Spotted Night. Ray A. Young Bear. HATNAP

In the Blooming Time o'th' year. Silvio's Complaint: A Song, to a Fine Scotch Tune. Aphra Behn. KTR

In the blossom-land Japan. An Old Song. "Yehoash," *tr. fr. Yiddish by* Marie Syrkin. AWP

In the bloud of Adam death was taken. Charm: Bleeding. *Unknown.* FaBoUs

In the blue air. Bats. Mary Oliver. HeIP

In the blue distance. Nelly Sachs, *tr. fr. German by* Ruth Mead *and* Matthew Mead. BoWoP

In the blue eye of the medievalist there is a cart in the road. Another November. Stanley Plumly. AnAn

In the blue hubbub of the same-through-wealth sky. Geography. Kenneth Koch. NoAM

In the blue night. Pine Tree Tops. Gary Snyder. ArNa; NOBA; PoBeRe; Prf

In the bluebell forest. Bluebells. Olive Enoch. BoTP

In the blurring low-blood-pressure. The Judgment. Kathleen Spivack. BoWoP

In the body-and-soul-stinking town of Cologne. *(LL)* On My Joyful Departure from the City of Cologne. Samuel Taylor Coleridge. FaBoCo; InvP; OBTV

In the *Boston Sunday Herald* just three lines. To an American Poet Just Dead. Richard Wilbur. HCAP; NBLV; NoP

In the bottom of my mind. *(LL)* The Goat Paths. James Stephens. AWP; CH; GoJo; LiTB; SCGP; UnPo

In the bowl of buildings alias the back yard. Milk at the Bottom of the Sea. Oscar Williams. LiTA

In the branches of the lonely trees. *(LL)* Wind Tossed Dragons. Hsieh Ngao. OHMPC

In the Breeze. Boris Pasternak, *tr. fr. Russian by* C. M. Bowra. TrJP

In the bridal suite there was a black, cosmic cold. The Wedding. Maria Banus, *tr. fr. Romanian by* Brenda Walker *and* Andrea Deletant. VBLP

In the bright bay of your morning, O God. Claire Goll, *tr. fr. German by* Babette Deutsch *and* Avrahm Yarmolinsky. TrJP

In the bright broad Swiss glare I stand listening. Recessional. Thomas MacGreevy. CIP

In the bright summer morning. Heine. RiWo

In the broken light, in owl weather. Colloquy. Weldon Kees. NaP; NYBP

In the burned-/ out highway. Beer Bottle. Ted Kooser. SM

In the cafe, the chandelier hangs from the ceiling. Spain, 1929. Ai. *Fr.* He Kept On Burning. AnAn

In the Cage. Robert Lowell. FF; NOBA; SM; Son

In the calm of the autumn night. By the Open Window. C. P. Cavafy, *tr. fr. Greek by* Rae Dalven. ArNa

In the Canyon of Echo, there's a railroad begun. Echo Canyon. *Unknown.* AmFP

In the Capability. Sam Abrams. Jaz

In the capital Spring comes late. Buying Flowers. Po Chü-i, *tr. fr. Chinese by* Robert Payne. TAL

In the Carolinas. Wallace Stevens. SAmP; VGW

In the Case of Lobsters. Petra von Morstein, *tr. fr. German by* Rosemarie Waldrop. BoWoP

In the casket of the Hours. *Unknown, tr. fr. Arabic. Fr.* Meditations, The. TAL, *tr. by* Reynold A. Nicholson, *sts.* I–XX

In the Castle. Joseph Freiherr von Eichendorff, *tr. fr. German by* Philip L. Miller. RiWo

In the Cathedral. Patricia Beer. OxBC

In the Cathedral Close. Edward Dowden. EBVV; IIP; PeIV

In the cathedral the acolytes are praying. The Habeas Corpus Blues. Conrad Aiken. NYBP

In the cedar canoe gliding and paddling. Geese Gone Beyond. Gary Snyder. NoAM

In the cedar limbs. (LL) Thirteen Ways of Looking at a Blackbird. Wallace Stevens. BLPL; CMoP; HCAP; HeIL; HeIP; InPK; InPS; LiTM; MoP; NAAL-2; NoAM; NOBA; NoP; PoE; Poetr; RB; SAmP; SOTW; TAP; TFi

In the Cemetery. Thomas Hardy. *Fr.* Satires of Circumstance. InPK; Son

In the cemetery on North Hill. Mourning. Kuan P'an-p'an, *tr. fr. Chinese by* Kenneth Rexroth *and* Ling Chung. WPC

In the censer the coals are high. Final Prayer. Enheduanna, *tr. fr. Sumerian by* Aliki *and* Willis Barnstone. BoWoP

In the centre of the poster, Napoleon. A Poster of Our Dazzling Victory at Saarbrucken. Rimbaud, *tr. by* Robert Lowell. *Fr.* Eighteen-Seventy. FaBoPV; OBWP

In the chamber. Margaret Witter Fuller. *Fr.* Memoirs, I. CrSp

In the chaos of the autumn sun. The Smell of Old Newspapers Is Always Stronger after Sleeping in the Sun. Mike Lowery. Poetsp

In the cheap room. Episode. Cassiano Nunes, *tr. fr. Spanish by* E. A. Lacey. PeHV

In the cherry blossom's shade. Issa, *tr. fr. Japanese by* Stephen Mitchell. EnIH

In the Children's Hospital. "Hugh MacDiarmid." NAEL-2; NoP

In the chorus of memories a blessing in disguise. Declension. Stephen Sandy. PoA

In the church fallen like dancers. Enfidaville. Keith Douglas. PoWW

In the Church of I AM she hears there is a time to heal. Do What You Can. Lawrence Joseph. PBCAP

In the Churchyard. Detlev von Liliencron, *tr. fr. German by* Philip L. Miller. RiWo

In the Churchyard. Eleanor Ross Taylor. UnPo

In the Churchyard at Cambridge. Longfellow. AmPP; PoEL-5; TAP

In the citadel of Jade Gate Pass, elm leaves early scatter yellow. Wang Ch'ang-ling, *tr. by* Ronald C. Miao. *Fr.* Following the Army on Campaign. SuSp

In the City. Israel Zangwill. WGRP

In the city of Marseilles, there lived a beautiful lady. The Lowly Peasant. *Unknown, tr. by* Rina Benmayor. PBWP

In the city of St. Francis they have taken down the statue of St. Francis. Afterwards, They Shall Dance. Bob Kaufman. PoNe; TwCP; VGW

In the clear dusk upon the fields below. Sunset. Lizette Woodworth Reese. AmWP

In the clear gold of sunlight, stretching their backs. White Cats. Paul Valéry, *tr. fr. French by* David Paul. OFC; SoCa

In the clear light that confuses everything. The Laurel Tree. Louis Simpson. NNaP

In the clear water by the beach. Bianor, *tr. fr. Greek by* Robin Skelton. GrAn

In the clear world. Blue Specks. Nurunnessa Choudhury, *tr. fr. Bengali by the author* and Paul Joseph Thompson. AIW

In the clearing stands. Missionaries in the Jungle. Linda Piper. BlSi

In the cliff over the frog pond. The Fossils. Galway Kinnell. NYBP

In the close covert of a grove. The Geranium. Sheridan. BoLoP; ErPo

In the Cloud of Unknowing. Carol Rumens. DiPo

In the Coach, *sels.* Thomas Edward Brown. Conjergal Rights. PeVV

In the cold barn before sunrise. Morning, Milking. Herbert Scott. NGP

In the cold, cold parlor. First Death in Nova Scotia. Elizabeth Bishop. CoAP; FaBoWP; LCAP; NOBA; NYBP

In the cold dome of the college observatory. Conjunctions. Eamon Grennan. PBCIP

In the cold shed sharpening saws. Sixth-Month Song in the Foothills. Gary Snyder. HCAP

In the cool future. The Old Causes. Donald Revell. BAP-90

In the cool soft evening I lie on my trailer bed. Campground. Elliot Fried. NGP

In the cool waters of the river. Woman. Malangatana Ngwenya, *tr. fr. Portuguese by* Philippa Rumsey. PeSAV

In the cool waters of the river. Woman. Valente Malangatana, *tr. fr. Portuguese by* Dorothy Guedes *and* Philippa Rumsey. PBA; TTY

In the copper marsh. Heron. Philip Booth. Poetsp

In the corner, doubled up, black PVC. What to Say When You Talk to Yourself. Stephen Knight. CBCK

In the corner of a flower-shop. Twelve. Rossana Ombres, *tr. fr. Italian by* Ruth Feldman. NeIt

In the corner of the living room was an album of unbearable photos. Dead in Frock Coats, The. Carlos Drummond de Andrade, *tr. fr. Portuguese by* Mark Strand. AnRep

In the corner the fire made a place. Two Women. Tania van Zyl. PeSA

In the Counselor's Waiting Room. Bettie M. Sellers. InPK

In the Country. Lu Yu, *tr. fr. Chinese by* Kenneth Rexroth. OHMPC

In the Country. Ssu-k'ung Shu, *tr. fr. Chinese by* Hellmut Wilhelm. SuSp

In the county of Essex there lived a squire. The Wandering Shepherdess. *Unknown.* OBET

In the County Tyrone, in [*or near*] the town of Dungannon. The Old [*or Ould*] Orange Flute. *Unknown.* FaBoBa; GBP; OxBoLi; WTO

In the courtyard is a marvelous tree. *Unknown, tr. fr. Chinese by* Charles Hartman. SuSp

In the Covenant's Radiance. Uri Zvi Greenberg, *tr. fr. Hebrew by* Ruth Finer Mintz. MHP

In the covenant's radiance that moment had come. In the Covenant's Radiance. Uri Zvi Greenberg, *tr. fr. Hebrew by* Ruth Finer Mintz. MHP

In the cowslip's peeps I lie. Clock-a-Clay. John Clare. EBEV; EBVV; EnVR; FaPON; LiTB; NAEL-2; OAEL-2; OBAP; OBNC; PoEL-4 (Clock-o'-Clay.) TrGrPo

In the cream gilded cabin of his steam yacht. Mr. Nixon. Ezra Pound. *Fr.* Hugh Selwyn Mauberly. (Life and Contacts). AmPP; CMoP; InPS; LiTA; LiTM; MoAmPo; NoAM; NOBA; NoP; TAP

In the crimson of the morning, in the whiteness of the noon. The Coming of His Feet. Lyman W. Allen. BLPA

In the cross field. Out West. Gary Snyder. NNaP

In the Cross of Christ I Glory. Sir John Bowring. WGRP

In the crowd's multitudinous mind. Crucifixion. Eva Gore-Booth. WGRP

In the curious phenomenon of your occipital horn. (LL) To a Snail. Marianne Moore. CMoP; FaBoMo; FaBoWP; MeMAP; NAAL-2; NALW

In the Cyclops face of the future. (LL) Teleology. May Swenson. VCAP

In the daisied lap of summer. The Season's Lovers. Miriam Waddington. MoCV

In the damp brown evening of early winter. Nadezhda Mandelstam. Michael O'Loughlin. *Fr.* Two Women. IB

In the dank halls of Buchenwald. Juliek's Violin. Michael C. Blumenthal. BTR

In the Dark. Sophie Jewett. TrPWD

In the Dark. James Merrill. LCAP

In the dark. The Black Jewel. W. S. Merwin. CAPP; LCAP

In the Dark. Patrick Williams. PNI

In the dark aisles of Bruckner's symphonies. Bruckner. James Camp. MAT

In the dark and narrow street. When the Night and Morning Meet. Dora Greenwell. EBVV

In the dark at first, we see things in their sleep. Girandole. Dorothy Donnelly. NYBP

In the dark church of music. Vivaldi. Delmore Schwartz. NYBP

In the Dark Museum. Tracey Herd. NWP

In the dark mystery of my daughter's face. (LL) Sunday Afternoon at the State Hospital. Marilyn J. Boe. LoHo

In the dark Naomi. A Horror Story Written for the Cover of a Matchbook. Chuck Wachtel. UL

In the Dark None Dainty. Robert Herrick. CaPo

In the dark of December. (LL) I Heard a Bird Sing. Oliver Herford. NTCP; PDV; PoLF; SiSoPo

In the dark womb where I began. C. L. M. John Masefield. LiTM; MoBrPo; OxBTC

In the darkening church. Rufus Prays. L. A. G. Strong. MoBrPo

In the darkness east of Chicago. A Valedictory to Standard Oil of Indiana. David Wagoner. NYBP

In the darkness/ of the house of the white brother. Indian School. Norman H. Russell. MAT

In the dating bar, the potted ferns lean down. A History of Civilization. Albert Goldbarth. HCAP

In the Dawn. Odell Shepard. WGRP

In the dawn-dirty light, in the biggest snow of the year. Roe Deer. Ted Hughes. NoAM; OxAEP-2

In the dawning of the day. (LL) My Delight and Thy Delight. Robert Bridges. CMoP; NOBE; OBEV; PoEL-5

In the days before the high tide. A Sea Song. Digby Mackworth Dolben. EBVV

In the days of Caesar Augustus. Christmas Day; the Family Sitting. John Meade Falkner. ChIV-2; NOCV; OxBTC

In the days of mild Jerry Ford. *Unknown.* PeLi

In the heydays of 'forty-five. For George Santayana. Robert Lowell. CMoP; NAAL-2; VGW

In the high cool country. Driving through Sawmill Towns. Les A. Murray. FaBoMA

In the high corridors. Corridor. Federico García Lorca, tr. fr. Spanish. CBNP

In the high, high grass of Guinea. Country Graveyard. Charles Pressoir, tr. fr. French by Edna Worthley Underwood. NegPo

In the high jungle where Assam meets Tibet. Moschus Moschiferus. A. D. Hope. CBAP; GrPl

In the high seat, before-dawn dark. Why Log Truck Drivers Rise Earlier than Students of Zen. Gary Snyder. NNaP; SOTW

In the Highlands. Robert Louis Stevenson. FaBoCh; FaBV; OBEV; OxBS; SCGP

In the Hills. Wang Wei, tr. fr. Chinese by Robert Payne. TAL

In the holy cause to fall. (LL) The Young American. Alexander Hill Everett. VPP

In the Holy Nativity of Our Lord God. (Come we shepheards whose blest sight.) Richard Crashaw. GeHe; PoEL-2; SeCV-1 Sels.
"My darling, my love." CIP
"When the clouds' swoln bosoms echo back the shouts of the many and strong." ChIV-1; CMoP; LiTM; NoAM; OxBTC
"Wintertime nighs." NoAM; OAEL-2; SCGP
Shepherds' Hymn, The. NOBE
Shepherd's Hymn, The "We saw Thee in Thy balmy nest". TrGrPo, 3 sts.
(Verses from the Shepherd's Hymn.) OBEV

In the Home of the Scholar Wu Su-chiang. Wu Tsao, tr. fr. Chinese by Kenneth Rexroth and Ling Chung. BoWoP; WPC; WPOW

In the Hospital. Arthur Guiterman. WGRP

In the Hospital. Laura Jensen. AmPA

In the Hospital Near the End. Sharon Olds. NIP

In the Hospital of the Holy Physician. Nancy Willard. IHMS

In the hour before the Metro opens. The Fugitive. Michael O'Loughlin. IB

In the hour of death, after this life's whim. Dominus Illuminatio Mea. Richard Doddridge Blackmore. OBEV

In the hour [or houre] of my distress [or distresse]. His Litany to the Holy Spirit. Robert Herrick. BeJo; BLPL; ELP; JCP; NOSC; PeECV; PoLF; TEP
(His Letanie, to the Holy Spirit.) SeCV-1
(Litany to the Holy Spirit.) OBEV

In the hour of reckoning. The Reckoning. Marie Syrkin. BTR

In the Hours of Darkness. James Flexner. FaPON

In the house. A Marriage of Mutes. Ana Castillo. ETG

In the House of the Aylors. Albery Allson Whitman. Fr. Not a Man and Yet a Man. AAP

In the House of the Dying. Jane Cooper. CrSp; NMM

In the house of the hangman. The Hangman's Love Song. Stanley Moss. VGW

In the house with the tortoise chair. Poem to Ease Birth. Unknown, tr. fr. Aztec Indian by Anselm Hollo. BoWoP; STP

In the huge, rectangular room, the ceiling. My Mother, Who Came from China, Where She Never Saw Snow. Laureen Mar. CrSp; WPOW

In the huge, wide-open, sleeping eye of the mountain. The Bear. Ted Hughes. FaBoMo

In the human cities, never again to. Despisals. Muriel Rukeyser, tr. fr. Greek by Edmund Keeley. AnAn; NMM; Prf

In the Huon Valley. James McAuley. CBAP

In the ideal American. In Ancient December. Alice Notley. UL

In the Inner City. Lucille Clifton. HeIP

In the interim, how the children should be educated. Allen Curnow. Fr. Small Room with Large Windows, A. PeNZ

In the Interstices. Ruth Stone. ErPo

In the Isle of Dogs. John Davidson. OBNC

In the Isle of Great Britain long since famous known. Epitaph on Charles II. The Earl of Rochester. FaBoEH
(On Charles II.) IHNG

In the Jackdaw folder of "Historical Genitalia." Politics of Envy. Duncan Forbes. FaBoBl; PeLV

In the Jeta Pavilion of the Setting Sun. Drinking at Night in the Western Pavilion of the Fa-hua Temple. Liu Tsung-yüan, tr. fr. Chinese by Jan W. Walls. SuSp

In the Jewish Synagogue at Newport. Emma Lazarus. AmWP

In the joys of a living love. (LL) I Love You. Ella Wheeler Wilcox. BLPA; FaBoBe

In the Jury Room. Hodding Carter. MAT

In the Khamsin, sels. Yitzhak Lamdan, tr. fr. Hebrew by Ruth Finer Mintz. "Distant soughing of pine forests caresses my ear, The." MHP

"How little of God's grace caresses you, Massadah." MHP
"On roads beyond the camp the Khamsin struck me." MHP
"Why did Hagar weep over Ishmael when he thirsted." MHP

In the Kingdom of the Cross, sels. Uri Zvi Greenberg, tr. fr. Yiddish by Leonard Wolf.

In the Kitchen. Bible, Apocrypha, tr. fr. French. TSaS, tr. by Denise Levertov

In the Kitchen. Mary Leapor. Fr. Crumble Hall. ECWP

In the kitchen/ making dishes with a brush. A Plea to My Sister. James Cunningham. JB

In the knot there's no untying. (LL) Freedom and Love. Thomas Campbell. GTBS; GTBS-P

In the Laboratory. Dan Pagis, tr. fr. Hebrew by Robert Friend. PoSu

In the laboratory waiting room. Through a Glass Eye, Lightly. Carolyn Kizer. BoWoP

In the Ladies' Room at the Bus Terminal. William Zaranka. BXAP

In the lake of oblivion. (LL) To _____. Hsiung-hung. WPC

In the lamplight falling. Night. Peter Everwine. NNaP

In the land. In the Land Where Tanks. Leonid Martyrov, tr. fr. Russian by George Reavey. PAW

In the land o' the leal. (LL) The Land o' the Leal. Lady Nairne. GTBS; GTBS-P; OBEV; OxBS; ScCV; WBLP; WGRP

In the Land of Art. Anselm Hollo. NGP

In the land of dwarfs. Forugh Farrokhzad, tr. fr. Persian by Girdhard Tikku. BoWoP

In the land of God. Cecil County. Ron Welburn. PoBA

In the Land of Magic, sels. Henri Michaux, tr. fr. French.
"Hunchback, The. A poor wretch, unconsciously obsessed by paternity." AnRep, tr. by Richard Ellmann
"Suddenly you feel a touch." AnRep

In the land of mists. Land of Mists. Kwang-kyu Kim, tr. fr. Korean. TSaS, tr. by Brother Anthony

In the land of Tao-chou. The People of Tao-chou. Po Chü-i, tr. fr. Chinese by Arthur Waley. ChTr

In the land of turkeys in turkey weather. Dance of the Macabre Mice. Wallace Stevens. CMoP; NOBA; OxBA

In the Land Where Tanks. Leonid Martyrov, tr. fr. Russian by George Reavey. PAW

In the Land Where We Were Dreaming. Daniel B. Lucas. PAH

In the last days. Apocalypse. Francis Ernest Kobina Parkes. PBA

In the Last Few Moments Came the Old German Cleaning Woman. Jane Cooper. SM

In the last letter that I had from France. Easter Monday. Eleanor Farjeon. PAW

In the last minutes he said more to her. Seamus Heaney. Fr. Clearances. CIP; PBCIP; PNI

In the last storm, when hawks. The Epitaph Ending in And. William Stafford. LCAP; NaP

In the Late Afternoon. Nancy Condee. PRA

In the Lebanese Mountains. Nadia Tuéni. TSaS, tr. by Samuel Hazo

In the Lecture Room. James K. Baxter. Fr. Cressida. PeLV

In the Library. Michael Patrick Hearn. NTCP

In the Library. Ed Ochester. Poetsp

In the licorice fields at Pontefract. The Licorice Fields at Pontefract. Sir John Betjeman. CMoP

In the life we live [or lead] together every paradise is lost. Against Botticelli. Robert Hass. AmPA

In the light like rain. Easter Monday. Ralph Hawkins. VaA

In the little cage of Song! (LL) Birds. Richard Henry Stoddard. AnAmPo

In the little courtyard, by the side window. Li Ch'ing-chao, tr. by Eugene Eoyang. Fr. Tune: "Sand of Silk-washing Stream." SuSp

In the little port half hidden by the headlines of Pentire. War. S. S. Hunt. NSI

In the lives of their friends. (LL) Beware: Do Not Read This Poem. Ishmael Reed. BPo; NIP; NoP; PoBA

In the living room where slipcovers. Sunday and the Cigarette Salesman. Barbara Helfgott Hyett. ETG

In the Local Museum. Walter de la Mare. HAP

In the log dugout hidden by osiers. The Sighs of the Gunner from Dakar. Guillaume Apollinaire, tr. fr. French by Anne Hyde Greet. PeFWW

In the lonesome latter years. The Promissory Note. Bayard Taylor. AnAmPo; BXAP

In the long ago. (LL) An End. Christina Rossetti. CBLP; FaBoRV; GBL

In the long embrace of the sea. (LL) Rain to River to The Sea. Sister Mary Norbert Körte. SRLS

In the long journey out of the self. Journey to the Interior. Theodore Roethke. LCAP; NYBP; TRP; VGW

In the long night. Sermon on the Mount. Jeff Wright. UL

In the long, sleepless watches of the night. The Cross of Snow. Longfellow. HeIP; MeMAP; NOBA; OxBA; TAP

In the Longhouse, Oneida Museum. Roberta Hill Whiteman. NoAM

In the look of the black child. *(LL)* Note on a Shop in the Muceque. Geraldo Bessa Victor. PeSAV

In the Lord put I my trust. Bible, *O.T.*, *paraphrased by* Sir Thomas Wyatt. *Fr.* Psalms.
     (Psalm XI: "Since I do trust Jehova still," *paraphrased by* Sir Philip Sidney.) OBVE

In the Lost Province. Tom Paulin. PBCIP

In the love his beauty bringeth. *(LL)* The Singing Cat. Stevie Smith. CRH; OFC; OxBTC

In the love of home and country and the flag of Uncle Sam. Loyalty to the Flag. L. A. J. Moorer. CBWP-3

In the lovely month of May. Poet's Love. Heine, *tr. fr. German by* Philip L. Miller. RiWo

In the Lungs. Milo De Angelis, *tr. fr. Italian by* Lawrence Venuti. NeIt

In the Lybian desert I. Modo and Alciphron. Sylvia Townsend Warner. MoBrPo

In the Madison Zoo. Roberta Hill Whiteman. CDW

In the main sea the isle of Crete doth lie. Virgil, *tr. fr. Latin by* Robert Fitzgerald. *Fr.* Aeneid [*or* Eneados], The. NAWM-1; SiPSBD, *tr. by* Sir Walter Ralegh

In the mandolin air of pistons. Couch Fantasy. Adrian C. Louis. NAmP90

In the manger of course were cows and the Child Himself. Pig. Anthony Hecht. OxBC

In the maple-sugar bush. March. Elizabeth J. Coatsworth. PDV

In the Marble Quarry. James Dickey. NoP

In the market, in the cloister — only God I saw. Baba Kuhi of Shiraz, *tr. fr. Persian by* R. A. Nicholson. TOF

In the market, women are buying spring. *(LL)* The Window in the Cliff. Bei Dao. SpMi

In the marketplace they are piling the dry sticks. Witch Burning. Sylvia Plath. CAPP

In the marketplace where St Florian. She Looked At the Sun. Tadeusz Rózewicz, *tr. fr. Polish by* Magnus F. Krynski. PoSu

In the Memory of the Most Worthy Benjamin Jonson, *sels.* William Cartwright.
     "Where shall we find a Muse like thine, that can." EPCY

In the men's room on upper campus. Hit in the Head. Charles B. Stetler. NGP

In the merry month of May. Nicholas Breton. *Fr.* Honourable Entertainment Given to the Queen's Majesty in Progress at Elvetham, 1591, The. EBEvV; NoSic
     (Pastoral, A.) TrGrPo
     (Phillida and Coridon.) OBEV; TTTS
     (Phyllida and Corydon.) EIL
     (Ploughman's Song, The.) NOBE

In the merry month of May. The Sound of the Drum. *Unknown.* OBET

In the merry month of May from my home I started. The Rocky Road to Dublin. *Unknown.* FaBoBa

In the Middle of Life. Tadeusz Rózewicz, *tr. fr. Polish by* Czeslaw Milosz.

In the middle of nowhere. A Town I Have Heard of. Anne Carson. *Fr.* Life of Towns, The. BAP-90

In the middle of our times. Middle. Jimmie Durham. HATNAP

In the middle of the harbour. Derek Walcott. *Fr.* Sea-Chantey, A. RB; TTY

In the middle of the journey of our life. The Dark Wood. Dante, *tr. fr. Italian by* Seamus Heaney. *Fr.* Divina Commedia. BiHa; MeMAP; NAWM-1, *tr. by* John Ciardi

In the middle of the night. In Childbed. Thomas Hardy. NAs

In the middle of the night. Philodemus, *tr. fr. Greek by* Kenneth Rexroth. PGA

In the middle of the night he started up. Silver Wedding. Ralph Hodgson. CBLP; OxBTC; TrGrPo

In the middle of the night I slipped away from my husband. Philodemus, *tr. fr. Greek by* Barbara Hughes Fowler. *Fr.* Epigrams. HePo

In the middle of the night in the next room. The Cell of Himself. Arthur Freeman. TwCP

In the Middle of the Party. Carl Dennis. CBNP

In the middle of the sea. *Unknown, tr. fr. Chippewa Indian by* Jerome K. Rothenberg. STP

In the middle of the Southeast Asian war. The Pure Products of America. Alicia Ostriker. NGP

In the middle of the wood I set sail. Amhrán na mBréag. Pearse Hutchinson. PBCIP

In the Middle of Things, Begin. Beckian Fritz Goldberg. NAmP90

In the middle silences of this night's course the blackthorn. David Jones. *Fr.* Mabinog's Liturgy. OxAEP-2

In the Midst of Life. Tadeusz Rózewicz. *See* After the end of the world.

In the midst of my garden. The Palm Tree. Abd-ar-Rahman I, *tr. fr. Arabic by* J. B. Trend. AWP

In the midst of words your wordless image. The Heart. Harvey Shapiro. HoPM

In the mighty British Army. Rumour. Owen Rutter. *Fr.* Song of Tiadatha, The. NSI

In the Mirror. Elizabeth Fleming. BoTP

In the mirror it's plain to see. Bald. Bill Zavatsky. UL

In the mirror of his eyes I saw ever my own beauty mirrored. *(LL)* The Disciple. Oscar Wilde. OAEL-2

In the Miscroscope. Miroslav Holub, *tr. fr. Czech by* Ian Milner *and* Jarmila Milner. PoSu

In the Missouri Ozarks. Mona Van Duyn. NGP

In the month of Averil. The Cuckoo. *Unknown.* FaBoVe

In the month of February. *Unknown.* BoTP

In the Month of Green Fire. Sophie Himmell. GoYe

In the month of June the grass grows high. Reading the Book of Hills and Seas. T'ao Ch'ien, *tr. fr. Chinese by* Arthur Waley. ArNa

In the month of the long decline of roses. Hendecasyllabics. Swinburne. FaBoRV

In the moonlight. Anecdote of the Prince of Peacocks. Wallace Stevens. SOTW

In the Moonlight. Thomas Hardy. *Fr.* Satires of Circumstance. NoAM

In the Morgue. Israel Zangwill. TrJP

In the Morning. Jayne Cortez. BCF; BlSi

In the Morning. Paul Laurence Dunbar. BPo

In the morning and at night. T'ao Ch'ien, *tr. by* Eugene Eoyang. *Fr.* Seasons Come and Go, The. SuSp

In the morning he steps out. The Crier. Philip Kahclamet, *tr. fr. Wishram Chinook Indian by* Dell Hymes. STP

In the morning I didn't know. Comfortable Strangers. Terence Winch. UL

In the Morning I Look for You. Solomon ibn Gabirol, *tr. fr. Hebrew by* David Goldstein. TOF

In the Morning I Will Pray. William Henry Furness. AH

In the morning in the blue snow. Annual Gaiety. Wallace Stevens. MoAB; MoAmPo

In the morning, in the morning. A. E. Housman. CBLP

In the morning light a line. The Morning Light. Louis Simpson. NNaP

In the morning make me on with the light. *(LL)* At night make me one with the darkness. Wendell Berry. EaPr

In the morning the city. City [San Francisco]. Langston Hughes. PDV

In the morning the Jews were lined up by an officer. Charles Reznikoff. *Fr.* Mass Graves. BTR

In the morning, very early. Barefoot Days. Rachel Field. FaPON

In the mornings we're in the dark. More Blues and the Abstract Truth. C. D. Wright. NAmP90

In the mountain temple they beat the Dharma Drum. Dawn at Chiao Mountain, Seeing Off K'un-lun on His Way Back to Ching-k'ou. Wang Shih-chieng, *tr. fr. Chinese by* Richard John Lynn. SuSp

In the Mountain Tent. James Dickey. CAPP; MT

In the Mountain Village. Wang Hung Kung, *tr. fr. Chinese by* Kenneth Rexroth. OHMPC

In the mountain where you are unworshiped. Inanna and Ebih. Enheduanna, *tr. fr. Sumerian.* BoWoP, *ad. by* Aliki *and* Willis Barnstone

In the Mountains. Ssu-k'ung Shu, *tr. fr. Chinese by* Edward H. Schafer. SuSp

In the Mountains. Wang An-shih, *tr. fr. Chinese by* Jan W. Walls. SuSp

In the Mountains., *sels.* Wu Wen, *tr. fr. Chinese by* Irving Lo.

In the Mountains as Autumn Begins. Wen T'ing-yün, *tr. fr. Chinese by* Kenneth Rexroth. OHMPC

In the mountains o' the west. The Maid o' the West. John Clare. OAEL-2

In the Mountains on a Summer Day. Li Po, *tr. fr. Chinese by* Robert Payne. TAL

In the Mountains on a Summer Day. Li Po, *tr. fr. Chinese by* Arthur Waley. AWP

In the Mourning Time. Robert Hayden. BPo

In the mouths of everybody. *(LL)* Athena in the Front Lines. Marge Piercy. SRLS

In the mud of the Cambrian main. A Ballade of Evolution. Grant Allen. EBVV

In the multitude of counsellors. Kyrielle: Party Politics. Frederick Macartney. NOBAu

In the Museum. Isabella Gardner. CAPP; NYBP; SoSe

In the museum of translucent. In the Dark Museum. Tracey Herd. NWP

In the music of the morns. A Call. Thomas Holley Chivers. Poetr

In the mustardseed sun. Poem on His Birthday. Dylan Thomas. NAs

In the Naked Bed, in Plato's Cave. Delmore Schwartz. LiTA; LiTM; MoAB; MoAmPo; NoAM; NOBA; PoA; VGW

In the naked tree an enormous crow. Winter Longing. Gu Cheng, *tr. fr. Chinese by* Donald Finkel *with* Yi Jinsheng. SpMi

In the name of Allah, the Merciful the Compassionate! Love Charm. *Malay Oral Tradition, tr. by* R. O. Winstedt. WTO

In the name of God, the merciful, the compassionate! Of Iron Am I. *Malay Oral Tradition, tr. by* W. W. Skeat. WTO

In the name of Love. (*LL*) Sirventes. Paul Blackburn. NeAP; PoM

In the name of the Father full of virtue. Exodus to Connacht. Fear Dorcha O'Meallain, *tr. fr. Irish by* Thomas Kinsella. FaBoPV; TIRV

In the name of the God of strangers, we beg you. Damagetus, *tr. fr. Greek by* John Heath-Stubbs *and* Carol A. Whiteside. GrAn

In the name of the people. Matsemela Manaka. Fr. Pula. PeSAV

In the nativity of time. Love Made in the First Age: To Chloris. Richard Lovelace. BeJo; CaPo; JCP; NAEL-1; OAEL-1; SeCP

In the natural year come two thanksgivings. The Sabbath of Mutual Respect. Marge Piercy. CrSp; SRLS

In the negro gardens negro birds. To Eliza, Duchess of Dorset. Joseph Deericks Bennett. LiTA

In the Neolithic Age. Kipling. NOBVV

Sels.

Wide, Wide World, The. OtMeF

In the New Sun. Philip Levine. NNaP

In the Night. Elizabeth Jennings. NYBP

In the Night. James Stephens. OBMV

in the night. (*LL*) My Love's Guardian Angel. William Barnes. GBL; PoEL-4

In the night. The Peaks. Stephen Crane. *Fr.* War Is Kind. WGRP

In the Night. *Unknown.* FaBoNo; NBLV

In the night accompanies my playing. (*LL*) In the Mountains as Autumn Begins. Wen T'ing-yün. OHMPC

In the night, awash with symbols. Night. Duo Duo, *tr. fr. Chinese by* Donald Finkel *with* Li Guohua. SpMi

In the night/ Gray, heavy clouds muffled the valleys. The Peaks. Stephen Crane. *Fr.* War Is Kind. WGRP

In the Night of the Full Moon. Carl Busse, *tr. fr. German by* Jethro Bithell. AWP

In the Night She Came. Thomas Hardy. OxBM

In the night the agile mole. The Unfortunate Mole. Mary Kennedy. GoYe

In the night the house is thin and blue. House. Sue May. NBrP

In the night the man could hear the wind walking. Harvest. Gene Shuford. GoYe

In the night the night. After Time. John Seed. VaA

In the night the struggle of men is not heard. Pentecost. John Riley. VaA

In the night there was a murder in the street. Of Autumn. Veronica Porumbacu, *tr. fr. Romanian by* Willis Barnstone *and* Matei Calinescu. BoWoP

In the night we shall go in. The Stolen Branch. Pablo Neruda, *tr. fr. Spanish by* Donald Devenish Walsh. ArNa

In The Nighttime Someone. Luigi Fontanella, *tr. fr. Italian by* Michael Palma. NeIt

In the nighttime someone in my place. In The Nighttime Someone. Luigi Fontanella, *tr. fr. Italian by* Michael Palma. NeIt

In the North. Kung Liu, *tr. fr. Chinese.* LHF, *tr. by* Hualing Nieh

In the north the cloud flower blossoms. The Cloud-Flower Lullaby. *Unknown, tr. fr. Tewa Indian by* H. J. Spinden. WTO

In the northern hemisphere. Kangaroo. D. H. Lawrence. EBEV; InPS; MeMBP; OBTV; OxBTC

In the northwest there is a drifting cloud. Ts'ao P'i, *tr. fr. Chinese by* Ronald C. Miao. SuSp

In the numb, numberless days. The Burning. N. Scott Momaday. HATNAP

In the Nuptial Chamber. Thomas Hardy. *Fr.* Satires of Circumstance. InPK

In the ocean there's a very sad turtle. Jack Kerouac. *Fr.* Mexico City Blues. PoM

In the offing scatterest foam, thy white sails crowding. (*LL*) A Passer-by. Robert Bridges. CMoP; EBEvV; ImPo; LiTB; LiTM; MoAB; MoBrPo; OAEL-2; OBEV; OBNC; OxBTC; SCGP; WiR

In the old age black was not counted fair. Shakespeare. *Fr.* Sonnets. OxAEP-1

In the old back streets o' Pimlico. The Rambling Sailor. Charlotte Mew. PoRA

In the Old City. Jacob Fichman, *tr. fr. Hebrew by* Sholom J. Kahn. TrJP

In the old days. Scorpion. Linda Hogan. SRLS

In the old days (a custom laid aside). Abraham Davenport. Whittier. AmPP; NoP

In the old days back when. Death Crown. Robert Morgan. MT

In the old days with married women's stockings. The Libertine. Louis MacNeice. MoP; NoAM

In the old neighborhood, each funeral parlor. Teach Us to Number Our Days. Rita Dove. NoAM

In the old, old days when the West was young. The Texas Ranger. Margie B. Boswell. AiP

In the old park, deserted and frozen. Sentimental Colloquy. Paul Verlaine, *tr. fr. French by* Philip L. Miller. RiWo

In the old stone pool. Basho, *tr. fr. Japanese by* Cid Corman. InPK

In the Old Theatre, Fiesole. Thomas Hardy. OBTV

In the old time, by the forks of the Santiam. A Kalapuya Prophecy. *Unknown, tr. fr. Kalapuya Indian by* Jarold Ramsey. STP

In the old time women's cunts had teeth in them. How Her Teeth Were Pulled. *Unknown, tr. fr. Paiute Indian by* Jarold Ramsey. STP

In the old way and raise our heritage. (*LL*) Poem from Llanybri. Lynette Roberts. AngWe

In the olive darkness of the sally-trees. The Bull. Judith Wright. GrPl

In the one cool room of the house. Developing a Wife. Andrew Taylor. CBAP

In the one light on. First Aid at 4 A.M. Christopher Bursk. InPK

In the one-two domestic goose one-two one-two step. Henry Beissel. *Fr.* New Wings for Icarus. MoCV

In the only free. In the Ladies' Room at the Bus Terminal. William Zaranka. BXAP

In the Operating Room. Alden Nowlan. NOBC

In the Orchard. Ibsen, *tr. fr. Norwegian by* Sir Edmund Gosse. AWP

In the Orchard. Muriel Stuart. EBNV; ErPo; FF; OxBTC

In the Orchard. Swinburne. BoLoP

In the orchestra it matters. Beards. Pure Valentine. Connie Deanovich. UTF

In the Orpheum Building. Kit Robinson. UL

In the other gardens. Autumn Fires. Robert Louis Stevenson. NTP

In the Outhouse. Mitsuye Yamada. *Fr.* Camp Notes. WPOW

In the outlying districts where we know something. Everyman's Library. John Ashbery. NoP

In the painkilling cold that wrapped. Snow. David Wevill. MoCV

In the painting. Up against the Wall. D. C. Berry. BXAP

In the Palais Royale Ballroom in 1948. John Engels. Jaz

In the pale splendour of the winter sun. (*LL*) Schoolboys in Winter. John Clare. InvP; PoEL-4

In the palm. A Guerrilla Handbook. Amiri Baraka. PoBA

In the Pantry. "Hugh MacDiarmid." NoAM

In the pantry the dear dense cheeses. O Cheese. Donald Hall. DiPo

In the parading square. Medusa on Skyros. Alison Fell. NBrP

In the Paralelo a one-legged. Entered in the Minutes. Louis MacNeice. LiTB

In the Park. Gwen Harwood. CBAP; FaBoMA

In the parlour of the shanty where the lives have all gone wrong. Will Yer Write It Down for Me? Henry Lawson. CBAP

In the Past. Trumbull Stickney. AnAmPo; NOBA; OxBA

In the past I brought trouble upon myself when I sought rank and honor. Tune: "Wild Geese Have Come Down; Song of Victory." *Unknown, tr. fr. Chinese by* Sherwin S. S. Fu. SuSp

In the pathway of the sun. Penelope. Dorothy Parker. PAW

In the Pauper's Turnip-Field. Herman Melville. OxBSP; PoEL-5

In the pause. Wallflower to a Moonbeam. Louis Untermeyer. BXAP

In the Pea Patch. Maxine W. Kumin. CAPP

In the Person of Woman Kind (A Song Apologetic). Ben Jonson. BeJo; SeCP; SeCV-1

In the Person of Womankind (In Defense of Their Inconstancy). Ben Jonson. BeJo; NAEL-1

In the pharmacy a nude cadaver evaporates. (*LL*) Charlie's Sad Date. Rafael Alberti. AnAn; CBNP

In the photograph he stands alone. Chinese Camp, Kamloops (circa 1883). Andrew Suknaski. NOBC

In the picture the people stroll and stroll all day. Public Holiday: Paris. Joyce Horner. GoYe

In the pinch of time, facing. Victorian Grandmother. Margo Lockwood. Poetsp

In the Pines. *Unknown.* AmFP

In the Pinewoods, Crows and Owl. Mary Oliver. Poetr

In the Pink. Siegfried Sassoon. CMoP

In the place where. Judy Grahn. *Fr.* Edward the Dyke and Other Poems. NALW; PeHV

In the placid summer midnight. Street Scene. W. E. Henley. BoTP

In the pleasant pastime of temple viewing. Manners. Edith Marcombe Shiffert. WPE

In the pond in the park. Water Picture. May Swenson. BoNaP

In the pond of our new garden. Visiting Hour. Stewart Conn. PWE

In the Poppy Field. James Stephens. PoRA

In the Praise of Music. Humphrey Gifford. NoSic

In the pride of Human Nature when its pants begin to go. *(LL)* When Your Pants Begin to Go. Henry Lawson. NOBAu

In the Prison Pen. Herman Melville. PoEL-5; TAP

In the Proscenium. Gene Derwood. LiTA

In the Pub. Peter Riley. *Fr.* One Day. VaA

In the Public Garden. Marianne Moore. NOBA

In the Public Gardens. Sir John Betjeman. NYBP

In the Public Theater lobby, I wait for Marie. Marilyn Hacker. *Fr.* Taking Notice. VCAP

In the purple light, heavy with redwood, the slopes drop seaward. Apology for Bad Dreams. Robinson Jeffers. AmPP; LiTA; MoAB; MoAmPo; NOBA; OxBA

In the pushcart market, on Sunday. Galway Kinnell. *Fr.* Avenue Bearing the Initial of Christ into the New World, The. NaP

In the quarter of the Negroes. Cultural Exchange. Langston Hughes. BPo; PoBA; PoNe

In the Queen's Room. Norman Cameron. *Fr.* Three Love Poems. FaBoTw; GTBS-P; OxBTC

In the quiet arms of grief. *(LL)* If All the Skies Were Sunshine. Henry van Dyke. WBLP; WGRP

In the quiet before cockcrow when the cricket's. Dear Men and Women. John Hall Wheelock. IMW; NYBP; Prf

In the quiet time. Ghostly Love. Valerie Sinason. DT

In the quiet waters. Fafnir and the Knights. Stevie Smith. Mes

In the R-Mitage. Great Birthday Blaublau with Rhymework and Assonance. Paul Celan, *tr. fr. German.* CBNP

In the rain in a yard in Cessnock. Ruth Silcock. PeLi

In the rain that has passed by. Lost City. Ingrid Jonker, *tr. fr. Afrikaans by* Jack Cope *and* Ruth Miller. PeSA

In the rain, the bark of the plane trees shines. Rain. Martha Collins. FoLa

In the rain, the naked old father is dancing, he will get wet. Natural History. Robert Penn Warren. FF; NAAL-2

In the rains of winter the pa children. The Dark Welcome. James K. Baxter. *Fr.* Five Sestinas. PeNZ

In the rain's push and the wind's hand. From My Thought. Daniel Smythe. GoYe

In the reading room in the New York Public Library. Reading Room, The New York Public Library. Richard Eberhart. GOYP

In the Red Grove. Andrew Duncan. NBrP

In the Refectory. Alcuin, *tr. fr. Latin by* Helen Waddell. MLL

In the Restaurant. Thomas Hardy. *Fr.* Satires of Circumstance. MoAB; MoBrPo

In the revolutionary shout. A White Mess. Anthony Barnett. VaA

In the right with two or three. *(LL)* Stanzas on Freedom. James Russell Lowell. GN, 2 *sts.*; OHIP; PoNe

In the ring of high hills. Feodosia. Osip Mandelstam, *tr. fr. Russian by* W. S. Merwin *and* Clarence Brown. AnAn

In the Ringwood. Thomas Kinsella. CMoP; PBCIP

In the ripest days of August, sunflowers. The Whisper. Eugene Gloria. OpBo

In the riprap. Mussels. Mary Oliver. NU

In the river bank, an empty sandpit. Frankfurt. János Pilinszky, *tr. fr. Hungarian by* János Csokits *and* Ted Hughes. PoSu

In the Room. James Thomson ("B. V."). NOBVV; PeVV

In the Room of the Bride-Elect. Thomas Hardy. *Fr.* Satires of Circumstance. InPK

In the Root Cellar. Maxine W. Kumin. FaBoWP

In the rude age when scyence was not so rife. The Earl of Surrey. AAS (Another Tribute to Wyatt.) SiPS

In the Rue Monsieur le Prince. Song for "Buvez les Vins du Postillion" — Advt. Jean Garrigue. TAP

In the rush odour of Danish meadows. Peter Huchel, *tr. fr. German by* Michael Hamburger. PoSu

In the sad spirit. To the Unknown Light. Edward Shanks. TrPWD

In the same blood you closed your eyes to. *(LL)* The Morning They Shot Tony Lopez, Barber and Pusher Who Went Too Far, 1958. Gary Soto. PBCAP

In the Same Boat. H. Crawford. FaBoEH

In the same post, the Old Fox receives. Negotiation. Alan Brownjohn. PeLV

In the same sweet eternity of love. *(LL)* Love What It Is. Robert Herrick. ArLo; FaBoEE; GBL

In the same way that the sea. The Morning Train. W. S. Merwin. BAP-90

In the sand I grew, by the rocky sea-wall. The Husband's Message. *Unknown, tr. fr. Anglo-Saxon by* Charles W. Kennedy. AnOE

(Now that we are on our own I can explain this secret stave.) ASW

In the satin shade of an olive tree. Achilles and the Tortoise. Miroslav Holub, *tr. fr. Czech by* Stuart Friebert *and* Dana Hábová. PoSu

In the scented bud of the morning — O. The Daisies. James Stephens. AWP

In the school auditorium. Bully. Martín Espada. AfAz

In the Sea. Brendan Kennelly. BiHa

In the sea. *(LL)* Little Fish. D. H. Lawrence. OxBTC; RB; SOTW; Spl; TTTS

In the sea, Biscayne, there prinks. Homunculus et la Belle Étoile. Wallace Stevens. MoAB; MoAmPo

In the Sea of Tears. Naomi Replansky. BrRo

In the Secret House. Christopher Middleton. FaBoMo

In the sedge beyond Chalco. The Flowering War. *Unknown, tr. fr. Aztec Indian by* Jerome K. Rothenberg. STP

In the Seminole darkness of your singing eyes. Poem to a Redskin. Wendy Rose. CDW

In the Seraglio. David R. Slavitt. ErPo; PeHV

In the Servants' Quarters. Thomas Hardy. FaBoVe; MoAB; MoBrPo

In the Seven Woods. W. B. Yeats. CMoP; NoAM

In the Seventh Month. Shih Ching, *tr. fr. Chinese by* Irving Y. Lo. SuSp

In the seventh month the Fire-star declines. In the Seventh Month. Shih Ching, *tr. fr. Chinese by* Irving Y. Lo. SuSp

In the shabby train no seat is vacant. The Refugees. Randall Jarrell. MoAB; MoAmPo

In the shade of a metaphor. Patrizia Cavalli, *tr. fr. Italian by* Robert McCracken *with* Patrizia Cavalli. NeIt

In the shadow of a stand. Wimbledon Veteran. Lawrence Sutton. FaBoBl

In the Shadow of My Curls. Paul Johann Ludwig Heyse, *tr. fr. German by* Philip L. Miller. RiWo

In the Shadow of the Valley of Death. Abu-Qasim al-Shabbi. DL

In the Shadows, *sels.* David Gray.
"If it must be; if it must be, O God!" OxBS

In the shaking of the sieve, the refuse. The Test of Men. Bible, Apocrypha. *Fr.* Ecclesiasticus. TrJP

In the shambles of love, they kill only the best, Jalal al-Din Rumi, *tr. fr. Persian by* Coleman Barks *and* John Moyne. *Fr.* Four Quatrains. RaBo

In the shape of this night, in the still fall of snow, Father. At the New Year. Kenneth Patchen. LiTM

In the Shire of Phestos hard by Cnossus dwelt of yore. Ovid, *tr. by* Arthur Golding. *Fr.* Metamorphoses. PeHV

In the shop in the muceque. Note on a Shop in the Muceque. Geraldo Bessa Victor, *tr. fr. Portuguese by* Donald Burness. PeSAV

In the Shreve High football stadium. Autumn Begins in Martins Ferry, Ohio. James Wright. CAPP; HCAP; HeIP; InPK; InPS; NaP; NoAM; VCAP; WeW

In the shut drawer, even now, they rave and grieve. Packet of Letters. Louise Bogan. GrPl

In the sightless air I dwell. Song of a Spirit. Ann Radcliffe. ECWP

In the Silence. Stephany Fuller. BPo

In the silence and the dark. Armageddon. Georgia Douglas Johnson. ShDr

In the silence and the gloom. *(LL)* Aftermath. Longfellow. NAAL-1; NOBA; TAP

In the silence that falls on my spirit. My Father's Voice in Prayer. May Hastings Nottage. BLRP

In the silence that prolongs the span. Black Jackets. Thom Gunn. HeIP; NAEL-2; TwCP

In the Silent Night. Isaac Leibush Peretz, *tr. fr. Yiddish by* Joseph Leftwich. TrJP

In the six-acre field. Lost. Millen Brand. NYBP

In the sky above the clouds. It Could Have Been More. Ralph Angel. FoLa

In the sky the Milky Way turns. Tune: "Southern Song, A." Li Ch'ing-chao, *tr. fr. Chinese by* Eugene Eoyang. SuSp

In the sky there is a moon and stars. Proportion. Amy Lowell. BoWoP

In the sky was final above. The Sweeping Gesture. John Ash. BAP-90

In the slime of desolate moors the floods of autumn whitened. *(LL)* The Liang Terrace. Li Ho. PLT

In the sludge drawer of animals in arms. Rules of Sleep. Howard Moss. VCAP

In the Slums. George Campbell. PBCV

In the small beauty of the forest. George Oppen. NNaP

In the Smoking-Car. Richard Wilbur. LiTM; MoAmPo

In the smoky outhouses of the court of love. In the Queen's Room. Norman Cameron. *Fr.* Three Love Poems. FaBoTw; GTBS-P; OxBTC

In the Snack-Bar. Edwin Morgan. FF

In the Snake Park. William Plomer. NYBP; OxBTC

In the Snowfall. Gwerfyl Mechain, *tr. fr. Welsh by* Willis Barnstone. BoWoP

In the sod with songs. *(LL)* At the Cemetery. Jean Richepin. RiWo

In the soft air perfumed with blooming May. Lines to Mount Glen. George Marion McClellan. AAP

In the Soul Hour. Robert Mezey. AmPA; NaP

In the South be drooping trees. Chou and the South. *Unknown, tr. by* Ezra Pound. *Fr. Shi King.* CTC

In the South be drooping trees. Confucius, *tr. fr. Chinese by* Ezra Pound. *Fr.* Chou and the South. CTC

In the south, sleeping against. Legacy. Amiri Baraka. MoP; NoAM; NOBA; PoBA

In the South there is a saying. Why Are Daddies So Mean? Jane Chambers. GLP

In the southern land many birds sing. The South. Wang Chien, *tr. fr. Chinese by* Arthur Waley. AWP

In the southern village the boy who minds the ox. The Herd Boy. Lu Yu, *tr. fr. Chinese by* Arthur Waley. ChTr

In the spaces between the stars still water dances. David Ignatow. *Fr.* Leaving the Door Open. CAPP

In the splendor of the morning. Ganymede. Goethe, *tr. fr. German by* Philip L. Miller. RiWo

In the Spring. William Barnes. GBL

In the Spring. Meleager, *tr. fr. Greek by* Andrew Lang. AWP

In the Spring. Tennyson. *Fr.* Locksley Hall. BLPL; BoNaP; EBEV; EBVVPR; EnVR; FaBoBe; ImPo; NAEL-2; OAEL-2

In the spring, by the big shuck-pile. Burning the Cat. W. S. Merwin. NIP

In the spring of the year, in the spring of the year. The Spring and the Fall. Edna St. Vincent Millay. ArLo

In the Spring, on the trees. Fluttering Leaves. Rodney Bennett. BoTP

In the Spring the quince and the. Ibycus, *tr. fr. Greek by* Kenneth Rexroth. PGA

In the spring woods, how good it is to see. Aspects of the World like Coral Reefs. William Bronk. VGW

In the square of a lighted window. Observation of a Bee. Leah Goldberg, *tr. fr. Hebrew by* Stephen Mitchell. WPOW

In the stagnant pride of an outworn race. Santiago. Thomas A. Janvier. PAH

In the state of old Kentucky. The Death of Samuel Adams. *Unknown.* AmFP

In the State of "Old Palmetto," from the town of Eutawville. The Eutawville Lynching. L. A. J. Moorer. CBWP-3

In the States. Robert Louis Stevenson. AiP; OHCV

In the steamy, stuffy Midlands, 'neath an English summer sky. Switzerland. Alfred Denis Godley. OBTV

In the steel room. Birth. George Ella Lyon. CrSp

In the still air the music lies unheard. The Master's Touch. Horatius Bonar. TrPWD

In the still-blistering late afternoon. The Farmer. Ellen Bryant Voigt. MT; WeW

In the still jungle of the senses lay. The Tiger. Ella Wheeler Wilcox. AmWP

In the still morning when you move. Tropics. Ellen Bryant Voigt. SM

In the stillness. Expectant Mother. Penelope Shuttle. BrRo

In the strange city of life. Nostalgia. Walter de la Mare. LiTM

In the Stravinsky book by Lillian Libman. Reading in the Night. Roy Fuller. OxBC

In the Street. John Shaw Neilson. CBAP

In the streetcar conductor's uniform. Portrait: The Freedom Fighter. George Jonas. NOBC

In the Style of Han Shan and Shih Te, *sels.* Wang An-shih, *tr. fr. Chinese.*
  "Had I been an ox or horse." SuSp
  "Wind blew, a tile fell from the roof, The." SuSp

In the Suburbs. Michael O'Loughlin. IB

In the Suburbs. Louis Simpson. CAPP; MAT; TRP

In the summer heat and fever crackling. The Boy; or, Son of Rip-off. Malcolm Glass. BXAP

In the summer months on every crossing to Piraeus. Watching for Dolphins. David Constantine. OBTV; PWE; SCBI

In the summer of the first year of Chia-yu (A.D. 1056). The Cicada. Ou-yang Hsiu, *tr. fr. Chinese by* Arthur Waley. AWP

In the sunny orchard closes. In the Orchard. Ibsen, *tr. fr. Norwegian by* Sir Edmund Gosse. AWP

In the sunny Spring of March and April. Spring Song. Meng Chu, *tr. fr. Chinese by* Kenneth Rexroth *and* Ling Chung. WPC

In the sun's path. Dawn in the Valley. Fily-Dabo Sissoko, *tr. fr. French by* Ellen Conroy Kennedy. NegPo

In the supreme hashish of our dream. *(LL)* Uses of Poetry. Lawrence Ferlinghetti. PoBeRe

In the swaddling clothes. *(LL)* When the herd[s] were watching. William Canton. OHIP

In the swamp in secluded recesses. Walt Whitman. *Fr.* Memories of President Lincoln. AmPP; AWP; HAP; LiTA; MeMAP; MoAmPo; NAAL-1; NOBA; NoP; OxBA; PoEL-5; PoRA; PPP; RFM; SAmP; TAP; TFi; TrGrPo

In the Sweet Dark. John Seed. VaA

In the sweet shire of Cardigan. Simon Lee. Wordsworth. EnRP; NAEL-2 (Simon Lee the Old Huntsman.) GTBS; GTBS-P

In the sweetness of our Lord. *(LL)* The All-embracing. Frederick William Faber. BLRP

In the Tail of the Scorpion. Genevieve Taggard. VGW

In the tall quiet pines of Washington. For Tom Numkena, Hopi/Spokane. Harold Littlebird. VoR

In the Tank. Thom Gunn. NoAM

In the Tavernas. C. P. Cavafy, *tr. fr. Greek by* Edmund Keeley *and* Philip Sherrard. AnAn

In the television's pale square of light. Back in the Twilight Zone. Martha Hollander. UTF

In the Theatre. Dannie Abse. NoAM

In the third-class seat sat the journeying boy. Midnight on the Great Western. Thomas Hardy. CH; NOBE; OxAEP-2

In the third day of May. The Boy and the Mantle. *Unknown.* ESPB; OxBB

In the third decade of March. Where Art Is a Midwife. Tom Paulin. SCBI

In the Third Month. David Ray. RaBo

In the third month, a sudden flow of blood. The Vow. Anthony Hecht. InPK; Prf

In the tides of the warm south wind it lay. Verazzano. Hezekiah Butterworth. PAH

In the time it takes. Andrew Crozier. *Fr.* High Zero. NBrP

In the time of old sin without sadness. Variations on [*or of*] an Air: After [Algernon Charles] Swinburne. G. K. Chesteron. FaBoPa; NOBL

In the Time of Revolution. Julius Lester. PoBA
  Sels.
  "It cannot be/ reasoned with."
  "One needs a lyric poet in these."

In the Time of Trouble. Leslie Savage Clark. TrPWD

In the tiny village. What She Said. Vayilanrevan, *tr. fr. Tamil by* A. K. Ramanujan. PLW

In the tiny world of lovers' arms and/ challenge time. *(LL)* To His Coy Mistress. John Flood. BXAP; FaBoPa

In the top and front of a bus, eager to meet his fate. Figure of Eight. Louis MacNeice. OxBSP

In the Touch of This Bosom There Worketh a Spell. Samuel Taylor Coleridge. *Fr.* Christabel. CH, ll. 1-65; EnRP; FHYEP; OAEL-2; RB

In the tower the bell. The Bell. Richard Jones. NAmP90

In the Town. *Unknown, tr. fr. French by* Eleanor Farjeon. OBCP; PChr

In the town of Athy one Jeremy Lanigan. Lanigan's Ball. *Unknown.* OxBoLi

In the town of Odessa. Dvonya. Louis Simpson. NNaP; NOBA

In the town where every man is king. Josephine Miles. NALW

In the Town With Cat-/ Shaped Maze. Kanai Mieko, *tr. fr. Japanese by* Kenneth Rexroth *and* Ikuko Atsumi. WPJ

In the Train. James Thomson ("B. V."). *See* As we rush, as we rush in the train.

In the tranced dancing of men. *(LL)* The Bear on the Delhi Road. Earle Birney. HeIP; MoCV; NoAM; NOBC; NoP; NYBP; PrIm

In the Tree House at Night. James Dickey. NoP

In the tree the luminous sap ascends. *(LL)* Horse and Tree. Rita Dove. TRP

In the Tree-Top. Lucy Larcom. OBCA

In the Trenches. Richard Aldington. PeFWW

In the tunnel of woods, as the road. Last Things. William Meredith. NoAM

In the twelfth month of this Eighth Year. Bitter Cold, Living in the Village. Po Chü-i, *tr. fr. Chinese by* Irving Lo. SuSp

In the Twentieth Century. James McAuley. ChIV-2

In the Twenty-Fifth Year of Marriage, It Goes On. Alicia Ostriker. PBCAP

In the twilight hour all is still. Night Vigil. Evangelina Vigil. BCF

In the universal Sun. *(LL)* The Invitation. Shelley. GTBS; GTBS-P; OBEV

In the unmade light I can see the world. West Wall. W. S. Merwin. RaBo

In the unnavigable dusk, when. Owl. Peter Kane Dufault. NYBP

In the usual way of the young/ we made appointments. I Say Goodbye to Fan An-ch'eng. Shen Yüeh, *tr. fr. Chinese by* Lenore Mayhew *and* William McNaughton. SuSp

In vain to me the smiling mornings shine. Sonnet on the Death of Mr. Richard West. Thomas Gray. EnRP; NOEC; NoP; OBD; PeHV; PoE; PoEL-3
(On the Death of Mr. Richard West.) NOBE; Son; TrGrPo

In vain we grant, if she refuse. (LL) Advice to the Old Beaux. Sir Charles Sedley. FaBoUs; SeCV-2

In vain your bangles cast. Abiku. Wole Soyinka. PBA

In vain fair[e] sorceress[e], thy eyes speak[e] charm[e]s. To a Wanton. William Habington. NOSC; SeCP

In valleys green and still. A. E. Housman. FaBoTw; OAEL-2; SCV

In Vienna there are ten young girls. Little Viennese Waltz. Federico García Lorca, tr. fr. Spanish by William B. Logan. SOTW

In Vietnam. Militerotics. Chuck Ortleb. GLP

In villages from which their childhoods came. The City. W. H. Auden. Fr. Quest, The. Son

In Vinculis, sels. Wilfrid Scawen Blunt.
Deeds That Might Have Been, The. TrGrPo

In Violet. Debora Greger. BAP-89

In Virginia. Beauty Kills. Charlie Smith. PFL

In Virgyne the sweltrie sun gan sheene. An Excelente Balade of Charitie. Thomas Chatterton. EBEV; EnRP; NOEC; OxAEP-1
(Excellente Balade of Charity.) LiTB

In Wakefield there lives a jolly pinder. The Jolly Pinder of Wakefield. Unknown. ESPB, A vers.

In Wales there is a borough town. Tale of a Friar and A Shoemaker's Wife, A. Thomas Churchyard. NoSic

In walking naked. (LL) A Coat. W. B. Yeats. CMoP; EPCY; IIP; LiTM; NAEL-2; NoAM; OxAEP-2; OxBSP; PoEL-5

In War. Mason Jordan Mason. PoNe

In warm night air. (LL) Little by little. Gary Lawless. EaPr

In warm war-sun they erupt. Mules. Ted Walker. NYBP

In Waste Places. James Stephens. MoAB; MoBrPo; SCGP

In water-heavy nights behind grandmother's porch. Adolescence — I. Rita Dove. NoAM; VBLP

In water nothing is mean. The fugitive. Patience. Elaine Feinstein. BrRo; FaBoWP

In waves still as the skillful yachts pass over. (LL) The Yachts. William Carlos Williams. AmPP; CMoP; HeIP; ImPo; LiTA; LiTM; MeMAP; MoAB; MoAmPo; MoP; NoAM; NOBA; NoP; OxBA; PoE; PPP; SAmP; TFi

In Weather. Robert Hass. AmPA

In Western Massachusetts, Sixteen Months Sober. Joan Larkin. LoHo

In western skies. Sunset. H. Cordelia Ray. Fr. Idyl. BlSi; CBWP-3

In Westminster Abbey. Sir John Betjeman. CMoP; FaBoCo; FaBoEH; InPK; NBLV; NIP; NoAM; NOBL; OAEL-2; OBSV; OxAEP-2; PlP; TOF

In Westminster not long ago. The Ratcatcher's Daughter. Unknown. ChTr; GBP; OxBoLi

In wet green midspring, midnight and the wind. Mrs. Walpurga. Muriel Rukeyser. NMM

In wet May, in the months of change. An Exequy. Peter Porter. NoAM; OxBC

In what a silence princes pass away. On the Death of a Prince; a Meditation. Thomas Philipott. JCP

In what cave in the love of love. Douglas Oliver. VaA

In what dark silent grove. Cogitabo Pro Peccato Meo. William Habington. ChIV-1

In what estate so ever I be. Timor Mortis. Unknown. FF; NoP

In what finite tendon dost thou rise? Spirituality. Samuel Greenberg. LiTA

In what house, the jade flute that sends these dark notes drifting. Spring Night in Lo-Yang — Hearing a Flute. Li Po, tr. fr. Chinese by Burton Watson. TTTS

In what I say: it is his praise I sing. (LL) As When Some Hungry Fledgling Hears and Sees. Vittoria da Colonna. BoWoP, tr. by Barbara Howes; PBWP, tr. by Lynne Lawner

In What Manner the Soule Is United to the Body. Sir John Davies. Fr. Nosce Teipsum. LiTB; NoSic, abr.; PoEL-2; SiPS

In what order or what degree. Be True to Your Condition in Life. John Audelay [or Awdelay]. MeEL

In what recesses of the brain. Memory, a Poem. Laetitia Pilkington. ECWP

In what soft language shall my thoughts get free. Upon the Death of Her Husband. Elizabeth Rowe. ECWP

In what torn [or torne] ship soever I embark [or embarke]. A Hymne to Christ, at the Author's Last Going into Germany. John Donne. EBEV; EnRePo; ESCV; LiTB; MeLP; NAEL-1; NOSC; OxAEP-1; PeECV; SeCV-1

In which being there together is enough. (LL) Final Soliloquy of the Interior Paramour. Wallace Stevens. HAP; HCAP; LCAP

In which if they turn and twist, it is neither with volition nor consciousness. (LL) A Grave. Marianne Moore. CMoP; FaBoWP; HAP; HeIP; LiTA; MeMAP; MoP; NAAL-2; NoAM; NOBA; PoE; Poetr; TAP; TFi; TRP; UnPo; WeW; WPE

In Which Roosevelt Is Compared to Saul. Vachel Lindsay. ChIV-1

In Which She Satisfies a Fear with the Rhetoric of Tears. Sister Juana Inés de la Cruz, tr. by Aliki and Willis Barnstone. BoWoP

In which we all begin. (LL) History. Gary Soto. PBCAP

In White. Robert Frost. TRP

In white robes I'm joined by a. Martin Robbins. See As summer ends and leaves fall like dust.

In white Siberia where the fallen have risen. Diary of a Tashkent Jew. Gloria Glickstein. BTR

In Whitman's day there were the secret bathers. Devolution of the Nude. Lynne McMahon. NAmP90

In whom the Lord of Hosts did pitch his tent! (LL) Ana(Mary-Army)gram. George Herbert. ChIV-2; GeHe; OAEL-1

In Whom We Trust. Harry Clifton. IB

In whose will is our peace? Thou happiness. J. V. Cunningham. VGW

In wild flight. Unknown, tr. fr. Sioux Indian by James Koller. Fr. Sioux Metamorphoses. STP

In wind from Asia and a wanton rain. (LL) The Way a Ghost Dissolves. Richard Hugo. NAAL-2; NoAM; NoP; SM

In Windsor Castle. The Earl of Surrey. See So cruel [or cruell or crewell] prison how could betide [or howe coulde betyde], alas.

In winged-tip shoes. The Cigarette Salesman. Barbara Helfgott Hyett. ETG

In wings and starched. Chana Bloch. Fr. Sacrifice, The. CrSp

In Winter. William Dunbar. OxBLMV

In winter. (LL) Ode to My Socks. Pablo Neruda. RaBo; TRP

In Winter. Robert Wallace. BoNaP

In winter I get up at night. Bed in Summer. Robert Louis Stevenson. GoJo; NBLV; OTCP; OxBChV; PFP

In winter I remember. All Winter. Linda Hogan. ETG

In winter in my room. Emily Dickinson. AmPP; ErPo; LiTA; MoP; NAAL-1; NALW; NoAM; NOBA; OxBA; Poetr

In Winter in the Woods Alone. Robert Frost. HeIP

In winter my mothers goes away. Desert. Del Marie Rogers. MDDM

In winter on her hearth lighting some coal. Antipater of Thessalonica, tr. fr. Greek by Alistair Elliot. GrAn

In winter, those first mornings after my father died. The Pier. Garrett Kaoru Hongo. OpBo

In winter when it's/ Zero. John Travers Moore and Margaret Moore and Margaret Moore. SiSoPo

In winter, when the fields are white. "Lewis Carroll." Fr. Through the Looking-Glass. EBEV; NOBVV
(Humpty Dumpty's Poem.) Mes
(Humpty Dumpty's Poetic Recitation.) CBNP
(Humpty Dumpty's Recitation.) ChTr; FaBoCo; FaBoNo; FiBHP; OBSP; PeVV
(Humpty Dumpty's Song.) GTBS-P; OxBChV; OxBoLi; PeLV

In winter when the nights are long. The Beggar Wind. Mary Austin. BoNaP

In winter when the rain rain'd cauld. Tak' Your Auld Cloak about Ye. Unknown. OxBS

In winter woe befell me. Christopher Marlowe, tr. fr. Latin by A. R. Myers. FaBoEH

In winter's just return, when Boreas gan his reign. The Earl of Surrey. AAS; SiPS; SiPSBD

In wintertime I have such fun. Quoits. Mary Effie Lee Newsome. CDC

In Wintry Midnight, o'er a Stormy Main. Petrarch, tr. fr. Italian by William Barnes. ChTr

In wiser days, my darling rosebud, blown. To My Daughter Betty. Thomas Michael Kettle. TIRV

In wit, as nature, what affects our hearts. Pope. Fr. Essay on Criticism. HAP; PoEL-3

In with them, and tore down the slaughterhouse. (LL) Reuben Bright. E. A. Robinson. AnAmPo; MeMAP; MoAB; MoAmPo; NOBA; NoP; PFP; Son; TAP; TrGrPo

In wizened old terminal birth. Back Always. Clark Coolidge. UL

In wonted walkes. Sir Philip Sidney. PoEL-1

In woods still winter bare. Shadbush. Christina Rainsford. GoYe

In Worcester, Massachusetts. In the Waiting Room. Elizabeth Bishop. FaBoWP; HeIP; InPS; LCAP; NAAL-2; NALW; NoAM; NOBA; PoE; Prf; VCAP

In Word and Will I am a friend to you. On Himself. William Oldys. FaBoEE

In wrath and grief away the Paynims fly. Unknown, tr. by Dorothy L. Sayers. Fr. Song of Roland, The. NAWM-1, tr. by Frederick Goldin, abr.; OBWP

Incline Thine ear, O God. Therefore, We Thank Thee, God. Reuben Grossman, *tr. fr. Hebrew by* L. V. Snowman. TrJP

Inclusiveness. Dante Gabriel Rossetti. *Fr.* House of Life, The. NAEL-2

Incognita. Austin Dobson. EBVV; OHCV

Incomparable treasure, heart's blood spilt. The Poetry of Gerard Manley Hopkins. Monk Gibbon. TIRV

Incompleteness. H. Cordelia Ray. AmWP; CBWP-3

Incomprehensible, The. Isaac Watts. WGRP

Inconclusive Evening, An. Frances Bellerby. FaBoTw

Inconstancy Reproved. Sir Robert Ayton. *See* I do confess thou'rt smooth and fair.

Inconstancy's the Greatest of Sins. Lord Herbert of Cherbury. OxBSP

Inconstant Dawn, thou tak'st thy time. Meleager, *tr. fr. Greek by* Peter Whigham. GrAn

Incontestably sang, and the people were beautiful. *(LL)* The Unpredicted. John Heath-Stubbs. BoLoP; OxBC

Incontinence, and the mind going. Where? Nursing Home. Philip Martin. FaBoMA

Inconvenience, An. John Raven. BPo; CRP

Increasing moonlight drifts across my bed, The. Fredericksburg. Thomas Bailey Aldrich. AnAmPo; PAH

Incredible Vistas. David Chaloner. VaA

Incrusted in his island home that lies beyond the sea. The Neutral British Gentleman. "Orpheus C. Kerr." OBAL

Indecent, self-soiled, bilious. Geocentric. Pattiann Rogers. NAmP90

Indeed, good Sir, you're quite mistaken. Verses Designed to Be Sent to Mr. Adams. Elizabeth Frances Amherst. ECWP

Indeed I must confess. Platonic[k] Love. Abraham Cowley. *Fr.* Mistress, The. BeJo; NoP; SeCV-1

Indeed Indeed, I Cannot Tell. Thoreau. RaBo

Indeed, it will soon be over, I shall be done. Intimations of Mortality. Stanley Kunitz. MoAmPo

Indeed, Sir Peter, I could wish, I own. On Clergymen Preaching Politics. John Byrom. ECEV

Indeed then, it was your own courage. Anyte, *tr. fr. Greek by* John Heath-Stubbs *and* Carol A. Whiteside. GrAn

Indeed will I, quo' Findlay. *(LL)* Wha Is That at My Bower-Door? Burns. ErPo; InvP

Indelible lust (for you). From Malay. David Shapiro. UL

Independance. Louise Bennett. FaBoVe; PBCV

Independence. Nancy Cato. WPE

Independence. Adebayo Faleti, *tr. fr. Yoruba by* Bakare Gbadamosi *and* Ulli Beier. PBA

Independence. *Somali Oral Tradition, tr. by* B. W. Andrzejewski *and* I. M. Lewis. WTO

Independence Bell — July 4, 1776. *Unknown.* BLPA; FaBoBe

Independence Day. William Jay Smith. TwCP

Independence Day. Royall Tyler. PAH

Independence Day: Eureka. Cornel Lengyel. BTR

Independence tun Big-Smady! Independence Twenty-One. Louise Bennett. PBCV

Independence Twenty-One. Louise Bennett. PBCV

Independent, The. Phyllis McGinley. FaBoEE

Independent Squire. Samuel Butler. *Fr.* Hudibras. NOBE

Index. Paul Violi. EOEF

India. W. J. Turner. MoBrPo; OBAP; PDV

India Guide, The; or, Journal of a Voyage to the East Indies in 1780, *sels.* Sir George Dallas.
     "If you my dear mother, had e'er been at sea." OBTV
     Miss Emily Brittle Sails for India. NOEC

India that one read about, The. I Wonder What Happened to Him. Noël Coward. FaBoEH

Indian. Laura Jensen. AmPA

Indian Bagman's Toast. *Unknown.* FaBoVe

Indian Boarding School: The Runaways. Louise Erdrich. HATNAP; NoAM

Indian Burying Ground, The. Philip Freneau. AmPP; AnAmPo; EAP; HAP; LiTA; NAAL-1; NOBA; NoP; OBD, *abr.*; OxBA; PoEL-4; PoLF; TAP; TFi

Indian Camp. Janet Reed McFatter. GrPl

Indian Cave Jerry Ramsey Found, the. William Stafford. NoAM

Indian chief who, fam'd of yore, The. The Prophecy of King Tammany. Philip Freneau. GOA

Indian College Blues. Adrian C. Louis. NAmP90

Indian Convert, The. Philip Freneau. TAP

Indian Elephant, The. C. J. Kaberry. FiBHP

Indian Emperor, The, *sels.* Dryden.
     Ah, Fading Joy. ChTr
     (Song: "Ah fading joy, how quickly art thou past!") NoP

Indian Girl's Song, The. Shelley. *See* I arise from dreams of thee.

Indian Hunter, The. Eliza Cook. BLPA

Indian, Indian, lived in a tent. *Unknown.* RoPo

Indian Lass, The. *Unknown.* OBET

Indian Love Song. Lew Blockcolski. VoR

Indian Maid, The; Demararie, Oct. 27, 1781. Edward Thompson. NOEC; OBTV

Indian Mother about to Destroy Her Child, An. James Montgomery. VPP

Indian Names. Lydia Huntley Sigourney. FaPON; GOA; OBCA ; PAH; PoLF

Indian Queen, The, *sels.* Sir Robert Howard *and* John Dryden.
     "Poor mortals that are clogged with earth below." TEP

Indian Reservation: Caughnawaga. A. M. Klein. LiTM; NOBC; NoP

Indian River, The. Sebastian Barry. IB

Indian Rock, Bainbridge Island, Washington. Duane Niatum. CDW

Indian Ruins along Rio de Flag. Greg Pape. PBCAP

Indian School. Norman H. Russell. MAT

Indian Serenade, The. Shelley. AWP; BLPL; CBLP; EnRP; HoPM; ImPo; LiTB; MeMBP; OBEV; PIP; RaBo; TrGrPo; TTTS

Indian Singing in 20th Century America. Gail Tremblay. HATNAP

Indian Song: Survival. Leslie Silko. CDW; VoR

Indian Student; or, Force of Nature, The. Philip Freneau. AnAmPo; OxBA

Indian Summer. Wilfred Campbell. NOBC

Indian Summer. Emily Dickinson. *See* These are the days when birds come back.

Indian Summer. Barbara Howes. IHMS

Indian Summer. Dorothy Parker. NIP

Indian Summer at Land's End. Stanley Kunitz. CAPP

Indian Summer Day on the Prairie, An. Vachel Lindsay. RFM

Indian Summer: Montana, 1956. W. M. Ransom. CDW

Indian upon God, The [*or* An]. W. B. Yeats. MoBrPo; WGRP

Indian war was over, The. The Captive's Hymn. Edna Dean Proctor. PAH

Indian weed [now] withered quite, The. Religious Use of [Taking] Tobacco. Robert Wisdome. EIL; SCGP
     (Pipe and Can, I "The Indian weed withered quite".) OBEV

Indian, who lived at Muskingum, remote, An. The Indian Convert. Philip Freneau. TAP

Indians. John Fandel. NYBP

Indians, The. Roberto Sosa, *tr. fr. Spanish.* TSaS, *tr. by* Jim Lindsey

Indians. Charles Sprague. GN

Indians at the Guthrie. Gerald Vizenor. VoR

Indian's Bride, The. Edward Coote Pinkney. AnAmPo

Indians Come Down from Mixco, The. Miguel Angel Asturias, *tr. fr. Spanish by* Donald Devenish Walsh. FaPON

Indians count of men as dogs, The. Roger Williams. SCAP

Indians have mostly gone, The. Like Ghosts of Eagles. Robert Francis. GOA; LCAP

Indians prize not English gold, The. Roger Williams. SCAP

Indians stole fair Annie, The. Fair Annie. *Unknown.* CH; ESPB, A, B, *and* E *vers.*; FaBoBa; OxBB

Indictment of Senior Officers. Sharon Olds. PBCAP

Indies, The, *sels.* Edouard Glissant, *tr. fr. French by* Ellen Conroy Kennedy.
     "Child climbs to the island's highest point, The." NegPo
     "O Sun! O age-old labor mutely mixed with ocean." NegPo
     "One of them, taking advantage of the crew's momentary carelessness." NegPo
     "They fastened a people to merchant ships." NegPo

Indifference. Harry Graham. NBLV

Indifference, The. Sir Charles Sedley. SeCV-2

Indifference. G. A. Studdert-Kennedy. TrCP

Indifferences and success had crowned them all. *(LL)* On First Looking into Loeb's Horace. Lawrence Durrell. FaBoMo; LiTM

Indifferent, The, *sels.* John Donne. BoLoP; CBLP; ESCV; NAEL-1; NAWM-1; NOSC; SeCV-1; SoSe; TEP
     I Can Love Both Fair and Brown. CBCK

Indifferent or unaware. *(LL)* Cortège. Paul Verlaine. AWP; OBVE

Indigestion of the Vampire, The. W. S. Merwin. NaP

Indignant at the fumbling wits, the obscure spite. Paudeen. W. B. Yeats. HAP; OxBSP; PoEL-5

Indignation Dinner, An. James David Corrothers. PoNe

Indigo. Chitra Divakaruni. OpBo

Indigo against ocher, Atlantic. Acadian Lane. David St. John. SM

Indigo Glass in the Grass, The. Wallace Stevens. PoA

Indigo, magenta, color of ghee. Whitebeard on Videotape. James Merrill. NoP

Individualist Speaks, The. Louis MacNeice. OBMV

Individuality. Ella Wheeler Wilcox. AmWP

Indolence. Vernon Watkins. FaBoTw

Indolent and kitten-eyed. Cheetah. Charles Eglington. OBAP

Indolent Gardener, The. Mary Kennedy. BoNaP

Indolent Housewife — in Daisies — lain! (*LL*) How many times these low feet staggered. Emily Dickinson. AmPP; HAP; NAAL-1; PoEL-5; WeW

Indolent vicar of Bray, An. Langford Reed. PeLi

Indoors. George Johnston. PoA

Indoors the tang of a tiny oil lamp. Outdoors. House on a Cliff. Louis MacNeice. NOIV

Indra, the Supreme God, *Fr.* Rig Veda. *Unknown, tr. fr. Sanskrit by* Romesh Dutt. *Fr.* Vedic Hymns. AWP

Induction, The. Milton. *See* Of man's first disobedience, and the fruit.

Induction, The. Thomas Sackville. *Fr.* Induction to "A Mirror for Magistrates". AAS; NoSic

Induction to "A Mirror for Magistrates." Thomas Sackville. AAS *Sels.*
  "Poor mortals that are clogged with earth below." TEP
  Induction, The. NoSic
  Midnight ("Midnight was come, when every vital thing.") CH
  Shield of War, The.

Indulge thy smiling scorn, if smiling still. The Fish Turns Into a Man, and Then Into a Spirit, and Again Speaks. Leigh Hunt. *Fr.* Fish, the Man, and the Spirit, The. ChTr; EnRP; FM; GGP; HAP; NOBL; NTP; OBEV; PoEL-4

Indulgent Nature on each kind bestows. On Dr. Evans Cutting Down a Row of Trees. *Unknown.* FaBoEE

Industrial Childhood. Sharon Stevenson. TSaS

Industrial Evils. Joseph Cottle. *Fr.* Malvern Hills. NOEC

Industrial Size. Jeff Wright. UL

Industrious, unfatigued in faction's cause. The Character of a Certain Whig. William Shippen. APAS

Industrious young obstetrician, An. Isaac Asimov. PeLi

Industry undressing in front of Agriculture. Ecologue. Michael Hofmann. SCBI

Inebriety. George Crabbe. BXAP

Ineffable Dou, The. Sydney Goodsir Smith. OxBS

Inept young person, Miss Muffet, The. Dean Walley. PeLi

Inertia. Kirti Chaudhari, *tr. by* Leonard Nathan. WPOW

Inertia. Vivienne Finch. BrRo

Inevitable. Sir John Betjeman. MoBrPo

Inevitable, The. Sarah Knowles Bolton. WGRP

Inevitable, of course. Very old now, she. Elegy for Delina. Albert Rowe. CRH

Inexhaustible. Israel Zangwill. TrJP

Inexorable. William Drummond of Hawthornden. *See* Like the Idalian Queen[e].

Inexorable. William Drummond of Hawthornden. *See* My thoughts hold mortal[l] strife.

Inexpensive Progress. Sir John Betjeman. IHNG

Inextinguishable Blaze. Charles Wesley. *See* O thou who camest from above.

Infamous Doctrine. Paul Evans. NBrP

Infancy. Carlos Drummond de Andrade, *tr. fr. Portuguese by* Elizabeth Bishop. ArLo

Infancy! fearless, lustful, happy, nestling for delight. Blake. *Fr.* Visions of the Daughters of Albion. OAEL-2; OxAEP-2

Infant and the Pearl, The, *sels.* Douglas Oliver.
  "We followed the river to Fortune's Wheel." NBrP

Infant Diseases and Their Treatment. M. Saint-Marthe, *tr. fr. French. Fr.* Paedotrophiae; or, The Art of Bringing Up Children. FaBoUs

Infant Innocence. A. E. Housman. FaBoNo; NOBL

Infant Innocence. A. E. Housman. MeMBP

Infant Innocence. A. E. Housman. ChTr; FaBoCh; FaBoCo; FaBoNo; ImPo; LiTB; NOBL; OxBoLi; PeLV; Spl

Infant Joy. Blake. *Fr.* Songs of Innocence. FaPON; FHYEP; GoJo; NAEL-2; NAs; NTP; OxAEP-2; OxBSP; PoLF; TEP

Infant she played in the shadow. Anne and the Peacock. Noel Welch. FF

Infant Song. Charles Causley. NAs; OxBC

Infant Sorrow. Blake. *Fr.* Songs of Experience. EBEvV; FHYEP; InPS; NAEL-2; NAs; OBNC; OxAEP-2; OxBM; OxBSP; PoEL-4; RB

Infant — wailing in maneless fear, An. Life. Ella Wheeler Wilcox. PoToHe

Infantry. Alun Lewis. PoWW

Infantryman, The. *Unknown.* NSI

Infelice. Stevie Smith. FaBoWP

Infelix. Adah Isaacs Menken. AAP; AmWP; CBWP-1

Infernal Regions and the Invisible Girl. Alfred Corn. BAP-91

Inferno. Dante, *tr. fr. Italian. Fr.* Divina Commedia. MeMAP; NAWM-1, *tr. by* John Ciardi.

Infidel Reclaimed, The. Edward Young. *Fr.* Night Thoughts. NOEC

Infidelity. Olga Berggolts, *tr. fr. Russian by* Daniel Weissbort. BoWoP; IMW

Infidelity. Théophile Gautier, *tr. fr. French by* Philip L. Miller. RiWo

Infidelity. Stanley Plumly. NAmP90

Infidelity. Louis Untermeyer. TrJP

Infield Outfield. Asa Benveniste. NBrP

Infinite, The. Giacomo Leopardi, *tr. fr. Italian by* William Jay Smith. ArNa

Infinite, The. John Boyle O'Reilly. TIRV

Infinite consanguinity it bears. Hart Crane. *Fr.* Voyages (I – VI). CMoP; MeMAP; NoAM; NOBA; NoP; OxBA; TAP

Infinite grief! amazing woe! Look on Him Whom They Pierced, and Mourn. Isaac Watts. NOCV

Infinite Portugal, June eleventh, nineteen hundred and fifteen . . . Salutationi to Walt Whitman. Fernando Pessoa, *tr. fr. Portuguese by* Edwin Honig. AnRep

Infinite power essenciall, The. Mary, Queen of Heaven. *Unknown.* MeEL

Infinite Power, eternal Lord. The Comparison and Complaint. Isaac Watts. TrPWD

Infinite speaks in our silent hearts, The. Reason. Elizabeth Oakes Smith. *Fr.* Atheism. AmWP

Infinite Spirit, when I pray each day. Jennie Frost Butler. EaPr

Infinite task of the human heart," The. (*LL*) For the One Who Would Take Man's Life in His Hands. Delmore Schwartz. LiTA; LiTM; MoAB; MoAmPo; VGW

"Infinite," The. Word horrible! at feud. Legem Tuam Dilexi. Coventry Patmore. *Fr.* Unknown Eros, The. PoEL-5

Infinite Truth and Might! whose love. Thy Name We Bless and Magnify. John Power. BLRP

Infinito, L'. Giacomo Leopardi, *tr. fr. Italian by* Lorna De' Lucchi. AWP

Infinity Effect at the Hôtel Soubise. Alfred Corn. EOEF

Infinity, when all things it beheld. Edward Taylor. *Fr.* God's Determinations [touching his Elect]. AmPP; EAP; HAP; MeMAP; NAAL-1; NOBA; OxBA; SCAP

Infinity, when all things it beheld. The Preface. Edward Taylor. *Fr.* Preparatory Meditations Before My Approach to the Lord's Supper. NOSC

Infir Taris. *Unknown.* ChTr; ISE; OxNR

Infirm and aged, doth he sit. The Old Year. Priscilla Jane Thompson. CBWP-2

Infirmity. Theodore Roethke. CoAP; NAAL-2; NYBP

Inflammable Woman, The. James K. Baxter. OxBC

Inflatable Globe, The. Theodore Spencer. LiTA; PAW

Inflation. Charles O. Hartman. PoA

Inflation. Heather McHugh. NAmP90

Influence. Sarah Knowles Bolton. PWR

Influence of Local Attachment, The, *sels.* Richard Polwhele.
  Visit to the Author's Paternal Seat, A. NOEC

Influence of Natural Objects, The. James Simmons. PNI

Influence of Natural Objects. Wordsworth. *Fr.* Prelude [or, Growth of a Poet's Mind], The. AWP; CH; EnRP; GN; HAP; NOBE; NoP; NU; OAEL-2; OBNC; OxAEP-2; PoE; SCV

Influence of Time on Grief. William Lisle Bowles. *See* O Time! who know'st a lenient hand to lay.

Influencing Machines. Nick Totton. VaA

Inform the Lakedaimonians, friend — we rest. Simonides. *See* Go tell at Sparta, traveler passing by.

Informer, art thou in the tree. On the Meetings of the Scotch Covenanters. *Unknown.* FaBoEE

Informing a correct compassion, that performs its love, and makes it live. (*LL*) A Correct Compassion. James Kirkup. FaBoTw; OxBTC

Informing Spirit, The. Emerson. AWP

Infusorial earthmounds of the Upper Amazon, The. Lost Explorer. Edmund Pennant. GoYe

Ingenious god was old Zeus, An. Deus "Sex" Machina. Harriet Mandelbaum. PeLi

Ingenious insect, but of ruthless mold. To the Spider. Thomas Russell. Son

Ingenious Little Old Man, The. John Bennett. FaPON

Inglis archeris schot sa fast, The. John Barbour. *Fr.* Bruce, The. ScCV

Inglorious friend! most confident I am. Sonnet to a Clam. John Godfrey Saxe. AnAmPo

Inglorious Milton, The. Francis Letters. NOBAu

Ingmar Bergman's "Seventh Seal." Robert Duncan. CAPP; PoE

Ingoldsby Legends, The, *sels.* "Thomas Ingoldsby."
  Cynotaph, The. FM
  Not a Sous Had He Got. FaBoCo
  Jackdaw of Rheims, The. EBNV; FaBoCo; OBNV; OBSP; VPP

Ingrateful[l] Beauty Threatened. Thomas Carew. BeJo; CaPo; HeIL; InvP; MeLP; OBEV; SeCP; SeCV-1

Ingratitude. Anna Seward. ECWP; NOEC

Ingrown. James Berry. PBCV

Inhabitants of heavenly land. The Countess of Pembroke. *Fr.* Psalms of David, The. SiPSBD

Inheritors, The. Gary Geddes. NOBC

Inheritors, The. William Peskett. PNI

Inhuman, The. Eugenio Montale, *tr. fr. Italian by* G. Singh. OBD

Inhuman Henry. A. E. Housman. FiBHP; NBLV

Inimitably quick. Static Autumn. Yvor Winters. PoA

Iniquity of the Fathers upon the Children, The. Christina Rossetti. FaBoVe

Inis Fal. Egan O'Rahilly, *tr. fr. Irish by* James Stephens. BIrV; OBMV

Initiate, The. W. S. Merwin. NNaP

Initiate, The. Charles Simic. BAP-90

Initiation. Jayne Cortez. PoBA

Initiation. Rainer Maria Rilke, *tr. fr. German by* C. F. MacIntyre. TrJP

Initiations, *sels.* Paul Niger, *tr. fr. French by* Ellen Conroy Kennedy. "What?/ a rhythm." NegPo

Injian Ocean sets an' smiles, The. For to Admire. Kipling. MoBrPo

Injure Tinglit. Busk, Pierce. Maggie O'Sullivan. NBrP

Injured Maple. Ronald G. Everson. NOBC

Injurious Hermia, most ungrateful maid. Shakespeare. *Fr.* Midsummer Night's Dream, A. OBF

Injustice of the Courts. L. A. J. Moorer. CBWP-3

Ink, a-bink, a bottle of ink. *Unknown.* RoPo

Ink runs from the corners of my mouth. Eating Poetry. Mark Strand. CAPP; GrPl; MAT; MoP; NoAM; PPP; TAP

Inky gloss of your mane, The. *Unknown, tr. fr. Greek by* W. G. Shepherd. GrAn

Inland City. John Crowe Ransom. CMoP

Inland,/ far inland go my thoughts. Song of the Rejected Woman. Kibkarjuk, *tr. fr. Eskimo into Danish by* Knud Rasmussen; *English vers. by* Tom Lowenstein. WPOW

Inland Lighthouse, The. James McMichael. AmPA

Inland, within a hollow Vale, I stood. Near Dover, September 1802. Wordsworth. EnRP
  (September, 1802: Near Dover.) MeMBP

Inlet, The. Jean Pedrick. ETG

Inmate, An. Peter Kocan. NOBAu

Inn, The. Wilhelm Müller, *tr. fr. German by* Philip L. Miller. *Fr.* Winter's Journey, The. RiWo

Inn of Earth, The. Sara Teasdale. LiTA

Inn That Missed Its Chance, The. Amos R. Wells. TrCP

Inner Ear. T. R. Hummer. MT

Inner greet. Greenberg said it. Columbus. Muriel Rukeyser. GOA

Inner Light, The. F.W.H. Myers. *Fr.* Saint Paul. WGRP

Inner Mongolia — The Grasslands. Sibyl James. LoHo

Inner Part, The. Louis Simpson. PBCV; RaBo

Inner Realm, The. Priscilla Jane Thompson. CBWP-2

Inner Source, The. Andrei Codrescu. UL

Inner Temple Masque, The, *sels.* William Browne.
  Sirens' Song, The. NOBE; OBEV
  (Song of the Sirens.) EiL
  (Song of the Syrens.) ChTr
  (Syrens' Song, The.) GBL

Inner Tube. Michael Ondaatje. NoAM

Inner Vision, The. Wordsworth. *See* Most Sweet It Is with Unuplifted Eyes.

Inniskeen Road: July Evening. Patrick Kavanagh. CIP; IPY; MoP; NoAM; NoP; Poetr

Innkeeper's Wife, The. Clive Sansom. OBCP

Innocence, The. Robert Creeley. NeAP

Innocence. Thom Gunn. LiTM

Innocence. Patrick Kavanagh. RB

Innocence. Anne Spencer. CDC; ShDr

Innocence. Wislawa Szymborska, *tr. fr. Polish by* Jan Darowski. PoSu

Innocence. Thomas Traherne. ChIV-2; ESCV; MiEL; NOSC

Innocence, girlhood, beauty. (*LL*) In Whom We Trust. Harry Clifton. IB

Innocence in the creases of my soul. (*LL*) Blue, so blue that eye of sky. Jacques Rabémanganjara. NegPo

Innocence of her, The. The Innocent Breasts. Joel Oppenheimer. PoM

Innocence of Radium, The. Lavinia Greenlaw. NWP

Innocence? Soon as you try putting your finger on it. 1966. David Rivard. PBCAP

Innocent Breasts, The. Joel Oppenheimer. PoM

Innocent bride from the Mission, An. *Unknown.* PeLi

Innocent Country-Maid's Delight; or, A Description of the Lives of the Lasses of London, The. *Unknown.* CoMu

Innocent decision: to enjoy. Triple Feature. Denise Levertov. FF; NoP

Innocent eyes not ours. All Things Wait upon Thee. Christina Rossetti. GN

Innocent Ill, The. Abraham Cowley. OPOP

Innocent Landscape. Elinor Wylie. OxBA

Innocent maiden of Gloucester, An. *Unknown.* PeLi

Innocent Mistress, The, *sels.* Mary Pix.
  "When I languish'd, and wish'd you wou'd something bestow." KTR

Innocent of history. (*LL*) Latitude 5°N. Harry Clifton. IB

Innocent Play. Isaac Watts. NOEC

Innocent Spring, The. Edith Sitwell. *See* In the great gardens, after bright spring rain.

Innocent's Song. Charles Causley. GTBS-P; OBCP

Innominatus. Sir Walter Scott. *See* Breathes There the [*or* a] Man [with Soul So Dead].

Inns are not residences. (*LL*) Silence. Marianne Moore. AnAmPo; CMoP; CoGr; FaBoMo; FaBoWP; InPS; LiTA; NALW; NOBA; TRP

Innsbruck, now I must depart. *Unknown, tr. fr. German by* Ingrid Waløe-Engel. GePo

Innumerable City knights we know. On Lord Mayors. Daniel Defoe. *Fr.* True-born Englishman, The. APAS; IHNG

Innumerable Beauties, thou white haire. Lord Herbert of Cherbury. PoEL-2

Innumerable Christ, The. "Hugh MacDiarmid." EBEV; NoP; OxAEP-2; OxBS

Innumerable worlds! We dream of them. Contemplation of the Heavens. Bill Manhire. PeNZ

Inordinate Love. *Unknown. See* I shall say what inordinat[e] love is.

Inquest, The. W. H. Davies. AngWe; GTBS-P; NOBE; OxBTC; RB

Inquietude. Pauli Murray. BISi

Inquietude of a Particular Matter, The. Alberto A. Ríos. NAmP90

Inquirers, trailing printed liberty. (*LL*) Scholar II. Seamus Deane. CIP; NOIV

Inquisitive Bridegroom, The. William Somervile. ECEV

Inquisitors, The. Robinson Jeffers. MoAmPo

Insatiable Love. Eduard Friedrich Mörike, *tr. fr. German by* Philip L. Miller. RiWo

Insatiable Priest, The. Matthew Prior. OxBSP

Insatiableness. Thomas Traherne. NOSC

Insatiate. Mae V. Cowdery. ShDr

Inscribed on a Painting. Cheng Hsieh, *tr. fr. Chinese by* Irving Y. Lo. SuSp

Inscribed in Melrose Abbey. *Unknown.* FaBoEE; FaBoRV

Inscribed on a Lichen-Covered Wall in My Hut, *sels.* Chin Nung, *tr. fr. Chinese by* Jonathan Chaves.

Inscribed on a Painting. Shen Chou, *tr. fr. Chinese by* Daniel Bryant. SuSp

Inscribed on a Painting. Shen Chou, *tr. fr. Chinese by* Irving Y. Lo. SuSp

Inscribed on a Painting. T'ang Yin, *tr. fr. Chinese by* Chiang Yee. SuSp

Inscribed on a Painting of a Cock. T'ang Yin, *tr. fr. Chinese by* Chiang Yee. SuSp

Inscribed on a Painting of Bamboo Presented to Lec, *sels.* Yang Shih-ch'i, *tr. fr. Chinese by* Jonathan Chaves.

Inscribed on a Painting of Windy Bamboo, to Be Presented to Tzu-kan. Hsü Wei, *tr. fr. Chinese by* Chiang Yee. SuSp

Inscribed on a Scroll "Plum Blossoms by the Water." Huang T'ing-chien, *tr. fr. Chinese by* Michael E. Workman. SuSp

Inscribed on a Statue of Hermes. *Unknown, tr. fr. Greek by* Peter Jay. GrAn

Inscribed on Byron's Poetic Works. Su Man-shu, *tr. fr. Chinese by* Wu-chi Liu. SuSp

Inscribed on My Grass-script Calligraphy Written While Drunk. Lu Yu, *tr. fr. Chinese by* Irving Y. Lo. SuSp

Inscribed on the Arbor of the Old Drunkard (Tsui-weng-t'ing) at Ch'u-chou. Ou-yang Hsiu, *tr. fr. Chinese by* Irving Y. Lo. SuSp

Inscribed on the Fan of a Wealthy Old Man. Shen Chou, *tr. fr. Chinese by* Irving Y. Lo. SuSp

Inscribed on the Painting of "Garden for Retirement": Pavilion of Sincerity, on Rocky Mountain. Chu Yi-tsun, *tr. fr. Chinese by* Chang Yin-nan *and* Lewis C. Walmsley. SuSp

Inscribed on the Painting "Pleasures of the Lute by the River." Lin Hung, *tr. fr. Chinese by* Irving Y. Lo. SuSp

Inscriptio. Pope. OxBSP

Inscription: "Eagle, stooping from yon snow-blown peaks, The." Whittier. GOA

Inscription: "For one long term, or e'er her trial came." George Canning *and* John Hookham Frere. FaBoCo; FaBoEE

Inscription, An: "Grass of levity." *Unknown.* CBCK; EiL

Is ancient hair; Grandma's hair, secret, let down only here. (*LL*) The Boy who Dreamed the Country Night. Christopher Koch. NOBAu

Is anyone waiting for you at the end of the road? Traveling Star. Ljubomir Simovic, *tr. fr. Serbo-Croatian by* Charles Simic. HSix

Is anything central? The One Thing That Can Save America. John Ashbery. AiP; NoAM; NOBA

Is bare: I, Angelo, will sit and eat. (*LL*) Angelo Orders His Dinner. Bayard Taylor. AnAmPo; BXAP

Is being bandied like dust. (*LL*) Because we suspected/ the pillow would say "I know." Lady Ise. AIW; BoWoP

Is better for man and for woman than cycles of blossoming Spring. (*LL*) Magdalen Walks. Oscar Wilde. EBVV; MoBrPo

Is beyond the value of money. (*LL*) A Song of White Hair. Chuo Wen-chün. WPC

Is both my physick and my sword. (*LL*) Conscience. George Herbert. ESCV

Is broken, be admitted in. (*LL*) Shadows in the Water. Thomas Traherne. GeHe; HAP; LiTB; NoP; OAEL-1; PoEL-2; SCGP; SeCP

Is burning, burning the unbired grain. (*LL*) Children of Light. Robert Lowell. CMoP; MoAB; NAAL-2; OxBA

Is bury me not in a land of slaves. (*LL*) Bury Me in a Free Land. Frances E. W. Harper. AAP; AmWP; BPo

Is but a child's balloon, forgotten after play. (*LL*) Above the Dock. T. E. Hulme. FaBoMo; GTBS-P; NTP

Is but a one-day house of prayer. (*LL*) The Church in the Heart. Morris Abel Beer. PoToHe

Is by his hand alone that guides nature and fate. (*LL*) In Memory of My Dear Grandchild Elizabeth Bradstreet Who Deceased August, 1665, Being a Year and a Half Old. Anne Bradstreet. EAP; NAAL-1; NOCV; SCAP; WPE

Is cat instead of rabbit, you must answer, '*Tant mi-eux*'! (*LL*) To Henrietta, on Her Departure for Calais. Thomas Hood. OBTV; OxBChV

Is Cathleen, the daughter of Houlihan. (*LL*) Red Hanrahan's Song about Ireland. W. B. Yeats. CMoP; FaBoCh; IIP; NOIV

Is clean in vain. (*LL*) All heavy minds. Sir Thomas Wyatt. SiPS

Is come, my love is come to me. (*LL*) A Birthday. Christina Rossetti. AWP; BLPL; CH; CoGr; EBEvV; ImPo; InvP; LiTB; MeMBP; NAEL-2; NALW; NOBE; NOBVV; OAEL-2; OBEV; OHCV; PeVV; PoE; TFi; TrGrPo; TTTS; UV; WiR; WPE

Is corpse and dust, shadow and nothingness. (*LL*) This coloured counterfeit that thou beholdest. Sister Juana Inés de la Cruz. PBWP

Is cruel to thy cruelty. (*LL*) Limits. Emerson. FM; OxBSP; PoEL-4

Is dead and awa'. (*LL*) The Baron of Braikley. *Unknown*. OxBB

Is diabetes catching, he asks. Identifying Things. Wendy Barker. PFL

Is drowning in its own blood. (*LL*) Cross Country. Rod Moran. NOBAu

Is dry as dust. (*LL*) My Creed. Alice Cary. AmWP; WGRP

Is each neat niplet of her breast. (*LL*) Upon the Nipples of Julia's Breast. Robert Herrick. CaPo; ErPo; NAEL-1; NOSC; PeLV

Is easily guessed. (*LL*) Dora versus Rose. Austin Dobson. NOBL; PDV

Is even more fun than going to San Sebastian, Irún, Hendaye. Having a Coke with You. Frank O'Hara. GLP; VCAP

Is every creature. (*LL*) Apprehend God in all things. *Unknown*. EaPr

Is fair and wise and good and gay. (*LL*) Birthdays. Mother Goose. BLPA; BLPL; BoTP; FaBoBe; FaBoCh; MoShBr; NBLV; OTCP; OxNR; PYC

Is fame (the breath of popular applause). (*LL*) Fame Makes Us Forward. Robert Herrick. CaPo

Is far away, beyond the reach of man. (*LL*) By T'ing Yang Waterfall. Hsieh Ling-yün. OHMPC

Is far less comfortable than his tears? (*LL*) The Resolute Courtier. Thomas Shipman. ErPo; GBL

Is far too good for thee. (*LL*) Jellon Grame. *Unknown*. EBEV; ESPB; OxBB

Is Friends fled, or Love grown cold? An Epistle. Mary Mollineux. KTR

Is gazing at the moon again. The Selenologist. Bill Manhire. PeNZ

Is God invisible? This very room. Adele Greeff. GoYe

Is God mad? Was Christ. Third Person Neuter. Heather McHugh. NAmP90; PFL

I's gonna shine. *Unknown*. WTO

Is gratitude enough for all the sunshine of spring? (*LL*) Wanderer's Song. Meng Chiao. PLT

Is greater than any nightingales. (*LL*) The Moon. W. H. Davies. MoBrPo

Is he painting with tips. Grace Lake. VBLP

Is heaven a place where pearly streams. What Is Heaven? Philip James Bailey. PWR

Is his cane growing roots. (*LL*) Botanical Fanaticism. Thylias Moss. TRP

Is holy. (*LL*) Psalm III. Allen Ginsberg. CAPP; ChIV-1

Is hows to hump a cows. (*LL*) The Way to Hump a Cow Is Not. E. E. Cummings. NoAM; NOBA; OxBA

Is immortal diamond. (*LL*) That Nature Is a Heraclitean Fire and of the Comfort of the Resurrection. Gerard Manley Hopkins. EnlH; EnVR; FaBoMo; FaBoVe; GTBS-P; LiTB; MeMBP; MoAB; NoP; OAEL-2; PoE; PoEL-5; TEP

Is in death's end. (*LL*) A Penny for You. Uri Zvi Greenberg. MHP

Is it a dream. For My Husband. Ellen Bryant Voigt. NoP

Is It a Dream? G. A. Studdert-Kennedy. PoToHe

Is it a happiness? On a Birth. Geoffrey Grigson. NAs

Is It a Month. J. M. Synge. ArLo; BIrV

Is it a Sin to Love Thee? *Unknown*. BLPA

Is it an idle fantasy. The Mist Maiden. H. Cordelia Ray. CBWP-3

Is it any better in Heaven, my friend Ford. To Ford Madox Ford in Heaven. William Carlos Williams. AmPP; NOBA

Is it bad to have come here. Gallant Château. Wallace Stevens. MoAB; MoAmPo

Is It Because of Some Dear Grace. Louis Golding. TrJP

Is it birthday weather for you, dear soul? Birthday Poem for Thomas Hardy. C. Day Lewis. EBEvV; EPCY

Is it children we are killing now? My God. Victor Hugo. *Fr*. Recollection of the Night of the Fourth, A. OBD

Is it enough? I'm Here. Theodore Roethke. *Fr*. Meditations of an Old Woman. CoAP; NaP; NYBP

Is it enough to think to-day. Memorial Day. Annette Wynne. OHIP

"Is it far to the town?" said the poet. The Coming Poet. Francis Ledwidge. PeIV

Is it foolhardy to hope. Zeugma. Christopher Reid. CBLP

Is it God? (*LL*) In a Year. Robert Browning. CBLP

Is it illusion? or does there a spirit from perfecter ages. Arthur Hugh Clough. *Fr*. Amours de Voyage. EBEV; NOBVV; OxAEP-2 (Spirit from Perfecter Ages.) OBNC

Is it ironical, a fool enigma. Dartmoor: Sunset at Chagford. Thomas Edward Brown. NOBVV

Is it just like picking a lock. The Bomb Disposal. Ciaran Carson. CIP; IIP

Is it my clothes, my way of walking. Disembarking at Quebec. Margaret Atwood. PoE

Is it naught? Is it naught. Cuba. Edmund Clarence Stedman. PAH

Is it no dream that I am he. Walter Savage Landor. GBL

Is it not fine to fling against loaded dice. Hughie at the Inn. Elinor Wylie. NYBP; WPE

Is it not fit the mold and frame. A Dedication of My First Son. Mildmay Fane, 2d Earl of Westmorland. BeJo

Is it not in yr service that I wear myself out. The Loba Addresses the Goddess/ or The Poet as Priestess Addresses the Loba-Goddess. Diane Di Prima. *Fr*. Loba. SRLS

Is it not strange that men can die. Reflection. W. J. Turner. OBMV

Is it not sure a deadly pain. *Unknown*. EnLoPo

Is it not sweet to die? for, what is death. Death Sweet. Thomas Lovell Beddoes. NOBVV

Is it not the same. Home Cooking. Alan Chong Lau. BCF

Is It Not You, Lord! Padraig de Brun. TIRV

Is It Nothing to You? May Probyn. OBEV

Is it poetry I'm after those moments when. Vocation. Carol Rumens. DiPo

Is it possible. The Tomatoes. Teresa Moszkowicz-Syrop. BTR

Is It Possible. Sir Thomas Wyatt. ELP; EnRePo; GBL; NoP; NoSic; SiPS; SiPSBD

Is it raining. Mary, can you see? Wildflowers. Richard Howard. NoAM

Is it really so very unthinkable. Basil Ransome-Davies. PeLi

Is It Really Worth the While? *Unknown*. BLPA

Is it serious, or funny. B. Larry Eigner. NeAP

Is it strange if I start to cry with joy? (*LL*) The Mother's Song. *Unknown*. OBCP; WTO

Is it the duty. Another Book on the Holocaust. J. R. Solonche. BTR

Is It the Morning? Is It the Little Morning? Delmore Schwartz. ArNa

Is it the wind of the dawn that I hear. Duet. Tennyson. *Fr*. Becket. GBL

Is it the wind, the many-tongued, the weird. The Draft Riot. Charles de Kay. PAH

Is it, then, regret for buried time. Tennyson. *Fr*. In Memoriam A. H. H. EBVV, *abr*.; FHYEP; OAEL-2, *abr*.; PeECV, *abr*.

"Is it thou?" "Ay," cries Fra Lippo Lippi. Gerard Benson. PeLi

Is It Thy Wil, Thy Image Should Keepe Open. Shakespeare. *Fr*. Sonnets. PoEL-2

Is it time now? (*LL*) Death of a Vermont Farm Woman. Barbara Howes. MoAmPo; SM

Is the age of pisces/ check it out. *(LL)* 12 Gates to the City. Nikki Giovanni. IHMS; PoBA

Is the Ahkond of Swat! *(LL)* The A[h]kond of Swat. Edward Lear. CBNP; FaBoCh; FaBoCo; FaBoNo; FiBHP; PeLi, 5 *ll. only*

Is the applause always plausible that applauds the bosses. The Tasty 'Tanjarines' of Inhambane. José Craveirinha, *tr. fr. Portuguese by* Michael Wolfers. PeSAV

Is the ball very stupid ma mignonne? At the Ball! Charles H. Webb. OBAL

Is the burden of my song. *(LL)* Love Me Little, Love Me Long. Robert Herrick. BLPA; CaPo; CBLP; EiL; FaBoBe; NoP; SCGP

Is the clock wound up, is it wound? The Insect Kitchen. Nicki Jackowska. BrRo

Is the darling for me. *(LL)* The Streams of Lovely Nancy. *Unknown.* FaBoBa; OBET; OxBoLi

Is the/ dinner/ ready. I Ask. Novica Tadic, *tr. fr. Serbo-Croatian by* Charles Simic. HSix

Is the ending of my song. *(LL)* The Seven Virgins. *Unknown.* CH; ChTr; GBP; OBET; OBEV

Is the evening twilight. *(LL)* Bless Adonai. Rami M. Shapiro. EaPr

Is the fish ready? You're a tedious while. Dialogue between a Squeamish Cotting Mechanic and His Sluttish Wife, in the Kitchen. Edward Ward. *Fr. Nuptial Dialogues.* NOEC

Is the hand that rules the world. *(LL)* The Hand That Rocks the Cradle Is the Hand That Rules the World. William Ross Wallace. BLPL; PoLF; WBLP

Is the kitchen tap still dripping? Guest. D. J. Enright. Mes; OxBC

Is the lass in the Female Factory. *(LL)* The Lass in the Female Factory. *Unknown.* NOBAu

Is the least decent. *(LL)* On Thomas Moore's Poems. *Unknown.* FaBoCo; FiBHP

Is the Moon Tired? Christina Rossetti. BoTP; OTCP

Is the one frog we dwell upon. *(LL)* A Frog's Fate. Christina Rossetti. NOBVV

Is the one I choose. *(LL)* A Charm against a Magpie. *Unknown.* ChTr

Is the one who thinks he can. *(LL)* Thinking. Walter D. Wintle. WBLP

Is the prayer of poor Skin the Goat. *(LL)* Skin the Goat's Curse on Carey. *Unknown.* BIrV

Is the pride of thus dying for thee. *(LL)* Pro Patria Mori. Thomas Moore. GTBS; GTBS-P; HoPM; OxAEP-2

Is the reader leaning late and reading there. *(LL)* The House Was Quiet and the World Was Calm. Wallace Stevens. AiP; HAP; NoP; PFP; SAmP; VGW

Is the snow on Kurakake mountain. *(LL)* The Snow on Saddle Mountain. Miyazawa Kenji. NoAM; NOBA

Is the soul solid, like iron? Some Question You Might Ask. Mary Oliver. BAP-89

Is the stringing together of so many little passings. *(LL)* Life and death. Rami M. Shapiro. EaPr

Is the struggle and strife. Let the Rest of the World Go By. J. Keirn Brennan. UnPo

Is the symbol of my birth in You. *(LL)* O Lord,/ One tiny bit of water rests on the palm of my hand. Ishpriya. EaPr

Is the total black, being spoken. Coal. Audre Lorde. BlSi; NALW; NBV; NoAM; NoP; PoBA; VCAP

Is the university of hunger the wide waste. University of Hunger. Martin Carter. PBCV

Is the way o'ercast with shadows? Jesus Understands. *Unknown.* BLRP

Is there a cause why we should wake the dead? The Yew-Tree. Vernon Watkins. LiTB

Is there a great green commonwealth of Thought. John Masefield. *Fr.* Sonnets. LiTM; MoBrPo

Is there a hand-rail to the stairs? *(LL)* Had We Two Met. Walter Savage Landor. FaBoEE; OxBSP

Is there a solitary wretch who hies. On Being Cautioned against Walking on an Headland Overlooking the Sea, because It Was Frequented by a Lunatic. Charlotte Smith. ECWP; WoRP

Is There a Voice. Philip Appleman. BXAP

Is there an imagination that sits enthroned. Wallace Stevens. *Fr.* Auroras of Autumn, The. CMoP; HCAP

"Is there anybody there?" said the traveller. The Listeners. Walter de la Mare. AWP; BLPL; ClHu; CMoP; CoGr; EBEvV; FaPoB; FaPON; GGP; HAP; HeIP; HoPM; ImPo; InPK; InvP; LiTB; LiTM; MoAB; MoBrPo; MoP; NoAM; NOBE; NoP; NTP; OBMV; OBSP; OtMeF; OxAEP-2; PlP; Poetr; PoRA; SoSe; TFi; TrGrPo

Is there anything as I can do ashore for you. A Valediction (Liverpool Docks). John Masefield. OBMV

Is there anything I can do. The Key to Everything. May Swenson. IHMS

Is there anything in Spring so fair. Apple Blossoms. Henry Adams Parker. BoTP

Is there ever a new beginning when every. Marriage. Elaine Feinstein. AIW

Is there for honest poverty. For A' That [and A' That] Burns. EnRP; FaBoBe; FaBoPV; FaPoR; LiTB; NAEL-2; OAEL-1; OxAEP-2; TEP; TFi; UV; WBLP
  (Man's a Man for A' That, A.) ImPo; OxBS; SWP; TrGrPo
  (Song: For A' That and A' That.) NOEC; OPOP

Is, there is not a word of fear. *(LL)* Death Stands above Me. Walter Savage Landor. EnRP; LiTB; NOBE; NoP; OBNC; OxBSP; PoEL-4

Is there never a man in all Scotland. Johnie Armstrong. *Unknown.* ESPB

Is There No Balm in Christian Lands? *Unknown.* AH

Is there no secret place on the face of the earth. The Moneyless Men. Henry T. Stanton. BLPA

Is there no vision in a lovely place? William Montgomerie. *Fr.* Kinfauns Castle. OxBS

Is there not one spark of pity for five poor unhappy men. Execution of Five Pirates for Murder. *Unknown.* OxBSS

Is there not pardon for the brave. The Brave. G. K. Chesteron. OtMeF

Is there nothing to be said about the cockroach which is kind? Cockroach. Mary Ann Hoberman. *Fr.* Bugs. OBCA

Is there one desires to heat. Epilogue. William Larminie. *Fr.* Fand. PeIV

Is there ony room at your head, Saunders? *Unknown. Fr.* Clerk Saunders. EBNV; OBD

Is there really a new Mr. Nixon. T. Griffiths. PeLi

Is there still any shadow there, on the rainwet window of the coffee pot. Memo. Kenneth Fearing. CMoP; PoE

Is this a dagger which I see before me. Shakespeare. *Fr.* Macbeth. EBEvV

Is this a fast, to keep. To Keep a True Lent. Robert Herrick. TrCP
  (True Lent, A.) OHIP

Is this a holy thing to see. Holy Thursday. Blake. *Fr.* Songs of Experience. EnRP; FF; FHYEP; InPS; NAEL-2; NOEC; NoP; OAEL-2; TEP

Is This Africa. Roland Tombekai Dempster. PBA

Is this all there is? Yehuda Amichai, *tr. fr. Hebrew by* Chana Bloch. *Fr.* Seven Laments for the War — Dead. CBCK

Is this man turning angel as he stares. The Messengers. Thom Gunn. PoA

Is this me? Shuang-ch'ing? *(LL)* To the Tune "A Watered Silk Dress." Ho Shuang-ch'ing. WPC

Is this rapture that your rums have filled me with. Marie Galante. Guy Tirolien, *tr. fr. French by* Ellen Conroy Kennedy. NegPo

Is this really the failure. Masaccio's Expulsion. Jorie Graham. AnAn

Is this the monument of Leonato? Shakespeare. *Fr.* Much Ado about Nothing. OxAEP-1

Is this the movie in which James Mason. A Gothic Gesture. Steve Levine. UL

Is this the object. Judith Kroll. AmPA; SM

Is this the price of beauty! Fairest, thou. Charleston. Richard Watson Gilder. PAH

Is this the region, this the soil, the clime. Milton. *Fr.* Paradise Lost. EPCY; TEP
  (Satan as Rebel-Liberator.) FF, *ll.* 242 – 255

Is this the Seine? An Ode to Spring in the Metropolis. Sir Owen Seaman. FiBHP

Is this the self I thought I knew, within. Reflections. Vivian Smith. CBAP

Is this the street? Never a sign of life. Stormy Night. W. R. Rodgers. PNI

Is This the Time to Sound Retreat? *Unknown.* BLRP

Is this the ultimate exile no man born. Ultimate Exile IV. Ralph Nixon Currey. PeSA

Is this the way my Father. Matin Hymn. Josephine D. Henderson Heard. CBWP-4

Is this where idealism ends. Guerrillas. Roger McTair. PBCV

Is this where people are buried? In Painswick Churchyard. Frances Horovitz. NBrP

Is this where Tasso walked? Old Sant'Onofrio. Pure Dust. Maria Luisa Spaziani, *tr. fr. Italian by* Beverly Allen. NeIt

Is this your special light. Six Nations Museum Onchiota, New York — January. Wendy Rose. HATNAP

Is thy face like thy mother's, my fair child! Byron. *Fr.* Childe Harold's Pilgrimage. EnRP; OAEL-2, *abr.*

Is thy first breath, and mans eternall Prime. *(LL)* The Evening-Watch. Henry Vaughan *and* Thomas Stanley. ESCV

Is thy sun obscured to-day. My Grace Is Sufficient. Josephine D. Henderson Heard. CBWP-4

Is Time? I cannot bite the day to the core. *(LL)* The Glory. Edward Thomas. OxBTC; PAW; TOF

Is too precise in every part. (*LL*) Delight in Disorder. Robert Herrick. BeJo; CaPo; ClHu; EBEV; EBEvV; EnLoPo; ErPo; FaBV; FF; GGP; GTBS; GTBS-P; HAP; HeIP; InPK; InPS; JCP; LiTB; NAEL-1; NIP; NOBE; NoP; NOSC; OAEL-1; OBEV; OxAEP-1; PeLV; PoE; Poetr; PoRA; PPP; PrIm; SCGP; SeCP; SeCV-1; TEP; TFi; TrGrPo; TRP; WeW

Is welling up in my heart. (*LL*) Praise the world to the angel, not the unutterable world. Rainer Maria Rilke. EaPr

Is wetter water, slimier slime! (*LL*) Heaven. Rupert Brooke. EBEV; HoPM; LiTB; LiTM; MoBrPo; NOBE; NSI; PFP; PoRA; WGRP

Is what it feels like. (*LL*) Before the [*or* a] Cashier's Window in a Department Store. James Wright. CoAP; MAT; NYBP

Is what the sea-birds know. (*LL*) An Inscription by the Sea. E. A. Robinson, *after* Glaucus. AWP; ChTr; FaBoEE

Is what to make of a diminished thing. (*LL*) The Oven Bird. Robert Frost. AmPP; AWP; HeIP; MeMAP; MoP; NAAL-2; NoAM; NOBA; NoP; OxBA; PoE; PPP; Son; TAP

Is what you first see, stepping off the train. Welcome to Hiroshima. Mary Jo Salter. ArOW; DiPo; NIP

Is with me at thy farewell, joyous Bark! (*LL*) Where Lies the Land. Wordsworth. EnRP; MeMBP; OBNC; PoEL-4

Is without world. The Howling of Wolves. Ted Hughes. OxBTC; PlP

Is Wolly's wife now dead and gone? A Jacobite Scot in Satire on England's Unparalleled Loss. *Unknown.* APAS

Is won with flesh, not drapery. (*LL*) Clothes Do but Cheat and Cozen Us. Robert Herrick. CaPo; ErPo

Is yo eye so empty. Signals. Jewel C. Latimore. PoBA

Is your crop of millet. What Her Friend Said to Her, before the Rains. Kapilar, *tr. fr. Tamil by* A. K. Ramanujan. PLW

Is your place a small place? Your Place. John Oxenham. BLRP

Isaac. Amir Gilboa, *tr. fr. Hebrew by* Ruth Finer Mintz. MHP

Isaac: a Poise. Peter Cole. ChIV-1

Isaac and Archibald. E. A. Robinson. OxBA

Isaac Singer (you probably know). Peter Brookes. PeLi

Isaac's Marriage. Henry Vaughan. ChIV-1

Isabel. Richard Hovey. AnAmPo

Isabel met an enormous bear. Adventures of Isabel. Ogden Nash. MoAmPo; MoShBr; NTCP; OBAL; OBCA; PDV; SiSoPo, 3 *sts. only*

Isabella; or, The Morning, *sels.* Sir Charles Hanbury Williams. "Monkey, lap-dog, parrot, and her Grace, The." NOEC

Isabella; or, The Pot of Basil. Keats. EnRP

Isabella spits at Spain. Bourbons. Walter Savage Landor. OBSV

Isabelle. James Hogg. BXAP

Isaiah, *sels.* Bible, *O.T.*
　All Flesh Is Grass. TrJP
　Bravery of Their Tinkling Ornaments, The. CBCK
　"Comfort ye, comfort ye my people." OBVE, *sts.* 1 – 8; TrJP, (1-5)
　Downfall of the Tyrant. TrGrPo
　"Earth dries up and withers, The." EaPr
　For Zion's Sake. TrJP
　God's Vengeance. FM
　Hear the Word of the Lord. TrJP
　How Beautiful upon the Mountains. TrJP
　I Waste Away. TrJP
　In the End of Days. TrJP
　Israel, My Servant. TrJP
　Let Me Sing of My Well-beloved. TrJP
　Messiah, The. AWP
　My Thoughts Are Not Your Thoughts. TrJP
　"People that walked in darkness, The." PAW
　Rod of Jesse, The. AWP; OBVE; TrJP
　Song of the Harlot. TrJP
　Song of The Suffering Servant, The. NAWM-1
　Vision of the Day of Judgment. WGRP
　Watchman, What of the Night? AWP
　Whom Shall One Teach. TrJP
　"Wilderness and the solitarie place shall be glad for them, The." OBVE
　"Wolf also shall dwell with the lamb, The." PDV
　　(God's Rule.) FM
　　(Peaceable Kingdom.) FaPON

Isaiah by Kerosene Lantern Light. Robert Harris. ChIV-1; NOBAu

Isaiah: Chapter 66. David Rosenberg. ChIV-1

Isaiah 66.11. Francis Quarles. ChIV-1

Isatou died. Lenrie Peters. HBAPE

I'se been upon de karpet. Old Maid's Soliloquy. Maggie Pogue Johnson. CBWP-4

I'se got a gal in the Sourwood Mountain. Sourwood Mountain. *Unknown.* AmFP

I'se wild Nigger Bill. Wild Negro Bill. *Unknown.* BPo

Ishmael. Herbert Edward Palmer. OBEV

Ishtar. Judith Wright. NALW; NoAM

Isiah said would be the serpent's meat. (*LL*) On Falling Asleep by Firelight. William Meredith. ChIV-1; NoAM; NYBP

Isias my love, with your scented breath. Argentarius, *tr. fr. Greek by* Fleur Adcock. GrAn

Isidor. Louis Simpson. NNaP

Isis Wanderer. Kathleen Raine. NALW; OxBS

Island, The. James Dickey. SM

Island. Langston Hughes. HCAP

Island, The. Brendan Kennelly. PBCIP

Island, The. Edwin Muir. OAEL-2

Island. Meredith Stricker. LoHo

Island, The. George Woodcock. MoCV

Island, The. George Woodcock. MoCV

Island Funeral. Frank Stanford. MT

Island Girls. David Trinidad. BAP-91

Island in the Evening, The. Fairfield Porter. PoA

Island in the Moon, An, *sels.* Blake.
　Good English Hospitality. CoMu
　(Mayors, The.) CH; CoGr
　"Hail Matrimony, made of Love!" CBLP
　"Hang that," said Suction; "let us have a song." CBNP
　In Obtuse Angle's Study. FaBoNo
　Sipsop's Song. FaBoNo
　Suction's Anthem. CBNP; FaBoNo
　"When old corruption first begun." RB
　　(Quid the Cynic's Song.) FaBoNo

Island Mary. Lucille Clifton. NALW

Island Muse. John C. M. Lyons. NBrP

Island of the Living, The. Aleida Rodríguez. ETG

Island of the Three Marias. Alberto A. Ríos. NoAM

Island off the main, An. Tycoon, Poet, Saint. Abdur-Rahman Slade Hopkinson. PBCV

Island on Sunday Afternoons, The. Mary Ann Larkin. LPA

Island Quarry. Hart Crane. PPP

Island that had flowered to the sun, The. The Coming of Dusk upon a Village in Haiti. Henry Rago. HoPM

Island was a word he woke upon, The. Settler. Stewart Lindh. PoA

Island Waters. Tony Beyer. PeNZ

Islanders, Inlanders. Michael Mott. PoA

Islandman. Brenda Chamberlain. AngWe; OBWVE

Islands, The. Hilda Doolittle ("H. D."). MoAmPo

Islands. Nicholas Hasluck. NOBAu

Islands and peninsulas, continents and capes. Geography. Eleanor Farjeon. FaPON

Islands are green. Alaskan Fragments June 1981 — Summer Solstice. Wendy Rose. HATNAP

Islands move inward. The Name of Our Country. Dennis Schmitz. AmPA

Islands of the Sea, The. George Edward Woodberry. PAH

Island's Prince, of frame more than celestial, The. The All-seeing Intellect. Phineas Fletcher. *Fr. Purple Island, The.* JCP

Islands Where I Was Born, The. Gloria Rawlinson. PeNZ

Islands which have. Islands. Nicholas Hasluck. NOBAu

Islands which whisper to the ambitious, The. At Epidaurus. Lawrence Durrell. LiTB; OBTV

Isle!/ Island of the syllables of flame! Jacques Rabémanganjara, *tr. fr. French by* Ellen Conroy Kennedy. NegPo

Isle Juan Fernandez off Valparaiso Bay, The. Battle of the Falkland Isles. I. C. NSI

Isle of a summer sea. Cuba. Harvey Rice. PAH

Isle of Man, The. *Unknown.* GBP

Isle of Man is the true explanation! (*LL*) There Was a Young Lady of Station. "Lewis Carroll." FaBoNo; PeLi

Isle of Man Shore, The. *Unknown.* AmFP

Isle of Portland, The. A. E. Housman. *Fr. Shropshire Lad, A.* FaPoB; MoBrPo

Isle of Streams; or, the Jamaica Hermit, The. William Hosack. PBCV
　Sels.
　"Blazing noon, fierce, unrelenting noon!, The."
　"But hark! The sharp beat of the Afric drum."

Isle of the Long Ago, The. Benjamin Franklin Taylor. WBLP

Isle of the ocean, say, whence comest thou? Sabrina. Lucretia Davidson. AmWP

Isles of Greece, The. Demetrios Capetanakis. GTBS-P

Isles of Greece, the isles of Greece, The. Byron. *Fr. Don Juan.* AWP; ChTr; FaPoB; FaPoR; LiTB; NOBE; OBEV; OBTV; OxAEP-2

Islet the Dachs. George Meredith. —

Isn't it a blooming shame? (*LL*) She Was Poor but She Was Honest. *Unknown.* ErPo; FaBoCo; FiBHP; GBP; NOBL

Isn't It Funny? Essex Hemphill. GLP

Isn't it good she asked as. Rhyme. James Laughlin. WeW

Isn't it nice that everyone has a grocery list. Population. Mark Halliday. NAmP90

Isn't it plain the sheets of moss except that. Landscape. Mary Oliver. HeIP

Isn't it so? In spite of fools and schemers. Paul Verlaine, tr. fr. French by Philip L. Miller. RiWo

Isn't it strange. A Bag of Tools. R. L. Sharpe. BLPA; PoToHe

Isn't it strange some people make. Some People. Rachel Field. FaPON; NTCP; PDV

Isn't it wonderful, when you think. Wonderful. Julian S. Cutler. PWR

Isn't ligature — or is it ligament? — a lovely word? Rupert Brooke. NSI

Isn't she soft and still? Captive. Marion Strobel. ErPo

Isn't the violet a dear little flower? And the daisy, too. The Lay Preacher Ponders. Idris Davies. OxBTC

Isolation. Martha Sansom. UnDi

Isolation. Arthur Symons. OxBSP

Isolation of exile is a gutted, The. Waiting. Arthur Nortje. HBAPE

Isolation of Genius, The. Byron. WBLP

Israel. Yitzhak Lamdan, tr. fr. Hebrew by Ruth Finer Mintz. MHP

Israel. Carl Rakosi. ChIV-1

Israel. Israel Zangwill. TrJP

Israel I. Charles Reznikoff. ChIV-1

Israel II. Charles Reznikoff. ChIV-1

Israel Freyer's Bid for Gold. Edmund Clarence Stedman. PAH

Israel in ancient days. Old-Testament Gospel. William Cowper. ChIV-2; TrCP

Israel, My Servant. Bible, O.T. Fr. Isaiah. TrJP

Israel's Duration. Judah Halevi, tr. fr. Hebrew by Nina Davis Salaman. TrJP

Israfel. Poe. AmPP; AWP; BLPL; ImPo; LiTA; MeMAP; NAAL-1; NOBA; OxBA; PoE; PoEL-4; TAP

Issue of great Jove, draw near you Muses nine, The. The Garden. Nicholas Grimald. OAEL-1

Issues from the hand of God, the simple soul. Animula. T. S. Eliot. CRP; LiTB; NAs

Issues of the Fall. Sydney Lea. SM

Is't here the fairies haunt the place. On a Nook Called Fairyland. H. Cordelia Ray. CBWP-3

Istanbul. 21 March. I woke today. The Thousand and Second Night. James Merrill. NYBP

Isuba. Jim Barnes. Fr. Four Things Choctaw. HATNAP

It. Gary Snyder. LCAP

It ain't forever, Gimme! (LL) Preference. Langston Hughes. HCAP; NOBA

It ain't gonna rain, it ain't gonna snow. Ain't Gonna Rain. Unknown. AS

It Ain't Neccessarily So. Ira Gershwin. OBAL

It ain't no use to grumble and complain. Rain. James Whitcomb Riley. BoNaP

It ain't the failures he may meet. The Quitter. Unknown. BLPA; WBLP

It ain't the guns nor armament. Co-operation. J. Mason Knox. BLPA

It all began so easy. Christina. Louis MacNeice. BoLoP

It All Comes Together Outside the Restroom in Hogansville. James Seay. MT

It all happened on the water. Miracle. Susan Griffin. CrSp

It all happened so fast. Fenya was in the straight chair. Norman Dubie. AmPA

It all wears out. I keep telling myself this, but. Down by the Station, Early in the Morning. John Ashbery. HCAP

It always comes, and when it comes they know. Women in Love. Donald Justice. SM

It always felt to me — a wrong. Emily Dickinson. ChIV-1

It always rains against the front door. But It May Be So. Ralph Hawkins. VaA

It Always Seems. A. M. Sayers. BXAP

It appears to be the pampas. The Man in the Dream Is Death. Lynne Butler. IHMS

It asked a crumb — of Me. (LL) Hope is the thing with feathers. Emily Dickinson. AmPP; BLPL; MeMAP; MoAB; MoAmPo; MoShBr; NOBA; OxBA; SAmP; TAP

It asked for bread and butter first. The Perfect Child. Adrian Porter. NBLV

It baffles the foreigner like an idiom. Drug Store. Karl Shapiro. CMoP; OxBA; TwCP

It be as short as yours. (LL) Life. George Herbert. ESCV; FaBoRV; GeHe; JCP; LiTB; MeLP; NoP; NOSC; SeCP; SeCV-1

It beat the shapes of harps into the air. (LL) Shopping for Meat in Winter. Oscar Williams. LiTA; LiTM

It beats me. I feel it done to me, and ache. (LL) Odi et Amo. Catullus. CTC, tr. by Ezra Pound

It befell at Martynmas. Captain Car; or, Edom o Gordon. Unknown. ESPB

It began as a joke: she did not like to leave the house. Another Poem about the Madness of Women. Tom Wayman. NOBC

It began in her pram. The Renaming. Valerie Sinason. BrRo

It began/ reasonably enough. The Man Who Owned Cars. Elliot Fried. GOYP

It began/ When God popped His head. Noah's Ark. Roger McGough. OBSP

It begins again, the nocturnal pulse. The Assassination. Donald Justice. CAPP; VCAP

It begins quietly. The Deviation. Louise Glück. Fr. Dedication to Hunger. AnAn

It begins with an easy voice saying. Nightmare. Lyall Wilkes. OBD

It begins with my dog, now dead, who all his long life. The Retrieval System. Maxine W. Kumin. FaBoWP; WeW

It begins with one or two soldiers. Truce. Paul Muldoon. PBCIP; PNI

It belongs, has always belonged, to you? (LL) Desire. Kathy Fagan. UTF

It bends far over Yell'ham Plain. The Comet at Yell'ham. Thomas Hardy. CMoP; GBL

It blows like a spouting whale. (LL) Song: The Railway Train. Unknown. NOBAu

It breaks up green moss ground. Pond in a Basin. Tu Mu, tr. fr. Chinese by Eddie Tsang. SuSp

It burneth yet, alas, my heart's desire. Sir Thomas Wyatt. SiPSBD

It burns in the void. The World. Kathleen Raine. OxBTC

It cam from Pizzeria. Around the World. Gary Lenhart. UL

It came/ Out of the blackness of the spaces between galaxies. The Second Coming. Carl Clark. JB

It came today to visit. The Visitor. Jack Prelutsky. OTCP

It Came upon the Midnight Clear. Edmund Hamilton Sears. AH; FaPON

It came upon the noontide air. Bishop James A. Shorter. Josephine D. Henderson Heard. CBWP-4

It Can Be Done. Unknown. PoToHe

It can be so tedious, a bore. Moods of Rain. Vernon Scannell. BoNaP

It can kill a man. (LL) Poetry Is a Destructive Force. Wallace Stevens. AnAmPo; MeMAP; OxBA; RaBo

It can never fly from you. (LL) A E I O U. Swift. BoTP

It can never fly from you. (LL) On the Vowels — a Riddle. Swift. FaBoUs

It can not be, the baffled heart, in vain. The Bard. Elizabeth Oakes Smith. AmWP

It cannot be/ reasoned with. Julius Lester. Fr. In the Time of Revolution. PoBA

It cannot be that men who are the seed. Our First Century. George Edward Woodberry. PAH

It cannot be. Where is that mighty joy. The Temper. George Herbert. GeHe

It cannot come. Balboa, the Entertainer. Amiri Baraka. NoAM

It can't be the passing of time that casts. Rip. James Wright. NaP

It can't keep a-goin'. If The War Keeps On. Bernard Gilbert. NSI

It caught his image as he flew. (LL) L'Oiseau Bleu. Mary Elizabeth Coleridge. BoTP

It ceased to hurt me, though so slow. Emily Dickinson. SAmP

It certainly is the smell. Circe. Gavin Ewart. FaBoBl

It chanced his lips did meet her forehead cool. George Meredith. Fr. Modern Love. CBLP; EnVR; NOBVV

It chanced to be our washing day. Oliver Wendell Holmes. Fr. September Gale, The. FiBHP

It chaunced me on day beside the shore. The Ruines of Time. Spenser. OxAEP-1

It comes about that the drifting of these curtains. The Curtains in the House of the Metaphysician. Wallace Stevens. PoA

It comes back. Deceased. Cid Corman. VGW

It comes, the blast of death! that sudden glare. The Simoom. Martin Farquhar Tupper. OBTV

It comes to me more and more. The Love of the Father. Unknown. BLRP

It comes to this. Revelations. David Meltzer. NeAP

It consisted of 8 to 10 pages of short essays. Her Application to Elysium. Kathleen Norris. IHMS

It could be a clip, it could be a comb. Obsessive. Marvin Bell. Fr. Escape into You, The. SM

It could be a jaw-bone. Viking Dublin; Trial Pieces. Seamus Heaney. IPY

It Could Be a Wonderful World. Hy Zaret. SWP

It could go on for ever so; the giving. Alison Brackenbury. SCBI

It Could Have Been More. Ralph Angel. FoLa

It could not have been. Negative Capability. John Drew. PWE

It could resurrect us all. (*LL*) Resurrection. Joy Harjo. HATNAP

It Couldn't Be Done. Edgar A. Guest. BLPA; FaBoBe; WBLP

It crawled away from 'neath my feet. That Hill. Blanche Taylor Dickinson. CDC

It Depends on You. "Angelus Silesius," *tr. fr. German by* Stephen Mitchell. EnlH

It Did. Robert Lowell. NoAM

It did not last; the Devil howling Ho. J. C. Squire. FaBoCo; FaBoEE; FaBoEH

It did not seem important at the time. As It Was. John Mander. Mes

It didn't require great character at all. The Power of Taste. Zbigniew Herbert, *tr. fr. Polish by* John Carpenter *and* Bogdana Carpenter. AnAn; PoSu

It dies hard, the notion of a just people. Atlantis. David Constantine. SCBI

It does, it does, I have seen it. America Bleeds. Angelo Lewis. PoBA

It does not care yet to be only the void at its heart. (*LL*) A Withered Tree. Han Yü. PLT

It does not happen. That love, removes. Audubon, Drafted. Amiri Baraka. PPP; TTY

It does not worry me that this verse has three stresses. The Eumenides at Home. James Agate. BXAP

It doesn't always do to let a mug know everything. Charlie Piecan. L. Murray *and* F. Leigh. OxBoLi

It doesn't do to do much talking. Not Much Talking. *Unknown.* PWR

It don't seem hordly right, John. Jonathan to John. James Russell Lowell. *Fr.* Biglow Papers, The. PAH

It dropped so low — in my regard. Emily Dickinson. CMoP; HAP; HeIP; InPK; OxBA; OxBSP

It drowned the amber-colored flesh with blood. (*LL*) The Jewels. Baudelaire. BoLoP, *tr. by* Roy Campbell; ErPo, *tr. by* Paul Blackburn; NAWM-2, *tr. by* David Paul

It dwindles in the west. (*LL*) Aeroplane. Pudjipangu. NOBAu

It embarrasses. Personal Poem. Ingrid Wendt. NMM

It ended, and the morrow brought the task. George Meredith. *Fr.* Modern Love. EnVR

It ended when he popped one of the three of the order. Rock, Scissors, Paper. Deborah Digges. NAmP90

It faced the north with a roar, then. Passage. Geoffrey Fraser Dutton. PWE

It faces west, and round the back and sides. Domicilium. Thomas Hardy. FaBoPP

It faded on the crowing of the cock. Shakespeare. *Fr.* Hamlet. NAWM-1; PeECV, *sect.* I, i; TOF

It faints and withers, and is done. (*LL*) Evening Primrose. John Clare. CH; TrGrPo

It falles me here to write of Chastity. The Legend of Britomartis, or of Chastitie. Spenser. *Fr.* Faerie Queene, The. NAEL-1, *much abr.*

It falls and riseth aside beside my reach. (*LL*) The Author, of His Own Fortune. Sir John Harington. FaBoEE

It feels a shame to be Alive. Emily Dickinson. PAW

It feels good as it is without the giant. Wallace Stevens. *Fr.* Notes toward a Supreme Fiction. NOBA

It feels like a bear eating me. Divorce. Adam Koehn. AiP

It fell about the Lammbass tide. Bonny Lizie Baillie. *Unknown.* ESPB

It fell about the Lammas time. Lord Livingston. *Unknown.* ESPB; OxBB

It fell about the Martinmas. Jamie Telfer of [*or* in] the Fair Dodhead. *Unknown.* ESPB; IBB; OxBB

It fell about the Martinmas time. Get Up and Bar the Door. *Unknown.* ESPB; FaBoBa; HeIL; HeIP; NoP; OxBS; PDV; TrGrPo

It fell about the Martinmas[s] time. Edom o' Gordon. *Unknown.* OxBB (Captain Car.) ESPB; FaBoBa

It fell ageyns the next nyght. The Fox and the Goose. *Unknown.* OxBLMV

It fell in the ancient periods. Uriel. Emerson. LiTA; NAAL-1; NOBA; OxBA

It fell on a day, and a bonnie simmer [*or* bonny summer] day. The Bonnie House o' Airlie. *Unknown.* ESPB; OBEV; OxBB; OxBS

It Fell on a Summer's Day. Thomas Campion. ErPo; HAP

It Fell upon a Holy [*or* Holly] Eve. Spenser. *Fr.* Shepheardes [*or* Shepeards *or* Shepherd's] Calender, The. CBLP; InvP

It fell upon a Wednesday. A Gest of Robyn Hode. *Unknown.* OxBLMV

It fell upon a Wodensday [*or* Wednesday]. Brown Robyn's [*or* Robin's] Confession. *Unknown.* CH; ESPB; GBP

It fell upon the Lammas time. Young Ronald. *Unknown.* ESPB

It fell upon us like a crushing woe. Colonel Ellsworth. Richard Henry Stoddard. PAH

It fell when I was sleeping. In my dream. The Land-Mine. George MacBeth. OBWP

It felt like the zero in brook ice. The Funeral. Norman Dubie. InPK; NoAM

It fill the sky to beat on an airy shell. (*LL*) Bell Tower. Léonie Adams. MoAB; MoAmPo

It first began when sitting in the huge auditorium. On Having Been an Experimental Sacred Cow for Four Years, and a Token African on Faculty. Kofi Awoonor. HBAPE

It flows through old hushed Egypt and its sands. The Nile. Leigh Hunt. EBEV; EnRP; NOBE; OBNC

It follows now you are to prove. Ben Jonson. *Fr.* Pleasure Reconciled to Virtue. NAEL-1; OAEL-1

It fortuned (as faire it then befell). Spenser. *Fr.* Faerie Queene, The. OAEL-1

It gets awful lonely. Lonely. Bloke Modisane. PBA

It gives a lovely light! (*LL*) Figs from Thistles. Edna St. Vincent Millay. CoGr; FaBV; NoP; PoA

It gives such divine materials to men, and accepts such leavings from them at last. (*LL*) This Compost. Walt Whitman. AWP; LiTA; MoAmPo; NAAL-1

It gives tho' bound, tho' bound 'tis free! (*LL*) Christ Crucified. Richard Crashaw. OBEV

It glimmers like a wakeful lake in the dusk narrowing room. The Mirror. Isaac Rosenberg. NoAM

It got beyond all orders an' it got beyond all 'ope. Kipling. *Fr.* That Day. PlP

It gradually became a different country. Morning in America. John Koethe. BAP-91

It grows too fast! I cannot keep pace with it! Ado. Mary Ursula Bethell. ArNa

It had a velvet cap. John Skelton. *Fr.* Phyllyp Sparowe [*or* Philip Sparrow]. AAS; OBF; PoEL-1

It had to be a big book to be a whale. Publishing 2001. Bob Rosenthal. UL

It hain't no use to grumble and complane [*or* complain]. Wet-Weather Talk. James Whitcomb Riley. AnAmPo (Rain frogs.) BoNaP

It hangs from heaven to earth. Tapestry. Charles Simic. LCAP; VCAP

It happen sometimes; a pair of eyes a profile. Almost Love. Magaly Sánchez, *tr. fr. Spanish by* Margaret Randall. AIW

It happened in Jacksboro in the year of 'seventy-three. The Buffalo Skinners. *Unknown.* AmFP

It happened in some peasant land. Bloody Fable. Desanka Maksimovic, *tr. fr. Serbo-Croatian by* Charles Simic. HSix

It happened, it happened all on a Saturday night. Johnny Dyers. *Unknown.* AmFP

It happened not far away. Clonfeacle. Paul Muldoon. CIP

It happened once, before the duller. Green Slates. Thomas Hardy. FaBoPP

It happened once upon a time. James Hatley. *Unknown.* ESPB

It happened to be on one certain day. The Wreck of the *Rambler.* *Unknown.* OxBSS

It happens hundreds of times each year. Glance. Peter Schmitt. NGP

It happens lonely — no one. The Moment. William Stafford. NNaP

It happens through the blond window, the trees. Ascension. Denis Devlin. BIrV; ChIV-2

It happens. Will it go on? Paralytic. Sylvia Plath. FaBoWP

It has a head like a cat, feet like a cat. *Unknown.* NTCP (Riddle.) RoPo

It has all/ come back today. From Gloucester Out. Edward Dorn. NOBA; PoM

It has become light. (*LL*) Day has risen, The. *Unknown.* EaPr

It has been a month since I gave up shaving. House Plants. David McFadden. NOBC

It has been eaten by the bear. (*LL*) Infant Innocence. A. E. Housman. FaBoNo; NOBL

It has been raining now since. Rain Downriver. Philip Levine. VCAP

It has been thrown until today. (*LL*) A Song of the Dice. *Unknown.* WPC

It has circles of light fragments. Cartography of the Subtle Heart. Jeni Couzyn. NBrP

It has done its work — I toss it carelessly to fall where it may. (*LL*) From Pent-up Aching Rivers. Walt Whitman. BoLoP; NAAL-1; NOBA

It has done its work — I toss it carelessly to fall where it may. (*LL*) Spontaneous Me. Walt Whitman. NAAL-1; OxBA

It has gone with me as with a child. Heinrich von Morungen, *tr. fr. German by* Frederick Goldin. GePo

It has hardened. Momcilo Nastasijevic, *tr. fr. Serbo Croatian by* Charles Simic. *Fr.* Deaf Things. HSix, *sect.* 2

It has lighted on you, this shape of air. Shape of Air. Robert Wells. SCBI

It has never been confined to one locality. (*LL*) England. Marianne Moore. LiTA; MeMAP; MoAB; MoAmPo

It has no wings. Loneliness and July Ninth. Claribel Alegría, *tr. fr. Spanish by* Aliki *and* Willis Barnstone. BoWoP

It has not been given me to have a friend. Friend Who Never Came. William Stafford. SM

It Has Snowed Repeatedly and We Can Count On a Good Crop of Wheat and Barley. Lu Yu, *tr. fr. Chinese by* Burton Watson. SuSp

It has to be a hill. The Person as Dreamer: We Talk about the Future. Michael Hartnett. PBCIP

It has to be the end of the day. Surf-casting. W. S. Merwin. NOBA

It has turned cold. Autumn. Wang Wei, *tr. fr. Chinese by* Kenneth Rexroth. OHMPC

It has turned crystal clear lately. The Autumn Brook. Hsüeh T'ao, *tr. fr. Chinese by* Kenneth Rexroth *and* Ling Chung. WPC

It hath been said of old that plays are feasts. To the Reader of Master William Davenant's Play, The Wits. Thomas Carew. CaPo

It hurries down to wither on the strand. (*LL*) Memory. Walter Savage Landor. EBEV; NOBVV; OAEL-2

It hurts, the things of old. Inside. Kim Chiha, *tr. fr. Korean*. TSaS, *tr. by* Kim Uchang

It Is a Beauteous Evening[, Calm and Free]. Wordsworth. AWP; BLPL; ChTr; EnRP; FaBoPP; FaBoRV; FHYEP; HeIP; ImPo; LiTB; LPA; MeMBP; NAEL-2; NIP; NoP; OAEL-2; OBTV; OxAEP-2; PoEL-4; PoLF; PPP; SCGP; Son; TEP; TFi

It is a being somewhat like a well. Woman. Kora Rumiko, *tr. fr. Japanese by* Kenneth Rexroth *and* Ikuko Atsumi. WPJ

It is a blessed heritage. Heritage. Mae V. Cowdery. ShDr

It is a bright house. Bright House. Fukao Sumako, *tr. fr. Japanese by* Kenneth Rexroth *and* Ikuko Atsumi. UnAS; WPJ

It is a clearing deep in a forest: overhanging boughs. Johnson's Cabinet Watched by Ants. Robert Bly. MoP; NOBA

It is a clever pushbutton you have, Juan Trippe. What Bright Pushbutton? Samuel Allen. PoNe

It is a cold and snowy night. The main street is deserted. Driving to Town Late to Mail a Letter. Robert Bly. BoNaP; CAPP; HeIP; InPK; NaP; VGW

It is a cramped little state with no foreign policy. Shame. Richard Wilbur. FaBoMo; OxBC

It is a fearful thing to fall into the hands of the living God. The Hands of God. D. H. Lawrence. ChIV-2

It is a flower. On this mountainside it is dying. (*LL*) Flower Herding on Mount Monadnock. Galway Kinnell. HeIP; LCAP; NaP; NoAM; NOBA

It is a funny thing, but true. Folks and Me. Lucile Crites. PWR; WBLP

It is a God-damned lie to say that these. Another Epitaph on an Army of Mercenaries. "Hugh MacDiarmid." InPK; MoP; NAEL-2; NoAM; NSI; OBWP; PAW; RB

It is a green globe like a vegetable light bulb. Avocado. John Logan. CAPP

It is a huge spider, which can no longer move. The Spider. César Vallejo, *tr. fr. Spanish by* Robert Bly. RaBo

It is a kind of shadow. The Umbrella. Ann Stanford. NYBP

It is a land with neither night nor day. Cobwebs. Christina Rossetti. NAEL-2; NALW

It Is a Lie. John Fowles. AnAn

It is a lie – their Priests, their Pope. The Confessional. Robert Browning. OtMeF

It is a long time since I flapped my wings. The Angels of 1912 and 1972. Richard Jackson. NAmP90

It is a lost road into the air. An Airstrip in Essex, 1960. Donald Hall. LCAP; LiTM; PAW

It is a matter of interest to see. On Our Modern World. Edward Bond. IHNG

It is a month, and isna mair. The White Fisher. *Unknown*. ESPB

It is a new America. Brown River, Smile. Jean Toomer. *Fr*. Blue Meridian, The. PoBA; PoNe

It is a pilgrim coming from the East. The Pilgrim from the East. Gustave Kahn, *tr. fr. French by* Jethro Bithell. TrJP

It is a place where poets crowned may feel the heart's decaying. Cowper's Grave. Elizabeth Barrett Browning. OxAEP-2

It Is a Pleasant Day. *Unknown*. BoTP

It is a satisfaction. Portrait of a Woman at Her Bath. William Carlos Williams. ArLo

It is a shame that this beautiful green ribbon. With the Green Lute-Ribbon. Wilhelm Müller, *tr. fr. German by* Philip L. Miller. *Fr*. Beautiful Maid of the Mill, The. RiWo

It is a simple ritual. My Brother. Patricia Parker. GLP

It is a sin. *Unknown*. RoPo

It is a solemn evening, golden-clear. The After-Glow. Mathilde Blind. OBNC

It is a sultry day; the sun has drunk. Summer Wind. Bryant. PoEL-4

It is a test you have to pass. Essie Parrish in New York. Essie Parrish, *tr. fr. Kashia Pomo Indian by* George Quasha. STP

It is a theatre floating through the clouds. Wallace Stevens. *Fr*. Auroras of Autumn, The. CMoP; HCAP

It is a thought breaking the granite heart. On the Death of Her Body. James K. Baxter. PeNZ

It is a tide pool, shallow, water coming in. Looking into a Tide Pool. Robert Bly. CAPP; MAT

It is a time of hunger. Personal Song. Arnatkoak, *tr. fr. Eskimo*. WTO

It is a very curious fact. Lines for a Worthy Person Who Has Drifted by Accident into a Chelsea Revel. A. P. Herbert. NOBL

It is a warm grey afternoon in August. Out of Control; the Quarry. Christopher Dewdney. NOBC

It is a water hand, this right one. Look to the Back of the Hand. Judith Minty. PoA

It is a willow when summer is over. Willow Poem. William Carlos Williams. NAAL-2

It is a windy day. Weather. Marchette Chute. SiSoPo

It is a winter night. Fever and chill. A Winter's Tale. Robert Patrick Dana. NYBP

It is a winter's tale. A Winter's Tale. Dylan Thomas. CMoP; LiTB; MeMBP

It is a wonder foam is so beautiful. Spray. D. H. Lawrence. BoNaP

It is a year of good harvest. Harvesting Wheat for the Public Share. Li Chü, *tr. fr. Chinese by* Kenneth Rexroth *and* Ling Chung. BoWoP; PBWP; WPC

It is again. "Stephany." NBV

It is all a rhythm. The Rhythm. Robert Creeley. LiTM

It is all blood and breaking. She Understands Me. Lucille Clifton. CAPP

It is all right. All they do. To the Muse. James Wright. NAAL-2; NNaP; NoP

It is almost time to grow up. (*LL*) Movin' with Nancy. David Trinidad. UTF

It is almost time to grow up. Movin' with Nancy. David Trinidad. UTF

It is almost too long ago to remember. That Moment. Sharon Olds. Poetr

It is already late, it is growing cold. Dialogue in the Forest. Joseph Freiherr von Eichendorff, *tr. fr. German by* Philip L. Miller. RiWo

It is already so late at night. Ise Tayu, *tr. fr. Japanese by* Kenneth Rexroth *and* Ikuko Atsumi. WPJ

It is always a temptation to an armed and agile nation. Dane-Geld. Kipling. FaBoEH; OxBTC

It is always night here. Star & Garter Theater. Dennis Schmitz. LCAP

It is always so: the declining. Returning from Harvest. Vernon Watkins. NYBP

It is always the quiet ones. Rite de Passage. Michele Roberts. NBrP

It is always there. The Little Place. Anneliese Wagner. BTR

It is an ancestral castle. Life in the Castle. Anne Hébert, *tr. fr. French by* Aliki *and* Willis Barnstone. BoWoP

It is an ancient Mariner. The Ancient Mariner: The Wedding Guest's Version of the Affair from His Point of View. *Unknown*. FaBoPa

It is an auncient waggonere. The Rime of the Auncient Waggonere. William Maginn. BXAP; ClHu

It is an honorable thought. Emily Dickinson. NOCV

It is an image of irreversible loss. The Sorrow Garden. Thomas McCarthy. BiHa; IB

It is as if they are ashamed. The Elephants Dying. Michael C. Blumenthal. NoAM

It is as true as strange, else trial feigns. John Davies of Hereford. EiL

It is Ash Wednesday and Christ is waiting. The Campesino's Lament. Judith Ortiz Cofer. AfAz

It Is at Moments after I Have Dreamed. E. E. Cummings. OxBA

It is at morning, twilight they expire. After Midnight. Charles Vildrac, *tr. fr. French by* Jethro Bithell. AWP

It is because you always hope, my heart. Yosano Akiko, *tr. fr. Japanese by* Kenneth Rexroth *and* Ikuko Atsumi. WPJ

It Is Becoming Now to Declare My Allegiance. C. Day Lewis. LiTM

It is best to turn on the set. Violence on Television. Louis Jenkins. NU

It is better. Abandoning Your Car in a Snowstorm: Rosslyn, Virginia. Michael C. Blumenthal. NoAM

It Is Better . . . . Bible, *O.T. Fr*. Ecclesiastes. TrJP

It is better this year. If the Birds Knew. John Ashbery. PoA

It Is Better to Be Together. Ruth Miller. PeSA

It is blue-butterfly day here in spring. Blue-Butterfly Day. Robert Frost. RFM

It is building music. (*LL*) Then. Muriel Rukeyser. GLP; LCAP

It is, but hadn't ought to be. *(LL)* Mrs. Judge Jenkins (Being the Only Genuine Sequel to "Maud Muller.") Bret Harte. BXAP; FiBHP

It is Christmas Day in the workhouse, and the cold, bare walls are bright. Christmas Day in the Workhouse. George R. Sims. BeLS; BLPA; EBNV
  (In the Workhouse: Christmas Day.) VPP
  (In the Workhouse.) OBCP

It is Christmas in the mansion. Christmas in the Heart. *Unknown.* OHIP

It is clear that Napoleon's Queen. Moss Rich. PeLi

It is cold, bitter as a penny. Who Will Know Us? Gary Soto. AfAz

It is cold here. The Moths. W. S. Merwin. HeIP

It is cold, the snow is deep. Poor North. Mark Strand. AnAn

It is colder now. Epistle to Be Left in the Earth. Archibald MacLeish. CMoP; MoAB; MoAmPo; NoBA; TrGrPo

It is coming up. Landfall. David Campbell. FaBoMA

It is common knowledge to every schoolboy and even. Portrait of the Artist as a Prematurely Old Man. Ogden Nash. BLPL; ImPo; InPS; LiTA; LiTM

It is dangerous for a woman to defy the gods. Letter to My Sister. Anne Spencer. BlSi; PoBA; PoNe; ShDr

It Is Dangerous to Read Newspapers. Margaret Atwood. CrSp; HeIP; OBWP

It is dark. The Last Bus. Mark Strand. TwCP

It is dark and. Kaddish. Catherine de Vinck. BTR

It is dark, now, and grave. Melting Pot. Michael Echeruo. TTY

It is dark up here on the heights. Le Sacré-Coeur. Charlotte Mew. OBTV

It is daybreak everywhere. *(LL)* The Bells of San Blas. Longfellow. MeMAP; OxBA

It is decided, dear Theramenes. Phaedra. Jean Racine, *tr. fr. French by* Kenneth Muir. NAWM-2

It is deep going from here. Edward Dorn. BCF

It is deep summer. Far out. There. Robert Mezey. NaP

It Is Difficult Now to Speak of Poetry. George Oppen. *Fr.* Of Being Numerous. NNaP

It is difficult to imagine how vulnerable they are. The Birds. David Posner. NYBP

It is difficult to keep sane in it. Rain Forest. Eric Rolls. NOBAu

It is disastrous to be a wounded deer. Hello. Gregory Corso. PoM

It is done! Laus Deo! Whittier. AmPP; PAH

It is done by us all, as God disposes, from. The Excrement Poem. Maxine W. Kumin. CAPP; FaBoWP

It is done to the sound of muffled drums. The Soldier. Adelbert von Chamisso, *tr. fr. German by* Philip L. Miller. RiWo

It is early dawn. The city forty miles away draws airplanes. Written Forty Miles South of a Spreading City. Robert Bly. NNaP

It is early, yet. The Grand Canyon. James Merrill. TAP

It is easier to forgive an enemy than to forgive a friend. Blake. *Fr.* Jerusalem. OAEL-2

It is easily forgotten, year to. Memorial Day. Michael Anania. NoAM

It is easy enough to be pleasant. Worthwhile. Ella Wheeler Wilcox. BLPA; EBEvV; PoToHe

It is easy enough to love flowers but these. Giant Decorative Dahlias. Molly Holden. OxBTC

It is easy to be young. (Everybody is). How to Be Old. May Swenson. MAT; UnPo

It Is Enough. Philip Appleman. BXAP

It is enough and as good as a feast. *(LL)* Vain excess of flattering fortune's gifts, The. George Gascoigne. EnRePo

It is enough for me. Old Man Told Me. Lance Henson. VoR

It is enough! My feeble sense. Dying Song. Anton Ulrich, *tr. fr. German by* George C. Schoolfield. GePo

It is equal to living in a tragic land. Dry Loaf. Wallace Stevens. MeMAP; NOBA; OxBA; PoRA; RaBo

It is essential I remember. Man White, Brown Girl and All That Jazz. Gloria C. Oden. PoBA

It is eternally winter. Asclepiades, *tr. fr. Greek by* Sam Hamill. InMo

It is evening. One bat dances. A Soul. Randall Jarrell. CMoP

It is far from just between us. *Unknown.* NOIV

It is far to Assisi. The Mental Hospital Garden. William Carlos Williams. *Fr.* Garden, The. CRP; FYAP

It is February in the mountains. Maurya Simon. *Fr.* Spellbound: An Alphabet. FoLa

It is finished. The enormous dust-cloud over Europe. Armistice. Paul Dehn. OxBTC; PAW

"It is finished." The last nail. Tenebrae. David Gascoyne. PeECV

It is fitting that you be here. *(LL)* On Seeing Two Brown Boys in a Catholic Church. Frank Horne. CDC; PoBA; PoNe; TTY

It is fitting that you be here. On Seeing Two Brown Boys in a Catholic Church. Frank Horne. CDC; PoBA; PoNe; TTY

It is for my Self who shall not be I. *(LL)* Like This before You. Yocheved Bat-Miriam. MHP

It is for us/ to praise the Lord of all. The Kingdom of God. Rab, *tr. fr. Hebrew.* TrJP

It is for you, my mother fair. For You. James Harvey Spencer. PWR

It is four in the afternoon. Time still for a poem. Public Journal. Phyllis McGinley. NBLV

It is four times as big as the bush!' *(LL)* There was an old man who said, "Hush!" Edward Lear. FaBoCo; GoJo; NOBL; OxBChV; OxBoLi; PeLi; PeLV; TEP

It is friday. We have come. Forgiving My Father. Lucille Clifton. CAPP

It is from the ideas of you that you emerge. Correspondences. Robert Duncan. PoM

It is fun to ride the horse. Horse. Kenneth Rexroth. *Fr.* Bestiary, A. NNaP; OBAL

It is going to be a splendid summer. Future Work. Fleur Adcock. DiPo

It is going to rain. She Thinks of Her Beloved. Lu Chi, *tr. fr. Chinese by* Kenneth Rexroth. OHMPC

It is good sometimes to grasp our helplessness. The Flood. Charles G. Bell. GrPl

It is good to be out on the road, and going one knows not where. Tewkesbury Road. John Masefield. BoTP

It is hanging/ in the edge of sunshine. *Unknown, tr. fr. Chippewa Indian by* Frances Densmore. *Fr.* Poems for the Game of Silence. STP

It is hard. Being a Giant. Robert Mezey. GrPl

It is hard as diamonds; it wants to destroy us all. *(LL)* The Unbeliever. Elizabeth Bishop. LiTA; NAAL-2; NoAM

It is hard going to the door. The Door. Robert Creeley. NaP; NeAP; NoAM; PoM; VGW

It is hard, inland. In Winter. Robert Wallace. BoNaP

It is hard, loving this way. *Unknown, tr. fr. Chinese by* Kenneth Rexroth *and* Ling Chung. *Fr.* Courtesan's Songs. WPC

It is hard to beat a good meal. Thomas Kinsella. *Fr.* Technical Supplement, A. CIP

It Is Hard to Catch Trout. Piuvkaq, *tr. fr. Eskimo.* WTO

It is hard to keep going. *(LL)* For a Woman Murdered While Running at Land's End, October 1979. Patricia Kirkpatrick. LoHo

It is hard to remember parents at their loving. Train Song. Fiona Kidman. PeNZ

It Is He. Eduard Friedrich Mörike, *tr. fr. German by* Philip L. Miller. RiWo

It Is Her Cousin's Death. Gail Fox. NOBC

It is her eyes. In Her Own Image. Eavan Boland. PBCIP

It is I, America, calling! A Call to Arms. Mary Raymond Shipman Andrews. PAH

It Is Important. Gail Tremblay. WeW

It is impossible to find anything good. Flood. Mary Grant Charles. GoYe

It is in captivity. The Bull. William Carlos Williams. LiTM; NoP; TwCP

It is in the rock, but not in the stone. *Unknown.* ChTr; ISE

It Is in Vain, the Sorrow. Paul Fleming, *tr. fr. German by* J. W. Thomas. GePo

It is Isis the mystery. Don Juan. D. H. Lawrence. PoA

It is June, it is June. Andraitx — Pomegranate Flowers. D. H. Lawrence. NoP

It is languorous ecstasy. It Is the Ecstasy of Languor. Paul Verlaine, *tr. fr. French by* Philip L. Miller. RiWo

It is late at night and still I am losing. In Dives' Dive. Robert Frost. VGW

It is late in the day of the world. Latter Day Lysistrata. Lauris Edmond. PeNZ

It is late in the Winter night. Winter Night. Yüan Mei, *tr. fr. Chinese by* Kenneth Rexroth. OHMPC

It is late in the year. Night in the House by the River. Tu Fu, *tr. fr. Chinese by* Kenneth Rexroth. NaP

It is late last night the dog was speaking of you. Donal Og. *Unknown, tr. fr. Irish by* Lady Augusta Gregory. RB
  (Grief of a Girl's Heart, The.) ChTr

It is late, late. *Unknown. Fr.* Week-End of Dermot and Grace, The. PeIV

It is Leviathan, mountain and world. History. Robert Fitzgerald. FYAP

It is like the plot of an ol/ novel. Instructions to a Princess. Ishmael Reed. PoBA

It is likely enough that lions and scorpions. Ante Mortem. Robinson Jeffers. MoAmPo

It is little I repair to the matches of the Southron folk. At Lord's. Francis Thompson. CoGr; EBVV; OxBSP; PeLV

It is lovely indeed, it is lovely indeed. Susanne Anderson. EaPr

It is lovely indeed, it is lovely indeed. *(LL)* It is lovely indeed, it is lovely indeed. Susanne Anderson. EaPr

It is lovely to walk fields of tall grass. Anacreon, *tr. fr. Greek by* Sam Hamill. InMo

It Is March ("It is March and black dust falls out of the books.") W. S. Merwin. NaP

It is Margaret you mourn for. (*LL*) Spring and Fall. Gerard Manley Hopkins. ArNa; CMoP; EBEV; ELP; FaBoUs; FF; GTBS-P; HAP; HeIP; HoPM; InPK; InPS; LiTM; MAT; NAEL-2; NIP; NoAM; NOBE; NoP; OBD; PeVV; PoE; PoEL-5; Poetr; PPP; RB; SCGP; SCV; SOTW; TEP; TFi; TOF; TRP

It Is Marvellous . . . Elizabeth Bishop. BAP-89

It is May on every hand. Bird Song. William Carlos Williams. SAmP

It is midnight. Poem at Thirty. Sonia Sanchez. BlSi; BPo; NMM; NTP; PoBA

It is midnight. The Mailman. Mark Strand. CAPP

It is midnite. The room is blue. Death Songs. L. V. Mack. PoBA

It Is Mine, This Country Wide. *Unknown.* GOA

It is miserable. Líadan and Cuirithir. *Unknown.* NOIV

It is Monday morning. The Goldfish Wife. Sandra Hochman. NYBP; UnPo

It is morning, Chrysilla. Some time ago the clarion cock. Antipater of Thessalonica, *tr. fr. Greek by* W. G. Shepherd. GrAn

It is morning darling look the sun. Aubade: N.Y.C. Robert Wallace. HoPM

It is morning now. The light whitens her face more than ever. (*LL*) The Chorus Speaks Her Words as She Dances. Linda Gregg. AnAn

It is morning, Senlin says, and in the morning. Conrad Aiken. *Fr.* Senlin; a Biography. LiTM; NoAM
(Morning Song of Senlin.) ImPo; LiTA; MoAmPo; OxBA
(Morning Song.) CMoP; MoAB; TrGrPo

It is most true that eyes are formed to serve. Sir Philip Sidney. *Fr.* Astrophel and Stella. AAS; ESo, *sl. abr.*; GGP; HeIL, *Sonnets,* I–CVIII *and 11 Songs*; NAEL-1; NoSic; OAEL-1; Poetr; SCGP, *Sonnets,* I–CVIII *and 11 Songs*; SiPS, *Sonnets,* I–CVIII *and 11 Songs*; SiPSBD, *Sonnets,* I–CVIII *and 11 Songs*; Son

It is most true that God to Israel. Bible, *O.T., paraphrased by* Sir Thomas Wyatt. *Fr.* Psalms. NoSic, *paraphrased by* the Countess of Pembroke

It is much like ocean the way it opens. Open Country. Richard Hugo. LCAP

It is much to late. (*LL*) My Mother on an Evening in Late Summer. Mark Strand. FYAP

It is my first Scotch tinkling. Christmas Party. Kate Daniels. NAmP90

It is myself. To a Dog Injured in the Street. William Carlos Williams. LCAP; LiTM; MoAB; SAmP

It Is Near Toussaints. Ivor Gurney. OBD; PeFWW

It is necessary that things. Anixamander, *tr. fr. Greek by* Kenneth Rexroth. PGA

It is neither spring nor summer: it is Always. All Morning. Theodore Roethke. EaPr

It is never enough to know what you want. "Wish to Be Believed," The. Mona Van Duyn. PoA

It Is New. Al-Hutay'a, *tr. fr. Arabic by* Omar S. Pound. ArPe

It is New Year's Day. Best Loved of Africa. Margaret Danner. PoBA; PoNe

It is night again. Tzu Yeh, *tr. fr. Chinese by* Kenneth Rexroth *and* Ling Chung. WPC; WPOW

It is night and the barbarians have not come. Poem Beginning with a Line by Cavafy. Derek Mahon. PNI

It is night like a red rag. A Moment of War. Laurie Lee. OBWP; PAW

It is nine o'clock where you are breakfasting. Here Today Here Tomorrow. David Chaloner. VaA

It Is No Dream of Mine. Thoreau. ImGa

It is no fault to be deformed. To a Hunchback. Ibn al-Rumi, *tr. fr. Arabic by* Omar S. Pound. ArPe

It is no flaming lustre made of light. The Celestial City. Giles Fletcher the Younger. *Fr.* Christ's Victory and Triumph. OBD
(In midst of this city celestial.) NOBE

It is no idle fabulous tale, nor is it fayned newes. Newes from Virginia. Richard Rich. PAH

It is no longer as it once was. Atong and His Goodbye. Benilda S. Santos, *tr. fr. Spanish.* TSaS, *tr. by* Ramón C. Sunico

It is no madness to say. Hilda Doolittle ("H. D."). *Fr.* Flowering of the Rod, The. FaBoMo

It is no vulgar nature I have wived. George Meredith. *Fr.* Modern Love. NAEL-2

It is noble country where we dwell. Our Country. Thoreau. GOA

It is not a chariot. (*LL*) Thunder. Fu Hsüan. OHMPC

It Is Not Always May. Longfellow. PWR

It is not anything he says. Kavin Again. Richard Hovey. AnAmPo

It is not bad. Let them play. The Bloody Sire. Robinson Jeffers. CMoP; ImPo; LiTM; PoA

It is not Beauty I Demand. George Darley. GGP; OAEL-2
(Loveliness of Love, The.) GTBS; GTBS-P; OxAEP-2
(Song, A: "It is not beauty I demand.") OBNC

It is not, Celia, in our power. To a Lady Asking Him How Long He Would Love Her. Sir George Etherege. OBEV

It is not cosy to live. From the Chinese. Michael Smith. CIP; PBCIP

It is not death, that sometime in a sigh. Thomas Hood. OBNC

It is not dusk. Response. Linda Pastan. BTR

It is not enough. The Prophet's Warning or Shoot to Kill. Ebon Dooley. PoBA

It is not enough to drink. "When the Wild Goose Finds Food He Calls His Comrades" — *I Ching.* Jan Kemp. PeNZ

It is not far to my place. Visit. A. R. Ammons. CoAP; GrPl; TwCP

It is not four years ago. Proffered Love Rejected. Sir John Suckling. ErPo

It Is Not Growing Like a Tree. Ben Jonson. *Fr.* To the Immortal[l] Memory [*or* Memorie] and Friendship of That Noble Pair[e], Sir Lucius Cary and Sir Henry Morrison. BeJo; ChTr; ImPo; LiTB; NOBE; NoP; OAEL-1; PoEL-2; SeCP; SeCV-1

It is not gunfire I hear, but a hunting horn. (*LL*) Aristocrats. Keith Douglas. FaBoMo; NAEL-2; NoAM; OBWP

It is not I, ever or now. (*LL*) The Pebble. Elinor Wylie. ChIV-1; MoAmPo

It is not — I swear it by every fiery omen to be seen these nights. Readings, Forecasts, Personal Guidance. Kenneth Fearing. MoAmPo

It is not in the shining, nor yet in the dead. (*LL*) It is in the rock, but not in the stone. *Unknown.* ChTr; ISE

It Is Not, Lord, the Sound of Many Words. Henry Lok. *Fr.* Sundry Christian Passions Contained in Two Hundred. Son

It is not mine to run, with eager feet. Not Mine. Julia Caroline Ripley Dorr. PWR

It is not right to judge a man. First Impressions. Alfred Grant Walton. PoToHe

It is not safe to know. (*LL*) Lover and Philosopher. Sir William Davenant. NOBE; OBEV; Prf

It is not so much. Outrage. Lucille Iverson. CrSp

It is not so much the image of the man. Photograph of Haymaker, 1890. Molly Holden. OxBTC

It is not that the sea lanes. Stone and Fern. Leslie Norris. AngWe

It is not the earth that I worship. Earth Song. Thomas Love Peacock. VoR

It is not the fear of death. André's Request to Washington. *Unknown.* PAH

It is not the hunter who is cunning. First Lessons. Marilyn Chin. LoHo

It is not the moon, I tell you. Mock Orange. Louise Glück. LPA; NoAM; VCAP

It is not the weight of the jewel or plate. The Perfect Gift. Edmund Vance Cooke. PChr

It is not the young whom we find feeding the pigeons. The Pigeon-Feeders in Battery Park. Julia Cooley Altrocchi. GoYe

It Is Not to Be Thought Of [That the Flood]. Wordsworth. EnRP

It is not what they built. It is what they knocked down. A German Requiem. James Fenton. NAEL-2; NoAM; SCBI

It is not wine that makes me reel/ Not juice of grape I crave. Agathias, *tr. fr. Greek by* Peter Whigham. GrAn

It is nothing new. Demonstration. W. S. Merwin. PRA

It is nothing to me, the beauty said. Nothing and Something. Frances E. W. Harper. PWR

It is now my brave boys we are clear of the sea. The Antarctic Muse. Thomas Perry. OBTV

It is now that I weep. (*LL*) Great-great-grandmother. Guy Butler. PeSAV

It is — Occasionally. (*LL*) We do not play on graves. Emily Dickinson. NIP; PoEL-5

It is of a fearless Irishman a story I will tell. Brennan on the Moor. *Unknown.* AmFP; FaBoBa; GBP

It is of a fine frigate, dare not mention her name. The Fancy Frigate. *Unknown.* OxBSS

It is of a flash packet, she's a packet of fame. The *Dreadnought. Unknown.* OxBSS

It is, of course, the wrong house. The Houses of Emily Dickinson. Larry Rubin. NIP

It is one that most people should be prepared to be blank upon. (*LL*) Ignorance of Death. William Empson. CMoP; LiTM; NoAM; OBD

It is only in ourselves united. (*LL*) Brothers of the sea. *Unknown.* EaPr

It is only that this warmth and movement are like. The Woman in Sunshine. Wallace Stevens. ArLo

It is other people who have separated. Lady Otomo no Sakanoe, *tr. fr. Japanese by* Arthur Waley. TAL

It is our quiet time. Nancy Wood. EaPr

It is overdue time. Ron Welburn. NBV

It is the soul that sees; the outward eyes. George Crabbe. *Fr.* Lover's Journey, The. OxAEP-1

It Is the Stars That Govern Us. Michael Magee. PoA

It is the things we have that go. *(LL)* Wisdom. Sara Teasdale. AnAmPo; MoAmPo

It is the thirty-first of March. Peter Bell. John Hamilton Reynolds. OBNC

It is the time of rain and snow. Lady Izumi Shikibu, *tr. fr. Japanese by* Kenneth Rexroth. WPOW

It is the way of a pleasant path. Green Frog at Roadstead, Wisconsin. James Schevill. TAP

It is the white of faces from which the sunburn has been suddenly scared away. Driftwood from a Ship. Galway Kinnell. AnAn

It is the wife, it is the home. *(LL)* Who Drags the Fiery Artist Down? Clarence Day. FaBoCo; NBLV

It is the year's end, the winds are blasting, and I. December 30th. Ivor Gurney. NAEL-2

It is their way to find the surface. Poem by the Charles River. Robin Blaser. NeAP

It Is There. Muriel Rukeyser. WoWa

It is this deep blankness is the real thing strange. Let It Go. William Empson. FaBoMo; OPOP; OxBSP; OxBTC

It Is This Way with Men. C. K. Williams. CAPP; RaBo; VCAP

It is three o'clock in the morning. Trials of a Tourist. Anne Tibble. FaBoCo; NBLV

It is time. The Moon Rises Slowly Over the Ocean. Xu De-min, *tr. fr. Chinese.* TSaS, *tr. by* Edward Morin *and* Dennis Ding

It Is Time for Me to Go Up into the House of Paradise. *Unknown, tr. fr. Gaelic.* ScCV

It is time for the others to come. The Magus. James Dickey. NAs

It is time to be old. Terminus. Emerson. AmPP; AWP; MeMAP; NOBA; OxBA; PoEL-4; PoLF; TAP

It is to a goodly child well fitting. A Goodly Child. *Unknown.* OxBChV

It is to have a sharper's thanks! *(LL)* A Bad Break! W. T. Goodge. NOBAu

It is tomorrow now. Morning Star. Thomas Hornsby Ferril. VGW

It Is Too Late. Longfellow. *Fr.* Morituri Salutamus. BLPL; PoLF

It is true--/ I've always loved. Alice Walker. *Fr.* Once. BlSi; NMM; PoBA

It is true, Martin Heidegger, as you have written. The Envelope. Maxine W. Kumin. CrSp; NALW

It is true, modern life is complicated. For the Market. Jane Mayhall. TAP

It is true, that even in the best-run state. The Murder of William Remington. Howard Nemerov. CMoP; CoAP

It is true that I held Thero fair. Meleager, *tr. fr. Greek by* Peter Whigham. GrAn; PeHV

It is true true, that older than man and ages to outlast him. Gray Weather. Robinson Jeffers. CMoP

It is 12:20 in New York a Friday. The Day Lady Died. Frank O'Hara. CAPP; HCAP; Jaz; LCAP; MoP; NAAL-2; NeAP; NoAM; NOBA; NoP; PoBeRe; PoEt; PoM; RaBo; SOTW; TRP; VCAP

It is twenty years. The Piper. W. S. Merwin. NAAL-2

It is unfortunately understandable enough. Royal Wedding Gifts. "Hugh MacDiarmid." IHNG

It is unreasonable to ask my tears. Daughter of Shunzei, *tr. fr. Japanese by* Kenneth Rexroth *and* Ikuko Atsumi. WPJ

It is up to us to receive and transmit our Torah. Rami M. Shapiro. EaPr

It is very aggravating. The Truth about Horace. Eugene Field. AnAmPo

It is very early now, no light yet, nor. La Brea. Richard Kenney. DiPo

It is waking in the night. Fix. Michael Dransfield. NOBAu

It is well for small birds that can rise up on high. *Unknown, tr. fr. Irish by* Thomas Kinsella. NOIV

It is what he does not know. On a Squirrel Crossing the Road in Autumn, in New England. Richard Eberhart. HeIP; LiTM; Poetsp

It is whatever day, whatever time it is. Sunday Morning. Wayne Moreland. PoBA

It is when I hear Mozart. Deafness. Richard Ryan. BIrV; PBCIP

It is windy today. A wall of wind crashes against. Cloudy Day. Jimmy Santiago Baca. InPS

It is wine-harvest, summer, the year's heart. A Poem for Maurice O'Shea. Geoffrey Lehmann. NOBAu

It is winter again. Stopping to Take Notes. Michael Smith. PBCIP

It is Winter, and the clerk. Apropos of the Falling Sleet. Harry Clifton. IB

It is winter and the new year. The New Year. Mark Strand. *Fr.* Elegy for My Father. HCAP; LCAP; UnPo

It Is Winter, I Know. Merrill Moore. MoAmPo

It is winter in California, and outside. California Winter. Karl Shapiro. AiP

It is with curiosity, finally. Not Dachau. Aaron Miller. BTR

It is written in the skyline of the city. Pact. Kenneth Fearing. CMoP

It is written that a hurricane holds the power. An Antipastoral Memory of One Summer. Dave Jeddie Smith. MT

It is you, matter, that I bless. *(LL)* Blessed be you, harsh matter, barren soil, stubborn rock. Pierre Teilhard de Chardin. EaPr

It is your last day and hour and you are alone. Who. Edwin Honig. TAP

It is yourself you seek. Man Alone. Louise Bogan. NYBP

It isn't a game for girls. Reaching Yellow River. Roberta Hill Whiteman. HATNAP

It isn't a very big cake. Poets. Gavin Ewart. PeLV

It isn't any worse than war. Anxiety about Dying. Alicia Ostriker. CrSp

It isn't as if I never enjoyed good wine. I'm Not Complaining. Philip Schultz. SoSe

It isn't pleasant. The Inhuman. Eugenio Montale, *tr. fr. Italian by* G. Singh. OBD

It isn't raining rain to me. April Rain. Robert Loveman. BoTP; TrJP (Rain Song.) WBLP

It isn't such a bad thing. Everyone Knows Whom the Saved Envy. James Galvin. FoLa

It isn't that the threat of the bomb is great. Cocoon. Ishigaki Rin, *tr. fr. Japanese by* Ayusawa Takako. WPOW

It isn't the church — it's *you.* *(LL)* It Isn't the Church — It's You. *Unknown.* BLPA; WBLP

It Isn't the Church — It's You. *Unknown.* BLPA; WBLP

It isn't the poppies. Toward Umbria. Stanley Plumly. NAmP90

It isn't the thing you do, dear. At Sunset. Margaret E. M. Sangster. PWR (Sin of Omission, The.) BLPA; PoToHe

It Isn't the Town, It's You. R. W. Glover. BLPA

It isn't winter that brings it. Earth. Margaret Atwood. PoE

It keeps eternal whisperings around. On the Sea. Keats. EnRP; FF; LiTB; MeMBP; NoP; OAEL-2; TEP; TrGrPo (Sonnet on the Sea.) 09SeCePo

It killed the lilac bushes and the weight may pull the phone lines down. *(LL)* Anticipation. Sheila Richter. LoHo

It later befell in the years that followed. The Fire-Dragon and the Treasure. *Unknown, tr. by* Charles W. Kennedy. *Fr.* Beowulf. AnOE; ASW, *tr. by* Kevin Crossley-Holland.

It lay, dark in the corner of the field. Suicide Pond. Kathy McLaughlin. PoA

It leaves its moisture thick and thin. *(LL)* A Candle. Sir John Suckling. ErPo

It leaves no stain upon the shrine. *(LL)* Art thou afraid the adorer's prayer. Walter Savage Landor. GBL

It left upon her tender flesh no trace. A Woman's Death-wound. Helen Hunt Jackson. AmWP

It lies around us like a cloud. The Other World. Harriet Beecher Stowe. WGRP

It lies not in our power to love, or hate. Christopher Marlowe. *Fr.* Hero and Leander. AAS; EBEvV; NoP; TrGrPo (Who Ever Loved, That Loved Not at First Sight?) BLPL; ImPo; LiTB

It lies not on the sunlit hill. The White Peace. "Fiona Macleod." FaBoBe

It listened to all the jokes and it laughed. *(LL)* Periphery. Ruth Stone. NALW

It little profits that an idle king. Ulysses. Tennyson. AWP; ClHu; EBEV; EBVVPR; EnVR; FaPoB; FaPoR; FF; FHYEP; HAP; HeIL; HeIP; HoPM; ImPo; InPK; InPS; LiTB; MeMBP; NAEL-2; NAWM-2; NIP; NOBE; NOBVV; NoP; OAEL-2; OxAEP-2; PoE; Poetr; PoRA; PPP; PrIm; SCGP; SCV; SoSe; TEP; TFi; TrGrPo; TRP; UnPo; WeW

It looked extremely rocky for the Mudville nine that day. Casey at the Bat. Ernest Lawrence Thayer. AnAmPo; BeLS; BLPA; FaBoBe; PoRA

It looks for grasshopper, goanna, thin one. *(LL)* Goanna. *Unknown.* NOBAu

It looks like any building. The Library. Barbara A. Huff. FaPON

It looks that way. But I dunno. *(LL)* To Be or Not to Be. *Unknown.* FaBoCo; MoShBr

It Makes a Change. Mervyn Laurence Peake. OTCP

It makes us uncomfortable: the pillars. Early Views of Manchester and Paris: First View. John Ash. SCBI

It matters little where I was born. What Does It Matter? Noah Barker. PWR

It matters not if the pasture is far. Cowherd, The; a Song. Ch'u Kuang-hsi, *tr. fr. Chinese by* Joseph J. Lee. SuSp

It may be good, like it who list. Sir Thomas Wyatt. EnRePo; FaBoPV; SiPS; SiPSBD

It may be these things never did occur. Kinnereth. Rachel, *tr. fr. Hebrew by* A. M. Klein. TrJP

It may be/ they dare to. Whitewash. Léon Damas, *tr. fr. French by* Ellen Conroy Kennedy. NegPo

It may be 'tis observ'd, I want relations. George Wither. *Fr.* Tired Petitioner, The. SeCV-1

It may be when the sunlight strikes the sill. In Your Absence. Elizabeth Baxter. PoToHe

It may bring to thee. (*LL*) From the Arabic; an Imitation. Shelley. OBEV

It may have been the pride in me for aught. The Corridor. E. A. Robinson. AnAmPo

It may indeed be phantasy, when I. To Nature. Samuel Taylor Coleridge. ArNa; OAEL-2

It May Not Always Be So. E. E. Cummings. *Fr.* Sonnets — Unrealities. BoLoP; FaBV

It may of course be John his father-in-law. The Stone Face. Harri Webb. AngWe

It means everything. Sizeline. Felix Mnthali. PeSAV

It melts and seethes, the chaos that shall grow. The Rose Enthroned. Lucy Larcom. AmWP

It midnights, not a moon is out. The Midnightmouse. Christian Morgenstern, *tr. fr. German by* W. D. Snodgrass *and* Lore Segal. CBNP; RB

It Might Be a Lump of Amber. Walter de la Mare. FaBoNo

It might be any night. These Days. Andrew Motion. DiPo

It might be anywhere. A Lighthouse in Maine. Derek Mahon. OBTV

It might be lonelier. Emily Dickinson. SAmP

It Might Have Been Worse. G. J. Russell. PoToHe

It mounts at sea, a concave wall. From the Wave. Thom Gunn. NAEL-2; NoP

It Must Be. Linda Hogan. SRLS

It must be/ deeeeep. (*LL*) Jesus Was Crucified or: It Must Be Deep. Carolyn M. Rodgers. BlSi; PoBA

It must be done, my soul, but 'tis a strange. The Meditation. John Norris. NOSC

It must be hunky dory on Venus. The synapse. Jeremy. Jeffrey Miller. UL

It must be mine! no other heart could prove. The Returned Heart. Sarah Dixon. ECWP

It must be so--Plato, thou reason'st well. Cato's Soliloquy. Joseph Addison. *Fr.* Cato. WBLP

It must have been a single thread of tears. Meng Chiao, *tr. by* Stephen Owen. *Fr.* Apricots Die Young. SuSp

It must have been a year. Fire, Hair, Meat and Bone. Fred Johnson. PoBA

It must have been for one of us, my own. Not Thou but I. Philip Bourke Marston. BLPA; BLPL

It must have been one o'clock at night. To Remain. C. P. Cavafy, *tr. fr. Modern Greek by* John Mavrogordato. ErPo

It must have been one or one-thirty. To Remain. C. P. Cavafy, *tr. fr. Modern Greek by* Nikos Stangos *and* Stephen Spender. BoLoP

It must have seemed the apex of dreams. Adonis Theater. Mark Doty. NAmP90

It must've been lousy. (*LL*) Elizabethans Called It Dying, The. James Schuyler. NeAP; PoM

It needn't have ribaldry's taint. Don Marquis. PeLi

It never occurred to me, never. The Meeting. Howard Moss. GOYP; NYBP

It nods and curtseys and recovers. A. E. Housman. *Fr.* Shropshire Lad, A. FaPoB; NOBVV

It occurred when she crossed the Atlantic. *Unknown.* PeLi

It occurs to me now. The Lesson. Charles Simic. HCAP

It often falss (as here it erst befell). Spenser. *Fr.* Faerie Queene, The. OBF

It ofttimes has been told, that the British seamen bold. The *Constitution* and the *Guerrière. Unknown.* AmFP

It once might have been, once only. Youth and Art. Robert Browning. CTC; MeMBP; NAEL-2; NOBVV

It only can live underground. (*LL*) The Rabbit. *Unknown.* FaBoCo; FiBHP

It Out-Herods Herod. Pray You, Avoid It. Anthony Hecht. CoAP; NIP; NoAM; NOBA; OxBC

It pays to advertise! (*LL*) Advertisement. *Unknown.* FaBoUs

It plunges into itself, stone-white, mottled with. Waterfall. David Wagoner. ArNa

It put forth buds at the end of the Nine Splendors. The Fragrant Tree. Shen Yüeh, *tr. fr. Chinese by* Richard B. Mather. SuSp

It puts itself right. (*LL*) Cat and the Weather. May Swenson. HAP; OFC; SoCa; WeW

It quicknd next a toyful Ape, and so. John Donne. *Fr.* Progress[e] of the Soul[e], The. PoEL-2

It raindrops on the cold. Introit. Padraic Fiacc. CIP

It rained all day. Now a single bird. After Clouds and Rain. Sam Hamill. ArNa

It rained in my sleep. September. Linda Pastan. Poetsp

It rained quite a lot, that spring. You woke in the morning. Metropolitan Nightmare. Stephen Vincent Benét. NYBP

It rained; through the windows thrown open. Rain. Vittoria Aganoor Pompilj, *tr. fr. Italian by* Philip L. Miller. RiWo

It rained toward day. The morning came sad and white. Colder Fire. Robert Penn Warren. *Fr.* To a Little Girl, One Year Old, in a Ruined Fortress. LiTM

It rains across the country I remember. (*LL*) Mnemosyne. Trumbull Stickney. LiTA; NOBA; OxBA

It Rains ("It rains, and nothing stirs within the fence.") Edward Thomas. OxBTC; PlP; PoE

It rains, it pains. *Unknown.* ISE

It rains, it rains in merry Lincoln. Little Sir Hugh. *Unknown.* OBET

It rains on my friends' faces. Rain on a Battlefield. Yehuda Amichai, *tr. fr. Hebrew by* Assia Gutmann. AnRep

It Really Is the Heart. Denise Riley. NBrP

It Really Must Be Nice. E. E. Cummings. AnAmPo

"It relaxes me," he said. Six Reasons for Drinking. Vernon Scannell. OxBC

It rests me to be among beautiful women. Tame Cat. Ezra Pound. OBAL

It results in a permanent slo. (*LL*) Cautionary Limerick. *Unknown.* FaBoUs; NBLV

It returns to the same nest. Bird-Watcher. Clive Wilmer. SCBI

It rises over the lake, the farms. The Kite. Mark Strand. NYBP

It rolls on. (*LL*) To the Terrestrial Globe. W. S. Gilbert. FaBoNo; NBLV; TrGrPo

It rose dark as a stack of peat. Suilven. Andrew Young. OxBS

It said "Come home, here is an end, a goal." Woodrow Wilson. Robinson Jeffers. FaBoPV

It said welcome. The Second Coming. John William Corrington. HoPM

It sat between my husband and my children. Seele im Raum. Randall Jarrell. LCAP

It seconds the crickets of the province. The Rocking Chair. A. M. Klein. HeIP; NoP

It seemed as though the heavens. Moonlit Night. Joseph Freiherr von Eichendorff, *tr. fr. German by* Philip L. Miller. RiWo

It seemed corrival of the world's great prime. A Fallen Yew. Francis Thompson. MoAB; MoBrPo

It seemed that out of the battle I escaped. Strange Meeting. Wilfred Owen. CMoP; EBEvV; FaBoMo; FaBoRV; FaPoB; GGP; GTBS-P; HeIP; HoPM; ImPo; LiTB; MeMBP; MoAB; MoBrPo; MoP; NAEL-2; NoAM; NOBE; NoP; OAEL-2; OBF; OBWP; OxAEP-2; PeFWW; PoE; PoWW; RB; SCV; TFi; TrGrPo

It seemed to us all a stupid trick. (*LL*) The Inflatable Globe. Theodore Spencer. LiTA; PAW

It seems a certain time ago: a-maybe. One Time. Douglas Livingstone. PeSA

It seems a day. Nutting. Wordsworth. EnRP; NAEL-2; NU; OAEL-2; PFP; Poetr; RB

It seems a flower, but not a flower. A Flower. Po Chü-i, *tr. fr. Chinese by* Robert Payne. TAL

It seems a trick of lighting, his legs lost. Legless Boy Climbing In and Out of Chair. Michael Pettit. NAmP90

It seems better that we kept alive. (*LL*) Old Apple Trees. W. D. Snodgrass. CAPP; FYAP; SV

It seems, for a moment, the river ceases flowing. (*LL*) Summer near the River. Carolyn Kizer. CoAP; VGW

It seems high time/ I challenged you to song-contest! A Dispute between Women. *Unknown, tr. fr. Eskimo by* Tom Lowenstein. STP

It seems I have no tears left. They should have fallen. Tears. Edward Thomas. GTBS-P; LiTB; NAEL-2

It seems I impregnated Marge. *Unknown.* PeLi

It seems like a dream. An Autumn Morning. *Unknown.* BoTP

It seems like a dream — that sweet wooing of old. Bachelor Hall. Eugene Field. BLPA

It seems no day passes now. A Family Procession. J. P. Clark Bekederemo. HBAPE

It seems no work of man's creative hand. Pedra. John William Burgon. BLPA

It seems now far off and foolish, a memory. Lot Later. Howard Nemerov. HoPM

It seems so simple now, that life of thine. Washington. Geraldine Meyrich. OHIP

It Seems That God Bestowed Somehow. Amanda Benjamin Hall. AH

It seems that I hear that beauty who. Lament of the Lovely Helmet-Dealer. Villon, *tr. fr. French by* Hubert Creekmore. ErPo

It seems to be a flower, yet not a flower. Tune: "Water Dragon's Chang" after Chang Chi-fu's Lyric on the Willow Catkin. Su Shih, *tr. fr. Chinese by* James J. Y. Liu. SuSp

It was a funky deal. *(LL)* It Was a Funky Deal. Etheridge Knight. BPo; NBV; PoBA

It Was a Funky Deal. Etheridge Knight. BPo; NBV; PoBA

It was a gallant sailor man. The Two Anchors. Richard Henry Stoddard. BeLS

It Was a Goodly Co. E. E. Cummings. LiTA; LiTM

It was a graveyard scene. The crescent moon. "Great Unaffected Vampires and the Moon." Stevie Smith. NoAM

It was a hand. God looked at it. The Hand. R. S. Thomas. NOCV; OxBC

It was a hard thing to undo this knot. Gerard Manley Hopkins. NOBVV (At a Welsh Waterfall.) FaBoPP

It was a hard thing to undo this knot. *(LL)* It was a hard thing to undo this knot. Gerard Manley Hopkins. NOBVV

It was a heartfelt game, when it began. Portrait. Judith Wright. OxBSP; SoSe

It was a hot day thrown suddenly cool. Real Life. Bob Arnold. ETG

It was a house of female habitation. A House of Mercy. Stevie Smith. FaBoWP

It was a kind and northern face. Praise for an Urn. Hart Crane. AWP; CMoP; HAP; LiTM; MeMAP; MoAB; MoAmPo; NoAM; NOBA; OxBA; PPP; WeW

It was a Knight in Scotland borne. The Fair Flower of Northumberland. *Unknown.* ESPB; OxBB

It was a lady of the north she lov'd a gentleman. Room for a Jovial Tinker: Old Brass to Mend. *Unknown.* CoMu; OxBB

It was a letter. 1945, The Silence. Burton D. Wasserman. BTR

It was a little captive cat. The Singing Cat. Stevie Smith. CRH; OFC; OxBTC

It was a long time ago. As I Grew Older. Langston Hughes. AmPP

It Was a Long Time Before. Leslie Silko. NoAM

It Was a Lording's Daughter. *At. to* Shakespeare Shakespeare. *Fr.* Passionate Pilgrim, The. EIL

It was a lovely night. W. R. Rodgers. *Fr.* Resurrection: An Easter Sequence. PNI

It was a lover and his lass. Shakespeare. *Fr.* As You Like It. AWP; CBLP; CH; EIL; ELP; GBL; GTBS; GTBS-P; HeIL; ImPo; InPS; LiTB; NAEL-1; NOBE; NoP; NoSic; OBEV; RB; SCGP; TFi; TTTS (Country Song.) TrGrPo
(Song: "It was a lover and his lass.") OxAEP-1; EBEvV; CTC; 09FiP

It was a maid of brenten arse. A Maid of Brenten Arse. *Unknown.* GBP

It was a Maine lobster town. Water. Robert Lowell. CMoP; HeIP; LCAP; NOBA; NoP; PFP; PoE; SM

It was a mighty monarch's child. Mir träumte von einem Königskind. Heine, *tr. fr. German by* Richard Garnett. AWP

It was a mile of greenest grass. The Occasional Yarrow. Stevie Smith. FaBoNo

It was a miniature country once. Japan. Anthony Hecht. LiTM

It was a mischievous wind that pushed him; a murderous gust that jarred young Jan from the scaffold. Monument. A. M. Sullivan. GoYe

It was a moment, sudden as snowflakes. 2 Wren Street. Christian McEwen. VBLP

It was a mother and a maid. The Milk White Doe. *Unknown, tr. fr. French by* Andrew Lang. AWP

It Was a Navy Boy. Wilfred Owen. NSI

It was a navy boy, so prim, so trim. It Was a Navy Boy. Wilfred Owen. NSI

It was a night in winter. Clive Sansom. *Fr.* Witnesses, The. PChr

It was a night of early spring. Wisdom. Sara Teasdale. AnAmPo; MoAmPo

It was a noble Roman. On Fort Sumter. *Unknown.* PAH

It was a noble Roman. Where There's a Will There's a Way. John Godfrey Saxe. AnAmPo

It was a patch of pain. Back Garden. Cliff Beynon. AngWe

It was a Phrygian king. Telestes, *tr. fr. Greek by* Sam Hamill. InMo

It was a Phrygian, Pelops. Telestes, *tr. fr. Greek by* Sam Hamill. InMo

It was a place where apples sprouted teeth. Childhood. Chitra Divakaruni. OpBo

It was/ a policeman's ball. The Policeman's Ball. Martín Espada. UTF

It was a puritanicall ladd. Off a Puritane. *Unknown.* CoMu

It was a quiet way. Emily Dickinson. LPA

It was a rainbow impossibly. Prisms. Philip Dacey. Poetsp

It was a real well, real. Old Wives' Tales. Constance Urdang. PBCAP

It was a rich merchant man. The Merchant and the Fidler's Wife. *Unknown.* CoMu; OxBB

It was a robber's daughter, and her name was Alice Brown. Gentle Alice Brown. W. S. Gilbert. FaBoCo; FiBHP

It was a summer evening. Sentences While Remembering Hiraethog. T. Glynne Davies, *tr. fr. Welsh by* R. Gerallt Jones. OBWVE

It was a summer evening in an Alabama city. Prelude. René Depestre, *tr. fr. French by* Ellen Conroy Kennedy. *Fr.* Epiphanies of the Voodoo Gods. NegPo

It was a summer's night, a close warm night. Wordsworth. *Fr.* Prelude [or, Growth of a Poet's Mind], The. EnRP; OAEL-2; PoEL-4

It was a tall young oysterman lived by the river-side. The Ballad of the Oysterman. Oliver Wendell Holmes. AnAmPo; MoShBr

It was a testimony. Gregory's House. David Huddle. PBCAP

It was a tortoise aspiring to fly. Improvisations on Aesop. Anthony Hecht. OBAL

It was a violent time. Wheels, racks, and fires. A Mirror for Poets. Thom Gunn. LiTM

It was a wasp, or an imprudent bee. The Wasp. Daryl Hine. NYBP

It was a way of punishing the house, setting it a blaze. Interior at Petworth: From Turner. Rosanna Warren. NoAM

It was a winter's morning. Harry Graham. *Fr.* Battue of Berlin, The. UV

It was a wondrous realm beguiled. Alfred Domett. *Fr.* Ranolf and Amohia. OBTV

It was about the deep of night. A Ballad of Christmas. Walter de la Mare. OBCP

It was about the Martinmas time. Barbara Allan. *Unknown.* EnSB

It was after vespers one evening. Low Church. Stanley J. Sharpless. NBLV; PeLV

It was all different; that, at least, seemed sure. Mutability. W. D. Snodgrass. DiPo

It Was All Very Tidy. Robert Graves. OxBTC; RB

It was almost easy to say goodby. The Soldiers Returning. Richard Shelton. GOYP

It was always. Hose and Iron. Greg Kuzma. MAT

It was always peaceful. After Claude Lanzmann's Shoah. Liliane Richman. BTR

It was an accident." *(LL)* The Dolls. W. B. Yeats. CMoP; NoAM; PoE

It was an adventure much could be made of. Orpheus Alone. Mark Strand. BAP-90

It Was an April Morning. Wordsworth. FaBoPP

It was an English ladye bright. Song of Albert Graeme. Sir Walter Scott. *Fr.* Lay of the Last Minstrel, The. EnRP

It was an evening in November. The Pig. *Unknown.* FaBoEE

It was an hill placed in an open plain. The Dance of the Graces. Spenser. *Fr.* Faerie Queene, The. (Dance, The.) TrGrPo

It was an icy day. Complete Destruction. William Carlos Williams. SAmP

It was an intellectual face. A Beauty. John Ash. SCBI

It was an international rage. Royston Ellis. *Fr.* Cherry Boy, The. PeHV

It was an old, old, old, old lady. One, Two, Three. H. C. Bunner. FaPON; PoLF

It was announced in the *Daily Times*, the *New Nigerian*. Launching Our Community Developement Fund. Tanure Ojaide. HBAPE

It was another race. Panoptics. Chris Wallace-Crabbe. FaBoMA

It was April in the year Kuei-mao. The Lament of the Lady of Ch'in. Wei Chuang, *tr. fr. Chinese by* Robin D. S. Yates. SuSp

It was as if. Spring Song. Peter Fallon. CIP; PBCIP

It was as if the devil of evil had got. García Lorca. Louis Dudek. MoCV; NOBC

It was at dinner as they sat. The Laird of Wariston. *Unknown.* ESPB

It was at the very date to which we have come. An Anniversary. Thomas Hardy. OxBTC

It was awful long ago. The Anxious Farmer. Burges Johnson. BoNaP

It was beautiful as God. The White Tiger. R. S. Thomas. AngWe

It was before. *(LL)* The Term. William Carlos Williams. InvP; LiTA

It Was Beginning Winter. Theodore Roethke. *Fr.* Lost Son, The. HAP; HCAP; LiTM; NAAL-2; VGW

It was better when we were. For My Mother. Louise Glück. UnPo

It was between the night and day. Evening by the Sea. Swinburne. FaBoPP

It was boss cook's fault. He left. The Tip. Belle Waring. PBCAP

It was but a little thing. The Peace-Offering. Thomas Hardy. OxBSP

It was Captain Pierce of the *Lion* who strode the streets of London. The First Thanksgiving. Clinton Scollard. PAH

It was cold, and all they gave him to wear. Back in the States. Louis Simpson. PBCV

It was cold in that room, after the cold hours. My Grandmother Died in the Early Hours of the Morning. T. Harri Jones. AngWe

It was cold then in the cautious hours. Curtain. Lance Henson. VoR

It was dark and frosty, pain congealed into ice. Deportation. "M. B.," *tr. fr. Polish by* A. Glanz-Leyeles. TrJP

It was dark when we came home. Runaway. Linda France. NWP

It was death, and death indeed. *(LL)* There was a man of double deed. *Unknown.* CoGr; GBP; OxNR; RB

It was December. Even There. Lyn Lifshin. IHMS

It was down in old Joe's barroom. Those Gambler's Blues. *Unknown*. AS

It was Earl Haldan's daughter. Charles Kingsley. GN

It was early, early in the spring. The Croppy Boy. *Unknown*. AmFP; FaBoBa; NOIV; OxBoLi

It was early, early one mornin'. Stagolee. *Unknown*. TTY

It was early in the month of cold December. On Board the *Leicester Castle*. *Unknown*. OxBSS

It was early in the season, the fall of 'sixty-three. Michigan-I-O. *Unknown*. AmFP

It was early last December. The Drunkard and the Pig. *Unknown*. OBAL

It was early Monday morning Willie Leonard arose. Willie Leonard; or, The Lake of Cold Finn. *Unknown*. AmFP

It was early Saturday, dawn. Meat. Michael van Walleghen. NAmP90

It was early Sunday mornin. Stagolee. *Unknown*. MAT; OxBoLi; TTY

It was early Sunday morning, in the year of sixty-four. *Kearsarge* and *Alabama*. *Unknown*. PAH

It was Easter as I walked in the public gardens. 1929. W. H. Auden. OxAEP-2; SOTW

It was easy enough. Circe. Hilda Doolittle ("H. D."). PoRA

It was $8,000 with a GI loan. Floor Plans. Maxine Scates. PBCAP

It was everything to me to think well of one man. Euripides, *tr*. by Rex Warner. *Fr*. Medea. NAWM-1; OxBM

It was exactly eleven. Pawiak 1943. Jerzy Ficowski, *tr. fr. Polish* by Frank J. Corliss, Jr., *and* Grazyna Sandel. PoSu

It was far in the night and the bairnies grat. Gerry Hamill. BXAP

It was far in the sameness of the wood. The Demiurge's Laugh. Robert Frost. OxBA

It Was Fever That Made the World. Jim Powell. NIP

It was for you that the mountains shook at Sinai. *Unknown*. TrJP

It was general conflagration. (*LL*) The Devil's Thoughts. Robert Southey *and* Samuel Taylor Coleridge. CBNP; CoGr, *abr*.; FaBoCo, *abr*.; IHNG, *abr*.; OBSV; OxBoLi, *abr*.; PeLV, *abr*.

It was good for the virgin mary. Poem for Unwed Mothers. Nikki Giovanni. OBAL

It was here Jhirka. Unanswerable Questions. Reva Sharon. BTR

It was his story. It would always be his story. In Memory of the Unknown Poet, Robert Boardman Vaughn. Donald Justice. CAPP; DiPo; NoAM

It was hurry and scurry at Monmouth town. Molly Pitcher. Kate Brownlee Sherwood. PAH

It was impossible for one to read. Holy Was Demeter Walking th' Corn Furrow. Edward Sanders. PoM

It was in Abomey that I felt. Dahomey. Audre Lorde. NAAL-2

It was in and about the Martinmas time. Bonny Barbara Allan ("In Scarlet Town where I was born.") *Unknown*. AWP; BoLoP; CH; ESPB; GGP; HeIP; InPK; LiTB; NAEL-1; NoP; OxBB; TrGrPo

It was in autumn that I met. A Picture. Dora Greenwell. EBVV

It was in June the eight and thirtieth day. John Taylor. *Fr*. Sir Gregory Nonsense's News from No Place. CBNP; NOSC

It was in October, a favorite season. Elegy for a Nature Poet. Howard Nemerov. BoNaP; HoPM

It was in October the woe began. The Fire of Frendraught. *Unknown*. ESPB

It was in the city of Expert. The Oxford Girl; or, Expert Town. *Unknown*. AmFP

It was in the lovely month of May. The Troubled Soldier. *Unknown*. AS

It was in the merry month of May. The Trail to Mexico. *Unknown*. AS

It was in the month of January the hills. Month of January. Frankie Armstrong. BrRo

It was in the Spring of 1825. Noel Petty. UV

It was in winter. Steeples, spires. The Fortunate Traveller. Derek Walcott. NoAM

It was intill a pleasant time. Earl Mar's Daughter. *Unknown*. GN (Earl of Mar's Daughter, The.) CH; ESPB; ScCV

It was Ips, Gips, and Johnson, as I've heard many say. The Three Butchers. *Unknown*. PeVV

It was June, and I was twenty. When I Was Twenty. Bliss Carman. AnAmPo

It was just before the last fierce charge, two soldiers drew a-rein. The Last Fierce Charge. *Unknown*. AmFP

It was Landor who first said. "Hugh MacDiarmid." *Fr*. In Memoriam James Joyce. FaBoPV

It was last Friday at ten to four. In Daylight Strange. Alan Brownjohn. OBAP

It was last Monday morning as I have heard them say. Lancashire Lads. *Unknown*. CoMu

It was last year. Fox Glove Song. Christina Beer. PeNZ

It was late in the night when the Squire came home. The Gipsy Laddie. *Unknown*. FaBoCh; OxBoLi

It was late last night when my lord come home. The Gypsy Davy. *Unknown*. AmFP

It was late last Saturday evening. Blow the Candle Out ("It was late one Saturday evening.") *Unknown*. FaBoBa

It was late — late in the silence. The Death Mazurka. Charles Fishman. BTR

It was late, we. Man and Wife. Mitchell Goodman. VGW

It was laughing time, and the tall giraffe. Laughing Time. William Jay Smith. FaPON

It was less than two thousand we numbered. With Corse at Allatoona. Samuel H. M. Byers. PAH

It was like a cave of snow, no. Merlin. David St. John. BAP-91

It was like a church to me. The Moor. R. S. Thomas. OBWVE

It was like feasting upon air. (*LL*) Morels. William Jay Smith. BoNaP; MAT; NYBP; RFM

It was like the moment when a bird decides not to eat from your hand. Part of Eve's Discussion. Marie Howe. NAmP90

It was lonely in the zero dark, Admetus. Alcestis. Isabel Williams Verry. GoYe

It was love that built the mountains. The Work of Love. Margaret E. Sangster. BLRP

It was many and many a year ago. A Poe-'em of Passion. Charles Fletcher Lummis. BXAP

It was many and many a year ago. Andrew M'Crie. Robert Fuller Murray. FaBoCo

It was many and many a year ago. Annabel Lee. Poe. AiP; AmPP; AnAmPo; AWP; BeLS; BLPA; CH; DL; EBEvV; FaPON; HeIL; HeIP; ImPo; LiTA; MeMAP; NAAL-1; NOBA; NoP; OBCA; OBSP; OPOP; OtMeF; OxBA; PrIm; TAP; TFi; TrGrPo; WBLP

It was many and many a year ago. Samuel Brown. Phoebe Cary. OBAL

It was midnight on the ocean. *Unknown*. RoPo

It Was Miss Scarlet with the Candlestick in the Billiard Room. Bernadette Mayer. UL

It was Murupaenga who brought me here. Slave Girl's Song. *Unknown, tr. fr. Maori* by Margaret Orbell. PeNZ

It was my bridal night I remember. I Remember. Stevie Smith. BoLoP; BoWoP; FaBoWP; InPK; OxBC

It was my choice, it was no chance, Sir Thomas Wyatt. EnRePo; SiPS; SiPSBD

It was my day to study. The Field. Heather McHugh. FoLa

It was my fate to help Billy Redanz learn how to read. The Story of My Life. Liz Rosenberg. PBCAP

It was my fifth year to heaven. Christopher Robin Changes Guard with Dylan Thomas. Bill Greenwell. UV

It was my thirtieth year to heaven. Poem in October. Dylan Thomas. AngWe; EBEvV; ImPo; LiTB; MeMBP; NAEL-2; NAs; NoAM; OxAEP-2; PoA; PoRA; PrIm; RB; SoSe; UV, *st.* 1 *only*

IT was near a thicky shade. The Description of the Shepherd and His Wife. Robert Greene. NoSic

It was near evening, the room was cold. The Oath. Allen Tate. FaBoMo; LiTM; OxBA; VGW

It was nearly morning when the giant. The Reason for Skylarks. Kenneth Patchen. NaP

It was never in the planning. For Virginia Chavez. Lorna Dee Cervantes. BCF

It was night-time! God, the Father Good. What the Devil Said. James Stephens. CMoP

It was no costume jewellery I sent. With a Gift of Rings. Robert Graves. GBL

It was no place for the faithless. Walking the Marshland. Stephen Dunn. NGP

It was no vast dynastic fate. A Father's Death. John Hewitt. PNI

It was not a very formal affair but. A Chinese Banquet. Kitty Tsui. GLP

It was not death, for I stood up. Emily Dickinson. MeMAP; NAAL-1; NOBA; NoP; SAmP

It was not death to me. The Kiss of God. G. A. Studdert-Kennedy. BLRP

It was not dying: everybody died. Losses. Randall Jarrell. HCAP; LCAP; LiTM; OxBA; PoA; TAP; UnPo

It was not I who began it. Eve to Her Daughters. Judith Wright. NALW

It Was Not in the Winter. Thomas Hood. ELP, *longer vers*.

It was not in their power to stop what the rabble they designed. (*LL*) The Boyne Water. *Unknown*. FaBoEH, *abr*.; FaPoR; IIP; NOIV

It was not like your great and gracious ways. Departure. Coventry Patmore. *Fr*. Unknown Eros, The. NOBE; OBEV; OBNC

It was not long e're he perceiv'd the skies. Michael Drayton. *Fr*. Moone-Calfe, The. PoEL-2

It was not meant for human eyes. The Combat. Edwin Muir. CMoP; LiTB; Mes; MoBrPo; NOBE

It was not our duty to question but to guard. Bread and a Pension. Louis Johnson. PeNZ

It was not th' first time. Rough Time in th' Barrio. José Montoya. ETG

It was not that I lost direction. Martha Sansom. ECWP

It Was Not You. André Spire, *tr. fr. French by* Jethro Bithell. TrJP

It was October. It was the Depression. Money. What Happened. Robert Penn Warren. *Fr.* Tale of Time. LCAP

It was on a cold winter's night. When Poor Mary Came Wandering Home. *Unknown.* AS

It was on a May, on a midsummer's day. Sir Hugh; or, The Jew's Daughter. *Unknown.* AmFP; ESPB

It was on a Wednesday night, the moon was shining bright. Jesse James. *Unknown.* AS; BeLS; FaBoBe; UnPo; WiR

It was on an evning sae saft and sae clear. The Broom of Cowdenknows. *Unknown.* ESPB

It was on one Monday morning,/ All in the month of May. Lisbon. *Unknown.* AmFP

It was on one Monday morning just about one o'clock. The *Titanic. Unknown.* AmFP

It was on the seventeenth, by break of day. The Battle of Bunker Hill. *Unknown.* PAH

It was on the twenty-first day of December. Ella Speed. *Unknown.* AmFP

It was once suggested by Brecht. After Brecht. D. J. Enright. AnAn

It was one summer's morning on the fourteenth day of May. The Mower. *Unknown.* CoMu

It was one Sunday morning of June the eighth day. Henry K. Sawyer. *Unknown.* AmFP

It was only a bird call at evening, unidentified. Ornithology in a World of Flux. Robert Penn Warren. PFP

It was only a small place and they had cheered us too much. St. Aubin d'Aubigne. Paul Dehn. OBWP

It was only a tiny seed. Only a Little Thing. M. P. Handy. PoToHe

It was only important. The Moss of His Skin. Anne Sexton. CoAP; IHMS; NALW; SM

It was only two fields away from the house. In Memoriam I, Elizabeth at Twenty. Richard Weber. ErPo

It was out on the Western frontier. The Clown's Baby. "Margaret Vandegrift." VPP

It was over Target Berlin the flak shot up our plane. World War II. Edward Field. ArOW; GLP

It was perfect. He could do. Other. R. S. Thomas. AngWe

It was plain to see the sense of being a woman. The Inflammable Woman. James K. Baxter. OxBC

It was planted early. Boundary. A. L. Hendricks. PBCV

It was pleasant and delightful on one midsummer's morn. Pleasant and Delightful. *Unknown.* OBET; OxBSS

It was pneumonia. Lament of the Virtues and Verses on Account of the Death of Don Guido. Antonio Machado Ruiz, *tr. fr. Spanish by* Charles Tomlinson *and* Henry Gifford. OBVE

It was Private Blair, of the regulars, before dread El Caney. Private Blair of the Regulars. Clinton Scollard. PAH

It was proper for them, awaking in ordered houses. Apology. Anthony Cronin. CIP

It was roses, roses, all the way. The Patriot. Robert Browning. FHYEP; TrGrPo

(Patriot, The; An Old Story.) PlP

It was running down to the great Atlantic. The Stream. Lula Lowe Weeden. CDC

It was said at the/ flirting creekwater's birth. To an Imaginary Father. Wendy Rose. CDW

It was/ Saturday. All the Women in Suburbia. Kurt Nimmo. NGP

It was shattered. The Battle of Maldon. *Unknown, tr. fr. Anglo-Saxon by* Kevin Crossley-Holland. ASW; OBWP

It was six men of Hindostan. The Blind Men and the Elephant. John Godfrey Saxe. BLPA; BoTP; FaBoBe; OBCA; OTCP; PoToHe; WBLP

It was something to see that their white was different. Holiday in Reality. Wallace Stevens. OxBA

It was such a bright morning. Beautiful Sunday. "Jake Falstaff." BoNaP

It was sudden. The Sea Fog. Josephine Jacobsen. NYBP

It was summer. Summer or Its Ending. Yehuda Amichai, *tr. fr. Hebrew by* Dennis Silk. PoSu

It was summer and thoughtfully calm. Incredible Vistas. David Chaloner. VaA

It was Sunday morning, I had the *New York Times.* First Love. Sharon Olds. FYAP

It was supposed to be Arts & Crafts for a week. At the Smithville Methodist Church. Stephen Dunn. NAmP90; NGP

It was taken some time ago. This Is a Photograph of Me. Margaret Atwood. NALW; NoAM; NoP; Poetr

It was that fierce contested field when Chickamauga lay. Thomas at Chickamauga. Kate Brownlee Sherwood. PAH

It was that rainy summer night. Jamming. Everett Hoagland. Jaz

It was the arrival of the kings. The Adoration of the Magi. Christopher Pilling. OBCP

It was the beginning of me. Look at My Face, a Collage. Carolyn M. Rodgers. JB

It was the busy hour of 4. Spring Arithmetic. *Unknown.* FiBHP

It was the calm and silent night! A Christmas Hymn. Alfred Domett. GN; WGRP

It was the charming month of May. Chloe. Burns. GN

It was the cooling hour, just when the rounded. Haidée and Don Juan. Byron. *Fr.* Don Juan. OBNC

It was the curtain, softly rising and falling. The Curtain. Judith Wright. FaBoMA

It was the dead who groaned within. *(LL)* The Sleeper. Poe. AmPP; AnAmPo; LiTA; MeMAP; NAAL-1; NOBA; OxBA; PoEL-4; TAP; TrGrPo

It was the departure, the sun was risen. Farewell Voyaging World! Conrad Aiken. NYBP

It was the dingiest bird. Robin Redbreast. Stanley Kunitz. Prf

It was the eve my mother died. The Reflection. Edith M. Thomas. AmWP

It was the first gift he ever gave her. The Black Lace Fan My Mother Gave Me. Eavan Boland. BiHa

It was the frog in the well. The Marriage of the Frog and the Mouse. *Unknown.* EBEV

It was the fruit on high. Soul's Kiss. Samuel Greenberg. LiTA

It was the garden of the golden apples. The Long Garden. Patrick Kavanagh. IPY

It was the generosity of delight. Love's Anniversaries. Maurice Lindsay. OxBM

It was the hole for looking in. It All Comes Together Outside the Restroom in Hogansville. James Seay. MT

It was the hour of night, when thus the Son. Milton. *Fr.* Paradise Regained [*or* Regain'd]. EBEV; PeECV

It was the house of childhood, the house of the dark wood. The House. Alison Brackenbury. SCBI

It Was the Last of the Parades. Louis Simpson. NYBP

It Was the Lovely Moon. John Freeman. BoNaP

It was the morning of that blessed day. Petrarch, *tr. fr. Italian. Fr.* Sonnets to Laura. NAWM-1

It was the morning of the first of May. *Unknown, tr. fr. Italian by* John Addington Symonds. *Fr.* Popular Songs of Tuscany. AWP

It was the rainbow gave thee birth. The Kingfisher. W. H. Davies. AngWe; NOBE; OBEV; OBWVE

It was the schooner *Hesperus.* Wreck of the *Hesperus,* The. Longfellow. AnAmPo; BeLS; BLPA; EBEvV; EBNV; FaBoBe; GN; OBCA; OBNV; PAH; VPP; WBLP

It was the season, when through all the land. Birds of Killingworth, The (The Poet's Tale). Longfellow. *Fr.* Tales of a Wayside Inn. MeMAP; OxBA

It was the stage-driver's story, as he stood with his back to the wheelers. The Stage-Driver's Story. Bret Harte. EBNV

It was the *Stately Southerner,* that carried the Stripes and Stars. The *Stately Southerner. Unknown.* AmFP

It Was the Time. Joachim du Bellay, *tr. fr. French by* Spenser. Son

It Was the Time of Roses. Thomas Hood. *See* It Was Not in the Winter.

It was the time when, granted from the gods. Virgil, *tr. fr. by* Henry Howards, Earl of Surrey. *Fr.* Aeneid [*or* Eneados], The. NAEL-1; NAWM-1; SiPSBD

It was the time when lilies blow. Lady Clare. Tennyson. BeLS; FaPON

It was the time, when rest, soft sliding downe. Joachim du Bellay, *tr. fr. French by* Spenser. *Fr.* Visions. AWP; Son

It was the utmost of his thirst. His Thirst. Robert Wells. SCBI

It was the very noon of night: the stars above the fold. The Story of the Shepherd. *Unknown, tr. fr. Spanish.* OHIP

It was the virgin Zennora, who dwelt. John Heath-Stubbs. *Fr.* Artorius. EBEV

It was the way/ things jutted up. Everything Juts Up in Europe. Wallace Stevens. *Fr.* Greenest Continent, The. CBCK

It was the west wind caught her up, as. The Ring Of. Charles Olson. NOBA; VGW

It was the wild midnight. The Death of Leonidas. George Croly. BeLS

It was the wind that gave them life. *Unknown, tr. fr. Navajo Indian.* EaPr

It was the winter I had to get away. Men Talk. Stephen P. Dunn. NIP

It was the winter wild[e]. Hymn on the Morning of Christ's Nativity [*or* On the Morning of Christ's Nativity]. Milton. *Fr.* On the Morning of Christ's Nativity. MeLP; NAEL-1; NAs; NOBE; NOCV; NoP; OBEV; OtMeF; PoEL-3; SCGP; WGRP

It was the worst party I'd ever been to. Hurting Small Animals. Lavinia Greenlaw. NWP

It was the [or a] worthy Lord of Lorn [or Learne]. The Lord of Lorn and the False [or Fals] Steward. *Unknown*. ESPB; OxBB

It was the year the Icondic. Ballad of the Icondic. John Ciardi. OBAL

It was their duty, and they did. (*LL*) Captain Reece. W. S. Gilbert. FiBHP; GN

It was then night: the sound[e] and quiet sleep [or slepe]. Virgil, *tr. by* Henry Howard, Earl of Surrey. *Fr*. Aeneid [or Eneados], The. NAWM-1; OAEL-1; PoEL-1; SiPSBD

It was then that destiny decided to take me by the hand. Destiny. Maria Luisa Spaziani, *tr. fr. Italian by* Beverly Allen. NeIt

It was this way. Rumoresque Senum Severiorum. Argentarius, *tr. fr. Greek by* Dudley Fitts. ErPo

It was Thomas Macdonough, as gallant a sailor. The Battle of Plattsburg Bay. Clinton Scollard. PAH

It was three slim does and a ten-tined buck in the bracken lay. The Revenge of Hamish. Sidney Lanier. EBNV; PoEL-5

It was Tiny's habit. Sketches of Harlem. David Henderson. PoNe

It was too lonely for her there. The Impulse. Robert Frost. *Fr*. Hill Wife, The. ArLo; CMoP; HAP; HoPM; InPS; LiTM; NoP; RaBo

It was too long ago — that Company which we served with. To One Who Was with Me in the War. Siegfried Sassoon. NSI

It was touching when I started. Aunt Nerissa's Muffin. Wallace Irwin. FiBHP

It was upon a Cristemesse night. The Dancers of Colbek. Robert Mannyng. *Fr*. Handling Sin. PoE

It was upon a Lammas night. The Rigs o' Barley. Burns. LiTB
(Corn Rigs Are Bonnie.) ErPo; OxBS
(Song: "It was upon a Lammas night.") BoLoP
(Song.) PeLV

It was upon a Shere [or Scere] Thorsday that vre [or oure] Loverd [or Lord] aros. *Unknown*. MiEL
(Judas.) PoE

It was upon the twilight of that day. Samuel Daniel. *Fr*. Civil Wars, The. OBWP

It was water I was trying to think of all the time. Appoggiatura. Donald Jeffrey Hayes. PoBA; PoNe

It was, we thought, blue. Goodbye to the Bay of Naples. Wendy Mulford. NBrP

It was when I said. On the Road Home. Wallace Stevens. NU

It was, when scarce had rang the morning bells. An Almanack for the Year of Our Lord, 1657. Samuel Bradstreet. SCAP

It was when the words on the covers of books. The Complete Introductory Lectures on Poetry. Bernadette Mayer. UL

It was when weather was Arabian I went. Allegory of the Adolescent and the Adult. George Barker. LiTB; MeMBP

It was wild. Assassination. Don L. Lee. FF; PoBA

"It Was Wrong to Do This" Said the Angel. Stephen Crane. *Fr*. Black Riders, The. LiTA; MeMAP

It was yesterday morning. Little Old Letter. Langston Hughes. SAmP

It was you, Atthis, who said. Sappho, *tr. fr. Greek by* Mary Barnard. PeHV

It was you:/ I could have crawled. Watching Salmon Jump. Simon J. Ortiz. CDW; ETG

It was you who understood; it is we who change. (*LL*) The Emancipators. Randall Jarrell. PoA

"It was your fault! It was your fault!" cried the Peacock. The Peacock and the Snake. John Heath-Stubbs. PRA

It was your mother wanted you. The Son. R. S. Thomas. NAs

It was your resting-place. (*LL*) Ah, Are You Digging on My Grave? Thomas Hardy. DL; MoAB; MoBrPo; NAEL-2; OBD; TEP

It was your smell that, for a day after, I carried with me. The Anniversary. William Dickey. GOYP

It Was Your Song. Steve Kowit. UL

It was your vision of the pilot. Adrienne Rich. *Fr*. Twenty-one Love Poems. GLP

It wasn't by chance that Marpessa preferred Idas over Apollo. Marpessa's Choice. Yannis Ritsos, *tr. fr. Greek by* Edmund Keeley. AnAn

It wasn't easy, inventing the wheel. Poem for Men Only. Tony Hoagland. NAmP90

It wasn't Ernest; it wasn't Scott. Song for the Squeeze-Box. Theodore Roethke. NBLV

It wasn't hysterical it was enigmatic. Hotel Tropicana. Michael Burkard. BAP-89

It wasn't in my time, or so I suppose. Responses to Montale. Brian Turner. PeNZ

It wasn't our battalion, but we lay alongside it. Sergeant-Major Money. Robert Graves. OBWP

It wasn't supposed to be this way. Pushing Forty. Alan Catlin. NGP

It wasn't that he loved her. No, that wasn't it at all. He was. Air. Cyn Zarco. BCF

It wasn't that she didn't recognize him in the light from the hearth. Penelope's Despair. Yannis Ritsos, *tr. fr. Greek by* Edmund Keeley. AnAn

It wasn't the daffodils so much. Daffodils. Michael Heffernan. SM

It wasn't the money or their silly. Delilah. Ellen Bryant Voigt. CrSp

It wastes us all, Jed, you. For Jed. X. J. Kennedy. PFL

It well may be. I do not think I would. (*LL*) Love is not all; it is not meat nor drink. Edna St. Vincent Millay. CMoP; HAP; HeIL; HeIP; MeMAP; NoAM; OxBA; TAP

It went and cut a pigeon's wing! (*LL*) Muddled Metaphors. Tom Hood.

It went many years. The Lockless Door. Robert Frost. NOBA

It were best to sleep. November 1956. Evan Jones. PBCV

It were my soul's desire. The Soul's Desire. *Unknown*, *tr. fr. Irish by* Eleanor Hull. TIRV

It wes in November an' aw nivor will forget. The Oakey Street Evictions. Thomas Armstrong. OBET

It wes upon a Shere [or Scere] Thorsday that ure [or oure] Louerd [or Lord] aros. *Unknown*. MiEL
(Judas Sells His Lord.) MeEL

It will be all the same in a hundred years. In a Hundred Years. *At. to* Elizabeth Doten. BLPA

It will be looked for, book[e], when some but see. To My Book. Ben Jonson. BeJo; FaBoVe; NAEL-1; SeCV-1

It will be strange. When the Vacation Is Over for Good. Mark Strand. NYBP

It will live it will grow it will last. (*LL*) Letter to Ellen Conroy Kennedy. Edouard J. Maunick. NegPo

It will look as though I am flying into myself. (*LL*) Death. William Knott. PBCAP

It will mean me. (*LL*) Everybody but Me. Margaret Goss Burroughs. BlSi

It will not always be like this. A Day in Autumn. R. S. Thomas. BoNaP

It will not be able to help us. (*LL*) The New Poem. Charles Wright. CAPP; HCAP

It will not be in our time. (*LL*) May-June, 1940. Robinson Jeffers. LiTA; MoAB; MoAmPo

It will not be long, love, till our wedding day. (*LL*) She Moved through the Fair. Padraic Colum. BIrV; InvP; NOIV

It will not hurt me when I am old. (*LL*) Moonlight. Sara Teasdale. GOYP; VGW

It will not hurt me when I am old. Moonlight. Sara Teasdale. GOYP; VGW

It will not resemble the sea. The New Poem. Charles Wright. CAPP; HCAP

It will not shine again. Emily Brontë. NOBVV

It will rain tonight. New Life. Joseph E. Kariuki. TTY

It will slide to the floor in a blue heap. (*LL*) Waiting. Yevgeny Yevtushenko. UnAS

It would be/ a mercy if. Phone Call to Rutherford. Paul Blackburn. PoM

It would be nice to simply melt away. Leavings. Gerard Benson. BXAP

It would be ordinary enough to live. After Christopher Wood. John James. NBrP; VaA

It would be painful to interfere. Memo. Charles G. Ballard. VoR

It would be very pleasant to die with a wolf woman. Yoldugu, *tr. fr. Tlingit Indian by* James Koller. STP

It would be wrong for us. It is not right. Sappho, *tr. fr. Greek by* Willis Barnstone. BoWoP

It would have been better that I slept. Akazome Emon, *tr. fr. Japanese by* Kenneth Rexroth *and* Ikuko Atsumi. WPJ

It would have been August, I think. Mississippi 1955 Confessional. Terry Hummer. NAmP90

It would never be morning, always evening. Memory of Brother Michael. Patrick Kavanagh. MoAB

It wouldn't be a good idea. Wendy Cope. FaBoBl

It wouldn't be so bad if he. In Extremis. Margaret Fishback. FiBHP

It wouldn't have lasted long anyway. In the Evening. C. P. Cavafy, *tr. fr. Greek by* Edmund Keeley *and* Philip Sherrard. AnAn

It wound through strange scarred hills, down cañons lone. The Old Santa Fe Trail. Richard Burton. PAH

It woz in April nineteen eighty-wan. Great Insohreckshan, Di. Linton Kwesi Johnson. FaBoPV

It wuz one day, I believe in May, when old Si Hubbard to me did say. Si Hubbard. *Unknown*. AS

Ita. Yolanda Ulloa, *tr. fr. Spanish by* Margaret Randall. AIW

Italia, Io Ti Saluto. Christina Rossetti. CoGr; OBTV; WPE

Italia! Oh Italia! thou who hast. Italy. Vincenzo da Filicaia, *tr. fr. Italian by* Byron. AWP

It's quiet in Hell just now, it's very tame. Lament of an Idle Demon. R. P. Lister. FiBHP; NOBL

It's Quiz Night at the Chamberlain Arms and Frank. Fifty Years On. Janet Fisher. NWP

Its radiance bursts forth in summer's bright light. Sunflower. Kao Ch'i, *tr. fr. Chinese* by Irving Y. Lo. SuSp

It's Raining. Guillaume Apollinaire, *tr. fr. French*. SOTW, *tr. by* Kenneth Koch; TTTS, *tr. by* Kenneth Koch

It's Raining. Lucha Corpi, *tr. fr. Spanish* by Catherine Rodriguez-Nieto. AfAz

It's raining, it's pouring. *Unknown*. ISE; OxNR; RoPo

It's raining, it's raining. *Unknown*. OxNR

It's raining today, a dark rain. Birthday. P. J. Kavanagh. NAs

Its rancid saliva can't fill up a shell. On a Snail. Su Shih, *tr. by* Irving Y. Lo. *Fr.* Two Poems on Insect Painting by Candidate Yin. SuSp

It's really something, the onion. Onion. Wislawa Szymborska, *tr. fr. Polish* by Grazyna Drabik *and* Sharon Olds. PoSu

Its retributions work like clockwork. Under the Eyes. Tom Paulin. CIP; PNI

It's right to call you son. That cursing alcoholic. Letter to an Absent Son. Madeline DeFrees. NMM

It's run an' jump an' hop an' skip. Owdham Footbo. Ammon Wrigley. FaBoVe

It's sad/ To be the Mayor of Jerusalem. Mayor. Yehuda Amichai, *tr. fr. Hebrew* by Assia Gutmann. PoSu

It's said you take a long time over a bath. Lucilius, *tr. fr. Greek* by Peter Porter. GrAn

It's Saturday afternoon at the edge of the world. Laguna Blues. Charles Wright. PRA

It's Saturday night, and I'm feeling reckless. Saturday Night. A. P. Herbert. NBLV

Its savage eyes, at whom do they glare? On a Toad. Su Shih, *tr. by* Irving Y. Lo. *Fr.* Two Poems on Insect Painting by Candidate Yin. SuSp

Its savage hammering. *(LL)* The Blood of one entire class . . . Duo Duo. SpMi

It's seldom wise to generalize. Homage to Texas. Robert Graves. LiTB

Its shadow upon life enough for thee. *(LL)* Aspecta Medusa. Dante Gabriel Rossetti. OxBSP

It's simple but I find it hard to explain. A Terminal Moraine. James Fenton. SCBI

It's Simply Great. Sidney Warren Mase. PoToHe

Its skirt of rain and wind and snow. Second Rondeau. Johann Nikolaus Götz, *tr. fr. German* by George C. Schoolfield. GePo

Its smile is stoned at our feet. *(LL)* Beyond Melody. Nathan Alterman. MHP

It's smoke, the star, a broom. Smoke. Rubén Bonitaz Nuño, *tr. fr. Spanish* by John Frederick Nims. STV

It's/ snowing defective. Self-Pity Is a Kind of Lying, Too. James Schuyler. PoM

It's snowing hard enough that the taxis aren't running. The Rites of Manhood. Alden Nowlan. RaBo

It's snowing this afternoon and there are no. Absences. Donald Justice. ArNa

It's so cold in here I can't do anything. Warming Up. Anne Waldman. PRA

It's so dark now. The Tip. Albert Goldbarth. HCAP

It's so good to talk with somebody. He Runs into an Old Acquaintance. Alden Nowlan. GOYP

It's Something Our Family Has Always Done. Wing Tek Lum. BCF

It's Spring. Eduard Friedrich Mörike. ArNa

It's spring and Jake toddles to the garden. Jake Addresses the World from the Garden. Jack Myers. NAmP90

It's Spring Returning, It's Spring and Love. *Unknown*. HAP

It's spring; the City, wrapped. To His Chi Mistress. George Starbuck. NYBP

It's starting to break my sleep. Kicking against the Walls. Katrina Porteous. NWP

It's step her to your weev'ly wheat. Weevily Wheat. *Unknown*. AS

It's still a good idea. To Friends Who Have Also Considered Suicide. Phyllis Webb. NOBC

It's still dark, my chest is hollow, and aches. Emergency. Jack Skelley. UTF

It's still inside me. My Mother's Death. Judith Hemschemeyer. MDDM

It's strange what the past brings back. Driving through Tennessee. Charles Wright. CAPP

Its strength, and struck. *(LL)* Eight o'Clock. A. E. Housman. CMoP; InPK; MoAB; MoBrPo; MoP; NoAM; NoP; OxBSP; PoE; Poetr; SoSe; TrGrPo

It's such a/ Bore. Ennui. Langston Hughes. OBAL; OBCA

It's such a little thing to weep. Emily Dickinson. RB (Life's Trades.) AnAmPo

It's such a static reference; looking. Epistrophe. Amiri Baraka. PoNe

It's summer now, or nearly. Out at the back door, my sister. Silent Night. Peter McDonald. PWE

Its surface glittering, the dawn, glancing from its glaze, oblique, relentless, unadorned. *(LL)* From My Window. C. K. Williams. CAPP; PRA; SV

Its teeth worked doubtfully. The Key. John Ormond. AngWe

It's ten. Evening. The room is in half light. My Sister. Alfonsina Storni, *tr. fr. Spanish* by Aliki *and* Willis Barnstone. BoWoP

It's that we're identical. Peter Philpott. VaA

It's the anarchy of poverty. The Poor. William Carlos Williams. MoAB; MoAmPo; NoP; PPP

It's the broken phrases, the fury inside him. Art Pepper. Edward Hirsch. NAmP90

It's the day of the penumbral eclipse and I'm driving. Ellington Indigos. Aleda Shirley. Jaz

It's the Enobarbus Complex. *Unknown, tr. fr. Greek* by Peter Porter. GrAn

It's the first night, I suppose. A First Night. Peter Kane Dufault. DiPo

It's the fourteenth of August, and I'm too hot. Too Much Heat, Too Much Work. Tu Fu. ArNa

It's the long road to Guinea. Guinea. Jacques Roumain, *tr. fr. French* by Langston Hughes. NegPo; TTY

It's the old rule that drunks have to argue. The New Rule. Jalal al-Din Rumi, *tr. fr. Persian* by Coleman Barks. RaBo

It's the poor first light of morning. The Obscure. Norman Dubie. NoAM

It's the sanest of vessels. *(LL)* A Mat to Weave. Tchicaya U Tam'si. NegPo

It's the stillness that fills me with peace. *(LL)* The Spell of the Yukon. Robert W. Service. BLPA; BLPL; FaBoBe

It's the sweeper with the torpid broom. Waiting for the Storm. Gerald Mangan. PWE

It's the Syme the Whole World Over. *Unknown*. AS

It's the Syme the Wide World Over. *Unknown*. *See* She was just a parson's daughter.

It's the willingness to sing. Mrs. Schneider in Church. Kathleen Norris. CrSp

It's the world's longest car, I swear. Longmobile. Shel Silverstein. AiP

It's there/ in the hole of the sea. The Hole in the Sea. Marvin Bell. NYBP

It's there you'll see confectioners with sugar sticks and dainties. Galway Races. *Unknown*. OxBoLi

It's this crazy weather we've been having. Crazy Weather. John Ashbery. AnAn; PoE

It's those helmets we remember. Trainride, Vienna — Bonn. Margaret Atwood. LCAP

"It's three No Trumps," the soldier said. It's Three No Trumps. Guy Innes. FiBHP

("It's Three No Trumps," the Soldier Said.) UV

It's through my mouth they'll say it. *(LL)* Canto I. Vincente Huidobro. EaPr

It's thus he does it of a winter night. *(LL)* An Old Man's Winter Night. Robert Frost. AWP; HAP; MoAB; MoAmPo; NAAL-2; NoAM; OxBA; VGW

It's time for wild cooking. Last Supper. Matthew Sweeney. IB

It's time, I believe. *Unknown*. ISE

It's time I told you why. The Hindoo: He Doesn't Hurt a Fly or a Spider Either. A. K. Ramanujan. OxBC

It's time little people were going to bed! *(LL)* Bed-time. Thomas Hood. BoTP

It's time to get back to the car. Already, at half-past three. Sunday in Great Tew. Peter McDonald. PNI

It's time to get him away. *(LL)* The Hunt Is Up. *Unknown*. CH; FaBoEH; GBP

It's time to make love. Douse the glim. Conrad Aiken. NBLV; PeLi (Limerick: "It's time to make love. Douse the glim.") FiBHP; PeLV (Limerick: "It's time to make love. Douse the glim.") FaBoNo

It's too dark to see black. A Mother Speaks: The Algiers Motel Incident, Detroit. Michael S. Harper. AmPA; BPo; NBV

"It's too easy." Malaria. Paolo Ruffilli, *tr. fr. Italian* by Felix Stefanile. NeIt

It's too good for them. Sex and the Over Forties. Peter Porter. CBLP

Its train with the posthumous scales a-glitter. *(LL)* Smoke. Rubén Bonitaz Nuño. STV

It's true I make books, but not often. Why I Never Answered Your Letter. Nancy Willard. CrSp

It's true I will die. So what do I care. Nicarchus of Alexandria, *tr. fr. Greek* by Sam Hamill. InMo

Its trunk as of dead silver cast. The Felled Plane Tree. Anna Hajnal, *tr. fr. Hungarian by* William Jay Smith. BoWoP

It's 12:21 in New York a Thursday. In Blue. D. C. Berry. BXAP

It's twenty years ago and more. In Moncur Street. Dorothy Hewett. NOBAu

It's two hours since you went to the river. Hours Ago, 1973. Thomas McCarthy. IB

It's under-sized; for God's sake throw it back! (*LL*) Farewell to New Zealand. Wynford Vaughan-Thomas. NOBL; OBTV

It's up the spout and Charley Wag. The Moral. W. E. Henley. OxAEP-2

It's Useless. Gloria Fuertes, *tr. fr. Spanish by* Philip Levine. AnAn

It's very hard to be polite. Under the Table Manners. *Unknown.* CRH

Its wednesday night baby. Master Charge Blues. Nikki Giovanni. OBAL

It's when things seem worst that you mustn't quit. (*LL*) Don't Quit. *Unknown.* BLPA

Its wingèd lion stands up straight to hide. Venice. Howard Moss. MoAB

It's wise to make the most. *Unknown, tr. fr. Greek by* Sam Hamill. InMo

It's wonderful how I jog. Animals Are Passing from Our Lives. Philip Levine. CAPP; CoAP; NOBA; Poetr; RaBo; SM; TAP

Its wrinkled foreskin, twisting open, opens. Morning Glory. Howard Moss. DiPo

It's you, it's you. Many Years. Bei Dao, *tr. fr. Chinese by* Donald Finkel *with* Chen Xueliang. SpMi

Its youth. The sea grows old in it. (*LL*) The Fish. Marianne Moore. AmPP; FaBoWP; MeMAP; MoAB; MoAmPo; MoP; NAAL-2; NoAM; OxBA; Poetr

Itself the more intact. (*LL*) Chiefly to Mind Appears. C. Day Lewis. MoAB; MoBrPo

Itself, until, at last, the cry concerns no one at all. (*LL*) The Course of a Particular. Wallace Stevens. HCAP

ITT Alcan Kaiser. I Fight Back. Lillian Allen. PBCV

Itt [*or* It] rely is ridikkelus. Bobby's First Poem. Norman Gale. FiBHP; MoShBr

Itum Paradisum all clothed in green. *Unknown.* GBP

Itylus. Swinburne. ChTr; EBVVPR; UV, *Sts.* I *and* II *only*

Ivanhoe, *sels.* Sir Walter Scott.
    Rebecca's Hymn. EnRP
    (When Israel, of the Lord Beloved.) ChIV-1

I've a Shooting Box In Scotland, *sels.* Cole Porter. Collections. CBCK

I've always been going somewhere — Vancouver. The Madwoman on the Train. Alfred W. Purdy. NoAM

I've always known that old age would arrive. Feeling Old Age. Liu Tsung-yüan, *tr. fr. Chinese by* Jan W. Walls. SuSp

I've always liked this lonely hill. The Infinite. Giacomo Leopardi, *tr. fr. Italian by* William Jay Smith. ArNa

I've always tried to be good. Goodness. Benny Andersen, *tr. fr. Danish. TSaS, tr. by* Alexander Taylor

I've always wanted one. Wanting a Mummy. Sandra McPherson. AmPA; LCAP

I've an ingle, shady ingle, near a dusky bosky dingle. Midsummer Jingle. Newman Levy. BoNaP

I've been a moonshiner for seventeen long years. Kentucky Moonshiner. *Unknown.* AS; OBAL

I've been after the exotic. The Ethnic Life. Daniel Halpern. AmPA

I've been cherishing. A Room with a View. Noël Coward. PeLV

I've been digging a hole in sunlight. Four Seasons of His Discontent. Roger Weingarten. NAmP90

I've been driving for hours. Looking for a Rest Area. Stephen Dunn. AmPA

I've been giving a lot of thought. Sea Things. Gwendolyn MacEwen. FaBoWP

I've been going around everywhere without any skin. Josephine Miles. IHMS

I've been in jail from slander. The Rocky Mountains. *Unknown.* AmFP

I've been in love for long. In Love for Long. Edwin Muir. ArLo; BoLoP; LiTM; MeMBP; MoBrPo

I've been in love. Who hasn't? I went out and got drunk. Philodemus, *tr. fr. Greek by* Barbara Hughes Fowler. *Fr.* Epigrams. HePo

I've been list'nin' to them lawyers. The Lawyers' Ways. Paul Laurence Dunbar. AnAmPo

I've been restless today. Haircut. Sue May. DT

I've been scarred and battered. Langston Hughes. *See* I been scarred and battered.

I've been sweating again, a symptom. Storms. Dean Young. NAmP90

I've Been to a Marvelous Party. Noël Coward. NBLV

I've been to Palestine. John Brown. Vachel Lindsay. *Fr.* Booker Washington Trilogy, The. MoAmPo

I've been trying for hours to figure out who I was reminded of. Combat. C. K. Williams. AnAn

I've been trying to fashion a wifely ideal. A Plea for Trigamy. Sir Owen Seaman. NOBL; PeLV

I've been watchin' of 'em, parson. Deacon Jones' Grievance. Paul Laurence Dunbar. AAP

I've bicycled out. Coyotes. Robert Vasquez. AfAz

I've brought you nuts and hops. October. Christina Rossetti. BoTP

I've built a castle in the sand. Castles in the Sand. Dorothy Baker. BoTP

I've changed stations: autumn remained behind and my bags. Leaf. Rade Drainac, *tr. fr. Serbo-Croatian by* Charles Simic. HSix

I've combed out my beard and I've found. Pauline Phillips. PeLi

I've come back. Past Love. Anne Keiter. GOYP

I've come back all skin and bone. The Diggins-Oh. *Unknown.* NOBAu

I've come back many times today. Gift from Kenya. May Miller. BlSi

I've come back to my city. These are my own old tears. Leningrad. Osip Mandelstam, *tr. fr. Russian by* W. S. Merwin *and* Clarence Brown. FaBoPV

I've come by the May-tree all times o' the year. The May Tree. William Barnes. LiTB

I've come this far to freedom and I won't turn back. Midway. Naomi Long Madgett. BlSi; BPo; PoNe

I've come to close your door, my handsome, my darling. Frances Bellerby. FaBoWP

I've come to give you fruit from out my orchard. The Crossed Apple. Louise Bogan. HeIP; NALW

I've come to see a stranger. Sunday Afternoon at the State Hospital. Marilyn J. Boe. LoHo

I've come to see Miss Jennian Jones. Miss Jennian Jones. *Unknown.* AmFP

I've decided to return to the emperor's court. The Return of the Proconsul. Zbigniew Herbert, *tr. fr. Polish by* Czeslaw Milosz. FaBoPV; PoSu

I've discovered a way to stay friends forever. Friendship. Shel Silverstein. NTCP

I've dispatch'd, my dear madam, this scrap of a letter. Sent to a Patient, with the Present of a Couple of Ducks. Edward Jenner. FaBoUs

I've done my bits of mindless aggro too. Tony Harrison. FaBoVe

I've dreamed of my first love, the subtle serpent. (*LL*) In Nature There Is neither Right nor Left nor Wrong. Randall Jarrell. CBLP; OxBC

I've dropped me swag in many camps. The Search. Charles Shaw. NOBAu

I've dug up all my garden. Sowing Seeds. Ursula Cornwall. BoTP

I've ever lost were. For Both of Us at Fisk. Sharon Scott. JB

I've found out why, that day, that suicide. John Berryman. PoE

I've gone and done. (*LL*) Hay for the Horses. Gary Snyder. CAPP; GrPl; NaP; TRP

I've got a bow and arrow. Robin Hood. Rachel MacAndrew. BoTP

I've got a different system. Wild Women Blues. Ida Cox. VBLP

I've Got a Home in That Rock. Raymond R. Patterson. FF; PoBA; PoNe

"I've got a lad and he's double double-jointed." *Unknown.* ISE

I've got a lovely home. Best of All. J. M. Westrup. BoTP

I've got a mule and her name is Sal. The Erie Canal. William S. Allen. AS
    (Low Bridge, Everybody Down.) SWP shorter

I've Got a New Book from My Grandfather Hyde. Leroy F. Jackson. FaPON

I've got a pony. The Pony. Rachel MacAndrew. BoTP

I've got a rocket. *Unknown.* RoPo

I've got a silk-worm. Theobald James. J. B. Morton. *Fr.* When We Were Very Silly. FaBoPa

I've Got No Use for the Women. *Unknown.* AmFP

I've Got the Giggles Today. A. P. Herbert. FiBHP

I've Gotten a Rock, I've Gotten a Reel. Susanna Blamire. ECWP

I've had enough. The Bridge Poem. Kate Rushin. GLP

I've Had Many an Aching Pain. John Clare. NOBVV

I've had my share of pastime, and I've done my share of toil. Adam Lindsay Gordon. *Fr.* Sick Stockrider, The. OtMeF

I've had tangled feelings about. Breakthrough. Carolyn M. Rodgers. BPo

I've Had the Wagon Hauled Out. Shih Ching, *tr. fr. Chinese by* C. H. Wang. SuSp

I've heard all about musicians. Saxophonetyx. Cyn Zarco. UL

I've heard it said that Sir Barnabas Beer. Endurance Test. Dacre Balsdon. FiBHP

I've heard that holy madness is a state. Buzzard. George Garrett. MT

I've heard the case for clarity. I know. Giant Killer. George Garrett. CRP

I've heard them lilting at loom and belting. C. Day Lewis. HAP; NoAM; OBMV

I've heard them [*or* the] lilting at our yewe [*or* yowe]-milking [*or* the ewe-milking]. The Flowers of the Forest. Jane (*or* Jean) Elliot. CH; CoGr; ECWP; FaBoCh; FaBoRV; OxBS; ScCV; SCGP; WPE
    (Lament for Flodden, The.) CoGr; GTBS; GTBS-P; OBEV

J

J. A. G. Julia Ward Howe. PAH

J. Alfred Prufrock to. Said. George Starbuck. OBAL

J. C. Lawson/ my great-grandfather. Town History, 1917. David Huddle. PBCAP

J haf latly, bing tw bysy. Sir Richard's Confession. Richard William. AngWe

J. J. Walter de la Mare. FaBoNo

J. M. W. Turner on Switzerland. Consolations of Art. Roy Fuller. OxBC

J. S. Mill. E. C. Bentley. See John Stuart Mill.

J. V. Cunningham Gets Hung Up on a Dirty, of All Things, Joke. Henry Taylor. BXAP

Ja-Nez — burro with the long ears. Burro with the Long Ears. Unknown, tr. fr. Navajo Indian by Hilda Faunce Wetherill. FaPON

Jabberwocky. "Lewis Carroll." Fr. Through the Looking-Glass. CBNP; ClHu; CoGr; EBEV; EBEvV; EBVV; FaBoBe; FaBoCo; FaBoNo; FaBV; FaPON; FF; FiBHP; GoJo; HeIP; HoPM; ImPo; InPK; InPS; LiTB; NAEL-2; NBLV; NoAM; NOBE; NOBL; NOBVV; NoP; NTCP; OAEL-2; OBSP; OHCV; OPOP; OxAEP-2; OxBChV; PeLV; PeVV; Poetr; PoRA; PPP; RB; TEP; TFi; TRP; TTTS; UV

Jacaranda. Roo Borson. NOBC

Jack. Louis Golding. TrJP

Jack. Charles Henry Ross. OxBChV; Spl

Jack, Afterwards. Philip Dacey. SM

Jack and Dinah Want Freedom. Unknown. BPo

Jack and Gill. Mother Goose. See Jack and Gill [or Jill] went up the hill.

Jack and Gill [or Jill] went up the hill. Mother Goose. CBNP; FaBoBe; OxBoLi; OxNR
  (Jack and Gill.) PeLV

Jack and Gye. Unknown. OxNR

Jack and His Fiddle. Mother Goose. See Jacky, come give me thy fiddle.

Jack and Jill. A. E. Housman. UV

Jack and Jill. Charles Battell Loomis. BXAP

Jack and Jill. Charles Powell. BXAP

Jack and Jill — as Kipling Might Have Written It. Anthony C. Deane. FaBoPa

Jack and Jill went up the hill/ To fetch some heavy water. Paul Dehn. Fr. Rhymes for a Modern Nursery. FiBHP; ReMoGo

Jack and Joan. Thomas Campion. See Jack and Joan they think no ill.

Jack and Joan they think no ill. Thomas Campion. AAS
  (Jack and Joan.) FaBoCh; FaPoR; PlP

Jack and Roger. At. to Benjamin Franklin. ChTr; FaBoEE; NOBL

Jack Barrett went to Quetta. The Story of Uriah. Kipling. NOBVV; PeVV; SCV

Jack be nimble. Mother Goose. OxNR; ReMoGo

Jack Creamer. James Jeffrey Roche. PAH

Jack, eating rotten cheese, did say. Jack and Roger. At. to Benjamin Franklin. ChTr; FaBoEE; NOBL
  (Impromptu.) NOBL
  (Sampson Imitated.) FaBoEE

Jack Ellyat Heard the Guns. Stephen Vincent Benét. Fr. John Brown's Body. PoLF

"Jack fell as he'd have wished," the Mother said. The Hero. Siegfried Sassoon. OBWP

Jack finds his wife a perfect beauty. (LL) The Double Transformation. Goldsmith. OBNV

Jack Frenchman's Defeat. Congreve. APAS

Jack Frenchman's Lamentation. Congreve. See Ye Commons and Peers.

Jack Frost. Cecily E. Pike. BoTP

Jack Frost. "Gabriel Setoun." BoTP

Jack Frost. Celia Laighton Thaxter. OBCA

Jack Frost in the Garden. John P. Smeeton. BoTP

Jack Frost was in the garden. Jack Frost in the Garden. John P. Smeeton. BoTP

Jack Giantkiller took and struck. Driving Cross-Country. X. J. Kennedy. TwCP

Jack Haggerty. Unknown. AmFP

Jack Hall. Unknown. OBET

Jack hammer! brain chiseller! come out! Men at Work. Richard Tipping. NOBAu

Jack, I never knew you. Sanity. Betty Wisoff. BTR

Jack in the Pulpit. Unknown. OxNR

Jack, Jack,/ Sat on a tack. Unknown. RoPo

Jack Jelf. Unknown. ReMoGo

Jack Jingle. Unknown. ReMoGo

Jack Monroe. Unknown. AmFP

Jack o' Diamonds, shorter vers. Unknown. AmFP

Jack o' the Inkpot. Algernon Blackwood. BoTP

Jack Robinson. Unknown. OBET

Jack scrubs the smell of hemp and tar from his hands. Traveling through Ports That Begin with "M." Christy Sheffield Sanford. UL

Jack Sprat could eat no fat. Mother Goose. FaBoBe; OxNR; ReMoGo

Jack Sprat's Cat ("Jack Sprat/ Had a cat.") Unknown. OxNR

Jack Steeplejack. Tall Story for Fred Dibnah. Geoffrey Summerfield. OTCP

Jack Tar. Emile Jacot. BoTP

Jack Tar. Unknown. OxBSS

Jack the Giant Queller; an Antique History. Henry Brooke. NOEC
  Sels.
  "Arise, arise, arise!"
  "For often my mammy has told."

Jack the Jolly Tar. Unknown. AmFP

Jack the Piper. Unknown. See As I was going up the hill.

Jack the Ripper. Allan M. Laing. FiBHP

Jackdaw of Rheims, The. Unknown. Fr. Ingoldsby Legends, The. EBNV; FaBoCo; OBNV; OBSP; VPP

Jackdaw sat on the Cardinal's chair, The. The Jackdaw of Rheims. Unknown. Fr. Ingoldsby Legends, The. EBNV; FaBoCo; OBNV; OBSP; VPP

Jackey Jackey gallops on a horse like a swallow. A Bushranger. Kenneth Slessor. CBAP; NOBAu

Jackfruit, The. Ho Xuan Huong, tr. fr. Vietnamese by Nguyen Ngoc Bich. PBWP; VBLP

Jackie. King D. Kuka. VoR

Jackie Faa. Unknown. See Gypsies [or Gipsies] they came to my Lord Cassilis' yett [or gate], The.

Jackie Kennedy Onassis, working at Woolworth's. Dream. Harold Witt. SM

Jackie Tar. Unknown. OxBSS

Jackie's gone a-sailing with trouble on his mind. Jack Monroe. Unknown. AmFP

Jackknife swandive gainer twist. Elegy for a Diver. Peter Meinke. Poetsp

Jacklight. Louise Erdrich. HATNAP; WeW

Jack's Postcards. Ken Smith. NBrP

Jackson. Unknown. AS

Jackson at New Orleans. Wallace Rice. PAH

Jackson Hotel. Lynda Hull. UTF

Jackson is on sea, Jackson is on shore. Jackson. Unknown. AS

Jackson Pollock had a quaint. Squeeze Play. Phyllis McGinley. Fr. Spectator's Guide to Contemporary Art. FaBoEE; OBSV

Jacky, come give me thy fiddle. Mother Goose. OxNR
  (Jack and His Fiddle.) ReMoGo

Jacob. Phoebe Cary. OBAL

Jacob. George Garrett. CRP

Jacob. Ruth Gilbert. Fr. Leah. PeNZ

Jacob. Delmore Schwartz. ChIV-1

Jacob and Esau. Else Lasker-Schüler, tr. fr. German by Rosemarie Waldrop. BoWoP

Jacob Epstein. Unknown. FaBoCo

Jacob Godbey. Edgar Lee Masters. Fr. Spoon River Anthology. LiTA

Jacob, hear! Jacob's Destiny. Richard Beer-Hofmann, tr. fr. German by Ida Bension Wynn. Fr. Jacob's Dream. TrJP

Jacob ("Jacob: a bull among his herd.") Else Lasker-Schüler, tr. by Rosemarie Waldrop. BoWoP

Jacob Wrestling with the Angel. Jones Very. ChIV-1

Jacobean. Clifton Fadiman. FiBHP

Jacobite Scot in Satire on England's Unparalleled Loss, A. Unknown. APAS

Jacobite Toast. John Byrom. FaBoCo; FaBoEE; OtMeF

Jacobite's Epitaph, A. Macaulay. FaBoEH; FaPoR; NOBE; OBEV; OBNC

Jacob's Destiny. Richard Beer-Hofmann, tr. fr. German by Ida Bension Wynn. Fr. Jacob's Dream. TrJP

Jacob's Dream, sels. Richard Beer-Hofmann, tr. fr. German by Ida Bension Wynn.
  Jacob's Destiny. TrJP

Jacob's Ladder, The. Denise Levertov. AmPP; CAPP; ChIV-1; PoM; PPP

Jacob's Pillow, and Pillar. Henry Vaughan. ChIV-1

Jacob's Well. Unknown. OBET

Jade. Janice Mirikitani. NGP

Jade dews deeply wilt and wound the maple woods. Tu Fu, tr. by Wu-chi Liu. Fr. Autumn Thoughts. SuSp

Jade faces of the girls on Yueh Stream, The. The Girls of Yueh. Li Po, tr. fr. Chinese by Robert Payne. TAL

Jade Flower Palace. Tu Fu, tr. fr. Chinese by Kenneth Rexroth. NaP

Jade, or the Medea within Us. Patrizia Vicinelli, *tr. fr. Italian by* Franco Beltramettii *and* Tom Raworth. VBLP

Jade Steps Plaint. Hsieh T'iao, *tr. fr. Chinese by* Ronald C. Miao. SuSp

Jade turns dull, flowers wilt. Farewell to Li. Nieh Sheng-ch'iung, *tr. fr. Chinese by* Kenneth Rexroth *and* Ling Chung. WPC

Jaffar. Leigh Hunt. BeLS

Jagged head. King & Queen. John Montague. PBCIP

Jaguar, The. Ted Hughes. LiTM

Jaguar, The. Dick King-Smith. OBAP

Jaguar lies secretly in trees, The. The Jaguar. Dick King-Smith. OBAP

Jah Son/ Another Way. Kendel Hippolyte. PBCV

Jahr der Seele, Das, *sels.* Stefan George, *tr. fr. German by* Daisy Broicher. "No way too long — no path too steep." AWP

Jailbird. Vernon Scannell. OxBC

Jain Bird Hospital in Delhi, The. William Meredith. VCAP

Jain dusent ware enny. Spelling It Out. Robert Maitre. FaBoBl

Jair the son of Manasseh went and seized the encampments. Place Names. Thomas Merton. ChIV-1

Jake Addresses the World from the Garden. Jack Myers. NAmP90

Jake Balokowsky, my biographer. Posterity. Philip Larkin. OxBC

Jake's store past Pindaric mountain. Purchase of a Blue, Green, or Orange Ode. Josephine Miles. NoP

Jake's Wharf. Philip Booth. NYBP

Jalan Thamrin in Denpasar. Walking down Jalan Thamrin. R. F. Brissenden. CBAP

Jalapeña Gypsies. Jay Wright. NBV

Jam Fish, The. Edward Abbott Parry. OxBChV

Jam on Gerry's Rock, The. *Unknown.* AmFP; AS; FaBoBa

Jam Trap, The. Charles Tomlinson. MoBrPo

Jamaica. Louis Simpson. PBCV

Jamaica, a Poem in Three Parts, Written in That Island in the Year 1776, *sels. Unknown.*
"And can the muse reflect her tear-stain'd eye." PBCV

Jamaica Market. Agnes Maxwell-Hall. TTY; WHSW

Jamaican Bus Ride. A. S. J. Tessimond. OBTV; OxBTC

Jamaican Fisherman. Philip Sherlock. PBCV

Jamboree. David McCord. SiSoPo
Sels.
"Rhyme for ham? Jam, A."

James. John Ennis. PeIV

James I. Kipling. FaBoEH

James Alan Park/ Came naked stark. Thomas, Lord Erskine. FaBoEE

James Bird. *Unknown.* AmFP

James Bond Movie, The. May Swenson. FaBoWP

James Cagney was the one up both our streets. Continuous. Tony Harrison. SCBI

James Grant. *Unknown.* ESPB

James Harris. *Unknown. See* "Well met, well met, my own true love."

James Harris. *Unknown. See* "O where [*or* whare] have you [*or* hae ye] been, my dear, dear [*or* dearest dear *or* long, long] love."

James Harris (The Daemon Lover). *Unknown.* ESPB

James Hatley. *Unknown.* ESPB

James Honeyman. W. H. Auden. MoBS

James Hugo Johnston. Maggie Pogue Johnson. CBWP-4

James James. Disobedience. A. A. Milne. NTCP; OTCP; TLR; UV, *ll.* 1–11

James Lee's Wife, *sels.* Robert Browning.
Among the Rocks. OxBSP

James Powell on Imagination. Larry Neal. BPo

James Rigg. James Hogg. BXAP

Sir James the Rose. *Unknown.* ESPB

James Wetherell. E. A. Robinson. MoAmPo

James Whaland. *Unknown.* AS

Jameson's Ride. Alfred Austin. FaBoEH; UV

Jameson's Ride, *sels.* Alfred Austin.
"Wrong! Is it wrong? Well, may be." UV

Jamestown. Randall Jarrell. GOA

Jamie Douglas. *Unknown.* ESPB

Jamie Douglas. *Unknown. See* Oh [*or* O] waly, waly, up the [*or* yon] bank.

Jamie Telfer of [*or* in] the Fair Dodhead. *Unknown.* ESPB; IBB; OxBB

Jamila. Nazik al-Mala'ika, *tr. fr. Arabic by* Kamal Boullata. WPOW

Jamming. Everett Hoagland. Jaz

Jamming together of fragments, The. Chet's Jazz. Richard Elman. Jaz

Jan van Hogspeuw staggers to the door. The Card-Players. Philip Larkin. OxBC

Jane Austen at the Window. Patricia Beer. FaBoWP

Jane awoke Ralph so gently on one morning. Morning. John Crowe Ransom. AnAmPo

Jane, Jane. *Unknown.* RoPo

Jane, Jane,/ Tall as a crane. Edith Sitwell. CMoP; MoAB; MoBrPo; MoP; NALW; NoAM; Poetr; PoRA

Jane looks down at her organdy skirt. In Bertram's Garden. Donald Justice. BoLoP; ErPo; MT; VGW

Jane Seagrim's Party. Leonard Nathan. GOYP

Jane Williams had a lover true. Shocking Rape and Murder of Two Lovers. *Unknown.* CoMu

Janet Waking. John Crowe Ransom. CMoP; InPK; MeMAP; MoAB; MoAmPo; MoP; NAAL-2; NoAM; NoP; OBD; PoE; Poetr; RB; TAP

Janie Swecker and Me and Gone with the Wind. David Huddle. GrPl

Janitor's Boy, The. Nathalia Crane. PoLF

Jankin. *Unknown. See* Kyrie, so kyrie.

Jankin, the Clerical Seducer. *Unknown. See* Kyrie, so kyrie.

Jankin, the Clerical Seducer. *Unknown.* MeEL

Janna. King D. Kuka. VoR

Jansenist Journey. Denis Devlin. IPY

Januar: by this fire [*or* thys fyre] I warme my handes. *Unknown.* EBEV (Labours of the Months.) GBP; OxBLMV

Januaries, Nature greets our eyes. Brazil, January 1, 1502. Elizabeth Bishop. FaBoWP; NoAM; VCAP

January. Anthony Barnett. VaA

January. Douglas Gibson. OBCP

January. John Heath-Stubbs. OBCP

January. Frances Horovitz. PWE

January. Weldon Kees. CoAP

January. H. Cordelia Ray. CBWP-3

January. John Updike. PDV

January. Ellen Bryant Voigt. NoP

January. William Carlos Williams. MoAB; MoAmPo

January, 1795. Mary Robinson. ECWP; WoRP

January Afternoon, with Billie Holiday. Lisel Mueller. Jaz

January brings the snow. The Garden Year. Sara Coleridge. FaBoBe; OTCP
(Months, The.) OxBChV

January cold and desolate. The Months. Christina Rossetti. FaPON

January Dandelion, A. George Marion McClellan. AAP

January 18, 1979. John Yau. UL

January falls the snow. Calendar Rhyme. Flora Willis Watson. BoTP

January 15 as a National Holiday. Carter Revard. VoR

January 1st. Anne Sexton. HCAP

January first isn't New Year's. Happy New Year, Anyway. Joanna Cole. NTCP

January Man. Dave Goulder. OBET

January Morning. William Carlos Williams. InPS; SOTW

January night, A. Moonlight. Significant Fevers. Alison Fell. BrRo

January 1940. Roy Fuller. LiTM

January, 1978. Ron Schreiber. ETG

January played. One Year. N. M. Bodecker. TLR

January snow falls, listen. (*LL*) Wild Strawberry. Maurice Kenny. HATNAP

January 3, 1970. Mae Jackson. PoBA

January 25th. Maxine W. Kumin. SM

Janus. Madeline Mason. GoYe

Janus. Laurence Perrine. InPK

Japan. Anthony Hecht. LiTM

Japanese Archery. Aleksander Wat, *tr. fr. Polish by* Richard Lourie. TOF

Japanese Beetles. X. J. Kennedy. OBAL

Japanese Birthday Wish, A. Thomas Burnett Swann. GoYe

Japanese Consulate, The. Frank Polite. UL

Japanese Fan. James Kirkup. GrPl

Japanese have funny things, The. A Rhyme Sheet of Other Lands. Hugh Chesterman. BoTP

Japanese Hokku. Lewis Alexander. CDC

Japanese Lovers, The. *Unknown.* BeLS; BLPA

Japanese Lullaby. Eugene Field. AnAmPo

Japanese Presentation, I & II. Jean Retallack. BAP-90

Japanese Print. Austin Clarke. IPY; NOIV

Japanesque. Oliver Herford. FiBHP

Jaquerie, The, *sels.* Sidney Lanier.

Jar, The. Peter Didsbury. PWE

Jar of cider and my pipe, A. The Sluggard. W. H. Davies. OBMV

Jar of Nations, The. A. E. Housman. LiTB

Jarring on the piles of broken shells. (*LL*) Shelly Beach. Christopher Koch. NOBAu

Jarring the air with rumour cool. Small Fountains. Lascelles Abercrombie. *Fr.* Emblems of Love. CH; MoBrPo

Jars with pussy-willow in them stand around the. Two Robin Croft. Andrew Crozier. VaA

Jasmattie live in bruk. Coolie Mother. David Dabydeen. NBrP

Jasmine. Kyongjoo Hong Ryou, *tr. fr. Korean.* TSaS

Jasmine. Chris Wallace-Crabbe. FaBoMA

Jaunty crop-haired graying, The. Poem about People. Robert Pinsky. VCAP

Jaunty traveller that comes to peer, The. Llyn y Gadair. T. H. Parry-Williams, *tr. fr. Welsh by* Anthony Conran. OBWVE

Javanese Dancers. Arthur Symons. OHCV

Jawbone is a platter for the face, The. Dog. D. C. Berry. BXAP

Jay a-Pass'd. William Barnes. NOBVV

Jay Gould's Daughter. *Unknown.* AS

Jay: I've one mouth but many voices. Unknown, formerly at. to Cynewulf, *tr. fr. Anglo-Saxon. Fr.* Riddles (Exeter Book). ASW, *tr. by* Kevin Crossley-Holland

Jaybird a-sitting on a hickory limb. *Unknown.* RoPo

Jazz. Frank London Brown. PoNe

Jazz. *(LL)* Jazz Chick. Bob Kaufman. PoBeRe

Jazz. Sybil Kein. Jaz

Jazz. Carolyn M. Rodgers. JB

Jazz Band in a Parisian Cabaret. Langston Hughes. MoAmPo

Jazz Chick. Bob Kaufman. PoBeRe

Jazz Dancer. Cornelius Eady. UTF

Jazz Drummer. Etheridge Knight. Jaz

Jazz Fantasia. Carl Sandburg. AiP; Jaz; MoAB; MoAmPo; Poetr; PoNe

Jazz Funeral. Maxine Cassin. *Fr.* Three Love Poems by a Native. Jaz

Jazz Impressions in the Garden. C. D. Wright. Jaz

Jazz Is My Religion. Ted Joans. Jaz

Jazz June. We/ Die soon. *(LL)* We Real Cool. Gwendolyn Brooks. CAPP; FF; HAP; HeIL; HeIP; HoPM; InPK; NALW; NoP; PoA; PoBA; PoE; PrIm; RaBo; SM; SoSe; TAP; TRP; TTY; WeW

Jazz — listen to it at your own risk. War Memoir. Bob Kaufman. Jaz

Jazz Must Be a Woman. Ted Joans. Jaz

Jazz must be a woman because its the only thing that. Jazz Must Be a Woman. Ted Joans. Jaz

Jazz Poem for the Girl Who Cried Wolf. James Nolan. Jaz

Jazz radio on a midnight kick. Round about Midnight. Bob Kaufman. PoBeRe

Jazz Station. Michael S. Harper. NoAM

Jazz to Jackson to John. Jerry W. Ward, Jr. Jaz

Jazzmen. Lee Meitzen Grue. Jaz

Jazzonia. Langston Hughes. Jaz

Je ne veux de personne aupres de ma tristesse. Henri de Regnier, *tr. fr. French by* "Seumas O'Sullivan." AWP

Je suis —/ I am a pot of jam;/ *Tu es —/* thou art a fool. *Unknown.* ISE

Je suis —/ I am a pot of jam;/ *Tu es —/* thou art a juicy fart. *Unknown.* ISE

Je T'Adore. Thomas Kinsella. MoP; NoAM

Jealosie. John Donne. *See* Fond woman, which would'st have thy husband die.

Jealous Adam. Itsik Manger, *tr. fr. Yiddish by* Jacob Sonntag. TrJP

Jealous Brothers, The. *Unknown.* AmFP

Jealous girls these sometimes were. How Marigolds Came Yellow. Robert Herrick. ChTr; TTTS

Jealous Lovers, The. Donald Hall. NYBP

Jealous Man, A. Robert Graves. CMoP

Jealous Wife, The. Vernon Scannell. ErPo

Jealousie Is the Rage of a Man. The Countess of Winchilsea. FM

Jealousy. Mei-Mei Berssenbrugge. BAP-90; OpBo; UL

Jealousy. Mary Elizabeth Coleridge. CH; EnLoPo; OBNC; WPE

Jealousy. John Donne. *Fr.* Elegies. FF

Jealousy. Esther Johnson. OxBSP

Jealousy. *Malay Oral Tradition, tr. by* R. J. Wilkinson *and* R. O. Winstedt. WTO

Jealousy. Valerie Sinason. DT

Jealousy. *Unknown, tr. fr. Irish by* Frank O'Connor. PeIV

Jealousy and Pride. Wilhelm Müller, *tr. fr. German by* Philip L. Miller. *Fr.* Beautiful Maid of the Mill, The. RiWo

Jealousy's an awful thing and foreign to my nature. I Can't Think What He Sees in Her. A. P. Herbert. FiBHP

Jean. Burns. *See* Of A' the Airts [the Wind Can Blaw].

Jean, death comes close to us all. The Child Bearers. Anne Sexton. BoWoP

Jean, Jean, Jean. Cat at the Cream. *Unknown.* GBP

Jean Maillard lies buried here. Epitaph for Jean Maillard. *Unknown, tr. fr. French.* PeHV

Jean Richepin's Song. Herbert Trench. OBMV

Jeanie, come tie my. *Unknown.* BoTP

Jeanie with the Light Brown Hair. Stephen Collins Foster. AnAmPo

Jeanne d'Arc. Susan Ludvigson. MT

Jeannette. Otto Julius Bierbaum, *tr. fr. German by* Jethro Bithell. AWP

Jeannette and Jeannot. Charles Jefferys. BLPA

Jeannot's Answer. Charles Jefferys. BLPA

Jeat Ring Sent, A. John Donne. *See* Thou art not so black as my heart.

Jeff Buckner. Frank Beddo. WTO

Jefferson and Liberty. *Unknown.* SWP

Jefferson D. Henry Sylvester Cornwell. PAH

Jefferson Davis. Walker Meriwether Bell. PAH

Jefferson Valley. John Hollander. PPP

Jehovah. Israel Zangwill. WGRP

Jehovah, God, Who Dwelt of Old. Lewis R. Amis. AH

Jehovah, Lord and Majesty. Conrad Weiser, *tr. fr. German by* Sheema Z. Buehne. AH

Jehovah Our Righteousness. William Cowper. NOCV

Jehu. Louis MacNeice. LiTM; MoAB

Jellicle Cats are black and white. The Song of the Jellicles. T. S. Eliot. EBEvV; FaBoCh; FaBoNo; ImGa; OFC; OxBChV

Jellon Grame. *Unknown.* EBEV; ESPB, A *vers.*; OxBB

Jellon Grame. *Unknown.* EBEV; ESPB; OxBB

Jelly in the bowl. *Unknown.* RoPo

Jelly Piece Song, The. Anne MacNaughton. NTP

Jellyfish, The. Ogden Nash. FaPON

Jellyfish, A. Marianne Moore. OxBSP

Jemima. *At. to* Mother Goose, *st.* 1; *sts.* 2 *and* 3, *Unknown, at. to* Longfellow. *See* There Was a Little Girl.

Jemmy Ball, a lucky digger. Moggy's Wedding. Charles Robert Thatcher. NOBAu

Jennie Jenkins. *Unknown.* AmFP

Jennie Lubell is In a Nursing Home in Provincetown, *sels.* Adeline Naiman. "My mother has died, but I visit her weekly." MDDM

Jennifer Gentle and Rosemary. *Unknown. See* There was a knicht riding frae the east.

Jenny. Dante Gabriel Rossetti. EnVR; PoEL-5

Jenny and Johnny. Dorothy King. BoTP

Jenny come tie my. The Bonny Cravet. Mother Goose. OxNR

Jenny gay and Johnny grim. Jenny and Johnny. Dorothy King. BoTP

Jenny got so angry. *Unknown.* RoPo

Jenny Hit Me. John Clarke. UV

Jenny hit me when we met. Jenny Hit Me. John Clarke. UV

Jenny kiss'd me in a dream. Such Stuff as Dreams. Franklin P. Adams. FiBHP

Jenny kiss'd me when we met. Paul Dehn. *Fr.* Leaden Treasury of English Verse, A. CBLP; FiBHP

Jenny kiss'd me when we met. Jenny Kiss'd [*or* Kissed] Me. Leigh Hunt. BLPA; CoGr; FaBoBe; ImPo; NBLV; NTCP; OBEV; OxAEP-2; PeLV; PoRA

(Jenny Kissed Me.) TFi; UV

(Rondeau, A: "Jenny kissed me when we met.") BLPA; EnRP; FaBV; FF; HoPM; InPK; NOBE; NOBVV; SCGP; TEP

Jenny Kiss'd [*or* Kissed] Me. Leigh Hunt. BLPA; CoGr; FaBoBe; ImPo; NBLV; NTCP; OBEV; OxAEP-2; PeLV; PoRA

Jenny Kissed Me. Leigh Hunt. *See* Jenny kiss'd me when we met.

Jenny kissed me! *(LL)* Jenny Kiss'd [*or* Kissed] Me. Leigh Hunt. BLPA; CoGr; FaBoBe; ImPo; NBLV; NTCP; OBEV; OxAEP-2; PeLV; PoRA

Jenny out from Hwome. William Barnes. SCGP

Jenny White and Johnny Black. Eleanor Farjeon. FaPON

Jenny Wren. W. H. Davies. MoBrPo

Jenny Wren. Mother Goose. *See* As little Jenny Wren/ Was sitting by the shed.

Jenny Wren fell sick. Ungrateful Jenny. Mother Goose. OxNR

Jenny Wren's got a house. The Secret. Elizabeth Fleming. BoTP

Jenny, your mind commands. Reading the Brothers Grimm to Jenny. Lisel Mueller. NYBP

Jephtah's Daughter, *sels.* Charles Heavysege.

Jephthah's Daughter. "Yehoash," *tr. fr. Yiddish by* Alter Brody. TrJP

Jeptha's Daughter. Byron. ChIV-1

Jerboa, The. Marianne Moore. FYAP; NALW *Sels.*

"Roman had an, A/ artist, a freedman." CMoP

Jeremiad. Oscar Williams. LiTA

Jeremiah, *sels.* Bible, O.T.

As Fowlers Lie in Wait. TrJP

But Fear Thou Not, O Jacob. TrJP
Cry of the Daughter of My People, The. TrJP
Cursed Be the Day. TrJP
"For Thus saith The Lord to the men of Judah and Jerusalem." OBVE
O Lord, Thou Hast Enticed Me. TrJP
Oh That I Were in the Wilderness. TrJP
Jeremiah. Stefan Zweig, *tr. fr. German by* Eden *and* Cedar Paul. TrJP
Sels.
Chosen of God.
Flowering Without End.
Jeremiah, blow the fire. *Unknown.* OxNR
Jeremiah Obadiah. *Unknown.* OTCP
Jeremiah Obadiah, puff, puff, puff. Jeremiah Obadiah. *Unknown.* OTCP
Jeremie .17. Bible, Apocrypha. ChIV-1
Jeremy. Jeffrey Miller. UL
Jeremy Hobbler. *Unknown.* BoTP
Jeremy Taylor: The Rule and Exercise of Holy Dying, 1663. Peter
    Scupham. *Fr.* Marginalia. SCBI
Jericho is on the inside. The Walls of Jericho. Blanche Taylor Dickinson.
    CDC
Jericho's Blind Beggar. Longfellow. WBLP
Jerking his head spasmodically as he is penetrated by invisible. Night
    Patrol. Ciaran Carson. PWE
Jerome. Randall Jarrell. PPP
Jerome in Solitude. James Wright. AnAn
Jeronimo's House. Elizabeth Bishop. NoP
Jerry, Go an' Ile That Car. *Unknown. See* Come all ye railroad section
    men.
Jerry, Go and Ile [*or* Oil] That Car. *Unknown.* SWP
Jerry Hall,/ He is so small. Mother Goose. OxNR; ReMoGo
Jersey Cattle. Ralph Nixon Currey. OxBTC
Jersey Marsh, The. David Galler. NYBP
Jerusalem. Yehuda Amichai, *tr. fr. Hebrew.* TSaS, *tr. by* Stephen Mitchell
Jerusalem, *sels.* Blake.
    "But still the thunder of Los peals loud and thus the thunder's cry."
        OAEL-2
    "England! awake! awake! awake!" EnRP; FHYEP; NoP
    (Prelude: "England! awake! awake! awake!") OBNC
    "Fearing that Albion should turn his back against the Divine Vision."
        OAEL-2
    Fields from Islington to Marybone, The. ChTr, 4 *sts.*; FaBoPV; OBNV
    (Prelude: "Fields from Islington to Marybone, The.") OBNC
    "I give you the end of a golden string." Spl
    (Epigraph.) OBNC
    (To the Christians.) EnRP; WGRP
    I Give You the End of a Golden String. NTP
    "It is easier to forgive an enemy than to forgive a friend." OAEL-2
    Male & Female Loves in Beulah. OBNC
    Monk, The. EnRP
    "Shuddring the Spectre howls, his howlings terrify the night." OAEL-2
Jerusalem. Blake. *See* And Did Those Feet in Ancient Time.
Jerusalem, *sels.* Uri Zvi Greenberg, *tr. fr. Hebrew by* Charles A. Cowen.
    Jerusalem the Dismembered. TrJP
Jerusalem. Judah Halevi, *tr. fr. Hebrew by* David Goldstein. TOF
Jerusalem. David Rokeah, *tr. fr. Hebrew by* Ruth Finer Mintz. MHP
Jerusalem. Julia Vinograd. SRLS
Jerusalem can celebrate herself. Celebration. Julia Vinograd. SRLS
Jerusalem going through her jewel-box of lives. Jerusalem's Jewel Box.
    Julia Vinograd. BCF
Jerusalem is weeping. Mourning. Julia Vinograd. BCF
Jerusalem, My Happy Home. *Unknown.* PoE
Jerusalem 1967, *sels.* Yehuda Amichai, *tr. fr. Hebrew by* Warren Bargad
    and Stanley F. Chyet.
Jerusalem rises from honor as from sleep. Jerusalem. Julia Vinograd.
    SRLS
Jerusalem Shadow. Melanie Kaye/Kantrowitz. LoHo
Jerusalem Sonnets, *sels.* James K. Baxter.
    "Bees that have been hiving above the church pond, The." PeNZ
    "Colin, you can tell my words are crippled now." PeNZ
    "Small grey cloudy louse that nests in my beard, The." NoP; PeNZ
    "Yesterday I planted garlic." PeNZ
Jerusalem the Dismembered. Uri Zvi Greenberg, *tr. fr. Hebrew by* Charles
    A. Cowen. *Fr.* Jerusalem. TrJP
Jerusalem the Golden. Bernard of Cluny, *tr. fr. Latin by* John Mason
    Neale. *Fr.* De Contemptu Mundi. WGRP
"Jerusalem," the Lord called softly. The Calling of Jerusalem. Julia
    Vinograd. BCF
Jerusalem washed her bitter hair, first in salt, then in perfumes. Anger.
    Julia Vinograd. SRLS
Jerusalem's Jewel Box. Julia Vinograd. BCF
Jervis Bay, The. *Unknown.* OxBSS

Jes 'fore Christmas be as good as yer kin be! (*LL*) Jest 'fore Christmas.
    Eugene Field. FaBV; FaPON; PoLF
Jes' smile, an' smile, an' smile. (*LL*) Smile. *Unknown.* BLPA; WBLP
Jesous Ahatonhia. Jesse Edgar Middleton. OBCP
Jesse James. William Rose Benét. FYAP; MoAmPo; TrGrPo
Jesse James. *Unknown.* AS; BeLS; FaBoBe; UnPo; WiR
Jesse James. *Unknown.* AmFP
Jesse James was a lad who [*or* that] killed many a man. Jesse James.
    Unknown. AmFP
Jesse James was a two-gun man. Jesse James. William Rose Benét.
    FYAP; MoAmPo; TrGrPo
Jessica Drew's Married Son. Tony Flynn. PWE
Jessica, Jessica, how could I ever. From a Saxon Monk to His Love.
    Christiania Whitehead. NWP
Jessie ("Jessie is both young and fair.") Bret Harte. GN
Jessie Mitchell's Mother. Gwendolyn Brooks. BoWoP; NALW; NAs;
    NMM
Jest, The. Austin Clarke. BIrV
Jest a-wearyin' for you. Wearyin' for You. Frank Lebby Stanton.
    AnAmPo
Jest 'fore Christmas. Eugene Field. FaBV; FaPON; PoLF
Jester shook his hood and bells, and leap'd upon a chair, The. The Jester's
    Sermon. George Walter Thornbury. BeLS
Jester walked in the garden, The. The Cap and Bells. W. B. Yeats.
    ChTr; MoAB; MoBrPo; NoAM; NoP; OtMeF; RB
Jester's Sermon, The. George Walter Thornbury. BeLS
Jesu. George Herbert. MeLP
Jesu Christ, My Leman Swete. Jesus, My Sweet Lover. *Unknown.* MeEL
Jesu, Come on Board. Johann C. Pyrlaeus, *tr. fr. German by* Sheema Z.
    Buehne. AH
Jesu Crist, heovene king. *Unknown.* MiEL
Jesu! for thy mercy endelesse. Jesu! Send Us Peace. *Unknown.* MeEL
Jesu, for thy muchele might. *Unknown.* MiEL
Jesu,/ if Thou wilt make. A Page's Road Song. William A. Percy.
    TrPWD
Jesu is in my heart, his sacred name. Jesu. George Herbert. MeLP
    (Iesu.) GeHe
Jesu, Joy of Man's Desiring. Robert Fitzgerald. NYBP
Jesu, Lord, welcom thou be. A Prayer to the Sacrament of the Altar.
    Unknown. MeEL
Jesu, Lorde, that madest me. A Hymn to Jesus. Richard of Caistre.
    MeEL
Jesu, no more! It is full tide. Richard Crashaw. *Fr.* On the Bleeding
    Wounds of Our Crucified Lord. SeCV-1; TrGrPo
Jesu our raunsoun. William Herebert. MiEL
Jesu! Send Us Peace. *Unknown.* MeEL
Jesu, sweete sone dear. The Virgin's Song. *Unknown.* NOBE
Jesu, that hast me dere iboght. A Devout Prayer of the Passion.
    Unknown. MeEL
Jesu that is most of might. *Unknown.* MiEL
Jesu, thie love within mee is soe maine. William Alabaster. *Fr.* Divine
    Meditations. ESCV; Son
JESU, thy love within me is so main. A Divine Sonnet. William
    Alabaster. NoSic
Jesu, to Thee My Heart I Bow. Nikolaus Ludwig, Graf von Zinzendorf, *tr.*
    fr. German by John Wesley. AH
Jesukin. *At. to* Saint Ita, *tr. fr. Irish.* TIRV, *tr. by* George Sigerson
Jesukin is on our breast. (*LL*) Jesukin. *At. to* Saint Ita. TIRV, *tr. by*
    George Sigerson
Jesus. Francis Lauderdale Adams. OxBS
Jesus. James McAuley. CBAP; ChIV-2; FaBoMA
Jesus. Novica Tadic, *tr. fr. Serbo-Croatian by* Charles Simic. HSix
Jesus a Child His Course Begun. Margaret Fuller. AH
Jesus absent on vacation, heaven closed till his return. (*LL*) The Preacher's
    Vacation. *Unknown.* BLPA; BLPL
Jesus, almighty King of Blis. The Nativity. *Unknown.* MeEL
Jesus and His Mother. Thom Gunn. OxBC
Jesus and I. Dan Crawford. BLRP
Jesus Bids Man Remember. *Unknown. See* Men rent me on rode.
Jesus Borned in Bethlea. *Unknown.* AmFP
Jesus Christ ("Jesus Christ was a man that travelled through the land.")
    Woody Guthrie. WTO
Jesus Comforts His Mother. *Unknown. See* Baby is born [*or* borne], us
    bliss [*or* blis] to bring, A.
Jesus Contrasts Man and Himself. *Unknown.* MeEL
Jesus Dies. Anne Sexton. CrSp
Jesus doth him bimene. Jesus Contrasts Man and Himself. *Unknown.*
    MeEL

John Charles Frémont. Charles Fletcher Lummis. PAH
John Cherokee. *Unknown.* GBP
John Clare. Jon Anderson. AmPA
John Clare. Mark Halperin. SM
John Coltrane. Lawson Fusao Inada. ETG
John Coltrane: An Impartial Review. Alfred B. Spellman. PoBA
John Connu Rider. Andrew Salkey. NTP
John Cook had a little grey mare. Mother Goose. OxNR
John didn't die. he hasn't. The Valley of Death. Ron Schreiber. PFL
John Donne. James Simmons. CIP
John Dory. *Unknown.* ESPB; OxBSS
John Endicott. Longfellow. PAH
  Sels.
  Proclamation, The.
  "To-night we strive to read, as we may best."
John Evereldown. E. A. Robinson. AnAmPo; CMoP; MeMAP; OxBA
John Fane Dingle. Glaucopis. Richard Hughes. OBMV
John Filson. William Henry Venable. PAH
John, founder of towns, - dweller in none; Bread-Word Giver. John
  Wheelwright. ChIV-2
John Gibson's Bat. Michael S. Harper. AnAn
John Gilbert Was a Bushranger. *Unknown.* NOBAu
John Gilpin. William Cowper. InvP
John Gorham. E. A. Robinson. MoAB; MoAmPo
John Greenleaf Whittier. Phoebe Cary. AmWP
John Grumlie. Allan Cunningham. GBP; PoLF
John Hardy. *Unknown.* AmFP; FaBoBa
John Hardy, that's the last of you. (*LL*) John Hardy. *Unknown.* AmFP;
  FaBoBa
John Harralson, John Harralson, you are a wretched creature. Two Appeals
  to John Harralson, Agent. *Unknown.* OBAL
John Henry. *Unknown.* AMFP; AS; BeLS; BPO; FaBoBa; FaBoBe;
  NOBA; OxBoLi; SWP; TrGrPo
John Henry tol' his cap'n. *Unknown. See* John Henry was a lil [*or* little]
  baby.
John Henry was a lil [*or* little] baby. John Henry. *Unknown.* FaBoBa;
  NOBA; OxBoLi; SWP; TrGrPo
  (John Henry tol' his cap'n.) AS; BeLS
  (When John Henry was a little babe [*or* fellow].) AmFP; BPo
  (When John Henry was nothin' but a baby.) FaBoBe
John Hielandman. *Unknown.* GBP
John, his mother and sister step from. John Kennedy Jr. at Twenty-One.
  Dennis Cooper. ETG
John. In the sound of that rebellious word. John. Ebenezer Elliot. Son
John J. Curtis. Joseph Gallagher. AmFP
John-John. Thomas MacDonagh. AWP; PeIV
John Jones. Swinburne. *Fr.* Heptalogia, The.
John Keats. Byron. *See* Who Kill'd John Keats?
John Keats. Dante Gabriel Rossetti. EPCY
John Keats rose at dawn. Nick Enright. PeLi
John Kennedy Jr. at Twenty-One. Dennis Cooper. ETG
John Kinsella's Lament for Mrs. Mary Moore. W. B. Yeats. CMoP;
  LiTM; MeMBP; MoAB; NoP; OAEL-2; RB
John Knox. Iain Crichton Smith. OxBS
John L. Sullivan Enters Heaven. Robert Frost. BXAP
John Landless Leads the Caravan. Iwan Goll, *tr. fr. French by* William
  Carlos Williams. TrJP
John, look what Mis' Nelson give me. The Easter Bonnet. Clara Ann
  Thompson. CBWP-2
John looks about him with enjoyment. What a Man Needs. Vikram Seth.
  CBCK
John loved Teresa who loved Raymond. Quadrille. Carlos Drummond de
  Andrade, *tr. fr. Portuguese by* Mark Strand. AnRep
John Masefield Relates the Story of Tom, Tom, the Piper's Son. Louis
  Untermeyer. *Fr.* Mother Goose Up-to-Date. MoAmPo
John Maynard. Horatio Alger, Jr.. BeLS; BLPA; FaBoBe
John Mouldy. Walter de la Mare. OxBChV; RB
John of Gaunt Speaks. Shakespeare. *Fr.* King Richard II. EBEvV;
  FaBoEH; FaBoPP; FaPoR
John of Gaunt's Dying Speech. Shakespeare. *Fr.* King Richard II.
  FaBoEH
John of Hazelgreen [*or* Haselgreen]. *Unknown.* ESPB
John of Tours. *Unknown, tr. fr. French by* Dante Gabriel Rossetti. AWP
John Peel. John Woodcock Graves. CH; OxBoLi
John Pelham. James Ryder Randall. PAH
John Percy/ Said to his nursy. John Percy. J. B. Morton. UV
John Quincy Adams. Rosemary *and* Stephen Vincent Benét. OBCA

John Rabbit, by Dame Eagle chased. The Eagle and the Beetle. La
  Fontaine, *tr. fr. French by* Elizur Wright. OBVE
Sir John Raynsford's Confession. John Harington. NoSic
John Rogers' Exhortation to His Children. *Unknown. Fr.* New England
  Primer, The. OBCA
Sir John Shagbag (Conservative, Nore). Victor Gray. PeLi
John Smith and His Son, John Smith. Wallace Stevens. TLR
John Smith, fellow fine. *Unknown.* OxNR
John Smith is my name. *Unknown.* FaBoUs
John Smith of His Friend Master John Taylor. John Smith. SCAP
John Smith's Approach to Jamestown. James Barron Hope. PAH
John spared his patient labouring ox. Adaios of Macedon, *tr. fr. Greek by*
  Robin Skelton. GrAn
John Stuart Mill. E. C. Bentley. *Fr.* Clerihews. FaBoCo; FiBHP
  (J. S. Mill.) OxBoLi; PeLV
John Sutter. Yvor Winters. MoAmPo; MoP; NoAM; NOBA
John Thomson and the Turk. *Unknown.* ESPB, A *and* B *vers.*
John, Tom, and James. Charles Henry Ross. NBLV; OxBChV
John Underhill. Whittier. PAH
John was a bad boy, and beat a poor cat. John, Tom, and James. Charles
  Henry Ross. NBLV; OxBChV
John Webster. Swinburne. *Fr.* Sonnets of English Dramatic Poets. InvP;
  Son
John Wesley Gaines. *Unknown.* FiBHP
John while swimming in the ocean. Brats. X. J. Kennedy. NBLV
John, you were figuring in the gay career. To John Lamb, Esq.: Of the
  South-Sea House. Charles Lamb. Son
Johnie Armstrang. *Unknown.* ESPB; IBB; OxBB
Johnie Armstrong. *Unknown.* ESPB, A *vers.*; FaBoBa; HoPM; NoP, A
  vers.; TrGrPo
Johnie Armstrong. *Unknown.* ESPB
Johnie Blunt. *Unknown.* OxBB
Johnie Cam to Our Toun. *Unknown.* GBP
Johnie Cock. *Unknown.* ESPB, A, B, *and* C *vers.*; FaBoBa
Johnie o' Cocklesmuir. *Unknown. See* Up Johnie raise in a May morning.
Johnie Scot. *Unknown.* ESPB
Johnna at the Windmill. Diane Glancy. CRP
Johnnie Cope. Adam Skirving. OxBS; ScCV
Johnnie Crack and Flossie Snail. Dylan Thomas. *Fr.* Under Milk Wood.
  FaPON; FiBHP; GoJo; OTCP; PDV
Johnnie Norrie. *Unknown.* OxNR
Johnny. W. H. Auden. PlP
Johnny and Jane and Jack and Lou. Children's Ball-Bouncing Song.
  Unknown. NOBAu
Johnny Appleseed. Vachel Lindsay. FaPON
Johnny Appleseed. William Henry Venable. PAH
Johnny Armstrong killed a calf. *Unknown.* OxNR
Johnny bum-bonny. *Unknown.* RoPo
Johnny Carroll's Camp. *Unknown.* AmFP
Johnny Cock, in a May morning. Johnie Cock. *Unknown.* ESPB, C *vers.*
Johnny Dow [*or* Doo]. *Unknown.* FaBoCo; FaBoEE; FiBHP
Johnny Dyers. *Unknown.* AmFP
Johnny Faa, the Lord of Little Egypt. *Unknown. See* Gypsies [*or* Gipsies]
  they came to my Lord Cassilis' yett [*or* gate], The.
Johnny Faa, the Lord of Little Egypt. *Unknown.* EnSB
Johnny Gallagher. *Unknown.* AmFP
Johnny German. *Unknown.* AmFP
Johnny had a little dove. Johnny's Farm. H. M. Adams. BoTP
Johnny he's risen up in the morn. Johnny of Cockley's Well. *Unknown.*
  EnSB
Johnny, I Hardly Knew Ye. *Unknown.* BIrV; ELP; FaBoBa; GBP; IIP;
  OxBoLi; WoWa
Johnny is a long-haired Blue. Three Cheers for the Black, White and Blue.
  Ruth Pitter. OFC
Johnny made a custard. Some Cook. John Ciardi. PDV
Johnny of Cockley's Well. *Unknown.* EnSB
Johnny on the woodpile. *Unknown.* RoPo
Johnny Raw and Polly Clark. *Unknown.* CoMu
Johnny Sands ("A man whose name was Johnny Sands.") *Unknown.*
  CoMu; OBET
Johnny Sands ("There was a man named Johnny Sands, who married Betty
  Hague.") *Unknown.* AmFP
Johnny shall have a new bonnet. Mother Goose. OxNR; ReMoGo
Johnny, since today is. Many Happy Returns. W. H. Auden. NAs
Johnny Tek Away Mi Wife. Slim Beckford *and* Sam Blackwood. PBCV
Johnny Thomson, so they say. Mrs. Vickers' Daughter. *Unknown.* AmFP
Johnny Weissmuller Dead in Acapulco. Clive James. NOBAu

3-31-70. BlSi
Journal, *sels.* Edna St. Vincent Millay.
Journal from France, A, *sels.* Gillian Clarke.
Seamstress at St. Léon. OBTV
Journal of Albion Moonlight, The. Kenneth Patchen. NaP
Sels.
"But there is no black jaw which cannot be broken by our word."
"I/ want you/ to listen."
Journal of Society, The. Godfrey Turner. NOBL; PeLV
Journal of the Laguna de San Ignacio. Nathaniel Tarn. FoLa
Sels.
"Immense architecture/ building in air."
Journal of the Storm. Greg Kuzma. AmPA
Journal to Stella. Morton Dauwen Zabel. PoA
Journey, The. Eavan Boland. BiHa
Journey, The. Aidan Clarke. BoTP
Journey. Gillian Clarke. SCBI
Journey. David Constantine. SCBI
Journey. Elizabeth Cook-Lynn. HATNAP
Sels.
Dream.
Memory.
Sacristans.
Journey. Roy Daniells. MoCV
Journey. Rodney Hall. NOBAu
Journey, The. David Ignatow. Poetsp
Journey, The. Maxine W. Kumin. MDDM
Journey. Judith Nicholls. OBSP
Journey, The. Mary Oliver. CrSp
Journey. Vasco [*or* Vasko] Popa, *tr. fr. Serbo-Croatian. Fr.* Besieged
Serenity. PoSu
Journey, The. Margaret Reckord. AIW
Journey. Diane Wakoski. IHMS
Journey, The. Franz Wright. LCAP
Journey, The. James Wright. CAPP; NoAM; PoE
Journey and Observations of a Countryman, The, *sels.* John Hawthorn.
Deathbed, A. NOEC
Journey, and the struggles of the moon, The. (*LL*) Ajanta. Muriel
Rukeyser. LiTA; LiTM; MoAB; MoAmPo; NNaP
Journey Back to Christmas. Gwen Dunn. OBCP
Journey Home, The. Irena Klepfisz. BTR
Journey in the Orient. Maria Luisa Spaziani, *tr. fr. Italian by* Ruth
Feldman. BoWoP
Journey into France, The. *Unknown.* CoMu; FaBoBa; OBTV
Journey Nears the Road-End, The. Rabindranath Tagore, *tr. fr. Bengali by*
Amiya Chakravarty. DL
Journey North. Tu Fu, *tr. fr. Chinese by* Hugh M. Stimson. SuSp
Journey of Life, The. Bryant. EAP
Journey of the Magi. T. S. Eliot. EBEvV; FaBoCh; FaBoMo; HAP; HeIP;
ImPo; InPK; LiTA; LiTM; MoAB; MoAmPo; NAEL-2; NIP; NOCV;
NoP; OBCP; OBMV; OxBTC; PChr; PoE; Poetr; TAP; TFi; TrGrPo;
TRP; TwCP
Journey Onwards, The. Thomas Moore. GTBS; GTBS-P; OxAEP-2
Journey round the World. Ingrid Jonker, *tr. fr. Afrikaans by* Jack Cope *and*
William Plomer. PBWP
Journey: the North Coast. Robert Gray. FaBoMA
Journey Through Hell. Nicanor Parra, *tr. fr. Spanish by* Miller Williams.
AnRep
Journey through the Moonlight, A. Russell Edson. LCAP
Journey to a Parallel. Bruce McM. Wright. PoNe
Journey to Hell, A; or, A Visit Paid to the Devil, *sels.* Edward Ward.
Parish Poor-Officers, The. NOEC
Journey to Iceland. W. H. Auden. OBTV; PoA
Journey to the Interior. Theodore Roethke. LCAP; NYBP; TRP; VGW
Journey to the Interior. William Jay Smith. DiPo; PFL
Journey to the Place of Ghosts. Jay Wright. VCAP
Journey toward Evening. Phyllis McGinley. GoYe; NYBP
Journeying by Stream: Following Chin-chu Torrent I Cross the Mountains.
Hsieh Ling-yün, *tr. fr. Chinese by* Francis Westbrook. SuSp
Journeying to Hsiang-yi. Ch'en Yu Yi, *tr. fr. Chinese by* Irving Y. Lo.
SuSp
Journeying to the Village. Wang Yü-ch'eng, *tr. fr. Chinese by* Irving Y.
Lo. SuSp
Journeys. Meg Campbell. PeNZ
Journeys. Gary Snyder. NU
Journey's End. Janet Fisher. NWP
Journey's End. Humbert Wolfe. TrJP

Journey's Formulae, The. Tomas Tranströmer, *tr. fr. Swedish by* Robin
Fulton. PWE
Jove descends in sleet and snow. The Storm. Alcaeus, *tr. fr. Greek by*
John Hermann Merivale. AWP
Jove, for Europa[e]s love took[e] shape of bull. Would I were Changed.
Barnabe Barnes. *Fr.* Parthenophil and Parthenophe. AAS; ESo;
FaBoBl
Jovial Beggar, The. *Unknown.* BoTP
Jovial Marriner; or, The Sea-Man's Renown, The. John Playford. CoMu
Jovial Shepheard's Song, The. Michael Drayton. *See* Near[e] to the silver
Trent.
Jovial Tinker; or, The Willing Couple, The. *Unknown.* CoMu
Jowl, Jowl and Listen. *Unknown.* OBET
Joy. Gavin Bantock. OxBTC
Joy. Robert Creeley. PPP
Joy. Clarissa Scott Delany. CDC; PoNe; ShDr
Joy. Robinson Jeffers. CMoP
Joy — a beginning. Anguish, ardor. Relearning the Alphabet. Denise
Levertov. NOBA
Joy! a heart so overflowing. Bernard de Ventadour, *tr. fr. French by* John
Frederick Nims. STV
Joy and Peace in Believing. William Cowper. NOCV
Joy and Pleasure. W. H. Davies. OBMV
Joy and Temperance. *Unknown.* SoSe
Joy and the soul are mates, as heart and sorrow. The Cruse. Louise
Townsend Nicholl. NYBP
Joy, did I [*or* I did] lock thee up; but some bad man. The Bunch of
Grapes. George Herbert. ChIV-1; ESCV; GeHe; NAEL-1; NOSC;
TOF
Joy for the sturdy trees. Tree-planting. Samuel Francis Smith. OHIP
Joy in rebel Plymouth town, in the spring of sixty-four. "Albemarle"
Cushing. James Jeffrey Roche. PAH
Joy is a partnership. Frederic Lawrence Knowles. *Fr.* Grief and Joy.
IMW
Joy is a trick in the air. Birth-Dues. Robinson Jeffers. MoAB; MoAmPo
Joy May Kill. Michelangelo, *tr. fr. Italian by* John Addington Symonds.
AWP
Joy of a Singer, The. Piuvkaq, *tr. fr. Eskimo.* WTO
Joy of Church Fellowship Rightly Attended, The. Edward Taylor. *Fr.*
God's Determinations [touching his Elect]. AmPP; EAP; MeMAP;
NAAL-1; OxBA; SCAP
Joy of Cooking, The, *sels.* David Mus.
Conserves. PoA
Joy of Fishes, The. Chuang Tzu, *tr. fr. Chinese by* Thomas Merton. Mes
Joy of Incompleteness, The. Albert Crowell. PoToHe
Joy of Knowledge. Isidor Schneider. TrJP
Joy of Life. Moses ibn Ezra, *tr. fr. Hebrew by* Solomon Solis-Cohen. *Fr.*
Book of Tarshish, The. TrJP
Joy of Love, The. Allan Dowling. ErPo
Joy of My Life! While Left Me Here. Henry Vaughan. GeHe; SeCV-1
Joy of the Morning. Edwin Markham. FaPON
Joy of the Poor, The, *sels.* Nathan Alterman, *tr. fr. Hebrew by* Ruth Finer
Mintz.
Convert Comes to the City, A. MHP
Introduction. MHP
Song to the Wife of His Youth, The. MHP
Joy of the poor knocked on the door, The. Introduction. Nathan Alterman,
tr. fr. Hebrew by Ruth Finer Mintz. *Fr.* Joy of the Poor, The. MHP
Joy of the Yiddish Word, The, *sels.* Jacob Glatstein, *tr. fr. Yiddish by*
Benjamin *and* Barbara Harshav.
Joy shakes me like the wind that lifts a sail. Joy. Clarissa Scott Delany.
CDC; PoNe; ShDr
Joy, shipmate, joy! (*LL*) Joy, Shipmate, Joy! Walt Whitman. MeMAP;
MoAmPo; OHIP; PFP; TAP
Joy, Shipmate, Joy! Walt Whitman. MeMAP; MoAmPo; OHIP; PFP; TAP
Joy so short alas, the pain so near, The. Sir Thomas Wyatt. SiPS; SiPSBD
Joy to Philip, he this day. Going into Breeches. Charles Lamb *and* Mary
Lamb. OxBChV
Joy to the bridegroom and the bride. The Milkmaid's Epithalamium.
Thomas Randolph. BoLoP
Joyce: By Herself and Her Friends. Joyce Grenfell. OBD
Joyce was afraid of thunder. Volcano. Derek Walcott. OxBC
Joyce's Repentance, The. *Unknown, tr. fr. Irish by* Douglas Hyde. TIRV
Joye and blisse were me newe. (*LL*) Brid one brere, brid, brid one brere.
Unknown. MiEL
Joyful at length may be my fare. (*LL*) When raging [*or* ragyng] love with
extreme pain [*or* payne]. The Earl of Surrey. NoSic; SiPSBD
Joyful [*or* Joyfull] New Ballad, A. Thomas Deloney. CoMu; OxBSS
Joyful Noise, A. Donald Finkel. CoAP

Joyful Sound It Is, A. George Strebeck. AH

Joyfully, Joyfully Onward I Move. William Hunter. AH

Joyless/ what I have done. Liadan Laments Cuirithir. *Unknown, tr. fr. Irish by* John Montague. BIrV; PBWP

Joyous birds, hid under greenewood shade, The. Tasso, *tr. fr. Italian by* Edward Fairfax. *Fr.* Godfrey of Bulloigne; or, The Recoverie of Jerusalem. OBVE

Joys. James Russell Lowell. BoTP

Joys of Mary, The. *Unknown.* AmFP

Joys of the Country: Seven Poems, *sels.* Wang Wei, *tr. fr. Chinese by* Burton Watson.

Joys of the Road, The. Bliss Carman. AnAmPo; GGP

Joys seldom yet attained by humankind! *(LL)* To an Unborn Pauper Child. Thomas Hardy. FaBoRV; GTBS-P; LiTB; MeMBP; NAs

Joys That Sting. C. S. Lewis. ArLo

J's the jumping Jay-walker. Phyllis McGinley. *Fr.* All around the Town. FaPON

Juan and Haiidée. Byron. *Fr.* Don Juan. EBNV

Juan de Juni the priest said. Aodh Ruadh O'Domhnaill. Thomas MacGreevy. CIP; OBMV

Juan in England. Byron. *Fr.* Don Juan. FaBoVe

Juan knew several languages — as well. Byron. *Fr.* Don Juan. OAEL-2

Juan Rulfo Moved Away. Alberto A. Ríos. UL

Juan, the moron next door. Report from the Correspondent They Fired. David McElroy. AmPA

Juana. Alfred de Musset, *tr. fr. French by* Andrew Lang. AWP

Juan's Song. Louise Bogan. NYBP

Jubilate Agno. Christopher Smart. FaBoVe

Sels.

"For I bless the Prince of Peace and pray that all the guns may be nail'd up." InPS

"For I prophesy that they will understand the blessing and virtue of the rain." ECEV

"For I prophesy that we shall have our horns again." ChIV-1

For I Will Consider My Cat Jeoffry. NTP; OBF; OFC; OxAEP-1; UV, sh. vers.

(For I Will Consider My Cat Jeoffry [or Jeoffrey].) CTC; FM; HAP; HeIP; NAEL-1; NOEC; NoP; OAEL-1; OBWVE; PoEL-3; PPP; Prf; SCV; TRP; TTTS; WeW

(My Cat Jeoffry.) ChTr; FaBoCh; LiTB; PoE; RB; SoCa; WiR

(Of Jeoffry, His Cat.) NU; PrIm

"For man is between the pinchers while his soul is shaping and purifying." ChIV-1

"For the air is purified by prayer which is made aloud." Prf

"For the doubling of flowers is the improvement of the gardners talent." ChIV-2; NOEC

"For the spiritual musick is as follows." NOEC

God Hath Sent Me to Sea for Pearls. CBCK

"Let Elizur[e] rejoice with the Partridge." OAEL-1; PoEL-3

"Let Ephah rejoice with Buprestis, the Lord endue us with temperance and humanity." NOEC

"Let Peter rejoice with the Moonfish who keeps up the life in the waters by night." ChIV-2

"Let Shobi rejoice with the Kastrel — blessed be the name Jesus." NOEC

Mineral Rejoicings. CBCK

Reflections on Sounds and Language

"Rejoice in God." PoE

Jubilate Canis. Erica Jong. PRA

Jubilate Herbis. Norma Farber. PChr

Jubilate Matteo. Gavin Ewart. UV

Jubilation T. Cornpone. Johnny Mercer. OBAL

Jubilee before Revolution. Andrew Lang. BXAP

Juce of lekes with gotes galle. *Unknown.* MiEL

Juchitán. Luis J. Rodriguez. AfAz

Judaeus Errans. Louis Golding. TrJP

Judah in Exile Wanders. George Sandys. AH; ChIV-1

Judas. Vassar Miller. ChIV-2; MoAmPo

Judas. *Unknown.* ESPB

Judas. *Unknown. See* It was upon a Shere [*or* Score] Thorsday that vre [*or* oure] Loverd [*or* Lord] aros.

Judas and the Profiteer. Sir Osbert Sitwell. NSI

Judas descended to this lower Hell. Judas and the Profiteer. Sir Osbert Sitwell. NSI

Judas Goat, The. Susan Musgrave. NOBC

Judas Iscariot. Countee Cullen. PoLF

Judas Iscariot. R. A. K. Mason. PeNZ

Judas Iscariot. Stephen Spender. MoAB; MoBrPo; NIP

Judas Iscariot/ sat in the upper. Judas Iscariot. R. A. K. Mason. PeNZ

Judas Maccabeus. Bible, Apocrypha. *Fr.* First Maccabees. TrJP

Judas Sells His Lord. *Unknown. See* It wes upon a Shere [*or* Score] Thorsday that ure [*or* oure] Louerd [*or* Lord] aros.

Judas Town. Anne Carson. *Fr.* Life of Towns, The. BAP-90

Jude. Carol Moldaw. UTF

Judeebug's Country. Joe Johnson. PoBA

Judge Commits Suicide, A. "Hugh MacDiarmid." IHNG

Judge gives negro 90 days in county jail. *(LL)* Ballad of the Landlord. Langston Hughes. HCAP; NOBA

Judge has sentenced himself to a suicide's grave?, A. A Judge Commits Suicide. "Hugh MacDiarmid." IHNG

Judge, judge, tell the judge. *Unknown.* OxBoLi; RoPo

Judge Me, O God. Joel Barlow. AH

Judge me, O God. Bible, *O.T., paraphrased by* Sir Thomas Wyatt. *Fr.* Psalms.

(Search, The, XLII *and* XLIII Moulton, *Modern Reader's Bible.*) WGRP

Judge Not. Josephine D. Henderson Heard. CBWP-4

Judge Not. Theodore Roethke. ChIV-2

Judge not a Princess' worth impeached hereby. Queen Katherine to Owen Tudor. Michael Drayton. *Fr.* England's Heroical Epistles. NoSic

Judge Not According to the Appearance. Christina Rossetti. TrPWD

Judge Not the Preacher; for He is Thy Judge. George Herbert. OxAEP-1

Judge of an abnormal stone. The Narrator. Milo De Angelis, *tr. fr. Italian by* Lawrence Venuti. NeIt

Judge said "Stand up, boy, and dry up your tears," The. Twenty-one Years. *Unknown.* AmFP

Judge Somers. Edgar Lee Masters. *Fr.* Spoon River Anthology. FaBoEE; OBSV

Judge tenderly of me! *(LL)* This is my letter to the world. Emily Dickinson. AmPP; HeIP; MeMAP; MoP; NAAL-1; NALW; NoAM; NOBA; OxBA; Poetr; SAmP; SCV; TAP; WPE

Judge then what debtor can keep touch truly. *(LL)* A Secret Love or Two I Must Confess[e]. Thomas Campion. AAS; ErPo

Judge whether I am happy, yea or no. *(LL)* The Deformed Mistress. Sir John Suckling. BXAP; ErPo

Judge, who lives impeccably upstairs, The. Upstairs Downstairs. Hervey Allen. PoA; PoNe

Judge with the Sore Rump, The. St. George Tucker. OBAL

Judged by my goddess' doom to endless pain. William Percy. *Fr.* Coelia. Son

Judged by the Company One Keeps. *Unknown.* BLPA; NBLV

Judgement. Ciaran Carson. PBCIP

Judgement. George Herbert. ESCV; GeHe; SeCP

Judgement Day. Odia Ofeimun. HBAPE

Judgement Day. *Unknown.* WTO

Judgement of God, The. William Morris. PeVV

Judgement of Tiresias, The. Hildebrand Jacob. NOEC

Judges, *sels.* Bible, *O.T.*

Song of Deborah, The. AWP; BoWoP; PBWP

(Then Sang Deborah and Barak.) TrJP

"Blessed above women/ shall Jael the wife of Heber the Kenite be" WPOW

Judges of the Little Box, The. Vasco [*or* Vasko] Popa, *tr. fr. Serbo-Croatian by* Charles Simic. AnRep; HSix

Judges so just, so knowing, and so kind. *(LL)* Epilogue Spoken by Mrs. Boutell. Dryden. SeCV-2

Judging Distances. Henry Reed. *Fr.* Lessons of the War. BoLoP; GTBS-P; HeIP; LiTB; MoAB; NIP; NOBE; NoP; OBWP; PAW; Poetr; PoWW

Judging Lear. Libby Houston. NBrP

Judgment. William Rose Benét. AnAmPo

Judgment, The. Kathleen Spivack BoWoP

Judgment Day. Robert Garioch, *after the Italian of* Giuseppe Belli. OBVE

Judgment Day, The. James Weldon Johnson. ChIV-2

Judgment Day. R. S. Thomas. CRP

Judgment in Heaven, A, *sels.* Francis Thompson.

"Heaven, which man's generations draws." MoAB; MoBrPo

Judgment of Paris, The. W. S. Merwin. NAAL-2; NNaP

Judgment of Paris, The. Ralph Schomberg. TrJP

Sels.

Ay or Nay?

Courtier's a Riddle, A

Like Birds of a Feather

Judgment of Paris, The. *Unknown. Fr.* Goddesses Three. OtMeF

Judgment of the May, The. Richard Watson Dixon. OBNC

Judicious Observation of That Dreadful Comet, A. Ichabod Wiswall. SCAP

Judith, *sels.* Lascelles Abercrombie.

"Balkis was in her marble town." MoBrPo

Judith. Eloise Bibb. CBWP-4

Judith, *sels.* Bible, Apocrypha.

With Timbrels. TrJP

Judith. Adah Isaacs Menken. AmWP; CBWP-1

Judith 2. Patti Smith. VBLP

Judith of Bethulia. John Crowe Ransom. FaBoMo; FYAP; LiTA; LiTM; MeMAP; NoAM; NOBA

Judith Recalls Holofernes. Maura Stanton. AmPA

Judy Jetson spins. In Outer Space. David Trinidad. BAP-91

Judy-One. Don L. Lee. TAP

Judy Sugden! Judy, I made you caper. Barnsley and District. Donald Davie. NoAM; OxBC

Jug Brook. Ellen Bryant Voigt. MT

Jug, jug! Fair fall the nightingal. The Nightingale. Richard Brathwaite [or Brathwait]. Fr. Nature's Embassy. EIL

Jug of water in the hand, and on, A. Dawn. Rachel, tr. fr. Hebrew by A. M. Klein. TrJP

Juggler. Lucien Stryk. CAPP

Juggler. Richard Wilbur. CMoP; LiTM; MoAB; NYBP; TAP

Juggler and the baron's daughter, The. Unknown. See Here beside dwelleth.

Juggling Jerry. George Meredith. BeLS

Juggy's Christening. Unknown. NOEC

Jugs, The. Paul Celan, tr. fr. German by Christopher Middleton. OBVE

Juice of apples climbs in me, The. The Forbidden. Phyllis Haring. PeSA

JuJu. Askia Muhammad Touré. PoBA

Juju of My Own, A. Lebert Bethune. PoBA; PoNe

Juke Box Love Song. Langston Hughes. GrPl; PoBA; SAmP; TTTS

Julia, how Irishly you sacrifice. Reproach to Julia. Robert Graves. FaBoEE

Julia, I bring. A Ring Presented to Julia. Robert Herrick. PeLV

Julia, if I chance to die. His Request to Julia. Robert Herrick. BeJo; CaPo; NOSC

Julia, my wife, has grown quite rude. From a Connecticut Newspaper. Levi Rockwell. FaBoUs

Julia, when thy Herrick dies. To Julia. Robert Herrick. CaPo; NOSC

Julian and Maddalo. Shelley. FHYEP; OAEL-2, abr.; OBTV

Julian Barely Misses Zimmer's Brains. Paul Zimmer. GOYP

Julian of Norwich. Kathleen Jamie. VBLP

Juliana, sels. Cynewulf, tr. fr. Anglo-Saxon by Charles W. Kennedy. "I have great need that the Saint grant help." AnOE

Julianus Sees a Bronze Statue of Icarus in a Public Bath. Julianus of Egypt, tr. fr. Greek by Lee T. Pearcy. GrAn

Julianus Sees a Magistrate's Axe. Julianus of Egypt, tr. fr. Greek by Lee T. Pearcy. GrAn

Julianus Sees the Chair of the Sophist Craterus. Julianus of Egypt, tr. fr. Greek by Lee T. Pearcy. GrAn

Julia's Petticoat. Robert Herrick. BeJo; CaPo

Julie, Pete and Linc. The Mod Squad. David Trinidad. BAP-91

Juliek's Violin. Michael C. Blumenthal. BTR

Juliet. Hilaire Belloc. ArLo; BoLoP; EnLoPo

Juliet, farewell. I would not be forgiven. Wilfrid Scawen Blunt. Fr. Love Sonnets of Proteus, The. TrGrPo

Julius Caesar, sels. Shakespeare. "Cowards die many times before their deaths." FF (That Men Should Fear.) TrGrPo "Friends, Romans, countrymen, lend me your ears." EBEvV (Antony's Oration [over Caesar's Body].) LiTB; TrGrPo (Mark Antony Addresses the Mob.) FaPoR "Friends, Romans, countrymen, lend me your ears." OxAEP-1 "How died my master, Strato?" OxAEP-1 "If you have tears, prepare to shed them now." OxAEP-1 "O mighty Cæsar! dost thou lie so low?" OxAEP-1 "O, pardon me, thou bleeding piece of earth." EBEvV; OxAEP-1 Portrait of Brutus. TrGrPo Portrait of Caesar. TrGrPo "Since Cassius first did whet me against Cæsar." OxAEP-1 "Who ever knew the heavens menace so?" OxAEP-1

Julius Caesar. Unknown. InPK; ISE

Julius Caesar and the Honey-Bee. Charles Tennyson Turner. FM

Julius Caesar made a law. Unknown. ISE

Julius Caesar said with a smile. Unknown. ISE

July. H. Cordelia Ray. CBWP-3

July. Folgore da San Geminiano, tr. fr. Italian by Dante Gabriel Rossetti. Fr. Sonnets of the Months. AWP

July. Susan Hartley Swett. GN

July 4, 1984: For Buck. June Jordan. NoAM

July 4th. May Swenson. PoA

July 4th. Anne Waldman. UL

July in Chicago. Lorri Jackson. NGP

July in Indiana. Robert Fitzgerald. AiP; NYBP

July in Washington. Robert Lowell. LCAP; NAAL-2; NaP; Prf

July 1914. "Anna Akhmatova," tr. fr. Russian by Stanley Kunitz and Max Hayward. PeFWW; WPOW, Pt. I only, tr. by Stanley Kunitz

July the First. Robert Currie. Poetsp

July the first, of a morning clear, one thousand six hundred and ninety. The Boyne Water. Unknown. FaBoEH, abr.; FaPoR; IIP; NOIV

July: The Succession of the Four Sweet Months. Robert Herrick. See First, April, she with mellow showers.

July the twenty-second day. The Descent on Middlesex. Peter St. John. PAH

July 31. Norman Jordan. PoBA

July 27. Norman Jordan. NBV

7,22,66. Sandra McPherson. AnAn

July Wakes. Richard Pomfret. OBET

Jumbled in the Common Box. W. H. Auden. PoRA

Jumblies, The. Edward Lear. BLPL; CBNP; ChTr; EBEV; EBEvV; FaBoBe; FaBoNo; GoJo; ImPo; LiTB; NAEL-2; OtMeF; OxBChV; OxBoLi; PeLV; PeVV; PoRA; SiSoPo; TEP; TFi; UV, sh. vers.; WiR

Jump back, honey, jump back. (LL) A Negro Love Song. Paul Laurence Dunbar. AAP; PoNe

Jump bigness upward. Mwilu/ or Poem for the Living. Don L. Lee. JB

Jump Cabling. Linda Pastan. InPK

Jump — jump — jump — Jump away. The Little Jumping Girls. Kate Greenaway. FaPON

Jump over the wall and come to me. Come to Me. Gond Oral Tradition, tr. by V. Elwin and S. Hivale. WTO

Jump-Rope Rhyme. Unknown. See "Hello, hello, hello, sir."

Jump stone hand leaf shadow sun. The Fire. Robert Duncan. Fr. Passages. VGW

Jump stop shake. (LL) Blackberry Sweet. Dudley Randall. HAP; InPS; SoSe; WeW

Jumping into Joy. Marg Yeo. DT

Juncture. Rea Lubar Duncan. PoNe

June. Elaine Feinstein. BrRo

June. Aileen Fisher. PDV

June. Mary Weston Fordham. CBWP-2

June. Francis Ledwidge. BIrV; NOIV; PeIV

June. Irene F. Pawsey. BoTP

June. H. Cordelia Ray. CBWP-3

June. Folgore da San Geminiano, tr. fr. Italian by Dante Gabriel Rossetti. Fr. Sonnets of the Months. AWP

June. Jane G. Stewart. BoTP

June and finally the snowpeas. What Makes the Grizzlies Dance. Sandra Alcosser. FoLa

June Bracken and Heather. Tennyson. EnLoPo

June, but the morning's cold, the wind. Porth Cwyfan. Roland Mathias. AngWe

June Fugue. Thomas W. Shapcott. NOBAu

June in her eyes, in her heart January. (LL) The Spring. Thomas Carew. BeJo; CaPo; GN; NoP; PFP; PoE; PoEL-3; SeCV-1; TEP; TrGrPo; WiR

June, 1915. Charlotte Mew. OxAEP-2

June 1940. Weldon Kees. ArOW

June sun in an orchard, A. My Mother's Burying. Sean O Riordain, tr. fr. Irish by Valentine Iremonger. TIRV

June 10. Magdalena de Rodriguez, tr. fr. Spanish by Nina Serrano. WPOW

June Thunder. Louis MacNeice. CMoP

June Twilight. John Masefield. GoYe

June Weather. James Russell Lowell. See For a cap and bells our lives we pay.

June ("What is so rare as a day in June?") James Russell Lowell. See What [or And what] Is So Rare as a Day in June?

June, yet the roses are still asleep in their black dormitory. Getting Dressed in the Dark. Vickie Karp. BAP-89

Junes were free and full, driving through tiny, The. June Thunder. Louis MacNeice. CMoP

Jungle, The. Diane Di Prima. PoM

Jungle. Phyllis Haring. PeSA

Jungle, The. Alun Lewis. AngWe; OBWVE

Jungle. Mary Carter Smith. PoNe

Jungle, The. Randolph Stow. Fr. Thailand Railway. CBAP

Jungle Book, The, sels. Kipling. Seal Lullaby. FaPON; OBAP (Seal Mother's Song.) ZA

Jungle Café, The. Gary Soto. NoAM

Jungle Gliders. Roger Weingarten. NAmP90

Jungle Husband, The. Stevie Smith. FaBoWP; NBLV; NIP; RB

Jungle Mammy Song. Unknown. AS

Jungle Rot and Open Arms. Janice Mirikitani. ETG

Just like the Travels of Captain Cook. (*LL*) The Pedlar's Caravan. William Brighty Rands. BoTP; OxBChV

Just Like This. D. A. Olney. BoTP

Just like unto a nest of boxes round. Of Many Worlds in This World. Margaret Cavendish, Duchess of Newcastle. NOSC

Just look at them, the shameless well-to-do. Palladas, *tr. fr. Greek by* Tony Harrison. GrAn

Just look, Manetto, at that wry-mouth'd minx. Sonnet: Of an Ill-Favored Lady. Cavalcanti, *tr. fr. Italian by* Dante Gabriel Rossetti. AWP

Just look, 'tis a quarter past six, love. The Coming Woman. Mary Weston Fordham. AmWP; CBWP-2

Just lost, when I was saved! Emily Dickinson. AmPP; NOBA; NOCV; Prf (Called Back.) MoAmPo

Just Making It. Richard W. Thomas. PoNe

Just man followed then his angel guide, The. Lot's Wife. "Anna Akhmatova," *tr. fr. Russian by* Richard Wilbur. BoWoP; PBWP

Just missed him! (*LL*) On a Squirrel Crossing the Road in Autumn, in New England. Richard Eberhart. HeIP; LiTM; Poetsp

Just now/ Out of the strange. The Warning. Adelaide Crapsey. Spl; WPE (Cinquain: A Warning.) WeW

Just now the lilac is in bloom. The Old Vicarage, Grantchester. Rupert Brooke. EBEvV; FaBoPP; FaBV; FaPoB; MoBrPo; OBTV; OxBTC; PFP; PoRA

Just off his motorbike. Going to Mass after Fifteen Years. Maxine Scates. PBCAP

Just off the highway to Rochester, Minnesota. A Blessing. James Wright. ArNa; CAPP; GoJo; GrPl; InPK; InPS; NAAL-2; NaP; NoAM; NOBA; NoP; PoE; Poetr; PPP; RaBo; TRP; TwCP; VCAP

Just One Book. *Unknown*. BLRP

Just one brief instant here. (*LL*) Could it be true we live on earth? Nezalhualcoyotl. EaPr

Just One Day. Susan E. Gammons. PWR

Just one more time. Only one. Needle, The: For a Friend Who Disappeared. Franz Wright. NAmP90

Just One Signal. *Unknown*. PAH

Just one too many times. Jazz Poem for the Girl Who Cried Wolf. James Nolan. Jaz

Just out of San Francisco one cold December day. The Dying Hobo. *Unknown*. AmFP

Just Passing. *Unknown*. BLRP

Just past the fading line I hold. (*LL*) Short Wave In Shanghai. Sibyl James. LoHo

Just quartering a Tree. (*LL*) Wind begun to rock the grass, The. Emily Dickinson. HAP; NAAL-1; WeW

Just sitting around smoking, drinking and telling stories. And with March a Decade in Bolinas. Joanne Kyger. UL

Just smiling. (*LL*) Try Smiling. *Unknown*. BLPA; PWR; WBLP

Just so it goes — the day, the night. An Ordinary Evening in Cleveland. Lewis Turco. NYBP

Just so long and long enough. (*LL*) As Freedom Is a Breakfastfood. E. E. Cummings. CMoP; LiTA; LiTM; MAT; NOBA; OxBA; TAP; VGW

Just-So Stories., *sels*. Kipling. Hump, The. OxBChV

Just stand aside and watch yourself go by. Watch Yourself Go By. Strickland W. Gillilan. BLPA; PoToHe (Cure for Fault Finding, A.) PWR; WBLP

Just such a happy Change, our Nation finds. Daniel Defoe. FaBoEH

Just Taking Note. Sharon Scott. JB

Just that way I wanted to touch you. No Hay Fronteras. Jan Clausen. ETG

Just the lessons given you now. Maxims in Rhyme for the Young. J. Clark. PWR

"Just the place for a Snark!" the Bellman cried. "Lewis Carroll." *Fr.* Hunting of the Snark, The. CBNP; EBEvV, *Pt.* 1 *only*; FaBoNo; FaPoB; FiBHP, *much abr*.; OBNC; OBNV; PoEL-5

Just the right age to take an interest in the job. To a Home-town Conscript Posted Overseas. Peter Bland. PAW

Just the Same Today. *Unknown*. BLRP; WBLP

Just the Two of Us. Tomioka Taeko, *tr. fr. Japanese*. WPOW, *tr. by* Harry *and* Lynn Guest *and* Kajima Shozo

Just then, forgetful of the strict command. Homer, *tr. by* William Cowper. *Fr.* Odyssey. NAWM-1; OBVE

Just there, in a corner of the whin-field. Our Lady of Ardboe. Paul Muldoon. BiHa; PBCIP

Just think how it's improved her French. (*LL*) Compensation. Harry Graham. CBNP; PeLV

Just to be is a blessing. Abraham Heschel. EaPr

Just to Be Needed. Mary Eversley. PoToHe

Just to be tender, just to be true. God's Will for Us. *Unknown*. BLRP; WBLP

(God's Will for You and Me.) SoSe

Just to keep her from the foggy, foggy dew. (*LL*) The Foggy, Foggy Dew. *Unknown*. AS; CoMu; ELP; GBP; LiTB; OBET; OxBoLi; PeLV; PIP

Just to live is holy. (*LL*) Just to be is a blessing. Abraham Heschel. EaPr

Just Try This. *Unknown*. WBLP

Just Try to Be the Fellow That Your Mother Thinks You Are. Will S. Adkin. WBLP

Just Walking Around. John Ashbery. NAAL-2

Just watch Melissa sweep a room! (*LL*) When Young Melissa Sweeps. Nancy Byrd Turner. FaPON; NTCP

Just when our drawing-rooms begin to blaze. Winter Evening ("Just when our drawing-rooms begin to blaze.") William Cowper. *Fr.* Task, The. NOEC

Just when you're able to admit. Corps d'Esprit. Heather McHugh. AmPA

Just where the Treasury's marble front. Pan in Wall Street. Edmund Clarence Stedman. AnAmPo

Justice. George Chapman. *Fr.* Euthymiae Raptus; or, The Teares of Peace. NOSC

Justice. Langston Hughes. BPo

Justice. Petra von Morstein, *tr. fr. German by* Rosemarie Waldrop. BoWoP

Justice Denied in Massachusetts. Edna St. Vincent Millay. AiP; GOA; MoAmPo

Justice Is Reason Enough. Diane Wakoski. AmPA

Justice of the Peace, The. Hilaire Belloc. IHNG; NOBVV; OBSV

Justice to Scotland. *At. to* Burns Burns. NBLV

Justification. William Strode. NOSC

Justified mother of men, The. (*LL*) Faces. Walt Whitman. PoEL-5

Justified Mother of Men, The. Walt Whitman. OHIP

Justify all those renowned generations. The Renowned Generations. W. B. Yeats. OxBoLi

Justiniano Lamé Has Been Killed. Jimmie Durham. HATNAP

Justus Quidem Tu Es, Domine. Gerard Manley Hopkins. *See* Thou Art Indeed Just, Lord, If I Contend.

Jute Mill Song, The. *Unknown*. OBET

Juventius, could you not find in this great crowd of men. Catullus, *tr. fr. Latin*. PeHV

Juventius, my honey, while you played. Catullus, *tr. fr. Latin by* James Michie. PeHV

Juxta. Grover Jacoby. GoYe

Juxtaposition. Arthur Hugh Clough. *Fr.* Amours de Voyage. NOBVV; OBNC

Juxtaposition is great, — but, you tell me, affinity greater. Claude to Eustace. Arthur Hugh Clough. *Fr.* Amours de Voyage. CBLP; NOBVV

K

K for the Klondyke, a country of gold. Hilaire Belloc. *Fr.* Moral Alphabet, A. NoAM

Ka 'Ba. Amiri Baraka. BPo; NBV; TAP

Ka-la-kaua, a great name. Praise Song for King Kalakaua. *Unknown, tr. fr. Hawaiian by* N. B. Emerson. WTO

Kabul town's by Kabul river. Ford o' Kabul River. Kipling. FaBoTw; PeVV

Kaddish. Catherine de Vinck. BTR

Kaddish. Allen Ginsberg. HCAP; NAAL-2; NeAP; NOBA; PoBeRe; PoM

Kaddish. David Ignatow. EaPr; NU; RaBo

Kaddish, *sels*. Melanie Kaye/Kantrowitz. "If I said kaddish for each one." BTR

Kaddish. Levi Yitzhok, *tr. fr. Yiddish by* Joseph Leftwich. TrJP

Kadia the Young Mother Speaks. Jessie E. Sampter. TrJP

Kafka's Semen. Carolyn Lau. BCF

Kafoozalum. *Unknown*. BeLS; BLPA

Kagwa hunted the lion. The Huntsman. Edward Lowbury. OBSP

Kaiser Bill. *Unknown*. NSI

Kaiser Bill went up the hill. Kaiser Bill. *Unknown*. NSI

Kaiser Dead. Matthew Arnold. FM

Kalahari Bushman fires flowing. Firebowl. Sydney Clouts. PeSAV

Kalaloch. Carolyn Forché. AmPA; AnAn; NoAM

Kalapuya Prophecy. A. *Unknown, tr. fr. Kalapuya Indian by* Jarold Ramsey. STP

Kaleidoscope, The. David Gill. OBTV

Kaleidoscope. G. K. Page. NoAM

Kaleidoscope, A. Sunfish Races. James Preston. InPK

Keep Thou My Way, O Lord. Fanny Crosby. TrPWD

Keep to the one path. Bacchylides, *tr. fr. Greek by* Sam Hamill. InMo

Keep to yourself your kisses. Taisigh Agat Fein Do Phog. *Unknown, tr. fr. Irish by* Maire Cruise O'Brien. BIrV

Keep Ye Holy Sabbath Rest. *Unknown, tr. fr. Hebrew by* Herbert Loewe. TrJP

Keep your copper coin, save your cup of wheat. Never Ask Me Why. Silvia Margolis. GoYe

Keep your eyes open when you kiss: do: when. John Berryman. BoLoP

Keep your kiss to yourself. *Unknown, tr. fr. Irish by* Thomas Kinsella. NOIV

Keep your whiskers crisp and clean. The King of Cats Sends a Postcard to His Wife. Nancy Willard. OBCA; OFC

Keeper, The. William Carpenter. Poetsp

Keeper of the Midnight Gate, The. George Mackay Brown. OxBC

Keeper who worked at the zoo, A. Frank Richards. PeLi

Keeping Christmas. Eleanor Farjeon. OBCP

Keeping Hair. Ramona Wilson. CrSp; VoR

Keeping On. Arthur Hugh Clough. *See* Say not the struggle nought [*or* naught] availeth.

Keeping Pacific Time. Aidan Carl Mathews. IB

Keeping Quiet. Pablo Neruda, *tr. by* Alastair Reed. EaPr

Keeping Their World Large. Marianne Moore. RaBo

Keeping Things Whole. Mark Strand. CoAP; HCAP; HeIP; LCAP; PPP; TAP; VCAP

Keeps on sleeping. (*LL*) Judith 2. Patti Smith. VBLP

Keeps the sleeping child from harms. (*LL*) Another. Robert Herrick. BeJo

Keepsake from Quinault. Dorothy Alyea. GoYe

Kehama's Curse. Robert Southey. *Fr.* Curse of Kehama, The. OBNC

Keine Lazarovitch, 1870-1959. Irving Layton. NIP

Keith Haring, Deceased. Ammon Wrigley. UnDi

Keith of Ravelston. Sydney Thompson Dobell. *See* Murmur of the mourning ghost, The.

Kelly on a Mountain. The Man from Strathbogie. Olive Mary Finnin. NOBAu

Kelly Square Smoke Shop closes its doors, The. Outside Baby Moon's. Paul Violi. UL

Kellyburnbraes. *Unknown.* OxBB

Kelly's kept an unlicensed bull, well away. The Outlaw. Seamus Heaney. MoP; OxBC

Kelp. Nora Dauenhauer. HATNAP

Kemp Owyne. Alice Cary. EnSB; ESPB; OHIP

Kemp Owyne. *Unknown.* EnSB; ESPB, A *and* B *vers.*

Kempion. *Unknown. See* "Come here, come here, you freely feed."

Ken when to spend and when to spare. *Unknown.* FaBoUs

Kenst doo hoo. The Miller's Wife's Lullaby. *Unknown.* GBP

Kent State, May 4, 1970. Paul Goodman. MAT

Kentucky, *sels.* Yisroel-Yankev Schwartz, *tr. fr. Yiddish by* Seymour Levitan.

Kentucky Belle. Constancè Fenimore Woolson. BeLS; BLPA; FaBoBe; PAH

Kentucky Moonshiner. *Unknown.* AS; OBAL

Kentucky Mountain Farm, *sels.* Robert Penn Warren.
   History among the Rocks. GOA; MoAmPo

Kentucky water, clear springs: a boy fleeing. The Swimmers. Allen Tate. InPS; MoAmPo; NoAM; NOBA

Kentucky Woman. Al Masarik. NGP

Kepe well X, and flee fro VII. *Unknown.* MiEL
   (Ten Commandments, Seven Deadly Sins, and Five Wits.) ChTr; FaBoEE

Kéramos, *sels.* Longfellow.
   Potter's Song, The. PoEL-5

Kerouac was born in the same town. Lowell, Mass. Billy Collins. NGP

Kerr's Ass. Patrick Kavanagh. NOIV; RB

Kerve thy brede note to thynne. Table Manners. *Unknown.* OxBLMV

Kettle sang the boy to a half-sleep, The. Halibut Cove Harvest. Kenneth Leslie. NOBC

Kettle's for the kitchen, A. John Travers Moore *and* Margaret Moore *and* Margaret Moore. SiSoPo

Kett's Rebellion. Keith Chandler. FaBoEH

Kevin Barry. *Unknown.* AS; SWP

Kevin Barry: Died for Ireland, 1st November, 1920. *Unknown.* FaBoBa

Key, The. John Ormond. AngWe

Key of the kingdom, The. *Unknown. See* This Is the Key.

Key (or Penis): "Strange thing hangs by man's hip, A." Unknown, formerly at. to Cynewulf, *tr. fr. Anglo-Saxon. Fr.* Riddles (Exeter Book). PeLV, *tr. by* Kevin Crossley-Holland

Key. The door. Open, A. Tom. James Schuyler. GLP

Key to Everything, The. May Swenson. IHMS

Key West. Hart Crane. CMoP

Keyhole in the Door, The. *Unknown.* CoMu

Keys of Canterbury, The. *Unknown.* AmFP

Keys of Morning, The. Walter de la Mare. NoP

Keyss lids acid and speed. (*LL*) Street Song. Thom Gunn. HeIP; NoP; OxBC

Khrushchev is coming on the right day! Frank O'Hara. NeAP; PoM

Kick a Little Stone. Dorothy Aldis. TLR

Kick at the rock, Sam Johnson, break your bones. Epistemology. Richard Wilbur. CRP; NoAM; NOBA; OxBSP

Kicking against the Walls. Katrina Porteous. NWP

Kicking his mother until she let go of his soul. Mundus et Infans. W. H. Auden. LiTB; LiTM; MeMAP; MoAB; MoBrPo; NAs; NoAM

Kicking Mule, The. *Unknown.* AmFP

Kicking the Leaves. Donald Hall. CAPP

(Kicks the Knife-grinder, overturns his wheel, and exit in a transport of Republican enthusiasm and universal philanthropy). (*LL*) The Friend of Humanity and the Knife Grinder. George Canning *and* John Hookham Frere. BXAP; FaBoCo; UV

Kid, The. Ai. NoAM

Kid, The, *sels.* Conrad Aiken.
   Proem to "The Kid." MoAB

Kid Has Gone to the Colors, The. William M. Herschell. PoLF

Kid Stuff. Frank Horne. PChr; PoBA; PoNe

Kid who wrote *fuck* everywhere kissed his mom, The. Vandal. Richard Robbins. NGP

Kidded in April above Glencolumbkille. Care. Richard Murphy. IPY

Kiddushin 4:12. *Unknown.* EaPr

Kidnap Poem. Nikki Giovanni. BPo; GOYP; Poetr; TAP

Kidnaper. Tess Gallagher. AmPA

Kidnapped. Bible, Apocrypha. BAP-89

Kidnapper. Tess Gallagher. *See* He motions me over with a question.

Kidnapping of Sims, The. John Pierpont. PAH

Kilaben Bay Song. *Unknown, tr. fr. Aborigine by* Perce Haslam. NOBAu

Kilbarchan now may say alas! The Life and Death of [Habbie Simson] the Piper of Kilbarchan. Robert Sempill. OxBS

Kilcash. *Unknown, tr. fr. Irish by* Frank O'Connor. BIrV; IIP; OBMV; PeIV

Kilfenora Teaboy, The. Paul Durcan. PBCIP

Kilkenny Cats, The. *Unknown.* CRH

Kill me not every day. Affliction ("Kill me not every day.") George Herbert. NOSC; TEP

Kill or be killed, the sergeant cried. The Killer Too. Walker Gibson. FF

Kill That Crowing Cock. *Unknown, tr. fr. Chinese by* Kenneth Rexroth. OHMPC

Kill yourselves with knives and poisoned gas. Strangers Are We All upon the Earth. Franz Werfel, *tr. fr. German by* Edith Abercrombie Snow. TrJP

Killed at the Ford. Longfellow. OHIP

Killed by an omnibus — why not? On a Man Run Over by an Omnibus. Henry Luttrell. FaBoEE

Killed in Action. Joseph Leftwich. NSI

Killed women, children, and defencelss men. (*LL*) The White Monster. W. H. Davies. LiTB

Killer, The. A'yunini, *tr. fr. Cherokee Indian by* Jerome K. Rothenberg. STP

Killer-cops, the San Diego three, The. Deadly James (For All the Victims of Police Brutality). James A. Emanuel. ETG

Killer Too, The. Walker Gibson. FF

Killers. Cordelia Candelaria. AfAz

Killers That Run, The. Leonard Cohen. NOBC

Killigrew Wood, The. Norman Dubie. AmPA

Killing. Samuel Greenberg. LiTA

Killing, The. George MacBeth. FaBoMo

Killing No Murder. Sylvia Townsend Warner. MoBrPo

Killing of the Birds, The. Shirley Williams. BoWoP

Killing Time. Tony Harrison. *Fr.* Art & Extinction. SCBI

Kilmeny. James Hogg. *Fr.* Queen's Wake, The. OBEV; OxAEP-2

Kilmeny. Alfred Noyes. NSI

Kilroy. Eugene McCarthy. AiP

Kilroy. Peter Viereck. ArOW; FF; MoAmPo

Kilroy is gone. Kilroy. Eugene McCarthy. AiP

Kilroy Was Here. Peter Viereck. *See* Also Ulysses once — that other war.

Kilruddery Hunt, The. Thomas Mozeen. BIrV

Kiltartan Legend. Padraic Fallon. NOIV

Kim, *sels.* Kipling.
   Prodigal Son, The. NoAM

Kimono, The. Don Gordon. PAW

Kin. Michael S. Harper. LCAP

Kin. C. K. Williams. PWE

Kin of my skin you are. (LL) I Go to Meet Him. Grace Nichols. VBLP

Kin: quiet grasses. Deborah as Scion. James Dickey. SV

Kind. A. R. Ammons. NoP; PrIm

Kind Are Her Answers. Thomas Campion. BoLoP; CBLP; ELP; TrGrPo

Kind country-men listen I pray. All Things Be Dear but Poor Mens Labour; or, The Sad Complaint of Poor People. Unknown. CoMu

Kind Deeds. Isaac Watts. BoTP

Kind friends, you must pity my horrible tale. The Dreary Black Hills. Unknown. AmFP

Kind gentlemen, will you be patient awhile? Robin Hood's Birth, Breeding, Valor, and Marriage. Unknown. ESPB

Kind Heaven, assist the trembling muse. The Wyoming Massacre. Uriah Terry. PAH

Kind Inn, A. George Dillon. GoYe

Kind Keeper, The, sels. Dryden.
  Song from the Italian, A. SeCV-2

Kind, kind, milk in the mind. Stars in Your Name. Olga Broumas. PFL

Kind lovers, love on. John Crowne. Fr. Calisto. InvP; OxBSP

Kind Miss. Unknown. AS

Kind Mousie, The. Natalie Joan. BoTP

Kind o'er the kinderbank leans Myfanwy. Myfanwy. Sir John Betjeman. BoLoP
  (KIND o're the kinderbank leans my Myfanwy.) FaPoB

Kind of Act Of, The. Robert Creeley. NeAP

Kind of an Ode to Duty. Ogden Nash. TrGrPo

Kind of change came in my fate, A. Byron. Fr. Prisoner of Chillon, The. BeLS; EnRP; NOBE; PoLF

Kind of empty in the way it sees everything, the earth gets to its feet. For John Clare. John Ashbery. FYAP

Kind of rain we knew is a thing of the past, The. Kinsale. Derek Mahon. BiHa

Kind of rose she wants called John F. Kennedy, The. Fourth Ode to Persephone. Robert Kelly. Fr. Book of Persephone, The. PoM

Kind of slant — the way a ball will glance, A. Gary Miranda. SM

KIND o're the kinderbank leans my Myfanwy. Sir John Betjeman. See Kind o'er the kinderbank leans Myfanwy.

Kind pity [or Kinde pitty] chokes my spleen[e]; brave scorn forbids. John Donne. Fr. Satires. EBEV; ESCV; FHYEP; JCP; OAEL-1; PoEL-2; SeCV-1
  (Religion.) NoP
  (Satyre [or Satire] III.) MeLP; OxAEP-1
  (Satyre III: On Religion.) NAEL-1; SeCP
  (Satyre: Of Religion.) PoE
  (Search for True Religion, The.) NoSic

Kind Saint! who loved the garden flowers. Saint Fiacre. John Irvine. TIRV

Kind Sir: These Woods ("Kind Sir: This is an old game.") Anne Sexton. GoYe

Kind to Gipsy Jane. (LL) Gipsy Jane. William Brighty Rands. BoTP; FaPON

Kind voice, A, calls, "Come, little ones." Crocuses. Anna M. Platt. BoTP

Kind was the hand that at the last. The Death Mask of John Clare. Edmund Blunden. EPCY

Kind Words Can Never Die. Abby Hutchinson. AH

Kinde Are Her Answeres. Thomas Campion. See Kind Are Her Answers.

Kindely is now my coming. Unknown. MiEL

Kinder- und Hausmärchen. Brian Alderson. Mes

Kindergarten children first come forth, The. The May Day Dancing. Howard Nemerov. NYBP; Poetr

Kindergarten Curse. Nina Zivančević, tr. fr. Serbo-Croatian by Charles Simic. HSix

Kindertotenlieder. Michael Longley. CIP

Kindle men's hearts with this, my Word. (LL) The Prophet. Pushkin. AWP

Kindle the Taper. Emma Lazarus. AH

Kindliest thing God ever made, The. The Shade. Theodosia Garrison. OHIP

Kindly Deed, A. Priscilla Jane Thompson. CBWP-2

Kindly I envy thy songs perfection. To Mr. R.W. John Donne. ESCV

Kindly Neighbor, The. Edgar A. Guest. PoToHe

Kindly Unhitch That Star, Buddy. Ogden Nash. LiTA

Kindly Vision. Otto Julius Bierbaum, tr. fr. German by Jethro Bithell. AWP

Kindly watcher by my bed, lift no voice in prayer. Music. George Du Maurier, after the French of Sully-Prudhomme. OBEV

Kindly word and a tender tone, A. A Gentle Word. Unknown. PoToHe

Kindness. Catherine Davis. NYBP

Kindness. T. Sturge Moore. OBMV

Kindness. Sylvia Plath. FaBoWP

Kindness. Mary E. Tucker. CBWP-1

Kindness glides about my house. Kindness. Sylvia Plath. FaBoWP

Kindness to Animals. Laura E. Richards. NTCP

Kindness to Animals. Unknown. BoTP; FaBoUs; WHSW

Kinds of Shel-fish. William Wood. SCAP

Kinds of Trees to Plant. Spenser. Fr. Faerie Queene, The. OHIP

Kineo Mountain. Celeste Turner Wright. Poetsp

Kinfauns Castle, sels. William Montgomerie.
  "Is there no vision in a lovely place?" OxBS

King, a pope, and a kaiser, A. The Ship. Charles MacKay. BLPA

King Alfred sensed among his country's words. Anglo-Saxon. Edward Leslie Mayo. BCF

King & Queen. John Montague. PBCIP

King and Queen of Cantelon. Babylon ("King and Queen of Cantelon.") Unknown. ChTr

King and Queen of the Pelicans we. The Pelican Chorus. Edward Lear. FaBoNo; OBSP

King Arthur, sels. Dryden.
  Harvest Home. PrIm
    (Song: "Your hay it is mow'd, and your corn is reap'd.") SeCV-2
  Song of Venus. OxBoLi; PoEL-3

King Arthur. Mother Goose. See When good King Arthur ruled this [or the] land.

King Arthur and King Cornwall. Unknown. ESPB

King Arthur Growing Very Tired Indeed. Mortimer Collins. See Salad: After Tennyson.

King Arthur made new knights to fill the gap. Pelleas and Ettarre. Tennyson. Fr. Idylls of the King. NAEL-2

King Arthur's Waes-hael. Robert Stephen Hawker. OBEV

King asked, The. The King's Breakfast. A. A. Milne. OTCP; OxBChV; UV, sts. I and II only

King Balak sat on his gaudy throne. Balaam. Charles Causley. EBNV

King Berdok. Unknown. OxBS

King Billy on the Walls. Sheenagh Pugh. AngWe

King Bruce of Scotland flung himself down. Try Again. Eliza Cook. BoTP

King but an' his nobles a', The. Brown Robin. Unknown. ESPB; OxBB

King Canute. Stanley J. Sharpless. BXAP

King Canute, sels. Thackeray.
  "King Canute was weary-hearted; he had reigned for years a score." FaBoEH

King Canute was weary-hearted; he had reigned for years a score. Thackeray. Fr. King Canute. FaBoEH

King Charles on [or upon] the Scaffold. Andrew Marvell. Fr. Horatian Ode upon Cromwell's [or Cromwel's] Return from Ireland, An. ChTr; EBEV; ESCV; FaBoRV; GeHe; GTBS; GTBS-P; HAP; IIP; InPS; JCP; NOBE; NoP; NOSC; OAEL-1; OBEV; OBWP; OxAEP-1; PoEL-2; SCGP; SeCP; SeCV-1; TFi

King Charles the First. Unknown. See As I was going by Charing Cross.

King Charles the First walked and talked. Unknown. OxNR

King Christian. Johannes Evald, tr. fr. Danish by Longfellow. AWP

King Cobra as Political Assassin, The. Ray A. Young Bear. HATNAP

King David. Stephen Vincent Benét. ChIV-1

King David and King Solomon. James Ball Naylor.
  (Authorship.) NBLV

King David Dances. John Berryman. ChIV-1; OxBC; OxBSP

King Duffus. Sylvia Townsend Warner. FaBoWP

King Easter has courted her for her gowd. Fause Foodrage. Unknown. ESPB
  (Fa'se Footrage.) OxBB

King Edward the Fourth and a Tanner of Tamworth. Unknown. ESPB

King Edward the Third, sels. Blake.
  War Song to Englishmen, A. CH
    (War Song, A.) OHIP

King Enjoys His Own Again, The. Martin Parker. FaBoCh; OxBoLi

King Estmere. Unknown. ESPB; OBNV; OxBB

King Ethelred the Unready. Bill Greenwell. BXAP

King Fisher courted Lady Bird. The King-Fisher [or King-Fisher's] Song. "Lewis Carroll." Fr. Sylvie and Bruno Concluded. CBNP; FaBoNo

King-Fisher [or King-Fisher's] Song, The. "Lewis Carroll." Fr. Sylvie and Bruno Concluded. CBNP; FaBoNo

King Francis was a hearty king, and loved a royal sport. The Glove and the Lions. Leigh Hunt. BeLS; FaPON; GN; WBLP

King George V. Charles W. Hayward. NOBAu

King George, observing with judicious eyes. Joseph Trapp. FaBoCo
  (King, observing with judicious eyes, The.) FaBoEE

King had been an hour asleep, The. *(LL)* Mazeppa. Byron. EnRP

King Hancock sat in regal state. A Song about Charleston. *Unknown.* PAH

King Harald's Trance. George Meredith. EBNV; PeVV

King Hart, *sels.* Gawin Douglas.
Hart's Castle. PoEL-1

King Hart, into his cumlye castell strang. Hart's Castle. Gawin Douglas. *Fr.* King Hart. PoEL-1

King has called for priest and cup, The. The Last Rhyme of True Thomas. Kipling. OtMeF

King has written a braid letter, The. Lord Derwentwater. *Unknown.* ESPB

King he hath been a prisoner, The. Willie o Winsbury. *Unknown.* ESPB

King he reigns on a throne of gold, The. The Leveller. "Barry Cornwall." OxAEP-2

King [he] sits in Dumferline [*or* Dumferling] town [*or* toune], The. Sir Patrick Spens [*or* Spence]. *Unknown.* AmFP; AWP; BXAP; CH; ClHu, *diff. vers.*; EBEV; ELP; EnRP; EnSB; ESPB; FaBoBa; FaBoCh; FaPoR; FF; GGP; GN; GoJo; HAP; HeIL; HoPM; InPK; InPS; InvP; LiTB; NAEL-1; NIP; NOBE; NoP; OAEL-1; OBEV; OBSP, *(diff. vers.)*; OtMeF; OxBB; OxBS; PoE; PoEL-1; PPP; PrIm; RB; ScCV; SCGP; TFi; TrGrPo; UnPo; WeW
(King sits in Dunfermlin town, The.) CoGr

King he wrote a love-letter, The. Lord Derwentwater. *Unknown.* AmFP

King Henry. *Unknown.* ESPB; OxBB

King Henry IV, Pt. I. Shakespeare. NAEL-1
Sels.
At My Nativity. NAs
"I have learn'd." OxAEP-1
"I know you all, and will awhile uphold"
"O, Harry! thou hast robb'd me of my youth." OxAEP-1
"Rebellion lay in his way, and he found it"
"So shaken as we are, so wan with care." OxAEP-1
Staff Officer. OtMeF
Villanious and Abominable Falstaff. CBCK

King Henry IV, Pt. II, *sels.* Shakespeare.
"But wherefore did he take away the crown?" OxAEP-1
Cares of Majesty, The. LiTB
(O Gentle Sleep.) FaBoRV
"I never thought to hear you speak again." FaBoEH
"This new and gorgeous garment, majesty." OxAEP-1

King Henry V, *sels.* Shakespeare.
Commonwealth of the Bees, The. GN
"King is full of grace and fair regard, The." OxAEP-1
"Now entertain conjecture of a time." OxAEP-1; RB
(Before Agincourt.) ChTr; EBEV
"From camp to camp, through the foul womb of time" FaBoRV
"O for a Muse of fire, that would ascend." OxAEP-1; SCV
(Muse of Fire, A.) ChTr
"O! that we now had here." OxAEP-1
(Before Agincourt.) PAW
"Once more unto the breach, dear friends, once more." EBEvV; FaBV; OxAEP-1
(Blast of War, The.) TrGrPo
(Henry V at the Siege of Harfleur.) PAW
"This day is called the Feast of Crispian." EBEvV; FaBoEH
(Henry V before Agincourt.) FaPoR
(St. Crispin's Day.) FF
"Thus far, with rough and all-unable pen." CTC
"Thus with imagin'd wing our swift scene flies." EBEV; OxAEP-1
"We few, we happy few, we band of brothers." UnPo
Yon Island Carrions Desperate of Their Bones. RB

King Henry Fifth's Conquest of France. *Unknown.* ESPB

King Henry VI, Pt. I, *sels.* Shakespeare.
"Hung be the heavens with black, yield day to night." OxAEP-1
(King Is Dead, A.) ChTr

King Henry VI, Pt. III, *sels.* Shakespeare.
"Owl shriek'd at thy birth, an evil sign, The." OxAEP-1

King Henry VIII, *sels.* John Fletcher *and* William Shakespeare.
Ambition. TrGrPo
Cranmer's Prophecy of Queen Elizabeth. WGRP
"I have ventur'd." FaBoEH
"Orpheus with his lute made trees." NOSC
(Music.) FaBoCh
(Orpheus with His Lute [Made Trees].) ChTr; EnRePo; GN; TrGrPo
(Orpheus.) EiL; OBEV
(Song: "Orpheus with his Lute made Trees.") PoEL-2
(Sweet Music's Power.) NOBE
This Royal Infant. NAs
Wolsey. FaBoRV
Wolsey's Farewell to His Greatness
(Cardinal Wolsey's Farewell.) LiTB
(Farewell to Greatness.) TrGrPo

King Henry the Eighth was a Tudor. Kirkham Talbot. PeLi

King I saw who walked a cloth of gold, The. Cloth of Gold. Francis Reginald. MoCV

King in May, The. Michael Dennis Browne. NYBP

King in Thule, The. Goethe, *tr. fr. German by* John Frederick Nims. STV

King Is Dead, A. Shakespeare. *See* Hung be the heavens with black, yield day to night.

King is full of grace and fair regard, The. Shakespeare. *Fr.* King Henry V. OxAEP-1

King is out a-hunting, The. The King's Wood. C. S. Holder. BoTP

King James and Brown. *Unknown.* ESPB

King Jamie hath made a vow. Flodden Field. *Unknown.* ESPB

King John, *sels.* Shakespeare.
"Grief fills the room up of my absent child." OBD
"Must you with hot irons burn out both mine eyes?" OxAEP-1
"O, I am scalded with my violent motion." FaBoEH
"This England never did, nor never shall." OxAEP-1
To Gild Refinèd Gold. ImPo; LiTB
"You are as fond of grief as of your child." IMW

King John and the Abbot of Canterbury. *Unknown.* BoTP; EnSB; GN; TrGrPo

King John and the Bishop. *Unknown.* ESPB, A *and* B vers.

King Killi in Combat. Cattantaiyar, *tr. fr.* Tamil *by* A. K. Ramanujan. PLW

King Lear. Peter Huchel, *tr. fr. German by* Michael Hamburger. PoSu

King Lear, *sels.* Shakespeare.
"Blow, winds, and crack your cheek! rage! blow!" OxAEP-1
(Blow, Winds.) TrGrPo
"Come on, sir; here's the place. Stand still." OxAEP-1
(Dover, the Samphire Cliff.) FaBoPP
Fool's prophecy, The. CBNP
"He wakes; speak to him." SCV
"How does my royal lord? How fares your Majesty?" Prf
"Here is the place, my lord; good my lord, enter." OxAEP-1
"Howl, howl, howl! O! you are men of stones." OBD; OxAEP-1
"I prithee, daughter, do not make me mad." OxAEP-1
Lear's Madness. CBNP
"O my dear father! Restoration, hang." OxAEP-1
"Please you, draw near. — Louder the music there!" EBEV
"Prithee go in thyself; seek thine own ease." FaPoB, *sect.* III, iv
Take Physic, Pomp. TrGrPo

King Lear's Wife, *sels.* Gordon Bottomley.
"Ah, you have always been a friend to me." NSI
Louse Crept Out of My Lady's Shift, A. ChTr

King Lot's Envoys. Drummond Allison. OxBSP

King Louis gave lessons in Class. *Unknown.* PeLi

King Louis on his bridge is he. Le Père Sévère. *Unknown, tr. fr.* French *by* Andrew Lang. AWP

King luikit owre his castle wa', The. Sir Colin. *Unknown.* OxBB

King Mark, Tristram, and Palamede. Swinburne. *Fr.* Tristram of Lyonesse. EBNV

King Midas. Howard Moss. CoAP; TAP

King Midas. Ovid, *tr. by* Arthur Golding. *Fr.* Metamorphoses. CTC

King must rule kingdom. Cities are seen from afar. Maxims (Cotton MS.). *Unknown, tr. fr.* Anglo-Saxon *by* Charles W. Kennedy. AnOE

King, observing with judicious eyes, The. Joseph Trapp. *See* King George, observing with judicious eyes.

King of Ai, The. Hyam Plutzik. LiTM

King of Brentford, The. Thackeray. OtMeF

King of Brentford's Testament *abr,* The. *Thackeray.* OBNV

King of Cats Sends a Postcard to His Wife, The. Nancy Willard. OBCA; OFC

King of Ch'in Drinks Wine, The. Li Ho, *tr. fr.* Chinese *by* A. C. Graham. PLT

King of Ch'in rides out on his tiger and roams to the Eight Bounds, The. The King of Ch'in Drinks Wine. Li Ho, *tr. fr.* Chinese *by* A. C. Graham. PLT

King of China's Daughter, The. Edith Sitwell. BoTP; FaBoMo; MoBrPo

King of Comforts! King of life! Praise. Henry Vaughan *and* Thomas Stanley. ESCV

King of Connacht, The. *Unknown, tr. fr.* Early Irish *by* Frank O'Connor. IIP; PeIV

King of Denmark's Ride, The. Caroline E. Norton. BeLS; GN

King of France, the king of France, The/ with forty thousand men. Mother Goose. OxNR
(King of France went up the hill, The.) ReMoGo

King of France went up the hill, The. Mother Goose. *See* King of France, the king of France, The/ with forty thousand men.

King of Glorie, King of Peace. Praise. George Herbert. ESCV

King of glorie, King of peace,/ With the one make warre to cease. L'Envoy. George Herbert. ESCV

King of Glory, King of Peace. Praise II. George Herbert. ChIV-1

King of Glory sends his Son, The. Miracles at the Birth of Christ. Isaac Watts. NOCV

King of Ireland's Cairn, The. "Ethna Carbery." WPE

King of Mercy, King of Love. Begging. Henry Vaughan *and* Thomas Stanley. ESCV

King of Owls, The. Louise Erdrich. NoAM

King of stars. The Open Door. *Unknown, tr. fr. Irish by* Frank O'Connor. IIP

King of the Beasts, deep in the wood, The. The Lion and the Echo. Brian Patten. OBSP

King of the Belgians. Marion Couthouy Smith. PAH

King of the Castle. *Unknown.* OxNR

King of the Cats is Dead, The. Peter Porter. NoAM

King of the Hobbledygoblins, The. Laura E. Richards. OBCA

King of the perennial holly-groves, the riven sandstone. Geoffrey Hill. *Fr.* Mercian Hymns. FaBoMo; HAP; NoAM

King of Thulé, The. Goethe, *tr. fr. German by* James Clarence Mangan. AWP

King of waters, the sea shouldering whale, The. William Wood. SCAP (Sea's Abundant Progeny, The.) NOSC

King of Yellow Butterflies, The. Vachel Lindsay. OBCA

King of Yvetot, The. Pierre Jean de Béranger, *tr. fr. French by* William Toynbee. AWP

King Oliver of New Orleans. Satchmo. Melvin B. Tolson. BPo (Lamda.) PoNe

King, once summoned his favorites, A. The King's Favorites. Priscilla Jane Thompson. CBWP-2

King Orfeo. *Unknown.* ESPB; OxBB; OxBoLi

King over shepherds; here he built his house, A. Median Palace. Robert Wells. SCBI

King Pellam's Launde. David Jones. *Fr.* In Parenthesis. OAEL-2

King Philip had vaunted his claims. A Ballad to Queen Elizabeth. Austin Dobson.
(Ballade of the Armada, A.) FaPoR

King Philip's Last Stand. Clinton Scollard. PAH

"King Rear was foorish man his girls make crazy." A Girdle round the Earth. Anthony Thwaite. PeLV

King Richard hearing of the pranks. The King's Disguise, and Friendship with Robin Hood. *Unknown.* ESPB

King Richard, in one of his rages. Amanda Benjamin Hall. PeLi

King Richard II, sels. Shakespeare.
"Alack, why am I sent for to a king." FaBoEH
"Draw near,/ And list what with our council we have done." OxAEP-1
John of Gaunt's Dying Speech. FaBoEH
    John of Gaunt Speaks EBEvV; FaBoPP; FaPoR
    (This Blessed Plot . . . This England.) FaBV
Let's Talk of Graves. FaBoBe
    Death of Kings, The
    "For God's sake, let us sit upon the ground" HoPM
"O, but they say the tongues of dying men." FaBoRV
    (Tongues of Dying Men, The.) FaBoRV
This England. BoTP; TrGrPo

King Richard III, sels. Shakespeare.
Dream of Wrecks, A. ChTr
"I have been studying how I may compare." OxAEP-1
Methought That I Had Broken from the Tower. RB
"Now is the winter of our discontent." EBEvV; PoE
    (Hate the Idle Pleasures.) TrGrPo
"Rescue, my Lord of Norfolk, rescue, rescue!" FaBoEH
"Tyrannous and bloody act is done, The." FaBoEH
"Where is the duke my father with his power?" OxAEP-1
"Who made thee then a bloody minister." FaBoEH
"Why looks your Grace so heavily today?" OxAEP-1

King Robert of Sicily (The Sicilian's Tale). Longfellow. *Fr.* Tales of a Wayside Inn. OHIP

King Saul and I. Yehuda Amichai, *tr. fr. Hebrew by* Assia Gutmann. PoSu

King Saul was disconcerted. David and Goliath. Priscilla Jane Thompson. CBWP-2

King scrapes the sweat, The. When a King Asks for a Chieftain's Daughter. Maturai Marutan Ilanakanar, *tr. fr. Tamil by* A. K. Ramanujan. PLW

King sent for his wise men all, The. W. W. James Reeves. ChTr; NTCP; SiSoPo

King sent his lady on the first Yule day, The. The Yule Days. *Unknown.* ChTr; GBP; NTP

King Shall Reign in Righteousness, A. Sebastian Streeter. AH

King Sigurd and King Eystein. Sheenagh Pugh. AngWe

King sits in Dunfermlin town, The. *Unknown. See* King [he] sits in Dumferline [*or* Dumferling] town [*or* toune], The.

King snake said to the rattlesnake, The. Rattlesnake Ceremony Song. *Unknown, tr. fr. Yokuts Indian by* A. L. Kroeber. OBAP

King Solomon and the Ants. Whittier. ChIV-1

King Solomon Vistas. Ian Wedde. PeNZ

King Solomon's Camel is a hypocritical creature. King Solomon's Camel. Natan Zach, *tr. fr. Hebrew by* Jon Silkin. PoSu

King Stephen, *sels.* Keats.
"Another sword! And what if I could seize." FaBoEH
"If shame can on a soldier's vein-swoll'n front." FaBoEH

King then left his coach, The. Priam and Achilles. Homer, *tr. fr. Greek. Fr.* Iliad, The. NOSC, *tr. by* George Chapman

King to Oxford sent a troop of horse, The. Sir William Browne. FaBoCo; FaBoEE

King Triumphant. Isaac Watts. *See* Jesus Shall Reign Where'er the Sun.

King walked in his garden green, The. The Three Singing Birds. James Reeves. PDV

King was on his throne, The. The Vision of Belshazzar. Byron. GN

King was sick, The. His cheek was red. The Enchanted Shirt. John Milton Hay. BLPA; GN; VPP

King William Was King George's Son. *Unknown.* AmFP

King William's Dispatch to Queen Augusta. Coventry Patmore. FaBoEE

King Winter sat in his Hall one day. Outside. Hugh Chesterman. BoTP

King with all his kingly train, The. Louis XV. John Sterling. BeLS

Kingcups. Sacheverell Sitwell. MoBrPo

Kingdom, The. Louis MacNeice. LiTM
Sels.
"Take this old man with the soldierly straight back"
"Under the surface of flux and of fear there is an underground movement"

Kingdom. Leopold Staff, *tr. fr. Polish by* Adam Czerniawski. PoSu

Kingdom, The. Jon Swan. NYBP

Kingdom of God, The. Rab, *tr. fr. Hebrew.* TrJP

Kingdom of God, The. Francis Thompson. FaPoR; GTBS-P; NOCV; PlP

Kingdom of God, The. Richard Chenevix Trench. WBLP

Kingdom of Heaven. Léonie Adams. MoAB; MoAmPo

Kingdom of Heaven Compared to a Grain of Mustard-Seed, The. Henry Vaughan. ChIV-2

Kingdom of heaven is likened unto a man which sowed good seed in his field, The. The Parable of the Good Seed. Bible, *N.T. Fr.* St. Matthew. InPK

Kingdom of Kali, The. May Sarton. *Fr.* Invocation to Kali, The. SRLS

Kingdom, or a cottage, or a grave, A. (*LL*) Were I a king, I could command content. Edward de Vere, Earl of Oxford. NoSic

Kingdoms. Alison Brackenbury. SCBI

Kingdoms fall in sequence, like the waves on the shore, The. The Sparrow's Skull. Ruth Pitter. FaBoWP

Kinge Arthur lives in merry Carleile. The Marriage of Sir Gawain. *Unknown.* ESPB

Kinges baneres beth forth ilad, The. *Unknown.* MiEL

Kingfisher, The. Amy Clampitt. HCAP; SM

Kingfisher, The. W. H. Davies. AngWe; NOBE; OBEV; OBWVE

Kingfisher, The. Dyneley Hussey. NSI

Kingfisher, The. John Lloyd. AngWe

Kingfisher, The. Andrew Marvell. *Fr.* Upon Appleton House, to My Lord Fairfax. ChTr; SeCP; SeCV-1

Kingfisher blue along a tangled bank. Poem to the Tune "Riverbank Willows." Yü Hsüan-chi, *tr. by* Geoffrey R. Waters. BoWoP

Kingfisher Flat. William Everson. PoM

Kingfisher green lines the deserted shore. Composed on the Theme "Willows by the Riverside." Yü Hsüan-chi, *tr. fr. Chinese by* Jan W. Walls. SuSp; WPOW

Kingfisher is a glorious thing, The. The Kingfisher. John Lloyd. AngWe

Kingfishers, The. Charles Olson. CMoP; InPS; NAAL-2; NeAP; NOBA; PoM; VCAP

Kingfisher's Boxing Gloves, The. James Fenton. NoAM; SCBI

Kingfisher's naked arc alight, A. Allen Curnow. *Fr.* Small Room with Large Windows, A. PeNZ

Kingfishers nest on South Sea islands. Ch'en Tzu-ang, *tr. by* Irving Y. Lo. *Fr.* Impressions of Things Encountered. SuSp

Kingis Quair, The, *sels.* James I, King of Scotland.
He Sees His Beloved. PoEL-1
"Now was there maid fast by the towris wall." EBEV
"Quhare in a lusty plane tuke I my way." ScCV

Kingly lyon, and the strong arm'd beare, The. William Wood. SCAP

Kingly vulture sat alone, A. The Wounded Vulture. Anne Lynch Botta. AmWP

Kings, The. Louise Imogen Guiney. AmWP

Kings. *Unknown, tr. fr. Sanskrit by* Arthur Ryder. *Fr.* Panchatantra, The. AWP

Kings and Queens of England, The. *Unknown.* FaBoUs

Kings and Queens of England after the Conquest, The. *Unknown. See* Willy, Willy, Harry, Ste.

Kings and Stars. John Erskine. TrCP

King's Breakfast, The. A. A. Milne. OTCP; OxBChV; UV, *sts.* I *and* II *only*

Kings Came Riding. Charles Williams. OBCP

Kings cast wreaths at your feet and fall upon their faces. At Your Feet, Jerusalem. Uri Zvi Greenberg, *tr. fr. Hebrew by* Ruth Finer Mintz. MHP

King's College Chapel. Charles Causley. PeECV; TOF

King's Daughter!/ Wouldst thou be all fair. Everymaid. John Oxenham. TrCP

Kings' Daughters, Home for Unwed Mothers, 1948. C. D. Wright. NAmP90

King's Disguise, The, *sels.* John Cleveland. "And why so coffined in this vile disguise." JCP

King's Disguise, and Friendship with Robin Hood, The. *Unknown.* ESPB

Kings do not touch doors. The Pleasures of the Door. Francis Ponge, *tr. fr. French by* Beth Archer. AnRep

King's Dochter Lady Jean, The. *Unknown.* AmFP; ESPB

Kings don't touch doors. The Delights of the Door. Francis Ponge, *tr. fr. French by* Robert Bly. NU; RaBo

King's Double Nature, A. Kakkai Patiniyar Naccellaiyar, *tr. fr. Tamil by* A. K. Ramanujan. PLW

King's Epitaph, The. The Earl of Rochester.

Kings even in captivity. (*LL*) Crossing the Plains. Joaquin Miller. AnAmPo; GN

King's Favorites, The. Priscilla Jane Thompson. CBWP-2

Kings from the East, The. Heine. *See* "Dear children," they asked in every town.

Kings go by with jeweled crowns, The. The Choice. John Masefield. *Fr.* Lollingdon Downs. LiTB, I–XV; MoAB; MoBrPo

King's Highway, The. John Masefield. BLRP

King's Highway to the Dare-Not-Know, The. Dreams Are the Royal Road to the Unconscious. Paul Goodman. PoA

King's Horses, The. John Hewitt. IIP

King's Last Words, A. Ceraman Kanaikkal Irumporai, *tr. fr. Tamil by* A. K. Ramanujan. PLW

Kings/ like golden gleams. A History Lesson. Miroslav Holub, *tr. fr. Czech by* George Theiner. PAW; PoSu; RB

King's Men, The. William Heyen. PoA

King's Missive, The. Whittier. PAH

King's most faithful Subjects we, The. England's Triumph. *Unknown.* CoMu

Kings of France. Mary W. Lincoln. BLPA

Kings of Peru were the Incas, The. *Unknown.* PeLi

Kings of the East, The. Katharine Lee Bates. WGRP

Kings of the sea, The. (*LL*) The Forsaken Merman. Matthew Arnold. BeLS; CoGr; EBEV; EBVVPR; FaBoCh; FaPoR; FHYEP; GN; NAEL-2; NTP; OBNV; OBSP; OHCV

Kings of the world are growing old, The. Rainer Maria Rilke, *tr. fr. German by* Robert Bly. NU

King's Own Regulars, The. *Unknown.* PAH

King's poet was his captain of horse in the wars, The. Mount Badon. Charles Williams. FaBoTw

Kings River Canyon. Kenneth Rexroth. NaP

King's Son, The. Thomas Boyd. OBMV

King's Speech, The. Howard Moss. *See* My food was pallid till I heard it ring.

Kings who have died. Guillaume Apollinaire, *tr. fr. French by* Roger Shattuck. *Fr.* Heart, Crown, and Mirror. TTTS

King's Wood, The. C. S. Holder. BoTP

King's young dochter was sitting in her window, The. The King's Dochter Lady Jean. *Unknown.* AmFP; ESPB

Kinkaiders, The. *Unknown.* AS

Kinkora. James Clarence Mangan. PeIV

Kinky Hair Blues. Una Marson. PBCV

Kinky young girl from Uttoxeter, A. Herbert Kretzmer. PeLi

Kinloch, *sels.* Dorothy Nash.

Kinmont Willie. *Unknown.* ESPB; IBB; OxBB

Kinned by hieroglyphic. Kinship. Seamus Heaney. IPY

Kinneret. John Hollander. BAP-89

Kinnereth. Rachel, *tr. fr. Hebrew by* A. M. Klein. TrJP

Kinsale. Derek Mahon. BiHa

Kinshasa, we feel, is not the place to reach. The Flight of the White South Africans. Christopher Hope. PeSAV

Kinship. Seamus Heaney. IPY

Kinship. Judith Wright. *Fr.* For a Pastoral Family. FaBoMA

Kiph. Walter de la Mare. CBNP

Kirilov on a Skyscraper. Randall Jarrell. CAPP

Kirk Bell, The. John Buchan. NSI

Kirk Lonegren's Home Movie Taking Place Just North of Prince George, with Sound. Sharon Thesen. NOBC

Kirk of the Birds, Beasts and Fishes, The. *Unknown.* GBP

Kirk's Alarm, The. Burns. OxBoLi

Kirkwall Auction Mart. David Scott. PWE

Kirkyaird by the Sea, The, *sels.* Douglas Young, *after the French of* Paul Valéry. "Steekit, consecrat, fou o fire but fuel." OBVE

Kirsten. Ted Berrigan. TTTS

Kisimiso. Musaemura Bonus Zimunya. HBAPE

Kiss, The. Thomas Moore. EnLoPo

Kiss, The. Ned O'Gorman. FYAP

Kiss, The. Coventry Patmore. *Fr.* Angel in the House, The. ArLo; BoLoP; EnLoPo; FiBHP; NOBVV

Kiss, The. Plato, *tr. fr. Greek by* John Frederick Nims. STV

Kiss, The. Dante Gabriel Rossetti. *Fr.* House of Life, The. NOBVV; Son

Kiss, The. (Wine pours, the singer's blood.) Carlyle Reedy. VBLP *Sels.*

Kiss, The. John Yau. UL

Kiss. Al Young. PoBA

Kiss, A. William Drummond of Hawthornden. EIL

Kiss, A. Robert Herrick. CaPo

Kiss, A. Mary E. Tucker. CBWP-1

Kiss? A. Pray tell me, what is in a kiss. A Kiss. Mary E. Tucker. CBWP-1

Kiss from Her, A. Rufinus Domesticus, *tr. fr. Greek by* John Frederick Nims. STV

Kiss from her! Her mouth, coming even close to your own, how, A. A Kiss from Her. Rufinus Domesticus, *tr. fr. Greek by* John Frederick Nims. STV

Kiss his weef, wife, woaf. (*LL*) Did You Ever, Ever, Ever. *Unknown.* AS; FaBoNo; GBP

Kiss I begged; but, smiling, she, A. Weeping and Kissing. Sir Edward Sherburne. NOSC

Kiss I never had, The. (*LL*) Midsummer. Sydney King Russell. BLPA; FaBoBe

Kiss, if you can: Resistance if she make. Ovid, *tr. by* Dryden. *Fr.* Art of Love, The. ErPo

Kiss in the Morning Early, A. *Unknown.* GBP

Kiss in the Rain, A. Samuel Minturn Peck. OBAL

Kiss in the Ring. *Unknown.* OxBoLi

Kiss me again, re-kiss and kiss me whole. Louise Labé, *tr. fr. French.* WPOW, *tr. by* Raymond Oliver (Sonnet XVIII: "Kiss me again, rekiss, kiss me more.") BoWoP, *tr. by* Willis Barnstone

Kiss me and hug me. *Unknown, tr. fr. Spanish by* Willis Barnstone. BoWoP

Kiss me good night. A Kiss Requested. Eda Lou Walton. ShDr

Kiss[e] me, sweet: the wary [*or* warie] Lover. To the Same. Ben Jonson. *Fr.* Volpone. AWP; BeJo; EIL; JCP; NOSC; OAEL-1; OBVE; SeCP; SeCV-1

Kiss me then, my merry May. *Unknown, tr. fr. French by* John Addington Symonds. AWP

"Kiss me there where pride is glistening." Aria. Delmore Schwartz. ErPo

Kiss my grey hair, oh, my love. Healing. Abraham Reisen, *tr. fr. Yiddish by* Joseph Leftwich. TrJP

Kiss of God, The. G. A. Studdert-Kennedy. BLRP

Kiss Requested, A. Eda Lou Walton. ShDr

Kiss, The 1656. To Mrs. C. Thomas Shipman. NOSC

Kiss'd Yestreen. *Unknown.* ErPo; GBP; OtMeF

Kisses. *At. to* Thomas Campion. EIL

Kisses. *Malay Oral Tradition, tr. by* R. J. Wilkinson *and* R. O. Winstedt. WTO

Kisses Desired. William Drummond of Hawthornden. EnLoPo

Kisses in the Train. D. H. Lawrence. MoAB; MoBrPo

Kisses Loathesome. Robert Herrick. CaPo; CBLP; FaBoBl; OxBSP

Kisses make men loth to go. (*LL*) Kisses. *At. to* Thomas Campion. EIL

Kissie Lee. Margaret Walker. BlSi; NALW; NMM

Kissin'. *Unknown.* FiBHP

Kissing. Lord Herbert of Cherbury. EnLoPo; NOSC

Kissing. Brian Mueller. LPA

Kissing Agathon, I found. Sokrates to Agathon. Plato, *tr. fr. Greek by* Peter Jay. GrAn

Kissing and bussing differ both in this. Kissing and Bussing. Robert Herrick. BeJo; CBLP

Kissing Game. Bob Rosenthal. UL

Kissing Helena. Plato, *tr. fr. Greek by* Shelley. OBVE

Kissing her hair, I sat against her feet. Swinburne. BLPL; FaBoBe

Kissing Hippomenes, I crave. Paulus Silentiarius, *tr. fr. Greek by* Andrew Miller. GrAn; PeHV

Kissing Natalia. Eldon Grier. NOBC

Kissing of My Dame. *Unknown.* GBP

Kissing out on the patio. You Make Everything Move Me. Jack Skelley. UTF

Kissing Stieglitz Goodbye. Gerald Stern. LCAP

Kissing, still unable to speak. (*LL*) All Legendary Obstacles. John Montague. BIrV; CIP; IPY; NOIV; PBCIP; PNI

Kissing the lover in the mouth of bread:/ lip to lip. (*LL*) Song of the Taste. Gary Snyder. CAPP; EaPr; LCAP

Kitchen. Laura Jensen. LCAP

Kitchen Door Blues. Tennessee Williams. GrPl; OBAL

Kitchen fire that wakes so soon, The. Fires. Elizabeth Fleming. BoTP

Kitchenette Building. Gwendolyn Brooks. *Fr.* Street in Bronzeville, A. BlSi; BPo; CAPP; FaBoWP; FF; NAAL-2; NMM; NoP; PoE; Poetr; PoNe; UnPo

Kitchen's old-fashioned planter's clock portrays, The. Nightfishing. Gjertrud Schnackenberg. WeW

Kitchie-Boy, The. *Unknown.* ESPB

Kite, The. Harry Behn. FaPON

Kite, The. Alexander Blok, *tr. fr. Russian by* David McDuff *and* Jon Silkin. PeFWW

Kite, The. Alexander Blok, *tr. fr. Russian by* Frances Cornford *and* Esther P. Salamon. PAW

Kite. Laura Jensen. LCAP

Kite. John Robert Lee. PBCV

Kite. David McCord. PDV

Kite, The. Pearl Forbes MacEwen. BoTP

Kite, The. Adelaide O'Keeffe. OxBChV

Kite, The. Mark Strand. NYBP

Kite, A, *sels.* Hsü Wei, *tr. fr. Chinese by* Jonathan Chaves.

Kite, completed thus, is borne along, The. Samuel Bowden. *Fr.* Paper Kite, The. NOEC

Kite-Flying. Kath McKay. DT

Kite Is a Victim, A. Leonard Cohen. NOBC

Kite Poem. James Merrill. TwCP

Kite!/ Summon not me to enter: there's no doubt. For a Lady's Summons of Non-Entry. William Drummond of Hawthornden. NOSC

Kithairon sang of cunning Kronos. Korinna, *tr. fr. Greek by* Willis Barnstone. BoWoP

Kitten, The. Joanna Baillie. OFC

Kitten, The. Ogden Nash. CRH; FaPON; MoShBr; OFC

Kitten, The. Mary Oliver. CAPP

Kitten, A. Eleanor Farjeon. CRH; OFC

Kitten and the Falling Leaves. (That way look, my Infant, lo!) Wordsworth. OFC; SoCa
Sels.
Kitten at Play, The. FaPON

Kitten at Play, The. Wordsworth. *Fr.* Kitten and the Falling Leaves, The. FaPON; OFC; SoCa

Kitten can, A. Where Knock Is Open Wide. Theodore Roethke. HAP; VGW

Kitten told the truth. Model Children. David Trinidad. BAP-91

Kitty. Doug McLeod. CRH

Kitty. Elizabeth Payson Prentiss. BoTP; MoShBr

Kitty Alone. *Unknown.* CBNP

Kitty and Bug. John Hollander. SoCa

Kitty and I. W. H. Davies. CBLP

Kitty-Cat Bird, The. Theodore Roethke. OBAL

Kitty Cornered. Eve Merriam. CRH

Kitty Kline. *Unknown.* AmFP

Kitty Morey. *Unknown.* AmFP

Kitty Returns to Auschwitz. David Ray. BTR

Kiwi Bird in the Kiwi Tree, The. Charles Bernstein. UL

Kleine Nachtmusik, *sels.* Jacob Glatstein, *tr. fr. Yiddish by* Chana Bloch.

Kleomedes. David Wright. MoP

Kleson's goat snorted all night through the dark. Erucius, *tr. fr. Greek by* Peter Levi. GrAn

Klockius so deeply hath sworne, ne'er more to come. Klockius. John Donne. PeLV

Klondike, The. E. A. Robinson. PAH

Knave of darkness, limber in the leaves, The. Death for the Dark Stranger. Thomas McGrath. VGW

Knave, the gull, the Jew, the blackamoor?, The. (*LL*) African Student. Noel H. Brettell. PeSAV

Kneading Bread. Teresa Anderson. LoHo

Knedneuch land. In the Pantry. "Hugh MacDiarmid." NoAM

Knee, The. Ciaran Carson. PNI

Knee, The. Christian Morgenstern, *tr. fr. German by* W. D. Snodgrass *and* Lore Segal. CBNP; RB

Knee-deep in June. James Whitcomb Riley. PFP

Knee on Its Own, The. Christian Morgenstern, *tr. fr. German by* R. F. L. Hull. FaBoNo

Kneegrows niggas. Be Cool, Baby. Rob Penny. PoBA

Kneeling Camel, The. Anna Temple Whitney. BLPA

Kneeling Down to Look into a Culvert. Robert Bly. NoAM

Knell, The. Muhammad al-Faituri, *tr. fr. Arabic by* Samir M. Zoghby. TTY

Knell for the onset! (*LL*) Pibroch of Donuil Dhu. Sir Walter Scott. EnRP; FaBoCh; OxBS; PoEL-4

Knew all that summer knows. (*LL*) Heritage. Dorothea MacKellar. NOBAu

Knew her themselves, through all her vailes. (*LL*) Ingrateful[l] Beauty Threatened. Thomas Carew. BeJo; CaPo; HeIL; InvP; MeLP; OBEV; SeCP; SeCV-1

Knicht had two sons o sma fame, A. Sir Lionel. *Unknown.* ESPB

Knife, The. Keith Douglas. NoAM

Knife, The. Milton Kaplan. TrJP

Knife, The. Richard Tillinghast. MT

Knife across her throat, A. (*LL*) Going Back Again. "Owen Meredith." FiBHP

Knife and a fork!, A. *Unknown.* RoPo

Knife like a precious bond, The. Journey. Rodney Hall. NOBAu

Knife steady, a precious bond, The. (*LL*) Journey. Rodney Hall. NOBAu

Knife's edge, moon's edge, water's edge. Edge. Robert David Fitzgerald. CBAP

Knight and a lady, A. *Unknown.* BoTP

Knight and a lady once met in a grove, A. Sympathy. Reginald Heber. BeLS

Knight and Shepherd's Daughter, The, A *vers. Unknown.* ESPB

Knight and the Lady, The. William Cornish. *See* Knight knocked at the castle gate, The.

Knight and the Shepherd's Daughter, The. *Unknown.* AmFP; ESPB, A *and* B *vers.*

Knight, Death, and the Devil, The. Randall Jarrell. WeW

Knight Errant, The. Louise Imogen Guiney. AmWP

Knight Fallen on Evil Days, The. Elinor Wylie. MoAmPo

Knight from the world's end, The. A Dream of Governors. Louis Simpson. NYBP

Knight had ridden down from Wensley Moor, The. Hart-Leap Well. Wordsworth. BeLS

Knight in the Bower, The. *Unknown. See* Heron [*or* Hern] flew east, the heron [*or* hern] flew west, The.

Knight in the Wood, The. Lord De Tabley. NOBVV; PeVV

Knight knocked at the castle gate, The. Desire. William Cornish. Mes (Knight and the Lady, The.) NOBE (You and I and Amyas.) NoSic

Knight Knocked at the Castle Gate, The. *Unknown.* OxBLMV

Knight of Curtesy, The, *sels. Unknown, tr. fr. Middle English by* Pearl London.
Eaten Heart, The. TrGrPo

Knight of Curtesy, The. *Unknown.* OxBLMV

Knight of Liddesdale, The. *Unknown.* ESPB

Knight of My Maiden Love. Priscilla Jane Thompson. CBWP-2

Knight of "silver tongue" and stately grace, A. Wendell Phillips. H. Cordelia Ray. CBWP-3

Knight of the Burning Pestle, The, *sels.* Beaumont *and* Fletcher *and* John Fletcher.
Come, You Whose Loves Are Dead. ElL
Jillian of Berry. ElL
Mirth. ElL
(Laugh and Sing.) TrGrPo
Month of May, The. ChTr
"Nose, nose, jolly red nose." FaBoCh; OxNR

Knight of the Grail, The. *Unknown. See* Lully, lullay, lully, lullay.

Knight Stained from Battle, The. William Herebert. *See* What is he, this lordling, that cometh from the fight?

Knight stands in the stable-door, The. Young Johnstone. *Unknown.* ESPB

Knight went down to the river's rim, A. Gerda Mayer. OBSP

Knight who came was Launcelot at good need, The. (*LL*) The Defense of Guenevere. William Morris. NAEL-2; TEP

L

La Toilette. Seamus Heaney. CBLP

La Tricoteuse. George Walter Thornbury. BeLS

La Tumba de Buenaventura Roig. Martín Espada. AfAz

La Vie C'est la Vie. Jessie Redmond Fauset. CDC; PoNe

La Vita Nuova. Weldon Kees. VGW

Laban, I curse you for this trick you played! Jacob. Ruth Gilbert. *Fr.* Leah. PeNZ

Labasheedy (the Silken Bed). Nuala Ni Dhomhnaill, *tr. fr. Irish by the Author.* CIP; VBLP

Labienus, each hair on your bosom that grows. To Labienus. Martial, *tr. fr. Latin.* PeHV

Labor Day. Louise Glück. NoAM

Labor raises honest sweat. The Dignity of Labor. Robert Bersohn. NBLV

Laboratory; Ancien Régime, The. Robert Browning. EnVR; NAEL-2; OBEV

Laboratory Poem. James Merrill. CAPP; InPK; MAT; TwCP

Laborer, The. Richard Dehmel, *tr. fr. German by Jethro Bithell.* AWP

Laborer, The. José-Maria de Heredia, *tr. fr. French by Wilfrid Thorley.* AWP

Laborers of Christ! Arise. Lydia Huntley Sigourney. AH

Laborers that shall not fail, when man is gone. (*LL*) Quiet Work. Matthew Arnold. FaBoBe; TrGrPo

Laborers Together with God. Lucy Alice Perkins. BLRP

Laboring and Heavy Laden. Jeremiah Eames Rankin. AH

Laboring men, please all attend. Free Silver. *Unknown.* AmFP

Laborintus, sels. Edoardo Sanguineti, *tr. fr. Italian by Lawrence R. Smith.*

Labors of Hercules, The. Marianne Moore. MeMAP; OxBA

Labour. M. Saint-Marthe, *tr. fr. French. Fr.* Paedotrophiae; or, The Art of Bringing Up Children. FaBoUs

Labour of the Brain, Ballad of the Body. Nicole Forman. NMM

Labour Pains. Yosano Akiko, *tr. fr. Japanese by Kenneth Rexroth and Ikuko Atsumi.* AIW; WPJ

Labourer, The. Toolsy Daby, *tr. fr. French.* TSaS

Labourer, The. Iolo Goch, *tr. fr. Welsh by Gwyn Williams.* OBWVE

Labourer is back from the field, The. The Labourer. Toolsy Daby, *tr. fr. French.* TSaS

Labourer's Wife, A. John Davidson. *Fr.* To the Street Piano. EBVV

Labouring Man, The. *Unknown.* OBET

Labouring man, that tills the fertile soil, The. Edward de Vere, Earl of Oxford. NoSic
(Pains and Gains.) EIL

Labouring poor, in spite of double pay, The. Daniel Defoe. *Fr.* True-born Englishman, The. APAS; NOBL

Labours of the Months. *Unknown. See* Januar: by this fire [*or* thys fyre] I warme my handes.

Labyrinth, The. W. H. Auden. LiTA

Labyrinth, The. Edwin Muir. CMoP; MeMBP; MoBrPo

Lace. Dean Young. NAmP90

Lace curtains at half mast, and the street. View from the Window. Christine McNeill. NWP

Lace Pedlar, The. Catherine A. Morin. BoTP

Lace Tell. *Unknown.* OBET

Lacemaker (Vermeer), The. Anne Marx. GoYe

Lachesis. Victor James Daley. CBAP

Lachesis. Hilaire Kirkland. *Fr.* Clotho, Lachesis, Atropos. PeNZ

Lachesis. Kathleen Raine. NYBP

Lachin y Gair. Byron. OxBS

Lachlan MacQuarie's First Language. Les A. Murray. FaBoMA

Lachrimae, sels. Geoffrey Hill.
Lachrimae Verae. NAEL-2; NoAM; NoP
Masque of Blackness, The. NoAM

Lachrimae Amantis. Geoffrey Hill. NOCV

Lachrimae Verae. Geoffrey Hill. *Fr.* Lachrimae. NAEL-2; NoAM; NoP

lackblockblackb. Ian Hamilton Finlay. TRP

Lacking grace/ beauty. Capito, *tr. fr. Greek by Peter Jay.* GrAn

Lacking my love, I go from place to place. Spenser. *Fr.* Amoretti. AAS; EIL; ESo, lacking epigrams I–IV; HeIL; NoSic

Lacking rich acres, thick grape-crops. Apollonides, *tr. fr. Greek by Peter Whigham.* GrAn

Lacking Sense, The. Thomas Hardy. CMoP; PoEL-5

Laconic as anglers and, like them, submissive. At the Ferry. U. A. Fanthorpe. FaBoWP

Lacquer dust and powdered bone and red cinnabar grains. An Arrowhead from the Ancient Battlefield of Ch'ang-p'ing. Li Ho, *tr. fr. Chinese by A. C. Graham.* PLT

Lacquer Liquor Locker, The. David McCord. FiBHP

Lacrimas or There Is a Need to Scream. K. Curtis Lyle. NBV; PoBA

Lacy mobile changing lazily, A. Watching a Cloud. Dannie Abse. OxBC; TEP

Lad came to the door at night, The. The True Lover. A. E. Housman. *Fr.* Shropshire Lad, A. EBNV; FaPoB

Lad I lo'e dearly, Tam Glen, The. (*LL*) Tam Glen. Burns. AWP; OxBS

Lad of Athens, faithful be. Emily Dickinson. FaBoEE

Lad of the brainier kind, A. Hymie Sneak. PeLi

Lad Philisides, The. A Country Song. Sir Philip Sidney. *Fr.* Arcadia. SiPS

Lad saw a rosebud, A. The Wild Rose. Goethe, *tr. fr. German by* Philip L. Miller. RiWo

Lad when at school, one day stole a pin, A. The Results of Stealing a Pin. *Unknown.* FaBoUs

Ladd I the dance a Midsomer Day. A Night with a Holy-Water Clerk. *Unknown.* MeEL

Laddie, little laddie, come with me over the hills. A Cry from the Canadian Hills. Lilian Leveridge. BLPA

Laddy tell I day, tell I do, laddy laddy tell I day. (*LL*) The Crafty Farmer. *Unknown.* AmFP; ESPB

Laden with my heavy sorrow. (*LL*) Spring Ends. Li Ch'ing-chao. WPC

Ladie stude in her bour-door, The. Young Hunting. *Unknown.* ESPB

Ladies, The. Kipling. MoBrPo; NAEL-2

Ladies' Aid, The. *Unknown.* PoLF

Ladies and gentlemen. Irish Sweaters. Shirley Graves Cochrane. IIP

Ladies and gentlemen come to supper. Hot Boiled Beans. *Unknown.* ReMoGo

Ladies and gentlemen:/ I have only one question. I Move the Meeting Be Adjourned. Nicanor Parra, *tr. fr. Spanish by Miller Williams. Fr.* Manifesto. HoPM

Ladies and Gentlemen,/ List to my song. Temperance Song. *Unknown.* FaBoUs

Ladies and gentlemen,/ Take my advice. *Unknown.* RoPo

Ladies and gentlemen, that is the end of the programme. Epilogue to a Poetry Reading. M. K. Joseph. PeNZ

Ladies and gentlemen:/ This broadcast comes to you from the city. Voice of the Studio Announcer. Archibald MacLeish. *Fr.* Fall of the City, The. HoPM

Ladies and gentlemen, this is High Wood. High Wood. Philip Johnstone. NSI; PAW

Ladies and Gentlemen This Little Girl. E. E. Cummings. CMoP; PoE

Ladies and gents, you are here assembled. James Joyce. *Fr.* Gas from a Burner. IIP

Ladies bow, and partners set, The. Soliloquy of a Maiden Aunt. Dollie Radford. NOBVV

Ladies' Home Journal, The. Sandra M. Gilbert. NIP

Ladies, I crave your indulgence for. The Young Laundryman. William Carlos Williams. SAmP

Ladies, I do here present you. A Present to a Lady. *Unknown.* ErPo; PeLV

Ladies of King Bolo's Court, The. Columbiad: Two Stanzos. T. S. Eliot. FaBoBl

Ladies of London, both wealthy and fair. Advice to the Ladies of London in the Choice of Their Husbands. *Unknown.* CoMu

Ladies of St. James's, The. Austin Dobson. PoRA

Ladies of the morning gauze their mouths, The. Canonical Hours. William Dickey. CoAP

Ladies Prayer to Cupid, A. Thomas Carew, *after* Giovanni Battista Guarini. *See* Since I must needs into thy school[e] return[e].

Ladies reading. Rites of the Eastern Star. Janine Pommy-Vega. UL

Ladies that have intelligence in love. Dante, *tr. fr. Italian by* Dante Gabriel Rossetti. *Fr.* Vita Nuova, La. AWP

Ladies, though so born your conquering eyes. Sir George Etherege. *Fr.* Comical Revenge, The. OxBSP

Ladies, to this advice give heed. A Maxim Revised. *Unknown.* BLPA; NBLV; WBLP

Ladies' Voices. Gertrude Stein. SOTW

Ladies, You See time Flieth. Thomas Morley. EnRePo

Ladies, you see time flieth. *Unknown.* NoSic

Ladles and jelly spoons. Smart Alec Oration. *Unknown.* RoPo

Lads and lasses gathering. The Willow-Boughs. Alexander Block. BoTP

Lads in Their Hundreds, The. A. E. Housman. *Fr.* Shropshire Lad, A. FaPoB; MeMBP; MoBrPo; OxBTC

Lads of the Village, The. Stevie Smith. OxBSP

Lads of Wamphray, The. *Unknown.* ESPB; IBB

Lady. Ted Berrigan. UL

Lady, The, sels. Christine de Pisan, *tr. fr. French by* Naomi Lewis.

Lady, A. Amy Lowell. AnAmPo; MoAmPo

Lady A. L., My Asylum in a Great Extremity, The. Richard Lovelace. CaPo

Lady Adeline Amundeville. Byron. *Fr.* Don Juan. MeMBP; PoEL-4

Lady Again Complains, The. The Earl of Surrey. *See* Good ladies, ye [or you] that have your pleasure in exile.

Lady Alice. *Unknown.* ESPB, A *vers.*

Lady Alice ("George Collins came home last Saturday night.") *Unknown.* AmFP

Lady Alice ("George Collins come home last Friday night.") *Unknown.* AmFP

Lady Alice ("Giles Collin he said to his mother one day.") *Unknown.* ESPB, C *vers.*

Lady Alice ("Giles Collins he said to his old mother.") *Unknown.* ESPB, B *vers.*

Lady Alice ("She says the coffin to be opened.") *Unknown.* AmFP

Lady Alice was sitting in her bower-window. Lady Alice. *Unknown.* ESPB, A *vers.*

Lady & Gentleman. Richard Weber. PeIV

Lady and gentlemen fays, come buy! The Elfin Pedlar. George Darley. BoTP

Lady and the Bear, The. Theodore Roethke. GoJo; NBLV

Lady and the Doctor, The. Helen Leigh. WoRP

Lady and the Gypsy, The. Vernon Scannell. Mes

Lady Anne Bathing. Anthony Delius. PeSA

Lady asks me, A. Canzone: Donna Mi Priegha. Cavalcanti, *tr. fr. Italian by* Ezra Pound. CTC

(Donna Mi Priegha.) OBVE

Lady at the Castle, The. John Hollander. NoAM

Lady,/ baby. *Unknown.* OxNR

Lady bird, lady bird, turn around. *Unknown.* RoPo

Lady Bug. *Unknown.* LPA

Lady bug, lady bug. Lady Bug. *Unknown.* LPA

Lady Byron's Reply to Lord Byron's "Fare Thee Well." *Unknown.* BLPA

Lady came to a bear by a stream, A. The Lady and the Bear. Theodore Roethke. GoJo; NBLV

Lady Charlotte Guest. Goronva Camlan. AngWe

Lady Cicely Wemyss. James I, King of England. NOSC

Lady Clare. Tennyson. BeLS; FaPON

Lady Comes to an Inn, A. Elizabeth J. Coatsworth. MoAmPo

Lady Diamond. *Unknown.* ESPB

Lady Elspat. *Unknown.* ESPB

Lady Erskine sits in her chamber. Child Owlet. *Unknown.* ESPB

Lady, farewell, whom I in silence serve. A Poem Put into My Lady Laiton's Pocket. Sir Walter Ralegh. SiPS

Lady Fortune is both friend and foe, The. Fortune. *Unknown.* HeIP

Lady Franklin's Lament for Her Husband. *Unknown.* OxBSS

Lady from near Rising Sun, A. Ogden Nash. PeLi

Lady from Vanity Fair, A. W. F. N. Watson. PeLi

Lady gave me a gift she had not, A. Sir Thomas Wyatt. SiPSBD

Lady Greensleeves. *Unknown.* GBL; PoEL-2

Lady Greensleeves. *Unknown. See* Greensleeves.

Lady, helpe! Jesu mercy! In His Utter Wretchedness. John Audelay [or Awdelay]. MeEL

Lady, how can I speak, my mouth silent. Our Lady. Janine Canan. SRLS

Lady I Know, A. Countee Cullen. *See* She even thinks that up in heaven.

Lady in a boat, A. *Unknown.* RoPo

Lady in a Distant Face. James Welch. AmPA

Lady in Kicking Horse Reservoir, The. Richard Hugo. CoAP; LCAP; NAAL-2; NoAM; NoP; VCAP

Lady in the Barbershop, The. Raphael Rudnik. NYBP

Lady in the Moon, The, *sels.* Li Shang-yin, *tr. fr. Chinese by* A. C. Graham.
"First calls of the migrant geese, no more cicadas." PLT
"Lamp glows deep in the mica screen." PLT

Lady in the Pink Mustang, The. Louise Erdrich. HATNAP

Lady Is a Tramp, The. Lorenz Hart. OBAL

Lady is a tramp, The. Le Sporting-Club de Monte Carlo. James Baldwin. Jaz

Lady is smarter than a gentleman, maybe, A. Trial and Error. Phyllis McGinley. PeLV

Lady Isabel. *Unknown.* ESPB

Lady Isabel and the Elf-Knight. *Unknown.* ESPB; FaBoBa

Lady Isabel and the Elf-Knight [or The Elfin Knight]. *Unknown.* FaBoBa; GBP

Lady Isabel and the Elf Knight (Pretty Polly). *Unknown.* AmFP

Lady Isabella's Tragedy, The. *Unknown.* GBP

Lady Jane. Sir Arthur Quiller-Couch. FiBHP; PeLV

Lady Jane, The; a Humorous Novel in Rhyme. Nathaniel Parker Willis. OBAL

Sels.
"If, in well-bred society, 'hear! hear!'"
"Some men, 'tis said, prefer a woman fat."

Lady Jane Grey, *sels.* John Webster.
"Thus like a nun, not like a princess born." FaBoEH

Lady, Lady. Anne Spencer. BlSi; PoBA; ShDr

Lady, lady, I saw your face. Lady, Lady. Anne Spencer. BlSi; PoBA; ShDr

Lady, lady, lady fair. The Suffolk Miracle. *Unknown.* AmFP

Lady, lady should you meet. Social Note. Dorothy Parker. *Fr.* Some Beautiful Letters. AnAmPo; FaBoUs

Lady Laments for Her Lost Lover, by Similitude of a Falcon, A. *Unknown,* *tr. fr. Italian by* Dante Gabriel Rossetti. AWP

Lady Lazarus. Sylvia Plath. CAPP; ChIV-2; FaBoWP; HCAP; MAT; MoP; NAAL-2; NALW; NaP; NIP; NoAM; NOBA; NoP; Poetr; PrIm; TAP; TRP; VCAP; VGW

Lady lived in Lancaster, A. Kate and the Cowhide. *Unknown.* AmFP

Lady Lost. John Crowe Ransom. MoAB; MoAmPo; TrGrPo; UnPo

Lady Love. Paul Éluard, *tr. fr. French.* ArLo; OBVE, *tr. by* Samuel Beckett

Lady, lovely lady. Vain and Careless. Robert Graves. NTP

Lady loves her will, The. (*LL*) Hart he loves the high wood, The. Mother Goose. FaBoCh; GBP; OxNR; ReMoGo

Lady Lowbodice. *Unknown.* FaBoBl; PeLi; PeLV

Lady Luck. Ann Gottlieb. NMM

Lady Maisdry was a lady fair. Lord Ingram and Chiel Wyet. *Unknown.* ESPB, A, B, *and* C *vers.*

(Lady Maisry.) OBET; OxBB

Lady Maisry. *Unknown.* ESPB, A *and* B *vers.*; OBET; OxBB

Lady Maisry. *Unknown. See* Lady Maisdry was a lady fair.

Lady Maisry lives intill a bower. Thomas o Yonderdale. *Unknown.* ESPB

Lady Maisry ("Oh she called to her little page boy.") *Unknown.* OBET

Lady Maisry ("The young lords o' the north country.") *Unknown.* ESPB; OxBB

Lady Margaret sat in her bower-door. Prince Heathen. *Unknown.* ESPB, A *and* B *vers.*

Lady Margaret sat in her bowry all alone. Sweet William's Ghost. *Unknown.* AWP; ESPB, A, B, F, *and* G *vers.*

Lady Margaret sits in her bower door. Hind Etin. *Unknown.* ESPB

Lady Margery May sits in her bower. Prince Heathen. *Unknown.* ESPB

Lady Maria, in you merit and distinction. Bieiris de Romans, *tr. fr. Provençal.* PeHV

Lady Mary Villiers lies, The. Epitaph on the Lady Mary Villiers. Thomas Carew. BeJo; CaPo; FaBoEE; NOBE; OBEV; SeCV-1

Lady Moon, The. Kate Louise Brown. BoTP

Lady Moon. Richard Monckton Milnes. BoTP; MoShBr; OxBChV

Lady Moon is sailing, The. The Lady Moon. Kate Louise Brown. BoTP

Lady Moon, Lady Moon, where are you roving. Lady Moon. Richard Monckton Milnes. BoTP; MoShBr; OxBChV

Lady Murasaki says. Murasaki Shikibu, *tr. fr. Japanese by* Kenneth Rexroth *and* Ikuko Atsumi. *Fr.* Tale of Genji, The. BoWoP; WPJ

Lady, my lady, come from out the garden. To a Certain Lady, in Her Garden. Sterling A. Brown. CDC

Lady My Treasure. Sir Philip Sidney. GBL

Lady never shakes free the ashes, The. Sonia at 32. Morrie Warshawski. BTR

Lady of all the divine attributes, resplendent light. Inanna and the Divine Essences. Enheduanna, *tr. fr. Sumerian by* W. W. Hallo *and* J. J. A. Van Dyck. VBLP

Lady of all the essences, full light. Inanna and the Divine Essences. Enheduanna, *tr. fr. Sumerian.* BoWoP, *ad. by* Aliki *and* Willis Barnstone

Lady, of anonymous flesh and face. J. V. Cunningham. HoPM

Lady of Arngosk, The. *Unknown.* ESPB

Lady of Carlisle, The. *Unknown.* AmFP

Lady of Castlenoire. Thomas Bailey Aldrich. BeLS

Lady of dusk-wood fastnesses. First Praise. William Carlos Williams. VGW

Lady of features cherubic, A. *Unknown.* PeLi

Lady of Heaven and earth, and therewithal. His Mother's Service to Our Lady. Villon, *tr. fr. French by* Dante Gabriel Rossetti. AWP; CTC

Lady of Heaven, Queen of the world. Villon's Prayer for His Mother to Say to the Virgin. Villon, *tr. fr. French by* Robert Lowell. OBD

Lady of Heaven, queen terrestrial. Ballade which Villon Made. Donagh MacDonagh. TIRV

Lady of heaven, Regent of the earth. Ballade Which Villon Wrote at the Request of His Mother to Pray to Our Lady. Villon, *tr. fr. French by* Philip L. Miller. RiWo

Lady of High Degree, A. *Unknown, tr. fr. French by* Andrew Lang. AWP

Lady of Miracles. Nina Cassian, tr. fr. Romanian by Laura Schiff. AIW; WPOW

Lady of Quality, A. Thomas Kinsella. PBCIP

Lady of Shalott, The. Tennyson. BeLS; BLPL; EBEvV; EBVVPR; FHYEP; GN; InPS; NAEL-2; NOBE; OAEL-2; OBEV; OBNV; OBSP; OxAEP-2; PoE; TEP; TFi; TOF; WiR

Lady of Shalott, The. (LL) The Lady of Shalott. Tennyson. BeLS; BLPL; EBEvV; EBVVPR; FHYEP; GN; InPS; NAEL-2; NOBE; OAEL-2; OBEV; OBNV; OBSP; OxAEP-2; PoE; TEP; TFi; TOF; WiR

Lady of Shalott: Ode, The. Veronica Forrest-Thomson. VaA

Lady of shrouding hair. Unknown. NOIV

Lady of the bright coils and curlings. Eire. David O'Bruadair, tr. fr. Irish by Austin Clarke. BIrV

Lady of the Ferry Inn. Gwerfyl Mechain, tr. fr. Welsh. BoWoP, tr. by Willis Barnstone

Lady of the house is on her benders, The. Five Domestic Interiors. Vernon Scannell. OxBC

Lady of the Lake, The, sels. Sir Walter Scott.
Alice Brand. BeLS
(Ballad: Alice Brand.) OxAEP-2
Chase, The. EnRP
Coronach. CH; EnRP; GTBS; GTBS-P; OHIP; OxAEP-2; SCGP; TrGrPo; WiR
Flowers and Trees. OxAEP-2
Gathering, The. OBNC
Hail to the Chief Who in Triumph Advances. EnRP; PoEL-4
(Boat Song.) OxAEP-2
Harp of the North, Farewell! The Hills Grow Dark. PFP
(Farewell Thou Minstrel Harp.) OBNC
(Harp of the North, Farewell!) OxAEP-2
Hymn to the Virgin. EnRP
"Now, yield thee, or by Him who made." OxBS
Soldier Rest! [Thy Warfare O'er.] AWP; GN; MoShBr; NOBE; PoRA; TrGrPo
(Song: "Soldier rest! thy warfare o'er.") OBNC
Toils Are Pitched, The. EnRP
Western Waves of Ebbing Day, The. PoEL-4

Lady of the Lambs, The. Alice Meynell. See She walks — the lady of my delight.

Lady of the legless world I have. Notes after Blacking Out. Gregory Corso. NeAP

Lady of the Manor, The. George Crabbe. Fr. Parish Register, The. NOBE; OAEL-1, abr.; OBNC

Lady of the Manor was dressing for the ball, The. The Highland Tinker. Unknown. CoMu

Lady of the Pearls, The, sels. Alexandre Dumas, tr. fr. French by Gerard Manley Hopkins.
"We set out yesterday upon a winter drive." TTY

Lady of the Pool, The. David Jones. Fr. Anathemata, The. AngWe

Lady of the Restaurant, The. Sean O'Meara. PeIV

Lady on a Bus. Jeanne Lohmann. CrSp

Lady on climbing Mount Shasta, A. Unknown. PeLi

Lady on Streetcar. Sandro Penna, tr. fr. Italian by John Frederick Nims. STV

Lady Pitcher, The. Cynthia MacDonald. Poetsp

Lady Poverty, The. Alice Meynell. NOBVV; OBMV; OHCV; PeVV

Lady Poverty was fair, The. The Lady Poverty. Alice Meynell. NOBVV; OBMV; OHCV; PeVV

Lady Prayeth the Return of Her Lover Abiding on the Seas, The. Unknown. EIL; GBL

Lady Queen Anne she sits in the sun. Unknown. OxNR

Lady Ralegh's Lament. Robert Lowell. OxBSP

Lady red upon the hill, A. Emily Dickinson. BoNaP; OHIP

Lady Resists the Lover's Pleas, The. At. to Alain Chartier, tr. fr. French by Sir Richard Ros. Fr. La Belle Dame sans Mercy. OxBLMV

Lady "Rogue" Singleton. Stevie Smith. FaBoWP; OxBSP

Lady Sings, The. Milton. See Sweet Echo, sweetest Nymph, that livest unseen.

Lady stands in her bower door, The. The Twa Magicians. Unknown. ESPB; GBP; OAEL-1; OxBB
(Two Magicians, The.) ChTr; OAEL-1; OxBoLi

Lady Stood, A. Dietmar von Aist, tr. fr. German by Jethro Bithell. AWP

Lady Stood Alone, A. Dietmar von Aist, tr. fr. German by J. W. Thomas. GePo

Lady Tactics. Anne Waldman. PoM

Lady, take this garland. Walther von der Vogelweide, tr. fr. German by Frederick Goldin. GePo

Lady T'ao Ch'ui-tse gave a farewell party in T'ao Jan. Ch'iu Chin, tr. fr. Chinese by Kenneth Rexroth and Ling Chung. Fr. Two Poems to the Tune "The Narcissus by the River". WPC

Lady, tell me, will you, pray. Found — Who Lost? Mary E. Tucker. CBWP-1

Lady that hast my heart within thy hand. Hafiz, tr. by Gertrude Lowthian Bell. Fr. Odes. AWP

Lady That in the Prime. Milton. Son

Lady that in the prime of earliest youth. Lady That in the Prime. Milton. Son
(Sonnet: Lady, That in the Prime.) ChIV-2

Lady, the shepherds have all gone. Ya Se Van Los Pastores. Dudley Fitts. FYAP

Lady there was in Antigua, A. Unknown. PeLi

Lady, there's fragrance in your sighs. Lines Written for a Blank Page of "The Keepsake." Winthrop Mackworth Praed. CBLP

Lady, those cherries plenty. Unknown. NoSic

Lady walked by the ocean strand, The. Strand-Thistle. Gustav Falke, tr. fr. German by Jethro Bithell. AWP

Lady walked down a roadbed, A. Gentle Heart, A: Two. Judith Johnson Sherwin. BoWoP

Lady was chasing her boy round the room, A. Unknown. RoPo

Lady, when your lovely head. On a Sleeping Friend. Hilaire Belloc. CoGr

Lady Who Offers Her Looking-Glass to Venus, The. Matthew Prior, after the Greek of Plato. AWP; FaBoEE; NOEC; OBEV; OxBSP

Lady who rules Fort Montgomery, A. Morris Bishop. PeLi

Lady, who signs herself "Vexed," A. Edward Gorey. OBAL; PeLi

Lady with a Falcon on Her Fist, A. Richard Lovelace. CaPo

Lady with Technique, The. Hughes Mearns. Fr. Later Antigonishes. FiBHP

Lady with the Unicorn, The. Vernon Watkins. LiTB; TwCP

Lady with thine eyes of beauty. The Valentine. Mary Weston Fordham. CBWP-2

Lady without Paragon, A. Chaucer. See Hide [or Hyd], Absalon, thy gilte tresses clere.

Lady, you are with beauties so enriched. Francis Davison. EIL

Lady, you think too much of speeds. Statistics. Stephen Spender. MoBrPo

Lady, you think you spite me. Unknown. NoSic

Lady,/ You, who are pattering to your carriage door. Genius. Louis Saunders Perkins. PeHV

Lady, your art or wit could ne'er devise. To a Lady Who Sent Me a Copy of Verses at My Going to Bed. Henry King. CBLP

Ladybird. Clive Sansom. GrPl

Ladybird. Unknown. FaBoVe

Ladybird, The. Unknown. GBP

Ladybird, Ladybird fly away home. Mother Goose. FaBoVe, diff. vers.; FaPON; ISE, diff. vers.; OxNR; ReMoGo, diff. vers.

Ladybug. Raymond Souster. MoCV

Ladybug, ladybug, fly away home. Unknown. RoPo

Ladybug's Christmas. Norma Farber. PChr

Lady's Complaint, The. John Heath-Stubbs. TwCP

Lady's Days. Larry Neal. NBV

Lady's Diary, The. Charles Dibdin. NOEC

Lady's Dressing Room, The. Swift. ErPo; FaBoBl; IHNG; NoP; TEP

Lady's love is gained, A. The Price of Disrespect. L. A. J. Moorer. CBWP-3

Lady's-Maid's Song, The. John Hollander. ErPo; LiTM; TwCP

Lady's Prayer to Cupid, A. Thomas Carew, after Giovanni Battista Guarini. CaPo

Lady's Receipt for a Beau's Dress, The. Unknown. CoMu

Lady's Resolve, The. Lady Mary Wortley Montagu. BoWoP; OxBSP

Lady's Song. Milton. See Sweet Echo, sweetest Nymph, that livest unseen.

Lady's Song in Leap Year, The. Unknown. GBP

Lady's Third Song, The. W. B. Yeats. Fr. Three Bushes, The. FaBoTw

Lady's "Yes," The. Elizabeth Barrett Browning. LPA

LaFayette. Samuel Taylor Coleridge. EnRP

Lafayette. Dolley Madison. AiP; PAH

Lagoons, Hanlan's Point. Raymond Souster. NOBC

L'Agulhas, A Walk. Wilma Stockenström, tr. fr. Afrikaans by Rosa Keet. PeSAV

Laguna. Paul Trachtenberg. NGP

Laguna Beach. Ruth Stone. FoLa

Laguna Blues. Charles Wright. PRA

Laguna man said. Wind and Glacier Voices. Simon J. Ortiz. HATNAP

Laid in My Quiet Bed. The Earl of Surrey. CH; EnRePo; InvP; SiPSBD

Laid in my quiet bed, in study as I were. Laid in My Quiet Bed. The Earl of Surrey. CH; EnRePo; InvP; SiPSBD
(How No Age Is Content with His Own Estate, shorter vers.) EIL
(How No Age Is Content.) LiTB
(Youth and Age.) SiPS

Laid many heavy loads on thee! (*LL*) On Sir John Vanbrugh [Architect]. Abel Evans. FaBoCo; FaBoEE; FaBoEH; FiBHP; IHNG

Laid on Thine Altar. *Unknown*. TrPWD

Laid out for dead, let thy last kindness be. To Robin Redbreast. Robert Herrick. PoE; TrGrPo

Laid with papyrus to catch fire. Martial, *tr. fr. Latin* by James Michie. FaBoEE

Laieikawai's Lament after Her Husband's Death. *Unknown, tr. fr. Hawaiian* by M. W. Beckwith. WTO

Laila Boasting. Laila Akhyaliyya, *tr. fr. Arabic* by Willis Barnstone. BoWoP

Laily Worm and the Machrel of the Sea, The. *Unknown*. ChTr; ESPB; InvP; OxBB; PoEL-1; SCGP

Laird, a lord, A. *Unknown*. OxNR

Laird o' Cockpen, The. Lady Nairne, 2 *added sts.* by Susan Ferrier. BeLS; WPE

Laird o Drum, The. *Unknown*. ESPB

Laird o' Logie, The. *Unknown*. CH; ESPB

Laird o' Logie, The. *Unknown*. CH; ESPB, A *and* B *vers.*

Laird o' Ochiltree Wa's, The. *Unknown*. OxBB

Laird of Bristoll's daughter was in the woods walking, The. Captain Wedderburn's Courtship. *Unknown*. ESPB

Laird of Leys is on to Edinbrugh [*or* Edinburgh], The. The Baron o [*or of*] Leys. *Unknown*. ESPB; OxBB

Laird of Wariston, The. *Unknown*. ESPB

Laird of Wariston, The. *Unknown*. ESPB

Lairdless Place, The. Kate Rennie Archer. GoYe

Lais. Hilda Doolittle ("H. D."). MoAmPo

Lais. Elaine Feinstein. FaBoWP

Lais, courtesan of Corinth, why has. Lais. Elaine Feinstein. FaBoWP

Lais' Mirror. Julianus of Egypt, *tr. fr. Greek* by Robin Skelton. GrAn

Lais' Mirror. *Unknown, tr. fr. Greek* by Peter Jay. GrAn

Lais now old, that erst attempting lass. *Unknown, after the Greek of* Plato. EnRePo; FaBoEE

Lais to Aphrodite. E. A. Robinson, *after* Plato. FaBoEE

Lais, who was a lovely flower. Pompeius, *tr. fr. Greek* by Dennis Schmitz. GrAn

Lak of Stedfastnesse. Chaucer. AWP

Lake, The. Matthew Arnold. *Fr.* Switzerland. EnVR

Lake. Martha Collins. FoLa

Lake, The. Louis O. Coxe. NYBP

Lake, The. Ted Hughes. FaBoTw; NYBP

Lake, The. Poe. MeMAP; NAAL-1

Lake, The. R. A. Simpson. CBAP

Lake, The. James Stephens. MoBrPo

Lake, The. Alma Villanueva. SRLS

Lake, A. Thomas Lovell Beddoes. NOBVV

Lake, A/ Is a river curled and asleep like a snake. A Lake. Thomas Lovell Beddoes. NOBVV

Lake blue below the hill, The. L'Oiseau Bleu. Mary Elizabeth Coleridge. BoTP

(Lake lay blue below the hill, The.) CH

Lake Chelan. William Stafford. NaP

Lake Chemo. James Wilton Rowe. AmFP

Lake Drummond Dream. Dave Jeddie Smith. VCAP

Lake has drifted from Persia, A. (*LL*) Summer in Monaghan. Michael O'Loughlin. IB

Lake is blue with morning, The; and the sky. Morning on the Shore. Wilfred Campbell. NOBC

Lake is deserted now, the. The Dispossessed. Thomas Kinsella. NOCV

Lake is known as West Branch Pond, The. The Ballad of Blossom. Mona Van Duyn. EOEF; SM

Lake is sharp along the shore, The. Lakeshore. F. R. Scott. MoCV; NOBC

Lake Isle, The. Ezra Pound. FaBoCo; FaBoPa; OxBSP; PoA

Lake Isle of Innisfree, The. W. B. Yeats. ArNa; ClHu; CMoP; CoGr; EBEvV; FaBoPP; FaBV; FaPoB; FaPON; FaPoR; HeIP; IIP; InPK; InPS; LiTM; MeMBP; MoAB; MoBrPo; MoP; NAEL-2; NoAM; NOBE; NoP; NTP; OBEV; OHCV; OxAEP-2; OxBTC; PlP; PoE; Poetr; PoRA; PrIm; TEP; TFi; TrGrPo; UV

Lake lay blue below the hill, The. Mary Elizabeth Coleridge. *See* Lake blue below the hill, The.

Lake Leman. Byron. *See* Lake Leman woos me with its crystal face.

Lake Leman ("Clear, placid Leman! thy contrasted lake.") Byron. *Fr.* Childe Harold's Pilgrimage. LiTB; MeMBP; OBNC, *sl. diff. sel.*

Lake Leman woos me with its crystal face. Byron. *Fr.* Childe Harold's Pilgrimage. InPS

(Lake Leman.) PoEL-4

Lake lies blind and glinting in the sun, The. Virginia Lake. James K. Baxter. PeNZ

Lake of Gaube, The. Swinburne. NAEL-2; OAEL-2

Lake of night is still in the valley, The. The Pine. Saunders Lewis, *tr. fr. Welsh* by Gwyn Morgan. OBWVE

Lake of pain, an absence, A. But What Is the Reader to Make of This? John Ashbery. InPS

Lake of the Caogama, The. *Unknown*. WTO

Lake of the Dismal Swamp, The. Thomas Moore. BLPA

Lake of the Woods, The. Richard Ryan. PBCIP

Lake of Zurich, The. Friedrich Gottlieb Klopstock, *tr. fr. German* by George C. Schoolfield. GePo

Lake Song. Jean Starr Untermeyer. TrJP

Lake Success. Robert Conquest. OxBC

Lake sunken among, A. Woman Skating. Margaret Atwood. FaBoWP; IHMS

Lake Superior. Lorine Niedecker. FaBoWP

Lake that held a mirror to the sun, The. Northamptonshire Fens. John Clare. *Fr.* Child Harold. FaBoPP

Lake water lifted a little and fell, The. Crab Orchard Sanctuary, Late October. Thomas Kinsella. IPY

Lakes. David Donnell. NoAM

Lakes of the Atchafalaya, The. Longfellow. *Fr.* Evangeline. BeLS; PoEL-5

Lakeshore. F. R. Scott. MoCV; NOBC

Lakeside Incident. Robin Skelton. NOBC

Lakshmi. Padraic Fallon. NOIV

Lalai (Dreamtime). Sam Woolagoodjah. NOBAu

Laleham: Matthew Arnold's Grave. Lionel Johnson. FaBoPP

Lalela Zulu. *Unknown, tr. fr. Zulu.* PeSA

Lalla Halima! Protect abandoned girls! Like Smoke. Mririda n'Ait Attik, *tr. fr. French* by Daniel Halpern *and* Paula Paley. PBWP

Lalla Rookh, *sels.* Thomas Moore.
  "Fly to the desert, fly with me." BIrV
  Golden Hour, The. OBNC
  Light of the Harem [*or* Haram], The. EnRP; TEP
  "Oh! ever thus from childhood's hour." UV
  Peri's Lament for Hinda, The. OBNC

Lalla Rookh/ Is a naughty book. On Thomas Moore's Poems. *Unknown*. FaBoCo; FiBHP

L'Allegro. (Hence, loathèd Melancholy.) Milton. AWP; FaPoB; FHYEP; GTBS; GTBS-P; HAP; HoPM; ImPo; JCP; LiTB; NoP; NOSC; OAEL-1; OBEV; PPP; TEP; TFi; TrGrPo

Sels.
  "Haste thee, nymph, and bring with thee." GN
  (Mirth, with Thee I Mean to Live. FaBV
  Mirth and Poetry. EPCY

Lama, The. Ogden Nash. *See* One-l lama, The.

Lama of Outer Mongolia, A. Ogden Nash. PeLi

Lamb, The. Blake. *Fr.* Songs of Innocence. BLPL; BoTP; CH; ChIV-2; EBEvV; EnRP; FaBoBe; FaBoCh; FaPON; FHYEP; GoJo; HeIL; HeIP; ImPo; InPS; LiTB; MeMBP; NAEL-2; NAWM-2; NIP; NOEC; NoP; OAEL-2; OxAEP-2; OxBChV; PoE; Poetr; SoSe; TEP; TFi; TrCP; TrGrPo; TRP; UnPo; WGRP

Lamb. Michael Dennis Browne. NU; RaBo

Lamb, The. Keith Wilson. Poetsp

Lamb indestructible lamb. Song to the Lamb. Novica Tadic, *tr. fr. Serbo-Croatian* by Charles Simic. HSix

Lamb of the shepherds, Child, how still you lie. (*LL*) The Holy Innocents. Robert Lowell. InvP; MoAB; MoAmPo; OBCP; OxBC

Lamb Was Bleating Softly, The. Juan Ramón Jiménez, *tr. fr. Spanish* by Robert Bly. NU; PChr

Lamba, *sels.* Jacques Rabémananjara, *tr. fr. French* by Ellen Conroy Kennedy.
  "In hermetic enclosure." NegPo

Lambeth Lyric. Lionel Johnson. NOBVV

Lambs at Play. Christina Rossetti. BoTP

Lambs bleat my lullaby. (*LL*) Daisy's Song. Keats. BoNaP

Lambs of Grasmere, 1860, The. Christina Rossetti. FM

Lambs that learn to walk in snow. First Sight. Philip Larkin. BoNaP; NTCP

Lamda. Melvin B. Tolson. Jaz; PoNe

Lamda. Melvin B. Tolson. *See* King Oliver of New Orleans.

Lame Beggar, A. John Donne. FF; NoSic; PeLV

Lame cat, A. Chinese Proverb. *Unknown*. OFC

Lame Waltzer, The. Matthew Sweeney. IB

Lament. Pindar, *tr. fr. Greek* by Willis Barnstone. ArLo

Lament. Dylan Thomas. *See* When I was a windy boy and a bit.

Lament. Georg Trakl, *tr. fr. German* by Michael Hamburger. PeFWW

Lament: "Blue, so blue that eye of sky." Jacques Rabémanganjara, *tr. fr. French by* Ellen Conroy Kennedy. NegPo

Lament: "Even beauty must die! That which subdues both gods and mortals." Schiller, *tr. fr. German.* OBD

Lament: "Farewell Mercy, farewell thy piteous grace." John Lydgate. *Fr.* Court of Sapience. PoEL-1

Lament: "Gizzard and some ruby inner parts, A." Margaret Avison. HAP

Lament: "I lie in darkness, as the dead shades gather." Matangi Hauroa, *tr. fr. Maori by* Barry Mitcalfe. WTO

Lament: "I turn to you high priests." Tadeusz Rózewicz, *tr. fr. Polish by* Magnus J. Krynski. PoSu

Lament: "In a dismal air; a light of breaking summer." G. S. Fraser. PoWW

Lament: "Listen, children:/ Your father is dead." Edna St. Vincent Millay. CrSp; DL; IMW; MeMAP

Lament: "My man is a bone ringèd with weed." Brenda Chamberlain. WPE; WPOW

Lament: "My old red Schwinn had a carrier over the back fender." George Roberts. GOYP

Lament: "Oh, everything is far." Rainer Maria Rilke, *tr. fr. German by* C. F. MacIntyre. TrJP

Lament, A: "O world! O life! O time!" Shelley. ChTr; EnRP; GTBS; GTBS-P; NAEL-2; NOBE; PoRA; TEP; TrGrPo

Lament: "One sore thing is the way." Gibbons Ruark. MT

Lament: "Someone is dead." Anne Sexton. WPE

Lament: "Spell, treasure-bearing spell, prop up the sky standing above." *Unknown, tr. fr. Maori by* Margaret Orbell. PeNZ

Lament: "Stars and the rivers, The." Pindar, *tr. fr. Greek by* Willis Barnstone. ArLo

Lament: "We who are left, how shall we look again." W. W. Gibson. NSI; OxBTC

Lament: "What face, in the water." William Carlos Williams. VGW

Lament: When He Wes Sek. William Dunbar. *See* I that in heill wes [*or* health was] and gladnes[s] [*or* gladiness].

Lament: "When I was a windy boy and a bit." Dylan Thomas. ErPo; OPOP; PPP

(Lament.) MeMBP

Lament: "Young men of the world, The." F. S. Flint. PeFWW

Lament: "Your dying was a difficult enterprise." Thom Gunn. GLP

Lament after Her Husband Bishr's Murder. Al-Khirniq, *tr. fr. Arabic by* Willis Barnstone. BoWoP

Lament City. Thomas Lux. AmPA

Lament, 1547, A, *abr.* Alexander Scott. *See* Depairt, depairt, depairt [*or* Departe, departe, departe].

Lament for a Brother. Al-Khansa, *tr. fr. Arabic by* Omar S. Pound. ArPe

Lament for a Cricket Eleven. Kenneth Allott. OxBTC

Lament for a Dead Lover. Siraad Haad, *tr. fr. Somali by* B. W. Andrzejewski *and* I. M. Lewis. WTO

Lament for a Husband. *Unknown, tr. fr. Papuan by* Don Laycock. BoWoP; VBLP

Lament for a Leg. John Ormond. AngWe; OBWVE

Lament for a Warrior. *Unknown, tr. fr. Sotho by* Dan Kunene *and* Jack Cope. PeSA

Lament for Adonis. Bion, *tr. fr. Greek by* John Addington Symonds. AWP

Lament for an Arab Encampment. Abid ibn al-Abras, *tr. fr. Arabic by* Omar S. Pound. ArPe

Lament for Apirana Ngata. Arnold Reedy, *tr. fr. Maori by* Barry Mitcalfe. WTO

Lament for Aquileia Destroyed, and Never to be Built Again. Paulinus of Aquileia, *tr. fr. Latin by* Helen Waddell. MLL

Lament for Art O Laoghaire, The, *sels.* Eibhlin Dubh O'Connell, *tr. fr. Irish by* Thomas Kinsella.
"My steadfast love!" NOIV

Lament for Art O'Leary, The. Eileen O'Leary, *tr. fr. Irish by* Frank O'Connor. PeIV

Lament for Arthur O'Leary, The, *sels.* *Unknown.*
"My love forever!" BIrV; PBWP; VBLP

Lament for Banba. *At.* to Egan O'Rahilly, *tr. by* James Clarence Mangan. AWP

Lament for Barney Flanagan. James K. Baxter. NoP

Lament for Bion. Moschus, *tr. fr. Greek by* George Chapman. AWP

Lament for Chaucer. Thomas Hoccleve. *Fr.* De Regimine Principum. OBEV; OxBLMV

Lament for Culloden. Burns. *See* Lovely Lass o' Inverness, The.

Lament for Damon. Milton, *tr. fr. Latin by* Helen Waddell. MLL

Lament for Fearghal Ruadh. Tadhg Og O'Huiginn. NOIV

Lament for Five Sons Lost in a Plague. Abu Dhu'ayb al-Hudhali, *tr. fr. Arabic by* Omar S. Pound. ArPe

Lament for Flodden, The. Jane (*or* Jean) Elliot. *See* I've heard them [*or* the] lilting at our yewe [*or* yowel]-milking [*or* the ewe-milking].

Lament for Glasgerion. Elinor Wylie. PoA

Lament for Hathimoda, Abbess of Gandesheim. *Unknown, tr. fr. Latin by* Helen Waddell. MLL

Lament for Hsieh T'iao. Shen Yüeh, *tr. fr. Chinese by* Lenore Mayhew *and* William McNaughton. SuSp

Lament for Ignacio Sánchez Mejías. Federico García Lorca, *tr. fr. Spanish.* NAWM-2, *tr. by* Stephen Spender *and* J. L. Gili; OBVE, *tr. by* A. L. Lloyd

Lament for Kepa Anaha Ehau. Arapeta Awatere, *tr. fr. Maori by the author.* PeNZ

Lament for Lleucu Llwyd. Llywelyn Goch ap Meurig Hen, *tr. fr. Welsh by* Joseph P. Clancy. OBWVE

Lament for Llywelyn ap Gruffudd. Gruffudd ab yr Ynad Coch, *tr. fr. Welsh by* Joseph P. Clancy. OBWVE

Lament for Lost Lodgings. Phyllis McGinley. NYBP

Lament for Lu Yin. Meng Chiao, *tr. fr. Chinese by* Stephen Owen. SuSp

Lament for Mafukuzela. *Zulu Oral Tradition, tr. by* H. Tracey. WTO

Lament for Maurice Bishop. Howard Fergus. PBCV

Lament for Myself, A, *sels.* Yün Shou-p'ing, *tr. fr. Chinese by* Jonathan Chaves.

Lament for Our Lady's Shrine at Walsingham, A. *Unknown. See* In the wracks of Walsingham.

Lament for Pasiphae. Robert Graves. FaBoTw

Lament for Siôn y Glyn. Lewis Glyn Cothi, *tr. fr. Welsh by* Joseph P. Clancy. OBWVE

Lament for Tadhg Cronin's Children. Michael Hartnett. PBCIP; RB

Lament for Taramoana. Makere, *tr. fr. Maori by* Barry Mitcalfe. WTO

Lament for Tawhiao. *Unknown, tr. fr. Maori by* Margaret Orbell. PeNZ

Lament for Te Heuheu Herea. Te Heuheu Tukino, *tr. fr. Maori by* Margaret Orbell. PeNZ

Lament for Te Iwi – ika. *Unknown, tr. fr. Maori by* Margaret Orbell. PeNZ

Lament for the Cuckoo. Alcuin, *tr. fr. Latin by* Helen Waddell. NAWM-1; PeHV

Lament for the Death of Eoghan Ruadh O'Neill. Thomas Osborne Davis. NOIV; PeIV

Lament for the Death of Thomas Davis. Sir Samuel Ferguson. BIrV; NOIV; PeIV

Lament for the Dorsets. Alfred W. Purdy. NoAM; NoP

Lament for the Drowned Country. Mary Durack. NOBAu

Lament for the Graham. Henry the Minstrel. *See* When they [*or* Quhen thai] him fand, and gude [*or* gud] Wallace him saw.

Lament for the Great Music, *sels.* "Hugh MacDiarmid."
"Yet there is no great problem in the world today." OxBTC

Lament for the Gypsies. Julius Balbin. BTR

Lament for the Makaris. William Dunbar. ChTr; EBEV; HAP; NoP; OxBS; ScCV

Lament for the Makers. William Dunbar. *See* I that in heill wes [*or* health was] and gladnes[s] [*or* gladiness].

Lament for the Murderers. A. D. Hope. FaBoMA

Lament for the O'Neills. John Montague. CIP

Lament for the People of Lung. P'i Jih-hsiu, *tr. fr. Chinese by* William H. Nienhauser. SuSp

Lament for the Poets: 1916. Francis Ledwidge. AWP

Lament for the Princes of Tyrone [*or* Tir-Owen] and Tyrconnel [*or* Tirconnell], A. James Clarence Mangan, *tr. fr. Irish by* James Clarence Mangan. PeIV

Lament for the Priory of Walsingham, A. *Unknown.* FaBoPP; GBP

Lament for the Two Brothers Slain by Each Other's Hand. Aeschylus, *tr. fr. Greek by* A. E. Housman. *Fr.* Seven against Thebes, The. AWP

Lament for the Woodlands. *Unknown, tr. fr. Irish by* Frank O'Connor. IIP

Lament for Thomas MacDonagh. Francis Ledwidge. BIrV

Lament for Timoleague. Sean O'Coileain, *tr. fr. Irish by* Sir Samuel Ferguson. TIRV

Lament for Troy. Hugh Primas of Orleans, *tr. fr. Latin by* Helen Waddell. MLL

Lament for Turlough O'Carolan. David Brendon Hopes. SM

Lament for Una, A, *sels.* Tomas Costello, *tr. fr. Gaelic by* Frank O'Connor.
"Young Una, you were a rose in a garden." WTO

Lament for Urien, The. *Unknown, tr. fr. Middle Welsh by* Ernest Rhys. *Fr.* Red Book of Hergest, The. OBMV

Lament for Yellow-haired Donough, The. *Unknown, tr. fr. Irish by* Frank O'Connor. PeIV

Lament for Ying, A. Ch'u Yüan, *tr. fr. Chinese by* Wu-chi Liu. SuSp

Lament him, Mauchline husbands a'. On a Wag in Mauchline. Burns. FiBHP

(Epitaph for James Smith.) EBEV

(On James Smith.) ScCV

Lament in rhyme, lament in prose. Poor Mailie's Elegy. Burns. FM

Lament, lament, Sir Isaac Heard. Epitaph on Tuft-Hunter. Thomas Moore. FaBoCo; FaBoEE

Lament my losse, my labor, and my payne. Sir Thomas Wyatt. AAS

Lament of a Man for His Son. *Unknown, tr. fr. Paiute Indian by* Mary Austin. AWP; IMW

Lament of a Slug-a-Bed's Wife. Stevie Smith. Mes

Lament of a Soldier's Wife. Kao Ch'i, *tr. fr. Chinese by* Irving Y. Lo. SuSp

Lament of a Subwayite. Eugene O'Neill. UV

Lament of a Woman Acorn-gatherer. P'i Jih-hsiu, *tr. fr. Chinese by* William H. Nienhauser. SuSp

Lament of a Young Man for His Son. *Unknown. See* Son, my son!

Lament of an Idle Demon. R. P. Lister. FiBHP; NOBL

Lament of Edward Blastock, The. Edith Sitwell. OBMV

Lament of Hsi-chün. Hsi-chün, *tr. fr. Chinese.* BoWoP, *tr. by* Arthur Waley

Lament of Maev Leith-Dherg, The. *Unknown, tr. fr. Middle Irish by* Thomas W. H. Rolleston. OBWP

Lament of One of the Old Regime. Emma Catherine Embury. AmWP

Lament of Swordy Well, The. John Clare. FaBoVe

Lament of the Banana Man, The. Evan Jones (b. 1927). PBCV

Lament of the Border Widow, The. *Unknown.* GBP; Mes; OxBB; ScCV

Lament of the Flowers, The. Jones Very. AnAmPo; NOBA; OxBA

Lament of the Flutes. Christopher Okigbo. PBA

Lament of the Frontier Guard. Li Po, *tr. fr. Chinese by* Ezra Pound. OBVE; OBWP; VGW

Lament of the Lady of Ch'in, The. Wei Chuang, *tr. fr. Chinese by* Robin D. S. Yates. SuSp

Lament of the Lovely Helmet-Dealer. Villon, *tr. fr. French by* Hubert Creekmore. ErPo

Lament of the Maister of Erskine. Alexander Scott. *See* Depairt, depairt, depairt [*or* Departe, departe, departe].

Lament of the Master of Erskine. Alexander Scott. GBL

Lament of the Sodomites. George Lestey. *Fr.* Fire and Brimstone; or, The Destruction of Sodom. PeHV

Lament of the Unmarried Girl, The. Brian Merriman, *tr. by* Frank O'Connor. *Fr.* Midnight Court, The. NOIV, *tr. by* Thomas Kinsella; OBVE

Lament of the Virtues and Verses on Account of the Death of Don Guido. Antonio Machado Ruiz, *tr. fr. Spanish by* Charles Tomlinson *and* Henry Gifford. OBVE

Lament of Toby the Learned Pig, The. Thomas Hood. CBNP

Lament over the Ruins of the Abbey of Teach Molaga. *Unknown, tr. fr. Irish by* James Clarence Mangan. NOIV

Lament to the Spirit of War. Enheduanna. WoWa, *ad. by* Daniela Gioseffi

Lament while Descending a Shaft. *Unknown.* AmFP

Lament, with Flesh and Blood. Sandra McPherson. SM

Lamentable Ballad of the Bloody Brook, The. Edward Everett Hale. PAH

Lamentable Case, A. Sir Charles Hanbury Williams. ErPo

Lamentation. Bible, *O.T. Fr.* Ezekiel. TrJP

Lamentation, The. Ts'ai Yen, *tr. fr. Chinese by* Yi-T'ung Wang. SuSp

Lamentation, A. Thomas Campion. CH; OHIP

Lamentation during His Most Painful Illness. Simon Dach, *tr. fr. German by* Ingrid Walsøe-Engel. GePo

Lamentation for Celin, The. *Unknown, tr. fr. Spanish by* John Gibson Lockhart. AWP

Lamentation of Chloris, The. *Unknown.* CoMu

Lamentation of Enion, The. Blake. *Fr.* Vala; or The Four Zoas. OBNC

Lamentation of Queen Elizabeth, A. Sir Thomas More. *See* O ye that put your trust and confidence.

Lamentation of the Old Pensioner, The. W. B. Yeats. HAP; PeVV; TRP; WeW

Lamentation of the Old Pensioner, The. W. B. Yeats. HAP; InPK; NoAM; TRP; WeW

Lamentation on My Dear Son Simon, A. John Saffin. SCAP

Lamentation on Ninety-Mile Beach. Barry Mitcalfe. PeNZ

Lamentation on the Death of the Duke of Wellington. *Unknown.* OBET

Lamentations, *sels.* Bible, *O.T.*
   Affliction. TrJP
   Desolation in Zion. TrJP
   How Is the Gold Become Dim. ChTr
   Misery of Jerusalem, The. AWP

Lamentations. Alter Brody. TrJP

Lamentations. Norman Dubie. NoAM

Lamentations. Louise Glück. BoWoP; HCAP; VCAP

Lamentations. Siegfried Sassoon. OBSV; OxAEP-2; PeFWW

Lamentations of an Au Pair Girl. Susan Feldman. AmPA

Lamentations of Jeremy, For the Most Part According to Tremelius, The. John Donne. ChIV-1

Lamentations of the Bronze Camels. Li Ho, *tr. fr. Chinese by* Irving Y. Lo. SuSp

Lamentations of the Fallen Angels. *Unknown, tr. fr. Anglo-Saxon by* Charles W. Kennedy. *Fr.* Christ and Satan. AnOE

Lamenting all her fallen sons! (*LL*) The High Tide at Gettysburg. Will Henry Thompson. AnAmPo; BeLS; BLPA; FaBoBe; PAH; VPP

Lamenting Maid, The. *Unknown.* OBET

Lamenting Tauba. Laila Akhyaliyya, *tr. fr. Arabic by* Willis Barnstone. BoWoP

Lamenting thru gipsies his fast suicide. (*LL*) Political Poem. Amiri Baraka. CoAP; MoP; NAAL-2; NoAM

Lamenting Yang Ch'uan. Lu Hsun, *tr. fr. Chinese by* William R. Schultz. SuSp

Lamento. Tomas Tranströmer, *tr. fr. Swedish.* TSaS, *tr. by* May Swenson *with* Leif Sjoberg

Laments. Rachel Hadas. UnDi

Laments of the Gorges, *sels.* Meng Chiao, *tr. fr. Chinese.*
   "Edges of the gorges hack up sun and moon, The." SuSp
   "Owls mimic human speech." SuSp

Laments on the War Dead, *sels.* Yehuda Amichai, *tr. fr. Hebrew by* Warren Bargad *and* Stanley F. Chyet.
   "Is all this sorrow? I don't know." PoSu

Lamia. (Upon a time, before the faery broods.) Keats. EnRP; FHYEP *Sels.*

Lamisca, who breathed her last in lamentable pangs of labor. Dioscorides, *tr. fr. Greek by* Barbara Hughes Fowler. *Fr.* Epigrams. HePo

L'Amitiè est l'Amour sans Ailes, *sels.* Byron.
   "Why should my anxious breast repine." OBF

L'Amitié et l'Amour. John Swanwick Drennan. BIrV

L'Amitie: To Mrs. M. Awbrey. Katherine Philips. KTR; NOSC

Lamkin. ("Bolakins was a very fine Mason"). *Unknown.* AmFP

Lamkin. (It's Lamkin was a mason good). *Unknown.* ESPB; FaBoBa; OxBB

Lammas Dream Poem. Robert Duncan. PRA

Lamp, The. Charles Whitehead. OBEV

Lamp are you, above all stars of night, A. The Pole Star. Coslett Coslett, *tr. fr. Welsh by* Kenneth Hurlstone Jackson. OBWVE

Lamp burns long in the cottage, The. There's Money in Mother and Father. Morris Bishop. FiBHP

Lamp burns sure, within, The. Emily Dickinson. LiTA

Lamp Flower, The. Margaret Cecilia Furse. BoTP

Lamp glows deep in the mica screen. Li Shang-yin, *tr. fr. Chinese by* A. C. Graham. *Fr.* Lady in the Moon, The. PLT

Lamp lit in the corner, A. The Eagle Bar. John Wieners. BCF

Lamp of heaven's crystal hall that brings the hours. William Drummond of Hawthornden. JCP

Lamp[e], The. Henry Vaughan. ChIV-2; ESCV

Lamplight. May Wedderburn Cannan. NSI

Lamplight from our kitchen window-pane. Again. Glyn Jones. OBWVE

Lamplighter, The. "Seumas O'Sullivan." BIrV

Lamplighter, The. Robert Louis Stevenson. *Fr.* Child's Garden of Verses, A. EBVV; OxBChV

Lamplighter, if you can't set two equally. Rufinus Domesticus, *tr. fr. Greek by* Barbara Hughes Fowler. *Fr.* Epigrams. HePo

Lamprey, glowing with uncommon fires, The. William Diaper, *after the Greek of* Oppian. *Fr.* Halieutica. ECEV; OBVE

Lampriskos, the dear Muses allow you. The Schoolmaster. Herodas, *tr. fr. Greek by* Barbara Hughes Fowler. HePo

Lamps Are Burning, The. Charles Reznikoff. TrJP

Lamps burn all the night. The Fifth Sense. Patricia Beer. MoBS

Lamps now glitter down the street, The. Armies in the Fire. Robert Louis Stevenson. *Fr.* Child's Garden of Verses, A. EBVV

L'An Trentiesme de Mon Eage. Archibald MacLeish. LiTM; MoP; NOBA

Lana Turner has collapsed! Frank O'Hara. CAPP; VGW

Lancashire Born. *Unknown.* GBP

Lancashire Lads. *Unknown.* CoMu

Lancashire Puritane, The. *Unknown.* CoMu

Lancashire Winter. Tony Connor. OxBTC

Lancelot. Arna Bontemps. CDC

Lancelot and Elaine. Tennyson. *Fr.* Idylls of the King.

Lancer. A. E. Housman. MoBrPo; OBWP

Lancet, The. Denis Devlin. NOIV

Land. Carroll Arnett. VoR

Land, The. Kipling. CoGr; MoBrPo

Last Love. Fyodor Tyutchev, *tr. fr. Russian.* BoLoP; LPA, *tr. by* Vladimir Nabokov

Last Man, The, *sels.* Thomas Lovell Beddoes. Crocodile, A. FM; NOBVV; OBTV; RB

Last Man, The. Thomas Campbell. EnRP

Last Man, The. Thom Gunn. OxAEP-2

Last Man's Club, The. James Galvin. AnAn

Last May-day fair I search'd to find a snail. John Gay. *Fr.* Shepherd's Week, The. FaBoUs; PoEL-3

Last meal together, Leeds, the Queen's Hotel. The Queen's English. Tony Harrison. DiPo

Last Meeting. Robert Penn Warren. DiPo

Last Meeting of Pocahontas and the Great Captain, The. Margaret Junkin Preston. PAH

Last Month. John Ashbery. CoAP

Last month in your little Roman house, The. On the Death of Keats. John Logan. Prf

Last month of the year, grass roots taste sweet. Li Ho, *tr. by* Irving Y. Lo. *Fr.* About Horse. SuSp

Last News about the Little Box. Vasco [*or* Vasko] Popa, *tr. fr. Serbo-Croatian by* Charles Simic. AnRep; HSix

Last Night, The. Alfred Austin. PeVV

Last Night. Ethel M. Caution. ShDr

Last Night. David Ignatow. VGW

Last Night. Antonio Machado Ruiz, *tr. fr. Spanish by* Robert Bly. RaBo

Last Night. Oku Onuora. PBCV

Last night . . . in sleep. (*LL*) I am of this world. *Unknown.* BoWoP; IMW

Last night a baby gargled in the throes. A Widow in Wintertime. Carolyn Kizer. CAPP; IMW

Last night a sword-light in the sky. Stone Trees. John Freeman. BoNaP

Last night, above the whistling wind. A Sanitary Message. Bret Harte. AnAmPo

Last night, ah, yesternight, betwixt her lips and mine. Non Sum Qualis Eram Bonae sub Regno Cynarae [*or* Cynara]. Ernest Dowson. AWP; BeLS; BLPA; BoLoP; CBLP; ClHu; EBVV; EnLoPo; FaBoBe; FaPoB; GBL; GTBS-P; HAP; HeIP; ImPo; LiTB; MoBrPo; NOBE; NoP; OAEL-2; OBEV; OBMV; OBNC; PeVV; PlP; PoRA; PrIm; TEP; TFi; TrGrPo; UnPo

(Cynara.) CoGr; GGP; NAEL-2; OtMeF

Last night along the river banks. The Boats Are Afloat. Chu Hsi, *tr. fr. Chinese by* Kenneth Rexroth. NaP

Last night, among his yellow roughs. Private of the Buffs; or, The British Soldier in China. Sir Francis Hastings Doyle. OBEV; OBTV; VPP

Last night and the night before. *Unknown.* RoPo

Last night as I lay beside you all the desire had gone out of me. House. Murray Edmond. PeNZ

Last night, as I was sleeping. Last Night. Antonio Machado Ruiz, *tr. fr. Spanish by* Robert Bly. RaBo

Last night, as I was washing up. The General. G. K. Menzies. NSI

Last night at black midnight I woke with a cry. The Ghosts of the Buffaloes. Vachel Lindsay. MeMAP; MoAmPo

Last night at my daughter's, near Blaine. Energy. Raymond Carver. ArLo

Last night I danced on the rim of the moon. Last Night. Ethel M. Caution. ShDr

Last night I did not fight for sleep. In Hospital: Poona, I. Alun Lewis. AngWe; OBWVE

Last night I dreamed a ghastly dream. Ballad of the Flood. Edwin Muir. MoBS

Last night I dreamed again about the horse. Dreamwork with Horses. Alison Deming. FoLa

Last night I dreamed of an old lover. Grandmother, Rocking. Eve Merriam. GrPl

Last night I dreamed you drank coffee. One More Sign. Roberta Hill Whiteman. HATNAP

Last night I dreamt of the Pittsburgh tunnels. After a Death. Jennifer Strauss. FaBoMA

Last night I had a dream bad 'cess to my dreaming. The Dream. *Unknown.* WTO

Last night I heard him in the woods. The Woodpecker. Joyce Sambrook. BoTP

Last night I lay a-sleeping. The Holy City. Frederic E. Weatherly. BLRP; WBLP

Last night I licked. In Celebration. Ellen Bass. NMM

Last night, I looked from the Island. Behind the Lights. Jeremy Hooker. SCBI

Last night I saw a silver road. The Silver Road. Hamish Hendry. BoTP

Last night I saw Merce Cunningham. Merce Cunningham and the Birds. Lisel Mueller. GrPl

Last night I saw the monster near; the big. The White Monster. W. H. Davies. LiTB

Last night I saw the savage world. Song for a Birth or a Death. Elizabeth Jennings. EBEV

Last night I saw you in the sky. Starfish. Winifred Welles. FaPON

Last night I saw your corpse. Joyce Mansour, *tr. fr. French by* Willis Barnstone. BoWoP

Last night I slew my wife. Necessity. Harry Graham. *Fr.* Some Ruthless Rhymes. PeLV

Last night I spoke to a dead woman with green face. Last Night. David Ignatow. VGW

Last night I supped on lobster; it nearly drove me mad. The Dream. *Unknown.* OxBoLi

Last night I tossed and could not sleep. God Prays. Angela Morgan. WGRP

Last night I watched my brothers play. The Brothers. Edwin Muir. GTBS-P; HeIP; Mes; NoP; NTP; PrIm

Last Night in Calcutta. Allen Ginsberg. NoAM

Last night in Fall River in Lafayette Park. How It Will Always Seem. David Rivard. PBCAP

Last night in La Plata an avalanche of stars. La Plata, Missouri: Clear November Night. Jim Barnes. HATNAP

Last night in stomped. Dardanelles 1916. Padraic Fallon. CIP

Last night in swirling colour we danced again. Dermot Bolger. *Fr.* Stardust Sequence, The. BiHa

Last night in the open shippen. Christmas Day. Andrew Young. OBCP

Last night, just before sleep, this: a bright. Willi, Home. Jean Valentine. PFL

Last night, late, a light rain. Pavlov's Dog. Michael Pettit. NAmP90

Last night my boy [*or* little boy] confessed to me. The Two Prayers. Andrew Gillies. BLRP

(Two Prayers.) PoToHe

Last night my friend — he says he is my friend. I Hear It Said. Barbara Young. BLPA

Last night my soul departed. Muireadach Albanach O'Dalaigh. NOIV

Last night my soul witihin a dream. Tune: "Gazing at the South." Li Yü, *tr. fr. Chinese by* Daniel Bryant. SuSp

Last night returning from my twilight walk. A Ballad of Past Meridian. George Meredith. OAEL-2; PeVV

Last night that she lived, The. Emily Dickinson. BoWoP; CMoP; HeIP; LiTA; MeMAP; NAAL-1; OxBA; PoEL-5; SOTW

Last night the carol-singers came. The Carol Singers. Margaret G. Rhodes. BoTP

Last night the cold wind and the rain blew. Sunday at the End of Summer. Howard Nemerov. BoNaP; ImGa

Last night the gypsies came. Gypsies. Rachel Field. BoTP

Last night the rainbow. Moon Shadow. George Bowering. MoCV

Last night the stars seemed not themselves. Atomic Psalm. Maurya Simon. FoLa

Last night, the wind blew down the apple tree. I Still Would Plant My Apple Tree. John Greening. PWE

Last night thin rain, gusty wind. Li Ch'ing-chao, *tr. fr. Chinese by* Willis Barnstone *and* Sun Chu-chin. BoWoP

Last night thou didst invite me home to eat. Upon Showbread: Epigram. Robert Herrick. CaPo

Last night watching the Pleiades. An Autumn Morning in Shokoku-ji. Gary Snyder. *Fr.* Four Poems for Robin. HAP; MoP; NNaP; NoAM; NOBA; NoP; SOTW; VGW; WeW

Last night we anchored in. Arrival, New York Harbor. Robert Peters. GOA

Last night we had a thunderstorm in style. Robert Louis Stevenson. NOBVV

Last night we started with some dry vermouth. Ballade of Liquid Refreshment. E. C. Bentley. FaBoCo

Last night when the yellow moon. Wadasa Nakamoon, Vietnam Memorial. Ray A. Young Bear. HATNAP

Last night, while I lay thinking here. Whatif. Shel Silverstein. OTCP

Last Night with Rafaella. David St. John. BAP-90

Last night, within my dreaming. Pine Music. Kate Louise Brown. BoTP

Last night you would not come. John Logan. CAPP

Last Night's Dream. Denise Levertov. NoAM

Last night's stars, last night's winds. Li Shang-yin, *tr. fr. Chinese by* A. C. Graham. PLT

Last o' the Tinkler, The. Violet Jacob. OxBS

Last of His Tribe, The. Henry Clarence Kendall. CBAP

Last of last words spoken is, Good-bye, The. Good-bye. Walter de la Mare. NoP

Last of the Fire Kings, The. Derek Mahon. FaBoPV; PNI

Last of the Poet's Car. Tony Connor. OxBTC

Last of the poets, first of the undead. The Mole. Dennis Schmitz. AmPA

Last of the Princes, The. A. K. Ramanujan. OxBC

Last on legs, last on sax. "Bird Lives": Charles Parker [in St. Louis]. Michael S. Harper. AmPA; Jaz

Last One, The. W. S. Merwin. FoLa; LCAP; NoAM; VGW

Last one, The/ to die here. Nelly Sachs, tr. fr. German by Arthur Wensinger. BoWoP

Last Ones, The. "Robin Hyde." PeNZ

Last Ones, The. Dan Pagis. See I am already quite scarce. For years [or now].

Last pale rank of poplar-trees, The. Aubade Triste. Agnes Mary Frances Robinson. NOBVV

Last Plea. Jean Starr Untermeyer. TrPWD

Last Poem. Margaret Atwood. LCAP

Last Poem. Ted Berrigan. UL

Last Poem. Charles Donnelly. BIrV

Last Poem. Po Chü-i, tr. fr. Chinese by Arthur Waley. OBD

Last Poems. A. E. Housman. PAW
   Sels.
   Epitaph on an Army of Mercenaries. CoGr; EBEvV; NSI; OtMeF; SCGP; SoSe

Last pose flickered, failed, The. Rain after a Vaudeville Show. Stephen Vincent Benét. MoAmPo

Last Prayer, A. Helen Hunt Jackson. TrPWD

Last Quarter Moon of the Dying Year, The. Jonathan Henderson Brooks. CDC

Last Quatrain of the Ballad of Emmett Till, The. Gwendolyn Brooks. LCAP; PoBA; WPE

Last Refuge, The. Augustus Young. BIrV

Last Republicans, The. Austin Clarke. CIP

Last Reservation, The. Walter Learned. PAH

Last Rhyme of True Thomas, The. Kipling. OtMeF

Last Ride Together, The. Robert Browning. BoLoP; FHYEP; LiTB; NAEL-2; OBEV; PoEL-5; UnPo

Last Ride Together (from Her Point of View), The. James Kenneth Stephen. BXAP; FaBoCo; UnPo

Last Rites. Christina Rossetti. FaBoVe; OxBChV

Last Rose of Summer, The. Thomas Moore. See 'Tis the Last Rose of Summer.

Last Round, The. Anna Wickham. MoBrPo

Last Scab of Hawarth, The. John Manifold. FaBoMA

Last Scene in the First Act. Marge Piercy. NoAM

Last settlement scraggled out with a barbed wire fence, The. The Flight in the Desert. William Everson. ChIV-2; VGW

Last Sheet. Roy Fuller. TEP

Last Sight of Xencha, The. Philip Gross. PWE

Last Snow. Andrew Young. OxBTC

Last Song. James Guthrie. PDV

Last Songs. Galway Kinnell. CAPP; VCAP

Last Statement. Vladimir Mayakovsky, tr. fr. Russian by Tom Paulin. FaBoPV; PBCIP

Last Statement for a Last Oracle. Alan Dugan. CAPP; NoAM

Last summer, in the blue heat. La Vita Nuova. Weldon Kees. VGW

Last sunbeam, The. Dirge for Two Veterans. Walt Whitman. AnAmPo; MoAmPo; PoEL-5
   (Two Veterans.) GN

Last Supper. Matthew Sweeney. IB

Last Supper, The. Oscar Williams. ImPo; LiTA; LiTM

Last Survivor's Speech, The. Unknown, tr. by Alfred David. Fr. Beowulf. ASW, tr. by Kevin Crossley-Holland; NAEL-1

Last thin acre of stalks that stood, The. Immortal. Mark Van Doren. MoAmPo

Last thing I remember are Yeats' po, The. Lissadell. Matthew Sweeney. IB

Last Thing I Say, The. Marvin Bell. CAPP

Last Things. William Meredith. NoAM

Last Things. Kathleen Raine. NYBP

Last Things, Black Pines at 4 a.m. Robert Lowell. NOBA

Last things/ the turning leaves slip in the wind. Vincent O'Sullivan. Fr. Brother Jonathan, Brother Kafka. PeNZ

Last time around the forest floor. Rainier. Jim Tollerud. VoR

Last time blues, The/ with no hesitations. (LL) Do Nothing till You Hear from Me. David Henderson. PoBA

Last time I saw Donald Armstrong, The. The Performance. James Dickey. ArOW; CAPP; CoAP; LiTM; MoP; NOBA; PoE

Last Time I Saw Jack, The. Carolyn Lau. BCF

Last time I slept with the Queen. Dylan Thomas. PeLi

Last time i was home, The. Mothers. Nikki Giovanni. UnPo

Last time you left. A Greeting to Lu Hung-Chien. Li Yeh, tr. fr. Chinese by Kenneth Rexroth and Ling Chung. WPC

Last Tournament, The. Tennyson. Fr. Idylls of the King.

Last trainees are climbing the diving tower, The. The Naval Trainees Learn How to Jump Overboard. David Wagoner. VCAP

Last truly foolish thing I did was some years ago, The. The Void. Gwendolyn MacEwen. Fr. T. E. Lawrence Poems, The. NOBC

Last twist of the knife., The. (LL) Rhapsody on a Windy Night. T. S. Eliot. CMoP; HeIP; InPS; PoE

Last two Februarys have passed, The. St. Bridget's Cross. Anne Hartigan. CIP

Last Utterance of the Delphic Oracle, The. Unknown, tr. fr. Greek by Kenneth Rexroth. OBVE

Last Verses. Thomas Chatterton. TrGrPo

Last Violet, The. Oliver Herford. OHIP

Last Visa for Palestine, The. Elaine Mott. BTR

Last Vision of Eoghan Rua Ó Súilleabháin, The. Michael Hartnett. PBCIP

Last Visit. Robert Finch. NOBC

Last War, The. Kingsley Amis. OBSV; OxBC

Last war was my favourite picture story, The. In September 1939. Bernard Gutteridge. PoWW

Last week a showing of Holocaust films. The familiar. Meditation after Hearing the Richard Yardumian Mass, "Come, Creator Spirit." Geraldine Clinton Little. BTR

Last week in March the rains come, The. A Scriptwriter's Discipline. Matthew Sweeney. IB

Last Will and Testament. Hans Magnus Enzensberger. PoSu

Last Will and Testament, A. Unknown. MeEL

Last Will and Testament, A. John Winstanley. FaBoVe; OBSV

Last winter we were/ short of firewood. A Letter to Hitler. James Laughlin. LiTA

Last Wish, The. "Owen Meredith." OxBSP

Last Word, The. Matthew Arnold. CoGr; NOBE; OAEL-2; OBNC; PoEL-5; SCGP; TrGrPo

Last Word, The. Peter Davison. InPK

Last Word, A. Ernest Dowson. MoBrPo

Last Word of a Bluebird, The. Robert Frost. FaPON; GoJo; GrPl

Last word this one spoke, The. Two Friends. Norman MacCaig. OBF

Last Words. Emily Brontë. WPE

Last Words. John Hollander. OBAL

Last Words. Richard Howard. Fr. Ithaca: The Palace at Four A.M. DiPo

Last Words, The. Maurice Maeterlinck, tr. fr. French by Frederick York Powell. AWP

Last Words. James Merrill. TAP

Last Words. Sylvia Plath. FYAP

Last Words before Winter. Louis Untermeyer. MoAmPo

Last Words, 1968. Lance Henson. CDW

Last Words of Don Henriquez, The. Zalman Schneour, tr. fr. Yiddish by Joseph Leftwich. TrJP

Last Words of My English Grandmother, The. William Carlos Williams. RaBo; RB; SAmP; SOTW

Last Words to a Dumb Friend. Thomas Hardy. FM; OBF; OFC; SoCa

Last Words to Miriam. D. H. Lawrence. CBLP

Last World, A. John Ashbery. PoM

Last year at the Feast of Lanterns. Lost. Chu Shu-chen, tr. fr. Chinese by Kenneth Rexroth. BoWoP; OHMPC

Last year changed its seasons. In Retrospect. Maya Angelou. UnAS

Last year he drew the harvest home. Commandeered. L.G. Moberley. NSI

Last year I lost an incisor. Poem on Losing One's Teeth. Han Yü, tr. fr. Chinese by Kenneth O. Hanson. SuSp

Last year, Orlando. The Political Orlando. George MacBeth. NOBL

Last year, scarce one short season back. In Memoriam J.H.H. C. J. Ronald. NSI

Last year the child died. Olive Senior. PBCV

Last year the war was in the northeast. War. Li Po, tr. fr. Chinese by Rewi Alley. ChTr

Last year we fought. They Fought South of the Walls. Li Po, tr. fr. Chinese by Joseph J. Lee. SuSp

Last year we fought by the springs of Sankan river. Fighting on the South Frontier. Li Po, tr. fr. Chinese by Robert Payne. TAL

Last year when I accompanied you. To a Traveler. Su Tung-p'o, tr. by Kenneth Rexroth. HoPM

Last Years, The. W. H. Davies. FM

Last year's decencies. Odysseus. Padraic Fallon. CIP

Last Year's Discussion: The Nobel Russian. Phyllis McGinley. FaBoEE

Last year's sunflower stalks blacken. Spring Planting. Gail Mazur. NAmP90

Lasting Influence. Susan Wheeler. BAP-91

Lastly came Winter cloathèd all in frize. Winter. Spenser. *Fr.* Faerie Queene, The. GN

Lastly, safely buried. *(LL)* Divination by a Daffadill [*or* Daffodil]. Robert Herrick. CaPo; SeCV-1

Lastly, stood war, in glittering arms yclad. The Shield of War. Thomas Sackville. *Fr.* Induction to "A Mirror for Magistrates." AAS

Lastly, with friends t' enjoy our days. *(LL)* Four Things Make Us Happy Here. Robert Herrick. CaPo

Lastness. Galway Kinnell. NNaP

Lastness, *sels.* Galway Kinnell.
"Black bear sits alone, A." RaBo

Lat never a man a wooing wend. King Henry. *Unknown.* ESPB; OxBB

Lat no man booste of conning not vertu. Transient as a Rose. John Lydgate. MeEL

Lat Take a Cat. Chaucer. *See* Lat take a cat, and fostre him wel with milk.

Lat take a cat, and fostre him wel with milk. Chaucer. *Fr.* Canterbury Tales, The. EnVB; OFC
(Lat Take a Cat.) ChTr

Latch was hiding, The. *(LL)* The Return. Sebastian Barry. IB

Late. Louise Bogan. PBWP; VGW

Late. Helen Salz. GoYe

Late afternoon in July, too early to begin, A. The Gypsy. Susan Stewart. NAmP90

Late Afternoon, Late in the Twentieth Century. Jeffrey Skinner. PBCAP

Late afternoon light slices through the dormer window. The Gun. Stephen Dobyns. AnAn

Late Annie in her bower lay. The Ballad of the Late Annie. Gwendolyn Brooks. *Fr.* Notes from the Childhood and the Girlhood. LCAP

Late April and you are three; today. W. D. Snodgrass. *Fr.* Heart's Needle. VCAP

Late April. Taking stock. Generalities. Robert Conquest. OxBC

Late at een, drinkin' the wine. The Dowie Houms o' Yarrow. *Unknown.* OBEV; OxBS
(Braes o' Yarrow, The.) ESPB

Late at Night. William Stafford. NNaP; RFM

Late at Night During a Visit of Friends. Robert Bly. InPS

Late at night I stood on a battlement. Der von Kürenberg, *tr. fr. German by* Frederick Goldin. GePo

Late Aubade, A. Richard Wilbur. Poetr; SM; SoSe

Late August, given heavy rain and sun. Blackberry-picking. Seamus Heaney. BoNaP

Late Autumn. May Sarton. CrSp

Late-born and woman-souled I dare not hope. Echoes. Emma Lazarus. AmWP

Late Bus (After a Series of Hold-Ups). Russell Atkins. ETG

Late Child. Robert Pinsky. *Fr.* Three on Luck. AnAn

Late Comer. Fanny de Groot Hastings. GoYe

Late Dandelions. Ben Belitt. NYBP

Late Evening Conversation with My Friend's Dog, Moses, after Watching Visconti's The Innocent. Luis Omar Salinas. AfAz

Late Express, The. Barbara Giles. OTCP

Late Fall Night. William Trowbridge. NGP

Late-flowering Lust. Sir John Betjeman. CMoP; ErPo

Late for Breakfast. Mary Dawson. TLR

Late Fragment. Raymond Carver. ArLo

Late Gothic. Phyllis Gotlieb. NOBC

Late Hour, The. Mark Strand. HCAP

Late in an evening forth as I went. Archie o Cawfield. *Unknown.* ESPB

Late in Fall. Ramona Wilson. VoR

Late in the afternoon. Spring Burning. Patrick Roland. PeSA

Late in the afternoon the light. Crepuscular. Richard Howard. TwCP

Late in the evening the ale graines and blood. Baits for Various Fish. Thomas Barker. *Fr.* Art of Angling, The. FaBoUs

Late in the fall. For a Woman Murdered While Running at Land's End, October 1979. Patricia Kirkpatrick. LoHo

Late in the Forest I did Cupid see. Mary Sidney Wroth, Countess of Montgomery. *Fr.* Urania. KTR; WPE

Late in the season the world digs in, the fat blossoms. Over and Over Stitch. Jorie Graham. HCAP; VCAP

Late it was in the night, with the wind. Lament for Turlough O'Carolan. David Brendon Hopes. SM

Late Lark, A. W. E. Henley. *See* Late lark twitters from the quiet skies, A.

Late lark twitters from the quiet skies, A. Margaritæ Sorori, [I. M.]. W. E. Henley. *Fr.* Echoes. MoBrPo; NOBE; OBEV; OBNC; PlP; TrGrPo; WGRP
(Late Lark, A.) PoRA

Late Last Night. Arthur Gregor. VGW

Late last night, a girl came. *Unknown, tr. fr. Greek by* Sam Hamill. InMo

Late last night I was a-making my rounds. Bad Man Ballad. *Unknown.* AmFP

Late, Last Rook, The. Ralph Hodgson. MoBrPo

Late lies the wintry sun a-bed. Winter Time. Robert Louis Stevenson. *Fr.* Child's Garden of Verses, A. EBVV; MoBrPo; OxBChV

Late Light. Edmund Blunden. EnLoPo

Late Light. Barbara Bellow Watson. NYBP

Late Miss H. came to us Wednesday at four, The. Swansong. Carol Muske. AmPA

Late Mother, The. Cynthia MacDonald. Poetsp

Late Naps. Marvin Bell. AnAn

Late night, with my bundle of new straws. The Burden of Decision. Peter Everwine. NNaP

Late Notebooks of Albrecht Dürer, The. Rita Dove. BAP-89

Late November. Sherod Santos. Son

Late November, driving to Wichita. For a Friend. Ted Kooser. GOYP

Late November in a Field. James Wright. CAPP; NAAL-2; NNaP

Late October. Sara King Carleton. GoYe

Late October sun. White Earth. Gerald Vizenor. HATNAP

Late one afternoon we walk along the flank of a hill. South Seas. Cesare Pavese, *tr. fr. Italian by* William Arrowsmith. AnAn

Late Passenger, The. C. S. Lewis. TrCP

Late, Passing Prairie Farm. William Stafford. GOYP

Late Reflections. Babette Deutsch. NYBP

Late Return. E. A. Markham. PBCV

Late Singer, The. William Carlos Williams. SAmP

Late singer of a sunless day. The Linnet in November. Francis Turner Palgrave. EBVV

Late Snow and Lumber Strike of the Summer of Fifty-four, The. Gary Snyder. NaP

Late Sonnet. Hayden Carruth. SM; Son

Late Spring. Fan Ch'eng-ta, *tr. by* Irving Y. Lo. *Fr.* Seasonal Poems on Fields and Gardens. SuSp

Late Spring. W. S. Merwin. AnAn

Late Spring. Yüan Chen, *tr. fr. Chinese by* Dell R. Hales. SuSp

Late Spring, A. James Scully. NYBP

Late Spring: Eastport, A. Philip Booth. Poetsp

Late Stravinsky Listening to Late Beethoven. Stephen Spender. AnAn

Late Summer. Theocritus [*or* Theokritus], *tr. fr. Greek by* Willis Barnstone. EaPr

Late summer, and at midnight. The Guttural Muse. Seamus Heaney. NOIV; NoP

Late Summer Storm. Christine Churches. FaBoMA

Late sun, the stream and the hills; the beauty. Tu Fu, *tr. fr. Chinese by* Jerome Seaton. SuSp

Late that summer. Surrendered Names. Gerald Vizenor. HATNAP

Late Train, The. Theodore Weiss. BTR

Late Tuesday afternoon the romantic self weaves. Seventh Avenue. Mark Halliday. NAmP90

Late Twentieth Century Pastoral. William Pitt Root. BTR

Late Twentieth-Century Prayer, A. Ernest Sandeen. WeW

Late Victorian Girl, The. Bill Manhire. PeNZ

Late, when it returns from the city wall. The Crow Cries at Night. Po Chü-i, *tr. fr. Chinese by* Irving Y. Lo. SuSp

Late Wisdom. George Crabbe. *Fr.* Reflections. OBEV; TrGrPo

Lately, Alas, I Knew a Gentle Boy. Thoreau. PeHV

Lately his haunch has grown stiff. Father. Jean Lipkin. AIW; PeSA

Lately I saw a sight most quaint. "Gross, Coarse, Hideous" (Police Description of My Pictures). D. H. Lawrence. FaBoEE

Lately, I think of my love for you and the rose. The Rose Growing into the House. Gibbons Ruark. InPK

Lately, I've become accustomed to the way. Preface to a Twenty Volume Suicide Note. Amiri Baraka. PoBA; PoM; PoNe; PPP; TTY

Lately I've become religious about atoms. Metamorpho I. Joe Rosenblatt. MoCV

Lately I've felt a grave concern. Beatrice, Countess de Die, *tr. fr. Provençal by* Willis Barnstone. BoWoP

Lately my neighbor wheezes. Running. Leslie Ullman. PBCAP

Lately Our Poets. Walter Savage Landor. LiTB; OAEL-2; PoEL-4

Lately our poets loitered in green lanes. Walter Savage Landor. *See* Lately Our Poets.

Lateness. Jonathan Galassi. PRA

Lateness is all that shimmers in the leaves. Lateness. Jonathan Galassi. PRA

Later, a cormorant. Cormorant. Peter Preece. AngWe

Later Antigonishes, *sels.* Hughes Mearns.

Law there is of ancient fame, A. Tit for Tat; a Tale. John Aikin. OxBChV

Law ever above kings, The. Morgan Llwyd. *Fr.* Charles, the last king of Britain. AngWe

Law! what is law? The wise and sage. Elymas Payson Rogers. *Fr.* Poem on the Fugitive Slave Law, A. AAP

Lawd, Dese Colored Chillum. Ruby C. Saunders. BlSi

Lawd, I'm broke and hungry, ragged and dirty, too. Ragged and Dirty. *Unknown.* AmFP

Lawlands o' Holland, The. *Unknown.* CH

Lawlands o' Holland, The. *Unknown. See* "My love has built a bonny ship, and set her on the sea."

Lawn as white as driven snow. Shakespeare. *Fr.* Winter's Tale, The. NoSic
  (Autolycus as Peddler.) OAEL-1
  (Come Buy! Come Buy!) CBCK; EIL
  (Pedlar, The.) WiR
  (Pedlar's Song, The.) CH

Lawn-Tennisonian Idyll, A. *Unknown.* FaBoPa

Lawns darken, evening broods in the black, The. Tennyson. Alan Ansen. CoAP

Lawns, the orientalia, The. *(LL)* A Setting. Donald Revell. UTF

Lawrence Bloomfield in Ireland, *sels.* William Allingham.
  Tenants at Will. PeIV

Lawrence Dooley. Note Slipped under a Door. Wilma Elizabeth McDaniel. ETG

Lawrence here for ever blames. D. H. Lawrence and James Joyce. Humbert Wolfe. FaBoEE

Lawrence — not the bearded one — the one. Any Complaints? Vernon Scannell. OxBTC

Lawrence, of virtuous father virtuous son. To Mr. Lawrence. Milton. AWP; GTBS; GTBS-P; OBEV; PoE
  (Sonnet.) OxAEP-1
  (Sonnet: "Lawrence, of virtuous father virtuous son.") NOSC
  (Sonnet to Edward Lawrence.) OBF

Lawrence O'Toole. Aidan Carl Mathews. IB

Laws-a-massey, what have you done? Negro Reel. *Unknown.* AS

Laws are the secret avengers, The. The Avengers. Edwin Markham. MoAmPo

Laws of God, The. A. E. Housman. *See* Laws of God, the Laws of Man, The.

Laws of God, the Laws of Man, The. A. E. Housman. MeMBP; MoAB; MoBrPo; NOBVV; NTP; OBSV; PeHV

Lawyer, The. John Gay. *See* Fox may steal your hens, sir, A.

Lawyer had a legal mouse, A. A Legal Mouse. L. A. J. Moorer. CBWP-3

Lawyers, Bob, know too much, The. The Lawyers Know Too Much. Carl Sandburg. CMoP; PoE

Lawyer's Invocation to Spring, The. Henry Howard Brownell. PoLF

Lawyers Know Too Much, The. Carl Sandburg. CMoP; PoE

Lawyers may revere that tree, The. Epigram on a Lawyer's Desiring One of the Tribe to Look with Respect to a Gibbet. Robert Fergusson. OxBS

Lawyers' Ways, The. Paul Laurence Dunbar. AnAmPo

Lay a garland on my hearse. Beaumont *and* Fletcher *and* John Fletcher. *Fr.* Maid's Tragedy, The. EIL; GBL; SCGP
  (Aspatia's Song.) AWP; HAP; NOBE; OBEV; TrGrPo
  (I Died True.) CH

Lay aside phrases; speak as in the night. This Is Not Death. Humbert Wolfe. MoBrPo

Lay busily hid. *(LL)* A Grasshopper. Richard Wilbur. HAP; HoPM

Lay down the axe; fling by the spade. Our Country's Call. Bryant. PAH

Lay down these words. Riprap. Gary Snyder. CAPP; HCAP; NAAL-2; NeAP; NoAM; NOBA; PoBeRe; PoM; VCAP

Lay him low! *(LL)* Dirge for a Soldier. George Henry Boker. AnAmPo; PAH

Lay his dear ashes where ye will. President Lincoln's Grave. Caroline A. B. Mason. OHIP

Lay in the house mostly living. Madness. James Dickey. NYBP

Lay lightly down, and slept. *(LL)* After Love. Maxine W. Kumin. CrSp; NMM; TAP; VBLP

Lay me down beneaf de willers in de grass. A Death Song. Paul Laurence Dunbar. CDC; PoLF; PoNe

Lay me in yon place, lad. The Last o' the Tinkler. Violet Jacob. OxBS

Lay me on an anvil, O God. Prayers of Steel. Carl Sandburg. CMoP; FaPON; MoAmPo; PDV; TrCP; TrPWD

Lay me on my true Love's body. *(LL)* Deirdre's [*or* Deidre's] Lament for the Sons of Usnach. *Unknown.* IIP; NOIV; PeIV

Lay me to sleep in [the] sheltering flame. The Mystic's Prayer. "Fiona Macleod." TrPWD; WGRP

Lay neither the scrawny. Rufinus, *tr. fr. Greek by* Alan Marshfield. GrAn

Lay not up for yourselves treasures upon the earth. Treasures. Bible, *N.T. Fr.* St. Matthew. TrGrPo

Lay of Finn, The. *Unknown, tr. by* Charles W. Kennedy. *Fr.* Beowulf. AnOE; ASW, *tr. by* Kevin Crossley-Holland

Lay of Ike, The. John Berryman. *Fr.* Dream Songs. LCAP

Lay of Real Life, A, *sels.* Thomas Hood.
  "Who, gratis, shared my social glass." OBF

Lay of St. Cuthbert, The. "Thomas Ingoldsby." OtMeF

Lay of the Battle of Tombland, The. Dunstan Thompson. LiTA

Lay of the Captive Count, The. Goethe, *tr. fr. German by* James Clarence Mangan. AWP

Lay of the Ettercap, The. John Leyden. BXAP

Lay of the Honeysuckle, The. Marie de France, *tr. fr. French by* Robin Johnson. WPE

Lay of the Last Minstrel, The, *sels.* Sir Walter Scott.
  "Breathes There the [*or* a] Man [with Soul So Dead]." BLPA; EBEvV; EnRP; OxBS; PlP; SoSe; TFi
  (Innominatus.) OBEV
  (Love of Country.) VPP; WBLP
  (My Native Land.) GN
  (Native Land.) TrGrPo
  (Patriot, The.) FaPoR; OBNC
  (Patriotism.) NOBE; OxAEP-2
  O Caledonia! FaBoPP
  Father's Notes of Woe, A. OBNC
  Hunting Song. EnRP; GN; GTBS; GTBS-P; SCGP; TrGrPo; WiR
  Love. OxAEP-2
  Melrose Abbey. FaBoPP; OxAEP-2
  (Sir William of Deloraine at the Wizard's Tomb.) OBNC
  Minstrel Responds to Flattery, The. OBNC
  (Nature's Sympathy with the Poet.) OxAEP-2
  Minstrel, The. OxAEP-2
  Rosabelle. BeLS; GTBS; GTBS-P
  (Harold's Song: Rosabelle.) EnRP
  Song of Albert Graeme. EnRP

Lay of the Lovelorn, The. William Edmonstoune Aytoun *and* Sir Theodore Martin. FaBoCo

Lay [*or* Short Lay] of Sigurd, The. *Unknown, tr. by* William Morris *and* Eirikr Magnusson. *Fr.* Elder Edda, The. AWP

Lay out the minutes, row on ordered row. Time Out. Frances Westgate Butterfield. GoYe

Lay Preacher Ponders, The. Idris Davies. OxBTC

Lay the cloth, knife and fork. *Unknown.* ISE

Lay to Eliza, The. Spenser. *See* Ye dainty nymphs, that in this blessed brook.

Lay wreaths upon the stone. Wreaths. Requiescat. Haim Guri, *tr. fr. Hebrew by* Ruth Finer Mintz. MHP

Lay Your Arms Aside. Pierce Ferriter, *tr. fr. Irish by* Eilean Ni Chuilleanain. BIrV

Lay Your Sleeping Head, My Love. W. H. Auden. *See* Lay your sleeping head, my love.

Lay your sleeping head, my love. Lullaby. W. H. Auden. CMoP; EBEvV; FaPoB; GLP; HAP; MoP; NAEL-2; NoAM; NOBE; OAEL-2; OxAEP-2; OxBTC; PoE; PPP; TFi; UnPo; WeW
  (Lay Your Sleeping Head, My Love.) BoLoP; LPA
  (Song XI: "Lay your sleeping head, my love.") EnLoPo

Lay your weapons down, young lady. Piaras Feiritear, *tr. fr. Irish by* Thomas Kinsella. NOIV

Laying the pen aside, when he had signed. Faustus. A. D. Hope. NOBAu

Lays of Ancient Rome, *sels.* Macaulay.
  Horatius. OBWP
  Horatius at the Bridge. BeLS; FaBoCh; FaPoR; OBNV, *abr.;* OBWP; PoLF
  (Horatius.) AnRep; CoGr; EBEvV, *abr.;* OxAEP-2
  (Lars Porsena of Clusium.) EBNV

Lays of Tom-cat Hiddigeigei. Joseph Victor von Scheffel, *tr. by* William Fitzgerald. OFC

Lazarus. Agnes Nemes Nagy, *tr. fr. Hungarian by* Frederic Will. PoSu

Lazarus, kindling at the breath of pain. The Second Life of Lazarus. Gwen Harwood. CBAP

Lazarus to Christ. David Constantine. PWE

Lazarus was heavy but she, little sister. Talitha Cumi. David Constantine. PWE

Lazily I stir a white feather fan. In the Mountains on a Summer Day. Li Po, *tr. fr. Chinese by* Robert Payne. TAL

Laziness and Silence. Robert Bly. PPP

Lazy. Lu Yu, *tr. fr. Chinese by* Kenneth Rexroth. OHMPC

Lazy-bones, lazy-bones, wake up and peep! Nonsense Verses. Charles Lamb. CBNP

Lazy deuks that sit i' the coal-neuks. *Unknown.* OxNR

Lazy laughing languid Jenny. Jenny. Dante Gabriel Rossetti. EnVR; PoEL-5

Lazy Man's Song. Po Chü-i, *tr. fr. Chinese by* Arthur Waley. OBVE

Lazy Marcus once dreamed. Lucilius, *tr. fr. Greek by* Peter Porter. GrAn

Lazy Mary. *Unknown.* AmFP

Lazy People, The. Shel Silverstein. NTCP

Lazy petals of magnolia-bloom float down the sluggish river. Elegy on a Nordic White Protestant. John Gould Fletcher. PoNe

Lazy Pussy, The. Palmer Cox. OBCA

Lazy sheep, pray tell me why. The Sheep. Ann Taylor. BoTP; OxBChV

Le Balcon. Baudelaire, *tr. fr. French by* Lord Alfred Douglas. AWP

Le Chariot. John Wieners. VGW

Le Hibou et la Poussiquette. Francis Steegmuller. NYBP

Le Jardin. Oscar Wilde. *Fr.* Impressions.

Le Jazz Hot. Anselm Hollo. PoM

Le Marais du Cygne. Whittier. PAH

Le Médecin Malgré Lui. William Carlos Williams. PoA

Le Monocle de Mon Oncle. Wallace Stevens. LiTM; MeMAP; MoAB

Le Père Sévère. *Unknown, tr. fr. French by* Andrew Lang. AWP

Le Sacré-Coeur. Charlotte Mew. OBTV

Le Sporting-Club de Monte Carlo. James Baldwin. Jaz

Le Tombeau de Frank O'Hara. Art Lange. UL

Le Tombeau de Pierre Falcon. James Reaney. MoCV

Lead. Jayne Cortez. PoBA

Lead & zinc company, The. Holes Commence Falling. David Huddle. PBCAP

Lead disc composed of black stuff for marking, A. Damocharis, *tr. fr. Greek by* John Heath-Stubbs *and* Carol A. Whiteside. GrAn

Lead gently, Lord, and slow. After Reading "Lead, Kindly Light." Paul Laurence Dunbar. TrPWD

Lead, Kindly Light. Cardinal Newman. PlP

Lead, Kindly Light, amid the encircling gloom. Lead, Kindly Light. Cardinal Newman. PlP
(Pillar of the Cloud, The.) ChIV-1; OHCV

Lead On, O King Eternal. Ernest W. Shurtleff. AH

Lead the black bull to slaughter, with the boar. Upon Master Walter Montagu's Return from Travel. Thomas Carew. CaPo

Lead us, Evolution, lead us. Evolutionary Hymn. C. S. Lewis. NOBL

Lead Us, O Father, in the Paths of Peace. William Henry Burleigh. AH

Leaden Echo and the Golden Echo, The. Gerard Manley Hopkins. CMoP; FaPoB; GTBS-P; ImPo; LiTB; LiTM; MeMBP; MoAB; MoBrPo; NOBVV; OBMV; OBNC; SOTW

Leaden-eyed, The. Vachel Lindsay. CMoP; CoGr; FaBoEE; ImPo; LiTA; OxBSP; PoE; RB

Leaden rapier in a golden sheath, A. *(LL)* Against Gaudy-Bragging-Undoughty Daccus. John Davies of Hereford. FaBoEE

Leaden Treasury of English Verse, A, *sels.* Paul Dehn.
"Jenny kiss'd me when we met." CBLP; FiBHP
"Nuclear wind, when wilt thou blow." FiBHP

Leader. Bruce Bennett. InPK

Leader, The. Dorothy Livesay. MoCV

Leaders. *Unknown.* WBLP

Leaders of the Crowd, The. W. B. Yeats. EBEV; MoAB; MoBrPo; OxAEP-2

Leading liot act to forage is activity. On Autumn Lake. John Ashbery. LCAP

Leaf. Rade Drainac, *tr. fr. Serbo-Croatian by* Charles Simic. HSix

Leaf, A. Ludwig Uhland, *tr. fr. German by* John S. Dwight. AWP

Leaf falls softly at my feet, A. A Leaf. Ludwig Uhland, *tr. fr. German by* John S. Dwight. AWP

Leaf floats in endless space, A. Seeking a Mooring. Wang Wei, *tr. fr. Chinese by* Kenneth Rexroth *and* Ling Chung. BoWoP; WPC; WPOW

Leaf From a French Bible (circa 1270). Peter Scupham. *Fr.* Marginalia. SCBI

Leaf from freedom's golden chaplet fair, A. To My Father. H. Cordelia Ray. AAP; BlSi; CBWP-3; Son

Leaf in Love and War, A. Veripatiya Kamakkanniyar, *tr. fr. Tamil by* A. K. Ramanujan. PLW

Leaf is not too little, A. A world may rest. At My Father's Grave. John Ciardi. SM

Leaf of a light boat, A. Tune: "Joy of Eternal Union" — Passing the Seven-league Shallows. Su Shih. *tr. fr. Chinese by* Irving Y. Lo. SuSp

Leaf of lehua and noni-tint, the Kona Sea. The Kona Sea. *Unknown, tr. fr. Hawaiian by* N. B. Emerson. WTO

Leaf on the grey sand-path, A. The Unreturning Spring. Laurence Binyon. NSI

Leaf [*or* Leafe] gold, Lord of thy golden wedge o'erlaid. Edward Taylor. *Fr.* Preparatory Meditations Before My Approach to the Lord's Supper. EAP; NAAL-1

Leaf-picking, The. Frédéric Mistral, *tr. fr. French by* Harriet Waters Preston. AWP

Leaf this boat, its light sail rolled, A. Tune: "Prelude to Allure Goddesses." Liu Yung, *tr. fr. Chinese by* Jerome P. Seaton. SuSp

Leaf-Treader, A. Robert Frost. MoAmPo

Leaf, treeless, A. Paul Celan, *tr. fr. German by* Michael Hamburger. PoSu

Leaf will wrinkle to decay, The. The Crest Jewel. James Stephens. MoAB; MoBrPo

Leafbud straggles forth, The. Upper Broadway. Adrienne Rich. HCAP; InPS

Leafless are the trees; their purple branches. The Golden Mile-Stone. Longfellow. PoEL-5

Leafless there by my door, trembled a sense of the rose. *(LL)* Earliest Spring. William Dean Howells. OBEV

Leafless Trees, Chickahominy Swamp. Dave Jeddie Smith. FoLa

Leafshade stirring on lichened bark. Culture and Anarchy. Adrienne Rich. NALW

Leafy the boughs — they also hide big fruit. *(LL)* Do Not Expect Again a Phoenix Hour. C. Day Lewis. CMoP; FaBoMo; LiTB; LiTM; MoAB; MoBrPo; NoAM; OxBTC; PoRA

Leafy-with-love banks and the green waters of the canal. Canal Bank Walk. Patrick Kavanagh. CIP; CMoP; FaBoTw; IPY; MoBrPo; NoAM

League and a league from the trenches, A — from the traversed maze of the lines. Headquarters. Gilbert Frankau. NSI

League of Nations, The. Mary Siegrist. PAH

Leah, *sels.* Ruth Gilbert.
Jacob. PeNZ

Leak in the Dike, The. Phoebe Cary. FaPON; VPP

Lean back, and get some minutes' peace. Faustine. Swinburne. BeLS; EBVVPR; PeHV

Lean bird circles, A. *(LL)* Legacy: My South. Dudley Randall. PoBA; PoNe

Lean Gaius, who was thinner than a straw. Lucilius, *tr. fr. Greek by* Peter Porter. GrAn; OBVE

Lean in the greenhood of my fearful years. Fool Song. Cornel Lengyel. GoYe

Lean is the ghost of Molly Means. *(LL)* Molly Means. Margaret Walker. BlSi; NALW; NMM; PoNe

Lean out the window: down the street. A Man with a Little Pleated Piano. Winifred Welles. FaPON

Lean Street. G. S. Fraser. OxBS

Lean to hear a secret chord that mine will bear. *(LL)* Trembling before Thine Awful Throne. Augustus Lucas Hillhouse. AH

Lean wizard, A. Lizard. Grace Nichols. OBAP

Lean wolf unmolested made her lair, The. *(LL)* Unguarded Gates. Thomas Bailey Aldrich. AnAmPo; PAH

Leander. Hugh Henry Brackenridge *and* Philip Freneau. *Fr.* Rising Glory of America, The. AiP

Leander Stormbound. Sydney Goodsir Smith. OxBS

Leander to the envious light. George Chapman. *Fr.* Hero and Leander. AAS; NoP; OAEL-1

Leander's Return. Christopher Marlowe, First *and* Second Sestiads, *completed by* George Chapman. *Fr.* Hero and Leander. AAS; EBNV; NoP

Leane, The. William Barnes. EBVV

Leaning against the golden undertow. Kenneth Slessor. *Fr.* Out of Time. CBAP

Leaning against the — Sun. *(LL)* I taste a liquor never brewed. Emily Dickinson. AmPP; CMoP; FaBV; FF; HeIP; LiTA; LiTM; MeMAP; MoAmPo; NAAL-1; NoAM; NOBA; NoP; OxBA; PoEL-5; SoSe; TAP; TFi; WPE

Leaning into the hill. Fyllr. Gavin Selerie. NBrP

Leaning/ on the parapet. My Father Spoke with Swans. Patrick Galvin. BiHa

Leaning Over. Janet Sutherland. DT

Leaning over the wall at Trafalgar Square. Cosmos in London. Arthur Nortje. HBAPE; PeSAV

Leaning together on the spring wind with the moonbeams for our toys? *(LL)* The Retired Official Yüan's High Pavilion. Tu Mu. PLT

Leap, The. James Dickey. NIP; Poetr

Leap before You Look. W. H. Auden. NoAM

Leap-Centuries. Paul Celan, *tr. fr. German by* Michael Hamburger. OBVE

Leap in the Dark. Roberta Hill Whiteman. WPOW

Leap of Faith. David St. John. NAmP90

Leap of the salmon, The. The Shannon Estuary Welcoming the Fish. Nuala Ni Dhomhnaill, *tr. fr. Irish by the author.* CIP

Leap out, chill water, over reeds and brakes. The River God. Sacheverell Sitwell. MoBrPo

Leap, plashless as they swim. *(LL)* Bird came down the walk, A. Emily Dickinson. AmPP; BLPL; CMoP; FaPON; FF; FM; GoJo; HeIP; InvP; LiTA; LiTM; MeMAP; Mes; MoAmPo; NAAL-1; NoAM; NOBA; NoP; NTCP; OBAL; OBCA; OxBA; PDV; PoLF; PoRA; SAmP; TFi

Leg in the Subway, The. Oscar Williams. LiTM

Leg over leg. Mother Goose. OxNR; ReMoGo

Legacies. Nikki Giovanni. CrSp

Legacies. Léon Laleau, *tr. fr. French by* Ellen Conroy Kennedy. *Fr.* Black Music. NegPo

Legacy. Amiri Baraka. MoP; NoAM; NOBA; PoBA

Legacy, The. Bible, *O.T. Fr.* Proverbs. TrJP

Legacy [or Legacie], The. John Donne. SeCP; TrGrPo

Legacy. Gena Ford. IHMS

Legacy, The. Heinrich von Morungen, *tr. fr. German by* F. C. Nicholson. GePo

Legacy. Maurice Kenny. HATNAP

Legacy: My South. Dudley Randall. PoBA; PoNe

Legacy of a Brother. Renaldo Fernandez. NBV

Legal Fiction. William Empson. CMoP; FaBoMo; ImPo; LiTB; LiTM; MoP; NoAM; NoP

Legal Mouse, A. L. A. J. Moorer. CBWP-3

Legate, I had the news last night — my Cohort ordered home. Kipling. *Fr.* Roman Centurion's Song, The. FaBoEH

Legem Tuam Dilexi. Coventry Patmore. *Fr.* Unknown Eros, The. PoEL-5

Legend. Charles Causley. TOF

Legend. Hart Crane. InPS; OxBA

Legend, The. Carol Ann Duffy. OBAP

Legend, The. Garrett Kaoru Hongo. NAmP90; OpBo; TRP

Legend. Jules Laforgue, *tr. fr. French by* Louis Simpson. Prf

Legend. Judith Wright. NOBAu; NTP; PAW; RB

Legend, A. *At. to* Peter Ilich Tchaikovsky, *tr. fr. Russian by* Nathan Haskell Dole. OHIP

Legend of Alhambra, A. Richard Chenevix Trench. OBTV

Legend of Britomartis, or of Chastitie, The. Spenser. *Fr.* Faerie Queene, The. NAEL-1, *much abr.*

Legend of Captain Jones, The, *sels.* David Lloyd.
  "'Twas well the wars wars done before." AngWe
  (Roses and tulips Flora gathers here.) AngWe

Legend of Felix is ended, the toiling of Felix is done, The. Henry van Dyke. *Fr.* Toiling of Felix, The. BLPA

Legend of Ghost Lagoon, The, *sels.* Joseph Schull.

Legend of Good Women: Prologue, The, *sels.* Chaucer.
  "Alas, that I ne had English, rhyme or prose." EPCY
  "And as for me, though that I konne [or can] but [or my wit be] lyte." CH; HeIP
  "Hide [or Hyd], Absalon, thy gilte tresses clere." AWP; ChTr; EBEV; EnVB; GBL; HAP; ImPo; NOBE; OAEL-1; OBEV; SCGP
  (Lady without Paragon, A.) MeEL

Legend of Hell, The. C. D. Wright. LCAP

Legend of His Lyre. Aaron Schmuller. GoYe

Legend of Montrose, The, *sels.* Sir Walter Scott.
  Annot Lyle's Song. EnRP

Legend of Paul Bunyan, A, *sels.* Arthur S. Bourinot.
  Paul Bunyan. FaPON

Legend of Robert, Duke of Normandy, The, *sels.* Michael Drayton.

Legend of St. Gingulph's Relict, The. Thomas Lovell Beddoes. *See* Whoever has heard of St. Gingo.

Legend of Success, The Salesman's Story, The. Louis Simpson. NYBP

Legend of the Admen, The. Everett W. Lord. BLPA

Legend of the Dead Soldier, The. Bertolt Brecht, *tr. fr. German by* Louis MacNeice. PAW

Legend of the Easter Eggs, The. Fitz-James O'Brien. BeLS

Legend of the Hive, A. Robert Stephen Hawker. EBVV

Legend of the Knight of the Red Crosse, or of Holinesse, The. Spenser. *Fr.* Faerie Queene, The. EPCY; FHYEP; NAEL-1; OAEL-1, *abr.*

Legend of the Northland, A. Phoebe Cary. OBCA; OBSP

Legend of the Organ-Builder, The. Julia Caroline Ripley Dorr. BeLS; BLPA; FaBoBe

Legend of the Panda, The. Anthony Stuart. OBAP

Legend of the Sea. Kung Liu, *tr. fr. Chinese.* LHF, *tr. by* Hualing Nieh

Legend of Versailles, A. Melvin B. Tolson. BPo

Legend of Walbach Tower, The. George Houghton. PAH

Legend of Waukulla, The. Hezekiah Butterworth. PAH

Legend: The god in the sun made two men. J. Michael Yates. *Fr.* Great Bear Lake Meditations, The. HoPM

Legend with Sea Breeze. Tess Gallagher. NGP

Legendary muscle that wants and grieves, The. The Hearts. Robert Pinsky. VCAP

Legends of Evil, I, The. Kipling. MoShBr

Legion Club, The, *sels.* Swift.
  "As I strole the city, oft I." BIrV
  On Irish Memebers of Parliament. IHNG

Legless Boy Climbing In and Out of Chair. Michael Pettit. NAmP90

Legree's big house was white and green. Simon Legree — a Negro Sermon. Vachel Lindsay. *Fr.* Booker Washington Trilogy, The. LiTA; MeMAP; TAP
  (Negro Sermon, A — Simon Legree.) MoAmPo

Legs, The. Robert Graves. ImPo; LiTB; LiTM; MeMBP; PeLV; RB

Legs are locked; the sky is dead, The. (*LL*) The Distant Runners. Mark Van Doren. GOA; LiTA; LiTM; MoAmPo

Legs!/ How we have suffered each other. Poem in Which My Legs Are Accepted. Kathleen Fraser. AmPA; NMM

Legs of the elk punctured the snow's crust, The. To Christ Our Lord. Galway Kinnell. HeIP; PrIm; RFM; SM; TwCP

Legsby, Lincolnshire. *Unknown.* GBP

Lehayyim, my brethren, Lehayyim, I say. Simhat Torah. Judah Leib Gordon, *tr. fr. Hebrew by* Alice Lucas *and* Helena Frank. TrJP

Lehmann does well with Largactil. Laprairie Hunger Strike. Ronald G. Everson. MoCV

Leicester Chambermaid. *Unknown.* CoMu

Leicester Chambermaid, The. *Unknown.* CoMu; OBET

Leichhardt in Theatre, *sels.* Francis Webb.

Leisure. W. H. Davies. AngWe; ArNa; AWP; BoNaP; BoTP; CH; CoGr; EBEvV; FaBoBe; FaPON; GGP; LiTB; LiTM; MoBrPo; MoShBr; NOBE; NTP; OBMV; OBMV; OtMeF; PoRA; TFi; TrGrPo

Leisurely Stroll, A, *sels.* Hsü Pen, *tr. fr. Chinese by* Jonathan Chaves.

Leisurely talk in low voices. Tune: *"Wu-t'ung* Leaves" — Written in Jest at a Banquet. Lu Chih, *tr. fr. Chinese by* Hellmut Wilhelm. SuSp

Leith police dismisseth us, The. *Unknown.* OxNR

Leith Races, *sels.* Robert Fergusson.
  My Winsome Dear. VGW

Leith Races. Allan Ramsay. ScCV

Lela's Charms. L. A. J. Moorer. CBWP-3

L'Elisir d'Amore. Dallas E. Wiebe. MAT

L'Embarquement pour Cythère. John Manifold. CBAP

Lementable New Ballad upon the Earle of Essex Death, A. *Unknown.* CoMu

Lemme be wid Casey Jones. Odyssey of Big Boy. Sterling A. Brown. CDC

Lemmings, The. John Masefield. CMoP; OBAP

Lemon and a pickle knocked at the door, A. *Unknown.* RoPo

Lemon Pie. Edgar A. Guest. OBAL

Lemonade. *Unknown.* GBP

Lemonade Stand. Myra Cohn Livingston. TLR

Lemons. Ted Walker. NYBP

Lemoshl: for example. A Few Words in the Mother Tongue. Irena Klepfisz. LoHo

Lemuel's Blessing. W. S. Merwin. NYBP

Lend me cruel light. To an Angry God. X. J. Kennedy. CRP

Lend me your arm. Little Song of the Maimed. Benjamin Péret, *tr. fr. French by* David Gascoyne. OBWP; PeFWW

Lend my thy mare to ride a mile. Money and the Mare. *Unknown.* ReMoGo

L'Enfant Glacé. Harry Graham. CBNP; FaBoCo; NBLV; PeLV

Length is now quite another thing; that is. From End to End. J. H. Prynne. VaA

Length o' days ageän do shrink, The. The Fall. William Barnes. PoEL-4

Length of an Arm, The. Melanie Silgardo. VBLP

Length of an arm is history, The. (*LL*) The Length of an Arm. Melanie Silgardo. VBLP

Length of Days. Horatius Bonar. PWR

Length of Life, The. Amos R. Wells. PWR

Length of Moon. Arna Bontemps. CDC; LiTM; PoNe

Lengthened shadow of my hand, The. Persephone Pauses. Carolyn Kizer. SRLS

Lengthening Days. *Unknown.* ReMoGo

Lengths of Time. Phyllis McGinley. SiSoPo

Lenin, *sels.* Dorothy Wellesley.
  "So I came down the steps to Lenin." OBMV

Leningrad. Osip Mandelstam, *tr. fr. Russian by* W. S. Merwin *and* Clarence Brown. FaBoPV

Leningrad Cemetery, Winter of 1941. Sharon Olds. NIP

Leningrad (1941–1943). Edward Hirsch. ArOW

Leningrad Romance. Carol Rumens. PWE

Lennox Island. David McFadden. NOBC

Lenore. Poe. AmPP; AnAmPo; LiTA

Lenox Avenue. Sidney Alexander. PoNe

Lenox Avenue is a big street. Keep on Pushing. David Henderson. PoBA

Lenox Avenue Mural. Langston Hughes. HoPM

Lest men suspect your tale untrue. The Painter Who Pleased Nobody and Everybody. John Gay. BeLS

Lest the fair cheeks begin their shrivelling. Homework. Mona Van Duyn. VCAP

Lest the ripple deceive us. Winter Pond. Ben Belitt. NYBP

Lest Thou Forget. William Leroy Stidger. PoToHe

Lest thou forget in the years between. Lest Thou Forget. William Leroy Stidger. PoToHe

Lest you should think that verse shall die. Pope, *tr. fr. Latin. Fr.* Odes. EPCY

(Immortality of Verse the.) AWP

Lestenyt, lordynges, both elde and yinge. Of a Rose, a Lovely Rose. *Unknown.* OBEV

Lester Leaps In. Al Young. SM

Lester Young. Ted Joans. Jaz

Let a broad man, stout and brawny. Alexander MacDonald, *tr. fr. Gaelic by* Rev. A. Macdonald. *Fr.* Birlinn of Clanranald, The. ScCV

Let a lewd judge come reeking from a wench. A True Englishman. *Unknown.* FaBoEH

Let Age no longer toil with feeble strife. The Poor. John Langhorne. *Fr.* Country Justice, The. NOEC

Let all chaste matrons, when they chance to see. Upon a Young Mother of Many Children. Robert Herrick. CaPo

Let All Created Things. Artis Seagrave. AH

Let all the family gather. Light Another Candle. Miriam Chaikin. NTCP

Let all the little poets be gathered together in classes. To School! Stevie Smith. FaBoEE

Let all the world in ev'ry corner sing. My God and King. George Herbert. PeECV

Let All Things Pass Away. W. B. Yeats. ChTr

Let all who will. Militant. Langston Hughes. PoBA

Let Allen's eyes be a jukebox of light plugged into the navel of Whitman's verb. Leaps over the Aisle of Syllogism. D. C. Berry. BXAP

Let America Be America Again. Langston Hughes. AiP; PoNe

Let Ancients boast no more. Barbara Palmer, Duchess of Cleveland. The Earl of Rochester. FaBoEH

Let angels speak, and heaven thy praises tell. (*LL*) Epitaph on Sir Philip Sidney. *At. to* Sir Walter Ralegh. SiPS

Let Aphrodite herself. Manifesto. Agathias, *tr. fr. Greek by* Dudley Fitts. GrAn

Let Archimedes loud his glasses' glory roar. Her Eyes. Daniel Casper von Lohenstein, *tr. fr. German by* George C. Schoolfield. GePo

Let azure eyes with coral lips unite. The Value of Dentistry. Solyman Brown. *Fr.* Dentologia; a Poem on the Diseases of the Teeth and Their Proper Remedies. FaBoUs

Let baths and wine-butts be November's due. November. Folgore da San Geminiano, *tr. fr. Italian by* Dante Gabriel Rossetti. *Fr.* Sonnets of the Months. AWP

Let Be. *Unknown.* WBLP

Let Bourbons fight for status quo. Status Quo. Binga Dismond. PoNe

Let but the son of earth. The Ages of Man. *At. to* Abraham ibn Ezra Abraham Ibn Ezra, *tr. fr. Hebrew by* Nina Davis Salaman. TrJP

Let but thy voice engender with the string. Upon Her Voice. Robert Herrick. CaPo

Let certain holdings of stocks and bonds. Codicil. Mabel MacDonald Carver. GoYe

Let Christian Hearts Rejoice Today. *Unknown, tr. fr. French by* Francis X. Curley. AH

Let Christmas celebrate greenly. For the fir is king. Jubilate Herbis. Norma Farber. PChr

Let clownish Cymon, in fond rustic strains. St. Anthony and His Pig; a Cantata. Frederick Forrest. NOEC

Let coffined eyes come to life in the electrified air. (*LL*) Frankenstein in the Markets. Dermot Bolger. IB

Let Cynics bark, and the stern Stagirite. The Paradox. *Unknown.* APAS

Let dainty wits cry on the sisters nine. Sir Philip Sidney. *Fr.* Astrophel and Stella. AAS; ESo, *sl. abr.*; GGP; HeIL; NoSic; OAEL-1; Poetr; SCGP; SiPS; SiPSBD; Son

Let day, let night, come no more. Auvaiyar, *tr. fr. Tamil by* A. K. Ramanujan. PLW

Let de peoples know (unnh). Blues for Bessie. Myron O'Higgins. PoNe

Let Dew, house of Dew rejoice with Xanthenes a precious stone of an amber colou r. Mineral Rejoicings. Christopher Smart. *Fr.* Jubilate Agno. CBCK; FaBoVe

Let dirty streets be paved with flow'ry green. *Unknown. Fr.* Comparison, The. NOEC

Let due civilities be strictly paid. John Gay. *Fr.* Trivia; or, The Art of Walking the Streets of London. OAEL-1

Let each fair maid, who fears to be disgraced. Soame Jenyns. *Fr.* Art of Dancing, The. ECEV; FaBoUs

Let each man first seek out his proper totem. A Joyful Noise. Donald Finkel. CoAP

Let Einstein be, restored the status quo. (*LL*) It did not last; the Devil howling Ho. J. C. Squire. FaBoCo; FaBoEE; FaBoEH

Let Elizur rejoice with the Partridge. Christopher Smart. *Fr.* Jubilate Agno. FaBoVe; OAEL-1; PoEL-3

Let 'em censure: what care I? In Imitation of Anacreon. Matthew Prior. FaBoEE

Let 'em take heed, they do not speed as they did they know when-a! (*LL*) Sir Francis Drake; or, Eighty-eight. *Unknown.* GBP

Let Ephah rejoice with Buprestis, the Lord endue us with temperance and humanity. Christopher Smart. *Fr.* Jubilate Agno. FaBoVe; NOEC

Let Erin Remember the Days of Old. Thomas Moore. EnRP

Let Evening Come. Jane Kenyon. ArNa; BAP-91

Let folly praise that fancy loves, I praise and love that Child. A Child My Choice. Robert Southwell. PeECV

Let fools great Cupid's yoke disdain. Song: The Willing Prisoner to His Mistress. Thomas Carew. CaPo

Let foreign nations of their language boast. George Herbert. *See* Let forrain nations of their language boast.

Let foreign nations of their language boast. The Son. George Herbert. *Fr.* Temple, The. GeHe; Son

Let forrain nations of their language boast. The Sonne. George Herbert. PeECV; SeCP

(Let foreign nations of their language boast.) AngWe

Let go of the present and death. Once Again. Liz Sohappy Bahe. CDW

Let Go the Whore of Babylon. Miles Coverdale. ChIV-2

Let Grace conduct thee to the paths of peace. Francis Quarles. *Fr.* Emblems. ESCV

Let hammer on anvil ring. The Armorer's Song. Harry Bache Smith. OHIP

Let Her Give Her Hand. *Unknown.* ELP

Let her go with her dreams yet unlived? (*LL*) Babouchka. Sophie Slingeland. LoHo

Let her lie naked here, my hand resting. News of the World III. George Barker. FaBoTw; LiTB; LiTM

Let her who walks in Paphos. Lais. Hilda Doolittle ("H. D."). MoAmPo

Let Heroes Account to Love. Alan Dugan. NoAM

Let him answer as he will. The Companion. E. A. Robinson. NoAM

Let Him Return. Leona Hill. PoToHe

Let him sit down and pick the meaning out. (*LL*) A Copy of Non Sequitors. *Unknown.* FaBoNo

Let him that will, ascend the tottering seat. Seneca. *See* Stand [*or* Stond] who so list upon the slipper top [*or* toppe].

Let him who may. To Be Recited to Flossie on Her Birthday. William Carlos Williams. VGW

Let Him with Kisses of His Mouth. *Unknown.* AH; ChIV-1

Let Horace blush, and Virgil too. (*LL*) Epitaph for One Who Would Not Be Buried in Westminster Abbey. Pope. FaBoEE; OBD

Let hound and horn in wintry woods and dells. Alfred Austin. *Fr.* Why England is Conservative. FaBoEH

Let it be alleys. Let it be a hall. A Lovely Love. Gwendolyn Brooks. BPo

Let it be anywhere. For Her. Mark Strand. GOYP

Let it be forgotten, as a flower is forgotten. Sara Teasdale. AnAmPo; MoAmPo; PoA; TrGrPo

Let it be Sabbath, Sabbath! Eternal Sabbath. Isaac Leibush Peretz, *tr. fr. Yiddish by* Joseph Leftwich. TrJP

Let it disturb no more at first. Fountain. Elizabeth Jennings. WPE

Let it end here where the blueprint. Making Chicago. Dennis Schmitz. LCAP

Let It Go. William Empson. FaBoMo; OPOP; OxBSP; OxBTC

Let it no longer be a forlorn hope. On the Baptized Ethiopian (*or* Aethiopian). Richard Crashaw. ChIV-2; FaBoEE; NoP; SeCV-1

Let it not come near me, let it not. Fragment for the Dark. Elizabeth Jennings. FaBoWP

Let it not come unto you, all ye that pass by. Desolation in Zion. Bible, *O.T. Fr.* Lamentations. TrJP

Let it not your wonder move. His Excuse for Loving. Ben Jonson. *Fr.* Celebration of Charis in Ten Lyric[k] Peeces [*or* pieces], A. BeJo; EnRePo; JCP; NOSC; OxAEP-1; PoEL-2; SeCP; SeCV-1

Let kings command, and do the best they may. The Power in the People. Robert Herrick. CaPo

Let love come under your roof. Carol for Advent. John Heath-Stubbs. OxBC

Let man's Soul [*or* Soule] be a Sphere [*or* Spheare], and then, in this. Good Friday [*or* Goodfriday], 1613. Riding Westward. John Donne. ChIV-2; EnRePo; ESCV; InPS; JCP; MeLP; NAEL-1; NOCV; NoP; NOSC; OAEL-1; PeECV; PoE; PoEL-2; PPP; SeCP; SeCV-1; TEP; TFi

Let me alone, alas, and drive him back to London. *(LL)* Thyrsis, Sleep'st Thou? *Unknown.* InvP; NoSic; OxBSP

Let me be. Hilda Doolittle ("H. D."). *Fr.* Sigil. AnAn

Let Me Be a Giver. Mary Carolyn Davies. PoToHe

Let me be a little kinder, let me be a little blinder. My Daily Creed. *Unknown.* PWR

Let me be at the place of the castle. Psalm Concerning the Castle. Denise Levertov. TwCP; WPE

Let me be buried as flesh, not burned, I say. Earth Buried. Kenneth Mackenzie. CBAP

Let me be buried in the rain. Helene Johnson. PoNe; ShDr

Let Me Be Held When the Longing Comes. Stephany Fuller. BPo

Let me be my own fool. A Counterpoint. Robert Creeley. NeAP

Let me be prodigal as sun in praising you. Geography of Music. Kenneth Patchen. UnAS

Let me be thankful, God, that I am not. Viscount Demos. William Kean Seymour. IHNG

Let me be that huge red peony. Peony. Jackie Kay. DT

Let me be what I am, as Virgil cold. Ben Jonson. PoEL-2; SeCP

Let Me Begin Again. Philip Levine. CAPP

Let me but live from year to year. The Zest of Life. Henry van Dyke. *Fr.* Three Best Things, The. WBLP

Let me call a ghost. Song of Three Smiles. W. S. Merwin. CoAP; NOBA; VGW

Let me celebrate you. I. A Dialogue of Watching. Kenneth Rexroth. UnAS

Let Me Confess That We Two Must Be Twain. Shakespeare. *Fr.* Sonnets. HeIP, *sect.* XXXVI; PeHV, *sect.* XXXVI

Let Me Die a Youngman's Death. Roger McGough. PeLV

Let me die and not tremble at death. Imploring to Be Resigned at Death. George Moses Horton. AAP

Let me die in the Spring, said a sweet young girl. The Time to Die. Matilda C. Edwards. PWR

Let me do my work each day. Max Ehrmann. BLPA; BLPL; FaBoBe (Prayer, A.) PoToHe

Let Me Enjoy [(Minor Key)]. Thomas Hardy. AWP; FaBV; NoAM

Let me feed full, till that I fart', says Jill. *(LL)* Upon Jack and Jill: Epigram. Robert Herrick. CaPo; NAEL-1

Let Me Flower as I Will. Lew Sarett. TrPWD

Let Me Gallop, Let Me Go. Shih Ching, *tr. fr. Chinese by* C. H. Wang. SuSp

Let Me Go. *Gond Oral Tradition, tr. by* V. Elwin *and* S. Hivale. WTO

Let Me Go Back. Mary E. Albright. BLRP

Let Me Go Down to Dust. Lew Sarett. TrPWD

Let me go forth, and share. Ode in May. Sir William Watson. OBEV; WGRP

Let Me Go Warm. Luis de Góngora y Argote, *tr. fr. Spanish by* Longfellow. AWP

Let Me Go Where Saints Are Going. Lewis Hartsough. AH

Let me go where'er I will. Music. Emerson. FaBV; WGRP

Let Me Grow Lovely. Karle Wilson Baker. BLPA; FaBoBe; TrPWD

Let me hide myself in thee. *(LL)* Rock of Ages. Augustus Montague Toplady. BLRP; FaPoR; NOCV; PIP; SCGP; WGRP

Let me lament the exodus of so many men from their. Recitative. Iwan Goll, *tr. fr. German by* Patrick Bridgwater. *Fr.* Requiem for the Dead of Europe. PeFWW

Let me lay it to you gently, Mr. Gone! Ray Bremser. *Fr.* Poem of Holy Madness. NeAP

Let me learn now where Beauty is. Questing. Anne Spencer. CDC

Let me live harmlessly; and near the brink. The Angler's Song. John Dennys. *Fr.* Secrets of Angling, The. EIL

Let me look at what I was, before I die. Jamestown. Randall Jarrell. GOA

Let me make the songs for the people. Songs for the People. Frances E. W. Harper. AAP; PWR

Let Me Not Die. Edith Lovejoy Pierce. TrPWD

Let me not die for ever, when I'm gone. A Wish. Fanny Kemble. WPE

Let me not die till death is due to come. Let Me Not Die. Edith Lovejoy Pierce. TrPWD

Let me not know how sins and sorrows glide. James Elroy Flecker. TrPWD

Let me not live, if I not love. Robert Herrick. *Fr.* On Himself[e]. CaPo

Let Me Not to the Marriage of True Minds. Shakespeare. *Fr.* Sonnets. ArLo; AWP; ClHu; EBEvV; EIL; EnLoPo; EnRePo; FaBV; FaPoB; GBL; GGP; HAP; HeIL; HeIP; InPS; InvP; LiTB; NAEL-1; NIP; NOBE; NoP; NoSic; OAEL-1; OBEV; OxAEP-1; OxBM; PeHV; PoE; PoEL-2; Poetr; PoRA; PPP; PrIm; SCGP; SCV; Son; SoSe; TEP; TFi; TrGrPo; TRP; UnPo; WeW

Let me now set down a picture of New England that will show it to you and explain it. Praise of New England. Thomas Caldecot Chubb. GoYe

Let me obtain forgiveness of thee, Samson. Milton. *Fr.* Samson Agonistes. EBEV; FHYEP; OAEL-1; PoEL-3

Let me open mama your 3 corner box. Blues for Franks Wooten. Tom Weatherly. NBV

Let Me Play the Fool. Shakespeare. *Fr.* Merchant of Venice, The. TrGrPo

Let me play to you tunes without measure or end. Bagpipe Music. "Hugh MacDiarmid." OAEL-2

Let me pour [*or* powre] forth. A Valediction: Of Weeping. John Donne. EnRePo; ESCV; FHYEP; HAP; HeIP; InPS; MeLP; NAEL-1; NoP; NOSC; OAEL-1; PoE; SCGP; SeCP; WeW

Let me repentant work for thee! *(LL)* A Last Prayer. Helen Hunt Jackson. TrPWD

Let me say (in anger) that since the day we were married. The Crisis. Robert Creeley. FF; PPP

Let me see if Philip can. The Story of Fidgety Philip. Heinrich Hoffmann, *tr. fr. German.* OxBChV

Let me see you. Mirabai, *tr. fr. Hindi by* Willis Barnstone *and* Usha Nilsson. BoWoP

Let me show you everything in the sky. Heartbeat. Jack Skelley. UTF

Let me show you my love. Webern. Thomas W. Shapcott. *Fr.* Piano Pieces. CBAP

Let Me Sing of My Well-beloved. Bible, *O.T. Fr.* Isaiah. TrJP

Let me speak, sir,/ For Heaven now bids me. Cranmer's Prophecy of Queen Elizabeth. John Fletcher *and* William Shakespeare. *Fr.* King Henry VIII. WGRP

Let me strap/ the baby in the seat. If He Let Us Go Now. Shirley Williams. BoWoP

Let me take this other glove off. In Westminster Abbey. Sir John Betjeman. CMoP; FaBoCo; FaBoEH; InPK; NBLV; NIP; NoAM; NOBL; OAEL-2; OBSV; OxAEP-2; PIP; TOF

Let me tell to you the story. Edith Agnew. PChr

Let me tell you a little story. Miss Gee. W. H. Auden. EBNV; OxBTC; UV, abr.

Let me tell you a little story/ About Miss Edith Gee. A Moral Tale. Roger Woddis. IHNG; UV

Let me tell you the story of how I began. Lift-Boy. Robert Graves. NTP; OxAEP-2

Let me today do something that will take. A Morning Prayer. Ella Wheeler Wilcox. PoToHe

Let me work. *(LL)* Grass. Carl Sandburg. AWP; BLPL; FaBV; MoAB; MoAmPo; MoP; NAAL-2; NoAM; NOBA; NoP; OBWP; OxBA; PeFWW; Poetr; PoLF; TFi; TrGrPo

Let me work and be glad. Theodosia Garrison. TrPWD

Let men take note of her, touching her shyness. The Gift of Song. Anthony Hecht. NYBP

Let Mine Eyes See Thee. St. Theresa of Avila, *tr. fr. Spanish by* Arthur Symons. AWP

Let mine not be the saddest fate of all. Uselessness. Ella Wheeler Wilcox. TrPWD

Let mother Earth now deck herself in flowers. Sir Philip Sidney. *Fr.* Arcadia. OxAEP-1; SiPS
(Epithalamium: "Let mother Earth.") SiPSBD

Let my people go. *(LL)* Go Down, Moses. *Unknown.* AnAmPo; BPo; PeECV; SWP

Let my sweet song be pleasing unto Thee. Judah Halevi, *tr. fr. Hebrew by* Nina Davis Salaman. TrJP

Let my words. Joseph Bruchac. ETG

Let Ninety-Nine Schools of Thought Contend. Mu Tan, *tr. fr. Chinese.* LHF, *tr. by* Hualing Nieh

Let no blame upon us fall. Poppies in Our Wheat. Edith M. Thomas. AmWP

Let no blasphemer till the sacred earth. Benediction. Mark Turbyfill. PoA

Let No Charitable Hope. Elinor Wylie. LiTA; LiTM; MoAB; MoAmPo; NAAL-2; NALW; OxBA; OxBSP; TrGrPo; VGW

Let no girl wait on you on that day when you bind your wild. The Alchemy of Day. Anne Hébert, *tr. fr. French by* A. Poulin, Jr. BoWoP

Let no man cum into this hall. Now Is the Time of Christmas. *Unknown.* MeEL

Let no man deem that he is free! *(LL)* The Storm Cone. Kipling. NoAM; OxBTC

Let Noah build an ark out of the old lady's shoe and. Third Psalm. Anne Sexton. *Fr.* O Ye Tongues. NALW

Let none but guests or clubbers hither come. Ben. Johnsons Sociable Rules for the Apollo. Ben Jonson, *tr. fr. Latin by* Alexander Brome. SeCV-1

Let not Death boast his conquering power. On Eleanor Freeman, Who Died 1650, Aged 21. *Unknown.* OBEV

Let not his humble vesture make thee blind. The Poor Scholar. Abraham ibn Chasdai, *tr. fr. Hebrew by* J. Chotzner. TrJP

Let not old age disgrace my high desire. Sir Philip Sidney. *Fr.* Arcadia. SiPSBD
(Old Age.) SiPS

Let not our naive labours have been in vain!" (*LL*) A Disused Shed in Co. Wexford. Derek Mahon. AnAn; BiHa; CIP; FaBoPV; NOIV; OxBC; PBCIP; PNI; SCBI

Let not the sluggish sleep. *Unknown.* OxBSP

Let not the title of my verse offend. The Natural Child. Helen Leigh. ECWP; WoRP

Let not thy beauty make thee proud. Aurelian Townshend. JCP; NOSC

Let not young souls be smothered out before. The Leaden-eyed. Vachel Lindsay. CMoP; CoGr; FaBoEE; ImPo; LiTA; OxBSP; PoE; RB

Let nothing disturb thee. Lines Written in Her Breviary. St. Theresa of Avila, *tr. fr. Spanish by* Longfellow. AWP
(Bookmark.) CTC; WPOW
(St. Theresa's Book-Mark.) PoEL-5

Let now thy power be great O Lord. Numeri XIII. John Hall. ChIV-1

Let Observation, Shuddering the While. F. Mullen. UV

Let Observation with extensive view. Samuel Johnson. *Fr.* Vanity of Human Wishes, The: The Tenth Satire of Juvenal Imitated. EBEV; ECEV; NOEC; NoP; OAEL-1; OxAEP-1; PoEL-3; PrIm; TEP; TFi; UV

Let oken club now strike, and poast of might. Seneca, *tr. fr. Latin by* Jasper Heywood. *Fr.* Hercules Furens. OBVE

Let other mount aloft, let other sore. Seneca, *tr. fr. Latin by* John Studley. *Fr.* Hercules Oetaeus. OBVE

Let other people come as streams. Charles Reznikoff. VGW

Let other poets raise a fracas. Scotch Drink. Burns. ChIV-1

Let others better mold the running Mass. The Sixth Book of the Aeneis. Virgil, *tr. by* Dryden. *Fr.* Aeneid [*or* Eneados], The. NAWM-1; SeCV-2

Let others chaunt a country praise. London Town. Lionel Johnson. FaBoPP; OHCV

Let others cheer the winning man. A Smile. *Unknown.* BLPA; WBLP

Let others creep by timid steps, and slow. A Certain Type of Scientist Speaks. Pope. *Fr.* Dunciad, The. ECEV

Let others draw from smiling skies their theme. The Vision of the Night. Philip Freneau. EAP

Let others from the town retire. Nonpareil. Matthew Prior. EnLoPo

Let others hail the holidays with laughter. Ausiàs March, *tr. fr. Catalan by* John Frederick Nims. STV

Let others of the world's decaying tell. William Alexander, Earl of Stirling. *Fr.* Aurora. ElL

Let others pile their yellow ingots high. A Pastoral Elegy. Tibullus, *tr. fr. Latin by* Sir Charles Abraham Elton. AWP

Let others pray for the passenger pigeon. Elegy for the Giant Tortoises. Margaret Atwood. BoWoP; EaPr; FoLa

Let others probe the mystery if they can. The Right Thing. Theodore Roethke. PeECV

Let others sing of knights and paladins [*or* palladines]. Samuel Daniel. *Fr.* To Delia. AAS; ESo; NOBE; NoP; NoSic; OBEV; SCGP
(Sonnet: "Let others sing of knights and paladin[e]s.") ElL

Let passion's swelling tide my senses drown! Ibnu 'L-Farid, *tr. fr. Persian by* R. A. Nicholson. TOF

Let Peter rejoice with the Moonfish who keeps up the life in the waters by night. Christopher Smart. *Fr.* Jubilate Agno. ChIV-2; FaBoVe

Let poets praise the softer winds of spring. J. B. Morton. FaBoEE

Let rain say nothing stays. (*LL*) Rain. Diana Der Hovanessian. VBLP

Let rhyme be my conclusion. (*LL*) The Chances of Rhyme. Charles Tomlinson. FaBoMo; PoA

Let rigid Cato read these lines of mine. (*LL*) When He Would Have His Verses Read. Robert Herrick. BeJo; CaPo; NOBE; NOSC; SCGP; SeCV-1

Let sailors watch the waning Pleiades. Cleonicos. Edward Cracroft Lefroy, *after the Greek of* Theocritus. *Fr.* Echoes from Theocritus. AWP

Let school-masters puzzle their brain. Goldsmith. *Fr.* She Stoops to Conquer. BIrV; NOIV
(Three Jolly Pigeons, The.) PoRA
(Three Pigeons, The.) ELP

Let scoffers mock, let unbelief deny. Albery Allson Whitman. *Fr.* Octoroon, The. AAP

Let Shobi rejoice with the Kastrel — blessed be the name Jesus. Christopher Smart. *Fr.* Jubilate Agno. FaBoVe; NOEC

Let sleep take her, let sleep take her, let sleep. Fourth Song the Night Nurse Sang. Robert Duncan. VGW

Let Sol his annual journeys run. Hint from Voiture. William Shenstone. EnLoPo

Let some in beer place their delight. The Dish of Tea. Philip Freneau. EAP

Let some sad trumpeter stand. Back on Times Square, Dreaming of Times Square. Allen Ginsberg. PoE

Let sordid mortals toil all day. Frederick Forrest. *Fr.* St. Anthony and His Pig: A Cantata. OBF

Let Sporus tremble — "What? That thing of silk." Pope. *Fr.* Epistle to Dr. Arbuthnot. FHYEP; InPS; NoP; OAEL-1; OxAEP-1; PoE; PoEL-3; SCV; TFi
(Sporus.) AWP; ChTr; NOBE; OBSV

Let that Diana shine, which all these gives. (*LL*) Praised be Diana's fair and harmless light. Sir Walter Ralegh. NoSic; SiPSBD

Let the arched knife. Pruning. John Philips. *Fr.* Cyder. FaBoUs

Let the ascetics sing of the garden of Paradise. Asadullah Khan Ghalib, *tr. fr. Urdu by* Jane Hirshfield. EnIH

Let the bells ring, and let the boys sing. John Fletcher. *Fr.* Spanish Curate, The. SCGP

Let the Bird of Earth, Fly! Meridel LeSueur. SRLS

Let the bird of loudest [*or* lowdest] lay. The Phoenix and the Turtle. Shakespeare. EnRePo; ImPo; LiTB; NOBE; NoP; NoSic; OAEL-1; OBEV; OxAEP-1; PeECV; PoEL-2; SCGP; TEP

Let the boy try along this bayonet-blade. Arms and the Boy. Wilfred Owen. CMoP; HAP; ImPo; LiTB; LiTM; MeMBP; MoAB; MoBrPo; OAEL-1; OAEL-2; OxBSP; PoE; Poetr; WeW

Let the crows go by hawking their caw and caw. River Roads. Carl Sandburg. VGW

Let the damned ride their earwigs to Hell, but let me not join them. Rock Pilgrim. Herbert Edward Palmer. OxBTC

Let the Day Perish [Wherein I Was Born]. Bible, *O.T. Fr.* Job. NAs, III; NAWM-1, *abr.*; OBVE, III: 3–26; TrJP, III

Let the Dead Depart in Peace. *Yoruba Oral Tradition, tr. by* Ulli Beier. WTO

Let the Deep Organ Swell. Constantine Pise. AH

Let the eugenist reach for his gun! Stanley J. Sharpless. PeLi

Let the eye remember the loved face. The Soul Remembers. Richard Burdick Eldridge. GoYe

Let the fire of my body. Prayer for a Tenspeed Heart. Barbara Hendryson. CrSp

Let the flowers make a journey. The Fury of Flowers and Worms. Anne Sexton. BoWoP

Let the four-clustered ivy flourish about you, Anacreon. Antipater of Sidon, *tr. fr. Greek by* Barbara Hughes Fowler. *Fr.* Epigrams. HePo

Let the greater praise belong. (*LL*) Lament for the Death of Thomas Davis. Sir Samuel Ferguson. BIrV; NOIV; PeIV

Let the hardened by a sharp soldier's life. III, 2. ("Angustam amice.") Horace, *tr. fr. Latin by* Austin Dobson. *Fr.* Odes.
(Disciplined in the school of hard campaigning.) OBWP, *tr. by* James Michie.

Let the knowing speak. Adjuration. Charles Enoch Wheeler. PoNe

Let the Light Enter. Frances E. W. Harper. AmWP; PoNe

Let the light of late afternoon. Let Evening Come. Jane Kenyon. ArNa; BAP-91

Let the limited years of life do nothing for the limitless years of death! (What do you suppose death will do, then?). (*LL*) Respondez! Walt Whitman. NoAM; PoEL-5

Let the lover be disgraceful, crazy, Jalal al-Din Rumi, *tr. by* John Moyne *and* Coleman Barks. *Fr.* Three Quatrains. RaBo

Let the male Poets their male *Phoebus* chuse. To the Excellent Orinda. "Philo-Philippa." KTR

Let the memorial hill remember, instead of me. Yehuda Amichai, *tr. fr. Hebrew. Fr.* Patriotic Songs. PoSu, *tr. by* Yehuda Amichai *and* Ted Hughes

Let the moon shine ne'er so bright. (*LL*) The Jolly Beggar. *At. to* James V, King of Scotland. CoMu; OxBB

Let the mountains stand forth! Hamilton Warren. GoYe

Let the Nations Be Glad. Bible, *O.T., paraphrased by* Sir Thomas Wyatt. *See* God be merciful unto us, and bless us.

Let the new cycle shame the old! (*LL*) Centennial Hymn. Whittier. PAH

Let the night keep. Night. William Rose Benét. MoAmPo

Let the Nile cloak his head in the clouds, and defy. On the Discoveries of Captain Lewis. Joel Barlow. AmPP; PAH

Let the only consistency. In the Fall. "Hugh MacDiarmid." *Fr.* In Memoriam James Joyce. FaBoMo; InPS

Let the pines rock in torment of the storm. Horatian Ode. Joseph Warren Beach. PoA

Let the poppy unfold itself let it intoxicate. Asger Schnack, *tr. fr. Danish. Fr.* Aqua. Jaz

Let the rain kiss you. April Rain Song. Langston Hughes. FaPON; ImGa; NTCP; OBCA; PDV; SiSoPo

Let the rain plunge radiant. The Way Through. Denise Levertov. NeAP; PoM

Let the reeds pander to the wayward wind. Huang Guobin. EaPr

Let the Rest of the World Go By. J. Keirn Brennan. UnPo

Let the rich man fill his belly. Antonio Machado Ruiz, *tr. fr. Spanish by* Havelock Ellis. *Fr.* Spanish Folk Songs. AWP

Let the shark keep to the shelves and closets of coral. From a Litany. Mark Strand. PPP

Let the snake wait under. A Sort of a Song. William Carlos Williams. HoPM; NAAL-2; NoP; OxBSP; TAP

Let the superstitious wife. Another. Robert Herrick. BeJo

Let the tale's sailor from a Christian voyage. Dylan Thomas. *Fr.* Altarwise by Owl-Light. CMoP; FaBoMo; LiTM; OAEL-2

Let the trees be consulted. John Wright. EaPr

Let the waters, who are goddesses, help me here and now. (*LL*) They who have the ocean as their eldest. EaPr

Let the wick burn low: and suddenly I remember. The Sleepers. Randolph Stow. *Fr.* Thailand Railway. CBAP

Let the wind blow, for many a man shall die. (*LL*) Nostalgia. Karl Shapiro. CMoP; CoAP; TrJP; TwCP

Let the Wind Blow High or Low. *Unknown.* OBET

Let the wood be pulled. Surprised by Me. Walter Darring. NYBP

Let the world's sharpness, like a clasping knife. Elizabeth Barrett Browning. *Fr.* Sonnets from the Portuguese. NOBVV

Let them bestow on every airt[h] a limb. On Himself, upon Hearing What Was His Sentence. James Graham, Marquess of Montrose. NOSC
(His Metrical Prayer.) ChIV-2; OxBS; PrIm
(Verses Composed on the Eve of His Execution.) ChTr; FaBoEE
(Written on the Eve of His Execution.) ScCV

Let them bury your big eyes. Edna St. Vincent Millay. *Fr.* Memorial to D. C. CMoP; MoAB; MoAmPo; PoRA
(O, loveliest throat of all sweet throats.) OxBA

Let Them Choose Paths. Odia Ofeimun. HBAPE

Let them count scalps under the barroom wall. Lying in a Yuma Saloon. Jim Barnes. CDW

Let them keep it. And Was Not Improved. Lerone Bennett, Jr.. PoBA

Let them lie perilous and beautiful. (*LL*) The Equilibrists. John Crowe Ransom. CMoP; HAP; LiTM; MeMAP; MoAB; MoP; NAAL-2; NoAM; NOBA; OxBA; PPP; TAP

Let them rest peacefully in ice. A Feather Plucked from the Tail of the Fiery Hen. Novica Tadic, *tr. fr. Serbo-Croatian by* Charles Simic. HSix

Let them say to my lover. Amor Mysticus. Sister Marcela de Carpio de San Felix, *tr. fr. Spanish by* John Hay. AWP

Let them, when they once get in. On Irish Memebers of Parliament. Swift. *Fr.* Legion Club, The. IHNG

Let there be commerce between us. (*LL*) A Pact. Ezra Pound. AmPP; AnAmPo; LiTA; MeMAP; MoP; NAAL-2; NoAM; NOBA; OxBA; TAP

Let there be laid, when I am dead. Posthumous Coquetry. Théophile Gautier, *tr. fr. French by* Arthur Symons. AWP; OBD; PeVV

Let there be life, said God. And what He wrought. The Power and the Glory. Siegfried Sassoon. OBMV

Let There Be Light! D. H. Lawrence. ChIV-1

Let There Be Light. William M. Vories. AH

"Let there be light!" said God, and there was light! Byron. *Fr.* Don Juan. OBWP

Let there be many windows to your soul. Progress. Ella Wheeler Wilcox. BLPA

Let there be no flowery banks. A Garden of Situations. Jack Anderson. PoA

Let there be peace, welfare and righteousness. Hagen Hasselbalch. EaPr

Let there be within these phantom walls. Dream House. Catherine Parmenter Newell. PoToHe

Let this life of worry. Palladas, *tr. fr. Greek by* Kenneth Rexroth. PGA

Let those toil for gold who please. Solitude: An Ode. James Grainger. ECEV

Let those who are in favour with their stars. Shakespeare. *Fr.* Sonnets. OxAEP-1; PAW; SCGP

Let those who from the frozen Arctos reach. The Advantages of Washing. John Armstrong. *Fr.* Art of Preserving Health, The. FaBoUs

Let those with cost deck their ill-fashioned clay. Thomas Rymer. OxBSP

Let thunder be heard over the six regions of the earth. (*LL*) Cover my earth mother four times with many flowers. *Unknown.* EaPr

Let thy gold be cast in the furnace. Cleansing Fires. Adelaide Anne Procter. WGRP

Let Thy Kingdom. *Unknown.* AH

Let thy tears, Le Vayer, let them flow. To Monsieur de la Mothe le Vayer. Molière, *tr. fr. French by* Austin Dobson. AWP

Let tigers. Wolf Town. Anne Carson. *Fr.* Life of Towns, The. BAP-90

Let Tyrants Shake Their Iron Rod. William Billings. AH

Let uh revolution come. uh. U Name This One. Carolyn M. Rodgers. BlSi; NMM; PoBA

Let us abandon then our gardens and go home. Justice Denied in Massachusetts. Edna St. Vincent Millay. AiP; GOA; MoAmPo

Let Us All Be Unhappy on Sunday. Lord Neaves. FaBoCo

Let Us All Speak Our Minds. William Brough. SWP

Let us ask ourselves some questions; for that man is truly wise. The Higher Catechism. Sam Walter Foss. WGRP

Let us await the great American novel! Critical Observations. Archibald MacLeish. OBAL

Let Us Be Frank. Alfred Cruickshank. PBCV

Let us be friends, said Walt. Communion. David Ignatow. CAPP

Let us be guests in one another's house. Any Wife or Husband. Carol Haynes. BLPA
(Any Husband or Wife.) PoToHe

Let us be still. To Usward. Gwendolyn B. Bennett. BlSi; ShDr

Let us be united. *Unknown, tr. fr. Sanskrit by* Romesh Dutt. *Fr.* Vedic Hymns. EaPr

Let us become the overhanging day. Shelley. *Fr.* Epipsychidion. EnRP; OAEL-2

Let us begin and carry up this corpse. A Grammarian's Funeral. Robert Browning. NAEL-2; NOBVV; PeECV; WGRP

Let us begin and portion out these sweets. A Girtonian Funeral. *Unknown.* FaBoCo

Let Us Believe. Hildegarde Flanner. WPE

Let Us Break Bread Together. *Unknown.* AH

Let us bring out those heavy dice. Birth. Gabriela Melinescu, *tr. fr. Romanian by* Willis Barnstone *and* Matei Calinescu. BoWoP

Let us celebrate the single-cloaked beings. Psalm to the Creatures. Gwilym R. Jones, *tr. fr. Welsh by* Joseph P. Clancy. OBWVE

Let Us Cheer the Weary Traveler. *Unknown.* AH

Let us come in to worship Jehovah. Come In. Isaiah Shembe, *tr. fr. Zulu by* H. Tracey. WTO

Let Us Consider Where the Great Men Are. Delmore Schwartz. *Fr.* Shenandoah. MoAB; MoAmPo

Let us dance and let us sing. The Fairy Ring. *Unknown.* BoTP

Let us deride the smugness of "The Times." On *The Times.* Wyndham Lewis. IHNG

Let us do, or die! (*LL*) Scots, wha hae wi' Wallace bled. Burns. EBeVV; EnRP; FaPoR; NAEL-2; OAEL-1; OxBS; PlP; ScCV; TEP

Let us do something grand. To the Poem. Frank O'Hara. SM

Let Us Drink. Alcaeus, *tr. fr. Greek by* John Hermann Merivale. AWP

Let Us Drink. Thomas Jordan. *See* Let us drink and be merry, dance, joke, and rejoice [*or* rejoyce].

Let us drink and be merry, dance, joke, and rejoice [*or* rejoyce]. The Careless Gallant. Thomas Jordan. CoMu; HAP; OxBoLi
(Coronemus Nos Rosis Antequam Marcescant.) CoGr; OBEV
(Epicure, The, Sung by One in the Habit of a Town Gallant.) NOBE; PeLV
(Let Us Drink.) GGP

Let us forgive Ty Kendricks. Southern Cop. Sterling A. Brown. SoSe

Let Us Gather at the River. Marge Piercy. SRLS

Let us gather hand in hand. A Medieval Poem of the Nativity. *Unknown.* TrCP

Let us gather up the sunbeams. Scatter Seeds of Kindness. May Riley Smith. WBLP

Let us give thanks to God above. Thanksgiving. L. A. J. Moorer. CBWP-3

Let us give up our trips. Direction. Barbara Guest. WPE

Let us go hence, my songs; she will not hear. A Leave-taking. Swinburne. CBLP; CH; CoGr; NOBE; NOBVV; OBNC; OPOP; PoEL-5; PoLF

Let us go hence: the night is now at hand. A Last Word. Ernest Dowson. MoBrPo

Let us go into the temple. Nossis, *tr. fr. Greek by* Kenneth Rexroth. PGA

Let us go then, you and I. The Love Song of J. Alfred Prufrock. T. S. Eliot. AmPP; AWP; ClHu; CMoP; EBEV; EBeVV; FaPoB; FF; HAP; HeIL; HeIP; HoPM; InPK; InPS; LiTB; LiTM; MoAB; MoAmPo; MoP; NAAL-2; NAEL-2; NAWM-2; NoAM; NOBA; NOBE; NoP; OAEL-2; OxAEP-2; OxBTC; PoA; PoE; Poetr; PoRA; PPP; PrIm; SoSe; SOTW; TAP; TFi; TrGrPo; TRP; TwCP; UV, *ll.* 1–36; WeW

Let us go to the temple. Nossis, *tr. fr. Greek by* Sally Purcell. GrAn

Let Us Go, Then, Exploring. Virginia Woolf. BoNaP

Let us have a rest about the sunset. To the Poets. *Unknown.* PeNZ

Let Us Have Peace. Nancy Byrd Turner. PoToHe

Let us have winter loving that the heart. Winter Love. Elizabeth Jennings. BoLoP

Let us honour if we can. W. H. Auden. PeLV

Let us lay, and dance, and sing. The Vision of Delight Presented at Court in Christmas, 1617. Ben Jonson. SeCV-1

Let us leave our island woods grown dim and blue. "Æ." TIRV

Let us leave talking of angelic hosts. Elinor Wylie. *Fr.* One Person. OxBA

Let us live our little day! (*LL*) The Fisherman's Story. H. Cordelia Ray. CBWP-3

Let us move the stone gentleman to the toadstool wood. The Stone Gentleman. James Reeves. OxBSP

Let us never forget the dance. Calling. Alma Villanueva. SRLS

Let us not make apologies. Instructions. Anita Skeen. IHMS

Let us not speak, for the love we bear one another. In a Bath Teashop. Sir John Betjeman. CBLP; EnLoPo

Let us now praise famous men. Bible, Apocrypha. *Fr.* Ecclesiasticus. ChTr; FaBoEH; OBVE
(Our Fathers.) TrJP

Let Us Now Praise Famous Men. C. Day Lewis. CMoP

Let us now praise famous men; and the children. Dostoievsky's Daughters. Michael Hamburger. NAs

Let us pause to consider the English. England Expects. Ogden Nash. PeLV

Let us play, and dance, and sing. The Vision of Delight. Ben Jonson. PoEL-2

Let us praise death that turns pink cheeks to ashes. Praise for Death. Donald Hall. BAP-90

Let us praise our Maker, with true passion extol Him. W. H. Auden. NOCV

Let us put on appropriate galoshes, letting them flap open. Walking in the Snow. David Wagoner. Poetr

Let us record/ The evenings when we were innocents of twenty. Winfield Townley Scott. *Fr.* Biography for Traman. ErPo

Let us rejoice on our cots, for His nocturnal miracles. Lauds. John Berryman. HAP

Let us remember the yellow. In the Month of Green Fire. Sophie Himmell. GoYe

Let us save the babies. The Babies. Mark Strand. NYBP

Let us say good-bye. Bags Packed and We Expected This. Ramona Wilson. VoR

Let us sing of Federation. Federation. W. T. Goodge. NOBAu

Let us sing of it ever and long. Song of Sukkaartik, the Assistant Spirit. Ajukutooq, *tr. fr. Eskimo.* WTO

Let us sit by the hissing steam radiator a winter's day, grey wind. Horses and Men in the Rain. Carl Sandburg. PoLF

Let us sleep now. (*LL*) Strange Meeting. Wilfred Owen. CMoP; EBEvV; FaBoMo; FaPoB; FaPoB; GGP; GTBS-P; HeIP; HoPM; ImPo; LiTB; MeMBP; MoAB; MoBrPo; MoP; NAEL-2; NoAM; NOBE; NoP; OAEL-2; OBF; OBWP; OxAEP-2; PeFWW; PoE; PoWW; RB; SCV; TFi; TrGrPo

Let Us Smile. Wilbur D. Nesbit. WBLP

Let us speak simply of. (*LL*) Asking for Ruthie. Judy Grahn. NMM

Let us stiffen. The Covenant. James Cunningham. JB

Let Us Strive to Do Something. Mrs. Henry Linden. CBWP-4

Let us suppose the mind. Barbara Moraff. IHMS

Let us suppose, valleys and such ago. John Berryman. *Fr.* Dream Songs. NaP; PPP

Let us synge unto the Lorde, for he is become glorious. Bible, *O.T., tr. by* William Tyndale. *Fr.* Exodus. OBVE

Let us take the road. The Highwaymen. John Gay. *Fr.* Beggar's Opera, The. OAEL-1; WiR

Let us take to our hearts a lesson. The Tapestry Weavers. Anson G. Chester. BLPA; BLRP; WBLP

Let us thank Almighty God. Creatrix. Anna Wickham. MoBrPo

Let us to-day. Song for Memorial Day. Clinton Scollard. OHIP

Let us, to pass the time as we cycle. Aristarchus and the Whale. Martin Johnston. FaBoMA

Let us try to save the babies. (*LL*) The Babies. Mark Strand. NYBP

Let us tunnel. Ronald Johnson. *Fr.* Letters to Walt Whitman. WH

Let us two a burden try. (*LL*) Robin Hood. Keats. AWP; EnRP; SCGP

Let us use it while [*or* whilst] we may. Of Beauty. Sir Richard Fanshawe, *after the Italian of* Giovanni Battista Guarini. *Fr.* Il Pastor Fido. BoLoP
(Beauty.) GBL
(Nymph's Song.) OxBSP

Let us walk in the white snow. Velvet Shoes. Elinor Wylie. CH; FaPON; GoJo; HeIL; MoAB; MoAmPo; TrGrPo; WHSW

Let us wash each other's body. Rufinus, *tr. fr. Greek by* Alan Marshfield. GrAn

Let us wax and wane. (*LL*) Easter Monday. Christina Rossetti. NOCV

Let Us with a Gladsome Mind. Milton. WGRP

Let War's Tempests Cease. Longfellow. OHIP

Let who so lyst with might mace to raygne. Seneca. *See* Stand [*or* Stond] who so list upon the slipper top [*or* toppe].

Let Wisdom Wear the Crown: Hymn for Gaia. Elsa Gidlow. SRLS

Let wits contest. The Posie. George Herbert. ChIV-1
(Posy, The.) NOSC

Let Words and Sense be set by thee. (*LL*) To Mr. Henry Lawes, Who Had Then Newly Set a Song of Mine in the Year 1635. Edmund Waller. BeJo; CTC; SeCP; SeCV-1

Let Y stand for you who says. You. Kenneth Rexroth. *Fr.* Bestiary, A. HoPM; OBAL

Let you drag me here, without demurring. To Belinda. Goethe, *tr. fr. German by* John Frederick Nims. STV

Let your eyes look at old people. In Respect of the Elderly. Thomas Love Peacock. VoR

Let your longing for me, my love. Sulpicia, *tr. fr. Latin by* John Dillon. PBWP

Let Zeus Record., sels. Hilda Doolittle ("H. D.").
"Stars wheel in purple, yours is not so rare." MoAmPo; NOBA; TAP

Let Zulu Be Heard. Isaiah Shembe, *tr. fr. Zulu by* G. C. Oosthuizen. WTO

Lethal Thought, The. Mary Boyd Wagner. GoYe

Lethargy. Donald Justice. CRP

Lethargy of evil in her eyes, The. A Dying Viper. "Michael Field." FM

Lethe. Hilda Doolittle ("H. D."). AnAmPo; CMoP; FaBoWP; LiTM; MoAmPo; PoRA; TrGrPo; VGW

Lethe. Georgia Douglas Johnson. CDC

Let's agree to meet in our dreams. You're So Far Away. Iyamide Hazeley. DT

Let's Be Merry. Christina Rossetti. *Fr.* Sing-Song. FaPON; TLR

Let's build bridges here and there. Interracial. Georgia Douglas Johnson. PoNe; TTY

Let's contend no more, Love. A Woman's Last Word. Robert Browning. BLPA; BLPL; FaBoBe; NAEL-2; TrGrPo

Let's count the bodies over again. Counting Small-boned Bodies. Robert Bly. CAPP; NaP

Let's Do It, *sels.* Noël Coward.
"Mr. Irving Berlin." UV

Let's Do It. Cole Porter. OBAL

Let's Do It, Let's Fall in Love. Cole Porter. *See* When the little blue-bird.

Let's Dress Up. Mary Ann Hoberman. TLR

Let's dress up in grown-up clothes. Let's Dress Up. Mary Ann Hoberman. TLR

Let's drink up: with wine, what original. Hedylos, *tr. fr. Greek by* William Moebius. GrAn

Let's enjoy, while the season invites us. "Giovinette, Che Fate All'Amore." Lorenzo da Ponte, *tr. fr. Italian by* Natalie MacFarren. *Fr.* Don Giovanni. TrJP

Let's enter the literary scene. *Unknown.* PeLi

Let's Forget. Charles L. H. Wagner. PoToHe

Let's forget the many troubles. Let's Forget. Charles L. H. Wagner. PoToHe

Let's Fuck, Dear Heart. Pietro Aretino, *tr. fr. Italian by* Alistair Elliot. FaBoBl

Let's get going. Leylâ Hanim, *tr. fr. Turkish by* Tâlat S. Halman. PBWP

Let's Go. Bei Dao, *tr. fr. Chinese by* Donald Finkel *with* Chen Xueliang. SpMi

Let's go back carefully the way we came. (*LL*) The Walk. Sebastian Barry. IB

Let's go home again. (*LL*) Marching Song. Robert Louis Stevenson. BoTP; FaPON

Let's go — much as that dog goes. Overland to the Islands. Denise Levertov. UnPo

Let's go rolling, rolling. Getting Dirty. Dorthi Charles. TLR

Let's Go to Bed. *Unknown.* ChTr

Let's go to sleep. (*LL*) If You Can't Eat You Got To. E. E. Cummings. CMoP; PrIm

Let's go to the wood, says this pig. *Unknown.* OxNR

Let's go up to the hillside today. Play Song. Peter Clarke. PBA

Let's have less nonsense from the friends of Joe. Less Nonsense. A. P. Herbert. OxBTC

Let's Hear It for Goliath. Jon Dressel. AngWe

Let's hope you won't think me too vicious. (*LL*) The Song of the Mischievous Dog. Dylan Thomas. GrPl

Let's keep it all with bankers she said giving a gut welcome. Remember Stortford, Birthplace of Rhodes. Douglas Oliver. VaA

Let's live, my Lesbia, and love. Lesbia. Catullus, *tr. fr. Latin by* Sheridan Baker. PrIm

Let's look. Confirmation. Art Lange. UL

Let's not be slow in knowing. On Calvary's Lonely Hill. Herbert Clark Johnson. PoNe

Let's Not Talk About Love, *sels.* Cole Porter.
Intellectual Discussion. CBCK

Letting the Puma Go. Stephen Dunn. BAP-89

Letting us know for certain you didn't want that kind of Jew. Fairy Straighttalk. Carl Morse. GLP

Letty's Globe. Charles Tennyson Turner. NOBVV; OBEV; OHCV; PeVV

Levant. Lawrence Durrell. OBTV

Levantine, A. William Plomer. OBMV

Levedy Fortune is bothe frend and fo, The. *Unknown*. MiEL

Levedy, ic thonke thee. *Unknown*. FaBoVe
(Thanks and a Plea to Mary.) MeEL; MiEL

Levee, The: Letter to No One. Lorna Dee Cervantes. AfAz

Levee Moan. *Unknown*. AS

Level and the Square, The. Robert Morris. BLPA

Level ocean lies immeasurably blind, The. The Flying Fish. Jack Cope. PeSA

Level slope of colored sea, The. Metaphysical. Robert Fitzgerald. PoA

Level with duty, days ride a city-express across the calendar page. Coin in the Fist. Florence Kerr Brownell. GoYe

Levelled Churchyard, The. Thomas Hardy. NOBL

Leveller, The. "Barry Cornwall." OxAEP-2

Leveller's Rant, The. Alexander Brome. FaBoEH

'Leven-cent cotton, forty-cent meat. Eleven Cent Cotton. Emma Dermer *and* Bob Miller *and* Bob Miller. SWP

Leviathan. Jay Macpherson. MoCV

Leviathan. W. S. Merwin. ChIV-1; MoP; NoAM; NOBA

Leviathan, *sels*. Peter Quennell.
"Music met Leviathan returning, A." MoBrPo

Leviathan, XLI: 1–21. Bible, *O.T.* See Canst thou draw out Leviathan with an hook[e]?

Leviathan; or, A Hymn to Poor Brother Ben. *Unknown*. APAS

Levin, on his way to Kitty's love. Secular Games. Richard Howard. PoA

Levivot. Saul Tchernichowsky, *tr. fr. Hebrew by* Ruth Finer Mintz. MHP

Lewesdon Hill, *sels*. William Crowe.
"Up to thy summit, Lewesdon, to the brow." NOEC

Lewis Carroll. Eleanor Farjeon. OxBChV

Lewis Has a Trumpet. Karla Kuskin. PDV

Lewis Mumford. George Buchanan. PNI

Lewti. Samuel Taylor Coleridge. EnRP

Lexington. Oliver Wendell Holmes. PAH

Lexington. Sidney Lanier. *Fr.* Psalm of the West. PAH

Lexington. Whittier. PAH

L'Homme Moyen Sensuel. Ezra Pound. OBSV
Sels.
"Alas, eheu, one question that sorely vexes."
"'Tis of my country that I would endite."

Li Po put it in a poem, this West-of-the-Waters Abbey. Tu Mu, *tr. fr. Chinese by* A. C. Graham. *Fr.* Recalling Former Travels. PLT

Li Sao, *sels*. Ch'u Yüan, *tr. fr. Chinese*.
"Descendant I am of Emperor Kao-yang, A." SuSp
"Oftentimes, I grew dejected and sobbed." SuSp

Liadain. *Unknown, tr. by* Frank O'Connor. PeIV; WPOW

Líadan and Cuirithir. NOIV

Liadan Laments Cuirithir. *Unknown, tr. fr. Irish by* John Montague. BIrV; PBWP

Liang Terrace, The. Li Ho, *tr. fr. Chinese by* A. C. Graham. PLT

Liar, The. Amiri Baraka. AmPP; NOBA

Liar and bragger. Peregrine. Elinor Wylie. BLPL

Liar, liar, lick spit. *Unknown*. ISE

'Lias! 'Lias! Bless de Lawd! In the Morning. Paul Laurence Dunbar. BPo

Libation./ Hey sisters, we the color of our men. Ceremony. Jewel C. Latimore. BlSi

Libation Bearers, The. Aeschylus, *tr. fr. Greek by* Robert Fagles. NAWM-1

Libationer Hu Became Ill from Eating Sunflowers, *sels*. Yang Shih-ch'i, *tr. fr. Chinese by* Jonathan Chaves.

Libel on the Reverend Dr. Delany, A, *sels*. Swift.
"Hail, happy Pope, whose generous mind." EPCY

Liber doth vaunt how chastely he hath liv'd. In Librum. Sir John Davies. FaBoEE

Libera nos, Domine – Deliver us, O Lord. Emancipation from British Dependence. Philip Freneau. PAH

Liberal arts lie eastward of this shore, The. The Seven Sleepers. Mark Van Doren. FYAP

Liberal, blue-eyed, shivering, trying not. The Blue-eyed Precinct Worker. Henri Coulette. MAT; PRA

Liberal, or Innocent by Definition. James McAuley. NOBAu

Liberals raised this in their finest hour. Norris Dam. Selden Rodman. PoNe

Liberation / Poem. Sonia Sanchez. NBV

Liberation. Ruth Stone. BoWoP

Liberation of Music, The. Grace Cavalieri. Jaz

Liberia?/ No micro-footnote in a bunioned book. On the Founding of Liberia. Melvin B. Tolson. *Fr.* Libretto for the Republic of Liberia. UnPo
(Do.) PoNe

Libertie, that wee'll enjoy to night, The. (*LL*) Inviting a Friend to Supper. Ben Jonson, *after* Martial. AWP; BeJo; EnRePo; JCP; LiTB; NOBE; NoP; NOSC; OAEL-1; OBF; OxBoLi; PeLV; PoEL-2; PPP; SeCP; SeCV-1

Liberties, The. Susan Howe. BCF

Libertine, The. Louis MacNeice. MoP; NoAM

Liberty, *sels*. Paul Éluard, *tr. fr. French by* W. S. Merwin.
"On my school notebooks." TTTS

Liberty, The. Sarah Fyge. KTR

Liberty. Archibald MacLeish. GOA

Liberty. Edward Thomas. MoAB; OAEL-2

Liberty, *sels*. Wordsworth.
"Beetle loves his unpretending track, The." FaBoCo; FiBHP

Liberty and Peace. Phillis Wheatley. AiP
Sels.
"Lo! Freedom comes. Th' prescient Muse foretold." BlSi

Liberty Bell in Philadelphia, The. Crazy Quilt. Jane Wilson Joyce. CrSp

Liberty Enlightening the World. Edmund Clarence Stedman. PAH

Liberty Pole, The. *Unknown*. PAH

Liberty Tree. Thomas Paine. PAH

Libra, September. John Taylor. NOSC

Librarian, The. Charles Olson. CAPP

Library, The. Barbara A. Huff. FaPON

Library. Louis Jenkins. NU; RaBo

Library, The. Aidan Carl Mathews. CIP

Libretto for the Republic of Liberia, *sels*. Melvin B. Tolson.
On the Founding of Liberia. UnPo
(Do.) PoNe

Lice Seekers, The. Rimbaud, *tr. by* Kenneth Koch *and* George Guy. *Fr.* Illuminations. SOTW

Licence to run my life. (*LL*) Drat my hateful birthday. Sulpicia. PBWP

Licentious Person, A. John Donne. PeLV

Licia, *sels*. Giles Fletcher the Elder.
Are Those Two Stars. Son
"As are the sandes (faire Licia) on the shore." ESo
"Chrystal streames, wherein my love did swimme, The." ESo
First Did I Fear. Son
"For if alone thou thinke to waft my love." ESo
"I live (sweete love) whereas the gentle winde." ESo
"I wish sometimes, although a worthlesse thing." AAS
"If (aged Charon), when my life shall end." ESo
In Time the Strong and Stately Turrets Fall. AAS; EBEV; ESo
(Time.) CBCK
"Like [*or* Lyke] Memnons rock, touched [*or* rocke toucht] with the rising sun[ne]." AAS; FF
(Sonnet: "Like Memnon's rock, touched with the rising sun.") EIL
"Sadde all alone, not long I musing satte." ESo
(Sad, All Alone, Not Long I Musing Sat.) Son
"When as her lute is tuned to her voyce." ESo

Lick your lips, X. darling, it may be the last. The Summer Ending. Glenway Wescott. PoA

Licorice Fields at Pontefract, The. Sir John Betjeman. CMoP

Liddell and Scott; on the Completion of Their Lexicon. Thomas Hardy. OxBoLi; PeLV

Liddesdale Crosiers hae ridden a race, The. The Death of Parcy Reed. *Unknown*. ESPB, A *vers*.
(God send the land deliverance.) IBB, *diff. vers*.

Lido, The. Edmund Wilson. ErPo

Lie, The. Kipling. NOBL

Lie, The. Alfred M. Lee. AmPA

Lie, The. Howard Moss. LiTM; MoAB

Lie, The. Sir Walter Ralegh. AAS; ChTr; CTC; EBEV; EnRePo; FaBoPV; HAP; ImPo; InvP; LiTB; NAEL-1; NOBE; NoP; NoSiC; OPOP; PoEL-2; RB; SCGP; SCV; SiPS; SiPSBD; TEP; TFi; TrGrPo; WGRP

Lie back, daughter, let your head. First Lesson. Philip Booth. SM; TwCP

Lie Easy in Your Secret Cradle. John Wain. *Fr.* Wildtrack. NAs

Lie for lie! (*LL*) The Goddess. Denise Levertov. LiTM; NALW; NeAP; NOBA; PoM; SRLS

Lie here, without a record of thy worth. Tribute to the Memory of the Same Dog. Wordsworth. FM

Lie on the mats and sweat in summer. Things to Do around Kyoto. Gary Snyder. NaP

Lie on your back on stone. Canyon de Chelly. Simon J. Ortiz. ETG; NGP

Life Story. *Unknown. See* Once — but no matter when.

Life Story. Tennessee Williams. GLP; PeHV

Life That Counts, The. "A. W. S.". WBLP

Life the hound. The Hound. Robert Francis. SoSe

Life to be understood turns into legend. Against the Dark. James McAuley. FaBoMA

Life to the bigot is a whip. Epitaph for a Bigot. Dorothy Vena Johnson. PoNe

Life today is hectic. What's Going to Happen to the Tots? Noël Coward. NBLV

Life we find is nevermore. Deception. Josephine D. Henderson Heard. CBWP-4

Life which now I lead is as a perfect death, The. Love Is Life and Death. Georg Rudolph Weckherlin, *tr. fr. German by* George C. Schoolfield. GePo

Life will keep hammering the grass blades into the ground. Force. Derek Walcott. OxBC

Life without Passion. Shakespeare. *See* They that have power to hurt[e], and will do[e] none.

Life would be an easy matter. Nixon Waterman. *Fr.* If We Didn't Have to Eat. FiBHP; OBAL

Lifeboat, The. George R. Sims. VPP

Lifeguard, The. James Dickey. NoP; NYBP; SoSe

Lifeguard's whistle organized our swimming, The. The River. Dabney Stuart. NYBP

Lifeless solitude — an angry waste, A. On the Telescopic Moon. John Swanwick Drennan. BIrV

Lifeline. Rachel Blake. NWP

Lifers file into the hall, The. In the Cage. Robert Lowell. FF; NOBA; SM; Son

Life's a Funny Proposition after All. George M. Cohan. PoLF

Life's a Game. *Unknown.* BLPA

Life's a performance. Either join in. Palladas, *tr. fr. Greek by* Tony Harrison. GrAn

Life's all getting and giving. The Wishing-Caps. Kipling. OtMeF

Life's an ocean crossing where winds howl. Palladas, *tr. fr. Greek by* Tony Harrison. GrAn

Life's Boundary. H. Cordelia Ray. AmWP; CBWP-3

Life's Circumnavigators. W. R. Rodgers. GTBS-P

Life's Common Duties. Minot Judson Savage. WBLP

Life's Common Things. Alice E. Allen. WBLP

Life's Evening. Dudley Foulke. WGRP

Life's Golden Sunset. Mrs. Henry Linden. CBWP-4

Life's Journey. Ella Wheeler Wilcox. PWR

Life's Lessons. *Unknown.* BLRP; PoLF

Life's Made up of Little Things. Mary R. Hartman. PoToHe

Life's Mirror. "Madeline Bridges." BLPA; FaBoBe; PoToHe; PWR; WBLP

Life's Morning. Howell Elvet Lewis, *tr. fr. Welsh by* H. Idris Bell. OBWVE

Life's Mystery. Alice Cary. AmWP

Life's Parallels, A. Christina Rossetti. MeMBP; NAEL-2; PoEL-5

Life's pathway to me is dreary. The Opium-Eater. Mary E. Tucker. AmWP; CBWP-1

Life's Progress. The Countess of Winchilsea. ECWP

Life's sadly solemn mystery. Life's Mystery. Alice Cary. AmWP

Life's Scars. Ella Wheeler Wilcox. BLPA

Life's spent guarding. What there is to guard, A. August the First: The Watchman Speaks. Marjorie Oludhe Macgoye. HBAPE

Life's stormy surge had scarcely touched. The Grafted Bud. Mary Weston Fordham. CBWP-2

Life's Testament., *sels.* William Baylebridge.

Life's Trades. Emily Dickinson. *See* It's such a little thing to weep.

Lifetime Devoted to Literature, A. Judith Rodriguez. NOBAu

Lifetime's teaching grammar come to this, A. Palladas, *tr. fr. Greek by* Tony Harrison. GrAn

Lift-Boy. Robert Graves. NTP; OxAEP-2

Lift Every Voice and Sing. James Weldon Johnson. FaBV; PoNe

Lift her up tenderly. Song of the Ballet. J. B. Morton. FiBHP

Lift latch, step in, be welcome, Sir. A Luncheon. Max Beerbohm. FaBoCo; NOBL; OBSV; OxBTC; PeLV

(Luncheon Thomas Hardy Entertains the Prince of Wales, A.) UV

Lift Me Higher. Mary E. Tucker. AmWP; CBWP-1

Lift me, O God, above myself. Per Ardua ad Astra. John Oxenham. TrPWD

Lift not the painted veil which those who live. Shelley. EnRP; OBNC, *sl. diff. vers.*; Son

(Sonnet: "Lift Not the Veil Which Those Who Live.") FHYEP, *diff. vers.*

Lift, O dark and glorious Wonder. A Hymn to God in Time of Stress. Max Eastman. TrPWD

Lift the nozzle. *Unknown.* RoPo

Lift up thy lips, turn round, look back for love. Hermaphroditus. Swinburne. TEP

Lift up, ye poor! your everlasting prayer! The Poor of London. William Forster. CBAP

Lift up your eyes on high. Erige Cor Tuum ad Me in Caelum. Hilda Doolittle ("H. D."). CMoP

Lift up your hartes and be glad. A Cheerful Welcome. *Unknown.* MeEL

Lift Up Your Heads. Bible, *O.T., paraphrased by* Sir Thomas Wyatt. *See* Earth is the Lord's, and the fullness thereof, The.

Lift Up Your Heads, Rejoice! Thomas T. Lynch. TrCP; WGRP

Lift your arms to the stars. Love and Liberation. John Hall Wheelock. MoAmPo

Lift Your Glad Voices in Triumph on High. Henry Ware, Jr.. AH

Lifted by a little breeze. Lucilius, *tr. fr. Greek by* Alistair Elliot. GrAn

Lifted by its tufts. The Shroud. Galway Kinnell. LCAP

"Lifted higher" — than life's cares. (*LL*) Lift Me Higher. Mary E. Tucker. AmWP; CBWP-1

Lifting and Leaning. Ella Wheeler Wilcox. BLPA; WBLP

Lifting, both hands pulling whitely. Grandpa's .45. W. M. Ransom. CDW

Lifting hands of Louisiana black. (*LL*) Second Language. Christine Dumaine. LoHo

Lifting his slowly trickling jaws. Tête-à-Tête. Edwin Honig. NoAM

Lifting Illegal Nets by Flashlight. William Stafford. NNaP

Lifting my fingers. Frozen Hands. Joseph Bruchac. CDW

Lifting of the Cloud, The. Thomas MacDonagh. TIRV

Lifts up her head expectantly. (*LL*) Police Sift New Clues in Search for Beauty. Vickie Karp. UTF

Ligeia, *sels.* Poe.
Conqueror Worm, The. AnAmPo; AWP; BLPL; ImPo; LiTA; MeMAP; NOBA; OBD
(Emperor Worm, The.) DL

Light./ Stage of dawn. Creation Story. Paula Gunn Allen. SRLS

Light. Frank Bidart. *Fr.* Elegy. HCAP

Light. Francis William Bourdillon. *See* Night Has a Thousand Eyes, The.

Light. Richard Kenney. Son

Light. Milton. *See* Hail, holy light, ofspring [*or* offspring] of Heav'n [*or* heaven] first born.

Light. Michael Ondaatje. NIP

Light. Still Life: In the Epidemic. Jean Valentine. PFL

Light a drum, The. (*LL*) Signs. Alejandra Pizarnik. VBLP

Light across the courtyard. Saint's Bridge. Lola Ridge. WPE

Light after darkness, gain after loss. Afterwards. Frances Ridley Havergal. BLRP

Light along the hills in the morning, The. Notice What This Poem Is Not Doing. William Stafford. LCAP

Light alternates, comes and goes, The. Peter Riley. VaA

Light and Rejoicing to Israel. *Unknown, tr. fr. Hebrew by* Israel Abrahams. TrJP

Light and the clear day and so simple a goal. (*LL*) The Face of the Waters. Robert David Fitzgerald. CBAP; FaBoMA

Light Another Candle. Miriam Chaikin. NTCP

Light became her grace and dwelt among, The. Ballatetta. Ezra Pound. VGW

Light Behind the Rain. Michael Longley. CBLP

Light Breaks Where No Sun Shines. Dylan Thomas. CMoP; ErPo; FaBoMo; ImPo; LiTB; LPA; MoAB; MoBrPo; OxAEP-2; OxBTC; PlP

Light Breather, A. Theodore Roethke. NoP

Light breeze rustles the reeds, A. Night Thoughts while Travelling. Tu Fu, *tr. fr. Chinese by* Kenneth Rexroth. NaP

Light chill on the knees, A. Poema Del Dity 2. Ron Padgett. ArNa

Light clouds above. Alois Jeitteles, *tr. by* Philip L. Miller. RiWo

Light collides with the walls, bounces off, The. Accident. Nina Cassian, *tr. fr. Romanian by* Fleur Adcock. VBLP

Light come from my head, A. The Island. James Dickey. SM

Light dances cheerily before me, A. Delusion. Wilhelm Müller, *tr. fr. German by* Philip L. Miller. *Fr.* Winter's Journey, The. RiWo

Light diffusing my likeness. Legend of His Lyre. Aaron Schmuller. GoYe

Light do I see within my Lady's eyes. Cavalcanti, *tr. fr. Italian by* Ezra Pound. CTC

Light Dress, The. Debora Greger. *Fr.* Afterlife, The. BAP-91

Light drizzle falling off, A. Taking a Captive/ 1984. Barney Bush. HATNAP

Light exists in spring, A. Emily Dickinson. BoWoP; EaPr; LiTA; NOBA; OxBA

Like a prowling wolf, I padded from door to door. The Return. Evan J. Thomas. AngWe

Like a rainstorm, he said, the braided colors. Worsening Situation. John Ashbery. NOBA

Like a ravaged sea/ this bed. Lady Ise, *tr. fr. Japanese by* Etsuko Terasaki *and* Irma Brandeis. BoWoP

Like a relentless milkman up the stairs. (*LL*) Living in Sin. Adrienne Rich. FF; IHMS; NIP; NoP; NYBP; Poetr; SoSe; TAP; UnPo

Like a revealed mineral, a new earth. (*LL*) In Piam Memoriam. Geoffrey Hill. OxBC

Like a rising flag. (*LL*) Unfinished Poem. Jiang He. SpMi

Like a river she was. The Memory. Robert Creeley. CAPP; VGW

Like a rock, Elly. Splash! David Trinidad. BAP-91

Like a round loaf, that's how small you were. To the Newborn. Judit Tóth, *tr. fr. Hungarian by* Laura Schiff. WPOW

Like a scared rabbit running over and. Jack Spicer. *Fr.* Graphemics. VGW

Like a scene in a classical painting. I-ch'ang. Ts'ai Ch'i-chiao, *tr. fr. Chinese.* LHF, *tr. by* Hualing Nieh

Like a she-camel with a large bell. Fortitude. *Somali Oral Tradition, tr. by* B. W. Andrzejewski *and* I. M. Lewis. WTO

Like a shell, and as it opens, cuts. (*LL*) Earliness at the Cape. Babette Deutsch. FYAP; NYBP

Like a silkworm weaving. Mahadevi, *tr. fr. Kannada by* A. K. Ramanujan. PBWP

Like a skein of loose silk blown against a wall. The Garden. Ezra Pound. AWP; HeIP; LiTA; MoAB; MoAmPo; NIP; NoP; OxBSP; PPP; SOTW; TwCP

Like a small gray/ coffee-pot. The Gray Squirrel. Humbert Wolfe. GoJo; MoBrPo

Like a small hamlet at a mountain's base. (*LL*) Giantess. Baudelaire. ErPo, *tr. by* Karl Shapiro; OBVE, *tr. by* Roy Campbell

Like a spider through ink, someone says, mocking: see it. Arabic Script. Anthony Thwaite. OBTV

Like a sweet apple reddening on the high. Sappho, *tr. fr. Greek by* Willis Barnstone. BoWoP

Like a sword on a shield. (*LL*) My Lover Will Soon Be Here. *Unknown.* OHMPC

Like a trapped bird. First Day at Boarding School. Prunella Power. Mes

Like a veiled dream thy memory comes. To a Loved One of Other Days. Matilda C. Edwards. PWR

Like a very fine, white dust snow was falling. Memories of December. Gizela Spunberg. BTR

Like a Whisper. Ethan Ayer. GoYe

Like a white candle through a shuttered hand. (*LL*) The Sisters. Roy Campbell. BoLoP; ErPo; FaBoTw; LPA; OBMV

Like a Wick, I Thought, a Woman. Eloise Klein Healy. ETG

Like a woman you've longed to make love to, and finally did. Pennsylvania Winter Indian 1974. Harold Littlebird. VoR

Like Achilles you had a goddess for mother. On Looking into E. V. Rieu's Homer. Patrick Kavanagh. NOIV

Like air on skin, coolness of yachts at mooring. Yachts on the Nile. Bernard Spencer. NoAM

Like all other impropagandula? (*LL*) Animula vagula blandula. Conrad Aiken. FaBoNo; OBAL

Like an Adventurous Seafarer Am I. Michael Drayton. *Fr.* Idea. ESo; NOSC; Son

Like an adversity. (*LL*) Drowning is not so pitiful. Emily Dickinson. CMoP; OxBSP

Like an Aerolith. Peter Philpott. VaA

Like an arrow shot/ To Death from Birth. Wine. Micah Joseph Lebensohn, *tr. fr. Hebrew by* A. M. Klein. TrJP

Like an elephant. Mahadevi, *tr. fr. Kannada by* A. K. Ramanujan. PBWP

Like an home-reared animal in a quiet nook. King Pellam's Launde. David Jones. *Fr.* In Parenthesis. OAEL-2

Like an intelligence. (*LL*) Upon Her Eyes. Robert Herrick. BeJo

Like an invader, not a guest. Winter's Troops. Charles Cotton. *Fr.* Winter. ChTr

Like an old stone tree. (*LL*) The Moss of His Skin. Anne Sexton. CoAP; IHMS; NALW; SM

Like an Orchid in Deep Muddy Water. Nilene O. A. Foxworth. AIW

Like an Oriental dagger. (*LL*) There Are Nights. Léon Damas. NegPo

Like Ana. Nina Cassian, *tr. fr. Romanian by* Nina Cassina. PoSu

Like Any Other Man. Gregory Orr. FF

Like as the armed knight. The Ballad Which Anne Askew Made and Sang When She Was in Newgate. Anne Askew. NoSic; WPE

Like as the Bay, that bears on branches sweet. In Praise of His Lady. Matthew Grove. *Fr.* Pelops and Hippodamia. ElL

Like as the bird in the cage enclosed. Sir Thomas Wyatt. SiPS; SiPSBD

Like as the damask rose you see. Man's Mortality. *At. to* Simon Wastell. *Fr.* Microbiblion. FaBoCh

Like as the divers-fretchled Butterfly. The Muse Reviving. Sir John Davies. SiPS

Like as the Dove. Sir Philip Sidney. SiPS

Like as the dumb solsequium, with care ourcome. The Solsequium. Alexander Montgomerie. NoP

Like as the fountain of all light created. Incarnatio Est Maximum Dei Donum [*or* Donum Dei]. William Alabaster. NoSic

Like as the rage of rain. The Uncertain State of a Lover. *Unknown.* EIL

Like as the swan towards her death. Sir Thomas Wyatt. SiPS; SiPSBD

Like as the tide that comes from th' Ocean main. Spenser. *Fr.* Faerie Queene, The. HoPM

Like as the waves make towards the pebbled shore. Shakespeare. *Fr.* Sonnets. ChTr; EBEV; EIL; EnRePo; FaPoB; LiTB; NIP; NOBE; NoSic; OxAEP-1; PeHV; PoRA; SCGP; Son; TEP; TFi; UnPo (Like as the Waves.) ImPo (Revolutions.) GTBS; GTBS-P

Like as, to make our appetites more keen. Shakespeare. *Fr.* Sonnets. SCGP

Like Attracts Like. Emmett Williams. WeW

Like battered old millhands, they stand in the orchard. Old Apple Trees. W. D. Snodgrass. CAPP; FYAP; SV

Like Bird or Balloon. David Trinidad. BAP-91

Like Birds of a Feather. Ralph Schomberg. *Fr.* Judgment of Paris, The. TrJP

Like birds when first light breaks. Children Waking: Indian Hill Station. Ralph Nixon Currey. PeSA

Like blood, like good, and like age. *Unknown.* FaBoUs

Like burnt-out torches by a sick man's bed. The Grave of Shelley. Oscar Wilde. OBTV

Like butterflies but lately come. Beautiful Creatures Brief as These. Douglas G. Jones. MoCV

Like Coleridge, I waltz. Under the Ice. Stewart Conn. PWE

Like Coney Island in winter. (*LL*) Ladies and Gentlemen This Little Girl. E. E. Cummings. CMoP; PoE

Like cud. (*LL*) Three Laments. Diane Di Prima. PoBeRe

Like cutting the dry rot out of a potato. Dark Conclusions. Ruth Stone. BoWoP

Like dives in the deeps of hell. Save the Boys. Frances E. W. Harper. AAP; PWR

Like Dolmens Round My Childhood, the Old People. John Montague. EBEV; IIP; IPY; PBCIP; PNI

Like dreams. (*LL*) Your Work. Jean-Joseph Rabéarivelo. NegPo

Like Etna's dread volcano see the ample forge. The Anchorsmiths. Charles Dibdin. NOEC

Like fabrics of enchantment piled to Heaven. (*LL*) Julian and Maddalo. Shelley. FHYEP; OAEL-2, *abr.*; OBTV

Like Father. Herbert Williams. AngWe

Like fire-flies that the peasant on the hill. Dante, *tr. by* Laurence Binyon. *Fr.* Divina Commedia. MeMAP; NAWM-1, *tr. by* John Ciardi; Prf

Like fire roses. (*LL*) Fire Roses. Cynthia Fuller. VBLP

Like Flowers We Spring. *Unknown.* EIL

Like foxgloves in the school of the grass moon. The Flower Master. Medbh McGuckian. PNI

Like Ghosts of Eagles. Robert Francis. GOA; LCAP

Like God's attention. Where nothing is diminished by perspective. (*LL*) Equanimity. Les A. Murray. NOBAu

Like Grandpa Paul/ The water is all of my mind. Louis Zukofsky. *Fr.* "A-12". ChIV-1

Like green fire. (*LL*) Former Barn Lot. Mark Van Doren. FaBV; MoAmPo; PDV

Like gript stick. The Sermon. Richard Hughes. OBMV

Like Groping Fingers. Abraham Sutzkever, *tr. fr. Yiddish by* Joseph Leftwich. TrJP

Like Gulliver. Nina Cassian, *tr. fr. Romanian by* Willis Barnstone *and* Matei Calinescu. BoWoP

Like Hamlet you began at thirty handing out. The Comedy of Art: Henri de Toulouse Lautrec. Richard Howard. AnAn

Like her, — because they love him. (*LL*) In School-Days. Whittier. AnAmPo; BLPA; FaBoBe; FaPON; OBCA; OxBChV

Like hibiscus. Like a Flower. Fily-Dabo Sissoko, *tr. fr. French by* Ellen Conroy Kennedy. NegPo

Like his hand, in fever, on my forehead. (*LL*) Out-of-the-Body Travel. Stanley Plumly. AmPA; LCAP

Like hooved up ground/ thats what. (*LL*) The Hermit Cackleberry Brown, on Human Vanity. Jonathan Williams. OBAL; PoM

Like inept soldiers. Scots Pines. Vuyelwa Carlin. NWP

Like it used to be, not even the future. (*LL*) Ö. Rita Dove. HCAP; WeW

Like John on Patmos, brooding on the Four. A Commination. A. D. Hope. ChIV-2

Like Jonah in the green belly of the whale. Emily Carr. Wilfred Watson. MoCV; NOBC

Like lamp of intricate stained glass which hangs. From Ancient Fangs. Peter Viereck. LiTA

Like leaves on trees the race of man is found. Homer, *tr. by* Pope. *Fr.* Iliad, The. OBVE

Like liquid gold the wheat-field lies. A Dakota Wheat-Field. Hamlin Garland. OBCA

Like Lise, moreover, my mother was white. The Black Man's Son. Oswald Durand, *tr. fr. French by* Edna Worthley Underwood. TTY, *tr. by* Ellen Conroy Kennedy
  (At twenty, I loved Lise. She was frail and white.) NegPo, *tr. by* Ellen Conroy Kennedy

Like lizards on rocks. (*LL*) Eastern guard tower. Etheridge Knight. BPo; MoP; SM; TAP

Like love & family romance, has neither beginning, middle nor end! (*LL*) My Guardian Angel Stein. Philip Schultz. InPS

Like Loving Chekhov. Denise Levertov. InPS

Like many a one, when you had gold. The Old Story. Argentarius, *tr. by* E. A. Robinson. AWP

Like many of us, born too late. Shut In. Robert B. Shaw. SoSe

Like many of us he was rather disgusting. Tennyson. Karl Shapiro. BAP-89

Like Melodies. Klaus Groth, *tr. fr. German by* Philip L. Miller. RiWo

Like [*or* Lyke] Memnons rock, touched [*or* rocke toucht] with the rising sun[ne]. Giles Fletcher the Elder. *Fr.* Licia. AAS; FF
  (Sonnet: "Like Memnon's rock, touched with the rising sun.") EIL

Like men riding. Nelly Trim. Sylvia Townsend Warner. ErPo; MoAB; MoBrPo

Like milk. What She Said. Kollan Alici, *tr. fr. Tamil by* A. K. Ramanujan. PLW

Like moss on water. What She Said. Paranar, *tr. fr. Tamil by* A. K. Ramanujan. PLW

Like Mother, like Son. Margaret Johnston Grafflin. *See* Do you know that your soul is of my soul such part.

Like mourning coaches when the funeral's done. (*LL*) Beppo; a Venetian Story. Byron. NOBL, *abr; OBNV, abr; OBSV*

Like musical instruments. Dispersion and Convergence. Tom Clark. TRP; UL

Like nae mair hooses ower piece-flinging height. (*LL*) The Jelly Piece Song. Anne MacNaughton. NTP

Like needles, crystals, you are happy. (*LL*) You Are Happy. Margaret Atwood. TRP

Like new, though ancient — will be found. (*LL*) How to Be Old. May Swenson. MAT; UnPo

Like Noah's Weary Dove. William Augustus Mühlenberg. AH

Like nothing else in Tennessee. (*LL*) Anecdote of the Jar. Wallace Stevens. AmPP; CMoP; HCAP; HeIP; HoPM; InPK; LiTA; MeMAP; MoAB; MoAmPo; MoP; NAAL-2; NAWM-2; NoAM; NOBA; NoP; OxBA; OxBSP; PoA; Poetr; PPP; PrIm; SAmP; SOTW; TAP; TFi; UnPo

Like Odysseus under the ram. Archilochus, *tr. fr. Latin by* Guy Davenport. OBVE

Like one of the grasses, like one of man. (*LL*) Will There Yet Come. Leah Goldberg. MHP

Like one of yours, ye multitudinous ocean. (*LL*) By That Long Scan of Waves. Walt Whitman. NAAL-1

Like one who'in her third widdowhood doth professe. To Mr. Rowland Woodward. John Donne. ESCV

Like our dawn in my throat. (*LL*) First Problem. Aimé Césaire. NegPo

Like our hope of success it has passed. (*LL*) Lines on the Back of a Confederate Note. Samuel Alroy Jonas. BLPA

Like Oxford colledge bells, to supp. (*LL*) On Westwall Downes [*or* On Westwell Downs]. William Strode. FaBoPP; GGP; JCP; NOSC; PoEL-2

Like pianos advancing on ice, each moment's. Trumpet Voluntary. Paul Hoover. UL

Like plump green floor plans. Rotation. Julian Bond. FF

Like priceless treasures sinking in the sand. (*LL*) America. Claude McKay. CDC; MoP; NIP; NoAM; PoBA; PoNe; TAP; TTY

Like Queen Christina. Kenneth Rexroth. ArNa

Like rain it sounded till it curved. Emily Dickinson. RB

Like Ripples on the Water. *Gond Oral Tradition, tr. by* V. Elwin *and* S. Hivale. WTO

Like rouge and powder. (*LL*) Flying Petals. Hsiao Kang. OHMPC

Like Rousseau. Amiri Baraka. PoA

Like ruminating cattle on the sands. Women Damned. Baudelaire, *tr. fr. French by* Joanna Richardson. PeHV

Like schoolgirls taking a boy's hand and swallowing their pride. (*LL*) The Woman's Daughter. Dermot Bolger. IB

Like shepherds at daybreak. (*LL*) On Her Brother. Al-Khansa. BoWoP

Like shuttles fleet the clouds, and after. Oxford Bells. Gerard Manley Hopkins. FaBoPP

Like silence into music, opening a way through time. (*LL*) Air. Kathleen Raine. MoAB; MoBrPo

Like silver dew are the tears of love. A. E. Coppard. OBMV

Like small curled feathers, white and soft. While Shepherds Watched Their Flocks by Night. Margaret Deland. GN

Like Smoke. Mririda n'Ait Attik, *tr. fr. French by* Daniel Halpern *and* Paula Paley. PBWP

Like smoke in a bottle, like. Poem for the Name Mary. Mark Cox. NAmP90

Like snakes of golden autumn fire. Nevada. Lawrence Gurney. GoYe

Like some awful animal. Windstorm. Sun Ching-hsuan, *tr. fr. Chinese. Fr.* Lyrics of the Forest. LHF, *tr. by* Hualing Nieh

Like some ill-fated butterfly, the literalists. John Hollander. *Fr.* Powers of Thirteen. VCAP

Like some one school master, kind in being stern. Unanswered Prayers. Ella Wheeler Wilcox. WGRP

Like sorrow or a tune. (*LL*) The Night Will Never Stay. Eleanor Farjeon. BoTP; CH; NTCP; OxBChV

Like South Sea stock, expressions rise and fall. Time's Changes. James Bramston. *Fr.* Art of Politics, The. NOEC

Like Stephen Vincent Benét, I have fallen in love with American names. Ill Met by Zenith. Ogden Nash. NYBP

Like sticks in a fire. (*LL*) Variations on an Air: After W. B. Yeats. G. K. Chesteron. BXAP; FaBoPa; NOBL

Like still seas, to vacant skies. (*LL*) Betty by the Sea. Ronald McCuaig. NOBAu

Like tall men with a battering-plank — the colt. Letter from Underground. Ronald G. Everson. MoCV

Like that. (*LL*) Poem for Flora. Nikki Giovanni. BPo; CrSp; PoBA

Like that dying woman in Mexico. If. Patrick Lane. NOBC

Like the beat beat beat of the tom-tom. Night and Day. Cole Porter. CBLP

Like the buffalo. To You. Elolongue Epanya Yondo, *tr. fr. French by* Ellen Conroy Kennedy. NegPo

Like the cadence of an old love song. Child Life. Mary E. Tucker. CBWP-1

Like the crash of the thunder. Zionist Marching Song. Naphtali Herz Imber, *tr. fr. Hebrew by* Israel Zangwill. TrJP

Like the dark germs across the filter clean. Loss. Charles Madge. FaBoMo

Like the eyes of a mild savior. (*LL*) The Blue Booby. James Tate. AmPA; NoAM; NoP

Like the Eyes of Wolves. Nachum Yud, *tr. fr. Yiddish by* Joseph Leftwich. TrJP

Like the heap of soil on the grave. (*LL*) A Poem. Mongane Wally Serote. PeSAV

Like the heaven above. (*LL*) Little Things. *At. to* Julia A. Fletcher Carney. BLPA; BLPL; FaBoBe; FaPON; OxBChV

Like the high fanning tufts on swift horses. What She Said ("Like the high fanning tufts on swift horses.") Orampokiyar, *tr. fr. Tamil by* A. K. Ramanujan. *Fr.* Five on the Riverside Cane. PLW

Like the honeycomb dropping honey. Hildegard von Bingen, *tr. fr. Latin by* Patrick Diehl. WPOW

Like the Idalian Queen[e]. William Drummond of Hawthornden. CBLP; NOSC; OAEL-1; SCGP
  (Inexorable.) NOBE; OBEV
  (Madrigal: "Like the Idalian Queen.") EIL; ELP; GBL; InvP; OBAL; PeLV; PoEL-2

Like the inflatable palm tree I gave to my lover. In Pompano Beach, Florida. Robin Becker. PBCAP

Like the leopard's. Through Eyes. Cole Swenson. UTF

Like the poor, they are with us always. Sparrows. Christopher Buckley. FoLa

Like the quiver of a Negro woman's eye-lids cupping tears. (*LL*) Negro Woman. Lewis Alexander. CDC; PoBA

Like the red flame. Peyanar, *tr. fr. Tamil by* A. K. Ramanujan. *Fr.* Seven Said by the Foster-Mother. PLW

Like the ringing of church bells. (*LL*) The Return. Nika Turbina. VBLP

Like the sound of horns, the sound of thousands of small wings. (*LL*) The Executive's Death. Robert Bly. CoAP; NaP

Like the stalks of wheat in the fields. Heine, *tr. fr. German. Fr.* North Sea, The. TrJP, *tr. by* Emma Lazarus

Limerick: "Connoisseurs of coition aver." *Unknown.* PeLi
Limerick: "Consider the Emperor Nero." *Unknown.* PeLi
Limerick: "Consider the lowering Lynx." Langford Reed. PeLi
Limerick: "Consistent disciples of Marx." A. Cinna. PeLi
Limerick: "Couple from old Aberystwyth, A." Stuart Woods. PeLi
Limerick: "Couple there was in Blefuscu, A." W. F. N. Watson. PeLi
Limerick: "Couturier from Haverford West, A." E. O. Parrott. PeLi
Limerick: "Creature of charm is the gerbil, A." *Unknown.* PeLi
Limerick: "Cried the maid: "You must marry me, Hume!"" P. W. R. Foot.
    PeLi
Limerick: "Crusader's wife slipped from the garrison, A." Ogden Nash.
    PeLi
Limerick: "Cryptic philosopher, Kant, The." E. F. C. PeLi
Limerick: "Cute secretary, none cuter, A." Ogden Nash. PeLi
Limerick: "Cynic says: Now that we know, A." Thomas Thorneley. PeLi
Limerick: "Cynical sage with a kink, A." Hassall Pitman. PeLi
Limerick: "Dad waited while Mum bought the ham." Coral E. Copping.
    PeLi
Limerick: "Daring young lady of Guam, A." *Unknown.* PeLi
Limerick: "Dear Albert, of Saxe-Coburg-Gotha." W. F. N. Watson. PeLi
Limerick: "Dear Sir, You're quite wrong about me." M. Trench. PeLi
Limerick: "Decrepit old gas man named Peter, A." *Unknown. See* Decrepit
    Old Gasman, A.
Limerick: "Democracy works (*entre nous*)." W. Stewart. PeLi
Limerick: "Desperate spinster of Clare, A." *Unknown.* PeLi
Limerick: "Devil, who plays a deep part, The." Little Billee. PeLi
Limerick: "Devil's no longer a myth, The." Little Billee. PeLi
Limerick: "Dickensian borough of Coketown, The." Martin Fagg. PeLi
Limerick: "Did Ophelia ask Hamlet to bed?" A. Cinna. PeLi
Limerick: "Divine by the name of McWhinners, A." *Unknown.* PeLi
Limerick: "Dr. Johnson, when sober or pissed." A. Cinna. PeLi
Limerick: "Don't thee think, Zurrr, I be zo amazin'." Elizabeth H. Lister.
    PeLi
Limerick: "Don't think it will fall to your lot." Leslie Johnson. PeLi
Limerick: "Dowager Duchess of Spout, The." Edward Gorey. PeLi; PeLV
Limerick: "Each Lon was a notable man." L. G. Udall. PeLi
Limerick: "Each night father fills me with dread." Edward Gorey. PeLi
Limerick: "Earnest young leftie named Tariq." Bernard Levin. PeLi
Limerick: "Elderly bride of Port Jervis, An." Ogden Nash. PeLi
Limerick: "Emperor Marcus Aurelius, The." Yorick. PeLi
Limerick: "English professor named Brooks, An." D. H. Cudmore. PeLi
Limerick: "Enjoyment of sex, although great, The." *Unknown.* PeLi
Limerick: "Epicure dining at Crewe, An." *Unknown.* PeLV
Limerick: "Ethnologists up with the Sioux." *Unknown.* PeLi
Limerick: "Evangelical vicar in want." Ronald Arbuthnott Knox. PeLi
Limerick: "Example of Kant's sterling wit, An." Victor Gray. PeLi
Limerick: "Exposing his plate to the air." Joyce Johnson. PeLi
Limerick: "Exquisite bartender at Sweeney's, The." *Unknown.* PeLi
Limerick: "Fabulous Wizard of Oz, The." *Unknown.* PeLi
Limerick: "Fact of the matter is, Jack, The." John Stanley. PeLi
Limerick: "Famed big-hitter in cricket, A." Douglas Catley. PeLi
Limerick: "Famous philosopher, Kant, The." C. S. Cook. PeLi
Limerick: "Famous theatrical actress, A." *Unknown.* PeLi
Limerick: "Far beyond all the girls of Pirelli." I. D. M. Morley. PeLi
Limerick: "Fascist, erect and irate, A." Thomas Thorneley. PeLi
Limerick: "Fat-tailed Dwarf Lemur, in bed, A." Gerry Hamill. PeLi
Limerick: "Fellow from far Erewhon, A." W. F. N. Watson. PeLi
Limerick: "Fellow who fucked but as few can, A." *Unknown.* PeLi
Limerick: "Feminine mouth in Utopia, The." W. F. N. Watson. PeLi
Limerick: "Fencing instructor named Fisk, A." *Unknown.* PeLi
Limerick: "Few people could hope to compare." J. Endersby. PeLi
Limerick: "Few things to desire can so prod us." W. F. N. Watson. PeLi
Limerick: "Figure is not anatomical, The." Thomas Thorneley. PeLi
Limerick: "Filthy young fellow called Lawrence, A." Bill Greenwell. PeLi
Limerick: "Finding God's taboos totalitarian." Basil Ransome-Davies. PeLi
Limerick: "Fire Island pixie called "Mary," A." *Unknown.* PeHV
Limerick: "First chap to fuck little Sophie, The." Victor Gray. PeLi
Limerick: "Flighty young lady from Loddon, A." Ida Thurtle. PeLi
Limerick: "Fly and a flea [flew up] in a flue, A." *Unknown.* RoPo
    (Flea and the Fly, The.) FaPON
Limerick: "For his Campbell's Soup screen-prints, society's." Bill
    Greenwell. PeLi
Limerick: "For hours my wife says "Goodbye."" Gelett Burgess. PeLi
Limerick: "For the tenth time, dull Daphnis," said Chloe." *Unknown.* PeLi
Limerick: For Travelers Going Sidereal. Robert Frost. *See* For Travelers
    Going Sidereal.

Limerick: "For Widower — wanted, house-keeper." *Unknown.* PeLi
Limerick: "French are a race among races, The." *Unknown.* PeLi
Limerick: "French poodle espied in the hall, A." *Unknown.* PeLi
Limerick: "From Number Nine, Penwiper Mews." Edward Gorey. PeLi
Limerick: "From the bathing machine came a din." Edward Gorey. OBAL;
    PeLi
Limerick: "From the crypt of the church of St. Giles." *Unknown.* PeLi
Limerick: "From the elephant paddock one day." Frank Richards. PeLi
Limerick: "From the west to the fabulous east." *Unknown.* PeLi
Limerick: "G. B. Shaw wrote to Yeats: "P'raps it's mad of me." W. A.
    Rathkey. PeLi
Limerick: "Gamekeeper of Lady Chatterley, The." Gerry Hamill. PeLi
Limerick: "Gay soccer spectator from Wix, A." Cyril Mountjoy. PeLi
Limerick: "General once lived named de Gaulle, A." Paul Bristow. PeLi
Limerick: "George Stephenson said: "These repairs." Frank Richards. PeLi
Limerick: "George Washington said to his dad." Frank Richards. PeLi
Limerick: "Giraffes, yes, even the strongest." Frank Davies. PeLi
Limerick: "Girl who was touring Zambesi, A." *Unknown.* PeLi
Limerick: "Given faith," sighed the vicar of Deneham." *Unknown.* PeLi
Limerick: "Glib little beer-buff from Troon, A." Bill Greenwell. PeLi
Limerick: "God brought perfect man to fruition." Douglas Catley. PeLi
Limerick: "Goddess capricious is Fame, A." Langford Reed. PeLi
Limerick: "God's plan made a hopeful beginning." *Unknown.* PeLi
Limerick: "Goliath was known for ferocity." Frank Richards. PeLi
Limerick: "Good mechanics are all of one mind." Douglas Catley. PeLi
Limerick: "Great-grandfather at Waterloo." Frank Richards. PeLi
Limerick: "G'uggery G'uggery Nunc." Sir John Betjeman. PeLi
Limerick: "Handsome young monk in a wood, A." *Unknown.* PeLi
Limerick: "Having rid Hamelin town of its vermin." Ted Thompson. PeLi
Limerick: "Headstrong young lady of Ealing, A." Edward Gorey. PeLi
Limerick: "Heart of O'Leary, S.J., The." David Phillips. PeLi
Limerick: "Henley's a special regatta." Jim Anthony. PeLi
Limerick: "Her husband was *hors de combat*." C. Vita-Finzi. PeLi
Limerick: "Her limp lover Maud couldn't pardon." Kit Wright. PeLi
Limerick: "Herder who hailed from Terre Haute, A." *Unknown.* PeLi
Limerick: "Hermaphrodite fairy of Kew, A." *Unknown.* PeHV
Limerick: "Hibiscus is flaming and frillier." Ruth Silcock. PeLi
Limerick: "Highly bored damsel called Brown, A." *Unknown.* PeLi
Limerick: "His sister named [*or* called] Lucy O'Finner." "Lewis Carroll."
    FaBoNo; PeLi
Limerick: "Honourable Winifred Wemyss, The." *Unknown.* PeLi
Limerick: "Hoover, in grim silence, sat, The." David Woodsford. PeLi
Limerick: "Hopeful old fellow called Rousseau, A." John Fay. PeLi
Limerick: "Horsewoman of charm at Uttoxeter, A." R. D. Condon. PeLi
Limerick: "How much," sighed the gentle Narcissus." Stephen Sylvester.
    PeLi
Limerick: "How often and often I wish." Frances Cornford. PeLi
Limerick: "How Socratic is Somerset Maugham!" R. B. S. Instone. PeLi
Limerick: "How varied the family Sen!" Roy Fuller. PeLi
Limerick: "Husband who lived in Tiberias, A." *Unknown.* PeLi
Limerick: "I admire your felicitous phrasing." A. M. Sayers. PeLi
Limerick: "I, Caesar, when I learned of the fame." *Unknown.* PeLi
Limerick: "I consider I really am through." Elizabeth H. Lister. PeLi
Limerick: "I fear, Mr. Lear, you're a clot." Eric Swainson. PeLi
Limerick: "I have heard," said a maid from Montclair." Morris Bishop.
    PeLi
Limerick: "I haven't a clue where I've been." Sydney Bernard Smith. PeLi
Limerick: "I must leave here," said Lady De Vere." *Unknown.* PeLi
Limerick: "I once had a cat called Maria." Paul Griffin. PeLi
Limerick: "I once knew a spinster of Staines." Plaiwon. PeLi
Limerick: "I once took my girl to Southend." Veronica Nicolson. PeLi
Limerick: "I sat next to the Duchess at tea." *Unknown.* SoSe
Limerick: "I spotted these daffs by the lake." E. O. Parrott. PeLi
Limerick: "I suppose I could try if I chose." E. F. C. PeLi
Limerick: "I was brought up on old Aristotle." C. S. Cook. PeLi
Limerick: "I was sitting there, taking my ease." Cyril Ray. PeLi
Limerick: "I was thrilled when I went to the Zoo." Victor Gray. PeLi
Limerick: "I went with the Duchess to tea." At. to Woodrow Wilson. PeLi
Limerick: "I wish that my room had a floor." Gelett Burgess. FiBHP;
    InvP; OBCA; PeLi
Limerick: "I wonder how King Arthur felt." Moss Rich. PeLi
Limerick: "I would doubt," said the Bishop of Balham." Terence Rattigan.
    PeLi
Limerick: "I wouldn't be bothered with drawers." *Unknown.* PeLi
Limerick: "I'd rather have fingers than toes." Gelett Burgess. FaPON; PeLi
Limerick: "If Eve hadn't eaten the apple." Wendy Cope. PeLi

Limerick: "There was an old person of Harrow." Edward Lear. FaBoNo

Limerick: "There was an old person of Hove." Edward Lear. FaBoNo

Limerick: "There was an Old Person of Hurst." Edward Lear. PeLi

Limerick: "There was an old person of Persia." William Plomer. PeLi

Limerick: "There was an old person of Philae." Edward Lear. CBNP; FaBoNo

Limerick: "There was an old person of Skye." Edward Lear. ChTr

Limerick: "There was an old person of Slough." George Robey. PeLi

Limerick: "There was an Old Person of Slough." Unknown. CBNP

Limerick: "There was an old person of Twickenham." Edward Lear. FaBoNo

Limerick: "There was an old person of Wick." Edward Lear. FaBoNo

Limerick: "There was an old person whose habits." Edward Lear. FaBoNo

Limerick: "There was an old sage of New Delhi." Joyce Parr. PeLi

Limerick: "There was an old Scot called McTavish." Unknown. PeLi

Limerick: "There was an old Welshman called Morgan." Ron Rubin. PeLi

Limerick: "There was an Old Woman of Gloster." Unknown. PeLi

Limerick: "There was an Old Woman of Lynn." Unknown. PeLi

Limerick: "There was an old woman of Wales." George Seferis, tr. fr. Greek by Peter Levi. CBNP

Limerick: "There was once a young man of Oporta." "Lewis Carroll." FaBoNo; PeLi

Limerick: "There we was, and wanting our tea." P. E. A. PeLi

Limerick: "There were once two young people of taste." Monica Curtis. PeLi

Limerick: "There were three little owls in a wood." Unknown. PeLi

Limerick: "There's a combative artist named Whistler." Dante Gabriel Rossetti. FaBoEE; PeLi

Limerick: "There's a fortunate priest of St. Paul's." Douglas Catley. PeLi

Limerick: "There's a notable family named Stein." Unknown. NOBL

Limerick: "There's a Portuguese person named Howell." At. to Dante Gabriel Rossetti. PeLi

Limerick: "There's a publishing party named Ellis." Dante Gabriel Rossetti. PeLi

Limerick: "There's a sensitive type in Tom's River." Unknown. PeLi

Limerick: "There's a slow tolling bell in the dark." Gavin Ewart. PeLi

Limerick: "There's a tiresome young man of Bay Shore." Morris Bishop. PeLi

Limerick: "There's a very prim girl called McDrood." Unknown. PeLi

Limerick: "There's a wonderful family called Stein." Unknown. PeLi

Limerick: "There's an emerald frog down the loo." Ruth Silcock. PeLi

Limerick: "There's an Irishman, Arthur O'Shaughnessy." Dante Gabriel Rossetti. PeLi

Limerick: "These days, the ubiquitous db." A. P. Cox. PeLi

Limerick: "They say that I was in my youth." Unknown. PeLi

Limerick: "Thomas Hobbes of Malmesbury thought." Peter Alexander. PeLi

Limerick: "Though clerical errors are fun." Unknown. PeLi

Limerick: "Though his plan, when he gave her a buzz." Unknown. PeLi

Limerick: "Though Sir James (God's-a-Formula) Jeans." R. J. P. Hewison. PeLi

Limerick: "Though the limerick can not be deaded." Unknown. PeLi

Limerick: "Though the music of love is Schubérty." Unknown. PeHV

Limerick: "Though your dreams may seem normal and right." J. C. B. Date. PeLi

Limerick: "Three Aldis, not one of them dim." Joyce Johnson. PeLi

Limerick: "Three scribblers whose names end in Bert." C. Vita-Finzi. PeLi

Limerick: "Three wonderful people called Ley." Tim Hopkins. PeLi

Limerick: "Three wonderful people called Wick." A. M. Sayers. PeLi

Limerick: "Throughout the whole world, experts say." Unknown. PeLi

Limerick: "Thus spake an old Chinese mandarin." Unknown. PeLi

Limerick: "'Tis strange how the newspapers honour." Eugene Field. PeLi

Limerick: "To Algebra God is inclined." J. C. B. Date. PeLi

Limerick: "To avoid matrimonial disasters." Martin Fagg. PeLi

Limerick: "To her friends, said the Bright one, in chatter." Arthur Buller. PeLi

Limerick: "To her gardener, a lady named Liliom." Unknown. PeLi

Limerick: "To his bride said a numbskull named Clarence." Unknown. PeLi

Limerick: "To his club-footed child said Lord Stipple." Edward Gorey. PeLi

Limerick: "To his Queen said the circumspect Burleigh." A. Cinna. PeLi

Limerick: "To his wife said the lynx-eyed detective." Langford Reed. PeLi

Limerick: "Tone-deaf old person of Tring, A." Unknown. PeLi

Limerick: "Toper who spies in the distance, A." Leslie Johnson. PeLi

Limerick: "Traveller to Timbuktu, A." Unknown. PeLi

Limerick: "Treatment by old Mr. Mears, The." Unknown. PeHV

Limerick: "Trouble with General Sherman, The." Basil Ransome-Davies. PeLi

Limerick: "Truth about truth is elusive, The." Unknown. PeLi

Limerick: "Try our Rubber Girl-Friend (air-inflatable)." Unknown. PeLi

Limerick: "Tutor who tooted a flute, A." Carolyn Wells. PeLi; SoSe

Limerick: "Two dykes went their separate routes." Unknown. PeHV

Limerick: "Two earnest young fellows named Wright." Basil Ransome-Davies. PeLi

Limerick: "Two middle-aged ladies from Fordham." Unknown. PeLi

Limerick: "Two playwrights called Beaumont and Fletcher." Fiona Pitt-Kethley. PeLi

Limerick: "Two she-camels spied on a goat." Unknown. PeLi

Limerick: "Undressing a maiden called Sue." Brian Allgar. PeLi

Limerick: "Unfortunate lad from Madrid, An." Unknown. PeLi

Limerick: "United States Constitution, The." Peter Alexander. PeLi

Limerick: "Unperson from West Oceania, An." C. Vita-Finzi. PeLi

Limerick: "Unpopular man of Cologne, An." Unknown. PeLi

Limerick: "Up the street sex is sold by the piece." Unknown. PeLi

Limerick: "Vain old Professor of Greek, A." Ron Rubin. PeLi

Limerick: "Van Gogh, feeling devil-may-care." Pibwob. PeLi

Limerick: "Very apt question struck me, A." Sydney Bernard Smith. PeLi

Limerick: "Vice most obscene and unsavoury, A." Unknown. NOBL; PeLV

Limerick: "Victoria said: "We've no quarrel." Frank Richards. PeLi

Limerick: "Victoria was bitterly short." Cyril Mountjoy. PeLi

Limerick: "Victorian gent said: "This dance," A." Frank Richards. PeLi

Limerick: "Viscount Stansgate, or Wedgwood, or Benn." Tim Hopkins. PeLi

Limerick: "Wandering tribe called the Siouxs, A." Charles Follen Adams. PeLi

Limerick: "Wanting children a couple once sat." G. W. Hanney. PeLi

Limerick: "Wanton young lady of Wimley, A." Unknown. PeLi

Limerick: "Watt's dream was the cream of steam engines." Bill Greenwell. PeLi

Limerick: "We all place a great deal of reliance." Unknown. PeLi

Limerick: "Wee Jamie, a canny young Scot." Joyce Johnson. PeLi

Limerick: "Well-bred young girl of Gomorrah, A." Unknown. PeHV

Limerick: "Well-buggered boy named Delpasse, A." Unknown. PeHV; PeLi

Limerick: "Well, I took your advice, Doc," said Knopp." Unknown. PeLi

Limerick: "Well, if it's a sin to like Guinness." Cyril Ray. PeLi

Limerick: "Well, it's partly the shape of the thing." Unknown. SoSe

Limerick: "We're not amused," said Victoria." Stanley J. Sharpless. PeLi

Limerick: "We've got a new maid called Chrysanthemum." Unknown. PeLi

Limerick: "We've socially-conscious biography." Unknown. PeLi

Limerick: "What have I done?" said Christine." Unknown. PeLi

Limerick: "What led to the crassness of Custer." Bill Greenwell. PeLi

Limerick: "What! Parted! Not even a kiss?" X. A. M. PeLi

Limerick: "What's the matter, old chap?" "Well, I came." Joyce Johnson. PeLi

Limerick: "When a feverish groom in Armenia." Morris Bishop. PeLi

Limerick: "When a friend said to Leda: "Come on." Peter Alexander. PeLi

Limerick: "When a friend told a typist called Eve." Gordon Harper. PeLi

Limerick: "When a man's too old even to toss off, he." Robert Conquest. PeLi

Limerick: "When an amorous youth from Atlantis." C. Vita-Finzi. PeLi

Limerick: "When an obstinate fellow of Fife." Allan M. Laing. PeLi

Limerick: "When approached by a person from Porlock." Richard Leighton Greene. PeLi

Limerick: "When Arthur was homeless and broke." Unknown. PeHV

Limerick: "When Daddy and Mum got quite plastered." Unknown. PeLi

Limerick: "When Gauguin was visiting Fiji." Victor Gray. NOBL

Limerick: "When he raped a young maid in a train." Unknown. PeLi

Limerick: "When I sit in the Churchyard at Stoke." A. M. Sayers. PeLi

Limerick: "When I thought of this Duchess affair." Unknown. PeLi

Limerick: "When Ireland was bloody and leaderless." Gina Berkeley. PeLi

Limerick: "When Jael crept in to see Sisera." Bill Greenwell. PeLi

Limerick: "When Keats was at work on Endymion." Victor Gray. PeLi

Limerick: "When Lazarus came back from the dead." Unknown. PeLi

Limerick: "When our dean took a pious young spinster." Victor Gray. NOBL; PeLi

Limerick: "When Pegotty found Barkis was willing." Douglas Catley. PeLi

Limerick: "When the census man called upon Gail." George McWilliam. PeLi

Limerick: "When the judge with his wife having sport." Unknown. PeLi

Limerick: "When the Prince, who was terribly smit." Joyce Johnson. PeLi

Limerick: "When your capitalist boss takes his toll." Dominic Fitzpatrick. PeLi

Limerick: "Whenever he got in a fury, a." Unknown. PeLi

Lines: "From fair Jamaica's fertile plains." "Ada." BlSi

Lines: "Here often, when a child, I lay reclined." Tennyson. FaBoPP

Lines: "His cock is big and red when I am there." Paul Goodman. PeHV

Lines: "How I love country you have heard." Samuel Alfred Beadle. AAP

Lines: "I have been cherish'd and forgiven." Hartley Coleridge. PoEL-4

Lines: I Praise God's Mankind in an Old Woman. Wilfred Watson. NOBC

Lines: Inspired by the Controversy on the Value or Otherwise of Old English Studies. Anthony Burgess. FaBoCo

Lines: "Nay, read it not, thou wouldst not know." Anne Lynch Botta. AmWP

Lines: "Singularly and in pairs the decade has been ripped by bullets." Herbert Martin. PoBA

Lines: To a Movement in Mozart's E-Flat Symphony. Thomas Hardy. ArLo; ELP; NoAM

Lines: "Wake not again the cannon's thundrous voice." Alfred Gibbs Campbell. AAP

Lines: "When the lamp is shattered." Shelley. See When the lamp is shattered.

Lines: "When youthful faith hath fled." John Gibson Lockhart. OBEV

Lines: "Whene'er the Muse pleases to grace my dull page." Lucretia Davidson. AmWP

Lines: "Where the dark primeval forests." Anne Lynch Botta. AmWP

Lines Addressed to Mr. Jefferson. Philip Freneau. EAP

Lines are cast and the nets are set and waiting, The. *Unknown, tr. fr. Greek by* Kenneth Rexroth. PGA

Lines are keen against today's bad sky, The. The Church on Comiaken Hill. Richard Hugo. Prf; SM

Lines Composed a Few Miles above Tintern Abbey [on Revisiting the Banks of the Wye during a Tour, July 13, 1798]. (Five years have passed [or past]; five summers, with the length.) Wordsworth. BLPL; EBEvV; EnRP; FaBoPP; FF; FHYEP; HeIP; InPS; LiTB; MeMBP; NoP; OAEL-2; OBNC; OxAEP-2; PoEL-4; Poetr; PPP; PrIm; SCGP; TEP; TFi; TrGrPo

Sels.

As a Beauty I Am Not a Star. InvP

"For I have learned." NU

"For thou art with me here upon the banks." Prf

"Sounding cataract, The/ Haunted me like a passion." WGRP

Lines Composed in a Wood on a Windy Day. Anne Brontë. EBVV

Lines Concerning the Unknown Soldier, sels. Osip Mandelstam, *tr. fr. Russian by* James Greene.

Arteries Juicy with Blood. NAs

Lines Descriptive of Thomson's Island. Benjamin Lynde. SCAP

Lines for a Bed at Kelmscott Manor. William Morris. *See* Wind's on the wold, The.

Lines for a Hard Time. Gena Ford. IHMS

Lines for a Painter. Anthony Cronin. PBCIP

Lines for a Worthy Person Who Has Drifted by Accident into a Chelsea Revel. A. P. Herbert. NOBL

Lines for a Young Wanderer in Mexico. John Logan. PoA

Lines for an Interment. Archibald MacLeish. CMoP; NOBA

Lines for an Old Man. T. S. Eliot. FaBoTw; RaBo; RB

Lines for Cuscuscaraway and Mirza Murad Ali Beg. T. S. Eliot. FiBHP; NBLV; NTP; OBAL; PeLV; UV

Lines for Marking Time. Roberta Hill Whiteman. BoWoP; CDW

Lines for Roethke Twenty Years after His Death. Duane Niatum. HATNAP

Lines for Those to Whom Tragedy Is Denied. Joyce Carol Oates. IHMS

Lines from Catullus. Sir Walter Ralegh, *after the Latin of* Catullus. *See* Sun [or Sunne] may set and rise, The.

Lines from Love Letters. Unknown. OBEV

Sels.

Arteries Juicy with Blood. NAs

"A celuy que plus eyme en mounde."

"A soun tres chere et special."

Lines from Love Letters, I. *Unknown. See* A celuy que pluys eyme en mounde.

Lines in a Roman Schoolbook, *sels.* Desmond O'Grady.

"In the valleys of the future we shall walk." PBCIP

"This introspective exile here today." PBCIP

Lines in Memory of My Father. Basil Payne. IIP; PeIV

Lines in old people's hands, The. The Memory of Horses. Rolf Jacobsen, *tr. fr.* Norwegian. TSaS, *tr. by* Roger Greenwald

Lines in the Corner of a Manuscript. *Unknown.* FaBoVe

Lines in Wasdale Head. John Seed. VaA

Lines Left at Mr. Theodore Hook's House in June, 1834. "Thomas Ingoldsby." FaBoUs

Lines Occasioned by the Burning of Some Letters. Sarah Dixon. ECWP; NOEC

Lines of the Hand, The. Julio Cortázar, *tr. by* Pal Blackburn. AnRep

Lines of this new song are nothing, The. Louis Zukofsky. VGW

Lines of your arteries, The. Robert. Wendy Rose. HATNAP

Lines on a Boer War Pin-up Girl Seen in the Falcon Hotel, Bude. Christopher Hope. PeSAV

Lines on a Dead Girl. Priscilla Jane Thompson. CBWP-2

Lines on a Purple Cap Received as a Present from My Brother. George Alsop. SCAP

Lines on a Young Lady's Photograph Album. Philip Larkin. EnLoPo; HAP; OAEL-2

Lines on Bounce. Pope. *See* Ah Bounce! ah gentle Beast! why wouldst thou dye.

Lines on Carmen Sylva. Emma Lazarus. TrJP

Lines on Hearing That Lady Byron Was Ill. Byron. EBEV; OxAEP-2

Lines on Hearing the Organ. Charles Stuart Calverley. FaBoCo; FiBHP; NOBL

Lines on His Companions Who Died in the Northern Seas. Thomas James. NOSC

Lines on Leaving a Scene in Bavaria. Thomas Campbell. OBNC

Lines on Milton. Dryden. *See* Three poets, in three distant ages born.

Lines on Receiving My Mother's Picture Out of Norfolk. William Cowper. *See* Oh [or O] that those lips had language! Life has passed [or pass'd].

Lines on Succession of the Kings of England. *Unknown.* FaBoUs

Lines on Swift's Ancestors. Pope. FaBoCo

Lines on Swinburne. Robert Browning. EPCY

Lines on the Arsehole. Paul Verlaine. *See* Dark, puckered hole: a purple carnation.

Lines on the Back of a Confederate Note. Samuel Alroy Jonas. BLPA

Lines on the Death of Bismarck. John Jay Chapman. PoEL-5

Lines on the Death of Mr P – R – C – V – L. Thomas Moore. FaBoEH

Lines on the Death of the Rev. S. K. Talmage. Mary E. Tucker. CBWP-1

Lines on the Execution of King Charles I. James Graham, Marquess of Montrose. *See* Great, good and just, could I but rate.

Lines on the Hundredth Anniversary of the Birth of W. Somerset Maugham. E. J. Thribb. PeLV

Lines on the Mermaid Tavern. *At. to* Keats. EnRP; FaBoEH, *st. 1 only*; FHYEP; PoRA; SCGP

Lines on the Return to Britain of Billy Graham. E. J. Thribb. PeLV

Lines on the Sea. Dilys Bennett Laing. NYBP

Lines on the Succession of the Kings of England (Reversed). *Unknown.* FaBoUs

Lines on the Tombs in Westminster. *At. to* Beaumont, Francis *and* William Basse Francis Beaumont *and to* William Basse. *Fr.* On the Tombs in Westminster Abbey. CH; FaPoR; GTBS; GTBS-P; NOBE; OBEV; PlP; SCGP; TrGrPo

Lines on Thomas Warton's Poems *or* Lines in Ridicule of Certain Poems Published in 1777. Samuel Johnson. EPCY; FaBoCo; FaBoEE

Lines parallel. The Room. De Leon Harrison. PoBA

Lines Printed under the Engraved Portrait of Milton [In Tonson's Folio of the "Paradise Lost"]. Dryden. InPK; OxAEP-1; SeCV-2

Lines Rhymed in a Letter Received (by J. H. R.) from Oxford. Keats. *See* Gothic looks solemn, The.

Lines to ———. Mary Weston Fordham. CBWP-2

Lines to a Don. Hilaire Belloc. FaBoCo; MoBrPo; OBSV; OtMeF

Lines to a Dragon-Fly. Walter Savage Landor. *See* Life (priest and poet say) is but a dream.

Lines to a Graduate. L. A. J. Moorer. CBWP-3

Lines to a Lady-Bird. Lord De Tabley. FM

Lines to a Nasturtium. Anne Spencer. CDC; PoNe; ShDr; VBLP

Lines to a Reviewer. Shelley. OxBSP

Lines to a Seagreen Lover. Isabella Gardner. CAPP

Lines to a Sophisticate. Mae V. Cowdery. ShDr

Lines to a World-famous Poet Who Failed to Complete a World-famous Poem; or, Come Clean, Mr. Guest! Ogden Nash. OBAL

Lines to Accompany Flowers for Eve. Carolyn Kizer. BoWoP

Lines to an Indian Air. Shelley. *See* I arise from dreams of thee.

Lines to an Old Dress. Mary E. Tucker. CBWP-1

Lines to an Old School-House. Priscilla Jane Thompson. CBWP-2

Lines to Be Embroidered on a Bib; or, The Child Is Father of the Man, but Not for Quite a While. Ogden Nash. FaBoUs

Lines to Caste. Samuel Alfred Beadle. AAP

Lines to Do with Youth. Witter Bynner. PoA

Lines to Emma. Priscilla Jane Thompson. CBWP-2

Lines to Florence. Mary Weston Fordham. CBWP-2

Lines to Mrs. Isabel Peace. Mary Weston Fordham. CBWP-2

Lines to Mrs. M. C. Turner. Eloise Bibb. CBWP-4

Lines to Mother. Rose M. Stein. PWR

Lines to Mount Glen. George Marion McClellan. AAP

Lines to My Grandfathers. Tony Harrison. *Fr.* School of Eloquence, The. NAEL-2; NoAM

Lines to Our Elders. Countee Cullen. CDC

Lines to Ralph Hodgson, Esqre. T. S. Eliot. NBLV; OBAL; PeLV

Lines to Ratclif. The Earl of Surrey. *See* My Ratclif [*or* Ratcliffe], when the retchlesse [*or* retchless *or* rechless] youth offendes.

Lines to the Black Oak. Oliver La Grone. NBV

Lines to the Blessed Sacrament. *Unknown, tr. fr. Irish by* Jeremiah J. Callanan. TIRV

Lines to the Hon. George L. Knox. Eloise Bibb. CBWP-4

Lines Where Beauty Lingers. Franklin P. Adams. OBAL

Lines Written among the Euganean Hills. Shelley. EnRP; GTBS; GTBS-P; PoEL-4

Lines Written at Bridgewater, 27 July 1797, *sels.* John Thelwall. "Day of my double birth, if such the year." NOEC

Lines Written at Cambridge, to W. R., Esquire. Phineas Fletcher. *Fr.* To My Ever-honoured Cousin W. R. Esquire. ElL

Lines Written at the Grave of Alexander [*or* Alexandre] Dumas. Gwendolyn B. Bennett. CDC; PoNe

Lines Written beneath a Picture. Byron. OxBSP

Lines Written by a Bear of Very Little Brain. A. A. Milne. FaBoNo

Lines Written During a Period of Insanity. William Cowper. *Fr.* Task, The. EBEV; FaBoRV; HAP; NOEC; NoP; OAEL-1; OPOP; PPP; Prf

Lines Written during the Time of the Spy System. Charles Lamb. FaBoEH

Lines Written for a Blank Page of "The Keepsake." Winthrop Mackworth Praed. CBLP

Lines Written for Gene Kelly to Dance To. Carl Sandburg. AiP

Lines Written Immediately after Parting from a Lady. Sir Samuel Egerton Brydges. NOEC

Lines Written in a Blank Leaf of the Prometheus Unbound. Thomas Lovell Beddoes. EPCY; OAEL-2

Lines Written in a Lincoln's Inn Boghouse. *Unknown.* FaBoEH

Lines Written in a Mausoleum. Lillian Grant. GoYe

Lines Written in Dejection. W. B. Yeats. NAs

Lines Written in Early Spring. Wordsworth. EnRP; FHYEP; GTBS; GTBS-P; NAEL-2; OAEL-2; PoLF

Lines Written in Her Breviary. St. Theresa of Avila, *tr. fr. Spanish by* Longfellow. AWP

Lines Written in Kensington Gardens. ("In this lone, open glade I lie.") Matthew Arnold. FaBoPP; FHYEP

Sels.
    Calm Soul of All Things! [Make It Mine]. TrPWD; WGRP

Lines Written in Oregon. Vladimir Nabokov. NYBP

Lines Written in Ridicule of Certain Poems. Samuel Johnson. *See* Wheresoe'er I turn my view.

Lines Written in the Album at Elbingerode, in the Hartz Forest. Samuel Taylor Coleridge. OBTV

Lines Written in the Bay of Lerici. Shelley. OAEL-2

Lines Written in the Bay of Lerici. Shelley. NAEL-2; OAEL-2

Lines Written in the Dog-Days. William Woty. NOEC

Lines Written in the Front of a Well-read Copy of Burns's *Songs:* To the Reader. *Unknown.* FaBoUs

Lines Written in Windsor Forest. Pope. EBEV

Lines Written near Linton, on Exmoor. Daniel Hoffman. BXAP

Lines Written Near San Francisco. Louis Simpson. PRA

Lines Written on a Farewell View of the Franconia Mountains at Twilight. H. Cordelia Ray. CBWP-3

Lines Written on a Seat on the Grand Canal, Dublin. Patrick Kavanagh. BIrV; CMoP; InPS; IPY; NOIV

Lines Written on a Very Boisterous Day in May, 1844. John Clare. OxBSP

Lines Written on a Window at The Leasowes. William Shenstone. OxBSP

Lines Written on New Year's Day, *sels.* Wen Cheng-ming, *tr. fr. Chinese by* Jonathan Chaves.

Lines Written on Seeing My Husband's Picture, Painted When He Was Young. Anna Sawyer. ECWP

Lines Written to Console Those Ladies Distressed by the Lines 'Men Never Make Passes, etc.' Ogden Nash. PeLV

Lines Written Under the Influence of Delerium. William Cowper. *See* Hatred and vengeance, my eternal portion.

Lines Written upon a Window-Shutter at Weston. William Cowper. NOEC

Lingam and the Yoni, The. A. D. Hope. MAT; NoAM

Linger not, stranger; shed no tear. Inscription for a War. A. D. Hope. FaBoMA

Lingo. Fred Voss. NGP

Lingua, *sels.* Thomas Tomkis.
    Gordion Knot, The. ElL

Linguist parrot flicked his flowery wings, The. Crinagoras, *tr. fr. Greek by* Alistair Elliot. GrAn

Linin' ub De Hymns, De. Daniel Webster Davis. AAP

Lining Track. *Unknown.* AmFP

Links. Turner Cassity. SM

Links are chance, the chain is fate, The. Mathematics of Love. Michael Hamburger. UnAS

Linnet, The. Robert Bridges. *See* I Heard a Linnet Courting.

Linnet, The. Walter de la Mare. LiTB

Linnet in November, The. Francis Turner Palgrave. EBVV

Linnet in the rocky dells, The. Emily Brontë. HAP; OBNC (My Lady's Grave.) OxAEP-2

Linnet who had lost her way, A. Tenebris Interlucentem. James Elroy Flecker. MoBrPo

Linnets. Larry Levis. LCAP

Linoleum: Breaking Down. Stanley Plumly. AnAn

Linstead Market. *Unknown.* FaBoVe; PBCV

Lint. Rita Dove. TRP

Lintie in a Cage. Alice V. Stuart. OxBS

Lion, The. Hilaire Belloc. MoBrPo; NBLV; WHSW

Lion, The. Mary Howitt. FaPON

Lion, The. Ogden Nash. TLR; WHSW

Lion. Kenneth Rexroth. *Fr.* Bestiary, A. HoPM; OBAL

Lion. May Swenson. LiTM

Lion, The. Ting Mang, *tr. fr. Chinese. Fr.* Sketch of the Zoo, The. LHF, *tr. by* Hualing Nieh

Lion, The. W. J. Turner. MoBrPo

Lion. *Unknown, tr. fr. Hottentot.* PeSA

Lion and Albert, The. Marriott Edgar. OBNV

Lion and his shadow the lioness, The. Girl with Pitcher. Ruth Dallas. PeNZ

Lion and the Cub, The. John Gay. *Fr.* Fables. GN

Lion and the Echo, The. Brian Patten. OBSP

Lion and the unicorn, The. Mother Goose. BoTP; OxBoLi; OxNR; ReMoGo

Lion and the Wave, The. William Allingham. FM

Lion ane his tamer, The. The Crunch. Gerda Mayer. OBSP

Lion Calls All the Beasts to His Parliment. Robert Henryson. *Fr.* Taille of the Sone and Air of the Foxe, The. CBCK

Lion cub, of sordid mind, A. The Lion and the Cub. John Gay. GN

Lion dishonoured bids death come, The. Reversionary. Stevie Smith. FaBoEE

Lion, even when full of mud, with burrs, The. Birds. Ruth Miller. PeSA

Lion for Real, The. Allen Ginsberg. GLP; HCAP; RB

Lion-Hunt, The. Thomas Pringle. OBTV

Lion Hunts. Patricia Beer. OxBTC

Lion in Love, The. Marianne Moore. VBLP

Lion is called the king, The. Lion. Kenneth Rexroth. *Fr.* Bestiary, A. HoPM; OBAL

Lion is never a lion in a royal hunt, A. Lion Hunts. Patricia Beer. OxBTC

Lion is the [*or* a] beast to fight, The. Sir Arthur Quiller-Couch. (Sage Counsel.) NBLV

Lion Named Passion, A. John Hollander. NoAM

Lion of my sun, my fiery joy. Psalm of St. The Priapus. James Richard Broughton. ErPo

Lion of Winter, The. Shakespeare. *See* Now the Hungry Lion Roars.

Lion over the Tomb of Leonidas, The. *Unknown, tr. fr. Greek by* Walter Leaf. AWP

Lion tamers wrestle with the lions in a cage, The. Apex. Nate Salsbury. NBLV

Lion, the Lion, he dwells in the waste, The. The Lion. Hilaire Belloc. MoBrPo; NBLV; WHSW

Lioness whelped, and the sturdy cub, The. The Eagle's Song. Richard Mansfield. PAH

Lions and tigers dominate. Jungle. Mary Carter Smith. PoNe

Lion's Bride, The. Gwen Harwood. BoWoP

Lion's disheveled mane is the color, The. The Lion. Ting Mang, *tr. fr. Chinese. Fr.* Sketch of the Zoo, The. LHF, *tr. by* Hualing Nieh

Lions of fire, The. Kenneth Patchen. VGW

Lions of the hill are gone, The. Deirdre's [*or* Deidre's] Lament for the Sons of Usnach. *Unknown, tr. fr. Irish by* Sir Samuel Ferguson. IIP; NOIV; PeIV

Lion's Skeleton, The. Charles Tennyson Turner. FM; NOBVV

Lions who ate the Christians on the sands of the arena, The. Sunt Leones. Stevie Smith. NoAM

Lip was a man who used his head. J. V. Cunningham. *Fr.* Five Epigrams. OBAL
(Lip.) ErPo

Lip which had once been stolid, now moving, A. Divine Love. Michael Benedikt. AmPA; CoAP

Lipman and Cohen, butchers, Hercules Lane. At the Jaffé Memorial Fountain, Botanic Gardens. Frank Ormsby. CIP

Lipper folk to Cresseid than can draw, The. Robert Henryson. *Fr. Testament of Cresseid, The.* OxBLMV; OxBS; ScCV

Lips, The. (*LL*) The Queen of Night Walks Her Thin Dog. Diane Wakoski. SRLS

Lips and Eyes. Giovanni Battista Marino, *tr. fr. Italian by* Thomas Carew. OBVE; OxBSP

Lips and Nose. Rodney Hall. *Fr.* Owner of My Face, The. CBAP

Lips and tongue. A Hand of Solo. Thomas Kinsella. CIP; NOIV

Lips of the one I love are my perpetual pleasure, The. Hafiz, *tr. fr. Persian by* Peter Avery *and* John Heath-Stubbs. BoLoP (Lord Be Praised, The.) LPA

Lips of the Wise, The. Bible, *O.T. Fr.* Proverbs. TrGrPo

Lips pressed against my heart. (*LL*) Evening Song. Jean Toomer. BPo; CDC

Lips That Touch Liquor. George W. Young. NBLV

Lips That Touch Liquor Shall Never Touch Mine, The. Harriet A. Glazebrook. VPP

Liquidity's a mystery; it's very rarely seen. The Accounting Cat. John Clarke. UV

Liquor, wages, automobiles, women, dope. Elegy for Llywelyn Humphries. Meic Stephens. AngWe

Liquor, you turn us into kings. What Matter? *Gond Oral Tradition, tr. by* V. Elwin *and* S. Hivale. WTO

Lisa's Ritual, Age 10. Grace Caroline Bridges. LoHo

Lisbon. *Unknown.* AmFP

Lisbon Earthquake, The, *sels.* Voltaire, *tr. fr. French by* Tobias Smollet. "Moralist still obstinate replies, The." OBD

Lisbon Packet, The. Byron. NBLV

Lischka stepped down through the pass without a permit. The Myth of Lischka. Sylvia Kantaris. PWE

Lisnagade. *Unknown.* WTO

Lisp of death was always on my father's lips, A. The Light That Made Him Whisper. Jill Young. NGP

Lisping young lady called Beth, A. *Unknown.* PeLi

Lissadell. Matthew Sweeney. IB

Lissom psychotic named Jane, A. *Unknown.* PeLi

List, The. Michael McClure. NU

List, I hear the church bells ring. The Church Bells. Mrs. Henry Linden. CBWP-4

List! list! the sleigh bells peal across the snow. December. H. Cordelia Ray. CBWP-3

List of small deformities passed unrecorded, The. Weather Markings. Siri Hustvedt. PRA

List the harp in window wailing. The Aeolian Harp. Herman Melville. AmPP

List to the sad wind, drearily moaning. Autumn ("List to the sad wind, drearily moaning.") Priscilla Jane Thompson. CBWP-2

List while the poet trolls. The Rival Curates. W. S. Gilbert. PeLV

Listen. Jessica Hagedorn. WPOW

Listen! Lilian Moore. ImGa; NTCP

Listen. Linda Lancione Moyer. CrSp

Listen, and when thy hand this paper presses. A Letter from a Girl to Her Own Old Age. Alice Meynell. FaBoRV; LiTB; MoBrPo

Listen awhile and I here will unfold. The Golden Voyage; or, The Prosperous Arrival of the *James and Mary. Unknown.* OxBSS

Listen awhile ye nations, and be dumb. (*LL*) Great Spirits Now on Earth. Keats. Son

Listen Children. Lucille Clifton. PoBA

Listen . . . / With faint dry sound. November Night. Adelaide Crapsey. ArNa; FaPON; Spl

Listen:/ There roams, far away, by the waters of Clead. Nikolai Gumilev, *tr. fr. Russian by* C. M. Bowra. *Fr.* Giraffe, The. FaPON

Listen!/ My friend. What the Girl Friend Said to the Foster-Mother. Kapilar, *tr. fr. Tamil by* A. K. Ramanujan. PLW

Listen!/ Listen to the witch! Listen! Lilian Moore. ImGa; NTCP

Listen, children:/ Your father is dead. Edna St. Vincent Millay. CrSp; DL; IMW; MeMAP

Listen, Comrades. David Diop, *tr. fr. French by* ELlen Conroy Kennedy. NegPo

Listen, comrades of the flaming centuries. Listen, Comrades. David Diop, *tr. fr. French by* ELlen Conroy Kennedy. NegPo

Listen, for example, to the thudding of the winter stream. An Inconclusive Evening. Frances Bellerby. FaBoTw

Listen, good people, and you shall hear. The Ballad of Barnaby. W. H. Auden. OBNV

Listen — help me! Ears. Sonja Åkesson, *tr. fr. Swedish by* Joanna Bankier. WPOW

Listen here, Joe. Without Benefit of Declaration. Langston Hughes. TTY

Listen I am just like. *Unknown, tr. fr. Japanese by* Kenneth Rexroth *and* Ikuko Atsumi. WPJ

Listen! I will describe the best of dreams. The Dream of the Rood. *Unknown, tr. fr. Anglo-Saxon by* Kevin Crossley-Holland. ASW

Listen! In the April rain. In the April Rain. Mary Anderson. BoTP

Listen! It is the summer's self that ambles. The Good Humor Man. Phyllis McGinley. MoShBr

Listen! I've a big surprise! Invitation. Myra Cohn Livingston. TLR

Listen, listen! The small song bird. Song to Imogen [in Basic English]. Richard Leighton Greene. BXAP

Listen! Listen to shopkeepers talking. Shopkeepers at the Party Meeting. Thomas McCarthy. BiHa; IB

Listen, lively lordings all. The Rising in the North. *Unknown.* ESPB

Listen, Lord — [a Prayer]. James Weldon Johnson. BPo

Listen, mad girl! for giving ear. Walter Savage Landor. CBLP

Listen more often. Breaths. Birago Diop, *tr. fr. French by* Anne Atik. TTY

Listen Mr. Oxford Don. John Agard. NBrP

Listen, my children, and you shall hear. Paul Revere's Ride (The Landlord's Tale). Longfellow. *Fr.* Tales of a Wayside Inn. AiP; AnAmPo; BeLS; BLPA; EBEvV; EBNV; FaBoBe; FaBoTw; FaBV; FaPON; FaPoR; ImGa; OBAL; OBCA; OBNV; PAH; PWR; TFi; TrGrPo; WBLP (Midnight Ride of Paul Revere, The.) VPP

Listen, my children, and you shall hear. *Unknown.* RoPo

Listen, my Dearest, hear the sweet night march! (*LL*) Meditation. Baudelaire. InPK; NAWM-2

Listen, my dearest, once this flesh of mine. Two Hearts Divided. R. Williams Parry, *tr. fr. Welsh by* Joseph P. Clancy. OBWVE

Listen natives of a dry place. The Old Boast. W. S. Merwin. NOBA

Listen, nephew/ When I opened the cantina. The Tale of Sunlight. Gary Soto. NoAM

Listen! Now I have come to step over your soul. Sacred Formula to Destroy Life. *Unknown, tr. by* James Mooney. LiTA

"Listen, now, verse should be as natural." Poetry for Supper. R. S. Thomas. OxBC

Listen old man listen. Sweat-House Ritual No. 1. *Unknown, tr. fr. Omaha Indian by* Jerome K. Rothenberg *from* Alia Fletcher *and* Francis La Flesche. STP

Listen. Put on Morning. W. S. Graham. FaBoTw; LiTM

Listen sweet Dove unto my song. Whitsunday. George Herbert. GeHe

Listen! The garbage pouring down the chutes. For David Shapiro. David Lehman. PoA

Listen, the hay-bells tinkle as the cart. The Holy Innocents. Robert Lowell. InvP; MoAB; MoAmPo; OBCP; OxBC

Listen! The night-raven's song. Nicarchus of Alexandria, *tr. fr. Greek by* Peter Porter. GrAn

Listen. These voices are under attack. Under Attack. Margaret Randall. AIW

Listen to me and you shall hear. The World is Turned Upside Down. *Unknown.* NOSC

Listen to me, as when ye heard our father. Canadian Boat Song. *At. to* John Galt *and also to* "Christopher North." BLPA; FaBoCh; FaPoR; OBEV; OBNC

Listen to the air. John Lame Deer. EaPr

Listen to the binding ties falling away which still hold you from above from below. (*LL*) It's Raining. Guillaume Apollinaire. SOTW, *tr. by* Kenneth Koch; TTTS, *tr. by* Kenneth Koch

Listen to the call of the muezzin. A Denunciation. Mahammed Abdille Hassan, *tr. fr. Somali by* B. W. Andrzejewski. WTO

Listen to the coal. In Memoriam John Coltrane. Michael Stillman. InPK; Jaz

Listen to the exhortation of the dawn! The Salutation of the Dawn. *Unknown.* PoLF

Listen to the Kitchen Clock. The Old Kitchen Clock. Ann Hawkshawe. BoTP

Listen to the phone calls they do not. Metaphor as Illness. Chuck Ortleb. GLP

Listen to the salutation to the dawn. *Unknown, tr. fr. Sanskrit.* EaPr

Listen to the song. Wandering Jack. Emile Jacot. BoTP

Listen to the story of Willie the Weeper. Willie the Weeper. *Unknown.* BeLS; BLPA; OBAL

Listen to the water-mill. The Water Mill. Sarah Doudney. BLPA; WGRP (Lesson of the Water Mill, The.) PoToHe

Listen to Things. Spirits. Birago Diop, *tr. fr. French by* Ellen Conroy Kennedy. NegPo

Listen to this story. This Island Mopsy. Victor Questel. PBCV

Listen, Will You Learn to Hear Me from Afar. Jules Supervielle, *tr. fr. French by* George Bogin. ArLo

Listen/ with the night falling we are saying thank you. W. S. Merwin. EaPr

Listen, you drawing men. Snapshots of the Cotton South. Frank Marshall Davis. PoBA

Listen, you know the pains of love. Meleager, *tr. fr. Greek by* Peter Whigham. PeHV

Listen Zulus. Lalela Zulu. *Unknown, tr. fr. Zulu.* PeSA

Listenen to Big Black at S. F. State. Sonia Sanchez. BPo

Listeners, The. Walter de la Mare. AWP; BLPL; ClHu; CMoP; CoGr; EBEvV; FaPoB; FaPON; GGP; HAP; HeIP; HoPM; ImPo; InPK; InvP; LiTB; LiTM; MoAB; MoBrPo; MoP; NoAM; NOBE; NoP; NTP; OBEV; OBMV; OBSP; OtMeF; OxAEP-2; PlP; Poetr; PoRA; SoSe; TFi; TrGrPo

Listener's Guide to the Birds, A. E. B. White. NYBP

Listening. Aileen Fisher. NTCP

Listening. William Stafford. RFM

Listening for the sound. Pinkie Gordon Lane. BlSi

Listening, listening; it is never still. The Märchen. Randall Jarrell. CMoP

Listening Nydia. H. Cordelia Ray. CBWP-3

Listening only to the lonely present. *(LL)* You delude yourself. Jean-Joseph Rabéarivelo. NegPo

Listening to a Monk from Shu Playing the Lute. Li Po, *tr. fr. Chinese by* Joseph J. Lee. SuSp

Listening to a Wanderer's "Water Melody." Wang Ch'ang-ling, *tr. fr. Chinese by* Joseph J. Lee. SuSp

Listening to Beethoven on the Oregon Coast. Henry Carlile. Poetsp

Listening to Grownups Quarreling. Ruth Whitman. NTCP

Listening to hard bop. Zimmer's Last Gig. Paul Zimmer. Jaz

Listening to Lester Young. William Matthews. Jaz

Listening to Sonny Rollins at the Five-Spot. Paul Blackburn. Jaz

Listening to the Köln Concert. Robert Bly. RaBo

Listening to the Music of Arsenio Rodríguez Is Moving Closer to Knowledge. Victor Hernandez Cruz. UL

Listening-to-the-Rain Studio. Chu Yi-tsun, *tr. fr. Chinese by* Chang Yin-nan *and* Lewis C. Walmsley. SuSp

Listening to the River. Su Tung-p'o, *tr. fr. Chinese by* Robert Payne. TAL

Listening to the Washblock in the Moonlight. Liu Ch'ang-ch'ing, *tr. fr. Chinese by* Dell R. Hales. SuSp

Listening, woman and man. Trial Marriage. Harry Clifton. IB

Listeth, lordes, in good entent [or intent]. Sir Thopas. Chaucer. *Fr.* Canterbury Tales, The. EnVB
　(Sir Thopas's Tale.) NAEL-1
　(Tale of Sir Thopas.) BXAP

Listing Attic, The, *sels.* Edward Gorey.
　"Gift was delivered to Laura, A." CBNP

Listless beauty of the hour, The. History. D. H. Lawrence. RaBo

Listless he eyes the palisades. In the Prison Pen. Herman Melville. PoEL-5; TAP

Listless the silent ladies sit. Music. William Bell Scott. NOBVV

Lists became shorter, The. Making Lists. Gladys Cardiff. HATNAP

Lists of Coventry, The. John Greening. PWE

Lisy's Parting with Her Cat. James Thomson. OFC

Lit by no skill of mine. *(LL)* Milton's Prayer for [or of] Patience. Elizabeth Lloyd Howell. WGRP

Lit Stations, The. Kathy Fagan. UTF

Litanie, The. (Father of heaven, and him, by whom.) John Donne. PoEL-2
　Sels.
　Father, The. NOCV
　Holy Ghost, The. NOCV
　Son, The. NOCV

Litanies, *sels.* Hertha Kräftner, *tr. fr. German by* Beth Bjorklund.

Litanies of Julia Pastrana (1832-1860), The. Thomas W. Shapcott. CBAP; FaBoMA; NOBAu

Litany. G. K. Chesteron. *Fr.* O God of Earth And Altar. OtMeF

Litany: "From a ruler that's a curse." Charles Cotton. OBSV

Litany, A: "Ring out your bells." Sir Philip Sidney. *See* Ring out your bells [or belles], let mourning shows [or shewes] be spread.

Litany: "When the sun rises on another day." Charles Angoff. TrPWD

Litany for All Souls Day. Johann Georg Jacobi, *tr. fr. German by* Philip L. Miller. RiWo

Litany for Dictatorships. Stephen Vincent Benét. OxBA

Litany for Latter-Day Mystics, A. Cale Young Rice. WGRP

Litany for Old Age, A. Una W. Harsen. TrPWD

Litany for Rain, A. John S. Mbiti. EaPr

Litany in Time of Plague, A. Thomas Nashe. *See* Adieu, Farewell, Earth's Bliss[e].

Litany of [or at] Atlanta, A. W. E. B. DuBois. CDC; PoNe

Litany of Sleep., *sels.* Tristan Corbière, *tr. fr. French by* Christopher Pilling.
　"You who snore with your sleeping wife so near." OBVE

Litany of the Dark People, The. Countee Cullen. TrPWD

Litany of the Heroes, *sels.* Vachel Lindsay.
　Lincoln. OHIP

Litany of the Little Bourgeois. Nicanor Parra, *tr. fr. Spanish by* James Laughlin. AnRep

Litany of the Rooms of the Dead. Franz Werfel, *tr. fr. German by* Edith Abercrombie Snow. TrJP

Litany to Our Lady. *Unknown, tr. fr. Irish by* Eugene O'Curry. TIRV

Litany to Satan. Baudelaire, *tr. fr. French by* James Elroy Flecker. AWP

Litany to the Holy Spirit. Robert Herrick. *See* In the hour [or houre] of my distress [or distresse].

Literally thin-skinned, I suppose, my face. Weathering. Fleur Adcock. DiPo

Literary Dinner, A. Vladimir Nabokov. FiBHP; OBAL; PeLV

Literary Importation. Philip Freneau. TAP

Literary Life in the Golden West. Philip Whalen. NAs

Literature and Action. Goronva Camlan. AngWe

Lithe poppies ran like torchmen with the wheat. *(LL)* Poppies in the Wheat. Helen Hunt Jackson.

Litrajure of Everyday Life, The. Michael C. Blumenthal. NoAM

Litter of little black foxes. And later, A. Foxes. Mary Ann Hoberman. SiSoPo

Little. Dorothy Aldis. FaPON; NTCP; WHSW

Little, A. *(LL)* The Ship's Whistle. Tarapada Ray. TSaS, *tr. by* Shyamasree Devi *and* P. Lal

Little Ah Sid. *Unknown.* AS

Little and Great. Charles MacKay. PoLF

Little baby bunting. *(LL)* Lullaby for My Mother. Blaga Dimitrova. VBLP

Little bat, little bat. To the Bat. Edith King. BoTP

Little Beach-Bird, The. Richard Henry Dana. AnAmPo

Little Beauty That I Was Allowed, The. Elinor Wylie. *Fr.* One Person. Son

Little bee returns with evening's gloom, The. A Summer Night in the Beehive. Charles Tennyson Turner. FM

Little Bell. Mary E. Tucker. CBWP-1

Little Bell. Thomas Westwood. GN

Little Benny sat one evening. Misplaced Sympathy. Charles Follen Adams. OBAL

Little Bessie. *Unknown.* AmFP

Little Betty Blue. Betty Blue. Mother Goose. OxNR; ReMoGo

Little Betty Blue. Agnes Grozier Herbertson. BoTP

Little Betty Pringle [or Winckle] she had a pig. Betty Pringle's Pig. Mother Goose. OxNR
　(Dirge, A.) CBNP

Little Big Horn. Ernest McGaffey. PAH

Little Billee. Thackeray. FaBoCh; FaBoCo; NOBL; OHCV; OxAEP-2; PlP

Little Billy. *Unknown.* GBP

Little Billy Breek. *Unknown.* OxNR

Little Birches. Mary Effie Lee Newsome. PoNe

Little Bird, The. Walter de la Mare. NAs

Little Bird, The. Mother Goose. *See* Once I saw a little bird.

Little bird! *(LL)* The Robber Bridegroom. Allen Tate. CBLP

Little Bird, The. *Unknown, tr. by* Rolf Italiaander. PBA

Little bird, The. *Unknown. Fr.* Four Glosses. NOIV

Little bird, a tender bird, A. The Siren Bird. H. Cordelia Ray. CBWP-3

Little bird flew through the dell, A. Autumn Song. Johann Ludwig Tieck, *tr. fr. German by* James Clarence Mangan. AWP

Little Bird I Am, A. Mme Guyon, *tr. fr. French by* T. C. Upham. WGRP

Little bird of paradise. *Unknown.* OxNR

Little bird with truthful throat. My Canary. Josephine D. Henderson Heard. CBWP-4

Little Birds. Jacob Sternberg, *tr. fr. Yiddish by* Joseph Leftwich. TrJP

Little Birds, The. *Unknown.* NTCP

Little birds in a row. Little Birds. Jacob Sternberg, *tr. fr. Yiddish by* Joseph Leftwich. TrJP

Little Birds ("Little birds are playing.") "Lewis Carroll." *Fr.* Sylvie and Bruno Concluded. FaBoNo; OxBoLi; PeLV

Little birds sit in their nest and beg, The. The Little Birds. *Unknown.* NTCP

Little birds sleep sweetly. Evening Song. Cecil Frances Alexander. OHIP

Little Bird's Song, A. Margaret Rose. BoTP

Little birds warble their song in the tree, The. The Bird Song. Mrs. Henry Linden. CBWP-4

Little bit of blowing, A. Thoughts for a Cold Day. *Unknown.* BoTP

Little-Bitty Man. Alfonsina Storni, *tr. fr. Spanish by* Marion Freeman. VBLP

Little bitty man, little bitty man. Little-Bitty Man. Alfonsina Storni, *tr. fr. Spanish by* Marion Freeman. VBLP

Little Black Boy, The. Blake. *Fr.* Songs of Innocence. AWP; CH; EnRP; FHYEP; HeIP; NAEL-2; NAWM-2; NOEC; NoP; OAEL-2; OBEV; OBNC; OxBChV; PeECV; PoE; PoEL-4; PoNe; SCGP; TFi; TrGrPo

Little Black boy. Nigger. Frank Horne. CDC

Little Black Boy's Prayer, A. Guy Tirolien, *tr. fr. French by* Ellen Conroy Kennedy. NegPo

Little Black Bug. Margaret Wise Brown. FaPON; NTCP

Little black bull kem down de medder, De. Hoosen Johnny. *Unknown.* AS; FaPON

Little Black Dog, The. Elizabeth Gardner Reynolds. PoLF

Little black dog ran round the house, The. *Unknown.* OxNR

Little Black-eyed Rebel, The. Will M. Carleton. FaPON; PAH

Little Black Rose, The. Aubrey Thomas De Vere. BIrV

Little Black Rose. *Unknown, tr. fr. Irish by* Thomas Kinsella. NOIV

Little Black Rose shall be red at last!, The. The Little Black Rose. Aubrey Thomas De Vere. BIrV

(Song.) PeIV

Little Black Sheep, The. Paul Laurence Dunbar. WBLP

Little black thing among the snow, A. The Chimney Sweeper ("A little black thing among the snow.") Blake. *Fr.* Songs of Experience. EBEvV; FHYEP; NAEL-2; NAWM-2; NOEC; OAEL-2; PPP; RB; TEP

Little Black Train, The. *Unknown.* AmFP

Little blessed Earth that turns, The. O Earth, Turn! George Johnston. MoCV

Little blood, more or less, he said, A. Great and Strong. Miroslav Holub, *tr. fr. Czech by* George Theiner. RB

Little Blue Apron. *Unknown.* BoTP

Little Blue Ben. *Unknown.* OxNR

Little Blue Ben, who lives in the glen. Little Blue Ben. *Unknown.* OxNR

Little Blue Betty. *Unknown.* OxNR

Little Blue Betty lived in a den. Little Blue Betty. *Unknown.* OxNR

Little Bo-Peep. Mother Goose. *See* Little Bo-Peep has lost her sheep.

Little Bo-Peep,/ Had lost her sheep. The Fairy Sleep and Little Bo-Peep. *Unknown.* BoTP

Little Bo-Peep has lost her sheep. Mother Goose. FaBoBe; OxNR; ReMoGo

(Little Bo-Peep.) WHSW

Little boat with stubby oars, and West Lake's good, A. Tune: "Song of Picking Mulberry" — Recollections of West Lake. Ou-yang Hsiu, *tr. fr. Chinese by* Jerome P. Seaton. SuSp

Little Bob Robin. Bob Robin. Mother Goose. OxNR

Little Bobby Snooks was fond of his books. Bobby Snooks. *Unknown.* ReMoGo

Little Box, The. Vasco [*or* Vasko] Popa, *tr. fr. Serbo-Croatian by* Anne Pennington *and* Charles Simic. CBNP; HSix

Little box grows [gets] her first teeth, The. The Little Box. Vasco [*or* Vasko] Popa, *tr. fr. Serbo-Croatian by* Anne Pennington *and* Charles Simic. CBNP; HSix

Little box which [that] contains the world, The. Last News about the Little Box. Vasco [*or* Vasko] Popa, *tr. fr. Serbo-Croatian by* Charles Simic. AnRep; HSix

Little Boy. Jacob Glatstein, *tr. fr. Yiddish by* Doris Vidaver. BTR

Little boy, The. The Junior Addict. Langston Hughes. BPo

Little Boy Blue. Eugene Field. AnAmPo; BeLS; FaPON; OBAL; OBCA; PoLF; SoSe; VPP

Little Boy Blue. John Crowe Ransom. LiTM

Little Boy Blue, come blow [up] your horn! Mother Goose. BoTP; FaBoBe; OxNR

Little Boy Found, The. Blake. *Fr.* Songs of Innocence. EnRP; FHYEP; NoP

Little boy is fishing, The. The Fisherman. David McCord. PDV

Little boy kneels at the foot of the bed. Vespers. A. A. Milne. OxBChV

Little boy, laid sick and low, A. The Dying Child's Request. Hannah Flagg Gould. OBCA

Little boy, little boy, where wast thou born? Lancashire Born. *Unknown.* GBP

Little Boy Lost, The. Stevie Smith. FaBoTw

Little Boy Lost, A ("Nought loves another as itself.") Blake. *Fr.* Songs of Experience. EnRP; FHYEP; PeECV

Little Boy Lost, The ("Father, father, where are you going?") Blake. *Fr.* Songs of Innocence. EnRP; FHYEP; NoP

Little boy lost in the lonely fen, The. The Little Boy Found. Blake. *Fr.* Songs of Innocence. EnRP; FHYEP; NoP

Little boy on August first night, A. Warren Phinney. Bernadette Mayer. UL

Little boy once played so loud, A. Extremes. James Whitcomb Riley. FaPON

Little Boy, to show his might and power, The. The Metamorphosis. Sir John Suckling. CaPo; FaBoEE

Little boy was looking for his voice, The. The Little Mute Boy. Federico García Lorca, *tr. fr. Spanish by* W. S. Merwin. RB

Little boy went into a barn, A. The Boy in the Barn. *Unknown.* ReMoGo

Little boy who would not say "Thank you" and "If you please," The. *Unknown.* FaBoUs

Little Boy with His Hands Up, The. Yala Korwin. BTR

Little Breeches. John Milton Hay. AnAmPo; BeLS; FaBoBe; VPP

Little Britain. *Unknown.* NOEC

Little Brother, The. James Reeves. OxBTC

Little Brother's Secret. Katherine Mansfield. FaPON; NAs

Little Brown Baby. Paul Laurence Dunbar. NoP; PoNe

Little brown baby wif spa'klin eyes! (*LL*) Little Brown Baby. Paul Laurence Dunbar. NoP; PoNe

Little brown boy. Helene Johnson. CDC; PoBA; ShDr

(Little brown boy.) VBLP

Little brown boy. Helene Johnson. *See* Little brown boy.

Little brown brother, oh! little brown brother. Baby Seed Song. E. Nesbit. FaPON

Little Brown Bulls, The. *Unknown.* AmFP

Little Brown Jug. *At. to* Joseph E. Winner. OBAL

Little Brown Seed. Rodney Bennett. BoTP

Little Brown Seed, The. Harriett Mulford Lothrop. PWR

Little brown squirrel hops in the corn, The. "Orpheus C. Kerr." *Fr.* Rejected "National Hymns," The. OBAL

Little bunches of/ grass pretend they are bushes. Stories from Kansas. William Stafford. RFM

Little buoy said, A, "Mother, deer." A Misspelled Tail. Elizabeth T. Corbett. OBCA

Little by little. Gary Lawless. EaPr

Little by Little. *Unknown.* PWR

Little by little my gender drifts away. Apostrophe to a Dead Friend. Maxine W. Kumin. CAPP

Little Candle. Carl Sandburg. GoYe

Little Car, The. Guillaume Apollinaire, *tr. fr. French.* SOTW, *tr. by* Ron Padgett *and others*

Little cares that fretted me, The. Out in the Fields with God. *At. to* Elizabeth Barrett Browning *and to* Louise Imogen Guiney. BLRP; WBLP; WGRP

(Song from Sylvan, A.) BLPA

Little Carol of the Virgin, A. Lope de Vega. PChr

Little Cat, The. *Unknown, tr. fr. Medieval Latin by* Helen Waddell. CRH

Little Cat Angel, The. Leontine Stanfield. BLPA

Little caterpillar creeps, The. Cocoon. David McCord. OBCA

Little cats walk with their tails up. Confidence. Martha Baird. OFC

Little Chap Who Follows Me, The. *Unknown.* PoToHe

Little Charlie Chipmunk. Helen Cowles LeCron. FaPON

Little Cheat. *Malay Oral Tradition, tr. by* R. J. Wilkinson *and* R. O. Winstedt. WTO

Little child, A. Puer Aeternus. Kathleen Raine. NYBP

Little child, I counsel you that ye. Customs Change. *Unknown.* OxBChV

Little child sat on the floor, A. Where Do School Days End? Josephine D. Henderson Heard. CBWP-4

Little children here ye may lere. Manners at Table When Away from Home. *Unknown.* OxBChV

Little children, never give. Kindness to Animals. *Unknown.* BoTP; FaBoUs; WHSW

Little children you will all go. Song of Man Chipping an Arrowhead. W. S. Merwin. InPK

Little Child's Faith, The. Louis E. Thayer. PoToHe

Little Chisel, The. N. P. van Wyk Louw, *tr. fr. Afrikaans by* Jack Cope *and* Uys Krige. PeSA

Little Clan, The. F. R. Higgins. OBMV

Little Clotilda. *Unknown.* BoTP

Little cock sparrow sat on a green tree, A. Mother Goose. OxNR

(Boy and the Sparrow.) ReMoGo

Little cock sparrow sat on a tree, A. *Unknown.* BoTP

Little colt, A — broncho, loaned to the farm. The Broncho That Would Not Be Broken. Vachel Lindsay. MeMAP

Little cousin is dead, by foul subtraction, The. Dead Boy. John Crowe Ransom. CMoP; FaBoMo; LiTA; MeMAP; Mes; NoAM; NoP; OBD; OxBA; PoE; TwCP

Little Cradle Rocks Tonight in Glory, The. *Unknown.* AmFP

Little hours: two lovers herd upstairs, The. Almost Aubade. Marilyn Hacker. NoAM

Little House, Big House. Medbh McGuckian. PNI

Little house there stood within a glen, A. A Deathbed. John Hawthorn. *Fr.* Journey and Observations of a Countryman, The. NOEC

Little Sir Hugh. *Unknown.* OBET

Little Hundred. *Unknown.* OxNR

Little Hunger. Richard Murphy. BIrV

Little Hymn to Mary, A. *Unknown.* MeEL

Little I ask; my wants are few. Contentment. Oliver Wendell Holmes. *Fr.* Autocrat of the Breakfast Table, The. AmPP; AnAmPo; OxBA; PWR

Little Indian, Sioux, or Crow. Foreign Children. Robert Louis Stevenson. BoTP

Little Infinite Poem. Federico García Lorca, *tr. fr. Spanish by* Robert Bly. RaBo

Little Ink More or Less, A. Stephen Crane. MeMAP

Little inmate, full of mirth. The Cricket. Vincent Bourne, *tr. fr. Latin by* William Cowper. PoLF

Little island whispered over his shoulder. A Wound. Brendan Kennelly. BiHa

Little Jack Dandy-prat. *Unknown.* OxNR

Little Jack Horner/ Sat in a corner. Mother Goose. FaBoEH; OxNR, *orig. and parody;* ReMoGo; SoSe

Little Jack Jelf. Jack Jelf. *Unknown.* ReMoGo

Little Jack Jingle. Jack Jingle. *Unknown.* ReMoGo

Little Jack Sprat/ Once had a pig. *Unknown.* OxNR

Little Jenny Wren. *Unknown.* BoTP; ReMoGo

Little Jesus came to town, The. A Christmas Folk-Song. Lizette Woodworth Reese. FaPON; OBCA; OHIP; TrCP

Little Jesus wast Thou shy. Ex Ore Infantium. Francis Thompson. BoTP; FaBV; OHIP; OxBChV
    (Child's Prayer, A.) OHIP

Little Jew lived in a little straw hut, A. Biography. A. M. Klein. TrJP

Little Jim. Edward Farmer. VPP

Little Jock Elliot. *Unknown.* IBB

Little joe gould has lost his teeth and doesn't know where. E. E. Cummings. NoAM

Little John a Begging. *Unknown.* ESPB

Little John Bottlejohn. Laura E. Richards. PDV

Little John Jiggy Jag. *Unknown.* OxNR

Little John Nobody. *Unknown.* CBNP; OxBoLi

Little Johnny wants to play. (*LL*) Rain, rain, go away. *Unknown.* ISE, diff. vers.; OxNR; ReMoGo; RoPo; SiSoPo

Little Josie buried under the bright moon. Half-Caste Girl. Judith Wright. NALW

Little Jumping Girls, The. Kate Greenaway. FaPON

Little Jumping Joan. Mother Goose. *See* Here am I, little jumping Joan.

Little King Boggen. *Unknown.* ReMoGo

Little King Pippin. Mother Goose. OxNR

Little Kingdom I Possess, A. Louisa May Alcott. AH

Little Kings and Queens of May. For Good Luck. Juliana Horatia Ewing. FaPON
    (Little Kings and Queens of the May.) BoTP

Little Kings and Queens of the May. Juliana Horatia Ewing. *See* Little Kings and Queens of May.

Little Knight, you are amusing. Song of the Enchanters. W. H. Auden. AnAn

Little Knowledge, A. Bible, *O.T. Fr.* Genesis. LPA

Little lad, little lad. *Unknown.* OxNR

Little ladies, white and green. Snowdrops. Laurence Alma-Tadema. BoTP

Little lady lairdie, The. *Unknown.* OxNR

Little Lady Wren. Tom Robinson. FaPON

Little Lamb. Pearl B. Sheridan. BTR

Little lamb, who made thee? The Lamb. Blake. *Fr.* Songs of Innocence. BLPL; BoTP; CH; ChIV-2; EBEvV; EnRP; FaBoBe; FaBoCh; FaPON; FHYEP; GoJo; HeIL; HeIP; ImPo; InPS; LiTB; MeMBP; NAEL-2; NAWM-2; NIP; NOEC; NoP; OAEL-2; OxAEP-2; OxBChV; PoE; Poetr; SoSe; TEP; TFi; TrCP; TrGrPo; TRP; UnPo; WGRP

Little lambs, little lambs. Baby Beds. *Unknown.* BoTP

Little lame tailor, The. The Starling. Robert Buchanan. FM

Little lamps of the dusk. Fireflies. Carolyn Hall. FaPON

Little Learning, A. Pope. *See* Little learning is a dangerous thing, A.

Little learning is a dangerous thing, A. Pope. *Fr.* Essay on Criticism. EBEvV; HAP; HoPM; PoEL-3; PoLF; TrGrPo
    (Little Learning, A.) ChTr; ImPo; LiTB; NOBE

Little less returned for him each spring, A. Anglais Mort a Florence. Wallace Stevens. SAmP

Little Libbie. Julia A. Moore. OBAL

Little Light. Jim Brodey. UL

Little light is going by, A. Firefly. Elizabeth Madox Roberts. GoJo; NTCP; PDV; SiSoPo

Little Lion Face. May Swenson. VBLP

Little lonely child am I, A. The Moon-Child. "Fiona Macleod." CH

Little Love-God, The. Meleager, *tr. fr. Greek by* Walter Headlam. AWP

Little Lucy Lavender. Lucy Lavender. Ivy O. Eastwick. BoTP

Little Lucy Lester. M. Steel. BoTP

Little Lullaby. Irving Feldman. NYBP

Little lute, when I am gone. Richard Corbett [*or* Corbet]. FaBoEE

Little Lyric (of Great Importance). Langston Hughes. NBLV; OBAL

Little Madness in the spring, A. Emily Dickinson. TAP

Little Maid, The. Anna Maria Wells. OBCA

Little Maid and the Cowslips, The. John Clare. BoTP

Little maid, pretty maid,/ Whither goest thou? Mother Goose. OxNR; ReMoGo

Little Man, The. Hughes Mearns. *See* As I was going up the stair.

Little man in coal pit. Putting On Nightgown. *Unknown.* OxNR

Little man of Teheran, A. *Unknown.* RoPo

Little Man That Had a Little Gun, The. "Lewis Carroll." *See* In stature, the Manlet was dwarfish.

Little Man Who Wasn't There, The. Hughes Mearns. FaPON

Little Marg'et sitting in her high hall door. Fair Margaret and Sweet William ("Little Marg'et sitting in her high hall door.") *Unknown.* AmFP

Little marsh-plant, yellow green, A. The Sundew. Swinburne. ELP; NoP; OBNC; PeVV

Little Mary Bell had a fairy in a nut. Long John Brown and Little Mary Bell. Blake. ECEV; RB

Little Men, The. William Allingham. *See* Up the airy mountain.

Little Men, The. Flora Fearne. BoTP

Little Milliner, The. Robert Buchanan. BeLS

Little Mimshi-tiger mixtures. (*LL*) The Mimshi Maiden. Hugh McCrae. NOBAu

Little Miss and Her Parrot. John Marchant. OxBChV

Little Miss Muffet. W. S. Brownlie. PeLi

Little Miss Muffet, *parody. Unknown.* BXAP; FaBoPa

Little Miss Muffet discovered a tuffet. The Embarrassing Episode of Little Miss Muffet. Guy Wetmore Carryl. FaPON; OBCA

Little Miss Muffet/ Sat on a tuffet. Mother Goose. FaBoBe; OxNR; ReMoGo

Little Mr. Browny Bee. Browny Bee. Irene F. Pawsey. BoTP

Little Mistress Comfort got up early one fine day. Mistress Comfort. Elizabeth Gould. BoTP

Little Mohea, The. *Unknown.* AmFP

Little monkey goes like a donkey that means to say, A. A Dog. Gertrude Stein. *Fr.* Tender Buttons. TTTS

Little Moon, The. Longfellow. BoTP

Little Moppet, The. Mother Goose. *See* I had a little moppet.

Little More about the Brothers and Sisters, A. Sharon Scott. JB

Little more kindness and a little less creed, A. World Needs, the. *Unknown.* PoToHe

Little more love for this one, and for each other, A. (*LL*) We seek a renewed stirring of life for the earth. Nancy Newhall. EaPr

Little more tired at the close of the Day, A. Growing Old [*or* Growing Older]. Rollin J. Wells. BLPA; WBLP
    (As We Grow Older.) PoToHe

Little More Traveling Music, A. Al Young. NBV

Little Morning Music, A. Delmore Schwartz. BoNaP; NYBP

Little moths are creeping, The. Interior. Padraic Colum. MoBrPo

Little mountain spring I found, A. The Spring. Rose Fyleman. FaPON

Little Mouse, The. *Unknown.* ReMoGo

Little Musgrave and Lady Barnard. *Unknown.* AmFP; ErPo; ESPB; FaBoBa; InvP; OBET; OxBB

Little mushroome table spred, A. Oberon's Feast. Robert Herrick. CBCK

Little Mute Boy, The. Federico García Lorca, *tr. fr. Spanish by* W. S. Merwin. RB

Little Nancy [*or* Nanny] Etticoat. Mother Goose. ChTr; OxNR

Little Nanny Etticoat. A Candle. Mother Goose. ReMoGo

Little nearer, this time, A. After the Second Operation. Patricia Goedicke. TAP

Little noises of the house, The. During a Bombardment by V-Weapons. Roy Fuller. OxBSP

Little Ode. Paul Goodman. PoA

Little of brilliance did they write or say. The Stricken Average. William Rose Benét. AnAmPo

Little of its loneliness?, A. (*LL*) On the Way. Ho Chi Minh. EaPr, *tr. by* Christopher Jenkins, Tran Khanh Tuget, *and* Hugh Sanh Thong

Little of myself do I remember. Patrizia Cavalli, *tr. fr. Italian by* Robert McCracken. NeIt

Little old-fashioned girl, The. At Grandfather's. Clara Doty Bates. OBCA

Little Old Lady, The. Rodney Bennett. BoTP

Little Old Lady in Lavender Silk, The. Dorothy Parker. NBLV

Little Old Letter. Langston Hughes. SAmP

Little old man of Derby, A. *Unknown.* OxNR; ReMoGo

Little old man of the sea, A. The Ingenious Little Old Man. John Bennett. FaPON

Little Old Sod Shanty. *Unknown.* AmFP; AS

Little old woman, A. Bramble Jam. Irene F. Pawsey. BoTP

Little one, come to my knee! A Night with a Wolf. Bayard Taylor. GN

Little one sleeps in its cradle, The. Walt Whitman. *Fr.* Song of Myself. AmPP; LiTA; MoAmPo, *abr.*; NOBA; OxBA; SAmP; SOTW, (*much abr.*); TrGrPo

Little Ones' A. B. C., The, *sels.* Noël Coward. "A. Stands for Absolutely Anything." NBLV

Little onward lend thy guiding hand, A. Milton. *Fr.* Samson Agonistes. FHYEP; OAEL-1; OxAEP-1; PoEL-3 (Samson before the Prison in Gaza.) FaBoPV

Little Orchids, The. Ai Ch'ing, *tr. fr. Chinese.* LHF, *tr. by* Hualing Nieh

Little orphan, Alice Fell!, The. (*LL*) Alice Fell; or, Poverty. Wordsworth. BeLS; OBNV

Little Orphan Annie. *Unknown.* RoPo

Little Orphant Annie. James Whitcomb Riley. AnAmPo; FaPON; MoShBr; NBLV; OBAL; OBCA; OxBChV; VPP

Little owl few through the night, The. On the Adequacy of Landscape. Wallace Stevens. SAmP

Little Papoose. Hilda Conkling. FaPON

Little, passionately, not at all, A? Villanelle of Marguerites. Ernest Dowson. MoBrPo

Little path dotted with red. Tune: "Treading on Grass." Yen Shu, *tr. fr. Chinese by* James J. Y. Liu. SuSp

Little Peach, The. Eugene Field. AnAmPo; OBAL

Little Peach Blossoms in the Garden. Li Shang-yin, *tr. fr. Chinese by* Eugene Eoyang *and* Irving Y. Lo. SuSp

Little People. Isaac Leibush Peretz, *tr. fr. Yiddish by* Joseph Leftwich. TrJP

Little Pets of Saint Mochua, The. John Irvine. TIRV

Little picks of the roosters, The. Ballad of Black Grief. Federico García Lorca, *tr. fr. Spanish by* John Frederick Nims. STV

Little Picture Catalogue. Novica Tadic, *tr. fr. Serbo-Croatian by* Charles Simic. HSix

Little Pig. *Unknown.* OxNR

Little pig lived in a sty, A. The Greedy Little Pig. Irene F. Pawsey. BoTP

Little Piggies, The. Thomas Hood. BoTP

Little Place, The. Anneliese Wagner. BTR

Little plum/ said the mother to her son. Hansel and Gretel. Anne Sexton. InPS

Little Poll Parrot. *Unknown.* OxNR

Little Polly Flinders. Mother Goose. OxNR; ReMoGo

Little poppies, little hell flames. Poppies in July. Sylvia Plath. FaBoWP; LCAP; NaP; RB

Little Prayer, A. Paul Goodman. LiTA

Little Pretty Bonny Lass, A. *Unknown.* CBLP; ElL

Little pretty Nancy girl. *Unknown.* OxNR

Little pretty nightingale, The. The Nightingale. *Unknown.* TrGrPo

Little priest of Felton, The. Priest of Felton. *Unknown.* OxNR

Little prince of long ago, A. Sons of the King. Joan Agnew. BoTP

Little Pudding. Mary M. Roberts. BXAP

Little Puppy. *Unknown, tr. fr. Navajo Indian by* Hilda Faunce Wetherill. FaPON

Little ragged girl, our ball-boy, A. A Game at Salzburg. Randall Jarrell. NoAM

Little Rain, The. Tu Fu, *tr. fr. Chinese by* L. Cranmer-Byng. FaPON

Little Raindrops. *At. to* Ann Hawkshawe *also to* Jane Euphemia Browne. BoTP; OxBChV

Little Random Creatures, The. *Unknown, tr. fr. Fox Indian by* Armand Schwerner. STP

Little red lark, The. Morning. Ivy O. Eastwick. BoTP

Little Red Riding Hood. Guy Wetmore Carryl. FiBHP

Little red wagon for d black bureaucrat, A. Catechism of d Neoamerican Hoodoo Church. Ishmael Reed. NBV

Little Rhyme and a Little Reason, A. Henry Anstadt. BLRP

Little Roads to Happiness. Wilhelmina Stitch. PoToHe

Little roads to happiness, they are not hard to find, The. Little Roads to Happiness. Wilhelmina Stitch. PoToHe

Little robber girl, you sleep. The Story of Good. Phyllis Janik. IHMS

Little robin grieves, The. When the Snow is on the Ground. *Unknown.* ReMoGo

Little Robin red breast/ I hear you sing your song. Robin Red Breast. Lula Lowe Weeden. CDC

Little Robin Redbreast. *Unknown.* BoTP

Little Robin Redbreast/ Came to visit me. Visitor. *Unknown.* OxNR

Little Robin Redbreast/ Sat upon a rail. Niddle Noddle. Mother Goose. OxNR

Little Robin Redbreast sat upon a tree. Catch. Mother Goose. OxNR; ReMoGo

Little Robin Redbreast sat upon a tree. Little Robin Redbreast. *Unknown.* BoTP

Little room, depressing, old, A. The Tailor. "S. Ansky," *tr. fr. Yiddish by* Joseph Leftwich. TrJP

Little Rose Tree, The. Rachel Field. FaPON

Little saint best fits a little shrine, A. A Ternarie of Littles, upon a Pipkin of Jellie [*or* Jelly] Sent to a Lady. Robert Herrick. BeJo; FaBoCh; FaBoUs; GoJo; PoEL-3 (Littles.) BoTP

Little Sally Water. *Unknown.* RoPo

Little Sally Waters, *sl. diff. vers. Unknown.* AmFP, 2 *vers.*

Little Sam Clemens, one night back in Hannibal, The. Last Laugh. Robert Penn Warren. MT

Little scavenger away. Flute Song. Hilda Doolittle ("H. D."). AnAmPo

Little Scotch-ee. *Unknown.* AS

Little sharp vexations, The. The Unfailing One. Phillips Brooks. BLRP

Little Shoes That Died, The. Mary Gilmore. NOBAu

Little Shon a [*or* Johnny] Morgan, shentleman [*or* gentleman] of Wales. Shon a Morgan. *Unknown.* GBP; OxNR

Little Shroud, The. Letitia Elizabeth Landon. VPP

Little Shrub Growing By, A. Ben Jonson. BeJo; EnRePo

Little Sleep's-Head Sprouting Hair in the Moonlight. Galway Kinnell. InPS; LCAP

Little Sleep's-Head Sprouting Hair in the Moonlight. Galway Kinnell. LCAP

Little slender lad, toad-headed. The Ambrosia of Dionysus and Semele. Robert Graves. NYBP

Little Snail. Hilda Conkling. FaPON; SiSoPo

Little snail,/ Dreaming you go. Snail. Langston Hughes. FaPON

Little snatch of an ancient song. Of an Old Song. William E. H. Lecky. WGRP

Little Son. Georgia Douglas Johnson. CDC

Little Song. Langston Hughes. TLR

Little Song, A. Charles O. Hartman. SM

Little Song of Life, A. Lizette Woodworth Reese. FaPON; OBCA

Little Song of the Maimed. Benjamin Péret, *tr. fr. French by* David Gascoyne. OBWP; PeFWW

Little Song of Work, A. Sarah Elizabeth Sprouse. BLRP

Little songs of summer are all gone today, The. End-of-Summer Poem. Rowena Bastin Bennett. FaPON

Little soul of little Ronsard. To His Soul. Pierre de Ronsard, *tr. fr. French by* Philip L. Miller. RiWo

Little soul so sleek and smiling. The Emperor Hadrian to His Soul. Emperor Hadrian, *tr. by* Stevie Smith. OBVE

Little sound, A. Many a Mickle. Walter de la Mare. FaBV

Little Sparrow. *Unknown.* AmFP

Little sparrows, The. William Carlos Williams. SAmP; TwCP

Little spinner, you are too clever. Birth-Prospectus; the End of Us. Peter Riley. VaA

Little sycamore, The. *Unknown, tr. fr. Egyptian by* J. E. Manchip White. TTY

Little Talk. Aileen Fisher. FaPON

Little Te Deum of the Commonplace, A, *sels.* John Oxenham. We Thank Thee, Lord. WBLP "With hearts responsive." TrPWD

Little Tee-wee. *Unknown.* OxNR

Little Testament. Eugenio Montale, *tr. fr. Italian by* William Arrowsmith. AnAn

Little Things. *At. to* Julia A. Fletcher Carney. BLPA; BLPL; FaBoBe; FaPON; OxBChV

Little Things, The. Elizabeth Isler. PoToHe

Little Things. Eileen Mathias. BoTP

Little Things. John Orrick. PoToHe

Little Things. James Stephens. FaPON; GoJo; MoBrPo; PDV; PoRA

Little Things. *Unknown.* PoToHe

Little Things That Happen, The. Marjorie Wilson. BoTP

Little things, that run, and quail. Little Things. James Stephens. FaPON; GoJo; MoBrPo; PDV; PoRA

Little thinkest thou, poor ant, who there. The Ant. Richard Flecknoe. NOSC

Little thinks, in the field, yon red-cloaked clown. Each and All. Emerson. AmPP; AnAmPo; AWP; BLPL; MeMAP; NAAL-1; NOBA; OxBA; TAP; WGRP

Little think'st thou, poor [or poore] flower. The Blossom [or Blossome]. John Donne. AWP; ESCV; ImPo; LiTB; MeLP; NAEL-1; SCGP; SeCP; UnPo

Little time for laughter, A. After. Philip Bourke Marston. NOBVV

Little toe, big toe, three toes between. Close Quarters. John Banister Tabb. OBAL

Little toe is attractive, The. The Time of Man. Phyllis Webb. MoCV

Little Tom Tittlemouse/ Lived in a bell-house. Unknown. OxNR

Little Tommy [or Tom] Tucker. Tommy Tucker. Mother Goose. OxNR; ReMoGo

Little Tommy Tacket. Unknown. OxNR

Little Tommy Tadpole began to weep and wail. Growing Up. C. J. Dennis. ZA

Little Tommy Tiddler. Paul Edmonds. BoTP

Little Tommy Tittlemouse/ Lived in a little house. Mother Goose. OxNR (Tommy Tittlemouse.) ReMoGo

Little Tommy Yesterday. Alex Glasgow. OBET

Little too abstract, a little too wise, A. Return. Robinson Jeffers. EaPr; GoYe

Little toy dog is covered with dust, The. Little Boy Blue. Eugene Field. AnAmPo; BeLS; FaPON; OBAL; OBCA; PoLF; SoSe; VPP

Little tree. E. E. Cummings. Fr. Chansons Innocentes. NTCP; OBCP; PChr; PDV

Little trotty hetty coat. Unknown. FaBoVe

Little Trotty Wagtail. John Clare. BoTP; FaPON; NTP; RB; SCGP; UnPo

Little Tumescence, A. Jonathan Williams. ErPo; NeAP; PoM

Little Turtle, The. Vachel Lindsay. FaPON; GoJo; NTCP; OBAL; OBCA; OBSP; PDV; SiSoPo

Little twig that Byron planted here, The. Byron's Oak at Newstead Abbey. Timothy Thomas Fortune. AAP

Little Vagabond, The. Blake. Fr. Songs of Experience. FHYEP; NBLV; OBSV

Little Viennese Waltz. Federico García Lorca, tr. fr. Spanish by William B. Logan. SOTW

Little Village, A. Mei Yao Ch'en, tr. fr. Chinese by Jonathan Chaves. SuSp

Little While, a Little While, A. Emily Brontë. EnVR; MeMBP; OBNC

Little while I still would linger here, A. (LL) Little while (my life is almost set!), A. Paul Hamilton Hayne. AnAmPo

Little while (my life is almost set!), A. Paul Hamilton Hayne. AnAmPo

Little while, that in me sings no more, A. (LL) What Lips My Lips Have Kissed. Edna St. Vincent Millay. BoLoP; FaBoBl; HeIL; HeIP; HoPM; LiTA; MeMAP; MoAB; MoAmPo; NAAL-2; NIP; PrIm; Son

Little Whistler, The. Frances Frost. PDV

Little white clouds are racing over the sky, The. Magdalen Walks. Oscar Wilde. EBVV; MoBrPo

Little white lilies, The. Widows' Rice. Okkur Macattanar, tr. fr. Tamil by A. K. Ramanujan. PLW

Little white mermaidens live in the sea, The. The Mermaidens. Laura E. Richards. OBCA

Little White Schoolhouse Blues. Florence Becker Lennon. PoNe

Little wild bird sometimes at my ear, A. Ballata: Of True and False Singing. Unknown, tr. fr. Italian by Dante Gabriel Rossetti. AWP

Little wild birds have come flying, The. Unknown, tr. fr. Russian by W. R. S. Ralston. AWP

Little Willie. Gerald Massey. VPP

Little Willie ("Little Willie from his mirror.") Unknown. MoShBr

Little Willie ("Willie saw some dynamite.") Unknown. FaPON

Little Wind. Kate Greenaway. GoJo

Little wind, blow off the rain. (LL) Little Wind. Kate Greenaway. GoJo

Little Word, The, sl. diff, 2 sts. only. Unknown. PWR

Little Words. Benjamin Keech. PoToHe

Little Work, A. George Du Maurier. Fr. Trilby. FaBoBe; PoLF

Little work, a little play, A. Unknown. PoToHe

Little world in folio, The. (LL) Home Travel. Joseph Hall. CBLP

Little Wren, A. Priscilla Jane Thompson. CBWP-2

Little Wren of tender mind, The. The Wren. Unknown. OxBChV

Little yellow buttercup, A. A Buttercup. Unknown. BoTP

Little young lambs, oh! why do you stay. The Wolf and the Lambs. Ivy O. Eastwick. BoTP

Littleblood. Ted Hughes. Fr. Crow. FF; PoE

Littles. Robert Herrick. See Little saint best fits a little shrine, A.

Liu Ch'e. Ezra Pound. OBVE; VGW

Live Acts. Charles Bernstein. UL

Live all thy sweet life thro.' A Summer Wish. Christina Rossetti. OBNC

Live Blindly. Trumbull Stickney. LiTA

Live Christ. John Oxenham. BLRP

Live ever here, Lorenzo? — shocking thought! Edward Young. Fr. Night Thoughts. EnRP

Live, Evil Veil. John Wheelwright. ChIV-1

Live fowl squatting on the grapefruit and bananas, The. Jamaican Bus Ride. A. S. J. Tessimond. OBTV; OxBTC

Live in these conquering leaves; live all the same. Richard Crashaw. Fr. Flaming Heart, The. LiTB; NAEL-1; OAEL-1, abr; OxAEP-1; PoEL-2; SeCV-1; TEP

Live large, man, and dream small. (LL) Lore. R. S. Thomas. OxBC; RB

Live, live with me, and thou shalt see. To Phyllis, to Love and Live with Him. Robert Herrick. CaPo

Live so that you. Certain Maxims of Archy. Don Marquis. OBAL

Live storm went through last night, The. Glad at the Cold (1955). Alan Dugan. NoAM

Live thy Life,/ Young and old. The Oak. Tennyson. FaPON; PFP

Live to that point I will, for which I am man. Ben Jonson. Fr. Epistle Answering to One That Asked to Be Sealed of the Tribe of Ben, An. OBF

Liveliest effigy of the human race. Ralph Chubb. Fr. Book of God's Madness, The. PeHV

Lively lark stretched forth her wing, The. Edward de Vere, Earl of Oxford. NoSic

Lively young turtle lived down by the banks, A. The Song of the Turtle and the Flamingo. James Thomas Fields. GN (Turtle and Flamingo, The.) AnAmPo

Liverockie, liverockie lee. The Lark. Unknown. GBP

Liverpool. Unknown. AmFP

Liverpool Girls. Unknown. OxBSS

Liverpool John. Phil and June Colclough and June Colclough. OxBSS

Lives. Derek Mahon. PBCIP

Lives. Henry Reed. BoNaP; LiTB

Lives ago, years past generations. Being the Third Song of Urias. Ken Smith. PWE

Lives and Times of John Keats, Percy Bysshe Shelley, and George Gordon Noel, Lord Byron, The. Dorothy Parker. Fr. Pig's-Eye View of Literature, A. NALW

Lives and times of Oedipus and Elektra, The. This One's on Me. Phyllis Gotlieb. MoCV; NOBC

Lives but in its own excess. (LL) For mercy, courage, kindness, mirth. Laurence Binyon. BoTP; MoBrPo

Lives in winter. Unknown. NTCP (Icicles, An.) ReMoGo

Lives of all that ever breathed most worthy the envying. (LL) First Love. Thomas Campion. GBL; OxBoLi

Lives of Great Men. Unknown.

Lives of great men all remind us. Life. Longfellow. Fr. Psalm of Life, A. FaBoBe; GN; OBCA; PoLF; PrIm; TAP; VPP; WBLP

Lives of great men all remind us/ As their pages o'er we turn. Lives of Great Men. Unknown. (After Longfellow.) NOBL

Lives of the Great Composers. Dana Gioia. EOEF

Lives of the Poets., sels. Richard O'Connell.

Lives there on Earth to whom I am unknown. Gilbert West. Fr. Triumphs of the Gout, The. ECEV

Lives thirteen floors above and runs a practice. Doctor Type. Wayne Koestenbaum. PFL

Livid sky on London, A. The Old Song. G. K. Chesteron. FaBoTw

Living, A. D. H. Lawrence. RFM

Living. Denise Levertov. PWE; VGW; WPE

Living. Harold Monro. ImPo; LiTB

Living, The. Robert Pinsky. NoAM

Living. Unknown. BLPA; FaBoBe

Living and dying. (LL) A Grammarian's Funeral. Robert Browning. NAEL-2; NOBVV; PeECV; WGRP

Living and Dying Prayer for the Holiest Believer in the World, A. Augustus Montague Toplady. See Rock of ages, cleft for me.

Living Apart. Maura Stanton. NAmP90

Living between heaven and earth. Tune: "Sprig of Flowers, A" — Written for My "Ugly Studio." Chung Ssu-ch'eng, tr. fr. Chinese by Sherwin S. S. Fu. SuSp

Living by the Red River. James Wright. NNaP

Living Color. Laurie Sheck. BAP-91

Living death is your piteous lot, A. (LL) 'Nkongane. W. C. Scully. PeSAV

Living God, The. Charlotte Perkins Gilman. WGRP

Living God, The. Abraham ibn Ezra, *tr. fr. Hebrew by* Alice Lucas. TrJP

Living God, The. Daniel ben Judah, *tr. fr. Hebrew by* Israel Zangwill. TrJP

Living God O magnify and bless, The. The Living God. Daniel ben Judah, *tr. fr. Hebrew by* Israel Zangwill. TrJP

Living here. *Unknown, tr. fr. Sanskrit by* W. S. Merwin *and* J. Moussaieff Masson. UnAS

Living in a Riverside Village — Miscellaneous Impressions, *sels.* Yang Chi, *tr. fr. Chinese by* Jonathan Chaves.

Living in a wide landscape are the flowers. Desert Flowers. Keith Douglas. FaBoTw

Living in Exile at Ch'ien-nan. Huang T'ing-chien, *tr. fr. Chinese by* Michael E. Workman. SuSp

Living in its shell. Conch. Raymond Queneau. OBD

Living in Master Fang's Garden, *sels.* Yang Chi, *tr. fr. Chinese by* Jonathan Chaves.

Living in retirement beyond the World. The Valley Wind. Lu Yün, *tr. fr. Chinese by* Arthur Waley. ArNa

Living in Sin. Adrienne Rich. FF; IHMS; NIP; NoP; NYBP; Poetr; SoSe; TAP; UnPo

Living in the Barn. Robin Becker. ETG

Living in the Cave. Adrienne Rich. AnAn

Living in the Country at Kou-ch'ü in Autumn — Miscellaneous Impressions, *sels.* Yang Chi, *tr. fr. Chinese by* Jonathan Chaves.

Living in the earth-deposits of our history. Power. Adrienne Rich. NALW; TAP

Living in the La Brea Tar Pits. Nancy Vieira Couto. PBCAP

Living in the Mountains. Tai Shu-lun, *tr. fr. Chinese by* William H. Nienhauser. SuSp

Living in the North one gets used to the cold nights. The North. Brian Higgins. IHNG

Living in the sea and drifting. The Seaweed. Ai Ch'ing, *tr. fr. Chinese. LHF, tr. by* Hualing Nieh

Living in the Summer Mountains. Yü Hsüan-chi, *tr. fr. Chinese by* Kenneth Rexroth *and* Ling Chung. WPC

Living in the Woods, *sels.* Wang Chiu-ssu, *tr. fr. Chinese by* Jonathan Chaves.

Living Juliet, The. Shakespeare. *See* He jests at scars [that never felt a wound].

Living long is containing. Rosina Alcona to Julius Brenzaida. Judith Wright. NALW

Living man is blind and drinks his drop, A. W. B. Yeats. *Fr.* Dialogue of Self and Soul, A. RaBo

Living Memory. Adrienne Rich. BAP-90; TRP

Living Mirror, The. Jason Shinder. UTF

Living mother-of-pearl of a salmon, The. A Hazel Stick for Catherine Ann. Seamus Heaney. NoAM

Living Near the Plaza of Thieves. Leslie Ullman. PBCAP

Living paradise of flowers, land of honey. Merioneth. John Machreth Rees, *tr. fr. Welsh by* Kenneth Hurlstone Jackson. OBWVE

Living Pearl, A. Kenneth Rexroth. LiTM

Living quality of, The. Haymaking. William Carlos Williams. *Fr.* Pictures from Brueghel. NoAM

Living Room. Michael Heffernan. NGP

Living Room, The. Gjertrud Schnackenberg. FYAP

Living someplace else is wrong. The Spring Offensive of the Snail. Marge Piercy. TAP

Living Tenderly. May Swenson. OBCA

Living Together. Jean Valentine. LCAP

Living Truth, The. Sterling Plumpp. PoBA

Living with Children. Jim Wayne Miller. GOYP

Living with the Boss. Ken Smith. NBrP

Living with You. Angela Langfield. FF

Livings, *sels.* Philip Larkin.
Seventy Feet Down. RB

Liza! call dat chile. Meal Time. Maggie Pogue Johnson. CBWP-4

Liza in the Summer Time (She Died on the Train). *Unknown.* AS

Liza Jane. *Unknown.* AS

Lizard. Jerome Kielly. PeIV

Lizard. D. H. Lawrence. NTP; RB

Lizard, The. Rona Murray. NOBC

Lizard. Grace Nichols. OBAP

Lizard. Bundgård Povlsen, *tr. fr. Danish by* Poul Borum. TSaS

Lizard, The. Theodore Roethke. GrPl

Lizard ran out on a rock and looked up, listening, A. Lizard. D. H. Lawrence. NTP; RB

Lizards and Snakes. Anthony Hecht. FaBoMo; TwCP

Lizards in Sardinia. Eamon Grennan. BiHa

Lizie Lindsay. *Unknown.* ESPB, A *and* B *vers.*

Lizie Wan. *Unknown.* AmFP

Lizie Wan sits at her father's bower door. *Unknown. See* Fair Lucy was sitting in her own cabin door.

Lizie. Nancy Vieira Couto. PBCAP

Lizzie and Joe Catch a Thief. Edward Cordle. PBCV

Lizzie and Joe in Court. Edward Cordle. PBCV

Lizzie Borden took an axe. *Unknown.*
(Crimes of Lizzie Borden, The.) FaBoCo

Lizzie Discourses on the Small-Pox. Edward Cordle. PBCV

Llama, The. Hilaire Belloc. FaBoCh; FaBoNo; FiBHP

Llanafan Unrevisited. T. Harri Jones. AngWe

Llangollen Vale., *sels.* Anna Seward.
"Now with a vestal lustre glows the Vale." PeHV

Llanrhaeadr Ym Mochnant. R. S. Thomas. AngWe

Llewellyn and the Tree. E. A. Robinson. BeLS

Lloyd George. *Unknown. See* Count not his broken pledges as a crime.

Lloyd George and Woodrow Wilson and Clemenceau. A Legend of Versailles. Melvin B. Tolson. BPo

Llyn y Gadair. T. H. Parry-Williams, *tr. fr. Welsh by* Anthony Conran. OBWVE

LMFBR. Gary Snyder. PoM

Lo! above the mournful chanting. Kol Nidra. Joseph Leiser. TrJP

Lo, alas, I look and seek. The Ageing Hunter. Avane, *tr. fr. Eskimo.* WTO

Lo & behold. Yes, peat bogs. Landscape for the Disappeared. Yusef Komunyakaa. NGP

Lo, as a careful housewife runs to catch. Shakespeare. *Fr.* Sonnets. SCGP

Lo as I pause in the alien vale of the airport. Twenty-third Flight. Earle Birney. HeIP; OxBC

Lo! As the Potter Mouldeth. *Unknown, tr. fr. Hebrew by* Elsie Davis. TrJP

Lo! Beauty flashed forth sweetly; from his eyes. Meleager, *tr. fr. Greek by* Sydney Oswald. PeHV

Lo, between the Myrtles Standing. Ann Griffiths, *tr. fr. Welsh by* H. Idris Bell. OBWVE

Lo! Death has reared himself a throne. The City in the Sea *or* The Doomed City. Poe. AmPP; AnAmPo; LiTA; MAT; MeMAP; NAAL-1; NOBA; NoP; OxBA; PoE; PoEL-4; SCV; TAP; TFi; TrGrPo; TRP

Lo, fainter now lie spread the shades of night. Morning Hymn. St. Gregory the Great, *tr. fr. Latin by* Edward Caswell. WGRP

Lo, for I to myself am unknown, now in God's name what must I do? Jalal al-Din Rumi, *tr. fr. Persian by* R. A. Nicholson. TOF

Lo! Freedom comes. Th' prescient Muse foretold. Phillis Wheatley. *Fr.* Liberty and Peace. AiP; BlSi

Lo from our loitering ship. Iceland First Seen. William Morris. OBTV

Lo here hath been dawning. Morning. Thomas Carlyle. PWR

Lo here I am lord, whither wilt thou send me? To Christ. William Alabaster. NoSic

Lo here I sit at holy head. Holyhead, Sept. 25th, 1727. Swift. BIrV
(Lo here I sit at Holyhead.) NOIV

Lo here I sit at Holyhead. Swift. *See* Lo here I sit at holy head.

Lo! Here the Gentle Lark. Shakespeare. *Fr.* Venus and Adonis. BeLS; ChTr

Lo! the gentle lark, weary of rest. Lo! Here the Gentle Lark. Shakespeare. *Fr.* Venus and Adonis. BeLS; ChTr
(Death of Adonis, The.) NoSic

Lo, here the state of every mortal wight. Respice Finem. Thomas Proctor. NoSic

Lo! here we come a-reaping, a-reaping. George Peele. *Fr.* Old Wives' [*or* Wife's] Tale, The. TrGrPo

Lo here, within the waters liquid womb. Third Day. Thomas Traherne. *Fr.* Meditations on the Six Days of the Creation. ChIV-1

Lo, how a rose is growing. *Unknown, tr. fr. German by* Gracia Grindal. GePo

Lo, how I seek and sue to have. Sir Thomas Wyatt. SiPS

Lo! how the lark soars upward and is gone. The Death of Leander. Thomas Hood. *Fr.* Hero and Leander. EnRP

Lo how the sailor in a stormy night. Sonnet: on Loss. Sir Robert Ayton. NOSC

Lo! Hymen passes through th' admiring crowds. *Unknown.* ECWP

"Lo, I am black but I am comely too." The Dark Brother. Lewis Alexander. CDC

Lo! I am come to autumn. Gold Leaves. G. K. Chesteron. OxBTC

Lo, I Am Stricken Dumb. *Unknown, tr. by* Theodor H. Gaster. *Fr.* Dead Sea Scrolls, The. TrJP

Lo, I have given thee wings wherewith to fly. To Kuvos. Theognis, *tr. fr. Greek by* G. Lowes Dickinson. PeHV

Locked In. Ingemar Leckius, *tr. fr. Swedish.* TSaS, *tr. by* May Swenson

Locked in Hippomenes' kisses. Paulus Silentiarius, *tr. fr. Greek by* Sam Hamill. InMo

Locked lagoon is ice, the lake beyond, The. Double Mock Sonnet. Charles O. Hartman. SM

Locked up in mother's chamber. *(LL)* Yankee Doodle. *At.* to Richard Shuckburg *and to* Edward Bangs. AmFP; AnAmPo; ChTr; FaPON; GBP; OBAL; OxNR, 4 *ll.*

Locket, The. John Montague. BiHa; PBCIP

Locking the Church. David Scott. PWE

Lockless Door, The. Robert Frost. NOBA

Locks. Kenneth Koch. CoAP

Locks and Bolts. *Unknown.* OBET

Locksley Hall. (Comrades, leave me here a little, while as yet 'tis early morn.) Tennyson. BLPL; EBEV; EBVVPR; EnVR; FaBoBe; ImPo; NAEL-2; OAEL-2
Sels.
For I Dipped [*or* Dipt] into the Future. PoLF
(Lines.) PAW
(Prophecy.) WBLP
"In the Spring." BoNaP
"Not in vain the distance beacons. Foreward, forward let us range." FaBoEH

Locksley Hall Sixty Years After, *sels.* Tennyson.
"Chaos! Cosmos! Cosmos, Chaos! who can tell how all will end?" FaBoEH

Locrine, *sels. At.* to Charles Tilney.

Locus, The. Cid Corman. VGW

Locus. Robert Hayden. FYAP

Locust, The. *Unknown, tr. fr. Malagasy.* FaPON, *tr. by* Frank Cushing; OBAP, *tr. by* A. Marre *and* Willard R. Trask; RB, *tr. by* A. Marre *and* Willard R. Trask

Locust, locust, playing a flute. The Coyote and the Locust. *Unknown.* AWP

Locust Tree in Flower, The. William Carlos Williams. SOTW; Spl; TTTS

Locust Trees. Margaret L. Thomas. ShDr

Locusts, or Appolyonists, The, *sels.* Phineas Fletcher.
"Of Men, nay Beasts: worse, Monsters: worst of all." SeCV-1
"Porter to th' infernal[l] gate is Sin, The." NOSC
"Say Muses, say; who now in those rich fields." ChIV-1

Lodestoned salmon, hurtling, The. Weir Bridge. Padraic Fallon. CIP

Lodgepole/ cone/seed waits for fire. Gary Snyder. *Fr.* Myths and Texts. NaP

Lodging for the Night, A. Elinor Wylie. ErPo

Lodging-House Fuchsias, The. Thomas Hardy. OxBSP

Lodging with the Old Man of the Stream. Po Chü-i, *tr. fr. Chinese by* Arthur Waley. AWP

Loe! formest of a rout that followd him. Virgil, *tr. by* the Earl of Surrey. *Fr.* Aeneid [*or* Eneados], The. NAWM-1; OBVE

Loe here a little volume but great booke. An Ode Which was Prefixed to a Prayer Booke Given to a Young Gentlewoman. Richard Crashaw. ESCV

Loe here the precious dust is laid. Epitaph on Maria Wentworth. Thomas Carew. PoEL-3

Loew's Bridge: A Broadway Idyl. (For hours I stood upon the bridge.) Mary E. Tucker. CBWP-1
Sels.
"Our City rulers pass in grand array." AmWP

Loft. Michael Dransfield. CBAP

Lofty elm-trees darkly dream, The. The Rookery at Sunrise. "Fiona Macleod." *Fr.* Transcripts from Nature. FM

Lofty ship from Salcombe came, A. The Salcombe Seaman's Flaunt to the Proud Pirate. *Unknown.* ChTr

Lofty trees, ten thousand or more trunks. Enjoying Coolness. Wang Wei, *tr. fr. Chinese by* Hugh M. Stimson. SuSp

Lofty young squire from Portsmouth he came, A. The Golden Glove. *Unknown.* AmFP

Log Jam, The. William Henry Drummond. NOBC

Logan at Peach Tree Creek. Hamlin Garland. PAH

Logan Braes. John Mayne. OxBS; ScCV

Loggia, The. Liz Cashdan. NWP

Logging. Gary Snyder. *Fr.* Myths and Texts.

Logic. *Unknown.* FaBoUs

Logic does well at school. Scholars. Walter de la Mare. NoAM; Poetr

Logical Song, A. *Unknown.* ErPo

Logic's hard lines have pressed. Judging Lear. Libby Houston. NBrP

Logitek 100. Spring Fever. Vuyelwa Carlin. NWP

Logs, at the door, by the fence; broadcast over the paddock. B. E. Baughan. *Fr.* Bush Section, A. PeNZ

L'Oiseau Bleu. Mary Elizabeth Coleridge. BoTP

Loitering With a Vacant Eye. A. E. Housman. *Fr.* Shropshire Lad, A. FaPoB; SoSe

Loke that none of you departe. Peniarth Poet, The. *Fr.* Drinking Song, A. AngWe

Lolek. John Jordan. TIRV

Lollay, Lollay, Littel Child. *Unknown.* EnVB

Lollay, lollay, littel child, why wepestow so sore? Lollay, Lollay, Littel Child. *Unknown.* EnVB
(Adult Lullaby, An.) MeEL

Lollingdon Downs. John Masefield. LiTB, I–XV
Sels.
Choice, The. MoAB; MoBrPo
"Here in the self is all that men can know." AWP
"I could not sleep for thinking of the sky." LiTM
"Night is on the downland, on the lonely moorland." GoYe; LiTM
(Night on the Downland.) MoBrPo

Lollipop Lady. John Agard. OTCP

Lollipops of the Pomeranian Baroque. James Fenton. PeLV

Lollocks. Robert Graves. ChTr; RB

Lolotte, who attires my hair. Noblesse Oblige. Jessie Redmond Fauset. CDC; VBLP

London ("I wander through each chartered street.") Blake. *Fr.* Songs of Experience. AWP; ChTr; ClHu; CoGr; EnRP; FaBoPP; FaBoPV; FF; FHYEP; GGP; HAP; HeIL; HeIP; InPK; InPS; LiTB; MAT; MeMBP; Mes; NAEL-2; NAWM-2; NIP; NOBE; NoP; OAEL-2; OBNC; OxAEP-2; PlP; PoE; PoEL-4; Poetr; PrIm; RB; SCGP; SCV; TEP; TFi; TRP; UnPo; WeW

London ("There souls of men are bought and sold.") Blake. *Fr.* Human Image, The. ChTr

London. John Davidson. MeMBP; NOBE; OBNC

London. Daniel Defoe. *Fr.* Reformation of Manners. NOEC

London. Samuel Johnson. PoEL-3; TEP

London. John Oldham. *Fr.* Satyr, A. NOSC

London. J. R. Rowland. CBAP

London: A Poem in Imitation of the Third Satire of Juvenal. Samuel Johnson. PoEL-3; TEP
Sels.
"By numbers here from shame or censure free." NOEC; OBSV; OxAEP-1
(Poverty in London.) ChTr
"Prepare for death, if here at night you roam." OAEL-1

London Adulterations. *Unknown.* OBET

London after the Great Fire, 1666. Dryden. *See* Methinks already, from this chymick flame.

London at Night. John Gay. *Fr.* Trivia; or, The Art of Walking the Streets of London. FaBoPP

London Bells. *Unknown. See* Gay go up and gay go down.

London Birds: a Lollipop. John Heath-Stubbs. *Fr.* Two Wedding Songs. NTP

London Bridge. Mother Goose. CBNP; CH; ChTr; FaBoVe, *diff. vers.*; GBP; OxBoLi; OxNR, *diff. vers.*; ReMoGo

London Bridge Is a-Burning Down. *Unknown.* AmFP

London Bridge is broken down. London Bridge. Mother Goose. CBNP; CH; ChTr; FaBoVe, *diff. vers.*; GBP; OxBoLi; OxNR, *diff. vers.*; ReMoGo

London Bridge was built. Stranger than the Worst. Babette Deutsch. WPE

London burnt like rotten sticks. *(LL)* William the Conqueror, ten sixty-six. *Unknown.* FaBoUs; OxNR

London City. *Unknown.* AS

London Despair. Frances Cornford. OBMV

London, 1802 ("Milton! thou should'st be living at this hour.") Wordsworth. AWP; EBEvV; EnRP; EPCY; FaBoPV; FaBV; FF; HAP; HeIP; InvP; LiTB; MeMBP; NAEL-2; NIP; NoP; OBNC; OxAEP-2; PoEL-4; PoRA; SCGP; Son; TEP; TFi; UV

London, MDCCCII ("O friend! I know not which way I must look.") Wordsworth. GTBS; GTBS-P

London Evening Post, *sels. Unknown.*
"Ye Beauties, Beaux, ye Pleaders at the Bar." FaBoUs

London Fete, A. Coventry Patmore. EBVV; EnVR; FaBoEH; HAP; PeVV

London, from Hampstead Heath. Wordsworth. *Fr.* Extempore Effusion upon the Death of James Hogg. EBEV; FaBoPP; FaBoRV; NOBE; NoP; OAEL-2; SCV

London, hast thou [*or* thow] accused me. The Earl of Surrey. SiPSBD
(Satire on London, A.) AAS; SiPS

London Impossibilities. *Unknown.* CBCK

London in 1646. Henry Vaughan. FaBoPP

London Is a Fine Town. *Unknown.* CoMu

London is full of chickens, on electric spits. Peter Porter. *Fr.* Annotations of Auschwitz. OxBTC

London is painted round them: burly railings. Street Performers, 1851. Terence Tiller. GTBS-P

London: John Lane, The Bodley Head. On the Imprint of the First English Edition of "The Works of Max Beerbohm." Max Beerbohm. InPK

London Lackpenny. *Unknown. See* In London there I was bent.

London Lackpenny. *Unknown. See* To London once my stepps [*or* steps] I bent.

London Lickpenny. *Unknown, tr. fr. Middle English.* CoMu; FaBoPP; OBSV

London Lyckpeny. *Unknown. See* To London once my stepps [*or* steps] I bent.

London Nightfall. John Gould Fletcher. MoAmPo

London, 1940. Frank Thompson. FaBoEH

London Pavement Artist. James Schevill. TAP

London Plane, The. John Greening. PWE

London Prentice, The. *Unknown.* CoMu

London Rain. Louis MacNeice. NoP; Poetr

London Snow. Robert Bridges. BoNaP; CH; ChTr; CMoP; EBEV; EBEvV; EBVV; FaBoPP; GTBS-P; LiTB; LiTM; MoAB; MoBrPo; MoP; NoAM; NOBE; NOBVV; OAEL-2; OBNC; OxAEP-2; OxBTC; PoEL-5; TFi; TrGrPo; WiR

London Spring. Antoni Slonimski, *tr. fr. Polish by* Frances Notley. TrJP

London Street, A. John Donne. *Fr.* Satires. NoSic

London Street-Scene, A. Edward Ward. *Fr.* Hudibras Redidivus. CBCK

London Suburbs. William Cowper. *Fr.* Retirement. FaBoPP

London Subverted by the Furies. Abraham Cowley. NOSC

London, thou art of townes. To the City of London [*or* In Honour of the City of London]. William Dunbar. ChTr; EBEV; FaBoPP; OBEV

London, thou art the flour of Cities all. (*LL*) To the City of London [*or* In Honour of the City of London]. William Dunbar. ChTr; EBEV; FaBoPP; OBEV

London to Folkestone. Dante Gabriel Rossetti. EnVR

London, to thee I do present the merry month of May. The Month of May. Beaumont *and* Fletcher *and* John Fletcher. *Fr.* Knight of the Burning Pestle, The. ChTr

London Town. Lionel Johnson. FaBoPP; OHCV

London Town. John Masefield. OtMeF

London Trees. Beryl Netherclift. BoTP

London under Bombardment. Greta Briggs. OtMeF; PlP

London University, The, *sels.* Winthrop Mackworth Praed. "Ye Dons and ye doctors, ye Provosts and Proctors." FaBoEH

London versus Epping Forest. John Clare. *Fr.* Child Harold. FaBoPP

London Voluntaries., *sels.* W. E. Henley.

London Zoo, The. C. H. Sisson. IHNG

Londoners Gent to the King do present, The. On the Lord Mayor and Court of Aldermen, Presenting the Late King and Duke of York Each with a Copy of Their Freedoms. Andrew Marvell. CoMu; FaBoBa (Upon His Majesty's Being Made Free of the City.) APAS

London's Resurrection., *sels.* Simon Ford. "Hail, glorious day; mayst thou be writ in gold." NOSC

London's Summer Morning. Mary Robinson. ECWP; WoRP

Lone am I, and would be. Christine de Pisan, *tr. fr. French by* Tom Vaughan. AIW

Lone and forgotten/ Through a long sleeping. The Lonely. "Æ." AWP

Lone and weary as I wander'd by the bleak shore of the sea. Lament for Timoleague. Sean O'Coileain, *tr. fr. Irish by* Sir Samuel Ferguson. TIRV

Lone Bather. A. M. Klein. HeIP

Lone boat, a sliver of moon facing the maple woods, A. Listening to a Wanderer's "Water Melody." Wang Ch'ang-ling, *tr. fr. Chinese by* Joseph J. Lee. SuSp

Lone Dog. Irene Rutherford McLeod. FaPON; OBAP; PDV

Lone figure is waving, A. A Postcard from North Antrim. Seamus Heaney. IPY; PBCIP; PNI

Lone Founts. Herman Melville. LiTA

Lone Freedom. Edith M. Thomas. AmWP

Lone Gentleman. Pablo Neruda, *tr. fr. Spanish by* Clayton Eshleman. ErPo

Lone Huntsman. Christie Jeffries. GoYe

Lone Kauri Road ("First time I looked seaward, westward.") Allen Curnow. *Fr.* Trees, Effigies, Moving Objects. PeNZ

Lone knee wanders through the world, A. The Knee on Its Own. Christian Morgenstern, *tr. fr. German by* R. F. L. Hull. FaBoNo

Lone listener to my spirit wild. (*LL*) On the Tower. Annette von Droste-Hülshoff. PBWP; WPOW

Lone, lone, and lone I stand. The Myall in Prison. Mary Gilmore. CBAP

Lone, phallic, Alet's get. Tour de Force. Peter Kane Dufault. ErPo

Lone seas are ominous. Lone Huntsman. Christie Jeffries. GoYe

Lone Star Trail, The. *Unknown.* AS

Lone Wild Fowl, The. H. R. MacFayden. AH

Lone Wild Goose, A. Lu Kuei-meng, *tr. fr. Chinese by* Robin D. S. Yates. SuSp

Loneliest voice I heard as a child, The. Overhearing. John Cassidy. PWE

Loneliness. Hayden Carruth. SM

Loneliness. Edwin Essex. TrPWD

Loneliness. Robert Frost. *Fr.* Hill Wife, The. CMoP; HAP; InPS; LiTM; NoP; VGW

Loneliness. Wilhelm Müller, *tr. fr. German by* Philip L. Miller. *Fr.* Winter's Journey, The. RiWo

Loneliness. Kenneth Rexroth. ArLo

Loneliness. Franz Werfel, *tr. fr. German by* Edith Abercrombie Snow. TrJP

Loneliness. Al Young. PoBA

Loneliness and July Ninth. Claribel Alegría, *tr. fr. Spanish by* Aliki *and* Willis Barnstone. BoWoP

Loneliness in the Tropics. Harry Clifton. IB

Lonely, The. "Æ." AWP

Lonely. Bloke Modisane. PBA

Lonely. André Spire, *tr. fr. French by* Jethro Bithell. AWP; TrJP

Lonely and bare and desolate. From Albert to Bapaume. Alec Waugh. NSI

Lonely and big. First Pregnancy. Alta. NMM

Lonely and dreary was the day. Heart's Ease. Mary E. Tucker. CBWP-1

Lonely Are the Fields of Sleep. Mary Newton Baldwin. GoYe

Lonely Beauty. Samuel Daniel. *Fr.* Complaint of Rosamond, The. CTC

Lonely Cloud of Care, The. Coventry Patmore. *Fr.* Victories of Love, The. FaBoRV

Lonely courtyard,/ once more slanting wind, misty rain. Tune: "Charm of Nien-nu, The." Li Ch'ing-chao, *tr. fr. Chinese by* Eugene Eoyang. SuSp

Lonely, desolate, the new literary scene. Hesitation. Lu Hsun, *tr. fr. Chinese by* William R. Schultz. SuSp

Lonely Dog, The. Margaret E. Bruner. PoToHe

Lonely Eagles. Marilyn Nelson Waniek. NAmP90

Lonely Farmer, The. R. S. Thomas. PlP

Lonely Hearts. Wendy Cope. OBF

Lonely House, The. Emily Dickinson. MoAB; MoAmPo; OxBA; PoRA

Lonely in the Regent Palace. The Flight from Bootle. Sir John Betjeman. PeLV

Lonely Isle, The. Claudian, *tr. fr. Latin by* Howard Mumford Jones. AWP

Lonely Land, The. A. J. M. Smith. NOBC

Lonely Love. Edmund Blunden. OxBTC

Lonely Man, The. Randall Jarrell. OxBC

Lonely moon loiters above the village, The. Sailing at Dusk from T'u-sung. Wu Wei-yeh, *tr. fr. Chinese by* Chang Yin-nan *and* Lewis C. Walmsley. SuSp

Lonely Mother, The. Fenton Johnson. PoNe

Lonely Night in Early Autumn. Po Chü-i, *tr. fr. Chinese by* Robert Payne. TAL

Lonely old maid named Loretta, A. *Unknown.* PeLi

Lonely pond in age-old stillness sleeps, A. Basho, *tr. fr. Japanese by* Curtis Hidden Page. AWP

Lonely Road. Peter Abrahams. PBA

Lonely rock above a midnight plain, A. Te Whetu Plains. Edward Tregear, *tr. by* Alan Myers. PeNZ

Lonely, save for a few faint stars, the sky. The Little Dancers. Laurence Binyon. BoTP; CH; MoBrPo; OxBTC

Lonely Scarecrow, The. James Kirkup. GrPl; PDV

Lonely season in lonely lands, when fled, The. November. Robert Bridges. OBNC; PoEL-5

Lonely Settler, The. Oliver Goldsmith, the Younger. *See* What noble courage must their hearts have fired.

Lonely Street, The. William Carlos Williams. PoA; TwCP

Lonely the Sea-Bird Lies at Her Rest. W. B. Yeats. RB

Lonely Traveller, The. Kwesi Brew. PBA; TTY

Lonely wanderer, wounded with iron, A. Shield: "Lonely wanderer, wounded with iron, A." Unknown, formerly at. to Cynewulf, *tr. by* Charles W. Kennedy. *Fr.* Riddles (Exeter Book). AnOE

Lonely Woman. Jayne Cortez. NBV

Lonely World. Mrs. Henry Linden. CBWP-4

Lonely young fellow of Eton, A. *Unknown.* PeLi

Lonely your friend wanders in the garden of spring blossoms. Adelaide. Friedrich von Matthison, *tr. fr. German by* Philip L. Miller. RiWo

Lonesome Dove, The. *Unknown.* AmFP

Lonesome Dream, The. Lisel Mueller. CoAP

Lonesome in the Country. Al Young. MAT

Lonesome scenes of winter incline to frost and snow, The. The Rejected Lover. *Unknown.* AmFP

Lonesome Water. Roy Helton. MoAmPo

Long after it was heard no more. (*LL*) The Solitary Reaper.
Wordsworth. AWP; BLPL; CH; ClHu; EBEvV; EnRP; FaBoCh; FaPoB;
FaPoR; FHYEP; GN; HAP; HeIP; ImPo; InPS; LiTB; MeMBP; NAEL-2;
NOBE; NoP; OAEL-2; OBEV; OBNC; OxAEP-2; PoEL-4; Poetr; PoRA;
PPP; SCGP; SCV; SoSe; TEP; TFi; TrGrPu; UnPo; WeW

Long after there were none of them alive. Recalled. E. A. Robinson.
MeMAP

Long after we've forgotten the fallen beneath? (*LL*) Between Seasons.
Li-Young Lee. TRP

Long after you have swung back. Losing Track. Denise Levertov. HeIP;
MoP; NaP; NOBA; PoE; PoM

Long afterward, Oedipus, old and blinded. Myth. Muriel Rukeyser. CrSp;
FaBoWP; IHMS; NALW; NNaP

Long afterwards. The Judgment of Paris. W. S. Merwin. NAAL-2; NNaP

Long ago. Harriet Kofalk. EaPr

Long ago/ We spoke a mother tongue. Mame-Loshen, Yiddish. Bernard S.
Mikofsky. BTR

Long Ago, The. Benjamin Franklin Taylor. *See* Oh [*or* O], a wonderful
stream is the River Time.

Long ago a young girl. The Sun Witness. Nurunnessa Choudhury, *tr. fr.
Bengali by* Nurunnessa Choudhury *and* Paul Joseph Thompson. AIW

Long ago at the end of Deborah's song. His Mother. Haim Guri, *tr. fr.
Hebrew by* Ruth Finer Mintz. MHP

Long ago her mother. What the Informant Said to Franz Boas in 1920.
Unknown, tr. fr. Keresan Indian by Armand Schwerner. STP

Long ago how fine was everything! Disillusion. *Unknown, tr. fr. Tewa
Indian by* H. J. Spinden. WTO

Long ago I learned how to sleep. Wind Song. Carl Sandburg. MoAB;
MoAmPo; MoShBr

Long ago, in Kentucky, I, a boy stood. Tell Me a Story. Robert Penn
Warren. *Fr.* Audubon. MT

Long ago, in the forests of southern Europe. The Stillness, the Dancing.
Linda Bierds. NAmP90

Long ago in the north. Songs in the Turtle Dance at Santa Clara.
Unknown, tr. fr. Tewa Indian by H. J. Spinden. WTO

Long ago powerful snake when men also. The Deluge. *Unknown, tr. by* C.
S. Rafinesque. *Fr.* Walam [*or* Wallum] Olum; or, Red Score. LiTA

Long ago there was an immortal man. Juan Chi, *tr. by* Charles Hartman.
Fr. Poems Expressing My Feelings. SuSp

Long ago you were perhaps. To the Waters of the Chia-ling. Yüan Chen,
tr. fr. Chinese by William H. Nienhauser. SuSp

Long and gray and gaunt he lies. At the Dog Show. Christopher Morley.
MoShBr

Long and Happy Life, A. Simon Schuchat. UL

Long and Lazy. Robert Herrick. FaBoEE

Long and Lonely Winter, The. Dave Goulder. OBET

Long & Short of It: A Letter to Brendan Galvin. George Garrett. NGP

Long and toneless chant, The. (*LL*) Francie-the-Possessed. Oswald
Durand. NegPo

Long anxiety and time of school, The. Childhood. Rainer Maria Rilke, *tr.
fr. German by* M. D. Herter Norton. SOTW

Long Approach, The. Maxine W. Kumin. NGP

Long are the shadows, slanting, dim. West Ch'Ang-an Street. Pien Chih-
lin, *tr. fr. Chinese*. LHF; PRA *tr. by* Hualing Nieh

Long as I can call to mind. A Childish Game. Reinmar von Hagenau, *tr.
fr. German by* Jethro Bithell. AWP

Long as the Darkening Cloud Abode. George Richards. AH

Long as thine art shall love true love. Dear Land of All My Love. Sidney
Lanier. *Fr.* Centennial Meditation of Columbia, The. GN; PAH

Long autumn grass under my body, The. Field Manoeuvres. Richard
Aldington. PeFWW

Long Barren. Christina Rossetti. PBWP; TrCP

Long beardes heartles. The English. *Unknown.* GBP

Long before a woman knows she's pregnant. Progression of the Species.
Brian W. Aldiss. FF

Long before I first left home, my father. Breakings. Henry Taylor. GrPl

Long before I hear it, Naples bright. Napoli Again. Richard Hugo. LCAP

Long before the adult flora of. The Grace of Animals. Richard Harteis.
GLP

Long before the father died. Himself. Peter Fallon. PBCIP

Long-billed Gannets. Frances D. Emery. GoYe

Long bound in ice and horrid hills of snow. After a Storm, Going a
Hawking. George Daniel. NOSC

Long canoe, The. Robert Silliman Hillyer. FaPON; ImGa

Long closed door, oh open it again, The. Judah al-Harizi, *tr. fr. Hebrew by*
Emma Lazarus. TrJP

Long day on the road, R. H., and three trips now. Note to R. H. from
Strongsville. Richard Hugo. AnAn

Long desired, the dead return. They Return. Jay Macpherson. *Fr.* Way
Down, The. NOBC; PoA

Long desired, the journey is begun. The suppliants. Landscapeople. John
Ashbery. HCAP

Long Distance. Tony Harrison. NAEL-2

Long Distance. Dana Naone. CDW

Long-eared beast, and a field-house for cattle, A. A Riddling Letter.
Unknown. CBNP

Long enough to be noticed. (*LL*) The Good Hands People Know Their
Bodies. "Lynn Doyle." UTF

Long-expected one and twenty. A Short Song of Congratulation [*or* To a
Young Heir]. Samuel Johnson. EBEV; ELP; HAP; InPK; InPS; InVP;
NOBE; NOEC; NoP; OBSV; OxAEP-1; PeLV; PlP; PoE; PoEL-3; TEP;
TFi; UnPo
(One-and-Twenty.) GGP
(To a Young Heir.) SCGP

Long farewell to all you universe-swivelling optics, A. Philip of
Thessalonica, *tr. fr. Greek by* Edwin Morgan. GrAn

Long Feud. Louis Untermeyer. MoAmPo

Long Garden, The. Patrick Kavanagh. IPY

Long Gone. Sterling A. Brown. BPo; CDC

Long had passed the hour of midnight. Dawn. *Malay Oral Tradition, tr.
by* R. J. Wilkinson. WTO

Long [had] the proud Spaniard [advanced to conquer us]. The Winning of
Cales. Thomas Deloney. CoMu; OBTV; OxBSS

Long Hair. Gary Snyder. NOBA

Long hair, endless curls trained by the devoted. Strato, *tr. fr. Greek by*
Teddy Hogge. GrAn; PeHV

Long-haired preachers come out every [*or* ev'ry] night. The Preacher and
the Slave. *At. to* Joe Hill. AS; SWP; WTO
(Pie in the Sky.) GBP

Long Harbour, The. Mary Ursula Bethell. PeNZ

Long hast thou, friend! been absent from thy soil. Mr. Pope's Welcome
from Greece. John Gay. EBEV, *abr.*; OxAEP-1; OxBoLi, *abr.*;
PoEL-3

Long hast thou slept unnoted. Nature stole. The Mother of Washington.
Lydia Huntley Sigourney. AmWP

Long hast thou slumber'd, O my sounding Lyre! Daniel Alexander Payne.
Fr. Pleasures, The. AAP

Long hath my sufferance labored to in force. Thomas Lodge. *Fr.* Phyllis.
ESo

Long have I beat with timid hands upon life's leaden door. The Suppliant.
Georgia Douglas Johnson. CDC; PoBA; PoNe; ShDr

Long have I framed weak phantasies of Thee. Agnosto Theo (To an
Unknown God). Thomas Hardy. WGRP

Long have I looked for my lost child. The Lost Child. James Reaney.
NOBC

Long have I loved the terrible clouds that loom. Prayer for Dreadful
Morning. E. Merrill Root. TrPWD

Long have I sighed for a calm; God grant I may find it at last! Tennyson.
Fr. Maud[: A Monodrama]. EBVVPR; EnVR

Long have I yearned and sought for beauty. I Sit and Wait for Beauty.
Mae V. Cowdery. BlSi

Long hears have left their writing on my brow. "George Eliot." *Fr.*
Brother and Sister. GN; NALW

Long Hill, The. Sara Teasdale. LiTA; MoAmPo

Long History of the Short Poem. Paul Hoover. UL

Long I followed [*or* follow'd] happy guides. Forerunners. Emerson.
OBEV; OxBA

Long I Have Loved to Stroll. T'ao Ch'ien, *tr. fr. Chinese by* William
Acker. ChTr

Long I have seen those eyes. To a Friend Condemned to Prison. James
Wright. PRA

Long I Thought That Knowledge Alone Would Suffice. Walt Whitman.
NOBA

Long in thy shackles, liberty. To Lucasta, from Prison. Richard Lovelace.
BeJo; CaPo

Long Interval, The. S. J. Litherland. NWP

Long is th' Impris'ment of the dead. (*LL*) In March birds couple, a new
birth. *At. to* Henry Vaughan *and* Thomas Stanley, *fr. the Welsh of*
Aneirin. FaBoEE; FaBoRV

Long is the night. Curriculum Vitae. Ingeborg Bachmann, *tr. fr. German
by* Jerome K. Rothenberg. BoWoP

Long Island. Marvin Bell. CAPP

Long Island Springs. Howard Moss. UnPo

Long John Brown and Little Mary Bell. Blake. ECEV; RB

Long John Nelson and Sweetie Pie. Margaret Walker. VBLP

Long Kiang, reaching heaven, The. (*LL*) Separation on the River Kiang.
Li Po. InPS; SOTW; UnPo

Long lay the ocean-paths from man conceal'd. The Inspiration. James Montgomery. *Fr.* West Indies, The. PAH; PBCV

Long-legged Fly. W. B. Yeats. CMoP; FaBoMo; FaBoTw; InPS; LiTM; MoP; NAEL-2; NoAM; NOBE; NoP; OPOP; PoE; TEP

Long legs, crooked thighs. Mother Goose. GBP; OxNR (Tongs.) ReMoGo

Long Lines. Paul Goodman. VGW

Long lines, clean and syllabic as knotted bamboo. / Yes! (*LL*) Poetics against the Angel of Death. Phyllis Webb. MoCV; NOBC

Long lines of cliff breaking have left a chasm. Enoch Arden. Tennyson. BeLS

Long Lines: Youth and Age. Paul Goodman. GLP; PeHV

Long live our dear and noble Queen. Edward Edwin Foot. *Fr.* On the Inauguration of the Memorial Statue. FaBoCo

"Long live the Republic," said Master McGrath. (*LL*) A Ballad of Master McGrath. Unknown. FaBoBa

Long Live the Weeds. Theodore Roethke. NoAM; NOBA; PoA

Long live the weeds and the wilderness yet. (*LL*) Inversnaid. Gerard Manley Hopkins. BLPL; CMoP; EnVR; FaBoPP; FaBoVe; GTBS-P; ImPo; LiTB; LiTM; MeMBP; MoAB; MoBrPo; NoAM; OAEL-2; PeVV; PoRA; RB; SCGP; TFi; UnPo

Long, long ago. (*LL*) Long, Long Ago. Unknown. FaPON; OHIP; PChr; PDV

Long, Long Ago. Unknown. FaPON; OHIP; PChr; PDV

Long, long ago, beyond the misty space. The Celts. Thomas D'Arcy Magee. PeIV; TIRV

Long long ago on Calvary. Victory. Unknown. CoMu; WGRP

Long long ago when the world was a wild place. Bedtime Story. George MacBeth. MoP; SoSe

Long, Long Be My Heart with Such Memories Filled. Thomas Moore. BLPL; FaBoBe

Long, between your hands you held the warrior's black face. Léopold Sédar Senghor, *tr. fr. French by* Ellen Conroy Kennedy. *Fr.* Songs for Signare. NegPo

Long Love, The. Sir Thomas Wyatt. SCGP

Long[e] love that in my thought doth harbour, The. Alas! So All Things Now Do Hold Their Peace. Petrarch, *tr. fr. Italian.* *Fr.* Sonnets to Laura. NAEL-1; NoP; OAEL-1; OBVE; SCGP
(Alas, so all things now do hold their peace.) NoSic, *tr. by the Earl of Surrey, sect.* CIX
(Alas, So All Things Now.) EnRePo
(Lover for Shamefastnesse Hideth His Desire within His Faithfull Hart, The.) AAS, 2 *ver.*

Long May. Rosalía de Castro, *tr. fr. Galician by* Benjamin M. Woodbridge, Jr. PBWP

Long may the lonely one wait for comfort. The Wanderer. Unknown, *tr. fr. Anglo-Saxon.* AnOE, *tr. by* Charles W. Kennedy; OAEL-1, *tr. by* Charles W. Kennedy; TEP, *tr. by* Mark Caldwell

Long Mountain, rise. Pocomania. Philip Sherlock. PBCV

Long my dull Muse in heavy slumbers lay. To My Lord Colrane, in Answer to His Complemental Verses Sent Me under the Name of Cleanor. Anne Killigrew. KTR

Long Nature travailed, till at last she bore. Nature's Travail. Unknown, *tr. fr. Greek by* Goldwin Smith. AWP

Long neglect has worn away. Emily Brontë. NOBVV
(Long Neglect Has Worn Away.) NoP; PFP; PoE

Long night of linden trees, your honey hands. The Figurehead. Maria Luisa Spaziani, *tr. fr. Italian by* Beverly Allen. NeIt

Long night succeeds thy little day. Margaret Love Peacock, for Her Tombstone, 1826. Thomas Love Peacock. OBNC; PIP

Long past midnight I sit here. Forsaken. Zalman Schneour, *tr. fr. Yiddish by* Joseph Leftwich. TrJP

Long path sap sludges up, The. New. William Matthews. FoLa

Long, perfect loveliness of sow, The. (*LL*) Saint Francis and the Sow. Galway Kinnell. CAPP; FYAP; InPK; RB

Long Person. Gladys Cardiff. CDW

Long Picnic, The. Russell Edson. LCAP

Long placid evening. Tune: The Butterfly Woos the Blossoms. Li Ch'ing-chao, *tr. by* C. H. Kwock *and* Vincent McHugh. PBWP

Long Plighted. Thomas Hardy. NOBVV

Long poles support the branches of the orchards in New Hampshire. Apples in New Hampshire. Marie Emilie Gilchrist. BoNaP

Long Prologue to a Short Play, A. Sir Henry Sheeres. APAS

Long rain falls on the empty forest. Smoke rises, The. After Long Rain. Wang Wei, *tr. fr. Chinese by* Robert Payne. TAL

Long River, The. Donald Hall. LCAP; SM

Long Road, The, *sels.* John Gray.
Gazelles and Unicorn. ChTr

Long road and a village, A. Holy Family. Muriel Rukeyser. ChIV-2; MoAmPo

Long rolling, The. The Main-Deep. James Stephens. MoBrPo; OBMV; UnPo

Long sea, how short-lasting, The. There Is No Land Yet. Laura Riding. ChIV-1

Long shadows. Jill Maughan. NWP

Long shines the line of wet lamps dark in gleaming. Rainy Midnight. Ivor Gurney. FaBoPP

Long since I heard the muttered anger of the reef. Long Since. Robert David Fitzgerald. FaBoMA

Long since I'd ceased to care. The Parrot. W. W. Gibson. OBMV

Long since, it was by me desir'd. To the Queen of Bohemia. "Eliza." KTR

Long Since Last. Ruth Miller. PeSA

Long slick black feller. Unknown. FaBoVe

Long, slim, slick fellow. Unknown. RoPo

Long Small Room, The. Edward Thomas. Mes; PIP

Long steel grass. Trio for Two Cats and a Trombone. Edith Sitwell. *Fr.* Façade. NAEL-2; PBWP

Long-Suffering of God. Christopher Smart. *Fr.* Hymns for the Amusement of Children. NOCV

Long Summer. Laurie Lee. BoNaP

Long-tailed pig, A. Mother Goose. OxNR

Long-tailed ponies go nosing the pine-lands. Parochial Theme. Wallace Stevens. LiTA

Long the flimsy skirts. Wang Chien, *tr. by* William H. Nienhauser. *Fr.* Palace Poems. SuSp

Long the loose wits of a degenerate age. Verses to Mr. Richardson on his History of Sir Charles Grandison. Anna Williams. ECWP

Long the tyrant of our coast. On the Capture of the *Guerrière*. Philip Freneau. PAH

Long they pine in weary woe, the nobles of our land. Kathaleen Ny-Houlahan [*or* Kathleen-Ni-Houlahan]. William Heffernan, *tr. fr. Irish by* James Clarence Mangan. IIP; NOIV

Long Time a Child. Hartley Coleridge. EnRP; PoEL-4; Son

Long time ago. (*LL*) Hoosen Johnny. Unknown. AS; FaPON

Long time ago, A. T'ao Ch'ien, *tr. fr. Chinese by* Arthur Waley. FaBoCh

Long Time Ago, A. Unknown. AmFP

Long time ago/ in the beginning. The Invention of White People. Leslie Silko. NoAM; STP

Long time back, a long way south, A. (*LL*) You Call Me by Old Names. Rhina P. Espaillat. LoHo

Long Time Coming. Daphne Marlatt. VBLP

Long time hath Christ, long time I must confess. Of the Reed That the Jews Set in Our Saviour's Hand. William Alabaster. NoSic

Long time he lay upon the sunny hill. Childhood. Edwin Muir. CMoP; HeIP; NoP

Long time I have lived with you, A. Nancy Wood. EaPr

Long time in some forgotten churchyard earth of Warwickshire. Who Were before Me. John Drinkwater. OBMV

Long time Plain Dealing in the haughty town. Plain Dealing's Downfall. Unknown. OBSV

Long time since it seems to-day, A. W. H. Auden. *Fr.* New Year Letter. GOA

Long time those gay and spotted hides. Your Chase Had a Beast in View. John Peale Bishop. LiTA

Long time yet, because you're strong as a mule, A. (*LL*) George. Dudley Randall. BPo; NoAM

Long Tom. W. W. Gibson. OxBTC

Long, Too Long America. Walt Whitman. GOA

Long Tour: The Country Music Star Explains Why He Put off the Bus and Fired a Good Lead Guitar in West Texas. James Whitehead. MT

Long Trail, The. Kipling. *See* There's a whisper down the field where the year has shot her yield.

Long tyme hathe Christ (long tyme I must confesse). On the Reed of Our Lord's Passion. William Alabaster. PoEL-2

Long Voyage, The. Malcolm Cowley. SoSe

Long War, The. Laurie Lee. PAW

Long war had ended, The. The Next War. Sir Osbert Sitwell. NSI; PAW; PoWW

Long Waters, The. Theodore Roethke. NYBP

Long waves glide in through the afternoon, The. Anniversary on the Island. W. S. Merwin. ArLo

Long Way after Ronsard, A. James Simmons. PBCIP

Long Way outside Yellowstone, A. Thomas McGrath. VGW

Long ways, A. A Remembrance of a Color inside a Forest. Ray A. Young Bear. CDW

Long, wet trajectory of the ferry's railing, The. Sketch of the Harbour. Robert Gray. FaBoMA

Long white barn, A. *Unknown.* ChTr; GBP

Long White Seam, The. Jean Ingelow. GN; NOBVV

Long wind coming from beyond the horizon. Commandeering the Wind. Su Shun-ch'in, *tr. fr. Chinese by* Irving Y. Lo. SuSp

Long years ago I wandered here. On Recrossing the Rocky Mountains after Many Years. John Charles Frémont. AiP

Long years ago the envoy of Han departed. Tune: "Pacifying the Western Barbarians." Wen T'ing-yün, *tr. fr. Chinese by* William R. Schultz. SuSp

Long years ago there came to me in sleep. The Beautiful. F. S. Woodley. PeHV

Long years beheld me PATTON's mansion grace. A Favourite Cat's Dying Soliloquy. Anna Seward. FM; OFC

Long years have passed since first a merry child. To One Who Sleepeth. Mary E. Tucker. CBWP-1

Long years of pleasant friendship may be broken. True to the Best. Benjamin Keech. PoToHe

Longed-for night! *(LL)* Secret Invitation. John Henry Mackay. RiWo

Longed-for summer goes, The. Now. Walter de la Mare. ArNa

Longer to muse. Sir Thomas Wyatt. SiPS

Longer we are together, The. Ripening. Wendell Berry. EaPr; RaBo

Longest and much the dearest. Book Review. Russell Davies. FaBoEE

Longest Journey, The. Shelley. *Fr.* Epipsychidion. EnRP; OtMeF; OxBM

Longest Night, The. Marge Piercy. SRLS

Longest Tyranny that ever sway'd, The. To My Friend, Dr. Charleton, on His Learned and Useful Works; and More Particularly This of Stone-Heng, by Him Restored to the True Founders. Dryden. SeCV-2

Longface Mahoney Discusses Heaven. Horace Gregory. VGW

Longfellow. H. Cordelia Ray. AAP; CBWP-3

Longfellow's Visit to Venice. Sir John Betjeman. NOBL

Longing. Matthew Arnold. PoLF; SoSe

Longing. *Gond Oral Tradition, tr. by* V. Elwin *and* S. Hivale. WTO

Longing. Judah Halevi, *tr. fr. Hebrew by* Nina Davis Salaman. TrJP

Longing. George Herbert. ESCV; SeCV-1; UV, *sl. sh. vers.*

Longing. James Russell Lowell. AnAmPo

Longing couple all that elder lovers know, The. *(LL)* Epithalamion, or a Song Celebrating the Nuptials of That Noble Gentleman, Mr. Jerome Weston. Ben Jonson. BeJo

Longing for Death because of Feebleness. Stevie Smith. OBD

Longing for Eternal Life, The. Liz Rosenberg. PBCAP

Longing for Heaven. Anne Bradstreet. *See* As Weary Pilgrim, Now at Rest.

Longing for Home. Jean Ingelow. *Fr.* Songs of Seven. WGRP

Longing for Jail, A. Edvard Kocbek, *tr. fr. Slovene by* Michael Scammell *and* Veno Taufer. PoSu

Longing for Jerusalem. Judah Halevi, *tr. fr. Hebrew by* Emma Lazarus. TrJP

Longing for that true comrade of my need. To Liebig. August, Graf von Platen, *tr. fr. German by* Reginald Bancroft Cooke. PeHV

Longing for you. Princess Nukada, *tr. fr. Japanese by* Kenneth Rexroth *and* Ikuko Atsumi. PRA; WPJ

Longing in My Heart. Wei Ying-wu, *tr. fr. Chinese by* Irving Y. Lo. SuSp

Longing to Be Saved, The. Maxine W. Kumin. CAPP

Longings. Mae V. Cowdery. ShDr

Longmobile. Shel Silverstein. AiP

Longobards, The. Zbigniew Herbert, *tr. fr. Polish by* Czeslaw Milosz. PoSu

Longon lights are far abeam, The. Old Australian Ways. Andrew Barton Paterson. NOBAu

Longshore Intellectual. Sean Lucy. CIP

Longsight Market. Valerie Bloom. NBrP

Lonnie said before this, "I'm." Commanding Elephants. Philip Levine. NaP

Loo! loo! Lulu! lulu! Loo! loo! Loot! loot! Kipling. *Fr.* Loot. UV

Loo-wit. Wendy Rose. HATNAP

Loo-wit sings and sings and sings! *(LL)* Loo-wit. Wendy Rose. HATNAP

Look, The. Elizabeth Barrett Browning. TrCP

Look/ There/ The smiling infant. Cold. Brian Coffey. CIP

Look, The. Elizabeth Daryush. PoA

Look! Stan Rice. IMW

Look, among the boughs. Those stars are men. The Star-Tribes. *Aborigine Oral Tradition, tr. by* Fred Biggs. NOBAu

Look and remember. Look upon this sky. Travelogue for Exiles. Karl Shapiro. MoAmPo; TrJP

Look Askance, A. James Merrill. AnAn

Look at her, calm and benign. A Bronze Statuette of Kwan-yin. Charles Wharton Stork. GoYe

Look at him, over there. Disillusion. Maureen Burge. AIW; BrRo

Look at him there in his stovepipe hat. American Primitive. William Jay Smith. FF; InPK; MoAmPo; OxBSP; RaBo; TwCP

Look at it well. This was the good town once. The Good Town. Edwin Muir. CMoP

Look at Jonah embarking from Joppa, deterred by. Tom Fool at Jamaica. Marianne Moore. NYBP

Look at me 8th. Sonia Sanchez. PoBA

Look at me move. The Amputee Soldier. Philip Dacey. GOYP

Look at me: my mouth unlearned complaining early. Mother of Fishermen. Henriëtte Roland-Holst, *tr. by* Ria Leigh-Loohuizen. PBWP

Look at me sleeping I am somewhat disfigured. Lachesis. Hilaire Kirkland. *Fr.* Clotho, Lachesis, Atropos. PeNZ

Look at my belt, how loose it hangs. *(LL)* I Can No Longer Untangle My Hair. *Unknown.* OHMPC

Look at my continent containing. Human Geography. Gloria Fuertes, *tr. fr. Spanish by* Willis Barnstone. BoWoP

Look at My Face, a Collage. Carolyn M. Rodgers. JB

Look at my footprints in the snow. *(LL)* Bitter Cold. *Unknown.* OHMPC

Look at my knees. I Wonder What It Feels Like to Be Drowned? Robert Graves. MoBrPo

Look at pretty little kitty. Kitty. Doug McLeod. CRH

Look at Six Eggs. Carl Sandburg. *Fr.* Prairie. FaPON

Look at That Gal. Julian Bond. PoNe; TTY

Look at the aeroplane. The Aeroplane. Jeannie Kirby. BoTP

Look at the horned goat of Dionysus. Anyte, *tr. fr. Greek by* Sally Purcell. GrAn

Look at the silly prince, with his little horse and little saddle. F. Jack Marshall. UL

Look at the stars! look, look up at the skies! The Starlight Night. Gerard Manley Hopkins. EnVR; GTBS-P; InPS; LiTM; MeMBP; MoAB; MoBrPo; NAEL-2; PoE; PPP

Look at these most wretched remains of a man. Philip of Thessalonica, *tr. fr. Greek by* Edwin Morgan. GrAn

Look at this, golden-horned moon. Argentarius, *tr. fr. Greek by* Fleur Adcock. GrAn

Look at this red pear. The Indigestion of the Vampire. W. S. Merwin. NaP

Look at this skin — at fourscore years. Robert Barnabas Brough. *Fr.* Marquis of Carabas, The. FiBHP

Look at this village boy, his head is stuffed. Farm Child. R. S. Thomas. BoNaP

Look at your corn in May. *Unknown.* FaBoUs

Look Away child. Susan Cavin. GLP

Look away! Look away! Look away! Dixie Land. *(LL)* Dixie. Daniel Decatur Emmett. AnAmPo; FaPON; TrGrPo

Look between the bow and the bowstring, beneath. Backgrounds to Italian Paintings: Fifteenth Century. Anne Ridler. WPE

Look Closely. Morton Marcus. FF

Look, Delia, how we [e]steem the half-blown rose. Samuel Daniel. *Fr.* To Delia. ESo; NoP; NoSic; SCGP

(Sonnet: "Look, Delia, how we esteem the half-blown rose.") EiL

Look down on me, a little one. A Child's Morning Prayer. Jeannie Kirby. BoTP

Look down. The dead have life. Gravestones. Vernon Watkins. TEP

Look, Edwin! Edna St. Vincent Millay. GoJo

Look for your other half. Antonio Machado Ruiz, *tr. by* Robert Bly. *Fr.* Moral Proverbs and Folk Songs. RaBo

Look forth and tell me what they do. Hammer and Anvil. Samuel Valentine Cole. PoLF

Look forward, truant, to your second childhood. The Death Room. Robert Graves. NYBP

Look from the sphere of endless day. Other Sheep I Have, Which Are Not of This Fold. Bryant. TrPWD

Look, God, I have never spoken to You. Conversion. Frances Angermayer. PoLF

Look, he is superfluous — for of what use was it to be born? Ovid, *tr. by* L. R. Lind. *Fr.* Tristium. NAs

Look he trusts it's good. Warning. Tadeusz Rózewicz, *tr. fr. Polish by* Magnus F. Krynski. PoSu

Look: Here our bodies lie in a long, long line. But We Shall Bloom. Haim Guri, *tr. fr. Hebrew by* David Kuselewitz. TrJP

Look here, Petah! whut's this here. The Examination. Priscilla Jane Thompson. CBWP-2

Look here, upon this picture, and on this. Shakespeare. *Fr.* Hamlet. NAWM-1; OxAEP-1

Look him. As quiet as a July river-/ bed. Grampa. Dennis Scott. NTP; PBCV

Look how harmless he is, have mercy on him. *(LL)* Menace of the Sick. Breyten Breytenbach. PeSAV

Look how her close defences laddered now. Apollo and Daphne. W. R. Rodgers. ErPo; LiTB

Look how peaceful these wooden figures are, going to their death. The War against the Jews. Gerald Stern. CAPP

Look/ how Selma holds. Selm . . . A Pot of Soup . . . A Bottle of Milk. Lodz, 1938. Kirtland Snyder. BTR

Look! how the clouds are flying south! The Snow-Man. "Marian Douglas." OBCA

Look how the industrious bee in fragrant May. The Bee. Charles Fitz-Geffry. *Fr.* Sir Francis Drake. EIL

Look how the lark soars upward and is gone. False Poets and True. Thomas Hood. EPCY

Look how yon lecher's legs are worn away. John Taylor. NOSC

Look in my face and see. *(LL)* A Denial. Elizabeth Barrett Browning. GBL; OBNC

Look in my face; my name is Might-have-been. A Superscription. Dante Gabriel Rossetti. *Fr.* House of Life, The. EBVV; GTBS-P; NAEL-2; NoP; OAEL-2; OBNC; PoEL-5

Look in the dark alcove under the stairs. Under the Stairs. Frank Ormsby. PBCIP

Look, in the Labyrinth of Memory. Delmore Schwartz. TrJP

Look in this crystal pool, and you will see. To —————, with an Ivory Hand-Glass. Lord Alfred Bruce Douglas. FaBoUs

Look in thy glass, and tell the face thou viewest. Shakespeare. *Fr.* Sonnets. EnRePo; ImPo; LiTB; NAEL-1; SCGP

Look! It is there! *(LL)* Not Marble nor the Gilded Monuments. Archibald MacLeish. BoLoP; CMoP; HoPM; MeMAP; MoAB; PoRA; TwCP

Look like somewhere else today. *(LL)* First Snow. Marie Louise Allen. SiSoPo

Look, Loig, behind. The Only Jealousy of Emer. *Unknown, tr. fr. Irish by* John Montague. BIrV

Look! Look at me! Tree Birthdays. Mary Carolyn Davies. OHIP

Look, look! rejoice and wonder! The Return of Astraea. Ben Jonson. NOBE

Look! look! the spring is come. First Spring Morning. Robert Bridges. BoNaP; BoTP

Look, Medusa!. Suniti Namjoshi. AIW

Look, No Hands. Pearse Hutchinson. PBCIP

Look: no one ever promised for sure. An Introduction to Some Poems. William Stafford. CAPP

Look north if you like: Map Reading. Raymond Garlick. AngWe

Look Not in My Eyes, for Fear. A. E. Housman. *Fr.* Shropshire Lad, A. FaPoB; PeHV; PoEL-5

Look Not Thou. Sir Walter Scott. *See* Look not thou on beauty's charming.

Look not thou on beauty's charming. Lucy Ashton's Song. Sir Walter Scott. *Fr.* Bride of Lammermoor, The. EnRP; NOBE; OBEV; OtMeF; OxAEP-2; OxBS
(Look Not Thou.) OxBSP

Look Not to Memories. Angela de Hoyos. AfAz

Look now, bride of God. In Praise of Virginity. Hroswitha, *tr. fr. Latin by* John Dillon. PBWP; VBLP

Look of sympathy, the gentle word, The. These Are Not Lost. Richard Metcalf. PoToHe

Look off, dear Love, across the sallow sand. Evening Song. Sidney Lanier. AnAmPo; UnPo

Look on Him Whom They Pierced, and Mourn. Isaac Watts. NOCV

Look on that form, once fit for the sculptor! Working and Waiting. Adah Isaacs Menken. CBWP-1

Look — on the topmost branches of the world. Sunday Evening in the Common. John Hall Wheelock. MoAmPo

Look on this cast, and know the hand. The Hand of Lincoln. Edmund Clarence Stedman. AnAmPo; OHIP

Look on this statue, traveller; look well. Theocritus *[or Theokritus], tr. fr. Greek by* Anthony Holden. GrAn

Look once more ere we leave this specular Mount. Milton. *Fr.* Paradise Regained *[or Regain'd].* OBTV, *ll.* 236–284; PeECV, *ll.* 236–271
(Athens.) NOSC, *bk.* IV, *ll.* 236–364

Look one way and the sun is going down. The Mockingbird. Randall Jarrell. NYBP; RFM

Look *[or Looke]* Home. Robert Southwell. ESCV; NOCV; NoSic

Look or You Leap. Jasper Heywood. EIL

Look our ransomed shores around. Additional Verses to Hail Columbia. Oliver Wendell Holmes. PAH

Look, our Spaniard's yawning. Antonio Machado Ruiz, *tr. fr. Spanish by* John Frederick Nims. STV

Look out how you use proud words. Primer Lesson. Carl Sandburg. FaPON; MoAmPo; MoShBr

Look out! look out! Jack Frost. Cecily E. Pike. BoTP

Look out! Look out, boys! Clear the track! Oliver Wendell Holmes. *Fr.* Broomstick Train, The. FaPON

Look out there. *Unknown.* NOIV

Look out upon the stars, my love. Edward Coote Pinkney. AnAmPo

Look round, brown moon, brown bird, as you rise to fly. God is Good. It Is a Beautiful Night. Wallace Stevens. SAmP

Look round our world; behold the chain of love. Pope. *Fr.* Essay on Man, An. FHYEP; OBD

Look round: You see a little supper room. De Coenatione Micae. Martial, *tr. fr. Latin by* Robert Louis Stevenson. FaBoCh

Look! she is dead: no candle can cover her: look. Look! Stan Rice. IMW

Look Sheila Seeing You've Asked Me. Vincent O'Sullivan. PeNZ

Look soul. Animula. W. S. Merwin. CAPP

Look sour, and hum a tune — as you may now. *(LL)* Epistle to Miss *[or* Miss Teresa*]* Blount, on Her Leaving the Town after the Coronation. Pope. BoLoP; EBEV; FHYEP; NAEL-1; NOBE; NOEC; NoP; OPOP; PoEL-3; PPP

Look, stranger, on this island now. On This Island. W. H. Auden. CMoP; NAEL-2; PAW; PoE
(Look, Stranger, on This Island.) InvP
(Look, Stranger.) MoAB; MoBrPo; TrGrPo
(Seascape.) GTBS-P

Look that is that uninvited. Vasco *[or Vasko]* Popa, *tr. fr. Serbo-Croatian. Fr.* Far Within Us. PoSu, *tr. by* Anne Pennington

Look. The land ends up. Some Grand River Blues. Daniel David Moses. HATNAP

Look, the trees. In Blackwater Woods. Mary Oliver. CAPP; CrSp

Look there at the star! Shepherd's Song at Christmas. Langston Hughes. PChr

Look thy last on all things shitty. Shitty. Kingsley Amis. OxBC

Look to the Back of the Hand. Judith Minty. PoA

Look to this day! Salutation to the Dawn. Kalidasa, *tr. fr. Sanskrit.* PoToHe

Look! Unlearn your bookish lore. Song of the Knight of the Mirrors. W. H. Auden. *Fr.* Man of La Mancha. AnAn

Look Up *or* Lend a Hand. Edward Everett Hale. FaBoBe

Look up and not down. Look Up *or* Lend a Hand. Edward Everett Hale. FaBoBe

Look up, and swear by the slain of the War that you'll never forget! *(LL)* Aftermath. Siegfried Sassoon. MoBrPo; NSI; PoWW; TrJP

Look up, dear one, nor be cast down. Truth. Josephine D. Henderson Heard. CBWP-4

Look up into the dome. Altitudes. Richard Wilbur. CMoP

Look up into the light of the lantern. Night Song. Louise Glück. SV

Look up, you men. Men there at the fire. Rainer Maria Rilke, *tr. fr. German by* M. D. Herter Norton. *Fr.* Annunciation over the Shepherds. PChr

Look wha' happen las' week at de Oval! Edward Kamau Brathwaite. *Fr.* Rites. FaBoVe

Look what a thousand blue thousand white. Town of My Farewell to You. Anne Carson. *Fr.* Life of Towns, The. BAP-90

Look where it's come from. *(LL)* Codex. Stephen Rodefer. UL

Look where the mist. Mist over Pukehina. *Maori Oral Tradition, tr. by* E. Shortland. WTO

Look you child, I signify three hundred years in swarm. Policeman Cleared in Jaywalking Case. Claire Harris. PBCV

Look, You Have Cast Out Love! Kipling. *Fr.* Plain Tales from the Hills. OxBSP

Look you, my simple friend, 'tis one of those. Arthur Hugh Clough. EnVR

Look'd up in perfect silence at the stars. *(LL)* When I Heard the Learn'd Astronomer. Walt Whitman. AmPP; AnAMPo; FF; HAP; MoAmPo; NAAL-1; NoP; OxBA; PAW; Poetr; SoSe; TAP; TrGrPo; WeW

Look[e] how the pale Queen[e] of the silent night. A Sonnet of the Moon. Charles Best. CH
(Of the Moon.) EIL

Looke well about, ye that lovers be. Against Women. *Unknown.* MeEL

Looker-On, The. Frank Kendon. PAW

Looking across/ The water we are. Twilight. Samuel Menashe. ArNa

Looking and lusting is not love. Argentarius, *tr. fr. Greek by* Sam Hamill. InMo

Looking as I've looked before, straight down the heart. The Stranger. Adrienne Rich. NNaP

Looking at a Dead Wren in My Hand. Robert Bly. NNaP

Looking at a Dry Canadian Thistle Brought In from the Snow. Robert Bly. NNaP

Lord Buddha, The. Hayashi Fumiko, *tr. fr. Japanese by* Kenneth Rexroth and Ikuko Atsumi. WPJ

Lord, but *how* much beauty was there/ Back in 1955! (*LL*) Betjeman, 1984. Charles Causley. FaBoCo; NOBL; OxBTC; PeLV; UV

Lord, by thy sweet and saving sign. *Howres for the Hours of Matines, The*. Richard Crashaw. PeECV

Lord Byron. John Clare. EPCY

"Lord Byron" was an Englishman. Sketch of Lord Byron's Life. Julia A. Moore. FiBHP; OBAL

Lord, can a crumb of dust the earth outweigh. Edward Taylor. *Fr.* Preparatory Meditations Before My Approach to the Lord's Supper. NAAL-1

(Prologue.) EAP

Lord Chancellours Villanies Discovered; or, His Rise and Fall in the Four Last Years, The. *Unknown*. CoMu

Lord Christ, we pray thy mercy on our table spread. In the Refectory. Alcuin, *tr. fr. Latin by* Helen Waddell. MLL

Lord Clive. E. C. Bentley. *See* What I like about Clive.

Lord, confound this surly sister. The Curse. J. M. Synge. ChTr; FaBoCo; FaBoEE; NOIV; PeIV

(To a Sister of an Enemy of the Author Who Disapproved of The Playboy.) IHNG

Lord Coningsby's Epitaph. Pope. FaBoEE

Lord Cozens Hardy. Sir John Betjeman. OxBTC

Lord Crashton: The Absentee Landlord. William Allingham. *Fr.* Laurence Bloomfield in Ireland. NOIV

Lord, Dear God! to Thy Attending. Heinrich Otto, *tr. fr. German by* Sheema Z. Buehne. AH

Lord Delamere. *Unknown*. ESPB

Lord, Deliver, Thou Canst Save. Eliza Lee Follen. AH

Lord deplored unwedded bliss, The. The Book of the Law. John Whitworth. FaBoBl

Lord Derwentwater. *Unknown*. AmFP; ESPB

Lord Descended from Above, The. Thomas Sternhold. AH

(Majesty of God, The.) WGRP

Lord Douglas. *Unknown*. *See* I was a lady of high renown.

Lord Douglas. *Unknown*. *See* Oh [*or* O] waly, waly, up the [*or* yon] bank.

Lord Erlinton had ae daughter. Erlinton. *Unknown*. ESPB, A *and* B *vers.*

Lord Finchley. Hilaire Belloc. FaBoCo; FaBoEE; FiBHP; NBLV; NoAM; NOBL; OxAEP-2; OxBoLi; PeLV

Lord Fluting Dreams of America on the Eve of His Departure from Liverpool. Paul Zimmer. VGW

Lord, for the erring thought. William Dean Howells. *Fr.* Thanksgiving, A. TrPWD; WGRP

Lord, for to-morrow and its needs. Just for To-Day. Ernest R. Wilberforce. PWR

Lord, Forgive a Spirit. Gerald Stern. CAPP

Lord Galloway. Burns. OxBoLi

Lord gie you chile de spirit. Gettin de Spirit. Una Marson. PBCV

Lord, give me vision that shall see. Beyond the Profit of Today. *Unknown*. PoToHe

Lord God, forgive white Europe! Léopold Sédar Senghor, *tr. fr. French by* Ellen Conroy Kennedy. *Fr.* Prayer for Peace. TTY, *tr. by* John Reed *and* Clive Wake, *sect.* II

Lord God, how full our cup of happiness! The Cup of Happiness. Gilbert Thomas. TrPWD

Lord God, I saw the son-of-a-bitch uncoil. The Rural Carrier Stops to Kill a Nine-Foot Cottonmouth. T. R. Hummer. Poetr; SM

Lord God in Paradise. Grace for Gardens. Louise Driscoll. TrPWD

Lord God of Heaven, who only are. The Prayer of Nehemiah. George Wither. ChIV-1

Lord God of Hosts. Shepherd Knapp. AH

Lord God of Hosts incline thine ear. The Century Prayer. James Ephriam McGirt. AAP

Lord, God of love, the wedded hearts.' The Sanctum. T. A. Daly. TrPWD

Lord God of the oak and the elm. George Villiers. TrPWD

Lord God of trajectory and blast. Man unto His Fellow Man. Norman Corwin. *Fr.* On a Note of Triumph. TrJP

Lord God Planted a Garden, The. Dorothy Frances Gurney. BLPA; EBEvV; FaBoBe; WGRP

Lord God! this was a stone. The Stone. Thomas Vaughan. OBWVE

Lord's jealous of yourself and me, The. (*LL*) Dread. J. M. Synge. BoLoP; MoBrPo; OxBSP

Lord Gorbals. Harry Graham. FaBoCo; PeLV

Lord, guard and guide the men who fly. Hymn for Airmen. M. C. D. H. NSI

Lord had a job for me, The. Get Somebody Else. Paul Laurence Dunbar. BLRP

(Too Busy.) WBLP

Lord Harry has written a novel. A Novel of High Life. Thomas Haynes Bayly. OxAEP-2

Lord Has a Child, The. Langston Hughes. AH

Lord, Have Mercy. Nahum Tate. TIRV

Lord, Have Mercy on Us. Thomas Nashe. *See* Adieu, Farewell, Earth's Bliss[e].

Lord Hay's Mask., *sels.* Thomas Campion.

Lord, he thought he'd make a man. Dese Bones Gwine to Rise Again. *Unknown*. AS; OxBoLi

Lord, Hear My Prayer. John Clare. ChIV-1; NOCV; NoP; TrCP

Lord, hear my prayer when trouble glooms. Lord, Hear My Prayer. John Clare. ChIV-1; NOCV; NoP; TrCP

Lord, help me live from day to day. Others. Charles D. Meigs. WBLP

Lord here my prayre and let my crye passe. Bible, *O.T.*, *paraphrased by* Sir Thomas Wyatt. *Fr.* Psalms. OBVE

Lord Heygate. Hilaire Belloc. OxBoLi

Lord High-Bo. Hilaire Belloc. FiBHP

Lord High Executioner's Song, The. W. S. Gilbert. *See* As some day it may happen that a victim must be found.

Lord Hippo. Hilaire Belloc. NoAM

Lord, how are they increased that trouble me! Bible, *O.T.*, *paraphrased by* Sir Thomas Wyatt. *Fr.* Psalms.

(Psalm III: "Lord how many are my foes," *paraphrased by* Milton.) OBVE

Lord, how can man preach thy eternal[l] word? The Windows. George Herbert. ESCV; GeHe; MeLP; NAEL-1; NOCV; NoP; PeECV; PoE; SeCP; SeCV-1; TrCP

Lord, how delightful 'tis to see. For the Lord's Day Evening. Isaac Watts. OxBChV

Lord, hush this ego as one stops a bell. Vassar Miller. *Fr.* Love's Bitten Tongue. MT

Lord, I also want to meet you, see. Second Coming. Adam Small, *tr. fr. Afrikaans by* Carrol Lasker. PeSAV

Lord, I am like to mistletoe. To God. Robert Herrick. TrPWD; WGRP

Lord, I am lonely. A Stranger in This Land. Cliff Ashby. NOCV

Lord I am not entirely selfish. Gavin Ewart. OxBC

Lord, I am poor; but it becomes. I Have a Roof. Ada Jackson. TrPWD

Lord, I Am Thine. Samuel Davies. AH

Lord, I don't want no more school. (*LL*) A Little Black Boy's Prayer. Guy Tirolien. NegPo

Lord, I give thanks! Thanksgiving. Susie Montgomery Best. TrPWD

Lord, I go softly all my years! (*LL*) The Quiet Pilgrim. Edith M. Thomas. AmWP

Lord, I have knelt and tried to pray to-night. Communion. Edward Dowden. TrPWD

Lord, I have not time to pray. Helene Magaret. *Fr.* Impiety. TrPWD

Lord, I Know Thy Grace Is nigh Me. Hervey Doddridge Ganse. AH

Lord, I long to be with thee! (*LL*) Guide Me, O Thou Great Jehovah. William Williams. OBWVE

Lord, I remember, and am sore amazed. Hymn of Weeping. Amittai ben Shefatiah, *tr. fr. Hebrew by* Nina Davis Salaman. TrJP

Lord, I say nothing: I profess. Christ, the Man. W. H. Davies. WGRP

Lord I Sleep and I Sleep. David Shapiro. ChIV-1

Lord, I Want to Be a Christian. *Unknown*. AH

Lord, if I loved her, count it not my shame. (*LL*) Of the Gentle Heart. Guido Guinicelli. AWP; CTC; OBVE

Lord! if in love, though fainting oft, I have tended thy gracious Vine. "Owen Meredith." *Fr.* Last Lines. OBVE

Lord, If Thou Art Not Present. John Gray. TrPWD

Lord, I'm done for: now Margot. Vincent Voiture, *tr. fr. French by* William Jay Smith. FiBHP

Lord, I'm tired. A Little Black Boy's Prayer. Guy Tirolien, *tr. fr. French by* Ellen Conroy Kennedy. NegPo

Lord in His wisdom made the fly, The. The Fly. Ogden Nash. FaPON

Lord, in my silence how do I despise. Frailty. George Herbert. NOCV

Lord, in this day of battle. Prayer during Battle. Hermann Hagedorn. TrPWD

Lord, in this dust Thy sovereign voice. A Thanksgiving. Cardinal Newman. TrPWD

Lord, in Thy Presence Here. Jesse L. Holman. AH

Lord Ingram and Chiel Wyet. *Unknown*. ESPB, A, B, *and* C *vers.*

Lord into His Garden Comes, The. *Unknown*. AH

Lord Is King, The. *Unknown, tr. fr. Hebrew by* Solomon Solis-Cohen. TrJP

Lord is my herd, nae want sal fa' me, The. Psalm XXIII. P. Hately Waddell. ChIV-1

Lord is my light and my salvation, The; whom shall I fear? Bible, *O.T.*, *paraphrased by* Sir Thomas Wyatt. *Fr.* Psalms.

(Deliverance of Jehovah, The.) WGRP

Lord is my shepherd, The. Bible, *O.T., paraphrased by* Sir Thomas Wyatt. *See* Lord is my shepherd, I shall not want, The.

Lord is my shepherd/ and keeps me from wanting, The. Bible, *O.T., paraphrased by* Sir Thomas Wyatt. *See* Lord is my shepherd, I shall not want, The.

Lord is my shepherd;/ I have everything I need, The. Bible, *O.T., paraphrased by* Sir Thomas Wyatt. *See* Lord is my shepherd, I shall not want, The.

Lord is my shepherd, I shall not, The. Neo-Thomist Poem. Ernest Hemingway. OBAL

Lord is my shepherd, I shall not want, The. Bible, *O.T., paraphrased by* Sir Thomas Wyatt. *Fr.* Psalms. AWP; BLPL; FaBoBe; FaPON; NAWM-1; NIP; OHIP; PoLF; TFi; TrGrPo; TrJP; TRP

(Psalm XXIII: "Lorde is my shepherde, The; therfore can I lack nothing.") OBVE, *tr. by* Miles Coverdale

(Lord is my shepherd/ and keeps me from wanting, The.) TRP, *tr. by* David Rosenberg

(Lord is my shepherd;/ I have everything I need, The.) TRP

(Lord is my shepherd, The.) FaPoB

(Lord to me a shepherd is, The.) OBCA

(Lord's my shepherd, I'll not want, The.) ScCV

(Lord's My Shepherd, The.) AH; WBLP, *ad. by* Francis Rous

(Protection of Jehovah, The.) WGRP

(Psalm XXIII: "Lord my shepherd, me His sheep, The," *paraphrased by* George Sandys.) JCP

Lord it is my chief complaint. William Cowper. *Fr.* Lovest Thou Me? TrPWD

Lord, it is not Life to live. Augustus Montague Toplady. *Fr.* Happiness Found. TrPWD

Lord: it is time. The huge summer has gone by. Rainer Maria Rilke. *See* Lord, it is time. The summer was too long.

Lord, it is time. The summer was too long. Autumn Day. Rainer Maria Rilke, *tr. fr. German by* C. F. MacIntyre. TrJP

(Lord: it is time. The huge summer has gone by.) ArNa

(Lord, it is time. The summer was very big.) EaPr, *tr. by* Tr: Stephen Mitchell

Lord Jesus, at the end of this book which I offer you. Léopold Sédar Senghor, *tr. fr. French by* Ellen Conroy Kennedy. *Fr.* Prayer for Peace. NegPo

Lord Jesus Christ, in whose hand is the breath. *Unknown, tr. fr. Latin by* Helen Waddell. MLL

Lord Jesus Christ, We Humbly Pray. Henry Eyster Jacobs. AH

Lord Jesus, make Thyself to me. My Prayer. *Unknown.* BLRP

Lord Jesus, Thou hast known. A Mother's Birthday. Henry van Dyke. OHIP

Lord Jesus, who would think that I am Thine? Christina Rossetti. NOBVV

Lord Jesus! with what sweetness and delights. Ascension-Day. Henry Vaughan. ESCV

Lord, knights, and squires, the num'rous band. To a Child of Quality of Five Years Old, the Author Supposed Forty. Matthew Prior. NOEC

Lord, lay the taste of prayer upon my tongue. The Taste of Prayer. Ralph W. Seager. TrPWD

Lord, lay your fingers on. Closing Prayer. Johnstone G. Patrick. TrPWD

Lord! Lead the Way the Saviour Went. William Croswell. AH

Lord, let me be the torch that springs to light. The Torch. Theodosia Garrison. BLPA

Lord, let me live like a Regular Man. Berton Braley. BLPA

Lord, let me live to serve and make a loan. Hydromel and Rue. George Marion McClellan. AAP

Lord, let me make this rule. School Days. Maltbie D. Babcock. PWR

Lord, let the angels praise thy name. Miserie. George Herbert. PoEL-2

Lord, let war's tempests cease. Let War's Tempests Cease. Longfellow. OHIP

Lord Livingston. *Unknown.* ESPB; OxBB

Lord, Lord, an East Virginia man. (*LL*) John Henry. *Unknown.* FaBoBa; NOBA; OxBoLi; TrGrPo

Lord, Lord to Thee. A Sailor's Prayer. George Hornell Morris. TrPWD

Lord Lovel. *Unknown.* ESPB

Lord Lovel. *Unknown.* AmFP; AS; BLPA; ESPB, B *and* D *vers.*; FaPON

Lord Lovel he stands at his stable-door. Lord Lovel. *Unknown.* AmFP; AS; BLPA; ESPB, B *and* D *vers.*; FaPON

(Tale of Lord Lovell, The.) NOBL

Lord Lovel ("Lord Lovel he stood at his castle gate.") *Unknown.* AmFP; AS; BLPA; ESPB, A, B, *and* D *vers.*; FaPON

Lord Lovel he stood at his castle gate. Lord Lovel ("Lord Lovel he stood at his castle gate.") *Unknown.* AmFP; AS; BLPA; ESPB, A, B, *and* D *vers.*; FaPON

Lord Lovell he stood at his own front door. The Tale of Lord Lovell. *Unknown.* NOBL; PeLV

Lord Lucky. Hilaire Belloc. NBLV

Lord Lundy. Hilaire Belloc. FaBoCo; OBSV; OxBoLi; PeLV

Lord Lundy from his earliest years. Lord Lundy. Hilaire Belloc. FaBoCo; OBSV; OxBoLi; PeLV

Lord, Make a Regular Man out of Me. Edgar A. Guest. BLPA; BLPL

Lord, make me an instrument of Thy Peace. Prayer of St. Francis of Assisi for Peace. St. Francis of Assisi, *tr. fr. Latin.* PoLF; PoToHe

Lord, make me coy and tender to offend. Unkindness. George Herbert. NOSC; OBF

Lord, make me sensitive to the sight. Barbara Marr. TrPWD

Lord, Make Me to Know Mine End. Bible, *O.T., paraphrased by* Sir Thomas Wyatt. *See* I said: "I will take heed to my ways."

Lord, make my soul. The Mirror. Blanche Mary Kelly. TrPWD

Lord make us mindful of the little things that grow and blossom. W. E. B. DuBois. EaPr

Lord, Many Times Thou Pleased Art. George Wither. AH

Lord Maxwell has te'n his last good-night. (*LL*) Lord Maxwell's Last Goodnight ("Good Lord of the Land . . . .") *Unknown.* ESPB, A *vers.*; OxBB

Lord Maxwell's Last Goodnight. *Unknown.* ESPB

Lord Maxwell's Last Goodnight ("Good Lord of the Land . . . .") *Unknown.* ESPB, A *vers.*; OxBB

Lord, may there be no moment in her life. Prayer of Any Husband. Mazie V. Caruthers. PoToHe

Lord, mine eye offended. Matthew V. 29-30. Derek Mahon. CIP

Lord, my mind is not noisy with desires. Bible, *O.T., paraphrased by* Sir Thomas Wyatt. *Fr.* Psalms. EnlH, *paraphrased by* Stephen Mitchell

Lord my shepherd, me His sheep, The. George Sandys. *Fr.* Paraphrase on the Psalms of David. JCP

Lord, My Weak Thought in Vain Would Climb. Ray Palmer. AH

Lord North's Recantation. *Unknown.* PAH

Lord, not for light in darkness do we pray. John Drinkwater. TrPWD; WGRP

Lord, now lettest thou thy servant depart in peace. Nunc Dimittis. Bible, *N.T. Fr.* St. Luke. WGRP

Lord of All Being, Throned Afar. Oliver Wendell Holmes. *Fr.* Professor at the Breakfast Table, The. AH

Lord of all, himself through all diffused, The. William Cowper. *Fr.* Task, The. OAEL-1

Lord of Each Soul. Paul Engle. AH

Lord of Heaven and Earth has made a feast, The. On a Feast. Francis Quarles. ChIV-2

Lord of Hosts, and God of Israel! The Prayer of Hezekiah. George Wither. ChIV-1

Lord of Life, All Praise Excelling. Clement Clarke Moore. AH

Lord of Lorn and the False [*or* Fals] Steward, The. *Unknown.* ESPB; OxBB

Lord of My Heart's Elation. Bliss Carman. AH; NOBC; TrPWD

Lord of my love, to whom in vassalage. Shakespeare. *Fr.* Sonnets. HeIP

Lord of my years, can life be bare. Common Blessings. Thomas Curtis Clark. TrPWD

Lord of Rosslyn's daughter gaed through the wud her lane, The. Captain Wedderburn's Courtship. *Unknown.* ESPB

Lord of Sea and Earth and Air. Prayer for a Pilot. Cecil Roberts. FaPON (Prayer for the Pilot.) TrPWD

Lord of the Dance. Sydney Carter. OBET

Lord of the Far Horizons. Bliss Carman. TrPWD

Lord of the grass and hill. Overlord. Bliss Carman. (Veni Creator.) WGRP

Lord of the Isle, The. Stefan George, *tr. fr. German by* Ludwig Lewisohn. AWP

Lord of the Mountain. Prayer to the Mountain Spirit. *Unknown, tr. by* G. W. Cronyn. WGRP

Lord of the pots and pipkins, since I have not time to be. The Divine Office of the Kitchen. Cecily Hallack. BLRP; PoLF

Lord of the River Hsiang. Ch'u Yüan, *tr. fr. Chinese by* Wu-chi Liu. SuSp

Lord of the Throne. Al-Tirimmah, *tr. fr. Arabic by* Omar S. Pound. ArPe

Lord of the Winds. Mary Elizabeth Coleridge. TrPWD

Lord of the winds! I feel thee nigh. The Hurricane. Bryant. EAP

Lord of the World. *Unknown, tr. fr. Hebrew by* D. A. de Sola. TrJP

Lord of the Worlds Below! James Freeman. AH

Lord of Tree, may I be blessed. (*LL*) May the axe be far away from you. *Unknown.* EaPr

Lord Our God Alone Is Strong, The. Caleb T. Winchester. AH

Lord over all! whose power the sceptre swayed. Lord of the World. *Unknown, tr. fr. Hebrew by* D. A. de Sola. TrJP

Lord over life and all the ways of breath. Ernest Dowson. *Fr.* De Amore. OBNC; TrPWD

Lord, pity such sinners. Monday afternoon. A Devotional Sonnet. Timothy Steele. CRP

Lord, purge our eyes to see. Judge Not According to the Appearance. Christina Rossetti. TrPWD

Lord Rameses of Egypt sighed. Birthright. John Drinkwater. CH; CoGr; OxBTC

Lord Randal. *Unknown.* AmFP; AWP; EBEV; EBEvV; EBNV; EnRP; ESPB, A, B, *and* J vers.; FaBoBa; FF; GGP; HAP; HeIL; HeIP; HoPM; ImPo; LiTB; NoP, (A vers.); NTP; OAEL-1; OxBB; OxBS; Poetr; SCGP; TFi; TrGrPo; TRP; WeW

Lord, receive my prayer. Evening Prayer. Thomas Merton. ChIV-1

Lord reigneth; he is apparelled with majesty, The. Bible, *O.T., paraphrased by* Sir Thomas Wyatt. *Fr.* Psalms. WGRP

Lord Saltoun and Auchanachie. *Unknown.* ESPB

Lord, Save Us, We Perish. Christina Rossetti. TrPWD

Lord, send what Thou wilt. Eduard Friedrich Mörike, *tr. fr. German by* Philip L. Miller. RiWo

Lord, shall I find it in Thy Holy Church. Truth. Claude McKay. BPo

Lord she's gone done left me done packed/ up and split. Feeling Fucked Up. Etheridge Knight. NNaP; PBCAP; RaBo

Lord, since it's hard to explain. J. E. Press. PeLi

Lord, since the strongest human hands I know. In the Dark. Sophie Jewett. TrPWD

Lord, speak to me, that I may speak. For Every Day. Frances Ridley Havergal. *Fr.* Teacher's Prayer, A. BLRP

Lord speaks, The/ this way. Isaiah: Chapter 66. David Rosenberg. ChIV-1

Lord survives the rainbow of His will, The. (LL) The Quaker Graveyard in Nantucket. Robert Lowell. CMoP; HAP; LiTM; MoAB; MoP; NAAL-2; NoAM; NOBA; NoP; OxBA; PeECV; Poetr; TAP; UnPo; VCAP

Lord, teach us how to pray! (LL) What Is Prayer? James Montgomery. BLRP; WGRP

Lord Tennyson and Lord Melchett. D. H. Lawrence. FaBoEE

Lord, the air smells good today, straight from the mysteries. Jalal al-Din Rumi, *tr. by* John Moyne *and* Colman Barks. EaPr

Lord, the Roman hyacinths are blooming in bowls. A Song for Simeon. T. S. Eliot. ChIV-2; LiTB; NAs; NOCV

Lord, the snowful sky. Sailor's Carol. Charles Causley. OBCP; PeECV

Lord, Thine humble servants hear. Hymn for Atonement Day. Judah Halevi, *tr. fr. Hebrew by* Solomon Solis-Cohen. TrJP

Lord, this woman who fell into many sins. Kassia, *tr. by* Aliki, Willis Barnstone, *and* Elene Kolb. BoWoP

Lord Thomas and Fair Annet. *Unknown.* ESPB

Lord Thomas and Lady Margaret. *Unknown.* ESPB

Lord Thomas is to the hunting gone. Lord Thomas and Lady Margaret. *Unknown.* ESPB

Lord Thomas Stuart. *Unknown.* ESPB

Lord, Thou art mine, and I am Thine. Clasping of Hands. George Herbert. PoEL-2

Lord, Thou Clepedest Me. *Unknown.* OxBSP

Lord, Thou Hast Been Our Dwelling Place. Bible, *O.T., paraphrased by* Sir Thomas Wyatt. *See*Psalm XC ("Lord, thou hast been our dwelling place in all generations.")

Lord, Thou hast given me a cell. A Thanksgiving to God for His House. Robert Herrick. BeJo; BLPL; ChTr; FaBoBe; HAP; NOSC; OHIP; PeECV; PoRA; SeCP; SeCV-1; TrCP; TrPWD; WGRP
(Thankful Heart, A.) PoToHe

Lord, Thou hast made this world below the shadow of a dream. McAndrew's Hymn. Kipling. OxBTC
(M'Andrew's Hymn.) OtMeF; PoEL-5

Lord, Thou Hast Promised. Samuel K. Cox. AH

Lord, Thou who art like the sea. The Night Prayer of Glückel of Hameln. Edouard Roditi. CRP

Lord, thus I sin, repent, and sin again. A Sinner's Lament. Lord Herbert of Cherbury. SeCP

Lord 'tis midnight. Three Phases of Africa. Francis Ernest Kobina Parkes. PBA

Lord to me a shepherd is, The. Bible, *O.T., paraphrased by* Sir Thomas Wyatt. *See* Lord is my shepherd, I shall not want, The.

Lord to me a shepherd is, The. *Unknown. Fr.* Bay Psalm Book, The. OBCA

Lord Ullin's Daughter. Thomas Campbell. BeLS; BoTP; EnRP; FaPON; FaPoR; GN; GTBS; GTBS-P; WBLP

Lord, very fair my lot and beautiful my story. Very Fair My Lot. Jacob David Kamzon, *tr. fr. Hebrew by* Sholom J. Kahn. TrJP

Lord Walter's Wife. Elizabeth Barrett Browning. BeLS; HAP

Lord Waterford. *Unknown.* ChTr; GBP

Lord, we come! (LL) The Reveille. Bret Harte. GN; OHIP; OtMeF; PAH

Lord, we look to once for all, The. The Heretic's Tragedy. Robert Browning. OAEL-2

Lord! what a busy [or busie] restles[s] thing. The Pursuit[e]. Henry Vaughan. AngWe; GeHe; NOSC; SeCP; TrCP; TrPWD

Lord, what a change within us one short hour. Richard Chenevix Trench. WBLP; WGRP
(Power of Prayer, The.) PoToHe
(Prevailing Prayer.) BLRP
(Sonnet.) TrPWD

Lord! what a goodly thing is want of shirts. John Cleveland. *Fr.* Rebel [or Rebell] Scot, The. OBSV

Lord, what a thoughtless wretch was I. *Unknown.* AmFP

Lord, what am I, that, with unceasing care. To-Morrow. Lope de Vega, *tr. fr. Spanish by* Longfellow. AWP; TrPWD

Lord, what are the sins. In a U-Haul North of Damascus. David Bottoms. FYAP; MT

Lord what is man, that he should find. Bible, *O.T., paraphrased by* Sir Thomas Wyatt. *Fr.* Psalms. AWP; NAWM-1

Lord, what is man? why should he cost thee [or you]. C[h]aritas Nimia; or, The Dear[e] Bargain. Richard Crashaw. ESCV; JCP; NOCV; NOSC

Lord, What Will the Earth Bring Forth. Paul Johann Ludwig Heyse, *tr. fr. German by* Philip L. Miller. RiWo

Lord, when I look at lovely things which pass. In the Fields. Charlotte Mew. ArNa; BoNaP; MoAB; MoBrPo; NTP; OxAEP-2

Lord, when I think. *Unknown.* CBLP

Lord, when the clock strikes. The Reader. Thomas Merton. CRP

Lord, when the sense of Thy sweet grace. Richard Crashaw. TrPWD
(Ecstacy, An.) OxAEP-1

Lord, when the wise men came from far[r]. Sidney Godolphin. BeJo; HAP; JCP; MeLP; NOCV; PeECV
(Meditation on the Nativity.) NOSC
(Wise Men and Shepherds.) BLPL; NOBE

Lord, when they kill me, let the job be thorough. Merthyr. Glyn Jones. AngWe

Lord! when thou didst thy self undress. The Incarnation and Passion. Henry Vaughan. GeHe; TrCP

Lord, Where Shall I Find Thee? Judah Halevi, *tr. fr. Hebrew by* Nina Davis Salaman. TrJP

Lord, While for All Mankind. John R. Wreford. TrPWD

Lord, who am I that they should stoop — these holy folk of thine? (LL) Good Company. Karle Wilson Baker. FaPON; WGRP

Lord, who am I to teach the way. The Teacher. Leslie Pinckney Hill. PoNe; TrPWD

Lord! Who Art Merciful as Well as Just. Robert Southey. TrPWD

Lord, who createdst man in wealth and store. Easter Wings. George Herbert. AngWe; ChIV-1; ESCV; FHYEP; GeHe; HAP; HeIP; InPK; InPS; LiTB; MeLP; NAEL-1; NIP; NoP; NOSC; OAEL-1; PoE; PoEL-2; Poetr; PPP; SeCP; TEP; TFi; TOF; TrCP; TRP; WeW

Lord, who hast formed me out of mud. Trinity Sunday. George Herbert. OxBSP

Lord who ordainst for mankind. The Mother's Hymn. Bryant. OHIP

Lord, Who's the Happy Man. Nahum Tate *and* Nicholas Brady. AH

Lord will answer, go below!, The. (LL) Steal not this book for fear of shame. *Unknown.* FaBoUs; ISE

Lord Will Happiness Divine, The. William Cowper. NOCV

Lord will see us through some day, The. (LL) We Shall Overcome. *Unknown.* AH

Lord William; or, Lord Lundy. *Unknown.* ESPB

Lord Willoughby. *Unknown.* CoMu

Lord, with glowing heart I'd praise thee. Francis Scott Key. TrPWD

Lord, with what care hast thou begirt us round! Sin. George Herbert. GeHe; NoP; OxAEP-1

Lord, with what glorie wast thou serv'd of old. Sion. George Herbert. ChIV-1; ESCV

Lord, within thy fold I be. Priscilla Jane Thompson. CBWP-2

Lord, You may not recognize me. The Gift. Louise Glück. FaBoWP

Lord! You Saved Me from Ur-Germany as I Fled. Uri Zvi Greenberg, *tr. fr. Hebrew by* Ruth Finer Mintz. MHP

Lord, you visited Paris on the day of your birth. Paris in the Snow. Léopold Sédar-Senghor, *tr. fr. French by* Ulli Beier. PBA

Lorde blesse the and kepe the, The. Bible, *O.T. See* Lord bless thee and keep thee, The.

Lordinges, listen, and hold you still. Durham Field. *Unknown.* ESPB

Lordings, Listen to Our Lay. *Unknown.* OHIP

"Lordings [or Lordinges or Lordynges]," quod he, "in chirches whan I preche." The Pardoner's Prologue. Chaucer. *Fr.* Canterbury Tales, The. EnVB; FHYEP; NAEL-1; NoP; OAEL-1; PoE
("In churches," said the Pardoner, "when I preach," *mod. vers. by* Theodore Morrison.) NAWM-1

Lordly and Isolate Satyrs, The. Charles Olson. CoAP; NeAP; PoM

Lordly Hudson, The. Paul Goodman. CoAP; VGW

Lord's Chameleons, The. Peter Klappert. AmPA

Lords do crave all, The. A Postscript to Verses on the History of France. *Unknown.* NOIV

Lords have been made whose hired robes have hidden. On the Relinquishment of a Title. Geoffrey Grigson. FaBoEE

Lords, knights, and squires, the numerous band. To a Child of Quality [Five Years Old, the Author Supposed Forty]. Matthew Prior. GN; LiTB; NOBE; NOEC; OBEV; PoEL-3

Lord's lost Him His mockingbird. Mourning Poem for the Queen of Sunday. Robert Hayden. HCAP; NoAM; NoP; PoBA

Lord's Mask, The, *sels.* Thomas Campion.

Lord's My Shepherd, The. Bible, *O.T., paraphrased by* Sir Thomas Wyatt. *See* Lord is my shepherd, I shall not want, The.

Lord's my shepherd, I'll not want, The. Bible, *O.T., paraphrased by* Sir Thomas Wyatt. *See* Lord is my shepherd, I shall not want, The.

Lord's name be praised, The. The Litanies of Julia Pastrana (1832-1860). Thomas W. Shapcott. CBAP; FaBoMA; NOBAu

Lords of Creation, The. *Unknown.* PoLF

Lords of life, the lords of life, The. Experience. Emerson. LiTA; MeMAP; PoEL-4; TAP

Lords of the Main, The. Joseph Stansbury. PAH

Lord's Prayer, The. Massillon Coicou, *tr. fr. French by* Ellen Conroy Kennedy. NegPo

Lord's Prayer. D. H. Lawrence. PeECV

Lord's Prayer in Verse, The. Aaron Hill. FaBoUs

Lore. R. S. Thomas. OxBC; RB

Lore and Language of Schoolchildren, *sels. Unknown.* "Masculine, Feminine, Neuter." CBNP

Lorelei. Alta. CrSp

Lorelei, The. Heine, *tr. fr. German by* Philip L. Miller. RiWo

Lorelei. Heine, *tr. fr. German.* TrJP, *tr. by* Emma Lazarus

Loreley, The. Heine. *See* I know not what spell is o'er me.

Lorena. H. D. L. Webster. BLPA

Lorenzo dwelt at Heighington. Fragment of a Song. "Lewis Carroll." FaBoNo

Lorenzo! Such the glories of the world! The Consolation. Edward Young. *Fr.* Night Thoughts. NOEC

Lorry made the windows shake, A. Bar Room Conversation. James K. Baxter. *Fr.* Cressida. PeLV

Los Mineros. Edward Dorn. PoM

Lose This Day Loitering. Goethe, *tr. fr. German. Fr.* Faust. PoLF, *tr. by* John Anster

Losers. Carl Sandburg. CMoP; MoAB; MoAmPo; NoAM; TrGrPo

Losing a Slave-Girl. Po Chü-i, *tr. fr. Chinese by* Arthur Waley. AWP

Losing altitude, you can see below you the flames. Death of Thomas Merton. Harry Clifton. IB; PBCIP

Losing its gust, and my ambition blind! *(LL)* To Fanny. Keats. BoLoP; EBEV; EnRP; PPP; Son; TrGrPo

Losing the Marbles. James Merrill. DiPo

Losing the relations. *(LL)* Benjamin Banneker Sends His *Almanac* to Thomas Jefferson. Jay Wright. VCAP

Losing the Straight Way, *sels.* Ian Wedde.

Losing Track. Denise Levertov. HeIP; MoP; NaP; NOBA; PoE; PoM

Loss. Charles Madge. FaBoMo

Loss./ Thank you. With You. Anthony Barnett. VaA

Loss falls from the air as the tables turn. Complaint. Joseph Deericks Bennett. LiTA

Loss in Delay. Robert Southwell. NoSic

Loss, my molester, at last patient be. Pamphilia's Sonnet. Mary Sidney Wroth, Countess of Montgomery. *Fr.* Urania. WPE

Loss of an Oil Tanker. Charles Causley. OxBC

Loss of our learning brought darkness, weakness and woe. *Unknown, tr. fr. Greek by* Thomas Kinsella. NOIV

Loss of something ever felt I, A. Emily Dickinson. ChIV-2; NALW; PFP

Loss of Strength, The. Austin Clarke. IPY

Loss of the *Amphitrite.* *Unknown.* OxBSS

Loss of the *Due Dispatch,* The. *Unknown.* AmFP

Loss of the *Evelyn Marie,* The. *Unknown.* OxBSS

Loss of the *New Columbia,* The. *Unknown.* AmFP

Loss of the *Royal George.* William Cowper. *See* Toll for the brave!

Losses. Randall Jarrell. HCAP; LCAP; LiTM; OxBA; PoA; TAP; UnPo

Losses. Edith M. Thomas. AmWP

Losses, The. Reed Whittemore. OBF

Losses and Recoveries. Chris Wallace-Crabbe. FaBoMA

Lost. Millen Brand. NYBP

Lost. Chu Shu-chen, *tr. fr. Chinese by* Kenneth Rexroth. BoWoP; OHMPC

Lost. James Godden. OBSP

Lost, The. *Malay Oral Tradition, tr. by* R. J. Wilkinson *and* R. O. Winstedt. WTO

Lost, The. *Malay Oral Tradition, tr. by* R. J. Wilkinson *and* R. O. Winstedt. WTO

Lost. Carl Sandburg. AmPP; CMoP; PDV

Lost, The. Jones Very. NOBA

Lost. David Wagoner. ArNa; FoLa; PoA

Lost Acres. Robert Graves. MeMBP; NoAM

Lost Anchors. E. A. Robinson. CMoP

Lost, and all mine, alll mine, forever. *(LL)* Dear Men and Women. John Hall Wheelock. IMW; NYBP; Prf

Lost and bewildered in the thickening mist. On the Great Fog in London, December 1762. James Eyre Weeks. NOEC

Lost and Found. George Macdonald. WGRP

Lost and found, in Sunset Land! *(LL)* The Vanishers. Whittier. AnAmPo

Lost Angel, The. Philip Levine. NOBA

Lost Baby, The. *Unknown.* AmFP

Lost Baby Poem, The. Lucille Clifton. BlSi; CAPP; WPE

Lost Bird. Chenjerai Hove. HBAPE

Lost Bride, The. Antiphanes, *tr. fr. Greek by* Dudley Fitts. GrAn

Lost Carnival, The. Fred Chappell. GOYP

Lost Cat, The. Emile Victor Rieu. CRH

Lost Child, The. James Reaney. NOBC

Lost Children, The. Randall Jarrell. CoAP; PrIm; TAP

Lost child's voice breaks in my throat: no time, The. U. Douglas Oliver. VaA

Lost Chord, The. D. B. Wyndham Lewis. UV

Lost Chord, The. Adelaide Anne Procter. EBEvV; UV, *sts.* I *and* II *only*; VPP; WGRP

Lost City. Harold Farmer. PeSAV

Lost City. Ingrid Jonker, *tr. fr. Afrikaans by* Jack Cope *and* Ruth Miller. PeSA

Lost Continent, The. Jenny Joseph. BrRo

Lost! Cupid!/ One lost Cupid! Meleager, *tr. fr. Greek by* Peter Whigham. GrAn

Lost Dancer, The. Jean Toomer. PoBA

Lost Days. Dante Gabriel Rossetti. *Fr.* House of Life, The. EnVR

Lost days of my life until to-day, The. Lost Days. Dante Gabriel Rossetti. *Fr.* House of Life, The. EnVR

Lost Desire. Meleager, *tr. fr. Greek by* William M. Hardinge. AWP

Lost Doll, The. Charles Kingsley. *Fr.* Water Babies, The. FaPON; MoShBr

Lost Explorer. Edmund Pennant. GoYe

Lost Fan, Hotel Californian, Fresno, 1923. Larry Levis. AnAn

Lost for a Rose's Sake. *Unknown, tr. by* Andrew Lang. AWP

Lost God, A, *sels.* Francis William Bourdillon. "Ah, happy who have seen Him, whom the world." WGRP

Lost Golf Ball, The. David Shapiro. BAP-89

Lost Heifer, The. Austin Clarke. BIrV

Lost in France Jo's Requiem. Ernest Rhys. PAW

Lost in Heaven. Robert Frost. MoAmPo

Lost in the distance, the peaceful time when the green palanquin passed. Crooked River. Li Shang-yin, *tr. fr. Chinese by* A. C. Graham. PLT

Lost, in the heart's worship, and the body's sleep. *(LL)* Yours is the face that the earth turns to me. Kathleen Raine. ArLo; LiTB; MoAB; MoBrPo

Lost in the Philippines. David Mura. ETG

Lost in the vastness of the void Pacific. Homecoming. Karl Shapiro. ArOW

Lost in Translation. James Merrill. FYAP; HCAP; LCAP; NAAL-2; NoAM; VCAP

Lost in wonder, love, and praise! *(LL)* Love Divine, All Loves Excelling. Charles Wesley. NOCV

Lost Jewel, The. Robert Graves. EnLoPo; NYBP

Lost Jimmie Whalen. *Unknown.* AmFP

Lost Johnny. *Unknown.* AmFP

Lost Lady, The, *sels.* Sir William Berkeley. "Where did you borrow that last sigh." OxBSP

Lost Lane. Dorothy Wellesley. WPE

Lost Leader, The. Robert Browning. EBEvV; EnVR; FaBoPV; FaPoB; FHYEP; IHNG; NAEL-2; OtMeF; PFP; PWR; SCGP; TrGrPo

Lost Letter to James Wright, with Thanks for a Map of Fano. Gibbons Ruark. MT

Lost life lost. Lost Monday. Martha Sansom. UnDi

Lost Lines from Chaucer's Prologue to "The Canterbury Tales." *Unknown.* PeHV

Lost Little Sister, The. William Barnes. PoEL-4

Lost! lost! lost! Advertisement of a Lost Day. Lydia Huntley Sigourney. WBLP

Lost! lost! lost! Anne Boleyn. Eloise Bibb. CBWP-4

Lost — lost — lost! Into the Depths. Adah Isaacs Menken. CBWP-1

Lost Love. Dick Allen. NIP

Lost Love. Robert Graves. AWP; CBLP; CH; CoGr; FaBoCh; Mes; MoAB; MoBrPo; NoP

Lost Love. Edward Rowland Sill. AnAmPo

Lost Love. *Unknown, tr. fr. Tewa Indian* by H. J. Spinden. WTO

Lost Love, The. Wordsworth. *See* She Dwelt among the Untrodden Ways.

Lost Lover, The, *sels.* Delariviere Manley.
  "Ah Dangerous Swain, tell me no more." KTR
  "First Adventurer for her fame I stand, The." KTR

Lost manor where I walk continually. The Pier-Glass. Robert Graves. CMoP; MoAB; NoAM

Lost Mistress, The. Robert Browning. BoLoP; NOBE; OBEV; OBNC

Lost Mohican Visits Hell's Kitchen, A. A. K. Redwing. VoR

Lost Moment. Hoyt W. Fuller. PoBA

Lost Moments. Glover Davis. SM

Lost Monday. Martha Sansom. UnDi

Lost Occasion, The. Whittier. BLPL; NOBA

Lost on a fogbound spit of sand. W. H. Auden. FaBoEE

Lost on Both Sides. Dante Gabriel Rossetti. *Fr.* House of Life, The. EnVR; NoP

Lost on Septemter Trail, 1967, *sels.* Alberto A. Ríos.
  There Was a Roof over Our Heads. AfAz; FYAP; ImGa

Lost on the outer rim of some. Written on Beginning Georg Büchner's *Lenz* & While Waiting a Return. John James. VaA

Lost, One Soul. Sandy McIntosh. AIW

Lost Opportunities. H. Cordelia Ray. AmWP; CBWP-3

Lost Orchard, The. Edgar Lee Masters. CMoP

Lost Parasol, The, *sels.* Sándor Weöres, *tr. fr. Hungarian* by Edwin Morgan.
  "Where metalled road invades light thinning air." OBVE

Lost Parents. Lawrence Ferlinghetti. PoM

Lost Pictures, The. Hollis Spurgeon Summers. HoPM

Lost Pilot, The. James Tate. ArOW; CoAP; GoJo; NoAM; NoP; OBWP; TwCP; UnPo

Lost Seed. Patrick Williams. PNI

Lost Shoe, The. *Unknown.* ReMoGo

Lost Silvertip. J. D. Reed. NYBP

Lost Sister. Cathy Song. NoAM

Lost Son, The. Theodore Roethke. HAP; HCAP; LiTM; VGW
Sels.
  Flight, The. NAAL-2; RB; TrGrPo; TRP
  Gibber, The. NAAL-2
  It Was Beginning Winter. NAAL-2
  Pit, The. NAAL-2
  Return, The. NAAL-2

Lost Soul, A. Jay Macpherson. NOBC

Lost Teddy Bear, The. Maggie Pogue Johnson. CBWP-4

Lost: The Original, Its Reason and Its Rhyme. Translation. Rika Lesser. PoA

Lost to the world; lost to myself; alone. On Himself. Robert Herrick. BeJo

Lost Tradition, A. John Montague. CIP; PBCIP

Lost traveller's dream under the hill, The. *(LL)* For the Sexes; the Gates of Paradise. Blake. LiTB; MeMBP; PoEL-4

Lost Tribe, The. Ruth Pitter. WPOW

Lost War-Sloop, The. Edna Dean Proctor. PAH

Lost Word of Jesus, A. Henry van Dyke. TrCP; WGRP

Lost World, A. Robert Graves. NYBP

Lost Youth. Sir Roger Casement. TIRV

Lot. David Helwig. NIP

Lot and His Daughters. A. D. Hope. ChIV-1

Lot and his two daughters and their sons: Man sat sozzled with his two wives, A. Unknown, formerly at. to Cynewulf, *tr. fr. Anglo-Saxon. Fr.* Riddles (Exeter Book). ASW, *tr.* by Kevin Crossley-Holland

Lot Later. Howard Nemerov. HoPM

Lot of love is chosen, The. I learnt that much. Chosen. W. B. Yeats. BoLoP; CMoP

Lot of Night Music, A. Anthony Hecht. OxBC; Poetr

Lot of the old folks here, A — all that's left. Reflections in a Slum. "Hugh MacDiarmid." FaBoTw

Lot of times I've thought about suicide, A. Testament. Bill Zavatsky. UL

Loth to depart, but yet at last, each one. The Parting Verse, the Feast There Ended. Robert Herrick. SeCV-1

Lotos Eating. Mortimer Collins. NOBVV

Lotos Eating, *sels.* Mortimer Collins.
  "Now and then a friend and some sauterne." OBF

Lots, *sels.* Lorna Dee Cervantes.
  Alley, The. ETG

Herself. ETG

Lots of empty. History. Art Lange. UL

Lots of truisms don't have to be repeated. The Anatomy of Happiness. Ogden Nash. LiTA; TAP

Lot's Wife. "Anna Akhmatova," *tr. fr. Russian* by Richard Wilbur. BoWoP; PBWP

Lot's Wife. Cherra S. Ransom. CrSp

Lotte Lenya. Michael O'Loughlin. *Fr.* Two Women. IB

Lottery & Requiem. Maggie O'Sullivan. NBrP

Lotus. Hsü Wei, *tr. fr. Chinese* by Irving Y. Lo. SuSp

Lotus-Eaters, The. ("Courage!" he said, and pointed toward the land.) Tennyson. ChTr, 5 *sts.*; EnVR; LiTB; MeMBP; NAEL-2; NoP; OAEL-2; PoEL-5; SCGP; TEP
Sels.
  Flight, The. NAAL-2; RB; TrGrPo; TRP
  There Is Sweet Music Here. FaBV
  (Choric Song of the Lotos-Eaters.) ImPo
  (Choric Song: "There is sweet music here that softer falls.") HeIP; OBNC
  (Song of the Lotus-Eaters.) GGP; NOBE; OBEV

Lotus Flower, The. Heine, *tr. fr. German* by Philip L. Miller. RiWo

Lotus-flower doth languish, The. Die Lotusblume ängstigt. Heine, *tr. fr. German* by James Thomson. AWP

Lotus flower is fretful. The Lotus Flower. Heine, *tr. fr. German* by Philip L. Miller. RiWo

Lotus Flowers, The. Ellen Bryant Voigt. MT

Lotus-gatherer's Song. Po Chü-i, *tr. fr. Chinese* by Irving Y. Lo. SuSp

Lotus Pond, The. Ts'ao P'i, *tr. fr. Chinese* by Ronald C. Miao. SuSp

Lotuses on the Crooked Pond. Lu Chao-lin, *tr. fr. Chinese* by Paul W. Kroll. SuSp

Loud drums are rolling, the mad trumpets blow, The! Battle Cry. William Henry Venable. PAH

Loud he sang the psalm of David! The Slave Singing at Midnight. Longfellow. GOA

Loud mockers in the roaring street. The Second Crucifixion. Richard Le Gallienne. WGRP

Loud report through Lybian cities goes, The. Virgil, *tr.* by Dryden. *Fr.* Aeneid [*or* Eneados], The. NAWM-1; OBVE

Loud roars the wind that shakes this wall. Ghost of Edward. Joanna Baillie. *Fr.* Night Scenes of Other Times. ECWP

Loud talk in the overlighted house. Ends. Robert Frost. TRP

Loud through the still November air. The Church of the Revolution. Hezekiah Butterworth. PAH

Loud were they, loud, as they rode o'er the hill. Charms for a Sudden Stitch. *Unknown, tr. fr. Anglo-Saxon* by Charles W. Kennedy. AnOE

Loudens the sea-wind, downward plunge the bows. To D'Annunzio: Lines from the Sea. Robert Nichols. OBMV

Louder than gulls the little children scream. The Beach. Robert Graves. OxBSP

Loudon Hill; or, Drumclog. *Unknown.* ESPB

Louerd, thu clepedest me. *Unknown.* MiEL

Lough Derg. Denis Devlin. BIrV; CIP; IPY; PeIV

Lough Derg. Patrick Kavanagh. PeIV

Louis B. Russell. Bruce Guernsey. InPK

Louis XV. John Sterling. BeLS

Louis i'm trying to understand what you were. For Lil Louis. Tom Dent. Jaz

Louisa. Wordsworth. EnRP; GBL

Louisburg. *Unknown.* PAH

Louise, have you forgotten yet. Old Loves. Henry Murger, *tr. fr. French* by Andrew Lang. AWP

Louise on the Door-Step. Charles MacKay. EBVV

Louisiana. Steve Crow. HATNAP

Louisiana Perch. Ron Padgett. UL

Louisiana Weekly #4, The. David Henderson. PoBA

Loulou and Her Cat. Frederick Locker-Lampson. OFC

Lounge in the shade of the luxuriant laurel's. Anyte, *tr. fr. Greek* by Willis Barnstone. BoWoP

Lourenço Marques. Charles Eglington. PeSA; PeSAV

Louse Crept Out of My Lady's Shift, A. Gordon Bottomley. *Fr.* King Lear's Wife. ChTr

Louse Hunting. Isaac Rosenberg. EBEV; NAEL-2; NoAM; NoP; NSI; OxAEP-2; OxBTC; PeFWW

Lousy Miner. *Unknown.* AmFP

Lousy parson, a nitty clerk, and a shabby congregation, A. *(LL)* Acton Beauchamp, Herefordshire. *Unknown.* FaBoPP; GBP

Lout, The. John Clare. EnVR

Love. Al-Abbas ibn al-Ahnaf, *tr. fr. Arabic* by Omar S. Pound. ArPe

Love cast! Meleager, *tr. fr. Greek by* Peter Whigham. GrAn

Love Charm. *Malay Oral Tradition, tr. by* R. O. Winstedt. WTO

Love Charm, The. *Unknown, tr. fr. Chippewa Indian by* Jerome K. Rothenberg. STP

Love Charm Songs., *sels. Unknown, tr. fr. Chippewa Indian by* Frances Densmore.

Love-Charms. Thomas Campion. *See* Thrice Toss [*or* Tosse] These Oaken Ashes in the Air [*or* Ayre].

Love Child — a Black Aesthetic. Everett Hoagland. BPo

Love comes without bounds. (*LL*) A Spring Song of Tzu-yeh. Hsiao Yen. SuSp

Love Constraining to Obedience. William Cowper. NOCV

Love Deposed. Thomas Stanley. NOSC

Love Dirge. *Unknown, tr. fr. Maori by* John White. WTO

Love Dislikes Nothing. Robert Herrick. CBCK

Love Divine, All Loves Excelling. Charles Wesley. NOCV

Love doth again. Sir Thomas Wyatt. SiPS

Love, Drink, and Debt. Alexander Brome. OtMeF

Love, drunk the other day, knocked at my breast. The Dual. Richard Lovelace. CaPo

Love Enthroned. Richard Lovelace. CaPo

Love Enthroned. Dante Gabriel Rossetti. *Fr.* House of Life, The. OBNC

Love Equals Swift and Slow. Thoreau. NoP

Love essential unto youth. Ninety. Mary Elizabeth Fullerton. CBAP

Love ever gives. Love's Prerogative. John Oxenham. BLRP

Love Ever Green. Henry VIII, King of England. MeEL

Love Feast, The. W. H. Auden. ErPo

Love fed Heliodora's fingernail and made. Meleager, *tr. fr. Greek by* Barbara Hughes Fowler. *Fr.* Epigrams. HePo

Love flies with bow unstrung when Time appears. Love and Age. Walter Savage Landor. GBL

Love Flows from God. Mechthild von Magdeburg, *tr. fr. German by* Lucy Menzies. WPOW

Love Flows Not from My Liver. George Chapman. *Fr.* Coronet for His Mistress Philosophy, A. Son

Love for a Beautiful Lady. *Unknown. See* Ichot a burde in boure bryht.

Love for a Hand. Karl Shapiro. CoAP; NYBP

Love for an Island. Phyllis Shand Allfrey. PBCV

Love for Enjoying. James Shirley. BeJo

Love for Love, *sels.* Congreve.
    Soldier and a Sailor, A. CoMu

Love for Patsy, A. John Thompson, Jr.. LiTA

Love for such a cherry lip. Thomas Middleton. *Fr.* Blurt, Master Constable. EIL

Love for you. (*LL*) Portrait of Malcolm X. Etheridge Knight. PoBA

Love from My Father. Carole Gregory Clemmons. PoBA

Love from that day's courting burns my heart to a coal. (*LL*) We Passed by Green Closes. John Clare. EnVR

Love from The North. Christina Rossetti. CBLP

Love, give me leave to serve thee, and be wise. Thomas Randolph. BeJo
    (Elegy, An: "Love, give me leave to serve thee, and be wise.") NOSC

Love gives its best. Love. John Oxenham. BLRP

Love God — / my mother said. The Will's Love. Besmilr Brigham. CrSp; IHMS

Love-goddess, saviour/ Of the sea-wrecked. *Unknown, tr. fr. Greek by* Edward Lucie-Smith. GrAn

Love Gone Cold. Lindsay MacRae. DT

Love-grip, first excited by the eye, The. In Panelled Rooms. Ruth Herschberger. LiTA

Love grows alone (though I my brain for counsel harrow). He Loves in Vain. Christian Hofmann von Hofmannswaldau, *tr. fr. German by* George C. Schoolfield. GePo

Love Guards [*or* Guides] the Roses of Thy Lips. Thomas Lodge. *Fr.* Phyllis. EIL; NoSic; Son

Love Has Eyes. William Forster. CBAP

Love has found out how to mix. Asclepiades, *tr. fr. Greek by* Kenneth Rexroth. GrAn; PGA

Love has gone and left me, and the days are all alike. Ashes of Life. Edna St. Vincent Millay. BLPL; FaBoBe

Love has its morn, its noon, its eve, and night. Too Late. Philip Bourke Marston. OBNC

Love has its secrets, joy has its revealings. The Love Secret. *Unknown, tr. fr. Arabic by* Wilfrid Scawen Blunt. AWP

Love has never read the Ave Maria. Love. Immanuel di Roma, *tr. fr. Italian by* J. Chotzner. TrJP

Love has seven names. Hadewijch, *tr. fr. Dutch by* Willis Barnstone *and* Elene Kolb. BoWoP

Love hath so long possessed me for his own. Dante, *tr. fr. Italian by* Dante Gabriel Rossetti. *Fr.* Vita Nuova, La. AWP

Love he to morrow, who lov'd never. *Unknown, tr. by* Thomas Stanley. *Fr.* Vigil of Venus, The. AWP, *tr. by* Thomas Stanley; GBL, *tr. by* Allen Tate; OBVE

Love heeds no more the sighing of the wind. The Garden of Shadow. Ernest Dowson. OBNC

Love her he doesn't but the thought he puts. John Berryman. *Fr.* Dream Songs. FaBoMo

Love him nor want him. (*LL*) Pretty I Am, But I Am Wretched. *Unknown.* VBLP

Love, how thou'rt tired out with rhyme! Margaret Cavendish, Duchess of Newcastle. EnLoPo

Love, I adore the contours of thy shape. To a Sicilian Boy. Theodore Wratislaw. PeHV

Love, I am sick for thee, sick with an absolute grief. The Grief of Love. *Unknown, tr. fr. Arabic by* Wilfrid Scawen Blunt. AWP

Love, I have lain awake by night. J. V. Cunningham Gets Hung Up on a Dirty, of All Things, Joke. Henry Taylor. BXAP

Love, I have warmed the car. News from the House. Michael Dennis Browne. NYBP

Love. I, in mine, celebrate the love-choir. (*LL*) Ovid in the Third Reich. Geoffrey Hill. FaBoMo; NoAM

Love I love whose lips I love, A. The Accomplices. Conrad Aiken. NOBA

Love, I should be content. Duality. Katherine Thayer Hobson. GoYe

Love, I think, is a disease. Maghnas O Domhnaill. NOIV

Love, in a humour, played the prodigal. Michael Drayton. *Fr.* Idea. ESo; NoSic

Love in a Life. Robert Browning. CBLP; EBVVPR; FHYEP; InvP; NOBE; NOBVV; OBNC

Love in a Valley., *sels.* George Meredith.
    White Owl, The. ChTr

Love in a Village., *sels.* Isaac Bickerstaffe.
    "There was a jolly miller once." EBEvV; OxNR

Love in a Warm Room in Winter. James Wright. OBAL

Love in America. Marianne Moore. AiP; GOA

Love in Exile, *sels.* Mathilde Blind.
    "Dost thou remember ever, for my sake." OBNC
    "I charge you, O winds of the West, O." TrJP

Love in fantastic [*or* fantastique] triumph sat [*or* sate *or* satt]. Aphra Behn. *Fr.* Abdelazer. NOBE; WPE
    (Love Armed.) NALW
    (Song: Love Armed.) NOSC; Poetr; WeW
    (Song: "Love in fantastic triumph sate.") OBEV; OxAEP-1; TrGrPo

Love in Her Eyes. John Gay. *Fr.* Acis and Galatea. ELP

Love in her sunny eyes does basking play. The Change. Abraham Cowley. *Fr.* Mistress, The. CBLP; MeLP; SeCP; SeCV-1

Love-in-Idleness. Shakespeare. *Fr.* Midsummer Night's Dream, A. TrGrPo

Love in July. Ivan V. Lalic, *tr. fr. Serbo-Croatian by* Charles Simic. HSix

Love in Labrador. Carl Sandburg. VGW

Love in May. Jean Passerat, *tr. fr. French by* Andrew Lang. AWP

Love in My Bosom. Thomas Lodge. *See* Love in my bosom[e] like a bee.

Love in my bosom like a bee. Rosalind's [*or* Rosalynd's] Madrigal[l]. Thomas Lodge. *Fr.* Rosalynde; or Euphues' Golden Legacy. CBLP; EIL; EnRePo; GGP; InvP; NOBE; NoP; NoSic; OBEV; PoEL-2; TrGrPo
    (Love in My Bosom.) SCGP

Love in silence shall. Meleager, *tr. fr. Greek by* Peter Whigham. GrAn

Love in the Air. J. H. Prynne. VaA

Love in the Dark Valley. Douglas Oliver. VaA

Love in the Museum. Adrienne Rich. NYBP

Love in the peaceful u.s.a. Love u.s.a. Kathleen Spivack. BoWoP

Love in the Valley. George Meredith. AWP; EBVV; EnVR; ErPo; LiTB; NOBE; OAEL-2; OBEV, *abr.; TrGrPo*

Love in Vain. Robert Johnson. UnPo

Love! in what poyson is thy Dart. Sir John Denham. *Fr.* Freindship and Single Life against Love and Marriage. OBF

Love Indestructible. Robert Southey. *Fr.* Curse of Kehama, The. OBNC

Love in's first infant days had's wardrobe full. To His Scornful Mistress. William Hammond. CBLP

Love: Intimacy. C. K. Williams. CBLP

Love Is. Ann Darr. GrPl

Love is a circle that doth restless[e] move. Love What It Is. Robert Herrick. ArLo; FaBoEE; GBL

Love Is a Flame. George Marion McClellan. AAP

Love is a flame that burns with sacred fire. Love Is a Flame. George Marion McClellan. AAP

Love is a funny thing. Love. *Unknown.* TTY

Love is a green girl. Michael Stillman. TLR

Love Is a Keeper of Swans. Humbert Wolfe. MoBrPo

Love Is a Law. *At. to* John Webster *and* William Rowley. *Fr.* Thracian Wonder, The. EIL; GBL

Love is a place. E. E. Cummings. FaBoEE

Love is a region full of fires. A Description of Love. Sir John Beaumont. NOSC

Love Is a Secret Feeding Fire. *Unknown.* ArLo; OxBSP

Love is a secret feeding fire that gives all. Love Is a Secret Feeding Fire. *Unknown.* ArLo; OxBSP

Love Is a Shark. *Unknown, tr. fr. Hawaiian by* N. B. Emerson. WTO

Love Is a Sickness. Samuel Daniel. *Fr.* Hymen's Triumph. ELP; NOBE; OBEV; PoEL-2

Love is a twin to death; it makes my senses dead. Love. "Angelus Silesius," *tr. fr. German. Fr.* Cherubical Wanderer, The. GePo, *tr. by* George C. Schoolfield

Love is a universal migraine. Symptoms of Love. Robert Graves. BoLoP

Love Is a Wound Within the Body. Marie de France, *tr. fr. French by* Helen R. Lane. VBLP

Love is all/ Unsatisfied. Crazy Jane on the Day of Judgment. W. B. Yeats. CMoP; SOTW

Love is and was my lord and king. Tennyson. *Fr.* In Memoriam A. H. H. EBVV, *abr.*; EBVVPR; NOBE; NOCV; OAEL-2, *abr.*; OBEV; OBNC; PeECV, *abr.*

(My Lord and King.) ChTr

Love is anterior to life. Emily Dickinson. CBLP

Love is begot by fancy, bred. Love. George Granville. BoLoP

Love is believable. Alta. *Fr.* 7 : 3. CrSp

Love is best. *(LL)* Love among the Ruins. Robert Browning. EnVR; FaBV; FHYEP; HAP; MeMBP; NAEL-2; NOBE; OAEL-2; OBEV; PoEL-5; PrIm; SCGP

Love Is Bitter. *Unknown.* PeSA

Love is boring and passe, all the old baggage. Blond Bombshell. Lynn Emanuel. NAmP90

Love Is Enough., *sels.* William Morris.

"Love is enough: though the World be a-waning." FaBV; OBEV; PoEL-5

Love is enough: though the World be a-waning. William Morris. *Fr.* Love Is Enough. FaBV; OBEV; PoEL-5

Love Is Kind. Benjamin Keech. PoToHe

Love is Life. Richard Rolle of Hampole. *Fr.* Song of the Love of Jesus, A. PoEL-1

Love Is Life and Death. Georg Rudolph Weckherlin, *tr. fr. German by* George C. Schoolfield. GePo

Love is like butter, Evans mused, and stuck. Pendydd. Kingsley Amis. *Fr.* Evans Country, The. FaBoBl; NOBL

Love is like the lion's tooth. *(LL)* Crazy Jane Grown Old Looks at the Dancers. W. B. Yeats. CMoP; EBEV

Love is like the wild rose-briar. Love and Friendship. Emily Brontë. EBVV; ELP; InPK; MeMBP; OBF; VBLP

Love is no fire. Poem of Apology. Tim Longville. VaA

Love is no more. Amor Vincit Omnia. Edgar Bowers. VCAP

Love Is Not All. Edna St. Vincent Millay. *Fr.* Fatal Interview. Son

Love is not all; it is not meat nor drink. Edna St. Vincent Millay. CMoP; HAP; HeIL; HeIP; MeMAP; NoAM; OxBA; TAP

(Love Is Not All.) InPS; PrIm

Love Is Not Blind. I See with Single Eye. Edna St. Vincent Millay. LPA

Love Is Not Concerned. Alice Walker. CrSp

Love is not just a function of the eyes. Argentarius, *tr. fr. Greek by* Fleur Adcock. GrAn

Love is not mocked whatever use. Jack Spicer. *Fr.* Graphemics. VGW

Love is not worth so much. Coda. James Tate. AmPA; NYBP

Love is soft, love is swete, love is goed sware. *Unknown.* MiEL

(Love Is Wele, [or Weal] Love Is Wo.) CBCK; CBLP

Love Is Teasing. *Unknown.* OBET

Love is that later thing than death. Emily Dickinson. LiTA

Love Is That Orbit. George Henry Boker. Son

Love is the blood of a deep wound. Wounds. Harriet Zinnes. WoWa

Love is the blossom where there blows. Wooing Song. Giles Fletcher the Younger. *Fr.* Christ's Victory and Triumph. EIL; OBEV

(Enchantress' Song, The.) NOSC

Love is the center and circumference. What Love Is. Ella Wheeler Wilcox. PWR

Love is the peace, whereto all thoughts do[e] strive. Fulke Greville. *Fr.* Caelica. AAS; NoSic

(Sonnet: "Love is the peace, whereto all thoughts do strive.") JCP

Love is the plant of peace and most precious of virtues. Et Incarnatus Est. William Langland. *Fr.* Vision of Piers Plowman, The. NOBE, Passus II C *text*

Love is too young to know what conscience is. Shakespeare. *Fr.* Sonnets. EBEV; HeIP; NoSic; OxAEP-1; PoE; PoEL-2

Love is unjust: justice is loveless. *(LL)* Jacob. Delmore Schwartz. ChIV-1

Love Is Wele, [or Weal] Love Is Wo. *Unknown. See* Love is soft, love is swete.

Love is what lacks then: but what does it mean to you? A Remonstrance. James Kenneth Stephen. NOBVV

Love, it is night. The orb of day. The Passionate Professor. Bert Leston Taylor. NBLV

Love It Is Pleasing. *Unknown.* OBET

Love, it was good to talk to you tonight. Rondeau after a Transatlantic Telephone Call. Marilyn Hacker. NoAM; SM

Love itself shall slumber on. *(LL)* Music, When Soft Voices Die. Shelley. CBLP; EBEvV; FaBV; GTBS; GTBS-P; ImPo; LiTB; MeMBP; NOBE; OBEV; OxAEP-2; OxBSP; TFi; TrGrPo

Love-Joy. George Herbert. OAEL-1

Love killed this man. No more but so. *(LL)* The Cruel Maid. Robert Herrick. CaPo

Love laid his sleepless head. Swinburne. TrGrPo

Love Leave to Urge. Mary Sidney Wroth, Countess of Montgomery. *Fr.* Urania. Son; WPE

Love-Lesson, A. Clément Marot, *tr. fr. French by* Leigh Hunt. AWP

Love, let us live as we have lived, nor lose. To His Wife. Ausonius, *tr. fr. Latin by* Helen Waddell. OxBM

Love Letter. W. H. Auden. CBLP

Love Letter. Carole C. Gregory. AIW; BlSi; VBLP

Love Letter. Sylvia Plath. NOBA

Love Letter. Karl Shapiro. *See* I love you first because your face is fair.

Love-letter, A. Mary E. Tucker. CBWP-1

Love Letter, A. *Unknown.* MeEL

Love Letter, A: Ruth Arbeiter to Major Paul Maxwell. Anne Stevenson. *Fr.* Correspondences. OxBM

Love-Letter One ("To C ———— her lover.") *Unknown.* PeHV

Love Letter to Elizabeth Thatcher, A. Thomas Thatcher. SCAP

Love-Letter Two. *Unknown.* PeHV

Love Letters. Josephine D. Henderson Heard. CBWP-4

Love Letters of the Dead. Douglas Street. PAW

Love-Life. Hugo Williams. CBLP

Love, like a bird, hath perched upon a spray. Love. Sir William Watson. *Fr.* Two Epigrams. TrGrPo

Love like a heavy wave. Meleager, *tr. fr. Greek by* Sam Hamill. InMo

Love, like a mountain-wind upon an oak. Love. Sappho, *tr. fr. Greek by* William Ellery Leonard. AWP

Love like heat and cold. Jealousy. *Unknown, tr. fr. Irish by* Frank O'Connor. PeIV

Love like ours can never die! *(LL)* The Lovers' Litany. Kipling. CBLP

Love Like War, A. Ruth Asher-Pettipher. VBLP

Love lives beyond. Loves Lives Beyond the Tomb. John Clare. ArLo; FHYEP

Love, loneliness and the face of death. *(LL)* Pain. Edith Södergran. PBWP; WPOW

Love long dormant showing itself. Palais des Arts. Louise Glück. AnAn; VCAP

Love-lorn microbe met by chance, A. The Microbe's Serenade. George Ade. OBAL

Love love. *(LL)* Finished. Kate Llewellyn. NOBAu

Love, love. What His Friend Said, Teasing the Man in Love. Milaipperun Kantan, *tr. fr. Tamil by* A. K. Ramanujan. PLW

Love, love, a lily's my care. Words for the Wind. Theodore Roethke. CoAP; NOBA

Love ("Love bade me welcome . . .") George Herbert. *See* Love bade me welcome; yet my soul drew back.

Love, love today, my dear. Charlotte Mew. MoBrPo

Love ("Love was before the light began.") *Unknown, tr. fr. Arabic by* E. Powys Mathers. *Fr.* Thousand and One Nights, The. AWP

Love, love! What nonsense it is. Natalya Gorbanevskaya, *tr. fr. Russian by* Daniel Weissbort. WPOW

Love, love, what wilt thou with this heart of mine? Jean Froissart, *tr. by* Longfellow. AWP

Love Made in the First Age: To Chloris. Richard Lovelace. BeJo; CaPo; JCP; NAEL-1; OAEL-1; SeCP

Love, Maybe. Audre Lorde. Poetr

Love Me! Stevie Smith. OxBSP

Love Me. Maria Wine, *tr. fr. Swedish by* Nadia Christensen. PBWP

Love Me Again. *Unknown.* EIl

Love me, and I'll love you. *(LL)* Curr dhoo, curr dhoo. Mother Goose. OxNR

Love me and leave me; what love bids retrieve me? John Jones. Swinburne. *Fr. Heptalogia, The.* (At the Piano.) FaBoNo

Love me broughte. *Unknown.* MiEL

Love Me, for I Love You. Christina Rossetti. *Fr. Monna Innominata.* Son

Love Me - I Love You. Christina Rossetti. BoTP

Love Me Little, Love Me Long. Robert Herrick. BLPA, *sh. vers.*; CaPo; CBLP, *sh. vers.*; EiL, *sh. vers.*; FaBoBe, *sh. vers.*; NoP, *sh. vers.*

Love me, Love me, I cried to the rocks and the trees. Love Me! Stevie Smith. OxBSP

Love me no more, now let the god depart. Edna St. Vincent Millay. HeIP

Love Me Not for Comely Grace. *Unknown. See* Love not me for comely grace.

Love Me, O Love, *Sometimes considered Sonnet CX of* Astrophel and Stella. Sir Philip Sidney. HeIP

Love Me or Not. Thomas Campion. EiL

Love me Sweet, with all thou art. A Man's Requirements. Elizabeth Barrett Browning. PFP; VBLP

Love me with the left hand. The Light Woman's Song. Judith Johnson Sherwin. TAP

Love Medicine, A. Louise Erdrich. HATNAP

Love, Meet Me in the Green Glen. John Clare. ELP

Love mocks us all. Then cast aside. I, 33. Albi, Ne Doleas. Horace, *tr. fr. Latin by* Austin Dobson. *Fr. Odes.* AWP, *tr. by* Austin Dobson

Love much. Earth has enough of bitter in it. Ella Wheeler Wilcox. PoToHe

Love my heart for an hour, but my bone for a day. Street Song. Edith Sitwell. CMoP

Love never lets you go. *(LL)* An Ever-Fixed Mark. Kingsley Amis. ErPo; MoP; NoAM; PeHV

Love not a loveliness too much. Ownership. Lizette Woodworth Reese. MoAmPo

Love Not Me. *Unknown.* BLPL; CH; EiL; ELP; ImPo; LiTB; PoLF (Love Me Not for Comely Grace.) GTBS; GTBS-P; OBEV; OxBSP

Love Note. Gwendolyn Brooks. VBLP

Love now no fire hath left him. Giovanni Battista Marino, *tr. fr. Italian by* Richard Crashaw. OBVE

Love of a woman, The. Robert Creeley. VCAP; VGW

Love of Country. Sir Walter Scott. *See* Breathes There the [*or* a] Man [with Soul So Dead].

Love of Fame, the Universal Passion. Edward Young. OBSV Sels.
"Britannia's daughters, much more fair than nice."
"Love of praise, howe'er concealed by art, The."
"See commons, peers, and ministers of state."
"These all their care expend on outward show."
"With what, O Codrus! is thy fancy smit?"

Love of God, The. Bernard Rascas, *tr. fr. Provençal by* Bryant. WGRP

Love of God, unutterable and perfect, The. Dante, *tr. fr. Italian. Fr. Divina Commedia.* EnlH, *tr. by* Stephen Mitchell; MeMAP

Love of Hell, The. Abraham Burstein. TrJP

Love of Lettuce, The. Marge Piercy. CAPP

Love of men for each other, The — so tender, heroic, constant. Edward Carpenter. *Fr. Mightier than Mammon, A.* PeHV

Love of Moses for his race soon found, The. Flight into Midian. Frances E. W. Harper. *Fr. Moses: A Story of the Nile.* AAP

Love of my life came not, The. The Deep-Sea Pearl. Edith M. Thomas. AmWP

Love of Nature. Mark Akenside. *Fr. Pleasure of Imagination, The.* NOEC

Love of Nature. Mark Akenside. *See* Oh! blest [*or* bless'd] of heav'n [*or* Heaven], whom not the languid songs.

Love of Older Men, The. James Kirkup. PeHV

Love of Our Country, The, *sels.* Evan Evans.
"Whatever clime we travel or explore." AngWe

Love of praise, howe'er concealed by art, The. Edward Young. *Fr.* Love of Fame, the Universal Passion. OBSV

Love of the Father, The. *Unknown.* BLRP

Love of the Quartz Pebble, The. Vasco [*or* Vasko] Popa, *tr. fr. Serbo-Croatian. Fr.* Quartz Pebble, The. PoSu, *tr. by* Anne Pennington

Love of the world, The. Peter Philpott. VaA

Love of this black prince with her derision, The. *(LL)* Ten Lines. Emile Roumer. NegPo

Love, of this clearest, frailest Glass. In a Glass-Window for Inconstancy. Lord Herbert of Cherbury. OxBSP; SeCP

Love, oh love, oh careless love. Careless Love. *Unknown.* AS; UnPo

Love on a day (wise poets tell). How Violets Came Blue. Robert Herrick. BeJo; CaPo; TTTS

Love on, and turn to love again? *(LL)* If, Lord, Thy Love for Me Is Strong. St. Theresa of Avila. AWP; PBWP

Love on the Farm. D. H. Lawrence. CBLP; CMoP; ErPo; FaBV; FF; MoAB; MoBrPo; NAEL-2; NoAM; SCGP; TrGrPo

Love One Another. Kahlil Gibran. *Fr.* Prophet, The. LPA; OxBM

Love one another, but make not a bond of love. Love One Another. Kahlil Gibran. *Fr.* Prophet, The. LPA; OxBM

Love one another or die. *(LL)* Lower the Standard: That's My Motto. Karl Shapiro. MoP; NoAM

Love opened a vista rare with stars. Love's Vista. H. Cordelia Ray. CBWP-3

Love Overgrows a Rock. Eric Roach. PBCV

Love Play. William Cavendish. ErPo

Love plays a lute, and Thought an organ grand. The Two Musicians. H. Cordelia Ray. CBWP-3

Love Poem: "And they have to get it right. We just need." John Ashbery. HCAP

Love Poem: "Black biplane crashes into [*or* through] the window, The." Gregory Orr. MAT

Love Poem, The: "In bed with our bodies so completely intertwined." Andrew Elliott. PNI

Love Poem: "I want to write you." Linda Pastan. NIP

Love Poem: "Kind of slant — the way a ball will glance, A." Gary Miranda. SM

Love Poem: Growing Down. Christian McEwen. VBLP

Love Poem: "Last night you would not come." John Logan. CAPP

Love Poem: "My child — Star — you gaze at the stars." Plato, *tr. fr. Greek by* Willis Barnstone. ArLo

Love Poem: "My clumsiest dear, whose hands shipwreck vases." John Frederick Nims. FF; HoPM; InPK

Love Poem: "My love the sun sets." Valerie Sinason. DT

Love Poem: "Rain smell comes with the wind." Leslie Silko. UnPo; VoR

Love Poem: "Six o'clock and/ the sun rises . . . ." Miller Williams. MAT

Love Poem: "Speak earth and bless me with what is richest." Audre Lorde. GLP; NoAM

Love Poem: "There is a white mare that my love keeps." Alex Comfort. *Fr.* Postures of Love, The. ErPo

Love Poem: "We have plenty of matches in our house." Ron Padgett. UL

Love Poem: "You wrote a poem." Lindsay MacRae. DT

Love Poem: "Yours is the face that the earth turns to me." Kathleen Raine. ArLo; LiTB; MoAB; MoBrPo

Love Poem for My Country, A. Frank Mkalawile Chipasula. HBAPE

Love Poem — 1940. Miriam Hershenson. GoYe

Love Poem on Theme by Whitman. Allen Ginsberg. CAPP; NaP

Love poems they read. Uses of Poetry. Winfield Townley Scott. PoA

Love poured her beauty into my warm veins. *(LL)* Fragment of a Sonnet. Pierre de Ronsard. AWP; OBVE

Love-prone Asclepias with eyes like a summer's day. Meleager, *tr. fr. Greek by* Barbara Hughes Fowler. *Fr.* Epigrams. HePo

Love Pursued. At. to John Webster *and* William Rowley. *See* Art Thou Gone in Haste?

Love ran with me, then walk'd, then sate. Walter Savage Landor. CBLP

Love, Reason, Hate, did once bespeak. A Barley-Break. Sir John Suckling. CaPo; SeCV-1

Love Recognized. Robert Penn Warren. ArLo

Love Redeemed, *sels.* William Baylebridge.
"Quiet moon, immaculate of face, The." CBAP

Love Rejected. Lucille Clifton. BPo

Love said, the garden is coolest in the morning. What Was Said. Edward Kleinschmidt. UnDi

Love scorch'd my finger, but did spare. Upon Love. Robert Herrick. SeCV-1

Love Scorns Degrees. Paul Hamilton Hayne. *Fr.* Mountain of the lovers, The. AnAmPo

Love Secret, The. *Unknown, tr. fr. Arabic by* Wilfrid Scawen Blunt. AWP

Love seeketh not itself to please. The Clod and the Pebble. Blake. *Fr.* Songs of Experience. EnLoPo; EnRP; FaBV; FHYEP; InPS; NAEL-2; NOBE; NoP; OBNC; OtMeF; OxAEP-2; OxBSP; PoE; PrIm; RB; SCGP; SCV; TEP; TFi; TrGrPo

Love Serviceable. Coventry Patmore. *Fr.* Angel in the House, The. EnLoPo

Love set you going like a fat gold watch. Morning Song. Sylvia Plath. BoWoP; HCAP; HeIP; IHMS; InPK; InPS; LCAP; LPA; NAAL-2; NAs; NIP; NOBA; NTP; PrIm; VCAP

Love shall live, although he dye. *(LL)* Love's Horoscope. Richard Crashaw. MeLP

Love Should Grow Up like a Wild Iris in the Fields. Susan Griffin. CrSp

Love should intend realities: good-bye! Exit Line. John Ciardi. WeW

Love: Shyness. C. K. Williams. CBLP

Love signed the contract blithe and leal. John Swanwick Drennan. BIrV

Love Sleeping. Plato, *tr. fr. Greek by* Thomas Stanley. AWP; FaBoEE

Love so alike, that none do slacken, none can die. (*LL*) The Good[-]Morrow. John Donne. AWP; BoLoP; CBLP; ClHu; EBEV; EIL; EnLoPo; EnRePo; ESCV; FaBoBe; FaBoVe; FaBV; FaPoB; FF; FHYEP; HoPM; ImPo; InPS; InvP; JCP; LiTB; MeLP; NAEL-1; NAWM-1; NoP; NOSC; OAEL-1; OxAEP-1; PoE; PoEL-2; Poetr; PoRA; PPP; SCV; SeCP; SeCV-1; SoSe; TEP; TFi; TrGrPo

Love Somebody, Yes I Do. *Unknown*. AS

Love-song: "Beautiful, delicate bright gazelle, The." W. J. Turner. OBMV

Love Song: "Beautiful is she, this woman." *Unknown, tr. by* Constance Lindsay Skinner. *Fr.* Three Songs from the Haida. AWP

Love Song: "By the fierce flames of love I'm in a sad taking." Royall Tyler. TAP

Love Song: "Come to me in the night — we shall sleep closely together [*or* Let us sleep entwined]." Else Lasker-Schüler, *tr. fr. German.* BoWoP, *tr. by* Michael Gillespie; TrJP, *tr. by* Michael Gillespie

Love Song: "Do not love me, my friend." Flavien Ranaivo, *tr. fr. French.* PBA

(Common Lover's Song, The.) NegPo, *tr. by* Ellen Conroy Kennedy

(Do not love me, cousin.) NegPo, *tr. by* Ellen Conroy Kennedy

Love Song: "Early I rose." *Unknown, tr. fr. Papago Indian by* Mary Austin. AWP; LiTA

Love Song: First Version, 1915, A. William Carlos Williams. Poetr

Love Song: "For what as easy." W. H. Auden. *See* For what as easy.

Love Song: "Had I concealed my love." Elinor Wylie. BLPL

Love Song: "I am a bunch of red roses." *Unknown, tr. fr. Turkish by* Reza Baraheni *and* Zahra-Soltan Shokoohtaezeh. BoWoP

Love Song: I and Thou. Alan Dugan. CAPP; FF; HoPM; InPK; MoP; NoAM

Love Song: "I lie here thinking of you." William Carlos Williams. ArLo; Poetr

Love Song: "I painted my eyes with black antimony." *Unknown, tr. fr. Bagirmi by* H. Gaden. BoWoP

Love Song: "I passed by the house of the young man who loves me." *Unknown, tr. fr. Egyptian by* J. E. Manchip White. TTY

Love Song: "Inside the late nights of last week." Edward Dorn. BCF

Love Song: "It is deep going from here." Edward Dorn. BCF

Love Song: "Let my sweet song be pleasing unto Thee." Judah Halevi, *tr. fr. Hebrew by* Nina Davis Salaman. TrJP

Love Song: "Little sycamore, The." *Unknown, tr. fr. Egyptian by* J. E. Manchip White. TTY

Love-Song: "Little wild birds have come flying, The." *Unknown, tr. fr. Russian by* W. R. S. Ralston. AWP

Love Song: "Long closed door, oh open it again, The." Judah al-Harizi, *tr. fr. Hebrew by* Emma Lazarus. TrJP

Love Song: "More pleasing sounds the song of the birds." Ludwig Heinrich Christoph Hölty, *tr. fr. German by* Philip L. Miller. RiWo

Love Song: "My boat sails downstream." *Unknown, tr. fr. Egyptian by* J. E. Manchip White. TTY

Love Song: "My love is a lotus blossom." *Unknown, tr. fr. Egyptian by* J. E. Manchip White. TTY

Love Song: "My loved one is unique, without a peer." *Unknown, tr. fr. Egyptian by* J. E. Manchip White. TTY

Love Song: "My speech is tinged." Edward Dorn. BCF

Love Song: "On the hill tops I visit the snares." *Unknown, tr. fr. Maori by* Margaret Orbell. PeNZ

Love Song: "One with eyes the fairest." Euripides, *tr. fr. Greek by* Shelley. *Fr.* Cyclops. AWP

Love Song: "Our roofs are adjacent." *Unknown, tr. fr. Turkish by* Reza Baraheni *and* Zahra-Soltan Shokoohtaezeh. BoWoP

Love-Song: "Out of one golden breath." Else Lasker-Schüler, *tr. fr. German by* Jethro Bithell. TrJP

Love Song: "Out of the blackthorn hedges." Ivor Gurney. EnLoPo

Love Song: "See'st thou o'er my shoulders falling." Judah Halevi, *tr. fr. Hebrew by* Emma Lazarus. TrJP

Love Song: "She is a reed swaying in blue." Earle Thompson. HATNAP

Love-Song, A: "Such a heart." *Unknown, tr. fr. Irish by* Brendan Kennelly. PeIV

Love Song: "Sweep the house clean." William Carlos Williams. MoAB; MoAmPo; SAmP

Love Song: "That haughty tyranny of thine." Luís de León, *tr. fr. Spanish by* Thomas Walsh. TrJP

Love Song: "Though to think/ Rejoiceth me." Margot Ruddock. OBMV

Love Song: "Tiny children." Yityangu Ejong, *tr. fr. Yindjibarndi by* Frank Wordick. CBAP

Love Song: "You've got nice knees." Gavin Ewart. OxBTC

Love Song During Riot with Many Voices. Lynda Hull. NAmP90

Love Song for the Future. Vassar Miller. PRA

Love-Song, A, *sels.* Thomas of Hales.

Where is Paris and Heleyne? ChTr

Love Song of Har Dyal, The. Kipling. OtMeF

Love Song of J. Alfred Prufrock, The, *sels.* T. S. Eliot.
And Would It Have Been Worth It? LPA

Love Song of J. Alfred Prufrock, The. T. S. Eliot. AmPP; AWP; ClHu; CMoP; EBEV; EBEvV; FaPoB; FF; HAP; HeIL; HeIP; HoPM; InPK; InPS; LiTB; LiTM; MoAB; MoAmPo; MoP; NAAL-2; NAEL-2; NAWM-2; NoAM; NOBA; NOBE; NoP; OAEL-2; OxAEP-2; OxBTC; PoA; PoE; Poetr; PoRA; PPP; PrIm; SoSe; SOTW; TAP; TFi; TrGrPo; TRP; TwCP; UV, *ll.* — 36; WeW

Love Song of J. Alfred Prufrock, The,, *Parody.* J. Walker. BXAP; PeLi

Love Song of the Empress Wu, A. Empress Wu Tse-t'ien, *tr. fr. Chinese by* Kenneth Rexroth *and* Ling Chung. WPC

Love Song of the Loba. Diane Di Prima. Di Pr. Loba. SRLS

Love-Song of the Water Carriers. *Unknown, tr. fr. Zulu.* PeSA

Love Song of Tommo Frogley. Roger Crawford. FaBoBl; UV

Love Song to a Stranger. Joan Baez. UnAS

Love Song to Eohippus. Peter Viereck. MoAmPo

Love Song to King Shu-Suen. Kubatum, *tr. fr. Sumerian by* Thorkild Jacobsen. WPOW

Love Song ("Your handkerchief should be blue.") *Unknown, tr. fr. Turkish by* Reza Baraheni *and* Zahra-Soltan Shokoohtaezeh. BoWoP

Love Songs. Mina Loy. VBLP; VGW; WPE, *abr*

Love-Songs, at Once Tender and Informative. Samuel Hoffenstein. OBAL

Love-songs, at Once Tender and Informative, *sels.* Samuel Hoffenstein.
"Your little panties." FiBHP; NBLV; TrJP

Love Songs (Dadaria). *Gond Oral Tradition, tr. by* V. Elwin *and* S. Hivale. WTO

Love Songs in Age. Philip Larkin. PPP

Love Songs to Joannes, *sels.* Mina Loy.
"Spawn of Fantasies." VBLP

Love Sonnet. John Updike. Son

Love Sonnet, A. George Wither. *See* I loved a lass, a fair one.

Love Sonnets. Zora Cross. CBAP
Sels.
"In me there is a vast and lonely place."
"What have you more than I, who crave you so?"

Love Sonnets of Proteus, The, *sels.* Wilfrid Scawen Blunt.
As to His Choice of Her. Son
Depreciating Her Beauty. OBMV
Farewell to Juliet.
Farewell to Juliet ("I see you, Juliet, still, with your straw hat").
BoLoP; EnLoPo; OxBTC
"Juliet, farewell. I would not be forgiven." TrGrPo
St. Valentine's Day. EnLoPo
Woman with a Past, A. Son

Love steered my course, while yet the sun rode high. Of Fiammetta Singing. Boccaccio, *tr. fr. Italian by* Dante Gabriel Rossetti. *Fr.* Sonnets. AWP

Love still has something of the sea. Love Still Has Something of the Sea. Sir Charles Sedley. GBL; NOBE; OxAEP-1; SeCV-2

Love Still Has Something of the Sea. Sir Charles Sedley. GBL; NOBE; OxAEP-1; SeCV-2

Love Story. Bei Dao, *tr. fr. Chinese by* Donald Finkel *with* Chen Xueliang. SpMi

Love Story. Adrian Henri. UnAS

Love Story, A. Robert Graves. CMoP; FaBoTw; LiTB; NAEL-2

Love Story (Part 2). Marsha Prescod. VBLP

Love, strong as Death, is dead. An End. Christina Rossetti. CBLP; FaBoRV; GBL

Love Suicides at Sonezaki, The, *sels.* Chikamatsu Monzaemon, *tr. fr. Japanese.*
"To this world, farewell."
(Farewell to the world, and to the night farewell.) DL

Love supreme, a love supreme, A. (*LL*) Dear John, Dear Coltrane. Michael S. Harper. AmPA; Jaz; NIP; VCAP

Love surfeits with rewards, his nurse is scorn. (*LL*) Disdain Me Still. The Earl of Pembroke. CBLP; EIL

Love, sweet love is the poet's theme. Love, Sweet Love. Felix McGlennon. VPP

Love-Talker, The. "Ethna Carbery." CH; WPE

Love Tells Us Who We Are. Donald T. Sanders. ArLo

Love, That Doth Reign [*or* Raine] and Live within My Thought. Petrarch, *tr. by* the Earl of Surrey. *Fr.* Sonnets to Laura. AAS; HeIP; NAEL-1; NoP; OAEL-1; OBVE; SiPSBD
(Complaint of a Lover Rebuked.) AWP; Son; TrGrPo
(Love that liveth and reigneth in my thought.) SiPS

Love, that drained her, drained him when she'd loved, though each. The Turtle Dove. Geoffrey Hill. FaBoTw

Love that I hae chosen, The. The Lawlands o' Holland. *Unknown.* CH

Love that is alone with love. Love and Language. Louisa S. Guggenberger. NOBVV

Love that is hoarded, moulds at last. Harold C. Sandall. PoToHe

Love that liveth and reigneth in my thought. Petrarch. *See* Love, That Doth Reign [*or* Raine] and Live Within My Thought.

Love that rose on stronger wings, The. Tennyson. *Fr.* In Memoriam A. H. H. EBVV, *abr.*; EBVVPR; OAEL-2, *abr.*; PeECV, *abr.*

Love that we have broken. (*LL*) Broken Dreams. Hugo Williams. CBLP

Love That's Pure, Itself Disdaining. Johann A. Gruber, *tr. fr. German by* Sheema Z. Buehne. AH

Love, the delight of all well-thinking minds. Fulke Greville. *Fr.* Caelica. GBL

Love, the great master of true eloquence. Love. Tasso, *tr. fr. Italian by* John Hermann Merivale. AWP

Love, the Light-Giver [*or* To Tommaso de' Cavalieri]. Michelangelo, *tr. fr. Italian by* John Addington Symonds. AWP; PeHV

Love the quick profit, the annual raise. Manifesto: the Mad Farmer Liberation Front. Wendell Berry. FoLa

Love the unholy, that frost which quickens summer. Didactic Sonnet. Melvin Walker La Follette. PoA

Love the Wild Swan. Robinson Jeffers. HeIL; MoAB; MoAmPo; NoAM; Son

Love thee? Yes, I'm sure I love thee. The City by the Sea. Josephine D. Henderson Heard. CBWP-4

Love, thou are absolute sole lord. Richard Crashaw. *Fr.* Hymn to the Name and Honour [*or* Honor] of the Admirable Saint[e] T[h]eresa, A. HAP; JCP; NOBE; NoP; NOSC; OBEV; PoEL-2; SeCV-1, *abr.* (Hymn to Saint Teresa.) EBEV; ESCV; GeHe; MeLP; WGRP

Love thou saist. Milton. *Fr.* Paradise Lost. EPCY; TOF

Love thy God and love Him only. Reality. Sir Aubrey De Vere. WGRP

Love Thy Neighbour. D. H. Lawrence. ChIV-2

Love to Death is gathered in. (*LL*) As Lambs into the Pen. Dorothy Wellesley. FaBoTw

Love to give law unto his subject hearts. Prologue. Sir Thomas Wyatt. *Fr.* Penitential Psalms. ChIV-1

Love to Hermes, Aphrodite the Friend, The. (*LL*) To the Fair Clarinda, Who Made Love to Me, Imagin'd More than Woman. Aphra Behn. NALW; VBLP

Love? Too dangerous. Fourth Wish. Alberta Turner. LCAP

Love Town. Anne Carson. *Fr.* Life of Towns, The. BAP-90

Love Triumphant., *sels.* Dryden. "As, when some treasurer lays down the stick." NOSC Prologue to "Love Triumphant." OxBoLi

Love tunes my Heart just to my strings. (*LL*) Love. Abraham Cowley, *after the Greek of* Anacreon. AWP; BeJo; OBVE

Love, 20 Cents the First Quarter Mile. Kenneth Fearing. HAP

Love twists. The Pressures. Amiri Baraka. BPo

Love Unfeigned. Chaucer. *Fr.* Troilus and Criseyde [*or* Criseide]. EnVB; NOBE; OBEV

Love Unfeigned, The. Chaucer. OBEV

Love Unknown. George Herbert. JCP; Prf

Love Unlike Love. *Unknown. See* Christ made [*or* maketh] to man a fair present.

Love unreturnd, howe'er [how ere] the flame. Constancy[e]. Sidney Godolphin. BeJo; NOSC

Love u.s.a. Kathleen Spivack. BoWoP

Love was before the light began. Love ("Love was before the light began.") *Unknown, tr. fr. Arabic by* E. Powys Mathers. *Fr.* Thousand and One Nights, The. AWP

Love, we curve downwards, we are set to night. After Midsummer. E. J. Scovell. OxBTC

Love we define for ourselves, The. Prothalamion. Michael Ryan. AmPA

Love we thought would never stop, The. Ending. Gavin Ewart. NBLV; OxBSP; SoSe

Love What It Is. Robert Herrick. ArLo; FaBoEE; GBL

Love Which Frees. Gloria Fuertes, *tr. fr. Spanish by* Philip Levine. WPOW

Love, which is least sure and most dared, the pure, keen. Peyton Houston. *Fr.* Sonnet Variations. Son

Love who points the swallow home. Who Points the Swallow. David Campbell. FaBoMA

Love Who Will, for I'll Love None. William Browne. NOSC

Love, Whose Month Was Ever May. Ulrich von Liechtenstein, *tr. fr. German by* Jethro Bithell. AWP

Love, why have you led me here. The Young Cordwainer. Robert Graves. MoBS

Love Will Find Out the Way. *Unknown.* FaBoCh; GBL; GN; GTBS; GTBS-P; OBEV; WiR

Love will find out the way! (*LL*) Love Will Find Out the Way. *Unknown.* FaBoCh; GBL; GN; GTBS; GTBS-P; OBEV; WiR

Love will not have me cry. Canzonetta: He Will Neither Boast nor Lament to His Lady. Jacopo da Lentino, *tr. fr. Italian by* Dante Gabriel Rossetti. AWP

Love Winged My Hopes. *Unknown. See* Love winged my hopes and taught me how to fly.

Love winged my hopes and taught me how to fly. *Unknown.* (Icarus.) OBEV (Love Winged My Hopes.) EIL; TrGrPo

Love without Hope. Robert Graves. BoLoP; ChTr; FaBoEE; GBL; GTBS-P; NAEL-2; NTP; OAEL-2; PlP; Spl

Love without Longing. *Unknown. See* I have a yong suster.

Love you dare but look I find, The. To Cleon's Eyes. Martha Sansom. ECWP

Love, You have struck me straight, my Lord! Resolution. Charles L. O'Donnell. TrPWD

"Love you?" said I, then I sighed, and then I gazed upon her sweetly. Ferdinando and Elvira, or the Gentle Pieman. W. S. Gilbert. FaBoCo; FaBoNo; FiBHP

Love Your Enemy. Yusef Iman. BPo; TTY

Love,/ your mother"/ Which is Naomi. (*LL*) Kaddish. Allen Ginsberg. HCAP; NAAL-2; NeAP; NOBA; PoBeRe; PoM

Love, You've Been a Villain. James Robinson Planché. NOBL

Loveact. Grace Nichols. VBLP

Lovebirds. William Jay Smith. ErPo

Loved by thee. (*LL*) A Woman's Last Word. Robert Browning. BLPA; BLPL; FaBoBe; NAEL-2; TrGrPo

Loved I am, and yet complain[e] of Love. Complaint of Love. Sir Philip Sidney. *Fr.* Arcadia. PoEL-1; SiPS

Loved I not Honor more. (*LL*) To Lucasta, Going to the Wars [*or* Warres]. Richard Lovelace. AWP; BeJo; CaPo; CBLP; ClHu; CoGr; EBEvV; ELP; EnLoPo; FaBoEH; FaBV; FF; GBL; GTBS; GTBS-P; HAP; HoPM; ImPo; InPS; JCP; LiTB; MeLP; NAEL-1; NIP; NOBE; NoP; OAEL-1; OBEV; OBWP; OxAEP-1; OxBSP; PAW; PoEL-3; Poetr; PoRA; SCV; SeCP; SeCV-1; TFi; TrGrPo; UV; WeW

Loved of My Soul. Israel Najara, *tr. fr. Hebrew by* Nina Davis Salaman. TrJP

Loved One, The. Joseph Hansen. NYBP

Loved stream, that meanders along. Memories of Childhood. Sir John Carr. *Fr.* Derwent; an Ode. NOEC

Loved thee and thy sad cry. (*LL*) The Aziola. Shelley. EBEV

Loveliest dawn of gold and rose. The Least of Carols. Sophie Jewett. OHIP

Loveliest girl in Vienna, The. Alma. Tom Lehrer. NBLV

Loveliest of Counties, Shropshire Now. Ian Sainsbury. BXAP

Loveliest of Pies. Peter De Vries. OBAL

Loveliest of Trees [the Cherry Now]. A. E. Housman. *Fr.* Shropshire Lad, A. ArNa; AWP; BLPL; BoNaP; ChTr; ClHu; CMoP; ELP; FaBoBe; FaBV; FaPoB; FF; HAP; InPK; LiTB; LiTM; MeMBP; MoAB; MoBrPo; MoP; NAs; NoAM; NoP; OAEL-2; OHIP; OxBTC; PoE; Poetr; PoLF; PrIm; RB; SoSe; TEP; TFi; TrGrPo

Loveliest of Trees, the Cherry Now. A. E. Housman. *See* Loveliest of Trees [the Cherry Now].

Loveliest of trees, the cherry now. A. E. Housman. *See* Loveliest of Trees [the Cherry Now].

Loveliest of trees, the cherry now. In a Town Garden. Donald Mattam. FiBHP; SCGP

Loveliest of what I leave. Adonis, Dying. Praxilla, *tr. fr. Greek by* Richard Lattimore. PBWP; WPOW

Loveliness. Christopher Smart. *Fr.* Hymns for the Amusement of Children. NOCV

Loveliness of Love, The. George Darley. *See* It is not Beauty I demand.

Lovel's Song. Ben Jonson. *See* It Was a Beauty That I Saw.

Lovely Albert. *Unknown.* IHNG

Lovely! all the essential parts. These Purists. William Carlos Williams. OBAL

Lovely are curves of the white owl sweeping. The White Owl. George Meredith. *Fr.* Love in a Valley. ChTr

Lovely body of the dead, The. Lament for Glasgerion. Elinor Wylie. PoA

Lovely cherries on the tree. Adjectives. Moishe Nadir, *tr. fr. Yiddish by* Joseph Leftwich. TrJP

Lovely courier of the sky. Anacreon's Dove. Samuel Johnson. AWP

Lovely Étan, The. *Unknown.* NOIV

Lovely fairy! Charming sprite! An Ode Composed in Sleep. Judith Madan. ECWP

Lovely Fia was the summer queen. A Mare. Kate Barnes. NYBP

Lovely form there sate beside my bed, A. Phantom or Fact. Samuel Taylor Coleridge. EnRP

Lovely ghost, A. (*LL*) The Bristol Channel. Thomas Edward Brown. NOBVV

Lovely girl, you look at me through the window. Praxilla, *tr. fr. Greek by* John Dillon. PBWP

Lovely grapes and apples. A Tabernacle Thought. Israel Zangwill. TrJP

Lovely Green Lady, A. The Green Lady. Charlotte Druitt Cole. BoTP

Lovely hill-torrents are. W. J. Turner. GoJo; MoBrPo

Lovely in the winter sunshine lies the Haslemere Hotel. John Betjeman's Brighton. Gavin Ewart. FaBoPa

Lovely Is the Modest Girl. Shih Ching, *tr. fr. Chinese by* Wu-chi Liu. SuSp

Lovely kind, and kindly loving. An Odd Conceit. Nicholas Breton. EIL

Lovely Lass o' Inverness, The. Burns.

Lovely Lass to a Friar Came, A. At. to The Earl of Rochester John Wilmot, 2d Earl of Rochester. CoMu

Lovely, lasting peace of mind! A Hymn to Contentment. Thomas Parnell. NOEC

Lovely Love, A. Gwendolyn Brooks. BPo

Lovely Maya, Hermes' mother. Barnabe Barnes. *Fr.* Parthenophil and Parthenophe. NoSic

Lovely of hair and breast and face. The Question. Norman Gale. FiBHP

Lovely Pamela, who found. Epitaph on a Party Girl. Richard Usborne. FaBoEE

Lovely Rivers and Lakes of Maine, The. George B. Wallis. BLPA

Lovely Rose Is Sprung, A. Unknown, *tr. fr. German by* Margarete Münsterberg. AWP

Lovely Shall Be Choosers, The. Robert Frost. MoAB; MoAmPo; NOBA; OxBA; PoE

Lovely Song for Jackson, A. V. R. Lang. VBLP

Lovely spot which thou dost see, The. Upon a Mole in Celia's Bosom. Thomas Carew. BeJo

Lovely thing to see, A. Heaven's River. Issa, *tr. fr. Japanese by* Harold G. Henderson. ArNa

Lovely Things. H. M. Sarson. BoTP

Lovely Village Fair; or, I Dont Mean to Tell You Her Name, The. *Unknown.* CoMu

Lovely viper, haste not on. A Song of the Cannibals. The Countess of Winchilsea. PoE

Lovely was the death. Samuel Taylor Coleridge. *Fr.* Religious Musings. EnRP

lovely weather — long way from home — . (*LL*) The Country Girl. Dermot Bolger. IB

Lovely White Flowers. C. P. Cavafy, *tr. fr. Greek by* Edmund Keeley *and* Philip Sherrard. OBD

Lovely whore though. Cathleen. *Unknown, tr. fr. Irish by* Thomas MacIntyre. BIrV

Lovely young lady I mourn in my rhymes, A. George John Cayley. FiBHP

Lovely Young Moor, A. *Unknown, tr. by* Willis Barnstone. BoWoP

Lovelye William. *Unknown.* AmFP

Lovemusic. Carolyn Kizer. ErPo

Lover, The. Robert Duncan. PeHV

Lover, The. "Eliza." KTR

Lover, The. Coventry Patmore. *Fr.* Angel in the House, The. OxAEP-2

Lover, The. Solveig von Schoultz, *tr. fr. Finnish by* Anne Born. VBLP

Lover. Isobel Thrilling. DT

Lover, The. C. K. Williams. PWE

Lover, The; a Ballad. Lady Mary Wortley Montagu. ECWP; GGP; NAEL-1; NoP

Lover Abused Renounceth Love, The, *sels.* George Turberville. "Was never day came on my head." EIL

Lover and Philosopher. Sir William Davenant. NOBE; OBEV; Prf

Lover and the Syringa-Bush, The. Herman Melville. AnAmPo; OBAL

Lover Comparath His State to a Ship in Perilous Storm Tossed on the Sea, The. Petrarch. *See* My galley [*or* gally] charged with forgetfulness.

Lover Compareth Himself to the Painful Falconer, The. *Unknown.* NoSic

Lover Complaineth, The. Sir Thomas Wyatt. *See* My lute, awake! Perform [the] last.

Lover Complaineth the Unkindness of His Love, The. Sir Thomas Wyatt. *See* My lute, awake! Perform [the] last.

Lover Consults with Reason, The. Thomas Carew. *See* Weep not, nor backward turn your beams.

Lover Deceived Writes to His Lady, The, *sels.* Thomas Howell. Who Would Have Thought. EIL

Lover for Shamefastnesse Hideth His Desire within His Faithfull Hart, The. Petrarch. *See* Long[e] love that in my thought doth harbour, The.

Lover Having Dreamed Enjoying of His Love, Complaineth That the Dreame Is Not either Longer or Truer, The. Sir Thomas Wyatt. AAS; SiPSBD

Lover in all Shapes, The. Goethe, *tr. fr. German by* Philip L. Miller. RiWo

Lover in Liberty Smileth at Them in Thraldom, That Sometime Scorned His Bondage, The. *Unknown.* EIL

Lover in Winter Plaineth for the Spring, The. *Unknown. See* Wester[n] wind, when will thou blow.

Lover is a slender, glowing urn, A. A Fantastic Simile. Thomas Lovell Beddoes. Son

Lover Left Alone, A. *Unknown.* MeEL

Lover Mourns for the Loss of Love, The. W. B. Yeats. LPA; WeW

Lover of mine, if upland you journey. Ave Atque Vale. Malay Oral Tradition, *tr. by* R. J. Wilkinson *and* R. O. Winstedt. WTO

Lover of swamps. To the Snipe. John Clare. FaBoPV; OBNC

Lover of the Lord. *Unknown.* AmFP

Lover of the moorland bare, A. To K[atharine de M]attos. Robert Louis Stevenson. OBNC

Lover Pleads with his Friend for Old Friends, The. W. B. Yeats. OBF

Lover Proved False, The. *Unknown.* AmFP

Lover Rejoiceth, The. Sir Thomas Wyatt. SiPS; TrGrPo

Lover Rejoiceth the Enjoying of His Love, The. Sir Thomas Wyatt. *See* Once, [*or* Ons] as methought [*or* me thought], fortune me kissed [*or* kist *or* kyst].

Lover Remembereth Such as He Sometimes Enjoyed and Showeth How He Would Like to Enjoy Her Again, The. Leon Stokesbury. SM

Lover Renounceth Love, The. Sir Thomas Wyatt. *See* Farewell, love, and all thy laws [*or* lawes] for ever.

Lover Showeth How He Is Forsaken of Such as He Sometime Enjoyed, The. Sir Thomas Wyatt. *See* They Flee [*or* Fle] from Me That Sometime Did Me Seek [*or* Seke].

Lover Tells of the Rose in His Heart, The. W. B. Yeats. CMoP

Lover that Durst Not Speak to His M[istress], A. James Shirley. NOSC

Lover to His Lady, The. At. to Plato, *tr. fr. Greek by* George Turberville. CTC; FaBoEE; FF; NoSic

Lover to the Thames of London, to Favour [*or* Favor] His Lady Passing Thereon, The. George Turberville. ChTr; EIL; NoP

Lover, under burthen of his mistress' love, The. Sir John Davies. *Fr.* Gulling[e] Sonnets, The. EIL; ESo; Son

Lover, upon an Accident Necessitating His Departure, Consults with Reason, A. Thomas Carew. CaPo

Lover Whose Mistress Feared a Mouse, The. George Turberville. NTP

Loverd, thou clepedest me. Wait a Little! *Unknown.* NOCV (Thole a Little.) EnVB

Lovers, The. Conrad Aiken. NYBP

Lovers, The. Alex Comfort. PoA

Lovers, The. W. R. Rodgers. BIrV; OxBSP; PNI

Lovers, The. William Jay Smith. MoAmPo

Lovers, The. Marya Zaturenska. MoAmPo

Lovers, and a Reflection. Charles Stuart Calverley. FaBoCo; FaBoPa

Lovers and madmen have such seething brains. The Lunatic, the Lover, and the Poet. Shakespeare. *Fr.* Midsummer Night's Dream, A. (Imagination.) ImPo; LiTB

Lover's Anger, A. Matthew Prior. ErPo

Lover's Appeal, The. Sir Thomas Wyatt. *See* And Wilt Thou Leave Me Thus?

Lover's Arithmetic, The. *Unknown.* CBNP; OxBoLi; PeLV

Lover's Confession, A. Charles, Duc d'Orléans. *See* My Ghostly Father, I me confess.

Lover's death, how regular, The. Stark Major. Hart Crane. MeMAP

Lovers' Debouchment. William Zaranka. BXAP

Lovers everywhere are bringing babies into the world. Make Love Not War. Howard Nemerov. NAs

Lover's eyes will gaze an eagle blind, A. Shakespeare. *Fr.* Love's Labour's Lost. GBL

Lover's Farewell, The. James Clarence Mangan. PeIV

Lovers, fast in their longing, The. March. William Everson. ErPo

Lovers, forget your love. Wind and Window Flower. Robert Frost. AnAmPo

Lovers Go Fly a Kite, The. W. D. Snodgrass. NYBP

Lovers How They Come and Part. Robert Herrick. GBL; OxBoLi; OxBSP; PoEL-3

Lovers in ladies' magazines. Thomas McGrath. VGW

Lovers in the act dispense. The Thieves. Robert Graves. BoLoP; CMoP; GTBS-P; LiTM; OAEL-2

Lovers in Winter. Robert Graves. FaBoEE; NYBP

Lovers' Infiniteness. John Donne. EIL; ESCV; LiTB; MeLP; NOSC; OAEL-1; PoEL-2; SeCP; SeCV-1

Lover's Journey, The, *sels.* George Crabbe. "It is the soul that sees; the outward eyes." OxAEP-1

Lover's Lament, The. *Unknown.* AS

Lover's Lament, A. *Unknown.* AmFP

Lover's Lament or The Willows by the Water Side, A. *Unknown, tr. fr. Tewa Indian by* H. J. Spinden. AWP

Lover's Lament for Her Sailor, The. *Unknown.* AmFP

Lover's Leap; a Tale, The. Andrew Macdonald. NOEC

Lovers, like wrestlers, when they do not lay. Samuel Butler. *Fr.* Love. ErPo

Lovers' Litany, The. Kipling. CBLP

Lover's Lullaby, A. George Gascoigne. *See* Sing lullaby [*or* lullabie] as women do[e].

Lovers' Mass, The. *Unknown.* OxBLMV

Lovers may find similitudes. The Cascade. Edgell Rickword. FaBoTw

Lover's Meeting. Ray Mathew. CBAP

Lover's Melancholy, The, *sels.* John Ford.
  Dawn. OBEV, V, i
  "If thou canst wake with me, forget to eate." PoEL-2
  "Minutes are numbered by the fall of sands." PoEL-2

Lover's New Year's Gift, A. John Lydgate. PoEL-1

Lovers of pleasure more than God. Lover of the Lord. *Unknown.* AmFP

Lovers of the Poor, The. Gwendolyn Brooks. CAPP; LCAP; MoP; NAAL-2; NoAM; NOBA; Poetr

Lover's Plea, A. Thomas Campion. *See* Shall I come, sweet love, to thee.

Lover's Posy, The. Rufinus Domesticus, *tr. fr. Greek by* W. H. D. Rouse. AWP

Lover's Prayer, The. *Malay Oral Tradition, tr. by* R. J. Wilkinson *and* R. O. Winstedt. WTO

Lover's Progress, The, *sels.* John Fletcher.
  Dead Host's Welcome, The. OxAEP-1; TrGrPo

Lovers' Quarrel, A. Robert Browning. EBVVPR

"Lover's quarrel" hah. *Reading the Facts about Frost in* The Norton Anthology. George Starbuck. BAP-89

Lover's quarrel will never rest his roots, A. (*LL*) Cosmos in London. Arthur Nortje. HBAPE; PeSAV

Lover's Question, A. James Baldwin. GLP

Lovers Rejoice! Beaumont *and* John Fletcher. *Fr.* Cupid's Revenge. EIL

Lover's Reply to Good Advice. Richard Hughes. MoBrPo

Lover's Resolution, A. George Wither. *See* Shall I, Wasting in Despair.

Lover's Return. Langston Hughes. SAmP

Lovers, scholars — the fervent, the austere. Cats. Baudelaire, *tr. fr. French by* Richard Howard. SoCa

Lovers think of death, The. (*LL*) Blindman's Buff. Peter Viereck. LiTM; MoAmPo

Lovers who are young indeed, and wish to know the sort of life. Love, You've Been a Villain. James Robinson Planché. NOBL

Lovers who/ came to me. Ghost Poem Five. Sister Mary Norbert Körte. IHMS

Lovers whose lifted hands are candles in winter. For a Child Expected. Anne Ridler. LiTM

Love's Alchemy [*or* Alchemie]. John Donne. ESCV; NAEL-1; NoP; OAEL-1; PoE; SeCP

Love's an headstrong wild desire. Love. Henry Baker. NOEC

Loves and sorrows of those who lose an orchard. The Lost Orchard. Edgar Lee Masters. CMoP

Love's Anniversaries. Maurice Lindsay. OxBM

Love's Apparition and Evanishment. Samuel Taylor Coleridge. EnRP

Love's as Warm as Tears. C. S. Lewis. TIRV

Love's awfulness. (*LL*) Self-Pity. Philip Hodgins. NOBAu

Love's Bitten Tongue, *sels.* Vassar Miller.
  "Lord, hush this ego as one stops a bell." MT

Love's Clock. Sir John Suckling. *See* That none beguiled be by time's quick flowing.

Love's Coming. Ella Wheeler Wilcox. AnAmPo

Love's Consolation., *sels.* Richard Watson Dixon.
  "All who have loved, be sure of this from me." OBNC

Love's Cure, *sels.* Beaumont *and* Fletcher *and* John Fletcher.
  "Turn, turn thy beauteous face away." NOSC; PoEL-2

Love's Deity [*or* Deitie]. John Donne. AWP; EiL; EnRePo; ESCV; GBL; ImPo; LiTB; SeCP; SeCV-1; SoSe

Love's Despair. Richard Lynche. *Fr.* Diella. EIL

Love's Despair. Shakespeare. *See* Come away, come away, death.

Love's domain, supernal Zion. Brynbwrla. Kingsley Amis. *Fr.* Evans Country, The. NOBL

Love's Emblem. John Clare. NIP

Love's Emblems. John Fletcher. *See* Now the Lusty Spring [Is Seen].

Loves End. Lord Herbert of Cherbury. SeCP

Love's Entreaty. Michelangelo. *See* Thou knowest, love, I know that thou dost know.

Love's Epitaph. William Cavendish. OxBSP

Love's Fancy. Dryden. *See* After the Pangs of a Desperate Lover.

Love's Farewell. Michael Drayton. *See* Since There's No Help, Come Let Us Kiss and Part.

Loves Feast. Sir John Suckling. CBLP

Love's Fidelity. Petrarch. *See* Set me whereas the sun doth parch the green [*or* sonne dothe perche the grene].

Love's First Approach. "Ephelia." KTR

Love's Flight. Else Lasker-Schüler, *tr. fr. German by* Jethro Bithell. TrJP

Love's Force. Thomas Carew. CaPo

Love's god is a boy. Cupid. *Unknown.* EIL

Love's Grave. George Meredith. *See* Mark where the pressing wind shoots javelin-like.

Love's Growth. John Donne. ESCV; JCP; NoP; NOSC; SeCV-1

Love's Guerdons. E. Nesbit. NOBVV

Love's hidden pearl is shining yet. Hafiz, *tr. fr. Persian by* R. A. Nicholson. TOF

Love's Horoscope. Richard Crashaw. MeLP

Love's Hue and Cry. James Shirley. BeJo

Love's Immaturity. E. J. Scovell. GBL; LiTB

Love's Innocence. Thomas Stanley. BeJo

Love's Justification. Michelangelo. *See* Yes! hope may with my strong desire keep pace.

Love's Labour Lost. Robert Tofte. *Fr.* Alba. EIL

Love's Labour's Lost, *sels.* Shakespeare.
  Heavenly Rhetoric, The. ImPo; LiTB; Son
  Holofernes's Letter. CBNP
  "If she be made of white and red." CTC
  "Lover's eyes will gaze an eagle blind, A." GBL
  On a Day — Alack the Day. EIL
    (Blossom, The.) OBEV
    (Love's Perjuries.) GTBS; GTBS-P
  So Sweet a Kiss. EIL; InvP
  Spring. EnRePo; FF; InPK; NAEL-1; NOBE; NoP; NoSic; PFP; PoRA; PrIm; TFi
    (Now daisies pied, and violets blue.) BoTP
    (Song: "When daisies pied and violets blue.") PoEL-2
    (Spring.) EIL; HAP; ImPo; NBLV; NIP; OAEL-1; OBEV; PoEL-2; SCGP; TEP; TrGrPo; UnPo
  "When icicles hang by the wall." TRP
  "When icicles hang by the wall." AWP; ClHu; FaPON; FF; GN; GoJo; InPK; InPS; LiTB; NAEL-1; NOBE; NoSic; PoRA; PrIm
    (Hiems.) FaBoCh
    (Merry Note, A.) WiR
    (Song: "When icicles hang by the wall.") PoEL-2
    (Tu-Whit To-Who.) CH
    (Winter.) BoNaP; ChTr; EIL; GTBS; GTBS-P; HAP; ImPo; NIP; OAEL-1; OBEV; SCGP; TEP; TFi; TrGrPo; UnPo; WeW

Love's Last Resource. Sadi, *tr. by* L. Cranmer-Byng. *Fr.* Gulistan, The. AWP

Love's like a Game at Tables, where your Dy. On Love. Sir Robert Ayton. ScCV

Love's Limit. *Unknown.* TrGrPo

Loves Lives Beyond the Tomb. John Clare. ArLo; FHYEP

Love's Martyr. Sir Robert Chester. EIL
  Sels.
  Her Hair.
  "O holy Love, religious saint!"

Love's Martyrs. John Ford. *See* Oh [*or* O], no more, no more, too late.

Love's Matrimony. William Cavendish. NOSC

Love's memories haunt my footsteps still. John Clare. NOBVV

Love's multitudinous boneyard. Jack Kerouac. *Fr.* Mexico City Blues. NeAP

Love's Mystery. Joseph Beaumont. NOSC

Love's night and a lamp. Meleager, *tr. fr. Greek by* Peter Whigham. BoLoP; GrAn

Loves of a little while ago, The. *Unknown, tr. fr. Japanese by* Kenneth Rexroth *and* Ikuko Atsumi. WPJ

Loves of the Birds. *Malay Oral Tradition, tr. by* R. J. Wilkinson *and* R. O. Winstedt. WTO

Loves of the Plants, The. Erasmus Darwin. *Fr.* Botanic Garden, The.

Loves of the Puppets. Richard Wilbur. OxBC

Loves of the Triangles, The, *sels.* John Hookham Frere.
  "Stay your rude steps, or e'er your feet invade." FaBoNo

Love's Offence. Sir John Suckling. CaPo; NOSC

Love's Old Sweet Song. G. Clifton Bingham. FaBoBe

Love's Omnipresence. *At. to* Joshua Sylvester. *See* Were I as Base as Is the Lowly Plain.

Love's Pains. John Clare. NOBVV

Love's pallor and the semblance of deep ruth. Dante, *tr. fr. Italian by* Dante Gabriel Rossetti. *Fr.* Vita Nuova, La. AWP

Love's Perjuries. Shakespeare. *See* On a Day — Alack the Day.

Love's Perversity. Coventry Patmore. *Fr.* Angel in the House, The. EnVR

Love's Philosophy. Shelley. ArLo; BLPA; BLPL; BoLoP; EnRP; FaBoBe; FaBV; FHYEP; GTBS; GTBS-P; HoPM; MeMBP; OxAEP-2; PoToHe; SCGP; TrGrPo

Love's Prerogative. John Oxenham. BLRP

Love's Primal Want. William Ellery Leonard. *Fr.* Two Lives. Son

Love's Progress. John Donne. *Fr.* Elegies. LiTB; OAEL-1

Love's Rebel. The Earl of Surrey. *See* When summer took in hand the winter to assail.

Love's Remorse. Edwin Muir. OxBTC

Love's Resume. Heine. *See* Rose and the lily, the moon and the dove, The.

Love's Résumé. Heine, *tr. by* J. F. C. TrJP

Love's Secret. Blake. *See* Never Seek to Tell Thy Love.

Loves serene, uncarnate Graces! Monotropa. Rose Terry Cooke. AmWP

Love's Siege. Sir John Suckling. *See* 'Tis Now, Since I Sat[e] Down Before.

Love's Stratagems. Donald Justice. NYBP

Love's Sun. William Cavendish. NOSC

Love's the boy stood on the burning deck. Casabianca. Elizabeth Bishop. CBCK; FaBoWP; OxBSP

Loves Triumph, must be Honours Funeral. *(LL)* Loving and Beloved. Sir John Suckling. BeJo; CaPo; NAEL-1

Love's tryst to keep, with truant Eve. *(LL)* The Lover and the Syringa-Bush. Herman Melville. AnAmPo; OBAL

Love's twilight wanes. *(LL)* Before Sunset. Swinburne. CBLP

Love's twilight wanes in heaven above. Before Sunset. Swinburne. CBLP

Loves Victory. Aurelian Townshend. *See* Victorious beauty, though your eyes.

Love's Vision. Edward Carpenter. WGRP

Love's Vista. H. Cordelia Ray. CBWP-3

Love's Votary. George Augustus Simcox. NOBVV

Loves who many years held all my mind, The. Walter Savage Landor. GBL

Love's Will. Lewis Warsh. UL

Love's Witchery. Thomas Lodge. EIL

Love's Witness. Aphra Behn. BoWoP

Loves World. Sir John Suckling. SeCV-1

Love's worshipers alone can know. Love and Folly. La Fontaine, *tr. fr. French by* Bryant. AWP

Loves you. *(LL)* Beginning with a Stain. Alice Notley. VBLP

Love's Young Dream. Thomas Moore. WBLP

Lovesickness — / What is the cure? Ma Chih-yüan, *tr. by* Sherwin S. S. Fu. *Fr.* Tune: "Song of Shou-yang". SuSp

Lovesickness is like a creditor. Tune: "Clear River, a Prelude" — Lovesickness. Hsu Tsai-ssu, *tr. fr. Chinese by* Sherwin S. S. Fu. SuSp

Lovesight. Dante Gabriel Rossetti. *Fr.* House of Life, The. EBVV; GTBS-P; NAEL-2; OBNC; TrGrPo

Lovesleep, The. Gavin Ewart. OxBC

Lovesong: "He loved her and she loved him." Ted Hughes. LPA

Lovest Thou Me?, *sels.* William Cowper. "Lord it is my chief complaint." TrPWD

Lovest Thou Me? William Cowper. ChIV-2

Lovewell's Fight. *Unknown.* PAH

Loving. Jane Stembridge. NMM

Loving and Beloved. Sir John Suckling. BeJo; CaPo; NAEL-1

Loving and Liking [Irregular Verses Addressed to a Child]. Dorothy Wordsworth. OxBChV; WoRP

Loving are the daring, The. *(LL)* The Song of the Camp. Bayard Taylor. AnAmPo; BeLS; GN; WBLP

Loving Henry. *Unknown.* AmFP

Loving in truth, and fain[e] in verse my loue to show. Sir Philip Sidney. *Fr.* Astrophel and Stella. AAS; AWP; BLPL; EBEV; EPCY; ESo, *sl. abr.*; GBL; GGP; HAP; HeIL, *(Sonnets,* 1–CVIII *and* 11 Songs); ImPo; InPS; LiTB; NAEL-1; NoP; NoSic; OAEL-1; OxAEP-1; PoE; Poetr; SCGP, *(Sonnets,* I–CVIII *and* 11 Songs); SiPS, *(Sonnets,* I–CVIII *and* 11 Songs); SiPSBD, *(Sonnets,* I–CVIII *and* 11 Songs); Son; TEP; TFi; TrGrPo

Loving Kind. A. D. Hope. FaBoMA

Loving Kind went by the way. Loving Kind. A. D. Hope. FaBoMA

Loving looks the large-eyed cow. A Christmas Prayer. George Macdonald. PChr

Loving Mad Tom. *Unknown. See* From the hag [*or* hagg] and hungry [*or* hungrie] goblin.

Loving Memory. Tony Harrison. *Fr.* Art & Extinction. SCBI

Loving My Enemies. Anna Kamienska, *tr. fr. Polish by* Susan Bassnett *and* Piotr Kuhiwczak. VBLP

Loving the rituals that keep men close. Palladas, *tr. fr. Greek by* Tony Harrison. OBVE

Loving this man who is far away. Like Loving Chekhov. Denise Levertov. InPS

Loving You Less than Life, a Little Less. Edna St. Vincent Millay. NAAL-2

Loving you was difficult. Dear John. Lindsay MacRae. DT

Loving your neighbor is all very fine when you have nice. Alta. *Fr.* 2 : 7. CrSp

Lovingly I turn me down. After Mass. "Michael Field." WPE

Low-anchored Cloud. Thoreau. *Fr.* Week on the Concord and Merrimack Rivers, A. ArNa; NoP

Low and brown barns thatched and repatched and tattered. The Wife of Flanders. G. K. Chesterton. NSI

Low Barometer. Robert Bridges. CMoP; LiTB; MoP; NoAM; NOCV; OBNC; Poetr; SCGP

Low beating of the tom-toms, The. African Dance. Langston Hughes. FaPON

Low Bridge, Everybody Down. William S. Allen. *See* I've got a mule and her name is Sal.

Low Church. Stanley J. Sharpless. NBLV; PeLV

Low clouds yellow in a mist wind. First Movement. Padraic Fiacc. PNI

Low Fields and Light. W. S. Merwin. LCAP

Low huts, groans muffled. The Midwives. Celia Gilbert. ChIV-1

Low in the eastern sky. To the Maiden in the East. Thoreau. AnAmPo; OxBA

Low in thy grave with thee. David's Lament for Jonathan. Peter Abelard, *tr. fr. Latin by* Helen Waddell. NAWM-1; PeHV

Low places where the rock-fish feed. *(LL)* Evening by the Sea. Swinburne. FaBoPP

Low prayer, a high prayer, I send through space, A. *Unknown, tr. by* Douglas Hyde. WTO

Low Road, The. Marge Piercy. CrSp

Low sandy beach and the thin scrub pine, The. Cape Cod. George Santayana. AnAmPo

Low Scene. Paul Verlaine, *tr. fr. French by* Alistair Elliot. FaBoBl

Low-set island this September, A. Tresco. Geoffrey Grigson. FaBoPP

Low spake the knight to the peasant maid. The Rose and the Gauntlet. "Christopher North." BeLS

Low sun whitens on the flying squalls, The. Rounding the Cape. Roy Campbell. PeSA

Low Tide on Grand Pré. Bliss Carman. NOBC

Low Trick, A. Gelett Burgess. OBCA

Low Volume. Reiner Kunze, *tr. fr. German by* Michael Hamburger. PoSu

Low was our pretty cot: our tallest rose. Reflections on Having Left a Place of Retirement. Samuel Taylor Coleridge. EnRP

Low ye hills in ocean lie. My Heart Is in Merioneth. *Unknown, tr. fr. Welsh by* Richard Llwyd. OBWVE

Lowdown Dirty Blues. *Unknown.* AmFP

Lowell. James Russell Lowell. *Fr.* Fable for Critics, A. AmPP; NOBA; OxBA; TAP

Lowell, Mass. Billy Collins. NGP

Lower Forms of Life. Mary Winter. GoYe

Lower the flags. Special Bulletin. Langston Hughes. PoBA

Lower the Standard: That's My Motto. Karl Shapiro. MoP; NoAM

Lower them and dream of home. *(LL)* Still Night Thoughts. Li Po. TTTS

Lowery Cot. L. A. G. Strong. MoBrPo

Lowest Place, The. Christina Rossetti. NOBVV; TrPWD

Lowest Trees Have Tops, The. Sir Edward Dyer. EnRePo; FaPoB; NoSic; OPOP; OxBSP; RB

Lowest trees have tops, the ant her gall, The. The Lowest Trees Have Tops. Sir Edward Dyer. EnRePo; FaPoB; NoSic; OPOP; OxBSP; RB (Modest Love, A.) SCGP

Lowlands. *Unknown.* ChTr; OxBoLi

Lowlands Away ("Lowlands, Lowlands away, my John,") *diff. versions. Unknown.* GBP

Lowlands o' [*or* of] Holland, The. *Unknown.* AmFP, *diff. vers.*; OxBB; ScCV, *(diff. vers.)*

Lowlands of Holland, The. *Unknown.* AmFP; OxBB

Lowliest duties on herself did lay, The. *(LL)* London, 1802 ("Milton! thou should'st be living at this hour.") Wordsworth. AWP; EBEvV; EnRP; EPCY; FaBoPV; FaBV; FF; HAP; HeIP; InvP; LiTB; MeMBP; NAEL-2; NIP; NoP; OBNC; OxAEP-2; PoEL-4; PoRA; SCGP; Son; TEP; TFi; UV

Lowly Peasant, The. *Unknown, tr. by* Rina Benmayor. PBWP

Lowveld, The. Charles Eglington. PeSA

Loyal General, The, *sels.* Nahum Tate. "If yet there be a few that take delight." SeCV-2

Loyal Hearts of London City, come I pray, and sing my ditty. The Dutchess of Monmouth's Lamentation for the Loss of Her Duke. *Unknown.* CoMu; FaBoBa

Loyal subject, thou, to that bright Queen, A. To W. L. G. on Reading His "Chosen Queen." Charlotte Forten. BlSi

Loyal Woman's No, A. Lucy Larcom. AmWP

Loyalty. Berton Braley. BLPA

Loyalty. Allan Cunningham. *See* Hame, Hame, Hame.

Loyalty Confin'd. Sir Roger L'Estrange.

Loyalty to the Flag. L. A. J. Moorer. CBWP-3

Lubber Breeze. T. Sturge Moore. CH

Lubin. *Unknown.* FaBoVe

Luca Signorelli to His Son. Eugene Lee-Hamilton. PeVV

Lucasia, Rosania and Orinda Parting at a Fountain, July 1663. Katherine Philips. KTR; PeHV

Lucasta, frown and let me die. To Lucasta: Her Reserved Looks. Richard Lovelace. CaPo; SeCV-1

Lucasta Laughing. Richard Lovelace. PoEL-3

Lucasta Replies to Lovelace. G. K. Chesteron. UV

Lucasta's Fan, with a Looking-Glass in It. Richard Lovelace. CaPo

Lucasta's World. Richard Lovelace. BeJo; CaPo; SeCP

Lucent lake was lit with sheen, The. A Thought of Lake Ontario. H. Cordelia Ray. CBWP-3

Lucia. Lucia Casalinvovo, *tr. fr. Italian.* TSaS

Lucifer. Ljiljana Djurdjic, *tr. fr. Serbo-Croatian by* Charles Simic. HSix

Lucifer has bad habits. Lucifer. Ljiljana Djurdjic, *tr. fr. Serbo-Croatian by* Charles Simic. HSix

Lucifer in Starlight. George Meredith. AWP; CH; ChIV-1; EBVV; EnVR; FF; GGP; HAP; ImPo; InPK; LiTB; Mes; NAEL-2; NOBE; NOBVV; NoP; OAEL-2; OBEV; OBNC; PoE; PoEL-5; SCGP; Son; TFi; TrGrPo; UnPo

Lucilia, wedded to Lucretius, found. Lucretius. Tennyson. EnVR; OAEL-2

Lucille. Steve Carey. UL

Lucille among the flamingos. Cameos. Rita Dove. NAmP90

Lucina, Care. Perses, *tr. fr. Greek by* Peter Whigham. GrAn

Lucina Schynning in Silence of the Nicht. Eiléan Ní Chuilleanáin. PWE

Lucinda Matlock. Edgar Lee Masters. *Fr.* Spoon River Anthology. CMoP; FaBV; FF; HAP; LiTA; LiTM; MoAmPo; MoP; NoAM; NOBA; OxBA

Lucindy, who you 'spose I seed. A Common Occurrence. Priscilla Jane Thompson. CBWP-2

Luck. W. W. Gibson. MoShBr; OBMV

Luck. Langston Hughes. SAmP

Luck. Dennis McHarrie. PAW

Luck has no songs, luck has no thoughts, luck has nothing. Pain. Edith Södergran, *tr. fr. Swedish by* Jaakko A. Ahokas. PBWP; WPOW

Luck? I am upset. My dog is ill. A Rune for C. Barbara Howes. NYBP; SM

Luck is something I do not understand. The Lover Remembereth Such as He Sometimes Enjoyed and Showeth How He Would Like to Enjoy Her Again. Leon Stokesbury. SM

Luck — 1932. Lucien Stryk. NGP

Luck of Edenhall, The. Ludwig Uhland, *tr. fr. German by* Longfellow. AWP

Luck Own. Anne Carson. *Fr.* Life of Towns, The. BAP-90

Luck, we've had it; our character the public's. It Did. Robert Lowell. NoAM

Luckes, my faire falcon, and your fellowes all. Sir Thomas Wyatt. *See* Lux my fair falcon, and your fellows all.

Luckily for us. (*LL*) Humming-Bird. D. H. Lawrence. CMoP; InPS; LiTB; LiTM; MeMBP; NoAM; RB

Luck's Shining Child. George Garrett. MT

Lucky bridegroom. Sappho, *tr. fr. Greek by* Josephine Balmer. AIW

Lucky Chance, The, *sels.* Aphra Behn. "Oh! Love, that stronger art than wine." WPE; WPOW

Lucky Eugene. Michael Foley. PNI

Lucky Lion! *Zulu Oral Tradition, tr. by* H. Tracey. WTO

Lucky Marriage, The. Thomas Blackburn. GTBS-P

Lucky Sailor; or, The Sailor's Invitation to Go with Admiral Anson, The. *Unknown.* OxBSS

Lucky shepherd, if only on the hill. Crinagoras, *tr. fr. Greek by* Alistair Elliot. GrAn

Lucky Spence's Last Advice. Allan Ramsay. FaBoBl

Lucky the husband. Mabel Kelly. Turlough Carolan, *tr. fr. Irish by* Austin Clarke. BIrV; CIP

Lucky the ones who were sick and in pain. Auschwitz. Harvey Shapiro. BTR

Lucky with day approaching, with leaning dawn. (*LL*) The Wanderer. W. H. Auden. CMoP; LiTB; MeMAP; MoP; NoAM; RB; SOTW; WeW

Lucrece's Death. Shakespeare. *Fr.* Rape of Lucrece, The. BeLS; NoSic

Lucretius. Tennyson. EnVR; OAEL-2

Lucretius could not credit centaurs. Invitation to Juno. William Empson. CBLP; CMoP; FaBoMo

Lucretius felt the change of the world in his time. Prescription of Painful Ends. Robinson Jeffers. LiTA; MoAB; MoAmPo; OxBA

Lucy. Walter de la Mare. CMoP

Lucy. (Strange fits of passion have I known.) Wordsworth. EBEV; EnRP; FHYEP; GBL; NOBE; OAEL-2; OBEV; OBNC; TrGrPo

Sels.
I Traveled [*or* travell'd] among Unknown Men. AWP; FaBV; GTBS; GTBS-P; SCGP; TFi

She Dwelt among the Untrodden Ways. AWP; BLPA; BoLoP; EBEvV; ELP; EnLoPo; FaBV; FF; HAP; HeIL; HeIP; ImPo; IMW; LiTB; MeMBP; NIP; NoP; OxAEP-2; OxBSP; Poetr; PPP; PrIm; PWR; SCGP; TEP; TFi; UnPo; UV; WeW

(Lost Love, The.) GTBS; GTBS-P

Slumber Did My Spirit Seal, A. AWP; BLPL; EBEvV; ELP; EnLoPo; FaBoCh; GGP; GTBS; GTBS-P; HAP; HeIP; ImPo; InPK; InPS; InvP; MeMBP; NoP; PoEL-4; PoRA; PPP; PrIm; SCGP; SCV; TEP; TFi; UnPo; WeW

Three Years She Grew in Sun and Shower. GN; HAP; NoP; PoEL-4; SCGP; TFi

(Education of Nature, The.) GTBS; GTBS-P

Lucy Ashton's Song. Sir Walter Scott. *Fr.* Bride of Lammermoor, The. EnRP; NOBE; OBEV; OtMeF; OxAEP-2; OxBS

Lucy goes down the celestial escalator in light. Lucy Taking Birth. Diana Scott. BrRo

Lucy Gray; or, Solitude. Wordsworth. BeLS; CH; EnRP; NAEL-2; OAEL-2; OxAEP-2; OxBChV; TEP

Lucy Lake. Newton Mackintosh. BXAP

Lucy Lavender. Ivy O. Eastwick. BoTP

Lucy Locket lost her pocket. Mother Goose. OxBoLi; OxNR; ReMoGo

Lucy Taking Birth. Diana Scott. BrRo

Lucy, you brightness[e] of our sphe[a]re, who are. To Lucy, Countess[e] of Bedford, with Mr. Donnes Satyres [*or* Satires]. Ben Jonson. BeJo; EPCY; SeCV-1

Lucy's Letter. James Berry. FaBoVe

Lud! what a group the motley scene discloses! Goldsmith. *Fr.* Epilogue to "The Sister." OBSV

Luef me were gome boute gile. (*LL*) In a frith as I con fare fremede. *Unknown.* MiEL

Lufthansa. John Tranter. NOBAu

Lugubriously enough they're playing. Bmp Bmp. William Matthews. Jaz

Lui et Elle. D. H. Lawrence. NoAM

Luis de Camões. Roy Campbell. FaBoTw; OxAEP-2; PeSA

Luke and John. Handwriting on the Wall. *Unknown.* AmFP

Luke XI: Blessed Be the Paps Which Thou Hast Sucked. Richard Crashaw. BXAP; JCP

Luke Havergal. E. A. Robinson. AmPP; AWP; GBL; LiTA; LiTM; MeMAP; MoAB; MoAmPo; NAAL-2; NoAM; NOBA; PoEL-5; TFi; UnPo

Luke Preach-Ill admires what we laymen can mean. The Insatiable Priest. Matthew Prior. OxBSP

Luke 6.25. Francis Quarles. ChIV-2

Luke 23. Jorge Luis Borges, *tr. fr. Spanish by* Irving Feldman. OBF

Lula Vires. *Unknown.* AmFP

Lulee, lullay. Janet Lewis. NOCV

Lull thee or lure, more fond thou wilt not find. (*LL*) Erotion. Swinburne. PoEL-5

Lulla, la lulla, lulla lullaby. Lulla, My Sweet Little Baby. William Byrd. ChIV-2

Lulla, My Sweet Little Baby. William Byrd. ChIV-2

Lullaby: "Beloved, may your sleep be sound." W. B. Yeats. BoLoP; FaBoTw; OBMV

Lullaby: "But who killed Johannes, mama . . . ?" Jeremy Cronin. PeSAV

Lullaby: "Close your sleepy eyes, or the pale moonlight will steal you." Aqua Laluah. ShDr

Lullaby: "Din of work is subdued, The." W. H. Auden. FaBoMo; GLP; NoAM

Lullaby: "For wars his life and half a world away." Randall Jarrell. HCAP; OxBC

Lullaby: "Golden slumbers kiss your eyes." Thomas Dekker *and others.* *See* Golden slumbers kiss your eyes.

Lullaby: "Here is the guillotine." Christopher Logue. IHNG

Lullaby: "Hush, lullay." Léonie Adams. MoAB; MoAmPo

Lullaby: "Hush ye, hush ye! honey, darlin'." Clara Ann Thompson. CBWP-2

"Rev'rend Father stood inculcating, The." PeSAV

"Shores are crown'd with people, The."

Luss! be for ever sunk beneath. Mercury; on Losing My Pocket Milton at Luss near Ben Lomond, and Other Mountains. Robert Andrews. NOEC

Lust in Action. Shakespeare. *See* Expense of spirit in a waste of shame, The [*or* Th'].

Lust it comes out, that gluttony went in. (*LL*) On Gut. Ben Jonson. JCP; NoP

Lust of Gold, The. James Montgomery. *Fr.* West Indies, The. PAH; PBCV

Lustily, Lustily. *Unknown. Fr.* Common Conditions. OxBSS

Lustra, *sels.* Ezra Pound.
   "Come, my songs, let me express our baser passions." PoA
   (Further Instructions.) TwCP
   "O helpless few in my country." MeMAP; PoA
   (Rest, The.) AmPP; MoAB; MoAmPo; NoAM; NOBA; OxBA

Lust's too genteel to let the weather in. In a Bed-Sitter. Hal Porter. NOBAu

Lusty Fryer of Flanders, The. *Unknown.* CoMu

Lusty Juventus. Charles Madge. FaBoMo

Lusty Juventus., *sels.* Robert Wever.
   "In a herber [*or* a harbour *or* an arbour] green [*or* grene], asleep [*or* aslepe] whereas [*or* where as *or* where] I lay."
   (In an Arbour Green.) ELP
   (In Youth Is Pleasure.) ChTr; NOBE; OBEV
   (Of Youth He Singeth.) CBLP; EiL

Lusty May. *Unknown.* OBEV

Lusty wench as nimble as an eel, A. John Taylor. NOSC

Lute and the pear are your half sisters, The. A Flock of Guinea Hens Seen from a Car. Eudora Welty. GrPl; NYBP; PrIm

Lute, companion of my calamity. Louise Labé, *tr. fr. French by* Aliki *and* Willis Barnstone. BoWoP

Lute Music. Kenneth Rexroth. TAP

Lute Song, The. Kung Tzu-chen, *tr. fr. Chinese by* An-yan Tang. SuSp

Lute without strings, A. Without You I Am. Diana Der Hovanessian. LoHo

Lutea Allison. Sir John Suckling. ErPo

Lutel wot it any mon. *Unknown.* MiEL

Luther, they say, was unwise; he didn't see how things were going. Arthur Hugh Clough. *Fr.* Amours de Voyage. FaBoVe; NOBVV

Luther to a Bluebottle Fly. Eugene Lee-Hamilton. *Fr.* Imaginary Sonnets. Son

Lutheran, Popish, Calvinistic, all of these confessions three. Faith. Friedrich von Logau, *tr. fr. German.* GePo, *tr. by* George C. Schoolfield

Lutra, the Fisher. James McMichael. AmPA

Luttrell, Master of Luttrellstown. Luttrell. Richard Murphy. *Fr.* Battle of Aughrim, The. PBCIP

Luvin' wumman is a licht, A. Love. "Hugh MacDiarmid." CMoP; PoE

Lux in Tenebris. Katharine Tynan. TrPWD

Lux my fair falcon, and your fellows all. Sir Thomas Wyatt. AAS; OBF; SiPS
   (Epigram: "Lux my fair falcon, and your fellows all.") SiPSBD
   (Luckes, my faire falcon, and your fellowes all.) AAS
   (Lux, My Falre Falcon.) OxBSP

Luxurious house had a huge mirror, The. The Mirror in the Front Hall. C. P. Cavafy, *tr. fr. Greek by* Edmund Keeley *and* Philip Sherrard. PeHV

Luxurious man, to bring his vice in use. The Mower against Gardens. Andrew Marvell. EBEV; ESCV; FaBoPV; LiTB; NAEL-1; NoP; NOSC; OAEL-1; OxAEP-1; PFP; PoE; PoEL-2; PPP; SeCV-1

Luxury. Yehuda Amichai, *tr. fr. Hebrew by* Assia Gutmann. PoSu

Luxury. Donald Justice. HeIP

Luxury diminishing death, A. (*LL*) Dancing the Shout to the True Gospel; or, The Song Movement Sisters Don't Want Me to Sing. Rita Mae Brown. CrSp; NMM; PeHV

Luxury, then, is a way of. Political Poem. Amiri Baraka. CoAP; MoP; NAAL-2; NoAM

Lwonesomeness. William Barnes. NOBVV

Lyarde is an old horse and can naught well draw. Lyarde. John Lydgate. PlP

Lyce. William Walsh. BoLoP

Lychee, The. Wang I, *tr. fr. Chinese by* Arthur Waley. FaBoCh

Lychees. Medbh McGuckian. PBCIP

Lycias. The Earl of Rochester. ErPo

Lycidas. (Yet once more, O ye laurels, and once more.) Milton. AWP; ChTr; ClHu; EBEV; EBEvV; FHYEP; GTBS; GTBS-P; HAP; ImPo; InPS; JCP; LiTB; NOBE; NoP; NOSC; OAEL-1; OBEV; OxAEP-1; PoEL-3; Poetr; PPP; PrIm; SCGP; TfI; TrGrPo; UnPo; WGRP

Sels.
   "Ay me! whilst thee the shores and sounding seas." Prf
   "Return Alpheus, the dread voice is past." PeECV
   "Weep no more, woful shepherds weep no more." FaBoRV

Lycidas and Moeris. Virgil, *tr. by* Dryden. *Fr.* Eclogues. AWP

Lycoris darling, once I burned for you. Martial, *tr. fr. Latin by* Peter Porter. BoLoP

Lydia. Charles Marie René Leconte de Lisle, *tr. fr. French by* Philip L. Miller. RiWo

Lydia, in Heavens Name. I, 8. "Lydia, in Heavens Name" ("Lydia, dic, per omnes.") Horace, *tr. by* Sir Richard Fanshawe. *Fr.* Odes. OBVE

Lydia Is Gone This Many a Year. Lizette Woodworth Reese. CH; GoJo

Lydia, on your rosy cheeks. Lydia. Charles Marie René Leconte de Lisle, *tr. fr. French by* Philip L. Miller. RiWo

Lydia Pinkham. *Unknown.* AS

Lydstep Caverns., *sels.* Sir Lewis Morris.
   "Here in these fretted caverns whence the sea." AngWe

Lye ye here, a husband to them a.' (*LL*) Lady Isabel and the Elf-Knight. *Unknown.* ESPB; FaBoBa

Lyf So Short, The. Palladas, *tr. fr. Greek by* Dudley Fitts. GrAn

Lying. Thomas Moore. FiBHP

Lying. Richard Wilbur. DiPo; HCAP; PeVV; Poetr; SV

Lying amber of the histories., The. (*LL*) For wars his life and half a world away. Randall Jarrell. HCAP; OxBC

Lying apart now, each in a separate bed. One Flesh. Elizabeth Jennings. AIW; FaBoWP; OxAEP-2; OxBTC; PBWP

Lying asleep between the strokes of night. Love and Sleep. Swinburne. BoLoP; CBLP

Lying at the bottom of water. The Crocodile. Ting Mang, *tr. fr. Chinese. Fr.* Sketch of the Zoo, The. LHF, *tr. by* Hualing Nieh

Lying Awake. Thomas Hardy. FaBoRV; FaBoVe

Lying Awake. W. D. Snodgrass. HoPM; MoAmPo; NYBP

Lying close to your heart-beat, my lips. Before Sleep. Fleur Adcock. *Fr.* Night-Piece. PeNZ

Lying Down. *Unknown, tr. fr. Bella Bella Indian by* Franz Boas. STP

Lying down in my father's grey dressing gown. Douglas Oliver. VaA

Lying down in the frugality of sleep. (*LL*) Märchenbilder. John Ashbery. LCAP; NOBA

Lying Hare's lip to this day, The. (*LL*) How Death Came. *Unknown.* PeSA; TTY

Lying here alone. Lady Izumi Shikibu, *tr. fr. Japanese.* WeW

Lying here quietly beside you. Quietly. Kenneth Rexroth. ErPo

Lying in a Hammock at a Friend's Farm in Pine Island, Minnesota. James Wright. *See* Over my head, I see the bronze butterfly.

Lying in a Hammock at William Duffy's Farm in Pine Island, Minnesota. James Wright. CAPP; HAP; HCAP; HoPM; NaP; NOBA; OPOP; Poetr; TRP; VCAP

Lying in a Yuma Saloon. Jim Barnes. CDW

Lying in bed I hear two come nose to nose. Drag Race. Dave Jeddie Smith. AnAn

Lying in bed in the dark, I hear the bray. Weather Ear. Norman Nicholson. OxBSP

Lying in the dark music. The Enigma Variations. Paul Petrie. NYBP

Lying in the dark together. One, Two. Mervyn Morris. PBCV

Lying in the Grass. Sir Edmund Gosse. EBVV

Lying in the sunshine among the buttercups and dandelions. Tribute to Grass. John James Ingalls. WBLP

Lying is an occupation. Laetitia Pilkington. WPE

Lying mouldering away. (*LL*) The Death of Queen Jane. *Unknown.* AmFP, 2 *vers.*; ESPB, (A *and* B *vers.*); OBET

Lying Muslims. *Yoruba Oral Tradition, tr. by* Ulli Beier. WTO

Lying on a Bridge. Van K. Brock. MT; SM

Lying quietly on the bed. David Ignatow. *Fr.* Leaving the Door Open. CAPP

Lying so primly propped. (*LL*) Bells for John Whiteside's Daughter. John Crowe Ransom. CMoP; FF; HAP; HeIP; HoPM; IMW; InPK; InPS; LiTA; LiTM; MeMAP; MoAB; MoAmPo; MoP; NAAL-2; NIP; NoAM; NOBA; NoP; OxBA; PoE; Poetr; PPP; PrIm; RB; TAP; TfI; UnPo; VGW; WeW

Lying south of sweet Northumber. Rhymed Mnemonic of the Forty Counties of England. Donald Monat. FaBoUs

Lying under the olive tree, O world, O death? (*LL*) Ultima Ratio Regum. Stephen Spender. CMoP; ImPo; LiTB; LiTM; OAEL-2; OBWP; PAW; PoWW

Lying under the stars. The Heart of Herakles. Kenneth Rexroth. *Fr.* Lights in the Sky are Stars, The. NU

Lying with my back on the slanted weir. Dream in an Afternoon. Rhyll McMaster. FaBoMA

Lying with unstable pego 'twixt a brace of vigorous boys. To Phoebus. Martial, *tr. fr. Latin.* PeHV

Lyk as the dum. The Solsequium. Alexander Montgomerie. NoP; OxBS

Lyke-Wake Dirge, The [*or* A]. *Unknown.* CH; ChTr; CoGr; EBEvV; FaBoCh; FaBoRV; GBP; HAP; HoPM; NOBE; NoP; NTP; OBEV; OtMeF; PeECV; PoEL-1; ScCV; TFi; WeW

Lyke wyse to think yt is not. (*LL*) Deme as Ye List Uppon Goode Cause. Sir Thomas Wyatt. PoEL-1

Lyle Donaghy, Poet, 1902-1949. George Buchanan. PNI

Lynched/ the lakes. Our Earth Will Not Die. Niyi Osundare. HBAPE

Lynched Negro. Maxwell Bodenheim. PoNe

Lynching, The. Claude McKay. PoBA

Lynching, The. Dorothea Matthews. ShDr

Lynching. L. A. J. Moorer. CBWP-3

Lynching and Burning. Primus St. John. PoBA

Lynn. Jeanne Foster. CrSp

Lynn Schmidt says. Epiphany. Pem Kremer. CrSp

Lynx, The. Charles Edward Eaton. DiPo

Lynx. Ben Howard. GrPl

Lyre neglected, and the tuneful lay, The. To Lysander. Judith Madan. ECWP

Lyre of the sonnet, that fully many a time. Written December 1790. Anna Seward. Son

Lyre Player, The. Stefan George, *tr. by* Carol North Valhope *and* Ernst Morowitz. PeHV

Lyrebirds. Judith Wright. GoJo

Lyric: "Absence, alas,/ Causeth me pass." Sir Thomas Wyatt. SiPSBD

Lyric: "Alone, Musing." Sir Thomas Wyatt. SiPSBD

Lyric: "Embodiment of what, The." Arthur Gregor. TAP

Lyric: "For want of will in woe I plain." Sir Thomas Wyatt. SiPSBD

Lyric: "From now on kill America out of your mind." James Agee. GOA

Lyric: "Horrible of hue, hideous to behold." Sir Thomas Wyatt. SiPSBD

Lyric: "I know not where my heavy sighs to hide." Sir Thomas Wyatt. SiPSBD

Lyric: "It burneth yet, alas, my heart's desire." Sir Thomas Wyatt. SiPSBD

Lyric: "O goodly hand." Sir Thomas Wyatt. SiPSBD

Lyric: "Pain of all pain, the most grievous pain." Sir Thomas Wyatt. SiPSBD

Lyric: "Sometime I sigh, sometime I sing." Sir Thomas Wyatt. SiPS; SiPSBD

Lyric: "When Dido feasted first the wandering Trojan knight." Sir Thomas Wyatt. SiPSBD

Lyric Afterwards, A. Tom Paulin. PNI; SCBI

Lyric Barber. Liboria E. Romano. GoYe

Lyric[k] for Legacies. Robert Herrick. BeJo; FaBoRV; JCP

Lyric from a Play, A. *Unknown.* MeEL

Lyric Meditation on Sour Locker Rooms, A. Dabney Stuart. *Fr.* Opposite Field, The. NGP

Lyric night of the lingering Indian Summer. September Midnight. Sara Teasdale. PoA

Lyric to Mirth, A. Robert Herrick. CaPo

Lyric to Spring. Joseph W. Stilwell. OBAL

Lyrics. James Agee. MoAmPo
Sels.

Lyrics of the Forest, *sels.* Sun Ching-hsuan.
   Night of the Forest. LHF, *tr. by* Hualing Nieh
   Pines, The. LHF, *tr. by* Hualing Nieh
   Purple Martin, The. LHF, *tr. by* Hualing Nieh
   Windstorm. LHF, *tr. by* Hualing Nieh

Lyrics shimmy like. Ron Welburn. NBV

Lysidice dedicated to you, Cypris. Asclepiades, *tr. fr. Greek by* Barbara Hughes Fowler. *Fr.* Epigrams. HePo

Lysidice, I'm anxious to find out the meaning. Antipater of Sidon, *tr. fr. Greek by* Tony Harrison. GrAn

Lysidike dedicates. Kenneth Rexroth, *after the Greek of* Asklepiades. NNaP; PGA

Lysimachus' cushion caught Antiochus' eye. Lucilius, *tr. fr. Greek by* Alistair Elliot. GrAn

Lysistrata. Aristophanes, *tr. fr. Greek by* B. B. Rogers. NAWM-1
Sels.

Lytell Treatyse for to Lerne Englysshe and Frens, A. *Unknown.* OxBLMV
Sels.
   For to Aske the Waye
   Pour demander le chemin

Lyth and listen, gentlemen. Robin Hood and the Beggar, II. *Unknown.* ESPB

Lytle turned with an oath — By God, it's true! (*LL*) The Oath. Allen Tate. FaBoMo; LiTM; OxBA; VGW

Lyve thowe gladly, yff so thowe may. Sir Thomas Wyatt. AAS

M

M. François le Vaillant Recalls His Travels to the Interior Parts of Africa. Patrick Cullinan. PeSAV

M, I, crooked letter, crooked letter, I. *Unknown.* RoPo

M. le professeur in prominent senility. My Neighbor in the Mirror. Louise Glück. Son

M. l'Epicier in his white hat. Soissons. Keith Douglas. NoAM

M. [*or* Mr.] Crashaw's Answer for Hope. Richard Crashaw. *See* Dear hope! Earth's dowry and heaven's debt!

M., Singing. Louise Bogan. GoJo; LiTA; NoAM

Ma. Paul Muldoon. PNI

Ma Canny Hinny. *Unknown.* FaBoPP; GBP

Ma dame, ye ben of all beauté shrine. Chaucer. *Fr.* To Rosemounde. EnVB

Ma-ha-mee!. (*LL*) My Mammy Was a Wall-eyed Goat. *Unknown.* ChTr; FaBoNo

Ma lass by munelicht fesht me frae the fail. The Deean Tractorman, Deleerit. Edith Anne Robertson. OxBS

Ma mammy bot me oot a shop. The Telling Part. Jackie Kay. NWP

Ma people, come an get ready. In Memoriam Ben Zwane. Wopko Jensma. PeSAV

Ma Rainey. Sterling A. Brown. Jaz

Ma sister, ma sister. A Brief Note to the Bag Lady, Ma Sister. Yusuf Eradam, *tr. fr. Turkish.* TSaS

Ma-wei. Li Shang-yin, *tr. fr. Chinese by* A. C. Graham. PLT

Mab. Ben Jonson. *See* This is Mab, the mistress-fairy.

Mab the Mistress-Fairy. Ben Jonson. *Fr.* Satyr, The. EIL

Mab will pinch her by the toe. (*LL*) The Fairies. Robert Herrick. FaPON

Mabel Kelly. Turlough Carolan, *tr. fr. Irish by* Austin Clarke. BIrV; CIP

Mabel, Mabel, set the table. *Unknown.* RoPo

Mabel Woo. Belle Randall. *Fr.* Hundred Ways of Playing Solitaire, A. CRP

Mabinog's Liturgy, *sels.* David Jones.
   "In the middle silences of this night's course the blackthorn." OxAEP-2

Mabrak. "Bongo Jerry." PBCV

Macadam, gun-grey as the tunny's belt. Van Winkle. Hart Crane. *Fr.* Bridge, The. AmPP; FaBV; LiTA; MoAB; MoAmPo; NAAL-2

McAfee's Confession. *Unknown.* AmFP

Macaffie's Confession. *Unknown.* BeLS

McAndrew's Hymn. Kipling. OxBTC

Macao. W. H. Auden. MeMAP

Macavity: The Mystery Cat. T. S. Eliot. CRH; FaBoCo; InPS; NBLV; NOBL; OBCA; OxBChV; PeLV; PoRA; RB; UV, *ll.* 1–36

Macaw preens upon a branch outspread, A. Decoration. Louise Bogan. MoAB; MoAmPo

Macbeth. Andrew of Wyntoun. OxBS

Macbeth, *sels.* Shakespeare.
   "Give sorrow words; the grief that does." IMW
   "Glamis thou art, and Cawdor; and shalt be." OxAEP-1
   "I have done the deed. Didst thou not hear a noise?" EBEV; OxAEP-1
   I Have Lived Long Enough. TrGrPo
   "If it were done when 'tis done, then 'twere well." EBEvV; OxAEP-1
   (If it were done when 'tis done, then 'twere well.) UnPo
   "Is this a dagger which I see before me." EBEvV
   "Now o'er the one half-world." OxAEP-1
   "Raven himself is hoarse, The." EBEvV
   "Scale of dragon, tooth of wolf." UV
   "Seyton! — I am sick at heart." OxAEP-1
   "She should have died hereafter." DL; SoSe
   (Out, Out, Brief Candle!) ChTr
   (Tomorrow, and Tomorrow, and Tomorrow.) FaBoRV; 09FaFP; FF; LiTB; 08MasP; 08PoPl; 08TRV; 08WHA; 08MasP; 08PoPl; 08TRV; 08WHA; TrGrPo, *sl. shorter sel.*
   Thrice the Brinded Cat Hath Mewed. InvP; RB
   (Charm, The.) EIL
   (Recipe for Hell-Broth, The.) CBCK
   "To-morrow, and to-morrow, and to-morrow." EBEvV; ImPo
   (Hang out our banners on the outward walls.) EBEV; OxAEP-1

Macbeth. Horace Smith *and* James Smith. BXAP

McCaffery. *Unknown.* OBET

McDonald's, New Hartford, NY. Valerie Worth. AiP

Macdonald's Raid. Paul Hamilton Hayne. PAH

McDonogh Day in New Orleans. Marcus B. Christian. PoNe

MacDuff. Charles Tomlinson. NAs; OxBC

MacFlecknoe; or, A Satire [*or* Satyr] upon the True-Blue [*or* -Blew]
  Protestant Poet T. S. Dryden. CBNP, *sl. abr.*; FHYEP; HAP, (*abr.*);
  NoP; OAEL-1; OBSV; OxBoLi; PeLV; Poetr; TEP; TFi
  Sels.
  "Give sorrow words; the grief that does." IMW
  "All human[e] things are subject to decay." NAEL-1; NOSC, *ll.* 1-30;
    PoE; PPP; SCV; SeCV-2; TrGrPo
  (Crown Prince of Dullness, The.) NOBE
  (Primacy of Dullness, The.) 09OBS
  "This is thy province, this thy wonderous way." EPCY
MacGregor's Gathering. Sir Walter Scott. OxBS
Machberoth. Immanuel di Roma, *tr. fr.* Hebrew by J. Chotzner. TrJP
  Sels.
  Oh, Let Thy Teachings
  Virtue
Macheath and Polly. John Gay. *See* Were I laid on Greenland's coast.
Machine-gun bullets, The. Mexico, August 20, 1940. Ai. NoAM
Machine gunner aims, A. El Alamein. Steve Crow. HATNAP
Machines of War. Nelly Sachs, *tr. fr.* German by Ruth Mead *and* Matthew
  Mead. WoWa
Machines of war set up. Machines of War. Nelly Sachs, *tr. fr.* German by
  Ruth Mead *and* Matthew Mead. WoWa
"Machines will raid at dawn," they say. Dawn. Day Jeffery. NSI
McIlrath of Malate. John Jerome Rooney. PAH
Mackenzie's shirtless. Déjeuner sur l'herbe. Anne Rouse. NWP
Mackerel-man drives down the street, The. A Pretty Ambition. Mary E.
  Wilkins Freeman. OBCA
Mackerel sky. *Unknown.* FaBoUs; OxNR
McKinley. *Unknown.* PAH
Mackinnon's Boat. Charles Tomlinson. AnAn
McLean's Welcome. James Hogg. OxBS
Macleod's Lament. Neil Munro. NSI
Macliammoir at Cappoquin. Thomas McCarthy. *Fr.* Neutral State, A. IB
McNaughtan. *Unknown.* OxBB
Macpherson's Farewell. Burns. OtMeF
Macrinus against Trees. "Michael Field." WPE
Macrocarpas. Michael Jackson. PeNZ
Mad, The. Robert Pinsky. *Fr.* Essay on Psychiatrists. NoAM
Mad Answer of a Madman, A. Robert Hayman. FF
Mad are predators, The. Too often lately they harbor. Geoffrey Hill. *Fr.*
  Mercian Hymns. NoP
Mad as the Mist and Snow. W. B. Yeats. ChTr; RaBo
Mad Berkeley believed, with his gay cavaliers. The Burning of Jamestown.
  Thomas Dunn English. PAH
Mad Day in March. Philip Levine. NYBP
Mad Dogs and Englishmen. Noël Coward. FiBHP; NBLV; NOBL; OBTV;
  PeLV
Mad Druggest, The. Robert Penn Warren. *Fr.* Tale of Time. LCAP
Mad Fight Song for William S. Carpenter, 1966, A. James Wright. NoAM
Mad Gardener's Song, The. "Lewis Carroll." *Fr.* Sylvie and Bruno.
  BLPL; CBNP; FaBoCo; FaBoNo; FiBHP, 6 *sts.*; OxBChV; WiR
Mad girl with the staring eyes and long white fingers, The. Cassandra.
  Robinson Jeffers. HeIP; LiTA; LiTM
Mad Hatter's Concert Song, The. "Lewis Carroll." *See* Twinkle, twinkle,
  little bat!
Mad Hatter's Song, The. "Lewis Carroll." *See* Twinkle, twinkle, little bat!
Mad is the poet men call Kit. Christopher Smart. Stanley Shaw. UV
Mad Lover, The, sels. John Fletcher.
  Arm, Arm, Arm, Arm! EIL
  "O divine star of heaven." GBL
  "Orpheus I am, come from the deeps below." GBL
Mad Maid's Song, The. Robert Herrick. AWP; CaPo; CH; EnLoPo;
  OAEL-1; OBEV; SeCV-1; TrGrPo; WiR
Mad Maudlin is Come. *Unknown.* CBNP
Mad Negro Soldier Confined at Munich, A. Robert Lowell. FaBoMo;
  OxBC
Mad Patsy said, he said to me. In the Poppy Field. James Stephens.
  PoRA
Mad Potter, The. John Hollander. VCAP
Mad Scene, The. James Merrill. CoAP; NOBA; PoA; PoE; TAP
Mad sculptor in our park, A. Helen. Peter Meinke. PBCAP
Mad Song. Blake. EnRP; MeMBP; NAEL-2; NOEC; OAEL-2; PoE;
  PoEL-4; PrIm; TEP; TrGrPo
Mad Song. Denise Levertov. TAP
Mad Sonnet 1. Michael McClure. PoM
Mad Talk of George III, The, sels. Jeffrey Wainwright.
  Hymn to Liberty, A. SCBI
  "Slow-worm from my orchard seeking me, The." SCBI

Mad Tom's Song. *Unknown. See* From the hag [*or* hagg] and hungry [*or*
  hungrie] goblin.
Mad Woman of Punnet's Town, The. L. A. G. Strong. MoBrPo
Mad Yak, The. Gregory Corso. PoBeRe
Madaket Beach. Isabel Harriss Barr. GoYe
Madam and Her Madam. Langston Hughes. SAmP
Madam and the Census Man. Langston Hughes. SAmP
Madam and the Minister. Langston Hughes. NOBA
Madam and the Rent Man. Langston Hughes. SAmP
Madam and the Wrong Visitor. Langston Hughes. SAmP
Madam Eglantine. Chaucer. *See* There [*or* Ther] was also a nun [*or*
  Nonne], a Prioress[e].
Madam,/ Reason is our soul's left hand, faith her right. To the Countess of
  Bedford ('Madam,/ Reason is Our Soul's Left Hand, Faith Her Right.
  John Donne. NOSC
Madame:/ Whilst that for which all virtue now is sold. Epistle to Elizabeth,
  Countess of Rutland. Ben Jonson. BeJo
Madam,/ I hope you'll think it's true. Strephon to Celia; a Modern
  Love-Letter. Mary Leapor. ECWP
Madam,/ If you're deceived, it is not by my cheat. A Very Heroical Epistle
  in Answer to Ephelia. The Earl of Rochester. APAS
Madam,/ Were you but only great, there are some men. To the Excellent
  Pattern of Beauty and Virtue, Lady Elizabeth, Countess of Ormonde.
  James Shirley. BeJo
Madam I praise you, 'cause you'r free. To a Friend for Her Naked
  Breasts. "Eliza." KTR
Madam Life. W. E. Henley. *See* Madam Life's a Piece in Bloom.
Madam Life's a Piece in Bloom. W. E. Henley. EBVV; NAEL-2; OPOP;
  PeVV
Madam Mouse Trots. Edith Sitwell. FaBoCh
Madam, no more! The time has come to eat. A. D. Hope. ErPo; NoP
Madam [*or* Madame], had all antiquity [*or* antiquitie] been lost. To Mary
  Lady Wroth. Ben Jonson. NOSC
Madam! permit a Muse, that has been long. To Madam Bhen. "Ephelia."
  KTR
Madam, the Lady Valeria is come to visit you. Shakespeare. *Fr.*
  Coriolanus. OxAEP-1
Madam, 'tis true, your beauties move. Sidney Godolphin. JCP
Madam, twice through the Muses Grove I walkt. Upon Mrs. Anne
  Bradstreet Her Poems. John Rogers. SCAP
Madam, withouten Many Words. Sir Thomas Wyatt. *See* Madame,
  withouten Many Wordes.
Madam would speak with me. So, now it comes. George Meredith. *Fr.*
  Modern Love. NOBVV
Madam, you are right, the fight was a great pity. To the Woman in Bond
  Street Station. Edward Weismiller. LiTA
Madam, your beauty and your lovely parts. Platonic Love. Lord Herbert of
  Cherbury. NOSC
Madam, your humble servant, Samuel Sewall." (*LL*) Samuel Sewall.
  Anthony Hecht. LiTM; NBLV; PeLV; PoRA; TwCP
Madame. George McWhirter. UnAS
Madame d'Albert's Laugh. Clément Marot, *tr. fr.* French by Leigh Hunt.
  AWP
Madame de Staël. Emma Catherine Embury. AmWP
Madame Dill. *Unknown.* FiBHP
Madame, his grace will not be absent long. Cyril Tourneur. *Fr.* Revenger's
  Tragedy, The. PoEL-2
Madame, I Have Come a-Courting. *Unknown.* AmFP
Madame Maynard of the hard pebble. Stranded in My Ontario. Ronald G.
  Everson. NOBC
Madame Orchidée. Sherod Santos. AnAn
Madame, withouten Many Wordes. Sir Thomas Wyatt. AAS; HeIL; OBVE
Madame, ye been [*or* ben] of alle [*or* all *or* al] beautee [*or* beaute] shrine [*or*
  shryne]. To Rosamond. Chaucer. NoP
  (Ballade to Rosamund. MeEL)
  (To Rosamound[e].) CBLP; OAEL-1; PoE
Madam's Calling Cards. Langston Hughes. SAmP
Madam's Past History. Langston Hughes. MoP; NoAM; SAmP
Madarika. Vince Gotera. OpBo
Madboy's Song. Muriel Rukeyser. MoAmPo; TrJP
Mädchen mit dem rothen Mündchen. Heine, *tr. fr.* German by Sir Theodore
  Martin. AWP
Maddam to you. (*LL*) Madam's Past History. Langston Hughes. MoP;
  NoAM; SAmP
Maddening moon, A. Niyi Osundare. *Fr.* Moonsongs. HBAPE, *sect.* XIX
Made her much in demand as a starter. (*LL*) There was a young girl of La
  Plata. *Unknown.* PeLi
Made him take up his shirt, lay down his sword. (*LL*) Upon Pagget.
  Robert Herrick. CaPo; FaBoCh

Made in Sweden: carts are my trade. (*LL*) A Carriage from Sweden. Marianne Moore. HAP; LiTA; LiTM; MoAB; TwCP

Made in the Hot Weather. W. E. Henley. *See* Fountains that frisk and sprinkle.

Made in the Tropics. Vijay Seshadri. UTF

Made love made children. (*LL*) The Children. Constance Urdang. CoAP; IHMS

Made marriage it was, A. Wedding at Aughrim, Galway 1900. Catherine Byron. VBLP

Made of stone, round, and very ugly. (*LL*) Audubon, Drafted. Amiri Baraka. PPP; TTY

Made pale by her lover's faithlessness. (*LL*) The Maiden Came from the Tryst. Johann Ludvig Runeberg. RiWo

Made palpable, a gift for us. (*LL*) Muse of the Golden Throne. Sappho. InMo

Made Shine. Josephine Miles. NoAM

Made this world a heaven for me. (*LL*) Dream, dream, my sweet life. Richard Dehmel. RiWo

Madeleine in Church., *sels.* Charlotte Mew.
'Find rest in Him!' One knows the parsons' tags. ChIV-2
"How old was Mary out of whom you cast." MoAB; MoBrPo

Madelon. Peter Scupham. *Fr.* Notes from a War Diary, H.J.B. 1914–19. SCBI

Mademoiselle — goddess instead. The Lion in Love. Marianne Moore. VBLP

Mademoiselle/She went to the well. *Unknown.* ISE

Madge Wildfire Sings. Sir Walter Scott. *See* Proud Maisie ("Proud Maisie is in the wood.")

Madge Wildfire's Song. Sir Walter Scott. *See* Proud Maisie ("Proud Maisie is in the wood.")

Madhouse. Calvin C. Hernton. ETG; PoNe

Meditation on the Nativity. Sidney Godolphin. *See* Lord, when the wise men came from far[r].

Madly Singing in the Mountains. Po Chü-i, *tr. fr. Chinese by* Arthur Waley. Mes

Madman, The. S. J. Pretorius, *tr. fr. Afrikaans by* Uys Krige *and* Jack Cope. PeSA

Madman and the Lethargist, The. Samuel Taylor Coleridge. CBNP

Madman has threatened my life, A. I mean. Blue Lights. Thomas Rabbitt. NAmP90

Madman saith He said so: it is strange, The. (*LL*) An Epistle Containing the Strange Medical Experience of Karshish, the Arab Physician. Robert Browning. ChIV-2; NAEL-2

Madman's Song, The. John Webster. *Fr.* Duchess of Malfi, The. EIL; NAEL-1

Madman's Song. Elinor Wylie. MoAB; MoAmPo; PoRA

Madness. John Armstrong. *Fr.* Art of Preserving Health, The. NOEC

Madness. James Dickey. NYBP

Madness. Yoshihara Sachiko, *tr. fr. Japanese by* James Kirkup *and* Shozo Tokunaga. BoWoP

Madness of King Goll, The. W. B. Yeats. NAEL-2

Madonna Natura. "Fiona Macleod." WGRP

Madonna of the Evening Flowers. Amy Lowell. NALW; PeHV; UnAS

Madras,/ 1965, and rain. Some Indian Uses of History on a Rainy Day. A. K. Ramanujan. OxBC

Madre Sofía. Alberto A. Ríos. NAmP90; NoAM

Madrid. "Pai Wei," *tr. fr. Chinese by* Kenneth Rexroth *and* Ling Chung. PBWP; WPC

Madrid. Jay Wright. BAP-89

Madrigal, A: "Crabbed age and youth." Shakespeare. *See* Crabbed age and youth cannot live together.

Madrigal: "Astrea in this time." William Drummond of Hawthornden. *Fr.* Urania, or Spiritual Poems. NOSC

Madrigal: "Ay me, alas, heigh ho, heigh ho!" Thomas Weelkes. FaBoCh; OxBoLi

Madrigal: "Beauty [*or* Beautie], and the life, The." William Drummond of Hawthornden. EIL; PoEL-2
(Her Passing.) OBEV

Madrigal: "Come let's begin to revel't out." *Unknown.* BoTP

Madrigal: "Daedal of my death, A." William Drummond of Hawthornden. NOSC

Madrigal: "Dear, when I did from you remove." Lord Herbert of Cherbury. EIL
(Another [Madrigal].) NOSC

Madrigal: "Ha ha! ha ha! This world doth pass." *At. to* Thomas Weelkes. CBNP; EIL; FaBoCh; FaBoCo; FaBoNo; OxBoLi; PeLV

Madrigal: "How should I love my best?" Lord Herbert of Cherbury. PoEL-2; SeCP

Madrigal: "I always loved to call my lady Rose." *Unknown.* EIL

Madrigal: "I am all bent to glean the golden ore." Cino da Pistoia, *tr. fr. Italian by* Dante Gabriel Rossetti. AWP

Madrigal: "I'm going to make a million some night." Bible, Apocrypha, *tr. fr. Spanish by* W. S. Merwin. AnRep

Madrigal: "Like the Idalian Queen[e]." William Drummond of Hawthornden. CBLP; EIL; ELP; GBL; InvP; NOSC; OBAL; OAEL-1; PeLV; PoEL-2; SCGP
(Inexorable.) NOBE; OBEV

Madrigal: "Love now no fire hath left him." Giovanni Battista Marino, *tr. fr. Italian by* Richard Crashaw. OBVE

Madrigal: "My mistress frowns when she should play." John Hilton. OxBoLi
(Fa La La.) CH

Madrigal: "My mistress is as fair as fine." Thomas Ravenscroft. CH; OxBoLi

Madrigal: "My thoughts hold mortal[l] strife." William Drummond of Hawthornden. EIL; GTBS; GTBS-P; NOSC; OxBSP
(Inexorable.) NOBE; OBEV

Madrigal: "Poor turtle! thou bemoans." William Drummond of Hawthornden. ScCV

Madrigal: "Ivory, coral, gold, The." William Drummond of Hawthornden. *See* Ivory, Coral, Gold, The.

Madrigal: "My love in her attire doth show her wit." *Unknown. See* My Love in her attire doth show her wit.

Madrigal: "Since Bonny-boots was dead, that so divinely." *Unknown. See* Since Bonny-Boots Was Dead.

Madrigal: "Sister, awake! close not your eyes." *Unknown. See* Sister, Awake!

Madrigal: "Some there are as fair to see." Francis Davison. *See* Some there are as fair to see to.

Madrigal: "Sound of thy sweet name, my dearest treasure, The." Francis Davison. EIL

Madrigal: "Tell me where is fancy bred." Shakespeare. *See* Tell Me Where Is Fancy [*or* Fancie] Bred.

Madrigal: "To be a whore, despite of grace." Charles Cotton. FaBoEE

Madrigal: "This life, which seems [*or* seemes] so fair [*or* faire]." William Drummond of Hawthornden. EIL; GTBS; GTBS-P; PAGL-1; SeCePo
(This Life.) CH; TrgrPo

Madrigal: "This world a hunting is." William Drummond of Hawthornden. OxBSP

Madrigal: "Unhappie [*or* Unhappy] Light." William Drummond of Hawthornden. NOSC

Madrigal: "When in her face mine eyes I fix." William Alexander, Earl of Stirling. *Fr.* Aurora. EIL

Madrigal: "Why dost thou haste away?" Sir Philip Sidney. *Fr.* Arcadia. NoSic; SiPS

Madrigal: "Your love is dead, lady, your love is dead." R. S. Thomas. BoLoP; EnLoPo

Madrigal de Verano. Federico García Lorca, *tr. fr. Spanish by* Paul Blackburn. ErPo

Madwoman at Rodmell. Michele Roberts. BrRo

Madwoman of Cork, The. Patrick Galvin. BiHa

Madwoman of Papine, The. Abdur-Rahman Slade Hopkinson. PBCV

Madwoman on the Train, The. Alfred W. Purdy. NoAM

Madwomen of the Plaza de Mayo, The. Eli W. Mandel. NOBC

Mae West. Edward Field. FYAP

Maen Madoc. Chris Torrance. AngWe

Mae's Rent Party. Ernest J. Wilson, Jr.. PoNe

Maesia's Song. Robert Greene. *Fr.* Farewell to Folly. CTC; UnPo

Mafukuzela, rain-giving clouds. Lament for Mafukuzela. *Zulu Oral Tradition, tr. by* H. Tracey. WTO

Mag Uidhir's Winter Campaign. Eochadh O'Hussey. NOIV

Magalu. Helene Johnson. BlSi; CDC; PoBA; PoNe; ShDr

Magda Goebbels. W. D. Snodgrass. ArOW

Magdalen at Michael's gate. At Glastonbury. Henry Kingsley. PoRA

Magdalen Walks. Oscar Wilde. EBVV; MoBrPo

Maggie. Duane Niatum. HATNAP

Maggie and Milly and Molly and May. E. E. Cummings. ImGa; MeMAP; NoAM; NOBA; RB

Maggie Lauder. At. to Francis Sempill. OxBS

Maggie Mac. *Unknown.* AmFP

Maggie Meek, the tail of a leek. *Unknown.* RoPo

Maggie's Star. Charles Tennyson Turner. FM

Maggot Song. *Unknown.* NOBAu

Magi, The. George Garrett. MT

Magi, The. Louise Glück. PoA

Magi, The. Ramon Guthrie. PoE

Magi, The. Milton. *Fr.* On the Morning of Christ's Nativity. ChTr; MeLP; NAs; NOCV; NoP; PoEL-3; SCGP; WGRP

Magi, The. W. B. Yeats. ChIV-2; CMoP; FaBoRV; HAP; InPK; NoAM; OAEL-2; OxAEP-2; PChr; PoA; PoE; TrCP; TRP

Magic. Aimé Césaire, *tr. fr. French by* Clayton Eshleman *and* Denis Kelly. NegPo

Magic. Ovid, *tr. fr. Latin. Fr.* Metamorphoses. AWP, *tr. by* Shakespeare

Magic. Dahlia Ravikovitch, *tr. fr. Hebrew.* TSaS, *tr. by* Chana Bloch *and* Ariel Bloch

Magic/ my man. Black Magic. Sonia Sanchez. BPo

Magic. Shakespeare. *See* Ye elves of hill(s), brooks, standing lakes, and groves.

Magic Apple Tree, The. Elaine Feinstein. BrRo

Magic Car Moved On, The. Shelley. *Fr.* Queen Mab. GN

Magic Casements. Keats. *Fr.* Ode to a Nightingale. AWP; BLRP; ClHu; EBEV; EnRP; FaBoBe; FaBV; FaPoB; GTBS; GTBS-P; HAP; HeIP; ImPo; InPS; LiTB; NAEL-2; NAWM-2; NOBE; NoP; OAEL-2; OBEV; OBNC; OPOP; PoE; PoEL-4; PoRA; PPP; PrIm; RB; SCGP; SoSe; TEP; TFi; TOF; TrGrPo; UnPo

Magic dance, The. After the Ball. Amiri Baraka. NAAL-2

Magic Flute, The. W. D. Snodgrass. NYBP

Magic Fox. James Welch. CDW; HATNAP; NoAM

Magic holds, The. Rain in New York. Eva Salzman. NWP

Magic Mist, A. Owen Roe O'Sullivan, *tr. fr. Irish by* Thomas Kinsella. NOIV

Magic Mountain, A. Czeslaw Milosz, *tr. fr. Polish by* Lillian Vallee. AnAn

Magic of the day is the morning, The. Ballad of the Morning Streets. Amiri Baraka. SOTW; TTTS

Magic Piper, The. E. L. Marsh. BoTP

Magic Strings. Li Ho, *tr. fr. Chinese by* A. C. Graham. PLT

Magic Whistle, The. Margaret Rose. BoTP

Magic Words. *Unknown, tr. fr. Eskimo.* ImGa, *tr. by* Edward Field; NU; RaBo; STP

Magic Words for Hunting Caribou. *Unknown, tr. fr. Eskimo by* Jerome K. Rothenberg *and* Johnny John. STP

Magic Words for Hunting Seal. *Unknown, tr. fr. Eskimo by* Edward Field. STP

Magic Words to Feel Better. Nakasuk, *tr. fr. Eskimo by* Jerome K. Rothenberg. STP

Magical Feelings. Friendship. Emily Marshall. OBF

Magician, The. Gary Miranda. SM

Magician and the Baron's Daughter, The. *Unknown. See* Draw me nere [*or* near], draw me nere [*or* near].

Magician and the Baron's Daughter, The. *Unknown.* MeEL

Magna Est Veritas. Coventry Patmore. *See* Here, in This Little Bay.

Magna Est Veritas. Stevie Smith. OxBC

Magnet. Thomas Stanley. NOBE

Magnet, The. Ruth Stone. MoAmPo

Magnet hung in a hardware shop, A. The Fable of the Magnet and the Churn. W. S. Gilbert. *Fr.* Patience. FaPON

Magnetic Mountain, The, *sels.* C. Day Lewis.
Nearing Again the Legendary Isle. FaBoTw; LiTB; MoAB; MoBrPo
Tempt Me No More. MoAB; MoBrPo; OBMV; PoA

Magnificat, The. Bible, *N.T. Fr.* St. Luke. BoWoP; WGRP

Magnificat. Chana Bloch. CrSp

Magnificat. Michele Roberts. BrRo; NBrP; VBLP

Magnificence, *sels.* John Skelton.
"Stow, birde, stow, stow!" NoSic
"Unto this process briefly compiled." NoSic

Magnificent Bull, The. *Dinka Oral Tradition.* TTTS

Magnolia. Mary Weston Fordham. CBWP-2

Magnolia's Shadow, The. Robert Lowell, *tr. fr. Italian by* Eugenio Montale. NaP

Magnum Vectigal Parsimonia. George Gascoigne. NoSic

Magpie. Peter Davison. GrPl

Magpie and Pines. Louis Johnson. PeNZ

Magpie, magpie, flutter and flee. *Unknown.* OxNR

Magpie Rhyme, Northumberland, A. *Unknown.* GBP

Magpie Song. *Unknown, tr. fr. Navajo Indian by* Washington Matthews. AnAmPo

Magpie! The Magpie! Here underneath, The. Magpie Song. *Unknown, tr. fr. Navajo Indian by* Washington Matthews. AnAmPo

Magpies, The. Denis Glover. NTP; PeNZ

Magpies in Picardy. T. P. Cameron Wilson. NSI; OtMeF; PAW

Magryme, The. William Dunbar. FaBoVe

Mag's Song. *Unknown.* AS

Maguire is not afraid of death, the Church will light him a candle. Patrick Kavanagh. *Fr.* Great Hunger, The. CIP

Magus, The. James Dickey. NAs

Magus, A. John Ciardi. MAT

Magwere, Who Waits Wondering. Kingsley Fairbridge. PeSAV

Mahabalipuram. Louis MacNeice. OBTV

Mahabharata, The, *sels. Unknown, tr. fr. Sanskrit by* Franklin Edgerton.
Sâvitrî; or, Love and Death. TAL, *tr. by* Sir Edwin Arnold
"So, pure and dutiful, she sought that place." DL

Maharani of midnight tresses, The. In the Seraglio. David R. Slavitt. ErPo; PeHV

Mahler, *sels.* Jonathan Williams.
Symphony No. 3, in D Minor. VGW

Mahratta Ghats, The. Alun Lewis. AngWe; OBTV; OBWVE; PoWW

Maid, The. Nathan Alterman, *tr. fr. Hebrew by* Ruth Finer Mintz. MHP

Maid, The. Theodore Goodridge Roberts. MoShBr

Maid and the Palmer, The. *Unknown.* ESPB

Maid Freed from the Gallows, The. *Unknown.* AS

Maid Freed from the Gallows, The. *Unknown.* AWP; ESPB

Maid, I dare not tell her name, A. The Nameless Maiden. *Unknown.* ErPo

Maid in the Mill, The, *sels.* John Fletcher *and* William Rowley.
"Now having leisure, and a happy wind." GBL

Maid Marian, *sels.* Thomas Love Peacock.
For the Slender Beech and the Sapling Oak. EnRP
(Song: "For the tender beech and the sapling oak.") OHIP
Over, Over. OxAEP-2
Robin Hood and the Grey Friars. OxAEP-2

Maid Marjory sits at the castle gate. *Unknown, tr. fr. French by* John Addington Symonds. *Fr.* Medieval Norman Song. AWP

Maid o' the West, The. John Clare. OAEL-2

Maid of Athens [Ere We Part]. Byron. EBEV; EnRP; FaBV; PrIm

Maid of Athens, ere we part. Maid of Athens [Ere We Part]. Byron. EBEV; EnRP; FaBV; PrIm
(Song.) FHYEP

Maid of Brenten Arse, A. *Unknown.* GBP

Maid of Ehrenthal, The. H. Cordelia Ray. CBWP-3

Maid of Honour, The, *sels.* Philip Massinger.

Maid of Kent, A. *Unknown.* CBLP; OxBoLi

Maid of Monterey, The. *Unknown.* AmFP

Maid of Neidpath, The. Thomas Campbell. GTBS; GTBS-P

Maid of Neidpath, The. Sir Walter Scott. BeLS; EnRP; GTBS; GTBS-P

Maid of Orleans, The. Schiller, *tr. fr. German by* James Clarence Mangan. AWP

Maid of the Moor, The; or, The Water-Fiends, *sels.* George Colman the Younger.
"Cold blows the blast — the night's obscure." NOEC

Maid of Tottenham, The. *Unknown.* CoMu

Maid she went to the well to wash[e], The. The Maid and the Palmer. *Unknown.* ESPB

Maid, where's my lawrel? Oh my rageing soul! The Enchantment. Theocritus [*or* Theokritus], *tr. by* Thomas Creech. *Fr.* Idylls. CTC; OBVE
(Where is my bay? Bring it, Thestylis. Where are my charms?) HePo, *tr. by* Barbara Hughes Fowler

Maid who binds her warrior's sash, The. The Brave at Home. Thomas Buchanan Read. AnAmPo

Maiden, The. Peter Hille, *tr. fr. German by* Jethro Bithell. AWP

Maiden, and mistress of the months and stars. Swinburne. *Fr.* Atalanta in Calydon. EnVR; PoEL-5

Maiden and River. Mary Weston Fordham. CBWP-2

Maiden at college called Breeze, A. Mrs. Mercy Warren. PeLi

Maiden Came from the Tryst, The. Johann Ludvig Runeberg, *tr. fr. Finnish by* Philip L. Miller. RiWo

Maiden caught me in the wild, The. The Crystal Cabinet. Blake. CH; FaBoCh; MeMBP; OAEL-2; OBNC; PoEL-4

Maiden has dropped her veil and broken it on the rock, The. The Fountain at Tzarskoye Selo. Pushkin, *tr. fr. Russian by* Philip L. Miller. RiWo

Maiden in the Moor [*or* Mor], A. *Unknown. See* Maiden in the mor lay.

Maiden in the mor lay. *Unknown.* MiEL; PoEL-1
(Maiden in the Moor [*or* Mor], A.) EnVB; PoEL-5
(Maiden Lay in the Wilds, The.) MeEL

Maiden Lay in the Wilds, The. *Unknown. See* Maiden in the mor lay.

Maiden Lies in Her Chamber, A. Heine, *tr. fr. German by* Louis Untermeyer. AWP

Maiden moder milde. *Unknown.* MiEL

Maiden Name. Philip Larkin. GTBS-P

Maiden, not to be greeted unbenignly. (*LL*) Hendecasyllabics. Tennyson. EBEV; FaBoCo; NOBL; PeLV

Maiden of the Smile, The. Alfred Austin. TEP

Maiden ran away to fetch the clothes, The. Deluge. John Clare. BoNaP

Maiden Speaks, The. Otto Friedrich Gruppe, tr. fr. German by Philip L. Miller. RiWo

Maiden There Lived, A. Unknown. NOBL; PeLV

Maidenhead. "Ephelia." KTR; WPE

Maidenhead: Written at the Request of a Friend. "Ephelia." See At your entreaty [or Intreaty], I at last have writ.

Maidenhood. Sir John Davies. Fr. Contention Betwixt a Wife, a Widow, and a Maid, A. CBCK

Maidenhood, maidenhood, where have you gone and left me? Bride: Maidenhood, Maidenhood. Sappho, tr. fr. Greek by Jane McIntosh Snyder. VBLP

Maiden's Best Adorning, The. Unknown. OxBChV

Maidens Blush, The, sels. Joshua Sylvester.
  "But, fair Iëmpsar (wife of Potiphar.") ChIV-1

Maidens Came, The. Unknown. GBL; PoEL-1
  (Bailey Beareth the Bell Away, The. CBNP; LiTB

Maiden's Denial, A. Unknown. ErPo

Maidens, kilt your skirts and go. Celia's Home-coming. Agnes Mary Frances Robinson. OBEV

Maidens of London's Brave Adventures, Or, a Boon Voyage Intended for the Sea, The. Laurence Price. NOSC

Maiden's Plight, The. Brian Merriman, tr. by Frank O'Connor. Fr. Midnight Court, The. BIrV; NOIV, tr. by Thomas Kinsella

Maidens shall weep at merry morn. The Summer Malison. Gerard Manley Hopkins. CMoP; PoEL-5

Maidens who this bursting [or burning] May. A Young Man's Song. William Bell. FaBoTw

Maidens, why spare ye? To Cupid. Michael Drayton. EIL

Maids. Aleksandar Ristovic, tr. fr. Serbo-Croatian by Charles Simic. HSix

Maids, and here strew violets. (LL) An Epitaph upon a Child. Robert Herrick. FaBoEE; SeCV-1

Maid's Complaint for Want of a Dil Doul, The. Unknown. CoMu

Maids Conjuring Book, The. Unknown. CoMu

Maid's Husband, The. Henry Carey. ECEV

Maid's Lament, The. Walter Savage Landor. Fr. Citation and Examination of William Shakespeare, The. OBEV; OBNC

Maids, not to you my mind doth change. "Michael Field." Fr. Variations on Sappho. PeHV

Maids of Honour, The. Unknown. CoMu

Maid's Thought, The. Robinson Jeffers. ErPo

Maids to bed and cover coal. The Bellman's Song. Unknown. EBEV; EIL; SCGP

Maid's Tragedy, The, sels. Beaumont and Fletcher and John Fletcher.
  Bridal Song ("Cynthia, to thy power"). OBEV
  Bridal Song ("Hold back thy hours"). EIL; ErPo; TrGrPo
  (Song: "Hold back thy hours, dark night, till we have done.") OxBSP
  "Lay a garland on my hearse." EIL; GBL; SCGP
  (Aspatia's Song.) AWP; HAP; NOBE; OBEV; TrGrPo
  (I Died True.) CH

Mail Boat, Leinster, The. Unknown. OxBSS

Mail Call. Randall Jarrell. ArOW

Mail-Coach, The. Wilhelm Müller, tr. fr. German by Philip L. Miller. Fr. Winter's Journey, The. RiWo

Mail Has Come, The. Mary E. Tucker. CBWP-1

Mailman, The. Mark Strand. CAPP

Maim[e]'d Debauchee, The. The Earl of Rochester. See As some brave admiral, in former war.

Main Character. Jimmy Santiago Baca. NAmP90

Main cook lies sick on a banquette, and his assistant, The. Restaurant. Maxine Hong Kingston. OpBo

Main-Deep, The. James Stephens. MoBrPo; OBMV; UnPo

Main-Truck; or, A Leap for Life, The. At. to George Pope Morris. AnAmPo; BLPL; PoLF; VPP

Maine. Elinor Nauen. UL

Maine Lake at Night. Harry Morris. CRP

Maine Vastly Covered with Much Snow. John Tagliabue. InPK

Mainly I was led to them, the casinos of aluminium. Painting Mount Taranaki. David Eggleton. PeNZ

Maintrunk Country Roadsong. Sam Hunt. PeNZ

Maisie. James Merrill. HeIP

Maja's Glance, The. Fernando Periquet Y Zuaznabar, tr. fr. Spanish by Philip L. Miller. RiWo

Majestic, from the most distant time. From the Most Distant Time. Emperor Wu of Han, tr. fr. Chinese by Kenneth Rexroth. OHMPC

Majestic Valley. Chu Yi-tsun, tr. fr. Chinese by Chang Yin-nan and Lewis C. Walmsley. SuSp

Majesty and Mercy of God, The. Sir Robert Grant. OHIP; WGRP

Majesty of God, The. Thomas Sternhold. See Lord Descended from Above, The.

Major abstraction is the idea of man, The. Wallace Stevens. Fr. Notes toward a Supreme Fiction. NOBA

Major André. Unknown. AmFP

Major Bowes' Diary. Amiri Baraka. NAAL-2

Major-General Scott. On to Richmond. John R. Thompson. PAH

Major is a fine cat. My Cat Major. Stevie Smith. OFC

Major Macroo. Stevie Smith. NBLV

Major Work, A. William Meredith. Poetr

Majuba Hill. Roy Macnab. PeSA

Makar, The. William Soutar. OxBS

Make a joyful noise unto the Lord, all ye lands. Bible, O.T., paraphrased by Sir Thomas Wyatt. Fr. Psalms. BLRP; OHIP
  (Be Thankful unto Him.) FaPON
  (Giving Thanks, 4.) BLRP
  (Hundredth Psalm, The.) BLRP; OtMeF
  (Old Hundredth, metrical vers. by William Kethe.) FaPoR; NOCV
  (Scotch Te Deum.) WGRP

Make a most infernal clatter, here the dinner comes! (LL) Going In to Dinner. Edward Shanks. OBMV; OxBTC

Make all your sorrow neat. The Young Wife. Derek Walcott. DiPo

Make Bright the Arrows. Edna St. Vincent Millay. ChIV-1

Make but the dear Amanda mine. (LL) For ever, Fortune, wilt thou prove. James Thomson. GTBS; GTBS-P

Make clay ascend more quick than light. (LL) Ascension Hymn ("Dust and clay.") Henry Vaughan. ESCV; GeHe; NOSC; SeCV-1; TrCP

Make company break. Advice of Housewives. Thomas Tusser. Fr. Five Hundred Points of Good Husbandry. NoSic

Make even feathered wings. (LL) Be Daedalus. Nanina Alba. PoBA; PoNe

Make every bargain clear and plain. Unknown. FaBoUs

Make friendship with the stars. The Stars. Lydia Huntley Sigourney. AmWP

Make haste away, and let one be. To His Book ("Make Haste Away, And Let One Be.") Robert Herrick. NOSC

Make haste away together. (LL) An Invitation to Lubberland. Unknown. FaBoNo; GBP

Make him afraid? (LL) Mantis. Ruth Miller. PeSAV

Make it ever flourishing. (LL) A Grace for Children. Robert Herrick. OxBChV

Make it sweet and delicate to eat. The Eaten Heart. Unknown, tr. fr. Middle English by Pearl London. Fr. Knight of Curtesy, The. TrGrPo

Make love at home, and go to bed betimes. (LL) Fatal Love. Matthew Prior. FaBoCo; NBLV

Make Love Not War. Howard Nemerov. NAs

Make me a bowl, a mighty bowl. The Cup. John Oldham. AWP

Make me a captive, Lord. Christian Freedom. George Matheson. TrPWD

Make me a grave where'er you will. Bury Me in a Free Land. Frances E. W. Harper. AAP; AmWP; BPo

Make me a handle as straight as the mast of a ship. To the Blacksmith with a Spade. Owen Roe O'Sullivan. IIP

Make me a heaven, and make me there. The Eye. Robert Herrick. CaPo

Make me a humble thing of love and the tears. (LL) "Multum Dilexit." Hartley Coleridge. EnRP

Make me a long coat of heavy cloth, tailor. Gingerbread Heart. Aleksandar Ristovic, tr. fr. Serbo-Croatian by Charles Simic. HSix

Make me content, O Lord, with daily bread. Prayer for Contentment. Edwin McNeill Poteat. TrPWD

Make me, dear Lord, polite and kind. A Child's Prayer. John Banister Tabb. FaPON

Make me immoderately wise. (LL) As pools beneath stone arches take. John Drinkwater. PoA

Make me, O Lord, thy spinning [or spining] wheel[e] complete [or compleat or compleate] [or of use for thee]. Huswifery. Edward Taylor. EAP; FaBV; LiTA; MeMAP; NAAL-1; NIP; NOBA; NOBE; NoP; OxBA; SCAP; TAP; TFi
  (Housewifery.) LiTA; NoP

Make me over, mother April. Spring Song. Bliss Carman. AnAmPo

Make me too brave to lie or be unkind. A Prayer for Every Day. Mary Carolyn Davies. BLPA; FaBoBe; PoToHe

Make men beleeve no Paradice. (LL) To Cynthia, on Concealment of Her Beauty. Sir Francis Kynaston. MeLP; NOBE

Make miniatures of the once-monstrous theme. A Short History of British India. Geoffrey Hill. OxBC

Make my cup with clay. Zonas, tr. fr. Greek by Sam Hamill. InMo

Make my mortal dreams come true. Whittier. Fr. Andrew Rykman's Prayer. TrPWD

Make new friends, but keep the old. New Friends and Old Friends. Joseph Parry. BLPA; BLPL; PoToHe

Make no mistake: if He rose at all. Seven Stanzas at Easter. John Updike. TrCP

Make no mistake; there will be no forgiveness. Easter Hymn. A. D. Hope. ChIV-2; FaBoMA

Make no sound, do not speak. Reading. Jean-Joseph Rabéarivelo, *tr. fr. French by* Ellen Conroy Kennedy. NegPo

Make once more my heart thy home! (*LL*) Rarely, Rarely, Comest Thou. Shelley. EnRP; OBNC; TrGrPo

Make one place ev'rywhere. (*LL*) The Temper, ("How should I praise Thee, Lord.") George Herbert. ESCV; GeHe; NOCV; NoP; PFP; PoEL-2

Make room, all ye kingdoms, in history renown'd. American Independence. Francis Hopkinson. PAH

Make room on our banner bright. Song of Texas. William Henry Cuyler Hosmer. PAH

Make sure that they are thoroughly cremated. (*LL*) Shipment to Maidanek. Ephim G. Fogel. BTR; OBWP; TrJP

Make the Earth Bright and Thanks. Meridel LeSueur. SRLS

Make this thing plain to us, O Lord! Clean Hands. Austin Dobson. TrPWD

Make three fourths of a cross, and a circle complete. *Unknown.* OxNR

Make-Up. Geraldine Monk. NBrP

Make up the King of Glory's Diadem. (*LL*) Christendom. Thomas Traherne. PoEL-2

Make us Thy mountaineers. The Last Defile. Amy Carmichael. TrCP

Make Way. Steven Lavoie. UL

Make Way! Ada Negri, *tr. fr. Italian by* Lynne Lawner. PBWP

Make way! From the Noisy ceilings of workshops. Make Way! Ada Negri, *tr. fr. Italian by* Lynne Lawner. PBWP

Make way, make way. The Stream's Song. Lascelles Abercrombie. OBMV

Make we mery bothe more and lasse. *Unknown.* MiEL

Make we mirth. Sing We Yule. *Unknown.* MeEL

Make Ye a Joyful Sounding Noise. *Unknown.* AH

Make yourself pure before you purify others. Tune: "As in a Dream; a Song." Su Shih, *tr. fr. Chinese by* Irving Y. Lo. SuSp

Maken pilgrimage to herself, walken. (*LL*) Present. Sonia Sanchez. WPOW

Maker of the trees. (*LL*) May all I say and all I think. *Unknown.* EaPr

Makers, The. David Galler. NYBP

Makers, The. Howard Nemerov. DiPo; FYAP

Makes a kwela for tomorrow. (*LL*) Kwela for Tomorrow. Rui Knopfli. PeSAV

Makes a man healthy, wealthy and wise. (*LL*) Early to bed and early to rise. *Unknown.* FaBoBe; FaBoUs

Makes countless thousands mourn. (*LL*) Man's Inhumanity to Man. Burns. BLPA

Makes lime for Mammon's tower. (*LL*) The Ravaged Villa. Herman Melville. CTC; NOBA; PoEL-5

Makes the Little Ones Dizzy. Samuel Hoffenstein. BXAP

Makes Time so vicious in his reaping. (*LL*) For a Dead Lady. E. A. Robinson. CMoP; DL; FYAP; HeIP; HoPM; InvP; LiTA; LiTM; MoAB; MoAmPo; MoP; NoAM; NOBA; OxBA; PoEL-5; PoRA; TFi

Makeup on Empty Space. Anne Waldman. SRLS

Makhno's Philosophers. John Manifold. CBAP; NOBAu

Makin' Jump Shots. Michael S. Harper. PoE

Making a Door. Dennis Schmitz. LCAP

Making a Man. Nixon Waterman. BLPA

Making a Season. Nicki Jackowska. DT

Making Camp. David Wagoner. VCAP

Making Chicago. Dennis Schmitz. LCAP

Making Contact. John Manifold. CBAP

Making Fools, than keeping Lovers. (*LL*) A Dialogue between Strephon and Daphne. The Earl of Rochester. SeCV-2

Making Hay. Philip Hodgins. NOBAu

Making his advances. Tortoise Gallantry. D. H. Lawrence. CMoP; MoP

Making It Simple December 8, 1969. David McElroy. AmPA

Making johnny-cakes round in the bend. (*LL*) The Springtime It Brings On the Shearing. E. J. Overbury. NOBAu

Making Lists. Gladys Cardiff. HATNAP

Making love down through the centuries. Here Today. Andrew Elliott. PNI

Making Love to Marilyn Monroe. Paul Groves. FaBoBl

Making Love to Myself. James L. White. GLP

Making Money: Drought Year in Minkler, California. Gary Soto. NoAM

Making of a Servant, The. J. J. R. Jolobe. PeSAV

Making of Birds, The. Katharine Tynan. TIRV

Making of Color, The. Hugh Seidman. AmPA

Making of Poems, The. Lucille Clifton. CrSp

Making of the Cross, The. William Everson. VGW

Making Old Bones. Alberta Turner. LCAP

Making Our Clowns Martyrs. Jack A. Mapanje. HBAPE

Making our pillows either down, or dust. (*LL*) Death. George Herbert. ESCV; GeHe; JCP; NAEL-1; NoP; SeCP; SeCV-1

Making Peace. Denise Levertov. WoWa

Making Poetry. Anne Stevenson. DiPo

Making Tens. M. M. Hutchinson. BoTP

Making the batter understand too late. (*LL*) Pitcher. Robert Francis. OxBSP; RaBo; WeW

Making the Jam without You. Maxine W. Kumin. NALW

Making the marmalade this year, I carve. Preserving. Roy Fuller. CBLP

Making the Move. Paul Muldoon. NoAM

Making these word things to. Report from a Far Place. William Stafford. CAPP

Making two one. (*LL*) The Search. George Herbert. ESCV; MiEL

Making Up for a Soul. David Wagoner. VGW

Making wild reference. (*LL*) White Poetess. Musaemura Bonus Zimunya. PeSAV

Makings of Happiness, The. Ronald Wallace. PBCAP

Malacoda. Samuel Beckett. CIP

Malady of Love Is Nerves, The. Petronius Arbiter, *tr. fr. Latin by* Howard Mumford Jones. AWP

Malady smote the earth one year, A. The Animals Sick of the Plague. Marianne Moore, *ad. fr. La* Fontaine. InPS

Malaga. Pearse Hutchinson. BIrV; PBCIP

Malaria. Paolo Ruffilli, *tr. fr. Italian by* Felix Stefanile. NeIt

Malcolm. Welton Smith. BPo

Malcolm Lowry. Malcolm Lowry. OBD

Malcolm X. Gwendolyn Brooks. PoBA; TTY

Malcolm X — an Autobiography. Larry Neal. BPo

Malcolm's Katie., *sels.* Isabella Valancy Crawford.

Malcontent, The, *sels.* John Marston.
    "I cannot sleepe, my eyes ill neighbouring lids." PoEL-2

Maldive Shark, The. Herman Melville. AmPP; AnAmPo; NAAL-1; NOBA; NoP; OxBA; PoE; PoEL-5; RB; TAP

Male & Female Loves in Beulah. Blake. *Fr.* Jerusalem. OBNC

Male child — ox abandoned to the vultures!, A. A War Song of the Basotho. *Unknown, tr. by* Daniel P. Kunene. PeSAV

Male Order. Robert Maitre. FaBoBl

Male Rage Poem. Pier Giorgio di Cicco. NOBC

Malefic Return, The. Ramón López Velarde, *tr. fr. Spanish by* Samuel Beckett. OBVE

Malemute Dog, A. Pat O'Cotter. BLPA

Malepractice and maleabsence issue is loneliness & limiting to-. Men and Birth: the Unexplainable. Don L. Lee. RaBo

Malest Cornifici Tuo Catullo. Allen Ginsberg. NeAP

Malfeasance, The. Alan Bold. OBSP

Malice of Innocence, The. Denise Levertov. NNaP

Malign my character, but do it under a willow. Direct Address. Amy Gerstler. UL

Malignant planets! do ye still combine. The Sow of Feeling. Robert Fergusson. NOEC

Malison of the Stone-chat. *Unknown.* GBP

Malisons, malisons more than ten. The Lark. *Unknown.* GBP

Mallard Lake Boating Songs, *sels.* Chu Yi-tsun, *tr. fr. Chinese by* Irving Lo.

Mallard's Going, The. John Logan. PRA

Malsum. Joseph Bruchac. ETG

Malta. John Forbes. NOBAu

Maltese Dog, A. Tymnes, *tr. by* Edmund Blunden. *Fr.* Epigrams. FaBoCh; FaBoEE; OBD; Spl

Malum Opus. James Appleton Morgan. FaBoCo

Malvern Hill. Herman Melville. AmPP; PAH; TAP

Malvern Hills, *sels.* Joseph Cottle.
    Industrial Evils. NOEC

Malvern Water, says Dr. John Wall. Malvern Waters. *Unknown.* FaBoEE

Malvern Waters. *Unknown.* FaBoEE

Mam-maw's losing touch at last: her face. Beside My Grandmother. Alfred M. Lee. SM

Mama and Daughter. Langston Hughes. UnPo

Mama, don't cry. (*LL*) Without Benefit of Declaration. Langston Hughes. TTY

Mama/ eats death/ tastes like fish. Monogram 4. Martina Werner, *tr. fr. German by* Rosemarie Waldrop. BoWoP

Mama Have You Heard the News. *Unknown.* AS

Mama/ I wish I were silver. Silly Song. Federico García Lorca, *tr. fr. Spanish by* M. D. Herter Norton. TTTS

Mama Julinda is let down into a hole. Island Funeral. Frank Stanford. MT

Mama Knows. Sharon Scott. JB

Mama, lying so far down. Unveiling. Hilary Sametz Lloyd. MDDM

Mama,/ papa,/ and us. An Inconvenience. John Raven. BPo; CRP

Mama, pick me up. Munich, 1955. Maurya Simon. BTR

Mama, please brush off my coat. Mama and Daughter. Langston Hughes. UnPo

Mama Rosanna's Last Bead-Clack. Laurel Speer. CrSp; PFL

Mama writes. Under Your Voice, among Legends. Phyllis Beauvais. NMM

Mamba the Bright-eyed, *sels.* George Gordon McCrae.

Mambojive collapse of occidental managerial class system. Autoincineration of the Right Stuff. Iván Argüelles. UL

Mame-Loshen, Yiddish. Bernard S. Mikofsky. BTR

Mame was singing. Queen of the Blues. Gwendolyn Brooks. NALW

Mamma!. Frank Horne. BPo

Mamma sent me to the spring, she told me not to stay. Chewing Chawing Gum. *Unknown.* AmFP

Mamma, there's Rachel making hay. The Mistake. *Unknown.* VPP

Mammon Marriage. George Macdonald. BoLoP; EBVV

Mammoth morning moved grey flanks and groaned, A. Walking Wounded. Vernon Scannell. OBWP

Mammy Hums. Carl Sandburg. PoNe

Mams, pig-sick of oilstains in the wash, The. Breaking the Chain. Tony Harrison. UV

Mamzelle. Mary Wilson. AIW

Man, The. Robert Creeley. OBAL

Man. Sir John Davies. *Fr.* Nosce Teipsum. EIL; NoSic, abr.; SiPS

Man. George Herbert. ESCV; GeHe; ImPo; NAEL-1; NoP; PoEL-2; SeCP; SeCV-1; TrGrPo; TrPWD, *abr*

Man. Bulat Okudzhava, *tr. fr. Russian by* George Reavey. PAW

Man. Pope. *See* Know then thyself, presume not God to scan.

Man. Swinburne. *See* Before the Beginning of Years.

Man. Henry Vaughan. ESCV; GeHe; MeLP; NOBE; NOCV; OBEV; PoEL-2; SCGP; SeCV-1

Man. Humbert Wolfe. MoBrPo

Man! A. Clinton Scollard. OHIP

Man, A. I think it is a man. My Dream About the Poet. Lucille Clifton. TRP

Man, a man, a kingdom for a man!, A. A Cynic Satire. John Marston. *Fr.* Satires. NoSic

Man, a man alive., A. *(LL)* The Reply. Theodore Roethke. NoP; NYBP

Man Adrift on a Slim Spar, A. Stephen Crane. NAAL-2

Man against the Sky, The. E. A. Robinson. AmPP; CMoP; LiTA; OxBA

Man All Grown Up Is Supposed To, A. Terry Stokes. AmPA

Man Alone. Louise Bogan. NYBP

Man Alone. Denise Levertov. CAPP

Man alone at the third-floor window, The. West Strand Visions. James Simmons. PBCIP

Man and Bat. D. H. Lawrence. RB

Man and Cows. Andrew Young. EBEV

Man and Dog. Edward Thomas. FM; PeFWW

Man and His Image, The. La Fontaine, *tr. fr. French by* Elizur Wright. OBVE

Man and Superman. Cameron Self. FaBoBl

Man and the Tree, The. Philip Mead. NOBAu

Man and the Weasel, The. Phaedrus, *tr. fr. Latin by* Christopher Smart. AWP

Man and Wife. Mitchell Goodman. VGW

Man and Wife. Robert Lowell. AmPP; BoLoP; CAPP; NAAL-2; VCAP

Man and Wife. Anne Sexton. CAPP

Man and Woman. Robert Conquest. OxBTC

Man and woman, A. The Woman's Dream. Frances Horovitz. BrRo

Man Arrested in Hacking Death Tells Police He Mistook Mother-in-Law for Raccoon. Susan Ludvigson. MT

Man asks, Time, The. Time Speaks. Shao Yen-hsiang, *tr. fr. Chinese.* LHF, *tr. by* Hualing Nieh

Man Asleep in a Child's Bed. Thomas Lux. AnAn

Man at the moment of departure, turning, A. Ritual of Departure. Thomas Kinsella. CIP; CMoP

Man behind the book may not be man, The. The Intellectual. Karl Shapiro. CMoP

Man bent over his guitar, The. Wallace Stevens. *Fr.* Man with the Blue Guitar, The. CMoP; LiTA; MoP; NoAM; RaBo

Man, bewar of thine wowing. *Unknown.* MiEL

Man blew away, A. The Blizzard. Roger McDonald. NOBAu

Man-brained and man-handed ground-ape, physically, The. Original Sin. Robinson Jeffers. MoAB; MoAmPo

Man called Andronicus (Titus), A. Paul Wigmore. PeLi

Man came into the store, A. Inventory. Frank Stanford. MT

Man came slowly from the setting sun, A. The Death of Cuchulain. W. B. Yeats. ChTr

Man Can Complain, Can't He?, A. Ogden Nash. NBLV

Man Cannot Name Himself. Luci Shaw. TrCP

Man Carrying Bale. Harold Monro. MoBrPo

Man Closing Up, The. Donald Justice. CoAP

Man comes and goes by himself. *(LL)* Returning by Night to Lu-Men. Meng Hao Jan. OHMPC

Man comes in, A, his suit is crumpled. Sergei Timofeyev, *tr. fr. Latvian.* TSaS, *tr. by* Irina Osadchaya *with* Lyn Hejinian

Man Coming toward You, The. Oscar Williams. LiTA

Man, could you in yourself the vermin all behold. The Abomination Of Evil. "Angelus Silesius," *tr. fr. German.* *Fr.* Cherubical Wanderer, The. GePo, *tr. by* George C. Schoolfield

Man Cursing the Sea. Miroslav Holub, *tr. fr. Czech by* Ian Milner *and* George Theiner. AnRep

Man dances with twelve girls, A. Kelvin Corcoran. NBrP

Man dat wahs de slickest tile, De. Appearances. Ben King. AnAmPo

Man did not make, and cannot mar. *(LL)* Lines Written in Kensington Gardens. Matthew Arnold. FaBoPP; FHYEP

Man differs more from Man, than Man from Beast. *(LL)* Were I, who to my cost already am. The Earl of Rochester. LiTB; NoP; NOSC; OAEL-1; OBSV; PoEL-3; SCV; SeCV-2

Man, dream[e] no more of curious mysteries. Fulke Greville. *Fr.* Caelica. EnRePo; NoSic

(Sonnet: "Man, dream[e] no more of curious mysteries." JCP; NOSC

Man enters hell without a golden bough. *(LL)* For the Word Is Flesh. Stanley Kunitz. VGW

Man Exalted. *Unknown.* MeEL; NoP

Man-Fate, The. William Everson. NoAM

Man feared that he might find an assassin, A. Stephen Crane. *Fr.* Black Riders, The. MeMAP; NAAL-2

Man fits a key into the door of an office in Chicago, A. A Bottomlands Farmer Suffers a Sea Change. Jo McDougall. NGP

Man Flammonde, from God knows where, The. Flammonde. E. A. Robinson. AmPP; CMoP; LiTA; LiTM; MeMAP; NoAM

Man! Foolish Man! On Exodus 3: 14: "I am that I am." Matthew Prior. ChIV-1; NOCV

Man fools about with self-analysis. The Collective Portrait. Robert Finch. MoCV

Man Frail, and God Eternal. Isaac Watts. *See* O God, Our Help in Ages Past.

Man from Changi, The. Graeme Hetherington. NOBAu

Man from Maputo and so on, A. J. H. Lee. PeLi

Man from Snowy River, The. Andrew Barton Paterson. CBAP

Man from Strathbogie, The. Olive Mary Finnin. NOBAu

Man from the Crowd, The. Sam Walter Foss. PoLF

Man from the *Washington Post*, A. Anthony Burgess. PeLi

Man from Washington, The. James Welch. CDW; HATNAP; NoAM; RaBo

Man had just married an automobile, A. The Automobile. Russell Edson. LCAP; RaBo

Man has been standing, A. The Tunnel. Mark Strand. HeIP; TwCP

Man has found no comfort in the grave, The. *(LL)* The Man Who Dreamed of Faeryland. W. B. Yeats. CMoP; NAEL-2; NoAM; NoP

Man has no roots, A. T'ao Ch'ien, *tr. fr. Chinese by* Eugene Eoyang. SuSp

Man has nought so much his own. The Bonds of Friendship. Simon Dach, *tr. fr. German by* Ingrid Walø e-Engel. GePo

Man He Killed, The. Thomas Hardy. CMoP; DL; FF; HAP; HeIP; LiTB; LiTM; MeMBP; MoAB; MoBrPo; NIP; OBWP; PAW; Poetr; RB; TFi; WeW

Man, hef in mind and mend thy mis. Remember the Last Things. *Unknown.* MeEL

Man hired by John Smith and Co., A. "Mark Twain." FaBoNo; InPK; PeLi

Man, husband existence: ne'er launch on the sea. Epitaph of Cleonicus. Theocritus [*or* Theokritus], *tr. fr. Greek by* Charles Stuart Calverley. FaBoEE

Man I had a love for, The. An Old Woman's Lamentations. Villon, *tr. fr. French by* J. M. Synge. MoBrPo; OBMV

Man I know brought me henna, A. Hennaing My Hair. Linda France. NWP

Man I saw in the forest, The. Dream 2: Brian the Still-Hunter. Margaret Atwood. BoWoP; CrSp

Man, if you God as balm, as light, and sweetness take. Take Therefore That You May Have. "Angelus Silesius," *tr. fr. German.* Fr. Cherubical Wanderer, The. GePo, *tr. by* George C. Schoolfield

Man, if your heart is gold, and if your soul is pure. The Spiritual Ark And The Manna-Vessel. "Angelus Silesius," *tr. fr. German.* Fr. Cherubical Wanderer, The. GePo, *tr. by* George C. Schoolfield

Man in a Window. Ralph Angel. NAmP90

Man in his secret shrine. Hymn in Columbus Circle. Stephen Vincent Benét. OBAL

Man in Our Town. *Unknown.* ReMoGo

Man in righteousness arrayed, The. Horace. *See* Virtue, dear friends, needs no 'defense.'

Man in righteousness arrayed, The. To Sally. John Quincy Adams, *after* Horace. AWP; OBAL

Man in terror of impotence, A. The Ninth Symphony of Beethoven Understood at Last as a Sexual Message. Adrienne Rich. NoP; TAP

Man in the black suit delivers a eulogy, The. The Eulogy. Carol Muske. PBCAP

Man in the Dead Machine, The. Donald Hall. ArOW; CAPP

Man in the Dream Is Death, The. Lynne Butler. IHMS

Man in the feed store called them mountain beavers, The. Looking for Mountain Beavers. David Wagoner. VGW

Man in the Land of the Houyhnhnms, A. W. S. Brownlie. PeLi

Man in the Mirror, The. Mark Strand. NYBP

Man in the Moon. Linda Hogan. HATNAP

Man in the Moon, The. *Unknown.* OTCP

Man in the Moon, as he sails the sky, The. The Man in the Moon. *Unknown.* OTCP

Man in the moon, The/ Came down too soon [or tumbling dow]. Man in the Moon. *Unknown.* CBNP; OxBoLi; OxNR

Man in the moon came tumbling down. Man in the Moon. *Unknown.* MeEL; OxBoLi; PYC; ReMoGo

Man in the moon drinks claret, The/ But he is a dull jack-a-dandy. Man in the Moon. *Unknown.* OxNR

Man in the Moon Drinks Clarret, The. *Unknown.* CoMu

Man in the Moon looked out of the moon, The. Bedtime. *Unknown.* ReMoGo

Man in the Moon ("Man in mone stond and strit.") *Unknown.* MeEL; MiEL; PYC

Man in the Moon ("Man in the moon cam tumbling down.") *Unknown.* MeEL; OxBoLi; PYC; ReMoGo

Man in the Moon ("Man in the moon/ Came down too soon.") *Unknown.* CBNP; OxBoLi; OxNR

Man in the Moon ("Man in the moon drinks claret, The.") *Unknown.* OxNR

Man in the Moon ("Man in the moon was caught in a trap.") *Unknown.* OxNR

Man in the Moon, The ("Mon in the mone stond and strit.") *Unknown.* MeEL

Man in the Moon Stayed up Too Late, The. J. R. R. Tolkien. OBSP

Man in the moon was caught in a trap, The. Man in the Moon. *Unknown.* OxNR

Man in the mune, The/ is making shune. *Unknown.* OxNR

Man in the Rain, The. Van K. Brock. MT

Man in the Recreation Room, The. Edward Harkness. SM

Man in the Street. Robert Penn Warren. OBAL

Man in the street is fed, The. Carl Sandburg. OxBA

Man in the Tree, The. Mark Strand. CBNP

Man in the wilderness asked [of] me [or said to me], The [or A]. Mother Goose. BoTP; CBNP; FaBoCh; FaBoCo; FaBoNo; GBP; OxNR; ReMoGo; Spl

Man in this Lapst Estate at very best. Edward Taylor. *See* O! Honour! Honour! Honour! Oh! the Gain!

Man, introverted man, having crossed. Science. Robinson Jeffers. NU; OxBA

Man is a lumpe, where all beasts kneaded bee. To Sir Edward Herbert at Julyers. John Donne. SeCV-1

Man is a sacred city built of marvelous earth. John Masefield. Fr. Tragedy of Pompey the Great, The. WGRP

Man Is a Spirit. Stevie Smith. OxBC

Man Is a Weaver. Moses ibn Ezra, *tr. fr. Hebrew by* Emma Lazarus. TrJP

Man is dear to man: the poorest poor. Wordsworth. PoToHe

Man Is in Pain. Philip Lamantia. NeAP

Man is leaning on a cold iron rail, A. The Man Who Loved Islands. Derek Walcott. NoAM

Man is more busie, bold, and free. (*LL*) A Drinking-Song, against All Sorts of Disputes in Drinking. William Wycherley. SeCV-2

Man is mowing between the rows of headstones, A. Sweat. Richard Hoffman. ETG

Man is no microcosm, and they detract. The Habitation. Ralph Knevet. NOSC

Man Is the Highest Thing. "Angelus Silesius," *tr. fr. German.* Fr. Cherubical Wanderer, The. GePo, *tr. by* George C. Schoolfield

Man Is What He Wills to Be. Mrs. Henry Linden. CBWP-4

Man knocked three times, A. Madam and the Wrong Visitor. Langston Hughes. SAmP

Man knows not love — such love as woman feels. Woman's Love. *Unknown.* WBLP

Man knows where first he ships himself, but he. Man's Dying-Place Uncertain. Robert Herrick. CaPo

Man Leavens the Batch. Mildmay Fane, 2d Earl of Westmorland. BeJo

Man leaves the world, A. Streets. Naomi Shihab Nye. NAmP90

Man, like others, formed by God, A. The Saxons of Flint. *Unknown, tr. fr. Welsh by* Mary C. Llewelyn. OBWVE

Man lives his life in a dust bowl. Han-shan, *tr. fr. Chinese by* Eugene Eoyang. SuSp

Man looking into the sea. A Grave. Marianne Moore. CMoP; FaBoWP; HAP; HeIP; LiTA; MeMAP; MoP; NAAL-2; NoAM; NOBA; PoE; Poetr; TAP; TFi; TRP; UnPo; WeW; WPE

Man loosened his shoe, A. The Hourglass. Russell Edson. AnAn

Man Lost by a River, A. Michael C. Blumenthal. RaBo

Man loved his Cat with a love quite fanatic, A. The Cat Metamorphosed into a Woman. Jean De la Fontaine, *tr. fr. French by* Norman B. Spector. OFC

Man Lying on a Wall. Michael Longley. PNI

Man-made bay, its fat weeds, The. Mission Bay. John Koethe. PoA

Man makes his spirit strong by lifting weights. With Steve Ovett in Preston Park. Eva Salzman. NWP

Man, Man, Man Is for the Woman Made. *Unknown. See* Man, Man, Man.

Man may make a Remark, A. Emily Dickinson. SAmP

Man may securely sinne, but safely never. (*LL*) Epode. Ben Jonson. BeJo; SeCP; SeCV-1

Man meye longe him lives wene. *Unknown.* MiEL

Man-Moth, The. Elizabeth Bishop. CAPP; CBNP; LiTA; LiTM; MAT; MoAB; MoAmPo; MoP; NALW; NoAM; NOBA; Poetr; PPP

Man Never Cries, A. José Craveirinha, *tr. fr. Bantu.* TSaS, *tr. by* Donald Burness

Man never knows precisely what is right. Essay on Man. *Unknown.* PoToHe

Man o' War Bird. Derek Walcott. TTY

Man of Action, A. Charles B. Stetler. GOYP

Man of Bombay, The. *Unknown.* ReMoGo

Man of bone confirms his throne, The. The New Ancient of Days. Herman Melville. OBAL

Man of Calvary, The, *sels.* "Sin-Killer" Griffin. "Roman soldiers come riding in full speed." AmFP

Man of God is drunken without wine, The. Jalal al-Din Rumi, *tr. fr. Persian.* Fr. Dīvāni Shamsi Tabrīz. TAL, *tr. by* Reynold A. Nicholson

Man of independent means, A. No Occupation. George Rostrevor Hamilton. FaBoEE

Man of Kerioth, The, *sels.* Robert Norwood.

Man of La Mancha. W. H. Auden. AnAn
Sels.
Don Quixote's Credo
Don Quixote's Farewell
Finale
Golden Age, The
Highway to Glory Song
Sancho Panza's Dream
Song of Dejection
Song of the Barber
Song of the Knight of the Mirrors
Song of the Quest

Man of Life Upright, The. Thomas Campion. AAS; CoGr; ElL; EnRePo; NoSic; PoRA

Man of marble holds the throne, A. The Roman Stage. Lionel Johnson. NOBVV

Man of massive meditation, A. Analogue of Unity in Multeity. Richard Eberhart. Poetr

Man of Peace, The, *abr. Bliss Carman. OHIP*

Man of Prayer, The. Christopher Smart. *See* Strong is the horse upon his speed.

Man of Qualities, A. Shakespeare. Fr. Much Ado about Nothing. CBCK

Man of Sense in Bedlam, I recount, A. His Petition to Mr. Speaker. James Carkesse. CBNP

Man of Sorrows. Steve Ellis. PWE

Man of Taste, The, *sels.* James Bramston.
"Huge commentators grace my learned shelves." FaBoCo
"Whoe'er he be that to a taste aspires." NOEC
Man of Taste, The. William Parsons. OBTV
Man of the House, The. Katharine Tynan. TIRV
Man of the House, The. David Wagoner. NoAM
Man of Thessaly, The. *Unknown.* CBNP; FaBoCo; FaBoNo; OxNR
Man of Tyre, The. D. H. Lawrence. TOF
Man of Valour to His Fair Lady, The. William Dunbar. *See* In secreit place, this hyndir [*or* hindir] nycht [*or* nicht].
Man-of-War's Garland, The. *Unknown.* OxBSS
Man of Words, A. John Ashbery. PoA
Man of Words, A. *Unknown.* CBNP; FF; OTCP
Man on a Roof. George Charlton. PWE
Man on his own in a car, A. Meditation on the A30. Sir John Betjeman. RB
Man on the dubious waves of error toss'd. William Cowper. *Fr.* Truth. NOCV
Man on the Dump, The. Wallace Stevens. HAP; NAWM-2; NoAM
Man on the Flying Trapeze, The. *At. to* George Leybourne. BeLS; BLPA; FaBoBe
Man on the Flying Trapeze, The. *Unknown.* BLPA; OxBoLi
Man on the Hotel Room Bed, The. Galway Kinnell. VCAP
Man on the phone says he is blind, The. The Power of Faith. Thomas Rabbitt. NAmP90
Man once married who hunts wife once more, A. *Unknown, tr. fr. Greek by* Alistair Elliot. GrAn
Man points with his umbrella, A. Paul Evans. *Fr.* Sofa Book, The. NBrP
Man pulling radishes, The. Issa, *tr. fr. Japanese by* Robert Hass. EnlH
Man raced wildly through a burning, The. Conflagration. John Blight. FaBoMA
Man Rapes 25 in fight. Up, Up, Home & Away. John Forbes. NOBAu
Man Ray is blowing out fuses in a French room. Time; or, How the Line about Chagall's Lovers Disappears. Jane Miller. SM
Man Root, The. Shiraishi Kazuko, *tr. fr. Japanese by* Kenneth Rexroth *and* Ikuko Atsumi. WPJ
Man Said to the Universe, A. Stephen Crane. *Fr.* War Is Kind. AmPP; FaBoEE; FF; LiTM; NAAL-2; OBAL; OBSV; PrIm; TAP; WeW
Man said unto his Angel, A. The Kings. Louise Imogen Guiney. AmWP
Man sat in the felon's tank, alone, A. In the Tank. Thom Gunn. NoAM
Man Saw a Ball of Gold [in the Sky], A. Stephen Crane. *Fr.* Black Riders, The. LiTA; MeMAP
Man, seated high on Learning's awful throne. Women of the Future. Mary Scott. ECWP
Man Seeking Experience Enquires His Way of a Drop of Water. Ted Hughes. OxAEP-2
Man Sentenced to Death, The, *sels.* Jean Genet, *tr. fr. French by* Steven Finch.
"Murderers of the wall wrap themselves in sunrise, The." PeHV
Man shot himself, A. Leader. Bruce Bennett. InPK
Man should never earn his living, A. A Living. D. H. Lawrence. RFM
Man should seek great glory, and not broad, A. (*LL*) To John Donne. Ben Jonson. BeJo; EPCY; JCP; NoP; SeCP; SeCV-1
Man sits in a timelessness, The. The Rescue. Robert Creeley. CAPP; CRP; VCAP
Man sits memorizing a naked woman. Aleph, Beth, Gimel, Daleth . . . Frederick Seidel. *Fr.* AIDS Days. BAP-90
Man Splitting Wood in the Daybreak, The. Galway Kinnell. AnAn; VCAP
Man, standing in the shadows of a, A. For H. W. Fuller. Carolyn M. Rodgers. BPo
Man standing next to molten steel, The. 29. Alta. CrSp
Man stands, A. Aram Saroyan. PRA
Man still light of foot, but ageing, took, A. Thinking of Mr. D. Thomas Kinsella. NoAM
Man stole fire, and Zeus created flame. Palladas, *tr. fr. Greek by* Tony Harrison. GrAn
Man stood in the laurel tree, A. Things. Louis Simpson. OxBC
Man stoops low on the overcast plain, A. He is earthing. Landscape and Figure. Thomas Kinsella. IPY
Man straps on her harness, A. On the Wings of the Wind. Elaine Mott. BTR
Man stumbled on some rat droppings, A. The Rat's Tight Schedule. Russell Edson. AnAn
Man talks/ the woman listens, The. The Meaningful Exchange. Marge Piercy. AIW
Man that had six mortal wounds, a man, A. Cuchulain Comforted. W. B. Yeats. CMoP; LiTM; OAEL-2; TOF
Man that hath a handsome wife, The. Things Forbidden. *Unknown.* NoSic

Man, that is borne of a woman is of a few dayes, and full of trouble. Bible, *O.T. Fr.* Job. ChTr, *sect.* XIV: 1–2; NAWM-1, *abr.*; OBVE (Immortality, XIV: 1–12.) WGRP
(Job Cries Out.) TrGrPo
(Job's Entreaty.) AWP
Man That Lives, The. *Unknown.* OBET
Man that mates wi' Poverty, The. Comfort in Puirtith. Helen B. Cruickshank. OxBS
Man that never will declare his thought, The. On the Deception of Appearances. Sadi, *tr. by* L. Cranmer-Byng. *Fr.* Gulistan, The. AWP
Man that sees by chance his picture made, A. Robert Bridges. *Fr.* Growth of Love, The. NoAM
Man That Waters the Worker's Beer, The. Paddy Ryan. SWP
Man, the egregious egoist. Cold-blooded Creatures. Elinor Wylie. OxBSP
Man the Enemy of Man. Sir Walter Scott. *Fr.* Rokeby. WBLP
Man the hare has met, The. The Names of the Hare. *Unknown, tr. fr. Middle English by* Seamus Heaney. RB
Man the Monarch. Mary Leapor. ECWP
Man, them revolutionary niggers is all. Just Taking Note. Sharon Scott. JB
Man Then Suddenly Stops Moving, A. Alberto A. Ríos. NoAM
Man (they say), A. Paulus Silentiarius, *tr. fr. Greek by* Andrew Miller. GrAn
Man Thinking about Woman. Don L. Lee. MoP
Man to the plough. Farmers. *Unknown.* OtMeF
Man too bad you don't notice that my eyes. Mississippi. Aimé Césaire, *tr. fr. French by* Clayton Eshleman *and* Denis Kelly. NegPo
Man torn from his home, A. Auschwitz #5. Alfred Van Loen. BTR
Man under the Bed, The. Erica Jong. AmPA
Man United. *Unknown.* FaBoVe
Man unto His Fellow Man. Norman Corwin. *Fr.* On a Note of Triumph. TrJP
Man upon mold, whatsoever thou be. *Unknown.* MiEL
(Money Is What Matters.) MeEL
Man Upright, The. Thomas MacDonagh. BIrV
Man walking on the street, A. In Memoriam. Adrienne Rich. PFL
Man walks beside them, A. White Oxen. Louis Simpson. NoAM
Man walks calmly on his legs in the grass, A. We Shall Overcome. Breyten Breytenbach, *tr. fr. Afrikaans by* Ernst van Heerden. PeSAV
Man walks into a room, A. There is a corpse on the floor. Gorg, a Detective Story. B. P. Nichol. NOBC
Man walks towards town, A. The Late Hour. Mark Strand. HCAP
Man wants but little here below. The Wants of Man. John Quincy Adams. OBAL, *abr.*; PoLF
Man was sitting underneath a tree, A. Seumas Beg. James Stephens. FaPON; GrPl; OxBTC
Man watched/ and though he was accustomed, The. Bringing It Down. Stephen P. Dunn. BAP-91
Man Watching, The. Rainer Maria Rilke, *tr. fr. German by* Robert Bly. NU; RaBo
Man waxy, The — he jogs along the fields. Napoleon after Sedan. Rimbaud, *tr. by* Robert Lowell. *Fr.* Eighteen-Seventy. FaBoPV; OBWP
Man went a-hunting at Reigate, A. *Unknown.* BoTP; ReMoGo
Man went forth one day at eve, A. Tragedy. "Æ." MoBrPo
Man went forth with gifts, A. Martin Luther King, Jr. Gwendolyn Brooks. PoBA
Man White, Brown Girl and All That Jazz. Gloria C. Oden. PoBA
Man Who Became Old, The. Alberto A. Ríos. NoAM
Man who buries his house in the sand, The. Houses. Agha Shahid Ali. NIP
Man who changed the paths of earth and sea, The. Thermopylai. Parmenion of Macedon, *tr. fr. Greek by* Peter Jay. GrAn
Man Who Closed Shop, The. Stephen P. Dunn. NIP
Man Who Dreamed of Faeryland, The. W. B. Yeats. CMoP; NAEL-2; NoAM; NoP
Man who drew his strength from all, A. The Lincoln Statue. W. F. Collins. OHIP
Man who feels not, more or less, somewhat, The. Sonnet: Of Love in Men and Devils. Cecco Angiolieri, da Siena, *tr. fr. Italian by* Dante Gabriel Rossetti. AWP
Man Who Finds That His Son Has Become a Thief, The. Raymond Souster. NOBC
Man who first built up with good strong words, The. Antipater of Thessalonica, *tr. fr. Greek by* Alistair Elliot. GrAn
Man Who Had Fallen among Thieves, A. E. E. Cummings. ChIV-2; HAP; LiTM; MeMAP; MoP; NoAM; NOBA; OxBA; TAP
Man who had lately declared, A. Thomas Thorneley. PeLi

Man, who had no rivals in the love, A. The Man and His Image. La Fontaine, *tr. fr. French by* Elizur Wright. OBVE

Man Who Had Singing Fits, The. Al Zolynas. NGP

Man Who Hid His Own Front Door, The. Elizabeth MacKinstry. FaPON

Man who in his life trusts in this world, A. *Unknown.* TrJP

Man who, in his youth in Poland, A. Unforgettable. Mark Pawlak. BTR

Man who invented the plastic rose, The. Sonnet on the Death of the Man Who Invented Plastic Roses. Peter Meinke. PBCAP

Man who keeps a diary, pays, A. Writing. William Allingham. NOBVV

Man who lies on his back under huge trees, The. Breathing Space July. Tomas Transt*r*ömer, *tr. fr. Swedish by* Robert Bly. RB

Man Who Loved Islands, The. Derek Walcott. NoAM

Man who loves hiking, A. Hiking. Joseph Bruchac. CDW

Man Who Married Magdalene, The. Anthony Hecht. ChIV-2; PeLV

Man Who Married Magdalene, The. Louis Simpson. MoP; NoAM; SM; TAP

Man who misses the fun, The. It Can Be Done. *Unknown.* PoToHe

Man, who once aganist thee fought, The. *(LL)* The Reprisal[l]. George Herbert. ESCV; GeHe

Man who once loved me, told me, A. Beetles. Lorna Dee Cervantes. ETG

Man Who Owned Cars, The. Elliot Fried. GOYP

Man Who Rode to Conemaugh, The. John Eliot Bowen. PAH

Man Who Sang the Sillies, The. John Ciardi. OBCA

Man who saw the light hanging on the tall end, The. The Borrower of Salt. Oscar Williams. *Fr.* Variations on a Theme. LiTA

Man who seeks one thing in life, and but one, The. One Thing. "Owen Meredith." WBLP

Man who sits on the bottom step, The. Rude Awakenings. Bob Rosenthal. UL

Man who sold his lawn to standard oil, The. The War against the Trees. Stanley Kunitz. CAPP; HAP

Man Who Stepped Out of Feeling, The. Dermot Bolger. IB

Man who stood beside me, The. Sweet Will. Philip Levine. LCAP; VCAP

Man who tells you which is the whiter wash, The. Love and How It Becomes Important in Our Day to Day Lives. Miller Williams. MT

Man Who Thinks He Can, The. Walter D. Wintle. *See* If you think you are beaten, you are.

Man who was asked out to dinner, A. Spike Milligan. PeLi

Man Who Wasn't There, The. Hughes Mearns. *See* As I was going up the stair.

Man Who Went Absent from the Native Literature, The. Anthony Cronin. CIP

Man who would woo a fair maid, A. W. S. Gilbert. *Fr.* Yeoman of the Guard. FaBoUs

Man whose height his fear improved he, The. Medgar Evers. Gwendolyn Brooks. NoP; PoBA

Man whose mind is rounded out to perfection, The. Chan-Jan. EaPr

Man whose name was Johnny Sands, A. Johnny Sands ("A man whose name was Johnny Sands.") *Unknown.* CoMu; OBET

Man whose work is hard, The. Night Stand. Lorna Dee Cervantes. AfAz

Man will keep a horse for prestige, A. Gateposts. Medbh McGuckian. BiHa; PBCIP

Man with a broken rabbit . . ., A. The Rabbit Story. Russell Edson. BAP-89

Man with a chip on his shoulder, The. *(LL)* A Chip on His Shoulder. *Unknown.* BLPA; WBLP

Man with a Little Pleated Piano, A. Winifred Welles. FaPON

Man with a marvelous mug, A. A Ballad in "G." Eugene Fitch Ware. PoLF

Man with a scythe: the torrent of his swing. Gardens No Emblems. Donald Davie. LiTM; OAEL-2

Man with a thousand hearts, The. Image-Nation 13 (the Telephone). Robin Blaser. PoM

Man with his burning soul. Truth. John Masefield. WGRP

Man with his lion under the shed of wars, The. The Song of the Borderguard. Robert Duncan. NeAP; PoM

Man With Night Sweats, The. Thom Gunn. PFL

Man with One Small Hand. P. K. Page. MoCV

Man with the Blue Guitar, The. Wallace Stevens. LiTA; RaBo
Sels.
 "I cannot bring a world quite round." CMoP
 "Man bent over his guitar, The." CMoP; MoP; NoAM
 "Tom-tom, c'est moi. The blue guitar." CMoP
 "Tune beyond us as we are, A." CMoP

Man with the camera comes, The. Reservation Special. Lew Blockcolski. VoR

Man with the Hoe, The. Edwin Markham. AnAmPo; BLPA; BLPL; LiTA; MoAmPo; PrIm; TFi; TrGrPo; WBLP; WGRP

Man with the Hollow Breast, The. Tania van Zyl. PeSA

Man with the Lepidoptera on His Ass, The. Albert Stainton. PRA

Man with the red hat, The. Glazunoviana. John Ashbery. LCAP; VCAP

Man without Food, A. Mari Evans. ETG

Man without Sense of Direction. John Crowe Ransom. LiTM; MeMAP; OxBA

Man you/ are/ a liar. Insult before Gift-Giving. Frank Bolton, *tr. fr. Tsimshian Indian by* Armand Schwerner. STP

Man, you are at the first door. The Seven Houses. George Mackay Brown. NAs

Man you know, assured and kind, The. Almost Human. C. Day Lewis. NoAM

Man, you too, aren't you, one of these rough followers of the criminal? In the Servants' Quarters. Thomas Hardy. FaBoVe; MoAB; MoBrPo

Managed as they say about such men. Peter Porter. *Fr.* Nine Points of the Law. PeLV

Manager, Perhaps? Brendan Kennelly. PWE

Manahatta . . . / A lovely name, he thought, and a lovely island. Early Dutch. Jennie M. Palen. GoYe

Manassas. Catherine Anne Warfield. PAH

Manchán's Prayer. Saint Manchán. NOIV

Manchester. Pamela Gillilan. PWE

Manchester Ship Canal, The. *Unknown.* OBET

Manciple's Tale, The. Chaucer. *Fr.* Canterbury Tales, The. EnVB

Mandalay. Kipling. CoGr; EBEvV; FaBV; LiTB; MoBrPo; NOBE; OBTV; OxAEP-2; TrGrPo

Mandarin/ in a silent film. The Yellow Bird. James W. Thompson. PoBA

Mandelstam. David Young. AmPA

Mandolin Serenade. Paul Verlaine, *tr. fr. French by* Philip L. Miller. RiWo

Mandoline. Paul Verlaine, *tr. fr. French by* Arthur Symons. AWP; OBMV

Mandorla. Paul Celan, *tr. fr. German by* Michael Hamburger. PoSu

Mandrake Hert, The. Sydney Goodsir Smith. OxBS

Mandrakes for Supper. James K. Baxter. OxBC

M'Andrew's Hymn. Kipling. *See* Lord, Thou hast made this world below the shadow of a dream.

Manfred: A Dramatic Poem. Byron. EnRP; NAEL-2
Sels.
 "Stars are forth, the moon above the tops, The." OAEL-2

Mango on the Mango Tree, The. Robert Penn Warren. *Fr.* Mexico Is a Foreign Country: Four Studies in Naturalism. MoP; NoAM

Mangoes. Richard Tipping. NOBAu

Mangoes are not cigarettes. Mangoes. Richard Tipping. NOBAu

Mangoes grow in clusters, The. So Close Should Be Our Love. *Gond Oral Tradition, tr. by* V. Elwin *and* S. Hivale. WTO

Mangoes like poetry. *(LL)* Mangoes. Richard Tipping. NOBAu

Mangrove. John Blight. FaBoMA; NOBAu

Manhattan. Lorenz Hart. OBAL

Manhattan. Osbert Lancaster. *Fr.* Afternoons with Baedeker. NOBL; PeLV

Manhattan faces and eyes forever for me. *(LL)* Give Me the Splendid Silent Sun. Walt Whitman. BoNaP; FaPON; HAP; MoAmPo; NOBA

Manhattan Lullaby. Norma Farber. TLR

Manhattan Lullaby. Rachel Field. TLR

Manhattan Menagerie. Joseph Cherwinski. GoYe

Manhole Covers. Karl Shapiro. GoJo; NoAM

Manhood. Sir Thomas More. *Fr.* Pageant Verses. EnRePo

Manhood am; therefore I am delight. Manhood. Sir Thomas More. *Fr.* Pageant Verses. EnRePo

Manichaeans, The. Gary Snyder. VGW

Manichean Geography I. Tom Paulin. PNI

Manicheans did no idols make, The. Fulke Greville. *Fr.* Caelica. NOCV

Manifest Destiny. Anita Endrezze-Danielson. CDW

Manifest Destiny. Anselm Hollo. UL

Manifest Destiny. Pearse Hutchinson. CIP

Manifesto. Agathias, *tr. fr. Greek by* Dudley Fitts. GrAn

Manifesto. D. H. Lawrence. CBLP

Manifesto, *sels.* Nicanor Parra, *tr. fr. Spanish by* Miller Williams. I Move the Meeting Be Adjourned. HoPM

Manifesto for the Faint-Hearted, A. Carole Oles. SM

Manifesto on Ars Poetica. Frank Mkalawile Chipasula. HBAPE

Manifesto: the Mad Farmer Liberation Front. Wendell Berry. FoLa

Manila. Eugene Fitch Ware. FiBHP

Manila Bay. Arthur Hale. PAH

Mankend I cale. Christ Calls Man Home. *Unknown.* MeEL

Mankind, *sels. Unknown.*

"Very fownder and begynner of owr fyrst creacyon, The." OxBLMV

Mankind should hope; in wedlock's state, A. Mary Savage. *Fr.* Letter to Miss E.B. on Marriage. ECWP

Mankind, you dismay me. Thoughts at Midnight. Thomas Hardy. IHNG

Manlet, The. "Lewis Carroll." BXAP

Manly Ferry. John Philip. NOBAu

Manly Heart, The. George Wither. *See* Shall I, Wasting in Despair.

Manly Man, The. *Unknown.* BLPA; WBLP

Mannahatta. Walt Whitman. GOA; MoAmPo

Manner of Her Will and What She Left to London and to All Those in It, at Her Departing, The. (I whole in body and in mind.) Isabella Whitney. NoSic *Sels.*

Manner of the World Nowadays, The, *sels.* John Skelton. "So many cloisters closed." PeECV

Mannerly Margery Mylk and Ale. John Skelton. AAS; FaBoNo; NAEL-1; NoP

Manners. Howard Nemerov. NBLV

Manners. Edith Marcombe Shiffert. WPE

Manners. Mariana Griswold van Rensselaer. FaPON

Manners at Table When Away from Home. *Unknown.* OxBChV

Manners [for a Child of 1918]. Elizabeth Bishop. GOYP; OxBC; RB

Manners in the dining-room. *Unknown.* OxNR

Manor Garden, The. Sylvia Plath. FaBoWP; LCAP

Manor Water. *Unknown.* GBP

Manos Karastefanís. James Merrill. TAP

"Man's a man, A," says Robert Burns. For A' That and A' That. *Unknown.* BXAP

Man's a Man for A' That, A. Burns. *See* Is there for honest poverty.

Man's a poor deluded bubble. Robert Dodsley. OxBSP

Man's [a] Sliding Mood, A. Mary Elizabeth Fullerton. CBAP; NOBAu

Man's Amazement. *Unknown.* CoMu

Man's an ass for a' that, The. (*LL*) More Luck to Honest Poverty. Shirley Brooks. BXAP

Man's and woman's bodies lay without souls. A Childish Prank. Ted Hughes. OAEL-2; OxBC

Man's body at auction, A. Walt Whitman. *Fr.* I Sing the Body Electric. CTC; SAmP, *Pt. I only*

Man's Civil War. Robert Southwell. NoSic

Man's Days. Eden Phillpotts. OBEV; OxBTC

Man's Dying-Place Uncertain. Robert Herrick. CaPo

Mans Fall, and Recovery. Henry Vaughan *and* Thomas Stanley. ESCV

Man's Going Hence. Samuel Rogers. *Fr.* Human Life. OBNC

Man's Inhumanity to Man. Burns. BLPA

Man's life is a hundred years' constant vexation, A. Sent to Recluse Ch'eng. Wang Chi, *tr. fr. Chinese by* Hellmut Wilhelm. SuSp

Man's life is death. Yet Christ endured to live. Wednesday in Holy Week. Christina Rossetti. TrCP

Man's life is laid in the loom of time. The Loom of Time. *Unknown.* BLPA

Man's life is like a rose that in spring. Meditation 9. Philip Pain. *Fr.* Meditations for July 26, 1666. NOBA; SCAP

Man's life is well compared to a feast. A Comparison of the Life of Man. Richard Barnfield. NoSic; OxBSP

Man's life's a tragedy: his mother's womb. De Morte. Sir Henry Wotton. NOSC; OxBSP

Man's Littleness in Presence of the Stars. Henry Kirke White. WBLP

Man's makeshift days would flash past at the best. Antiphanes, *tr. fr. Greek by* Edwin Morgan. GrAn

Man's Mortality. *At. to* Simon Wastell. *Fr.* Microbiblion. FaBoCh

Man's Need. *Gond Oral Tradition, tr. by* V. Elwin *and* S. Hivale. WTO

Man's Prayer, The. T. A. Daly. TrPWD

Man's Requirements, A. Elizabeth Barrett Browning. PFP; VBLP

Mans restlesse soule hath restlesse eyes and ears. Roger Williams. SCAP

Man's Song, about His Daughter, A. *Unknown, tr. fr. Eskimo by* Armand Schwerner. STP

Man's two people, well and sick, A. No Joke. William Scammell. FaBoBl

Man's Woman, A. Mary Carolyn Davies. PoLF

Manservants on the last trains. North to Milwaukee. Gerald Vizenor. VoR

Mansion of Rosamonde, The. Robert de Bonnières, *tr. fr. French by* Philip L. Miller. RiWo

Mansions of the concubines, The. Life in the Palace. Lady Hua Jui, *tr. fr. Chinese by* Kenneth Rexroth *and* Ling Chung. WPC

Mantatee Horde, The. Mtutuzeli Matshoba. PeSAV

Mantelpiece of Shells, A. Ruthven Todd. NYBP

Mantis. David McCord. OBAL

Mantis. Ruth Miller. PeSAV

Mantle So Green, The. *Unknown.* AmFP

Mantova. James Wright. NNaP

Manual, The. Larry Rubin. MT

Manuel Is Quiet Sometimes. Martín Espada. ETG

Manuelzinho. Elizabeth Bishop. FaBoWP; NYBP

Manufactured Gods. Carl Sandburg. WGRP

Manumission. Barbara Burford. DT

Manure Book, The. Russell Edson. AnAn

Manwolf, worse; and their packs infest the age. (*LL*) Tom's Garland: Upon the Unemployed. Gerard Manley Hopkins. EnVR; FaBoPV; Son

Many a fairer face than yours. To a Lady. Franklin P. Adams. FiBHP

Many a green isle needs must be. Lines Written among the Euganean Hills. Shelley. EnRP; GTBS; GTBS-P; PoEL-4

Many a hearth upon our dark globe sighs after many a vanish'd face. Vastness. Tennyson. OPOP

Many a lip is gaping for drink. Eliza Cook. *Fr.* Song of the Seaweed. FiBHP

Many a long, long year ago. The Alarmed Skipper. James Thomas Fields. AnAmPo; NBLV

Many a man gets bewitched by the elves. Heinrich von Morungen, *tr. fr. German by* Frederick Goldin. GePo

Many a Mickle. Walter de la Mare. FaBV

Many a mile of lonely stone; overpowering night. (*LL*) On the Banks of the Duero. Antonio Machado Ruiz. STV

Many a soldier's kiss dwells on these bearded lips.). (*LL*) The Wound-Dresser. Walt Whitman. AmPP; NAAL-1; NOBA; OBWP; PrIm; TAP

Many a summer is dead and buried, A. Spirits Everywhere. Ludwig Uhland, *tr. fr. German by* James Clarence Mangan. AWP

Many a swan-white breast. (*LL*) The Dead at Clonmacnois [*or* Clonmacnoise]. Angus O'Gillan. FaBoPP; OBEV; OBMV; PeIV

Many American flags, The. The Grand Entry. Gary Snyder. NoAM

Many and many a happy year. (*LL*) To the Rev. F. D. Maurice. Tennyson. GTBS-P; NOBVV; OBF; PeECV

Many and sharp the numerous ills. Man's Inhumanity to Man. Burns. BLPA

Many animals that our fathers killed in America. Fear Is What Quickens Me. James Wright. CAPP

Many Are Called. E. A. Robinson. MeMAP; OxBA

Many are making love. Privilege of Being. Robert Hass. NAmP90; NIP

Many are the joys. Intimations of Sublimity. Wordsworth. *Fr.* Prelude [*or,* Growth of a Poet's Mind], The. EnRP; OAEL-2; OBNC

Many are the wand-bearers. Evoe! Edith M. Thomas. AmWP

Many are the ways and many the recipes. Recipe: Hare. Archestratus, *tr. fr. Greek.* FaBoUs

Many a your tones, O Ocean. Sea Cadences. H. Cordelia Ray. AAP; CBWP-3

Many as noticed by the one, The. De Imagine Mundi. John Ashbery. FaBoMo

Many Birds. Anne Welsh. PeSA

Many by valour have deserved renown. Horace, *tr. fr. Latin by* Austin Dobson. *Fr.* Odes. SiPSBD, *tr. by* Sir Walter Ralegh

Many colors will take you to themselves. Never Seek to Tell Thy Love. John Ashbery. HCAP; InPS

Many days of sorrow, many nights of woe. Chain Gang Blues. *Unknown.* WTO

Many desire, but few or none deserve. The Advice. Sir Walter Ralegh. AAS; SiPS; SiPSBD

Many Die Here. Gayl Jones. BlSi

Many Happy Returns. W. H. Auden. NAs

Many happy returns and good luck. Verse for a Birthday Card. Wendy Cope. FaBoBl

Many-headed Hydra, or the People, The. The Common People. Rowland Watkyns. AngWe

Many husbands are missing tonight. The Beautiful Urinals of Paris. Charles David Wright. MT

Many in aftertimes will say of you. Christina Rossetti. *Fr.* Monna Innominata. OBNC

Many Indeed Must Perish in the Keel. Hugo von Hofmannsthal, *tr. fr. German by* Jethro Bithell. AWP; TrJP

Many ingenious lovely things are gone. W. B. Yeats. *Fr.* Nineteen Hundred and Nineteen. BIrV; LiTB; MoAB; PoE

Many little cuss words, bother, dash and blow. *Unknown.* FaBoUs

Many long years ago. (*LL*) Old Gray Mare. *Unknown.* AS; GBP

Many long years ago, I loved a youth. The Blight of Love. Mary E. Tucker. CBWP-1

Many love-happy songs. (*LL*) My Love is Green. Felix Schumann. RiWo

Many love music but for music's sake. On Music. Walter Savage Landor. GoJo

Many-maned scud-thumper, tub. Winter Ocean. John Updike. InPK; Poetr

Many, many things. Basho, tr. fr. Japanese by Harold G. Henderson. TAL

Many, monstrous, tumbled, dun-gray boulders, The. You Were Broken. Giuseppe Ungaretti, tr. fr. Italian by John Frederick Nims. STV

Many of the English. The English. Stevie Smith. IHNG

Many people have been frighted & died in cemeteries. My Gang. Jack Kerouac. PoM

Many people have gathered together. Foot Race Song. Unknown, tr. fr. Pima Indian by Frank Russell. NU; OBVE

Many people seem to think. Nonsense Quatrains. Gelett Burgess. FaBoNo (Parisian Nectar.) FaBoNo

Many poets great and gifted whom the muse's touch had blessed. My Childhood's Happy Days. Daniel Webster Davis. AAP

Many poplars and many elms shook overhead. Late Summer. Theocritus [or Theokritus], tr. fr. Greek by Willis Barnstone. EaPr

Many prophets have failed, their voices silent. Ode to Failure. Allen Ginsberg. CAPP; PoBeRe

Many red devils ran from my heart. Stephen Crane. Fr. Black Riders, The. MeMAP; TAP

Many setups. At least as many falls. Breaking and Entering. Ralph Angel. NAmP90

Many shapes of wings. Environs. Larry Eigner. NeAP

Many Sisters to Many Brothers. Rose Macaulay. NSI

Many tears from my eyes. The Deluge. Wilhelm Müller, tr. fr. German by Philip L. Miller. Fr. Winter's Journey, The. RiWo

Many Things. Oliver Wendell Holmes. PoToHe

Many things have come and gone. The Breezing Dawn of the New Day. Mongane Wally Serote. PeSAV

Many things I might have said today. Aprons of Silence. Carl Sandburg. NOBA

Many times the size of man. The Horse. Francis Ponge, tr. fr. French by Beth Archer. AnRep; NU

Many-volumned authoresses. Agatha Christie and Beatrix Potter. John Updike. AnAmPo

Many Wagons Ago. John Ashbery. HCAP

Many weary weeks divide me. The Ship's Cook, a Captive Sings. Hugo von Hofmannsthal, tr. fr. German by Charles Wharton Stork. TrJP

Many without Elegy. W. S. Graham. OxBS

Many women call on me to sleep with them. A Mourning-Song for Rangiaho. Te Heuheu Herea, tr. fr. Maori by Barry Mitcalfe. WTO

Many Workmen. Stephen Crane. Fr. Black Riders, The. LiTA; MeMAP; TAP

Many Worlds Are Walked Once. Kojo Laing. HBAPE

Many Years. Bei Dao, tr. fr. Chinese by Donald Finkel with Chen Xueliang. SpMi

Many years ago we were all white. The Legend of the Panda. Anthony Stuart. OBAP

Manyo Shu, Part 1 of 4, sels. Unknown, tr. fr. Japanese.
  "Because he is young." AWP
  "By way of pretext." AWP
  "Dress that my brother has put on is thin, The." AWP
  "Even a flaming fire can be snatched." WPJ
  "For my sister's sake." AWP

Manyo Shu, Part 2 of 4, sels. Unknown.
  "How will you manage." AWP
  "I am of this world." BoWoP; IMW
  "I wish I could lend a coat." AWP
  "May the men who are born." AWP; TAL
  "Men of valor, The." AWP; TAL

Manyo Shu, Part 3 of 4, sels. Unknown.
  "My heart, thinking." AWP
  "O boy cutting grass." AWP
  "O pine-tree standing." AWP; TAL
  "On the moor of Kasuga." AWP
  "On the shore of Nawa." AWP
  "Plum-blossom, The." AWP; TAL
  River of Heaven, The. AWP
  "Shall we make love." AWP
  Sudden Appearance of Cherry Blossoms, The. WPJ, tr. by Kenneth Rexroth and Ikuko Atsumi

Manyo Shu, Part 4 of 4, sels. Unknown.
  "Thousand years, you said, A." BoLoP
  "Unknown love/ Is as bitter a thing." AWP, tr. by Arthur Waley; PBWP, tr. by Arthur Waley
    (Unknown love/ is bitter.) BoWoP, tr. by Willis Barnstone
  "What am I to do with my sister?" AWP
  "When evening comes." AWP, tr. by Arthur Waley
  "When, loosened from the winter's bonds." PBWP

Manzanita, The. Yvor Winters. VGW

Manzini; Escape Artist. Gwendolyn MacEwen. NOBC

Mao Yen-shou, your painter's brush seems to move the gods. Wang Chao-chün. Li Shang-yin, tr. fr. Chinese by Irving Y. Lo. SuSp

Map, The. Elizabeth Bishop. NOBA

Map, The. Gloria C. Oden. PoNe

Map, The. Gary Soto. NoAM

Map, The. Mark Strand. NYBP

Map of Mock-Begger Hall, The. Unknown. CoMu

Map of Montana in Italy, A. Richard Hugo. LCAP

Map of My Country, A. John Holmes. AiP

Map of Places, The. Laura Riding. LiTA

Map of the City, A. Thom Gunn. NAEL-2; PoE

Map of the Western Part of the County of Essex in England, A. Denise Levertov. CoAP; NAAL-2

Map of tracks on frosted paper, A. The Wrong Shoes. Sebastian Barry. IB

Map Reading. Raymond Garlick. AngWe

Map shows me where it is you are, The. A Private Letter to Brazil. Gloria C. Oden. PoNe

Maple and Sumach. C. Day Lewis. FaBoMo; Son

Maple buds are red, are red, The. A Song of Waking. Katharine Lee Bates. OHIP

Maple is a dainty maid, The. Autumn Fancies. Unknown. FaPON

Maple Leaf. Shu Ting, tr. fr. Chinese by Carolyn Kizer with Y.H. Zhao. SpMi

Maple Leaves. Thomas Bailey Aldrich. GN

Maple Syrup. Donald Hall. CAPP

Maples. Philip Appleman. BXAP

Maples have turned, The. Fire snaps on my tongue. On a Recent Protest against Social Conditions. David Posner. NYBP

Mapmaker on His Art, The. Howard Nemerov. NYBP

Mapooram. Aborigine Oral Tradition, tr. by Fred Biggs. NOBAu

Mapped in a single word. (LL) Grit. Geoff Page. NOBAu

Maquillage. Lynda Hull. UTF

Maquillage. Arthur Symons. OxBSP

Maratea Porto: Saying Goodbye to the Vitolos. Richard Hugo. MAT

Marathon Runner, The. Fenton Johnson. CDC

Marathon runner's legs, A. Yagi Mikajo, tr. fr. Japanese by Kenneth Rexroth and Ikuko Atsumi. WPJ

Marban, a Hermit Speaks. Unknown, tr. fr. Irish by Michael Hartnett. BIrV; CIP

Marble Floor. Karol Wojtyla. CRP

Marble mausoleum solemnly holds the rich, A. Quatrains. Salah Jahin, tr. fr. Arabic by Samir M. Zoghby. TTY

Marble Nor Monuments whereof Then We Spoke. John Berryman. Fr. Sonnets. Son

Marble one so warmed would speak, A. (LL) To a Fair Lady Playing with a Snake. Edmund Waller. CBLP; EBEV; HoPM; NOSC; PoE

Marble Statuette Harpist. Sara Van Alstyne Allen. GoYe

Marble-streeted Town, The. Thomas Hardy. FaBoPP

Marble-Top. E. B. White. FiBHP; OBAL

Marble, weepe, for thou dost cover. On Margaret Ratcliffe. Ben Jonson. SeCP

Marcelia; or, Treacherous Friend, The, sels. Frances Boothby.
  "Oh, you powerful Gods, if I must be." KTR
  "What strange effects of Fortune do I prove!" KTR

Marceline, to Her Husband. Elizabeth Libbey. AmPA

March. Bryant. GN

March. Elizabeth J. Coatsworth. PDV; Spl

March. Hart Crane. BoNaP

March. William Everson. ErPo

March, sels. Daryl Hine.
  "Once when I was coming from art class they surprised me." GLP

March. A. E. Housman. FaBoCh

March. Roy McFadden. TIRV

March. William Morris. Fr. Earthly Paradise, The. OtMeF

March. H. Cordelia Ray. CBWP-3

March. Folgore da San Geminiano, tr. fr. Italian by Dante Gabriel Rossetti. Fr. Sonnets of the Months. AWP

March, The. J. C. Squire. OHIP

March. Unknown. GBP

March . . . someone has walked across the snow. Vacancy in the Park. Wallace Stevens. ArNa; LCAP; SAmP

March 4th Anno 1698/9; a Charracteristicall Satyre, diff. vers. John Saffin. See Should I thee ranke with Radamanthus fell.

March around and make a stand. (LL) The Dance. At. to Thomas Campion. EiL; FaBoCh

March beyond green outskirts. Girls' School. Alan Moore. BiHa

March Calf, A. Ted Hughes. NoP

March comes and water moves. Ghosts. Bob Arnold. ETG

March Evening. L. A. G. Strong. MoBrPo

March 1st. Kathleen Spivack. NYBP

March Hares. Walter de la Mare. FaBoNo

March Hares. Andrew Young. SAmP

March has come to the bridge head. Poem by the Bridge at Ten-shin. Li Po, tr. fr. Chinese by Ezra Pound. OBVE

March in the Ranks Hard-Prest, and the Road Unknown, A. Walt Whitman. AmPP; NAAL-1; OxBA

March into Virginia, The. Herman Melville. BLPL; HAP; ImPo; LiTA; NAAL-1; NoP; PoE; TAP; TrGrPo

March Journal. Charles Wright. LCAP

March, march, Ettrick and Teviotdale. Border Ballad. Sir Walter Scott. Fr. Monastery, The. GN
(Blue Bonnets over the Border.) OxBS
(Border March.) EnRP

March, march, head erect. Mother Goose. OxNR

March! March! March! from sunrise till it's dark. The Marching Song of Stark's Men. Edward Everett Hale. PAH

March, May, July, October; these are they. The Roman Calendar. Benjamin Hall Kennedy. FaBoUs

March Night. Alison Brackenbury. SCBI

March, 1941. Paul Goodman. LiTA

March 1979 and I am watching. The Jews That We Are. Richard Michelson. BTR

March of the Three Kings. Unknown. OHIP

March of the Women, The. Cicely Hamilton. BrRo

March (1), The. Robert Lowell. HCAP; NoP

March (2), The. Robert Lowell. NoP

March said to Averil. The Borrowing Days. Unknown. GBP

March Snow. Don McKay. NOBC

March strongly forth, my Muse, whilst yet the temperate air. Michael Drayton. Fr. Polyolbion. NOSC

March the 3rd. Edward Thomas. NAs

3-31-70. Gayl Jones. Fr. Journal. BlSi

March to Moscow, The. Robert Southey. FaBoCo

March, Upstate. William Bronk. NYBP

March Weather. Jon Swan. NYBP

March Wind, The. E. H. Henderson. BoTP

March Wind. Lewis Warsh. UL

March winds and April showers. Unknown. FaBoBe; OxNR; ReMoGo

March with his wind hath struck a cedar tall. On Queen Anne's Death. Unknown. EIL

March with its sharp pick. Landscape beyond Warsaw. Peter Huchel, tr. fr. German by Michael Hamburger. PoSu

March yeans the lammie. March. Unknown. GBP

Marchant was ther with a forked berd, A. Chaucer. Fr. Canterbury Tales, The. CTC, abr.; EnVB; FHYEP; NoP; OAEL-1; PPP, abr.

Märchen, The. Randall Jarrell. CMoP

Märchenbilder. John Ashbery. LCAP; NOBA

Marches. Philip Booth. PFL

Marching. Isaac Rosenberg. NSI; PeFWW

Marching Chant. Unknown. RoPo

Marching on Tanga, marching the parch'd plain. The Gift. Francis Brett Young. NSI

Marching 'round the Levee. Unknown. AmFP

Marching Song. Dana Burnet. PAH

Marching Song. Robert Louis Stevenson. BoTP; FaPON

Marching Song of Stark's Men, The. Edward Everett Hale. PAH

Marching through Georgia. Henry Clay Work. FaPoR; PAH

Marching to Quebec. Unknown. AmFP

Marching to Utah. Unknown. AmFP

Marchlyn. Ian Hughes. AngWe

Marcia and I went over the curve. Millions of Strawberries. Genevieve Taggard. FaPON; MoShBr

Marcia Thompane was light and compact. Dancing School. Jonathan Holden. Poetsp

Marco Bozzaris. Fitz-Greene Halleck. AnAmPo; BeLS; GN; WBLP
Sels.
"At midnight, in his guarded tent." HoPM

Marconi, whose ardour was tireless. Stanley J. Sharpless. PeLi

Marcus Antoninus Cui Cognomen Erat Aurelius. Burns Singer. OxBS

Marcus Aurelius. C. H. Sisson. OxBC

Marcus Curtius. Oliver St. John Gogarty. OBMV

Marcus in the armed hoplites' race. Lucilius, tr. fr. Greek by Peter Porter. GrAn

Mare, The. Vernon Watkins. OBWVE

Mare, A. Kate Barnes. NYBP

Mare Liberum. Henry van Dyke. PAH

Mare lies down in the grass where the nest of the skylark is hidden, The. The Mare. Vernon Watkins. OBWVE

Mare Nostrum. Joel Oppenheimer. NeAP

Mares of the Camargue, The. Frédéric Mistral, tr. by George Meredith. Fr. Mirèio. AWP

Mare's skeleton in the clearing: another sign of life, The. Adrienne Rich. Fr. Shooting Script. FaBoWP

Marezle toats. Unknown. FaBoNo

Margaret. Charles Cotton. See Marg'ret of Humbler Stature by the Head.

Margaret Are You Drug. George Starbuck. InPK; MAT

Margaret, are you grieving. Spring and Fall. Gerard Manley Hopkins. ArNa; CMoP; EBEV; ELP; FaBoUs; FF; GTBS-P; HAP; HeIP; HoPM; InPK; InPS; LiTM; MAT; NAEL-2; NIP; NoAM; NOBE; NoP; OBD; PeVV; PoE; PoEL-5; Poetr; PPP; RB; SCGP; SCV; SOTW; TEP; TFi; TOF; TRP
(Spring and Fall: To a Young Child.) ChTr; ClHu; GoJo; ImPo; IMW; LiTB; MeMBP; MoAB; OxAEP-2; PFP

Margaret Grady — I fear she will burn. The Witch. Katharine Tynan. NOBVV

Margaret Love Peacock, for Her Tombstone, 1826. Thomas Love Peacock. OBNC; PIP

Margaret, Margaret, has big eyes. Unknown. RoPo

Margaret mentioned Indians. Indians. John Fandel. NYBP

Margaret my sweetest, Margaret I must go. The Souldiers Farewel to His Love. Unknown. CoMu

Margaret wrote a letter. The Dusty Miller. Unknown. ReMoGo

Margarita first possest [or possessed]. The Chronicle; a Ballad. Abraham Cowley. OxAEP-1; SeCV-1

Margarite of America, A, sels. Thomas Lodge.
"O shady vales, O fair enriched meads." EIL

Margaritæ Sorori, [I. M.]. W. E. Henley. Fr. Echoes. MoBrPo; NOBE; OBEV; OBNC; PIP; TrGrPo; WGRP

Margery daw. The See-Saw. John Hollander. BAP-91

Margery Mutton-pie. Mother Goose. OxNR

Marginal Field, The. Stephen Spender. PoA

Marginalia, sels. W. H. Auden.
"Dead man, A/ who never caused others to die." OAEL-2

Marginalia, sels. Peter Scupham.
"Almanac's green vellum skin is rubbed." SCBI
Jeremy Taylor: The Rule and Exercise of Holy Dying, 1663. SCBI
Leaf From a French Bible (circa 1270). SCBI

Marginalia. Richard Wilbur. CMoP; PoA

Marg'ret of Humbler Stature by the Head. Charles Cotton. Fr. Resolution in Four Sonnets, of a Poetical Question Put to Me by a Friend, Concerning Four Rural Sisters. PoEL-5; Prf; Son

Marhue quet carante! (LL) Foreign Literature. Thackeray. FaBoNo

Mari Magno, sels. Arthur Hugh Clough.
"Have you the Giesbach seen? a fall." OBTV

Maria intended a letter to write. How to Write a Letter. Elizabeth Turner. MoShBr; OxBChV

Maria now I'll cease to sing. Verses Written in a London Churchyard. Christopher Smart. CBNP

Maria Olt. Ruth Whitman. BTR

Maria, she said. No city river. The Scuba Diver Recovers the Body of a Drowned Child. Gerald William Barrax. NBV

Maria to Henric. Unknown. KTR

Maria Wentworth. Thomas Carew. CaPo; JCP; MeLP; OBD; PeECV; SeCV-1

Mariachi beckon, their guitars, The. On Plaza Garibaldi. Nellie Wong. OpBo

Mariam. Lady Elizabeth Carey. WPE
Sels.
"Fairest action of our human life, The"
"How oft have I with publike voyce runne on?" KTR, act I, sc. 1
"Those mindes that wholy dote upon delight." KTR
"'Tis not enough for one that is a wife"

Mariana. Lucha Corpi. AfAz

Mariana. Tennyson. AWP; CBLP; CH; EBVVPR; EnVR; FHYEP; InPS; MeMBP; NAEL-2; NOBE; NoP; OAEL-2; OBEV; OBNC; OxAEP-2; PeVV; PoE; PoEL-5; SCGP; TEP; TFi; TrGrPo; UnPo; WiR

Marica Lart. W. S. Merwin. PRA

Maridunum. Douglas Phillips. AngWe

Marie antoinette / slice, The. After / the Moratorium Reading. Nigel Roberts. NOBAu

Marie Galante. Guy Tirolien, tr. fr. French by Ellen Conroy Kennedy. NegPo

Marie Hamilton's to the kirk gane. The Queen's Marie. Unknown. OBEV; ScCV

Marriage in Eden, The. William Williams, *tr. fr. Welsh* by Lewis Saunders *and* Gwyn Jones. *Fr.* View of Christ's Kingdom, A. OBWVE

Marriage in the 'Sixties. A. Adrienne Rich. TRP

Marriage is a lovely thing. Christine de Pisan, *tr. fr. French* by Joanna Bankier. WPOW

Marriage is a sweet state. In Praise of Marriage. Christine de Pisan, *tr. fr. French.* OxBM

Marriage is not/ a house or even a tent. Habitation. Margaret Atwood. BoWoP; FaBoWP; WeW

Marriage is where. Marriage as a Problem of Universals. Dick Davis. SCBI

Marriage Morning. Tennyson. GBL

Marriage of a Virgin, The. Dylan Thomas. *See* Waking [*or* Walking] alone in a multitude of loves when morning's light.

Marriage of a Virgin, The. Dylan Thomas. ChIV-2; ErPo

Marriage of Sir Gawain, The. *Unknown.* ESPB

Marriage of Heaven and Earth, The. Howard Nemerov. NYBP

Marriage of Heaven and Hell, The. Blake. EnRP; OAEL-2 *Sels.*
"In seed time learn, in harvest teach, in winter enjoy." FF (Proverbs of Hell.) MeMBP; NAEL-2
Memorable Fancy, A ("Angel came to me and said"). NU
Memorable Fancy, A ("As I was walking among the fires of hell"). NU
"Pride of the peacock is the glory of God, The." FF; RaBo
"Rintrah roars & shakes his fires in the burdend air." NAEL-2
Voice of the Devil, The. NU

Marriage of Hector and Andromache, The. Sappho, *tr. fr. Greek* by Guy Davenport. OBVE

Marriage of Mutes, A. Ana Castillo. ETG

Marriage of Pocahontas, The. Mary Morison Webster. PAH

Marriage of the Frog and the Mouse, The. *Unknown.* EBEV

Marriage of True Minds, The. Shakespeare. *See* Let Me Not to the Marriage of True Minds.

Marriage Portrait. James Applewhite. MT

Marriage Prospect, A. William Hurrell Mallock. NOBVV

Marriage Ring, A. George Crabbe. BoLoP; EnLoPo; OBEV; OxBM

Marriage Song. Judah Halevi, *tr. fr. Hebrew* by Alice Lucas. TrJP

Marriage Song. Carolyn Kizer. BAP-91

Marriage Vow. Mrs. Henry Linden. CBWP-4

Marriage, which might have been a mateship sweet. Elizabeth Wolstenholme-Elmy. *Fr.* Woman Free. BrRo

Marriage Wig, The. Ruth Whitman. IHMS

Marriages. George Crabbe. *Fr.* Parish Register, The.

Marriages. Anthony Thwaite. OxBM

Marrie dear. When in Rome. Mari Evans. SoSe

Married and Single Life. *Unknown.* AmFP

Married Blues. Kenneth Rexroth. *Fr.* Written to Music. Jaz

Married for one year. Making It Simple December 8, 1969. David McElroy. AmPA

Married life for a poor man. Cillactor, *tr. fr. Greek* by Barriss Mills. GrAn

Married Love. Kuan Tao Sheng, *tr. fr. Chinese* by Kenneth Rexroth *and* Ling Chung. OxBM; UnAS; WPC

Married Love. Sherod Santos. Son

Married Lover, The. Coventry Patmore. *Fr.* Angel in the House, The. OBEV; OxAEP-2; TrGrPo

Married man comes nearest to the dead, A. Samuel Butler. FaBoEE

Married, poor soul! your empire's over. Jane West. *Fr.* To a Friend on her Marriage. ECWP

Married the astronaut's daughter. Entries in a Diary. Matthew Sweeney. IB

Married to a Soldier. John Clare. SCGP

Marrow, The. Theodore Roethke. NYBP; PeECV

Marrow of My Bone. Mari Evans. BPo

Marrow of time; eternity in brief. Church Festivals. Christopher Harvey. NOSC

Marrows. Louis Johnson. PeNZ

Marry in Lent. *Unknown.* FaBoUs

Marry state affords but little Ease, A. Katherine Philips. KTR

Marrying left your maiden name disused. Maiden Name. Philip Larkin. GTBS-P

Marrying the Hangman. Margaret Atwood. NOBC

Mars. (*LL*) Moonpoem. Rosie Orr. VBLP

Mars is braw in crammasy. The Bonnie Broukit Bairn. "Hugh MacDiarmid." FaBoCh; FaBoVe; HAP; InPS

Marseillaise, The. Claude Joseph Rouget de Lisle, *tr.* by Charles H. Kerr. WBLP

Marsh, The. W. D. Snodgrass. BoNaP

Marsh, The. Marcia Southwick. FoLa

Marsh bank, lotus rank. Confucius, *tr. fr. Chinese* by Ezra Pound. *Fr.* Songs of Ch'en. CTC

Marsh flew through my flesh. (*LL*) Heron. Philip Booth. Poetsp

Marsh Leaf. David Wagoner. PoA

Marsh, New Year's Day, The. Peter Everwine. NNaP

Marsh Song — at Sunset. Sidney Lanier. NOBA

Marshalling Yard, The. Helen Dunmore. PWE

Marshes, The. Jane Mayhall. TAP

Marshes of Glynn, The. Sidney Lanier. AmPP; AnAmPo; ImPo; LiTA; NOBA; OxBA; PrIm; WGRP

Marshlands. Emily Pauline Johnson. NOBC

Marston. Stephen Spender. FaBoTw

Marta we found the little box. Protect Me, My Talisman. Milo De Angelis, *tr. fr. Italian* by Lawrence Venuti. NeIt

Martha. Walter de la Mare. MoBrPo

Martha/ Mary passed this morning. Mary Passed This Morning. Owen Dodson. PoBA

Martha Blake. Austin Clarke. TIRV

Martha Blake at Fifty-one. Austin Clarke. CIP; IPY; NOIV

Martha Graham. Elaine Equi. UTF

Martha Is Not So Tall. Charles Cotton. *Fr.* Resolution in Four Sonnets, of a Poetical Question Put to Me by a Friend, Concerning Four Rural Sisters. PoEL-2; Prf; Son

Marthe Away (She Is Away). Kenneth Rexroth. UnAS

Marthy Virginia's Hand. George Parsons Lathrop. PAH

Martial Cadenza. Wallace Stevens. MeMAP; OxBA; VGW

Martial [*or* Marshall *or* My Friend], the thing[e]s that do [*or* for to] attain [*or* attayne]. Martial, *tr.* by Henry Howard, Earl of Surrey. SiPSBD
(Happy Life, The.) NOBE; NoSic; OBVE; SiPS
(Means to Attain the Happy Life, The.) CBCK; EiL; EnRePo; FaBoEE; OBEV
(My Friend, the Things That Do Attain.) NAEL-1; NoP
(Things That Cause a Quiet Life, The.) TrGrPo

Martial Variations., *sels.* Amelia Rosselli, *tr. fr. Italian.*

Martian Sends a Postcard Home, A. Craig Raine. NAEL-2; NoAM; NoP

Martians sent to Earth disguised as humans. Returning to Arizona. Maura Stanton. NGP

Martin and His Man. *Unknown. See* Martin to His Man.

Martin Buber in the Pub. Max Harris. NOBAu

Martin cat long shaged of courage good, The. John Clare. FM

Martin, I wonder who makes all the songs. Child and Boatman. Jean Ingelow. *Fr.* Songs on the Voices of Birds. FM

Martin Luther King, Jr. Gwendolyn Brooks. PoBA

Martin said to his man. *Unknown. See* Martin to His Man.

Martin sat young upon his bed. St. Martin and the Beggar. Thom Gunn. Mes; MoBS

Martin to His Man. *Unknown.*
(Martin and His Man.) CBNP
(Martin said to his man.) FaBoNo

Martins. Mike Jenkins. AngWe

Martin's Blues. Michael S. Harper. HCAP; PoBA

Martyr. Mary Elizabeth Fullerton. CBAP

Martyr, The. Herman Melville. PoEL-5; TAP; TrGrPo

Martyrdom. "Rufus Learsi." TrJP

Martyrdom. Richard W. Thomas. PoBA

Martyrdom of Bishop Farrar, The. Ted Hughes. FaBoEH

Martyrdom of Brébeuf and Lalemant, 16 March 1649, The. E. J. Pratt. *Fr.* Brébeuf and His Brethren. NOBC

Martyrdom of St. Theresa, The. A. D. Hope. CBAP

Martyrdom of Two Pagans. Philip Whalen. NeAP

Martyred Democrat, The. C. J. Dennis. CBAP

Martyred Earth, The. Ewart Milne. BIrV

Martyred Saint, he lies upon his bier, A. Lincoln. Corinne Roosevelt Robinson. OHIP

Martyrs, The. Jay Macpherson. MoCV

Martyrs Are Calling, The. Ber Green, *tr. fr. Yiddish* by Aaron Kramer. BTR

Martyr's Death, A. Menahem ben Jacob, *tr. fr. Hebrew.* TrJP

Martyrs of the *Maine,* The. Rupert Hughes. PAH

Maru Mori brought me. Ode to My Socks. Pablo Neruda, *tr. fr. Spanish* by Robert Bly. RaBo; TRP

Marvel, The. Keith Douglas. RB

Marvel, A. Carolyn Wells. OBCA

Marvel at the/ awful many-armed/ Sea-god Octopus. Octopus. Valerie Worth. OBAP

Marvel No More. Sir Thomas Wyatt. *See* Marvel [*or* Marvaill] no more although [*or* all tho].

Marvel of Marvels. Christina Rossetti. NOBE; WGRP

Mask'd with such violet disallow their green? *(LL)* The Rainbow. Gerard Manley Hopkins. FaBoPP; OxBSP

Masks. Elizabeth Fenton. NMM

Masks! O Masks! Prayer to the Masks. Léopold Sédar Senghor, *tr. fr. French by* Ellen Conroy Kennedy. NegPo

Masochist, The. Maxine W. Kumin. IHMS; PoA

Mason, The. Robert Farren. PeIV

Mason lives, The. Symbolum. Goethe, *tr. fr. German by* Tom Paulin. FaBoPV

Mason's Trick. James Hayford. InPK

Masons, when they start upon a building. Scaffolding. Seamus Heaney. GOYP

Masque of Alfred, The, *sels.* James Thomson.
   "When Britain first at Heaven's command." FaBoEH

Masque of Blackness, The. Geoffrey Hill. *Fr.* Lachrimae. NoAM

Masque of Christmas, The. Ben Jonson. OxBoLi

Masque of Queens, The, *sels.* Ben Jonson.
   "Help, help all tongues, to celebrate this wonder." NOSC
   Witches' Charms, The. EiL
   Witches' Charm, The FaBoCh
   (Charme.) FM

Masque of the Inner Temple and Gray's Inne, The, *sels.* Francis Beaumont.
   "Shake off your heavy trance!" NTP; TrGrPo
   (Fit Only for Apollo.) ChTr
   (Song for a Dance.) EiL; FaBoCh
   "Ye [*or* You] should stay longer if we durst." TrGrPo
   (Fourth Song, The.) NOSC

Masque of the Middle Temple and Lincoln's Inn, The, *sels.* George Chapman.
   Bridal Song. EiL; OxBSP
   Descend, Fair Sun! EiL

Masque of the Twelve Months, The, *sels. At. to* George Chapman.
   Shine Out, Fair Sun, with All Your Heat. ChTr; ELP
   (Song: "Shine out, fair sun, with all your heat.") EiL

Masque of the Virtues against Love. Mary Monck. ECWP; NOEC

Masquerade. Carolyn M. Rodgers. BlSi

Mass at Dawn. Roy Campbell. OxAEP-2; PeSA

Mass for the Day of St. Thomas Didymus, *sels.* Denise Levertov.
   Credo. AIW; EaPr
   "God then." CrSp
   "Powers and principalities — all the gods." CrSp

Mass Graves, *sels.* Charles Reznikoff.
   "In the morning the Jews were lined up by an officer." BTR

Mass hysteria, wave after breaking wave. Willowware Cup. James Merrill. NoP; VCAP

Mass is Over, The. Sara Berkeley. PBCIP

Mass is over, they have gone in peace, The. The Mass is Over. Sara Berkeley. PBCIP

Massachusetts Song of Liberty. *At. to* Mrs. Mercy Warren. PAH

Massacre of the Innocents, The, *sels.* Giovanni Battista Marino, *tr. fr. Italian by* Richard Crashaw.
   "Yet on the other side, faine would he start." OBVE

Massacre of the Innocents. Tadeusz Rózewicz, *tr. fr. Polish by* Jan Darowski. OBD

Massacre of the Macpherson, The. William Edmonstoune Aytoun. BXAP; ChTr; FaBoCo; OtMeF

Massacres, *sels.* Charles Reznikoff.
   "Her father had a shop for selling leather." BTR

Massada, *sels.* Yitzhak Lamdan, *tr. fr. Hebrew by* A. C. Jacobs.

Massenet/ Never wrote a Mass in A. Antony Butts. FiBHP

Masses. César Vallejo, *tr. by* Robert Bly. *Fr.* España, Aparta de me Este Caliz. RB

Masses of flowers and plants envelop the riverbanks. Tu Fu, *tr. by* Irving Y. Lo. *Fr.* Strolling along the Riverbank, Looking for Flowers. SuSp

Masseuse, The. Olga Broumas. PFL

Massive engines lift beautifully from the deck. The Teeth Mother Naked at Last. Robert Bly. NNaP

Massive hills, numberless valleys, all point to Ching-men. Thoughts on Historical Sites: Wang Chao-chün. Tu Fu, *tr. fr. Chinese by* Irving Lo. SuSp

Mast Year, The. Medbh McGuckian. CIP

Master. Brendan Kennelly. BiHa

Master, The. Czeslaw Milosz, *tr. fr. Polish by the author.* AnRep

Master, The. E. A. Robinson. LiTA; LiTM; MoAB; MoAmPo; OHIP

Master and Boatswain. W. H. Auden. *See* At Dirty Dick's and Sloppy Joe's.

Master and mage, our prince of song, whom Time. To Lord Tennyson. Sir William Watson. EPCY

Master and Man. Mother Goose. OxNR; ReMoGo

Master and Man. Sir Henry Newbolt. OxBTC

Master Brunetto, this my little maid. Sonnet: To Brunetto Latini. Dante, *tr. fr. Italian by* Dante Gabriel Rossetti. AWP

Master, by Styx — which is the poets' oath. Bounce to Pope. A. D. Hope. OBF

Master Charge Blues. Nikki Giovanni. OBAL

Master City, The. Rose J. Orente. GoYe

Master dragon-tamer has fled the world, The. Li Ho, *tr. by* Irving Y. Lo. *Fr.* About Horse. SuSp

Master Francesco, I have come to thee. Petrarch. Giosuè Carducci, *tr. fr. Italian by* William Dudley Foulke. AWP

Master Francis Beaumont to Ben Johnson, *sels.* Beaumont *and* Fletcher *and* John Fletcher.
   "What things have we seen." FaBoEH

Master has come over Jordan, The. Christ and the Little Ones. Julia Gill. BLPA

Master Hugues of Saxe-Gotha. Robert Browning. OAEL-2

Master I have, and I am his man. Master and Man. Mother Goose. OxNR; ReMoGo

Master knows what he want, The. Paul Klee, *tr. fr. German.* CBNP

Master Liu Painted a Portrait of Me in My Old Age and Asked Me to Write a Poem About the Picture. Yang Wan-li, *tr. fr. Chinese by* Jonathan Chaves. SuSp

Master McGrath. *Unknown. See* Eighteen sixty nine being the date of the year [*or* and the year].

Master, No Offering. Edwin Pond Parker. AH

Master of Auschwitz, angel of death. For the Bones of Josef Mengele, Disinterred June 1985. Robert Bringhurst. NIP

Master of beauty, craftsman of the snowflake. John Berryman. *Fr.* Eleven Addresses to the Lord. OxBC; UnPo

Master of blood I am yours. Nocturnal Heart. Anne-Marie Kegels, *tr. fr. French by* W. S. Merwin. BoWoP

Master of human destinies am I! Opportunity. John James Ingalls. AnAmPo; PoLF; WBLP

Master of *The Monarch of the Glen,* The. An Unsagacious Animal. David Gascoyne. PeLV

Master-Player, The. Paul Laurence Dunbar. AnAmPo

Master Singers, The. Rhys Carpenter. WGRP

Master Sky-Lark, *sels.* John Bennett.

Master-songs are needed, and the man, The. Walt Whitman. E. A. Robinson. OxBA

Master stood in His garden, The. For the Master's Use. *Unknown.* BLPA
   (Watered Lilies, The.) BLRP

Master stood upon the mount, and taught, The. Progress. Matthew Arnold. ChIV-2

Master, the swabber, the boatswain and I, The. Shakespeare. *Fr.* Tempest, The. OAEL-1
   (Sea Song, A: "Master, the swabber, the boatswain and I, The.") NBLV
   (Sea Song, A.) PeLV
   (Song: "Master, the swabber, the boatswain and I, The.") FF; NOBL; OxBSP

Master, they say that when I seem. C. S. Lewis. TIRV; TrCP

Master, to do great work for Thee my hand. Life-Mosaic. Frances Ridley Havergal. TrPWD

Master Tung-p'o, in raising children, was afraid of their being clever. Rebuttal of Tung-p'o's Poem on "Bathing the Infant," A. Ch'ien Ch'ien-i, *tr. fr. Chinese by* Irving Y. Lo. SuSp

Masterful units of his siesta, and always did, The. *(LL)* The Perfection of Dentistry. Marvin Bell. AmPA; CoAP

Masters, be kind to the old house that must fall. Rockland. Julia Randall. WPE

Masters, in This Hall. William Morris. ChTr

Masters of the forests. The Praises of Baboon, the Totem Animal. *Unknown, tr. by* George Fortune. OBAP

Master's Touch, The. Horatius Bonar. TrPWD

Mastery. Sara Teasdale. WGRP

Masts at Dawn. Robert Penn Warren. FoLa; NAAL-2; VCAP

Mat to Weave, A. Tchicaya U Tam'si, *tr. fr. French by* Ellen Conroy Kennedy. NegPo

Matadors, The. Josephine Jacobsen. TAP

Matauwhi Bay V. Amanda Eason. DT

Match, The. Andrew Marvell. EBEV

Match, The. Henry Vaughan *and* Thomas Stanley. ESCV

Match, A. Swinburne. CBLP; ELP; GGP; NOBVV

Match at Football, A, *sels.* Matthew Concanen.

Match-bark of the younger dog sets fire to, The. Table-Birds. Kenneth Mackenzie. NOBAu

Match Me Such Marvel. William Basil Tickell Jones. UV

Match me such marvel save in Eastern clime. John William Burgon. *Fr.* Petra. UV

Maureen in England, Joseph in Guelph. The Wishbone. Paul Muldoon. CIP; PBCIP

Maurice was in an Exhibition Hall. Austin Clarke. *Fr.* Mnemosyne Lay in Dust. IPY; PoE

Maurus. Palladas, *tr. fr. Greek by* Tony Harrison. GrAn

Mauve. Leslie Ullman. NAmP90

Mavrone. Arthur Guiterman. BXAP; FiBHP

Maw Bonnie Lad. *Unknown.* GBP

Max Roach/ has fire and steel in his hands. Jazz Drummer. Etheridge Knight. Jaz

Max Schmitt in a Single Scull. Richmond Lattimore. AiP

Maxie Allen. Gwendolyn Brooks. NAAL-2

Maxim. Kipling. *Fr.* Certain Maxims of Hafiz. OtMeF

Maxim. Josephine Miles. CrSp

Maxim Revised, A. *Unknown.* BLPA; NBLV; WBLP

Maxims (Cotton MS.). *Unknown, tr. fr. Anglo-Saxon by* Charles W. Kennedy. AnOE

Maxims (Exeter Book). *Unknown, tr. fr. Anglo-Saxon by* Charles W. Kennedy. AnOE

Maxims in Rhyme for the Young. J. Clark. PWR

Maximus. D. H. Lawrence. TOF

Maximus Poems, The, *sels.* Charles Olson.
    Celestial Evening, October 1967. PoM
    Cole's Island. PoM
    "Colored pictures." NoAM
    I, Maximus of Gloucester, to You ("By ear, she sd"). NeAP
    I, Maximus of Gloucester, to You ("Off-shore, by islands hidden in the blood"). LiTM; NoAM; NOBA; PoM
    Later Note on Letter 15, A. CAPP
    Maximus from Dogtown-II. PRA
    Maximus, to Gloucester, Letter 2. NoAM
    Maximus, to Gloucester, Letter 19. CMoP
    Maximus, to Gloucester, Letter 27. NOBA; PoE
    Maximus, to Gloucester, Sunday, July 19. NAAL-2; TRP
    Maximus, to Himself. CAPP; CMoP; NeAP; NOBA; PoE; PoM; VGW
    Songs of Maximus. NeAP
      "Colored pictures/ of all things to eat: dirty" NoAM
      "This morning of the small snow"
      (All/ wrong.) NoAM, II

Maxixe. Sir Osbert Sitwell. PoA

Maxwell[l] ton['s] braes are bonnie. Annie Laurie. William Douglas, *rev. by* Lady Jane Scott. FaBoBe; FaBV; GN; ImPo; ScCV; WBLP

May. William Barnes. ChTr
    Sels.
    "Mother o' blossoms, and ov all"

May. Edward Hovell-Thurlow. OBEV

May. Mrs. Henry Linden. CBWP-4

May. John Shaw Neilson. NOBAu

May. Mary Oliver. Poetr

May. James Gates Percival. BoTP

May. H. Cordelia Ray. CBWP-3

May. Christina Rossetti. GBL; NOBVV

May. Spenser. *Fr.* Faerie Queene, The. GN

May. John Updike. *Fr.* Child's Calendar, A. OBCA

May All Earth Be Clothed in Light. George Hitchcock. VGW

May all I say and all I think. *Unknown, tr. fr. Chinook Indian.* EaPr

May all that dread the cruel feind of night. Warning to Travailers Seeking Accomodations at Mr. Devills Inn. Sarah Kemble Knight. SCAP

May all things move and be moved in me. *Unknown, tr. fr. Chinook Indian.* EaPr

May, and among the miles of leafing. May. Mary Oliver. Poetr

May and Death. Robert Browning. FaBoRV; IMW; NOBE

May, and the air is light. The Road's End. John Montague. *Fr.* Severed Head, A. IPY

May, and the wall was warm again. For miles. Winter's Cold. W. R. Rodgers. EnLoPo

May be opened for inspection. (*LL*) Epitaph for a Postal Clerk. X. J. Kennedy. NIP

May be refin'd, and join th' angelic train. (*LL*) On Being Brought from Africa to America. Phillis Wheatley. FF; GOA; NAAL-1; NALW; NOBA; NOEC; TAP; TTY; WPE

May! be thou never graced with birds that sing. [Epitaph] In Obitum M.S., X° Maij [or Maii], 1614. William Browne. EIL; FaBoEE; JCP; NOBE; OBEV

May become everlasting tomorrow. (*LL*) Tomorrow. John Collins. GTBS; GTBS-P

May blaze the virtue[or vertue] of their sires. (*LL*) A Nuptial[l] Song, or Epithalamie [or Epithalamy], on Sir Clipseby Crew and His Lady. Robert Herrick. BeJo; CaPo; CBLP; JCP; PoEL-3; SeCP; SeCV-1

May blow my ashes up and strike thee blind. (*LL*) Curse, The; a Song. Robert Herrick. CaPo

May Carol. *Unknown.* OBET

May cheer the herds with pasture memories. (*LL*) The Mowing. Sir Charles G. D. Roberts. NOBC

May Collin. Lady Isabel and the Elf-Knight. *Unknown.* ESPB

May Colven. *Unknown.* OxBB; TrGrPo

May come up with bird-din. Nuts in May. Louis MacNeice. MoAB; MoBrPo

May comes again, the meadows are in bloom. Alois Jeitteles, *tr. by* Philip L. Miller. RiWo

May crown thy Feet, that could not crown thy Head. (*LL*) The Coronet. Andrew Marvell. ESCV; FHYEP; GeHe; MeLP; NAEL-1; NOCV; NoP; NOSC; PoE; SCGP; SeCV-1; TOF

May-Day, *sels.* Emerson.
    April and May. GN; OHIP

May-Day. Aaron Hill. NOEC

May Day. Sara Teasdale. BoNaP

May-Day, A. Sir Henry Wotton. *See* And now all Nature seem'd in Love.

May-Day carol, A. Alfred Noyes. PFP

May Day Dancing, The. Howard Nemerov. NYBP; Poetr

May Day Rounds: Renfrew County, *sels.* Joan Finnigan.
    "Stoop on the log-house is brown with sweet rain-rot, The." WPE

May drink itself up, and forget to die. (*LL*) An Apology for the Foregoing Hymn. Richard Crashaw. JCP

May everything be known as the light of mutual love. (*LL*) Prayer of the Seven Galactic Directions. José Argüelles. EaPr

May 1506 (Christopher Columbus Speaking). Winfield Townley Scott. GOA

May 15th. Raymond Souster. MoCV

May filter in my daily songs. (*LL*) As I Sit Writing Here. Walt Whitman. NAAL-1

May 4th, 1926. Bill Foot. FaBoEH

May God be praised for woman. On Woman. W. B. Yeats. ChIV-1; CMoP

May God bless your home. Marriage Vow. Mrs. Henry Linden. CBWP-4

May God Give Strength. Peter van Wynen. BLRP

"May Grace be with you all" said the bishop. *Unknown, tr. fr. Greek by* Peter Jay. GrAn

May has come out from the showers. The Jewish May. Morris Jacob Rosenfeld, *tr. fr. Yiddish by* Rose Pastor Stokes *and* Helena Frank. TrJP

May have killed the cat; more likely. Curiosity. Alastair Reid. SoSe

May he fall in with beasts that scatter fire. Ballad against the Enemies of France. Villon, *tr. fr. French by* Swinburne. AWP

May he have new life like the fall. John Coltrane: An Impartial Review. Alfred B. Spellman. PoBA

May he lose his way on the cold sea. Archilochus, *tr. fr. Latin by* Guy Davenport. OBVE

May His Body make me safer. Thanksgiving after Communion. *Unknown, tr. fr. Gaelic by* Douglas Hyde. WTO

May his Counsels Sweet uphold you. God Be with You. *Unknown.* PoToHe

May, Home after a Year Away. Gail Mazur. NAmP90

May I Be Beautiful. *Malay Oral Tradition, tr. by* W. W. Skeat. WTO

May I be there to see! (*LL*) John Gilpin. William Cowper. InvP

May I come in? May I come in? Jean-Joseph Rabéarivelo, *tr. fr. French by* Ellen Conroy Kennedy. NegPo

May I Feel Said He. E. E. Cummings. BoLoP; ErPo; FF; HeIP; LiTA; NBLV; NOBE; OxBM; PeLV

May I find a woman fair. True Beauty. Francis Beaumont. EIL

May I forever a Muse-/ um. Vow. John Updike. NYBP; PeLV

May I learn the shape of that hurt. Don. Anthony McNeill. PBCV

May I truly appreciate this autumn day. (*LL*) Autumn Psalm of Contentment. Edward Hays. EaPr

May in the Green-Wood. *Unknown.* OBEV

May Is Building Her House. Richard Le Gallienne. OHIP

May is Mary's month, and I. The May Magnificat. Gerard Manley Hopkins. PeECV

May is the moneth maist amene. Of May. Alexander Scott. OxBS

May It Be. Boris Pasternak, *tr. fr. Russian by* C. M. Bowra. TrJP

May it be delightful my house. *Unknown, tr. fr. Navajo Indian.* EaPr

May it be so! (*LL*) Ballad of a Little Lamp. René Depestre. NegPo

May–June, 1940. Robinson Jeffers. LiTA; MoAB; MoAmPo

May lay my burden down. (*LL*) In the Town. *Unknown.* OBCP; PChr

May lie till eleven. He that would thrive must rise at five. *Unknown.* FaBoUs; OxNR

May look to heaven as I depart. (*LL*) To the Fringed Gentian. Bryant. AnAmPo; AWP; FaBoBe; GN; NoP; PoLF; TAP

May Magnificat, The. Gerard Manley Hopkins. PeECV

May Margret stood in her bouer door. Hind Etin. *Unknown.* ESPB, A *and* B *vers.;* OxBB

May My Heart Always. E. E. Cummings. OxBSP

May Night, The. Ludwig Heinrich Christoph Hölty, *tr. fr. German by* Philip L. Miller. RiWo

May 1968. Sharon Olds. NAmP90; NIP

May no man slepe in youre halle. *Unknown.* MiEL

May none of these waterburners by night have his rest! *(LL)* The Blacksmiths. *Unknown.*

May not be this poem. *(LL)* The Man in the Tree. Mark Strand. CBNP

May nothing evil cross this door. Prayer for This House. Louis Untermeyer. BLPL; FaPON; PoLF; PoToHe (Prayer for a New House.) TrPWD

May nothing I own be stolen or concealed. For the Theft of Cattle. *Unknown, tr. fr. Anglo-Saxon by* Kevin Crossley-Holland. ASW

May our corner of the earth join us. *Unknown, tr. fr. French by* Mary Rogers. EaPr

May peace be established throughout the land. Te Atairangikaahu. Kingi M. Ihaka, *tr. fr. Maori by* Kingi M. Ihaka. PeNZ

May poverty, without offense, approach. Nicholas James. *Fr.* Complaints of Poverty, The. NOEC

May Queen, The. Tennyson. PFP *Sels.* "You must wake and call me early, call me early, mother." EBEvV

May! queen of blossoms. May. Edward Hovell-Thurlow. OBEV

May rains! Sanpu, *tr. fr. Japanese by* Kenneth Koch *and* Harold Henderson. TTTS

May rest in the Fleet with you, Lord Collingwood. *(LL)* The Death of Nelson. *Unknown.* OxBoLi

May say Alas but cannot help or pardon. *(LL)* Spain 1937. W. H. Auden. FaBoPV; LiTB; NAEL-1; OBWP

May seven tears in every week. A Wish. J. M. Synge. FaBoEE

May Song. Goethe, *tr. fr. German by* John Frederick Nims. STV

May Song. *Unknown.* OBET

May steal my love away. *(LL)* Going to My Sweetheart. Josef Wenzig. RiWo

May steale a heart or two from you. *(LL)* To the Countesse of Salisbury. Aurelian Townshend. SeCP

May supple-footed theatre-growing ivy. Erucius, *tr. fr. Greek by* Peter Levi. GrAn

May 10th. Maxine W. Kumin. BoNaP; NYBP; RFM

May that greenwood of soul be in sight! *(LL)* The Isle of the Long Ago. Benjamin Franklin Taylor. WBLP

May the axe be far away from you. *Unknown.* EaPr

May the Babylonish curse. A Farewell to Tobacco. Charles Lamb. OxBoLi

May the earth continue to live. *Unknown.* EaPr

May the ethereal elements not rise up as enemies. Prayer for Guidance. *Unknown, tr. fr. Tibetan by* W. Y. Evans-Wentz. *Fr.* Tibetan Book of the Dead, The. OBD

May the grace of the Holy Ghost be gained by us. The Graces of the Holy Ghost. *Unknown, tr. fr. Irish by* Douglas Hyde. TIRV

May the harpoon rust, may the cold steel be gone. Blood on the Sails. Phil *and* June Colclough *and* June Colclough. OBET

May the Lord in His mercy be kind to Belfast. *(LL)* Ballad to a Traditional Refrain. Maurice James Craig. BIrV; TIRV

May the man who gained my trust yet did not come. Ryojin Hisho. BoWoP

May the man who has cruelly murdered his sire. A Counterblast against Garlic. Horace, *tr. by* Roswell Martin Field. *Fr.* Epodes. NBLV

May the men who are born. Hitomaro, *tr. fr. Japanese by* Arthur Waley. *Fr.* Manyo Shu, Part 2 of 4. AWP; TAL

May the Ocean of Salt, the Ocean of. *Unknown.* EaPr

May the Saddest Memory. Birthday Wishes to a Husband. L. A. J. Moorer. CBWP-3

May the soil cover/ your interred corpse. Ammianus, *tr. fr. Greek by* Peter Jay. GrAn

May the will come from Thee. Annul Wars. Rabbi Nahman of Bratzlav, *tr. fr. Hebrew by* Jacob Sloan. TrJP

May the wind blows sweetness. *Unknown, tr. fr. Sanskrit by* Romesh Dutt. *Fr.* Vedic Hymns. EaPr

May the wind put out everything for you. Curses. Ljubomir Simovic, *tr. fr. Serbo-Croatian by* Charles Simic. HSix

May the wrath of the heart of my god be pacified! Penitential Psalm to the Goddess Anunit. *Unknown, tr. fr. Babylonian.* WGRP

May their numbers increase. *(LL)* Ah Power that swirls us together. Gary Snyder. EaPr

May they come, may they come. Song of the Highest Tower. Rimbaud, *tr. fr. French by* Edgell Rickword. AWP

May they stumble [*or* wander], stage by stage. The Travel[l]er's Curse after Misdirection. Robert Graves. CMoP; FiBHP; HoPM; LiTM; MeMBP; MoAB; MoBrPo; NBLV

May thret thy cruell hert. *(LL)* What rage is this? what furor [*or* furour] of what kind [*or* kynd]? Sir Thomas Wyatt. AAS; EnLoPo; SiPS

May-Time. *Unknown.* BoTP

May toss him to my breast. *(LL)* The Pulley. George Herbert. AWP; ChIV-1; EBEvV; FHYEP; GeHe; GTBS; GTBS-P; HAP; HeIP; ImPo; InPK; InPS; LiTB; Mes; NAEL-1; NOBE; NOCV; NoP; NOSC; OAEL-1; OBEV; OtMeF; OxAEP-1; PPP; PrIm; SCGP; SeCP; SeCV-1; TEP; TFi; TrGrPo

May Tree, The. William Barnes. LiTB

May Trees in a Storm. Geoffrey Grigson. GBL

May trouble you more than ever, when you've nailed his coffin down! *(LL)* How Old Brown Took Harper's Ferry. Edmund Clarence Stedman. PAH; PoNe

May we be nourished that we may nourish life. *(LL)* Earth, water, air, and fire combined to make this food. *Unknown.* EaPr

May we now venture to be kind. *(LL)* Exit. E. A. Robinson. MoAmPo; OxBSP

May wish us of their choir. *(LL)* The Musical Strife, in a Pastoral Dialogue. Ben Jonson. BeJo

May with its light behaving. W. H. Auden. EBEV

May you be reborn in the supreme lotus, the realm of truth. Mourning My Son. Yüan Chen, *tr. fr. Chinese by* Angela Jung Palandri. SuSp

May you drink beer, or that adult' rate wine. To a Friend, Inviting Him to a Meeting upon Promise. William Habington. *Fr.* Castara. BeJo

May you live forever. In that eternity. A Curse on Herod. Amy Witting. ChIV-2; NOBAu

May you rejoice, Paeon lord, who rule. Women at the Temple. Herodas, *tr. fr. Greek by* Barbara Hughes Fowler. HePo

May your life be bright and sunny. *Unknown.* RoPo

Maya in the city has a dream. The Book of Ephraim. James Merrill. *Fr.* Changing Light at Sandover, The. NAAL-2

Mayakovsky was right. Kiss. Al Young. PoBA

Mayan Prophecy, A. Sharon Spencer. WoWa

Maybe all I saw was the mirror. Vision. Delmira Augustini, *tr. fr. Spanish by* Marti Moody. WPOW

Maybe Alone on My Bike. William Stafford. NYBP

Maybe because I was married and felt secure and dead. Visiting My Gravesite: Talbott Churchyard, West Virginia. Irene McKinney. PBCAP

Maybe Dats Your Pwoblem Too. Jim Hall. MT

Maybe for Love. John Holmes. LPA

Maybe he dreamed of/ new snow. Retired Farmer. David Allan Evans. Poetsp

Maybe I am what she always wanted. Why My Mother Made Me. Sharon Olds. Poetr

Maybe I'm seven in the open field. Sudden Journey. Tess Gallagher. NIP

Maybe it is the shyness of the pride. The Surge. Molly Peacock. NAmP90

Maybe it is true we have to return. Obsessions. Denise Levertov. LiTM; SM

Maybe it was the Bichot. Poetry Makes Rhythm in Philosophy. Ishmael Reed. Jaz

Maybe it was the way. Finding You. Virginia Gilbert. IHMS

Maybe it's really Bette Davis I want. Bette Davis. Jackie Kay. NWP

Maybe Love. Allen Ginsberg. PeHV

Maybe morning lightens over. For My Grandmother, Bridget Halpin. Michael Hartnett. BIrV; IIP; PBCIP

Maybe that is what he was after. Sweet Rain. Tony Hoagland. NAmP90

Maybe the jay resting on the eve right now. Maybe the Jay. Robin Behn. PFL

Maybe the street is tired of being a street. New Year. Naomi Shihab Nye. MT

Maybe they're angels. *(LL)* Extraterrestrial. Alicia Ostriker. VBLP

Maybe this is the final battle. No One's Land. Janet Dubé. DT

Maybe we knew each other better. Coda. Louis MacNeice. CBLP

Maybe we should have known. *(LL)* A Locked House. W. D. Snodgrass. VCAP

Maybe what Thomas means when he says grace. Reading Aquinas. Michael Heffernan. WeW

Maybe you ranted in the grove. Ezry. Archibald MacLeish. NOBA

Maybrick trial is over now, there's been a lot of jaw, The. Penal Servitude for Mrs. Maybrick. *Unknown.* OxBoLi

Mayday. Ed Roberson. PoBA

Mayde ther was, y-clept Joan Hunter Dunn, A. The Summonee's Tale. Stanley J. Sharpless. BXAP; FaBoPa

Mayde's Metamorphosis, The, *sels.* At. *to* John Lyly *and to* Thomas Ravenscroft.
  By the Moon ("By the moon we sport and play"). CH
    (Fairy Dances.) EIL
    (Urchin's Dance, The.) BoTP
  Elves' Dance, The. CH; FaPON
Mayflower, The. Erastus Wolcott Ellsworth. FaBoBe; PAH
Mayflower. John Boyle O'Reilly. PAH
Maynard cooked Vesti la Giubba. Ferguson's Conquistadores 77. Joy Walsh. Jaz
Mayor. Yehuda Amichai, *tr. fr. Hebrew by* Assia Gutmann. PoSu
Mayor couldn't be here, but he sends his grand whereases, The. State Poetry Day. Ronald Wallace. PBCAP
Mayor has angrily banished the seven deadly, The. The Exiles. Paul Ramsey. *Fr.* Three Epigrams. CRP
Mayor of Lagos. *Yoruba Oral Tradition, tr. by* Ulli Beier. WTO
Mayors, The. Blake. *See* This city and this country has brought forth many mayors.
Mayor's son had options. One was death, The. Tale of the Mayor's Son. Glyn Maxwell. PWE
Maypole is up, The. The Maypole. Robert Herrick. BeJo
May's Invocation after a Tardy Spring. H. Cordelia Ray. CBWP-3
May'st find thy Darling in an urn. *(LL)* Epitaph on the Lady Mary Villiers. Thomas Carew. BeJo; CaPo; FaBoEE; NOBE; OBEV; SeCV-1
Mayst thou die desp'rate in some dirty pool. An Adieu to My Landlady. George Farewell. NOEC
Maytide's evenen wer a-dyen, A. Light or Sheade. William Barnes. NOBVV
Maytime. Thomas Dekker *and others. See* O the month of May, the merry month of May.
Maytime. *Unknown, tr. by* L. Cranmer-Byng. *Fr.* Shi King. AWP
Maytime, loveliest season. Sadness in Spring. *Unknown, tr. fr. Welsh by* Gwyn Jones. OBWVE
Maze of Blood, A. N. C. G. Mathema. PeSAV
Maze of Decades, A. Martha Sansom. UnDi
Mazeppa. Byron. EnRP
Mazeppa's Ride. Byron. *See* 'Twas after dread Pultowa's day.
Mazilla and Mazura. *Unknown.* ChTr
Mbuyazi (Henry Francis Fynn). *Unknown.* PeSAV
Mbuyazi of the Bay! Mbuyazi (Henry Francis Fynn). *Unknown.* PeSAV
Mbuyazi of the Bay! Praises of Henry Francis Fynn. *Zulu Oral Tradition, tr. by* T. Cope. WTO
Me. Walter de la Mare. FaPON
Me a poet! My daughter with maimed limb. Self Justification. Tony Harrison. *Fr.* School of Eloquence, The. NAEL-2; NoAM
Me Alone. Lula Lowe Weeden. CDC
Me and Gib likes it here — always comes of a night. Tryst. Peter Reading. FaBoBl
Me and Marlene sit tight in her truck. Our Lady of the Laundromat. Belle Waring. PBCAP
Me and my brother. My Brother, Beautiful Shinault, That Goat. David Huddle. GrPl
Me and my brother would jump off the porch. Pushing. Christopher Gilbert. SoSe
Me and My Chauffeur Blues. "Memphis Millie." VBLP
Me and My Mother's Morphine. Joan Jobe Smith. NGP
Me and Rhonda draggin the strip. Norma at the A&W Drive-In. Jana Harris. NGP
Me and the World. James Simmons. PRA
Me and you be sisters. Sisters. Lucille Clifton. VBLP
Me/ As She/ or Her? Crowbar. Rachel Blau DuPlessis. VBLP
Me best of all, Maude Clare. *(LL)* Maude Clare. Christina Rossetti. BeLS; EBVV
Me clairvoyant. Old King Cole ("Me clairvoyant.") G. K. Chesteron. *Fr.* Variations on an Air Composed on Having to Appear in a Pageant as Old King Cole. BXAP; FaBoPa; NOBL; UV
Me, Colored. Peter Abrahams. *Fr.* Tell Freedom. PBA
Me! dutiful son going back to South Wales, this time afraid. Down the M4. Dannie Abse. OxBC
Me, for example. Say Girls in Shoe Ads: "I Go for a Man Who's Tall!" Robley Wilson, Jr. PBCAP
Me from myself — to banish. Emily Dickinson. NALW; TRP
Me from the womb the midwife Muse did take. Abraham Cowley. *Fr.* Destinie. EPCY
Me go to Morant Bay. Morant Bay. *Unknown.* FaBoVe
Me happy, night, night full of brightness. Ezra Pound. *Fr.* Homage to Sextus Propertius. MeMAP
  (Elegy VII.) ErPo; InvP; VGW

Me Heart. G. K. Chesteron. OtMeF
Me I like to putz in the kitchen and regard. Breeze in Translation. Belle Waring. NAmP90
Me, I like to putz in the kitchen and regard. Breeze in Translation. Belle Waring. PBCAP
Me I will throw away. The Self-slaved. Patrick Kavanagh. MoBrPo
Me Imperturbe. Walt Whitman. NOBA
Me, in Kulu Se and Karma. Carolyn M. Rodgers. PoBA
Me list no more to sing. Sir Thomas Wyatt. AAS; SiPS
Me liste drinke non ale. *(LL)* Care away, away, away,/ Murninge away! *Unknown.* MiEL
Me Lord? can'st Thou mispend. Phineas Fletcher. *Fr.* Divine Wooer, The. TOF; TrPWD
Me lover gone a Colon Bay. Colon Bay. *Unknown.* FaBoVe
Me lusteth no longer [or lenger] rotten boughs [boughes] to climb [or clymbe]. *(LL)* Farewell, love, and all thy laws [or lawes] for ever. Sir Thomas Wyatt. AAS; CBLP; LiTB; NAEL-1; NoSic; OAEL-1; SCGP; SiPS; SiPSBD
Me miserable! which way shall I fly. Milton. *Fr.* Paradise Lost. EPCY; PoE
Me, myself, and I. *Unknown.* RoPo
Me nappy hair dream child. Image in the Mirror. Peggy Susberry Kenner. JB
Me needeth not to boast; I am Eternity. Eternity. Sir Thomas More. *Fr.* Pageant Verses. EnRePo
Me no know. *Unknown.* RoPo
Me not no Oxford don. Listen Mr Oxford Don. John Agard. NBrP
Me now?" *(LL)* As I Was Walking. Robert Creeley. RaBo
Me — of Me? *(LL)* Me From Myself — to Banish. Emily Dickinson. NALW; TRP
"Me oh my," said the tiny, shiny ant. Big Little Boy. Eve Merriam. SiSoPo
Me one, way out in the crowd. Valley Prince. Mervyn Morris. PBCV
Me — Pirate. Clive Sansom. OTCP
Me Polytimus vexes and provokes. Martial, *tr. fr. Latin.* PeHV
Me Rueth, Mary. *Unknown. See* Now Goeth [or goth or goothe] Sun [or Sonne or Sunne] under Wood.
Me rueth, Mary, thy son and thee. *(LL)* Now Goeth [or goth or goothe] Sun [or Sonne or Sunne] under Wood. *Unknown.* MiEL; NoP
me sleeping. *(LL)* Sleeping Beauty. Olga Broumas. VBLP
Me so oft my fancy drew. The Choice. George Wither. OBEV
Me sooner starve than those can kill. *(LL)* The Frozen Zone; or, Julia Disdainful. Robert Herrick. CaPo
Me take my cutacoo. A Negro Song. *Unknown.* PBCV
Me Tarzan. Tony Harrison. *Fr.* School of Eloquence, The. NAEL-2; NoAM
Me that 'ave been what I've been. Chant-Pagan. Kipling. FaBoPV
Me thinks I see our mighty monarch stand. *Unknown. Fr.* Royal Angler, The. OBSV
Me thinks [or Methinks], I see, with what a busie [or busy] hast[e]. On Zacheus [or Zacchaeus]. Francis Quarles. HAP
Me to strike for your life's blood, and you to strike for mine. *(LL)* D.G.C. to J.A. Emily Brontë. BrRo, 1 *st.*; EnLoPo, (1 *st.*)
Me to You. Alastair Reid. NYBP
Me Up at Does. E. E. Cummings. NYBP; OxBSP; Poetr; WeW
Mea Culpa. "Ethna Carbery." TrPWD
Meadow, The. Peter Fallon. PBCIP
Meadow Bug. Rossana Ombres, *tr. fr. Italian by* Ruth Feldman. NeIt
Meadow Mouse, The. Theodore Roethke. HeIP; NaP; RB; TRP
Meadows, The. Ann Taylor. BoTP
Meadows again!, The. *(LL)* Old Song. Edward Fitzgerald. GN; OBEV; OxAEP-2
Meadowsweet. William Allingham. OBNC
Meal, The. Martha Sansom. UnDi
Meal Time. Maggie Pogue Johnson. CBWP-4
Mean and Stupid. Christopher Howell. NGP
Mean Drunk Poem. Sharon Thesen. NOBC
Mean mean mean to be free. *(LL)* Runagate Runagate. Robert Hayden. BPo; InPS; LCAP; PoBA; PoNe
Mean old Hermon. Lucilius, *tr. fr. Greek by* Peter Porter. GrAn
Meandering River., *sels.* Tu Fu, *tr. fr. Chinese.*
  "Returning from court day after day, I pawn my spring clothes." SuSp
  "Single petal swirling diminishes the spring, A." SuSp
Meandering Wye. Robert Bloomfield. *Fr.* Banks of Wye, The. OBNC
Meanest Gang in the Bronx, The. Terence Winch. BCF
Meanest trick I ever knew, The. A Low Trick. Gelett Burgess. OBCA
Meanin' of captivity!, The. *(LL)* Half-Ballad of Waterval. Kipling. PeSAV

Meaning Insomnia. John Hall. VaA
Meaning of a Letter, The. *Unknown.* PoToHe
Meaning of Africa, The. Abioseh Nicol. PBA
Meaning of Love, The. *Malay Oral Tradition, tr. by* R. O. Winstedt. WTO
Meaning of Simplicity, The. Yannis Ritsos, *tr. fr. Greek by* Edmund Keeley. TSaS
Meaning of the Look, The. Elizabeth Barrett Browning. TrCP
Meaningful Exchange, The. Marge Piercy. AIW
Meanings in the Pattern, The. Judy Grahn. UL
Means by which I waken into light, The. *(LL)* The Gateway. A. D. Hope. BoLoP; ErPo; FaBoMA
Means of Propulsion for Steam-Ships. Thomas Baker. *Fr.* Steam Engine; or, The Power of the Flame, The. FaBoUs
Means only those who broke — in life — thy peace. *(LL)* The Timber. Henry Vaughan. FaBoRV, *abr.*; GeHe, *abr.*; NoP; OBEV; SeCP; SeCV-1
Means to Attain the Happy Life, The. Martial. *See* Martial [*or* Marshall *or* My Friend], the thing[e]s that do [*or* for to] attain [*or* attayne].
Meanwhile. Joel Dailey. UL
Meanwhile . . . John Ashbery. BAP-89
Meanwhile, back home at the ranch. Victor Gray. PeLi
Meanwhile Cesario Dancing. Helen Kidd. VBLP
Meanwhile surely there must be something to say. The Constructed Space. W. S. Graham. PoA
Meanwhile the adversary of God and man. Milton. *Fr.* Paradise Lost. DL, *ll.* 629–841; EBEV, *ll.* 629–734; EPCY (Sin and Death.) OBNV, *ll.* 629–889
Meanwhile the choleric Captain strode wrathful away to the council. The War-Token. Longfellow. *Fr.* Courtship of Miles Standish, The. AiP, *st.* 1; BeLS; PAH
Meanwhile the heinous and despiteful act. Milton. *Fr.* Paradise Lost. EPCY; FHYEP
Meanwhile the troops beneath Patroclus' care. Homer, *tr. by* Pope. *Fr.* Iliad, The. OBVE
Meanwhile the woman, from her strawberry lips. Metamorphoses of the Vampire. Baudelaire, *tr. by* Jackson Mathews. ErPo
Meare's milk and deer's milk. A Witch's Spell [*or* Witch's Milking Charm]. *Unknown.* ChTr; GBP (Witch's Milking Charm.) GBP
Measles in the Ark. "Susan Coolidge." OxBChV
Measure. Gillian Eve Hanscombe *and* Suniti Namjoshi. DT
Measure, The. Patrick Lane. NOBC
Measure for Measure. Sipho Sepamla. PeSAV
Measure for Measure., *sels.* Shakespeare.
  "Ay[e], but to die, and go we know not where." OBD; RB
  Be Absolute for Death. FaBoRV
  "Sense of death is most in apprehension, The." OBD
  Take, O Take Those Lips Away. AWP; EBEV; EiL; ELP; EnLoPo; EnRePo; FaBV; GBL; ImPo; InPS; LiTB; NoP; NoSic; OAEL-1; OBEV; SCGP; TFi
    (At the Moated Grange.) NOBE
    (Seals of Love.) TrGrPo
    (Song: "Take, O take those lips away.") 09FiP; PoEL-2
  "'Tis one thing to be tempted, Escalus." OxBM
Measure his strides by the length of the arm's arc. Cool. Beverlyjean Smith. ETG
Measure Me, Sky. Leonora Speyer. FaPON
Measure of a Man, The. *Unknown.* BLPL; PoLF
Measure of Light at the Altar on the Day of the Dead, The. Rosemary Catacalos. AfAz
Measured blood beats out the year's delay, The. Simple Autumnal. Louise Bogan. MoAB; MoAmPo; Son
Meat. Michael van Walleghen. NAmP90
Mechanic, The. Robert Creeley. NaP
Mechanic, The. Richard Jones. NAmP90
Mechanic, The. Diane Wakoski. AmPA
Mechanical/ Oracles dot the sky. Gods in Vietnam. Eugene B. Redmond. PoBA
Mechanical Cow, The. Robley Wilson, Jr.. PBCAP
Mechanical digger wrecks the drill, A. At a Potato Digging. Seamus Heaney. CIP; IPY; PeIV
Mechanical marvel was Bill, A. *Unknown.* PeLi
Mechanism. A. R. Ammons. HAP
Mechanophilus, *sels.* Tennyson.
  "Dash back that ocean with a pier." FaBoCo
Mecklenburg Declaration, The. William C. Elam. PAH
Medal [*or* Medall], The, *sels.* Dryden.
  Vox Populi. NOBE
Medal, The. Tawfiq Rafat. PAW

Medal of John Bays; a Satire against Folly and Knavery, The. Thomas Shadwell. APAS
Medal Reversed, The. Elkanah Settle. APAS
Medallion. Sylvia Plath. HeIP; NoP; SM
Meddlesome Matty. Ann Taylor. OxBChV
Meddow Verse; or, Aniversary to Mistris Bridget Lowman, The. Robert Herrick. SeCV-1
Medea, *sels.* Lord De Tabley.
  "Sweet are the ways of death to weary feet." OBEV
Medea. (How I wish the Argo had never reached the land.) Euripides, *tr. by* Rex Warner. NAWM-1; OxBM
  Sels.
    "It was everything to me to think well of one man"
Medea. Seneca, *tr. fr. Latin by* John Studley. OBVE
  Sels.
    "Her chaunging lookes no colour longe can holde"
    "That Orpheus Calliops sonne who stayde the running brooke"
Medea in Athens., *sels.* Augusta Webster.
  "Oh smooth adder/ who with fanged kisses changedst my natural blood." BrRo
Medea's Incantation. Ovid, *tr. fr. Latin. Fr.* Metamorphoses. AWP, *tr. by* Shakespeare; OBVE, *tr. by* Arthur Golding
Medgar Evers. Gwendolyn Brooks. NoP; PoBA
Median Palace. Robert Wells. SCBI
Mediator, The. Elizabeth Barrett Browning. TrPWD
Mediatrix. David Haynes. NBrP
Medical Aid. Walter Hard. BXAP
Medical Science. Robin Becker. ETG; PBCAP
Medicina pro morbo caduco et le fevre. *Unknown.* MiEL
Medicine. Alice Walker. CrSp; NMM
Medicine Bearer. Gail Tremblay. HATNAP
Medieval Norman Song. *Unknown, tr. fr. French by* John Addington Symonds. AWP
  Sels.
    "Alas, poor heart, I pity thee"
    "Before my lady's window gay"
    "Beneath the branch of the green may"
    "Drink, gossips mine!"
    "Fair is her body, bright her eye"
    "I found at daybreak yester morn"
    "In this merry morn of May"
    "Maid Marjory sits at the castle gate"
    "My love for him shall be"
    "Now who is he on earth that lives"
    "O Love, my love, and perfect bliss!"
    "O nightingale of woodland gay"
    "Sweet flower, that art so fair and gay"
    "They have said evil of my dear"
    "They lied, those lying traitors all"
    "This month of May, one pleasant eventide"
Medieval Poem of the Nativity, A. *Unknown.* TrCP
Medieval town, with frieze, The. What Is Poetry. John Ashbery. LCAP
Medine in Turkey. Alison Brackenbury. SCBI
Mediocrity in Love Rejected. Thomas Carew. BeJo; PFP
Meditating at Olema. Jim Gove. NGP
Meditating on Star Light While Traveling Highway. Anita Endrezze-Danielson. HATNAP
Meditatio. Ezra Pound. FaBoCh; OBAL
Meditatio, *sels.* Francis Quarles.
  Why? What are Men? CBCK
Meditatio Septima. Francis Quarles. ChIV-1
Meditatio Tertia Decima. Francis Quarles. *Fr.* Job Militant. ChIV-1
Meditation. Baudelaire, *tr. fr. French by* Robert Lowell. InPK; NAWM-2
Meditation. Anne Bradstreet. *See* As Spring the Winter Doth Succeed.
Meditation, A. Richard Eberhart. LiTA
Meditation. Anthony Hecht. EOEF
Meditation, A. Herman Melville. GOA
Meditation, The. John Norris. NOSC
Meditation. Palladas, *tr. fr. Greek by* Dudley Fitts. GrAn
Meditation after Hearing the Richard Yardumian Mass, "Come, Creator Spirit." Geraldine Clinton Little. BTR
Meditation among Trees. Marbod of Rennnes, *tr. fr. Latin by* Helen Waddell. MLL
Meditation at Kew. Anna Wickham. FaBoTw; MoBrPo; NALW
Meditation at Lagunitas. Robert Hass. AnAn; NoP; VCAP
Meditation at Oyster River. Theodore Roethke. CAPP; CMoP; MoAmPo; NYBP
Meditation at Pearl Street. Bruce Weigl. NAmP90
Meditation 8. Philip Pain. NOBA; NOSC; OxBSP
Meditation Eight. Edward Taylor. ChIV-2

Meditation, Followed by Excellent Advice. Eratosthenes, *tr. fr. Greek by* Dudley Fitts. GrAn

Meditation for a Pickle Suite. Richard H. W. Dillard. HoPM; MT

Meditation for Christmas, A. Selwyn Image. OBEV

Meditation for His Mistress[e], A. Robert Herrick. CaPo; JCP; NOBE; NOSC; OBEV; SeCP

Meditation Hall. Liu Tsung-yüan, *tr. fr. Chinese by* Jan W. Walls. SuSp

Meditation in Seven Days, A. Alicia Ostriker. PBCAP

Meditation 9. Philip Pain. *Fr.* Meditations for July 26, 1666. NOBA; SCAP

Meditation of a Mariner. Dorothy Auchterlonie. CBAP

Meditation on a Bone. A. D. Hope. NoAM

Meditation on a News Item. John Updike. PeLV

Meditation on Communion with God. Judah Halevi, *tr. fr. Hebrew by* Solomon Solis-Cohen. TrJP

Meditation on Rhode Island Coal, A. Bryant. TAP

Meditation on Statistical Method. J. V. Cunningham. CoAP; VGW

Meditation on the A30. Sir John Betjeman. RB

Meditation on the Nativity. Elizabeth Jennings. NAs

Meditation 62. Philip Pain. NOBA

Meditation 10. Philip Pain. NOBA

Meditation 29. Philip Pain. *Fr.* Meditations for July 26, 1666. NOBA; SCAP

Meditations. Solomon ibn Gabirol, *tr. fr. Hebrew by* Emma Lazarus. TrJP

Meditations, The, *sels. Unknown, tr. fr. Arabic.*
"In the casket of the Hours." TAL, *tr. by* Reynold A. Nicholson, *sts.* I–XX

Meditations for August 1, 1666. Philip Pain. SCAP

Meditations for July 26, 1666. Philip Pain. NOBA; SCAP
Sels.
Meditation 9
Meditation 29

Meditations for July 19, 1666. Philip Pain. SCAP

Meditations for July 25, 1666. Philip Pain. SCAP

Meditations in an Emergency. Frank O'Hara. CAPP; TAP; VCAP

Meditations in Time of Civil War, *sels.* W. B. Yeats.
Ancestral Houses. LiTB; OAEL-2
I See Phantoms of Hatred and of the Heart's Fullness and of the Coming Emptiness. LiTB
My Descendants. LiTB
My House. LiTB
My Table. LiTB
Road at My Door, The. BIrV; LiTB; NOBE; PoE
Stare's Nest by My Window, The. BIrV; GTBS-P; InPS; LiTB; NOBE
(Bees in the crevices, The.) FaBoPV

Meditations of a Hindu Prince. Sir Alfred Comyn Lyall. WGRP

Meditations of a Parrot. John Ashbery. TTTS

Meditations of a Tortoise Dozing under a Rosetree Near a Beehive at Noon While a Dog Scampers About and a Cuckoo Calls from a Distant Wood. Emile Victor Rieu. FiBHP

Meditations of an Old Woman. Theodore Roethke. NaP
Sels.
First Meditation. LCAP; NOBA
I'm Here. CoAP; NYBP

Meditations of Man's Mortalitie; or, A Way to True Blessedness, *sels.* Alice Sutcliffe.
"Bacchus that drunken God from Hell comes forth." KTR
"Of all the Trees that in the Garden grew." KTR

Meditations on the Moon. Paula Gunn Allen. HATNAP

Meditations on the Sepulchre in the Garden. Philip Doddridge. NOCV; NOEC

Meditations on the Six Days of the Creation, *sels.* Thomas Traherne.
Third Day. ChIV-1

Meditatioun in Wyntir. William Dunbar. EnVB; OxBS

Mediterranean, The. Allen Tate. FaBoMo; GOA; HAP; ImPo; LiTA; LiTM; MoAB; MoAmPo; VGW

Mediterranean Snake Admitter. Lynn Lonidier. SRLS

Medium, The. Elaine Feinstein. BrRo

Medium. Marc Kaminsky. BTR

Medium IV: Sights, The. Carl Rakosi. InPS

Medium Poem. Eileen Myles. UL

Medlars and Sorb-Apples. D. H. Lawrence. FaBoVe; NoAM; OAEL-2

Medley of Southern and Northern Tunes — Scenic Tour of West Lake, *sels.* Kuan Yun-shih, *tr. fr. Chinese.*
Tune: "Butterflies." SuSp
Tune: "Chilly East Wind." SuSp
Tune: "Coda." SuSp
Tune: "Going Up Small Pavilion." SuSp
Tune: "Happy Events Approaching." SuSp
Tune: "Moth Fluttering Against Lamp." SuSp
Tune: "Moth Fluttering against Lamp." SuSp

Tune: "Pomegranate Blossoms." SuSp

Tune: "Squabbling Quails." SuSp

Medusa. Louise Bogan. AWP; BoWoP; HoPM; MoAB; MoAmPo; NALW; NoAM; NoP; Poetr; WPE

Medusa. Amy Clampitt. VCAP

Medusa. X. J. Kennedy. GoJo

Medusa. Sylvia Plath. NALW

Medusa living on a remote shore. Look, Medusa! Suniti Namjoshi. AIW

Medusa on Skyros. Alison Fell. NBrP

Medusa. Sit down. Take. Eve Meets Medusa. Michelene Wandor. AIW

Medusa's looks had what it takes. Medusa. X. J. Kennedy. GoJo

Mee-ow, mee-ow. Pussy-Cat and Puppy-Dog. Lilian McCrea. BoTP

Meek and the Proud, The. Abraham ibn Chasdai, *tr. fr. Hebrew by* J. Chotzner. TrJP

Meek dew shone, the grass lay prostrate, The. The Tree. Ilya Ehrenburg, *tr. fr. Russian by* Babette Deutsch. TrJP

Meek Francis lies here, friend, without stop or stay. Matthew Prior. FaBoEE

Meerkats go about in packs. The Meerkats of Africa. Gavin Ewart. OBAP

Meerkats of Africa, The. Gavin Ewart. OBAP

Meet Ladybug. I Want You to Meet. David McCord. SiSoPo

Meet Me in St. Louis, Louis. Andrew B. Sterling. OBAL

Meet Me in the Green Glen. John Clare. *See* Love, Meet Me in the Green Glen.

Meet me to-night, lover, meet me. Moonlight. *Unknown.* AS

Meet me tonight. Jackie. King D. Kuka. VoR

Meet me tonight as usual at nine. Love Poem — 1940. Miriam Hershenson. GoYe

Meet-on-the-Road. *Unknown.* TTTS

Meet Rabbi Shatz in his correct black homburg. Tales of Shatz. Dannie Abse. OxBC

Meet the Supremes. David Trinidad. UL; UTF

Meet was at "The Cock and Pye," The. John Masefield. *Fr.* Reynard the Fox. OxBTC

Meet women with tender bearing. The Voice of Experience. Goethe, *tr. fr. German by* Walter Kaufmann. ErPo

Meeting, The. Louise Bogan. NoAM; NYBP

Meeting. George Crabbe. OBEV

Meeting, A. C. Day Lewis. NYBP

Meeting. Charles-Jean Grandmougin, *tr. fr. French by* Philip L. Miller. *Fr.* Poem of a Day. RiWo

Meeting, The. Nicki Jackowska. BrRo

Meeting, The. Longfellow. OBF

Meeting, The. Pierre Louÿs, *tr. fr. French. Fr.* Chansons de Bilitis. PeHV

Meeting, The. Howard Moss. GOYP; NYBP

Meeting. Christina Rossetti. CBLP; GBL; Mes

Meeting, The. Muriel Rukeyser. MoAmPo; TrJP

Meeting, The. Kathleen Spivack. NMM

Meeting, The. Ramona Wilson. VoR

Meeting a Bear. David Wagoner. FoLa; HAP; WeW

Meeting a lovely boy face to face. Strato, *tr. fr. Greek by* W. G. Shepherd. GrAn

Meeting a monster of mourning wherever I go. Epistle I. George Barker. MeMBP

Meeting after Long Absence, *sels.* Lilla Cabot Perry.

Meeting after Separation. Marula, *tr. fr. Sanskrit by* Tambimuttu *and* G. V. Vaiyda. BoWoP

Meeting and Passing. Robert Frost. OxBA; PFP

Meeting at a Salesyard. John Ennis. CIP

Meeting at Night. Robert Browning. AWP; BoLoP; CBLP; EBEvV; ELP; EnVR; FaBoVe; FaBV; FF; FHYEP; GBL; HeIP; InPS; InvP; LPA; NAEL-2; NOBE; NOBVV; OBEV; OBNC; OHCV; OPOP; OxBSP; PeVV; PoRA; SCGP; SCV; SoSe; TFi; TrGrPo; UnPo

Meeting Bida. Fily-Dabo Sissoko, *tr. fr. French by* Ellen Conroy Kennedy. NegPo

Meeting-House Hill. Amy Lowell. MoAmPo; OxBA; PoRA

Meeting-house is not what it used to be, The. Elegy in a Presbyterian Burying-Ground. Robert Noble Denison Wilson. BIrV

Meeting Mescalito at Oak Hill Cemetery. Lorna Dee Cervantes. BCF; PBCAP

Meeting Mick Jagger. Robert Peters. BXAP

Meeting My Best Friend from the Eighth Grade. Gary Gildner. SM

Meeting of Cultures, A. Donald Davie. OBTV; OxBC

Meeting of the Susquehanna with the Lackawanna. Lydia Huntley Sigourney. AmWP

Meeting of the Waters, The. Thomas Moore. ArLo; IIP; NOIV; OxBoLi; PoEL-4

Meeting Point. Louis MacNeice. CBLP; PNI

Meeting the British. Paul Muldoon. BiHa; CIP; FaBoPV; NoAM; PNI

Meeting, the Departure, The. Goethe, *tr. fr. German by* John Frederick Nims. STV

Meeting the first time for many years. A Meeting. C. Day Lewis. NYBP

Meeting the Herdsmen. Mei Yao Ch'en, *tr. fr. Chinese by* Jonathan Chaves. SuSp

Meeting the Mountains. Gary Snyder. NoAM; TAP

Meeting the Reincarnation Analyst. Gary Gildner. AmPA

Meeting Together of Poles & Latitudes: In Prospect. Margaret Avison. NOBC

Meeting when all the world was in the bud. Loves of the Puppets. Richard Wilbur. OxBC

Meeting with Time, "Slack thing," said I. Time. George Herbert. NAEL-1; TEP

Meeting with Vilakazi, the Great Zulu Poet, A. Raymond Mazisi Kunene, *tr. fr. Zulu by the author.* PeSAV

Meeting You at an Underground Station. Gillian Allnutt. VBLP

Meetings meetings meetings. Yuh Lookin Good. Carolyn M. Rodgers. BPo

Meets our bouquet of death-and turns sharp right. (*LL*) Unseen Fire. Ralph Nixon Currey. OBWP; OxBTC; PoWW

Meg Merrilies [*or* Merrilees]. Keats. BoTP; ELP; FaBoCh; FaPON; OxBChV; PlP; TEP

Megaceph, chosen to serve the State. Ambrose Bierce. *Fr.* Devil's Dictionary, The. OBAL

Mehinaku Girl in Seclusion, A. Cathy Song. OpBo

Mehitabel and Her Kittens. Don Marquis. *Fr.* Archy and Mehitabel. SoCa

Mehitabel Tries Companionate Marriage. Don Marquis. *Fr.* Archy and Mehitabel. OFC

Mein Breast, mein Corset und mein Legs. Palladas, *tr. fr. Greek by* Tony Harrison. GrAn

Mein Herz, Mein Herz Ist Traurig. Heine, *tr. fr. German by* James Thomson. AWP

Mein Kind, wir waren Kinder. Heine. *See* My child, we were two children.

Mein Liebchen, wir sassen zusammen. Heine, *tr. fr. German by* James Thomson. AWP

Melampus. George Meredith. PoEL-5

Melancholetta, *sels.* "Lewis Carroll." "My dismal sister! Couldst thou know." FiBHP

Melancholia. Robert Bly. NoP

Melancholia. Robert Bridges. CMoP

Melancholy, The. E. E. Cummings. MeMAP

Melancholy. Joseph Freiherr von Eichendorff, *tr. fr. German by* Philip L. Miller. RiWo

Melancholy. John Fletcher. *Fr.* Nice Valor, The. GTBS; GTBS-P; OBEV

Melancholy. Thomas Middleton. NOSC

Melancholy. Edward Thomas. NoP

Melancholy days are come, the saddest of the year, The. The Death of the Flowers. Bryant. AnAmPo; BLPL; BoNaP; EAP; GN; OBCA; PoLF; WBLP

Melancholy days come once a year, The. A View on Death. Roy W. Watson. PWR

Melancholy days have come, The. Autumn Leaves. Charles H. Webb. OBAL

Melancholy desire of ancient things, A. On an Air of Rameau. Arthur Symons. OBNC

Melancholy face Charles Carville had, A. Charles Carville's Eyes. E. A. Robinson. AnAmPo; CMoP; MeMAP; OxBA; TAP

Melancholy inside Families. Pablo Neruda, *tr. fr. Spanish by* Robert Bly *and* James Wright. RaBo

Melancholy Knight, The, *sels.* Samuel Rowlands. "My dismal sister! Couldst thou know." FiBHP Poetaster, The. EIL Sir Eglamour. EIL; FaBoCh; FaBoNo; InvP

Melancholy Lay, A. Marjory Fleming. FaBoCh; FiBHP; NBLV

Melancholy Pig, The. "Lewis Carroll." *See* There was a Pig that sat alone.

Melancholy remembrances and vesperal. (*LL*) The Church of a Dream. Lionel Johnson. OAEL-2; OBMV

Melancholy slackening that ensued, The. Cambridge and the Alps. Wordsworth. *Fr.* Prelude [*or*, Growth of a Poet's Mind], The. EnRP; OAEL-2; PoEL-4

Melancholy Speech of Bluebell the Bogomil Dog. Tim Longville. VaA

Meleager. Ovid, *tr. by* Arthur Golding. *Fr.* Metamorphoses. CTC

Melhill Feast. William Barnes. OBNC

Melincourt, *sels.* Thomas Love Peacock.

Sun-Dial, The. OBNC

Melinda, who had never been. The Coquette. Aphra Behn. TrGrPo

Melinna herself! It *is* — see how kindly. Nossis, *tr. fr. Greek by* Sally Purcell. GrAn

Melissa means honeybee; yes, you're true. Argentarius, *tr. fr. Greek by* Fleur Adcock. GrAn

Melissa where is the golden. In Spite. Rufinus, *tr. fr. Greek by* Alan Marshfield. GrAn

Melissias. Rufinus, *tr. fr. Greek by* Alan Marshfield. GrAn

Melissias denies her love, but her body screams. Rufinus Domesticus, *tr. fr. Greek by* Barbara Hughes Fowler. *Fr.* Epigrams. HePo

Melissias denies she's in love. Melissias. Rufinus Domesticus, *tr. fr. Greek by* Alan Marshfield. GrAn

Mellifluous as bees, these brittle men. On First Looking in on Blodgett's Keats's "Chapman's Homer." George Starbuck. OBAL

Mellisandra. Harriet Rose. BrRo

Mellow as the glory roses. (*LL*) Gloire de Dijon. D. H. Lawrence. CMoP; ELP; EnLoPo; ErPo; GBL; NoAM

Mellow moon hangs golden in the sky, The. October. H. Cordelia Ray. CBWP-3

Mellow sunlight, soothing, warm. Autumn. Marjorie Marshall. ShDr

Mellow the moonlight to shine is beginning. The Spinning-Wheel. John Francis Waller. ChTr

Mellow year is hasting to its close, The. November. Hartley Coleridge. *Fr.* Sonnets to the Seasons. OBNC; PlP

Melmac Year, The. David Hilton. UL

Melodic Trains. John Ashbery. NoP

Melodies. "Lewis Carroll." CBNP

Melodies of Time, The. Thomas Hood. *Fr.* Plea of the Midsummer Fairies, The. OBNC

Melody, A. Lan Ling, *tr. fr. Chinese by* Kenneth Rexroth *and* Ling Chung. WPC

Melon-Slaughterer; or, A Sick Man's Praise for a Well Woman. Robert Peters. BXAP

Melpomene (at whose mischeifous tove). Carmen Elegiacum. Thomas Morton. SCAP

Melpomene, the Muse of tragic songs. Oenone's Complaint. George Peele. *Fr.* Arraignment of Paris, The. EIL

Melrose Abbey. Sir Walter Scott. *Fr.* Lay of the Last Minstrel, The. FaBoPP; OxAEP-2

Melt all the butter. What Her Girl Friend Said to Her Lover on His Return. Kakkai Patiniyar Naccellaiyar, *tr. fr. Tamil by* A. K. Ramanujan. PLW

Melting. Marjorie Appleman. WoWa

Melting, flowing into one. (*LL*) Thought. Christopher Pearse Cranch. WGRP

Melting in thin mist and heavy clouds. Li Ch'ing-chao, *tr. fr. Chinese by* J. P. Seaton. BoWoP

Melting melodious words to lutes of amber. (*LL*) Upon Julia's Voice. Robert Herrick. InPK; JCP; NOBE; SeCP; SoSe

Melting Pot. Michael Echeruo. TTY

Melting Pot, The. Dudley Randall. BPo; NBV

Melton Mowbray Pork Pie, A. Richard Le Gallienne. BXAP

Member of the modern great, A. John Cunningham. FaBoEE

Members of the Orchestra, The. Kevin Hart. NOBAu

Memento for Mortality, A. *At. to* Beaumont, Francis *and* William Basse. Francis Beaumont *and to* William Basse. *See* Mortality [*or* Mortalitie], behold and fear[e]!

Memento of Roads. Nathan Alterman, *tr. fr. Hebrew by* Ruth Finer Mintz. MHP

Mementos, I. W. D. Snodgrass. FF; MoAmPo; UnPo; VCAP

Memling. Roland Mathias. AngWe

Memo. Charles G. Ballard. VoR

Memo. Kenneth Fearing. CMoP; PoE

Memo. Hildegarde Flanner. NYBP

Memo. Charles Lynch. PoBA

Memo from the Desk of X. Donald Justice. TwCP

Memoir. Honor Moore. GLP; PFL

Memoir of a Queen. Helen Hunt Jackson. AmWP

Memoirs, The. Carl Rakosi. PoA

Memoirs, I, *sels.* Margaret Witter Fuller. "In the chamber." CrSp

Memoirs in Oxford., *sels.* F. T. Prince. "Somewhere in Mauriac a girl." PeSAV

Memoirs of a Spinach-Picker. Sylvia Plath. GrPl

Memoirs of a Turcoman Diplomat, *sels.* Denis Devlin. "Evenings ever more willing lapse into my world's evening." IPY; NOIV

Memorabilia. Robert Browning. FHYEP; NAEL-2; NOBVV; NoP; OAEL-2; OBNC; PoE; RB

Men with crew-cuts. Crew-cuts. Donald Hall. MAT

Men with much toil, and time, and pain. Female Wits, The: A Song by a Lady of Quality. *Unknown*. NOSC

Men with the heads of eagles. Margaret Atwood. *Fr.* Circe/ Mud Poems. NoAM

Men with ventilators of black straw, The. Confab. Kenneth Rosen. AmPA

Men would never have come to need an attic. Up There. W. H. Auden. OxBTC

Menace of the Sick. Breyten Breytenbach, *tr. fr. Afrikaans by* Stephen Gray *and* A. J. Coetzee. PeSAV

Menacing machine turns on and off, The. Terror Conduction. Philip Lamantia. NeAP

Ménage à Trois. Howard Moss. VCAP

Menagerie, The. William Vaughn Moody. AnAmPo

Menagerie came to Cape Race, A. *Unknown*. PeLi

Menaphon, *sels*. Robert Greene.
Doron's Description of Samela. PoEL-2
  (Samela.) ElL; GBL; NOBE; OBEV
Doron's Jigge. PoEL-2
  (Jig, A.) ElL
Of His Mistress. ElL
Sephestia's Song to Her Child[e]. ELP; EnRePo; NoSic; OxAEP-1; PoEL-2; TrGrPo
  (Sephestia's Lullaby.) NOBE; OBEV
  (Sephestia's Song.) NTP
  (Weep Not My Wanton.) ElL; SCGP

Mend my broken mood. Prayer for Song. Fay Lewis Noble. TrPWD

Mendacity. A. E. Coppard. OBMV

Mendelian Theory. *Unknown*. FaBoCo

Mending Crab Pots. Dave Jeddie Smith. MT

Mending his broken *tabi* without becoming a Nora. Sugita Hisajo, *tr. fr. Japanese by* Kenneth Rexroth *and* Ikuko Atsumi. WPJ

Mending Sump. Kenneth Koch. BXAP; InPK; MoP; NeAP; NoAM

Mending the Adobe. Hayden Carruth. Poetsp

Mending Wall. Robert Frost. AmPP; AnAmPo; ClHu; CMoP; CoGr; EBEvV; FaBoPV; FaBV; HAP; HeIP; HoPM; ImGa; InPS; LiTA; LiTM; MeMAP; MoAB; MoAmPo; MoP; NAAL-2; NoAM; NOBA; NoP; OtMeF; OxBA; PoE; Poetr; PrIm; SAmP; SCV; SoSe; TAP; TFi; VGW; WeW

Mendocino Rose. Garrett Kaoru Hongo. WeW

Mene, Mene, Tekel, Upharsin. Madison Cawein. PAH

Mennonites. Julia Kasdorf. LoHo; PBCAP

Menodotis. Leonidas of Alexandria, *tr. fr. Greek by* Richard Garnett. AWP

Menoitas of Lyktos. Callimachus, *tr. fr. Greek by* Peter Jay. GrAn

Men's hearts love gold and jade. Lodging with the Old Man of the Stream. Po Chü-i, *tr. fr. Chinese by* Arthur Waley. AWP

Men's Impotence. *Unknown, tr. fr. Eskimo*. WTO

Men's loving is a false affection. *Unknown*. NOIV

Men's Room in the College Chapel, The. W. D. Snodgrass. MoAmPo; PPP

Men's Voices. Inger Christensen, *tr. fr. Danish by* Nadia Christensen. BoWoP

Menstruation at Forty. Anne Sexton. CAPP

Mental Cases. Wilfred Owen. CMoP; FaBoMo; MeMBP; NoAM; PeFWW; PIP

Mental France. Molly Peacock. VBLP

Mental Hospital Garden, The. William Carlos Williams. *Fr.* Garden, The. CRP; FYAP

Mental Traveller, The. Blake. ChIV-2; EnRP; MeMBP; NAEL-2; OAEL-2; OPOP; PoE; PoEL-4

Mentorides, please tell us who. Antipater of Thessalonica, *tr. fr. Greek by* Alistair Elliot. GrAn

Menu. Edward Lear. FaBoNo

Menzi son of Ndaba! Senzangakhona. *Zulu Oral Tradition, tr. by* T. Cope. WTO

Mephisto, *sels*. Uri Zvi Greenberg, *tr. fr. Yiddish by* Robert Friend.

Mer-Man, and Marstig's Daughter, The. *Unknown, tr. fr. Danish by* Robert Jamieson. AWP

Mer-men, First-form. Mary E. O'Donnell. NWP

Mercado. Greg Pape. AmPA

Merce Cunningham and the Birds. Lisel Mueller. GrPl

Merce of Egypt. Charles Olson. NoP

Merced. Adrienne Rich. NOBA

Mercedes, Her Aloneness. Colette Inez. IHMS

Mercenaries & Minstrels. Jayne Cortez. BCF

Mercenary like Rolf Steiner, A. Mercenaries & Minstrels. Jayne Cortez. BCF

Merchant and the Fidler's Wife, The. *Unknown*. CoMu; OxBB

Merchant, as crafty a man is he, The. Do You Plan to Speak Bantu? Ogden Nash. FiBHP

Merchant at Yokohama, The. Osman Edwards. *Fr.* Residential Rhymes. OBTV

Merchant Marine. Josephine Miles. TAP; VGW

Merchant of Venice, The, *sels*. Shakespeare.
All That Glisters Is Not Gold. CTC
Fire Seven Times Tried This, The. CTC
"Go, draw aside the curtain, and discover." OxAEP-1
"How sweet the moonlight sleeps upon this bank!" FaBoRV; OxAEP-1; TrGrPo
"In sooth, I know not why I am so sad." OxAEP-1
Let Me Play the Fool. TrGrPo
"Moon shines bright, The. In such a night as this." GBL
  (In Such a Night.) ChTr
Power of Music, The. GN
"Quality of mercy is not strained, The." EBEvV; ImPo; LiTB
  (Mercy.) TrGrPo; WBLP
"Tell Me Where Is Fancy [or Fancie] Bred." CH; EIL; ELP; EnRePo; LiTB; NAEL-1; NoSic; OAEL-1; SCGP; TFi
  (Fancy.) FaPON; 08TreFS; TrGrPo
  (Love.) OBEV
  (Madrigal: "Tell me where is fancy bred.") GTBS; GTBS-P
  (Song: "Tell me where is fancy bred.") CTC; PoEL-2
  (Song.) EBEvV

Merchant Shipping Act, The. *Unknown*. OxBSS

Merchant, to secure his treasure, The. Matthew Prior. AWP; EnLoPo; GTBS; GTBS-P; NOEC; NoP; PoRA
  (Song: "Merchant, to secure his treasure, The." OBEV; TrGrPo

Merchants from Cathay. William Rose Benét. MoAmPo

Merchants have multiplied more than the stars of heaven. The Executive's Death. Robert Bly. CoAP; NaP

Merchants of London, The. Mother Goose. *See* Hey diddle dinkety, poppety, pet.

Merchant's Tale, The. Chaucer. *Fr.* Canterbury Tales, The. EnVB; OxBM

Mercian Hymns, *sels*. Geoffrey Hill.
"And it seemed, while we waited, he began to walk." NoAM; NoP
"At Pavia, a visitation of some sorrow. Boethius' dungeon." FaBoMo
"Brooding on the eightieth letter of *Fors Clavigera*." HAP; PoE
"Clash of salutation. As keels thrust into shingle." NoAM; NoP
"Coins handsome as Nero's; of good substance and weight." FaBoMo; HAP; NoAM
"Dismissing reports and men, he put pressure on the wax." HAP
"Gasholders, russet among fields." HAP; NoAM; NoP
"He adored the desk, its brown-oak inlaid with ebony." HAP; NoAM; NoP
"I was invested in mother-earth, the crypt of roots." NoAM
"King of the perennial holly-groves, the riven sandstone." FaBoMo; HAP; NoAM
"Mad are predators, The. Too often lately they harbor." NoP
"Not strangeness, but strange likeness." FaBoMo; HAP; NoAM
"On the morning of the crowning we chorused our remission from school." HAP
"Pet-name, a common name. Best-selling brand, curt, A." NoAM
"Princes of Mercia were badger and raven, The." HAP; NAEL-2; NoAM; NoP; PoE
"Processes of generation; deeds of settlement." NoP
"So much for the elves' wergild, the true governance." NoAM
"Strange church smelled a bit 'high,' of censers, The." PoE
"Their spades grafted through the variably-resistant." PoE
"Trim the lamp; polish the lens; draw, one by one, rare coins." FaBoMo
"We ran across the meadow scabbed with the cow-dung." HAP

Mercies of the Year, The. John Danforth. SCAP

Merciful Shore, The. Maria Luisa Spaziani, *tr. fr. Italian by* Beverly Allen. NeIt

Merciles[s] Beaute [*or* Beautée *or* Beauty]. Chaucer. CTC; EBEV; EnLoPo; HAP; NoP
Sels.
"And it seemed, while we waited, he began to walk." NoAM; NoP
Merciless Beauty. BoLoP; EnVB, *mod. vers.*; NAEL-1; SCGP, (*mod. vers.*)
  (Rondel of Merciles Beaute, A.) TrGrPo
  (Rondel of Merciless Beauty, A, (*mod. vers. by* Louis Untermeyer).) TrGrPo

Merciless love, whom nature hath denied. John Fletcher. *Fr.* Chances, The. GBL

Mercury. Naomi Segal. VBLP

Mercury and Cupid. Matthew Prior. PeLV

Mercury Bay Eclogue. M. K. Joseph. PeNZ

Mercury; on Losing My Pocket Milton at Luss near Ben Lomond, and Other Mountains. Robert Andrews. NOEC

Mercury shew'd Apollo, Bartas Book. Nathaniel Ward. SCAP

Mercury's Song [to Phaedra]. Dryden. *See* Fair Iris I love, and hourly I die.

Mercutio Describes Queen Mab. Shakespeare. *See* She is the fairies' midwife, and she comes.

Mercutio's Queen Mab Speech. Shakespeare. *See* O [*or* Oh], then, I see Queen Mab hath been with you.

Mercy. Olga Broumas. PFL

Mercy. Andrew Lansdown. NOBAu

Mercy. Shakespeare. *See* Quality of mercy is not strained, The.

Mercy, a Healing, Psalm 64, A. Daniel Berrigan. EaPr

Mercy abid and loke all day. *Unknown.* MiEL

Mercy and Love. Robert Herrick. SeCV-1

Mercy is whiter than laundry. Angels in Winter. Nancy Willard. LCAP

Mercy Pleads for Mankind. Giles Fletcher the Younger. *Fr.* Christ's Victory and Triumph. JCP

Mere ants and gnats and trivia with stings. Palladas, *tr. fr. Greek by* Tony Harrison. GrAn

Mere chance that the patterned lute has fifty strings. The Patterned Lute. Li Shang-yin, *tr. fr. Chinese by* A. C. Graham. PLT

Meredith Phyfe. Edgar Lee Masters. *Fr.* New Spoon River, The. GOA

Merida, 1969. William Matthews. EOEF

Meridian. David St. John. NAmP90

Meridians are a net. Objects. Richard Wilbur. FF; NoP

Merie sungen the muneches binnen Ely. Cnut's Song. *Unknown. Fr.* Canute at Ely. PoE

Merioneth. John Machreth Rees, *tr. fr. Welsh by* Kenneth Hurlstone Jackson. OBWVE

Merit of True Passion, The. *At. to* Sir Robert Ayton. *See* Wrong Not, Sweete Empress of My Heart.

Merit will live, though parties disagree! (*LL*) To Wordsworth. John Clare. OAEL-2; Son

Merlin. Emerson. AmPP; NOBA
Sels.
Merlin ("Rhyme of the poet, The"). AmPP; NOBA; PoEL-4
Merlin ("Thy trivial harp will never please"). AmPP; NAAL-2; NOBA; OxBA

Merlin. Geoffrey Hill. InPK; TRP

Merlin. Edwin Muir. FaBoTw; OxBS; RB

Merlin. David St. John. BAP-91

Merlin and the Gleam. Tennyson. FHYEP; NTP; OAEL-2

Merlin and the Snake's Egg. Leslie Norris. OBSP

Merlin and Vivien. Tennyson. *Fr.* Idylls of the King.

Merlin Enthralled. Richard Wilbur. CMoP; NYBP

Merlin's Riddling. Tennyson. *Fr.* Idylls of the King. FaBoRV

Mermaid, The. Ben King. AnAmPo; OBAL

Mermaid, The. Lisel Mueller. CrSp

Mermaid, The. Ogden Nash. Spl

Mermaid, The. Tennyson. BoTP, *ll.* 1–14; FaPON; GN

Mermaid, The ("As we lay musing in our beds"). *Unknown. See* As we lay musing in our beds.

Mermaid, The ("One Friday morn"). *Unknown.* AmFP; CH; ESPB

Mermaid, The ("To you fausse stream"). *Unknown.* CH

Mermaid Tavern, The. *At. to* Keats Keats. *See* Souls of poets dead and gone.

Mermaiden, A. Thomas Hennell. FaBoTw

Mermaidens, The. Laura E. Richards. OBCA

Mermaidens' Vesper-Hymn, The. George Darley. *Fr.* Syren Songs. GBL; NAEL-2; OBNC; PoEL-4

Mermaids, The. Spenser. *Fr.* Faerie Queene, The. ChTr

Merman, The. Tennyson. BoTP, *ll.* 1–20; FaPON; GN; UV, (*ll.* 1–20)

Merops. Emerson. OxBA

Merrily, merrily,/ All the spring. Merry Birds. Rodney Bennett. BoTP

Merrily swinging on brier and weed. Robert of Lincoln. Bryant. EAP; FaBoBe; FaPON; OBCA; WBLP, *abr*

Merritt Parkway. Denise Levertov. AmPP; NeAP; PoM

Merry Are the Bells. *Unknown.* MoShBr

Merry Bagpipes, The. *Unknown.* CoMu

Merry Birds. Rodney Bennett. BoTP

Merry Country Lad, The. Nicholas Breton. *Fr.* Passionate Shepherd, The. ElL; NoSic

Merry Cuckold, The. *Unknown.* CoMu

Merry-go-round. Langston Hughes. PoNe

Merry-go-round. Oliver Jenkins. GoYe

Merry-go-round. James McAuley. CBAP

Merry-go-round, The. Rainer Maria Rilke, *tr. fr. German by* C. F. MacIntyre. WeW

Merry have we met. A Party Song. *Unknown.* BoTP

Merry Hay-Makers; or, Pleasant Pastime between the Young-Men and Maids, in the Pleasant Meadows, The. *Unknown.* CoMu; ErPo

Merry Heart, The [*or* A]. Shakespeare. *See* Jog on, jog on, the footpath way.

Merry Hoastess, The. *Unknown.* CoMu

Merry It Is. *Unknown.* HAP
(How Long This Night Is, *medieval vers.*) MeEL
(Mirie it is, while sumer ilast.) HAP; MeEL; MiEL

Merry it is in May morning. By a Chapel as I Came. *Unknown.* ChTr; GBP

Merry it is. (*LL*) By a Chapel as I Came. *Unknown.* ChTr; GBP

Merry it is in the good greenwood. Alice Brand. Sir Walter Scott. *Fr.* Lady of the Lake, The. BeLS
(Ballad: Alice Brand.) OxAEP-2

Merry Jovial Beggar, The. Peter Casey, *tr. fr. Irish by* Douglas Hyde. TIRV; WTO

Merry Little Maid and Wicked Little Monk, The. *Unknown.* ErPo

Merry Little Men. Kathleen M. Chaplin. BoTP

Merry-ma-Tanzie, The. *Unknown.* GBP

Merry March wind is a boisterous fellow, The. The March Wind. E. H. Henderson. BoTP

Merry mate amongst the rest, of cloisterers thus told, A. A Tale of the Beginning of Friars and Cloisterers. William Warner. *Fr.* Albion's England. NoSic

Merry May the Keel Row. *Unknown.* GBP

Merry may the maid be. The Miller. Sir John Clerk. ChTr

Merry, merry sparrow! The Blossom. Blake. *Fr.* Songs of Innocence. FHYEP; GoJo

Merry Month of March, The. Wordsworth. *See* Cock is crowing, The.

Merry Note, A. Shakespeare. *See* When icicles hang by the wall.

Merry [*or* Mirry] Margaret,/ As midsummer flower. To Mistress [*or* Maystres] Margaret Hussey. John Skelton. *Fr.* Garland [*or* Garlande *or* Garlands] of Laurel[l], The. AAS; EBEV; EnLoPo; GGP; GN; GoJo; HoPM; InPS; NAEL-1; NBLV; NOBE; NoP; NoSic; NTP; OAEL-1; OBEV; OPOP; PeLV; PlP; PoE; PoEL-1; PoRA; PPP; SCGP; SCV; TFi; TrGrPo
(Mistress Margaret Hussey.) FaBoCh

Merry the green, the green hill shall be merry. Another Song. Donald Justice. VGW
(Tune for a Lonesome Fife.) NYBP

Merry wind danced over the hill, A. Such a Blustery Day! Elizabeth Gould. BoTP

Merry [*or* Merrie] World did on a day, The. The Quip. George Herbert. GeHe; JCP; LiTB; NOSC; OxAEP-1; SeCP; SeCV-1

Merthe of all this land, The. God Speed the Plough! *Unknown.* EnVB

Merthyr. Glyn Jones. AngWe

Mertill though my heart should break. To Mertill Who Desired Her to Speak to Clorinda of His Love. Elizabeth Taylor. KTR

Meru. W. B. Yeats. NoAM; OAEL-2; PoA

Mery Gest How a Sergeaunt Wolde Lerne to Be A Frere, A. Sir Thomas More. AAS

Mery it is in May morning. *Unknown.* MiEL

Mery it was in grene forest. Adam Bel [*or* Bell], Clym [*or* Clim] of the Clough[e], and Wyllyam [*or* William] of Cloudesle [*or* Cloudesly]. *Unknown.* ESPB; OxBB

Meseem'd that Love, with swifter feet than fire. An Utter Passion Uttered Utterly. John Todhunter. BXAP

Meseemeth I heard cry and groan. The Complaint of the Fair Armoress [*or* Armouress]. Villon, *tr. fr. French by* Swinburne. AWP; CTC; OBVE

Mesembryanthemum and Zauschneria. Sandra McPherson. FoLa

Mesh cast for mackerel. Fishermen. Basil Bunting. PoA

Meshed in a glow of nickel, glass. Ballad of the Drinker in His Pub. N. P. van Wyk Louw, *tr. fr. Afrikaans by* Uys Krige, Jack Cope, *and* Ruth Miller. PeSA

Mesnevi. Sadi, *tr. by* L. Cranmer-Byng. *Fr.* Gulistan, The. AWP

Mesón Brujo. E. A. Lacey. PeHV

Mesopotamia. Kipling. PoWW

Mess Deck. Alan Ross. PoWW

Mess of Love, The. D. H. Lawrence. ArLo; CBLP; OAEL-2

Message, A. Fleur Adcock. DiPo

Message, The. Jeni Couzyn. NBrP

Message, The. Georg Friedrich Daumer, *tr. fr. German by* Philip L. Miller. RiWo

Message, The. John Donne. ElL; MeLP

Message. Allen Ginsberg. NeAP; VGW

Message, The. Heine, *tr. fr. German by* Kate Freiligrath Kroeker. AWP

Message, A. George Ives. PeHV

Message. Renata Pallottini, *tr. fr. Portuguese by* Monique *and* Carlos Altschul. WPOW

Message, The. Jacques Prévert, tr. fr. French by John Frederick Nims. WeW

Message. Dorothy M. Richardson. PoA

Message, A. Elizabeth Stuart Phelps Ward. PAH

Message for Langston, A. "Kush." NBV

Message from a Cross. Max Harris. NOBAu

Message from a secretary tells me first, A. Elegy for Frank Stanford. Thomas Lux. AnAn

Message from her set his brain aflame, A. George Meredith. Fr. Modern Love. EnVR; NOBVV

Message from Home. Kathleen Raine. WPE

Message from Ohanapecosh Glacier. W. M. Ransom. CDW

Message of King Sakis and the Legend of the Twelve Dreams He Had in One Night, The. Unknown, tr. fr. Serbo-Croatian by Charles Simic. HSix

Message of Peace, A. Longfellow. Fr. Arsenal at Springfield, The. AmPP; WBLP

Message of the March Wind, The. William Morris. OBNC; WiR

Message of the men is linear, The. The Message. Jeni Couzyn. NBrP

Message on Cape Cod, The. Michael S. Weaver. PBCAP

Message to a Loved One Dead, A. Josephine D. Henderson Heard. CBWP-4

Message to Siberia. Pushkin, tr. fr. Russian by Max Eastman. AWP; TTY

Messages, The. W. W. Gibson. OHIP

Messages. Jack A. Mapanje. HBAPE

Messages. Francis Thompson. CH; OtMeF

Messages come through at last, The. Fort Wayne. Jack Spicer. CBNP

Messe of Nonsense, A. Unknown. CBNP; NOSC

Messenger, The. Frances Horovitz. BrRo

Messenger, The, sels. Thomas Kinsella. "Inside, it is bare but dimly alive." CIP

Messenger, The. Grace Schulman. AnAn

Messenger from Rome. A Defence of Poetry. Giolla Brighde Mac Con Midhe. NOIV

Messenger, hear what I say. Reinmar der Alte, tr. fr. German by J. W. Thomas. GePo

Messenger of Sympathy and Love. The Meaning of a Letter. Unknown. PoToHe

Messengers, The. Steve Chimombo. HBAPE

Messengers. Louise Glück. AnAn; HCAP; VCAP

Messengers, The. Thom Gunn. PoA

Messengers, The. H. Cordelia Ray. CBWP-3

Messengers finally arrived and said, The. Barbarians. Jovan Hristic, tr. fr. Serbo-Croatian by Charles Simic. HSix

Messiah, The. Bible, O.T. Fr. Isaiah. AWP

Messiah, sels. Pope. Rise, Crowned with Light Imperial Salem Rise. WGRP

Messiah, The. Virgil, tr. fr. Latin. Fr. Eclogues. AWP, tr. by Dryden

Messiah: A Sacred Eclogue in Imitation of Virgil's Pollio. Pope. ChIV-1

Messmates. Sir Henry Newbolt. CH; EBVV; OHCV; PeVV

Met in the milder shades of Purgatory. (LL) To Mr. H. Lawes on His Airs. Milton. AWP; NoP

Meta-A and the A of Absolutes. Jay Wright. TRP

Meta-social, The. Lecture. Anselm Hollo. UL

Metal I, the soul the hearth, the blaze that warms, The. The Spiritual Alchemy. "Angelus Silesius," tr. fr. German. Fr. Cherubical Wanderer, The. GePo, tr. by George C. Schoolfield

Metal of the footpath is, The. On Leaving the Footpath. John James. NBrP; VaA

Metal smokestack, The. Exercise No. 2. William Carlos Williams. SAmP

Metallic weight of iron, The. De Profundis. Walter de la Mare. OBD

Metamorpho I. Joe Rosenblatt. MoCV

Metamorphopsia, sels. Norma Cole. "I think of him as a house and as an ordeal." VBLP

Metamorphoses. Roy Fuller. OxBTC

Metamorphoses. Howard Nemerov. HCAP

Metamorphoses, sels. Ovid, tr. fr. Latin. Acteon. CTC "And from the Citie Tegea there came the Paragone." OBVE Baucis and Philemon. NOSC Ceyx and Alcyone. NoSic Daedalus. CTC; OBVE Daphne and Apollo. NOEC Death of Eurydice and Orpheus' Journey to Hell, The. JCP "Floods, by nature enemies to land, The." OBVE, tr. by Dryden Flood, The ChTr "I pray thee Nymph Penaeis stay, I chase not as a fo." OBVE "In the Shire of Phestos hard by Cnossus dwelt of yore." PeHV King Midas. CTC

Magic. AWP, tr. by Shakespeare Medea's Incantation OBVE, tr. by Arthur Golding Meleager. CTC "More whyght thou art than primrose leaf my Lady Galatee." OBVE, tr. by Arthur Golding (Cyclops.) CTC, tr. by Arthur Golding "My intention is to tell of bodies changed." NAWM-1 "Near the Cymmerians, in his dark abode." OBVE "Neare Enna walles there standes a Lake Pergusa is the name." OBVE "Northern breath, that freezes floods, he binds, The." OBVE "Not Pallas, not ev'n Spleen it self could blame." OBVE "Now have I brought a woork to end which neither Joves fierce [or feerce] wrath." OBVE (Conclusion.) CTC "Now whyle Hippomenes/ Debates theis things." OBVE, tr. by Arthur Golding Of the Pythagorean Philosophy "But this by sure experiment we know." FM "This let me further add, that nature knows" OBVE Philemon and Baucis. CTC "Heaven's power is infinite; earth, air, and sea" OAEL-1, tr. by Dryden "Then Lelex rose, an old experienced man" AWP, tr. by Dryden; OBVE, tr. by Dryden Phoenix Self-born, The. ChTr "Pygmalion seeing these to spend their times." OAEL-1, tr. by George Sandys Pygmalion's Statue Comes to Life. OAEL-1 "Seeing as the father saw the rosy morn." OBVE "Stones (a miracle to mortal view), The." OBVE "Then sprang up first the golden age, which of itself maintained." NAEL-1 (Golden Age, The.) OAEL-1 "Then thus the sire of gods, with look serene." OBD "There was a man here, Samian born, but he." NAWM-1 "To thee obeyeth all the East as far as Ganges goes." OBVE

Metamorphoses of M. John Peale Bishop. ErPo

Metamorphoses of the Vampire. Baudelaire, tr. by Jackson Mathews. ErPo

Metamorphosis. Sylvia Plath. PoA

Metamorphosis. Peter Porter. OxBTC

Metamorphosis. May Sarton. ArNa

Metamorphosis. Wallace Stevens. InPK; VGW

Metamorphosis, The. Sir John Suckling. CaPo; FaBoEE

Metamorphosis of Aunt Jemima, The. William Childress. MAT

Metamorphosis of Pygmalion's Image, The, sels. John Marston. "O gracious gods, take compassion." OAEL-1

Metamorphosis of the Carnation, sels. Rafael Alberti, tr. fr. Spanish by Mark Strand. "I went away." AnAn

Metaphor as Degeneration. Wallace Stevens. LCAP

Metaphor as Illness. Chuck Ortleb. GLP

Metaphor for My Son. John Holmes. ImGa

Metaphors. Sylvia Plath. HeIL; HeIP; InPK; Poetr; SoSe

Metaphors of a Magnifico. Wallace Stevens. SOTW

Metaphysic of Snow. Donald Finkel. PoA

Metaphysical. Robert Fitzgerald. PoA

Metaphysical Amorist, The. J. V. Cunningham. VGW

Metaphysical Sectarian, The. Samuel Butler. Fr. Hudibras. MeLP; PeLV

Metaphysician. Robert Fitzgerald. PoA

Metaphysics. Oliver Herford. CBNP

Metempsychosis. Kenneth Slessor. NOBAu

Meteor of the war., The. (LL) The Portent. Herman Melville. AmPP; AnAmPo; InPK; NAAL-1; NOBA; NoP; OBWP; OxBA; PoE; PoEL-5; PrIm; TAP; WiR

Meteor's arc of quiet, The; a voiceless rain. Faint Music. Walter de la Mare. FaBoCh

Metevsky said to the one side. The Profiteer. Ezra Pound. NSI

Methinks all things have travelled since you shined. On the Sun Coming Out in the Afternoon. Thoreau. OxBSP; PoEL-4

Methinks already, from this chymick flame. The New London. Dryden. Fr. Annus Mirabilis. FaBoCh (London after the Great Fire, 1666.) FaBoEH; NOBE

Methinks, dear Tom, I see thee stand demure. To the Revd. Mr. —— on His Drinking Sea-Water. John Winstanley. NOEC

Methinks Death like one laughing lyes. Epitaph. Caecil. Boulstr. Lord Herbert of Cherbury. SeCP

Methinks heroick poesie till now. To Sir William Davenant, Upon His Two First Books of Gondibert. Abraham Cowley. SeCV-1

Methinks How Dainty Sweet It Were. Charles Lamb. Son

Methinks I am a prophet new inspir'd. John of Gaunt's Dying Speech. Shakespeare. Fr. King Richard II. FaBoEH

Methinks I see great Diocletian walk. Great Diocletian. Abraham Cowley. *Fr.* Garden, The. ChTr

Methinks I See Some Crooked Mimic Jeer. Michael Drayton. *Fr.* Idea. ESo; Son

Methinks I see with what a busy haste. On Zacchaeus [*or* Zacheus]. Francis Quarles. NOSC; OxBSP

Methinks I spy Almighty holding in. Edward Taylor. *Fr.* Preparatory Meditations Before My Approach to the Lord's Supper. HAP

Methinks it is no journey. (*LL*) Tom o' Bedlam. *Unknown.* CH; CoGr; FaBoCh; PoRA

Methinks the poor town has been troubled too long. Charles Sackville. SeCV-2

Methinks This Heart. Emily Brontë. MeMBP

Methinks thou writhest as in rage. To a Worm Which the Author Accidentally Trode Upon. William Hawkins. FM

Methinks 'Tis Pretty Sport [to Hear a Child]. Thomas Bastard. ElL; InvP

Methinks, 'tis strange you can't afford. The Forsaken Wife. Elizabeth Thomas. ECWP

Method, The. J. D. McClatchy. EOEF

Method must be purest meat, The. On Burroughs' Work. Allen Ginsberg. NAAL-2; NOBA; PoBeRe

Method of Preserving Hay from Being Mow-Burnt, or Taking Fire, A. Robert Dodsley. *Fr.* Agriculture. FaBoUs

Methode Champenoise. Steve Carey. UL

Methodist, The. Thomas Chatterton. ECEV

Methodist, The, *sels.* Evan Lloyd.
   Religion and the Lower Classes. NOEC
   "Sons of War sometimes are known, The." OBSV

Methods of Cooking Trout. Thomas Barker. *Fr.* Art of Angling, The. FaBoUs

Methought I lived in the icy times forlorn. Great Britain Through the Ice: Or, Premature Patriotism. Charles Tennyson Turner. Son

Methought I saw/ Life swiftly treading over endless space. The Sea of Death. Thomas Hood. LiTB; OBNC; PoEL-4

Methought I Saw. Milton. *See* Methought I saw my late espoused saint.

Methought I saw, as I did dream in bed. Robert Herrick. *See* Methought I saw (as I did dream in bed).

Methought I saw (as I did dream in bed). The Vision. Robert Herrick. CaPo
   (Methought I saw, as I did dream in bed.) NOSC

Methought I saw my late espoused saint. On His Deceased Wife. Milton. BLPL; CBLP; ImPo; LiTB; OBEV; OxBM; PoE; SCV; TEP; TFi
   ("Methought I saw my late espoused saint.") BoLoP; EnLoPo; IMW; NAEL-1; PeECV; SCGP
   (Methought I Saw.) NoP; Son
   (On His Dead Wife.) GBL; HAP; NOBE; WeW
   (On His Late Wife.) PoEL-3
   (Sonnet: "Methought I saw my late espoused saint.") EBEV; NOSC; OAEL-1

Methought I saw the grave where Laura lay. A Vision upon This Conceit of the Faerie [*or* Fairy] Queene [*or* Queen]. Sir Walter Ralegh. *Fr.* Commendatory Verses to Edmund Spenser's Fairy Queen. NAEL-1; NoSic; SCGP; SiPSBD; Son
   (Of Spenser's Faery Queen.) SiPS

Methought I stood where trees of every clime. A Dream. Keats. *Fr.* Fall of Hyperion, The. OAEL-2; OBNC

Methought, one night, I saw, in trance sublime. A Vision of Sunday in Heaven. Victor James Daley. ChIV-2

Methought That I Had Broken from the Tower. Shakespeare. *Fr.* King Richard III. RB

Methuselah ("Methuselah ate what he found on his plate.") *Unknown.* BLPA; BLPL; FaBoBe

Meticulous, past midnight in clear rime. Hart Crane. *Fr.* Voyages (I–VI). CMoP; MeMAP; NAAL-2; NoAM; NOBA; NoP; PoE; TAP

Metonymy as an Approach to a Real World. William Bronk. VGW

Metre Colombian, The. *Unknown.* BXAP; UV

Metric Figure. William Carlos Williams. MoAB; MoAmPo

Metrical Feet. Samuel Taylor Coleridge. FaBoUs; FHYEP; NIP; OxBChV; Poetr, *ll.* 1–6 *only*

Metrical Index to the Bible, A, *sels.* Josiah Chorley.
   "All things created, Moses writes." FaBoUs

Metrical Version of the Bible, Said to Have Been Composed by a Negro Christian in the State of Massachusetts, and Published in Louisville, Kentucky, in 1858, A, *sels.* *Unknown.*
   "Adam was de first man and Eve was de udder." FaBoUs

Metropolitan/ Museum of/ Art, The. Miss Pimberton Of. Siv Cedering. PBCAP

Metropolitan Nightmare. Stephen Vincent Benét. NYBP

Metropolitan Railway, The. Sir John Betjeman. EBEV; OxAEP-2; OxBTC

Mew . . . mew . . . mew. (*LL*) The Mysterious Cat. Vachel Lindsay. ChTr; FaPON; GoJo; OBCA; OFC; SiSoPo; SoCa

Mews Flat Mona. William Plomer. FaBoTw

Mexican dwarfs can dance for miles, The. Maxixe. Sir Osbert Sitwell. PoA

Mexican hat dance is performed around a sombrero, a broad-, The. Hats Around the World. Maxine Chernoff. PRA

Mexican Serenade. Arthur Guiterman. FiBHP

Mexicans Begin Jogging. Gary Soto. NGP

Mexico, *sels.* Robert Lowell.
   "Difficulties, the impossibilities, The." HCAP
   "South of Boston, south of Washington." HCAP

Mexico, 1940. Ai. NoAM

Mexico, August 20, 1940. Ai. NoAM

Mexico City Blues., *sels.* Jack Kerouac.
   "And how sweet a story it is." PoBeRe
   "Big Engines, The." NeAP
   "Charlie Parker looked like Buddha." Jaz; PoBeRe
   "Essence of Existence, The." NeAP
   "Glenn Miller and I were heroes." NeAP
   "Got up and dressed up." NeAP
   "In the ocean there's a very sad turtle." PoM
   "Love's multitudinous boneyard." NeAP
   "Musically as important as Beethoven." PoBeRe
   "Nobody knows the other side." NeAP
   "Old Man Mose." Jaz; NeAP
   "Only awake to Universal Mind." NeAP
   "Praised be man, he is existing in milk." NeAP
   "Saints, I give myself up to thee." NeAP
   "Sound in your mind, The." PoBeRe
   "Void that's highly embraceable, The." NeAP
   "Wheel of the quivering Meat, The." NeAP; PoBeRe; PoM

Mexico Is a Foreign Country: Four Studies in Naturalism, *sels.* Robert Penn Warren.
   Mango on the Mango Tree, The. MoP; NoAM

Mezzo Cammin. Longfellow. NAAL-1; NoP; PoE; TAP

Mezzo Cammin. Judith Moffett. SM

Mezzo Forte. William Carlos Williams. SAmP

M'Fingal, *sels.* John Trumbull.
   "At once with resolution held." AmPP
   "Rise then, ere ruin swift surprize." GOA

Mia Carlotta. T. A. Daly. NBLV

Miami Rastas. Alurista. ETG

Mica, if you peel carefully. Earth Angel. Jeffrey Skinner. PBCAP

Mica shines on the beach. Extract. Paul Bowles. PoA

Micah, *sels.* Bible, *O.T.*
   "But in the last days it shall come to pass." PAW
   Woe Is Me! TrJP

Mice. Rose Fyleman. BoTP; FaPON; NTCP; PDV; SiSoPo

Mice in the garbage. For Rosa Yen, Who Lived Here. Greg Pape. AmPA

Mice in the Hay. Leslie Norris. OBCP; PChr

Mice masticate from crumb to tooth. Repast. Gertrude Tiemer-Wille. GoYe

Michael. Wordsworth. EnRP; FHYEP; NAEL-2; OAEL-2; OxAEP-2

Michael, Archangel of the King of Kings. A Sequence for Saint Michael. Alcuin, *tr. fr. Irish by* Helen Waddell. TIRV

Michael Met a Duck. J. Dupuy. BoTP

Michael Robartes and the Dancer. W. B. Yeats. OAEL-2

Michael Robartes Bids His Beloved Be at Peace. W. B. Yeats. MoP; NoAM

Michael wants to. Systems Alert. Marael Johnson. NGP

Michaelmas. Norman Nicholson. MoBrPo

Michael's Song. W. W. Gibson. BoTP; NTP

Michal her modest flames sought to conceal. Abraham Cowley. *Fr.* Davideis. ChIV-1

Micheál Mac Liammóir. Paul Durcan. PBCIP

Michigan Ghosttown, A. Brad Leithauser. NGP

Michigan-I-O. *Unknown.* AmFP

Micmac woman's body has been disinterred and her, The. Report on Her Remains. Daniel David Moses. HATNAP

Microbe's Serenade, The. George Ade. OBAL

Microbiblion, *sels.* At. to Simon Wastell.
   Man's Mortality. FaBoCh

Microcosmos. Susan Miles. OxBTC

Microcosmus, *sels.* Thomas Nabbes.

Micromutations. James Wright. NYBP

Microscope. Gwyn Thomas, *tr. fr. Welsh by* Joseph P. Clancy. OBWVE

Microscope in Winter, The. Sandra McPherson. LCAP; VCAP

'Mid all the ceaseless rush of life. Refuge. Mabel E. McCartney. BLRP

Mid-August at Sourdough Mountain Lookout. Gary Snyder. HAP; InPK; MAT; NaP; NoP; PoBeRe; TAP; VCAP

Mid-Country Blow. Theodore Roethke. BoNaP

Midst the fair range of buildings which, new-reared. George Keate. *Fr.* Burlesque Ode, on the Author's Clearing a New House of Some Workmen, A. NOEC

Midstream. D. J. Enright. OxBC

Midstream. Mao Tse-tung, *tr. fr. Chinese by* Earle Birney. MoCV

Midsummer. Claire Collett. Jaz

Midsummer. Robert Fitzgerald. PoA

Midsummer. Kevin Hart. FaBoMA

Midsummer. Thomas Kinsella. IPY

Midsummer. Sydney King Russell. BLPA; FaBoBe

Midsummer. James Scully. NYBP; TwCP

Midsummer. Derek Walcott. NAEL-2

Midsummer, *sels.* Derek Walcott.
"Rest, Christ! from tireless war. See, it's midsummer." TOF

Midsummer, *sels.* Derek Walcott.
"Camps held their distance of brown chestnuts and grey smoke, The." BTR

Midsummer Day in France. Alexander Hume. *Fr.* Of the Day Estivall. FaBoPP; NOCV; OxBS; ScCV

Midsummer Jingle. Newman Levy. BoNaP

Midsummer Moon. "E. M. G. R." BoTP

Midsummer Night. Elizabeth Gould. BoTP

"Midsummer Night's Dream, A" in Regent's Park. Derwent May. Mes

Midsummer Night's Dream, A, *sels.* Shakespeare.
Bottom's Dream. CBNP
Bottom's Song. CTC
Flower of This Purple Dye. CTC
Helena and Hermia. GN; OBF
"How now, spirit! whither wander you?" GN
"Injurious Hermia, most ungrateful maid." OBF
Love-in-Idleness. TrGrPo
"Lunatic, the lover, and the poet, The." EBEvV
(Asleep, My Love?) CTC
Lunatic, the Lover, and the Poet, The
(Imagination.) ImPo; LiTB
Now the Hungry Lion. CH; ChTr; CTC; EiL; EnRePo; LiTB
(Fairy Blessing, The.) OxBoLi
(Fairy Songs ("Now the hungry lion roars.").) TrGrPo
(Lion of Winter, The.) WiR
(Puck's Song.) MoShBr
Now, Until the Break of Day. NAs
(Fairy Songs ("Now, until the break of day.").) TrGrPo
"Ousel cock, so black of hue, The." NoSic
Over Hill, over Dale. EiL
(Fairy Land, 1.) OBEV
(Fairy Song ("Over hill, over dale").) NOBE; TrGrPo
(Fairy's Wander-Song.) FaPON
(Puck and the Fairy.) GN
(Song: "Over hill, over dale.") InvP
Poetic Frenzy. EPCY
Sunrise on the Sea. ChTr
Through the Forest Have I Gone. CTC
Through the House. CTC
(Oberon and Titania to the Fairy Train.) GN
Up and Down. CTC
Violet Bank, A. FaPON
(I know a place whereon the wild thyme blows.) BoNaP
(Where the Wild Thyme Blows.) TrGrPo
Yet but Three? CTC
"You spotted snakes [with double tongue]." BoTP; InvP; LiTB; NOBE; NoSic; PoRA; SCGP
(Fairies' Lullaby, The.) EiL
(Fairy Land, 2.) OBEV
(Fairy Lullaby.) FaPON
(Fairy Songs ("You spotted snakes with double tongue.").) TrGrPo
(Lullaby for Titania.) GN

Midsummer Song, A. Richard Watson Gilder. BoNaP

Midsummer stretches before me with a cat's yawn. Port of Spain. Derek Walcott. NoAM

Midway. Naomi Long Madgett. BlSi; BPo; PoNe

Midway between Mecca and Medina. To a Hero Dead at al-Safra. Hind bint Uthatha, *tr. fr. Arabic by* Bridget Connelly *and* Deirdre Lashgari. WPOW

Midway in our life's journey, I went astray. Inferno. Dante, *tr. fr. Italian. Fr.* Divina Commedia. MeMAP; NAWM-1, *tr. by* John Ciardi

Midway the hill of science, after steep. To Mr. S. T. Coleridge. Anna Laetitia Barbauld. NOEC; WoRP
(To Mr. C — ge.) ECWP

Midways of a walled garden. William Morris. *Fr.* Golden Wings. ChTr; OBNC

Midweek. Josephine Miles. NoP

Midwife Cat. Mark Van Doren. CRH

Midwife laid her hand on his thick skull, The. Thomas Shadwell the Poet. John Dryden *and* Nahum Tate. *Fr.* Absalom and Achitophel, Pt. II. ChTr

Midwife puts a rag in the dead woman's hand, The. Obedience of the Corpse. C. D. Wright. LCAP; MT

Midwife's Story; Two, A. Anne Szumigalski. NOBC

Midwinter. Margaret E. Bruner. PoToHe

Midwinter. John Townsend Trowbridge. AnAmPo; GN

Midwinter spring is its own season. Little Gidding. T. S. Eliot. *Fr.* Four Quartets. FaBoMo; FaBoPV; FaBoTw; GTBS-P; MoP; NAEL-2; NAWM-2; NoAM; NOBA; NOBE; OAEL-2; OxAEP-2; OxBTC; PeECV; PrIm; TAP; TFi

Midwives, The. Celia Gilbert. ChIV-1

Might and Right. Clarence Day. NBLV

Might as well bury her. Maumee Ruth. Sterling A. Brown. CDC

Might drop his arms, that he had held up all day since the dew. (*LL*) Wednesday. Marvin Bell. VCAP

Might find a sense of worth, a part to play. (*LL*) An Inmate. Peter Kocan. NOBAu

Might have been. This Place Rumord to Have Been Sodom. Robert Duncan. NeAP; NOBA; PoM; PPP

Might have known it. Unknown, *tr. fr. Chippewa Indian by* Jerome K. Rothenberg. STP

Might I but moor — Tonight — / In Thee! (*LL*) Wild nights — wild nights! Emily Dickinson. AmPP; CBLP; HeIP; LPA; NAAL-1; NALW; NIP; NoAM; NOBA; NoP; OxBA; PBWP; PFP; Poetr; RaBo; TAP; UnAS; WPE

Might I, if you can find it, be given. Saint Nicholas. Marianne Moore. NYBP; WPE

Might Is Right. Israel Zangwill. TrJP

Might of this pagoda seems to erupt upwards, The. On Climbing the Pagoda of the Temple of Gracious Benevolence with Kao Shih and Hsüeh Chü. Ts'en Shen, *tr. fr. Chinese by* Daniel Bryant. SuSp

Might rise from where they slept and go away. (*LL*) The Sheaves. E. A. Robinson. AWP; CMoP; FaBV; HAP; ImGa; MoAB; MoAmPo; MoP; NoAM; NOBA; OxBA; Poetr; SoSe; TAP

Might speak them. Then we heard them, every word. (*LL*) Charles Carville's Eyes. E. A. Robinson. AnAmPo; CMoP; MeMAP; OxBA; TAP

Might visit thee at will. (*LL*) Cold earth slept below, The. Shelley. EnRP

Might well have been the death of me. (*LL*) Not even my pride will suffer much. Edna St. Vincent Millay. VBLP

Mightier Storms than This. George Santayana. AnAmPo

Mightier storms than this are brewed on earth. George Santayana. *Fr.* Sonnets. AnAmPo

Mightier than Mammon, A, *sels.* Edward Carpenter.
"Love of men for each other, The — so tender, heroic, constant." PeHV

Mightier than the sword art thou. (*LL*) The Pen. Mary Weston Fordham. AmWP; CBWP-2

Mightier than the sword thou art. The Pen. Mary Weston Fordham. AmWP; CBWP-2

Mighty bell is six o'clock, A. Six to Six. Unknown, *tr. fr. Xhosa by* A. C. Jordan. PBA

Mighty change it is, and ominous, A. The Winter Shore. Thomas Wade. OAEL-2

Mighty creature is the germ, A. The Germ. Ogden Nash. MoShBr; RB

Mighty Fortress, A. Bible, O.T., *paraphrased by* Sir Thomas Wyatt. *See* He that dwelleth in the secret place of the most High.

Mighty Fortress Is Our God, A. Martin Luther, *tr. fr. German.* AWP; GePo; PWR, *tr. by* Frederick Henry Hedge

Mighty growth! The county side, A. The Old Oak Tree at Hatfield Broadoak. Frederick Locker-Lampson. OxAEP-2

Mighty Hunter, The. J. B. Worley. PoLF

Mighty Love. John Fletcher. *See* Hear, Ye Ladies [That Despise].

Mighty Mary, hear me. Muireadach Albanach O'Dalaigh. NOIV

Mighty mother, and her son who brings, The. Pope. *Fr.* Dunciad, The. OBSV; PoE
(To Dr. Jonathan Swift.) OxAEP-1

Mighty One, before Whose Face. Bryant. AH

Mighty, praised beyond compare. Rock of My Salvation. Mordecai ben Isaac, *tr. fr. Hebrew by* Solomon Solis-Cohen. TrJP

Mighty river flowing dark and deep, The. James Thomson ("B.V."). *Fr.* City of Dreadful Night, The. EBVV; EnVR; OBNC

Mighty Runner, A. E. A. Robinson. MeMAP; OBAL

Mighty shelde of doublenesse, A. (*LL*) The Duplicity of Women. John Lydgate. MeEL

Mighty spirit, and its power, which stains, The. Inebriety. George Crabbe. BXAP

Mighty Thoughts of an Old World, The. Thomas Lovell Beddoes. *Fr.* Ivory Gate, The. GoJo

Mighty wave rush'd o'er him as he spoke, A. Homer, *tr. by* Pope. *Fr.* Odyssey. NAWM-1; OBVE

Mighty you are, dark mouth. Dejection. Georg Trakl, *tr. fr. German by* Michael Hamburger. PeFWW

Mignon. Goethe, *tr. by* Robert Bly. *Fr.* Wilhelm Meister's Apprenticeship. NU

Mignon. H. Cordelia Ray. AmWP; CBWP-3

Migod, a picture window. The One-Night Stand: An Approach to the Bridge. Paul Blackburn. ErPo

Migrant, The. A. L. Hendricks. PBCV

Migrant's Lament: A Song. Alfred Temba Qabula. PeSAV

Migration. Carole Gregory Clemmons. *See* She stood hanging wash before sun.

Migration. Pinkie Gordon Lane. BlSi

Migration of the Grey Squirrels, The. William Howitt. OxBChV

Migratory bird flew with mirth. Lost Bird. Chenjerai Hove. HBAPE

Migratory Bird ("One day he perched. . .") Chenjerai Hove. HBAPE

Mikado, The, *sels.* W. S. Gilbert.
  Ko-Ko's Song ("As some day it may happen that a victim must be found"). LiTB
    (Lord High Executioner's Song, The.) CBCK
    (They'll None of 'Em Be Missed.) OHCV
  Ko-Ko's Winning Song. LiTB
    (Ko-Ko's Song.) ImPo
    (Titwillow.) NoP
  Mikado's Song, The. LiTB
  To Sit in Solemn Silence. FiBHP

Mikado's Song, The. W. S. Gilbert. *Fr.* Mikado, The. LiTB

Mike Howe's head with frozen frown. Hobart Town, Van Diemen's Land (11th June, 1837). Hal Porter. NOBAu

Mike 65. Lennox Raphael. PoBA

Miklos Radnoti. Willis Barnstone. BTR

Mild and peaceful spring glow, Cold Food Day. Li Ch'ing-chao, *tr. by* Eugene Eoyang. *Fr.* Tune: "Sand of Silk-washing Stream". SuSp

Mild and slow and young. Girl Help. Janet Lewis. HeIP; InPK

Mild is the parting year, and sweet. Walter Savage Landor. *Fr.* Ianthe. EnLoPo; TEP
  (Autumn.) TrGrPo

Mild man, God-fearing, A. Rural Idyll. Margaret Toms. PAW

Mild, melancholy, and sedate, he stands. The Hottentot. Thomas Pringle. OBTV

Mild, of sweet/ countenance. Paulus Silentiarius, *tr. fr. Greek by* Andrew Miller. GrAn

Mild offspring of a dark and sullen sire! To an Early Primrose. Henry Kirke White. OBNC

Mild the mist upon the hill. Emily Brontë. NOBVV

Mildmay Grove. Sue May. NBrP

Mildred's Doves. H. Cordelia Ray. CBWP-3

Mile an' a Bittock, A. Robert Louis Stevenson. NOBVV; OxBS

Mile and mile and mile; but no one would gather. The Sea. Francis Webb. CBAP

Mile Hill. Dennis Schmitz. LCAP

Mile more down the flat fast road, the homestead, A. Serpent Knowledge. Robert Pinsky. *Fr.* Explanation of America, An. NAAL-2

Mile out in the marshes, under a sky, A. The Town Dump. Howard Nemerov. CMoP; MAT

Mile with Me, A. Henry van Dyke. BLPA

Miles, and miles, and miles of desolation! Suffolk. Swinburne. *Fr.* By the North Sea. FaBoPP

Miles Davis. Lawson Fusao Inada. ETG

Miles Davis on a night off. The Fifties. Marvin Bell. Jaz

Miles' Delight ("Miles Davis.") Ted Joans. PoNe

Miles go sliding by, The. Walking Song. Ivor Gurney. NTP

Miles' house. Miles Davis. Lawson Fusao Inada. ETG

Miles Keogh's Horse. John Milton Hay. PAH

Miles of pram in the wind and Pam in the gorse track. Potpourri from a Surrey Garden. Sir John Betjeman. CBLP; FiBHP; NOBL

Militance of a Photograph in the Passbook of a Bantu under Detention, The. Michael S. Harper. VCAP

Militant. Langston Hughes. PoBA

Military Harpist, The. Ruth Pitter. FaBoTw; NALW

Military-Industrial Complex, The. Robley Wilson, Jr. PBCAP

Military Occupations., *sels.* Dionne Brand.
  "In the 5 a.m. dusk." PBCV

Militerotics. Chuck Ortleb. GLP

Militia, The. Dryden. *Fr.* Cymon and Iphigenia. EPCY; OBNV; OBSV

Milk all the way. (*LL*) To the Infant Martyrs. Richard Crashaw. ChIV-2; GeHe; NAEL-1; NoP; OxBSP; SeCV-1

Milk at the Bottom of the Sea. Oscar Williams. LiTA

Milk Bottle, The. Galway Kinnell. Poetr; PRA

Milk for the Cat. Harold Monro. BoTP; FaBoBe; MoBrPo; OBMV; OFC

Milk-white bird, A. *Unknown.* RoPo

Milk White Doe, The. *Unknown, tr. fr. French by* Andrew Lang. AWP

Milk-white Dove. *Unknown. See* Pew, pew,/ My minny me slew.

Milk white Hind, immortal and unchang'd, A. Dryden. *Fr.* Hind and the Panther, The. SeCV-2; UV

Milk-white Moon, Put the Cows to Sleep. Carl Sandburg. FaPON; ImGa

Milk-white mouse immortal and unchang'd, A. The Town Mouse and the Country Mouse. Matthew Prior. BXAP

Milke before wine, I would 'twere mine. *Unknown.* FaBoUs

Milkers lace their boots up at the farms, The. (*LL*) Cock-Crow. Edward Thomas. GTBS-P; MoAB; MoBrPo; NTP; OxBSP; RB

Milkfish. Eugene Gloria. OpBo

Milking before Dawn. Ruth Dallas. NTP; PeNZ

Milking-Maid, The. Christina Rossetti. BeLS

Milking Pails. *Unknown.* CH

Milking Shed, The. John Clare. CH

Milking Time. Elizabeth Madox Roberts. FaPON; GoJo; OBCA

Milkmaid. Laurie Lee. BoLoP; FaBoTw

Milkmaid, The. *Unknown.* AmFP

Milkmaid's Epithalamium, The. Thomas Randolph. BoLoP

Milkman, The. Isabella Gardner. CAPP

Milkman, The. Clive Sansom. BoTP

Milkman and His Son, The. Thomas Lux. LCAP

Milkweed. Philip Levine. LCAP

Milkweed. James Wright. LCAP; NaP; NOBA; NU; RaBo

Milkweed, A. Richard Wilbur. *Fr.* Two Voices in a Meadow. CRP

Milky-bell'd amaryllis blew, A. (*LL*) The Daisy. Tennyson. EnLoPo; NOBVV; OBNC; PoEL-5

Milky in the spring grotto stone fattens, sprouts goose-quills. Tu Mu, *tr. fr. Chinese by* A. C. Graham. *Fr.* Red Slope. PLT

Milky Way above, The. Fire Island. May Swenson. PoA; TAP

Mill, A. William Allingham. FaBoEE; OxBSP

Mill, The. E. A. Robinson. CMoP; DL; HAP; MeMAP; NAAL-2; NoAM; NoP; Poetr; PrIm; WeW

Mill, The. Richard Wilbur. Poetsp

Mill-Pond, The. Edward Thomas, *tr. fr. German.* RB

Mill sails on the heath a-going, The. (*LL*) Autumn ("I love the fitful gust.") John Clare. BoTP

Mill-stream, now that noises cease, The. A. E. Housman. GBL

Mill Valley. Myra Cohn Livingston. RFM

Mill Was Made of Marble, The. Joseph Glazer. SWP

Milla. *Unknown.* NOSC

Milla, the glory of whose beauteous rays. Milla. *Unknown.* NOSC

"Millennium," yes; "pandemonium!" Hometown Piece for Messrs. Alston and Reese. Marianne Moore. OBAL

Miller, The. Sir John Clerk. ChTr

Miller, The. John Cunningham. ECEV

Miller and His Sons, The. *Unknown.* OBET

Miller and the Brook, The. Wilhelm Müller, *tr. fr. German by* Philip L. Miller. *Fr.* Beautiful Maid of the Mill, The. RiWo

Miller, Miller. Ivy O. Eastwick. BoTP

Miller of Dee, The. *Unknown.* GBP

Miller was a stout carl, for the nones, The. Chaucer. *Fr.* Canterbury Tales, The. EnVB; FHYEP; NoP; OAEL-1; PPP, *abr.; TrGrPo*
  (Miller, stout and sturdy as the stones, The, *mod. vers. by* Louis Untermeyer.) TrGrPo

Miller's daughter, The. Spinning Song. Edith Sitwell. MoAB; MoBrPo

Miller's Daughter, The. Tennyson. OBEV; TrGrPo

Miller's Flowers, The. Wilhelm Müller, *tr. fr. German by* Philip L. Miller. *Fr.* Beautiful Maid of the Mill, The. RiWo

Miller's mill-dog lay at the mill-door, The. Bingo. *Unknown.* CH; TTTS

Miller's Prologue, The. Chaucer. *Fr.* Canterbury Tales, The. EnVB

Miller's [*or* Milleres] Tale, The. Chaucer. *Fr.* Canterbury Tales, The. EnVB; FaBoBl; NAEL-1; OAEL-1; OxBoLi; PeLV

Miller's Wife, The. The Mill. E. A. Robinson. CMoP; DL; HAP; MeMAP; NAAL-2; NoAM; NoP; Poetr; PrIm; WeW
  (Miller's Wife, The. TAP

Miller's Wife's Lullaby, The. *Unknown.* GBP

Millery, millery, dustipole. *Unknown.* ISE; OxNR

Million, The. Peter Redgrove. OxBC

Million billion trillion stars, A. (*LL*) A Man Who Had Fallen among Thieves. E. E. Cummings. ChIV-2; HAP; LiTM; MeMAP; MoP; NoAM; NOBA; OxBA; TAP

Million butterflies rose up from South America, A. Annual Legend. Winfield Townley Scott. CoAP; LiTA; LiTM

Million emeralds break from the ruby-budded lime, A. Tennyson. *Fr.* Maud[: A Monodrama]. EnVR

Million Pairs of Shoes, A. Aaron Kurtz, *tr. fr. Yiddish by* Aaron Kurtz *and* Olga Cabral. BTR

Million stars are dreaming out, A. Frank O'Hara. SM

Million years of death some star, A. Micromutations. James Wright. NYBP

Millionaire, filled with elation, A. Thomas Thorneley. PeLi

Millionaires, presidents — even kings. Everyday Things. Jean Ayer. BoTP

Millions of Strawberries. Genevieve Taggard. FaPON; MoShBr

Mills of the Gods, The. *Unknown.* BLPA

Milltown Union Bar, The. Richard Hugo. NoAM

Milne's Bar. Norman MacCaig. FaBoTw

Milo's from home; and, Milo being gone. Martial, *tr. fr. Latin by* Elijah Fenton. OBVE

Milton, *sels.* Blake.
  And Did Those Feet in Ancient Time. AWP; ClHu; EBEvV; EnRP; FaBoCh; FaBoPV; FaBV; HAP; HeIP; InPS; MAT; MeMBP; NAEL-2; NAWM-2; NoP; OAEL-2; PeECV; PlP; PoE; PoEL-4; PoRA; PrIm; SCGP; TFi; WGRP
  (And Did Those Feet.) ChIV-1
  (Jerusalem.) BoTP; FaPoR; FHYEP; NOBE; NOCV; OBEV; OtMeF; OxAEP-2; RB; UV
  (New Jerusalem, A.) CoGr; LiTB; SWP; TrGrPo
  (New Jerusalem, The.) ImPo
  (Prelude: "And did those feet in ancient time.") OBNC
  "And in the midst of the Great Assembly Palamabron pray'd." OBF
  "But turning toward Ololon in terrible majesty Milton." OxAEP-2
  "Daughters of Beulah! Muses who inspire the Poets Song." PeECV
  Reason and Imagination. EnRP
  "Then Milton rose up from the heaven of Albion ardorous!" OAEL-2
  "This wine-press is call'd war on earth." EBEV
  (Wine-Press of Los, The.) EnRP
  "Thou hearest the nightingale begin the song of spring"
  (Choir of Day, The.) EnRP
  (Lark's Song, The.) WiR
  (Vision of Beulah, The ("Thou hearest the nightingale begin the song of spring").) NOBE
  (Vision of the Lamentation of Beulah, A.) OBNC
  To Morning. EnRP; OxAEP-2
  Vision of Beulah, The ("There is a place where contrarieties are equally true"). OAEL-2
  Wild Thyme, The. WiR

Milton. Anne Lynch Botta. AmWP

Milton. Longfellow. AmPP; AWP; NoP; TAP; TrGrPo

Milton. H. Cordelia Ray. BlSi; CBWP-3

Milton. Tennyson. PeECV

Milton. Wordsworth. *See* Milton! thou should'st be living at this hour.

Milton: Alcaics. Tennyson. EPCY

Milton by Firelight. Gary Snyder. CAPP; CoAP; InPS; NAAL-2; PoBeRe; PPP

Milton: On the Busts of Milton, in Youth and Age. William Lisle Bowles. Son
  Sels.
  In Age.
  In Youth.

Milton, our noblest poet, in the grace. In Youth. William Lisle Bowles. *Fr.* Milton: On the Busts of Milton, in Youth and Age. Son

Milton, the airport driver, retired now. Becoming Milton. Coleman Barks. RaBo

Milton! thou should'st be living at this hour. London, 1802 ("Milton! thou should'st be living at this hour.") Wordsworth. AWP; EBEvV; EnRP; EPCY; FaBoPV; FaBV; FF; HAP; HeIP; InvP; LiTB; MeMBP; NAEL-2; NIP; NoP; OBNC; OxAEP-2; PoEL-4; PoRA; SCGP; Son; TEP; TFi; UV
  (England, 1802, II.) OBEV
  (Milton.) FaPoR
  (Same, The.) GTBS; GTBS-P
  (To Milton.) TrGrPo

Milton, who made his illiterate daughters. Eve of Easter. Bernadette Mayer. UL

Milton's Prayer for [*or* of] Patience. Elizabeth Lloyd Howell. WGRP

Milton's strong pinion now not heaven can bound. Pope. *Fr.* First Epistle of the Second Book of Horace, Imitation of. EPCY

Milton's the prince of poets — so we say. Byron. *Fr.* Don Juan. NOBL; OAEL-2

Milwaukee Fire, The. *Unknown.* AmFP

Mimic Muse, The, *sels.* Samuel Hoffenstein.
  "With rue my heart is laden." NBLV

Mimikòs. Luigi Fontanella, *tr. fr. Italian by* Michael Palma. NeIt

Mimnermus in Church. William Johnson Cory. CoGr; NOBE; OBEV

Mimnermus Incert. Walter Savage Landor. PoEL-4

Mimosas. Louis Aragon, *tr. fr. French.* CBNP

Mimshi Maiden, The. Hugh McCrae. NOBAu

Mina Bell's Cows. Wesley McNair. TRP

Mince-Python, The. Carolyn Wells. *Fr.* Baker's Dozen of Wild Beasts, A. OBCA

Mincemeat. Elizabeth Gould. BoTP

Mind. Jorie Graham. HCAP; Poetr

Mind, The, *sels.* Charles Swain.

Mind. Richard Wilbur. CMoP; HCAP; HoPM; OxBSP; PPP; SoSe; VCAP

Mind and Matter. *Unknown. See* There was a faith-healer of Deal.

Mind at peace, cassia flowers fall. Birdsong Brook. Wang Wei, *tr. fr. Chinese by* Irving Y. Lo. SuSp

Mind Content, A. Robert Greene. *See* Sweet are the thoughts that savo[u]r of content.

Mind Flying Afar. Edgar Lee Masters. PoA

Mind has its own level to find., The. (*LL*) Alpine. R. S. Thomas. BoNaP; RFM

Mind in its [*or* the] purest play is like some bat. Mind. Richard Wilbur. CMoP; HCAP; HoPM; OxBSP; PPP; SoSe; VCAP

Mind, Intractable Thing, The. Marianne Moore. LiTM; NYBP

Mind Is an Ancient and Famous Capital, The ("The mind is a city like London.") Delmore Schwartz. NoAM; TAP

Mind Is an Enchanting Thing, The. Marianne Moore. CMoP; HeIL; HeIP; InPK; InvP; MeMAP; MoAB; MoAmPo; NAAL-2; OxBA; PoE; PPP; WPOW

Mind is not, The. The Perishing Bird. Douglas G. Jones. MoCV

Mind knows no death. Life is the "first and last." Albery Allson Whitman. *Fr.* Octoroon, The. AAP

Mind of Absolute Trust, The. Seng-ts'an, *tr. fr. Chinese by* Stephen Mitchell. EnlH

Mind of Man is fram'd even like the breath, The. In Patterdale. Wordsworth. *Fr.* Prelude [or, Growth of a Poet's Mind], The. CH; EnRP; FaBoRV; GN; HAP; NOBE; NoP; NU; OAEL-2; OBNC; OxAEP-2; PoE; SCV

Mind of man is this world's true dimension, The. Fulke Greville. *Fr.* Treaty of Human Learning, A. NOSC

Mind of the people is like mud, The. Talking with Soldiers. W. J. Turner. MoBrPo

Mind Pictures. Beatrice Hastings. PeSAV

Mind-Reader, The. Richard Wilbur. LCAP; NAAL-2; NoAM
  Sels.
  "What should I tell them?" CRP

Mind will change, and change shall be relief, The. (*LL*) Amor Vincit Omnia. Edgar Bowers. VCAP

Mind, with its own eyes and ears, The. The Mind's Liberty. W. H. Davies. MoBrPo

Minding Ruth. Aidan Carl Mathews. BiHa; CIP; IB; PBCIP

Minding Things. Paul Hyland. PWE

Mindless this life is like water flowing east. (*LL*) Clouds and mountains all tangled together up to the blue sky. Han-shan. EaPr

Mindoro. Ramon C. Sunico, *tr. fr. Spanish.* TSaS, *tr. by the author.*

Mindoro, 1944. James Dickey. PRA

Minds awake in bodies that were asleep. Pandora and the Moon. Merrill Moore. MoAmPo

Mind's eye aches from Henry James, The. Satie, at the End of Term. Simon Curtis. NOBL; PeLV

Mind's immortal, but the man is dead, The. (*LL*) Time and the Garden. Yvor Winters. MoAmPo; NoAM; VGW

Mind's Liberty, The. W. H. Davies. MoBrPo

Mine. Tim Longville. VaA

Mine!. Wilhelm Müller, *tr. fr. German by* Philip L. Miller. *Fr.* Beautiful Maid of the Mill, The. RiWo

Mine. Frank Polite. NYBP

Mine. Mary E. Tucker. CBWP-1

Mine and the sea-wind's. (*LL*) The Rose. Theodore Roethke. NOBA; NYBP; TRP

Mine Argosy from Alexandria. Christopher Marlowe. *Fr.* Jew of Malta, The. ChTr

Mine be a cot beside the [*or* a] hill. A Wish. Samuel Rogers. FaPoR; GGP; GTBS; GTBS-P; NOBE; OBEV; OxAEP-2; PlP

Mine — by the right of the white election! Emily Dickinson. CBLP; NAAL-1; NALW; NoP

Mine Enemy Is Growing Old. Emily Dickinson. RaBo

Mine Eternal Heaven. (*LL*) During His Courtship. Charles Wesley. NOCV

Mine Eye and Heart Are at a Mortal War. Shakespeare. *Fr.* Sonnets. HeIP

Mine eye bewrays. Love Cannot Live. *Unknown*. EIL

Mine eye, mine [*or* myne] ear[e], my will, my wit[t], my h[e]art[e]. Sir John Davies. *Fr*. Gulling[e] Sonnets, The. ESo; Son

Mine eyes beheld the blessed pity spring. Dante, *tr. fr. Italian by* Dante Gabriel Rossetti. *Fr*. Vita Nuova, La. AWP

Mine eyes have seen the glory of the coming of the Lord. The Battle Hymn of the [American] Republic. Julia Ward Howe. AH; AmWP; AnAmPo; BLPA; CH; CoGr; EBEvV; FaBoBe; FaPON; FaPoR; GN; NOBA; NOCV; OBWP; OHIP; OtMeF; PAH; PWR; SCV; SWP; TAP; TFi; WBLP; WGRP; WPE
(Battle-Hymn of the Republic, The.) ImPo

Mine eyes, like clouds, were drizzling rain. Rainbow, The: or Curious Covenant. Robert Herrick. ChIV-1

Mine has opened its soul to me; therefore I love it. (*LL*) My Star. Robert Browning. FaPON; TrGrPo

Mine heart is desolate. (*LL*) Il Pleut Doucement sur la Ville. Paul Verlaine. AWP

Mine Heart's a Park or Chase of Sins. Edward Taylor. *Fr*. Preparatory Meditations Before My Approach to the Lord's Supper. CBCK

Mine high estate, power and auctority. Sir Thomas More. NoSic

Mine Host of "The Golden Apple." Thomas Westwood. GN; OHIP

Mine — long as Ages steal! (*LL*) Mine — by the right of the white election! Emily Dickinson. CBLP; NAAL-1; NALW; NoP

Mine, O thou lord of life, send my roots rain. (*LL*) Thou Art Indeed Just, Lord, If I Contend. Gerard Manley Hopkins. AWP; ChIV-1; CMoP; EBVV; GTBS-P; HAP; HoPM; inPK; LiTM; MoAB; MoBrPo; NAEL-2; NoAM; NOBE; NOBVV; NoP; OAEL-2; PeECV; SCGP; TOF; TrPWD; UnPo

Mine old dear enemy, my froward master. Petrarch, *tr. fr. Italian by* Sir Thomas Wyatt. SiPSBD
(Translation from Petrarch.) SiPS

Mine only died. (*LL*) [Epitaph] In Obitum M.S., X° Maij [*or* Maii], 1614. William Browne. EIL; FaBoEE; JCP; NOBE; OBEV

Mine Own John Poins [*or* Poyntz]. Sir Thomas Wyatt. *Fr*. Satires. AAS; NoP; NoSic; OBSV; OBVE; PoEL-1; SCGP; SiPS; SiPSBD

Mine owne enough betray me. (*LL*) Oh do[e] not wanton with those eyes. Ben Jonson. CBLP; SeCP; TEP

Mine owne good Bat, before thou hoyse up saile. Councell Given to Master Bartholmew Withipoll. George Gascoigne. AAS

Mine shall be to make believe. (*LL*) I Can't Hold You and I Can't Leave You. Sister Juana Inés de la Cruz. ArLo; PBWP; VBLP

Mine Sweepers 1914-18. Kipling. CoGr

Mine-Sweeping Trawlers. Edward Hilton, 1st Baron Kennet of the Dene Young. NSI

Mine was a Midwest home — you can keep your world. One Home. William Stafford. CoAP; VGW

Mine with inner, weather. (*LL*) Tree at My Window. Robert Frost. BLPL; BoNaP; FaBoBe; MeMAP; MoAB; MoAmPo; NoAM; OxBA; TAP; TrGrPo

Mined Country. Richard Wilbur. ArOW

Miner Boy, The. *Unknown*. AmFP

Miner Coming Home One Night, A. *Unknown*. GBP

Miner thus through perils digs his way, The. Thomas Yalden. *Fr*. To Sir Humphry Mackworth. ECEV

Mineral Rejoicings. Christopher Smart. *Fr*. Jubilate Agno. CBCK; FaBoVe

Minerals of Cornwall, Stones of Cornwall. Peter Redgrove. FaBoMo

Miners. Branko Miljkovic, *tr. fr. Serbo-Croatian by* Charles Simic. HSix

Miners. Wilfred Owen. MeMBP; MoAB; MoBrPo; NAEL-2; NOBE; NSI; OBWVE; OxAEP-2; PeFWW

Miner's Ballad, The. Lewis Morris. AngWe

Miner's Doom, The. *Unknown*. AmFP

Miner's Helmet, The. George MacBeth. OxBTC

Miner's Lament, The. *Unknown*. AmFP

Miner's Life, A. *Unknown*. OBET; SWP

Miners' Response, The. Dugald Sutherland MacColl. NSI

Miners' Wives. Joe Corrie. OxBS

Minesweeper Sunk, A. Edward Davison. NSI

Ming will be over to make way for the Ch'ing, The. Barbarian Suite. Marilyn Chin. OpBo

Mingle their dying light with the dawning day. (*LL*) Dawn. Paul Armand Silvestre. RiWo

Mingled/ breath and smell. Subway Rush Hour. Langston Hughes. InPK

Mingled the moonlight with daylight. Thomas Hardy. Walter de la Mare. NoAM

Mingled Yarns. X. J. Kennedy. OBCA

Mingling my prayer. Saigyo, *tr. fr. Japanese by* Arthur Waley. AWP

Mingus. Bob Kaufman. PoBA

Mini-Samizdat of New River Rhymes, A, *sels*. William Rossa Cole.

Miniature. Eden Phillpotts. OxBSP

Miniature. Yannis Ritsos, *tr. fr. Greek by* Edmund Keeley. AnRep

Miniatures IV. Lynn Strongin. IHMS

Minimal, The. Theodore Roethke. HCAP; MoP; NoAM; NOBA; RB

Mining in Killdeer Alley. Dabney Stuart. MT

Minion Wife, A. Nicholas Udall. *Fr*. Ralph Roister Doister. EIL

Minister at Chiuzenji, The. Osman Edwards. *Fr*. Residential Rhymes. OBTV

Minister of birds, islands, and pools. Cortege for Colette. Jean Garrigue. NYBP

Minister said it wad [*or* wald] dee, The. Last Lauch. Douglas Young. FaBoCo; NBLV; OxBS

Minister up in Vermont, A. *Unknown*. PeLi

Ministers who've sold the King. Are You Glad? *Mongol Oral Tradition*, *tr. by* C. R. Bawden. WTO

Miniver Cheevy. E. A. Robinson. AmPP; AWP; ChTr; ClHu; CMoP; EBEvV; FaBoCh; FaBV; FF; HeIP; ImPo; LiTA; LiTM; MoAB; MoAmPo; MoP; NAAL-2; NBLV; NoAM; NOBA; NoP; OBSV; OxBA; PeLV; PoEL-5; Poetr; PoLF; PoRA; RaBo; SCV; SoSe; TAP; TFi; TrGrPo

Miniver Cheevy, Jr., *parody*. David Fisher Parry. BXAP; NBLV

Minks, The. Toi Derricotte. NAmP90

Minneapolis Poem, The. James Wright. FYAP; NoAM; UnPo

Minnesota Thanksgiving. John Berryman. GOA

Minnie and a minnie and a ha ha ha! (*LL*) I Went Downtown. *Unknown*. ISE; RoPo; TLR

Minnie and Her Dove. Charles Tennyson Turner. FM

Minnie and Mattie. Christina Rossetti. *Fr*. Sing-Song. GoJo; InvP

Minnie and Mrs. Hoyne. Kenneth Fearing. PoRA

Minnie and Winnie. Tennyson. OxBChV; TTTS

Minnie, I canna caa my wheel. Douglas Young, *after the Greek of* Sappho. OBVE

Minnow, go to sleep and dream. Lullaby for the Cat. Elizabeth Bishop. OFC; SoCa

Minnows. Keats. *Fr*. I Stood Tiptoe [upon a Little Hill]. EnRP; FaPON; GN

Minoan Snake Goddess is flanked by a Chardin still-life, somber, The. The Postcards: A Triptych. Denise Levertov. SRLS

Minor Bird, A. Robert Frost. CMoP; SAmP

Minor Elegy. Henriqueta Lisboa, *tr. fr. Portuguese by* Willis Barnstone *and* Nelson Cerqueira. BoWoP

Minor Prophet, A, *sels*. "George Eliot."
Tide of Faith, The. WGRP

Minor Things. Heather Ross Miller. MT

Minor Tremor, A. Robert Duncan. BAP-89

Minority Poem. Wing Tek Lum. BCF

Minority Report. John Updike. GOA

Minotaur Next Door, The. Greg Pape. PBCAP

Minotaur Poems., *sels*. Eli W. Mandel.
"My father was always out in the garage." MoCV

Minster rings, The. (*LL*) On Christmas-Day. Thomas Traherne. PoEL-2

Minstrel, The, *sels*. James Beattie.
Youth of a Poet, The. NOEC

Minstrel, The. Goethe, *tr. fr. German by* James Clarence Mangan. AWP

Minstrel, The. Sir Walter Scott. *Fr*. Lay of the Last Minstrel, The. OxAEP-2

Minstrel and Genius, to whose songs or sighs. Autumnal Ode. Aubrey Thomas De Vere. OBNC

Minstrel Boy, The. Thomas Moore. FaBoBe; GN; OxAEP-2; PrIm

Minstrel Responds to Flattery, The. Sir Walter Scott. *Fr*. Lay of the Last Minstrel, The. OBNC

Minstrels and Maids. William Morris. *See* Outlanders, The.

Minstrel's Last Lay, The. John Barth. OBAL

Minstrels sing the jasmine songs. Peyanar, *tr. fr. Tamil by* A. K. Ramanujan. *Fr*. Seven Said by the Foster-Mother. PLW

Minstrel's Song. Thomas Chatterton. *See* Oh! sing unto my roundelay [*or* O! Synge untoe mie roundelaie].

Minstrel's Song. Ted Hughes. OBCP

Mint bed is in, The. Sunday. James Schuyler. TTTS

Minuet on Reaching the Age of Fifty, A. George Santayana. BLPL; ImPo

Minukha, Minukha, here comes your Faigl's Rukhl. Poem for My Grandmother's Grandmother. Lesléa Newman. LoHo

Minukha Minukha Minukha. (*LL*) Poem for My Grandmother's Grandmother. Lesléa Newman. LoHo

Minute flowers harden. Depend. Lilies of the Valley. Jon Silkin. NoAM

Minute-Guns, The. Celia Laighton Thaxter. AmWP

Minute I heard my first love story, The. Jalal al-Din Rumi, *tr. fr. Persian by* John Moyne *and* Coleman Barks. UnAS

Minute-Men of Northboro', The. Wallace Rice. PAH

Minutes are numbered by the fall of sands. John Ford. *Fr.* Lover's Melancholy, The. PoEL-2

Minutes grow tedious, Time too slowly moves. Maria to Henric. *Unknown.* KTR

Minutes of Gold. *Unknown.* PoToHe

Mips and ma the mooly moo. Theodore Roethke. *Fr.* Praise to the End! CBNP; InPS; NBLV; RB

Mir träumte von einem Königskind. Heine, *tr. fr. German by* Richard Garnett. AWP

Mir träumte wieder der alte Traum. Heine, *tr. fr. German by* James Thomson. AWP

Mira, as they dear Edward's senses grow. Ann Yearsley. *Fr.* To Mira, On the Care of her Infant. ECWP

Mira is dancing with bells tied on her ankles. Mirabai, *tr. fr. Hindi by* Willis Barnstone *and* Usha Nilsson. BoWoP

Mira to Octavia. Mary Leapor. ECWP

Mirabeau Bridge, The. Guillaume Apollinaire, *tr. fr. French.* ArLo, *tr. by* Richard Wilbur; BoLoP, *tr. by* Quentin Stevenson; LPA; OBVE, *tr. by* W. S. Merwin; PRA, *tr. by* Richard Wilbur

Mirabell: Books of Number, *sels.* James Merrill.
"And Maddening—it's all by someone else." NAAL-2
"It starts in the small hours. An interlude." NoAM
"World was everything that was the case?, The." HCAP

Mirabell's Books of Number. James Merrill. *Fr.* Changing Light at Sandover, The. NAAL-2

Miracle. Liberty Hyde Bailey. OHIP

Miracle, The. Walter de la Mare. LiTB; UnPo

Miracle, The. Allan Dowling. ErPo

Miracle, The. Emerson. FM

Miracle. Susan Griffin. CrSp

Miracle, The. Thom Gunn. FaBoBl

Miracle, The. Maureen Hawkins. AIW

Miracle, The. Sir John Suckling. CaPo

Miracle for Breakfast, A. Elizabeth Bishop. LiTA

Miracle Indeed, A. Swami Purohit. OBMV

Miracle Mart. Wislawa Szymborska, *tr. fr. Polish by* Adam Czerniawski. PoSu

Miracle of the children the brilliant. Exodus. George Oppen. ChIV-1

Miracle of the world, I never will deny. Henry Constable. *Fr.* Diana. ESo; SCGP

Miracle, this massive, drab constant of experience. (*LL*) The Constant. A. R. Ammons. HAP; WeW

Miracles. Conrad Aiken. MoAmPo

Miracles. Arna Bontemps. PoNe

Miracles. Julia Randall. CRP

Miracles. Walt Whitman. AnAmPo; PFP; SAmP

Miracles at the Birth of Christ. Isaac Watts. NOCV

Miraculous Dawn. R. Williams Parry, *tr. fr. Welsh by* Joseph P. Clancy. OBWVE

Miraculous love's wounding! *Unknown.* NoSic

Mirage, The. Avedik Issahakian, *tr. fr. Armenian by* Diana der Hovanessian. LPA

Mirage. Christina Rossetti. BoLoP; CoGr; PoRA

Mirage, The. Oscar Williams. LiTM

Miramar Beach. J. V. Cunningham. *Fr.* To What Strangers, What Welcome. NoAM; PoA

Miramichi Fire, The. *Unknown.* AmFP

Miranda. W. H. Auden. *Fr.* Sea and the Mirror, The. NoAM

Miranda, remember that Inn? John Stanley. PeLi

Mira's Picture, a Pastoral, *sels.* Mary Leapor.
Portrait of the Artist, A. ECWP

Mira's Will. Mary Leapor. ECWP; NOEC

Mirèio. Frédéric Mistral, *tr. fr. Provençal.* AWP
Sels.
Cocooning, The.
Mares of the Camargue, The.

Miriam, *sels.* Whittier.
Book Our Mothers Read, The. BLRP
(Knowledge.) PoToHe

Miriam and Horlick spend a great deal of time putting off going to bed. Goodnight. Stevie Smith. FaBoWP

Mirie it is, while sumer ilast. *Unknown. See* Merry It Is.

Mirror, The. Michael Davitt, *tr. fr. Irish by* Paul Muldoon. BiHa; CIP; PBCIP

Mirror. Peter De Vries. PoA

Mirror, The. Louise Glück. LPA

Mirror, The. Judah Halevi, *tr. fr. Hebrew by* Emma Lazarus. TrJP

Mirror, The. Blanche Mary Kelly. TrPWD

Mirror. James Merrill. CoAP; SM

Mirror, The. John N. Morris. PoA

Mirror. Sylvia Plath. FaBoWP; HAP; HeIL; NIP; NYBP

Mirror, The. Isaac Rosenberg. NoAM

Mirror. Tada Chimako, *tr. fr. Japanese by* Kenneth Rexroth *and* Ikuko Atsumi. BoWoP; WPJ

Mirror copies everything it sees, A. Reflections on Mirrors. Elder Olson. CRP

Mirror for Detractors, A. Esther Lewis. ECWP

Mirror for Poets, A. Thom Gunn. LiTM

Mirror for the Barnyard. Jack Myers. AmPA

Mirror in February. Thomas Kinsella. CIP; GTBS-P; NoAM

Mirror in the Front Hall, The. C. P. Cavafy, *tr. fr. Greek by* Edmund Keeley *and* Philip Sherrard. PeHV

Mirror in Which Two Are Seen as One, The. Adrienne Rich. NAAL-2; NNaP

Mirror, Mirror, The. Robert Graves. NTP

Mirror of a Day Chiming Marigold, The. Diane Wakoski. NALW

Mirror of Knighthood, The. Robert Parry. EIL
Sels.
Except I Love.
"Fond affection, hence, and leave me!"

Mirror of Matsuyama, The. Sharon Hashimoto. OpBo

Mirror of men's eyes delights me less, The. Laus Virginitatis. Arthur Symons. EnLoPo

Mirror of poets, mirror of our age. Upon Ben Johnson [*or* Jonson]. Edmund Waller. BeJo; EPCY; NOSC; SeCV-1

Mirror Perilous, The. Alan Dugan. LiTM; TwCP

Mirrorment. A. R. Ammons. SiSoPo

Mirrors, The. Sophia de Mello Breyner Andresen, *tr. fr. Portuguese by* Allan Francovich. PBWP

Mirrors, let us pass through the glass. The Flight into Egypt. W. H. Auden. *Fr.* For the Time Being; a Christmas Oratorio. OxBA

Mirrors, no one yet has really described. Rainer Maria Rilke, *tr. by* Christopher Hawthorne. *Fr.* Sonnets to Orpheus. SOTW

Mirrors of water, mirrors of ebony. Jorge Luis Borges. *Fr.* Poem of Quality. CBCK

Mirror's Song. Liz Lochhead. NBrP

Mirth. Beaumont *and* Fletcher *and* John Fletcher. *Fr.* Knight of the Burning Pestle, The. EIL

Mirth. Robert Herrick. LiTB

Mirth. Christopher Smart. *Fr.* Hymns for the Amusement of Children. OxBChV

Mirth and Melancholy. Margaret Cavendish, Duchess of Newcastle. WPE

Mirth and Poetry. Milton. *Fr.* L'Allegro. AWP; EPCY; FaPoB; FHYEP; GTBS; GTBS-P; HAP; HoPM; ImPo; JCP; LiTB; NoP; NOSC; OAEL-1; OBEV; PPP; TEP; TFi; TrGrPo

Mirth, Spring, to linger in a garden fair. Hafiz, *tr. fr. Persian by* Gertrude Lowthian Bell. *Fr.* Odes. AWP; TAL

Mirth, with thee I mean to live. (*LL*) L'Allegro. Milton. AWP; FaPoB; FHYEP; GTBS; GTBS-P; HAP; HoPM; ImPo; JCP; LiTB; NoP; NOSC; OAEL-1; OBEV; PPP; TEP; TFi; TrGrPo

Mirth, with Thee I Mean to Live. Milton. *See* Haste thee, nymph, and bring with thee.

Mirthful Lunacy. Thomas Tod Stoddart. *Fr.* Death-Wake, The; or, Lunacy. OBNC

Mis-shapen Time, copesmate of ugly Night. Shakespeare. *Fr.* Rape of Lucrece, The. BeLS; OAEL-1

Mis' Smith. Albert Bigelow Paine. PoLF

Misalliance. Ella Wheeler Wilcox. AmWP

Misanthropist, The. James M. Whitfield. AAP

Misanthropos, *sels.* Thom Gunn.
"Serving man, A. Curled my hair." OxBC

Misapprehension. Paul Laurence Dunbar. BPo

Miscarriage. Joseph P. Clancy. AngWe

Miscarriage. Robert Peters. ETG

Miscellaneous Poems on Lake Biwa, *sels.* Liu Ya-tzu, *tr. fr. Chinese.*
"Beyond the stream at Seta stretches an endless view." SuSp
"By Flower-and-Moon Pavilion, I stay my carriage." SuSp
"Cataracts flying down a thousand fathoms roll up a raging billow." SuSp

Miscellanies of the Year Chi-hai. Kung Tzu-chen, *tr. fr. Chinese by* Irving Y. Lo. SuSp

Misconception, A. James Russell Lowell. OBAL

Misconceptions. Robert Browning. EnVR; OBEV

Misconceptions. L. L. Zeigler. PRA

Mise en Scène. Robert Fitzgerald. NYBP; VGW

Miserable change now at my end, The. Shakespeare. *Fr.* Antony and Cleopatra. EBEV

Miserere, *sels.* David Gascoyne.

Ecce Homo. ChIV-2; LiTM; OBWP; PeECV

Ex Nihilo. GTBS-P

Miserere. William Pillen. BTR

Miserere, My Maker. *Unknown.* NOCV

Misericordia! James Lipton. NBLV

Misericordia. Margaret Mead. PoA

Miserie. George Herbert. PoEL-2

"Miseries of Courtiers" by Æneas Sylvius Ricolomini, The. Alexander Barclay. *Fr.* Eclogues.

Miserimus. Adah Isaacs Menken. CBWP-1

Misery. John Holmes. NYBP

Misery and Splendor. Robert Hass. VCAP

Misery etcetera. The Day of the Sentry. David St. John. AnAn

Misery is a good thing if misery is spread. Misery. John Holmes. NYBP

Misery of Jerusalem, The. Bible, *O.T. Fr.* Lamentations. AWP

Misery of Mechanics, The. Philip Booth. MAT

Misfortunes of Elphin, The, *sels.* Thomas Love Peacock.
  Song of the Four Winds, The. WiR
  War Song of Dinas Vawr, The. AWP; CoGr; EBEvV; EnRP; FaBoCh; FaPoR; GGP; HAP; InvP; NAEL-2; NOBE; NTP; OAEL-2; OxAEP-2; PrIm; WiR

Misgivings. Herman Melville. NAAL-1; NOBA; OxBA

Misguided. Harriet Brown. CrSp

Mishka. John Gray. NOBVV

Mishnah says I blind you with my hair, The. The Marriage Wig. Ruth Whitman. IHMS

Misled me to my ruin. (*LL*) The Queen of Hearts. Christina Rossetti. CBLP; PeVV

Misnomer really, A. With a few exceptions. Squares. Michael Hamburger. FF

Misogynist, The. Jean Morgan. FF

Misplaced Sympathy. Charles Follen Adams. OBAL

Misplacing — Mistaking. On Sir Nathaniel Wraxall the Historian. George Colman the Younger. FaBoEE

Miss Bailey's Ghost. George Colman the Younger. *See* Captain bold in [*or* from] Halifax, that [*or* who] dwelt in country quarters, A.

Miss Beale and Miss Buss. (*LL*) Miss Buss and Miss Beale. *Unknown.* FaBoEE; ISE

Miss Betty's Singing-Bird. John Winstanley. NOEC

Miss Bitter. N. M. Bodecker. NTCP

Miss Blues'es Child. Langston Hughes. SAmP; TTTS

Miss Brown, before these walls unquote. Notation in Haste. Elias Lieberman. GoYe

Miss Buss and Miss Beale. *Unknown.* FaBoEE; ISE

Miss Carney handed us out blank paper and marla. Model School, Inchicore. Thomas Kinsella. CIP

Miss Cho Composes in the Cafeteria. James Tate. SM; WeW

Miss Creighton. Henry Taylor. GrPl

Miss Dickinson is gone. A New England Sampler. John Malcolm Brinnin. GOA

Miss Ellen Gee of Kew. *Unknown.* FaBoNo

Miss Emily Brittle Sails for India. Sir George Dallas. *Fr.* India Guide, The; or, Journal of a Voyage to the East Indies in 1780. NOEC

Miss Euphemia. John Crowe Ransom. CMoP

Miss Fny M[—]t[—]y to Miss P[—]y B[—]s. Fanny (Frances) Macartney Greville. ECWP

Miss Flora McFlimsey, of Madison Square. Nothing to Wear. William Allen Butler. OBAL; PoLF

Miss Florence Jackson. David Huddle. PBCAP

Miss Foggerty's Cake. *Unknown.* BLPA; NBLV

Miss Gee. W. H. Auden. EBNV; OxBTC; UV, abr.

Miss Geeta. Margaret Reckord. AIW

Miss Grant. Freda Downie. FaBoWP

Miss Helen Slingsby was my maiden aunt. Aunt Helen. T. S. Eliot. AnAmPo; OBAL; PoA

Miss her, Catullus? don't be so inept to rail. Catullus, *tr. fr. Latin by* Celia *and* Louis Zukofsky. OBVE

Miss Ivy, tell me supmn. Wha Fe Call I'. Valerie Bloom. AIW; FaBoVe

Miss J. Hunter Dunn, Miss J. Hunter Dunn. A Subaltern's Love-Song. Sir John Betjeman. BoLoP; EBEvV; HAP; NoAM; NOBL; OxAEP-2; OxBTC; TwCP

Miss James. A. A. Milne. MoShBr

Miss Jennian Jones. *Unknown.* AmFP

Miss Kilmansegg and Her Precious Leg, *sels.* Thomas Hood.
  "Born in wealth and wealthily nursed." EBVV
  Her Accident. EBVV
  Her Christening. NOBVV
  Her Death. NOBVV
  Her Education. EBVV

Her Precious Leg. NOBVV
What Different Dooms Our Birthdays Bring! NAs
  (Miss Kilmansegg's Birth.) OxBoLi; PeLV

Miss Kilmansegg's Birth. Thomas Hood. *See* What Different Dooms Our Birthdays Bring!

Miss Lavender. Jon Stallworthy. OxBC

Miss Liza's Banjer. Daniel Webster Davis. AAP

Miss Loo. Walter de la Mare. CMoP; OxBTC

Miss Marnell. Austin Clarke. IPY

Miss Melerlee. John Wesley Holloway. PoNe

Miss Millay Says Something Too. Samuel Hoffenstein. BXAP; NBLV

Miss, miss, little miss, miss. *Unknown.* RoPo

Miss Muffett in a runaway ugly machine. I mean. Like that. (*LL*) W. W. Amiri Baraka. HeIL; HeIP; NOBA; PoBA

Miss Nancy Ellicott. Cousin Nancy. T. S. Eliot. AnAmPo; OBAL; OxBSP

Miss One, Two, and Three. *Unknown.* OxNR

Miss Penelope Burgess, Balling the Jack. Thomas McGrath. BCF

Miss Pheasant. Walter de la Mare. FaBoNo

Miss Pimberton Of. Siv Cedering. PBCAP

Miss R. looks at the mantel-piece, which must mean something. (*LL*) Evening in the Sanitarium. Louise Bogan. FaBoWP; FYAP; IHMS; NALW; TwCP

Miss Rafferty wore taffeta. The Private Dining Room. Ogden Nash. NYBP

Miss Ravenel's Conversion, *sels.* John William de Forest.

Miss Riley stands above me, fading fast. Bailey Gatzert: The First Grade, 1945. Lonny Kaneko. ETG

Miss Rosie. Lucille Clifton. AmPA; BlSi; CAPP; NMM; PoBA; Poetr; TwCP

Miss T. Walter de la Mare. FaBoBe; GoJo; GrPl; MoShBr; NTCP; PDV

Miss that fear because I survived it. (*LL*) The Winter Jacket. Sebastian Barry. IB

Miss Tourist. "Lord Kitchener." PBCV

Miss Tristram's *poulet* ended thus: 'Nota bene.' Mr. Placid's Flirtation. Frederick Locker-Lampson. PeVV

Miss Twye. Gavin Ewart. ErPo; FiBHP; NOBL

Miss Ulalume, there are questions that linger here. Abbreviated Interviews with a Few Disgruntled Literary Celebrities. Reed Whittemore. FiBHP

Miss Wagnalls, when I brought you here. The Girl I Took to the Cocktail Party. Trevor Williams. FiBHP

Miss You. David Cory. BLPA; FaBoBe

Miss You. *Unknown.* PoToHe

Missed a last shot. Gary Snyder. *Fr.* Myths and Texts. NaP; NOBA; NU

Missing. W. H. Auden. *See* From Scars Where Kestrels Hover.

Missing, The. Thom Gunn. PFL

Missing. A. A. Milne. MoShBr; PDV

Missing. John Pudney. OxBTC

Missing. John Banister Tabb. TrPWD

Missing. *Unknown.* WGRP

Missing Beat. Carolyn M. Rodgers. JB

Missing Dates. William Empson. CMoP; HAP; LiTB; LiTM; MoAB; MoBrPo; MoP; NoAM; NOBE; NoP; OAEL-2; PoE; UnPo

Missing from the map, the abandoned roads. Old Roads. Eiléan Ní Chuilleanáin. CIP; IIP; PWE

Missing Link. Sean Lucy. BiHa

Missing My Daughter. Stephen Spender. GTBS-P

Missing Patriarch, The. Michael S. Weaver. PBCAP

Missing Person, The. Donald Justice. CAPP; NYBP; Poetr

Missing so much and so much? (*LL*) To a Fat Lady Seen from the Train. Frances Cornford. BLPA; EBEvV; FaBoWP; GoJo; MoBrPo; OBMV; UV; WeW

Missing you. Love. Ted Berrigan. UL

Missing You. Shu Ting, *tr. fr. Chinese by* Carolyn Kizer *with* Y.H. Zhao. SpMi

Mission. *Unknown.* AmFP

Mission Bay. John Koethe. PoA

Mission of the Flowers, The. Frances E. W. Harper. BlSi

Mission to Linz. Richard Hugo. ArOW

Mission Work-Boat. *Unknown, tr. fr. Aborigine by* Mungayana Nundhirribala. NOBAu

Missionaries in the Jungle. Linda Piper. BlSi

Missionary, The. Mrs. Henry Linden. CBWP-4

Missionary at Karnizawa, The. Osman Edwards. *Fr.* Residential Rhymes. OBTV

Missionary from the Mau Mau told me, A. A Magus. John Ciardi. MAT

Missionary Hymm. James Burke. TIRV

Mitchells, The. Les A. Murray. FaBoMA

Mitching. Michael Smith. CIP

Mite, The. Boynton Merrill, Jr. CRP

Mites go up, The. Stalagmites and Stalactites. *Unknown.* FaBoUs

Mither's Lament, The. Sydney Goodsir Smith. OxBS

Mithraic Emblems, *sels.* Roy Campbell.

Mithras, God of the morning, our trumpets waken the wall! A Song to Mithras. Kipling. *Fr.* Puck of Pook's Hill. NoAM

Mithridates. Emerson. AnAmPo; NOBA

Mittelbergheim. Czeslaw Milosz, *tr. fr. Polish by the author* and Richard Lourie. AnRep

Mitten Song, The. Marie Louise Allen. NTCP

Mix a Pancake. Christina Rossetti. *Fr.* Sing-Song. NTCP

Mix in the box after the grinding of bones. (*LL*) November and Aunt Jemima. Thylias Moss. TRP

Mix up. Callaloo. Merle Collins. NBrP

Mixed Emotions. Huang Ching-jen, *tr. fr. Chinese by* Chang Yin-nan *and* Lewis C. Walmsley. SuSp

Mixed Feelings. John Ashbery. HAP; WeW

Mixed Marriage, The. Paul Muldoon. PNI

Mixed Singles. Liz Cashdan. NWP

Mixed Sketches. Don L. Lee. BPo; TAP

Mixed with age, she could foresee the future. Paul Evans. *Fr.* Two Sonnets. NBrP

Mixer, The. Louis MacNeice. FaBoTw

Mixing fresher air. (*LL*) It sounded as if the streets were running. Emily Dickinson. NAAL-1; OxBSP; PBWP

Mixture as Before, The. Phyllis McGinley. ArOW

Mixture of smells, The. A Bower of Roses. Louis Simpson. ArOW

Mizpah. Julia Aldrich Baker. BLPA; FaBoBe

Mnasylla, the daughter you lament. Perses, *tr. fr. Greek by* Peter Whigham. GrAn

Mnemosyne. Trumbull Stickney. LiTA; NOBA; OxBA

Mnemosyne Lay in Dust, *sels.* Austin Clarke.
"Maurice was in an Exhibition Hall." IPY; PoE
"Men were looking up." IPY
"One night he heard heart-breaking sound." CIP; CMoP; IPY
"Past the house where he was got." CMoP; IPY; PoE
"Rememorised, Maurice Devane." CMoP, (1970 ed.); IPY
"Straight-jacketing sprang to every lock." CMoP; IPY
"Summer was sauntering by." IPY
"Tall, handsome, tweeded Dr. Leeper." IPY

Mo Ghra Thu. Michael Hartnett. PeIV

Moanish Lady. *Unknown.* AS

Mob of dressing-tables is grazing, A. Duchesses. David Campbell. NOBAu

Mobile-Buck. James Edwin Campbell. AAP

Moby Dick, *sels.* Herman Melville.
Ribs and Terrors in the Whale, The.
(Ribs and Terrors, The.) ChIV-1
(Whale, The.) TrGrPo

Mock Charon, A. Richard Lovelace. CaPo

Mock-Epic Satire. Walter Harte. EPCY

Mock Invocation to Genius, A, *sels.* William Woty.
"I now solicit not the Muses nine." NOEC

Mock-Medicine. *Unknown.* MeEL

Mock On, Mock On, Voltaire, Rousseau. Blake. ChIV-1; EnRP; HAP; MeMBP; NAEL-2; NAWM-2; NoP; OAEL-2; OBNC; OxBSP; PeECV; PoE; PoEL-4; PPP; PrIm; SCGP; TFi

Mock Orange. Louise Glück. LPA; NoAM; VCAP

Mock Song, A. Richard Lovelace. BeJo; CaPo

Mock-Suns, The. Wilhelm Müller, *tr. fr. German by* Philip L. Miller. *Fr.* Winter's Journey, The. RiWo

Mock Turtle's Song, The. "Lewis Carroll." *See* "Will you walk a little faster?" said a [*or* the] whiting to a [*or* the] snail.

Mock up again, summer, the sooty altars. Spectacular Blossom. Allen Curnow. PeNZ

Mockado, Fustian, and Motley. John Taylor. *See* Sweet semi-circled Cynthia played at maw.

Mocking Bird, The. Paul Hamilton Hayne. AnAmPo

Mocking Bird, The. *Unknown.* AmFP

Mocking-bird on a branch, A. Wyncote, Pennsylvania: A Gloss. Thomas Kinsella. NOIV

Mocking Fairy, The. Walter de la Mare. MoBrPo; MoShBr

Mocking Song against Qaqortingneq. Piuvkaq, *tr. fr. Eskimo.* WTO

Mocking your untimely weeping. (*LL*) Dirge for the Year. Shelley. GN

Mockingbird, The. Randall Jarrell. NYBP; RFM

Mod Squad, The. David Trinidad. BAP-91

Model Children. David Trinidad. BAP-91

Model Church, The. John H. Yates. PWR

Model for the Laureate, A. W. B. Yeats. CMoP

Model School, Inchicore. Thomas Kinsella. CIP

Model Sermon, A. *Unknown.* FaBoUs

Moder Phoebe. *Unknown.* FaBoVe

Moderation. Robert Herrick. FaBoEE

Moderation. Horace, *tr. fr. Latin by* William Cowper. *Fr.* Odes. PoToHe

Moderation. Christopher Smart. *Fr.* Hymns for the Amusement of Children. NOCV

Modern Baby, The. William Croswell Doane. BLPA

Modern composer called Cage, A. Peter Alexander. PeLi

Modern Critics. Samuel Taylor Coleridge. FaBoEE

Modern Dragon, A. Rowena Bastin Bennett. PDV

Modern Fine Gentleman, The, *sels.* Soame Jenyns.
"Just broke from school, pert, impudent, and raw." ECEV; OBSV

Modern Fine Lady, The. Soame Jenyns. NOEC
Sels.
"But soon th'endearments of a husband cloy." ECEV
"For love no time has she, or inclination." OBSV

Modern Hiawatha, The. George A. Strong. *Fr.* Song of Milkanwatha, The. FaBoCo; FaBoPa; FaPON; FiBHP; MoShBr; PeLV; UV

Modern Jonas, The. *Unknown.* PAH

Modern Love. Keats. CBLP; OBNC; SCGP

Modern Love, *sels.* George Meredith.
"All other joys of life he strove to warm." EnVR
"Along the garden terrace, under which." NOBVV
"Am I failing? For no longer can I cast." EnVR; GBL; SCGP
"At dinner, she is hostess, I am host." EnVR; NOBVV; NoP; OHCV; PoE
(At Dinner, She Is Hostess.) Son
"But where began the change; and what's my crime?" PoEL-5
"By this he knew she wept with waking eyes." EnLoPo; EnVR; NAEL-2; NOBVV; NoP; OAEL-2; OHCV; OxBM; PoE; PoEL-5; Son
(End of Love, The.) HoPM
"He felt the wild beast in him betweenwhiles." EnVR; NOBVV
"He found her by the ocean's moaning verge." EnVR; NoP; OAEL-2
"Here Jack and Tom are paired with Moll and Meg." EnVR; InvP; PoEL-5
"I am to follow her. There is much grace." NAEL-2; NOBVV
"I play for seasons, not eternities." OBNC; SCGP
"I think she sleeps: it must be sleep, when low." NAEL-2
"In our old shipwrecked days there was an hour." BoLoP; EnVR; NOBVV
"It chanced his lips did meet her forehead cool." CBLP; EnVR; NOBVV
"It ended, and the morrow brought the task." EnVR
"It is no vulgar nature I have wived." NAEL-2
"It is the season of the sweet wild rose." GBL; PoEL-5
"Madam would speak with me. So, now it comes." NOBVV
"Mark where the pressing wind shoots javelin-like." EnLoPo; EnVR; GBL; NOBE; OBNC; PoEL-5; SCGP; TEP
(Love's Grave.) OBEV
"Message from her set his brain aflame, A." EnVR; NOBVV
"My lady unto Madam makes her bow." NOBVV
"Not solely that the future she destroys." GBL; TEP
"Out in the yellow meadows, where the bee." GBL
"She issues radiant from her dressing-room." EnVR; NOBVV
"Their sense is with their senses all mixed in." NAEL-2; NoP; OAEL-2; SCGP
"This golden head has wit in it. I live." NOBVV
"This was the woman; what now of the man?" EnVR; OHCV; Son
"Thus piteously Love closed what he begat." EBEV; EnLoPo; EnVR; GTBS-P; HAP; NOBE; NOBVV; NoP; OAEL-2; OBNC; OHCV; OxAEP-2; PoE; PoEL-5; SCGP; Son; TFi; TrGrPo
"'Tis Christmas weather, and a country house." NAEL-2; NOBVV
"We saw the swallows gathering in the sky." EnLoPo; GTBS-P; Mes; NOBE; NOBVV; OAEL-2; OBNC
(We Saw the Swallows.) ELP
"We three are on the cedar-shadowed lawn." NOBVV
"What are we first? First, animals; and next." GBL; HAP; NoP; PoEL-5
"Yet it was plain she struggled, and that salt." EnVR
"You like not that French novel? Tell me why." EnVR; NOBVV

Modern Love Poems. Somali Oral Tradition, *tr. by* B. W. Andrzejewski *and* M. Laurence. WTO

Modern Love Songs. *Unknown, tr. fr. Somali by* B. W. Andrzejewski *and* I. M. Lewis. TTY

Modern Major-General, The. W. S. Gilbert. *See* I Am the Very Model [*or* Pattern] of a Modern Major-General.

Modern malady of love is nerves, The. Nerves. Arthur Symons. FaBoTw

Modern Man I sing, The. (*LL*) One's-Self I Sing. Walt Whitman. FaBoPV; LPA; NOBA; OxBA

Modern Manners. Mary Alcock. ECWP

Modern Moses, or "My Policy" Man. James Madison Bell. AAP

Mondays sweating the flat smell. Days through Starch and Bluing. Alice Fulton. GOYP

Monet: "Les Nymphéas." W. D. Snodgrass. CoAP

Monet never knew. Monet's Lilies Shuddering. Lawrence Ferlinghetti. CAPP

Monet Refuses the Operation. Lisel Mueller. FYAP

Monet's Lilies Shuddering. Lawrence Ferlinghetti. CAPP

Monet's "Waterlilies." Robert Hayden. CAPP; Poetr

Money. Richard Armour. NBLV

Money. W. H. Davies. OBEV; OBMV

Money. Howard Nemerov. OxBC; VCAP; WeW

Money. C. H. Sisson. IHNG; OxBSP

Money. *Unknown.* AS

Money and a Friend. *Unknown.* BLPA

Money and the Mare. *Unknown.* ReMoGo

Money burns the pocket, pocket hurts. Seventh Street. Jean Toomer. NAAL-2

Money Cry, The. Peter Davison. FYAP

Money Gets the Mastery. Robert Herrick. CaPo

Money Is What Matters. *Unknown. See* Man upon mold, whatsoever thou be.

Money Isn't Everything! Oscar Hammerstein II. OBAL

Money Makes the Mirth. Robert Herrick. CaPo

Money men collect in high rise, The. Thumbing Old Magazines. Gerald Vizenor. VoR

Money! Money! *Yoruba Oral Tradition,* tr. by O. Ogunba. WTO

Money, money, now hay goode day! *Unknown.* MiEL

Money, thou bane of bliss and source of woe. Avarice. George Herbert. FaBoRV; LiTB

Money thou ow'st me; prithee fix a day. Upon Bunce: Epigram. Robert Herrick. CaPo

Money was anything that came to hand. La Malinche. Laura Moriarty. BAP-90

Money was once well known, like a townhall or the sky. Behaviour of Money. Bernard Spencer. LiTB

Moneyless Men, The. Henry T. Stanton. BLPA

Mongol in the Woods. Douglas Oliver. VaA

Mongoloid boy is astounded, The. In the Dome Car of the "Canadian." Sid Marty. NOBC

Mongoloid Child Handling Shells on the Beach, A. Richard Snyder. InPK

'Mongst all the hard names that denote reproach. Burnet's Character. *Unknown.* APAS

Mongst all the palaces in Hells command. Sospetto d'Herode. Giovanni Battista Marino, *tr. fr. Italian by* Richard Crashaw. *Fr.* Strage degli innocenti, La. SeCV-1

Monk, The. Blake. *Fr.* Jerusalem. EnRP

Monk and His Pet Cat, The. *Unknown, tr. fr. Old Irish.* CH

Monk and the Peasant, The. Margaret E. Bruner. PoToHe

Monk Arnulphus uncorked his ink, The. The Court Historian. George Walter Thornbury. CoGr; PeVV

Monk from Shu, carrying a precious lute. Listening to a Monk from Shu Playing the Lute. Li Po, *tr. fr. Chinese by* Joseph J. Lee. SuSp

Monk in the Kitchen, The. Anna Hempstead Branch. MoAmPo

Monk of Auspicious Fortune Monastery Asking Me to Name a Pavilion, A. Su Shih, *tr. fr. Chinese by* Chiang Yee. SuSp

Monk of Casal-Maggiore, The (The Sicilian's Tale). Longfellow. *Fr.* Tales of a Wayside Inn. AmPP; OxBA

Monk of Great Renown, The. *Unknown.* CoMu

Monk sat in his den, The. The Weak Monk. Stevie Smith. BoWoP; FaBoTw

Monk, step further off. *Unknown.* NOIV

Monk ther was, a fair for the maistrye [*or* maistrie], A. Chaucer. *Fr.* Canterbury Tales, The. CTC, *abr.;* EnVB; FHYEP; NoP; OAEL-1; PPP, *abr.;* TrGrPo

(Monk ther was, a monk of mastery, A.) TrGrPo

Monk there was, a monk of mastery, A. Chaucer. *See* Monk ther was, a fair for the maistrye [*or* maistrie], A.

Monkey, The. Mary Howitt. GN

Monkey. Josephine Miles. LiTM

Monkey Difference. Barbara Howes. AnAn

Monkey exclaimed with great glee, A. Frank Richards. PeLi

Monkey, lap-dog, parrot, and her Grace, The. Sir Charles Hanbury Williams. *Fr.* Isabella; or, The Morning. NOEC

Monkey, little merry fellow. The Monkey. Mary Howitt. GN

Monkey married the Baboon's sister, The. The Monkey's Wedding. *Unknown.* AS; BLPA

Monkey, monkey, bottle of pop. *Unknown.* RoPo

Monkey, monkey, sittin' on a rail. *Unknown.* RoPo

Monkey see, monkey do. *Unknown.* RoPo

Monkeyland. Sándor Weöres, *tr. fr. Hungarian by* Edwin Morgan. RB

Monkeys. Frank A. Collymore. PBCV

Monkeys. Padraic Colum. Mes; OxBTC

Monkeys. Klara Koettner-Benign, *tr. fr. German.* TSaS, *tr. by* Herbert Kuhner

Monkeys, The. Marianne Moore. CMoP; LiTA; MeMAP; NOBA; OxBA

Monkeys and the Crocodile, The. Laura E. Richards. FaPON

Monkeys gibbering by our bridal bed., The. (*LL*) The Puritan on His Honeymoon. Robert Bly. FF

Monkeys in a forest. Where. Walter de la Mare. GoJo; NYBP

Monkeys on Mt. Hiei. Edith Marcombe Shiffert. WPE

Monkey's Wedding, The. *Unknown.* AS; BLPA

Monkeys winked too much and were afraid of snakes, The. The Monkeys. Marianne Moore. LiTA; OxBA

Monks. Palladas, *tr. fr. Greek by* Peter Jay. GrAn

Monk's Dream. Art Lange. Jaz

Monk's gone. Bluehawk. Anne Waldman. Jaz

Monk's Mood. Sascha Feinstein. Jaz

Monk's Point. Art Lange. Jaz

Monk's robe hangs in a cloister in the hills, A. Paying a Visit to Monk Yung's Cloister. Meng Hao Jan, *tr. fr. Chinese by* Joseph J. Lee. SuSp

Monmouth Degraded. *Unknown.* FaBoEH

Monna Innominata., *sels.* Christina Rossetti.
"I love you first: but afterwards your love." VBLP
I Wish I Could Remember. Son
(First Day, The.) BLPL; BoLoP; FaBoBe; GBL; LPA
Love Me, for I Love You. Son
"Many in aftertimes will say of you." OBNC
"Youth gone, and beauty gone if ever there." GBL; OBNC; Son

Monochrome. Louise Imogen Guiney. AmWP

Monody. Herman Melville. LiTA; NAAL-1; OxBSP; PoE; PoEL-5

Monody on the Death of Chatterton, *sels.* Samuel Taylor Coleridge.
"Elate of heart and confidence of fame." EPCY

Monody to the Sound of Zithers. Kay Boyle. PoA

Monogamy, *sels.* Gerald Gould.
"You were young – but that was scarcely to your credit." OxBTC

Monogram 4. Martina Werner, *tr. fr. German by* Rosemarie Waldrop. BoWoP

Monogram 23. Martina Werner, *tr. fr. German by* Rosemarie Waldrop. BoWoP

Monogram 29. Martina Werner, *tr. fr. German by* Rosemarie Waldrop. BoWoP

Monologue. Hone Tuwhare. PeNZ

Monologue for Cassandra. Wislawa Szymborska, *tr. fr. Polish by* Grazyna Drabik *and* Sharon Olds. PoSu

Monologue in a Rand Hospital. William Elijah Hunter. PeSAV

Monologue of a Dying Beast. Mark Ameen. GLP

Monologue of the Crazed Mastodon. Paul Scheerbart. CBNP

Monostichs de la Guerre de Petite-Sparte, *sels.* Ian Hamilton Finlay.

Monotropa. Rose Terry Cooke. AmWP

Monsieur Etienne de Silhouette. Some Frenchmen. John Updike. FaBoCo; NBLV

Monsieur Ezra Pound croit que. Another Canto. J. B. Morton. FaBoPa; UV

Monsieur Gaston. A. M. Klein. MoCV

Monsieur Gauguin? 'E's gone to Tahiti. Stanley J. Sharpless. PeLi

Monsoon. Beckian Fritz Goldberg. NAmP90

Monsoon. David Wevill. NYBP

Monsoon Girl. Harry Clifton. BiHa; IB; PBCIP

Monster, The. Greg Kuzma. AmPA

Monster, The. Henry Rago. PoA

Monster has escaped from the dungeon, The. Frankenstein. Edward Field. FF

Monster, in a course of vice grown old, A. The Monument. Samuel Wesley. OxBSP

Monstering horror swallows, A. Thanksgiving (1956). E. E. Cummings. FaBoPV; IHNG

Monsters. Vuyelwa Carlin. NWP

Monstrance. János Pilinszky, *tr. fr. Hungarian by* Peter Jay. PoSu

Mont Blanc. Shelley. EnRP; InPS; NAEL-2; NIP; NoP; OAEL-2; OBTV; TEP

Montague Michael. *Unknown.* CRH; OTCP

Montalbert, *sels.* Charlotte Smith.
"Swift fleet the billowy clouds along the sky." BoWoP; WPE

Montana Eclogue. William Stafford. NYBP

Montana Fifty Years Ago. J. V. Cunningham. Prf

Montana Pastoral. J. V. Cunningham. MAT; MoAmPo; PrIm; VGW

Montana Ranch Abandoned. Richard Hugo. CAPP

Montanus' Sonnet. Thomas Lodge. *Fr.* Rosalynde; or Euphues' Golden Legacy. PoEL-2

Montcalm and Wolfe. *Unknown.* AmFP

Montecastelli Poem. Sophie Behrens. NBrP

Monterey. Charles Fenno Hoffman. AnAmPo; FaBoBe; PAH

Montgomery. Sam Cornish. PoBA; Poetsp

Montgomery at Quebec. Clinton Scollard. PAH

Month is amber, The. October. John Updike. PDV

Month of great men. February. Lolly Quinones. IMW

Month of January. Frankie Armstrong. BrRo

Month of January has flown Past, The. Joseph Brodsky, *tr. fr. Russian by* George L. Kline. AnAn

Month of leaves. June. Irene F. Pawsey. BoTP

Month of May, The. Beaumont *and* Fletcher *and* John Fletcher. *Fr.* Knight of the Burning Pestle, The. ChTr

Month of September, The. Sir John Davies. *Fr.* Hymns of Astræa [in Acrostic Verse]. SiPSBD

Month of the drowned dog, The. After long rain the land. November. Ted Hughes. CMoP; GTBS-P; NoP

Month or twain to live on honeycomb, A. Before Parting. Swinburne. CBLP; NOBVV

Months, The. Sara Coleridge. *See* January brings the snow.

Months, The. Christina Rossetti. FaPON

Months, The. *Unknown.* OxBLMV

Months, The. *Unknown. See* By this [*or* thys] fire [*or* fyre] I warm[e] my handes [*or* handys].

Months after the Muse. The Illustration — a Footnote. Denise Levertov. PoA

Months Go By, The. *Unknown, tr. fr. Chinese by* Kenneth Rexroth. OHMPC

Months go by like water in a waterfall, The. The Months Go By. *Unknown, tr. fr. Chinese by* Kenneth Rexroth. OHMPC

Months of the Year, The. Richard Grafton. *See* Thirty days hath November.

Months of the Year, The. *Unknown.* FaBoUs

Monticello. Robert Hass. AnAn

Monticello. May Sarton. GOA

Montjuich. Philip Levine. AnAn

Montrachet — le — Jardin, *sels.* Wallace Stevens. Ascetic Trove of Responsive Fact, The. CBCK

Montreal. A. M. Klein. MoCV

Monument, The. Elizabeth Bishop. HCAP; LiTA; NoAM; NOBA; Poetr; TRP

Monument, A. Charles Madge. FaBoMo

Monument. A. M. Sullivan. GoYe

Monument, The. Samuel Wesley. OxBSP

Monument Mountain. Bryant. BeLS; EAP

Monument of Cleita, The. Edward Cracroft Lefroy, *after the Greek of* Theocritus. *Fr.* Echoes from Theocritus. AWP

Monumental Memorial of Marine Mercy, A. Richard Steere. SCAP

Monuments for a Friendly Girl at a Tenth Grade Party. William Stafford. NoAM

Monuments of Hiroshima, The. D. J. Enright. OxBSP; PAW

Monumentum Aere, Etc. Ezra Pound. NOBA

Mony ane talks o the grass, the grass. Willie and Earl Richard's Daughter. *Unknown.* ESPB

Mony klyf he overclambe in contrayes straunge. *Unknown, tr. fr. Middle English by* Brian Stone. *Fr.* Sir Gawain and the Green Knight. FaBoVe; OAEL-1

Moo! Robert Silliman Hillyer. OBAL

Moo-Cow-Moo, The. Edmund Vance Cooke. MoShBr

Moochie ("Moochie likes to keep on playing.") Eloise Greenfield. NTCP

Mood, The. Quandra Prettyman. PoBA

Mood Apart, A. Robert Frost. OxBSP

Mood Indigo. William Matthews. WeW

Mood of Vichy, The. Hildebert, *tr. fr. Latin by* Helen Waddell. MLL

Moods. Leyb Kvitko, *tr. fr. Yiddish by* Joseph Leftwich. TrJP

Moods. W. B. Yeats. CTC; EBVVPR

Moods and Tenses. *Unknown.* ISE

Moods of Rain. Vernon Scannell. BoNaP

Mooimeisjes. Perceval Gibbon. PeSAV

Moolie Besom, A. "Hugh MacDiarmid." IHNG

Mooly cow, mooly cow, home from the wood. The Cow-Boy's Song. Anna Maria Wells. OBCA

Moon. Nathan Alterman, *tr. fr. Hebrew by* Ruth Finer Mintz. MHP

Moon, The. Robert Creeley. VGW

Moon, The. W. H. Davies. MoBrPo

Moon, The. Emily Dickinson. BoTP

Moon. Frances Horovitz. BrRo

Moon, The. Hsüeh T'ao, *tr. fr. Chinese by* Eric W. Johnson. SuSp

Moon, The. (*LL*) In Mornigan's park there is a deer. *Unknown.* GBP

Moon, The. Wendy Mulford. NBrP

Moon. Henry Rowe. OBEV

Moon, The. Shelley. *See* And, like a dying lady, lean and pale.

Moon, The. William Jay Smith. CRH; PDV

Moon, The. Robert Louis Stevenson. PWR; TLR

Moon, The. *Unknown.* FaBoVe

Moon. Derek Walcott. MoP

Moon, a sweeping scimitar, dipped in the stormy straits, The. Winged Man. Stephen Vincent Benét. MoAmPo

Moon above the milky field, The. Night-Piece. Léonie Adams. MoAB; MoAmPo

Moon all over Ch'ang-an. Song of Wu at Midnight. Li Po, *tr. fr. Chinese.* LHF, *tr. by* Hualing Nieh

Moon and a Cloud, The. W. H. Davies. RB

Moon and Candle-light. William Renton. NOBVV

Moon and clouds are the same. Wu-Men. EnlH

Moon and seven Pleiades have set, The. Alone. Sappho, *tr. fr. Greek by* William Ellery Leonard. AWP

Moon and the Night and the Men, The. John Berryman. ArOW; CoAP; VCAP; VGW

Moon and the Nightingale, The. Milton. *See* Now came still evening on, and twilight gray.

Moon and the Salt Flats, The. Mary di Michele. NOBC

Moon and the Yew Tree, The. Sylvia Plath. CoAP; FaBoMo; FaBoWP; NaP; NYBP; PlP; PPP; VGW; WPE; WPOW

Moon as Medusa. Vinnie-Marie D'Ambrosio. IHMS

Moon at Three A.M. Lance Henson. CDW

Moon beams and yams. Rapping Along with Ronda Davis. James Cunningham. JB

Moon behind High Tranquil Leaves, The. Robert Nichols. OBMV

Moon behind the Hill, The. *Unknown.* WTO

Moon blackens, geese fly high. Lu Lun, *tr. by* Ronald C. Miao. *Fr.* Frontier Songs. SuSp

Moon-Bone Song [*or* Cycle]. *Aborigine Oral Tradition, tr. by* R. M. Berndt. CBAP

Sels.

Birds, The. WTO

Evening Star, The. WTO

New Moon. WTO

Moon Bound. Raymond Washington. NBV

Moon came to the forge, The. Ballad of Luna, Luna. Federico García Lorca, *tr. fr. Spanish by* William B. Logan. SOTW

Moon-Child, The. "Fiona Macleod." CH

Moon comes down amongst men, The. (*LL*) Night on the Great River. Meng Hao Jan. OHMPC

Moon does shine as bright as day. (*LL*) Namby-Pamby. Henry Carey. CBNP; FaBoNo; FaBoPa; NOEC; OBSV; UV, *sh. vers.*

Moon drops one or two feathers into the field, The. Beginning. James Wright. VCAP

Moon Eclipse Exorcism. *Unknown, tr. fr. Alsea Indian by* Armand Schwerner. STP

Moon-faced baby with cocaine arms. Blues for Sister Sally. Lenore Kandel. NMM

Moon Festival. Tu Fu, *tr. fr. Chinese by* Kenneth Rexroth. NaP

Moon Fishing. Lisel Mueller. CoAP

Moon, Flowers, Man. Su Tung-p'o, *tr. fr. Chinese by* Kenneth Rexroth. NaP

Moon goes over the water, The. Half Moon. Federico García Lorca, *tr. fr. Spanish by* W. S. Merwin. RFM

Moon had a courtyard, The. The Enemy. Bettina Wegner, *tr. fr. German by* Agnes Stein. PAW

Moon had climbed the highest hill, The. The Banks of Dee. *Unknown.* AmFP

Moon had risen an hour or more, The. Crescent Moon. William Renton. NOBVV

Moon had risen on the eastern hill, The. The Sailor and His Bride. *Unknown.* AmFP

Moon has a face like the clock in the hall, The. The Moon. Robert Louis Stevenson. PWR; TLR

Moon Has Complained, The. Paul Johann Ludwig Heyse, *tr. fr. German by* Philip L. Miller. RiWo

Moon has gone to her rest, The. Wilfrid Scawen Blunt. OBMV

Moon has lodged a grievous complaint, The. The Moon Has Complained. Paul Johann Ludwig Heyse, *tr. fr. German by* Philip L. Miller. RiWo

Moon Has Set, The. Sappho, *tr. fr. Greek.* ChTr; PGA

Moonmoth and grasshopper that flee our page. A Name for All. Hart Crane. VGW

Moonpoem. Rosie Orr. VBLP

Moonrise. Hilda Doolittle ("H. D."). PoA

Moonrise. Gerard Manley Hopkins. EnVR; FaBoPP; MoAB; MoBrPo; NOBVV; RB

Moonrise. D. H. Lawrence. LiTM; PoA

Moonrise Over Battlefield. Edgell Rickword. NSI; PoWW

Moons. Peter Fallon. BiHa

Moon's a devil jester, The. The Traveler. Vachel Lindsay. MoAmPo

Moon's a little arch, The. A Classic Case. Gilbert Sorrentino. NeAP

Moon's a path, The. Hansel, Gretel and Ruby Redlips. Anita Endrezze-Danielson. HATNAP

Moon's glow by seven fold multiplied, turned red. After Reading St. John the Divine. Gene Derwood. ImPo; LiTM; WPE

Moon's greygolden meshes make, The. Alone. James Joyce. InvP

Moon's little skullcap, The. Front Street. Howard Moss. NYBP

Moon's my constant mistress, The. Tom o' Bedlam. *Unknown.* CH; CoGr; FaBoCh; PoRA

Moon's on the lake, and the mist's on the brae, The. MacGregor's Gathering. Sir Walter Scott. OxBS

Moon's the North Wind's Cooky, The. Vachel Lindsay. FaPON; OBCA; PDV

Moon's up-riding makes a line, The. Night Scenes. Robert Duncan. VGW

Moonset. Sir Henry Newbolt. EBVV

Moonset, Gloucester, December 1, 1957, 1:58 A.M. Charles Olson. CAPP

Moonsheep, The. Christian Morgenstern, *tr. fr.* German by Hugh Haughton. CBNP, *tr. by* Geoffrey Grigson; FaBoNo, *tr. by* Geoffrey Grigson

Moonshine. Walter de la Mare. FiBHP

Moonshot Sonnet. Mary Ellen Solt. BoWoP

Moonsongs, *sels.* Niyi Osundare.
"Frantic as a prentice poet," sect V. HBAPE
"Maddening moon, A," sect. XIX. HBAPE
"Moon is an exile, The," sect. XVIII. HBAPE
"We called the statue." HBAPE

Moonstruck. "Hugh MacDiarmid." NAEL-2

Moontan. Mark Strand. NYBP

Moonwalk. John Engels. MAT

Moor, The. Ralph Hodgson. MoBrPo

Moor, The. R. S. Thomas. OBWVE

Moorhen. William Logan. DiPo

Mooring at K'ou-ch'üeh, *sels.* Pien Kung, *tr. fr.* Chinese by Jonathan Chaves.

Mooring in the Evening at Plum Village, *sels.* P'eng Sun-yü, *tr. fr.* Chinese by Daniel Bryant.

Moorings. Norman MacCaig. OxBTC

Moorish Cloth, The. Manuel de Falla, *tr. fr.* Spanish by Philip L. Miller. RiWo

Moorland fires are gathered up, The. Tune: "Big String of Words A" — The Great Wall. Na-lan Hsing-te, *tr. fr.* Chinese by Lenore Mayhew *and* William McNaughton. SuSp

Moorland sheep is frightened and amazed, The. Philosophy Is Born. Christian Morgenstern, *tr. fr.* German by Geoffrey Grigson. FaBoNo

Moors, The. John Clare. EnVR

Moose, The. Elizabeth Bishop. DiPo; FaBoWP; NAAL-2; NALW

Mooses. Ted Hughes. OBAP

Mop-eyed I am, as some have said. Upon Himself. Robert Herrick. OxBSP

Moral, The. W. E. Henley. OxAEP-2

Moral, The. Theodore Weiss. Prf

Moral Alphabet, A, *sels.* Hilaire Belloc.
"A stands for Archibald who told no lies." NoAM
"B stands for Bear. When bears are seen." NoAM
"Dreadful Dinotherium he, The." NOBL
"E stands for egg." NoAM
"K for the Klondyke, a country of gold." NoAM
"R the reviewer, reviewing my book." NoAM

moral: "Behave." (*LL*) Rules and Regulations. "Lewis Carroll." FaBoUs; NOBVV; PeVV

Moral climbs whose name should be a wreath, A. (*LL*) Mr. Pope. Allen Tate. MoAB; NoAM; NOBA; TwCP; VGW

Moral Essays, *sels.* Pope.
Coxcomb Bird, The. ImPo
Duke of Buckingham, The. NOBE
Epistle to a Lady: Of the Characters of Women. NAEL-1; NOEC; OAEL-1; OxBoLi, *shorter sel.*
"Men, some to bus'ness, some to pleasure take." OBSV
"Yet Chloe [*or* Cloe] sure was formed without a spot." ErPo; OBSV (Chloe.) AWP; NOBE

To Richard Boyle, Earl of Burlington: Of the Uses of Riches. NOEC; OAEL-1; OBSV; PoEL-3; PPP
"At Timon's villa let us pass a day."
(Of the Use of Riches.) ECEV
(Timon's Villa.) PoE

Moral is — Take care how you light, The. (*LL*) Darius Green and His Flying-Machine. John Townsend Trowbridge. AnAmPo; BeLS; BLPL; FaBoBe; MoShBr; OBAL; OBCA; OxBChV; PoLF

Moral Poem, A. J. V. Cunningham. VGW

Moral Poem Freely Accepted from Sappho, A. James Wright. CAPP

Moral Proverbs and Folk Songs, *sels.* Antonio Machado Ruiz, *tr. fr.* Spanish.
"But look in your mirror for the other one." RaBo
"Don't trace out your profile." RaBo
"Look for your other half." RaBo
"Narcissism/ is an ugly fault." RaBo

Moral says; mix water with your wine, The. (*LL*) Great Bacchus: From the Greek. Matthew Prior. FaBoCo

Moral Story II. David Wright. PeSA

Moral Tale, A. Roger Woddis. IHNG; UV

Moral Taxi Ride, The. Erich Kästner, *tr. fr.* German by Jerome K. Rothenberg. ErPo

Moral Tetrastich, A. Sir William Jones, *after the Sanskrit of* Kalidasa. *See* On parent knees, a naked new-born child.

Moral. You can *see* it's immoral. (*LL*) Are Flowers Whores? Elizabeth Smart. VBLP

Moralist still obstinate replies, The. Voltaire, *tr. fr.* French by Tobias Smollet. *Fr.* Lisbon Earthquake, The. OBD

Morality, thou deadly bane. Burns. *Fr.* Dedication to G**** H******* Esq., A. OBSV

Morals. James Thurber. *Fr.* Further Fables for Our Time. FaBV

Morant Bay. *Unknown.* FaBoVe

Mordant and decadent Youth, A. Thomas Thorneley. PeLi

More. Philip Appleman. BXAP

More. Gertrude Stein. *Fr.* Tender Buttons. PBWP

More. (*LL*) The Execution of Madame du Barry. J. J. Bray. NOBAu

More Abandoned, The More Divine, The. "Angelus Silesius," *tr. fr.* German. *Fr.* Cherubical Wanderer, The. GePo, *tr. by* George C. Schoolfield

More amazed than anything. The Kitten. Mary Oliver. CAPP

More amorous than Solomon. (*LL*) A Worm Fed on the Heart of Corinth. Isaac Rosenberg. OAEL-2; PeFWW; PoWW

More Ancient Mariner, A. Bliss Carman. AnAmPo; OBAL

More Animals, *sels.* Oliver Herford.

More Astonishing. Khosrovidought Koghtnatsi, *tr. fr.* Armenian by Diana Der Hovanessian. VBLP

More astonishing to me. More Astonishing. Khosrovidought Koghtnatsi, *tr. fr.* Armenian by Diana Der Hovanessian. VBLP

More Bagpipe Music. E. O. Parrott. UV

More Ballads! here's a spick and span new Supplication. A Free Parliament Litany. *Unknown.* OxBoLi

More beautiful and soft than any moth. The Landscape near an Aerodrome. Stephen Spender. LiTM; MoAB; MoBrPo; NoAM; OxBTC

More beautiful than any gift you gave. The Token. F. T. Prince. FaBoTw; OxBTC

More beautiful than the notable moon and its ennobled light. To the Sun. Ingeborg Bachmann, *tr. fr.* German. BoNaP, *tr. by* Michael Hamburger

More Best Jokes of the Delphic Oracle. William Knott. UL

More Blues and the Abstract Truth. C. D. Wright. NAmP90

More brave than me: more blond than you. (*LL*) I Sing of Olaf Glad and Big. E. E. Cummings. HeIP; LiTM; MeMAP; MoP; NAAL-2; NoAM; NOBA; NoP; OBSV; OBWP; PoWW; VGW

More bright and large than this. (*LL*) An Answer to Another Persuading a Lady to Marriage. Katherine Philips. HAP; VBLP; WeW

More Clues. Muriel Rukeyser. IHMS

More dear, both for themselves, and for thy sake. (*LL*) Lines Composed a Few Miles above Tintern Abbey [on Revisiting the Banks of the Wye during a Tour, July 13, 1798]. Wordsworth. BLPL; EBEvV; EnRP; FaBoPP; FF; FHYEP; HeIP; InPS; LiTB; MeMBP; NoP; OAEL-2; OBNC; OxAEP-2; PoEL-4; Poetr; PPP; PrIm; SCGP; TEP; TFi; TrGrPo

More discontents I never had. Discontents in Devon. Robert Herrick. BeJo; CaPo; OxBSP; SeCV-1

More diseases than textbooks. Serpent to Zymurgy. Iain Sinclair. VaA

More distant than the dead sea. Nadia Tuéni, *tr. fr.* French by Carol Cosman. PBWP

More essential thing., A. (*LL*) Pedigree of honey, The. Emily Dickinson. BLPL; FaBV; MoP; NOBA; SAmP

More everyday. (*LL*) Brown Lullaby. Adam Small. PeSAV

More gaily, dance. Quick-Step. Robert Creeley. VGW

More geese than swans now live, more fools than wise. (*LL*) The Silver Swan. *At. to* Orlando Gibbons. ChTr; EiL; ELP; EnRePo; FaBoCh; HAP; HeIP; IMW; InPK; NAEL-1; NoP; OBD; OxBSP

More grotesque than a row of laundromats. The Novelty Shop. Duane Niatum. CDW

More hard than any ghost there is or any man there/ was! (*LL*) The Looking Glass. Kipling. FaBoEH; FaBoTw; NTP; OBMV

More harmless vanity?, A. (*LL*) On an Infant Dying as Soon as Born. Charles Lamb. GTBS; GTBS-P; IMW; OBEV

More haughty than the rest, the wolfish race. The Presbyterians. Dryden. *Fr.* Hind and the Panther, The. NOSC

More hope to perish soon. (*LL*) The End of May. William Morris. NOBVV

More humane Mikado never, A. The Mikado's Song. W. S. Gilbert. *Fr.* Mikado, The. LiTB

More I beat my wife, The. (*LL*) When Adam Day by Day. A. E. Housman. FiBHP

More ill at ease was never man than Walbach, that Lord's day. The Legend of Walbach Tower. George Houghton. PAH

More Islands. Eiléan Ní Chuilleanáin. PWE

More It Snows, The. A. A. Milne. NTCP; PYC; SiSoPo

More Joy in Heaven. Howard Nemerov. NoAM

More kicks than pence. To Hell with Commonsense. Patrick Kavanagh. FaBoTw

More Lessons from a Mirror. Thylias Moss. ETG

More Light! More Light! Anthony Hecht. ArOW; BTR; CoAP; HAP; NoAM; NOBA; NoP; OBWP; Poetr; RB; SM; TwCP; UnPo; VCAP; VGW

More like a stock than like a vine. (*LL*) The Vine. Robert Herrick. BeJo; CaPo; ErPo; FaBoBl; NAEL-2; NoP

More liked by her, or loved by me. (*LL*) To the Most Fair and Lovely Mistress Anne Soame, Now Lady Abdie [*or* Abdy]. Robert Herrick. CaPo; NOBE; NOSC

More Love. *Unknown.* AH

More love ore more disdain I crave. Against Indifference. Charles Webbe. OBEV

More Love to Thee, O Christ. Elizabeth Payson Prentiss. AH

More Loving One, The. W. H. Auden, *tr. by the author.* ArLo; HoPM; TOF

More Luck to Honest Poverty. Shirley Brooks. BXAP; UV

More Nudes for Florence. Harold Witt. ErPo

More of a Corpse than a Woman. Muriel Rukeyser. NALW; NMM

More of Thee. Horatius Bonar. BLRP

More oft than once Death whispered in mine ear. Sonnet: Death's Last Will. William Drummond of Hawthornden. JCP
(Redeem Time Past.) OxAEP-1

More On George IV. *Unknown.* IHNG

More pleasing sounds the song of the birds. Ludwig Heinrich Christoph Hölty, *tr. fr. German by* Philip L. Miller. RiWo

More Power. Egan O'Rahilly, *tr. fr. Modern Irish by* John Montague. BIrV

More Reformation., *sels.* Daniel Defoe.
"To sin's a vice in nature, and we find." OBSV

More reminiscent than distressed, you say. To a Blind Student Who Taught Me to See. Samuel Hazo. GOYP

More rich than Cleopatra's tomb. (*LL*) The Amber Bead. Robert Herrick. BeJo; CaPo; ChTr

More she had spoke, but yawn'd — All nature nods. Pope. *Fr.* Dunciad, The. FHYEP

More Shrines. David Kirby. NGP

More Songs from Vagabondia, *sels.* Richard Hovey.

More Sonnets at Christmas. Allen Tate. LiTA; LiTM
Sels.
"Gay citizen, myself, and thoughtful friend."

More sound in France — that, too, he secret keeps. (*LL*) A Private. Edward Thomas. GTBS-P; NSI; PeFWW

More Stanzas Applied to Spiritual Things. St. John of the Cross, *tr. fr. Spanish by* K. Kavanaugh *and* O. Rodrigues. TOF

More Strong Than Time. Victor Hugo, *tr. fr. French by* Andrew Lang. AWP

More than a King's my Word dos rule to day. To a Young Lady That Desired a Verse of My Being Servant One Day and Mistress Another. Elizabeth Tipper. *Fr.* Pilgrim's Viaticum; or, The Destitute, But Not Forlorn. KTR; NOSC

More than Apollo's golden lyre. Meleager, *tr. fr. Greek by* Peter Whigham. GrAn

More than leaves, more than flakes. More. Philip Appleman. BXAP

More than Morgan, I desire to eat people. Morgan. John Blight. CBAP

More than most fair, full of that heavenly fire. Fulke Greville. *Fr.* Caelica. EiL

More Than Most People. Eldon Grier. MoCV

More than novelty crooked its finger — silent, austere. Melissa Green. DiPo

More than the gems/ locked away and treasured. Sent from the Capital to Her Elder Daughter. Lady Otomo no Sakanoe, *tr. fr. Japanese by* Geoffrey Bownas *and* Anthony Thwaite. AIW; BoWoP; MDDM; WPOW

More than the moment. Two Mexicanos Lynched in Santa Cruz, California, May 3, 1877. Martín Espada. AfAz

More than the shortest distance. A Barbed Wire Fence Meditates upon the Goldfinch. Don McKay. NOBC

More than thirty years have rushed. On His Thirty-Third Birthday. Ch'ang Kuo Fan, *tr. fr. Chinese by* Kenneth Rexroth. OHMPC

More than this I scarce can die. (*LL*) Fare Thee Well. Byron. BLPA; CBLP; EnRP; MeMBP; OBNC; PoEL-4

More than thyself to love thy neighbor. (*LL*) The Latest Decalogue. Arthur Hugh Clough. ChIV-1; ChTr; CoGr; EBEV; EBVV; EBVVPR; EnVR; FaBoCo; FaBoEE; FF; GTBS-P; HAP; HeIL; HoPM; IHNG; NAEL-2; NOBE; NOBVV; OAEL-2; OBNC; OBSV; OPOP; OtMeF; PeECV; PlP; PPP; SCGP; TFi; WeW; WGRP

More than We Ask. Faith Wells. BLRP

More then of eithers manners, wit, or face! (*LL*) Let me be what I am, as Virgil cold. Ben Jonson. PoEL-2; SeCP

More things are wrought by prayer. Tennyson, *incorporated in* Idylls of the King *with changes, as* The Passing of Arthur. *Fr.* Morte d'Arthur. BLRP; DL; EBVVPR; FaBoBe; FaBoRV; NIP; NOBVV; OAEL-2; OBNV; PoEL-5

More to be pleased than innocent. (*LL*) I Pressed Her Rebel Lips. *Unknown.* BoLoP; ErPo

More touching is the deathbed than the bier! (*LL*) Old Ruralities: A Regret. Charles Tennyson Turner. EBVV; Son

More vicious than stoat or weasel. Ferret. Stewart Conn. PWE

More ways to set the selfsame welkin ringing? (*LL*) The Canadian Authors Meet. F. R. Scott. NOBC

More we live, more brief appear, The. The River of Life. Thomas Campbell. GTBS; GTBS-P; ImPo; LiTB
(Thought Suggested by the New Year, A.) OBNC

More wealth brings in than all those three. (*LL*) The Four Sweet Months. Robert Herrick. BoTP; WiR

More white than whitest Lillies far. To Electra. Robert Herrick. CBCK

More whyght thou art than primrose leaf my lady Galatee. Ovid, *tr. fr. Latin. Fr.* Metamorphoses. OBVE, *tr. by* Arthur Golding (Cyclops.) CTC, *tr. by* Arthur Golding

More ye desire her, the sooner ye miss, The. How to Obtain Her. *Unknown.* NoSic

More years ago than I can state. My Last Illusion. John Kaye Kendall. FiBHP

Morea's Sonnet. Mary Sidney Wroth, Countess of Montgomery. *Fr.* Urania. WPE

Morels. William Jay Smith. BoNaP; MAT; NYBP; RFM

Moreover the Lord answered Job, and said. Bible, *O.T. Fr.* Job. NAWM-1, *abr.*; OBVE

Moreover the LORD saith, Because the daughters of Zion are haughty. The Bravery of Their Tinkling Ornaments. Bible, *O.T. Fr.* Isaiah. CBCK

Moreton Bay. *Unknown.* CBAP

Morgan. John Blight. CBAP

Morgan Stanwood. Hiram Rich. PAH

Morgan's Country. Francis Webb. FaBoMA

Morgan's curls are matted. Henry Morgan's March on Panama. A. G. Prys-Jones. AngWe

Morgante Maggiore, Il, *sels.* Luigi Pulci, *tr. fr. Italian.* Prophecy. PAH

Morituri Salutamus., *sels.* Longfellow.
"For age is opportunity no less." PoToHe
It Is Too Late. BLPL; PoLF
(Too Late?) WBLP

Moriturus. "Marie Madelaine," *tr. fr. French by* Ferdinand E. Kappey. PeHV

Moriturus. Edna St. Vincent Millay. LiTA; MeMAP

Morley's light went out. Power Failure. Michael Dennis Browne. AmPA

Mormons, led by Colonel Cooke, The. On the Road to California; or, The Buffalo Bullfight. *Unknown.* AmFP

Morn. Josephine D. Henderson Heard. CBWP-4

Morn hath risen clear and bright, The. The Expulsion of Hagar. Eloise Bibb. CBWP-4

Morn was cloudy and dark and gray, The. The Battle of Morris' Island. *Unknown.* PAH

Morning. Joanna Baillie. *Fr.* Winter Day, A. ECWP

Morning. Blake. FaBoCh; OAEL-2

Morning. William Browne. *See* Muses' friend, The (grey-eyed Aurora), yet.

Morning. Charles Stuart Calverley. FiBHP

Morning. Thomas Carlyle. PWR

Morning. Chu Shu-chen, *tr. fr. Chinese* by Kenneth Rexroth. BoWoP

Morning. Harry Clifton. IB

Morning. John Cunningham. NOEC

Morning. (LL) Curriculum Vitae. Robert Gray. NOBAu

Morning. Emily Dickinson. *See* Will there really be a morning?

Morning. Tove Ditlevsen, *tr. fr. Danish* by Nadia Christensen. PBWP

Morning. Ivy O. Eastwick. BoTP

Morning. Glyn Jones. AngWe

Morning. Keats. *See* Now Morning from her orient chamber came.

Morning/ broods. Strawberrying. Maurice Kenny. HATNAP

Morning. John Crowe Ransom. AnAmPo

Morning. Unknown. NOEC

Morning. Wang Wei, *tr. fr. Chinese* by Robert Payne. TAL

Morning, A. Mark Strand. HCAP

Morning: a polished knifeblade. Jalal al-Din Rumi, *tr. fr. Persian* by Coleman Barks *with* A. J. Arberry. EnlH

Morning After, The. Tony Harrison. FaBoEH

Morning After, The. Heine, *tr. fr. German* by Louis Untermeyer. ErPo

Morning After. Langston Hughes. Jaz; MoP; NAAL-2; NBLV; NoAM

Morning After, The. Dorothy Wellesley. OBMV

Morning after morning, to be close to floating fame. (LL) Wandering on Mount Chung-nan. Meng Chiao. PLT

Morning after . . . Love, The. Kattie M. Cumbo. BlSi

Morning again, nothing has to be done. Second Poem. Peter Orlovsky. NeAP

Morning and evening. Christina Rossetti. *Fr.* Goblin Market. BoTP; EBEV; EBEvV, *ll.* 1–31; NAEL-2; NALW; NOBVV; OBNV; OxAEP-2 (Worrying Fruit.) CBCK

Morning and Evening. Antoni Slonimski, *tr. fr. Polish* by Watson Kirkconnell. TrJP

Morning and evening, drunk and singing. For Kuo Hsiang. Yü Hsüan-chi, *tr. fr. Chinese* by Geoffrey R. Waters. BoWoP

Morning and evening in the corn. (LL) Country Summer. Léonie Adams. GoJo; LiTM; MoAB; MoAmPo; TrGrPo

Morning and evening, sleep she drove away. The Spinning Woman. Leonidas of Tarentum, *tr. by* Andrew Lang. *Fr.* Epigrams. AWP

Morning and Evening Star. Plato. *See* Thou wert the morning star among the living.

Morning and night I bring. Cottage Song. John Drinkwater. UV

Morning and night I found. Same Cottage — But Another Song, of Another Season. Max Beerbohm. UV

Morning, and streaks of heavenly blue. London Spring. Antoni Slonimski, *tr. fr. Polish* by Frances Notley. TrJP

Morning, and the poet up again and out and about. The Poet's Day. Richard Weber. CIP

Morning and the snow might fall forever. Going to Remake This World. James Welch. CDW

Morning arises stormy and pale. Tennyson. *Fr.* Maud[: A Monodrama]. EBVVPR; EnVR

Morning at nine, seven ultra-masculine men. In Your Bad Dream. Richard Hugo. LCAP

Morning at Point Dume. May Swenson. DiPo

Morning at the Window. T. S. Eliot. AWP; PoA

Morning Athletes. Marge Piercy. AIW

Morning Bird Songs. Tomas Transtromer, *tr. fr. Swedish* by Robert Bly. InPS

Morning: blue, cold, and still. January. Weldon Kees. CoAP

Morning breaks like a pomegranate, The. Wedding Morn. D. H. Lawrence. MoAB; MoBrPo

Morning Bright, with Rosy Light, The. Thomas O. Summers. AH

Morning broke like an egg. Eggs. Susan Wood. SoSe

Morning Call. Richard Murphy. BiHa

Morning comes and now is!, The. Unknown. EaPr

Morning comes, and thickening clouds prevail, The. The Clouded Morning. Jones Very. NOBA

Morning comes, the night decays, the watchmen leave their stations, The. Empire Is No More. Blake. *Fr.* America; a Prophecy. EnRP; OAEL-2

Morning comes. The old woman, a spot, The. Grief. Wendell Berry. MT

Morning comes to consciousness, The. T. S. Eliot. *Fr.* Preludes (I–IV). HeIP; LiTA; NoP; OBMV; PPP; SOTW; TwCP; UnPo; VGW; WeW

Morning Compliments. Sydney Dayre. OxBChV

Morning drum-call on my eager ear, The. Robert Louis Stevenson. NOBVV

Morning. Eleven. The billiard table has been slept on. The Billiard Table. Roy Fisher. VaA

Morning Exercises. Nina Cassian, *tr. fr. Romanian* by Andrea Deletant *and* Brenda Walker. PoSu

Morning. Fifteen books beside a window. Two Brothers Up. Sebastian Barry. IB

Morning finds the self-sequester'd man, The. William Cowper. *See* I was a stricken deer, that left the herd.

Morning-Glory, The. Maria White Lowell. AmWP

Morning Glory. Howard Moss. DiPo

Morning Glory. Ruth Pitter. FaBoWP

Morning Glory. Siegfried Sassoon. TrCP

Morning Glory, The. Unknown, *tr. by* Helen Waddell. *Fr.* Shi King. AWP

Morning-Glory, The. Sarah Helen Whitman. AmWP

Morning Greeting. Wilhelm Müller, *tr. fr. German* by Philip L. Miller. *Fr.* Beautiful Maid of the Mill, The. RiWo

Morning Harvest. Gerald Stern. LCAP

Morning has broken like the first morning. Eleanor Farjeon. EaPr

Morning Has No House. Rosemarie Waldrop. MAT

Morning Hours. Rossana Ombres, *tr. fr. Italian* by Robert McCracken *and* Pietro Pedace. *Fr.* Excursion to Ravenna of A Young Girl with Her Parents. NeIt

Morning hovers in a state of panic, The. Evaporation of a Dream. Andrew Crozier. VaA

Morning Hymn. Joseph Beaumont. TrPWD

Morning Hymn. St. Gregory the Great, *tr. fr. Latin* by Edward Caswell. WGRP

Morning Hymn. John Keble. *See* New every morning.

Morning Hymn. Thomas Ken. NOSC

Morning Hymn. Charles Wesley. TOF

Morning Hymn, A. Christopher Smart. OxBChV

Morning Hymn of Adam. Milton. *See* These are thy glorious works, Parent of good.

Morning, if this late withered light can claim. The Zonnebeke Road. Edmund Blunden. OBWP; PeFWW

Morning in America. John Koethe. BAP-91

Morning in My City. Avraham Shlonsky, *tr. fr. Hebrew* by Ruth Finer Mintz. MHP

Morning in Spring. Louis Ginsberg. GoYe

Morning in the Hills. Bliss Carman. NOBC

Morning Inscription. Miodrag Pavlović, *tr. fr. Serbo-Croatian* by Charles Simic. HSix

Morning is clean and blue and the wind blows up the clouds, The. John Gould Fletcher. *Fr.* Irradiations. MoAmPo

Morning is lost in a maze. We're OK. Gloria Fuertes, *tr. fr. Spanish* by Philip Levine. WPOW

Morning is quiet with unanswered questions, The. Reading the Sky. Rebecca Gonzales. AfAz

Morning is the gate of day, The. The Sentinel. Unknown. BLRP

Morning Letter, A. Robert Duncan. PoA

Morning Light. Mary Effie Lee Newsome. CDC; PoBA; PoNe; ShDr

Morning Light, The. Louis Simpson. NNaP

Morning light creaks down again!, The. (LL) Jane, Jane,/ Tall as a crane. Edith Sitwell. CMoP; MoAB; MoBrPo; MoP; NALW; NoAM; Poetr; PoRA

Morning Light Is Breaking, The. Samuel Francis Smith. AH; WGRP

Morning Light Song. Philip Lamantia. NeAP

Morning, Milking. Herbert Scott. NGP

Morning, Noon, and. Hawley Truax. NYBP

Morning of our rest has come, The. The Poor Man's Sunday Walk. Charles MacKay. EBVV

Morning, on a beach. A man & woman sitting by fire. Moon Is to Blood. Richard Duerden. NeAP

Morning on the St. John's. Jane Cooper. NYBP

Morning on the Shore. Wilfred Campbell. NOBC

Morning ought not. Pas de Deux for Lovers. Michael Dransfield. CBAP

Morning-Piece; or, An Hymn for the Hay-Makers, A. Christopher Smart. NOEC

Morning Prayer. Aua, *tr. fr. Eskimo.* WTO

Morning Prayer. Geoffrey Mac Briain Mac an Bhaird, *tr. fr. Irish* by the Earl of Longford. TIRV

Morning Prayer. Ogden Nash. GrPl; OxBChV

Morning Prayer. Unknown. PoToHe

Morning Prayer, A. Ella Wheeler Wilcox. PoToHe

Morning Quatrains. The. Charles Cotton. NOSC; PeECV

Morning rain of Wei city wets the white dust, The. A Song for Wei City. Wang Wei, *tr. fr. Chinese* by Robert Payne. TAL

Morning Roar of the City, The. Slavko Mihalic, *tr. by* Charles Simic. PoSu

Morning, Rosamonde. Anne Batten Cristall. ECWP

Morning service! parson preaches. The House of God. A. D. Hope. OxBC

Morning sky glitters, The. De Civitate Hominum. Thomas MacGreevy. CIP

Morning Song. Conrad Aiken. *See* It is morning, Senlin says, and in the morning.

Morning Song. Sir William Davenant. *See* Lark Now Leaves His Watery [or Wat'ry] Nest.

Morning Song. A. A. Fet, *tr. fr. Russian by* Max Eastman. AWP

Morning Song. Sylvia Plath. BoWoP; HCAP; HeIP; IHMS; InPK; InPS; LCAP; LPA; NAAL-2; NAs; NIP; NOBA; NTP; PrIm; VCAP

Morning Song. Solomon ibn Gabirol, *tr. fr. Hebrew by* Nina Davis Salaman. TrJP

Morning Song. Kurt M. Stein. FiBHP

Morning Song. Sara Teasdale. AnAmPo

Morning Song, A. Shakespeare. *See* Hark! hark! the lark at heaven's gate sings.

Morning Song in the Jungle. Kipling. NoAM

Morning Song of Senlin. Conrad Aiken. *See* It is morning, Senlin says, and in the morning.

Morning spent looking for my calendar. Losing the Marbles. James Merrill. DiPo

Morning spreads over. May All Earth Be Clothed in Light. George Hitchcock. VGW

Morning Star, The. Emily Brontë. ChTr

Morning Star. Thomas Hornsby Ferril. VGW

Morning Star, The. Primus St. John. PoBA

Morning star goes under cover, The. Der von Kürenberg, *tr. fr. German by* Frederick Goldin. GePo

Morning Star, O Cheering Sight! *Unknown.* AH

Morning Sun. Louis MacNeice. MoAB; MoBrPo; TwCP

Morning sun, The. Poem for Myself and Mei: Abortion. Leslie Silko. VoR

Morning Sun Shines, The. Emperor Wu of Liang, *tr. fr. Chinese by* Kenneth Rexroth. OHMPC

Morning Swim. Maxine W. Kumin. CAPP; Poetr; SM; WPE

Morning Thanksgiving. John Drinkwater. BoTP

Morning: the soft release. Meditation for a Pickle Suite. Richard H. W. Dillard. HoPM; MT

Morning: The World in the Lake. Linda Hogan. SRLS

Morning They Shot Tony Lopez, Barber and Pusher Who Went Too Far, 1958, The. Gary Soto. PBCAP

Morning to Remember, A; or, E Pluribus Unum. Edward Dorn. NoAM

Morning Track, The. Edward Parone. NYBP

Morning Train, The. W. S. Merwin. BAP-90

Morning uptown, quiet on the street. Song Form. Amiri Baraka. SOTW; TTTS

Morning Vigil. Phillip William George. VoR

Morning Watch, The. Henry Vaughan. AngWe; ESCV; GeHe; LiTB; NOSC; NTP; PeECV

Morning Work. D. H. Lawrence. MoAB; MoBrPo

Morning would find me gone." (*LL*) Sam. Walter de la Mare. FaBV; MoAB; MoBrPo

Mornings/ I got up early. The Way It Was. Lucille Clifton. WPE

Mornings. Alice Notley. VBLP

Mornings/ before the sun's liquid. Lagoons, Hanlan's Point. Raymond Souster. NOBC

Mornings are his, The. Waterwings. Cathy Song. NoAM

Morning's at seven. Pippa Passes, But I Can't Get Around This Truck. Margaret Blaker. NBLV

Mornings everything is grey. Morning Has No House. Rosemarie Waldrop. MAT

Mornings I see the Wu Mountain recumbent. At the Heng-ts'ui Pavilion of Fa-hui Monastery. Su Shih, *tr. fr. Chinese by* Irving Y. Lo. SuSp

Mornings I wonder if I. Mornings. Alice Notley. VBLP

Morning's mask of cool, The. Just Deserts. David Chaloner. VaA

Mornings of dew. I Go to Meet Him. Grace Nichols. VBLP

Mornings run their course, clear and deserted, The. Grappa in September. Cesare Pavese, *tr. fr. Italian by* William Arrowsmith. RaBo

Mornings the sparrow twitters seeking food. Han Yü, *tr. fr. Chinese by* Kenneth Hanson. SuSp

Morning's underplayed resistance, The. White Zombie. Harrison Fisher. UL

Mornings when sky is white as dried gristle. The Onion. Margaret Gibson. MT

Morningside Lady, A. A Morningside Lady named Alice. *Unknown.* FaBoBl

Morningside Lady named Alice, A. *Unknown.* FaBoBl

Mornin's Mornin, The. Gerald Brennan. BLPA

Morns are meeker than they were, The. Emily Dickinson. BoNaP; FaPON; ImGa; OBCA; SAmP

Moro Assassinato, *sels.* Allen Curnow. Urban Guerrilla, An. PeNZ

Moroccans with the carpets, The. Patrizia Cavalli, *tr. fr. Italian by* Kenneth Koch. NeIt

Morpheus, the humble god, that dwells. Sir John Denham. NOSC

Morrigan, The. *Unknown, tr. fr. Irish by* Thomas Kinsella. BIrV

Morrissey and the Russian Sailor. *Unknown.* AS

Mors et Vita. James Edwin Campbell. AAP

Mors mihi ærumnarum Requies. (*LL*) Dummer the shepherd sacrific'd. Cotton Mather. SCAP

Morse. Les A. Murray. NTP

Morse signal sounds the end of transmission, A. (*LL*) Dog Fight. Eric Rolls. NOBAu

Mort aux Chats. Peter Porter. OxBC

Mortal Combat. Countess Alice Fay di Castagnola. GoYe

Mortal flesh is full of grief. The Vanity of the World. Siôn Cent, *tr. fr. Welsh by* Joseph P. Clancy. OBWVE

Mortal mixed of middle clay. Guy. Emerson. NOBA

Mortal my mate, bearing my rock-a-heart. To His Watch. Gerard Manley Hopkins. MoAB; MoBrPo

Mortal never won to view thee. Hafiz, *tr. fr. Persian by* R. A. Nicholson. TOF

Mortal Prudence, handmaid of divine Providence. The Testament of Perpetual Change. William Carlos Williams. GOA

Mortal, Sneer Not at the Devil. Heine, *tr. by* Emma Lazarus. *Fr.* Homeward Bound. TrJP

Mortal though I be, yea ephemeral, if but a moment. Ptolemy, *tr. fr. Greek by* Robert Bridges. GrAn

Mortality. Naomi Long Madgett. PoBA; PoNe

Mortality [or Mortalitie], behold and fear[e]! Lines on the Tombs in Westminster. *At. to* Beaumont, Francis *and to* William Basse. *Fr. On the Tombs in Westminster Abbey.* CH; FaPoR; GTBS; GTBS-P; NOBE; OBEV; PlP; SCGP; TrGrPo
(Memento for Mortality, A.) EIL; FaBoCh; HAP
(On the Tombs in Westminster Abbey.) CoGr; OxAEP-1

Mortally smitten by a feather'd dart. The Wounded Bird. La Fontaine, *tr. fr. French by* Edward Marsh. OBD

Mortar Salvos. Jaroslav Seifert, *tr. fr. Czech by* Jeffrey Fiskin *and* Erik Vestville. AnAn

Morte d'Arthur. Tennyson, *incorporated in* Idylls of the King *with changes, as* The Passing of Arthur. DL; EBVVPR; FaBoBe; FaBoRV; NIP; NOBVV; OAEL-2; OBNV; PoEL-5
Sels.
"And answer made King Arthur, breathing hard." EBEV
"But now farewell. I am going a long way."
"More things are wrought by prayer." BLRP
Sir Gawain Encounters Sir Priamus. PoEL-1
"So all day long the noise of battle rolled." EBNV; EnVR; OxAEP-2
"Then loudly cried the bold Sir Bedivere." TOF
"Then saw they how there hove a dusky barge." FaPoB

Mortgage. Angie Gilligan. NBrP

Morticia snipped off. With a Little Grin. David Trinidad. BAP-91

Mortification. George Herbert. ESCV; GeHe; NOSC; SeCP

Mortified Genius, The. James Graeme. NOEC

Mortmain, *sels.* Robert Penn Warren.
"In Time's concatenation and/ Carnal conventicle." NOBA; Prf

Mosaic Worker, The. Arthur Wallace Peach. BLRP

Mosby at Hamilton. Madison Cawein. PAH

Moschus Moschiferus. A. D. Hope. CBAP; GrPl

Moscow/ like a Christmas-tree. Capitals. Raymond Garlick. AngWe

Moses. Amir Gilboa, *tr. fr. Hebrew by* Ruth Finer Mintz. MHP

Moses, *sels.* Isaac Rosenberg.
"Fine! Fine!" PeFWW

Moses. Sydney Tremayne. OxBS

Moses. *Unknown.* ISE; OxNR

Moses: A Story of the Nile, *sels.* Frances E. W. Harper.
Death of Moses, The. AAP
Flight into Midian. AAP

Moses and Jesus. Israel Zangwill. TrJP

Moses, from whose loins I sprung. The Jew. Isaac Rosenberg. ChIV-1; MoBrPo

Moses His Birth and Miracles, *sels.* Michael Drayton.
"In time the Princess playing with the child." ChIV-1

Moses in Infancy. Jones Very. ChIV-1

Moses supposes his toeses are roses. Moses. *Unknown.* ISE; OxNR

Moses was a holy man. *Unknown.* ISE

Moses, what a smash! *(LL)* How We Drove the Trotter. W. T. Goodge. NOBAu

Moses, who is there to save us. Late Evening Conversation with My Friend's Dog, Moses, after Watching Visconti's *The Innocent*. Luis Omar Salinas. AfAz

Moses, who spake with God as with his friend. The Death of Moses. "George Eliot." ChIV-1

Mosque is the Earth, and as holy it is. Alamsaeen. EaPr

Mosques into snow-palaces; banks, bagnios. City Under Snow. Gwyn Williams. AngWe

Mosquito, The. Rodney Jones. MT

Mosquito, The. D. H. Lawrence. RB

Mosquito. John Updike. AnAmPo

Mosquito Knows, The. D. H. Lawrence. *See* When did you start your tricks.

Mosquito, may you fly, a swift courier for me. Meleager, *tr. fr. Greek by* Barbara Hughes Fowler. *Fr.* Epigrams. HePo

Mosquito was heard to complain, A. *Unknown.* PeLi

Mosquitoes. P'i Jih-hsiu, *tr. fr. Chinese by* William H. Nienhauser. SuSp

Mosquitoes. Franz Wright. LCAP

Mosquitoes, shameless and shrill of voice, sucking the blood. Meleager, *tr. fr. Greek by* Barbara Hughes Fowler. *Fr.* Epigrams. HePo

Moss covered paths between scarlet peonies. Visit to the Hermit Ts'ui. Ch'ien Ch'i, *tr. fr. Chinese by* Kenneth Rexroth. OHMPC

Moss covers his stone bed fresh. Weeping for the Zen Master Po-yen. Chia Tao, *tr. fr. Chinese by* Stephen Owen. SuSp

Moss-gathering. Theodore Roethke. RFM; VGW

Moss of His Skin, The. Anne Sexton. CoAP; IHMS; NALW; SM

Mossbawn Sunlight. Seamus Heaney. *Fr.* Mossbawn: Two Poems in Dedication. BIrV; CIP; PNI

Mossbawn: Two Poems in Dedication. Seamus Heaney. CIP; PNI *Sels.*

    Mossbawn Sunlight. BIrV

    (Sunlight.) NoP

    Seed Cutters, The

Most Acceptable Gift, The. Matthias Claudius, *tr. fr. German by* J. M. Campbell. BLRP

Most alluring clouds that mount the sky, The. Wordsworth. NOBVV

Most are innocent, shy, will not undress. Angels. Dannie Abse. PoA

Most are sleeping, some. Birdsong. David Constantine. PWE

Most at home with what is Real. *(LL)* Doggerel by a Senior Citizen. W. H. Auden. IHNG; NBLV; NOBL

Most Beautiful, The. Guido Gozzano, *tr. fr. Italian by* Victoria Pesce. TTTS

Most Beautiful Girl in the World, The. Lorenz Hart. OBAL

Most beautiful is the object, The. Study of the Object. Zbigniew Herbert, *tr. fr. Polish by* Czeslaw Milosz *and* Peter Dale Scott. AnRep

Most beautiful of things I leave is sunlight. Praxilla, *tr. fr. Greek by* Willis Barnstone. BoWoP

Most beautiful power in the world has buttocks, The. Perfection Eludes Us. Frederick Seidel. *Fr.* AIDS Days. BAP-90

Most beautiful! the red-flowering eucalyptus. The Torso: Passages 18. Robert Duncan. CAPP

Most Beautiful Woman at My Highschool Reunion, The. Ellen Marie Bissert. GLP; PeHV

Most beds are beds. Sylvia Plath. *Fr.* Bed Book, The. PYC

Most Excellent Song Which Was Solomon's, The, *sels.* Michael Drayton. "By night within my bed, I roamed here and there." ChIV-1

Most explicit —. Age. Robert Creeley. BAP-89

Most folks believe in doctors, but there's my old girl she don't. Household Remedies. *Unknown.* OBET

Most glorious lord of life that on this day. Spenser. *Fr.* Amoretti. AAS; ChIV-2; EIL; EnRePo; ESo, lacking epigrams I–IV; HAP; HeIL; InPS; LiTB; NAEL-1; NOCV; NoP; NoSic; PoE; Son; TrPWD

    (Easter Morning.) OHIP

    (Easter.) NOBE; OBEV; PeECV

    (Most Glorious Lord of lyfe, that on this day.) PeECV

Most glorious of all the Undying, many-named, girt round with awe! Hymn to Zeus. Cleanthes, *tr. fr. Greek by* Edward H. Plumptre. WGRP

Most Gracious Queen, we thee implore. On Queen Caroline. *Unknown.* FaBoEE

    (On Queen Caroline.) FaBoEH

"Most happy letters framed by skilfull trade." Spenser. *Fr.* Amoretti. AAS; ESo, lacking epigrams I–IV; HeIL; NAEL-1

Most high, all-powerful sweet Lord. Canticle of the Sun. St. Francis of Assisi, *tr. fr. Italian by* Stephen Mitchell. EnIH

Most high Lord. Cantico del Sole. St. Francis of Assisi, *tr. fr. Italian by* Ezra Pound. CTC

Most Holy Night, that still dost keep. The Night. Hilaire Belloc. OBEV

Most holy Satyr. Holy Satyr. Hilda Doolittle ("H. D."). MoAmPo

Most honoured Hera, who descends from heaven. Nossis, *tr. fr. Greek by* Sally Purcell. GrAn

Most I riden by Ribbesdale. *Unknown.* MiEL

Most inexplicable the wiles of boys I deem. Rhianus, *tr. fr. Greek by* Sydney Oswald. PeHV

Most Ingenious Paradox, A. W. S. Gilbert. *Fr.* Pirates of Penzance, The. NAs

Most is your name the name of this dark stone. Rainy Mountain Cemetery. N. Scott Momaday. CDW; HATNAP

Most Lovely Shade ("Most lovely dark, my Æthiopia born.") Edith Sitwell. FaBoTw; GTBS-P

Most Men Know Love. Henry Timrod. *See* Most Men Know Love But as a Part of Life.

Most men know love but as a part of life. Quatorzain. Henry Timrod. AnAmPo

Most Men Know Love But as a Part of Life. Henry Timrod.

Most men use/ their eyes. The Mechanic. Diane Wakoski. AmPA

Most miserably wise. *(LL)* Phillis for Shame Let Us Improve. Charles Sackville.

Most modern nature lovers have a personal scale of values that tells them. William Wordsworth (1770-1850). Gavin Ewart. NoAM

Most mornings we go running side by side. Morning Athletes. Marge Piercy. AIW

Most musical of mourners, weep again! Shelley. *Fr.* Adonais; an Elegy on the Death of John Keats. EBEV; EnRP; EPCY; FHYEP; HoPM; ImPo; MeMBP; NoP; OAEL-2; PoEL-4; TrGPo

Most near, most far, most loved and most far. Sonnet to My Mother. George Barker. ImPo; LiTB; MoAB; RaBo

    (Piers Plowman.) FaBoEH

    (To My Mother.) FaBoMo; FF; LiTM; MeMBP; OxAEP-2; OxBTC; PoWW; Son; TwCP

Most needy aren oure neighebores, The. The Poor. William Langland. *Fr.* Vision of Piers Plowman, The. PoEL-1

    (Poor, The.) FaBoEH

Most noble empress, you have heard of me? Shakespeare. *Fr.* Antony and Cleopatra. OxAEP-1

Most noble prince of cristen princes alle. To the King on his Coronation. *At. to* John Lydgate. FaBoEH

Most, O maid's child, thy choice and worthy the winning. *(LL)* Spring. Gerard Manley Hopkins. BoNaP; EBVV; FaBV; HAP; InvP; LiTM; MeMBP; MoAB; MoBrPo; NAEL-2; NoAM; NOBE; NOBVV; OAEL-2; OBMV; OBNC; RB; TFi; TrCP

Most of his friends, as expected. As Expected. Thom Gunn. GLP

Most of It, The. Robert Frost. EaPr; HAP; NAAL-2; NoP; NU; TOF; TRP; WeW

Most of my days are passed away, yet my heart is still impure. The Worthless Heart. Immanuel di Roma, *tr. fr. Hebrew.* TrJP

Most of my friends and all of my past. The Gifts. David Craig Austin. PFL

Most of the mornings here, when we awaken. For a Suicide, a Little Early Morning Music. Gibbons Ruark. MT

Most of the past is lost. Switchblade. Michael Ryan. BAP-90; NAmP90

Most of the walls. Taranto. James Wright. AnAn

Most of your life we have kept our separate places. Discovering My Daughter. Dabney Stuart. SM

Most people expect their sons to be clever. Bathing the Infant. Su Shih, *tr. fr. Chinese by* Irving Y. Lo. SuSp

Most poets to a muse that is stone-deaf cry. On the Oxford Book of Victorian Verse. "Hugh MacDiarmid." MoBrPo

Most precious treasure is never fully known, The. Bubbles on the Water. Yang Wan-li, *tr. fr. Chinese by* Jonathan Chaves. SuSp

Most present of all the watchers where we camped, The. When We Looked Back. William Stafford. NYBP

Most Quietly at Times. Cäsar Flaischlen, *tr. fr. German by* Jethro Bithell. AWP

Most reverend Father, I have borne all wrong. Two Souls. Marjorie Pickthall. NOBC

Most reverend lords, the church's joy and wonder. On Calamy's Imprisonment and Wild's Poetry. *Unknown.* APAS

Most Saturday afternoons. The Weepies. Paul Muldoon. NoAM; PNI

Most souls, 'tis true, but peep out once an age. Pope. *Fr.* Elegy to the Memory of an Unfortunate Lady. CH; ECEV; NOBE; NOEC; OAEL-1; OBD; OBEV; SCGP; TEP

    (Dull, Sullen Prisoners.) FaBoRV

Most Sovereign Lady. *Unknown.* MeEL

Most stupendous show they ever gave, The. In Memory of the Circus Ship Euzkera. *Walker Gibson.* FiBHP

Most Sweet It Is with Unuplifted Eyes. Wordsworth. EnRP

Most terrible was our hero in battle blows. From the Irish. James Simmons. PBCIP; PNI

Most that can be said, The. Parade's End. Barbara Guest. PoM

Most that I know but one. Care. Josephine Miles. NYBP

Most things are colorful things — the sky, earth, and sea. White Things. Anne Spencer. ShDr

Most truly honoured, and as truly dear. To Her Father with Some Verses. Anne Bradstreet. NALW

Most Vital Thing in Life, The. Grenville Kleiser. PoToHe; SoSe

Most weeds, whilst young. Francis Daniel Pastorius. SCAP

Most whale-like human friends. (LL) Whale Wisdom Peace Illumination. Jeff Poniewaz. EaPr

Most who die, the more we live, The. (LL) What If a Much of a Which of a Wind. E. E. Cummings. BLPL; ImPo; LiTA; LiTM; MeMAP; MoAmPo; NAAL-2; NOBA; NoP; OxBA; PoA; PoRA; PPP

Most women get married, 'tis true. Barney Blackley. PeLi

Most worthy of praise were the virtuous ways. Little Red Riding Hood. Guy Wetmore Carryl. FiBHP

Most worthye she is in towne, The. In Praise of Ivy. Unknown. MeEL

Most wounds can Time repair. At Ease. Walter de la Mare. GTBS-P

Most wretched heart, most miserable. Sir Thomas Wyatt. SiPS

Mostly in the trees was starlings. Shooting Crows. David Huddle. GOYP

Mot eran dous miei cossir. Arnaut Daniel, tr. by Harriet Waters Preston. AWP

Mote it is to trouble the mind's eye, A. Shakespeare. Fr. Hamlet. NAWM-1; OxAEP-1

Motel. William Mills. MT

Motet: "I am a young girl." Unknown, tr. fr. French by Carol Cosman. PBWP

Motet: "Stranger here, as all my fathers were, A." John Amner. OxBSP

Motets, The, sels. Eugenio Montale, tr. fr. Italian by Dana Gioia.

Moth. Lance Henson. VoR

Moth, The. Vernon Scannell. OxBC

Moth, A. Henry Bellyse Baildon. NOBVV

Moth, A. Confusion. Victor Hernandez Cruz. UL

Moth ate a word. To me it seemed, A. Book Moth: "A moth ate a word. To me it seemed." Unknown, formerly att. to Cynewulf, tr. by Charles W. Kennedy. Fr. Riddles (Exeter Book). AnOE

(Bookmoth: Moth devoured words, A. When I heard.) ASW, tr. by Kevin Crossley-Holland

Moth flew a bee-line, The. Mothy Monologue. Ralph Gustafson. NOBC

Moth-force a small town always has. The Strength of Fields. James Dickey. VCAP

Moth has got into it, The. The Moth. Vernon Scannell. OxBC

Moth-Terror. Benjamin de Casseres. TrJP

Moth under the eaves, The. Prelude to Winter. William Carlos Williams. SAmP

Mother,/ You did not leave me an inheritance of necklaces for a wedding. Mother's Inheritance. Fawziyya Abu Khalid, tr. fr. Arabic by Kamal Boullata. WPOW

Mother, The. Gwendolyn Brooks. Fr. Street in Bronzeville, A. BlSi; BPo; CAPP; CrSp; FaBoWP; MDDM; NALW; NMM

Mother! (LL) Because they are traitors, your eyes. Manuel de Falla. RiWo

Mother, sels. Sharon Doubiago.
"My mother is a poem I'll never be able to write." MDDM

Mother. Max Ehrmann. PoToHe

Mother. Hermann Hagedorn. See For such as you, I do believe.

Mother. Seamus Heaney. NAs

Mother. Josephine D. Henderson Heard. CBWP-4

Mother. Theresa Helburn. FaPON; OHIP

Mother. Vladimir Holan, tr. fr. Czech by Ian Milner and Jarmila Milner. PoSu

Mother, A. Issa. SiSoPo

Mother. Rudy Kikel. NGP

Mother. Sharon Mayer Libera. CrSp; IHMS

Mother/ Deer/ Lady. Harold Littlebird. VoR

Mother. Bea Liu. LoHo

Mother, The. Catulle Mendès, tr. fr. French by W. J. Robertson. TrJP

Mother. Nancy Morejón, tr. fr. Spanish by Kathleen Weaver. AIW

Mother. Nagase Kiyoko, tr. fr. Japanese by Kenneth Rexroth and Ikuko Atsumi. AIW; BoWoP; WPJ

Mother, The. Sharon Olds. PBCAP

Mother, The. Padraic Pearse. PeIV; TIRV

Mother. Hettye Rayburn Ramsey. PWR

Mother, The. W. D. Snodgrass. CAPP

Mother! (LL) All that I have comes from my Mother! Luisah Teish. EaPr

Mother,/ If I am where I am. From an Asylum; Kathy Chattle to Her Mother, Ruth Arbeiter. Anne Stevenson. BrRo

Mother. Unknown. PoToHe

Mother, The. Unknown, tr. fr. Chinese by George Barrow. OHIP

Mother. Rosanna Warren. Fr. Funerary Portraits. NoAM

Mother. Whittier. Fr. Snow-bound; a Winter Idyl [or Idyll]. AmPP; GN; NOBA; OHIP; OxBA; TAP; WiR

Mother, a father, a boy child, two maybe, A. Holy Family. Peter Cooley. NAmP90

Mother, among the Dustbins. Stevie Smith. PBWP

Mother and Child. Penelope Shuttle. AIW

Mother and Her Son on the Cross, The. Unknown. See "Stond well, moder, under Rode."

Mother and listener is, but she does not listen. The Question. Muriel Rukeyser. IHMS; WPOW

Mother and Poet. Elizabeth Barrett Browning. NAEL-2; NALW

Mother and Son. Alden Nowlan. RaBo

Mother and Son. Allen Tate. LiTA; MoAB; MoAmPo

Mother and the Father are One, The. (LL) I sing to the Mother Gaia. Unknown. EaPr

Mother Asks What I'm Put To. Julia Alvarez. Fr. 33. Son

Mother at Shannon, waving to her young, A. Throwing the Beads. Sean Dunne. BiHa

Mother, because you never spoke to me. More Clues. Muriel Rukeyser. IHMS

Mother Bombie, sels. John Lyly.
O Cupid! Monarch over Kings. CBLP; ElL
(Fools in Love's College.) TrGrPo

Mother Cat. John Montague. AnAn; NOIV

Mother Country, The. Benjamin Franklin. AiP; PAH

Mother Crab and Her Family, The. L. T. Manyase, tr. fr. Xhosa by Jack Cope and C. M. Mcanyangwa. PeSA

Mother Dark. Francesca Yetunde Pereira. PBA

Mother darling, I cannot work the loom. Sappho, tr. fr. Greek by Willis Barnstone. BoWoP

Mother dear. Unknown. RoPo

Mother dear, may I go downtown. Ballad of Birmingham. Dudley Randall. BPo; HeIL; HeIP; InPK; MoP; NIP; NoAM; Poetr; SoSe

Mother Dear, O! Pray for Me. Unknown. AH

Mother does knitting, The. Familial. Jacques Prévert, tr. fr. French by D. J. Enright. OBD

Mother Doesn't Want a Dog. Judith Viorst. NBLV

Mother Doorstep. Victor James Daley. NOBAu

Mother Duck. Unknown. BoTP

Mother Earth; Her Whales. Gary Snyder. LCAP; PoBeRe

Mother, Father, God, Universal Power. Jo Poore. EaPr

Mother, for months a mist has been before me. Light in Darkness. Mary E. Tucker. CBWP-1

Mother, The ("From out the south the genial breezes sigh.") Unknown, tr. fr. Chinese by George Barrow. OHIP

Mother Glacier. Iain Sinclair. VaA

Mother Goose Rhyme. Kenneth Rexroth. ErPo

Mother Goose Sonnets, sels. Harriet S. Morgridge.

Mother Goose Up-to-Date, sels. Louis Untermeyer.
Archibald MacLeish Suspends the Five Little Pigs. MoAmPo
Edgar A. Guest Considers "The Good Old Woman Who Lived in a Shoe" and the Good Old Truths Simultaneously
(Edgar A. Guest Considers "The Old Woman Who Lived in a Shoe" and the Good Old Verities at the Same Time.) FiBHP; MoAmPo; OBAL
Edna St. Vincent Millay Exhorts Little Boy Blue. MoAmPo
John Masefield Relates the Story of Tom, Tom, the Piper's Son. MoAmPo
Walter de la Mare Tells the Listener about Jack and Jill. MoAmPo

Mother Goose's Garland. Archibald MacLeish. AnAmPo; OBAL

Mother Goose's Melody, sels. Unknown.
Learned Song, A. FaBoUs

Mother has lupus. Dear World. Paula Gunn Allen. HATNAP

Mother, here there are shadowy salmon. Letter from Oregon. William Stafford. NaP

Mother, Home, Heaven. William Goldsmith Brown. FaBoBe

Mother horse, A. A Mother. Issa. SiSoPo

Mother Hubbard's Tale, sels. Spenser.
Fox and the Ape Go to Court, The. NoSic

Mother, I am something more. Looking Out. Helen Chasin. NMM

Mother, I Cannot Mind My Wheel. Walter Savage Landor, first st. paraphrased fr. the Greek of Sappho. AWP, st. 1; BoLoP; EnRP; GBL; NAEL-2; NOBE; OBEV; OBVE; TEP; TrGrPo

Mother, I long to get married. Whistle, Daughter, Whistle. Unknown. AIW; AmFP; ErPo; OBET; OxNR, shorter vers.; ReMoGo
(Mother, I longs to get married.) ErPo
(O mother, I longs to get married.) OBET

Mother, I longs to get married. *Unknown.* *See* Mother, I long to get married.

Mother, I love you so. Human Affection. Stevie Smith. NALW

Mother, I may do violence to you. Mother. Sharon Mayer Libera. CrSp; IHMS

Mother, I want to go. *Unknown, tr. fr. Spanish* by Willis Barnstone. BoWoP

Mother, I will have a husband. Thomas Vautor. *Fr.* Songs of Divers Airs and Natures. CBLP

Mother in gladness, Mother in sorrow. W. Dayton Wedgefarth. PoToHe

Mother-in-Law of the Marquis de Sade, The. Jennifer Maiden. NOBAu

Mother in the House, The. Hermann Hagedorn. OHIP

Mother in the Snow-Storm, The. Sebald Smithon. VPP

Mother is dead. Motherdeath. Julia Vinograd. SRLS

Mother is drinking to forget a man. Frying Trout While Drunk. Lynn Emanuel. ETG; NAmP90

Mother is gone. Bird songs wouldn't let her breathe. William Stafford. NaP

Mother, is this the darkness of the end. For "Our Lady of the Rocks." Dante Gabriel Rossetti. EBEV

Mother, it pains me that I must confide. Winter Offerings. Frank Ormsby. PNI

Mother it's snowing in the mountain. Invitation. *Unknown, tr.* by Ruth Padel. VBLP

Mother Land/ Long lain asleep. Mother Dark. Francesca Yetunde Pereira. PBA

Mother, let me congratulate you on/ the birthday of your son. Birthday. Yevgeny Yevtushenko, *tr. fr. Russian* by Peter Levi *and* Robin Milner-Gulland. NAs

Mother, let me go! (*LL*) A Frosty Night. Robert Graves. CH; MoAB; MoBrPo; MoBS; OxBTC

Mother looms up on the prarie out there. Believe it or Not. Nicolai Kantchev, *tr. fr. Bulgarian.* TSaS, *tr.* by Alexander Shurbanov

Mother Love. Stevie Smith. Spl

Mother love is a mighty benefaction. Mother Love. Stevie Smith. Spl

Mother made a seedy cake. *Unknown.* ISE

Mother Maudlin the Witch. Ben Jonson. *Fr.* Sad Shepherd, The. ChTr

Mother, May I? Alma Villanueva. WPOW

Mother, May I Go Out to Swim? *Unknown.* FaPON; OxNR

Mother, may I stay up tonight? Conversation. David McCord. GrPl

Mother might have drowned me. The Bath. Ira Sadoff. NAmP90

Mother mortgaged the piano. Mortgage. Angie Gilligan. NBrP

Mother, Mother, Are You All There? Felicia Lamport. NBLV

Mother, Mother, I am ill! *Unknown.* ISE

Mother, mother, I feel sick. *Unknown.* OBD

Mother, Mother, Make My Bed. *Unknown.* ELP

Mother, mother, mother, pin a rose on me. *Unknown.* RoPo

Mother Mother shave me. *Unknown, tr. fr. Nyasa* by Ulli Beier. BoWoP

Mother, mother, what illbred aunt. The Disquieting Muses. Sylvia Plath. NALW; NMM

Mother, mother,/ Why is it not you? The One Who Struggles. Ernst Toller, *tr. fr. German* by E. Ellis Roberts. TrJP

Mother Nature gave bulls horns. Anacreon, *tr. fr. Greek* by Sam Hamill. InMo

Mother Nature, how fair has your invention's grace. The Lake of Zurich. Friedrich Gottlieb Klopstock, *tr. fr. German* by George C. Schoolfield. GePo

Mother Nature's Bloomers. Leonard Barras. IHNG

Mother, never mourn. (*LL*) Mater Dolorosa. William Barnes. CH; NOBE; OBEV

Mother Night. James Weldon Johnson. Son

Mother o' blossoms, and ov all. William Barnes. *Fr.* May. ChTr

Mother o' Mine. Kipling. *Fr.* Light That Failed, The. WBLP

Mother of all. Invocation to the Mayan Moon Goddess. Sharon Spencer. WoWa

Mother of Fishermen. Henriëtte Roland-Holst, *tr.* by Ria Leigh-Loohuizen. PBWP

Mother of God, The. W. B. Yeats. ChIV-2

Mother of God! no lady thou. Our Lady. Mary Elizabeth Coleridge. OBEV; OBMV; WPE

Mother of God! Our Lady! For Eleanor and Bill Monahan. William Carlos Williams. CRP, *abr.*; VGW

Mother of God that's Lady of the Heavens. Prayer of the Old Woman. Villon, *tr. fr. French* by J. M. Synge. MoBrPo; PeECV

Mother of gods. Meleager, *tr. fr. Greek* by Peter Whigham. GrAn

Mother of heaven, regina of the clouds. Le Monocle de Mon Oncle. Wallace Stevens. LiTM; MeMAP; MoAB

Mother of Hermes! and still youthful Maia! Fragment of an Ode to Maia Written on May Day, 1818. Keats. EnRP; OAEL-2; OBEV; PoEL-4

Mother of Man. Vesna Parun, *tr. fr. Croatian* by Mary Coote. PBWP

Mother of memories! O mistress-queen! Le Balcon. Baudelaire, *tr. fr. French* by Lord Alfred Douglas. AWP

Mother of musings, contemplation sage. Thomas Warton the Younger. *Fr.* Pleasures of Melancholy, The. EnRP

Mother of my birth, for how long were we together. Kaddish. David Ignatow. EaPr; NU; RaBo

Mother of roots, you have not seeded. Goodbye to the Poetry of Calcium. James Wright. CAPP

Mother of the Groom. Seamus Heaney. OxBSP

Mother of the muses, we are taught, The. Memory. Walter Savage Landor. EBEV; NOBVV; OAEL-2

Mother of Washington, The. Lydia Huntley Sigourney. AmWP

Mother, oh mother! where shall we hide us? Others. James Reeves. Spl

Mother Parrot's Advice to Her Children. *Unknown, tr.* by A. K. Nyabongo. OBAP

Mother Poem. Joel Oppenheimer. PoM

Mother Poem (two), The. Jackie Kay. NBrP

Mother presses her head to her hand, already, The. Mother. Rosanna Warren. *Fr.* Funerary Portraits. NoAM

Mother Said. Barbara Drake. NGP

Mother said: Come now, say your prayers, The. The Lord's Prayer. Massillon Coicou, *tr. fr. French* by Ellen Conroy Kennedy. NegPo

Mother said, Don't do it. Mother Said. Barbara Drake. NGP

Mother said if I wore this hat. My Hat. Stevie Smith. BrRo; CBNP

Mother said thirty years ago. Miss Florence Jackson. David Huddle. PBCAP

Mother said to call her if the H bomb exploded. Belief. Josephine Miles. FaBoWP; MoP; NoAM; TAP

Mother Sarah's Lullaby ("Mother Sarah rocks the cradle."). Itsik Manger, *tr. fr. Yiddish* by Jacob Sonntag. TrJP

Mother sat/ with hunger on her hands. Child's Parliment. Chenjerai Hove. HBAPE

Mother, saying Anne good night. William Empson. CBNP

Mother says I'm not to go. Big Black Dog. Carol Michael. ZA

Mother shake the cherry-tree. Let's Be Merry. Christina Rossetti. *Fr.* Sing-Song. FaPON; TLR

Mother Shipton's Prophecies. *At.* to Charles Hindley. BLPA

Mother Speaks: The Algiers Motel Incident, Detroit, A. Michael S. Harper. AmPA; BPo; NBV

Mother Tabbyskins. Elizabeth Anna Hart. OFC; OxBChV

Mother, the Nurse, and the Fairy, The. John Gay. *Fr.* Fables. PeLV

Mother the Wardrobe Is Full of Infantrymen. Roger McGough. MAT

Mother then must suck the Son, The. (*LL*) Luke XI: Blessed Be the Paps Which Thou Hast Sucked. Richard Crashaw. BXAP; JCP

Mother, they say we never really leave you. Skin. Sari Friedman. BTR

Mother to Her Waking Infant, A. Joanna Baillie. ECWP; NOEC; WoRP

Mother to Son. Langston Hughes. CDC; HeIL; NAAL-2; NTCP; OBCA; PoNe; SAmP; TTY

Mother Tongue, The. Carolina Hospital. LoHo

Mother Tongue. Jon Stallworthy. NoAM

Mother turned and wept. (*LL*) Mother Wept. Joseph Skipsey. EBVV

Mother Wept. Joseph Skipsey. EBVV

Mother wept, A: where were You, God. Calvary. Libby Stopple. GoYe

Mother, what trick of light. The Mirror of Matsuyama. Sharon Hashimoto. OpBo

Mother, while you were at the shops. The Snowman. Roger McGough. OTCP

Mother Who Gave Me Life. Gwen Harwood. FaBoMA

Mother, you know there is a place somewhere called Paris. The Right Meaning. César Vallejo, *tr. fr. Spanish* by Robert Bly. RaBo

Motherdeath. Julia Vinograd. SRLS

Motherhood. Charles Stuart Calverley. FM

Motherhood. Georgia Douglas Johnson. ShDr

Motherhood. Agnes Lee. BLPA

Motherhood. May Swenson. CoAP

Mothers. Auvaiyar, *tr. fr. Tamil* by A. K. Ramanujan. PLW

Mothers. Nikki Giovanni. UnPo

Mothers/ cranking the machine. The Greater Friendship Baptist Church. Carole C. Gregory. BISi

Mothers,/ That hope of yours, your joyful burden. To the Mothers. Ernst Toller, *tr. fr. German* by E. Ellis Roberts. TrJP

Mothers. Kakkai Patiniyar Naccellaiyar, *tr. fr. Tamil* by A. K. Ramanujan. PLW

Mothers. Kavarpentu, *tr. fr. Tamil* by A. K. Ramanujan. PLW

Mothers. Maturaipputan Ilanakanar, *tr. fr. Tamil* by A. K. Ramanujan. PLW

Mountain is a tiger burning fiercely beside the sea of chaos, The. Nuo-ri-lang. Yang Lian, *tr. fr. Chinese by* Donald Finkel *with* Li Guohua. SpMi

Mountain/ Is earth's mouth, A. Of Earth. Mae V. Cowdery. ShDr

Mountain Lion. D. H. Lawrence. FaBoVe; Mes; OBTV; OxBTC; RB; RFM

Mountain looks gaunt, The. Tune: "Celebration in the Eastern Plain" — Replying to a Lyric Song by the Senior Poet Ma Chih-yüan. *Unknown, tr. fr. Chinese by* Sherwin S. S. Fu. SuSp

Mountain Meadows. Martha Keller. BoNaP

Mountain moon shines on a cloudless sky, The. Written at Mauve Garden: Pine Wind Terrace. Chu Yi-tsun, *tr. fr. Chinese by* Chang Yin-nan *and* Lewis C. Walmsley. SuSp

Mountain of the lovers, The, *sels.* Paul Hamilton Hayne. Love Scorns Degrees. AnAmPo

Mountain over Aberdare, The. Alun Lewis. AngWe

Mountain over the town. (*LL*) Higashi Hongwanji. Gary Snyder. PoBeRe

Mountain path is steep, The. Sending Spring Love to Tzu-an. Yü Hsüan-chi, *tr. fr. Chinese by* Kenneth Rexroth *and* Ling Chung. UnAS; WPC

Mountain road is steep, the stone steps are dangerous, The. Spring Thoughts Sent to Tzu-an. Yü Hsüan-chi, *tr. by* Geoffrey R. Waters. BoWoP

Mountain sat upon the plain, The. Emily Dickinson. FaBV

Mountain sheep are sweeter, The. The War Song of Dinas Vawr. Thomas Love Peacock. *Fr.* Misfortunes of Elphin, The. AWP; CoGr; EBEvV; EnRP; FaBoCh; FaPoR; GGP; HAP; InvP; NAEL-2; NOBE; NTP; OAEL-2; OxAEP-2; PrIm; WiR

Mountain snow. Seasons in Santa Fe. Gerald Vizenor. HATNAP

Mountain Spring, A. Ch'u Ch'uang I, *tr. fr. Chinese by* Kenneth Rexroth. OHMPC

Mountain Stream, The. John Ceiriog Hughes, *tr. fr. Welsh by* Kenneth Hurlstone Jackson. OBWVE

Mountain Study. Peter van Toorn. NOBC

Mountain summits sleep, The: glens, cliffs, and caves. Sleep Upon the World. Alcman, *tr. by* Thomas Campbell. ChTr
    (Fragment: "Mountain summits sleep, glens, cliffs, and caves, The.") AWP

Mountain Talk. A. R. Ammons. HCAP

Mountain Tambourine. Peter van Toorn. TSaS

Mountain teeth, tips of anemious rippled stone. On the Subject of Waves. Eldon Grier. MoCV

Mountain temple dim and far away, its back against the setting sun, A. Tune: "Sand of Silk-washing Stream." Wang Kuo-wei, *tr. fr. Chinese by* Ching-i Tu. SuSp

Mountain Tops. L. A. J. Moorer. CBWP-3

Mountain Town — Mexico. Eldon Grier. NOBC

Mountain was in great distress and loud, A. The Mountain in Labor. Aesop, *tr. fr. Greek by* William Ellery Leonard. AWP

Mountain Whippoorwill, The. Stephen Vincent Benét. TrGrPo

Mountain Wind, A. "Æ." AWP

Mountaineer, The. Robert Nathan. TrJP

Mountaineer is working with his Bible, The. Quatrina. Joseph Deericks Bennett. LiTA

Mountains. W. H. Auden. FaBoPV

Mountains. Lucy Larcom. WBLP

Mountains and mountains and mountains. Autumn Leaves. James Schuyler. ArLo

Mountains and rivers lie in the opening sun. Spring. Tu Fu, *tr. fr. Chinese by* Robert Payne. TAL

Mountains and Rivers without End: The Market, *sels.* Gary Snyder. "Seventy-five feet hoed rows equals." NaP

Mountains and seas. Whip-the-World. "Hugh MacDiarmid." FaBoVe

Mountains, and the lonely death at last, The. To a Traveler. Lionel Johnson. MoBrPo

Mountains are clouds, lightning, but no rain, The. (*LL*) Utah. Anne Stevenson. FaBoVe

Mountains are moving, rivers. The Redwoods. Louis Simpson. CoAP

Mountains are steadfast but the mountain streams. Hwang Chin-i, *tr. fr. Korean by* Peter H. Lee. PBWP

Mountains carry snow, the season fails, The. The Homer Mitchell Place. John Engels. SM

Mountains Covered With Cats, *sels.* Wallace Stevens. Too Commodious. CBCK

Mountains grow unnoticed, The. Emily Dickinson. MoAB; MoAmPo; TrGrPo

Mountains, I become part of it, The. *Unknown, tr. fr. Navajo Indian.* EaPr

Mountains lie quietly together, The. Rebel Camp in the Hindu Kush. Gu Cheng, *tr. fr. Chinese by* Donald Finkel *with* Chang Sheng-Tai. SpMi

Mountains loom upon the path we take. Song to the Mountains. *Unknown, tr. fr. Pawnee Indian by* Alice C. Fletcher. AWP

Mountains, macadam, presents a strange and willful country. (*LL*) Into Mexico. Mona Van Duyn. VCAP

Mountains rubbed by light clouds. Tune: "Courtyard Full of Fragrance." Ch'in Kuan, *tr. fr. Chinese by* James J. Y. Liu. SuSp

Mountains surround the ancient kingdom in a massive circle. Chin-ling. Liu Yu Hsi, *tr. fr. Chinese by* Paul Kroll. SuSp

Mountains will go with me, The. (*LL*) On Returning. Brigitte Frase. LoHo

Mountebank of Mourne, The. Roger Woddis. IHNG

Mountebank's Mask, The, *sels.* Thomas Campion. Hours of Sleepy Night, The. EIL

Mountown! thou sweet retreat from Dublin cares. William King. *Fr.* Mully of Mountown. FaBoPP; OBTV

Mourn for Yourself. Geoffrey Keating, *tr. fr. Irish by* Sean Lucy. BIrV

Mourn, hapless Caledonia, mourn. The Tears of Scotland. Tobias Smollett. ECEV; NOEC

Mourn No More. *At. to* John Fletcher. *See* Weep No More.

Mourn Not for Adonais. Shelley. *See* Peace, peace! he is not dead, he doth not sleep.

Mourn not, friends, mourn not, bereaved. Lines on the Death of the Rev. S. K. Talmage. Mary E. Tucker. CBWP-1

Mourned by scholars who dream of the ghosts of Greek boys. (*LL*) The Funeral. Stephen Spender. CMoP; MoAB; MoBrPo; NoAM

Mourners, The. Bevil Higgons. APAS

Mournful Dove, The. *Unknown.* AmFP

Mournful is the remembrance which awakes. William Haygarth. *Fr.* Greece. OBTV

Mourning. Kuan P'an-p'an, *tr. fr. Chinese by* Kenneth Rexroth *and* Ling Chung. WPC

Mourning. Andrew Marvell. SeCP

Mourning. Julia Vinograd. BCF

Mourning Bride, The, *sels.* Congreve. Music. OxAEP-1

Mourning Conquest; or, The Woman's Sad Complaint, and Doleful Cry to See Her Love in Fainting Fits to Lye, The. *Unknown.* CoMu

Mourning for Lü Hui-chiu, *sels.* Yün Shou-p'ing, *tr. fr. Chinese by* Jonathan Chaves.

Mourning for My Son Jun-erh, *sels.* Cheng Hsieh, *tr. fr. Chinese by* Jonathan Chaves.

Mourning for My Wife. Mei Yao Ch'en, *tr. fr. Chinese by* Jonathan Chaves. SuSp

Mourning Letter from Paris, A. Conrad Kent Rivers. BPo

Mourning My Son. Yüan Chen, *tr. fr. Chinese by* Angela Jung Palandri. SuSp

Mourning Pablo Neruda. Robert Bly. LCAP

Mourning Picture. Adrienne Rich. CoAP

Mourning Pictures, *sels.* Honor Moore.

Mourning Poem for the Queen of Sunday. Robert Hayden. HCAP; NoAM; NoP; PoBA

Mourning Song. Robert Pearl, *tr. fr. Tsimshian Indian by* Armand Schwerner. STP

Mourning-Song for Rangiaho, A. Te Heuheu Herea, *tr. fr. Maori by* Barry Mitcalfe. WTO

Mourning the Dying American Female Names. Hunt Hawkins. NGP

Mourning the first and last to love me. (*LL*) I Would Like My Love to Die. Samuel Beckett. BIrV; CIP; IIP; NOIV

Mouse, The. Elizabeth J. Coatsworth. BoTP; FaPON; MoShBr; OBCA

Mouse, The. Jean Garrigue. TwCP

Mouse, The. Laura E. Richards. OBCA

Mouse, The. Thirza Wakley. BoTP

Mouse and the Cake, The. Eliza Cook. OxBChV

Mouse Ate the Bait, The. Mildred Luton. ZA

Mouse-brown foal that fain had fed, The. The Foal. William Renton. NOBVV

Mouse crawled through it, The. Hole. Leonard Nathan. PBCAP

Mouse Dinner. Aileen Fisher, *tr. fr. Armenian by* Aileen Fisher. TLR

Mouse Dinners. Russell Edson. *See* Woman prepared a mouse for her husband's dinner, A.

Mouse doesn't dine, A. Mouse Dinner. Aileen Fisher, *tr. fr. Armenian by* Aileen Fisher. TLR

Mouse found a beautiful piece of plum cake, A. The Mouse and the Cake. Eliza Cook. OxBChV

Mouse, The Frog and The Little Red Hen, The. *Unknown.* BoTP

Mouse in Her Room, A. *Unknown.* TLR

Mouse in her room woke Miss Dowd, A. A Mouse in Her Room. *Unknown.* TLR

Mouse in the Wainscot, The. Ian Serraillier. OTCP; PDV

Mouse the trap had slapped on, but not caught, A. Ballad of the Mouse. Robert Wallace. NYBP

Mouse Whose Name Is Time, The. Robert Francis. TLR

Mousemeal. Howard Nemerov. TwCP

Mouse's Lullaby, The. Palmer Cox. OBCA; TLR

Mouse's Nest. John Clare. ChTr; InPK; LiTB; NAEL-2; RB

Mouse's Petition, The. Anna Laetitia Barbauld. ECWP; FM; OxBChV

Mouse's Tale, The. "Lewis Carroll." *See* Fury Said to a Mouse.

Mousetrap, The. Callimachus, *tr. fr. Greek by* Barbara Hughes Fowler. HePo

Mousetrap Incantation. Eduard Friedrich Mörike, *tr. fr. German by* Philip L. Miller. RiWo

Mouse)Won. E. E. Cummings. MeMAP

Mouse—young, inexperienced, A. The Old Cat and the Young Mouse. La Fontaine, *tr. fr. French by* Norman R. Shapiro. SoCa

Mousie, mousie. Conversation. Rose Fyleman. BoTP

Mousōnios built this solid, windproof mansion, and built it well. A House in Byzantium. Agathias, *tr. fr. Greek by* Fleur Adcock. GrAn

Mouth, The. Ciaran Carson. PNI

Mouth. Dennis Scott. PBCV

Mouth and the Ears, The. Shem-Tob ben Joseph Palquera, *tr. fr. Hebrew by* J. Chotzner. TrJP

Mouth. Can blow or breathe, A. Cardinal Ideograms. May Swenson. OBCA

Mouth like old silk soft with use, A. A Levantine. William Plomer. OBMV

Mouth of the Hudson, The. Robert Lowell. AiP; NaP; VCAP

Mouth of the Wolf. Susan Stewart. NAmP90

Mouth takes food, The. *(LL)* Russians Breathing. Philip Hammial. NOBAu

Mouth to mouth joined we lie, her naked breasts. Tantalos. Paulus Silentiarius, *tr. fr. Greek by* Dudley Fitts. ErPo

Move Continuing, The. Al Young. PoBA

Move him into the sun. Futility. Wilfred Owen. CMoP; FaBoMo; GTBS-P; MeMBP; MoAB; MoBrPo; NAEL-2; NoAM; NoP; NSI; OBWP; PAW; PeFWW; RB; TrGrPo

Move into/ the past tense. Grammar Lesson. Linda Pastan. Poetsp

Move over, Ali Baba! Now there comes. Autosonic Door. Dorothy Brown Thompson. GoYe

Move over, ham. Hiding Place. Richard Armour. NIP

Moved. *(LL)* Unconscious Came a Beauty. May Swenson. VCAP

Moved on. None heeded, and few heard. *(LL)* Cassandra. E. A. Robinson. CMoP; ImPo; LiTA; LiTM; MeMAP; NoAM; OxBA

Moved on the darkness of the formless Deep! *(LL)* To the Reverend W. L. Bowles. Samuel Taylor Coleridge. EnRP; Son

Movement of Fish, The. James Dickey. NYBP; VGW

Movement of the sea, The. *(LL)* Reasons for Music. Archibald MacLeish. MeMAP

Movement one: genesis. Jazz to Jackson to John. Jerry W. Ward, Jr. Jaz

Movement, she explained, would bring poetry to the rich, The. Ralph Hodgson. *Fr.* Flying Scrolls. FaBoTw

Movement Song. Audre Lorde. VCAP

Movements. Norman MacCaig. OxBC

Moves small beyond it. *(LL)* The Door. Robert Creeley. NaP; NeAP; NoAM; PoM; VGW

Moves the calm spirit, but disturbs it not. *(LL)* The Ocean. Moschus. AWP; OBVE

Moves with the numbers which she hears. *(LL)* The Dancer. Edmund Waller. CBLP; TrGrPo

Movie. Bob Perelman. BAP-89

Movie. Patricia Storace. BAP-89

Movie Actors Scribbling Letters Very Fast in Crucial Scenes. Jean Garrigue. TAP

Movie-Going. John Hollander. CoAP

Movie House. John Updike. PeLV

Movie Run Backward, The. Robert Creeley. CAPP

Movies and the magazines are all of them liars, The. Love Letter. W. H. Auden. CBLP

Movies are badder. Saturday Afternoon at the Movies. John Logan. NNaP

Movies for the Home. Howard Moss. NYBP

Movies, Left to Right. Robert Sward. NYBP

Movies wouldn't buy it, The. Are We Ready for the Jimi Hendrix Story? Connie Deanovich. UTF

Movies you wouldn't let them see when they were young. *(LL)* Ave Maria. Frank O'Hara. HCAP; NAAL-2; NNaP; NoP; PoM; VCAP

Movin' with Nancy. David Trinidad. UTF

Moving. Jeanne Foster. CrSp

Moving. Darrell Gray. UL

Moving. Janet Reed McFatter. GrPl

Moving. Frank Steele. GOYP

Moving Ahead. Rainer Maria Rilke, *tr. fr. German by* Robert Bly. NU

Moving at summer's pace. *(LL)* Cut Grass. Philip Larkin. NoAM; NTP; OxBC; PrIm; RB

Moving between Beloit and Monroe. Bink Noll. GrPl

Moving deep. "Stephany." NBV

Moving Finger writes; and, having writ, The. Omar Khayyám, *tr. fr. Persian by* Edward Fitzgerald. *Fr.* Rubáiyát of Omar Khayyám of Naishápúr, The. AWP; EBVV, *abr.*; FaBoBe; FaBoRV, *abr.*; FaPoR, *abr.*; HAP, *abr.*; LiTB; NAEL-2; NoP; PoEL-5; PrIm, *abr.*; TrGrPo; TRP

Moving from Cheer to Joy, from Joy to All. Next Day. Randall Jarrell. HAP; HCAP; MoP; NAAL-2; NoAM; NoP; NYBP; Poetr; VCAP; WeW

Moving from the bus at the Loop it's possible suddenly. Seeing St. James's. Ray Mathew. NOBAu

Moving In. Paul Engle. PoA

Moving In. Josephine Miles. NoP

Moving In. Frank Ormsby. PeIV

Moving In. Karl Shapiro. NAs

Moving like women: Justice, Truth, such figures. *(LL)* Another September. Thomas Kinsella. BIrV; CIP

Moving Occupations, The. Wayne Koestenbaum. UTF

Moving of stones, that sly jockeying thrust, The. Stones. Maxine W. Kumin. CAPP

Moving on or going back to where you came from. A Procession at Candlemas. Amy Clampitt. FaBoWP; HCAP; Poetr

Moving out. Thing Poem. Petra von Morstein, *tr. fr. German by* Rosemarie Waldrop. BoWoP

Moving over the hills, crossing the irrigation. Some San Francisco Poems. George Oppen. NNaP

Moving river shall swallow it!, The. *(LL)* Nozizwe. Mazisi Kunene. PeSAV

Moving shadows, The. Virgil Hutton. InPK

Moving slowly sweating a lot. Post the Lake Poets Ballad. Frank O'Hara. PoBeRe

Moving sun-shapes on the spray, The. Going and Staying. Thomas Hardy. CMoP; NoAM

Moving through the silent crowd. Unemployed. Stephen Spender. FaBoEH; NOBE

Moving to Her New House. Nellie Wong. ETG

Moving to the Cottage of Pine and Bamboo, *sels.* Chang Wen-t'ao, *tr. fr. Chinese by* William Schultz.

Moving towards Home. June Jordan. WoWa

Mower, The. *Unknown.* CoMu; OBET

Mower against Gardens, The. Andrew Marvell. EBEV; ESCV; FaBoPV; LiTB; NAEL-1; NoP; NOSC; OAEL-1; OxAEP-1; PFP; PoE; PoEL-2; PPP; SeCV-1

Mower to the Glo-Worms, The. Andrew Marvell. *See* Ye living lamps, by whose dear light.

Mower to the Glow-Worms [*or* Glowworms], The. Andrew Marvell. AWP; ELP; FHYEP; GeHe; InvP; NAEL-1; NOBE; NoP; OAEL-1; OxBoLi; PeLV; PPP; SCGP; TFi; TrGrPo

Mowers: An Antication of the Cholera, 1848, The. Charles MacKay. EBVV; OHCV

Mowers begin, The. Watchers. W. S. Merwin. NaP

Mower's Song, The. Andrew Marvell. CBLP; ESCV; NAEL-1; NOSC; PFP; PoEL-2; PPP; SeCP; SeCV-1

Mowers, weary and brown, and blithe. Scythe Song. Andrew Lang. GN

Mowing. Robert Frost. AnAmPo; BLPL; CMoP; HoPM; LiTA; NAAL-2; NOBA; OxBA; PoP; TRP; VGW

Mowing, The. Sir Charles G. D. Roberts. NOBC

Mowing his three acres with a tractor. On the Turning Up of Unidentified Black Female Corpses. Toi Derricotte. NAmP90

Mown from the harvest's middle floor. *(LL)* August. Swinburne. WiR

Moxford Book of English Verse, The, *sels.* Archibald Stodart-Walker.

Moytura, *sels.* William Larminie.
 Sword of Tethra, The. PeIV

Mozart. John Heath-Stubbs. EBEV

Mozart, Goethe, and the Duke of Wellington. The Augsburg Adoration. Randall Jarrell. NYBP

Mozart's Grave. Paul Scott Mowrer. GoYe

Mr. and Mrs. Wendy Mulford. NBrP

Mr. Jones. Harry Graham. *See* 'There's been an accident!' they said.

Mr. Lear, I'm the Akond of Swat. Ethel Talbot Scheffauer. PeLi
 (Reply from the Akond of Swat, A.) FiBHP

Mr. L'Estrange's Verses in the Prison at Lynn. Sir Roger L'Estrange. *See* Beat on, proud billow[e]s! Boreas blow!

Mr. T./ bareheaded. The Artist. William Carlos Williams. InPS; LCAP; NYBP; RB; SAmP

Mummies, The. Maxine W. Kumin. Poetsp

Mummy is singing at breakfast and dancing!/ So big! *(LL)* Eskimo Occasion. Judith Rodriguez. CBAP; FaBoWP; NOBAu

Mummy of a Lady Named Jemutesonekh XXI Dynasty. Thomas James. AmPA; SM

Mummy Slept Late and Daddy Fixed Breakfast. John Ciardi. PDV

Mumpaty, mumpaty, mump. *(LL)* Roger and Dolly. Henry Carey. CBNP; CoMu; NOEC; OxNR, *sl. diff. vers.*

Mumps. Elizabeth Madox Roberts. FaPON

Munching a plum on/ the street. To a Poor Old Woman. William Carlos Williams. AnAmPo; MeMAP; OBAL; SOTW; TAP; TTTS

Mundaka Upanishad. *Unknown, tr. fr. Hindi. Fr.* Upanishads, The.

Mundus et Infans. W. H. Auden. LiTB; LiTM; MeMAP; MoAB; MoBrPo; NAs; NoAM

Mundus Muliebris. Mary Evelyn. NOSC

Mundus Muliebris, *sels.* Mary Evelyn.
"In Pin-up Ruffles now she flaunts." KTR

Mundus Qualis. Joshua Sylvester. FaBoEE

Munich: Elegy No. 1. George Barker. MeMBP

Munich Mannequins, The. Sylvia Plath. CAPP; NaP

Munich, 1955. Maurya Simon. BTR

Municipal. Kipling. BXAP

Municipal Gallery Revisited, The. W. B. Yeats. GTBS-P; LiTB; MeMBP; OxBTC

Muntch, muntch. Nycey! *(LL)* The Cannibals' Grace before Meat. Charles Dickens. FaBoNo

Muppim and Huppim! Strike blows on your drums! The Dance of Despair. Hayyim Nahman Bialik, *tr. fr. Hebrew by* A. M. Klein. TrJP

Mural, *sels.* Vincente Rodríguez Nietzche, *tr. fr. Spanish by* Julio Marzán.

Murder. Gertrud Kolmar, *tr. fr. German by* Henry A. Smith. WoWa

Murder in the Cathedral, *sels.* T. S. Eliot.
"We do not wish anything to happen." OxBTC
"We have not been happy, my Lord, we have not been too happy." OxBTC
"Where is Becket, the traitor to the king?" FaBoEH
"You see, my Lord, I do not wait upon ceremony." OBF

Murder of a Spanish Lady by a Pirate. Richard Henry Dana. AnAmPo

Murder of Goins, The. *Unknown.* AmFP

Murder of Maria Marten, The. W. Corder. CoMu; OBET

Murder of William Remington, The. Howard Nemerov. CMoP; CoAP

Murder self slowly. And die like ants shuffling up under. Reckoning A.M. Thursday. Doris Turner. JB

Murder Trial, The. Perseus Adams. PeSA

Murdered City, The. Anne Hébert, *tr. fr. French by* A. Poulin, Jr. WoWa

Murdered Girl Is Found on a Bridge, The. Jane Hayman. NYBP

Murdered himself, to show some manful deed. *(LL)* Assyrian [*or* Assyrians'] King in peace, with foul desire, The [*or* Th']. The Earl of Surrey. NoSiC; SiPSBD

Murdered, I went, risen. The Life. James Wright. LCAP; NaP

Murdered Little Bird. *Unknown.* FiBHP

Murderer, The. Paul Petrie. NYBP

Murderer, The. Stevie Smith. FaBoWP; OxBSP; TEP

Murderer & Sarapis, The. Palladas, *tr. fr. Greek by* Tony Harrison. GrAn

Murderer spread his palliasse, A. The Murderer & Sarapis. Palladas, *tr. fr. Greek by* Tony Harrison. GrAn

Murderers/ of Emmett Till. Salute. Oliver Pitcher. PoBA

Murderers are loose! The; They search the world. Murder. Gertrud Kolmar, *tr. fr. German by* Henry A. Smith. WoWa

Murderers of Kings, The. Zbigniew Herbert, *tr. fr. Polish by* John Carpenter *and* Bogdana Carpenter. AnAn

Murderers of the wall wrap themselves in sunrise, The. Jean Genet, *tr. fr. French by* Steven Finch. *Fr.* Man Sentenced to Death, The. PeHV

Murge with your white stones and green olives. Second Image Sequence. Umberto Piersanti, *tr. fr. Italian by* Stephen Sartarelli. NeIt

Murie Sing. Archibald Y. Campbell. FaBoPa

Murmur of a bee, The. Emily Dickinson. MoAmPo

Murmur of the mourning ghost, The. The Ballad of Keith of Ravelston. Sydney Thompson Dobell. *Fr.* Nuptial Eve, A. CH; OBEV; OBNC (Keith of Ravelston.) CH

Murmur of voices behind the ploughman, A. The Journey's Formulae. Tomas Tranströmer, *tr. fr. Swedish by* Robin Fulton. PWE

Murmurers, The. Josephine Jacobsen. GrPl

Murmuring Esk; may Roses shade the place, The. *(LL)* To Sir William Alexander. William Drummond of Hawthornden.

Murmuring from Glaramara's inmost caves. *(LL)* Yew Trees. Wordsworth. EnRP; UnPo

Murmuring in empty shells, A. The Relic. Robert Silliman Hillyer. GoYe

Murmuring, in her sleep as it seemed, the ancient slogan/ *Noblesse oblige.* *(LL)* Belief. Josephine Miles. FaBoWP; MoP; NoAM; TAP

Murukan: His Places. Nakkiranar, *tr. fr. Tamil by* A. K. Ramanujan. PLW

Murukan, the Red One. Nakkiranar, *tr. fr. Tamil by* A. K. Ramanujan. PLW

Musa, Musae,/ The Gods were at tea. The Muses. *Unknown.* FaBoNo

Muscovy Drake, The. E. A. S. Lesoro, *tr. fr. Sotho by* Dan Kunene *and* Jack Cope. PeSA

Muse, The. Abraham Cowley. EPCY

Muse, The. Barry Spacks. MAT

Muse. David Wagoner. PoA

Muse and Poet. Robert Bridges. OBMV

Muse as Medusa, The. May Sarton. NALW

Muse, bid the morne awake. To His Valentine. Michael Drayton. PoEL-2

Muse, disgusted at an age and clime, The. On the Prospect of Planting Arts and Learning in America. George Berkeley. AiP; ImPo; NOEC; OBTV; TrGrPo

Muse, first of Arden tell, whose footsteps yet are found. The Dwindling Forest of Arden. Michael Drayton. *Fr.* Polyolbion.

Muse forgot, and thou beloved no more!, The. *(LL)* Elegy to the Memory of an Unfortunate Lady. Pope. ECEV; NOBE; NOEC; OAEL-1; OBD; OBEV; SCGP; TEP

Muse in Late November. Jonathan Henderson Brooks. ChIV-1; PoNe

Muse in the New World, The. Walt Whitman. *Fr.* Song of the Exposition. MoAmPo

Muse Is Always the Other Woman, The. Constance Urdang. PBCAP

Muse is still in ure, The. *(LL)* An Ode Written in the Peak[e]. Michael Drayton. FaBoPP; NOSC

Muse, June, Related, *sels.* Brian Coffey.
"Blooms such as wither at finger-touch." BIrV

Muse of Amergin, The. *Unknown, tr. fr. Irish by* John Montague. BIrV; IIP

Muse of Distance, The. Alan Williamson. BAP-89

Muse of Fire, A. Shakespeare. *See* O for a Muse of fire, that would ascend.

Muse of my Spenser, who so well could sing. George Crabbe. *Fr.* Birth of Flattery, The. EPCY

Muse of native land! loftiest Muse! Keats. *Fr.* Endymion [a Poetic Romance]. EnRP

Muse of Poetry came down one day, The. In Memoriam Paul Laurence Dunbar. H. Cordelia Ray. CBWP-3
(In Memoriam.) AmWP

Muse of the fields, oft have I said farewell. John Clare. *Fr.* To the Rural Muse. EPCY

Muse of the Golden Throne. Sappho, *tr. fr. Greek by* Sam Hamill. InMo

Muse of the many-twinkling feet! whose charms. Byron. *Fr.* Waltz, The. OBSV

Muse of Water, A. Carolyn Kizer. NMM; VCAP

Muse Poem. Kathryn van Spanckeren. FF

Muse Reviving, The. Sir John Davies. SiPS

Muse should be sprightly, The. A Skeltoniad. Michael Drayton. PoEL-2

Muse, sing the stir that happy Whitbread made. George III Visits Whitbread's Brewery. "Peter Pindar." *Fr.* Instructions to a Celebrated Laureat. NOEC

Muse that stirs my blood, The. Bird and the Muse. Marya Zaturenska. PoA

Muse to an Unknown Poet, The. Paul Potts. FaBoTw

Muse with the hero's brave deeds being fired, The. Captain Death. *Unknown.* CoMu

Muse, you have left me at last. How did I come. Cooking Eggs. Dave Jeddie Smith. AnAn

Musée des Beaux Arts. W. H. Auden. ClHu; CMoP; FF; GTBS-P; HAP; HeIL; HeIP; ImPo; InPK; InPS; LiTB; LiTM; MeMAP; MoAB; MoP; NAEL-2; NoAM; NOBE; NoP; OxAEP-2; PoE; Poetr; PoRA; PPP; PrIm; RaBo; SCV; SoSe; TEP; TFi; TrCP; TrGrPo; TRP; TwCP

Muses, The. *Unknown.* FaBoNo

Muse's Answer, The. Gibbons Ruark. MT

Muses are turned gossips; they have lost, The. Washing-Day. Anna Laetitia Barbauld. ECWP; WoRP

Muses' Elysium [*or* Elizium], *sels.* Michael Drayton.
"Clear [*or* Cleere] had the day been [*or* bin] from the dawn [*or* dawne]." BoTP
(Fine Day, A.) GN
Description of Elizium, The. OAEL-1
(Poet's Paradise, The.) WiR, *much abr.*
Tenth Nimphall, The. JCP

Muses evening, as their morning-starre, The. *(LL)* To Lucy, Countess[e] of Bedford, with Mr. Donnes Satyres [*or* Satires]. Ben Jonson. BeJo; EPCY; SeCV-1

Muses' fairest light in no dark time, The. On Ben Jonson. Sidney Godolphin. BeJo; EPCY

Muse's Favor, The. Priscilla Jane Thompson. AAP; CBWP-2

Musmee, The. Sir Edwin Arnold. OBTV

Musophilus; or, Defence of All Learning, *sels.* Samuel Daniel.
  "Behold how every man, drawn with delight." NoSic
  "But yet in all this interchange of all." EPCY
  "Fond man, Musophilus, that thus dost spend." NoSic
  "O blessed letters, that combine in one." EPCY
    (O Blessed Letters.) FaBoRV
  Poetry in England. EPCY; NoSic
    (Heavenly Eloquence.) NOBE
  "Sacred Religion, mother of form and fear." NoSic

Muspilli. *Unknown, tr. fr. German by* Carroll Hightower. GePo

Mussel Hunter at Rock Harbor. Sylvia Plath. NYBP

Mussel Rock/Lowtide — Santa Cruz, California 1959. Jeff Tagami. OpBo

Musselburgh Field. *Unknown.* ESPB

Mussels. Mary Oliver. NU

Must all successful rebels grow. 1912–1952, Full Cycle. Peter Viereck. OBAL

Must be always best. *(LL)* God Knoweth Best. *Unknown.* WBLP

Must Be Freed. L. A. J. Moorer. CBWP-3

Must be some girl from the villages. Sappho, *tr. fr. Greek by* Sam Hamill. InMo

Must both remain as strangers still to you. *(LL)* Yourself. Jones Very. NOBA; OxBA; PoEL-4; Son

Must ever love the autumn wind. *(LL)* The Autumn Wind. John Clare. BoNaP

Must gulp it down at Closing Time. *(LL)* To His Not-so-coy Mistress. Wynford Vaughan-Thomas. BXAP; NOBL

Must hapless man, in ignorance sedate. Celestial Wisdom. Juvenal, *tr. by* Samuel Johnson. *Fr.* Satires. AWP

Must I die now? Is this a part of life? *(LL)* A Cut Flower. Karl Shapiro. BoNaP; HAP; WeW

Must I go bound and you go free. *Unknown.* WTO

Must I lament the time that's gone because I've been cast aside? Ch'ien Ch'ien-i, *tr. by* Irving Y. Lo. *Fr.* Willow Branch Songs. SuSp

Must I shoot thee. Watts. Conrad Kent Rivers. PoBA

Must I tell again. The Daemon. Louise Bogan. NYBP

Must I then see, alas! eternal night. Elegy over a Tomb. Lord Herbert of Cherbury. EIL; GGP; MeLP; NOBE; OBEV; OBWVE; PoEL-2

Must leash'd t' himself with him a-hunting go. *(LL)* Cupid Far Gone. Richard Lovelace. CaPo; OPOP

Must look on Thrale at Thirty-five. *(LL)* To Mrs. Thrale [on Her Thirty-fifth Birthday]. Samuel Johnson. FaBoEE; NAs

Must noble Hastings immaturely die. Upon the Death of the Lord Hastings. Dryden. SeCV-2

Must not be numbred in the year. *(LL)* Christ's Nativity. Henry Vaughan. ESCV

Must pine neglected and alone. *(LL)* The Captive Dove. Anne Brontë. EBVV; OHCV; PIP

Must plough the wave no more. *(LL)* On the Loss of the *Royal George.* William Cowper. EBEV; GN; NOBE; TrGrPo

Must soon partake his grave. *(LL)* Epitaph on a Hare. William Cowper. CoGr; FM; HAP; NOEC; PoEL-3

Must surely have belonged to him. *(LL)* Aleister Crowley Slept Here. Elaine Equi. UTF

Must we part, Von Hügel, though much alike. W. B. Yeats. *Fr.* Vacillation. NoAM; OBMV

Must you alone then, happy flowers. To a Nosegay in Pancharilla's Breast. Soame Jenyns. ECEV

Must you deny me a bite of your raisin? *(LL)* Brief Autumnal. *Unknown.* GrAn; WeW

Must you leave, John Holmes, with the prayers and psalms. Somewhere in Africa. Anne Sexton. NALW

Must you with hot irons burn out both mine eyes? Shakespeare. *Fr.* King John. OxAEP-1

Mustacheless Bard, A. J. Gordon Coogler. OBAL

Mustapha, *sels.* Fulke Greville.
  Chorus Primus of Bashaws or Cadis. NOSC
  Chorus Sacerdotum. HAP; InvP; JCP; LiTB; NAEL-1; NOBE; OAEL-1; PoEL-1; PPP
    (Chorus of Priests.) NoSic; OxAEP-1
  Eternity's Speech against Time.

Mutability. Shelley. EnRP; NAEL-2; NoP; OBNC; PFP

Mutability. W. D. Snodgrass. DiPo

Mutability. Spenser. *Fr.* Faerie Queene, The. PoEL-1

Mutability. Wordsworth. *Fr.* Ecclesiastical Sonnets. EBEV; EnRP; HeIP; InPK; LiTB; MeMBP; NOBE; NoP; OAEL-2; OBEV; PoEL-4; PrIm

Mutability Claims to Rule the World. Spenser. *Fr.* Faerie Queene, The. NoSic

Mutation. Bryant. EAP

Mutations of the Phoenix, *sels.* Sir Herbert Read.

"Phoenix, bird of terrible pride." FaBoTw

Mute/ the hand moves from the heart. Miniatures IV. Lynn Strongin. IHMS

Mute he sat in the saddle — mute 'midst our full acclaim. A Christopher of the Shenandoah. Edith M. Thomas. PAH

Mute Opinion. Thomas Hardy. CMoP

Muted. Paul Verlaine, *tr. fr. French.* RiWo, *tr. by* Philip L. Miller; UnAS, *tr. by* C. F. MacIntyre.

Muted Screen of Graham Greene, The. Phyllis McGinley. FaBoEE

Muted wood-wind is one noise of the traffic, and there is a second. The Empire Clock. Bernard Spencer. OBTV

Mutes, The. Denise Levertov. IHMS; NALW; NaP; NOBA; PWE

Mutilated choir boys, The. Heine, *tr. fr. German by* Ezra Pound. *Fr.* Heimkehr, Die. AWP

Mutineer's Ballad, The. Peter Kocan. NOBAu

Mutoscope. Elizabeth Spires. NAmP90

Mutterings over the Crib of a Deaf Child. James Wright. LCAP

Mutton. *Unknown.* BXAP

Mutton and Leather. *Unknown.* CoMu

Mutton Bird Man. Rhyll McMaster. NOBAu

Mutual Congratulations of the Poets Anna Seward and Hayley, The. Richard Porson. FaBoEE; OBSV

Mutual Forgiveness of each vice. For the Sexes; the Gates of Paradise. Blake. LiTB; MeMBP; PoEL-4

Mutual Love. William Hammond. JCP

Mutual Problem. William Cole. OBAL

Mutual Subjection. Christopher Smart. *Fr.* Hymns for the Amusement of Children. NOCV

Muu's Way; or Pictures from the Uterine World. *Unknown, tr. fr. Cuna Indian by* Jerome K. Rothenberg. STP

Muvver was barfin' 'er biby one night, A. Dahn the Plug'ole. *Unknown, tr. by* Robert Bly. RB
  ("Biby's" Epitaph.) FiBHP

Muzak spreading like ice. *(LL)* Planes Landing. Jamie Grant. NOBAu

Muzik of blood. Bass Culture. Linton Kwesi Johnson. PBCV

Muzzle and jowl and beastly brow. Fearfull Symmetry. Basil Bunting. PoA

Muzzy with drink, I let my humor recline. The Ghost of an Education. James Michie. NYBP

Mwilu/ or Poem for the Living. Don L. Lee. JB

My/ father/ dreams. The Eyes of Flesh. Sandra Hochman. NMM

My Acts. William Meredith. *Fr.* Consequences. VCAP

My Africa. Michael Dei-Anang. PBA

My Afternoon. Robert Adamson. FaBoMA

My age fallen away like white swaddling. Age. Philip Larkin. CMoP

My age is three hundred and seventy-two. The Sleepy Giant. Charles Edward Carryl. OTCP

My aged friend, Miss Wilkinson. The Bards. Walter de la Mare. FaBoNo; NOBL

My Aim. George Linnaeus Banks. *See* I live for those who love me.

My Ain Countree. Mary Lee Demarest. WGRP

My Ain Fireside. Elizabeth Hamilton. FaBoBe

My Alba. Allen Ginsberg. NOBA

My ambition as I remember and. Love at Roblin Lake. Alfred W. Purdy. NoP

My analyst hints at amnesia impending. *(LL)* A Right-of-Way: 1865. William Plomer. PeLV

My ancestor was called on to go out. The Wind at Your Door. Robert David Fitzgerald. FaBoMA; NOBAu

My ancestors are nearer. Ancestral Poem. Olive Senior. PBCV

My ancestors weren't hippies, cotton. Botanical Fanaticism. Thylias Moss. TRP

My Angel. Jonathan Henderson Brooks. PoNe

My Angeline. Harry Bache Smith. NBLV

My angry blood for a thousand years will be emeralds under the earth! *(LL)* Autumn Comes. Li Ho. PLT

My Answer. Ralph Adamo. MT

My answer would have to be music. The Medium. Elaine Feinstein. BrRo

My ardours for emprize nigh lost. On an Invitation to the United States. Thomas Hardy. AiP; AWP

My Arkansas. Maya Angelou. BlSi

My arm sweeps down. Gesture. Donald Finkel. InPK

My arms are round you, and I lean. To the Oaks of Glencree. J. M. Synge. MoBrPo; NOIV; PeIV

My arms have mutinied against me — brutes! Wild with All Regrets. Wilfred Owen. SCGP

My arms smell good. Think. Please Forward. James Welch. CDW

My ash spear is my barley bread. Archilochus, *tr. fr. Greek by* Guy Davenport. GrAn

My aspens dear, whose airy cages quelled. Binsey Poplars (Felled 1879). Gerard Manley Hopkins. BoNaP; EBVV; ELP; EnVR; FaBoPP; InPS; Mes; NAEL-2; NoAM; NoP; RB

My attention is a wild/ animal. Pet Panther. A. R. Ammons. NoP

My Atthis, although our dear Anaktoria. Sappho, *tr. fr. Greek by* Willis Barnstone. BoWoP

My attire is noiseless when I tread the earth. Wild Swan: "My attire is noiseless when I tread the earth." Unknown, formerly at. to Cynewulf, *tr. fr. Anglo-Saxon. Fr.* Riddles (Exeter Book). AnOE, *tr. by* Charles W. Kennedy

My Auld Wife. *Unknown.* GBP

My Aunt. Oliver Wendell Holmes. AmPP; TAP

My Aunt Bebe. The Aga Khan. Steve Orlen. Poetsp

My Aunt Jane. *Unknown.* FaBoVe

My Aunt Louise subscribed to *Photoplay.* Heartthrobs. Joan Jobe Smith. NGP

My aunt! my dear unmarried aunt! My Aunt. Oliver Wendell Holmes. AmPP; TAP

My aunt she died a month ago. Death of My Aunt. *Unknown.* OxBoLi

My aunt was an herb doctor, one-eyed with crooked yellow teeth. To-ta Ti-om. Peter Blue Cloud. HATNAP

My aunts washed dishes while the uncles. Paper Matches. Paulette Jiles. Mes; NIP; NOBC

My author and disposer, what thou biddest. Milton. *Fr.* Paradise Lost. EPCY

(Thus Eve to Adam.) FaBV

My baby/ loves flowers. William J. Harris. NBV

My Baby Has No Name Yet. Kim Nam Jo, *tr. fr. Korean by* Ko Won. AIW; ArLo; PBWP

My bands of silk and miniver. Full Moon. Elinor Wylie. MoAB; NALW

My banks they are furnished with bees. William Shenstone. *Fr.* Pastoral Ballad. BoNaP

(Shepherd's Home, The.) GN

My Baptismal Birthday. Samuel Taylor Coleridge. ChIV-2; NOCV

My bar is somewhat further down the street. (*LL*) Third Avenue in Sunlight. Anthony Hecht. CoAP; PGP; VCAP

My beak is bent downward, I burrow below. Plow: "My beak is bent downward, I burrow below." Unknown, formerly at. to Cynewulf, *tr. fr. Anglo-Saxon. Fr.* Riddles (Exeter Book). AnOE

My beard's overcrowded. Now that. Richard Unwin. PeLi

My beautiful black baby, sleep. (*LL*) Lullaby. Elolongue Epanya Yondo. NegPo

My beautiful boy you have killed me. (*LL*) Ballygrand Widow. Deborah Randell. VBLP

My beautiful! my beautiful! that standest meekly by. The Arab to His Favorite Steed. Caroline E. Norton. BeLS

(Arab's Farewell to His Horse, The.) BLPA

(Arab's Farewell to His Steed, The.) VPP

My beautiful picture of pirates and treasure. Jigsaw Puzzle. Russell Hoban. NTCP

My beautiful trembler! how wildly she shrinks! Ellen Learning to Walk. Frances Sargent Osgood. AmWP

My beauty is not weak to me. The Song of the Narcissus. *Unknown, tr. fr. Arabic by* E. Powys Mathers. *Fr.* Thousand and One Nights, The. AWP

My Bed Is a Boat ("My bed is like a little boat.") Robert Louis Stevenson. PeVV; PWR

My bed is so empty that I keep on waking up. Winter Night. Chien Wen-Ti. ArNa

My behavior,/ not barely perceptible. Habeas Corpus. Anthony Barnett. VaA

My bell is Charlie Parker's. Saxophone. Christopher Gilbert. *Fr.* Horizontal Cosmology. Jaz

My Beloved. Ammon Wrigley. UnDi

My beloved hath a vineyard. The Vineyard of My Beloved. Priscilla Jane Thompson. AAP; CBWP-2

My Beloved Is Mine, and I Am His; He Feedeth among the Lillies. Francis Quarles. *Fr.* Emblems. MeLP; NOBE; OBEV; TrGrPo, *abr.*

My beloved land. Minority Report. John Updike. GOA

My beloved little billiard balls. Poem to Some of my Recent Poems. James Tate. NoAM

My beloved spake, and said unto me. Song of Songs. Bible, *O.T. Fr.* Song of Solomon, The. ArNa

My beloved's eyes. Secret. Goethe, *tr. fr. German by* Philip L. Miller. RiWo

My Ben! Robert Herrick. BeJo

My best belovit brother of the band. To R. Hudson. Alexander Montgomerie. OxBS

My better half, why turn a peevish scold. Martial, *tr. fr. Latin.* PeHV

My biggest worry is this. In a Time of Sickness. Orpingalik, *tr. fr. Eskimo by* Edward Field. STP

My Birds. Solomon Mutswairo, *tr. fr. Shona by* Solomon Mutswairo *and* Donald E. Herdeck. PeSAV

My Birth. Minot Judson Savage. WGRP

My Birthday. George Crabbe. OxBSP

My black-eyed lover broke my back. The Masochist. Maxine W. Kumin. IHMS; PoA

My black face fades. Facing It. Yusef Komunyakaa. BAP-90; MT; TRP

My black hills have never seen the sun rising. Shancoduff. Patrick Kavanagh. BIrV; CIP; FaBoTw; IIP; IPY; NoP; PeIV

My black mothers I hear them singing. Black Star Line. Henry Dumas. PoBA

My black self. Another. Vers Negre. Richard Caddel. NBrP

My Blackness Is the Beauty of This Land. Lance Jeffers. PoBA

My Blessed Lord, how doth thy Beautious Spouse. Edward Taylor. *Fr.* Preparatory Meditations Before My Approach to the Lord's Supper. SCAP

My blessed mother dozing in her chair. A Valentine to My Mother. Christina Rossetti. OHIP

My Blood Brother. Frank Mkalawile Chipasula. HBAPE

My blood sits upright in a chair. Blood. Franz Wright. LCAP

My blood so red. The Call. *Unknown.* OBEV

My bloodstream chokes on gall and spleen. Barend Toerien, *tr. fr. Afrikaans by the author.* PeSA

My blueveined child. (*LL*) A Flower Given to My Daughter. James Joyce. OBMV; RaBo; RB

My board and blanket were Navajo. In Memory of Crossing the Columbia. Elizabeth Woody. BCF

My boat goes west, yours east. Ch'ao Li-houa, *tr. fr. Chinese by* J. P. Seaton. BoWoP

My boat is on the shore. To Thomas Moore. Byron. EnRP

My Boat Moored on a River. Yen Yu, *tr. fr. Chinese by* Irving Y. Lo. SuSp

My boat sails downstream. *Unknown, tr. fr. Egyptian by* J. E. Manchip White. TTY

My body. What She Said ("My body.") Ammuvanar, *tr. fr. Tamil by* A. K. Ramanujan. PLW

My body/ she says. Cleopatra. Mary Mackey. AIW

My body a rounded stone. Living Tenderly. May Swenson. OBCA

My body being dead, my limbs [*or* lims] unknown. The Preparative. Thomas Traherne. ESCV; GeHe; PoEL-2

My body, eh? Friend Death, how now? Habeas Corpus. Helen Hunt Jackson. WGRP

My body heavy with poverty (starch). Today's News. Ted Berrigan. UL

My body holds its shape. The genius is intact. Mummy of a Lady Named Jemutesonekh XXI Dynasty. Thomas James. AmPA; SM

My Body in the Walls Captived. Sir Walter Ralegh. SiPS; SiPSBD

My body is like/ a field wasted by winter. On Seeing the Field Being Singed. Lady Ise, *tr. fr. Japanese by* Etsuko Terasaki *and* Irma Brandeis. BoWoP

My body is one with the earth. (*LL*) Sowing the seed. Wendell Berry. EaPr

My body is weary to death of my mischievous brain. Nebuchadnezzar. Elinor Wylie. ChIV-1; MoAmPo

My body knows it will never bear children. Waiting. Jane Cooper. CrSp; TAP

My body opens over San Francisco like the daylight. Splittings. Adrienne Rich. CAPP

My Bonnie Mary. Burns. *See* Go fetch to me a pint o'wine.

My Bonny Black Bess. *Unknown. See* Dick Turpin's Ride ("Dick Turpin bold! Dick, hie away.")

My bonny keel laddie, my canny keel laddie. The Bonny Keel Laddie. *Unknown.* GBP

My bonny lass, thine eye. Love's Witchery. Thomas Lodge. EIL

My bonny moorhen, my bonny moorhen. The Bonny Moorhen. *Unknown.* GBP

My book is largely growing. Introductory to Second Edition. Alfred Islay Walden. AAP

My boy friend's name is Jello. *Unknown.* RoPo

My Boy Jack. Kipling. OtMeF

My Boy Tammy. Hector MacNeill. CH

My boy was scarcely ten years auld. Leesome Brand. *Unknown.* ESPB

My boy, what do you think that I can tell you? Oom Gert's Story. C. Louis Leipoldt, *tr. fr. Afrikaans by* C. J. D. Harvey. PeSAV

My brain dried like spread turf, my stomach. Seamus Heaney. *Fr.* Station Island. CIP

My brain is like the ravaged shores — the sand. At Night. Frances Cornford. MoBrPo

My country, 'tis of thee. Assembly: Harlem School. Eugene T. Maleska. GoYe

My Country, to Thy Shore. Theodore Chickering Williams. AH

My countryman, the poet, wears a Stetson. David Wright. *Fr.* Seven South African Poems. PeSA

My countrymen have now become too base. April 1962. Paul Goodman. VGW

My Cousin Agueda [*or* Agatha]. Ramón López Velarde, *tr. fr. Spanish.* OBVE

My Cousin German came from France. *Unknown.* FaBoCh

My Cousin Muriel. Amy Clampitt. BAP-90

My Creed. Alice Cary. AmWP; WGRP

My Creed. Jeanette Leonard Gilder. WGRP

My Creed. Samuel Ellsworth Kiser. PoToHe

My Creed. Howard Arnold Walter. PoLF; WBLP

My crown desired, my true love and joy. A Love Letter to Elizabeth Thatcher. Thomas Thatcher. SCAP

My curse be on the day when first I saw. Sonnet: To the Lady Pietra degli Scrovigni. Dante, *tr. fr. Italian by* Dante Gabriel Rossetti. AWP

My cuticles are a mess. Oh honey, by the way. The Motorcyclists. James Tate. NoAM

My dad had done the same. (*LL*) Epitaph on a Pessimist. Thomas Hardy. FaBoEE; FF; TRP

My dad was a fisherman bold and he lived till he grew old. The Candlelight Fisherman. *Unknown.* OxBSS

My Dad was worried about his brother. Lucilius, *tr. fr. Greek by* Peter Porter. GrAn

My Daddy baptized me. A Testimony. George Ella Lyon. GOYP

My daddy come home this morning. Don't Fish in My Sea. Gertrude Rainey. VBLP

My Daddy has paid the rent. Good Times. Lucille Clifton. AmPA; BPo; FF; GoJo; GrPl; InPS; PoBA; SoSe; TAP; TRP; TwCP

My daddy is an engineer. Wanderin'. *Unknown.* AS

My daddy played the market. January 1st. Anne Sexton. HCAP

My daddy rides me piggy-back. Piggy-back. Langston Hughes. TLR

My Daddy, Whenever He Went Some Place. David Huddle. PBCAP

My daddy's dressing up as Father Christmas. Now We Are Six. "Sagittarius." PAW

My Dad's Dinner Pail. Edward Harrigan. BLPA

My daily affairs are quite ordinary. Layman P'ang, *tr. fr. Chinese by* Stephen Mitchell. EnlH

My Daily Creed. *Unknown.* PWR

My Daily Prayer. Grenville Kleiser. BLRP

My dame hath a lame tame crane. *Unknown.* OxNR

My Damon, I am sick. (*LL*) Ipecacuanha. George Canning. ChTr; FaBoNo

My Damon was the first to wake. Meeting. George Crabbe. OBEV

My Dancing Day. *Unknown.* OxBoLi

My dancing is, in my opinion, good. Of Dancing. Alan Brownjohn. FaBoMo

My Daphne's hair is twisted gold. John Lyly. *Fr.* Midas. NoSic (Daphne.) EIL

My dark and sultry love. (*LL*) The Invention of Comics. Amiri Baraka. CRP; LiTM; PoBA

My Dark Fathers. Brendan Kennelly. BIrV; CIP; PBCIP; PeIV

My Dark Rosaleen! (*LL*) Dark Rosaleen. *At.* to Owen Roe MacWard *and* to Hugh O'Donnell. AWP; BIrV; CH; EnRP; IIP; NOIV; OBEV; OxAEP-2; PeIV

My darkling child the stars have obeyed. George Barker. *Fr.* To My Son. TwCP

My Darling Dear, My Daisy Flower. John Skelton. *See* With lullay, lullay, like a child [*or* childe].

My darling is hotter than midsummer night. (*LL*) All Year Long. *Unknown.* OHMPC

My darling, my love. Desmond O'Grady, *tr. fr. Irish by the author. Fr.* In the Greenwood. CIP

My darling, we sat together. Mein Liebchen, wir sassen zusammen. Heine, *tr. fr. German by* James Thomson. AWP

My darling where His lambs do feed! (*LL*) The Ghona Widow's Lullaby. Thomas Pringle. PeSAV

My darling, you know how much I like to see the light on a. The Black Hairs. Heinz Pasman, *tr. fr. German by* Robert Bly. RaBo

My Darling's on the Deep Blue Sea. *Unknown.* AmFP

My daughter, all is not vanity. The Song to the Wife of His Youth. Nathan Alterman, *tr. fr. Hebrew by* Ruth Finer Mintz. *Fr.* Joy of the Poor, The. MHP

My daughter, at eleven. Little Girl, My Stringbean, My Lovely Woman. Anne Sexton. NYBP

My daughter, by a German Mother. Christine McNeill. NWP

My Daughter Considers Her Body. Floyd Skloot. SM

My daughter cries when we have to talk about money. The Money Cry. Peter Davison. FYAP

My daughter has turned against eggs. Age six. Eggs. Sharon Olds. CrSp

My daughter makes songs from the words. Riding Hood. Betsy Sholl. CrSp

My daughter of the Mabinogion name. Rhiannon. T. Harri Jones. AngWe

My daughter plays on the floor. Spelling. Margaret Atwood. NALW; NoAM; NoP

My daughter's dear child here I hold on my lap. After the Inscription on a Greek Stele of a Woman Holding Her Grandchild on Her Knees. *Unknown, tr. fr. Greek by* Stephen Spender. GrAn

My days among the dead are past. Robert Southey. EnRP; TEP (Among His Books.) OxAEP-2 (His Books.) OBEV

My Days are Gliding Swiftly By. David Nelson. AH

My day's delight, my springtime joys for[e]done. Sir Walter Ralegh. *Fr.* Ocean's Love to Cynthia, The. SiPSBD (Poem Entreating of Sorrow, A.) SiPS

My Days of Love Are Over. Byron. *Fr.* Don Juan. OBNC

My Dead. Frederick L. Hosmer. WGRP

My dead friend's face as well. (*LL*) Pour out your light, O stars. Ivor Gurney. FaBoEE; FaBoTw

My dead Love came to me, and said. The Apparition. Stephen Phillips. OBEV

My dead, my living child! (*LL*) The Gray Swan. Alice Cary. BeLS; GN

My dear,/ Today a letter from Berlin. A Letter from Berlin. Jon Stallworthy. MoP; OBWP; OxBC

My Dear and Only Love. James Graham, Marquess of Montrose. BeJo; JCP

Sels.
"Swift fleet the billowy clouds along the sky." BoWoP; WPE
I Wish I Could Remember. Son
Touch, The. OtMeF

My dear Antenor now give ore. To My Antenor, March 16, 1661/2. Katherine Philips. KTR

My dear brother Ned. The *South Carolina. Unknown.* PAH

My dear Brother, wt courage bear the crosse. A Sonnet sent to Blackness to Mr. John Welsch, by the Lady Culross. Elizabeth Melvill, Lady Culross. KTR

My dear child, first thyself enable. The Boy Serving at Table. John Lydgate. OxBChV

My dear Daddie bought a mansion. The Little Bird. Walter de la Mare. NAs

My dear, darkened in sleep turned from the moon. To Judith Asleep. John Ciardi. LiTM; LPA

My dear deaf father, how I loved him then. Sir John Betjeman. *Fr.* Summoned by Bells. OxBTC

My dear, do you know. Babes in the Wood, The ("My dear, do you know.") *Unknown.* OxBChV

My dear, do you remember that country. Remember That Country. Jean Garrigue. VGW

My dear, dumb friend, low lying there. To My Dog "Blanco." Josiah Gilbert Holland. PoLF

"My dear fellow!" said the great poet. Fiction: A Message. Gavin Ewart. OxBC

My dear, I wonder if before the end. To D — —, Dead by Her Own Hand. Howard Nemerov. PoA

My Dear Lady. *Unknown.* EIL

My dear Magritte, I have been ill. Again. Personal Values. Richard Howard. SM

My dear Mr. Murray. Epistle to Mr. Murray. Byron. FaBoUs

My dear Mrs. Bloomer. Part of a True Story. Marilyn Hacker. Poetr

My dear mistress has a heart. The Earl of Rochester. SeCV-2

My dear, my dear, I know. To a Young Girl. W. B. Yeats. EBEV

My dear, naïve, ingenuous child. Don't Say You Like Tchaikowsky. Paul Rosner. FiBHP

My dear one is mine as mirrors are lonely. Miranda. W. H. Auden. *Fr.* Sea and the Mirror, The. NoAM

My dear ones, at those moments. Titian: Assumption (Detail). Sarah Pelham. UnDi

My dear Orange brothers, have you heard of the news. The Orange Lily. *Unknown.* NOIV

My Dear Son John's deceas'd ah! gone from hence. A Brief Elegie on My Dear Son John. John Saffin. SCAP

My dear! this morning we will take a ride. The Tête à Tête; or, Fashionable Pair: an Eclogue. Ann Murry. ECWP

My dear, what you said was one thing. Marge Piercy. *Fr.* My Mother's Body. MDDM

My dear young friend, whose shining wit. Comic Miseries. John Godfrey Saxe. AnAmPo

My dearest Boy,/ Since time begun. To a School-Boy at Eton, Yes and No. Mary Savage. ECWP

My dearest dear, the time draws near. The Lover's Lament. *Unknown.* AS

My dearest dust, could not thy hasty day. Epitaph on the Monument of Sir William Dyer at Colmworth, 1641. Lady Catherine Dyer. *Fr.* Sir William Dyer, Knight. BoLoP; EnLoPo; OxBM

My dearest friend is struck, and I must stern beware. He Loves. David Schirmer, *tr. fr. German by* George C. Schoolfield. GePo

My Dearest Mistress. William Corkine. EnRePo

My Dearest Rival, lest [*or* least]] Our Love. Sir John Suckling. BeJo; MeLP

My dearest, to let you or the world know. The Forfeiture. Henry King. NOSC

My dearly loved friend how oft have we. To My Most Dearly-loved Friend, Henry Reynolds, Esquire, of Poets and Poesy. Michael Drayton. (First Steps Up Parnassus.) NOBE, *abr.*

My dears, 'tis said in days of old. The Bee, the Ant, and the Sparrow. Nathaniel Cotton. OxBChV

My Death. Carl Zuckmayer, *tr. fr. German by* E. B. Ashton. TrJP

My death was arranged by special plans in Heaven. A New England Bachelor. Richard Eberhart. MoAmPo; NoAM

My deep red song will never die. (*LL*) Testament of a Rebel. Breyten Breytenbach. PeSAV

My Deery Honey. *Unknown.* PBCV

My Delight and Thy Delight. Robert Bridges. CMoP; NOBE; OBEV; PoEL-5

My demands upon life are quite modest. Robert Conquest. PeLi

My Descendants. W. B. Yeats. *Fr.* Meditations in Time of Civil War. LiTB

My desire for revenge, the bitterness. Till Death Do Us Part. Leila Miccolis, *tr. fr. Portuguese by* Willis Barnstone *and* Nelson Cerqueira. BoWoP

My desk, most loyal friend. Marina Tsvetayeva, *tr. fr. Russian by* Elaine Feinstein. *Fr.* Desk. OBF

My desolation does begin to make. Shakespeare. *Fr.* Antony and Cleopatra. OBD

My destiny has been to prune one tree. They. Marvin Bell. CAPP

My Detached Villa. Li Shan-fu, *tr. by* Edward H. Schafer. SuSp

My deth I love, my lif ich hate. *Unknown.* MeEL; MiEL

My dismal sister! Couldst thou know. "Lewis Carroll." *Fr.* Melancholetta. FiBHP

My disordered perfumed clouds are still damp. Cloud Hairdress. Chao Luan-luan, *tr. fr. Chinese by* Kenneth Rexroth *and* Ling Chung. WPC

My Dog. John Kendrick Bangs. BLPA; BLPL; FaBoBe

My Dog. Marchette Chute. FaPON; ImGa; PDV; WHSW

My Dog. Emily Lewis. OTCP

My Dog Dash. John Ruskin. FM

My dog lay dead five days without a grave. The Pardon. Richard Wilbur. MoP; NoAM; NOBA; NoP; OBD; Poetr

My Dog Ponto. Edgar Lee Masters. FM

My Dog, Spot. Rodney Bennett. BoTP

My dog went mad and bit my hand. D is for Dog. W. H. Davies. OxBSP

My Doggie. C. Nurton. BoTP

My dog's so furry I've not seen. The Hairy Dog. Herbert Asquith. FaPON; PDV

My dolour is ane cup. Ressaif My Saul. R. Crombie Saunders. OxBS

My Dolphin, you only guide me by surprise. Dolphin. Robert Lowell. NoAM; NOBA; VCAP

My donkey has a bridle. The Donkey. Rose Fyleman. BoTP

My donkey stops. At Her Grave. Kuthaiyir, *tr. fr. Arabic by* Omar S. Pound. ArPe

My Double. Heine, *tr. fr. German by* Philip L. Miller. RiWo

My Dove, My Beautiful One. James Joyce. ChIV-1

My downfall: those pink articulate lips. Dioscorides, *tr. fr. Greek by* Peter Whigham. GrAn

My Dream. Lew Blockcolski. VoR

My Dream. Christina Rossetti. BrRo

My dream a drink with Lonnie Johnson. Ted Berrigan. NoAM

My Dream about the Cows. Lucille Clifton. TRP

My Dream about the Poet. Lucille Clifton. TRP

My dream is the dream of a pond. Gifts. Shu Ting, *tr. fr. Chinese by* Carolyn Kizer *with* Y.H. Zhao. SpMi

My dreams are lucid. Dreams. Anne Bloch. Mes

My dreams are of a field afar. A. E. Housman. PeVV

My Dreams by Henry James. Michael Ryan. SV

My Dreams, My Works, Must Wait Till after Hell. Gwendolyn Brooks. NoP

My Dressing Mirror is a Humpbacked Cat. Jung Tzu, *tr. fr. Chinese by* Kenneth Rexroth *and* Ling Chung. WPC

My Drinking Song. Richard Dehmel, *tr. fr. German by* Ludwig Lewisohn. AWP

My drum, hollowed out thru the thin slit. La Chute. Charles Olson. InPK

My duchess was the werst she laffed she bitte. Ernest Walsh. ErPo

My dugout canoe goes. Paddling Song. *Unknown, tr. fr. Bantu by* Max Exner. PBA

My dumb ox loyalty is. Remember Medusa? Eunice De Souza. AIW

My eager waiting heart can bear no more. He Comes Not To-night. Josephine D. Henderson Heard. CBWP-4

My earliest flame, to whom I owe. A Letter from a Captain in Country Quarters to his Corinna in Town. Isaac Hawkins Browne. ECEV

My Early Home. John Clare. BoTP; PoLF

My early home was this. (*LL*) My Early Home. John Clare. BoTP; PoLF

My early manhood. (*LL*) The Dirty Word. Karl Shapiro. CoAP; InPK; PoA

My early Mistress, now my ancient Muse. Preface to The Progress of Learning. Sir John Denham. NOSC; OxBSP

My Easter Dove. H. Cordelia Ray. CBWP-3

My elder,/ Born into death like a message into a bottle. To My Brother Hanson. W. S. Merwin. NAAL-2

My eldest sister arrived home that morning. Cuba. Paul Muldoon. CIP; PNI

My embarrassment at his nakedness. The Pool. Robert Creeley. CoAP

My enemy came nigh. Hate. James Stephens. MoAB; MoBrPo

My enemy had bidden me as guest. The Compassionate Fool. Norman Cameron. GTBS-P; OxBSP; OxBTC; RB

My energy is going, been spent. Old Man. Faye Kicknosway. UL

My Epitaph. H. J. Daniel. FaBoEE

My Epitaph. David Gray. EBVV

My Epitaph. Alexis Piron, *tr. fr. French.* OBD

My epitaph write on your heart. Love's Epitaph. William Cavendish. OxBSP

My Erotic Double. John Ashbery. LCAP; PoE; VCAP

My Esmeralda. Vijay Seshadri. UTF

My Estate. John Norris. NOSC

My Evening Prayer. Charles H. Gabriel. BLPA; FaBoBe

My eye cried and woke me. The Night. Al-Khansa, *tr. fr. Arabic by* Willis Barnstone. BoWoP

My eye descending from the Hill, surveys. Sir John Denham. *Fr.* Cooper's Hill. BeJo; OAEL-1; OxAEP-1; SeCP; SeCV-1

My eyelids red and heavy are. A Poor Scholar of the 'Forties. Padraic Colum. NOIV

My eyes already touch the sunny hill. A Walk. Rainer Maria Rilke, *tr. fr. German by* Robert Bly. RaBo

My eyes are filmed, my beard is grey. The Time of the Barmecides. James Clarence Mangan. EnRP; PeIV

My eyes are the enemy's eyes. The Enemy's Eyes. Emma Lee Warrior. HATNAP

My eyes are thirsty. Mirabai, *tr. fr. Hindi by* Willis Barnstone *and* Usha Nilsson. BoWoP

My eyes are white stones. River God's Song. Anne Ridler. NYBP

My eyes catch ruddy necks. Marching. Isaac Rosenberg. NSI; PeFWW

My eyes filled with tears. (*LL*) For the Record. "Ping Hsin." WPC

My Eyes Have Seen and Chosen. Meinloh von Sevelingen, *tr. fr. German by* J. W. Thomas. GePo

My eyes have seen and chosen for me a handsome youth. My Eyes Have Seen and Chosen. Meinloh von Sevelingen, *tr. fr. German by* J. W. Thomas. GePo

My eyes want to kiss your face. The Lover. Solveig von Schoultz, *tr. fr. Finnish by* Anne Born. VBLP

My eyes went away from me. The Fickle One. Pablo Neruda, *tr. fr. Spanish by* Donald Devenish Walsh. FF

My Face. Anthony Euwer. *See* As a Beauty I Am Not a Star.

My face is black. See the moon? My eyes. Crystal. Faye Kicknosway. IHMS

My face is grass. Legacy. Maurice Kenny. HATNAP

My face is Mrs. Heyward's. A Poem about Faith. Kathleen Norris. CrSp

My face is wet with rain. Walking at Night. Amory Hare. PoLF

My faint spirit was sitting in the light. From the Arabic; an Imitation. Shelley. OBEV

My fair-haired child dancing in the dunes. Poem for Melissa. Nuala Ni Dhomhnaill. BiHa

My Fair Lady. *Unknown.* EnLoPo; PoEL-1

My fairest child, I have no song to give you. Charles Kingsley. BLPA; EBVV; GN; OxBChV

My fairest child, I have no song to sing thee. A Farewell, To C. E. G. Charles Kingsley. BoTP

My Fairy. "Lewis Carroll." CBNP; FaBoNo

My Faith. Ananda Acharya. WGRP

My Faith Looks Up to Thee. Ray Palmer. AH; WGRP

My faithful friend, if you can see. Impossibilities to His Friend. Robert Herrick. OxBSP

My Faithful Mother Tongue. Czeslaw Milosz. PRA

My falling tears wet the double gates. (LL) Old Poem. Unknown. AWP, tr. by Arthur Waley

My Familiar. John Godfrey Saxe. AnAmPo

My family complains like cackling geese. Borrowing Rice from Ju-hui. Mei Yao Ch'en, tr. fr. Chinese by Jonathan Chaves. SuSp

My family slept those level miles. Across Kansas. William Stafford. CAPP

My family tree is mist and darkness. Family History. Irving Feldman. VCAP

My Fancy. "Lewis Carroll." See I painted her a gushing thing.

My fate. (LL) The Soldier's Bride. Aleksei Nikolayevich Pleshcheyev. RiWo

My Father. James Berry. PBCV

My Father. Rae Dalven. GoYe

My Father/ Against the victories of age. Plaisir d'Amour. Patrick Galvin. BiHa

My Father, sels. H. Leivick, tr. fr. Yiddish by Benjamin and Barbara Harshav.

My Father — Is the Root, sels. Itamar Ya'oz-kest, tr. fr. Hebrew by Bernhard Frank.

My Father after Work. Gary Gildner. Poetsp

My father and mother, my brother and sister. The Sightseers. Paul Muldoon. BiHa; CIP

My father and mother (what ails 'em?). The Rural Lass. Catherine Jemmat. ECWP; NOEC

My father and my mother. (LL) Carry Me. Flavien Ranaivo. NegPo

My father and my mother never quarrelled. Because. James McAuley. CBAP; NOBAu

My father asks me how I stand it all. Parents. Vincent Buckley. CBAP

My Father at 85. Robert Bly. BAP-89

My father at the dictionary-stand. Supernatural Love. Gjertrud Schnackenberg. DiPo; NoAM; VCAP

My father beat the robins. Exiles. Judy F. Ham. LoHo

My father bequeathed me no wide estates. Heirloom. A. M. Klein. NOBC; TrJP

My father brought that dog home. Bony. Simon J. Ortiz. CDW

My father brought the emigrant bundle. Europe and America. David Ignatow. NNaP; UnPo

My father by some strange conjunction had mice for sons. In All the Days of My Childhood. Russell Edson. AmPA

My father came in the darkness. Hyena. Unknown, tr. fr. Hurutsche by George Economou. TTY

My father could go down a mountain faster than I. That Dark Other Mountain. Robert Francis. CRP

My father could hear a little animal step. Listening. William Stafford. RFM

My father died a month ago. Unknown. OxNR (Bequests.) CBCK

My father died near evening, having spent. The Truth. Frankie Paino. NAmP90

My father died nine months before. Birth of a Son. Sam Hunt. PeNZ

My Father Died This Spring. Joanne Kyger. PoM

My father entered the kingdom of roots. 1933. Philip Levine. LCAP

My father found it after the war. The House on Buder Street. Gary Gildner. TAP

My father, gasping, in his white calked shoes. The Course. Robert Huff. CoAP

My father got on his horse and went to the field. Infancy. Carlos Drummond de Andrade, tr. fr. Portuguese by Elizabeth Bishop. ArLo

My father had a glass eye. My Father's Eye. Eléni Vakaló, tr. fr. Modern Greek by Kimon Friar. BoWoP

My father had a lot of friendly enemies. Father-Sequence. Luigi Fontanella, tr. fr. Italian by Michael Palma. NeIt

My father had terrible words for you. For My Brother Jesus. Irving Layton. NoP

My father he died, but I can't tell you how. Mother Goose. CBNP; OxNR

My father, he was a mountaineer. The Ballad of William Sycamore. Stephen Vincent Benét. MoAmPo; PoRA

My father, his mouth full of nails. Nails. Gary Gildner. PBCAP; TAP

My father, in a 1956 gray suit. Dance of the Letters. Vince Gotera. OpBo

My Father in the Night Commanding No. Louis Simpson. CoAP; HeIP; NoAM; NOBA; NYBP; SM; TAP; TwCP; VGW

My father is a hand-/ some guy. A Daddy Poem. William J. Harris. NBV

My father is a knight and a man of high renown. Bold Dragoon, The ("My father is a knight and a man of high renown.") Unknown. OBET

My father is a quiet man. Fruit of the Flower. Countee Cullen. PoLF

My father is clearing the first Party shrine: Party Shrine. Thomas McCarthy. BiHa; IB

My father is dead. Song of the Bush-Shrike. Unknown, tr. fr. Zulu. PeSA

My father is dead and there is nothing left. Not Saying Much. Linda Gregg. AiP

My father is lying in a green. At Mt. Auburn Cemetery. Diana Der Hovanessian. LoHo

My father is sleeping. His noble face. The Distant Footsteps. César Vallejo, tr. fr. Spanish by James Wright and John Knoepfle. RaBo

My Father Kept a Horse. Unknown. GBP

My Father Knows. Wilbur Fisk Tillett. BLRP

My father leaves us in the car. Signal Hill. Sharon Doubiago. ETG; NGP

My father left his English home. Song of the Bounder, THe. Edgar Wallace. PeSAV

My father left me three acres of land. Sing Ivy. Unknown. BoTP; OxNR

My father, let no similes eclipse. In Memoriam. Michael Longley. PNI

My father lies black and hushed. The Worker. Richard W. Thomas. PoBA; PoNe

My father lives by the ocean. Certain People. Richard Jones. NAmP90

My father, looking for trouble, would find it. The Man of the House. David Wagoner. NoAM

My father made a synagogue of a boat. Two Fishermen. Stanley Moss. CoAP

My Father Moved through Dooms of Love. E. E. Cummings. CMoP; FYAP; HAP; LiTA; MeMAP; MoAB; MoP; NAAL-2; NoAM; NOBA; NoP; OxBA; TAP; UnPo

My father moves through the South hunting duck. Treetops. Marvin Bell. AmPA

My Father, My Son. John Malcolm Brinnin. NYBP

My Father; October 1942. William Stafford. CAPP; NaP

My father owns the butcher shop. Unknown. RoPo

My father paces the upstairs hall. Spree. Maxine W. Kumin. NoAM

My Father Paints the Summer. Richard Wilbur. NOBA

My father played the melodion. Patrick Kavanagh. Fr. Christmas Childhood, A. IIP; IPY; PChr; RB

My father put me in my mother. Where I Came From. Ruth Stone. NAmP90

My father remembered what it was to be small. In the Giant's Castle. Ruth Dallas. PeNZ

My Father Scything. Sam Hunt. PeNZ

My father sensed Christmas approaching, like a pip on a radar. The Family at Christmas. John Norton. BCF

My father smiled this morning when. Keep Smiling. Unknown. WBLP

My Father Spoke with Swans. Patrick Galvin. BiHa

My father stands in the warm evening. Starlight. Philip Levine. CAPP

My father the hawk. Latvian Songs. Johannes Bobrowski, tr. fr. German by Ruth Mead and Matthew Mead. AnRep

My father, the least happy. The Cage. John Montague. CIP; PNI

My father thought that fact was dull. Garland for a Storyteller. Jessie Farnham. GoYe

My Father Today. Sam Hunt. PeNZ

My father tore out his native roots. My Father. Rae Dalven. GoYe

My father used to say. Silence. Marianne Moore. AnAmPo; CMoP; CoGr; FaBoMo; InPS; LiTA; NALW; NOBA; TRP

My father was a barber-surgeon. The Worker (We Own Two Houses). Charles Fort. NGP

My father was a Cornish customs officer. Naturalised. Cyril Hodges. AngWe

My father was a farmer gay. One-and-Twenty. Unknown. AmFP

My father was a Frenchman. Unknown. OxNR

My father was a sailor. Antonio Machado Ruiz, tr. fr. Spanish by Havelock Ellis. Fr. Spanish Folk Songs. AWP

My father was a servant boy. The Mixed Marriage. Paul Muldoon. PNI

My father was always out in the garage. Eli W. Mandel. Fr. Minotaur Poems. MoCV

My father was four years at their war. Yehuda Amichai, tr. fr. Hebrew by Ruth Finer Mintz. Fr. Here We Loved. MHP

My father was sixty when I was born. My Father Scything. Sam Hunt. PeNZ

My Father Washes His Hands. Fred Chappell. MT

My Father Went to Funerals. Howard Nelson. RaBo

My father! when I saw thee last. To Father. Mary E. Tucker. CBWP-1

My father who found the English landscape tame. Woods. Louis MacNeice. IIP

My father, who works with stone. A Story of How a Wall Stands. Simon J. Ortiz. HATNAP

My father won't talk about the numbers. Tattoo. Gregg Shapiro. BTR

My father wore it working coal at Shotts. The Miner's Helmet. George MacBeth. OxBTC

My father worked with a horse-plough. Follower. Seamus Heaney. IIP; IPY; PNI

My father, you say. Reply. Reiner Kunze, tr. fr. German by Ewald Osers. PoSu

My Father's a Still Day. Geoffrey Lehmann. Fr. Ross's Poems. CBAP

My Father's Back. Edward Hirsch. VCAP

My father's body was a globe of fear. Letters & Other Worlds. Michael Ondaatje. NoAM; NOBC; NoP

My father's brother brought it home. My Grandmother's African Grey. Matt Simpson. PWE

My father's brother has a farm in the forest. Meditation among Trees. Marbod of Rennnes, tr. fr. Latin by Helen Waddell. MLL

My Father's Close. Unknown, tr. fr. French by Dante Gabriel Rossetti. AWP

My Father's Cot, sels. J. C. Squire.
  "I left thee with a courage high." BXAP

My Father's Country. Joyce Lee. NOBAu

My Father's Death. Constance Urdang. PBCAP

My Father's Eye. Eléni Vakaló, tr. fr. Modern Greek by Kimon Friar. BoWoP

My father's face is brown with sun. Father. Frances Frost. FaPON

My Father's Father. Alun Rees. AngWe

My Father's Fights. Stuart Dybek. PBCAP

My Father's First Baseball Game. Michael S. Weaver. PBCAP

My Father's Football Game. David Wagoner. NGP

My father's friend came once to tea. A Recollection. Frances Cornford. FaBoWP; NTP

My Father's Garden. David Wagoner. DiPo; NIP

My Father's Geography. Michael S. Weaver. PBCAP

My Father's Hands. Jeni Couzyn. PeSAV

My father's heart is on television. Medical Science. Robin Becker. ETG; PBCAP

My father's in business, takes it a day at a time. Ballade of the Back Road. Ron Block. SM

My Father's Leaving. Ira Sadoff. AmPA

My father's life is alchemy. Words and Legacy. Cyril Dabydeen. PBCV

My Father's Loveletters. Yusef Komunyakaa. NAmP90

My Father's Martial Art. Stephen Shu Ning Liu. InPK

My Father's Memorial Day. Yehuda Amichai, tr. fr. Hebrew by the author and Ted Hughes. OBD

My father's name is Frankenstein. Father and Mother. X. J. Kennedy. GrPl

My Father's Song. Simon J. Ortiz. HATNAP

My Father's Story. Priscilla Jane Thompson. CBWP-2

My Father's Voice in Prayer. May Hastings Nottage. BLRP

My Father's Wars. Colleen J. McElroy. BCF

My Father's Wedding. Robert Bly. CAPP; InPS; NoAM; RaBo

My favorite student lately is the one who wrote about feeling clumbsy. The Spell against Spelling. George Starbuck. FYAP

My favorite things. A Coltrane/ Poem. Sonia Sanchez. Jaz

My Favorite Word. Lucia M. and James L. Hymes, Jr. and James L. Hymes. SiSoPo

My favourite view of people. Fish Shop Windows. Geoffrey Dutton. NOBAu

My Fear in the Crowd. Josephine Miles. BCF

My feelings like a knifeblade's wound. (LL) Failing the Examination. Meng Chiao. SuSp

My feet are elms, roots in the earth. They Tell Me I Am Lost. Maurice Kenny. HATNAP

My feet have felt the sands. Determination. John Henrik Clarke. PoBA

My feet taste funny. Why I Didn't Go to Delphi. James Welch. CDW

My feet two hundred years old. (LL) Montgomery. Sam Cornish. PoBA; Poetsp

My female friends, whose tender hearts. Swift. Fr. Verses on the Death of Doctor Swift [D.S.P.D., Occasioned by Reading a Maxim in Rochefoucauld]. NOBL

My Fever. (LL) Charm me asleep, and melt me so. Robert Herrick. BeJo; CaPo; GoJo; OBEV; SeCV-1

My Fiddle. James Whitcomb Riley. AnAmPo

My fiftieth year had come and gone. W. B. Yeats. Fr. Vacillation. NoAM; RaBo

My 50th year having arrived. On the Birth of Dan Goldman. Daniel Berrigan. NAs

My fighting days are done. Mnasalcas, tr. fr. Greek by Edward Lucie-Smith. GrAn

My fine web sparkles. The Christmas Spider. Michael Richards. Spl

My fingers are but stragglers at the rear. Stragglers. Pietro Aretino, tr. fr. Italian by Samuel Putnam. ErPo

My finger's wet. Unknown. ISE

My first big love was cosmically correct. My Chakabuku Mama. Jewelle Gomez. GLP

My First Forty Years. Kevin Ireland. PeNZ

My first lesson: you won't even let me touch. School of Music. Theodore Deppe. BTR

My First Love. Harry Graham. FiBHP

My first love sighed for brooches. Prices. Louis Ginsberg. TrJP

My First Memory, Switzerland, Circa 1947. Joan Dobbie. LoHo

My First Proper Girlfriend. Robert Adamson. FaBoMA

My first thought was, he lied in every word. Childe Roland to the Dark Tower Came. Robert Browning. EnVR; NAEL-2; NOBVV; NoP; OAEL-2; OBNV; OtMeF; PeVV; PoE; PPP

My Five Gentlemen. Elizabeth Bartlett. IHNG

My fixed abode is Glen Bolcain. Suibne Geilt. NOIV

My flesh be consigned to the tomb. (LL) Ah! Lovely Appearance of Death! Charles Wesley. AH

My flesh is at a distance from me. The Virgin. Laura Riding Jackson. ChIV-2

My flock feeds [or flocks feed] not, my ewe[s] breed[s] not. The Unknown Shepherd's Complaint. Richard Barnfield. EIL

My flowery and green age was passing away. Petrarch, tr. fr. Italian. Fr. Sonnets to Laura. OBMV, tr. by J. M. Synge
  (He Understands the Great Cruelty of Death.) BIrV

My foamlesss heart, the bloodleap at my wrist. (LL) Rattler, Alert. Brewster Ghiselin. HAP; WeW

My folk, now answere me. Unknown. MiEL
  (Jesus Reproaches His People.) MeEL

My folk, what habbe I do thee. Unknown. MiEL

My folks could beg or borrow. (LL) Saturday's Child. Countee Cullen. LiTM; NAs; PoBA

My food was pallid till I heard it ring. King Midas. Howard Moss. CoAP; TAP
  (King's Speech, The.) PoA

My footsteps in this street. Here. Octavio Paz, tr. fr. Spanish by John Frederick Nims. STV
  (My steps along this street.) ArNa, tr. by Charles Tomlinson

My foster-brother and foster-sister. The Golden Sea-Otter. Wakarpa, tr. by Arthur Waley. Fr. Kutune Shirka (The Ainu Epic). WTO

My Foster-Mother-Land. (LL) An Answer. Perceval Gibbon. PeSAV

My foundling, my fondling, my frolic first-footer. A Blason. A. D. Hope. NOBAu

My frame of nature is a ruffled sea. The Hurry of the Spirits, in a Fever and Nervous Disorders. Isaac Watts. NOEC

My frenzies you call wildflowers. Jude. Carol Moldaw. UTF

My freshmen/ settle in. Achilles. Freshmen. Barry Spacks. NYBP

My Friend. Philip Appleman. BXAP

My friend. We Laughed. Rochelle Kraut. UL

My friend from Asia has powers and magic. Credo. Robinson Jeffers. EaPr; MoAB; MoAmPo

My friend, have you heard of the town of Nogood. The Town of Nogood. W. E. Penny. BLPA

My friend is always doing good. Faith and Works. Muriel Spark. OxBSP

My friend is dwelling in the eastern mountain. To Tan Ch'iu. Li Po, tr. fr. Chinese by Robert Payne. TAL

My friend is lodging high in the Eastern Range. To Tan Ch'iu. Li Po, tr. fr. Chinese by Arthur Waley. AWP

My friend, judge not me. Unknown. NOSC

My friend laughs at me behind my back. Ghazals in the Void. Henrietta O'Neill. UnDi

My friend must be a bird. Emily Dickinson. TAP

My friend says I was not a good son. Yesterday. W. S. Merwin. FYAP; LCAP; RaBo

My friend, speak always once, but listen twice. The Mouth and the Ears. Shem-Tob ben Joseph Palquera, tr. fr. Hebrew by J. Chotzner. TrJP

My Friend, the Things That Do Attain. Martial. See Martial [or Marshall or My Friend], the thing[e]s that do [attain or to] attain [or attyne]

My Friend the Wind. King D. Kuka. VoR

My friend, this body is His lute. He tightens the strings and plays its songs. Kabir, tr. fr. Hindi by Robert Bly. EnIH

My friend, this body is made of bone. The Origin of the Praise of God. Robert Bly. NU

My friend thy beauty seemeth good. The Penurious Quaker; or, The High Priz'd Harlot. *Unknown.* CoMu; FaBoBl

My friend who married the girl I. Watts. Shirley Kaufman. NMM

My friend, who was a heroin addict. Certain Choices. Richard Shelton. Poetsp

My friend, you don't understand. My Friend. Philip Appleman. BXAP

My friend, your face. Who Is My Brother? Pinkie Gordon Lane. BlSi

My Friendly People. Frank Mkalawile Chipasula. HBAPE

My friends,/ I am amazed. Acceptance Speech. Marvin Bell. AmPA

My friends & I speak mostly to one another's machine. The Answering Machine. Philip Schultz. NAmP90

My friends are borne to one another. Martin Buber in the Pub. Max Harris. NOBAu

My Friends Are Little Lamps to Me. Elizabeth Whittemore. PoToHe

My friends are real, though very few. (*LL*) Money. W. H. Davies. OBEV; OBMV

My friend's knife by my side. On the Gift of a Knife. Muireadach Albanach O'Dalaigh. NOIV

My friends, let us give thanks for Wonder. Rami M. Shapiro. EaPr

My friends, my sweet barbarians. A Breakfast for Barbarians. Gwendolyn MacEwen. NOBC

My friends, our race is ostracised. Ajax' Conclusion. Frank Barbour Coffin. AAP

My friend's sweet love came into town. Song to Hymen: 1942. Anthony Richardson. PoWW

My Friends the Pigeons. Richard Katrovas. NAmP90

My funeral-shaft, and marble shapes that dwell. Baucis. Erinna, *tr. fr. Greek by* Richard Garnett. AWP

My future will not copy fair my past. Elizabeth Barrett Browning. *Fr.* Sonnets from the Portuguese. EnVR

My galleon of adventure. San Francisco. Walter Adolphe Roberts. PoNe

My Galley. Petrarch, *tr. fr. Italian by* Sir Thomas Wyatt. InPS; NAEL-1

My galley [*or* galy] charged with forgetfulness. My Galley ("My galley charged with forgetfulness.") Petrarch, *tr. fr. Italian. Fr.* Sonnets to Laura. AAS; HAP; NoP; OAEL-1; OBVE; PPP; SCGP; SiPS; SiPSBD; Son; WeW

(Lover Comparath His State to a Ship in Perilous Storm Tossed on the Sea, The.) EIL; GBL; 09HeIP; PoEL-1

My Gang. Jack Kerouac. PoM

My garage is a structure of excessive plainness. Detail. Mary Ursula Bethell. PeNZ

My Garden. Thomas Edward Brown. BLPL; EBEvV; FaBV; InPK; OBEV; PoLF; UV; WBLP; WGRP

My Garden. W. H. Davies. BoNaP

My Garden. P. R. Hines. UV

My Garden. Norah E. Hussey. BoTP

My Garden, *parody.* J. A. Lindon. InPK

My Garden. Janice Appleby Succorsa. HoPM

My garden is a pleasant place. Louise Driscoll. BLPA; FaBoBe

My Garden, My Daylight. Jorie Graham. HCAP; Poetr

My Gartmore friends a blessing on ye. Epistle to Her Friends at Gartmore. Susanna Blamire. ECWP

My generous muse, assistance lend. The Favourite Swain. Elizabeth Hands. WoRP

My gentle child, behold this horse. The Racing-Man. A. P. Herbert. FiBHP

My gentle father. Feliks Skrzynecki. Peter Skrzynecki. CBAP

My gentle son is performing tricks for me on his bicycle. Visitation Rites. Jack Myers. NAmP90

My ghost pets are like shadows on the wall. Ghost Pet. Horatio Colony. GoYe

My Ghostly Father, I me confess. Charles, Duc d'Orléans. BoLoP

(Confession of a Stolen Kiss.) MeEL

(Confession.) ChTr

(Lover's Confession, A.) NOBE

(My Ghostly Fader.) EnVB

(My ghostly fadir, I me confess.) EnVB; GBL

(My Gostly Fader, I Me Confesse.) EnLoPo; MiEL

My Gift. Christina Rossetti. *Fr.* Christmas Carol, A. ChTr; FaPON; InPS; NOBVV; OHIP; PChr

My girl friend is a lulu. *Unknown.* RoPo

My girl hath violet eyes and yellow hair. The Little Milliner. Robert Buchanan. BeLS

My girl says she'll take no one else as a lover. Catullus, *tr. fr. Latin by* John Frederick Nims. STV

My girl, thou gazest much. The Lover to His Lady. *At.* to Plato, *tr. fr. Greek by* George Turberville. CTC; FaBoEE; FF; NoSic

My girlhood was surrounded by flickering screens. The Grand Tradition of Western Culture. Julia Stein. LoHo

My glad feet shod with the glittering steel. The Skater. Sir Charles G. D. Roberts. NOBC

My Glass Shall Not Persuade Me I Am Old. Shakespeare. *Fr.* Sonnets. Son, *sect.* XXII

My glittering sky, high, clear, profound. The Lovers. Marya Zaturenska. MoAmPo

My glory, honor, all depend. The Gentleman. Menahem ben Judah Lonzano, *tr. fr. Hebrew by* A. B. Rhine. TrJP

My Glumdalclitch, come here and sit with me. A Tryst in Brobdingnag. Adrienne Rich. NYBP

My God. Solomon ibn Gabirol, *tr. by* Alice Lucas. *Fr.* Royal Crown, The. AWP, *tr. by* Israel Zangwill; TrJP

My God, a verse is not a crown. The Quidditie. George Herbert. GeHe; PoEL-2

(Quiddity, The.) NOSC

My God and King! to thee. Anguish. Henry Vaughan. OxAEP-1

My God and love Thee so. (*LL*) The Lowest Place. Christina Rossetti. NOBVV; TrPWD

My God, how gracious art thou! I had slipt. The Relapse. Henry Vaughan. ESCV; TrCP

My God, how perfect are thy ways! Jehovah Our Righteousness. William Cowper. NOCV

My God, How Wonderful Thou Art. Frederick William Faber. *Fr.* Our Heavenly Father. TrPWD

My God, I heard this day. Man. George Herbert. ESCV; GeHe; ImPo; NAEL-1; NoP; PoEL-2; SeCP; SeCV-1; TrGrPo; TrPWD, *abr*

My God, I know that those who plead. My God. Solomon ibn Gabirol, *tr. by* Alice Lucas. *Fr.* Royal Crown, The. AWP, *tr. by* Israel Zangwill; TrJP

My God, I love thee, not because. St. Francis Xavier, *tr. fr. Latin.* WGRP

My God, I mean my sinful heart. (*LL*) The Dwelling-Place. Henry Vaughan. GeHe; MeLP; NOSC; PeECV; TrPWD; WGRP

My God, I Thank Thee. Andrews Norton. AH

My God, I thank Thee who hast made. Thankfulness. Adelaide Anne Procter. TrPWD

My God, if writings may. Obedience. George Herbert. ESCV; GeHe

My God, I'm wounded by my sin. To God: An Anthem, Sung In The Chapel at White-Hall, Before the King. Robert Herrick. ChIV-1

My God is just, yes he is. *Unknown, tr. fr. Pashto by* Saduddin Shpoon. PBWP

My God is not a chiselled stone. True Knowledge. Panatattu, *tr. fr. Sanskrit.* WGRP

My God! looke on me with thine eye. His Ejaculation to God. Robert Herrick. SeCV-1

My God, my God, have mercy on my sin. Ash Wednesday. Christina Rossetti. TrCP

My God, My God, he cried. Eli, Eli. Miriam Kessler. CrSp

My God, my God, let me for once look on thee. Robert Browning. *Fr.* Pauline. TrPWD

My God, My God, Look upon Me. Chad Walsh. *Fr.* Psalm of Christ, The. TrCP

My God, my god, what queer corner am I in? In the Deep Museum. Anne Sexton. MoAmPo; Prf

My God, my God, why hast thou forsaken me? Bible, *O.T., paraphrased by* Sir Thomas Wyatt. *Fr.* Psalms.

(Cry in Distress, A.) TrGrPo

My God, my Lord, my help, my health. The Countess of Pembroke. *See* "O Lord God of My Salvation."

My God (oh, let me call Thee mine). Anne Brontë. TrPWD

My God, prepare me for that hour. Written a Few Hours before the Birth of a Child. Jane Cave. ECWP

My God shall raise me up, I trust. (*LL*) Even Such Is Time. Sir Walter Ralegh. BLPL; ChTr; CoGr; EIL; EnRePo; HAP; ImPo; LiTB; NTP; OxBSP; PoRA; RB; SiPS; TFi

My God, sometimes I cannot pray. Unuttered Prayer. Josephine D. Henderson Heard. CBWP-4

My God, the bitter-tasting mouth was me. Homage. R. J. Schoeck. GoYe

My God, thou that didst dye for me. Henry Vaughan *and* Thomas Stanley. ESCV

My God, till I received thy stroke. Ephraim Repenting. William Cowper. ChIV-1

My God, what a dream I had. Us Two. Nina Cassian, *tr. fr. Romanian by* Nina Cassian. PoSu

My God, when I walk [*or* walke] in those groves. Religion. Henry Vaughan. ESCV; NOCV; OAEL-1; OxAEP-1; PeECV; TOF

My God, where is that ancient heat towards Thee. George Herbert. ESCV; GeHe; NOSC; OAEL-1

My God would give a Sun-shine after raine. *(LL)* The Shower [*or* Showre]. Henry Vaughan. BoNaP; ChTr; ESCV; FaBoPP; GeHe; LiTB; SeCP

My godmother invited my cousin. My Cousin Agueda [*or* Agatha]. Ramón López Velarde, *tr. fr. Spanish.* OBVE

My gold six-pointed star. I Am Babi Yar. Ginger Porter. BTR

My golden cat has dappled sides. The Golden Cat. Eleanor Farjeon. OFC

My good blade carves the casques of men. Sir Galahad [*or* The Purple Heart]. Tennyson. OHCV

My Gostly Fader, I Me Confesse. Charles, Duc d'Orléans. *See* My Ghostly Father, I me confess.

My Grace Is Sufficient. Josephine D. Henderson Heard. CBWP-4

My Grace Is Sufficient for Thee. *Unknown.* BLRP

My gracious Lord, I would thee glory doe. Edward Taylor. *Fr.* Preparatory Meditations Before My Approach to the Lord's Supper. EAP; SCAP

My graduation mass. Christmas Mass. Elizabeth Wood. NGP

My Grandaddy Mostly with His Knife. David Huddle. GrPl

My Grandfather. Joanne Hotchkiss. CrSp

My Grandfather and His Apple-Tree. John Ormond. AngWe

My grandfather had the right-hand side of his seat inscribed. Exhorting Myself. Ssu-k'ung Shu, *tr. fr. Chinese by* Hellmut Wilhelm. SuSp

My Grandfather in Search of Moonshine. George Ella Lyon. GOYP

My grandfather placed wood. Mythology. Earle Thompson. HATNAP

My grandfather said to me. Manners [for a Child of 1918]. Elizabeth Bishop. GOYP; OxBC; RB

My grandfather sits in front of the house and leaves fall. The War. Vesna Parun, *tr. fr. Yugoslavian by* Ivana Spalatin *and* Daniela Gioseffi. WoWa

My grandfather used to pray. The Wicked Neighbor. "Zelda," *tr. fr. Hebrew by* Hannah Hoffman. WPOW

My grandfather was always sad. The Last Man's Club. James Galvin. AnAn

My grandfather was an elegant gentleman. David Wright. *Fr.* Seven South African Poems. PeSA

My grandfather worked when he was very young. An Old Man's Advice. *Unknown.* OBET

My Grandfather's Church Goes Up. Fred Chappell. SM

My grandfather's clock was too large for the shelf. Grandfather's Clock. Henry Clay Work. BLPA

My Grandfather's Days. *Unknown.* OBET

My Grandfather's Death. Vicente Aleixandre, *tr. fr. Spanish by* Stephen Kessler. IMW

My Grandfather's Funeral. James Applewhite. MT

My grandfather's painted grandfather. Cracked Portraits. Agha Shahid Ali. OpBo

My grandma thinks only of me. Grandmother. Fily-Dabo Sissoko, *tr. fr. French by* Ellen Conroy Kennedy. NegPo

My Grandmama/ dont believe they walked in space. It's All the Same. Thadious M. Davis. BlSi

My Grandmother. Perseus Adams. PeSA

My Grandmother. Karl Shapiro. VGW

My grandmother. This Is the Poem I Never Meant to Write. Colleen J. McElroy. BCF

My Grandmother Died in the Early Hours of the Morning. T. Harri Jones. AngWe

My grandmother, dying, thought my. Tim Longville. VaA

My Grandmother Green. *Unknown.* AmFP

My grandmother grew tiny grapes and tiger-lilies. Her Garden. Freda Downie. FaBoWP

My grandmother had braids. Keeping Hair. Ramona Wilson. CrSp; VoR

My grandmother is an ivory chord. Trilogy. Cecile Hamermesh. BTR

My grandmother lived in yonder little lane. Grandma's Advice. *Unknown.* OBET

My grandmother lived on yonder green. My Grandmother Green. *Unknown.* AmFP
(Grandma's Advice, *sl. diff. vers.*) OBET

My grandmother moves to my mind in context of sorrow. My Grandmother. Karl Shapiro. VGW

My Grandmother said, "Now isn't it queer." Wonders of Nature. *Unknown.* OTCP

My grandmother sent me a new-fashioned three-cornered cambric country-cut handkerchief. *Unknown.* BLPA

My grandmother, she, at the age of eighty-three. Grandmother's Old Armchair. *Unknown.* BLPA

My grandmother used it, Dutch Cleanser. Dutch Cleanser. John Updike. PRA

My grandmother was a wrinkled little girl. Genealogy. Eléni Vakaló, *tr. fr. Modern Greek by* Paul Merchant. PBWP

My Grandmother was buried here. Epitaph in a Churchyard at Thetford, in Norfolk. *Unknown.* FaBoUs

My Grandmother Washes Her Feet. Fred Chappell. MT

My Grandmother Washes Her Vessels. Fred Chappell. MT

My Grandmother's African Grey. Matt Simpson. PWE

My Grandmother's Burial Ground. Elizabeth Cook-Lynn. HATNAP

My Grandmother's Funeral. Thomas Lux. WeW

My Grandmother's Ghost. James Wright. Son

My Grandmother's Love Letters. Hart Crane. BLPL; CMoP; FaBoBe; InPK; MoAB; NoAM; NOBA; NoP; Poetr

My grandmothers were strong. Lineage. Margaret Walker. BlSi; CrSp; NALW; NMM; PBWP; PoBA

My grandmother's/ brother here. At a Chinaman's Grave. Wing Tek Lum. BCF

My Grandpa lives in a wonderful house. The Painted Ceiling. Amy Lowell. OBAL

My grandparents lived to a great age in the cold. Cold. Dorothy Roberts. NOBC

My Granny. Robert Adamson. FaBoMA

My granny used to say that if a shadow. August the First: The Shadow. Patel Speaks. Marjorie Oludhe Macgoye. HBAPE

My great-aunt Elizabeth Fortune. Strawberry Moon. Mary Oliver. InPS

My great brother. A Psalm Praising the Hair of Man's Body. Denise Levertov. CAPP

My Great Grand Uncle. Tarapada Ray, *tr. fr. Hindi.* TSaS

My great grand uncle had a peculiar hobby. My Great Grand Uncle. Tarapada Ray, *tr. fr. Hindi.* TSaS

My great-grandfather hunted elephants. A Ballad of Hunters. C. J. Driver. PeSAV

My great-grandfather spoke to Edmund Burke. The Seven Sages. W. B. Yeats. NOIV

My great-grandmother. The Woman in the Moon. Mary Mackey. SRLS

My great-grandmother's native. Heirloom. Cinda Thompson. LoHo

My Great Great etc. Uncle Patrick Henry. James Tate. OBAL

My great wars close. Treaties. A. R. Ammons. HCAP

My green leaves are more beautiful. Leaves. Frank Asch. NTCP

My grey-eyed father kept pigs on his farm. The Pigs. Geoffrey Lehmann. CBAP

My grief, my grief, maid without sin. The Body's Speech. *Unknown, tr. fr. Irish by* Frank O'Connor. PeIV

My grief on the ocean. *Unknown, tr. fr. Irish by* Thomas Kinsella. NOIV

My Grief on the Sea. Biddy Cussrooee, *tr. fr. Modern Irish by* Douglas Hyde. OBEV; WTO

My grief, quoth I, is called Ignorance. Rachel Speght. *Fr.* Dream, A. KTR; WPE

My Guardian Angel Stein. Philip Schultz. InPS

My gudame wes a gay wif, bot scho wes ryght gend. The Ballad of Kynd Kittok. William Dunbar. OxBoLi; PeLV

My guest! I have not led you thro'. Interlude. Walter Savage Landor. GTBS-P

My Hair. Francisco Alarcon. AfAz

My hair has dried. Self Dirge. Wendy Rose. CDW

My hair is springy like the forest grasses. Black Woman. Naomi Long Madgett. BlSi; LPA; PoBA; VBLP

My Hairt Is Heich Aboif. *Unknown.* OxBS

My half-sister comes to me to be painted. The Sitting. Medbh McGuckian. PNI

My hammer will topple a small statue. Deconstructions. Liz Cashdan. NWP

My hand. Comparison of Hands One Day Late Summer El Sobrante. Wendy Rose. HATNAP

My hand is dirty. The Dirty Hand. Carlos Drummond de Andrade, *tr. fr. Portuguese by* Mark Strand. AnRep

My hand is lonely for your clasping, dear. You and I. Henry Alford. BLPA; FaBoBe

My hand is longing. *(LL)* Revelation. Edith Södergran. VBLP

My hand is steady. Towards the End of a Century. E. A. Markham. NBrP

My hand is weary with [*or* has a pain from] writing. St. Columcille the Scribe. *At. to* St. Columcille Saint Columcille, *tr. by* Kuno Meyer. BIrV, *tr. by* Flann O'Brien

My hand strays out and picks off one sick leaf. *(LL)* The Secret Garden. Thomas Kinsella. IPY; TwCP

My hands/ Open the curtains of your being. Touch. Octavio Paz, *tr. fr. Spanish.* BoLoP; LPA, *tr. by* Charles Tomlinson

My hands are murder-red. Many a plump head. Strawberrying. May Swenson. VCAP

My hands are tender feathers. Calypso's Song to Ulyssess. Adrian Mitchell. GBL

My Hero. Benjamin Brawley. PoNe

My hoary locks I dye with care. Self-Defense. Santob de Carrion, *tr. fr. Spanish by* George Ticknor. TrJP

My Holocaust Songs. William Heyen. BTR

My Home. Ludwig Rellstab, *tr. fr.* German *by* Philip L. Miller. RiWo

My home is a house. The Country Child. Irene Thompson. BoTP

My home is the mountain. Akhtar Amiri, *tr. fr. Farsi by* Fereshte Mahamadi. *Fr.* I Am a Woman. WPOW

My home was at Cold Mountain from the start. Han-shan, *tr. fr.* Chinese *by* Gary Snyder. EnlH

My home's in Montana, I wear a bandanna. Cowboy's Lament, The Smoky Mountains. *Unknown.* AmFP

My homestead's with lightning aflame. The Meaning of Love. *Malay Oral Tradition, tr. by* R. O. Winstedt. WTO

My Honey, My Love. Joel Chandler Harris. *Fr.* Uncle Remus and His Friends. FaBoBe

My Honeyed Languor. "Eduard Bagritzky," *tr. fr. Russian by* Babette Deutsch. TrJP

My hope, alas, hath me abused. Sir Thomas Wyatt. SiPS; SiPSBD

My hope and treasure lies above. (*LL*) Some Verses upon the Burning of Our House, July 10th, 1666. Anne Bradstreet. NOBA; PFP; TAP

My hope is on what is to come. Anthem for Doomed Youth. Raymond Garlick. AngWe

My Hope, My Love. *Unknown, tr. fr.* Irish *by* Edward Walsh. BIrV

My hopes retire; my wishes as before. Walter Savage Landor. *Fr.* Ianthe. GBL; OBNC

My horny feet are cutting through the fog. Satyr. Charles Gullans. PoA

My horse threads the mountain path as chrysanthemums begin to yellow. Journeying to the Village. Wang Yü-ch'eng, *tr. fr. Chinese by* Irving Y. Lo. SuSp

My horse whinnies again and again. (*LL*) Passing a Ruined Palace. Wen T'ing-yün. OHMPC

My horse whose tail is like a trailing black cloud. (*LL*) The War God's Horse Song. *Unknown.* LiTA, *tr. by* Dane Coolidge *and* Mary Roberts Coolidge; RB, *tr. by* Louis Watchman; TTTS

My horse's feet beside the lake. A Farewell. Matthew Arnold. *Fr.* Switzerland. EnVR; MeMBP

My hour switched on the cameras take. The Voice of America, 1961. James Liddy. CIP

My House. Robert Adamson. CBAP

My House. George Bruce. OxBS

My House. Claude McKay. CDC

My House. W. B. Yeats. *Fr.* Meditations in Time of Civil War. LiTB

My house, I say. But hark to the sunny doves. Robert Louis Stevenson. FM; NOBVV

My house is a boat. Houseboat Mouse. Charles Sullivan. ImGa

My House Is Bugged. Mafika Pascal Gwala. PeSAV

My house is empty but for a pair of boots. The Flooded Valley. Roland Mathias. AngWe

My house is granite. My House. George Bruce. OxBS

My house is not quiet, I am not loud. Fish in River: "My house is not quiet, I am not loud." *Unknown,* formerly at. to Cynewulf, *tr. by* Charles W. Kennedy. *Fr.* Riddles (Exeter Book). AnOE

My house is red — a little house. A Happy Child. Kate Greenaway. BoTP

My house is simple, lying beside the sea. Antipater of Sidon, *tr. fr.* Greek *by* Sam Hamill. InMo

My house, my fairy/ palace. Jeronimo's House. Elizabeth Bishop. NoP

My hovering thoughts would fly to heaven. Man's Civil War. Robert Southwell. NoSic

My human heart on Thee! (*LL*) The Eternal Goodness. Whittier. PFP; WGRP

My humble Muse sad, and in lonely state. To His Excellency Joseph Dudley. John Saffin. SCAP

My hunger is infinite and my hands always empty. Rade Drainac, *tr. fr. Serbo-Croatian by* Charles Simic. HSix

My hunter of dragonflies. Chiyojo, *tr. fr. Japanese by* Kenneth Rexroth *and* Ikuko Atsumi. WPJ

My Husband. *Unknown.* CoMu

My husband gives me an A. Marks. Linda Pastan. NIP

My husband is the same man who first pierced me. Silabhattarika. *See* My husband is the same who took my maidenhead.

My husband is the same who took my maidenhead. Silabhattarika, *tr. by* Daniel H. H. Ingalls. *Fr.* Wanton. PBWP

(My husband is the same man who first pierced me.) BoWoP, *tr. by* Willis Barnstone

My husband never desired the official seal of a marquis. Lament of a Soldier's Wife. Kao Ch'i, *tr. fr. Chinese by* Irving Y. Lo. SuSp

My husband, our opened home has broken my heart. The Slighted Wife. Aaron Hodza, *tr. fr.* Shona *by* George Fortune. PeSAV

My Husband Says. Alice Walker. MT

My husband smiles in sleep beside me. Charlotte Nicholls. Jack R. Clemo. NAs

My husband was a whure maister, the hugeast in erd. William Dunbar. *Fr.* Tretis of the Twa Mariit Wemen and the Wedow, The. FaBoBl, *sect.* II

My husband's a jockey, a jockey, a jockey. My Husband. *Unknown.* CoMu

My Husband's Birthday. Josephine D. Henderson Heard. CBWP-4

My Hut. Eileen Mathias. BoTP

My Iambic Pentameter Lines. Robert Crawford. InPK

My Illness and Other Animals. Maria Jastrzebska. NBrP

My Infelice's face, her brow, her eye. A Portrait. Thomas Dekker *and others.* OxAEP-1

My infinite child, hold me to sleep. David Ignatow. *Fr.* Sunlight: A Sequence for My Daughter. CAPP

My Infundibuliform Hat. Charles Follen Adams. OBAL

My Inmost Hope. Sarah Copia Sullam, *tr. fr. Italian.* TrJP

My Inside-Self. Rachel Field. FaPON

My insignificance seeks significance. My True Desire. Tommy McClennan. UnD

My intention is to tell of bodies changed. Ovid, *tr. by* Rolfe Humphries. *Fr.* Metamorphoses. NAWM-1

My jade body, like my gold hairpins. Spring Night. Chu Shu-chen, *tr. fr. Chinese by* Kenneth Rexroth *and* Ling Chung. WPC

My Jesus, as Thou wilt! Consecration. Benjamin Schmolck. BLRP

My Johnny. *Unknown.* OBET

My Joy, My Jockey, My Gabriel. George Barker. *Fr.* First Cycle of Love Poems. ErPo; MoBrPo

My Joy, my Life, my Crown! A True Hymn. George Herbert. GeHe; InvP; NOCV

My Kate. Elizabeth Barrett Browning. WBLP

My Kate. (*LL*) My Kate. Elizabeth Barrett Browning. WBLP

My ketch must lead into the fray. Parting at Dawn. *Malay Oral Tradition, tr. by* R. J. Wilkinson *and* R. O. Winstedt. WTO

"My King and Country needed me," to fight. Afterwards. H. B. K. Allpass. NSI

My kingdom for a horse! Kingdom. Leopold Staff, *tr. fr. Polish by* Adam Czerniawski. PoSu

My Kinsman Hanamel. Letter Written in the Year of the Carrying Away to Babylon. Rose Drachler. BCF

My kite is three feet broad, and six feet long. The Kite. Adelaide O'Keeffe. OxBChV

My Kitten. Mother Goose. *See* Hey, my kitten, my kitten.

My kitty cat has nine lives. Nine Lives. *Unknown.* CRH

My ladies haire is threeds [*or* threads] of beaten gold. Bartholomew Griffin. *Fr.* Fidessa, More Chaste than Kind[e]. AAS; ESo

My Lady Carenza of the lovely body. *Unknown, tr. fr. Provençal by* Willis Barnstone. BoWoP

My lady/ fair with. A Token. Robert Creeley. VGW

My lady carries love within her eyes. Dante, *tr. fr. Italian by* Dante Gabriel Rossetti. *Fr.* Vita Nuova, La. AWP

My Lady Greensleeves. *Unknown. See* Alas! my love, you [*or* ye] do me wrong.

My Lady Has the Grace of Death. Joseph Mary Plunkett. PeIV

My Lady Is a Pretty One. *Unknown.* OxBoLi

My lady looks so gentle and so pure. Dante, *tr. fr. Italian by* Dante Gabriel Rossetti. *Fr.* Vita Nuova, La. AWP

My Lady mine, I send. Canzonetta: Of His Lady, and of His Making Her Likeness. Jacopo da Lentino, *tr. fr. Italian by* Dante Gabriel Rossetti. AWP

My Lady Pleases Me. Robert Bridges. *Fr.* Growth of Love, The. Son

My Lady Is a Pretty One. *Unknown.* OxBoLi

My Lady Spring. *Unknown.* BoTP

My lady unto Madam makes her bow. George Meredith. *Fr.* Modern Love. NOBVV

My lady walks her morning round. The Henchman. Whittier. OBEV

My lady went to Canterbury [*or* Caunterbury]. *Unknown.* FaBoCo; FaBoNo (Nonsense Song, A.) OxBLMV

My lady woke upon a morning fair. On His Lady's Waking. Pierre de Ronsard, *tr. fr. French by* Andrew Lang. AWP

My Lady's face it is they worship there. Sonetto XXXV: To Guido Orlando. Cavalcanti, *tr. fr. Italian by* Ezra Pound. CTC

My Lady's Grave. Emily Brontë. *See* Linnet in the rocky dells, The.

My lady's presence makes the roses red. Henry Constable. *Fr.* Diana. EIL; ESo; NIP

My Lady's Tears. *Unknown. See* I Saw My Lady Weep.

My Lai/ Remuera/ Ponsonby. David Mitchell. PeNZ

My lamp and life, both shall in Thee abide. (*LL*) The Morning Watch. Henry Vaughan. AngWe; ESCV; GeHe; LiTB; NOSC; NTP; PeECV

My lamp, full charged with its sweet oil, still burns. Hero Entombed I. Peter Quennell. LiTB

My land is bare of chattering folk. Sanctuary. Dorothy Parker. NBLV

My land is fair for any eyes to see. Jesse Stuart. FaPON

My lank limp lily, my long lithe lily. A Maudle-in Ballad. *Unknown.* BXAP; FaBoPa

My Last Afternoon with Uncle Devereux Winslow. Robert Lowell. NAAL-2; NoP; VGW

My Last Duchess. Robert Browning. AWP; BeLS; ClHu; EBNV; EBVV; FaBoPV; FF; FHYEP; GGP; GTBS-P; HAP; HeIL; HeIP; HoPM; ImPo; InPK; InPS; LiTB; MAT; MeMBP; NAEL-2; NIP; NOBE; NOBVV; NoP; OAEL-2; OBNC; OHCV; OtMeF; PeVV; PoE; PoEL-5; Poetr; PoLF; PPP; Prlm; SCGP; SCV; SoSe; TEP; TFi; TrGrPo; TRP

My Last Illusion. John Kaye Kendall. FiBHP

My Last Will. Robert Fergusson. ScCV

My Latest Sun Is Sinking Fast. Jefferson Haskell. AH

My least height flowers late with buds. Where Unimaginably Bright. Oliver Hale. GoYe

My lefe is faren in a lond. The One I Love Is Gone Away. *Unknown.* MeEL

  (Separated Lovers.) OAEL-1

My left eye is blind and jogs like. Sketch for a Job Application Blank. James Harrison. AmPA; MoP

My Legs Half Round Your Neck. Pietro Aretino, *tr. fr. Italian by* Alistair Elliot. FaBoBl

My legs swollen from pressing pedals. I'm A Worker. Jayne Cortez. NBV

My lemmon she shal be. (*LL*) The Hawthorn. *Unknown.* ChTr; EnVB; GBP; MiEL

My Lesbia let us love and live. Catullus, *tr. fr. Latin by* Wordsworth. OBVE

My Lessons in the Jail. Miriam Waddington. MoCV

My letters! all dead paper, mute and white. Elizabeth Barrett Browning. *Fr.* Sonnets from the Portuguese. HAP; OxAEP-2

My Lief Is Faren in Londe. *Unknown.* NAEL-1

My Life. Mark Strand. NoAM

My life/ is/ a/ bald headed match. Black Taffy. Peggy Susberry Kenner. JB

My life belongs to the world. I will do what I can. (*LL*) The Strength of Fields. James Dickey. VCAP

My life closed twice before its close. Emily Dickinson. AmPP; BoLoP; BoWoP; EBEvV; GBL; HeIP; ImGa; MoAB; MeMAP; MoAmPo; MoP; NAAL-1; NIP; NoAM; NOBA; OxBA; OxBSP; Poetr; PPP; SAmP; SCV; TFi; TrGrPo

My life had stood — a loaded gun. Emily Dickinson. AmPP; HAP; HeIP; InPK; NAAL-1; NALW; NAWM-2; NIP; NoP; Poetr; SAmP; TRP; WeW; WPOW

My life had taken the shape of the small square. The Small Square. Sophia de Mello Breyner Andresen, *tr. fr. Portuguese by* Alexis Levitin. WPOW

My life has crept so long on a broken wing. Tennyson. *Fr.* Maud[: A Monodrama]. EnVR; OAEL-2; OBWP

My Life Is a Bowl. May Riley Smith. BLPA

My life is a wearisome journey. The End of the Way. Harriet Cole. BLRP

My life is cast. Sifting. Victor Emanuel Beck. GoYe

My life is done, yet all remains. Robert the Bruce. Edwin Muir. OxBS

My life is engraved on my poems. Of Myself. Leah Goldberg, *tr. fr. Hebrew by* Ramah Commanday. BoWoP

My life is like a stroll upon the beach. The Fisher's Boy. Thoreau. ChTr

My Life Is like the Summer Rose. Richard Henry Wilde. AnAmPo

My life is measur'd by this glass[e], this glass[e]. On an Hour[e]-Glass[e]. John Hall. MeLP; OPOP

My life must touch a million lives in some way ere I go. My Prayer. *Unknown.* BLRP

My Life, my Strength, my Joy, my All. (*LL*) A Hymn to My God in a Night of My Late Sickness[e]. Sir Henry Wotton. MeLP; NOSC

My life, she said at last, quietly. The Gift. Luada Sandler. BTR

My Life, the Quality of Which. Etheridge Knight. NNaP

My life — to Discontent a prey. Rhymes (?). Henry S. Leigh. NOBL

My life, very much like life, is flowing on. (*LL*) Pause. Octavio Paz. STV

My life was never so precious. Inscription for the Tank. James Wright. TwCP

My life, your light green eyes. Last Words. James Merrill. TAP

My Life's Delight. Thomas Campion. EiL; InVP; TrGrPo

My light will tip tankards of fire in the sky. A Constant Labor. James W. Thompson. BPo

My limping mule brayed all the way. (*LL*) Remembering Min Ch'e. Su Tung-p'o. OHMPC

My lips from this day forgot how to smile. Auguste Lacaussade, *tr. fr. French.* *Fr.* Salaziennes, Les. TTY

My lips (the inconstancy of man!). Rupert Brooke. NSI

My little Ben, whilst thou art young. To His Son Bennet. John Hoskyns. FaBoEE

My Little Bird. Bunyan.

My Little Birds. *Unknown, tr. fr. Arabic by* Henrietta Siksek-Su'ad. FaPON

My little breath, under the willows by the water-side we used to sit. A Lover's Lament *or* The Willows by the Water Side. *Unknown, tr. fr. Tewa Indian by* H. J. Spinden. AWP
  (Willows by the Water Side, The.) WTO

My little cousin, if you'll be. To My Youngest Kinsman, R. L. Abraham Chear. OxBChV

My little cup, go now and taste. Leontios, *tr. fr. Greek by* Sam Hamill. InMo

My little dears, who learn to read, pray early learn to shun. Cautionary Verses to Youth of Both Sexes. Theodore Hook. OxBChV
  (Address to Children.) FaBoUs

My Little Dog. Pearl Forbes MacEwen. BoTP

My Little Dreams. Georgia Douglas Johnson. BlSi; CDC; PoNe

My Little House. J. M. Westrup. BoTP

My Little Lize. James Martinez. PBCV

My little lord, methinks 'tis strange. A Prognostication on Will Laud, Late Archbishop of Canterbury. *Unknown.* OxBoLi

My Little Love Lies on the Ground. Larin Paraske, *tr. fr. Finnish by* Jaakko A. Ahokas. PBWP

My Little Maid. *Unknown.* ReMoGo

My little old man and I fell out. Mother Goose. OxNR
  (Quarrle, The.) ReMoGo

My little pretty patch of wilderness. Touching Heartsease. Janet Sutherland. DT; NBrP

My little scholar, to thy book inclined. A Schoolmaster's Precepts. John Penkethman. OxBChV

My little son enters. Transformations. Tadeusz Rózewicz, *tr. fr. Polish by* Czeslaw Milosz. TSaS

My little son, I have cast you out. Choosing a Name. Anne Ridler. NOBE

My little son, when you could command marvels. Geoffrey Hill. *Fr.* Funeral Music. NoAM

My little son, who looked from thoughtful eyes. The Toys. Coventry Patmore. *Fr.* Unknown Eros, The. BeLS; EBEV; EBVV; NOBVV; OBEV; OHCV; OxAEP-2; PlP; PoToHe, *sl. diff.*; SoSe; TrGrPo; TrPWD

My Live Story. Lan Nguyen, *tr. fr. Vietnamese.* TSaS

My lizard, my lively writher. Wish for a Young Wife. Theodore Roethke. MoP; NAAL-2; NoAM; NoP; OxBSP; TAP

My locker, green steel. Game Resumed. Richmond Lattimore. NYBP

My lodging it is on the cold ground. Sir William Davenant. *Fr.* Rivals, The. JCP

My loneliness relieves. (*LL*) The Autumn Robin. John Clare. BoTP

My long scythe whispered and left the hay to make. (*LL*) Mowing. Robert Frost. AnAmPo; BLPL; CMoP; HoPM; LiTA; NAAL-2; NOBA; OxBA; PPP; TRP; VGW

My long two-pointed ladder's sticking through a tree. After Apple-picking. Robert Frost. AmPP; AnAmPo; CMoP; InPS; LiTA; MeMAP; MoAB; MoAmPo; MoP; NAAL-2; NoAM; NOBA; NTP; NU; OxBA; PoE; Poetr; PPP; Prlm; SAmP; SoSe; TAP; TFi; TRP; UnPo

My lookalike passed muster in the morgue. Horst Wessel on Alcatraz. Douglas Houston. PWE

My Lord and King. Tennyson. *See* Love is and was my lord and king.

My Lord Archbishop, what a scold you are. *Unknown.* FaBoEH

My lord, as I was sewing in my closet. Shakespeare. *Fr.* Hamlet. NAWM-1; OxAEP-1

My lord contemplates a pool. The Bamboo Shaded Pool. Chang Wên-chi, *tr. fr. Chinese by* Kenneth Rexroth and Ling Chung. WPC

My Lord, fallen, sin-stained. Sticheron for Matins, Wednesday of Holy Week. Kassia, *tr. fr. Greek by* Patrick Diehl. WPOW

My lord has great shoulders. A Woman in Love with a Captive King. Nakkannaiyar, *tr. fr. Tamil by* A. K. Ramanujan. PLW

My lord hath called for my sonne. Wretten by Me att the Same Tyme; on the Death of My 4th, & Only Child, Robert Payler. Mary Carey. KTR

My lord, I was accustomed to swill about the sky. The Dove Apologizes to His God for Being Caught by a Cat. Anthony Eaton. PeSA

My Lord/ if I worship Thee from fear of Hell. Rabi'a al-Adawiyya, *tr. fr. Arabic by* Margaret Smith. WPOW, *ad. by* Deirdre Lashgari

My lord is all a-glow. *Unknown, tr. fr. Chinese by* Arthur Waley.
  (My Lord Summons Me.) OxBM

My Lord Is Full of Delight. *Unknown, tr. fr. Chinese* by Robert Payne. TAL

My Lord, my life, can envy ever bee. Edward Taylor. *Fr.* Preparatory Meditations Before My Approach to the Lord's Supper. PoEL-3

My Lord raised a flag of surrender. The Emperor Asks Why My Husband Surrendered. Lady Hua Jui, *tr. fr. Chinese* by Kenneth Rexroth *and* Ling Chung. WPC

My lord said to my lady. Lamkin. *Unknown.* ESPB

My Lord Summons Me. *Unknown. See* My lord is all a-glow.

My Lord Tomnoddy. Robert Barnabas Brough. FiBHP; PeLV; PIP

My Lord, What a Morning. Waring Cuney. TTY

My Lord, what a morning when de stars begin to fall. Judgement Day. *Unknown.* WTO

My lord, you only want to. To the Tune "Plucking a Cinnamon Branch." Huang O, *tr. fr. Chinese* by Kenneth Rexroth *and* Ling Chung. WPC

My Lords the Judges laugh, and you're dismissed. *(LL)* The First Satire of the Second Book of Horace. Pope. OAEL-1; PPP

My lords, with your leave. A New War Song by Sir Peter Parker. *Unknown.* PAH

My Lost Youth. Longfellow. AmPP; AnAmPo; AWP; FaBoBe; FaBV; FaPoR; GoJo; ImGa; LiTA; MeMAP; NAAL-1; NOBA; OBEV; OxBA; PoEL-5; PoLf; PoRA; TAP; TFi

My loud machine for making hay. An Old Field Mowed. William Meredith. NYBP

My lov'd, my honour'd, much respected friend! The Cotter's Saturday Night. Burns. EnRP

My Love. E. E. Cummings. ErPo; LiTM; VGW

My Love. Bartholomew Griffin. *See* Faire Is My Love.

My Love. James Russell Lowell. BLPL; FaBoBe

My love/ Is like the grasses. Ono no Yoshiki, *tr.* by Arthur Waley. *Fr.* Kokin Shu. AWP; TAL

My Love. Richard Shelton. GOYP

My Love. *Unknown.* ReMoGo

My love and I for kisses played [*or* play'd]. William Strode. FaBoEE; NOSC

My love and my delight. The Lament for Art O'Leary. Eileen O'Leary, *tr. fr. Irish* by Frank O'Connor. PeIV

My love bound me with a kiss. Kisses. *At.* to Thomas Campion. EIL

My love came back to me. All Souls' Night. Frances Cornford. EnLoPo; OBD; OxBSP; OxBTC

My Love Eats an Apple. Ralph Gustafson. MoCV

My love for him shall be. *Unknown, tr. fr. French* by John Addington Symonds. *Fr.* Medieval Norman Song. AWP

My Love For You. *Unknown.* Spl

"My love for you has faded" — thus the Bad. Versions of Love. Roy Fuller. CBLP; LiTM

My love for you will never fail. *Unknown.* RoPo

My love forever! *Unknown, tr. fr. Irish* by Eilis Dillon. *Fr.* Lament for Arthur O'Leary, The. BIrV; PBWP; VBLP

My love has built a bonny ship, and set her on the sea. The Lowlands o' [*or* of] Holland. *Unknown.* AmFP, *diff. vers.*; OxBB; ScCV, *diff. vers.*

(Lawlands o' Holland, The.) CH

My love has gone down to his garden. Bible, *O.T. Fr.* Song of Solomon, The. BoWoP, *ad.* by Willis Barnstone

My love has left me has gone from me. Souvenirs. Dudley Randall. ArLo; BPo

My love he built me a bonnie bower. The Lament of the Border Widow. *Unknown.* GBP; Mes; OxBB; ScCV

(Bonnie Bower, The.) CH

My love he is fairer than a summer day. The Drynaun Dhun. *Unknown.* GBP

My love he was a fisher lad and when he came on shore. The Fisher Lad of Whitby. *Unknown.* OxBSS

My love, how could your heart consider. Motet. *Unknown, tr. fr. Old French* by Carol Cosman. PBWP

My love hurts me because you cannot know. Lady Otomo no Sakanoe, *tr. fr. Japanese* by Kenneth Rexroth *and* Ikuko Atsumi. WPJ

My Love, I cannot thy rare beauties place. William Smith. *Fr.* Chloris [*or* the Complaint of the Passionate Despised Shepheard]. EIL; ESo; InvP

My Love I Gave for Hate. *Unknown, tr. fr. Irish* by George Hay. BIrV

My love I give to you a threefold thing. Branwell's Sestina. James Reaney. *Fr.* Suit of Nettles, A. MoCV

My love I learned. Poem for a Marriage. Christine Craig. AIW

My love, if I write a song for you. Veronica Forrest-Thomson. VBLP

My Love in Her Attire. *Unknown.* BLPL; CoGr; FF; GTBS; GTBS-P; HeIP; ImPo; LiTB; NIP; OxBSP; TFi

(Madrigal: "My love in her attire doth show her wit.") ArLo; BoLoP; EIL; NAEL-1; NOBE; OBEV

My love is a lotus blossom. *Unknown, tr. fr. Egyptian* by J. E. Manchip White. TTY

My love is as a fever [*or* feaver], longing still. Shakespeare. *Fr.* Sonnets. EBEV; HoPM; NAEL-1; OxAEP-1; PoEL-2; TEP

My love is but a shepherd lad. The Shepherd and the Shepherdess. *Unknown.* OBET

My Love Is Dead. Thomas Chatterton. *See* Oh! sing unto my roundelay [*or* O! Synge untoe mie roundelaie].

My love is falle upon a may. *Unknown.* MiEL

My Love is Green. Felix Schumann, *tr. fr. German* by Philip L. Miller. RiWo

My love is green like the lilac bush. My Love is Green. Felix Schumann, *tr. fr. German* by Philip L. Miller. RiWo

My love is in my house. Mirabai, *tr. fr. Hindi* by Willis Barnstone *and* Usha Nilsson. BoWoP

My Love is Like a Myrtle. Moses ibn Ezra, *tr. fr. Hebrew* by Solomon Solis-Cohen. TrJP

My Love is Like a Red Red Rose. Burns. *See* Oh, My Love Is Like a Red, Red Rose.

My love is like a red, red rose. Burns. *See* O my luve is [*or* luve's] like a red, red rose.

My love is like Mies van der Rohe's. Dea ex Machina. John Updike. UV

My Love Is Like to Ice. Spenser. *Fr.* Amoretti. AAS; ErPo; ESo; IV; FF; HeIL; ImPo; LiTB; TrGrPo

My Love Is Neither Young Nor Old. At. to Robert Jones. EnRePo

My love is no short year's sentence. Love. *Unknown, tr. fr. Irish* by John Montague. BIrV

My love is o' comely height, an' straight. White an' Blue. William Barnes. GBL; GTBS-P

My love is of a birth as rare. The Definition of Love. Andrew Marvell. BLPL; BoLoP; CBLP; EBEV; ESCV; FHYEP; GBL; GeHe; HoPM; ImPo; InPS; JCP; LiTB; MeLP; NAEL-1; NOBE; NoP; NOSC; OAEL-1; OBEV; PoEL-2; SCGP; SeCP; SeCV-1; TEP; TFi; TrGrPo; UnPo

My Love is Past. Thomas Watson. NoSic

My love is playing on a fiddle. *Gond Oral Tradition, tr.* by V. Elwin *and* S. Hivale. WTO

My Love Is Strengthen'd, Though More Weak In Seeming. Shakespeare. *Fr.* Sonnets. AWP; EiL; OBEV

My love is tasting the fragrance. *Unknown, tr. fr. Pashto* by Saduddin Shpoon. PBWP

My love is the maid ov all maidens. In the Spring. William Barnes. GBL

My love is white and ruddy. Bible, *O.T. Fr.* Song of Solomon, The. BoWoP, *ad.* by Willis Barnstone

My Love Is Young. Earle Birney. NOBC

My love lies in the gates of foam. The Churchyard on the Sands. Lord De Tabley. CH, *abr.;* FaBoPP; GBL; OBNC

My love lies underground. Hymn to Priapus. D. H. Lawrence. CMoP; MoAB; OBMV; PoE; SCGP

My love, like my hair, is pure. A Song of White Hair. Chuo Wen-chün, *tr. fr. Chinese* by Kenneth Rexroth *and* Ling Chung. WPC

My love looks like a girl to-night. The Bride. D. H. Lawrence. NoAM; OxBTC

My Love, My Love. *(LL)* Poem for Francis Harvey. Madge Herron. VBLP

My love on Wednesday letting fall her body. In Crisis. Lawrence Durrell. LiTM

My love says. Alibi. Eunice De Souza. VBLP

My love sent me a chicken without e'er a bone. *Unknown.* OxNR

My love she is a gentlewoman. Auld Matrons. *Unknown.* ESPB

My Love She Passed Me By. *Unknown.* AmFP

My love she was born in the north country wide. Molly of the North Country. *Unknown.* OBET

My Love-Song. Else Lasker-Schüler, *tr. fr. German* by Jethro Bithell. TrJP

My love takes an apple to bed. Evesong. Maureen Duffy. PeHV

My love the sun sets. Valerie Sinason. DT

My love, this is the bitterest, that thou. Any Wife to Any Husband. Robert Browning. OBNC; OtMeF

My love took scorn my service to retain. Sir Thomas Wyatt. SiPS

My Love Was Lead. Tennessee Williams. PoA

My Love When This Is Past. Stephany Fuller. BPo

My love whose bangles. What He Said. Ammuvanar, *tr. fr. Tamil* by A. K. Ramanujan. PLW

My love will come. Waiting. Yevgeny Yevtushenko, *tr. fr. Russian* by Robin Milner-Gulland *and* Peter Levi. UnAS

My loved one is unique, without a peer. *Unknown, tr. fr. Egyptian* by J. E. Manchip White. TTY

My lover capable of terrible lies. Kaccipettu Nannakaiyar, *tr. fr. Tamil* by A. K. Ramanujan. BoWoP; PBWP; WPOW

My lover is the old poet, Gabriel. Vida. Judith Ortiz Cofer. AfAz

My lover never danced with me. Lines to a Seagreen Lover. Isabella Gardner. CAPP

My Lover Will Soon Be Here. *Unknown, tr. fr. Chinese by* Kenneth Rexroth. OHMPC

My lovers/ (Simple chaps). Ode: To My Lovers. Paul Verlaine, *tr. fr. French by* J. Murat *and* W. Gunn. PeHV

My lover's a cowboy, wild broncos he breaks. Bucking Bronco. *Unknown.* AmFP

My lovers come, not from the floating classes: they're. A Thousand and Three. Paul Verlaine, *tr. fr. French by* Alistair Elliot. FaBoBl

My lovers do not belong to the two rich classes. Thousands and Three. Paul Verlaine, *tr. fr. French by* François Pirou. PeHV

My love's eyes are red as the sargasso. The Talking Fish. Ruth Stone. BoWoP

My Love's Guardian Angel. William Barnes. GBL; PoEL-4

My Love's in Germany. Thomas Traill. ScCV

My love's manners in bed. The Way. Robert Creeley. BoLoP; LiTM; NeAP; PPP

My Lowlands a-ray. (*LL*) Lowlands. *Unknown.* ChTr; OxBoLi

My Lufe Murnis for Me. *Unknown.* ScCV

My lufe murnis for me, for me. My Lufe Murnis for Me. *Unknown.* ScCV

My Lulu. *Unknown.* AS

My lute and I. Sir Thomas Wyatt. MeEl; SiPS

My Lute Awake! Perform [the] last. Sir Thomas Wyatt.NoSic; SiPSBD; TFi
  (Lover Complaineth the Unkindness of His Love, The.) AAS; EBEV; EIL; ELP; GBL; HAP; InPS; NAEL-1; NoP; OAEL-1; PoEL-1; SiPS
  (Lover Complaineth, The.) TrGrPo
  (My Lute and I.) MeEl; SiPS
  (My Lute Awake.) EnRePo; SCGP
  (To His Lute.) BoLoP; NOBE; OBEV

My lute, be as thou wast [*or* wert] when thou didst grow. William Drummond of Hawthornden. EIL; NOSC; SCGP; Son
  (To His Lute.) GTBS; GTBS-P

My lute, be still, for I have done. (*LL*) My lute, awake! Perform [the] last. Sir Thomas Wyatt. NoSic; SiPSBD; TFi

My Luve. Burns. *See* O my luve is [*or* luve's] like a red, red rose.

My luve is like a red, red rose. Burns. EBEvV; EnRP; FaBoBe; HoPM

My luve she lives in Lincolnshire. Alison and Willie. *Unknown.* ESPB

My Luve's in Germany. *Unknown.* CH

My luve's [*or* luve is] like a red, red rose. My luve is like a red, red rose. Burns. EBEvV; EnRP; FaBoBe; HoPM

My lyre, and become a poem. (*LL*) Come, holy tortoise shell. Sappho. BoWoP

My madman bathes in the golden tank. The Right True End. *Gond Oral Tradition, tr. by* V. Elwin *and* S. Hivale. WTO

My madness is dear to me. Mad Song. Denise Levertov. TAP

My Madonna. Robert W. Service. BLPA

My maid Mary,/ She minds the dairy. Mother Goose. OxNR; ReMoGo

My Maisters all attend you. Turners Dish of Lentten Stuffe or A Galymaufery. William Turner. CoMu

My Maker shunneth me. Spiritual Isolation. Isaac Rosenberg. TrJP

My Makeup. Rochelle Kraut. UL

My Mall, I mark that when you mean to prove me. The Author to His Wife, of a Woman's Eloquence. Sir John Harington. BoLoP; ErPo; LPA; OxBM

My Mama Moved among the Days. Lucille Clifton. BlSi; PoBA

My Mamma is a mean old sing. Insulted. Priscilla Jane Thompson. CBWP-2

My mamma is dead and she's buried. My Darling's on the Deep Blue Sea. *Unknown.* AmFP

My mammy she told me to open the door. Old Gray Beard a-Shaking. *Unknown.* AmFP

My Mammy Was a Wall-eyed Goat. *Unknown.* ChTr; FaBoNo

My mammy's in the cold, cold ground. Po' Boy. *Unknown.* AS

My man is a bone ringèd with weed. Brenda Chamberlain. WPE; WPOW

My man is a bone ringèd with weed. (*LL*) My man is a bone ringèd with weed. Brenda Chamberlain. WPE; WPOW

My Man John. *Unknown.* OBET

My man loved me so much. So Long. Jayne Cortez. BoWoP

My man smiles at me. (*LL*) Cloud Hairdress. Chao Luan-luan. WPC

My Many-Coated Man. Laurie Lee. NYBP

My Mary. William Cowper. *See* Twentieth year is well-nigh past, The.

My Mary! (*LL*) To Mary. William Cowper. EnLoPo; EnRP; NOEC; UV, *sl. sh. vers.*

My Maryland. James Ryder Randall. AnAmPo; FaBoBe; PAH

My Master and I. *Unknown.* CoMu; OBET

My Master Hath a Garden. *Unknown.* CH; CoGr

My master hath a garden, full-filled with divers flowers. My Master Hath a Garden. *Unknown.* CH; CoGr

My masters all, Good day to you. (*LL*) The Bellman. Robert Herrick. CaPo; CH

My masters twain made me a bed. Said the Canoe. Isabella Valancy Crawford. NOBC

My meaning passes like wild nightbirds. Credo. Brewster Ghiselin. PoA

My microscopic cushion shows its claws. (*LL*) The Microscope in Winter. Sandra McPherson. LCAP; VCAP

"My milk-white doo," said the young man. The Young Man and the Young Nun. Albert D. Mackie. OxBS

My mill grinds pepper and spice. *Unknown.* OxNR

My mind i th' mines of rich Philosophy. On My Lord Bacon. John Danforth. SCAP

My mind is intact, but the shapes. Riddle in the Garden. Robert Penn Warren. NoAM

My mind is sad and weary thinking how. Odell. James Stephens. MoAB; MoBrPo

My mind is stuffed with tablecloths. Poland/ 1931 "The Wedding." Jerome Rothenberg. PoM; Prf

My mind is worn out, my features grown sharp and gaunt. Sitting at Night with My Nephew Who Has Just Come from Afar. Su Tung-p'o, *tr. fr. Chinese by* Robert Payne. TAL

My mind lets go a thousand things. Memory. Thomas Bailey Aldrich. AnAmPo; BoNaP; GGP; PoLF

My mind [*or* minde *or* mynde] to me a kingdom [*or* kyngdome] is. My Mind to Me a Kingdom Is. *Unknown, wr. at. to* Sir Edward Dyer. BLPL; EBEvV; EIL; EnRePo; FaBoBe; GGP; ImPo; LiTB; NOBE; PoEL-1; SCGP; TrGrPo; WGRP
  (In Praise of a Contented Mind.) NoSic; NAEL-1

My mind shrugs off his threadbare winter poems. Time Out. Donald Finkel. HoPM

My Mind to Me a Kingdom Is. *Unknown, wr. at. to* Sir Edward Dyer. BLPL; EBEvV; EIL; EnRePo; FaBoBe; GGP; ImPo; LiTB; NOBE; PoEL-1; SCGP; TrGrPo; WGRP

My mind was once the true survey. The Mower's Song. Andrew Marvell. CBLP; ESCV; NAEL-1; NOSC; PFP; PoEL-2; PPP; SeCP; SeCV-1

My mirror is always a little taller than I am. Mirror. Tada Chimako, *tr. fr. Japanese by* Kenneth Rexroth *and* Ikuko Atsumi. BoWoP; WPJ

My Mistress. Thomas Lodge. *Fr.* Life and Death of William Longbeard, The. TrGrPo

My Mistress. William Warner. EIL

My mistress' eyes are nothing like the sun. Shakespeare. *Fr.* Sonnets. AWP; BoLoP; EBEV; FF; HAP; HeIP; HoPM; ImPo; InPK; InPS; InvP; LiTB; NAEL-1; NIP; NoP; NoSic; OAEL-1; OtMeF; OxAEP-1; PlP; PoE; Poetr; PPP; Prlm; Son; SoSe; TEP; TFi; WeW

My mistress frowns when she should play. John Hilton. OxBoLi
  (Fa La La.) CH

My Mistress is a paragon. My Mistress. William Warner. EIL

My mistress is as fair as fine. Thomas Ravenscroft. CH; OxBoLi

My mistress loves no woodcocks. *Unknown.* NOSC

My mistress said I'd robbed her. I was straightway sent to gaol. (*LL*) The Sheffield Apprentice. *Unknown.* OBET

My mistress sayes she'll marry none but me. Catullus, *tr. fr. Latin. Fr.* Carmina. OBVE, *tr. by* Richard Lovelace

My mither sent me to the well. Whistle o'er the Lave o't. *Unknown.* GBP

My moccasins are black obsidian. The Song of the Black Bear. *Unknown, tr. fr. Navajo.* RaBo

My Mocking Bird. Josephine D. Henderson Heard. CBWP-4

My money! O, my money! Mavimbela, *tr. fr. Zulu by* H. Tracey. WTO

My most distinguished guest and learnèd friend. Edna St. Vincent Millay. VGW

My Mother. Josephine Rice Creelman. OHIP

My Mother. Francis Ledwidge. OHIP; TIRV

My Mother. Robert Mezey. NaP; SM

My Mother. Ann Taylor. BLPA; BLPL; OHIP; OxBChV; VPP

My Mother? (*LL*) My Mother. Ann Taylor. BLPA; BLPL; OHIP; OxBChV; VPP

My Mother. John Wieners. GLP

My mother always said. My Mother's Homeland. Belkis Cuza Malé, *tr. fr. Spanish by* Pamela Carmell. LoHo

My mother always said. Sappho, *tr. fr. Greek by* Willis Barnstone. BoWoP

My mother and I debate. The Black Walnut Tree. Mary Oliver. CAPP

My mother and your mother. *Unknown.* OxNR; RoPo

My Mother at Evening. Harry Humes. NGP

My mother bathes alone. Miscarriage. Robert Peters. ETG

My mother bids me bind my hair. A Pastoral Song. Anne Hunter. ECWP

My mountains, God has company in heaven. In High Places. Harriet Monroe. PoA

My mouth is a horse's mouth. Remembering. Xue Di, *tr. fr. Chinese.* TSaS, *tr. by* Iona Cook *and* Keith Waldrop

My mouth is daubed with black and green! Summer in Monaghan. Michael O'Loughlin. IB

My mouth is often joined against his mouth. Rimbaud, *tr. fr. French by* François Pirou. PeHV

My mouth slightly open. (*LL*) Clams. Ishigaki Rin. PBWP

My mouth, steer our lost bodies carefully downward. (*LL*) Who's Most Afraid of Death? Thou. E. E. Cummings. CMoP; PoE; VGW

My movable empire between Athens and Megara. Damastes (Also Known As Procrustes) Speaks. Zbigniew Herbert, *tr. fr. Polish by* John Carpenter *and* Bogdana Carpenter. PoSu

My Muse bade, Bedford write, and that was shee. (*LL*) On Lucy Countesse of Bedford. Ben Jonson. BeJo; EnRePo; NOSC; SeCP; SeCV-1

My muse came up from the creek. Virginian Arcady. Anne Rouse. NWP

My Muse had plowed with his that sung A-jax. (*LL*) On the Famous Voyage. Ben Jonson. BeJo

My muse in meads has spent her many hours. To Mistress Katherine Bradshaw, the Lovely, That Crowned Him with Laurel. Robert Herrick. CaPo

My muse is in the sulks to-day. Knitting. Mary E. Tucker. CBWP-1

My Muse, though airy, glides softly along. The Song of the Pen. Judah al-Harizi, *tr. fr. Hebrew by* J. Chotzner. TrJP

My muse, what ails this ardour? Sappho, *tr. fr. Greek by* Sir Philip Sidney. OBVE

My Muse will now by chymistry draw forth. To the Learned and Reverend Mr. Cotton Mather, on His Excellent Magnalia. Grindall Rawson. SCAP

My Naked Aunt. Archibald MacLeish. MeMAP

My naked simple life was I. My Spirit. Thomas Traherne. GeHe; SeCV-2

My Name and I. Robert Graves. Mes; NoAM; NYBP

My name engraved herein. A Valediction: Of My Name in the Window. John Donne. EnRePo

My Name Is. Pauline Clarke. SiSoPo

My Name Is Afrika. Keorapetse Kgositsile. PoBA

My name is Captain Hall. Captain Hall. *Unknown.* GBP

My name is Captain Kid, who has sailed. Captain Kid's Farewell to the Seas; or, The Famous Pirate's Lament. *Unknown.* OxBSS

My name is Colin Clout. The Prelates. John Skelton. *Fr.* Colin Clout. TrGrPo

My name is David Lowston, I did seal, I did seal. David Lowston. *Unknown.* PeNZ

My name is Edgar Poe and I was born. On the Edge. Philip Levine. CoAP; TAP

My name is Edward Hollander, as you may understand. The *Flying Cloud.* *Unknown.* AmFP; OBET; OxBSS

My name is Eteocles. The sea seduced me from my farm. Isidorus, *tr. fr. Greek by* Edwin Morgan. GrAn

My name is Fermin. Tobera. Jeff Tagami. OpBo

My name is Frank Taylor [*or* Frank Bolar] a [*or* 'nole] bachelor I am. Starving to Death on a Government Claim. *Unknown.* AmFP; OBAL (Lane County Bachelor, The.) AS

My name is George Nathaniel Curzon. John William Mackail *and* Cecil Arthur Spring-Rice, *and* Cecil Arthur Spring-Rice. *Fr.* Balliol Rhymes. FaBoCo; FaBoEE; NOBL; PeLV

My name is Henri. Listen. It's morning. Work Song. Mark Levine. BAP-91

My name is "I am living." I Have Bowed before the Sun. Anna Walters. WPOW

My name is James A. Wright, and I was born. At the Executed Murderer's Grave. James Wright. HCAP; VCAP

My name is Jesus, I am Mary's son. D. H. Lawrence. PeECV

My name is John J. Curtis. John J. Curtis. Joseph Gallagher. AmFP

My name is Johnson. Madam's Past History. Langston Hughes. MoP; NoAM; SAmP

My name is Judith meaning. Judy Grahn. *Fr.* Confrontations with the Devil in the Form of Love. VBLP

My name is O'Kelly, I've heard the Revelly. Shillin' a Day. Kipling. NoAM

My name is Parrot, a bird [*or* byrd] of paradise. John Skelton. *Fr.* Speak [*or* Speke], Parrot. NoSic; OxBoLi (Parrot's Soliloquy.) PoEL-1

My name is Peter Emily. Peter Amberley. John Calhoun. AmFP

My name is Phyllis Janik. In the Field. Phyllis Janik. IHMS

My name is Saartjie Baartman and I come from Kat Rivier. Hottentot Venus. Stephen Gray. PeSAV

My name is Samuel Hall, Samuel Hall. Sam Hall. *Unknown.* AmFP

(Samuel Hall.) ChTr

My name is Sanford Barney, and I came from Little Rock town. Sanford Barney. *Unknown.* AmFP

My name is Sluggery-wuggery. My Name Is. Pauline Clarke. SiSoPo

My name is Solomon Levi. An Old Cracked Tune. Stanley Kunitz. SM

My name it is Jack Hall, chimney sweep, chimney sweep. Jack Hall. *Unknown.* OBET

My name is [*or* is] Joe Bowers, I have [*or* I've got] a brother Ike. Joe Bowers. *Unknown.* AmFP

My name — my country — what are they to thee? No Matter. Paulus Silentiarius, *tr. fr. Greek by* William Cowper. AWP
(Epitaph: "My name — my country — what are they to thee.") FaBoEE; OBVE

My name was Pnytagoras; I died by drowning. Argentarius, *tr. fr. Greek by* Fleur Adcock. GrAn

My name's Polly Parker I come o'er. The Collier Lass. Frankie Armstrong. BrRo

My Nannie's Awa'. Burns. GN

My native clay. Growing in Grace. Jack R. Clemo. NOCV

My Native Land. Sir Walter Scott. *See* Breathes There the [*or* a] Man [with Soul So Dead]

My Native Land, thy Puritanic stock. "Orpheus C. Kerr." *Fr.* Rejected "National Hymns," The. OBAL

My nature singing in me is your nature singing. Singing & Doubling Together. A. R. Ammons. NAAL-2; NoAM

My necktie, my gloves. Charlie's Sad Date. Rafael Alberti, *tr. fr. Spanish by* Mark Strand. AnAn; CBNP

My neighbor, a scientist and art-collector, telephones me. The Burning of Paper instead of Children. Adrienne Rich. LCAP; NAAL-2; VCAP

My neighbor brings me bottom fish. My Garden, My Daylight. Jorie Graham. HCAP; Poetr

My neighbor frets about his lawn. Summer. Lucien Stryk. CAPP

My neighbor Hunks's house and mine. Near Neighbors. Martial, *tr. fr. Latin by* Swift. AWP

My Neighbor in the Mirror. Louise Glück. Son

My neighbor runs to me with. In the Country. Lu Yu, *tr. fr. Chinese by* Kenneth Rexroth. OHMPC

My Neighborhood. Stuart Dybek. PBCAP

My neighbor's boy has lifted his father's shotgun and stolen. Snowy Egret. Bruce Weigl. FoLa

My Neighbor's Child Cries in the Middle of the Night. Kung Tzu-chen, *tr. fr. Chinese by* Wu-chi Liu. SuSp

My Neighbor's Reply. *Unknown.* PoToHe

My Neighbor's Roses. Abraham L. Gruber. BLPA; PoToHe

My neighbor's willow sways its frail. The Willow. Tu Fu, *tr. fr. Chinese by* Kenneth Rexroth. NaP

My nephew, who is six years old, is called "Tortoise." Children. Po Chü-i, *tr. fr. Chinese by* Arthur Waley. ArLo

My-ness. Czeslaw Milosz, *tr. fr. Polish by* Czeslaw Milosz *and* Robert Hass. ArLo

My net/ Is heavy with weed. The Disappointed Shrimper. P. A. Ropes. BoTP

My new-cut ashlar takes the light. Kipling. PoEL-5

My New Friend. Helen Hunt Jackson. AmWP

My new friend finds buffets and matinees and bruches. Hospitals. Rachel Hadas. UnDi

My New Garden Field. *Unknown.* AmFP

My new province is a land of bamboo-groves. Eating Bamboo-Shoots. Po Chü-i, *tr. fr. Chinese by* Arthur Waley. OBVE

My New Rabbit. Elizabeth Gould. BoTP; OTCP

My New Umbrella. M. M. Hutchinson. BoTP

My newly rented home commands a view of the temple hall. A Solitary Falcon above the Buddha Hall of the Monastery of universal Purity. Mei Yao Ch'en, *tr. fr. Chinese by* Jonathan Chaves. SuSp

My nights are haunted by footsteps. The Terrified Meadows. William Pillen. BTR

My Nkosi you loved me. I Am the Beginning. Isaiah Shembe, *tr. fr. Zulu by* G. C. Oosthuizen. WTO

My noble, lovely, little Peggy. A Letter to the Honourable Lady Miss Margaret Cavendish Holles-Harley. Matthew Prior. NoAM; NOEC; NoP; OxBC; OxBSP
(Letter to Lady Margaret Cavendish Holles-Harley, When a Child, A.) NOBE; OBEV
(Letter to the Child Lady Margaret Cavendish Holles-Harley, A.) OxBChV

My normal dwelling is the lungs of swine. Autobiography of a Lungworm. Roy Fuller. MoP; NoAM; NoP; OxBC

My northern pines are good enough for me. Boston. E. A. Robinson. AnAmPo

My November Guest. Robert Frost. BLPL; OxBA; PoLF

My poor old bones — I've only two. The Lonely Scarecrow. James Kirkup. GrPl; PDV

My poor true heart, all comfortless. (*LL*) If in the World There Be More Woe. Sir Thomas Wyatt. EiL; SiPS; SiPSBD

My poplars are like ladies trim. The Poplars. Theodosia Garrison. OHIP

My portion is defeat — today. Emily Dickinson. OBWP

My Portrait. Moyshe-Leyb Halpern, *tr. fr. Yiddish by* Joseph Leftwich. TrJP

My Prairies. Hamlin Garland. FaPON

My Prayer. Horatius Bonar. BLRP

My Prayer. Patrick O'Connor. TIRV

My Prayer. *Unknown.* BLRP

My prayer is that I have friends. My Prayer. Patrick O'Connor. TIRV

My precious life I spent considering. Take the Crust. Sadi, *tr. by* L. Cranmer-Byng. *Fr.* Gulistan, The. AWP

My Pretty [Little] Pink. *Unknown.* AmFP; AS

My pretty Marten, my winter friend. The Dead Marten. Walter Savage Landor. FM

My Pretty Rose Tree. Blake. *Fr.* Songs of Experience. BoLoP; FHYEP; NAEL-2

My prime of youth is but a frost of cares. Tichborne's Elegy. Chidiock Tichborne. EiL; FaBoRV; FF; HAP; HeIP; InPS; NoP; NoSic; OAEL-1; OBD; TFi
 (Elegy for Himself.) PlP; RB
 (Elegy: "My Prime of Youth Is But a Frost of Cares.") ChTr; EBEV; NOBE; SCGP; WeW
 (Elegy, Written with His Own Hand in the Tower before His Execution.) DL; InPK
 (On the Eve of His Execution.) TrGrPo
 (Written on the Eve of Execution.) LiTB
 (Written the Night before His Execution.) SCV

My private protonotary? (*LL*) To His Conscience. Robert Herrick. BeJo; ChIV-1; NAEL-1; NoP; PoEL-3

My prize possession's peace. My Beloved. Ammon Wrigley. UnDi

My Proposal Is That. Miguel Algarin. BCF

My puberty tree swayed big, saw-edged leaves. The Puberty Tree. D. M. Thomas. TOF

My pulses rushed, and, quick, to saddle! The Meeting, the Departure. Goethe, *tr. fr. German by* John Frederick Nims. STV

My purpose is to tell my own true tale. The Seafarer. *Unknown, tr. by* John Wain. EBEV

My purpose was purely corrective. Leslie Johnson. PeLi

My Purse. *Unknown.* EBEV

My Queen her sceptre did lay down. Regina. Mary Elizabeth Coleridge. NALW

My quiet kin, must I affront you. Preliminary to Classroom Lecture. Josephine Miles. MoP; NoAM

My quiet prison guards, much tried. My beloved. Pictures of the Jews. Haim Guri, *tr. fr. Hebrew by* Ruth Finer Mintz. MHP

My quietness has a man in it, he is transparent. In Memory of My Feelings. Frank O'Hara. NAAL-2; NeAP; PoM

My quill is charged with fire. Song of Hate. Jacob ben David Frances, *tr. fr. Hebrew by* A. B. Rhine. TrJP

My Race. Helene Johnson. ShDr

My race began as the sea began. Names. Derek Walcott. AnAn

My Ratclif [*or* Ratcliffe], when the retchlesse [*or* retchless *or* rechless] youth offendes. The Earl of Surrey. AAS; SiPSBD
 (Exhortation to Learn of Others' Trouble.) FaBoEE
 (Lines to Ratclif.) SiPS

My ravist spreit in that desart terribill. Nightmare. Gawin Douglas. *Fr.* Palace [*or* Palice] of Honor [*or* Honour], The. PoEL-1

My reckless race is run, green youth and pride be past, A Gloze Upon This Text, *Dominus iis opus habet.* George Gascoigne. ChIV-2

My red engine goes chuff-chuff-choo! chuff-chuff-choo! My Toys. Lilian McCrea. BoTP

My reflection. Ray A. Young Bear. STP

My Regrets. Michael Andre. UL

My relatives are dead. As for my friends. Silence. René Maran, *tr. fr. French by* Ellen Conroy Kennedy. NegPo

My rent His Son should pay if I believed. (*LL*) My Country Audit. Mildmay Fane, 2d Earl of Westmorland. BeJo; NOSC

My report is not of schools. Return from Luluabourg. Michael Jackson. PeNZ

My reproach is like the mottled bamboo. Complaint of a Neglected Wife. Meng Chiao, *tr. fr. Chinese by* A. C. Graham. PLT

My rifle cocked, in savage calm. The Hunter's Song at Nightfall. Goethe, *tr. fr. German by* John Frederick Nims. STV

My Right Hand Don't Leave Me No More. Carter Revard. HATNAP

My Rival. Kipling. OxBTC

My Roaring Boy. Deborah Randall. PWE

My roaring boy comes home. My Roaring Boy. Deborah Randall. PWE

My room in Florence was the color of air. Above the Arno. May Swenson. NYBP

My room is blue, the carpet's blue. The Blue Room. Richard Edwards. Spl

My room is so small. Leah Goldberg, *tr. fr. Hebrew by* Ramah Commanday. *Fr.* Nameless Journey. BoWoP

My room's a square and candle-lighted boat. The Country Bedroom. Frances Cornford. MoBrPo

My room's bigger than a coffin. On Saint-Urbain Street. Milton Acorn. NOBC

My rug is red. My couch, whereon I deal. The Map. Gloria C. Oden. PoNe

My sack of tiny. An Armenian Looking at Newsphotos of the Cambodian Deathwatch. Diana Der Hovanessian. WoWa

My Sad Captains. Thom Gunn. CMoP; FaBoMo; LiTM; NAEL-2; NoAM

My Sad Self. Allen Ginsberg. Poetr; UnPo; VCAP

My Sadness Sits around Me. June Jordan. BPo

My sange es in sihting. A Song of Love for Jesus. Richard Rolle. MeEL

My saull and lyfe, stand up and see. Ane Sang of the Birth of Christ, with the Tune of Baw Lula Low. Martin Luther, *tr. fr. German by* John Wedderburn. ChTr

My Savior, let me hear Thy voice tonight. I'll Follow Thee. Clara Ann Thompson. CBWP-2

My second in the sea. (*LL*) Phenomenal Survivals of Death in Nantucket. Louise Glück. AmPA; SM

My secrets cry aloud. Open House. Theodore Roethke. NoAM; NOBA; NoP

My self to die, and prove mine owne. (*LL*) The Garden. James Shirley. BeJo; NOSC

My selves dissolving, old whore petticoats _____/ To Paradise. (*LL*) Fever 103°. Sylvia Plath. CMoP; FaBoWP; NoAM; NOBA; VCAP; VGW

My serious son! I see thee look. Before a Saint's Picture. Walter Savage Landor. OxBChV

My service thus is growne into disdayne. (*LL*) In Cipres springes [*or* Cyprus springs] (wheras [*or* whereas] dame Venus dwelt.) The Earl of Surrey. AAS; SiPS

My seven sons came back from Indonesia. Homecoming. Peter Viereck. CoAP

My seven year old friend. The World Is with Me Just Enough. Sam Abrams. UL

My 71st Year. Walt Whitman. NAs

My sexual feats. Fred Apollus at Fava's. Nicholas Moore. ErPo

My Shadow. W. Hodgson Burnett. UV

My Shadow. Robert Louis Stevenson. FaBoBe; FaBV; FaPON; OTCP; OxBChV; PDV; PFP; PWR; TEP; UV

My shag-hair Cyclops, come, lets ply. Vulcan's Song. John Lyly. *Fr.* Sapho and Phao. EBEV; EiL
 (Song in Making of the Arrows, The.) NoSic

My Share. Salih Bolat, *tr. fr. Turkish.* TSaS, *tr. by* Yusuf Eradam

My Shattered Sister. Naomi Quinonez. AfAz

My shattred phancy stole away from mee. Edward Taylor. *Fr.* Preparatory Meditations Before My Approach to the Lord's Supper. EAP; NOSC; SCAP

My Sheep Are Thoughts. Sir Philip Sidney. *Fr.* Arcadia. NoSic; SiPS; SiPSBD

My Shepherd Is the Living Lord. Thomas Sternhold. AH

My Shepherd's unkind; alas, what shall I do? The Lamentation of Chloris. *Unknown.* CoMu

My Ship Does Not Need a Helmsman. Alan Chong Lau. OpBo

My Ships. Ella Wheeler Wilcox. PoLF

My shoes./ I have just taken them off. 17. IV. 71. Paul Blackburn. PoM

My Shoes. Charles Simic. CoAP; HCAP; VCAP

My shoes are almost dead. Caesar. W. S. Merwin. LCAP; NaP

My shrink told me it was unnatural to be. Invisible History. Walta Borawski. GLP

My signs are a rain-proof coat, good shoes, a staff cut from the woods. Walt Whitman. *Fr.* Song of Myself. AmPP; LiTA; MoAmPo, *abr.*; NOBA; OxBA; Prf; SOTW, *much abr.*

My Silks and Fine Array. Blake. *See* My silks and fine array.

My silks and fine array. Blake. EnRP; OBNC; SCGP; TrGrPo
 (My Silks and Fine Array.) ChTr; ELP; GBL; TEP; UnPo

My sin! my sin, my God, these cursed dregs. Edward Taylor. *Fr.* Preparatory Meditations Before My Approach to the Lord's Supper. EAP; SCAP

My sins, and my contrition. (*LL*) Lord! Who Art Merciful as Well as Just. Robert Southey. TrPWD

My sins in their completeness. Mael Isu O Brolchain. NOIV

My Sister. Abba Kovner, *tr. fr. Hebrew by* T. Carmi. TOF

My Sister. Alfonsina Storni, *tr. fr. Spanish by* Aliki *and* Willis Barnstone. BoWoP

My sister and I. Plans. Helen Morgan Brooks. PoNe

My sister doesn't write poems. In Praise of My Sister. Wislawa Szymborska, *tr. fr. Polish by* Adam Czerniawski. PoSu

My sister in her well-tailored silk blouse hands me. The Photos. Diane Wakoski. NIP

My Sister Laura. Spike Milligan. NTCP

My sister Laura's bigger than me. My Sister Laura. Spike Milligan. NTCP

My sister! my sweet sister! if a name. Epistle to Augusta. Byron. EnRP; FHYEP

My sister rubs the doll's face in mud. The Kid. Ai. NoAM

My sister singing the Kyrie. Near Burning. Kathleen Peirce. PBCAP

My sister, you are a stranger to this place. God Hasn't Made Room. Mririda n'Ait Attik, *tr. by* Daniel Halpern *and* Paula Paley. PBWP

My Sisters. Bill Kushner. UL

My Sisters, O My Sisters. May Sarton. NALW

My Sister's Sleep. Dante Gabriel Rossetti. EnVR; NAEL-2

My Six Toothbrushes. Phyllis McGinley. GoYe

My skin is black, my arms are long. Four Women. Nina Simone. MAT

My skin is pumiced to a fault. Fado Singer. Wole Soyinka. HBAPE

My slain! Oh silver-hoof! Oh clover breath! Unbridled Now. Laura Lourene LeGear. GoYe

My Socks Are Thin. Duane Big Eagle. ETG

My softness heaves its spiral canopy. Snail. Elisabeth Eybers, *tr. fr. Afrikaans by* Elisabeth Eybers. PeSA; PeSAV

My Son. James D. Hughes. BLPA

My Son. Ruth Stone. WPE

My Son and I. Rosemary Norman. BrRo

My son and I ride bikes. Little Family. Ammon Wrigley. UnDi

My Son Asks. Mila D. Anguilar. WoWa

My son, come pierce my soul with a sword. Ballad of the Scarecrow Christ. Elder Olson. ChIV-2

My Son, Forsake Your Art. Mahon O'Heffernan, *tr. fr. Irish by* Maire Cruise O'Brien. BIrV

My son has birds in his head. Daedalus. Alastair Reid. NYBP

My son invites me to witness with him. Mousemeal. Howard Nemerov. TwCP

My son John. *(LL)* Diddle, diddle, dumpling, my son John. Mother Goose. BoTP; OxNR; ReMoGo

My son, keep well thy tongue, and keep thy friend. Controlling the Tongue. Chaucer. *Fr.* Canterbury Tales, The. EnVB; OxBChV

My Son, My Executioner. Donald Hall. CAPP; LPA; SM; TRP

My son, my son, here, please put it on." *(LL)* Family History. Irving Feldman. VCAP

"My son my son" the Blakean figure mourns and affirms. Brian Coffey. *Fr.* Advent. BiHa

My son squats in the snow in his blue snowsuit. Illuminations. Louise Glück. NALW

My son squirms in the pit of his shoes. Now It Is Time. James Lewisohn. ETG

My son tells his aunt. A San Diego Poem. Simon J. Ortiz. CDW

My son was killed while laughing at some jest. A Son. Kipling. *Fr.* Epitaphs of the War, 1914–1918. FaBoEE; NoP; OBWP; PeFWW

My son wears a nappy. My Son and I. Rosemary Norman. BrRo

"My son!" What simple, beautiful words! To My Unborn Son. Cyril Morton Thorne. BLPA

My son, where is your soul? And If the Angel Should Ask. Hayyim Nahman Bialik, *tr. fr. Hebrew by* Ruth Finer Mintz. MHP

My Song. King D. Kuka. VoR

My Song. James Ephriam McGirt. AAP

My Song. Rabindranath Tagore. OHIP

My Song Is Love Unknown. Samuel Crossman. OxBChV

My Song to the Jewish People. Leib Olitski, *tr. fr. Yiddish by* Jacob Sonntag. TrJP

My song today is the storm-cock's song. The Storm-Cock's Song. "Hugh MacDiarmid." OxBTC

My Songs Are Poisoned ("My songs, they say, are poisoned.") Heine, *tr. fr. German by* Louis Untermeyer. AWP

My sons/ sometimes I can. Efficiency Apartment. Gerald William Barrax. PoBA

My Sons. Ron Loewinsohn. NeAP

My son's eyes plead for expense I should otherwise. Mongol in the Woods. Douglas Oliver. VaA

My son's father is Kiowa-Comanche. Super-Brave. Teresa Whitman. LoHo

My son's image. Song for a Son. Robert Peters. ETG

My Son's One-Year Test: Improvised, *sels.* Wen Cheng-ming, *tr. fr. Chinese by* Jonathan Chaves.

My sorrow, Donncha, my thousand-cherished. Padraig O Heigeartaigh, *tr. fr. Irish by* Thomas Kinsella. NOIV

My sorrow is so wide. Kings River Canyon. Kenneth Rexroth. NaP

My sorrow that I am not by the little dún. The Starling Lake. "Seumas O'Sullivan." AWP

My sorrow, when she's here with me. My November Guest. Robert Frost. BLPL; OxBA; PoLF

My soul . . ., turn we to survey. Goldsmith. *Fr.* Travel[l]er; or, A Prospect of Society, The. FHYEP

My soul, be not disturbed. Address to My Soul. Elinor Wylie. AWP; LiTM; OxBA

My Soul before Thee Prostrate Lies. C. F. Richter, *tr. fr. German by* John Wesley. AH

My soul, calm sister, towards thy brow, whereon scarce grieves. Sigh. Stéphane Mallarmé, *tr. fr. French by* Arthur Symons. AWP

My soul doth magnify the Lord, The Song of the Virgin Mary. Miles Coverdale. ChIV-2

My Soul Doth Pant towards Thee. Jeremy Taylor. TrPWD

My soul, dread not the pestilence that hags. Preparations for Victory. Edmund Blunden. PeFWW

My soul from a mother's old arm-chair. *(LL)* The Old Arm-Chair. Eliza Cook. AnAmPo; BrRo; InPK; Poetr, *St. 1 only*; VPP; WBLP

My soul has grown deep like the rivers. *(LL)* The Negro Speaks of Rivers. Langston Hughes. AiP; BPo; CDC; EaPr; HAP; HCAP; HeIP; NAAL-2; NIP; NoAM; NOBA; NoP; OBCA; PoBA; Poetr; PoNe; RaBo; TAP; TFi; TTY; WeW

My soul has solitudes. Loneliness. Edwin Essex. TrPWD

My Soul in the Bundle of Life. *Unknown, tr. by* E. Margaret Rowley. *Fr.* Dead Sea Scrolls, The. TrJP

My soul is awakened, my spirit is soaring. Lines Composed in a Wood on a Windy Day. Anne Brontë. EBVV

My soul is enchanted boat. Shelley. *Fr.* Prometheus Unbound. EnRP; FHYEP; OAEL-2

My soul is like the oar that momently. Struggle. Sidney Lanier. LiTA; OxBA

My soul is the veil of his love. Hafiz, *tr. fr. Persian by* R. A. Nicholson. TOF

My soul looked down from a vague height, with Death. The Show. Wilfred Owen. ImPo; LiTB; LiTM; MoAB; MoBrPo; NSI; OBWVE; OxBTC; PeFWW

My soul magnifies the Lord. The Magnificat. Bible, *N.T. Fr.* St. Luke. BoWoP; WGRP

(And Marie said, My soule doth magnifie the Lord.) OBVE

My soul, my pleasant soul and witty. Animula Vagula, Blandula. Emperor Hadrian, *tr. fr. Latin by* Henry Vaughan. FaBoRV

My soul shall spurn them evermore. *(LL)* The Holy Office. James Joyce. FaBoTw; NoAM; OxBTC

My Soul, Sit Thou a Patient Looker-on. Francis Quarles. *See* My soul, sit thou a patient looker-on.

My soul, sit thou a patient looker-on. Francis Quarles. NOBE; PoToHe

(Epigram: Respice Finem.) OBEV

(My Soul, Sit Thou a Patient Looker-on.) NIP

My soul stands at the window of my room. Nostalgia. Karl Shapiro. CMoP; CoAP; TrJP; TwCP

My soul surcharged with grief now loud complains. Rachel Morpurgo, *tr. fr. Hebrew by* Nina Davis Salaman. TrJP

My Soul, there is a country [*or* countrie]. Peace. Henry Vaughan. AWP; ChTr; EBEV; ELP; ESCV; FaBoCh; GeHe; GN; HAP; NOBE; NOCV; OBD; OBEV; OxAEP-1; PlP; PoE; SCGP; SeCV-1; TEP; TFi; TrCP; WeW; WGRP

My Soul Thirsteth for God. Bible, *O.T., paraphrased by* Sir Thomas Wyatt. *See* As the hart panteth after the water brooks.

My Soul Thirsts for God. William Cowper. TrCP

My soul, thy love is dear: 'twas thought a good. Francis Quarles. *Fr.* Emblems. OAEL-1

My soul thy sacrifice! I choose thee out. Poems of the Arabic. *Unknown, tr. by* Sir Richard Burton. *Fr.* Thousand and One Nights, The. ErPo

My soul to-day. Drifting. Thomas Buchanan Read. AnAmPo; GN

My soul was an old horse. Pegasus. Patrick Kavanagh. MoAB

My Soul, Weigh Not Thy Life. Leonard Swain. AH

My soul, what's lighter than a feather? Wind. Francis Quarles. FaBoEE

My Soul Would Fain Indulge a Hope. Joseph Steward. AH

My soule a world is by Contraccion. William Alabaster. *Fr.* Divine Meditations. ESCV; Son

My soul I'll [*or* Ile] pour[e] into thee. *(LL)* The Night-Piece [*or* Nightpiece], to Julia. Robert Herrick. BeJo; CaPo; CBLP; CH; EBEvV; ELP; HeIL; InvP; JCP; LiTB; NAEL-1; NoP; NOSC; OAEL-1; OBEV; PoE; PoEL-3; PoRA; SCGP; SeCP; SeCV-1; TEP; TFi

My Soule is like a Bird; my Flesh, the Cage. Francis Quarles. *Fr.* Emblems. ESCV

My South. Don West. PoNe

My sovereign is as sweet and fair. *(LL)* Give beauty all her right. Thomas Campion. AAS

My specialty is living said. E. E. Cummings. NOBA

My Spectre around Me Night and Day. Blake. OAEL-2

My speech is tinged. Edward Dorn. BCF

My Spirit. Thomas Traherne. GeHe; SeCV-2

My spirit and flesh, parting now. At the End. Richard Ryan. PBCIP

My spirit is a pestilential city. Desolate. Claude McKay. CDC

My spirit is too weak — mortality. On Seeing the Elgin Marbles. Keats. BLPL; EnRP; ImPo; LiTB; MeMBP; NAEL-2; NIP; PrIm; TrGrPo

My spirit leans in joyousness tow'rd thine. Lines. "Ada." BlSi

My Spirit Longeth for Thee. John Byrom. BLPL; NOBE
(Desiderium.) OxAEP-1
(Desponding Soul's Wish, The.) TrPWD

My spirit loves with thine in peace to dwell. *(LL)* Wilt Thou not visit me? Jones Very. OxBA; TrCP; TrPWD

My spirit may come to you without shame. *(LL)* O Great Spirit. *Unknown.* EaPr

My spirit to yours dear brother, To Him That Was Crucified. Walt Whitman. ChIV-2

My Spirit Will Not Haunt the Mound. Thomas Hardy. FaBoVe; MoBrPo; OBNC

My Spirit's Complement. H. Cordelia Ray. AAP; CBWP-3

My Spoon Was Lifted. Naomi Replansky. WoWa

My spoon was lifted when the bomb came down. My Spoon Was Lifted. Naomi Replansky. WoWa

My spotless love hovers, with purest wings. Samuel Daniel. *Fr.* To Delia. ESo; OBEV

My spouse, Chunaychunay. *Unknown, tr. fr. Quechua (Peru) by* W. S. Merwin. BoWoP

My Spring Thing. Everett Hoagland. BPo

My Springs. Sidney Lanier. UnPo

My Star. Robert Browning. FaPON; TrGrPo

My star, star-gazing? — If only I could be. Aster. Plato, *tr. fr. Greek by* Peter Jay. GrAn; PeHV

My steadfast love! Eibhlin Dubh O'Connell, *tr. fr. Irish by* Thomas Kinsella. *Fr.* Lament for Art O Laoghaire, The. NOIV

My Stearine Candles. James Henry. NOBVV

My steps along this street. Here. Octavio Paz, *tr. fr. Spanish by* Charles Tomlinson. ArNa

My steps along this street. Octavio Paz. *See* My footsteps in this street.

My stick fingers click with a snicker. Player Piano. John Updike. Poetr; WeW

My stock lies dead, and no increase. Grace. George Herbert. ChIV-1; GeHe; JCP; SeCV-1

My stocking's where. David McCord. *Fr.* Christmas Package, A. PChr

My stomach is of many minds. Stomach. Kathleen Norris. OBAL

My Story. *Unknown, tr. fr. Irish by* Brendan Kennelly. PeIV

My story would have been longer. *(LL)* There Was a King. *Unknown.* CBNP; NBLV; OxBoLi

My story would have been longer. *(LL)* Three wise men of Gotham. Mother Goose. CBNP; FaBoBe; FaBoNo; OxNR; ReMoGo; Spl

My straying thoughts, reduced stay. Anne Collins. WPE

My students look at me expectantly. The Mountain. Louise Glück. NoAM

My Students Who Stand in Snow. Michael S. Harper. AnAn

My Sun,/ You smile at the granite of Milton. The Street of Named Houses. Robert David Cohen. NYBP

My Sun-killed Tree. Marguerite Harris. GoYe

My sunlight came pre-packaged. Nomen. Naomi Long Madgett. BlSi

My supermarket is bigger than your supermarket. That's. Supermarket. Peter Meinke. PBCAP

My Sweet Deare Lord, for thee I'le Live, Dy, Fight. Extasy of Joy Let in by This Reply Returned In Admiration. Edward Taylor. *Fr.* God's Determinations [touching his Elect]. EAP

My sweet did sweetly sleep. Stolen Pleasure. William Drummond of Hawthornden. EnLoPo

My sweet-faced, tattle-tale brother was born blind. The Twins. Mona Van Duyn. VCAP

My Sweet Gazelle! Immanuel di Roma, *tr. fr. Italian.* TrJP

My Sweet Old Etcetera. E. E. Cummings. AmPP; AnAmPo; CMoP; FF; HeIP; InPS; OBAL; OBWP; OxBA; PeFWW; PPP; SOTW

My Sweet Parthenope, within thy face. Barnabe Barnes. *Fr.* Parthenophil and Parthenophe. ESo

My Sweet Sweeting. *Unknown.* CH

"My sweetest Dorothy," said John. Dorothy's Dower. Phoebe Cary. AmWP

My sweetest Elpis. Letter from Ephesos. Rufinus, *tr. fr. Greek by* Alan Marshfield. GrAn

My Sweetest Lesbia [Let Us Live and Love]. Thomas Campion, *after the Latin of* Catullus. AAS; AWP; EIL; EnRePo; FF; GBL; HAP; HeIP; InPS; NAEL-1; NoP; NoSic; OAEL-1; OBVE; PoE; PoRA; PrIm; SCGP; TEP; TFi; TrGrPo; WeW

My sweetheart in the rippling hills of sand. *Unknown, tr. fr. Hawaiian by* S. H. Elbert *and* N. Mahoe. WTO

My Sweetheart's Dainty Lips. Judah Halevi, *tr. fr. Hebrew by* Emma Lazarus. TrJP

My sweetheart's the Mule in the Mines. *Unknown. See* My Sweetie's a Mule in the Mine.

My Sweetie's a Mule in the Mine. *Unknown.* AmFP

My swirling wants. Your frozen lips. A Valediction Forbidding Mourning. Adrienne Rich. NAAL-2; NoAM; NoP

My sword I shook. The Sword. Abu Bakr, *tr. fr. Arabic by* A. J. Arberry. TTY

My Table. W. B. Yeats. *Fr.* Meditations in Time of Civil War. LiTB

My tailor is against parting. Against Parting. Natan Zach, *tr. fr. Hebrew by* Jon Silkin. PoSu, *tr. by* Peter Everwine *and* Shulamit Yasny-Starkman

My Task. Maude Louise Ray. PWR

My tea is nearly ready and the sun has left the sky. The Lamplighter. Robert Louis Stevenson. *Fr.* Child's Garden of Verses, A. EBVV; OxBChV

My teachers are dead men. I was too young. Autopsy. Arthur Nortje. HBAPE

My tears were Orion's splendor with sextuple suns. Tears. Edith Sitwell. CMoP

My teeth dare not trust you. Bridgework. Annette Lynch. FF

My temples throb, my pulses boil. To Minerva. Thomas Hood. ChTr; FaBoCo; FaBoNo; FiBHP; NBLV; NOBL; OxBoLi; PeLV

My tender bottom is sore all day long. *(LL)* To the Tune "Washing Silk in the Stream." Ho Shuang-ch'ing. WPC

My tender parents brought me here. The Wexford Girl. *Unknown.* AmFP

My Thing Is My Own. *Unknown.* CoMu

My Thirty Years. Juan Fransico Manzano, *tr. fr. Spanish by* Oliver Cobarn *and* Ursula Lehrburger. TTY

My thought awaked me with Thy Name. Meditation on Communion with God. Judah Halevi, *tr. fr. Hebrew by* Solomon Solis-Cohen. TrJP

My thought is caught in the eyes of love. Entanglement. Francis Sparshott. MoCV

My thoughts are as a garden-plot, that knows. Thy Garden. Don Johnson, *tr. fr. Arabic by* Dulcie L. Smith. AWP

My thoughts are crowded with death. In Time of Plague. Thom Gunn. PFL

My Thoughts Are Not Your Thoughts. Bible, *O.T. Fr.* Isaiah. TrJP

My thoughts are of thee love though thou thinkest not of me. Song — Molly Magee. John Clare. EnVR

My thoughts are winged with hopes. *At. to* Sir Walter Ralegh *and to* George Clifford. EIL; GBL

My thoughts are with a boat. Hitomaro, *tr. fr. Japanese by* Arthur Waley. TAL

My Thoughts Do Harbour. Shakespeare. *Fr.* Two Gentlemen of Verona, The. CTC

My thoughts hold mortal[l] strife. William Drummond of Hawthornden. EIL; GTBS; GTBS-P; NOSC; OxBSP
(Inexorable.) NOBE; OBEV

My thoughts impelled me to the resting-place. Moses ibn Ezra, *tr. fr. Hebrew by* Emma Lazarus. TrJP

My thoughts, like sailors becalmed in Cape Town harbor. Sailor's Harbor. Henry Reed. MoAB; MoBrPo

My thoughts, my grief! are without strength. A Poem Written in Time of Trouble by an Irish Priest Who Had Taken Orders in France. *Unknown, tr. fr. Irish by* Lady Augusta Gregory. OBMV

My Thread. David Hofshteyn, *tr. fr. Yiddish by* Joseph Leftwich. TrJP

My three sisters are sitting. Women. Adrienne Rich. NMM; TRP

My Three Wives. *Unknown, after* Etienne Pasquier. FaBoEE

My tidings for you: the stag bells. Summer Is Gone. *Unknown, tr. fr. Old Irish by* Kuno Meyer. FaBoCh

My tiger! My clarity! My small. Peter Philpott. VaA

My time he said was not my own. Private But Sulphurous. Tom Matthews. PNI

My time, my monster, who will be able. The Age. Osip Mandelstam, *tr. fr. Russian by* Peter Russell. AnAn

My Times Are in Thy Hand. Anna L. Waring. PWR

My tongue enjoys inside my mouth. *(LL)* Wordless Day. Chang Shiang-Lua. TSaS, *tr. by* Stephen L. Smith *with* Naomi Shihab Nye

My Tongue-tied Muse In Manners Holds Her Still. Shakespeare. *Fr.* Sonnets. Son

N

Name all the shadows astride & back from the street. Take the Toys from the Boys. Ulli Freer. NBrP

Name as the Shadow of the Predator's Wing. Robert Hass. NGP

Name for All, A. Hart Crane. VGW

Name Giveaway. Phillip William George. VoR

Name in block letters. *None that signified. A Form of Epitaph. Laurence Whistler.* GTBS-P; Mes

Name is hard, The. On the 25th Anniversary of the Liberation of Auschwitz. Eli W. Mandel. NOBC

Name of a Place, The. Norbert Krapf. BTR

Name of "Gêlert's Grave," The. *(LL)* Beth Gêlert. William Robert Spencer. BeLS

Name of it is "Autumn," The. Emily Dickinson.
(Name — of it — is "Autumn," The.) InPS

Name of Jesus, The. (How sweet the name of Jesus sounds.) John Newton. ECEV; NOEC
Sels.
Burning. NeAP; PoM
"Jesus! my Shepherd, Husband, Friend." TrPWD

Name of my heroine, simply "Rose." The Tale of a Pony. Bret Harte. OBNV

Name of Old Glory, The. James Whitcomb Riley. GN

Name of Our Country, The. Dennis Schmitz. AmPA

Name of Robert Burns? The. *(LL)* Burns. Fitz-Greene Halleck. AnAmPo

Name of the product I tested is "Life," The. A Consumer's Report. Peter Porter. FaBoCo; NOBL; NTP

Name of this poem is, The. Cameo No. II. June Jordan. BPo

Name only once. America. Kofi Awoonor. HBAPE

Name stained in colored glass. Joshua Clark. Maurice Kenny. BCF

Named them. Orpheus. Donald Davie. TEP

Nameless Doon [*or* Dun], The. William Larminie. BIrV; PeIV

Nameless Epitaph, A. Matthew Arnold. FaBoEE

Nameless Journey., sels. Leah Goldberg, tr. fr. Hebrew by Ramah Commanday.
"My room is so small." BoWoP

Nameless Maiden, The. *Unknown.* ErPo

Nameless One, The. James Clarence Mangan. BIrV; EnRP; GGP; IIP; NOIV; OBEV; PeIV

Nameless One, A. Margaret Avison. HeIP; NOBC

Nameless Ones, The. Conrad Aiken. AnAmPo; OxBA

Nameless Saints, The. Edward Everett Hale. WGRP

Names. Gerald Dawe. IIP; PNI

Names. D. J. Enright. FaBoCo

Names. Jalal al-Din Rumi. *See* You should try to hear the name.

Names. Derek Walcott. AnAn

Names and Order of the Books of the Old Testament, The. Thomas Russell. BLPA

Names for everything I touch. The Hollow Thesaurus. Roger McDonald. CBAP

Names in Monterchi: To Rachel. James Wright. AnAn; NNaP

Names of Georgian Women, The. Bella Akhmadulina, tr. fr. *Russian.* BoWoP, tr. by Stanley Noyes *and* Olga Carlisle

Names of Horses. Donald Hall. CAPP; FoLa; HAP; InPK; SoSe; TRP

Names of the dead, The. Naming the Elements. Michael Klein. PFL

Names of the Hare, The. *Unknown, tr. fr. Middle English by* Seamus Heaney. RB

Names of the Humble, The. Les A. Murray. CBAP

Names of the Sea-trout, The. Tom Rawling. OBAP

Names of things, The — sparks! Resigning from a Job in a Defense Industry. Sandra McPherson. LCAP

Naming Day, A. Odia Ofeimun. HBAPE

Naming of Cats, The. T. S. Eliot. NBLV; PFP; SoCa

Naming of Parts. Henry Reed. *Fr. Lessons of the War.* CoGr; EBEvV; FaBoEH; FF; GoJo; HeIP; HoPM; ImPo; InPS; LiTB; MoAB; MoBrPo; NOBE; NoP; OBWP; OxBTC; PAW; Poetr; PoRA; PrIm; RaBo; SoSe; TFi; TrGrPo; UnPo; UV

Naming of Private Parts. John Lloyd Williams. BXAP; FaBoPa

Naming of the Beasts, The. Francis Sparshott. NOBC

Naming Souls. Uri Zvi Greenberg, tr. fr. *Hebrew by* Jon Silkin *and* Ezra Spicehandler. PeFWW

Naming the Animals. Anthony Hecht. ChIV-1

Naming the Elements. Michael Klein. PFL

Naming the House. Ann Lauterbach. PRA

Nan-Chin Gorge. Ts'ai Ch'i-chiao, tr. fr. *Chinese.* LHF, tr. by Hualing Nieh

Nanak and the Sikhs, sels. *Unknown, tr. fr. Hindustani.*
"How shall I address Thee, O God? how shall I praise Thee?" WGRP

Nancibel. Bliss Carman. AnAmPo

Nancy Dawson. *Unknown.* ReMoGo

Nancy Hanks. Rosemary *and* Stephen Vincent Benét *and* Stephen Vincent Benét. FaBV; FaPON; NTCP

Nancy Hanks. Harriet Monroe. OHIP

Nancy Hanks dreams by the fire. Fire-Logs. Carl Sandburg. AnAmPo

Nancy Hanks, Mother of Abraham Lincoln. Vachel Lindsay. CMoP

Nancy, Jimmy, Larry, Frank, and Berdie. Lady. Ted Berrigan. UL

Nancy, the hogs don't know us. Mirror for the Barnyard. Jack Myers. AmPA

Nane of them durst cum neir his Hald. *(LL)* Johnie Armstrang. *Unknown.* ESPB; IBB; OxBB

Nani. Alberto A. Ríos. SM; SoSe

Nani Worries about Her Father's Happiness in the Afterlife. Ana Castillo. AfAz

Nano's Song. Ben Jonson. *See* Fools, They Are the Only Nation.

Nanta was nominated for a W(hore). Aenigma on the Six Cases. *Unknown.* FaBoUs

Nantucket. William Carlos Williams. AnAmPo; HAP; InPS; OxBA; SOTW; TAP; TRP; WeW

Nantucket Honeymoon. David Mura. ETG

Naomi. Gwendolyn Brooks. NAAL-2

Naomi and Ruth. Bible, *O.T. Fr.* Ruth. TrJP

Naomi (Omie) Wise. *Unknown.* AmFP

Napa, California. Ana Castillo. WPOW

Nape. Jane Epton Seale. CrSp

Napkin and Stone. Vernon Watkins. NYBP

Naples. Samuel Rogers. OBTV

Naples Again. Arthur Freeman. NYBP

Napoleon. Walter de la Mare. FaBoCh; FaBoTw; NOBE; OtMeF; RB; Spl

Napoleon. Miroslav Holub, *tr. fr. Czech by* Káča Poláčková. PoSu, *tr. by* Kaca Polackova; TSaS, *tr. by* Kaca Polackova

Napoleon after Sedan. Rimbaud, *tr. by* Robert Lowell. *Fr.* Eighteen-Seventy. FaBoPV; OBWP

Napoleon and the British Sailor. Thomas Campbell. BeLS

Napoleon hoped that all the world would fall beneath his sway. *Unknown.* FaBoCo

Napoleon is standing with his pants upon the floor. The Poor Old Prurient Interest Blues. John Hartford. MAT

Napoli Again. Richard Hugo. LCAP

Napolo has spoken: Death. The Messengers. Steve Chimombo. HBAPE

Nappy Edges (A Cross Country Sojourn). Ntozake Shange. BlSi

Narcissa. Gwendolyn Brooks. GrPl; NTCP

Narcissism/ is an ugly fault. Antonio Machado Ruiz, *tr. by* Robert Bly. *Fr.* Moral Proverbs and Folk Songs. RaBo

Narcissus. Paul Valéry, *tr. fr. French by* Joseph T. Shipley. AWP

Narcissus and Echo. Fred Chappell. MT

Narcissus, Come Kiss Us! *Unknown.* ErPo

Narcissus in a Cocktail Glass. Frances Minturn Howard. GoYe

Narcissus in Camden. Helen Gray Cone. BXAP

Narcissus: To Himself. David Galler. PoA

Narcolepsy. Maureen Owen. TTTS

Narrative. Russell Atkins. PoBA

Narrative. Elisabeth Eybers, *tr. fr. Afrikaans by the author.* PeSA; PeSAV

Narrative Hooper and L.D.O. Sestina with a Long Last Line, The. James Whitehead. HoPM

Narrative. How we tell. How is told. Tenth Matter: Story. Robert Kelly. BCF

Narrative of the Life of an American Slave, sels. Frederick Douglass.
"Just God! and these are they." NAAL-1
Parody, A. NAAL-1; NAWM-2

Narrator. W. H. Auden. *See* Well so that is that. Now we must dismantle the tree.

Narrator, The. Milo De Angelis, *tr. fr. Italian by* Lawrence Venuti. NeIt

Narrator's Trance, The. James Cunningham. JB
Sels.
"And birds came crying."
"Song thumbed down a cruiser for a ride, A."
"There were blood spots on the skirt."
"Woods are overhead over everywhere, The."

Narrow Fellow in the Grass, A. Emily Dickinson. AmPP; BoWoP; ClHu; CMoP; FM; GoJo; HAP; HeIP; HoPM; LiTA; LiTM; MeMAP; MoAB; NAAL-1; NALW; NIP; NoAM; NOBA; NoP; NTP; OBCA; OxBA; PoE; PoEL-5; Poetr; PoLF; PPP; RB; SAmP; SoSe; TAP; TFi; TRP; WeW

Narrow glade unfolded, such as Spring, A. An Interview near Florence. Samuel Rogers. *Fr.* Italy. OBNC

Narrow Sea, The. Robert Graves. FaBoEE; FaBoMo

Narrowed down to a spyhole, a globed eyelid closing. *(LL)* Dublin Girl, Mountjoy, 1984. Dermot Bolger. BiHa; IB

Nature That Framed Us of Four Elements. Christopher Marlowe. *Fr.* Tamburlaine the Great. PoEL-2; TrGrPo

Nature, That Washed [*or* Washt] Her Hands in Milk[e]. Sir Walter Ralegh. EnRePo; NoP

Nature, which is the vast creation's soul. To Mr. Henry Lawes. Katherine Philips. WPE

Nature withheld Cassandra in the skies. Fragment of a Sonnet. Pierre de Ronsard, *tr. fr. French by* Keats. AWP; OBVE

Nature's confectioner, the bee. Fuscara, or the Bee Errant. John Cleveland. CBLP

Nature's Cook, *sels.* Margaret Cavendish, Duchess of Newcastle. "Death is the cook of nature, and we find." CBCK; PBWP

Nature's Creed. *Unknown.* OHIP

Nature's Easter Music. Lucy Larcom. OHIP

Nature's Embassy., *sels.* Richard Brathwaite [*or* Brathwait]. Nightingale, The. EIL

Nature's first green is gold. Nothing Gold Can Stay. Robert Frost. AmPP; GrPl; MoAB; MoAmPo; NAAL-2; NOBA; Poetr; PPP; SoSe; TAP; VGW

Nature's Influence on Man. Mark Akenside. *Fr.* Pleasures of Imagination, The. NOEC

Nature's lay idiot [*or* Ideot], I taught thee to love. John Donne. *Fr.* Elegies. CBLP; NoP; PeLV
(Elegie: "Nature's lay ideot, I taught thee to love." OxAEP-1; SeCP

Nature's Lineaments. Robert Graves. FaBoTw; RB

Nature's Minor Chords. H. Cordelia Ray. CBWP-3

Nature's Praise of God. Christian Fürchtegott Gellert, *tr. fr. German by* Philip L. Miller. RiWo

Nature's Questioning. Thomas Hardy. EnVR; PFP; TEP

Nature's Reply to Mutability. Spenser. *Fr.* Faerie Queene, The. NOBE

Nature's Sympathy with the Poet. Sir Walter Scott. *See* Call it not vain; they do not err.

Nature's Travail. *Unknown, tr. fr. Greek by* Goldwin Smith. AWP

Nature's Uplifting. H. Cordelia Ray. CBWP-3

Naught in the world keeps an immortal stay. Juvencus, *tr. fr. Latin by* Helen Waddell. MLL

Naughty Boy. Robert Creeley. HeIP; NoAM; NOBA

Naughty Lord and the Gay Young Lady Damages, $10,000, The. *Unknown.* CoMu

Naughty Paughty Jack-a-Dandy. Namby-Pamby; or, A Panegyric on the New Versification. Henry Carey. FaBoNo; FaBoPa; NOEC, *abr.;* OBSV
(Nauty Pauty Jack-a-Dandy.) OxNR

Naughty Preposition, The. Morris Bishop. FiBHP; NBLV; NYBP; PeLV

Nausicäa. Irving Layton. ErPo

Nautical Ballad, A. Charles Edward Carryl. *See* Capital ship for an ocean trip, A.

Nautilus Island's hermit. Skunk Hour. Robert Lowell. AmPP; CAPP; CMoP; CoAP; FaBoMo; HAP; HCAP; HeIP; InPK; InPS; LCAP; MoAmPo; MoP; NAAL-2; NIP; NoAM; NOBA; NoP; OPOP; OxBC; PFP; PoE; Poetr; PPP; PrIm; SCV; TAP; TFi; TRP; VCAP

Nauvoo. Bayard Taylor. OBAL

Naval Trainees Learn How to Jump Overboard, The. David Wagoner. VCAP

Navel. Dennis Schmitz. AnAn

Navigation. Ralph Knevet. NOSC

Navigator. May Sarton. ArOW

Navigators, The. W. J. Turner. OBMV

Nay, but of such an one. *Unknown, tr. by* Sir Edwin Arnold. *Fr.* Bhagavad-Gita, The. TOF

Nay but you, who do not love her. Song: ("Nay but you, who do not love her.") Robert Browning. MeMBP; TrGrPo

Nay do not smile: my lips shall rather dwell. One Desiring Me to Read, But Slept It Out, Wakening. George Daniel. OxBSP

Nay fie, Platonics, still adoring. Epithalamy. Alexander Brome. NOSC

Nay, gather not that filbert, Nicholas. The Filbert. Robert Southey. FM

Nay, he could sail a yacht both nigh and large. The Cabin-Boy. George Villiers. NOSC

Nay, Ivy, Nay. *Unknown. See* Holly and Ivy ("Holly stand in the hall.")

Nay, Ivy, Nay. *Unknown. See* Holy stond in the hall [*or* halle].

Nay, lady, one frown is enough. To Helen in a Huff. Nathaniel Parker Willis. AnAmPo; OBAL

Nay, lady, sit; if I but wave this wand. Milton. *Fr.* Comus; a Masque Presented at Ludlow Castle. FHYEP; OAEL-1; OxAEP-1

Nay, lady, smile! (*LL*) To Helen in a Huff. Nathaniel Parker Willis. AnAmPo; OBAL

Nay, Lord, not thus! white lilies in the spring. Sonnet on Hearing the *Dies Irae* Sung in the Sistine Chapel. Oscar Wilde. TrPWD

Nay! Nay! Ivy! Holly against Ivy. *Unknown.* MeEL

Nay, nay, my boy — 'tis not for me. Horace. *See* Boy, I have their empty shouts.

May, 1945. Peter Porter. OxBC

Nay, painter, if thou dar'st design that fight. The Second Advice to a Painter. Andrew Marvell. APAS

Nay, pish; nay, phew! nay, faith and will you? fie! A Maiden's Denial. *Unknown.* ErPo

Nay, prethee [*or* prithee] dear, draw nigher. A Loose Saraband. Richard Lovelace. BeJo; CaPo; PoEL-3

Nay, prithee tell me, Love, when I behold. The Transfiguration of Beauty. Michelangelo, *tr. fr. Italian by* John Addington Symonds. AWP

Nay, read it not, thou wouldst not know. Anne Lynch Botta. AmWP

Nay, start not at the name — America! (*LL*) Tribute to America. Shelley. AiP

Nay, tempt me not to love again. Thomas Moore. *Fr.* Odes to Nea. OBNC

Nay, thank me not again for those. Reproof of Thanks. Walter Savage Landor. CBLP

Nay then, farewell, if this be so. To Avisa. Henry Willoby. *Fr.* Willobie His Avisa. CBLP; EIL

Nay, thou art my eternal attribute. Whym Chow. "Michael Field." FM

Nay, Xanthias, feel unashamed. II, 4. Ad Xanthiam Phoceum ("Ne sit ancillae.") Horace, *tr. fr. Latin by* Austin Dobson. *Fr.* Odes. AWP, *tr. by* Franklin P. Adams

Nazi in the Dock, at Sixty, The. Larry Rubin. BTR

Nazis/ and friends. Seriatim. Robert A. Frauenglas. BTR

Nazis. Ira Sadoff. NAmP90

Ndaaya, I, am so poor. Citèkù Ndaaya, *tr. after French-Luba texts by* Judith Gleason. *Fr.* Ndaaya's Kàsàlà. PBWP

Ndaaya's Kàsàlà, *sels.* Citèkù Ndaaya, *tr. after French-Luba texts by* Judith Gleason.
"Ndaaya, I, am so poor." PBWP

"Ne crede colori," the Poet erst sang. Prejudice against Colour. Langham Dale. PeSAV

Ne Plus Ultra. Samuel Taylor Coleridge. OAEL-2

Ne thence the Irishe Rivers absent were. The Rivers of Ireland. Spenser. *Fr.* Faerie Queene, The. CBCK

Ne trellisses, no vines. Iron Landscapes (and the Statue of Liberty). Thom Gunn. FaBoPV; OBTV

Neaera when I'm there is adamant. J. V. Cunningham, *after the Latin of* George Buchanan. OBVE

Neap-tide and the ebbing days slide. A Song of Sickness. Hine Tangikuku, *tr. fr. Maori by* Barry Mitcalfe. WTO

Near a shady wall a rose once grew. The Rose Still Grows beyond the Wall. A. L. Frink. BLPA

Near a Waterfall at Ryumon. Lady Ise, *tr. fr. Japanese by* Etsuko Terasaki *and* Irma Brandeis. BoWoP

Near an Old Prison. Frances Cornford. OBMV

Near and Dear, The. Cynthia Zarin. UTF

Near Avalon. William Morris. OAEL-2

Near Burning. Kathleen Peirce. PBCAP

Near Circe's House. Robert Duncan. BCF

Near Damascus. W. S. Di Piero. ChIV-2

Near Death. Stef Pixner. AIW

Near Dover, September 1802. Wordsworth. EnRP

Near Dusk. Joseph Auslander. FaPON

Near Hartington. Roy Fisher. *Fr.* Wonders of Obligation. NBrP

Near Helikon. Trumbull Stickney. LiTA

Near-Johannesburg Boy, The. Gwendolyn Brooks. ETG

Near Lanivet, 1872. Thomas Hardy. AWP; CMoP; NoAM

Near Neighbors. Martial, *tr. fr. Latin by* Swift. AWP

Near-neighboured by a blandly boisterous Dean. The Blues at Lord's. Siegfried Sassoon. PeLV

Near Perigord. Ezra Pound. FaBoMo; LiTA; LiTM

Near Rhydcymerau. Rhydcymerau. David Gwenallt Jones, *tr. fr. Welsh by* Anthony Conran. OBWVE

Near Roscoe and Coldwater. Amy Uyematsu. OpBo

Near-sighted fellow named Walter, A. *Unknown.* PeLi

Near-Sightedness. Edmond Yi-Teh Chang. OpBo

Near the Border of Insanities. Dannie Abse. PoA

Near the Bravo 20 Bombing Range. Gary Short. NGP

Near the celebrated Lido where the breeze is fresh and free. Longfellow's Visit to Venice. Sir John Betjeman. NOBL

Near the City of Petersburg. The V. N. and C. I. Maggie Pogue Johnson. CBWP-4

Near the Cymmerians, in his dark abode. Ovid, *tr. by* Dryden. *Fr.* Metamorphoses. OBVE

Near the dry river's water-mark we found. A Note Left in Jimmy Leonard's Shack. James Wright. HCAP; NoP

Ne'er walked the earth a greater man than he. (*LL*) Dante. Michelangelo. AWP

Negation is the spectre, the reasoning power in man, The. Reason and Imagination. Blake. *Fr*. Milton. EnRP

Negative Capability. John Drew. PWE

Negative Passage. Michael Newman. PoA

Negative tree, you are belief. Bound. Theodore Roethke. PoA

Negatives. Charles Wright. PoA

Negev. David Rokeah, *tr. fr. Hebrew by* Ruth Finer Mintz. MHP

Neglect. C. K. Williams. PWE

Neglected, leaves a dreary waste behind. (*LL*) A Comparison. William Cowper. OxBSP

Neglected long had been my useless lyre. On the Defeat at Ticonderoga or Carilong. *Unknown*. PAH

Neglectful Edward. Robert Graves. MoBrPo

Neglecting thy derision. (*LL*) To Fortune. Robert Herrick. OxBSP; SeCV-1

Negotiation. Alan Brownjohn. PeLV

Negritude. James A. Emanuel. BPo

Negro, The. James A. Emanuel. HoPM; InPK

Negro/ With the trumpet at his lips, The. Trumpet Player. Langston Hughes. NAAL-2; TTY

Negro Ballot, The. L. A. J. Moorer. CBWP-3

Negro Boy, The. David Samwell. AngWe

Negro Cemetery Next to a White One, A. Howard Nemerov. OxBSP

Negro Dreams. Doughtry Long, Jr.. PoBA

Negro Has a Chance, The. Maggie Pogue Johnson. CBWP-4

Negro Hero. Gwendolyn Brooks. CAPP

Negro Heroines. L. A. J. Moorer. CBWP-3

Negro holds firmly the reins of his four horses, The. The Drayman. Walt Whitman. *Fr*. Song of Myself. AmPP; LiTA; MoAmPo, *abr*.; NOBA; OxBA; PoNe; SOTW, (*much abr*.)

Negro Laughs Back, The. Mary Jenness. ShDr

Negro Laughter. Anita Scott Coleman. ShDr

Negro Love Song, A. Paul Laurence Dunbar. AAP; PoNe

Negro Mask. Léopold Sédar Senghor, *tr. fr. French by* Ellen Conroy Kennedy. NegPo

Negro Meets to Pray, The. Daniel Webster Davis. AAP

Negro peddler of revolt. Jacques Roumain, *tr. fr. French by* Ellen Conroy Kennedy. *Fr*. Ebony Wood. NegPo

Negro Reel. *Unknown*. AS

Negro Schools, The. L. A. J. Moorer. CBWP-3

Negro Sermon, A — Simon Legree. Vachel Lindsay. *See* Legree's big house was white and green.

Negro Servant. Langston Hughes. VGW

Negro Soldier's Civil War Chant. *Unknown*. BPo

Negro Soldier's Viet Nam Diary, A. Herbert Martin. PoBA

Negro Song, A. *Unknown*. PBCV

Negro Song at Cornwall. *Unknown*. PBCV

Negro Speaks of Rivers, The. Langston Hughes. AiP; BPo; CDC; EaPr; HAP; HCAP; HeIP; NAAL-2; NIP; NoAM; NOBA; NoP; OBCA; PoBA; Poetr; PoNe; RaBo; TAP; TFi; TTY; WeW

Negro Spiritual. Perient Trott. PoNe

Negro Spirituals. Rosemary *and* Stephen Vincent Benét *and* Stephen Vincent Benét. FaPON

Negro sprouts from the pavement like an asparagus, A. Stumpfoot on 42nd Street. Louis Simpson. NNaP; UnPo; VGW

Negro Tramp. David Diop, *tr. fr. French by* Ellen Conroy Kennedy. NegPo

Negro Woman. Lewis Alexander. CDC; PoBA

Negro Woman, A/ carrying a bunch of marigolds. William Carlos Williams. SAmP

Negroes. Maxwell Bodenheim. PoNe

Negroes/ Sweet and docile. Warning. Langston Hughes. BPo

Negroes, labouring, The. Guadalupe, W.I. Nicolás Guillén, *tr. fr. Spanish by* Anselm Hollo. TTY

Negro's Complaint, The. William Cowper. FaBoEH

Negro's Lament, The. John Willis Menard. AAP

Negro's Tragedy, The. Claude McKay. BPo

Neighbor thought that they, A. The Planetary Arc-Light. August Derleth. GoYe

Neighborhood House, The. Jay Wright. NBV

Neighbors. A. R. Ammons. CAPP

Neighbors. Maura Dooley. PWE

Neighbors. David Allan Evans. Poetsp

Neighbors. Marilyn Francis. GoYe

Neighbors. Anne Spencer. CDC

Neighbors. James Tate. LCAP

Neighbors of Bethlehem, The. *Unknown, tr. fr. French*. OHIP

Neighbour. Christine Churches. FaBoMA

Neighbour mine not long ago there was, A. Sir Philip Sidney. *Fr*. Arcadia. SiPSBD

(Tale for Husbands, A.) SiPS

Neighbour's Pear Tree. Tony Curtis. AngWe

Neither blemish this book, nor the leaves double down. *Unknown*. FaBoUs

Neither can you crack a nut. (*LL*) Mountain and the squirrel, the. Emerson. AmPP; AnAmPo; BeLS; BLPL; BoTP; FaBoBe; FaBV; FaPON; GoJo; ImPo; LiTA; MeMAP; NBLV; OBAL; OBCA; TFi

Neither Durst Any Man From That Day Ask Him Any More Questions. Richard Crashaw. ChIV-2

Neither father nor lover. (*LL*) Elegy for Jane. Theodore Roethke. AmPP; CAPP; CoAP; FF; HAP; HCAP; IMW; InPR; InPS; LiTM; MoAB; MoAmPo; NoP; PoE; Poetr; TAP; TFi; TRP; TwCP; WeW

Neither fruit, nor leaf behind thee. (*LL*) Autumnus. Joshua Sylvester. ElL

Neither had said they were going to climb to it. The Source. David Wagoner. VCAP

Neither Here nor There. W. R. Rodgers. ImPo; LiTB; LiTM; MoAB; MoBrPo

Neither in idleness consume thy days. Walter Savage Landor. FaBoEE

Neither legs nor arms have I. The Snake Song. John S. Mbiti. OBAP

Neither love, the subtlety of refinement. The Presence. William Everson. ErPo

Neither of them was better than the other. From Plane to Plane. Robert Frost. MoAmPo

Neither on horseback nor seated. Walt Whitman at Bear Mountain. Louis Simpson. CAPP; LiTM; TRP

Neither our vices nor our virtues. Poetry, a Natural Thing. Robert Duncan. CAPP; NoAM; NOBA; TRP

Neither Out Far nor In Deep. Robert Frost. AmPP; ChTr; HAP; LiTA; MeMAP; MoAB; MoP; NAAL-2; NoAM; NOBA; NoP; Poetr; TAP; TRP; WeW

Neither Poverty nor Riches. Bible, *O.T. Fr*. Proverbs. TrJP

Neither Shadow of Turning. Jack R. Clemo. NOCV

Neither snow, nor rain. On Their Appointed Rounds. *Unknown*. FaPON

Neither the actors nor the audience knew what was coming next. Amnesia. David Lehman. EOEF

Neither the harps nor the crowns amused, nor the. The Return of the Children. Kipling. OBD

Neither the paths determine, nor the goal. The Command. Avraham Huss, *tr. fr. Hebrew by* Ruth Finer Mintz. MHP

Neither war, nor cyclones, nor earthquakes. Antipater of Thessalonica, *tr. fr. Greek by* Kenneth Rexroth. GrAn; PGA

Neither will I put myself forward as others may do. Eternal Masculine. William Rose Benét. AWP; MoAmPo

Neither wish death, nor fear his might. (*LL*) Martial [*or* Marshall *or* My Friend], the thing[e]s that do [*or* for to] attain [*or* attayne]. Martial. SiPSBD

Neither you nor I would imagine gardens. Ogata Kōrin on His Field of Irises. Martha Hollander. UTF

Nell. Raymond Knister. *Fr*. Row of Stalls, A. Mes; NOBC

Nell. Charles Marie René Leconte de Lisle, *tr. fr. French by* Philip L. Miller. RiWo

Nell Gwynne. *Unknown*. FaBoEH

Nellie Bligh caught a fly. *Unknown*. ISE

Nellie Rakerfield. Nell. Raymond Knister. *Fr*. Row of Stalls, A. Mes; NOBC

Nelly Kelly loved baseball games. Take Me Out to the Ball Game. Jack Norworth. OBAL

Nelly, methinks, 'twixt thee and me. To a Cat. Hartley Coleridge. FM

Nelly Trim. Sylvia Townsend Warner. ErPo; MoAB; MoBrPo

Nelson, Pitt, Fox. Sir Walter Scott. *Fr*. Marmion. OBEV

Nelson's Death. *Unknown*. OBET

Nelson's Death and Victory. *Unknown*. OxBSS

Nemea. Lawrence Durrell. FaBoTw; GTBS-P

Nemean Odes, *sels*. Pindar, *tr. fr. Greek by* Richmond Lattimore.

Nemesis. Emerson. NOBA

Neo-Classical Urn, The. Robert Lowell. NAAL-2

Neo-Thomist Poem. Ernest Hemingway. OBAL

Neocolonialism. Felix Mnthali. PeSAV

Neon sign blinked red, A. Something Old, Something New. Carl H. Greene. NBV

Neonbright orange. Robben Island Sequence. Dennis Brutus. HBAPE

Nepenthe, *sels*. George Darley.
 Hundred-gated Thebes. NOBE
 In Dreamy Swoon. OBNC; PeIV
 O Blest Unfabled Incense Tree. BIrV; FaBoCh; FaBoRV

(Hundred-sunned Phenix.) OBNC
(O fast her amber blood doth flow.) OBEV
(Phoenix, The.) ChTr; NOBE; OAEL-2; WiR
Onward to Far Ida. OBNC
"Solitary wayfarer!"
  (Hoopoe.) OBNC
Unicorn, The. ChTr; OBNC; PoEL-4
Nephelidia. Swinburne. *Fr.* Heptalogia, The. BXAP; EnVR; FaBoCo; FaBoNo; FaBoPa; HoPM, *ll.* 1–16; PeVV
Neptune and Mars in council sate. Louisburg. *Unknown.* PAH
Neptune Goes to the Greeks. Homer, *tr. fr. Greek.* *Fr.* Iliad, The. NOSC, *tr. by* George Chapman
Neptune — Polka. Edith Sitwell. NOBE
Neptune's Triumph, *sels.* Ben Jonson.
Ne'r may Prophetique *Daphne* crown my Brow. (*LL*) The Welcome to Sack. Robert Herrick. BeJo; CaPo; SeCP; SeCV-1
Nereides; or, Sea-Eclogues, *sels.* William Diaper.
Nerve pivots and that space, A. Finite Intuition. Milo De Angelis, *tr. fr. Italian by* Lawrence Venuti.
  (?) NeIt
Nerves. David Huddle. *Fr.* Tour of Duty. Son
Nerves. Mark Rudman. PFL
Nerves. "Sagittarius." OxBTC
Nerves. Arthur Symons. FaBoTw
Nervous hose is dribbling on the tar, A. The Roof Garden. Howard Moss. MAT
Nervous Miracles. Jim Gustafson. UL
Nervous Prostration. Anna Wickham. AIW; FaBoWP; VBLP
Nervy with neons, the main drag. At Barstow. Charles Tomlinson. MoP; NoAM; TwCP
Nessun Dorma. Francis Webb. FaBoMA
Nest, The. Marvin Bell. CAPP
Nest, The. Andrew Young. Spl
Nest Eggs. Robert Louis Stevenson. FM
Nest in a Wall, A. Richard Murphy. BiHa; CIP
Nestle-down Cottage. Mary Weston Fordham. CBWP-2
Nests of golden porridge shattered in the silky-oak trees. Equanimity. Les A. Murray. NOBAu
Nests well hidden. Secret Places. Irene Thompson. BoTP
Nestucca River Poem. Tom Crawford. NGP
Nestus Gurley. Randall Jarrell. HeIP; TwCP
Net, A. (*LL*) Notes on the City of the Sun. Bei Dao. SpMi
Net, The. Fleur Adcock. PeNZ
Net, The. W. R. Rodgers. BoLoP; CIP; ErPo; PeIV; PNI
Net and the Sword, The. Douglas Le Pan. NOBC
Net for a Night Raven, A. *Unknown.* OxBSS
Net from my shoulder in the wet forest. Cassibus Impositis Venor. Sebastian Barry. IB
Net of Moon, The. *Unknown, tr. fr. Pawnee Indian by* Jerome K. Rothenberg. STP
Net rests on the water's surface, The. Elena Clementelli, *tr. fr. Italian by* Ruth Feldman *and* Brian Swann. *Fr.* Etruscan Notebook. PBWP
Net to Snare the Moonlight, A. Vachel Lindsay. PoLF
Netherlands, The. Samuel Taylor Coleridge. OBTV
Netley Abbey. William Lisle Bowles. Son
Netley Abbey; Midnight. William Sotheby. NOEC
Nets are real, The. — heroin (sniffed) clears them. For Artaud. Michael McClure. NeAP
Nets to Catch the Wind. John Webster. *See* All the flowers of the spring.
Nettles, The. Thomas Hardy. OxBSP
Nettles in May. Euros Bowen, *tr. fr. Welsh by the author.* OBWVE
Network, The. Arthur Sze. AiP; OpBo
Network of the Imaginary Mother, The, *sels.* Robin Morgan.
  "And this is the fragrance, almost forgotten." CrSp
  "As it was in the beginning." CrSp
  "Blessed be my brain." CrSp
  "Little heart, little heart." CrSp
  Self, The. SRLS
Neurasthenia. Agnes Mary Frances Robinson. NOBVV
Neutral British Gentleman, The. "Orpheus C. Kerr." OBAL
Neutral State, A, *sels.* Thomas McCarthy.
  Lights of Dunleary, The. IB
  Macliammoir at Cappoquin. IB
Neutral Tones. Thomas Hardy. CMoP; EBVV; EnVR; HAP; HeIP; InPK; InPS; MeMBP; MoBrPo; MoP; NAEL-2; NoAM; NOBVV; OAEL-2; PPP; TEP; TFi; UnPo
Neutrality. Sidney Keyes. MoAB; MoBrPo
Neutrality Loathsome. Robert Herrick. ChIV-1; LiTB; NoP
Nevada. Lawrence Gurney. GoYe

Never. George Reavey. BIrV
Never a careworn wife but shows. Wives in the Sere. Thomas Hardy. NOBE; NOBVV
Never a day, never a day passes. Europe's Prisoners. Sidney Keyes. PoWW
Never a ploughman. Never a one. (*LL*) Ha'nacker Mill. Hilaire Belloc. CoGr; FaPoR; MoBrPo; OxBTC; PlP; RB
Never a trial that He is not there. Moment by Moment. Daniel W. Whittle. BLRP
Never able to enter. Farmers. Kathleen Peirce. PBCAP
Never afflict yourself to know the cause. Refrain. Mary Jo Salter. EOEF
Never Again. Richard Henry Stoddard. *See* There Are Gains for All Our Losses.
Never again, Orpheus. Antipater of Sidon, *tr. fr. Greek by* Kenneth Rexroth. GrAn; OBVE; PGA
Never again rising at dawn. A Cock. Anyte, *tr. fr. Greek by* Sally Purcell. GrAn
Never Again to Go to You. Georg Friedrich Daumer, *tr. fr. German by* Philip L. Miller. RiWo
Never Again Would Birds' Song Be the Same. Robert Frost. FYAP; HAP; InPK; NIP; NoAM; NoP; Son; SoSe; VGW
Never and never, my girl riding far and near. In Country Sleep. Dylan Thomas. LiTB
Never any more. In a Year. Robert Browning. CBLP
Never Ask Me Why. Silvia Margolis. GoYe
Never ask of money spent. The Hardship of Accounting. Robert Frost. FaBoCh; FaBoCo; OBAL
Never believe all you hear. Wolf. Kenneth Rexroth. *Fr.* Bestiary, A. NNaP; OBAL
Never believe I leave you. Hiding Our Love. Carolyn Kizer. UnAS
Never, believe me/ Appear the Immortals. The Visit of the Gods. Schiller, *tr. fr. German by* Samuel Taylor Coleridge. OBVE
Never could I think/ Our love a worldly commonplace. Lady Izumi Shikibu, *tr. fr. Japanese by* Edwin A. Cranston. PBWP
Never dies. (*LL*) Rose Solitude. Jayne Cortez. Jaz; VBLP
Never doubt that the world of men can share this knowledge. (*LL*) The Walls of Emerald. Li Shang-yin. PLT
Never — forever! (*LL*) The Old Clock on the Stairs. Longfellow. PWR; WBLP
Never forget who brings the rain. Turn of the Moon. Robert Graves. TEP
Never forgetting him that kept coming constantly so near. (*LL*) The World as Meditation. Wallace Stevens. HeIP; LCAP; MoAB; PPP
Never Get Out! John Galsworthy. OtMeF
Never get up till the sun gets up. Mother Parrot's Advice to Her Children. *Unknown, tr. by* A. K. Nyabongo. OBAP
Never Give a Bum an Even Break. James Welch. NoAM
Never Give All the Heart. W. B. Yeats. BoLoP; CMoP
Never have I seen the sky more clear. Depressed by the Death of the Horse That He Bought from Robert Bly. Henry Taylor. BXAP
Never in My Life. Walter McDonald. MT
Never look back, simply resume. (*LL*) Trial Marriage. Harry Clifton. IB
Never May the Fruit Be Plucked. Edna St. Vincent Millay. NAAL-2; OxBSP
Never mind the clouds which gather. I Have Always Found It So. Birdie Bell. BLRP
Never mind the day we left, or the way the women clung to us. The Klondike. E. A. Robinson. PAH
Never more will the wind. Hilda Doolittle ("H. D."). *Fr.* Hymen. CTC; TrGrPo
Never, my partridge, O patient heart. Partridge. Agathias, *tr. fr. Greek by* Guy Davenport. GrAn
Never, Never Can Nothingness Come. Norma Keating. GoYe
Never, never let your gun. A Rule for Shooting. *Unknown.* FaBoUs
Never, never may the fruit be plucked from the bough. Never May the Fruit Be Plucked. Edna St. Vincent Millay. NAAL-2; OxBSP
Never, never would she wear out. (*LL*) Vocation. Judith Herzberg. WPOW
Never on this side of the grave again. A Life's Parallels. Christina Rossetti. MeMBP; NAEL-2; PoEL-5
Never once — since the world began. God's Sunshine. John Oxenham. WBLP
Never our lips, our hands. (*LL*) Evening Song. Sidney Lanier. AnAmPo; UnPo
Never Pain to Tell Thy Love. Blake. *See* Never Seek to Tell Thy Love.
Never pass a nun. How to Walk in a Crowd. Robert Hershon. FF
Never presume that in this marble stable. The Brass Horse. Drummond Allison. FaBoTw
Never Said a Mumbalin' Word. *Unknown.* GBP
Never saw him. The Negro. James A. Emanuel. HoPM; InPK

Never Say Fail. *Unknown.* PWR

Never Seek to Tell Thy Love. John Ashbery. HCAP; InPS

Never Seek to Tell Thy Love. Blake. CBLP; ELP; EnLoPo; EnRP; FaBV; InPS; NOBE; OBNC; PoEL-4; SCGP

Never shall a young man. For Anne Gregory. W. B. Yeats. CMoP; ImPo; LiTM; MeMBP; NAEL-2; OxAEP-2; Poetr; SOTW

Never shepherd sung the like. (*LL*) On a hill there grows a flower. Nicholas Breton. EiL

Never such innocence again. (*LL*) MCMXIV. Philip Larkin. EBEV; FaBoEH; NAEL-2; NoAM; NSI; OBWP; OxAEP-2

Never Such Love. Robert Graves. BoLoP

Never talk down to a glowworm. Glowworm. David McCord. NTCP

Never Tell. *Unknown,* tr. fr. *Welsh by* Anthony Conran. OBWVE

Never the Time and the Place. Robert Browning. EnLoPo

Never the tramp of foot or horse. Farewell to Anactoria. Sappho, tr. fr. *Greek by* Allen Tate. AWP

Never think she loves him wholly. Appraisal. Sara Teasdale. MoAmPo

Never think you fortune can bear the sway. On Fortune. Elizabeth I, Queen of England. PBWP; WPE

Never to be lonely like that. Face to Face. Adrienne Rich. LiTM; NAAL-2; NoAM; NoP

Never to part more. (*LL*) Meeting. Christina Rossetti. CBLP; GBL; Mes

Never to rise again, oh! (*LL*) Open the Door to Me, Oh! Burns. PoEL-4; SCGP

Never to see a nation born. James Russell Lowell. *Fr.* Under the Old Elm. GOA

Never to see ghosts? Then to be. Ghosts. Alastair Reid. NYBP

Never to see her or hear her. Sigh. Sully-Prudhomme, tr. fr. *French by* Philip L. Miller. RiWo

Never Too Late., *sels.* Robert Greene.
Palmer's Ode, The. CTC; EnRePo; NoSic; SCGP

Never too many fish in a swift creek, Jalal al-Din Rumi, tr. by John Moyne *and* Coleman Barks. *Fr.* Three Quatrains. RaBo

Never trust any woman more than you know. (*LL*) Lord, when I think. *Unknown.* CBLP

Never twice that river. By the River Eden. Kathleen Raine. NYBP

Never until the mankind making. A Refusal to Mourn the Death, by Fire, of a Child in London. Dylan Thomas. BLPL; CMoP; EBEV; FaBoMo; FF; GTBS-P; HeIP; HoPM; ImPo; LiTB; LiTM; MeMBP; MoAB; MoBrPo; MoP; NoAM; NOBE; NoP; OAEL-2; OBWVE; OxAEP-2; OxBTC; PAW; PoE; PoWW; TEP; TFi; TwCP; UnPo

Never was always will be. First Song / Bankei / 1653 /. Stephen Berg. BAP-90

Never we needed Thee so sore. In Time of Need. Katharine Tynan. TrPWD

Never weather-beaten sail[e] more willing bent to shore. Thomas Campion. ChTr; EiL; OAEL-1; OxAEP-1; OxBSP; PoEL-2
(O Come Quickly!) NOBE; OBEV

Never without ill-fame to him who gives her birth. (*LL*) Lausanne. Thomas Hardy. FaBoRV; FaBoTw; OBTV

Never would I seek. Lines to a Sophisticate. Mae V. Cowdery. ShDr

Never Your Captive! (*LL*) Blues Note. Bob Kaufman. PoBA

Never Your Captive! (*LL*) How High the Moon. Lance Jeffers. PoBA

Nevermore/ Shall the shepherds of Arcady follow. The God-Maker, Man. Don Marquis. WGRP

Nevermore shall you leave this wood! (*LL*) Dialogue in the Forest. Joseph Freiherr von Eichendorff. RiWo

Nevertheless. Gustav Davidson. GoYe

Nevertheless. Marianne Moore. CMoP; MeMAP; MoAB; NAAL-2; OxBA; SoSe

Nevertheless I prefer. . . . 1968 . . . . Petra von Morstein, tr. fr. *German by* Rosemarie Waldrop. BoWoP

Nevertheless you've seen a strawberry. Nevertheless. Marianne Moore. CMoP; MoAB; OxBA; SoSe

New. William Matthews. FoLa

New Age, The. Stevie Smith. NAEL-2

New air has come around us. Dakota: October, 1822, Hunkpapa Warrior. Rod Taylor. WeW

New Ancient of Days, The. Herman Melville. OBAL

New; and you. E. E. Cummings. *See* She Being Brand.

New Apartment, Minneapolis, The. Linda Hogan. HATNAP

New Approach Needed. Kingsley Amis. NoAM; OxBTC

New Ark Space. Amiri Baraka. *Fr.* Poem of Destiny, A. NGP

New Army Education. *Unknown.* NSI

New Ballad, A. Arthur Mainwaring. APAS

New Ballad, A ("I'm a senseless thing"). *Unknown.* APAS

New Ballad, A ("Rouse, Britons! at lengh"). *Unknown.* PAH

New Ballad, to an Old Tune, Called, I Am the Duke of Norfolk, A. *Unknown.* APAS

New Ballade of the Marigolde, A. William Forrest. CoMu

New Balow, The. *Unknown.* CoMu

New Bamboo in the North Garden at Ch'ang-ku. Li Ho, tr. fr. *Chinese by* Irving Y. Lo. SuSp

New Bath Guide, The, *sels.* Christopher Anstey.
"Hearken, Lady Betty, hearken." NOEC
"This morning, dear mother, as soon as 'twas light." ECEV

New Birth, The. Jones Very. NOBA

New Brooms. Robert Wilson. *Fr.* Three Ladies of London, The. EiL

New Bundling Song, A. *Unknown.* ErPo

New Bury Loom, The. *Unknown. See* As I walked between Bolton and Bury.

New Canaans Genius; Epilogus. Thomas Morton. SCAP

New Cantata, A. Clara Reeve. ECWP

New Carpentry. Chris Wallace-Crabbe. FaBoMA

New Catch in Praise of the Reverend Bishops, A. *Unknown.* APAS; FaBoEH

New Cecilia, The. Thomas Lovell Beddoes. OAEL-2

New Chitons for Old Gods, *sels.* David McCord.

New-Chum's First Trip, The. *Unknown.* FaBoBa

New Church Organ, The. Will M. Carleton. PoLF

New cinematic emporium, The. *Unknown.* PeLi

New Coasts and Poseidon's Son. Homer, tr. by Robert Fitzgerald. *Fr.* Odyssey. NAWM-1; WTO

New Colossus, The. Emma Lazarus. AiP; AmWP; FaBV; FaPON; PoLF; PrIm; Son; WPE

New-come buckra/ He get sick. *Unknown. Fr.* Songs. PBCV

New-come Chief, The. James Russell Lowell. *Fr.* Under the Old Elm. PAH

New Courtly Sonnet of the Lady Greensleeves, A. *Unknown. See* Alas! my love, you [*or* ye] do me wrong.

New Courtly Sonnet of the Lady Greensleeves, A. *Unknown. See* Greensleeves.

New Cup and Saucer, A. Gertrude Stein. *Fr.* Tender Buttons. TTTS

New curtains darken the room all day. Clouds and Windows. Andrew Crozier. VaA

New-dated from the terms that reappear. To Oxford. Gerard Manley Hopkins. FaBoPP

New Dawn, The. Mafika Pascal Gwala. PeSAV

New Day, The, *sels.* Richard Watson Gilder.
"Night was dark, though sometimes a faint star, The." PoLF

New Day. Naomi Long Madgett. BlSi

New decade, the teacher cried, A. My Mother's Young Sister. Roy McFadden. PNI

New Dial, The. *Unknown.* OBET

New Diary, A. Dannie Abse. AngWe; NoAM

New Dodo: Isabrand's Song, The. Thomas Lovell Beddoes. CBNP

New doth the sun appear. Change Should Breed Change. William Drummond of Hawthornden. OBEV

New Dress, A. Ruth Dallas. TSaS

New Dress, The. Tony Flynn. PWE

New Duckling, The. Alfred Noyes. BoTP; FaPON

New Emigration, The. Kay Boyle. WPE

New England. Anne Bradstreet. *Fr.* Dialogue between Old England and New, A. KTR

New England. E. A. Robinson. GOA; HeIP; MeMAP; MoAB; MoAmPo; NAAL-2; NOBA; NoP; OxBA; PFP; TAP

New England Bachelor, A. Richard Eberhart. MoAmPo; NoAM

New-England Boy's Song about Thanksgiving Day, The. Lydia Maria Child. *See* Over the river and through the wood.

New England Church, A. Wilson Agnew Barrett. WGRP

New England Is New England Is New England. Brenda Heloise Green. GoYe

New England Primer, The, *sels. Unknown.*
"In Adam's fall/ We sinned all." OBCA
(ABC, An.) GBP
John Rogers' Exhortation to His Children. OBCA

New England Sampler, A. John Malcolm Brinnin. GOA

New England Verses, *sels.* Wallace Stevens.

New England's Annoyances. *Unknown.* PAH

New England's Chevy Chase. Edward Everett Hale. PAH

New-Englands Crisis. Benjamin Tompson. SCAP

New England's Growth. William Bradford. PAH

New England's Mountain-child. Frances Sargent Osgood. AmWP

New English Canaan; Prologue. Thomas Morton. SCAP

New every morning. John Keble. FaPoR

New every morning is the love. Prime. Donald Davie. *Fr.* Horae Canonicae. CRP

New every morning now the clerk docks off. Summer Holidays. W. R. Rodgers. LiTB

New Ezekiel, The. Emma Lazarus. AmWP

New Face. Alice Walker. AIW

New Faces, The. W. B. Yeats. GTBS-P

New Farm Tractor. Carl Sandburg. FaPON

New-fashioned Farmer, The. *Unknown.* OBET

New Fashions. George Moses Horton. OBAL

New feet within my garden go — . Emily Dickinson. MeMAP

New follies spring; and now we must be taught. Picturesque; a Fragment. John Aikin. NOEC

New Friends and Old Friends. Joseph Parry. BLPA; BLPL; PoToHe

New from Ethiopia and the Sudan, The. J. P. Clark Bekedereme. HBAPE

New Garden Fields. *Unknown.* OBET

New God, The. Witter Bynner. *Fr.* New World, The. WGRP

New God, The. James Oppenheim. WGRP

New Guinea. James McAuley. NOCV

New Guinea Time. Louis Johnson. PeNZ

New Hampshire. T. S. Eliot. *Fr.* Landscapes. FaBoCh; GTBS-P; NoAM; RB; WeW

New Hampshire, *sels.* Robert Frost.
  "If I must choose which I would elevate." UV

New Hampshire. Donald Hall. LCAP

New Hampshire Farm Woman. Rachel Graham. GoYe

New Hampshire, February. Richard Eberhart. LiTM; TwCP

New Heart, The. *Unknown, tr. fr. Chinese.* WGRP

New Heaven and Earth. D. H. Lawrence. CMoP

New Heaven, New War[re]. Robert Southwell. ChIV-2; ESCV; NOBE; NoP

New Holland is a barren place, in it there grows no grain. The Lowlands of Holland. *Unknown.* OxBB

New House, A. Bertolt Brecht, *tr. fr. German by* Michael Hamburger. AnAn

New House, The. Vern Rutsala. GOYP

New House, The. Edward Thomas. EBEV; MoAB; MoBrPo; NOBE; OBEV; OBWVE

New Household, A. Longfellow. *Fr.* Hanging of the Crane, The. GN

New Hunting Song, A. *Unknown.* CoMu; OBET

New Hymns for Solitude, *sels.* Edward Dowden.
  "I found Thee in my heart, O Lord." TrPWD

New Improved Sonnet XVIII. Peter Titheradge. FaBoPa

New Incidents in the Life of Shelley, *sels.* Robert Johnstone.
  "Not from our dreams, not from our daft cadres." PNI

New Indian Medicine. Emma Lee Warrior. HATNAP

New Inn, The, *sels.* Ben Jonson.
  It Was a Beauty That I Saw. BeJo
  (Lovel's Song.) TrGrPo
  (Vision of Beauty.) NOSC

New Jail. *Unknown.* AmFP

New Jersey. Will Bennett. UL

New Jersey Turnpike. Richard Cumbie. NBLV

New Jerusalem, The. Bible, *N.T. Fr.* Revelation. TrGrPo

New Jerusalem, The. Blake. *See* And Did Those Feet in Ancient Time.

New Jerusalem, The. Allan M. Laing. UV

New Jerusalem, The. *Unknown. See* Hierusalem, my happy [*or* happie] home.

New Jewish Hospital at Hamburg, The. Heine, *tr. fr. German by* Charles Godfrey Leland. TrJP

"New King Arrives in His Capital by Air . . . " — Daily Newspaper. Sir John Betjeman. OxBoLi

New Knighthood, The. Kipling. UV

New knowledge of reality, A. (*LL*) Not Ideas about the Thing but the Thing Itself. Wallace Stevens. HAP; HCAP; LCAP; MeMAP; SAmP; TAP

New Leaf, A [*or* The]. *At. to* Helen Field Fischer, *at. to* Kathleen Wheeler. BLRP; PoToHe; WBLP

New Life. Joseph E. Kariuki. TTY

New Light, A. William Hawkins. MoCV

New light gives new directions, fortunes new. George Chapman. *Fr.* Hero and Leander. AAS; NoP; NoSic; OAEL-1

New light on a slant. Pouring. Making everything new, The. (*LL*) Water./ Lakes and rivers. Paula Gunn Allen. EaPr

New Lines for Cuscuscaraway and Mirza Murad Ali Beg. Louis Simpson. OBAL

New Litany, The. Rita Mae Brown. PeHV

New Litany in the Year 1684, A. *Unknown.* APAS

New Litany, Occasioned by an Invitation to a Wedding, A. Elizabeth Thomas. ECWP

New Little Boy, The. Harry Behn. TLR

New little boy moved in next door, A. The New Little Boy. Harry Behn. TLR

New little foxes are shivering in the rain, The/ Step softly. (*LL*) Four Little Foxes. Lew Sarett. FaPON; PDV; RFM

New London, The. Dryden. *Fr.* Annus Mirabilis. FaBoCh

New Love and the Gentle Heart. Dante. RaBo

New love and the gentle heart are the same thing. New Love and the Gentle Heart. Dante. RaBo

New Man, The. Jones Very. NOBA

New man flies in from Manchester, A. A New Poet Arrives. Gavin Ewart. OxBTC

New man in the ovens., the. (*LL*) A Black Man. Sam Cornish. PoBA

New Married Couple; or, A Friendly Debate between the Country Farmer and His Buxome Wife, The. *Unknown.* CoMu

New Maths. Tom Lehrer. FaBoUs

New mercies, new blessings, new light on the way. A New Year Wish. Frances Ridley Havergal. BLRP

New Mexican Mountain. Robinson Jeffers. GOA; InPS; MoP; NoAM

New Mistress, The. A. E. Housman. *Fr.* Shropshire Lad, A. FaPoB; MoBrPo

New Moon. *Aborigine Oral Tradition, tr. by* R. M. Berndt. *Fr.* Moon-Bone Song [*or* Cycle]. CBAP; WTO

New Moon. D. H. Lawrence. BoNaP

New moon hangs like an ivory bugle, The. The Penny Whistle. Edward Thomas. MoAB; MoBrPo

New moon has come up and the autumn dew is light, A. Song of Autumn Night. Wang Yu, *tr. fr. Chinese by* Irving Y. Lo. SuSp

New moon, new moon, I hail thee! *Unknown.* FaBoUs

New moon, of no importance, The. New Moon. D. H. Lawrence. BoNaP

New Morality, *sels.* George Canning *and* John Hookham Frere.
  "From mental mists to purge a nation's eyes." NOEC
  "Give me the avowed, erect and manly foe." OBF

New Mother. Sharon Olds. CrSp

New-mown hay smell and wind of the plain. Population Drifts. Carl Sandburg. OxBA

New Music. Gwen Harwood. CBAP

New National Hymn. Francis Marion Crawford. PAH

New Navigation, The. John Freeth. OBET

New Negro, The. James Edward McCall. CDC

New Negro Sermon. Jacques Roumain, *tr. fr. French by* Ellen Conroy Kennedy. NegPo

New Night Thoughts on Death; a Parody. William Whitehead. NOEC

New Notebook, The. Maria Banus, *tr. fr. Romanian by* Laura Schiff *and* Dana Beldiman. AIW; PBWP

New Nutcracker Suite, The, *sels.* Ogden Nash.
  "Little girl marched around her Christmas tree, A." PChr

New Orleans. Maxine Cassin. *Fr.* Three Love Poems by a Native. Jaz

New Orleans. Joy Harjo. HATNAP

New parties in the corporate hill. (*LL*) Indians at the Guthrie. Gerald Vizenor. VoR

New Pastoral, The, *sels.* Thomas Buchanan Read.
  Blennerhassett's Island. PAH

New peach blossoms are glowing, The. Flying Petals. Hsiao Kang, *tr. fr. Chinese by* Kenneth Rexroth. OHMPC

New penny vanishing over my head, A. (*LL*) Crabbing for Blue-claws. James Ulmer. UTF

New periods of pain. (*LL*) Pain — has an element of blank. Emily Dickinson. HeIP; LiTA; LiTM; MoAB; MoAmPo; NAAL-1; PPP

New Pietà: For the Mothers and Children of Detroit, The. June Jordan. PoBA

New Poem, A. Robert Duncan. NNaP; PoM

New Poem, The. Charles Wright. CAPP; HCAP

New Poet Arrives, A. Gavin Ewart. OxBTC

New presbyter is but old priest writ large. (*LL*) On the New Forcers of Conscience Under the Long Parliament. Milton. FaBoEH; FaBoPV; NAEL-1; NOSC; Son

New Prince, New Pomp[e]. Robert Southwell. ELP; ESCV; GN; NOBE; NOCV; NoSic; OHIP; TrCP

New Proverb. Shirley Brooks. FaBoNo

New Reality Is Better Than a New Movie!, A. Amiri Baraka. NoAM

New Reforms, The. Jack Roberts. BAP-91

New Refugee, A. Marisella Veiga. LoHo

New River Head, a Fragment, The. E. Dower. NOEC

New road runs into, The. Directions. William Matthews. AmPA

New road unfolds from the heart of downtown, The. The Change to One-Way after Repaving. Richard Robbins. NGP

New Roof, The. Francis Hopkinson. PAH

New Rule, The. Jalal al-Din Rumi, *tr. fr. Persian* by Coleman Barks. RaBo

New Saddhus, The. Robert Pinsky. NAmP90

New St. Louis Blues. Sterling A. Brown. Jaz

New Sculptor, A. Julia Ward Howe. AmWP

New Sea Song. *Unknown.* OxBSS

New Season. Michael S. Harper. CAPP

New season brought sure the visible good. Restoration. Woodridge Spears. GoYe

New Shoes. John Agard. OTCP

New shoes, new shoes. Choosing Shoes. Ffrida Wolfe. PYC

New Sights. *Unknown.* BoTP

New-slain Knight, The. *Unknown.* ESPB

New Song, A. Seamus Heaney. CIP; FaBoTw

New Song, A. Joseph Stansbury. PAH

New Song, A. *Unknown.* PAH

New Song, A. Thomas, Lord Wharton. *See* Ho! brother [*or* broder] Teague, dost hear de decree.

New Song called The Curling of the Hair, A. *Unknown.* CoMu

New Song, Called the Frolicsome Sea Captain; or, Tit for Tat, A. *Unknown.* OxBSS

New Song Called the Gaspee, A. *Unknown.* PAH

New Song Called the *Victory*, A, *with music. Unknown.* OxBSS

New Song Composed on the Death of Lord Nelson, A. *Unknown. See* Come all gallant [*or* you gallant] seamen that unite a meeting.

New Song Entitled the Warming Pan, A. *Unknown.* CoMu

New Song of an Orange, A. *Unknown.* CoMu; FaBoEH

New Song of Mary, A. *Unknown.* MeEL

New Song of New Similies, A. John Gay. CBNP; FaBoCo; NOBL

New Song of Wood's Halfpence, A. *At. to* Swift Swift. OxBoLi

New Song on the Birth of the Prince of Wales, A. *At. to* John Harkness. CoMu; FaBoBa; FaBoEH; NOBVV

New Song on the *Blandford* Privateer, A, *with music. Unknown.* OxBSS

New Song on the Taxes, A. *Unknown.* WTO

New Song on the Total Defeat of the French Fleet, A,. *Unknown.* OxBSS

New Song to an Old Tune, A. *Unknown.* PAH

New songs of Praise to CHRIST our KING. (*LL*) Once More, Our God, Vouchsafe to Shine! Samuel Sewall. AH

New Speaker. James Berry. NBrP

New Spoon River, The, *sels.* Edgar Lee Masters.
    Benjamin Franklin Hazard. GOA
    Marx the Sign Painter. NoAM; TAP
    Meredith Phyfe. GOA
    Unknown Soldiers, A. NoAM; TAP

New Spring, A. Albert D. Mackie. OxBS

New Strain. George Starbuck. TwCP

New Style, The. David O'Bruadair, *tr. fr. Irish* by John Montague. BIrV

New styles of architecture, a change of heart. (*LL*) Petition. W. H. Auden. CMoP; LiTB; MeMAP; NAEL-2; Son

New Suit, The. Nidia Sanabria de Romero, *tr. fr. Spanish.* TSaS, *tr. by* Arnaldo D. Larrosa Morán *with* Naomi Shihab Nye

New Tarantella. Paul Griffin. UV

New Tenants, The. E. A. Robinson. NoAM

New Territory. Eavan Boland. PeIV

New Testament, The. *Unknown.* FaBoUs

New things for the word's caress. (*LL*) A Sweet Disorder in the Dress. Harry Hooton. NOBAu

New things succeed, as former things grow old. (*LL*) Ceremonies for Candlemas[se] Eve. Robert Herrick. BeJo; CaPo; JCP

New ties, fifteen each, ten. Ties. Raymond Souster. MoCV

New Time. *Unknown.* BLRP

New Vestments, The. Edward Lear. NOBVV

New Vicar of Bray, The. Colin Ellis. NOBL

New Victory, The. Margaret Widdemer. WGRP

New volcano has erupted, A. Crusoe in England. Elizabeth Bishop. FaBoVe; HCAP

New War Song by Sir Peter Parker, A. *Unknown.* PAH

New Wife. *Gond Oral Tradition, tr. by* V. Elwin *and* S. Hivale. WTO

New Wife, The. Ng Shao, *tr. fr. Chinese* by Kenneth Rexroth. OHMPC

New Wings for Icarus, *sels.* Henry Beissel.
    "In the one-two domestic goose one-two one-two step." MoCV

New Words, *sels.* Coleman Barks.
    "So it is." CRP

New World, The. Amiri Baraka. NoAM; NoP

New World, The, *sels.* Louis James Block.
    Final Struggle, The. PAH

New World, The, *sels.* Witter Bynner.

New God, The. WGRP

New World. Sally Roberts Jones. AngWe

New World, The, *sels.* Edgar Lee Masters.

New World. Derek Walcott. OxBC

New World, A. Shelley. *See* World's great age begins anew, The.

New World Symphony, A. Kit Wright. NBLV; PeLV

New Year, The. Homera Homer-Dixon. BLRP

New Year. Naomi Shihab Nye. MT

New Year, The. Horatio Nelson Powers. *See* Flower unblown; a book unread; A.

New Year. Stephen Spender. AWP

New Year, The. Mark Strand. *Fr.* Elegy for My Father. HCAP; LCAP; UnPo

New Year, The ("Here we bring new water"). *Unknown. See* Here we bring new water.

New Year, The ("I am the live New Year"). *Unknown.* BoTP

New Year Ballad. "Anna Akhmatova." OBF

New-year bells are wrangling with the snow, The. (*LL*) Year's End. Richard Wilbur. CAPP; CoAP; HeIP; LiTM; NAAL-2; SM

New Year Carol, A. *Unknown.* BoTP; CH; OxBoLi

New year, forth looking out of Janus' gate. Spenser. *Fr.* Amoretti. AAS; ESo, lacking epigrams I–IV; HeIL; NoSic

New Year Gift to the Queen Mary When She First Came Home, 1562, A. Alexander Scott. ScCV

New year has dawned and we meet it with gladness, The. New Year's Morning; or, the First Day of the Year. Mrs. Henry Linden. CBWP-4

New Year Letter., *sels.* W. H. Auden.
    "Long time since it seems to-day, A." GOA
    "Our news is seldom good: the heart." FaBoRV
    "Self-educated WILLIAM BLAKE." EPCY

New Year on Dartmoor. Sylvia Plath. FaBoWP

New Year Party. Matthew Sweeney. IB

New Year Wish, A. Frances Ridley Havergal. BLRP

New Year Wish, A. *Unknown.* BLRP

New yeares, expect new gifts: Sister, your Harpe. Ben Jonson. SeCP

New-Yeares-Gift Sung to King Charles, 1635, A. Ben Jonson. SeCP

New Year's. (Solid houses in the mist, The.) Charles Reznikoff. VGW *Sels.*

New Year's Carol. *Unknown.* OBET

New Year's Day. Richard Crashaw. JCP

New Year's Day. Robert Lowell. AmPP; LiTM; TRP

New Year's Day Song. Nahum Tate. FaBoEH

New Year's Days. Celia Standish. BoTP

New Year's Eve. John Berryman. LiTM

New Year's Eve. Boethius, *tr. fr. Latin. Fr.* Consolation of Philosophy, The. MLL, *tr. by* Helen Waddell

New Year's Eve., *sels.* John Davidson.
    Imagination. ArNa; MeMBP; MoBrPo

New Year's Eve. Thomas Hardy. MoBrPo; NoAM

New Year's Eve. D. H. Lawrence. BoLoP; ErPo

New Year's Eve. David Trinidad. BAP-91

New Year's Eve in Solitude. Robert Mezey. NaP

New Year's Eve Poem 1965. Peter Levi. OxAEP-2

New Year's Gift, A. William Cartwright. BeJo

New Year's Gift, A. William Cartwright. *See* Now that the Village-Reverence doth lye [*or* lie] hid.

New-Year's Gift Sent to Sir Simeon Steward, A. Robert Herrick. CaPo

New-Years-Gift to Brian Lord Bishop of Sarum, A. William Cartwright.

New Year's Morning; or, the First Day of the Year. Mrs. Henry Linden. CBWP-4

New Year's Poem. Margaret Avison. LiTM; NOBC

New Year's Promise, A. *Unknown.* BLRP

New Year's Sacrifice: To Lucinda, A. Thomas Carew. CaPo

New Year's [*or* Year] Song. Ted Hughes. OBCP

New Year's Water. *See* Here we bring new water.

New Year's Wish, A. "J. H. S." BLRP

New Year's Wishes. Frances Ridley Havergal. BLRP

New-Yeeres Gift, or Circumcisions Song, Sung to the King in the Presence at White Hall, The. Robert Herrick. SeCV-1

New York. "Æ." OBMV

New York. Federico García Lorca, *tr. fr. Spanish* by Robert Bly. NU; RaBo

New York, *sels.* A. Leyeles, *tr. fr. Yiddish* by Benjamin *and* Barbara Harshav.

New York. William Logan. EOEF

New York. Marianne Moore. NAAL-2

New York. Léopold Sédar-Senghor. *See* New York! At first I was confused by your beauty, by those great golden long-legged girls.

New York! At first I was confused by your beauty, by those great golden long-legged girls. To New York. Léopold Sédar-Senghor, *tr. fr. French by Ulli Beier.* PBA

(New York.) Jaz

(New York! At first I was confused by your beauty, those tall long-legged golden girls.) NegPo, *tr. by Ellen Conroy Kennedy*

New York! At first I was confused by your beauty, those tall long-legged golden girls. Léopold Sédar-Senghor. *See* New York! At first I was confused by your beauty, by those great golden long-legged girls.

New York City. George Abbe. GoYe

New York City. Helen Waddell. MLL

New York City Mira Mira Blues. Gloria Vando. LoHo

New York City 1970. Audre Lorde. NBV

New York City — 1935. Gregory Corso. Poetsp

New York City World's Fairs, 1939 and 1964, The. Judith Baumel. UTF

New York Everywhere., *sels.* Berysh Vaynshteyn, *tr. fr. Yiddish by Benjamin and Barbara Harshav.*

New York has had it, newsmen all proclaim. New York Sonnet. Judith Rodriguez. NOBAu

New York Sonnet. Judith Rodriguez. NOBAu

New York Woman, The. L. E. Sissman. MAT

New Zealand. James K. Baxter. NoP

Newark Abbey. Thomas Love Peacock. NOBE; OBNC; PlP

Newark, for Now (68). Carolyn M. Rodgers. PoBA

Newark Public Library Reading Room, The. Sotère Torregian. NBV

Newberry. *Unknown.* AmFP

Newborn greylag geese follow anyone who moves. The Romance of Imprinting. Christy Sheffield Sanford. UL

Newborn, on the naked sand. *Unknown, tr. fr. Grande Pueblo Indian by Mary Austin.* EaPr

(Song for the Newborn.) WPE

Newcombe at the Croydon Gallery. Arthur Nortje. HBAPE

Newcomer's Wife, The. Thomas Hardy. BoLoP; OxBTC

Newer headstones tense against the cold, The. Churchyard under Snow. David Scott. PWE

Newes from Virginia. Richard Rich. PAH

Newest Banana Plant Leaf, The. Ingrid Wendt. NMM

Newgate's Garland. John Gay. ECEV; FaBoBa; PeLV

Newletter from My Mother. Michael S. Harper. PoBA

Newly Discovered "Homeric" Hymn, A. Charles Olson. MoP; NeAP; NoAM; PoM

Newly Pressed Suit, The. Roger McGough. MoP

Newly shaven, your eyes only slightly bloodshot. Desires. Connie Bensley. FaBoWP

Newlyweds, The. Cloyd Mann Criswell. PoLF

Newmarket Song, The. *Unknown.* APAS

Newport, 1930. Herbert Morris. PRA

News. Louis Dudek. *Fr. Provincetown.* MoCV

News, The. Tuini Ngawai, *tr. fr. Maori by Kumeroa Ngoingoi Pewhairangi.* PeNZ

News, The. John Godfrey Saxe. NBLV

News. Thomas Traherne. *Fr. Third Century, The.* NOBE; OBEV; SeCV-2

News for the Delphic Oracle. W. B. Yeats. CMoP; FaBoMo; LiTB; LiTM; MeMBP; NoAM

News from a foreign [*or* forein *or* forrein] country came. News. Thomas Traherne. *Fr. Third Century, The.* NOBE; OBEV; SeCV-2

(On News.) ESCV; GeHe

News from a Pacified Area. James K. Baxter. OxBC

News from abroad does a secret reveal, The. An Excellent New Song Called "Mat's Peace." Arthur Mainwaring. APAS

News from Mount Amiata. Robert Lowell, *tr. fr. Italian by Eugenio Montale.* NaP

News from Norwood. Christopher Middleton. FaBoMo; PRA

News from the Cabin. May Swenson. NYBP

News from the House. Michael Dennis Browne. NYBP

News from Yorktown. Lewis Worthington Smith. PAH

News, Indeed! — pray do you call it news, The. The News. John Godfrey Saxe. NBLV

News is of camps, outpost, little progress, The. Lecturing on the Theme of Motherhood. Michael S. Harper. AnAn

News Item. Dorothy Parker. *Fr. Some Beautiful Letters.* FaBoUs; NALW; OBAL

News of Dorham's, The. Elegy for Kenny Dorham. Joel Wolk. Jaz

News of the Occluded Cyclone. Alice Fulton. WeW

News of the palace. Lady Ise, *tr. fr. Japanese by Etsuko Terasaki and Irma Brandeis.* BoWoP

News of the Phoenix. A. J. M. Smith. MoCV

News of the World I ("Cold shuttered loveless star, skulker in clouds.") George Barker. LiTB; MeMBP

News of the World II. George Barker. FaBoTw; LiTB

News of the World III. George Barker. FaBoTw; LiTB; LiTM

News Photos of Bombed Children. Rose Graubart. WoWa

News Reel. David Ross. GoYe

News Report. David Ignatow. ErPo; TwCP

Newspaper is a collection of half injustices, A. A Newspaper [Is a Collection of Half-Injustices]. Stephen Crane. *Fr.* War Is Kind. AmPP; MeMAP; NAAL-2

Newspaper [Is a Collection of Half-Injustices], A. Stephen Crane. *Fr.* War Is Kind. AmPP; MeMAP; NAAL-2

Newspapers aged the couch. Marina Tsvetayeva. Derek Walcott. AnAn

Newsreel. C. Day Lewis. MoAB; MoBrPo

Newsreel. Adrienne Rich. *Fr.* Shooting Script. FaBoWP; HCAP

Newsvendor with his hut and crutch, The. The Imprisoned. Robert Fitzgerald. TwCP

Newton to Einstein. Jeannette Chappell. GoYe

Newton's Statue. Wordsworth. *See* Evangelist St. John my patron was, The.

Next Act, The. Debora Greger. *Fr.* Afterlife, The. BAP-91

Next after comes coyote, Stretched-out-in-Dew. Scalp Dance Song. *Unknown, tr. fr. Tewa Indian by H. J. Spinden.* WTO

Next bidding all draw near on bended knees. Idle Pursuits. Pope. *Fr.* Dunciad, The. ECEV; OBSV

Next came one/ Who mourn'd in earnest. Milton. *Fr.* Paradise Lost. EBEV; EPCY

Next comes the dull disciple of thy school. Byron. *Fr.* English Bards and Scotch Reviewers. EPCY

Next conquest shall be thine, The. (LL) A Song of Dalliance. William Cartwright. ErPo; JCP; NOSC

Next darkness already forming inside it, The. (LL) The Man on the Hotel Room Bed. Galway Kinnell. VCAP

Next Day. Randall Jarrell. HAP; HCAP; MoP; NAAL-2; NoAM; NoP; NYBP; Poetr; VCAP; WeW

Next day I couldn't remember his name, The. The Dragon Lady Considers Dinner. Colleen J. McElroy. BCF

Next day they rambled round the town, and swore. James Bisset. *Fr.* Ramble of the Gods through Birmingham. NOEC

Next died the Lady, who yon Hall possess'd. The Lady of the Manor. George Crabbe. *Fr.* Parish Register, The. NOBE; OAEL-1, *abr.;* OBNC

Next grand adjunct to our Hero's cause, The. The Electric Telegraph. Thomas Baker. *Fr.* Steam Engine; or, The Power of the Flame, The. FaBoUs

Next Heaven, my vows to thee, O sacred Muse! Upon the Saying That My Verses Were Made by Another. Anne Killigrew. KTR; NALW; WPE

Next him Jack Squire through his own tear-drops sploshes. Roy Campbell. *Fr.* Georgiad, The. OxBTC

Next, in a low-browed cave, a little hell. William Thompson. *Fr.* Sickness. ECEV

Next is your lot, fair, to be numbered one. To His Kinswoman, Mistress Penelope Wheeler. Robert Herrick. CaPo

Next millennium you'll have to search quite hard. Five. Tony Harrison. PWE

Next, Please. Philip Larkin. MoBrPo

Next Poem, The. Dana Gioia. DiPo

Next step up is sky, The. (LL) How To Tell the Top of a Hill. John Ciardi. SiSoPo

Next Story, The. Pattiann Rogers. NAmP90

Next Table, The. C. P. Cavafy, *tr. fr. Greek by John Mavrogordato.* PeHV

Next These, a troop of busy [*or* buisy] spirits press. John Dryden *and* Nahum Tate. *Fr.* Absalom and Achitophel, Pt. II. PPP; SeCV-2

Next they leave it leagues behind, The. (LL) Anno 1829. Heine. AWP; OBVE

Next thing, I wake up in a swaying bunk. Journey: the North Coast. Robert Gray. FaBoMA

Next time 1930 rolls around. (LL) This One's on Me. Phyllis Gotlieb. MoCV; NOBC

Next to my best friend I woke up. Old-fashioned. Dara Wier. NAmP90

Next to my counsels an attention pay. Hesiod, *tr. fr. Greek by Thomas Cooke. Fr.* Works and Days. FaBoUs

Next to of Course God America I. E. E. Cummings. *See* Next to of course god america i.

Next to of course god america i. E. E. Cummings. AmPP; FaBoPV; HeIL; InPK; LiTM; MeMAP; NAAL-2; NBLV; NoP; OBWP; OPOP; OxBA; PAW; PoWW; TAP; VGW

(Next to of Course God America I.) EBEvV; RaBo; TFi

Next to the fresh grave of my beloved grandmother. Ireland 1972. Paul Durcan. PBCIP

Next to will/ I value reason. Swimming Pool. Maria Teresa Horta, *tr. fr. Portuguese* by Suzette Macedo. PBWP

Next unto God, to whom I owe. To Retiredness. Mildmay Fane, 2d Earl of Westmorland. BeJo; NOSC

Next War, The. Wilfred Owen, *tr. fr. Turkish.* MeMBP; OBD; Son

Next War, The. Sir Osbert Sitwell. NSI; PAW; PoWW

Next, who 'as leave to domineer, The. Alicia D'Anvers. *Fr.* Academia; or The Humours of the University of Oxford. KTR

Next whose fortune 't was a tale to tell, The. Fitz Adam's Story. James Russell Lowell. AmPP

Next Year. Nora Perry. PoToHe

"Next year, next year," we say. Next Year. Nora Perry. PoToHe

Next year the grave grass will cover us. Street Corner College. Kenneth Patchen. MoAmPo

Next year we are to bring the soldiers home. Homage to a Government. Philip Larkin. EBEV; FaBoPV; NoAM

Ngaa . . . now then. Paddy Biran's Song. Paddy Biran, *tr. fr. Girramay* by R. M. W. Dixon. CBAP

Ngoni Burial Song. *Unknown, tr. fr. Zulu.* PeSA

Niagara Falls. Alan Dugan. PoA

Nialls' cottage had one, The. Hearth Song. John Montague. PNI

Nibble, nibble, little sheep. Sheep. Samuel Hoffenstein. TrJP

Nicander, ooh, your leg's got hairs! Epigram. Alcaeus, *tr. fr. Greek* by Tony Harrison. GrAn; PeHV

Nice Day for a Lynching. Kenneth Patchen. PoNe

Nice mice to an untimely death. (*LL*) Cruel, Clever Cat. Geoffrey Taylor. ChTr; FaBoEE

Nice Mrs. Eberle early had been told. La Donna E Perpetuum Mobile. Irwin Edman. FiBHP; NYBP

Nice of you, white. Red. Gerald William Barrax. *Fr.* Old Gory, The. NBV

Nice Part of Town, A. Alfred Hayes. NYBP

Nice pot of gold that was mari, A. Arthur Shaw. PeLi

Nice Valor, The, *sels.* John Fletcher.
Melancholy. GTBS; GTBS-P; OBEV
(O Sweetest Melancholy.) TrGrPo
(Song: "Hence all you vaine delights.") PoEL-2

Nice young man about the town, A. I've Got the Giggles Today. A. P. Herbert. FiBHP

Nicest child I ever knew, The. Charles Augustus Fortescue. Hilaire Belloc. NoAM

Nicest in the town, The. (*LL*) Chook, chook, chook, chook, chook. *Unknown.* OxNR

Nicest Phantasies Are Shared, The. Brian Coffey. CIP

Nicetes begins with gentle declamation. Automedon, *tr. fr. Greek* by Frederick Garber. GrAn

Nichita Stanescu. Brian Turner. PeNZ

Nicholas Ned. Laura E. Richards. NTCP; SiSoPo

Nicholas Nye. Walter de la Mare. BoTP

Nick and the Candlestick. Sylvia Plath. CAPP; CoAP; LCAP; NALW; PBWP; Poetr

Nickleplate moon, The. Kansas City West Bottoms. Edward Dahlberg. PoA

Nicky, the word has come to the West Coast. Smoke. Charles Wright. NYBP

Nicole may have been a beauty long ago. Nicarchus of Alexandria, *tr. fr. Greek* by Sam Hamill. InMo

Niconoë has just inched past her prime. Nicarchus of Alexandria, *tr. fr. Greek* by Peter Porter. GrAn

Nico's bedroom talents entice men. *Unknown, tr. fr. Greek* by Sam Hamill. InMo

Nid-nod through shuttered streets at dead of night. The Last Bus. E. V. Knox. BXAP

Niddle Noddle. Mother Goose. OxNR

Niemand. Marie Syrkin. BTR

Nietzsche is pietsche. Graffiti. "James." NBLV

Nievie nievie nick nack. *Unknown.* OxNR

Niger Ferry, The. Harry Clifton. IB

Nigeria in the Year 1999. Catherine Obianuju Acholonu. HBAPE

Nigga Section, The. Welton Smith. BPo

Nigger/ Can you kill. True Import of Present Dialogue, Black vs. The Negro. Nikki Giovanni. BPo; PoBA

Nigger. Frank Horne. CDC

Nigger. Sonia Sanchez. BPo

Nigger. Karl Shapiro. OxBA

Nigger . . . nigger. (*LL*) Nigger. Frank Horne. CDC

Nigger Song: An Odyssey. Rita Dove. AmPA

Niggerlips. Martín Espada. AfAz

Niggerlips was the high school name. Niggerlips. Martín Espada. AfAz

Nigger's Got to Go, De. Daniel Webster Davis. AAP

Nigger's Leap, New England. Judith Wright. NOBAu

Night, The. Al-Khansa, *tr. fr. Arabic* by Willis Barnstone. BoWoP

Night, The. Hilaire Belloc. OBEV

Night. William Rose Benét. MoAmPo

Night. Hayyim Nahman Bialik, *tr. fr. Hebrew* by Maurice Samuel. AWP

Night. Blake. *Fr.* Songs of Innocence. BLPL; BoNaP; BoTP; CH; EnRP; FaBoBe; FaPON; FHYEP; MeMBP; OBEV; OxBChV; PoLF; WiR

Night II (Enion's Lament). Blake. *See* I am made to sow the thistle for wheat, the nettle for a nourishing dainty.

Night VIII (The Eternal Man). Blake. *Fr.* Vala; or The Four Zoas. PoE

Night. Robert Bly. NaP

Night. Louise Bogan. Poetr; UnPo

Night. Henri de Regnier, *tr. fr. French* by "Seumas O'Sullivan". AWP

Night. Duo Duo, *tr. fr. Chinese* by Donald Finkel *with* Li Guohua. SpMi

Night. Peter Everwine. NNaP

Night, The. Herman von Gilm zu Rosenegg, *tr. fr. German* by Philip L. Miller. RiWo

Night. Donald Jeffrey Hayes. CDC

Night. Josephine D. Henderson Heard. CBWP-4

Night. Hermann Hesse, *tr. fr. German* by Ludwig Lewisohn. AWP

Night. Patricia Hubbell. PDV

Night. Solomon ibn Gabirol, *tr. fr. Hebrew* by Emma Lazarus. TrJP

Night. Robinson Jeffers. AWP; LiTA; MoAmPo; NOBA; OxBA

Night, The. Helen Leuty. BoTP

Night, The. (Through that pure virgin-shrine.) Henry Vaughan. ChIV-2; EBEV; ESCV; GeHe; LiTB; MeLP; NAEL-1; NOBE; NOCV; NoP; OAEL-1; OBEV; OBWVE; OxAEP-1; PoEL-2; SCGP; SeCV-1; TFi; TOF
Sels.
"Dear Night! this world's defeat." TrGrPo
(Diversely Holy Darkness.) CBCK

Night. (*LL*) The Sentry. Alun Lewis. AngWe; PoWW

Night, The. Myra Cohn Livingston. PDV; TLR

Night. Richard Lovelace. CaPo

Night,/ And the yellow pleasure of candlelight. Song of the Rain. Hugh McCrae. CBAP; PAW

Night. Ada Negri, *tr. fr. Italian* by Philip L. Miller. RiWo

Night. Ann Radcliffe. WPE

Night. Shelley. *See* Swiftly walk o'er the western wave.

Night. Sir Philip Sidney. *See* O night, the ease of care, the pledge of pleasure.

Night. Robert Southey. GN

"Night" . . . "Good night." (*LL*) In the Orchard. Muriel Stuart. EBNV; ErPo; FF; OxBTC

Night, The. James Stephens. BoTP

Night. S. D. R. Sutu, *tr. fr. Sotho* by Dan Kunene *and* Jack Cope. PeSA; TTY

Night. Sara Teasdale. FaPON

Night. Georg Trakl, *tr. fr. German* by David McDuff, Jon Silkin, *and* R. S. Furness. PeFWW

Night. Tu Fu, *tr. fr. Chinese* by Jan W. Walls. SuSp

Night, The. Tu Fu, *tr. fr. Chinese* by Hualing Nieh. LHF

Night. *Unknown.* BoTP

Night, A: mysterious, tender, quiet, deep. A Common Inference. Charlotte Perkins Gilman. WGRP

Night a Sailor Came to Me in a Dream, The. Diane Wakoski. TAP; VGW

Night after night. Desire. Dinah Livingstone. AIW

Night after night from my small bed. Hooters. Meic Stephens. AngWe

Night after night from our camp on Sugar Loaf Hill. The Influence of Natural Objects. James Simmons. PNI

Night after night, it was very nearly enough. A Whippoorwill in the Woods. Amy Clampitt. BAP-91

Night along the Mackinac Bridge. Roberta Hill Whiteman. CDW

Night; an Epistle to Robert Lloyd, *sels.* Charles Churchill.
Nut, a World, a Squirrel, and a King, A. FaBoRV
"Spectators only on this bustling stage." OBSV

Night and a Distant Church. Russell Atkins. PoBA

Night and a starless sky. Shipwreck. Mary Weston Fordham, *tr. by* Mary Ann Caws. CBWP-2

Night and Day. Michael Drayton. *See* Deare [*or* Dear], why should you command [*or* commaund] me to my rest.

Night and Day. Linda Hogan. BCF

Night and Day. Cole Porter. CBLP

Night and day arrive, and day after day goes by. For My Son, Noah, Ten Years Old. Robert Bly. CAPP; InPS; RaBo

Night and day under the rind of me. Parodies of Cole Porter's "Night and Day." Ring Lardner. OBAL

Night & Fog Decree:, The. God Teaches Us How to Forgive, but We Forget. Louis Phillips. BTR

Night/ and in the warm blackness. Upon Your Leaving. Etheridge Knight. NNaP

Night, and its muffled creakings, as the wheels. The Shako. Robert Lowell. Son

Night and mist, what bones you have eaten. Leonidas of Tarentum, tr. fr. Greek by Peter Levi. GrAn

Night and Morning. Austin Clarke. CIP; IPY; MoAB

Night and Morning. Unknown, tr. fr. Welsh by R. S. Thomas. OBWVE

Night and Night's longing. Meleager, tr. fr. Greek by Peter Whigham. GrAn

Night, and on all sides only the folding quiet. Night. S. D. R. Sutu, tr. fr. Sotho by Dan Kunene and Jack Cope. PeSA; TTY

Night, and one single ridge of narrow path. Robert Browning. Fr. Pauline. EBVVPR

Night and Sleep. Coventry Patmore. EBVV

Night, and the down by the sea. Rain on the Down. Arthur Symons. Fr. At Dieppe. OBNC

Night, and the heavens beam serene with peace. Night. Solomon ibn Gabirol, tr. fr. Hebrew by Emma Lazarus. TrJP

Night and the hood. Conrad Kent Rivers. PoBA

Night and we heard heavy and cadenced hoofbeats. The Return. John Peale Bishop. ImPo; LiTA; OxBA

Night and wine, his face wavering on the glass. (LL) A Poem for Maurice O'Shea. Geoffrey Lehmann. NOBAu

Night, and your frail. A Mother's Death. Tony Flynn. PWE

Night arches England, and the winds are still. Peace. Walter de la Mare. MoAB; MoBrPo

Night at an Airport. David Ignatow. NNaP

Night at Anchor by Maple Bridge. Chang Chi, tr. fr. Chinese by Kenneth Rexroth. OHMPC

Night at Gettysburg. Don C. Seitz. OHIP

Night attendant, a B.U. sophomore, The. Waking in the Blue. Robert Lowell. CoAP; HCAP; MoAmPo; UnPo

Night before Christmas, The. Clement Clarke Moore. See 'Twas the night before Christmas, when all through the house.

Night before Larry Was Stretched, The. Unknown. BIrV; FaBoBa; GBP; NOBL; NOIV; OxBoLi; PeIV

Night before my uncle Carter got shot, The. Support Your Local Police Dog. Carter Revard. VoR

Night before the Battle of Waterloo, The. Byron. See There was a sound of revelry by night.

Night before the day of our wedding, The. The Double Bubble of Infinity. Kate Farrell. ArLo

Night before they meant to pluck his eyes, The. Among Philistines. R. S. Gwynn. MT

Night before Waterloo, The. Byron. See There was a sound of revelry by night.

Night-blooming Cereus, The. Robert Hayden. CAPP; NoP; NU

Night Braid, sels. Faye Kicknosway.

Night breaths, short ones. In the Hospital. Laura Jensen. AmPA

Night by nightfall more benighted. Garcia Lorca Murdered in Granada. John Manifold. CBAP

Night by the Sea, A. Heine, tr. by Howard Mumford Jones. Fr. North Sea, The. AWP

Night Catch. Heather McHugh. AmPA

Night Chill. Li Shang-yin, tr. fr. Chinese by Eugene Eoyang and Irving Y. Lo. SuSp

Night Clouds. Amy Lowell. AnAmPo; MoAmPo

Night Club. Louis MacNeice. OxBSP

Night Club. F. R. Scott. NOBC

Night comes. Day runs for its life into my eyes. Gil Orlovitz. Fr. Art of the Sonnet. PoA

Night comes to the man who can pray. New Year's Eve in Solitude. Robert Mezey. NaP

Night Comes Walking. Esther Popel. ShDr

Night comes walking out our way. Night Comes Walking. Esther Popel. ShDr

Night Creature. Lilian Moore. SiSoPo

Night, The/ creeps in. The Night. Myra Cohn Livingston. PDV; TLR

Night Cries, Wakari Hospital, sels. Charles Brasch. Winter Anemones. PeNZ

Night Crossing. Sylvia Kantaris. PWE

Night Crow. Theodore Roethke. HoPM; InPK; OxBSP; VGW

Night crushes you so I look for you, The. No. José Hidalgo, tr. fr. Spanish by Stephen Berg. IMW

Night Dances, The. Sylvia Plath. LCAP; LPA

Night dark as leopard-flower. (LL) When my love becomes/ All-powerful. Ono no Komachi. PBWP

Night, Death, Mississippi. Robert Hayden. CAPP; FF; LCAP; VCAP; VGW

Night Don Juan came to pay his fees, The. Don Juan in Hell. Baudelaire, tr. fr. French by James Elroy Flecker. AWP

Night falls/ and after night, darkness. Couple. Forugh Farrokhzad, tr. fr. Farsi by Hasan Javadi and Susan Sallée. VBLP

Night Feeding. Muriel Rukeyser. MDDM; NMM; WPE

Night Ferry. Mark Doty. NAmP90

Night Flight. Marion Alexopoulos. NOBAu

Night Flower. Geoffrey Lehmann. NOBAu

Night found me so flushed with wine. Tune: "Telling of Innermost Feelings." Li Ch'ing-chao, tr. fr. Chinese by Eugene Eoyang. SuSp

Night full of talking that hurts, A. Jalal al-Din Rumi, tr. by John Moyne and Coleman Barks. Fr. Three Quatrains. RaBo

Night Fun. Judith Viorst. TLR

Night Funeral in Harlem. Langston Hughes. InPS

Night Game of the Maker of Faces, The. Novica Tadic, tr. fr. Serbo-Croatian by Charles Simic. HSix

Night gathers. Outside. Kinder- und Hausmärchen. Brian Alderson. Mes

Night Gives Old Woman the Word. Gail Tremblay. HATNAP

Night Gives Us the Next Day. Minnie Bruce Pratt. ETG

Night Has a Thousand Eyes, The. Francis William Bourdillon. ArLo; BoLoP; CoGr; OBEV; OxBSP; PoToHe; WBLP

Night has come on like a woman sleeping, the. Moon Poems. John Wieners. VGW

Night has driven the shadow. The Shadow Inside Me. Tommy Olofsson, tr. fr. Swedish. TSaS, tr. by Jean Pearson

Night has secreted us. Amen. Richard W. Thomas. PoBA

Night he died, earth's images all came, The. Poet. Peter Viereck. HoPM; MoAmPo

Night held me as I crawled and scrambled near. The Turkish Trench Dog. Geoffrey Dearmer. Mes; NSI

Night-herding Song. Harry Stephens. NTP

Night here, a covert. Gary Snyder. Fr. Myths and Texts. NaP; NeAP; PoM

Night Herons. Judith Wright. OBAP

Night hides our thefts; all faults then pardoned be. In the Dark None Dainty. Robert Herrick. CaPo

Night Highway Ninety-Nine. Gary Snyder. PoBeRe

Night huddled our town. In Dear Detail, by Ideal Light. William Stafford. NaP

Night hung o'er Virginia's forest wild, The. Capt. Smith and Pocahontas. Eloise Bibb. CBWP-4

Night, I know you are powerful and artistic. For Bill Hawkins, a Black Militant. William J. Harris. PoBA

Night I lost you, The. The Five Stages of Grief. Linda Pastan. IMW

Night I seldom remember, A. Obeah Night. Jean Rhys. PBCV

Night in a Village, A. Ivan Savvich Nikitin, tr. fr. Russian by P. E. Matheson. AWP

Night in June, A. Wordsworth. BoTP

Night in Odessa, A. Louis Simpson. NNaP

Night in Shanghai is incredible, The. Shanghai Serenade II. Kung Liu, tr. fr. Chinese. Fr. Shanghai Lyrics. LHF, tr. by Hualing Nieh

Night in soft slumbers rolled gently away, The. Miss F[——]ny M[——] t[——]y to Miss P[——]y B[——]s. Fanny (Frances) Macartney Greville. ECWP

Night in Spring. Joseph Freiherr von Eichendorff, tr. fr. German by Philip L. Miller. RiWo

Night in the bloodstained snow: the wind is chill. Hialmar Speaks to the Raven. Charles Marie René Leconte de Lisle, tr. fr. French by James Elroy Flecker. AWP

Night in the Forest. Galway Kinnell. TAP

Night in the House by the River. Tu Fu, tr. fr. Chinese by Kenneth Rexroth. NaP

Night in the Red Sea, A. Sir Alfred Comyn Lyall. OBTV

Night in the Royal Ontario Museum, A. Margaret Atwood. PBWP

Night in the Villa by the River. Tu Fu, tr. fr. Chinese by Robert Payne. TAL

Night is a furrow, a queasy, insistent wound, The. Nightletter. Charles Wright. PoA

Night is a purple pumpkin. Night. Patricia Hubbell. PDV

Night Is a Space of White Marble, The. Philip Lamantia. PoBeRe

Night is beautiful, The. Langston Hughes. CDC

Night is black swan wholly adrift. Hotel in Paris. Dennis Trudell. PoA

Night is calm, the cygnet's down, The. On a Calm Summer's Night. John Nicholson. EnLoPo

Night is cold and frosty, The. A Winter Night. Priscilla Jane Thompson. CBWP-2

Night is cold on the Great Bog, The. *Unknown. Fr.* Toward Winter. NOIV

Night is come, but not too soon, The. The Little Moon. Longfellow. BoTP
(Light of Stars.) PFP

Night is come. The land is wrapt in sleep., The. *(LL)* Storm is over, the land hushes to rest, The. Robert Bridges. GTBS-P

Night is dark, The. And Yet. Errol B. Sloan. BLRP

Night is dark, the wind has dashed, The. Midnight Prayer. Hayyim Nahman Bialik, *tr. fr. Hebrew by* Helena Frank. TrJP

Night Is Darkening round Me. Emily Brontë. MeMBP; NOBVV; OBNC; PoEL-5

Night Is Freezing Fast, The. A. E. Housman. CMoP; LiTM; MeMBP; OxBSP; PrIm

Night is full of storm clouds, The. Freezing Night. T'ao Hung Ching, *tr. fr. Chinese by* Kenneth Rexroth. OHMPC

Night is like an avalanche. Bessie Mayle. ShDr

Night is long, The. Grandpa Bear's Lullaby. Jane Yolen. SiSoPo

Night is long, she cannot sleep, The. Song of Tzu-yeh. *Unknown, tr. fr. Chinese by* Ronald C. Miao. SuSp

Night is my sister, and how deep in love. Edna St. Vincent Millay. HAP

Night Is Near [*or* Neir] Gone, The. Alexander Montgomerie. OBEV; OxBS

Night is neir gone, The. *(LL)* The Night Is Near [*or* Neir] Gone. Alexander Montgomerie. OBEV; OxBS

Night is o'er England, and the winds are still. Peace. Walter de la Mare. MoAB; MoBrPo; PAW

Night is on the downland, on the lonely moorland. John Masefield. *Fr.* Lollingdon Downs. GoYe; LiTB, I–XV; LiTM
(Night on the Downland.) MoBrPo

Night is still. The unfailing surf, The. Miramar Beach. J. V. Cunningham. *Fr.* To What Strangers, What Welcome. NoAM; PoA

Night is very dark, The. Assassination Poems. John Ridland. MAT

Night is warm and clear and without wind, The. Poem after Leopardi. Mark Strand. AnAn

Night is white, The. Birch Trees. John Richard Moreland. OHIP

Night it was a holy night, The. Godly Girzie. Burns. CoMu; ErPo; FaBoBl

Night it was horribly dark, The. Measles in the Ark. "Susan Coolidge." OxBChV

Night John Henry is born an ax, The. The Birth of John Henry. Melvin B. Tolson. *Fr.* Harlem Gallery. BPo; TTY

Night Journey. Theodore Roethke. GOA; NYBP

Night Letter. Marge Piercy. NMM

Night-life. Letters, journals, bourbon. Origins and History of Consciousness. Adrienne Rich. NIP; Poetr

Night Light. Nancy Willard. LCAP

Night, lighter than day! Night, more than brilliant night. On the Birth of Jesus. Andreas Gryphius, *tr. fr. German by* George C. Schoolfield. GePo

Night like purple flakes of snow. Night. Donald Jeffrey Hayes. CDC

Night! loathèd jailor of the locked-up sun. Night. Richard Lovelace. CaPo

Night long and wintry/ the Pleiades half set. Asclepiades, *tr. fr. Greek by* Alan Marshfield. GrAn

Night Mail, The. W. H. Auden. ChTr; GrPl; OxBTC

Night Mail North, The. Henry Cholmondeley-Pennell. EBVV; OHCV

Night makes no difference 'twixt the priest and clerk. No Difference in the Dark. Robert Herrick. CaPo

Night-March, The. Herman Melville. LiTA

Night Mirror, The. John Hollander. NYBP; Prf; VCAP

Night mist leaves us yearnng for a new location, The. Floating Houses. David Wojahn. SM

Night-Music. Philip Larkin. InPS

Night music slanted. Cell Song. Etheridge Knight. NNaP; PoBA

Night Nurse Goes Her Round, The. John Gray. OBNC

Night of Battle. Yvor Winters. PoA

Night of Death, The. Frances E. W. Harper. PWR

Night of Forebeing, The, *sels.* Francis Thompson.
Ode after Easter, An. OtMeF

Night of gentle thunder fells a thousand catkins, A. Spring Rain. Ch'in Kuan, *tr. fr. Chinese by* Stephen West. SuSp

Night of iron wheels and rain, A. The Red Flag. Michael Jackson. PeNZ

Night of our parting in the red tower is enough for sorrow, The. Tune: "Deva-like Barbarian." Wei Chuang, *tr. fr. Chinese by* Lois M. Fusek. SuSp

Night of Rattlesnake Chili, The. Walter McDonald. NGP

Night of Sine. Léopold Sédar-Senghor, *tr. fr. French.* PBA

Night of Souls. Ann Stanford. WPE

Night of Spring. Thomas Westwood. BoTP

Night of the eclipse we're parallel, The. Total Eclipse. Michael J. Rosen. DiPo

Night of the Forest. Sun Ching-hsuan, *tr. fr. Chinese. Fr.* Lyrics of the Forest. LHF, *tr. by* Hualing Nieh

Night of the Moths, The. Douglas Stewart. FaBoMA

Night of the Shirts, The. W. S. Merwin. VCAP

Night of Trafalgar, The. Thomas Hardy. *Fr.* Dynasts, The. ChTr; FaBoCh; MoBrPo; OBMV

Night of utter silences, A. Shadows. "Yehoash," *tr. fr. Yiddish by* Elias Lieberman. TrJP

Night of Wind. Frances Frost. FaPON

Night on Clinton. Robert Mezey. AmPA; NaP

Night on earth and sky. A Terrible Thought. Eliezer Steinbarg, *tr. fr. Yiddish by* Joseph Leftwich. TrJP

Night on Goat Haunt, A. Sandra Alcosser. FoLa

Night on the Conroy. Siegfried Sassoon. NSI

Night on the Downland. John Masefield. *See* Night is on the downland, on the lonely moorland.

Night on the Great River. Meng Hao Jan, *tr. fr. Chinese by* Kenneth Rexroth. OHMPC

Night on the Prairies. Walt Whitman. RFM, *ll.* 1–5

Night opens like an almond. Yvonne Caroutch, *tr. fr. French by* Elene Margot Kolb. BoWoP

Night Operations, Coastal Command RAF. Howard Nemerov. ArOW

Night, our [*or* the] black summer, simplifies her smells. Nights in the Gardens of Port of Spain. Derek Walcott. NAEL-2; OxBC

Night outside is the theatre of our patience. Peter Riley. *Fr.* Eight Preludes. VaA

Night passd and Enitharmon eer the dawn returnd in bliss. Song of Enitharmon. Blake. *Fr.* Vala; or The Four Zoas. OAEL-2

Night Patrol. Ciaran Carson. PWE

Night Patrol, The. Arthur Graeme West. NSI

Night-Piece. Léonie Adams. MoAB; MoAmPo

Night-Piece, *sels.* Fleur Adcock.
Before Sleep. PeNZ

Night Piece. John Manifold. LiTM; MoBrPo

Night-Piece. Raymond R. Patterson. PoBA

Night-Piece, A. Wordsworth. EnRP

Night Piece on Death. (By the blue taper's trembling light.) Thomas Parnell. NOEC
Sels.
"How deep yon azure dyes the sky!" OxAEP-1
"Up yonder hill, behold how sadly slow." OBD

Night-Piece; or, Modern Philosophy, A. Christopher Smart. NOEC

Night-Piece [*or* Nightpiece], to Julia, The. Robert Herrick. BeJo; CaPo; CBLP; CH; EBEvV; ELP; HeIL; InvP; JCP; LiTB; NAEL-1; NoP; NOSC; OAEL-1; OBEV; PoE; PoEL-3; PoRA; SCGP; SeCP; SeCV-1; TEP; TFi

Night Plane. Frances Frost. FaPON; PDV

Night Post, The. Matthew Sweeney. IB

Night Prayer. *Unknown, tr. fr. Irish by* Douglas Hyde. TIRV

Night Prayer, A. Alcuin, *tr. fr. Latin by* Helen Waddell. MLL

Night Prayer of Glückel of Hameln, The. Edouard Roditi. CRP

Night Prayers. Dinah Livingstone. DT

Night Quarters. Henry Howard Brownell. GN

Night Raid. Desmond Hawkins. PoWW

Night Rains: to my Wife up North. Li Shang-yin, *tr. fr. Chinese by* A. C. Graham. PLT

Night rests like a ball of fur on my tongue. *(LL)* Adolescence — II. Rita Dove. AmPA; HCAP; NoAM; VCAP

Night-Ride, The. Kenneth Slessor. FaBoMA

Night sank upon the dusky beach, and on the purple sea. Macaulay. *Fr.* Armada, The. BeLS; CoGr; EBEvV; FaBoCh; FaBoEH; FaPoR; GN; OBNC; PeVV; WBLP

Night saw the crew like pedlars with their packs. Lunar Stanzas. Henry Coggswell Knight. CBNP; FaBoNo

Night, say all, was made for rest, The. Upon Visiting His Lady by Moonlight. "A. W." CTC

Night Scenes. Robert Duncan. VGW

Night Scenes of Other Times, *sels.* Joanna Baillie.
Ghost of Edward. ECWP

Night sea quickens, The. On the shoal or rock. Lighthouses. Dorothy Wellesley. WPE

Night Serene, The. Luís de León, *tr. fr. Spanish by* Thomas Walsh. TrJP

Night Shift at the Fruit Cannery. Ilze Mueller. LoHo

Night Shore. Barry O. Higgs. PeSA

Night Sits in This Chair, The. Alice Notley. UL

Nightingale, The. ("Little, pretty nightingale, The"). *Unknown*. TrGrPo

Nightingale, The. *Unknown*. TrGrPo

Nightingale as soone as Aprill bringeth, The. Sir Philip Sidney. EnRePo; SiPSBD
(Nightingale, The.) SCGP
(Philomela.) OxAEP-1

Nightingale, in dead of night, The. The Happy Nightingale. *Unknown*. OxBChV

Nightingale near the House, The. Harold Monro. MoBrPo

Nightingale Poem. John Drew. PWE

Nightingale, whose happy noble hart, The. The Steele Glas. George Gascoigne. AAS

Nightingales. Robert Bridges. CMoP; GGP; ImPo; LiTB; LiTM; MoAB; MoBrPo; NOBE; OAEL-2; OBEV; OBMV; OBNC; SCGP; TFi; TrGrPo; UnPo

Nightingales. Samuel Taylor Coleridge. *Fr.* Nightingale, The. ChTr; EnRP; FM

Nightingales, The. Harri Webb. AngWe

Nightingales in America. Jane Flanders. CrSp

Nightingales of Spring, The. *Unknown*. AmFP

Nightingales, the nightingales!, The. *(LL)* Bianca among the Nightingales. Elizabeth Barrett Browning. BrRo; GTBS-P

Nightingales' tongues, your majesty? Figgie Hobbin. Charles Causley. NTP

Nightingales warbled without. In the Garden at Swainston. Tennyson. OBEV; OBNC

Nightjar, The. Sir Henry Newbolt. Mes; PlP

Nightletter. Charles Wright. PoA

Nightline: An Interview with the General. Ronald Wallace. PBCAP

Nightly the watchman's rattle startles my sleep. Ch'ien Ch'ien-i, *tr. by* Irving Y. Lo. *Fr.* Poems Written in Prison. SuSp

Nightly tormented by returning doubt. The Struggle. Sully-Prudhomme, *tr. fr. French by* Arthur O'Shaughnessy. AWP

Nightmare, The. Van K. Brock. BTR

Nightmare. Erasmus Darwin. *Fr.* Botanic Garden, The. NOEC

Nightmare. Gawin Douglas. *Fr.* Palace [*or* Palice] of Honor [*or* Honour], The. PoEL-1

Nightmare. James A. Emanuel. BPo

Nightmare. Isabella Gardner. CoAP

Nightmare. Lyall Wilkes. OBD

Nightmare, [A]. W. S. Gilbert. *Fr.* Iolanthe. NOBL; NoP; NTP; OxBoLi; PoRA

Nightmare Abbey., *sels*. Thomas Love Peacock.
Song by Mr. Cypress. OAEL-2; OBNC
Wise Men of Gotham, The. BXAP; CBNP; FaBoNo
(Men of Gotham, The.) CH
(Seamen Three.) WiR
(Three Men of Gotham.) FaBoCh; OBEV; OxAEP-2

Nightmare at Noon. Stephen Vincent Benét. OxBA

Nightmare Begins Responsibility. Michael S. Harper. CAPP; HCAP; LCAP; TAP; VCAP

Nightmare begins responsibility. *(LL)* Nightmare Begins Responsibility. Michael S. Harper. CAPP; HCAP; LCAP; TAP; VCAP

Nightmare Factory, The. Maxine W. Kumin. WoWa

Nightmare leaves fatigue. Louis MacNeice. *Fr.* Autumn Journal. BIrV; CIP; PNI

Nightmare Number Three. Stephen Vincent Benét. MoAmPo

Nightmare of beasthood, snorting, how to wake. Moly. Thom Gunn. HAP; MoP; NoAM; Poetr; PrIm

Nightmare shower room, The. My tormentor leers. Days of 1941 and '44. James Merrill. GLP

Nightmare, with Angels. Stephen Vincent Benét. MAT

Nightpiece. James Joyce. PoA

Nights. Cyn Zarco. UL

Nights along the River. Charles Sullivan. AiP

Night's bible-black darkness prevails. V. R. Ormerod. PeLi

Nights bring you the fever. Prometheus. Jenny Mastoraki, *tr. fr. Modern Greek by* Nikos Germanakos. BoWoP

Night's Delights. Kaspar Stieler, *tr. fr. German by* Ingrid Waløe-Engel. GePo

Night's diadem around thy head. Fairest of Freedom's Daughters. Jeremiah Eames Rankin. PAH

Night's drifts, The. A Winter Daybreak above Vence. James Wright. InPS; LCAP; VCAP

Night's first sweet silence fell, and on my bed. The Malady of Love Is Nerves. Petronius Arbiter, *tr. fr. Latin by* Howard Mumford Jones. AWP

Nights in the Gardens of Port of Spain. Derek Walcott. NAEL-2; OxBC

Nights in the Iron Hotel. Michael Hofmann. SCBI

Nights of 1964-66: The Old Reliable. Marilyn Hacker. VCAP

Nights of 1965: the Old Reliable. Marilyn Hacker. PFL

Nights passed very darkly, The. The Healing. Yannis Ritsos, *tr. fr. Greek*. TSaS, *tr. by* Edmund Keeley

Night's Protégé. Marjorie Marshall. ShDr

Night's ride's over. Anselm Hollo. UL

Nights when there is nothing downstairs. Upstairs Child. Harry Clifton. IB

Nightsea and violet wave. A Storm of Love. Hilary Corke. NYBP

Nightshift. John Seed. VaA

Nightshift Workers. George Charlton. PWE

Nightsong, *sels*. Frank Mkalawile Chipasula.
Dusk. HBAPE

Nightsong. Louis O. Coxe. FYAP

Nightsong. Jacob Glatstein. *See* Strangers' eyes don't see.

Nightsong: City. Dennis Brutus. HBAPE

Nighttime. The faithful prison guard. Bedtime Story. Lou Lipsitz. VGW

Nightwalker. (Mindful of the/ shambles of the day.) Thomas Kinsella. IPY
Sels.
"Foot of the tower. An angle where the darkness, The." PBCIP
"I must lie down with them all soon and sleep." BIrV

Nightwatch, *sels*. Khairi Mansour, *tr. fr. Arabic by* Lena Jayyusi.

Nightwatcher:/ Fast falls the night unfurling its vile veil. Dusk. Frank Mkalawile Chipasula. *Fr.* Nightsong. HBAPE

Nightwatchman. Deborah Randall. PWE

Nightwind sings and rustles through the reeds, The. Nocturne in G Minor. Karl Gustav Vollmoeller, *tr. fr. German by* Ludwig Lewisohn. AWP

Nightwood. William Jay Smith. PoA

Nihilist as Hero, The. Robert Lowell. VCAP

Nijinsky. Parker Tyler. PoA

Nikarete's face, sweetly moistened. Asclepiades, *tr. fr. Greek by* Alan Marshfield. GrAn

Nikki-Rosa. Nikki Giovanni. AIW; BlSi; CrSp; HeIP; IHMS; MoP; PoBA; TAP

Nikolina. Celia Laighton Thaxter. GN

Nile, The. Albert Goldbarth. NAmP90

Nile, The. Leigh Hunt. EBEV; EnRP; NOBE; OBNC

Nile the Hermit. *Unknown*, *tr. fr. Greek by* Guy Davenport. GrAn

Nima, The. Jorge Isaacs, *tr. fr. Spanish by* Alice Jane McVan. TrJP

Nimble as dolphins to. Gimboling. Isabella Gardner. ErPo

Nimble cat and lazy maid, A. On Maids and Cats. Henricus Selyns. SCAP

Nimble sigh, on thy warm wings. To Amoret. Henry Vaughan. EnLoPo

Nimble swan plays in the river pool, The. Presented as a Farewell to Secretary Fu. Pao Chao, *tr. fr. Chinese by* Daniel Bryant. SuSp

Nimbler race of mice, A. *(LL)* On a Cat Aging. Sir Alexander Gray. OFC

Nimbus. Douglas Le Pan. MoCV

Nîmes, August, 1966, and I. The Survivor. Philip Levine. BTR

Nimium Fortunatus. Robert Bridges. *See* I have lain in the sun.

Nimmers, The. John Byrom. OxAEP-1

Nimphs Reply to the Sheepheard, The. Sir Walter Ralegh. *See* If all the world and love were young.

Nimrod gazed across the plain. The Tower of Babel. Laurance Wieder. ChIV-1

Nina and John: there are spaceships circling above us. Extraterrestrial. Alicia Ostriker. VBLP

Nina loved compromising. Three Women. Alan Dienstag. ErPo

Nina Simone. Paulette C. White. Jaz

Nine, The. John Sheffield, Duke of Buckingham and Normandy. APAS

Nine adulteries, 12 liaisons, 64 fornications and something approaching a rape. The Temperaments. Ezra Pound. BoLoP; ErPo; FaBoBl; MeMAP; NoAM; NOBA

Nine Below. Joy Harjo. VBLP

Nine Birds. E. E. Cummings. UnPo

Nine drops of water bead the jessamine. A Wet August. Thomas Hardy. PPP

Nine grenadiers, with bayonets in their guns. The Dream of a Boy Who Lived at Nine Elms. William Brighty Rands. OxBChV

999 Call. Elizabeth Bartlett. FaBoWP

Nine Inch Will Please a Lady. Burns. ErPo

Nine Little Goblins, The. James Whitcomb Riley. OBCA

Nine Lives. *Unknown*. CRH

Nine Lyric Poets, The. *Unknown*, *tr. fr. Greek by* Peter Jay. GrAn

Nine Men's Morris. Peter Philpott. VaA

Nine months I waited in the dark beneath. Pro Sua Vita. Robert Penn Warren. MoAmPo

Nine Nectarines and Other Porcelain. Marianne Moore. OxBA

Nine o'Clock. Katharine Pyle. *Fr.* Wonder Clock, The. OBCA

Nine-o'clock Bell! School-Bell. Eleanor Farjeon. FaPON

9 o'clock. The bells come floating in. The Journey. Franz Wright. LCAP

Nine on Happy Reunion. Peyanar, *tr. fr. Tamil* by A. K. Ramanujan. PLW

Sels.
What He Said "As the deer begin to hide."
What He Said ("As wild oxen bellowed.")
What He Said ("Because peacocks moved like you.")
What He Said ("In this time of rain and thunder.")
What He Said ("The red earth.")
What Her Girl Friend Said ("As the cassias blossom.")
What Her Girl Friend Said ("Her eyes lined with kohl.")
What Her Girl Friend Said ("Saying to himself.")
What Her Girl Friend Said ("Your arms are beautiful again.")

Nine Poems for the Unborn Child, *sels.* Muriel Rukeyser.
They Came to Me and Said, "There Is a Child." Son

Nine Points of the Law, *sels.* Peter Porter.
"Managed as they say about such men." PeLV

Nine Reasons Why. Deborah Levy. DT

Nine Songs, *sels.* Ch'u Yüan, *tr. fr. Chinese* by Burton Watson.

Nine swallows sat on a telephone wire. The Swallows. Elizabeth J. Coatsworth. TLR

Nine Times. James Michie. DiPo

Nine Times a Night. *Unknown.* OBET

Nine times out of ten. Airs and Graces. Peter Fallon. PBCIP

Nine times the sun his yearly course had run. Elizabeth Thomas. *Fr.* Jill, A Pindaric Ode. ECWP

9 Verses of the Same Song, *sels.* Wendell Berry.

Nine white chickens come. A Black November Turkey. Richard Wilbur. LCAP; MoAB; NAAL-2

Nineteen. Lucha Corpi, *tr. fr. Spanish* by Catherine Rodriguez-Nieto. AfAz

1918-1941. Robert David Fitzgerald. CBAP

1985 — In a Small American Town. Judith Irwin. BTR

1915. Roger McDonald. NOBAu

Nineteen Fifty-five. Sherod Santos. NAmP90

1951. Frank O'Hara. LCAP

1956. Maxine Scates. PBCAP

1905. David Ignatow. BTR

1940. Sir John Betjeman. PAW

1945. Sheila Cussons, *tr. fr. Afrikaans* by Jack Cope *and* Uys Krige. PeSA

1945. Bernard S. Mikofsky. BTR

1945. Sir Herbert Read. OxBTC

1945, The Silence. Burton D. Wasserman. BTR

1947. That winter they talk of. Freeze-frame. Alison Fell. NBrP

1943. Sandra McPherson. FaBoWP

1904. Frederick Morgan. WeW

1914, *sels.* Rupert Brooke.
Dead, The ("Blow out, you bugles, over the rich dead!"). WGRP
Dead, The ("These hearts were woven"). CH; LiTB; OtMeF; PeFWW; PoA; SoSe
Peace. OBWP; PAW; PoA; WGRP
Safety. EnLoPo
Soldier, The. CoGr; EBEvV; FaBoEH; FaBV; FaPoB; FaPoR; FF; HeIP; LiTB; LiTM; MoBrPo; NAEL-2; NOBE; NoP; NSI; OBEV; OBWP; OxBTC; PAW; PeFWW; PlP; PoA; PoLF; PoRA; PoWW; Son; TEP; TFi; TrGrPo; UV

MCMXIV. Philip Larkin. EBEV; FaBoEH; NAEL-2; NoAM; NSI; OBWP; OxAEP-2

1914. J. C. Squire. FaBoEH

Nineteen Hundred and Nineteen, *sels.* W. B. Yeats.
Come Let Us Mock at the Great. IHNG
"Many ingenious lovely things are gone." BIrV; LiTB; MoAB; PoE
"Some moralist or mythological poet." PoE

1966. Dermot Bolger. IB

Nineteen long lines hanging over my door. Lace Tell. *Unknown.* OBET

Nineteen Old Poems of the Han, *sels.* Mei Sheng *and* Fu I, *tr. fr. Chinese* by Burton Watson.

Nineteen Pieces for Love, *sels.* Susan Griffin.

1974. Marilyn Hacker. GLP

1974 — The Sounds. Christina Beer. PeNZ

1916. R. S. Gwynn. MT

1916 Seen from 1921. Edmund Blunden. PeFWW

1964 and I'm parked. White. Christopher Buckley. NGP

1967 – 1971. Michael Hofmann. SCBI

1966. David Rivard. PBCAP

1935. Stephen Vincent Benét. MoAmPo

Nineteen Thirty-Nine, *sels.* Charles Brasch.

1939. Elaine Terranova. BTR

1933. Philip Levine. LCAP

1930's. Robert Lowell. NoP

1912 – 1952, Full Cycle. Peter Viereck. OBAL

1925. Edwin Honig. *Fr.* To Restore a Dead Child. NoAM

1929. W. H. Auden. OxAEP-2; SOTW

1901, *sels.* Noël Coward.
"When Queen Victoria died." FaBoEH

Nineteenth Century and After, The. W. B. Yeats. FaBoEE

Nineteenth of April, The. Lucy Larcom. PAH

Ninetieth Psalm, The. Isaac Watts. *See* O God, Our Help in Ages Past.

Ninety. Mary Elizabeth Fullerton. CBAP

Ninety-fifth. Isaac Watts. AmFP

Ninety-nine. (*LL*) Night Highway Ninety-Nine. Gary Snyder. PoBeRe

90 North. Randall Jarrell. CAPP; CoAP; FYAP; MoAB; MT; NAAL-2; NoAM; NOBA; TAP; VCAP

Ninety percent of the mass of the Universe. Certainty before Lunch. John Berryman. LCAP; OxBC

Ninety summers — and never a platitude. Stanley J. Sharpless. PeLi

Nino, the Wonder Dog. Roy Fuller. FF

Ninth Canticle, The. George Wither. ChIV-1

9th July, 1932. Mary Ursula Bethell. PeNZ

Ninth Matter: Shape. Robert Kelly. BCF

Ninth Month. Robert Lowell. *Fr.* Marriage. NAs

Ninth of Av. Myra Sklarew. CRP

Ninth of July, The. John Hollander. CoAP

Ninth Symphony of Beethoven Understood at Last as a Sexual Message, The. Adrienne Rich. NoP; TAP

Niobe, *sels.* Aeschylus, *tr. fr. Greek* by C. M. Bowra.
"Alone of gods death has no love for gifts." OBD

Niobe. H. Cordelia Ray. CBWP-3

Niobe. *Unknown, tr. fr. Greek* by Peter Jay. GrAn

Niobe is very old now. Bus Ride. Kate Daniels. PBCAP

Niobe lives in the desert, too. Ethiopia. Kate Daniels. PBCAP

Niobe on Phrygian sands. The Wish. Thomas Stanley. AWP

Nip for new, A. *Unknown.* ISE

Nip in the blossom all our hopes and thee. (*LL*) The Picture of Little T. C. in a Prospect of Flowers. Andrew Marvell. ESCV; GeHe; JCP; LiTB; MeLP; NAEL-1; NOBE; NoP; OAEL-1; OBEV; OxAEP-1; PoE; PPP; PrIm; SCGP; SeCP; SeCV-1; TFi

Niplets. *Unknown, tr. fr. Greek* by Wallace Rice. ErPo

Nipping chill, the frost killed spring. Meng Chiao, *tr. by* Stephen Owen. *Fr.* Apricots Die Young. SuSp

Nirvana. John Hall Wheelock. MoAmPo

Nisei: Second Generation Japanese-American. Jim Mitsui. OpBo

'Nkongane. W. C. Scully. PeSAV

No! Eliza Cook. PoToHe

No,/ I cannot/ turn from love. To Turn from Love. Sarah Webster Fabio. BlSi

No. José Hidalgo, *tr. fr. Spanish* by Stephen Berg. IMW

No! Thomas Hood. CBCK; ChTr; FiBHP; GN

No. (*LL*) Overheard on a Saltmarsh. Harold Monro. BoTP; CH; FaPON; GoJo; Mes; MoShBr

No/ No/ No/ I am not doing. Our Lives. Sharon Scott. JB

No Admittance. Chris Daly. NGP

No alien dust covers your tomb. Simonides, *tr. fr. Greek* by Peter Jay. GrAn

No ancestral bones of ours. A Visit to the Village. Michael Smith. PBCIP

No angel has descended here. The Visitation. Jan Owen. NOBAu

No argument, no anger, no remorse. Hedges Freaked with Snow. Robert Graves. OxBTC

No Bargains Today. Peggy Susberry Kenner. JB

No bars are set too close, no mesh too fine. The Sparrow in the Zoo. Howard Nemerov. MoP
(Epigram: Political Reflection. NIP

No beggar she in the mighty hall where her bay-crowned sisters wait. Arizona. Sharlot M. Hall. PAH

No bells rang in her house. The silver plate. Miss Marnell. Austin Clarke. IPY

No berserk thirst of blood had they. Lexington. Whittier. PAH

No better lost than any other woman. Marilyn Hacker. NoAM

No bird, no fabled fowl it is. Little Cheat. *Malay Oral Tradition, tr. by* R. J. Wilkinson *and* R. O. Winstedt. WTO

No bitterness: our ancestors did it. Ave Caesar. Robinson Jeffers. FaBoPV; MoP; NoAM; NOBA; OxBA; OxBSP

No black and swirling cloak, no faceless grin. Waiting for the Post. Dorothy Auchterlonie. CBAP

No blacker than others in winter, but. Burning Mountain. W. S. Merwin. NYBP

No Blacks, No Irish, *sels.* Gabriel Gbadamosi.
Scene 6 The Boat Passage. NBrP

No blame lies with the rat for what it did. (*LL*) The Man from Changi. Graeme Hetherington. NOBAu

No blooming youth shall ever make me err. Katherine Philips. KTR

No bottom,/ Mark four. *Unknown.* AmFP

No bounds to human woe. *(LL)* Ode to Winter. Thomas Campbell. GTBS; GTBS-P

No branch nor the last grass. Fossil. E. D. Blodgett. NOBC

No burning leaf; prithee, let no bird call. *(LL)* God's World. Edna St. Vincent Millay. BLPL; CMoP; FaBoBe; FaBV; MoAmPo; TrCP

No, but lovely in that way. *(LL)* Part of Plenty. Bernard Spencer. ErPo; GBL; LiTB; LiTM

No butler, no second maid, no blood upon the stair. Crime Club. Weldon Kees. NaP

No Buyers; a Street Scene. Thomas Hardy. LiTB; MeMBP; NoP

No camellia. Yosano Akiko, *tr. fr. Japanese by* Geoffrey Bownas *and* Anthony Thwaite. PBWP

No Categories! Stevie Smith. NoP

No Change in Me. *Unknown.* AmFP

No Change of Place. W. H. Auden. *See* Who Will Endure.

No changes of support — only. Last Month. John Ashbery. CoAP

No charm. Kapitonos, *tr. fr. Greek by* Sam Hamill. InMo

No charm can stay, no medicine can assuage. Walter Savage Landor. FaBoEE

No Child. Padraic Colum. OBMV

No, children, my trips are over. The Engineer's Story. *Unknown.* BeLS

No citizen is melancholy. Joie de Vivre. Joel Dailey. UL

No city in the spacious universe. London. Daniel Defoe. *Fr.* Reformation of Manners. NOEC

No city is more inclined than Eusapia to enjoy life and flee care. Italo Calvino, *tr. fr. Italian. Fr.* Cities and the Dead. AnRep, *tr. by* William Weaver

No city primness train'd my feet. Rustic Childhood. William Barnes. OBNC

No cloud can hide the glow of living faith. The Light of Faith. Edgar Dupree. BLRP

No cloud, no relique of the sunken day. Samuel Taylor Coleridge. *Fr.* Nightingale, The. EnRP; FM (Nightingale, The.) FHYEP

No clouds are in the morning sky. Going a-Nutting. Edmund Clarence Stedman. GN

No Cold Approach. *Unknown.* EBEV

No Coming to God without Christ. Robert Herrick. OxBSP

No Complaints. Anselm Hollo. UL

No conozco la palabra to say I sometimes miss you *en español.* Invisible Boundaries. Maureen Hurley. LoHo

No Continuing City. Michael Longley. PNI

No Country You Remember. Robert Mezey. FF

No coward soul is mine. Emily Brontë. BrRo; EBEvV; EBVV; EnVR; LiTB; MeMBP; NALW; NoP; OBNC; PoEL-5; TrCP; TRP; TrPWD (Last Lines.) OxAEP-2; PlP

No Coward's Song. James Elroy Flecker. OxBSP

No creature, no least being but catches fire from him. *(LL)* Heavens bespeak the glory of God, The. Daniel Berrigan. EaPr

No Credit. Kenneth Fearing. CMoP

No crooked leg, no bleared eye. Written in Her French Psalter. Elizabeth I, Queen of England. PBWP; WPE

No cry. *(LL)* The Starry Night. Anne Sexton. NoAM; PoE; VCAP

No, Daisy! lift not up thy ear. To a Spaniel. Walter Savage Landor. FM

No Dawns. Julianne Perry. PoBA

No day was sad as the day Sakhr. On Her Brother Sakhr. Al-Khansa, *tr. fr. Arabic.* BoWoP, *tr. by* Willis Barnstone

No days that dawn can match for her. Rachel. Lizette Woodworth Reese. AmWP

No deed of mine shall shame thee, gentle name. *(LL)* The Family Name. Charles Lamb. Son

No Delicacies. Ingeborg Bachmann, *tr. fr. Hebrew by* Mark Anderson. PoSu

No Deposit. Earle Thompson. HATNAP

No, dere ain't no use r workin' in de blazin' summertime. When de Sun Shines Hot. James Ephriam McGirt. AAP

No Difference in the Dark. Robert Herrick. CaPo

No different, I said, from rat's or chicken's. Not to Be Born. David Sutton. OBD; OxBM

No dignity without a chromium. Ballad of Faith. William Carlos Williams. OBAL

No Discharge. Arthur Waley. OBD

No doubt he well invented, nobly felt. Swift. *Fr.* Run Upon the Bankers, The. EPCY

No doubt in the mind of Brébeuf that this was the last. The Martyrdom of Brébeuf and Lalemant, 16 March 1649. E. J. Pratt. *Fr.* Brébeuf and His Brethren. NOBC

No doubt this way is best. No Use. W. D. Snodgrass. BoLoP

No doubt to-morrow I will hide. At Mass. Vachel Lindsay. VGW

No dream of mortal joy. Love and Lust. Isaac Rosenberg. TrJP

No drums they wished, whose thoughts were tied. Epitaph on a New Army. Michael Thwaites. PAW

No dust have I to cover me. An Inscription by the Sea. E. A. Robinson, *after* Glaucus. AWP; ChTr; FaBoEE

No ears could hear then the mutter of the Milky Way. Prophecy. Eileen Duggan. PeNZ

No earthquake. Chapped, a lifting in this field. Dead Center. Chester Kallman. PoA

No Easy Harbour. Anne Hartigan. CIP

No easy thing to bear, the weight of sweetness. The Weight of Sweetness. Li-Young Lee. RaBo

No end in sight to the days of my wandering. Written on the Thirtieth Day, Ninth Month, Second Year of the Ta-li Reign [767]. Tu Fu, *tr. fr. Chinese by* Irving Y. Lo. SuSp

No End of No-Story. George Macdonald. NOBVV

No end of sea. *(LL)* Antarctica. Carole Forman. EaPr

No Escape. Harriet L. Delafield. GoYe

No "fan is in his hand" for these. The Threshing Machine. Alice Meynell. WPE

No feet. Snow. The Arctic Fox. Ted Hughes. OBAP

No fence will keep a growing boy outside. Father of the Man. Elizabeth Mabel Bryan. GoYe

No fine white bone-sheen now. A Buffalo Skull. Ted Kooser. FoLa

No first-class war can now be fought. Civil Defense. Kenneth Burke. OBAL

No fledgling feeds the fatherbird. Child Labor. Charlotte Perkins Gilman. AnAmPo

No, for I'll save it! Seven years since. Apparent Failure. Robert Browning. EBVVPR; NAEL-2; NOBE

No, for spring's passion there is no simile. *(LL)* Dawn in Stone City. Li Ho. PLT

No for you, my queyn, will I prepare. The Real Muse. Tom Scott. PoA

No forward soul, ambition stung. After Reading Bryant's Lines to a Waterfowl. Eloise Bibb Thompson. ShDr

No Foundation. John Hollander. OBAL

No Friend Like Music. Daniel Whitehead Hicky. PoToHe

No friendly shade thy shade shall company! *(LL)* Achtung. Sappho. CTC; OBVE

No fruits, no flowers, no leaves, no birds — November! *(LL)* No! Thomas Hood. ChTr; FiBHP; GN

No Funeral Gloom. Ellen Terry. BLPA

No funeral gloom, my dears, when I am gone. William Allingham. NOBVV

No future hope, no fear for evermore. *(LL)* Cobwebs. Christina Rossetti. NAEL-2; NALW

No Ghost Is True. Leslie A. Fiedler. PoA

No glittering chaplet brought from other lands! Abraham Lincoln. Alice Cary. AmWP

No, go back into your exile, go back quick. After Wiriyamu Village Massacre by Protuguese. Jack A. Mapanje. PeSAV

No, go back until our anger has simmered. *(LL)* After Wiriyamu Village Massacre by Protuguese. Jack A. Mapanje. PeSAV

No gorgeous coat has he. My Mocking Bird. Josephine D. Henderson Heard. CBWP-4

No great house is finer. An Ivied Tree-Top. *Unknown.* NOIV

No Great Matter. David Lawson. VGW

No Greener Pastures. Brenda Hillman. BAP-90

No hand has been allowed to touch. Inscription on a Chemise. *Unknown, tr. fr. Arabic by* E. Powys Mathers. *Fr.* Thousand and One Nights, The. ErPo

No Hast But Good. George Gascoigne. *See* In haste poste haste, when first my wandering [*or* wandring] mind[e].

No haste but good, where wisdome makes the waye. *(LL)* For why? the gaines doth seldome quitte the charge. George Gascoigne. AAS

No haste but good, where wisdome makes the waye. George Gascoigne. *Fr.* Gascoigne's Memories. AAS; EnRePo; Son

No hawk hangs over in this air. The Snow Storm. Edna St. Vincent Millay. NAAL-2; PoA

No Hay Fronteras. Jan Clausen. ETG

No, He is too quick. We never. Getting Inside the Miracle. Luci Shaw. TrCP

"No!" He Said. Wole Soyinka. HBAPE

No Head for Heights. Ralph Hawkins. VaA

No head-ropes or dung. Lament for an Arab Encampment. Abid ibn al-Abras, *tr. fr. Arabic by* Omar S. Pound. ArPe

No help I'll call till I'm put in the narrow coffin. Egan O'Rahilly, *tr. fr. Irish by* Thomas Kinsella. NOIV

No Hiding Place Down There. *Unknown.* GBP

No hint upon the hill top shows. Inspiration. John Banister Tabb. WGRP

"No home, no home," cried an orphan girl. The Orphan Girl. *Unknown.* AmFP; AS

No honey, ah suspect you-all/ Of bein' intellectual. Intellectual Discussion. Cole Porter. *Fr.* Let's Not Talk About Love. CBCK

No, Honoria, I am greatly flattered. Time's Revenges. Sir Owen Seaman. FaBoUs

No hope deceives it, and no doubt divides it; The Purified Soul. Francis Quarles. *Fr.* Emblems. CBCK

No hope have I to live a deathless name. Poietes Apoietes. Hartley Coleridge. OBNC

No hope, unless your mercy work me loose. *(LL)* Day's in dread of losing her bright features, The. Ausiàs March. STV

No horror hounds him, and he feels no pain. *(LL)* Tell Me, Love. Ingeborg Bachmann. VBLP

No house of stone. The Elements. W. H. Davies. MoBrPo

No hungr hawke poore patridge to devoure. Mr. Thomas Shepeard. Edward Johnson. SCAP

No: I am neither seeking to change nor keep myself. A Brown Aesthete Speaks. Mae V. Cowdery. ShDr

No, I Am Not as Others Are. Villon, *tr. fr. French by* Arthur Symons. AWP

No, I am through and you can call in vain. Admonition. Philip Stack. BLPA

No, I cannot write the poem of war. Poem in 1944. Robert Conquest. PAW

No! I don't begrudge en his life. The Bachelor. William Barnes. PeVV

No, I don't love you. Anti-Love Poems. Elizabeth Brewster. NOBC

No, I don't think we would. More Shrines. David Kirby. NGP

No, I had set no prohibiting sign. Trespass. Robert Frost. FaBV

No, I have never found. Places, Loved Ones. Philip Larkin. CMoP

No, I have tempered haste. The Mount. Léonie Adams. MoAB; MoAmPo

No — I'll endure ten thousand deaths. Chaste Florimel. Matthew Prior. BoLoP; ErPo

No, I'm Not Afraid. Irina Ratushinskaya, *tr. fr. Russian by* David McDuff. PWE

No, I'm not afraid: after a year. No, I'm Not Afraid. Irina Ratushinskaya, *tr. fr. Russian by* David McDuff. PWE

No, I'm not going to. De Souza Prabhu. Eunice De Souza. FaBoVe

No Images. Waring Cuney. CDC; MAT; NIP; TTY

No imagination to forestall woe. *(LL)* Charleston in the 1860s. Adrienne Rich. CoAP; NAAL-2

No! Indeed. Sir Thomas Wyatt. *See* What no, Perdy [*or* Perdie]! ye may be sure!

No Irish Need Apply. John F. Poole. SWP; WTO

No! is my answer from this cold, bleak ridge. A Loyal Woman's No. Lucy Larcom. AmWP

No, it isn't so bad being. Later History. David Rivard. NAmP90

No, it was only a touch of dysentery, he said. He was doing fine. The Taking of the Koppie. Uys Krige. PeSAV

No, it's a tenement. "It's a Whole World, the Body. A Whole World!" — Swami Satchidananda. David Young. FF

No. It's an impudent falsehood. Men did not. On a Vulgar Error. C. S. Lewis. OxBTC

No Joke. William Scammell. FaBoBl

No lake is so still but that it has its wave. *Unknown, tr. fr. Chinese by* Arthur Waley. Spl

No leaf is left unmoistened by the dew. Prayer by Moonlight. Roberta Teale Swartz. TrPWD

No less fabulous than the carved marble inner. Leap of Faith. David St. John. NAmP90

No Less than Prisoners. Frederick Macartney. CBAP

No, let it stay. It speaks but truth. The First Grey Hair. Mary E. Tucker. CBWP-1

No Letter. Mary E. Tucker. CBWP-1

No lifeless thing of iron and stone. Brooklyn Bridge. Sir Charles G. D. Roberts. PAH

No light except the stars, but from the cliff. The Sea Birds. Van K. Brock. NYBP; SM

No light to guide but the moon's pallid ray. Contrition. Henry More. *Fr.* Psychozoia, or, the Life of the Soul. NOSC

No, listen, there's this albatross. Bill Greenwell. PeLi

No Loathsomnesse in Love. Robert Herrick. BeJo; GBL

No Lock against Lechery. Robert Herrick. CaPo

No locust grows alone. Locust Trees. Margaret L. Thomas. ShDr

No Longer. Roberta Hill Whiteman. ETG

No longer any man needs me. Widow. Dorothy Livesay. IMW

No longer are the forests green. Storms. Steel Usurps the Forests; Silence Dethrones Dialogue. Bible, Apocrypha. HBAPE

No longer, as before, will you wake at dawn and flap. Anyte, *tr. fr. Greek by* Barbara Hughes Fowler. *Fr.* Epigrams. HePo

No longer casual hand to lip. Blind, I Speak to the Cigarette. Joanne de Longchamps. GoYe

No longer, cricket, sitting. Mnasalcas, *tr. fr. Greek by* Edward Lucie-Smith. GrAn

No longer glimpsing a few beer cans that glint. The Bottles. Alexander Craig. *Fr.* Sea Change. FaBoMA

No longer mourn for me when I am dead. Shakespeare. *Fr.* Sonnets. AWP; EBEV; EIL; EnRePo; FaBoRV; GBL; HAP; HeIP; ImPo; IMW; LiTB; NAEL-1; NoP; NoSic; OxAEP-1; PoRA; SCGP; Son; TEP; TFi; TrGrPo

(Triumph of Death, The.) GTBS; GTBS-P

No longer shall I exult in the floating seas and arch. Anyte, *tr. fr. Greek by* Barbara Hughes Fowler. *Fr.* Epigrams. HePo

No longer students and not likely to succeed. Sonnet for the Class of '58. James Simmons. PWE

No longer the feather. Guilt. Lorenzo Thomas. UL

No longer throne of a goddess to whom we pray. Full Moon. Robert Hayden. BPo

No longer to lie reading Strauss's *Life.* Memories of Aunt Maria-Martha. William Zaranka. BXAP

No longer to lie reading *Tess of the d'Urbervilles.* The Lesson. Robert Lowell. CMoP; LCAP

No longer truth, though shown in verse, disdain. George Crabbe. *Fr.* Village, The. OxAEP-1

No, Lord: Thou wilt accept a broken heart. *(LL)* Are all such off'rings, as are crusht, and bruis'd. Francis Quarles. FaBoEE

No, Love Is Not Dead. Robert Desnos, *tr. fr. French by* Bill Zavatsky. UnAS

"No love," quothe he, "but vanity, sets love a task like that". *(LL)* The Glove and the Lions. Leigh Hunt. BeLS; FaPON; GN; WBLP

No Love, to Love of Man and Wife. Richard Eedes. InvP

No lovelier city than all of this. Toast. Thomas McCarthy. PBCIP

No lover saith, I love, nor any other. The Paradox. John Donne. NOSC

No McTavish. Genealogical Reflection. Ogden Nash. OBAL

No man can bid a fool or sage. The Power of Thought. Süsskind von Trimberg, *tr. fr. Middle High German.* TrJP

No man can serve two masters. Bible, *N.T. Fr.* St. Matthew. OBVE

No man could have been more unfaithful. The Turkish Carpet. Paul Durcan. CIP

No man could have that woman, Mouth-of-the-River. The Boy Who Became Sky. David Wagoner. AnAn

No man could think base thoughts who looked on her. *(LL)* Sonnet: He Will Praise His Lady. Guido Guinicelli. AWP

No man had ever heard a nightingale. Critic and Poet. Emma Lazarus. AmWP

No Man, if Men Are Gods. E. E. Cummings. InvP; VGW

No Man Knoweth His Sepulchre. Bryant. AnAmPo

No man knows. When A Woman Gets Blue. Norman Jordan. NBV

No Man Knows War. Edwin Rolfe. TrJP

No man may disregard. *(LL)* God's Controversy with New-England. Michael Wigglesworth. EAP; SCAP

No man outlives the grief of war. The Permanence of the Young Men. William Soutar. OxBS

No man takes the farm. John Masefield. UV

No man's forever fully satisfied. Nicarchus of Alexandria, *tr. fr. Greek by* Sam Hamill. InMo

No-Man's-Land. H. d'A. B. NSI

No Man's Land. Eric Bogle. OBET

No Man's Land. Gloria Escoffery. PBCV

No man's trust let woman claim. The Roman Earl. *Unknown, tr. fr. Irish by* Douglas Hyde. OBVE

No Marvel Is It. Bernard de Ventadour, *tr. fr. Provençal by* Harriet Waters Preston. AWP

No, Master, Never! Joshua McCarter Simpson. AAP

No Matter. Paulus Silentiarius, *tr. fr. Greek by* William Cowper. AWP

No matter by what hand or trick. *(LL)* Of thee (kind boy) I ask no red and white. Sir John Suckling. BeJo; CaPo; MeLP; NoP; NOSC; OxBoLi; SeCP; SeCV-1

No matter how hard I listen, the wind speaks. For Zbigniew Herbert, Summer, 1971, Los Angeles. Larry Levis. FYAP

No matter what life you lead. Snow White and the Seven Dwarfs. Anne Sexton. HCAP

No matter where it's going. *(LL)* Travel. Edna St. Vincent Millay. FaPON; MoShBr; OBCA; PDV

No matter why, nor whence, nor when she came. The Story of the Ashes and the Flame. E. A. Robinson. AnAmPo; MeMAP

No Mean City. Patrick MacDonogh. BIrV; OxBSP

No memory is here of things once done. The Mood of Vichy. Hildebert, *tr. fr. Latin* by Helen Waddell. MLL

No. Merely to have writ. Peruke of Poets. William Zaranka. BXAP

No mo meetings. Listenen to Big Black at S. F. State. Sonia Sanchez. BPo

No monarch more blest than the man of the mill. (*LL*) The Miller. John Cunningham. ECEV

No Money in Art. Jim Gustafson. UL

No money to bury him. Ballad of the Man Who's Gone. Langston Hughes. SAmP

No monuments or landmarks guide the stranger. A Country without a Mythology. Douglas Le Pan. MoCV; NOBC

No moon, no chance to meet. Ono no Komachi, *tr. fr. Japanese* by Rob Swigart. WPOW

No Moon, No Star. Babette Deutsch. NYBP

No More. Carl Clark. JB

No More. (*LL*) Comfort to a Youth That Had Lost His Love. Robert Herrick. NOBE; OBEV

No more — no more — Oh! never more on me. My Days of Love Are Over. Byron. *Fr.* Don Juan. OBNC

No more alone sleeping, no more alone waking. Marriage. Mary Elizabeth Coleridge. NALW; PeHV

No more, America, in mournful strain. Phillis Wheatley. *Fr.* To the Right Honourable William, Earl of Dartmouth. AmPP; WPOW

No More Auction Block. *Unknown.* BPo; RaBo; SWP

No more auction block for me. No More Auction Block. *Unknown.* BPo; RaBo; SWP

No more be grieved at that which thou hast done. Shakespeare. *Fr.* Sonnets. HeIP; ImPo; NAEL-1; NoSic; OxAEP-1; PeHV; PoE; SCGP; TEP; UnPo

No More Beneath the Oppressive Hand. *Unknown.* AH

No More Booze. *Unknown.* OBAL

No more chant your old rhymes about bold Robin Hood. General Ludd's Triumph. *Unknown.* OBET

(Chant no more your old rhymes about bold Robin Hood.) FaBoEH

No More Crying Out. Giuseppe Ungaretti, *tr. fr. Italian* by Jon Silkin. PeFWW

No more exercises of style for him. A Younger Poet. Peter Schjeldahl. PoA

No more for sin's dark stain the debt of death to pay. (*LL*) The Garden. Jones Very. OxBA; TAP

No more for them shall evening's rose unclose. Epicedium. J. Corson Miller. PAH

No more in any house can I be at peace. A Dream. Charles Williams. OBEV

No more in delightful chase through buoyant seas. On a Dolphin. Anyte, *tr. fr. Greek* by John Heath-Stubbs *and* Carol A. Whiteside. GrAn

No More Kissing — AIDS Everywhere. Michael C. Blumenthal. PFL

No more let Greece her bolder fables tell. On the Famous Voyage. Ben Jonson. BeJo

No More Lewd Lays. Barnabe Barnes. *Fr.* Divine Century of Spiritual Sonnets, A. Son

No More Love Poems #1. Ntozake Shange. *Fr.* For Colored Girls Who Have Considered Suicide When the Rainbow Is Enuf. BlSi

"No more mistresses," King Edward said. Frank Richards. PeLi

No more moaning, no more moaning. Oh, Freedom. *Unknown.* SWP

No More, My Dear, No More These Counsels Try. Sir Philip Sidney. *Fr.* Astrophel and Stella. AAS; ESo, GGP; Poetr; SCGP, SiPS, SiPSBD

No more, my Stella, to the sighing shades. To Stella. Hester Mulso. ECWP

No more my visionary soul shall dwell. Pantisocracy. Samuel Taylor Coleridge. EnRP

No more ne will I wicked be. *Unknown.* MiEL

No more, no more,/ We are already pined [pin'd]. Alexander Brome. NOSC

No More, O My Spirit. Euripides, *tr. by* Hilda Doolittle ("H. D."). *Fr.* Hippolytus. AWP; NAWM-1, *tr. by* Rex Warner

No more of I and thou. Hitler Speaks. Helen Waddell. MLL

No more of talk where God or Angel Guest. Milton. *Fr.* Paradise Lost, *Bk.* IX. EPCY, *ll.* 1–47; NAEL-1, *ll.* 1–1189; NAWM-1; NoP; TOF, *ll.* 1–47

(Higher Argument.) NOSC, *ll.* 1–47

No more of your titled acquaintances boast. Burns. FaBoEE

No more — Oh never more! (*LL*) Lament, A: "O world! O life! O time!" Shelley. ChTr; EnRP; GTBS; GTBS-P; NAEL-2; NOBE; PoRA; TEP; TrGrPo

No more shall I see. Frithiof's Farewell. Esaias Tegnér, *tr. fr. Swedish* by Longfellow. *Fr.* Frithiof's Saga. AWP

No more shall I, since I am driven hence. To Larr [*or* Lar]. Robert Herrick. CaPo; SeCV-1

No more shall walls, no more shall walls confine. Hosanna. Thomas Traherne. ChIV-2; PoEL-2; SeCV-2

No More Soft Talk. Diane Wakoski. FF; IHMS

No more talk where God or angel guest. Milton. *See* Thus saying, from her husband's hand her hand.

No More than Five. Fred Levinson. AmPA

No more the English girls may go. High Germany. Edward Shanks. OBMV

No more/ The feel of your hand. Mae V. Cowdery. ShDr

No more the highschool land. Canada: Case History: 1973. Earle Birney. PeLV

No more the swanboat on the artificial lake. Blind Date. Conrad Aiken. DL

No More the Thunder of Cannon. Julia Caroline Ripley Dorr. OHIP

No more to feel man's wrath or dread his chain. (*LL*) The Fugitive Slaves. Jones Very. TAP

No more unto My Thoughts Appear. Sidney Godolphin. BeJo

No more walks in the wood. An Old-Fashioned Song. John Hollander. BAP-90

No more was heard of lowing, died. (*LL*) Aristeides. Antipater of Sidon. AWP

No more with candied words infect mine ears. Tell Me No More. William Drummond of Hawthornden. TrGrPo

No more with overflowing light. For a Dead Lady. E. A. Robinson. CMoP; DL; FYAP; HeIP; HoPM; InvP; LiTA; LiTM; MoAB; MoAmPo; MoP; NoAM; NOBA; OxBA; PoEL-5; PoRA; TFi

No More Words. Franklin Lushington. PAH

No more words! To the field, to arms. Veronica Franco, *tr. fr. Italian* by Lynne Lawner. PBWP

No more work and no more play. Good Night. Ruth Ainsworth. BoTP

No mortal man beneath the sky. Epitaph for George Moore. Thomas Hardy. FaBoEE

No mortal thing enthralled these longing eyes. Celestial Love. Michelangelo, *tr. fr. Italian* by John Addington Symonds. AWP

No mountain and no forest, land nor sea. To Arno of Salzburg. Alcuin, *tr. fr. Latin* by Helen Waddell. MLL

No mountains or ocean, but we had orchards. Produce. Debra Allbery. PBCAP

No need for confusion if we but recall. Rhyme for Remembering the Date of Easter. Justin Richardson. FaBoUs

No need to get home early. Father's voice. William Stafford. RFM

No! never such a draught was poured. A Ballad of the Boston Tea-Party. Oliver Wendell Holmes. PAH

No, Never Think. Pushkin, *tr. fr. Russian* by Babette Deutsch. ErPo

No new delights to our desire. Singers to Come. Alice Meynell. WPE

No New Music. Stanley Crouch. PoBA

No New Thing. Vincent Buckley. CBAP

No News at All. Jack Butler. MT

No News from the Old Country. Andrew Motion. SCBI

No news of navies burnt at seas. A New-Year's Gift Sent to Sir Simeon Steward. Robert Herrick. CaPo

No, no, don't, please. Crimes of Passion: The Phone Caller. Terry Stokes. AmPA

No, no, fair heretic[k], it needs must be. Sir John Suckling. *Fr.* Aglaura. BeJo; CaPo; PrIm

No, no; for my virginity. A True Maid. Matthew Prior. ErPo; FaBoCo; FaBoEE; NAEL-1; NIP; NOEC; PeLV

No, no! Go from me. I have left her lately. A Virginal. Ezra Pound. CMoP; MeMAP; MoAB; MoAmPo; NAAL-2; NIP; NOBA; OxBA; Poetr; Son; TAP

No, no, go not to Lethe, neither twist. Ode on Melancholy. Keats. EnRP; FHYEP; HAP; ImPo; InPK; InPS; LiTB; MAT; MeMBP; NAEL-2; NAWM-2; NOBE; NoP; OAEL-2; OBEV; OBNC; OxAEP-2; PIP; PoE; PoEL-4; Poetr; PoRA; PPP; PrIm; SCGP; TEP; TFi; TrGrPo

No, no I did not bargain for so much. Too Much. Edwin Muir. LiTB

No, no I don't want my heart broken again today. Have a Nice Day. Jack Myers. NAmP90

No, no, it cannot be; for who e'er set. Beauty and Denial. William Cartwright. BeJo

No, No, Nigella! Thomas Morley. EnRePo

No, no, no, I know I was not important as I moved. Come Dance with Kitty Stobling. Patrick Kavanagh. MoP; NoAM; Poetr

No, no, no, no, I cannot hate my foe. Sir Philip Sidney. SiPS

No, No, Poor Suffering Heart. Dryden. *Fr.* Cleomenes. LiTB

No no: they definitely were. Testimony. Dan Pagis, *tr. fr. Hebrew by* Stephen Mitchell. PoSu

No, not earth, nor a stone slab. Glaukos, *tr. fr. Greek by* Clive Sansom. GrAn

No, not tonight. In Teesdale. Andrew Young. FaBoPP; OxBSP

No, not writers for Heaven's sake. That bunch of slobbers. Brothers and Sisters. Michael Foley. PNI

No occasion to. *(LL)* The British Journalist. Humbert Wolfe. FaBoEE; FiBHP; IHNG; OxBTC

No Occupation. George Rostrevor Hamilton. FaBoEE

No Offence. D. J. Enright. OxBTC

No One. Lilian Moore. TLR

No one asks/ wher I am from. Jorge the Church Janitor Finally Quits. Martín Espada. AfAz

No one believes them. Their windows get broken. The Police. Sean O'Brien. PWE

No one can communicate to you. Face of Poverty. Lucy Smith. PoNe

No one can hurt me. They've tried to kill me. Alone. "Anna Akhmatova," *tr. fr. Russian by* Stephen Berg. BoWoP

No One Cares Less Than I. Edward Thomas. NSI

No one coming home. Loneliness in the Tropics. Harry Clifton. IB

No one could have a blacker tail. Othello Jones Dresses for Dinner. Ed Roberson. PoBA; PoNe

No one ever walking this our only earth. Muriel Rukeyser. NNaP

No one for spelling at a loss is. What's the Plural? *Unknown.* FaBoUs

No one goes there now. The Tune of Seven Towers. William Morris. EnVR

No one has ever loved but you and I. *(LL)* The Ragged Wood. W. B. Yeats. CBLP; GBL

No one has sung "Let the world know!" Antiphonal Hymn in Praise of Inanna. Enheduanna, *tr. fr. Sumerian. by* Aliki *and* Willis Barnstone

No one has yet looked at. *(LL)* Beach Glass. Amy Clampitt. FaBoWP; NoAM; VCAP

No One Heard Him Call. Dorothy Aldis. TLR

No one in the garden. Laughter. Olive Enoch. BoTP

No one invited me. Tune: "Magnolia Blossoms, Abbreviated." Chu Tun-ju, *tr. fr. Chinese by* James J. Y. Liu. SuSp

No one kneads us again out of earth and clay. Paul Celan, *tr. fr. German by* Joachim Neugroschel.
(No one moulds us again out of earth and clay.) AnReP; OBVE, *tr. by* Michael Hamburger; PoSu, *tr. by* John Felstiner

No one knew the secret of my flutes. Something Whispered in the *Shakuhachi.* Garrett Kaoru Hongo. InPS

No one knows it or guesses it. The Silent Girl. Joseph Freiherr von Eichendorff, *tr. fr. German by* Philip L. Miller. RiWo

No one knows the way out of his mother. String. Dennis Schmitz. LCAP

No one knows what you mean. *(LL)* Nails. Gary Gildner. PBCAP; TAP

No one knows why you killed yourself. To John Garfield, for Whom the Postman Only Rang Once. Charles B. Stetler. NGP

No one lives past a hundred. Wang Fun-chih, *tr. fr. Chinese by* Eugene Eoyang. SuSp

No one moulds us again out of earth and clay. Paul Celan. *See* No one kneads us again out of earth and clay.

No one need feel alone looking up at leaves. Looking Up at Leaves. Barbara Howes. BoNaP

No one needs to ask. Reinmar der Alte, *tr. fr. German by* Frederick Goldin. GePo

No one, not even Cambridge, was to blame. A. E. Housman. W. H. Auden. OxAEP-2

No one, not even God, can put back a leaf on to a tree. Fatality. D. H. Lawrence. PeECV

No One Remembers [Abandoning] the Village of White Fir. Duane Niatum. CDW; ETG

No one saw her afterwards. *(LL)* The Leaving. Margot Fortunato. LoHo

No One So Much as You. Edward Thomas. GBL

No one spoke. Ryota, *tr. fr. Japanese by* Kenneth Rexroth. TTTS

No one understands the Windigo, his voice like. Windigo. Paulette Jiles. NOBC

No one walks when the guardian drum sounds. Thinking of My Brothers on a Moonlit Night. Tu Fu, *tr. fr. Chinese by* Robert Payne. TAL

No one wants to hear about the war. Nam. Mike Lowery. Poetsp

No one was in the fields. Tom's Angel. Walter de la Mare. Mes

No one will take it. *(LL)* Seguidilla of Murcia. Manuel de Falla. RiWo

No one will write poetry anymore. No One Will Write Poetry. Matija Beckovic, *tr. fr. Serbo-Croatian by* Charles Simic. HSix

No one, wise Kublai, knows better than you. Italo Calvino, *tr. fr. Italian. Fr.* Cities and Signs. AnRep, *tr. by* William Weaver

No one's been told. Black Study. Michael S. Harper. CAPP

No one's fated or doomed to love anyone. Adrienne Rich. *Fr.* Twenty-one Love Poems. GLP

No one's going to read. A Dance for Militant Dilettantes. Al Young. NBV; PoBA

No One's Land. Janet Dubé. DT

No Ordinary Sun. Hone Tuwhare. PeNZ

No Other Choice. At. *to* Tobias Hume. *See* Fain Would I Change That Note.

No other name but thine. *(LL)* Praise for the Fountain Opened. William Cowper. InPK

No palace too great, no cottage too small. *(LL)* Christmas Everywhere. Phillips Brooks. BLRP; PWR; WBLP

No Passenger was known to flee. Emily Dickinson. SAmP

No pavement chalks the plain with memories. Beginning the Year at Rosebud, S. D. Roberta Hill Whiteman. CDW

No peace or quiet in the countryside. Farewell of an Old Man. Tu Fu, *tr. fr. Chinese by* Michael E. Workman. SuSp

No people are uninteresting. People. Yevgeny Yevtushenko, *tr. fr. Russian by* Robin Milner-Gulland *and* Peter Levi. DL

No Place Like Home. Llawdden, *tr. fr. Welsh by* Gwyn Jones. OBWVE

No place seemed farther than your death. And I Am Old to Know. Pauline Hanson. TAP

No Place So Grand. *Unknown.* WTO

No place was like your father's house. I followed. Your Father's House. Vincent Buckley. FaBoMA

No Platonic [or Platonique] Love. William Cartwright. BeJo; ErPo; GBL; ImPo; InvP; JCP; LiTB; NOSC; OAEL-1; PoEL-2

No, please don't. On Thinking of Photographing My Fantasies. Nellie Wong. OpBo

No pleasure in the loveless air. *(LL)* To see the lark, delighted, dare. Bernard de Ventadour. STV

No Pleasure without Some Pain. Thomas, Lord Vaux. EiL; EnRePo

No poem you send. Buson, *tr. fr. Japanese by* Harold G. Henderson. TAL

No point now my friend in telling. Heemi. Hone Tuwhare. PeNZ

No population, roofs that move. Unusual View of the Town. J. P. Ward. AngWe

No porter guards the passage of your door. Dryden. *Fr.* To My Honour'd Kinsman, John Driden, of Chesterton. EBEV

No Portuguese Lady Is Nautical. Sydney Hoffman. PeLi

No Possum, No Sop, No Taters. Wallace Stevens. HCAP; MeMAP; OxBA; TAP; VGW

No private grudge they need, no personal spite. Modern Critics. Samuel Taylor Coleridge. FaBoEE

No quirt — right? — nor spur. To My Mouse-colored Mare. Tristan Corbière, *tr. fr. French by* C. F. MacIntyre. ErPo

No rack can torture me. Emily Dickinson. MeMAP; MoAB; NALW

No Regret. Rochelle Kraut. UL

No Remedy. Drummond Allison. OxBTC

No rest! No rest on this bleak earth for me. Crazed. Mary E. Tucker. CBWP-1

No resurrection in the minds of men. *(LL)* It is not death, that sometime in a sigh. Thomas Hood. OBNC

No rice — In that hour. Basho, *tr. fr. Japanese by* Harold G. Henderson. TAL

No riches from his scanty store. A Song. Helen Maria Williams. WoRP

No Road. Philip Larkin. CBLP; EBEV; MoBrPo; OxAEP-2

No rock along the road but knows. Poet. Donald Jeffrey Hayes. PoNe

No room for mourning: he's gone out. William Wordsworth. Sidney Keyes. OxBTC

No room in the inn, of course. What the Donkey Saw. U. A. Fanthorpe. OBCP

No rooster wakes them. A donkey brays. In the Madison Zoo. Roberta Hill Whiteman. CDW

No round-shouldered pitchers here, no stewards. Cana Revisited. Seamus Heaney. FaBoMo

No runner clears the final fence. The Unfinished Race. Norman Cameron. OxBS

"No," said Charles Peace. E. C. Bentley. *Fr.* Clerihews. NOBL

No saint on a disc of snow. Emily Dickinson Postage Stamp. Lynn Strongin. NMM

No Second Troy. W. B. Yeats. CMoP; EnLoPo; GTBS-P; MoP; NAEL-2; NoAM; NOBE; OAEL-2; OxAEP-2; OxBTC; PoEL-5; PPP; TFi; WeW

No Sects in Heaven. Elizabeth H. Jocelyn Cleavland. BLPA

No sense like the strong magnetic feel. Noh Play. Jim Brodey. UL

No shade on the golden ground. *(LL)* Aria. Rolfe Humphries. NYBP

No ship of all that under sail or steam. Immigrants. Robert Frost. GOA

No Shop Does the Bird Use. Elizabeth J. Coatsworth. OBCA

No shrine along the way. *(LL)* Prayer for a Thief. Phil DuPlessis. PeSAV

No sickness worse than secret love. *Unknown.* NOIV

No sign is made while empires pass. Continuity. "Æ." MoBrPo

No single hour can stand for naught. John Clare. OBNC

No Single Thing Abides. Lucretius, *tr. by* W. H. Mallock. *Fr.* De Rerum Natura (On the Nature of Things). AWP

No sir: empty head. (*LL*) Look, our Spaniard's yawning. Antonio Machado Ruiz. STV

No, Sir, No. *Unknown.* AmFP

"No, sir," said General Sherman. E. C. Bentley. *Fr.* Clerihews. NOBL

No sleep for twelve days. What Happened to a Young man in a Place Where He Turned to Water. *Unknown, tr. fr. Apache Indian by* Anselm Hollo. STP

No sleep. The sultriness pervades the air. The House-Top. Herman Melville. LiTA; NAAL-1; NOBA; Prf

No sleep tonight. Summary. Sonia Sanchez. BPo

No Sleepe so sweet as thine, no rest so sure. (*LL*) A Good-Night. Francis Quarles. TrGrPo

No So. Not So. Anne Sexton. CrSp

No Social Stuff for Mehitabel. Don Marquis. *Fr.* Archy and Mehitabel. OFC

No song of a soldier riding down. The Ride of Collins Graves. John Boyle O'Reilly. PAH

No sooner came, [*or* come] but gone, and fall'n asleep. On My Dear Grandchild Simon Bradstreet, [Who Died on 16 November, 1669, Being But A Month, And One Day Old]. Anne Bradstreet. EAP; KTR; NAAL-1; SCAP

No sooner did the Cymbrians overcommer. The Antidoted Fanfreluches: or, a Galimatia of Extravagant Conceits Found in an Ancient Monument. Rabelais, *tr. fr. French by* Sir Thomas Urquhart. CBNP

No sound is dissonant which tells of Life. (*LL*) This Lime-Tree Bower My Prison. Samuel Taylor Coleridge. EnRP; FaBoPP; FHYEP; HeIP; MeMBP; NAEL-2; OxAEP-2; PoE; PoEL-4; TOF

No sound of any storm that shakes. Hillcrest. E. A. Robinson. MeMAP; MoAB; OxBA

No sound — yet my room fills up with thunder. The Peeper. Peter Davison. ErPo

No specious splendour of this stone. The Cornelian. Byron. PeHV

No Speech from the Scaffold. Thom Gunn. OxBTC

No Spices wanting, when I'm laid by thee. (*LL*) To Anthea. Robert Herrick. PoEL-3

No spot of earth where men have so fiercely for ages of time. Antrim. Robinson Jeffers. BIrV; IIP; NOBA; VGW

No Spring, nor Summer Beauty hath such grace. The Autumnal[l]. John Donne. *Fr.* Elegies. InPS; JCP; NOSC; PoEL-2; SeCV-1; TEP

No stab thy soul can kill. (*LL*) The Lie. Sir Walter Ralegh. AAS; ChTr; CTC; EBEV; EnRePo; FaBoPV; HAP; ImPo; InVP; LiTB; NAEL-1; NOBE; NoP; NoSic; OPOP; PoEL-2; RB; SCGP; SCV; SiPS; SiPSBD; TEP; TFi; TrGrPo; WGRP

No Stars Her Eyes. Thomas Lodge. *Fr.* Phyllis. Son

No stately column marks the hallowed place. Alamance. Seymour W. Whiting. PAH

No Stewart art thou, Galloway. On Lord Galloway. Burns. FaBoEE

No stir in the air, no stir in the sea. The Inchcape Rock. Robert Southey. BeLS; ChTr; EBEvV; EBNV; FaBoBe; GN; OBNV; OBSP; OxAEP-2; VPP

No store of spirits against fainting. (*LL*) Mundus Muliebris. Mary Evelyn. NOSC

No stranger has ever owned. (*LL*) Summerfield. Jim Barnes. HATNAP, *sect.* i; NGP, *sect.* i

No strength of Nature can suffice. Love Constraining to Obedience. William Cowper. NOCV

No sun — no moon! No! Thomas Hood. CBCK; ChTr; FiBHP; GN (November.) ChTr

No sunny ray, no silver night. Threnody. Thomas Lovell Beddoes. EnRP

No Swan So Fine. Marianne Moore. AnAmPo; MeMAP; NALW; NoP; OxBA; PFP; PoA; PrIm; UnPo

No table there is spread. John Derricke. *Fr.* Image of Irelande, The. OBTV

No, thank you, John. (*LL*) "No, Thank You, John." Christina Rossetti. NAEL-2; TEP

No, Thank You, John. Christina Rossetti. NAEL-2; TEP

No, the cards don't lie! (*LL*) The Fortune-Teller. Adelbert von Chamisso. RiWo

No, the Christian faith, as at any rate I understood it. Claude to Eustace ("No, The Christian Faith.") Arthur Hugh Clough. *Fr.* Amours de Voyage. EnVR; NOBVV

No, the serpent did not. Theology. Ted Hughes. FaBoMo; NAEL-2; NoAM

No, the serpent was not. Reveille. Ted Hughes. PPP

No Theory. David Ignatow. NNaP; RaBo

No thing/ no-thing. Cathexis. Frederick Bryant, Jr.. NBV; PoBA

No Thoroughfare. Ruth Holmes. BoTP

No! those days are gone away. Robin Hood. Keats. AWP; EnRP; SCGP

No, thou hast never griev'd but I griev'd too. Walter Savage Landor. GBL

No thought but lifts, none furrowing the clay. (*LL*) Not so with me as with the little page. Ausiàs March. STV

No; thou'rt a fool, I'll swear, if e'er thou grant. Against Fruition. Abraham Cowley. *Fr.* Mistress, The. BeJo; NOSC

No thunder blasts Jove's plant, nor can. Occasioned by Seeing a Walk of Bay Trees. Mildmay Fane, 2d Earl of Westmorland. BeJo; NOSC; OxBSP

No thyng is to man so dere. Praise of Women. Robert Mannyng. OBEV

No Time Ago. E. E. Cummings. OxBSP

No Time for God. Norman L. Trott. BLRP

No Time for Lamentation Now. Milton. *See* Come, come, no time for lamentation now.

No time, no time. The Suburb. Anne Stevenson. NMM

No, Time, thou shalt not boast that I do change. Shakespeare. *Fr.* Sonnets. OxAEP-1; Son; TrGrPo

No touch, but forever and ever this. (*LL*) At Baia. Hilda Doolittle ("H. D."). LiTA; LPA; NAAL-2; NOBA

No tree but the banyan. The Banyan Tree. Ts'ai Ch'i-chiao, *tr. fr. Chinese.* LHF, *tr. by* Hualing Nieh

No tricks/ nothing doing. Tune: "Greeting the Immortal Guest." Yun-K'an Tzu, *tr. fr. Chinese by* Jerome P. Seaton. SuSp

No trumpets announce. Rebellion Suite/Straight. No Chaser. Askia Muhammad Touré. BCF

No two eyes gaze alike. Janus. Madeline Mason. GoYe

No Use. W. D. Snodgrass. BoLoP

No use . . . Under his jacket nothing but maggots and ribs . . . No use. (*LL*) Bringing a Dead Man Back into Life. Russell Edson. TRP

No use in my going. Blue Monday. Langston Hughes. SAmP

No use, no use, now, begging Recognize! Amnesiac. Sylvia Plath. NYBP

No use waiting for it to stop. Apples. Shirley Kaufman. CrSp; MDDM; NMM

No voice but that of gladness. Emma Catherine Embury. AmWP

No Voice of Man. Raymond Falconer. GGP

No walls confine! Can nothing hold my mind? Insatiableness. Thomas Traherne. NOSC

No War. Judith Kazantzis. AIW

No warm, downy pillow His sweet head pressed. The Heavenly Stranger. Ada Blenkhorn. BLRP

No water is still, on top. The Movement of Fish. James Dickey. NYBP; VGW

No water so still as the/ dead fountains of Versailles. No Swan So Fine. Marianne Moore. AnAmPo; MeMAP; NALW; NoP; OxBA; PFP; PoA; PrIm; UnPo

No Way of Knowing. John Ashbery. AnAn

No way too long — no path too steep. Stefan George, *tr. fr. German by* Daisy Broicher. *Fr.* Jahr der Seele, Das. AWP

No, we will not make vows to the ever-winning goddess. What She Said to Her Girl Friend. Korran, *tr. fr. Tamil by* A. K. Ramanujan. PLW

No weather is ill. *Unknown.* FaBoVe

No Welcome. Matthew Sweeney. IB

No? Well, then the next time you're passin'; and ask after Dow, — and that's me. (*LL*) Dow's Flat. Bret Harte. AnAmPo; FaBoBe

No winter shall abate the spring's increase. (*LL*) Love's Growth. John Donne. ESCV; JCP; NoP; NOSC; SeCV-1

No woman's pleasure did I feel. Evidence at the Witch Trials. James K. Baxter. OxBC

No wonder I slipped, being soaked. Dionysius, *tr. fr. Greek by* Barriss Mills. GrAn

No Word. Tu Fu, *tr. fr. Chinese by* Eugene Eoyang. SuSp

No words, no tears can mend. (*LL*) Father and Child. Gwen Harwood. CBAP; WPE

No, worldling no, 'tis not thy gold. The Second Rapture. Thomas Carew. CaPo; OPOP

No worst, there is none. Pitched past pitch of grief. Gerard Manley Hopkins. CMoP; EBVV; EnVR; FaBoMo; GTBS-P; HeIP; InPS; LiTB; LiTM; MeMBP; MoAB; MoBrPo; MoP; NAEL-2; NoAM; NOBE; NOBVV; NoP; OAEL-2; OPOP; OxAEP-2; PeVV; PoE; PoEL-5; Poetr; PPP

(No Worst, There Is None.) TFi

(Sonnet: "No worst, there is none.") OBNC

No Worst, There Is None. Gerard Manley Hopkins. *See* No worst, there is none. Pitched past pitch of grief.

No you. (*LL*) You sit down on a hill top, or anywhere high enough for you. *Unknown.* EaPr

Noah. Wayne Brown. PBCV

Noah. Roy Daniells. Mes

Noah. Gerda Mayer. OTCP

Noah. James Reeves. OTCP

Noah, *sels. Unknown.*
  "I thank thee, Lord so dere, that wold vowchsayf." PoE

Noah an' Jonah an' Cap'n John Smith. Don Marquis. PoLF

Noah was an Admiral. Noah. James Reeves. OTCP

Noah's Ark. Roger McGough. OBSP

Noah's Ark. Marguerite Young. WPE

Noah's Flood. Caedmon, *tr.* by C. W. Kennedy. *Fr.* Genesis. AnOE

Noah's Flood, *sels.* Michael Drayton.
  "By this the sun had sucked up the vast deep." NOSC
  "Eternall and all-working God, which wast." PoEL-2
  "Hundred years the Ark in the building was, A." ChIV-1

Noah's Prayer. Carmen Bernos de Gasztold, *tr. fr. French* by Rumer Godden. TrCP

Noah's Raven. W. S. Merwin. ChIV-1; HCAP

Nobility. Alice Cary. WBLP

Noble, The. Wordsworth. *Fr.* Prelude [or, Growth of a Poet's Mind], The. ChTr; EnRP; OAEL-2

Noble ambition spans the four seas, A. T'ao Ch'ien, *tr. fr. Chinese* by Eugene Eoyang. SuSp

Noble Balm, The. Ben Jonson. OBEV

Noble [*or* Brave Old] Duke of York, The. *Unknown.* GBP

Noble Fisherman; or, Robin Hood's Preferment, The. *Unknown.* ESPB

Noble hart, that harbours vertuous [*or* virtuous] thought, The. The Fight of the Red Cross Knight and the Heathen Sansjoy. Spenser. *Fr.* Faerie Queene, The. FHYEP; NoSic

Noble horse with courage in his eye, The. Aristocrats. Keith Douglas. FaBoMo; NAEL-2; NoAM; OBWP

Noble in the sound which. Love. J. H. Prynne. VaA

Noble King of Brentford, The. The King of Brentford's Testament *abr.* Thackeray. OBNV

Noble Mayde, still standing, all this vewd, The. Spenser. *Fr.* Faerie Queene, The. NoP; PoEL-1

Noble, nasty course he ran, A. Epitaph on the Late King of the Sandwich Isles. Winthrop Mackworth Praed. FiBHP

Noble Nature, The. Ben Jonson. *See* It Is Not Growing Like a Tree.

Noble range it was, of many a rood, A. Leigh Hunt. *Fr.* Story of Rimini, The. EnRP

Noble Ritter Hugo, Der. Ballad by Hans Breitmann. Charles Godfrey Leland. BXAP; NOBL
  (Ballad of the Mermaid.) FiBHP

Noble Sidney with this last arose, The. Michael Drayton. *Fr.* To Henry Reynolds, of Poets and Poesy. EPCY

Noble six hundred! (*LL*) The Charge of the Light Brigade. Tennyson. BeLS; BLPA; EBEvV; EnVR; FaBoBe; FaBoEH; FaBV; FaPON; FaPoR; FHYEP; GN; HoPM; NAEL-2; NOBVV; OBWP; OxAEP-2; PeVV; PrIm; TEP; TFi; UV; VPP; WBLP

Nobleman and Thresherman, The ("Nobleman lived in a valley of late.") *Unknown.* OBET

Nobleman's House, A, *sels.* May Sarton.

Nobler funeral pyre!, A. (*LL*) John Maynard. Horatio Alger, Jr.. BeLS; BLPA; FaBoBe

Nobles and heralds, by your leave. On Himself. Matthew Prior. FaBoEE
  (Prior's Epitaph.) TrGrPo

Noblesse Oblige. Jessie Redmond Fauset. CDC; VBLP

Noblesse Oblige. Celeste Turner Wright. Poetsp

Noblest bodies are but gilded clay. Samuel Harding. NOSC

Noblest Charis, you that are. His Discourse with Cupid. Ben Jonson. *Fr.* Celebration of Charis in Ten Lyric[k] Peeces [*or* pieces], A. BeJo; OxAEP-1; SeCP

Noblest of men, woo't die? Shakespeare. *Fr.* Antony and Cleopatra. IMW, *act* V, *sc.* 1; OxAEP-1, *sect.* IV, xiii

Nobly Born, The. Frances E. W. Harper. PWR

Nobly, nobly Cape Saint Vincent to the northwest died away. Home Thoughts, from the Sea. Robert Browning. EBEvV; NAEL-2; SCGP

Nobody. Shel Silverstein. OTCP

Nobody. Novica Tadic, *tr. fr. Serbo-Croatian* by Charles Simic. HSix

Nobody ain't Christmas shoppin.' Crowded Out. Rosalie Jonas. ShDr

Nobody asked you, sir, she said. (*LL*) "Where are you going [to], my pretty maid?" Mother Goose. OxNR; ReMoGo

Nobody but Lester let Lester leap. Lester Leaps In. Al Young. SM

Nobody comes up from the sea as late as this. You Will Know When You Get There. Allen Curnow. PeNZ

Nobody else can have as much fun as. The Twenty Grand (Saturday Night on the Block). Naomi Long Madgett. NBV

Nobody heard him, the dead man. Not Waving but Drowning. Stevie Smith. CoGr; FaBoWP; FaPoB; FF; GTBS-P; HAP; HeIP; MoP;

NAEL-2; NALW; NoAM; NOBE; NoP; OAEL-2; OxAEP-2; OxBTC; PoE; Poetr; PPP; PrIm; TEP; TFi; UV; WeW

Nobody in the lane, and nothing, nothing but blackberries. Blackberrying. Sylvia Plath. HAP; HCAP; NAAL-2; NoAM; NOBA; NYBP

Nobody is dead yet and won't be. Right. A Local Contractor Flees His Winter Trouble and Saves Some Lives in a Knoxville Motel Room. James Whitehead. MT

Nobody is going to slap him around. (*LL*) Hedgehog. Chu Chen Po. OHMPC

Nobody knew when it would start again. Schizophrenic. P. K. Page. HeIP

Nobody knows/ Whither our delirium. The Need. Siegfried Sassoon. TrPWD

Nobody Knows but Mother. Mary Morrison. BLPA

Nobody Knows de Trouble I've Seen, *Unknown.* AH

Nobody knows the other side. Jack Kerouac. *Fr.* Mexico City Blues. NeAP

Nobody knows the world but me. Professor Noctutus. George Macdonald. NOBVV

Nobody knows what love is anymore. For a Masseuse and Prostitute. Kenneth Rexroth. NNaP

Nobody knows what's growing in Bridget. The Bulge. George Johnston. MoCV

Nobody lives in the cottage now. Fairy Feet. Phyllis L. Garlick. BoTP

Nobody Loses All the Time. E. E. Cummings. CMoP; DL; FaBoCo; FF; LiTM; NAAL-2; NBLV; NOBA; RB; TwCP

Nobody loves me. Nobody. Shel Silverstein. OTCP

Nobody loves me/ Everybody hates me. *Unknown.* ISE

Nobody loves you Chloe, you sly minx. To His Coy Mistress. Edward Bird. BXAP; FaBoPa

Nobody noogers the shaft of a sloo. On a Flimmering Floom You Shall Ride. Carl Sandburg. GoYe; OBAL

Nobody, not even the rain, has such small hands. (*LL*) Somewhere I Have Never Travelled[, Gladly Beyond]. E. E. Cummings. ArLo; BoLoP; InPS; LiTA; LiTM; LPA; MoAB; MoAmPo; NAAL-2; NoP; Poetr; SOTW; TrGrPo; TwCP; UnAS; VGW

Nobody on earth has a book of matches. Race of the Kingfishers. Ray A. Young Bear. HATNAP

Nobody painted Mrs. Aherne's store. Dakota: Five Times Six. Joseph Hansen. NYBP

Nobody picks a red rose when the winter wind. Red and White. Carl Sandburg. ArNa

Nobody planted roses, he recalls. "Summertime and the Living." Robert Hayden. PoBA; PPP; TwCP

Nobody put their hand out. All Clear. Roger Woddis. PeLV

Nobody read him, the poor sod. Not Wavell but Browning. Gavin Ewart. UV

Nobody Riding the Roads Today. June Jordan. BPo; NoAM

Nobody sings. (*LL*) They've lost it, lost it. Aaron Kramer. EaPr

Nobody stays here long. Not in the Guide-Books. Elizabeth Jennings. LiTM

Nobody stuffs the world in at your eyes. Snow. Margaret Avison. NOBC

Nobody Thinks Hard Enough for Poetry. Kelvin Corcoran. NBrP

Nobody wanted this infant born. Burial. Mark Van Doren. MoBS

Nobody will open the door for you. Blanca Varela, *tr. fr. Spanish* by Willis Barnstone. BoWoP

Nobody will quarrel with the woodcock. Quarrel. *Yoruba Oral Tradition*, *tr.* by Ulli Beier. WTO

Nobody will sing a mass. Anniversary. Heine, *tr. fr. German* by Alistair Elliot. OBD

Nobody's chasing me. (*LL*) Nobody's Chasing Me. Cole Porter. CBLP

Nobody's Chasing Me. Cole Porter. CBLP

Nochebuena. Rosario Caicedo. LoHo

Nocht o' Mortal Sicht. Bessie J. B. Macarthur. OxBS

Noctambule. George Johnston. MoCV

Nocturn at the Institute. David McElroy. Poetsp

Nocturnal Heart. Anne-Marie Kegels, *tr. fr. French* by W. S. Merwin. BoWoP

Nocturnal honey that glides down from the flanks, The. White on White. Maria Luisa Spaziani, *tr. fr. Italian* by Beverly Allen. NeIt

Nocturnal Landscape. Malcolm Cowley. PoA

Nocturnal Landscape. Anton Schnack, *tr. fr. German* by Christopher Middleton. PeFWW

Nocturnal, my panther, has eyes that spark, The. Tuvia Rivner, *tr. fr. Hebrew* by Ruth Finer Mintz. MHP

Nocturnal Reverie, A. The Countess of Winchilsea. EBEV; ECEV; ECWP; NAEL-1; NALW; NOEC; NoP; OxAEP-1; PBWP; PoE; PoEL-3; Poetr; WPE

Nocturnal Sketch, A. Thomas Hood. FaBoCo; FiBHP; PeLV

Nocturnal Sounds. Kattie M. Cumbo. BlSi

Nocturnal water, primaeval silences. Useless Day. Rosario Castellanos, tr. by Maureen Ahern. WPOW

Nocturnal[1] upon Saint Lucy's [or S. Lucies] Day, Being the Shortest Day, A. John Donne. EBEV; EnRePo; ESCV; FHYEP; GBL; JCP; LiTB; MeLP; NAEL-1; NOBE; NoP; NOSC; OAEL-1; OxAEP-1; PoE; PoEL-2; PPP; SCGP; SeCP; SeCV-1; TEP; TFi

Nocturne: "After a friend has gone." Eavan Boland. NBrP

Nocturne: "Be thou at peace this night." Edward Davison. CH

Nocturne: "Blade of a knife, The." Richard Murphy. IPY

Nocturne: "Dismal as a toad's domed eye, a cloud." John Cassidy. PWE

Nocturne: "I see the local satyr stand." Gerda Mayer. FaBoBl

Nocturne: "If the deep word is haunted." Robert Silliman Hillyer, tr. by John Moyne and Coleman Barks. FYAP; UnAS

Nocturne: "Listening for the sound." Pinkie Gordon Lane. BlSi

Nocturne: "Moon has gone to her rest, The." Wilfrid Scawen Blunt. OBMV

Nocturne: "Over New England now, the snow." Frances Frost. BoNaP

Nocturne: "Red flame flowers bloom and die, The." Crosbie Garstin. CH

Nocturne: "Softly blow lightly." Donald Jeffrey Hayes. CDC

Nocturne: "This cool night is strange." Gwendolyn B. Bennett. ShDr

Nocturne: "Wildness of haggard flights." Roussan Camille, tr. fr. French by Seth L. Wolitz. TTY

Nocturne at Bethesda. Arna Bontemps. CDC; ChIV-2; PoNe

Nocturne at Danieli's, A. Sir Owen Seaman. UV

Nocturne by Ben Shahn. R. S. Thomas. OxAEP-2

Nocturne for October 31st, A. Yvor Winters. PoA

Nocturne in a Deserted Brickyard. Carl Sandburg. MoAmPo

Nocturne in G Minor. Karl Gustav Vollmoeller, tr. fr. German by Ludwig Lewisohn. AWP

Nocturne in the Women's Prison. Maria Beneyto, tr. fr. Spanish by Catherine Rodriguez-Nieto. WPOW

Nocturne of the Self-evident Presence. Thomas MacGreevy. BIrV; CIP

Nocturne of the Wharves. Arna Bontemps. BPo; LPA; PoNe

Nocturne Varial. Lewis Alexander. PoBA; PoNe

Nod. Will Bennett. UL

Nod. Walter de la Mare. BoTP; MoAB; MoBrPo; OxBTC; PFP

Nodding and beckoning across, observed of Attaché and Guardsman. Arthur Hugh Clough. Fr. Bothie of Tober-na-Vuolich, The [A Long-Vacation Pastoral]. FaBoPV; OBF

Nodding, its great head rattling like a gourd. Original Sin; a Short Story. Robert Penn Warren. HoPM; LiTA; LiTM; NOCV; PPP; SM; TAP

Noe more unto my thoughts appeare. Sidney Godolphin. MeLP

Noël. Hilaire Belloc. UV

Noel; Christmas Eve, 1913. Robert Bridges. LiTB; NOCV; OBCP; PoEL-5

Noel, noel, noel. Out of Your Sleep Arise and Wake. Unknown. NoP

Noel of the marvelous night. To Noel. Gabriela Mistral, tr. fr. Spanish by Doris Dana. PChr

Noël Tragique. Ramon Guthrie. ErPo

Noh Play. Jim Brodey. UL

Noise began in my belly, The. For Carlos Charles Bucillio. Alice Sadongei. HATNAP

Noise Grimaced. Larry Eigner. NeAP

Noise of hammers once I heard. The Hammers. Ralph Hodgson. GoJo; MoBrPo; NOBE; OxBTC

Noise of the Village, The. Unknown, tr. fr. Chippewa Indian by Frances Densmore. OBVE

Noise of water teased his literal ears, The. Persistent Explorer. John Crowe Ransom. OxBA

Noise That Time Makes, The. Merrill Moore. MoAmPo; TrGrPo

Noiseless Patient Spider, A. Walt Whitman. AmPP; AnAmPo; AWP; BLPL; FF; HAP; HeIL; HeIP; ImPo; InPK; InPS; LiTA; MoAmPo; NAAL-1; NOBE; NoP; NTP; OxBA; OxBSP; PoE; Poetr; SAmP; SCV; TAP; TFi; TrGrPo; WiR

Noiselessly, the mountain stream. A Sketch of Mount Chung. Wang An-shih, tr. fr. Chinese by Jan W. Walls. SuSp

Noises in the Night. Lilian McCrea. BoTP

Noises in the Night. Thomas Middleton. See Midnight's bell goes ting, ting, ting, ting, ting.

Noises of the harbour die, the smoke is petrified, The. The Statue. John Fuller. NOBE

Noises round my house, The. On cobbles bounding. Regent's Park Terrace. Bernard Spencer. FaBoPP

Noisy politicians confuse the world. Rhyming with a Friend. Yü Hsüan-chi, tr. by Geoffrey R. Waters. BoWoP

Noisy urchins scampered round, The. Much Distressed. Unknown. CBAP

Nokes went, he thought, to Styles's wife to bed. A Case to the Civilians. Unknown. FaBoEE

Noll's soul and Ireton's live within him yet. (LL) An Acrostic on Wharton. Unknown. FaBoEH; OBSV

Noman, the King of Hira, sat one day. The Abdication of Noman. Richard Henry Stoddard. AnAmPo

Nomen. Naomi Long Madgett. BlSi

Nomenclature. Stephen Vincent Benét. AnAmPo

Nominativo hic gallant asse. The Declining of a Gallant. Unknown. FaBoUs

Nomine Domini/ Theotocopoulos. High Renaissance. George Starbuck. NBLV; OBAL

Non Amo Te. Thomas Brown, after the Latin of Martial. See I do not love [or like] thee, Doctor Fell.

Non Dolet. Oliver St. John Gogarty. OBMV

Non Fit. Rose Terry Cooke. AmWP

Non-native plantings stuck into lawns. Cougar. Brendan Galvin. FoLa

Non Nobis. Henry Cust. OBEV

Non Piangere, Liù. Peter Porter. CBLP; FaBoMA; OxBC

Non Que Je Veuille Ôter la Liberté. Pernette de Guillet, tr. fr. French by Raymond Oliver. WPOW

Non-sense. Unknown. See Oh that my lungs could bleat like butter'd pease.

Non Sequitor [or Sequitur], A. Richard Corbett [or Corbet]. CBNP; FaBoNo

Non Sum Qualis Eram Bonae sub Regno Cynarae [or Cynara]. Ernest Dowson. AWP; BeLS; BLPA; BoLoP; CBLP; ClHu; EBVV; EnLoPo; FaBoBe; FaPoB; GBL; GTBS-P; HAP; HeIP; ImPo; LiTB; MoBrPo; NOBE; NoP; OAEL-2; OBEV; OBMV; OBNC; PeVV; PlP; PoRA; PrIm; TEP; TFi; TrGrPo; UnPo

Non Sum Qualis Eram in Bona Urbe Nordica Illa. John Hollander. ErPo

Non Ti Fidar. Louis Zukofsky. VGW

Non ti scordar di me! (LL) Aux Italiens. "Owen Meredith." BeLS; BLPA; BLPL; FaBoBe

Nona poured oil on the water and saw the eye. The Evil Eye. John Ciardi. MoBS; NAs

Nondescript, The. Peter Scupham. SCBI

Nondescript express in from the South, A. Gare du Midi. W. H. Auden. OxBSP

None. (LL) As I was going to St. Ives. Mother Goose. NTCP; OFC; OxNR; ReMoGo

None. Josephine Miles. VGW

None are like you, Shulamite. (LL) The Hebrew of Your Poets, Zion. Charles Reznikoff. ChIV-1; VGW

None but a Muse in love, can tell. On Fruition. Sir Charles Sedley. ErPo; NOSC

None but the mouse-brown wren. The Young Martins. Andrew Young. FM

None but them, and leave the rest. (LL) To Sickness. Ben Jonson. BeJo

None but Zion's children know. (LL) Glorious Things of Thee Are Spoken. John Newton. NOCV; WGRP

None could better our sex limousine. Unknown. PeLi

None could ever say that she. True or False. Catullus, tr. fr. Latin by Walter Savage Landor. AWP; OBVE

None ever liv'd more just, none more abused. (LL) Where are all thy beauties now, all hearts enchaining? Thomas Campion. GBL

None ever was in love with me but grief. "My True Love Hath My Heart and I Have His." Mary Elizabeth Coleridge. BoLoP

None Is Happy. Hartmann von Aue, tr. fr. German by Jethro Bithell. AWP

None is, slight things do lightly please. (LL) His Grange, or Private Wealth. Robert Herrick. BeJo; CaPo; FM; GoJo; SeCV-1

None is the Same as Another. Iain Crichton Smith. NTP

None of it true; for Christ's sake, spill the ink. "Robin Hyde." Fr. Houses, The. PeNZ

None of my ancestors sat for their portraits. Descendant. Elisaveta Bagriana, tr. fr. Bulgarian by Maxine W. Kumin. VBLP

None of Self and All of Thee. Theodore Monod. BLRP

None of Us are as Young. W. H. Auden. ArLo

None other fame mine unambitious muse. Samuel Daniel. Fr. To Delia. AAS; ESo

None Other Lamb None Other Name. Christina Rossetti. TrPWD

None saw their spirits' shadow shake the grass. Isaac Rosenberg. Fr. Dead Man's Dump. FaBoMo; GTBS-P; LiTM; NAEL-2; NoAM; NoP; NSI; OBD; OBWP; PeFWW; PoWW; TrJP

None shall gainsay me. I will lie on the floor. Gloriana Dying. Sylvia Townsend Warner. FaBoEH; FaBoWP

None walked behind that shoddy rain-swept hearse. Mozart's Grave. Paul Scott Mowrer. GoYe

None'll come, and then a lot'll. (LL) On Tomato Ketchup. Unknown. FaBoUs; NBLV

Nonpareil. Matthew Prior. EnLoPo

Nonsense [or Nonsence]. Richard Corbett [or Corbet]. *See* Like to the Thundering Tone.

Nonsense. Thomas Moore. FaBoEE

Nonsense: ("Oh that my lungs could bleat like butter'd pease"). *Unknown*. *See* Oh that my lungs could bleat like butter'd pease.

Nonsense Quatrains. Gelett Burgess. FaBoNo

Nonsense Song, A. Stephen Vincent Benét. OBAL

Nonsense Song, A: ("My lady went to Canterbury"). *Unknown*. *See* My lady went to Canterbury [or Caunterbury].

Nonsense Song: ("My heart of gold"). *Unknown*. CBNP; OxBLMV

Nonsense Verses. Charles Lamb. CBNP

Noodle-Vendor's Flute, The. D. J. Enright. NoP

Nooksack Valley. Gary Snyder. NaP

Noon. John Clare. OxAEP-2

Noon. "Michael Field." NOBVV

Noon. Robinson Jeffers. MoAmPo

Noon heat in the yard, The. Hen Woman. Thomas Kinsella. CIP; IPY; PBCIP

Noon is beautiful, The: the perfect wheel. Yvor Winters. VGW

Noon of the Sunbather. Marge Piercy. NMM

Noon on the mountain! Walt Whitman. Emanuel Carnevali. PoA

Noon sun beats down the leaf; The noon. Grapes Making. Léonie Adams. FYAP; UnPo

Noon. The luminous tide. Ballydavid Pier. Thomas Kinsella. BIrV

Noonday Sun. Kathryn Jackson *and* Byron Jackson. FaPON

Noonday Thought. H. Cordelia Ray. *Fr.* Group of Musings, A. CBWP-3

Noonlight is sudden full of the spirits. The Storm. Robert Wallace. NYBP

Noon's Dream-Song. Eugene Lee-Hamilton. NOBVV

Noontide. H. Cordelia Ray. *Fr.* Idyl. CBWP-3

Nooo!/ me nah call him. Wasting Time. Opal Palmer. FaBoVe

Nooses of double meanings swing. Conversation Piece. Arthur Freeman. ErPo

Nor a chair to sit doon. (*LL*) Buchlyvie. *Unknown*. GBP

Nor all earth's flowers, how fair. (*LL*) Slim Cunning Hands. Walter de la Mare. FaBoEE; NIP; WeW

Nor all, that glisters, gold. (*LL*) Ode on [or On] the Death of a Favourite [or Favorite] Cat, Drowned in a Tub [or Bowl] of Gold Fishes. Thomas Gray. ClHu; EBEV; ECEV; FaBoBe; FHYEP; FM; HoPM; NAEL-1; NBLV; NOBE; NOBL; NOEC; NoP; OAEL-1; OFC; PeLV; PoE; PoEL-3; PPP; SoCa; TEP; TFi

Nor antlers through the thickness of his curls. (*LL*) Arms and the Boy. Wilfred Owen. CMoP; HAP; ImPo; LiTB; LiTM; MeMBP; MoAB; MoBrPo; OAEL-1; OAEL-2; OxBSP; PoE; Poetr; WeW

Nor any bird of the air. (*LL*) The Deserted House. Mary Elizabeth Coleridge. BoTP; CH

Nor beauty's want my first good will remove. (*LL*) To His Friend, Promising That Though Her Beauty Fade, Yet His Love Shall Last. George Turberville.

Nor bring, to see me cease to live. A Wish. Matthew Arnold. IHNG

Nor, by God, shall we neglect. Diogenes Laertius, *tr. fr. Greek by* Robin Skelton. GrAn

Nor can I for my soul delight. Soame Jenyns. *Fr.* Epistle Written in the Country to the Right Honourable the Lord Lovelace, An. ECEV

Nor delayed the winged saint. Raphael's Descent. Milton. *Fr.* Paradise Lost. EPCY; NOSC

Nor did the peach complain. (*LL*) The Blue-Fly. Robert Graves. CMoP; NAEL-2; NoAM; NYBP

Nor do these gentle creatures wrong. (*LL*) Kindness to Animals. *Unknown*. BoTP; FaBoUs; WHSW

Nor doth the sliver-tonguèd Melicert. Henry Chettle. FaBoEH

Nor dread nor hope attend. Death. W. B. Yeats. OxAEP-2; OxBSP

Nor even dying. (*LL*) Dartmoor: Sunset at Chagford. Thomas Edward Brown. NOBVV

Nor ever did a wise one. (*LL*) Epitaph on Charles II. The Earl of Rochester. FaBoCo; FiBHP; SCGP; TrGrPo

Nor ever did a wise one. (*LL*) Impromptu on Charles II. The Earl of Rochester. ChTr; FaBoEE; NBLV; NOBL; NTP; OBSV; OxAEP-1; PeLV

Nor ever shall be. (*LL*) Fortunatus Nimium. Robert Bridges.

Nor exults he nor complains he; silent bears whate'er befalls him. Ever Watchful. Ta' Abbata Sharra, *tr. fr. Arabic by* W. G. Palgrave. AWP

Nor fear thy latest day, nor wish therefor. (*LL*) Things that make the happier life, are these, The. Martial. CBCK; FaBoEE; OBVE

Nor feare, or wish your dying day. (*LL*) A Country Life: To His Brother, Master Thomas Herrick. Robert Herrick. CaPo; SeCP; SeCV-1

Nor feel the heart-break in the heart of things? (*LL*) We who are left, how shall we look again. W. W. Gibson. NSI; OxBTC

Nor for the crabbed state-creed, wayward wight. James Hogg. *Fr.* To The Right Honourable Lord Byron. EPCY

Nor God, nor man, the image thou dost see. Hildebert, *tr. fr. Latin by* Helen Waddell. MLL

Nor had that sweet fa-laing. (*LL*) Since Bonny-Boots Was Dead. *Unknown*. PoEL-2

Nor Hammond's love nor Shenstone's was sincere. John Maclaurin. NOEC

Nor happiness, nor majesty, nor fame. Political Greatness. Shelley. EnRP

Nor he with my review. (*LL*) Browning. Robert Louis Stevenson. NOBVV

Nor heed my craft or art. (*LL*) In My Craft or Sullen Art. Dylan Thomas. AngWe; BoLoP; CMoP; GTBS-P; HAP; HeIL; HeIP; InvP; LiTM; LPA; MAT; MeMBP; MoP; NIP; NoAM; NoP; PoE; Poetr; RaBo; WeW

Nor hymn, nor prayer, nor church. (*LL*) The Bohemian Hymn. Emerson. WGRP

Nor is it essential to be young. (*LL*) Late Sonnet. Hayden Carruth. SM; Son

Nor Is It Written. Laura Riding. *Fr.* Three Sermons to the Dead. LiTA

Nor Jests wilt thou afford me more. (*LL*) Animula Vagula, Blandula. Emperor Hadrian. FaBoRV

Nor kith nor kin nor ox nor ass nor anything. (*LL*) Mind Pictures. Beatrice Hastings. PeSAV

Nor knows he makes the shadow he pursues! (*LL*) Constancy to an Ideal Object. Samuel Taylor Coleridge. MeMBP; NAEL-2

Nor lingered Paris in the lofty house. Homer, *tr. by* Tennyson. *Fr.* Iliad, The. OBVE

Nor long the trench or lofty walls oppose. Homer, *tr. by* Pope. *Fr.* Iliad, The. OBVE

Nor maid, nor honour, sure no honesty. (*LL*) On a Maid [or Maide] of Honour Seen by a Scholar in Somerset Garden. Thomas Randolph. JCP

Nor my titanic tears, the seas, be dried." (*LL*) The End. Wilfred Owen. CH; ChIV-1; FaBoRV; PAW

Nor over ground. (*LL*) For the Company Underground. Francis MacNamara. NOBAu

Nor Pirate, though a Prince he be. (*LL*) Upon Kind[e] and True Love. Aurelian Townshend. MeLP; NOSC; PlP

Nor practising virtue nor committing crime. Geoffrey Taylor. FaBoEE

Nor second he, that rode sublime. Thomas Gray. *Fr.* Progress of Poesy, The. EPCY

Nor shall my verse that elder bard forget. James Thomson. *Fr.* Seasons, The. EPCY

Nor shall you for your fields neglect your stock. Young Stock. V. Sackville-West. OxBTC

Nor, Shenstone, thou/ Shalt pass withou thy meed, thou son of peace! William Mason. *Fr.* English Garden, The. EPCY

Nor skin nor hide nor fleece. Lethe. Hilda Doolittle ("H. D."). AnAmPo; CMoP; FaBoWP; LiTM; MoAmPo; PoRA; TrGrPo; VGW

Nor sought in me much more than thou couldst find. (*LL*) I never cared for Life: Life cared for me. Thomas Hardy. FaBoEE; FaBoRV

Nor speaks nor sings. (*LL*) Lines Written at the Grave of Alexander [or Alexandre] Dumas. Gwendolyn B. Bennett. CDC; PoNe

Nor success make proud. (*LL*) Rock and Hawk. Robinson Jeffers. NoAM; NOBA; OxBA; Poetr

Nor the endless harvest of speech. (*LL*) Desperate Message #2. Mark Svenvold. UTF

Nor their noise, nor their noise. (*LL*) The Death of Admiral Benbow. *Unknown*. CoMu; GBP

Nor think, in nature's state they blindly trod. Pope. *Fr.* Essay on Man, An. OAEL-1

Nor thirteen pence a day. (*LL*) Grenadier. A. E. Housman. OBMV; OBWP

Nor trusteth man to this weal, the wheel it turneth so. (*LL*) Fortune. *Unknown*. HeIP

Nor truth nor good did they know. Gloss. Padraic Fiacc. CIP; PNI

Nor used this complaint, nor have thought the day to be so long. (*LL*) Constant Penelope sends to thee, careless Ulysses. Ovid. EnLoPo; GBL; NAEL-1; NoSic; OAEL-1

Nor was this fellowship vouchsaf'd to me. Wordsworth Skates on Esthwaite Water. Wordsworth. *Fr.* Prelude [or, Growth of a Poet's Mind], The. CH; EnRP; FaBoPP; GN; HAP; NOBE; NoP; NU; OAEL-2; OBNC; OxAEP-2; PoE; SCV

Nor what God blessed once, prove accursed. (*LL*) Apparent Failure. Robert Browning. EBVVPR; NAEL-2; NOBE

Nor what I "wished to say" a while ago. (*LL*) A Grievance. James Kenneth Stephen. BXAP; FaBoPa

Nor when the youthful pair more closely join. Concerning the Nature of Love. Lucretius, *tr. by* Dryden. *Fr.* De Rerum Natura (On the Nature of Things). ErPo

(I Know Myself a Man.) ChTr
"I know my soul hath power to know all things."
"Strongest and the noblest argument, The."
What Is This Knowledge? FaBoRV
(Much Knowledge, Little Reason.) ChTr
Nose, The. Iain Crichton Smith. OBSP; RB
Nose, nose, jolly red nose. Beaumont *and* Fletcher *and* John Fletcher. *Fr.* Knight of the Burning Pestle, The. FaBoCh; OxNR
Nose of the pick-up lifted, The. Scattering Ashes. David Scott. PWE
Nose only above water. Sandra: At the Beaver Trap. Michael S. Harper. NoAM
Nose went away, by itself, The. The Nose. Iain Crichton Smith. OBSP; RB
Nosegay. Elizabeth J. Coatsworth. *See* Violets, Daffodils.
Nosegay. Elizabeth J. Coatsworth. OBCA
Nosegay, A. John Reynolds. OBEV
Nosegay Always Sweet, for Lovers to Send for Tokens of Love at New Year's Tide, or for Fairings, A ("Nosegay, lacking flowers fresh,") William Hunnis. EIL
Nosobame, The. Christian Morgenstern. CBNP
Nostalgia. Walter de la Mare. LiTM
Nostalgia. D. H. Lawrence. PoA
Nostalgia. Amy Lowell. AnAmPo
Nostalgia. Louis MacNeice. OxAEP-2
Nostalgia. Marjorie Marshall. ShDr
Nostalgia. Bin Ramke. MT
Nostalgia. Karl Shapiro. CMoP; CoAP; TrJP; TwCP
Nostalgia and Complaint of the Grandparents. Donald Justice. *See* Our diaries squatted, toad-like [*or* toadlike].
Nostalgia is the elixir drained. Lyn Hejinian. UL
Nostoi. Rodolfo Di Biasio, *tr. fr. Italian by* Stephen Sartarelli. NeIt
Not a breeze. Rest, My Soul. Karl Henkell, *tr. fr. German by* Philip L. Miller. RiWo
Not a cage but an organ. Elevator Man, 1949. Rita Dove. NAmP90
Not a crumb of leavened. Passover Night 1942. Yala Korwin. BTR
Not a day goes by without my thinking of you. To One in Beirut. Karen Alkalay-Gut. WoWa
Not a Dream, Just Thoughts. Marion Cohen. BTR
Not a drum was heard, not a funeral note. The Burial of Sir John Moore [after (*or* at) Corunna]. Charles Wolfe. ChTr; EBEvV; EnRP; FaBoEH; FaBoPa; FaBoRV; FaPoB; FaPoR; GN; GTBS; GTBS-P; NOBE; NTP; OBEV; OBWP; OxAEP-2; PeIV; PlP; PoRA; PWR; TFi; UV; VPP; WBLP
Not a Herod's oath that cannot change. (*LL*) The Mind Is an Enchanting Thing. Marianne Moore. CMoP; HeIL; HeIP; InPK; InvP; MeMAP; MoAB; MoAmPo; NAAL-2; OxBA; PoE; PPP; WPOW
Not a late hour not unlit rows. Judas Town. Anne Carson. *Fr.* Life of Towns, The. BAP-90
Not a laugh was heard, not a frivolous note. The Burial of the Bachelor. *Unknown.* FaBoPa
Not a line of her writing have I. Thoughts of Phena [at News of Her Death]. Thomas Hardy. EBVV; NoP; OxBTC
Not a Man and Yet a Man, *sels.* Albery Allson Whitman.
End of the Whole Matter, The. AAP
Flight of Leeona. AAP
In the House of the Aylors. AAP
Old Sac Village, The. AAP
Runaway, The. AAP
Saville in Trouble. AAP
Not a roof but a field of stars. (*LL*) Rent. Jane Cooper. FYAP; TAP
Not a shank of the long lane upwards. Brechfa Chapel. Roland Mathias. AngWe
Not a single flower. Evening View at the Western Palace. Liu Sha-ho, *tr. fr. Chinese. Fr.* Two Poems of Peking. LHF, *tr. by* Hualing Nieh
Not a soul, only. As a Thousand Years. Jeremy Hooker. AngWe
Not a Sous Had He Got. "Thomas Ingoldsby." R. H. Barham. *Fr.* Ingoldsby Legends, The. FaBoCo; FM; UV
Not a thing on the river McCluskey did fear. The Little Brown Bulls. *Unknown.* AmFP
Not a tree but the tree. There Is Only One of Everything. Margaret Atwood. NOBC
Not a twig or a leaf on the old tree. A Withered Tree. Han Yü, *tr. fr. Chinese by* A. C. Graham. PLT
Not a Very Cheerful Song, I'm Afraid. Adrian Mitchell. OTCP
Not a word! not a word. Flamingo. Eleanor Farjeon. OBAP
Not a word, not a word, not a word. (*LL*) Crucifixion. *Unknown.* BPo; TAP; TrGrPo
Not a word, or to the knowing. Ecstatic Longing. Goethe, *tr. fr. German by* John Frederick Nims. STV

Not a word to each other; we kept the great pace. Robert Browning. *Fr.* How They Brought the Good News from Ghent to Aix. Poetr, *St.* 2 *only*
Not Adlestrop. Dannie Abse. AngWe; NoAM
Not all can nick it that will, heigho! (*LL*) Ballad[e] of Ladies' Love, Number Two. Villon. ErPo
Not All Immaculate. Laura Riding. *Fr.* Three Sermons to the Dead. LiTA
Not all of them were human. The Village of Tudda. Kenneth Patchen. VGW
Not all of us were warm, not all of us. Spring. James Still. GrPl; MT
Not all pale Hecate's direful charms. Lines Occasioned by the Burning of Some Letters. Sarah Dixon. ECWP; NOEC
Not All There. Robert Frost. FaBoCo
Not all thy flushing suns are set. An Ode to Master Endymion Porter, upon His Brother's Death. Robert Herrick. CaPo
Not all trees are felled by storms. Also All. Shu Ting, *tr. fr. Chinese by* Donald Finkel *with* Yi Jinsheng. SpMi
Not Alone for Mighty Empire. William Pierson Merrill. AH; TrPWD
Not alwayes give a melting kiss. Johannes Secundus, *tr. fr. Latin by* Thomas Stanley. *Fr.* Basia. OBVE
Not always as the whirlwind's rush. The Call of the Christian. Whittier. NOCV
Not always to the swift race. The Law of Averages. "Troubadour." FiBHP
Not among men. (*LL*) You ask. Li Po. EaPr
Not an avenue and not a bower. Seamus Heaney. *Fr.* Crossings. BAP-90
Not an editorial-writer, bereaved with bartlett. Portrait of the Poet as Landscape. A. M. Klein. NoAM; NOBC
Not and tries last once tries tries AH, GOD. (*LL*) Falling. James Dickey. LCAP; MT; NoAM; NYBP
Not any higher stands the Grave. Emily Dickinson. AnAmPo; SAmP
Not as all other women are. My Love. James Russell Lowell. BLPL; FaBoBe
Not as Black Douglas, bannered, trumpeted. Two Wise Generals. Ted Hughes. MoBS
Not as height rises into lightness. Breadth. Circle. Desert. Monarch. Month. Wisdom. John Hollander. PoA
Not as she is, but as she fills his dream. (*LL*) In an Artist's Studio. Christina Rossetti. NAEL-2; NALW; NoP; Poetr
Not as the thirsty soyle desires soft showres. Francis Quarles. *Fr.* Emblems. ESCV
Not as the white nations. The Black Madonna. Albert Rice. CDC
Not as things. (*LL*) Angry Dusk. Jack Lindsay. NOBAu
Not as we are but as we must appear. Geoffrey Hill. *Fr.* Funeral Music. NoAM
Not as when some great Captain falls. Abraham Lincoln. Richard Henry Stoddard. AnAmPo; FaBoBe; GN; OHIP; PAH
Not as Wont. Joseph Skipsey. NOBVV
Not at midnight, not at morning, O sweet city. Caryatid. Léonie Adams. LiTM
Not because of his eyes. The Turtle. William Carlos Williams. RaBo; SAmP
Not because of victories. Te Deum. Charles Reznikoff. ChIV-1; TrJP
Not because of you, not because of me, just that. Natalya Gorbanevskaya, *tr. fr. Russian by* Daniel Weissbort. BoWoP
Not because you didn't call. The Heart Has Its Reasons. Felice Picano. PeHV
Not because you suck/ off a sugar-cane. Distaste. Ammianus, *tr. fr. Greek by* Peter Jay. GrAn
Not being Breedlove, whose immortal skid. To Dorothy on Her Exclusion from the *Guinness Book of World Records.* X. J. Kennedy. Poetsp
Not Being Oedipus. John Heath-Stubbs. OxBC; TEP
Not-Being was not, Being was not then. Brahma, the World Idea. *Unknown, tr. fr. Sanskrit by* Romesh Dutt. *Fr.* Vedic Hymns. WGRP
Not blest, but lonely. (*LL*) Sometimes I wish that I were Helen-fair. Lesbia Harford. NOBAu
Not born to the forest are we. Song of the Camels. Elizabeth J. Coatsworth. FaPON
Not British; certainly. Expatriates. R. S. Thomas. AngWe
Not but they die, the teasers and the dreams. The Teasers. William Empson. OxBTC
Not by Amphialus. (*LL*) Oh! [*or* O!] for some honest lover's ghost. Sir John Suckling. BeJo; BXAP; JCP; MeLP; PoEL-3; SeCP; SeCV-1
Not by Bread Alone. *Unknown, tr. fr. Greek by* James Terry White. PoLF
Not by hammering the furious word. Harlem Riot, 1943. Pauli Murray. PoBA
Not by lost killers stranded. The Biggest Killing. Edward Dorn. VGW
Not by the city bells that chime the hours. A Summer Day. Florence Harrison. BoTP

Not by the poets. Discovery of This Time. Archibald MacLeish. LiTA

Not by wayout hairdos, bulbous Afro blowouts and certainly. Only in This Way. Margaret Goss Burroughs. BlSi

Not Caesar's deeds, nor all his honours won. To Clement Edmonds, on His *Caesar's Commentaries* Observed, and Translated. Ben Jonson. NOSC

Not caring to observe the Wind. Of Loving at First Sight. Edmund Waller. NOSC; SeCP

Not, Celia, that I juster am. Sir Charles Sedley. GTBS; GTBS-P (To Celia. AWP; NOBE; OBEV

Not comin' back tonight, matey. Matey. Patrick MacGill. NSI; PoWW

Not Dachau. Aaron Miller. BTR

Not Dead, but Sleeping. Clara Ann Thompson. CBWP-2

Not drunk but with a buzz on maybe, he. In Memory of W. H. Auden. David R. Slavitt. SM

Not easy to state the change you made. Love Letter. Sylvia Plath. NOBA

Not even. Albert Speer. W. D. Snodgrass. NoAM

Not even a lynx could see a gap at all. (*LL*) Divided. Walter de la Mare. CBLP

Not even an hour. (*LL*) Sent from the Capital to Her Elder Daughter. Lady Otomo no Sakanoe. AIW; BoWoP; MDDM; WPOW

Not Even Because You Have Pearl-White Teeth. Angela de Hoyos. AfAz

Not even for a moment. He knew, for one thing, what he was. Leda. Mona Van Duyn. NMM

Not even I — would undo me so! (*LL*) The Going. Thomas Hardy. CBLP; EBEV; ELP; LiTB; MeMBP; NOBE; OxAEP-2; SCGP; UnPo

Not even in a dream. The Victims of the Little Box. Vasco [*or* Vasko] Popa, *tr. fr. Serbo-Croatian by* Charles Simic. AnRep; HSix

Not even in death can I. Archias of Byzantium, *tr. fr. Greek by* Clive Sansom. GrAn

Not even in dreams/ Can I meet him anymore. Lady Ise, *tr. fr. Japanese by* Donald Keene. WPOW

Not even my pride will suffer much. Edna St. Vincent Millay. *Fr.* Theme and Variations. VBLP

Not even the cops who can do anything could do this. Laundry. Bruce Smith. Son

Not even the sherpas have heard. The River's Elegy. Aidan Carl Mathews. IB

Not ever knowing what she does in the shower. A Fixture. Bill Berkson. UL

Not Every Day Fit for Verse. Robert Herrick. BeJo; PoRA

Not every man has gentians in his house. Bavarian Gentians. D. H. Lawrence. CMoP; FaBoCh; FaBoMo; GoJo; GTBS-P; HAP; ImPo; InPK; InPS; LiTB; MeMBP; MoP; NAEL-2; NoAM; NOBE; NoP; OAEL-2, 2 *ver.*; PoE; Poetr; SOTW; TFi; TRP; TTTS

Not every man knows what he shall sing at the end. The End. Mark Strand. TRP

Not every skin-teeth. Skin-Teeth. Grace Nichols. AIW

Not excluding mr u. (*LL*) Mr. U Will Not Be Missed. E. E. Cummings. FaBoEE; VGW

Not far advanc'd was morning day. Battle, The ("Not far advanc'd was morning day.") Sir Walter Scott. *Fr.* Marmion. EnRP

Not far beyond the town wild flowers grow. Sanctuary. Clifford Dyment. PoA

Not far from Belsen the countryside. Late Twentieth Century Pastoral. William Pitt Root. BTR

Not far from Circe's house I met a man. Near Circe's House. Robert Duncan. BCF

Not far from the estuary's grey window. Leningrad Romance. Carol Rumens. PWE

Not Flesh of Brass. Bible, *O.T. Fr.* Job. NAWM-1, *abr.*; TrJP

Not for all of beauty. Commentary Applied to Spiritual Things. St. John of the Cross, *tr. fr. Spanish by* K. Kavanaugh *and* O. Rodrigues. TOF

Not for Its Own Sake. Hazel Littlefield. GoYe

Not for me! (*LL*) Bat. D. H. Lawrence. GTBS-P; HAP; OAEL-1; OAEL-2; OBTV

Not for me a giantess. Requirements. Niarchus, *tr. fr. Greek by* Wallace Rice. ErPo

Not for That City. Charlotte Mew. ChIV-2; MoBrPo

Not for the promise of the laboured field. Ode to the Poppy. Henrietta Oneil. ECWP; WPE

Not for these lovely blooms that prank your chambers did I come. Rendezvous. Edna St. Vincent Millay. NALW

Not for us alone did the god, Nicias. Hylas. Theocritus [*or* Theokritus], *tr. fr. Greek by* Barbara Hughes Fowler. *Fr.* Idylls. HePo

Not Fortune's worshipper, nor Fashion's fool. Apologia pro Vita Sua. Pope. *Fr.* Epistle to Dr. Arbuthnot. FHYEP; InPS; NOBE; NoP; OAEL-1; OxAEP-1; PoE; PoEL-3; TFi

Not from my reverent sires hath come. Poet's Prayer. Adelaide Love. TrPWD

Not from our dreams, not from our daft cadres. Robert Johnstone. *Fr.* New Incidents in the Life of Shelley. PNI

Not from successful love alone. Halcyon Days. Walt Whitman. OxBA

Not from that/ could you get it. The City. Robert Creeley. LCAP

Not from the earth, or skies. Health of Body Dependent on Soul. Jones Very. WGRP

Not From the Stars Do I My Judgement Pluck. Shakespeare. *Fr.* Sonnets. Son, *sect.* XIV

Not from the unmapped valleys of darkness, nor. Hall of Ocean Life. John Hollander. PoA

Not from This Anger. Dylan Thomas. LiTB

Not from Titania's Court do I. Hob Gobbling's Song. James Russell Lowell. OBCA

Not furred nor wet, the pointing words yet make. Beaver Pond. Anne Marriott. NOBC

Not glad, like those that have new hopes or suits. To the Same [Robert, Earl of Salisbury] Upon the Accension of the Treasureship to Him. Ben Jonson. NOSC

Not gold, but only man can make. Wr. at. to Emerson Emerson. *Fr.* Nation's Strength, A. FaPON

Not greatly moved with awe am I. The Two Deserts. Coventry Patmore. BoNaP

Not guns, not thunder, but a flutter of clouded drums. Fireworks. Babette Deutsch. NYBP; Poetr

Not happy with what he has. What Her Girl Friend Said to Her. Palaipatiya Perunkatunko, *tr. fr. Tamil by* A. K. Ramanujan. PLW

Not he who holds the sceptre high atop the eagle's throne. Why the Resurrection Was Revealed to Women. Catharina Regina von Greiffenberg, *tr. fr. German by* Michael Hamburger. PBWP

Not hell but a street, not. 209 Canal. Richard Howard. TAP

Not Here. Edmund Wilson. PoA

Not Here, O Apollo. Matthew Arnold. *See* Through the black, rushing smoke-burst.

Not his clothes, but their chimerical creases. In This His Suit. Mark Cox. NAmP90

Not honey/ not the plunder of the bee. Hilda Doolittle ("H. D."). NAAL-2

Not — "How did he die?" But — "How did he live?" The Measure of a Man. *Unknown.* BLPL; PoLF

Not I. (*LL*) Not I. Robert Louis Stevenson. NOBL

Not I. Robert Louis Stevenson. NOBL

Not I ("Not I, but Christ.") *Unknown.* BLRP

Not I, not I, but the wind that blows through me! D. H. Lawrence. *Fr.* Song of a Man Who Has Come Through. CMoP; FaBoMo; GTBS-P; InPS; LiTM; MeMBP; OxBTC; PeFWW; PoE; RaBo; TRP

Not, I/ said pushing. Uncertain Steps. Richard Caddel. NBrP

Not Ideas about the Thing but the Thing Itself. Wallace Stevens. HAP; HCAP; LCAP; MeMAP; SAmP; TAP

Not idly hast thou builded on a rock. To Peter, Bishop of Poitiers, Who Withstood William of Aquitaine and Died in Exile. Hildebert, *tr. fr. Latin by* Helen Waddell. MLL

Not if men's tongues and angels' all in one. Shakespeare. Swinburne. EPCY; TrGrPo

Not, I'll not, carrion comfort, Despair, not feast on thee. Carrion Comfort. Gerard Manley Hopkins. CMoP; EnVR; HeIP; LiTB; MeMBP; NAEL-2; NoAM; NoP; OAEL-2; PoE; PoEL-5; PPP; Son; TEP; TFi; TOF

(Sonnet: Not, I'll not, carrion comfort, Despair, not feast on thee.) OBNC

Not in a silver casket cool with pearls. Edna St. Vincent Millay. CMoP; VGW

Not in Another Photo. Douglas Oliver. VaA

Not in Dumb Resignation. John Milton Hay. WGRP

Not in my saddle, but above it. Indian Summer: Montana, 1956. W. M. Ransom. CDW

Not in our time, O Lord. Hilda Doolittle ("H. D."). *Fr.* Tribute to the Angels. NOBA

Not in rich furniture, or fine array. The H. Communion. George Herbert. ChIV-1; ESCV; MiEL

Not in sleep did I dream this. Pleasant Reverie. Otto Julius Bierbaum, *tr. fr. German by* Philip L. Miller. RiWo

Not in sleep I saw it, but in daylight. Kindly Vision. Otto Julius Bierbaum, *tr. fr. German by* Jethro Bithell. AWP

Not in the city, Philoterus. Nicaenetus, *tr. fr. Greek by* Peter Whigham. GrAn

Not in the crises of events. The Spirit's Epochs. Coventry Patmore. *Fr.* Angel in the House, The. EBEV; GBL; OxBSP

Not in the days of Adam and Eve, but when Adam. In the Days of Prismatic Colour. Marianne Moore. MeMAP

Not in the dire, ensanguined front of war. The Men of the *Maine*. Clinton Scollard. PAH

Not in the Guide-Books. Elizabeth Jennings. LiTM

Not in the poet is the poem or. George Barker. OxAEP-2; OxBSP

Not in the sepulchre Thou art. Passiontide Communion. Katharine Tynan. TrPWD

Not in the silence only. My Prayer. Horatius Bonar. BLRP

Not in the solitude. Hymn of the City. Bryant. EAP

Not in those climes where I have late been straying. Dedication: To Ianthe. Byron. *Fr.* Childe Harold's Pilgrimage. OBNC

Not in thy body is thy life at all. Life-in-Love. Dante Gabriel Rossetti. *Fr.* House of Life, The. HAP

Not in Vain. *Unknown.* BLRP

Not in vain the distance beacons. Foreward, forward let us range. Tennyson. *Fr.* Locksley Hall. BLPL; EBEV; EBVVPR; EnVR; FaBoBe; FaBoEH; ImPo; NAEL-2; OAEL-2

Not just folklore, or. Fast Ball. Jonathan Williams. NeAP

Not Just for the Ride. *At.* to Cosmo Monkhouse. *See* There Was a Young Lady of Niger.

Not just here, but everywhere. (*LL*) The City. Michael O'Loughlin. IB

Not just my patter, my mind's oblique. A Speech for the Clown. James Simmons. PWE

Not just the sizes named (like miniatures). Taxonomical Note. David Sutton. Mes

Not Just Yet. Carter Revard. VoR

Not knowing in what season this again. Parting: 1940. John Frederick Nims. PoA

Not knowing where he was or how he got there. A Bewilderment at the Entrance of the Fat Boy into Eden. Daryl Hine. NOBC

Not last night but the night before. *Unknown.* ISE

Not less because in purple I descended. Tea at the Palaz of Hoon. Wallace Stevens. FaBoMo; PoA

Not less delighted do I call to mind. Recollections of a Day's Journey in Spain. Robert Southey. OBTV

Not less light shall the gold and the green lie. O Who Will Speak from a Womb or a Cloud? George Barker. MeMBP

Not like a suddenly-extinguished light. Triumphs. Petrarch, *tr. fr. Italian by* Morris Bishop. OBD

Not like the brazen giant of Greek fame. The New Colossus. Emma Lazarus. AiP; AmWP; FaBV; FaPON; PoLF; PrIm; Son; WPE

Not like we used to with pipes. Bubbles. George Garrett. MT

Not Long Ago. Charles D'Orléans. EnVB

Not long ago a man was smoking on a balcony. Birth of the Cool. Charles David Wright. MT

Not long ago from hence I went. The Lusty Fryer of Flanders. *Unknown.* CoMu

Not long ago I hied me apace. Not Long Ago. Charles D'Orléans. EnVB

Not long wet and not long dry. (*LL*) Mackerel sky. *Unknown.* FaBoUs; OxNR

Not lorst, but gorn before!' (*LL*) Dahn the Plug'ole. *Unknown.* RB

Not Lost, but Gone Before. Caroline E. Norton. BLRP; VPP; WBLP

Not lost or won but above all endeavor. Fidelity. Trumbull Stickney. LiTA

Not Lotte. Katherine Hoskins. ErPo

Not magnitude, not lavishness. Greek Architecture. Herman Melville. NoP

Not Marble nor the Gilded Monuments. Archibald MacLeish. BoLoP; CMoP; HoPM; MeMAP; MoAB; PoRA; TwCP

Not Marble, nor the Gilded Monuments. Shakespeare. *Fr.* Sonnets. AWP; BLPL; CTC; EnRePo; EPCY; FF; HeIL; HeIP; ImPo; LiTB; LPA; NAEL-1; NIP; NOBE; NoP; NoSic; OAEL-1; OxAEP-1; PeHV; PoE; PoEL-2; Poetr; PoRA; SCGP; Son; TEP; TrGrPo

Not Marching Away to Be Killed. Jean Overton Fuller. FF

Not Me. Shel Silverstein. *See* Slithergadee, The.

Not midst the lightning of the stormy fight. Stonewall Jackson. Henry Lynden Flash. PAH

Not Mine. Julia Caroline Ripley Dorr. PWR

Not mine own fears nor the prophetic soul. Shakespeare. *Fr.* Sonnets. AWP; CTC; EBEV; HAP; ImPo; LiTB; NAEL-1; NoP; NoSic; OAEL-1; OxAEP-1; SCGP

Not more blue at the dawn of the world. Autumn on the Beaches. Sara Teasdale. ArNa

Not more of light I ask, O God. Understanding. *Unknown.* PoToHe

"Not mortal?'' said he. "Lingering — worse,'' said I. (*LL*) The Burghers. Thomas Hardy. EBNV

Not much. (*LL*) Their Thing. Léon Damas. NegPo

Not much more than being. Louis Zukofsky. *Fr.* 29 Poems. PoE

Not Much Talking. *Unknown.* PWR

Not My Best Side. U. A. Fanthorpe. FaBoWP

Not my hands but green across you now. The Lady in Kicking Horse Reservoir. Richard Hugo. CoAP; LCAP; NAAL-2; NoAM; NoP; VCAP

Not now, but in the coming years. Some Time We'll Understand. Maxwell N. Cornelius. BLRP; WBLP

Not o'er thy dust let there be spent. Whittier. Paul Laurence Dunbar. AnAmPo

Not of All My Eyes See. Gerard Manley Hopkins. OxBSP

Not, of course, the monster hunched downtown. Dome Poem. Dave Jeddie Smith. PoA

Not of Gennesareth, but Thames! (*LL*) The Kingdom of God. Francis Thompson. FaPoR; GTBS-P; NOCV; PlP

Not of itself, but thee. (*LL*) To Celia ("Drink to me only with thine eyes.'') Ben Jonson. BoLoP; CBLP; EBEvV; EnLoPo; FaBoBe; FaBV; GGP; GTBS; GTBS-P; ImPo; InPK; LiTB; NOBE; OBEV; OBVE; PlP; PoLF; SCGP; TEP; TrGrPo

Not of Itself but Thee. *Unknown, tr. fr. Greek by* Richard Garnett. AWP

Not of Itself, But Thee. *Unknown, tr. fr. Greek by* Dudley Fitts. GrAn

Not of ourselves are we free. Heritage. Mary Gilmore. CBAP

Not of the princes and prelates with periwigged charioteers. A Consecration. John Masefield. MoAB; MoBrPo; OtMeF

Not often *con brio,* but *andante, andante.* Stanley Matthews. Alan Ross. OxBTC

Not on an altar shall mine eyes behold thee. Real Presence. Ivan Adair. WGRP

Not on our golden fortunes builded high. The Forgotten Man. Edwin Markham. BLPL; PoLF

Not one poem about an animal, she said. Florida. Dannie Abse. OxBC

Not one single light. (*LL*) Rebel Camp in the Hindu Kush. Gu Cheng. SpMi

Not one whisper. Momcilo Nastasijevic, *tr. fr. Serbo Croatian by* Charles Simic. *Fr.* Deaf Things. HSix

Not one would be faultless to. (*LL*) A Hot Day In Sydney. *Unknown.* NOBAu

Not Only around Our Infancy. James Russell Lowell. *Fr.* Vision of Sir Launfal, The. ImPo

Not only how far away, but the way that you say it. Judging Distances. Henry Reed. *Fr.* Lessons of the War. BoLoP; GTBS-P; HeIP; LiTB; MoAB; NIP; NOBE; NoP; OBWP; PAW; Poetr; PoWW

Not only the cultivated ones in parks. Thanks to Flowers. Kate Farrell. ArNa

Not only their money. A Few More Things about the Holocaust. Leatrice H. Lifshitz. BTR

Not only we, the latest seed of Time. Godiva. Tennyson. BeLS; FaBoEH

Not only when you go to bed/ And sleep. (*LL*) Knoxville, Tennessee. Nikki Giovanni. BlSi; BPo; PoBA; SiSoPo

Not Only Where God's Free Winds Blow. Shepherd Knapp. AH

Not only with no sense of shame. Tennyson. FaBoEE

Not oriental Indus' crystal streams. Lady Cicely Wemyss. James I, King of England. NOSC

Not ours the fighter's glow. Mine-Sweeping Trawlers. Edward Hilton, 1st Baron Kennet of the Dene Young. NSI

Not owning a cart, my father. Weights. Les A. Murray. TSaS

Not Palaces [an Era's Crown]. Stephen Spender. CMoP; FaBoMo; LiTB; LiTM; MoAB; MoBrPo; NoAM; NoP

Not pall, but shadows. My Words. William Hathaway. EOEF

Not Pallas, not ev'n Spleen it self could blame. Ovid, *tr.* by John Gay. *Fr.* Metamorphoses. OBVE

Not perched on the top of the hill. At Mrs. Alefounder's. Barbara Howes. AnAn

Not picnics or pageants or the improbable. Terror. Robert Penn Warren. PoA

Not power nor the storied hand of God. Allen Tate. *Fr.* Sonnets of the Blood. PoA

Not public like mountains' but private like companions.' (*LL*) On a Painting by Patient B of the Independence State Hospital for the Insane. Donald Justice. CoAP; NoAM

Not quite sleep, but nearly all we want of it — . Movie. Patricia Storace. BAP-89

Not Ragged-and-Tough. *Unknown.* ChTr; FaBoNo

Not realizing. Six Feet Under. Janet Campbell Hale. VoR

Not recognize a sister? (*LL*) The Eel. Eugenio Montale. STV; WeW

Not "Revelation'' — 'tis — that waits. Emily Dickinson. EnlH

Not Rice, Not Water. Mocikiranar, *tr. fr. Tamil by* A. K. Ramanujan. PLW

Not rose of death. Rose in the Afternoon. Jenny Joseph. BrRo

Not say, "Alas! I did not know him at all.'' (*LL*) The U. S. Sailor with the Japanese Skull. Winfield Townley Scott. ArOW; LiTM

Not Saying Much. Linda Gregg. AiP

Not Seeing Is Believing. Paul Petrie. TAP

Not Sending Cards This Year. Sean O'Brien. PWE

Not Sense. Gail Tremblay. WeW

Not serious about drugs. Angel. John Forbes. NOBAu

Not serried ranks with flags unfurled. What Makes a Nation Great? Alexander Blackburn. WBLP

Not she with traitorous kiss her Saviour stung. Woman. Eaton Stannard Barrett. TIRV

Not Singing. Kate Daniels. PBCAP

Not Slipping into Something More Comfortable. Nick Totton. VaA

Not slowly wrought, nor treasured for their form. Snowflakes. Howard Nemerov. HCAP

Not so, for living yet are those. A Dead Past. *At. to* C. C. Munson. BLRP; WBLP

Not-so-good Earth, The. Bruce Dawe. CBAP

Not so much Rose, as Wreathe. (*LL*) Upon a Virgin Kissing a Rose. Robert Herrick. SeCP; SeCV-1

Not so much the whole arm as of the movement from the heart. (*LL*) Meanwhile Cesario Dancing. Helen Kidd. VBLP

"Not so!" rang the spirit, "Not so!" (*LL*) Columbia U Poesy Reading — 1975. Gregory Corso. PoBeRe

Not so with me as with the little page. Ausiàs March, *tr. fr. Catalan by* John Frederick Nims. STV

Not solely that the future she destroys. George Meredith. *Fr.* Modern Love. GBL; TEP

Not soon shall I forget — a sheet. Katharine Tynan. CH

Not speaking of the way. Yosano Akiko, *tr. fr. Japanese by* Kenneth Rexroth. UnAS

Not steal one thought from thee. (*LL*) Song. William Shenstone. GGP

Not stitched to air or water but to both. Definition of a Waterfall. John Ormond. AngWe

Not strangeness, but strange likeness. Geoffrey Hill. *Fr.* Mercian Hymns. FaBoMo; HAP; NoAM

Not Such Your Burden. Agathias, *tr. fr. Greek by* William M. Hardinge. AWP

Not that a cease-fire. Wildpeace. Yehuda Amichai, *tr. fr. Hebrew.* TSaS, *tr. by* Chana Bloch

Not that by this disdain. The Repulse. Thomas Stanley. BeJo; MeLP

Not That Far. May Miller. BlSi

Not that he promised not to windowshop. One Man's Wife. Philip Booth. VGW

Not that her blooms are marked with beauty's hue. To Mr. Gray. Thomas Warton the Younger. EPCY; Son

Not that I could choose. (*LL*) I'm the Way I Am. Jacques Prévert. STV

Not that I wish to take the liberty. Non Que Je Veuille Ôter la Liberté. Pernette de Guillet, *tr. fr. French by* Raymond Oliver. WPOW

Not that in colour it was like thy hair. The Bracelet. John Donne. NoSic

Not that it always transpired. Cyril Ray. PeLi

Not that miracles are. Janet Gray. VBLP

Not that night, anyway. (*LL*) For My Mother, Who Lives. Lorraine Duggin. LoHo

Not that the earth is changing, O my God! On Refusal of Aid between Nations. Dante Gabriel Rossetti. EBEV; OxAEP-2; SCGP

Not that the Pines were darker there. The Long Voyage. Malcolm Cowley. SoSe

Not that they die, but that they die like sheep. (*LL*) The Leaden-eyed. Vachel Lindsay. CMoP; CoGr; FaBoEE; ImPo; LiTA; OxBSP; PoE; RB

Not that they shall, but if they must. Song of the Cornish Wreckers. D. M. Thomas. FaBoEH

Not that we are weary. In the Trenches. Richard Aldington. PeFWW

Not the Arms Race. Sam Abrams. UL

Not the attendance of stones. Black Maps. Mark Strand. PoA

Not the beautiful youth with features of bloom & brightness. Beauty. Walt Whitman. WeW

Not the blue-fountained Florida hotel. Eclogue of the Shepherd and the Townie. Anthony Hecht. BAP-90

Not the dead today shall praise you, God! Of Those Who Go, Not to Return. Benyamin Galai, *tr. fr. Hebrew by* Ruth Finer Mintz. MHP

Not the dumb earth, wherein they set their graves. (*LL*) Cassandra. Louise Bogan. HAP; MoAmPo; NALW; PBWP; VGW

Not the end of the world. Desperate Message #2. Mark Svenvold. UTF

Not the End of the World. Michael Ryan. NAmP90

Not the glittering shudder in the ear, the high whine of the wasp. Applause. Carol Muske. PFL

Not the intimacy of your forehead clear as a celebration. Amorous Anticipation. Jorge Luis Borges, *tr. fr. Spanish by* Perry Higman. ArLo

Not the round natural world, not the deep mind. Frederick Goddard Tuckerman. *Fr.* Sonnets. NoP

Not the songs that nobly tell. Stanzas on the Psalms. Thomas, the Elder Warton. ChIV-1

Not the wild olive, not the fatal stones. Euphorion, *tr. fr. Greek by* Alistair Elliot. GrAn

Not There. Tess Gallagher. NIP

Not these appal/ The soul. Faith's Difficulty. Theodore Maynard. TrPWD

Not thick, unwholesome, shuffling, as 'tis here. (*LL*) The Pleasant Life in Newfoundland. Robert Hayman. NOBC

Not Thinking of America. Judith Kroll. AmPA

Not Thinking of Himself. Jack Myers. NAmP90

Not this with cataracts and creeks. (*LL*) The Waterfall [*or* Water-Fall]. Henry Vaughan. AngWe; ESCV; FaBoPP; GeHe; MeLP; NAEL-1; NOBE; NOCV; NoP; NOSC; OBWVE; OxAEP-1; PoEL-2; PrIm; SeCV-1; WiR

Not thither, Caesar, yet. Cornelia's Defiance. Katherine Philips. *Fr.* Corneille's Pompey. NOSC

Not those patient men who knocked and were unheeded. 1918-1941. Robert David Fitzgerald. CBAP

Not Thou but I. Philip Bourke Marston. BLPA; BLPL

Not to Be Born. David Sutton. OBD; OxBM

Not to be born, or, being born, to die? (*LL*) The Life of Man. Francis Bacon. EIL; GTBS; NoSic

Not to Be Ministered To. Maltbie D. Babcock. TrPWD

Not to believe the phoebes wept. (*LL*) The Need of Being Versed in Country Things. Robert Frost. NoAM; NOBA; OxBA; PFP; SAmP; TRP; UnPo

Not to dance with her. A Triviality. Waring Cuney. CDC

Not to do but work. The Sum of Life. Ben King. CTC

Not to Forget Miss Dickinson. Marshall Schacht. LiTM

Not to forget not to ever forget so long as you live. Chant for All the People on Earth. Leslie Woolf Hedley. BTR

Not to Keep. Robert Frost. CMoP; OxBA; Poetr

Not to know vice at all, and keepe true state. Epode. Ben Jonson. BeJo; SeCP; SeCV-1

Not to lose the feel of the mountains. The Double-headed Snake. John Newlove. MoCV

Not to Love. Robert Herrick. CaPo

Not to meddle with my toys. (*LL*) When I am grown to man's estate. Robert Louis Stevenson.

Not to say what everyone else was saying. Different. Clere Parsons. FaBoTw

Not to sigh and to be tender. Aphra Behn. BoWoP

Not to the butcher did he pass. The Old Ox. George Rostrevor Hamilton, *after the Greek of* Addaios of Makedon. FaBoEE

Not to the weak alone. The Call to the Strong. William Pierson Merrill. BLRP

Not to Us, Not unto Us, Lord. *Unknown.* AH

Not tomorrow night. Not Yet. Joanne Kyger. UL

Not Tonight, Josephine. Colin Curzon. ErPo

Not too chary, not too fast. Requirements ("Not too chary, not too fast.") Rufinus, *tr. by* Wallace Rice. ErPo

Not too far north from where I write set dawn. Hint for the Incomplete Angler. Kendrick Smithyman. PeNZ

Not too lean, and not too fat. Requirements ("Not too lean, and not too fat.") Rufinus, *tr. by* Wallace Rice. ErPo

Not too old, and not too young. Requirements ("Not too old, and not too young.") Honestus, *tr. by* Wallace Rice. ErPo

Not too pallid, as if bleacht. Requirements ("Not too pallid, as if bleacht.") Xenos Palaestes, *tr. by* Wallace Rice. ErPo

Not Ulysses, no, nor any other man. Louise Labé, *tr. fr. Italian by* Willis Barnstone. BoWoP

Not Understood. Thomas Bracken. BLPA

Not unto us, O Lord. Non Nobis. Henry Cust. OBEV

Not upon earth, as you suppose. "Tu Non Se' in Terra, Si Come Tu Credi." Kathleen Raine. WPE

Not us, I say, not us. Bible, *O.T., paraphrased by* Sir Thomas Wyatt. *Fr.* Psalms.
(Psalm CXV: "Not unto us, O Lord, not unto us," *paraphrased by* the Countess of Pembroke.) NOCV

Not waking, in my dreams, my dreams. Infidelity. Olga Berggolts, *tr. fr. Russian by* Daniel Weissbort. BoWoP; IMW

Not Wavell but Browning. Gavin Ewart. UV

Not Waving but Drowning. Stevie Smith. CoGr; FaBoWP; FaPoB; FF; GTBS-P; HAP; HeIP; MoP; NAEL-2; NALW; NoAM; NOBE; NoP; OAEL-2; OxAEP-2; OxBTC; PoE; Poetr; PPP; PrIm; TEP; TFi; UV; WeW

Not weaned yet, without comprehension loving. Love's Immaturity. E. J. Scovell. GBL; LiTB

Not wept for and not buried *in this tomb.* Philip at Kynoskephalai. Alcaeus, *tr. fr. Greek by* Alistair Elliot. GrAn

Not what, but Whom, I do believe. Credo. John Oxenham. BLRP

Not what I am, O Lord, but what Thou art. More of Thee. Horatius Bonar. BLRP

Not what you'd imagine, not posh. Kathleen Jamie. *Fr.* Katie's Poems. PWE

Not when leaves are brown and sere. When I Would Die. Josephine D. Henderson Heard. CBWP-4

Not when, with self dissatisfied. With Self Dissatisfied. Frederick L. Hosmer. TrPWD

Not where the battle red. On the Death of "Jackson." *Unknown.* PAH

Not while, but long after he had told me. Each Bird Walking. Tess Gallagher. CrSp; FaBoWP; NAmP90; SV

Not whitening in the sky. *(LL)* I arise from rest with movements swift. *Unknown.* EaPr

Not winds to voyagers at sea. The Resurrection. Abraham Cowley. ChIV-2

Not with a bang but a whimper. *(LL)* The Hollow Men. T. S. Eliot. FaPoB; ImPo; InPS; LiTA; LiTM; MoAB; MoAmPo; NAAL-2; OAEL-2; OBMV

Not with a club the heart is broken. Emily Dickinson. LiTA

Not with Libations, but with Shouts and Laughter. Edna St. Vincent Millay. MeMAP

Not with more glories, in th'ethereal plain. Pope. *Fr.* Rape of the Lock, The. EBEV; EBNV; ECEV; FHYEP; HAP; ImPo; NOEC; NoP; OAEL-1; OBNV; OxAEP-1; PeLV; PoEL-3; TEP; TrGrPo (Voyage on the Thames, The.) NOBE

Not with my hands. Benediction. Donald Jeffrey Hayes. EaPr; PoNe

Not with slow, funereal sound. An Ode, on the Unveiling of the Shaw Memorial on Boston Common, May 31st, 1897. Thomas Bailey Aldrich. PAH

Not with snow only, east of Buchenwald. *(LL)* A Letter from Berlin. Jon Stallworthy. MoP; OBWP; OxBC

Not with the cheer of battle in the throat. The Birkenhead. Sir Henry Yule. OtMeF

Not without hope we suffer and we mourn. *(LL)* Elegiac Stanzas Suggested by a Picture of Peele Castle, in a Storm [Painted by Sir George Beaumont]. Wordsworth. EnRP; FaBoPP; GTBS; GTBS-P; NAEL-2; NoP; OAEL-2; OBNC; PoE

Not wooing, no longer shall wooing, voice that has outgrown it, Rainer Maria Rilke, *tr. fr. German by* Stephen Mitchell. *Fr.* Duino Elegies. EnlH, *tr. by* Stephen Mitchell

Not Working. Henry Taylor. Poetr

Not working, not breathing. Autumn. Bella Akhmadulina, *tr. fr. Russian by* Barbara Einzig. BoWoP

Not worth anyone's glance, lost in the vague colorless drifting dead. *(LL)* On a Lady Indifferent to Poetry. Sappho. STV

Not wrongly moved by this dismaying scene. William Empson. LiTM

Not Yet. Joanne Kyger. UL

Not yet. Summer. Jayanta Mahapatra, *tr. fr. Hindi.* TSaS

Not Yet 40, My Beard is Already White. Lew Welch. PoBeRe

Not yet dead, not yet alone. Osip Mandelstam, *tr. fr. Russian by* James Greene. OBVE

Not yet enslaved, not wholly vile. O My Mother Isle! ("Not yet enslaved, not wholly vile.") Samuel Taylor Coleridge. *Fr.* Ode on the Departing Year. FaBoPP

Not yet five, and the light. After Hours. Robert Mezey. NaP

Not yet had History's Ætna smoked the skies. George Meredith. *Fr.* Revolution, The. FaPoB, *sect.* I–V

Not yet in sight. 'Twere well to step aside. At the Polo-Ground. Sir Samuel Ferguson. NOIV

Not yet long a bride? *(LL)* The Maiden Speaks. Otto Friedrich Gruppe. RiWo

Not yet, not yet. The Tree. Joel Sloman. VGW

"Not yet. Not yet," between the lines. Boy Reading. John Holmes. ImGa

"Not yet, not yet; steady, steady!" Bunker Hill. George Henry Calvert. BeLS; FaBoBe; PAH

Not yet will those measureless fields be green again. The Cenotaph. Charlotte Mew. OxAEP-2; WPE

Not you, lean quarterlies and swarthy periodicals. To the Film Industry in Crisis. Frank O'Hara. NOBA; OBAL; SOTW

Not young, and not renewable, but man. *(LL)* Mirror in February. Thomas Kinsella. CIP; GTBS-P; NoAM

Not your winged lust but his must now change suit. William Empson. *Fr.* Death of the King's Canary, The. UV

Nota: man is the intelligence of his soil. The Comedian as the Letter C. Wallace Stevens. OxBA

Notable Dinner, A. L. A. J. Moorer. CBWP-3

Notably fond of music, I dote on a sweeter tone. The Clink of the Ice. Eugene Field. AnMPo

Notation in Gold. Ljubomir Simovic, *tr. fr. Serbo-Croatian by* Charles Simic. HSix

Notation in Haste. Elias Lieberman. GoYe

Note-Book of a European Tramp, The, *sels.* Michael Hamburger.

Note Delivered by a Female Impersonator. Heather McHugh. AmPA

Note in a Bottle. Gerald McCarthy. NGP

Note is sad, yet music for a king, The. *(LL)* Sion. George Herbert. ChIV-1; ESCV

Note Left in Jimmy Leonard's Shack, A. James Wright. HCAP; NoP

Note of Humility, A. Arna Bontemps. PoNe

Note on a Shop in the Muceque. Geraldo Bessa Victor, *tr. fr. Portuguese by* Donald Burness. PeSAV

Note on Feeding. *Unknown.* FaBoUs

Note on Intellectuals. W. H. Auden. FiBHP

Note on Local Flora. William Empson. EBEV; FaBoMo; OxAEP-2

Note on Propertius I.5. Fleur Adcock. BoLoP; PeNZ

Note on the Iliad. Raymond Garlick. AngWe

Note on the Latin Gerunds, A. Richard Porson. FaBoCo; FaBoEE

Note on Wyatt, A. Kingsley Amis. WeW

Note Slipped under a Door. Wilma Elizabeth McDaniel. ETG

Note that the fire. The Fire Poem. Theodore Enslin. CRP

Note the stump, a peach tree. We had to cut it down. Places and Ways to Live. Richard Hugo. NIP

Note this survivor, bearing the mark of the violator. Swedenborg's Skull. Vernon Watkins. FaBoTw

Note to Olga, A. Denise Levertov. NALW

Note to R. H. from Strongsville. Richard Hugo. AnAn

Note to the Difficult One, A. W. S. Graham. AnAn

Note to the Previous Tenants. John Updike. GOYP

Note to Wang Wei. John Berryman. NYBP

Notes after Blacking Out. Gregory Corso. NeAP

Notes for a History of Poetry. David Daiches. PoA

Notes for a Lecture. David Ignatow. NNaP

Notes for a Movie Script. M. Carl Holman. PoBA; PoNe

Notes for a Revised Sonnet. Edward Pygge. BXAP

Notes for a Sonnet. Edward Pygge. BXAP

Notes for a Southern Road Map. Phyllis McGinley. NBLV

Notes for an Elegy: for John Gardner. Linda Pastan. AnAn

Notes for My Son. Alex Comfort. *Fr.* Song of Lazarus, The. LiTM; MoBrPo

Notes for the Chart in 306. Ogden Nash. NYBP

Notes for the Legend of Salad Woman. Michael Ondaatje. NoAM

Notes from a War Diary, H.J.B. 1914–19, *sels.* Peter Scupham. Madelon. SCBI

Notes from a Youngest Daughter, *sels,* Betsy Sholl. "This old woman." MDDM

Notes from an Analyst's Couch. Anita Endrezze-Danielson. CDW

Notes from the Air. John Ashbery. BAP-90

Notes from the Childhood and the Girlhood. Gwendolyn Brooks. LCAP *Sels.*
 Ballad of the Late Annie, The.
 Do Not Be Afraid of No.
 Old Relative.
 Parents: People Like Our Marriage Maxie and Andrew, The.
 Pygmies Are Pygmies Still, Though Percht on Alps. PoNe
 Sunday Chicken.
 Throwing Out the Flowers.

Notes I count drop from the farthest sky, The. *(LL)* An Excursion to the Dragon Pool Temple on Chung-nan. Meng Chiao. PLT

Notes Made in the Piazza San Marco. May Swenson. CoAP

Notes on a Girl. Peter Kane Dufault. ErPo

Notes on a Life to Be Lived. Robert Penn Warren. NYBP

Notes on My Father., *sels.* Katerina Anghelaki-Rooke. "Old man moved into his night, The." PBWP

Notes on the Book of Defeat, *sels.* Nizar Qabbani, *tr. fr. Arabic by* Diana Der Hovanessian *and* Lena Jayyusi.

Notes on the City of the Sun. Bei Dao, *tr. fr. Chinese by* Donald Finkel *with* Chen Xueliang. SpMi

Notes on the Peanut. June Jordan. NoAM

Notes to the Reader. Robert Bringhurst. NOBC

Notes toward a Supreme Fiction, *sels.* Wallace Stevens.
 "And for what, except for you, do I feel love?" NOBA
 "Begin, ephebe, by perceiving the idea." NOBA
 "Bethou me, said sparrow, to the crackled blade." LiTM
 "First idea was not our own, The. Adam." NOBA
 Great Statue of the General Du Puy, The. LiTA
 "It feels good as it is without the giant." NOBA
 "Major abstraction is the idea of man, The." NOBA
 President Ordains the Bee to Be, The. LiTA
 Soldier, There Is a War between the Mind. LiTM; NoAM
 Two Things of Opposite Natures Seem to Depend. MeMAP

Whistle Aloud, Too Weedy Wren. LiTA

Notes towards a Poem That Can Never Be Written. Margaret Atwood. NOBC

Notes Written in Obory, *sels.* Aleksander Wat, *tr. fr. Polish* by Czeslaw Milosz.
"X was asked." CBNP

Nother mule be in your stall. *(LL)* Don't Fish in My Sea. Gertrude Rainey. VBLP

Nothing. Julia de Burgos, *tr. by* Aliki *and* Willis Barnstone. BoWoP

Nothing. Tom Raworth. NBrP

Nothing. Charles Simic. NNaP

Nothing. Burns Singer. OxBS

Nothing about the emptied family.y. *(LL)* Eviction. Lucille Clifton. NTCP

Nothing ades to Loves fond fire. Elizabeth Wilmot, Countess of Rochester. KTR

Nothing and Something. Frances E. W. Harper. PWR

Nothing at All. I. A. Richards. CRP

Nothing at all. *(LL)* Army, Navy. *Unknown.* OxNR

Nothing but a hovel now. The Ruin. Dafydd ap Gwilym, *tr. fr. Welsh by* Rolfe Humphries. OBWVE

Nothing but a man. Nadia Tuéni, *tr. fr. French by* Willis Barnstone. BoWoP

Nothing but an assemblage. The Detective Examines the Body. Martha Hollander. UTF

Nothing but laughter, nothing. Glycon, *tr. fr. Greek by* Kenneth Rexroth. PGA

Nothing but no and I, and I and no. Michael Drayton. *Fr.* Idea. ESo; GBL; PoEL-2

Nothing can be done about the rain in your meal. The Same Corpse. Kojo Laing. HBAPE

Nothing can oppose the cloud. Landscape. Laura Jensen. FoLa

Nothing Could Take Away the Bear-King's Image. Ray A. Young Bear. HATNAP

Nothing delights me as I sit. Somewhere East of Suez. H. W. Berry. NSI

Nothing derivative here. The Litrajure of Everyday Life. Michael C. Blumenthal. NoAM

Nothing Elegant. Gertrude Stein. *Fr.* Tender Buttons. PBWP

Nothing else. *(LL)* The Story of Our Lives. Mark Strand. VCAP

Nothing — except thirty-three. *(LL)* On My Thirty-third Birthday. Byron. FaBoEE; NAs

Nothing for a dirty man. All That Is Lovely in Men. Robert Creeley. NaP; RaBo

Nothing for sale in/ Stupidity Street. *(LL)* Stupidity Street. Ralph Hodgson. CH; IHNG; LiTM; MoAB; MoBrPo; OBD; OxBTC; PDV

Nothing for Tears. Milton. *Fr.* Samson Agonistes. FHYEP; OAEL-1; OtMeF; PoEL-3

Nothing from a straight line swerves. Samuel Hoffenstein. *Fr.* Songs about Life and Brighter Things Yet. NBLV

Nothing Gold Can Stay. Robert Frost. AmPP; GrPl; MoAB; MoAmPo; NAAL-2; NOBA; Poetr; PPP; SoSe; TAP; VGW

Nothing gold can stay. *(LL)* Nothing Gold Can Stay. Robert Frost. AmPP; GrPl; MoAB; MoAmPo; NAAL-2; NOBA; Poetr; PPP; SoSe; TAP; VGW

Nothing grows in vain. Use plants to heal. Creed of Mr. Nicholas Culpeper. Patricia Beer. OxBC

Nothing Happened. Belle Waring. PBCAP

Nothing happens now, except when. Small Wants. Bibhu Padhi, *tr. fr. Hindi.* TSaS

Nothing has changed. Torture. Wislawa Szymborska. WoWa

Nothing here is bitter. Wisdom. Phyllis Hanson. GoYe

Nothing I do will take the war. Prologue: Salvadoran Woman's Lament. Demetria Martinez. AfAz

Nothing in Heaven Functions as It Ought. X. J. Kennedy. SM; Son

Nothing in this bright region melts or shifts. From the Highest Camp. Thom Gunn. Son; TwCP

Nothing Is. Sun-Ra. PoBA

Nothing is better, I well think. The Leper. Swinburne. GBL; NOBVV

Nothing Is Enough. Laurence Binyon. MoBrPo

Nothing is here for tears, nothing to wail. Nothing For Tears. Milton. *Fr.* Samson Agonistes. FHYEP; OAEL-1; OtMeF; PoEL-3

Nothing is left but glistening snow petals. *(LL)* Visiting. Chung Ling. WPC

Nothing Is Lost. Anne Ridler. WPE

Nothing is lost more completely than. Urban Renewal, Baltimore. David Bergman. NGP

Nothing is new: we walk where others went. Nothing New. Robert Herrick. CaPo

Nothing is plumb, level or square. Love Song: I and Thou. Alan Dugan. CAPP; FF; HoPM; InPK; MoP; NoAM

Nothing is quite alien or quite recognizable at this speed. Barbie's Ferrari. Lynne McMahon. BAP-90; NAmP90

Nothing is quite so quiet and clean. Snow in Town. Rickman Mark. BoTP

Nothing is real but the fog. *(LL)* Here. Octavio Paz. STV

Nothing is so beautiful as spring. Spring. Gerard Manley Hopkins. BoNaP; EBVV; FaBV; HAP; InvP; LiTM; MeMBP; MoAB; MoBrPo; NAEL-2; NoAM; NOBE; NOBVV; OAEL-2; OBMV; OBNC; RB; TFi; TrCP

Nothing Is Sweeter Than Eros. Nossis of Locri, *tr. fr. Greek by* Jane McIntosh Snyder. VBLP

Nothing is sweeter than love. Nossis, *tr. fr. Greek by* Kenneth Rexroth. PGA

Nothing is sweeter than love, all other blessings. Nossis, *tr. fr. Greek by* Peter Jay. GrAn

Nothing like that road runs from me. A Cabin in Minnesota. Marvin Bell. HoPM

Nothing move thee. St. Theresa of Avila, *tr. fr. Spanish by* Yvor Winters. CRP

"Nothing much here!" they say. With careless glance. Auction Sale — Household Furnishings. Adele DeLeeuw. PoToHe

Nothing nastier than a white person! The Great Palaces of Versailles. Rita Dove. NoAM

Nothing New. Robert Herrick. CaPo

Nothing now to mark the spot. Rachel Field. *Fr.* Circus Garland, A. OBCA

Nothing older than stone but the soil and the sea and the sky. The Mason. Robert Farren. PeIV

Nothing on earth can make me believe them. Spirituals, Gospels. Gerald William Barrax. NGP

Nothing [*or* Nothin'] very bad hapen to me lately. Henry's Confession. John Berryman. *Fr.* Dream Songs. LCAP; MoP; NAAL-2; NoAM; PoE; TwCP; VCAP

Nothing out of which to create a new, A. None. Josephine Miles. VGW

Nothing pleases me anymore. No Delicacies. Ingeborg Bachmann, *tr. fr. Hebrew by* Mark Anderson. PoSu

Nothing remains, see, leaves, flowers, village elders. Wind's Foam. Al Mahmud, *tr. fr. Bengali.* TSaS, *tr. by* Marian Maddern

Nothing Sacred. Roger Woddis. NOBL

Nothing so difficult as a beginning. Romantic to Burlesque. Byron. *Fr.* Don Juan. EnRP; OAEL-2

Nothing so sharply reminds a man he is mortal. Departure in the Dark. C. Day Lewis. TwCP

Nothing so startles us as tumbleweeds in December. Weeds. Ann Stanford. GrPl

Nothing so true as what you once let fall. Epistle to a Lady: Of the Characters of Women. Pope. *Fr.* Moral Essays. NAEL-1; NOEC; OAEL-1; OxBoLi, *shorter sel.*

Nothing So Wise. Jeanne Lohmann. CrSp

Nothing Stays Put. Amy Clampitt. FoLa

Nothing/ substance utters or time. The Word. Basil Bunting. PoA

Nothing that could save him. *(LL)* Sweet Everlasting. Ellen Bryant Voigt. AnAn; MT

Nothing that is not there and the nothing that is. *(LL)* The Snow Man. Wallace Stevens. CMoP; EnlH; GoJo; HAP; HCAP; HeIP; MAT; NAAL-2; NoAM; NoP; NU; PoE; Poetr; PrIm; SoSe; TRP; WeW

Nothing that is said or done. At First. C. H. Sisson. OxBC

Nothing: the nothing for which there's no reward. *(LL)* Thinking of the Lost World. Randall Jarrell. NoAM; NOBA

Nothing! thou elder brother ev'n [*or* even] to shade. Upon Nothing. The Earl of Rochester. NOSC; OBSV; OxAEP-1; PoEL-3; TrGrPo

Nothing to Be Said. Philip Larkin. OxBTC

Nothing to be said about it, and everything. Dying. Robert Pinsky. HCAP; VCAP

Nothing to bury but dead. *(LL)* The Pessimist. Ben King. AnAmPo; BLPA; CoGr; FaBoCo; FaBoNo; NBLV; OBAL

Nothing to Do. James Ephriam McGirt. AAP

Nothing to do but work. The Pessimist. Ben King. AnAmPo; BLPA; CoGr; FaBoCo; FaBoNo; NBLV; OBAL
(Sum of Life, The, *abr..* CTC

Nothing to Fear. Kingsley Amis. ErPo; OxBC

Nothing to Save. D. H. Lawrence. SOTW

Nothing to say? Then we'll say nothing. Conrad Aiken. *Fr.* Preludes for Memnon; or, Preludes to Attitude. LiTA

Nothing to Wear. William Allen Butler. OBAL; PoLF

Nothing was changed and nothing was the same. *(LL)* The Beast with Two Backs. Andrew Taylor. NOBAu

Nothing was left of me. A Dream of Burial. James Wright. NaP

Nothing Will Die. Tennyson. ArNa

Nothing will ever change beside this river. Changeless Shore. Sarah Leeds Ash. GoYe

Nothing will fill the salt caves our youth wore. Alone. E. J. Scovell. GBL

Nothing would sleep in that cellar, dank as a ditch. Root Cellar. Theodore Roethke. AmPP; AnAmPo; BoNaP; HeIP; InPK; NoP; PPP; VCAP

Nothing you could ask me to. (LL) I Was Born at Birth of Blossoms. Rosalía de Castro. STV

Nothing you could know, or name, or say. Peppergrass. Stanley Plumly. LCAP

Nothingness, for the, The. Paul Celan, tr. fr. German by Beth Bjorklund. PoSu, tr. by John Felstiner

Nothing's going to become of anyone. Play. A. R. Ammons. PoA

Notice. Robert Lowell. NoAM

Notice at the factory gate, The. Hands. Alex Glasgow. OBET

Notice the Convulsed Orange Inch of Moon. E. E. Cummings. VGW

Notice the oak, the high. Baii. Jim Barnes. Fr. Four Things Choctaw. HATNAP

Notice What This Poem Is Not Doing. William Stafford. LCAP

Noticing from what they talk about, and how they stand, or walk. Remembering Lunch. Douglas Dunn. OxBC

Notify someone of authority. If You See This Man. Thomas Lux. AmPA

Notions of freedom are tied up with drink. The Drunkards. Malcolm Lowry. NYBP

NOTl. Max Beerbohm and William Rothenstein. UV

Notorious Glutton, The. Ann Taylor. OxBChV

Notre Dame. Osip Mandelstam, tr. fr. Russian by James Greene. OBVE

Not's good-night to one and all, A. (LL) Villon's Good-Night. W. E. Henley. CBNP

Nottamun Town. Unknown. CBNP; FaBoNo; OxBoLi

Nottingham Fair. Unknown. AmFP

Nottinghamshire Poacher, The. Unknown. OBET

Nought is on earth more sacred or divine. Spenser. Fr. Faerie Queene, The. OAEL-1

Nought is there under heav'ns wide hollownesse. Spenser. Fr. Faerie Queene, The. FHYEP

Nought loves another as itself. Little Boy Lost, A ("Nought loves another as itself.") Blake. Fr. Songs of Experience. EnRP; FHYEP; PeECV

Nought may endure but mutability. (LL) Mutability. Shelley. EnRP; NAEL-2; NoP; OBNC; TEP

Nought vnder heauen so strongly doth allure. Spenser. Fr. Faerie Queene, The. NoSic

Nova. Robinson Jeffers. CMoP; HAP

Novas. Van K. Brock. MT

Novel, The, sels. Paul Hoover. Twenty-Five. BAP-89

Novel of High Life, A. Thomas Haynes Bayly. OxAEP-2

Novelettes, sels. Louis MacNeice. Gardener, The. IIP

Novelist. W. H. Auden. MeMAP

Novelist, flushed with success, a. Thomas Thorneley. PeLi

Novelist of the Absurd, A. Ogden Nash. PeLi

Novella. Adrienne Rich. PPP

Novelty Shop, The. Duane Niatum. CDW

November. Margaret Atwood. NOBC

November. Robert Bridges. OBNC; PoEL-5

November. Bryant. AnAmPo; Son

November. Alice Cary. OBCA

November. Hartley Coleridge. Fr. Sonnets to the Seasons. OBNC; PlP

November. Frederick William Harvey. OxBTC

November. Linda Hogan. BCF; SRLS

November. Thomas Hood. See No sun — no moon!

November. Ted Hughes. CMoP; GTBS-P; NoP

November. Kathleen Jamie. PWE

November. John Keble. Fr. Forest Leaves in Autumn. OBEV

November. Lucy Larcom. AmWP

November. William Morris. Fr. Earthly Paradise, The. EnVR

November. H. Cordelia Ray. CBWP-3

November. Margaret Rose. BoTP

November. Folgore da San Geminiano, tr. fr. Italian by Dante Gabriel Rossetti. Fr. Sonnets of the Months. AWP

November. Spenser. Fr. Shepheardes [or Shepeards or Shepherd's] Calender, The. PoEL-1

November. Frederick Goddard Tuckerman. NOBA

November and Aunt Jemima. Thylias Moss. TRP

November Blue. Alice Meynell. MoBrPo

November Calf. Jane Kenyon. InPS

November Cotton Flower. Jean Toomer. CDC; MoP; NoAM; UnPo

November dawns and dewy-glooming downs. November in the Isle of Wight. Tennyson. Fr. Enoch Arden. BeLS; FaBoPP

November Day at McClure's. Robert Bly. NU

November, 1806. Wordsworth. OBWP

November Fugitive. Henry Morton Robinson. GoYe

November Harvest. Anita Endrezze-Danielson. HATNAP

November in Boston. Thomas McCarthy. BiHa

November in the Isle of Wight. Tennyson. Fr. Enoch Arden. BeLS; FaBoPP

November is a spinner. November. Margaret Rose. BoTP

November Landscape, A. Sarah Helen Whitman. AmWP

November Night. Adelaide Crapsey. ArNa; FaPON; Spl

November 1956. Evan Jones (b. 1927). PBCV

November 1968. Adrienne Rich. CAPP; NMM

November Poppies. Hilary Corke. NYBP

November Sky. Edward Thomas. PlP

November Song. Mark Vinz. Poetsp

November Sunday Morning. Alvin Feinman. CoAP

November Surf. Robinson Jeffers. NAAL-2; OxBA

November the 1st. Gold leaves. Autumn. Charles Wright. FoLa

November through a Giant Copper Beech. Edwin Honig. NoAM; NYBP

November Twenty-sixth Nineteen Hundred and Sixty-three. Wendell Berry. LiTM

November woods are bare and still. Down to Sleep. Helen Hunt Jackson. GN

November, zinnias late. Día de los Muertos. Robert Vasquez. AfAz

November's days are thirty. November Sky. Edward Thomas. PlP

Novembers or Straight Life. Maureen Owen. UL

November's sky is chill and drear. Ettrick Forest in November. Sir Walter Scott. Fr. Marmion. FaBoPP

Novice, The. Jakob Nikolaus von Craigher de Jachelutta, tr. fr. German by Philip L. Miller. RiWo

Novice, The. Edward Davison. ErPo

Novice was sitting on a cornice, a. Illustration. John Ashbery. NAAL-2

Novice when I came beneath thy gaze, A. Stanzas Concerning Love. Stefan George, tr. fr. German by Ludwig Lewisohn. AWP

Novices, The. Denise Levertov. NaP

Now. Sarah Knowles Bolton. PWR

Now. Walter de la Mare. ArNa

Now. Marica Lart. W. S. Merwin. PRA

Now. William Stafford. NNaP

Now. Unknown. PWR

Now a slight meniscus floats on the moral. The Ideal Star-Fighter. J. H. Prynne. VaA

Now a young porcupine. The Personable Porcupine. Wilbur G. Howcroft. ZA

Now, after a party with the consul and our best friend. Summer, 1970. Daniel Halpern. AmPA

Now after David had lived seventy years. The Death of David. Hayyim Nahman Bialik, tr. fr. Hebrew by Herbert Danby. TrJP, ad. by Sholom J. Kahn

Now Ain't That Love? Carolyn M. Rodgers. BPo

Now all aloud the wind and rain. The Watercress Seller. Thomas Miller. OxBChV

Now all day long the man who is not dead. Mother and Son. Allen Tate. LiTA; MoAB; MoAmPo

Now all is one, and one is all. (LL) No Love, to Love of Man and Wife. Richard Eedes. InvP

Now all of change. Sir Thomas Wyatt. SiPS

Now all our hurries that hung up on hooks. War-Time. W. R. Rodgers. OxBSP

Now all that sound of laughter, sound of singing. Rosalía de Castro, tr. fr. Galician by John Frederick Nims. BoWoP; STV

Now all the dogs with folded paws. Suburban Song. Elizabeth Riddell. CBAP; NOBAu

Now all the doors and windows. Philosophy in Warm Weather. Jane Kenyon. ArNa

Now all the lights of Dublin. The Lights of Dublin. Patrick O'Connor. TIRV

Now all the peacefull regents of the night. George Chapman. Fr. Bussy d'Ambois. PoEL-2

Now all the truth is out. To a Friend Whose Work Has Come to Nothing. W. B. Yeats. AWP; InPK; LiTM; MoAB; MoBrPo; OAEL-2; OBMV; OxAEP-2; PoA

Now all the world she knew is dead. House of Rest. Sir John Betjeman. OxAEP-2

Now and Afterwards. Dinah Maria Mulock Craik. PoLF; WGRP

Now and, I fear, again. Table Talk. Donald Mattam. FiBHP

Now and Then. David Chaloner. VaA

Now and then a friend and some sauterne. Mortimer Collins. *Fr.* Lotos Eating. OBF

Now and then concentrating. Observation. William Hart-Smith. FaBoMA

Now and then there will arise. *Unknown, tr. fr. Chippewa Indian by* Frances Densmore. OBVE

Now another day is breaking. Morning Prayer. Ogden Nash. GrPl; OxBChV

Now are our labours crowned with their reward. Hops along the Medway. Christopher Smart. *Fr.* Hop-Garden, The. FaBoPP

Now are our prayers divided, now. At the "Ye That Do Truly." Charles Williams. NOCV

Now are you a marsupial? Are You a Marsupial? John Becker. ZA

Now Arethusa from her snow couches arises. Shelley's "Arethusa" Set to New Measures. Robert Duncan. CMoP

Now art thou fair, Diodorus. Strato, *tr. fr. Greek by* Sydney Oswald. PeHV

Now as at all times I can see in the mind's eye. The Magi. W. B. Yeats. ChIV-2; CMoP; FaBoRV; HAP; InPK; NoAM; OAEL-2; OxAEP-2; PChr; PoA; PoE; TrCP; TRP

Now as even's warning bell. Solitude. John Clare. EnRP

Now as I took a walk down Grand Street I stepped into Paddy West's house. Paddy West. *Unknown.* OxBSS

Now as I was young and easy under the apple boughs. Fern Hill. Dylan Thomas. AngWe; ClHu; CMoP; FaBoPP; FaBV; FaPoB; GoJo; GTBS-P; HAP; HeIL; HeIP; ImPo; InPK; InPS; LiTB; LiTM; MeMBP; MoAB; MoBrPo; MoP; NAEL-2; NIP; NoAM; NOBE; NoP; NTP; OAEL-2; OBWVE; OxBTC; PoE; Poetr; PoLF; PoRA; PPP; SoSe; TFi; TrGrPo; TRP; TwCP

Now as I watch the progress of the plague. The Missing. Thom Gunn. PFL

Now as the train bears west. Night Journey. Theodore Roethke. GOA; NYBP

Now, as we cross this ancient threshold. Parting. Gu Cheng, *tr. fr. Chinese by* Donald Finkel *with* Yi Jinsheng. SpMi

Now as we cross this white page together. The Escape. William Stafford. NNaP

Now at the dark's perpetual descent. By the Beautiful Ohio. Joan LaBombard. SM

Now, at the time that was before agreed. Spenser. *Fr.* Faerie Queene, The. OAEL-1

Now at the turn of the year this coil of clay. The Mad Potter. John Hollander. VCAP

Now austere lips are laid. The Hard Lovers. George Dillon. PoA

Now Autumn comes, the wise fool of the year. Autumn. Frances Winwar. GoYe

Now Be the Gospel Banner. Thomas Hastings. AH

Now be ye lords or commoners. The Tod's Hole. *Unknown.* GBP

Now beginneth Glutton [*or* biginneth Glotoun] for to go to shrift[e]. The Glutton [*or* Glutton in the Tavern]. William Langland. *Fr.* Vision of Piers Plowman, The. PoE

Now Behold the Saviour Pleading. John Leland. AH '

Now being arrived at his Colledge. Alicia D'Anvers. *Fr.* Academia; or The Humours of the University of Oxford. KTR

Now, being invisible, I walk without mantilla. The Souls of Women at Night. Wallace Stevens. CMoP

Now Bekotsidi, that am I. For them I make. The Song of Bekotsidi. *Unknown, tr. fr. Navajo Indian by* Washington Matthews. OBVE

Now bernes, buirdes, bolde and blithe. *Unknown.* MiEL

Now bitter bitter grown to me. (*LL*) Grown and Flown. Christina Rossetti. NOBVV

Now Blue October. Robert Nathan. FYAP

Now bold Robin Hood to the north would go. Robin Hood and the Scotchman. *Unknown.* ESPB

Now burley's curing in the high-tiered barn. Squirrel Stand. Jim Wayne Miller. MT

Now burst above the city's cold twilight. Six o'Clock. Trumbull Stickney. AnAmPo; OxBA

Now, by one year, time and our frailty have. Elegy on D. D. Sidney Godolphin. BeJo

Now call to mind Edom, remember well. The Church of England's Glory. *Unknown.* APAS

Now calumnies arise, and black reproach. Mary Latter. *Fr.* Soliloquies on Temporal Indigence. ECWP

Now Came Still Evening On. Milton. *See* Uriel to his charge/ Returned on that bright beam.

Now came still evening on, and twilight gray. Milton. *Fr.* Paradise Lost. EPCY; PeECV, *ll.* 598–688

(Evening in Paradise.) GN, *ll.* 598–609; NOBE, *ll.* 598–656

(Moon and the Nightingale, The.) ChTr

Now can you see the monument? It is of wood. The Monument. Elizabeth Bishop. HCAP; LiTA; NoAM; NOBA; Poetr; TRP

Now Cape Clear it is in sight. Whip Jamboree. *Unknown.* OxBSS

Now chaos has pitched a tent. Revival. George Garrett. MT

Now children may. May. John Updike. *Fr.* Child's Calendar, A. OBCA

Now Christmas Day is drawing near at hand. Christmas Now Is Drawing Near. *Unknown.* OBET

Now Christmas is come. *Unknown.* PChr

Now Clear the Triple Region of the Air. Christopher Marlowe. *Fr.* Tamburlaine the Great. TrGrPo

Now close your eyes. Wedding Reception. Melinda Goodman. GLP

Now coldness comes sifting down, layer after layer. Flute Notes from a Reedy Pond. Sylvia Plath. FaBoMo

Now Come Along Mary. Paul Johann Ludwig Heyse, *tr. fr. German by* Philip L. Miller. RiWo

Now come young men and list to me. Macaffie's Confession. *Unknown.* BeLS

Now comes the evening of the mind. The Evening of the Mind. Donald Justice. VCAP

Now Comes the Good Rain Farmers Pray for (and). E. E. Cummings. NoAM

Now comes the happy morning long desired. The Village Fair. James Hurdis. *Fr.* Village Curate, The. ECEV

Now cometh alle ye that ben ibroght. Huc omnes pariter. Boethius, *tr. by* John Walton. *Fr.* Consolation of Philosophy, The. OBMV

Now corn pushes past the foam. Ode to a Dead Dodge. David McElroy. AmPA

Now crouch, ye kings of greatest Asia. The Bloody Conquests of Mighty Tamburlaine. Christopher Marlowe. *Fr.* Tamburlaine the Great. ChTr (Emperor of the Threefold World. TrGrPo

Now Cunningham, who rhymed by fits and starts. Terse Elegy for J.V. Cunningham. X. J. Kennedy. DiPo

Now Curll his shop from rubbish drains. Swift. *Fr.* Verses on the Death of Doctor Swift [D.S.P.D., Occasioned by Reading a Maxim in Rochefoucauld]. PeLV

Now Cynthia shone serene, and ev'ry star. The Daventry Wonder. "Agricola." NOEC

Now daisies pied, and violets blue. Shakespeare. *See* When daisies pied and violets Blue.

Now, damn you, you're stiff, uptight —. Private Poem. Strato, *tr. fr. Greek by* Teddy Hogge. GrAn

Now day and night sit balanced. Spring Equinox. Peter Blue Cloud. *Fr.* Within the Seasons. HATNAP

Now do our eyes behold. Lament for the Two Brothers Slain by Each Other's Hand. Aeschylus, *tr. fr. Greek by* A. E. Housman. *Fr.* Seven against Thebes, The. AWP

Now Does Our World Descend. E. E. Cummings. NYBP

Now, does she still want to live? Babouchka. Sophie Slingeland. LoHo

Now does Spains Fleet her spatious wings unfold. Andrew Marvell. *Fr.* On the Victory Obtained by *Blake* over the *Spaniards*, in the Bay of *Sanctacruze*, in the Island of *Tenerif.* 1657. FaBoEH

Now Dreary Dawns the Eastern Light. A. E. Housman. CMoP

Now each creature joys the other. Samuel Daniel. ElL; NoSic

Now Endymion dedicates/ his cold bed's failure to the moon. Isidorus, *tr. fr. Greek by* Robin Skelton. GrAn

Now entertain conjecture of a time. Shakespeare. *Fr.* King Henry V. OxAEP-1; RB
(Before Agincourt.) ChTr; EBEV

Now especially, each flower moves. Variation on the Gothic Spiral. W. S. Merwin. PoA

Now Evening Puts Amen to Day. Paul Horgan. AH

Now every man at my request. *Unknown.* OBCP

Now every thing that shadowy thought. In Festubert. Edmund Blunden. OBMV

Now ev'ning fades! her pensive step retires. Night. Ann Radcliffe. WPE

Now Fade the Rose and Lily-Flower. *Unknown, tr. fr. Middle English by* Brian Stone. NOCV

Now fades the last long streak of snow. Tennyson. *Fr.* In Memoriam A. H. H. EBVV, *abr.*; FaBoRV; FHYEP; GTBS-P; NOBE; OAEL-2, *abr.*; OBNC; PeECV, *abr.*

Now faintly the falling sun. Chengtu. Tu Fu, *tr. fr. Chinese by* Robert Payne. TAL

Now, Fanny, 'tis too bad, you teazèn maïd! A Bit o' Sly Coorten. William Barnes. PeLV

Now ferkes to the firthe thees fresche men of armes. Sir Gawain Encounters Sir Priamus. Tennyson, *incorporated in* Idylls of the King *with changes, as* The Passing of Arthur. *Fr.* Morte d'Arthur. DL; EBVVPR; FaBoBe; FaBoRV; NIP; NOBVV; OAEL-2; OBNV; PoEL-1; PoEL-5

Now, fie on foolish love! It not befits. Fie on Love. James Shirley. OxBSP

Now fie upon that everlasting life, I dye! Valiant Love. Richard Lovelace. SeCP

Now fine mists envelope the towers and terraces. *(LL)* A Song of Chin Men District. Hsueh Ch'iung. WPC

Now first, as I shut the door. The New House. Edward Thomas. EBEV; MoAB; MoBrPo; NOBE; OBEV; OBWVE

Now first of all he means the night. A Song for the Middle of the Night. James Wright. SM; WeW

Now for a brisk and cheerful fight! The Fight at [the] San Jacinto. John Williamson Palmer. PAH

Now for a little I have fed on loneliness. Fruit of Loneliness. May Sarton. PoA

Now for I see the fields in flower. From the Provençal of William of Poitiers. William of Aquitaine, *tr. fr. Provençal by* Helen Waddell. MLL

Now for the spirit of the people. Here. W. H. Auden. *Fr.* Letter to Lord Byron. FaBoPV

Now for your sixtieth birthday am I to send you. To Wystan Auden. Geoffrey Grigson. NAs

Now from each van. War Poetry. John Philips. *Fr.* Blenheim. NOEC

Now from Labor and from Care. Thomas Hastings. AH

Now from Leander's place she rose, and found. George Chapman. *Fr.* Hero and Leander. AAS; EBEV; NoP

Now from the east. Masahongva, *tr. fr. Hopi Indian by* Natalie Curtis. WTO

Now from their slumber waking. Comrades. Henry R. Dorr. PAH

Now front to front the hostile armies stand. Homer, *tr. by* Pope. *Fr.* Iliad, The. OBVE

Now gather round, you stroppy Jacks who serve the peacetime Andrew. The Kola Run. D. S. Goodbrand. OxBSS

Now gently winding up the fair ascent. Homer, *tr. by* Pope. *Fr.* Odyssey. NAWM-1; OBVE

Now get thee back, retreat, depart, O Serpent. He Overcometh the Serpent of Evil in the Name of Ra. *Unknown, tr. fr. Egyptian by* Robert Hillyer. *Fr.* Book of the Dead. AWP

Now Gilderoy was a bonny boy, and he would not the ribbons wear. Gilderoy. *Unknown.* OBET
(My Handsome Gilderoy.) CH

Now ginnes this goodly frame of temperaunce. The Bower of Bliss. Spenser. *Fr.* Faerie Queene, The. PoEL-1

Now glory to the Lord of Hosts, from whom all glories are! Ivry. Macaulay. FaBV; GN
(Battle of Ivry, The.) WBLP

Now go trouble maker go. *(LL)* Migrant's Lament: A Song. Alfred Temba Qabula. PeSAV

Now, God be thanked Who has matched us with His hour. Peace. Rupert Brooke. *Fr.* 1914. OBWP; PAW; PoA; WGRP

Now God is truly naught, and if He aught may be. God Is Nothing Physical. "Angelus Silesius," *tr. fr. German. Fr.* Cherubical Wanderer, The. GePo; *tr. by* George C. Schoolfield

Now God preserve, as you well do deserve. The Masque of Christmas. Ben Jonson. OxBoLi

Now God Stand Up for Bastards. Brian Merriman, *tr. by* Arland Ussher. *Fr.* Midnight Court, The. BIrV; NOIV, *tr. by* Thomas Kinsella

Now Goeth [*or* goth *or* goothe] Sun [*or* Sonne *or* Sunne] under Wood. *Unknown.* MiEL; NoP

Now Good-night. Good Night. Eleanor Farjeon. NTP; OTCP

Now gowans sprout, an' lavrocks sing. Ode to Mr. F — [*or* Mr. Forbes]. Allan Ramsay, *after* Horace. NOEC; OBVE

Now gracious plenty rules the board. Thanksgiving. Florence Earle Coates. TrPWD

Now grapes are plush upon the vines. Contrary Theses (I). Wallace Stevens. OxBA; SAmP

Now Green, Now Burning. Muriel Rukeyser. *Fr.* Tenth Elegy. Elegy in Joy. LPA

Now green, now burning, I make a way for peace. Now Green, Now Burning. Muriel Rukeyser. *Fr.* Tenth Elegy. Elegy in Joy. LPA

Now grimy April comes again. For City Spring. Stephen Vincent Benét. BXAP; NBLV

Now gypsy fires burn bright in every tree. October. Isabel Neill. ShDr

Now had th' Almighty Father from above. Milton. *Fr.* Paradise Lost. EPCY; NIP

Now hand in hand, you little maidens, walk. Spring. André Spire, *tr. fr. French by* Jethro Bithell. AWP

Now hands to seedsheet, boys! The Sower's Song. Thomas Carlyle. SCGP

Now hardly here and there a hackney-coach. A Description of the Morning. Swift. EBEV; ECEV; FF; HAP; HeIP; InPS; NOBE; NOEC; NoP; OAEL-1; OxAEP-1; Poetr; PPP; Prf; SoSe; TEP; TFi

Now has ended the battle of Saul. Saul. Nathan Alterman, *tr. fr. Hebrew by* Dov Vardi. TrJP

Now haste, my Muse, pursue thy destined way. Soame Jenyns. *Fr.* Art of Dancing, The. ECEV; FaBoUs

Now hath my life across a stormy sea. On the Brink of Death. Michelangelo, *tr. fr. Italian by* John Addington Symonds. AWP

Now haud your tongue, baith wife and carle. Red Harlaw. Sir Walter Scott. *Fr.* Antiquary, The. OxBB

Now have I brought a woork to end which neither Joves fierce [*or* feerce] wrath. Ovid, *tr. by* Arthur Golding. *Fr.* Metamorphoses. OBVE (Conclusion.) CTC

Now have I see, in Graisivaudan's vale. From Grenoble. James Elroy Flecker. OBTV

Now having leisure, and a happy wind. John Fletcher *and* William Rowley. *Fr.* Maid in the Mill, The. GBL

Now hawk, wind's jockey, sitting tight. Kite. John Robert Lee. PBCV

Now he comes! will he come? alas, no, no! *(LL)* O happy [*or* happie] dames, that may embrace. The Earl of Surrey. NoSic; SCGP; SiPSBD

Now he has seen the girl Hsiang-Hsiang. Chinese Ballad. Mao Tse-tung, *tr. fr. Chinese by* William Empson. Mes

Now he is gone and we had not understood one another. The Year's Ending. St. J. Page Yako, *tr. fr. Xhosa by* C. M. Mcanyangwa *and* Jack Cope. PeSA

Now he who knows old Christmas. Old Christmas. Mary Howitt. GN

Now Help Us, Lord. *Unknown.* AH, *ad. by* Charles E. Ives

Now here, now there, lightheaded, crazed with grief. A Psalm of the Early Buddhist Sisters. *Unknown.* WGRP

Now he's in the plughole, swimming against the tide. *(LL)* Soldiers' Chorus from Faust. *Unknown.* NOBAu

Now high and low, where leaves renew. Autet e bas. Daniel Arnaut, *tr. fr. Provençal by* Ezra Pound. CTC

Now his nose's bridge is broken, one eye. On Hurricane Jackson. Alan Dugan. CoAP; TRP

Now hollow fires burn out to black. A. E. Housman. *Fr.* Shropshire Lad, A. FaPoB; NOBVV

Now homing tradesmen scatter through the streets. Place Pigalle. Richard Wilbur. ArOW; HeIP

Now I again see such fountains and valleys. At Rundane. Aasmund Olavsen Vinje, *tr. fr. Norwegian by* Philip L. Miller. RiWo

Now I am dead you sing to me. An Upbraiding. Thomas Hardy. OPOP

Now I am dry bones and my face a stony skull staring in yellow surprise at the sun. *(LL)* Between the World and Me. Richard Wright. LiTM; MoP; PoBA

Now I am getting light as cotton candy. Snakebite. Thomas James. SM

Now I am old and free from time. Winter Paradise. Kathleen Raine. ArNa

Now I am slow and placid, fond of sun. With Child. Genevieve Taggard. AIW; MoAmPo

Now I Become Myself. May Sarton. CrSp

Now I become myself. It's taken. Now I Become Myself. May Sarton. CrSp

Now I believe tradition, which doth call. Upon the Author; by a Known Friend. Benjamin Woodbridge. SCAP

Now I board up the streets between me and then. *(LL)* Too Bad. Gig Ryan. NOBAu

Now I can be sure of my sleep. On the Hill below the Lighthouse. James Dickey. SM

Now I can stand, walk, open my mouth. Winter Morning. Lauris Edmond. PWE

Now I Do Believe. B. W. Vilakazi, *tr. fr. Zulu by* Cherie Maclean. PeSAV

Now I do believe that he has died. Now I Do Believe. B. W. Vilakazi, *tr. fr. Zulu by* Cherie Maclean. PeSAV

Now I find thy looks were feigned. Thomas Lodge. *Fr.* Phyllis. ElL; EnRePo

Now I go down here and bring up a moon. Auctioneer. Carl Sandburg. PDV

Now I have come from the Berg String Quartet Opus 3. Adoration. Jane Miller. BAP-90

Now I have come to reason. C. Day Lewis. CMoP

Now I have found thee, I will ever more. William Alabaster. *Fr.* Divine Meditations. ESCV; Son

Now I have found thee I will evermore. Upon the Crucifix. William Alabaster. NoSic; PoEL-2

Now I have known, O Lord. Al-Junaid, *tr. by* A. J. Arberry. TOF

Now I have lost you, I must scatter. Farewell, Sweet Dust. Elinor Wylie. LiTA

Now I Have Nothing. Stella Benson. OxBTC

Now I knew I lost her. Emily Dickinson. PeHV

Now I know I never shall. Ted Hughes. *Fr.* Prometheus on His Crag. AnAn

Now I lay me down to sleep. Compline. Donald Davie. *Fr.* Horae Canonicae. CRP

Now I Lay Me Down to Sleep. Eugene Henry Pullen. FaBoBe

Now I Lay me Down to Sleep. *Unknown.* CoGr; OBD

Now I lay me down to sleep,/ A bag of peanuts at my feet. *Unknown.* RoPo

Now I Lay Me Down to Take My Sleep, *diff. versions. Unknown.* BLRP; GBP; OxNR

Now I must betray myself. Prothalamion. Delmore Schwartz. OxBA

Now I no longer need anything. *(LL)* Letter to a Dead Father. Richard Shelton. PBCAP

Now I notice for the first time how tired I am. Rest. Wilhelm Müller, *tr. fr. German by Philip L. Miller. Fr.* Winter's Journey, The. RiWo

Now I out walking. Away! Robert Frost. NOBA

Now I pray the man who may love this lay. Cynewulf, *tr. fr. Anglo-Saxon by Charles W. Kennedy. Fr.* Fates of the Apostles. AnOE

Now I remember: in our town the druggist. Serving with Gideon. William Stafford. LCAP

Now I see its whiteness. The Dead Butterfly. Denise Levertov. NoP

Now I see lotus-pickers singing the lotus-pickers' song. Tune: "Pomegranate Blossoms." Kuan Yun-shih, *tr. by Richard John Lynn. Fr.* Medley of Southern and Northern Tunes — Scenic Tour of West Lake. SuSp

Now I shall reach over. With Lilacs in My Eye. Lucile Coleman. GoYe

Now I wake and see the light. Eugene Henry Pullen. BLRP

Now I walk with you through the ruins of the city. Some Walks with You. John Hollander. NoAM

Now I wear my named pants. Glose. Michael Malinowitz. EOEF

Now I will ask for one true word beyond. Grandfather and Grandmother in Love. David Mura. ETG; TRP

Now I will do nothing but listen. Walt Whitman. *Fr.* Song of Myself. AmPP; HoPM; LiTA; MoAmPo, *abr.*; NOBA; OxBA; SAmP; SOTW, *much abr.*

Now I will fashion the tale of a fish. The Whale. *Unknown, tr. fr. Anglo-Saxon. Fr.* Physiologus. AnOE, *tr. by Charles Kennedy* (Now I will sing about a kind of fish.) ASW, *tr. by Kevin Crossley-Holland*

Now I will make fat puddings. Advent. Anne Hartigan. CIP

Now I Will Only Believe. B. W. Vilakazi. PeSAV

Now I will sing about a kind of fish. *Unknown. See* Now I will fashion the tale of a fish.

Now I would remind you, brethren. Bible, *N.T. Fr.* First Corinthians. DL

Now ich see blostme springe. Of Jesu Christ I Sing. *Unknown.* PoE

Now if all of you were gone. Alice Zeno Talking, and Her Son George Lewis the Jazz Clarinetist in Attendance. William Matthews. Jaz

Now if ever it is time to cleanse Helicon. Ezra Pound. *Fr.* Homage to Sextus Propertius. VGW

Now, if I could, its whirling vacuum. *(LL)* Elegy for My Father. Howard Moss. CoAP; LiTM

Now if the first woman God ever made. Sojourner Truth. Sojourner Truth. WoWa

Now if thou hast one dram of grace. Nahum Tate, *after the Latin of Catullus.* OBVE

Now if you want an onion, just consider. Recipe: Onions. Philemon, *tr. fr. Greek.* FaBoUs

Now if you will listen I'll tell you a story. The New-Chum's First Trip. *Unknown.* FaBoBa

Now I'm Easy. Eric Bogle. OBET

Now I'm leaving old England, the land that I love. The First of the Emigrants. *Unknown.* OxBSS

Now I'm undernourished, too! *(LL)* Dear Husband. Yamba Ouloguem. NegPo

Now in a thought, now in a shadowed word. E. A. Robinson. TrCP

Now in her green mantle blythe nature arrays. My Nannie's Awa.' Burns. GN

Now in midsummer come and all fools slaughtered. Credences of Summer. Wallace Stevens. MeMAP

Now in my/ heart I/ see clearly. Sappho, *tr. fr. Greek by Willis Barnstone.* BoWoP

Now in my Samarkand of blue enamels. Journey in the Orient. Maria Luisa Spaziani, *tr. fr. Italian by Ruth Feldman.* BoWoP

Now in the Bloom. Florence Kiper Frank. GoYe

Now in the dawn before it dies, the eagle swings. The Story of a Well-made Shield. N. Scott Momaday. CDW; GrPl; HATNAP

Now in the grace of the world and always. *(LL)* A Lyric Afterwards. Tom Paulin. PNI; SCBI

Now in the Palace Gardens. Trumbull Stickney. *Fr.* Eride. LiTA

Now in the patron's mansion see the wight. Richard Savage. *Fr.* Progress of a Divine, The. OBSV

Now in the people. Hildegard von Bingen, *tr. fr. Latin.* CrSp

Now in the suburbs and the falling light. Father and Son. Stanley Kunitz. CAPP; MoP; Poetr; TwCP

Now in the third voice. W. S. Graham. *Fr.* Dark Dialogues, The. OxBS

Now in this mirthful tyme of May. Four May Poems, II. *Unknown.* OxBS

Now in this while gan Daedalus a wearinesse to take. Daedalus. Ovid, *tr. by Arthur Golding. Fr.* Metamorphoses. CTC; OBVE

Now in thy dazzling half-oped eye. A Mother to Her Waking Infant. Joanna Baillie. ECWP; NOEC; WoRP

Now, innocent, within the deep. M., Singing. Louise Bogan. GoJo; LiTA; NoAM

Now is a bursting in me. Argent Solipsism. Howard Blake. PoA

Now is a Ship. E. E. Cummings. Spl

Now is a ship. Now is a Ship. E. E. Cummings. Spl

Now is Ingland all in fight. The State of the Nation. *Unknown.* CBCK

Now is it most like as if on ocean. The Voyage of Life. Cynewulf, *tr. fr. Anglo-Saxon by Charles W. Kennedy. Fr.* Christ 2. AnOE

Now is it pleasant in the summer-eve. George Crabbe. *Fr.* Borough, The. FM

Now is killing me. *(LL)* Latin is a dead tongue. *Unknown.* ChTr; FaBoVe; ISE

Now is mon hol and soint. When Death Comes. *Unknown.* MeEL

Now is my father. Poem for My Father's Ghost. Mary Oliver. InPS

Now is Past. John Clare. Mes

Now is the fox drevin to hole! hoo to hym, hoo, hoo! *Unknown.* OxBLMV

Now is the globe shrunk tight. Snowdrop. Ted Hughes. FaBoMo

Now is the hour when, swinging in the breeze. Harmonie du Soir. Baudelaire, *tr. fr. French by Lord Alfred Douglas.* AWP

Now Is the Time. Fukui Hisako, *tr. fr. Japanese by Kenneth Rexroth and Ikuko Atsumi.* WPJ

Now is the time for mirth. To Live Merrily, and to Trust to Good Verses. Robert Herrick. AWP; BeJo; CaPo; InvP; NOSC; SeCP; SeCV-1

Now is the time for the burning of the leaves. Laurence Binyon. *Fr.* Burning of the Leaves, The. GTBS-P; NOBE; OxBTC; PlP

Now Is the Time of Christmas. *Unknown.* MeEL

Now is the time, when all the lights wax dim. To Anthea. Robert Herrick. PoEL-3

Now is the winter of our discontent. Shakespeare. *Fr.* King Richard III. EBEvV; PoE
(Hate the Idle Pleasures.) TrGrPo

Now is the world withdrawn all. Carol. Howard Nemerov. TrCP

Now Israel may say, and that truly. Bible, *O.T., paraphrased by* Sir Thomas Wyatt. *See* If it had not been the Lord who was on our side.

Now Israel May Say, and That Truly. William Whittingham. AH

Now it appears very clear. Hilda Doolittle ("H. D."). *Fr.* Walls Do Not Fall, The. NAAL-2

Now it belongs not to my care. Richard Baxter. NOSC

Now it grows dark. Hymn to Night. Melville Cane. MoAmPo

Now it is almost night, from the bronzey soft sky. Storm in the Black Forest. D. H. Lawrence. FaBoVe

Now it is autumn and the falling fruit. The Ship of Death. D. H. Lawrence. CMoP; FaBoRV; FaBoTw; GTBS-P; LiTB; MeMBP; MoAB; MoBrPo; MoP; NAEL-2; NoAM; NoP; OAEL-2; OxAEP-2; PrIm

Now it is fifteen years you have lain in the meadow. Lines for an Interment. Archibald MacLeish. CMoP; NOBA

Now it is only hours before you wake. Letter to My Daughter at the End of Her Second Year. Donald Finkel. CoAP

Now it is September and the web is woven. The Dwarf. Wallace Stevens. MeMAP

Now It Is Time. James Lewisohn. ETG

Now it is time for a nation. 'It's Nation Time.' Michael McClure. PoBeRe

Now it is winter and the fallen snow. Los Mineros. Edward Dorn. PoM

Now it seems an old forgotten fable. H. M. S. *Glory* at Sydney. Charles Causley. OBTV

Now it was Spring. Grant at Appomattox. Gertrude Claytor. GoYe

Now it was that the Morrigan settled in bird shape. The Morrigan. *Unknown, tr. fr. Irish by* Thomas Kinsella. BIrV

Now it's July, hot and sleepy and still. Summer Journey. W. R. Rodgers. OBTV

Now it's styrofoam pellets. White Trash. Jim Hall. MT

Now, it's three long years since we made her pay. The Final Trawl. Archie Fisher. OxBSS

Now Jentil Belly Down. *Unknown.* GBP

Now Johnson would go up to join the great simulacra of men. Up Rising. Robert Duncan. *Fr.* Passages. NNaP

Now, jolly Swains! the harvest of your cares. How to Shear Sheep. John Dyer. *Fr.* Fleece, The. FaBoUs

Now Jones had left his new-wed bride. A Code of Morals. Kipling. FaBoCo

Now, Joy is born of parents poor. Joy and Pleasure. W. H. Davies. OBMV

Now Kindness. Peter Viereck. LiTA

Now kisse me, lovely Ganimed, for see. Jupiter and Ganimede. Thomas Heywood. PeHV

Now, ladies, if you'll listen, a story I'll relate. Pearl Bryan. *Unknown.* AmFP

Now leave the check-reins slack. To the Man after the Harrow. Patrick Kavanagh. CIP; GTBS-P

Now let no charitable hope. Let No Charitable Hope. Elinor Wylie. LiTA; LiTM; MoAB; MoAmPo; NAAL-2; NALW; OxBA; OxBSP; TrGrPo; VGW

Now Let Our Hearts Their Glory Wake. Elizabeth Scott. AH

Now let the cycle sweep us here and there. Hilda Doolittle ("H. D."). *Fr.* Sigil. AnAn; VGW

Now let the legless boy show the great lady. In the Children's Hospital. "Hugh MacDiarmid." NAEL-2; NoP

Now let us celebrate the day. Squirrel. Lucile Adler. FoLa

Now Liddesdale [*or* Liddisdale] has ridden a raid. Jock o' the Side. *Unknown.* ESPB; IBB; OxBB

Now Liddesdale [*or* Liddesdale] has lain long [*or* layen lang] in. Dick o' the Cow. *Unknown.* ESPB; IBB; OxBB

Now lies in the Abbey. (*LL*) Epitaph for William Pitt. Byron. FaBoEE

Now light the candles; one; two; there's a moth. Repression of War Experience. Siegfried Sassoon. CMoP; NoAM; NSI; PeFWW; PoE

Now lighted windows climb the dark. Manhattan Lullaby. Rachel Field. TLR

Now, like the gods, he is invulnerable. On the Death of Francisco López Merino. Jorge Luis Borges, *tr. fr. Spanish by* Norman Thomas di Giovanni. OBD

Now list and lithe, you gentlemen. Northumberland Betray[e]d by Douglas [*or* Dowglas]. *Unknown.* ESPB; OxBB

Now list you, lithe you, gentlemen. Robin Hood and Queen Katherine. *Unknown.* ESPB

Now listen to boasting which leaves the heart dazed. Al-Samau'al Ibn Adiya, *tr. fr. Arabic by* Hartwig Hirschfeld. *Fr.* Are We Not the People. TrJP

Now, listen, Ye who established the Great League. Memorial Ode. John Buck. GOA

Now Little Billy is gone to the kirk. Little Billy. *Unknown.* GBP

Now look, you see, it's this way like. The Road to Hogan's Gap. Andrew Barton Paterson. CBAP

Now, Lord, or never, they'll believe on Thee. On the Miracle of Loaves. Richard Crashaw. OxBSP

Now lufferis cummis with larges lowd. The Petition of the Gray Horse, Auld Dunbar. William Dunbar. OxBS

Now, lusty lords now, not by chance of war. Christopher Marlowe. *Fr.* Edward the Second. FaBoEH

Now majesty into a pump so deep. "Peter Pindar." *Fr.* Mr. Whitebead's Brewhouse. FaBoEH

Now, Mamma, couldn't you? (*LL*) A Lesson for Mamma. Sydney Dayre. OBCA; OxBChV

Now manhood and garbroyls I chaunt. Virgil, *tr. by* Richard Stanyhurst. *Fr.* Aeneid [*or* Eneados], The. BIrV; NAWM-1; OBVE

Now may we turn aside and dry our tears. Inis Fal. Egan O'Rahilly, *tr. fr. Irish by* James Stephens. BIrV; OBMV

Now milkmaids' pails are deckt with flowers. Stool Ball. *Unknown.* CH

Now, miners, if you'll listen, I'll tell you quite a tale. Coming around the Horn. John A. Stone. AmFP

Now mirk December's dowie face. The Daft Days. Robert Fergusson. NOEC; OxAEP-1; ScCV

Now Mister Johnson had troubles of his own. The Cat Came Back. *Unknown.* CRH

Now more admir'd in being understood. (*LL*) The Copernican System. Thomas Chatterton. FaBoUs

Now more and more on my concern with the lifted waves of genius gaining. On the Ocean Floor. "Hugh MacDiarmid." FaBoMo; HAP

Now more toward that. (*LL*) Then. Diane Glancy. LoHo

Now Morn her rosy steps in the eastern clime. Milton. *Fr.* Paradise Lost. EPCY; NAEL-1; OAEL-1

Now Morning from her orient chamber came. Imitation of Spenser. Keats. EnRP

(Morning.) GN

Now Muse assist me, aptly to describe. A. D. Hope. *Fr.* Dunciad Minor. BXAP

Now must all satisfaction. Certain Mercies. Robert Graves. GTBS-P

Now must I learn to live [*or* lerne to lyve] at rest. Sir Thomas Wyatt. AAS; SiPS

Now must I mend my manners. Marbod of Rennnes, *tr. fr. Latin by* Helen Waddell. MLL

Now must I these three praise. Friends. W. B. Yeats. IIP; MoP; NoAM

Now must I wait. The Blank Book Letter. Samuel Greenberg. LiTA

Now my charms are all o'erthrown. Shakespeare. *Fr.* Tempest, The. CTC; OAEL-1

Now my fair'st friend. Some Flowers o' the Spring. Shakespeare. *Fr.* Winter's Tale, The. ChTr; GBL

Now my heart turns to and fro. Hatshepsut, *tr. fr. Egyptian by* Mariam Lichtheim. *Fr.* Obelisk Inscriptions. WPOW

Now my kinching-cove is gone. The Rum Mort's Praise of Her Faithless Maunder. *Unknown.* CBNP

Now my legs begin to walk. Thaw in the City. Lou Lipsitz. MAT

Now My Life Has Gained Some Meaning. Walther von der Vogelweide, *tr. fr. German by* J. W. Thomas. GePo

Now my mind's been brought to such a state – and it's your fault. Catullus, *tr. fr. Latin by* John Frederick Nims. STV

Now my old bawd is dead? (*LL*) John Kinsella's Lament for Mrs. Mary Moore. W. B. Yeats. CMoP; LiTM; MeMBP; MoAB; NoP; OAEL-2; RB

Now, my son, is life for you. Wishes for My Son. Thomas MacDonagh. TIRV

Now, My Usefullness Over. Edwin Honig. NoAM

Now neghes the New Yere and the night passes. *Unknown, tr. fr. Middle English by* Brian Stone. *Fr.* Sir Gawain and the Green Knight. EnVB; OAEL-1

Now new-vamped silks the mercer's window shows. A Description of Spring in London. *Unknown.* NOEC

Now, not a tear begun. A Woman Mourned by Daughters. Adrienne Rich. IHMS; IMW; Poetr

Now, now the world. Deciduous Spring. Robert Penn Warren. ArNa

Now, now's the time so oft by Truth. An Epithalamy to Sir Thomas Southwell and His Lady. Robert Herrick. CaPo

Now o'er the one half-world. Shakespeare. *Fr.* Macbeth. OxAEP-1

Now o'er the sea from her old love comes she. Ad Auroram, Ne Properet. Ovid, *tr. fr. Latin by* Christopher Marlowe. *Fr.* Amores. NoSic

Now of all the trees by the king's highway. Aunt Mary. Robert Stephen Hawker. OHIP

Now of that vision I, bereaven. Francis Thompson. *Fr.* Grace of the Way. MoAB; MoBrPo

Now, on the day before my daughter's. The Death of Kin Chuen Louie. Michael McClure. PoBeRe

Now on the verge of spring the icy silver leaf. Return to Spring. Florence Ripley Mastin. GoYe

Now on their coasts our conquering navy rides. Dryden. *Fr.* Annus Mirabilis. OxAEP-1

Now once again the gloomy scene explore. The Pauper's Funeral. George Crabbe. *Fr.* Village, The. OBNC

Now once upon a time the King of Astrakhan, at that. The Lacquer Liquor Locker. David McCord. FiBHP

Now one and all, you roses. A Wood Song. Ralph Hodgson. GoJo

Now or Never. Astra. AIW; BrRo

Now or Never. Judith Moffett. SM; Son

Now [*or* The Moment Eternal]. Robert Browning. CBLP

Now orange blossoms filigree. Ain't Nature Commonplace! Arthur Guiterman. FiBHP

Now ore the sea from her old love comes she. Ovid, *tr. by* Christopher Marlowe. *Fr.* Amores. OBVE

Now, Parrot, my sweet bird, speak our yet once again. John Skelton. *Fr.* Speak [*or* Speke], Parrot. NoSic

Now Phillipa Is Gone. Anne Ridler. FaBoTw

Now Phoebus did the world with frowns survey. Abigail's Lamentation for the Loss of Mr. Harley. William Walsh. APAS

Now Poem. For Us. Sonia Sanchez. PoBA

Now polish the crucible. Hilda Doolittle ("H. D."). *Fr.* Tribute to the Angels. NALW

Now ponder well, you parents dear. Babes in the Wood, The ("Now ponder well your parents dear.") *Unknown.* OBNV; OxAEP-1 (Children in the Wood, The.) EnSB

Now Pontius Pilate is to judge the cause. Emilia Lanier. *Fr.* Salve Deus Rex Judaeorum. NALW; NOSC

"Now, pray, where are you going, child?" said Meet-on-the-Road. Meet-on-the-Road. *Unknown.* OBSP; OTCP ("Now pray, where are you going, child?") OBSP; OTCP

Now, Priam's Son, thou may'st be mute. Allan Ramsay. ScCV

Now that the barbarians have got as far as Picra. Translation. Roy Fuller. NOBE; OxBTC

Now that the day is done. Centaur Song. Hilda Doolittle ("H. D."). VGW

Now That the Flowers. Cullen Jones. GoYe

Now that the harth [or hearth] is crown'd with smiling fire. Ode to Sir William Sydney, on His Birth-Day. Ben Jonson. BeJo; NAs (Another Birthday.) WiR

Now that the men have gone off to the choleric wars. The Stay Behind. Andrew Elliott. PNI

Now that the midd day heate doth scorch my shame. William Alabaster. Fr. Divine Meditations. ESCV; Son

Now that the others are gone, all of them, forever. Tomorrow. Kenneth Fearing. CMoP

Now, that the public sorrow doth subside. To the Pious Memory of C. W. Esquire. Henry Vaughan. PeECV

Now that the red glare of thy fall is blown. Francis Thompson. Fr. Ode to the Setting Sun. OBNC

Now that the time has come wherein. Advice from Poor Robin's Almanack. Unknown. OBCP

Now THAT the triumphant march has entered the last street. Come Thunder. Christopher Okigbo. HBAPE

Now That the Truth Is Tried. Thomas Whythorne. EIL

Now that the Village-Reverence doth lye [or lie] hid. A New-Years-Gift to Brian Lord Bishop of Sarum. William Cartwright. (New Year's Gift, A.) OxAEP-1

Now that the winter's gone, the earth hath lost. The Spring. Thomas Carew. BeJo; CaPo; GN; NoP; PFP; PoE; PoEL-3; SeCV-1; TEP; TrGrPo; WiR

Now that the world is all in a maze. The Unconcerned. Thomas Flatman. FaBoCh
(Unconcerned, The: Song.) NOSC

Now that the young buds are tipped with a falling sun. Early Spring. Sidney Keyes. MoBrPo

Now that these wings to speed my wish ascend. The Philosophic Flight. Giordano Bruno, tr. fr. Italian by John Addington Symonds. AWP

Now that time seems all mine. Patrizia Cavalli, tr. fr. Italian by Judith Baumel. NeIt

Now that we are on our own I can explain this secret stave. Unknown. See In the sand I grew, by the rocky sea-wall.

Now that we're almost settled in our house. In Memory of Major Robert Gregory. W. B. Yeats. EBEV; OAEL-2; OBF; SCGP

Now that we're alone we can talk prince man to man. Elegy of Fortinbras. Zbigniew Herbert, tr. fr. Polish by Czeslaw Milosz. FaBoPV; PoSu

Now that we've come to the end. The Avenue. Paul Muldoon. PBCIP

Now that we've done our best and worst, and parted. The Busy Heart. Rupert Brooke. MoBrPo

Now the bat circles on the breeze of eve. Ann Radcliffe. WPE

Now the bitter pangs of hope deferred. The Mail Has Come. Mary E. Tucker. CBWP-1

Now the bright crocus flames, and now. In the Spring. Meleager, tr. fr. Greek by Andrew Lang. AWP

Now the bright morning star, day's [or dayes] harbinger. Song on [or of] May Morning. Milton. BoNaP; CH; GN; PFP; TrGrPo

Now the crops grow green and the fields flourish with life. Request for Meat and Drink. Sedulius Scottus, tr. fr. Latin. NOIV

Now the day is over. Sabine Baring-Gould. OxBChV; WHSW

Now the declining fulgent orb of day. J. C. Squire. Fr. Doris and Philemon. BXAP

Now the declining sun 'gan downwards bend. The Nightingale. William Strode, after the Latin of Famianus Strada. OBVE

Now the dreary winter's over. Spring Song. Nahum, tr. fr. Hebrew by Emma Lazarus. TrJP

Now the earth spins. (LL) And now I wish to pray and perform. David Ignatow. EaPr

Now the Earth, the Skies, the Air. Unknown. EIL

Now the eyes of my eyes are opened. (LL) I Thank You God for Most This Amazing. E. E. Cummings. ArNa; EaPr; MeMAP; MoAB; PAW; TAP

Now the fingers and toes are formed. Magnificat. Chana Bloch. CrSp

Now the first silly bastard he got in an aeroplane. Ops in a Wimpey. Unknown. CoMu

Now the Four-way Lodge is opened, now the Hunting Winds are loose. The Feet of the Young Men. Kipling. OtMeF

Now the frog, all lean and weak. The Sweet o' the Year. George Meredith. BoNaP

Now the golden morn aloft. Thomas Gray. Fr. Ode on the Pleasure Arising from Vicissitude. GTBS; GTBS-P; NOEC

Now the good man's away from home. Sally Sweetbread. Henry Carey. CoMu

Now the green plane-tree hides the lovers, hides the lovers'/ rites. Thallus, tr. fr. Greek by Edwin Morgan. GrAn

Now the hard margin bears us on, while steam. Dante, tr. by Dorothy L. Sayers. Fr. Divina Commedia. MeMAP; NAWM-1, tr. by John Ciardi; PeHV

Now the heart sings with all its thousand voices. The Gateway. A. D. Hope. BoLoP; ErPo; FaBoMA

Now the Holy Lamp of Love. Patrick MacDonogh. BIrV

Now the Hungry Lion. Shakespeare. Fr. Midsummer Night's Dream, A. CH; ChTr; CTC; EIL; EnRePo; LiTB

Now the Hungry Lion Roars. Now the Hungry Lion. Shakespeare. Fr. Midsummer Night's Dream, A. CH; ChTr; CTC; EIL; EnRePo; LiTB
(Fairy Blessing, The.) OxBoLi
(Fairy Songs ("Now the hungry lion roars.").) TrGrPo
(Lion of Winter, The.) WiR
(Puck's Song.) MoShBr

Now the ice lays its smooth claws on the sill. Scotland's Winter. Edwin Muir. OxBS; OxBTC

Now the joys of the road are chiefly these. The Joys of the Road. Bliss Carman. AnAmPo; GGP

Now the Laborer's Task Is O'er. John Lodge Ellerton. BLPA; WGRP

Now the late fruits are in. For a Wine Festival. Vernon Watkins. OxBTC

Now the Leaves Are Falling Fast. W. H. Auden. CMoP

Now the light o' the west is a-turn'd to gloom. Evenen in the Village. William Barnes. EBVV

Now the little green blackbird liked a mouse. Because It's Good to Keep Things Straight. Kenneth Patchen. CBNP

Now the lotuses in the imperial lake. Wang Ch'ing-hui, tr. fr. Chinese by Kenneth Rexroth and Ling Chung. BoWoP

Now the Lusty Spring [Is Seen]. John Fletcher. Fr. Tragedy of Valentinian, The. ELP; ErPo; FF

Now the moisty wood discloses. Spring Morning. Frances Cornford. BoTP

Now the Most High Is Born. James Ryman. MeEL

Now the narrowing track. The Look. Elizabeth Daryush. PoA

Now the New Moon is hanging, having cast away his bone. New Moon. Aborigine Oral Tradition, tr. by R. M. Berndt. Fr. Moon-Bone Song [or Cycle]. CBAP; WTO

Now the People Have the Light. Charles G. Ballard. VoR

Now the Philistines fought against Israel. Bible, O.T. Fr. First Samuel. OBF

Now the pines lift. Burning the Tomato Worms. Carolyn Forché. AmPA

Now the pumpkin is ripe. A Letter to a Son. Charles Mungoshi. PeSAV

Now the quietude of earth. The Hermit. "Æ." OHCV

Now the rain is falling, freshly, in the intervals between sunlight. Spring Rain. Robert Hass. FoLa

Now! The Red Tobacco has come to strike your soul. Unknown, tr. fr. Cherokee Indian. Fr. Run toward the Nightland. STP

Now the rich cherry, whose sleek wood. Country Summer. Léonie Adams. GoJo; LiTM; MoAB; MoAmPo; TrGrPo

Now the river is rich, but her voice is low. The River in March. Ted Hughes. OxBC

Now the riverbed is lined with concrete. Our Mothers Were Sisters. Marilyn Johnson. NGP

Now the seasons are closing their files. Year's End. Ted Kooser. PBCAP

Now the shadow flee and vanish. William Williams. AngWe

Now the shiades o' the elems da stratch muore an muore. Evening, and Maidens. William Barnes. OBEV

Now the smallest creatures, who do not know. The First of May. Anne Porter. ArNa

Now the storm begins to lower. The Fatal Sisters. Thomas Gray, after the Icelandic. EnRP

Now the sun's gane out o' sight. Up in the Air. Allan Ramsay. NOEC; ScCV

Now the thinkers our old ones remember. Dance of the Rain Gods. Unknown, tr. fr. Cora Indian by Anselm Hollo. STP

Now the trouble with SETting down a: written calypso. Calypsomania. Anthony Brode. FiBHP; PeLV

Now the vapour hot and damp. Song of the Evil Spirit of the Woods. Thomas Moore. OBTV

Now the white violet blooms and narcissus that loves. Meleager, tr. fr. Greek by Barbara Hughes Fowler. Fr. Epigrams. HePo

Now the wild bees that hive in the rocks. The Brown Bear. Mary Austin. FaPON

Now the winds are riding by. And It Was Windy Weather. James Stephens. ArNa

Now the winter is gone and the summer is come. As I Walked through the Meadows. Unknown. OBET

Now Thebes stood in good estate, now Cadmus might thou say. Acteon. Ovid, tr. by Arthur Golding. Fr. Metamorphoses. CTC

Now then, take your seats! for Glasgow and the North. The Night Mail North. Henry Cholmondeley-Pennell. EBVV; OHCV

Now then, what are you up to, Dai? Langwell. Kingsley Amis. *Fr.* Evans Country, The. NOBL; OxBC

Now there are gold reflections on the water. In Time of Gold. Hilda Doolittle ("H. D."). PoA

Now there are no bonds except the flesh; listen. Manzini; Escape Artist. Gwendolyn MacEwen. NOBC

Now there comes/ The Christmas rose. New Year's [*or* Year] Song. Ted Hughes. OBCP

Now there's many fool things a woman will do. Gold Tooth Blues. Tennessee Williams. OBAL

Now they are married Nature breathes once more. (*LL*) Summer Storm. Louis Simpson. ErPo; OxBC

Now they are resting. Fine Work with Pitch and Copper. William Carlos Williams. OxBA

Now they have two cars to clean. Do It Yrself. Larry Eigner. NeAP; PoM

Now they're pillaging the last coast. The Vandals. Jenny Mastoraki, *tr. fr. Modern Greek by Nikos Germanakos.* BoWoP

Now, thirty years on, I shift. Headmaster. John Tripp. AngWe

Now this bloody war is over. George Barker. PeLV

Now this day, my Sun Father. *Unknown, tr. fr. Egyptian.* EaPr

Now this is my first counsel. Counsels of Sigrdrifa. *Unknown, tr. fr. Old Norse by* William Morris *and* Eirikr Magnusson. *Fr.* Elder Edda, The. AWP
(Part of the Lay of Sigrdrifa.) OBVE

Now this is new: that I (habitué). First Day of Teaching. Bonaro W. Overstreet. TrPWD

Now this is the Law of the Jungle — as old and as true as the sky. The Law of the Jungle. Kipling. LiTB; PoEL-5

Now this particular girl. Spinster. Sylvia Plath. FaBoWP; SoSe

Now this the Law of the Jungle — as old and as true as the sky. Kipling. *Fr.* Second Jungle Book, The. OBAP

Now those that are low spirited I hope won't think it wrong. A New Hunting Song. *Unknown.* CoMu; OBET

Now thou art dead, no eye shall ever see. Upon His Spaniel[l] Tracie [*or* Tracy]. Robert Herrick. BeJo; FM

Now thou hast lov'd me one whole day. Woman's Constancy. John Donne. ESCV; NBLV; NoP; NOSC; SeCV-1

Now, though the pages are brittle with dirt. (*LL*) After the Flood. John Foulcher. NOBAu

Now Thrice Welcome Christmas. *Unknown.* OHIP

Now through Night's Caressing Grip. W. H. Auden. PoRA

Now through the ocean in great haste they flunder. Camões, *tr. fr. Portuguese by* Sir Richard Fanshawe. *Fr.* Lusiads, The. OBVE

Now tidings of Arab unrest dismay connoisseurs in the West. Arabesque. "Sagittarius." IHNG

Now Time's Andromeda on this rock rude. Andromeda. Gerard Manley Hopkins. EBEV; FaBoMo; LiTB; MeMBP; OxAEP-2; SCGP

Now to be clean he must abandon himself. The Swan Bathing. Ruth Pitter. MoBrPo

Now to Blackwall Docks we bid adieu. Homeward Bound. *Unknown.* OxBSS

Now to dispose the dead, the care remains. Homer, *tr. by* Pope. *Fr.* Odyssey. NAWM-1; OBVE

Now to Great Britain we must make our way. Of England, and of Its Marvels. Fazio degli Uberti, *tr. fr. Italian by* Dante Gabriel Rossetti. AWP

Now, to tense stillness as the door is slammed. Their Thoughts Cling to Everything They See on the Way. Allen Afterman. NOBAu

Now to you my Country wench I'le bringe. The 4th Sheppard Speakes This. Lady Jane Cavendish *and* Lady Elizabeth Brackley. *Fr.* Pastorall, A. KTR

Now toils the Heroe; trees on trees o'erthrown. Homer, *tr. by* Pope. *Fr.* Odyssey. NAWM-1; OBVE

Now Tomlinson gave up the ghost in his house in Berkeley Square. Tomlinson. Kipling. BeLS; OtMeF

Now touch the air softly. A Pavane for the Nursery. William Jay Smith. GoJo; MoAmPo

Now tow'rd the Hunter's gloomy sides we came. The Hospital Prison Ship. Philip Freneau. *Fr.* British Prison Ship, The. AmPP

Now twenty springs had clothed the park with green. The Toilette. John Gay *and* Alexander Pope. ECEV

Now, Until the Break of Day. Shakespeare. *Fr.* Midsummer Night's Dream, A. NAs

Now upon sale, a bankrupt island. John Byrom. *Fr.* Four Epigrams on the Naturalization Bill. NOBL

Now upon this piteous year. The Stranger. Jean Garrigue. LiTA; LiTM; NOBA; TwCP

Now van to van the foremost squadrons meet. Dryden. *Fr.* Annus Mirabilis. OBWP

Now Venus is an evening star. Waiting. Hilary Corke. ErPo

Now Voyager/ how do you see — . Elegy for Jack Moffat. Charlotte Painter. IMW

Now — wagon full of thunder. Wagon Full of Thunder. Louis Oliver. HATNAP

Now war and vengeance claim. The Death of Sohráb. Firdausi, *tr. fr. Persian. Fr.* Shahnamah, The. TAL, *tr. by* James Atkinson

Now war is all the world about. Ode on His Majesty's Proclamation. Sir Richard Fanshawe, *after the Italian of* Giovanni Battista Guarini. *Fr.* Il Pastor Fido. NOBE

Now was there maid fast by the towris wall. James I, King of Scotland. *Fr.* Kingis Quair, The. EBEV

Now watch this autumn that arrives. Song at the Beginning of Autumn. Elizabeth Jennings. OxBTC

Now we are back to normal, now the mind is. Louis MacNeice. *Fr.* Autumn Journal. OxAEP-2

Now we are civilized, the old men die. Old Men's Ward. Elma Dean. GoYe

Now we are left out. Funeral Song. *Unknown, tr. fr. Sotho by* Dan Kunene *and* Jack Cope. PeSA

Now We Are Sick. J. B. Morton. *Fr.* When We Were Very Silly. FaBoPa

Now We Are Six. "Sagittarius." PAW

Now we are thirty-five we no longer enjoy red neon. Literary Life in the Golden West. Philip Whalen. NAs

Now we begin another day together. Prayer at Dawn. Edwin McNeill Poteat. TrPWD

Now we can burn a gesture into stone. Hieronymus Bosch, We Can Do It. Paul Coltman. PAW

Now we enter a strange world, where the Hessian Christmas. After the Industrial Revolution, All Things Happen at Once. Robert Bly. CoAP

Now we flourish/ as others have/ before. *Unknown, tr. fr. Greek by* Peter Jay. GrAn

Now we have always with us these men — these men! Memo. Hildegarde Flanner. NYBP

Now we have buried the face we never knew. Easter, 1968. May Sarton. CrSp

Now We Have Present Made. Sir Walter Ralegh. SiPSBD

Now we must get up quickly. Two Lines from the Brothers Grimm. Gregory Orr. AmPA

Now we must praise the Guardian of Heaven. Cædmon's Hymn. *Unknown, tr. fr. Anglo-Saxon by* Kevin Crossley-Holland. ASW

Now weary labourers perceivem well pleased. Evening. Joanna Baillie. *Fr.* Summer Day, A. ECWP

Now Welcom[e], Somer [*or* Summer]. Chaucer. *Fr.* Parlement of Foules, The. HAP

Now we'll never, etc. (*LL*) Sheath and Knife. *Unknown.* CH; ESPB

Now we're met, my brethren Benchers. The Humours of the King's Bench Prison, a Ballad. Leonard Howard. NOEC

Now we're stuck there. Heaving the Lead Line. *Unknown.* AmFP

Now westward Sol had spent the richest beam[e]s. Music[k]'s Duel[l]. Richard Crashaw. GeHe; OAEL-1; SeCP; SeCV-1

Now we've made a child. And What About the Children. Audre Lorde. PoBA

Now what do you think. *Unknown.* OxNR

Now what in the world shall we dioux. The Sioux. Eugene Field. FiBHP

Now what was the name of this scholar? (*LL*) As I was a-walking on Westminster Bridge. *Unknown.* OxNR

Now what will we do for timber. Cill Chais. *Unknown, tr. fr. Irish by* Thomas Kinsella. NOIV

Now what's here a Hee cave, as was a Shee. The 3d Sheppard Speakes This to the Rest. Lady Jane Cavendish *and* Lady Elizabeth Brackley. *Fr.* Pastorall, A. KTR

Now when I have thrust my body. To Forget Me. Theodore Weiss. CoAP

Now when I walk around at lunchtime. Personal Poem. Frank O'Hara. PoBeRe

Now, when the cheerless empire of the sky. Winter ("Now, when the cheerless empire of the sky.") James Thomson. *Fr.* Seasons, The. OxBA

Now when the solemn rites of pray'r were past. Homer, *tr. by* Dryden. *Fr.* Iliad, The. OBVE

Now, when thou hast decreed to seize their stores. The Care of Bees. Virgil, *tr. by* Dryden. *Fr.* Georgics. FaBoUs

Now, when twelve days complete had run their race. Homer, *tr. by* Dryden. *Fr.* Iliad, The. OBVE

Now where's a song for our small dear. The Unwritten Song. Ford Madox Ford. BoTP

Now whether folks are Methodists. The Radio Religion. William Ludlum. WBLP

Now, whether it were by peculiar grace. Wordsworth. *Fr.* Resolution and Independence. BoNaP; EBEV; EnRP; FHYEP; HAP; InPS; LiTB; MAT; MeMBP; NOBE; NOCV; NoP; OAEL-2; OBNC; OxAEP-2; PoEL-4; PPP; TEP; TFi; UV

Now which is wrong or right? Too glib we talk. Falkland at Newbury, 1643. Hugh Conway. EBVV

Now, amid those dainty downs and dales. To His Pandora, from England. Alexander Craig. Son

Now, while the birds thus sing a joyous song. Wordsworth. *Fr.* Ode: Intimations of Immortality from Recollections of Early Childhood. AWP; BLPL; EnRP; FaBoRV; FHYEP; HAP; HeIP; InvP; LiTB; MeMBP; NAs; NOBE; NoP; OAEL-2; OBEV; OBNC; PoE; PoEL-4; PPP; Prf; PrIm; TEP; TrGrPo

Now, while thou hast the wondrous power of word. The Gift of Speech. Sadi, *tr.* by L. Cranmer-Byng. *Fr.* Gulistan, The. AWP

Now Whitehall's in the grave. A Mock Song. Richard Lovelace. BeJo; CaPo

Now who is he on earth that lives. *Unknown, tr. fr. French by* John Addington Symonds. *Fr.* Medieval Norman Song. AWP

Now whyle Hippomenes/ Debates theis things. Ovid, *tr. fr. Latin. Fr.* Metamorphoses. OBVE, *tr.* by Arthur Golding

Now will I a lover be. The Combat. Thomas Stanley. AWP

Now will I open unto thee — whose heart. *Unknown, tr.* by Sir Edward Arnold. *Fr.* Bhagavad-Gita, The. TAL

Now will you stand for me, in this cool light. Love in the Museum. Adrienne Rich. NYBP

Now winedrinkers, this way to an airy shrine. A Musical Wine-Jar. Hedylos, *tr. fr. Greek by* William Moebius. GrAn

Now winter downs the dying of the year. Year's End. Richard Wilbur. CAPP; CoAP; HeIP; LiTM; NAAL-2; SM
(At Year's End.) NYBP

Now Winter Nights Enlarge. Thomas Campion. AAS; EBEV; EIL; ELP; EnRePo; NoP; NTP; OxAEP-1; TEP

Now, winter's dolorous days are o'er. Thomas Caulfield Irwin. PeIV

Now, winter's dolorous days are o'er, and through. Now, Winter's Dolorous Days Are O'er. Thomas Caulfield Irwin. PeIV

Now Winter's winds are banished from the sky. Spring. Meleager, *tr. fr. Greek by* William M. Hardinge. AWP

Now with a vestal lustre glows the Vale. Anna Seward. *Fr.* Llangollen Vale. PeHV

Now with earth riven and a bloodied sun. We Shall Say. Miriam Allen DeFord. GoYe

Now/ with your head thrown back. I Tell of Another Young Death. César Tiempo, *tr. fr. Spanish by* Donald Devenish Walsh. TrJP

Now, with your palms on the blades of my shoulders. Dead Still. Andrei Voznesensky, *tr. fr. Russian by* Richard Wilbur. BoLoP

Now Wolde. A. Godwin. *See* Now wolde I fayne sum merthis [*or* faine some merthis] mak[e].

Now wolde I fayne sum merthis [*or* faine some merthes] mak[e]. A. Godwin. MiEL
(Now Wolde.) CH
(Song for My Lady.) OxBoLi
(Song in His Lady's Absence, A.) MeEL

Now would to God swift ships had ne'er been made! Sopolis. Callimachus, *tr. fr. Greek by* William M. Hardinge. AWP

Now, wouldn't it be funny. Wouldn't It Be Funny? Pixie O'Harris. ZA

Now, yield thee, or by Him who made. Sir Walter Scott. *Fr.* Lady of the Lake, The. OxBS

Now, yields you, with some sighs, our explanation. (*LL*) To R. B. Gerard Manley Hopkins. CMoP; EnVR; EPCY; GTBS-P; InvP; OAEL-2; OxAEP-2

Now you are going, what can I do but wish you. The Poet's Farewell to His Teeth. William Dickey. PoA

Now you are holding my skull in your hand. A Meditation. Richard Eberhart. LiTA

Now you are one with us, you know our tears. To America, on Her First Sons Fallen in the Great War. E. M. Walker. PAH

Now you are standing face to face with the clear light. Prayer for the Little Daughter between Death and Burial. Diana Scott. BrRo

Now you can see him, exactly as he came. Herakles. Parrhasios, *tr. fr. Greek by* Peter Jay. GrAn

Now you come again. Happiness of 6 A.M. Harvey Shapiro. NYBP

Now you depart, and though your way may lead. To a Friend Going on a Journey. Mahammed Abdille Hassan, *tr. fr. Somali by* M. Laurence. WTO

Now, you great stanza, you heroic mold. Single Sonnet. Louise Bogan. Son

Now You Have Burned. John Thompson. NOBC

Now you have come, The Foot-Washing. A. R. Ammons. ChIV-2

Now you have freely given me leave to love. To a Lady That Desired I Would Love Her. Thomas Carew. BeJo; CaPo; CBLP; MeLP; SCGP; SeCV-1

Now you have stabbed her good. Kreutzer Sonata. Ted Hughes. FaBoMo

Now you have to promise. Cousin Ella Goes to Town. George Ella Lyon. ETG

Now you lie — a grape-offering. Moiro, *tr. fr. Greek by* Fleur Adcock. GrAn

Now you love me. Divorce Song. *Unknown, tr. fr. Tsimshian Indian by* Carl Cary. STP

"Now you must die," the young one said. The Rite. Dudley Randall. HoPM

Now you take ol Rufus. He beat drums. For Freckle-faced Gerald. Etheridge Knight. BPo

Now you think that is right, sah? Talk the truth. The Carpenter's Complaint. Edward Baugh. PBCV

Now You're Content. André Spire, *tr. fr. French by* Stanley Burnshaw. TrJP

Nowadays it's rather nobby. Collections. Cole Porter. *Fr.* I've a Shooting Box In Scotland. CBCK

Nowadays the mess is everywhere. The Survivors. Daryl Hine. TwCP

Nowel! (*LL*) Man Exalted. *Unknown.* MeEL; NoP

Nowel! nowel! Man Exalted. *Unknown.* MeEL

Nowel! nowel! nowel! Mary Is with Child. *Unknown.* MeEL

Nowell . . (*LL*) The First Nowell. *Unknown.* LiTB; PChr; PlP

Nowhere. John Berryman. AnAn

Nowhere else but on the mouth. How He Should Like to Be Kissed. Paul Fleming, *tr. fr. German by* Harold B. Segel. GePo

Nowhere else does screened porch wire. Marriage Portrait. James Applewhite. MT

Nowhere, not among the warriors at their festival. Atimantiyar, *tr. fr. Tamil by* A. K. Ramanujan. WPOW

Now's the time for mirth and play. For Saturday. Christopher Smart. *Fr.* Hymns for the Amusement of Children. FaBoCh; NOEC; OxBChV
(Hymn for Saturday.) OxBChV
(Lark's Nest, A.) FaBoCh

Nox Nocti Indicat Scientiam. William Habington. *Fr.* Castara. BeJo; JCP; MeLP; NOBE; OBEV; SCGP

Nox was lit by lux of Luna, The. Carmen Possum. *Unknown.* BLPA; NBLV

Nozizwe. Mazisi Kunene, *tr. fr. Zulu by the author.* PeSAV

Ntabuu/ Ntabuu Selina and. The Sisters. Alexis De Veaux. GLP; VBLP

Nu-numma-kwiten formerly sang. The Song of Nu-Numma-Kwiten. *Unknown, tr. fr. Bushman.* PeSA

Nu thu, unsely body, upon bere list. *Unknown.* MiEL

Nuances not effective in point form. Town Just Before the Lightning Flash. Anne Carson. *Fr.* Life of Towns, The. BAP-90

Nuances of a Theme by Williams. Wallace Stevens. CMoP; LiTA

Nuchal, a Fragment. Thomas Kinsella. PBCIP

Nuclear ecstasy on the picket line. Cheap Replicas of the Eiffel Tower. Elton Glaser. PBCAP

Nuclear Unit. Valerie Sinason. DT

Nuclear wind, when wilt thou blow. Paul Dehn. *Fr.* Leaden Treasury of English Verse, A. FiBHP

Nude. Duncan Forbes. FaBoBl

Nude. Harold Witt. ErPo

Nude Descending a Staircase. X. J. Kennedy. CoAP; HoPM; NIP; OxBSP; PoA; SM

Nude ghosts seeking each other out in the silence. (*LL*) Love Poem on Theme by Whitman. Allen Ginsberg. CAPP; NaP

Nude in a Fountain. Norman MacCaig. OxBS

Nude Kneeling in Sand. John Logan. ErPo

Nude on the Bathroom Wall, The. Gena Ford. IHMS

Nude Reclining at Word Processor, in Pastel. Carl Conover. GOYP

Nude Swim, The. Anne Sexton. WPE

Nudes — stark and glistening. Louse Hunting. Isaac Rosenberg. EBEV; NAEL-2; NoAM; NoP; NSI; OxAEP-2; OxBTC; PeFWW

Nudities. André Spire, *tr.* by Jethro Bithell. AWP; ErPo

Nudities. André Spire, *tr. fr. French by* Stanley Burnshaw. TrJP

Nudus Redibo. Thomas Flatman. OxBSP

Nuit Blanche: North End. Conrad Aiken. OxBA

Nulla Fides. Patrick Carey. SCGP

Numb, stiff, broken by no sleep. Night Thoughts over a Sick Child. Philip Levine. SM

Number Four. Doughtry Long, Jr.. PoBA

Number One/ I slouch in bed. Two Hangovers. James Wright. LCAP

Number one is a good clean number, The. The Million. Peter Redgrove. OxBC

Number Song. Anne Waldman. UL

Number Two! (*LL*) The Wail of the Waiter. Marcus Clarke. NOBAu

Number, Weight, and Measure. Abraham Cowley. *See* Tell me, O[h] Muse (for thou, or none canst tell.)

Numbered but twenty that answered "Here!". (*LL*) Roll-Call. Nathaniel Graham Shepherd. OHIP

Numbers, *sels.* Bible, *O.T.*
  Balaam's Blessing. TrGrPo
  (How goodly are the tentes of Jacob and thine habitacions Israel.) OBVE, *tr.* by William Tyndale
  Benediction. TrGrPo
  (Blessing of the Priests.) TrJP
  (Lorde blesse the and kepe the, The,.) OBVE, *tr.* by William Tyndale, VI: 24–27
  Song of the Well. TrJP

Numbers. Norah Reap. BTR

Numbers and Faces., *sels.* W. H. Auden.

Numbers in ass, The. Strato, *tr. fr. Greek* by Thomas Meyer. GrAn

Numbers, Letters. Amiri Baraka. BPo; NOBA

Numbness. Wilhelm Müller, *tr. fr. German* by Philip L. Miller. *Fr.* Winter's Journey, The. RiWo

Numeri XIII. John Hall. ChIV-1

Numerous Celts. J. C. Squire. BXAP

Numerous host of dreaming saints succeed, A. Zimri: The Duke of Buckingham. Dryden. *Fr.* Absalom and Achitophel, Pt. I. NOBE; NoP; OAEL-1; OBSV; SeCV-2
  (Zimri: "Numerous host of dreaming saints succeed.") AWP

Nummum et secalis sacculum cantate! Four and Twenty Merulae. J. Moyr Smith. FaBoNo

Nun, The. Edward Moore. ECEV

Nun walked on her prayer, The. The Friar and the Nun. *Unknown.* GBP

Nunaptigne . . . In our land — ahe, ahe, ee, ee, iee. The Wind Has Wings. *Unknown, tr.* by Raymond de Coccola *and* Paul King. GrPl

Nunc Dimittis. Bible, *N.T. Fr.* St. Luke. WGRP

Nunc Viridant Segetes. Sedulius Scottus, *tr. fr. Medieval Latin* by Helen Waddell. BIrV; NAWM-1

Nunnery, The. Anna Williams. ECWP

Nuns at Eve. John Malcolm Brinnin. MoAB; TwCP

Nuns Fret Not at Their Convent's Narrow Room. Wordsworth. EBEV; EnRP; NIP; NoP; Poetr; Son

Nuns, his nieces, bring the priest in the next. A Far Cry after a Close Call. Richard Howard. NYBP; UnPo

Nuns in the Wind. Muriel Rukeyser. NNaP

Nun's Priest's Prologue, The. Chaucer. *Fr.* Canterbury Tales, The. EnVB; FHYEP; OAEL-1

Nun's Priest's Tale, The. Chaucer. *Fr.* Canterbury Tales, The. EnVB; FHYEP; NAEL-1; NoP; OAEL-1; PoEL-1; TrGrPo, *orig. and mod. vers.* by Frank Ernest Hill

Nuo-ri-lang. Yang Lian, *tr. fr. Chinese* by Donald Finkel *with* Li Guohua. SpMi

Nuptial Dialogues., *sels.* Edward Ward.
  Dialogue between a Squeamish Cotting Mechanic and His Sluttish Wife, in the Kitchen. NOEC

Nuptial Eve, A. Sydney Thompson Dobell. OBNC
  Sels.
  Ballad of Keith of Ravelston, The. CH; OBEV
  (Keith of Ravelston.) CH

Nuptial Hymn. Henry Peacham. *Fr.* Period of Mourning, The. ElL

Nuptial Sleep. Dante Gabriel Rossetti. *Fr.* House of Life, The. EBVV; EnVR; NAEL-2; NOBVV

Nuptial Song. Lord De Tabley. GTBS-P; PeVV

Nuptial Song. Henricus Selyns. *See* O Christmas Night.

Nuptial Torches, The. Tony Harrison. SCBI

Nuptial[l] Song, or Epithalamie [*or* Epithalamy], on Sir Clipseby Crew and His Lady, A. Robert Herrick. BeJo; CaPo; CBLP; JCP; PoEL-3; SeCP; SeCV-1

Nuptials of Attila, The, *sels.* George Meredith.
  "Flat as to an eagle's eye." PeVV
  "Square along the couch, and stark." PeVV

Nuremberg. Longfellow. AmPP

Nurse, The. G. M. Mitchell. NSI

Nurse believed the sick man slept, The. Charlotte Brontë. NOBVV

Nurse coming off her shift at the psychiatric ward, The. Night Subway. Katha Pollitt. BAP-91

Nurse-life wheat, within his greene huske growing, The. Fulke Greville. *Fr.* Caelica. AAS; EnRePo
  (Sonnet: "Nurse-life wheat within his green husk growing, The.") JCP

Nursery, The. Fanny Howe. UL

Nursery boast, The. On Seeing My Birthplace from a Jet Aircraft. John Pudney. NYBP

Nursery Rhyme. Kenneth Burke. OBAL

Nursery Rhyme. Gavin Ewart. UV

Nursery Rhyme. Leo Hamalian. PAW

Nursery Rhyme 1984. Paul Coltman. PAW

Nursery Rhyme of Innocence and Experience. Charles Causley. GoJo; NTP

Nursery Rhymes. (*LL*) Ding Dong. Arthur Clement Hilton. BXAP

Nursery Rhymes for the Tender-hearted, *sels.* Christopher Morley.

Nurses, The. Kipling. *Fr.* Land and Sea Tales. NoAM

Nurse's Dole in the Medea, The. Byron. OBVE

Nurse's Lament, The. Mary Elizabeth Coleridge. NOBVV; OxBSP

Nurse's Song. Blake. *Fr.* Songs of Experience. EnRP; FF; FHYEP

Nurse's Song. Blake. *Fr.* Songs of Innocence. AWP; BLPL; CH; EnRP; FaBoBe; FHYEP; NAEL-2; OxBChV; PeLV; SCGP

Nurse's Song. *Unknown. See* Sleep, baby, sleep.

Nursing Home. Philip Martin. FaBoMA

Nursing: Mother, *sels.* Marie Ponsot.
  "Tranquilized, she speaks or does not speak." MDDM

Nursing your nerves. The Afterwake. Adrienne Rich. NOBA; Prf

Nut, a World, a Squirrel, and a King, A. Charles Churchill. *Fr.* Night; an Epistle to Robert Lloyd. FaBoRV

Nut-brown Maid, The. *Unknown.* NoSic; OBEV

Nut Tree, The. Julius Mosen, *tr. fr. German* by Philip L. Miller. RiWo

Nut Tree, A. *Unknown.* TTTS

Nut tree grows in front of the house, A. The Nut Tree. Julius Mosen, *tr. fr. German* by Philip L. Miller. RiWo

Nutcrackers and the Sugar-Tongs, The. Edward Lear. BLPL; Mes; PoLF

Nutcrackers sate by a plate on the table, The. The Nutcrackers and the Sugar-Tongs. Edward Lear. BLPL; Mes; PoLF

Nuts in May. "Hugh MacDiarmid." IHNG

Nuts in May. Louis MacNeice. MoAB; MoBrPo

Nutting. Wordsworth. EnRP; NAEL-2; NU; OAEL-2; PFP; Poetr; RB

NW5 and N6. Sir John Betjeman. SCV

N.Y. to L.A. by Jet Plane. Sonya Dorman. GOA

Nyanu was appointed. Early Losses; a Requiem. Alice Walker. BlSi

Nymph and Her Fawn, The. Andrew Marvell. *Fr.* Nymph Complaining for the Death of Her Faun, the. CH; FaBoCh; FM; HeIP; OAEL-1; PoEL-2; SeCP; SeCV-1

Nymph and shepherd raise electric tridents. Chances "R." Allen Ginsberg. HCAP

Nymph Complaining for the Death of Her Faun, The. Andrew Marvell. CH; FM; HeIP; OAEL-1; PoEL-2; SeCP; SeCV-1
  Sels.
  Nymph and Her Fawn, The. FaBoCh
  (Girl and Her Fawn, The.) BoTP

Nymph Fanarett, supposed to be. A Penance. Francis Daniel Pastorius. NOSC

Nymph I come once more awooing. Ay or Nay? Ralph Schomberg. *Fr.* Judgment of Paris, The. TrJP

Nymph in vain bestows her pains, The. The Countess of Winchilsea. OxBSP

Nymph, nymph, what are your beads? Overheard on a Saltmarsh. Harold Monro. BoTP; CH; FaPON; GoJo; Mes; MoShBr

Nymph turnd home, The. He fell to felling downe. Homer, *tr.* by George Chapman. *Fr.* Odyssey. NAWM-1; OBVE

Nymphidia, *sels.* Michael Drayton.
  Pigwiggin Arms Himself. MoShBr
  (Arming of Pigwiggen, The.) GN

Nymphs, The, *sels.* Leigh Hunt.
  "There are the fair-limbed nymphs o' the woods." OBNC

Nymphs and Shepherds. Milton. *Fr.* Arcades. ELP

Nymph's Disdain of Love, A. *Unknown.* ElL

Nymphs of Fiesole, *sels.* Boccaccio, *tr. fr. Italian* by Joseph Tusiani.

Nymphs of sea and land, away. Nuptial Hymn. Henry Peacham. *Fr.* Period of Mourning, The. ElL

Nymphs of the surface, whom Hermokreon gave. Hermocreon, *tr. fr. Greek* by Alistair Elliot. GrAn

Nymphs of water, daughters of Doros. Leonidas of Tarentum, *tr. fr. Greek* by Peter Levi. GrAn

Nymph's Reply to the Shepherd, The. Sir Walter Ralegh. ArLo; ClHu; CTC; EBEvV; EIL; FF; HAP; HeIL; HeIP; HoPM; ImPo; InPK; InPS; LiTB; NAEL-1; NBLV; NIP; NOBE; NoP; NoSic; PIP; PoE; Poetr; PPP; RB; SCGP; SiPS; SiPSBD; TFi; TrGrPo; TRP; WeW

Nymph's Secret, A. Ben Jonson. BeJo; OBEV

Nymph's Song. Sir Richard Fanshawe, *after the Italian of* Giovanni Battista Guarini. *See* Let us use it while [*or* whilst] we may.

Nymph's Song to Hylas, The. William Morris. *See* I know a little garden-close.

Nymphs! your fine hands ethereal floods amass. The Action of Electricity. Erasmus Darwin. *Fr.* Economy of Vegetation, The. FaBoUs

Nzingha Revisited. Askia Muhammad Touré. BCF

O

Ö. Rita Dove. HCAP; WeW

O! Marge Piercy. SRLS

O. Laura Rosenthal. UL

O. Richard Wilbur. LiTA

O, a dainty plant is the Ivy green. The Ivy Green. Charles Dickens. *Fr. Pickwick Papers, The.* BoNaP

O a little lonely in Cambridge all that first Fall. Transit. John Berryman. AnAn

O' a' the waters that can hobble. Called Oysters. Robert Fergusson. ScCV

O a year from tomorrow I left my own people. Clonmel Jail. *Unknown, tr. fr. Irish by* Valentin Iremonger. BIrV

O Abishag, my little serving-maid. Abishag. André Spire, *tr. fr. French by* Emanuel Eisenberg. TrJP

O Africa! *(LL)* A Wreath for Africa. Bernard Dadié. NegPo

O ah drove three mules foh Gawge McVane. Mule Skinner's Song. *Unknown.* AS

O Alison Gross, that lives in yon tower [*or* tow'r]. Alison [*or* Allison] Gross. *Unknown.* CH; ESPB; FaBoCh; OxBB

O All Down within the Pretty Meadow. Kenneth Patchen. HAP; WeW

O all the problems other people face. Alcoholic. John Berryman. NOCV

O all ye fair ladies with your colours and your graces. The Revenant. Walter de la Mare. GBL

O all you little blackey tops. Scaring Crows. *Unknown.* BoTP; OxNR

O all your ages at the mercy of my loves. John Berryman. *Fr.* Homage to Mistress Bradstreet. NOBA

O Alva hills is bonny. The Braes o' Menstrie. *Unknown.* ScCV

O amiable prospect! New Lines for Cuscuscaraway and Mirza Murad Ali Beg. Louis Simpson. OBAL

O an old King in a story. After W. B. Yeats. G. K. Chesterton. NOBL

O antique city on St. Lawrence shore. Quebec. H. Cordelia Ray. CBWP-3

O apple blossoms. Japanese Hokku. Lewis Alexander. CDC

O! Are Ye Sleepin [*or* Sleeping], Maggie? Robert Tannahill. OxBS

O Artemis and your virgin girls. Telesilla, *tr. fr. Greek by* Willis Barnstone. BoWoP

O Atthis. Ezra Pound. PoA

O Autumn, laden with fruit, and stained. To Autumn. Blake. BoNaP; NAEL-2; WiR

O baby, where you been so long? Lord, Lord, Lord, Lord. Levee Moan. *Unknown.* AS

O bards! weak heritors of passion and of pain! Miserimus. Adah Isaacs Menken. CBWP-1

O, be my friend, and teach me to be thine! *(LL)* Forbearance. Emerson. AnAmPo; GN; LiTA; MeMAP; TAP; TrGrPo; WGRP

O, Be Not Too Hasty, My Dearest. "Orpheus C. Kerr." PoRA

O be swift. The Helmsman. Hilda Doolittle ("H. D."). CMoP; OxBA

O! bear me witness, night. Shakespeare. *Fr.* Antony and Cleopatra. OxAEP-1

O beato solitudo! where have I flown to? High. Philip Lamantia. PoBeRe

O Beautful, My Country. Frederick L. Hosmer. AH

O beautiful calm. Tu-kehu *and* Wetea, *tr. fr. Maori by* J. C. Andersen. WTO

O beautiful for spacious skies. America the Beautiful. Katharine Lee Bates. BLPA; EaPr, *st. 1 only;* EBEvV; FaBoBe; FaBV; FaPON; GOA; TAP; WBLP; WGRP

O Beautiful Forever! I Saw Eternity. Louise Bogan. LiTA

O beech, unbind your yellow leaf, for deep. Ghostly Tree. Léonie Adams. MoAB; MoAmPo

O benign Jesu, my sovereign Lord and King. John Skelton. *Fr.* To the Second Person. SCGP

O Bessie Bell and Mary Gray. Bessy [*or* Bessie] Bell and Mary Gray. *Unknown.* ESPB; OxBB; ScCV

O Billie, billie, bonny billie. The Battle of Bothwell Bridge. *Unknown.* OxBB, *with music* (Bothwell Bridge.) ESPB

O Billows Bounding Far. A. E. Housman. BoNaP

O Bird at night, who, hearing, could forget. Bird at Night. Marion Ethel Hamilton. GoYe

O Bird, So Lovely. Louis Golding. TrJP

O bird's singing! Mitsuhashi Takajo, *tr. fr. Japanese by* Kenneth Rexroth *and* Ikuko Atsumi. WPJ

O Black and Unknown Bards. James Weldon Johnson. BPo; HeIP; PoBA; PoNe; TTY; UnPo

O black winter of savage death. On a Young Wife. Julianus of Egypt, *tr. fr. Greek by* Willis Barnstone. GrAn

O blackbird! sing me something well. The Blackbird. Tennyson. FM

O Blackbird, what a boy you are! Vespers. Thomas Edward Brown. BoTP

O blazing Sun, how happy you are there. Louise Labé, *tr. fr. French by* Willis Barnstone. BoWoP

O bless this people, Lord, who seek their own face. Léopold Sédar Senghor, *tr. fr. French by* Ellen Conroy Kennedy. *Fr.* Prayer for Peace. EaPr, *tr. by* John Reed *and* Clive Wake

O blessed bodie! Whither art thou thrown? Sepulchre. George Herbert. ESCV; MiEL

O blessed breeding sun! draw from the earth. Shakespeare. *Fr.* Timon of Athens. OxAEP-1

O Blessèd House, That Cheerfully Receiveth. Karl Johann Philipp Spitta, *tr. fr. German by* Charles William Schaeffer. TrPWD

O blessed letters, that combine in one. Samuel Daniel. *Fr.* Musophilus; or, Defence of All Learning. EPCY (O Blessed Letters.) FaBoRV

O blessed man, that in th' advice. Bible, O.T., *paraphrased by* Sir Thomas Wyatt. *See* Blessed is the man that walketh not in the counsel of the ungodly [*or* wicked].

O Blessed man, that in th'advice. *Unknown. Fr.* Bay Psalm Book, The. SCAP

O Blest Estate, Blest from Above. George Sandys. AH

O Blest Unfabled Incense Tree. George Darley. *Fr.* Nepenthe. BIrV; FaBoCh; FaBoRV

O blisful light, of which the beames clere. Wooing of Criseide, The, III. Chaucer. *Fr.* Troilus and Criseyde [*or* Criseide]. EnVB; PoEL-1

O blithe new-comer! I have heard. To the Cuckoo. Wordsworth. BoTP; EBEvV; ELP; EnRP; GTBS; GTBS-P; PoLF; TrGrPo; UV, *st.* 1 *only*

O blue is such a fatal colour. September Blue. Barbara Burford. DT

O Blush Not So! O Blush Not So! Keats. ArLo

O Bonny Baby Livingston. Bonny Baby Livingston. *Unknown.* ESPB

O bonny, bonny sang the bird. The Unquiet Grave. *Unknown.* EnSB

O, born in luckless hour, with every muse. To the Editor of Mr. Pope's Works. Thomas Edwards. Son

O Boston, though thou now art grown. Of Boston in New England. William Bradford. SCAP

O Boston wives and maids, draw near and see. To the Boston Women. *Unknown.* PAH

O boy cutting grass. Hitomaro, *tr. by* Arthur Waley. *Fr.* Manyo Shu, Part 3 of 4. AWP

O boys, O strong of heart in vain. Virgil, *tr. fr. Latin by* Robert Fitzgerald. *Fr.* Aeneid [*or* Eneados], The. MLL, *tr. by* Helen Waddell; NAWM-1

O Brazil, the Isle of the Blest. Gerald Griffin.

O brightness/ of peony's buds. Hoshino Tatsuko, *tr. fr. Japanese by* Kenneth Rexroth *and* Ikuko Atsumi. WPJ

O [*or* Oh], Brignal[l] banks are wild and fair. Brignall Banks. Sir Walter Scott. *Fr.* Rokeby. EnRP; OBEV (Edmund's Song.) PoRA (Outlaw, The.) GTBS; GTBS-P; OtMeF (Song: Brignall Banks.) OxAEP-2

O broad-breasted queen among nations! Boston. John Boyle O'Reilly. PAH

O bronco that would not be broken of dancing. *(LL)* The Broncho That Would Not Be Broken. Vachel Lindsay. MeMAP

O brother, as you've given me so much. Bride's Farewell: Two Songs. *Gond Oral Tradition, tr. by* V. Elwin *and* S. Hivale. WTO

O brother, lift a cry, a long world cry. Peace. Edwin Markham. WBLP

O brothers mine, take care! Take care! The White Witch. James Weldon Johnson. CDC

O brothers, why do you talk. Mahadevi, *tr. fr. Kannada by* A. K. Ramanujan. WPOW

O Bury Me Beneath the Willow. *Unknown.* AS

O [*or* Oh] bury me not on the lone prairie. Bury Me Not on the Lone Prairie. *Unknown.* AS; FaBV (Dying Cowboy, The.) FaBoBe

O, but how white is white, white from shadows come. Music of Colours: The Blossom Scattered. Vernon Watkins. AngWe; LiTB

O but there is wisdom. Consolation. W. B. Yeats. OxBSP

O, but they say the tongues of dying men. Shakespeare. *Fr.* King Richard II. FaBoRV (Tongues of Dying Men, The.) FaBoRV

O but we talked at large before. Sixteen Dead Men. W. B. Yeats. FaBoPV; OBWP

O By the By. E. E. Cummings. OxBA

O Caledonia! Sir Walter Scott. *Fr.* Lay of the Last Minstrel, The. BLPA; EBEvV; EnRP; FaBoPP; OxBS; PlP; SoSe; TFi

O cam ye in by the House o Rodes. John Thomson and the Turk. *Unknown.* ESPB, A *and* B *vers.*

O Cambridge, attend. Satire upon the Heads. Thomas Gray. FaBoCo

O camp of flowers, with poplars girdled round. Memory. Erik Johann Stagnelius, *tr. fr. Swedish* by Sir Edmund Gosse. AWP

O Canningate! poor elritch Hole. Elegy on Lucky Wood in the Canongate, May 1717. Allan Ramsay. ScCV

O Captain! My Captain! Walt Whitman. *Fr.* Memories of President Lincoln. EBEvV; FaBoBe; FaBoCh; FaBV; FaPON; FaPoR; GN; GOA; ImPo; InPK; LiTA; MeMAP; MoAmPo; OBCA; OHIP; PAH; PIP; PoLF; SAmP; TAP; TFi; TrGrPo

O Carib Isle! Hart Crane. NoAM; PoA; VGW

O Cat of Carlishkind. John Skelton. *Fr.* Phyllyp Sparowe [*or* Philip Sparrow]. AAS; ChTr; PoEL-1

O chansons foregoing. Ezra Pound. OxBA

O Charnwood, be thou called the choicest of thy kind. Charnwood Forest. Michael Drayton. *Fr.* Polyolbion. FaBoPP

O Chatterton, how very sad thy fate! To Chatterton. Keats. EPCY

O Cheese. Donald Hall. DiPo

O Child of Lowly Manger Birth. Ferdinand Q. Blanchard. AH

O Children, Would You Cherish? Christopher Dock, *tr. fr. German* by Samuel W. Pennypacker. AH

O child's tremble. Forming Child Poems. Simon J. Ortiz. CDW

O chillen, run, Cunjah man. Cunjah Man, De. James Edwin Campbell. AAP

O Christ of Bethlehem. H. Glenn Lanier. AH

O Christ of God! whose life and death. Vesta. Whittier. TrPWD

O Christ of Olivet, you hushed the wars. Edwin Markham. *Fr.* Christ of the Andes, The. TrPWD

O Christ, receive these souls in thy Mother's house. Hibernicus Exul, *tr. fr. Latin* by Helen Waddell. MLL

O Christ, Thou Art within Me Like a Sea. Edith Lovejoy Pierce. TrPWD

O Christ, Who Died. John Calvin Slemp. TrPWD

O Christ, who in Gethsemane. H. Cordelia Ray. CBWP-3

O Christmas Night. Henricus Selyns, *tr. fr. Dutch* by Howard Murphy. AH, *sts.* 1, 2, 4, 6

O city metropole, isle riverain! Montreal. A. M. Klein. MoCV

O city of the world, with sacred splendor blest. Longing for Jerusalem. Judah Halevi, *tr. fr. Hebrew* by Emma Lazarus. TrJP

O cloud that wants to be the sky's arrow. Rosario Castellanos, *tr. fr. Spanish* by Willis Barnstone. BoWoP

O Columbia, the gem of the ocean. Columbia, the Gem of the Ocean. *Unknown.* FaBoBe
(Red, White and Blue.) WBLP

O Come, All Ye Faithful. *Unknown, tr. fr. Latin* by Frederick Oakeley. AH

O come and take thou me/ Beneath thy wing. Beneath Thy Wing. Hayyim Nahman Bialik, *tr. fr. Hebrew* by Helena Frank. TrJP

O, come erlong, come erlong. Mobile-Buck. James Edwin Campbell. AAP

O come let us sing unto the Lord [*or* Jehovah]. Bible, *O.T., paraphrased* by Sir Thomas Wyatt. *Fr.* Psalms. AWP; BLRP; *OHIP, abr.*

O come Lord *Jesus* quickly! (*LL*) Burial. Henry Vaughan. GeHe; SeCV-1

O come, my body is alone. Come Laugh with Me. *Gond Oral Tradition, tr.* by V. Elwin *and* S. Hivale. WTO

O come, our Lord and Saviour. *Unknown.* BLRP

O Come Quickly! Thomas Campion. *See* Never weather-beaten sail[e] more willing bent to shore.

O! come quickly, glorious Lord, and raise my spright to thee. (*LL*) Never weather-beaten sail[e] more willing bent to shore. Thomas Campion. ChTr; EiL; OAEL-1; OxAEP-1; OxBSP; PoEL-2

O come, soft rest of cares, come Night. Bridal Song. George Chapman. *Fr.* Hero and Leander. AAS; NOBE; NoP; OBEV

O come to me in my dreams love! Lines to ————. Mary Weston Fordham. CBWP-2

O come to me, my brother Green, for I am shot and bleeding. Brother Green. *Unknown.* AmFP

O come with me, thus ran the song. Emily Brontë. NOBVV

O come you pious youth! adore. Jupiter Hammon. *Fr.* Address to Miss Phillis Wheatley, An. AmPP

O commemorate me where there is water. Lines Written on a Seat on the Grand Canal, Dublin. Patrick Kavanagh. BIrV; CMoP; InPS; IPY; NOIV

O comrades, come gather and join in my ditty. The *Cumberland's* Crew. *Unknown.* AmFP

"O Cormac, grandson of Conn," said Carbery. *Unknown, tr. fr. Irish* by Kuno Meyer. *Fr.* Instructions of King Cormac, The. BIrV

O Could I Find from Day to Day. Benjamin Cleavland. AH

O could I flow like thee, and make thy stream. Sir John Denham. *Fr.* Cooper's Hill. EPCY

"O could I love!" and stops, God writeth, "Loved." (*LL*) A True Hymn. George Herbert. GeHe; InvP; NOCV

O! could my sweet plaint lull to rest. Nightingale. Christian Carstairs. ECWP

O Country People. John Hewitt. IIP

O country people, you of the hill farms. O Country People. John Hewitt. IIP

O courteous Christkind guest, most gracious host. To a Crucifix. Anna Wickham. MoBrPo

O cricket, from your cheery cry. Basho, *tr. fr. Japanese* by Curtis Hidden Page. AWP

O crimson blood. Hildegard von Bingen, *tr. fr. Latin* by Patrick Diehl. WPOW

O crownless soul of Ishmael! Hemlock in the Furrows. Adah Isaacs Menken. CBWP-1

O cruel! — could thy infant bosom find. To a Little Boy, Who Had Destroyed a Nest of Young Birds. *Unknown.* FaBoUs

O cruel Death, give three things back. Three Things. W. B. Yeats. OBMV

O cruel Death! thou hast cut down. Epitaph — on the Wife of Dr. Greenwood. Dr. ———— Greenwood. FaBoUs

O cruel Love! on thee I lay. John Lyly. *Fr.* Sapho and Phao. NoSic

O cruell love, why dothe thow sore assayle. William Fowler. *Fr.* Tarantula of Love, The. ScCV

O Cuckoo. *Unknown, tr. by* Arthur Waley. *Fr.* Kokin Shu. AWP

O Cuckoo! shall I call thee Bird. F. H. Townsend. UV
(To the Cuckoo.) ChTr; FaBoNo

O cuckoo that sang to us and art fled. Lament for the Cuckoo. Alcuin, *tr. fr. Latin* by Helen Waddell. NAWM-1; PeHV

O Cupid! Monarch over Kings. John Lyly. *Fr.* Mother Bombie. CBLP; EiL

O cut the sweet apple and share it! (*LL*) O Blush Not So! O Blush Not So! Keats. ArLo

O Daedalus, Fly Away Home. Robert Hayden. HAP; PoBA; PoNe

O Dandelion. *Unknown.* BoTP

O David, highest in the list. Christopher Smart. *Fr.* Song to David, A. ChTr; EBEV; NAEL-1; NOBE, *abr.*; NOEC; OAEL-1; PoEL-3; TrGrPo, *abr.*

O David, if I had. That Harp You Play So Well. Marianne Moore. MoAB; MoAmPo; PoA

O day!/ With sun glowing. Exultation. Mae V. Cowdery. ShDr

O Day! he cannot die. An Death Scene. Emily Brontë. OxAEP-2

O Day most calm, most bright. Sunday. George Herbert. GeHe; PeECV; SeCV-1; TrCP

O Day of God, Draw Nigh. Robert Balgarnie Young Scott. AH

O Day of Light and Gladness. Frederick L. Hosmer. AH

O Day of Rest and Gladness. Christopher Wordsworth. WGRP

O days and hours, your work is this. Tennyson. *Fr.* In Memoriam A. H. H. EBVV, *abr.*; OAEL-2, *abr.*; PeECV, *abr.*

O' de wurl' ain't flat! Northboun.' Lucy Ariel Williams Holloway. BlSi; CDC; PoNe; ShDr

O dear and loving God. Prayer for Living and Dying. Christopher La Farge. TrPWD

O dear! I cannot choose but write. Eve. Oliver Herford. OBAL

O Dear Life, When Shall It Be? Sir Philip Sidney. EnRePo

O Dear O. *Unknown.* ErPo

O dearest, canst thou tell me why. Warum sind denn die Rosen so blass. Heine, *tr. fr. German* by Richard Garnett. AWP

O Dearest Dread, most glorious King. A Prayer unto Christ the Judge of the World. Michael Wigglesworth. SCAP

O dearest life! joy's sweet! O sweetest love! (*LL*) And Is It Night? Are they thine eyes that shine? *Unknown.* CBLP; EiL; GBL

O Death. Bible, Apocrypha. *Fr.* Ecclesiasticus. TrJP

O Death, Rock Me Asleep. *At. to* George Boleyn. EiL; FaBoRV; FF; TrGrPo; WPE

O Death, Rock Me on Sleep. *At. to* George Boleyn. *See* O Death, Rock Me Asleep.

O death, thy certainty is such. Henry Luttrell. FaBoEE

O Death! where is thy Sting. (*LL*) Vital spark of heavenly flame! Pope, *par. fr. the Latin of* Emperor Hadrian. BLPL; ImPo; LiTB

O Death! Why dost thou steal the great. In Memoriam Frederick Douglass. Eloise Bibb. CBWP-4

O deep-blue sea, O god Uli! Prayer of the Fishing Net. *Unknown, tr. fr. Hawaiian* by N. B. Emerson. WTO

O deep, creating Light. Eagle Song. Gordon Bottomley. *Fr.* Suilven and the Eagle. MoBrPo

O Deep River, O Dark Stream. Deep River. Eugène Marais, *tr. fr. Afrikaans* by Hugh Finn. PeSAV

O Deus, Ego Amo Te. Gerard Manley Hopkins. TrPWD

O Did you ever hear of the brave Earl Brand. Earl Brand. *Unknown.* OxBB

O Diodorus, in a storm of spring. *Unknown, tr. fr. Greek* by Sydney Oswald. PeHV

O Dirty Bird Yr Gizzard's Too Big & Full of Sand. James Koller. PoM

O distant Christ, the crowded, darkening years. Doubt. Margaret Deland. TrPWD

O divine star of heaven. John Fletcher. *Fr. Mad Lover, The.* GBL

O do not grieve, Dear Heart, nor shed a tear. Margaret Cavendish, Duchess of Newcastle. EnLoPo

O Do Not Sing. Pushkin, *tr. fr. Russian* by Philip L. Miller. RiWo

O do not sing, beautiful maiden. O Do Not Sing. Pushkin, *tr. fr. Russian* by Philip L. Miller. RiWo

O do not use me/ After my sinnes! Sighs and Grones. George Herbert. PoEL-2

O Doctor Dear My Love. Anne Halley. NMM

O Domine Deus! Speravi in te. Prayer before Execution. Mary Queen of Scots, *tr. fr. Latin* by John Fawcett. WGRP

O Donal Oge, if you go across the sea. Donal[l] Oge [*or* Og]: Grief of a Girl's Heart. *Unknown, tr. fr. Modern Irish* by Lady Augusta Gregory. GBL; PBWP; RB

O don't, don't ever ask me for alms. Death and the Plowman. Sidney Keyes. OxBTC

O! don't you wish that you were me? (*LL*) Foreign Children. Robert Louis Stevenson. BoTP

O down in the orchard. Apple Harvest. Helen Leuty. BoTP

O dream from the blackness. Sappho, *tr. fr. Greek* by Willis Barnstone. BoWoP

O dream, where art thou now? Emily Brontë. NOBVV

O Dreams, O Destinations. C. Day Lewis. *see* Oh Dreams, Oh Destinations.

O dull, cold northern sky. Robert Louis Stevenson. EBVV

O Duty,/ Why hast thou not the visage of a sweetie or a cutie? Kind of an Ode to Duty. Ogden Nash. TrGrPo

O Earl Rothes, an thou wert mine. Earl Rothes. *Unknown.* ESPB

O early one morning I walked out like Agag. The Streets of Laredo. Louis MacNeice. ChTr; MoBS; OBWP

O Earnest Be. *Unknown.* AH

O Earth, adore creative power. Creation. Mary Weston Fordham. CBWP-2

O earth, lie heavily upon her eyes. Rest. Christina Rossetti. MeMBP; NOBE; OAEL-2; OBEV; OBNC; TrGrPo

O Earth, O dewy mother, breathe on us. Archibald Lampman. TrPWD

O Earth, thou hast not any wind that blows. The Word. Richard Realf. WGRP

O Earth, throughout thy borders. Easter Carol. George Newell Lovejoy. OHIP

O Earth, Turn! George Johnston. MoCV

O Earth, Unhappy Planet Born to Die. Edna St. Vincent Millay. HeIP; WoWa

"O Echo!" (still the children call) "Where are you? where?" . . . "Air . . . ." (*LL*) Echo. Viscountess Grey of Fallodon. CH

O elephant, possessor of a savings-basket full of money. Salute to the Elephant. Odeniyi Apolebieji, *tr. fr. Yoruba* by S. A. Babalola. WTO

O eloquent and caustic sage. Frederick Douglass. Joseph S. Cotter, Sr. AAP

O England, Country of My Heart's Desire. E. V. Lucas. BoTP

O Englishwoman on the Pincian. Thomas Edward Brown. *Fr.* Roman Women. NOBVV; OBNC

O eternal grass. On the Meadow. "Katri Vala," *tr. fr. Finnish* by Jaakko A. Ahokas. PBWP

O Eternal, in thy majesty ride. Jewish Arabic Liturgies. *Unknown, tr. fr. Arabic* by Hartwig Hirschfeld. TrJP

O eterne God of power infinyt. A Prayer against the Plague. Robert Henryson. ScCV

O everie living warldly wight. Of Gods Omnipotencie. Alexander Hume. NOCV

O everlasting Kingdom of the Scepter. He Maketh Himself One with the Only God, Whose Limbs Are the Many Gods. *Unknown, tr. fr. Egyptian* by Robert Hillyer. *Fr.* Book of the Dead. AWP

O evermore great Psalm spring forth! spring forth anew! (*LL*) While Northward the hot sun was sinking o'er the trees. Robert Bridges. FaBoTw; LiTB

O evil Angel, set me free! (*LL*) A Clever Woman. Mary Elizabeth Coleridge. BrRo

O excellent sovereigne, most semely to see. *Unknown.* MiEL

O eye, weep for a rider. Rain to the Tribe. Al-Khansa, *tr. fr. Arabic* by Willis Barnstone *and* Tony Nawfal. BoWoP

O eyes clear with beauty, O tender gaze. Louise Labé, *tr. fr. French* by Willis Barnstone. BoWoP

O fair is our Lord's own city. Fair is Our Lord's Own City. *Unknown, tr. fr. Irish* by Coslett Quin. TIRV

O fair! O sweet! when I do look on thee. Sir Philip Sidney. SiPS

O faithless thorn. *Gond Oral Tradition, tr.* by V. Elwin *and* S. Hivale. WTO

O faithless world, and thy more faithless part. A Poem Written by Sir Henry Wotton, in His Youth. Sir Henry Wotton. NoSic

O, Falmouth is a fine town with ships in the bay. Home *or* Falmouth. W. E. Henley. GN; MoBrPo; PoLF

O false and treacherous Probability. Fulke Greville. *Fr.* Caelica. AAS

O fan of white silk. Fan-Piece, for Her Imperial Lord. Ezra Pound. MoAB

O far withdrawn into the lonely West. To K. H. Thomas Edward Brown. OBNC

O fare ye weel, my auld wife! My Auld Wife. *Unknown.* GBP

O fare you well, my darling. Ten Thousand Miles. *Unknown.* AmFP

O! farewell, my country — my kindred — my lover. The Exile of Erin. *Unknown.* NOBAu

O farther, farther, farther sail! (*LL*) Passage to India. Walt Whitman. AmPP; NAAL-1; PoEL-5

O fast her amber blood doth flow. George Darley. *See* O Blest Unfabled Incense Tree.

O, fastidious mind, gorging on absolutes, remember. Promises. Ruth Forbes Sherry. GoYe

O Father, give the spirit power to climb. Boethius, *tr. fr. Latin. Fr.* Consolation of Philosophy, The. MLL, *tr.* by Helen Waddell

"O Father, I acknowledge, " Job replied. George Sandys. *Fr.* Paraphrase Upon Job, A. ChIV-1

O Father of all lights, to thee. (*LL*) Psalm CXXXIX. The Countess of Pembroke. NOCV; WPE

O Father, we approach Thy throne. Adam's Hymn in Paradise. Joost van den Vondel, *tr. fr. Dutch* by Sir John Bowring. WGRP

O, father's gone to market town, he was up before the day. A Midsummer Song. Richard Watson Gilder. BoNaP

O favorable spirit, propitious guest. Milton. *Fr.* Paradise Lost. EPCY (Adam Unfallen.) NOCV

O fearfull, frowning nemesis. Samuel Daniel. *Fr.* Cleopatra. PoEL-2

O first created and creating source. Ode to the Sea. Howard Baker. OxBA

O Flame of Living Love. St. John of the Cross, *tr. fr. Spanish.* AWP, *tr.* by Arthur Symons

O flower fawn. Five Flower World Variations. *Unknown, tr. fr. Yaqui Indian* by Jerome K. Rothenberg. STP

O flower garment!/ when I take it off. Sugita Hisajo, *tr. fr. Japanese* by Kenneth Rexroth *and* Ikuko Atsumi. WPJ

O flower of all wind-flowers and sea-flowers. Sark. Swinburne. *Fr.* Garden of Cymodoce, The. FaBoPP

O flowers of Mekhmekh, give us peace! *Unknown, tr. fr. Egyptian hieroglyphics* by Ezra Pound *and* Noel Stock. BoWoP

O Flowery Mountain slopes. On the Slope of Hua Mountain. *Unknown, tr. fr. Chinese* by Kenneth Rexroth *and* Ling Chung. WPC

O fly away home fly away. (*LL*) O Daedalus, Fly Away Home. Robert Hayden. HAP; PoBA; PoNe

O fond, but fickle and untrue. Walter Savage Landor. CBLP; GBL

O foolish tears, go back! In Vain. Adah Isaacs Menken. CBWP-1

O foolishnes of men! that hind their ears. Comus's Praise of Nature. Milton. *Fr.* Comus; a Masque Presented at Ludlow Castle. FHYEP; OAEL-1; PoEL-3

O foot, O leg, O thighs for which I rightly died. Philodemus, *tr. fr. Greek* by Barbara Hughes Fowler. *Fr.* Epigrams. HePo

O for a Booke. *Unknown.* CH

O! [*or* Oh] for a bowl of fat canary. John Lyly. *Fr.* Alexander and Campaspe. NoSic

(Oh, for a Bowl of Fat Canary.) NoP

(Serving Men's Song, A.) NOBE

O [*or* Oh] for a Closer Walk with God. William Cowper. *See* Oh! for a closer walk with God.

O for a faith that will not shrink. Unshrinking Faith. W. H. Balhurst. BLRP

O for a ferryman to steer my yearning. Home-Sickness. Hedwig Lachmann, *tr. fr. German* by Jethro Bithell. TrJP

O for a muse of fire, a sack of dough. Sonnet with a Different Letter at the End of Every Line. George Starbuck. OBAL

O for a Muse of fire, that would ascend. Shakespeare. *Fr.* King Henry V. OxAEP-1; SCV

(Muse of Fire, A.) ChTr

O for a rope of Onions from Saint Omers. John Taylor. *Fr.* Odcomb's Complaint. CBNP

O for a sculptor's hand. Balaam. John Keble. OBNC

O for a toe, such as the funeral pyre. Sir Thomas Browne. FaBoEE

O for doors to be open and an invite with gilded edges. W. H. Auden. PeLV

O! For my sake do you with Fortune chide. Shakespeare. *Fr.* Sonnets. OxAEP-1

O for one minute hark what we are saying! F.W.H. Myers. TrPWD

O for our upland meads. Shepherd and Shepherdess. Thomas Hennell. FaBoTw

O for ten years, that I may overwhelm. Keats. *Fr.* Sleep and Poetry. EnRP; NAEL-2; OAEL-2

O for that warning voice, which he who saw. Milton. *Fr.* Paradise Lost. EPCY; OAEL-1; OxAEP-1, *ll.* 1–535; TEP, *ll.* 1–324 (Prospect of Eden, The. PoEL-3, *ll.* 1–775

O for the Happy Hour. George Washington Bethune. AH

O for the perfumes that arise. Non Sum Qualis Eram in Bona Urbe Nordica Illa. John Hollander. ErPo

O for the time when I shall sleep. Emily Brontë. *Fr.* Enough of Thought, Philosopher. OBD

O for the Wings of a Dove. Euripides, *tr.* by Gilbert Murray. *Fr.* Hippolytus. AWP; NAWM-1, *tr.* by Rex Warner

O fortunate, O happy day. A New Household. Longfellow. *Fr.* Hanging of the Crane, The. GN

O Fortune. *Unknown, tr. fr. Latin. Fr.* Carmina Burana. MLL, *tr.* by Helen Waddell

O fountain of Bandusia. III, 13. To the Fountain[s] of Bandusia ("O fons Bandusiae.") Horace, *tr.* by Eugene Field. *Fr.* Odes. AWP

O Frail Adam. Epitaph for Mr. Moses Levy. *Unknown.* TrJP

O frail flower. Alcaeus, *tr. fr. Greek by* Sam Hamill. InMo

O Freedom! Freedom! O! how oft. Charles Lewis Reason. *Fr.* Freedom. AAP

O Friend! I know not which way I must look. Written in London, September, 1802. Wordsworth. FaBoPV; TrGrPo
(England, 1802, I.) OBEV
(In London, September, 1802.) EnRP
(London, MDCCCII.) GTBS; GTBS-P
('O Friend! I Know No Which Way I Must Look'.) CoGr

O friends! who have accompanied thus far. Walter Savage Landor. GBL

O Friendship! Friendship! the shell of Aphrodite. Walter Savage Landor. GBL

O! From what power hast thou this powerful might. Shakespeare. *Fr.* Sonnets. OxAEP-1; SCGP

O furrowed plaintive face. The Hurrier. Harold Monro. MoBrPo

O Future bards. A Prophecy. Allen Ginsberg. TAP

O gallant brothers of the generous South. Henry Peterson. *Fr.* Ode for Decoration Day. FaBoBe; OHIP

O generation of the thoroughly smug and thoroughly uncomfortable. Salutation. Ezra Pound. HeIP; MeMAP; MoAB; MoAmPo; NOBA; OxBA; TAP; VGW

O gentle, gentle land. Night Sowing. David Campbell. CBAP

O gentle, gentle summer rain. Invocation to Rain in Summer. William Cox Bennett. GN

O Gentle Love. George Peele. *Fr.* Arraignment of Paris, The. EIL

O gentle Love, do not forsake the guide. Upon Some Alterations in My Mistress, after My Departure into France. Thomas Carew. CaPo

O Gentle Ships. Meleager, *tr. fr. Greek by* Andrew Lang. AWP

O Gentle Sleep. Shakespeare. *See* How many thousand of my poorest subjects.

O gentle Sleep, come, wave thine opiate wing. On Dreams, October 15, 1782. Sir Samuel Egerton Brydges. Son

O gentle sleep! do they belong to thee. To Sleep ('O gentle sleep! do they belong to thee'). Wordsworth. Son

O gie the lass her fairin' lad. Gie the Lass her Fairin.' Burns. CoMu; ErPo

O gin a body meet a body. Comin' Throu the Rye. Burns. FaBoBl, diff. vers.

O Gin My Love Were Yon Red Rose. *Unknown.* GBP

O girl, you torment me, you are so deceiving. *Gond Oral Tradition, tr. by* V. Elwin *and* S. Hivale. WTO

O give thanks unto the Lord, for He is good. Bible, *O.T., paraphrased by* Sir Thomas Wyatt. *Fr.* Psalms.
(O give yee thanks unto the Lord.) SCAP

O give thanks unto the Lord, for He is good/ because his mercy endureth forever. Bible, *O.T., paraphrased by* Sir Thomas Wyatt. *Fr.* Psalms. TrJP

O give thanks unto the Lord; for he is good;/ for his mercy endureth forever. Bible, *O.T., paraphrased by* Sir Thomas Wyatt. *Fr.* Psalms. AWP; OHIP, *abr.*

O give yee thanks unto the Lord. Bible, *O.T., paraphrased by* Sir Thomas Wyatt. *See* O give thanks unto the Lord, for He is good.

O Give yee thanks unto the Lord. *Unknown. Fr.* Bay Psalm Book, The. SCAP

O Glorious Childbearer. Joseph Campbell. TIRV

O Glorious Christ of God; I live. Cotton Mather. SCAP

O God,/ forever I turn in this hard crystal. The Prayer of the Goldfish. Carmen Bernos de Gasztold. PDV

O God,/ creator of our land. *Unknown, tr. fr. Ashanti.* EaPr

O god above, relent. Here Followeth the Songe of the Death of Mr. Thewlis. *Unknown.* CoMu

O God, above the Drifting Years. John Wright Buckham. AH

O God, Accept the Sacred Hour. Samuel Gilman. AH

O God, for as much as without Thee. Ronald Arbuthnott Knox. PeLi

O God, Great Father, Lord, and King. E. Embree Hoss. AH

O God! Have Mercy, in This Dreadful Hour. Robert Southey. TrPWD

O God! have mercy on the mariner! (*LL*) O God! Have Mercy, in This Dreadful Hour. Robert Southey. TrPWD

O God, I Cried, No Dark Disguise. Edna St. Vincent Millay. AH

O God, I love thee, I love thee. O Deus, Ego Amo Te. Gerard Manley Hopkins. TrPWD

O God, I thank thee. George Appleton. EaPr

O God! if this indeed be all. If This Be All. Anne Brontë. TrPWD

O God, in Restless Living. Harry Emerson Fosdick. TrPWD

O God, in the dream the terrible horse began. The Dream. Louise Bogan. InPK; LiTA; LiTM; MAT; MoAB; MoAmPo; NALW; NoAM

O God, in whom my deepest being dwells. Edmund Blunden. TrPWD

O God, in Whom the Flow of Days. Donald C. Babcock. AH

O God, in whom we half believe. Offertorium. C. Day Lewis. *Fr.* Requiem for the Living. TIRV

O God, in Whose Great Purpose. James G. Gilkey. AH

O God, keep not thou silence. Bible, *O.T., paraphrased by* Sir Thomas Wyatt. *Fr.* Psalms.
(Keep Not Thou Silence.) TrJP

O God, my dream! I dreamed that you were dead. On the Threshold. Amy Levy. NOBVV

O God, my master God, look down and see. The Artisan. Alice Brown. TrPWD

O God, my mother, my father, lord of the. Kekchi Maya. EaPr

O God! O Montreal! Samuel Butler. FaBoCo; OBSV; OxBoLi; PeLV

O God! O Montreal. (*LL*) O God! O Montreal! Samuel Butler. FaBoCo; OBSV; OxBoLi; PeLV

O God, O Venus, O Mercury, patron of thieves. The Lake Isle. Ezra Pound. FaBoCo; FaBoPa; OxBSP; PoA

O God of battles, who art still. On the Eve of War. Danske Bedinger Dandridge. PAH

O God of Bethel. Philip Doddridge *and* John Logan. WTO

O God of Calvary and Bethlehem. The Hem of His Garment. Anna Elizabeth Hamilton. TrPWD

O God of Earth and Altar, *sels.* G. K. Chesteron.
Wildness. EaPr; OtMeF
Fight in the Centre, The. OtMeF
Litany. OtMeF

O God of goodness, forwardness, and fulness. Doris Hedges. GoYe

O God of life. (*LL*) How lovely are thy holy groves. *Unknown.* EaPr

O God of love unbounded! Lord supreme! Prayer to God. "Placido," *tr. fr. Spanish by* Raoul Abdul. TTY

O God of Mercy. God of Mercy. Kadya Molodovsky, *tr. fr. Yiddish by* Irving Howe. WPOW

O God of My Salvation, Hear. Joel Barlow. AH

O God of Stars and Distant Space. John Franzen. AH

O God of Youth. Bates G. Burt. AH

O God, Our Help in Ages Past. Isaac Watts. FaPoR; WGRP

O God, our loving Father, help us. A Christmas Prayer. Robert Louis Stevenson. TrCP

O God, scatterer of ignorance and darkness. *Unknown, tr. fr. Sanskrit by* Romesh Dutt. *Fr.* Vedic Hymns. EaPr

O God, Send Men. Elizabeth Burrowes. AH

O God that art the only hope of the world. Prayer of the Venerable Bede. The Venerable Bede, *tr. fr. Latin by* Helen Waddell. MLL

O God, the heathen are come into Thine inheritance. Bible, *O.T., paraphrased by* Sir Thomas Wyatt. *Fr.* Psalms.
(Heathen Are Come into Thine Inheritance, The.) TrJP

O God, the Rock of Ages. Edward H. Bickersteth. BLPA

O God, though Countless Worlds of Light. James D. Knowles. AH

O God thy Judgments unto sinfull eye. On the Death of My Deare Sister the Countesse of Bridgewater. Lady Elizabeth Brackley. KTR

O God, unknown, invisible, secure. John Addington Symonds. *Fr.* Invocation, An. TrPWD

O God, when You send for me, let it be. Prayer to Go to Paradise with the Asses. Francis Jammes, *tr. fr. French by* Jethro Bithell. AWP

O God, where do they tend — these struggling aims? Robert Browning. *Fr.* Pauline. WGRP

O God, who made me. The Prayer of the Donkey. Carmen Bernos de Gasztold. PChr

O God, whose daylight leadeth down. George Macdonald. *Fr.* Evening Hymn. TrPWD

O God Whose Presence Glows in All. Nathaniel Langdon Frothingham. AH

O God! whose thunder shakes the sky. Resignation. Thomas Chatterton. TrCP

O God, why hast thou cast us off for ever? Bible, *O.T., paraphrased by* Sir Thomas Wyatt. *Fr.* Psalms.
(Psalm LXXIV: "O God, why hast thou cast us off for ever?," *paraphrased by* the Countess of Pembroke.) NOCV

O Goddess! hear these tuneless numbers, wrung. Ode to Psyche. Keats. EnRP; FHYEP; InPS; LiTB; MeMBP; NAEL-2; NOBE; NoP; OAEL-2; OBEV; OBNC; OxAEP-2; PFP; PoE; PoEL-4; PPP; TFi; TOF

O goddess Laka! Altar Prayers. *Unknown, tr. fr. Hawaiian by* N. B. Emerson. WTO

O Golden Fleece ("O golden fleece she is where she lies tonight.") George Barker. *Fr.* Secular Elegies. ErPo; LiTM; MoAB; MoBrPo

O golden fleece she is where she lies tonight. O Golden Fleece. George Barker. *Fr.* Secular Elegies. ErPo; LiTM; MoAB; MoBrPo
(Secular Elegy V.) MeMBP

O golden-tongued romance, with serene lute! On Sitting Down to Read "King Lear" Once Again. Keats. EBEV; EnRP; EPCY; NAEL-2; NoP

O Gongyla, my darling rose. Sappho, *tr. fr. Greek by* Willis Barnstone. BoWoP

O good Lord Judge, and sweet Lord. *Unknown. See* Slack your rope, hangs – a – man.

O good Lord Judge, and sweet Lord Judge. The Maid Freed from the Gallows. *Unknown.* AWP; ESPB

O! good my lord, tax not so bad a voice. Shakespeare. *Fr.* Much Ado about Nothing. OxAEP-1

O good painter, tell me true. An Order for a Picture. Alice Cary. BLPA

O good sun. Song for Fine Weather. *Unknown, tr. by* Constance Lindsay Skinner. *Fr.* Three Songs from the Haida. AWP

O good Sun,/ Look thou down upon us. Song for Fine Weather. *Unknown, tr. fr. Haida Indian by* Constance Lindsay Skinner. AWP

O goodly golden chaine, wherewith yfere. Spenser. *Fr.* Faerie Queene, The. FHYEP

O Goodly Hand. Sir Thomas Wyatt. InvP; SiPS

O goodly hand. Sir Thomas Wyatt. SiPSBD

O Gracious Father of Mankind. Henry Hallam Tweedy. AH

O gracious God, how far have we. Dryden. *Fr.* To the Pious Memory of the Accomplished Young Lady, Mrs. Anne Killigrew. EPCY

O gracious gods, take compassion. John Marston. *Fr.* Metamorphosis of Pygmalion's Image, The. OAEL-1

O Gracious Jesus, Blessed Lord! Andrew Fowler. AH

O grandest of the Angels, and most wise. Litany to Satan. Baudelaire, *tr. fr. French by* James Elroy Flecker. AWP

O Grant. Keats. *See* O grant that like to Peter I.

O grant that like to Peter I. Keats. CBNP
(O Grant.) ChIV-2

O grasses wet with dew, yellow fallen leaves. A Glimpse. Frances Cornford. OBMV

O Great Mary. Litany to Our Lady. *Unknown, tr. fr. Irish by* Eugene O'Curry. TIRV

O Great Queen Whom I idolize. Jeffery Littman. PeLi

O Great Spirit! A Voyager's Prayer. *Unknown, tr. fr. Chippewa Indian by* Tanner. WGRP

O Great Spirit. *Unknown.* EaPr

O Great Spirit of the East. Gaia's Alchemy: Ruin and Renewal of the Elements. Ralph Metzner. EaPr

O great tone-master! low thy massive head. Beethoven. H. Cordelia Ray. CBWP-3

O grief! even on the bud that fairly flowered. O Grief! *Unknown.* EiL

O' gude Braid Claith. *(LL)* Braid Claith. Robert Fergusson. NOEC; OxBS

O guide my judgment and my taste. Taste. Christopher Smart. *Fr.* Hymns for the Amusement of Children. ChIV-1; NOCV

O guns, fall silent till the dead men hear. The Anxious Dead. John McCrae. OHIP

O had truth power the guiltless could not fall. His Petition to Queen Anne of Denmark (1618). Sir Walter Ralegh. SiPS
(Sir Walter Ralegh's Petition to the Queen. 1618.) SiPSBD

O hame, hame, hame, to my ain countree! *(LL)* Hame, Hame, Hame. Allan Cunningham. CH; OBEV

O handsome chestnut eyes, evasive gaze. Louise Labé, *tr. fr. French by* Willis Barnstone. BoWoP

O Happie Death. Alexander Hume. ScCV

O happie death, to life the readie way. O Happie Death. Alexander Hume. ScCV

O happie Tems, that didst my *Stella* beare. Sir Philip Sidney. *Fr.* Astrophel and Stella. AAS; ESo, *sl. abr.*; GGP; HeIL, *Sonnets, I–CVIII and 11 Songs*; OxAEP-1; Poetr; SCGP, *Sonnets, I–CVIII and 11 Songs*; SiPS, *Sonnets, I–CVIII and 11 Songs*; SiPSBD, *Sonnets, I–CVIII and 11 Songs*

O happiness! *(LL)* Released. Richard Dehmel. RiWo

O happy hour. *Unknown, tr. fr. Latin. Fr.* Carmina Burana. MLL, *tr. by* Helen Waddell

O happy hour, and happier hours. Tennyson. *Fr.* In Memoriam A. H. H. EBVV, *abr.*; EnVR; OAEL-2, *abr.*; PeECV, *abr.*

O happy [*or* happie] dames, that may embrace. The Earl of Surrey. NoSic; SCGP; SiPSBD
(Complaint of the Absence of Her Lover Being upon the Sea.) AAS; EBEV; EiL; ELP; GBL; NOBE; OBEV
(Seafarer, The.) SiPS

O Happy people, where good princes reign. The Tower of Babel. Joshua Sylvester. *Fr.* Divine Weeks and Works of Guillaume de Saluste Sieur Du Bartas, The. NoSic

O happy Tithon! if thou know'st thy harp. William Alexander, Earl of Stirling. *Fr.* Aurora. OBEV

O hark, the drums do beat, my love, I can no longer stay. The Banks of the Nile. *Unknown.* OBET

O hark! 'tis the note of the Schmaltztenor! Schmaltztenor! M. W. Branch. FiBHP

O Hark to the Herald. Eleazar ben Kalir, *tr. fr. Hebrew by* Israel Zangwill. TrJP

O harmless feast. Barten Holyday. *Fr.* Technogamia. EiL

O Harry Heine, curses be. Translator to Translated. Ezra Pound. FaBoEE

O, Harry! thou hast robb'd me of my youth. Shakespeare. *Fr.* King Henry IV, Pt. I. NAEL-1; OxAEP-1

O hate me not for my grey hair. A Song: In the Name of a Lover, to His Mistress; Who Said, She Hated Him for His Grey Hairs, Which He Had at Thirty. William Wycherley. SeCV-2

O, have ye been in love, me boys. I Met Her in the Garden Where the Praties Grow. *Unknown.* AS

O have ye na heard o' the fause Sakelde? Kinmont Willie. *Unknown.* ESPB; IBB; OxBB

O Have You Caught the Tiger? A. E. Housman. BXAP; FaBoNo

O, have you seen the leper healed. The Healing of the Leper. Vernon Watkins. FaBoTw

O have you seen the Stratton flood. Stratton Water. Dante Gabriel Rossetti. OxBB

O Hear My Prayer, Lord. John Craig. AH

O hear ye that foul and fiendish laughter. War! James Gilchrist Lawson. WBLP

O heard ye never of Wat o' the Cleuch? Walsinghame's Song. James Hogg. BXAP

O heard ye of a silly Harper. The Lochmaben Harper. *Unknown.* OxBB

O heard ye of Sir James the Rose. Sir James the Rose. *Unknown.* ESPB

O hearken and hear, and I will you tell. Friar in the Well. *Unknown.* ESPB

O heart/ sorrowing. A Young Warrior. Ponmutiyar, *tr. fr. Tamil by* A. K. Ramanujan. PLW

O heart of mine, we shouldn't worry so! Just Be Glad. James Whitcomb Riley. WBLP

O Heart! the equal poise of love's both parts. Richard Crashaw. *Fr.* Flaming Heart, The. GeHe; LiTB; NAEL-1; OAEL-1, *abr*; PoEL-2; SeCV-1; TEP; TrGrPo

O heart, why dost thou sigh, and wilt not break? When He Thought Himself Contemned. Thomas Howell. EiL

O Heaven Indulge. Stephen Tilden. AH

O heavenly color, London town. November Blue. Alice Meynell. MoBrPo

O heavy day! oh day of woe! The Lament of Toby the Learned Pig. Thomas Hood. CBNP

O Heavy Step of Slow Monotony. Ernst Toller, *tr. fr. German by* Ashley Dukes. TrJP

O Hector, thou wert rooted in my heart. Helen's Lamentation. Homer, *tr. by* Congreve. *Fr.* Iliad, The. OBVE

O Heitsi-Eibib. Hunter's Prayer. *Unknown, tr. fr. Hottentot.* PeSA

O helpless few in my country. Ezra Pound. *Fr.* Lustra. MeMAP; PoA
(Rest, The.) AmPP; MoAB; MoAmPo; NoAM; NOBA; OxBA

O hermitage well found. The Young Pilgrim Finds Refuge with the Goatherds. Luis de Góngora y Argote, *tr. fr. Spanish by* Edward Meryon Wilson. *Fr.* First Solitude, The. OBVE

O Hesperus! thou bringest all good things. Evening. Byron. *Fr.* Don Juan. TrGrPo
(Hesperus the Bringer.) AWP

O Hidden Life vibrant in every atom. Annie Besant. EaPr

O hideous little bat, the size of snot. The Fly. Karl Shapiro. LiTM; MoP; NoAM; SoSe

O, hits time fur de plantin' ur de co'n. Song of the Corn. James Edwin Campbell. AAP

O Holy Aether, and swift-wingèd Wings. The Wail of Prometheus Bound. Aeschylus, *tr. fr. Greek by* Elizabeth Barrett Browning. *Fr.* Prometheus Bound. WGRP

O Holy City Seen of John. Walter Russell Bowie. AH

O Holy Ghost. Stephen Langton, *tr. fr. Latin by* Helen Waddell. MLL

O Holy Ghost, O faithful Paraclete. For Whitsuntide. Hildebert, *tr. fr. Latin by* Helen Waddell. MLL

O Holy Ghost, whose temple I. The Holy Ghost. John Donne. *Fr.* Litanie, The. NOCV; PoEL-2

O Holy, Holy, Holy, Lord. James Wallis Eastburn. AH

O holy Jerusalem, Vision of peace. *Unknown, tr. fr. Anglo-Saxon by* Charles W. Kennedy. *Fr.* Christ 1. AnOE

O holy Love, religious saint! Sir Robert Chester. *Fr.* Love's Martyr. EllL

O Holy Mother, thou who still dost send. At the Tomb of Rachel. "Yehoash," *tr. fr. Yiddish by* Isidore Goldstick. TrJP

O holy night as it was in the beginning. Canticle for Xmas Eve. David Wagoner. SM

O Holy One. (LL) Blessed be the works of your hands. Diann Neu. EaPr

O Holy One, I ran through the fields and gathered flowers of a thousand colors. Sandhya. Ishpriya. EaPr

O holy talk show host. The Wish Foundation. Carol Muske. PBCAP

O holy virgin! clad in purest white. To Morning. Blake. *Fr.* Milton. EnRP; OxAEP-2

O Holy Water. Margot Ruddock. OBMV

O/ Holy/ Wood. Sister Mary Madeleva. CRP

O! Honour! Honour! Honour! Oh! the Gain! God's Selecting Love in the Decree. Edward Taylor. *Fr.* God's Determinations [touching his Elect]. PoEL-3, *sl. shorter vers.*
(Man in this Lapst Estate at very best.) EAP

O how beautiful is Thy world. In the Evening Glow. Franz Kugler, *tr. fr. German by* Philip L. Miller. RiWo

O how canst thou renounce the boundless store. The Youth of a Poet. James Beattie. *Fr.* Minstrel, The. NOEC

O! How I faint when I of you do write. Shakespeare. *Fr.* Sonnets. OxAEP-1

O how lightly in youth we achieved our disinterested. Friends. Richard Moore. SM

O [or Oh], How Much More Doth Beauty Beauteous Seem. Shakespeare. *Fr.* Sonnets. AWP; EllL; OBEV; PoE; SCGP

O how my mind. Confusion. Christopher Hervey. BXAP; UV

O! How shall I picture, in delicate strain. Miss Emily Brittle Sails for India. Sir George Dallas. *Fr.* India Guide, The; or, Journal of a Voyage to the East Indies in 1780. NOEC

O, how sick and weary I. In a Myrtle Shade. Blake. ChIV-1

O How Sweet Are Thy Words! Anne Steele. BLRP

O how that glittering taketh me! (LL) Upon Julia's Clothes. Robert Herrick. AWP; BeJo; CaPo; ChTr; ClHu; EBEV; EnLoPo; FaBV; FF; GBL; HAP; HeIL; HeIP; HoPM; ImPo; InPS; JCP; LiTB; NAEL-1; NBLV; NIP; NOBE; NoP; NOSC; OAEL-1; OBEV; OPOP; OxAEP-1; OxBSP; PeLV; PoE; PoEL-3; Poetr; PPP; SCGP; SeCP; SeCV-1; TFi; TrGrPo; TRP; TTTS; UV; WeW

O, how this spring of love resembleth. This Spring of Love. Shakespeare. *Fr.* Two Gentlemen of Verona, The. ChTr

O how this sullen, careless world. The Idiot. John Ashbery. *Fr.* Two Sonnets. VGW

O, hungry heart. Heart-Hungry. Josephine D. Henderson Heard. CBWP-4

O hurry where by water among the trees. The Ragged Wood. W. B. Yeats. CBLP; GBL

O, hush thee, my babie [or baby], thy sire was a knight. Lullaby of an Infant Chief. Sir Walter Scott. EnRP; FaPON; OxBChV

O! hush thee, my darling, sleep soundly my son. *Unknown, tr. fr. Yiddish by* Alice Lucas. TrJP

O hushed October morning mild. October. Robert Frost. GoJo

O Hymen! O Hymenee! Walt Whitman. ErPo

O hymned in many a poet's strain. A Legend of Alhambra. Richard Chenevix Trench. OBTV

O, I am scalded with my violent motion. Shakespeare. *Fr.* King John. FaBoEH

O! I do love thee, meek simplicity. To Simplicity. Samuel Taylor Coleridge. *Fr.* Sonnets Attempted in the Manner of Contemporary Writers. FaBoPa; Son

O, I don't give a shit. On the Death of Robert Lowell. Eileen Myles. UL

O I forbid you, maidens a' [or all]. Tam Lin. *Unknown.* ESPB; FaBoBa; NOBE; OBEV; OBNV; OxBB; OxBS

O I had a future. I Had a Future. Patrick Kavanagh. BIrV; NoAM

O I had been to sunny Spain. On First Looking into Chapman's Homer. T. Griffiths. BXAP

O, I hae come from far away. The Witch's Ballad. William Bell Scott. CoGr; NOBVV; OBEV; PeVV
(Witches' Ballad, The.) CH

O I hae tint my rosy cheek. *Unknown.* FaBoVe

O, I remember you. The Removal of Our Village, KwaBhanya. Mbuyiseni Oswald Mtshali, *tr. fr. Zulu by the author.* PeSAV

O, I wad like to ken — to the beggar-wife says I. The Spaewife. Robert Louis Stevenson. OxBS

O I went into the stable. Our Goodman. *Unknown.* AmFP; ESPB, A *and* B *vers.*

O I will sing to you a sang. The Clerk's Twa Sons o Owsenford. *Unknown.* ESPB

O, I yearn to go back to the Cam! E. O. Parrott. PeLi

O if all the young maidens was blackbirds and thrushes. Blackbirds and Thrushes. *Unknown.* GBP

O, insatiable monster! Could'st thou not. Mary Weston Fordham. CBWP-2

O interminable desires, O futile hope. Louise Labé, *tr. fr. French by* Willis Barnstone. BoWoP

O Isis, Mother of God, to thee I pray! Prayer to Isis. Christina Walsh. BrRo

O "Isles" (as Byron said) "of Greece!" The Schoolmaster Abroad. Sir Owen Seaman. OBTV

O islets green, Nature's immortal gems. Hymn to the Thousand Islands. H. Cordelia Ray. CBWP-3

O it fell out upon a day. The Laird o Drum. *Unknown.* ESPB

O, it is hard to work for God. The Right Must Win. Frederick William Faber. PWR

O it is terrible to dream of angels. (LL) The Gardener. Sidney Keyes. MoAB; MoBrPo

O Italy, I see the lonely towers. To Italy. Giacomo Leopardi, *tr. fr. Italian by* Romilda Rendel. AWP

O it's best to be a total boor. David O'Bruadair, *tr. fr. Irish by* Thomas Kinsella. NOIV

O it's up in the Highlands. *Unknown. See* Hie upon Hielands [*or* High up on highland*or* High upon Highlands].

O it's up in the Highlands, and along the sweet Tay. Bonnie James Campbell. *Unknown.* ESPB

O-Jazz-O. Bob Kaufman. PoBeRe

O Jealous Night [*or* A Night Piece *or* To Night]. *Unknown.* EllL

O Jean Baptiste, pourquoi. Pourquoi You Greased. *Unknown.* ChTr

O Jean, my Jean, when the bell ca's the congregation. Tam i' the Kirk. Violet Jacob. GBL; OtMeF

O Jellon Grame sat in Silver Wood. Jellon Grame. *Unknown.* EBEV; ESPB; OxBB

O Jenny Dear. Susanna Blamire. ECWP

O Jenny dear, lay by your pride. O Jenny Dear. Susanna Blamire. ECWP

O Jenny, don't sobby! vor I shall be true. A Zong. William Barnes. BoLoP

O Jesus Christ, True Light of God. John F. Ernst. AH

O Jesus, drink of me. (LL) A Better Resurrection. Christina Rossetti. NOBVV; TrPWD

O Jesus, I have promised. To the End. John E. Bode. BLRP

O Jesus, My Savior, I Know Thou Art Mine. Caleb J. Taylor. AH

O John "Doctor" Donne, O John "Doctor" Donne. Death Again. T. Hope. BXAP

O Johney was as brave a knight. Johnie Scot. *Unknown.* ESPB

O Jojina my love, I always miss you. Jojina, My Love. *Zulu Oral Tradition, tr. by* H. Tracey. WTO

O joy of creation. What the Bullet Sang. Bret Harte. GGP; OBEV

O joy! that in our embers. Wordsworth. *Fr.* Ode: Intimations of Immortality from Recollections of Early Childhood. AWP; BLPL; EnRP; FaBoRV; FHYEP; HAP; HeIP; InvP; LiTB; MeMBP; NAs; NOBE; NoP; OAEL-2; OBEV; OBNC; PoE; PoEL-4; PPP; Prf; PrIm; TEP; TrGrPo

O joy, too high for my low stile to show. Sir Philip Sidney. *Fr.* Astrophel and Stella. AAS; ESo, *sl. abr.*; GGP; HeIL, *Sonnets,* I–CVIII *and 11 Songs*; NAEL-1; OxAEP-1; Poetr; SCGP, *Sonnets,* I–CVIII *and 11 Songs*; SiPS, *Sonnets,* I–CVIII *and 11 Songs*; SiPSBD, *Sonnets,* I–CVIII *and 11 Songs*; TrGrPo

O Kane, O Ku-ka-Pao. Old Creation Chant. *Unknown, tr. fr. Hawaiian.* WTO

O Kane, O Lono of the blue sea. *Unknown, tr. fr. Hawaiian by* N. B. Emerson. WTO

O Kané! Transform the earth. *Unknown, tr. fr. Hawaiian.* EaPr

O keen pellucid air! nothing can lurk. A Brilliant Day. Charles Tennyson Turner. NOBVV

O Kentucky! my parents were driving. A Poem of the Forty-eight States. Kenneth Koch. NNaP; OBAL

O King, give Angilbert thy rest. Angilbert, *tr. fr. Latin by* Helen Waddell. MLL

O King, I know you gave me poison. Mirabai, *tr. fr. Medieval Hindi by* Usha Nilsson. PBWP; WPOW

O King of Saints, We Give Thee Praise and Glory. Mary A. Thomson. AH

O King of the Friday. *Unknown, tr. fr. Irish by* Douglas Hyde. BIrV

O King of the World. *Unknown, tr. fr. Gaelic by* Douglas Hyde. WTO

O King that was born. Christmas 1915. Padraic Pearse. PeIV

O knit me, that am crumbled dust! the heape. Distraction. Henry Vaughan. GeHe; SeCP

O Lady amorous,/ Merciless lady. Canzonetta: A Bitter Song to His Lady. Pier Moronelli da Fiorenza, *tr. fr. Italian by* Dante Gabriel Rossetti. AWP; OBVE

O lady full of guile. Geoffrey Keating, *tr. fr. Irish by* Thomas Kinsella. NOIV

O Lady Moon. Christina Rossetti. OxBChV

O lady of all truths bright light going forth. Enheduanna, *tr. fr. Sumerian by* Anne Draffkorn Kilmer. *Fr.* Inanna Exalted. WPOW

O Lady, rock never your young son young. Young Hunting. *Unknown.* ESPB; OxBB

O Lady/ the hem of whose garment. The Poet Prays to the Loba. Diane Di Prima. *Fr.* Loba. EaPr; SRLS

O Lamb Give Me My Salt. *Unknown, tr. fr. Ibo by* Dennis C. Osadebay. PBA

O Land Beloved. George Edward Woodberry. *Fr.* My Country. PAH

O Land, of every land the best. Peace. Phoebe Cary. AmWP; PAH

O Lapwing! Blake. ChTr; FaBoEE

O lapwing, thou fliest around the heath. O Lapwing! Blake. ChTr; FaBoEE

O laugh it out, you laughsters! Incantation by Laughter. Velimir Khlebnikov, *tr. fr. Russian by* Gary Kern. CBNP

O, Lay Thy Hand in Mine, Dear! Gerald Massey. EBVV

O leafy yellowness you create for me. October. Patrick Kavanagh. CIP; GTBS-P

O! Lest the world should task you to recite. Shakespeare. *Fr.* Sonnets. OxAEP-1

O let me be in loving nice. Punctilio. Mary Elizabeth Coleridge. OBEV

O let me pull and taste them. (LL) Lady, those cherries plenty. *Unknown.* NoSic

O let the solid ground. Tennyson. *Fr.* Maud[: A Monodrama]. EnVR; NAEL-2; NOBVV

O Liberty! my spirit felt thee there. (LL) France; an Ode. Samuel Taylor Coleridge. EnRP

O Life! O Sun! (LL) Escape. Robert Graves. MoBrPo

O, Life of Dreams! O, Dreams of Life! Timothy Thomas Fortune. *Fr.* Dreams of Life. AAP

O Life That Maketh All Things New. Samuel Longfellow. AH

O Life, thou Nothing's younger brother! Life and Fame. Abraham Cowley. BOEP

O, Lift One Thought. Samuel Taylor Coleridge. *See* Stop, Christian passer-by! — Stop, child of God.

O Light Invisible, we praise Thee! T. S. Eliot. *Fr.* Rock, The. TrPWD

O Light, 'tis I, who from death's other shores. Helen. Paul Valéry, *tr. fr. French.* OBVE, *tr. by* Robert Lowell

O lily of the King! low lies the silver wing. Lillium Regis. Francis Thompson. WGRP

O lips full of lust and of laughter. Swinburne. *Fr.* Dolores. UV

O, listen for a moment, lads, and hear me tell my tale. Jim Jones. *Unknown.* CBAP

(Jim Jones at Botany Bay. GBP

O listen, gude peopell, to my tale. The Laird o' Logie. *Unknown.* CH; ESPB, A *and* B vers.

O [or Oh] listen, listen, ladies gay! Rosabelle. Sir Walter Scott. *Fr.* Lay of the Last Minstrel, The. BeLS; GTBS; GTBS-P

(Harold's Song: Rosabelle. EnRP

O little broken doll, dropped in the well. The Broken Doll. Nuala Ni Dhomhnaill, *tr. fr. Irish by* John Montague. BiHa

"O little cloud," the virgin said, "I charge thee tell to me." Blake. *Fr.* Book of Thel, The. EnRP; MeMBP; NAEL-2; NoP; OAEL-2; OBD; OBNC; PoE; PoEL-4; TEP

O little fleet! that on thy quest divine. Columbus and the Mayflower. Richard Monckton Milnes. PAH

O little friend, your nose is ready; you sniff. Dog. Harold Monro. MoBrPo

O little Land of lapping seas. The Promised Land. Jessie E. Sampter. TrJP

O little mouse, so frightened of each sound. O Pity Our Small Size. Benjamin Rosenbaum. TrJP

O little self, within whose smallness lies. John Masefield. *Fr.* Sonnets. WGRP

O little soldier with the golden helmet. Dandelion. Hilda Conkling. FaPON; PDV

O Little Town of Bethlehem. Phillips Brooks. AH; AnAmPo; BLRP; FaPON; GN; OHIP; WBLP; WGRP

O little well, you give no water. *Gond Oral Tradition, tr. by* V. Elwin *and* S. Hivale. WTO

O littleblood, hiding from the mountains in the mountains. Littleblood. Ted Hughes. *Fr.* Crow. FF; PoE

O Living Always, Always Dying. Walt Whitman. NOBA

O living will that shalt endure. Tennyson. *Fr.* In Memoriam A. H. H. EBVV, *abr.*; EBVVPR; FaBoBe; MeMBP; OAEL-2, *abr.*; PeECV, *abr.* (Prayer, The: "O living will that shalt endure." WGRP

O Lizard/ chinking up the new made wall. Lizard. Jerome Kielly. PeIV

O loathsome place, where I. The Earl of Surrey. SiPSBD

O loathsome rodent with your endless squeaking. To the Rats. E.J.L.. NSI

O London is a dainty place. London Is a Fine Town. *Unknown.* CoMu

O lonely bay of Trinity. The Cable Hymn. Whittier. PAH

O lonely workman, standing there. In the Moonlight. Thomas Hardy. *Fr.* Satires of Circumstance. NoAM

O lonesome sea-gull, floating far. Sea-Birds. Elizabeth Akers Allen. FaBoBe

O look how the loops and balloons of bloom. Stormy Day. W. R. Rodgers. LiTB

O look not, lady, with disdain! The Tooth. Rebekah Carmichael. ECWP

O Lord. Ishpriya. EaPr

O Lord,/ One tiny bit of water rests on the palm of my hand. Ishpriya. EaPr

O, Lord/ If in life eternal. "Ping Hsin," *tr. fr. Chinese by* Kai-yu Hsu. *Fr.* Spring Waters. WPOW

O Lord, Almighty God. *Unknown.* AH

O Lord, at Joseph's humble bench. The Carpenter. George Macdonald. TrPWD

O Lord, Bow Down Thine Ear. Thomas Prince. AH

O Lord God of My Salvation. The Countess of Pembroke. *Fr.* Psalms of David, The.

O Lord, grant each his own, his own death indeed. Rainer Maria Rilke, *tr. by* J. B. Leishman. *Fr.* Book of Hours, The. OBD

O Lord, How Lovely Is the Place. *Unknown.* AH, *ad. by* Francis Hopkinson

O Lord, how lovely it is to be your guest. Gregory Petrov. EaPr

O Lord, I been a-working. Trifling Women. *Unknown.* AmFP

O Lord, I Come Pleading. James Gilchrist Lawson. BLRP

O Lord, I pray: that for each happiness. Petition. John Drinkwater. TrPWD

O Lord, I pray/ That for this day. Not to Be Ministered To. Maltbie D. Babcock. TrPWD

O Lord I shall be whole in deed. Jeremie .17. Bible, Apocrypha. ChIV-1

O Lord, I wonder at thy lov. Thomas Traherne. *Fr.* Approach, The. TrPWD

O Lord, in me there lieth nought. Bible, *O.T., paraphrased by* Sir Thomas Wyatt. *See* O Lord, thou hast searched me.

O Lord, in me there lieth nought. Psalm CXXXIX. The Countess of Pembroke. NOCV; WPE

O Lord! methought, what pain it was to drown! A Dream of Wrecks. Shakespeare. *Fr.* King Richard III. ChTr

O Lord my sinne doth over-charge thy brest. Sinnes Heavie Loade. Robert Southwell. ESCV

O Lord of Life. Washington Gladden. AH

O Lord, our God, Thy mighty hand. Peace Hymn of the Republic. Henry van Dyke. AH

O Lord our Lord, how excellent is thy name. Bible, *O.T., paraphrased by* Sir Thomas Wyatt. *Fr.* Psalms. AWP; NAWM-1

(How Glorious Is Thy Name. TrJP

(Psalm VIII: "O Lorde oure governoure, howe excellent is thy name.") OBVE, *tr. by* Miles Coverdale

(Psalm VIII: "O Lord, that rul'st the human heart," *paraphrased by* Christopher Smart.) OBVE

(What Is Man?) TrGrPo

O lord, oure lord, thy name how merveilous. Chaucer. *See* There was in Asia, in a great city.

O Lord, rebuke me not in thine anger. Bible, *O.T., paraphrased by* Sir Thomas Wyatt. *Fr.* Psalms.

(Psalm VI: "O lord, I dred, and that I did not dred.") OBVE, *ad. by* Sir Thomas Wyatt

O Lord, Save We Beseech Thee. *Unknown.* TrJP

O Lord, seek us, O Lord, find us. Lord, Save Us, We Perish. Christina Rossetti. TrPWD

O Lord, since we have feasted thus. Grace after Dinner. Burns. FaBoEE

O Lord, sir, let me live, or let me see my death! Shakespeare. *Fr.* All's Well That Ends Well. OxAEP-1

O Lord, spare him the Call. Salvation. George Ella Lyon. CrSp

O Lord, That Art My God and King. John Craig. AH

O Lord, the hard-won miles. Paul Laurence Dunbar. TrPWD

O Lord, Thou art on the sandbanks. *Unknown, tr. fr. Sanskrit by* Romesh Dutt. *Fr.* Vedic Hymns. EaPr

O Lord, Thou Hast Been to the Land. *Unknown.* AH

O Lord, Thou Hast Enticed Me. Bible, O.T. *Fr.* Jeremiah. TrJP

O Lord, thou hast searched me. Bible, O.T., *paraphrased by* Sir Thomas Wyatt. *Fr.* Psalms.
(Psalm CXXXIX: "O Lord, in me there lieth nought," *paraphrased by the* Countess of Pembroke.) NOCV; OBVE, (7-10)
(O Lord, in me there lieth nought.) NoSic, *sect.* CXXXIX
(Psalm CXXXIX: Domine, Probasti.) WPE

O Lord thou seest my wrongs abound. Ode XV. Thomas Stanley. ChIV-1

O Lord, Turn Not Away Thy Face. *At. to* John Marckant. AH

O Lord two things I thee require. Proverb, XXX. John Hall. ChIV-1

O Lord, we come this morning. Listen, Lord — [a Prayer]. James Weldon Johnson. BPo

O Lord! who seest from yon starry height. The Image of God. Francesco de Aldana, *tr. fr. Spanish by* Longfellow. WGRP

O Lord whose mercy never fails. Pro Libra Mea. Joseph I. C. Clarke. TrPWD

O Lord, why must thy poets peak and pine. Priest or Poet. Shane Leslie. WGRP

O Lord, you know my inmost hope and thought. My Inmost Hope. Sarah Copia Sullam, *tr. fr. Italian.* TrJP

O Loss of sight, of thee I most complain. The Blindness of Samson. Milton. *Fr.* Samson Agonistes. FHYEP; ImPo; LiTB; OAEL-1; PoEL-3

O lost moon sisters. Ave. Diane Di Prima. *Fr.* Loba. SRLS

O love, be fed with apples while you may. Sick Love. Robert Graves. BoLoP; CMoP; EBEV; GTBS-P; HAP; NOBE; OAEL-2; OxAEP-2
(O Love in Me. FaBoMo

O Love Divine, That Stooped to Share. Oliver Wendell Holmes. *Fr.* Professor at the Breakfast Table, The. AH

O Love, give me a passionate heart. A Prayer. Irene Rutherford McLeod. TrPWD

O Love, how strangely sweet. John Marston. EIL

O love, how thou art tired out with rhyme! Of the Theme of Love. Margaret Cavendish, Duchess of Newcastle. OxBSP
(Love and Poetry. VBLP

O love, I never, never thought. Juan II, of Castile, *tr. fr. Spanish by* George Ticknor. AWP

O Love in Me. Robert Graves. *See* O love, be fed with apples while you may.

O, love, in your sweet name enough. Anne Finch. *Fr.* Essay on Marriage. FaBoTw

O Love, Love, Love! O withering might! Fatima. Tennyson. GBL; UnPo

O Love, my love, and perfect bliss! *Unknown, tr. fr. French by* John Addington Symonds. *Fr.* Medieval Norman Song. AWP

O love! O glory! what are you who fly. Byron. *Fr.* Don Juan. OAEL-2

O Love, O thou that, for my fealty. Sonnet: To Love, In Great Bitterness. Cino da Pistoia, *tr. fr. Italian by* Dante Gabriel Rossetti. AWP

O Love of God incarnate. Incarnate Love. Wilbur Fisk Tillett. BLRP

O Love, That Dost with Goodness Crown. John White Chadwick. TrPWD

O Love That Lights the Eastern Sky. Louis FitzGerald Benson. AH

O Love That Wilt Not Let Me Go. George Matheson. TrPWD; WGRP

O love, the interest itself in thoughtless heaven. W. H. Auden. EBEV; FaBoMo

O love triumphant over guilt and sin. Frederic Lawrence Knowles. TrPWD

O love, turn from the unchanging sea, and gaze. October. William Morris. *Fr.* Earthly Paradise, The. EnVR; OBNC

O Love! what art thou, Love? the ace of hearts. Love. Thomas Hood. CBLP

O love, what hours were thine and mine. The Daisy. Tennyson. EnLoPo; NOBVV; OBNC; PoEL-5

O Love, when in my day of doom. The Gardener. Laurence Housman. TrPWD

O Love, who all this while hast urged me on. Canzone: To Love and to His Lady. Guido Delle Colonne, *tr. fr. Italian by* Dante Gabriel Rossetti. AWP

O Love, whose patient pilgrim feet. The Golden Wedding. David Gray. FaBoBe

O, loveliest throat of all sweet throats. Edna St. Vincent Millay. *See* Let them bury your big eyes.

O lovely age of gold! Tasso, *tr. fr. Italian. Fr.* Aminta. OBVE, *tr. by* Leigh Hunt
(Golden Age, The.) AWP, *tr. by* Leigh Hunt

(Pastoral[1], A: "Oh [*or* O] happy golden age.") OAEL-1, *tr. by* Samuel Daniel; PoEL-2, *tr. by* Samuel Daniel

O lovely April, rich and bright. Gustave Kahn, *tr. fr. French by* Ludwig Lewisohn. TrJP

O lovely maiden, thou hast drawn my heart. The Unhappy Lover. Judah al-Harizi, *tr. fr. Hebrew by* J. Chotzner. TrJP

O lovely O most charming pug. A Sonnet on a Monkey. Marjory Fleming. FaBoCo; FiBHP
(Sonnet, A: "O lovely O most charming pug.") FaBoCo; NBLV

O [*or* Oh], lovers' eyes are sharp to see. The Maid of Neidpath. Sir Walter Scott. BeLS; EnRP; GTBS; GTBS-P

O ludicrous and pensive trinity. Romeo and Juliet. H. Phelps Putnam. ErPo

O luely, luely, cam she in. The Tryst [*or* Trysting Place]. William Soutar. EBEV; ErPo; OxBS
(Trysting Place, The.) BoLoP

O Lusty May, with Flora queen! Lusty May. *Unknown.* OBEV
(Four May Poems.) OxBS

O luxury! Thou curst by Heaven's decree. Goldsmith. *Fr.* Deserted Village, The. BeLS; BIrV; EnRP; NOEC; NoP; OAEL-1; PoEL-3; TEP

O Lyric Love. Winfield Townley Scott. VGW

O madam, I will give to thee a new silk gown. My Man John. *Unknown.* OBET

O madam, I will give to you the keys of Canterbury. The Keys of Canterbury. *Unknown.* AmFP

O Magnificent and Many. Shih Ching, *tr. fr. Chinese by* C. H. Wang. SuSp

O maister deere and fader reverent! Thomas Hoccleve. *Fr.* De Regimine Principum. EBEV

O Maistres Myn. *Unknown. See* O Mistress Mine ("O mistress mine, till you I me commend.")

O make me a mask and a well to shut from your spies. Dylan Thomas. PoA

O Maker of the starry world. Boethius, *tr. fr. Latin. Fr.* Consolation of Philosophy, The. MLL, *tr. by* Helen Waddell

O Mally's Meek, Mally's Sweet. Burns. GN

O Man of mine own people, I alone. The Jew to Jesus. Florence Kiper Frank. WGRP

O man of the seashore. What Her Girl Friend Said to Him When He Wanted to Come by Day. Ammuvanar, *tr. fr. Tamil by* A. K. Ramanujan. PLW

O! Mankinde. *See!* Here, My Heart. *Unknown.* MeEL

O Marduk, lord of countries, terrible one. *Unknown, tr. fr. Assyrian. Fr.* Hymn to Marduk. WGRP

O, Mare Atlanticum. The Sleep of My Lions. Douglas Livingstone. PeSAV

O Margie, Marge, Dear Margaret. Oswald von Wolkenstein, *tr. fr. German by* J. W. Thomas. GePo

O Martyred Spirit. George Santayana. TrPWD

O [*or* Oh] Mary, at the window be. Mary Morison. Burns. EnRP; GTBS; GTBS-P; OBEV; OxBS; TrGrPo
(Song: Mary Morison.) AWP

O [*or* Oh] Mary, go and call the cattle home. The Sands of Dee. Charles Kingsley. *Fr.* Alton Locke. BeLS; CH; EBEvV; EBVV; FaBoPP; FaPON; FaPoR; GN; OxAEP-2; PlP; WBLP

O Mary Hamilton to the kirk is gane. Mary Hamilton. *Unknown.* NOBE; OxBB

O Mary Mary lying on the wheel. Visitor's Parking. Anne Szumigalski. NOBC

O Mary sing thy songs to me. John Clare. CBLP

O master dear, and father reverent! An Admirer's Lament of Chaucer. Thomas Hoccleve. *Fr.* Regiment of Princes. EPCY

O Master, Let Me Walk with Thee. Washington Gladden. AH; PWR; WGRP

O Master Masons. Ernst Toller, *tr. fr. German by* Ashley Dukes. TrJP

O Master of the heart, whose magic skill. To the Author of Clarissa. Thomas Edwards. Son

O Master-Workman of the Race. Jay Thomas Stocking. AH

O May I Join the Choir Invisible. "George Eliot." OHCV

O [*or* Oh] may I join the choir invisible. O May I Join the Choir Invisible. "George Eliot." OHCV
(Choir Invisible, The.) EBVV; OBD; OBNC; WBLP; WGRP

O may I with myself agree. John Dyer. *Fr.* Grongar Hill. AngWe; ChTr; EnRP; FaBoPP; NOEC; NoP; OxAEP-1; PoEL-3; TrGrPo

O May she comes, and May she goes. The Bonny Hind. *Unknown.* ESPB
(Bonny Heyn, The.) OxBB

O me, oh my, oh you. Does the Spearmint Lose Its Flavor on the Bedpost Overnight? Billy Rose. OBAL

O Me! What Eyes Hath Love Put In My Head. (Blind Love.). Shakespeare. *Fr.* Sonnets. GTBS; GTBS-P

O 'Melia, my dear, this does everything crown! The Ruined Maid. Thomas Hardy. BoLoP; CMoP; ErPo; FaBoBl; FaBoVe; FiBHP; HeIL; HeIP; LiTB; MeMBP; NAEL-2; NBLV; NOBL; NoP; OxBTC; PeLV; PeVV; SCV; TEP; TFi; TRP

O Meliwa, I come, a messenger of the Beautiful Ones. "Advice" to a Young Poet. Mazisi Kunene, *tr. fr. Zulu by the author.* PeSAV

O memory, could I but loose thee now. Lindamira's Complaint. Mary Sidney Wroth, Countess of Montgomery. *Fr.* Urania. WPE

O Memory, Thou Fond Deceiver.' Goldsmith. *Fr.* Captivity, The. OxBSP

O men from the fields! A Cradle Song. Padraic Colum. TIRV (Lullaby. WTO

O men, the beautiful world is going to be spoiled. Suez Crisis. *Somali Oral Tradition, tr. by* B. W. Andrzejewski. WTO

O men, walk on the hills. Maxwell Bodenheim. TrJP

O merciful Father, my hope is in thee! Prayer Before Execution. Mary Queen of Scots, *tr. by* John Fawcett. WGRP

O merciful God, hear this our request. A Prayer to Be Said When Thou Goest to Bed. Francis Seager. OxBChV

O Merlin in your crystal cave. Merlin. Edwin Muir. FaBoTw; OxBS; RB

O! mestress, why. *Unknown.* MiEL (Distant as the Duchess of Savoy.) MeEL

O Michael, servant of the eternal King. Dedication to St. Michael. Alcuin, *tr. fr. Latin by* Helen Waddell. MLL

O Michael, you are at once the enemy. Garden-Lion. Mary Ursula Bethell. ArNa; ChTr

O mickle yeuks the keckle doup. Justice to Scotland. *At. to* Burns Burns. NBLV

O might some verse with happiest skill persuade. William Collins. *Fr.* Epistle, An, Addressed to Sir Thomas Hanmer, on His Edition of Shakespeares Works. EPCY

O might those sighes and teares returne againe. John Donne. *Fr.* Holy Sonnets. ESCV

O mighty Cæsar! dost thou lie so low? Shakespeare. *Fr.* Julius Caesar. OxAEP-1

O mighty lady, our leading / to have. Ieuan ap Hywel Swrdwal. *Fr.* Hymn to the Virgin, The. AngWe

O mighty-mouthed inventor of harmonies. Milton: Alcaics. Tennyson. EPCY

O mighty-mouthed inventory of harmonies. Milton. Tennyson. PeECV

O Mighty Nothing! unto thee. And He Answered Them Nothing. Richard Crashaw. ChIV-2

O Mighty, powerful, strong one of Ashur. *Unknown, tr. fr. Assyrian. Fr.* Hymn to Marduk. WGRP

O mighty river! strong, eternal Will. The Great River. Henry van Dyke. TrPWD

O mild Christ. Ellen Bryant Voigt. *Fr.* Feast Day. CrSp

O Mind of God, Broad as the Sky. Oliver Huckel. TrPWD

O mine own sweet heart. Simon and Susan. *Unknown.* OxBoLi

O miserable sorrow, withouten cure. Sir Thomas Wyatt. SiPS

O miss, I'll give you a paper of pins. *Unknown. See* "I'll give to you a paper of pins."

O Mistress Mine. Shakespeare. *Fr.* Twelfth Night. AWP; BoLoP; ClHu; CoGr; CTC; EIL; ELP; FaBV; GBL; GoJo; HAP; ImPo; LiTB; NAEL-1; NBLV; NOBE; NoP; NoSic; OAEL-1; OxBoLi; OxBSP; PFP; PoRA; SCGP; TFi; TrGrPo

O Mistress Mine ("O mistress mine, till you I me commend.") *Unknown.* MeEL

O mistress mine! till you I me commend. *(LL)* O Mistress Mine ("O mistress mine, till you I me commend.") *Unknown.* MeEL

O money is the meat in the cocoanut. Money. *Unknown.* AS

O months of blossoming, months of transfigurations. The Lilacs and the Roses. Louis Aragon, *tr. fr. French by* Louis MacNeice. OBWP

O Moon, Mr. Moon. Mr. Moon. Bliss Carman. FaPON

O Moon! the oldest shades 'mong oldest trees. Keats. *Fr.* Endymion [a Poetic Romance]. EnRP

O more, and more! this was so well. Ben Jonson. *Fr.* Pleasure Reconciled to Virtue. NAEL-1; OAEL-1

O Morning-Maker, deign that ray. Plea for Hope. Francis Carlin. TrPWD

O Mors! Quam Amara Est Memoria Tua Homini Pacem Habenti in Substantiis Suis. Ernest Dowson. OBMV

O mortal folk you may behold and see. The Epitaph of Graunde [*or* La Graunde] Amoure. Stephen Hawes. *Fr.* Pastime of Pleasure, The. ChTr; CoGr; EBEV; FaBoRV; NoSic; OBEV; TrGrPo
(Epitaph, An.) OtMeF
(Epitaphy of la Graunde Amoure.) FaBoEE

O mortal man, that lives by bread. *At. to* Julius Caeser Ibbetson. ChTr; FaBoEE

O Mother Dear, Jerusalem. "F. B. P." WGRP

O Mother-heart! when fast the arrows flew. Niobe. H. Cordelia Ray. CBWP-3

O mother, I longs to get married. *Unknown. See* Mother, I long to get married.

O mother, I longs to get married. Whistle, Daughter, Whistle. *Unknown.* OBET

O mother, lay your hand on my brow! The Sick Child. Robert Louis Stevenson. CH

O Mr. Cromek, how do ye do? *(LL)* A Petty Sneaking Knave. Blake. PeLV

O mud, mud, how fluid! Words Heard, by Accident, over the Phone. Sylvia Plath. AnAn

O [*or* Oh] my aged uncle Arly! Incidents in the Life of My Uncle Arly. Edward Lear. CBNP; FaBoNo; MoShBr; OAEL-2; OxBoLi; TrGrPo

O My Belly. *Unknown.* GBP

O my body! I dare not desert the likes of you in other men and women, nor the likes of the parts of you. Walt Whitman. *Fr.* I Sing the Body Electric. CTC; ErPo; SAmP, *Pt.* I *only*

O, my bonnie &c. *(LL)* As I Came O'er Cairney Mount. Burns. CoMu

O My Bonny, Bonny May. *Unknown.* GBP

O my brother I heard u. Before/ and After. Jewel C. Latimore. JB

O my brothers of the wilderness. Mary Austin. EaPr

O my chief good. Good Friday. George Herbert. GeHe

O my chief good! The Passion. Henry Vaughan *and* Thomas Stanley. ESCV

O my comrade, it is cold. Cold and Heat. *Unknown, tr. fr. Hawaiian by* M. W. Beckwith. WTO

O my coy darling, still. Ode to a Dressmaker's Dummy. Donald Justice. NoAM

O [*or* Oh] my dark Rosaleen. Dark Rosaleen. *At. to* Owen Roe MacWard *and to* Hugh O'Donnell, *tr. fr. Irish by* James Clarence Mangan. AWP; BIrV; CH; EnRP; IIP; NOIV; OBEV; OxAEP-2; PeIV

O my daughters. Behold This and Always Love It. Meridel Le Sueur. SRLS

O my dear father! Restoration, hang. Shakespeare. *Fr.* King Lear. OxAEP-1

O my dear, O my dear. *(LL)* The Three Bushes. W. B. Yeats. EBNV

O my deerest I shall grieve thee. The Complement. Thomas Carew. CBLP

O my deir hert, young Jesus sweit. Balulalow. John James *and* Robert Wedderburn. OBEV

O my earliest love, who, ere I number'd. First Love. Charles Stuart Calverley. FiBHP

O my eyes hurt and the bottle. Peter Riley. VaA

O my fair warrior! Shakespeare. *Fr.* Othello. OxAEP-1

O my friends. Mirabai, *tr. fr. Hindi by* Jane Hirshfield. EnlH

O my God, let it be thine! *(LL)* Begging. Henry Vaughan *and* Thomas Stanley. ESCV

O my God, thou hast wounded me with love. A Confession. Paul Verlaine, *tr. fr. French by* Arthur Symons. WGRP

O, My Heart Is Woe. *Unknown.* ChIV-2

O my Heart, my Mother, my Heart, my Mother. He Approacheth the Hall of Judgment. *Unknown, tr. fr. Egyptian by* Robert Hillyer. *Fr.* Book of the Dead. AWP

O My Honey, Take Me Back. *Unknown.* AS

O my hornbill husband, you have a bad smell. Lament for a Husband. *Unknown, tr. fr. Papuan by* Don Laycock. BoWoP; VBLP

O my Hornby and my Barlow long ago! *(LL)* At Lord's. Francis Thompson. CoGr; EBVV; OxBSP; PeLV

O My Invisible Estate. Bruce Smith. Son

O my Joseph, Jacob's son, *Unknown, tr. fr. Anglo-Saxon. Fr.* Christ 1. AnOE; ASW, *tr. by* Kevin Crossley-Holland

O my lady, the Anunna, the great gods. Inanna and the Anunna. Enheduanna, *tr. fr. Sumerian.* BoWoP, *ad. by* Aliki *and* Willis Barnstone

O my land! O my love! Lament for Banba. *At. to* Egan O'Rahilly, *tr. by* James Clarence Mangan. AWP

O my lord, blue beast. Love Song of the Loba. Diane Di Prima. *Fr.* Loba. SRLS

O my Lord, if I worship you from fear of Hell. Rabi'a al-Adawiyya, *tr. fr. Arabic by* Willis Barnstone. BoWoP

O my Lord, the stars glitter and eyes of men are closed. Rabi'a al-Adawiyya. BoWoP

O my lost husband! let me ever mourn. Andromache's Lamentation. Homer, *tr. by* Congreve. *Fr.* Iliad, The. OBVE

O my love/ The pretty towns. Kenneth Patchen. VGW

O my love, my wife! Shakespeare. *Fr.* Romeo and Juliet. OBD; OxAEP-1

O my lover, blind me. The Tired Woman. Anna Wickham. MoBrPo

O my Lucasia, let us speak our love. To My Lucasia, in Defence of Declared Friendship. Katherine Philips. MeLP

O my luve is [*or* luve's] like a red, red rose. A Red, Red Rose. Burns. ArLo; AWP; BoLoP; CBLP; ChTr; FaBV; FF; GBL; HAP; HeIP; ImPo;

O Powers Celestial, with what sophistry. Barnabe Barnes. *Fr.* Parthenophil and Parthenophe. EnLoPo

O pr/ gress verily thou art m. E. E. Cummings. UV

O, praise an' tanks! De Lord he come. Song of the Negro Boatman. Whittier. *Fr.* At Port Royal. GN; PAH

O praise God in his holiness: praise him in the firmament of his power. Bible, *O.T., paraphrased by* Sir Thomas Wyatt. *Fr.* Psalms. (Laudate Dominum.) ChTr

O pray! Example take too, and have care. *(LL)* After the Pleasure Party. Herman Melville. NAAL-1; PoEL-5

O pray! Example take too, and have care. *(LL)* After the Pleasure Party. Herman Melville. PoEL-5

O praying one, who long has prayed. Ask, and Ye Shall Receive. Mrs. Havens. BLRP

O precious codex [*or* code], volume, tome. To a Thesaurus. Franklin P. Adams. BLPL; NBLV

O prett'ly warbled from a sweet sweet throat. *(LL)* Pretty Wantons. *Unknown.* EiL

O Prince of Life, Thy Life hath tuned. The Prince of Life. John Oxenham. TrPWD

O pumpkins! O periwinkles! Wet Weather at Cannes. Edward Lear. FaBoNo

O quick quick quick, quick hear the song sparrow. Cape Ann. T. S. Eliot. *Fr.* Landscapes. GoJo; NAEL-2; NoAM; RB

O quiet quiet as the fox through the bush. The Fox and the Flood. Lucile Adler. FoLa

O quondam pre-and-post-bellum. The Bitch-Kitty. Jonathan Williams. PoM

O Rab an' Dave an' rantin' Jim. Jock, to the First Army. Violet Jacob. NSI

O radiant luminary of light interminable. A Prayer to the Father of [*or* in] Heaven. John Skelton. HoPM; TrPWD

O radiant you sunflowers abound. Unexpected Sunflowers. Paul Goodman. ArNa

O raging seas, and mighty Neptune's reign! Coming Homeward out of Spain. Barnabe Googe. EiL; NoSic

O rain at seven. Virginia. Hart Crane. *Fr.* Bridge, The. LiTA; NAAL-2

O rain, depart with blessings. Song of the Dew. *Unknown, tr. fr. Hebrew by* Solomon Solis-Cohen. TrJP

O Rair/ Preclair/ Most fair. To His Mistress. John Stewart. ScCV

O! raise the woefull Pillalu. An Irish Lamentation. Goethe, *tr. fr. German by* James Clarence Mangan. AWP

O Rama Kam! *(LL)* Rama Kam. David Diop. NegPo

O [*or* Oh] rare Harry Parry. Harry Parry. *Unknown.* GBP; OxNR

O rare Narcissus! sunny-haired! Echo's Complaint. H. Cordelia Ray. CBWP-3

O Reader! hast thou ever stood to see. The Holly Tree. Robert Southey. EnRP

O Realm Bejewelled. Forugh Farrokhzad, *tr. fr. Farsi by* Jascha Kessler *and* Amin Banani. WPOW

O resplendent Night. *Unknown, tr. fr. Sanskrit by* Romesh Dutt. *Fr.* Vedic Hymns. EaPr

O, rest in peace, for the Lord doth care. *(LL)* God Cares. "Marianne Farningham." BLRP; WBLP

O, rest ye, brother mariners, we will not wander more. *(LL)* The Lotus-Eaters. Tennyson. ChTr, 5 *sts.*; EnVR; LiTB; MeMBP; NAAL-2; NoP; OAEL-2; PoEL-5; SCGP; TEP

O restless, caressing eyes. *Unknown, tr. fr. Greek by* Kenneth Rexroth. PGA

O Restless Heart, Be Still! H. Cordelia Ray. CBWP-3

O Ride On, Jesus. *Unknown.* AH

O Risen Lord upon the Throne. Louis FitzGerald Benson. AH

O River, green and still. Boy in Ice. Laurie Lee. NYBP

O road in dizzy moonlight bleak and blue. La Quinque Rue. Edmund Blunden. PeFWW

O rocking boat, rocking boat poised on the wave. Boat Song. H. Cordelia Ray. CBWP-3

O Roger, Mackerel, Riley, Ned, Nellie, Chester, Lady Ghost. *(LL)* Names of Horses. Donald Hall. CAPP; FoLa; HAP; InPK; SoSe; TRP

O Rose the Red and White Lil[l]y. Rose the Red and White Lil[l]y. *Unknown.* ESPB; OxBB

O Rose, thou art sick! The Sick Rose. Blake. *Fr.* Songs of Experience. AWP; BoLoP; ChTr; ClHu; CoGr; EBEvV; ELP; EnLoPo; FHYEP; HAP; HeIP; InPK; InPS; MeMBP; NAEL-2; NAWM-2; NIP; NOBE; NOEC; NoP; OAEL-2; OBNC; OxAEP-2; OxBSP; PoE; PoEL-4; Poetr; PPP; PrIm; RB; SCGP; SoSe; TFi; TrGrPo; TRP; WeW

O Ross, thou wale of hearty cocks. To Mr. Alexander Ross. James Beattie. OxBS

O rosy red, O torrent splendour. Come On, My Lucky Lads. Edmund Blunden. PeFWW

O Rourk's noble fare. The Description of an Irish Feast. Hugh MacGowran, *tr. fr. Irish by* Swift. NOIV

O ruddier than the cherry! John Gay. *Fr.* Acis and Galatea. CBLP; EBEvV; ELP; NAEL-1; NOEC (Song: "O ruddier than the cherry." NOBE

O ruined father dead, long sweetly rotten. For the Word Is Flesh. Stanley Kunitz. VGW

O rural diversions, too long has the chace. Song in Praise of Gowfing. Andrew Duncan. FaBoEH

O sacred head, now wounded. Paul Gerhardt, *tr. fr. German.* GePo

O sacred poesie, thou spirit of artes. Ben Jonson. *Fr.* Poetaster, The. PoEL-2

O sacred Providence, who from end to end. George Herbert. *Fr.* Providence. AngWe

O sacred season of Autumn, be my teacher. Autumn Psalm of Contentment. Edward Hays. EaPr

O sage of the stage, Shaw of Shaws! Harold Ellis. PeLi

O sailing stars! Star Song. H. Cordelia Ray. CBWP-3

O sailor, come ashore. Christina Rossetti. *Fr.* Sing-Song. BoTP; FM

O sailor, tell me, tell me true. Elihu. Alice Cary. VPP

O Sally my dear, shall I come up to see you? Hares on the Mountain. *Unknown.* ErPo; OBET

O salty sea, how much of your salt. The Portuguese Sea. Fernando Pessoa. PeSAV

O Saviour of a World Undone. Leonard Withington. AH

O, saw ye bonny Lesley. Bonnie Lesley. Burns. CTC; GTBS; GTBS-P; NOBE; OBEV (Saw Ye Bonny Lesley.) OxBS

O saw ye my father? or saw ye my mother? The Grey Cock, or, Saw You My Father? *Unknown.* ELP; ESPB; FaBoBa; OBET

O saw ye not fair Ines? Fair Ines. Thomas Hood. EnRP; OBEV

O, Saw Ye the Lass. Richard Ryan. FaBoBe

O say can u see. On Watching a World Series Game. Sonia Sanchez. NBV

O [*or* Oh], say, can you see, by the dawn's early light. The Star-spangled Banner. Francis Scott Key. AiP; AnAmPo; BLPA; EBEvV; FaBoBe; FaPON; PAH; TAP; UV, abr.; WBLP

O say, have you seen at the Willows so green. The Ballad of the Emeu. Bret Harte. NBLV

O say what is that thing call'd Light. The Blind Boy. Colley Cibber. GTBS; GTBS-P; NOEC; OxBChV

O sea goddess Nuliajuk. Magic Words for Hunting Seal. *Unknown, tr. fr. Eskimo by* Edward Field. STP

O sea-gulls that are crying. *Unknown, tr. fr. Japanese by* Arthur Waley. TAL

O sea, take all, since thou hast taken him. Henry I to the Sea. Eugene Lee-Hamilton. PeVV

O search the heart and belly you may find. Forebears. Elizabeth Riddell. FaBoMA

O see how narrow are our days. Prayer of the Maidens to Mary. Rainer Maria Rilke, *tr. fr. German by* Jethro Bithell. AWP

O Seeded grass, you army of little men. John Gould Fletcher. *Fr.* Irradiations. MoAmPo

O, Seeger, the night you tied the cabbie. Quarry/Rock. Paul Mariah. GLP; PeHV

O self-born mockers of man's enterprise. *(LL)* Among School Children. W. B. Yeats. BLPL; CMoP; GTBS-P; HAP; ImPo; InPS; LiTB; LiTM; MeMBP; MoAB; MoBrPo; MoP; NAEL-2; NAWM-2; NIP; NoAM; NOBE; NoP; OAEL-2; OxBTC; PoE; Poetr; PPP; PrIm; SCGP; TFi; TrGrPo; TRP

O! sely anker, that in thy celle. Go, Sad Complaint. Charles, Duc d'Orléans. EnVB; MeEL

O shady vales, O fair enriched meads. Thomas Lodge. *Fr.* Margarite of America, A. EiL

O Shannadore, I love your daughter. The Wide Mizzoura. *Unknown.* AS

O she looked out of the window. The Two Magicians. *Unknown.* ChTr; OAEL-1; OxBoLi

O she pulled him down. *(LL)* Every Bush New Springing. *Unknown.* PoEL-2

O she was full of loving fuss. One of the Principal Causes of War. "Hugh MacDiarmid." OxBSP

O sight of pity, shame and dole! The Singer in the Prison. Walt Whitman. BeLS

O Silent God, Thou whose voice afar in mist and mystery. A Litany of [*or* at] Atlanta. W. E. B. DuBois. CDC; PoNe

O silent wood, I enter thee. A Silent Wood. Elizabeth Siddal. NOBVV

O silver splendor, marvelous! A Vision of Moonlight. H. Cordelia Ray. CBWP-3

O [*or* Oh] silver-throated swan. The Dying Swan. T. Sturge Moore. OBMV

O Simplicitas. Madeleine L'Engle. *Fr.* Three Songs of Mary. OBCP; PChr

O Sing to Me of Heaven. Mary Stanley Bunce Dana. AH

O [*or* Oh] sing unto the Lord [*or* Jehovah] a new song. Bible, *O.T.*, *paraphrased by* Sir Thomas Wyatt. *Fr.* Psalms. TrJP
(Floods Clap Their Hands, The.) TrGrPo
(Sing unto Jehovah.) BLRP

O! sing ye a dirge for the loved and the lost. Tribute to a Lost Steamer. Mary Weston Fordham. CBWP-2

O singer of Persephone! Theocritus. Oscar Wilde. NOBE

O singing wind. The Fir-Tree. Edith M. Thomas. OHIP

O sink, o sink your sorrow, my child. Faithful Love. Robert Reinick, *tr. fr. German by* Philip L. Miller. RiWo

O Sion, Haste, Thy Mission High Fulfilling. Mary A. Thomson. AH

O! sisters too. The Coventry Carol. *Unknown.* MeEL

O sleep, my babe, hear not the rippling wave. Sara Coleridge. *Fr.* Phantasmion. OBNC

O Sleep, O tranquil son of noiseless Night. To Sleep. Giovanni della Casa, *tr. fr. Italian by* John Addington Symonds. AWP

O sleeper rise, if thou would'st see. Sleeper Rise. *Gond Oral Tradition, tr. by* V. Elwin *and* S. Hivale. WTO

O sleepy city of reeling wheelchairs. The Wheelchair Butterfly. James Tate. LCAP; NoAM

O smooth flatterers, go over sea. Reflection and Advice. Ezra Pound. OBSV

O [*or* Oh] snatch'd away in beauty's bloom! Byron. EnRP; GTBS; GTBS-P

O snowflake clouds, O feath'ry clouds. Cloud Song. H. Cordelia Ray. CBWP-3

O soft embalmer of the still midnight. To Sleep. Keats. ChTr; EBEvV; EnRP; FaBoRV; MeMBP; NIP; OBEV; PIP; PoEL-4; PrIm; Son; TEP (Sonnet to Sleep.) NAEL-2

O soldier, O soldier, won't you marry me now. Soldier, Won't You Marry Me? *Unknown.* AmFP; OxBoLi; PeLV

O soldiers, soldiers, get ye back, I pray! Saved. Adah Isaacs Menken. CBWP-1

O Solitude! if I must with thee dwell. Solitude. Keats. EnRP
(To Solitude.) PFP

O solo mio, hot diggety, nix "I wather think I can." Frank O'Hara. TTTS

O! Solomon! let us try again." (*LL*) Solomon and the Witch. W. B. Yeats. ChIV-1; NoAM

O sometimes in the street, or in the Paris Metro. Remembrance. Antoni Slonimski, *tr. fr. Polish by* Frances Notley. TrJP

O Son of God, it would be sweet. St. Columcille. NOIV

O Son of God, who seeing two things. The Son. John Donne. *Fr.* Litanie, The. NOCV; PoEL-2

O son of man, by lying tongues adored. On the Russian Persecution of the Jews. Swinburne. Son

O Son of Man, Thou Madest Known. Milton S. Littlefield. AH; TrPWD

O son of man, when thou findest wine. Five Arabic Verses in Praise of Wine. *Unknown, tr. fr. Arabic by* Hartwig Hirschfeld. TrJP

O son of mine, when dusk shall find thee bending. From Generation to Generation. Sir Henry Newbolt. FaBoTw

O Son of the living God. Manchán's Prayer. Saint Manchán. NOIV

O song as yet unsung! A Song as Yet Unsung. "Yehoash," *tr. fr. Yiddish by* Isidore Goldstick. TrJP

O sons of men. *Unknown, tr. fr. Arabic by* E. Powys Mathers. *Fr.* Thousand and One Nights, The. OBD

O sons of men, that toil, and love with tears! The Fair Maid and the Sun. Arthur O'Shaughnessy. BeLS

O! sop of sorrow, sonkin into cair. Cresseid's Complaint against Fortune. Robert Henryson. *Fr.* Testament of Cresseid, The. MeEL; OxBLMV; OxBS

O Sorrow! Keats. *See* O Sorrow,/ Why dost borrow.

O sorrow, cruel fellowship. Tennyson. *Fr.* In Memoriam A. H. H. EBVV, *abr.*; EBVVPR; EnVR; HAP; OAEL-2, *abr.*; PeECV, *abr.*

O sorrow! He is one who jumps. Springbok. *Unknown, tr. fr. Hottentot.* PeSA

O Sorrow,/ Why dost borrow. Song of the Indian Maid. Keats. *Fr.* Endymion [a Poetic Romance]. NOBE; OBEV
(O Sorrow!) CH

O soul, canst thou not understand. Aridity. "Michael Field." OBMV

O soul, 'tis thine in season meet. Ode on Theoxenos. Pindar, *tr. fr. Greek.* PeHV, *tr. by* John Addington Symonds

O soul, why shouldst thou downcast be? Hope Thou in God. Josephine D. Henderson Heard. CBWP-4

O Soul, with Storms Beset. Solomon ibn Gabirol, *tr. fr. Hebrew by* Alice Lucas. TrJP

O sovereign power of love! O grief! O balm! Keats. *Fr.* Endymion [a Poetic Romance]. EnRP; OBNC

O spare a tear for poor Tom Hood. Elegy on Thomas Hood. Martin Fagg. FaBoPa; NOBL; UV
(Elegy: "O spare a tear for poor Tom Hood.") BXAP

O sperm, testes, paradidymus! o scrotum, septum, and rectum! Gay Epiphany. James Mitchell. PeHV

O spirit of Venus whom I adore. *Unknown, tr. fr. Latin.* PeHV

O spread agen your leaves an' flow'rs. The Woodlands. William Barnes. BoNaP

O Spring, thou youthful beauty of the year. Spring. Giovanni Battista Guarini, *tr. fr. Italian by* Leigh Hunt. AWP

O stagnant east-wind, palsied mare. A Room on a Garden. Wallace Stevens. NoP

O Star (the fairest one in sight). Choose Something like a Star. Robert Frost. MoAB; MoAmPo

O starry Temple of unvalted space. William Alabaster. *Fr.* Divine Meditations. ESCV; Son

O! Start a Revolution. D. H. Lawrence. FaBoEE

O Stay, Sweet Love. *Unknown.* TrGrPo

O stay that covetous hand! First turn all eye. Upon the Curtain of Lucasta's Picture It Was Thus Wrought. Richard Lovelace. CaPo

O stealthily-creeping *Merrimac.* The Victory-Wreck. Will M. Carleton. PAH

O stiffly shapen houses that change not. Suburbs on a Hazy Day. D. H. Lawrence. OBMV

O still, small voice of calm! (*LL*) The Brewing of Soma. Whittier. PoEL-4

O still their Tongues till morning comes! (*LL*) Resentments Composed because of the Clamor of Town Topers Outside My Apartment. Sarah Kemble Knight. AiP; SCAP

O stony grey soil of Monaghan. Stony Grey Soil. Patrick Kavanagh. CIP

O stop, Jade Rabbit! The Fall of Moon Lady. Chung Ling, *tr. fr. Chinese by* Kenneth Rexroth *and* Ling Chung. WPC

O strategic map of disasters, hungry America. On Walt Whitman's Birthday. Anne Waldman. UL

O sublime art, I thank you for it! (*LL*) To Music. Franz von Schober. RiWo

O sublime art, in how many gray hours. To Music. Franz von Schober, *tr. fr. German by* Philip L. Miller. RiWo

O such a commotion under the ground. Flower Chorus. Emerson. BoTP

O Suen, the usurper Lugalanne means nothing to me! Appeal to the Moongod Nanna-Suen to Throw Out Lugalanne. Enheduanna, *tr. fr. Sumerian by* Aliki *and* Willis Barnstone. BoWoP

O suitably-attired-in-leather-boots. Fragment of a Greek Tragedy. A. E. Housman. FaBoNo; NOBL; PeLV

O sun, and moonlight shining in the woods. Carmen Saeculare. C. H. Sisson, *after the Latin of* Horace. OBVE

O sun, be his protection. Branwen's Starling. R. Williams Parry, *tr. fr. Welsh by* Gwyn Jones. OBWVE

O Sun! O age-old labor mutely mixed with ocean. Edouard Glissant, *tr. fr. French by* Ellen Conroy Kennedy. *Fr.* Indies, The. NegPo

O Sun, when I stand in my green leaves. To the Sun from a Flower. Guido Gezelle, *tr. fr. Flemish by* Jethro Bithell. FaPON

O sundew, not remembering her. (*LL*) The Sundew. Swinburne. ELP; NoP; OBNC; PeVV

O suns [*or* sun] and skies and clouds of June. October's Bright Blue Weather. Helen Hunt Jackson. BLPA; BLPL; FaBoBe; GN

O supercilious delicious Rhodope. Irenaius, *tr. fr. Greek by* Andrew Miller. GrAn

O Swallow, Swallow. Tennyson. SCGP

"O Swallow, Swallow, flying, flying south. O Swallow, Swallow. Tennyson. SCGP

O Swallow, Swallow, flying, flying South. Tennyson. *Fr.* Princess, The. CBLP; PIP

O swan, come slowly from the sky. Song of Poverty. *Gond Oral Tradition, tr. by* V. Elwin *and* S. Hivale. WTO

O, sweep of stars over Harlem streets. Stars. Langston Hughes. GLP

O sweet and bitter monuments of pain. Upon the Ensigns of Christ's Crucifying. William Alabaster. NoSic

O sweet are tropic lands for waking dreams. North and South. Claude McKay. AmPP

O sweet delight, O more than human bliss. Song. Thomas Campion. CBLP

O sweet everlasting voices be still. The Everlasting Voices. W. B. Yeats. AWP; MeMBP

O sweet frustrations, I shall be back for more. (*LL*) A Voice from under the Table. Richard Wilbur. AmPP; HAP; NOBA

O sweet, sad, singing river. H. Cordelia Ray. CBWP-3

O sweet St. Bride of the. The Kye-Song of St. Bride. "Fiona Macleod." OtMeF

O sweet September! thy first breezes bring. Sweet September. George Arnold. GN

O Sweet Spontaneous. E. E. Cummings. MoP; NAAL-2; NoAM; NoP; PFP; Poetr; PrIm; RaBo

O Sweet Woods. Sir Philip Sidney. *See* O sweet woods, the delight of solitariness.

O sweet woods, the delight of solitariness. Sir Philip Sidney. *Fr.* Arcadia. NoSic; SiPSBD
  (Delight of Solitariness, The.) LiTB
  (O Sweet Woods.) FaBoRV; PoEL-1
  (Solitariness.) SCGP; SiPS

O sweete and bitter monuments of paine. William Alabaster. *Fr.* Divine Meditations. ESCV; Son

O Sweetest Melancholy. John Fletcher. *See* Hence all you vain delights.

O swiftly, re-light the flame. Hilda Doolittle ("H. D."). *Fr.* Tribute to the Angels. NALW

O sylvan priest of nature! rightly thou. A Thought at Walden. H. Cordelia Ray. CBWP-3

O Sylvan prophet, whose eternal fame. Hymn for St. John's Eve. *Unknown, tr. fr. Latin by* Dryden. AWP

O Sylvia, Sylvia. Sylvia's Death. Anne Sexton. LCAP; NAAL-2; NALW

O take me back to Gondwanaland. Gondwanaland. Gavin Ewart. OBAP

O take me to the sullen flats. From the Righteous Man Even the Wild Beasts Run Away. David Bromwich. PoA

O Taste and See. Denise Levertov. ChIV-1; CrSp; FoLa; NoP; PBWP; PPP; TAP

O tell me, little children, have you seen her. Nikolina. Celia Laighton Thaxter. GN

O tell me, pretty river! The River. *Unknown.* PWR

O tell me whence that joy doth spring. The Queer. Henry Vaughan. PoEL-2

O tender-heartedness right bitter grown. Fragmenti. Ezra Pound. PoA

O Tender under Her Right Breast. George Barker. *Fr.* Second Cycle of Love Poems. MoAB; MoBrPo

O tenderly the haughty day. Emerson. GN

O terrible is the highest thing. Kenneth Patchen. VGW

O Thalassa! Thalassa! Where, where. The Singers. George Bruce. OxBS

O that I could a sin once see! Sin. George Herbert. NoP; OxBSP

O, That I Had Some Secret Place. *Unknown.* AmFP

O That I Knew the Way Back. Klaus Groth, *tr. fr. German by* Philip L. Miller. RiWo

O that I were all soule that I might prove. On Platonic Love, to Mistress Cicely Crofts, Maid of Honour. Sir Robert Ayton. ScCV

O that it were possible we might. John Webster. *Fr.* Duchess of Malfi, The. IMW; NAEL-1

O that mastering tune! And up in the bed. In the Nuptial Chamber. Thomas Hardy. *Fr.* Satires of Circumstance. InPK

O that mine eyes might closed be. Thomas Elwood. PWR

O That My Love Were in My Arms. *Malay Oral Tradition, tr. by* R. J. Wilkinson *and* R. O. Winstedt. WTO

O that our dreamings all, of sleep or wake. Keats. *Fr.* Epistle to John Hamilton Reynolds. OAEL-2; OBNC

O, that the Holy Angels would indite. The Quarto Centennial. Josephine D. Henderson Heard. CBWP-4

O that the rain would come — the rain in big battalions. Precursors. Louis MacNeice. OxBSP

O, that the years had language! time would/ tell. Judith. Eloise Bibb. CBWP-4

O! that this too too solid flesh would melt. Shakespeare. *Fr.* Hamlet. NAWM-1; OxAEP-1; SCV
  (Frailty, Thy Name is Woman.) TrGrPo
  (O, that this too too sullied flesh would melt.) IMW

O, that this too too sullied flesh would melt. Shakespeare. *See* O! that this too too solid flesh would melt.

O [*or* Oh] that 'twere possible. Tennyson. *Fr.* Maud[: A Monodrama]. BoLoP; CBLP; EnVR; IMW; NAEL-2; NOBE; NOBVV; OAEL-2; OBEV; PoE

O! that we now had here. Shakespeare. *Fr.* King Henry V. OxAEP-1
  (Before Agincourt.) PAW

O the aching of that long, long night. Sundered. John Barford. PeHV

O the cuckoo she's a pretty bird. The Cuckoo. *Unknown.* GBP; RB

O, the days gone by! O, the days gone by! The Days Gone By. James Whitcomb Riley. OBCA

O the days of the Messiah are at hand, are at hand! Ballad of the Days of the Messiah. A. M. Klein. TrJP

O the evening's for the fair, bonny lassie O! Bonny Lassie O! John Clare. CH

O [*or* Oh] the French are on the sea. The Shan Van Vocht. *Unknown.* FaBoPV; GBP; OxBoLi

O the goose and the gander walk'd over the green. The Goose and the Gander. *Unknown.* GBP; RB

O, the grand old Duke of York. *Unknown. See* Oh [*or* O], the noble [*or* brave *or* grand old] duke of York.

O the green glimmer of apples in the orchard. Ballad of Another Ophelia. D. H. Lawrence. ChTr

O the green things growing, the green things growing. Green Things Growing. Dinah Maria Mulock Craik. GN; OHIP

O the hog-eye men are all the go. The Hog-Eye Man. *Unknown.* AS

O, the hurt, the hurt, and the hurt of love! The Hurt of Love. George Macdonald. TrCP

O the little rusty dusty miller. *Unknown.* OxNR

O, the lovely rivers and lakes of Maine! The Lovely Rivers and Lakes of Maine. George B. Wallis. BLPA

O, the Month of May. Thomas Dekker *and others. See* O the month of May, the merry month of May.

O the month of May, the merry month of May. Thomas Dekker *and others. Fr.* Shoemaker's Holiday, The. NoSic
  (Maytime.) TrGrPo
  (O, the Month of May.) EIL

O, the noble [*or* brave *or* grand old] duke of York. The Noble [*or* Brave Old] Duke of York. *Unknown.* GBP
  (Brave Old Duke of York, The) OxNR

O the opal and the sapphire of that wandering western sea. Beeny Cliff. Thomas Hardy. OBNC; OxAEP-2; RB

O the Ploughboy was a-ploughing. The Simple Ploughboy. *Unknown.* FaBoCh

O the pride of Portsmouth water. The Lost War-Sloop. Edna Dean Proctor. PAH

O the Raggedy Man! He works for Pa. The Raggedy Man. James Whitcomb Riley. FaPON; OBCA; OxBChV

O, the rain, the weary, dreary rain. Twenty Golden Years Ago. James Clarence Mangan. NOBVV; PeIV

O the sad day! The Sad Day. Thomas Flatman. OBEV

O the Spring will come. The Spring Will Come. H. D. Lowry. BoNaP

O the times will never be again. Lament of One of the Old Regime. Emma Catherine Embury. AmWP

O the treacherous Scots revengd hee'd be. (*LL*) Johnie Armstrong. *Unknown.* ESPB, A *vers.*; FaBoBa; HoPM; NoP, A *vers.*; TrGrPo

O the valley in the summer where I and my John. Johnny. W. H. Auden. PlP

O the warm, sweet, mellow summer noon. The Favorite Flower. Celia Laighton Thaxter. AiP

O [*or* Oh], then, I see Queen Mab hath been with you. Shakespeare. *Fr.* Romeo and Juliet.
  (Mercutio's Queen Mab Speech.) LiTB
  (Queen Mab.) FaPON

O there are lands. Limited Aggression. Mari Evans. ETG

O, there are times/ When all this fret. Daily Trials. Oliver Wendell Holmes. PoEL-5

O, there be many things. Many Things. Oliver Wendell Holmes. PoToHe

O [*or* Oh] there was a woman, and she was a widow. Flowers in the Valley. *Unknown.* OxBoLi

O [*or* Oh] there was an old soldier and he had a wooden leg. There Was an Old Soldier. *Unknown.* AS

O these wakeful wounds of thine! On the Wounds of Our Crucified Lord. Richard Crashaw. NAEL-1

O Thirsty Wind. *Unknown, tr. fr. Hawaiian by* N. B. Emerson. WTO

O this weather! this weather! A Hot Day In Sydney. *Unknown.* NOBAu

O thou afflicted, drunken not with wine! Dirge for the Ninth of Ab. *Unknown, tr. fr. Hebrew by* Nina Davis Salaman. TrJP

O thou all-eloquent, whose mighty mind. Man's Going Hence. Samuel Rogers. *Fr.* Human Life. OBNC

O Thou almighty will. Strength, Love, Light. Robert II, King of France. WGRP

O thou bright jewel in my aim I strive. On Virtue. Phillis Wheatley. TAP

O thou, by Nature taught. Ode to Simplicity. William Collins. EnRP; NOBE; OBEV; OxAEP-1; TEP

O, Thou Eternal One! Gavril Romanovich Derzhavin, *tr. fr. Russian by* Sir John Bowring. WGRP

O Thou Eternal Source of Life. Rolland W. Schloerb. TrPWD

O Thou Eternal Victim Slain. Charles Wesley. NOCV

O Thou/ God of all long desirous roaming. Rupert Brooke. *Fr.* Song of the Pilgrims, The. TrPWD

O Thou great being! what Thou art. A Prayer under the Pressure of Violent Anguish. Burns. ScCV; TrPWD

O Thou great Friend to all the sons of men. The Way, the Truth, and the Life. Theodore Parker. TrPWD; WGRP

O thou Great Mantle which envelops us. Great Hymn. Ntsikana Gaba, *tr. fr. Xhosa by* Thomas Pringle. PeSAV

O Thou Immortal Deity. Shelley. TrPWD

O thou in heaven and earth the only place. Milton. *Fr.* Paradise Lost. EPCY
(Plan of Salvation, The.) WGRP

O thou Moor of Morería. Abenamar, Abenamar. *Unknown, tr. fr. Spanish by* Robert Southey. AWP

O Thou Most High Who Rulest All. Anne Bradstreet. AH
(Upon My Dear and Loving Husband His going into England Jan. 16, 1661.) EAP

O Thou, My Lovely Boy, Who In Thy Power. Shakespeare. *Fr.* Sonnets. HeIP; NAEL-1

O Thou my soule, Jehovah blesse. *Unknown. Fr.* Bay Psalm Book, The. SCAP

O Thou my soule, Jehovah blesse, *Bay Psalm Book.* Bible, *O.T., paraphrased by* Sir Thomas Wyatt. *See* Bless the Lord, O my soul: and all that is within me.

O thou newcomer who seek'st Rome in Rome. Rome. Joachim du Bellay, *tr. fr. French by* Ezra Pound. AWP

O Thou not made with hands. The City of God. Francis Turner Palgrave. WGRP

O thou of little faith. Hitherto Hath the Lord Helped. *Unknown.* BLRP

O thou that after toil and storm. Tennyson. *Fr.* In Memoriam A. H. H. EBVV, *abr.;* OAEL-2, *abr.;* PeECV, *abr.*

O Thou, that dost cover the heavens. Song of the Wind and the Rain. Solomon ibn Gabirol, *tr. fr. Hebrew by* Solomon Solis-Cohen. TrJP

O thou that from thy mansion. For My Funeral. A. E. Housman. CMoP; TrPWD

O thou that held'st the blessed Veda dry. Hymn to Vishnu. Jayadeva, *tr. by* Sir Edwin Arnold. *Fr.* Gita Govinda, The. AWP

O Thou, that in the heavens does dwell. Holy Willie's Prayer. Burns. EBEV; FaBoBl; NOEC; OBSV; OxBS; PoE; PoEL-4; PPP; TFi
(O Thou, wha in the heavens dost dwell.) EnRP; InPS; NoP; OAEL-1; OxBoLi; ScCV
(O THOU, wha in the Heavens dost dwell.) FaPoB

O thou that lovest a pure, and whitend soul! Dressing. Henry Vaughan *and* Thomas Stanley. ESCV

O thou that often hast within thine eyes. Sonnet: He Speaks of a Third Love of His. Cavalcanti, *tr. fr. Italian by* Dante Gabriel Rossetti. AWP

O thou, that sendest out the man. England and America in 1782. Tennyson. PAH

O thou, that sitst [*or* sit'st] upon a throne. Christopher Smart. *Fr.* Song to David, A. ChTr; EBEV; NAEL-1; NOBE, *abr.;* OAEL-1; OBWVE; OxAEP-1, 25 *sts.;* PoE; PoEL-3; TrGrPo, *abr.*
(Song to David, A.) ImPo

O Thou That Sleep'st like Pig in Straw. Sir William Davenant. InvP; NOSC

O [*or* Oh] thou that swing'st [*or* swingest] upon the waving hair [*or* haire *or* ear *or* eare]. The Grasshopper. Richard Lovelace. BeJo; CaPo; EBEV; FaBoPV; JCP; NAEL-1; NOBE; NoP; NOSC; OAEL-1; OBEV; PPP; SCGP; SeCV-1; TFi
(Grasse-Hopper, The.) MeLP
(To the Grasshopper.) OxAEP-1

O thou that with surpassing glory crown'd. Milton. *Fr.* Paradise Lost. EPCY
(Satan's Soliloquy.) LiTB

O Thou! the first fruits of the dead. Burial. Henry Vaughan. GeHe; SeCV-1

O Thou, the first, the greatest friend. The First Six Verses of the Ninetieth Psalm. Burns. ChIV-1

O thou, the wonder of all days! The Dirge of Jephthah's Daughter. Robert Herrick. ChIV-1

O thou undaunted daughter of desires! Richard Crashaw. *Fr.* Flaming Heart, The. HAP; LiTB; NAEL-1; OAEL-1, *abr.;* PoEL-2; SeCV-1; TEP
(Upon the Book and Picture of the Seraphical Saint Teresa.) NOBE; OBEV

O Thou unknown, Almighty Cause. A Prayer in the Prospect of Death. Burns. TrPWD; WGRP

O THOU, wha in the Heavens dost dwell. Burns. *See* O Thou, that in the heavens does dwell.

O Thou, wha in the heavens dost dwell. Burns. *See* O Thou, that in the heavens does dwell.

O thou! whatever title suit thee. Address to the Deil. Burns. EnRP; NOEC; OAEL-1; OxBS; PoEL-4

O thou who art of all that is. Through Unknown Paths. Frederick L. Hosmer. TrPWD

O Thou who bidst the torrent flow. Whittier. *Fr.* Hymn from the French of Lamartine. TrPWD

O thou who camest from above. Charles Wesley. TrPWD
(Inextinguishable Blaze.) NOEC

O thou who didst furnish. Hymn to Moloch. Ralph Hodgson. OxBTC

O Thou, Who Didst Ordain the Word. Edwin Hubbell Chapin. AH

O thou, who lately closed my eyes. A Morning Hymn. Christopher Smart. OxBChV

O thou who never harbored fear. Eloise Bibb. CBWP-4

O thou, who passest through our valleys in. To Summer. Blake. WiR

O thou, who plumed with strong desire. The Two Spirits [an Allegory]. Shelley. CH; OAEL-2; Prf; WiR

O Thou who speedest Time's advancing wing. He Asketh Absolution of God. *Unknown, tr. fr. Egyptian by* Robert Hillyer. *Fr.* Book of the Dead. AWP

O tuou whom Poetry [*or* Poesy] abhors. On Elphinston's Translation of Martial. Burns. FaBoCo; FaBoEE

O Thou whose equal purpose runs. Wendell Phillips Stafford. TrPWD

O thou, whose eyes were closed in death's pale night. Epitaph on a Child Killed by Procured Abortion. *Unknown.* NOEC

O thou whose face hath felt the Winter's wind. What the Thrush Said. Keats. EBEV; PFP

O thou! whose fancies from afar are brought. To H. C. Wordsworth. EnRP; MeMBP; PoEL-4

O Thou Whose Feet Have Climbed Life's Hill. Louis FitzGerald Benson. AH

O Thou, whose glorious orbs on high. Hymn of the West. Edmund Clarence Stedman. PAH
(Hymn to the West.) TrPWD

O Thou Whose Gracious Presence Blest. Louis FitzGerald Benson. TrPWD

O Thou Whose Gracious Presence Shone. Marion Franklin Ham. AH

O Thou Whose Image. Arthur Hugh Clough. TrPWD

O thou, whose mighty palace roof doth hang. Hymn to Pan. Keats. *Fr.* Endymion [a Poetic Romance]. MeMBP; PoEL-4

O thou whose name shatters the universe. Eli the Thatcher. Max Beerbohm *and* William Rothenstein. FaBoNo

O Thou Whose Own Vast Temple Stands. Bryant. AH

O thou whose pow'r o'er moving worlds presides. Boethius, *tr. by* Samuel Johnson. *Fr.* Consolation of Philosophy, The. OBVE; TrPWD

O Thou! Whose Presence Went Before. Whittier. AH

O Thou whose reason guides the universe. Boethius, *tr. fr. Latin. Fr.* Consolation of Philosophy, The. MLL, *tr. by* Helen Waddell

O thou, with dewy locks who lookest down. To Spring. Blake. BLPL; BoNaP; BoTP; EnRP; MeMBP; NAEL-2; NOEC; OAEL-2; OBEV; PoEL-4; PoLF; PPP; SCGP; WiR

O Thought I! Dorothy Wordsworth. NTP

O thow archbishop and metropolitan. *Unknown. Fr.* Letter Sent by the Mayor and Inhabitants of the, A. NOIV

O thow Lucyna, qwene and empyresse. On the Departing of Thomas Chaucer. John Lydgate. OxBLMV

O [*or* Oh] thy bright eyes must answer now. Plead for Me. Emily Brontë. MeMBP; PoEL-5
(God of Visions.) TrGrPo
(O Thy Bright Eyes Must Answer Now.) BrRo

O Tim, my own Tim I must call 'ee — I will! Thomas Hardy. *Fr.* Bride-Night Fire, The. FaBoVe

O Time the fatal wrack of mortal things. Anne Bradstreet. *Fr.* Contemplations. AmPP; EAP; PBWP; PoEL-3, *abr.;* SCAP; WPE, *abr.;* WPOW

O Time, whence comes the Mother's moody look amid her labours. The Lacking Sense. Thomas Hardy. CMoP; PoEL-5

O Time! who know'st a lenient hand to lay. Time and Grief. William Lisle Bowles. OBEV
(Influence of Time on Grief.) EnRP

O times most bad. Upon the Troublesome Time. Robert Herrick. CaPo

O to abide in the desert with thee! (*LL*) The Skylark. James Hogg. GN

O to Be a Dragon. Marianne Moore. ChIV-1; CTC; GoYe; NALW; PFP

O to be blind! The Blind Man at the Fair. Joseph Campbell. AWP

O to break loose, like the chinook. Waking Early Sunday Morning. Robert Lowell. FaBoMo; HCAP; NOBA; OxBC; VCAP

O [*or* Oh], to have a little house! An Old Woman of the Roads. Padraic Colum. BoTP; CH; CoGr; FaBoBe; FaPON; FYAP; MoBrPo; NOIV; OBEV; PoRA; TIRV

O To Scuttle From the Battle. Justin Richardson. *See* O to scuttle from the battle and to settle on an atoll far from brutal mortal neath a wattle portal!

O to scuttle from the battle and to settle on an atoll far from brutal mortal neath a wattle portal! Justin Richardson. FiBHP
(O To Scuttle From the Battle.) UV

O Trade! O Trade! would thou wert dead! The Symphony. Sidney Lanier. AmPP; LiTA

O tragic hours when lovers leave each other! Partings. Charles Guérin, *tr. fr. French by* Jethro Bithell. AWP

O treacherous scent, O thorny sight. Another for the Briar Rose. William Morris. NOBVV

O trees, to whom the darkness is a child. Advice to a Forest. Maxwell Bodenheim. TrJP

O tremble, all ye earthly princes. The Revolutionaries. R. P. Lister. NOBL

O Troy Muir, my lily-flower. The Queen of Scotland. *Unknown.* ESPB

O trusty Christ that wearest a crown. Ieuan ap Hywel Swrdwal. *Fr.* Hymn to the Virgin, The. AngWe

O. T.'s Blues. Waring Cuney. MAT

O [*or* Oh] turn away those cruel eyes. The Relapse. Thomas Stanley. BeJo; NOSC; OBEV

O Turn Ye, O Turn Ye. Josiah Hopkins. AH

O 'twas on a bright mornin' in summer. Who's the Pretty Girl Milkin' the Cow? *Unknown.* AS

O Tweed! a stranger, that with wandering feet. The Tweed Visited. William Lisle Bowles. Son

O two-horned moon, you love the parties that last all night. Philodemus, *tr. fr. Greek by* Barbara Hughes Fowler. *Fr.* Epigrams. HePo

O-U-G-H. Charles Battell Loomis. NBLV

O — U — T, etc. (*LL*) Ex and Squarey. *Unknown.* ChTr; GBP, 1 *st.*

O, U, T, spells out! (*LL*) Out goes the rat. *Unknown.* RoPo

O uncreated Lord of all creation. Prayer to God the Father. Marbod of Rennnes, *tr. fr. Latin by* Helen Waddell. MLL

O universal Mother, who dost keep. Hymn to Earth the Mother of All. *Unknown, tr. fr. Greek by* Shelley. *Fr.* Homeric Hymns. AWP

O Urizen! Creator of men! mistaken Demon of heaven! Take Thy Bliss, O Man. Blake. *Fr.* Visions of the Daughters of Albion. EnRP; OAEL-2

O valiant Hearts, who to your glory came. The Supreme Sacrifice. John S. Arkwright. WGRP

O Virgin. *Unknown, tr. fr. Gaelic by* Douglas Hyde. WTO

O Virtuous Light. Elinor Wylie. MoAB; MoAmPo

O Visionary who adjust your lens. The Higher Empiricism. Francis C. Golffing. PoA

O wad this braw hie-heapit toun. The Prows o' Reekie. Lewis Spence. OxBS

O Wahkonda (Master of Life) pity me! A Dance Chant. *Unknown, tr. by* D. G. Brinton. WGRP

O walk not in the wind! (*LL*) To the Maids Not to Walk in the Wind. Oliver St. John Gogarty. ErPo

O wall-flower! or ever thy bright leaves fade. The Wall-Flower. Henrik Arnold Thaulov Wergeland, *tr. fr. Norwegian by* Sir Edmund Gosse. AWP

O Waly, Waly. *Unknown. See* Oh [*or* O] waly, waly, up the [*or* yon] bank.

O waly, waly, my gay goss-hawk. The Gay Goshawk [*or* Goss-Hawk]. At. to Anna Gordon Brown. ESPB, A *and* E *vers.;* GN; OxBB; WPE

O waly waly waly waly. The Holloe Menn. Harrison Everard. BXAP

O warm, enthusiastic maid. Joseph Warton. *Fr.* Ode to Fancy. NOEC

O, was it you? (*LL*) A Bowl of Roses. W. E. Henley. MoBrPo

O, Wast Thou with Me, Dearest, Then. Tennyson. *Fr.* In Memoriam A. H. H. EBVV, *abr.;* MeMBP; OAEL-2, *abr.;* PeECV, *abr.*

O wastfull riot, never well content. Lucan, *tr. by* Sir Walter Ralegh. *Fr.* Pharsalia. OBVE

O water-girl! with tinkling anklets. Water-Girl. *Gond Oral Tradition, tr. by* V. Elwin *and* S. Hivale. WTO

O Wave God who broke through me today. Burning Island. Gary Snyder. VCAP

O! we know not we know not, what future joys. There's a Silvery Lining to Every Cloud. Matilda C. Edwards. PWR

O, we loved long and happily, God knows! The Custom of the World. Louis Simpson. BoLoP

O we sailed to Virginia and thence to New York. The Death of Admiral Benbow. *Unknown.* OxBSS

O we were sisters seven, Maisry. Fair Mary of Wallington. *Unknown.* ESPB
(Bonny Earl of Livingston, The.) OxBB

O we were sisters, sisters seven. Earl Crawford. *Unknown.* ESPB

O weary Champion of the Cross, lie still. Cardinal Newman. Christina Rossetti. NAEL-2

O Weary Pilgrims. Robert Bridges. *Fr.* Growth of Love, The. MoAB; MoBrPo

O weel may the boatie row and better may she speed. The Boatie Rows. *Unknown.* OxBSS, *ad. by* John Ewen

O wen, wen, O little wennikins. A Charm. *Unknown, tr. fr. Anglo-Saxon by* Richard Hammer. RB

O Wendy, Arthur. Maurice Kenny. HATNAP

O Were My Love Yon Lilac Fair. Burns. ChTr; GBL; OBEV

O Wert Thou in the Cauld Blast. Burns. FaBoVe; OxAEP-2

O [*or* Oh], Wert Thou in the Cauld Blast. Burns. EBEV; ELP; EnRP; HAP; NOBE; NoP; OxBS; ScCV; SCGP; TrGrPo

O Western Wind. *Unknown.* CoGr; ImPo

O western wind when wilt thou blow. O Western Wind. *Unknown.* CoGr; ImPo

O wha my babie-clouts will buy? The Rantin' Dog, the Daddie o't. Burns. FaBoVe; OxBoLi; PeLV; PPP

O wha will bake my bridal bread. Fair Annie. *Unknown.* ESPB

O wha will shoe my bonny foot? Fair Isabell of Rochroyall. *Unknown.* OxBB

O wha will shoe my fair foot? The Lass of Roch Royal. *Unknown.* AmFP; ESPB

O wha would [*or* wou'd] wish the win to blaw. Brown Adam. *Unknown.* ESPB; OxBB

O whare are ye gaun? [*or* O where are you going?]. The False Knight upon [*or* on] the Road. *Unknown.* AmFP; CH; EnSB; ESPB; GBP
(False Knight and the Wee Boy, The.) FaBoCh; OxBoLi; OxBS

O whare hae ye been a' day, Lord Donald, my son? Lord Randal. *Unknown.* ESPB

O [*or* Oh] whare hae ye been a' day, my bonnie wee croodlin dow? Lord Randal. *Unknown.* EnSB; ESPB, J *vers.*

O whare hae ye been, my dearest dear. Carpenter's Wife, The ("O whare hae ye been, my dearest dear.") *Unknown.* OAEL-1; OxBB

O whare hae ye been, Peggy? Young Peggy. *Unknown.* ESPB

O Wha's the Bride? "Hugh MacDiarmid." RaBo

O wha's the bride that carries the bunch. O Wha's the Bride? "Hugh MacDiarmid." RaBo

O [*or* Oh] what a cunning guest. Confession. George Herbert. ESCV; JCP

O what a loud and fearful shriek was there. Koskiusko. Samuel Taylor Coleridge. EnRP

O, what a round of applause! (*LL*) The Coup de Grace. Edward Rowland Sill. PPP

O what a strange parcel of creatures are we. On an Unsociable Family. Elizabeth Hands. ECWP; WoRP

O what a tangled web we weave. A Word of Encouragement. J. R. Pope. FiBHP; NBLV; NOBL

O what a world of beauty lies within. The Garden. Emma Catherine Embury. AmWP

O, what can ail thee, knight at arms. Answer to a Kind Enquiry. Mary Holtby. UV

O, [*or* Oh *or* Ah] what can ail thee, knight-at-arms [*or* wretched wight]. La Belle Dame sans Merci. Keats. AWP; BeLS; BLPA; CH; ChTr; ClHu; CoGr; EBEvV; ELP; EnRP; FaBoBe; FaBoCh; FHYEP; GoJo; GTBS; GTBS-P; HAP; HeIP; ImPo; InPS; InvP; LiTB; MeMBP; NAEL-2; NAWM-2; NOBE; NoP; NTP; OAEL-2; OBEV; OBNC; OBSP; OtMeF; OxAEP-2; PoE; PoEL-4; Poetr; PoRA; Prf; PrIm; RB; SCGP; SCV; SoSe; TEP; TFi, *sl. sh. vers.;* TrGrPo; TRP; UnPo; UV, *sl. sh. vers.*

O, what can be the matter with thee, Knight-at-arms. La Belle Dame sans Merci. T. Griffiths. BXAP

O what can you give me? Idris Davies. AngWe

O what could be more nice. Light Listened. Theodore Roethke. MoAmPo

O what harper could worthily harp it. The Schoolmaster Abroad with His Son. Charles Stuart Calverley. NOBL; PeLV

O What Is That Sound [Which So Thrills the Ear]. W. H. Auden. FaBoPV; LiTB; MeMAP; PoE
(Ballad: "O what is that sound . . . .") MoAB; MoBrPo
(Quarry, The.) CMoP

O What Is That Sound [Which So Thrills the Ear]. W. H. Auden. FaBoPV; LiTB; MeMAP; PoE

O what their joy and their glory must be. Hymn for the Close of the Week. Peter Abelard, *tr. fr. Latin.* TrCP

O what transparent waves, what a tranquil sea. Vittoria da Colonna, *tr. fr. Italian by* Lynne Lawner. PBWP

O what's the blood that's [*or* 'at's] on your sword. Son David. *Unknown.* OxBB; OxBS

O what's the weather in a beard? Dinky. Theodore Roethke. OBAL; OBCA; SM

O, when I hear at sea. Wind and Wave. Charles Warren Stoddard. AnAmPo

O [*or* Oh] when our clergy at the dreadful day. On Those That Deserve It. Francis Quarles. NOCV; NOSC

O when, through ev'ry province, shall be raised. The Happy Workhouse and the Good Effects of Industry. John Dyer. *Fr.* Fleece, The. NOEC

O where are Mina Bell's cows who gave no milk. Mina Bell's Cows. Wesley McNair. TRP

O where are you going? said reader to rider. W. H. Auden. *Fr.* Orators, The. CMoP; CoGr; LiTB; MeMAP; NOBE; UV
(Epilogue: " 'O where are you going?' said reader to rider.") FaBoCh
(Five Songs.) LiTM; NoAM
(Song: " 'O Where Are You Going?' said reader to rider.") OAEL-2

O [*or* Oh] where are you going? says [*or* said] Milder to Malder. The Cutty Wren. *Unknown.* GBP; OxBoLi; SWP; UV, *abr.;* WiR

O where have you been all day. In the Woods. Dorothy Baker. BoTP

O [or Oh] where have [or ha or hae] you [or ye] been, Lord Randal [or Rendal or Randall] my son? Lord Randall[l]. *Unknown.* AmFP; AWP; EBEV; EBEvV; EBNV; EnRP; ESPB, A, B, *and* J *vers.*; FaBoBa; FF; GGP; HAP; HeIL; HeIP; HoPM; InPo; LiTB; NoP, A *vers.*; NTP; OAEL-1; OxBB; OxBS; Poetr; SCGP; TFi; TrGrPo; TRP; WeW

"O where [or whare] have you [or hae ye] been, my dear, dear [or dearest dear or long, long] love." The Demon Lover. *Unknown.* EnSB; HAP; LiTB; MAT; SCGP; TFi; UnPo; WeW

(Carpenter's Wife, The.) OAEL-1; OBET, *diff. vers.*; OxBB, *with music*

(Daemon Lover, The.) NU

(House Carpenter, The.) AmFP; AS,

(James Harris.) ESPB, A, D, *and* F *vers.*; FaBoBa

O where is tiny Hewe? The Goblin's Song. James Telfer. ChTr

O, where, Kinkora! is Brian the Great? Kinkora. James Clarence Mangan. PeIV

O Where, Tell Me Where. Ann Grant. ScCV

O where, tell me where, is your Highland laddie gone? O Where, Tell Me Where. Ann Grant. ScCV

O, Where Were We Before Time Was. Max Dunn. NOBAu

O where were ye, my milk-white steed. The Broomfield Hill. *Unknown.* CH

O, where, where are the winter grounds of angels. The Angels. Marguerite Young. WPE

O wherefore thus, apart with drooping wings. Renunciation. Helen Hunt Jackson. AmWP

O while within a Jewish breast. Hatikvah — a Song of Hope. Naphtali Herz Imber, *tr. fr. Hebrew by* Henry Snowman. TrJP

O whisper, O my soul! The afternoon. The Tired Worker. Claude McKay. BPo

O whistle, and I'll come to you [or ye], my lad. Whistle, and I'll Come to You, My Lad. Burns. CBLP; OtMeF; OxAEP-2; OxBoLi

O, whither sail you, Sir John Franklin? A Ballad of Sir John Franklin. George Henry Boker. AnAmPo

O who can ever praise enough. Poem. W. H. Auden. PoA

O who rides by night thro' the woodland so wild? The Erl-King. Goethe, *tr. fr. German by* Sir Walter Scott. AWP; OBVE

(Invisible King, The.) NU, *tr. by* Robert Bly

(Who spurs on the road when day is done.) STV, *tr. by* John Frederick Nims

O [or Oh] who shall, from this dungeon, raise. A Dialogue between the Soul and [the] Body. Andrew Marvell. ESCV; GeHe; HAP; InPS; JCP; MeLP; NAEL-1; NoP; OAEL-1; OxAEP-1; PoEL-2; PPP; SeCP; SeCV-1; SoSe; TEP; TFi

O, who will drive the chariot when she comes? She'll Be Comin' Round the Mountain. *Unknown.* AS, A *and* B *vers.*

O who will shoe my fair foot. Fair Annie of Lochryan. *Unknown.* AS

O who will shoe my little feet. The Lass of Roch Royal. *Unknown.* AmFP

O who will shoe your pretty little foot. Who Will Shoe Your Pretty Little Foot? *Unknown.* AS

O who will show me those delights on high? Heaven. George Herbert. ESCV; GeHe; SeCP; TrCP; TrGrPo; TTTS

O Who Will Speak from a Womb or a Cloud? George Barker. MeMBP

O who will walk a mile with me. A Mile with Me. Henry van Dyke. BLPA

O who would not sleep with the brave? (*LL*) Lancer. A. E. Housman. MoBrPo; OBWP

O who'll get me a healthy child. A Practical Woman. Thomas Hardy. NAs

O why do you walk through the fields in gloves. To a Fat Lady Seen from the Train. Frances Cornford. BLPA; EBEvV; FaBoWP; GoJo; MoBrPo; OBMV; UV; WeW

O, why should we the dead deplore. African Dirge. M. J. Chapman. PBCV

O wild-reävèn west winds, as you do roar on. Jenny out from Hwome. William Barnes. SCGP

O wild West Wind, thou breath of Autumn's being. Ode to the West Wind. Shelley. AWP; BoNaP; CH; ClHu; EBEV; EnRP; FaBoBe; FaBV; FHYEP; GGP; GTBS; GTBS-P; HAP; HeIL; HeIP; InPo; InPS; LiTB; MeMBP; NAEL-2; NAWM-2; NIP; NOBE; NoP; OAEL-2; OBEV; OBNC; OxAEP-2; PeECV; PoE; PoEL-4; Poetr; PoLF; PoRA; PPP; PrIm; SCGP; TEP; TFi; TrGrPo; TRP; WeW

O William Shakespeare. Hugh Holland. *See* Those hands which you so clapt [or clapped], go now and wring.

O Willie brew'd a peck o' maut. Willie Brew'd [or Brewed] a Peck o' Maut. Burns. AWP; EnRP; OxBS

O Willie's large o' limb and lith. The Birth of Robin Hood. *Unknown.* OAEL-1; OxBB

(Willie and Earl Richard's Daughter.) ESPB

O Willy was as brave a lord. Willie o Douglas Dale. *Unknown.* ESPB

O wind, rend open the heat. Heat. Hilda Doolittle ("H. D."). *Fr.* Garden, The. ArNa; CMoP; HeIL; HeIP; InPK; LiTA; MoAmPo; NoAM; OxBA; PrIm; TAP; TRP; UnPo

O wind, that sings so loud a song! (*LL*) The Wind. Robert Louis Stevenson. BoTP; GN; OHCV

O Winter! bar thine adamantine doors. To Winter. Blake. WiR

O winter wind, lat grievin be. Margaret Winefride Simpson. OxBS

O, winter, your gesture. Winter. Bella Akhmadulina, *tr. fr. Russian by* Barbara Einzig. BoWoP

O Winter's a beautiful time of the year. Winter. Enid Blyton. BoTP

O wistful eyes that haunt the gloom of sleep. Unborn. John Le Gay Brereton. NOBAu

O with what key. Skeleton Key. John Hollander. NoP

O woe, woe,/ People are born and die. Mr. Housman's Message. Ezra Pound. FaBoEE; FaBoPa

O! woful wretche! O! wretche, lesse ones thy speche! (*LL*) Come, Death — My Lady Is Dead. At. *to* Charles, Duc d'Orléans Charles, Duc d' Orléans. MeEL

O woman of the piercing wail. A Lament for the Princes of Tyrone [or Tir-Owen] and Tyrconnel [or Tirconnell]. James Clarence Mangan, *tr. fr. Irish by* James Clarence Mangan. PeIV

O Woman of Three Cows, agra [or agragh]! The Woman of Three Cows. *Unknown, tr. fr. Irish by* James Clarence Mangan. EnRP; NOIV; PeIV

O Woman, Shapely as the Swan. *Unknown. See* For thee I shall not die.

O wonder!/ How many goodly creatures are there here! Brave New World. Shakespeare. *Fr.* Tempest, The. OAEL-1; TrGrPo

O wonderful nonsense of lotions of Lucky Tiger. Haircut. Karl Shapiro. TwCP

O Wonderous Universe! Allen Grossman. *Fr.* Ether Dome (an Entertainment), The. BAP-91

O, wondrous depth to which my soul is stirr'd. Music. Josephine D. Henderson Heard. CBWP-4

O wondrous universe! O beautiful one! O Wonderous Universe! Allen Grossman. *Fr.* Ether Dome (an Entertainment), The. BAP-91

O words are lightly spoken. The Rose Tree. W. B. Yeats. CMoP; ELP; FaBoPV; OBMV

O words, which fall like summer dew on me! Sir Philip Sidney. *Fr.* Arcadia. SiPSBD

(Rural Poesy.) EIL

O world, I cannot hold thee close enough! God's World. Edna St. Vincent Millay. BLPL; CMoP; FaBoBe; FaBV; MoAmPo; TrCP

O world invisible, we view thee. The Kingdom of God. Francis Thompson. FaPoR; GTBS-P; NOCV; PlP

(In No Strange Land.) HAP; LiTB; MoAB; MoBrPo; NOBE; OBEV; TrCP; TrGrPo; WGRP

O world! O life! O time! Lament, A: "O world! O life! O time!" Shelley. ChTr; EnRP; GTBS; GTBS-P; NAEL-2; NOBE; PoRA; TEP; TrGrPo

O world, thou choosest not the better part! George Santayana. *Fr.* Sonnets. AnAmPo; TrGrPo

(Faith.) WGRP

O world, thy slippery turns! Friends now fast sworn. Shakespeare. *Fr.* Coriolanus. OBF

O worthi noble kyng, Henry the ferthe. John Gower. *Fr.* Address to the King, An. FaBoEH

O would I were where I would be! Suspiria. *Unknown.* OBEV

O wretch! hath madness cured thy dire despair? On Seeing an Officer's Widow Distracted. Mary Barber. ECWP; NOEC

O wretched offspring! O unhappy state. Death the Consequence of the Fall. Dryden. *Fr.* State of Innocence, The. NOCV

O ye, all ye that walk in Willowwood. Willowwood ("O ye, all ye that walk in Willowwood.") Dante Gabriel Rossetti. *Fr.* House of Life, The. NAEL-2; OAEL-2

O ye that put your trust and confidence. A Rueful Lamentation on the Death of Queen Elizabeth. Sir Thomas More. AAS; FaBoRV; LiTB

(Lamentation of Queen Elizabeth, A.) NoSic

O Ye That Would Swallow the Needy. Bible, *O.T. Fr.* Amos. TrJP

O Ye Tongues, *sels.* Anne Sexton. NALW

Third Psalm. NALW

O [or A or Oh] ye wha are sae guid yoursel. Address to the Unco Guid, or the Rigidly Righteous. Burns. ChIV-1; EnRP; NOBE; NOCV; NoP; OxBS; TrGrPo

O ye who tread the Narrow Way. Buddha at Kamakura. Francis Hastings Kipling. OBTV

O ye wretched Scots. John Skelton. *Fr.* How the Doughty Duke of Albany like a Coward Knight Ran Away Shamefully. OBSV

O Year, grow slowly. Exquisite, holy. Slow Spring. Katharine Tynan. BoTP

O years! and age! farewell. Eternity. Robert Herrick. OBD, *tr. by* Clarence Brown *and* W. S. Merwin

O yee, whome lorde of lande and waters wyde. Seneca, *tr. by* Jasper Heywood. *Fr.* Thyestes. OBVE

O yes, I love you, and with all my heart. Individuality. Ella Wheeler Wilcox. AmWP

O yes, I love you, book of my confessions. Water under the Earth. Robert Bly. NNaP

O yes, O yes! if any maid. Cupid's Indictment. John Lyly. *Fr.* Galathea. EIL

O yes, we've seen your girl friend, haven't we? Six Said by the Concubines to Him. Ammuvanar, *tr. fr. Tamil by* A. K. Ramanujan. PLW

O yes — you understand, I say. Hilda Doolittle ("H. D."). *Fr.* Tribute to the Angels. NALW

O yesterday the cutting edge drank thirstily and deep. To-morrow. John Masefield. MoBrPo; OtMeF; TrGrPo

O [*or* Oh], yet we trust that somehow good. Tennyson. *See* Oh yet we trust that somehow good.

O Yonge fresshe folks, he or she. The Love Unfeigned. Chaucer. OBEV

O you,/ Who came upon me once. Carrefour. Amy Lowell. BoWoP

O You among Women. F. R. Higgins. BIrV

O you are a rajah in your rage. Courage for the Pusillanimous. Paul Roche. GoYe

O you chorus of indolent reviewers. Hendecasyllabics. Tennyson. EBEV; FaBoCo; NOBL; PeLV

O you gods, think I, what need we have any friends. Shakespeare. *Fr.* Timon of Athens. OBF

O you hollow-cheeked offspring. Baboon. *Zulu Oral Tradition, tr. by* C. and W. Leslav. WTO

O you lovers that are so gentle, step occasionally. Rainer Maria Rilke, *tr. by* Robert Bly. *Fr.* Sonnets to Orpheus. RaBo

O you not only worshipful but dear. Credo. Zona Gale. TrPWD

O, you plant the pain in my heart with your wistful eyes. An Irish Love Song. John Todhunter. IIP

O you so long dead. To My Brother. Louise Bogan. AiP; NYBP

O you that strike will never flinch. Secret. Mary Jenness. ShDr

O you who come to me — alas! Laieikawai's Lament after Her Husband's Death. *Unknown, tr. fr. Hawaiian by* M. W. Beckwith. WTO

O you would clothe me in silken frocks. The Wild Goat. Claude McKay. CDC

O you, you wear flowers of gold. What She Said to Her Girl Friend ("O you, you wear flowers of gold.") Kapilar, *tr. fr. Tamil by* A. K. Ramanujan. PLW

O young Mariner. Merlin and the Gleam. Tennyson. FHYEP; NTP; OAEL-2

O younge [*or* yonge] fres[s]he folkes, he or she. Love Unfeigned. Chaucer. *Fr.* Troilus and Criseyde [*or* Criseide]. EnVB; NOBE; OBEV

O youngest, best-loved daughter of Hsieh. Yüan Chen, *tr. fr. Chinese by* Witter Bynner. IMW

"O your hair," he said. What She Said (" 'O your hair,' he said.") Kapilar, *tr. fr. Tamil by* A. K. Ramanujan. PLW

O, you're braw wi' your pearls and your diamonds. Lassie, What Mair Wad You Hae? Heine, *tr. fr. German into Scottish by* Alexander Gray. OxBS

O yr facing reality now. Broken Back Blues. Robert Creeley. Jaz

O zummer clote! when the brook's a-glidèn [*or* a-sliden]. The Clote (Water-Lily.) William Barnes. ELP; FaBoVe; PoEL-4

O' zummer night, as day did gleam. The Lost Little Sister. William Barnes. PoEL-4

Oa! hoy! awe! ba! mey! Canedolia. Edwin Morgan. FaBoCo

Oak, The. Dryden. OHIP

Oak, The. Tennyson. FaPON; PFP

Oak and Lily. Ben Jonson. *See* It Is Not Growing Like a Tree.

Oak and the Ash, The. *Unknown.* FaBoCh
(Fair Country Maid, The.) OBET

Oak and the Olive, The. George Barker. FaBoMo; OBTV

Oak Chrome. Iain Sinclair. VaA

Oak Inns Creak in Their Joints as Light Declines, The. Derek Walcott. NoAM

Oak is called the king of trees, The. Trees. Sara Coleridge. BoTP; OHIP; OxBChV

Oak now resembles which lightning hath blasted, The. (*LL*) Chloris and Hilas. Made to a Saraban. Edmund Waller. SeCV-1

Oak toad and the red-spotted toad love their love. The Power of Toads. Pattiann Rogers. NAmP90

Oaken, broken elbow-chair, An. True and Faithful Inventory of the Goods Belonging to Dr. Swift, Vicar of Laracor, A; upon Lending His House to the Bishop of Meath, till His Palace Was Rebuilt. Swift. FaBoUs

Oakey Street Evictions, The. Thomas Armstrong. OBET

Oaks and Squirrels. Anne Porter. ChIV-1

Oaks, how subtle and marine, The. Bearded Oaks. Robert Penn Warren. LiTM; MoAmPo; MoP; NAAL-2; NoAM; NOBA; PoA; PoE; TAP; TwCP

Oaks shone, The. Lightning. Mary Oliver. Poetr

Oaks written across tongues of rose, The. Childhood Lane. Rachel Blake. NWP

Oars fell from our hands, The. The Island. George Woodcock. MoCV

Oasis, light incarnate. (*LL*) "A World without Objects Is a Sensible Emptiness." Richard Wilbur. LiTM; MoAmPo; MoP; NAAL-2; NoAM; NOBA; PoA

Oasis Motel, The. William Olsen. NAmP90

Oasis of Sidi Khaled, The. Wilfrid Scawen Blunt. OBTV

Oath, The. Allen Tate. FaBoMo; LiTM; OxBA; VGW

Oath of Friendship. *Unknown, tr. fr. Chinese.* ArLo, *tr. by* Arthur Waley; OBF; TTTS, *tr. by* Arthur Waley

Oath of the Canting Crew, The. *Unknown.* CBNP

Oatmeal was in their blood and in their names. The Gathering. E. J. Pratt. *Fr.* Towards the Last Spike. MoCV

Ob all de subjects I kin read. Men Folks ob Today, De. Maggie Pogue Johnson. CBWP-4

Obatala, the Creator. *Yoruba Oral Tradition, tr. by* Ulli Beier. WTO

Obeah Night. Jean Rhys. PBCV

Obedience. George Herbert. ESCV; GeHe

Obedience. George Macdonald. BLRP; WGRP

Obedience of the Corpse. C. D. Wright. LCAP; MT

Obelisk Inscriptions., *sels.* Hatshepsut, *tr. fr. Egyptian by* Mariam Lichtheim.
"Now my heart turns to and fro." WPOW

Obermann Once More, *sels.* Matthew Arnold.
East, The. OtMeF

Obermann Once More. Matthew Arnold. PoEL-5

Oberon and Titania to the Fairy Train. Shakespeare. *See* Through the House.

Oberon, the Fairy Prince, *sels.* Ben Jonson.
Buz[z], Quoth the Blue Fly. CBNP; TEP
(Buzz, quoth the blue fly, *sl. diff. vers.*) OxNR
(Catch, A.) EIL
(Satyrs' Catch, The.) FaBoNo; FM

Oberon's Feast. Robert Herrick. BeJo; CaPo; CBCK; NOSC; SeCV-1; TrGrPo

Obese man with a goiter, The. The Flood. Dara Wier. NAmP90

Obit. Robert Lowell. HCAP; VCAP

Obit on Parnassus. F. Scott Fitzgerald. NBLV; NYBP; PrIm

Obituary. Conrad Aiken. OBAL

Obituary. Anthony Brode. FiBHP

Obituary. Steve Chimombo. HBAPE

Obituary. Kenneth Fearing. VGW

Object, The. Alma Villanueva. SRLS

Object among dreams, you sit here with your shoes off, An. A Girl in a Library. Randall Jarrell. NAAL-2; NoAM; NOBA; NoP

Objection to Being Stepped On, The. Robert Frost. NBLV

Objects. Richard Wilbur. FF; NoP

Objects in Mirror are Closer than They Appear. Jeffrey Skinner. PBCAP

Objets d'Art. Cynthia MacDonald. NMM

Oblique light on the trite, on brick and tile. Courtyards in Delft. Derek Mahon. CIP; PBCIP; PNI; SCBI

Obliterate/ mythology as you unwind. The Cavern. Charles Tomlinson. CMoP

Oblivion. Jessie Redmond Fauset, *fr. the French of* Massillon Coicou. NegPo; PoNe

Oblivion. Ellis Ayitey Komey. PBA

Oblivion! Skin. Nelly Sachs, *tr. fr. German by* Michael Roloff. PBWP

Oblivion — the shroud and envelope of happiness. (*LL*) Oblivion. Jessie Redmond Fauset, *fr. the French of* Massillon Coicou. NegPo; PoNe

Oboe. Laurence McKinney. NBLV

Obon: Festival of the Dead. Mitsuye Yamada. LoHo

O'Bruadair. David O'Bruadair, *tr. fr. Irish by* James Stephens. BIrV

Obscene Caller, The. Philip Dacey. AmPA

Obscure, The. Norman Dubie. NoAM

Obscure Night of the Soul, The. St. John of the Cross, *tr. by* Arthur Symons. AWP; OBMV

Obscure Night of the Soul, The. St. John of the Cross. *See* Once in the dark of night.

Obscured Prince; or, The Black Box Boxed, The. *Unknown.* APAS

Obscurely yet most surely called to praise. Praise in Summer. Richard Wilbur. CAPP; FoLa; NoP

Obscurest night involved [*or* involv'd] the sky. The Castaway. William Cowper. ELP; EnRP; NAEL-1; NOBE; NOEC; NoP; OAEL-1; PoE; PoEL-3; PPP; TRP

Obscurity has its tale to tell. Focus. Adrienne Rich. FaBoWP

Obsequies of Stuart. John Randolph Thompson. PAH

Obsequy for Dylan Thomas. James K. Baxter. PeLV

Observant of the way she told. Tact. E. A. Robinson. NoAM

Observation. William Hart-Smith. FaBoMA; FaBoUs

Observation. Robert Herrick. ChIV-2; FaBoUs

Observation. Dorothy Parker. *Fr.* Some Beautiful Letters. FiBHP

Observation Car. A. D. Hope. MoP; NoAM

Observation Car and Cigar. William Stafford. LCAP

Observation of a Bee. Leah Goldberg, *tr. fr. Hebrew by* Stephen Mitchell. WPOW

Observations. Hilaire Kirkland. PeNZ
Sels.
"Arranged on the opposite porch is a male."
"Daily the neighbour's dog is withdrawn to the park."
"Turn again, maiden, twice slain and rotten."

Observations in a Cornish Teashop. Kenneth Rexroth. OBAL

Observations of the Life of Epictetus. Elizabeth Tipper. *Fr.* Pilgrim's Viaticum; or, The Destitute, But Not Forlorn. KTR

Observe how he negotiates his way. Swimmer. Robert Francis. WeW

Observe! I turn the key in this new door. After the Blitz, 1941. J. R. Ackerley. PeHV

Observe the Cat upon this page. The Cat. Oliver Herford. FaBV

Observe the daily circle of the sun. Virgil, *tr. by* Dryden. *Fr.* Georgics. FaBoUs

Observe the weary birds ere night be done. Orinda to Lucasia. Katherine Philips. NOSC; PeHV

Observe the young and tender frond. Conversation in the Bush. A. R. D. Fairburn. *Fr.* Album Leaves. PeNZ

Observe these pirates bold and gay. On the Dangers Attending Altruism on the High Seas. G. K. Chesteron. FaBoNo

Obsessed by betrayal. Palm Leaf of Mary Magdalene. Cheryl Clarke. GLP

Obsession. Léon Damas, *tr. fr. French by* Ellen Conroy Kennedy. NegPo

Obsessions. Denise Levertov. LiTM; SM

Obsessive. Marvin Bell. *Fr.* Escape into You, The. SM

Obsidian Butterfly. Octavio Paz, *tr. fr. Spanish by* Eliot Weinberger. AnRep

Obsidian Mountain, The. John Harkness. UnDi

Obtuse Angle, Scopprell, Aradobo, and Tilly Lally. In Obtuse Angle's Study. Blake. *Fr.* Island in the Moon, An. FaBoNo

Obvious, The. (*LL*) Jazz Dancer. Cornelius Eady. UTF

Obvious is difficult, The. The White Room. Charles Simic. BAP-89

Occam's Razor Starts in Massachusetts. Edward Pygge. BXAP

Occasional Poem. A. E. Housman. *See* When Adam Day by Day.

Occasional Poem, A. Lu Yu, *tr. fr. Chinese by* Chiang Yee. SuSp

Occasional Poem, An. Ssu-k'ung Shu, *tr. fr. Chinese by* Irving Y. Lo. SuSp

Occasional Poem ("Ancient annals strewn left and right.") Han Yü, *tr. fr. Chinese by* Charles Hartman. SuSp

Occasional Verse. Wang Ts'an, *tr. fr. Chinese by* Ronald C. Miao. SuSp

Occasional Verses. Marilyn Hacker. Son

Occasional Yarrow, The. Stevie Smith. FaBoNo

Occasioned by General Washington's Arrival in Philadelphia, on His Way to His Residence in Virginia. Philip Freneau. PAH

Occasioned by Seeing a Walk of Bay Trees. Mildmay Fane, 2d Earl of Westmorland. BeJo; NOSC; OxBSP

Occasional Poem: Upon Seeing Lotuses Bloom in a Vase. Wang Shih-chieng, *tr. fr. Chinese by* Richard John Lynn. SuSp

Occupation: Housewife. Phyllis McGinley. *Fr.* I Know a Village. WPE

Occupations of Hell. Milton. *Fr.* Paradise Lost. EPCY; NOSC

Ocean, The. Bible, O.T., *paraphrased by* Sir Thomas Wyatt. *See* They That Go Down to the Sea.

Ocean, The. Byron. *See* There is a pleasure in the pathless woods.

Ocean, The. Louis Dudek. *Fr.* Provincetown. MoCV

Ocean, The. Moschus, *tr. fr. Greek by* Shelley. AWP; OBVE

Ocean-Fight, The. *Unknown.* PAH

Ocean has not been so quiet for a long while, The. Evening Ebb. Robinson Jeffers. NoAM

Ocean is a strange, The. Laura St. Martin. FF

Ocean Is like a Wreath, The. Kuapakaa, *tr. fr. Hawaiian.* WTO

Ocean Musing, An. H. Cordelia Ray. CBWP-3

Ocean of Light. Phineas Fletcher. NOSC

Ocean to Cynthia, The. Sir Walter Ralegh. *See* Sufficeth it to you [*or* yow] my joys [*or* joyes] interred.

Ocean too has winter-views serene, The. Winter Views Serene. George Crabbe. *Fr.* Borough, The. OBNC

Oceana and Britannia. John Ayloffe. APAS

Oceans. Juan Ramón Jiménez, *tr. by* Robert Bly. NU

Ocean's Love to Cynthia, The, *sels.* Sir Walter Ralegh.
"My day's delight[s], my springtime joys for[e]done." SiPSBD
(Poem Entreating of Sorrow, A.) SiPS

"Sufficeth it to you [*or* yow] my joys [*or* joyes] interred." SiPS, *sl. abr.*
(VIth and Last Book of the Ocean to Cynthia.) SiPSBD
(Ocean to Cynthia, The.) NoSic

Och hey! for the splendour of tartans! The Return. Pittendrigh Macgillivray. OxBS

Och hon for somebody! Somebody. *Unknown.* OxBS

Och, Johnny, I hardly knew ye!' (*LL*) Johnny, I Hardly Knew Ye. *Unknown.* BIrV; ELP; FaBoBa; GBP; IIP; OxBoLi; WoWa

Och! what will [*or* shall] we do for linen? What Will We Do for Linen? *Unknown.* GBP; WTO

Oche Iron. Peter Blue Cloud. HATNAP

Ock Gurney and old Pete were there. John Masefield. *Fr.* Reynard the Fox. CMoP

October. Mary Weston Fordham. CBWP-2

October. Robert Frost. GoJo

October. Rachel Hadas. UnDi

October. Rodney Hall. *Fr.* Black Bagatelles. CBAP

October. Patrick Kavanagh. CIP; GTBS-P

October. Denise Levertov. TRP

October. Audre Lorde. SRLS

October. William Morris. *Fr.* Earthly Paradise, The. EnVR; OBNC

October. Isabel Neill. ShDr

October. Greg Pape. AmPA

October. H. Cordelia Ray. CBWP-3

October. Christina Rossetti. BoTP

October. James Schuyler. ArNa

October. Barry Spacks. PoA; SM

October. Spenser. *Fr.* Shepheardes [*or* Shepeards *or* Shepherd's] Calender, The. NAEL-1; OAEL-1

October. Spenser. *Fr.* Shepherd's Garden, The.

October. Edward Thomas. NoAM

October. John Updike. PDV

October. S. W. Whitman. BoTP

October. Charles Wright. MT

October and November. Robert Lowell. MAT

October: and the fires go out along the coast. October. Rodney Hall. *Fr.* Black Bagatelles. CBAP

October at last has come! The thicket has shaken. Autumn. Pushkin, *tr. fr. Russian by* Max Eastman. AWP

October Cycle. John Peck, *tr. fr. Italian.* AnAn

October 1803. Wordsworth. EnRP

October Elegy. Margaret Gibson. FYAP

October 1. Karl Shapiro. MoAB; MoAmPo; PoA

October gave a party. October's Party. George Cooper. BoTP; PoLF

October in the Country: [1983]. James Simmons. BiHa; CIP

October is a piper. Autumn Song. Margaret Rose. BoTP

October Is Here. Mrs. Henry Linden. CBWP-4

October Journey. Margaret Walker. PoBA; PoNe

October Magic. Myra Cohn Livingston. PDV

October 1936. Milly Harris. FaBoEH

October Redbreast, The. Alice Meynell. MoBrPo

October Robin, An. Ted Hughes. NTP

October robin kept, An. An October Robin. Ted Hughes. NTP

October 16: The Raid. Langston Hughes. PoBA

October. They decide it is time to move. Sestina for the House. Ronald Wallace. PBCAP

October Thursdays. Circle of pale men. October. Rachel Hadas. UnDi

October turned my maple's leaves to gold. Maple Leaves. Thomas Bailey Aldrich. GN

October 21st, 9 P.M. (Autumn She Don't Waste no Time!). Carmen Tafolla. ETG

October XXIX, 1795. William Stanley Braithwaite. CDC

October's Bright Blue Weather. Helen Hunt Jackson. BLPA; BLPL; FaBoBe; GN

October's bright blue weather. (*LL*) October's Bright Blue Weather. Helen Hunt Jackson. BLPA; BLPL; FaBoBe; GN

October's gold is dim — the forests rot. David Gray. OxAEP-2

October's Party. George Cooper. BoTP; PoLF

Octopus. Arthur Clement Hilton. BXAP; FaBoCo; FaBoPa; UV

Octopus, The. James Merrill. CAPP; CoAP

Octopus, The. Ogden Nash. RB

Octopus. Valerie Worth. OBAP

Octopussycat, The. Kenyon Cox. FaPON

Octoroon, The, *sels.* Albery Allson Whitman.
"Before the world, I hold that none of these." AAP
"But, "if a man die, shall he live again?" AAP
"If it be shame to love a pretty woman." AAP
"Let scoffers mock, let unbelief deny." AAP

"Mind knows no death. Life is the "first and last." AAP

"These creatures of the languid Orient." AAP

"When genial Spring first bears the mating thrush." AAP

Octoroon eating a macaroon, An. Whalefeathers. Paul Violi. UL

'Od, lassie, what mair wad you hae? (*LL*) Lassie, What Mair Wad You Hae? Heine. OxBS

Odcomb's Complaint., *sels.* John Taylor.
  "O for a rope of Onions from Saint Omers." CBNP
  "Sweet semi-circled Cynthia played at maw." EIL
  (Mockado, Fustian, and Motley.) FaBoNo
  (Sonnet in Praise of Mr. Thomas the Deceased.) CBNP

Odd but True. *Unknown.* FaBoCo

Odd Conceit, An. Nicholas Breton. EIL

Odd day, An. For the first time in years. The View from a Cab. Henry Taylor. NBLV

Odd rot it what a shame it is. To Miss B. John Clare. NOBVV

Odd silence, An/ Falls as we enter. Dreams of Water. Donald Justice. LCAP; NYBP

Odd way you comb your hair, The. Lady in a Distant Face. James Welch. AmPA

"Odds and sods," cried the empty hod. The Building Site. Gwyneth Lewis. NWP

Ode: "Absence, Hear Thou My Protestation." *At.* to John Hoskyns, *sometimes at.* to John Donne. *See* Absence, hear thou my [*or* heare my] protestation.

Ode: Against War. John Scott of Amwell. *See* I hate that drum's discordant sound.

Ode: "Ah poor Olinda never boast." Elizabeth Taylor. KTR

Ode, An: "As it fell upon a day." Richard Barnfield. *See* As it fell upon a day.

Ode: "At her fair hands how have I grace entreated." Walter Davison. *See* At Her Fair Hands.

Ode: Autumn. Thomas Hood. *See* I saw old Autumn in the misty morn.

Ode: "Bards of passion and of mirth." Keats. EnRP; OBEV
  (Ode on the Poets.) GTBS; GTBS-P
  (Ode.) FHYEP; OxAEP-2

Ode: Dying Christian to His Soul, The. Pope, *par. fr. the Latin of* Emperor Hadrian. *See* Vital spark of heavenly flame!

Ode: First of April, The, *sels.* Thomas Warton the Younger.

Ode: "God save the Rights of Man!" Philip Freneau. GOA

Ode: "Grandma stuffed her fur coat . . . ." Philip Schultz. NAmP90

Ode: Hastening His Friend into the Country. Eldred Revett. NOSC

Ode: "How sleep the brave, who sink to rest." William Collins. *See* How sleep the brave who sink to rest.

Ode: "I hate that drum's discordant sound." John Scott of Amwell. NIP; NOEC; OxAEP-1
  (Drum, The.) PAW; PeFWW
  (Ode: Against War.) ECEV

Ode: "I sing a song of sixpence, and of rye." Anthony C. Deane. NOBL

Ode: "Idea of justice may be precious, An." Frank O'Hara. NeAP

Ode: "I'm going to write a novel, hey." John Updike. FiBHP

Ode: Intimations of Immortality from Recollections of Early Childhood. Wordsworth. AWP; BLPL; EnRP; FaBoRV; FHYEP; HAP; HeIP; InvP; LiTB; MeMBP; NAs; NOBE; NoP; OAEL-2; OBEV; OBNC; PoE; PoEL-4; PPP; PrIm; TEP; TrGrPo
  Sels.
  "O gallant brothers of the generous South." FaBoBe
  "Now, while the birds thus sing a joyous song." Prf
  "O joy! that in our embers." Prf
  "Our birth is but a sleep and a forgetting." WGRP
  (Intimations of Immortality.) ChTr
  (Our Birth Is But a Sleep.) FaBV
  "There was a time when meadow, grove and stream." HeIL; ImPo; NAEL-2; SCGP; TFi; TOF; TRP
  "There was a time when meadow, grove, and stream." FaPoB

Ode: "Merchant, to secure his treasure, The." Matthew Prior. AWP; EnLoPo; GTBS; GTBS-P; NOEC; NoP; PoRA
  (Song: "Merchant, to secure his treasure, The.") OBEV; TrGrPo

Ode: "Midnight moonlight mobbed Dante's bridge." Bill Berkson. UL

Ode: "Mistah Berrybones, you daid?" William Zaranka. BXAP

Ode: "Now each creature joys the other." Samuel Daniel. EIL; NoSic

Ode: "Now I find thy looks were feigned." Thomas Lodge. *Fr.* Phyllis. EIL; EnRePo

Ode XV: "O Lord, thou seest my wrongs abound." Thomas Stanley. ChIV-1

Ode: "O tenderly the haughty day." Emerson. GN

Ode: Of Wit. Abraham Cowley. BeJo; MeLP; NAEL-1; NOSC; OAEL-1; SeCP; SeCV-1

Ode: On First Looking into Chapman's Homer. Keats. *See* Much have I travell'd [*or* travelled *or* traveled] in the realms of gold.

Ode: Rule, Brittania! James Thomson *and* David Mallet. *See* When Britain first, at heaven's command.

Ode: Salute to the French Negro Poets. Frank O'Hara. GLP; NeAP; NNaP; PoM; PoNe

Ode: "Sleep sweetly in your humble graves." Henry Timrod. GOA; NOBA; OxBA; TAP
  (At Magnolia Cemetery.) AnAmPo
  (Ode: "Sleep sweetly . . . .") GOA; NOBA; OxBA; TAP
  (Sleep Sweetly.) AH

Ode: "Spacious firmament on high, The." Joseph Addison. BLPA; ChIV-1; ECEV; ELP; FaBoBe; FaPoR; GN; NOCV; NOEC; PoEL-3; TOF

Ode: Spirit Wooed, The. Richard Watson Dixon. OBNC

Ode: "That I have often been in love, deep love." "Peter Pindar." NOEC

Ode: "They journeyed,/ When the darkness of night." Ibn al-Arabi, *tr. fr. Arabic by* R. A. Nicholson. AWP

Ode: To Miss Margaret Pulteney. Ambrose Philips. OxAEP-1; Poetr; UV

Ode: To My Lovers. Paul Verlaine, *tr. fr. French by* J. Murat *and* W. Gunn. PeHV

Ode: To My Pupils. W. H. Auden. MoBrPo

Ode: "To orisons, the midnight bell." William Beckford. OBTV

Ode: "To read our few poets." Hugh Maxton. PBCIP

Ode: To the Cuckoo. Michael Bruce, *rev. by* John Logan. *See* Hail, beauteous stranger of the grove [*or* wood]!

Ode: "Trees have their doubts but we have ours." Paul Evans. NBrP

Ode: "Until thine hands clasp girdlewise the waist of the Belov'd." Sadi, *tr. fr. Persian by* R. A. Nicholson. AWP

Ode: "Weep, ah weep love's losing, love's with its dwelling place." Imr el Kais, *tr. fr. Arabic by* Lady Anne Blunt *and* Wilfrid Scawen Blunt. *Fr.* Mu'allaqat, The. AWP; TAL

Ode: "Who can support the anguish of love?" Ibn al-Arabi, *tr. fr. Arabic by* R. A. Nicholson. AWP

Ode: "Why doth heaven bear a sun." Barnabe Barnes. *Fr.* Parthenophil and Parthenophe. EIL

Ode: "Why will they never sleep." John Peale Bishop. LiTA; LiTM

Ode: Written after Reading Some Modern Love-Verses. John Scott of Amwell. ECEV

Ode: "You brave heroic [*or* heroique] minds." Michael Drayton. AiP, *sl. abr.*; EnRePo; FaBoEH, *sl. abr.*; HAP; NAEL-1; NOBE; NOSC; OBEV; PAH; PoEL-2; SCGP, *sl. abr.*; TEP

Ode after Easter, An. Francis Thompson. *Fr.* Night of Forebeing, The. OtMeF

Ode against St. Cecilia's Day. George Barker. PoA

Ode and elegy and sonnet. (*LL*) Lines on Thomas Warton's Poems *or* Lines in Ridicule of Certain Poems Published in 1777. Samuel Johnson. EPCY; FaBoCo; FaBoEE

Ode Composed in Sleep, An. Judith Madan. ECWP

Ode for a Social Meeting. Oliver Wendell Holmes. OBAL

Ode for Ben Jonson, An. Robert Herrick. AWP; BeJo; EPCY; InvP; OBF; SCGP; SeCP; TrGrPo

Ode for Decoration Day. Henry Peterson. OHIP
  Sels.
  "O gallant brothers of the generous South." FaBoBe

Ode for Him, An. Robert Herrick. *See* Ah, Ben!/ Say how, or when.

Ode for Soft Voice. Michael McClure. NeAP

Ode for the American Dead in Asia. Thomas McGrath. *See* God love you now, if no one else will ever.

Ode for the American Dead in Korea. Thomas McGrath. VGW

Ode for the Burial of a Citizen. John Ciardi. LiTM

Ode for the New Year, An. *At.* to John Gay. OxBoLi

Ode for Three Koras and Balaphong, *sels.* Léopold Sédar Senghor, *tr. fr. French by* Ellen Conroy Kennedy.
  "After this day's hope — see how the Somme, the Seine, and the wild Slav." NegPo

Ode Humbly Inscrib'd to the Queen, A, *sels.* Matthew Prior.
  "But, Greatest *Anna*! while Thy Arms pursue." FaBoEH

Ode in May. Sir William Watson. OBEV; WGRP

Ode in Memory of the American Volunteers Fallen for France. Alan Seeger. PAH

Ode in 1,000 Lines, *sels.* Takahashi Mutsuo, *tr. fr. Japanese by* Hiroaki Sato.

Ode in Time of Hesitation, An. William Vaughn Moody. AnAmPo; OxBA; PAH

Ode Inscribed to W. H. Channing. Emerson. AmPP; HAP; MeMAP; NAAL-1; NOBA; NoP; OxBA; TAP

Ode Occasioned by the Death of Mr. Thomson. William Collins. EPCY; NOEC; PoE

Ode of Signs, *sels.* Muhammad Abd al-Hayy, *tr. fr. Arabic by* Matthew Sorenson *and* Alistair Elliot.

Ode of the Birth of Our Saviour, An, *sels.* Robert Herrick.

Ode to Psyche. Keats. EnRP; FHYEP; InPS; LiTB; MeMBP; NAEL-2; NOBE; NoP; OAEL-2; OBEV; OBNC; OxAEP-2; PFP; PoE; PoEL-4; PPP; TFi; TOF

Ode to Rhys ap Maredudd of Tywyn. Dafydd Nanmor, *tr. fr. Welsh by* H. Idris Bell. OBWVE

Ode to Salt. Pablo Neruda, *tr. fr. Spanish by* Robert Bly. NU

Ode to Sappho. Elizabeth Oakes Smith. AmWP

Ode to Simplicity. William Collins. EnRP; NOBE; OBEV; OxAEP-1; TEP

Ode to Society, An. Hester Lynch Thrale. ECWP

Ode to Spring. Anna Laetitia Barbauld. OxAEP-1

Ode to Spring in the Metropolis, An. Sir Owen Seaman. FiBHP

Ode to Stephen Dowling Bots, Dec'd. "Mark Twain." *See* And did young Stephen sicken.

Ode to Suburbia. Eavan Boland. PBCIP

Ode to Swansea. Vernon Watkins. OBWVE

Ode to Tennis. Paul Evans. NBrP

Ode to Terminus. W. H. Auden. HAP

Ode to the Cameleopard. Thomas Hood. FaBoNo

Ode to the Confederate Dead. Allen Tate. AiP; FaBoMo; HeIP; LiTA; LiTM; MoAB; MoAmPo; MoP; NAAL-2; NoAM; NOBA; NoP; OBD, *ll.* 1–9; OBWP; OxBA; PrIm; TAP; TFi; UnPO

Ode to the Departing Year. Samuel Taylor Coleridge. EnRP

Ode to the Diencephalon. W. H. Auden. OxAEP-2

Ode to the End of Summer. Phyllis McGinley. NBLV

Ode to the Evening Star. Mark Akenside.

Ode to the Framers of the Frame Bill, An. Byron. CoMu

Ode to the German Drama. *Unknown.* NOEC

Ode to the Gowdspink. Robert Fergusson. ScCV

Ode to the Human Heart. Edward Laman Blanchard. NOBL

Ode to the Inhabitants of Pennsylvania. Longfellow. PAH

Ode to the Lake of Geneva. William Parsons. OBTV

Ode to the Last Pot of Marmalade. "John." OBTV

Ode to the Maguire. Eochadh O'Hussey. *See* Where is my Chief, my Master, this bleak night, *mavrone!*

Ode to the Medieval Poets. W. H. Auden. PoA

Ode to the Northeast Wind. Charles Kingsley. FaPoR; GN; OxAEP-2; PlP

Ode to the Pious Memory of the Accomplished Young Lady, Mrs. Anne Killigrew. Dryden. *See* Thou youngest virgin-daughter of the skies.

Ode to the Poppy. Henrietta Oneil. ECWP; WPE

Ode to the Protestant Poets. Paul Hoover. UL

Ode to the Sea. Howard Baker. OxBA

Ode to the Setting Sun, *sels.* Francis Thompson.
"Now that the red glare of thy fall is blown." OBNC
Sun, The. MoAB; MoBrPo

Ode to the Spirit of Earth in Autumn. George Meredith. TEP

Ode to the Sun. Eloise Bibb. CBWP-4

Ode to the Watermelon. Pablo Neruda, *tr. fr. Spanish by* Robert Bly. NU

Ode to the West Wind. Shelley. AWP; BoNaP; CH; ClHu; EBEV; EnRP; FaBoBe; FaBV; FHYEP; GGP; GTBS; GTBS-P; HAP; HeIL; HeIP; ImPo; InPS; LiTB; MeMBP; NAEL-2; NAWM-2; NIP; NOBE; NoP; OAEL-2; OBEV; OBNC; OxAEP-2; PoE; PoEL-4; Poetr; PoLF; PoRA; PPP; PrIm; SCGP; TEP; TFi; TrGrPo; TRP; WeW

Ode to Tobacco. Charles Stuart Calverley. FaBoCo; FiBHP

Ode to Truth. Mary Whateley. ECWP

Ode to Two Sisters in the Sun. Nellie Wong. SRLS

Ode to Walt Whitman. Federico García Lorca, *tr. fr. Spanish.* PeHV

Ode to Sir William Sydney, on His Birth-Day. Ben Jonson. BeJo; NAs

Ode to Winter. Thomas Campbell. GTBS; GTBS-P

Ode to Wisdom. Elizabeth Carter. ECWP

Ode to Wit. Abraham Cowley. *See* Tell me, O[h] tell, what kind[e] of thing is wit.

Ode to Zion. Judah Halevi, *tr. fr. Hebrew by* Nina Davis Salaman. TrJP

Ode, upon a Question Moved, Whether Love Should Continue Forever? An. Lord Herbert of Cherbury. JCP; MeLP; NOBE; OxAEP-1; SeCP

Ode upon Doctor Harvey. Abraham Cowley. PoEL-2

Ode Which was Prefixed to a Prayer Booke Given to a Young Gentlewoman, An. Richard Crashaw. ESCV

Ode Written during the War with America, 1814, *sels.* Robert Southey.
Bower of Peace, The. PAH

Ode Written in 1746. William Collins. *See* How sleep the brave who sink to rest.

Ode Written in the Beginning of the Year 1746. William Collins. *See* How sleep the brave who sink to rest.

Ode Written in the Peak[e], An. Michael Drayton. FaBoPP; NOSC

Odell. James Stephens. MoAB; MoBrPo

Odes, *sels.* Anacreon.
"Of late, what time the Bear turned round." NoSic

Odes. Hafiz, *tr. fr. Persian.* AWP

Sels.
Bower of Peace, The. PAH
"Comrades, the morning breaks, the sun is up."
"Days of spring are here, The! the eglantine."
"Flower-tinted cheek, the flowery close, A." TAL
"From Canaan Joseph shall return, whose face." TAL
"Grievous folly shames my sixtieth year, A."
"I cease not from desire till my desire." TAL
"I have borne the anguish of love, which ask me not to describe."
"I said to heaven that glowed above."
"Jewel of the secret treasury, The."
"Lady that hast my heart within thy hand."
"Mirth, Spring, to linger in a garden fair." TAL
"Oft have I said, I say it once more."
"Rose has flushed red, the bud has burst, The." TAL
"Rose is not the rose unless thou see, The."
"Saki, for God's love, come and fill my glass."
"What is wrought in the forge of the living and life." TAL
"Where is my ruined life, and where the fame." TAL
"Wind from the east, oh Lapwing of the day." TAL

Odes, *sels.* Horace, *tr. fr. Latin by* Austin Dobson.
"Brasen tower with doors close barred, The." SiPSBD
Carthaginian Peace, The. MLL, *tr. by* Helen Waddell
I, 3. To the Ship on Which Virgil Sailed to Athens ("Sic te diva potens Cyri"). AWP, *tr. by* Dryden
I, 4. Ode: "Hold! pale death, at the poor man's shack and the pasha's palace." OBD, *tr. by* James Michie
I, 5. "What slender youth bedewed with liquid odours" ("Quis multa gracilis"). OBVE, *tr. by* Milton
(Another to the Same.) OAEL-1, *tr. by* William Browne; WiR
(Fifth Ode of Horace, The.) EBEV, *tr. by* Milton; EnLoPo, *tr. by* Milton; PoEL-3, *tr. by* Milton
(Pyrrha, what slender well-shap'd beau.) OBVE, *tr. by* Anthony Horneck
(Say what slim youth, with moist perfumes.) OBVE, *tr. by* Christopher Smart
(Tell me, Pyrrha, what fine youth.) OAEL-1, *tr. by* William Browne; WiR, *tr. by* William Browne
(To a Girl.) WiR, *tr. by* Milton
(To Pyrrha.) AWP, *tr. by* Milton
(To whom now, Pyrrha, art thou kind?) OBVE, *tr. by* Abraham Cowley
(What stripling now thee discomposes.) OBVE, *tr. by* Sir Richard Fanshawe
I, 8. "Lydia, in Heavens Name" ("Lydia, dic, per omnes"). OBVE
I, 9. "Behold yon mountain's hoary height." ("Vides ut alta"). OBVE, *tr. by* Dryden
(To Thaliarchus ("Thou seest the hills").) OBVE, *tr. by* Sir Richard Fanshawe
(You see how, white with snows to the north of us.) STV, *tr. by* John Frederick Nims
I, 11. "Seek not, Leuconöe, to know how long you're going to live yet"
(Ad Leuconoen.) AWP, *tr. by* F. P. Adams
(Don't ask — knowing's taboo — what's in the cards, darling, for you, for me.) STV, *tr. by* John Frederick Nims
I, 14. Ship of State, The ("O navis, referent"). AWP, *tr. by* William Ewart Gladstone
I, 21. To Apollo and Diana ("Dianam tenerae dicite virgines"). OBVE, *tr. by* Branwell Brontë
(Invocation: "Maidens young and virgins tender.") AWP, *tr. by* Louis Untermeyer
I, 22. "Virtue, dear friend, needs no 'defence' " ("Integer vitae"). OBVE, *tr. by* the Earl of Roscommon
(Man in righteousness arrayed, The.) AWP, *tr. by* John Quincy Adams
(To Aristius Fuscus.) OBVE, *tr. by* Samuel Johnson
(To man, my friend, whose conscious heart.) OBVE, *tr. by* Samuel Johnson
(To Sally.) AWP, *tr. by* John Quincy Adams
I, 25. Ribald Romeos Less and Less Berattle ("Parcius iunctas quatiunt fenestras"). MAT, *tr. by* John Frederick Nims; STV, *tr. by* John Frederick Nims
(Bloods and bucks of this lewd town, The.) OBVE, *tr. by* the Young Gentlemen of Mr. Rule's Academy at Islington
(To Lydia.) OBVE, *tr. by* Philip Francis
(Young bloods come round less often now, The.) BoLoP, *tr. by* James Michie
I, 31. By the Flat Cup ("Quid dedicatum"). CTC, *tr. by* Ezra Pound
I, 33. Albi, Ne Doleas. AWP, *tr. by* Austin Dobson
I, 38. Simplicity. InPK; NBLV
(Ah child, no Persian — perfect art.) OBVE, *tr. by* Gerard Manley Hopkins
(Boy, I detest the Persian pomp.) InPK; NBLV
(Chicago Analogue.) NBLV, *tr. by* Keith Preston
(Davus, I detest.) NBLV, *tr. by* Austin Dobson
(Dear Lucy, you know what my wish is.) NBLV, *tr. by* Thackeray

Oedipus. Edwin Muir. CMoP

Oedipus at Colonus., *sels.* Sophocles, *tr. fr. Greek.*
Colonus' Praise. OBVE
"Endure what life God gives and ask no longer span." OBMV
"What man is he that yearneth." AWP

Oedipus said to the Sphinx. Victor Gray. PeLi

Oedipus the King [*or* Oedipus Rex]. (Oh my children, the new blood of ancient Thebes.) Sophocles, *tr. fr. Greek by* Robert Fagles. NAWM-1 *Sels.*
"Oh, may my constant feet not fail." WGRP

Oenone and Paris. George Peele. *See* Fair and Fair.

Oenone's Complaint. George Peele. *Fr.* Arraignment of Paris, The. EIL

O'er a low couch the setting sun had thrown its latest ray. The Baron's Last Banquet. Albert Gorton Greene, *tr. by* Alice C. Fletcher. AnAmPo; BeLS

O'er a small suburban borough. The Domineering Eagle and the Inventive Bratling. Guy Wetmore Carryl. OBAL

O'er all the hill-tops. Goethe, *tr. fr. German. Fr.* Wanderer's Night-Songs. AWP
(Second Poem the Night-Walker Wrote, The.) NU, *tr. by* Robert Bly

O'er Cambridge shot the yeoman's mark. Lexington. Sidney Lanier. *Fr.* Psalm of the West. PAH

O'er Continent and Ocean. John Haynes Holmes. AH

O'er desert plains, and rushy meers. Song. William Shenstone. GGP

O'er English dust. A broken heart lies here. (*LL*) A Jacobite's Epitaph. Macaulay. FaBoEH; FaPoR; NOBE; OBEV; OBNC

O'er golden sands my waters flow. The Enchanted Spring. George Darley. BoNaP

O'er Huron's wave the sun was low. The Battle of Bridgewater. *Unknown.* PAH

O'er me, alas! thou dost to much prevail. The Power of Spleen. The Countess of Winchilsea. *Fr.* Spleen, a Pindaric Poem, The. ECWP

O'er the high and o'er the lowly. Our National Banner. Dexter Smith. PAH

O'er the land of the free, and the home of the brave. (*LL*) The Star-spangled Banner. Francis Scott Key. AiP; AnAmPo; BLPA; EBEvV; FaBoBe; FaPON; PAH; TAP; UV, abr.; WBLP

O'er the level plains, where mountains greet me as I go. Time's Song. Winthrop Mackworth Praed. EnRP

O'er the men of Ethiopia she would pour her cornucopia. Husband and Heathen. Sam Walter Foss. OBAL

O'er the rough main, with flowing sheet. The *Bonhomme Richard* and *Serapis.* Philip Freneau. PAH

O'er the rugged mountain's brow. Harry Graham. *Fr.* Some Ruthless Rhymes.
(Calculating Clara.) PeLV

O'er [*or* O're] the smooth enameled green. Milton. *Fr.* Arcades. OBEV; TrGrPo
(Song: "O'er The smooth enamelled green.") OxBSP

O'er the snow, through the air, to the mountain. Alpine Spirit's Song. Thomas Lovell Beddoes. OBNC; OBTV

O'er the warm kettles, and the savoury streams. In the Kitchen. Mary Leapor. *Fr.* Crumble Hall. ECWP

O'er the warrior gauntlet grim. Parricide. Julia Ward Howe. PAH

O'er the waste of waters cruising. Philip Freneau. PAH

O'er the Water to Charlie. Burns. FaBoCh

O'er the Wild Gannet's Bath. George Darley. *Fr.* Ethelstan. ChTr; PoEL-4

O'er this wide extended country. To the White People of America. Joshua McCarter Simpson. AAP

O'er town and cottage, vale and height. Valley Forge. Thomas Buchanan Read. *Fr.* Wagoner of the Alleghanies, The. PAH

O'er Waiting Harp-Strings of the Mind. Mary Baker Eddy. AH

O'erspread the list'ning choir. (*LL*) The Adventurous Muse. Isaac Watts. NOEC

Of. Debora Greger. EOEF

Of a brazier's daughter who lived near. The Betrayed Maiden. *Unknown.* OBET

Of a brother back to bed. (*LL*) Brother. Mary Ann Hoberman. SiSoPo

Of a Contented Mind. Thomas, Lord Vaux. EIL; EnRePo

Of a Country Life., *sels.* James Thomson.
"How sweet and innocent are country sports." UV

Of a dark dial in a sunless place. (*LL*) The Sea of Death. Thomas Hood. LiTB; OBNC; PoEL-4

Of a day I had rued. (*LL*) Dust of Snow. Robert Frost. CMoP; MoShBr; OxBA; OxBSP; PDV; PrIm; SAmP; SoSe; TAP; UnPo; WeW

Of a demon in my view. (*LL*) From Childhood's Hour. Poe. MeMAP; PoEL-4

Of a Fair Lady Playing with a Snake. Edmund Waller. *See* Strange, that such horror and such grace.

Of a Fair Shrew. Sir John Harington, *after the Latin of* Martial. *See* Fair, Rich, and Young.

Of a Faire Woman: Translated out of Casaneus His Catalogus Gloriae Mundi. Sir John Harington. *Fr.* Epigrams. CBCK

Of a fallen sparrow, the prairie dog first softens. Gnawing the Breast. Sandra McPherson. LCAP

Of a Good Prince and an Evil. Timothy Kendall. NoSic

Of a good universe next door; let's go. (*LL*) Pity This Busy Monster, Manunkind. E. E. Cummings. AmPP; LiTA; LiTM; MeMAP; NAAL-2; NOBA; OxBA; PPP; TAP

Of a green so palely, recessively matched to the forest floor. Fringecups. Sandra McPherson. FoLa

Of a horse shoe nail. (*LL*) For want of a nail. Mother Goose. FaBoBe; OxNR; ReMoGo

Of a hungry devil. (*LL*) I dreamed I held/ A sword against my flesh. Kasa no Iratsume. BoWoP; WPOW

Of a Husbandman. Joshua Sylvester. NOSC

Of a lady fair to see. Lines to Mrs. M. C. Turner. Eloise Bibb. CBWP-4

Of a Lady That Refused to Dance with Him. The Earl of Surrey. *See* Each beast can choose his fere according to his mind.

Of a little love. (*LL*) At a Window. Carl Sandburg. FaBoBe; PoToHe; TrPWD

Of a little take a little. *Unknown.* OxNR

Of a love or a season? (*LL*) Reluctance. Robert Frost. CMoP; MoAB; MoAmPo; NOBA; OxBA

Of a mighty forest oak. (*LL*) The Acorn. *Unknown.* BoTP

Of a mon Matheu thoghte. *Unknown.* MiEL

Of a morning sun. (*LL*) Four Glimpses of Night. Frank Marshall Davis. NoP; PoBA; PoNe

Of a pendulum's mildness, with her feet up. A Timepiece. James Merrill. HoPM

Of a Rose, a Lovely Rose. *Unknown.* OBEV

Of a Spider. Wilfred Thornley. FaPON; PDV

Of a straight society to validate us. (*LL*) Christmas in the Midwest. Maureen Seaton. LoHo

Of a sudden, the great prima donna. *Unknown.* PeLi

Of a tall stature and of sable hue. Charles II. *Unknown.* FaBoEE
(Historical Poem, An.) APAS

Of A' the Airts [the Wind Can Blow]. Burns. AWP; EnRP; NoP; OxBS

Of a' the maids o' fair Scotland. Young Benjie. *Unknown.* ESPB; OxBB

Of a time gone by. (*LL*) The Piteous Maja. Fernando Periquet Y Zuaznabar. RiWo

Of a vanished subsistence, a consummate libation. (*LL*) Burial in the East. Pablo Neruda. TRP

Of a Zealous Lady. Sir John Harington, *after the Latin of* Martial. FaBoEE

Of Adam's first wife, Lilith, it is told. Body's Beauty. Dante Gabriel Rossetti. *Fr.* House of Life, The. OAEL-2; Son; TrGrPo
(Lilith.) PoEL-5

Of aid from them — She was the Universe. (*LL*) Darkness. Byron. EnRP; LiTB; MeMBP; NAEL-2; OAEL-2; OPOP; PoE; PoEL-4; TEP

Of airplane light, embroidering above him, alive. (*LL*) Where We Are. Julia Kasdorf. LoHo

Of al this world ne give ich a pese! (*LL*) All Too Late. *Unknown.* EBEV; OAEL-1

Of al this world ne give ich a pese! (*LL*) When mine eynen misteth. *Unknown.* EBEV

Of all amusements for the mind. Wishing. John Godfrey Saxe. AnAmPo

Of all are living, or have been. (*LL*) Queens. J. M. Synge. ChTr; GBL; MoBrPo; OBMV; PeIV; PeVV

Of all creatures women be best. What Women Are Not. *Unknown.* MeEL; MiEL

Of All Garments. Dhu'l-Rumma, *tr. fr. Arabic by* Omar S. Pound. ArPe

Of all God's jokes none is bluer. A. Cinna. PeLi

Of all interpreters read Nature True. (*LL*) Death's Lecture at the Funeral of a Young Gentleman. Richard Crashaw. SeCP

Of all our bath-house thieves the cleverest one. Catullus, *tr. fr. Latin by* James Michie. PeHV

Of all sad words of tongue or pen. The Saddest Words. Whittier. *Fr.* Maud Muller. ImPo

Of all sins of the flesh, that reprobate. Hangover Mass. X. J. Kennedy. DiPo

Of all that God has shown me. Mechthild von Magdeburg, *tr. fr. German by* Jane Hirshfield. EnIH

Of all that Orient lands can vaunt. The Haschish. Whittier. AnAmPo; OBAL

Of all the actors in this town, I loved Wilkes Booth the best. (*LL*) Booth Killed Lincoln. *Unknown.* AmFP

Of all the birds I know, few can. The Toucan. Pyke Johnson, Jr.. NTCP; ZA

Of course I always knew who you were. I. On First Looking into Raymond Chandler. Linda France. NWP

Of course, I don't know very much. Aunt Chloe's Politics. Frances E. W. Harper. AmWP; NALW

Of course I prayed. Emily Dickinson. BoWoP; MoAmPo

Of course I tried to tell him. Poets Hitchhiking on the Highway. Gregory Corso. NeAP; PoM

Of course, she's only a digestive tube, like all of us. A Dialogue between the Head and Heart. Gavin Ewart. CBLP

Of course, the entire effort is to put myself. Thoughts during an Air Raid. Stephen Spender. MoBrPo

Of course, the familiar rustling of programs. Peripeteia. Anthony Hecht. VCAP

Of course, We Would Wish. Irving Feldman. *Fr.* All of Us Here. VCAP

Of course when someone leaves you forever. Back. Angela McCabe. AmPA

Of course you saw the Villa d'Este Gardens. Villa d'Este Gardens. Siegfried Sassoon. OBTV

Of course Zimmer was late for the gig. The Duke Ellington Dream. Paul Zimmer. Jaz; PBCAP

Of Courtesy. Arthur Guiterman. Spl

Of Courtesy, it is much less. Courtesy. Hilaire Belloc. OtMeF

Of Cupid. Henry Chettle. *See* Trust not his wanton tears.

Of Dancing. Alan Brownjohn. FaBoMo

Of Dandelions & Tourists. Joe Rosenblatt. NOBC

Of danger. (*LL*) Remembering Mexico, 1969. Barbara Lau. LoHo

Of dark habits,/ Keeping their difficult balance. (*LL*) Love Calls Us to the Things of This World. Richard Wilbur. AmPP; CAPP; CMoP; HAP; HeIL; HeIP; InPS; MoAmPo; NIP; NoAM; PoE; Poetr; PoRA; PPP; TAP; TFi; TrGrPo; UnPo; VCAP; VGW

Of De Witt Williams on His Way to Lincoln Cemetery. Gwendolyn Brooks. *Fr.* Street in Bronzeville, A. BlSi; BPo; CAPP; FaBoWP; NMM; NoAM; NOBA

Of Death. The Countess of Pembroke. *Fr.* Antonius. EIL

Of Difference Does It Make. Tom Paulin. BiHa

Of Disdainful Daphne. M. H. Nowell. EIL

Of diverse monsters I have sometimes read. Strange Monsters. Rowland Watkyns. FaBoEE

Of double death can die. (*LL*) At last withdraw your cruelty. Sir Thomas Wyatt. SiPS

Of Dreams and Dreaming. John Ashbery. BAP-91

Of Drunkenness. George Turberville. NBLV; NoP

Of dust the primal Adam came. Kosmos. Julia Ward Howe. AmWP

Of Dying Beauty. Louis Zukofsky. PoA

Of dying is love. (*LL*) Little Sleep's-Head Sprouting Hair in the Moonlight. Galway Kinnell. InPS; LCAP

Of each bruised and heart-/ Shaped petal. (*LL*) The Wild Dog Rose. John Montague. BIrV; CIP; IPY; PBCIP; PoE

Of eager and extravagant anger. (*LL*) The Lovers. W. R. Rodgers. BIrV; OxBSP; PNI

Of Earth. Mae V. Cowdery. ShDr

Of earth-born passion dies. (*LL*) Thou, whose unmeasured temple stands. Bryant. BLRP

Of Earth's first blood, have titles manifold. (*LL*) It Is Not to Be Thought Of [That the Flood]. Wordsworth. EnRP

Of Edenhall the youthful lord. The Luck of Edenhall. Ludwig Uhland, *tr. fr. German by* Longfellow. AWP

Of elephop and telephony!). (*LL*) Eletelephony. Laura E. Richards. FaPON; GoJo; ImGa; MoShBr; NBLV; NTCP; OBCA; OxBChV; PDV; PYC; SiSoPo

Of Elizabeth, frigidly stretched. (*LL*) This Houre Her Vigill. Valentin Iremonger. CIP; NOIV; OxBTC

Of England, and of Its Marvels. Fazio degli Uberti, *tr. fr. Italian by* Dante Gabriel Rossetti. AWP

Of English Verse. Edmund Waller. BeJo; NAEL-1; NOSC; OAEL-1; PoE; SeCP

Of Eternal Love. Josef Wenzig, *tr. fr. German by* Philip L. Miller. RiWo

Of every kinne [*or* everykune] tree, of every kinne [*or* everykune] tree. The Hawthorn. *Unknown.* ChTr; EnVB; GBP; MiEL

Of every vice pursued by those. Gambling. Royall Tyler. TAP

Of feathered fouls, that fan the buxom air. Fashioned After the Manner of Master Geoffrey Chaucer in His Assembly of Fowls. Thomas, the Elder Warton. ChIV-1

Of February, 1918. (*LL*) In the Waiting Room. Elizabeth Bishop. FaBoWP; HeIP; InPS; LCAP; NAAL-2; NALW; NoAM; NOBA; PoE; Prf; VCAP

Of few words, Sir, you seem to be. *Unknown.* SiPS

Of Fiammetta Singing. Boccaccio, *tr. fr. Italian by* Dante Gabriel Rossetti. *Fr.* Sonnets. AWP

Of finite hearts that yearn. (*LL*) Two in the Campagna. Robert Browning. EBEV; EBVV; ELP; EnVR; FHYEP; GTBS-P; MeMBP; NAEL-2; NOBE; NOBVV; NoP; OAEL-2; OBNC; OxAEP-2; OxBM; PFP; PoE; PoEL-5; SCGP; TFi; TOF; TrGrPo

Of Flaxie and Althea. Cheryl Clarke. *See* In 1943 Althea was a welder.

Of flesh. O star of men! (*LL*) A Camp in the Prussian Forest. Randall Jarrell. BTR; CMoP; MoAmPo; OBWP; OxBC; PoWW

Of foam cast up, like spit, upon the shore. (*LL*) When the Tom-Tom Beats. Jacques Roumain. NegPo

Of footsteps over the gravel? (*LL*) Elegy for a Five Year Old. Aidan Carl Mathews. IB

Of Fortune, *abr.* Thomas Kyd. *Fr.* Cornelia. EIL

Of fret, of dark, of thorn, of chill. Opposition. Sidney Lanier. AnAmPo; LiTA

Of gasoline and desert air. (*LL*) At Barstow. Charles Tomlinson. MoP; NoAM; TwCP

Of genius art at home. Once the Sole Province. Douglas Crase. EOEF

Of gift from God. And here's my creed. (*LL*) His Creed. Robert Herrick. BeJo

Of glassy runnels bubbling over rocks. (*LL*) The Dead Eagle. Thomas Campbell. EnRP; OBTV

Of glassy taxidermy, moping on. (*LL*) Walking to Sleep. Richard Wilbur. NYBP; VCAP

Of Glotons and Dronkardes. Alexander Barclay. *Fr.* Ship of Fools, The. OxBLMV

Of God we ask one favor. Emily Dickinson. MeMAP

Of Gods Omnipotencie. Alexander Hume. NOCV

Of God's son. (*LL*) Earth is at the same time, The. Hildegard von Bingen. EaPr

Of gold or gowns my mother had not much. She Would Have Roses. Nicholas Lloyd Ingraham. PWR

Of gold then but now locked in brass. Epitaph: Chryseomallus the Mime. Paulus Silentiarius, *tr. fr. Greek by* Andrew Miller. GrAn

Of Grief, *sels.* May Sarton.
"I did not weep my father." MDDM

Of Growing Old. D. J. Enright. AnAn

Of hacked, beheaded coconuts toward home. (*LL*) Nights in the Gardens of Port of Spain. Derek Walcott. NAEL-2; OxBC

Of heaven, and hope to have it after all. (*LL*) The Argument of His Book. Robert Herrick. AWP; BeJo; CaPo; EBEV; HAP; ImPo; InvP; JCP; NAEL-1; NoP; NOSC; OAEL-1; OxAEP-1; PeECV; PoE; PoEL-3; PoRA; SeCP; SeCV-1; TEP; TFi; TrGrPo; TTTS

Of heaven and let us in. (*LL*) There Is a Green Hill Far Away. Cecil Frances Alexander. BLRP; OxBChV; TIRV; WGRP

Of heaven, and, waking in the darkness, screams. (*LL*) Nerves. Arthur Symons. FaBoTw

Of Heaven Considered as a Tomb. Wallace Stevens. PoA

Of Heaven or Hell I have no power to sing. An Apology. William Morris. *Fr.* Earthly Paradise, The. AWP; EBVV; EnVR; LiTB; NAEL-2; NoP; OAEL-2; OBNC; OPOP
(Prologue.) OtMeF

Of Her Justice. Sir John Davies. *Fr.* Hymns of Astræa [in Acrostic Verse]. SiPSBD

Of Her Magnanimity. Sir John Davies. *Fr.* Hymns of Astræa [in Acrostic Verse]. SiPSBD

Of Her Memory. Sir John Davies. *Fr.* Hymns of Astræa [in Acrostic Verse]. SiPSBD

Of Her Mind. Sir John Davies. *Fr.* Hymns of Astræa [in Acrostic Verse]. SiPSBD

Of Her Moderation. Sir John Davies. *Fr.* Hymns of Astræa [in Acrostic Verse]. SiPSBD

Of her peroration. whereupon she slapped me again. (*LL*) Elizabeth in Italy. Richard Weber. BoLoP

Of her soft armory. (*LL*) The Catch. Richard Wilbur. DiPo; WeW

Of Her Will. Sir John Davies. *Fr.* Hymns of Astræa [in Acrostic Verse]. SiPSBD

Of Her Wisdom. Sir John Davies. *Fr.* Hymns of Astræa [in Acrostic Verse]. SiPSBD

Of Her Wit. Sir John Davies. *Fr.* Hymns of Astræa [in Acrostic Verse]. SiPSBD

Of heroes and statesmen I'll just mention. Paul Jones — a New Song. *Unknown.* PAH

Of him he loved so well. (*LL*) The Burial of Moses. Cecil Frances Alexander. BeLS; BLPA; BLRP; GN; WBLP

Of Himself. Meleager, *tr. fr. Greek by* Richard Garnett. AWP

Of himself to think this: she does not. Lady & Gentleman. Richard Weber. PeIV

Of hireling wolves whose gospel is their maw. (*LL*) To the Lord General Cromwell. Milton. FaBoEH; FaBoPV; IIP; NAEL-1; NoP; NOSC; SCGP; Son; TrGrPo

Of My Dear Son Gervaise. Sir John Beaumont. *See* Can I, who have for others oft compil'd.

Of My Dear Son [*or* Deare Sonne], Gervase Beaumont. Sir John Beaumont. JCP; NOBE; PiP

Of My Dear Son, Gervase Beaumont. Sir John Beaumont. JCP; NOBE *Sels.*

Of His Dear Son, Gervase. OBEV

Of my fond heart, hath made me poor. (*LL*) A Complaint. Wordsworth. NOBE; PoEL-4

Of my great grief the great excess. (*LL*) Farewell, all my welfare. Sir Thomas Wyatt. GBL; SiPS; SiPSBD

Of my husband I do not ask much. *Unknown.* PeLi

Of My Lady Isabella Playing on the Lute. Edmund Waller. HAP

Of my lady, wel me rejoise I may. A Description of His Ugly Lady. Thomas Hoccleve. MeEL

Of my life/ toward home. (*LL*) I Am Singing the Cold Rain. Lance Henson. HATNAP; STP

Of my shoulder and quickly, too quickly, I am gone? (*LL*) Angel Surrounded by Paysans. Wallace Stevens. HCAP; LCAP; PPP

Of my true image. (*LL*) My Dressing Mirror is a Humpbacked Cat. Jung Tzu. WPC

Of Myself. Leah Goldberg, *tr. fr. Hebrew by* Ramah Commanday. BoWoP

Of nearness to her sundered things. Emily Dickinson. PoE

Of Necco Wafers, Nibs, and Juju Beads. (*LL*) Ex-Basketball Player. John Updike. InPK; NYBP; SM; TRP

Of Nelson and the North. Battle of the Baltic. Thomas Campbell. EnRP; FaPoR; GN; GTBS; GTBS-P; OBEV

Of Neptune's empire let us sing. A Hymn[e] in Praise [*or* Prayse] of Neptune. Thomas Campion. BoNaP; NOBE; OBEV; WiR

Of no removes! (*LL*) Fine Knacks for Ladies. *Unknown.* CH; EBEV; EiL; EnRePo; HAP; LiTB; NoP; NoSic

Of Nobility. Fulke Greville. *Fr.* Treatise of Monarchy, A.

Of now done darkness I wretch lay wrestling with (my God!) my God. (*LL*) Carrion Comfort. Gerard Manley Hopkins. CMoP; EnVR; HeiP; LiTB; MeMBP; NAEL-2; NoAM; NoP; OAEL-2; PoE; PoEL-5; PPP; Son; TEP; TFi; TOF

Of Objects Considered as Fortresses in a Baleful Place. Hyam Plutzik. VGW

Of old ecstasies. (*LL*) Illegitimate Things. William Carlos Williams. MoAB; MoAmPo

Of Old Sat Freedom on the Heights. Tennyson. MeMBP; OHCV

Of old when folk lay sick and sorely tried. On Hygiene. Hilaire Belloc. MoBrPo

Of old when Nature, in her verve defiant. The Giantess. Baudelaire, *tr. fr. French by* Roy Campbell. OBVE

Of old, when Scarron his companions invited. Goldsmith. *Fr.* Retaliation. NOIV; OxBoLi

Of on that is so fair and bright. A Hymn to Mary. *Unknown.* MeEL

Of One Dead. Tennyson. *See* If one should bring me this report.

Of One Dying. Philip Owens. AngWe

Of one man's breath. in the Capability. Sam Abrams. Jaz

Of one mirror, gazing on herself at last. (*LL*) A Ceremony. Robin Morgan. SRLS

Of One Self-slain. Charles Hanson Towne. WGRP

Of One That Died of the Wind-Colic. *Unknown.* CBNP

Of One That Had a Great Nose. George Turberville, *after the Greek of* Trajan. FaBoEE

Of one that longs for love in vain. (*LL*) The Wife's Lament. *Unknown.* AnOE, *tr. by* Charles W. Kennedy

Of one that longs for love in vain. (*LL*) Wife's Lament. *Unknown.* PBWP; PoE

Of one who grew up at Gallipoli. War Story. Jon Stallworthy. OxBC

Of other days around me. (*LL*) Oft, in the Stilly Night. Thomas Moore. EBEvV; EnRP; FaBoBe; IMW; LiTB; OBNC; PoEL-4; Prf; SCGP

Of our desires and needs. (*LL*) O! Marge Piercy. SRLS

Of our lives. (*LL*) Love Amidst the War. Jean Binta Breeze. VBLP

Of our love. (*LL*) And Sunday Morning. Christian McEwen. VBLP

Of our mortal truth. (*LL*) Loving My Enemies. Anna Kamienska. VBLP

Of Oxfordshire and Gloucestershire. (*LL*) Adlestrop. Edward Thomas. CH; EBEvV; FaBoPP; FaPoB; GGP; GoJo; HAP; LiTB; NAEL-2; NOBE; OBEV; OxBTC; PiP; UV

Of paradise. (*LL*) Original Mind. Nancy Paddock. LoHo

Of paradise. (*LL*) Plantings. Catalina Cariaga. LoHo

Of paradise. (*LL*) The Politics of Paradise. Alma Villanueva. SRLS

Of Paul and Silas it is said. Emily Dickinson. ChIV-2

Of Peace. Fulke Greville. *Fr.* Treatise of Monarchy, A.

Of Peculation shine again!' (*LL*) Tory Pledges. Thomas Moore. FaBoCo; OBSV

Of people running down the street. A Picture. Howard Nemerov. OxBC

Of Perfect Friendship. Henry Cheke. EiL

Of person rare, strong limbs, and manly shape. A Sonnet Written upon My Lord Admiral Seymour. John Harington. NoSic

Of Phyllis. William Drummond of Hawthornden. CBLP; EiL; GN

Of poison in. (*LL*) Loveact. Grace Nichols. VBLP

Of Politics, & Art. Norman Dubie. BAP-90

Of Poor B.B. Bertolt Brecht, *tr. fr. German by* Michael Hamburger. RB

Of precious pearls a glorious crown. (*LL*) For Saint Stephen's Day. Luke Wadding. TIRV

Of priests we can offer a charmin' variety. Father O'Flynn. A. P. Graves. PeIV

Of Promises and Prophecy. Steve Chimombo. HBAPE

Of proselytes of one another's trade. (*LL*) Greatest saints and sinners have been made, The. Samuel Butler. FaBoEE

Of purpose Love chose first for to be blind. Sir Thomas Wyatt. SiPSBD

Of Rama. Herman Melville. LiTA

Of red berries. Will he wake? (*LL*) Scenes from the Life of the Peppertrees. Denise Levertov. LiTM; NeAP; NoP; PoM

Of remembrance, whispers out of time. (*LL*) Self-Portrait in a Convex Mirror. John Ashbery. HCAP; NAAL-2

Of repentance for the false day that's fled. (*LL*) White Christmas. W. R. Rodgers. LiTM; MoAB; MoBrPo

Of Robert Frost. Gwendolyn Brooks. MoP; NoAM; NOBA

Of rocks in springtime blown about the skies. (*LL*) Erinna. Antipater of Sidon. AWP

Of Rome. Herman Melville. *Fr.* Clarel. OxBA

Of room to lodge th' inhabitant. (*LL*) Another [Epitaph on the Lady Mary Villiers]. Thomas Carew. BeJo; CaPo; SeCV-1

Of roses thrown on marble stairs. (*LL*) The Gift of God. E. A. Robinson. MoAB; MoAmPo; OxBA

Of Sarah Byng the tale is told. Hilaire Belloc. *See* Some years ago you heard me sing.

Of scarlet poppies. (*LL*) Let's Go. Bei Dao. SpMi

Of schoolgirls hastening down the way. (*LL*) Schoolgirls Hastening. John Shaw Neilson. NOBAu

Of Scolding Wives and the Third Day Ague. Henricus Selyns. AiP; SCAP

Of service which thou renderest. (*LL*) Reward of Service. Elizabeth Barrett Browning. BLPA; FaBoBe

Of shadow. (*LL*) Crowbar. Rachel Blau DuPlessis. VBLP

Of sharing a meal. (*LL*) My friends, let us give thanks for Wonder. Rami M. Shapiro. EaPr

Of simple choice they are the villagers; their clothes come. Adrienne Rich. *Fr.* Shooting Script. HCAP

Of sky. (*LL*) The Left Eye of Odin. Regina DeCormier-Shekejian. LoHo

Of Solitude, *sels.* Abraham Cowley.
Solitude and Reason, in the Village. FaBoPP

Of Solitude. Abraham Cowley.

Of Spenser's Faery Queen. Sir Walter Ralegh. *See* Methought I saw the grave where Laura lay.

Of spinach and gammon. The Right Heart in the Wrong Place. James Joyce. FaBoPV

Of St Stephen. Francis Quarles. NOSC

Of Stars. Margaret Cavendish, Duchess of Newcastle. NOSC

Of statue feet. (*LL*) They Came That Night. Léon Damas. NegPo

Of stone. (*LL*) The Reason. Chris Van Wyk. PeSAV

Of such a wit the world should have no more. (*LL*) An Ode for Ben Jonson. Robert Herrick. AWP; BeJo; EPCY; InvP; OBF; SCGP; SeCP; TrGrPo

Of such a wit the world should have no more. (*LL*) My Ben! Robert Herrick. BeJo

Of Suicide. John Berryman. NoAM

Of Tact. Arthur Guiterman. MoShBr

Of Taste; an Essay, *sels.* James Cawthorn.
"Time was, a [wealthy] Englishman would join." NOEC
(Englishman at the Table, The.) ECEV

Of th' others) as his own was known... (*LL*) On Mr. Abraham Cowley, His Death and Burial amongst the Ancient Poets. Sir John Denham. BeJo; SeCV-1

Of that loving majo who was my glory. The Piteous Maja. Fernando Periquet Y Zuaznabar, *tr. fr. Spanish by* Philip L. Miller. RiWo

Of that Paternal Soul. (*LL*) Abraham Lincoln. Richard Henry Stoddard. AnAmPo; FaBoBe; GN; OHIP; PAH

Of that short roll of friends writ in my heart. To Mr. I. L. John Donne. OBF

Of that table in the café. Cafe. Czeslaw Milosz, *tr. fr. Polish by* Jan Darowski. PoSu

Of that wherein thou art a questioner. To Dante Alighieri: He Interprets Dante Alighieri's Dream. Dante da Maiano, *tr. fr. Italian by* Dante Gabriel Rossetti. AWP

Of the Scythians. Katha Pollitt. DiPo; InPS; SM

Of the sea again. (*LL*) Stages on a Journey Westward. James Wright. LCAP; NaP

Of the snow, and the new year. (*LL*) New Year's Poem. Margaret Avison. LiTM; NOBC

Of the stars. (*LL*) At the Jewish Museum. Olga Cabral. BTR

Of the Sunbeams of Her Mind. Sir John Davies. *Fr.* Hymns of Astræa [in Acrostic Verse]. SiPSBD

Of the Swan, or the Bird in Hand. (*LL*) Homage to the Canal People. Andrew Sant. NOBAu

Of the tallest oak. (*LL*) The Trees. Adrienne Rich. CoAP; NOBA; WPE

Of the Theme of Love. Margaret Cavendish, Duchess of Newcastle. OxBSP

Of the thousands and thousands of years. The Garden. Jacques Prévert, *tr. fr. French* by Harriet Zinnes. ArLo

Of the three Wise Men. Carol of the Brown King. Langston Hughes. PChr

Of the toy's purchase with the length of life. (*LL*) Bacchus. Emerson. AmPP; AWP; LiTA; NOBA; OBEV; OxBA; PoEL-4

Of the toy's purchase with the length of life. (*LL*) Blight. Emerson. NOBA; NoP

Of the two kinds of wing-shaped rings on his desk. The Ring. Atsumi Ikuko, *tr. fr. Japanese* by Kenneth Rexroth and Ikuko Atsumi. WPJ

Of the underworld. (*LL*) The Savior Is Abducted in Puerto Rico. Martín Espada. TRP

Of the unended in the speed of. Anne-Marie Albiach, *tr. fr. French* by Paul Auster. *Fr.* État. PBWP

Of the unnamed poor. (*LL*) The Minneapolis Poem. James Wright. FYAP; NoAM; UnPo

Of the Use of Riches. Pope. *See* At Timon's villa let us pass a day.

Of the Wars in Ireland. John Harington. NoSic

Of the workers and their misery. (*LL*) Beans, Bacon, and Gravy. *Unknown.* SWP

Of thee (kind boy) I ask no red and white. Sir John Suckling. BeJo; CaPo; MeLP; NoP; NOSC; OxBoLi; SeCP; SeCV-1

Of thee one hour, than all else ever. (*LL*) A Fever. John Donne. OAEL-1

Of thee one hour, than all else ever. (*LL*) The Fever. Rosemary Dobson. FaBoWP

Of their *Red Sea,* a *Spring;* I wash, they wade. (*LL*) Mans Fall, and Recovery. Henry Vaughan and Thomas Stanley. ESCV

Of their unthinking drums. (*LL*) I Dreaded That First Robin So. Emily Dickinson. AmPP; HAP; MeMAP; MoAmPo; NAAL-1

Of them all — those laboring who knew my first name. At the Sign-Painter's. Jared Carter. FYAP

Of thes four letters purpose I. A New Song of Mary. *Unknown.* MeEL

Of thes Frer Minours me thenkes moch wonder. Friars' Enormities. *Unknown.* MeEL

Of these houses. San Martino del Carso. Giuseppe Ungaretti, *tr. fr. Italian* by David McDuff and Jon Silkin. PeFWW

Of these the false Achitophel was first. Dryden. *Fr.* Absalom and Achitophel, Pt. I. FaBoEH; HAP; InPS; NoP; OAEL-1; PoEL-3; SeCV-2

(Achitophel: The Earl of Shaftsbury.) NOBE

(Achitophel.) AWP

(Achitophel.) AWP

(Shaft[e]sbury.) NOSC; O9OBS

Of th'eternal silence. (*LL*) Noel; Christmas Eve, 1913. Robert Bridges. LiTB; NOCV; OBCP; PoEL-5

Of this bad world the loveliest and the best. On a Dead Hostess. Hilaire Belloc. MoBrPo

Of this fair volume which we World do[e] name. The Book. William Drummond of Hawthornden. CH; ChIV-1

(Lessons of Nature, The.) GTBS-P

Of those around thee there is none who heeds. To Bülow. August, Graf von Platen, *tr. fr. German* by Reginald Bancroft Cooke. PeHV

Of those calm solitudes, is there. (*LL*) Oh [*or* O] Fairest of the Rural Maids. Bryant. TAP

Of those few fools, who with ill stars are cursed. Congreve. *Fr.* Way of the World, The. NAEL-1

Of those rebellions that we start in jest. Fear Test: Integrity of Heroes. James Simmons. CIP

Of those, thou woundest with thy Dart! (*LL*) The Wounded Cupid. Robert Herrick. AWP; OBVE

Of Those Who Go, Not to Return. Benyamin Galai, *tr. fr. Hebrew* by Ruth Finer Mintz. MHP

Of those whom I have known, the few and fatal friends. Largo. Dunstan Thompson. LiTA

Of three eyes, I would still give two for one. The Third Eye. Jay Macpherson. MoCV

Of Three Friendly Warnings This Is the Second. *Unknown, tr. fr. Seneca Indian* by Jerome K. Rothenberg and Richard Johnny John. STP

Of Three Friendly Warnings This Is the Third. *Unknown, tr. fr. Seneca Indian* by Jerome K. Rothenberg and Richard Johnny John. STP

Of Three Girls and of Their Talk. Boccaccio, *tr. fr. Italian* by Dante Gabriel Rossetti. *Fr.* Sonnets. AWP

Of Thule, at midnight when the mice are still. (*LL*) My Father in the Night Commanding No. Louis Simpson. CoAP; HeIP; NoAM; NOBA; NYBP; SM; TAP; TwCP; VGW

Of thy departure, when thou wentest forth, it went out/ after thee. (*LL*) Parting. Judah Halevi. AWP; TrJP

Of thy life [*or* lyfe], Thomas, this compass[e] well mark. The Golden Mean. The Earl of Surrey, *after* Horace. OBVE; SiPS

Of thy life [life], Thomas, this compass well mark. Horace. *See* Receive, dear friend, the truths I teach.

Of thy meek nature! (*LL*) To the Daisy ("With little here to do or see.") Wordsworth. GTBS; GTBS-P

Of Time and the Line. Charles Bernstein. UL

Of times when equilibrium is born. (*LL*) The Hours. David Diop. NegPo

Of Treason. Sir John Harington. FaBoEE; FF; InPK; NoSic; OxBoLi; SoSe

Of truth into the heart again. (*LL*) In a Hard Intellectual Light. Richard Eberhart. CMoP; LiTM

Of twice ten thousand warriors slain. (*LL*) All That Is Left. Basho. AWP

Of two fair virgins, modest, though admired. On a Nun. Jacopo Vittorelli, *tr. fr. Italian* by Byron. AWP

Of Tyndarus, That Frumped a Gentlewoman. *Unknown, tr. fr. Latin.* BIrV, *tr.* by Richard Stanyhurst

Of unapplauding hands and broken song. (*LL*) My Dark Fathers. Brendan Kennelly. BIrV; CIP; PBCIP; PeIV

Of underground streams, what I see is a limestone landscape. (*LL*) In Praise of Limestone. W. H. Auden. CMoP; FaBoPV; FYAP; HAP; MoAB; MoP; NAEL-2; NoAM; NoP; OAEL-2; PPP

Of unknown lovers, featureless with flame. (*LL*) Terra Australis. James McAuley. NOBAu

Of unremembered seas. (*LL*) So I Said I Am Ezra. A. R. Ammons. NAAL-2; NoAM; NOBA; NoP

Of us/ not much is known. Degli Sposi. Rika Lesser. FYAP; UnAS

Of Use. John Heywood. FaBoEE

Of value? Have you left anything behind? (*LL*) On Motel Walls. David Wagoner. DiPo

Of Verbal Criticism., sels. David Mallet.

"Pride of his own, and wonder of his age." EPCY

Of vines crawls into the spilled body of a plane. (*LL*) New Hampshire. Donald Hall. LCAP

Of violets, and my soul's forgotten gleam. (*LL*) I had no thought of violets of late. Alice Dunbar Nelson. BlSi; CDC; PoBA; PoNe; Son

Of virtues I most warmly bless. Gerard Manley Hopkins. FaBoEE

Of water: I do not know him: he does not know me. (*LL*) Out Fishing. Barbara Howes. WPE

Of water, water, water. (*LL*) The Lifeguard. James Dickey. NoP; NYBP; SoSe

Of western New York state. As You Came from the Holy Land. John Ashbery. CAPP

Of what a quality is courage made. Donagh MacDonagh. *Fr.* Charles Donnelly. CIP

Of what from thee I learn. (*LL*) Anecdote for Fathers. Wordsworth. EnRP

Of what good can Paradise be. Paradise. Immanuel di Roma, *tr. fr. Hebrew* by J. Chotzner. TrJP

Of what mould did Nature frame me? The Tinder. Thomas Carew. CaPo

Of what you were, than what you are, express. (*LL*) Elegy on D. D. Sidney Godolphin. BeJo

Of white and tawny, black as ink. Variation on a Sentence. Louise Bogan. FM

Of Why He Is Unhanged. Cecco Angiolieri, da Siena, *tr. fr. Italian* by Dante Gabriel Rossetti.

Of wilding in his hand. (*LL*) The Two April Mornings. Wordsworth. EBEV; EnRP; GTBS; GTBS-P; NAEL-2

Of wisdom and of might through all eternity. (*LL*) The Eternity of Nature. John Clare. EBEV

Of woman and wine, of woods and spring. Inexhaustible. Israel Zangwill. TrJP

Of Women. Richard Edwards. EIL

Of Women. *Unknown, tr. fr. Arabic* by E. Powys Mathers. *Fr.* Thousand and One Nights, The. ErPo

Of woods, of plains, of hills and dales. Upon a Rich Country Gentleman. *Unknown.* FaBoEE

Of worthy Captain Lovewell I purpose now to sing. Lovewell's Fight. *Unknown.* PAH

Of writing many books there is no end! Elizabeth Barrett Browning. *Fr.* Aurora Leigh. NOBVV

Of years past. (*LL*) Cherry Blossoms. Basho. ArNa

Of your beloved in sleep. (*LL*) He Hears the Cry of the Sedge. W. B. Yeats. OxBTC; RB

Of your everlasting arms. Amen. (*LL*) Great mystery of sleep. *Unknown*. EaPr

Of your faire eies whereby the light is lost. (*LL*) I never saw you madam, lay [*or* sawe my Ladye] laye apart. The Earl of Surrey. AAS; SiPS; SiPSBD

Of Your Father's Indiscretions and the Train to California. Lynn Emanuel. NAmP90

Of your hand I could say this. Dawn. Jeni Couzyn. NBrP

Of your horses all knot-free. (*LL*) Another Charm for Stables. Robert Herrick. BeJo

Of your horses, all knot-free. (*LL*) Charmes. Robert Herrick. BeJo

Of your making, tell them I am. (*LL*) The Hand. R. S. Thomas. NOCV; OxBC

Of your swelling rage. (*LL*) Black Ore. René Depestre. NegPo

Of your trouble, Ben, to ease me. Her Man Described by Her Own(e) Dictamen. Ben Jonson. *Fr.* Celebration of Charis in Ten Lyric[k] Peeces [*or* pieces], A. BeJo; OxAEP-1; SeCP

Of your white hand, they are mine. (*LL*) On Mr. G. [*or* George] Herbert's Book[e] Intituled [*or* Entitled] the Temple of Sacred Poems, Sent to a Gentle-woman. Richard Crashaw. EPCY; ESCV; GeHe; SeCV-1

Of yours, which is not you. Which is. (*LL*) To Laura Phelan: 1880-1906. Leon Stokesbury. MT

Of Youth He Singeth. Robert Wever. *See* In a herber [*or* a harbour *or* an arbour] green [*or* grene], asleep [*or* aslepe] whereas [*or* where as *or* where] I lay.

Ofatedo/ seek it out upon the skin of Africa. Edouard J. Maunick, *tr. fr. French by* Ellen Conroy Kennedy. *Fr.* As Far as Yoruba Land. NegPo

Off a Puritane. *Unknown*. CoMu

Off all the lords in faire Scottland. The Heir of Linne. *Unknown*. ESPB

Off an ancient story Ile tell you anon. King John and the Bishop. *Unknown*. ESPB

Off Brighton Pier. Alan Ross. OBWP

Off Broadway, where they sell those photographs. Manhattan Menagerie. Joseph Cherwinski. GoYe

Off Coronel. Austin Threlfall Nankivell. NSI

Off Crane's Neck the sun. The Spirit of Wrath. William Heyen. AmPA

Off Februar the fyiftene nycht. William Dunbar. MiEL
(Dance of the Sevin Deidly Synnis, The.) OxBS; PoE

Off from Boston. *Unknown*. PAH

Off Havana the ocean is green this morning. Havana Birth. Susan Mitchell. BAP-90; NAmP90

Off Highway 106. Cherrylog Road. James Dickey. CoAP; HAP; HCAP; InPS; MT; NAAL-2; NIP; NYBP; Poetr; PrIm; TwCP; WeW

Off in the forest. Found. Goethe, *tr. fr. German by* John Frederick Nims. STV

Off in the twilight hung the low full moon. Full Moon. Sappho, *tr. fr. Greek by* William Ellery Leonard. AWP

Off in the wilderness bare and level. The Temptations of Saint Anthony. Phyllis McGinley. OxBSP

Off Manilly. Edmund Vance Cooke. PAH

Off-shore, by islands hidden in the blood. I, Maximus of Gloucester, to You ("Off-shore, by islands hidden in the blood.") Charles Olson. *Fr.* Maximus Poems, The. LiTM; NoAM; NOBA; PoM

Off that landspit of stony mouth-plugs. Medusa. Sylvia Plath. NALW

Off the Aleutian Chain. Linda Bierds. NAmP90

Off the Back of a Lorry. Tom Paulin. PBCIP

Off the coast of Hispaniola. Columbus and the Mermaids. Elizabeth J. Coatsworth. GOA

Off the Map. Lavinia Greenlaw. NWP

Off the Map. David Malouf. FaBoMA

Off the track/ I blew. Phoenix. Carolyn M. Rodgers. JB

Off to bed. (*LL*) Alphabet ("A, B, C, D, E, F, G.") *Unknown*. FaBoUs

Off to Patagonia. Theodore Weiss. AnAn; TAP

Off to Sea Once More. *Unknown*. OxBSS

Off We Go to Market. Gwen A. Smith. BoTP

Off with sleep, love, up from bed. Love in May. Jean Passerat, *tr. fr. French by* Andrew Lang. AWP

Off with the fetters. Vagabondia. Richard Hovey. AnAmPo

Off with you, boy! Pretended prude! Strato, *tr. fr. Greek by* Edward Lucie-Smith. GrAn

Off Womanheid Ane Flour Delice. *Unknown*. OxBS

Offal. And new cities raven and distend, The. (*LL*) A Lion Named Passion. John Hollander. NoAM

Offended, The. Anne Hébert, *tr. fr. French by* Willis Barnstone. BoWoP

Offensive, The. (Stars dead heroes in the sky, The.) Keith Douglas. PoWW

Offer, An. Arthur Guiterman. TrJP

Offer it up plank it down. Ooftish. Samuel Beckett. NoAM

Offer no angles to the wind. (*LL*) Cats No Less Liquid Than Their Shadows. A. S. J. Tessimond. OBAP

Offer varied attractions to Whistler. (*LL*) There's a combative artist named Whistler. Dante Gabriel Rossetti. FaBoEE; PeLi

Offer'd up by Her, to Thee. (*LL*) Upon Prudence Baldwin Her Sickness. Robert Herrick. JCP; SeCV-1

Offered across the table. (*LL*) She Drives. Sophie Cabot Black. LoHo

Offered to a Man Who Sells Pines. Yü Wu-ling, *tr. fr. Chinese by* Edward H. Schafer. SuSp

Offering. Debra Allbery. PBCAP

Offering. Thomas McGrath. RaBo

Offering. *Unknown, Tr. fr. Zuni Indian by* Ruth Bunzel; *ad. by* Robert Bly. EaPr; NU

Offering, An. Eloise Bibb. CBWP-4

Offering of the Heart Tapestry from Arras, XV Century, The. Rolfe Humphries. FYAP

Offering: Part One, The. Mary Lee, Lady Chudleigh. WPE

Offers the boon of Death. (*LL*) Compensation. Paul Laurence Dunbar. BPo; PoNe

Offers thee gold. (*LL*) And She Washed His Feet with Her Tear[e]s, and Wiped Them with the Hairs of Her Head. Sir Edward Sherburne, *after the Italian of* Giambattista Marina. ChTr; MeLP; NOSC

Offertorium. C. Day Lewis. *Fr.* Requiem for the Living. TIRV

Offertory. John F. Deane. TIRV

Office feels like a sealed glass case today, The. What Grandma Knew. Edward Field. Poetsp

Office Friendships. Gavin Ewart. PeLV

Office Party. Phyllis McGinley. OBSV

Office Window. Llewelyn Wyn Griffith. AngWe

Officer at the Rapids, The. Han Yü, *tr. fr. Chinese by* Charles Hartman. SuSp

Officer, I broke your gun. (*LL*) A Mother Speaks: The Algiers Motel Incident, Detroit. Michael S. Harper. AmPA; BPo; NBV

Officers. Josephine Miles. FaBoWP

Officers' kit and the long low limbers, The. Cookers, The: A Song of the Transport. A. P. Herbert. NSI

Officers' Mess. Gavin Ewart. OxBTC

Official document blows through a forest, An. The Long Picnic. Russell Edson. LCAP

Offshore, islanded. Ireland. Harry Clifton. IB

Offspring. Naomi Long Madgett. CrSp; SoSe

Offspring of modern poetry, attend. Morning. *Unknown*. NOEC

Offspring of this Miscellaneous Crowd, The. The True-Born Englishman. Daniel Defoe. *Fr.* True-born Englishman, The. APAS; FaBoEH

Oft am I by the women told. Age. Abraham Cowley. AWP

Oft as at pensive eve I pass the brook. Sonnet on Passing the Bridge of Alcantra, near Lisbon. William Julius Mickle. OBTV

Oft, as we run the weary way. Courage. Stopford Brooke. WGRP

Oft did I hear our eyes the passage were. Sir John Davies. *Fr.* Sonnets to Philomel. SiPS

Oft do I return/ To my little song. The Song of the Trout Fisher. Ikinilik, *tr. fr. Eskimo.* WTO

Oft has our Poet wisht, this happy Seat. Epilogue Spoken by Mrs. Boutell. Dryden. SeCV-2

Oft has this planet rolled around the sun. Sir Samuel Garth. *Fr.* Dispensary, The. OBSV

Oft have I heard my lief[e] Corydon [*or* Coridon] report on a love-day. Hexametra Alexis in Laudem Rosamundi. Robert Greene. *Fr.* Greene's Mourning Garment. EIL; GBL; PoEL-2

Oft have I heard thee mourn the wretched lot. Charles Churchill. *Fr.* Prophecy of Famine, The. OBSV

Oft Have I Mused. Sir Philip Sidney. EIL; EnRePo; GBL; NOBE; SiPS

Oft have I played at cards and dice. The Rantin Laddie. *Unknown*. AmFP; ESPB; HAP; OxBA; TAP

Oft have I said, I say it once more. Hafiz, *tr. by* Emerson. *Fr.* Odes. AWP

Oft have I said, the praise of doing well. Matthew Prior. *Fr.* Pleasure: The Second Book of Solomon on the Vanity of the World. ChIV-1

Oft have I seen, ere Time had ploughed my cheek. Decay of Piety. Wordsworth. TrCP

Oft have I seen, when that renewing breath. Resurrection and Immortality. Henry Vaughan *and* Thomas Stanley. ESCV

Oft have I walked these woodland paths. Under the Leaves. Albert Laighton. OHIP

Oft have we heard of impious sons before. The Female Parricide. *Unknown.* APAS

Oft I had heard of Lucy Gray. Lucy Gray; or, Solitude. Wordsworth. BeLS; CH; EnRP; NAEL-2; OAEL-2; OxBChV; TEP

Oft I must strive with wind and wave. Anchor: "Oft I must strive with wind and wave." Unknown, formerly at. to Cynewulf, *tr.* by Charles W. Kennedy. *Fr.* Riddles (Exeter Book). AnOE

Oft in danger yet alive. To Mrs. Thrale [on Her Thirty-fifth Birthday]. Samuel Johnson. FaBoEE; NAs

Oft in My Thought. Charles, Duc d'Orléans. NoP

Oft in the hall I have heard my people. *Unknown*, *tr.* by Charles W. Kennedy. *Fr.* Beowulf. ASW, *tr.* by Kevin Crossley-Holland; HeIP

Oft in the lone church-yard at night I've seen. Robert Blair. *Fr.* Grave, The. OBD; OxAEP-1

Oft, in the silence of the night. Our Little Ghost. Louisa May Alcott. OBCA

Oft in the Silent Night. Otto Julius Bierbaum, *tr. fr. German* by Ludwig Lewisohn. AWP

Oft, in the Stilly Night. Thomas Moore. EBEvV; EnRP; FaBoBe; IMW; LiTB; OBNC; PoEL-4; Prf; SCGP

Oft it befalls by the grace of God. Fates of Men (Exeter Book). *Unknown*, *tr. fr. Old English* by Charles W. Kennedy. AnOE

Oft mighty elephants by little Moors are led. Powerful Servants. Friedrich von Logau, *tr. fr. German*. GePo, *tr.* by George C. Schoolfield

Oft o'er my brain does that strange fancy roll. Composed on a Journey Homeward; the Author Having Received Intelligence of the Birth of a Son. Samuel Taylor Coleridge. Son

Oft-Repeated Dream, The. Robert Frost. *Fr.* Hill Wife, The. CMoP; HAP; InPS; LiTM; NoP; Poetr

Oft shall the soldier think of thee. Ben Milam. William H. Wharton. PAH

Oft Thou Hast with Greedy Ear. John Cooper. EnRePo

Ofte to the Wanderer, weary of exile. The Wanderer. *Unknown*, *tr. fr. Anglo-Saxon* by Charles W. Kennedy. AnOE; NAWM-1; OAEL-1

Oft when I'm sitting without anything to read. Lines to a World-famous Poet Who Failed to Complete a World-famous Poem; or, Come Clean, Mr. Guest! Ogden Nash. OBAL

"Oft when my spirit doth spread her bolder wings." Spenser. *Fr.* Amoretti. AAS; ESo, lacking epigrams I–IV; HeIL; Son

Often a friend will greet me thus. Hartmann von Aue, *tr. fr. German* by Frederick Goldin. GePo

Often, among the night-sounds, I've heard. Death in January. Vincent Buckley. FaBoMA

Often beneath the wave, wide from this ledge. At Melville's Tomb. Hart Crane. HAP; MoAmPo; MoP; NAAL-2; NoAM; NoP; PoA; TAP; UnPo; VGW

Often had I found her fair. A. D. Hope. ErPo

Often, half-way to sleep. In Procession. Robert Graves. TwCP

Often I Am Permitted to Return to a Meadow. Robert Duncan. CAPP; CMoP; NOBA; NU

Often I compare my lord to heaven. Gaspara Stampa, *tr. fr. Italian* by Lynne Lawner. PBWP

Often I dream of you, young. Thirteen Ways to Look at a Son. Stephen Knight. UnDi

Often I saw, as on my balcony. Christ Church Meadows, Oxford. Donald Hall. NYBP

Often I sit in the sun and brooding over the city, always. Dennis Lee. *Fr.* Civil Elegies. NOBC

Often I talk to men, on this or that. Talk. Philip A. Stalker. FiBHP

Often I think of my Jewish friends. The Pripet Marshes. Irving Feldman. BTR

Often I think of the beautiful town. My Lost Youth. Longfellow. AmPP; AnAmPo; AWP; FaBoBe; FaBV; FaPoR; GoJo; ImGa; LiTA; MeMAP; NAAL-1; NOBA; OBEV; OxBA; PoEL-5; PoLF; PoRA; TAP; TFi (Sea Memories.) FaPON

Often I would stand at the window. Grandmother. Louise Glück. *Fr.* Dedication to Hunger. AnAn

Often in summer, on a tarred bridge plank standing. Wild Bees. James K. Baxter. NoP

Often in the morning the fog is thick over Jersey. A View of Jersey. Edward Field. NeAP

Often, in these blue meadows. Pursuit from Under. James Dickey. HAP; PPP

Often I've wished that I'd been born a woman. A Wish. Laurence David Lerner. FF; OxBTC

Often on this her daughter's tomb did Cleina grieve. Anyte, *tr. fr. Greek* by Barbara Hughes Fowler. *Fr.* Epigrams. HePo

Often rebuked, yet always back returning. Stanzas ("Often rebuked, yet always back returning.") *At.* to Emily Brontë, *also at.* to Charlotte Brontë. LiTB; MeMBP; NOBVV; OAEL-2; OBNC; OHCV; PBWP; SCGP

(Stanza.) OBEV

(Stanzas.) NALW; PFP

Often/ Stepping so delicately through the shrubbery of learning. Salt. Monk Gibbon. PeIV

Often the western wind has sung to me. Lord Alfred Bruce Douglas. TrPWD

Often this thought wakens me unawares. Night. Hermann Hesse, *tr. fr. German* by Ludwig Lewisohn. AWP

Often waking/ before the sun decreed. Author of *Christine*, The. Richard Howard. CoAP

Often when alone I liken my lord/ to the cosmos. Gaspara Stampa, *tr. fr. Italian* by J. Vitiello. BoWoP

Often, when o'er tree and turret. Hic Vir, Hic Est. Charles Stuart Calverley. OxBoLi; PeLV

Often when the night is come. To a Maid Demure. Edward Rowland Sill. AnAmPo

Often you see them sitting, solitary, on a dune. The Beach Homos. Forrest Anderson. PeHV

Often you walked at night, houselights made. In Sepia. Jon Anderson. PoA

Oftener Seen, the More I Lust, The. Barnabe Googe. *See* Oftener seen, the more I lust, The.

Oftener seen, the more I lust, The. Out of Sight, Out of Mind. Barnabe Googe. EIL; EnRePo; InPS

(Oftener Seen, the More I Lust, The.) InvP; OPOP

Oftentimes, I grew dejected and sobbed. Ch'u Yüan, *tr.* by Wu-chi Liu. *Fr.* Li Sao. SuSp

Oftimes I wish that I could be. Poplar Tree. Mae V. Cowdery. ShDr

Ofttimes have I heard you speak of one who commits a. Crime and Punishment. Kahlil Gibran. *Fr.* Prophet, The. PoToHe

Og [and Doeg]. John Dryden *and* Nahum Tate. *Fr.* Absalom and Achitophel, Pt. II. AWP

Ogata Kōrin on His Field of Irises. Martha Hollander. UTF

Oggy! Oggy! Oggy! Land of Song. Nigel Jenkins. AngWe

O'Grady lived in Shantytown. O'Grady's Goat. Will S. Hays. PoLF

O'Grady's Goat. Will S. Hays. PoLF

Ogre does what ogres can, The. August 1968. W. H. Auden. OxBSP

Ogres and Pygmies. Robert Graves. CMoP; FaBoMo; LiTB; LiTM; MeMBP; MoP; NoAM

Ogun's Friend. Jayne Cortez. BCF

Oh, a capital ship for an ocean trip. Charles Edward Carryl. *See* Capital ship for an ocean trip, A.

Oh, a day in the city-square, there is no such pleasure in life! (*LL*) Up at a Villa — Down in the City. Robert Browning. CoGr; FaBoPP; FHYEP; GTBS-P; InPS; NOBE; OBTV; PoRA; PPP

Oh, a far cry to Heaven! (*LL*) A Far Cry to Heaven. Edith M. Thomas. WGRP

Oh, a hidden power is in my breast. Song of the Moon. Priscilla Jane Thompson. CBWP-2

Oh a high holiday, on a high holiday. Little Musgrave and Lady Barnard. *Unknown.* AmFP

Oh, a poor aviator lay dying. A Poor Aviator Lay Dying. *Unknown.* NSI

Oh! a private buffoon is a light-hearted loon. The Family Fool. W. S. Gilbert. *Fr.* Yeoman of the Guard. NBLV

Oh, a sailor's life is the life for me. The Warrior's Lament. Sir Owen Seaman. FiBHP

Oh a shantyman's life is a wearisome [*or* drearisome] life. A Shantyman's Life. *Unknown.* AmFP; AS

Oh, a ship she was rigged and ready for sea. The Fishes. *Unknown.* GBP

Oh, a soldier told me, before he died. The Soldier's Tale. *Unknown.* PeLV

Oh [*or* O], a wonderful stream is the River Time. The Isle of the Long Ago. Benjamin Franklin Taylor. WBLP

(Long Ago, The.) BLPA

Oh, about the joy of owning a crab hut at Sung-chiang! Chang Chih-ho, *tr.* by Hellmut Wilhelm. *Fr.* Fisherman's Songs. SuSp

Oh Achilles of the moleskins. To "Chick." Frank Horne. *Fr.* Letters [*or* Notes] Found near a Suicide. BPo; CDC; PoBA; PoNe

Oh all ye, who passe by, whose eyes and minde. The Sacrifice. George Herbert. GeHe; PoEL-2

Oh, always mine. (*LL*) The Piteous Maja. Fernando Periquet Y Zuaznabar. RiWo

Oh angels! will ye never sweep the drifts from my door? Drifts That Bar My Door. Adah Isaacs Menken. CBWP-1

Oh, as I went down to Derby Town. The Derby Ram. *Unknown.* AmFP

(As I was going to Derby.) OxNR

Oh, Athelstane, the faithful! Athelstane. Priscilla Jane Thompson. CBWP-2

Oh author of my being! — far more dear. To Charles Burney. Frances Burney. ECWP

Oh, away down South where I was born. Roll the Cotton Down. *Unknown.* AmFP

Oh, baby, baby, baby dear. E. Nesbit. NOBVV

Oh bard! what though upon thy mortal eyes. Milton. Anne Lynch Botta. AmWP

Oh, be but still, you half-part of my breast! Departure Aria. Johann Christian Günther, *tr. fr. German by* George C. Schoolfield. GePo

Oh be thou blest with all that Heav'n can send. To Mrs. M. B. on Her Birthday. Pope. EnLoPo

Oh Beverly, do you remember. September 7. Ellen Bass. NMM

Oh, black Persian cat! Mujer. William Carlos Williams. SAmP

Oh! blame not the bard, if he fly to the bowers. Thomas Moore. NOIV

Oh Blast France. On France. Wyndham Lewis. IHNG

Oh blessed Lord! and wouldst thou die. On the Death of Our Lord. Richard Flecknoe. TIRV

Oh! blest [*or* bless'd] of heav'n [*or* Heaven], whom not the languid songs. Nature's Influence on Man. Mark Akenside. *Fr.* Pleasures of Imagination, The. NOEC
(Love of Nature.) NOEC

Oh! blest with temper, whose unclouded ray. Heaven's Last Best Work. Pope. *Fr.* Of the Characters of Women. PIP

Oh, blush not so, oh, blush not so. Keats. CBLP

Oh blythely [*or* blithely] shines the bonnie [*or* bonny] sun. We'll Go to Sea No More. *Unknown.* ChTr; GBP

Oh Boney was a warrior. Boney. *Unknown.* FaBoVe

Oh Boney's on the sea. The Shan Van Vocht. *Unknown.* OxBoLi

Oh, Bonnie is the little cow. Midnight in Bonnie's Stall. Siddie Joe Johnson. PChr

Oh Book! infinite sweetnesse! let my heart. The H. Scriptures. George Herbert. ChIV-1; ESCV; MiEL

Oh, Boston, Boston, thou hast nought to boast on. Boston, Lincolnshire. *Unknown.* FaBoPP; GBP

Oh, bow your head, Tom Dooley. Tom Dooley. *Unknown.* AmFP

Oh boy oh boy four years to go before. 40. Paul Monette. PFL

Oh, Breathe Not His Name! Thomas Moore. EnRP

Oh! breathe upon this hapless world. Ode to Peace. *Unknown.* PAH

Oh bright-glancing Silver, who marriage has made. Stroll-Joy. Johann Klaj, *tr. fr. German by* George C. Schoolfield. GePo

Oh Britannia's got a baby, a baby, a baby. Britannia's Baby. D. H. Lawrence. NAs

Oh, brother, oh, brother, can you play ball. The Two Brothers. *Unknown.* AmFP

Oh bury me not on the lone prairie. (*LL*) Bury Me Not on the Lone Prairie. *Unknown.* AS; FaBV

Oh, but it is dirty! Filling Station. Elizabeth Bishop. FaBoMo; HAP; HCAP; InPK; NoP; NYBP; VCAP; WeW

Oh but it Was Good. Harold Littlebird. VoR

Oh, call my brother back to me. The Child's First Grief. Felicia Dorothea Hemans. BLPA
(First Grief, The.) CH

Oh, can we love and live? Pray, let us die. Love's Sun. William Cavendish. NOSC

Oh, cease, my wandering soul. Fulfillment. William Augustus Mühlenberg. WGRP

Oh! Celia, Celia, Celia shits! (*LL*) Cassinus and Peter. Swift. OAEL-1; PPP

Oh, Charlie's sweet and Charlie's neat. Weevily Wheat. *Unknown.* AmFP; AS

Oh, cheetie-pussie-cattie, O! (*LL*) There was a wee bit mousikie. *Unknown.* MoShBr; SoCa

Oh child, do you know, do you know. Our Child. Pablo Neruda, *tr. fr. Spanish by* Perry Higman. ArLo

Oh children think about the Good times. (*LL*) Good Times. Lucille Clifton. AmPA; BPo; FF; GoJo; GrPl; InPS; PoBA; SoSe; TAP; TRP; TwCP

Oh come and listen to my song. The Oxford and Hampton Railway. *Unknown.* OBET

Oh, come let us welcome sweet Sabbath the Queen! Welcome, Queen Sabbath. Zalman Schneour, *tr. fr. Hebrew by* Harry H. Fein. TrJP

Oh Come, Little Children. Phyllis McGinley. FaBV

Oh, Come to Me When Daylight Sets. Thomas Moore. EnRP

Oh, come with me in my little canoe. Ossian's Serenade. Calder Campbell. BLPA

Oh, come with old Khayyám and leave the Wise. Omar Khayyám, *tr. fr. Persian by* Edward Fitzgerald. *Fr.* Rubáiyát of Omar Khayyám of Naishápúr, The. AWP; EBVV, *abr.*; FaBoBe; FaBoRV, *abr.*; FaPoR, *abr.*; HAP, *abr.*; LiTB; NAEL-2; NoP; PIP; PoEL-5; PrIm, *abr.*; TrGrPo; UV

Oh, could I but sing as the minstrels of old! Lines to Emma. Priscilla Jane Thompson. CBWP-2

Oh! could I hope the wise and pure in heart. Hymn to Death. Bryant. EAP

Oh cruel death. The Piteous Maja ("Oh cruel death.") Fernando Periquet Y Zuaznabar, *tr. fr. Spanish by* Philip L. Miller. RiWo

Oh Cruel Was the Press-Gang. *Unknown.* GBP

Oh (cry'd the Goddess) for some pedant Reign! Pope. *Fr.* Dunciad, The. FaBoEH

Oh, cut the sweet apple and share it! (*LL*) Oh, blush not so, oh, blush not so. Keats. CBLP

Oh, Day of Days. LeRoy V. Brant. AH

Oh, de boll weevil am a little black bug. Boll Weevil Song. *Unknown.* AS
(Boll Weevil, The.) SWP, *sl. diff.*

Oh, de good ole chariot swing so low. Swing Low, Sweet Chariot. *Unknown.* AnAmPo

Oh, de grubbin'-hoe's a-rustin' in de co'nah. The Deserted Plantation. Paul Laurence Dunbar. AnAmPo

Oh, de ole sheep, dey know de road. Ole Sheep Dey Know de Road, De. *Unknown.* BPo

Oh, de white gal ride in a automobile. Black Girl, De. *Unknown.* GBP

Oh! Dear! *Unknown. See* Oh [*or* O], Dear! What Can the Matter Be?

Oh dear me! *Unknown.* ISE

Oh dear me, the mill's ga'in' fast. The Jute Mill Song. *Unknown.* OBET

Oh dear, my heart was ready to burst! (*LL*) As I was going by Charing Cross. *Unknown.* CH; FaBoCh; OxNR

Oh [*or* O], Dear! What Can the Matter Be? *Unknown.* CBLP; OxNR; ReMoGo

Oh, dear, what can the matter be?/ Two old women got up in an apple-tree. *Unknown.* FaBoNo
(Bunch of Blue Ribbons, The.) ReMoGo

Oh! dearer by far than the land of our birth. Richard Henry Wilde. GOA

"Oh, dearest grandpa, come and see." The Dead Sister. Caroline Gilman. OBCA

Oh! Death. *Unknown.* AmFP

Oh! Death will find me, long before I tire. Rupert Brooke. PoRA
(Sonnet: Death Will Find Me.) MoBrPo; Son

Oh, dere's lots o'keer an' trouble. A Banjo Song. Paul Laurence Dunbar. AnAmPo

Oh, dewy was the morning, upon the first of May. Manila. Eugene Fitch Ware. FiBHP

Oh, dey whupped him up de hill, up de hill, up de hill. Never Said a Mumbalin' Word. *Unknown.* GBP

Oh, did you go to see the show. The Orange Lily. *Unknown.* FaBoPV; GBP

Oh Did You Hear? Shel Silverstein. SiSoPo

Oh! Did you ne'er hear of Kate Kearney? Kate Kearney. Lady Morgan. BLPA; FaBoBe

Oh, do buzz off, you bumptious Sun. Busy Old Fool. Ian Kelso. BXAP

Oh do not die, for I shall hate. A Fever. John Donne. OAEL-1

Oh, do you remember sweet Betsey from Pike. Sweet Betsey from Pike. *Unknown.* AmFP; AS; FaBoBa; OBAL; OxBoLi

"Oh doe not die," says Donne, "for I shall hate," Joys That Sting. C. S. Lewis. ArLo

Oh do not wanton with those eyes. Ben Jonson. CBLP; SeCP; TEP

Oh! don't you see the turtle-dove. The Turtle-Dove. *Unknown.* OxBoLi

Oh! doo dah day! (*LL*) The Camptown Races. Stephen Collins Foster. AnAmPo

Oh [*or* O] Dreams, Oh [*or* O] Destinations, *sels.* C. Day Lewis. Symbols of Gross Experience. Son
"To travel like a bird." GTBS-P

Oh! Dublin sure there is no doubtin.' No Place So Grand. *Unknown.* WTO

Oh, early in the evenin', just after dark. The Blackleg Miners. *Unknown.* GBP; OBET

Oh East is East, and West is West, and never the twain shall meet. The Ballad of East and West. Kipling. BeLS; BLPL; FaBoBe; FaBV; FaPoR; OBNV

Oh effervescent palisades of ferns in drippage. From Rome, for More Public Fountains in New York City. Alan Dugan. Prf

Oh, Eleazar Wheelock was a very pious man. Eleazar Wheelock. Richard Hovey. OBAL

Oh Eliza look at your Uncle Jim! Soldiers' Chorus from Faust. *Unknown.* NOBAu

Oh, England is a pleasant place for them that's rich and high. The Last Buccaneer. Charles Kingsley. BeLS; EBEvV; EBVV; FaBoBe
(Last Buccanier, The.) PeVV
(Old Buccaneer, The.) MoShBr

Oh, England./ Sick in head and sick in heart. England. *Unknown.* FaBoEE; OxBSP

Oh! Erin my country, my ancestor's home! Song to Erin. Mary Weston Fordham. CBWP-2

Oh, ever skilled to war the form we love! Sonnet to Hope. Helen Maria Williams. ECWP

Oh! ever thus from childhood's hour. Thomas Moore. *Fr. Lalla Rookh.* UV

Oh, ever thus from childhood's hour, I've seen my fondest hopes recede. Muddled Metaphors. Tom Hood.
(Few Muddled Metaphors by Moore-ose Melodist.) FaBoNo

Oh, everything is far. Rainer Maria Rilke, *tr. fr. German by* C. F. MacIntyre. TrJP

Oh, face to face with trouble. Margaret E. M. Sangster. PoToHe

Oh, Fair to See. Christina Rossetti. *Fr. Sing-Song.* FaPON; OHIP

Oh [*or* O] fair[e] sweet face, oh [*or* O] eyes celestial[l] bright. John Fletcher. *Fr. Women Pleased.* PoEL-2
(To His Sleeping Mistress.) NOSC

Oh [*or* O] Fairest of the Rural Maids. Bryant. TAP

Oh, fairest of the rural maids! Bryant. EAP

Oh, fare you well, my darling. Fare You Well, My Darling. *Unknown.* AmFP

Oh! Farewell to the end of my Nose! (*LL*) There Was a Young Lady Whose Nose. Edward Lear. EBEV; FaPON

Oh Father. Wendy Rose. CDW

Oh father, answer me. Dialogue. Howard Nemerov. NYBP

Oh Father — if Thou wouldst indeed. Father. Arthur Davison Ficke. TrPWD

Oh father, let us hence — for hark. A Presentiment. Bryant. AnAmPo

Oh father, now that I have touched. Oh Father. Wendy Rose. CDW

Oh feet, oh legs, oh thighs/ that formed the deathrow. Philodemus, *tr. fr. Greek by* William Moebius. GrAn

Oh, fields of wonder. Birth. Langston Hughes. NAs

Oh flame falling, as shaken, as the stories. The Fire. Robert Creeley. NOBA

Oh, fond attempt to give a deathless lot. On Observing Some Names of Little Note Recorded in the "Biographia Britannica." William Cowper. OBD

Oh, for a book and a shady nook. Open Sesame. *Unknown.* BoTP

Oh, for a Bowl of Fat Canary. John Lyly. *See* O! [*or* Oh] for a bowl of fat canary.

Oh! for a closer walk with God. Walking with God. William Cowper. ECEV; EnRP; NOCV; NOEC; PeECV; PoEL-3; TEP; TOF; SCGP

Oh, for a drink, to-night. Charmion's Lament. Eloise Bibb. CBWP-4

Oh for a lodge in some vast wilderness. The Time-Piece. William Cowper. *Fr. Task, The.* EnRP
(Against Slavery.) NOEC

Oh for a pleasant book to cheat the sway. Winter Fields. John Clare. EnVR

Oh for a poet — for a beacon bright. Oh for a Poet — for a Beacon Bright. E. A. Robinson. OxBA

Oh for a Poet — for a Beacon Bright. E. A. Robinson. OxBA

Oh! for a thousand tongues to sing. The Farmer's Soliloquy. Robert Charles O'Hara Benjamin. AAP

Oh for boyhood's painless play. Whittier. *Fr. Barefoot Boy, The.* AiP; FaBoBe; GGP; GN; LiTA; OBAL; OBCA; PoLF; WBLP, *abr*

Oh for far-off monkeyland. Monkeyland. Sándor Weöres, *tr. fr. Hungarian by* Edwin Morgan. RB

Oh for His face! hidden by the veil of each breath! (*LL*) Behind the Veil. Andrew Lansdown. NOBAu

Oh for one hour of youthful joy! The Old Man Dreams. Oliver Wendell Holmes. AnAmPo; BLPL; PoLF

Oh! [*or* O!] for some honest lover's ghost. Sir John Suckling. BeJo; BXAP; JCP; MeLP; PoEL-3; SeCP; SeCV-1
(Doubt of Martyrdom, A.) BoLoP; CaPo; NOBE; OBEV

Oh fortune, [how] thy wresting wavering state. Elizabeth I, Queen of England. FaBoEH
(Written on a Wall at Woodstock.) PBWP; WPE

Oh, foully slighted Ethiope maid! Priscilla Jane Thompson. CBWP-2

Oh, Freedom. *Unknown.* SWP

Oh friend, we arrived too late. Friedrich Hölderlin, *tr. fr. German by* Robert Bly. *Fr. Bread and Wine.* NU; RaBo

Oh! fye upon care. The Ranting Wanton's Resolution; 1672. *Unknown.* CoMu

Oh gallant was our galley from her carven steering-wheel. The Galley-Slave. Kipling. PeVV

Oh, gallant was the first love, and glittering and fine. Pictures in the Smoke. Dorothy Parker. CoGr; NBLV

Oh, gallantly they fared forth in khaki and in blue. America's Welcome Home. Henry van Dyke. AiP

Oh [*or* O] Galuppi, Baldassaro, this is very sad to find! A Toccata of Galuppi's. Robert Browning. EBVV; EBVVPR; EnVR; FaBoVe;

FaPoB; GTBS-P; HAP; LiTB; Mes; NAEL-2; NOBE; NOBVV; NoP; OAEL-2; OtMeF; TEP; UV

Oh, gentle one, thy birthday sun should rise. The Twenty-Seventh of March. Bryant. EAP

Oh, Georgie Wedlock is my name. Georgie Wedlock. *Unknown.* AmFP

Oh, get you forth, my son Willy. Marm Grayson's Guests. Mary E. Wilkins Freeman. OBCA

Oh, Ghingeli, my bleeding heart. Oh, Ghingeli [*or* Gingilee], my bleeding heart. Moyshe-Leyb Halpern, *tr. fr. Yiddish.* TrJP, *tr. by* Joseph Leftwich

Oh gin I were a doo. Gin I Were a Doo. *Unknown.* GBP

Oh give attention, you maidens dear. Constance Kent. *Unknown.* OBET

Oh give me a home where the buffalo roam. A Home on the Range. *Unknown.* FaBoBe

Oh, Give Me the Hills. *Unknown.* AmFP

Oh! give to me of the bright green leaves. I Am Fashion's Toy. Mary E. Tucker. CBWP-1

Oh, Give Us Back the Days of Old! John Mason Neale. NOCV

Oh, give us pleasure in the flowers today. A Prayer in Spring. Robert Frost. TrCP; TrPWD
(Oh, Give Us Pleasure in the Flowers Today.) AH

Oh, Give Us Pleasure in the Flowers Today. Robert Frost. *See* Oh, give us pleasure in the flowers today.

Oh glorious spirits, who after all your bands. To All Angels and Saints. George Herbert. SeCV-1

Oh, go to old Ireland and then you will know. Go to Old Ireland. *Unknown.* AmFP

Oh, God, beneath thy guiding hand. The Pilgrim Fathers. Leonard Bacon. AH; WGRP

Oh God Forbid. Freddie Greenfield. GLP

Oh God I really went and did it this time. Went and picked up. The Blake Mistake. Sandie Castle. UL

Oh God! It's great! Chocolate Milk. Ron Padgett. TTTS

Oh, God, let me be beautiful in death. Last Plea. Jean Starr Untermeyer. TrPWD

Oh God made a trance on Sunday. God Made a Trance. *Unknown.* OBET

Oh God! my heart is thine. In the Valley. Priscilla Jane Thompson. CBWP-2

Oh God, she said. Song My. Susan Griffin. NMM; WPOW

Oh God, that I were dead! (*LL*) Mariana. Tennyson. AWP; CBLP; CH; EBVVPR; EnVR; FHYEP; InPS; MeMBP; NAEL-2; NOBE; NoP; OAEL-2; OBEV; OBNC; OxAEP-2; PeVV; PoE; PoEL-5; SCGP; TEP; TFi; TrGrPo; UnPo; WiR

Oh, golden flower opened up. A Poem to the Mother of the Gods. *Unknown, tr. fr. Aztec Indian by* Edward Kissam. STP

Oh golden life, waken! Fortunate night! Johann Klaj, *tr. fr. German by* George C. Schoolfield. GePo

Oh! Golden Rose! Oh. Glittering Lilly White. Edward Taylor. *Fr. Preparatory Meditations Before My Approach to the Lord's Supper.* SCAP

Oh, good gigantic smile o' the brown old earth. Among the Rocks. Robert Browning. *Fr. James Lee's Wife.* OxBSP

Oh! Good, good, good, my Lord. What more love yet. Edward Taylor. *Fr. Preparatory Meditations Before My Approach to the Lord's Supper.* NOBA

Oh Great Spirit of the North. Diann Neu. EaPr

Oh, greenly and fair in the lands of the sun. The Pumpkin. Whittier. OHIP

Oh grief that Earth's best hopes rest all with thee! (*LL*) England! the time is come when thou shouldst wean. Wordsworth. Son

Oh! had I now an overcoat. Wish for an Overcoat. Alfred Islay Walden. AAP

"Oh, halt!" cried Virginia, "Enough!" Otto Watteau. PeLi

Oh hame cam his guid horse, but never cam he. (*LL*) Bonnie [*or* Bonny] George [*or* James] Campbell. *Unknown.* AmFP; CH; ELP; EnRP; ESPB; FaBoBa; GBP; NoP; OxBB; OxBoLi; SCGP

Oh, hangman, hangman, slacken your rope. The Sycamore Tree. *Unknown.* AmFP

Oh, hapless sire, distraught with cares. The Yoke. Kalonymos ben Kalonymos, *tr. fr. Hebrew by* J. Chotzner. *Fr. Touchstone, The.* TrJP

Oh happy hero come, oh enter, worthy groom. To Be Read above the Castle-Gate, When His Princely Highness Rode in to His Marriage Bed. Simon Dach, *tr. fr. German by* George C. Schoolfield. GePo

Oh happy shades! to me unblest. The Shrubbery. William Cowper. FaBoRV; NOBE

Oh happy trees that we plant today. Tree Planting. *Unknown.* OHIP

Oh, hark the dogs are barking, love. The Banks of the Condamine. *Unknown.* FaBoBa; GBP; NOBAu

Oh, have you heard of lates'. Ballit of de Boll Weevil, De. *Unknown.* NOBA

Oh, have you seen the Tattlesnake. The Journal of Society. Godfrey Turner. NOBL; PeLV

Oh! He is a majo, a majo is he. (LL) The Discreet Majo. Fernando Periquet Y Zuaznabar. RiWo

Oh, he was a handsome trotter, and he couldn't be completer. How We Drove the Trotter. W. T. Goodge. NOBAu

Oh! hear a pensive prisoner's prayer. The Mouse's Petition. Anna Laetitia Barbauld. ECWP; FM; OxBChV

"Oh, hear you a horn, mother, behind the hill?" The Horn. James Reeves. OTCP

Oh heart rejoice! For I Have Done a Good and Kindly Deed. Franz Werfel, tr. fr. German by Edith Abercrombie Snow. TrJP

Oh, heavens! the weakness of my unkind father! The Obscured Prince; or, The Black Box Boxed. Unknown. APAS

Oh Heav'ns! I'm choack'd with smoak, I'm burn'd with fire. Lament of the Sodomites. George Lestey. Fr. Fire and Brimstone; or, The Destruction of Sodom. PeHV

Oh hell, what do mine eyes. Milton by Firelight. Gary Snyder. CAPP; CoAP; InPS; NAAL-2; PoBeRe; PPP

Oh, her beauty — the tender maid! Its brilliance gives light. Ibn al-Arabi, tr. fr. Persian by R. A. Nicholson. TOF

Oh, here's a jolly lark. The Old Marquis and His Blooming Wife. Unknown. CoMu

Oh hold me, for I am afraid. (LL) Woman to Man. Judith Wright. CBAP; FaBoMA; WPE

Oh, Hollow! Hollow! Hollow! W. S. Gilbert. Fr. Patience. FaBoNo

Oh, holy cause/ That points the grass. Sung on a Sunny Morning. Jean Starr Untermeyer. TrPWD

Oh how black the night is. The Old Man at the Window. Anthony Harvey. Mes

Oh, how can I live in a torture so wild. Disappointment. Mary E. Tucker. CBWP-1

Oh [or O] how comely it is and how reviving. Milton. Fr. Samson Agonistes. FHYEP; NOBE; NOCV; OAEL-1; OBEV; OxAEP-1; PoEL-3

Oh! How his pointed language, like a dart. Cant. 5.6 & c. Elizabeth Singer. ChIV-1; KTR

Oh, how I hope. (LL) Sinking. Lin Ling. WPC

Oh, how I love Humanity. The World State. G. K. Chesteron. IHNG

Oh how I wish that an embargo. The Nurse's Dole in the Medea. Byron. OBVE

Oh, how my love/ With a whirling power. Tu-kehu, tr. fr. Maori by J. C. Andersen. WTO

Oh how oft I wake and find. To My God. George Macdonald. TrPWD

Oh how real to me you are! (LL) Auburn. Paul Verlaine. ErPo

Oh hush thee, little Dear-my-soul. Christmas Eve. Eugene Field. OHIP

Oh! hush thee, my baby, the night is behind us. Seal Lullaby. Kipling. Fr. Jungle Book, The. FaPON; OBAP
(Seal Mother's Song.) ZA

Oh! hush Thee, oh! hush Thee, my Baby so small. Cradle Song at Bethlehem. E. J. Falconer. BoTP

Oh hush up. Breakfast. Everette Maddox. MT

Oh! I admit I'm dull and poor. The Claim. E. Nesbit. NOBVV

Oh I am a cat that likes to/ Gallop. The Galloping Cat. Stevie Smith. BrRo; CoGr; OFC

Oh, I am a Texas cowboy, just off the Texas plains. The Texas Cowboy. Unknown. AmFP

Oh, I am wild — wild! Sale of Souls. Adah Isaacs Menken. CBWP-1

Oh, I be vun of the useful troibe. A Rustic Song. Anthony C. Deane. FiBHP

Oh, I can hear you, God, above the cry. Wind in the Pine. Lew Sarett. TrPWD

Oh, I can smile for you, and tilt my head. A Certain Lady. Dorothy Parker. NIP

Oh I can't decide between my two loves ei!. Women's Songs. Unknown, tr. fr. Maori by Margaret Orbell. PeNZ

Oh, I don't want to be a gambler. I Don't Want to Be a Gambler. Unknown. AS

Oh I got up and went to work. On a Seven-Day Diary. Alan Dugan. OBAL

Oh, I had a bird and the bird pleased me. The Barnyard. Unknown. AmFP

Oh, I had a horse and his name was Bill. The Horse Named Bill. Unknown. AS

Oh I have grown so shrivelled and sere. Body of John. R. A. K. Mason. PeNZ

Oh, I have no illusions as to what. Penelope. James Harrison. NIP

Oh, I have slipped the surly bonds of earth. High Flight. John Gillespie Magee, Jr.. FaPON; ImGa; PoWW

Oh, I laugh to hear what grown folk. Mrs. Kriss Kringle. Edith M. Thomas. OBCA

Oh! I love to travel far and near throughout my native land. Wizard Oil. Unknown. AS

Oh I loved you Pete Brown. And you were a brother. Hayden Carruth. Fr. Paragraphs. Jaz

Oh, I never had but one true love. The Unquiet Grave. Unknown. AmFP

Oh, I should love to be like one of those. The Youth Dreams. Rainer Maria Rilke, tr. fr. German by Ludwig Lewisohn. AWP; TrJP

Oh I suppose I should. Le Médecin Malgré Lui. William Carlos Williams. PoA

Oh, I used to sing a song. The Endless Song. Ruth McEnery Stuart. OBAL

Oh! I vu'st know'd o' my true love. Heedless o' My Love. William Barnes. GBL

Oh, I went to California in the spring of seventy-six. Root, Hog, or Die. Unknown. AmFP

Oh! I wish I were a tiny brown bird from out the south. Valentine's Day. Charles Kingsley. BoTP

Oh, I Wish I Were Single Again. Unknown. AmFP

Oh, I wonder where my lost Johnny's gone. Lost Johnny. Unknown. AmFP

Oh, I woud I wee a cose, cose fiend. Sim Ines. Jane Stubbs. FiBHP

Oh, if but a single hour. Permanence in Change. Goethe, tr. fr. German. HoPM, tr. by John Frederick Nims

Oh! if by any unfortunate chance I should happen to die. The Soldier. J. Y. Watson. BXAP

Oh, if I could only make you see. Her Mother. Alice Cary. OHIP

Oh, if my power might equal my desire. Lady Charlotte Guest. Goronva Camlan. AngWe

Oh if only all. Scimitar for Brenda Lewis. Kenward Elmslie. UL

Oh, If They Only Knew! Edith L. Mapes. BLRP; WBLP

Oh, If Thou Knew'st How Thou Thyself Dost Harm. William Alexander, Earl of Stirling. Fr. Aurora. Son

Oh, ill-starred Ethiopia. Address to Ethiopia. Priscilla Jane Thompson. CBWP-2

Oh, I'm a good old Rebel. The Rebel. Innes Randolph. NBLV; OBAL; OxBoLi

Oh I'm Dirty Dan, the world's dirtiest man. The Dirtiest Man in the World. Shel Silverstein. OBCA

Oh I'm in love with the janitor's boy. The Janitor's Boy. Nathalia Crane. PoLF

Oh, I'm mad for Don Juan. How to Tell Juan Don from Another. Gardner E. Lewis. FiBHP

Oh! I'm the New Year. The New Year. Unknown. BoTP

Oh in eighteen hundred and forty-one. Poor Paddy Works on the Railway. Unknown. AS

Oh, in eighteen hundred and sixty-one. Roll, Alabama, Roll. Unknown. OxBSS

Oh, in the fourteenth the faith landed. The Land Is Gone. Unknown, tr. fr. Maori by Margaret Orbell. PeNZ

Oh, in the merry month of May. Bonny Barbara Allan. Unknown. AWP, A and B vers.; BoLoP, A and B vers.; CH, A and B vers.; ESPB, A and B vers.; HeIP; LiTB; NoP; OxBB

Oh in the Stonegut Sugar Works. Ballad of the Stonegut Sugar Works. James K. Baxter. PeNZ

Oh is it the jar of nations. The Jar of Nations. A. E. Housman. LiTB

Oh, is it, then, Utopian. De Profundis. Dorothy Parker. ErPo; NAAL-2

Oh, is not this a holy spot? On Laying the Corner-Stone of the Bunker Hill Monument. John Pierpont. PAH

Oh, it is done, my love, my death, my life, my prize. To the Superhuman Adelmund, When She Would Undo the Kiss Already Done. Philipp von Zesen, tr. fr. German by George C. Schoolfield. GePo

Oh it was a fine and pleasant day. The Shoals of Herring. Ewan MacColl. OxBSS

Oh, it was not a pheasant cock. The Drowned Lady. Unknown. ChTr

Oh it's all under the leaves and the leaves of life. The Leaves of Life. Unknown. OBET

Oh, it's fiddle-de-dum and fiddle-de-dee. The Dancing Bear. Albert Bigelow Paine. OBCA

Oh, it's H-A-P-P-Y I am, and it's F-R-double-E. The Bells. Unknown. FiBHP

Oh, it's hard to grow up at the way-station side! A Boatman's Song. Wang Chien, tr. fr. Chinese by William H. Nienhauser. SuSp

Oh, it's Hynde Horn fair, and it's Hynde Horn free. Hynde Horn. Unknown. GN

Oh, It's Nine Years Ago I Was Digging in the Land. Unknown. AmFP

Oh, it's twenty gallant gentlemen. The Last Hunt. William Roscoe Thayer. FaBoBe

Oh, I've got no use for the women. I've Got No Use for the Women. *Unknown.* AmFP

Oh, I've ridden plenty of horses. Noonday Sun. Kathryn Jackson *and* Byron Jackson. FaPON

Oh! joy it was for her, and joy for me! *(LL)* Among All Lovely Things My Love Had Been. Wordsworth. CoGr; GBL

Oh [*or* O] joys [*or* joyes]! Infinite sweetness! with what flowers [*or* flowres]. The Morning Watch. Henry Vaughan. AngWe; ESCV; GeHe; LiTB; NOSC; NTP; PeECV

Oh! kangaroos, sequins, chocolate sodas! Today. Frank O'Hara. TTTS

Oh King of grief! (a title strange, yet true). The Thanksgiving. George Herbert. ESCV; GeHe

Oh King of Saints, how great's thy work, say we. Edward Johnson. SCAP

Oh King of stars! Hospitality in Ancient Ireland. *Unknown, tr. fr. Irish by* Kuno Meyer. TIRV

Oh king, whose head alone can rule Earth's company. Concerning the King of Sweden. Georg Rudolph Weckherlin, *tr. fr. German by* George C. Schoolfield. GePo

Oh! Ladies and gentlemen, please to draw near. Down, Down Derry Down. *Unknown.* AS

Oh last Thursday morning while playing at ball. Willie. *Unknown.* AmFP

Oh Lawd have mussy now upon us. Blessing without Company. *Unknown.* BPo

Oh leaden heeld. Lord, give, forgive I pray. Edward Taylor. *Fr.* Preparatory Meditations Before My Approach to the Lord's Supper. SCAP

Oh, let me lay my head tonight upon your breast. I Am Your Wife. *Unknown.* PoToHe

Oh, let me not be last to fall asleep! *(LL)* Insomnia. Edith M. Thomas. AmWP

Oh, let me run and hide. Spring Ecstasy. Lizette Woodworth Reese. MoAmPo

Oh let that day from time be blotted quite. Lord General Fairfax. FaBoEH

Oh! let that day from time be blotted quite. On the Fatal Day January 30, 1648. Thomas Fairfax, Baron Fairfax. NOSC

Oh, Let Thy Teachings. Immanuel di Roma, *tr. fr. Hebrew by* J. Chotzner. *Fr.* Machberoth. TrJP

Oh, let us do so too. *(LL)* Good-night. James Shirley. BeJo

Oh, let us howl some heavy note. The Madman's Song. John Webster. *Fr.* Duchess of Malfi, The. EIL; NAEL-1 (Song: "O, let us howl some heavy note.") InvP

Oh, let's fix us a julep and kick us a houn.' Boogie-woogie Ballads. St. Clair McKelway. PoNe

Oh, let's go up the hill and scare ourselves. The Bonfire. Robert Frost. InvP

Oh, life is a glorious cycle of song. Comment. Dorothy Parker. *Fr.* Some Beautiful Letters. AnAmPo; NBLV; NIP; OBAL; VBLP

Oh, like a tree. The Tree. John Freeman. BoTP

Oh List to My Song!. Clara Ann Thompson. CBWP-2

Oh! Listen, man! Immortality. Richard Henry Dana. WGRP

Oh little boat with the red sail. *(LL)* Love Poem: Growing Down. Christian McEwen. VBLP

Oh, little body, do not die. *(LL)* A Child Ill. Sir John Betjeman. PIP

Oh, little body, do not die. A Child Ill. Sir John Betjeman. PIP

Oh little island. "Ping Hsin," *tr. fr. Chinese by* Kenneth Rexroth *and* Ling Chung. *Fr.* Multitudinous Stars. WPC

Oh Living Lord, I still will laud thy name. An Other Song of the Faithful, for the Mercies of God. Michael Drayton. ChIV-1

Oh loathsome place! where I. The Earl of Surrey. SiPS

Oh London Town's a fine town, and London sights are rare. London Town. John Masefield. OtMeF

Oh, lonely heart! why do thy pulses beat. Remembered Music. Sarah Helen Whitman. AmWP

Oh! lonely is our old green fort. Old Fort Meigs. *Unknown.* PAH

Oh, long, long/ The snow has possessed the mountains. The Grass on the Mountain. *Unknown, tr. fr. Paiute Indian by* Mary Austin. AWP; FaPON; GOA

Oh! Look at the Moon. Eliza Lee Follen. BoTP

Oh Lord Cozens Hardy. Lord Cozens Hardy. Sir John Betjeman. OxBTC

Oh, Lord! I lift my heart. Priscilla Jane Thompson. CBWP-2

Oh Lord! thou hast known me, and searched me out. An Hymn on the Omnipresence. John Byrom. TrPWD

Oh Lord upon whose will dependeth my welfare. Psalm 88. The Earl of Surrey. SiPSBD

Oh, Lord, we call to you from our apartment. A Gay Psalm from Fort Valley. Louie Crew. GLP

Oh Lord, when all our bones are thrust. Supplication. Edgar Lee Masters. TrCP; TrPWD

Oh lordy, lord, oh lordy, lord. Worried Life Blues. *Unknown.* AmFP

Oh, love me truly! *(LL)* You say you love, but with a voice. Keats. CBLP

Oh love! no habitant of earth art. Byron. *Fr.* Childe Harold's Pilgrimage. CBLP (Fatal Spell, The.) OBNC

Oh! Love, that stronger art than wine. Aphra Behn. *Fr.* Lucky Chance, The. WPE; WPOW

"Oh! Love," they said, "is King of Kings." Rupert Brooke. ArLo; PFP

Oh, love this house, and make of it a Home —. For a New Home. Rosa Zagnoni Marinoni. PoToHe

Oh Lovely Fishermaiden. Heine, *tr. fr. German by* Louis Untermeyer. AWP

Oh, Lovely, Lovely, Lovely! *Unknown.* CRH

Oh, Lovely Rock. Robinson Jeffers. NU

Oh! lovely voices of the sky. Hymn for Christmas. Felicia Dorothea Hemans. GN

Oh Lucky Jim! *Unknown.* ChTr; GBP

Oh lucky Jim, how I envy him! *(LL)* Oh Lucky Jim! *Unknown.* ChTr; GBP

Oh lyre divine, what daring spirit. Thomas Gray. *Fr.* Progress of Poesy, The. EPCY

Oh Madame Curie. While Dissecting Frogs in Biology Class Scrut Discovers the Intricacies of the Scooped Neckline in His Lab Partner's Dress. George Roberts. GOYP

Oh majo of my life. The Piteous Maja. Fernando Periquet Y Zuaznabar, *tr. fr. Spanish by* Philip L. Miller. RiWo

Oh, make me, sphere-descended Queen. A Wykehamist's Address to Learning. P. N. Shuttleworth. FaBoCo

Oh, Mammy, Mammy, now I'm married. Will the Weaver. *Unknown.* AmFP

Oh man, be born of God: for at His Godhead's throne. Only His Son Is With God. "Angelus Silesius," *tr. fr. German.* *Fr.* Cherubical Wanderer, The. GePo, *tr. by* George C. Schoolfield

'Oh man, don't make a noise' the officer. Waterloo. Patricia Beer. PAW

Oh [*or* O] many a day have I made good ale in the glen. The Outlaw of Loch Lene. *Unknown, tr. fr. Modern Irish by* Jeremiah Joseph Callanan. BIrV; CH; GBL; NTP; OBEV; PeIV

Oh, Mary and the Baby, sweet Lamb. Mary and the Baby, Sweet Lamb. *Unknown.* AmFP

Oh, Mary, this Enoch's a wonderful sight. The Mountebank of Mourne. Roger Woddis. IHNG

Oh May, bonnie May is to the Yowe buchts gane. The Laird o' Ochiltree Wa's. *Unknown.* OxBB

Oh, may my constant feet not fail. Sophocles, *tr. by* Robert Whitelaw. *Fr.* Oedipus the King [*or* Oedipus Rex]. NAWM-1; WGRP

Oh may you bless your happy lot that lies secure on shore. The Banks of Newfoundland ("Oh may you bless your happy lot that lies secure on shore.") *Unknown.* OxBSS

Oh me good friend, Mr. Wilberforce, make we free! Song of the King of the Eboes. *Unknown.* PBCV

Oh me/ is that the ambulance chasing out of town? Alan Brunton. PeNZ

Oh me, the time is come to part. Mary Sidney Wroth, Countess of Montgomery. *Fr.* Urania. NOSC; WPE

Oh, meet me tonight in the moonlight. New Jail. *Unknown.* AmFP

Oh men are beaten, beaten, beaten down. The Land Laws. Merimeri Penfold, *tr. fr. Maori by* Margaret Orbell. PeNZ

Oh Menelaus. On Hearing the First Cuckoo. Richard Church. OBMV

Oh, mighty America, hast thou come to this? Fare Thee Well. Eli Siegel. GOA

Oh mighty city of New York! you are wonderful to behold. Jottings of New York. William McGonagall. OBTV

Oh, Miss Bailey! unfortunate Miss Bailey! *(LL)* Unfortunate Miss Bailey. George Colman the Younger. FiBHP; GBP

Oh, Mr. Cross! Address to Mr. Cross, of Exeter 'Change, on the Death of the Elephant. Thomas Hood. FM

"Oh, Mrs. McGrath," the sergeant said. Mrs. McGrath. *Unknown.* FaBoBa

Oh [*or* O] mistress mine, where are you roaming? O Mistress Mine. Shakespeare. *Fr.* Twelfth Night. AWP; BoLoP; ClHu; CoGr; CTC; EIL; ELP; FaBV; GBL; GoJo; HAP; ImPo; InPS; LiTB; NAEL-1; NBLV; NOBE; NoP; NoSic; OAEL-1; OxBoLi; OxBSP; PFP; PoRA; SCGP; TFi; TrGrPo (Carpe Diem.) GTBS; GTBS-P (Sweet-and-Twenty.) OBEV; PoE

Oh modest, lovely child of spring. With a Violet. John Olaf Paulsen, *tr. fr. Danish by* Philip L. Miller. RiWo

Oh, Molly, oh, Molly, I've told you before. Red Whiskey. *Unknown.* AmFP

Oh moon, oh moon! *Unknown, tr. fr. Papuan by* Mari Marase. BoWoP

Oh Moon! when I look on thy beautiful face. Poetic Thought. *Unknown.* FiBHP

Oh, most high, almighty, good Lord God. Canticle of the Sun. St. Francis of Assisi, *tr. fr. Italian.* WGRP, *tr. by* Maurice Francis Egan

Oh mother, holiest mother, mother night! To Night, the Mother of Sleep and Death. John Addington Symonds. Son

Oh, mother, I shall be married to Mr. Punchinello. To Mr. Punchinello. *Unknown.* OxNR
(Mr. Punchinello.) CBNP

Oh mother my mouth is full of stars. Song of the Dying Gunner A.A.1. Charles Causley. PoWW

Oh mother of a mighty race. Bryant. EAP; FaBoBe; PAH

Oh! mourn not for Anacreon dead. On Tom Moore's Translation of Anacreon. Thomas, Lord Erskine. FaBoEE

Oh Muse! I crave a favor. The Muse's Favor. Priscilla Jane Thompson. AAP; CBWP-2

Oh, Musgrove, he persuaded me. Musgrove. *Unknown.* AmFP

Oh, my beloved, have you thought of this. Sonnet. Edna St. Vincent Millay. HeIP

Oh My Black Soul. John Donne. *See* Oh my black[e] soul[e]! now thou art summoned.

Oh my black soul[e]! now thou art summoned. John Donne. *Fr.* Holy Sonnets. EBEV; ESCV; JCP; OAEL-1; OxAEP-1; Son; TEP; TOF
(Oh My Black Soul.) Poetr

Oh my boy: Jesus. The Confession Stone. Owen Dodson. TTY

Oh my bride, my bride. (*LL*) I Remember. Stevie Smith. BoLoP; BoWoP; FaBoWP; InPK; OxBC

Oh, My Darling Clementine. *At. to* Percy Montross. AnAmPo; FaBoBe

Oh my God, screamed Mommy, you went and ate the baby. The Snack. L. L. Zeigler. BXAP

Oh, my house is bugged. (*LL*) My House Is Bugged. Mafika Pascal Gwala. PeSAV

Oh, my Lord. My Lord, What a Morning. Waring Cuney. TTY

Oh, My Love Is Like a Red, Red Rose. Burns. InPK; LiTB

Oh, my love's in Germany, send him hame, send him hame. My Love's in Germany. Thomas Traill. ScCV

Oh, my mother's moaning by the river. The Lonely Mother. Fenton Johnson. PoNe

Oh, my name is Diamond Lily. Diamond Lily. *Unknown.* FaBoBl

Oh [*or* O], my name it is Sam [*or* Samuel] Hall, it is Sam [*or* Samuel] Hall. Sam [*or* Samuel] Hall. *Unknown.* ChTr; UnPo

Oh, my name was Robert Kidd, as I sailed, as I sailed. Captain Kidd ("Oh, my name was Robert Kidd, as I sailed, as I sailed.") *Unknown.* MoShBr

Oh My Own Little Daughter, Four Years Old. *Unknown.* ECWP

Oh My People I Remember. Wendy Rose. CDW

Oh, my Plutonian restaurateur! Revving Up la Rêve. Joel Dailey. UL

Oh, my pretty cock, oh, my handsome cock. Cock-A-Doodle-Do. *Unknown.* ReMoGo

Oh, Nancy, my heart. To Milk in the Valley Below. *Unknown.* OBET

Oh, neighbours! what had I a-do for to marry! Hooly and Fairly. Joanna Baillie. WoRP

Oh, never before have I known, among. Love. Takasaki Masakazei, *tr. fr. Japanese by* Miyamori Asataro. LPA

Oh never marry Ishmael! Song for Unbound Hair. Genevieve Taggard. PoRA

Oh never on my youthful ear. My Mother's Voice. Mary E. Tucker. CBWP-1

Oh, never say that you have reached the very end. We Survive! Hirsch Glick, *tr. fr. Yiddish by* Ruth Rubin. TrJP

Oh never weep for love that's dead. Dead Love. Elizabeth Siddal. NOBVV

Oh nimber, nimber Will-o! Chuck Will's Widow Song. *Unknown.* BPo

Oh! ninna and anninia! Sleep, Baby Boy. *Unknown.* FaPON

Oh No. Robert Creeley. HeIP; InPK; NaP; SM

Oh, no. By Jove! There comes the white hippocampus. (*LL*) The Mermaid. Ben King. AnAmPo; OBAL

Oh No More, No More. John Ford. *See* Oh [*or* O], no more, no more, too late.

Oh [*or* O], no more, no more, too late. John Ford. *Fr.* Broken Heart, The. GBL; NOSC; PoEL-2
(Love's Martyrs.) NOBE
(Oh No More, No More.) ELP
(Song: "Oh no more, no more, too late.") OxBSP

Oh, no one can deny. Self's the Man. Philip Larkin. NOBL; PeLV

Oh! no, Poll, no! Since they've a-took. The Common a-Took In. William Barnes. EnVR

Oh, no! they just sold them for bioux. (*LL*) The American Indian. *Unknown.* FaBoCo; FiBHP; NBLV

Oh, No! We Never Mention Her. Thomas Haynes Bayly. VPP

Oh, no! we never mention her, her name is never heard. Oh, No! We Never Mention Her. Thomas Haynes Bayly. VPP

Oh, Noa, Noa! William Cole. NBLV

Oh, Northern men — true hearts and bold. Cast Down, but Not Destroyed. *Unknown.* PAH

"Oh not so fast," my ravished mistress cries. Thomas Nashe. *Fr.* Choice of Valentines, The. FaBoBl

Oh, not to be in England. Abroad Thoughts. Edward Blishen. NOBL

Oh, Nothing. John Ashbery. NAAL-2

Oh, now I've come back to you, Mother. The Cripple for Life; or, The Poor Volunteer. *Unknown.* AmFP

Oh, now we're leaving home, me boys; to Ottawa we're goin'. The Lake of the Caogama. *Unknown.* WTO

Oh! Oh! Should They Take Away My Stove . . . My Inexhaustible Ode to Joy. Miron Bialoszewski. *See* I have a stove.

Oh, oh, you will be sorry for that word! Edna St. Vincent Millay. BoWoP; HeIP; NALW

Oh, on an early morning I think I shall live forever! Poem in Three Parts. Robert Bly. CAPP; NaP; NOBA

Oh, once I lived in Cottonwood and owned a little farm. Once I Lived in Cottonwood. *Unknown.* AmFP

Oh, once I was a policeman young and merry (young and merry). A Policeman's Lot. Wendy Cope. FaBoWP

Oh once I was a shepherd boy. Once I Was a Shepherd Boy. *Unknown.* OBET

Oh, open the door, my hinnie, my heart. The Padda Song. *Unknown.* GBP

Oh, open the door, some pity to shew. Open the Door to Me, Oh! Burns. PoEL-4; SCGP
(O, Open the Door to Me, O!) FaBoCh

Oh, our manhood's prime vigour! no spirit feels waste. Robert Browning. *Fr.* Saul. OtMeF

Oh our Mother the Earth oh our Father the Sky. Song of the Sky Loom. *Unknown, tr. fr. Tewa Indian by* Herbert J. Spinden. WTO

Oh, Paddy dear! and did ye hear the news that's goin' round? The Wearin' o' the Green. *Unknown.* NOIV

Oh, Passage town is of great renown. The Town of Passage. *Unknown.* OxBoLi

Oh, passer-by, should you inquire. Epitaph on Pegasus, a Limping Gay. "Panormitanus," *tr. fr. Latin.* FaBoBl; PeHV

Oh photograph me thus! (*LL*) The Oneness of the Philosopher with Nature. G. K. Chesterton. CBNP; FaBoNo

Oh pile of white shirts who is coming. The Night of the Shirts. W. S. Merwin. VCAP

Oh, Pillykin Willykin Winky Wee! Punkydoodle and Jollapin. Laura E. Richards. OBCA

Oh pleasant eventide! Twilight Calm. Christina Rossetti. BoNaP; OBNC

Oh poesy is on the wane. Decay. John Clare. EnVR

Oh, Poet of Our Race. Poet of Our Race. Maggie Pogue Johnson. CBWP-4

Oh! poverty is a weary thing, 'tis full of grief and pain. The Sale of the Pet Lamb. Mary Howitt. CH

Oh praise Him, praise Him, praise without an end or aim. Zealous Admonition to Praise. Catharina Regina von Greiffenberg, *tr. fr. German by* George C. Schoolfield. GePo

Oh, pray come in. Rather Too Good, Little Peggy! Adelaide O'Keeffe. FaBoUs

Oh, Priest Pangeivi, you let go. Funeral Eva. Koroneu. RaBo

Oh princess of your land, whom Holstein cousin names. To the Great City of Moscow, as He Was Leaving June 25, 1636. Paul Fleming, *tr. fr. German by* George C. Schoolfield. GePo

Oh, pure and sportive little child. To a Little Colored Boy. Priscilla Jane Thompson. CBWP-2

Oh, river! gently as a wayward child. To the Hudson. Elizabeth Oakes Smith. AmWP

Oh, rock-a-by, baby mouse, rock-a-by, so! The Mouse's Lullaby. Palmer Cox. OBCA; TLR

Oh roses for the flush of youth. Christina Rossetti. ELP; GTBS-P; NOBVV

Oh, rouse you, rouse you, men at arms. The Great Swamp Fight. Caroline Hazard. PAH

Oh sacred Time! how soon thou'rt gone! Midnight Thought, A [on the Death of Mrs. *E. H.* and Her Little Daughter]. Elizabeth Thomas. KTR; NOSC

Oh, Sally Brown, of New York City. Sally Brown. *Unknown.* AmFP

Oh say, kid! *Unknown.* RoPo

Oh say not that my heart is cold. Charles Wolfe. OxAEP-2

Oh, say you can hear/ On the Watergate tapes. Final Curtain. Roger Woddis. FaBoPa; UV

Oh, says the linnet, if I sing. Birds' Lament. John Clare. PoEL-4

Oh, the gen'ral raised the devil with the kernel, so 'tis said. Bugs. Will Stokes. MoShBr

Oh, the girl that I loved she was handsome. The Man on the Flying Trapeze. *Unknown.* BLPA; OxBoLi

Oh! the Golden Age. The Golden Age. William Browne. *Fr.* Britannia's Pastorals. NOSC

Oh, the golden bauble of your rising. O! Marge Piercy. SRLS

Oh, the gorgeous leaves of autumn! Autumn Leaves. Clara Ann Thompson. CBWP-2

Oh the gray cat piddled in the white cat's eye. *Unknown.* ISE

Oh, the green and the graceful — the cocoa-nut tree! The Cocoa-nut Tree. Frances Sargent Osgood. AmWP

Oh, the hireling sun in a slipshod way. The Field of the Cloth of Gold. P. J. Hartigan. NOBAu

Oh the Inconstant. N. P. van Wyk Louw, *tr. fr.* Afrikaans by Uys Krige *and* Jack Cope. PeSA

Oh the January man he walks abroad in woollen coat and boots of leather. January Man. Dave Goulder. OBET

Oh! the king's gane gyte. Cophetua. "Hugh MacDiarmid." OxBS

Oh the maggots marched down Pitt Street. Maggot Song. *Unknown.* NOBAu

Oh the many joys of a harlot's wedding. Hail Wedded Love! Jay Macpherson. MoCV

Oh the Miller, the dusty, musty Miller. A Ballad of All the Trades. *Unknown.* CoMu; ErPo

Oh the noble fleet of whalers out sailing from Dundee. The *Balena.* *Unknown.* OxBSS

Oh the north countree is a hard countree. The Ballad of Yukon Jake. Edward E. Paramore, Jr.. BeLS; BLPA

Oh, the old gray mare, she ain't what she used to be. Old Gray Mare. *Unknown.* AS; GBP

Oh! the old swimmin'-hole! whare the crick so still and deep. The Old Swimmin'-Hole. James Whitcomb Riley. AnAmPo; BeLS

Oh, the Pilliwinks lived by the portals of Loo. The Cooky-Nut Trees. Albert Bigelow Paine. OBCA

Oh, the praties they grow small. The Praties. *Unknown.* WTO (Famine Song.) WTO

Oh, the Rifles have stolen my dear jewel away. The Rifles. *Unknown.* OBET

Oh the rocks and the thimble. Meditations of a Parrot. John Ashbery. TTTS

Oh the rose of keenest thorn! The Iniquity of the Fathers upon the Children. Christina Rossetti. FaBoVe

Oh the sad day. Death. Thomas Flatman. OBD

Oh, the sea is deep. Song for a Suicide. Langston Hughes. PoNe

Oh, the shambling sea is a sexton old. The Gravedigger. Bliss Carman. BoNaP

Oh the shores, the forests are turning. The Han River in the Fog. Ts'ai Ch'i-chiao, *tr. fr. Chinese. Fr.* Han River, The. LHF, *tr.* by Hualing Nieh

Oh, the slimy, squirmy, slithery eel! Song of Hate for Eels. Arthur Guiterman. OBAL

Oh! the snow, the beautiful snow. The Beautiful Snow. John Whittaker Watson. BLPA; WBLP

Oh the SS *Irwell* left this port the stormy sea to cross. The Manchester Ship Canal. *Unknown.* OBET

Oh the streams of lovely Nancy are divided into three parts. The Streams of Lovely Nancy. *Unknown.* FaBoBa; OBET; OxBoLi

Oh, the sun sets red, the moon shines white. The *Armstrong* at Fayal. Wallace Rice. PAH

Oh, the sweet contentment. Coridon's Song. John Chalkhill. NOSC

Oh! the time that is past. *Unknown.* BoLoP

Oh, the times are hard and the wages low. Across the Western Ocean *or* Leave Her, Bullies, Leave Her. *Unknown.* AS; OxBSS, *with music* (Leave Her, Johnny, Leave Her.) OxBSS

Oh, the train's off the track. The Train Is Off the Track. *Unknown.* AmFP

Oh the trawler wharf in Aberdeen. Deep Sea Tug. Harry Robertson. OxBSS

Oh, the white house, the bride's house. The Bride's Song. William Johnson Cory. OBTV

Oh, the white sea-gull, the wild sea-gull. The Sea-Gull. Mary Howitt. BoTP; OxBChV

Oh, the wild joys of living! the leaping from rock up to rock. Robert Browning. *Fr.* Saul. BoTP; FaBV (Youth.) BoTP

Oh! then remember me. *(LL)* Go Where Glory Waits Thee. Thomas Moore. OBNC; PlP

Oh! then tell me, Shawn O'Ferrall. The Rising of the Moon A.D. 1798. John Keegan Casey. PeIV

Oh *[or* O] there is a blessing in this gentle breeze. Wordsworth. *Fr.* Prelude [or, Growth of a Poet's Mind], The. CH; EnRP; FHYEP; GN; HAP; NOBE; NoP; NU; OAEL-2; OBNC; OxAEP-2; PoE; SCV

Oh, there once was a Puffin. There Once Was a Puffin. Florence Page Jaques. NTCP

Oh there was a jolly ship built in Nazi Germany. The Sinking of the *Graf Spee. Unknown.* OxBSS

Oh! there was a moanish lady. Moanish Lady. *Unknown.* AS

Oh, there was a youth and a noble youth. The Bailiff's Daughter of Islington. *Unknown.* AmFP; ESPB; FaBoBa; GN; OBET; OxBB; OxBoLi

Oh, there were fifteen men in green. Men in Green. David Campbell. (There were fifteen men in green.) FaBoMA

Oh, there's not much sense. *Unknown.* RoPo

Oh! they found a bit of iron what. They Called Them RAF 2C's. *Unknown.* NSI

Oh, Think Not I Am Faithful to a Vow! Edna St. Vincent Millay. FaBV

Oh this is the animal that never was. Rainer Maria Rilke, *tr. fr. German by* Stephen Mitchell. *Fr.* Unicorn, The. TTTS

Oh, this is the tale of John Cherokee. John Cherokee. *Unknown.* GBP

Oh this man. Magnificat. Michele Roberts. BrRo; NBrP; VBLP

Oh those were happy days, heaped up with wineskins. Silenus in Proteus. Thomas Lovell Beddoes. EnRP

Oh, those West Virginia Hills, so majestic and so grand. West Virginia Hills. Walter Seacrist. SWP

Oh! thou dead/ And everlasting witness! whose unsinking. Byron. *Fr.* Cain: A Mystery. ChIV-1

Oh *[or* O] thou great Power, in whom I move. A Hymn to My God in a Night of My Late Sickness[e]. Sir Henry Wotton. MeLP; NOSC

Oh, thou immortal bard! Byron. J. Gordon Coogler. OBAL

Oh, thou! in Hellas deemed of heavenly birth. Byron. *Fr.* Childe Harold's Pilgrimage. NAEL-2, *much abr.*

Oh thou, that dear and happy isle. Andrew Marvell. *Fr.* Upon Appleton House, to My Lord Fairfax. OxBoLi; SeCP; SeCV-1

Oh, Thou! Who Dry'st the Mourner's Tear. Thomas Moore. TrPWD

Oh! thou — whose great imperial mind could raise. *Unknown.* OBTV

Oh, 'tis my delight on a shining night, in the season of the year. *(LL)* The Lincolnshire Poacher. *Unknown.* FaBoEH; GBP; OxBoLi; PeLV

Oh! 'tis pretty to be in Ballinderry. Ballinderry. *Unknown.* WTO

Oh, 'tisn't manly, of course, 'tisn't manly, this method of/ wooing; Arthur Hugh Clough. *Fr.* Amours de Voyage. EBVVPR, *canto* II, xiv; NOBVV

Oh to be a bride. The Bride. Bella Akhmadulina, *tr. fr. Russian.* AIW; BoWoP, *tr. by* Stephan Stepanchev

Oh to be at Crowdieknowe. Crowdieknowe. "Hugh MacDiarmid." InPS; NoP; OxBS

Oh *[or* O] to be in England. Home Thoughts from Abroad. Robert Browning. ArNa; AWP; BoNaP; BoTP; ClHu; CoGr; EBEvV; EBVV; FaBoBe; FaBV; FaPoB; FaPON; FaPoR; FHYEP; GN; HeIL; HeIP; ImPo; LiTB; MeMBP; NAEL-2; NOBE; NOBVV; NoP; OBEV; OBNC; OBTV; OHCV; OtMeF; PlP; PoLF; PoRA; PrIm; TEP; TFi; TrGrPo; UV (April in England.) GN

Oh, to be in England. Home Truths from Abroad. *Unknown.* UV

Oh to be in England now that Winston's out. Ezra Pound. *Fr.* Cantos. IHNG; PoA

Oh to be Odd! Ogden Nash. CBNP

Oh, to feel the fresh breeze blowing. The Song of the Forest Ranger. Herbert Bashford. OHIP

Oh! to have hidden in the undergrowth. King Lot's Envoys. Drummond Allison. OxBSP

Oh, to those who know no better. That Little Lump of Coal. *Unknown.* AmFP

Oh, to vex me, contraries [or contraryes] meet in one. John Donne. *Fr.* Holy Sonnets. ESCV; NOSC; OAEL-1; PoEL-2; Son (Oh, to vex me, two contraries meet in one.) ChIV-2

Oh, to vex me, two contraries meet in one. John Donne. *See* Oh, to vex me, contraries [or contraryes] meet in one.

Oh Trial. *Unknown.* FaBoVe

Oh! true was his heart while he breathed. The King of Thulé. Goethe, *tr. fr. German by* James Clarence Mangan. AWP

Oh very early all in the spring. Early, Early in the Spring. *Unknown.* OBET

Oh virgin queen of mountain-side and woodland. III, 22. Pine Tree for Diana, The ("Montium custos nemorumque.") Horace, *tr. fr. Latin by* Austin Dobson. *Fr.* Odes. AWP, *tr. by* Louis Untermeyer

Oh *[or* O] waly, waly, up the [or yon] bank. Waly, Waly. *Unknown.* EnLoPo; EnSB; FaBoBa; GBP; HAP; NOSC; OBEV; OxBS; TFi (Forsaken Bride, The.) GTBS; GTBS-P

(Jamie Douglas.) ESPB

(Lord Douglas.) OxBB

(O Waly, Waly.) ELP; ScCV

(Waly, Waly, Love Be Bonny.) PrIm

Oh! water for me! Bright water for me! The Water-Drinker. Edward Jonson. BXAP

Oh! waves in the sunlight gleaming. Sonnet to My First Born. Mary Weston Fordham. CBWP-2

Oh, way down South where I was born. Roll the Cotton Down. *Unknown.* AmFP

Oh, we are the men of the Steelworkers' Union. United Steelworkers Are We. M. T. Montgomery. SWP

Oh, we come on the sloop *John B.* The John B. Sails. *Unknown.* AS

Oh [or O] wearisome condition of humanity. Chorus Sacerdotum. Fulke Greville. *Fr.* Mustapha. HAP; InvP; JCP; LiTB; NAEL-1; NOBE; OAEL-1; PoEL-1; PPP

(Chorus of Priests.) NoSic; OxAEP-1

Oh, weep for Columbia! oh, weep for the time! The Patriot's Lament. Joseph Cephas Holly. AAP

Oh, weep for Mr. and Mrs. Bryan! The Lion. Ogden Nash. TLR; WHSW

Oh! Weep for Those. Byron. ChIV-1

Oh! weep for those that wept by Babel's stream. Oh! Weep for Those. Byron. ChIV-1

Oh! weep with me the changing scene. A Letter to My Love — All Alone, Past 12, in the Dumps. "Amorous Lady, The." ECWP

Oh well done Lord E — — n! and better done R — — r! An Ode to the Framers of the Frame Bill. Byron. CoMu

Oh, we'll rally 'round the flag, boys, we'll rally once again. The Battle Cry [or Battle-Cry] of Freedom. George Frederick Root. AnAmPo; FaBoBe; PAH

Oh well tonight or some other night. Te Kaha. Rachel McAlpine. PeNZ

Oh, Wellington (or 'Vilainton' — for Fame). Byron. *See* Oh Wellington! (Or "Villainton," for Fame).

Oh Wellington! (Or "Villainton," for Fame). Byron. *Fr.* Don Juan. OBSV; OxBoLi

(Oh, Wellington or 'Vilainton' — for Fame.) OxAEP-2

Oh were I at the moss house, where the birds do increase. The Streams of Bunclody. *Unknown.* BIrV

Oh, whare ha'e ye been all day, Lord Donald, my son? Lord Donald. *Unknown.* ScCV

Oh! what a cruel wicked thing. Poem for Children, A; or, On Cruelty to the Irrational Creation. Jane Cave. ECWP

Oh, what a dawn of day! A Lovers' Quarrel. Robert Browning. EBVVPR

Oh, what a dreary place this was when first the Mormons found it. St. George. Charlie Walker. AmFP

Oh what a gay, what a rambling life a Settler's leading. Polyglot Medley. Andrew Geddes Bain. PeSAV

Oh what a host of questions in one rose. Back Again for the Holidays. Sir John Betjeman. *Fr.* Summoned by Bells. FaBoPP

Oh what a lad was Zimmer. A Zimmershire Lad. Paul Zimmer. SM

Oh [or O!] what a plague is Love! Phillida Flouts Me [or The Disdainful Shepherdess]. *Unknown.* CoMu; ElL; InvP; OBEV; PlP; TrGrPo

Oh! what a thing is man? Lord, who am I? Edward Taylor. *Fr.* Preparatory Meditations Before My Approach to the Lord's Supper. MeMAP; NAAL-1; NOBA; OxBA

Oh, what can be more pleasant. Chorus of Scyrian Maidens. Philip Bainbrigge. *Fr.* Achilles in Scyros. PeHV

Oh! what has caused this great commotion. Tippecanoe and Tyler Too. Alexander Coffman Ross. AnAmPo

Oh, what have you got for dinner, Mrs. Bond? Dilly Dilly. *Unknown.* OxNR

Oh, so merry, so merry, heigh-ho! The Light-hearted Fairy. *Unknown.* BoTP; FaPON

Oh! what is that comes gliding in. Sally Simpkin's Lament, [or John Jones's Kit-Cat-astrophe]. Thomas Hood. CBNP; EnRP

Oh, what is that I see yonder coming, coming, coming. Union Train. *Unknown.* SWP

Oh! What is the matter? *Unknown, tr. fr.* Greek *by* Kenneth Rexroth. PGA

"Oh! what shall I do?" sobbed a tiny mole. Who'll Help a Fairy? *Unknown.* BoTP

Oh, what was your name in the States? What Was Your Name in the States? *Unknown.* AS

Oh what wonders, what novels in this age there be. *Unknown.* FaBoEH

Oh, what's that stain on your shirt sleeve? Edward. *Unknown.* AmFP

Oh, what's the matter wi' [or with] you, my lass. Jimmy's Enlisted; or, The Recruited Collier. *Unknown.* CoMu; EBEV; OBET

(Recruited Collier, The.) OBET

Oh, what's the way to Arcady. The Way to Arcady. H. C. Bunner. AnAmPo

Oh, when I come to die. Give Me Jesus. *Unknown.* BPo

Oh when I think of my long-suffering race. Enslaved. Claude McKay. BPo

Oh, When I Was in Love with You. A. E. Housman. *Fr.* Shropshire Lad, A. BoLoP; CBLP; FaBV; FaPoB; LiTB; MeMBP; MoBrPo; TTTS

Oh, when I was in love with you. Oh, When I Was in Love with You. A. E. Housman. *Fr.* Shropshire Lad, A. BoLoP; CBLP; FaBV; FaPoB; LiTB; MeMBP; MoBrPo; TTTS

Oh, when I was single, oh then, oh then! I Wish I Were [or Was] Single Again. *Unknown.* AmFP, 2 *vers.*; AS

(Single Girl, The.) AmFP

Oh, when I'm in trouble. Do, Lord, Remember Me. *Unknown.* AmFP

Oh, When Shall I See Jesus? *Unknown.* AH, *with music*

(Ecstasy, , 1 *st., at. to* John Leland.) AmFP

Oh when the early morning at the seaside. East Anglian Bathe. Sir John Betjeman. NoP

Oh, when this earthly tenement. "Ada." BlSi

Oh, when we going to marry, to marry, to marry. Buffalo Boy. *Unknown.* AmFP

Oh, Whence Comes the Gladness? Priscilla Jane Thompson. CBWP-2

Oh whence do you come, my dear friend, to me. The Poor Ghost. Christina Rossetti. GBL

Oh, where are you going, my kind old husband. The Best Old Fellow in the World. *Unknown.* AmFP

Oh, where are you going, my little maiden fair. The Milkmaid. *Unknown.* AmFP

Oh, where are you going to, my pretty little dear. Dabbling in the Dew. *Unknown.* CH

Oh where are you going with your lovelocks [love-locks] flowing. Amor Mundi. Christina Rossetti. MeMBP; NoP; PoEL-5; Poetr

Oh, where do you come from. Little Raindrops. *At. to* Ann Hawkshawe *also to* Jane Euphemia Browne. BoTP; OxBChV

Oh, where have you been, Billy boy, Billy boy? Billy Boy. *Unknown.* AmFP; BLPA; HoPM; OBET

(Where have ye [or you] been all the day,/ Billy Boy?) OxNR

Oh, where have you been, my blue-eyed son? A Hard Rain's A-Gonna Fall. Bob Dylan. PoBeRe

Oh where, oh where has my little dog gone? Where Is He? Mother Goose. OxNR

Oh! where shall I bury my poor dog Tray. The Cynotaph. "Thomas Ingoldsby." *Fr.* Ingoldsby Legends, The. FM

Oh, where the white quince blossom swings. Japanesque. Oliver Herford. FiBHP

Oh, where will you hurry my dearest? The Press-gang. Charles Dibdin. FaBoEH

Oh! wherefore come ye forth, in triumph from the North. The Battle of Naseby. Macaulay. FaBoEH; OtMeF; OxAEP-2

Oh, where's the maid that I can love. One to Love. Alfred Islay Walden. AAP

Oh! where's the slave so lowly. Thomas Moore. NOIV

Oh, whiffaree an' a-whiffo-rye. Honey, Take a Whiff on Me. *Unknown.* OxBoLi

Oh, While I Sleep. Victor Hugo, *tr. fr.* French *by* Philip L. Miller. RiWo

Oh, while I sleep, come to my bedside. Oh, While I Sleep. Victor Hugo, *tr. fr.* French *by* Philip L. Miller. RiWo

Oh, whisky here, and whisky there. Whisky, Johnny. *Unknown.* AmFP

Oh, who crumbles up the heavens! Song of the Snow. Zalman Schneour, *tr. fr.* Hebrew *by* Ruth Finer Mintz. MHP

Oh, who has not heard of the Northmen of yore. America. Arthur Cleveland Coxe. PAH

Oh, who has not heard of the Wooyeo Ball. The Wooyeo Ball. *Unknown.* NOBAu

Oh who is/ so cosy with. The End of the Day. Robert Creeley. ArNa

Oh, who is so merry, so merry, heigh ho! The Light-hearted Fairy. *Unknown.* FaPON

Oh Who Is That Young Sinner with the Handcuffs on His Wrists?. A. E. Housman. FaBoTw; NOBVV; PeHV; SoSe

Oh! who is there of us that has not felt. November. Frederick Goddard Tuckerman. NOBA

Oh, Who Regards. *Unknown.* ElL

Oh, who regards a wounded soul's lamenting. Oh, Who Regards. *Unknown.* ElL

Oh who that ever lived and loved. The Egg. Clarence Day. NBLV

Oh, who will follow old Ben Milam into San Antonio? The Valor of Ben Milam. Clinton Scollard. PAH

"Oh, who will shoe your feet, my love." The Mournful Dove. *Unknown.* AmFP

Oh! who would live if this be death! (*LL*) The Geranium. Sheridan. BoLoP; ErPo

Oh who'll replace this old miner. The Old Miner. *Unknown.* OBET

Oh, why did God,/ Creator wise. Milton. *Fr.* Paradise Lost. EPCY

(Adam Speaks.) NU

Oh, why does the white man follow my path. The Indian Hunter. Eliza Cook. BLPA

Oh, why don't you [*or* I] work like other men do? Hallelujah, I'm a Bum. *Unknown.* AS; SWP, *with music*

(Hallelujah, Bum Again.) GBP

Oh [*or* O]! Why Should the Spirit of Mortal Be Proud? William Knox. BLPA; WBLP; WGRP

Oh! why should the spirit of mortal be proud?. (*LL*) Oh [*or* O]! Why Should the Spirit of Mortal Be Proud? William Knox. BLPA; WBLP; WGRP

Oh Wide and Sad Land. N. P. van Wyk Louw, *tr. fr. Afrikaans by* Adam Small. PeSAV

Oh wide and sad land, alone. Oh Wide and Sad Land. N. P. van Wyk Louw, *tr. fr. Afrikaans by* Adam Small. PeSAV

Oh! Wilberforce, our star of hope. Golden Jubilee of Wilberforce. Mrs. Henry Linden. CBWP-4

Oh, will you wear red? I'll Wear Me a Cotton Dress. *Unknown.* BPo

Oh Woman, Blessed Woman!. Mrs. Henry Linden. CBWP-4

Oh, women dear, and did ye hear the news that's going round. The Purple, White and Green. L. E. Morgan-Browne. BrRo

Oh! wondrous force of sympathy. The Triumvirate. Elizabeth Thomas. ECWP

Oh wond'rous power of words, how sweet they are. The Young Wordsworth's London. Wordsworth. *Fr.* Prelude [or, Growth of a Poet's Mind], The. EnRP; FaBoPP; HAP, *short sel.*; OAEL-2; PoEL-4, *sl. shorter*

"Oh [*or* O], World-God, give me Wealth!" the Egyptian cried. Gifts. Emma Lazarus. TrJP; WGRP

Oh, worship the King all glorious above. The Majesty and Mercy of God. Sir Robert Grant. OHIP; WGRP

Oh would I could subdue the flesh. Senex. Sir John Betjeman. RB

Oh, Would That I Knew. Al-Samau'al Ibn Adiya, *tr. fr. Arabic.* TrJP

Oh, would that I knew, the day my loss is lamented. Oh, Would That I Knew. Al-Samau'al Ibn Adiya, *tr. fr. Arabic.* TrJP

Oh would that I were a reliable spirit careering around. Longing for Death because of Feebleness. Stevie Smith. OBD

Oh would you know why Henry sleeps. Inhuman Henry. A. E. Housman. FiBHP; NBLV

Oh wretched World, but wretched above all. Fidelia Arguing with Her Self on the Difficulty of Finding the True Religion. Jane Barker. KTR

Oh, Ye Censurers. Al-Samau'al Ibn Adiya, *tr. fr. Arabic by* Hartwig Hirschfeld. TrJP

Oh, ye lost ones, ye departed, who have passed that silent shore. Beyond. *Unknown.* PWR

Oh ye! who teach the ingenuous youth of nations. Byron. *Fr.* Don Juan. EnRP

Oh — Yeah! Sharon Scott. JB

Oh Yes. William Matthews. AmPA

Oh yes I want to live colourfully once more. (*LL*) When I Lost Slum Life. Sipho Sepamla. PeSAV

Oh yes, we are so thankful. The Black Army. S. E. K. Mqhayi, *tr. fr. Xhosa by* C. M. Mcanyangwa *and* Jack Cope. PeSA

Oh yes/ We got Mr. President Roosevelt. President Roosevelt. Big Joe Williams. FaBoPV

Oh! yet a few short years of useful life. Wordsworth. *Fr.* Prelude [or, Growth of a Poet's Mind], The. EBEV; EnRP; OAEL-2; OBNC; PoEL-4

Oh Yet We Trust. Tennyson. *Fr.* In Memoriam A. H. H. EBVV, *abr.*; EBVVPR; ImPo; LiTB; NoP; OAEL-2, *abr.*; OBNC; PeECV, *abr.*; TrGrPo

Oh yet we trust that somehow good. Oh Yet We Trust. Tennyson. *Fr.* In Memoriam A. H. H. EBVV, *abr.*; EBVVPR; ImPo; LiTB; NoP; OAEL-2, *abr.*; OBNC; PeECV, *abr.*; TrGrPo

(Larger Hope, The.) WGRP

(O [*or* Oh], yet we trust that somehow good.) EnVR; FHYEP; MeMBP

Oh, you are a kilt which a young dandy set out to choose. Woman Sings of Her Love. *Somali Oral Tradition*, *tr. by* B. W. Andrzejewski *and* I. M. Lewis. WTO

Oh, you come along, boys, you listen to my tale. The Old Chisholm Trail. *Unknown.* AmFP

Oh, you may drive a horse to water. *Unknown.* RoPo

Oh, you must answer my questions nine. The Devil's Nine Questions. *Unknown.* AmFP

Oh you, my wheat field. The Harvest of Sorrow. A. K. Tolstoy, *tr. fr. Russian by* Philip L. Miller. RiWo

Oh, you never see a feather. *Unknown.* RoPo

Oh, you powerful Gods, if I must be. Frances Boothby. *Fr.* Marcelia; or, Treacherous Friend, The. KTR

Oh, You Wholly Rectangular. Eugene Roger Cole. GoYe

Oh You Young Men. George Orwell. FaBoEH

Oh [*or* O], young Lochinvar is come out of the west. Lochinvar. Sir Walter Scott. *Fr.* Marmion. BeLS; BoTP; EBEvV; EBNV; EnRP; FaBoBe; FaBV; FaPON; GN; NOBE; OBNV; OtMeF; OxAEP-2; OxBS; PoRA; TFi; VPP

(Young Lochinvar.) NTP; OBNV

Oh! young Lochinvar is come out of the West. Young Lochinvar. *Unknown.* FiBHP

Oh, your sweetness, softness, smoothness! Lassitude. Paul Verlaine, *tr. fr. French by* Lawrence M. Bensky. ErPo

Ohakune Fires. Lauris Edmond, *tr. fr. Maori by* Margaret Orbell. PeNZ

Ohé, long-haired beauty! Distress. Flavien Ranaivo, *tr. fr. French by* Ellen Conroy Kennedy. NegPo

Ohhh break love with white things. Sacred Chant for the Return of Black Spirit and Power. Amiri Baraka. NBV

Ohio Is the Iroquois Word for Beautiful. Helen Ruggieri. LoHo

Ohio Valley Swains. James Wright. NNaP

Ohioan Pastoral. James Wright. LCAP

Ohnedaruth's Day Begun. Nathaniel Mackey. Jaz

Oho for the woods where I used to grow. The Song of the Christmas Tree. Blanche Elizabeth Wade. OHIP

O'Hussey's Ode to the Maguire. Eochadh O'Hussey, *tr. fr. Irish by* James Clarence Mangan. NOIV; PeIV

Oil. Hansjörg Mayer. WeW

Oil/ refinery stink raging. El Paso Sex. Belinda Subraman. NGP

Oileus by his brother's side stood close. Homer, *tr. by* George Chapman. *Fr.* Iliad, The. OBVE

Oiseaurie. Margaret Widdemer. BXAP

Oisin. *Unknown*, *tr. fr. Irish by* Frank O'Connor. PeIV

Ojibwa War Songs. *Unknown*, *tr. fr. Ojibwa Indian by* H. H. Schoolcraft. AWP

Ojichan was a fisherman/farmer. The Fisherman. Janice Mirikitani. OpBo

Ojistoh. Emily Pauline Johnson. NOBC

O.K. Ann Ziety. DT

OK, it's imperishable or a world as Will. The Same Old Jazz. Philip Whalen. NeAP

OK. So she got back the baby. Onesided Dialog. June Jordan. NoAM

Okay. Sharon Scott. JB

Okay "Negroes." June Jordan. BPo

Okay, Prince, we understand the instructions. First Actor to Hamlet. Ivan V. Lalic, *tr. fr. Serbo-Croatian by* Charles Simic. HSix

Okay, so the wheel bit was a grinding bore. Eve: Night Thoughts. Judson Jerome. SM

Okeechobee. John Allison. GrPl

Oklahoma Ligno and Lithograph Co., The. Corporate Entity. Archibald MacLeish. OBAL

Ol' Bunk's Band. William Carlos Williams. Jaz; NOBA

Ol' Clothes. *Unknown.* PoToHe

Ol' Doc' Hyar. James Edwin Campbell. AAP

Ol' plantation wither. For Consciousness. Mervyn Morris. PBCV

Old, *sels.* Rosario Morales.
"Crow's wings not feet — pinions." ETG
"Skin/ practicing to be old." ETG

Old, The. Franz Wright. LCAP

Old Abram Brown is dead and gone. Abram Brown. *Unknown.* OxNR

Old Adam. Thomas Lovell Beddoes. *See* Old Adam, the Carrion Crow.

Old Adam, The. Denise Levertov. NaP; UnPo

Old Adam. *Unknown.* AS

Old Adam, the Carrion Crow. Thomas Lovell Beddoes. *Fr.* Death's Jest Book. EBEV; EnRP; GGP; LiTB; NAEL-2; OAEL-2; PoEL-4; TFi

Old Age. Al-Aswad, Son of Ya'fur, *tr. fr. Arabic by* Sir Charles Lyall. *Fr.* Mufaddaliyat, The. AWP

Old Age. *Gond Oral Tradition*, *tr. by* V. Elwin *and* S. Hivale. WTO

Old Age. E. Keary. NOBVV

Old Age. Mang Ke, *tr. fr. Chinese by* Donald Finkel *with* Chang Sheng-Tai. SpMi

Old Age. John Morris-Jones, *tr. fr. Welsh by* Anthony Conran. OBWVE

Old Age. Sir Philip Sidney. *See* Let not old age disgrace my high desire.

Old Age. Frederick Tennyson. NOBVV

Old Age. Edmund Waller. *See* Seas are quiet when the winds give o'er, The.

Old Age. *Zulu Oral Tradition*, *tr. by* H. Tracey. WTO

Old Age am I, with lockës thin and hoar. Age. Sir Thomas More. *Fr.* Pageant Verses. EnRePo

Old Age Compensation. James Wright. NNaP

Old Age Gets Up. Ted Hughes. NoAM

Old age has come, my head is shaking. Once I Played and Danced in My Parents' Kingdom. *Gond Oral Tradition*, *tr. by* V. Elwin *and* S. Hivale. WTO

(Folk Song, A.) AIW

Old Age in His Ailing. Herman Melville. TAP

Old age in the towns. War. Miguel Hernández, tr. fr. Spanish by Hardie St. Martin. RaBo

Old age is. To Waken an Old Lady. William Carlos Williams. HAP; InPK; NoP; SoSe; WeW

"Old age never comes alone" — it brings sighs. Old Age. John Morris-Jones, tr. fr. Welsh by Anthony Conran. OBWVE

Old Age of Michelangelo, The. F. T. Prince. PeSA

Old Age, on tiptoe, lays her jewelled hand. A Minuet on Reaching the Age of Fifty. George Santayana. BLPL; ImPo

Old Age Sticks. E. E. Cummings. InPS

Old am I in years and wisdom and. Old I Am. Herman Charles Bosman. PeSA

Old Amusement Park. Marianne Moore. NYBP

Old and abandoned by each venal friend. On Lord Holland's Seat near Margate, Kent. Thomas Gray. NOEC; OAEL-1; OPOP

Old and alone sit we. The Old Men. Walter de la Mare. MoAB; MoBrPo

Old and gnarled; wizened faces dreaming of. Grandparents. Sheila Bramfit. OxBM

Old and New. Unknown. BLRP

Old and New ("She went up the mountain to pluck wild herbs.") Unknown, tr. fr. Chinese by Arthur Waley. AWP

Old and New Year Ditties, sels. Christina Rossetti. Passing Away. MeMBP; NoP; OAEL-2; OBNC; PFP; WPE

Old and sick, many strange broodings. Meng Chiao, tr. by Stephen Owen. Fr. Autumn Meditations. SuSp

Old and sick, you turn away from mirrors, whether. Late Reflections. Babette Deutsch. NYBP

Old and the New, The. Clara Ann Thompson. CBWP-2

Old and the New Courtier, The. Unknown. CoMu

Old and young, everyone's asleep. The Cold Lantern. Yang Wan-li, tr. fr. Chinese by Jonathan Chaves. SuSp

Old Anguish, The. Chu Shu-chen, tr. fr. Chinese by Kenneth Rexroth. BoWoP

Old Apple-Tree, The. Paul Laurence Dunbar. AnAmPo

Old Apple Trees. W. D. Snodgrass. CAPP; FYAP; SV

Old archaeologist, Throstle, An. Unknown. PeLi

Old arguments that it's injurious. On the Low Status of Masturbation. Charles Thomson. FaBoBl

Old Arm-Chair, The. Eliza Cook. AnAmPo; BrRo; InPK; Poetr, St. 1 only; VPP; WBLP

Old Ash Tree on Ching Hill. Ai Ch'ing, tr. fr. Chinese. LHF, tr. by Hualing Nieh

Old astronomer there was, An. A Marvel. Carolyn Wells. OBCA

Old Astronomer to His Pupil, The. Sarah Williams. BLPA

Old Australian Ways. Andrew Barton Paterson. NOBAu

Old Barbarossa. Sleeping Heroes. Edward Shanks. OBMV

Old Battalion, The. Unknown. OBET

Old battle field, fresh with Spring flowers again. All That Is Left. Basho, tr. fr. Japanese by Curtis Hidden Page. AWP
(Old battle field, fresh with Spring flowers again.) AWP

Old battle field, fresh with Spring flowers again. Basho. See Old battle field, fresh with Spring flowers again.

Old Beauty, The. Phyllis McGinley. FaBoEE

Old Ben Bailey. Done For. Walter de la Mare. CoGr

Old black born on a strand of silk, An. Wise Owl. Patricia Goedicke. SM

Old black dog comes in one evening, The. First Snow. Ted Kooser. GrPl

Old Black ladies. Weeksville Women. Elouise Loftin. PoBA

Old Black Men. Georgia Douglas Johnson. CDC; PoBA; PoNe

Old Black Men Say. James A. Emanuel. PoBA

Old blanket. The crumbs of rubbed wool turning up, The. Adrienne Rich. Fr. Shooting Script. HCAP

Old Boards. Robert Bly. NaP

Old Boast, The. W. S. Merwin. NOBA

Old Boatman of Death's River, The. R. Williams Parry, tr. fr. Welsh by Joseph P. Clancy. OBWVE

Old Boniface he loved good cheer. Unknown. OxNR

Old Bones, The. Vernon Scannell. OxBC

Old boys, the cracked boards spread before. Bread. James Dickey. LCAP

Old Brass Wagon. Unknown. AS

Old brown hen and the old blue sky, The. Continual Conversation with a Silent Man. Wallace Stevens. LiTM; NoP

Old Brown Horse, The. W. F. Holmes. BoTP

Old brown thorn-trees break in two high over Cummen Strand, The. Red Hanrahan's Song about Ireland. W. B. Yeats. CMoP; FaBoCh; IIP; NOIV

Old Brown's Daughter. Unknown. OBET

Old Buccaneer, The. Charles Kingsley. See Oh, England is a pleasant place for them that's rich and high.

Old Business: The Drowned Bride. Ken Smith. PWE

Old Cabin, The. Paul Laurence Dunbar. PoLF

Old calypsonian sings, The. Politics Kaiso. Roger McTair. PBCV

Old canoe in, The. Sunrise. Jim Tollerud. VoR

Old Cat and the Young Mouse, The. La Fontaine, tr. fr. French by Norman R. Shapiro. SoCa

Old Cat Care. Richard Hughes. OBMV

Old cat whose calm, The. Her Seventeenth Winter. John Leax. CRP

Old Cat's Confessions, An. Christopher Pearse Cranch. OBCA

Old Cat's Dying Soliloquy, An. Anna Seward. ECWP; NOEC

Old Causes, The. Donald Revell. BAP-90

Old Charcoal Seller, An. Po Chü-i, tr. fr. Chinese by Eugene Eoyang. SuSp

Old Chaucer, like the morning Star. On Mr. Abraham Cowley, His Death and Burial amongst the Ancient Poets. Sir John Denham. BeJo; SeCV-1

Old cheer; a flourish without permanence. (LL) Last Days in the Party. Thomas McCarthy. IB

Old Children. R. A. Simpson. FaBoMA

Old Chisholm Trail, The. Unknown. AmFP; BeLS; FaBoBe; SWP

Old Christmas. Mary Howitt. GN

Old Christmas. Unknown. OHIP

Old Christmas Greeting, An. Unknown. See Sing, hey! Sing, hey!/ For Christmas Day.

Old Christmas Morning. Roy Helton. MoAmPo

Old Christmas Returned. Unknown. GN; OHIP

Old Churchyard of Bonchurch, The. Philip Bourke Marston. EBVV; OBNC

Old City, The. Ruth Manning-Sanders. CH

Old Clock on the Stairs, The. Longfellow. PWR; WBLP

Old Clothes. Phil Hey. GOYP

Old cloud passes mourning her daughter. Sunset after Rain. W. S. Merwin. PoA

Old Counsel. Herman Melville. FaBoRV

Old Countryside. Louise Bogan. HAP; LiTA; WPE

Old Couple, The. F. Pratt Green. OxBTC

Old Couple. Charles Simic. HCAP

Old Cove, The. Henry Howard Brownell. PAH

Old Cowboy, The. Kao Ch'i, tr. fr. Chinese by Kenneth Rexroth. OHMPC

Old Coyote . . . "If he hadn't looked back." Telling about Coyote. Simon J. Ortiz. STP

Old Crabbed Men. James Reeves. ErPo

Old Cracked Tune, An. Stanley Kunitz. SM

Old cradle of an infant world. Ode to Jamestown. James Kirke Paulding. PAH

Old Creation Chant. Unknown, tr. fr. Hawaiian. WTO

Old Crib, The. Mary E. Tucker. CBWP-1

Old crow of Shang Mountain, you are cruel! Song of the Crow Pecking at My Scarred Donkey. Wang Yü-ch'eng, tr. fr. Chinese by Jonathan Chaves. SuSp

Old Crow, upon the tall tree-top. The Crow. Mrs. —— Alexander. BoTP

Old Cumberland Beggar, The. Wordsworth. EnRP

Old Dan Tucker went to town. Unknown. RoPo

Old Danish jester named Yorick, An. Ogden Nash. PeLi

Old Dan'l. L. A. G. Strong. MoBrPo

Old daughter, small traveler. Making the Jam without You. Maxine W. Kumin. NALW

Old Davis owned a solid mica mountain. A Fountain, a Bottle, a Donkey's Ears and Some Books. Robert Frost. VGW

Old dears gardening in fur coats. The House Next Door. Douglas Dunn. OxBC

Old Doc. Mark Vinz. Poetsp

Old Doctor Foster. Unknown. OxNR

Old dog barks backward without getting up, The. The Span of Life. Robert Frost. HoPM; LiTM; SoSe

Old dog bends his head listening, The. Robert Bly. Poetr

Old Dog in the Ruins of the Graves at Arles, The. James Wright. NNaP

Old dog used to herd me through the street, The. Turnabout. Linda Pastan. NIP

Old dream comes again to me, The. Mir träumte wieder der alte Traum. Heine, tr. fr. German by James Thomson. AWP

Old Dutch Woman, The. Gary Snyder. NAAL-2

Old earth, how she sulks. Jacaranda. Roo Borson. NOBC

Old East End worker called Jock, An. Victor Gray. NOBL

Old Eben Flood, climbing alone one night. Mr. Flood's Party. E. A. Robinson. AmPP; AWP; BLPL; ClHu; CMoP; EBNV; FF; GGP; HAP; HeIL; HeIP; HoPM; LiTA; LiTM; MAT; MeMAP; MoAB; MoAmPo; MoP; NAAL-2; NIP; NoAM; NOBA; NoP; OBF; OxBA; PoE; Poetr; PoRA; PPP; PrIm; SoSe; TAP; TFi; TrGrPo; TRP; UnPo; WeW

Old Eddie's face, wrinkled with river lights. The Glory Trumpeter. Derek Walcott. NAEL-2

Old Egyptians hid their wit, The. On Mr. Nash's Picture at Full Length. Jane Brereton. WPE

Old Ellen Sullivan. Winifred Welles. FaPON

Old elm that murmured in our chimney top. The Fallen Elm. John Clare. FaBoPV; FHYEP

Old Emily. Hyacinthe Hill. GoYe

Old England. Anne Bradstreet. *Fr.* Dialogue between Old England and New, A. KTR

Old England. Nahum Tate. APAS

Old England Forever and Do It No More. *Unknown.* GBP

Old England has not lost her prayer. Robert Lloyd. *Fr.* Poetry Professors, The. ECEV

Old England is eaten by Knaves. Alexander McLachlan. *Fr.* Emigrant, The. NOBC

Old England's long-expected heavy news from our fleet. Nelson's Death. *Unknown.* OBET

Old escapes into the new, The. *(LL)* At start of spring I open a trench. Wendell Berry. EaPr

Old Essex Door. Agnes MacCarthy Hickey. GoYe

Old evil songs, The. Heine, *tr. fr. German by* Philip L. Miller. RiWo

Old faiths light their candles all about, The. Truth. Lizette Woodworth Reese. AmWP

Old Familiar Faces, The. Charles Lamb. AWP; BLPA; CoGr; EnRP; FaBoBe; FaBoRV; FaPoR; GTBS; GTBS-P; NOBE; OBEV; OBF; OxAEP-2; PlP; RB

Old Farmer Giles. *Unknown.* OxNR

Old farmer, nearing death, asked, The. Field Day. W. R. Rodgers. BIrV; IIP; PNI

Old Farmer Oats and his son Ned. John Jay Chapman. PoEL-5

Old-fashioned. Dara Wier. NAmP90

Old-fashioned sketchbook, An. Good News Bad News. Keith Abbott. UL

Old-Fashioned Song, An. John Hollander. BAP-90

Old Father Greybeard. *Unknown.* OxNR

Old father tongue sticking out. Rehearsal. Cyril Dabydeen. PBCV

Old Fellow. Ernest Walsh. ErPo

Old fellow, old one. Poem For My Father. Graham Allen. AngWe

Old Fence Post. Leigh Hanes. GoYe

Old/ Few years more attend me, I am redundant. Ago. Elizabeth Jennings. GOYP

Old Field Mowed, An. William Meredith. NYBP

Old fish fiddle with their fins and glide, The. Aquarium. George T. Wright. NYBP

Old Fisherman with Guitar. George Mackay Brown. OxBC

Old Fitz, who from your suburb grange. To E. Fitzgerald. Tennyson. NOBVV; OBF; PoEL-5

Old Flag. W. S. Merwin. AnAn

Old Flame, The. Robert Lowell. BoLoP; CBLP; HeIL; NoAM; NOBA

Old Flood Ireson! all too long. A Plea for Flood Ireson. Charles Timothy Brooks. PAH

Old Florist. Theodore Roethke. OxBSP

Old Folk, The. Tove Ditlevsen, *tr. fr. Danish by* Nadia Christensen. PBWP

Old Folks at Home, The. Stephen Collins Foster. AnAmPo; FaBoBe; WBLP

Old forms are like birdhouses that, The. Poetry. Greg Kuzma. PoA

Old Fort Meigs. *Unknown.* PAH

Old Fortunatus, *sels.* Thomas Dekker *and others.*
Fortune. OBSC
Fortune and Virtue. NoSic
"Virtue's branches wither, virtue pines." NoSic
(Song: "Virtue's branches wither, virtue pines.") EiI

Old Forty-five Per Cent. *Unknown.* FaBoEE

Old Freedman, The. Priscilla Jane Thompson. CBWP-2

Old friend, kind friend! lightly down. To My Old Schoolmaster. Whittier. NOBA

Old friend, you. Back from the Word-Processing Course, I Say to My Old Typewriter. Michael C. Blumenthal. GOYP; NoAM

Old friend, your place is empty now. No more. To Scott. Winifred M. Letts. PoLF

Old friends know what I like. T'ao Ch'ien, *tr. by* Wu-chi Liu. *Fr.* Drinking Wine. SuSp

Old friends sigh at long separation. Saying Farewell to Magistrate Ch'en Ta-yu. Lin Hung, *tr. fr. Chinese by* Irving Y. Lo. SuSp

Old Fritz, on this rotating bed. A Flat One. W. D. Snodgrass. CAPP; LiTM; SM

Old Furniture. Thomas Hardy. OxBTC

Old garden walks, old roses, and old loves. *(LL)* Old Mothers. Charles Sarsfield Ross. PoToHe

Old Gardens Are Not Relevant. Mary E. O'Donnell. NWP

Old Ghost, The. Thomas Lovell Beddoes. WiR

Old gilt vane and spire receive, The. The Late, Last Rook. Ralph Hodgson. MoBrPo

Old Girl, The. Gary Lenhart. UL

Old Glory! say, who. The Name of Old Glory. James Whitcomb Riley. GN

Old Gory, The. Gerald William Barrax. NBV
Sels.
Blue.
Red.
White.

Old gourmet who's grown somewhat stout, An. Yorick. PeLi

Old Grahame he is to Carlisle gone. Bewick and Graham. *Unknown.* ESPB

Old Gramophone Records. James Kirkup. NYBP

Old Grandpaw Yet. *Unknown.* AmFP

Old Gray Beard a-Shaking. *Unknown.* AmFP

Old Gray Goose, The. *Unknown.* AmFP; GBP

Old Gray Mare. *Unknown.* AS; GBP

Old Green River knife had to be scraped, An. Canst Thou Draw Out Leviathan with an Hook. Allen Curnow. PeNZ

Old Grey Goose, The. *Unknown.* ChTr

Old grey hearse goes rolling by, The. The Hearse Song. *Unknown.* AS, A *and* B *vers., with music*; OxBoLi; RB

Old Grimes. Albert Gorton Greene. BeLS; ReMoGo

Old Guitar, The. John Hollander. DiPo

Old Gumbie Cat, The. T. S. Eliot. PFP

Old guy put down his beer, The. Do the Dead Know What Time It Is? Kenneth Patchen. HoPM; MoAmPo

Old hag in. No surer thing, The. *(LL)* Another to Bring In the Witch. Robert Herrick. BeJo

Old hare and the chilled frog weep the sky's sheen, The. A Dream of Heaven. Li Ho, *tr. fr. Chinese by* A. C. Graham. PLT

Old Harem, The. Li Shang-yin, *tr. fr. Chinese by* Kenneth Rexroth. OHMPC

Old harem is quiet and deserted, The. The Old Harem. Li Shang-yin, *tr. fr. Chinese by* Kenneth Rexroth. OHMPC

Old Haven. Jean Garrigue. WPE

Old Hecuba young Helen. *(LL)* Artificial Beauty. Lucianus. AWP

Old Helen. Judy Grahn. BCF

Old hen sat on turkey eggs, The. *Unknown.* RoPo

Old hill town in northern Pennsylvania, a missed connection for a, An. Neglect. C. K. Williams. PWE

Old Hogan's Goat. *Unknown.* ZA

Old Hokum Buncombe, The. Robert E. Sherwood. NBLV

Old House. Judith Wright. FaBoMA

Old house felt unfriendly, The. The Empty House. Max Williams. CBAP

Old house stands deserted, gray, The. The Deserted House. Lizette Woodworth Reese. AmWP

Old house this — wide, yellowed, An. The Welcome House. Mary E. O'Donnell. NWP

Old house with trees and twisting river, An. A Visit to Bridge House. Richard Weber. BIrV

Old Houses. Homer D'Lettuso. PoToHe

Old Houses. Jennie Romano. PoToHe

Old Houses of Flanders, The. Ford Madox Ford. CTC

Old houses were scaffolding once. Image. T. E. Hulme. InPK; OxBTC

Old Humpy. *Unknown.* AmFP

Old Hundredth. William Kethe. FaPoR

Old Hundredth, *metrical vers. by* William Kethe. Bible, *O.T., paraphrased by* Sir Thomas Wyatt. *See* Make a joyful noise unto the Lord, all ye lands.

Old Husband Suspects Adultery, An. Gavin Ewart. NoAM

Old Hymns, The. Frank Lebby Stanton. BLRP

Old I Am. Herman Charles Bosman. PeSA

Old I Am. Thomas Stanley, *after the Greek of* Anacreon. AWP

Old Indian chief, Running B'ar, An. Mary Rita Hurley. PeLi

Old Inmate, An. Kenneth Mackenzie. FaBoMA

Old Ireland. Walt Whitman. IIP

Old Ironsides. Oliver Wendell Holmes. AiP; AnAmPo; BLPA; EBEvV; FaBoBe; FaPON; GN; GOA; NAAL-1; PAH; PWR; TAP; TFi

Old Ironsides at anchor lay. The Main-Truck; or, A Leap for Life. *At. to* George Pope Morris. AnAmPo; BLPL; PoLF; VPP

Old Italians Dying, The, *sels.* Lawrence Ferlinghetti. "For years the old Italians have been dying." NGP

Old Jason, the Argonaut, The. Denis Glover. PeNZ

Old Jockey, The. F. R. Higgins. OBMV; OxBTC

Old Joe. *Unknown.* OxBoLi

Old Joe Jones. Laura E. Richards. TLR

Old Joe Jones and his old dog Bones. Old Joe Jones. Laura E. Richards. TLR

Old jokes aren't as funny as they were, The. Husband and Wife. Bruce Dawe. FaBoMA

Old Kimball. *Unknown.* AmFP

Old King Cabbage. Richard Kendall Munkittrick. OBCA

Old King Cole. G. K. Chesteron. *See* Who smoke-snorts toasts o' My Lady Nicotine.

Old King Cole ("Me clairvoyant.") G. K. Chesteron. *Fr.* Variations on an Air Composed on Having to Appear in a Pageant as Old King Cole. BXAP; FaBoPa; NOBL; UV

Old King Cole ("Of an old king in a story.") G. K. Chesteron. *Fr.* Variations on an Air Composed on Having to Appear in a Pageant as Old King Cole. BXAP; FaBoPa; NOBL

Old King Cole was a merry old soul. Mother Goose. FaBoBe; OTCP; OxNR; ReMoGo

Old Kitchen Clock, The. Ann Hawkshawe. BoTP

Old Knight, The. George Peele. *See* His golden locks time hath to siluer turn'd.

Old Ladies. Will Allen Dromgoole. WeW

Old Ladies, The. Colin Ellis. OxBTC

Old Lady Fry. *Unknown.* RoPo

Old lady, I now celebrate. John Montague. *Fr.* Leaping Fire, The. CIP; IPY

(Little Flower's Disciple, The. IPY; TIRV

Old Lady of Harrow, An. *Unknown.* PeLi

Old Lady of London, The. *Unknown.* AmFP

Old Lady Sitting in the Dining Room. *Unknown.* AmFP

Old lady writes me in a spidery style, An. A Letter from Brooklyn. Derek Walcott. OxBTC

Old Lady's Lament for Her Youth, The. Villon, *tr. fr. French by* Robert Lowell. BoLoP

Old Lambro pass'd unseen a private gate. Byron. *Fr. Don Juan.* EnRP

Old leaves, the perfume of moldering. Looking Both Ways. Jane O. Wayne. GOYP

Old Lem. Sterling A. Brown. BPo; PoBA; PoNe; TTY

Old Liberia Is Not the Place for Me. Joshua McCarter Simpson. AAP

Old light & owl-light. 2nd Light Poem: For Diane Wakoski. Jackson MacLow. PoM

Old Log House. James S. Tippett. FaPON

Old-Long-Syne. *Unknown.*

Old Love Butchered (Colorado Springs and Huachuca). Lance Jeffers. NBV

Old Loves. Henry Murger, *tr. fr. French by* Andrew Lang. AWP

Old Lutheran Bells at Home, The. Wallace Stevens. NoAM

Old Ma Bell. *Unknown.* SWP

Old Ma Bell, she ain't what she used to be. Old Ma Bell. *Unknown.* SWP

Old, mad, blind, despised, and dying king, An. England in 1819. Shelley. EnRP; FaBoEH; FaBoPV; FF; MAT; NAEL-2; NAWM-2; NOBE; NoP; OAEL-2; OxAEP-2; Poetr; Son; TFi; TrGrPo; UnPo (Sonnet: England in 1819.) CBCK; PPP

Old Magic. Grace Nichols. PBCV

Old maid, an old maid, An. *Unknown.* OxNR

Old Maid Early, An. Blake. OxBSP

Old Maids. *Unknown.* AmFP

Old Maid's Soliloquy. Maggie Pogue Johnson. CBWP-4

Old Maid's Song. *Unknown.* AmFP

Old Malediction, An. Anthony Hecht, *after* Horace. IHNG; NoAM

Old Man, The. He Was Lucky. Anna Swirszczynska, *tr. by* Magnus J. Krynski *and* Robert A. Maguire. PoSu

Old Man. James Henry. NOBVV

Old Man. Faye Kicknosway. UL

Old Man. Edward Thomas. LiTM; SCV

Old Man [*or* Old Man Travelling], An. Wordsworth. FaBoCh; OBWP

Old Man and the Cow. Edward Lear. *See* There was an old man who said: "How."

Old Man and Young Wife, The. *Unknown.* CoMu

Old Man at the Crossing, The. L. A. G. Strong. OBMV

Old Man at the Window, The. Anthony Harvey. Mes

Old man bending I come among new faces, An. The Wound-Dresser. Walt Whitman. AmPP; NAAL-1; NOBA; OBWP; PrIm; TAP

Old man Brown. The Cheerful Chilterns. Frank Sidgwick. BXAP

Old man Chang, sick three years, finally up and died. The Rain Cleared and the Breeze and Sunshine Are Superb as I Stroll Outside the Gate. Lu Yu, *tr. fr. Chinese by* Burton Watson. SuSp

Old man comes out on the hill, The. Good. R. S. Thomas. PAW

Old Man Daisy. *Unknown.* RoPo

Old Man Dreams, The. Oliver Wendell Holmes. AnAmPo; BLPL; PoLF

Old man from Darjeeling. *Unknown.* NTCP

Old man from Hsin-feng, eighty-eight years old, An. The Old Man of Hsin-feng witih the Broken Arm. Po Chü-i, *tr. fr. Chinese by* Eugene Eoyang. SuSp

Old man from [*or of*] Peru. *Unknown. See* There was an old man of [*or* from] Peru/ Who dreamt [*or* dreamed] he was eating his shoe.

Old Man from Peru, An. *Unknown. See* There was an old man of [*or* from] Peru/ Who dreamt [*or* dreamed] he was eating his shoe.

Old man going a lone highway, An. Building the Bridge. Will Allen Dromgoole. WeW

(Bridge-Builder, The.) PoToHe

Old Man He Courted Me, An. *Unknown.* OBET

Old man in a lodge within a park, An. Chaucer. Longfellow. AWP; HeIP; InvP; MeMAP; NOBA; NoP; OBEV; OxBA; PoE; PoRA; PrIm; Son; TAP; TFi; TrGrPo

Old Man in a Moon Loft. T. Glynne Davies, *tr. fr. Welsh by the author.* OBWVE

Old Man in New Country. James Berry. NBrP

Old man in the crystal morning after snow. Delmore Schwartz. PoA

Old man in white, An. Alice Walker. *Fr.* Love. NMM

Old Man Know-All. *Unknown.* BPo

Old man leaning on a gate, An. From My Window. Mary Elizabeth Coleridge. OBNC

Old man/ man black man. Tony Get the Boys. D. L. Graham. PoBA

Old Man Mose. Jack Kerouac. *Fr.* Mexico City Blues. Jaz; NeAP

Old man moved into his night, The. Katerina Anghelaki-Rooke. *Fr.* Notes on My Father. PBWP

Old man mumbling in his dotage, or crying child, unborn? (*LL*) For Malcolm X. Margaret Walker. BPo; PoBA; Son

Old Man Ocean. Russell Hoban. TLR

Old Man Ocean, how do you pound. Old Man Ocean. Russell Hoban. TLR

Old Man of Hsin-feng witih the Broken Arm, The. Po Chü-i, *tr. fr. Chinese by* Eugene Eoyang. SuSp

Old Man of Nantucket, The. *Unknown.* PeLi

Old Man of Verona, The. Claudian, *tr. fr. Latin by* Abraham Cowley. AWP; MML, *tr. by* Helen Waddell; OBVE, *tr. by* Abraham Cowley.

Old Man, or Lad's-Love, – in the name there's nothing. Old Man. Edward Thomas. LiTM; SCV

Old Man Platypus. Andrew Barton Paterson. OBAP; ZA

Old Man Playing with Children. John Crowe Ransom. MeMAP

Old Man Pondered. John Crowe Ransom. MoAmPo

Old Man Potchikoo. Louise Erdrich. HATNAP
Sels.
Birth of Potchikoo, The.
Death of Potchikoo, The.
How Potchikoo Got Old.
Potchikoo Marries.

Old Man Remembers, An. Frances Horovitz. VBLP

Old Man Said, The. Carroll Arnett. ETG, *ll.* 1–8

Old man Sargent sitting at the desk. The Winnsboro Cotton Mill Blues. *Unknown.* SWP

Old man sits in wrinkled reverie, An. An Evasion. Douglas Livingstone. PeSA

Old Man Stirs the Fire to a Blaze, An. W. B. Yeats. *Fr.* Wanderings of Oisin, The. RB

Old Man, the Sweat Lodge. Phillip William George. GrPl

Old Man Told Me. Lance Henson. VoR

Old man went to meetin', for the day was bright and fair, The. The Preacher's Vacation. *Unknown.* BLPA; BLPL

Old Man Who Lived in a Wood, The. *Unknown. See* There was an old man who [*or* that] lived in the [*or* a] wood [*or* woods].

Old man who seined. Lorine Niedecker. VGW

Old man whose black face, An. The Rainwalkers. Denise Levertov. PPP

Old Man with a Beard. Edward Lear. *See* There Was an Old Man with a Beard.

Old Man with a Mowing Machine. May Carleton Lord. GoYe

Old Man's Advice, An. *Unknown.* OBET

Old Man's Comforts and How He Gained Them, The. Robert Southey. EBEvV; HoPM; OxBChV; UnPo; UV; VPP

Old Man's Complaint, The. *Unknown.* OxBSP

Old Man's Counsel, The. Bryant. EAP

Old Man's Darling, The. Phoebe Cary. AmWP

Old man's eagle mind., An. *(LL)* An Acre of Grass. W. B. Yeats. CMoP; NoAM

Old man's fair-haired consort, whole dewy axle-tree, The. Lente, Lente. Ovid, tr. by Kirby Flower Smith. *Fr.* Elegies. AWP

Old Man's Lazy, The. Peter Blue Cloud. HATNAP

Old Man's Son, An. Russell Edson. LCAP

Old Man's Song, about His Wife, The. *Unknown, tr. fr. Eskimo by* Armand Schwerner. STP

Old Man's Tale, The. Brian Merriman, *tr. by* David Marcus. *Fr.* Midnight Court, The. BIrV; NOIV, *tr. by* Thomas Kinsella

Old Man's Winter Night, An. Robert Frost. AWP; HAP; MoAB; MoAmPo; NAAL-2; NoAM; OxBA; VGW

Old Man's Wish, The. Walter Pope. CoMu; NOSC

Old Mansion. John Crowe Ransom. HeIP; MeMAP; NOBA; OxBA

Old Maps and New. Norman MacCaig. OxBC

Old Mare, The. Elizabeth J. Coatsworth. MoAmPo

Old Marlborough Road, The. Thoreau. PoEL-4

Old Marquis and His Blooming Wife, The. *Unknown.* CoMu

Old-Marrieds, The. Gwendolyn Brooks. PoBA

Old Marse John. *Unknown.* TTY

Old master always said. "No, Master, Never!" Joshua McCarter Simpson. AAP

Old master yourself now, Auden, An. As You Like It. Theodore Weiss. TAP

Old May Song. *Unknown.* BoTP; CH

Old mayor climbed the belfry tower, The. The High Tide on the Coast of Lincolnshire (1571). Jean Ingelow. BeLS; EBVV; FaBoPP; GN; Mes, *abr.*; OtMeF; OxAEP-2; VPP

Old Meg. Keats. *See* Old Meg she was a gipsy [*or* gypsy].

Old Meg she was a gipsy [*or* gypsy]. Meg Merrilies [*or* Merrilees]. Keats. BoTP; ELP; FaBoCh; FaPON; OxBChV; PlP; TEP (Old Meg.) FHYEP

Old Memories of Earth. R. A. K. Mason. PeNZ

Old Men, The. Walter de la Mare. MoAB; MoBrPo

Old Men, The. Irving Feldman. TwCP

Old Men, The. Alexander Javitz. TrJP

Old Men, The. Kipling. OBSV

Old Men. Ogden Nash. AnAmPo; InPS; RB

Old Men Admiring Themselves in the Water, The. W. B. Yeats. CMoP; FaBoCh; GoJo

Old Men and Old Women Going Home on the Street Car. Merrill Moore. MoAmPo

Old men in blue: and heavily encumbered. Pihsien Road. "Robin Hyde." WPE

Old Men on the Courthouse Lawn, Murray, Kentucky. James Galvin. AnAn

Old men sleeping. The List. Michael McClure. NU

Old men, white-haired, beside the ancestral graves. Basho, *tr. fr. Japanese by* Curtis Hidden Page. AWP

Old Menalcas on a day. The Palmer's Ode. Robert Greene. *Fr.* Never Too Late. CTC; EnRePo; NoSic; SCGP

Old Men's Ward. Elma Dean. GoYe

Old Merina Theme. Flavien Ranaivo, *tr. fr. French by* Ellen Conroy Kennedy. NegPo

Old Miner, The. *Unknown.* OBET

Old Miner's Refrain, The. *Unknown.* AmFP

Old Mrs. Jarvis. Elizabeth Fleming. BoTP

Old Mrs. Lazibones. Gerda Mayer. OTCP

Old Mrs. Thing-um-e-bob. Charles Causley. OTCP

Old Mrs. Tressider/ Over at Winches. The Scarf. Ivy O. Eastwick. BoTP

Old moder Phoebe how happy you be. Moder Phoebe. *Unknown.* FaBoVe

Old Mog comes in and sits on the newspaper. Cat. Joan Aiken. OFC

Old Moke. Harold Littlebird. VoR

Old Molly Means was a hag and a witch. Molly Means. Margaret Walker. BlSi; NALW; NMM; PoNe

Old monk perches, A.

Old moon is tarnished, The. Sea Lullaby. Elinor Wylie. BoNaP

Old moon my eyes are new moon with human footprint. Poem Rocket. Allen Ginsberg. VGW

Old Morgan. G. D. Roberts. BoTP

Old Mortality, *sels.* Sir Walter Scott.
And What though Winter Will Pinch Severe. EnRP
Sound, Sound the Clarion. FaBoEE; FaPoR; NOBE; OxAEP-2

(Call, The.) OBEV
(One Crowded Hour.) TrGrPo

Old mortality, these evening doorways into rooms, An. Birthday. Stanley Plumly. NAmP90

Old Mother, The. *Unknown.* PoToHe

Old Mother Doorstep had nursed him well. *(LL)* Mother Doorstep. Victor James Daley. NOBAu

Old Mother Duck has hatched a brood. Mother Duck. *Unknown.* BoTP

Old Mother Earth woke up from her sleep. A Spring Song. *Unknown.* PoLF

Old Mother Goose. Mother Goose. BoTP

Old Mother Goose/ When she wanted to wander. Mother Goose. OxNR; ReMoGo

Old Mother Hubbard. Sarah Catherine Martin. FaBoBe; OxNR; ReMoGo (Comic Adventures of Old Mother Hubbard and Her Dog, The.) CBNP; OxBChV

Old Mother Niddity Nod. *Unknown.* OxNR

Old Mother Shuttle. *Unknown.* OxNR

Old Mother Twitchett had [*or* has] but one eye. Mother Goose. NTCP; OxNR; ReMoGo

Old Mothers. Charles Sarsfield Ross. PoToHe

Old Motif. Aleksandar Ristovic, *tr. fr. Serbo-Croatian by* Charles Simic. HSix

Old Mountain Road. Charles Simic. FYAP

Old Mountains Want to Turn to Sand. Tommy Olofsson, *tr. fr. Swedish by* Jean Pearson. TSaS

Old Movies. John Cotton. FF

Old Navy, The. Frederick Marryat. *See* Captain Stood on the Carronade, The.

Old Nelly's Birthday. Ruth Pitter. NALW

Old newspapers nobody's ever got to read again. *(LL)* Twenty-Year Marriage. Ai. BoWoP; NoAM

Old Nick, who taught the village school. The Retort. George Pope Morris. AnAmPo

Old Nico brought wreaths to the tomb of Melite. Philip of Thessalonica, *tr. fr. Greek by* Edwin Morgan. GrAn

Old Noah he had an ostrich farm and fowls on the largest scale. Wine and Water. G. K. Chesteron. *Fr.* Flying Inn, The. ChIV-1; FaBoCo; FiBHP; MoBrPo

Old Noah once he built an ark. Old Noah's Ark. *Unknown.* ImGa

Old Noah's Ark. *Unknown.* ImGa

Old Nobility, The. Friedrich von Logau, *tr. fr. German.* GePo, *tr. by* George C. Schoolfield

Old now. Benjamin Banneker Sends His *Almanac* to Thomas Jefferson. Jay Wright. VCAP

Old oak, old timber, sunk and rooted. G. M. B. Donald Davie. OxBC

Old Oak Tree at Hatfield Broadoak, The. Frederick Locker-Lampson. OxAEP-2

Old Oaken Bucket, The, *parody. Unknown.* BLPA; WBLP

Old Oaken Bucket, The. Samuel Woodworth. AnAmPo; BLPA; FaBoBe; FaPON; VPP; WBLP

Old Obadiah. *Unknown.* RoPo

Old Obadiah jumped in the fire. Old Obadiah. *Unknown.* RoPo

Old, odd man, An. *(LL)* Cassibus Impositis Venor. Sebastian Barry. IB

Old, old/ To live on, wretched to behold. Owen Gruffydd, *tr. fr. Welsh by* Anthony Conran. *Fr.* Men That Once Were, The. OBWVE

Old One and the Wind, The. Clarice Short. IHMS

Old ones go to each other's funerals, The. Burials. Geoffrey Grigson. PoA

Old ones to the side. Charles Simic. AmPA; LCAP

Old [*or* Ould] Orange Flute, The. *Unknown.* FaBoBa; GBP; OxBoLi; WTO

Old orchard, full of smoking air, The. Wild Grapes. Kenneth Slessor. FaBoMA

Old Ox, The. George Rostrevor Hamilton, *after the Greek of* Addaios of Makedon. FaBoEE

Old Pack, The. *Unknown.* APAS

Old Paintings on Italian Walls. Kathleen Raine. NYBP

Old Parson Beanes hunts six days of the week. Upon Parson Beanes. Robert Herrick. BeJo

Old Penobscot Indian, The. Flux. Richard Eberhart. Poetsp; VGW

Old People. Michael Davitt, *tr. fr. Irish by* Michael Hartnett. PBCIP

Old people are like birds. City Pigeons. Helen Chasin. WeW

Old People Dozing. Denise Levertov. AIW

Old People on the Nursing Home Porch. Mark Strand. CAPP

Old People Speak of Death, The. Quincy Troupe. BCF

Old person of Troy, An. Ogden Nash. PeLi

Old Peter Grimes made fishing his employ. Peter Grimes. George Crabbe. *Fr.* Borough, The. EBNV; ECEV; EnRP; FHYEP; OBNV; PoEL-4; TEP (Poor of the Borough, The; Peter Grimes.) NoP

Old Peter Prairie-Dog. Prairie-Dog Town. Mary Austin. FaPON

Old photographs would have her bookish, sitting. Ma. Paul Muldoon. PNI

Old Picture, An. Howard Nemerov. OxBSP

Old Pilot, The. Donald Hall. LCAP

Old Pine, An. Wang An-shih, *tr. fr. Chinese by* Jan W. Walls. SuSp

Old Place, The. B. E. Baughan. PeNZ

Old Platthis often thrust away her morning's sleep. Leonidas of Tarentum, *tr. fr. Greek by* Barbara Hughes Fowler. *Fr.* Epigrams. HePo

Old Poem. Octavio Paz, *tr. fr. Spanish by* Eliot Weinberger. AnRep

Old Poem. *Unknown, tr. fr. Chinese.* AWP, *tr. by* Arthur Waley

Old Poem. *Unknown, tr. fr. Chinese by* Arthur Waley. AWP; BoWoP

Old Poem to Yän ChÅF/, An. Hsüeh T'ao, *tr. fr. Chinese by* Kenneth Rexroth *and* Ling Chung. WPC

Old pond,/ frog jumps in. Basho, *tr. fr. Japanese by* Burton Watson. *Fr.* Seventy-six Hokku. EnlH, *tr. by* Michael Katz; TAL; *tr. by* Harold G. Henderson.

Old Post Grill. John DeWitt. NGP

Old Priest, The. Vladimir Holan, *tr. fr. Czech by* George Theiner. PoSu

Old priest Peter Gilligan, The. The Ballad of Father Gilligan. W. B. Yeats. EBVV; MoBrPo; PoRA

Old professor of zoology, The. The Parrot. James Elroy Flecker. FaBoTw

Old Pro's Lament, The. Paul Petrie. TAP

Old Python Nose with the wind-rolling ears. To a Dead Elephant. Douglas Livingstone. PeSA

Old question. Will not God do right?, The. *(LL)* The Leper. Swinburne. GBL; NOBVV

Old Relative. Gwendolyn Brooks. *Fr.* Notes from the Childhood and the Girlhood. LCAP

Old Rhyme, An. *Unknown.* BoTP

Old ridiculous partner is back again, The. The She Wolf. Muriel Spark. NYBP

Old River Road. Blanche Whiting Keysner. GoYe

Old Roads. Eiléan Ní Chuilleanáin. CIP; IIP; PWE

Old Robin of Portingale. *Unknown.* ESPB

Old Roger. *Unknown.* OxBoLi

Old Room, The. W. S. Merwin. NYBP

Old Ross, Cockburn, and Cochrane too. The Battle of Baltimore. *Unknown.* PAH

Old rude church, with bare, bald tower, is here, The. Wordsworth's Grave. Sir William Watson. OBNC

Old Rugged Cross, The. George Bennard. AH

Old Ruralities: A Regret. Charles Tennyson Turner. EBVV; Son

Old Russian spits up a plum, The. A Man Then Suddenly Stops Moving. Alberto A. Ríos. NoAM

Old Rustic Mill, The. George Sands Johnson. PWR

Old Sac Village, The. Albery Allson Whitman. *Fr.* Not a Man and Yet a Man. AAP

Old Sailor Looking at a Container Ship. Robert Carson. AiP

Old Saint's Prayer, The. Priscilla Jane Thompson. CBWP-2

Old Sam's Wife. *Unknown.* ChTr

Old sandpiper contemplates his age, The. Summer's Early End at Hudson Bay. Hayden Carruth. NYBP

Old Santa Fe Trail, The. Richard Burton. PAH

Old-Saxon Fragment. *Unknown.* CBNP

Old Scent of the Plum Tree. Ietaka, *tr. fr. Japanese by* E. Powys Mathers. AWP

Old Scottish Cavalier, The. William Edmonstoune Aytoun. GN

Old sea-dog on a sailor's log, An. The Powerful Eyes o' Jeremy Tait. Wallace Irwin. FiBHP

Old Section Boss, The. *Unknown.* BPo

Old Sergeant, The. Forceythe Willson. BeLS

Old Shellover. Walter de la Mare. BoTP; OxBChV

Old Shepherd's Prayer. Charlotte Mew. MoAB; MoBrPo; OxBTC; WPE

Old Ships, The. James Elroy Flecker. CH; CoGr; FaBoRV; MoBrPo; OBMV; OtMeF; PoRA

Old shoe, an old pot, an old skin, An. Autumn Sequence. Adrienne Rich. VGW

Old Sir Simon the king. *Unknown.* OxNR

Old Sipsey Valley Road, The. Thomas Rabbitt. MT

Old Skinflint. W. W. Gibson. OBMV

Old Slave Woman, An. Joyce Sims Carrington. ShDr

Old snake, old hole in the corner man. A Dead Weasel. David Helwig. NOBC

Old Snapshot. Ronald G. Everson. MoCV

Old snow gets up and moves taking its, The. December among the Vanished. W. S. Merwin. NaP

Old soak from Stoke, An. C. J. Parker. PeLi

Old Soldier. Padraic Colum. OBMV

Old — some eighty, or thereabouts. 'Nkongane. W. C. Scully. PeSAV

Old Song, The. G. K. Chesteron. FaBoTw

Old Song. Robert Creeley. ArLo

Old Song. Edward Fitzgerald. GN; OBEV; OxAEP-2

Old Song. *Unknown.* RaBo

Old Song, An. "Yehoash," *tr. fr. Yiddish by* Marie Syrkin. AWP

Old Song Ended, An. Dante Gabriel Rossetti. BoLoP; EBVV

Old song made by an old aged pate, An. The Old and the New Courtier. *Unknown.* CoMu

Old Song of Rejoicing, An. *Unknown, tr. fr. Maori by* Margaret Orbell. PeNZ

Old Song Re-sung, An. John Masefield. LiTB

Old Song Resung, An. W. B. Yeats. *See* Down by the Salley Gardens.

Old Song Written during Washington's Life. *Unknown.* OHIP

Old Song, Wrote by One of Our First New-England Planters, An. *Unknown. See* New England's Annoyances.

Old Souldier of the Queens, An. *Unknown.* FaBoEH

Old South Boston Aquarium stands, The. For the Union Dead. Robert Lowell. AmPP; CoAP; FaBoPV; FYAP; HAP; HCAP; HeIP; InPS; LCAP; LiTM; MoP; NAAL-2; NaP; NoAM; NOBA; NoP; OBWP; PoE; Poetr; SCV; TFi; TRP; TwCP; UnPo; VCAP; WeW

Old spoon, An. The Spoon. Charles Simic. NNaP

Old Squire, The. Wilfrid Scawen Blunt. FaPoR; OBEV; SCGP

Old Stephen. Charles Tennyson Turner. EBVV

Old Stoic, The. Emily Brontë. FaPoR; MeMBP; NALW; NOBE; OBEV; OBNC; OxAEP-2; PIP; PoLF; TrGrPo

Old stories of a Tyler sing. Tom Tiler; or, The Nurse. *Unknown.* APAS

Old Story, The. Argentarius, *tr. by* E. A. Robinson. AWP

Old Story. Lance Henson. VoR

Old Story, The. Louis MacNeice. GBL

Old Story, An. E. A. Robinson. AnAmPo; MoAmPo; OxBSP

Old Summerhouse, The. Walter de la Mare. CMoP; FaBoPP; FaBoRV; GTBS-P

Old Susan. Walter de la Mare. CMoP; MoBrPo

Old Sussex Road, The. Ian Serraillier. NTCP

Old Sweetheart of Mine, An. James Whitcomb Riley. BeLS; BLPA

Old Swimmin'-Hole, The. James Whitcomb Riley. AnAmPo; BeLS

Old tales were told of Sigemund's daring. The Tale of Sigemund. *Unknown, tr. by* Charles W. Kennedy. *Fr.* Beowulf. AnOE; ASW, *tr. by* Kevin Crossley-Holland

Old temple leans against the green hillside, An. Tune: "Stretch of Cloud over Mount Wu, A." Li Hsün, *tr. fr. Chinese by* Hellmut Wilhelm. SuSp

Old Testament Contents. *Unknown.* BLPA

Old-Testament Gospel. William Cowper. ChIV-2; TrCP

Old, the curator wields his heavy. Tolquhon Castle. Margaret Toms. PAW

Old, the mad, the blind have fairest daughters, The. The Beauty of Job's Daughters. Jay Macpherson. ChIV-1; MoCV; NOBC

Old Thought for a New Couple, An. E. A. Markham. PBCV

Old Tiger. Marianne Moore. AnAn

Old-Time Childhood in Kentucky. Robert Penn Warren. AiP

Old Time is lame and halt. Wie langsam kriechet sie dahin. Heine, *tr. fr. German by* Richard Monckton Milnes. AWP

Old Timers. Carl Sandburg. NoAM

Old Times. Daniel Mark Epstein. DiPo

Old times unqueen thee, and old loves endear thee. *(LL)* To a Lofty Beauty, from Her Poor Kinsman. Hartley Coleridge. OxAEP-2

Old Tippecanoe. *Unknown.* PAH

Old Tongue, The. Herbert Williams. AngWe

Old town lies afar, An. There Is an Old City. Karl Bulcke, *tr. fr. German by* Ludwig Lewisohn. AWP

Old Toyota, green as a frog, coughs and clanks, The. Talking in the Woods with Karl Amorelli. Etheridge Knight. BCF

Old Trail Town, Cody, Wyoming.sie. John Garmon. BoLoP; EnLoPo; HAP; InPS; JCP; LiTB; MeLP; NOBE; NoP; OAEL-1; OBEV; PoEL-2; PrIm; SeCP; SeCV-1; TEP; TrGrPo

Old Tree, The. Andrew Young. GoJo

Old Triton Time. Vernon Watkins. OxBSP

Old Trouper, The. Don Marquis. *Fr.* Archy and Mehitabel. FaBoCo

Old Tubal Cain was a man of might. Tubal Cain. Charles MacKay. WBLP

Old Tune, An. Gérard de Nerval, *tr. fr. French by* Andrew Lang. AWP

Old Uncle Jim was as blind as a mole. Echoes of Childhood. Alice Corbin. PoNe

OLD UNCLE TOM COBLEIGH AND ALL. (*LL*) Widdecombe [*or* Widdicombe] Fair. *Unknown.* CH; MoShBr

Old Vicarage, Grantchester, The. Rupert Brooke. EBEvV; FaBoPP; FaBV; FaPoB; MoBrPo; OBTV; OxBTC; PFP; PoRA

Old violence is not too old to beget new values. (*LL*) The Bloody Sire. Robinson Jeffers. CMoP; ImPo; LiTM; PoA

Old virgin, your airs are proper. To an Elderly Virgin. Mael Isu O Brolchain, *tr. fr. Old Irish by* Thomas Kinsella. NOIV

Old Virginny. James A. Bland. *See* Carry Me Back to Old Virginny.

Old Voyager. Walter Blackstock. GoYe

Old Walking Song, The. J. R. R. Tolkien. RFM

Old walls creak. Restoring the Ancestral House. Katerina Te Hei Koko Mataira, *tr. fr. Maori by* Katerina Te Hei Koko Mataira. PeNZ

Old Walt. Langston Hughes. HeIP

Old War-Dreams. Walt Whitman. AnAmPo; OxBSP

Old warder of these buried bones. Tennyson. *Fr.* In Memoriam A. H. H. EBVV, *abr.*; OAEL-2, *abr.*; PeECV, *abr.*; PoEL-5

Old watch, The: their/ thick eyes. Vapor Trail Reflected in the Frog Pond. Galway Kinnell. CAPP; NoP; OBWP; VCAP; VGW

Old West, the old time, The. Spanish Johnny. Willa Cather. AiP; FaPON

Old Whim Horse, The. Edward Dyson. CBAP

Old Whore Speaks to a Young Poet, The. Dave Jeddie Smith. SM

Old Whorehouse, An. Mary Oliver. CAPP

Old Wichet. *Unknown.* GBP

Old Wife, The. Rolly Kent. FF

Old Wife and the Ghost, The. James Reeves. OTCP; PDV; SiSoPo

Old Wife in High Spirits. "Hugh MacDiarmid." CMoP; OxBTC; PoE

Old Wife Speaks, The. Gerda Mayer. DT

Old Winter. Thomas Noel. GN

Old Witherington. Dudley Randall. NBV; NoAM

Old Wives Prayer, The. Robert Herrick. SeCV-1

Old Wives' [*or* Wife's] Tale, The, *sels.* George Peele.
Fair Maiden.
  Gently Dip. ELP; InPS
  (Fair Maiden.) PoEL-2
  (Song for the Head.) RB
  (Voice from the Well [of Life Speaks to the Maiden], The.) ChTr; GGP; NOBE; NoSic
Harvester's Song. TrGrPo
  "Lo! here we come a-reaping, a-reaping."
Spell, A. ChTr
  "Spread, table, spread." NoSic
  "Three merry men, and three merry men." NoSic
Voice [Speaks] from the Well, A. CBNP; FaBoCh; NOBE; OxBoLi
  "Whenas [*or* When as] the Rye [Reach to the Chin]." CBLP; ELP; EnLoPo; FaBoCh; GBL; InvP; NoP; NoSic; TEP; TFi
  (Song: "When as [*or* whenas] the rye [*or* rie] reach to the chin.") CBNP; ElL; FaBoVe; OxBoLi; PoEL-2
  (Summer Song, A.) NOBE; OBEV

Old Wives' Tales. Constance Urdang. PBCAP

Old Woman, The. Joseph Campbell. AWP; MoBrPo; OxBTC; PoToHe

Old Woman, An. David Gwenallt Jones, *tr. fr. Welsh by* H. Idris Bell. OBWVE

Old Woman, The. Beatrix Potter. GoJo; NTCP; PDV

Old Woman, An. Charles Henry Ross. OxBChV

Old Woman. Iain Crichton Smith. FaBoTw; OxBTC

Old Woman. *Unknown.* AmFP

Old woman across the way, The. The Whipping. Robert Hayden. GrPl; PoBA; PoE; SoSe

Old Woman and the Pedlar, The. Mother Goose. *See* There was an old [*or* little woman], as I've heard tell.

Old Woman and the Sandwiches, The. Libby Houston. OBSP

Old woman at the pond, The. Close-Up. Christine McNeill. NWP

Old Woman Awaiting the Greyhound Bus. Duane Niatum. CDW

Old woman, blue eyed and sun burned. Leah Goldberg, *tr. fr. Hebrew by* Ruth Finer Mintz. *Fr.* On Blossoming. MHP

Old woman dried an egg, The. The Egg. Jean Follain, *tr. fr. French by* W. S. Merwin. AnRep

Old Woman from France, The. *Unknown.* ReMoGo

Old woman, her butt spread on the stoop, An. Rapunzel. Faye Kicknosway. UL

Old woman, I hope that at least. Ray A. Young Bear. *Fr.* Three translated Poems for October. ETG

Old woman in me walks patiently to the hospital, An. Revelation. Carole C. Gregory. BlSi

Old woman likes to melt her husband. She puts him in a, An. Feeding the Dog. Russell Edson. RaBo

Old woman must stand, The. *Unknown.* OxNR

Old Woman Nature. Gary Snyder. NoAM; RaBo

Old Woman of Beare, The. *Unknown, tr. fr. Irish by* Brendan Kennelly. PeIV

Old Woman of Beare Regrets Lost Youth, The. *Unknown, tr. fr. Irish by* Frank O'Connor. OBMV

Old Woman of Gloucester, The. *Unknown.* ReMoGo

Old Woman of Harrow. *Unknown.* FaBoNo; ReMoGo

Old Woman of Leeds, The. *Unknown.* ReMoGo

Old Woman of Surrey. Mother Goose. *See* There was an old woman in Surrey.

Old Woman of the Roads, An. Padraic Colum. BoTP; CH; CoGr; FaBoBe; FaPON; FYAP; MoBrPo; NOIV; OBEV; PoRA; TIRV

Old woman, old woman. Mother Goose. ReMoGo

Old woman, old woman, are you fond of carding? Old Woman. *Unknown.* AmFP

Old woman, old woman,/ Shall we go a-shearing? Mother Goose. OxNR (Shall We Go A-Shearing?) PeEV

Old Woman out of Iowa. Colette Inez. ETG

Old Woman, Outside the Abbey Theater, An. L. A. G. Strong. FiBHP; MoBrPo

Old Woman Remembers, An. Sterling A. Brown. PoBA

Old woman sits on a bench before the door and quarrels, The. Fawn's Foster-Mother. Robinson Jeffers. MoP; NoAM; NOBA

Old Woman Speaks of the Moon, An. Ruth Pitter. WPE

Old woman, time and your own. To Grandmother on Her Going. Gail Tremblay. HATNAP

Old woman went to market and bought a pig, An. *Unknown.* OxNR

Old Woman who lived in the Shoe, The. Joyce Johnson. PeLi

Old woman's hair, The. Mothers. Punkanuttiraiyar, *tr. fr. Tamil by* A. K. Ramanujan. PLW

Old Woman's Lamentations, An. Villon, *tr. fr. French by* J. M. Synge. MoBrPo; OBMV

Old woman's shoulders, The. Mothers. Kakkai Patiniyar Naccellaiyar, *tr. fr. Tamil by* A. K. Ramanujan. PLW

Old Woman's Song, An. Akjartoq, *tr. fr. Eskimo into Danish by* Knud Rasmussen; *English vers. by* Tom Lowenstein. WPOW

Old Women, The. George Mackay Brown. OxBS

Old women all their lives, they're a mixture of whitelime and brine. Women at the Market. Angela Figueroa-Aymerich, *tr. fr. Spanish by* Hardie St. Martin. PBWP

Old Women beside a Church. Keith Wilson. Poetsp

Old Women of Toronto. Miriam Waddington. NOBC

Old women say that men don't know. Becoming a Dad. Edgar A. Guest. BLPL; PoLF

Old wooden house a soft, The. Brass Tacks. Denise Levertov. InPS

Old wooden steps to the front door, The. A Time Past. Denise Levertov. NoAM

Old Words, The. David Wagoner. ArLo

Old, worn harp that had been played, An. The Master-Player. Paul Laurence Dunbar. AnAmPo

Old wound in my ass, The. Fabrication of Ancestors. Alan Dugan. CAPP; NoAM

Old Year, The. John Clare. NOBVV; OBCP

Old Year, The. Priscilla Jane Thompson. CBWP-2

Old Year, The. Clarence Urmy. PoToHe

Old Year and the New, The. Annie Johnson Flint. BLRP

Old year's gone away, The. The Old Year. John Clare. NOBVV; OBCP

Old yellow stucco, The. Winter Nightfall. J. C. Squire. OxBTC

Old yew, which graspest at the stones. Tennyson. *Fr.* In Memoriam A. H. H. EBVV, *abr.*; EBVVPR; ELP; EnVR; GTBS-P; NOBE; NoP; OAEL-2, *abr.*; OBNC; PeECV, *abr.*; PoEL-5; UnPo

Olden Scrapple Sonnet. Kenward Elmslie. UL

Older American, The. Cheryl Clarke. GLP

Older Men. Alfred Corn. GLP

Older than the ancient Greeks. Pigeons. Marianne Moore. PoA

Older than the anus with which it shares. Navel. Dennis Schmitz. AnAn

Older than this psalm I'm singing right to the end. (*LL*) Old ones to the side. Charles Simic. AmPA; LCAP

Older women were Sunbeams and I guess we, The. Nightingales in America. Jane Flanders. CrSp

Oldest human fossil, The. Fire. Mark O'Connor. NOBAu

Oldest man in the world wears shoes, The. Passage. Billy Marshall-Stoneking. NOBAu

Oldest of us burst into tears and cried, The. Allen Curnow. *Fr.* Tomb of an Ancestor. PeNZ

Oldest Place, The. Thomas Kinsella. PBCIP

Ole Abe (God bless 'is ole soul!) Negro Soldier's Civil War Chant. *Unknown.* BPo
(Black Soldier's Civil War Chant.) TAP

Ole Aunt Dinah, she's jes lak me. Jack and Dinah Want Freedom. *Unknown.* BPo

Ole Sheep Dey Know de Road, De. *Unknown.* BPo

Oleander on the wall, The. By the Arno. Oscar Wilde. EBVV

Oleaster, The. Robert Graves. OBTV

Olga Poems. Denise Levertov. LCAP; NNaP

Olga Poems, *sels.* Denise Levertov.
"Everything flows." NAAL-2

Olive, The. A. E. Housman. NoAM

Olive garden for the nightingales, The. (*LL*) Painted Head. John Crowe Ransom. LiTA; LiTM; MeMAP; NoAM; NOBA; OxBA

Olive journeys. Journey round the World. Ingrid Jonker, *tr. fr. Afrikaans by* Jack Cope *and* William Plomer. PBWP

Olive Tree, The. Sabine Baring-Gould. GN

Olive Trees. Bernard Spencer. NoAM

Oliver Cromwell and Beethoven both. Peter Daines at a Party. Alan Brownjohn. OBF

Oliver Singing. Israel Zangwill. NSI

Oliver Twist. Marlene Philip. PBCV

Oliver's singing. Oliver Singing. Israel Zangwill. NSI

Olives and Mountains. Elizabeth Barrett Browning. *Fr.* Aurora Leigh. FaBoPP; OBTV

Olivia. Elijah Fenton. ECEV

Olivia. Tennyson. *Fr.* Talking Oak, The. GN

Olivia's Face. Shakespeare. *Fr.* Twelfth Night. CBCK

Olivia's lewd, but looks devout. Olivia. Elijah Fenton. ECEV

Olivier Metra's Waltz of Roses. La Mélinite: Moulin-Rouge. Arthur Symons. PeVV

Ollie, Answer Me. Stephen Berg. NaP

Ollie McGee. Edgar Lee Masters. OBD

Olmutz, Moravia: Wittgenstein. Wittgenstein and Engelmann. Gwen Harwood. OBF

Ol'Tunes, The. Paul Laurence Dunbar. AnAmPo

Olympic Girl, The. Sir John Betjeman. ArLo

Olympicus, the welter-weight. Lucilius, *tr. fr. Greek by* Peter Porter. GrAn

Olympikos, with your ugly face. Lucilius, *tr. fr. Greek by* Sam Hamill. InMo

Om. *Malay Oral Tradition, tr. by* R. O. Winstedt. WTO

Omagh Post Office Rhyme. *Unknown.* FaBoVe

Ombre and basset laid aside. A Song on the South Sea. The Countess of Winchilsea. ECWP; NOEC

Omelet of A MacLeish, The. Edmund Wilson. NYBP

Omen. Birago Diop, *tr. fr. French by* Ellen Conroy Kennedy. NegPo

Omens. *Unknown, tr. fr. Gaelic by* Alexander Carmichael. RB

Omens of the Morning. Faustin Charles. NBrP

Omera. Marjorie Oludhe Macgoye. HBAPE

Omeros. Derek Walcott. BAP-91

Omeyn. (*LL*) Jerusalem Shadow. Melanie Kaye/Kantrowitz. LoHo

Ominous length uncoiling and thin, An. The Rattlesnake. Alfred W. Purdy. OBAP

Omit needless words! Preface Shrink Lit: Elements of Style. Maurice Sagoff. NBLV

Omnes gentes plaudite. A Last Drink. *Unknown.* MiEL

Omnes Gentes Plaudite!. *Unknown.* OxBSP

Omnia Exeunt in Mysterium. George Sterling. WGRP

Omnia Somnia. Joshua Sylvester. FaBoEE

Omnibus across the bridge, An. Symphony in Yellow. Oscar Wilde. EBVV; FaBoPP; MoBrPo; NoAM; NOBVV; OxBSP

Omnipotence. Johann Ladislaus von Felsö-Eör Pyrker, *tr. fr. German by* Philip L. Miller. RiWo

Omnipotent and steadfast God. John Brown's Prayer. Stephen Vincent Benét. *Fr.* John Brown's Body. PoNe

Omnipotent confederate of all good. Amos N. Wilder. TrPWD

Omnipresence. Edward Everett Hale. WGRP

Omniscience. Blanche Mary Kelly. TrPWD

On. Bob Kaufman. PoBeRe

On a Bank [*or* Banck] asl I Sat [*or* Sate] a-Fishing; a Description of the Spring. Sir Henry Wotton. NOSC; SeCP

On a Bank [*or* Banck] as I Sate [*or* Sat] a-Fishing; a Description of the Spring. Sir Henry Wotton. SeCP

On a Bath-House in which Both Men and Women Bathe. Paulus Silentiarius, *tr. fr. Greek by* Andrew Miller. GrAn

On a Bed of Guernsey Lilies. Christopher Smart. NOEC

On a bed. Orgasms came and went like tiny birds. (*LL*) 2 Wren Street. Christian McEwen. VBLP

On a Bicycle, *sels.* Yevgeny Yevtushenko, *tr. fr. Russian by* Robin Milner-Gulland *and* Peter Levi.

On a Birth. Geoffrey Grigson. NAs

On a Birthday. J. M. Synge. ChTr; GBL; OBMV; PeIV

On a Blind Girl. Baha Ad-din Zuhayr, *tr. fr. Arabic by* E. H. Palmer. AWP

On a board of raspberry and pure gold. Osip Mandelstam, *tr. fr. Russian by* W. S. Merwin *and* Clarence Brown. AnAn

On a Bougainvillaea Vine at the Summer Palace [*or* in Haiti]. Barbara Howes. MoAmPo; NYBP

On a branch covered with jade-green moss. Tune: "Sparse Shadows" — Plum Blossoms. Chiang K'uei, *tr. fr. Chinese by* An-yan Tang. SuSp

On a Bright and Summer's Morning. *Unknown.* AmFP

On a Bust of Lincoln. Clinton Scollard. OHIP

On a Calm Summer's Night. John Nicholson. EnLoPo

On a Carrier Who Died of Drunkenness. Byron. NBLV

On a Cat Aging. Sir Alexander Gray. OFC

On a Catholic Childhood. Janet Campbell Hall. VoR

On a Celtic Mask by Henry Moore. Horace Gregory. PoA

On a Certain Alderman. John Cunningham, *after the Greek of* Simonides. FaBoEE

On a Certain Effeminate Peer. John Winstanley. FaBoEE

On a Certain Lady at Court. Pope. NOBE; NOEC; OBEV; OBF; OxBSP; TrGrPo

On a Certain Lord Giving Some Thousand Pounds for a House. David Garrick. FaBoEE

On a Certain Occasion for the Year 1790. William Cowper. NOCV

On a Child Who Lived One Minute. X. J. Kennedy. HoPM; NYBP; Poetr

On a clear day, the jealous. The Danger of Loss. Robert Bly. LPA

On a clear night in Live Oak you can see. Walking Down the Road. Adrienne Rich. NIP

On a Clergyman's Horse Biting Him. *Unknown.* FaBoCo; FaBoEE; NBLV; OxBoLi

On a Cock at Rochester. Sir Charles Sedley. FaBoEE; NOSC; OPOP

On a Cold Autumn Day. Bonnie Nims. TLR

On a cold night. Solitary. Lance Henson. HATNAP

On a cold night I came through the cold rain. J. V. Cunningham. HAP; TRP; VCAP

On a cold winter day the snow came down. Proud Little Spruce Fir. Jeannie Kirby. BoTP

On a Contentious Companion. John Hoskyns. FaBoEE

On a C.P.R. packet. (*LL*) Gin the Goodwife Stint. Basil Bunting. CTC

On a Crab. P'i Jih-hsiu, *tr. fr. Chinese by* William H. Nienhauser. SuSp

On a Curate's Complaint of Hard Duty. Swift. SCGP; TIRV

On a dark and stormy night. The Wreck of the Royal Palm. *Unknown.* AmFP

On a Dark Night. John F. Deane. BiHa

On a Dark Road. Robert Herrick. *See* Her eyes the glow-worm[e] lend thee.

On a date with a charming young bird. *Unknown.* PeLi

On a Day--Alack the Day. Shakespeare. *Fr.* Love's Labour's Lost. ElL

On a day long and wet we fall upon. Arriving. Daniel Halpern. HoPM

On a day of ripped cloud. From a Pill-Box on the Solent. Jeremy Hooker. SCBI

On a Dead Babe. James Whitcomb Riley. AnAmPo

On a Dead Child. Robert Bridges. CMoP; EBEV; LiTB; LiTM; NoAM; NOBE; NOBVV; OBMV; OBNC; OxAEP-2; SCGP

On a Dead Hostess. Hilaire Belloc. MoBrPo

On a dead man's toe. (*LL*) Latin Night at the Pawnshop. Martín Espada. TRP

On a Dead Poet. William Rose Benét. AnAmPo

On a Dead Poet. Frances Sargent Osgood.

On a Dead Scholar, *sels.* St. Columcille, *tr. fr. Old Irish by* Robin Flower.

On a Death's Head. Elizabeth Tollet. ECWP

On a Discovery Made Too Late. Samuel Taylor Coleridge. EnRP; Son

On a Distant Prospect of an Absconding Bookmaker. George Rostrevor Hamilton. FaBoCo

On a Distinguished Politician. J. E. Thorold Rogers. FaBoEE

On a Doctor of Divinity. Richard Porson. *See* Here lies a Doctor of Divinity.

On a Dog of Lord Eglinton's. Burns. OxBSP

On a Dolphin. Anyte, *tr. fr. Greek by* John Heath-Stubbs *and* Carol A. Whiteside. GrAn

On a Drawing by Flavio. Philip Levine. BTR

On a Dream. Keats. EnRP

On a Drop of Dew. Andrew Marvell. ESCV; GeHe; HAP; JCP; LiTB; MeLP; NOSC; PFP; SCGP; SeCP; SeCV-1; TEP

On a Fair Beggar. Philip Ayres. EnLoPo

On a Fair Lady, Looking in the Glass. Richard Leigh. NOSC

On a Favorite Cat Drowned in a Tub of Gold Fishes. Thomas Gray. *See* 'Twas on a lofty vase's side.

On a Feast. Francis Quarles. ChIV-2

On a Female Rope-Dancer. *Unknown.* NOEC

On a Field Trip at Fredericksburg. Dave Jeddie Smith. HCAP

On a Fifteenth-Century Flemish Angel. David Ray. CRP

On a flat road runs the well-train'd runner. The Runner. Walt Whitman. InPK; InPS; SAmP

On a flimmering floom you shall ride. *(LL)* On a Flimmering Floom You Shall Ride. Carl Sandburg. GoYe; OBAL

On a Flimmering Floom You Shall Ride. Carl Sandburg. GoYe; OBAL

On a Fly Drinking out of [*or* from] His Cup. William Oldys. ImPo; OBEV; OxAEP-1; TrGrPo

On a Forsaken Lark's Nest. Mathilde Blind. FM

On a Fortification at Boston Begun by Women. Benjamin Tompson. GOA; NOSC; PAH; SCAP

On a Fowler. Isidorus, *tr. fr. Greek by* William Cowper. AWP

On a Frightful Dream. John Codrington Bampfylde. NOEC

On a General Election. Hilaire Belloc. FaBoCo; FaBoEE; NOBE; NOBL; OBSV; OxBTC

On a General Election. W. B. Yeats. IHNG

On a Gentleman Marrying His Cook. Colin Ellis. FaBoEE

On a Gentleman's Complaining to a Lady That He Could Not Eat Meat. *Unknown.* ECWP

On a Gentlewoman that Sung and Played upon a Lute. William Strode. NOSC

On a Gentlewoman Walking in the Snow. William Strode. *See* I saw fair[e] Chloris [*or* Cloris] walk alone.

On a German Tour. Richard Porson. FiBHP

On a Girdle. Edmund Waller. AWP; BeJo; BLPL; FF; GTBS; GTBS-P; ImPo; InPK; LiTB; NAEL-1; NoP; NOSC; OBEV; PoE; PoRA; SCGP; SeCV-1; TFi; TrGrPo

On a Gloomy Easter. Alice Freeman Palmer. OHIP

On a gnarled and naked tree. *(LL)* Song for a Dark Girl. Langston Hughes. AmPP; CDC; NAAL-2; PoBA; SAmP

On a Goldfinch Starved to Death in His Cage. William Cowper. OBD

On a Good Leg and Foot. William Strode. NOSC

On a Government Surveyor. Albert Brodrick. PeSAV

On a Great Election. Hilaire Belloc. *See* Accursed power which stands on Privilege, The.

On a green island in the Main Street traffic. Pro Patria. Constance Carrier. NYBP; WPE

On a Grey-haired Old Lady Knitting at an Orchestral Concert. Suzanne Gardinier. CBAP

On a High House in Byzantium. Paulus Silentiarius, *tr. fr. Greek by* Andrew Miller. GrAn

On a highway over the marshland. Flames and Dangling Wire. Robert Gray. NOBAu

On a hill above the town. The Whistle Column. John Haines. AnAn

On a hill far away. The Old Rugged Cross. George Bennard. AH

On a hill in Frisco. Irrational. Philip Lamantia. UL

On a hill near Petersburg. James Hugo Johnston. Maggie Pogue Johnson. CBWP-4

On a hill there blooms a palm. Hayyim Nahman Bialik, *tr. fr. Hebrew by* Maurice Samuel. *Fr.* Songs of the People. AWP

On a hill there grows a flower. Nicholas Breton. EIL (Phyllida and Corydon. TrGrPo

On a hillside in Jerusalem. Maria Olt. Ruth Whitman. BTR

On a holy day when sails were blowing southward. The Straying Student. Austin Clarke. BIrV; CIP; IPY; MoAB; NOIV; PeIV

On a Honey Bee [*or* To a Honey Bee]. Philip Freneau. TAP

On a Hopeful Youth. Owen Feltham [*or* Feltham]. NOSC

On a hot summer Sunday. The Cemetery at Academy, California. Philip Levine. NaP

On a Hound. Simonides, *tr. fr. Greek by* Kenneth Rexroth. PGA

On a Japanese Beach. Nina Cassian, *tr. fr. Romanian by* Daniela Gioseffi *and the author.* WoWa

On *a* Juniper-Tree, Cut Down to Make Busks. Aphra Behn. KTR

On a Lady Indifferent to Poetry. Sappho, *tr. fr. Greek by* John Frederick Nims. STV

On a Lady, Preached into the Colic, by One of Her Lovers. Aaron Hill. ECEV

On a Lady Who Beat Her Husband. *Unknown.* FiBHP

On a Lady Who P-ssed at the Tragedy of Cato. Pope. OxBSP

On a Line in Sandburg. R. S. Thomas. NAs

On a Little Bird. Martin Armstrong. CH

On a Little Boy's Endeavouring to Catch a Snake. Thomas Foxton. OxBChV

On a little green knoll. Old Log House. James S. Tippett. FaPON

On a little piece of wood. Mr. and Mrs. Spikky Sparrow. Edward Lear. OxBChV

On a Lord. Samuel Taylor Coleridge. FaBoCo; FiBHP

On a lorry the centre of a gaping crowd. W. H. Auden. *Fr.* Happy New Year, A. OBSV

On a Lover of Books. Geoffrey Grigson. FaBoEE

On a Magazine Sonnet. Russell Hillard Loines. OBAL

On a Maid [*or* Maide] of Honour Seen by a Scholar in Somerset Garden. Thomas Randolph. JCP

On a Man Run Over by an Omnibus. Henry Luttrell. FaBoEE

On a man that died for me. *(LL)* Jim Bludso of the Prairie Belle. John Milton Hay. AnAmPo; BeLS; FaBoBe; VPP

On a mid-December day. Since. W. H. Auden. CBLP; InPS

On a Midsummer Eve. Thomas Hardy. FaBoVe

On a midsummer night, on a night that was eerie with stars. August Night. Sara Teasdale. MoAmPo; VBLP

On a Miscellany of Poems, *sels.* John Gay.
"When Pope's harmonious Muse with pleasure roves." EPCY

On a Monday mornin' it began to rain. Jay Gould's Daughter. *Unknown.* AS

On a Monday Morning. Cyril Tawney. OBET

On a Monday morning early as my wandering steps did lead me. The Boys of Mullabaun [*or* Mullaghbawn]. *Unknown.* BIrV; GBP

On a Monday morning it began to rain. On the Charlie So Long. *Unknown.* AS

On a Monument to Martí. Walter Adolphe Roberts. PBCV; TTY

On a Moonlit Night, Sent to my Brothers and Sisters. Po Chü-i, *tr. fr. Chinese by* Irving Lo. SuSp

On a morning like this one, when the mist is lit from within. Who We Are. Daniel Hoffman. BAP-91

On a morning such as this. Veteran. Lola Ridge. WPE

On a mossy bank reclined. The Stolen Kiss. Robert Dodsley. ECEV

On a mountain of sugar-candy. Arno Holz, *tr. by* Babette Deutsch. *Fr.* Phantasus. AWP; PChr

On a never-ending journey, what a miracle to be! *(LL)* Clouds are flowing in the river, waves are flying in the sky. Eveline Beumkes. EaPr

On a New Duke. *Unknown.* FaBoEE

On a night of mist and rain. Phyllis. Sydney King Russell. ErPo

On a Night of Snow. Elizabeth J. Coatsworth. CRH; MoAmPo; MoShBr; OBCA; OFC

On a Night of the Full Moon. Audre Lorde. AIW; NALW; UnAS

On a Noisy Polemic. Burns. FaBoEE

On a Nomination to the Legion of Honour. *Unknown.* FaBoEE

On a Nook Called Fairyland. H. Cordelia Ray. CBWP-3

On a Note of Triumph., *sels.* Norman Corwin.
Man unto His Fellow Man. TrJP

On a Nun. Jacopo Vittorelli, *tr. fr. Italian by* Byron. AWP

On a Painted Woman. Shelley. FaBoCo; NBLV

On a Painting by Hsia Kuei Entitled "Returning in Wind and Snow to a Village Home." Kao Ch'i, *tr. fr. Chinese by* Irving Y. Lo. SuSp

On a Painting by Patient B of the Independence State Hospital for the Insane. Donald Justice. CoAP; NoAM

On a Painting of a Woman Shown Half-Length, *sels.* T'ang Yin, *tr. fr. Chinese by* Jonathan Chaves.

On a Painting of Ants and Butterflies. Huang T'ing-chien, *tr. fr. Chinese by* Michael E. Workman. SuSp

On a Painting of the Radiant Emperor's Night Revels by Candlelight. Kao Ch'i, *tr. fr. Chinese by* Irving Y. Lo. SuSp

On a Pair of Garters. Sir John Davies. OPOP; SiPS

On a Parisian Boulevard. James Kenneth Stephen. *Fr.* England and America. NOBL

On a patrician evening in Ireland. The Woman of the House. Richard Murphy. IPY

On a Pet Grasshopper. Aristodicus of Rhodes, *tr. fr. Greek by* Kenneth Rexroth. PGA

On a Photo of Sgt. Ciardi a Year Later. John Ciardi. AiP; ArOW

On a Photograph of My Mother at Seventeen. Miller Williams. MT

On a Picture by J. M. Wright, Esq. Robert Southey. FM

On a Picture by Michele Da Verona, of Arion as a Boy Riding upon a Dolphin. Anne Ridler. PoA

On a Picture by Pippin, Called "The Den." Selden Rodman. PoNe

On a Picture by Poussin Representing Shepherds in Arcadia. John Addington Symonds. FaBoBe

On a Picture of Your House. Douglas G. Jones. NOBC

On a Picture Painted by Herself[, Representing Two Nimphs of Diana's]. Anne Killigrew. KTR; NOSC

On a piece of our honeymoon. Honeymoon. Barry Goldensohn. NAmP90

On a Piece of Unwrought Pipeclay. John Frederick Bryant. NOEC

On a Pig's Head. Charles Tomlinson. NoAM

On a Poet. Henry Parrot. FaBoEE

On a poet's lips I slept. Shelley. *Fr.* Prometheus Unbound. ELP; EnRP; EPCY; OAEL-2; TOF
(Poet's Dream, The.) GTBS; GTBS-P

On a Political Prisoner. W. B. Yeats. FaBoPV; IIP; OAEL-2; OBMV

On a Portrait of Wordsworth by B. R. Haydon. Elizabeth Barrett Browning. EPCY; HeIP

On a Prayer Book Sent to Mrs. M.R, *sels.* Richard Crashaw. "Dear soul be strong!" ErPo

On a Puritan. Hilaire Belloc. FaBoEE

On a Puritanicall Lock-Smith. William Camden. FaBoEE

On a Quiet Conscience. Charles I, King of England. CH

On a Recent Protest against Social Conditions. David Posner. NYBP

On a Recollected Road. Amir Gilboa, *tr. fr. Hebrew* by Ruth Finer Mintz. MHP

On a red, red river. *(LL)* Omen. Birago Diop. NegPo

On a Rhine Steamer. James Kenneth Stephen. *Fr.* England and America. NOBL; NOBVV; OBTV; PeLV

On a Ring. Asclepiades, *tr. fr. Greek* by Alan Marshfield. GrAn

On a rock, Bishop of Cloyne. Berkeley. Mairtin O Direain. BiHa

On a Romantic Lady. Mary Monck. ECWP; NOEC

On a roof in the Old City. Jerusalem. Yehuda Amichai, *tr. fr. Hebrew.* TSaS, *tr. by* Stephen Mitchell

On a Rose in December. Ebenezer Elliot. FaBoEE

On a Royal Demise. Thomas Hood. FiBHP

On a Ruined House in a Romantic Country. Samuel Taylor Coleridge. *Fr.* Sonnets Attempted in the Manner of Contemporary Writers. FaBoPa; Son

On a Sabbath eve, at dusk on a summer day. A Song of Lies on Sabbath Eve. Yehuda Amichai, *tr. fr. Hebrew* by Chana Bloch. PoSu

On a saddle without a horse. Journey Through Hell. Nicanor Parra, *tr. fr. Spanish* by Miller Williams. AnRep

On a Saturday afternoon in the football season. Laziness and Silence. Robert Bly. PPP

On a Schoolmaster in Cleish Parish, Fifeshire. Burns. *See* Here lie Willie Michie's [*or* M — hie's] banes.

On a Scooter. Desmond A. Greig. PeSA

On a Sea-Grape Leaf. Katherine Garrison Chapin. GrPl

On a Sea-Storm nigh the Coast. Richard Steere. SCAP

On a Seal. Plato, *tr. fr. Greek* by Thomas Stanley. AWP; FaBoEE

On a Sermon Preach'd Sept. the 6th, 1697. on These Words: You Have Sold Your Selves for Nought. Sarah Fyge. KTR

On a Seven-Day Diary. Alan Dugan. OBAL

On a Shipmate, Pero Moniz, Dying at Sea. Camões, *tr. fr. Portuguese* by Roy Campbell. PeSAV

On a Similar Occasion for the Year 1792. William Cowper. NOCV

On a Sleeping Friend. Hilaire Belloc. CoGr

On a sleepless night. Teresa Moszkowicz-Syrop. BTR

On a slow wheel, sharpening fins/ Give glints. *(LL)* Fish and Chips on the Merry-Go-Round. K. O. Arvidson. PeNZ

On a Small Bath. *Unknown, tr. fr. Greek* by Robin Skelton. GrAn

On a small six-acre farm dwelt John Grist the miller. Under the Drooping Willow Tree. *Unknown.* OxBoLi

On a Snail. Su Shih, *tr. by* Irving Y. Lo. *Fr.* Two Poems on Insect Painting by Candidate Yin. SuSp

On a Snowy Day. Dorothy Aldis. PDV

On a Soldier Fallen in the Philippines. William Vaughn Moody. AnAmPo; NOBA; PAH

On a Soldier Killed in the Great War. R. Williams Parry, *tr. fr. Welsh* by H. Idris Bell. OBWVE

On a Spaniel Called Beau Killing a Young Bird. William Cowper. FaBoCh

On a Splendud Match. James Whitcomb Riley. AnAmPo

On a squeaking cart, they push the usual stuff. A Removal from Terry Street. Douglas Dunn. FaBoMo; FaBoVe; OxBC

On a Squinting Poetess. Thomas Moore. FaBoCo

On a Squirrel Crossing the Road in Autumn, in New England. Richard Eberhart. HeIP; LiTM; Poetsp

On a starless night and still. On Being Asked to Write a School Hymn. Charles Causley. OxAEP-2

On a starred [*or* starr'd] night Prince Lucifer uprose. Lucifer in Starlight. George Meredith. AWP; CH; ChIV-1; EBVV; EnVR; FF; GGP; HAP; ImPo; InPK; LiTB; Mes; NAEL-2; NOBE; NOBVV; NoP; OAEL-2; OBEV; OBNC; PoE; PoEL-5; SCGP; Son; TFi; TrGrPo; UnPo

On a starry, wintry night. The Christ Child. Mary Weston Fordham. CBWP-2

On a Statue of Sir Arthur Sullivan. George Rostrevor Hamilton. FaBoCo

On a Statue of Pan. *Unknown, tr. fr. Greek by* W. G. Shepherd. GrAn

On a Steamer. Dorothy W. Baruch. FaPON

On a still calm night when the bugs begin to bite. *Unknown.* ISE

On a Stingy Beau. John Winstanley. FaBoEE

On a Stone Thrown at a Very Great Man, But Which Missed Him. "Peter Pindar." NBLV

On a straw-colored day. Dream. Solomon Edwards. PoNe

On a street in Knoxville. Street Scene — 1946. Kenneth Porter. PoNe

On a Stupendous Leg of Granite, Discovered Standing by Itself in the Deserts of Egypt, with the Inscription Inserted Below. Horace Smith. PrIm

On a summer day in the month of May. The Big Rock Candy Mountains. *Unknown.* NOBA

On a summer night in Odessa. *(LL)* Dvonya. Louis Simpson. NNaP; NOBA

On a summer's day when the sea [*or* wave] was rippled. The Ship That Never Returned. Henry Clay Work. BLPA
(On a summer's day while the waves were rippling, with a quiet and gentle breeze.) AS

On a summer's day while the waves were rippling, with a quiet and gentle breeze. Henry Clay Work. *See* On a summer's day when the sea [*or* wave] was rippled.

On a Sunbeam. Thomas Heyrick. NOSC

On a Sundial. Hilaire Belloc. FaBoEE

On a sunny brae alone I lay. A Day Dream. Emily Brontë. NALW

On a throne of new gold the Son of the Sky. The Emperor. Tu Fu, *tr. fr. Chinese* by E. Powys Mathers. AWP

On a Time the Amorous Silvy. *Unknown.* GBL
(Parting at Dawn.) OtMeF
(Wakening, The.) OBEV

On a Toad. Su Shih, *tr. by* Irving Y. Lo. *Fr.* Two Poems on Insect Painting by Candidate Yin. SuSp

On a towering Christmas tree. *(LL)* City Lights. Rachel Field. FaPON; PDV

On a train in Texas German prisoners eat. Defeat. Witter Bynner. PoNe

On a tree by a river, a little tom-tit. Ko-Ko's Winning Song. W. S. Gilbert. *Fr.* Mikado, The. LiTB
(Ko-Ko's Song.) ImPo
(Titwillow.) NoP

On a Tree Fallen across the Road. Robert Frost. RB

On a tributary of the Amazon. The Lass of Aughrim. Paul Muldoon. NoAM; PBCIP

On a Vase of Gold-Fish. Charles Tennyson Turner. NOBVV

On a verdant summer islet. Burial of a Fairy Queen. Mary E. Tucker. CBWP-1

On a very fine gander. *(LL)* Old Mother Goose/ When she wanted to wander. Mother Goose. OxNR; ReMoGo

On a very hot Independence Day. Sonnet No. 21. Mark Ameen. GLP

On a Violet in Her Breast. Thomas Stanley. NOSC

On a Virtuous Young Gentlewoman That Died Suddenly. William Cartwright. HAP; OBEV

On a Virtuous Young Gentlewoman That Died Suddenly. William Cartwright. HAP

On a Visit to Ch'ung Chen Taoist Temple. Yü Hsüan-chi, *tr. by* Kenneth Rexroth *and* Ling Chung. PBWP; WPC

On a Vulgar Error. C. S. Lewis. OxBTC

On a Wag in Mauchline. Burns. FiBHP

On a War-worker, 1916. Arundell James Kennedy Esdaile. NSI

On a Wet Day. Franco Sacchetti. *See* As I walk'd thinking through a little grove.

On a wet night, laden with books for luggage. The Poet on the Island. Richard Murphy. CIP; PeIV

On a Wet Summer. John Codrington Bampfylde. NOEC

On a white field. The Sower. R. Olivares Figueroa, *tr. fr. Spanish* by Dudley Fitts. FaPON

On a Whore. John Hoskyns. FaBoEE

On A Wife. Francis Burdett Money-Coutts. OxBSP

On a winter's night long time ago. Noël. Hilaire Belloc. UV

On a withered branch. Basho, *tr. fr. Japanese* by Harold G. Henderson. TAL

On a Woman. Robert Williams, *tr. fr. Welsh* by H. Idris Bell. OBWVE

On A Woman's Inconstancy. Sir Robert Ayton. EIL

On a Worthless Politician. *Unknown, tr. fr. Greek by* Peter Jay. GrAn

On a Young Man and an Old Man. Edward May. OxBSP

On a Young Wife. Julianus of Egypt, *tr. fr. Greek by* Willis Barnstone. GrAn

On Addison. Pope. *See* Peace to all such! but were there one whose fires.

On Addy Road. May Swenson. GOYP

On Aesthetics, More or Less. Peter Kane Dufault. NYBP

On African Writing. Jack A. Mapanje. HBAPE

On afternoons of drowsy calm. Afternoon Service at Mellstock. Thomas Hardy. PeECV

On Ageing. Maya Angelou. AIW

On Alexander and Aristotle, on a Black-on-Red Greek Plate. Alan Dugan. PPP

On Alexis. Plato, tr. fr. Greek by Thomas Stanley. AWP

On alien ground, breathing an alien air. Where a Roman Villa Stood, above Freiburg. Mary Elizabeth Coleridge. OBNC; OBTV

On all graves silently it thawed: Recovered. (LL) In the Churchyard. Detlev von Liliencron. RiWo

On all the brightness of the common day. (LL) These Are the Gifts I Ask. Henry van Dyke. FaBoBe

On Allgood Road two miles off Georgia 41, you round a curve. The Window. David Bottoms. NGP

On America. Allen Ginsberg. See America I've given you all and now I'm nothing.

On American Politicians. Unknown. IHNG

On an Aberdeen Favourite. Unknown. FaBoPP

On an Air of Rameau. Arthur Symons. OBNC

On an Ancient Tomb East of the Village. Po Chü-i, tr. fr. Chinese by Robert Payne. TAL

On an Anniversary. J. M. Synge. FaBoEE; NOIV; OBMV; PeIV

On an apple-ripe September morning. Patrick Kavanagh. Fr. Tarry Flynn. IPY

On an early Sunday in April, a feeble day. An Extract from Addresses to the Academy of Fine Ideas. Wallace Stevens. LiTA; LiTM

On an Engraving by Casserius. A. D. Hope. CBAP

On an Hour-Glass[e]. John Hall. MeLP; OPOP

On an Indian Tomineois, the Least of Birds. Thomas Heyrick. FM; NOSC

On an Infant Dying as Soon as Born. Charles Lamb. GTBS; GTBS-P; IMW; OBEV

On an Infant Which Died before Baptism. Samuel Taylor Coleridge. OBD

On an Invitation to the United States. Thomas Hardy. AiP; AWP

On an Inyanga Road. Noel H. Brettell. PeSAV

On an Island. "Ethna Carbery." WPE

On an Island. J. M. Synge. BIrV; FaBoVe; MoBrPo; OxBSP; PeVV

On an oak in autumn. Survivor. Archibald MacLeish. PrIm

On an ocher island in an aqua ocean. (LL) The Swinging Goddess — / Sally Ride; First American Woman Astronaut. Lynn Lonidier. SRLS

On an Old Horn. Wallace Stevens. LiTA

On An Old Painting. Eduard Friedrich Mörike, tr. fr. German by Philip L. Miller. RiWo

On an Old Woman. Lucilius, tr. fr. Greek by William Cowper. AWP

On an outing with seventeen Czechs. Unknown. PeLi

On an Unsociable Family. Elizabeth Hands. ECWP; WoRP

On an unsuspecting Wednesday in October 1347. And Who Will Look Upon Our Testimony. Edward Hirsch. PFL

On and On for Ever. Li Ho, tr. fr. Chinese by A. C. Graham. PLT

On and on in the white clouds. Sent to the Taoist of Dragon Mountain, Hsü Fa-leng. Liu Ch'ang-ch'ing, tr. fr. Chinese by William H. Nienhauser. SuSp

On Angels. W. W. Eustace Ross. MoCV

On Another's Sorrow. Blake. Fr. Songs of Innocence. AWP; EnRP; FaBV; FHYEP; OxAEP-2; PoEL-4

On Apples. David Ross. NYBP

On Approaching My Birthday. Vassar Miller. IHMS; NMM

On Archaeanassa. Plato, tr. fr. Greek by Thomas Stanley. AWP

On Arrival. Richard Howard. TAP

On Arthur Hugh Clough. Swinburne. FaBoEE

On Australian Hills, sels. Ada Cambridge.

On Authors and Booksellers [or Publishers]. Pope. FaBoEE; IHNG

On Autumn Lake. John Ashbery. LCAP

On Balaam's Ass. Francis Quarles. ChIV-1

On Ballycastle Beach. Medbh McGuckian. PBCIP

On Barclay's Apology for the Quakers. Matthew Green. NOEC

On Bassa. Martial, tr. fr. Latin. PeHV

On beaches washed by seas. What She Said to Her Girl-Friend. Venmanipputi, tr. fr. Tamil by A. K. Ramanujan. PBWP

On Beauety, sels. James Thomson and David Mallet. "This happy place with all delights abounds." UV

On Beer. Emperor Julian, tr. fr. Greek by Kenneth Rexroth. PGA

On Behalf of Some Irishmen Not Followers of Tradition. "Æ." IIP; PeIV

On Being a Householder. Alan Dugan. NoAM

On Being a Poet in Sierra Leone. Syl Cheney-Coker. HBAPE

On Being a Woman. Dorothy Parker. AnAmPo; PoLF

On Being Asked for a Peace Poem. Howard Nemerov. OxBC

On Being Asked for a War Poem. W. B. Yeats. NIP; OBWP; OxAEP-2; PAW; PoWW

On Being Asked to Write a School Hymn. Charles Causley. OxAEP-2

On Being Brought from Africa to America. Phillis Wheatley. FF; GOA; NAAL-1; NALW; NOBA; NOEC; TAP; TTY; WPE

On Being Cautioned against Walking on an Headland Overlooking the Sea, because It Was Frequented by a Lunatic. Charlotte Smith. ECWP; WoRP

On Being Charged with Writing Incorrectly. "Amorous Lady, The." ECWP

On Being Head of the English Department. Pinkie Gordon Lane. BlSi

On Being Much Better Than Most and Yet Not Quite Good Enough. John Ciardi. GOYP

On Being Sixty. Po Chü-i, tr. fr. Chinese by Arthur Waley. AWP

On Ben Dorain. Duncan Ban MacIntyre, tr. fr. Gaelic by Robert Buchanan. Fr. Last Farewell to the Hills.

On Ben Jonson. Sidney Godolphin. BeJo; EPCY

On Ben Jonson. Mildmay Fane, 2d Earl of Westmorland. See He who began from brick and lime.

On Bertrand Russell's "Portraits from Memory." Donald Davie. FaBoTw

On better days, I bath with Wallace Stevens: dreaming his good. Another Word for Blue. John Engman. NAmP90

On Bishop Burnet's Being Set on Fire in His Closet. Thomas Parnell. ECEV

On black bare trees a stale cream moon. Eau-Forte. F. S. Flint. OxBTC

On blood, smoke, and the dead. Who Knows Where. Detlev von Liliencron, tr. fr. German by Ludwig Lewisohn. AWP

On Blood's Stealing the Crown. Andrew Marvell. FaBoEH

On Blossoming, sels. Leah Goldberg, tr. fr. Hebrew by Ruth Finer Mintz. "How shall we bring our dying heart up." MHP "Old woman, blue eyed and sun burned." MHP "Scarlet, warm and heavy in black velvet leaves." MHP "That death in his windows would rise." MHP

On blue summer evenings I'll go down the pathways. Sensation. Rimbaud, tr. fr. French by Kenneth Koch. SOTW; TTTS

On Board Ship. C. P. Cavafy, tr. fr. Greek by Edmund Keeley and Philip Sherrard. AnAn

On Board Starship Enterprise. Unknown. PeLi

On Board the Cumberland. George Henry Boker. PAH

On Board the Leicester Castle. Unknown. OxBSS

On board the noble Ann, twenty-seventh of March, from Shields to Greenland we set sail. The Greenland Men. Unknown. OxBSS

On Bond the Usurer. Unknown. NOSC

On Botching. John Heywood. FaBoCo; FaBoEE

On buds of late almond. (LL) Hands Full of Sun. David Rokeah. MHP

On Burroughs' Work. Allen Ginsberg. NAAL-2; NOBA; PoBeRe

On Butler who can think without rage. John Oldham. Fr. Satire, A. OBSV

On Button the Grave-Maker. Unknown. FaBoEE

On Buying a Dog. Edgar Klauber. NTCP

On Buying a Horse. Unknown. NBLV; RB

On Calamy's Imprisonment and Wild's Poetry. Unknown. APAS

On Calvary's Lonely Hill. Herbert Clark Johnson. PoNe

On Calvert's plains new faction reigns. Maryland Resolvesland. Unknown. PAH

On Captiva Island I sit on a ledge beside palmettos. Dreams of Snakes, Chocolate and Men. Christy Sheffield Sanford. UL

On Cardinal Wolsey. Unknown. FaBoCo

On Catania and Syracuse Swallowed Up by an Earthquake, from the Italian of Filicaja. Anna Seward. Son

On Catullus. Walter Savage Landor. OBEV

On Certain Ladies. Pope. See When other fair ones [or ladies] to the shades [or groves] go down.

On Certain Mornings Everything Is Sensual. David Jauss. GOYP

On certain nights I hear within the screeching of the horn. Legacies. Léon Laleau, tr. fr. French by Ellen Conroy Kennedy. Fr. Black Music. NegPo

On Certain Wits. Howard Nemerov. HCAP; OxBC

On Change of Weathers. Francis Quarles. OxBSP

On Chao Ch'ang's Flower Paintings in Wang Po-yang's Collection, sels. Su Shih, tr. fr. Chinese. Hibiscus. SuSp Plum Blossoms. SuSp Sunflower. SuSp

On Charles II. The Earl of Rochester. See In the Isle of Great Britain long since famous known.

On charts they fall like lace. Delos. Lawrence Durrell. OxAEP-2

On Children. Kahlil Gibran. Fr. Prophet, The. OxBM; PoToHe

On Chloris Walking in the Snow. William Strode. ELP; JCP; OAEL-1

On Christians, Mercy Will Fall. *Unknown, tr. fr. Welsh by* D. Myrddin Lloyd. OBWVE

On Christmas Day. the Earl of Orrery. TIRV

On Christmas-Day. Thomas Traherne. PoEL-2

On Christmas Day. *Unknown.* OBET

On Christmas Day I weep. Christmas Mourning. Vassar Miller. ChIV-2; MoAmPo

On Christmas-day in seventy-six. The Battle of Trenton. *Unknown.* PAH

On Christmas Day in the morning. *(LL)* As I Sat on a Sunny Bank. *Unknown.* ChTr; OxBoLi, *abr.*; OxNR, *(abr.)*

On Christmas day in the morning. *(LL)* Dame, get up and bake your pies. *Unknown.* BoTP; OxNR

On Christmas Day it happened so. On Christmas Day. *Unknown.* OBET

On Christmas Day to My Heart. Clement Paman. NOSC

On Christmas Eve I turned the spit. *Unknown.* OxNR

On Christmas Eve my mother read. Christmas Eve. Edna Kingsley Walla. BoTP

On Christmas Eve the little stars. Christmas Eve. Charlotte Druitt Cole. BoTP

On Christmas Morn. *Unknown. See* Shall I tell you who [*or* what] will come.

On Christmas morn awake did I. He Sports by Himself. Susan Miles. BXAP

On Christ's Sunday at morn! *(LL)* As I Sat under a Sycamore Tree. *Unknown.* LiTB

On City Streets. Margaret E. Bruner. PoToHe

On Clarastella walking in Her Garden. Robert Heath. NOSC

On Clergymen Preaching Politics. John Byrom. ECEV

On Climbing the Heights on the Ninth Day of the Ninth Moon. Tu Fu, *tr. fr. Chinese by* Robert Payne. TAL

On Climbing the Pagoda of the Temple of Gracious Benevolence with Kao Shih and Hsüeh Chü. Ts'en Shen, *tr. fr. Chinese by* Daniel Bryant. SuSp

On Climbing the Phoenix Tower at Chinling. Li Po, *tr. fr. Chinese by* Robert Payne. TAL

On Clouds. Douglas Livingstone. PeSAV

On cold winter mornings. Winter Morning. Frank Flynn. OTCP

On Commonwealth, on Marlborough. Technologies. George Starbuck. NYBP

On Communists. Ebenezer Elliot. *See* What is a communist? One who hath yearnings.

On Consulting "Contemporary Poets of the English Language." Anthony Thwaite. PeLV

On Court-Worme. Ben Jonson. SeCP

On Covering the Bones of Chang Chin, the Hired Man. Liu Tsung-yüan, *tr. fr. Chinese by* Jan W. Walls. SuSp

On Critics. Burns. IHNG

On crystal rims, they wheel in space. Snowflakes. Alice Behrend. GoYe

On Cupid's bow how are my heart-strings bent. Sir Philip Sidney. *Fr.* Astrophel and Stella. AAS; ESo, *sl. abr.*; GGP; HeIL, *Sonnets,* I–CVIII *and 11 Songs*; NoSic; Poetr; SCGP, *Sonnets,* I–CVIII *and 11 Songs*; SiPS, *Sonnets,* I–CVIII *and 11 Songs*; SiPSBD, *Sonnets,* I–CVIII *and 11 Songs*

On dark nights, when thoughts fly like nightbirds. It Is Important. Gail Tremblay. WeW

On days when I go out. My Illness and Other Animals. Maria Jastrzebska. NBrP

On Dean Inge. Humbert Wolfe. *See* Hark! the herald angels sing/ timidly.

On Death. Anne Killigrew. BoWoP; ChIV-1; KTR

On Death. Walter Savage Landor. *See* Death Stands above Me.

On Death. Francis Quarles. *Fr.* Divine Fancies. PeECV

On Death, *sels.* Shelley.
　"Who telleth a tale of unspeaking death?" OBD

On death and beauty — till a bullet stopped his song. *(LL)* All Day It Has Rained. Alun Lewis. AngWe; GTBS-P; NAEL-2; NOBE; OBWP; OBWVE; OxBTC; PAW

On Death and Love. Janet Campbell Hale. VoR

On Death, thy murd'rer, this revenge I take. An Epitaph upon My Dear Brother, Francis Beaumont. Sir John Beaumont. JCP

On Death's domain intent I fix my eyes. To a Gentleman and Lady on the Death of the Lady's Brother and Sister, and a Child of the Name Avis, Aged One Year. Phillis Wheatley. BlSi

On death's side of the bed. *(LL)* Eyes Fastened with Pins. Charles Simic. VCAP

On December, the sixth. Trenton and Princeton. *Unknown.* PAH

On Dennis. Pope. FaBoEE

On Descending the River Po. William Parsons. OBTV

On Destiny. Tanikawa Shuntaro, *tr. fr. Japanese.* TSaS, *tr. by* Harold Wright

On Dewdrop. Wei Ying-wu, *tr. fr. Chinese by* Irving Y. Lo. SuSp

On Digital Extremities. Gelett Burgess. FaPON; PeLi

On Dinah. Francis Quarles. ChIV-1

On Diogenes the Cynic. Antiphilus, *tr. fr. Greek by* W. S. Merwin. GrAn

On Disbanding the Army. David Humphreys. PAH

On Discovering a Butterfly. Vladimir Nabokov. NYBP

On Diverse Deviations. Maya Angelou. BlSi

On Dr. Evans Cutting Down a Row of Trees. *Unknown.* FaBoEE

On Dr. Isaac Letsome. *Unknown.* FaBoCo

On Dr. Keene, Bishop of Chester. Thomas Gray. FaBoEE

On Dr. Lettsom. *Unknown.* FaBoEE

On Dr. Samuel Ogden. R. P. Arden. FaBoCo

On Don Juan del Norte, Not Don Juan Tenorio del Sur. Alan Dugan. ErPo

On Don Surly. Ben Jonson. FaBoEE; NAEL-1

On Donne's Poem "To a Flea." Samuel Taylor Coleridge. FM

On Donne's Poetry. Samuel Taylor Coleridge. EPCY; InvP; MeMBP; NAEL-2; NoP; OAEL-2; UV

On Dorinda. Charles Sackville. *See* Dorinda's sparkling wit, and eyes.

On Double Creek. James Still. MT

On, dour! Oh, Mayflower! But enough of that. Ode to the Protestant Poets. Paul Hoover. UL

On Drawing-Room Amenities. Gelett Burgess. FaBoNo

On Dreams. Swift. BIrV

On Dreams, October 15, 1782. Sir Samuel Egerton Brydges. Son

On Dublin. Oliver St. John Gogarty. *Fr.* Elegy on the Archpoet William Butler Yeats Lately Dead. IHNG

On Dulcina. *At. to* Sir Walter Ralegh. CoMu

On dull mornings. Mrs. Busk. Sir Osbert Sitwell. OxBTC

On Dullness. Pope. OxBSP

On Duty. Frederick D'Aguiar. PBCV

On Dwelling. Robert Graves. CMoP; FaBoMo; OxBSP

On ear and ear two noises too old to end. The Sea and the Skylark. Gerard Manley Hopkins. FM; LiTB; MeMBP; OBMV

On Earth. Forugh Farrokhzad, *tr. fr. Persian by* Girdhard Tikku. BoWoP

On Earth There Is a Lamb So Small. Nikolaus Ludwig, Graf von Zinzendorf, *tr. fr. German by* Sheema Z. Buehne. AH

On Easter Day. Celia Laighton Thaxter. FaPON

On Easter Morning. Eben E. Rexford. BLRP

On Eastnor Knoll. John Masefield. CH

On Editing Scott Fitzgerald's Papers. Edmund Wilson. NYBP

On Education, December 1789. Elizabeth Bentley. WoRP

On either side the river lie. The Lady of Shalott. Tennyson. BeLS; BLPL; EBEvV; EBVVPR; FHYEP; GN; InPS; NAEL-2; NOBE; OAEL-2; OBEV; OBNV; OBSP; OxAEP-2; PoE; TEP; TFi; TOF; WiR

On Eleanor Freeman, Who Died 1650, Aged 21. *Unknown.* OBEV

On Elizabeth Ireland. *Unknown.* FaBoEE

On Elphinston's Translation of Martial. Burns. FaBoCo; FaBoEE

On Enclosures. *Unknown. See* 'Tis bad enough in man or woman.

On English Monsieur. Ben Jonson. NBLV; NoP

On Epicurus and Themistokles. Menander, *tr. fr. Greek by* Alan Marshfield. GrAn

On Epiktetos the Stoic. *Unknown, tr. fr. Greek by* Peter Jay. GrAn

On every schoolhouse, ship, and staff. Half-Mast. Lloyd Mifflin. PAH

On every trip away from these islands. It's Something Our Family Has Always Done. Wing Tek Lum. BCF

On Evolution. John Ciardi. OBAL

On Exodus 3: 14: "I am that I am." Matthew Prior. ChIV-1; NOCV

On fair Augusta's towers and trees. A Tale of Drury Lane. Horace Smith. FaBoCo

On Fairford Windows. William Strode. NOSC

On Falling Asleep by Firelight. William Meredith. ChIV-1; NoAM; NYBP

On Fame. Juvenal, *tr. by* John Dryden. *Fr.* Satires. IHNG

On Fanny Godwin. Shelley. OBNC

On festal days; or when their work is done. James Grainger. *Fr.* Sugar Cane, The. PBCV

On File. John Kendrick Bangs. PoToHe; WBLP

On Finding a Small Fly Crushed in a Book. Charles Tennyson Turner. FM

On Finding Out that the One You Slept with the Night Before Was Murdered the Next Day. Chuck Ortleb. GLP

On Finding the Tree of Life. Alan Dugan. CAPP

On Finding the Truth. Jones Very. TrCP

On fire. *(LL)* Watching the Stolen Rose. Michael McClure. PoBeRe

On First Looking in on Blodgett's Keats's "Chapman's Homer." George Starbuck. OBAL

On First Looking into Chapman's Hesiod. Peter Porter. NOBAu

On First Looking into Chapman's Homer. W. S. Brownlie. BXAP

On First Looking into Chapman's Homer. T. Griffiths. BXAP

On First Looking into Chapman's Homer. Keats. BLPA; CH; ChTr; ClHu; CoGr; EBEvV; EnRP; EPCY; FaBoBe; FaBoCh; FaBV; FaPoB; FF; FHYEP; GN; GTBS; GTBS-P; HAP; HeIL; HeIP; HoPM; ImPo; InPK; LiTB; MeMBP; NAWM-2; NIP; NOBE; NoP; OAEL-2; OBAL; OBEV; OBNC; OxAEP-2; PlP; PoE; PoEL-4; Poetr; PPP; PrIm; SCGP; Son; SoSe; TEP; TFi; TrGrPo; TRP

On First Looking into Chapman's Homer II. Peter Peterson. BXAP

On First Looking into Krafft-Ebing's *Psychopathosexualis* [or Psychopathia Sexualis]. Oliver St. John Gogarty. FaBoBl; IHNG; UV

On First Looking into Loeb's Horace. Lawrence Durrell. FaBoMo; LiTM

On First Looking into Michael Grant's *Cities of Vesuvius*. Gavin Ewart. OBTV

On First Looking into Raymond Chandler. Linda France. NWP

On flute/ spinning spinning spinning. For Eric Dolphy. Etheridge Knight. Jaz

On Fort Sumter. *Unknown*. PAH

On Fortune. Elizabeth I, Queen of England. PBWP; WPE

On four-horse coach, whose luggage pierced the sky. Past and Present. R. E. Egerton Warburton. NOBVV

On France. Wyndham Lewis. IHNG

On Francis Drake. *Unknown*. *See* Sir Drake, whom well the world's end knew.

On Freedom. James Russell Lowell. *See* They are slaves who fear to speak.

On Freedom and Ambition. Goldsmith. *Fr.* Travel[l]er; or, A Prospect of Society, The. NOIV

On Fridays he'd open a can of Jax. My Father's Loveletters. Yusef Komunyakaa. NAmP90

On from the image entertained. (*LL*) Drawing You, Heavy With Sleep. Sylvia Townsend Warner. VBLP

On Frosty Days. David Campbell. CBAP

On Frozen Fields. Galway Kinnell. CAPP

On Fruition. Sir Charles Sedley. ErPo; NOSC

On Galveston Beach. Barbara Howes. MoAmPo

On Garland Sunday, the weaver told me. Garland Sunday. Padraic Colum. GoYe

On gay Anacreon's joy-inspiring line. On the Translation of Anacreon. Horace Walpole. FaBoEE

On Gay Wallpaper. William Carlos Williams. MeMAP; MoAB; MoAmPo; TAP

On General Paoli and the Corsican Struggle for Liberty. Anna Laetitia Barbauld. *Fr.* Corsica. ECWP

On Genessarett. Josephine D. Henderson Heard. CBWP-4

On George I. *Unknown*. IHNG

On George III. "Peter Pindar." IHNG

On George IV. *Unknown*. IHNG

On George Herbert's "The Temple" Sent to a Gentlewoman. Richard Crashaw. *See* Know you fair[e], on what you look[e].

On getting a card. William Carlos Williams. VGW

On Getting a Natural. Dudley Randall. PoBA

On Gibson Lane, Sagaponack. Diana Chang. ETG

On Giles and Joan. Ben Jonson. NAEL-1; NOBL; TEP

On Giving Up Smoking. Lawrence Spooner. *Fr.* Looking-Glass for Smokers, A. NOEC

On Glaister's Hill, *sels.* William Jeffrey. Carlyle on Burns. OxBS

On God's Favour. Francis Quarles. *Fr.* Divine Fancies. PeECV

On God's Law. Francis Quarles. ChIV-1

On Going Home. Marjorie L. Agnew. GoYe

On Gold. Samuel Johnson. *Fr.* Vanity of Human Wishes, The: The Tenth Satire of Juvenal Imitated. EBEV; ECEV; IHNG; NOEC; NoP; OAEL-1; OxAEP-1; PoEL-3; PrIm; TEP; TFi

On golden seas of drink, so the Greek poet said. Alcohol. Louis MacNeice. LiTM

On Groin. Ben Jonson. NOSC

On Growing Old. John Masefield. CMoP; ImPo; LiTB; LiTM; MoAB; MoBrPo; PoLF; PoRA

On Gustavus Adolphus, King of Sweden. Sir Thomas Roe. FaBoEE

On Gut. Ben Jonson. JCP; NoP

On gypsum slabs of preternatural whiteness. Animal, Vegetable and Mineral. Louise Bogan. FM

On Hallowe'en the old ghosts come. Hallowe'en. Eleanor Farjeon. Mes

On Hardscrabble Mountain. Galway Kinnell. RFM

On Harting Down. T. Sturge Moore. OxBTC

On Having Been an Experimental Sacred Cow for Four Years, and a Token African on Faculty. Kofi Awoonor. HBAPE

On Having Piles. Sir Walter Scott. FaBoEE

On Hearing a Lady Praise a Certain Rev. Doctor's Eyes. George Outram. EBVV

On Hearing a Symphony of Beethoven. Harry M. Meacham. LiTA; LiTM; MoAB; MoAmPo; TrGrPo

On Hearing It Has Been Ordered in the Chapterhouse of Ireland That the Friars Make No More Songs or Verses. Padraigin Haicead, *tr. fr. Irish by* Thomas Kinsella. NOIV

On Hearing James W. Riley Read. Joseph S. Cotter, Sr.. AAP

On Hearing Michael Hartnett Read His Poetry in Irish. Michael O'Loughlin. IB

On Hearing of the Intention of a Gentleman to Purchase the Poet's Freedom. George Moses Horton. AAP

On Hearing Peace Has Been Declared. Argentina Daley, *tr. fr. Spanish by* Susana Stettri. WoWa

On Hearing Prokofieff's Grotesque for Two Bassoons, Concertina and Snare-Drums. Louis Untermeyer. BXAP

On Hearing that Holders of the *Chin-shih* Degree Are Dealing in Tea. Mei Yao Ch'en, *tr. fr. Chinese by* Jonathan Chaves. SuSp

On Hearing That the Students of Our New University Have Joined the Agitation against Immoral Literature. W. B. Yeats. MoP; NoAM

On Hearing That Torture Was Suppressed throughout the Austrian Dominions. John Codrington Bampfylde. Son

On Hearing the Airlines Will Use a Psychological Profile to Catch Potential Skyjackers. Stephen Dunn. AmPA

On Hearing the First Cuckoo. Richard Church. OBMV

On Hearing the Marsh Bird's Water Cry. Duane Niatum. CDW

On Hearing the News of the Japanese Surrender. Liu Ya-tzu, *tr. fr. Chinese by* Wu-chi Liu. SuSp

On Heaven. Ford Madox Ford. CTC

On Hellespont, guilty of true love's blood. Christopher Marlowe. *Fr.* Hero and Leander. AAS; NoP; NoSic; OAEL-1; PoE; PoEL-2; TEP

On Sir Henry Clinton's Recall. *Unknown*. PAH

On her beautiful face there are smiles of grace. A Pretty Girl. J. Gordon Coogler. OBAL

On her behalf. (*LL*) Her heart so stricken, Helen. Alcaeus. InMo

On Her Blindness. Priscilla Pointon. *Fr.* To the Critics. ECWP

On Her Brother. Al-Khansa, *tr. fr. Arabic by* Willis Barnstone. BoWoP

On Her Brother Sakhr. Al-Khansa, *tr. fr. Arabic*. BoWoP, *tr. by* Willis Barnstone

On her good name. (*LL*) Her Eyes. John Crowe Ransom. LiTM; MeMAP; OBAL

On her head. (*LL*) Eight Sandbars on the Takano River. Gary Snyder. NOBA; NoP; VGW

On Her Loving Two Equally. Aphra Behn. NALW; NIP

On Her Own Birthday. Judith Madan. ECWP

On Her Phantasy. Sir John Davies. *Fr.* Hymns of Astræa [in Acrostic Verse]. SiPSBD

On her side, reclining on her elbow. So-and-So Reclining on Her Couch. Wallace Stevens. AmP; LiTM; NOBA

On him the unpetitioned heavens descend. A Counsel of Moderation. Francis Thompson. MoBrPo

On Himself. Callimachus, *tr. fr. Greek by* Peter Jay. GrAn

On Himself. Robert Herrick. BeJo

On Himself[e], *sels.* Robert Herrick.
"Born[e] I was to meet with ages." ChTr; FaBoEE; SeCV-1
"Here down my wearied limbs I'll lay." CaPo
"I fear no earthly powers." CaPo
"I will no longer kiss." CaPo
"I'll write no more of love, but now repent." CaPo
"Let me not live, if I not love." CaPo
"Weep for the dead, for they have lost this light." FaBoEE
(On Himself.) NOSC
"Work [or Worke] is done, The. Young men and maidens, set." CaPo; SeCP

On Himself. Robert Herrick. *See* Weep for the dead, for they have lost this light.

On Himself. Walter Savage Landor. FaBoEE

On Himself. William Oldys. FaBoEE

On Himself. Matthew Prior. FaBoEE

On Himself. Dante Gabriel Rossetti. FaBoEE

On Himself, upon Hearing What Was His Sentence. James Graham, Marquess of Montrose. NOSC

On his airy perch among the branches. The Fox and the Crow. La Fontaine, *tr. fr. French by* Marianne Moore. NAWM-2; OBVE; PPP

On His Blindness. Milton. FaPoB; HeIL; InPK; NAEL-1; PoE; Poetr

On His Blindness. Milton. *See* When I consider how my light is spent.

On His Books. Hilaire Belloc. FaBoCo; FaBoEE; MoBrPo; NBLV; OxBoLi; WeW

On His Dead Wife. Milton. *See* Methought I saw my late espoused saint.

On his death-bed poor Lubin lies. A Reasonable Affliction. Matthew Prior. NOEC; NoP; TrGrPo
(Cause and Effect.) NBLV

On His Deceased Wife. Milton. BLPL; CBLP; ImPo; LiTB; OBEV; OxBM; PoE; SCV; TEP; TFi

On his dripping tunnels the combers wreck. *(LL)* Song to Be Written on a Wave. José Emilio Pacheco. STV

On his free weekends he took. The Military-Industrial Complex. Robley Wilson, Jr.. PBCAP

On His Friend Megistias, Who Died at Thermopylai. Simonides, *tr. fr. Greek by* Peter Jay. GrAn

On His Garden Book. Francis Daniel Pastorius. SCAP

On His Lady's Waking. Pierre de Ronsard, *tr. fr. French by* Andrew Lang. AWP

On his last swing around. Field Work. Doug Cockrell. Poetsp

On His Late Wife. Milton. *See* Methought I saw my late espoused saint.

On His Mistress. *At.* to Henry Noel *and to* William Strode. *See* Gaze not on Swans, in whose soft breast.

On His Mistress Drown'd. Thomas Spratt. EnLoPo

On His Mistress Going from Home [Song]. *Unknown.* NOSC

On His Mistress Looking in a Glass. Thomas Carew. CaPo

On His Mistress [*or* Mistris]. John Donne. *Fr.* Elegies. BoLoP; CBLP; EBEV; ESCV; LiTB; NAEL-1; NoSic; PoEL-2

On his morning rounds the Master. Incident Characteristic of a Favourite Dog. Wordsworth. FM

On His Ninth Decade. Walter Savage Landor. *See* To My Ninth Decade I Have Tottered On.

On His Own Deafness. Swift. BIrV; FaBoEE

On His Own Poetry. Charles Churchill. *Fr.* Prophecy of Famine, The. NOEC

On His Queerness. Christopher Isherwood. OxBTC; PeHV

On His Seventy-fifth Birthday. Walter Savage Landor. *See* I strove with none, for none was worth my strife.

On His Thirty-Third Birthday. Ch'ang Kuo Fan, *tr. fr. Chinese by* Kenneth Rexroth. OHMPC

On his way to the open hearth where white-hot steel. My Father's Garden. David Wagoner. DiPo; NIP

On His Writing Verses. John Hawthorn. NOEC

On Honour. Bernard Mandeville. NOEC

On Hope. Abraham Cowley. *See* Hope, whose weak being ruined is.

On Hope. Richard Crashaw. *See* Dear hope! Earth's dowry and heaven's debt!

On Hot Days. James Reiss. AmPA

On hot summer mornings my aunt set glasses. Water. Leslie Norris. AngWe; OBWVE

On How the Cobler. *Unknown.* SCAP

On humming rubber along this white concrete. Driving in Oklahoma. Carter Revard. HATNAP; VoR

On Hurricane Jackson. Alan Dugan. CoAP; TRP

On Hygiene. Hilaire Belloc. MoBrPo

On Imagination. Phillis Wheatley. AmPP; BlSi; PoNe

On Imitation. Samuel Taylor Coleridge. OxBSP

On Inclosures. *Unknown.* FaBoCo

On Independence. Jonathan Mitchell Sewall. PAH

On Inhabiting an Orange. Josephine Miles. NoAM; PoA

On Installing an American Kitchen in Lower Austria. W. H. Auden. NYBP

On Irish Memebers of Parliament. Swift. *Fr.* Legion Club, The. IHNG

On its ridge of burning stone. *(LL)* Ein Fichtenbaum steht einsam. Heine. AWP

On Its Way. May Swenson. SoSe; WPE

On its way I see. Kathleen Raine. NALW

On J. M. S. Gent. Pope. FaBoEE

On J. W. Ward. Samuel Rogers. FaBoEE

On Jacob Tonson, His Publisher. Dryden. ChTr; FaBoEE; OBSV

On Jacobinism. George Canning. IHNG

On Jacob's Purchase. Francis Quarles. ChIV-1

On Jam. Hilaire Belloc. NBLV

On James Smith. Burns. *See* Lament him, Mauchline husbands a.'

On Jessy Watson's Elopement. Marjory Fleming. Mes

On Jocky Bell. *Unknown.* FaBoEE

On John Donne's Book of Poems. John Marriot. CH

On John So. *Unknown.* FaBoEE

On Sir John Vanbrugh [Architect]. Abel Evans. FaBoCo; FaBoEE; FaBoEH; FiBHP; IHNG

On Jordan's Bank. Byron. ChIV-1

On Jordan's stormy banks I stand. The Promised Land. Samuel Stennett. AmFP

On Judas Iscariot. Francis Quarles. FaBoEE

On July 5 the Associated Press gave the news to the world. Harangue on the Death of Hayyim Nahman Bialik. César Tiempo, *tr. fr. Spanish by* Donald Devenish Walsh. TrJP

On Keats. Shelley. FaBoEE

On Keats, 18 January, 1948 (Eve of St Agnes). Christina Rossetti. EPCY

On King Arthur's Round Table, at Winchester. Thomas Warton the Younger. Son

On King Richard the Third, Who Lies Buried under Leicester Bridge. Sir John Suckling. CaPo

On Knighthood. Folgore da San Geminiano, *tr. fr. Italian by* John Addington Symonds. AWP

On Knowing the Difference Between Prejudice, Discrimination, and Oppression. Tom Leonard. NBrP

On Kriton the Miser. Lucilius, *tr. fr. Greek by* Dudley Fitts. GrAn

On Ladies' Accomplishments. *Unknown.* FaBoUs

On Lady Anne Hamilton. Sheridan. FaBoEE

On Lady Poltagrue, a Public Peril. Hilaire Belloc. FaBoCo; MoBrPo

On Lake Pend Oreille. Richard Shelton. NYBP

On Late-acquired Wealth *or* Riches. *Unknown, tr. fr. Greek by* William Cowper. OBVE

On Laying the Corner-Stone of the Bunker Hill Monument. John Pierpont. PAH

On Laying Up Treasure. Lois Smith Hiers. GoYe

On Lazarus Raised From Death. Henry Colman. ChIV-2

On Leander's Swimming over the Hellespont to Hero. Thomas Warton the Younger, *after* Martial. FaBoEE

On Leaping over the Moon. Thomas Traherne. GeHe; ImPo; LiTB; Mes; NAEL-1; SeCV-2

On Learning. Elizabeth Teft. ECWP

On Learning to Adjust to Things. John Ciardi. OBCA

On Leave. John Buchan. NSI

On Leaving. Gertrudis Gomez de Avellaneda, *tr. fr. Spanish by* Frederick Sweet. PBWP

On Leaving Baltimore. Duane Niatum. CDW

On Leaving Cuba, Her Native Land. Gertrudis Gomez de Avellaneda, *tr. fr. Spanish by* Catherine Rodriguez-Nieto. WPOW

On Leaving Holland, *sels.* Mark Akenside. "Farewell to Leyden's lonely bound." OBTV

On Leaving the Footpath. John James. NBrP; VaA

On Leaving Town. Alan Dugan. CAPP

On Liberty and Slavery. George Moses Horton. AAP; PoNe

On Lien-ch'ang Palace. Yüan Chen, *tr. fr. Chinese by* Angela Jung Palandri. SuSp

On Lieutenant Shift. Ben Jonson. OBSV

On life and extinction with sea wind changes. Open-Eyed Angel. David Rokeah, *tr. fr. Hebrew by* Ruth Finer Mintz. MHP

On Linden, when the sun was low. Hohenlinden. Thomas Campbell. BeLS; CH; ChTr; EnRP; FaBoCh; FaBoRV; FaPoR; GN; GTBS; GTBS-P; NOBE; OBNC; OBWP; PAW; TFi; WBLP (Battle of Hohenlinden, The.) VPP

On Listening to a Bus Conductor. Anne Bloch. Mes

On Listening to the Spirituals. Lance Jeffers. PoBA

On Literature, *sels.* Chang Wen-t'ao, *tr. fr. Chinese by* Irving Lo. SuSp

On Loch Leven. Christian Carstairs. ECWP

On Lolham Brigs in wild and lonely mood. The Flood. John Clare. RB

On London fell a clearer light. Summer in England, 1914. Alice Meynell. BrRo; SoSe; WPE

On lonely poet corners of low lying leaves & moist prophet eyes. *(LL)* On. Bob Kaufman. PoBeRe

On lonely river-mud a heron alone. The Heron. Phoebe Hesketh. OBAP

On Long Island, they moved my clapboard house. Whitman. Larry Levis. Jaz

On longer evenings. Coming. Philip Larkin. MoBrPo; OxBTC; PlP

On Looking in the Looking Glass. Isabella Gardner. CAPP

On Looking into E. V. Rieu's Homer. Patrick Kavanagh. NOIV

On Looking Up by Chance at the Constellations. Robert Frost. CMoP; MeMAP

On Lookout Mountain. Robert Hayden. PoE

On Lord Chesterfield and His Son. *Unknown.* FaBoCo

On Lord Galloway. Burns. FaBoEE

On Lord Holland's Seat near Margate, Kent. Thomas Gray. NOEC; OAEL-1; OPOP

On Lord Mayors. Daniel Defoe. *Fr.* True-born Englishman, The. APAS; IHNG

On Lot's Wife Turned to Salt. Agathias, *tr. fr. Greek by* Dudley Fitts. GrAn

On Love. Sir Robert Ayton. ScCV

On love was written. The Phoenix Reborn from Its Ashes. Louis Aragon, *tr. fr. French.* CBNP

On love's worst ugly day. First Meditation. Theodore Roethke. *Fr.* Meditations of an Old Woman. LCAP; NaP; NOBA

On Lucretia Borgia's Hair. Walter Savage Landor. *See* Borgia, thou once wert [*or* were] almost too august.

On Lucy Countesse of Bedford. Ben Jonson. BeJo; EnRePo; NOSC; SeCP; SeCV-1

On Lydia Distracted. Philip Ayres. EnLoPo; Son

On Maids and Cats. Henricus Selyns. SCAP

On Malverne Hilles, the Place of Piers Plowman's Vision. William Langland. *See* In a summer [*or* somer] season, when soft[e] was the sun [*or* sunne *or* sonne].

On Mammon. Herman Melville. *Fr.* Clarel. OxBA

On Man. Walter Savage Landor. OBNC

On Man. The Earl of Rochester. *See* Be Judge your self, I'll bring it to the test.

On man, on nature, and on human life. Prospectus. Wordsworth. *Fr.* Excursion, The. EnRP; NoP; OAEL-2
(Prospectus [*incl. in* The Excursion].) FHYEP

On Man, on Nature, and on Human Life. Wordsworth. *Fr.* Recluse, The. EPCY; OAEL-2
(Prospectus [*incl. in* The Excursion].) EnRP; NoP; PoE

On Margaret Ratcliffe. Ben Jonson. SeCP

On Maricopa Road. Rita Magdaleno. AfAz

On Marriage. Richard Crashaw. FaBoEE

On Marriage. Thomas Flatman. FaBoUs; FiBHP; NOBL; PeLV

On Mary Magdalene. William Drummond of Hawthornden. OAEL-1

On May Day, the girls of Penzance. *Unknown.* PeLi

On May-day, when the lark began to rise. *Unknown. Fr.* Court of Love, The. NoSic

On Mayday we dance. *Unknown.* BoTP

On Mayon Volcano. Gwyneth Lewis. NWP

On me and, renewed. (*LL*) I Am a Black Woman. Mari Evans. NMM

On Meeting——, Esq., in St. James's Park. *Unknown.* ECWP

On Meeting a Gentlewoman in the Dark. *Unknown.* FaBoEE

On Melancholy. *Unknown.* NOSC

On Mercenary and Unjust Bailiffs. Henricus Selyns. SCAP

On Mike O'Day. *Unknown.* FaBoEE

On Miles Platting Station. Simon Armitage. PWE

On miserable Nearchos' bones lie lightly, earth. Last Lines. X. J. Kennedy. OBAL

On Miss Eleanor Ambrose, a Celebrated Beauty in Dublin. Earl of Chesterfield. FaBoEE

On Mr. Abraham Cowley, His Death and Burial amongst the Ancient Poets, *sels.* Sir John Denham.
"His English stream so pure did flow." EPCY

On Mr. Abraham Cowley, His Death and Burial amongst the Ancient Poets. Sir John Denham. BeJo; SeCV-1

On Mr. Dryden, Renegade. Aphra Behn. FaBoVe

On Mr. Edward Howard, upon His British Princes. Charles Sackville. OBSV

On Mr. G. [*or* George] Herbert's Book[e] Intituled [*or* Entitled] the Temple of Sacred Poems, Sent to a Gentle-woman. Richard Crashaw. EPCY; ESCV; GeHe; SeCV-1

On Mr. Hobbs, and His Writings. John Sheffield, Duke of Buckingham and Normandy. PoEL-3

On Mr. Milton's Paradise Lost. Andrew Marvell. EPCY; JCP; NOSC

On Mr. Nash's Picture at Full Length. Jane Brereton. WPE

On Mr. Nash's Present of His Own Picture at Full Length. Earl of Chesterfield. NOEC

On Mr. Paine's Rights of Man. Philip Freneau. NAAL-1

On Mr. Pitt's Hair-Powder Tax. Burns. FaBoEE

On Mr. Pricke. *Unknown.* FaBoEE

On Mr. Rice the Manciple of Christ Church in Oxford. Richard Corbett [*or* Corbet]. NOSC

On Mr. Shirley's Poems. Thomas Stanley. BeJo

On Mrs. Montagu. Ann Yearsley. ECWP

On Mrs. Reynolds's Cat. Keats. *See* Cat! who hast pass'd thy grand climacteric.

On Mrs. W——. Nicolas Bentley. FiBHP

On Mites; to a Lady. Stephen Duck. FM

On Monday man gave God. Adam and God. Anne Wilkinson. MoCV

On Monday morning as we set sail. Bold General Wolfe. *Unknown.* OBET

On Monday, when the sun is hot. Lines Written by a Bear of Very Little Brain. A. A. Milne. FaBoNo

On Money. George Orwell. IHNG

On Monsieur's Departure. Elizabeth I, Queen of England. NAEL-1; NALW; VBLP; WPE

On moon-washed apples of wonder. (*LL*) Moonlit Apples. John Drinkwater. BoNaP; BoTP; EBEvV; FaPoB; OBMV; OxBTC; PlP; PoRA

On moonlight bushes. Nightingales. Samuel Taylor Coleridge. *Fr.* Nightingale, The. ChTr; EnRP; FM

On Moonlit Heath and Lonesome Bank. A. E. Housman. *Fr.* Shropshire Lad, A. CMoP; FaPoB; SCGP

On moony nights the dogs bark shrill. Night Song. Frances Cornford. FM

On moors where people get lost and die of air. Water. Ted Hughes. OxBSP

On Mortality. Henry Colman. ChIV-1

On Motel Walls. David Wagoner. DiPo

On Mother's Day. Aileen Fisher. NTCP

On Mount Ching. Meng Chiao, *tr. fr. Chinese by* A. C. Graham. PLT

On Mousehold Heath they gathered. Kett's Rebellion. Keith Chandler. FaBoEH

On Mundane Acquaintances. Hilaire Belloc. FaBoEE; FiBHP; OxBTC

On Music. Walter Savage Landor. GoJo

On my ancestral tree. (*LL*) My Aunt. Oliver Wendell Holmes. AmPP; TAP

On My Bed I Sought Him. Bible, *O.T. Fr.* Song of Solomon, The. TrJP; VBLP

On my bedroom wall is a big poster. Angela Davis. Jackie Kay. NWP

On My Birthday. Yehuda Amichai, *tr. fr. Hebrew by* Ruth Finer Mintz. MHP

On My Birthday. Farhad Mazhar, *tr. fr. Bengali.* TSaS, *tr. by* Kabir Chowdhury *and* Naomi Shihab

On My Birthday, July 21. Matthew Prior. OBEV

On My Boy Henry. Lady Elizabeth Brackley. KTR

On my cheeks I wear. My Makeup. Rochelle Kraut. UL

On My Child's Death. Joseph Freiherr von Eichendorff, *tr. fr. German by* W. D. Snodgrass. IMW

On My Dear Grandchild Simon Bradstreet, [Who Died on 16 November, 1669, Being But A Month, And One Day Old]. Anne Bradstreet. EAP; KTR; NAAL-1; SCAP

On my desk, a set of labels. City Gent. Craig Raine. NoAM

On my father's memorial day. My Father's Memorial Day. Yehuda Amichai, *tr. fr. Hebrew by the author* and Ted Hughes. OBD

On My First Daughter. Ben Jonson. BeJo; EBEV; EnRePo; FaBoEE; HoPM; InPS; JCP; NAEL-1; NOBE; NoP; NOSC; PoE; SeCP; SeCV-1; TEP

On My First Son [*or* Sonne]. Ben Jonson. AWP; BeJo; ClHu; CoGr; EBEV; ElL; EnRePo; FaBoEE; FF; HAP; HoPM; IMW; InPK; InPS; JCP; LiTB; NAEL-1; NIP; NoP; NOSC; OAEL-1; OBD; OxBSP; PFP; PoE; PoEL-2; Poetr; RaBo; RB; SCGP; SeCP; SeCV-1; TEP; TFi; TRP; WeW

On My Fortieth Birthday. John Tripp. AngWe; NAs

On my hearth? (*LL*) Windy Monday. Sylvia Kantaris. PWE

On My Joyful Departure from the City of Cologne. Samuel Taylor Coleridge. FaBoCo; InvP; OBTV

On My Joyful Departure from the Same City. Samuel Taylor Coleridge. *See* As I am a Rhymer.

On my knees to cry, Who the hell are you, kid? (*LL*) The Roundhouse Voices. Dave Jeddie Smith. MT; NoAM; VCAP

On My Lady Isabella Playing on the Lute. Edmund Waller. *See* Such moving sounds from such a careless touch.

On my land grew a green tree. The Possessor. A. R. D. Fairburn. *Fr.* Album Leaves. PeNZ

On My Late Dear Wife. Jonathan Richardson. NOEC

On My Leaving London, June the 29. Sarah Fyge. KTR

On my little guitar. On My Old Ramkiekie. C. Louis Leipoldt, *tr. fr. Afrikaans by* Anthony Delius. PeSA

On my little magic whistle I will play to you all day. The Magic Whistle. Margaret Rose. BoTP

On my livingroom wall hangs a Navajo rug. Storm Pattern. Greg Pape. NGP; PBCAP

On My Lord Bacon. John Danforth. SCAP

On my Northwest coast in the midst of the night. The Torch. Walt Whitman. SAmP

On my old battledress tonight, my sweet. (*LL*) Goodbye. Alun Lewis. AngWe; BoLoP; NAEL-2; OBWP; OxBM; OxBTC; PoWW

On My Old Ramkiekie. C. Louis Leipoldt, *tr. fr. Afrikaans by* Anthony Delius. PeSA

On My Own. Philip Levine. FYAP

On My Pretty Marten. Charles Cotton. FM

On my school notebooks. Paul Éluard, *tr. fr. French by* W. S. Merwin. *Fr.* Liberty. TTTS

On My Son. Ben Jonson. *See* Farewell, thou child of my right hand, and joy.

On Reading Dr. Young's Satires, Called *The Universal Passion*, by Which He Means Pride. Swift. EPCY

On Reading Poems to a Senior Class at South High. D. C. Berry. SoSe

On Receiving a Crown of Ivy from the Same. Leigh Hunt. Son

On Receiving News of the War. Isaac Rosenberg. MoBrPo; NSI; OBWP; OxAEP-2; PeFWW; PeSAV; PoWW

On Recrossing the Rocky Mountains after Many Years. John Charles Frémont. AiP

On Reelection Night the news was bad. Into a Cordless Phone. Robert McDowell. UTF

On Refusal of Aid between Nations. Dante Gabriel Rossetti. EBEV; OxAEP-2; SCGP

On Regret Road we must not tarry. (*LL*) Exile's Letter: After the Failed Revolution. Marilyn Chin. LoHo

On Returning. Brigitte Frase. LoHo

On Returning to My Garden and Field, sels. T'ao Ch'ien, *tr. fr. Chinese.* "I plant beans at the foot of the southern hill." SuSp
"When I was young, I did not fit into the common mold." SuSp

On Returning to Sung Mountain. Wang Wei, *tr. fr. Chinese by* Paul W. Kroll. SuSp

On Revisiting Cintra after the Death of Catarina. Camões, *tr. fr. Spanish by* Richard Garnett. AWP

On Rhyme, *sels.* Robert Lloyd.
"Some, Milton-mad (an affectation)." EPCY

On Richard Hind. Francis Jeffrey. *See* Here lies the body of Richard Hind.

On Riding to See Dean Swift in the Mist of the Morning. Pope *and* Thomas Parnell. FaBoEE

On roads beyond the camp the Khamsin struck me. Yitzhak Lamdan, *tr. fr. Hebrew by* Ruth Finer Mintz. *Fr.* In the Khamsin. MHP

On Robert Buchanan, Who Attacked Him under the Pseudonym of "Thomas Maitland." Dante Gabriel Rossetti. FaBoEE

On Sir Robert Cotton the Antiquary. Thomas Randolph. NOSC

On Roman Feet my stumbling Muse declines. An Elegiack Verse on Mr. Elijah Corlet. Nehemiah Walter. SCAP

On Roofs of Terry Street. Douglas Dunn. OxBTC

On Rosania's Apostasy, and Lucasia's Friendship. Katherine Philips. KTR

On Ryñeveld, an Unpopular Dutch Judge. *Unknown.* FaBoEE

On S. John the Baptist. Thomas Stanley. ChIV-2

On St. Brigid's Day the new life could be entered. Seamus Heaney. *Fr.* Crossings. BAP-90

On Saint David's Day. Jeremy Hooker. SCBI

On St. James's Park, as Lately Improved by His Majesty. Edmund Waller. BeJo; NOSC

On St. Martin's evening green. Nuns at Eve. John Malcolm Brinnin. MoAB; TwCP

On Saint-Urbain Street. Milton Acorn. NOBC

On Saturday night shall be [all] my care. Mother Goose. OxNR (Saturday, Sunday.) ReMoGo

On Saturday with joy Bill dubs his half. The Linen Weaver. *Unknown.* NOEC

On Saturn the sexes are three. *Unknown.* PeLi

On Saul and David. Francis Quarles. ChIV-1

On Scafell Pike. Ted Walker. NYBP

On Scotia's plains, in days of yore. Elegy on the Death of Scots Music. Robert Fergusson. ScCV

On Scott's Poem "The Field of Waterloo." Thomas, Lord Erskine. FaBoCo; FiBHP; NBLV

On sea and land alike. Poseidippus, *tr. fr. Greek by* Edward Lucie-Smith. GrAn

On Seein an Aik-Tree Sprent Wi Galls. Robert Garioch. OxBS

On Seeing a Butterfly in the Street. Robert Fergusson. ScCV

On Seeing a Fine Frigate at Anchor in a Bay off Mount Edgecumbe, sels. N. T. Carrington.
"Is she not beautiful? reposing there." FaBoPP

On Seeing a Hair of Lucretia Borgia. Walter Savage Landor. HAP; WeW

On Seeing a Lady's Garter. *Unknown.* ErPo

On Seeing a Little Child Spin a Coin of Alexander the Great. Charles Tennyson Turner. NOBVV

On Seeing a Painting of Plants and Insects by Chü-ning. Mei Yao Ch'en, *tr. fr. Chinese by* Jonathan Chaves. SuSp

On Seeing a Piece of Our Artillery Brought into Action. Wilfred Owen. MeMBP

On Seeing a Pigeon Make Love. Leigh Hunt. FM

On Seeing a Poet of the First World War on the Station at Abbeville. Charles Causley. LiTM

On Seeing a Tapestry Chair-Bottom Beautifully Worked by His Daughter for Mrs Holroyd. Richard Owen Cambridge. ECEV

On Seeing a Torn Out Coin Telephone. Martin Robbins. MAT

On Seeing an Officer's Widow Distracted. Mary Barber. ECWP; NOEC

On Seeing an Old Poet in the Café Royal. Sir John Betjeman. UV

On Seeing Francis Jeffrey Riding on a Donkey. *At. to* Sydney Smith. FaBoEE

On Seeing My Birthplace from a Jet Aircraft. John Pudney. NYBP

On Seeing the Black Male as #1 Sex Object in America. Etheridge Knight. BCF

On Seeing the Elgin Marbles. Keats. BLPL; EnRP; ImPo; LiTB; MeMBP; NAEL-2; NIP; PrIm; TrGrPo

On Seeing the Field Being Singed. Lady Ise, *tr. fr. Japanese by* Etsuko Terasaki *and* Irma Brandeis. BoWoP

On Seeing the Speaker Asleep in His Chair. Winthrop Mackworth Praed. EnRP

On Seeing Two Brown Boys in a Catholic Church. Frank Horne. CDC; PoBA; PoNe; TTY

On Seeming to Presume. Lawrence Durrell. LiTM

On Shakespeare. Milton. EPCY; HeIL; InvP; MeLP; NAEL-1; NoP; NOSC; PoE; PoRA; SCGP; TrGrPo

On Shakespeare and Voltaire. Thomas Holcroft. NOEC

On Shakespeare Critics. A. D. Hope. *Fr.* Dunciad Minor. OxBC

On shallow straw, in shadeless glass. Take One Home for the Kiddies. Philip Larkin. OBD; OxBTC

On Shiloh's dark and bloody ground. The Drummer Boy of Shiloh. *Unknown.* AmFP

On shining heights where Thought with stately tread. Emerson. H. Cordelia Ray. CBWP-3

On Shooting a Swallow in Early Youth. Charles Tennyson Turner. FM; NOBVV

On Shooting Particles beyond the World. Richard Eberhart. LiTA; LiTM

On Sight of a Gentlewoman's Face in the Water. Thomas Carew. CaPo; SeCV-1

On Sin. Francis Quarles. *Fr.* Divine Fancies, The. CBCK

On Sir J—— S—— Saying in a Sarcastic Manner, My Books Would Make Me Mad; an Ode. Elizabeth Thomas. ECWP

On Sir John Calf. *Unknown.* FaBoEE

On Sir John Fenwick. Henry Hall. APAS

On Sir John Hill, M. D., Playwright. David Garrick. FaBoCo; FaBoEE; NBLV

On Sitting Down to Read "King Lear" Once Again. Keats. EBEV; EnRP; EPCY; NAEL-2; NoP

On Slieve Gullion. Michael Longley. BiHa

On Slieve Gullion 'men and mountain meet.' On Slieve Gullion. Michael Longley. BiHa

On Snow, *sels.* Li K'ai-hsien, *tr. fr. Chinese by* Jonathan Chaves.

On Snuff-Taking. Elizabeth Teft. ECWP

On Solitude. Abraham Cowley. *See* Hail, old patrician trees, so great and good!

On Solomon Pavy, a Child of Queen Elizabeth's Chapel. Ben Jonson. *See* Weep [or Weepe] with me, all you that read.

On Some Humming-Birds in a Glass Cage. Charles Tennyson Turner. FM

On some island I long to be. St. Columcille, *tr. fr. Irish by* John Montague. BIrV

On some park bench. (*LL*) Sleepless Night. Léon Damas. NegPo

On Some Shells Found Inland. Trumbull Stickney. LiTA; Son

On Some South African Novelists. Roy Campbell. FaBoCo; FaBoEE; GTBS-P; InPK; MoBrPo; NOBL; OxAEP-2; OxBTC; PeLV

On some Vermont road. Mating the Goats. Aliki Barnstone. BoWoP

On Something, That Walks [or Walkes] Somewhere. Ben Jonson. BeJo; NAEL-1; OxBSP; PoE; SCGP; SeCP; SeCV-1

On Sound. Wei Ying-wu, *tr. fr. Chinese by* Irving Y. Lo. SuSp

On Spadina Avenue. Emily Grosholz. VBLP

On Spies. Ben Jonson. BeJo; FaBoVe; NoP; OxBSP

On Springfield Mountain there did dwell. Springfield Mountain. *Unknown.* AmFP

On starry heights. The Conflict of Convictions. Herman Melville. NOBA

On stars that brighter beam, when most we need their love. (*LL*) The Tree. Jones Very. GN; OHIP

On Stella's Birthday, [1718] 1719. Swift. *See* Stella this day is thirty-four.

On still black waters where the stars lie sleeping. Ophelia. Rimbaud, *tr. fr. French by* Brian Hill. ChTr

On Stopping Late in the Afternoon for Steamed Dumplings. Toi Derricotte. InPS

On street corners east and west. The Girl from Flower Mountain. Han Yü, *tr. fr. Chinese by* Charles Hartman. SuSp

On Sturminster Foot-Bridge. Thomas Hardy. FaBoPP; OxBSP

On such a day as this. Soundings. Paula Gunn Allen. HATNAP

On such a day as this I think. An April Day. Joseph S. Cotter, Sr.. CDC

On such a morning as this. In Memory of Basil, Marquess of Dufferin and Ava. Sir John Betjeman. OBWP

On such as care to attend.' (*LL*) Eddi's Service. Kipling. CoGr; OBCP

On Summer. George Moses Horton. AAP

On summer afternoons I sit. La Vie C'est la Vie. Jessie Redmond Fauset. CDC; PoNe

On summer evenings blue, pricked by the wheat. Sensation. Rimbaud, *tr. fr. French.* AWP, *tr.* by Jethro Bithell

On Sunday Afternoons. Sunday Afternoons. Anthony Thwaite. OxBTC

On Sunday Morning. Paul Johann Ludwig Heyse, *tr. fr. German by* Philip L. Miller. RiWo

On Sunday morning, dressed in your best. On Sunday Morning. Paul Johann Ludwig Heyse, *tr. fr. German by* Philip L. Miller. RiWo

On Sunday morning, then he comes. Mr. Wells. Elizabeth Madox Roberts. FaPON

On Sunday morning well I knew. *Unknown, tr. fr. Italian by* John Addington Symonds. *Fr. Popular Songs of Tuscany.* AWP

On Sunday the hawk fell on Bigging. The Hawk. George Mackay Brown. RB

On Sunday we buried the icons. Great Serbian Migration 1690. Milorad Pavic, *tr. fr. Serbo-Croatian by* Charles Simic. HSix

On sunny summer Sunday afternoons in Harlem. Passing. Langston Hughes. SAmP

On Sweet Killen Hill. Tom MacIntyre. CIP

On Sympathisers with the American Revolution. Charles Wesley. NOCV

On Tara's hill the daylight dies. The Paschal Fire. Denis Florence MacCarthy. TIRV

On taut air — bells; lifted, adoring eyes. Immolation. Robert Farren. TIRV

On Teaching the Young. Yvor Winters. NoAM; NOBA

On tears, and sighs, and groans, and brains, and blood. *(LL)* The Flying Tailor. James Hogg. BXAP

On Ternissa's Death. Walter Savage Landor. *See* Ternissa! You Are Fled.

On Thanksgiving for a National Victory. Burns. *See* Ye hypocrites! are these your pranks?

On that big estate there is no rain. Monangamba. Antonio Jacinto, *tr. fr. Portuguese.* TTY, *tr.* by Alan Ryder

On that day when I brought wine to Red Bridge. Occasional Poem: Upon Seeing Lotuses Bloom in a Vase. Wang Shih-chieng, *tr. fr. Chinese by* Richard John Lynn. SuSp

On that great, that awful day, Dies Iræ. Macaulay. ChIV-2

On that last night before we went. Tennyson. *Fr.* In Memoriam A. H. H. EBVV, *abr.*; OAEL-2, *abr.*; PeECV, *abr.*; PoEL-5

On that morning when the Unknown Revolutionary rises. Revolutionary Frescoes — the Ascension. Thomas McGrath. BCF

On that unfashionable gyre again. *(LL)* The Gyres. W. B. Yeats. GTBS-P; HAP; NoAM

On that which is always about to be revealed. *(LL)* Soundwaves. Andrew Sant. NOBAu

On the Adequacy of Landscape. Wallace Stevens. SAmP

On the advice of Praxilla. Aristophanes, *tr. fr. Greek by* Sam Hamill. InMo

On the Ambivalence of Male Contact Sports. Gavin Ewart. FaBoBl

On the American Rivers. James Smith. FaBoUs

On the Antiquity of Microbes. Strickland W. Gillilan. NBLV

On the Apparition of Oneself. William Burford. PoA

On the Appeal from the Race of Sheba: II. Léopold Sédar Senghor, *tr. fr. French by* John Reed *and* Clive Wake. TTY

On the Army of Spartans, Who Died at Thermopylae. Simonides. *See* Tell them in Lacedaemon [*or* Lakedaimon], passer-by.

On the Assumption. Richard Crashaw. *See* Hark! she is call'd, the parting houre is come.

On the Astrologer and Almanac Maker, John Partridge. Swift. FaBoEE

On the Asylum Road. Charlotte Mew. MoBrPo

On the Athenians Who Died at the Hellespont, 440–39 B.C. *Unknown, tr. fr. Greek by* Peter Jay. GrAn

On the Author of the *Treatise of Human Nature.* James Hay Beattie. FaBoCo

On the Author's Husband Desiring Her to Write Some Verses. Mary Whateley. ECWP

On the avenue the faces change each day. Hope. F. D. Reeve. PoA

On the Babel-Builders. Francis Quarles. ChIV-1

On the Back of a Photograph. János Pilinszky, *tr. fr. Hungarian by* Peter Jay. PoSu

On the Balcony. D. H. Lawrence. GBL

On the Bangor-bound platform, the crowd became one. The Self-Exposed. X. J. Kennedy. FaBoBl

On the Banisters. Margaret E. Gibbs. BoTP

On the bank of Lake Rouge a chestnut steed treads proudly. Su Man-shu, *tr.* by Wu-chi Liu. *Fr.* Poems Written during My Sojourn in Japan. SuSp

On the Banks of Salee. *Unknown.* AmFP

On the banks of the Condamine. *(LL)* The Banks of the Condamine. *Unknown.* FaBoBa; GBP; NOBAu

On the Banks of the Duero. Antonio Machado Ruiz, *tr. fr. Spanish by* John Frederick Nims. STV

On the Banks of the Little Eau Pleine. *Unknown.* AmFP

On the banks of the Potomac there's an army so grand. The Red, White and Red. *Unknown.* AmFP

On the Baptized Ethiopian (*or* Aethiopian). Richard Crashaw. ChIV-2; FaBoEE; NoP; SeCV-1

On the bare mountain. Distant View. Uys Krige, *tr. fr. Afrikaans by* Uys Krige *and* Jack Cope. PeSA

On the bare, sunlit stage the hungers could begin. *(LL)* Faust. John Ashbery. NoP; TwCP

On the bare veld where nothing ever grows. A Veld Eclogue: The Pioneers. Roy Campbell. OBSV

On the Bath of Pallas. Callimachus, *tr. fr. Greek by* Barbara Hughes Fowler. *Fr.* Hymns. HePo

On the Beach. Charles Stuart Calverley. FiBHP

On the Beach. John Corben. Spl

On the Beach at Fontana. James Joyce. MoBrPo; OBMV; PoA; RaBo; RB

On the Beach at Night. Walt Whitman. AmPP; AWP; ChTr; MoAmPo; NOBA; NoP; OxBA; SAmP

On the Beach at Night Alone. Walt Whitman. TAP

"On the beach," said John sadly, "there's such." Isaac Asimov. PeLi

On the beach where we had been idly. Gracious Goodness. Marge Piercy. Poetsp

On the Bearing of Waitresses. Rodney Jones. BAP-90

On the Benefactions in the Late Frost. Pope. NOEC; OxBSP

On the beryl-rimmed rebecs of Ruby. Lily Adair. Thomas Holley Chivers. OBAL

On the Bible. Thomas Traherne. ChIV-1

On the Bible. *Unknown.* NOSC

On the Big Horn. Whittier. PAH

On the Birth of a Posthumous Child, Born in Peculiar Circumstances of Family Distress. Burns. NAs

On the Birth of Dan Goldman. Daniel Berrigan. NAs

On the Birth of His Son. Su Tung-p'o, *tr. fr. Chinese by* Arthur Waley. AWP; OBVE

On the Birth of Jesus. Andreas Gryphius, *tr. fr. German by* George C. Schoolfield. GePo

On the Birth of My Son, Malcolm Coltrane. Julius Lester. PoBA

On the black tarmac playground dark. Deaf-and-Dumb School. Anthony Delius. PeSA

On the blank stones of the landing. *(LL)* The Colossus. Sylvia Plath. CAPP; FaBoWP; HCAP; LiTM; NALW; NoAM; NOBA; NoP; Poetr; TAP; VCAP

On the Bleeding Wounds of Our Crucified Lord. Richard Crashaw. SeCV-1

Sels.
"Is she not beautiful? reposing there." FaBoPP
"Jesu, no more! It is full tide." TrGrPo

On the Blessed Virgin's Bashfulness. Richard Crashaw. HAP; OxBSP

On the bloody field of Monmouth. Captain Molly. William Collins. ImGa

On the bluff of the Little Big Horn. Miles Keogh's Horse. John Milton Hay. PAH

On the boats all day. We Fish Our Lives Out. Jana Harris. NGP

On the bog road the blackthorn flowers, the turf-stacks. Anthony Cronin. *Fr.* R.M.S. *Titanic.* BIrV

On the bonnie banks o' Fordie. *(LL)* Babylon; or, The Bonnie Banks o' Fordie. *Unknown.* AmFP; ESPB; OxBB

On the border. Gaby at the U.N. Observation Post. Susan Tichy. BTR

On the Border, First Series, sels. Tu Fu, *tr. fr. Chinese by* Burton Watson.

On the bottom of the sky. Burning Shewolf. Vasco [*or* Vasko] Popa, *tr. fr. Serbo-Croatian by* Charles Simic. HSix

On the branches of a fallen tree. A Fallen Tree. Mang Ke, *tr. fr. Chinese by* Donald Finkel *with* Li Guohua. SpMi

On the Bridge of Sighs. Byron. *See* I stood in Venice on the Bridge of Sighs.

On the Bright Side. Carter Revard. VoR

On the Brink of Death. Michelangelo, *tr. fr. Italian by* John Addington Symonds. AWP

On the British Invasion. Philip Freneau. PAH

On the British King's Speech. Philip Freneau. PAH

On the broad River Huai, dotted with islets, a village suddenly appears. A Little Village. Mei Yao Ch'en, *tr. fr. Chinese by* Jonathan Chaves. SuSp

On the brown dry/ forest-bed. *(LL)* If Ice. W. W. Eustace Ross. NOBC

On the Building of a New Church. *Unknown. See* They built the front, upon my word.

On the mantelpiece. Studio Poem. Cilla McQueen. PeNZ

On the Margin, *sels*. David Wright.
Anniversary Approaches, An; of the Birth of God. NAs

On the Marginal Way. Richard Wilbur. CoAP; NOBA

On the Marriage of a Virgin. Dylan Thomas. EnLoPo; MeMBP; OxBM

On the Marriage of T. K. and C. C., the Morning Stormy. Thomas Carew. BoLoP

On the Masquerades. Christopher Pitt. ECEV; NOEC

On the Meadow. "Katri Vala," *tr. fr. Finnish by* Jaakko A. Ahokas. PBWP

On the Meatwheel. Dick Gallup. UL

On the Meetings of the Scotch Covenanters. *Unknown.* FaBoEE

On the Melting Lake. Chung Ling, *tr. fr. Chinese by* Kenneth Rexroth *and* Ling Chung. WPC

On the Memorial building's. Under Cancer. John Hollander. CoAP

On the Memory of Mr. Edward King, Drowned in the Irish Seas. John Cleveland. OAEL-1; SeCP

On the merry morning of May! (*LL*) The Padstow Night Song. *Unknown.* ChTr; GBP

On the mid stairs, between the light and dark. King Mark, Tristram, and Palamede. Swinburne. *Fr.* Tristram of Lyonesse. EBNV

On the Miracle of Loaves. Richard Crashaw. OxBSP

On the Miracle of Multiplied Loaves. Richard Crashaw. OxBSP

On the moor of Kasuga. Hitomaro, *tr. by* Arthur Waley. *Fr.* Manyo Shu, Part 3 of 4. AWP

On the Morning of Christ's Nativity. (This is the month and this the happy morn.) Milton. MeLP; NAs; NOCV; NoP; PoEL-3; SCGP; WGRP
Sels.
Anniversary Approaches, An; of the Birth of God. NAs
"But peaceful was the night." FaBoCh
Hymn on the Morning of Christ's Nativity [*or* On the Morning of Christ's Nativity]. NAEL-1; NOBE; OBEV; OtMeF
Magi, The. ChTr

On the morning of the crowning we chorused our remission from school. Geoffrey Hill. *Fr.* Mercian Hymns. HAP

On the Morning of the Third Night above Nisqually. W. M. Ransom. CDW; NU

On the Motor Bus. Alfred Denis Godley. *See* What is this that roareth thus?

On the Mountain. Neidhart von Reuental, *tr. fr. German by* Jethro Bithell. AWP

On the Mountain. Ruth Stone. BoWoP

On the mountain, Epicydes the hunter seeks. Callimachus, *tr. fr. Greek. Fr.* Epigrams. HePo

On the Mountain of Boiled Rice I met Tu Fu. To Tu Fu. Li Po, *tr. fr. Chinese by* Robert Payne. TAL

On the mountain peak, called "Going-to-the-Sun." The Apple-Barrel of Johnny Appleseed. Vachel Lindsay. OxBA

On the Move. Thom Gunn. CMoP; HAP; LiTM; NoP; OAEL-2; OxAEP-2; OxBTC; PoE; PPP; TRP; TwCP

On the Murder of Sir Edmund Berry Godfrey. *Unknown.* APAS

On the murky earth. (*LL*) Ecstatic Longing. Goethe. STV

On the Name of Jesus. Richard Crashaw. *See* I sing the Name which none can say.

On the Nativity of Our Saviour. Thomas Philipott. JCP

On the Nature of Food. Alberta Turner. LCAP

On the navel of the Boer's domain. Lesotho. Bennett Makalo Khaketla, *tr. fr. Sotho by* Dan Kunene *and* Jack Cope. PeSA

On the Needle of a Sundial. Francis Quarles. TrGrPo

On the New Forcers of Conscience Under the Long Parliament. Milton. FaBoEH; FaBoPV; NAEL-1; NOSC; Son

On *The New Inn*: Ode, To Himself. Ben Jonson. *See* Come leave the loathed stage.

On the New Jersey shore he met her. Blue Springs, Georgia. Ree Young. GOYP

On the New Laureate. *Unknown.* FaBoCo

On the new sand. What Her Girl Friend Said, the Lover within Earshot, behind a Fence. Uloccanar, *tr. fr. Tamil by* A. K. Ramanujan. PLW

On the Night. Ivor Gurney. OxBSP

On the night beach, quiet beside the blue. Morning. Glyn Jones. AngWe

On the Night in Question. Patricia Goedicke. TAP

On the night journey there would be talk. The Lights of Dunleary. Thomas McCarthy. *Fr.* Neutral State, A. IB

On the night of the Belgian surrender the moon rose. The Moon and the Night and the Men. John Berryman. ArOW; CoAP; VCAP; VGW

On the Night of the Fifteenth Day of the First Month I Go Out and Return. Mei Yao Ch'en, *tr. fr. Chinese by* Jonathan Chaves. SuSp

On the night road from El Rama the cows. Second Poem from Nicaragua Libre: War Zone. June Jordan. NoAM

On the Ninth Day of the Month, Thinking of Ch'eng, *sels.* Wu Chia-chi, *tr. fr. Chinese by* John E. Wills, Jr.

On the 9th of August I'll transform. On My Birthday. Farhad Mazhar, *tr. fr. Bengali.* TSaS, *tr. by* Kabir Chowdhury *and* Naomi Shihab

On the ninth of November by the dawning of the day. Farewell to Kingsbridge. *Unknown.* ECEV

On the North Shore a reptile lay asleep. The Precambrian [*or* Pre-Cambrian] Shield. E. J. Pratt. *Fr.* Towards the Last Spike. MoCV; NOBC

On the Numerous Access of the English to Wait upon the King in Flanders. Katherine Philips. *See* Hasten (great prince) unto thy British Isles.

On the Numerous Accesse of the English to Waite upon the King in Holland. Katherine Philips. KTR

On the Ocean Floor. "Hugh MacDiarmid." FaBoMo; HAP

On the ocean that hollows the rocks where ye dwell. O Brazil, the Isle of the Blest. Gerald Griffin.
(Hy-Brasail – the Isle of the Blest.) BLPA

On the old submarine. (*LL*) Charlie Chaplin went to France. *At. to* Carl Withers. MoShBr; RoPo

On the one-ton temple bell. Buson, *tr. fr. Japanese.* InPK

On the Open Side. Roy Fisher. NBrP

On the Oregon Coast. Galway Kinnell. NoAM

On the Origin of Evil. John Byrom. NOEC

On the Other Side. Czeslaw Milosz, *tr. fr. Polish by* Jan Darowski. OBD; PoSu

On the other side. Ohioan Pastoral. James Wright. LCAP

On the other side/ of my world. To the Man I Live With. Ann Menebroker. IHMS

On the other side of the world I heard. Elegy for a Schoolmate. Vincent O'Sullivan. PeNZ

On the outermost far-flung ridge of ice and snow. Inspiration. W. W. Gibson. WGRP

On the outskirts, dumplings of mud. Wang Fun-chih, *tr. fr. Chinese by* Eugene Eoyang. SuSp

On the Oxford Book of Victorian Verse. "Hugh MacDiarmid." MoBrPo

On the Painter Val Prinsep. Dante Gabriel Rossetti. FaBoEE

On the Painting "Joys of Village Life," *sels.* Yün Shou-p'ing, *tr. fr. Chinese by* Jonathan Chaves.

On the Painting "Mist over Ten Thousand Mountains," *sels.* Yün Shou-p'ing, *tr. fr. Chinese by* Jonathan Chaves.

On the path. Under the Maud Moon. Galway Kinnell. CAPP; NNaP

On the path winding. The Path among the Stones. Galway Kinnell. NNaP; NOBA; Prf

On the pathway mica glints. Water and Worship: An Open-Air Service on the Gatineau River. Margaret Avison. HAP

On the Phoenix. Jean Adams. ECWP

On the phonograph, the voice. Reunion. Carolyn Forché. NoAM

On the Picture of a Child. H. Cordelia Ray. CBWP-3

On the Pilgrim's Way in Kent, as It Leads to the Coldrum Stones. "Asphodel." BrRo

On the plain that town flat like an iron sheet. A Naked Town. Zbigniew Herbert, *tr. fr. Polish by* Czeslaw Milosz *and* Peter Dale Scott. AnRep

On the Planet of Flies. Christian Morgenstern, *tr. fr. German by* Geoffrey Grigson. FaBoNo

On the Ploughman [*or* Plough-Man]. Francis Quarles. NOSC

On the Poet O'Shaughnessy. Dante Gabriel Rossetti. ChTr

On the Portrait of a Girl. Erinna, *tr. fr. Greek by* Lenore Mayhew. GrAn

On the Portrait of a Woman about to Be Hanged. Thomas Hardy. CMoP

On the Prince's Death, to the King. Sir Robert Ayton. NOSC; ScCV

On the promising young robber, the lieutenant of his band. (*LL*) Gentle Alice Brown. W. S. Gilbert. FaBoCo; FiBHP

On the Proposed Seizure of Twelve Graves in a Colonial Cemetery. X. J. Kennedy. NGP

On the Prorogation. *Unknown.* APAS

On the Prospect from Westminster Bridge. Elizabeth Tollet. ECWP

On the Prospect of Peace, *sels.* Thomas Tickell.
"Ah! curst Ambition, to thy lures we owe." ECEV

On the Prospect of Planting Arts and Learning in America. George Berkeley. AiP; ImPo; NOEC; OBTV; TrGrPo

On the prow. The Landing. Daniel Halpern. AmPA

On the quays of Papeete, the dawdling white-ducked colonists. Gauguin. Derek Walcott. NoAM

On the Queen's Return from the Low Countries. William Cartwright. OBEV

On the rank harvest of betrayal they feed. The Rank Harvest of Betrayal. Wilma Stockenström, *tr. fr. Afrikaans by* Rosa Keet. PeSAV

On the rapids of the St. Lawrence. H. Cordelia Ray. CBWP-3

On the Receipt of My Mother's Picture out of Norfolk [the Gift of My Cousin Ann Bodham]. William Cowper. EnRP; NOEC

On the summer road that ran by our front porch. Lizards and Snakes. Anthony Hecht. FaBoMo; TwCP

On the Sun Coming Out in the Afternoon. Thoreau. OxBSP; PoEL-4

On the Supposed Author of a Late Poem "In Defense of Satire." The Earl of Rochester. APAS

On the Swag. R. A. K. Mason. PeNZ

On the Symbolic Consideration of Hands and the Significance of Death. Miller Williams. InPK

On the Tack. Thomas Hearne. ECEV

On the tall hill. What She Said to Her Girl Friend ("On the tall hill.") Paranar, tr. fr. Tamil by A. K. Ramanujan. PLW

On the tallest day in time, the dead came back. V-J Day. John Ciardi. ArOW

On the tedious ferry crossing through the obscure night. "If Only I Knew the Truth, I Swear I Would Act on it." Paul Goodman. ArLo

On the Telescopic Moon. John Swanwick Drennan. BIrV

On the temple bell. Spring Scene. Buson, tr. fr. Japanese by Kenneth Koch and Harold Henderson. TTTS

On the temple porch of Syrian Astarte. To Astarte. Unknown, tr. fr. Greek by Guy Davenport. GrAn

On the tenth day of December. Musselburgh Field. Unknown. ESPB

On the Tercentenary of Milton's Death. Gavin Ewart. OxBC

On the Thessalians Who Fought at Marathon. Aeschylus, tr. fr. Greek by Edwin Morgan. GrAn

On the third day of the third month, in fresh weather. The Elegant Women. Tu Fu, tr. fr. Chinese by Mark Perlberg. SuSp

On the third day rose Arp. Resurrection of Arp. A. J. M. Smith. MoCV; NOBC

On the third finger of my left hand. Ceremony. William Stafford. FoLa; LCAP

On the third planet too, life is found. Excerpt from a Report to the Galactic Council. Robert Conquest. OxBC

On the Thirteenth Day of Christmas. Charles Causley. OBCP

On the Thirteenth Day of the Eleventh Month I Went to the Granary for the First Time since My Illness. Mei Yao Ch'en, tr. fr. Chinese by Jonathan Chaves. SuSp

On the 31st day of the month of August 1914. The Little Car. Guillaume Apollinaire, tr. fr. French. SOTW, tr. by Ron Padgett and others

On the Three Children in the Fiery Furnace. Henry Colman. ChIV-1

On the Threshold. Karl Kraus, tr. fr. German by Albert Bloch. TrJP

On the Threshold. Amy Levy. NOBVV

On the Threshold. Unknown. BLPA

On the threshold of heaven, the figures in the street. To an Old Philosopher in Rome. Wallace Stevens. EnlH; MeMAP; MoP; NoAM; NOBA; Poetr

On the tidal mud, just before sunset. Daybreak. Galway Kinnell. FoLa

On the tiles, all through the night. (LL) To the Tune "The Fair Maid of Yu." Chiang Chieh. OHMPC

On The Times. Wyndham Lewis. IHNG

On the Tomb of Orpheus. Damagetus, tr. fr. Greek by John Heath-Stubbs and Carol A. Whiteside. GrAn

On the Tomb of the Spartan Dead at Thermopylae. Unknown. PAW

On the Tombs in Westminster Abbey, sels. At. to Beaumont, Francis and William Basse Francis Beaumont and to William Basse.
"Here's a world of pomp and state." PIP
Lines on the Tombs in Westminster. CH; FaPoR; GTBS; GTBS-P; NOBE; OBEV; PIP; SCGP; TrGrPo
(Memento for Mortality, A.) EIL; FaBoCh; HAP
(On the Tombs in Westminster Abbey.) CoGr; OxAEP-1

On the Tombs in Westminster Abbey. At. to Beaumont, Francis and William Basse Francis Beaumont and to William Basse. See Mortality [or Mortalitie], behold and fear[e]!

On the top of the Crumpetty Tree. The Quangle Wangle's Hat. Edward Lear. CBNP; EBEV; PeVV

On the Tower. Annette von Droste-Hülshoff, tr. fr. German by James Edward Tobin. PBWP; WPOW

On the Tower of Gathering Remoteness. Su Tung-p'o, tr. fr. Chinese by Robert Payne. TAL

On the Town's Honest Man. Ben Jonson. NOSC

On the train/ old ladies playing football. Going Uptown to Visit Miriam. Victor Hernandez Cruz. FF; MAT

On the Translation of Anacreon. Horace Walpole. FaBoEE

On the Treasury of the True Dharma Eye. Dogen. EnlH

On the Triumph of Rationalism. Alfred Ainger. FaBoCo

On the Turning Up of Unidentified Black Female Corpses. Toi Derricotte. NAmP90

On the 25th Anniversary of the Liberation of Auschwitz. Eli W. Mandel. NOBC

On the Twenty-fifth of July. David Cornel DeJong. NYBP

On the Twenty-fourth: Improvisations, sels. Liu E, tr. fr. Chinese by Jonathan Chaves.

On the Twenty-fourth of the Third Month, in the Year Ting-wei Sailed across Lake T'ai from Behind the Mountain. Wu Wei-yeh, tr. fr. Chinese by Chang Yin-nan and Lewis C. Walmsley. SuSp

On the twenty-sixth of August, our fatal moss gave way. The Donibristle Moss Moran Disaster. Unknown. WTO

On the Two Great Floods. Francis Quarles. ChIV-1

On the unbreathing sides of hills. Squatter's Children. Elizabeth Bishop. NoP

On the Uniformity and Perfection of Nature. Philip Freneau. AmPP; EAP

On the Union. Swift. See Queen has lately lost a part, The.

On the Universality and Other Attributes of the God of Nature. Philip Freneau. EAP

On the University Carrier (Who Sickn'd [or Sickened] in the Time of His Vacancy) [being Forbid to go to London, by Reason of the Plague]. Milton. EBEV; FaBoCh; FaBoEE; NOSC; OxAEP-1; PrIm

On the University of Cambridge's Burning the Duke of Monmouth's Picture. George Stepney. APAS

On the Unusual Cold and Rainy [or Rainie] Weather in the Summer, 1648. Robert Heath. NOSC

On the unyielding flint. (LL) Art. Théophile Gautier. AWP

On the up-platform at Morpeth station. The Complaint of the Morpethshire Farmer. Basil Bunting. CTC

On the Use of Jayshus. Oliver St. John Gogarty. FaBoEE

On the Use of New and Old Words in Poetry. Anna Seward. Son

On the Vanity of Earthly Greatness. Arthur Guiterman. BXAP; HeIP; HoPM; OBCA; TrJP

On the vast plains, with night and rain coming on. (LL) Independence. Nancy Cato. WPE

On the verandah. A War-time picnic. Mimi Khalvati. NWP

On the Victory Obtained by Blake over the Spaniards, in the Bay of Sanctacruze, in the Island of Tenerif. 1657, sels. Andrew Marvell. "Now does Spains Fleet her spatious wings unfold." FaBoEH

On the Village Green. William Somervile. Fr. Hobbinol. ECEV

On the volcanic hill. Precarious Ground. Leah Bodine Drake. GoYe

On the Vowels — a Riddle. Swift. FaBoUs

On the Wall. Immanuel di Roma, tr. fr. Hebrew by Solomon Solis-Cohen. TrJP

On the wall by the bathtub there clings. Things Grow Up out of the Dark. Joan Dobbie. LoHo

On the Wall of a KZ-Lager. János Pilinszky, tr. fr. Hungarian by János Csokits and Ted Hughes. PoSu

On the wan sea-strand. Evening Twilight. Heine, tr. by John Todhunter. Fr. North Sea, The. AWP

On the warm July river. Inner Tube. Michael Ondaatje. NoAM

On the Water of Our Lord's Baptism. Richard Crashaw. GeHe

On the water the first wind. Spring. W. S. Merwin. NaP

On the Waterfront. Michael Foley. PNI

On the Watergate Women. Robin Morgan. GLP

On the Way. Ho Chi Minh. EaPr, tr. by Christopher Jenkins, Tran Khanh Tuget, and Hugh Sanh Thong

On the way down. The Way Down. Philip Levine. NOBA

On the way home from the University, I saw. Bible Bob Responds to a Jesus Honker. D. H. Lloyd. NGP

On the Way to Huang-ch'ang River. Wang Shih-chieng, tr. fr. Chinese by Richard John Lynn. SuSp

On the Way to Kew. W. E. Henley. Fr. Echoes. MoBrPo; TrGrPo

On the Way to Mind. Milo De Angelis, tr. fr. Italian by Lawrence Venuti. NeIt

On the way to school I tell my son. These words Are Synonymous, Now. Juan Felipe Herrera. AfAz

On the way to see a friend. For David. Frankie Paino. PFL

On the way to the evening reading. The Shrine and the Burning Wheel. Mark Jarman. NAmP90

On the Way to the Island. David Ferry. PRA

On the Way to the Mission. Duncan Campbell Scott. NOBC

On the Way to the Reunion. Rita Magdaleno. AfAz

On the way to the reunion in copper country. On the Way to the Reunion. Rita Magdaleno. AfAz

On the way up from Sheet I met some children. To Edward Thomas. Alun Lewis. PoWW

On the Welch. Unknown. AngWe

On the Welsh Language. Katherine Philips. NOSC

On the Welsh Marches. Walter Stone. NYBP

On the western hills the sun sets, the eastern hills darken. A Piece for Magic Strings. Li Ho, tr. fr. Chinese by A. C. Graham. PLT

On the wet sand the queen emerged from forest. Theseus: A Trilogy. Yvor Winters. NOBA

On the white throat of the useless passion. Ad Finem. Ella Wheeler Wilcox. BLPA

On the whole goddam town. *(LL)* The Memory. Robert Creeley. CAPP; VGW

On the Wide Heath. Edna St. Vincent Millay. CMoP; WPE

On the wide level of a mountain's head. Time, Real and Imaginary. Samuel Taylor Coleridge. EnRP; MeMBP; NOBE; OBEV; OxBSP; PFP

On the wind, a drifting echo. Christmas Night. Lawrence Sail. OBCP

On the wind of January. The Wind of January. Christina Rossetti. BoTP

On the wings of the buck and wing. *(LL)* Buckdancer's Choice. James Dickey. HeIP; NoAM; NOBA; NoP; NYBP; PoNe

On the Wings of the Morning. Day Jeffery. NSI

On the Wings of the Wind. Elaine Mott. BTR

On the World. Francis Quarles. HAP

On the Wounds of Our Crucified Lord. Richard Crashaw. NAEL-1

On the Yangtze. Wang An-shih, *tr. fr. Chinese by* Jan W. Walls. SuSp

On the Yard. Etheridge Knight. RaBo

On the Young Statesmen. Charles Sackville. APAS

On thee thou must take a long journey. *Unknown. Fr.* Everyman. NAEL-1; NAWM-1; OAEL-1; OBD; OxBLMV; PoEL-1

On Their Appointed Rounds. *Unknown.* FaPON

On Theodoros. Simonides. *See* Someone is glad that I, Theodorus, am dead.

On these ancient discs, smooth-backed, severe. Old Gramophone Records. James Kirkup. NYBP

On these hands," he grins proudly. *(LL)* Perfecto Flores. Jimmy Santiago Baca. TRP

On these occasions, the feelings surprise. Father and Son. Delmore Schwartz. LiTA

On these white cliffs, that calm above the flood. At Dover Cliffs. William Lisle Bowles. EnRP
(Dover Cliffs.) OxAEP-2

On things asleep, no balm. North American Sequence. Theodore Roethke. NaP

On Things Seen, *sels.* Tsung Ch'en, *tr. fr. Chinese by* Jonathan Chaves.

On Thinking of Photographing My Fantasies. Nellie Wong. OpBo

On Third Street there's a naked spot. The Ballad of Mary Baldwin. Stephen Sandy. MAT

On this bald hill the new year hones its edge. Parliament Hill Fields. Sylvia Plath. HCAP; NALW

On This Day. M. B. Goffstein. NTCP

On This Day. Leah Goldberg, *tr. fr. Hebrew by* Ruth Finer Mintz. MHP

On This Day I Complete My Fortieth Year. Peter Porter. NAs

On This Day I Complete My Thirty-sixth Year. Byron. EnRP; FHYEP; MeMBP; NAs; NoP; OAEL-2; OBWP; PoE

On this day man's disgust is known. On Shooting Particles beyond the World. Richard Eberhart. LiTA; LiTM

On this day they break bread. On This Day. Leah Goldberg, *tr. fr. Hebrew by* Ruth Finer Mintz. MHP

On this day when you have needed to sleep forever. Healing Animal. Joy Harjo. ETG

On this feast day, oh, cursèd day and hour! Love at First Sight. Christopher Marlowe. *Fr.* Hero and Leander. AAS; NOBE; NoP

On this ground I may look for rest. My Detached Villa. Li Shan-fu, *tr. by* Edward H. Schafer. SuSp

On this her daughter's tomb. Anyte, *tr. fr. Greek by* Sally Purcell. GrAn

On this high hill in a year's turning. *(LL)* Poem in October. Dylan Thomas. AngWe; EBEvV; ImPo; LiTB; MeMBP; NAEL-2; NAs; NoAM; OxAEP-2; PoA; PoRA; PrIm; RB; SoSe; UV, *st. 1 only*

On this hill crossed. Galway Kinnell. NaP

On this hotel, their rumpled royalties. The West Forties: Morning, Noon, and Night. L. E. Sissman. CoAP; NYBP

On This Island. W. H. Auden. CMoP; NAEL-2; PAW; PoE

On this lone Isle, whose rugged rocks affright. Sonnet: Suppos'd to Be Written at Lemnos. Thomas Russell. NOEC

On this map white. A state thick as a fist. A Map of Montana in Italy. Richard Hugo. LCAP

On this primeval strip of western land. Destroyers. Sir Henry Head. NSI

On this resemblance, where we find. On a Death's Head. Elizabeth Tollet. ECWP

On this side, and on that, men see their friends. All Impelled Onward Alike. Robert Blair. *Fr.* Grave, The. OxAEP-1

On this side of the tapestry. The Tapestry. Howard Nemerov. Prf

On this tiny planet. Tune: "Full River Red" — A Reply to Kuo Mo-jo. Mao Tse-tung, *tr. fr. Chinese by* Eugene Eoyang. SuSp

On this tree thrown up. Spindrift. Galway Kinnell. NaP; NYBP

On this winter night. Lady Izumi Shikibu, *tr. fr. Japanese by* Willis Barnstone. BoWoP

On Thomas Moore's Poems. *Unknown.* FaBoCo; FiBHP

On Thomas, Second Earl of Onslow. *Unknown.* FaBoCo

On Those That Deserve It. Francis Quarles. NOCV; NOSC

On Those That Hated *The Playboy of the Western World.* W. B. Yeats. NOIV

On three crosses of a tree. A Charm Rhyme. *Unknown.* FaBoVe

On three sides/ the sea's. On a High House in Byzantium. Paulus Silentiarius, *tr. fr. Greek by* Andrew Miller. GrAn

On thrones from China to Peru. A Model for the Laureate. W. B. Yeats. CMoP

On thy fair bosom, silver lake. To Senaca Lake. James Gates Percival. BoTP

On thy stars below in Frederick town! *(LL)* Barbara Frietchie. Whittier. AiP; AnAmPo; BeLS; BoTP; CTC; EBNV; FaBoBe; FaBV; FaPON; FaPoR; FF; GN; NOBA; OBAL; OBCA; PAH; PoLF; TFi; TrGrPo; VPP; WBLP

On Time. Richard Hughes. MoBrPo

On Time. Milton. BLPL; ImPo; LiTB; OBEV; SCGP

On Tintock-Tap there is a mist. Tintock. *Unknown.* GBP

On to, dear God, well trodden ground. *(LL)* In Memory, 1978. Judith Kazantzis. AIW; BrRo

On to Richmond. John R. Thompson. PAH

On to the beach the quiet waters crept. The Quiet Tide near Ardossan. Charles Tennyson Turner. FaBoPP

On, to the City of God. *(LL)* Rugby Chapel. Matthew Arnold. EBVVPR; EnVR; FaBoEH; PeECV; PoEL-5; WGRP

On to the Morgue. *Unknown.* AS

On to the Source. James Tate. AnAn

On Tobacco. Charles Cotton. OBSV

On Tobacco. Thomas Pestel. EIL

On Tom Holland and Nell Cotton. *Unknown.* FaBoEE

On Tom Moore's Translation of Anacreon. Thomas, Lord Erskine. FaBoEE

On Tom-o-Combe. *Unknown.* FaBoEE

On Tom Onslow, Earl of Onslow. *Unknown. See* What can Tommy Onslow [*or* little T. O.] do?

On Tomato Ketchup. *Unknown.* FaBoUs; NBLV

On top of that if you know me I pronounce you an ignu. Ignu. Allen Ginsberg. NaP

On top of the Crumpetty Tree. The Quangle Wangle's Hat. Edward Lear. OTCP

On Tour. Richard Howard. PRA

On tour he motored into the enchanted place. Macliammoir at Cappoquin. Thomas McCarthy. *Fr.* Neutral State, A. IB

On Treason. Sir John Harington. *See* Treason doth never prosper [*or* Treason never prospers]; what's the reason?

On tree-topped hill, on tufted green. Tree-topped Hill. *Unknown.* NOEC

On Trees. Alan Dugan. NoAM

On Tuesday I and my lover spent all night in a wood. Dawn Song. *Unknown, tr. fr. French by* Willard R. Trask. VBLP

On Tuesday morn at half-past six o'clock. James Rigg. James Hogg. BXAP

On Twisting River Is the Old Home of My Father, *sels.* Chin Nung, *tr. fr. Chinese by* Jonathan Chaves.

On Two Brothers. Simonides, *tr. fr. Greek by* W. H. D. Rouse. AWP

On Two Monopolists. John Byrom. FaBoCo; FaBoEE

On Ullswater. Wordsworth. *Fr.* Prelude [*or*, Growth of a Poet's Mind], The. CH; EnRP; FaBoPP; GN; HAP; NOBE; NoP; NU; OAEL-2; OBNC; OxAEP-2; PoE; RB; SCV

On Vacation. Robert Creeley. CAPP

On Venus, time passes slowly because. Here. Marvin Bell. AmPA

On Viewing Her Sleeping Infant. Maria Frances Cecelia Cowper. ECWP

On Viewing Herself in a Glass. Elizabeth Teft. ECWP

On village green, whose smooth and well-worn sod. A Disappointment. Joanna Baillie. NOEC; WoRP

On Virtue. Phillis Wheatley. TAP

On Visiting My Son, Port Angeles, Washington. Duane Niatum. CDW

On Visiting the Graves of Hawthorne and Thoreau. Jones Very. TAP

On Waking. Alida Carey Gulick. GoYe

On Waking after Dreaming of Raoul. Lynn Emanuel. NAmP90

On Walt Whitman's Birthday. Anne Waldman. UL

On Sir Walter Rawleigh at His Execution. *Unknown. See* Great heart, who taught thee so to dye?

On wan dark night on Lac St. Pierre. The Wreck of the *Julie Plante* [*or* The *Julie Plante*]. William Henry Drummond. BeLS; BLPA; FaBoBe; FaPON

On Watching a World Series Game. Sonia Sanchez. NBV

On Watching *Heritage: Civilization and the Jews.* Deborah Hanan. BTR

On Watching Politicians Perform at Martin Luther King's Funeral. Etheridge Knight. NNaP

On water the Man-Fisher walks. (*LL*) The Drunken Fisherman. Robert Lowell. AmPP; ChIV-2; CMoP; ImPo; LiTA; LiTM; NOBA; OxBA; VGW

On Waterloo's ensanguined plain. On Scott's Poem "The Field of Waterloo." Thomas, Lord Erskine. FaBoCo; FiBHP; NBLV

On Wednesday night. Wednesday Night Prayer Meeting. Jay Wright. PoBA

On Wellington ("You are 'the best of cut-throats' .") Byron. *See* You are 'the best of cut-throats:' — do not start.

On Wenlock Edge the Wood's in Trouble. A. E. Housman. *Fr.* Shropshire Lad, A. CoGr; FaPoB; GTBS-P; LiTB; MeMBP; Mes; MoAB; MoBrPo; NAEL-2; NOBE; NoP; OBNC; OxAEP-2; OxBTC; PlP; PoEL-5; PoRA; PrIm; RB; SCGP; TFi

On went She, and due north her journey took. (*LL*) With Ships the Sea Was Sprinkled Far and Nigh. Wordsworth. EnRP; SCGP

On Westwall Downes [*or* On Westwell Downs]. William Strode. FaBoPP; GGP; JCP; NOSC; PoEL-2

On what a brave and curious whim. Clocks. Louis Ginsberg. TrJP

On what foundation stands the warrior's pride. Samuel Johnson. *Fr.* Vanity of Human Wishes, The: The Tenth Satire of Juvenal Imitated. EBEV; ECEV; NOEC; NoP; OAEL-1; OBWP; OxAEP-1; PoEL-3; PrIm; TEP; TFi

(Charles XII of Sweden.) NOBE

On which it should be touch'd would melt away! (*LL*) Admonition to a Traveller. Wordsworth. GTBS; GTBS-P

On which so much depends will clear the moon. (*LL*) Bitter Harvest. Alistair Campbell. PeNZ

On Whitsunday morning. Dunt Dunt Dunt Pittie Pattie. *Unknown.* FaBoVe

On ["Who Wrote Icon Basilike" by Dr.] Christopher Wordsworth, Master of Trinity. Benjamin Hall Kennedy. FaBoCo; FaBoEE

On Will Smith. *Unknown.* FaBoCo

On William Prynne. Samuel Butler. *See* Here lies the corpse of William Prynne.

On William Wilson, Tailor. *Unknown.* FaBoEE

On Windermere; Bowness Bay and Belle Isle. Wordsworth. *Fr.* Prelude [or, Growth of a Poet's Mind], The. CH; EnRP; FaBoPP; GN; HAP; NOBE; NoP; NU; OAEL-2; OBNC; OxAEP-2; PoE; SCV

On windy days. Clothes on the Washing Line. Frank Flynn. OTCP

On windy days the mill. The Unfortunate Miller. A. E. Coppard. FaBoTw

On Wings of Song. Heine, *tr. fr. German by* Philip L. Miller. RiWo

On Winter Evenings; 1912, *sels.* David Hofshteyn, *tr. fr. Yiddish by* Robert Friend.

On winter nights. The Car Cemetery. Ciaran Carson. CIP

On Witch Moutain the fireflies flit in the autumn night. Upon Seeing the Fireflies. Tu Fu, *tr. fr. Chinese by* Wu-chi Liu. SuSp

On Wodin's day, sixth of December, thirty-nine. *In re* Solomon Warshawer. A. M. Klein. MoCV

On Woman. W. B. Yeats. ChIV-1; CMoP

On Women ("Britannia's daughters.") Edward Young. *Fr.* Satires. ECEV

On Women ("Lavinia is polite.") Edward Young. *Fr.* Satires. ECEV

On wool-soft feet he peeps and creeps. Santa Claus. Walter de la Mare. PChr

On Words and Concepts and Things. Paul Ramsey. CRP

On Wordsworth. Hartley Coleridge. *See* He Lived amidst th' Untrodden Ways.

On Work. Kahlil Gibran. *Fr.* Prophet, The. PoToHe, *abr.*

On Worldly Prelates. Charles Wesley. ChIV-2

On Writing for the Stage. John Sheffield, Duke of Buckingham and Normandy. *Fr.* Essay on Poetry. FaBoUs

On yardbird corners of embryonic hopes, drowned in a heroin tear. On. Bob Kaufman. PoBeRe

On ye both; good night to all. (*LL*) The Good-Night, or Blessing. Robert Herrick. CaPo

On Yes Tor. Sir Edmund Gosse. CH

On yon hill's top which this sweet plain commands. Invites His Nymph to His Cottage. Philip Ayres. EnLoPo

On yonder hill there is a red deer. *Unknown.* ChTr; GBP

On yonder hill there stands a creature. O, No, John [*or* No John] [*or* The One Answer]. *Unknown.* ErPo; OBET; PDV; PeLV

On yonder oak, upon its lordliest height. Mistletoe. Mary E. Tucker. CBWP-1

On your breast. Vague Apprehension. Lin Ling, *tr. fr. Chinese by* Kenneth Rexroth *and* Ling Chung. WPC

On your dazzling throne, Aphrodite. Sappho, *tr. fr. Greek by* Willis Barnstone. BoWoP

On your outstretched hand. (*LL*) Unfamiliar Shore. Bei Dao. SpMi

On your slender body. For the Courtesan Ch'ing Lin. Wu Tsao, *tr. fr. Chinese by* Kenneth Rexroth *and* Ling Chung. BoWoP; VBLP; WPC; WPOW

On your street, whose name means "roundabout" in Dutch. Tulips: A Selected History. Vickie Karp. UTF

On your throne, a marvel of art, immortal. Sappho, *tr. fr. Greek by* John Frederick Nims. STV

On Zacchaeus [*or* Zacheus]. Francis Quarles. HAP; NOSC; OxBSP

On Zion and on Lebanon. Henry Ustic Onderdonk. AH

Once. Eric N. Batterham. CH

Once. George Ives. PeHV

Once. *Unknown.* CH

Once. Alice Walker. BlSi

Sels.
"Green lawn/ a picket fence." PoBA
"I/ never liked/ white folks." PoBA
"It is true — / I've always loved." NMM; PoBA

Once. Siv Widerberg, *tr. fr. Swedish by* Verne Moberg. NTCP

Once a Big Molicepan. *Unknown.* FaPON

Once a boy beheld a bright. The Rose. Goethe, *tr. fr. German by* James Clarence Mangan. AWP

Once a day the rocks, with little warning. Naskeag. Alfred Corn. VCAP

Once a dream did weave a shade. A Dream. Blake. *Fr.* Songs of Innocence. CH; EnRP; FHYEP

Once a jolly swagman camped by a billabong. Waltzing Matilda. Andrew Barton Paterson. CBAP; ChTr; GBP

Once a Kansas zephyr strayed. Zephyr. Eugene Fitch Ware. PoLF

Once, a lady of the O Moores. Parthenogenesis. Nuala Ni Dhomhnaill, *tr. fr. Irish by* Michael Hartnett. CIP

Once a little baby lay. The First Christmas. Emilie Poulsson. OHIP

Once a little boy, Jack, was, oh! ever so good. The Sad Story of a Little boy That Cried. *Unknown.* OBSP

Once a little boy was dreaming. Parables, I. Antonio Machado Ruiz, *tr. fr. Spanish by* John Frederick Nims. STV

Once a man is born he has to die. All Intents. Larry Eigner. VGW

Once a mouse, a frog, and a little red hen. The Mouse, The Frog and The Little Red Hen. *Unknown.* BoTP

Once a pallid vestal. The Vestal. Nathalia Crane. TrJP

Once a poor widow, aging year by year, (*mod. vers. by* Theodore Morrison). Chaucer. *See* Poore [*or* Povre] widwe [*or* widow], somdeel [*or* somedel *or* somedel] stape in age, A.

Once a raven from Pluto's dark shore. The True Facts of the Case. Anthony Euwer. OBAL; PeLi

Once a red vixen. Wintermusik. Sarah Kirsch, *tr. fr. German by* Wendy Mulford *and* Anthony Vivis. VBLP

Once a wife in Bethlehem. A Prayer for a Sleeping Child. Mary Carolyn Davies. OHIP

Once, after long-drawn revel at The Mermaid. The Craftsman. Kipling. CoGr

Once Again. Liz Sohappy Bahe. CDW

Once again a spring has come around. A Natural Theology. James Whitehead. MT

Once again a yellow twilight. To the Tune "The Pain of Lovesickness." Wu Tsao, *tr. fr. Chinese by* Kenneth Rexroth *and* Ling Chung. WPC

Once again I saw winter flee before the spring. Spring. Aasmund Olavsen Vinje, *tr. fr. Norwegian by* Philip L. Miller. RiWo

Once again the scurry of feet[]those myriads. The Face of the Waters. Robert David Fitzgerald. CBAP; FaBoMA

Once again the wind is howling and you, Rufus. At the Bridge with Rufus. Kenneth McClane. Jaz

Once Alien Here. John Hewitt. CIP; PNI

Once alien here my fathers built their house. Once Alien Here. John Hewitt. CIP; PNI

Once Allen Ginsberg stopped to pee at a bookstore in New Jersey. Allen Ginsberg. Toi Derricotte. PBCAP

Once an ant. *Unknown.* RoPo

Once an ex-con told me. The Rape Poem. Tommi Avicolli. GLP

Once, and but once found in thy company. The Perfume. John Donne. *Fr.* Elegies. ESCV; NoSic; SeCP

Once and Upon. Madeline Gleason. NeAP

Once, as a child, I ate raspberries. And forgot. Raspberries. Laurence David Lerner. EBEV

Once as a child I loved to hop. Adam's Footprint. Vassar Miller. MT

Once as Congress sat in session. The Reagan. Richard Quick. FaBoPa

Once as I in my study sat and saw. The Hourglass. Joseph Beaumont. NOSC

Once as I travelled through a quiet evening. Egrets. Judith Wright. GoJo; OBAP

Once as I went by rail to Epping Street. The Wasp. John Davidson. FM

Once as it was morning and I was in the field. Poppies. Zalman Schneour, *tr. fr. Hebrew by* Ruth Finer Mintz. MHP

Once, [or Ons] as methought [or me thought], fortune me kissed [or kist or kyst]. Sir Thomas Wyatt. SiPSBD

(Lover Rejoiceth the Enjoying of His Love, The.) 08FaBoEn; AAS; BoLoP; SiPS

Once, as old Lord Gorbals motored. Lord Gorbals. Harry Graham. FaBoCo; PeLV

Once as we were sitting by. Spring 1942. Roy Fuller. LiTM; OxBTC; PAW

Once at a merry wedding feast. St. George Tucker. *Fr.* Cynic, The. NBLV; OBAL

Once at Swanage. Thomas Hardy. CBLP; FaBoPP

Once between us the Atlantic. Sundered. Israel Zangwill. TrJP

Once Bitten, Twice Bitten; Once Shy, Twice Shy. Peter Porter. FaBoMA

Once — but no matter when. A Chronicle. *Unknown.* BLPL; CBNP

(Life Story.) OBSP

Once by the Pacific. Robert Frost. CMoP; HAP; HeIP; LiTA; LiTM; MeMAP; MoAB; MoAmPo; NAAL-2; NOBA; PrIm; Son; TRP; VGW; WeW

Once came an exile, longing to be free. Blennerhassett's Island. Thomas Buchanan Read. *Fr.* New Pastoral, The. PAH

Once Cypris sent to Europa a sweet dream. Europa. Moschus, *tr. fr. Greek by* Barbara Hughes Fowler. HePo

Once Delpho read — sage Delpho, learned and wise. The Patrons of My Early Song. Mary Leapor. *Fr.* Epistle to Artemisia. ECWP

Once did my Philomel reflect on me. Sir John Davies. *Fr.* Sonnets to Philomel. SiPS

Once Did My Thoughts. *Unknown.* EBEV; ELP

Once did she hold the gorgeous east in fee. On the Extinction of the Venetian Republic. Wordsworth. EnRP; FaBoRV; GTBS; GTBS-P; NOBE; NoP; OBEV; OBNC; TrGrPo

Once down on my knees to growing plants. A Mood Apart. Robert Frost. OxBSP

Once, for a dare. After the Deluge. Wole Soyinka. HBAPE

Once for thin walls, once for the sound of time. (*LL*) Fall Wind. William Stafford. FoLa

Once fully enslaved, no nation, state, city of this earth, ever after ward resumes its liberty. (*LL*) To the States. Walt Whitman. CTC; NAAL-1; RaBo

Once, grave Laodicean profiteer. Lourenço Marques. Charles Eglington. PeSA; PeSAV

Once he followed simple rules. My Father's Wars. Colleen J. McElroy. BCF

Once he puts out the light. The Hermit Has a Visitor. Maxine W. Kumin. BoWoP

Once he will miss, twice he will miss. Death ("Once he will miss, twice he will miss.") *Unknown, tr. fr. Arabic by* E. Powys Mathers. *Fr.* Thousand and One Nights, The. AWP

Once heard, hear the voice: It's late! come home. (*LL*) What Voice at Moth-Hour. Robert Penn Warren. DiPo; ImGa; MT; SM

Once I am sure there's nothing going on. Church Going. Philip Larkin. CMoP; GTBS-P; HeIP; LiTM; MoBrPo; MoP; NAEL-2; NIP; NoAM; NoP; OAEL-2; Poetr; PPP; PrIm; SCV; SoSe; TFi; TwCP; UnPo

Once I belonged to Achaimenides. A Field. *Unknown, tr. fr. Greek by* Peter Jay. GrAn

Once I came across/ some beardless doctors. Strato, *tr. fr. Greek by* Thomas Meyer. GrAn

Once I courted a fair beauty bride. The Fair Beauty Bride. *Unknown.* AmFP

Once I cried for new songs to sing. I Sing No New Songs. Frank Marshall Davis. PoBA; PoNe

Once I entered. Like Ana. Nina Cassian, *tr. fr. Romanian by* Nina Cassina. PoSu

Once I followed horses. Thistledown. Denis Glover. *Fr.* Sings Harry. PeNZ

Once I got a postcard from the Fiji Islands. Jaan Kaplinski, *tr. fr. Estonian by* Jann Kaplinski, Riina Tamm, *and* Sam Hamill. TSaS

Once I heard an old bachelor say. The Bachelor's Complaint. *Unknown.* AmFP

Once I heard him play. At the Half-Note Café. Ira Sadoff. Jaz; NAmP90

Once I lay down with Hermione. Asclepiades, *tr. fr. Greek by* Sam Hamill. InMo

Once I learnt in wilful hour. On A Wife. Francis Burdett Money-Coutts. OxBSP

Once I liked pablum. Once. Siv Widerberg, *tr. fr. Swedish by* Verne Moberg. NTCP

Once I Lived in Cottonwood. *Unknown.* AmFP

Once I loved a sailor, who often enjoyed my charms. What'll the Neighbours Say? Sandra Kerr. AIW

Once I loved a spider. The Spider and the Ghost of the Fly. Vachel Lindsay. VGW

Once I Pass'd through a Populous City. Walt Whitman. AmPP; AnAmPo; NAAL-1; OxBA; RaBo; SAmP

Once I Pass'd through a populous city imprinting my brain. Once I Pass'd through a Populous City. Walt Whitman. AmPP; AnAmPo; NAAL-1; OxBA; RaBo; SAmP

Once I Played and Danced in My Parents' Kingdom. *Gond Oral Tradition, tr. by* V. Elwin *and* S. Hivale. WTO

Once I read a story. The Story. Dan Pagis, *tr. fr. Hebrew by* Stephen Mitchell. PoSu

Once I saw a little bird. Mother Goose. OxNR

(Little Bird, The.) ReMoGo

Once I saw a little bird going hop, hop, hop. *Unknown.* BoTP

Once I seen a human ruin. Ambrose Bierce. *Fr.* Devil's Dictionary, The. OBAL

Once I stood in a green bough. Portrait of the Father. Lindy Hough. IHMS

Once I Thought to Die for Love. *Unknown.* EIl

Once I was a boy and I sat in a meadow with flowers in it. Time Passes. R. P. Lister. NYBP

Once I was a grape nehi. Richwood. Bob Henry Baber. ETG

Once I was a little boy. The Foggy Dew. *Unknown.* OBET

Once I was a monarch's daughter. Once. *Unknown.* CH

Once I was a schoolboy and stayed at home with ease. The Smacksman. Sam Larner. OxBSS

Once I Was a Shepherd Boy. *Unknown.* OBET

Once I was a young horse all in my youthful prime. Poor Old Horse. *Unknown.* NTP; OBET

Once I was good like the Virgin Mary and the Minister's wife. The Scarlet Woman. Fenton Johnson. PoBA; PoNe

Once I was happy, but now I'm forlorn. The Man on the Flying Trapeze. *At. to* George Leybourne. BeLS; BLPA; FaBoBe

Once I was in love. Who's been exempted? Philodemus, *tr. fr. Greek by* William Moebius. GrAn

Once I was jealous of lovers. Now I am. The Valley. Stanley Moss. NYBP

Once I was reading Hesiod. Argentarius, *tr. fr. Greek by* Alistair Elliot. GrAn

Once/ I went for an ocean trip. On a Steamer. Dorothy W. Baruch. FaPON

Once I went through the lanes, over the sharp. Spring. V. Sackville-West. *Fr.* Land, The. PeHV

Once in a dream I saw the flowers. Paradise. Christina Rossetti. WGRP

Once, in a finesse of fiddles found I ecstasy. The Embankment [or Fantasia of a Fallen Gentleman]. T. E. Hulme. EBEV; FaBoMo; GTBS-P; OxBSP; OxBTC

Once, in a foreign country, I was suddenly ill. The Widening Spell of the Leaves. Larry Levis. NAmP90; PBCAP

Once in a hundred years the lemmings come. The Lemmings. John Masefield. CMoP; OBAP

Once in a Lifetime, Snow. Les A. Murray. CBAP

Once in a lifetime, we may see the veil. Midnight — September 19, 1881. John Boyle O'Reilly. PAH

Once in a saintly passion. Once in a Saintly Passion. James Thomson ("B.V."). FF; NOBVV

Once in a Saintly Passion. James Thomson ("B.V."). FF; NOBVV

Once in a While a Protest Poem. David B. Axelrod. InPK

Once in a while/ we'd find a patch. The Children. William Carlos Williams. SAmP

Once in Canandaigua, hitchhiking from Ann Arbor. Faces. John Ciardi. WeW

Once, in hiding, we went open-. In Hiding. Helen Degan Cohen. BTR

Once in Mexico an old man was. Visions. William Stafford. NoAM

Once in our lives,/ Let us drink to our wives. *Unknown.* FaBoEE

Once in Persia reigned a King. Even This Shall Pass Away. Theodore Tilton. BLPA; WGRP

Once in Royal David's City. Cecil Frances Alexander. OxBChV; PlP

Once in the dark of night. The Dark Night. St. John of the Cross, *tr. fr. Spanish.* STV, *tr. by* John Frederick Nims; WeW, *tr. by* John Frederick Nims

(Obscure Night of the Soul, The.) AWP, *tr. by* Arthur Symons; OBMV, *tr. by* Arthur Symons

Once in the dear dead days beyond recall. Love's Old Sweet Song. G. Clifton Bingham. FaBoBe

Once, in the Giant's Ring, I closed my eyes. Home. Frank Ormsby. PBCIP; PNI

Once in the Jurassic, about 150 million years ago. Smokey the Bear Sutra. Gary Snyder. MAT; PoBeRe

Once in the Phoenix tower the phoenix made her nest. On Climbing the Phoenix Tower at Chinling. Li Po, *tr. fr. Chinese by* Robert Payne. TAL

Once in the winter. The Forsaken. Duncan Campbell Scott. NOBC

Once, in this Tuscan garden, noon's huge ball. A Snail's Derby. Eugene Lee-Hamilton. FM

Once in this vast sky. The Sky Is Vast. Pramila Khadun, *tr. fr. French.* TSaS

Once it had gorged itself. On a Pig's Head. Charles Tomlinson. NoAM

Once, it happened I'd been dining, on my couch I slept reclining. The Goblin Goose. *Unknown.* FaBoPa

Once it smiled a silent dell. The Valley of Unrest. Poe. AmPP; NAAL-1; PoEL-4

Once it was cards on the table. In Memory of Elizabeth Kearney, Blasket-Islander. Michael Davitt, *tr. fr. Irish by the author.* BiHa

Once it was enough simply. Reaching the Horizon. Robert Mezey. NaP

Once, long ago. (*LL*) Brooms. Charles Simic. AmPA; NNaP, *early vers.*

Once, long ago, a friend gave me a book. The Gift. Margaret E. Bruner. PoToHe

Once, long ago, set close beside a wood. Chaucer. *See* Poore [*or* Povre] widwe [*or* widow], somdel [*or* somedeal *or* somedel] stape in age, A.

Once looked Gudrun. Gudrun Laments over Sigurd. *Unknown, tr. by* William Morris *and* Eirikr Magnusson. *Fr.* Elder Edda, The. AWP; OBVE

Once Mr. Daddy Long-legs. The Daddy Long-legs and the Fly. Edward Lear. CBNP

Once More. Forugh Farrokhzad, *tr. by* Jascha Kessler *and* Amin Banani. BoWoP

Once More a-Lumbering Go. *Unknown.* AmFP

Once more around should do it, the man confided. Flight of the Roller Coaster. Raymond Souster. NOBC

Once more beneath my thumb the globe turns. Childhood. Donald Justice. AnAn; LCAP

Once more by the brook the alder leaves. Hayden Carruth. NNaP

Once more, Cesario. Shakespeare. *Fr.* Twelfth Night. SCV

Once More Fields and Gardens. T'ao Ch'ien, *tr. fr. Chinese by* Amy Lowell *and* Florence Ayscough. AWP

Once more I came to Sarum Close. The Cathedral Close. Coventry Patmore. *Fr.* Angel in the House, The. EBVV
(Salisbury; the Cathedral Close.) EBVV; FaBoPP

Once more I come to the white page of art. The Cost of Seriousness. Peter Porter. NoAM

Once more I move among you, dear familiar places. Amagansett Beach Revisited. John Hall Wheelock. NYBP

Once more I visited the place. Female's Lamentations, The; or, The Village in Mourning. Hannah Wallis. ECWP

Once more, listening to the wind and rain. The Return. Arna Bontemps. CDC; PoBA; PoNe

Once more my deeper life goes on with more strength. Moving Ahead. Rainer Maria Rilke, *tr. fr. German by* Robert Bly. NU

Once More, O Lord. George Washington Doane. AH

Once More, Our God, Vouchsafe to Shine! Samuel Sewall. AH

Once, more than you wanted. To My Daughter Riding in the Circus Parade. Joan LaBombard. GOYP

Once more the Ancient Wonder. Easter, 1923. John G. Neihardt. OHIP

Once more the changed year's turning wheel returns. Barren Spring. Dante Gabriel Rossetti. *Fr.* House of Life, The. EBVV; IMW; NoP; OAEL-2; OBNC; PoEL-5

Once more the cuckoo's call I hear. Spring. Aubrey Thomas De Vere. *Fr.* Year of Sorrow, A. OBNC

Once more the flower of Essex is marching to the wars. Essex Regiment March. George Edward Woodberry. PAH

Once more the leaves. Seattle, Autumn, 1933. Alfred Encarnacion. OpBo

Once more the liberal year laughs out. Harvest Hymn. Whittier. *Fr.* For an Autumn Festival. OHIP

Once more the perfect pattern falls asleep. Replica, the. Vernon Watkins. AngWe

Once More, the Round. Theodore Roethke. ArLo

Once more the searchlights beckon from the night. Return. John Ciardi. ArOW

Once more the storm is howling, and half hid. A Prayer for My Daughter. W. B. Yeats. BLPL; CMoP; HAP; LiTB; LiTM; MeMBP; MoAB; MoP; NAEL-2; NAs; NoAM; NoP; OxBTC; PoA; PoLF; PoRA; PrIm; RaBo; TEP; TFi

Once more, through God's high will and grace. Spring. Aubrey Thomas De Vere. *Fr.* Year of Sorrow, A. PeIV

Once more upon the breach, dear friends, once more. Shakespeare. *Fr.* King Henry V. EBEvV; FaBV; OxAEP-1
(Blast of War, The.) TrGrPo
(Henry V at the Siege of Harfleur.) PAW

Once more upon the waters! yet once more! Byron. *Fr.* Childe Harold's Pilgrimage. FHYEP, *shorter sel.*

Once more we are alone, among the bathers. "You Must Know Everything." Allen Grossman. *Fr.* Ether Dome (an Entertainment), The. BAP-91

Once Musing as I Sat. Barnabe Googe. NoP

Once, my braids swung heavy as ropes. The Butcher's Wife. Louise Erdrich. HATNAP

Once, my father got invited. The Age of Reason. Michael van Walleghen. NAmP90

Once my parents were older. Chiyojo, *tr. fr. Japanese by* David Ray. BoWoP

Once noble custom was: by blood on battleground. The Old Nobility. Friedrich von Logau, *tr. fr. German.* GePo, *tr. by* George C. Schoolfield

Once older than me, now certainly younger. A Portrait by Bronzino. Maura Stanton. NAmP90

Once on a charger there was laid. Salome. Charles Lamb. ChIV-2

Once on a morning of sweet recreation. The Blackbird. *Unknown.* NOIV

Once on a time, a monarch, tired with whooping. The Apple Dumplings and a King. "Peter Pindar." OBSV

Once on a time a thousand different men. James Henry. NOBVV

Once on a time did Eucritus and I. Harvest-Home. Theocritus [*or* Theokritus], *tr. by* Charles Stuart Calverley. *Fr.* Idylls. AWP
(There was a time when Eucritus and I were going.) HePo, *tr. by* Barbara Hughes Fowler

Once on a time I used to be. Harlot's Catch. Robert Nichols. ErPo; FaBoTw

Once on a time, it came to pass. The Fable of the Piece of Glass and the Piece of Ice. John Hookham Frere. OxBChV

Once on a time, some centuries ago. Monk of Casal-Maggiore, The (The Sicilian's Tale). Longfellow. *Fr.* Tales of a Wayside Inn. AmPP; OxBA

Once on a time there was a pool. Rev. Homer Wilbur's "Festina Lente." James Russell Lowell. *Fr.* Biglow Papers, The. OBAL

Once, once, in Washington. Patriotic Tour and Postulate of Joy. Robert Penn Warren. AiP; NYBP

Once . . . once upon a time. Martha. Walter de la Mare. MoBrPo

Once, one of my students read a book we had. Untitled Poem. Alan Dugan. CAPP

Once only by the garden gate. Youth and Love. Robert Louis Stevenson. PFP

Once or twice he eyed me oddly. Once. Temptations of St. Antony by His Housekeeper. Elizabeth Smither. PeNZ

Once-over, The. Paul Blackburn. ErPo; NeAP; PoM

Once, playing cricket, beneath a toast-dry hill. Curriculum Vitae. Robert Gray. NOBAu

Once riding in Old Baltimore. Incident. Countee Cullen. BPo; CDC; FF; NAAL-2; NoAM; NTCP; OBCA; PoBA; Poetr; PoNe; VGW

Once she was the reason for his festivals. What Her Girl Friend Said, When the Woman Was About to Take Back Her Unfaithful Husband. Orampokiyar, *tr. fr. Tamil by* A. K. Ramanujan. PLW

Once, so long ago. For Paddy Mac. Padraic Fallon. CIP; IIP

Once some people were visiting Chekhov. Chocolates. Louis Simpson. InPS; Mes; OxBC

Once the Days. Denis Glover. *Fr.* Sings Harry. PeNZ

Once, the mighty waves of ocean. The Precious Pearl. Priscilla Jane Thompson. CBWP-2

Once the nation's chief was honored by the company of one. A Notable Dinner. L. A. J. Moorer. CBWP-3

Once the Sole Province. Douglas Crase. EOEF

Once the stone god turned its. For D. S. Christine Craig. AIW

Once the voice has quietly spoken, every knight must ride alone. Song of the Quest. W. H. Auden. *Fr.* Man of La Mancha. AnAn

Once the world was waiting for a song. The History of Poetry. Peter Cooley. NAmP90

Once There Came a Man. Stephen Crane. AnAmPo

Once there lived a little man. *Unknown.* BoTP

Once there was a bridegroom named Mr Ormantude whose. The Strange Case of Mr. Ormantude's Bride. Ogden Nash. OxBM

Once there was a fence here. Former Barn Lot. Mark Van Doren. FaBV; MoAmPo; PDV

Once there was a little boy. Switch on the Night. Ray Bradbury. OBSP

Once there was a little boy whose name was Robert Reese. An Overworked Elocutionist. Carolyn Wells. BLPA; BLPL

Once there was a little Kitty. Kitty. Elizabeth Payson Prentiss. BoTP; MoShBr

Once there was a man named Mr. Artesian and his activity was tremendous. Mr. Artesian's Conscientiousness. Ogden Nash. NBLV

Once there was a snowman. The Snowman. *Unknown.* OTCP

Once there was a woman went out to pick beans. The Hairy Toe. *Unknown.* OBSP; PYC

Once there was an elephant. Eletelephony. Laura E. Richards. FaPON; GoJo; ImGa; MoShBr; NBLV; NTCP; OBCA; OxBChV; PDV; PYC; SiSoPo

Once there were none and the dark air was dumb. The Nightingales. Harri Webb. AngWe

Once there were 3 little Indian girls. Charité Espérance et Foi. Earle Birney. OxBC

Once there were three stones sitting in a patch of soft. The Death of Potchikoo. Louise Erdrich. Fr. Old Man Potchikoo. HATNAP

Once this soft turf, this rivulet's sands. The Battle-Field. Bryant. AnAmPo; PoLF

Once to Every Man and Nation. James Russell Lowell. Fr. Present Crisis, The. FaPoR

Once to life I said, yes! To Life I Said Yes. Chaim Grade, tr. fr. Yiddish by Joseph Leftwich. TrJP

Once to my Fancy's hall a stranger came. A New Sculptor. Julia Ward Howe. AmWP

Once, Twice, Thrice. Unknown. ErPo

Once, twice, thrice/ I give thee warning. Unknown. OxNR

Once up u hurl a stone. Mike 65. Lennox Raphael. PoBA

Once upon a colony. Can. Hist. Earle Birney. OxBC

Once upon a midnight dreary, eerie, scary. Ravin's of Piute Poet Poe. C. L. Edson. BXAP

Once upon a midnight dreary, while I pondered [or ponder'd], weak and weary. The Raven. Poe. AmPP; AnAmPo; BeLS; BLPA; CH; CoGr; EBEvV; EBNV; FaBoBe; FaBoCh; FaBV; GGP; GN; GoJo; HeIP; ImGa; LiTA; NAAL-1; NIP; NOBA; OBCA; OBNV; OxBA; PoRA; PWR; TAP; TFi; UV, abr.; VPP; WBLP

Once upon a Time. Gabriel Okara. PBA

Once upon a time/ I composed a witty rhyme. The Minstrel's Last Lay. John Barth. OBAL

Once upon a time,/ In the realm of Dewajing. Zong Belegt Baatar. Mongol Oral Tradition, tr. by C. R. Bawden. WTO

Once upon a time/ Old Mr. Pyme. Mr. Pyme. Harry Behn. PDV

Once upon a time/ I caught a little rhyme. Catch a Little Rhyme. Eve Merriam. OBCA; PDV

Once upon a time/ there was a lonely wolf. János Pilinszky, tr. fr. Hungarian by Ted Hughes and János Csokits. OBVE; PoSu; RB

Once upon a time/ A monkey drank some wine. Unknown. RoPo

Once upon a time, children. Storytime. Judith Nicholls. OBSP

Once upon a time I was. To the Tune "The Fall of a Little Wild Goose." Huang O, tr. fr. Chinese by Kenneth Rexroth and Ling Chung. AIW; WPC; WPOW

Once upon a time in California. A Friend of the Family. Louis Simpson. NNaP

Once upon a time, the goddesses settled down. First Merseburg Spell. Unknown, tr. fr. German by Carroll Hightower. GePo

Once upon a time there was a girl called Annabell. Annabell and the Witches. Mick Gowar. OBSP

Once upon a time there was a number. Forgetful Number. Vasco [or Vasko] Popa, tr. fr. Serbo-Croatian. Fr. Yawn of Yawns, The. AnRep, tr. by Charles Simic; HSix, tr. by Charles Simic

Once upon a time there was a story. The Story of a Story. Vasco [or Vasko] Popa, tr. fr. Serbo-Croatian by Anne Pennington. CBNP

Once upon a time there was a tale. The Tale About a Tale. Vasco [or Vasko] Popa, tr. fr. Serbo-Croatian. Fr. Yawn of Yawns, The. AnRep, tr. by Charles Simic; HSix

Once upon a time there was a triangle. A Wise Triangle. Vasco [or Vasko] Popa, tr. fr. Serbo-Croatian. Fr. Yawn of Yawns, The. CBNP, tr. by Anne Pennington and Charles Simic; CoGr, tr. by Anne Pennington and Charles Simic; PoSu, tr. by Anne Pennington

Once upon a time there was a yawn. The Yawn of Yawns. Vasco [or Vasko] Popa, tr. fr. Serbo-Croatian. Fr. Yawn of Yawns, The. AnRep, tr. by Charles Simic; PoSu, tr. by Anne Pennington

Once upon a time there was an error. Proud Error. Vasco [or Vasko] Popa, tr. fr. Serbo-Croatian. Fr. Yawn of Yawns, The. AnRep, tr. by Charles Simic; HSix, tr. by Charles Simic

Once upon a time there was an infinity of echoes. Petrified Echoes. Vasco [or Vasko] Popa, tr. fr. Serbo-Croatian. Fr. Yawn of Yawns, The. PoSu, tr. by Anne Pennington

Once upon a time there was an Italian. Columbus. Ogden Nash. NoP

Once upon a time there were so many echoes. Echo Turned to Stone. Vasco [or Vasko] Popa, tr. fr. Serbo-Croatian by Charles Simic. AnRep

Once upon a time there were three little foxes. The Three Foxes. A. A. Milne. GoJo; GrPl; MoShBr; OxBChV

Once, walking home, I passed beneath a tree. The Music of a Tree. W. J. Turner. MoBrPo

Once, walking in the woods. Getting at the Root of the Matter. Henry Taylor. BXAP

Once was every woman the witch. Witches. Ted Hughes. GoYe

Once, we dreamed. Uncharted. Mary E. O'Donnell. NWP

Once we dreamed of eagles. Reading Indian Poetry. Ramona Wilson. VoR

Once we had a knocker. Lazy. Lu Yu, tr. fr. Chinese by Kenneth Rexroth. OHMPC

Once we had a little retriever. Pets. Daniel Pettiward. ZA

Once when by Trent's pellucid streams. Elves and Fairies. John Gilbert Cooper. Fr. Call of Aristippus, The. ECEV

Once when Grandma moved her hand. A Railroad Happening. Daniil Kharms, tr. fr. Russian by Vladimir Markov and Merrill Sparks. CBNP

Once, when Heracles was ten months old, Alcmena. Little Heracles. Theocritus [or Theokritus], tr. fr. Greek by Barbara Hughes Fowler. Fr. Idylls. HePo

Once when I walked into a room. Between Ourselves. Audre Lorde. WPOW

Once when I was coming from art class they surprised me. Daryl Hine. Fr. March. GLP

Once when I was in the fifth grade. The Meanest Gang in the Bronx. Terence Winch. BCF

Once when I was very scared. Charlotte Zolotow. NTCP

Once when I was young, Juanito. The Mother's Tale. Ai. BCF

Once, when midnight smote the air. On Those That Hated The Playboy of the Western World. W. B. Yeats. NOIV

Once when my heart was passion free. Communion. John Banister Tabb. WGRP

Once when our eyes were clean as noon, our rooms. Thomas Merton. See "This beginning of miracles did."

Once when the moon was out about three quarters. White Clover. Marvin Bell. CAPP; VCAP

Once when the snow of the year was beginning to fall. The Runaway. Robert Frost. AWP; CH; CoGr; FaBoCh; FaPON; GoJo; MoAB; MoAmPo; PDV; SAmP; TwCP; VGW

Once, when their hearts were wild with joy. On Harting Down. T. Sturge Moore. OxBTC

Once when young I lay and listened. To the Tune "The Fair Maid of Yu." Chiang Chieh, tr. fr. Chinese by Kenneth Rexroth. OHMPC

Once, with a certain pride, we kept attempts. Spot the Ball. Frank Ormsby. CIP; PBCIP; PNI

Once, years after your death, I dreamt. The Dream. Irving Feldman. VCAP

Once you said joking slyly, "If I'm killed." The Faithful. Jane Cooper. SM

Once you shone among the living as the morning star. Plato. OBD

Once your name was Bimbircokak. Dear Husband. Yamba Ouloguem, tr. fr. French by Ellen Conroy Kennedy. NegPo

Ondt and the Gracehoper, The. James Joyce. Fr. Finnegans Wake. BIrV

One, The. Gillian Conoley. Jaz

One, The. Patrick Kavanagh. MoBrPo; TIRV

One. Carolyn M. Rodgers. BPo

One . . . two . . . three . . . four. (LL) Long canoe, The. Robert Silliman Hillyer. FaPON; ImGa

One after another. Stories and Poems. Susan Griffin. CrSp

One after the other. Granada (1000 A.D.). Abu Ishaq al-Ilbin, tr. fr. Arabic by Omar S. Pound. ArPe

One afternoon in my room. A True Story. Marvin Bell. SV

One afternoon the last week in April. Axe Handles. Gary Snyder. CAPP; NoAM; PoBeRe; VCAP

One among friends who stood above your grave. Auden's Funeral. Stephen Spender. AnAn

One, and then another, they settled before me like flakes of air. Mining in Killdeer Alley. Dabney Stuart. MT

One-And-Twenty, sels. Samuel Johnson. "Wealth, my lad, was made to wander." OtMeF

One-and-Twenty. Samuel Johnson. See Long-expected one and twenty.

One-and-Twenty. Unknown. AmFP

One arch of the sky. Love in Labrador. Carl Sandburg. VGW

One arm hooked around the frayed strap. Yellow Light. Garrett Kaoru Hongo. InPS; OpBo

One-Armed Man in the Undergrowth, The. Bertolt Brecht, tr. fr. German by Derek Bowman. PoSu

One Art. Elizabeth Bishop. CAPP; DiPo; HAP; NAAL-2; NALW; NoAM; PFP; PoE; SM; SoSe; VCAP

One asked a madman if a wife he had. A Mad Answer of a Madman. Robert Hayman. FF

One asked a sign from God; and day by day. The Seekers. Victor Starbuck. WGRP

One assumes the poets' songs will be denied. (LL) On the Death of Ludwig Erhard. Hal Colebatch. NOBAu

One day we took our lunches. The Circus Parade. Katharine Pyle. OBCA

One day, when childhood tumbled the spongy tufts. Crane. Joseph Langland. NYBP

One day when Coyote. One for Coyote. *Unknown, tr. fr. Skagit Indian by* Carl Cary. STP

One day when I was a child, long ago. Grace Paley. NMM

One day, when sunny fields lay warm and still. Covert. Helen Hunt Jackson. AmWP

One day, while in a lonesome grove. Newberry. *Unknown.* AmFP

One day you finally knew. The Journey. Mary Oliver. CrSp

One day/ You gonna walk in this house. Seduction. Nikki Giovanni. NMM

One day, you wake. Blue. Harry Clifton. IB

One day you'll have to go to the City of the Dead. Elephants May Parade before Your House. *Gond Oral Tradition, tr. by* V. Elwin *and* S. Hivale. WTO

One deaf man went to law with. Nicarchus of Alexandria. *tr. fr. Greek by* Kenneth Rexroth. PGA

One Desiring Me to Read, But Slept It Out, Wakening. George Daniel. OxBSP

One died, and the soul was wrenched out. Street Musicians. John Ashbery. CAPP; HCAP

One dignity delays for all. Emily Dickinson. MeMAP

One disappearing, The. The Fool. Novica Tadic, *tr. fr. Serbo-Croatian by* Charles Simic. HSix

One door alone is shut, one chamber still. (LL) Gone. Mary Elizabeth Coleridge. OBEV; OBNC

One doth not stroke me, nor the other strike. (LL) To Fool, or Knave. Ben Jonson. FaBoEE; NoP

One dove has its head turned. Girl with Doves. Stephen Gray. PeSA

One dripping trophy! (LL) In a Garret. Herman Melville. AnAmPo; OBAL

One duck stood on my toes. Feeding Ducks. Norman MacCaig. OxBS

I, 8. "Lydia, in Heavens Name" ("Lydia, dic, per omnes.") Horace, *tr. by* Sir Richard Fanshawe. *Fr. Odes.* OBVE

I, 11. "Seek not, Leuconöe, to know how long you're going to live yet." Horace, *tr. fr. Latin by* Austin Dobson. *Fr. Odes.*

One end is moo, the other, milk. (LL) The Cow. Ogden Nash. NBLV; NoP; RB

One ends in ignominy because one begins mistakenly. Precious Mettle. Lewis Warsh. UL

One-erum, two-erum. *Unknown.* OxNR

One-ery, Ore-ery, Ickery, Ann. *Unknown. Fr. Counting-out Rhymes.* CBNP; FaPON; ImGa; OxNR

One-ery, two-ery, tickery, seven. *Unknown.* OxNR

One-ery, two-ery/ Ziccary zan. One-ery, Two-ery. *Unknown.* CBNP; ISE

One Evening. Ljubomir Simovic, *tr. fr. Serbo-Croatian by* Charles Simic. HSix

One evening a young lady fair, her estate rode out to see. On the Banks of Salee. *Unknown.* AmFP

One evening as the sun went down [*or* when the sun was low]. The Big Rock Candy Mountains. *Unknown.* AmFP; ChTr; GBP; OBAL; TTTS, *shorter vers.*

One evening bright stars they were shining. The Brooklyn Theater Fire. *Unknown.* AmFP

One evening in August, the light already failing. Elegy for the Unknown Soldier. Michael O'Loughlin. PBCIP

One evening in February I came near to dying here. Alone. Tomas Tranströmer, *tr. fr. Swedish by* Robin Fulton. PWE

One evening in November I happened for to stray. Johnny Carroll's Camp. *Unknown.* AmFP

One evening last June as I rambled. On the Banks of the Little Eau Pleine. *Unknown.* AmFP

One evening (surely I was led by her). On Ullswater. Wordsworth. *Fr.* Prelude [*or*, Growth of a Poet's Mind], The. CH; EnRP; FaBoPP; GN; HAP; NOBE; NoP; NU; OAEL-2; OBNC; OxAEP-2; PoE; RB; SCV

One evening, when the sun was just gone down. On the Death of Old Bennet the News-Crier. *Unknown.* NOEC

One evening when we were lounging in his apartment in a relaxed mood. Rain. Anselm Hollo. PoM

One evening, while the cooler shade she sought. Dryden. *Fr.* Hind and the Panther, The. PoEL-3

One ever hangs where shelled roads part. At a Calvary Near the Ancre. Wilfred Owen. ChIV-2

One everlasting night. (LL) Sun [*or* Sunne] may set and rise, The. Sir Walter Ralegh, *after the Latin of* Catullus. FaBoEE; NoSic; OBVE

One ewe. Shepherd's Night Count. Jane Yolen. TLR

One eye without a head to wear it. On the Farther Wall, Marc Chagall. Phyllis McGinley. *Fr.* Spectator's Guide to Contemporary Art. OBSV

One Eyed Black Man in Nebraska. Sam Cornish. PoBA

One-Eyed Seller of Arrows: Creature came shuffling where there sat, A. Unknown, formerly at. to Cynewulf, *tr. fr. Anglo-Saxon. Fr.* Riddles (Exeter Book). ASW, *tr. by* Kevin Crossley-Holland

One face looks out from all his canvases. In an Artist's Studio. Christina Rossetti. NAEL-2; NALW; NoP; Poetr

One Faith and No Faith. Friedrich von Logau, *tr. fr. German.* GePo, *tr. by* George C. Schoolfield

One fall not far from Ozark, Arkansas. The Narrative Hooper and L.D.O. Sestina with a Long Last Line. James Whitehead. HoPM

One fantee wave. Edith Sitwell. *Fr.* Gold Coast Customs. OBMV

One fatal mistake that is made today is gossip. Gossip. Mrs. Henry Linden. CBWP-4

One fear is that. September Town. Anne Carson. *Fr.* Life of Towns, The. BAP-90

One feather is a bird. The Voice. Theodore Roethke. VGW

One Final Fling. Kemal Khojandi, *tr. fr. Persian by* Omar S. Pound. ArPe

One finds in every boarding school. "Tropicals." René Maran, *tr. fr. French by* Ellen Conroy Kennedy. NegPo

One Fine Day. János Pilinszky, *tr. fr. Hungarian by* Peter Jay. PoSu

One fine day in the middle of the night. *Unknown.* ISE

One fine morning, in the country on a very gentle people. Royalty. Rimbaud, *tr. fr. French by* Enid Rhodes Peschal. SOTW

One fine night in a witch's cavern. Gobbolino, the Witch's Cat. G. C. Westcott. CRH

One-fingering my way through. Monk's Mood. Sascha Feinstein. Jaz

One Flesh. Elizabeth Jennings. AIW; FaBoWP; OxAEP-2; OxBTC; PBWP

One flew over the cuckoo's nest. (LL) Hinty, minty, cuty, corn. *Unknown.* FaPON; ImGa

One Flight Up. Bob Holman. UL

One flower at a time, please. Bouquets. Robert Francis. ArNa

One flutter of memory, then all becomes. Burning the Letters. Gwendolyn Grew. HoPM

One Foot in Eden. Edwin Muir. CMoP; GTBS-P; MeMBP; NoAM; NOBE; OPOP

One foot in Eden still, I stand. One Foot in Eden. Edwin Muir. CMoP; GTBS-P; MeMBP; NoAM; NOBE; OPOP

One Foot in the Door. Anne Elder. CBAP

One for another were designed. (LL) To Amoret, Walking in a Starry Evening. Henry Vaughan. BeJo

One for Coyote. *Unknown, tr. fr. Skagit Indian by* Carl Cary. STP

One for money. *Unknown.* OxNR
  (One for the money. RoPo

One for sorrow, two for joy. *Unknown.* OxNR

One for the cutworm. *Unknown.* RoPo

One for the heart, one for the head. (LL) Forked Tongue. Helen Ruggieri. LoHo

One for [the] money. *Unknown. See* One for money.

One for the Road. Martin Edmunds. UTF

One forfeit more from life the current claimed. At the Discharge of Cannon Rise the Drowned. Hubert Witheford. PeNZ

One Friday morn when we set sail. The Mermaid. *Unknown.* CH; ESPB

One from One Leaves Two, sels. Ogden Nash.
  "I pray the Lord my soul to take." NBLV

One Furrow, The. R. S. Thomas. HoPM; OxBC

One garland. Divorcing. Denise Levertov. NALW

One Generation Passeth Away. Jones Very. ChIV-1

One gets a wife, one gets a house. The Cat. Ogden Nash. CRH; OFC

One Girl. Sappho, *tr. fr. Greek by* Dante Gabriel Rossetti. AWP

One Girl at the Boys Party, The. Sharon Olds. InPK

One good crucifixion and he rose from the dead. Easter. C. H. Sisson. OxBSP

One good thing about music. Trenchtown Rock. Bob Marley. PBCV

One goodness ruleth by its single will. Alcuin, *tr. fr. Latin by* Helen Waddell. MLL

One got peace of heart at last, the dark march over. After War. Ivor Gurney. OxBSP

One grand boulevard with trees. Recipe for Happiness Khabarovsk or Anyplace. Lawrence Ferlinghetti. ArLo

One granite ridge. Piute Creek. Gary Snyder. CoAP; FoLa; NAAL-2; NaP; NOBA

One great truth in life I've found. Those We Love the Best. Ella Wheeler Wilcox. PoToHe

One had a lovely face. Memory. W. B. Yeats. BIrV; PoE

One half of me was up and dressed. The Gentle Check. Joseph Beaumont. NOSC

One hand is smaller than the other. It. Man with One Small Hand. P. K. Page. MoCV

One hand, two hands. Nothing more. Sphinxes Inclined to Be. Olga Orozco, *tr. fr. Spanish by* Leslie Keffer. WPOW

One hand washes the other. (*LL*) He Was a Man of Jokes outside Office. Oswald Basize Dube. PeSAV

One Happy Moment. Dryden. *See* No, No, Poor Suffering Heart.

One Happy Swede. Donna Shwarzrock. SWP

One Hard Look. Robert Graves. *See* Small gnats that fly.

One has a feeling it is all coming to an end. The Feeling. William Bronk. VGW

One, he loves; two, he loves. *Unknown*. ReMoGo

One heart should harden and another bleed. (*LL*) To One Unequally Matched. Walter Savage Landor. CBLP

One heifer and one fleecy sheep. Aristeides. Antipater of Sidon, *tr. fr. Greek by* Charles Whibley. AWP

One held the resined pinebranch. Altamira. William Hart-Smith. FaBoMA

One hesitates to bring a child into this world without fixing. Alta. *Fr.* 3 : 6. CrSp

One higher-pitched doth set his soaring thought. Joseph Hall. *Fr.* Virgidemiarum. EPCY

One holy church of God appears. The Church Universal. Samuel Longfellow. WGRP

One Home. William Stafford. CoAP; VGW

One Hope, The. Dante Gabriel Rossetti. *Fr.* House of Life, The. NAEL-2; OAEL-2; PFP

One-horned Ewe, The. *Unknown*. GBP

One Horse Chay, The. *Unknown*. OxBoLi

One hue of our flag is taken. "Orpheus C. Kerr." *Fr.* Rejected "National Hymns," The. OBAL

One hugs me. In the Village of My Forefathers. Vasco [*or* Vasko] Popa, *tr. fr. Serbo-Croatian. Fr.* Raw Flesh. PoSu, *tr. by* Anne Pennington 108 Tales of a Po 'Buckra, *sels.* Will Inman. "Dark brother touches me, The." GLP

One hundred feet from off the ground. Long-Suffering of God. Christopher Smart. *Fr.* Hymns for the Amusement of Children. NOCV 104. Alta. CrSp

104 Boulevard Saint-Germain. Kenneth Pitchford. NYBP

One Hundred Haiku in Free Form, *sels.* Hosai, *tr. fr. Japanese by* Hiroaki Sato.

One Hundred Lines for the Coast. Kojo Laing. HBAPE

One hundred men. Voices. Ronald William Pies. BTR

107 Poems. Roy Fisher. VaA

110 Year Old House. Ed Ochester. Poetsp

One I love. *Unknown*. OxNR; RoPo

One I Love Is Gone Away, The. *Unknown*. MeEL

One . . . / I smelt the weird Atlantic. Thomas Kinsella. *See* I . . . /One . . . / I smelt the weird Atlantic.

One imagines the lives of the Prince. Winter in Étienburgh. Stephen Parker. NYBP

One in the boat cried out. The Door. L. A. G. Strong. MoBrPo

One inch of love is an inch of ashes. (*LL*) East wind sighs, the fine rains come, The. Li Shang-yin. PLT

One Inch Tall. Shel Silverstein. OBCA

One instant is eternity. Wu-Men, *tr. fr. Chinese by* Stephen Mitchell. EnlH

One is a bitch with stinking. The Furies. Donald Justice. AnAn

One is a child and clings and slowly grows. The Green Wall. Rachel Hadas. UnDi

One is always nearer by not keeping still. (*LL*) On the Move. Thom Gunn. CMoP; HAP; LiTM; NoP; OAEL-2; OxAEP-2; OxBTC; PoE; PPP; TRP; TwCP

One is an ex-professor of biology. Dykes in the Garden. Sharon Barba. PeHV

One is enough, she cried. Technicalities for Jack Spicer. Philip Whalen. PoM

One is in the cellar. Maids. Aleksandar Ristovic, *tr. fr. Serbo-Croatian by* Charles Simic. HSix

One is not hale until one inhales. On Apples. David Ross. NYBP

One is reminded of a certain person. Kite Poem. James Merrill. TwCP

One is so seldom struck by lightning. For the Poet Who Said Poets Are Struck by Lightning Only Two or Three Times. Peter Klappert. NBLV

One keeps searchest for me. The Secret. Mary Morison Webster. PeSA

One king's daughter said to anither. Sheath and Knife. *Unknown*. CH; ESPB

One kitchen match to light her way back. (*LL*) The Crossroads. Carol Moldaw. UTF

One knight loves both, and both in thee remain. (*LL*) To His Friend Master R.L., In Praise of Music and Poetry. Richard Barnfield. AAS; EIL; EPCY; Son

One Knows Not What One Is. "Angelus Silesius," *tr. fr. German. Fr.* Cherubical Wanderer, The. GePo, *tr. by* George C. Schoolfield

One-l lama, The. Ogden Nash. FaBoCh (Lama, The.) FaPON; FiBHP

One last look at your hills, Lysander. Learning Destiny. Herman Charles Bosman. PeSA

One Last Word. John Glassco. NOBC

One late spring evening in Bohemia. The Cloud. Edwin Muir. OBTV

One Leaf. David Ignatow. EaPr

One leaf left on a branch. One Leaf. David Ignatow. EaPr

One Leg. *Unknown*. NTP

One Leg and Peers. Tim Longville. VaA

One leg in front of the other. One Leg. *Unknown*. NTP

One-legged Man, The. Siegfried Sassoon. CMoP

One-legged starling pecks at dust, The. One Leg and Peers. Tim Longville. VaA

One lesson from the cleanlier beast. (*LL*) A Quarrelsome Bishop. Walter Savage Landor. FaBoEE

One lesson, Nature, let me learn of [*or* from] thee. Quiet Work. Matthew Arnold. FaBoBe; TrGrPo

One Life. Dinah Butler. AIW

One Life. Andrew Motion. SCBI

One little dicky-bird. Ten Little Dicky-Birds. A. W. I. Baldwin. BoTP

One little Indian boy making a canoe. Ten Little Indian Boys. M. M. Hutchinson. BoTP

One little mess of whelks, so he may 'scape!. (*LL*) Caliban upon Setebos; or, Natural Theology in the Island. Robert Browning. AWP; EBEV; EnVR; FHYEP; NAEL-2; NOBVV; NoP; OAEL-2; OxAEP-2; PeVV; WGRP

One little noise of life remained — I heard. On the Eclipse of the Moon of October 1865. Charles Tennyson Turner. OBNC

One looks from the train. The Orient Express. Randall Jarrell. CMoP; CoAP; NOBA; PoE

One Lost, The. Isaac Rosenberg. MoBrPo

One lovely summer afternoon when balmy breezes blew. To Clements' Ferry. Josephine D. Henderson Heard. CBWP-4

One man/ Two times larger than life. Untranslatable Factual Items. E. L. T. Mesens, *tr. fr. French*. CBNP

One man except, the only son of light. The Flood. Milton. *Fr.* Paradise Lost. EPCY; NOSC

One man in a thousand, Solomon says. The Thousandth Man. Kipling. ArLo; FaPoB

One man shall smile one day and say goodbye. Cambodia. James Fenton. SCBI

One Man's Family. Rosemary Catacalos. AfAz

One Man's Wife. Philip Booth. VGW

One midnight, after a day when lilies. Digging. Donald Hall. CAPP

One midnight, deep in starlight still. Bankrupt. Cortlandt W. Sayres. PoLF; PoToHe

One midnight, old D. G. Rossetti. Victor Gray. PeLi

One might as well conceive this story in the cirrose. Richard Kenney. *Fr.* Encantadas, The. EOEF

One Minute of Night Sky. John Engman. NAmP90

One Mr. B,/ A joker he. Repartée. Charles Follen Adams. OBAL

One misty, moisty morning. Mother Goose. FaBoBe; OxNR

One misty moisty morning. *Unknown*. BoTP; ReMoGo

One Modern Poet. Carl Sandburg. OBAL

One moment past our bodies cast. Morning Song in the Jungle. Kipling. NoAM

One moonless night I bring three yarrow stalks. The Crossroads. Carol Moldaw. UTF

One more day gone. Again. Robert Creeley. VCAP

One More Day's Work for Jesus. Anna B. Warner. AH

One more hour to remember, one less sip. Insomnia. Ivan V. Lalic, *tr. fr. Serbo-Croatian by* Charles Simic. HSix

One more little spirit to Heaven has flown. Little Libbie. Julia A. Moore. OBAL

One More New Botched Beginning. Stephen Spender. CMoP; NoAM; NYBP

One more night my blood. O Wendy, Arthur. Maurice Kenny. HATNAP

One more rendezvous. John G. Neihardt. *Fr.* Song of Jed Smith, The. FYAP

One More Sign. Roberta Hill Whiteman. HATNAP

One more unfortunate. The Bridge of Sighs. Thomas Hood. BeLS; CoGr; EBEV; EnRP; FaPoR; GTBS; GTBS-P; OBEV; OxAEP-2; WBLP

One morn before me were three figures seen. Ode on Indolence. Keats. EnRP; LiTB; MeMBP; NAEL-2; OBNC

One morn I rose and looked upon the world. The Dawn. *Unknown*. PoToHe

One morn I watch'd the rain subside. Devonshire Scenes. Coventry Patmore. *Fr.* Tamerton Church-Tower or First Love. FaBoPP

One Morning. Timothy Steele. CRP

One morning a weasel came swimming. The Weasel. *Unknown.* ChTr; CoGr

One morning as I rambled. The Miner Boy. *Unknown.* AmFP

One morning de captain wake. Itanami. *Unknown.* PBCV

One morning ere [*or* before] Titan had thought to stir [*or* thought of stirring] his feet. The Vision. Egan O'Rahilly, *tr. fr. Irish by* Thomas Kinsella. NOIV

    (Reverie at Dawn.) FaBoPV, *tr. by* Frank O'Connor

One morning I got up. The Little Bird. *Unknown, tr. by* Rolf Italiaander. PBA

One morning I shall find. Maisie. James Merrill. HeIP

One Morning in May [*or* The Nightingale]. *Unknown.* AS

One Morning in May; or, The Young Girl Cut Down in Her Prime. *Unknown.* AmFP

One morning in spring. Fife Tune. John Manifold. CBAP; FaBoMA; GoJo; ImPo; InPS; LiTB; LiTM; Mes; NBLV; NOBAu

One morning in the month of June. The Royal Fisherman. *Unknown.* ChTr; GBP

One morning in the month of May. Just as the Tide Was a-Flowing. *Unknown.* OBET

One Morning, Oh, So Early! Jean Ingelow. OxBChV

One morning old Wilfrid Scawen Blunt. Victor Gray. NOBL

One morning, one morning, one morning in May. One Morning in May [*or* The Nightingale]. *Unknown.* AS

    (Nightingale, The.) AmFP

    (Rebel Soldier, The.) OxBoLi

One morning, one morning, one morning in Spring. I'll Be Fourteen Next Sunday. *Unknown.* AmFP

One morning the Monarch said: "When." D. W. Barker. PeLi

One Morning We Brought Them Order. Alfred M. Lee. FF

One morning when I went downtown. Morning in Spring. Louis Ginsberg. GoYe

One morning with a 12-gauge my brother shot what he said was a linnet. Linnets. Larry Levis. LCAP

One mouse adds up to many mice. Singular Indeed. David McCord. OBCA

One must have a mind of winter. The Snow Man. Wallace Stevens. CMoP; EnlH; GoJo; HAP; HCAP; HeIP; MAT; NAAL-2; NoAM; NoP; NU; PoE; Poetr; PrIm; SoSe; TRP; WeW

One Mystery, The. James Clarence Mangan. PeIV

One narcissus among the ordinary beautiful. Persephone, Falling. Rita Dove. NAmP90

One need not be a Chamber — to be Haunted. Emily Dickinson. NALW

One needs a lyric poet in these. Julius Lester. *Fr.* In the Time of Revolution. PoBA

One needs sand from the sea, we have known. Morning Hours. Rossana Ombres, *tr. fr. Italian by* Robert McCracken *and* Pietro Pedace. *Fr.* Excursion to Ravenna of A Young Girl with Her Parents. NeIt

"One night," a doctor said, "last fall." Ambrose Bierce. *Fr.* Devil's Dictionary, The. OBAL

One night a score of Erris men. Danny. J. M. Synge. PeVV

One night all tired with the weary day. The Gnat. Joseph Beaumont. FM; NOSC

One night as Dick lay fast asleep. Full Moon. Walter de la Mare. BoNaP

One night as I lay on my bed. Death. *Unknown, tr. fr. Welsh by* Aneirin Talfan Davies. OBWVE; RB

One night, as I was pondering of late. John Oldham. *Fr.* Satyr, A. NOSC

One night as Polly Oliver was lying in her bed. Polly Oliver's Rambles. *Unknown.* OBET

One night before a gig. Choofa. Mandy Sayer. Jaz

One night, being pressed by his old friend Chubb. The Undertakers' Club. *Unknown.* GBP

One night came on a hurricane. The Sailor's Consolation. *Unknown, wr. at. to* William Pitt. BeLS; FaBoCo

One-Night Expensive Hotel. Ronald G. Everson. NOBC

One-Night Fair. Nancy Price. GOYP

One night from the stern I thought, as I watched. Braemar. Galway Kinnell. PoA

One night he dreamed he was a. The Young Man Who Loved the Girl Who Took Care of Her Aged Father. Greg Kuzma. AmPA

One night he heard heart-breaking sound. Austin Clarke. *Fr.* Mnemosyne Lay in Dust. CIP; CMoP; IPY

One night, I saw a woman. Unlocking the Doors. Jill Breckenridge. LoHo

One night i' th' yeare [*or* in the year], my dearest Beauties, come. To His Lovely Mistresses. Robert Herrick. CaPo; CTC; SeCP

One night in late October. Judged by the Company One Keeps. *Unknown.* BLPA; NBLV

One night Jake telephoned. 26th Precinct Station. Louis Simpson. EOEF

One night of tempest I arose and went. Night and Morning. *Unknown, tr. fr. Welsh by* R. S. Thomas. OBWVE

One night quite bang up to the mark, ri tol de lol. Johnny Raw and Polly Clark. *Unknown.* CoMu

One Night Stand. Amiri Baraka. NeAP

One-Night Stand: An Approach to the Bridge, The. Paul Blackburn. ErPo

One night the Brownies reached a mound. The Brownies' Celebration. Palmer Cox. OBCA

One night when I was in the House of Death. Birth. Harold Monro. *Fr.* Strange Meetings. PoA

One night when I was walking. Let the Wind Blow High or Low. *Unknown.* OBET

One night when I went down. The Heap of Rags. W. H. Davies. NSI

One night, your mother is listening to the walls. How You Get Born. Erica Jong. UnPo

One night's east wind made a thousand trees burst into flower. Tune: "Green Jade Cup" — Lantern Festival. Hsin Ch'i-chi, *tr. fr. Chinese by* Irving Y. Lo. SuSp

One No. 7. John Frederick Frank. GoYe

One noonday, at my window in the town. Ball's Bluff. Herman Melville. OBWP

One o'Clock. Katharine Pyle. *Fr.* Wonder Clock, The. OBCA

One o'clock in the letter-box. The Meeting. Muriel Rukeyser. MoAmPo; TrJP

One of King Henry's favourites began. A Groom of the Chamber's Religion in King Henry the Eighth's Time. John Harington. NoSic

One of Many. Stevie Smith. OxBC

One of my father; he stands. Photographs. Charles Wright. HoPM

One of my friends has green fingers. Some Friends. Arthur Yap. OBF

One of my legs will not obey. Cuckold. Mary E. O'Donnell. NWP

One of my poems kept me awake at night. The Thieves. Martin Sorescu, *tr. fr. Romanian by* Michael Hamburger. PWE

One of our race's great lights has gone out to the world. Paul Laurence Dunbar. Mrs. Henry Linden. CBWP-4

One of our race's greatest needs in this country today. The Y. M. C. A. Mrs. Henry Linden. CBWP-4

One of the Boys. James Simmons. PNI

One of the clock, and silence deep. One o'Clock. Katharine Pyle. *Fr.* Wonder Clock, The. OBCA

One of the Dead Speaks. Cahit Sitki Taranci, *tr. fr. Turkish by* Nermin Menemencioglu. OBD

One of the difficulties is in being. Russian Asylum. Marilyn Bowering. NOBC

One of the first things we learn in school is. Raising My Hand. "Antler." ETG

One of the Gang. Tracey Herd. NWP

One of the Jews. C. P. Cavafy, *tr. fr. Greek.* TrJP

One of the more intelligent members. For the Fly-Leaf of a School-Book. Norman Cameron. OxBS

One of the neat ones in your awkward squad. (*LL*) Forgive Me, Sire. Norman Cameron. FaBoEE; GTBS-P; OxBS; OxBSP

One of the Principal Causes of War. "Hugh MacDiarmid." OxBSP

One of the visiting dignitaries. Eli 1943. R. M. Cooper. BTR

"One of the wits of the school" your chum would say. Your Birthday in Wisconsin You Are 140. John Berryman. NAs

"One of them takes himself to be an ox. Tune: "Song of Divination"Using Quotations from *Chuang-tzu.* Hsin Ch'i-chi, *tr. fr. Chinese by* Irving Y. Lo. SuSp

One of them, taking advantage of the crew's momentary carelessness. Edouard Glissant, *tr. fr. French by* Ellen Conroy Kennedy. *Fr.* Indies, The. NegPo

One of these days. A Swell Idea. Steve Kowit. UL

One of these days I'm gonna write a real performance poem. Playing the Invisible Saxophone en el Combo de las Estrellas. Harryette Mullen. Jaz

One of these mornings bright and fair. Great Day. *Unknown.* SWP

One of these nights about twelve o'clock. The Heavenly Aeroplane. *Unknown.* NOCV

One of those lubricious teenage latin beauties. Renewal. Steve Kowit. UL

One of those two-bit luncheonettes on nothing. A Candystore in Washington Heights. James Reiss. AnAn

One of Three Musicians. Steve Jonas. Jaz

One of us said, how odd, Hilda Doolittle ("H. D."). *Fr.* Tribute to the Angels. NALW

One of Us Two. Ella Wheeler Wilcox. PoToHe

One of us/ will/ be. Devils. Norman Mailer. OBAL

One old Oxford ox opening oysters. One Old Oxford Ox. *Unknown.* CBNP

    (One Old Ox.) ChTr; FaBoNo

One, or a thousand voices? — filling noon. The Crickets in the Fields. Edward Rowland Sill. AnAmPo

One or two per second died. The Faucets. Van K. Brock. ArOW

One, The Other, And. NMM

One perfect rose. (LL) One Perfect Rose. Dorothy Parker. FiBHP; NALW; NBLV; NIP; NoP; OBAL; Poetr; VBLP

One Perfect Rose. Dorothy Parker. FiBHP; NALW; NBLV; NIP; NoP; OBAL; Poetr; VBLP

One person. Issa, tr. fr. Japanese by Kenneth Koch and Harold Henderson. TTTS

One Person, sels. Elinor Wylie.
  "I hereby swear that to uphold your house." LiTA; MoAB; NAAL-2; OxBA; Son
  (I Hereby Swear.) ImPo
  (Sonnet from "One Person.") LiTA; MoAmPo
  "In our content, before the autumn came." NAAL-2; NALW
  "Let us leave talking of angelic hosts." OxBA
  Little Beauty That I Was Allowed, The. Son

One pillar holding up consolation. César Vallejo, tr. fr. Spanish by James Wright. AnAn

One plays the saxophone. 33⅓ RPM. George Economou. Jaz

1 Poem 2 Voices A Song. Sherley Anne Williams. Jaz

One potato, two potato. Unknown. Fr. Counting-out Rhymes. FaPON; ImGa; RoPo

One Presenting a Rare Book to Madame Hull. John Saffin. SCAP

One rainy night that year we saw our wives. Our Wives. Jonathan Galassi. EOEF

One Reason for Stars. Jack Butler. MT

One recognizes oneself. (LL) Mr. T. S. Eliot Cooking Pasta. József Tornai. GrPl

One remains, the many change and pass, The. Shelley. Fr. Adonais; an Elegy on the Death of John Keats. EBEV; EnRP; FHYEP; HoPM; ImPo; MeMBP; NoP; OAEL-2; PoEL-4; SCV; TrGrPo

One road leads to London. Roadways. John Masefield. BoTP; OTCP

One Rose of Stone. Keith Wilson. GOYP

One, round the candytuft. I Spy. Norah E. Hussey. BoTP

One Saturday night as we set sail. The Mermaid. Unknown. AmFP

One scene as I bow to pour her coffee. Vacation. William Stafford. Poetsp

One Season. Tony Hoagland. NAmP90

One seem'd all dark and red — a tract of sand. Tennyson. Fr. Palace of Art, The. UnPo

One sees — " '. . . indomitable that/ obelisk of a beard admonishes the heavens." (LL) For Malcolm X. Nanina Alba. PoBA

One set on the highway to sing. Li Po, tr. fr. Chinese by Ezra Pound. OxBA

One ship drives east and another drives west. The Winds of Fate. Ella Wheeler Wilcox. AnAmPo; BLPA; WBLP

One showing the eggs unbroken. (LL) The Explosion. Philip Larkin. EBEV; FaBoMo; HAP; NAEL-2; NoAM; OxAEP-2; OxBC; PeECV; RB; SCV; WeW

One shuts one eye. Before Play. Vasco [or Vasko] Popa, tr. fr. Serbo-Croatian by Anne Pennington. Fr. Games. RB

One side of his world is always missing. Riding a One-eyed Horse. Henry Taylor. HeIP; InPK

One Sided Shoot-out. Don L. Lee. BPo; NBV; PoBA

One silent night of late. The Cheat of Cupid; or, The Ungentle Guest. Robert Herrick, after Anacreon. AWP; OBVE

One single word of heartfelt kindness. Kindness. Mary E. Tucker. CBWP-1

One slit's enough to let adultery in.' (LL) Upon Scobble [Epigram]. Robert Herrick. BeJo; CaPo; FaBoEE; NoP

One small grave is all he gets. (LL) Cui Bono? Thomas Carlyle. WGRP

One Song, The. Mark Strand. CAPP

One sore thing is the way. Gibbons Ruark. MT

One sound. Then the hiss and whir. The Garden. Louise Glück. AmPA; HCAP; NAAL-2; VCAP

One star fell and another as we walked. Conrad Aiken. Fr. Preludes for Memnon; or, Preludes to Attitude. MoAmPo

One star in the dark pass of the houses. The Evening Star. Rainer Maria Rilke, tr. fr. German by Randall Jarrell. ArNa

One star that I loved ere the fields went brown. (LL) A Winter Twilight. Angelina Weld Grimké. CDC; PoBA; PoNe; ShDr

One Step at a Time. Unknown. WBLP

One step twix't me and death, (twas Davids speech). Roger Williams. SCAP

One stone. Inventory. Jacques Prévert, tr. fr. French by John Frederick Nims. STV

One stone sufficeth (lo what death can do). On a Whore. John Hoskyns. FaBoEE

One stood still, looking stupid. The other. The Willets. May Swenson. WPE

One stormy morn I chanced to meet. A Kiss in the Rain. Samuel Minturn Peck. OBAL

One student (white). Images. Naomi Long Madgett. ETG

One Summer Evening ("One summer evening (led by her) I found.") Wordsworth. Fr. Prelude [or, Growth of a Poet's Mind], The. CH; EnRP; GN; HAP; NOBE; NoP; NU; OAEL-2; OBNC; OxAEP-2; PoE; SCV

One summer he stole the jade buttons. Of Your Father's Indiscretions and the Train to California. Lynn Emanuel. NAmP90

One summer, high in Wyoming. Before the Storm. Kenneth O. Hanson. CoAP

One summer I stayed. The Two Families. Joyce L. Brisley. BoTP

One summer morning a daring band. The Ballad of Ishmael Day. Unknown. PAH

One summer only grant me, you powerful fates. To the Fates. Friedrich Hölderlin, tr. fr. German by Michael Hamburger. OBD

One Sunday morning as I went walking, by Brisbane waters I chanced to stray. Moreton Bay. Unknown. CBAP

One Sunday morning soft and fine. Brigadier. A. J. M. Smith. MoCV

One surely tires eventually of the frequent references — the gossip. Reading the Unpublished Manuscripts of Louis MacNeice at Kinsale Harbour. Desmond O'Grady. PBCIP

One swallow did not follow. To the Tune "A Dream Song." Wu Tsao, tr. fr. Chinese by Kenneth Rexroth and Ling Chung. WPC

One sweetly solemn thought. Nearer Home. Phoebe Cary. BLRP; PWR; WBLP; WGRP
  (One Sweetly Solemn Thought.) AH

One Sweetly Solemn Thought, with music. Phoebe Cary. See One sweetly solemn thought.

One Talent, The. William Cutler. PWR

One that is ever kind said yesterday. The Folly of Being Comforted. W. B. Yeats. GBL; HeIL; HeIP; NAEL-2

One they hunt by night, The. I Am Ham Melanite. William Millett. GoYe

One Thing. "Owen Meredith." WBLP

One Thing at a Time. M. A. Stodart. PoToHe

One thing at a time. Unknown. OxNR

One thing has a shelving bank. A Drumlin Woodchuck. Robert Frost. GoYe; NoAM; NOBA

One thing in all things have I seen. The Secret. "Æ." MoBrPo

One thing is sure. The Pulse. Mark Van Doren. MoAmPo

One Thing Needful, The. Max Isaac Reich. BLRP

One thing not to do is worry. Between the River and the Sea. Tim Longville. VaA

One Thing That Can Save America, The. John Ashbery. AiP; NoAM; NOBA

One thing that literature would be greatly the better for. Very like a Whale. Ogden Nash. BLPL; HAP; InPK; InPS; PoLF; TrGrPo

One thing you left with us, Jack Johnson. Strange Legacies. Sterling A. Brown. PoBA; TTY

One thought the recurring "image" in the poet's song. Handbook of Versification. Gilbert Sorrentino. PoA

One thousand eight hundred and twenty-four. The Greenland Whale Fishery. Unknown. AmFP

One Thousand Fearful Words for Fidel Castro. Lawrence Ferlinghetti. PoBeRe; VGW

1,000 Illustrations and a Complete Concordance. Michael Andre. UL

One thousand saxophones infiltrate the city. Battle Report. Bob Kaufman. Jaz; TTY

One Time. Douglas Livingstone. PeSA

One time/ Columbus said this island and the seas. Time of Turtles. Grace Perry. NOBAu

One Time Henry Dreamed the Number. Doughtry Long, Jr.. BPo; PoBA

One time I wanted two moons. Jacob Nibenegenesabe, tr. fr. Cree Indian by Howard Norman. Fr. Wishing Bone Cycle, The. STP

One time in Alexandria, in wicked Alexandria. Thaïs. Newman Levy. FiBHP; PeLV

One time my friend Tergvinder brought a large round boulder. Tergvinder's Stone. W. S. Merwin. CAPP

One time, to a coast of light. (LL) Flames and Dangling Wire. Robert Gray. NOBAu

One Times One, sels. E. E. Cummings.
  Plato Told. ArOW; CTC

One to destroy, is murder by the law. Edward Young. FF

One to Grieve, The. Rudy Thomas. GOYP

One to Love. Alfred Islay Walden. AAP

One to make ready. The Start. Unknown. OxNR

One to Nothing. Carolyn Kizer. OBAL

One to One. Alfred Corn. PRA

One to Ten. *Unknown.* ReMoGo

One Too Many Mornings. David Rivard. PBCAP

One Tourist's Cologne. Hal Colebatch. NOBAu

One Tuesday in Summer. James McAuley. FaBoMA

One, Two. Mervyn Morris. PBCV

One, two,/ Buckle my shoe. Mother Goose. BoTP; OxNR; ReMoGo

One, two, Buckle my shoe. The Late Mother. Cynthia MacDonald. Poetsp

One, Two, Three. H. C. Bunner. FaPON; PoLF

One, Two, Three. Michael Rosen. OTCP

One — Two — Three. Hannah Senesh, *tr. fr. Hungarian by* Peter Hay. WPOW

One, two, three, a-lary,/ I spy Mistress Mary. *Unknown.* RoPo

One, two, three, a-lary,/ My first name is Mary. *Unknown.* RoPo

One, two, three, a nation. *Unknown.* RoPo

1, 2, 3, 4, 5!/ I caught a hare alive. One to Ten. *Unknown.* ReMoGo

One, two, three, four, five/ [Once] I caught a fish alive. *Unknown.* OxNR; ReMoGo; RoPo

ONE/ TWO/ THREE/ FOUR/ FIVE/ SIX/ SEVEN. *Unknown.* ISE

One, two, three, four,/ I spy Eleanor. *Unknown.* RoPo

One, two, three, four,/ Mary at the cottage door. Mother Goose. OxNR

One, Two, Three — Gough! Eve Merriam. NTCP

One, two, three,/ I love coffee. *Unknown.* OxNR

One, two, three,/ Johnny caught a flea! *Unknown.* RoPo

1-2-3 was the number he played but today the number came 3-2-1. Kenneth Fearing. FF; HoPM; NIP; PoRA; RB; TrJP

One, two, tie your shoe. *Unknown.* RoPo

One, two, tree/ All de same. *Unknown. Fr.* Songs. PBCV

One, two, whatever you do. *Unknown.* OxNR

One ugly trick has often spoiled. Meddlesome Matty. Ann Taylor. OxBChV

One unkind word in the early morn. The Boomerang. Carrie May Nichols. PoToHe

One-Upmanship. Miriam Chaikin. NTCP

One wading a fall meadow finds on all sides. The Beautiful Changes. Richard Wilbur. CMoP; CoAP; HCAP; InPS; PoE

One wants a Teller in a time like this. Gwendolyn Brooks. *Fr.* Womanhood, The. WPE

One was fifteen years old, the other sixteen, The. Pensionnaires. Paul Verlaine, *tr. fr. French by* François Pirou. PeHV

One was kicked in the stomach. Gangrene. Philip Levine. VGW

One watch had passed, and still sweet slumber shed. The Birth of Sohráb. Firdausi, *tr. fr. Persian. Fr.* Shahnamah, The. TAL, *tr. by* James Atkinson

One Way at Any Time. J. H. Prynne. VaA

One Way of Looking at It. A. J. Munby. NOBVV

One Way of Love. Robert Browning. OtMeF

One-Way Song, *sels.* Wyndham Lewis.
"I would set all things whatsoever front to back." CTC

One way the world. Whale Wisdom Peace Illumination. Jeff Poniewaz. EaPr

One We Knew. Thomas Hardy. NAEL-2

One went spinning down the plughole. Yesterday the House was Full of Flies. Geoffrey Summerfield. OTCP

One wept whose only child was dead. Maternity. Alice Meynell. OxBSP

One whistle, a short husky breath. Not There. Tess Gallagher. NIP

One white flower. *(LL)* Summer Freezes Here. Hsiung-hung. WPC

One white foot, hm him for your life. How to Choose a Horse. *Unknown.* FaBoUs

One white foot, try him. On Buying a Horse. *Unknown.* NBLV; RB

One who does not love me, The. Song of Abuse. *Yoruba Oral Tradition, tr. by* Ulli Beier *and* B. Gbadamosi. WTO

One who gave the warning with his wings, The. Exile. Karl Shapiro. *Fr.* Adam and Eve. CRP

One who has loved the hills and died, a man. Pony Rock. Archibald MacLeish. MeMAP

One who has pulled his oar in a start of storm, The. Simile. Agnes Nemes Nagy, *tr. fr. Hungarian by* Frederic Will. PoSu

One Who Is at Home, The. Franciso Albanez, *tr. fr. Spanish by* Robert Bly. RaBo

One who is not, we see: but one, whom we see not, is. The Higher Pantheism in a Nutshell. Swinburne. *Fr.* Heptalogia, The. BXAP; CBNP; EnVR; FaBoNo; OHCV; PeVV

One who sees corn and is glad. Chicken. *Unknown, tr. fr. Yoruba by* Ulli Beier. *Fr.* Hunter Poems of the Yoruba. RB

One who should drownn him too. *(LL)* I Looked Up from My Writing. Thomas Hardy. NoAM; PAW

One Who Struggles, The. Ernst Toller, *tr. fr. German by* E. Ellis Roberts. TrJP

One Who Watches. Siegfried Sassoon. TrJP

One who will remain standing when I die, The. *(LL)* I Am Not I. Juan Ramón Jiménez. RaBo

One whom I knew, a student and a poet. Alex Comfort. MoBrPo

One whose love will never end. Accompanying a Gift ("One whose love will never end.") L. A. J. Moorer. CBWP-3

One whose majestic presence ever here. In Memoriam Frederick Douglass. H. Cordelia Ray. CBWP-3

One Wife for One Man. Frank Aig-Imoukhede. PBA

One will walk to-day! *(LL)* I have not told my garden yet. Emily Dickinson. AnAmPo

One Winter Night in August. X. J. Kennedy. OBCA; OBSP

One with eyes the fairest. Euripides, *tr. fr. Greek by* Shelley. *Fr.* Cyclops. AWP

One with this world! *(LL)* My words are tied in one. *Unknown.* EaPr

One without looks in to-night [*or* tonight]. The Fallow Deer at the Lonely House. Thomas Hardy. AWP; CH; CMoP; OBAP; OxBSP; RB; TTTS

One Word Is Too Often Profaned. Shelley. BLPL; BoLoP; CBLP; EBEvV; ELP; EnRP; FaBV; GTBS; GTBS-P; ImPo; LiTB; MeMBP; NOBE; OBEV; OBNC; OPOP; OxAEP-2; PoLF; PPP; TFi; TrGrPo

One Word More. (There they are, my fifty men and women.) Robert Browning. EnVR; MeMBP; OtMeF; PoEL-5
Sels.
"I shall never, in the years remaining." EPCY
Phases of the Moon. ChTr

One word, "nacreous." Shéhérazade. Wayne Koestenbaum. UTF

One would be in less danger. Family Court. Ogden Nash. CoGr; FiBHP; PeLV

One would continue to contend with one's ideas. *(LL)* The Glass of Water. Wallace Stevens. MeMAP; MoAB; MoAmPo; OxBA; TAP

One would never assume, from the toy bulldogs taking the air. A Nice Part of Town. Alfred Hayes. NYBP

One would never suspect there were so many vices. The Destruction of Sodom. Daryl Hine. ChIV-1

One writes, that "other friends remain." Tennyson. *Fr.* In Memoriam A. H. H. EBVV, *abr.*; EnVR; OAEL-2, *abr.*; OBF, *first two sts.*; PeECV, *abr.*; PoEL-5

One Writing against His Prick. *Unknown.* NOSC

One X. E. E. Cummings. FaBoMo

One Year. N. M. Bodecker. TLR

One Year Ago. Adah Isaacs Menken. CBWP-1

One year there were too many/ frogs. Calendar. Cecil Bodker, *tr. fr. Danish by* Nadia Christensen *and* Alexander Taylor. BoWoP

One Year to Live. Mary Davis Reed. PoToHe

Onely the Reverend Grave and Godly Mr. Buckly Remaines. Edward Johnson. SCAP

Oneness of the Philosopher with Nature, The. G. K. Chesteron. CBNP; FaBoNo

One's grand flights, one's Sunday baths. The Sense of the Sleight-of-Hand Man. Wallace Stevens. HAP; ImPo; LiTM; MoAB; MoAmPo; NoAM; NOBA; PoA; TwCP; WeW

One's none. Little Hundred. *Unknown.* OxNR

One's-Self I Sing. Walt Whitman. FaBoPV; LPA; NOBA; OxBA

Ones you fear most of all: ask where you were, The. *(LL)* For the Record. Adrienne Rich. CAPP; NIP; VCAP

Oneself a living armoury? *(LL)* The Dead Crab. Andrew Young. FaBoTw; FM; OBD; RB

Oneself Miss Grant. Miss Grant. Freda Downie. FaBoWP

Onesided Dialog. June Jordan. NoAM

Onesided, stripped of its ghosts. Eccles Street, Bloomsday, 1982. Harry Clifton. PBCIP

Ongoing Story, The. John Ashbery. HCAP

Onion, The. Margaret Gibson. MT

Onion. Katha Pollitt. RaBo

Onion. Wislawa Szymborska, *tr. fr. Polish by* Grazyna Drabik *and* Sharon Olds. PoSu

Onion, The. John Thompson. NOBC

Onion Bucket. Lorenzo Thomas. PoBA

Onion, Memory, The. Craig Raine. NAEL-2; NoAM; NoP

Onion (or Penis): "I'm a Strange Creature, for I Satisfy Women." Unknown, formerly at. to Cynewulf. *See* I'm a strange creature, for I satisfy women.

Onkel Fritz Is Sitting. David Koenig. BTR

Only a baby, fair, and small. George Washington. *Unknown.* OHIP

Only a Baby Small. Matthias Barr. VPP

Only a Blush. Mary E. Tucker. CBWP-1

Only a cloud or two hangs here and there. (*LL*) Another ("As I beheld a winters evening air.") Richard Lovelace. SeCP

Only a few will really understand. One Sided Shoot-out. Don L. Lee. BPo; NBV; PoBA

Only a fool would eat his heart out so. Ballad of the Bushman. Ellen Duggan. PeNZ

Only a fool would fail. God's Praises. *Unknown, tr. fr. Irish by* Brendan Kennelly. PeIV; TIRV

Only a hint of light reflected in the snow. Going Home. James Lewisohn. ETG

Only a knee, no more. (*LL*) The Knee. Christian Morgenstern. CBNP; RB

Only a Litlle Thing. M. P. Handy. PoToHe

Only a man harrowing clods. In Time of "The Breaking of Nations." Thomas Hardy. BoLoP; ChIV-1; CMoP; CoGr; EBEV; EBEvV; HAP; LiTB; LiTM; MeMBP; MoAB; MoBrPo; MoP; NAEL-2; NoAM; NOBE; NoP; OAEL-2; OBEV; OBWP; OxAEP-2; PAW; Poetr; PoWW; PPP; RB; TFi; WeW

Only a Miner. *Unknown.* AmFP

Only a Pin. Isaac Hinton Brown. PWR

Only a tender little thing. A Snowdrop. Harriet Prescott Spofford. GN

Only a Thought. Charles MacKay. Poetr

Only a woman of this measure. Tatiana Kalatschova. William Logan. SM

Only accidents preserve. Athena in the Front Lines. Marge Piercy. SRLS

Only after a couple of months of hard. Ice River. David Baker. SM

Only awake to Universal Mind. Jack Kerouac. *Fr.* Mexico City Blues. NeAP

Only Bar in Dixon, The. James Welch. AmPA; FF

Only Be Willing to Search for Poetry. Yüan Mei, *tr. fr. Chinese.* PDV

Only believe your eyes. No need of faith. (*LL*) Let others hail the holidays with laughter. Ausiàs March. STV

Only better. (*LL*) Lisa's Ritual, Age 10. Grace Caroline Bridges. LoHo

Only brooms. Brooms. Charles Simic. AmPA; NNaP, *early vers.*

Only by the sound of his own voice. (*LL*) Deer on pine mountain, The. Yoshinobu. PoBeRe

Only call in, not dare to rest. (*LL*) To Mr. W. B., at the Birth of His First Child. William Cartwright. BeJo

Only calm here is the trees, waiting, The. A Girl Named Spring. Betsy Sholl. PBCAP

Only casually invited, and that several months ago. (*LL*) Eager note on my door said 'Call me,' The. Frank O'Hara. CAPP; NoAM; NOBA; Poetr

Only Child. Barbara Soretsky. NGP

Only consonants and vowels. (*LL*) Survey of Literature. John Crowe Ransom. FaBoCh; LiTA; MeMAP; NBLV; OBAL; TAP; TwCP; VGW

Only Daughter, The. *Unknown.* OBET

Only depression if I stay at home. On the Night of the Fifteenth Day of the First Month I Go Out and Return. Mei Yao Ch'en, *tr. fr. Chinese by* Jonathan Chaves. SuSp

Only emperor is the emperor of ice-cream, The. (*LL*) The Emperor of Ice-Cream. Wallace Stevens. AmPP; AnAmPo; CBNP; CMoP; FaBoMo; FF; HAP; HCAP; HeIP; InPK; LiTA; MeMAP; MoP; NAAL-2; NAWM-2; NIP; NoAM; NOBA; OPOP; OxBA; PoE; Poetr; TAP; TFi; TRP; WeW

Only for these I pray. Two Prayers. Charlotte Perkins Gilman. WGRP

Only function of the red-cupped fruit, The. Second Witness. Pattiann Rogers. FoLa

Only head in the sky, The. Giraffe. Stanley Plumly. AmPA

Only His Son Is With God. "Angelus Silesius," *tr. fr. German.* Fr. Cherubical Wanderer, The. GePo, *tr. by* George C. Schoolfield

Only I have directions. (*LL*) Let the reeds pander to the wayward wind. Huang Guobin. EaPr

Only I that mourn out. (*LL*) The Courtier's Good-Morrow to His Mistress. *Unknown.* EiL

Only in sleep. The Old Wife Speaks. Gerda Mayer. DT

Only in This Way. Margaret Goss Burroughs. BISi

Only Jealousy of Emer, The. *Unknown, tr. fr. Irish by* John Montague. BIrV

Only Jealousy of Emer, The, *sels.* W. B. Yeats.
"Woman's beauty is like a white, A." MoAB

Only joy, now here you are. Sir Philip Sidney. *Fr.* Astrophel and Stella. AAS; EIL; EnRePo; ESo, *sl. abr.*; GBL; GGP; HAP; HeIL, (*Sonnets, I–CVIII and 11 Songs*); InvP; NAEL-1; NoP; NoSic; Poetr; SCGP, (*Sonnets, I–CVIII and 11 Songs*); SiPS, (*Sonnets, I–CVIII and 11 Songs*); SiPSBD, (*Sonnets, I–CVIII and 11 Songs*)

Only kid, An! an only kid. Had Gadyaa Kid, a Kid. *Unknown, tr. fr. Hebrew.* TrJP

Only last week, walking the hushed fields. Father and Son. F. R. Higgins. BIrV; OBMV

Only lasting part of me, The. (*LL*) To Violet [with Prewar Poems]. Basil Bunting. FaBoMo; PoA

Only let me know your feeling, your true feeling! (*LL*) Never Again to Go to You. Georg Friedrich Daumer. RiWo

Only major city, one would hope, The. U-24 Anchors off New Orleans. Turner Cassity. ArOW; MT

Only monarch all obey, The. (*LL*) Written for My Son, and Spoken by Him at His First Putting on Breeches. Mary Barber. ECEV; ECWP; NOEC

Only mother he could afford was a skinny old man, The. Because They Were Very Poor That Winter. Kenneth Patchen. NaP

Only My Opinion. Monica Shannon. FaPON

Only news I know, The. Emily Dickinson. NOCV

Only now that my hair is gray. Anacreon, *tr. fr. Greek by* Sam Hamill. InMo

Only, of course, they can't sustain the part. (*LL*) Fireflies in the Garden. Robert Frost. OxBSP; SAmP

Only of Myself I Knew How to Tell. Rachel, *tr. fr. Hebrew by* Ruth Finer Mintz. MHP

Only on the rarest occasions, when the blue air. The Mountain. W. S. Merwin. VGW

Only one drifter down in the patrol! A Minesweeper Sunk. Edward Davison. NSI

Only one guy and. Issa, *tr. fr. Japanese by* Cid Corman. InPK

Only one kiss. Good-bye, my dear. (*LL*) Jenny. Dante Gabriel Rossetti. EnVR; PoEL-5

Only One Mother. George Cooper. OHIP

Only One Way. Ella Wheeler Wilcox. *See* However the battle is ended.

Only [*or* Onely] a little more. His Poetry His Pillar. Robert Herrick. BeJo; CaPo; JCP; NOSC
(His Poetrie His Pillar.) SeCP

Only [*or* Onley] to feed her pride. (*LL*) 'Tis Now, Since I Sat[e] Down Before. Sir John Suckling. PoEL-3; SeCV-1

Only real airship, The. The Dirigible. Ralph Wilhelm Bergengren. FaPON

Only record of our great affection, The. A Gravestone at Corinth. *Unknown, tr. fr. Greek by* Peter Jay. GrAn

Only relics left are those long, The. Monuments for a Friendly Girl at a Tenth Grade Party. William Stafford. NoAM

Only response, The. William Knott. InPK

Only responsible people keep cows. If you buy near cattle. To Carry All of Us. Maggie Anderson. ETG

Only ribbon round it. (*LL*) Lucy Locket lost her pocket. Mother Goose. OxBoLi; OxNR; ReMoGo

Only rule is enjoy yourself, The. *Unknown, tr. fr. Greek by* Peter Porter. GrAn

Only Seven. Henry S. Leigh. BXAP

Only "special" children wear a star. I am a Star. Inge Auerbacher. BTR

Only strains of love. (*LL*) To His Lyre. Franz von Bruchmann. RiWo

Only, sweet Love, afford me but thy heart. For Her Heart Only. *Unknown.* EIL

Only teaching on Tuesdays, book-worming. Memories of West Street and Lepke. Robert Lowell. AmPP; ArOW; CAPP; CMoP; InPS; NAAL-2; NaP; NoAM; NOBA; PoE; VCAP

Only temple He delights to fill, The. (*LL*) Enoch. Jones Very. ChIV-1; HAP

Only the air-spirits know. Solitary Song. *Unknown, tr. fr. Eskimo.* WTO

Only the casket left, the jewel gone. Charles Sumner. Charlotte L. Forten Grimke. AAP

Only the clouds were new. The Beast with Two Backs. Andrew Taylor. NOBAu

Only the Dead. Reed Whittemore. NYBP

Only the deep well. I Break the Sky. Owen Dodson. PoBA

Only the dim-witted say it's evening. What She Said ("Only the dim-witted say it's evening.") Milaipperun Kantan, *tr. fr. Tamil by* A. K. Ramanujan. PLW

Only the foreground's green. Love Overgrows a Rock. Eric Roach. PBCV

Only the grace from simple stone. (*LL*) Elegy before Death. Edna St. Vincent Millay. CMoP; LiTA; LiTM; MeMAP

Only/ the gray wind. Something for Supper. Carroll Arnett. VoR

Only the illegitimate are beautiful. Thesis. Edward Dorn. NOBA

Only the lion and the cock. After Galen. Oliver St. John Gogarty. FaBoEE; OBMV; PoRA

Only the lure of a rattler kept us. The Night of Rattlesnake Chili. Walter McDonald. NGP

Only, the Nations shall be great and free. (*LL*) Near Dover, September 1802. Wordsworth. EnRP

Only the Polished Skeleton. Countee Cullen. PrIm; VGW

Only the sand, only the sand. El Alamein Revisited. Roy Macnab. PeSA

Only the short, broad, splayed feet. Young Shepherd Bathing His Feet. Peter Clarke. PBA

Only the thief was there, no one else. What She Said ("Only the thief was there, no one else.") Kapilar, *tr. fr. Tamil by* A. K. Ramanujan. PLW

Only the wanderer. Ivor Gurney. FaBoPP

Only the waning morning moon/ visits my garden. Ise Tayu, *tr. fr. Japanese by* Kenneth Rexroth *and* Ikuko Atsumi. WPJ

Only the wholesomest foods you eat. Samuel Hoffenstein. *Fr.* Poems in Praise of Practically Nothing. FiBHP; TrJP

Only the wind sings. Mary Celeste. Judith Nicholls. OBSP

Only the winds of spring. Walt Franklin. EaPr

Only thing I have of Jane MacNaughton, The. The Leap. James Dickey. NIP; Poetr

Only thing that can be relied on, The. The Snow on Saddle Mountain. Miyazawa Kenji, *tr. fr. Japanese by* Gary Snyder. NoAM; NOBA

Only thing we know is the thing, The. Red Light. Amiri Baraka. SOTW

Only think, dearest Louisa, what fearful scenes we have witnessed! Arthur Hugh Clough. *Fr.* Amours de Voyage. EBVV; NOBVV

Only thirty years to come down human. *(LL)* A Picture of Okinawa. Dennis Schmitz. LCAP

Only this evening I saw again low in the sky. Martial Cadenza. Wallace Stevens. MeMAP; OxBA; VGW

Only Thy Dust. Don Marquis. PoLF

Only to fail again! *(LL)* I never hear the word "escape." Emily Dickinson. CMoP; NOBA; SAmP

Only to fright us at the gate. *(LL)* A Deposition from Love. Thomas Carew. BeJo; CaPo; MeLP

Only to have a grief. Peeling Onions. Adrienne Rich. BoWoP; HCAP; TAP

Only to say, Here I am in person. *(LL)* Stumpfoot on 42nd Street. Louis Simpson. NNaP; UnPo; VGW

Only to sing thy elegy. *(LL)* The Falcon. Richard Lovelace. CaPo

Only to think she came and went. *(LL)* She Came and Went. James Russell Lowell. AnAmPo

Only to wring my hands raw as soon as I was alone. *(LL)* On Sunday Morning. Paul Johann Ludwig Heyse. RiWo

Only today and just for this minute. The Withdrawal. Robert Lowell. NoP

Only Tourist in Havana Turns His Thoughts Homeward, The. Leonard Cohen. MoCV; MoP

Only true likeness of myself., The. *(LL)* My Shoes. Charles Simic. CoAP; HCAP; VCAP

Only two patient eyes to stare. Faded Pictures. William Vaughn Moody. AnAmPo

Only until this cigarette is ended. Sonnet. Edna St. Vincent Millay. HeIP

Only Waiting. Frances Laughton Mace. BLPA

Only way to be quiet, The. Poetry. Frank O'Hara. HCAP

Only Way to Have a Friend, The. *Unknown.* PoToHe

Only way to save 'em from our arses, The. *(LL)* Cibber! write all thy verses upon glasses. Pope. FaBoEE

Only Way to Win, The. *Unknown.* WBLP

Only, we die in earnest — that's no jest. *(LL)* What Is Our Life? Sir Walter Ralegh. EBEV; EnRePo; FaBoEE; NoSic; OxBSP; SCGP; SiPS; SoSe

Only what I bring to this room will exist here. At the Jewish Museum. Olga Cabral. BTR

Only what is heroic and courageious moves our blood. The Flowers of Politics, II. Michael McClure. NeAP

Only When My Heart Freezes. Alden Nowlan. RaBo

Only when she left. Pig. Vasco [*or Vasko*] Popa, *tr. fr. Romanian by* Anne Pennington. OBD

Only with seasons and the cold crasy moon. *(LL)* Plowman. Sidney Keyes. MoAB; PoRA

Only Years. Kenneth Rexroth. TAP

Ons in your grace I knowe I was. What Once I Was. Sir Thomas Wyatt. MeEL

Onset, The. Robert Frost. CMoP; MoAB; MoAmPo; OxBA; PPP

Onto the empty fields. *(LL)* On Hearing Michael Hartnett Read His Poetry in Irish. Michael O'Loughlin. IB

Onto the hallowit steid bryng in, thai cry. Virgil, *tr. by* Gavin Douglas. *Fr.* Aeneid [*or* Eneados], The. NAWM-1; OBVE

Ontogeny. Jarold Ramsey. NIP

Onward, Christian Soldiers. Sabine Baring-Gould. FaBoBe; FaPoR; WGRP

Onward flies the rushing train. The Engine Driver. "G. S. O." BoTP

Onward led the road again. Hell Gate. A. E. Housman. NoAM; SCGP; UnPo

Onward, Onward, Men of Heaven. Lydia Huntley Sigourney. AH

Onward to Far Ida. George Darley. *Fr.* Nepenthe. PeIV

Onyons. Swift. *Fr.* Verses for Fruitwomen. BIrV; FaBoUs

Oocuck, The. Justin Richardson. FiBHP

Ooftish. Samuel Beckett. NoAM

Oom Gert's Story. C. Louis Leipoldt, *tr. fr. Afrikaans by* C. J. D. Harvey. PeSAV

Oor best-lo'ed makar has but late grown cauld. Carlyle on Burns. William Jeffrey. *Fr.* On Glaister's Hill. OxBS

Opa the Watchmaker. Arlene Maass. BTR

Opal. Amy Lowell. NALW

Opal ring and a holly tree, An. Sailor's Woman. Annette Patton Cornell. GoYe

Ope, aged Atlas, open then thy lap. Ben Jonson. *Fr.* Pleasure Reconciled to Virtue. NAEL-1; OAEL-1

Open. Larry Eigner. NeAP

Open all the ways to me of this long river. *(LL)* Viaticum. Tchicaya U Tam'si. NegPo

Open as experience, this day, this. Tomarata. Kendrick Smithyman. PeNZ

Open-backed dumpy junktruck. In Passing. Gerald Jonas. GrPl

Open Country. Richard Hugo. LCAP

Open Door, The. Elizabeth J. Coatsworth. TLR

Open Door, The. *Unknown, tr. fr. Irish by* Frank O'Connor. IIP

Open-Eyed Angel. David Rokeah, *tr. fr. Hebrew by* Ruth Finer Mintz. MHP

Open Gate, The. Tracey Herd. NWP

Open House. Theodore Roethke. NoAM; NOBA; NoP

Open hull nudging reeds and sand, An. Transmarine. Carol Moldaw. UTF

Open Letter from a Constant Reader. Mona Van Duyn. PoA

Open little box. The Prisoners of the Little Box. Vasco [*or Vasko*] Popa, *tr. fr. Serbo-Croatian by* Charles Simic. AnRep; HSix

Open me like a meadow lily. The Seduction. Suzanne Berger Rioff. NMM

Open! Open! But softly, my child. Adolf Friedrich Graf von Schack, *tr. fr. German by* Philip L. Miller. RiWo

Open Range. Kathryn Jackson *and* Byron Jackson. FaPON

Open Sea, The. William Meredith. CoAP; GoJo; GrPl; TAP; UnPo

Open Sesame. *Unknown.* BoTP

Open Shelves. Marilyn Kitchell. UL

Open Shutter, The. Karl Krolow, *tr. fr. German.* TSaS, *tr. by* Kevin Perryman

Open the book of tales you knew. Living Memory. Adrienne Rich. BAP-90; TRP

Open the Door. *Malay Oral Tradition, tr. by* R. J. Wilkinson *and* R. O. Winstedt. WTO

Open the Door. *Unknown.* ElI; GBL

Open the Door to Me, Oh! Burns. PoEL-4; SCGP

Open the door, who's there within? Open the Door. *Unknown.* ElI; GBL

Open the gates. The Bonny Earl of Murray. *Unknown.* ESPB

Open the Gates. *Unknown, tr. fr. Hebrew by* Israel Zangwill. TrJP

Open the window on the high. Earth Tremor in Lugano. James Kirkup. NYBP

Open this evening like a letter. Love in July. Ivan V. Lalic, *tr. fr. Serbo-Croatian by* Charles Simic. HSix

Open Thy Doors, O Lebanon. Bible, *O.T. Fr.* Zechariah. AWP

Open thy gates. To Heaven. Robert Herrick. ChIV-2

Open, Time. Louise Imogen Guiney. AmWP

Open to Me! He Commandeth a Fair Wind. *Unknown, tr. fr. Egyptian by* Robert Hillyer. *Fr.* Book of the Dead. AWP

Open up to me, I'm tired of waiting. *(LL)* Old Merina Theme. Flavien Ranaivo. NegPo

Open Waters. Jack R. Clemo. PWE

Open Windows. Marilyn Hacker. Poetr

Open wound which has been healed anew, An. Richard Chenevix Trench. TrPWD

Open your closed eyelids. The Phantom of the Rose. Théophile Gautier, *tr. fr. French by* Philip L. Miller. RiWo

Open Your Eyes. Emma Bridge Whisenand. PoToHe

Open your eyes and stare. Haka: Hinemotu. Te Aomuhurangi Te Maaka. PeNZ

Open your eyes that you may see. Open Your Eyes. Emma Bridge Whisenand. PoToHe

Open your mouth and shut your eyes. *Unknown.* RoPo

Opened, clear as a child's geography. The Summer Countries. Henry Rago. VGW

Opened my eyes, and was wide awake. *(LL)* The Midnight Court. Brian Merriman. PeIV

Opening of a door., The. *(LL)* Elysium is as far as to. Emily Dickinson. GrPl; MoAB; MoAmPo; OxBA; WPE

Opening of the Indian and Colonial Exhibition by the Queen. Tennyson. EBVVPR

Opening Service, An. Clara Ann Thompson. CBWP-2

Opening the knots of your braid. Memory of the Present. David Shapiro. UL

Opening Year, The. *Unknown, tr. fr. Latin by* F. Pott. BLRP

Openly send word to Algol and Procyon. (*LL*) For Heather, Entering Kindergarten. Roberta Hill Whiteman. HATNAP; NoAM

Openly, yes,/ with the naturalness. Black Earth. Marianne Moore. FaBoMo

Opens blue and cool on a hot morning. (*LL*) Pleasures. Denise Levertov. CAPP; NeAP; NoAM; NOBA; PoE; Poetr

Opens his throat to the moon. (*LL*) One for the Road. Martin Edmunds. UTF

Opens small notebook. The Terrorist Smiles. Anselm Hollo. UL

Opera Teacher neemed Enna, An. Moss Rich. PeLi

Operation, The. Robert Creeley. NaP

Operation, The. W. D. Snodgrass. InPK; TAP

Operation Memory. David Lehman. NAmP90

Operative No. 174 Resigns. Kenneth Fearing. NYBP

OPG right on the state line, The. Old Post Grill. John DeWitt. NGP

Ophelia. Rimbaud, *tr. fr. French by* Brian Hill. ChTr

Ophelia's Death. Shakespeare. *See* There is a willow grows aslant a brook.

Ophelia's Song. Shakespeare. *Fr.* Hamlet. EBEV; EBEvV; EnLoPo; LiTB; Mes; NAWM-1; NoSic; PoRA; SCGP

Ophelia's Songs, 2 ("And will he not come again."). Shakespeare. *See* And will he [*or* a'] not come again?

Ophra. Judah Halevi, *tr. fr. Hebrew by* Nina Davis Salaman. TrJP

Opinion is a flitting thing. Emily Dickinson. SAmP

Opinion is not worth a rush. Michael Robartes and the Dancer. W. B. Yeats. OAEL-2

Opinions of the New Student. Regino Pedroso, *tr. fr. Spanish by* Langston Hughes. TTY

Opium-Den. *Malay Oral Tradition, tr. by* R. J. Wilkinson *and* R. O. Winstedt. WTO

Opium-Eater, The. Mary E. Tucker. AmWP; CBWP-1

Opium Fantasy, An. Maria White Lowell. AmWP; AnAmPo; InPK

Oppenheimer/ I could have loved you. La Jornada. Antionia Quintana Pigno. AfAz

Opportunity. Berton Braley. WBLP

Opportunity. Harry Graham. FaBoCo; PeLV

Opportunity. John James Ingalls. AnAmPo; PoLF; WBLP

Opportunity. Machiavelli, *tr. fr. Italian by* James Elroy Flecker. AWP

Opportunity. Walter Malone. BLPA; BLPL; FaBoBe; PWR; WBLP

Opportunity. Shakespeare. *Fr.* Rape of Lucrece, The. BeLS; LiTB; PoEL-2

Opportunity. Edward Rowland Sill. AnAmPo; BLPA; GN; WGRP

Opposite Field, The, *sels.* Dabney Stuart.
 "I had no thought to find." NGP
 Lyric Meditation on Sour Locker Rooms, A. NGP

Opposite House, The. Robert Lowell. CMoP

Opposite to Melancholy. William Strode. NOSC

Opposition. Sidney Lanier. AnAmPo; LiTA

Oppressed and few, but freemen yet. The Mecklenburg Declaration. William C. Elam. PAH

Ops in a Wimpey. *Unknown.* CoMu

Optimism. Ella Wheeler Wilcox. BLPA; BLPL; FaBoBe; PWR

Optimist, The. *Unknown.* BLPA

Optimist fell ten stories, The. The Optimist. *Unknown.* BLPA

Options. "O. Henry." FiBHP

Opulent oracle — it's a terrible thing! It's a Terrible Thing! Everett Hoagland. BPo

Opus III, *sels.* Rade Drainac, *tr. fr. Serbo-Croatian by* Charles Simic.
 "Dreams worn out like small coins taken out of circulation." HSix

Opus Nil. Hans Arp, *tr. fr. German by* Michael Hamburger. CBNP

Opusculum paedagogum. Study of Two Pears. Wallace Stevens. InPS; NAAL-2; NoAM; NU; OxBA

Or. Ali Darwish, *tr. fr. Arabic.* TSaS, *tr. by* Darwish Ali

Or a crippled sloop falters, about to go under. The Volume. Robert Pinsky. AnAn

Or a loss of blood whitened your small hands. (*LL*) The Rarest Thyme. Thomas McCarthy. IB

Or an old man upon a winter's night. (*LL*) On Being Asked for a War Poem. W. B. Yeats. NIP; OBWP; OxAEP-2; PAW; PoWW

Or any other reason why. (*LL*) If all be true that I do think. Henry Aldrich. FaBoEE; FF

Or as we wheel. John James. VaA

Or banquet that I ever went to. (*LL*) Marble-Top. E. B. White. FiBHP; OBAL

Or come again. My Ben! Robert Herrick. BeJo

Or, conversely, hungers. Beethoven, Opus 111. Amy Clampitt. NIP

Or curtained close such scene from ev'ry future view. (*LL*) Ode on the Poetical Character. William Collins. EnRP; NAEL-1; NOEC; OAEL-1; PoE; PoEL-3; TEP

Or did one see what one looked at? (*LL*) Did one look at what one saw. Hart Crane. AnAn

Or die and so forget what love ere meant. (*LL*) On Monsieur's Departure. Elizabeth I, Queen of England. NAEL-1; NALW; VBLP; WPE

Or die by self-denial. (*LL*) The Greater Trial. The Countess of Winchilsea. TrGrPo

Or drown in despair when his days darken. (*LL*) The Answer. Robinson Jeffers. CMoP; GoYe

Or ells with gret shame your game wilbe sene. (*LL*) The Auncient Acquaintance, Madam. John Skelton. AAS; PoEL-1

Or else he would forgo his mortal nature. (*LL*) The Human Seasons. Keats. EnRP; GTBS; GTBS-P; WiR

Or else his dear papa is poor. (*LL*) System. Robert Louis Stevenson. PWR; TEP

Or else I'll have your liver and light. (*LL*) Crow, crow, get out of my sight. *Unknown.* ISE

Or else it will be. (*LL*) Say Goodbye to Big Daddy. Randall Jarrell. PoNe

Or else quite extinguish mine. (*LL*) A Prayer to the Wind. Thomas Carew. BeJo

Or else, there's no wife in the case. The Spoils of Youth. Robert Browning. *Fr.* Likeness, A. CBCK

Or else with thee to take me to the skie. (*LL*) Sinnes Heavie Loade. Robert Southwell. ESCV

Or else you break a faithful heart. (*LL*) To a Lady on Her Passion for Old China. John Gay. GGP; ImPo; LiTB; SCGP

Or Ever God Created Adam. *Malay Oral Tradition, tr. by* R. J. Wilkinson. WTO

Or ever the knightly years were gone. When I Was a King in Babylon. W. E. Henley. VPP

Or every man be blind. (*LL*) Tell all the truth but tell it slant. Emily Dickinson. AmPP; HeIL; HeIP; LiTA; NAAL-1; NALW; NAWM-2; NoAM; NOBA; NoP; PFP; Poetr; PPP; TAP; UnPo; WeW

Or find a grave. (*LL*) Battle Song. Ebenezer Elliot. OxAEP-2

Or flaw, and curls about her neck. (*LL*) At a Reading. Thomas Bailey Aldrich. AnAmPo; OBAL

Or gathers seaward, ebbing out of mind. (*LL*) The Slow Pacific Swell. Yvor Winters. NOBA

Or give the mittee will, or give the gode man power. (*LL*) An Excelente Balade of Charitie. Thomas Chatterton. EBEV; EnRP; NOEC; OxAEP-1

Or hanged thou shouldst be. (*LL*) Queen Eleanor's Confession. *Unknown.* ESPB, A *and* B *vers.*; OBET; PrIm

Or hear old Triton blow his wreathèd horn. (*LL*) The World Is Too Much with Us. Wordsworth. AWP; ChTr; ClHu; CoGr; EBEvV; EnRP; FaPoB; FaPoR; FHYEP; GTBS; GTBS-P; HAP; HeIL; HeIP; HoPM; ImPo; InPK; InPS; LiTB; MAT; MeMBP; NAEL-2; NAWM-2; NOBE; NoP; OAEL-2; OBNC; PoE; PoEL-4; Poetr; PoLF; PoRA; PPP; PrIm; RaBo; Son; SoSe; TEP; TFi; TrGrPo; TRP; WeW; WGRP

Or help to half-a-crown. (*LL*) The Man He Killed. Thomas Hardy. CMoP; DL; FF; HeIL; HeIP; LiTB; LiTM; MeMBP; MoAB; MoBrPo; NIP; OBWP; PAW; Poetr; RB; TFi; WeW

Or her kisses where a serpent hides. (*LL*) Returning, We Hear the Larks. Isaac Rosenberg. FaBoMo; NAEL-2; NoAM; NSI; OAEL-2; OBWP; PeFWW; PoWW

Or hope relief. (*LL*) Elegy over a Tomb. Lord Herbert of Cherbury. EIL; GGP; MeLP; NOBE; OBEV; OBWVE; PoEL-2

Or how beloved above all else that dies. (*LL*) And You as Well Must Die, Beloved Dust. Edna St. Vincent Millay. PoLF; PoRA; TAP

Or 'hurl their lances at the Sun' — (for 'lance' read 'assegai'.). (*LL*) Shu' Shu' of Delgo. Albert Brodrick. PeSAV

Or I of her a sinner. (*LL*) Pious Selinda [*or* Celinda]. Congreve. ELP; ErPo; NOBE

Or I shall live your epitaph to make. Shakespeare. *Fr.* Sonnets. OxAEP-1

Or I wouldn't be here. (*LL*) Birdie McReynolds. Samuel Hoffenstein. BXAP; NBLV

Or if I would delight my privat hours. Milton. *Fr.* Paradise Regained [*or* Regain'd]. PeECV, *bk.* IV, *ll.* 331–349

Or if the nightingale should die. (*LL*) By the Arno. Oscar Wilde. EBVV

Or in front, and I following her just the same. (*LL*) To the Garden the World. Walt Whitman. ChIV-1

Or in the dusk, the garden, one night bird. (*LL*) Return from Luluabourg. Michael Jackson. PeNZ

Or is the Caucasian played out? (*LL*) Further Language from Truthful James. Bret Harte. FaBoCo; NOBL

Or it goes to the backyard and stands like an old horse cold in the pasture. (*LL*) Original Sin; a Short Story. Robert Penn Warren. HoPM; LiTA; LiTM; NOCV; PPP; SM; TAP

Or just some human sleep. *(LL)* After Apple-picking. Robert Frost. AmPP; AnAmPo; CMoP; InPS; LiTA; MeMAP; MoAB; MoAmPo; MoP; NAAL-2; NoAM; NOBA; NTP; NU; OxBA; PoE; Poetr; PPP; PrIm; SAmP; SoSe; TAP; TFi; TRP; UnPo

Or kettle whispering its faint undersong. *(LL)* Personal Talk. Wordsworth. EnRP; NOBE

Or known what death could do. *(LL)* Carentan O Carentan. Louis Simpson. ArOW; CoAP; MoBS; NOBA; OBWP; PoE; PrIm; RB

Or lament that the pleasure is ended? *(LL)* Epigram: To Papilus. Martial. PeHV

Or lily on the water. *(LL)* Winter Rain. Christina Rossetti. BoNaP; WiR

Or look in a gipsy's eye. *(LL)* Where Do the Gipsies Come From? Sir Henry Howarth Bashford. CH; CoGr

Or looked I back unto the times hence flown. To Master Denham, on His Prospective Poem. Robert Herrick. BeJo

Or love me [*or mee*] less [*or lesse*], or love me [*or mee*] more. Sidney Godolphin. BeJo; JCP
(Song: "Or love me less, or love me more." NOSC

Or make a heart that's like our own! *(LL)* A Sonnet Made on Isabella Markham. John Harington. EIL

Or man a woman half so fair. *(LL)* There Is None, O None but You. Thomas Campion. EIL

Or many things adulterate. Tristan Corbière, *tr. fr. French by* Joseph T. Shipley. AWP

Or maybe I will stay a child. *(LL)* The Question. Karla Kuskin. NTCP; PDV

Or *me* anymore. *(LL)* Growing Up. Harry Behn. PDV

Or Medway smooth, or royal towred Thame. *(LL)* Rivers Arise; a Fragment. Milton. ChTr

Or mists the Apennine. *(LL)* Thought beneath so slight a film, The. Emily Dickinson. AmPP; OxBA

Or Mother Dunch's Buttocks — which? *(LL)* On an Inyanga Road. Noel H. Brettell. PeSAV

Or Nature's DARKLING of this mossy shed? *(LL)* The Contrast; the Parrot and the Wren. Wordsworth. FM

Or noon-in Mazarin? *(LL)* I found the phrase [*or words*] to every thought. Emily Dickinson. AmPP

Or not untrue or not unkind. *(LL)* Talking in Bed. Philip Larkin. BoLoP; CBLP; NAEL-2; NoP; OxBM

Or one that is coming to birth. *(LL)* Arthur O'Shaughnessy. CoGr; FaPoR; IIP; OBEV; PeIV; PlP; TrGrPo

Or only the delights, which you did give? *(LL)* To a Lady Who Did Sing Excellently. Lord Herbert of Cherbury. SeCP

Or other names. *(LL)* Leaving the Motel. W. D. Snodgrass. FF; NIP

Or out of time will correct this. *(LL)* The Country Clergy. R. S. Thomas. GTBS-P; OxBTC; PeECV

Or overrated thy designs. *(LL)* Great God, I Ask Thee for No Meaner Pelf. Thoreau. NOBA; PFP; TrPWD

Or placed thy friends above her stern decrees? *(LL)* The Complaint. Mark Akenside. OBEV

Or prove as false as thou art now. *(LL)* The Message. John Donne. EIL; MeLP

Or rather make no Thine and Mine! *(LL)* Clasping of Hands. George Herbert. PoEL-2

Or rather the sacred fish with the golden faces. Callimachus, *tr. fr. Greek by* Barbara Hughes Fowler. *Fr.* Galataea. HePo

Or, Round the world? *(LL)* American jump, American jump. *Unknown.* OxNR

Or scorn[e] or pity [*or pittie*] on me take. The Dream[e]. Ben Jonson. BeJo; CBLP; NOBE; NOSC; PoEL-2

Or send it backe to me. *(LL)* The Crier. Michael Drayton. EIL; InvP; NOSC

Or so they say. Or so he should. *(LL)* God's Love. Vikram Seth. TRP

Or so very little longer! *(LL)* The Lost Mistress. Robert Browning. BoLoP; NOBE; OBEV; OBNC

Or softly drop so poor a shame. *(LL)* "Died . . . ." Elizabeth Barrett Browning. NOBVV

Or Southey, or Barrow. *(LL)* Who Kill'd John Keats? Byron. EnRP

Or stain a point with blood. *(LL)* Ghostly Tree. Léonie Adams. MoAB; MoAmPo

Or stand all night watering roses, his feet blue in rubber boots. *(LL)* Old Florist. Theodore Roethke. OxBSP

Or teeth. *(LL)* Small Animal. Alberta Turner. FoLa

Or that of my Alexis, I am lost. *(LL)* On Her Loving Two Equally. Aphra Behn. NALW; NIP

Or the *Chaplain,* (for 'tis his *Trade*) as in Duty bound, shall ever *Pray.* *(LL)* To Their Excellencies the Lords Justices of Ireland, the Humble Petition of Frances Harris, Who Must Starve, and Die a Maid if It Miscarries. Swift. NOEC; PoEL-3

Or the day's vanity, the night's remorse. *(LL)* The Choice. W. B. Yeats. CMoP; NoAM; OxBSP; OxBTC

Or the dazzling crystal. *(LL)* What I Expected [Was]. Stephen Spender. MoAB; MoBrPo; NoAM; NOBE; OxAEP-2

Or the fox from his lair in the morning. *(LL)* John Peel. John Woodcock Graves. CH; OxBoLi

Or the image-kingdom's idol of the past generation. Saul Tchernichowsky, *tr. fr. Hebrew by* Ruth Finer Mintz. *Fr.* To the Sun. MHP

Or the light, or the. The Firmament Doth Shake. Ken Edwards. NBrP

Or the Persians and Xerxes? His judges or Socrates? Pilate or Christ? *(LL)* Io Victis! William Wetmore Story. WGRP

Or the price of grass-seed? *(LL)* The Other Side. Seamus Heaney. CIP; PNI

Or the prophetic sibillance of song. *(LL)* The Mad Potter. John Hollander. VCAP

Or the radiant sisters the Pleiades. *(LL)* On the Beach at Night. Walt Whitman. AmPP; AWP; ChTr; MoAmPo; NOBA; NoP; OxBA; SAmP

Or the rest will be wanting one too! *(LL)* An Epicure, Dining at Crewe. *Unknown.* NTCP; PeLi

Or the rest will be wanting one, too! *(LL)* I Raised a Great Hullabaloo. *Unknown.* PDV

Or the yeasty spirit dies. Here happiness is blest. *(LL)* Penelope Sets Up House with Odysseus. Jane Oliensis. UTF

Or Thebes half buried in the desert sand. *(LL)* The Rock of Cashel. Sir Aubrey De Vere. IIP; PeIV

Or they had now been here. *(LL)* Fair Margaret and Sweet William ("As it fell out in a long summer's day.") *Unknown.* ESPB, A *vers.*; OxBB

Or Think We'e Met subhuman rights Before. *(LL)* A Salesman Is an It That Stinks Excuse. E. E. Cummings. NoAM; OxBA; Poetr

Or this doll of death, hideous, we treasure. The Doll. Peyton Houston. *Fr.* Sonnet Variations. Son

Or till blossomed stalks cannot weave a spell. *(LL)* Spraying the Potatoes. Patrick Kavanagh. BIrV; IIP; IPY; NoP

Or to seal up the sun. *(LL)* To Daisies, Not to Shut So Soon[e]. Robert Herrick. BeJo; CaPo; CH; ELP; GBL; OBEV; OxBSP; SeCV-1; TrGrPo

Or, trying simple charms and spells. John Clare. *Fr.* Shepherd's [*or* Shepheards] Calendar, The. FaBoUs

Or wants for anything (but cash). *(LL)* Hail South Australia! *Unknown.* NOBAu

Or was myself — too small? *(LL)* I took my Power in my Hand. Emily Dickinson. ChIV-1; SAmP

Or what death I should dee. *(LL)* Mary Hamilton. *Unknown.* NOBE; OxBB

Or what, Faustine? *(LL)* Faustine. Swinburne. BeLS; EBVVPR; PeHV

Or what is closer to the truth. When I Buy Pictures. Marianne Moore. OxBA

Or whether doth in my mind, being crowned with you. Shakespeare. *Fr.* Sonnets. SCGP

Or whether we shall be victorious, or utterly quell'd and defeated. *(LL)* As I Lay with My Head in Your Lap Camerado. Walt Whitman. AnAmPo; NAAL-1; OxBA

Or whistling, I am not a little boy. *(LL)* The Ball Poem. John Berryman. CoAP; FF; MoAmPo; NoAM; NOBA; NoP; Poetr

Or winding path? The edge is what I have. *(LL)* In a dark time, the eye begins to see. Theodore Roethke. CAPP; HAP; HeIP; MAT; MoAmPo; MoP; NAAL-2; NoAM; NOBA; NoP; NYBP; PeECV; PoE; Poetr; PPP; RaBo, 2 *sts. only*; TAP; TFi; VCAP

Or withoute quiete to have huge labour. *(LL)* I shall say what inordinat[e] love is. *Unknown.* MiEL

Or wrong. He just wins or loses. *(LL)* My Father; October 1942. William Stafford. CAPP; NaP

Or yield or die's the word, what could he mean. Ignotum per Ignotius, or a Furious Hodge-Podge of Nonsense; a Pindaric. *Unknown.* CBNP; NOEC

Or you may guess. *(LL)* Winter: My Secret. Christina Rossetti. BrRo; NAEL-2; NOBVV; TEP

Oracle. *Yoruba Oral Tradition, tr. by* Ulli Beier. WTO

Oracle of the Drawned, The. Douglas Oliver. NBrP

Oracles, The. A. E. Housman. HAP

Oracular Portcullis, The. James Reaney. ErPo

Oradour-sur-Glane. Silence. Lucia Cordell Getsi. LoHo

Oraga Haru, *sels.* Issa, *tr. fr. Japanese by* Nobuyuki Yuasa.

Oral Messages, *sels.* Lawrence Ferlinghetti.
"I am waiting for my case to come up." AiP; CAPP; GOA

Oral Tradition, The. Eavan Boland. NBrP; PBCIP

Orang-utan. Judith Nicholls. OBAP

Orange. Barbara Ferland. PBCV

Orange, The. Matthew Prior. PeLV

Orange air grows fetid with smoke, The. The uneasy dark. Mess Deck Casualty. Alan Ross.
  (Epilogue: " 'O where are you going?' said reader to rider.") (Five Songs.) FaBoCh; LiTM
Orange and blue and then grey. Like Queen Christina. Kenneth Rexroth. ArNa
Orange Bears, The. Kenneth Patchen. NaP
Orange Buds by Mail from Florida. Walt Whitman. NAAL-1
Orange Chiffon. Jayne Cortez. BlSi
Orange in the middle of a table. Against Still Life. Margaret Atwood. MoCV; NMM
Orange leaves are gone. Lady Izumi Shikibu, tr. fr. Japanese by Willis Barnstone. BoWoP
Orange Lily, The. Unknown. NOIV
Orange Lily, The. Unknown. FaBoPV; GBP
Orange line splits the sky, An. The Flint Hills. Lew Blockcolski. VoR
Orange March. Richard Murphy. Fr. Battle of Aughrim, The. NOIV
Orange of Cloves, An. Alison Brackenbury. SCBI
Orange on its way. On Its Way. May Swenson. SoSe; WPE
Orange on the table, An. Alicante. Jacques Prévert, tr. fr. French by Lawrence Ferlinghetti. BoLoP
Orange rivers and red dogs of Paul Gauguin, The. Slag. Charles David Wright. MT
Orange Tree, The. John Shaw Neilson. CBAP; FaBoMA
Orange tree, The. Lady Otomo no Sakanoe, tr. fr. Japanese by Kenneth Rexroth and Ikuko Atsumi. WPJ
Orange Tree, The. Ellen Pearce. IHMS
Oranges, The. Abu Dharr, tr. fr. Arabic by A. J. Arberry. TTY
Oranges. Gary Soto. NoAM; WeW
Oranges Are Ripe, The. Bei Dao, tr. fr. Chinese by Donald Finkel with Chen Xueliang. SpMi
Orara. Henry Clarence Kendall. CBAP
Orator. Emerson. Fr. Quatrains. OxBA
Orator dismal of Nottinghamshire, An. An Excellent New Song, Being the Intended Speech of a Famous Orator against Peace. Swift. APAS
Orator Flaccus can commit solecisms. Lucilius, tr. fr. Greek by Peter Porter. GrAn
Orator from Rhetorick gardens picks, The. Edward Taylor. Fr. Preparatory Meditations Before My Approach to the Lord's Supper. EAP
Orator Prigg. Blake. OBSV
Orators, The, sels. W. H. Auden.
  "O where are you going? said reader to rider." CMoP; CoGr; LiTB; MeMAP; NOBE; UV
  (Epilogue: " 'O where are you going?' said reader to rider.") FaBoCh (Five Songs.) LiTM; NoAM
  (Song: " 'O Where Are You Going?' said reader to rider.") OAEL-2 Of The Enemy. CBCK
Orator's Epitaph, The. Lord Brougham. NBLV
Orbit I describe in my environment, The. Orbits. Nina Cassian, tr. fr. Romanian by Naomi Lazard. PoSu
Orbiting, the sun itself has a sun. The Great Dark. Martin Carter. PBCV
Orbits. Nina Cassian, tr. fr. Romanian by Naomi Lazard. PoSu
Orchard. Hilda Doolittle ("H. D."). CMoP; LiTA; LiTM; MoAmPo; OxBA
Orchard and the Heath, The. George Meredith. OBNC
Orchard at Avignon, An. Agnes Mary Frances Robinson. NOBVV; OBTV
Orchard-Pit, The. Dante Gabriel Rossetti. EnLoPo; NAEL-2; OAEL-2; PeVV; PoEL-5; SCV
Orchards, we linger here because. For a Second Marriage. James Merrill. (Upon a Second Marriage.) NoP
Orchestra, The. William Carlos Williams. HAP
Orchestra; or, A Poem[e] of Da[u]ncing. (Where lives the man that never yet did hear.) Sir John Davies. NoSiC, abr.; SiPS; SiPSBD
  Sels.
  Dance of Love, The. EIL
  Dancing Sea, The. ChTr
  "Dauncing (bright Lady) then began to bee." PoEL-2 (Praise of Dancing, The.) NOBE
  Dedications, I: To His Very Friend, Master Richard Martin
  Dedications, II: To the Prince
  "Sole heir of virtue, and of beauty both." NAEL-1
  "What eye doth see the heaven but doth admire." PeECV
Orchestra tunes up, each instrument, The. Meditation. Anthony Hecht. EOEF
Orchid-lipped, loose-jointed, purplish, indolent flowers. Himalayan Balsam. Anne Stevenson. FaBoWP; OxAEP-2; VBLP
Orchids. Theodore Roethke. CMoP; TRP
Orchids grow through spring and summer. Ch'en Tzu-ang, tr. by William H. Nienhauser. Fr. Impressions of Things Encountered. SuSp
Orcio and Fiasco. Judith Baumel. UTF

Ordained I was a beggar. The File-Hewer's Lamentation. Joseph Mather. FaBoPV; NOEC
Ordeal. Nina Cassian, tr. fr. Romanian by Michael Impey and Brian Swann. PBWP
Ordeal by Fire, The, sels. Edmund Clarence Stedman.
  "Thou, who dost feel Life's vessel strand." WGRP
Ordeal by Fire, sels. Itamar Ya'oz-kest, tr. fr. Hebrew by Bernhard Frank.
Order, but the sum of things, The. (LL) Fame. Robert Herrick. FaBoEE
Order for a Picture, An. Alice Cary. BLPA
Order in the gallery! Unknown. ISE
Order is a lovely thing. The Monk in the Kitchen. Anna Hempstead Branch. MoAmPo
Order of the Dead, The. J. P. Clark Bekedereme. HBAPE
Order the ground? Versions. Robert Kelly. Fr. Book of Persephone, The. PoM
Ordered ocean of flags swaying at dawn, An. 1966. Dermot Bolger. IB
Ordinary, The, sels. William Cartwright.
  Saint Francis and Saint Benedight
  (House Blessing, A.) ChTr
Ordinary Evening in Cleveland, An. Lewis Turco. NYBP
Ordinary people are peculiar too. Conversation. Louis MacNeice. TEP
Ordinary Women, The. Wallace Stevens. OxBA
Ordnance Survey Map 178. Douglas Oliver. VaA
Ore is waiting in the tubs, the snow's upon the fells, The. Fourpence a Day. At. to Thomas Raine. OBET; SWP
Oread. Hilda Doolittle ("H. D."). AWP; CMoP; GoJo; HeIP; InPS; MoAmPo; MoP; NAAL-2; NALW; NoAM; NOBA; OxBA; Poetr; TAP
Oregon Message, An. William Stafford. CoAP
Oregon Trail, The. Arthur Guiterman. FaPON
Orf. Ted Hughes. NoAM
Sir Orfeo. Unknown. EnVB
Organist, The. George W. Stevens. BLPA
Orgasm completely, The. Tom Clark. CoAP
Orgy. Norman MacCaig. OxBC
Orgy (That Is, Vegetable Market, at Sarno). Gina Labriola, tr. fr. Italian by Edgar Pauk. WPOW
Orgy was held on the lawn, The. Unknown. PeLi
Orient Express, The. Randall Jarrell. CMoP; CoAP; NOBA; PoE
Oriental Apologue, An. James Russell Lowell. PoEL-5
Oriflamme. Jessie Redmond Fauset. BlSi; PoBA; ShDr
Origin of Didactic Poetry, The. James Russell Lowell. PoEL-5
Origin of the Praise of God, The. Robert Bly. NU
Origin of the Skagit Indians, The. Lucy Williams, tr. fr. Skagit Indian by Carl Cary. STP
Origin, Signification, dread Daysman, Consummator. (LL) Midnight. Mary Ursula Bethell. PeNZ
Original./ Ragged-round. Malcolm X. Gwendolyn Brooks. PoBA; TTY
Original Child Bomb, sels. Thomas Merton.
  In the Year 1945 an Original Child Was Born. NAs
Original Epitaph on a Drunkard. Royall Tyler. OBAL
Original Mind. Nancy Paddock. LoHo
Original Sequence. Philip Booth. ChIV-1
Original Sin. Robinson Jeffers. MoAB; MoAmPo
Original Sin. Alexander Kinnan Laing. NYBP
Original Sin; a Short Story. Robert Penn Warren. HoPM; LiTA; LiTM; NOCV; PPP; SM; TAP
Original Strawberry. Nancy Willard. LCAP
Origins. Keorapetse Kgositsile. PoBA
Origins and History of Consciousness. Adrienne Rich. NIP; Poetr
Oriki Erinle. Unknown, tr. fr. Yoruba by Ulli Beier. PBA; TTY
Orinda, and the Fair Astrea gone. To the Author of Agnes de Castro. Delariviere Manley. KTR
Orinda to Lucasia. Katherine Philips. NOSC; PeHV
Orinoco, 1561, The. Ai. Fr. Gilded Man, The. AnAn
Orioles warble/ And flowers dance. Tune: "Telling of Innermost Feelings." Wen T'ing-yün, tr. fr. Chinese by William R. Schultz. SuSp
Orion. Adrienne Rich. MoP; NAAL-2; NIP; NoAM; NoP; Poetr; WPE
Orisha. Jayne Cortez. BlSi
Orlando Commercial, The. George MacBeth. NOBL; PeLV
Orlando Furioso., sels. Ariosto, tr. fr. Italian.
  "Alcyna met them at the outer gate." OBVE
  "Blessed angell not a word replies, The." OBVE
  "Go soule, go sweetest soule for ever blest." OBVE
  "Soon after, he a crystal stream espying." NoSic
  "Thus much he prayed, and thence away he went." NoSic
Orlando's Rhymes. Shakespeare. Fr. As You Like It. CTC
Ormerod was deeply troubled. Distractions and the Human Crowd. Stevie Smith. OxBC

Ormsby Slatter. Mr. Slatter. N. M. Bodecker. TLR

Ornamental bung, An. Gargoyle. Robert B. Shaw. CRP

Ornamental Hermits, The. Peter Scupham. SCBI

Ornaments. Frank Ormsby. CIP

Ornithology in a World of Flux. Robert Penn Warren. PFP

Ornithorhynchus Paradoxus. (LL) The Platypus. Oliver Herford. FiBHP; PeLV

Orotava Road, The. Basil Bunting. NoAM

O'Rourke's Feast. Hugh MacGowran, tr. fr. Irish. BIrV, tr. by Charles Wilson

Orphan, The. Muhammad al-Maghut, tr. fr. Arabic. TSaS, tr. by May Jayyusi and Naomi Shihab Nye

Orphan, The. Unknown, tr. fr. Chinese by Arthur Waley. PoA

Orphan beat of my heart, The. "Ping Hsin," tr. fr. Chinese by Kenneth Rexroth and Ling Chung. BoWoP

Orphan boat of my heart, The. "Ping Hsin," tr. fr. Chinese by Kenneth Rexroth and Ling Chung. Fr. Multitudinous Stars. WPC

Orphan Born. Robert J. Burdette. OBAL

Orphan Boy, The. Unknown. OBET

Orphan Boy's Tale, The. Amelia Alderson Opie. VPP

Orphan Girl, The. Unknown. AmFP; AS

Orphan Girl, An. Mrs. Henry Linden. CBWP-4

"Orphan Hours, the Year is dead." Dirge for the Year. Shelley. GN

Orphan jazz appears sobbing, sobbing, sobbing, An. (LL) Joal. Léopold Sédar Senghor. NegPo

Orphan, yes, An. But not. Fragment Reflection I. Doris Turner. JB

Orphanage in the rain. Promises of Leniency and Forgiveness. Charles Simic. LCAP

Orphanage of possibility, The. Sea Mouse. Amy Clampitt. FoLa

Orphan's Song, The. Sydney Thompson Dobell. CH; ELP; OBNC

Orpheus. Donald Davie. TEP

Orpheus. John Fletcher and William Shakespeare. See Orpheus with his lute made trees.

Orpheus. Robert Herrick. CaPo

Orpheus. Elizabeth Madox Roberts. MoAmPo

Orpheus. Yvor Winters. NOBA; VGW

Orpheus Alone. Mark Strand. BAP-90

Orpheus and Eurydice. Robert Browning. CTC

Orpheus and Eurydice. Jorie Graham. VCAP

Orpheus and Eurydice. Geoffrey Hill. TRP

Orpheus and Eurydice. Jean Valentine. FaBoWP; LCAP

Orpheus, dying, not all Music died. Leontios, tr. fr. Greek by Peter Whigham. GrAn

Orpheus he went (as poets tell). Orpheus. Robert Herrick. CaPo

Orpheus I am, come from the deeps below. John Fletcher. Fr. Mad Lover, The. GBL

Orpheus in the Underworld. David Gascoyne. FaBoTw

Orpheus liked the glad personal quality. Syringa. John Ashbery. HCAP; NoAM; VCAP

Orpheus to Beasts. Richard Lovelace. CaPo

Orpheus to Woods. Richard Lovelace. CaPo

Orpheus with His Lute [Made Trees]. John Fletcher and William Shakespeare. See Orpheus with his lute made trees.

Orpheus with his lute made trees. John Fletcher and William Shakespeare. Fr. King Henry VIII. NOSC
(Music.) FaBoCh
(Orpheus with His Lute [Made Trees].) ChTr; EnRePo; GN; TrGrPo
(Orpheus.) EiL; OBEV
(Song: "Orpheus with his lute made trees.") PoEL-2
(Sweet Music's Power.) NOBE

Orthodox, Orthodox, wha believe in John Knox. The Kirk's Alarm. Burns. OxBoLi

Orthodoxy's staunch adherent. To Dr. Kipling. Richard Porson. FaBoCo

Ortho's Epitaph. Theocritus [or Theokritus], tr. fr. Greek by Charles Stuart Calverley. FaBoEE

Ortiz. Hezekiah Butterworth. PAH

Orts, sels. Ted Hughes.
Buzz in the Window. NoAM

Ortus. Ezra Pound. LiTA

O's Song: ("How should I your true love know.") Shakespeare. See How should I your true love know.

Oscar Wilde. Ulick O'Connor. PeIV

Oscar Wilde. Dorothy Parker. Fr. Pig's-Eye View of Literature, A. NALW

Oscar Wilde. Swinburne. OHCV; PeVV

Osceola. Walt Whitman. NAAL-1

Oshun, the River Goddess. Yoruba Oral Tradition, tr. by Ulli Beier. WTO

Osip Mandelstam. Seamus Deane. BiHa; PBCIP

Ospita. Peter Riley. NBrP

Ossawatomie. Carl Sandburg. CMoP; OxBA

Ossian's Serenade. Calder Campbell. BLPA

Ostella forth of Town: To My Heart. John Tatham. NOSC

'Ostler Joe. George R. Sims. BeLS; BLPA

Ostrich. Alan Brownjohn. OBAP

Ostrich is a Silly Bird, The. Mary E. Wilkins Freeman. FaPON; OBCA

Ostriches and Grandmothers! Amiri Baraka. NeAP

O'Sullivan Rua to Mary Lavell. W. B. Yeats. See When my arms wrap you round I press.

Othello, sels. Shakespeare.
Farewell content. TrGrPo
"Her father lov'd me; oft invited me." EBEV; OxAEP-1; SCV
"I had been happy, if the general camp." OxBM
"I will in Cassio's lodging lose this napkin." OxAEP-1
"It is the cause, it is the cause, my soul." EBEV
"O my fair warrior!" OxAEP-1
"Soft you; a word or two before you go." OxAEP-1

Othello Jones Dresses for Dinner. Ed Roberson. PoBA; PoNe

Othello loved Desdemona. A. Cinna. PeLi

Other, The. Ruth Fainlight. BrRo

Other. Lance Henson. VoR

Other. R. S. Thomas. AngWe

Other, An. Thomas Carew. See This little vault, this narrow room.

Other bright days of action have seemed great. John Masefield. Fr. Biography. OxBTC

Other day a partridge, The. The Talk of the Town. Ed Fisher. FiBHP

Other day all thirty shillings' worth, The. Thomas Campey and the Copernican System. Tony Harrison. SCBI

Other day, when I looked at a tree, The. Roots. Louis Ginsberg. TrJP

Other Fabrics, Other Mores! Anna Maria Lenngren, tr. fr. Swedish by Nadia Christensen and Marianne Tiblin. AIW; PBWP

Other Fellow's Job, The. Strickland W. Gillilan. WBLP

Other Forms of Slaughter. Catherine Obianuju Acholonu. HBAPE

Other help for him there 's none, there 's none I know. (LL) The Unknown Shepherd's Complaint. Richard Barnfield. EiL

Other Life, the. Nina Cassian, tr. fr. Romanian by Cristian Andrei and Daniel Weissbort. PoSu

Other Little Tune, T'. Mother Goose. See I won't be my father's Jack.

Other Lives of the Romantics. Jane Flanders. PBCAP

Other loves I have known. Proof. Bessie Calhoun Bird. BlSi

Other loves may sink and settle, other loves may loose and slack. The Strange Music. G. K. Chesteron. OtMeF

Other men are thorn. Mahadevi, tr. fr. Kannada by A. K. Ramanujan. BoWoP

Other never read, The. (LL) Epigram on One Who Made Long Epitaphs. Pope. FaBoEE

Other Obit. Dean Young. NAmP90

Other oxen have long curly horns. The Old Cowboy. Kao Ch'i, tr. fr. Chinese by Kenneth Rexroth. OHMPC

Other patients are ill otherwise, and do. The Mad. Robert Pinsky. Fr. Essay on Psychiatrists. NoAM

Other props are gone, The. Je T'Adore. Thomas Kinsella. MoP; NoAM

Other remains, the/ passive today. (LL) Classic Scene. William Carlos Williams. NAAL-2; OxBA

Other Sheep I Have, Which Are Not of This Fold. Bryant. TrPWD

Other Side, The. Roy Fuller. OxBC

Other Side, The. Natalie Hardwick. IIP

Other Side, The. Seamus Heaney. CIP; PNI

Other Side, The. Linda Hogan. ETG

Other Side, The. Meredith Stricker. LoHo

Other Side of a Mirror, The. Mary Elizabeth Coleridge. BoWoP; NALW

Other Side of the River, The. Charles Wright. MT; VCAP

Other Song of the Faithful, for the Mercies of God, An. Michael Drayton. ChIV-1

Other Syllabus, The. Chenjerai Hove. HBAPE

Other Voice, The. Tom Paulin. PNI

Other way Satan went down, Th.' Milton. Fr. Paradise Lost. EPCY; NAEL-1

Other World, The. Harriet Beecher Stowe. WGRP

Other World, The. Unknown, tr. fr. Egyptian by Robert Hillyer. Fr. Book of the Dead. AWP; OBD

Others. Roger McDonald. FaBoMA

Others. Charles D. Meigs. WBLP

Others. James Reeves. Spl

Others abide our question. Thou art free. Shakespeare. Matthew Arnold. EBVVPR; EPCY; FHYEP; HeIP; InvP; NoP; OBEV; OxAEP-2; SCGP; Son; TrGrPo

Others again here lived in my days. Chapman the Translator. Michael Drayton. *Fr.* To Henry Reynolds, of Poets and Poesy. EPCY

Others because you did not keep. A Deep-sworn Vow. W. B. Yeats. CMoP; OAEL-2; PFP; PoE; UnPo

Others have pleasantness and praise. Love's Votary. George Augustus Simcox. NOBVV

Others Hunters in the North the Cree, The. Jerome Rothenberg. PoM

Others, I Am Not the First. A. E. Housman. *Fr.* Shropshire Lad, A. CMoP; FaPoB; LiTB; MeMBP; MoBrPo; NOBVV; OxBTC; PoE; PPP

Others, I am not the first. Others, I Am Not the First. A. E. Housman. *Fr.* Shropshire Lad, A. CMoP; FaPoB; LiTB; MeMBP; MoBrPo; NOBVV; OxBTC; PoE; PPP

Others, many others, must have known. Leaving Buffalo. Charles Martin. PoA

Others stand in their imported, The. Giving Up Butterflies. Geraldine Kudaka. ETG

Others taunt me with having knelt at well-curbs. For Once, Then, Something. Robert Frost. NoAM; NOBA

Others trap in the snarl of frenzy.' *(LL)* Attis. Catullus. OBVE

Others weary of the noise. Mothers — and Others. Amos R. Wells. WBLP

Otherwise kill me. *(LL)* Prayer before Birth. Louis MacNeice. EBEvV; FaBoVe; GTBS-P; LiTB; NAs; PAW; PNI; TIRV; TwCP

Otherwise you pay for it later!]. *(LL)* The Trout. Christian David Schubart. RiWo

Otis. Lorenzo Thomas. UL

O'Toole, Hodain, ye Bruthers Dogg. *(LL)* Ye Bruthers Dogg. Jon Anderson. NBLV

Ottava Rima would, I know, be proper. W. H. Auden. *Fr.* Letter to Lord Byron. NOBL

Otter, The. Seamus Heaney. IPY; NoAM; PNI

Otter, An. Ted Hughes. CMoP; MoP; NoAM

Otter is known, The. Lutra, the Fisher. James McMichael. AmPA

Otter, Redewetter. Colin Simms. NBrP

Otto. Gwendolyn Brooks. PChr; PDV

Ought to be told to come and take him in. *(LL)* The Runaway. Robert Frost. AWP; CH; CoGr; FaBoCh; FaPON; GoJo; MoAB; MoAmPo; PDV; SAmP; TwCP; VGW

Ought we to interfere? *(LL)* John Gilbert Was a Bushranger. Unknown. NOBAu

Oui Papa. Delano Abdul Malik de Coteau. PBCV

Our age bereft of nobility. A Poem for Painters. John Wieners. NeAP; PoM

Our ambassador to Venus, Mz Abner. Unknown. PeHV

Our anguish and our anodyne. *(LL)* From the Corpse Woodpiles, from the Ashes. Robert Hayden. CAPP

Our author by experience finds it true. Dryden. *Fr.* Aureng-Zebe. OxBoLi; SeCV-2

Our Backs Are to the Cypress. Leah Goldberg, *tr. fr. Hebrew by* Ramah Commanday. BoWoP

Our backyards touched somewhere upon the hill. Neighbors. Marilyn Francis. GoYe

Our Ball. Winthrop Mackworth Praed. *Fr.* Letters from Teignmouth. EnRP

Our band is few but true and tried. Song of Marion's Men. Bryant. AnAmPo; PAH

Our bark was out — far, far from land. The Sailor's Grave. *At. to* Eliza Cook. BLPA

Our beauty is to us that which to men. Sir Richard Fanshawe, *after the Italian of* Giovanni Battista Guarini. *Fr.* Il Pastor Fido. OBVE

Our bed adrift on morning's river. *(LL)* Widow offers her broken tears to an idol, A. Bei Dao. SpMi

Our beds are at a hospital distance. Nights in the Iron Hotel. Michael Hofmann. SCBI

Our best singers. The Blues (in Two Parts). Val Ferdinand. NBV

Our Bias. W. H. Auden. MoP; NoP; Poetr

Our Biggest Fish. Eugene Field. AnAmPo

Our Birth Is But a Sleep. Wordsworth. *See* Our birth is but a sleep and a forgetting.

Our birth is but a sleep and a forgetting. Wordsworth. *Fr.* Ode: Intimations of Immortality from Recollections of Early Childhood. AWP; BLPL; EnRP; FaBoRV; FHYEP; HAP; HeIP; InvP; LiTB; MeMBP; NAs; NOBE; NoP; OAEL-2; OBEV; OBNC; PoE; PoEL-4; PPP; PrIm; TEP; TrGrPo; WGRP

(Intimations of Immortality.) ChTr

(Our Birth Is But a Sleep.) FaBV

Our blue boat drifts. Birdwatching at Fan Lake. Anita Endrezze-Danielson. HATNAP

Our boat is asleep on Serchio's stream. Shelley. *Fr.* Boat on the Serchio, The. Mes

Our boat touches the bank. Thomas A. Clark. *Fr.* Sixteen Sonnets. NBrP

Our boats were moored where Luxor throws. Written on the Plain of Thebes. John William Burgon. OBTV

Our boatswain calls out for his bold British heroes. New Sea Song. Unknown. OxBSS

Our Bodies. Denise Levertov. NaP; PPP; VBLP

Our bodies. Every day we separate. *(LL)* Every day our bodies separate. Marilyn Hacker. AmPA; SM

Our bodyes, not wee move. *(LL)* Soules joy, now I am gone. *At. to* The Earl of Pembroke William Herbert, Earl of Pembroke. ESCV

Our Bog is Dood. Stevie Smith. CBNP; FaBoNo; NAEL-2; NBLV; PoE; WeW

Our bomber flying home. Hubris, off the White Cliffs. Martin Stokes. PWE

Our Bondage It Shall End. *At. to* Peter Cartwright. AH

Our brains ache, in the merciless iced east winds that knive us. Exposure. Wilfred Owen. FaBoMo; FaPoB; InPS; MeMBP; NoAM; OBWP; PAW; PeFWW; PIP; PoWW; RB

Our broadcast day is over, I've unplugged. Archaic Torso of My Uncle Phil. Mark Cox. NAmP90

Our brother Clarence goes to school. Big Brother. Elizabeth Madox Roberts. FaPON

Our brown canal was endless to my thought. "George Eliot." *Fr.* Brother and Sister. NALW; NOBVV

Our bugles sang truce, for the night-cloud had lowered [*or* lower'd]. The Soldier's Dream. Thomas Campbell. BeLS; EnRP; FaPoR; GTBS; GTBS-P; OxAEP-2; PIP

Our camp-fires shone bright on the mountain. Sherman's March to the Sea. Samuel H. M. Byers. PAH

Our candles, lit, re-lit, have gone down now. Twelfth Night. Peter Scupham. OBCP

Our Canoe Idles in the Idling Current. Kenneth Rexroth. ErPo

Our Captain Cried All Hands. Unknown. OBET

Our captain stood upon the deck, a spyglass in his hand. Captain Bunker. Unknown. AmFP

Our Caribbean/ a bandolier. Our Home. Jan Carew. PBCV

Our cat she crossed the road. Unknown. RoPo

Our caves do not go Boom! and make one nervy. Sterkfontein. Ruth Miller. PeSA; PeSAV

Our cherished dualism gone? Journal to Stella. Morton Dauwen Zabel. PoA

Our Child. Pablo Neruda, *tr. fr. Spanish by* Perry Higman. ArLo

Our children came for our hands. Rituals. Pat Mora. AfAz

Our children have eaten supper. Nightfall, Midwinter, Missouri. Brian Coffey. *Fr.* Missouri Sequence. CIP

Our Christian savages expect. He Shook off the Beast. Charles Wesley. ChIV-2

Our Christmas pudding was made in November. Pudding Charms. Charlotte Druitt Cole. BoTP

Our city declines, the world is still bleak. Beginnings. Peter Sirr. PBCIP

Our City rulers pass in grand array. Mary E. Tucker. *Fr.* Loew's Bridge: A Broadway Idyl. AmWP; CBWP-1

Our city's sons and daughters. School Days in New Amsterdam. Arthur Guiterman. FaPON

Our Club Work. Mrs. Henry Linden. CBWP-4

Our collective wastebin. In the Outhouse. Mitsuye Yamada. *Fr.* Camp Notes. WPOW

Our couch shall be roses all spangled with dew. A Sensible Girl's Reply to Moore's. Walter Savage Landor. FaBoEE

Our Country. Julia Ward Howe. PAH

Our Country. Thoreau. GOA

Our country, in fenced areas, in cool shady streets. *(LL)* The One Thing That Can Save America. John Ashbery. AiP; NoAM; NOBA

Our Country Is Divided. Faarah Nuur, *tr. fr. Somali by* B. W. Andrzejewski *and* I. M. Lewis. WTO

Our Country's Call. Bryant. PAH

Our Country's Emblem. Unknown. WBLP

Our cup of joy was overfilled. A Dialogue. L. A. J. Moorer. CBWP-3

Our darling's now completely frappé! *(LL)* L'Enfant Glacé. Harry Graham. CBNP; FaBoCo; NBLV; PeLV

Our day was composed of resemblances, take. Sail Away. Robert Adamson. CBAP

Our days, alas! our mortal days. The Shortness and Misery of Life. Isaac Watts. NOCV

Our days were a joy, and our paths through flowers. *(LL)* After a Journey. Thomas Hardy. CBLP; CMoP; EBEV; ELP; EnLoPo; FaBoPP; GBL; GTBS-P; MeMBP; OBNC; OxAEP-2; OxBTC; PoE; PoEL-5

Our Dead. Robert Nichols. WGRP

Our diaries squatted, toad-like [*or* toadlike]. Complaint of the Grandparents. Donald Justice. CAPP
(Nostalgia and Complaint of the Grandparents.) LCAP; NoAM

Our Dog Chasing Swifts. U. A. Fanthorpe. Spl

Our dog Fred. The Diners in the Kitchen. James Whitcomb Riley. OBAL

Our doom is in our being. We began. James Agee. *Fr.* Sonnets. MoAmPo

Our Dust. C. D. Wright. NAmP90

Our eager parties, when the lunar light. Clubs and Social Meetings. George Crabbe. *Fr.* Borough, The. OBF

Our ears were stunned with noisy drum. To Laura, on the French Fleet Parading before Plymouth. Ann Thomas. ECWP

Our earth in 1969. Doggerel by a Senior Citizen. W. H. Auden. IHNG; NBLV; NOBL

Our Earth Mother. *Unknown, tr. fr. Zuni Indian by* R. Bunzel. WTO

Our Earth Will Not Die. Niyi Osundare. HBAPE

Our eldest son is like Ishmael, Jacob is like you. Isreal I. Charles Reznikoff. ChIV-1

Our end is Life. Put out to sea. (*LL*) Thalassa. Louis MacNeice. BIrV; FaBoMo; FaBoRV; NOBE

Our England is a garden that is full of stately views. The Glory of the Garden. Kipling. ArNa

Our English gamesters scorne to stake. Roger Williams. SCAP

Our epoch takes a voluptuous satisfaction. Hypocrite Auteur. Archibald MacLeish. AmPP

Our Ernest. "Elmo." PWR

Our existence would be that much grimmer ex-. Robert Conquest. PeLi

Our eyes are holden that we do not see. Faith and Sight. Anna M. King. BLRP

Our eyes have viewed the burnished vineyards where. Letter to a Friend. Robert Penn Warren. MoAmPo

Our Fadder, Which are in Heaben! He Paid Me Seven. *Unknown.* BPo

Our fairest garland, made of Beauty's flowers. Contention between Four Maids Concerning That Which Addeth Most Perfection to That Sex. Sir John Davies. SiPS

Our Family Tree. Joseph Cephas Holly. AAP

Our family tree is in the sear. Our Family Tree. Joseph Cephas Holly. AAP

Our famous Harvey hath made good. The Circulation. Thomas Washbourne. NOCV

Our fancies are but joys all unexprest. H. Cordelia Ray. CBWP-3

Our fate was settled centuries ago. The Dance Half Done. Mary Ann Larkin. IIP

Our Father. James Schuyler. ChIV-2

Our Father, by Whose Name. F. Bland Tucker. AH

Our Father, God. Adoniram Judson. AH

Our Father, grant us to lie down in peace. Evening Prayer. *Unknown, tr. fr. Hebrew by* Solomon Solis-Cohen. TrJP

Our Father in Heaven. Sarah Josepha Hale. AH

Our Father, Our King. *Unknown.* TrJP

Our Father which [*or* who] art in heaven. Bible, *N.T. Fr.* St. Matthew. PoLF; TrGrPo
(Father our, he-who is at-the-height, name Thy let-it-be.) PeSAV
(Prayer of-Lord, *Tswana vers.*) PeSAV, *tr. by* Sol T. Plaatje

Our Father! While Our Hearts Unlearn. Oliver Wendell Holmes. AH

Our Father, whose creative Will. W. H. Auden. *Fr.* For the Time Being; a Christmas Oratorio. TrPWD

Our father works in us. Father of Women, A [Ad Sororem E. B.]. Alice Meynell. BrRo; NALW; WPE

Our Fathers. Bible, Apocrypha. *See* Let us now praise famous men.

Our fathers all were poor. The Fathers. Edwin Muir. OxBS

Our Fathers' God. Benjamin Copeland. AH

Our fathers' God! from out whose hand. Centennial Hymn. Whittier. PAH

Our Father's Hand. Annie Johnson Flint. BLRP

Our fathers took oaths as of old they took wives. Thomas Brown. FaBoEE

Our fathers were saved from the deaths. Babylon: 539 B.C.E. Charles Reznikoff. ChIV-1

Our fathers, who were wondrous wise. *Unknown.* FaBoUs

Our fathers wrung their bread from stocks and stones. Children of Light. Robert Lowell. CMoP; MoAB; NAAL-2; OxBA

Our feet have wandered from thy path. Wanderers. Thomas Curtis Clark. TrPWD

Our feet meet the earth in this place. Marble Floor. Karol Wojtyla. CRP

Our first ancestor (Abram) alone received his religion from Heaven. Therefore We Preserve Life. Shen Ch'üan, *tr. fr. Chinese by* William C. White. TrJP

Our First Century. George Edward Woodberry. PAH

Our flesh that was a battle-ground. Countee Cullen. *See* Our flesh was a battle-ground.

Our flesh was a battle-ground. The Litany of the Dark People. Countee Cullen. TrPWD
(Our flesh that was a battle-ground. ChIV-2

Our footprints. (*LL*) Day we die, The. *Unknown.* EaPr

Our foot's in the door. (*LL*) Mushrooms. Sylvia Plath. BoNaP; FaBoWP; RB; WPOW

Our friends go with us as we go. Non Dolet. Oliver St. John Gogarty. OBMV

Our friends, in life, in love, the lucky break. (*LL*) Guide to the Perplexed. David Malouf. NOBAu

Our friends on earth, fairer in death on high. (*LL*) Celestial Love. Michelangelo. AWP

Our friendship, Robert, firm through twenty years. A Letter to Robert Frost. Robert Silliman Hillyer. MoAmPo

Our garden's very near the trains. Trains. Hope Shepherd. BoTP

Our general was the greatest and bravest of generals. An Inscription for Dog River. Kenneth Slessor. FaBoMA

Our geodesic dome-shaped lodge. The Personification of a Name. Ray A. Young Bear. HATNAP

Our ghastly fears are dead. (*LL*) The Beleaguered City. Longfellow. AnAmPo

Our God and Father surely knows. The Father Knows. "F. L. H." BLRP

Our God and God of our fathers. Prayer for Dew. Eleazar ben Kalir, *tr. fr. Hebrew by* Israel Zangwill. TrJP

Our God and soldiers we alike adore. Francis Quarles. FaBoEE
(Of Common Devotion. OxBSP

Our God, for evermore. (*LL*) The Abiding Love. John White Chadwick. BLPA; FaBoBe; WGRP

Our God, Our Help. Isaac Watts. NoP; OBVE; PlP; PWR; TOF
(Man Frail, and God Eternal. ECEV

Our God, Our Help in Ages Past. Isaac Watts. OBVE; PlP; PWR; TOF

Our God's forgotten, and our soldiers slighted. (*LL*) Our God and soldiers we alike adore. Francis Quarles. FaBoEE

Our golden age was then, when lamp and rug. Family Prime. Mark Van Doren. VGW

Our Good President. Phoebe Cary. AmWP

Our goodly ship was loaded deep. Captain Mansfield's Fight with the Turks at Sea. *Unknown.* OxBSS

Our Goodman. *Unknown.* AmFP; ESPB, A *and* B *vers.*

Our gracious Queen. Thomas Deloney. FaBoEH

Our guest's wound went unnoticed. Callimachus, *tr. fr. Greek by* Peter Jay. GrAn

Our guns are a league behind us, our target a mile below. Eyes in the Air. Gilbert Frankau. NSI

Our guttural muse. Traditions. Seamus Heaney. FaBoMo

Our Hamster's Life. Kit Wright. OTCP

Our Hands in the Garden. Anne Hébert, *tr. fr. French by* A. Poulin, Jr. BoWoP

Our haughty life is crowned with darkness. London, from Hampstead Heath. Wordsworth. *Fr.* Extempore Effusion upon the Death of James Hogg. EBEV; FaBoPP; FaBoRV; NOBE; NoP; OAEL-2; SCV

Our heads on fire. (*LL*) Paper Matches. Paulette Jiles. Mes; NIP; NOBC

Our headteacher has a golden. Goldfish. Barrie Wade. OTCP

Our hearths are gone out, and our hearts are broken. The Raven Days. Sidney Lanier. AnAmPo; OxBA

Our hearts are filled with pride to-day. Welcome to Hon. Frederick Douglass. Josephine D. Henderson Heard. CBWP-4

Our hearts beat prouder for the blood we inherit. (*LL*) Memorial Wreath. Dudley Randall. PoBA; PoNe

Our Heavenly Father., *sels.* Frederick William Faber.
My God, How Wonderful Thou Art. TrPWD

Our heritage the sea. (*LL*) Wet sheet and a flowing sea, A. Allan Cunningham. EnRP; GTBS; GTBS-P; OxAEP-2; VPP

Our Heroes. Phoebe Cary. BLPA

Our Hired Man (And His Daughter, Too). Monica Shannon. FaPON

Our hired man is the kindest man. The Hired Man's Way. John Kendrick Bangs. OBCA

Our History. Catherine Cate Coblentz. FaPON

Our history is grave noble and tragic. Men. Archibald MacLeish. MoAB

Our history sings of centuries. Our History. Catherine Cate Coblentz. FaPON

Our Home. Jan Carew. PBCV

Our home, and all we know. (*LL*) A Prayer for a Little Home. Florence Bone. BLPA; FaBoBe

Our homes are eaten out by time. The Town Betrayed. Edwin Muir. CMoP

Our honeymoon. Bridal Piece. Louise Glück. SM

Our hope's sheet-anchor of salvation. (LL) My Observation at Sea. Mildmay Fane, 2d Earl of Westmorland. BeJo

Our horse fell down the well around behind the stable. Good-By Liza Jane. Unknown. AS

Our house had filled with moths. The Moths. Michael Jackson. PeNZ

Our house had wings for children, chandeliers. The Exile. Larry Rubin. GoYe

Our Houses. Linda Hogan. CrSp

Our houses are open tombs that will survive us. Concert-Going in Vienna. Michael O'Loughlin. Fr. Shards, The. IB

Our Hunting Fathers. W. H. Auden. FaBoMo; MoP; NoAM

Our hut puffs streaks of hope. Country Life. Chenjerai Hove. HBAPE

Our indolence was despair. We were still at times struck. An Interlude. John Peale Bishop. LiTA

Our Insufficiency to Praise God Suitably for His Mercy. Edward Taylor. LiTA

Our Islet out of Helgoland, dismissed. Islet the Dachs. George Meredith. FM

Our journey had advanced. Emily Dickinson. LiTA; LiTM; MoAB; NOCV; PoEL-5; SoSe

Our joy, a rampart to the mind. (LL) The Passing Strange. John Masefield. LiTB; MoAB; MoBrPo; OBEV

Our Joy that hath no end. Amen. (LL) The Day of Resurrection. Saint John of Damascus. TrCP

Our Joyful Feast. George Wither. See So now is come our joyful'st feast.

Our keels are furred with tropic weed that clogs the crawling tides. The Captive Ships at Manila. Dorothy Paul. PAH

Our Kind Creator. Solomon Howe. AH

Our king went forth to Normandy. The Agincourt Carol. Unknown. OAEL-1; OBET
    (Carol of Agincourt, A.) MeEL

Our king has wrote a lang letter. Lord Derwentwater. Unknown. ESPB

Our king he has a secret to tell. The Bonny Lass of Anglesey. Unknown. ESPB, A and B vers.

Our king he kept a false steward. Sir Aldingar. Unknown. ESPB, A, B, and C vers.; OxBB

Our king lay at Westminster. Hugh Spencer's Feats in France. Unknown. ESPB

Our King returned, and banished peace restored. George Granville. EPCY

Our[e] king[e] went forth to Normandy. The Agincourt Carol. Unknown. OAEL-1; OBET
    (Carol of Agincourt, A.) MeEL
    (Deo Gracias, Anglia.) EBEV

Our King went up upon a hill high. Henry before Agincourt: October 25, 1415. John Lydgate. CH

Our kisses/ Rhodope/ let us steal. Paulus Silentiarius, tr. fr. Greek by Andrew Miller. GrAn

Our knowledge is historical, flowing, and flown. (LL) At the Fishhouses. Elizabeth Bishop. CoAP; FaBoWP; HAP; HCAP; LCAP; LiTM; NAAL-2; NALW; NoP; NYBP; Poetr; PoRA; VCAP

Our Lady. Janine Canan. SRLS

Our Lady. Mary Elizabeth Coleridge. OBEV; OBMV; WPE

Our Lady of Ardboe. Paul Muldoon. BiHa; PBCIP

Our Lady of the Laundromat. Belle Waring. PBCAP

Our Lady's Expectation, sels. Frederick William Faber.

Our Lady's Song. Unknown. OBEV

Our Land. Yannis Ritsos, tr. fr. Greek by Edmund Keeley. AnAn

Our last bridge. Marina Tsvetayeva, tr. fr. Russian by Paul Schmidt. Fr. Daughter of Jairus, The. BoWoP

Our last free summer we mooned about at odd hours. Chrysalides. Thomas Kinsella. BIrV

Our last morning in that long room. In the Last Few Moments Came the Old German Cleaning Woman. Jane Cooper. SM

Our Left. Francis Orrery Ticknor. PAH

Our left and right show red and green: mute phonics. Flying Friendly Skies. Turner Cassity. MT

Our life in the world is only a great dream. Awakening from Drunkenness on a Spring Day. Li Po, tr. fr. Chinese by Robert Payne. TAL

Our life is changed; their coming our beginning. (LL) Horses, The ("Barely a twelvemonth after.") Edwin Muir. CMoP; GGP; HAP; HeIP; MoBrPo; MoP; NoAM; NOBE; NoP; OAEL-2; OxBTC; PAW; PoE; Poetr; RB; TEP; TRP; WeW

Our Life Is Hid with Christ in God. George Herbert. OAEL-1

Our life is like a forest, where the sun. Charles Sangster. Fr. Sonnets Written in the Orillia Woods. NOBC

Our life is two-fold: Sleep hath its own world. The Dream. Byron. BeLS; TEP

Our life's the model of a winter's day. On the Life of Man. Francis Quarles. Fr. Divine Fancies. PeECV

Our Light Afflictions. Unknown. BLRP

Our Lips and Ears. Unknown. BLPA; WBLP

Our lips will meet. (LL) The Doubt. Nestor Vasilyevich Kukolnik. RiWo

Our little bird in his full day of health. The Vacant Cage. Charles Tennyson Turner. FM

Our little fleet in July first. The Armada, 1588. John Wilson. OxBChV

Our Little Ghost. Louisa May Alcott. OBCA

Our little kinsmen after rain. Emily Dickinson. FaPON

Our Little Sister is Worried. Unknown, tr. fr. Chinese by Kenneth Rexroth. OHMPC

Our little tantrum, flushed and misery-hollow. Rebeca in a Mirror. Judith Rodriguez. CBAP

Our Lives. Sharon Scott. JB

Our lives again. (LL) The Goldfish Wife. Sandra Hochman. NYBP; UnPo

Our lives are Swiss. Emily Dickinson. NOBA; TAP

Our lives float on quiet waters. Quiet Waters. Blanche Shoemaker Wagstaff. BLPA

Our lives no longer feel ground under them. The Stalin Epigram. Osip Mandelstam, tr. fr. Russian by W. S. Merwin and Clarence Brown. FaBoPV

Our lives, that angel-vision. (LL) Life Sculpture. George Washington Doane. BLPA; WBLP

Our lives we consecrate to thee, our guide the Might of Right. (LL) Land of the Free. Arthur Nicholas Hosking. BLPA

Our lives were only half gone. Poem for Pekoe. Robert Phillips. SoCa

Our Lord, Immanuel. (LL) O Little Town of Bethlehem. Phillips Brooks. AH; AnAmPo; BLRP; FaPON; GN; OHIP; WBLP; WGRP

Our lords are to the mountains gane. Hughie Graham. Unknown. OxBB

Our loss of courtly grace cohabits. In the Pub. Peter Riley. Fr. One Day. VaA

Our love calls tiny as a tuning fork. (LL) Summer Home. Seamus Heaney. IPY; PBCIP

Our love has been dying for years. Parting. Anna Swirszczynska, tr. fr. Polish by Czeslaw Milosz and Leonard Nathan. ArLo

Our love has chosen its appropriate gesture. Lesson. Bill Knott. PRA

Our love was conceived in silence and must live silently. At the Dark Hour. Paul Dehn. BoLoP

Our love was pure. Song of Snow-white Heads. Chuo Wen-chün, tr. by Arthur Waley. BoWoP

Our love will not come back on fortune's wheel. Obit. Robert Lowell. HCAP; VCAP

Our man of the seashore. What Her Girl Friend Said on Her Wedding Day. Ammuvanar, tr. fr. Tamil by A. K. Ramanujan. PLW

Our March. Vladimir Mayakovsky, tr. fr. Russian by Babette Deutsch and Avrahm Yarmolinsky. AWP

Our mariner's last landfall was this shore. Richard Davis. Dick Davis. SCBI

Our Martyr-Chief. James Russell Lowell. OHIP

Our Master. Whittier. BLRP; WBLP

Our medieval fathers simply named. Hedge-Sparrows and House-Sparrows. Roy Fuller. AnAn

Our Modest Doughboys. Albert Charlton Andrews. PAH

Our morning-glory beautiful twine round our dear Lord's knee. (LL) The Morning-Glory. Maria White Lowell. AmWP

Our Mother. George Cooper. See Hundreds of stars in the pretty sky.

Our mother bade us keep the trodden ways. "George Eliot." Fr. Brother and Sister. GN; NALW

Our mother, the pride of us all. Mugford's Victory. John White Chadwick. PAH

Our Mother Tongue. Richard Monckton Milnes. GN

Our mother was the pussy-cat, our father was the owl. The Children of the Owl and the Pussy-Cat. Edward Lear. FaBoNo

Our mother, while she turned her wheel. Mother. Whittier. Fr. Snowbound; a Winter Idyl [or Idyll]. AmPP; GN; NOBA; OHIP; OxBA; TAP; WiR

Our Mothers Were Sisters. Marilyn Johnson. NGP

Our moulting days are in the twilight stage. Garnishing the Aviary. Margaret Danner. Fr. Far from Africa: Four Poems. BPo; PoBA

Our names do not appear. (LL) Diving into the Wreck. Adrienne Rich. CAPP; HCAP; HeIP; InPK; InPS; MoP; NAAL-2; NALW; NIP; NoAM; NOBA; NoP; Poetr

Our Nation Forever. Wallace Bruce. OHIP

Our National Banner. Dexter Smith. PAH

Our Nation's birth gave history your name. Washington. John A. Prentice. OHIP

Our natural tongue is rude. John Skelton. Fr. Phyllyp Sparowe [or Philip Sparrow]. AAS; EPCY; PoEL-1

Our Naughty Time. Friedrich von Logau, tr. fr. German. GePo, tr. by George C. Schoolfield

Our new clothes fool no one. Yom Kippur. Chana Bloch. CrSp

Our news is seldom good: the heart. W. H. Auden. *Fr.* New Year Letter. FaBoRV

Our Noble Booker T. Washington. Mrs. Henry Linden. CBWP-4

Our Norman betters. Lines: Inspired by the Controversy on the Value or Otherwise of Old English Studies. Anthony Burgess. FaBoCo

Our novels get longa and longa. H. G. Wells. PeLi

Our Number. Martin Carter. PBCV

Our nuns come out to shop in the afternoon. Intercessors. Austin Clarke. CMoP

Our Own. Margaret E. M. Sangster. BLPA; PoToHe

Our own calm journey on for human sake. (*LL*) The Nile. Leigh Hunt. EBEV; EnRP; NOBE; OBNC

Our own shadows disappear as the feet of thousand. Poem for South AFrican Women. June Jordan. MDDM

Our Padre. Sir John Betjeman. PeLV

Our padre is an old sky pilot. Our Padre. Sir John Betjeman. PeLV

Our Paris part of Belfast has. Intimate Letter 1973. Padraic Fiacc. PNI

Our Parodies are Ended. Horace Twiss. UV

Our parodies are ended. These our authors. Our Parodies are Ended. Horace Twiss. UV

Our passions are most like to floods and streams. To His Mistress. Sir Walter Ralegh. SiPS
(Sir Walter Ralegh to the Queen.) NoSic; SiPSBD

Our Past. Anne Waldman. PoBeRe

Our pastures are bitten and bare. Joseph Gordon MacLeod. *Fr.* Men of the Rocks. OxBS

Our paths began at distant points in space. Juncture. Rea Lubar Duncan. PoNe

Our perverse old *pisatel'* Vladimir. Something for My Russian Friends. Edmund Wilson. OBAL

Our Photograph. Frederick Locker-Lampson. NBLV; NOBL; PeLV

Our places are assigned. (*LL*) As by Fire. Ella Wheeler Wilcox. AmWP; AnAmPo

Our Poet tells me I am very pretty. Delariviere Manley. *Fr.* Royal Mischeif, The. KTR

Our Pope, they say, once entertained the whim. George Crabbe. *Fr.* Patron, The. EPCY

Our portion of fire. The Manichaeans. Gary Snyder. VGW

Our Presidents. *Unknown.* BLPA

Our prize fish is done! Hedylos. *tr. fr. Greek by* William Moebius. GrAn

Our quin's seek, an very seek. Queen Eleanor's Confession. *Unknown.* ESPB, A *and* B *vers.*; OBET; PrIm

Our revels now are ended. These our actors. Shakespeare. *Fr.* Tempest, The. FaPoB; ImPo; LiTB; OAEL-1; RB
(Epilogue.) UV
(Stuff of Dreams, The.) FaBV
(Such Stuff as Dreams Are Made On.) TrGrPo

Our Richard Allen in his early youth. Rt. Rev. Richard Allen. Josephine D. Henderson Heard. CBWP-4

Our roads are ridden. For Sammy Younge. Charlie Cobb. PoBA

Our Rock with loving care. Grace after Meals. *Unknown, tr. fr. Hebrew by* Alice Lucas. TrJP

Our rocks and pine trees speak for us. (*LL*) In protecting the earth, we found good pine needles and harsh. C. T. Mukpo. EaPr

Our roofs are adjacent. Love Song ("Our roofs are adjacent.") *Unknown, tr. fr. Turkish by* Reza Baraheni *and* Zahra-Soltan Shokoohtaezeh. BoWoP

Our sacred earth in our day is our curse. (*LL*) The Dead in Europe. Robert Lowell. LiTM; OxBA; OxBC

Our sacred Muse, of Israel's Singer sings. Michael Drayton. *Fr.* David and Goliath. ChIV-1

Our saints are poets, Milton and Blake. Encounter. Denis Devlin. BIrV

Our sardine fishermen work at night in the dark of the moon. The Purse-Seine. Robinson Jeffers. CMoP; HAP; NoAM; NOBA; NoP; OxBA; Poetr; PrIm; WeW

Our Savior Christ tracing the bordering hills, Thomas Deloney. *Fr.* Destruction of Jerusalem, The. ChIV-2

Our Saviour/ (Paterne of true holinesse). Ensamples of Our Savior. Robert Southwell. PoEL-2

Our Saviour's Golden Rule. Isaac Watts. OxBChV

Our Saviour's Love. *Unknown.* OBET

Our scene shifts to a hunting lodge in which. The Queer Assayers of the Frontier. Peter Porter. *Fr.* Baroque Quatrains. AnAn

Our School Now Closes Out. Edmund Dumas. AH

Our senses, without reason, are naught worth. Owen's Bracelet. Robert Hayman. *Fr.* Owen's Epigrams. NOSC

Our shadows lean across. Long shadows. Jill Maughan. NWP

Our shells clacked on the plates. Oysters. Seamus Heaney. UV

Our shepherds all. Boots and Saddles. Nicolas Saboly, *tr. fr. Provençal.* OHIP

Our Ship She Lies in Harbour. *Unknown.* NTP; OBET

Our ship, the Sea Smithy, swerved out of the tradewinds. On the Congo. Harry Edmund Martinson, *tr. fr. Swedish by* Robert Bly. RB

Our short fat, lord bishop. Bad Bishop Jegon. *Unknown.* GBP

Our Silly Little Sister. Dorothy Aldis. FaPON

Our single purpose was to walk through snow. Polar Exploration. Stephen Spender. MoAB; NoAM
(North, The. FaBoMo

Our smiles wrapped in lace. (*LL*) Love-Life. Hugo Williams. CBLP

Our Smoke Has Gone Four Ways. Lance Henson. CDW

Our song together. (*LL*) Eadwacer. *Unknown.* PBWP, *tr. by* Kemp Malone; WPE

Our soprano is on the wind tonight. Autumn Song on Perry Street. Lloyd Frankenberg. GrPI

Our sorrow sends its shadow round the earth. J. A. G. Julia Ward Howe. PAH

Our standard with the eagle stands for us. Standards in Hopeful Anticipation of the Bicentenery of the National Emblem of the United States of America. Tony Harrison. *Fr.* Art & Extinction. SCBI

Our Stars Come from Ireland. Wallace Stevens. GOA

Our States, O Lord. John Mycall. AH

Our steps are scattered far. In the Wilderness. Edith Lovejoy Pierce. TrPWD

Our storm is past, and that storm[e]'s tyrannous rage. The Calm[e]. John Donne. NoSic

Our story isn't a file of photographs. For an Album. Adrienne Rich. VCAP

Our street is known as the street of widows. Bruce Beaver. *Fr.* Letters to Live Poets. CBAP; FaBoMA

Our suffering life the dream. (*LL*) The Other World. Harriet Beecher Stowe. WGRP

Our sun hath gone down at the noonday. Our Good President. Phoebe Cary. AmWP

Our Sunday morning when dawn-priests were applying. John Berryman. BoLoP

Our tarin' Dan O'Connell sure he was a mighty man. Cushendall. *Unknown.* WTO

Our Task. H. Cordelia Ray. CBWP-3

Our task is done! on Gunga's breast. An Evening Walk in Bengal. Reginald Heber. OBTV

Our Tense and Wintry Minds. Hayden Carruth. AH

Our thanks to Mother Earth who lies here. (*LL*) Behold! Our Mother Earth is lying here. *Unknown.* EaPr

Our Tree. Marchette Chute. SiSoPo

Our tropic fruits, nurs'd 'neath a torrid sky. *Unknown. Fr.* Poetical Epistle, from the Island of Jamaica, to, A. PBCV

Our trust is now in thee, Beauregard! Beauregard. Catherine Anne Warfield. PAH

Our two soules therefore, which are one. John Donne. *Fr.* Valediction: Forbidding Mourning, A. UV

Our Two Worthies. John Crowe Ransom. OBAL

Our vernal signs the RAM begins. The Signs of the Zodiac. Ebenezer Cobham Brewer. FaBoUs

Our view of sky, jungle, and fields constricts. The Insert. R. L. Barth. InPK

Our Village. Thomas Hood. *See* Our Village, that's to say not Miss Mitford's.

Our Village — by a Villager. Thomas Hood. FaBoVe; OBSV

Our Village, that's to say not Miss Mitford's. Our Village — by a Villager. Thomas Hood. FaBoVe; OBSV
(Our Village. PoEL-4

Our voices poured out through. The House Made of Rain. Naomi Shihab Nye. NAmP90

Our way of life. It's a Woman's World. Eavan Boland. CIP

Our window is a drifting smoke. Watercourse. Ruth Padel. VBLP

Our window-panes enthral our summer bees. The Bee-Wisp. Charles Tennyson Turner. FM

Our Wives. Jonathan Galassi. EOEF

Our Youth. John Ashbery. SOTW; VGW

Our youth was gay but rough. One of the Boys. James Simmons. PNI

Our youth was happy: why repine. Walter Savage Landor. FaBoEE

Oure Hoste gan to swere as he were wood. The Introduction to the Pardoner's Prologue. Chaucer. *Fr.* Canterbury Tales, The. EnVB; FHYEP; NAEL-1; NoP

Ours are the streets where Bess first met her/ cancer. Bess. William Stafford. NNaP; NoP

Ours cannot be separated. (LL) Water Lilies Bloom. Emperor Wu of Liang. OHMPC

Ours is the ancient story: For Daughters of Magdalen. Countee Cullen. ChIV-2

Ourselves become our own best sacrifice! (LL) In the Holy Nativity of Our Lord God. Richard Crashaw. GeHe; PoEL-2; SeCV-1

Ourselves we do inter with sweet derision. Emily Dickinson. FaBoEE

Ourselves were wed one summer — dear. Emily Dickinson. PeHV

Ousel cock, so black of hue, The. Shakespeare. Fr. Midsummer Night's Dream, A. NoSic

Out. (LL) For the Last Wolverine. James Dickey. FoLa

Out. (LL) Whirlwinds. Fily-Dabo Sissoko. NegPo

Out and Fight. Charles Godfrey Leland. PAH

Out beside the highway, first thing in the morning. North Coast Town. Robert Gray. FaBoMA

Out beyond ideas of wrongdoing and rightdoing. Jalal al-Din Rumi, tr. fr. Persian by Coleman Barks and John Moyne. EnlH

Out Fishin'. Edgar A. Guest. BLPL; PoLF

Out Fishing. Barbara Howes. WPE

Out for a walk, after a week in bed. An Urban Convalescence. James Merrill. CoAP; NAAL-2; NOBA

Out for a walk the other day. A Mystic Song. Unknown, tr. fr. French by Percy Allen. WGRP

Out for the Elements. Andrew Waterman. SCBI

Out from Jerusalem. King Solomon and the Ants. Whittier. ChIV-1

Out from the harbor of Amsterdam. Henry Hudson's Quest. Burton Egbert Stevenson. PAH

Out — goes — he. (LL) Hickety pickety i sillickety [or i-silicity]. Unknown. GBP; OxNR

Out goes the rat. Unknown. RoPo
(Counting-out Rhymes.) FaPON

Out goes the rat. Unknown. Fr. Counting-out Rhymes. FaPON; ImGa

Out here on Cottage Grove it matters. The galloping. Pyrography. John Ashbery. PoM; VCAP

Out here there are no hearthstones. Sleep in the Mojave Desert. Sylvia Plath. AiP; NoP

Out here where the crows turn around. Country Wisdoms. Maggie Anderson. PBCAP

Out in a world of death, far to the northward lying. The Winter Lakes. Wilfred Campbell. BoNaP; NOBC

Out in the blustering darkness, on the deck. Night on the Conroy. Siegfried Sassoon. NSI

Out in the Cold. George Starbuck. NYBP

Out in the Dark. Edward Thomas. ArNa; CH; GTBS-P; LiTM; MoAB; MoBrPo; NOBE; OBWVE; RB

Out in the dark over the snow. Out in the Dark. Edward Thomas. ArNa; CH; GTBS-P; LiTM; MoAB; MoBrPo; NOBE; OBWVE; RB

Out in the Desert. Josephine D. Henderson Heard. CBWP-4

Out in the fields which were green last May. Child's Thought of Harvest, A.' "Susan Coolidge." OHIP

Out in the Fields with God. At. to Elizabeth Barrett Browning and to Louise Imogen Guiney. BLRP; WBLP; WGRP

Out in the fields with God. (LL) Out in the Fields with God. At. to Elizabeth Barrett Browning and to Louise Imogen Guiney. BLRP; WBLP; WGRP

Out in the garden. Bubbles. L. Nicholson. BoTP

Out in the garden. The Blackbird. Phyllis Drayson. BoTP

Out in the garden. The Pigeons. Rodney Bennett. BoTP

Out in the garden, sunny and still. Freedom. Joan Agnew. BoTP

Out in the harbor breaths of smoke. Mercy. Olga Broumas. PFL

Out in the late amber afternoon. In Shadow. Hart Crane. NOBA

Out in the Open. Aleksandar Ristovic, tr. fr. Serbo-Croatian by Charles Simic. HSix

Out in the rain a world is growing green. Easter Monday. Christina Rossetti. NOCV

Out in the silent Rockies. The Outcast. P. G. Wodehouse. UV

Out in the sky the great dark clouds are massing. Ships That Pass in the Night. Paul Laurence Dunbar. AnAmPo; CDC

Out in the smoke of every gig I play. Get the Hell off My Note. Rod Jellema. Fr. Four Voices Ending on Some Lines from Old Jazz Records. Jaz

Out in the Snow, Spending the Night at the New Stockade, Extremely Depressed. Huang T'ing-chien, tr. fr. Chinese by Michael E. Workman. SuSp

Out in the woods at play! (LL) The Curliest Thing. Unknown. BoTP

Out in the yellow meadows, where the bee. George Meredith. Fr. Modern Love. GBL

Out in this desert we are testing bombs. Trying to Talk with a Man. Adrienne Rich. HCAP

Out-island once, on a south slope. Deer Isle. Philip Booth. VGW

Out it fell! (LL) The Squirrel. Unknown. BoTP; OxNR

Out it spake Lizee Linzee. Lizie Lindsay. Unknown. ESPB, A and B vers.
(Donald of the Isles.) OxBB

Out of a brown-paper cocoon. The Light Dress. Debora Greger. Fr. Afterlife, The. BAP-91

Out of a dream of ease and indolence. Highway to Glory Song. W. H. Auden. Fr. Man of La Mancha. AnAn

Out of a fired ship, which, by no way. A Burnt Ship. John Donne. EBEV; InPK; OBWP

Out of a gothic North, the pallid children. Good-bye to the Mezzogiorno. W. H. Auden. OxBTC

Out of a government grant to poets, I paid. Economics. Mona Van Duyn. SM

Out of a Northern city's bay. Cruise of the Monitor, The. George Henry Boker. PAH

Out of a sheer, sunlit countryside. I Remember Coming into Warsaw, a Child. Helen Degan Cohen. BTR

Out of a War of Wits. Dylan Thomas. PoA

Out of adult hearing. A Picture of Okinawa. Dennis Schmitz. LCAP

Out of all our enemies, all the catastrophes of nations. Shoes. Victor Martinez. AfAz

Out of brightness, a brightness out of brightness. The Waltz. Hilary Corke. NYBP

Out of burlap sacks, out of bearing butter. They Feed They Lion. Philip Levine. CAPP; LCAP; MAT; MoP; NNaP; NoAM; NOBA; Prf; VCAP

Out of Chaos Out of Order Out. Michele Roberts. BrRo

Out of Control; the Quarry. Christopher Dewdney. NOBC

Out of Doors. E. North. BoTP

Out-of-Doors. Robert Whitaker. TrPWD

Out of French. Sir Charles Sedley. FaBoEE

Out of friendship and a slow retreat of the blood. Ascending Red Cedar Moon. Duane Niatum. CDW

Out of gas south. Autumn. Philip Levine. NNaP

Out of heaven on your bugles blown! (LL) England, My England. W. E. Henley. BLPL; MoBrPo; OBEV; PoLF

Out of Hellas if you please, Aristarchean pedants. Herodicus, tr. fr. Greek by Peter Jay. GrAn

Out of her house she crept. Miss Euphemia. John Crowe Ransom. CMoP

Out of her mouth came forth strawberry, strawberry froth. (LL) Hexameter and Pentameter. Unknown. ChTr; FaBoNo

Out of her own body she pushed. Grandmother. Paula Gunn Allen. MDDM; SRLS

Out of her womb of pain my mother spat me. Audre Lorde. Fr. Story Books on a Kitchen Table. MDDM

Out of him that I loved. Our Stars Come from Ireland. Wallace Stevens. GOA

Out of hir swouh whan she did abraide. The Letter of Compleynt of Canace. John Lydgate. Fr. Fall of Princes, The. OxBLMV

Out of his cottage to the sun. Old Dan'l. L. A. G. Strong. MoBrPo

Out of Horace. James Wright. NOSC

Out of it steps the future of the poor. The Door. W. H. Auden. Fr. Quest, The. Son

Out of Luck. Abraham ibn Ezra, tr. fr. Hebrew by Solomon Solis-Cohen. TrJP

Out of me unworthy and unknown. Anne Rutledge. Edgar Lee Masters. Fr. Spoon River Anthology. CMoP; HAP; ImPo; LiTA; LiTM; MoAmPo; MoP; NoAM; NOBA; OxBA; TFi; TrGrPo

Out of Midsummer's Blazing Most Not Night. E. E. Cummings. NoAM

Out of my clothes, I ran past the boathouse. Under the Boathouse. David Bottoms. MT

Out of my flesh that hungers. On a Night of the Full Moon. Audre Lorde. AIW; NALW; UnAS

Out Of My Great Afflictions. Heine, tr. fr. German by Philip L. Miller. RiWo

Out of my heart, one day, I wrote a song. Misapprehension. Paul Laurence Dunbar. BPo

Out of my longing, dusk-aware. Candle Song. Anna Elizabeth Bennett. GoYe

Out of my mother's womb. Job. I. John Hall. ChIV-1

Out of my own great woe. Heine, tr. fr. German by Elizabeth Barrett Browning. AWP

Out of my poverty. Conversation by the Body's Light. Jane Cooper. UnDi; VBLP

Out of my window high as aerie. Russia 1914/Bolinas 1988. Gail Shafarman. LoHo

Out of my window I could see. Blossoms. Frank Dempster Sherman. OBCA

Out of my window late at night I gape. In the Night. Elizabeth Jennings. NYBP

Out of one golden breath. Love-Song. Else Lasker-Schüler, tr. fr. German by Jethro Bithell. TrJP

Out of our daylight into death you burn. Paper Anarchist Addresses the Shade of Nancy Ling Perry. George Woodcock. NOBC

Out of Our Shame. Norman Rosten. TrJP

Out of Sight in the Direction of My Body. Paul Éluard, tr. fr. French by Samuel Beckett. CBCK

Out of Sight, Out of Mind. Barnabe Googe. EIL; EnRePo; InPS

Out of that nothing, what remains to Thee? (LL) On the Life of Man. Francis Quarles. ChIV-2

Out of the blackthorn hedges. Ivor Gurney. EnLoPo

Out-of-the-Body Travel. Stanley Plumly. AmPA; LCAP

Out of the bosom of the air. Snow-Flakes. Longfellow. ArNa; ChTr; FaBoRV; NOBA; NoP; PoEL-5; TAP; UnPo; WiR (Snow.) BoTP

Out of the church she followed [or follow'd] them. Maude Clare. Christina Rossetti. BeLS; EBVV

Out of the clover and blue-eyed grass. Driving Home the Cows. Kate Putnam Osgood. BeLS; PAH

Out of the complicated house, come I. The Hills. Frances Cornford. MoBrPo

Out of the corpse-warm vestibule of heaven steps the sun. Ingeborg Bachmann, tr. fr. German by Janice Orion. BoWoP

Out of the Cradle Endlessly Rocking. Walt Whitman. AmPP; AnAmPo; AWP; HAP; HeIL; HeIP; ImPo; MeMAP; MoAmPo; NAAL-1; NAWM-2; NOBA; NoP; OxBA; PFP; PoE; PoEL-5; PrIm; SAmP; TAP; TRP

Out of the crowd, I have seen you travelling south of Pardoo. The Witch Doctor's Magic Flight. Smiler Narautjarri, tr. by Georg von Brandenstein. NOBAu

Out of the dark. The Open Door. Elizabeth J. Coatsworth. TLR

Out of the dark raw earth. Alabama. Julia Fields. PoBA; PoNe

Out of the Darkness. Frankie Armstrong. BrRo

Out of the Darkness. Gertrud Kolmar, tr. fr. German by Michael Hamburger. WPOW

Out of the darkness/ on a dark path. Lady Izumi Shikibu, tr. fr. Japanese by Kenneth Rexroth and Ikuko Atsumi. WPJ

Out of the Deep. Clara Ann Thompson. CBWP-2

Out of the deep and the dark. The Poet. Yone Noguchi. WGRP

Out of the deeps I cry to thee, O God! Richard Le Gallienne. TrPWD

Out of the Depths. Frederic Lawrence Knowles. TrPWD

Out of the depths [or deep] have I cried [or called] (unto) Thee, O Lord. Bible, O.T., paraphrased by Sir Thomas Wyatt. Fr. Psalms. TrJP (De Profundis.) BLRP; WGRP
(Deep sunk in floods of grief.) ScCV
(Psalm CXXX: "Ffrom depth off sinn and from a diepe dispaire," paraphrased by Sir Thomas Wyatt.) OBVE
(F[f]rom depth of[f] sin[n] and from a deep [or diepe] despair [or dispaire].) NoSic
(Song of Supplication, A.) TrGrPo

Out of the depths of a heart of love. A Valentine. Priscilla Jane Thompson. CBWP-2

Out of the earth. I Sing for the Animals. Teton Sioux Oral Tradition, tr. fr. Teton Sioux Indian. EaPr; TTTS

Out of the earth beneath the water. The Mud Turtle. Howard Nemerov. NYBP

Out of the earth, out of the air, out of the water. Rapparees. Richard Murphy. Fr. Battle of Aughrim, The. BlrV; NOIV; PBCIP

Out of the earth to rest or range. The Passing Strange. John Masefield. LiTB; MoAB; MoBrPo; OBEV

Out of the East there came a hard man. Cod-Liver Oil and the Orange Juice. Hamish Imlach. FaBoBl

Out of the east window a storm. Wednesday of Holy Week, 1940. Kenneth Rexroth. ChIV-1

Out of the eyes of a hundred flowers. (LL) Talking in Their Sleep. Edith M. Thomas. BoNaP; OHIP

Out of the factory chimney, tall. Smoke Animals. Rowena Bastin Bennett. PDV

Out of the fields I see them pass. Youth's Own. John Galsworthy. NSI

Out of the focal and foremost fire. Little Giffen. Francis Orrery Ticknor. GOA; PAH
(Little Giffen of Tennessee. AnAmPo

Out of the fog. The Fog Dream. Sandra M. Gilbert. PoA

Out of the forest steals the night. The Night. Herman von Gilm zu Rosenegg, tr. fr. German by Philip L. Miller. RiWo

Out of the Frying Pan into the Fire. James Henry. NOBVV

Out of the garden comes the tree. Because Thou Did'st Give. Harry Morris. CRP

Out of the ghetto streets where a Jewboy. Autobiographical. A. M. Klein. MoCV; NoAM

Out of the golden remote wild west where the sea without shore is. Hesperia. Swinburne. OBNC

Out of the grey air grew snow and more snow. Snow. W. R. Rodgers. LiTM

Out of the hills of Habersham. Song of the Chattahoochee. Sidney Lanier. AnAmPo; BoNaP; FaBoBe; FaBV; LiTA

Out of the Hitherwhere. James Whitcomb Riley. BLPA

Out of the hitherwhere into the yon. (LL) Out of the Hitherwhere. James Whitcomb Riley. BLPA

Out of the Hurly-Burly. "Max Adeler." See Death-angel smote Alexander McGlue, The.

Out of the Italian; a Song. Richard Crashaw. SeCV-1

Out of the "Kalevala," sels. Anselm Hollo.

Out of the lamplight. Mice in the Hay. Leslie Norris. OBCP; PChr

Out of the Land of Heaven. Leonard Cohen. MoCV

Out of the light that dazzles me. My Captain. Dorothea Day. BLPA

Out of the marbled underwaters. Music by the Waters. John Hay. FoLa

Out of the melting pot, into the mint. Ten Pence Story. Simon Armitage. PWE

Out of the midnight sky a great dawn broke. The Shepherd Speaks. John Erskine. TrCP

Out of the morning dark, the pale. Terra Incognita. Sherod Santos. AnAn

Out of the mud two strangers came. Two Tramps in Mud Time. Robert Frost. BLPL; CMoP; HeIL; ImPo; LiTA; LiTM; MeMAP; MoAB; MoAmPo; MoP; NAAL-2; NoAM; PrIm; SAmP; TrGrPo

Out of the night of the sea. At Carbis Bay. Arthur Symons. FaBoPP

Out of the night that covers me. Invictus. W. E. Henley. Fr. Echoes. BLPA; CoGr; EBEvV; FaBoBe; FaBV; FaPoR; GGP; HoPM; ImPo; LiTB; MoBrPo; NOBE; OBEV; OBMV; OBNC; OHCV; OtMeF; TEP; TrGrPo

Out of the North the wild news came. The Rising. Thomas Buchanan Read. Fr. Wagoner of the Alleghanies, The. PAH

Out of the Northeast. The White Horse. Tu Fu, tr. fr. Chinese by Rewi Alley. ChTr

Out of the old fairy tales. Heine. RiWo

Out of the Sea, Early. May Swenson. RFM

Out of the shadow, I am come in to you whole a black holy man. Study Peace. Amiri Baraka. PoBA

Out of the smoke of men's wrath. The Face (Guillemont). Frederic Manning. NSI

Out of the strong, sweetness. Charles Reznikoff. Fr. Inscriptions: 1944–1956. BTR

Out of the swirling shadow host. Chatterton. Rina Hands. Mes

Out of the table endlessly rocking. Just Friends. Robert Creeley. NeAP

Out of the tense awed darkness, my Frangepani comes. Rainy Season Love Song. Gladys May Casely Hayford. CDC; ShDr

Out of the terra cotta still a voice. Etruscan Warrior's Head. Helen Rowe Henze. GoYe

Out of the tomb we bring Badroulbadour. (LL) The Worms at Heaven's Gate. Wallace Stevens. NoAM; OBD

Out of the tomb, we bring Badroulbadour. The Worms at Heaven's Gate. Wallace Stevens. NoAM; OBD

Out of the utmost pitch of wilderment. De Profundis. Amos N. Wilder. TrPWD

Out of the Vastness that is God. A Litany for Latter-Day Mystics. Cale Young Rice. WGRP

Out of the water that bore us all here. (LL) Elegy in an Abandoned Boatyard. Dave Jeddie Smith. VCAP

Out of the whim of data. True Solar Holiday. Douglas Crase. BAP-89

Out of the Whirlwind. Bible, O.T. Fr. Job. AWP; NAWM-1, abr.; OBVE

Out of the wild sweet grape, I have trampled a wine. On Laying Up Treasure. Lois Smith Hiers. GoYe

Out of the Wilderness. Ulrich Troubetzkoy. GoYe

Out of the wind's and the rain's way. (LL) An Old Woman of the Roads. Padraic Colum. BoTP; CH; CoGr; FaBoBe; FaPON; FYAP; MoBrPo; NOIV; OBEV; PoRA; TIRV

Out of the wine-pot cry'd the fly. The Fly. Philip Ayres, after the Spanish of Quevedo. OBVE

Out of the wood of thoughts that grows by night. Cock-Crow. Edward Thomas. GTBS-P; MoAB; MoBrPo; NTP; OxBSP; RB

Out of them that is my life on the boats. (LL) Fauviste. Donald Revell. UTF

Out of these depths. De Profundis. David Gascoyne. PoWW

Out of these thin, thin cups I drink pale tea. Bone China. R. P. Lister. NYBP

Out of this ugliness may come. Glasgow Street. William Montgomerie. OxBS

Out of Three or Four in a Room. Yehuda Amichai, *tr. fr. Hebrew by* Assia Gutmann. AnRep

Out of Time, *sels.* Kenneth Slessor.
"Leaning against the golden undertow." CBAP

Out of Tune. W. E. Henley. MoBrPo

Out of what calms and pools the cool shell grows. The Atoll in the Mind. Alex Comfort. LiTB; LiTM

Out of wild roses down from the switching road between pools. A Guide to Dungeness Spit. David Wagoner. FoLa

Out of Your Sleep Arise and Wake! *Unknown.* NoP; OxBLMV

Out of your slepe arise and wake. Man Exalted. *Unknown.* MeEL; NoP

Out of your whole life give but a moment! Now [*or* The Moment Eternal]. Robert Browning. CBLP

Out off the south thai saw quhar at the queyn. Henry the Minstrel. *Fr.* Sir William Wallace. ScCV

Out on a limb and frantically sawing. Martyrdom of Two Pagans. Philip Whalen. NeAP

Out on Killiney Hill that night, you said. Spring Night. Richard Kell. PeIV

Out on the bare grey roads, I pass. Touch It. Robert Mezey. NaP

Out on the board the old shearer stands. Click Go the Shears, Boys. *Unknown.*
(Click Go the Shears.) NOBAu

Out on the high "bird islands," Ciboux and Hertford. Cape Breton. Elizabeth Bishop. InPS

Out on the lawn I lie in bed. A Summer Night. W. H. Auden. FaBoRV

Out on the ocean, dreary and cold. Swell My Net Full. *Unknown.* OxBSS

Out on the ocean, great wide ocean. Great *Titanic. Unknown.* AmFP

Out on the tormented, midnight sea. Poem and Message. Dannie Abse. TEP

Out on the wastes of the Never Never. Where the Dead Men Lie. Barcroft Henry Boake. CBAP

Out on the windy hill. The Shepherd's Dog. Leslie Norris. OBCP

"Out, Out." Robert Frost. DL; FF; HAP; HeIP; NAAL-2; OxBA; Poetr; RB; SoSe; TRP; UnPo; VGW

Out, Out, Brief Candle! Shakespeare. *See* She should have died hereafter.

Out over the sea. (*LL*) A Bird Cried. Vilhelm Andreas Wexels Krag. RiWo

Out past Sylvan Beach is the place. Northwest Passage. Vern Rutsala. NGP

Out past the window two trees in splendor. Sentiments at Autumn. Han Yü, *tr. fr. Chinese by* Charles Hartman. SuSp

Out-sane men have walked, The. From Star to Sun We Are Going. Fatisha. Jaz

Out scouting for sound counsels? How to prosper? Ausiàs March, *tr. fr. Catalan by* John Frederick Nims. STV

Out shopping, little Julia spied. The Coconut. "Ande." FiBHP

Out springs the bubble, dazzling bright. The Bubble. Lydia Huntley Sigourney. AmWP

Out that black hole of bush. Third World Snapshots. John Robert Lee. PBCV

Out that door. Dennis. Dan Sicoli. NGP

Out the back of its eye. (*LL*) Through Eyes. Cole Swenson. UTF

Out the Greywolf valley. Gary Snyder. *Fr.* Myths and Texts. NaP

Out the window, Colombia, out the window. Sharon Doubiago. *Fr.* South America Mi Hija. PBCAP

"Out the window with the window!" (*LL*) The Whole Mess . . . Almost. Gregory Corso. PoBeRe

Out the You of Yesterday. Liliane Lijn. VBLP

Out there, beyond the boundary fence, beyond. The Singing Bones. Randolph Stow. CBAP

Out There Somewhere. Henry Herbert Knibbs. BLPA

Out there, we've walked [*or* talked] quite friendly up to death. The Next War. Wilfred Owen, *tr. fr. Turkish.* MeMBP; OBD; Son

Out there, with little else to do. Robben Island. Robert Dederick. PeSA

Out through the fields and the woods. Reluctance. Robert Frost. CMoP; MoAB; MoAmPo; NOBA; OxBA

Out till 4 o'clock dancing, they're. Anne Rouse. NWP

"Out To Lunch." Eric Dolphy. Anne Waldman. Jaz

Out to Old Aunt Mary's. James Whitcomb Riley. PFP

Out under the sky. (*LL*) I Wonder as I Wander. *Unknown.* PChr

Out upon it! I have loved [*or* lov'd]. Sir John Suckling. BeJo; EBEvV; NBLV; PeLV; PoE
(Constant Lover, A.) OxAEP-1
(Constant Lover, The.) CBLP; GGP; ImPo; NOSC

Out, upon the deep old ocean. On Genessarett. Josephine D. Henderson Heard. CBWP-4

Out upon you California. Pennsylvania Places. T. A. Daly. OBAL

Out walking in the frozen swamp one gray [*or* grey] day. The Wood-Pile. Robert Frost. AnAmPo; InPK; LiTA; NAAL-2; NoAM; NoP; SAmP; VGW

Out walking ties left over from a track. Cross Ties. X. J. Kennedy. HoPM

Out West. Gary Snyder. NNaP

Out where the grey streams glide. Buffalo Country. A. B. Paterson. OBAP

Out Where the West Begins ("Out where the hand-clasp's a little stronger.") Arthur Chapman. AiP; BLPA; FaBoBe

Out where yr going. (*LL*) I Know a Man. Robert Creeley. CAPP; InPS; MAT; NIP; NOBA; OxBSP; PoM; PPP; VCAP

Out with the mountain moon, stinging clear. Mill Valley. Myra Cohn Livingston. RFM

Outbound, your bark awaits you. Were I one. Godspeed. Whittier. Son

Outbreak. Bill Anderson. VGW

Outcast[, The]. "Æ." OxBSP

Outcast, The. John Davidson. MeMBP

Outcast, The. Josephine D. Henderson Heard. CBWP-4

Outcast. Claude McKay. PoBA

Outcast, The. James Stephens. MoBrPo

Outcast, The. P. G. Wodehouse. UV

Outcome, The? Conflicting rumours. After a War. Michael Hamburger. PAW

Outcome was/ unexpected, The. You Go to My Head. Elaine Equi. UTF

Outcrop stone is miserly. Still-Life. Ted Hughes. NYBP

Outcry upon Opportunity, An. Shakespeare. *See* O, Opportunity, thy guilt is great.

Outdoor Litany, An. Louise Imogen Guiney. TrPWD

Outgoing Sabbath. *Unknown, tr. fr. Yiddish by* Joseph Leftwich. TrJP

Outhouse. Aleksandar Ristovic, *tr. fr. Serbo-Croatian by* Charles Simic. HSix

Outlanders, The. Andrew Glaze. NYBP

Outlanders, The. William Morris. *Fr.* Earthly Paradise, The. EBVV

Outlandish Knight, The. *Unknown.* OBET

Outlaw, The. Seamus Heaney. MoP; OxBC

Outlaw, The. Sir Walter Scott. *See* O [*or* Oh], Brignal[l] banks are wild and fair.

Outlaw Murray, The. *Unknown.* ESPB; OxBB

Outlaw of Loch Lene, The. *Unknown, tr. fr. Modern Irish by* Jeremiah Joseph Callanan. BIrV; CH; GBL; NTP; OBEV; PeIV

Outlaw's Song, The. Joanna Baillie. OBEV

Outlines. Audre Lorde. GLP

Outlook wasn't brilliant for the Mudville nine that day, The. Casey at the Bat. Ernest Lawrence Thayer. AiP; AnAmPo; BeLS; BLPA; FaBoBe; FaPON; OBAL; OBCA; PoRA; VPP

Outpost, The. Tomas Tranströmer, *tr. fr. Swedish by* Robin Fulton. PWE

Outrage. Lucille Iverson. CrSp

Outroars a dead lion. (*LL*) Koheleth. Louis Untermeyer. ChIV-1; TrJP

Outside. Phyllis Beauvais. IHMS

Outside. Hugh Chesterman. BoTP

Outside. Robert Creeley. CAPP

Outside, a delicate arch. The Curse. John Hollander. UnPo

Outside, affectionate eyes. Ursula. David Ray. VGW

Outside Baby Moon's. Paul Violi. UL

Outside Bristol Rovers Football Ground. The Ballad of Billy Rose. Leslie Norris. AngWe; MoBS

Outside Fargo, North Dakota. James Wright. LCAP; NNaP

Outside: forecasts of humiliating storms. A Night with Cindy at Heitman's. Richard Hugo. AnAn

Outside, in fact, there wasn't any change. Patrizia Cavalli, *tr. fr. Italian by* Judith Baumel. NeIt

Outside my door the city waits. City/Country. Hester Wyat. UnDi

Outside my window a lorry misses gear. Weekend at Home. John Pook. AngWe

Outside New York, a high place where with one glance. Schubertiana. Tomas Tranströmer, *tr. fr. Swedish by* Robert Bly. NU

Outside/ outside myself/ there is a world. William Carlos Williams. *Fr.* Paterson. NoAM
(Sunday in the Park.) NAAL-2

Outside Pisa. Chitra Divakaruni. OpBo

Outside that bulbous Babylon. English Beach Memory: Mr. Thuddock. Sir Osbert Sitwell. NYBP

Outside the Capsule, *sels.* Andre Hodeir.
"By salt and by mercury." Jaz

Outside the cats are wailing. Leah Goldberg, *tr. fr. Hebrew by* Robert Alter. *Fr.* Symposium, The. PBWP

Outside the children play like flames. The Fever. Rosemary Dobson. FaBoWP

Outside the courtroom. Sharpeville Inquiry. Anne Welsh. PeSA

Outside the door! (*LL*) Spring Morning. D. H. Lawrence. ArNa; CMoP; MoAB; MoBrPo

Outside, the freezing desert night. Jalal al-Din Rumi, *tr. fr. Persian by* Coleman Barks *and* John Moyne. EnlH

Outside the Holy City. James G. Gilkey. AH

Outside the hotel window, unenlightened pigeons. The Jain Bird Hospital in Delhi. William Meredith. VCAP

Outside, the last kids holler. Leaving the Motel. W. D. Snodgrass. FF; NIP

Outside the office of the principal. (*LL*) Zimmer in Grade School. Paul Zimmer. PBCAP

Outside the precinct, the continents sway. Police Sift New Clues in Search for Beauty. Vickie Karp. UTF

Outside, the rain, pinafore of gray water, dresses the town. Child Beater. Ai. BoWoP

Outside the screen rain drips and splashes. Tune: "Ripples Sifting Sand: A Song." Li Yü, *tr. fr. Chinese by* Daniel Bryant. SuSp

Outside the second grade room. The Girl Who Loved the Sky. Anita Endrezze-Danielson. HATNAP

Outside the Supermarket. Roy Fuller. OxBC

Outside, the visible gale's. Storm Warning. Howard Moss, *tr. fr. Italian by* William Arrowsmith. AnAn

Outside the whistled gang-call, Twelfth Street Rag. Me Tarzan. Tony Harrison. *Fr.* School of Eloquence, The. NAEL-2; NoAM

Outside the world crackles like a daily. A lion. A Room I Once Knew. Henry Birnbaum. GoYe

Outside the world was full, plural. The Christmas Tree. Patricia Beer. OBCP

Outsider, The. Syl Cheney-Coker. HBAPE

Outspoken buttocks in pink beads. National Winter Garden. Hart Crane. *Fr.* Bridge, The. ErPo; InPS; LiTA; LiTM; NAAL-2; OxBA

Outvieing all the buds in Flora's diadem. (*LL*) Imitation of Spenser. Keats. EnRP

Outward. Louis Simpson. NYBP

Outward Bound. James Simmons. CIP; PWE

Outward Bound. Edward Sydney Tylee. PAH

Outward Man Accused, The. Edward Taylor. LiTA; MeMAP

Outwardly splendid as of old. The Church Today. Sir William Watson. WGRP

Outwit me, Lord, if ever hence. Security. Charles L. O'Donnell. TrPWD

Outwitted. Edwin Markham. BLPA; MoAmPo; PoToHe

Ov all the meäds wi shoals an' pools. Leeburn Mill. William Barnes. EnVR

Ovals of opal on dislustred seas. Memoriter. Charles Spear. PeNZ

Oven Bird, The. Robert Frost. AmPP; AWP; HeIP; MeMAP; MoP; NAAL-2; NoAM; NOBA; NoP; OxBA; PoE; PPP; Son; TAP

Oven Loves the TV Set, The. Heather McHugh.

Over. R. S. Thomas. FF

Over & over, bamming it in while I cry out your name I do love you/ please Master. (*LL*) Please Master. Allen Ginsberg. GLP; PeHV

Over a bloomy land, untrod. In Dreamy Swoon. George Darley. *Fr.* Nepenthe. OBNC; PeIV

Over a slow-dying fire. Lachesis. Victor James Daley. CBAP

Over a wild and stormy sea. Mother Shipton's Prophecies. *At. to* Charles Hindley. BLPA

Over Abbey ploughland. Pitts Deep. Jeremy Hooker. SCBI

Over against the treasury. His Gift and Mine. *Unknown.* BLRP

Over-all picture is winter, The. The Hunters in the Snow. William Carlos Williams. *Fr.* Pictures from Brueghel. LCAP

Over all the hills now. Song of the Traveler at Evening. Goethe, *tr. fr. German by* John Frederick Nims. STV

Over all the mountain peaks. Wanderer's Night Song. Goethe, *tr. fr. German by* Philip L. Miller. RiWo
(Over every peak. ArNa, *tr. by* John White)

Over an ash-fawn beach fronting a sea which keeps. Fiascherino. Charles Tomlinson. NoAM

Over and back. At Ithaca. Hilda Doolittle ("H. D."). VGW

Over and over again. (*LL*) To the Tune "The Pain of Lovesickness." Wu Tsao. WPC

Over and over again I order my students. The Widow Teaches Poetry Writing. Nell Altizer. IMW

Over and over again the papers print. Once in a While a Protest Poem. David B. Axelrod. InPK

Over and over again to people. The Limits of Submission. Faarah Nuur, *tr. fr. Somali.* TTY, *tr. by* B. W. Andrzejewski *and* I. M. Lewis; WTO, *tr. by* B. W. Andrzejewski *and* I. M. Lewis

Over and over I have heard. Portrait. Edna St. Vincent Millay. LPA

Over and Over Stitch. Jorie Graham. HCAP; VCAP

Over and over, when the wayside dust had grayed us. To Be Said at the Seder. Karl Wolfskehl, *tr. fr. German by* Carol North Valhope *and* Ernst Morowitz. TrJP

Over back where they speak of life as staying. The Investment. Robert Frost. CMoP; OxBA

Over beyond the village. The Hurdy-Gurdy Man. Wilhelm Müller, *tr. fr. German by* Philip L. Miller. *Fr.* Winter's Journey, The. RiWo

Over Bright Summer Seas. Robert Silliman Hillyer. NYBP

Over Case's Door. John Case. FaBoUs

Over cherry blossoms. Spring. Tanikawa Shuntaro, *tr. fr. Japanese by* Harold Wright. EaPr

Over deep cushions, drenched with drowsy scents. Damned Women. Baudelaire, *tr. fr. French by* Roy Campbell. BoLoP

Over every elm, the. You Too Lie down. Dennis Lee. TLR

Over every peak. Goethe. *See* Over all the mountain peaks.

Over-Heart, The. Whittier. ChIV-2; NOCV; WGRP

Over her beautiful eyes. (*LL*) The Morning Sun Shines. Emperor Wu of Liang. OHMPC

Over here in England I'm helpin' wi' the hay. Corrymeela. "Moira O'Neill." AWP

Over here, over here. (*LL*) The Praties. *Unknown.* WTO

Over Hill, over Dale. Shakespeare. *Fr.* Midsummer Night's Dream, A. EII

Over hills and high mountains. The Wandering Maiden; or, True Love at Length United. *Unknown.* CoMu

Over his keys the musing organist. James Russell Lowell. *Fr.* Vision of Sir Launfal, The. LiTA

Over his millions Death has lawful power. On the Death of M. D'Ossoli and His Wife, Margaret Fuller. Walter Savage Landor. PAH

Over in the Meadow. Oliver A. Wadsworth. MoShBr

Over Sir John's Hill. Dylan Thomas. AngWe; LiTB; MoAB; TOF

Over misted blue hills and distant water. To Judge Han Ch'o at Yang-chou. Tu Mu, *tr. fr. Chinese by* A. C. Graham. PLT

Over my district north to south, when will my days in office end? Out in the Snow, Spending the Night at the New Stockade, Extremely Depressed. Huang T'ing-chien, *tr. fr. Chinese by* Michael E. Workman. SuSp

Over my head, I see the bronze butterfly. Lying in a Hammock at William Duffy's Farm in Pine Island, Minnesota. James Wright. CAPP; HAP; HCAP; HoPM; NaP; NOBA; OPOP; Poetr; TRP; VCAP
(Lying in a Hammock at a Friend's Farm in Pine Island, Minnesota.) PRA

Over my head the woodland wall. The Scribe. *Unknown, tr. fr. Irish.* TIRV, *tr. by* Robin Flower

Over New England now, the snow. Frances Frost. BoNaP

Over North Mountain. On the Death of the Emperor Temmu. Empress Jito, *tr. fr. Japanese by* Kenneth Rexroth *and* Ikuko Atsumi. WPJ

Over northeast mountains. Voyeur's Dream. Barney Bush. HATNAP

Over oceans sped he, Attis, in the speediest of the ships. Attis. Catullus, *tr. fr. Latin by* John Frederick Nims. STV

Over, oh over/ the thorn. (*LL*) No one kneads us again out of earth and clay. Paul Celan.

Over on the hill there's a big red bull. *Unknown.* RoPo

Over our heads the missiles ran. Loss of an Oil Tanker. Charles Causley. OxBC

Over our naked guilt. (*LL*) The Net. W. R. Rodgers. BoLoP; CIP; ErPo; PeIV; PNI

Over, Over. Thomas Love Peacock. *Fr.* Maid Marian. OxAEP-2

Over Peter Taylor's. Long & Short of It: A Letter to Brendan Galvin. George Garrett. NGP

Over rips and tears and/ thin places. (*LL*) A Nameless One. Margaret Avison. HeIP; NOBC

Over rock and wrinkled ground. Beagles. W. R. Rodgers. FaBoTw

Over sheer banks a menacing wind moves. Night. Tu Fu, *tr. fr. Chinese by* Jan W. Walls. SuSp

Over that morn hung heaviness, until. Seascape. Francis Brett Young. OxBTC

Over that silly scent Willie sent Millicent. (*LL*) Limerick. *Unknown.* PeLi

Over the Arafura sea, the China sea. For John Chappell. Gary Snyder. NNaP

Over the ball of it. Pisgah-Sights. I & II. Robert Browning. ChIV-1

Over the bay. *Unknown.* RoPo

Over the black mountain, across the black bay, into the/ black night and beyond. Encounter. Uys Krige, *tr. fr. Afrikaans by the author.* PeSA

Over the bleak and barren snow. Tony O! Colin Francis. CH; CoGr; FaBoCo

Over the bridge. Crossing Portsmouth Bridge. Alan Chong Lau. BCF

Over the briny wave I go. The Kayak. *Unknown.* FaPON

Over the clay-laden estuary a. Bye Bye Blackbird. John James. VaA

Over the cradle the mother hung. Where Shall the Baby's Dimple Be. Josiah Gilbert Holland. BLPA

Over the dark highway. Winter Twilight. Lou Lipsitz. GOYP

Over the dark water. A Kayak Song. Lucy Diamond. BoTP

Over the Dark World Flies the Wind. Tennyson. FaBoRV

Over the downs there were birds flying. On the South Downs. Sara Teasdale. MoAmPo

Over the Edge. Fleur Adcock. PeNZ

Over the edge of the purple down. The City of Sleep. Kipling. NTP

Over the empty fields a black kite hovers. The Kite. Alexander Blok, *tr. fr. Russian by* Frances Cornford *and* Esther P. Salamon. PAW

Over the fence. Emily Dickinson. FaBoVe

Over the Fields. Adeline White. BoTP

Over the flat slope of St Eloi. Trenches: St Eloi. T. E. Hulme. PeFWW

Over, the four long years! And now there rings. Oxford. Lionel Johnson. FaBoPP; OBNC

Over the garden, through the breezes. Night in Spring. Joseph Freiherr von Eichendorff, *tr. fr. German by* Philip L. Miller. RiWo

Over the Great City. Edward Carpenter. WGRP

Over the half-finished houses. The Roofwalker. Adrienne Rich. CoAP; NAAL-2; PPP

Over the heather the wet wind blows. Roman Wall Blues. W. H. Auden. FaBoEH; NTP

Over the Hill and over the Dale. Dawlish Fair. Keats. NTP; PeLV

Over the hill came horsemen, horsemen whistling. A Stared Story. William Stafford. Son

Over the hill I have watched the dawning. Dawning. Richard Watson Dixon. NOBVV

Over the hill the farm-boy goes. Evening at [*or* on] the Farm. John Townsend Trowbridge. FaPON; GN (Evening on the Farm. MoShBr)

Over the Hill to the Poor-House. Will M. Carleton. BeLS; BLPA; VPP

Over the Hills and Far Away. John Gay. *See* Were I laid on Greenland's coast.

"Over the hills and far away." and a crescent moon. (*LL*) The Gypsy. Edward Thomas. NoAM; NoP

Over the hills the loose clouds rambled. The Subjection of Women. Austin Clarke. CIP

Over the hills/ Where the edge of the light. The Witches' Ride. Karla Kuskin. PDV; TLR

Over the land freckled with snow half-thawed. Thaw. Edward Thomas. ArNa; EBEV; FaBoTw; FM; GTBS-P; MoAB; MoBrPo; NTP; OxAEP-2; OxBSP; OxBTC; Spl

Over the lids of thine eye. Images. Richard Schaukal, *tr. fr. German by* Ludwig Lewisohn. AWP

Over the low, barnacled, elephant-colored rocks. Meditation at Oyster River. Theodore Roethke. CAPP; CMoP; MoAmPo; NYBP

Over the low lope of the bass, the highhat's chatter. Elegy for Professor Longhair. Elton Glaser. Jaz

Over the Medes and light Sabaeans reigns. Claudian. *Fr.* Against Eutropius. SiPSBD, *tr. by* Sir Walter Ralegh

Over the monstrous shambling sea. Marsh Song — at Sunset. Sidney Lanier. NOBA

Over the month of June the rain is falling. The Rain is Falling. Homero Aridjis, *tr. fr. Spanish by* John Frederick Nims. STV

Over the mountains/ And over the waves. Love Will Find Out the Way. *Unknown.* FaBoCh; GBL; GN; GTBS; GTBS-P; OBEV; WiR (Great Adventure, The.) GTBS-P

Over the mountains/ Over the plains. Trains. James S. Tippett. FaPON

Over the ocean. *Unknown.* RoPo

Over the one-strand river. (*LL*) Gray [*or* Grey] Goose and Gander. *Unknown.* GBP; OxBoLi; OxNR

Over the quarry the children went rambling. The Fossil Raindrops. Harriet Prescott Spofford. OBCA

Over the rainy day mountain. Wishes. Patty L. Harjo. VoR

Over the right/ triangle formed. The Slogan. Paul Blackburn. PoM

Over the rim of the glass. The Ghost in the Martini. Anthony Hecht. DiPo; OxBC

Over the river and through the wood. Thanksgiving Day. Lydia Maria Child. FaPON; ImGa; NTCP; OHIP; WHSW (New-England Boy's Song about Thanksgiving Day, The. OBCA

Over the roof-tops race the shadows of clouds. John Gould Fletcher. *Fr.* Irradiations. MoAmPo

Over the rough roads of pennsylvania. Sketches near Youngstown Ohio. Lance Henson. ETG

Over the sea. *Unknown.* RoPo

Over the sea our galleys went. The Wanderers. Robert Browning. *Fr.* Paracelsus. OBEV

Over the shoulders and slopes of the dune. The Daisies. Bliss Carman. AnAmPo; BoNaP

Over the Steppe. Aleksei Nikolayevich Pleshcheyev, *tr. fr. Russian by* Philip L. Miller. RiWo

Over the steppe I trudge. Over the Steppe. Aleksei Nikolayevich Pleshcheyev, *tr. fr. Russian by* Philip L. Miller. RiWo

Over the stern, my sad heart, drool. The Tortured Heart. Rimbaud, *tr. fr. French.* PeHV

Over the stones still rattling, up Pall Mall. Byron. *Fr.* Don Juan. NOBL

Over! the sweet summer closes. Tennyson. *Fr.* Becket. GBL

Over the tender, bow'd locks of the corn. (*LL*) Summer Dawn. William Morris. Mes; NOBE; NOBVV; OAEL-2; OBEV; OBNC; OxAEP-2

Over the top! The wire's thin here, unbarbed. The Night Patrol. Arthur Graeme West. NSI

Over the Top with Pershing. Zelda Sayre Fitzgerald. AiP

Over the treetops and the fields of grain. Secret Love. Joseph Freiherr von Eichendorff, *tr. fr. German by* Philip L. Miller. RiWo

Over the turret, shut in his ironclad tower. Craven. Sir Henry Newbolt. PAH

Over the utmost hill at length I sped. Shelley. *Fr.* Revolt of Islam, The. OBWP

Over the Wall: Berlin, May 1975. C. H. Sisson. OBTV; OxBC

Over the warts on the bumpy. Sadie's Playhouse. Margaret Danner. PoBA

Over the water an old ghost strode. The Old Ghost. Thomas Lovell Beddoes. WiR

Over the water and over the lea [*or* sea]. *Unknown.* OxNR; ReMoGo

Over the water/ and under the water. A Ship's Nail. *Unknown.* ReMoGo

Over the west side of the mountain. Lyrebirds. Judith Wright. GoJo

Over the wintry. Natsume Soseki, *tr. fr. Japanese by* Henry Behn. PDV

Over the wintry fields the snow drifts; falling, falling. Winter Evening. Walter de la Mare. FaBoRV

Over their edge of earth. The Little Clan. F. R. Higgins. OBMV

"Over their graves!" (*LL*) Over Their Graves. Henry Jerome Stockard. OHIP

Over Their Graves. Henry Jerome Stockard. OHIP

Over their iron stile. And still don't sleep. (*LL*) Zoo Keeper's Wife. Sylvia Plath. VBLP

Over there are faith, life, virtue in the sun. (*LL*) Report on Experience. Edmund Blunden. CoGr; FaBoTw; GTBS-P; NOBE; OBMV; OBWP; PeFWW; PlP

Over there in your fields you have. Rains for the Harvest. *Unknown, tr. fr. Tewa Indian by* H. J. Spinden. WTO

Over there?/ Where?. (*LL*) Cafe: 3 A.M. Langston Hughes. GLP; HCAP

Over These Brooks. Sir Philip Sidney. *Fr.* Arcadia. SiPSBD

Over these brooks, trusting to ease mine eyes. Over These Brooks. Sir Philip Sidney. *Fr.* Arcadia. SiPSBD

Over this battered track. Express Train. Karl Kraus, *tr. fr. German by* Albert Bloch. TrJP

Over thresholds of welcome dream with wet and moonlit skin. (*LL*) Elegy for Drowned Children. Bruce Dawe. NOBAu

Over to your place. (*LL*) The Poem You Asked For. Larry Levis. AmPA; GOYP; PBCAP

Over two shadowless waters, adrift as a pinnace in peril. Evening on the Broads. Swinburne. TEP

Over 2000 Illustrations and a Complete Concordance. Elizabeth Bishop. HCAP; LCAP; NAAL-2; NoAM; VCAP

Over us, like a candle, was the moon. (*LL*) The Abandoned. Nathan Alterman. MHP

Over which your glass slippers so ignorantly danced! (*LL*) On the Way to the Island. David Ferry. PRA

Over worn-out hands — oh! beautiful sleep! (*LL*) Beautiful Things. Ellen Palmer Allerton. BLPA; PWR; WBLP

Over yonder's a park, which is newly begun. The Corpus Christi Carol. *Unknown.* GBP

Over your body the clouds go. Gulliver. Sylvia Plath. NOBA

Overcoated throughout what we called summer. Harry the Black. Alun Rees. AngWe

Overcoats are gone from Central Park, The. "Grandfather" in Winter. Frederick Feirstein. BTR

Overdose of beautiful words, An. 12th Raga: For John Wieners. David Meltzer. *Fr.* Ragas. NeAP

Overdue Balance Sheet. Thérèse Plantier, *tr. fr. French by* Maxine W. Kumin *and* Judith Kumin. BoWoP

Overhanging Cloud. Robert Lowell. *Fr.* Marriage. NAs

Overhead on a wing under heaven, treading. To Father Gerard Manley Hopkins, S.J. George Barker. MeMBP

Overhead, the match burns out. Disregard. Ai. NoAM

Overhead the sky merges through windows. The Life Class. Andrew Crozier. VaA

Overheard/ a brother saying. July 27. Norman Jordan. NBV

Overheard. Denise Levertov. PoM

Overheard in an Orchard. Elizabeth Cheney. BLRP

Overheard on a Saltmarsh. Harold Monro. BoTP; CH; FaPON; GoJo; Mes; MoShBr

Overheard over S. E. Asia. Denise Levertov. BoWoP

Overhearing. John Cassidy. PWE

Overjoyed at Soviet Russia's Entry into the War. Liu Ya-tzu, tr. fr. Chinese by Wu-chi Liu. SuSp

Overland to the Islands. Denise Levertov. UnPo

Overlander, The. Unknown. NOBAu

Overloaded circuit, An — lightning. Shimmering Pediment. John Yau. UL

Overlooking the River Stour. Thomas Hardy. FaBoPP

Overlord. Bliss Carman.

Overnight Guest. Ramona Wilson. VoR

Overnight in the Apartment by the River. Tu Fu, tr. fr. Chinese by William Hung. ChTr

Overnight, very/ whitely, discreetly. Mushrooms. Sylvia Plath. BoNaP; FaBoWP; RB; WPOW

Overripe Fruit. Kasmuneh, tr. fr. Arabic. TrJP

Overture for Bubble-Gum and Flute. Alistair Paterson. PeNZ

Overture to Strangers. Phyllis Haring. PeSA

Overtures to Death, sels. C. Day Lewis.
"For us, born into a still." CMoP

Overwhelm my heart. (LL) Who Stops the Dance? Hsiung-hung. WPC

Overwhelmed the entire city. (LL) The Poor. William Carlos Williams. MoAB; MoAmPo; NoP; PPP

Overwhelmed with passion. (LL) To the Tune "A Floating Cloud Crosses Enchanted Mountain." Huang O. AIW; BoWoP; WPC

Overworked Elocutionist, An. Carolyn Wells. BLPA; BLPL

Ovibos, The. Robert Beverly Hale. FiBHP

Ovid in the Third Reich. Geoffrey Hill. FaBoMo; NoAM

Ovid is the surest guide. Written in an Ovid. Matthew Prior. FaBoEE; FaBoUs

Ovid, Meet a Metamorphodite. Jonathan Williams. PoM

Ovid on the Dacian Coast. Dunstan Thompson. NYBP

Ovid Twice Exiled. Jerzy Ficowski, tr. fr. Polish by Frank J. Corliss, Jr., and Grazyna Sandel. PoSu

Ovid would never have guessed how far. Brueghel in Naples. Dannie Abse. NIP

Ovid's Banquet of Sense, sels. George Chapman.
Ear's Delight, The. NoSic
"In a loose robe of tinsel forth [or tynsell foorth] she came." OxAEP-1

Oviparous Tailor, The. Thomas Lovell Beddoes. CBNP; WiR

Ow much poun fi di yellow yam? Longsight Market. Valerie Bloom. NBrP

Owdham Footbo.' Ammon Wrigley. FaBoVe

Owed to America. Lawrence Durrell. OBTV

Owed to New York. Byron Rufus Newton. BLPA; NBLV

Owen of Carron., sels. John Langhorne.
"Does nature bear a tyrant's breast?" FaBoCo

Owen Tudor. Hugh Holland. AngWe

Owen Tudor to Queen Katherine. Michael Drayton. Fr. England's Heroical Epistles. NoSic

Owen's Bracelet. Robert Hayman. Fr. Owen's Epigrams. NOSC

Owen's Epigrams., sels. Robert Hayman.
Owen's Bracelet. NOSC
Saturn's Three Sons. NOSC

Owen's praise demands my song. The Triumphs of Owen. Thomas Gray. EnRP; PoEL-3

Ower the grey sentinel hills. No Voice of Man. Raymond Falconer. GGP

Ower t'ills o Bingley. Blake Morrison. Fr. Ballad of the Yorkshire Ripper, The. FaBoVe

Owl, The. Thorkild Bjornvig, tr. fr. Danish by Robert Bly. NU

Owl, The. Edward Davison. PoA

Owl, The. Walter de la Mare. OxBSP

Owl. Peter Kane Dufault. NYBP

Owl, The. W. S. Merwin. PPP

Owl, The. William Jay Smith. PDV

Owl, The. Tennyson. BoTP; FaBoCh; FaPON; GoJo; MoShBr

Owl, The. Edward Thomas. ChTr; EBEV; FaBoRV; FaBoTw; FF; GTBS-P; LiTB; MoP; NAEL-2; NIP; NoAM; NOBE; NoP; OAEL-2; OBWVE; OxAEP-2; PeFWW; PlP; PoE; Poetr; RB; SCGP; TFi; TRP; UnPo

Owl, The. Robert Penn Warren. MoAmPo

Owl and the Crow, The. Ben King. AnAmPo

Owl and the Eel and the Warming-Pan, The. Laura E. Richards. OBCA

Owl and the Fox, The. Unknown. BLPA

Owl and the Nightingale, The, sels. At. to Nicholas de Guildford Nicholas De Guildford.

Owl and the Pussy-Cat, The. Edward Lear. BeLS; BoTP; CBNP; EBEvV; FaBoBe; FaBoCh; FaBoNo; FaPON; GoJo; GTBS-P; MoShBr; NBLV; NOBE; NoP; NTCP; NTP; OBSP, St. 1 only; OFC; OHCV; OTCP; OtMeF; OxBChV; OxBM, (St. 1 only); OxBoLi; PDV; PeLV; PlP, St. 1 only; PoLF; PoRA; PYC; SoCa; TFi; TLR; TrGrPo; TTTS

Owl-Critic, The. James Thomas Fields. BLPA; OBAL; WBLP

Owl expires, The! Death gave the dreadful word. On the Death of a Lady's Owl. Moses Mendes. TrJP

Owl has come, The/ Right into my house. Eyes. W. H. Davies. FM

Owl in the Oak, The. Unknown. FaBoNo

Owl in the Sarcophagus, The. Wallace Stevens. FaBoMo

Owl is a broad, the bat and the toad, The. The Witches' Charm. Ben Jonson. Fr. Masque of Queens, The. EiL; FaBoCh (Charme.) FM

Owl is abroad, the bat and the toad, The. Witches' Chasm. Ben Jonson. RB

Owl Is an Only Bird of Poetry, An. Robert Duncan. NeAP; PoM

Owl of the Greenwood. Patricia Hubbell. OTCP

Owl, owl/ I've a secret. Lulu, Lulu, I've a Lilo. Charlotte Pomerantz. SiSoPo

Owl shriek'd at thy birth, an evil sign, The. Shakespeare. Fr. King Henry VI, Pt. III. OxAEP-1

Owl that lives in the old oak tree, The. The Owl. William Jay Smith. PDV

Owl to her mate is calling, The. The Fate of the Oak. "Barry Cornwall." OHIP

Owl/ Who? Owl of the Greenwood. Patricia Hubbell. OTCP

Owl/ whose home was in the hemlock, The. Unknown, tr. fr. Seneca Indian by Jerome K. Rothenberg and Richard Johnny John. STP

Owl winks in the shadows, An. Mother Earth; Her Whales. Gary Snyder. LCAP; PoBeRe

Owl Wives. Nigel Wells. AngWe

Owl Woman's Death Song. Unknown, tr. fr. Papago Indian by Ruth Underhill. BoWoP

Owle, The, sels. Michael Drayton.
"And every bird shew'd in his proper kind." FM

Owls. Louise Erdrich. TRP

Owls. W. D. Snodgrass. Poetsp

Owls have feathers lined with down, The. The Hedgehog and His Coat. Elizabeth Fleming. BoTP

Owls mimic human speech. Meng Chiao, tr. by Stephen Owen. Fr. Laments of the Gorges. SuSp

Owls roost like gray lamps up there, The. Brobdingnag. Adrien Stoutenburg. NYBP

Own ways. (LL) Again did the. Diana Lee Moomey. EaPr

Owned her father all the fact'ries. The Pariah. James Edwin Campbell. AAP

Owner of My Face, The. Rodney Hall. CBAP
Sels.
After a Sultry Morning.
Lips and Nose.
Some Magnetism in the Sea.

Owners of the Little Box, The. Vasco [or Vasko] Popa, tr. fr. Serbo-Croatian by Charles Simic. HSix

Ownership. Lizette Woodworth Reese. MoAmPo

Owslebury Lads, The. Unknown. OBET

Owt of your slepe aryse and wake. Out of Your Sleep Arise and Wake! Unknown. OxBLMV

Ox, The. Russell Edson. RaBo

Ox, The. Mary Morison Webster. PeSA

Ox-Bow. Donald Davie. DiPo

Ox Cart Man. Donald Hall. CAPP; FYAP; InPS; LCAP

Ox-fed orating ominous octastiches. (LL) The King's Breakfast. A. A. Milne. OTCP; OxBChV; UV, sts. I and II only

Ox-Tamer, The. Walt Whitman. RB

Oxen, The. Thomas Hardy. BoTP; CMoP; EBEV; HAP; InPK; LiTM; MeMBP; MoAB; MoBrPo; MoP; NoAM; NOBE; NTP; OAEL-2; OBCP; OxAEP-2; OxBTC; PChr; PeECV; Poetr; PPP; RB; SoSe; TFi; TOF; TRP; WeW

Oxen: Ploughing at Fiesole. Charles Tomlinson. OxBTC

Oxen that rattle the yoke and chain or halt in the leafy shade. Walt Whitman. Fr. Song of Myself. AmPP; FM; LiTA; MoAmPo, abr.; NOBA; OxBA; PoNe; SOTW, much abr.

Oxford. W. H. Auden. OxAEP-2

Oxford, sels. Edward Dorn.
Comforted by Limestone. NOBA

P

Pain of too poignant beauty fills the heart. The World's Desire. William Rose Benét. TrPWD

Pain Paint. Peter Minck. FaBoUs

Pain/ so it turned black. Momcilo Nastasijevic, tr. fr. Serbo Croatian by Charles Simic. Fr. Deaf Things. HSix

Pain we have to suffer seems so broad, The. Belief. Ella Wheeler Wilcox. PWR

"Pain, who made thee?" thus I said once. Pain. James Henry. NOBVV

Painful husbandman with sweaty brows, The. The Husbandman. George Wither. Fr. Collection of Emblemes, Ancient and Moderne, A. NOSC

Painful Plough, The. Unknown. OBET

Pain's a cup of honey in the pelvis. Sheila Na Gig At Kilpeck. Gillian Clarke. SCBI

Pains and Gains. Edward de Vere, Earl of Oxford. See Labouring man, that tills the fertile soil, The.

Pains of Education, The. Charles Churchill. Fr. Author, The. FaBoCo

Pains of insecurity surround me. Back Again, Home. Don L. Lee. BPo

Pains of Sleep, The. Samuel Taylor Coleridge. EnRP; FHYEP; NAEL-2; OBNC; TEP

Pains the sharp sentence the heart in whose wrath it was uttered. Pardon. Julia Ward Howe. PAH

Paint Castlemaine in colours that will hold. Andrew Marvell. Fr. Last Instructions to a Painter, The. APAS; OBSV

Paint-flaken, it is paint-flaken. March, Upstate. William Bronk. NYBP

Paint last the King, and a dead shade of night. Andrew Marvell. Fr. Last Instructions to a Painter, The. APAS; OBSV

Paint me a cavernous waste shore. Sweeney Erect. T. S. Eliot. OxBTC; VGW

Painted autumn overwhelms, The. John Meade Falkner. FaBoPP

Painted Ceiling, The. Amy Lowell. OBAL

Painted Cup, The. Bryant. EAP

Painted Head. John Crowe Ransom. LiTA; LiTM; MeMAP; NoAM; NOBA; OxBA

Painted Lady, The. Margaret Danner. BPo

Painted streets alive with hum of noon, The. Sir Edwin Arnold. Fr. Light of Asia, The. OBTV

Painted whore, the mask of deadly sin, A. William Lithgow. OBTV

Painted with one fish, a cucumber. Japanese Fan. James Kirkup. GrPl

Painter, The. John Ashbery. HCAP; NOBA; NoP; PoE; SOTW

Painter and poet, runner and disk-thrower. One of the Jews. C. P. Cavafy, tr. fr. Greek. TrJP

Painter, by unmatch'd desert. The Picture. Anacreon, tr. fr. Greek by Thomas Stanley. AWP

Painter, encumbered with cash, A. Thomas Thorneley. PeLi

Painter in the Lion Cage, The. Betti Alver, tr. fr. Estonian by Willis Barnstone and Felix Oinas. BoWoP

Painter of Dante's awful ferry-ride, The. Babette Deutsch. PoA

Painter Who Pleased Nobody and Everybody, The. John Gay. BeLS

Painters, The. Judith Hemschemeyer. Poetsp

Painting: A Head. John Crowe Ransom. MoAB; MoAmPo

Painting: A Head. John Crowe Ransom. See By dark severance the apparition head.

Painting a picture of the same shrimp boat. Discovering Your Subject. Pattiann Rogers. MT

Painting Bamboo, a Song. Po Chü-i, tr. fr. Chinese by Irving Lo. SuSp

Painting Mount Taranaki. David Eggleton. PeNZ

Painting of My Father. Padraic Fallon. NOIV

Painting of Water Buffaloes, A, sels. Yang Shih-ch'i, tr. fr. Chinese by Jonathan Chaves.

Painting the Gate. May Swenson. TLR; WeW

Painting with a Knife. Iain Sinclair. NBrP

Painting with a knife the Invader. Painting with a Knife. Iain Sinclair. NBrP

Painting with Words, sels. Nizar Qabbani, tr. fr. Arabic by Diana Der Hovanessian and Lena Jayyusi.

Painting would have been the best way to get things over, A. In Memoriam. Martin Johnston. NOBAu

Paintings, sels. Chang Yü, tr. fr. Chinese by Jonathan Chaves.

Paintings, sels. Pien Kung, tr. fr. Chinese by Jonathan Chaves.

Paintings of Fishermen, sels. Wu Chen, tr. fr. Chinese by Jonathan Chaves.

Paintings of Ladies Engaged in Four Springtime Occupations, sels. Yang Chi, tr. fr. Chinese by Jonathan Chaves.

Paintings with stiff. Primitives. Dudley Randall. BPo; NBV

Painture. Richard Lovelace. CaPo

Pair, A. May Swenson. RFM

Pair of angels, A. Café. Hala Baykov. Mes

Pair of blackbirds, A. In Modern Dress. Craig Raine. NoAM

Pair of brothers love me, A. Strato, tr. fr. Greek by Teddy Hogge. GrAn

Pair of dark blue panties, A. Familiar Music. Bill Berkson. UL

Pair of funnels stroll by night, A. The Funnels. Christian Morgenstern, tr. fr. German by Geoffrey Grigson. FaBoNo

Pair of green-painted eyebrows, A. Wang Chien, tr. by William H. Nienhauser. Fr. Palace Poems. SuSp

Pair of Shoes, A. Theodore Weiss. NoAM

Pair of soft, black eyes, A. A Home Greeting. Priscilla Jane Thompson. CBWP-2

Pair of Wings, A. Stephen Hawes. MeEL

Pair-Royal of Coxcombs, The, sels. "Ephelia."
"Gallants,/ If, as you say, you Love Varietie." KTR

Paired Lives. W. R. Rodgers. CIP; IIP

Paisley Ceiling, The. Lila Arnold. IHMS

Paiute Ponies. Jim Barnes. CDW

Pajaro the men thigh deep in mud. Song of Pajaro. Jeff Tagami. OpBo

Paki Go Home. Himani Bannerji. AIW

Pal, in the Pals of Death Club. This Is a Poem for the Fathers and for Michael Ryan. Thomas Lux. AmPA

Palabras Grandiosas. Bayard Taylor. AnAmPo; OBAL

Palace, The. Charles Stuart Calverley. EBVV

Palace, The. Rita Dove. Fr. Parsley. NoAM; VCAP

Palace at dusk, the pearl blind is lowered. Jade Steps Plaint. Hsieh T'iao, tr. fr. Chinese by Ronald C. Miao. SuSp

Palace girls up early. Wang Chien, tr. by William H. Nienhauser. Fr. Palace Poems. SuSp

Palace great is builded rich and round. Tasso, tr. fr. Italian by Edward Fairfax. Fr. Godfrey of Bulloigne; or, The Recoverie of Jerusalem. NoSic

Palace of Art, The. Tennyson. EnVR

Palace of Art, The, sels. Tennyson.
Lincolnshire Shores ("A still salt pool locked in with bars of sand"). FaBoPP
"One seem'd all dark and red — a tract of sand." UnPo

Palace [or Palice] of Honor [or Honour], The, sels. Gawin Douglas.
Calliope's Nymph Brings the Poet to the Palace to Honour. OxBLMV
Nightmare. PoEL-1

Palace of humbug, The. "Lewis Carroll." CBNP; FaBoNo

Palace of Pleasant Regard, The. Lady of the Assembly. Fr. Assembly of Ladies, The. WPE

Palace of Rocks, The. Yuan Chieh, tr. fr. Chinese by William H. Nienhauser. SuSp

Palace Poem. Chu Ch'ing-yu, tr. fr. Chinese by Irving Y. Lo. SuSp

Palace Poem. Wang Yu, tr. fr. Chinese by Irving Y. Lo. SuSp

Palace Poems, sels. Wang Chien, tr. fr. Chinese.
"At home I loved to wear old clothes." SuSp
"Early autumn, white rabbits." SuSp
"Her silken gown rustles." SuSp
"Long the flimsy skirts." SuSp
"Pair of green-painted eyebrows, A." SuSp
"Palace girls up early." SuSp
"Red lantern calls the spring clouds from my sleep, A." SuSp
"Spring breeze blows the rain, A." SuSp
"Wanting to welcome the emperor." SuSp

Palace seemed the lodging of a baker, The. (LL) The Apple Dumplings and a King. "Peter Pindar." OBSV

Palaces of Gold. Leon Rosselson. OBET

Palaces of the dead are lined with diarrhea memories, The. Diarrhea Sestina. Edward Kleinschmidt. UnDi

Palais des Arts. Louise Glück. AnAn; VCAP

Palamon and Arcite., sels. Dryden.
Parts of the Whole Are We; but God the Whole. NAs

Palaver is silly. (LL) Air: Sentir avec Ardeur. Marie-Françoise-Catherine de, Marquise de Boufflers Beauveau. CTC; WPOW

Pale amber sunlight falls across. Autumnal. Ernest Dowson. EBVV; OBNC

Pale beech and pine so blue. Thomas Hardy. See Pale beech and pine-tree blue.

Pale beech and pine-tree blue. In a Wood. Thomas Hardy. OBNC
(Pale beech and pine so blue. EnVR

Pale, beyond porch and portal. Proserpine. Swinburne. Fr. Garden of Proserpine, The. AWP; BLPA; BLPL; ChTr; FaBoRV; FaBV; FaPoR; HAP; LiTB; NAEL-2; NOBE; NOBVV; NoP; OBNC; PoE; PoEL-5; PoRA; SCV; TrGrPo

Pale Blue Casket, The. Oliver Pitcher. PoBA; TTY

Pale Boy and the Old Woman, The. Rachel Blake. NWP

Pale brown Moses went down to Egypt land. Benediction. Bob Kaufman. PoNe

Pale brows, still hands and dim hair. The Lover Mourns for the Loss of Love. W. B. Yeats. LPA; WeW

Pale/ by the road to the North. North Russian Town. Johannes Bobrowski, *tr. fr. German by* Ruth Mead *and* Matthew Mead. AnRep

Pale darts still quivering, crocuses. Poem at Equinox. Hilary Corke. NYBP

Pale, drooping girl and the swaggering soldier, The. Just an Old Sweet Song. Donagh MacDonagh. CIP

Pale-faced rat! To Noël Coward. Noël Coward. FaBoPa

Pale Fire. Vladimir Nabokov. OBD

Pale grey, her guns hooded, decks clear of all impediment. H. M. S. Hero. Michael Roberts. OxBTC

Pale hands I love beside the Shalimar. Kashmiri Song. "Laurence Hope." BLPA; BLPL; FaBoBe

Pale Heinrich he came sauntering by. The Window-Glance. Heine, *tr. fr. German by* John Todhunter. AWP

Pale morning in June 4 AM, A. Country Roads. Rolf Jacobsen, *tr. by* Robert Bly. NU

Pale nuns of St. Joseph are here, The. Island of the Three Marias. Alberto A. Ríos. NoAM

Pale old man/ in the faded caftan, The. The Spoor in the Sand. Johannes Bobrowski, *tr. fr.* Ruth Mead *and* Matthew Mead. AnRep

Pale pink and green lights flush on white. Tangier: Hotel Rif. Donald Thomas. OBTV

Pale ravener of horrible meat. (LL) The Maldive Shark. Herman Melville. AmPP; AnAmPo; NAAL-1; NOBA; NoP; OxBA; PoE; PoEL-5; RB; TAP

Palely intent, he urged his keel. At the Cannon's Mouth. Herman Melville. PAH

Paleness of hunger, The. The Mutineer's Ballad. Peter Kocan. NOBAu

Palestine. Whittier. WBLP

Palindrome. Lisel Mueller. IHMS; WeW

Palinode. Oliver St. John Gogarty. OBMV

Palinode, A. Edmund Bolton. ElL; InvP; NoSic; PoEL-2; PrIm

Palinode, A. Robert Greene. *Fr.* Greene's Groatsworth of Wit.

Palinodia. Winthrop Mackworth Praed. CBLP

Palladium. Matthew Arnold. GTBS-P; OAEL-2; OBNC; PPP

Pallas and/ golden-shoed Hera. Rufinus, *tr. fr. Greek by* Alan Marshfield. GrAn

Pallid and moonlike in the smog. A Man Can Complain, Can't He? Ogden Nash. NBLV

Pallid Cuckoo. David Campbell. CBAP

Pallid, mis-shapen he stands. The World's grimed thumb. In the Dock. Walter de la Mare. LiTM

Pallid the leash-men! (LL) The Return. Ezra Pound. AmPP; CMoP; HAP; MoAB; MoAmPo; MoP; NoAM; NOBA; OxBA; PoE; Poetr; RB; TRP; VGW; WeW

Pallor. Agnes Mary Frances Robinson. NOBVV

Palm, The. Roy Campbell. MoBrPo

Palm at the end of the mind, The. Of Mere Being. Wallace Stevens. HCAP

Palm Leaf of Mary Magdalene. Cheryl Clarke. GLP

Palm of the Hand. Rainer Maria Rilke, *tr. fr. German by* Robert Bly. NU

Palm of the hand, The,/ is not aware of dying. Fumi Saito, *tr. fr. Japanese by* Edith Marcombe Shiffert *and* Yuki Sawa. BoWoP

Palm-Sunday Hymn, A. William Herebert. MeEL

Palm-Sunday Hymn, A. William Herebert. *See* Wele, herying and worship be to Crist [*or* Christ] that dere us [*or* ous] boughte.

Palm Sunday: Naples. Arthur Symons. PeVV

Palm the head just so. Then. How It's Done. Alvin Aubert. MT

Palm Tree, The. Abd-ar-Rahman I, *tr. fr. Arabic by* J. B. Trend. AWP

Palm-tree, The. Henry Vaughan *and* Thomas Stanley. ESCV

Palm tree grows in the far bush, The. Election Songs. *Yoruba Oral Tradition, tr. by* Ulli Beier. WTO

Palm Trees. Rex Warner. OBTV

Palm Wine Seller, The. Gladys May Casely Hayford. ShDr

Palmer, The. Robert Greene. NoSic

Palmer's Ode, The. Robert Greene. *Fr.* Never Too Late. CTC; EnRePo; NoSic; SCGP

Palms, The. David Knight. MoCV

Palms and Myrtles. Eleazar ben Kalir, *tr. fr. Hebrew by* Alice Lucas. TrJP

Palmstroem in Animal Costume. Christian Morgenstern, *tr. fr. German by* Hugh Haughton. CBNP

Palmstroem loves to ape the animals. Palmstroem in Animal Costume. Christian Morgenstern, *tr. fr. German by* Hugh Haughton. CBNP

Palsy shakes my pen, while I intend, A. To His Honored Friend Thomas Stanley Esquire, Upon His Elegant Poems. James Shirley. BeJo

Paltry Nude Starts on a Spring Voyage, The. Wallace Stevens. HCAP

Pampered Philainion stabbed me, The. Asclepiades, *tr. fr. Greek by* Alan Marshfield. GrAn

Pampered steed, of swiftness proud. The. The Horse and the Mule. John Huddlestone Wynne. OxBChV

Pamphilia to Amphilanthus. Mary Sidney Wroth, Countess of Montgomery. *Fr.* Urania. WPE

Pamphilia's Sonnet. Mary Sidney Wroth, Countess of Montgomery. *Fr.* Urania. WPE

Pan and the Cherries. Paul Fort, *tr. fr. French by* Jethro Bithell. AWP

Pan and the Nymphs. Glaukos, *tr. fr. Greek by* Dudley Fitts. GrAn

Pan Asks about Daphnis. Diodorus Zonas, *tr. fr. Greek by* Alistair Elliot. GrAn

Pan came out of the woods one day. Pan with Us. Robert Frost. OxBA

Pan Cogito on Virtue. Zbigniew Herbert, *tr. fr. Polish by* Adam Czerniawski. PoSu

Pan Cogito's Thoughts on Hell. Zbigniew Herbert, *tr. fr. Polish by* Adam Czerniawski. FaBoPV

Pan, grant that I may never prove. Song by the Wavering Nymph. Aphra Behn. VBLP

Pan-gu crouched up there. Dividing the Sky. Jiang He, *tr. fr. Chinese by* Donald Finkel *with* Li Guohua. SpMi

Pan-gu drifted to sleep while the moon foretold a heavenly spring. (LL) Dividing the Sky. Jiang He. SpMi

Pan in Battle. *Unknown.* PeNZ

Pan in Wall Street. Edmund Clarence Stedman. AnAmPo

Pan leave piping, the gods have done feasting. The Green-Gown. *Unknown.* CoMu

Pan loved his neighbour Echo — but that child. Moschus, *tr. fr. Greek by* Shelley. OBVE

Pan Piping. Plato, *tr. fr. Greek by* Thomas Stanley. FaBoEE

Pan Recipe. John Agard. PBCV

Pan with Us. Robert Frost. OxBA

Panama. Amanda T. Jones. PAH

Panama. James Jeffrey Roche. PAH

Pancake, The. Christina Rossetti. *See* Mix a Pancake.

Pancake Collector, The. Jack Prelutsky. OBCA

Pancake Day. Mother Goose. *See* Great A, little a.

Pancakes for the Queen of Babylon, sels. Peter Levi. "City built in darkness and cold air, A." CRP

Panchatantra, The. *Unknown, tr. fr. Sanskrit by* Arthur Ryder. AWP
Sels.
Fool and False.
Kings.
Penalty of Virtue, The.
Poverty.
True Friendship.

Pancho, the barrio idiot. Jimmy Santiago Baca. BCF

Pandora and the Moon. Merrill Moore. MoAmPo

Pandora Speaks. William Vaughn Moody. *See* I Stood within the Heart of God.

Pandosto, *sels.* Robert Greene.
Ah Were She Pitiful. TrGrPo, *abr*
(Fawnia.) OBEV
(In Praise of His Loving and Best-beloved Fawnia.) PoEL-2

Panegyric, A. *Unknown.* APAS

Panegyric on the Author of "Absalom and Achitophel," A. *Unknown.* APAS

Panegyric to Sir Lewis Pemberton, A. Robert Herrick. CaPo

Panegyric[k] to My Lord Protector, A, *sels.* Edmund Waller. "While with a strong and yet a gentle hand." JCP; SeCV-1

Panegyric upon Oates, A. Richard Duke. APAS

Panes of light cracking. A Wet Night. Richard Ryan. CIP

Pang of the long century of rains, The. The Lament of Edward Blastock. Edith Sitwell. OBMV

Pangloss's Song [A Comic-Opera Lyric]. Richard Wilbur. IHNG; MoP; NBLV; NoAM

Pangolin, The. Marianne Moore. HAP; NoAM; NOBA; PBWP; Poetr

Pangur Bán. *Unknown, tr. fr. Gaelic by* Robin Flower. CRH; FaBoCh; OFC; RB

Pangur Bán. *Unknown.* NOIV

Panic. Archibald MacLeish. MoAmPo
Sels.
Final Chorus.
Panic "Slowly the thing comes."

Panic ("Slowly the thing comes.") Archibald MacLeish. *Fr.* Panic. MoAmPo

Pannyra of the Golden Heel. Albert Samain, *tr. fr. French by* James Elroy Flecker. AWP

Panope. Edith Sitwell. MoAB; MoBrPo

Panoptics. Chris Wallace-Crabbe. FaBoMA

Pans at Carnival. Henry Beissel. PBCV

"He ended; and thus Adam last replied." HeIP
  (Retreat from Paradise, The.) PoEL-3
"He scarce had ceas't [or ceased] when the superior fiend."
  (Satan and the Fallen Angels.) LiTB; 09OBS
  (Satan's Summons.) NOSC, *bk.* I, *ll.* 283–313
"He stood and call'd/ His legions, angel forms, who lay intranced."
  (Satan's Legions and the Beech Leaves of the Casentino.) FaBoPP
"Heaven opened wide." ChIV-1
"Her long with ardent look his eye pursu'd." UnPo
"High in front advanced." EBEvV
"High on a throne of royal state, which far." FHYEP; NIP; OAEL-1, *ll.*
  1–309; OxAEP-1
"His pride/ Had cast him out from Heaven, with all his host."
  (Satan ("His pride/ Had cast him out from Heaven, with all his host").)
  TrGrPo
"How shall I behold the face." TOF
"How to th' ascent of that steep savage hill."
  (Satan Journey's to the Garden of Eden.) ChTr
"If thou beest he; but O how fall'n! how chang'd." SCV
"In bower and field he sought, where any tuft." TEP
"Into thir inmost bower." FF, *ll.* 738–757; TOF, *ll.* 738–775
"Is this the region, this the soil, the clime." TEP
  (Satan as Rebel-Liberator.) FF, *ll.* 242–255
"Love thou saist." TOF
"Me miserable! which way shall I fly." PoE
"Meanwhile the adversary of God and man." DL, *ll.* 629–841; EBEV, *ll.*
  629–734
  (Sin and Death.) OBNV, *ll.* 629–889
"Meanwhile the heinous and despiteful act." FHYEP
Mulciber. NOSC
"My author and disposer, what thou biddest."
  (Thus Eve to Adam.) FaBV
"Next came one/ Who mourn'd in earnest." EBEV
"No more of talk where God or Angel Guest." NAEL-1, *ll.* 1–1189;
  NAWM-1; NoP; TOF, *ll.* 1–47
  (Higher Argument.) NOSC, *ll.* 1–47
"Now came still evening on, and twilight gray." PeECV, *ll.* 598–688
  (Evening in Paradise.) GN, *ll.* 598–609; NOBE, *ll.* 598–656
  (Moon and the Nightingale, The.) ChTr
"Now had th' Almighty Father from above." NIP
"Now Morn her rosy steps in the eastern clime." NAEL-1; OAEL-1
"O favorable spirit, propitious guest"
  (Adam Unfallen.) NOCV
"O for that warning voice, which he who saw." OAEL-1; OxAEP-1, *ll.*
  1–535; TEP, *ll.* 1–324
  (Prospect of Eden, The.) PoEL-3, *ll.* 1–775
"O thou in heaven and earth the only place."
  (Plan of Salvation, The.) WGRP
"O thou that with surpassing glory crown'd."
  (Satan's Soliloquy.) LiTB
Occupations of Hell. NOSC
"Of man's first disobedience, and the fruit." EBEV, *ll.* 1–270; EBEvV,
  ll. 1–26; FaBoRV, *ll.* 1–26; FaPoB, *ll.* 1–74; FHYEP; NAEL-1;
  NAWM-1; NIP, *ll.* 1–49; NoP, *ll.* 1–26; OAEL-1, *ll.* 1–375;
  OxAEP-1; PeECV, *ll.* 1–26; TOF, *ll.* 1–26
  (Induction, The.) PoE, *ll.* 1–26
  (Invocation: "Of man's first disobedience, and the fruit.") NOSC, *ll.*
  1–26; PoEL-3, *ll.* 1–26
"Oh, why did God,/ Creator wise."
  (Adam Speaks.) NU
"Other way Satan went down, Th.'" NAEL-1
Paradise. PIP
Paradise. NOSC
"Pensive here I sat." OBD
"Pleasing was his shape." EBNV
Raphael's Descent. NOSC
Satan's Journey. NOSC
"She, as a veil down to the slender waist." ErPo
"So passed they naked on, nor shunned the sight." PeECV, *ll.* 319–334
"So Satan spake, and him Beëlzebub."
  (Council of Satan, The.) PoEL-3
"So spake our Mother Eve, and Adam heard."
  (Banishment, The.) NOBE
  (Exile.) NOSC, *ll.* 624–49
  (Exit from Eden, The.) FaBoRV
"So spake th' archangel Michael; then paused." FaBoPV, *ll.* 466–551;
  NAEL-1; OAEL-1
"So spake the enemy of mankind, enclosed." FM
"So spake the godlike power, and thus our sire." NAEL-1
"So stretched out huge in length the Arch-Fiend lay." TEP
"So to the sylvan lodge." NAEL-1
Standing on Earth ("Standing on Earth, not rapt above the Pole"). ChTr
"Stygian council thus dissolved; and forth, The." OAEL-1
"Such was thir song." PeECV, *ll.* 648–691
"Sweet is the breath of Morn, her rising sweet."
  (World Beautiful, The.) GN

Tempter Disarmed, The. NOSC
"Then both ourselves and seed at once to free." OBD
"There stood a hill not far whose grisly top." OAEL-1
"There the companions of his fall, o'erwhelmed."
  (Immortal Hate.) NOBE
"These are thy glorious works, Parent of good."
  (Adam's Morning Hymn.) WGRP
  (Morning Hymn of Adam.) TrPWD
"They ended parle, and both addressed for fight." OBWP
"This having learnt, thou hast attaind the summe." SCV
"This most afflicts me, that departing hence." PeECV, *ll.* 315–333
"Thus Adam himself lamented loud." OAEL-1
"Thus began/ Outrage from lifeless things; but Discord first." NAEL-1
"Thus Belial with words clothed in reason's garb." FaBoPV
"Thus God the heav'n created, thus the earth." PeECV, *ll.* 232–242
"Thus saying, from her husband's hand her hand."
  (Fall, The.) PoEL-3
  (No more talk where God or angel guest.) FHYEP, *bk.* IX
"Thus saying, from her side the fatal key." EBEV
"Thus talking hand in hand alone they pass'd." EBEV
"Thus they in Heav'n, above the starry sphear." EBEV
"Thus was this place." PeECV, *ll.* 246–275
"Thus with the year/ Seasons return." PIP, *ll.* 40–55
"To the Nuptial Bowre." OxBM
"To whom the Father, without cloud, serene." PeECV, *ll.* 45–66
"To whom thus also th' angel last replied." OxAEP-1; PeECV
"To whom thus Michael. Justly thou abhorr'st." FaBoPV
"To whom thus Michael. Those whom last thou saw'st." FaBoPV
"Two of far nobler shape erect and tall." PeECV, *ll.* 288–299
Uncloistered Virtue. NOSC
"Uriel to his charge/ Returned on that bright beam."
  (Now Came Still Evening On.) FaBoRV
What Words Have Passed. TrCP
"While thus he spake, th' Angelic Squadron bright." SCV
"With thee conversing, I forget all time." UV; WiR
  (Eve Speaks to Adam.) ArLo; ChTr; GBL
  (Eve to Adam.) TrGrPo

Paradise Lost. Stanley J. Sharpless. BXAP
Paradise Lost, Book V: An Epitome. Anthony Hecht. NBLV
Paradise Lost, Book IV, lines 639–654. Leslie Johnson. UV
Paradise of Birds, The, *sels.* William John Courthope.
  Dodoism. OtMeF
Paradise on earth is found, A. The Description of Elizium. Michael
  Drayton. *Fr.* Muses' Elysium [*or* Elizium]. OAEL-1
  (Poet's Paradise, The.) WiR, *much abr.*
Paradise Re-entered. D. H. Lawrence. ChIV-2
Paradise Regained [*or* Regain'd], *sels.* Milton.
  "At thy nativity a glorious quire." PChr
Banquet, The. NOSC
  "I who erewhile the happy Garden sung." PeECV, *ll.* 1–7
  "It was the hour of night, when thus the Son." EBEV; PeECV
  "Look once more ere we leave this specular Mount." OBTV, *ll.* 236–
  284; PeECV, *ll.* 236–271
  (Athens.) NOSC, *bk.* IV, *ll.* 236–364
  "Or if I would delight my privat hours." PeECV, *bk.* IV, *ll.* 331–349
Parthians, The
  (Parthian Powers.) NOSC, *bk.* III, *ll.* 310–43
Rome. NOSC
Satan's Guile ("Whom thus answer'd th' Arch Fiend now undisguis'd").
  LiTB
  "Set women in his eye and in his walk." PeECV, *bk.* II, *ll.* 153–162
  "So spake our morning star then in his rise." PeECV, *ll.* 294–320
  "So they in Heav'n their odes and vigils tun'd." PeECV, *bk.* I, *ll.* 182–
  195
  "Sometimes they thought he might be only shewn." PeECV, *bk.* II, *ll.*
  13–29
Table Richly Spread, A. FaBoCh
  "Therefore let pass, as they are transitory." OAEL-1
  "To whom the fiend with fear abasht repli'd." PeECV, *bk.* IV, *ll.* 195–
  203
  "To whom the Tempter impudent replied." ChIV-2, *ll.* 155-232, 285-352
True and False Glory ("To whom our Saviour calmly thus reply'd").
  LiTB
Paradise reserved for me, A. (*LL*) Meditations on the Sepulchre in the
  Garden. Philip Doddridge. NOCV; NOEC
Paradise Saved. A. D. Hope. OxBC
Paradiso. Dante, *tr. fr. Italian. Fr.* Divina Commedia. MeMAP
Paradox, The. John Donne. NOSC
Paradox, The. Paul Laurence Dunbar. AAP; PoBA
Paradox. Angelina Weld Grimké. CDC
Paradox, The. Francesca Yetunde Pereira. PBA
Paradox, The. *Unknown.* APAS
Paradox, A. The Earl of Pembroke. ElL
Paradox, A. Aurelian Townshend. SeCP

Parnell. W. B. Yeats. CMoP

Parochial Theme. Wallace Stevens. LiTA

Parodie, A. George Herbert.

Parodie, A. George Herbert. *See* Souls joy, when thou art gone.

Parodies of Cole Porter's "Night and Day." Ring Lardner. OBAL

Parody. Martha Paley Francescato, *tr. fr. Spanish by* Willis Barnstone. BoWoP

Parody, A. Frederick Douglass. *Fr.* Narrative of the Life of an American Slave. NAAL-1; NAWM-2

Parody on "A Psalm of Life," A. *At. to* Oliver Wendell Holmes. BLPA

Parody on Thomas Hood's "The Bridge of Sighs." *Unknown.* FiBHP

Parricide. Julia Ward Howe. PAH

Parrot, The. Thomas Campbell. FM

Parrot, The. Thomas Campbell. FM

Parrot, The. James Elroy Flecker. FaBoTw

Parrot, The. W. W. Gibson. OBMV

Parrot. Po Chü-i, *tr. fr. Chinese by* Irving Y. Lo. SuSp

Parrot can only copy the talk of others, The. Imagination. Li Pai-feng, *tr. fr. Chinese. Fr.* Pearls and Earth. LHF, *tr. by* Hualing Nieh

Parrot Cry, The. "Hugh MacDiarmid." OxBS

Parrot Fish, The. James Merrill. NOBA

Parrot, from the Spanish main, A. The Parrot. Thomas Campbell. FM

Parrot, if I had your wings. The Boy and the Parrot. John Hookham Frere. OxBChV

Parrot, The/ Is eating a carrot. Who Killed Lawless Lean? Stevie Smith. CBNP; TEP

Parrot was what, A. Why There Are No Cats in the Forest. Simeon Dumdum. TSaS

Parrots, The. W. W. Gibson. CH

Parrots. Neil Paech. OBAP

Parrots dwell in the west country. Han-shan, *tr. fr. Chinese by* Edward H. Schafer. SuSp

Parrot's Soliloquy. John Skelton. *See* My name is Parrot, a bird [*or* byrd] of paradise.

Parrot's voice snaps out, The. "Psittachus Eois Imitatrix Ales ab Indis." Sacheverell Sitwell. MoBrPo

Parrots/ with vermilion bands and beak. Parrots. Neil Paech. OBAP

Parry, of all my friends the best. The Invitation. Goronwy Owen, *tr. fr. Welsh by* George Borrow. OBWVE

Parsley, *sels.* Rita Dove.
   Cane Fields, The. HCAP; NoAM; VCAP
   Palace, The. NoAM; VCAP

Parsnips, those rabbis, The. In the Root Cellar. Maxine W. Kumin. FaBoWP

Parson Allen's Ride. Wallace Bruce. PAH

Parson Grocer, The. *Unknown.* CoMu

Parson of a country town was he, The. Chaucer. *See* Good man was there [*or* ther] of religion [*or* religioun], A.

Parson says, 'Contented be, and you will heaven gain', The. (*LL*) A New Hunting Song. *Unknown.* CoMu; OBET

Parson sung a Psalm, The. (*LL*) The Presbyterian Wedding. *Unknown.* CoMu; ErPo; FaBoBl

Parson, these things in thy possessing. The Happy Life of a Country Parson. Pope. BXAP; UV

Parson's Case, The, *sels.* Swift.
   "Thy curate's place, thy fruitful wife." UV

Parson's Looks, The. Burns. OxBoLi

Parson's Pleasure. Barry O. Higgs. PeSA

Parson's Prologue, The. Chaucer. *Fr.* Canterbury Tales, The. EnVB; NAEL-1

Part eye, part tear, unwilling to recognize us. (*LL*) Stone Canyon Nocturne. Charles Wright. HCAP; LCAP; VCAP

Part for the Whole. Robert Francis. PoA

Part of a Bird. Nina Cassian, *tr. fr. Romanian by* Andrea Deletant *and* Brenda Walker. PoSu

Part of a Letter. Richard Wilbur. CMoP

Part of a Novel, Part of a Poem, Part of a Play, *sels.* Marianne Moore.
   Hero, The. CMoP; NOBA; OxBA; PoA
   Steeple-Jack, The. BoWoP; CMoP; FaBoMo; FaBoWP; HAP; InPS; NoAM; NOBA; NoP; OxBA; PBWP; Poetr; WPE

Part of a True Story. Marilyn Hacker. Poetr

Part of an Ode, A. Ben Jonson. *See* It Is Not Growing Like a Tree.

Part of Eve's Discussion. Marie Howe. NAmP90

Part of him is on my side, A. (*LL*) Two in Bed. Abram Bunn Ross. FaPON; NTCP

Part of Plenty. Bernard Spencer. ErPo; GBL; LiTB; LiTM

Part of the Darkness. Isabella Gardner. CAPP

Part of the Lay of Sigrdrifa. *Unknown. See* Now this is my first counsel.

Part of the mottled mood of summer's whole. (*LL*) Credences of Summer. Wallace Stevens. MeMAP

Part of the universe is missing. The Lost Golf Ball. David Shapiro. BAP-89

Part of the work remains; one part is past. The End of His Work. Robert Herrick. CaPo

Part-Sequence for Change, A. Robert Duncan. VGW

Parta Quies. A. E. Housman. NOBE; TEP

Parted. Alice Meynell. PeVV

Parted. Clara Ann Thompson. CBWP-2

Parted by death, we swallow remorse. Tu Fu, *tr. by* Eugene Eoyang. *Fr.* Dreaming of Li Po. SuSp

Parted me leaf and leaf, divided me, eyelid and eyelid of slumber. (*LL*) Moonrise. Gerard Manley Hopkins. EnVR; FaBoPP; MoAB; MoBrPo; NOBVV; RB

Parted Souls. Lord Herbert of Cherbury. SeCP

Parterre, The. E. Harriet Palmer. FaBoCo; NOBL; PeLV

Parthenogenesis. Nuala Ni Dhomhnaill, *tr. fr. Irish by* Michael Hartnett. CIP

Parthenon, The. John Heath-Stubbs. OBTV

Parthenophil and Parthenope, *sels.* Barnabe Barnes.
   "Ah, sweet Content! where is thy mylde abode?" AAS; ESo
     (Sonnet: "Ah, sweet Content! where is thy mild abode.") EiL
   "Ah sweet content, where is thy mylde abode?" ESo
   "And thus continuing with outrageous fier." ESo
   "But pitie which sometimes doth Lyon's move." ESo
   "Lovely Maya, Hermes' mother." NoSic
   Mistress, Behold, in This True-Speaking Glass. Son
   "My Sweet Parthenope, within thy face." ESo
   "O Powers Celestial, with what sophistry." EnLoPo
   "Oh that I had no hart, as I have none." ESo
   "Soft, lovely, rose-like lips, conjoined with mine." EnLoPo
   "Then first with locks dishevelled and bare." NoSic
   "When I was yong, indewd'd with nature's graces." ESo
   "Whilst some the Troiane warres in verse recount." ESo
   "Why doth heaven bear a sun." EiL
   Would I were Changed. AAS; ESo; FaBoBl
   Write! Write! Help! Help! Son

Parthian Powers. Milton. *See* He look't [*or* looked] and saw what numbers numberless.

Parthians, The. Milton. *Fr.* Paradise Regained [*or* Regain'd].

Partholan went out one day. The First Lawcase. *Unknown, tr. fr. Irish by* John Montague. BIrV

Partial Accounts. William Meredith. GLP

Partial Comfort. Dorothy Parker. FaBoCo; OBAL; OBD

Partial Explanation, The. Charles Simic. NoP

Partial History of Poppies, A. Rosemary Catacalos. AfAz

Partial Luetic History of an Individual at Risk. J. M. Regan. GLP

Partial Resemblance. Denise Levertov. CoAP; NaP

Particulars. Thomas McCarthy. IB

Parties drilled for the election. "Sagittarius." FaBoEH

Parting. A. R. Ammons. NoAM

Parting. Matthew Arnold. *Fr.* Switzerland. EnVR

Parting, The. Sara Berkeley. PBCIP

Parting, The. Buson, *tr. fr. Japanese by* Harold G. Henderson. ArLo

Parting, The. Michael Drayton. *See* Since There's No Help, Come Let Us Kiss and Part.

Parting. Gu Cheng, *tr. fr. Chinese by* Donald Finkel *with* Yi Jinsheng. SpMi

Parting. Rachel Hadas. *Fr.* Elegy Variations. UnDi

Parting. Judah Halevi, *tr. fr. Hebrew by* Nina Davis Salaman. AWP; TrJP

Parting, The. Josephine D. Henderson Heard. CBWP-4

Parting. *Malay Oral Tradition, tr. by* R. J. Wilkinson *and* R. O. Winstedt. WTO

Parting. Thomas Middleton. *Fr.* Chaste Maid in Cheapside, A. EiL

Parting. Eduard Friedrich Mörike, *tr. fr. German by* Philip L. Miller. RiWo

Parting. Coventry Patmore. PoToHe

Parting. Anna Swirszczynska, *tr. fr. Polish by* Czeslaw Milosz *and* Leonard Nathan. ArLo

Parting. Edward Thomas. Mes

Parting. W. B. Yeats. FaBoTw

Parting; a Game. Lynn Sukenick. NMM

Parting, a thousand cups won't wash away the sorrow. To Tzu-an. Yü Hsüan-chi, *tr. by* Geoffrey R. Waters. BoWoP

Parting as Descent. John Berryman. LiTA; MoAmPo

Parting at Dawn. *Malay Oral Tradition, tr. by* R. J. Wilkinson *and* R. O. Winstedt. WTO

Parting at Dawn. John Crowe Ransom. AnAmPo

Parting at Dawn. *Unknown. See* On a Time the Amorous Silvy.

Parting at Morning. Robert Browning. AWP; EBEvV; EnVR; FaBV; FF; FHYEP; HeIP; ImPo; InPS; NAEL-2; NOBE; OBEV; OBNC; OHCV; OxBSP; PFP; SCGP; SoSe; TFi; UnPo; WiR

Parting at Morning. Dietmar von Aist, *tr. fr. German by* Frank C. Nicholson. AWP

Parting from Liu Nan-chou, *sels.* Hsieh Chin, *tr. fr. Chinese by* Jonathan Chaves.

Parting from Wang Wei. Meng Hao Jan, *tr. fr. Chinese by* Daniel Bryant. SuSp

Parting Gift. Elinor Wylie. OxBA

Parting Hymn, A. Charlotte Forten. BlSi

Parting Hymn We Sing, A. Aaron R. Wolfe. AH

Parting in Wartime. Frances Cornford. CoGr; FaBoWP; NIP

Parting Is Hard. *Unknown, tr. fr. Chinese by* Geoffrey R. Waters. BoWoP

Parting Kiss, The. Josephine D. Henderson Heard. CBWP-4

Parting Lovers, The. Mrs. Henry Linden. CBWP-4

Parting: 1940. John Frederick Nims. PoA

Parting of the Red Sea, The. *Unknown, tr. fr. Anglo-Saxon by* Charles W. Kennedy. *Fr.* Exodus. AnOE

Parting of the Ways, The. Joseph B. Gilder. PAH

Parting of Venus and Old Age, The. John Gower. *Fr.* Confessio Amantis. PoEL-1

Parting Roundel. Jemal Sharah. NOBAu

Parting slightly off-centre, like Oscar Wilde's, A. Boys' Own. Michael Hofmann. SCBI

Parting sorrow shattered/ Beyond the gauze window. Tune: "Full River Red." Hsin Ch'i-chi, *tr. fr. Chinese by* Irving Y. Lo. SuSp

Parting. To ———. Robert Frost. AnAmPo

Parting Verse, the Feast There Ended, The. Robert Herrick. SeCV-1

Parting with Lucasia; a Song. Katherine Philips. CBLP; PeHV

Parting, without a Sequel. John Crowe Ransom. MeMAP; MoAB; MoAmPo; OxBA; SoSe

Partings. Charles Guérin, *tr. fr. French by* Jethro Bithell. AWP

Partings. Maria Jane Jewsbury. OxBChV

Partition. W. H. Auden. FaBoEH

Partly Because. Ursula Laird. Mes

Partly to My Cat. Ellen Bass. NMM

Partridge. Agathias, *tr. fr. Greek by* Guy Davenport. GrAn

Partridge in a pear tree, A. (*LL*) The Twelve Days of Christmas. *Unknown.* AmFP; OxBoLi; OxNR; PChr

Partridges. John Masefield. OxBTC

Parts of Speech, The. *Unknown.* FaBoUs

Parts of the Whole Are We; but God the Whole. Dryden. *Fr.* Palamon and Arcite. NAs

Party, The. Margaret Avison. PoA

Party. Cynthia Huntington. NAmP90

Party, The. W. R. Rodgers. BIrV; PNI

Party, The. Jerome Sala. UL

Party, The. Reed Whittemore. CoAP

Party at Hydra. Irving Layton. HeIP

Party Favour. Daniel David Moses. HATNAP

Party finished early, 'twas on the stroke of nine, The. The Keyhole in the Door. *Unknown.* CoMu

Party is going strong, The. Tribute to Kafka for Someone Taken. Alan Dugan. CAPP

Party Knee. John Updike. FiBHP

Party Piece. Brian Patten. BoLoP

Party Shrine. Thomas McCarthy. BiHa; IB

Party Song, A. *Unknown.* BoTP

Partying by a river near Ellwood City, Pennsylvania. Coming Home in March. Harold Littlebird. VoR

Pas de Deux for Lovers. Michael Dransfield. CBAP

Pascal. Louise Imogen Guiney. AmWP

Paschal Fire, The. Denis Florence MacCarthy. TIRV

Pasha Bailey Ben., *sels.* W. S. Gilbert.
    Diverse Gifts of Pasha Bailey Ben, The. CBCK

Pasquin to the Queen's Statue at St. Paul's. William Shippen. APAS

Pass. Edmund Vance Cooke. PWR

Pass by, pass by. Death and the Maiden. Matthias Claudius, *tr. fr. German by* Philip L. Miller. RiWo

Pass forth, my wonted cries. Sir Thomas Wyatt. SiPS; SiPSBD

Pass It On. Henry Burton. BLRP; PWR

Pass it on. (*LL*) Listen Children. Lucille Clifton. PoBA

Pass it on. (*LL*) Motherdeath. Julia Vinograd. SRLS

Pass me the sweet earthenware jug. Zonas, *tr. fr. Greek by* Kenneth Rexroth. PGA

Pass not, but wonder, and amazed stand. Upon the Much Lamented Death of the Right Honourable, the Lady Elizabeth Langham. Bathsua Pell Makin. KTR

Pass Office Song. *Unknown, tr. fr. Afrikaans.* PBA, *tr. by* Peggy Rutherford; TTY, *tr. by* Peggy Rutherford; WTO, *tr. by* H. Tracey

Pass on! for the bright torch of glory is beaming. To the Vermont Cadets. Lucretia Davidson. AmWP

Pass rascal deer, strike me the largest doe. (*LL*) La Bella Bona Roba. Richard Lovelace. BeJo; CaPo; CBLP; EBEV; NOSC; OAEL-1; PoEL-3; SeCP

"Pass the biscuits," said Pappy, pursing his lips. A Short History of the New South. R. S. Gwynn. NGP

Pass the tambourine, let me bash out praises. The Way We Live. Kathleen Jamie. PWE

Pass to thy rendezvous of light. Emily Dickinson. NAWM-2

Pass we the ills, which each man feels or dreads. Matthew Prior. *Fr.* Solomon on the Vanity of the World. NOEC; PoEL-3

Passage. Hart Crane. CMoP; NOBA; PoE

Passage. Geoffrey Fraser Dutton. PWE

Passage. Denise Levertov. CAPP

Passage. Billy Marshall-Stoneking. NOBAu

Passage. John M. Roderick. GOYP

Passage of a Year, The. *Unknown, tr. fr. Middle English by* Brian Stone. *Fr.* Sir Gawain and the Green Knight. OAEL-1; PoEL-1

Passage of the Mountain of St. Gothard, The. Georgiana Cavendish, Duchess of Devonshire. ECWP

Passage over Water. Robert Duncan. NoAM; NOBA

Passage to India. Walt Whitman. AmPP; NAAL-1; PoEL-5

Passage to India. Walt Whitman. AmPP; PoEL-5
Sels.
    "Ah, more than any priest, O soul, we too believe in God." WGRP
    "Bathe me O God in thee, mounting to thee." TrPWD

Passages, *sels.* Robert Duncan.
    At the Loom. VGW
    Fire, The. VGW
    "Good Night, at last." VGW
    Tribal Memories. NOBA
    Up Rising. NNaP

Passages. Larry Eigner. NeAP

Passages. Aidan Carl Mathews. IB

Passed Ruin'd Ilion. Walter Savage Landor. *See* Past ruin'd [*or* ruined] Ilion Helen lives.

Passenger Pigeons. Robert Morgan. MT

Passengers, The. David Antin. NYBP

Passengers. Denis Johnson. SM

Passengers afloat on many thousand feet. Night Flight. Marion Alexopoulos. NOBAu

Passenjare, The. Isaac H. Bromley. FiBHP

Passer-by, A. Robert Bridges. CMoP; EBEvV; ImPo; LiTB; LiTM; MoAB; MoBrPo; OAEL-2; OBEV; OBNC; OxBTC; SCGP; WiR

Passer-by, don't blame this memorial. Carphyllides, *tr. fr. Greek by* Alistair Elliot. GrAn

Passer Mortuus Est. Edna St. Vincent Millay. CMoP; FaBoWP; MoAmPo; OBD; OxBA

Passerby being fair about sacrifice, A. Chickens the Weasel Killed. William Stafford. NaP

Passes are blocked by snow, The. Persia. V. Sackville-West. WPE

Passing. Langston Hughes. SAmP

Passing a dull red college-block. A Walk in Würzburg. William Plomer. NYBP

Passing a Ruined Palace. Wen T'ing-yün, *tr. fr. Chinese by* Kenneth Rexroth. OHMPC

Passing across the billowy sea. *Unknown, tr. fr. Italian by* John Addington Symonds. *Fr.* Popular Songs of Tuscany. AWP

Passing an Orchard by Train. Robert Bly. CAPP

Passing and Glassing. Christina Rossetti. OBNC

Passing Away. Christina Rossetti. *Fr.* Old and New Year Ditties. MeMBP; NoP; OAEL-2; OBNC; PFP; WPE

Passing Bell, The. Thomas Heywood. *Fr.* Rape of Lucrece, The. FaBoRV

Passing between the stumbling generations. The Wandering Jew Comes to the Wall. Edmond Fleg, *tr. fr. French by* Humbert Wolfe. *Fr.* Wall of Weeping, The. TrJP

Passing by a Mountain Village: Evening. Chia Tao, *tr. fr. Chinese by* Stephen Owen. SuSp

Passing By, *abr. At. to* Thomas Ford. *See* There Is a Lady Sweet and Kind.

Passing by Kamata. Su Man-shu, *tr. fr. Chinese by* Wu-chi Liu. SuSp

Passing by the Hot Springs at Hua-ch'ing Palace, *sels.* Yüan Hung-tao, *tr. fr. Chinese by* Jonathan Chaves.

Passing By Waterwheel Bay. Yang Wan-li, *tr. fr. Chinese* by Jonathan Chaves. SuSp

Passing Ch'ien-hsi as Military Adviser in the Third Month of the Year Yi-ssu. T'ao Ch'ien, *tr. fr. Chinese* by Eugene Eoyang. SuSp

Passing Hung-fu Monastery with Yüan-ming: Inscribed in Jest. Huang T'ing-chien, *tr. fr. Chinese* by Michael E. Workman. SuSp

Passing into Storm. Patrick Lane. NOBC

Passing like a Strauss waltz. The Hoofer. A. K. Redwing. VoR

Passing of a dream, The. John Clare. NOBVV

Passing of Arthur, The. Layamon. *Fr.* Brut, The. PoE

Passing of Arthur, The. J. C. Squire. BXAP

Passing of Arthur, The. Tennyson. *Fr.* Idylls of the King. FHYEP; NAEL-2; OBNC

Passing of Sorrow, The. Mary Jane Moffat. IMW

Passing of Tennyson, The. Ernest Dowson. EPCY

Passing of the Forest, The. William Pember Reeves. PeNZ

Passing of the Old Year. Mary Weston Fordham. CBWP-2

Passing of the Poets, The. Fearflatha O'Gnive. NOIV

Passing of the Shee, The. J. M. Synge. BIrV; FaBoEE

Passing out of the shadow. Just Passing. *Unknown.* BLRP

Passing Strange. Alan Bernheimer. UL

Passing Strange, The. John Masefield. LiTB; MoAB; MoBrPo; OBEV

Passing stranger! you do not know how longingly I look upon you. To a Stranger. Walt Whitman. NOBA; SAmP

Passing the American graveyard, for my birthday. Poem for My Twentieth Birthday. Kenneth Koch. PoA

Passing the central Palace (called 'of Reason'). Il Palazzo della Ragione. Clive Wilmer. SCBI

Passing the flower-stalls there did I perceive. Strato, *tr. fr. Greek* by Sydney Oswald. PeHV

Passing the great plane tree in the square. The Beginning of the End. Jon Stallworthy. OxBC

Passing the Night on a River in Chien-te. Meng Hao Jan, *tr. fr. Chinese* by Paul W. Kroll. SuSp

Passing this tomb with no smile on his face. Thermopylai. Hegemon, *tr. fr. Greek* by Peter Jay. GrAn

Passing Through. Annie Johnson Flint. BLRP

Passing Through. Patrick Williams. PNI

Passing through Albuquerque where I'd read poetry. Second Prelude. Reality in Albuquerque: The Son. John Logan. *Fr.* Poem in Progress. CAPP

Passing through huddled and ugly walls. The Harbor. Carl Sandburg. TAP

Passing through My Shih-ning Estate. Hsieh Ling-yün, *tr. fr. Chinese* by Francis Westbrook. SuSp

Passing Visit to Helen. D. H. Lawrence. CMoP

Passing White Banks Pavilion. Hsieh Ling-yün, *tr. fr. Chinese* by Francis Westbrook. SuSp

Passion, The. Ralph Knevet. JCP

Passion. Jena Lengold, *tr.* by Richard Burns. VBLP

Passion. Sue May. DT

Passion. Susan Prospere. AnAn

Passion. Henry Vaughan *and* Thomas Stanley. ESCV

Passion. Diane Ward. VBLP

Passion and Exaltation of Christ, The. Isaac Watts. NOCV

Passion and oracle. Nineteen. Lucha Corpi, *tr. fr. Spanish* by Catherine Rodriguez-Nieto. AfAz

Passion, and then the anguish. And with whom. Reconciliation. Goethe, *tr. fr. German* by John Frederick Nims. *Fr.* Trilogy of Passion. STV

Passion Drinker, The. Anita Endrezze-Danielson. VoR

Passion of Christ, The. Denis Devlin. IPY

Passion of Jesus, The. *Unknown.* MeEL

Passion of Ravensbrück. János Pilinszky, *tr. fr. Hungarian* by Ted Hughes *and* Janos Csokits. PoSu

Passion of M'Phail, The, *sels.* Horace Gregory.
They Were All like Geniuses. NYBP
This Is the Place to Wait. MoAmPo

Passion Shaved beneath the Grain-Silo. Peter Finch. NBrP

Passion too deep seems like none. Tu Mu, *tr. fr. Chinese* by A. C. Graham. *Fr.* Farewell Poem. PLT

Passionate angels serenaded today in Jerusalem. Passover in Jerusalem. Avigdor Hame'iri, *tr. fr. Hebrew* by Ruth Finer Mintz. MHP

Passionate love is temporary. Landscape with Leaves and Figure. Olga Broumas. BoWoP

Passionate Man's Pilgrimage, The. Sir Walter Ralegh. AAS; ChIV-2, *st. 1 only;* ChTr; EBEvV, *st. 1 only;* EIL; EnRePo; LiTB; NOBE; NoP; NoSic; PeECV; PoE; PoEL-2; PoRA; RB; SCGP, *st. 1 only;* SiPSBD; TFi, *st. 1 only;* TrGrPo

Passionate pages of his earlier years, The. Thomas Hardy. *Fr.* Singer Asleep, A (Algernon Charles Swinburne). EPCY

Passionate Pilgrim, The, *sels.* Shakespeare *and others.*
"As it fell upon a day." GBL
(Nightingale, The.) AWP; GTBS; GTBS-P
(Ode, An.) EIL
(Philomel.) CH; NOBE; OBEV
Crabbed Age and Youth. EBEvV; GBL; InPS; LiTB; NoSic; OBEV
(Age and Youth.) EIL
(Madrigal, A: "Crabbed age and youth.") GTBS; GTBS-P; InPS
Fair Is My Love. EIL
It Was a Lording's Daughter. EIL
Sweet Rose, Fair Flower. EIL

Passionate Professor, The. Bert Leston Taylor. NBLV

Passionate Shepherd, The, *sels.* Nicholas Breton.
Merry Country Lad, The. EIL; NoSic
(Happy Countryman, The, *shorter sel.*) CH
(Pastoral: "Who can live in heart so glad.") ELP
Pretty Twinkling Starry Eyes. EIL

Passionate Shepherd to His Love, The. Christopher Marlowe. AAS; ArLo; AWP; BoLoP; CBLP; ClHu; CoGr; CTC; EBEvV; EIL; ELP; FaBoBe; FF; GGP; GTBS; GTBS-P; HAP; HeIL; HeIP; HoPM; ImPo; InPK; InPS; LiTB; NAEL-1; NBLV; NIP; NOBE; NoP; NoSic; OAEL-1; OBEV; OxAEP-1; PoE; Poetr; PoLF; PoRA; PPP; RB; SCV; SiPSBD; TFi; TrGrPo; TRP; TTTS; WeW

Passionate Shepherd to His Love, The. Delmore Schwartz. PlP; SCGP

Passionate Sword, The. Jean Starr Untermeyer. TrJP; TrPWD

Passionately joined to all things visible. Invisible Work. Margaret Gibson. MT

Passions, an Ode for [*or* to] Music, The. William Collins. GTBS; GTBS-P

Passions are liken'd best to floods and streams. Sir Walter Ralegh. *Fr.* Silent Lover, The. EIL; LiTB; OBEV, *abr.*

Passion's excess for thee we need no fear. Sidney Godolphin. *Fr.* Elegy on John Donne. EPCY

Passiontide Communion. Katharine Tynan. TrPWD

Passive Participle's Petition, The. John Byrom. ECEV

Passover at Auschwitz. Laurence Josephs. BTR

Passover Eve. Fania Kruger. GoYe

Passover in Jerusalem. Avigdor Hame'iri, *tr. fr. Hebrew* by Ruth Finer Mintz. MHP

Passover Night 1942. Yala Korwin. BTR

Passport Officer, The. Basil Bunting. IHNG

Past, The. Emerson. FaBoCh; LiTA; MeMAP; PoEL-4; TAP

Past, The. Mary Weston Fordham. CBWP-2

Past, The. William Oandasan. BCF

Past, The. Stevie Smith. IHNG

Past, The. Sarah Helen Whitman. AmWP

Past, a glacier, gripped the mountain wall, The. Full Moon at Tierz; before the Storming of Huesca. John Cornford. OBWP

Past all accident. (*LL*) The Ivy Crown. William Carlos Williams. NAAL-2; NoAM; NoP; PrIm

Past and Present. Thomas Hood. *See* I Remember, I Remember.

Past and Present. R. E. Egerton Warburton. NOBVV

Past bush paths tarred by tireless treading. Excursion. Niyi Osundare. HBAPE

Past exchanges have left orbits of rain around my face. An Apology. Diane Wakoski. TAP

Past factory workshops, empty. Marina Tsvetayeva, *tr. fr. Russian* by Paul Schmidt. *Fr.* Daughter of Jairus, The. BoWoP

Past Fairy Hill, range above range, ten thousand mountains rise. (*LL*) Coming was an empty promise, you have gone, and left no footprint. Li Shang-yin. PLT

Past/ fences the first sheepmen. To the Republic. James Galvin. BAP-90

Past fifty and cloyed at last. Philetas, *tr. fr. Greek* by Kenneth Rexroth. GrAn; PGA

Past hovering as it revisits the light, The. (*LL*) It Rains ("It rains, and nothing stirs within the fence.") Edward Thomas. OxBTC; PlP; PoE

Past is a strange land, most strange, The. Parting. Edward Thomas. Mes

Past is best forgotten., The. (*LL*) Custer Lives in Humbolt County. Janet Campbell Hale. VoR

Past/ Is but the cinders, The. The Search. Kwesi Brew. PBA

Past Is Dark with Sin and Shame, The. Thomas Wentworth Higginson. AH

Past is past, and if one. Salute. James Schuyler. FYAP; NeAP

Past is such a curious creature, The. Emily Dickinson. Mes

Past Is the Present, The. Marianne Moore. MeMAP; NAAL-2

Past Lives. Robyn Selman. BAP-91

Past Love. Anne Keiter. GOYP

Past my grave each night shall file,. (*LL*) When I Die. Fenton Johnson. CDC; PoNe

Past One O'Clock. Vladimir Mayakovsky, *tr. fr. Russian* by George Reavey. ArLo

Past one o'clock. You must have gone to bed. Past One O'Clock. Vladimir Mayakovsky, *tr. fr. Russian by* George Reavey. ArLo

Past ploughed and fallow, at the top. Glenarm. John Lyle Donaghy.
(Ianthe.) LiTB; PoEL-4
(Past Ruin'd Ilion.) AWP
(To Ianthe.) NOBE
(Verse: "Past ruin'd [*or* ruined] Ilion Helen lives.") OBEV

Past Ruin'd Ilion. John Lyle Donaghy. *See* Past ploughed and fallow, at the top.

Past ruin'd [*or* ruined] Ilion Helen lives. Walter Savage Landor. *Fr.* Ianthe. CTC; ELP; EnLoPo; EnRP; GBL; HAP; NAEL-2; NoP; OBNC; PoRA; TFi; TrGrPo; WeW
(Ianthe.) LiTB; PoEL-4
(Passed Ruin'd Ilion.) AWP; SCGP
(To Ianthe.) NOBE
(Verse: "Past ruin'd Ilion . . . .") OBEV

Past scenic laybys and stag warning signs. History Classes. Tony Harrison. *Fr.* School of Eloquence, The. NAEL-2; NoAM

Past second cock-crow yacht masts in the harbor go slowly white. Masts at Dawn. Robert Penn Warren. FoLa; NAAL-2; VCAP

Past seven o'clock: time to be gone. Moonset. Sir Henry Newbolt. EBVV

Past six o'clock. I have prayed. No one is sleeping. Nessun Dorma. Francis Webb. FaBoMA

Past the angular maguey fields, a ride on the optic nerve. Into Mexico. Mona Van Duyn. VCAP

Past the house where he was got. Austin Clarke. *Fr.* Mnemosyne Lay in Dust. CMoP; IPY; PoE

Past the school and down. Directions to the Nomad. James Welch. CDW

Past them he strode. The Hinds of Kerry. William S. Wabnitz. GoYe

Past Thinking of Solomon. Francis Thompson. ChIV-1

"Past two o'clock and Cornwallis is taken." News from Yorktown. Lewis Worthington Smith. PAH

Pastel: Masks and Faces. Arthur Symons. NOBVV

Pastel the flowers, the wreaths in the pastel gardens. Moon Mattress. Diane Di Prima. NMM

Pastiche. Elinor Wylie. NALW

Pastime. Henry VIII, King of England. *See* Pastime with good company.

Pastime of Pleasure, The, *sels.* Stephen Hawes.
Dame Music. PoEL-1
Epitaph of Graunde [*or* La Graunde] Amoure, The. ChTr; CoGr; EBEV; FaBoRV; NoSic; OBEV; TrGrPo
(Epitaph, An.) OtMeF
(Epitaphy of la Graunde Amoure.) FaBoEE
Seven Deadly Sins, The. PoEL-1
Time and Eternity. PoEL-1
True Knight [*or* True Knighthood], The. OBEV; TrGrPo

Pastime with good company. Henry VIII, King of England. NoSic
(Good Company.) TrGrPo
(Pastime.) CTC; EBEV

Pastoral: "Afternoon wears on, The." David Wright. NYBP

Pastoral: "Annette came through the meadows." H. Cordelia Ray. CBWP-3

Pastoral: "By the side of a green stagnate pool." George Alexander Stevens. CoMu; ErPo

Pastoral: "Death./ The death of a million." Ron Loewinsohn. NeAP

Pastoral: "Dominic Francis Xavier Brotherton-Chancery." Gavin Ewart. OxBC

Pastoral: "Dove walks with sticky feet, The." Kenneth Patchen. NaP

Pastoral: "I came to a field." Charles Simic. NNaP

Pastoral: "I don't know much about sheep, don't know." Janet Holmes. FoLa

Pastoral, "In the merry month of May." A. Nicholas Breton. *See* In the merry month of May.

Pastoral: "It all happened so fast. Fenya was in the straight chair." Norman Dubie. AmPA

Pastoral: "Little sparrows, The." William Carlos Williams. SAmP; TwCP

Pastoral: "Lumpish trollop, The !" D. B. Wyndham Lewis. UV

Pastoral[l], A: "Oh [*or* O] happy golden age." Tasso. *See* O lovely age of gold!

Pastoral: "On a hill there grows a flower." Nicholas Breton. ElL
(Phyllida and Corydon. TrGrPo

Pastoral: "So soft in the hemlock wood." Robert Silliman Hillyer. MoAmPo

Pastoral, A: "Sweet Bird! that sit and sing amid the shady valleys." Nicholas Breton. *See* Sweet birds! that sit and sing amid the shady valleys.

Pastoral: "There went out in the dawning light." *Unknown, tr. fr. Latin by* John Addington Symonds. AWP

Pastoral: "They are our creatures, clover, and they love us." Veronica Forrest-Thomson. VaA

Pastoral: "This is a place of ease." Marion Strobel. PoA

Pastoral: "Today in Peru, this first day of summer." Lawrence Raab. AmPA

Pastoral: "When I was younger." William Carlos Williams. AmPP; OxBA; SAmP

Pastoral: "Wise old apple tree in spring, The." Robert Silliman Hillyer. BoNaP

Pastoral Ballad., *sels.* William Shenstone.
"My banks they are furnished with bees." BoNaP
(Shepherd's Home, The.) GN

Pastoral Ballad by John Bull, A. Thomas Moore. BIrV; OBSV

Pastoral Dialogue between Two Shepherdesses, A. The Countess of Winchilsea. ECWP

Pastoral Eclogue upon the Death of Sir Philip Sidney Knight, A. Lodowick Bryskett. NoSic

Pastoral Elegy. Sir Philip Sidney. *Fr.* Arcadia. SiPSBD

Pastoral Elegy, A. Tibullus, *tr. fr. Latin by* Sir Charles Abraham Elton. AWP

Pastoral; in the Modern Style, A. "Worcester." NOEC

Pastoral Lives. Judith Wright. *Fr.* For a Pastoral Family. FaBoMA

Pastoral Muses once were scattered, The. Artemidorus, *tr. fr. Greek by* Anthony Holden. GrAn

Pastoral on the King's Death, The; [Written in 1648]. Alexander Brome. NOSC

Pastoral Poetry. John Clare. *See* True poesy is not in words.

Pastoral Song, A. Anne Hunter. ECWP

Pastoral: "Who can live in heart so glad." Nicholas Breton. *See* Who can live in heart so glad.

Pastorall, A, *sels.* Lady Jane Cavendish *and* Lady Elizabeth Brackley.
2 Antemasque, The: Two Countrye Wives, the Songe. KTR
3 Sad Sheppards Sings This in Parts, The. KTR
3d Sheppard Speakes This to the Rest, The. KTR
4th Sheppard Speakes This, The. KTR
Antemasque, The: Witches the Number Beinge Five. KTR
Songs Anthome. KTR

Pastorall Dialogue, A. Thomas Carew. CaPo; GBL; SeCP

Pastoral[l] Hymn[e], A. John Hall. MeLP; TrPWD

Pastorals, *sels.* Pope.
Sylvan Delights. NOBE

Pastor M'Gadi's startling blackness. Halo. Ralph Nixon Currey. PeSA

Pasture, The. Robert Frost. BLPL; CMoP; FaPoB; FaPON; GoJo; MoAB; MoAmPo; MoShBr; NAAL-2; NOBA; OxBA; PDV; PoE; SAmP; TLR; TRP; TTTS; WHSW

Pasture is a faded white, The. Breakfast. Robert Wells. SCBI

Pasture, stone wall, and steeple. Question in a Field. Louise Bogan. NYBP

Pastures of Plenty. Woody Guthrie. WTO

Pat-a-cake, pat-a-cake, baker's man. Mother Goose. OxNR; ReMoGo

Pat Cloherty's Version of *The Maisie*. *Richard Murphy. IPY; RB*

Pat Dugan . . . .my grandfather . . . .throat cancer . . . .1947. People Who Died. Ted Berrigan. UL

Pat of Butter, A. Sarah Helen Whitman. AmWP

Pat Works on the Railway. *Unknown.* SWP

Patapan. Bernard de la Monnoye, *tr. fr. French.* PChr

Patch of Old Snow, A. Robert Frost. CMoP; OxBSP; WeW

Patch-Shaneen. J. M. Synge. FaBoVe

Patches. Thomas Russell Shelton. PWR

Patches of it. The Luminous. Barbara Guest. PoM

Patches of Sky. Debora Greger. ImGa

Patching Together, A, *sels.* Murray Edmond.
Cell Lay Inside Her Body, The. NAs

Patchwork Quilt, The. Elizabeth Fleming. BoTP

Patchy sunlight, The. (*LL*) Tall/ lush. Joseph Richey. EaPr

Patent No. 1. Kay Hargreaves. Mes

Pater and *Ave* for my peace. (*LL*) Posthumous Coquetry. Théophile Gautier. AWP; OBD; PeVV

Pater Filio. Robert Bridges. CMoP; OBEV

Paternal, *sels.* Mariella Bettarini, *tr. fr. Italian by* Muriel Kittel.

Paternal. Ernest J. Wilson, Jr.. PoNe

Pater's Bathe. Edward Abbott Parry. OxBChV

Paterson, *sels.* William Carlos Williams.
"Beautiful thing/ I saw you." CMoP
"Edward/ Paterson has grown older." NoAM
Episode 17. OxBA
"I remember." MeMAP
"Outside/ outside myself/ there is a world." NoAM
(Sunday in the Park.) NAAL-2
"Paterson lies in the valley under the Passaic Falls." MeMAP; TAP
(Delineaments of the Giants, The.) NoAM
"Rigor of beauty is the quest. But how will you find beauty when it is locked." NoAM

Paul Laurence Dunbar. Robert Hayden. NoP

Paul Laurence Dunbar. Mrs. Henry Linden. CBWP-4

Paul Revere's Ride (The Landlord's Tale). Longfellow. *Fr.* Tales of a Wayside Inn. AiP; AnAmPo; BeLS; BLPA; EBEvV; EBNV; FaBoBe; FaBoTw; FaBV; FaPON; FaPoR; ImGa; OBAL; OBCA; OBNV; PAH; PWR; TFi; TrGrPo; WBLP

Paul Robeson. Gwendolyn Brooks. PoBA

Paul Stewart from the college was black (was the point). Stop-time. Rod Jellema. Jaz

Paula Becker to Clara Westhoff. Adrienne Rich. NAAL-2; VCAP

Pauline, *sels.* Robert Browning.
"My God, my God, let me for once look on thee." TrPWD
"Night, and one single ridge of narrow path." EBVVPR
"O God, where do they tend — these struggling aims?" WGRP
"Sun-treader, life and light be thine for ever!" EPCY
"Thou wilt remember. Thou art not more dear." OAEL-2

Paul's clock struck twelve, 'twas time to go to bed. The Midnight Ramble. Charles Woodward. NOEC

Paul's Wife. Robert Frost. EBNV

Pauper, A. Allen Tate. LiTM

Pauper Woodland. Ronald G. Everson. NOBC

Pauper's Drive, The. Thomas Noel. VPP

Pauper's Funeral, The. George Crabbe. *Fr.* Village, The. OBNC

Pause. Mary Ursula Bethell. PeNZ

Pause. Witter Bynner. IMW

Pause. Wilhelm Müller, *tr. fr. German by* Philip L. Miller. *Fr.* Beautiful Maid of the Mill, The. RiWo

Pause. Octavio Paz, *tr. fr. Spanish by* John Frederick Nims. STV

Pause for Breath, A. Ted Hughes. NYBP

Pause of Thought, A. Christina Rossetti. CoGr; NOBE; OBNC

Pavane for a Dead Cat. Tim Longville. VaA

Pavane for the Nursery, A. William Jay Smith. GoJo; MoAmPo

Pavement slippery, people sneezing. January, 1795. Mary Robinson. ECWP; WoRP

Pavlov. Naomi Long Madgett. BPo

Pavlov's Dog. Michael Pettit. NAmP90

Pawiak 1943. Jerzy Ficowski, *tr. fr. Polish by* Frank J. Corliss, Jr., *and* Grazyna Sandel. PoSu

Pawing us who dealt them war and madness. (*LL*) Mental Cases. Wilfred Owen. CMoP; FaBoMo; MeMBP; NoAM; PeFWW; PIP

Pawky auld carle cam[e] ower [*or* owre *or* o'er] the lea [*or* lee], The. The Gaberlunzie Man. *Unknown.* EnSB; OxBB; OxBS

Pawnshop Window. R. H. Grenville. GoYe

Pawntickets. John C. Ryan. IIP

Pax. D. H. Lawrence. EnlH; PeECV; TrCP

Pax Anima, *sels.* Manuel Gutiérrez Nájera, *tr. fr. Spanish by* Samuel Beckett.

"Pax vobis", quod the fox. *Unknown.* MiEL

Pay Day [*or* Payday] at Coal Creek. *Unknown.* AmFP

Pay-off. Kenneth Fearing. CMoP

Pay Your Debts. Mrs. Henry Linden. CBWP-4

Paying a Visit to Monk Yung's Cloister. Meng Hao Jan, *tr. fr. Chinese by* Joseph J. Lee. SuSp

Paying calls. Thomas Hardy. OBF

Paysage Choisi. Francis Sparshott. MoCV

Paysage Moralisé. W. H. Auden. *See* Hearing of Harvests Rotting in the Valleys.

Paysage Moralisé. John Hollander. ErPo

P.C. Plod versus the Dale St. Dog Strangler. Roger McGough. MoP; OBSP

P.C., X, 36. Max Beerbohm. *See* Then it's collar 'im tight.

Pcheek pcheek pcheek pcheek pcheek. Galway Kinnell. *Fr.* Avenue Bearing the Initial of Christ into the New World, The. LiTM

Pea-Fields, The. Sir Charles G. D. Roberts. *Fr.* Songs of the Common Day. NOBC

Peace. Bhartrihari, *tr. fr. Sanskrit by* Paul Elmer More. AWP

Peace. Rupert Brooke. *Fr.* 1914. OBWP; PAW; PoA; WGRP

Peace. Charles Stuart Calverley. EBVV

Peace. Phoebe Cary. AmWP; PAH

Peace. Walter de la Mare. MoAB; MoBrPo; PAW

Peace. Irwin Edman. TrJP

Peace. George Herbert. AWP; ChTr; ELP; ESCV; GeHe; NOCV; NOSC; TEP

Peace. Gerard Manley Hopkins. ELP; GTBS-P; OxBSP; TrCP

Peace. Langston Hughes. BPo

Peace. Patrick Kavanagh. IIP

Peace. Mazisi Kunene, *tr. fr. Zulu.* PAW

Peace. D. H. Lawrence. FaBoPP

Peace. Michael Longley. BiHa; CIP; PBCIP; PNI

Peace. Edwin Markham. WBLP

Peace. *Unknown. See* Pees maketh plente.

Peace. Henry Vaughan. AWP; ChTr; EBEV; ELP; ESCV; FaBoCh; GeHe; GN; HAP; NOBE; NOCV; OBD; OBEV; OxAEP-1; PIP; PoE; SCGP; SeCV-1; TEP; TFi; TOF; TrCP; WeW; WGRP

Peace. Adeline D. T. Whitney. PAH

Peace: A Study. Charles Stuart Calverley. *See* He stood, a worn-out City clerk.

Peace and goodwill, to all mankind. (*LL*) Time draws near the birth of Christ, The. Tennyson. EBVV, *abr.*; EBVVPR, *sect.* XXVIII; FaBoRV, *sect.* XXVIII; FHYEP, *sect.* XXVIII; NOCV, *sect.* XXVIII; OAEL-2, *abr.*; PChr, *sect.* XXVIII; PeECV, *abr.*; SoSe, *sect.* XXVIII

Peace and Love. Ella Wheeler Wilcox. PWR

Peace and Mercy and Jonathan. First Thanksgiving of All. Nancy Byrd Turner. FaPON

Peace and safety we shall find. (*LL*) Hail, Columbia. Joseph Hopkinson. AnAmPo; FaBoBe; PAH

Peace, and this Cot, and thee, heart-honored Maid! (*LL*) The Eolian [*or* Aeolian] Harp. Samuel Taylor Coleridge. EnRP; FHYEP; NAEL-2; NoP; OAEL-2

Peace and War. Rowland Watkyns. AngWe

Peace at the Goal. Ella Wheeler Wilcox. PWR

Peace, Be at Peace, O Thou My Heaviness. Baudelaire, *tr. fr. French by* Lord Alfred Douglas. InPK

Peace be to earth and to airy space! *Unknown, tr. fr. Sanskrit by* Romesh Dutt. *Fr.* Vedic Hymns. EaPr

Peace be unto you, Penglima Lenggang Laut! Invitation to a Spirit. *Malay Oral Tradition, tr. by* W. W. Skeat. WTO

Peace be unto you,/ Ye ministering angels. Shalom Aleichem. *Unknown, tr. fr. Hebrew.* TrJP

Peace be with you, gentle scrivener. Sholom Aleichem. Elias Lieberman. TrJP

Peace be with you, O Tin-ore. Tin-Ore. *Malay Oral Tradition, tr. by* W. W. Skeat. WTO

Peace; come away: the song of woe. Tennyson. *Fr.* In Memoriam A. H. H. EBVV, *abr.*; EBVVPR; EnVR; FHYEP; IMW; OAEL-2, *abr.*; PeECV, *abr.*

Peace Delegate. Douglas Livingstone. PeSA

Peace Discovers the Poet. George Chapman. *Fr.* Euthymiae Raptus; or, The Teares of Peace. NOSC

Peace Hymn of the Republic. Henry van Dyke. AH

Peace in the sober house of Jonas dwelt. Jonas Kindred's Household. George Crabbe. *Fr.* Tales. OBNC

Peace in the Welsh Hills. Vernon Watkins. GTBS-P; OxBTC

Peace in the western sky. The Breaking. Edwin Muir. PIP

Peace in the World. John Galsworthy. PoLF

Peace in This Green Field. Kenneth Patchen. ArNa

Peace in thy hands. The Ghost. Walter de la Mare. CMoP; ELP; EnLoPo; LiTM; MoAB; MoBrPo; NOBE; OAEL-2; OxBTC

Peace is declared, and I return. The Return. Kipling. MoBrPo

Peace is like salt which seasons all our meat. Peace and War. Rowland Watkyns. AngWe

Peace is made with a warlike man. *Unknown, tr. fr. Irish by* John Montague. BIrV

Peace is the men not marching away to be killed. Not Marching Away to Be Killed. Jean Overton Fuller. FF

Peace Is the Mind's Old Wilderness. John Holmes. AH

Peace is the next in order, first in end. Fulke Greville. *Fr.* Treatise of Monarchy, A. NOSC

Peace is written on the doorstep. Peace. D. H. Lawrence. FaBoPP

Peace Maketh Plenty. *Unknown.* OxBSP

Peace Message, The. Burton Egbert Stevenson. PAH

Peace, my heart's blab! Be ever dumb: Silence: A Sonnet. Henry King. NOSC

Peace of a Good Mind, The. Sir Thomas More. *Fr.* Twelve Weapons of Spiritual Battle, The. EnRePo; FaBoRV

Peace of Death, The. George Chapman. *Fr.* Euthymiae Raptus; or, The Teares of Peace. NOSC

Peace of great doors be for you, The. For You. Carl Sandburg. MoAmPo

Peace of Wild Things, The. Wendell Berry. ArNa; EaPr; MT; NU; VGW

Peace-Offering, The. Thomas Hardy. OxBSP

Peace on Earth. Bacchylides, *tr. fr. Greek by* John Addington Symonds. AWP

Peace on Earth. William Carlos Williams. LiTA

Peace on New England, on the shingled white houses, on golden. Jehu. Louis MacNeice. LiTM; MoAB

Peace, peace! he is not dead, he doth not sleep. Shelley. *Fr.* Adonais; an Elegy on the Death of John Keats. EBEV; EnRP; FHYEP; HoPM; ImPo; MeMBP; NoP; OAEL-2; OBD; PoEL-4; TrGrPo

(Elegy on the Death of John Keats, An.) OBNC

(Mourn Not for Adonais.) NOBE

Peace, peace, my friend; these subjects fly. George Crabbe. *Fr.* Sir Eustace Grey. PoEL-4

Peace, peace, my hony [*or* honey], do not cry. Christ's Reply. Edward Taylor. *Fr.* God's Determinations [touching his Elect]. EAP; NAAL-1; PoEL-3

(Christ's Reply "I am a Captain to Your Will".) EAP

Peace, peace, peace, make no noise. A Ditty. John Day. *Fr.* Humour Out of Breath. EiL

Peace, Perfect Peace. Edward H. Bickersteth. BLRP; WGRP

Peace Poem. Maturai Velacan, *tr. fr. Tamil by* A. K. Ramanujan. PLW

Peace pratler, do not lowre. Conscience. George Herbert. ESCV

Peace Project (5). Eric Mottram. NBrP

Peace, Shepherd, peace! What boots it singing on? Genius Loci. Margaret L. Woods. OBEV

Peace that hallows rudest ways. (*LL*) Forerunners. Emerson. OBEV; OxBA

Peace the End of the Good Man. Robert Blair. *Fr.* Grave, The. OxAEP-1

Peace! The perfect word is sounding, like a universal hymn. In the Dawn. Odell Shepard. WGRP

Peace, the wild valley streaked with torrents. The Straw. Robert Graves. OxBTC

Peace-Time. Mervyn Morris. PBCV

Peace to all such! but were there one whose fires. Atticus ("Peace to all such! but were there one whose fires.") Pope. *Fr.* Epistle to Dr. Arbuthnot. AWP; FHYEP; InPK; InPS; NOBE; NoP; OAEL-1; OxAEP-1; PoE; PoEL-3; TFi; TRP

(On Addison.) IHNG

Peace to-night, heroic spirit! Requiem for a Young Soldier. Florence Earle Coates. OHIP

Peace to Swift's faults! his wit hath made them pass. Byron. *Fr.* Hints from Horace. EPCY

Peace to these little broken leaves. Leaves. W. H. Davies. MoBrPo

"Peace upon earth!" was said. We sing it. Christmas: 1924. Thomas Hardy. FaBoEE; OBCP

Peace Walk. William Stafford. Poetsp

Peace, war, religion. This Tokyo. Gary Snyder. NeAP

Peace! where art thou to be found? Enquiry after Peace. A Fragment. The Countess of Winchilsea. ECWP; PoE

Peace, you ungracious clamours! peace, rude sounds! Shakespeare. *Fr.* Troilus and Cressida. OxAEP-1

Peaceable Kingdom. Bible, *O.T. See* Wolf also shall dwell with the lamb, The.

Peaceable Kingdom, The. Marge Piercy. TwCP

Peaceful and young, Herculean silence bore. The Peace of Death. George Chapman. *Fr.* Euthymiae Raptus; or, The Teares of Peace. NOSC

Peaceful life, A — just toil and rest. Lincoln. James Whitcomb Riley. OHIP

Peaceful Our Valley, Fair and Green. Dorothy Wordsworth. NALW

Peaceful prince of earth and heaven, The. (*LL*) A Christmas Hymn. Alfred Domett. GN; WGRP

Peaceful Shepherd, The. Robert Frost. *Fr.* Sky Pair, A. MoAB; MoAmPo

Peaceful Western Wind, The. Bible, Apocrypha. EnRePo

Peacefully upon its plantlike stem. (*LL*) Flowers by the Sea. William Carlos Williams. CMoP; GoJo; MoAB; MoAmPo; NoAM; RB; TAP

Peach and plum blossoms, speechless, keep swaying in the wind. Huang T'ing-chien, *tr. by* Michael E. Workman. *Fr.* In My Study in Monastery, Rising after a Nap. SuSp

Peach Tree with Fruit. Padraic Colum. BoNaP

Peachblossom is redded because rain fell overnight, The. Morning. Wang Wei, *tr. fr. Chinese by* Robert Payne. TAL

Peaches. Siv Cedering Fox. PBCAP; PRA

Peachstone. Dannie Abse. AngWe; OxBC; WeW

Peacock. D. H. Lawrence. TTTS

Peacock and the Snake, The. John Heath-Stubbs. PRA

Peacock "At Home," The. Catherine Ann Dorset. OxBChV

"Peacock colored tears and rotten oranges." Midnight on Front Street. Roberta Hill Whiteman. CDW

Peacock drags its tail with its long golden threads, The. Tune: "Eight-beat Barbarian Tune." Sun Kuang-hsien, *tr. fr. Chinese by* Hellmut Wilhelm. SuSp

Peacock Poems, The, *sels.* Sherley Anne Williams.

"I never thought to see us." MDDM

Peacocks. Walter Adolphe Roberts. PBCV

Peacock's Feather, A. Seamus Heaney. DiPo

Peak and Puke. Walter de la Mare. Mes

Peaks, The. Stephen Crane. *Fr.* War Is Kind. WGRP

Pealing again, prolonged the roar. (*LL*) In Romney Marsh. John Davidson. EBVV; FaBoPP; MeMBP; OxBTC

Peals which will soon be felt. (*LL*) The Praises of Field-marshal J. C. Smuts. Nongejeni Zuma. PeSAV

Peanut Sat on a Railroad Track, A. *Unknown. See* Peanut sat on a railroad track, A.

Peanut sat on a railroad track, A. *Unknown.* RoPo

(Peanut Sat on a Railroad Track, A. TLR

Pear Tree. Hilda Doolittle ("H. D."). BoWoP; CMoP; MoAmPo; NOBA; PoE; UnPo

Pear-Tree, The. Iwan Goll, *tr. fr. German by* Babette Deutsch *and* Avrahm Yarmolinsky. TrJP

Pear Tree, The. Edna St. Vincent Millay. MoAmPo

Pear-Tree, The. *Unknown, tr. by* Allen Upward. *Fr.* Shi King. AWP

Pear-Tree, The. *Unknown. See* I have a newe gardin.

Pear tree, more dead than alive, The. Markers. Frank Steele. GOYP

Pear tree that last year, The. Shimmer. James Schuyler. VCAP

Pearl, The. George Herbert. EBEV; FHYEP; GeHe; HAP; JCP; NOCV; OAEL-1; PoEL-2; SeCP

Pearl, *sels. Unknown.*

"Dubbement dere of down and dales, The." EnVB

"Perle, plesaunte to prynces paye." EBEV, *sts.* 1–5

Pearl, A. Fawziyya Abu Khalid, *tr. fr. Arabic.* TSaS, *tr. by* Salwa Jabsheh *and* John Heath-Stubbs

Pearl Avenue runs past the high-school lot. Ex-Basketball Player. John Updike. InPK; NYBP; SM; TRP

Pearl Bryan. *Unknown.* AmFP

Pearl Bryan. *Unknown.* AmFP

Pearl Harbor. Robinson Jeffers. ArOW

Pearl-Hen, The. Christian Morgenstern, *tr. fr. German by* Hugh Haughton. CBNP

Pearl-hen counts; one, two, three, four, The. The Pearl-Hen. Christian Morgenstern, *tr. fr. German by* Hugh Haughton. CBNP

Pearl, Matt. 13:45, The. George Herbert. *See* I know the ways [*or* wayes] of learning: both the head.

Pearl, The. Matth. 13. George Herbert. *See* I know the ways [*or* wayes] of learning: both the head.

Pearl of the sea! Star of the West! On Leaving Cuba, Her Native Land. Gertrudis Gomez de Avellaneda, *tr. fr. Spanish by* Catherine Rodriguez-Nieto. WPOW

Pearl pellets, resplendent young dandies. On the Street of Lo-yang. Meng Hao Jan, *tr. fr. Chinese by* Paul W. Kroll. SuSp

Pearl Perch. John Blight. CBAP

Pearlised shadows/ under the Tilley lamp. Eeling. Rhyll McMaster. FaBoMA

Pearls. Alan Gould. NOBAu

Pearls and Earth., *sels.* Li Pai-feng.

Imagination. LHF, *tr. by* Hualing Nieh

Pearls and Earth ("Water Imagines That Its Bibbles, The"). LHF, *tr. by* Hualing Nieh

Song for the Subjectivist. LHF, *tr. by* Hualing Nieh

Song for the Yesman. LHF, *tr. by* Hualing Nieh

Pearls and Earth ("Water Imagines That Its Bibbles, The.") Li Pai-feng, *tr. fr. Chinese.* Pearls and Earth. LHF, *tr. by* Hualing Nieh

Pearly and opaque boy, it was to you. For My Brother Who Died before I Was Born. Baron Wormser. GOYP

Pearly Beads. Gond Oral Tradition, *tr. by* V. Elwin *and* S. Hivale. WTO

Pears Soap. Cynthia Zarin. UTF

Peas. *Unknown. See* I eat my peas with honey.

Peasant. W. S. Merwin. NYBP

Peasant, The. Leonard Wolf. NYBP

Peasant, A. R. S. Thomas. AngWe; OBWVE; PWE

Peasant and the Sheep, The. I. A. Kriloff, *tr. fr. Russian by* C. Fillingham Coxwell. AWP

Peasant Declares His Love, The. Emile Roumer, *tr. fr. French by* John Peale Bishop. ErPo; NegPo; TTY

Peasant haled a sheep to court, A. The Peasant and the Sheep. I. A. Kriloff, *tr. fr. Russian by* C. Fillingham Coxwell. AWP

Peasant once unthinkingly, A. The Monk and the Peasant. Margaret E. Bruner. PoToHe

Peasant oppressed by sorrow and misery, A. Song of a Farmer. P'i Jih-hsiu, *tr. fr. Chinese by* William H. Nienhauser. SuSp

Peasant Poet, The. John Clare. FHYEP; OAEL-2; OBNC; WGRP

Peasants, The. Alun Lewis. LiTM; PoWW

Peasants at Work. James Hurdis. *Fr.* Favourite Village, The. ECEV

Peasant's Revolt, The, *sels. Unknown.*

"Camping Provencial. Notices: (1)." PeLV

"Tax has tenet us alle." FaBoEH

Travelogue

Peasant's Song, The. *Unknown. See* When Adam delf [*or* dalf]/ and Eve span.

Pease porridge [*or* pudding] hot. Mother Goose. ISE; OxNR, 2 *vers.*; ReMoGo

Peatbog Soldiers, The. *Unknown.* SWP

Pebble, The. Francis Ponge, *tr. fr. French by* Cid Corman. AnRep

Pebble, The. Elinor Wylie. ChIV-1; MoAmPo

Pebble is not an easy thing to define adequately, The. The Pebble. Francis Ponge, *tr. fr. French by* Cid Corman. AnRep

Pebbles. Edith King. BoTP

Pebbles are beneath, but we stand softly. Sea-Marge. Ivor Gurney. NTP

Pebbles skipping off the window woke me. Dawn Raid on an Orchard. Tom Pickard. NBrP

Pecan, The Toucan, The. Robert Williams Wood. NBLV

Peck of Gold, A. Robert Frost. PDV

Peck out a living from the farmyard. (*LL*) Australorp. Edith Speers. NOBAu

Peculiar name flickers in the mirror, and then disappears, A. (*LL*) Picture of Little Letters. John Koethe. PRA

Pedalling between lectures, spokes throwing off. Cricket at Oxford. Alan Ross. PeLV

Peddler and His Wife, The. *Unknown.* AmFP

Peddler's Song, A. *Unknown. See* Fine knacks for ladies, cheap, choice, brave and new!

Pedestal ashtray next to the son who hadn't seen, A. Father Hunger and Son. Roger Weingarten. NAmP90

Pedestrian Woman, The. Robin Morgan. CrSp

Pediatrics. Carol Muske. PBCAP

Pedigree of honey, The. Emily Dickinson. BLPL; FaBV; MoP; NOBA; SAmP

Pedlar. Confucius, *tr. fr. Chinese by* Ezra Pound. *Fr.* Wei Wind. CTC; OBVE

Pedlar, The. Shakespeare. *See* Lawn as white as driven snow.

Pedlar Jim. Florence Hoare. BoTP

Pedlar of Small-Wares, A ("A pedlar I am, that take great care.") Sir John Suckling. CaPo

Pedlar's Caravan, The. William Brighty Rands. BoTP; OxBChV

Pedlar's Song, The. Shakespeare. *See* Lawn as white as driven snow.

Pedlar's Song, The. Shakespeare. *See* When Daffodils Begin to Peer.

Pedra. John William Burgon. BLPA

Pedro. Phoebe W. Hoffman. GoYe

Pedro. Luis Omar Salinas. FF

Peekaboo, I Almost See You. Ogden Nash. EBEvV; PeLV; PoLF

Peeking in through. Praxilla, *tr. fr. Greek by* Sam Hamill. InMo

Peeking into her own clasped hands. (*LL*) Preface to a Twenty Volume Suicide Note. Amiri Baraka. PoBA; PoM; PPP; TTY

Peeler's Lament, The. *Unknown.* WTO

Peeling Onions. Adrienne Rich. BoWoP; HCAP; TAP

Peeling Pippins. Mary TallMountain. HATNAP

Peeper, The. Peter Davison. ErPo

Peepin' through the knothole. Go Get the Axe. *Unknown.* AS

Peeping Tom. Francis Hope. ErPo

Peeps a maple-sugar child. (*LL*) This Little House Is Sugar. Langston Hughes. NTCP

Peeps the daisy white. (*LL*) Buttercups and Daisies. Mary Howitt. BoTP; OHIP; OxBChV

Peepshow Girl, The. Marion Lomax. PWE

Peer of the gods is that man, who. Sappho, *tr. fr. Greek by* William Carlos Williams. OBVE

Peer of the golden gods is he to Sappho. Ode to Anactoria. Sappho, *tr. fr. Greek by* William Ellery Leonard. AWP

Peering into the depths of the stream. T'ao Ch'ien, *tr. by* Eugene Eoyang. *Fr.* Seasons Come and Go, The. SuSp

Peerless yet hopeless maid of Q. Miss Ellen Gee of Kew. *Unknown.* FaBoNo

Pees maketh plente. *Unknown.* MiEL

(Peace.) MeEL

Peeter a Whitfeild he hath slaine. Jock o' the Side. *Unknown.* ESPB

Peg of Limavaddy. Thackeray. OBTV

Pegasos are steaming, The. Winter Rains: Cataluña. Philip Levine. NaP

Pegasus. Patrick Kavanagh. MoAB

Pegasus Lost. Elinor Wylie. MoAmPo

Peggy. Allan Ramsay. *See* My Peggy is a young thing.

Peggy Browne. Turlough Carolan, *tr. fr. Irish by* Austin Clarke. BIrV

Peggy Said Good Morning. John Clare. ELP

Pelagius. Gwyn Williams. AngWe

Pelican, The. Greg Kuzma. AmPA

Pelican Chorus, The. Edward Lear. FaBoNo; OBSP

Pelicans. Robinson Jeffers. FM; MoAmPo

Pelicans in the Wilderness (A Grave near Halfa). Kipling. *Fr.* Epitaphs of the War, 1914–1918. NoP; OBWP; PeFWW

Pelleas and Ettarre. Tennyson. *Fr.* Idylls of the King. NAEL-2

Pelops and Hippodamia, *sels.* Matthew Grove. In Praise of His Lady. EIL

Pelters of Pyramids. Richard Henry Horne. OBTV

Pen, The. Muhammad al-Ghuzzi, *tr. fr. Arabic by* May Jayyusi *and* John Heath-Stubbs. TSaS

Pen, The. Mary Weston Fordham. AmWP; CBWP-2

Pen and four fingers: I watched four fair creatures. Unknown, formerly at. to Cynewulf, *tr. fr. Anglo-Saxon. Fr.* Riddles (Exeter Book). ASW, *tr. by* Kevin Crossley-Holland

Pen-guin sits up-on the shore, The. A Penguin. Oliver Herford. FiBHP

Pen-guin. The Sword-fish, The. Robert Williams Wood. NBLV

Pen Hy Cane ("Pen Hyrogliphic Cane.") Mason Jordan Mason. PoNe

Pen is an index finger, The. Castration of the Pen. Erica Jong. NALW

"Pen is mightier than the sword, The." A Feather's Weight. George Parsons Lathrop. FaBoUs

Pen-knife, quills, ink-horn, books, paper, table-books, caps; take. Verses to Be Repeated by an Attorney Leaving His Lodging to Wait upon Judges Riding the Circuits from One County to Another, Least He Forget Some Necessary Thing. John Willis. FaBoUs

Pen slides, The. Valerio Magrelli, *tr. fr. Italian by* Dana Gioia. NeIt

Penal Law. Austin Clarke. BoLoP; GTBS-P; IPY; NOIV

Penal Servitude for Mrs. Maybrick. *Unknown.* OxBoLi

Penalties of Baldness, The. Sir Owen Seaman. FiBHP

Penalty of Virtue, The. *Unknown, tr. fr. Sanskrit by* Arthur Ryder. *Fr.* Panchatantra, The. AWP

Penance, A. Francis Daniel Pastorius. NOSC

Pencil and Paint. Eleanor Farjeon. PDV

Pencilled by the Rain. Peter Hooper. PeNZ

Pencil's Dream, The. Tymoteusz Karpowicz, *tr. fr. Polish by* Czeslaw Milosz.

Pencil's Sleep, The. Tymoteusz Karpowicz. *See* When the pencil undresses for sleep.

Pendant Watch. Madeline DeFrees. NMM

Pendydd. Kingsley Amis. *Fr.* Evans Country, The. FaBoBl; NOBL

Penelope. Janet Dubé. DT

Penelope. James Harrison. NIP

Penelope. Monique Laederach, *tr. fr. French by* Charles Guenther. BoWoP *Sels.*
   "And so I speak/ in place of that primordial cry."
   "Leaving the island, she believes, to go to the child."

Penelope. Dorothy Parker. PAW

Penelope as a *garçon manqué. Mythology.* Marilyn Hacker. NoAM

Penelope pulls home. Kiltartan Legend. Padraic Fallon. NOIV

Penelope Sets Up House with Odysseus. Jane Oliensis. UTF

Penelope, That Longèd for the Sight. William Byrd. EnRePo

Penelope this slow Epistle sends. Anne Wharton. *Fr.* Penelope to Ulysses. KTR

Penelope to Ulysses, *sels.* Anne Wharton.
   "Penelope this slow Epistle sends." KTR

Penelope's Despair. Yannis Ritsos, *tr. fr. Greek by* Edmund Keeley. AnAn

Penguin. Michael Richards. OBAP

Penguin, The. Ricardo Yáñez, *tr. fr. Spanish.* TSaS, *tr. by* Raúl Aceves *and* Arturo Súarez, *with* Jane Taylor

Penguin, A. Oliver Herford. FiBHP

Penguin hailed me at the door, A. Penguins in the Home. Helen Smith Bevington. OBAL

Penguin, isn't meat, fish or bird, The. The Penguin. Ricardo Yáñez, *tr. fr. Spanish.* TSaS, *tr. by* Raúl Aceves *and* Arturo Súarez, *with* Jane Taylor

Penguin on the Beach. Ruth Miller. PeSA

Penguins. Artur Miedzyrzecki, *tr. fr. Polish by* Artur Miedzyrzecki *and* John Batki. PoSu

Penguins in the Home. Helen Smith Bevington. OBAL

Peninsula, The. Seamus Heaney. IIP

Penis envy, they call it. Alta. NMM

Penitent, The. Edna St. Vincent Millay. AnAmPo

Penitent Considers Another Coming of Mary, A. Gwendolyn Brooks. NoAM; PChr

Penitent Nun, The. John Lockman. ErPo

Penitential Psalm. *Unknown, tr. fr. Babylonian.* WGRP

Penitential Psalm to the Goddess Anunit. *Unknown, tr. fr. Babylonian.* WGRP

Penitential Psalms., *sels.* Sir Thomas Wyatt. Prologue. ChIV-1

Penniless Indian fakirs and their camels, The. Avarice. Anthony Hecht. OxBSP

Pennines in April. Ted Hughes. PPP

Pennsylvania Deutsch. Christopher Morley. NBLV

Pennsylvania Places. T. A. Daly. OBAL

Pennsylvania Song. *Unknown.* PAH

Pennsylvania spiders. Morning Harvest. Gerald Stern. LCAP

Pennsylvania Winter Indian 1974. Harold Littlebird. VoR

Penny. *Unknown.* EnVB; FaBoVe; MiEL

Penny and penny. *Unknown.* OxNR

Penny for You, A. Uri Zvi Greenberg, *tr. fr. Hebrew by* Ruth Finer Mintz. MHP

Penny for you, philosophers of eternity, A. A Penny for You. Uri Zvi Greenberg, *tr. fr. Hebrew by* Ruth Finer Mintz. MHP

Penny lost in the lak, The. *Unknown. Fr.* Colkelbie Sow. OxBS

Penny Trumpet. Raphael Rudnik. MAT; NYBP

Penny Whistle, The. Edward Thomas. MoAB; MoBrPo

Penny Wish, A. Irene Thompson. BoTP

Pennycandystore beyond the El, The. Lawrence Ferlinghetti. *Fr.* Coney Island of the Mind, A. CAPP; HeIL; HeIP; PoM; TAP

Penological Study: Southern Exposure, *sels.* Robert Penn Warren. Wet Hair: If Now His Mother Should Come. NoAM

Pensioners. Winifred M. Letts.

Pensionnaires. Paul Verlaine, *tr. fr. French by* François Pirou. PeHV

Pensive at Eve. Samuel Taylor Coleridge. *Fr.* Sonnets Attempted in the Manner of Contemporary Writers. FaBoPa; Son

Pensive Eliza lately sate. The Triple League to Mrs. Susan Dove. Elizabeth Thomas. KTR

Pensive gnu, the staid aardvark, The. For an Amorous Lady. Theodore Roethke. ArLo; NBLV

Pensive here I sat. Milton. *Fr.* Paradise Lost. EPCY; OBD

Pensive, on Her Dead Gazing, I Heard the Mother of All. Walt Whitman. RB

Pensive they sit, and roll their languid eyes. Keats. CBNP

Pentagonia. G. E. Bates. NYBP

Pentecost. Adelbert Sumpter Coats. TrPWD

Pentecost. John Riley. VaA

Pentecost Castle, The. Geoffrey Hill. HAP

Pentelogia, *sels.* Francis Quarles.
"Can he be fair that withers at a blast." PeECV

Penthesileia. Robert Graves. OBD

Pentland Hills, The. *Unknown.* GBP

Pentucket. Whittier. PAH

Penumbra. Pierre Louÿs, *tr. fr. French. Fr.* Chansons de Bilitis. PeHV

Penurious Quaker; or, The High Priz'd Harlot, The. *Unknown.* CoMu; FaBoBl

Peonage System, The. L. A. J. Moorer. CBWP-3

Peonies. Li Shang-yin, *tr. fr. Chinese by* A. C. Graham. PLT

Peonies bloom, white and pink, The. By the Peonies. Czeslaw Milosz, *tr. fr. Polish by* Czeslaw Milosz. ArNa

Peonies/ The strange pink colour of Chinese porcelains. Afterglow. Amy Lowell. ArNa

Peony. Jackie Kay. DT

Peony for Apollo, A. Charles Edward Eaton. GoYe

People, The. Tomasso Campanella, *tr. fr. Italian by* John Addington Symonds. AWP

People, The. Robert Creeley. VGW

People. Lois Lenski. FaPON

People, The. Elizabeth Madox Roberts. GoJo

People, The. W. B. Yeats. CMoP

People. Yevgeny Yevtushenko, *tr. fr. Russian by* Robin Milner-Gulland *and* Peter Levi. DL

People all talk about serving the King of Emptiness. Sent to the Ch'an Master Wu-hsiang. Lo Yin, *tr. fr. Chinese by* Geoffrey R. Waters. SuSp

People along the sand, The. Neither Out Far nor In Deep. Robert Frost. AmPP; ChTr; HAP; LiTA; MeMAP; MoAB; MoP; NAAL-2; NoAM; NOBA; NoP; Poetr; TAP; TRP; WeW

People always say to me. The Question. Karla Kuskin. NTCP; PDV

People are making a camp of branches in that country at Arnhem Bay, The. Song Cycle of the Moon-Bone. *Unknown, tr. fr. Aborigine by* Ronald M. Berndt. NOBAu

People are of two kinds, and he. Tribute on the Passing of a Very Real Person. *Unknown.* PoToHe

People are putting up storm windows now. Storm Windows. Howard Nemerov. InPK; VCAP

People are saying that I am your enemy, The. To Julia de Burgos. Julia de Burgos, *tr. fr. Spanish by* Grace Schulman. BoWoP; PBWP

People arrive to worship in their church. The Church. Jules Romains, *tr. fr. French by* Jethro Bithell. WGRP

People Buy a Lot of Things. Annette Wynne. PDV

People came to listen, The. Chartist Meeting. Mike Jenkins. AngWe

People chained to aurora, A. Civilization and Its Discontents. John Ashbery. LCAP; TwCP

People come from all over to consult me, bringing their limbs. Margaret Atwood. *Fr.* Circe/ Mud Poems. NALW

People did die in our neighborhood. Suburban. H. R. Coursen. GOYP

People die from loneliness. One. Carolyn M. Rodgers. BPo

People do gossip. Sappho, *tr. fr. Greek by* Mary Barnard. PBWP

People expect old men to die. Old Men. Ogden Nash. AnAmPo; InPS; RB

People Getting Divorced. Lawrence Ferlinghetti. NoAM

People going straight up to heaven. Amazing Grace. Anselm Hollo. PoM

People I love the best, The. To Be of Use. Marge Piercy. CAPP; CrSp

People is a beast of muddy brain, The. The People. Tomasso Campanella, *tr. fr. Italian by* John Addington Symonds. AWP

People know, The. A Little More about the Brothers and Sisters. Sharon Scott. JB

People live forever in Jacksonville and St. Petersburg and Tampa. Come On in, the Senility Is Fine. Ogden Nash. AiP

People love each other and the light. Of Love. William Meredith. *Fr.* Consequences. VCAP

People,/ male and female. Mahadevi, *tr. fr. Kannada by* A. K. Ramanujan. BoWoP

"People need poetry, The." Osip Mandelstam. Seamus Deane. BiHa; PBCIP

People Next Door, The. Louis Simpson. BAP-89

People, No, The. Vicki Raymond. NOBAu

People of Blakeney, The. *Unknown.* GBP

People of Spain think Cervantes, The. E. C. Bentley. *Fr.* Clerihews. FiBHP

People of Tao-chou, The. Po Chü-i, *tr. fr. Chinese by* Arthur Waley. ChTr

People of the Future. Ted Berrigan. UL

People of the Harvest. Naomi Quinonez. AfAz

People of the South Wind. William Stafford. NNaP

People, people, have you heard? *Unknown.* RoPo

People — people of my kind, my own, The. To the Lacedemonians. Allen Tate. NAAL-2; NoAM

People say the chameleon can take on the hue. The Chameleon. John Gardner. ZA

People say they have a hard time. For de Lawd. Lucille Clifton. IMW; PoBA; TAP; TwCP

People stopped coming here to pray. The Chapel Snake. Lavinia Greenlaw. NWP

People that walked in darkness, The. Bible, *O.T. Fr.* Isaiah. PAW

People the Churches love best, The. Patrick Braybrook. PeLi

People Trying to Love. Stephen Berg. NaP

People vs. the People, The. Kenneth Fearing. MoAmPo

People walk upon their heads, The. Topsy-turvy Land. H. E. Wilkinson. BoTP

People were bathing and posturing themselves on the beach. The Gods! The Gods! D. H. Lawrence. CMoP

People were those who. *Unknown. See* They were the people, those who.

People who are always praising the past. The Past. Stevie Smith. IHNG

People Who Died. Ted Berrigan. UL

People who have no children can be hard. The Children of the Poor. Gwendolyn Brooks. *Fr.* Womanhood, The. PoA, *complete*; WPE, (1 *and* 2)

People Who Must. Carl Sandburg. PDV

People who want to live beside the ocean are fundamentalists. Lakes. David Donnell. NoAM

People will live on, The. Carl Sandburg. *Fr.* People, Yes, The. MoAB; MoAmPo; NoAM; NOBA; OxBA; TrGrPo

People Will Talk. Samuel Dodge. WBLP

People, Yes, The, *sels.* Carl Sandburg.
"Englishman in the old days, An." FYAP
"From the four corners of the earth." CMoP
"People will live on, The." MoAB; MoAmPo; NoAM; NOBA; OxBA; TrGrPo
"They have yarns." LiTA; MoAmPo
"What the people learn out of lifting and hauling." OBAL
"Who shall speak for the people?" OxBA
"Why did the children." OBAL
"Why repeat? I heard you the first time." OBAL

People's Literary, De. Maggie Pogue Johnson. CBWP-4

People's [or Worker's] flag is deepest red, The. The Red Flag. Jim Connell. SWP

People's Surroundings. Marianne Moore. CBCK

Peotry Was Like This. Al Mahmud, *tr. fr. Bengali by* Kabir Chowdhury. TSaS

Pep. Grace G. Bostwick. WBLP

Pepita, my paragon, bright star of Arragon. Saragossa. Henry S. Leigh. FaBoCo

Pepper in ashes, cassia branches broken, the good man grows old, The. Sending Off O.E. Who Brought an Orchid Home to Japan. Lu Hsun, *tr. fr. Chinese by* William R. Schultz. SuSp

Peppergrass. Stanley Plumly. LCAP

Peppertrees, the peppertrees, The! Scenes from the Life of the Peppertrees. Denise Levertov. LiTM; NeAP; NoP; PoM

Peppery Man, The. Arthur Macy. FaPON

Pepsi Generation. Walasse Ting. MAT

Per Ardua ad Astra. John Oxenham. TrPWD

Per Iter Tenebricosum. Oliver St. John Gogarty. OBMV

Per Pacem ad Lucem. Adelaide Anne Procter. TrPWD

Perambulator Poems, I-VII, *sels.* David McCord.
When I Was Christened. OBCA

Perceived she stirred, but did not see. (*LL*) Seeing Her Dancing. Robert Heath. NOSC; OxBSP

Perception of an object costs. Emily Dickinson. NOBA

Perchance in days to come. Strange Love. Moses ibn Ezra, *tr. fr. Hebrew by* Solomon Solis-Cohen. TrJP

Perchance she died in age — surviving all. Rome by Metella's Tomb. Byron. *Fr.* Childe Harold's Pilgrimage. FaBoPP

Perchance some coming after. Strato, *tr. fr. Greek by* Sydney Oswald. PeHV

Perchance that I might learn what pity is. A Prayer for Purification. Michelangelo, *tr. fr. Italian by* John Addington Symonds. AWP

Perchance, the friend who cheered thy early years. Judge Not. Josephine D. Henderson Heard. CBWP-4

Perched in a tower of this ancestral wall. At the Great Wall of China. Edmund Blunden. GTBS-P

Percivale's Quest. Tennyson. *Fr.* Idylls of the King. OAEL-2

Percussive, furious, this wind. Mistral. Barbara Howes. NYBP

Percy Bysshe Shelley: Inscription for the Couch, Still Preserved, on which He Passed the Last Night of His Life. Dante Gabriel Rossetti. EPCY

Percy Shelley. John Peale Bishop. ErPo

Perdam Sapientiam Sapientum. William Habington. ChIV-2

Perdie [*or* Perdye], I Said[e] It [*or* Yt] Not. Sir Thomas Wyatt. *See* Perdy [*or* Perdie *or* Perdye]! I said[e] it [*or* yt] not.

Perdita. Louis MacNeice. PoA

Perdy [*or* Perdie *or* Perdye]! I said[e] it [*or* yt] not. Constancy. Sir Thomas Wyatt. SiPS
(Perdie [*or* Perdye], I Said[e] It [*or* Yt] Not.) EnRePo
(Perdye I Saide Yt Not.) PoEL-1

Perdye I Saide Yt Not. Sir Thomas Wyatt. *See* Perdy [*or* Perdie *or* Perdye]! I said[e] it [*or* yt] not.

Père Lalement. Marjorie Pickthall. NOBC

Peregrine. Elinor Wylie. BLPL

Peregrine Prykke's Pilgrimage, *sels.* Clive James.
"Blood has soaked the bone which hides the stone, The." FaBoPa

Peregrine White and Virginia Dare. Rosemary *and* Stephen Vincent Benét *and* Stephen Vincent Benét. OBCA

Peregrine's Sunday Song. Elinor Wylie. NYBP

Perennial tears descend in gems. (*LL*) The Valley of Unrest. Poe. AmPP; NAAL-1; PoEL-4

Perfect. "Hugh MacDiarmid." RB

Perfect breakfast, all must own, The. Breakfast. Harry Graham. EBNV

Perfect Child, The. Adrian Porter. NBLV

Perfect Day, A. Carrie Jacobs Bond. WBLP

Perfect Disc of the Moon, The. Richard Kenney. Son

Perfect Gift, The. Edmund Vance Cooke. PChr

Perfect Husband, The. Ogden Nash. FaBoUs; Poetr

Perfect is the word I can never hear. Rhymes. Charles Tomlinson. DiPo

Perfect little body, without fault or stain on thee. On a Dead Child. Robert Bridges. CMoP; EBEV; LiTB; LiTM; NoAM; NOBE; NOBVV; OBMV; OBNC; OxAEP-2; SCGP

Perfect love is nourished by despair, A. George Santayana. *Fr.* Sonnets. AnAmPo

Perfect Orchestra, The. H. Cordelia Ray. CBWP-3

Perfect order trusted to the dead, The. (*LL*) The Astronomers of Mont Blanc. Edgar Bowers. PoA

Perfect Reactionary, The. Hughes Mearns. NTCP

Perfect Woman. Wordsworth. *See* She Was a Phantom of Delight.

Perfected whiteness. For Stephen Procter. Frances Horovitz. PWE

Perfectest of all created things, The. Maidenhood. Sir John Davies. *Fr.* Contention Betwixt a Wife, a Widow, and a Maid, A. CBCK

Perfection. Yevgeny Yevtushenko, *tr. fr. Russian by* Tina Tupinkina-Glaessner, Geoffrey Dutton, *and* Igor Mezhakoff-Koriakin. ArNa

Perfection Eludes Us. Frederick Seidel. *Fr.* AIDS Days. BAP-90

Perfection, if't hath been attayned. In the Due Honor of the Author Master Robert Norton. John Smith. SCAP

Perfection is terrible, it cannot have children. The Munich Mannequins. Sylvia Plath. CAPP; NaP

Perfection, of a kind, was what he was after. Epitaph on a Tyrant. W. H. Auden. HeIP; MeMAP; NoAM; OxBSP; PAW; RB

Perfection of Dentistry, The. Marvin Bell. AmPA; CoAP

Perfectly beautiful, perfectly ignorant of it. (*LL*) Piazza di Spagna, Early Morning. Richard Wilbur. GrPl; InPS; OxBSP; SM; VGW

Perfectly happy now, he looked at his estate. Voltaire at Ferney. W. H. Auden. LiTA; LiTM; PoA

Perfecto Flores. Jimmy Santiago Baca. TRP

Perfervid Roc, sitting on candle light, The. The Roc. Richard Eberhart. CMoP

Perfidia. David Lehman. NAmP90

Perfidious, The. Walter Savage Landor. CBLP

Perforated Spirit, The. Morris Bishop. FiBHP

Perforce, like those whom Gideon schooled with briars. (*LL*) Buonaparte. Tennyson. Son

Performance, The. James Dickey. ArOW; CAPP; CoAP; LiTM; MoP; NOBA; PoE

Performance at Hog Theater, A. Russell Edson. AmPA

Performances, assortments, résumés. The Tunnel. Hart Crane. *Fr.* Bridge, The. CMoP; LiTA; MAT; MoAB; MoAmPo; NAAL-2; OxBA

Performing Seal, The. Rachel Field. *Fr.* Circus Garland, A. OBCA

Perfume, The. John Donne. *Fr.* Elegies. ESCV; NoSic; SeCP

Perfume, The. Robert Herrick. CaPo

Perfume / of Flowers!, The. Charles Olson. RaBo

Perfume/ of flowers! A haw, The. The Perfume / of Flowers! Charles Olson. RaBo

Perfume remained in his room, perhaps only, A. Final Hour. Yannis Ritsos, *tr. fr. Greek by* Paul Merchant. AnRep

Perfume sweet I send you. Not of Itself, But Thee. *Unknown, tr. fr. Greek by* Dudley Fitts. GrAn

Perhaps. Lucille Clifton. CAPP

Perhaps. Sydney Thompson Dobell. NOBVV

Perhaps he does . . . O Lord, that House in stratford! (*LL*) Ben Jonson Entertains a Man from Stratford. E. A. Robinson. AmPP; MoAB; MoAmPo

Perhaps he was found at the Throne. (*LL*) William Blake. James Thomson ("B.V."). EPCY

Perhaps he was your father. (*LL*) On a Wag in Mauchline. Burns. FiBHP

Perhaps he will fall. (*LL*) Wilderness Gothic. Alfred W. Purdy. HeIP; MoCV; NOBC; NoP

Perhaps I always knew what they were saying. The Prophets. W. H. Auden. CBLP

Perhaps I am one of them. (*LL*) Midnight. Jên Jui. WPC

Perhaps I don't care if I do: you may give me the same, Jim — no sugar. (*LL*) The Stage-Driver's Story. Bret Harte. EBNV

Perhaps I killed a man to-day. The Question. Alexander McKee. PAW

Perhaps I may allow, the Dean. Swift. *Fr.* Verses on the Death of Doctor Swift [D.S.P.D., Occasioned by Reading a Maxim in Rochefoucauld]. EPCY; NOBE; PeLV

Perhaps, if you/ Are very good. Hob the Elf. Norman M. Johnson. BoTP

Perhaps in the dead of some different night. Of the Knowledge of Good and Evil. George Bradley. BAP-89

Perhaps it is to avoid some great sadness. Sleeping on the Wing. Frank O'Hara. InPS; NAAL-2; SOTW

Perhaps It's as You Say. Peter Everwine. NNaP

Perhaps my mother murdered me. (*LL*) The Inquest. W. H. Davies. AngWe; GTBS-P; NOBE; OxBTC; RB

Perhaps on a sunday. Day Song. Lance Henson. HATNAP

Perhaps one day men would be more spiritual. (*LL*) The Ghostly Father. Peter Redgrove. MoBS

Perhaps she said, lively at first but once. Farmer Goes Beserk. Anne Elder. CBAP

Perhaps something ought to be said about how deadpan. Great Stone Face. George Bradley. BAP-91

Perhaps the earth is floating. The Poet of Ignorance. Anne Sexton. PRA

Perhaps the Socrates he had never read. Why Hast Thou Forsaken Me? Chad Walsh. *Fr.* Psalm of Christ, The. TrCP

Perhaps the time has come. Testament. Bei Dao, *tr. fr. Chinese by* Donald Finkel *with* Chen Xueliang. SpMi

Perhaps there is a better night than this or better dream. Etchings. James William Chichetto. BTR

Perhaps/ This is the way. Antigone I. Herbert Martin. PoBA

Perhaps this valley too leads into the head of long-ago days. Grand Abacus. John Ashbery. PoA

Perhaps we would never have known what to say to each. Two Girls. Sallie Bingham. NGP

Perhaps — well/ It may not matter! Men's Impotence. *Unknown, tr. fr. Eskimo.* WTO

Perhaps you expected a face that was free from tears. Narcissus. Paul Valéry, *tr. fr. French by* Joseph T. Shipley. AWP

Perhaps/ You will remember/ John Brown. October 16: The Raid. Langston Hughes. PoBA

Pericles, *sels.* Shakespeare.
 "Terrible child-bed hast thou had, my dear, A." EBEV; OxAEP-1
 Thou God of This Great Vast, Rebuke These Surges. NAs

Pericles and Aspasia, *sels.* Walter Savage Landor.
 Behold, O Aspasia! I Send You Verses. OBNC; SCGP
 Corinna, from Athens, to Tanagra. OBEV
 (Corinna, to Tanagra, from Athens.) NOBE; OBTV
 (Corinna to Tanagra.) OBNC
 Death of Artemidora, The. EnRP; OBNC
 Dirce. AWP; CTC; EBEV; EnRP; FaBoEE; GBL; HAP; LiTB; NOBE; NoP; OAEL-2; OBEV; OBNC; OxAEP-2; OxBSP; PoEL-4; PoRA; SCGP; TFi; TrGrPo; WeW
 (Stand Close Around.) ChTr

Perils and the dangers of the voyage being past, The. Jack Robinson. *Unknown.* OBET

Perils of Obesity, The. Harry Graham. FiBHP

Perimedes [*or* Perimedes, the Blacksmith], *sels.* Robert Greene.
 Coridon and Phillis
 (Phillis and Coridon.) NoSic
 Fair Is My Love. EiL

Period of Mourning, The, *sels.* Henry Peacham.
 Nuptial Hymn. EiL

Peripatetic Letter to Isabella Fey, A, *sels.* David Wright.
 "This was as far as I had got." PeSAV

Peripeteia. Anthony Hecht. VCAP

Periphery. A. R. Ammons. NOBA

Periphery. Ruth Stone. NALW

Peri's Lament for Hinda, The. Thomas Moore. *Fr.* Lalla Rookh. OBNC

Perish th' illiberal thought which would debase. Hannah More. *Fr.* Slavery, a Poem. ECWP

Perish'd all on the coast of Spain. (*LL*) Carpenter's Wife, The ("O whare hae ye been, my dearest dear.") *Unknown.* OAEL-1; OxBB

Perishing Bird, The. Douglas G. Jones. MoCV

Periwig, A. Rowland Watkyns. NOSC

Perle, plesaunte to prynces paye. *Unknown. Fr.* Pearl. EBEV, *sts.* 1–5

Permanence in Change. Goethe, *tr. by* John Frederick Nims. HoPM; STV

Permanence in Change. Goethe, *tr. fr. German.* HoPM, *tr. by* John Frederick Nims

Permanence of the Young Men, The. William Soutar. OxBS

Permanent City, The. Matthew Sweeney. IB

Permanent Face. Laura Rosenthal. UL

Permanent occasion, A. Winter Garden. Donald Britton. EOEF

Permanent Tourists, The. P. K. Page. LiTM; NOBC

Permanent Wave. Andrew Crozier. NBrP

Permanently. Kenneth Koch. CoAP; GoJo; NoP; PoA; PoM; PPP

Permanently, seriously/ Without thought. (*LL*) At the Ball Game. William Carlos Williams. CMoP; MoP; NoAM; NOBA; OxBA; PoE

Permit me here a simple brief aside. To Calliope. Robert Graves. CMoP

Permit Me Voyage. James Agee. MoAmPo

Permit Us, Lord, to Consecrate. Joseph Green. AH

Permitted to assist you, let me see. St. Valentine. Marianne Moore. NYBP

Peroration, Concerning Genius. Robert Pinsky. *Fr.* Essay on Psychiatrists. NoAM

Perpetuall blush to thine, A. (*LL*) Good Counsel [*or* Counsell] to a Young Maid. Thomas Carew.

Perpetuum Immobile. Bruce Dawe. CBAP

Perplex'd with trifles thro' the vale of life. A Nut, a World, a Squirrel, and a King. Charles Churchill. *Fr.* Night; an Epistle to Robert Lloyd. FaBoRV

Perplexe him in his hinder-parts. (*LL*) To His Book[e] ("Who with thy leaves . . .") Robert Herrick. FaBoUs; JCP

Perplexity: A Poem. Elizabeth Hands. WoRP

Perry's Victory. *Unknown.* PAH

Perry's Victory — A Song. *Unknown.* PAH

Perse owt of Northombarlande, The. Chevy Chase. *Unknown.* EnSB, *sl. diff vers.*; OxBB, *sl. diff vers.*
 (Hunting of the Cheviot, The.) EnVB

Persecuted, poor, and old. (*LL*) Once. *Unknown.* CH

Persephone. Keith Abbott. UL

Persephone. Robert Duncan. NOBA

Persephone, *sels.* Jenny Joseph.
 "Those who turn their face to the wall." PWE
 "You see this rain." PWE

Persephone. Michael Longley. PBCIP

Persephone and Dis, Dis, have mercy upon her. Ezra Pound. *Fr.* Homage to Sextus Propertius. MeMAP

Persephone, Falling. Rita Dove. NAmP90

Persephone, 5, Outside. Keith Abbott. UL

Persephone in Armenia. Carol Rumens. PWE

Persephone is the woman buried. Robert Kelly. *Fr.* Book of Persephone, The. PoM

Persephone Pauses. Carolyn Kizer. SRLS

Persephone Underground. Rita Dove. NAmP90

Perseus. Robert Hayden. NoAM

Perseus. Louis MacNeice. LiTM

Pershing at the Tomb of Lafayette. Amelia Josephine Burr. PAH

Persia. V. Sackville-West. WPE

Persian, The. Stevie Smith. FaBoWP

Persian flummery. Horace. *See* Boy, I have their empty shouts.

Persian Fopperies. Horace. *See* Boy, I have their empty shouts.

Persian Miniature. William Jay Smith. CoAP

Persian on his throne!, The. (*LL*) The Vision of Belshazzar. Byron. GN

Persian Parables., *sels.* Aleksander Wat, *tr. fr. Polish by* Czeslaw Milosz.

Persian pomps, boy, ever I renounce them. Horace. *See* Boy, I have their empty shouts.

Persian Song of Hafiz, A. Hafiz, *tr. fr. Persian by* Sir William Jones. AWP

Persian Version, The. Robert Graves. CMoP; FaBoCo; LiTB; LiTM; MoP; NoAM; NOBL; OBWP; WeW

Persians, The, *sels.* Aeschylus, *tr. fr. Greek by* G. M. Cookson.
 "Word was given, and, instantaneously, The." PAW

Persicos Odi: Pocket Version. Horace. *See* Boy, I have their empty shouts.

Persimmon Tree, The. *Unknown.* GBP

Persimmons. Li-Young Lee. NIP

Persimmons and Plums. Elizabeth Hodges. GrPl

Persistence of Nature in Our Lives, The. Andrew Hudgins. DiPo; FoLa; WeW

Persistent Explorer. John Crowe Ransom. OxBA

Person as Dreamer: We Talk about the Future, The. Michael Hartnett. PBCIP

Person from Porlock, A. R. S. Thomas. TOF

Person Is Accidentally Rejuvenated in Old Age, A. Gavin Ewart. FaBoBl

Person is very self-conscious about his head, A. Thoughts on One's Head. William Meredith. HAP; VCAP

Person to Person. Gwen Harwood. FaBoMA

Person who can do, The. Alan Dugan. ErPo

Personable Porcupine, The. Wilbur G. Howcroft. ZA

Personal. Langston Hughes. NOBA; NTP; PoNe

Personal. Samuel Yellen. NYBP

Personal Advertisement. Kit Wright. FaBoBl

Personal Column. Basil Bunting. ArLo

Personal Column. Tom Paulin. PNI

Personal Helicon. Seamus Heaney. IPY

Personal Poem. Frank O'Hara. PoBeRe

Personal Poem. Ingrid Wendt. NMM

Personal Reflections., *sels.* Ahmad al-Mushari al-Udwani, *tr. fr. Arabic by* Hilary Kilpatrick *and* Charles Doria.

Personal Song. Arnatkoak, *tr. fr. Eskimo.* WTO

Personal Talk. Wordsworth. EnRP; NOBE

Personal Values. Richard Howard. SM

Personality Sketch: Bill, A. Ronda Davis. JB

Personification of a Name, The. Ray A. Young Bear. HATNAP

Persons Unknown. Aidan Carl Mathews. BiHa

Perspective. Coventry Patmore. *Fr.* Angel in the House, The. FaBoEE; GBL

Perspective never withers from their eyes. Quaker Hill. Hart Crane. *Fr.* Bridge, The. LiTA; LiTM; NAAL-2

Perspective of Co-ordination. Arthur Davison Ficke. PoA

Perspectives. Aidan Carl Mathews. IB

Perspectives Are Precipices. John Peale Bishop. LiTA

Persuasions to Enjoy. Thomas Carew. BeJo; CaPo; NOBE; OBEV; SeCP; SeCV-1

Persuasions to Joy; a Song. Thomas Carew. *See* If the quick spirits in your eye.

Perturbations of Uranus, The. Roy Fuller. ErPo

Peru, 1955. Ai. *Fr.* He Kept On Burning. AnAn

Peruke of Poets. William Zaranka. BXAP

Perverse Custom, A. *Unknown, tr. fr. Latin by* John Boswell. PeHV

Perverse habit of cat goddesses, A. Cat Goddesses. Robert Graves. NYBP; OxBSP

Perversion interests me. Note Delivered by a Female Impersonator. Heather McHugh. AmPA

Pervigilium Veneris. Suzanne Noguere. PoA

Pesach Has Come to the Ghetto Again. Binem Heller, *tr. fr. Yiddish by* Max Rosenfeld. TrJP

Pesci Misti. Leonard Aaronson. FaBoTw

Pessimist, The. Ben King. AnAmPo; BLPA; CoGr; FaBoCo; FaBoNo; NBLV; OBAL

Pessimist, The. *Unknown.* PoToHe

Pessimist's a cheerless man, The. The Pessimist. *Unknown.* PoToHe

Pet Lamb, The. Wordsworth. OxBChV

Pet-name, a common name. Best-selling brand, curt, A. Geoffrey Hill. *Fr.* Mercian Hymns. NoAM

Pet Panther. A. R. Ammons. NoP

Pet was never mourned as you. Last Words to a Dumb Friend. Thomas Hardy. FM; OBF; OFC; SoCa

Petal/ Yasmin/ Vlodostk. Frolic. Deborah Levy. DT

Petals fall from Heliodora's image, The. Meleager, *tr. fr. Greek by* Peter Whigham. GrAn

Petals fall in the fountain, The. Ts'ai Chi'h. Ezra Pound. NoP

Petals on a wet, black bough. (*LL*) In a Station of the Metro. Ezra Pound. AmPP; HAP; HeIL; HeIP; InPK; MeMAP; MoAB; MoAmPo; MoP; NAAL-2; NIP; NoAM; NOBA; NoP; OxBA; PoE; Poetr; TAP; TFi; UnPo; VGW; WeW

Petals on the ground are her likeness still beneath the tower where she fell. (*LL*) Shih Ch'ung's 'Golden Valley' Garden. Tu Mu. PLT

Petals red and purple turn to mud, and mud to dust. Fallen Blossoms. Yang Wan-li, *tr. fr. Chinese by* Sherwin S. S. Fu. SuSp

Petals step their fragrance off the shelf. In a Hot Country. Wendy Mulford. NBrP

Pete at the Zoo. Gwendolyn Brooks. PDV; TLR

Pete Peterson, before this bit, a professional entertainer. Vaudeville. Lincoln Kirstein. MoP

Pete Rousecastle the sailor's son. Rousecastle. David Wright. MoBS

Peter. Michael Dennis Browne. NYBP

Peter. Marianne Moore. CMoP; NAAL-2; NoP; OxBA; SoCa

Peter Amberley. John Calhoun. AmFP

Peter and John. Elinor Wylie. MoAB; MoAmPo; MoBS

Peter and Michael were two little menikin. *Unknown.* BoTP

Peter Bell. John Hamilton Reynolds. OBNC

Peter Bell the Third, *sels.* Shelley.
  "All things that Peter saw and felt." EPCY
  "Devil now knew his proper cue, The." OBSV
  "He was a might poet — and." EPCY
  "Hell is a city much like London." OBD; OBSV

Peter broke the ragged branch to push his nostrils closer. West Paddocks. Arthur Davies. NOBAu

Peter Daines at a Party. Alan Brownjohn. OBF

Peter died in a paper tiara cut. Tiara. Mark Doty. PFL

Peter Grimes. George Crabbe. *Fr.* Borough, The. EBNV; ECEV; EnRP; FHYEP; OBNV; PoEL-4; TEP

Peter Grimes at Aldeburgh. George Crabbe. *Fr.* Borough, The. EBNV; ECEV; EnRP; FaBoPP; FHYEP; OBNV; PoEL-4; TEP

Peter had experienced the tight, nauseous desire. The Wickedness of Peter Shannon. Alden Nowlan. MoCV

Peter Hath Lost His Purse. *Unknown.* FF

Peter-Penny, The. Robert Herrick. CaPo

Peter, Peter, pumpkin eater. Mother Goose. FaBoBe; OxNR (Pumpkin-Eater, The.) ReMoGo

Peter Piper picked a peck of pickled pepper[s]. Mother Goose. FaBoBe; FaPON; OTCP; OxNR; ReMoGo

Peter Quince at the Clavier. Wallace Stevens. AmPP; CMoP; HeIP; InPK; InPS; LiTM; MeMAP; MoAB; MoAmPo; NAWM-2; NoAM; NOBA; OxBA; PoE; PPP; SAmP; TAP; TFi; TrGrPo; TwCP

Peter Rabbit. Sandra McPherson. LCAP

Peter sleep-walks. Peter. Michael Dennis Browne. NYBP

Peter Stuyvesant's New Year's Call. Edmund Clarence Stedman. PAH

Peter White will ne'er go right. Mother Goose. OxBoLi; OxNR

Peterhead in May. Burns Singer. OxBS

Peterhof. Edmund Wilson. GoJo

Peter's not friendly. He gives me sideways looks. John Berryman. *Fr.* Dream Songs. CAPP (Dream Song 55.) ChIV-2

Peter's Pop kept a lollipop shop. *Unknown.* ISE

Petit, the Poet. Edgar Lee Masters. *Fr.* Spoon River Anthology. CMoP; MoAmPo; NoAM; NOBA; OxBA; TAP

Petite Histoire of Red Fascism, A. Andrei Codrescu. UL

Petition. W. H. Auden. CMoP; LiTB; MeMAP; NAEL-2; Son

Petition, The. Thomas Beedome. NOSC

Petition. John Drinkwater. TrPWD

Petition. Eleanor Slater. TrPWD

Petition. R. S. Thomas. FaBoMo

Petition for an Absolute Retreat, The. The Countess of Winchilsea. PoEL-3; WPE, *abr.*
  Sels.
  "Give me, O indulgent fate!" ECWP; NOSC; TrGrPo

Petition for Reconciliation. Cynddelw Brydydd Mawr, *tr. fr. Welsh by* Joseph P. Clancy. OBWVE

Petition from the Chain Gang at Newcastle to Captain Furlong the Superintendent, A. Francis MacNamara. NOBAu

Petition of the Gray Horse, Auld Dunbar, The. William Dunbar. OxBS

Petition of the Orangemen of Ireland, The. Thomas Moore. NOIV

Petitioners are full of prayers. The Lament of Swordy Well. John Clare. FaBoVe

Petra, *sels.* John William Burgon.
  "Match me such marvel save in Eastern clime." UV

Petrarch. Giosuè Carducci, *tr. fr. Italian by* William Dudley Foulke. AWP

Petrarch. Walter Holland. PFL

Petrarch, *sels.* Nicholas Kilmer.
  "In my first gentle days." PeECV

Petrarch must have known why we and the goldfinch. To Michael. Norman Dubie. AnAn

Petrifaction toward the core, the geode's rigor? (*LL*) Medusa. Amy Clampitt. VCAP

Petrified Echoes. Vasco [*or* Vasko] Popa, *tr. fr. Serbo-Croatian. Fr.* Yawn of Yawns, The. PoSu, *tr. by* Anne Pennington

Petrified Minute. Zoltán Zelk, *tr. fr. Hungarian by* Barbara Howes. TSaS

Petroglyph. Joy Harjo. NAmP90

Petrol. Kathleen Jamie. PWE

Petropolis. Osip Mandelstam, *tr. fr. Russian by* David McDuff. PeFWW

Petrushka's valentine pivots on its pin." (*LL*) The Wine Menagerie. Hart Crane. NoAM; NOBA; OxBA; VGW

Pets. Ted Hughes. CRH

Pets. Daniel Pettiward. ZA

Petticoat, A. Gertrude Stein. *Fr.* Tender Buttons. TTTS

Pettitoes are little feet, The. *Unknown.* OxNR

Petty Sneaking Knave, A. Blake. PeLV

Petty sneaking knave I knew, A. A Petty Sneaking Knave. Blake. PeLV (Mr. Cromek [*or* On Cromek].) ChTr; FaBoEE

Petulance is purple. Spectrum. Mari Evans. BPo

Peveril of the Peak, *sels.* Sir Walter Scott.
  "Speak not of niceness, when there's chance of wreck." FaBoEE

Pew, pew,/ My minny me slew. Song of the Murdered Child. *Unknown.* GBP (Milk-white Dove.) ChTr

Pewits Nest. John Clare. FaBoVe

Peyote Poem. Michael McClure. PoBeRe; PoM, I *only*
  Sels.
  "Clear — the senses bright — sitting in the black chair — Rocker." NeAP, I *only*

Peyote Vision. Lew Blockcolski. VoR

Phaedra. Osip Mandelstam, *tr. fr. Russian by* James Greene. OBVE

Phaedra. Jean Racine, *tr. fr. French by* Kenneth Muir. NAWM-2

Phaenomena, *sels.* Aratus, *tr. fr. Greek by* Barbara Hughes Fowler.
  "Beneath both the feet of Boötes you may see." HePo
  Proem. HePo
  Weather Signs. HePo

Phallic Root. Shiraishi Kazuko. WPOW

Phallus. Shiraishi Kazuko, *tr. by* Ikuko Atsumi. BoWoP

Phantasia for Elvira Shatayev. Adrienne Rich. NALW

Phantasmagorillaorgasmiasmacharismamama. Poem in Nueva York. Cyn Zarco. UL

Phantasmion, *sels.* Sara Coleridge.
  "O sleep, my babe, hear not the rippling wave." OBNC

Phantasus. Arno Holz, *tr. fr. German by* Ludwig Lewisohn. AWP
  Sels.
  "On a mountain of sugar-candy." PChr

Phantom. *Unknown, sometimes at. to* Samuel Taylor Coleridge. MeMBP; NAEL-2; OAEL-2; OxBSP; PoEL-4

Phantom Bark, The. Hart Crane. CMoP

Phantom Horsewoman, The. Thomas Hardy. CMoP; FaBoPP; MeMBP; NOBE; PoEL-5

Phlegmatic winter on a bed of snow. Born in Winter. Francis Quarles. NOSC

Phoebe Dawson, *sels.* George Crabbe.
  "Lo! now with red rent cloak and bonnet black." EBEV

Phoebe in a Rosebush. Clyde Watson. NTCP

Phoebe sate,/ Sweet she sate. Montanus' Sonnet. Thomas Lodge. *Fr.*
  Rosalynde; or Euphues' Golden Legacy. PoEL-2

Phoebus, accept this dinner that I bring you. Automedon, *tr. fr. Greek by*
  Frederick Garber. GrAn

Phoebus, Arise. William Drummond of Hawthornden. EIL

Phoebus farewell, a sweeter saint I serve. Sir Philip Sidney. *Fr.* Arcadia.
  SiPSBD
  (Sweeter Saint I Serve, A.) SiPS

Phoebus, make haste: the day's too long; be gone. A Letter to Her
  Husband. Anne Bradstreet. AnAmPo; LiTA

Phoebus red crashing wall of cloud. The Incantation. Sarah Kirsch, *tr. fr.*
  German by Anthony Vivis. VBLP

Phoebus, the goddess variant and changeable. Christine de Pisan, *tr. fr.*
  French by Joan Keefe. *Fr.* Epistle of Othea to Hector (A Lytil Bibell
  of Knyghthod), The. PBWP

Phoebus was a herdsman. Antipater of Thessalonica, *tr. fr. Greek by*
  Alistair Elliot. GrAn

Phoebus with Admetus. George Meredith. NOBE; OBEV

Phoenicians first (if Fame may credit have). Lucan, *tr. fr. Latin. Fr.*
  Pharsalia. SiPSBD, *tr. by* Sir Walter Ralegh

Phoenix, The. A. C. Benson. OBEV

Phoenix, The. George Darley. *See* O Blest Unfabled Incense Tree.

Phoenix, The. Howard Nemerov. LiTM

Phoenix. Carolyn M. Rodgers. JB

Phoenix, The. Siegfried Sassoon. ChTr

Phoenix, The, *sels. Unknown, tr. fr. Anglo-Saxon.*
  "I have heard that far from here." ASW, *tr. by* Kevin Crossley-Holland
  "Lo! I have learned of the loveliest of lands." AnOE; OAEL-1
  "When the wind is asleep and the weather set fair." ASW, *tr. by* Kevin
    Crossley-Holland

Phoenix and the Turtle, The. Shakespeare. EnRePo; ImPo; LiTB; NOBE;
  NoP; NoSic; OAEL-1; OBEV; OxAEP-1; PeECV; PoEL-2; SCGP; TEP

Phoenix at Fifty, A. Lawrence Ferlinghetti. NAs

Phoenix, bird of terrible pride. Sir Herbert Read. *Fr.* Mutations of the
  Phoenix. FaBoTw

Phoenix birds once frolicked on Phoenix Terrace, The. Climbing Phoenix
  Terrace at Chin-ling. Li Po, *tr. fr. Chinese by* Joseph J. Lee. SuSp

Phoenix comes of flame and dust, The. The Phoenix. Howard Nemerov.
  LiTM

Phoenix on the hot sirocco's breath. Herbert B. Mallalieu. PoA

Phoenix Reborn from Its Ashes, The. Louis Aragon, *tr. fr. French.* CBNP

Phoenix Self-born, The. Ovid, *tr. by* Dryden. *Fr.* Metamorphoses. ChTr

Phoenix tail on scented silk, flimsy layer on layer. Li Shang-yin, *tr. fr.*
  Chinese by A. C. Graham. PLT

Phol and Wotan rode through the forest. Second Merseburg Spell.
  Unknown, tr. fr. German by Carroll Hightower. GePo

Phone-call takes him, A. Terrorist's Wife. Angela Greene. NWP

Phone Call to Rutherford. Paul Blackburn. PoM

Phone duet over the radio, A. The Louisiana Weekly #4. David
  Henderson. PoBA

Phone for the fish-knives, Norman. How to Get On in Society. Sir John
  Betjeman. NOBL; OBSV; OxBTC; UV

Phone Number. Jack Collom. UL

Phone vibrates all winter. The. Exterminator. Lucien Stryk. CAPP

Phonic. Gail Mazur. NAmP90

'Phoning. Peter Sirr. BiHa

Photo of Emily, The. Lawrence Ferlinghetti. CAPP

Photo of someone else's childhood, A. The Old Adam. Denise Levertov.
  NaP; UnPo

Photo shows me, The. The Others Hunters in the North the Cree. Jerome
  Rothenberg. PoM

Photo That Watches, The. Carlota Caulfield, *tr. fr. Spanish* by Carol
  Maier. LoHo

Photograph. Sue May. DT

Photograph. Quandra Prettyman. PoBA

Photograph at the Cloisters: April 1972. Helen Chasin. NMM

Photograph: families looking of all things shy. Stephen Berg. *Fr.*
  Memory. BTR

Photograph in a Stockholm Newspaper for March 13, 1910. Don Coles.
  NOBC

Photograph of a Child, Japanese-American Evacuation, Bainbridge Island,
  Washington, March 30, 1942. Jim Mitsui. OpBo

Photograph of Haymaker, 1890. Molly Holden. OxBTC

Photograph of Myself, The. Jon Anderson. AmPA

Photograph of Ramona Posing While Father Sketches Her in Charcoal, The.
  Lynn Emanuel. ETG

Photograph: Sheepshearing. Jo Shapcott. PWE

Photograph the Cat Licks, The. Beatrice Walter. NMM

Photographs. Charles Wright. HoPM

Photographs: A Vision of Massacre. Michael S. Harper. PoBA

Photographs, fading already, recall my discomfort. Getting It Wrong,
  Again. Steve Griffiths. AngWe

Photographs of Pioneer Women. Ruth Dallas. PeNZ

Photos, The. Diane Wakoski. NIP

Photos of a Salt Mine. P. K. Page. NIP; NoAM; NOBC

Phrasal. Anthony Barnett. VaA

Phraseology. Jayne Cortez. BISi

Phryne. John Donne. FaBoEE

Phryne whom he loved, The. (*LL*) Praxiteles and Phryne. William
  Wetmore Story. BeLS

Phyllida and Corydon. Nicholas Breton. *See* In the merry month of May.

Phyllida and Corydon. Nicholas Breton. *See* On a hill there grows a
  flower.

Phyllida flouts me. (*LL*) Phillida Flouts Me [*or* The Disdainful
  Shepherdess]. *Unknown.* CoMu; EIL; InvP; OBEV; PIP; TrGrPo

Phyllida Flouts Me, *sels. Unknown.*
  Shepherd's Enticements, The. CBCK

Phyllidula. Ezra Pound. FaBoTw

Phyllis. Nicholas Breton. TrGrPo

Phyllis. William Drummond of Hawthornden. *See* In petticoat of green.

Phyllis, *sels.* Thomas Lodge.
  "?" ESo
    (I Hope and Fear.) Son
  "Devoide of reason, thrale to foolish ire." AAS
  "Faire art thou Phillis, I, so faire (sweet mayd)." ESo
  "I would in rich and golden coloured raine." AAS; ESo
  "Long hath my sufferance labored to in force." ESo
  Love Guards [*or* Guides] the Roses of Thy Lips. EIL; NoSic; Son
    (Phillis 2.) OBEV
  No Stars Her Eyes. Son
  "Now I find thy looks were feigned." EIL; EnRePo
  O Pleasing Thoughts. Son
  Phillis ("My Phillis hath the morning sun.")
    (Phillis 1.) OBEV
    (Phyllis.) EIL

Phyllis. Thomas Randolph. BoLoP

Phyllis. Sydney King Russell. ErPo

Phyllis Corydon clutched to him. Catullus, *tr. fr. Latin* by Peter Whigham.
  BoLoP

Phyllis, for shame, let us improve. The Advice. Thomas Sackville. GGP

Phyllis, loving Demophoon. Cometas, *tr. fr. Greek* by Sam Hamill. InMo

Phyllis; or, The Progress of Love. Swift. OAEL-1; OBSV; PoE

Phyllis! why should we delay. To Phyllis. Edmund Waller. BeJo; TrGrPo

Phyllis's Age. Matthew Prior. *See* How old may Phillis *or* Phyllis be, you
  ask.

Phyllyp Sparowe [*or* Philip Sparrow]. John Skelton. AAS; OxBoLi;
  PoEL-1
  Sels.
  "It had a velvet cap." OBF
  O Cat of Carlishkind. ChTr
    (Churlyshe Cat, The.) SoCa
  "Our natural tongue is rude." EPCY
  "*Pla ce bo!* Who is there, who?" CBNP; NOBE; NoSic; OAEL-1;
    OxBoLi, *abr.*
  "When I remember again."
    (Sparrow's Dirge, The.) FaBoCh
  "Yet one thing is behind." EPCY

Physical Universe. Louis Simpson. CAPP; InPS

Physician of eminence, some years ago, A. The Lady and the Doctor.
  Helen Leigh. WoRP

Physicians' Fortune, The. Friedrich von Logau, *tr. fr. German.* GePo, *tr.*
  by George C. Schoolfield

Physics. Chase Twichell. VBLP

Physics of Ochun, The. Victor Hernandez Cruz. UL

Physiologus. Josephine Miles. BCF

Physiologus, *sels. Unknown, tr. fr. Anglo-Saxon.*
  Whale, The. AnOE, *tr.* by Charles Kennedy
    (Now I will sing about a kind of fish.) ASW, *tr.* by Kevin Crossley-
    Holland
  Whale, The EBEV

π. Wislawa Szymborska, *tr. fr. Polish* by Adam Czerniawski. PoSu

π deserves our full admiration. π. Wislawa Szymborska, *tr. fr. Polish* by
  Adam Czerniawski. PoSu

P'i-p'a begins the dance, midst changing new sounds, The. Wang Ch'ang-ling, *tr. by* Ronald C. Miao. *Fr.* Following the Army on Campaign. SuSp

Piaf and Holiday Go Out. Carole Bergé. Jaz

Piano, The. Frank Daley. NOBC

Piano. D. H. Lawrence. BLPL; CMoP; FaPoB; GrPl; GTBS-P; HAP; HeIL; HeIP; InPK; InvP; LiTB; MoAB; MoBrPo; MoP; NAEL-2; NoAM; NOBE; NoP; OAEL-2; OxBSP; PoE; Poetr; PPP; RB; SCGP; TFi; TRP; UnPo; WeW

Piano, The. D. H. Lawrence. WeW

Piano, A. Gertrude Stein. *Fr.* Tender Buttons. PBWP

Piano and Drums. Gabriel Okara. NIP; PBA; TTY

Piano at Evening. Palea, *tr. fr. Hawaiian by* M. K. Pukui *and* A. L. Korn. WTO

Piano di Sorrento. Robert Browning. *Fr.* Englishman in Italy, The. FaBoPP; PoEL-5

Piano hums, The. Effendi. Michael S. Harper. PoBA

Piano Pieces. Thomas W. Shapcott. CBAP
Sels.
Schoenberg Op. 11.
Webern.

Piano Practice. Howard Moss. NYBP

Piano Solo. Nicanor Parra, *tr. fr. Spanish by* William Carlos Williams. AnRep

Piano tuner spoke to me, that tenderest, The. Pyrargyrite Metal, 9. Cecília Meireles, *tr. fr. Portuguese by* James Merrill. PBWP

Piano Tuner's Wife, The. Karl Shapiro. NoAM

Piarco. Eric Roach. PBCV

Piazza di Spagna. Willard M. Grimes. GoYe

Piazza di Spagna, Early Morning. Richard Wilbur. GrPl; InPS; OxBSP; SM; VGW

Piazza Piece. John Crowe Ransom. AnAmPo; BoLoP; CoGr; ErPo; HeIP; MeMAP; MoAB; MoAmPo; MoP; NAAL-2; NoAM; NOBA; NoP; OPOP; OxBA; Poetr; Son; TAP; TFi; TrGrPo

Piazza Tragedy, A. Eugene Field. FiBHP; NBLV

Piazzas. Barbara Guest. NeAP

Pibroch. Ted Hughes. FaBoMo; OAEL-2

Pibroch. Sir Walter Scott. *See* Pibroch of Donuil Dhu.

Pibroch of Donuil Dhu. Sir Walter Scott. EnRP; FaBoCh; OxBS; PoEL-4

Picaro. Harry Clifton. IB

Piccadilly. Ezra Pound. AnAmPo

Piccola Commedia. Richard Wilbur. PRA

Piccolomini, The, *sels.* Schiller, *tr. fr. German by* Samuel Taylor Coleridge. Thekla's Song. AWP

Pick a fern, pick a fern, ferns are high. Ezra Pound, after the Chinese. OBVE

Pick and Poke. Gerald Stern. AnAn

Pick on somebody your own size. (*LL*) Way Down South. *Unknown.* RoPo

Pickaxes, pickaxes swinging today. Bam, Bam, Bam. Eve Merriam. PDV

Picked offhand by the angels to demonstrate. Saint Ursula of Llangwyryfon. Gwyn Williams. AngWe

Picket Fence, The. Christian Morgenstern, *tr. fr. German by* Max Knight. GrPl

Picket-Guard, The. *At. to* Ethel Lynn Beers, *sometimes at. to* Lamar Fontaine. *See* All Quiet along the Potomac.

Picketing Supermarkets. Tom Wayman. NIP

Picket's off duty forever!, The. (*LL*) All Quiet along the Potomac. *At. to* Ethel Lynn Beers, *sometimes at. to* Lamar Fontaine. AnAmPo; BeLS; FaBoBe; VPP

Pickety fence, The. David McCord. NTCP

Pickin Em Up and Layin Em Down. Maya Angelou. CBLP; NBLV

Picking Lilies. *Unknown.* OBET

Picking Tea: A Ballad. Kao Ch'i, *tr. fr. Chinese by* Irving Y. Lo. SuSp

Pickpockets. John Gay. *See* Where the mob gathers, swiftly shoot along.

Pickup in Tony's Hashhouse. Kenneth Pitchford. *Fr.* Good for Nothing Man. ErPo

Pickwick Papers, The, *sels.* Charles Dickens.
Ivy Green, The. BoNaP

Picnic. Hugh Lofting. GoJo; OTCP

Picnic, The. John Logan. TRP

Picnic. Douglas Oliver. VaA

Picnic. Nellie Wong. OpBo

Picnic Remembered. Robert Penn Warren. NAAL-2

Picnic Rhyme. *Unknown. See* Lemonade.

Picnic: the Liberated. M. Carl Holman. PoBA; PoNe

Picnic to the Earth. Tanikawa Shuntaro, *tr. fr. Japanese.* TSaS, *tr. by* Harold Wright

Picnics. *Unknown.* BoTP

Pico della Mirandola. Mason Jordan Mason. PoNe

Pict Song, A. Kipling. *Fr.* Puck of Pook's Hill. NoAM

Pictor Ignotus. Robert Browning. CTC; TEP

Picture, The. Anacreon, *tr. fr. Greek by* Thomas Stanley. AWP

Picture, A. Dora Greenwell. EBVV

Picture, A. Howard Nemerov. OxBC

Picture, A. H. Cordelia Ray. CBWP-3

Picture and book remain. An Acre of Grass. W. B. Yeats. CMoP; NoAM

Picture Bride. Cathy Song. AiP

Picture Collection. Marjorie Welish. UL

Picture from the Blitz. Lois Clark. PAW

Picture me as a heroine from some lurid rag. Cheap Thrills. Eva Salzman. NWP

Picture memory brings to me, A. Whittier. *Fr.* My Trust. OHIP

Picture of a Fine Gentleman, The. Lady Sophia Burrell. ECWP

Picture of a Girl. James Lasdun. PRA

Picture of a Japanese Farmer, Woodland, California, May 20, 1942. Jim Mitsui. OpBo

Picture of a Nativity. Geoffrey Hill. NoAM; OxBC

Picture of Dorian Gray, The, *sels.* Oscar Wilde.
"Artist is the creator of beautiful things, The." NAEL-2

Picture of J. T. in a Prospect of Stone, The. Charles Tomlinson. PPP

Picture of Little J.A. in a Prospect of Flowers, The. John Ashbery. CAPP; PPP

Picture of Little Letters. John Koethe. PRA

Picture of Little T. C. in a Prospect of Flowers, The. Andrew Marvell. ESCV; GeHe; JCP; LiTB; MeLP; NAEL-1; NOBE; NoP; OAEL-1; OBEV; OxAEP-1; PoE; PPP; PrIm; SCGP; SeCP; SeCV-1; TFi

Picture of Loot. Alan Sillitoe. OxBTC

Picture of My Mother's Family, A. Wing Tek Lum. OpBo

Picture of Okinawa, A. Dennis Schmitz. LCAP

Picture of the Body, The. Ben Jonson. NOSC

Picture of the Times, A. Philip Freneau. EAP

Picture Postcard of a Zoo. Oscar Williams. Son

Picture-Show. Siegfried Sassoon. CMoP; NSI

Picture show, three-and-a-half hours of it, The. The Trailing Consequence: A Triptych. Tino Villanueva. AfAz

Picture this. Polygamist. Charlotte M. Wright. NGP

Pictures. F. Ann Elliott. BoTP

Pictures at an Exhibition. Nathan Rosenbaum. GoYe

Pictures from Brueghel, *sels.* William Carlos Williams.
Corn Harvest, The. ArNa; PPP
Haymaking. NoAM
Hunters in the Snow, The. LCAP
Landscape with the Fall of Icarus. LCAP; NAAL-2; NoAM; PPP
Self-Portrait. LCAP

Pictures in the Smoke. Dorothy Parker. CoGr; NBLV

Pictures of a Gone World, *sels.* Lawrence Ferlinghetti.
"Away above a harborful." BoLoP; ErPo; PoM
"Dada would have liked a day like this." NeAP
"Sarolla's women in their picture hats." NeAP; PoM

Pictures of Memory. Alice Cary. *See* Among the beautiful pictures.

Pictures of the Jews. Haim Guri, *tr. fr. Hebrew by* Ruth Finer Mintz. MHP

Pictures of the Rhine. George Meredith. OBTV

Picturesque; a Fragment. John Aikin. NOEC

Piddle-paddling race of critics, rhizome-fanciers. Antiphanes, *tr. fr. Greek by* Edwin Morgan. GrAn

Pie in the Sky. *At. to* Joe Hill. *See* Long-haired preachers come out every [or ev'ry] night.

Pie sat on a pear tree, A. Hop't She. *Unknown.* GBP

Piece by piece I seem. Necessities of Life. Adrienne Rich. HCAP; NOBA; Poetr

Piece for Magic Strings, A. Li Ho, *tr. fr. Chinese by* A. C. Graham. PLT

Piece of art, a scene, a poem, A. Silence, an Eloquent Applause. Leona Gregory. TrCP

Piece of Black Bread, A. "Eduard Bagritzky," *tr. fr. Russian by* C. M. Bowra. TrJP

Piece of Brooklyn sky, A. Methode Champenoise. Steve Carey. UL

Piece of Earth, A. Douglas Livingstone. PeSAV

Piece of forest, A. Still Life. Raymond Garlick. AngWe

Piece of fossil ivory, A. A Song of the Dice. *Unknown, tr. fr. Chinese by* Kenneth Rexroth *and* Ling Chung. WPC

Piece of green pepper, A. Haiku Ambulance. Richard Brautigan. InPK

Piece of Zinc! (*LL*) An Alphabet. Edward Lear. OxBChV

Piecemeal the summer dies. Exeunt. Richard Wilbur. BoNaP; HeIP; Poetsp; PoLF

Pieces. Duane Niatum. HATNAP

Pieces of a green/ Bottle. (*LL*) Between Walls. William Carlos Williams. HoPM; SOTW; TAP; VGW

Pieces of Coal. Huw Menai. *Fr.* Back in the Return. AngWe

Pieces of coal, hewn from the deeps of earth. Pieces of Coal. Huw Menai. *Fr.* Back in the Return. AngWe

Pieces of Snot. *Unknown, tr. fr. Bella Bella Indian by* Franz Boas. STP

Pied à Terre. Anne Bloch. Mes

Pied Beauty. Gerard Manley Hopkins. ArNa; AWP; CBCK; ClHu; CMoP; EaPr; EBEvV; EBVV; EnlH; EnVR; FaBoMo; FaPoB; GGP; GoJo; GTBS-P; HAP; HeIP; HoPM; ImPo; InPK; InPS; InvP; LiTB; LiTM; LPA; MeMBP; MoAB; MoBrPo; MoP; NAEL-2; NoAM; NOBE; NOBVV; NoP; NTP; OAEL-2; OBEV; OBMV; OBNC; OxAEP-2; OxBSP; PFP; PoE; Poetr; PoRA; PPP; PrIm; RaBo; RB; SCGP; SCV; SoSe; SOTW; TEP; TFi; TrGrPo; TTTS; UV; WeW

Pied Beauty. Stanley J. Sharpless. UV

Pied Piper of Hamelin, The. (Hamelin Town's in Brunswick.) Robert Browning. BeLS; BLPL; EBNV; FaBoBe; FaBoCh; GN; OBNV; OBSP; OtMeF; OxBChV; PeLV

Sels.

"Into the street the Piper stept." BoTP; OxAEP-2

Pien River Blocked by Ice. Tu Mu, *tr. fr. Chinese by* A. C. Graham. PLT

Pier, The. Garrett Kaoru Hongo. OpBo

Pier delle Vigne. Dante, *tr. by* John Ciardi. *Fr.* Divina Commedia. HoPM; MeMAP; NAWM-1, *tr. by* John Ciardi

Pier-Glass, The. Robert Graves. CMoP; MoAB; NoAM

Pier: Under Pisces, The. James Merrill. LCAP; NoAM

Piercing brightness of the living ray, The. Dante, *tr. fr. Italian. Fr.* Divina Commedia. MeMAP; TOF, *tr. by* Dorothy L. Sayers *and* Barbara Reynolds

Piercing Chill I Feel, The. Buson, *tr. fr. Japanese by* Harold G. Henderson. InPK

Piercing winter frost, and winds, and darkened air, The. (*LL*) November. Bryant. AnAmPo; Son

Piere Vidal Old. Ezra Pound. MoAB

Piero's name is a secret. (*LL*) Names in Monterchi: To Rachel. James Wright. AnAn; NNaP

Pierre Falcon. Le Tombeau de Pierre Falcon. James Reaney. MoCV

Pierrot, no sentimental swain. Pantomime. Paul Verlaine, *tr. fr. French by* Arthur Symons. AWP

Piers are pummelled by the waves, The. The Fall of Rome. W. H. Auden. InPS; MAT; OAEL-2; OxBTC; UnPo

Piers Gaveston., *sels.* Michael Drayton.

"This Edward in the Aprill of his age." PeHV

Piers Plainness' Seven Years' Prenticeship, *sels.* Henry Chettle. Aeliana's Ditty (Of Cupid.) ElL

Piers Plowman. George Barker. *See* Most near, most dear, most loved and most far.

Pietà. Allen Afterman. NOBAu

Pietà. James McAuley. CBAP

Pieta, The, Rhenish, 14th C., The Cloisters. Mona Van Duyn. Prf

Pietà's Over, The. Paul Durcan. PBCIP

Pietà's Over — and, now, my dear, droll, husband, The. The Pietà's Over. Paul Durcan. PBCIP

Pig. Paul Éluard, *tr. fr. French by* Kenneth Koch. TTTS

Pig. Anthony Hecht. OxBC

Pig, The. Ogden Nash. RB

Pig. Vasco [*or* Vasko] Popa, *tr. fr. Romanian by* Anne Pennington. OBD

Pig, The. *Unknown.* FaBoEE

Pig, if I am not mistaken, The. The Pig. Ogden Nash. RB

Pig Island Letters, *sels.* James K. Baxter. "From an old house shaded with macrocarpas." PeNZ "When I was only semen in a gland." PeNZ

Pig lay on a barrow dead, The. View of a Pig. Ted Hughes. LiTM; OxAEP-2; OxBTC; TwCP

Pig Song. Margaret Atwood. NoP

Pig stands squarely, The. Transubstantiation. Gary Geddes. NOBC

Pig-Tale, A. "Lewis Carroll." *Fr.* Sylvie and Bruno Concluded. WiR

Pig Tale, A. James Reeves. SiSoPo

"Pig'back" she brought me where the lake surrounded. Kineo Mountain. Celeste Turner Wright. Poetsp

Pigeon-Feeders in Battery Park, The. Julia Cooley Altrocchi. GoYe

Pigeon purrs in the wood; the wodd has gone, The. Idylls of the King. Geoffrey Hill. *Fr.* Apology for the Revival of Christian Architecture in England, An. FaBoRV; NoAM; PoE

Pigeons, The. Rodney Bennett. BoTP

Pigeons. Tim Longville. VaA

Pigeons. Bert Meyers. BTR

Pigeons. Marianne Moore. PoA

Pigeons. Alastair Reid. NYBP; TwCP

Pigeons are city folk. Pigeons. Marianne Moore. PoA

Pigeons flutter'd fieldward, one and all, The. Gout and Wings. Charles Tennyson Turner. NOBVV

Pigeons on the grass alas. Gertrude Stein. *Fr.* Four Saints in Three Acts. TAP

Pigeons shake their wings on the copper church roof. Fourth Floor, Dawn, Up All Night Writing Letters. Allen Ginsberg. CAPP; PoBeRe

Pigeon's Story, The. Jeannie Kirby. BoTP

Pigeons that peck at the grass in Trinity Churchyard, The. Trinity Place. Phyllis McGinley. MoAmPo; OxBSP; SoSe

Piggy-back. Langston Hughes. TLR

Piggy on the railway, picking up stones. *Unknown.* ISE

Piggy-wig found he had four little feet. What Piggy-Wig Found. Enid Blyton. BoTP

Pigmies and Cranes. Walter Savage Landor. NOBVV

Pigs, The. Geoffrey Lehmann. CBAP

Pigs, The. Jane Taylor. FM

Pig's-Eye View of Literature, A, *sels.* Dorothy Parker. Alfred, Lord Tennyson. NALW D. G. Rossetti. NALW George Sand. FiBHP; NALW Harriet Beecher Stowe. NALW Lives and Times of John Keats, Percy Bysshe Shelley, and George Gordon Noel, Lord Byron, The. NALW Oscar Wilde. NALW Thomas Carlyle. FiBHP; NALW Walter Savage Landor. NALW

Pigs for Circe in May, The. Joanne Kyger. PoM

Pig's leg fills the plate, wine overflowing the cups, A. Rejoicing the Spirits. Fan Ch'eng-ta, *tr. by* Wu-chi Liu. *Fr.* Four Songs in Imitation of Wang Chien. SuSp

Pigs like mud. *Unknown.* RoPo

Pigs o' Pelton. *Unknown.* GBP

Pig's Tail, The. Norman Ault. BoTP

Pigsty did not reek, The. The Barn-yard. Sheila Cussons, *tr. fr. Afrikaans by* Johann de Lange. PeSAV

Pigtail. Tadeusz Różewicz, *tr. fr. Polish by* Adam Czerniawski. PoSu

Pigtail dangled down my back, A. Ballad of the Dreamy Girl. Edith Roseveare, *tr. fr. Chinese.* Mes

Pigtail hangs behind him, The. (*LL*) A Tragic Story. Adelbert von Chamisso. BoTP; FaPON; MoShBr

Pigwiggen. Michael Drayton. BoTP

Pigwiggin Arms Himself. Michael Drayton. *Fr.* Nymphidia. MoShBr

Pihsien Road. "Robin Hyde." WPE

Pike, The. Edmund Blunden. LiTM

Pike. Ted Hughes. CMoP; FaBoMo; HAP; HeIL; HeIP; InPS; LiTM; MAT; NAEL-2; OxBTC; PoE

Pilate Remembers. William E. Brooks. ChIV-2

Pilate Tapes, The, *sels.* Vincent O'Sullivan.

Pile the bodies high at Austerlitz and Waterloo. Grass. Carl Sandburg. AWP; BLPL; FaBV; MoAB; MoAmPo; MoP; NAAL-2; NoAM; NOBA; NoP; OBWP; OxBA; PeFWW; Poetr; PoLF; TFi; TrGrPo

Piled deep below the screening apple-branch. The Orchard-Pit. Dante Gabriel Rossetti. EnLoPo; NAEL-2; OAEL-2; PeVV; PoEL-5; SCV

Piled on a loading dock where I walked. Desks. Dave Jeddie Smith. HCAP

Pilgrim, The. Bunyan. *See* Who would true valour see.

Pilgrim, The. Emma Catherine Embury. OBCA

Pilgrim, The. Brendan Kennelly. TIRV

Pilgrim, The. Nicanor Parra, *tr. fr. Spanish by* W. S. Merwin. AnRep

Pilgrim, The. Richard Wightman. WGRP

Pilgrim, The. W. B. Yeats. RB

Pilgrim Cranes, The. Lord De Tabley. EBVV

Pilgrim Fathers, The. Leonard Bacon. AH; WGRP

Pilgrim Fathers, The. Felicia Dorothea Hemans. *See* Breaking waves dashed high, The.

Pilgrim Fathers, The. John Pierpont. PAH

Pilgrim Fathers, The. Wordsworth. AiP, *abr.*; PAH

Pilgrim Fathers, The — where are they? The Pilgrim Fathers. John Pierpont. PAH

Pilgrim from the East, The. Gustave Kahn, *tr. fr. French by* Jethro Bithell. TrJP

Pilgrim Song, The. Bunyan. *See* Who would true valour see.

Pilgrim Song. Florence Earle Coates. OHIP

Pilgrimage. Austin Clarke. CIP; IPY; TIRV

Pilgrimage, The. George Herbert. ChTr; ESCV; FaBoRV; GeHe; NAEL-1; NOSC; PoE

Place Me in the Breach. Yehuda Karni, *tr. fr. Hebrew by* Sholom J. Kahn. TrJP

Place Names. Thomas Merton. ChIV-1

Place-Names of China. Alan Bennett. FaBoPa; NOBL; UV

Place of Backs, The. W. S. Merwin. HoPM

Place of Fire. Johannes Bobrowski, *tr. fr. German by* Ruth Mead *and* Matthew Mead. PoSu

Place of O, The. Ray A. Young Bear. VoR

Place of Rest, The. "Æ." WGRP

Place of the Damn'd [*or* Damned], The. Swift. CBCK; ChIV-2; FaBoEE; OBSV

Place of the Fian is bare tonight, The. *Unknown.* NOIV

Place of V, The. Ray A. Young Bear. VoR

Place on a Grave. Frank Stanford. MT

Place on the table the fragrant mignonettes. All Souls' Day. Herman von Gilm zu Rosenegg, *tr. fr. German by* Philip L. Miller. RiWo

Place Pigalle. Richard Wilbur. ArOW; HeIP

Place there is, where proudly raised there stands, A. Samuel Daniel. *Fr.* Civil Wars, The. NoSic

Place to Begin, The. Judith Sornberger. MDDM

Place to begin is not your death, The. The Place to Begin. Judith Sornberger. MDDM

Place we could never enter hides away still, The. Last Visit. Robert Finch. NOBC

Place Where a Great City Stands, The. Walt Whitman. *Fr.* Song of the Broad-Ax [*or* Broad-Axe]. ImGa

Place where a great city stands is not the place of stretch'd wharves, docks, The. The Place Where a Great City Stands. Walt Whitman. *Fr.* Song of the Broad-Ax [*or* Broad-Axe]. ImGa

Place where our two gardens meet, The. The Wall. Henry Reed. LiTB

Place where she would die, The. (*LL*) My Mother's Homeland. Belkis Cuza Malé. LoHo

Place where soon I think to lie, The. Walter Savage Landor. CBLP

Place Where the Rainbow Ends, The. Paul Laurence Dunbar. PWR

Place Where Things Got. Heather McHugh. NAmP90

Place which the flying birds do not reach, A. An Excursion to the Dragon Pool Temple on Chung-nan. Meng Chiao, *tr. fr. Chinese by* A. C. Graham. PLT

Pla ce bo,/ Who is there, who? Phyllyp Sparowe. John Skelton. AAS; OxBoLi

(Philip Sparrow. NOBE; OAEL-1; PeLV; PoEL-1

Placed in the west, Manukau spreads out. Tamaki of a Hundred Lovers. Merimeri Penfold, *tr. fr. Maori by* Margaret Orbell. PeNZ

Placed in walnut shells. (*LL*) Mary Arnold the Female Monster. *Unknown.* GBP; OBET

Placed midst the tempest, whose conflicting waves. On the Death of the Rev. Dr. Kippis. Helen Maria Williams. ECWP

Placed on this isthmus of a middle state. Pope. *Fr.* Essay on Man, An. WeW

Placed out in the afternoon sun. (*LL*) Meditation for a Pickle Suite. Richard H. W. Dillard. HoPM; MT

Placed these worlds in us. (*LL*) The Lost Pilot. James Tate. ArOW; CoAP; GoJo; NoAM; NoP; OBWP; TwCP; UnPo

Places and Ways to Live. Richard Hugo. NIP

Places, Loved Ones. Philip Larkin. CMoP

Placid Man's Epitaph, A. Thomas Hardy. MoBrPo

Placid, rotted harbour has no voice, The. Arrival and Departure. Charles Eglington. PeSA

Placing a $2 Bet for a Man Who Will Never Go to the Horse Races Any More. Diane Wakoski. UnPo

Placing our emotion on a field, I said, became a nucleus of space. The Star Field. Mei-Mei Berssenbrugge. VBLP

Plague, The. Marvin Bell. PFL

Plague. Robert Creeley. PFL

Plague and Hospice. Harry Clifton. IB

Plague is Love, a plague, A! but yet. The Little Love-God. Meleager, *tr. fr. Greek by* Walter Headlam. AWP

Plague of Dead Sharks. Alan Dugan. LiTM; NoAM

Plague of Starlings, A. Robert Hayden. NoAM

Plague take all your pedants, say I! Sibrandus Schafnaburgensis. Robert Browning. *Fr.* Garden Fancies. CTC; EBVV; TEP

Plague take them, every female! The Girls of Llanbadarn. Dafydd ap Gwilym, *tr. fr. Welsh by* Leslie Norris. DiPo

Plague to thy husband, scandal to thy sex. To Marina. Sarah Fyge Egerton. ECWP

Plain be the phrase, yet apt the verse. A Utilitarian View of the *Monitor's* Fight. Herman Melville. AmPP; NAAL-1; UnPo

Plain Dealing. Alexander Brome. NOSC

Plain Dealing's Downfall. *Unknown.* OBSV

Plain Fare. Daryl Hine. CoAP

Plain Humour, shown with her whole various face. John Oldham. *Fr.* Upon the Works of Ben Joson. EPCY

Plain is alive with shadow: rout of rags, The. Cissbury Ring. Paul Coltman. PAW

Plain Language from Truthful James. Bret Harte. AnAmPo; BeLS; BLPA; CTC; EBNV; FaBoBe; NOBL; OBAL; PeLV; UV

Plain Language from Truthful James. Bret Harte. *See* I reside at Table Mountain and my name is Truthful James.

Plain of Adoration, The. *Unknown, tr. fr. Irish by* John Montague. BIrV

Plain Sense of Things, The. Wallace Stevens. HCAP; NoAM

Plain Song. Craig Raine. TOF

Plain Song Talk. Richard Eberhart. PoA

Plain Tales from the Hills, *sels.* Kipling.
  By the Hoof of the Wild Goat. OBNC
  Look, You Have Cast Out Love! OxBSP
  There Is a Tide. OxBSP

Plain Talk. William Jay Smith. FiBHP; MoAmPo

Plain truth would never serve. Take It from Me. Kenneth O. Hanson. CoAP

Plain verse to start, no tricky stuff. The Poet's Progress. Chris Mann. PeSAV

Plain was grassy, wild and bare, The. The Dying Swan. Tennyson. WiR

Plainer Dubliners amaze us, The. On the Use of Jayshus. Oliver St. John Gogarty. FaBoEE

Plainness. Jorge Luis Borges, *tr. fr. Spanish by* Norman Thomas di Giovanni. NYBP

Plains of Waterloo, The. *Unknown.* OBET

Plaint. Ebenezer Elliot. OBD; OBEV

Plaint of Flowers, A. Ernest Sandeen. CRP

Plaint of the Camel, The. Charles Edward Carryl. *See* Canary-birds feed on sugar and seed.

Plaint of the Wife, The. *Unknown, tr. fr. Russian by* W. R. S. Ralston. AWP

Plainview: 3. N. Scott Momaday. CDW

Plaisir d'Amour. Patrick Galvin. BiHa

Plaiting a dark red love-knot into her long black hair. (*LL*) The Highwayman. Alfred Noyes. BeLS; EBEvV; EBNV; FaBV; FaPON, *abr.; NTP; OBNV; OBSP; PoLF*

Plaits. Tabitha Tuckett. Mes

Plan of Salvation, The. Milton. *See* O thou in heaven and earth the only place.

Plane: Earth, The. Sun-Ra. PoBA

Plane Geometer. David McCord. NYBP

Plane tilts to Nashville, The. The Homecoming Singer. Jay Wright. PoBA; VCAP

Plane Wreck at Los Gatos (Deportee). Woody Guthrie. PrIm; WTO

Planes Landing. Jamie Grant. NOBAu

"Planet doesn't explode of itself, A," said drily. Earth ("Planet doesn't explode, A.") John Hall Wheelock. LiTM; OBD; SoSe

Planet is ours, The: and the blue and the desert spaces. The Jungle. Randolph Stow. *Fr.* Thailand Railway. CBAP

Planet of Descendance, A. William Frederick Stevenson. NOBVV

Planet of Nothing fills the sky, The. The Day You Are Reading This. William Stafford. PoA

Planet on the Table, The. Wallace Stevens. HAP; HCAP; SAmP

Planet that we plant upon, The. Imagine Grass. Knute Skinner. SM

Planetarium. Adrienne Rich. CAPP; FaBoWP; HCAP; MoP; NAAL-2; NALW; NIP; NoAM; NOBA; Poetr; VCAP

Planetary Arc-Light, The. August Derleth. GoYe

Planets of air. Invisibility O. Víctor Hernández Cruz. AfAz

Planh, *sels.* Ray DiPalma.

Plankton. Ruth Miller. PeSA

Plans. Helen Morgan Brooks. PoNe

Plans. Brendan Kennelly. BiHa

Plans. Maxine W. Kumin. TLR

Plans for Altering the River. Richard Hugo. FYAP

Plant a Tree. Lucy Larcom. WBLP

Plant the 'ahi'a and cause it to propagate. The Crawlers. Keaulumoku, *tr. fr. Hawaiian by* M. W. Beckwith. *Fr.* Kumulipo, The; a Creation Chant. WTO

Plant without moisture sweet, A. Rising in the Morning. Hugh Rhodes. OxBChV

Plantation Bitters. *Unknown.* FaBoUs

Planted alternately? (*LL*) Lazy. Lu Yu. OHMPC

Planted Heel, The. Sir Arthur Quiller-Couch. EBVV

Planted in me. (*LL*) Frailty. George Herbert. NOCV

Planter. Richard Murphy. *Fr.* Battle of Aughrim, The. BIrV

Planter's Daughter, The. Austin Clarke. CIP; OxBTC

Planticru, The. Robert Rendall. OxBS

Planting. George Wither. *Fr.* Collection of Emblemes, Ancient and Moderne, A. NOSC

Planting a Cedar. Linda Hogan. BCF

Planting Bamboos. Po Chü-i, *tr. fr. Chinese by* Arthur Waley. ArNa

Planting Flowers on the Eastern Embankment. Po Chü-i, *tr. by* Arthur Waley. BoNaP

Planting of the Apple-Tree, The. Bryant. GN; OHIP

Planting Onions. Jane Flanders. CrSp

Planting Rice. *Unknown.* SWP

Planting rice is never fun. Planting Rice. *Unknown.* SWP

Planting the Poplar. Louise Imogen Guiney. AmWP

Planting Trees. Violet Helen Friedlaender. BoNaP

Planting Trout in the Chicago River. Dennis Schmitz. AnAn

Plantings. Catalina Cariaga. LoHo

Plants and Animals in the Garden. Wendy Johnson. EaPr

Plants don't talk, people say. Rosalía de Castro, *tr. fr. Spanish by* Doris Earnshaw. WPOW

Plants grow. Old Merina Theme. Flavien Ranaivo, *tr. fr. French by* Ellen Conroy Kennedy. NegPo

Plaque, *sels.* Harry Mathews.
 ABC From the Store. CBCK

Plaque in the Reading Room for My Classmates Killed in Korea, The. F. D. Reeve. GOA

Plashes the Fountain. Paul Celan, *tr. fr. German by* Michael Hamburger. OBVE

Plashes the tree-trunk lost in the river. Remember Thou Me. *Malay Oral Tradition, tr. by* R. J. Wilkinson *and* R. O. Winstedt. WTO

Platform. Rachel Hadas. UnDi

Platinum blonde, Goldilocks, A. Fiona Pitt-Kethley. PeLi

Plato, despair! Meditation on Statistical Method. J. V. Cunningham. CoAP; VGW

Plato Told. E. E. Cummings. *Fr.* One Times One. ArOW; CTC

Plato Told Him. E. E. Cummings. AmPP; CTC; MoP; NoAM; NOBA; OxBA; PoE

Plato told/ him. Plato Told Him. E. E. Cummings. AmPP; CTC; MoP; NoAM; NOBA; OxBA; PoE

Plato told/ him:he couldn't. Plato Told. E. E. Cummings. *Fr.* One Times One. ArOW; CTC

Platonic. Dudley North. NOSC

Platonic is a pretty name. Platonic. Dudley North. NOSC

Platonic Lady, The. The Earl of Rochester. NOSC

Platonic Love. Lord Herbert of Cherbury. NOSC

Platonic love! — a pretty name. On Platonic Love. Samuel Boyse. ECEV

Platonic[k] Love. Abraham Cowley. *Fr.* Mistress, The. BeJo; NoP; SeCV-1

Plato's great longing, my foot helplessly kicking space. (*LL*) First Night. Michael Hofman. CBLP

Plato's Tomb. *Unknown. See* Eagle! why soarest thou above that tomb?

Platted quite neat to catch applause, with a sliding noose at the end. (*LL*) Her Whole Life Is an Epigram. Blake. FaBoEE; InPK; OAEL-2

Platypus, The. *Aborigine Oral Tradition.* NOBAu

Platypus, The. Oliver Herford. FiBHP; PeLV

Plaudite, or End of Life, The. Robert Herrick. CaPo

Play. A. R. Ammons. PoA

Play. Frank Asch. NTCP

Play-acting. Frances Barber. GoYe

Play I could once; but, gentle friend, you see. To His Friend, on the Untunable. Robert Herrick. CaPo

Play is done, The; the curtain drops. The End of the Play. Thackeray. *Fr.* Dr. Birch and His Young Friends. GN

Play it once. Saturday Night. Langston Hughes. MoAmPo

Play of the Four P.P., The, *sels.* John Heywood.

Play of the Weather, The, *sels.* John Heywood.

Play, Phoebus, on thy lute. A Canticle to Apollo. Robert Herrick. CaPo

Play Song. Peter Clarke. PBA

Play that thing. Jazz Band in a Parisian Cabaret. Langston Hughes. MoAmPo

Play their offensive and defensive parts. Good Christians. Robert Herrick. LiTB

Play Time. Blake. *See* When the voices of children are heard on the green/ And laughing is heard on the hill.

Play Up! Play Up! Sir Henry Newbolt. *See* There's a breathless hush in the Close tonight.

Play up! play up! and play the game! (*LL*) Vitaï Lampada. Sir Henry Newbolt. BLPA; EBEvV; FaBoEH; FaPoR; NSI; OBWP; PlP; UV; VPP

Play Way, The. Seamus Heaney. NoP

Playboy. Richard Wilbur. FF; MoP; NoAM; NOBA; NoP

Playboy of the Demi-World[: 1938], The. William Plomer. IHNG; OxBTC; PeHV; UV

Played backwards on his grandson's eyes. (*LL*) Grandfather. Michael S. Harper. CAPP; LCAP; TAP; VCAP

Played with the brook, all day till twilight. At Clear Brook in Ch'ih-chou. Tu Mu, *tr. fr. Chinese by* A. C. Graham. PLT

Player Piano, The. Randall Jarrell. MT; NAAL-2

Player Piano. John Updike. Poetr; WeW

Playful monkey frisks with grand, A. Retinue. Paul Verlaine, *tr. fr. French by* C. F. MacIntyre. ErPo

Playgrounds. Laurence Alma-Tadema. BoTP

Playhouse, The. Joseph Addison. ECEV

Playhouse Key, The. Rachel Field. BoTP; FaPON

Playhouse Musings. James Smith. OxAEP-2

Playing All a Summer's Day by the Lake. Chu Shu-chen, *tr. fr. Chinese by* Kenneth Rexroth *and* Ling Chung. WPC

Playing at Cards. Belle Randall. CRP

Playing Cards, The. Pope. *Fr.* Rape of the Lock, The. ChTr; FHYEP; HAP; ImPo; NoP; OAEL-1; OBNV; PeLV; PoEL-3; TEP; TrGrPo

Playing Monopoly's. It's a Bit Rich. Max Fatchen. OTCP

Playing once with facile. Asclepiades, *tr. fr. Greek by* Kenneth Rexroth. PGA

Playing Pocahontas. Lew Blockcolski. VoR

Playing the Game. *Unknown.* PWR

Playing the Invisible Saxophone en el Combo de las Estrellas. Harryette Mullen. Jaz

Playing the 7th. 48 Words for a Woman's Dance Song. Jerome Rothenberg. PoM

Playing Through Old Games of Chess. Andrew Waterman. SCBI

Playing with Fire. James Simmons. CIP

Playing with friends one time. What Her Girl Friend Said to Him (on Her Behalf) When He Came by Daylight. *Unknown, tr. fr. Tamil by* A. K. Ramanujan. PLW

Playing your trumpets. Mosquitoes. Franz Wright. LCAP

Playmates. Lillian Everts. GoYe

Plays. Walter Savage Landor. EnRP; NBLV; NoP; OxBoLi; OxBSP; PeLV

Playwright, convict of public wrongs to men. On Playwright. Ben Jonson. NoP

Plea. John Ciardi. OxBSP

Plea for a Captive. W. S. Merwin. NoAM; NYBP

Plea for a Navy., *sels. Unknown.*
 "Trewe process of English polycye, The." FaBoEH

Plea for Flood Ireson, A. Charles Timothy Brooks. PAH

Plea for Hope. Francis Carlin. TrPWD

Plea for Mercy, A. Elizabeth Bartlett. FaBoBl

Plea for Mercy, A. Kwesi Brew. PBA

Plea for Peace. Frank Prewett. HATNAP

Plea for Tolerance. Margaret E. Bruner. PoToHe

Plea for Trigamy, A. Sir Owen Seaman. NOBL; PeLV

Plea for Workmen's Compensation, A. William Wantling. Jaz

Plea of the Midsummer Fairies, The. Thomas Hood. OBNC
 Sels.
 Fairy's Reply to Saturn, The.
 Green Dryad's Plea, The.
 Melodies of Time, The.
 Shakespeare: The Fairies' Advocate.

Plea to Boys and Girls, A. Robert Graves. GTBS-P; NAEL-2

Plea to My Sister, A. James Cunningham. JB

Plea to Those Who Matter. James Welch. AmPA

Plead for Me. Emily Brontë. MeMBP; PoEL-5

Pleaders, The. Peter Davison. NYBP

Pleading image of his native land, The. (*LL*) Wellington. Charles Harpur. NOBAu

Pleasant and Delightful. *Unknown.* OBET; OxBSS

Pleasant Changes. Jane Euphemia Browne. OxBChV

Pleasant Comedy of Patient Grissell [*or* Grissel *or* Grissill], The, *sels.* Thomas Dekker *and others.*
 "Art thou poor, yet hast thou golden slumbers?" HAP; InPS; NoSic; SCGP; UnPo
 (Basket-Maker's Song, The.) TrGrPo
 (Happy Heart, The.) GTBS; GTBS-P; RB; SCGP
 (Sweet Content.) CH; EiL; GGP; OBEV; OtMeF
 Beauty, Arise! EIL
 (Bridal Song, A ("Beauty arise, show forth thy glorious shining!").) TrGrPo
 Golden Slumbers. ELP; NoSic; OxAEP-1; SCGP

Ploughman, The. Karle Wilson Baker. WGRP

Ploughman. Patrick Kavanagh. TIRV

Ploughman, The. *Unknown.* CoMu; GBP

Ploughman at the Plough. Louis Golding. OHIP

Ploughman he comes home at night, The. The Ploughman. *Unknown.* GBP

Ploughman he's a bonnie lad, The. The Ploughman. *Unknown.* CoMu

Ploughman, in Imitation of Milton, The. Samuel Jones. NOEC

Ploughman: In Welsh Uplands, The. A. G. Prys-Jones. AngWe

Ploughman ploughing a level field. To a Schoolboy. *Unknown, tr. fr. Serbian* by Anne Pennington. RB

Ploughman Singing. John Clare. EnVR

Ploughman's Horse, The. Robert Bloomfield. *Fr.* Winter. ECEV

Ploughman's Song, The. Nicholas Breton. *See* In the merry month of May.

Plow, Maro, the plains. *Unknown, tr. fr. Serbo-Croatian* by Charles Simic. HSix

Plow: "My beak is bent downward, I burrow below." Unknown, formerly at. to Cynewulf, *tr. fr. Anglo-Saxon. Fr.* Riddles (Exeter Book). AnOE

Plower, The. Padraic Colum. MoBrPo

Plowman. Sidney Keyes. MoAB; PoRA

Plowman, The. *Unknown.* APAS

Pluck the Fruit and Taste the Pleasure. Thomas Lodge. *Fr.* Robert, Second Duke of Normandy. EiL; EnRePo; OxAEP-1

Pluck Wins. *Unknown.* PWR

Plucke the fruite and tast the pleasure. Pluck the Fruit and Taste the Pleasure. Thomas Lodge. *Fr.* Robert, Second Duke of Normandy. EiL; EnRePo; OxAEP-1

Plucking Out a Rhythm. Lawson Fusao Inada. AmPA; Jaz

Plucking the flowers of the abyss. *(LL)* On the Death of Her Body. James K. Baxter. PeNZ

Plucking the Rushes. *Unknown, tr. fr. Chinese.* BoLoP; Mes; OBVE

Plug. Edmund Vance Cooke. PWR

Plum. Liu Sha-ho. *Fr.* Family of Plants, A. LHF, *tr.* by Hualing Nieh

Plum-blossom, The. Akahito, *tr. fr. Japanese* by Arthur Waley. *Fr.* Manyo Shu, Part 3 of 4. AWP; TAL

Plum Blossoms. Chu Shu-chen, *tr.* by Kenneth Rexroth *and* Ling Chung. PBWP; WPC

Plum Blossoms. Su Shih, *tr.* by Irving Y. Lo. *Fr.* On Chao Ch'ang's Flower Paintings in Wang Po-yang's Collection. SuSp

Plum Blossoms on Solitary Hill. Wang An-shih, *tr. fr. Chinese* by Jan W. Walls. SuSp

Plum blossoms will be hard to come by. *(LL)* Tune: "Pure Serene Music." Li Ch'ing-chao. SuSp, *tr.* by Eugene Eoyang

Plum flowers all fallen and gone. *Unknown, tr.* by Michael E. Workman. *Fr.* Tzu-yeh Songs of the Four Seasons. SuSp

Plum Pudding, A. Mother Goose. *See* Flour of England, fruit of Spain.

Plum-pudding, goose, capon, minced pies, and roast beef. *(LL)* Old Christmas Returned. *Unknown.* GN; OHIP

Plum tree breaks out in bees, The. April. Charles Wright. CAPP; MT

Plum Tree by the House, The. Oliver St. John Gogarty. OBEV; PoRA

Plum Trees. Ranko, *tr. fr. Japanese.* FaPON

Plumber from Lowater Creek, A. *Unknown.* PeLi

Plumber is icumen in. Murie Sing. Archibald Y. Campbell. FaBoPa

Plumber may be a poet, but a poet is not likely, A. The Difference. Stoddard King. OBAL

Plumes of love are black, The! Mad Sonnet 1. Michael McClure. PoM

Plumpuppets, The. Christopher Morley. FaPON

Plums. Joseph Bruchac. ETG

Plums. Gillian Clarke. SCBI

Plums leave their tartness, weakening my teeth. Early Summer Waking from a Nap. Yang Wan-li, *tr. fr. Chinese* by Sherwin S. S. Fu. SuSp

Plunging and labouring on in a tide of visions. In Front of the Landscape. Thomas Hardy. OBNC

Plunging downward through the slimy water. Death by Drowning. Elizabeth Brewster. NOBC

Plunging towards Phrygia over violent water. Attis. Catullus, *tr. fr. Latin* by Peter Whigham. OBVE

Pluralist and Old Soldier, The. John Collier. NOEC

"Plus Ça Change . . ." Philip Whalen. PoBeRe

Plush bees above a bed of dahlias. England. A. S. J. Tessimond. IHNG (England, Autumn 1938. FaBoEH

Plush juice of, The. For Geraldine. Tony Baker. NBrP

Plutarch. Agathias, *tr. fr. Greek* by Dryden. AWP

Plying our trades, in hopes of a good drowing. *(LL)* Marginalia. Richard Wilbur. CMoP; PoA

Pneumoconiosis. Duncan Bush. AngWe

Po' Boy. *Unknown.* AS

Po Chu-i, balding old politician. As I Step over a Puddle at the End of Winter, I Think of an Ancient Chinese Governor. James Wright. CAPP; NaP

Po' lil' brack sheep dat strayed away. The Little Black Sheep. Paul Laurence Dunbar. WBLP

Po' los' boy, bebby,/ Evahmo.' *(LL)* Southern Road. Sterling A. Brown. BPo; PoBA

Po, po, po, po. *Unknown.* MiEL

Po, the unrivalled poet. To Li Po on a Spring Day. Tu Fu, *tr. fr. Chinese* by Robert Payne. TAL

Poacher, The. Gregory Orfalea. BTR

Poacher, The. *Unknown. See* When I was bound apprentice, in famous Lincolnshire.

Poaching in Excelsis. G. K. Menzies. FaBoCo

Pobble Who Has No Toes, The. Edward Lear. CBNP; FaBoCh; FaBoCo; FaBoNo; MoShBr; OTCP; OxBChV

Pocahontas. George Pope Morris. PAH

Pocahontas. Thackeray. FaPON; GN; PAH

Pocahontas, sels. Thackeray. "Wearied arm, and broken sword." AiP

Pock-marked player of the accordion, The. Wedding Party. Donald Hall. LCAP

Pocket, it is Poems by Pierre Reverdy. *(LL)* A Step Away from Them. Frank O'Hara. HCAP; InPS; NAAL-2; VCAP; VGW

Pocket Watch. Novica Tadic, *tr. fr. Serbo-Croatian* by Charles Simic. HSix

Pockets of our greatcoats full of barley, The. Requiem for the Croppies. Seamus Heaney. BIrV; CIP; FaBoMo; OBWP

Pocomania. Philip Sherlock. PBCV

Pod of the Milkweed. Robert Frost. *See* Calling all butterflies of every race.

Pods of summer crowd around the door. Fall Wind. William Stafford. FoLa

P.O.E. Lincoln Kirstein. PoWW

Poe. James Russell Lowell. *See* There comes Poe, with his raven, like Barnaby Rudge.

Poe, a very sick man in Baltimore. The Poets of Hell. Karl Shapiro. NYBP

Poe and Longfellow. James Russell Lowell. *Fr.* Fable for Critics, A. AmPP; NOBA; OxBA; TAP

Poe-'em of Passion, A. Charles Fletcher Lummis. BXAP

Poem: To the Coast Indian. Steve Carey. UL

Poem: "About the size of an old-style dollar bill." Elizabeth Bishop. FYAP; HCAP; NoAM; VCAP

Poem: "Ah, I know what happiness is!" Blanche Taylor Dickinson. CDC

Poem: "All the mirrors in the world." Frank O'Hara. CAPP

Poem: "And when I pay death's duty." Robin Blaser. NeAP

Poem: "As the cat." William Carlos Williams. FaPON; InPS; InvP; NoP; OFC; PDV; SoCa; SoSe; TTTS

Poem: "At night Chinamen jump." Frank O'Hara. CBNP; NoAM; NOBA; SM

Poem: "Clitoris is a kind of brain, A." Alice Notley. UL

Poem: "Country, The/ was back in the hands of the patriots." Fred Levinson. AmPA

Poem: "Disturbing to have a person." Barbara Guest. FaBoWP

Poem: "Eager note on my door said 'Call me,' The." Frank O'Hara. CAPP; NoAM; NOBA; Poetr

Poem: "Every morning I forget how it is." Charles Simic. NNaP

Poem: "Father of all! in Death's relentless claim." Oliver Wendell Holmes. TrPWD

Poem: "Figures in the fields against the sky!" Antonio Machado Ruiz, *tr. fr. Spanish* by John Dos Passos. AWP

Poem: "First day of May Jack." Tony Baker. NBrP

Poem: "For years I've heard." Robin Blaser. NeAP

Poem: "Form is the woods: the beast." James Harrison. FoLa; VGW

Poem: "Frail sound of a tunic trailing, A." Antonio Machado Ruiz, *tr. fr. Spanish* by John Dos Passos. AWP

Poem: "Geranium, houseleek, laid in oblong beds." John Gray. NOBVV

Poem: "Hate is only one of many responses." Frank O'Hara. NeAP; SOTW

Poem: "He lying spilt like water from a bowl." Alison Boodson. ErPo

Poem: "He watched with all his organs of concern." W. H. Auden. PoA

Poem: "Here we are again together." Frank O'Hara. ArLo

Poem: "I believe the yellow flowers think with me." Alice Notley. UL

Poem: "I cannot tell, not I, why she." Walter Savage Landor. GBL; OAEL-2

Poem: "I do not want only." Colleen Thibaudeau. NOBC

Poem: "I don't know as I get what D.H. Lawarence is driving at." Frank O'Hara. LCAP

Poem: "I had never heard of the whiteness." David Schloss. PoA

Poem: "I have brought it to my heart to be a still point." John Riley. VaA

Poem "I knew a woman." Theodore Roethke. *See* I knew a woman, lovely in her bones.

Poem: "I lived in the first century of world wars." Muriel Rukeyser. UnPo

Poem: "I love the old melodious lays." Whittier. AnAmPo; NoP; OxBA; TAP

Poem: "I loved my friend." Langston Hughes. NTCP; SiSoPo

Poem: "I sing th' adventures of mine worthy wights." Thomas Morton. SCAP

Poem: "I think that I shall never read." Tom Disch. UV

Poem: "I watched an armory combing its bronze bricks." Frank O'Hara. NoP

Poem: "I'm like all lovers, wanting love to be." Lesbia Harford. NOBAu

Poem: "In its going down, the moon." Robert Hoggra. MoCV

Poem: "In the early evening, as now, a man is bending." Louise Glück. HCAP

(Poem: "In the early evening, as now, a man is bending.") Poetr

Poem: "In the earnest path of duty." Charlotte Forten. BlSi

Poem: "It's a dull poem." Steve Jonas. PeHV

Poem: "Khrushchev is coming on the right day!" Frank O'Hara. NeAP; PoM

Poem: "Lana Turner has collapsed!" Frank O'Hara. CAPP; VGW

Poem: "Little brown boy." Helene Johnson. CDC; PoBA; ShDr

(Little brown Boy.) VBLP

Poem: "Look at me 8th." Sonia Sanchez. PoBA

Poem: "Naked is the earth." Antonio Machado Ruiz, *tr. fr. Spanish by* John Dos Passos. AWP

Poem: "Night is beautiful, The." Langston Hughes. CDC

Poem: "Nothing move thee." St. Theresa of Avila, *tr. fr. Spanish by* Yvor Winters. CRP

Poem: "O men, walk on the hills." Maxwell Bodenheim. TrJP

Poem: "O solo mio, hot diggety, nix "I wather think I can." Frank O'Hara. TTTS

Poem: "Of old, when Scarron his companions invited." Goldsmith. *Fr.* Retaliation. NOIV; OxBoLi

Poem: "Old man in the crystal morning after snow." Delmore Schwartz. PoA

Poem: "On getting a card." William Carlos Williams. VGW

Poem: "On this hill crossed." Galway Kinnell. NaP

Poem: "Only response, The." William Knott. InPK

Poem: "Painter of Dante's awful ferry-ride, The." Babette Deutsch. PoA

Poem: "Person who can do, The." Alan Dugan. ErPo

Poem: "Puriri moth's wing, A." Jan Kemp. PeNZ

Poem: "Rise Oedipus, and if thou canst unfould." Thomas Morton. SCAP

Poem: "Rose fades/ and is renewed again, The." William Carlos Williams. Poetr

Poem: "Roses every one were red, The." John Gray. NOBVV

Poem: "So many pigeons at Columbus." Arthur Gregor. VGW

Poem: "So they begin. With two years gone." Boris Pasternak, *tr. fr. Russian by* C. M. Bowra. TrJP

Poem: "Some who are uncertain compel me." Art Lange. UL

Poem: "Sometimes I wish that I were Helen-fair." Lesbia Harford. NOBAu

Poem: "There I could never be a boy." Frank O'Hara. NNaP

Poem: "Thing, The/ To do/ Is organize." Kenneth Koch. CAPP

Poem: "This beauty that I see." James Schuyler. PoA

Poem: "This life like no other." Gregory Orr. AmPA

Poem: "This poem is not addressed to you." Donald Justice. CAPP

Poem: "Time and the weather wear away." Donald Justice. *See* Time and the weather wear away.

Poem: "Upended, it crouches on broken limbs." Charles Tomlinson. CMoP

Poem: "We think to create festivals." Antonio Machado Ruiz, *tr. fr. Spanish by* John Dos Passos. AWP

Poem: "Were I a king, I could command content." Edward de Vere, Earl of Oxford. NoSic

(Doubtful Choice, A.) ElL

(Epigram: "Were I a king, I could command content.") FaBoEE; OxBSP

(Epigram.) GGP

(Were I a King.) NTP

Poem: "What ailes Pigmalion? Is it lunacy." Thomas Morton. SCAP

Poem: "What's the balm." Alan Dugan. CAPP; SM

Poem: "When I was still a child." Lesbia Harford. NOBAu

Poem: "You are ill and so I lead you away." Alfred W. Purdy. NOBC

Poem: "Your face,/so pale now it is blue." David St. John. AmPA

Poem about a Ball in the Nineteenth Century. William Empson. CBNP

Poem about a Seashell. Ranice Henderson Crosby. NMM

Poem about a Wolf Maybe Two Wolves, A. *Unknown, tr. fr. Seneca Indian by* Jerome K. Rothenberg *and* Richard Johnny John. STP

Poem about Breasts, A. James Wright. TAP

Poem about Breath. David Wagoner. NoAM

Poem about Faith, A. Kathleen Norris. CrSp

Poem about Morning. William Meredith. NYBP

Poem about My Rights. June Jordan. GLP; NoAM

Poem about People. Robert Pinsky. VCAP

Poem about Poems about Vietnam, A. Jon Stallworthy. NoAM

Poem about the Future. Hans Magnus Enzensberger. PoSu

Poem, after A. E. Housman. Hugh Kingsmill. *See* What, still alive at twenty–two.

Poem after Apollinaire. Ira Sadoff. AmPA

Poem after Leopardi. Mark Strand. AnAn

Poem against Catholics. James Fenton *and* John Fuller. OBSV; PeLV

Poem against Rats, A. Fred Levinson. AmPA

Poem against the Rich. Robert Bly. NOBA

Poem and Message. Dannie Abse. TEP

Poem as Light, The. John Riley. VaA

Poem As Mask, The. Muriel Rukeyser. CrSp; NALW

Poem ascends, The. (*LL*) The Jacob's Ladder. Denise Levertov. AmPP; CAPP; ChIV-1; PoM; PPP

Poem at Equinox. Hilary Corke. NYBP

Poem at Thirty. Sonia Sanchez. BlSi; BPo; NMM; NTP; PoBA

Poem at Thirty-nine. Alice Walker. CrSp

Poem before Departure. Jean Burden. WPE

Poem Beginning with a Line by Cavafy. Derek Mahon. PNI

Poem Beginning with a Line by Pindar, A. Robert Duncan. NeAP; NNaP; PoM; VCAP

Poem: "Between rebellion as a private study and the public." Charles Donnelly. *See* Between rebellion as a private study and the public.

Poem by a Perfectly Furious Academician. Shirley Brooks. FiBHP; NOBVV; PeLV

Poem by a Yellow Woman. Sook Lyol Ryu. WoWa

Poem by the Bridge at Ten-shin. Li Po, *tr. fr. Chinese by* Ezra Pound. OBVE

Poem by the Charles River. Robin Blaser. NeAP

Poem: "By the road to the contagious hospital." William Carlos Williams. *See* By the road to the contagious hospital.

Poem Called Poem. James Whitehead. GrPl

Poem Circling Hamtramck, Michigan All Night in Search of You, The. Philip Levine. NNaP

Poem Containing Some Remarks on the Present War, A. *Unknown.* PAH

Poem Dedicated to Mrs. Blennerhasset, the Only Female Member of the Limerick Hell Fire Club, A. Daniel Hayes. IIP

Poem Ended by a Death. Fleur Adcock. PeNZ

Poem Entitled the Day and the War, A, *sels.* James Madison Bell. "Though Tennyson,the poet king." AAP

Poem Entreating of Sorrow, A. Sir Walter Ralegh. *See* My day's delight[s], my springtime joys for[e]done.

Poem for a Chorus. Marie Cartier. CrSp

Poem for a Dead Poet. Roger McGough. NTP

Poem . . . For a Lover. Mae V. Cowdery. ShDr

Poem for a Marriage. Christine Craig. AIW

Poem for a Poet, A. Don L. Lee. PoBA

Poem for a Poet, A. Audre Lorde. NMM

Poem for Aretha. Nikki Giovanni. BPo; PoBA

Poem for August — or for My Birthday. Geraldine Monk. NBrP

Poem for Ben Barney. Leslie Silko. CDW; VoR

Poem for Black Boys. Nikki Giovanni. BPo

Poem for Black Hearts, A. Amiri Baraka. PoBA; PoM; SOTW

Poem For Buddy. June Jordan. PFL

Poem for Carroll, Descendant of Chiefs. Lance Henson. VoR

Poem for Children, A; or, On Cruelty to the Irrational Creation. Jane Cave. ECWP

Poem for Christmas, A. C. A. Snodgrass. PoToHe

Poem for Diane Wakoski, A. Ray A. Young Bear. CDW

Poem for Easter. Robert Kelly. VGW

Poem for Emily, A. Miller Williams. MT; WeW

Poem for Etheridge. Sonia Sanchez. BPo

Poem for Flora. Nikki Giovanni. BPo; CrSp; PoBA

Poem for Francis Harvey. Madge Herron. VBLP

Poem for Friends. Quincy Troupe. PoBA

Poem for Garcia Lorca. George Woodcock. NOBC

Poem for George Helm: Aloha Week 1980. Eric Chock. OpBo

Poem for Gerard. Edward Leslie Mayo. BCF

Poem for Half White College Students. Amiri Baraka. BPo; TAP; UnPo

Poem for Integration, A. Alvin Saxon. PoBA

Poem for Jacqueline Hill. *Unknown.* BrRo

Poems of the Arabic. *Unknown, tr. by* Sir Richard Burton. *Fr.* Thousand and One Nights, The. ErPo

Poems of the Hundred Flowers Blooming. Ch'en Hsiao-keng, *tr. fr. Chinese.* LHF, *tr. by* Hualing Nieh

Poems of the Yellow Patch, *sels.* H. Leivick, *tr. fr. Yiddish by* Benjamin *and* Barbara Harshav.

Poems of Z, *sels.* Paul Hyland.
"I am a puppet." PWE
"I do not listen much." PWE

Poems on the Ch'i-huai, *sels.* Wang Shih-chieng, *tr. fr. Chinese by* Daniel Bryant.

Poems on Yi Garden: Written for Mr. Juan-t'ing, *sels.* Wu Wen, *tr. fr. Chinese by* Chang Yin-nan.

Poems to a Brown Cricket. James Wright. NaP; NYBP

Poems We Can Understand. Paul Hoover. EOEF

Poems Written at the Construction Site of the Ming Tombs Dam, *sels.* Pien Chih-lin.
Dialogue at the Ground-Breaking Ceremony, A. LHF, *tr. by* Hualing Nieh
Embrace the Flood. LHF, *tr. by* Hualing Nieh
Goggles and Telescopes. LHF, *tr. by* Hualing Nieh
Salute to the Construction of the Dam. LHF, *tr. by* Hualing Nieh
View From the Ming Tombs, The. LHF, *tr. by* Hualing Nieh

Poems Written during My Sojourn in Japan, *sels.* Su Man-shu, *tr. fr. Chinese.*
"On the bank of Lake Rouge a chestnut steed treads proudly." SuSp
"She puts on a silken blouse and comes down from the western chamber." SuSp
"Shouldn't I pilfer wantonly this famed fragrance of a foreign land?" SuSp

Poems Written in Prison, *sels.* Ch'ien Ch'ien-i, *tr. fr. Chinese.*
"Fishing cove and long lines of fishermen's huts, A." SuSp
"Nightly the watchman's rattle startles my sleep." SuSp
"Spluttering burnt-out lamp blazes in the dusk." SuSp

Poesy to Prove Affection is Not Love, A. Sir Walter Ralegh. *See* Conceit Begotten by the Eyes.

Poet, The. Ai Ch'ing, *tr. fr. Chinese.* LHF, *tr. by* Hualing Nieh

Poet, The. Joel Benton. WGRP

Poet, The. Elizabeth Barrett Browning. EPCY; WGRP

Poet, The. Bryant. EAP; NAAL-1; TAP

Poet, The. Witter Bynner. WGRP

Poet, The. Paul Laurence Dunbar. AAP; BPo

Poet. Emerson. *Fr.* Quatrains. OxBA; OxBSP; Spl

Poet, The. Padraic Fiacc. CIP

Poet, The. Goethe, *tr. fr. German by* Philip L. Miller. RiWo

Poet. Donald Jeffrey Hayes. PoNe

Poet, The. Amy Lowell. WGRP

Poet, The. Edwin Markham. WGRP

Poet, The. Angela Morgan. WGRP
Sels.
"Why hast thou breathed, O God, upon my thoughts." TrPWD

Poet, The. Thomas Randolph. OxBSP

Poet. Karl Shapiro. CMoP; LiTM; MoAB; MoAmPo; NoAM

Poet, The. Elizabeth Oakes Smith. AmWP

Poet. Peter Viereck. HoPM; MoAmPo

Poet, The. Sir William Watson. *Fr.* Two Epigrams. TrGrPo

Poet, The. Walt Whitman. *Fr.* By Blue Ontario's Shore. MoAmPo

Poet, The. Yone Noguchi. WGRP

Poet, A. Thomas Hardy. NoAM

Poet, A! — He Hath Put His Heart to School. Wordsworth. EnRP; EPCY

Poet alone in my country, A. On Being a Poet in Sierra Leone. Syl Cheney-Coker. HBAPE

Poet and His Book, The. Edna St. Vincent Millay. MoAmPo

Poet and His Patron, The. Edward Moore. ECEV
Sels.
"Why, Celia, is your spreading waist"

Poet and his song, The. *(LL)* Auspex. James Russell Lowell. PoEL-5; TAP

Poet and His Songs, The. Longfellow. AnAmPo

Poet and priest, keeping my pride secret. *(LL)* Daedalus, The Maker. Thomas McCarthy. IB

Poet and Saint! to thee alone are given. On the Death of Mr. Crashaw. Abraham Cowley. BeJo; EPCY; MeLP; SeCP; SeCV-1

Poet and the Rose, The. John Gay. *Fr.* Fables. PeLV; TEP

Poet and the Schizophrenic, The. Andrew Duncan. NBrP

Poet and War, The. Albert Ehrenstein, *tr. fr. German by* Christopher Middleton. PeFWW

Poet, as Epilogue, The. Wilhelm Müller, *tr. fr. German by* Philip L. Miller. *Fr.* Beautiful Maid of the Mill, The. RiWo

Poet as King of Gotham, The. Charles Churchill. *Fr.* Gotham. NOEC

Poet, as Prologue, The. Wilhelm Müller, *tr. fr. German by* Philip L. Miller. *Fr.* Beautiful Maid of the Mill, The. RiWo

Poet at Fifty, The. Laurence David Lerner. PeSA

Poet at Night-Fall, The. Glenway Wescott. PoA

Poet at Seven, The. Donald Justice. MT; WeW

Poet at Seven, The. Robert Lowell, *tr. fr. French.* NaP, *ad. by* Rimbaud

Poet at Seventy. Czeslaw Milosz, *tr. fr. Polish by the author.* AnAn

Poet at the Breakfast Table, The, *sels.* Oliver Wendell Holmes.

Poet came to our games one day, A. Cerealius, *tr. fr. Greek by* Sam Hamill. InMo

Poet, cast your careful eye. On Seeing a Poet of the First World War on the Station at Abbeville. Charles Causley. LiTM

Poet Defended, A. Paul Ramsey. InPK

Poet felt the rain, The. Rain. Margiad Evans. OBWVE

Poet first his owne high prayses sings, The. The Argument of the Fourth Booke. Lucretius, *tr. fr. Latin.* *Fr.* De Rerum Natura (On the Nature of Things). KTR, *tr. by* Lucy Hutchinson

Poet from Cheltenham Spa, A. Betty Morris. PeLi

Poet gathers fruit from every tree, The. The Poet. Sir William Watson. *Fr.* Two Epigrams. TrGrPo

Poet has died, A. Alcaeus, *tr. fr. Greek by* Sam Hamill. InMo

Poet hath a realm within, and throne, The. Albery Allson Whitman. *Fr.* Twasinta's Seminoles; Or Rape of Florida. AAP

Poet hath the child's sight in his breast, The. The Poet. Elizabeth Barrett Browning. EPCY; WGRP

Poet Holds His Future in His Hand, The. B. S. Johnson. FaBoBl

Poet honed, The. Lyric Barber. Liboria E. Romano. GoYe

Poet I am neither borne, nor bred, A. Margaret Cavendish, Duchess of Newcastle. KTR

Poet! I come to touch thy lance with mine. Wapentake. Longfellow. EPCY

Poet! I like not mealy fruit; give me. Walter Savage Landor. FaBoEE

Poet in his joy, A. *(LL)* The Peasant Poet. John Clare. FHYEP; OAEL-2; OBNC; WGRP

Poet in his lone yet genial hour, The. Apologia Pro Vita Sua. Samuel Taylor Coleridge. EnRP; OxBSP

Poet in Old Age Fishing at Evening, The. Desmond O'Grady. CIP

Poet in Residence at a Country School. Don Welch. GOYP

Poet in Winter. Edward Lucie-Smith. TwCP

Poet Is Dead, The. William Everson. NoAM; NoP

Poet Is Not a Jukebox, A. Dudley Randall. NoAM

Poet is priest. Death to Van Gogh's Ear! Allen Ginsberg. NaP; VGW

Poet is the dreamer, The. Loneliness. Al Young. PoBA

Poet Laments the Coming of Old Age, The. Edith Sitwell. NAEL-2; NoAM

Poet, let passion sleep. Art, II. Alfred Noyes. OBEV

Poet Lets His Tongue Hang Down, The. Edward Dorn. PRA

Poet Lied, The. Odia Ofeimun. HBAPE

Poet lived in Galilee, A. The Poet. Witter Bynner. WGRP

Poet Loves a Mistress, but Not to Marry, The. Robert Herrick. CaPo; ErPo

Poet of Bray, The. John Heath-Stubbs. NOBL

Poet of Ignorance, The. Anne Sexton. PRA

Poet of nature, thou hast wept to know. To Wordsworth. Shelley. EnRP; EPCY; FHYEP; NoP; PFP; Son

Poet of Our Race. Maggie Pogue Johnson. CBWP-4

Poet of the dead leaves driven like ghosts. Shelley. Charles Simic. TRP

Poet of the Mountains, The. Thomas McCarthy. CIP

Poet of the serene and thoughful lay! Wordsworth. Charlotte L. Forten Grimke. AAP

Poet of the Streets. Jack Micheline. PoBeRe

Poet on the Island, The. Richard Murphy. CIP; PeIV

Poet Prays, The. Grace Noll Crowell. TrPWD

Poet Prays to the Loba, The. Diane Di Prima. *Fr.* Loba. EaPr; SRLS

Poet, Professor, Autocrat of Wit's own Breakfast-Table. *(LL)* Filling an Order. John Townsend Trowbridge. AnAmPo; OBAL

Poet Questions Peace, The. George Chapman. *Fr.* Euthymiae Raptus; or, The Teares of Peace. JCP

Poet Recognizing the Echo of the Voice, A. Diane Wakoski. NIP

Poet Speaks from the Visitors' Gallery, A. Archibald MacLeish. NYBP

Poet spilled my gin, The. Tropisms on John Berryman. Gerald Vizenor. VoR

Poet suffers making poems, A. Seeing Off Master Tan. Meng Chiao, *tr. fr. Chinese by* Stephen Owen. SuSp

Poet the Chief of Artists, The. Mark Akenside. *Fr.* Pleasures of Imagination, The. EPCY

Poet the Dreamer, The. Norman Jordan. NBV

Poet Thinks, A. Lui Chi, *tr. fr. Chinese by* E. Powys Mathers. AWP

Poet to a Dancer, A. Auvaiyar, *tr. fr. Tamil by* A. K. Ramanujan. PLW

Poet to a Painter, A. Aubrey Thomas De Vere. Son

Poet to the Birds, The. Alice Meynell. FM

Poet to the Sleeping Saki, The. Goethe, *tr. fr. German by* John Weiss. PeHV

Poet to Tiger. May Swenson. GLP
Sels.
Dream, The.
Hair, The.
Salt, The.
Sand, The.

Poet, to whose mighty heart, The. Matthew Arnold. *Fr.* Resignation. EPCY; FHYEP

Poet told me if I was serious, The. Instruction from Bly. Cynthia MacDonald. NMM

Poet-Tree. Earle Birney. OxBC

Poet, Trying to Surprise God. Peter Meinke. PBCAP

Poet, trying to surprise his God, The. Poet, Trying to Surprise God. Peter Meinke. PBCAP

Poet vs. Parson. Ebenezer Elliot. Son

Poet was busted by a topless judge, A. Sermonette. Ishmael Reed. PoBA

Poet went to the Isthmian games, A. Cerealius, *tr. fr. Greek by* Peter Jay. GrAn

Poet Who Talks to Himself, The. Edward Leslie Mayo. BCF

Poet, whoe'er thou art, God damn thee. The Earl of Rochester. FaBoEE

Poet Wondering What He Is Up To. D. J. Enright. OxBC

Poeta Fit, Non Nascitur. "Lewis Carroll." FaBoNo; OBSV

Poeta Loquitur. Swinburne. OAEL-2

Poetaster, The, *sels.* Ben Jonson.
"If I freely may discover." BeJo; EIL
"O sacred poesie, thou spirit of artes." PoEL-2
"Swell me a bowl with lusty wine." BeJo
"There is no bountie to be shew'd to such." PoEL-2

Poetaster, The. Samuel Rowlands. *Fr.* Melancholy Knight, The. EIL

Poète Manqué. Ernest Sandeen. CRP

Poetess Kō Ōgimi, The. Helen Chasin. NMM

Poetess's Bouts-Rimés, The. *Unknown.* NOEC

Poetic Frenzy. Shakespeare. *Fr.* Midsummer Night's Dream, A. EPCY

Poetic Genius. Mark Akenside. *Fr.* Pleasures of Imagination, The. NOEC

Poetic Thought. *Unknown.* FiBHP

Poetic wit. Abraham Cowley. *See* Tell me, O[h] tell, what kind[e] of thing is wit.

Poetical Commandments. Byron. *Fr.* Don Juan. OxBoLi, *sect.* I; PeLV, *sect.* II

Poetical Economy. Harry Graham. FaBoCo; Mes

Poetical Epistle, from the Island of Jamaica, to, A, *sels. Unknown.*
"Our tropic fruits, nurs'd 'neath a torrid sky." PBCV

Poetical Epistle tae Cullybackey Auld Nummer. Thomas Given. FaBoVe

Poetical Philander only thought to love. Philander. Donald Hall. ErPo

Poetics. A. R. Ammons. NoP

Poetics. Diane Di Prima. PoBeRe

Poetics. Tom Weatherly. UL

Poetics against the Angel of Death. Phyllis Webb. MoCV; NOBC

Poetresses Hasty Resolution, The. Margaret Cavendish, Duchess of Newcastle. KTR

Poetresses Petition, The. Margaret Cavendish, Duchess of Newcastle. KTR

Poetry. Mary Elizabeth Fullerton. NOBAu

Poetry. Ella Heath. WGRP

Poetry. Greg Kuzma. PoA

Poetry. Marianne Moore. AmPP; BLPL; BoWoP; CMoP; FaBoWP; FF; HAP; HeIL; HeIP; ImGa; ImPo; LiTA; LiTM; MoAB; MoAmPo; MoP; NAAL-2; NALW; NIP; NoAM; NOBA; NoP; OxBA; PoE; Poetr; TAP; TFi; UnPo

Poetry. Frank O'Hara. HCAP

Poetry. "Peter," *tr. by* Edmund Keeley *and* Philip Sherrard. Mes

Poetry, a Natural Thing. Robert Duncan. CAPP; NoAM; NOBA; TRP

Poetry, almost blind like a camera. Imaginary Elegies, I-IV. Jack Spicer. NeAP

Poetry and the Melancholy Man. Milton. *Fr.* Il Penseroso. AWP; EPCY; FHYEP; GTBS; GTBS-P; HAP; HoPM; ImPo; JCP; LiTB; NoP; NOSC; OAEL-1; OBEV; PPP; TEP; TFi; TrGrPo

Poetry and the Poet. H. C. Bunner. OBAL

Poetry Concert. Michael S. Harper. TAP

Poetry Defined. John Holmes. GrPl

Poetry, Emily. Brief History. Olga Hampel Briggs. GoYe

Poetry for Supper. R. S. Thomas. OxBC

Poetry in England. Samuel Daniel. *Fr.* Musophilus; or, Defence of All Learning. EPCY; NoSic

Poetry Is a Destructive Force. Wallace Stevens. AnAmPo; MeMAP; OxBA; RaBo

Poetry is a projection across silence of cadences arranged to break the silence. Ten Definitions of Poetry. Carl Sandburg. MoAmPo

Poetry is an applied science. Parapoetics. Eugene B. Redmond. NBV

Poetry Is Death Cast Out. Sydney Clouts. PeSA

Poetry is poetry. Poetry. "Peter," *tr. by* Edmund Keeley *and* Philip Sherrard. Mes

Poetry is the supreme fiction, madame. A High-toned Old Christian Woman. Wallace Stevens. CMoP; MoP; NAAL-2; NoAM; NOBA; Poetr; PPP; TAP

Poetry? It's a hobby. What the Chairman Told Tom. Basil Bunting. OxBTC

Poetry Makes Rhythm in Philosophy. Ishmael Reed. Jaz

Poetry of Departures. (Sometimes you hear, fifth-hand.) Philip Larkin. CMoP; FF; HeIP; OxBC; PoE; PrIm; TwCP
Sels.

Poetry of Earth, The. Keats. *See* Poetry of earth is never dead, The.

Poetry of earth is never dead, The. On the Grasshopper and [the] Cricket. Keats. ArNa; BoTP; CoGr; EnRP; FaBoBe; FHYEP; GN; ImPo; LiTB; MeMBP; NIP; OAEL-2; OxAEP-2; Poetr; Son; TrGrPo; TTTS (Poetry of Earth, The.) WiR

Poetry of Gerard Manley Hopkins, The. Monk Gibbon. TIRV

Poetry of Motion, The. Raymond Garlick. AngWe

Poetry Perpetuates the Poet. Robert Herrick. BeJo; FaBoEE

Poetry Professors, The, *sels.* Robert Lloyd.
"Old England has not lost her prayer." ECEV
"Yet matter must be gravely planned." ECEV

Poetry Reading. Eileen Myles. UL

Poetry Reading. Vernon Scannell. NOBL

Poetry was the memory of adolescence. Peotry Was Like This. Al Mahmud, *tr. fr. Bengali by* Kabir Chowdhury. TSaS

Poetry's a gift wherein but few excell. Nathaniel Ward. SCAP

Poetry's a tree. Yes, the Secret Mind Whispers. Al Young. PoBA

Poets. Kay Boyle. UL

Poets. Gavin Ewart. PeLV

Poets. Joyce Kilmer. WGRP

Poets, *sels.* Joseph Rolnik, *tr. fr. Yiddish by* Irving Feldman.

Poet's age is sad, The: for why? Robert Browning. *Fr.* Asolando. EnVR; OAEL-2

Poets Agree to Be Quiet by the Swamp, The. David Wagoner. CoAP; VGW

Poets and parents say he cannot die. Yet Another Poem about a Dying Child. Janet Frame. PeNZ

Poet's Arbour in the Birchwood, The. Edward Williams, *tr. fr. Welsh by* Kenneth Hurlstone Jackson. OBWVE

Poets/ are queer people. Definition. Wilma Elizabeth McDaniel. ETG

Poets are usually pure, rugged. Lament for Lu Yin. Meng Chiao, *tr. fr. Chinese by* Stephen Owen. SuSp

Poets at Tea, The, *sels.* Barry Pain.

Poet's Call, The. Thomas Curtis Clark. WGRP

Poet's cat, sedate and grave, A. The Retired Cat. William Cowper. FM; OFC

Poets' Corner. Robert Graves. FaBoEE

Poet's Counsel, A ("You come from the line of a Cola king.") Kovur Kilar, *tr. fr. Tamil by* A. K. Ramanujan. PLW

Poet's Counsel, A ("Your enemy is not the kind who wears.") Kovur Kilar, *tr. fr. Tamil by* A. K. Ramanujan. PLW

Poet's daily chore, The. Lens. Anne Wilkinson. MoCV; NOBC

Poet's Day, The. Richard Weber. CIP

Poets detained by Thought Police. Paul Evans. *Fr.* Sofa Book, The. NBrP

Poet's Dream, The. William Dunbar. *Fr.* Golden [or Goldyn] Targe, The. OxBS; PoEL-1

Poet's Dream, The. Shelley. *See* On a poet's lips I slept.

Poet's Epitaph, A. Wordsworth. EnRP

Poet's eye, in a fine frenzy rolling, The. Poetic Frenzy. Shakespeare. *Fr.* Midsummer Night's Dream, A. EPCY

Poet's Farewell to His Teeth, The. William Dickey. PoA

Poet's Fate, The. Thomas Hood. FaBoEE; FiBHP

Poet's Final Instructions, The. John Berryman. SM; Son; VGW

Poets for deciduous language., The. (*LL*) Postscript. R. S. Thomas. FaBoMo; OxBC

Poet's Grace, A. Burns. TrPWD

Poets have muddied all the little fountains, The. Abla. Antar, *tr. by* E. Powys Mathers. *Fr.* Mu'allaqat, The. AWP

Poets Have Their Ear to the Ground. Peter De Vries. UV

Poets have their ear to the ground more than most people. Poets Have Their Ear to the Ground. Peter De Vries. UV

Poet's heart is wrenched and wrenched again until his head turns white, A. Yuan Hao-wen, *tr. by* Irving Y. Lo. *Fr.* On Poetry. SuSp

Poets Hitchhiking on the Highway. Gregory Corso. NeAP; PoM

Poet's Hope, A, *sels*. William Ellery Channing.

Poets, I want to follow them all. On Originality. Bill Manhire. PeNZ

Poet's Ideal, The. H. Cordelia Ray. CBWP-3

Poet's Journal, The, *sels*. Bayard Taylor.
"God, to whom we look up blindly." TrPWD

Poet's Lament on the Death of His Wife. Raage Ugaas. *See* Like the yu'ub wood bell tied to gelded camels that are running away.

Poets Light But Lamps, The. Emily Dickinson. HeIL; HeIP

Poets like shepherds on green hills. The Shepherds. Beren van Slyke. GoYe

Poet's Lot, The. Oliver Wendell Holmes. PoEL-5

Poet's Love. Heine, *tr. fr. German by* Philip L. Miller. RiWo

Poets Love Nature. John Clare. OAEL-2

Poet's Loves, The. Hywel ab Owain Gwynedd, *tr. fr. Welsh by* Gwyn Williams. OBWVE

Poets make pets of pretty, docile words. Pretty Words. Elinor Wylie. NAAL-2

Poets may boast, as safely vain. Of English Verse. Edmund Waller. BeJo; NAEL-1; NOSC; OAEL-1; PoE; SeCP

Poets may sing of their Helicon streams. The Federal Constitution. William Milns. PAH

Poet's Memory Is Counsel, A. Kallil Attiraiyanar, *tr. fr. Tamil by* A. K. Ramanujan. PLW

Poet's Ministrants, The. H. Cordelia Ray. CBWP-3

Poets, minor or major, should arrange to remain slender. Poets. Kay Boyle. UL

Poets of Hell, The. Karl Shapiro. NYBP

Poet's Paradise, The. Michael Drayton. *See* Paradise on earth is found, A.

Poet's Place, The. Yannis Ritsos, *tr. fr. Greek by* Paul Merchant. AnRep

Poet's Prayer. Adelaide Love. TrPWD

Poet's Prayer, The. Stephen Philipps. WGRP

Poet's Prayer, The. *Unknown*. OBSV

Poet's Progress, The. Chris Mann. PeSAV

Poet's Request, The. *Unknown, tr. fr. Irish by* John Montague. BIrV

Poet's Sabbath, The, *sels*. John Critchley Prince.

Poets Seven Years Old. Rimbaud, *tr. fr. French by* Kenneth Koch *and* Georges Guy. SOTW

Poet's Simple Faith, The. Victor Hugo, *tr. fr. French by* Edward Dowden. WGRP

Poet's Song, The. Tennyson. EBVV; ELP; EPCY

Poets tell us of an age of unalloyed felicity, The. The Golden Age. W. H. Auden. *Fr.* Man of La Mancha. AnAn

Poet's Terror at the Bailiffs of Exeter, The. Andrew Brice. *Fr.* Freedom; a Poem, Written in Time of Recess from the Rapacious Claws of Bailiffs. NOEC

Poet's thoughts are full of might, The. Non Fit. Rose Terry Cooke. AmWP

Poets to Come. Walt Whitman. FF; LiTA; TrGrPo

Poet's Voice, The. Blake. *See* Hear the voice of the Bard!

Poet's Welcome to His Love-begotten Daughter, A. Burns. LiTB; NAs; NOEC; OxBoLi; PoEL-4

Poet's Wish. Valery Larbaud, *tr. fr. French by* William Jay Smith. GrPl

Poet's Wish; an Ode, The. Allan Ramsay, *after* Horace. OBVE

Poet's words are winged with fire, The. The Poet. Joel Benton. WGRP

Poet's yes obscenely seeing, The. Lawrence Ferlinghetti. *Fr.* Coney Island of the Mind, A. LiTM

Poggio. Lawrence Durrell. OxBTC

Poh! did ever one see such a troublesome bear? Delia Very Angry. *Unknown*. NOEC

Poietes Apoietes. Hartley Coleridge. OBNC

Poinsettia petal drops, A. The rain pastes twisted flowing drapery. Family Reunion. Hollis Spurgeon Summers. GoYe

Point, The. Evan Jones (b. 1927). NOBAu

Point, The. John Montague. IPY; PNI

Point, greatly enlarged, The. Thomas Kinsella. *Fr.* Technical Supplement, A. BiHa; IPY

Point Grey. Daryl Hine. NOBC

Point, I imagine, is, The. The Point. Evan Jones (b. 1927). NOBAu

Point Lobos: Animism. Michael McClure. PoBeRe

Point no scornful finger at Yoruba Land. Edouard J. Maunick, *tr. fr. French by* Ellen Conroy Kennedy. *Fr.* As Far as Yoruba Land. NegPo

Point of No Return. Robert Graves. BIrV

Point Shirley. Sylvia Plath. NIP; NoP; Poetr

Point their faces to the sky. (*LL*) The Town of Don't-You-Worry. I. J. Barlett. BLPA; WBLP

Point your nose to the sun. Trajan, *tr. fr. Greek by* Peter Jay. GrAn

Pointed clouds have become fixed in the heaven, The. A Stormy Day. *Unknown, tr. fr. Hawaiian*. WTO

Pointed houses lean so you would swear, The. Amsterdam. Francis Jammes, *tr. fr. French by* Jethro Bithell. AWP; FaPON, *ll*. 1–20

Pointed People, The. Rachel Field. FaPON

Pointless Pride of Man, The. *Unknown*. *See* When Adam delf [*or* dalf]/ and Eve span.

Points between A and B, The. (*LL*) Passion. Diane Ward. VBLP

Poise of my hands reminded me of yours. (*LL*) It is the pain, it is the pain, endures. William Empson. CBLP; CMoP; EnLoPo; MoP; NoAM; OAEL-2; PoE; TRP

Poised between going on and back, pulled. The Base Stealer. Robert Francis. GoJo; NTCP

Poison Tree, A. Blake. *Fr.* Songs of Experience. AWP; EnRP; FHYEP; HAP; HoPM; ImPo; LiTB; MeMBP; NAEL-2; NoP; NTP; OtMeF; OxAEP-2; PoEL-4; PPP; RB; SCV; SoSe; TFi; TrGrPo; WeW

Poisonous Mushroom. Liu Sha-ho, *tr. fr. Chinese*. *Fr.* Family of Plants, A. LHF, *tr. by* Hualing Nieh

Poke-Pole Fishing. Dennis Schmitz. AmPA

Poland/ 1931 "The Wedding." Jerome Rothenberg. PoM; Prf

Poland works nicely. The Story So Far. John Clarke. UV

Polar Bear. William Jay Smith. TLR

Polar Bear. *Unknown, tr. fr. Eskimo by* T. Lowenstein. OBAP

Polar Bear never makes his bed, The. Polar Bear. William Jay Smith. TLR

Polar DEW has just warned that, The. Your Attention Please. Peter Porter. OBWP; OxBTC; PAW

Polar Exploration. Stephen Spender. MoAB; NoAM

Polarities. Kenneth Slessor. CBAP

Polaroid, *sels*. Clark Coolidge.

Pole Star, The. Coslett Coslett, *tr. fr. Welsh by* Kenneth Hurlstone Jackson. OBWVE

Pole Star for This Year. Archibald MacLeish. MeMAP; OxBA

Poled high on his cactus over a cliff of desert island, the osprey. Song at San Carlos Bay. Brewster Ghiselin. FoLa

Poles are flying where the two eyes set, The. Discoveries. Vernon Watkins. ImPo; LiTM

Poles rode out from Warsaw against the German, The. The Abnormal Is Not Courage. Jack Gilbert. CoAP

Police. Greg Kuzma. NGP

Police, The. Sean O'Brien. PWE

Police are called *Syncromesh*, The. In Silvertown, Chasing the Dragon. Ken Smith. PWE

Police arrived early, The; I woke and heard. Police. Greg Kuzma. NGP

Police Inquiry, The. Christian Morgenstern, *tr. fr. German by* Max Knight. CBNP

Police Manual, A. David Wagoner. AnAn

Police Sift New Clues in Search for Beauty. Vickie Karp. UTF

Police Station Ditties. Max Beerbohm. NOBL

Police Station Ditty, A. Max Beerbohm. *See* Then it's collar 'im tight.

Policeman, A/ is a pig. Definition for Blk/Children. Sonia Sanchez. PoBA

Policeman buys shoes slow and careful, The. Psalm of Those Who Go Forth before Daylight. Carl Sandburg. MoShBr; OxBA

Policeman Cleared in Jaywalking Case. Claire Harris. PBCV

Policeman from Nottingham Junction, A. *Unknown*. PeLi

Policeman, policeman, don't catch me! *Unknown*. RoPo

Policeman, policeman, don't take me. I Stole Brass. *Unknown*. ChTr

Policeman walks with heavy tread, The. Action Rhyme. E. H. Adams. BoTP

Policeman's Ball, The. Martín Espada. UTF

Policeman's Lot, A. Wendy Cope. FaBoWP

Policeman's Lot, A [*or* The]. W. S. Gilbert. *Fr.* Pirates of Penzance, The. NOBL; PeLV; TrGrPo

Polish Eagle, The. Kornel Ujejski, *tr. fr. Polish by* Helen Waddell. MLL

Politeness. Una Marson. PBCV

Politeness. A. A. Milne. SiSoPo

Political Activist Living Alone. Pat Arrowsmith. AIW; BrRo

Political Despatch, A. George Canning. FaBoCo

Political Greatness. Shelley. EnRP

Political House that Jack Built, The, *sels*. *Unknown*.
"This is the man — all shaven and shorn." FaBoEH

Political Meeting. A. M. Klein. MoCV

Political Orlando, The. George MacBeth. NOBL

Political Poem. Amiri Baraka. CoAP; MoP; NAAL-2; NoAM

Political Relations. Audre Lorde. GLP

Political Studies Class, The. Mu Tan, *tr. fr. Chinese*. LHF, *tr. by* Hualing Nieh

"Political women," thought Yeats. R. K. R. Thornton. PeLi

Politician, A. E. E. Cummings. InPK

Politician Is an Arse Upon, A. E. E. Cummings. *See* Politician, A.

Politician's elephantine conk's, The. Maurus. Palladas, *tr. fr. Greek by* Tony Harrison. GrAn

Politicians, heart and soul. Poll Star. Felicia Lamport. NBLV

Politics. Tom Marshall. NOBC

Politics. *Unknown.* RoPo

Politics. W. B. Yeats. CBLP; CMoP; FF; HeIP; InPS; OxBTC; PoE; SCV

Politics Kaiso. Roger McTair. PBCV

Politics of Envy. Duncan Forbes. FaBoBl; PeLV

Politics of Paradise, The. Alma Villanueva. SRLS

Politics of Rich Painters, The. Amiri Baraka. VGW

Polka. John Fuller. *Fr.* Fox-Trot. PeLV

Polka. Edith Sitwell. CBNP

Polkas they danced at the Wooyeo Ball, The. *(LL)* The Wooyeo Ball. *Unknown.* NOBAu

Poll. Ed Roberson. PoBA

Poll Star. Felicia Lamport. NBLV

Polly; an Opera, *sels.* John Gay.
    Air. NOEC
    "Honour plays a bubble's part." PeLV
    "Woman's like the flatt'ring ocean." PeLV

Polly and Sukey. Mother Goose. *See* Polly put the kettle on.

Polly Be-en Upzides wi' Tom. William Barnes. NOBVV

Polly Oliver's Rambles. *Unknown.* OBET

Polly Perkins. *Unknown.* ELP; OxBoLi; PeLV; PlP

Polly put the kettle on. Mother Goose. OxNR
    (Polly and Sukey.) ReMoGo

Polly Vaughn. *Unknown.* AmFP

Polo. Manuel de Falla, *tr. fr. Spanish by* Philip L. Miller. RiWo

Polo Grounds. Rolfe Humphries. HoPM

Polo season would start early in April, The. Animal Days. Lee Harwood. NBrP

Polonius' Advice to Laertes. Shakespeare. *Fr.* Hamlet. NAWM-1

Polonius to Laertes. Shakespeare. *See* There, — my blessing with you [*or* thee]!

Polwart on the Green. Allan Ramsay. NOEC

Polyaenus' daughter, Scyllis, came to the wide gates. Diotimus, *tr. fr. Greek by* Barbara Hughes Fowler. *Fr.* Epigrams. HePo

Polychromatic springtime's gay cadenza. Vernal Equinox. Martin Johnston. CBAP

Polydamas, your depth in augry. Hector's Defiance. Homer, *tr. fr. Greek. Fr.* Iliad, The. NOSC, *tr. by* George Chapman

Polygamist. Charlotte M. Wright. NGP

Polyglot Medley. Andrew Geddes Bain. PeSAV

Polyhymnia, *sels.* George Peele.
    His Golden Lock[e]s [Time Hath to Silver Turned]. ElL; EnRePo; FaBoRV; NIP; NoP; SCGP; TFi
    (Farewell to Arms, A.) NOBE; OBEV; OBWP; OxAEP-1; PoRA
    (Farewell to the Court.) NoSic
    (Old Knight, The.) ChTr; TrGrPo
    (Sonnet, A: "His golden locks time hath to silver turned.") ELP; InPS; PoEL-2
    "Then proudly shocks amid the martial throng." FaBoEH

Polynesia. Allen Curnow. PeNZ

Polyolbion, *sels.* Michael Drayton.
    "And, now that every thing may in the proper place." FM
    "By thine own named town made famous in thy fall." NOSC
    Charnwood Forest. FaBoPP
    "Duck, and Mallard first, the falconers onely sport, The." FM
    (Birds in the Fens.) ChTr
    Dwindling Forest of Arden, The. FaBoPP
    Fen-Men of Lincolnshire's Holland, The. FaBoPP
    Fools Gaze at Painted Courts. ChTr
    Lincolnshire's Holland Speaks of Her Waterfowl. FaBoPP
    "March strongly forth, my Muse, whilst yet the temperate air." NOSC
    Stonehenge. FaBoPP
    "Then Frome (a nobler flood) the Muses doth implore." NOSC
    Trent Again, The. FaBoPP
    "Where she, of all the plains of Britain that doth bear." NOSC
    "With solitude what sorts, that here's not wondrous rife?" NOSC

Polyphemus. Virgil, *tr. fr. Latin by* Richard Stanyhurst. *Fr.* Aeneid [*or* Eneados], The. NAWM-1; NoSic

"Polyphemus, Galatea with apples pelts your flocks." Damoetas and Daphnis. Theocritus [*or* Theokritus], *tr. fr. Greek by* Barbara Hughes Fowler. *Fr.* Idylls. HePo

Pomegranate just splitting, a peach just furry, A. Diodorus Zonas, *tr. fr. Greek by* Alistair Elliot. GrAn

Pomegranate speaks, The. *Unknown, tr. fr. Egyptian hieroglyphics by* Ezra Pound *and* Noel Stock. BoWoP

Pomegranate surprise was a New Deal, The. Fruit and Government. Mira Teru Kurka. UL

Pomme arac. Derek Walcott. *Fr.* Sainte Lucie. FaBoVe

Pommes de Terre. Kathleen Norris. NGP

Pomona. William Morris. NOBVV; WiR

Pomp of Egypt's elder day. The Egyptian Tomb. William Lisle Bowles. OBTV

Pompadour, The. George Walter Thornbury. BeLS

Pompeius, best of all my comrades, you and I. II, 7. "Pompeius, best of all my comrades, you and I" ("O saepe mecum.") Horace, *tr. fr. Latin by* Austin Dobson. *Fr.* Odes.
    (Pompeius, chief of all my friends, with whom.) OBWP, *tr. by* James Michie

Pompeius, chief of all my friends, with whom. Horace. *See* Pompeius, best of all my comrades, you and I.

Pomposo (insolent and loud). Charles Churchill. *Fr.* Ghost, The. OBSV

Pon was born of an egg. Birth. Henri Michaux, *tr. fr. French by* Richard Ellmann. AnRep

Ponce de Leon. Edith M. Thomas. PAH

Ponce de León: A Morning Walk. Al Young. HoPM

Pond, The. Anthony Thwaite. MAT; NYBP

Pond-chestnuts poke through floating chickweed on the green brocade pool. The Pool behind Ch'i-an. Tu Mu, *tr. fr. Chinese by* A. C. Graham. PLT

Pond in a Basin. Tu Mu, *tr. fr. Chinese by* Eddie Tsang. SuSp

Pond in a Bowl, The. Han Yü, *tr. fr. Chinese by* Kenneth O. Hanson. SuSp

Pond in a Jardiniere, A, *sels.* Han Yü, *tr. fr. Chinese by* Burton Watson.

Ponder, Darling, These Busted Statues. E. E. Cummings. CMoP; NIP; PoE

Ponder my words, if so that any be. Request to the Graces. Robert Herrick. NOSC

Ponder thy cares, and sum them all in one. Sir David Murray. *Fr.* Caelia. EIL

Pondicherry Blues. Josephine Jacobsen. GoJo

Pond'rous projectiles, hurl'd by heavy hands. "Orpheus C. Kerr." *Fr.* Rejected "National Hymns," The. OBAL

Pondy Woods. Robert Penn Warren. MoAmPo

Ponies, Twynyrodyn. Meic Stephens. AngWe

Pont and Blyth. *Unknown.* GBP

Pont y Caniedydd. Alun Llywelyn-Williams, *tr. fr. Welsh by* Joseph R. Clancy. OBWVE

Pont-y-Wern. Arthur Hugh Clough. *Fr.* Ambarvalia. FaBoPP

Pontoon-Bridge Miracle, The. Vachel Lindsay. MeMAP

Pontoosuce. Herman Melville. NOBA

Pontypool. Richard Hall. AngWe

Pontypool! thou dirtiest of dirty places. Pontypool. Richard Hall. AngWe

Pony, The. Rachel MacAndrew. BoTP

Pony air, wild wheat, The. The End of the Indian Poems. Stanley Plumly. GOA

Pony Farm. Laura Jensen. LCAP

Pony Rock. Archibald MacLeish. MeMAP

Pooh!. Walter de la Mare. FiBHP; HAP

Pooh!. Walter de la Mare. HAP; PeLV

Pool. Wanda Barford. Mes

Pool, The. Hayyim Nahman Bialik, *tr. fr. Hebrew by* Ruth Finer Mintz. MHP

Pool, The. Robert Creeley. CoAP

Pool, The. Hilda Doolittle ("H. D."). CMoP

Pool. Cynthia Fuller. NWP

Pool, A. Thomas Whitbread. NYBP

Pool behind Ch'i-an, The. Tu Mu, *tr. fr. Chinese by* A. C. Graham. PLT

Pool players, The. We Real Cool. Gwendolyn Brooks. CAPP; FF; HAP; HeIL; HeIP; HoPM; InPK; NALW; NoP; PoA; PoBA; PoE; PrIm; RaBo; SM; SoSe; TAP; TRP; TTY; WeW
    (We Real Cool. We. NTP; Poetr; TFi

Poor, The. John Langhorne. *Fr.* Country Justice, The. NOEC

Poor, The. William Langland. *Fr.* Vision of Piers Plowman, The. PoEL-1

Poor, The. Emile Verhaeren, *tr. fr. French by* Ludwig Lewisohn. AWP

Poor, The. William Carlos Williams. MoAB; MoAmPo; NoP; PPP

Poor Adam and Eve were from Eden turned out. *Unknown.* Spl

Poor, and the dazed, and the idiots, The. Hurrying Away from the Earth. Robert Bly. NaP; PoA

Poor Aviator Lay Dying, A. *Unknown.* NSI

Poor beggars! — they'll never see 'ome! *(LL)* The Widow at Windsor. Kipling. FaBoEH; NAEL-2; NoAM; NoP

Poor [or Poore] bird! I do not envy thee. The Robin. George Daniel. FaBoRV

(Poore bird! I doe not envie thee. FM

Poor Boy: Portrait of a Painting. John Ash. SCBI

Poor But Honest. *Unknown. See* She Was Poor but She Was Honest.

Poor Calpurnius, the most Schweikian soldier in the land. Lucilius, *tr. fr. Greek by* Peter Porter. GrAn

Poor Children, The. Victor Hugo, *tr. fr. French by* Swinburne. AWP

Poor Christian Looks at the Ghetto, A. Czeslaw Milosz, *tr. fr. Polish by the author.* AnRep; PoSu

Poor chum, dear chum, so here you lie at rest. Monologue in a Rand Hospital. William Elijah Hunter. PeSAV

Poor Cotton Weaver, The. *Unknown.* OBET

Poor crawlin' bodies, sair neglectit. John Learmont. *Fr.* Address to the Plebeians, An. NOEC

Poor credulous and simple maid! Phyllis. Thomas Randolph. BoLoP

Poor Crow! Mary Mapes Dodge. OBCA

Poor Cupid sits and blows his nails for cold. *(LL)* Blame not my cheeks, though pale with love they be. Thomas Campion. AAS; SCGP; UnPo

Poor Dad he got five years or more as everybody knows. Stir the Wallaby Stew. *Unknown.* FaBoBa

Poor *Damon!* Art thou caught? Is't ev'n so? A Letter to a Brother of the Pen in Tribulation. Aphra Behn. KTR

Poor dear dead have been laid out in vain, The. Thomas Hood. FaBoEE

Poor degenerate from the ape, A. First Philosopher's Song. Aldous Huxley. AWP

Poor devil that I am, being so attacked. Palladas, *tr. fr. Greek by* Tony Harrison. OBVE

Poor Dick! though first thy airs provoke. Dick Hairbrain Learns the Social Graces. John Trumbull. *Fr.* Progress of Dulness, The. AmPP

Poor Doctor Blow went out of church. Queen Anne's Musicians. Thomas Hennell. FaBoTw

Poor drunkards, poor drunkards, take warning by me. John Adkins' Farewell. *Unknown.* AmFP

Poor Ellen Smith. *Unknown.* AmFP

Poor Epictetus, born the Slave of Fate. Observations of the Life of Epictetus. Elizabeth Tipper. *Fr.* Pilgrim's Viaticum; or, The Destitute, But Not Forlorn. KTR

Poor Estate, The. Robert Greene. *See* Sweet are the thoughts that savo[u]r of content.

Poor fawn about to die. Image. Anna de Noailles, *tr. fr. French by* Carol Cosman. PBWP

Poor fellow, what is it to you. Sir Charles Hanbury Williams. OBWVE

Poor for Our Sakes. Mary Brainerd Smith. BLRP

Poor French Sailor's Scottish Sweetheart, A. William Johnson Cory. EBVV

Poor George. George III. Robert Lowell. FaBoPV

Poor Ghost, The. Christina Rossetti. GBL

Poor Girl's Meditation, The. *Unknown, tr. fr. Irish by* Padraic Colum. BIrV; OBMV

Poor girls, neglected. *(LL)* To Violets. Robert Herrick. CaPo; JCP; OBEV; PFP; SeCP; TrGrPo

Poor Hal caught his death standing under a spout. Fatal Love. Matthew Prior. FaBoCo; NBLV

Poor have hands, and feet, and eyes, The. The Poor Man and His Parish Church. Robert Stephen Hawker. EBVV

Poor heart, unsatisfied! Shadow and Sunrise. H. Cordelia Ray. CBWP-3

Poor hill farmer astray in the grass. The Lonely Farmer. R. S. Thomas. PIP

Poor-House, The. George Crabbe. *Fr.* Village, The. ECEV

Poor humble roach. To a Humble Bug. Linda Lyon van Voorhis. GoYe

Poor, impious Soul! that fixes its high hopes. Aspiration. Adah Isaacs Menken. AAP; AmWP; CBWP-1

Poor in my youth, and in life's later scenes. On Late-acquired Wealth *or* Riches. *Unknown, tr. fr. Greek by* William Cowper. OBVE (Riches.) AWP

Poor in spirit on their rosary rounds, The. Lough Derg. Denis Devlin. BIrV; CIP; IPY; PeIV

Poor is cold feet in the morning, cold floor. Linoleum: Breaking Down. Stanley Plumly. AnAn

Poor Is the Life That Misses. *Unknown.* EiI

Poor Jack. Charles Dibdin. BeLS

Poor Jane Higgins. A Pig Tale. James Reeves. SiSoPo

Poor Jim Jay. *(LL)* Jim Jay. Walter de la Mare. CBNP

Poor john, who joined in make of wrong. Welcome the Wrath. Stanley Kunitz. VGW

Poor Johnny looked exceeding blue. Thomas Love Peacock. *Fr.* Sir Proteus, a Satirical Ballad. CBNP

Poor Johnny was bended well nigh double. Apple-Seed John. Lydia Maria Child. OHIP

Poor Kid. William Cole. OBAL

Poor Kitty Popcorn. *Unknown.* AS

Poor lad once and a lad so trim, A. Jean Richepin's Song. Herbert Trench. OBMV

Poor Lil' Brack Sheep. Ethel M. C. Brazelton. BLPA

Poor little donkey! It's no joke. Palladas, *tr. fr. Greek by* Tony Harrison. GrAn

Poor little foal of an oppressèd race! To a Young Ass. Samuel Taylor Coleridge. EnRP; OxAEP-2

Poor little Jenny she blushed quite red. *(LL)* A, B, C, D, E, F, G, Little Robin Redbreast. *Unknown.* OxNR

Poor Little Johnny. *Unknown.* AmFP

"Poor little pigs, they see the wind." *(LL)* The Unknown Color. Countee Cullen. FaPON; OBCA

Poor little, pretty, fluttering [or flutt'ring] thing. Adriani Morientis ad Animam Suam. Emperor Hadrian, *tr. by* Matthew Prior. OBVE; OxBSP

Poor little Willie. Little Willie. Gerald Massey. VPP

Poor lone Hannah. Hannah Binding Shoes. Lucy Larcom. GN

Poor Lonesome Cowboy. *Unknown.* AS

Poor Losers. Keith A. Dodson. NGP

Poor Lucy Lake was overgrown. Lucy Lake. Newton Mackintosh. BXAP

Poor Mailie's Elegy. Burns. FM

Poor Man and His Parish Church, The. Robert Stephen Hawker. EBVV

Poor Man and The Rich (On the Sabbath), The. Thomas Love Peacock. *See* Poor man's sins are glaring.

"Poor man, oh, poor man, come tell to me true." The Jolly Thresherman. *Unknown.* AmFP

Poor Man's Pig, The. Edmund Blunden. MoBrPo

Poor Man's Province, The. John Wright. NOEC

Poor man's sins are glaring, The. Rich and Poor; or, Saint and Sinner. Thomas Love Peacock. FaBoCo; NOBE; NOBL; OBSV; PeLV (Poor Man and The Rich On the Sabbath, The.) IHNG

Poor Man's Sunday Walk, The. Charles MacKay. EBVV

Poor Man's Work Is Never Done, A. *Unknown.* OBET

Poor Matthias. Matthew Arnold. FM; PoEL-5

Sels.

"Poor Matthias! Wouldst thou have." OFC

Poor Matthias! Wouldst thou have. Matthew Arnold. *Fr.* Poor Matthias. FM; OFC; PoEL-5

Poor Me. *Unknown, tr. fr. French by* Richard Beaumont. ErPo

Poor Mrs. Prior. Gerda Mayer. OTCP

Poor mortals that are clogged with earth below. Sir Robert Howard *and* John Dryden. *Fr.* Indian Queen, The. TEP

Poor Movies. Will Bennett. UL

Poor naked wretches, wheresoe'er you are. Take Physic, Pomp. Shakespeare. *Fr.* King Lear. TrGrPo

Poor nation, whose sweet sap and juice. The Jews. George Herbert. JCP

Poor North. Mark Strand. AnAn

Poor of London, The. William Forster. CBAP

Poor of the Borough, The; Peter Grimes. George Crabbe. *See* Old Peter Grimes made fishing his employ.

Poor Old Fat Woman. C.M. Donald. AIW

Poor Old Horse. *Unknown.* CH; CoGr; NTP; OBET

Poor old horse: poor old horse. (LL) Poor Old Horse. *Unknown.* CH; CoGr; OBET

Poor old Jonathan Bing. Jonathan Bing. Beatrice Curtis Brown. FaPON; PDV

Poor Old Lady. *Unknown.* OBCA

Poor old lady, set her aside. The Old Mother. *Unknown.* PoToHe

Poor old man, The. *(LL)* A Note Left in Jimmy Leonard's Shack. James Wright. HCAP; NoP

Poor old Mr. Bidery. Mr. Bidery's Spidery Garden. David McCord. OTCP

Poor Old Pilgrim Misery. Thomas Lovell Beddoes. *Fr.* Bride's Tragedy, The. EnRP

Poor Old Prurient Interest Blues, The. John Hartford. MAT

Poor old Reuben Ranzo. Reuben Ranzo. *Unknown.* AmFP

Poor old Robinson Crusoe! Mother Goose. BoTP; OxNR; ReMoGo

Poor old Robinson Crusoe! *(LL)* Poor old Robinson Crusoe! Mother Goose. BoTP; OxNR; ReMoGo

Poor old Widow in her weeds, A. A Widow's Weeds. Walter de la Mare. FaBV

Poor old woodman with a leafy load, A. Death and the Woodman. La Fontaine, *tr. fr. French by* Edward Marsh. OBD

Poor Omie. *Unknown.* PrIm

Poor Ophelia sighed: "I deplore." Frank Richards. PeLi

Poor Paddy Maguire, a fourteen-hour day. Patrick Kavanagh. *Fr.* Great Hunger, The. IPY

Poor Paddy Works on the Railway. *Unknown.* AS

Poor painter captures, The. Lucianus, *tr. fr. Greek by* Sam Hamill. InMo

Poor painters oft with silly poets join. Cupid. Sir Philip Sidney. *Fr.* Arcadia. SiPS
(Against Cupid.) SiPSBD

Poor Parson, The. Chaucer. *Fr.* Canterbury Tales, The. EnVB; FHYEP; NOCV; NoP; OAEL-1; PPP, *abr.*

Poor Ploughman to a Gentleman for Whom He Had Taken a Little Pains, A. George Turberville. NoSic

Poor Poet-Ape, that would be thought our chief. On Poet-Ape. Ben Jonson. Son

Poor Poll. Robert Bridges. EBEV; OxBoLi; OxBTC

Poor restless dove, I pity thee. The Captive Dove. Anne Brontë. EBVV; OHCV; PlP

Poor savage, doubting that a river flows. Watching the Dance. James Merrill. NIP

Poor Scholar, The. Abraham ibn Chasdai, *tr. fr. Hebrew by* J. Chotzner. TrJP

Poor Scholar of the 'Forties, A. Padraic Colum. NOIV

Poor Snail, The. J. M. Westrup. BoTP

Poor Snow. Denise Riley. NBrP

Poor song. The Tape. Myra Cohn Livingston. NTCP

Poor soul, in this thy flesh what dost thou know? John Donne. *Fr.* Of the Progres[se] of the Soule; the Second Anniversarie. ESCV; OAEL-1; SeCP

Poor[e] soul[e] sat[e] sighing by a sycamore [*or* sicamore] tree, The. The Green Willow. *Unknown.* EBEvV; SCGP
(Complaint of a Lover Forsaken of His Love, The.) CoMu

Poor[e] soul[e], the centre of my sinful[l] earth. Shakespeare. *Fr.* Sonnets. AWP; EiL; EnRePo; HAP; HeIP; ImPo; InPS; LiTB; NAEL-1; NOBE; NOCV; NoP; OAEL-1; OBEV; OxAEP-1; PoE; PoEL-2; PPP; SCGP; Son; TFi; TrGrPo
(Soul and Body.) GTBS; GTBS-P

Poor South! Her books get fewer and fewer. J. Gordon Coogler. FaBoCo; FiBHP

Poor Swann, death, you know, is shy. Death says. The Duchess after the Burial. Norman Dubie. *Fr.* Duchess' Red Shoes, The. AnAn

Poor thing. Poor crippled measure. The Question Mark. Gevorg Emin, *tr. fr. Armenian by* Diana Der Hovanessian. TSaS

Poor tired Tim! It's sad for him. (*LL*) Tired Tim. Walter de la Mare. BoTP; FaPON; MoShBr; NTCP

Poor tired Tim! It's sad for him. Tired Tim. Walter de la Mare. BoTP; FaPON; MoShBr; NTCP

Poor Tom. Charles Dibdin. NOEC; OxBoLi

Poor Tom will injure nothing. (*LL*) Tom o' Bedlam's Song. *Unknown.* ChTr; GGP; ImPo; InvP; LiTB; Mes; OtMeF; PoEL-2; TFi; TrGrPo

Poor turtle! thou bemoans. William Drummond of Hawthornden. ScCV

Poor Uncle Joe. Sartorial Solecism. R. E. C. Stringer. FiBHP

Poor vaunting earth, gloss'd with uncertain pride. George Alsop. SCAP

"Poor wanderer," said the leaden sky. The Subalterns. Thomas Hardy. CMoP; MeMBP; MoAB; MoBrPo; MoP; NoAM; NOBVV; OAEL-2; Poetr; PPP; TEP

Poor Wayfaring Stranger. *Unknown.* AmFP

Poor weaver, with the hopeless brow. How Different! Ebenezer Elliot. EBEV

Poor who begs with bated breath, The. The Price of Begging. Emmanuel ben David Frances, *tr. fr. Hebrew by* A. B. Rhine. TrJP

Poor Wolf Speaks. Poor Wolf. NU

Poor Women in a City Church. Seamus Heaney. TIRV

Poor Working Girl, The. *Unknown.* AS

Poore bird! I doe not envie thee. George Daniel. *See* Poor [*or* Poore] bird! I do not envy thee.

Poore [*or* Poor] Man Payes [*or* Pays] for All, The. *Unknown.* CoMu; OBET

Poore [*or* Povre] widwe [*or* widow], somdeel [*or* somedeal *or* somedel] stape in age, A. The Nun's Priest's Tale. Chaucer. *Fr.* Canterbury Tales, The. EnVB; FHYEP; NAEL-1; NoP; OAEL-1; PoEL-1; TrGrPo, *orig. and mod. vers. by* Frank Ernest Hill
(Cock and the Hen, The.) OBNV
(Once a poor widow, aging year by year, *mod. vers. by* Theodore Morrison.) NAWM-1
(Once, long ago, set close beside a wood.) TrGrPo
(There liv'd, as authors tell, in days of yore.) OBVE

Poore wench was sighing, and weeping amaine, A. The Bard. James Shirley. ErPo

Pop-bottles pop! (*LL*) Song of the Pop-Bottlers. Morris Bishop. FaPON; FiBHP

Pop bottles pop-bottles. Song of the Pop-Bottlers. Morris Bishop. FaPON; FiBHP

Pop Corn Song, A. Nancy Byrd Turner. FaPON; SiSoPo

Pop Goes the Weasel! At. to W. R. Mardale. FaBoNo; OxNR

Pop Sociologist. J. P. Sullivan. IHNG

Popcorn is greasy, and I forgot to bring a Kleenex, The. The James Bond Movie. May Swenson. FaBoWP

Popcorn peanuts clams and gum. Bar-Room Matins. Louis MacNeice. NYBP

Pope Alexander VI. Geoffrey Lehmann. NOBAu

Pope from penance purgatorial, The. J. V. Cunningham, *after the Latin of* George Buchanan. OBVE

Popeye went down in the cellar. *Unknown.* RoPo

Poplar. Liu Sha-ho, *tr. fr. Chinese. Fr.* Family of Plants, A. LHF, *tr. by* Hualing Nieh

Poplar Field, The. William Cowper. CH; ChTr; ELP; FaBoPP; FaBoRV; FHYEP; GTBS; GTBS-P; HAP; NOBE; NOEC; PoEL-3; TrGrPo; WiR

Poplar is a French tree, The. The Trees. Christopher Morley. OHIP

Poplar is a lonely tree, The. The Poplars. Edward Bliss Reed. OHIP

Poplar Tree. Mae V. Cowdery. ShDr

Poplars, The. Theodosia Garrison. OHIP

Poplars. Helen Leuty. BoTP

Poplars. Edward Bliss Reed. OHIP

Poplars are fell'd [*or* felled], farewell to the shade, The. The Poplar Field. William Cowper. CH; ChTr; ELP; FaBoPP; FaBoRV; FHYEP; GTBS; GTBS-P; HAP; NOBE; NOEC; PoEL-3; TrGrPo; WiR

Poplars are standing there still as death. Southern Mansion. Arna Bontemps. AiP; FF; LiTM; PoBA; PoNe; TTY

Poplar's Shadow, The. May Swenson. NYBP

Popol Vuh, The. *Unknown, tr. fr. Mayan by* Munro Edmonson. STP
Sels.
Alligator's Struggles with the 400 sons
Beginnings

Poppies. P. A. Ropes. BoTP

Poppies. Zalman Schneour, *tr. fr. Hebrew by* Ruth Finer Mintz. MHP

Poppies in July. Sylvia Plath. FaBoWP; LCAP; NaP; RB

Poppies in October. Sylvia Plath. FaBoWP; HCAP; LCAP; NoAM

Poppies in Our Wheat. Edith M. Thomas. AmWP

Poppies in the Garden, The. Ffrida Wolfe. BoTP

Poppies on the Wheat. Helen Hunt Jackson. *See* Along Ancona's hills the shimmering heat.

Poppy, The. Francis Thompson. MoBrPo

Pop's tops! Bill Greenwell. PeLi

Popular. Tennyson. NOBL

Popular Functionary, A. Charles Dibdin. NOEC

Popular leader, national hero. Finn's Wishes. Desmond O'Grady, *tr. fr. Irish by the author.* CIP

Popular Negro Song, A. *Unknown.* PBCV

Popular Personage at Home, A. Thomas Hardy. ArNa; FM

Popular, popular, unpopular! Popular. Tennyson. NOBL

Popular Romance, A. Kevin Ireland. PeNZ

Popular Songs of Tuscany. *Unknown, tr. fr. Italian by* John Addington Symonds. AWP
Sels.
"I see the dawn e'en now begin to peer."
"I would I were a bird so free."
"It was the morning of the first of May."
"On Sunday morning well I knew."
"Passing across the billowy sea."
"Sleeping or waking, thou sweet face."
"Strew me with blossoms when I die."
"What time I see you passing by."

Popularity. Robert Browning. OAEL-2

Population. Mark Halliday. NAmP90

Population. George Oppen. PoA

Population center of the USA, The. Found Poem. Howard Nemerov. NGP

Population Drifts. Carl Sandburg. OxBA

Poquito Allá. Carmen Tafolla. AfAz

Pora, The. W. H. Auden. *See* How he survived them they could never understand.

"Porcelain is personal," he smiles. For His Ring and Watch on the Night Stand. Gladys Cardiff. HATNAP

Porch, The. Gary Gildner. NGP

Porch, The. Philip Pain. SCAP

Porch, The. R. S. Thomas. NOCV

Porch diminishes the fat men, The. The Fat Men. Cyril Dabydeen. PBCV

Porch swing hangs fixed in a morning sun, The. Porch Swing in September. Ted Kooser. FoLa

Porch Swing in September. Ted Kooser. FoLa

Porchlight coming on again, The. 1926. Weldon Kees. CoAP; NaP

Porcupine, The. Galway Kinnell. FoLa; NaP; NOBA

Porgy, Maria, and Bess. DuBose Heyward. PoNe

Poring on Caesar's death with earnest eye. Julius Caesar and the Honey-Bee. Charles Tennyson Turner. FM

Porirua Friday Night. Sam Hunt. PeNZ

Pornographer changes sheets, The. Blue. Ron Koertge. NGP

Porous. William Carlos Williams. NYBP

Porphyria's Lover. Robert Browning. AWP; BeLS; CBLP; EnVR; FHYEP; HAP; MeMBP; NAEL-2; OBEV; TEP; TrGrPo

Porpoises spout amid the waves. Tune: "Song of Shou-yang." Kuan Yun-shih, tr. fr. Chinese by Richard John Lynn. SuSp

Porque tú no eres ni gringa ni hispana. (LL) Santos and Stones. J. Delayne Barber. LoHo

Porson on German Scholarship. Richard Porson. FaBoCo; FaBoEE

Porson on His Majesty's Government. Richard Porson. FaBoCo

Porson's Visit to the Continent. Richard Porson. FaBoCo; FaBoEE

Port Bou. Stephen Spender. OBTV; TwCP

Port Jefferson. Louis Simpson. CAPP

Port of Call: Brazil. Alun Lewis. OBTV

Port of Holy Peter. John Masefield. OBMV

Port of Many Ships. John Masefield. OBMV

Port of Spain. Derek Walcott. NoAM

Port Talbot. John Davies. AngWe

Portent, The. Herman Melville. AmPP; AnAmPo; InPK; NAAL-1; NOBA; NoP; OBWP; OxBA; PoE; PoEL-5; PrIm; TAP; WiR

Portents, The. Phyllis McGinley. ArOW

Portents over Coffee. David Campbell. FaBoMA

Porter and keepers, when they're civil. His Rule of Behaviour: If You Are Civil, I Am Sober. James Carkesse. NOSC

Porter to th' infernal[l] gate is Sin, The. Phineas Fletcher. Fr. Locusts, or Appolyonists, The. NOSC

Porth Cwyfan. Roland Mathias. AngWe

Portion of the glorious sky, A. (LL) Earth's Children Cleave to Earth. Bryant. AnAmPo

Portion of this yew. Transformations. Thomas Hardy. PPP; RB; TEP; TRP

Portland County Jail. Unknown. AS

"Portland" Going Out, The. W. S. Merwin. NYBP

Portly he was, in carriage somewhat grand. The Bunch of Larks. Robert Leighton. EBVV

Portly prince, and goodly to the sight, A. Dryden. Fr. Hind and the Panther, The. OBSV

Portly pusher of waves, wind-slave. (LL) Winter Ocean. John Updike. InPK; Poetr

Portly Roman Senator was sipping his Rock and Rye, A. A War Bird's Burlesque. Unknown. AS

Portola Valley. Amy Clampitt. EOEF

Portrait. George Leonard Allen. CDC

Portrait. Timothy Brownlow. PeIV

Portrait. E. E. Cummings. See Buffalo Bill's.

Portrait. John Lyle Donaghy. BIrV

Portrait. Kenneth Fearing. MoAmPo

Portrait. Gail Fox. NOBC

Portrait, The. Robert Graves. CMoP

Portrait, The. Stanley Kunitz. CAPP; IMW; Poetsp; RaBo

Portrait. Antonio Machado Ruiz, tr. fr. Spanish by Robert Bly. RaBo; STV

Portrait. Edna St. Vincent Millay. LPA

Portrait. Beverly Acuff Momoi. LoHo

Portrait. Adèle Naudé. PeSA

Portrait. Brenda Marie Osbey. MT

Portrait, The. Christina Rossetti. OHCV

Portrait. Leopold Staff, tr. fr. Polish by Adam Czerniawski. PoSu

Portrait. Judith Wright. OxBSP; SoSe

Portrait, A. Walter de la Mare. NoAM

Portrait, A. Thomas Dekker and others. OxAEP-1

Portrait, A. Keats. BXAP

Portrait by a Neighbor. Edna St. Vincent Millay. FaPON; MoShBr; OBCA; PDV

Portrait by Bronzino, A. Maura Stanton. NAmP90

Portrait d'une Femme. Ezra Pound. CMoP; FF; InPS; MeMAP; MoAB; MoAmPo; MoP; NAAL-2; NoAM; NOBA; NoP; Poetr; PPP; TAP; TwCP

Portrait from the Infantry. Alan Dugan. ArOW

Portrait in Black Paint, with a Very Sparing Use of Whitewash. Elinor Wylie. NALW

Portrait in Georgia. Jean Toomer. NAAL-2; NoP

Portrait in the Guards, A. Laurence Whistler. GTBS-P

Portrait in the next room, A. Of One Dying. Philip Owens. AngWe

Portrait in Winter. Katherine Garrison Chapin. GoYe

Portrait is where you, The. Robert Creeley Also Watches. D. C. Berry. BXAP

Portrait: My Wife. John Holmes. LPA; UnAS

Portrait of a Bishop. Evan Lloyd. AngWe

Portrait of a Girl. Conrad Aiken. See This Is the Shape of the Leaf.

Portrait of a House Detective. Hans Magnus Enzensberger. PoSu

Portrait of a Jew Old Country Style. Jerome Rothenberg. NNaP

Portrait of a Lady. T. S. Eliot. TwCP

Portrait of a Lady. Elizabeth Nannestad. PeNZ

Portrait of a Lady. William Carlos Williams. AmPP; ArLo; CMoP; MoP; NAAL-2; NoAM; NOBA; OxBA

Portrait of a Lady in the Exhibition of the Royal Academy. Winthrop Mackworth Praed. Fr. Every-Day Characters. NOBL; PeLV; PoEL-4

Portrait of a Machine. Louis Untermeyer. MoAmPo

Portrait of a Man. Alan Bernheimer. UL

Portrait of a Married Couple. Margaret Scott. NOBAu

Portrait of a Nun. Bobi Jones, tr. fr. Welsh by Joseph P. Clancy. OBWVE

Portrait of a Pregnant Woman. Bobi Jones, tr. fr. Welsh by Joseph P. Clancy. OBWVE

Portrait of a Stupid Teacher of Rhetoric. Unknown, tr. fr. Greek by Peter Jay. GrAn

Portrait of a Woman (and a Man). John Figueroa. PBCV

Portrait of a Woman at Her Bath. William Carlos Williams. ArLo

Portrait of a Young Girl Raped at a Suburban Party. Brian Patten. OxBTC

Portrait of an Artist. Barbara Howes. IHMS

Portrait of an Engine Driver. Bobi Jones, tr. fr. Welsh by Joseph P. Clancy. OBWVE

Portrait of Auntie Blodwen. Elwyn Davies. AngWe

Portrait of Brutus. Shakespeare. Fr. Julius Caesar. TrGrPo

Portrait of Caesar. Shakespeare. Fr. Julius Caesar. TrGrPo

Portrait of Cressida. Shakespeare. Fr. Troilus and Cressida. TrGrPo

Portrait of Helen. Shakespeare. Fr. Troilus and Cressida. TrGrPo

Portrait of Henri III, A. Théodore Agrippa d' Aubigné, tr. fr. French. Fr. Tragiques, Les. PeHV

Portrait of Hudibras. Samuel Butler. See He was in logic[k] a great critic.

Portrait of Malcolm X. Etheridge Knight. PoBA

Portrait of Sidrophel. Samuel Butler. Fr. Hudibras. PoEL-3

Portrait of the Artist, A. Mary Leapor. Fr. Mira's Picture, a Pastoral. ECWP

Portrait of the Artist as a Prematurely Old Man. Ogden Nash. BLPL; ImPo; InPS; LiTA; LiTM

Portrait of the Artist as an Old Man. Michael Dransfield. CBAP

Portrait of the Autist as a New World Driver. Les A. Murray. CBAP

Portrait of the Boy as Artist. Barbara Howes. MoAmPo

Portrait of the Father. Lindy Hough. IHMS

Portrait of the Poet as Landscape. A. M. Klein. NoAM; NOBC

Portrait of the Pornographer. G. W. Jones. BXAP

Portrait Philippines. Alfred A. Duckett. PoNe

Portrait: The Freedom Fighter. George Jonas. NOBC

Portrait with Background. Oliver St. John Gogarty. OBMV

Portraits, The. Anna Maria Lenngren, tr. fr. Swedish by C. W. Stork. WPOW

Portraits and Repetition, sels. Gertrude Stein. "How do you like what you have." AiP

Portraits of Tudor Statesmen. U. A. Fanthorpe. FaBoEH

Portraiture. Anita Scott Coleman. ShDr

Portrush. Walking dead streets in the dark. The Archæologist. James Simmons. PBCIP

Portuguese Sea, The. Fernando Pessoa. PeSAV

Posie, The. George Herbert. ChIV-1

Posing on the sloped rock. Horned Lizard. Charles Molesworth. GrPl

Position. Léon Damas, tr. fr. French by Ellen Conroy Kennedy. NegPo

Position is so well-known, The. Inside Diameter. Clarence Major. UL

Position is where you. The Window. Robert Creeley. CAPP; NoAM; NOBA; TAP; VGW

Position of Praise, The. Brendan Kennelly. BiHa

Positive. Michael Klein. PFL

Positives. Jewel C. Latimore. PoBA

Positives for Sterling Plumpp. Don L. Lee. JB; PoBA

Positivists, The. Mortimer Collins. EBVV

Positivists ever talk in s-/Uch an epic style as Dawkins. John William Mackail. Fr. Balliol Rhymes. FaBoEE

Possessed shaman with the spear, The. Murukan, the Red One. Nakkiranar, tr. fr. Tamil by A. K. Ramanujan. PLW

Possession. Richard Aldington. MoBrPo

Possession. Lynne Lawner. ErPo

Possession. Marie Ponsot. VGW

Possession. *Unknown*. BLRP

Possessions. Ivor Gurney. FaBoPP

Possessor, The. A. R. D. Fairburn. *Fr.* Album Leaves. PeNZ

Possessor. Things. W. S. Merwin. HAP

Possibilities. Sir Richard Blackmore. Poetr
Sels.
"In the wide womb of possibility."

Possibilities. Peter Kane Dufault. NYBP

Possibilities, The. Beckian Fritz Goldberg. NAmP90

Possibilities. Longfellow. MeMAP

Possibility That Has Been Overlooked Is the Future, The. Michael
Hartnett. NOIV

Possible Salvation of Continuous Motion, The. Pattiann Rogers. MT

Possibly. Lesléa Newman. VBLP

Possibly they thought of it. Passover at Auschwitz. Laurence Josephs.
BTR

Possum pie is made of rye. *Unknown*. RoPo

Possums. Ann Coleridge. OBAP

Possum's a greasy critter, The. Roast Possum. Rita Dove. Poetr

Post-boy drove with fierce career, The. Alice Fell; or, Poverty.
Wordsworth. BeLS; OBNV

Post-Coitum Tristesse: A Sonnet. Brad Leithauser. EOEF

Post-Meridian, *sels*. Wendell Phillips Garrison.

Post Mortem. Robinson Jeffers. MoAmPo; TrGrPo

Post Mortem. A. J. Munby. NOBVV

Post Mortem. Shakespeare. *See* If Thou Survive My Well-contented Day.

Post Mortem as Angels. Barry Goldensohn. NAmP90

Post-Obits and the Poets. Martial, *tr. fr. Latin by* Byron. AWP; FaBoEE;
OBVE

Post-obits rarely reach a poet. (*LL*) Post-Obits and the Poets. Martial.
AWP; FaBoEE; OBVE

Post-Rail Song. *Unknown*. AS

Post-Recessional. G. K. Chesterton. UV

Post the Lake Poets Ballad. Frank O'Hara. PoBeRe

Post-War. Libby Houston. PAW

Postcard. Margaret Atwood. NoAM

Postcard (Found on His body after He Was Killed by the Nazis). Miklós
Radnóti, *tr. fr. Hungarian by* Steven Polgar, Stephen Berg, *and* S. J.
Marks. RaBo

Postcard from Berlin, A. Derek Mahon. BiHa

Postcard from Mexico, 16.X.1973. Andrew Salkey. PBCV

Postcard from North Antrim, A. Seamus Heaney. IPY; PBCIP; PNI

Postcard from the Garden. Marge Piercy. NoAM

Postcard from the Volcano, A. Wallace Stevens. HAP; HCAP; LiTA;
MeMAP; NoAM; SAmP; WeW

Postcard from Trakl. John Yau. OpBo

Postcard to Send to Sumer, A. William Bronk. VGW

Postcards: A Triptych, The. Denise Levertov. SRLS

Postcard's caption says twilight, The. Twilight on the River Cam. Tracey
Herd. NWP

Postcards from Kodai. Kevin Crossley-Holland. OBTV

Posted. John Masefield. Son

Poster Girl, The. Carolyn Wells. BXAP

Poster of Our Dazzling Victory at Saarbrucken, A. Rimbaud, *tr. by* Robert
Lowell. *Fr.* Eighteen-Seventy. FaBoPV; OBWP

Poster with my picture on it, The. Unwanted. Edward Field. GLP; Poetsp

Posterity. Philip Larkin. OxBC

Posterity hath many fates bemoaned. On Sir Robert Cotton the Antiquary.
Thomas Randolph. NOSC

Posterity, thy name is Samuel Johnson. A Dream of Judgement. Douglas
Dunn. OxBC

Posterity will ne'er survey. An Epitaph for Castlereagh. Byron.
(Epitaph: "Posterity will ne'er survey.") FaBoEE

Posthumous. Michael O'Loughlin. IB; PBCIP

Posthumous Coquetry. Théophile Gautier, *tr. fr. French by* Arthur Symons.
AWP; OBD; PeVV

Posthumous Keats. Stanley Plumly. SV

Posthumous Rehabilitation. Tadeusz Rózewicz, *tr. fr. Polish by* Adam
Czerniawski. FaBoPV

Postilion Has Been Struck by Lightning, The. Patricia Beer. OxBC

Postman, The. Clive Sansom. BoTP

Postman, The. Alice Todd. BoTP

Postman, The. *Unknown*. FaPON

Postman comes when I am still in bed, The. A Sick Child. Randall
Jarrell. InPK; InvP; OxBC; VGW

Postman, Postman, at the gate. February 14th — Valentine's Day.
Unknown. ISE

Postman's Bell Is Answered Everywhere, The. Horace Gregory. MoAmPo;
NYBP

Postman's Knock. Rodney Bennett. BoTP

Postmaster-General cried: 'Arsehole!', The. Victor Gray. PeLi

Postponement. Thomas Hardy. EnVR

Postscript. Henri Coulette. DiPo

Postscript. Sandra Hochman. NMM

Postscript. R. S. Thomas. FaBoMo; OxBC

Postscript, 1984. John Hewitt. BiHa

Postscript for Gweno. Alun Lewis. AngWe; BoLoP; GTBS-P

Postscript to a Pettiness. A. S. J. Tessimond. OxBSP

Postscript to an Elegy. Gibbons Ruark. MT

Postscript to Orwell's *Animal Farm*, A. Miadesnia. PeLi

Postscript to Verses on the History of France, A. *Unknown*. NOIV

Postscripts 2. Dennis Brutus. HBAPE

Posture of the tree, The. Lovers in Winter. Robert Graves. FaBoEE;
NYBP

Postures of Love, The, *sels*. Alex Comfort.
"There is a white mare that my love keeps." ErPo

Posy: "Dear love, I am resolved with thee to live." Sir Robert Ayton.
NOSC

Posy, The: "Let wits contest." George Herbert. *See* Let wits contest.

Posy of Thyme, The. *Unknown*. OBET

Posy Ring, The. Clément Marot, *tr. fr. French by* Ford Madox Ford.
AWP

Pot itself was half the story, The. Cactus. Irena Klepfisz. ETG

Pot lilac,/ pet thorn/ flick/ nest. Lottery & Requiem. Maggie O'Sullivan.
NBrP

Pot of Tea, A. Robert W. Service. NSI; PoWW

Pot of wine among flowers, A. Drinking Alone in the Moonlight. Li Po,
tr. fr. Chinese by Amy Lowell *and* Florence Ayscough. AWP

Pot of wine among the flowers, A. Li Po, *tr. by* Irving Lo. *Fr.* Drinking
Alone beneath the Moon. SuSp

Pot Poured Out, A. Samuel Menashe. Mes

Pot Shot. Padraic Fallon. CIP

Potage au Petit Puss. Menu. Edward Lear. FaBoNo

Potato. Richard Wilbur. CAPP; LiTA; MoAB; TrGrPo

Potato Clock. Roger McGough. OTCP

Potato clock, a potato clock, A. Potato Clock. Roger McGough. OTCP

Potato Harvest, The. Sir Charles G. D. Roberts. NOBC

Potato Song. Stanley Moss. NGP

Potato was deep in the dark under ground. The Tryst. John Banister
Tabb. OBAL

Potatoes. David Donnell. NIP; NOBC

Potatoes come out of the earth bright, The. Seal Run. Helen Dunmore.
PWE

Potatoes' Dance, The. Vachel Lindsay. FaPON

Potatoes of the corner store sing, The. At Kino Viejo, Mexico. Alberto A.
Ríos. NoAM

Potchikoo Marries. Louise Erdrich. *Fr.* Old Man Potchikoo. HATNAP

Potent behind a cart with Mary Ann? (*LL*) On First Looking into Krafft-
Ebing's *Psychopathosexualis* [*or* Psychopathia Sexualis]. Oliver St.
John Gogarty. FaBoBl; IHNG; UV

Potflower on the windowsill says to me, The. The Power of Suicide.
Muriel Rukeyser. NALW

Potpourri from a Surrey Garden. Sir John Betjeman. CBLP; FiBHP; NOBL

Potter, The. *Unknown, tr. fr. Geez by* Halim El-Dabh. TTY

Potter,/ O potter. An Urn for Burial. *Unknown, tr. fr. Tamil by* A. K.
Ramanujan. PLW

Potter's Song, The. Longfellow. *Fr.* Kéramos. PoEL-5

Poulterer, The. Mimi Khalvati. NWP

Poultry. Diana Der Hovanessian. GrPl

Pound at Spoleto. Lawrence Ferlinghetti. PoM

Pound-note was the best kind of passport, A. The Emigration Trains.
Thomas McCarthy. PBCIP

Pounded spice [*or* spise] both taste [*or* tast] and scent [*or* sent] doth please,
The. At Fotheringay. Robert Southwell. PoEL-2
(Decease Release. NoSic

Pound's Gentility. Reed Bye. UL

Pour and say again and again and yet again. Meleager, *tr. fr. Greek by*
Barbara Hughes Fowler. *Fr.* Epigrams. HePo

Pour Commencer. Jon Stallworthy. NoAM

Pour demander le chemin. *Unknown*. *Fr.* Lytell Treatyse for to Lerne
Englysshe and Frens, A. OxBLMV

Pour for Heliodora Persuasion and pour for Cypris. Meleager, *tr. fr. Greek
by* Barbara Hughes Fowler. *Fr.* Epigrams. HePo

Pour l'Election de Son Sepulchre, I-V. Ezra Pound. *See* For three years, out of key with his time.

Pour O pour that parting soul in song. Song of the Son. Jean Toomer. CDC; NIP; PoBA

Pour out the dark wine, Miriamne. Romancero. Lex Banning. NOBAu

Pour out your light, O stars. Ivor Gurney. FaBoEE; FaBoTw

Pour this wine. Meleager, *tr. fr. Greek by* Peter Whigham. GrAn

Pour Us Wine. Ibn Kolthum, *tr. by* E. Powys Mathers. *Fr.* Mu'allaqat, The. AWP

Pouring its full life out into its scent. *(LL)* Cracked Looking Glass. Jean Garrigue. VCAP

Pourquoi You Greased. *Unknown.* ChTr

Pours into us . . . ding ding! *(LL)* Esanzo. Antoine-Roger Bolamba. NegPo

Poussie, poussie, baudrons. *Unknown.* OxNR

Poverty. Charles Simic. MAT

Poverty. Theognis, *tr. fr. Greek by* John Hookham Frere. AWP

Poverty. Thomas Traherne. Prf; TEP; TrCP

Poverty. *Unknown*, *tr. fr. Sanskrit by* Arthur Ryder. *Fr.* Panchatantra, The. AWP

Poverty, in Imitation of Milton. Samuel Jones. NOEC

Poverty in London. Samuel Johnson. *See* By numbers here from shame or censure free.

Poverty Knock. *Unknown.* FaBoVe; OBET

Poverty on the Bank. Mei Yao Ch'en, *tr. fr. Chinese by* Jonathan Chaves. SuSp

Poverty, remorseless spectre. Christmas Eve, South, 1865. Mary E. Tucker. CBWP-1

Poverty? wealth? seek neither. Kassia, *tr. fr. Greek by* Patrick Diehl. WPOW

Poverty's the worst savage crime. Alcaeus, *tr. fr. Greek by* Sam Hamill. InMo

Povre Ame Amoureuse. Louise Labé, *tr. fr. French by* Robert Bridges. AWP

Powder and scent and silence. The young dwarf. Clair de Lune. Anthony Hecht. NYBP

Powder-light let dust lie/ On Musa, who had blue eyes. Epitaph in the Borghese Gardens. *Unknown*, *tr. fr. Greek by* Peter Whigham. GrAn

Powder of Sympathy, The. James Tate. AnAn

Power. Hart Crane. *See* Nasal whine of power whips a new universe.

Power. Audre Lorde. GLP; NoAM

Power. Adrienne Rich. NALW; TAP

Power. Alma Villanueva. AfAz

Power above powers, O heavenly Eloquence. Poetry in England. Samuel Daniel. *Fr.* Musophilus; or, Defence of All Learning. EPCY; NoSic (Heavenly Eloquence.) NOBE

Power and Light. James Dickey. NAAL-2

Power and Peace. Robert Herrick. CaPo

Power and the Glory, The. Siegfried Sassoon. OBMV

Power Cut. Seamus Deane. PBCIP

Power Failure. Michael Dennis Browne. AmPA

Power Games. Eva Salzman. NWP

Power-house, A. Classic Scene. William Carlos Williams. NAAL-2; OxBA

Power in the People, The. Robert Herrick. CaPo

Power lies in my hand. The Sibyl. Joan LaBombard. GoYe

Power of Destiny, The. Mary Whateley. CaPo

Power of Faith, The. Thomas Rabbitt. NAmP90

Power of Fancy, The. Philip Freneau. AmPP

Power of Innocence, The. "C. G. H." NOEC

Power of Interval, The. Lord De Tabley. NOBVV; OxBSP

Power of Love He Wants Shih (Everything), The. Rochelle Owens. NMM

Power of Maples, The. Gerald Stern. NU

Power of Music, The. Thomas Lisle. NOBL; PlP

Power of Music, The. Shakespeare. *Fr.* Merchant of Venice, The. GN

Power of My Mother, The. Sharon Olds. MDDM

Power of Numbers, The. Abraham Cowley. *Fr.* Davideis.

Power of Prayer, The. Samuel Johnson. *Fr.* Vanity of Human Wishes, The: The Tenth Satire of Juvenal Imitated. EBEV; ECEV; NOBE; NOEC; NoP; OAEL-1; OxAEP-1; PoEL-3; PrIm; TEP; TFi

Power of Prayer, The. Richard Chenevix Trench. *See* Lord, what a change within us one short hour.

Power of raven be thine. Good Wish. *Unknown*, *tr. fr. Gaelic by* Alexander Carmichael. FaBoCh

Power of Ridicule, The. Pope. *See* Ask you what provocation I have had?

Power of Spleen, The. The Countess of Winchilsea. *Fr.* Spleen, a Pindaric Poem, The. ECWP

Power of Suicide, The. Muriel Rukeyser. NALW

Power of Taste, The. Zbigniew Herbert, *tr. fr. Polish by* John Carpenter *and* Bogdana Carpenter. AnAn; PoSu

Power of the Dog, The. Kipling. BLPA; BLPL

Power of Thought, The. Süsskind von Trimberg, *tr. fr. Middle High German.* TrJP

Power of Time, The. Swift. FaBoEE

Power of Toads, The. Pattiann Rogers. NAmP90

Power of Women, The. Matilda Betham-Edwards. ECWP

Power speaks only out of sleep and blackness, The. Below Loughrigg. Fleur Adcock. PeNZ; PWE

Power, that gives with liberal hand, The. On the Religion of Nature. Philip Freneau. AmPP; EAP; NAAL-1

Power Transformer. Ian Wedde. *Fr.* Earthly: Sonnets for Carlos. PeNZ

Powerful Eyes o' Jeremy Tait, The. Wallace Irwin. FiBHP

Powerful Servants. Friedrich von Logau, *tr. fr. German.* GePo, *tr. by* George C. Schoolfield

Powerless emperor, The. The Hard Listener. William Carlos Williams. OxBSP

Powerline Incarnation, The. Les A. Murray. CBAP

Powers and principalities — all the gods. Denise Levertov. *Fr.* Mass for the Day of St. Thomas Didymus. CrSp

Powers of Congress. Alice Fulton. BAP-89; NAmP90

Powers of Darkness. Abraham Cowley. NOSC

Powers of the Pen, The, *sels.* Evan Lloyd.
Helen like the Rose. OBWVE
(Powers of the Pen, The.) AngWe

Powers of the Pen, The. Evan Lloyd. *See* Drawn by old Homer's hand, the rose.

Powers of Thirteen., *sels.* John Hollander.
"After the midwinter marriages — the bride of snow." VCAP
"Like some ill-fated butterfly, the literalists." VCAP
"So we came at last to meet, after the lights were out." VCAP
"These two tales I tell of myself and the life I led." VCAP
"What she and I had between us once, America." VCAP
"Yes, go on! This is plain talk of plainer feelings now,." VCAP

Powhatan's Daughter. Hart Crane. *Fr.* Bridge, The. LiTA; NAAL-2

Pow'r must it maintain, A. *(LL)* An Horatian Ode upon Cromwell's [*or* Cromwell's] Return from Ireland. Andrew Marvell. EBEV; ESCV; GeHe; GTBS; GTBS-P; HAP; IIP; InPS; JCP; NOBE; NoP; NOSC; OAEL-1; OBEV; OBWP; OxAEP-1; PoEL-2; SCGP; SeCP; SeCV-1; TFi

Powte's Complaint, The. *Unknown.* GBP

Powwow. W. D. Snodgrass. GrPl; NYBP; SoSe

Powwow remnants. Lew Blockcolski. VoR

Pox of the statesman that's witty, A. The Cabal at Nickey Nackey's. Aphra Behn. NOSC

Pox of this fooling and plotting of late, A. The Careless Good Fellow. John Oldham. APAS; SeCV-2

Pox on't, says Time to Thomas Hearne. *Unknown.* FaBoEE

Practical Concerns. William J. Harris. PoBA

Practical Woman, A. Thomas Hardy. NAs

Practically all you newspaper people. The Clown. Donald Hall. NYBP

Practice Board. Linda Saunders. NWP

Practice of Magical Evocation, The. Diane Di Prima. PoBeRe; PoM

Practice resurrection. *(LL)* So, friends, every day do something. Wendell Berry. EaPr

Practising Not Dying. Vincent Buckley. *Fr.* Golden Builders. FaBoMA

Præfatory Poem to the Little Book, Entituled, Christianus per Ignem, A. Nicholas Noyes. SCAP

Prague is a famous, ancient, kingly seat. John Taylor. *Fr.* Taylor's Travels from London to Prague. OBTV

Prague Spring. Tony Harrison. OBTV

Prairie, *sels.* Carl Sandburg.
Look at Six Eggs. FaPON

Prairie child,/ Brief as dew. Nancy Hanks. Harriet Monroe. OHIP

Prairie-Dog Town. Mary Austin. FaPON

Prairie Fires. Hamlin Garland. OBCA

Prairie goes to the mountain. Open Range. Kathryn Jackson *and* Byron Jackson. FaPON

Prairie Graveyard. Anne Marriott. NOBC

Prairie Waters by Night. Carl Sandburg. NAAL-2

Prairie wind blew harder than it could, The. Swallows. Thomas Hornsby Ferril. RFM

Prairies, The. Bryant. AmPP; EAP; NAAL-1; NOBA; OxBA; PoEL-4; TAP

Praise. Mary Anderson. BoTP

Praise. Jane Cooper. TAP

Praise. R. H. Grenville. PoToHe

Praise. George Herbert. ESCV

Praise II. George Herbert. ChIV-1

Praise. Dinah Livingstone. AIW

Praise. William Matthews. AmPA

Praise. Rainer Maria Rilke, *tr. fr. German*. ChTr

Praise. Christopher Smart. OxBChV

Praise. Henry Vaughan *and* Thomas Stanley. ESCV

Praise and extol Him for ever and ever. (*LL*) All you big things, bless the Lord. *Unknown*. EaPr

Praise and Prayer. Sir William Davenant. *Fr*. Gondibert. OBEV

Praise for an Urn. Hart Crane. AWP; CMoP; HAP; LiTM; MeMAP; MoAB; MoAmPo; NoAM; OxBA; PPP; WeW

Praise for Death. Donald Hall. BAP-90

Praise for Mercies Spiritual and Temporal. Isaac Watts. NOEC

Praise for Sick Women. Gary Snyder. NeAP; PoBeRe

Praise for the Fountain Opened. William Cowper. InPK

Praise God, now, for an English war. The English War. Dorothy L. Sayers. OtMeF

"Praise God" said Spenser, "You live where you choose. The Position of Praise. Brendan Kennelly. BiHa

Praise Hearst, from whom all blessings flow! Doxology. Bert Leston Taylor. OBAL

Praise him. (*LL*) Pied Beauty. Gerard Manley Hopkins. ArNa; AWP; CBCK; ClHu; CMoP; EaPr; EBEvV; EBVV; EnlH; EnVR; FaBoMo; FaPoB; GGP; GoJo; GTBS-P; HAP; HeIP; HoPM; ImPo; InPK; InPS; InvP; LiTB; LiTM; LPA; MeMBP; MoAB; MoBrPo; MoP; NAEL-2; NoAM; NOBE; NOBVV; NoP; NTP; OAEL-2; OBEV; OBMV; OBNC; OxAEP-2; OxBSP; PFP; PoE; Poetr; PoRA; PPP; PrIm; RaBo; RB; SCGP; SCV; SoSe; SOTW; TEP; TFi; TrGrPo; TTTS; UV; WeW

Praise him all creatures! (*LL*) Cantico del Sole. St. Francis of Assisi. CTC

Praise him for the place he picked. Death in the Aquarium. Richard Hugo. AnAn

Praise him that aye. Laudate Dominum. The Countess of Pembroke. ChIV-1

Praise Him Who Makes Us Happy. Mark Van Doren. AH

Praise in Summer. Richard Wilbur. CAPP; FoLa; NoP

Praise is a quiet and a gracious thing. Praise. R. H. Grenville. PoToHe

Praise is devotion fit for mighty minds. Praise and Prayer. Sir William Davenant. *Fr*. Gondibert. OBEV

Praise it who list, I like it not. (*LL*) Give place all ye that doth rejoice. Sir Thomas Wyatt. SiPS

Praise memory and forgetfulness! Macedonius, *tr. fr. Greek* by Barriss Mills. GrAn

Praise Now Your God. H. P. Brucker. AH

Praise, O my heart, with praise from depth and height. Adam's Song of the Visible World. Ridgely Torrence. TrPWD

Praise of a Child. *Yoruba Oral Tradition, tr. by* Ulli Beier *and* B. Gbadamosi. WTO

Praise of a Collie. Norman MacCaig. RB

Praise of a Train. *Zulu Oral Tradition, tr. by* B. W. Vilakazi. WTO

Praise of a Yellow Skin, The, or An Elizabeth in Gold. John Collop. NOSC

Praise of Amen Ra! Hymn to Amen Ra, the Sun God. *Unknown, tr. fr. Egyptian by* Frank Lloyd Griffith. WGRP

Praise of Ceres. Thomas Heywood. *Fr*. Silver Age, The. ElL

Praise, of course, is best: plain speech breeds hate. Meditation. Palladas, *tr. fr. Greek by* Dudley Fitts. GrAn

Praise of Created Things. St. Francis of Assisi. FaPON

Praise of Creation. George Moses Horton. AAP

Praise of Dancing, The. Sir John Davies. *See* Daungcing (bright Lady) then began to bee.

Praise of Dust, The. G. K. Chesteron. MoBrPo; OtMeF

Praise of Faith, The. John Hall. ChIV-2

Praise of Fionn, The. *Unknown, tr. fr. Irish by* Frank O'Connor. PeIV; TIRV

Praise of God. *Unknown*. NOIV

Praise of Godly Love Out of 1 John. 4, The. John Hall. ChIV-2

Praise of His Lady, A. *At. to* John Heywood. ElL; OBEV

Praise of His Love, Wherein He Reproveth Them That Compare Their Ladies with His, A. The Earl of Surrey. *See* Give place, ye lovers (here before).

Praise of Ibikunle. *Yoruba Oral Tradition, tr. by* B. Awe. WTO

Praise of Little Women. Juan Ruiz, Archpriest of Hita, *tr. fr. Spanish by* Longfellow. AWP

Praise of meaner wits this work like profit brings, The. Another of the Same. *See* Sir Walter Ralegh. SiPS; SiPSBD

Praise of Neptune's empery, The. (*LL*) A Hymn[e] in Praise [*or* Prayse] of Neptune. Thomas Campion. BoNaP; NOBE; OBEV; WiR

Praise of New England. Thomas Caldecot Chubb. GoYe

Praise of New Netherland, The. Jacob Steendam. PAH

Praise of Philip Sparrow, The, *sels*. George Gascoigne. Of All the Birds That I Do Know. CH

Praise of Sailors, The. *Unknown*. OxBSS

Praise of Spenser. William Browne. OxAEP-1

Praise of Waterford, The, *sels*. *Unknown*. "God of his goodnes, praysed that he be." NOIV

Praise of Women. Robert Mannyng. OBEV

Praise one appearing. Rice Grass. Jeremy Hooker. SCBI

Praise Song for King Kalakaua. *Unknown, tr. fr. Hawaiian by* N. B. Emerson. WTO

Praise the Lord. Milton. *See* Let Us with a Gladsome Mind.

Praise the Lord for all the seasons. Praise. Mary Anderson. BoTP

Praise the Lord in your infinite variety all creatures. Ernesto Cardenal. EaPr

Praise the world to the angel, not the unutterable world. Rainer Maria Rilke, *tr. fr. German*. EaPr

Praise to the emptiness that blanks out existence. Existence. Jalal al-Din Rumi, *tr. fr. Persian by* Coleman Barks *and* John Moyne. EnlH

Praise to the End! Theodore Roethke. InPS

  Sels.

  "Mips and ma the mooly moo." CBNP; NBLV; RB

Praise to the Holiest in the height. Cardinal Newman. *Fr*. Dream of Gerontius, The. PlP

  (Chorus of Angels.) NOCV; PoEL-5

  (Fifth Choir of Angelicals.) NOBVV

Praise we the Lord/ of Heaven's kingdom. Caedmon's Hymn. Caedmon, *tr. fr. Anglo-Saxon*. EBEV, *tr. by* Sally Purcell; OAEL-1, *tr. by* Walter Kendrick; TEP, *tr. by* Walter Kendrick

Praise wet snow. Denise Levertov. EaPr

Praise ye the Lord!/ For it is good to sing praises unto our God. Bible, *O.T., paraphrased by* Sir Thomas Wyatt. *Fr*. Psalms.

  (Psalm CXLVII: "Praise ye the Lord," *paraphrased by* the Countess of Pembroke.) NOCV

  (Hallelujah/ Praise ye the Lord . . . .) TrJP

  (Psalm CXLVII: "Praise ye the Lord," *paraphrased by* Christopher Smart.) NOCV

  (Sing unto the Lord with thanksgiving.) OHIP

Praise ye the Lord for the avenging of Israel. The Song of Deborah. Bible, *O.T. Fr*. Judges. AWP; BoWoP; PBWP

  (Then Sang Deborah and Barak.) TrJP

Praise Ye the Lord, O Celebrate His Fame. Peleg Folger. AH; ChIV-1

Praise ye the Lord/ Praise ye the Lord. Bible, *O.T., paraphrased by* Sir Thomas Wyatt. *Fr*. Psalms. TrJP

  (Psalm CXLVIII: "Hallelujah! kneel and sing," *paraphrased by* Christopher Smart.) OBVE, *ll*. 1–10

  (Song of Praise, A.) TrGrPo

"Praise ye the Lord!" The psalm to-day. The Thanksgiving in Boston Harbor. Hezekiah Butterworth. OHIP; PAH

Praise you, "All these were lovely"; say, "He loved." (*LL*) The Great Lover. Rupert Brooke. HoPM; ImPo; LiTB; LiTM; MoBrPo; PAW; PoRA; TrGrPo

Praise youth's hot blood if you will, I think that happiness. Age in Prospect. Robinson Jeffers. MoAB; MoAmPo

Praised be Diana's fair and harmless light. Sir Walter Ralegh. NoSic; SiPSBD

  (Homage to Diana.) WiR

  (Shepherd's Praise of Diana, The.) SiPS

Praised be man, he is existing in milk. Jack Kerouac. *Fr*. Mexico City Blues. NeAP

Praised be the name of the Lord, who created the wine. Five Arabic Verses in Praise of Wine. *Unknown, tr. fr. Arabic by* Hartwig Hirschfeld. TrJP

Praised beyond all Enids be. In Morfudd's Arms. Dafydd ap Gwilym, *tr. fr. Welsh by* Rolfe Humphries. OBWVE

Praisers of women in their proud and beautiful poems, The. "Not Marble nor the Gilded Monuments." Archibald MacLeish. BoLoP; CMoP; HoPM; MeMAP; MoAB; PoRA; TwCP

Praises. Thomas McGrath. FoLa

Praises, The. Charles Olson. VGW

Praises of a Country Life, The. Ben Jonson. OBVE; SeCP

Praises of Baboon, the Totem Animal, The. *Unknown, tr. by* George Fortune. OBAP

Praises of Field-marshal J. C. Smuts, The. Nongejeni Zuma, *tr. fr. Zulu by* Harry C. Lugg. PeSAV

Praises of Henry Francis Fynn. *Zulu Oral Tradition, tr. by* T. Cope. WTO

Praises of King George VI. A. Z. Ngani, *tr. fr. Xhosa by* Jack Cope. PeSA

Praises of the Canna, The. *Unknown*, Thomas Arbonset; *Eng. vers. by* John Croumbie Brown. PeSAV

Praises of the King Dingana (Vesi). *Unknown, tr. fr. Zulu*. PeSA

Praises of the King of Oyo. *Yoruba Oral Tradition*, tr. by Ulli Beier. WTO

Praises of the King Tshaka. *Unknown, tr. fr. Zulu.* PeSA

Praises of the Train. Demetrius Segooa, tr. fr. Sotho. PeSA

Praises, Tamalpais. Song of the Turkey Buzzard. Lew Welch. PoM

Praises to Him for aye. *(LL)* For Deliverance from a Fever. Anne Bradstreet. NAAL-1; NALW

Praises to those who can wait. Zealots of Yearning. David Rokeah, tr. fr. *Hebrew* by I. M. Lask. TrJP

Praties, The. *Unknown.* WTO

Praxinoa at home? Gorgo and Praxinoa. Theocritus [or Theokritus], tr. fr. *Greek* by Barbara Hughes Fowler. *Fr. Idylls.* HePo

Praxiteles and Phryne. William Wetmore Story. BeLS

Pray!. Irene Arnold. BLRP

Pray Billy Pitt explain thy rigs. On Mr. Pitt's Hair-Powder Tax. Burns. FaBoEE

Pray but one prayer for me 'twixt thy closed lips. Summer Dawn. William Morris. Mes; NOBE; NOBVV; OAEL-2; OBEV; OBNC; OxAEP-2

Pray for my soul. More things are wrought by prayer. Prayer: "Pray for my soul. More things are wrought by prayer." Tennyson. *Fr.* Idylls of the King. FHYEP; NAEL-2; OBNC; WGRP

Pray for the soul of Maire Og at dawning of the day! *(LL)* The Love-Talker. "Ethna Carbery." CH; WPE

Pray — Give — Go. Annie Johnson Flint. BLRP

Pray God, pardon us out of His grace. *(LL)* Ballad of the Gibbet. Villon. AWP

Pray how did she look? Was she pale, was she wan? On Lady Anne Hamilton. Sheridan. FaBoEE

Pray in the early morning. Pray! Irene Arnold. BLRP

Pray keep them safe at home. *(LL)* Three children sliding on the ice. At. to John Gay. OxNR; ReMoGo

Pray let us carry on our shoulders with love! With their world's song. *(LL)* Lord! You Saved Me from Ur-Germany as I Fled. Uri Zvi Greenberg. MHP

Pray Remember the Poor. Christopher Smart. NOEC

Pray — reveal yourself, my bereaved soul is weary. *(LL)* Before Your Wonders I Stand, My World. Shimon Halkin. MHP

Pray steal me not, I'm Mrs. Dingley's. On the Collar of Mrs. Dingley's Lap-Dog. Swift. FaBoEE; FM

Pray tell me, sir, whose dog are you? *(LL)* Epigram Engraved on the Collar of a Dog Given [or Which I Gave] to His Royal Highness. Pope. CoGr; FaBoCo; FaBoEE; FM; InPK; NOEC; NTCP; OxBSP

Pray tell your querist if he may. Charm: Corns. *Unknown.* FaBoUs

Pray thee, take care, that tak'st my book[e] in hand. To the Reader. Ben Jonson. BeJo; NoP; PoE; SeCV-1

Pray to What Earth Does This Sweet Cold Belong. Thoreau. UnPo

Pray, where are the little bluebells gone. About the Fairies. Jean Ingelow. BoTP

Pray where would lamb and lion be. Nature Be Damned. Anne Wilkinson. NOBC

Pray who lies here? why don't you know. Original Epitaph on a Drunkard. Royall Tyler. OBAL

Pray why are you so bare, so bare. The Haunted Oak. Paul Laurence Dunbar. AAP; UnPo

Pray without Ceasing. Ophelia Guyon Browning. BLPA; BLPL

Prayer: "As I walk through the streets." F. S. Flint. TrPWD

Prayer: "Be thou my vision, O Lord of my heart." *Unknown, tr. fr. Irish by* Eleanor Hull. TIRV

Prayer: "Bear with me, Master, when I turn from Thee." Edith Lovejoy Pierce. TrPWD

Prayer: "Each day I walk with wonder." Clinton Scollard. TrPWD

Prayer: "Eternal God, our life is but." "Yehoash," tr. fr. *Yiddish* by Isidore Goldstick. TrJP

Prayer: "Father in Heaven! from whom the simplest flower." Felicia Dorothea Hemans. TrPWD

Prayer: "Fear of death disturbs me constantly, The." Gabrielle de Coignard, tr. fr. *French* by Raymond Oliver. WPOW

Prayer: "Forgive me, you whom they cast in a name." Avraham Shlonsky, tr. fr. *Hebrew* by Francis Landy. MHP, tr. by Ruth Finer Mintz

Prayer: "Give me a death like Buddha's. Let me fall." Stanley Moss. SM

Prayer: "God, I need a job because I need money." Alan Dugan. CAPP; NoAM

Prayer: "God, is it sinful if I feel." Mary Dixon Thayer. TrPWD

Prayer: "God, listen through my words to the beating of my heart." Margueritte Harmon Bro. TrPWD

Prayer: "God of light and blossom." James P. Mousley. GoYe

Prayer: "God, though [or although] this life is but a wraith." Louis Untermeyer. MoAmPo; TrJP; WGRP

Prayer: "Grant that no Hobgoblins fright me." John Day. Spl

Prayer: "I ask good things that I detest." Robert Louis Stevenson. TrPWD

Prayer: "I ask you this." Langston Hughes. CDC

Prayer: "I had thought of putting an/ altar." Isabella Maria Brown. PoNe

Prayer: "I kneel not now to pray that Thou." Harry Hibbard Kemp. WGRP

Prayer: "I know not by what methods rare." Eliza M. Hickock. BLRP

Prayer: "I praise Thee, Christ, that on Thy breast." Muireadhach Albannach, tr. fr. *Gaelic* by Nigel MacNeill. ScCV

Prayer: "I pray not for the joy that knows." Marion Franklin Ham. TrPWD

Prayer: "I pray Thee O Lord." Julian Tuwim, tr. fr. *Polish* by Wanda Dynowska. TrJP

Prayer: "I want a god." Francisco Alarcon. AfAz

Prayer: "If I must of my senses lose." Theodore Roethke. TwCP

Prayer: "If I popped in at Downing Street." Max Beerbohm. UV

Prayer: "If on a Spring night I went by." John Galsworthy. OtMeF
(Prayer, The.) UV

Prayer: "If you really exist — show up." Nina Cassian, tr. fr. *Romanian by* Brenda Walker *and* Andrea Deletant. VBLP

Prayer: "In the bright bay of your morning, O God." Claire Goll, tr. fr. *German by* Babette Deutsch *and* Avrahm Yarmolinsky. TrJP

Prayer: "Let me do my work each day." Max Ehrmann. BLPA; BLPL; FaBoBe
(Prayer, A.) PoToHe

Prayer: "Let me not know how sins and sorrows glide." James Elroy Flecker. TrPWD

Prayer: "Let me work and be glad." Theodosia Garrison. TrPWD

Prayer: "Let my words." Joseph Bruchac. ETG

Prayer: "Let us leave our island woods grown dim and blue." "Æ." TIRV

Prayer: "Lord, as thou wilt, bestow." Eduard Friedrich Mörike, tr. fr. *German by* John Drinkwater. TrPWD

Prayer: "Lord, for the erring thought." William Dean Howells. *Fr.* Thanksgiving, A. TrPWD; WGRP

Prayer: "Lord God of the oak and the elm." George Villiers. TrPWD

Prayer: "Lord I am not entirely selfish." Gavin Ewart. OxBC

Prayer: "Lord, let me live like a Regular Man." Berton Braley. BLPA

Prayer: "Lord, make me sensitive to the sight." Barbara Marr. TrPWD

Prayer: "Lord, not for light in darkness do we pray." John Drinkwater. TrPWD; WGRP

Prayer: "Lord, send what Thou wilt." Eduard Friedrich Mörike, tr. fr. *German by* Philip L. Miller. RiWo

Prayer: "Lord, what a change within us one short hour." Richard Chenevix Trench. WBLP; WGRP
(Power of Prayer, The.) PoToHe
(Prevailing Prayer.) BLRP
(Sonnet.) TrPWD

Prayer: "Master, they say that when I seem." C. S. Lewis. TIRV; TrCP

Prayer: "More things are wrought by prayer." Tennyson, *incorporated in* Idylls of the King *with changes, as* The Passing of Arthur. *Fr.* Morte d'Arthur. BLRP; DL; EBVVPR; FaBoBe; FaBoRV; NIP; NOBVV; OAEL-2; OBNV; PoEL-5

Prayer: "My God (oh, let me call Thee mine)." Anne Brontë. TrPWD

Prayer: "O Christ, who in Gethsemane." H. Cordelia Ray. CBWP-3

Prayer: "O Earth, O dewy mother, breathe on us." Archibald Lampman. TrPWD

Prayer: "O for one minute hark what we are saying!" F.W.H. Myers. TrPWD

Prayer: "O God of goodness, forwardness, and fulness." Doris Hedges. GoYe

Prayer: "O Lord, the hard-won miles." Paul Laurence Dunbar. TrPWD

Prayer: "O that mine eyes might closed be." Thomas Elwood. PWR

Prayer: "Often the western wind has sung to me." Lord Alfred Bruce Douglas. TrPWD

Prayer: "Oh, Lord! I lift my heart." Priscilla Jane Thompson. CBWP-2

Prayer: "Oh! that mine eye might closed be." Thomas Ellwood. WGRP

Prayer: "Omnipotent confederate of all good." Amos N. Wilder. TrPWD

Prayer: "Out of the deeps I cry to thee, O God!" Richard Le Gallienne. TrPWD

Prayer: "Pray for my soul. More things are wrought by prayer." Tennyson. *Fr.* Idylls of the King. FHYEP; NAEL-2; OBNC; WGRP

Prayer: "Prayer, the Church's banquet, Angels' age." George Herbert. *See* Prayer the churches banquet, angel's [or angels] age.

Prayer: "Searcher of souls, you who in heaven abide." Samuel Butler. FaBoEE

Prayer: "Take from the earth its tragic hunger, Lord." Hazel J. Fowler. TrPWD

Prayer: "Teach me, Father, how to go." Edwin Markham. BoTP; TrPWD; WGRP

Prayer: "Tend me my birds, and bring again." Norman Gale. TrPWD

Prayer: "These are the gifts I ask." Henry van Dyke. *See* These Are the Gifts I Ask.

Prayer: "Those who love Thee may they find." George F. Chawner. BLRP

Prayer: "Through every minute of this day." John Oxenham. BLRP

Prayer: "Thy blessing on the boys — for time has come." Haim Guri, tr. fr. Hebrew by Ruth H. Lask. TrJP

Prayer: "To Thy continual Presence, in me wrought." William Ellery Channing. TrPWD

Prayer: "Until I lose my soul and lie." Sara Teasdale. TrPWD

Prayer: "What a commanding power." Thomas Washbourne. WGRP

Prayer: "What do you take." Bill Manhire. PeNZ

Prayer: "When I look back upon my life nigh spent." George Macdonald. TrPWD

Prayer: "Wilt Thou not visit me?" Jones Very. OxBA; TrCP; TrPWD

Prayer: "You may be right, divinity." Francis Sullivan. CRP

Prayer after Illness, A. Violet Alleyn Storey. TrPWD

Prayer after World War. Carl Sandburg. VGW

Prayer against Indifference. Joy Davidman. TrPWD

Prayer against the Plague, A. Robert Henryson. ScCV

Prayer at Dawn. Edwin McNeill Poteat. TrPWD

Prayer at Night ("Fountain of light.") Alcuin, tr. fr. Latin by Helen Waddell. MLL

Prayer at Night ("He lay with quiet heart.") Alcuin, tr. fr. Latin by Helen Waddell. MLL

Prayer before Birth. Louis MacNeice. EBEvV; FaBoVe; GTBS-P; LiTB; NAs; PAW; PNI; TIRV; TwCP

Prayer Before Execution. Mary Queen of Scots, tr. by John Fawcett. WGRP

Prayer before Execution. Mary Queen of Scots, tr. fr. Latin by John Fawcett. WGRP

Prayer before Meat. Una W. Harsen. TrPWD

Prayer before Sleep. Alice Lucas. TrJP

Prayer before Study. Theodore Roethke. TrPWD

Prayer by Moonlight. Roberta Teale Swartz. TrPWD

Prayer: "Clother of the lily, feeder of the sparrow." Christina Rossetti. See Clother of the lily, feeder of the sparrow.

Prayer during Battle. Hermann Hagedorn. TrPWD

Prayer for a Day's Walk. Grace Noll Crowell. PoToHe

Prayer for a Happy New Year, A. Andrew Stuart Currie Clarke. BLRP

Prayer for a Little Home, A. Florence Bone. BLPA; FaBoBe

Prayer for a Marriage, A. Mary Carolyn Davies. TrPWD

Prayer for a New House. Louis Untermeyer. See May nothing evil cross this door.

Prayer for a Pilot. Cecil Roberts. FaPON

Prayer for a Play House. Elinor Lennen. TrPWD

Prayer for a Preacher, A. Edward Shillito. TrPWD

Prayer for a Second Flood. "Hugh MacDiarmid." EBEV

Prayer for a Sleeping Child, A. Mary Carolyn Davies. OHIP

Prayer for a Tenspeed Heart. Barbara Hendryson. CrSp

Prayer for a Thief. Phil DuPlessis, tr. fr. Afrikaans by the author. PeSAV

Prayer for a Very New Angel. Violet Alleyn Storey. BLPA

Prayer for All Poets at This Time. Irwin Edman. TrPWD

Prayer for Broken Little Families, A. Violet Alleyn Storey. PoToHe

Prayer for Charity, A. Edwin O. Kennedy. TrPWD

Prayer for Contentment. Edwin McNeill Poteat. TrPWD

Prayer for Dew. Eleazar ben Kalir, tr. fr. Hebrew by Israel Zangwill. TrJP

Prayer for Dreadful Morning. E. Merrill Root. TrPWD

Prayer for Every Day, A. Mary Carolyn Davies. BLPA; FaBoBe; PoToHe

Prayer for Every Day. Unknown, tr. fr. Fanti by Kweku Martin. PBA

Prayer for Faith. Alfred Norris. See I would not ask Thee that my days.

Prayer for Faith, A. Margaret E. Sangster. PoToHe

Prayer for Forgiveness, A. Aengus the Culdee, tr. fr. Irish by Eoin Neeson. TIRV

Prayer for Gentleness to All Creatures. John Galsworthy. BoTP

Prayer for Guidance. Unknown, tr. fr. Tibetan by W. Y. Evans-Wentz. Fr. Tibetan Book of the Dead, The. OBD

Prayer for Indifference, A. (Oft I've implored the gods in vain.) Fanny (Frances) Macartney Greville. ECWP; NOEC

Sels.
"I ask no kind return of love." OBEV

Prayer for Light. Stanton A. Coblentz. TrPWD

Prayer for Living and Dying. Christopher La Farge. TrPWD

Prayer for My Daughter, A. W. B. Yeats. BLPL; CMoP; HAP; LiTB; LiTM; MeMBP; MoAB; MoP; NAEL-2; NAs; NoAM; NoP; OxBTC; PoA; PoLF; PoRA; PrIm; RaBo; TEP; TFi

Prayer for My Son, A. Yvor Winters. TrPWD

Prayer for My Son, A. W. B. Yeats. EBEV; NAs; OxAEP-2; RaBo; TIRV

Prayer for Old Age, A. W. B. Yeats. IIP

Prayer for Pain. John G. Neihardt. TrPWD; WGRP

Prayer for Peace. Johnstone G. Patrick. TrPWD

Prayer for Peace., sels. Léopold Sédar Senghor, tr. fr. French by Ellen Conroy Kennedy.
"Lord God, forgive white Europe!" TTY, tr. by John Reed and Clive Wake, sect. II
"Lord Jesus, at the end of this book which I offer you." NegPo
"O bless this people, Lord, who seek their own face." EaPr, tr. by John Reed and Clive Wake

Prayer for Peace, A. Edward Rowland Sill. TrPWD

Prayer for Pentecost, A. Catherine Bernard Brown. BLRP

Prayer for Purification, A. Michelangelo, tr. fr. Italian by John Addington Symonds. AWP

Prayer for Rain. Sheikh Aquib Abdullahi Jama, tr. fr. Somali by B. W. Andrzejewski. WTO

Prayer for Rain. Unknown, tr. fr. Finnish. WGRP

Prayer for Recollection, A. Unknown, tr. fr. Irish by Frank O'Connor. PeIV

Prayer for Redemption. Unknown. TrJP

Prayer for Reptiles. Patricia Hubbell. PDV

Prayer for Revolutionary Love. Denise Levertov. CrSp

Prayer for Rivers, A. Keith Wilson. GOYP

Prayer for Shut-Ins. Ruth Winant Wheeler. PoToHe

Prayer for Song. Fay Lewis Noble. TrPWD

Prayer for Strength. Margaret E. Bruner. PoToHe

Prayer for Thanksgiving, A. Joseph Auslander. TrPWD

Prayer for the Age. Myron H. Broomell. TrPWD

Prayer for the Great Family. Gary Snyder. EaPr; HAP; WeW

Prayer for the Little City. Sydney Lea. NAmP90

Prayer for the Little Daughter between Death and Burial. Diana Scott. BrRo

Prayer for the New Year, A. Violet Alleyn Storey. TrPWD

Prayer for the New Year, A. Unknown. BLRP

Prayer for the Old Courage, A. Charles Hanson Towne. TrPWD

Prayer for the Pilot. Cecil Roberts. See Lord of Sea and Earth and Air.

Prayer for the Self, A. John Berryman. Fr. Eleven Addresses to the Lord. OxBC; PPP

Prayer for the Speedy End of Three Great Misfortunes. Unknown, tr. fr. Irish by Frank O'Connor. OBMV

Prayer for the Useless Days. Edith Lovejoy Pierce. TrPWD

Prayer for This Day. Hildegarde Flanner. TrPWD

Prayer for This House. Louis Untermeyer. BLPL; FaPON; PoLF; PoToHe

Prayer Found in Chester Cathedral, A. Thomas H. B. Webb. See Give me a good digestion, Lord,/ And also something to digest.

Prayer from 1936, A. Siegfried Sassoon. TrPWD

Prayer in a Country Church. Ruth B. Van Dusen. TrPWD

Prayer in Affliction. Violet Alleyn Storey. TrPWD

Prayer in April. Sara Henderson Hay. TrPWD

Prayer in Darkness, A. G. K. Chesterton. MoBrPo; PoLF; TrGrPo

Prayer in Late Autumn, A. Violet Alleyn Storey. TrPWD

Prayer in Spring, A. Robert Frost. TrCP; TrPWD

Prayer in the Prospect of Death, A. Burns. TrPWD; WGRP

Prayer in Time of Blindness, A. Clement Wood. TrPWD

Prayer is the soul's sincere desire. What Is Prayer? James Montgomery. BLRP; WGRP

Prayer, Living and Dying, A. Augustus Montague Toplady. See Rock of ages, cleft for me.

Prayer: "Matthew, Mark, Luke, and John." Unknown. See Matthew, Mark, Luke, and John/ Bless the bed that I lie on.

Prayer, The: "O living will that shalt endure." Tennyson. See O living will that shalt endure.

Prayer of a Beginning Teacher. Ouida Smith Dunnam. TrPWD

Prayer of a Pagan Woman. Cothrai Gogan. TIRV

Prayer of a Teacher. Dorothy Littlewort. TrPWD

Prayer of an Unbeliever. Lizette Woodworth Reese. TrPWD

Prayer of an Unemployed Man. W. C. Ackerly. PoToHe

Prayer of Any Husband. Mazie V. Caruthers. PoToHe

Prayer of Columbus. (Batter'd, wrecked old man, A.) Walt Whitman. AmPP; WGRP
Sels.
"Thou knowest my years entire, my life." TrPWD

Prayer of Hezekiah, The. George Wither. ChIV-1

Prayer of Jabez, The. Jones Very. ChIV-1

Prayer of-Lord, Tswana vers. Bible, N.T. See Our Father which [or who] art in heaven.

Prayer of Nehemiah, The. George Wither. ChIV-1

Prayer of St. Francis of Assisi for Peace. St. Francis of Assisi, tr. fr. Latin. PoLF; PoToHe

Prayer of St. Francis Xavier. Pope. TrPWD

Prayer of the Arab Physician, The. Monk Gibbon. TIRV

Prayer of the Cat, The. Carmen Bernos de Gasztold, tr. fr. French by Rumer Godden. CRH; PDV

Prayer of the Donkey, The. Carmen Bernos de Gasztold. PChr

Prayer of the Fishing Net. Unknown, tr. fr. Hawaiian by N. B. Emerson. WTO

Prayer of the Goldfish, The. Carmen Bernos de Gasztold. PDV

Prayer of the Little Ducks, The. Carmen Bernos de Gasztold, tr. fr. French by Rumer Godden. PDV; SiSoPo

Prayer of the Maidens to Mary. Rainer Maria Rilke, tr. fr. German by Jethro Bithell. AWP

Prayer of the Mouse, The. Carmen Bernos de Gasztold. PDV

Prayer of the Old Horse, The. Carmen Bernos de Gasztold. PDV

Prayer of the Old Woman. Villon, tr. fr. French by J. M. Synge. MoBrPo; PeECV

Prayer of the Peoples, A. Percy MacKaye. WGRP
Sels.
God of us who kill our kind! TrPWD, 3 sts.

Prayer of the Seven Galactic Directions. José Arguëlles. EaPr

Prayer of the Venerable Bede. The Venerable Bede, tr. fr. Latin by Helen Waddell. MLL

Prayer of the Young Stoic. Stephen P. Dunn. TrPWD

Prayer on Making a Canoe. Unknown, tr. fr. Hawaiian by N. B. Emerson. WTO

Prayer-Poem, A. Mary S. Edgar. BLRP

Prayer the churches banquet, angel's [or angels] age. George Herbert. Fr. Temple, The. AngWe; BLPL; CBCK; CoGr; EBEV; ELP; GeHe; InPS; JCP; NAEL-1; NOBE; NoP; NOSC; OAEL-1; OBWVE; OxAEP-1; PeECV; PoE; PoEL-2; SeCV-1; Son; TFi; TOF
(Prayer: "Prayer, the Church's banquet, angels' age.") EnlH

Prayer to Be Said When Thou Goest to Bed, A. Francis Seager. OxBChV

Prayer to Be Sung., sels. Miriam Yalan-Shteklis, tr. fr. Hebrew by Bernhard Frank.

Prayer to Escape from the Market Place, A. James Wright. NaP

Prayer to Go to Paradise with the Asses. Francis Jammes, tr. fr. French by Jethro Bithell. AWP

Prayer to Go to Paradise with the Donkeys, A. Jammes Francis, tr. fr. French by Richard Wilbur. RB

Prayer to God. "Placido," tr. fr. Spanish by Raoul Abdul. TTY

Prayer to God the Father. Hildebert, tr. fr. Latin by Helen Waddell. MLL

Prayer to God the Father. Marbod of Rennnes, tr. fr. Latin by Helen Waddell. MLL

Prayer to Hermes. Robert Creeley. PoM

Prayer to Isis. Christina Walsh. BrRo

Prayer to Mother Mary. Padraic Pearse. TIRV

Prayer to the Father of [or in] Heaven, A. John Skelton. HoPM; TrPWD

Prayer to the God Thot. Unknown, tr. fr. Egyptian by Ulli Beier. TTY

Prayer to the Holy Trinity, A. Richard Stanyhurst. EiL; PoEL-2

Prayer to the Hunting Star, Canopus. Unknown, tr. fr. Bushman by W. H. I. Bleek and Jack Cope. PeSA

Prayer to the Lord Ramakrishna, A. James Wright. NNaP

Prayer to the Masks. Léopold Sédar Senghor, tr. fr. French by Ellen Conroy Kennedy. NegPo

Prayer to the Mountain Spirit. Unknown, tr. by G. W. Cronyn. WGRP

Prayer to the Pacific. Leslie Silko. CDW; NoP; VoR; WeW

Prayer to the Sacrament of the Altar, A. Unknown. MeEL

Prayer to the Sun, A. Geoffrey Hill. PRA

Prayer to the Trinity, A. Unknown. MeEL

Prayer to the Trinity [or Trinitie], A. Richard Stanyhurst. See Trinity [or Trinitee] blessed, deity [or deitee] coequal.

Prayer to the Virgin. St. Columcille, tr. fr. Irish by Kuno Meyer and John Strachan. TIRV

Prayer to the Wind, A. Thomas Carew. BeJo

Prayer to the Young Moon. Unknown, tr. fr. Bushman by W. H. I. Bleek and Jack Cope. PeSA

Prayer to Venus. Lucretius. See Great Venus, Queene [or Queen] of Beautie [or Beauty] and of grace.

Prayer to Venus. Spenser. See Address to Venus.

Prayer under the Pressure of Violent Anguish, A. Burns. ScCV; TrPWD

Prayer unsaid, and mass unsung. The Sea-Ritual. George Darley. Fr. Syren Songs. BIrV; OBNC; WiR
(Deadman's Dirge.) CH

Prayer unto Christ the Judge of the World, A. Michael Wigglesworth. SCAP

Prayer yo Hymen. Unknown. NOSC

Prayers. Henry Charles Beeching. BoTP; OBEV

Prayers, Dorcas, Fellowship, and Children's Groups! Gwladys Rhys. W. J. Gruffydd, tr. fr. Welsh by Myrddin Lloyd. OBWVE

Prayers, goodnights. (LL) Plague and Hospice. Harry Clifton. IB

Prayers I make will then be sweet indeed, The. For Inspiration. Michelangelo, tr. by Wordsworth. WGRP
(To the Supreme Being. AWP; TrPWD

Prayers Must Have Poise. Robert Herrick. LiTB

Prayers of Steel. Carl Sandburg. CMoP; FaPON; MoAmPo; PDV; TrCP; TrPWD

Prayerwheel: 2. David Meltzer. NeAP

Praying. P. J. Kavanagh. OxBSP

Praying and to be married? It was rare. Isaac's Marriage. Henry Vaughan. ChIV-1

Praying in tounges. (LL) If I Stand in My Window. Lucille Clifton. BPo; CAPP

Praying mantis doesn't pray, The. Mantis. David McCord. OBAL

Praying Mantis Visits a Penthouse, The ("The praying mantis with its length of straw.") Oscar Williams. LiTM

Praying to you can be talking to the sea. Element. Peter Steele. FaBoMA

Pre-admonisheth the writer. The Flight of the Bucket. Kipling. BXAP

Pre Domina. Jean Lipkin. PeSA

Pre-Existence. Paul Hamilton Hayne. AnAmPo

Pre-Raphaelite Notebook, A. Geoffrey Hill. NoAM

Preacher, The. Al-Mahdi, tr. fr. Arabic by A. J. Arberry. TTY

Preacher and the Slave, The. At. to Joe Hill. AS; SWP; WTO

Preacher quoted, and the cranks, The. A Bad Break! W. T. Goodge. NOBAu

Preacher's Mistake, The. William Croswell Doane. BLPA; PoToHe

Preacher's Vacation, The. Unknown. BLPA; BLPL

Precambrian [or Pre-Cambrian] Shield, The. E. J. Pratt. Fr. Towards the Last Spike. MoCV; NOBC

Precarious Ground. Leah Bodine Drake. GoYe

Precede me into this elusive country. The Caravan. Gwendolyn MacEwen. MoCV

Precede us, O Lord, with Thy Grace. Frank R. McManus. PeLi

Precept of Silence, The. Lionel Johnson. MoBrPo

Precepts He Gave His Folk. Elijah ben Menahem Hazaken, of Le Mans, tr. fr. Hebrew by Israel Zangwill. TrJP

Precinct Station, The. Louis Simpson. EOEF

Preciosa and the Wind. Federico García Lorca, tr. fr. Spanish by John Frederick Nims. STV

Precious Child, So Sweetly Sleeping. Anna Hoppe. AH

Precious dry rose-geranium smell, The. Eiléan Ní Chuilleanáin. Fr. Rose-Geranium, The. CIP

Precious Five. W. H. Auden. PeECV

Precious in the Sight of the Lord. Unknown. BLRP

Precious Jewish child. Little Boy. Jacob Glatstein, tr. fr. Yiddish by Doris Vidaver. BTR

Precious Mettle. Lewis Warsh. UL

Precious Moments. Carl Sandburg. MoAmPo

Precious night-blooming cereus. Remembering Fannie Lou Hamer. Thadious M. Davis. BISi

Precious, oh, how precious is that blessed sleep. Precious in the Sight of the Lord. Unknown. BLRP

Precious Pearl, The. Priscilla Jane Thompson. CBWP-2

Precious Things. Unknown. See Hold my rooster, hold my hen.

Precious thought, my Father knoweth. God Knoweth Best. Unknown. WBLP
(Your Father Knoweth.) BLRP

Precious to me — she still shall be. Emily Dickinson. PeHV

Precious treasure, thou art mine. (LL) Holy Bible, Book Divine. John Burton. BLRP; WBLP

Precipice, The. Ts'ai Ch'i-chiao, tr. fr. Chinese. LHF, tr. by Hualing Nieh

Precise counterpart, The. The Orchestra. William Carlos Williams. HAP

Precisely down invisible threads these oak leaves. October Elegy. Margaret Gibson. FYAP

Precursors. Louis MacNeice. OxBSP

Predator's gleam a-gleam, The. (LL) Deep. Timothy Holmes. PeSAV

Predestination and Free Will. Dryden. Fr. State of Innocence, The. NOCV

Predicament: a corner of/ a room. Tenant at Number 9. John Blight. CBAP

Predicter of Famine, The. William Carlos Williams. VGW

Prediction, The. Mark Strand. LCAP; VCAP

Preface, The. Edward Taylor. Fr. Preparatory Meditations Before My Approach to the Lord's Supper. NOSC

Preface: "Aged catch their breath, The." W. H. Auden. Fr. Sea and the Mirror, The. LiTA

Preface: "Artist is the creator of beautiful things, The." Oscar Wilde. Fr. Picture of Dorian Gray, The. NAEL-2

Preface: "Infinity, when all things it beheld." Edward Taylor. *Fr.* God's Determinations [touching his Elect]. AmPP; EAP; HAP; MeMAP; NAAL-1; NOBA; OxBA; SCAP

Preface: "Rigor of beauty is the quest. But how will you find beauty when it is locked." William Carlos Williams. *Fr.* Paterson. NoAM

Preface: "Sonja Henie, the young girl." Theodore Weiss. VGW

Preface: "To make a start." William Carlos Williams. *Fr.* Paterson. CMoP; NoAM; NOBA

Preface Shrink Lit: Elements of Style. Maurice Sagoff. NBLV

Preface to a Twenty Volume Suicide Note. Amiri Baraka. PoBA; PoM; PoNe; PPP; TTY

Preface to *Divine Songs and Meditacions*, The. Anne Collins. KTR

Preface to the Memoirs, A. James Merrill. NOBA

Preface to *The Progress of Learning*. Sir John Denham. NOSC; OxBSP

Prefatory Epistle, A. Maria Falconar. ECWP

Prefatory Poem, on . . . *Magnalia Christi Americana*. Nicholas Noyes. SCAP

Prefer the cherry when the fruit hangs thick. Under the Boughs. Gene Baro. BoNaP

Preference. Langston Hughes. HCAP; NOBA

Preference Declared, The. Horace. *See* Boy, I have their empty shouts.

Prefix. Robert Kelly. BCF

Pregnancy. Sandra McPherson. BoWoP; NMM

Pregnant girl, under sorrow's sign, A. Under Sorrow's Sign. Gofraidh Fionn O'Dalaigh, *tr. fr. Irish by* John Montague. BIrV

Pregnant Woman. Ingrid Jonker, *tr. fr. Afrikaans.* PeSA, *tr. by* Jack Cope *and* Uys Krige

Prehistoric Burials. Siegfried Sassoon. MoBrPo

Prehistories. Peter Scupham. SCBI

Prehtys whilom dwelled in oure citee, A. The Cook's Tale. Chaucer. *Fr.* Canterbury Tales, The. BXAP; EnVB

Preiching of the Swallow, The. Robert Henryson. EnVB; OxBS

Prejudice. Georgia Douglas Johnson. PoBA; ShDr

Prejudice. L. A. J. Moorer. CBWP-3

Prejudice against Colour. Langham Dale. PeSAV

Prejudice against the Past, The. Wallace Stevens. LiTM

Prelates, The. John Skelton. *Fr.* Colin Clout. TrGrPo

Preliminary Poem. John Heath-Stubbs. OxBC

Preliminary to Classroom Lecture. Josephine Miles. MoP; NoAM

Prelude. René Depestre, *tr. fr. French by* Ellen Conroy Kennedy. *Fr.* Epiphanies of the Voodoo Gods. NegPo

Prelude: "Along the roadside, like the flowers of gold." Whittier. *Fr.* Among the Hills. NAAL-1; OxBA; PoEL-4

Prelude: "And did those feet in ancient time." Blake. *See* And Did Those Feet in Ancient Time.

Prelude: "As one, at midnight, wakened by the call." W. W. Gibson. MoBrPo

Prelude VII: "Beloved, let us once more praise the rain." Conrad Aiken. *Fr.* Preludes for Memnon; or, Preludes to Attitude. LiTA; UnPo

Prelude: "England! awake! awake! awake!" Blake. *See* England! awake! awake! awake!

Prelude XXI: "First note, simple, The; the second note, distinct." Conrad Aiken. *Fr.* Preludes for Memnon; or, Preludes to Attitude. LiTA

Prelude: "Fields from Islington to Marybone, The." Blake. *See* Fields from Islington to Marybone, The.

Prelude: "Give us another poem, he said." Patrick Kavanagh. IPY; PeIV

Prelude: "I am the bird of the wayside." Christine Ama Ata Aidoo. PBWP

Prelude: "It wouldn't be a good idea." Wendy Cope. FaBoBl

Prelude XLII: "Keep in the heart the journal nature keeps." Conrad Aiken. *Fr.* Preludes for Memnon; or, Preludes to Attitude. CMoP; OxBA

Prelude: "Night and the hood." Conrad Kent Rivers. PoBA

Prelude: "Night was dark, though sometimes a faint star, The." Richard Watson Gilder. *Fr.* New Day, The. PoLF

Prelude LIII: "Nothing to say? Then we'll say nothing." Conrad Aiken. *Fr.* Preludes for Memnon; or, Preludes to Attitude. LiTA

Prelude LVII: "One star fell and another as we walked." Conrad Aiken. *Fr.* Preludes for Memnon; or, Preludes to Attitude. MoAmPo

Prelude LVI: "Rimbaud and Verlaine, precious pair of poets." Conrad Aiken. *Fr.* Preludes for Memnon; or, Preludes to Attitude. FaBoMo; LiTA; LiTM; NoAM; TwCP

Prelude III: "Sleep: and between the closed eyelids of sleep." Conrad Aiken. *Fr.* Preludes for Memnon; or, Preludes to Attitude. LiTA

Prelude XX: "So, in the evening, to the simple cloister." Conrad Aiken. *Fr.* Preludes for Memnon; or, Preludes to Attitude. LiTA

(Cloister.) MoAB; MoAmPo

Prelude LII: "Stood, at the closed door." Conrad Aiken. *Fr.* Preludes for Memnon; or, Preludes to Attitude. LiTM

Prelude: "Still south I went and west and south again." J. M. Synge. AWP; BoNaP; ChTr; FaBoPP; IIP; MoBrPo; OBMV; PeIV

Prelude XXXIII: "Then came I to the shoreless shore of silence." Conrad Aiken. *Fr.* Preludes for Memnon; or, Preludes to Attitude. LiTA; OxBA

Prelude: "This fugitive between the Earth and Sky." Tu Fu, *tr. fr. Chinese by* Robert Payne. TAL

Prelude VI: "This is not you? These phrases are not you?" Conrad Aiken. *Fr.* Preludes for Memnon; or, Preludes to Attitude. MoAB; MoAmPo

Prelude: "This short straight sword." R. A. K. Mason. PeNZ

Prelude: "To live always as on the brink of leaving — but Goethe said." John Riley. VaA

Prelude: Troops, The. Siegfried Sassoon. *See* Dim, gradual thinning of the shapeless gloom.

Prelude II: "Two coffees in the Español, the last." Conrad Aiken. *Fr.* Preludes for Memnon; or, Preludes to Attitude. FYAP; LiTA; NoAM

Prelude XIX: "Watch long enough, and you will see the leaf." Conrad Aiken. *Fr.* Preludes for Memnon; or, Preludes to Attitude. CMoP; OxBA

Prelude XXIX: "What shall we do — what shall we think — what shall we say?" Conrad Aiken. *Fr.* Preludes for Memnon; or, Preludes to Attitude. FaBoMo

Prelude: "What makes a plenteous harvest." Virgil, *tr. by* Dryden. *Fr.* Georgics. AWP

Prelude I: "Winter for a moment takes the mind; the snow." Conrad Aiken. *Fr.* Preludes for Memnon; or, Preludes to Attitude. LiTA; LiTM; OxBA

Prelude: "Woman, Woman, let us say these things to each other." Conrad Aiken. NYBP

Prelude XIV: "You went to the verge, you say, and came back safely." Conrad Aiken. *Fr.* Preludes for Memnon; or, Preludes to Attitude. FaBoMo; LiTA; TwCP

Prelude [or, Growth of a Poet's Mind], The. Wordsworth. EnRP; OAEL-2 *Sels.*

Books

There Was a Boy "There was a boy, ye knew him well". FaBoCh; FaBoRV; FHYEP; MeMBP

"Thirteen years."

Cambridge and the Alps. PoEL-4

"But 'twas a time when Europe was rejoiced." FaBoPV

"Far different dejection once was mine." OBTV

(Crossing the Alps.) RB, *sl. shorter*

"I, too, have been a Wanderer; but, alas!"

Types and Symbols of Eternity. CBCK

"When from the Vallais we had turned."

Childhood and School-Time. CH; GN; HAP; NOBE; NoP; NU; OBNC; OxAEP-2; PoE; SCV

(Introduction — Childhood and School-Time.) PoEL-4

(On the Solitary Fells around Hawkshead.) FaBoPP

"Dust as we are, the immortal spirit grows."

In Patterdale. FaBoRV

Influence of Natural Objects. AWP

"Oh [*or* O] there is a blessing in this gentle breeze." FHYEP

On the Frozen Lake. FaBoCh; PIP

On Ullswater. FaBoPP

On Windermere; Bowness Bay and Belle Isle. FaBoPP

One Summer Evening ("One summer evening (led by her) I found"). Skating.

"So through the darkness and the cold we flew."

Was It for This.

"Wisdom and spirit of the universe!"

Wordsworth Skates on Esthwaite Water. FaBoPP

Conclusion ("It was a close, warm, breezeless summer night"). PoEL-4

"Child of my parents! Sister of my soul!"

"In one of these excursions, travelling then/ Through Wales on foot." PeECV

(Climb to Snowdon, The.) FaBoRV

(Snowdon Sunrise, The.) FaBoPP

"It was a summer's night, a close warm night."

"Oh! yet a few short years of useful life." EBEV

France

"O pleasant exercise of hope and joy!" HAP

(France leered me forth; the realm that I had crossed.) FaBoPV

(Residence in France [Continued].) PoEL-4

One Christmas-Time.

To Coleridge in Sicily

"I have thought/ Of thee, thy learning, gorgeous eloquence." EPCY

Imagination and Taste, How Impaired and Restored. PoE; PoEL-4, XII, *abr.*; TOF

Imagination, How Impaired and Restored

In One of Those Excursions. MeMBP

Residence at Cambridge. FaBoPP; HAP; OxAEP-2, *abr.*

"Caverns there were within my mind, which sun."

"Evangelist St. John my patron was, The."

(Newton's Statue.) FaBoRV

Gentle Spenser. EPCY

Residence in France.
  "Cheered with this hope, to Paris I returned."
  "I quitted, and betook myself to France."
  Noble, The. ChTr
Residence in France and French Revolution OBTV, *sl. shorter*
  "State, as if to stamp the final seal." FaBoPV
  "When the proud fleet that bears the red-cross flag." FaBoPV
Residence in London. HAP, *short sel.*; PoEL-4, *sl. shorter*
  Fair below Helvellyn, The. FaBoPP
  "From these sights/ Take one, — that ancient festival, the Fair."
  "Genius of Burke! forgive the pen seduced." FaBoPV
  "Rise up, thou monstrous ant-hill on the plain."
  "Those days are now."
  Young Wordsworth's London, The. FaBoPP
Retrospect — Love of Nature Leading to Love of Mankind
  Shepherd, The.
School-Time.
  "Blest the infant Babe."
  "But who shall parcel out."
  Intimations of Sublimity.
  "Thus far, O friend! have we, though leaving much." FHYEP
Summer Vacation. PoEL-4
  Consummate Happiness.
  "In a throng,/ A festival company." EBEV
  "That heartless chase."
  "While thus I wander'd, step by step led on."
'Tis Sweet. MeMBP
Wordsworth Reading Chaucer. EPCY; FaBoPP; HAP; OxAEP-2, *abr.*

Prelude to Akwasidae. *Unknown, tr. fr. Twi by* Halim El-Dabh. TTY

Prelude to an Evening. John Crowe Ransom. MoAB; MoAmPo; OxBA

Prelude to Commencement. Marie De L. Welch. NYBP

Prelude to Memorial Song: 100 Years Later. Phillip William George. VoR

Prelude to Winter. William Carlos Williams. SAmP

Preludes (I–IV). T. S. Eliot. HeIP; LiTA; NoP; OBMV; PPP; SOTW; TwCP; UnPo; VGW; WeW
  Sels.
  "His soul stretched tight across the skies."
  "Morning comes to consciousness, The."
  "Winter evening settles down, The." MoShBr; Poetr
  "You tossed a blanket from the bed."

Preludes for Memnon; or, Preludes to Attitude, *sels.* Conrad Aiken.
  "Beloved, let us once more praise the rain." LiTA; UnPo
  "First note, simple, The; the second note, distinct." LiTA
  "Keep in the heart the journal nature keeps." CMoP; OxBA
  "Nothing to say? Then we'll say nothing." LiTA
  "One star fell and another as we walked." MoAmPo
  "Rimbaud and Verlaine, precious pair of poets." FaBoMo; LiTA; LiTM; NoAM; TwCP
  "Sleep: and between the closed eyelids of sleep." LiTA
  "So, in the evening, to the simple cloister." LiTA
  (Cloister.) MoAB; MoAmPo
  "Stood, at the closed door." LiTM
  "Then came I to the shoreless shore of silence." LiTA; OxBA
  "This is not you? These phrases are not you?" MoAB; MoAmPo
  "Time has come, the clock says time has come, The." LiTA; OxBA
  "Two coffees in the Español, the last." FYAP; LiTA; NoAM
  "Watch long enough, and you will see the leaf." CMoP; OxBA
  "What shall we do — what shall we think — what shall we say?" FaBoMo
  "Winter for a moment takes the mind; the snow." LiTA; LiTM; OxBA
  "You went to the verge, you say, and came back safely." FaBoMo; LiTA; TwCP

Prelusive. Herman Melville. *Fr. Clarel.* AmPP

Premeditations. Geoff Page. NOBAu

Premonition. Richard Hovey. AnAmPo

Premonition, The. Theodore Roethke. CAPP

'Prentice Boy, The. *Unknown.* AmFP

Preparation. Thomas Edward Brown. OBEV

Preparations. Leslie Silko. VoR

Preparations. *Unknown. See* Yet if his majesty, our sovereign [*or* soveraign] Lord.

Preparations for Victory. Edmund Blunden. PeFWW

Preparative, The. Thomas Traherne. ESCV; GeHe; PoEL-2

Preparatory Meditations Before My Approach to the Lord's Supper, *sels.* Edward Taylor.
  "All Dull, my Lord, my Spirits flat, and dead." EAP; NOSC
  "Am I thy gold? or purse, Lord, for thy wealth." EAP; LiTA; MeMAP; NOSC; OxBA; TAP
  "Apples of gold, in silver pictures shrined." NAAL-1
  Art, Nature's Ape. CBCK
  "Bran, a chaff, a very barley [y]awn, A." ChIV-2; NOSC
  "Deity of Love Incorporate, A." TAP
  "Dull. Dull indeed! What shall it e'er be thus?" ChIV-1

"Guilty, my Lord, what can I more declare?" ChIV-1, *Division* II, *sect.* XXV
"Halfe Dead: and rotten at the Coare: my Lord!" EAP
"I kenning [*or* kening] through astronomy divine." AmPP; EAP; LiTA; MeMAP; NAAL-1; NOBA; NoP; OxBA; PoEL-3; SCAP; TAP
"Inamoring Rayes, thy Sparkles, Pearle of Price." EAP
  (Return, The.) EAP
"Leaf [*or* Leafe] gold, Lord of thy golden wedge o'erlaid." EAP; NAAL-1
"Like to the marigold, I blushing close." ChIV-2; SCAP
"Lord, art thou at the table head above." AmPP; MeMAP; OxBA
  (Reflexion, The.) AmPP; ChIV-1, *Division* I, *sect.* IV; OxBA
"Lord, can a crumb of dust the earth outweigh." NAAL-1
  (Prologue.) EAP
"Methinks I spy Almighty holding in." HAP
Mine Heart's a Park or Chase of Sins. CBCK
"My Blessed Lord, how doth thy Beautious Spouse." SCAP
"My gracious Lord, I would thee glory doe." EAP; SCAP
"My Lord, my life, can envy ever bee." PoEL-3
"My shattred phancy stole away from mee." EAP; NOSC; SCAP
"My sin! my sin, my God, these cursed dregs." EAP; SCAP
"Oh! Golden Rose! Oh. Glittering Lilly White." SCAP
"Oh! Good, good, good, my Lord. What more love yet." NOBA
"Oh leaden heeld. Lord, give, forgive I pray." SCAP
"Oh! that I alwayes breath'd in such an aire."
  (Experience, The.) AmPP; EAP
"Oh that I was the Bird of Paradise!" NOCV
"Oh! what a thing is man? Lord, who am I?" MeMAP; NAAL-1; NOBA; OxBA
"Orator from Rhetorick gardens picks, The." EAP
Preface, The. NOSC
Should I with Silver Tooles Delve through the Hill. ChIV-2, *sect.* II, lvi; EAP, *sect.* LVI; MeMAP; OxBA, *sect.* LVI; SCAP, *sect.* LVI
"State, a state, oh! dungeon state indeed, A." ChIV-1, *Division* II, *sect.* LXXVII; EAP
"Still I complain; I am complaining still." MeMAP; OxBA; PoEL-3
  (Was Ever Heart Like Mine?) CBCK
"Stupendious love! all saints astonishment." EAP; MeMAP; OxBA
"Thy grace, dear Lord's my golden wrack I find." EAP; NoP; SCAP
"Thy human frame, my glorious Lord, I spy." ChIV-1, (*Division* I); LiTA; MeMAP
"Unclean, unclean: my Lord, undone, all vile." NAAL-1
"View, all ye eyes above, this sight which flings." NOSC
"What Glory's this, my Lord? Should one small Point." EAP
"What love is this of thine, that cannot be." AmPP; NOCV; PoEL-3; SCAP
"What shall a Mote up to a Monarch rise?" EAP
"What shall I say, my Deare Deare Lord?" EAP
"What shall I say, my Lord? With what begin?" ChIV-2; HAP
"When thy bright beams, my Lord, so strike mine eye." NAAL-1
"Why should my bells, which chime thy praise, when thou." ChIV-2
"Would God I in that Golden City were." EAP
"Ye angells bright, pluck from your wings a quill." ChIV-2; PoEL-3

Prepare for death. But how can you prepare. Speculation. Howard Nemerov. TAP

Prepare for death, if here at night you roam. Samuel Johnson. *Fr.* London: A Poem in Imitation of the Third Satire of Juvenal. OAEL-1; PoEL-3; TEP

Prepare for Songs; He's come, He's come. The New-Yeeres Gift, or Circumcisions Song, Sung to the King in the Presence at White Hall. Robert Herrick. SeCV-1

Prepare, prepare the iron helm of war. A War Song to Englishmen. Blake. *Fr.* King Edward the Third. CH
(War Song, A. OHIP

Prepare to meet the King of Terrors, cried. Ebenezer Elliot. NOBVV

Prepare us for the service that we should render. (*LL*) O God,/ creator of our land. *Unknown.* EaPr

Preparedness. Edwin Markham. MoAmPo

Preparing to live for ever. (*LL*) A Lifetime Devoted to Literature. Judith Rodriguez. NOBAu

Preposterous. Jim Hall. MT

Preposterously swimming back and forth. (*LL*) Reculver Bay. Vicki Raymond. NOBAu

Presage and caveat not only seem. The Window Sill. Robert Graves. EnLoPo

Presaging. Rainer Maria Rilke, *tr. fr. German by* Jessie Lemont. AWP; TrJP

Presbyterian Knight, The. Samuel Butler. *See* When civil fury first grew high.

Presbyterian Study. Tom Paulin. PBCIP

Presbyterian Wedding, The. *Unknown.* CoMu; ErPo; FaBoBl

Presbyterians, The. Dryden. *Fr.* Hind and the Panther, The. NOSC

Prescience. Donald Jeffrey Hayes. PoNe

Prescott, press my Ascot waistcoat. Ascot Waistcoat. David McCord. FiBHP; NBLV (Sportif.) NYBP

Prescription of Painful Ends. Robinson Jeffers. LiTA; MoAB; MoAmPo; OxBA

Presence, The. William Everson. ErPo

Presence, The. Maxine W. Kumin. RFM; WPE

Presence, The. Denise Levertov. NaP

Presence, The. Medbh McGuckian. PNI

Presence, The. Dana Naone. CDW

Presence, The. Jones Very. HAP

Presence — how can you name a smell?, A. Jasmine. Chris Wallace-Crabbe. FaBoMA

Presence of Snow. Melville Cane. GoYe

Presence that so strangely rose beside the waters, The. New York City. Helen Waddell. MLL

Presences. Michael Dransfield. FaBoMA

Presences. Donald Justice. CAPP

Presences. Zoé Karélli, *tr. fr. Modern Greek by* Kimon Friar. PBWP

Presences Perfected. Siegfried Sassoon. MoBrPo

Present, The. Adelaide Anne Procter. WGRP

Present. Sonia Sanchez. WPOW

Present Age, The. Arthur Cleveland Coxe. BLPA

Present Age, The. Frances E. W. Harper. AAP; PWR

Present Crisis, The, *sels.* James Russell Lowell.
    "Count me o'er earth's chosen heroes — they were souls that stood alone." WGRP
    Once to Every Man and Nation. FaPoR

Present day we cannot spend, The. Isabella Whitney. *Fr.* Sweet Nosegay, A, or Pleasant Posy. WPE

Present from the Emperor's New Concubine, A. Lady Pan, *tr. fr. Chinese by* Kenneth Rexroth. BoWoP; OHMPC

Present of Butter, A. Tadhg Dall O'Huiginn, *tr. fr. Irish by* the Earl of Longford. BIrV

Present reigned supreme, The. Home Coming. Lenrie Peters. HBAPE

Present to a Lady, A. *Unknown.* ErPo; PeLV

Presentation of Two Birds to My Son, A. James Wright. PPP

Presentation Piece. Marilyn Hacker. AmPA

Presented as a Farewell to Secretary Fu. Pao Chao, *tr. fr. Chinese by* Daniel Bryant. SuSp

Presented to a Lady within the Palace. Chang Yü, *tr. fr. Chinese by* Ronald C. Miao. SuSp

Presentiment, A. Bryant. AnAmPo

Presentiment is that long shadow on the lawn. Emily Dickinson. HeIP; ImPo; OxBA

Presenting Eustacia Beauchaud: Ward 3. James Nolan. Jaz

Presently at our touch the teacup stirred. Voices from the Other World. James Merrill. TwCP; VCAP

Preserve a respectful demeanor. To a Baked Fish. Carolyn Wells. FiBHP

Preserve that old kettle, so blackened and worn. My Dad's Dinner Pail. Edward Harrigan. BLPA

Preserve thy sighs, unthrifty girl[e]. The Soldier Going to the Field. Sir William Davenant. NOBE; OBWP

Preserves. Jack Butler. MT

Preserves us, not for specialists. (*LL*) April Inventory. W. D. Snodgrass. CAPP; CoAP; HAP; LiTM; NoAM; NoP; Poetr; TAP; TRP; TwCP; VCAP

Preserving. Roy Fuller. CBLP

Preserving remnants of a model ship. (*LL*) The Glass Blower. James Scully. NYBP; TwCP

President Garfield. Longfellow. PAH

President has thus disclosed, The. The Door of Hope. L. A. J. Moorer. CBWP-3

President is Up before the first vendor, The. Ernesto Trejo. AfAz

President Lincoln's Grave. Caroline A. B. Mason. OHIP

President Lincoln's Proclamation of Freedom. Frances E. W. Harper. AmWP

President Ordains the Bee to Be, The. Wallace Stevens. *Fr.* Notes toward a Supreme Fiction. LiTA

President Parker. *Unknown.* OxBSS

President Roosevelt. Big Joe Williams. FaBoPV

President Slumming, The. James Tate. OBAL

Presidents, The. L. A. J. Moorer. CBWP-3

President's Men, The. Thomas McCarthy. IB

Presidents of the United States. *Unknown.* FaBoUs

Presiding over a Formica counter. The Latin Deli. Judith Ortiz Cofer. AfAz

Press, The. Thomas Phipson. PeSAV

Press, The. *Unknown.* VPP

Press——the Press——the glorious Press, The. The Press. *Unknown.* VPP

Press ahead, beloved children. Uncle Rube to the Young People. Clara Ann Thompson. CBWP-2

Press-gang, The. Charles Dibdin. FaBoEH

Press-Gang, The. *Unknown. See* Here's the Tender Coming.

Press [*or* Presse] me not to take more pleasure. The Rose. George Herbert. LiTB; PoEL-2

Press of the Spoon River *Clarion* was wrecked, The. Carl Hamblin. Edgar Lee Masters. *Fr.* Spoon River Anthology. CMoP; LiTA; LiTM; OBSV

Press often for, (nor, than at this time, more). Vox Oppressi, to the Lady Phipps. Richard Henchman. SCAP

Pressed by the Moon, Mute Arbitress of Tides. Charlotte Smith. NALW

Pressed to the wall, dying, but fighting back! (*LL*) If We Must Die. Claude McKay. AmPP; BPo; FaBV; MoP; NoAM; PBCV; PoBA; Poetr; PoNe; PPP; Son; TFi; TTY; UnPo

Pressing for Tax Payment. Fan Ch'eng-ta, *tr. by* Wu-chi Liu. *Fr.* Four Songs in Imitation of Wang Chien. SuSp

Pressure. Anne Waldman. PoM

Pressure Drop. Oku Onuora. PBCV

Pressure lamp hisses into the silence, The. African Student. Noel H. Brettell. PeSAV

Pressure of sun on the rockslide. Water. Gary Snyder. LCAP

Pressures, The. Amiri Baraka. BPo

Prestidigitator [1], The. Al Young. NBV

Prestidigitator [2], The. Al Young. NBV

Prestidigitator makes things disappear, A. The Prestidigitator [1]. Al Young. NBV

Presto, pronto! Two boys, two horses. Boy Riding Forward Backward. Robert Francis. LCAP

Preston. *Unknown.* GBP

Preston. *Unknown.* FaBoVe

Pretences. Ibn Rashiq, *tr. fr. Arabic by* A. J. Arberry. TTY

Pretext. Stephen Rodefer. UL

Prettiest girl, The. Sucking Cider through a Straw. *Unknown.* AS; GBP

Prettiest lady that ever I've seen, The. Pretty Lady. Rose Fyleman. BoTP

Pretty. Stevie Smith. NAEL-2; NoAM; NoP; TEP

Pretty a Day, A. E. E. Cummings. CMoP

Pretty Ambition, A. Mary E. Wilkins Freeman. OBCA

Pretty Bonnie, you are quick as a rabbit. Giving Rabbit to My Cat Bonnie. Anne Stevenson. FaBoWP

Pretty Fair Maid, A. *Unknown.* AS

Pretty game, my girl, A. The Flirt. W. H. Davies. EnLoPo

Pretty Girl, A. J. Gordon Coogler. OBAL

Pretty girls of the fall, The. The Falls. F. D. Reeve. NYBP

Pretty I Am, But I Am Wretched. *Unknown, tr. fr. Provençal.* VBLP

Pretty John Watts. Mother Goose. OxNR; ReMoGo

Pretty Lady. Rose Fyleman. BoTP

Pretty Lady Carenza. Tenson. Carenza *and* Iselda, *tr. fr. Provençal by* Bridget Connelly *and* Doris Earnshaw. WPOW

Pretty little crocus, in your cosy bed. Waking Up. *Unknown.* BoTP

Pretty loxia weaves, The. (*LL*) Namaqualand after Rain. William Plomer. PeSAV

Pretty Maid, The. Paul Fort. *See* Pretty maid she died, she died, in love-bed as she lay, The.

Pretty maid both kind and fair, A. The Very Pretty Maid of This Town, and the Amorous 'Squire Not One Hundred Miles from the Place. *Unknown.* CoMu

Pretty Maid Marion. Ivy O. Eastwick. BoTP

Pretty maid, pretty maid,/ Where have you been? Gift for the Queen. *Unknown.* OxNR

Pretty maid she died, she died, in love-bed as she lay, The. Paul Fort, *tr. fr. French by* Frederick York Powell. AWP
    (Pretty Maid, The.) OBMV

Pretty Maids Beware!!! *Unknown.* CoMu

Pretty Miss Apathy. Pooh! Walter de la Mare. FiBHP; HAP

Pretty party for people, A. And. Robert Creeley. LCAP

Pretty Ploughboy, The. *Unknown.* GBP

Pretty Polly. *Unknown.* AS

Pretty Polly. *Unknown. See* In Gosport of late a young damsel did dwell.

Pretty Polly of Topsham. *Unknown.* AmFP

Pretty prating poll. Little Miss and Her Parrot. John Marchant. OxBChV

Pretty red squirrel lives up in a tree, The. The Squirrel. Mary Howitt. BoTP

Pretty Saro. *Unknown.* AmFP

Pretty Saro. *Unknown.* AmFP

Pretty song, this coming spring, A. Miss Betty's Singing-Bird. John Winstanley. NOEC

Pretty Sport. William Habington. *See* Fine Young Folly.

Pretty Twinkling Starry Eyes. Nicholas Breton. *Fr.* Passionate Shepherd, The. EIL

Pretty Vomit. Bob Rosenthal. UL

Pretty Wantons. *Unknown.* EIL

Pretty white city. Precious white city. The Idea of San Francisco. Jim Gustafson. UL

Pretty Woman, A. Simon J. Ortiz. CDW

Pretty Words. Elinor Wylie. NAAL-2

Prevailing Prayer. Richard Chenevix Trench. *See* Lord, what a change within us one short hour.

Prevailing winds lied in intent, The. Statuary. John Ashbery. NoAM

Prevalent Poetry. Charles Follen Adams. PeLi

Prevention of Stacy Miller, The. Peter Miller. MoCV

Previsioning death in advance, our doom is delayed. Foresight. Lincoln Kirstein. ArOW; OBWP; PoWW

Prewar Late October Sea Breeze. Robert Grenier. UL

Prey for us the Prince of Pees. A Song to John, Christ's Friend. *Unknown.* MeEL

Prey swooped up, the iron love seat shudders. Up and Down. James Merrill. GLP

Prey to Prey. David Rowbotham. CBAP

Preyful princess pierc'd and prick'd a pretty pleasing pricket, The. Holofernes's Letter. Shakespeare. *Fr.* Love's Labour's Lost. CBNP

Priam and Achilles. Homer, *tr. fr. Greek. Fr.* Iliad, The. NOSC, *tr. by* George Chapman

Priapos of the Harbor. Antipater of Sidon, *tr. fr. Greek by* Dudley Fitts. GrAn

Priapus and the Pool, *sels.* Conrad Aiken.
　This Is the Shape of the Leaf. CMoP; NOBA; OxBA; TrGrPo
　(Portrait of a Girl.) GoJo; MoAB; MoAmPo
　"When trout swim down Great Ormond Street." NoAM; NOBA

Priapus seeing Kimon with a stand. Antipater of Thessalonica, *tr. fr. Greek by* Alistair Elliot. GrAn

Priapus the Scarecrow. Antistius Vetus, *tr. fr. Greek by* Alistair Elliot. GrAn

Price, The. John Davidson. EBVV

Price, The. Anne Stevenson. DiPo

Price He Paid, The. Ella Wheeler Wilcox. WBLP

Price of a Drink. Josephine Pollard. VPP

Price of Begging, The. Emmanuel ben David Frances, *tr. fr. Hebrew by* A. B. Rhine. TrJP

Price of Disrespect, The. L. A. J. Moorer. CBWP-3

Price of Experience, The. Blake. *Fr.* Vala; or The Four Zoas. EnRP; Prf

Price of Giving Too Much, The. Vanparanar, *tr. fr. Tamil by* A. K. Ramanujan. PLW

Price of Rice, The, *sels.* Shu Wei, *tr. fr. Chinese by* Irving Lo.

Price of Wisdom. Bible, *O.T. See* "Surely there is a mine for silver."

Price seemed reasonable, location, The. Telephone Conversation. Wole Soyinka. TTY

Price she pays for, The. (*LL*) Invisibility Poem: Lesbian. Ilze Mueller. LoHo

Prices. Louis Ginsberg. TrJP

Prick a maiden nether holly. W. J. Webster. BXAP

Prickle a lamb. Conjuring Roethke. James Tate. OBAL

Pride. Violet Jacob. OxBS

Pride, The. John Newlove. MoCV; NOBC

Pride. Dahlia Ravikovitch, *tr. fr. Hebrew.* TSaS, *tr. by* Chana Bloch *and* Ariel Bloch

Pride cannot see itself by mid-day light. Barten Holyday. FaBoEE

Pride got passed at the breakfast table. The Lesson. Kathleen Cain. LoHo

Pride is his pity, artifice his praise. *Unknown.* FaBoEE

Pride Is the Canker. *Unknown. See* Do Not, Oh, Do Not Prize.

Pride, lust, ambition, and the people's hate. The Downfall of the Chancellor. *Unknown.* APAS

Pride, Malice, Folly, against Dryden rose. Pope. *Fr.* Essay on Criticism. EPCY; PoEL-3

Pride of a Jew, The. Judah Halevi, *tr. fr. Hebrew by* Israel Cohen. TrJP

Pride of all the village, The. Married to a Soldier. John Clare. SCGP

Pride of Ancestry. Robert Frost. OBAL

Pride of his own, and wonder of his age. David Mallet. *Fr.* Of Verbal Criticism. EPCY

Pride of Kildare, The. *Unknown.* OBET

Pride of Ladies, A. Anne Halley. NMM

Pride of the peacock is the glory of God, The. Blake. *Fr.* Marriage of Heaven and Hell, The. EnRP; FF; OAEL-2; RaBo

Pride of wrights, the joy of smiths abide, The. The Junk Shop. Henri Coulette. NYBP

Pride of Youth. Dante Gabriel Rossetti. *Fr.* House of Life, The. OBNC

Pride of Youth, The. Sir Walter Scott. *See* Proud Maisie ("Proud Maisie is in the wood.")

Prided the running main as it had been — . (*LL*) I walked [*or* walk'd] along a stream for pureness rare. *At. to* Gervase Markham. CTC

Priest and the Mulberry-Tree, The. Thomas Love Peacock. *Fr.* Crotchet Castle. BoTP; GN; OxAEP-2

Priest attending, found he spoke at times, The. George Crabbe. *Fr.* Borough, The. EBNV; ECEV; EnRP; FHYEP; OBNV; PoE; PoEL-4; TEP

Priest in the Sabbath Dawn Addresses His Somnolent Mistress, A. Peter Didsbury. PWE

Priest Lake. William Stafford. PoA

Priest of Felton. *Unknown.* OxNR

Priest or Poet. Shane Leslie. WGRP

Priest Rediscovers His Psalm-Book, The. *Unknown, tr. fr. Irish by* Frank O'Connor. PeIV

Priesthood, The. George Herbert. ESCV

Priestin' of Father John, The. John D. Sheridan. TIRV

Priest's Chant, The. John Fletcher. *Fr.* Faithful Shepherdess, The.

Priests of Apollo, sacred be the room[e]. The Sacrifice to Apollo. Michael Drayton. NOSC

Priests, the elders, and the scribes, The. Death and Resurrection. Priscilla Jane Thompson. CBWP-2

"*Priez pour lui.*". (*LL*) Battlefield. Richard Aldington. OBWP

Prig offered Pig the first chance at dessert. Manners. Howard Nemerov. NBLV

Primacy of Dullness, The. Dryden. *See* All human[e] things are subject to decay.

Primaleon of Greece., *sels.* Anthony Munday.
　"Beauty sat bathing by a spring." EBEvV
　(Beauty Bathing.) NOBE; OBEV
　(Beauty Sat Bathing by a Spring.) EIL
　(Colin.) GTBS; GTBS-P

Primary Ground, A. Adrienne Rich. NNaP

Primary Lesson: The Second Class Citizens. Sun-Ra. PoBA

Primavera. David Miller. NBrP

Prime. W. H. Auden. *Fr.* Horae Canonicae. CMoP; PoE

Prime. Donald Davie. *Fr.* Horae Canonicae. CRP

Prime. Langston Hughes. PoBA

Primer for Schoolchildren, A. Richard Weber. CIP

Primer Lesson. Carl Sandburg. FaPON; MoAmPo; MoShBr

Primer of Plato. Jean Garrigue. NOBA

Primer of the Daily Round, A. Howard Nemerov. NYBP; SM; WeW

Primeval Forest, The. Longfellow. *See* This is the forest primeval. The murmuring pines and the hemlocks.

Primitive, The. Don L. Lee. BPo

Primitive like an Orb, A. Wallace Stevens. NOBA

Primitive Pithecanthropus erectus, The. Heredity. Arthur Guiterman. OBAL; PeLi

Primitives. Dudley Randall. BPo; NBV

Primo Vere. Giosuè Carducci, *tr. fr. Italian by* John Bailey. AWP

Primos. Elizabeth Spires. BAP-90

Primrose, The. *At. to* Robert Herrick. CBLP; FaBoUs; OBEV; PFP

Primrose Bed, The. Robert Graves. TEP

Primrose, Being at Montgomery Castle, upon the Hill, on Which It Is Situate, The. John Donne. FaBoPP; GBL

Primrose Hill. Rose Fyleman. BoTP

Primroses; salutations; the miry skull. A Pre-Raphaelite Notebook. Geoffrey Hill. NoAM

Prince Absalom and Sir Rotherham Redde. Evening. Edith Sitwell. MoBS

Prince Alfrid's Itinerary, *sels. Unknown, tr. fr. Middle Irish by* James Clarence Mangan.
　"I found in Munster, unfettered of any." BIrV

Prince-Archbishop, Father Adelhard. To Adelhard, Archbishop of Canterbury. Alcuin, *tr. fr. Latin by* Helen Waddell. MLL

Prince Charles in his Welsh principality. Bernard Levin. PeLi

Prince Enters the Forest, The. Henri Cole. DiPo

Prince Hamlet thought Uncle a traitor. Hamlet. Stanley J. Sharpless. BXAP; NBLV; PeLi

Prince Heathen. *Unknown.* ESPB, A *and* B *vers.*

Prince Henry the Navigator. Sydney Clouts. PeSA

Prince Is Dead, The. Helen Hunt Jackson. AmWP

Prince New Year, welcome to thy throne. To the New Year. Priscilla Jane Thompson. CBWP-2

Prince of Life, The. John Oxenham. TrPWD

Prince of Love, The. Blake. *See* How sweet I roamed from field to field.

Prince of Peace, The. Harry Emerson Fosdick. *See* Prince of Peace His Banner Spreads, The.

Prince of Peace His Banner Spreads, The. Harry Emerson Fosdick. AH

Prince of Wales' Marriage. *Unknown*. CoMu

Prince Robert. *Unknown*. AmFP; ESPB, A *and* B *vers*.; OxBB

Prince Sumiya. *Mongol Oral Tradition*, tr. by C. R. Bawden. WTO

Prince Wen Hui's cook. Cutting up an Ox. Chuang Tzu, tr. fr. *Chinese by* Thomas Merton. EnlH

Prince William, of the Brunswick race. The Royal Adventurer. Philip Freneau. PAH

Prince, with wonder, sees the stately tow'rs, The. Virgil, tr. by Dryden. *Fr*. Aeneid [*or* Eneados], The. NAWM-1; OBVE

Princely Ditty in Praise of the English Rose, A. Thomas Deloney. BoTP

Princely eagle, and the soaring hawke, The. William Wood. SCAP

Princes and kings decay and die. Philip Freneau. GOA

Princes of Mercia were badger and raven, The. Geoffrey Hill. *Fr*. Mercian Hymns. HAP; NAEL-2; NoAM; NoP; PoE

Prince's Progress, The, *sels*. Christina Rossetti.
  Bride Song. OBEV; WPE
  (Too Late.) OtMeF

Princess, The. Bjørnstjerne Bjørnson, tr. fr. *Norwegian by* Philip L. Miller. RiWo

Princess, The, *sels*. Tennyson.
  As thro' the Land at Eve. LiTB
    (As Thro' the Land at Eve We Went.) ImPo
    (As through the Land.) SCGP
    (We Kiss'd Again with Tears.) PoToHe
  Ask Me No More [the Moon May Draw the Sea]. CBLP; GBL; LiTB; MeMBP; NAEL-2; OBNC; PoEL-5; TrGrPo
    (Ask Me No More.) ImPo
  "Blame not thyself too much," I said, "nor blame." NAEL-2
  "Bright is the moon on the deep." PIP
  Come Down, O Maid, [from Yonder Mountain Height]. EBVV; FF; GTBS-P; MeMBP; NAEL-2; NOBVV; OAEL-2; OBEV; OBNC; PIP; SCGP
    (Idyl, An.) TrGrPo
  "Home they brought her warrior dead." OxAEP-2; TrGrPo
  Now Sleeps the Crimson Petal, Now the White. ArLo; BoLoP; CBLP; ChTr; CoGr; EBEV; EBVV; ELP; FaPoB; FHYEP; GBL; GTBS-P; MeMBP; NAEL-2; NOBE; NoP; OBNC; OxAEP-2; PIP; PoEL-5; PPP; SCGP; SCV; TFi; TrGrPo
    (Song: "Now sleeps the crimson petal, now the white.") BLPL; FaBoBe
    (Summer Night.) OBEV
  "O Swallow, Swallow, flying, flying South." CBLP; PIP
  Sir Walter Vivian's House. CBCK
  Spirit Haunts the Year's Last Hours, A. InvP; MeMBP
    (Song: "Spirit haunts the last year's hours, A.") GTBS-P; HeIP; OBNC
  "Splendor falls on castle walls, The." AWP; CH; ClHu; EBEvV; EBVV; ELP; FaBoCh; FaBV; FHYEP; GoJo; GTBS-P; HeIL; HeIP; InPK; MeMBP; NAEL-2; NoP; OAEL-2; OBNC; PeVV; PoEL-5; PrIm; TrGrPo
    (Blow, Bugle, Blow.) BLPL; ChTr; ImPo; LiTB; NOBE; OBEV; UnPo; WiR
    (Bugle Song.) FaPON; GN
    (He Hears the Bugle at Killarney.) FaBoPP
    (Splendour Falls, The.) CoGr; TFi
  Sweet and Low [Sweet and Low]. BLPL; BoTP; FaBoBe; FaPON; FHYEP; NAEL-2; OxBChV; PIP; SCGP; TrGrPo
    (Lullaby: "Sweet and low, sweet and low.") PoLF
  Tears, Idle Tears. AWP; EBEvV; EBVV; ELP; EnVR; FaBoRV; FaPoR; GTBS-P; HAP; ImPo; InPS; InvP; LiTB; MeMBP; NAEL-2; NIP; NOBE; NoP; OAEL-2; OBNC; OxAEP-2; PIP; PoE; PoEL-5; Poetr; PPP; SCGP; TEP; TFi; TrGrPo; UnPo
  "Thy voice is heard through rolling drums." TrGrPo

Princess Elizabeth of Bohemia, as Perdita. Frank O'Hara. PoA

Princess Ida, *sels*. W. S. Gilbert.
  Arac's Song. FiBHP

Princess of the nights, be welcome. Night's Delights. Kaspar Stieler, tr. fr. *German by* Ingrid Waløe-Engel. GePo

Princess Sabbath. Heine, tr. fr. *German by* Charles Godfrey Leland. TrJP

"Princess," said the Frog, "Do not wince." Gina Berkeley. PeLi

Princess sat high up in her bower, The. The Princess. BjØornstjerne Bjørnson, tr. fr. *Norwegian by* Philip L. Miller. RiWo

Principal and Principle. *Unknown*. FaBoUs

Principal British Writers. Edward B. Goodwin. FaBoUs

Principal pal of the principal, The. Principal and Principle. *Unknown*. FaBoUs

Print, with his hand, his eye, was more than print. Hiroshige. Mark Perlberg. NYBP

Printed Words. Liz Sohappy Bahe. CDW

Printers. Denis Glover. PeNZ

Printer's Error. P. G. Wodehouse. FiBHP

Printing Bibles is Jenny's daily chore. Printing Jenny. Matthew Mitchell. OxBTC

Printing Jenny. Matthew Mitchell. OxBTC

Printing of these rhymes afflicts me more. A Panegyric on the Author of "Absalom and Achitophel." *Unknown*. APAS

Printing the stones. (*LL*) The Otter. Seamus Heaney. IPY; NoAM; PNI

Prioress, The. Chaucer. *Fr*. Canterbury Tales, The. CTC, *abr*.; EnVB; FHYEP; NoP; OAEL-1; PPP, *abr*.

Prioress's Tale, The. Chaucer. *Fr*. Canterbury Tales, The. EnVB

Prior's Epitaph. Matthew Prior. *See* Nobles and heralds, by your leave.

Priory of St. Saviour, Glendalough, The. Donald Davie. OxBC

Pripet Marshes, The. Irving Feldman. BTR

Pripyat River flows on, we assure you, The. The International Meteorological Committee Reports. Suzanne Gardinier. UTF

Prisms. Philip Dacey. Poetsp

Prison Cell, The. Mahmoud Darwish, tr. fr. *Arabic*. TSaS, tr. by Ben Bennani

Prison House, The. Alan Paton. PeSA

Prison-house in which I live, The. Renewal of Strength. Frances E. W. Harper. PWR

Prison in Windsor Castle. The Earl of Surrey. *See* So cruel [*or* cruell *or* crewell] prison how could betide [*or* howe coulde betyde], alas.

Prison looks like houses or usual Youre nothing going in, A. Into Prison. Bill Griffiths. NBrP

Prison Song. Alan Dugan. PoA

Prisoned in Windsor, He Recounteth His Pleasure There Passed. The Earl of Surrey. *Fr*. Windsor Castle. NAEL-1

Prisoner, The. Emily Brontë. NOBE; NoP; OBEV
  Sels.
    "He comes with western winds, with evening's wandering airs." ELP
    "In the dungeon-crypts, idly did I stray." NALW; NOBVV
    "Still, let my tyrants know, I am not doomed to wear." OBNC

Prisoner. Marguerite George. GoYe

Prisoner, The. Eduard Friedrich Mörike, tr. fr. *German by* Christopher Middleton. CBNP

Prisoner, The. William Plomer. PeSA

Prisoner of Chillon, The. Byron. BeLS; EnRP; PoLF
  Sels.
    "Kind of change came in my fate, A." NOBE
    Sonnet on Chillon. LiTB; MeMBP; TrGrPo
    (On the Castle of Chillon. GTBS; GTBS-P

Prisoner of Los Angeles (2). Wanda Coleman. NGP

Prisoner of War. Gertrude May Lutz. GoYe

Prisoner of Zenda, The. Richard Wilbur. NBLV

Prisoners, The. Robert Hayden. CAPP

Prisoners. Randall Jarrell. OxBA

Prisoners. Denise Levertov. NoAM; VCAP

Prisoners, The. Stephen Spender. FaBoMo; MoAB; MoBrPo

Prisoners. *Unknown*. EiL

Prisoners at Fort Marion: 1875-1878. Duane Niatum. *Fr*. Warrior Artists of the Southern Plains. NGP, *sect*. I

Prisoners of the Little Box, The. Vasco [*or* Vasko] Popa, tr. fr. *Serbo-Croatian by* Charles Simic. AnRep; HSix

Prisons Are Full of Convicts, The. Yang Yi, tr. fr. *Chinese by* Jonathan Chaves. SuSp

Pristine, orphic; obmutescent. (*LL*) The Diary of a Silence. Michael O'Loughlin. IB

Prithee die and set me free. Martial, tr. fr. *Latin by* Sir John Denham. OBVE

Prithee, fine lady, come under my bush. (*LL*) Draw a pail of water. *Unknown*. BoTP; FaBoVe; MoShBr; OxNR

Prithee go in thyself; seek thine own ease. Shakespeare. *Fr*. King Lear. FaPoB, *sect*. III, iv

Prithee leave me, crafty hussy. The Cupbearer Speaks. Goethe, tr. fr. *German by* John Weiss. *Fr*. West-Easterly Divan. PeHV

Prithee, let no raindrop fall. A. M. Sayers. BXAP

Prithee, no more, how can love sail? To Her Questioning His Estate. William Hammond. JCP

Prithee now, fond fool, give o'er. A Dialogue between Strephon and Daphne. The Earl of Rochester. SeCV-2

Prithee, say aye or no. The Resolute Courtier. Thomas Shipman. ErPo; GBL

Private, A. Edward Thomas. GTBS-P; NSI; PeFWW

Private Blair of the Regulars. Clinton Scollard. PAH

Private But Sulphurous. Tom Matthews. PNI

Private Conference of Harry Fat, The. James K. Baxter. PeLV

Private Dining Room, The. Ogden Nash. NYBP

Private faces in public places. W. H. Auden. FaBoEE

(Dedication.) PeLV

Private Judgement Condemned. Dryden. *Fr.* Hind and the Panther, The.

Private Letter to Brazil, A. Gloria C. Oden. PoNe

Private madness has prevailed, A. O Virtuous Light. Elinor Wylie. MoAB; MoAmPo

Private Means Is Dead. Stevie Smith. OxBC

Private Meeting Place, The. James Wright. NYBP

Private of the Buffs; or, The British Soldier in China. Sir Francis Hastings Doyle. OBEV; OBTV; VPP

Private Pain in Time of Trouble. Kathleen Spivack. AmPA

Private Pantomime. Ruth Stone. PoA

Private Person, A. William Stafford. PRA

Private Poem. Strato, *tr. fr. Greek by* Teddy Hogge. GrAn

Private Transport. Adrian Mitchell. FaBoEE

Private Willis's Song. W. S. Gilbert. *See* When all night long a chap remains.

Privilege of Being. Robert Hass. NAmP90; NIP

Privilege to die, The. (*LL*) Heart asks pleasure — first, The. Emily Dickinson. AmPP; CMoP; MeMAP; MoAB; MoAmPo; NAAL-1; NOBA; NoP; OxBA; PPP; PrIm; TrGrPo; WPE

Privileged prisoners in a haunted land. (*LL*) Picnic: the Liberated. M. Carl Holman. PoBA; PoNe

Privy-Love for My Landlady. George Farewell. NOEC

Prize, The. Edwin Muir. MeMBP

Prize Cat, The. E. J. Pratt. MoP

Prize for Good Conduct. Kenneth Allott. OBWP

Prize-giving. Gwen Harwood. CBAP; FaBoMA

Prize giving Speech. James K. Baxter. IHNG

Prize of the *Margaretta*, The. Will M. Carleton. PAH

"Prize" Poem, A. Shirley Brooks. FaBoCo; FaBoNo

Prize Riddle on Herself When 24, A. Elizabeth Frances Amherst. ECWP

Prize they do aim at they do procure, The. (*LL*) Upon the [*or* a] Snail. Bunyan. ChTr; OxBSP

Prize-winning Limerick, A. R. Rhodes. FaBoUs

Prizefighter's Prayer, The. Menotti Vincent Caprani. TIRV

Pro and Con. Judith Wright. FaBoMA

Pro Femina, *sels.* Carolyn Kizer.
"From Sappho to myself, consider the fate of women." NMM; VCAP
"I take as my theme, "The Independent Woman."" MAT; NMM; VCAP
"I will speak about women of letters, for I'm in the racket." CAPP; MAT; NALW; NMM

Pro Libra Mea. Joseph I. C. Clarke. TrPWD

Pro Patria. Constance Carrier. NYBP; WPE

Pro Patria. Adah Isaacs Menken. CBWP-1

Pro patria mori. (*LL*) Dulce et Decorum Est. Wilfred Owen. CMoP; DL; FaBoEH; FaBoPV; FaBoTw; FaBV; FaPoB; FF; HeIL; HeIP; HoPM; InPK; InvP; LiTB; LiTM; MeMBP; MoAB; MoBrPo; NAEL-2; NIP; NoAM; NoP; OAEL-2; OBWP; PAW; PeFWW; PoE; Poetr; PoWW; PPP; PrIm; RaBo; TFi; TRP; UnPo

Pro Patria Mori. Thomas Moore. GTBS; GTBS-P; HoPM; OxAEP-2

Pro Sua Vita. Robert Penn Warren. MoAmPo

Probable volume of dreams, think so. (*LL*) Treetops. Marvin Bell. AmPA

Probably. Keith Preston. NBLV

Probably the Farmer. Laura Jensen. AnAn

Probatioun Officeres Tale, The. Gerard Benson. BXAP; NBLV

Problem, The. Paul Blackburn. NeAP

Problem, The. (I like a church; I like a cowl.) Emerson. AmPP; AnAmPo; AWP; LiTA; MeMAP; NAAL-1; NOBA; NoP; OxBA; TAP; WGRP *Sels.*

Problem in History, A. Robert Wallace. CRP

Problem in Morals, A. Howard Moss. ErPo

Problem in Social Geometry — the Inverted Square! Ray Durem. PoBA

Problem is the dissection problem, The. On Nothing. *Unknown.* BAP-90

Problem the grass under the saplings, The. David Chaloner. VaA

Problems. Alexander Scott. FF

Problems of a Journalist. Weldon Kees. NaP

Problems of translation are, perhaps, not so great. XifEWRRWA. John Ash. BAP-91

Procedures for Underground. Margaret Atwood. NALW

Proceed from want of Judgement and of Wit? (*LL*) An Allusion to Horace; the Tenth Satire of the First Book. The Earl of Rochester. APAS

Proceeding eighty miles into the northwest wind. Italo Calvino, *tr. fr. Italian. Fr.* Trading Cities. AnRep, *tr. by* William Weaver

Proceeding still in the westward face, and like. As It Were an Attendant. J. H. Prynne. VaA

Process, The. Tom Clark. UL

Process. Aidan Carl Mathews. IB

Process. John Montague. CIP

Process. Charles L. O'Donnell. TrPWD

Process calls for twenty heads to stare, The. Colorizing: Turner Broadcasting Enterprises, Computer Graphics Division, Burbank, California, 1987. David Wojahn. *Fr.* Mystery Train: A Sequence. PBCAP

Process in the Weather of the Heart, A. Dylan Thomas. MoAB

Process of time worketh such wonder. Sir Thomas Wyatt. SiPS; SiPSBD

Processes of generation; deeds of settlement. Geoffrey Hill. *Fr.* Mercian Hymns. NoP

Procession, The: a New Protestant Ballad. *Unknown.* APAS

Procession at Candlemas, A. Amy Clampitt. FaBoWP; HCAP; Poetr

Procession of ghosts shuffles by, The. Carnival at the River. Robert Greacen. PNI

Procession of honest men, A. Selah. R. S. Thomas. FaBoMo

Procession of the Flowers, The. Sydney Thompson Dobell. *See* First came the primrose.

Processions that lack high stilts have nothing that catches the eye. High Talk. W. B. Yeats. CBNP; FaBoVe; RaBo

Proclaim the Lofty Praise. Sarah Judson. AH

Proclaim: "The Lord is come." (*LL*) The Morning Light Is Breaking. Samuel Francis Smith. AH; WGRP

Proclaims the winter by. (*LL*) Crows in Spring. John Clare. EnRP

Proclamation, The. Longfellow. *Fr.* John Endicott. PAH

Proclamation, The. Whittier. PAH

Proclamation, A. *Unknown.* PAH

Proclamation/ From Sleep, Arise. Carolyn M. Rodgers. JB

Proclamation, or Paper Bomb, The. F. W. Reitz, *tr. fr. Afrikaans by* F. W. Reitz. PeSAV

Procne. Peter Quennell. LiTB; LiTM; MoBrPo

Procne, Philomela, and Itylus. Philomela. John Crowe Ransom. ChTr; CMoP; FaBoPP; NAAL-2; NoAM; NOBA; OBAL; OBSV; OxBA

Proconsul of Bithynia. To Petronius Arbiter. Oliver St. John Gogarty. OBMV

Procrastination. Martial, *tr. by* Abraham Cowley. AWP; FaBoEE; OBVE

Procuress, The. Herodas, *tr. fr. Greek by* Barbara Hughes Fowler. HePo

Prodigal, The. Elizabeth Bishop. ChIV-2; CoAP; InvP; LCAP; LiTM; MoAB; NYBP; PPP; TwCP

Prodigal Son, The. Robert Bly. ChIV-2

Prodigal Son, The. Kipling. *Fr.* Kim. NoAM

Prodigal Son, The. E. A. Robinson. MoAmPo

Prodigal Son is kneeling in the husks, The. The Prodigal Son. Robert Bly. ChIV-2

Prodigy. Charles Simic. VCAP

Prodike. Rufinus, *tr. fr. Greek by* Alan Marshfield. GrAn

Produce. Debra Allbery. PBCAP

Produce the urn that Hannibal contains. Hannibal ("Produce the urn that Hannibal contains.") Juvenal, *tr. by* William Gifford. *Fr.* Satires. OBVE

Producify by exclusioness. Disinterment. James Sherry. UL

Product of peoples on two sides of a narrow sea, The. Lyle Donaghy, Poet, 1902-1949. George Buchanan. PNI

Proem: "Lo, thus, as prostrate, "In the dust I write." James Thomson ("B.V."). *Fr.* City of Dreadful Night, The. OBNC; OxBS (City, The.) NOBE

Proem: "Out of my own great woe." Heine, *tr. fr. German by* Elizabeth Barrett Browning. AWP

Proem: "There is no rhyme that is half so sweet." Madison Cawein. BoNaP

Proem: To Brooklyn Bridge. Hart Crane. *See* How many dawns, chill from his rippling rest.

Proem to "The Kid." Conrad Aiken. *Fr.* Kid, The. MoAB

Profane, The. Horace. *See* Tread back — and back, the lewd and lay.

Professional, The. David Ignatow. NNaP

Professionals. Turner Cassity. MT

Professionals, The. Geoffrey Grigson. PoA

Professor at the Breakfast Table, The, *sels.* Oliver Wendell Holmes.
Lord of All Being, Throned Afar. AH
(Sun-Day Hymn.) TrPWD; WGRP
O Love Divine, That Stooped to Share. AH
(Hymn of Trust.) TrPWD

Professor Burke's symphony, "Colorado Vistas." Cultural Notes. Kenneth Fearing. CMoP; PoE

Professor Eisenbart, asked to attend. Prize-giving. Gwen Harwood. CBAP; FaBoMA

Professor Eisenbart, with grim distaste. Panther and Peacock. Gwen Harwood. CBAP

Professor Gratt. Donald Hall. OBAL

"Then Jonson came, instructed from the school." EPCY

Prologue [Spoken by Mr. Garrick] [at the Opening of the Theatre in Drury-Lane, 1747]. Samuel Johnson. EBEV; EPCY, *ll.* 1–8; NAEL-1; NOEC; NoP; OxAEP-1

Prologue: The Wanderers. William Morris. *Fr.* Earthly Paradise, The. EBVV

Prologue to Book VII, The. Virgil, *tr.* by Gavin Douglas. *Fr.* Aeneid [*or* Eneados], The. NAWM-1; OxBLMV; OxBS

Prologue to General Hamley, *sels.* Tennyson. Green Sussex. FaBoPP

Prologue to [Hugh Kelly's] "A Word to the Wise." Samuel Johnson. EBEV; FaPoR; OxAEP-1

Prologue to "Love Triumphant." Dryden. *Fr.* Love Triumphant. OxBoLi

Prologue to Responsibilities. W. B. Yeats. *See* Pardon, old fathers, if you still remain.

Prologue to the Avowis of Alexander. John Barbour. *Fr.* Buik of Alexander, The. OxBS

Prologue to the First Satire. Persius, *tr. fr. Latin* by Dryden. *Fr.* Satires. AWP

Prologue to "The Lakers; a Comic Opera," *sels.* James Plumptre. "Where Cumbria's mountains in the north arise." NOEC

Prologue to the Miller's Tale. Chaucer. *Fr.* Canterbury Tales, The. EnVB; NAWM-1

Prologue to the Second Nun's Tale, The. Chaucer. *Fr.* Canterbury Tales, The. EnVB

Prologue to "The Tempest." Dryden. NoP

Prologue to the Wife of Bath's Tale, The. Chaucer. *See* Experience, though noon auctoritee.

Prologue to Sir Thopas. Chaucer. *Fr.* Canterbury Tales, The. EnVB

Prelude XIX: "Watch long enough, and you will see the leaf." Conrad Aiken. *Fr.* Preludes for Memnon; or, Preludes to Attitude. CMoP; OxBA

Prologue: "We Who with Songs Beguile Your Pilgrimage. James Elroy Flecker. *See* We who with songs beguile your pilgrimage.

Prologues are over, The. It is a question, now. Asides on the Oboe. Wallace Stevens. FaBoMo; MoAB; MoAmPo

Prolonged Sonnet: In the Last Days of the Emperor Henry VII. Simone dall' Antella, *tr. fr. Italian* by Dante Gabriel Rossetti. AWP

Prolonged Sonnet: When the Troops Were Returning from Milan [*or* When The Troops Were Returning from Milan]. Niccolò degli Albizzi, *tr. fr. Italian* by Dante Gabriel Rossetti. AWP; OBVE

Promachus hangs here. Mnasalcas, *tr. fr. Greek* by Edward Lucie-Smith. GrAn

Promenade. David Ignatow. TrJP

Promenade, The. Tchicaya U Tam'si, *tr. fr. French* by Ellen Conroy Kennedy. NegPo

Promenading their/ skirted galleons of sex. The Return to Work. William Carlos Williams. NYBP

Prometheus. Byron. EnRP; InPS; NOBE; NoP; OAEL-2; OxAEP-2; Poetr

Prometheus. Goethe, *tr. fr. German* AWP; *tr.* by John S. Dwight.

Prometheus. Goethe, *tr. fr. German* RiWo; *tr.* by Philip L. Miller.

Prometheus. Jenny Mastoraki, *tr. fr. Modern Greek* by Nikos Germanakos. BoWoP

Prometheus. Swift. FaBoPV

Prometheus Bound, *sels.* Aeschylus, *tr. fr. Greek* by Elizabeth Barrett Browning.
"But Fortune governed all their works till when." SiPSBD, *tr.* by Sir Walter Ralegh
Wail of Prometheus Bound, The. WGRP

Prometheus on His Crag. Ted Hughes. AnAn
Sels.
"Now I know I never shall."
"Prometheus on his crag/ began to admire the vulture."
"Prometheus on his crag/ heard the cry of the wombs."

Prometheus on his crag/ began to admire the vulture. Ted Hughes. *Fr.* Prometheus on His Crag. AnAn

Prometheus on his crag/ heard the cry of the wombs. Ted Hughes. *Fr.* Prometheus on His Crag. AnAn

Prometheus Unbound. A. D. Hope. OxBC

Prometheus Unbound. Shelley. EnRP; OAEL-2
Sels.
"As I have said, I floated to the earth." FHYEP
"Crawling glaciers pierce me with the spears." FHYEP
Life of Life. CH; MeMBP; NOBE; PoE; PoEL-4
(Hymn to the Spirit of Nature.) GTBS; GTBS-P
"Monarch of Gods and Dæmons, and all Spirits." NAEL-2
"My soul is enchanted boat." FHYEP
"On a poet's lips I slept." ELP; EPCY; TOF
(Poet's Dream, The.) GTBS; GTBS-P
"This is the day, which down the void abysm." FHYEP
"Thou, Earth, calm empire of a happy soul." FaBoRV; PeECV

"Thou knowest that toads and snakes and loathly worms." PoE

Prometheus, when first from heaven high. Sir Edward Dyer. NoSic

Promiscuous lovers/ Pine to have. A Problem in Morals. Howard Moss. ErPo

Promise, The. Johari M. Kunjufu. BISi

Promise. Florence Lacey. BoTP

Promise me no promises. Promises like Pie-Crust. Christina Rossetti. NOBVV

Promise of a Constant Lover, The. *Unknown.* EIL

Promise of Peace. Robinson Jeffers. LiTA; LiTM; MoAB; MoAmPo

Promise was broken too freely, The. Galway Kinnell. *Fr.* Avenue Bearing the Initial of Christ into the New World, The. NaP

Promised Land, The. Jessie E. Sampter. TrJP

Promised Land, The. Samuel Stennett. AmFP

Promises. Ruth Forbes Sherry. GoYe

Promises, *sels.* Robert Penn Warren.
Founding Fathers, Nineteenth-Century Style. NoAM

Promises like Pie-Crust. Christina Rossetti. NOBVV

Promises of Freedom. *Unknown.* BPo

Promises of Leniency and Forgiveness. Charles Simic. LCAP

Promises of mother, The. I Hear You. Shirley Kaufman. MDDM

Promises of the World, The. Moses ibn Ezra, *tr. fr. Hebrew* by Solomon Solis-Cohen. *Fr.* World's Illusion, The. TrJP

Promising Author. Carolyn Kizer. NGP

Promissory Note, The. Bayard Taylor. AnAmPo; BXAP

Promontory Moment, The. May Swenson. NYBP

Prone couple still sleeps, A. First Light. Thomas Kinsella. BIrV; CMoP; PoE

Proof, The. W. H. Auden. OAEL-2

Proof. Bessie Calhoun Bird. BISi

Proof. Brendan Kennelly. CIP; PBCIP

Proof, The. Czeslaw Milosz, *tr. fr. Polish by the author.* TOF

Proof, The. Richard Wilbur. CRP; OxBSP

Proofs. Tadeusz Różewicz, *tr. fr. Polish* by Adam Czerniawski. PoSu

Proofs of Buddha's Existence. *Unknown.* WGRP

Prope ripam fluvii solus. Malum Opus. James Appleton Morgan. FaBoCo

Proper Clay. Mark Van Doren. PoRA; TrGrPo

Proper Distance and Proper Time. Judith Baumel. UTF

Proper Names. Martin Sorescu, *tr. fr. Romanian* by D. J. Enright *and* Ioana Russell-Gebbett. PWE

Proper New Ballad, Intitled The Fairies' Farewell, A. Richard Corbett [*or* Corbett]. PeLV; SCGP

Proper New Song, A, *sels.* Thomas Richardson.
Take Heed of Gazing Overmuch. EIL

Proper Pride. D. H. Lawrence. FaBoEE

Proper scale would pat you on the head, The. The Scales. William Empson. CBLP; CMoP; FaBoMo; LiTM

Proper Song, Entitled: Fain Would I Have a Pretty Thing to Give unto My Lady, A. *Unknown.* CoMu; EIL; InvP; NoSic

Proper Sonnet, How Time Consumeth All Earthly Things, A. *At.* to Thomas Proctor. FaBoRV

Proper Study of Mankind, The. Pope. *See* Know then thyself, presume not God to scan.

Proper way to eat a fig, in society, The. Figs. D. H. Lawrence. OAEL-2

Properte of every shire, The. The Properties of the Shires of England. *Unknown.* FaBoPP; GBP

Properties of a Good Greyhound, The. Dame Juliana Berners. RB

Properties of the Shires of England, The. *Unknown.* FaBoPP; GBP

Property! Property! Let us extend. On Property. Louis MacNeice. *Fr.* Jigsaws. IHNG

Prophecia Merlini Doctoris Perfecti. *Unknown.* OxBLMV

Prophecy. Eileen Duggan. PeNZ

Prophecy, The. Will Lilly. FaBoEH

Prophecy. Luigi Pulci, *tr. fr. Italian.* *Fr.* Morgante Maggiore, Il. PAH

Prophecy. Tennyson. *See* For I Dipped [*or* Dipt] into the Future.

"Prophecy." Gulian Verplanck. PAH

Prophecy. Elinor Wylie. BLPL; BoWoP; FaBoWP; NTP; PrIm; VGW

Prophecy, A. Blake. *Fr.* America. FaBoEH

Prophecy, A. Allen Ginsberg. TAP

Prophecy, A. Arthur Lee. PAH

Prophecy, A. Christopher Levenson. ErPo

Prophecy of Cuauhtémoc, *sels.* Ignacio Rodríguez Galván, *tr. fr. Spanish* by Samuel Beckett.

Prophecy of Famine, The, *sels.* Charles Churchill.
"Oft have I heard thee mourn the wretched lot." OBSV
On His Own Poetry. NOEC
"Two boys, whose birth beyond all question springs." OBSV

Prophecy of King Tammany, The. Philip Freneau. GOA

Prophecy on Lethe. Stanley Kunitz. PoA

Prophecy Sublime, The. Frederick L. Hosmer. *See* Thy Kingdom Come, O Lord.

Prophesie When Asses Shall Grow Elephants, A. Sir John Harington. CBCK

Prophet, The. Abraham Cowley. JCP; TrGrPo

Prophet, The, *sels.* Kahlil Gibran.
　Crime and Punishment. PoToHe
　Love One Another. LPA; OxBM
　Of Love. PoLF
　On Children. OxBM; PoToHe
　On Work. PoToHe, *abr.*
　"Then Almitra spoke, saying, We would ask now of Death." DL

Prophet. Omens of the Morning. Faustin Charles. NBrP

Prophet, The. Pushkin, *tr. fr. Russian tr.* by Babette Deutsch *and* Avrahm Yarmolinsky. AWP; WGRP, *tr.* by Babette Deutsch.

Prophet, The. "Yehoash," *tr. fr. Yiddish* by Isidore Goldstick. TrJP

Prophet, Go, Flee! Hayyim Nahman Bialik, *tr. fr. Hebrew* by Ruth Finer Mintz. MHP

Prophet Jeremiah and the Personification of Israel, The. *At. to* Eleazar ben Kalir, *tr. fr. Hebrew* by Nina Davis Salaman. TrJP

Prophet of the body's roving. Walt Whitman. Edwin Honig. TAP

Prophet speaks, The. Saint Malcolm. Jewel C. Latimore. BPo

Prophetess, The. Dorothy Livesay. MoCV

Prophets, The. W. H. Auden. CBLP

Prophets, The. Richard Shelton. NYBP

Prophets at street corners, in neat grey suits. Saturday Night. Antigone Kefala. CBAP

Prophets for a New Day. Margaret Walker. BPo

Prophets, preaching in new stars. The Pontoon-Bridge Miracle. Vachel Lindsay. MeMAP

Prophet's Warning or Shoot to Kill, The. Ebon Dooley. PoBA

Proportion. Amy Lowell. BoWoP

Proportion'd to their sweetness. *(LL)* The River of Life. Thomas Campbell. GTBS; GTBS-P; ImPo; LiTB

Propos of the Wet Snow, A, *sels.* N. A. Nekrasov, *tr. fr. Russian* by Juliet Soskice.
　"When from dark error's subjugation." NAWM-2

Proposition, The. Paul Blackburn. ErPo

Proposition. Nicolás Guillén, *tr. fr. Spanish* by Langston Hughes. FaPON; TTY

Proposition. Robert Pinsky. *Fr.* Essay on Psychiatrists. HCAP; NoAM

Proposition and Invocation. Homer, *tr. fr. Greek. Fr.* Iliad, The. NOSC

Proposition II. Keith Waldrop. InPK

Propositions. Phyllis Webb. MoCV

Propped against the crowded bar. Trane. Edward Kamau Brathwaite. Jaz

Propped boughs are heavy with apples. In the Huon Valley. James McAuley. CBAP

Propped on a stick he viewed the August weald. The One-legged Man. Siegfried Sassoon. CMoP

Prorogued on prorogation — damned rogues and whores! On the Prorogation. *Unknown.* APAS

Pros-pectin' round about one day. Joe's Luck. Albert Brodrick. PeSAV

Prosaic miles of streets stretch all round. Seder-Night. Israel Zangwill. TrJP

Prose. Bernard Welt. EOEF

Prose for Des Esseintes. Donald Davie, *after the French of* Stéphane Mallarmé. OBVE

Proserpine. Swinburne. *Fr.* Garden of Proserpine, The. AWP; BLPA; BLPL; ChTr; FaBoRV; FaBV; FaPoR; HAP; LiTB; NAEL-2; NOBE; NOBVV; NoP; ONBC; PoE; PoEL-5; PoRA; SCV; TrGrPo

Proserpine may pull her flowers. Song of the Stygian Naiades. Thomas Lovell Beddoes. EnRP; OAEL-2

Proserpine's Ragout. Mary Leapor. ECWP

Prospect, The. Timothy Dwight. *Fr.* Greenfield Hill. EAP

Prospect. Louis MacNeice. IIP

Prospect Beach. Lou Lipsitz. VGW

Prospect of Eden, The. Milton. *See* O for that warning voice, which he who saw.

Prospect of Heaven, A. Isaac Watts. *See* There is a land of pure delight.

Prospect of Heaven Makes Death Easy, A. Isaac Watts. *See* There is a land of pure delight.

Prospect of the Future, The. Mrs. Henry Linden. CBWP-4

Prospect of the Future Glory of America. John Trumbull. AmPP

Prospecting Dream. *Unknown.* AmFP

Prospective Immigrants Please Note. Adrienne Rich. AiP; GOA; VGW

Prospects. Tim Longville. VaA

Prospectus. Wordsworth. *Fr.* Excursion, The. EnRP; NoP; OAEL-2

Prospectus *[incl. in* The Excursion]. Wordsworth. *See* On man, on nature, and on human life.

Prospectus *[incl. in* The Excursion]. Wordsworth. *See* On Man, on Nature, and on Human Life.

Prospice. Robert Browning. BLPL; DL; FaBV; FHYEP; ImPo; LiTB; MeMBP; NAEL-2; OBD; PlP; PoLF; PoRA; TrCP; TrGrPo; WGRP

Prostate Operation. Robert Pinsky. *Fr.* Three on Luck. AnAn

Prostitute living in London, A. Douglas Catley. PeLi

Prostitutes at Smiller's Bar beside the dusty road, The. The Cheerful Girls at Smiller's Bar. Jack A. Mapanje. HBAPE; PeSAV

Prostitutes have clients, wives have husbands. My Five Gentlemen. Elizabeth Bartlett. IHNG

Protect Me, My Talisman. Milo De Angelis, *tr. tr. Italian by* Lawrence Venuti. NeIt

Protecting the sea-cliffs. *(LL)* Her Longing. Theodore Roethke. NAAL-2; NU

Protection of a cheap coat suffices, The. Parmenion of Macedon, *tr. fr. Greek* by Peter Jay. GrAn

Protection of Jehovah, The. Bible, *O.T., paraphrased by* Sir Thomas Wyatt. *See* Lord is my shepherd, I shall not want, The.

Protection of Plants, The. Erasmus Darwin. *Fr.* Economy of Vegetation, The. FaBoUs

Protective Grigri, The. Ted Joans. PoBA

Protective instinct among the Emperor penguins, The. Penguins. Artur Miedzyrzecki, *tr. fr. Polish by* Artur Miedzyrzecki *and* John Batki. PoSu

Protects the lingering dew-drop from the sun. *(LL)* To a Child. Wordsworth. OxBSP

Protégés will come. The True Protocol of Poets. Kapilar, *tr. fr. Tamil by* A. K. Ramanujan. PLW

Protest. Countee Cullen. CDC

Protest, A. Sir Thomas Wyatt. *See* Heaven and earth, and all that hear me plain.

Protest against the Ballot. Wordsworth. FaBoEH

Protest and Survive. *(LL)* What Would Tom Paine Do? Edward Sanders. PoBeRe

Protest in the Sixth Year of Ch'ien Fu, A. Ts'ao Sung, *tr. fr. Chinese by* Arthur Waley. FaBV

Protest of the Illiterate, The, *sels.* Gelett Burgess.
　"I seen a dunce of a poet once, a-writin' a little book." FiBHP

Protestant graveyard was a forbidden place, The. The Weeping Headstones of the Isaac Becketts. Paul Durcan. PBCIP

Prothalamion. (Calm was the day, and through the trembling air.) Spenser. AAS; AWP; ChTr; EBEV; ElL; FaBoPP; GTBS; GTBS-P; HAP; LiTB; Mes; NoP; NoSic; OBEV; PPP; TFi
Sels.
　"Calm was the day, and through the trembling air." EBEvV, *Pts.* I *and* II *only*; EnRePo; ImPo; SCGP
　(Calme was the day, and through the trembling ayre.) OxAEP-1

Prothalamion *sels.* Robert Silliman Hillyer.
　"Hills turn hugely in their sleep, The." MoAmPo

Prothalamion. Maxine W. Kumin. NYBP

Prothalamion. Michael Ryan. AmPA

Prothalamion. Delmore Schwartz. OxBA

Prothalamium. Donagh MacDonagh. BIrV

Protocols. Randall Jarrell. LCAP; OxBC; VGW

Protocols. Vikram Seth. OBF

Protracted Episode. A. F. Moritz. BAP-91

Proud and beautiful city of Moscow, The. History Lessons. Seamus Deane. BiHa; PBCIP; PNI

Proud and rest-ive Chim-pan-zee, The. Having a Wonderful Time. D. B. Wyndham Lewis. FiBHP

Proud as Apollo on his forked hill. Bufo. Pope. *Fr.* Epistle to Dr. Arbuthnot. FHYEP; InPS; NoP; OAEL-1; OBSV; OxAEP-1; PoE; PoEL-3; TFi

Proud Egyptian Queen, The. Sir Edward Sherburne, *after the Italian of* Giambattista Marina. *See* Proud Egyptian [*or* Aegyptian] queen, her Roman guest, The.

Proud Egyptian [*or* Aegyptian] queen, her Roman guest, The. And She Washed His Feet with Her Tear[e]s, and Wiped Them with the Hairs of Her Head. Sir Edward Sherburne, *after the Italian of* Giambattista Marina. ChTr; MeLP; NOSC
　(Proud Egyptian Queen, The. OxBSP

Proud Error. Vasco [*or* Vasko] Popa, *tr. fr. Serbo-Croatian. Fr.* Yawn of Yawns, The. AnRep, *tr.* by Charles Simic; HSix, *tr.* by Charles Simic

Proud fountains, wave your plumes. Fountains ("Proud fountains, wave your plumes.") Sir Osbert Sitwell. MoBrPo

Proud in Thy Love. *Unknown. Fr.* Zepheria. Son

Proud inclination of the flesh. Dilys Bennett Laing. ErPo

Proud Lady Margaret. *Unknown. See* Fair Margret was a young ladye.

Proud Little Spruce Fir. Jeannie Kirby. BoTP

Proud Maisie ("Proud Maisie is in the wood.") Sir Walter Scott. *Fr.* Heart of Midlothian, The. CH; ChTr; EnRP; FaBoCh; FF; Mes; NAEL-2; OAEL-2; OBEV; OxBS; PoEL-4; SCGP; TEP; TFi; TrGrPo; UnPo

Proud, majestic Southern sun, The. The Husband's Return. Priscilla Jane Thompson. CBWP-2

Proud Margret. *Unknown.* OxBB

Proud monument that doth enclose my jewel. *(LL)* They say that shadow[e]s of deceased ghosts. Joshua Sylvester. ElL

Proud of my music, let me often make. Stéphane Mallarmé, *tr. fr. French by* Aldous Huxley. *Fr.* Après-midi d'un Faune, L'. AWP; ErPo

Proud of my pride. A Tale Told by a Head. Lois Moyles. NYBP

Proud Preston poor people. Preston. *Unknown.* FaBoVe

Proud Preston, poor people. Preston. *Unknown.* GBP

Proud Songsters. Thomas Hardy. MoP

Proud who never loved, The. Sublimation. Alex Comfort. ErPo

Proud with success, richly pleased. Alexander Jannai. C. P. Cavafy, *tr. fr. Greek by* Simon Chasen. TrJP

Proud word you never spoke, but you will speak. Walter Savage Landor. *Fr.* Ianthe. CBLP; EnLoPo; GBL; OBEV

Proudful and barefoot I stride the street. For a Man Who Walked Sideways. Martin Carter. PBCV

Proudly the note of the trumpet is sounding. O'Donnell Aboo. Michael Joseph McCann. PeIV

Proust's Madeleine. Kenneth Rexroth. NoAM; TRP

Prove every fool to be a poet. *(LL)* Yes, every poet is a fool. Matthew Prior. FaBoEE

Proverb. *Unknown.* FaBoBe; ISE; OxNR; ReMoGo

Proverb: "Needles and pins, needles and pins." *Unknown. See* Needles and pins, needles and pins.

Proverb reporteth, no man can deny, The. *Unknown. Fr.* Tom Tyler and His Wife. ElL

Proverbial Advice on Marriage. *Unknown. See* Who weds a sot to get his cot.

Proverbial Philosophy: Of Reading. Charles Stuart Calverley. FaBoCo

Proverbios Morales, *sels.* Santob de Carrion.
  Friend, A. TrJP

Proverbs, *sels.* Bible, *O.T.*
  Drunkard, The. TrJP
  Fear of the Lord, The. TrJP
  Foolish Woman, A. TrGrPo
  Go to the Ant [Thou Sluggard]. FaPON; TrJP
  (Reproof, A.) TrGrPo
  Happy Is the Man. TrJP
  Hay Appeareth, The. FaPON
  He That Is Slow to Anger. FaPON
  House of Wisdom, The. TrGrPo
  Legacy, The. TrJP
  Lips of the Wise, The. TrGrPo
  Neither Poverty nor Riches. TrJP
  Seven Evils. TrGrPo
  She of the Impudent Face. TrJP
  "Who can find a virtuous woman? for her price is far above rubies"
    (Good Wife, The.) TrGrPo
    (Virtuous Woman, The.) TrJP
  Word Fitly Spoken, A. FaPON
  Words of Agur, The
  Too Wonderful. TrJP

Proverbs. Samuel Ha-Nagid, *tr. fr. Hebrew by* Israel Abrahams. TrJP

Proverbs of Alfred, The. *At. to* Alfred, King of England. PoE
  Sels.
  "Thus queth Alvred:/ 'Idelschipe and overprute, that lereth yong wif üvel thewes'. "
  "Thus queth Alvred:/ 'If thu havest seorewe, ne seyethu hit than arewe'. "
  "Thus queth Alvred:/ 'Ne schaltu nevere thi wif by hire wlyte choose'. "
  "Thus queth Alvred:/ 'Ne würth thu never so wod ne so wyn-drunke'. "
  "Thus queth Alvred:/ 'Nevre thu, bi thine lyve, the word of thine wyve'. "

Proverbs of Hell. Blake. *See* In seed time learn, in harvest teach, in winter enjoy.

Proverbs 6:6. David Curzon. ChIV-1

Proves Care's confessor at the last. *(LL)* The Sea Hath Many Thousand Sands. *Unknown.* ElL; LiTB

Provide for our starving children an abundance of daily bread. *(LL)* Here we are, God — a planet at prayer. Attune our spirits. Joan Metzner. EaPr

Provide, Provide. Robert Frost. AmPP; ChIV-1; CMoP; HAP; MoAB; MoP; NAAL-2; NoAM; NOBA; NoP; OPOP; PoE; Poetr; PPP; TAP; TFi; TwCP; UnPo; WeW

Providence. Reginald Heber. GN; OHIP

Providence, *sels.* George Herbert.
  "O sacred Providence, who from end to end." AngWe

Province has set up shrines, The. Parihaka. W. H. Oliver. PeNZ

Province I govern is humble and remote, The. To Li Chien. Po Chü-i, *tr. fr. Chinese by* Arthur Waley. AWP

Province of the Saved, The. Emily Dickinson. TRP

Provinces. C. D. Wright. LCAP

Provincetown. Louis Dudek. MoCV
  Sels.
  Avant Garde.
  Fishing Village.
  News.
  Ocean, The.

Provincetown, Mass. Harvey Shapiro. PoA

Provincia Deserta. Ezra Pound. OxBA

Provincial Adolescence. A. Michael Foley. PNI

Proving. Georgia Douglas Johnson. CDC

Proving to Death that Love is so and so. *(LL)* Goodby Betty, Don't Remember Me. E. E. Cummings. CMoP; PoE

Provisions. Margaret Atwood. IHMS

Prowling wolf, whose shaggy skin, A. The Wolf and the Dog. La Fontaine, *tr. fr. French by* Elizur Wright. OBVE

Prows o' Reekie, The. Lewis Spence. OxBS

Prudence. Emerson. OBAL

Prudent Simplicity. William Cowper. FaBoEE

Prudish old lady called Muir, A. *Unknown.* PeLi

Prue, my dearest maid, is sick. Upon Prudence Baldwin Her Sickness. Robert Herrick. JCP; SeCV-1

Pruned Tree, The. Howard Moss. NYBP; VCAP

Pruning, The. Adam David Miller. NBV

Pruning. John Philips. *Fr.* Cyder. FaBoUs

Prytherch is dead. We have no right. Dai, Live. Jon Dressel. AngWe

Psalm VI: "And on that day, upon the heavenly scarp." A. M. Klein. *Fr.* Psalter of Avram Haktani, The. PoA

Psalm XLII: "As the hart panteth after the water brooks." Bible, *O.T.*, *paraphrased by* Sir Thomas Wyatt. *Fr.* Psalms. AWP; TrJP

Psalm CXXXIII: "Behold, how good and how pleasant . . . ." Bible, *O.T.*, *paraphrased by* Sir Thomas Wyatt. *Fr.* Psalms. AWP

Psalm CXXXIII: "Beholde, how good and joyfull a thinge it is." Bible, *O.T.*, *paraphrased by* Sir Thomas Wyatt. *See* Behold, how good and how pleasant it is.

Psalm CIII: "Bless the Lord, O my soul . . . ." Bible, *O.T.*, *paraphrased by* Sir Thomas Wyatt. *Fr.* Psalms. AWP

Psalm CIV: "Bless the Lord, O my soul . . . ." Bible, *O.T.*, *paraphrased by* Sir Thomas Wyatt. *Fr.* Psalms. NAWM-1; OHIP, *abr.;* TrJP

Psalm I: "Blessed is the man . . . ." Bible, *O.T.*, *paraphrased by* Sir Thomas Wyatt. *Fr.* Psalms. AWP

Psalm LV: Exaudi, Deus: "My God most glad to look, most prone to hear," *paraphrased by* the Countess of Pembroke. Bible, *O.T.*, *paraphrased by* Sir Thomas Wyatt. *See* Give ear to my prayer, O God.

Psalm CXXXIX: Domine, Probasti. Bible, *O.T.*, *paraphrased by* Sir Thomas Wyatt. *See* O Lord, thou hast searched me.

Psalm LVIII: "Do ye indeed speak righteousness . . . ." Bible, *O.T.*, *paraphrased by* Sir Thomas Wyatt. *Fr.* Psalms.

Psalm LVIII: "Do ye indeed speak righteousness, O congregation?" *paraphrased by* the Countess of Pembroke. Bible, *O.T.*, *paraphrased by* Sir Thomas Wyatt. *See* Do ye indeed speak righteousness, O congregation?

Psalm XXIV: "Earth is the Lord's, The." Bible, *O.T.*, *paraphrased by* Sir Thomas Wyatt. *Fr.* Psalms. AWP; FaPON, *sts.* 1–4; TrJP

Psalm CXXVII: "Except the Lord build the house . . . ." Bible, *O.T.*, *paraphrased by* Sir Thomas Wyatt. *Fr.* Psalms. TrJP

Psalm XIV: "Fool hath said in his heart, The." Bible, *O.T.*, *paraphrased by* Sir Thomas Wyatt. *Fr.* Psalms. TrJP

Psalm CXIV: Fountain from Wilderness Stone, A. Bible, *O.T.* CRP

Psalm XXXVII: "Fret not thyself . . . ." Bible, *O.T.*, *paraphrased by* Sir Thomas Wyatt. *Fr.* Psalms.

Psalm CXXX: "From depth off sinn and from a diepe dispaire," *paraphrased by* Sir Thomas Wyatt. Bible, *O.T.*, *paraphrased by* Sir Thomas Wyatt. *See* Out of the depths [*or* deep] have I cried [*or* called] (unto) Thee, O Lord.

Psalm LXXVIII: "Give ear, O my people, to my law . . . ." Bible, *O.T.*, *paraphrased by* Sir Thomas Wyatt. *Fr.* Psalms.

Psalm LV: "Give ear to my prayer . . . ." Bible, *O.T.*, *paraphrased by* Sir Thomas Wyatt. *Fr.* Psalms. AWP

Psalm LXXII: "Give the king thy judgments . . . ." Bible, *O.T.*, *paraphrased by* Sir Thomas Wyatt. *Fr.* Psalms.

Psalm XXIX: "Give unto the Lord . . . ." Bible, *O.T.*, *paraphrased by* Sir Thomas Wyatt. *Fr.* Psalms. AWP

Psalm LXVII: "God be merciful unto us . . . ." Bible, *O.T.*, *paraphrased by* Sir Thomas Wyatt. *Fr.* Psalms.

Psalm XLVI: "God is our refuge and strength . . . ." Bible, *O.T.*, *paraphrased by* Sir Thomas Wyatt. *Fr.* Psalms. AWP

Psalm CXLVIII: "Hallelujah! kneel and sing," *paraphrased by* Christopher Smart. Bible, *O.T.*, *paraphrased by* Sir Thomas Wyatt. *See* Praise ye the Lord/ Praise ye the Lord.

Psalm CXLVI ("Hallelujah./ Praise the Lord, O my soul.") Bible, *O.T.*, *paraphrased by* Sir Thomas Wyatt. *Fr.* Psalms. TrJP

Psalm: "Happy is the man whom Thou hast set apart." "Yehoash," *tr. fr.* Yiddish by Isidore Goldstick. TrJP

Psalm XCI: "He that dwelleth . . . ." Bible, *O.T., paraphrased by* Sir Thomas Wyatt. *Fr.* Psalms. AWP

Psalm XVII: "Hear the right O Lord . . . ." Bible, *O.T., paraphrased by* Sir Thomas Wyatt. *Fr.* Psalms.

Psalm XIX: "Heavenly frame sets forth the fame, The," *paraphrased by* Philip Sidney. Bible, *O.T., paraphrased by* Sir Thomas Wyatt. *See* Law of Jehovah is perfect, restoring the soul, The.

Psalm XIX: "Heavens declare the glory of God, The." Bible, *O.T., paraphrased by* Sir Thomas Wyatt. *Fr.* Psalms. AWP; FaPON, *sts.* 1–4; NAWM-1; OBVE, *tr. by* Miles Coverdale; WBLP

Psalm 19: "Heavens doe declare/ The majesty of God, The." *Unknown. Fr.* Bay Psalm Book, The. SCAP

Psalm LXXXIV: "How amiable are thy tabernacles . . . ." Bible, *O.T., paraphrased by* Sir Thomas Wyatt. *Fr.* Psalms. FaPON; TrJP

Psalm XIII: "How long, O Lord, shall I forgotten be?," *paraphrased by* Philip Sidney. Bible, *O.T., paraphrased by* Sir Thomas Wyatt. *See* How long wilt thou forget me O Lord.

Psalm XIII: "How long wilt thou forget me O Lord . . . ." Bible, *O.T., paraphrased by* Sir Thomas Wyatt. *Fr.* Psalms.

Psalm LXXXIV: "How lovely are thy dwellings fair!," *paraphrased by* Milton. Bible, *O.T., paraphrased by* Sir Thomas Wyatt. *See* How amiable are thy tabernacles, O Lord of hosts!

Psalm LXXVII: "I cried unto God with my voice . . . ." Bible, *O.T., paraphrased by* Sir Thomas Wyatt. *Fr.* Psalms. AWP

Psalm XXXIX: "I said: 'I will take heed to my ways' ." Bible, *O.T., paraphrased by* Sir Thomas Wyatt. *Fr.* Psalms.

Psalm 121: "I to the hills lift up mine eyes." *Unknown. Fr.* Bay Psalm Book, The. OBCA

Psalm CXXXI: "I will lift up mine eyes unto the hills." Bible, *O.T., tr. fr.* German by Paul Gerhardt. *Fr.* Psalms. AWP; FaPON

Psalm IX: "I will praise thee, O Lord . . . ." Bible, *O.T., paraphrased by* Sir Thomas Wyatt. *Fr.* Psalms.

Psalm XI: "In the Lord put I my trust . . . ." Bible, *O.T., paraphrased by* Sir Thomas Wyatt. *Fr.* Psalms.

Psalm: "In the small beauty of the forest." George Oppen. NNaP

Psalm XCII: "Jehovah's Immovable Throne." Bible, *O.T., paraphrased by* Sir Thomas Wyatt. *Fr.* Psalms. WGRP

Psalm XLIII: "Judge me, o God . . . ." Bible, *O.T., paraphrased by* Sir Thomas Wyatt. *Fr.* Psalms.

Psalm LXXII: "Looke how the woods, where enterlaced trees," *paraphrased by* the Countess of Pembroke. Bible, *O.T., paraphrased by* Sir Thomas Wyatt. *See* Give the king thy judgments, O God.

Psalm CII: "Lord here my prayre and let my crye passe." Bible, *O.T., paraphrased by* Sir Thomas Wyatt. *Fr.* Psalms. OBVE

Psalm III: "Lord, how are they increased that trouble me!" Bible, *O.T., paraphrased by* Sir Thomas Wyatt. *Fr.* Psalms.

Psalm III: "Lord how many are my foes," *paraphrased by* Milton. Bible, *O.T., paraphrased by* Sir Thomas Wyatt. *See* Lord, how are they increased that trouble me!

Psalm XXVII: "Lord is my light, The" Bible, *O.T., paraphrased by* Sir Thomas Wyatt. *Fr.* Psalms.

Psalm XXIII: "Lord is my shepherd, The." Bible, *O.T., paraphrased by* Sir Thomas Wyatt. *Fr.* Psalms. AWP; BLPL; FaBoBe; FaPON; NAWM-1; OHIP; PoLF; TFi; TrGrPo; TrJP; TRP

Psalm XXIII: "Lord my shepherd, me His sheep, The." George Sandys. *Fr.* Paraphrase on the Psalms of David. JCP

Psalm XXIII: "Lord my shepherd, me His sheep, The," *paraphrased by* George Sandys. Bible, *O.T., paraphrased by* Sir Thomas Wyatt. *See* Lord is my shepherd, I shall not want, The.

Psalm XC: "Lord, thou hast been our dwelling place in all generations." Bible, *O.T., paraphrased by* Sir Thomas Wyatt. *Fr.* Psalms.

Psalm 23: "Lord to me a shepherd is, The." *Unknown. Fr.* Bay Psalm Book, The. OBCA

Psalm XXIII: "Lorde is my shepherde, The; therfore can I lack nothing." Bible, *O.T., paraphrased by* Sir Thomas Wyatt. *See* Lord is my shepherd, I shall not want, The.

Psalm C: "Make a joyful noise . . . ." Bible, *O.T., paraphrased by* Sir Thomas Wyatt. *Fr.* Psalms. BLRP; OHIP

Psalm XXII: "My God, my God . . . ." Bible, *O.T., paraphrased by* Sir Thomas Wyatt. *Fr.* Psalms.

Psalm XVII: "My suite is just, just lord to my suite hark," *paraphrased by* Sir Philip Sidney. Bible, *O.T., paraphrased by* Sir Thomas Wyatt. *See* Psalm XVII ("Hear the right O Lord . . . .")

Psalm: "No one kneads us again out of earth and clay." Paul Celan, *tr. fr.* German by Joachim Neugroschel.
(No one moulds us again out of earth and clay.) AnReP; OBVE, *tr. by* Michael Hamburger; PoSu, *tr. by* John Felstiner.

Psalm CXV: "Not unto us, O Lord . . . ." Bible, *O.T., paraphrased by* Sir Thomas Wyatt. *Fr.* Psalms.

Psalm CXV: "Not unto us, O Lord, not unto us," *paraphrased by* the Countess of Pembroke. Bible, *O.T., paraphrased by* Sir Thomas Wyatt. *See* Not us, I say, not us.

Psalm 100. 'O Be Joyful in the Lord, All Ye Lands.' William Kethe. *See* All people that on earth do dwell.

Psalm 1: "O Blessed man, that in th'advice." *Unknown. Fr.* Bay Psalm Book, The. SCAP

Psalm XCV: "O come let us sing unto the Lord." Bible, *O.T., paraphrased by* Sir Thomas Wyatt. *Fr.* Psalms. AWP; BLRP, *abr.; OHIP, abr.*

Psalm CVII: "O give thanks . . . ." Bible, *O.T., paraphrased by* Sir Thomas Wyatt. *Fr.* Psalms.

Psalm CXVIII: " 'O give thanks unto the Lord . . . ' ." Bible, *O.T., paraphrased by* Sir Thomas Wyatt. *Fr.* Psalms. TrJP

Psalm CXXXVI: "O give thanks unto the Lord; for he is good." Bible, *O.T., paraphrased by* Sir Thomas Wyatt. *Fr.* Psalms. AWP; OHIP, *abr.*

Psalm 107: "O Give yee thanks unto the Lord." *Unknown. Fr.* Bay Psalm Book, The. SCAP

Psalm: "O God, in whom my deepest being dwells." Edmund Blunden. TrPWD

Psalm LXXXIII: "O God, keep not Thou silence." Bible, *O.T., paraphrased by* Sir Thomas Wyatt. *Fr.* Psalms.

Psalm LXXIX: "O God, the heathen are come into Thine inheritance." Bible, *O.T., paraphrased by* Sir Thomas Wyatt. *Fr.* Psalms.

Psalm LXXIV: "O God, why hast thou cast us off . . . ." Bible, *O.T., paraphrased by* Sir Thomas Wyatt. *Fr.* Psalms.

Psalm LXXIV: "O God, why hast thou cast us off for ever?," *paraphrased by* the Countess of Pembroke. Bible, *O.T., paraphrased by* Sir Thomas Wyatt. *See* O God, why hast thou cast us off for ever?

Psalm VI: "O lord, I dred, and that I did not dred." Bible, *O.T., paraphrased by* Sir Thomas Wyatt. *See* O Lord, rebuke me not in thine anger.

Psalm CXXXIX: "O Lord, in me there lieth nought," *paraphrased by* the Countess of Pembroke. Bible, *O.T., paraphrased by* Sir Thomas Wyatt. *See* O Lord, thou hast searched me.

Psalm VIII: "O Lord our Lord, how excellent is thy name . . . ." Bible, *O.T., paraphrased by* Sir Thomas Wyatt. *Fr.* Psalms. AWP; NAWM-1

Psalm VI: "O Lord rebuke me not in thine anger . . . ." Bible, *O.T., paraphrased by* Sir Thomas Wyatt. *Fr.* Psalms.

Psalm VIII: "O Lord, that rul'st the human heart," *paraphrased by* Christopher Smart. Bible, *O.T., paraphrased by* Sir Thomas Wyatt. *See* O Lord our Lord, how excellent is thy name.

Psalm CXXXIX ("O Lord, thou hast searched me . . . .") Bible, *O.T., paraphrased by* Sir Thomas Wyatt. *Fr.* Psalms.

Psalm VIII: "O Lorde oure governoure, howe excellent is thy name." Bible, *O.T., paraphrased by* Sir Thomas Wyatt. *See* O Lord our Lord, how excellent is thy name.

Psalm CL ("O praise God in his holiness . . . .") Bible, *O.T., paraphrased by* Sir Thomas Wyatt. *Fr.* Psalms.

Psalm XCVIII: "O sing unto the Lord . . . ." Bible, *O.T., paraphrased by* Sir Thomas Wyatt. *Fr.* Psalms. TrJP

Psalm 103: "O Thou my soule, Jehovah blesse." *Unknown. Fr.* Bay Psalm Book, The. SCAP

Psalm: "Old ones to the side." Charles Simic. AmPA; LCAP

Psalm CXXX: "Out of the depths . . . ." Bible, *O.T., paraphrased by* Sir Thomas Wyatt. *Fr.* Psalms. TrJP

Psalm CIII: "Praise the Lord, O my soul," *paraphrased by* Henry Francis Lyte. Bible, *O.T., paraphrased by* Sir Thomas Wyatt. *See* Bless the Lord, O my soul: and all that is within me.

Psalm CXLVII ("Praise the Lord.") Bible, *O.T., paraphrased by* Sir Thomas Wyatt. *Fr.* Psalms.

Psalm CXLVIII ("Praise ye the Lord . . . .") Bible, *O.T., paraphrased by* Sir Thomas Wyatt. *Fr.* Psalms. TrJP

Psalm CXLVII: "Praise ye the Lord." Christopher Smart. NOCV

Psalm CXLVII: "Praise ye the Lord," *paraphrased by* Christopher Smart. Bible, *O.T., paraphrased by* Sir Thomas Wyatt. *See* Praise ye the Lord!/ For it is good to sing praises unto our God.

Psalm CXLVII: "Praise ye the Lord," *paraphrased by* the Countess of Pembroke. Bible, *O.T., paraphrased by* Sir Thomas Wyatt. *See* Praise ye the Lord!/ For it is good to sing praises unto our God.

Psalm CXLVII: "Praise ye the Lord." The Countess of Pembroke. NOCV

Psalm LVIII: Si Vere Utique: "And call ye this to utter what is just," *paraphrased by* the Countess of Pembroke. Bible, *O.T., paraphrased* by Sir Thomas Wyatt. *See* Do ye indeed speak righteousness, O congregation.

Psalm XI: "Since I do trust Jehova still," *paraphrased by* Sir Philip Sidney. Bible, *O.T.*, *paraphrased by* Sir Thomas Wyatt. *See* In the Lord put I my trust.

Psalm XIX: "Spacious firmament on high, The." Bible, *O.T.*, *paraphrased by* Sir Thomas Wyatt. *See* Law of Jehovah is perfect, restoring the soul, The.

Psalm LXXVIII: "There where the deepe did show his sandy flore," *paraphrased by* the Countess of Pembroke. Bible, *O.T.*, *paraphrased by* Sir Thomas Wyatt. *See* Give ear, O my people, to my law.

Psalm LXV: "Thou visitest the earth . . . ." Bible, *O.T.*, *paraphrased by* Sir Thomas Wyatt. Fr. Psalms. OHIP, *abr.*

Psalm LXII: "Truly my soul waiteth . . . ." Bible, *O.T.*, *paraphrased by* Sir Thomas Wyatt. Fr. Psalms.

Psalm LII: "Tyrant, why swel'st thou thus," *paraphrased by* the Countess of Pembroke. Bible, *O.T.*, *paraphrased by* Sir Thomas Wyatt. *See* Why boastest thou thyself in mischief, O mighty man?

Psalm CXIV: "When Israel came from Egypt's coast," *paraphrased by* Christopher Smart. Bible, *O.T.*, *paraphrased by* Sir Thomas Wyatt. *See* When Israel went out of Egypt.

Psalm CXIV: "When Israel went out of Egypt . . . ." Bible, *O.T.*, *paraphrased by* Sir Thomas Wyatt. Fr. Psalms.

Psalm CXXVI: "When the Lord brought back . . . ." Bible, *O.T.*, *paraphrased by* Sir Thomas Wyatt. Fr. Psalms.

Psalm LII: "Why boastest thou thyself in mischief . . . ." Bible, *O.T.*, *paraphrased by* Sir Thomas Wyatt. Fr. Psalms.

Psalm II: "Why do the Gentiles tumult," (*par. by* Milton). Bible, *O.T.*, *paraphrased by* Sir Thomas Wyatt. *See* Why do the heathen rage.

Psalm II: "Why do the heathen rage . . . ." Bible, *O.T.*, *paraphrased by* Sir Thomas Wyatt. Fr. Psalms. NAAL-1, *par. by* Edward Taylor

Psalm LXII: "Yet shall my soule in silence still," *paraphrased by* the Countess of Pembroke. Bible, *O.T.*, *paraphrased by* Sir Thomas Wyatt. *See* Truly my soul waiteth upon God.

Psalm and Lament. Donald Justice. DiPo

Psalm Concerning the Castle. Denise Levertov. TwCP; WPE

Psalm of Battle. *Unknown, tr. fr.* Arabic by E. Powys Mathers. Fr. Thousand and One Nights, The. AWP

Psalm of Christ, The. Chad Walsh. TrCP
Sels.
"Great-hearted Christ, importunate and mild."
My God, My God, Look upon Me.
There Is None to Help.
Why Hast Thou Forsaken Me?

Psalm of Life, A. Longfellow. AH; AnAmPo; EBEvV; FaBoBe; NAAL-1; OBCA; PlP; PoLF; PrIm; PWR; TAP; WBLP

Psalm of Life, A. (Tell me not in mournful numbers.) Longfellow. FaBoBe; OBCA; PoLF; PrIm; TAP; VPP; WBLP
Sels.
Life. GN
Tell Me Not in Mournful Numbers. AH

"Psalm of Life" for thee is o'er, The. Longfellow. H. Cordelia Ray. AAP; CBWP-3

Psalm of Marriage. Phoebe Cary. PWR

Psalm of Montreal, A. Samuel Butler. *See* Stowed away in a Montreal lumber room.

Psalm of Praise, A, *sels.* Richard Baxter.
"Ye holy Angels bright." NOCV

Psalm of St. The Priapus. James Richard Broughton. ErPo

Psalm of the Early Buddhist Sisters, A. *Unknown.* WGRP

Psalm of the West. Sidney Lanier. PAH
Sels.
Land of the Wilful Gospel.
Lexington.
Story of Vinland, The.
Triumph, The.

Psalm of Those Who Go Forth before Daylight. Carl Sandburg. MoShBr; OxBA

Psalm 119.37. Francis Quarles. ChIV-1

Psalm 137. Thomas Carew. ChIV-1

Psalm Praising the Hair of Man's Body, A. Denise Levertov. CAPP

Psalm to My Beloved. Eunice Tietjens. ErPo

Psalm: "While Northward the hot sun was sinking o'er the trees." Robert Bridges. FaBoTw; LiTB

Psalm to the Creatures. Gwilym R. Jones, *tr. fr.* Welsh by Joseph P. Clancy. OBWVE

Psalm to the Holy Spirit. A. M. Sullivan. TrPWD

Psalm to the Son, A. Marguerite Wilkinson. TrPWD

Psalm 23 to the Singer's Nectar, *sels.* Ali al-Sharqawi, *tr. fr.* Arabic by Lena Jayyusi and Naomi Shihab Nye.

Psalms, *sels.* Bible, *O.T.*, *paraphrased by* Sir Thomas Wyatt.
Psalm I ("Blessed is the man . . . "). AWP
  (Blessed are the man and the woman.) EnlH
  (Happy Is the Man.) TrJP
  (O blessed man, that in th' advice.) SCAP
  (Tree and the Chaff, The.) WGRP
Psalm II ("Why do the heathen rage . . . "). NAAL-1, (*par. by* Edward Taylor)
  (Psalm II: "Why do the Gentiles tumult," *par. by* Milton.) OBVE
Psalm III ("Lord, how are they increased that trouble me!").
  (Psalm III: "Lord how many are my foes," *paraphrased by* Milton.) OBVE
Psalm VI ("O Lord rebuke me not in thine anger . . . ").
  (Psalm VI: "O Lord, I dred, and that I did not dred.") OBVE, *ad. by* Sir Thomas Wyatt
Psalm VIII ("O Lord our Lord, how excellent is thy name . . . "). AWP; NAWM-1
  (How Glorious Is Thy Name.) TrJP
  (Psalm VIII: "O Lorde oure governoure, howe excellent is thy name.") OBVE, *tr. by* Miles Coverdale
  (Psalm VIII: "O Lord, that rul'st the human heart," *paraphrased by* Christopher Smart.) OBVE
  (What Is Man?) TrGrPo
  "Lord what is man, that he should find."
  When I Consider Thy Heavens FaPON, *sts.* 3 – 5
Psalm IX ("I will prase thee, O Lord . . . ").
  (I will Sing Praise.) FaPON
Psalm XI ("In the Lord put I my trust . . . ").
  (Psalm XI: "Since I do trust Jehova still," *paraphrased by* Sir Philip Sidney.) OBVE
Psalm XIII ("How long wilt thou forget me O Lord . . . ").
  (How long, O Lord, shall I forgotten be?) NoSic, *sect.* XIII
  (Psalm XIII: "How long, O Lord, shall I forgotten be?," *paraphrased by* Sir Philip Sidney.) OBVE
Psalm XIV ("The fool hath said in his heart . . . "). TrJP
Psalm XVII ("Hear the right O Lord . . . ").
  (Psalm XVII: "My suite is just, just lord to my suite hark," *paraphrased by* Sir Philip Sidney.) OBVE
Psalm XIX ("The heavens declare the glory of God"). AWP; FaPON, *sts.* 1 – 4; NAWM-1; OBVE, *tr. by* Miles Coverdale; WBLP
  (Heavens declare God's glory, The.) EnlH
  God's Precepts Perfect. BLRP
  (Psalm XIX: "Heavenly frame sets forth the fame, The," *paraphrased by* Sir Philip Sidney.) OBVE
  (Glory of God, The.) TrJP
  (God's Glory.) TrGrPo
  (Heavens Above and the Law Within, The.) WGRP
  (Heavens doe declare, The.) SCAP
  (Heavens, The.) ChTr, 1 – 6
  (Psalm XIX: "Spacious firmament on high, The.") WGRP
Psalm XXII ("My God, my God . . . ").
  (Cry in Distress, A.) TrGrPo
Psalm XXIII ("The Lord is my shepherd . . . "). AWP; BLPL; FaBoBe; FaPON; NAWM-1; NIP; OHIP; PoLF; TFi; TrGrPo; TrJP; TRP
  (Psalm XXIII: "Lorde is my shepherde, The; therfore can I lack nothing.") OBVE, *tr. by* Miles Coverdale
  (Lord is my shepherd/ and keeps me from wanting, The.) TRP, *tr. by* David Rosenberg
  (Lord is my shepherd;/ I have everything I need, The.) TRP
  (Lord is my shepherd, The.) FaPoB
  (Lord to me a shepherd is, The.) OBCA
  (Lord's my shepherd, I'll not want, The.) ScCV
  (Lord's My Shepherd, The.) AH; WBLP, *ad. by* Francis Rous
  (Protection of Jehovah, The.) WGRP
  (Psalm XXIII: "Lord my shepherd, me His sheep, The," *paraphrased by* George Sandys.) JCP
Psalm XXIV ("The Earth is the Lord's . . . "). AWP; FaPON, *sts.* 1 – 4; TrJP
  (Lift Up Your Heads.) TrGrPo
Psalm XXVII ("The Lord is my light . . . ")
  (Deliverance of Jehovah, The.) WGRP
  Serenity of Faith, The. BLRP
Psalm XXIX ("Give unto the Lord . . . "). AWP
Psalm XXXVII ("Fret not thyself . . . ").
  (Trust in the Lord, *paraphrased by* Charles Frederic Sheldon.) BLRP, 1 – 7
Psalm XXXIX ("I said: 'I will take heed to my ways' ").
  (Lord, Make Me to Know Mine End.) TrJP
Psalm XLII ("As the hart panteth after the water brooks"). AWP; TrJP
  (My Soul Thirsteth for God.) TrGrPo
  (Search, The, XLII *and* XLIII *Moulton, Modern Reader's Bible.*) WGRP
Psalm XLIII ("Judge me, O God . . . ").
  (Search, The, XLII *and* XLIII *Moulton, Modern Reader's Bible.*) WGRP
Psalm XLVI ("God is our refuge and strength . . . "). AWP

(Though the Earth Be Removed.) TrGrPo
Psalm LII ("Why boastest thou thyself in mischief . . . ").
   (Psalm LII: "Tyrant, why swel'st thou thus," *paraphrased by* the
      Countess of Pembroke.) OBVE
   (Tyrant, why swell'st thou thus.) NoSic, *sect.* LII
"Save me from such as me assail." NoSic, (*paraphrased by* the Countess
   of Pembroke)
"You that Jehovah's servants are." NoSic, (*par. by* the Countess of
   Pembroke)
Psalm LV ("Give ear to my prayer . . . "). AWP
   (Psalm LV: Exaudi, Deus: "My God most glad to look, most prone to
      hear," *paraphrased by* the Countess of Pembroke.) OBVE, *sts.* 1–4;
      WPE
   Wings. FaPON, *ll.* 6–7
Psalm LVIII ("Do ye indeed speak righteousness . . . ").
   (And call ye this to utter what is just.) NoSic, *sect.* LVIII
   (Psalm LVIII: "Do ye indeed speak righteousness, O congregation?,"
      paraphrased by the Countess of Pembroke.) NOCV
   (Psalm LVIII: Si Vere Utique: "And call ye this to utter what is just,"
      paraphrased by the Countess of Pembroke.) BoWoP; NAEL-1; WPE
Psalm LXII ("Truly my soul waiteth . . . ").
   (Psalm LXII: "Yet shall my soule in silence still," *paraphrased by* the
      Countess of Pembroke.) PBWP
Psalm LXV ("Thou visitest the earth . . . "). OHIP, *abr.*
Psalm LXVII ("God be merciful unto us . . . ").
   (Let the Nations Be Glad.) FaPON
Psalm LXXII ("Give the king thy judgments . . . ").
   (Psalm LXXII: "Looke how the woods, where enterlaced trees,"
      paraphrased by the Countess of Pembroke.) OBVE
Psalm LXXIV ("O God, why hast thou cast us off . . . ").
   (Psalm LXXIV: "O God, why hast thou cast us off for ever?,"
      paraphrased by the Countess of Pembroke.) NOCV
Psalm LXXVII ("I cried unto God with my voice . . . "). AWP
Psalm LXXVIII ("Give ear, O my people, to my law . . . ").
   (Psalm LXXVIII: "There where the deepe did show his sandy flore,"
      paraphrased by the Countess of Pembroke.) OBVE
Psalm LXXIX ("O God, the heathen are come into Thine inheritance").
   (Heathen Are Come into Thine Inheritance, The.) TrJP
Psalm LXXXIII ("O God, keep not Thou silence").
   (Keep Not Thou Silence.) TrJP
Psalm LXXXIV ("How amiable are thy tabernacles . . . "). FaPON; TrJP
   (Psalm LXXXIV: "How lovely are thy dwellings fair!," *paraphrased by*
      Milton.) TrPWD
   How Lovely Are Thy Tabernacles.
   Sparrow, The.
Psalm XC ("Lord, thou hast been our dwelling place in all generations").
   (Lord, Thou Hast Been Our Dwelling Place.) AWP; DL
Psalm XCI ("He that dwelleth . . . "). AWP
   (Everlasting Arms, The, *Moulton, Modern Reader's Bible.*) WGRP
   (Mighty Fortress, A.) TrGrPo
Psalm XCII ("Jehovah's Immovable Throne." WGRP
Psalm XCV ("O come let us sing unto the Lord"). AWP; BLRP, *abr.*;
   OHIP, *abr.*
Psalm XCVIII ("O sing unto the Lord . . . "). TrJP
   (Floods Clap Their Hands, The.) TrGrPo
   (Sing unto Jehovah.) BLRP
Psalm C ("Make a joyful noise . . . "). BLRP; OHIP
   (Be Thankful unto Him.) FaPON
   (Giving Thanks, 4.) BLRP
   (Hundredth Psalm, The.) BLRP; OtMeF
   (Old Hundredth, *metrical vers.* by William Kethe.) FaPoR; NOCV
   (Scotch Te Deum.) WGRP
Psalm CII ("Lord here my prayre and let my crye passe"). OBVE
Psalm CIII ("Bless the Lord, O my soul . . . "). AWP
   (Psalm CIII: "Praise the Lord, O my soul," *paraphrased by* Henry
      Francis Lyte.) NOCV
   (O Thou my soule, Jehovah blesse, *Bay Psalm Book.*) SCAP
Psalm CIV ("Bless the Lord, O my soul . . ."). NAWM-1; OHIP, *abr.*;
   TrJP
   (Hymn of the World Without.) WGRP
   (Unnamable God, you are fathomless.) EnlH
Psalm CVII ("O give thanks . . . ").
   (O give yee thanks unto the Lord.) SCAP
   They That Go Down to the Sea. ChTr, *ll.* 23–31; FaPON, (23-24)
   (Ocean, The.) WGRP, (23-33)
Psalm CXIV ("When Israel went out of Egypt . . . ").
   (Psalm CXIV: "When Israel came from Egypt's coast," *paraphrased by*
      Christopher Smart.) OBVE
   (When Israel Came Forth out of Egypt.) TrJP
Psalm CXV ("Not unto us, O Lord . . . ").
   (Psalm CXV: "Not unto us, O Lord, not unto us," *paraphrased by* the
      Countess of Pembroke.) NOCV
Psalm CXVIII (" 'O give thanks unto the Lord . . . ' "). TrJP
Psalm CXXI ("I will lift up mine eyes unto the hills"). AWP; FaPON
   (I to the hills lift up mine eyes.) OBCA
   (121st Psalm of David, The.) GePo

(Pilgrim's Song, The.) WGRP
(Song of Trust, A.) TrGrPo
Psalm CXXVI ("When the Lord brought back . . . ").
   (Like unto Them That Dream.) TrJP
Psalm CXXVII ("Except the Lord build the house . . . "). TrJP
Psalm CXXX ("Out of the depths . . . "). TrJP
   (De Profundis.) BLRP; WGRP
   (Deep sunk in floods of grief.) ScCV
   (Psalm CXXX: "Ffrom depth off sinn and from a diepe dispaire,"
      paraphrased by Sir Thomas Wyatt.) OBVE
   (F[f]rom depth of[f] sin[n] and from a deep [*or* diepe] despair [*or*
      dispaire].) NoSic
   (Song of Supplication, A.) TrGrPo
Psalm CXXXIII ("Behold, how good and how pleasant . . . "). AWP
   (Psalm CXXXIII: "Beholde, how good and joyfull a thinge it is.")
      OBVE, *tr.* by Miles Coverdale
   (To Dwell Together in Unity.) TrJP
Psalm CXXXVI ("O give thanks unto the Lord; for he is good"). AWP;
   OHIP, *abr.*
Psalm CXXXVII. AWP; NAWM-1; OAEL-1; OBVE; TrJP
   Song of Exile, A.
Psalm CXXXIX ("O Lord, thou hast searched me . . . ").
   (Psalm CXXXIX: "O Lord, in me there lieth nought," *paraphrased by*
      the Countess of Pembroke.) NOCV; OBVE, (7-10)
   (O Lord, in me there lieth nought.) NoSic, *sect.* CXXXIX
   (Psalm CXXXIX: Domine, Probasti.) WPE
Psalm CXLVI ("Hallelujah./ Praise the Lord, O my soul"). TrJP
Psalm CXLVII ("Praise ye the Lord").
   (Psalm CXLVII: "Praise ye the Lord," *paraphrased by* the Countess of
      Pembroke.) NOCV
   (Hallelujah/ Praise ye the Lord . . . .) TrJP
   (Psalm CXLVII: "Praise ye the Lord," *paraphrased by* Christopher
      Smart.) NOCV
   (Sing unto the Lord with thanksgiving.) OHIP
   Who Maketh the Grass to Grow. FaPON, (*greatly abr.*)
Psalm CXLVIII ("Praise ye the Lord . . . "). TrJP
   (Psalm CXLVIII: "Hallelujah! kneel and sing," *paraphrased by*
      Christopher Smart.) OBVE, *ll.* 1–10
   (Song of Praise, A.) TrGrPo
Psalm CL ("O praise God in his holiness . . . "). TrJP
   (Laudate Dominium.) ChTr
Psalms of David, The, *sels.* The Countess of Pembroke.
   Dedicatory poem: To the Angel Spirit of the Most Excellent Sir Philip
      Sidney. SiPSBD
   "From the depth of grief." SiPSBD
   "Inhabitants of heavenly land." SiPSBD
   "O Lord God of My Salvation."
      (My God, my Lord, my help, my health.) SiPSBD, *par.* by the
      Countess of Pembroke
Psalms of Love. Peter Baum, *tr. fr.* German by Jethro Bithell. AWP
Psalter of Avram Haktani, The, *sels.* A. M. Klein.
   Upon the Heavenly Scarp. PoA
Psittachus Eois Imitatrix Ales ab Indis. Sacheverell Sitwell. MoBrPo
Psss, the beard is a bit too long. Faces. D. C. Berry. BXAP
Psst, psst. Kitty Cornered. Eve Merriam. CRH
Psyche. Samuel Taylor Coleridge. MeMBP
Psyche. Corneille, *tr. fr. French by* Philip L. Miller. RiWo
Psyche to Cupid: Her Ditty. James Richard Broughton. ErPo
Psyche's Dream. Ann Lauterbach. EOEF
Psychiatrist. Peter De Vries. OBAL
Psychiatrist fellow from Rye, A. Stephen Cass. PeLi
Psychiatrist's Office Was Filled with Crazy People, The. Terence Winch.
   BCF
Psychic researcher's elation, A. Cyril Mountjoy. PeLi
Psycho. Peter Olds. PeNZ
Psychoanalysis. Gavin Ewart. NYBP
Psychoanalysis, *sels.* Judah Leib Teller, *tr. fr.* Yiddish by Benjamin *and*
   Barbara Harshav.
Psychologists, psychiatrists. Basic. Ray Durem. PoNe
Psycholophon. Gelett Burgess. CBNP
Psychonaut Sonnets: Jones, The. Albert Goldbarth. SM
Psychopathology of Everyday Life, The. William Matthews. AnAn; NIP
Psychozoia, or, the Life of the Soul, *sels.* Henry More.
   Contrition. NOSC
Psyllus lies here. Procuring was his trade. Argentarius, *tr. fr.* Greek by
   Fleur Adcock. GrAn
P'u — Hua Fei Hua. Po Chü-i, *tr. fr. Chinese by* Duncan Mackintosh.
   IMW
P'u-Shen Sheng Man. Li Ch'ing-chao, *tr. fr. Chinese by* Duncan
   Mackintosh. IMW

Purest soul that e'er was sent, The. Another [Epitaph on the Lady Mary Villiers]. Thomas Carew. BeJo; CaPo; SeCV-1

Purgatorial soul in the world. (LL) Solo for Two Voices. Octavio Paz. STV

Purgatorio. Dante, tr. fr. Italian. Fr. Divina Commedia. MeMAP

Purgatory. W. B. Yeats. CMoP

Purgatory of Hell., sels. Edoardo Sanguineti, tr. fr. Italian by Lawrence R. Smith.

Purgatory of Suicides, The, sels. Thomas Cooper.

Purge, The, sels. Michael Hartnett.
  "Hartnett, the poet, might as well be dead." BiHa

Purified Soul, The. Francis Quarles. Fr. Emblems. CBCK

Puriri moth's wing, A. Jan Kemp. PeNZ

Purist, The. Ogden Nash. FiBHP; GoJo; MoAmPo; MoShBr; NBLV; OBCA

Puritan, The. Karl Shapiro. MoAmPo

Puritan Lady, A. Lizette Woodworth Reese. MoAmPo

Puritan on His Honeymoon, The. Robert Bly. FF

Puritan Sonnet, IV. Elinor Wylie. See Down to the Puritan marrow of my bones.

Purity. Avigdor Hame'iri, tr. fr. Hebrew by Ruth Finer Mintz. MHP

Purity of Heart. John Keble. BLRP

Purple butterflies/ fly at night through my dreams. Yosano Akiko, tr. fr. Japanese by Kenneth Rexroth and Ikuko Atsumi. WPJ

Purple Clover. Emily Dickinson. MoAmPo

Purple Cow, The. Gelett Burgess. CBNP; FaBoCo; FaBoNo; FaPON; FiBHP; GrPl; NBLV; NTCP; OBAL; OBCA; PDV; PoLF; TFi; TLR

Purple headland over yonder. Afternoon. Louisa S. Guggenberger. NOBVV

Purple Indians pas de bourrée. Lord Fluting Dreams of America on the Eve of His Departure from Liverpool. Paul Zimmer. VGW

Purple Island, The, sels. Phineas Fletcher.
  All-seeing Intellect, The. JCP
  "With her, her sister went, a warlike maid." NOSC

Purple Martin, The. Sun Ching-hsuan, tr. fr. Chinese. Fr. Lyrics of the Forest. LHF, tr. by Hualing Nieh

Purple sky, the down's long spine, the. The Novice. Edward Davison. ErPo

Purple, White and Green, The. L. E. Morgan-Browne. BrRo

Purple William or The Liar's Doom. A. E. Housman. CBNP

Purple, yellow, red and green. Unknown. OxNR

Purpose. Desmond O'Grady. PBCIP

Purpose of Altar Boys, The. Alberto A. Ríos. AfAz

Purpose of Fable-writing, The. Phaedrus, tr. fr. Latin by Christopher Smart. AWP

Purr, says the cat. (LL) Dame Trot and her cat. Mother Goose. BoTP; OxNR; ReMoGo

Purrs all day. (LL) January. John Updike. PDV

Purse, dirk, cloak, night-cap, kerchief, shoeing-horn, buget, and shoes. Memorial Verses for Travellers. Sir Anthony Fitzherbert. Fr. Husbandry. FaBoUs

Purse-Seine, The. Robinson Jeffers. CMoP; HAP; NoAM; NOBA; NoP; OxBA; Poetr; PrIm; WeW

Purse, who'll not know you have a poet's been. A Parley with His Empty Purse. Thomas Randolph. JCP

Pursued his road. (LL) Half-way, for One Commandment Broken. A. E. Housman. OxBSP; PeHV

Pursuing beauty, men descry. Song. Thomas Southerne. NOSC

Pursuit. Hilda Doolittle ("H. D."). WPE

Pursuit. Julian Tuwim, tr. fr. Polish by Watson Kirkconnell. TrJP

Pursuit. Robert Penn Warren. HAP; LiTA; MoAmPo; TwCP

Pursuit from Under. James Dickey. HAP; PPP

Pursuit of Love. At. to John Webster and William Rowley. See Art Thou Gone in Haste?

Pursuit[e], The. Henry Vaughan. AngWe; GeHe; NOSC; SeCP; TrCP; TrPWD

Pusey Hughes, a low-grade voter. Unfortunate Occurrence at Cwm-Cadno. A. G. Prys-Jones. AngWe

Push, The. Kevin Killian. ETG

Push about the brisk bowl, 'twill enliven the heart. The Ass. Moses Mendes. Fr. Chaplet, The. TrJP

Push, push the heavy door. Skeleton House. Laurence Smith. OTCP

Pushan, God of golden day. Pushan, God of Pasture. Unknown, tr. fr. Sanskrit by Romesh Dutt. Fr. Vedic Hymns. AWP

Pushan, God of Pasture, Fr. Rig Veda. Unknown, tr. fr. Sanskrit by Romesh Dutt. Fr. Vedic Hymns. AWP

Pushed out of the earth. Canna Lily. Nancy Willard. FoLa

Pushing. Christopher Gilbert. SoSe

Pushing Forty. Alan Catlin. NGP

Pushing the shining rod into the ground. (LL) Windmill At Mandanthanunguna. Pambardu. NOBAu

Pushing young man in Patchogue, A. Morris Bishop. PeLi

Pushkin. "Anna Akhmatova," tr. fr. Russian by Stanley Kunitz with Max Hayward. AnAn

Pushkin Town. Anne Carson. Fr. Life of Towns, The. BAP-90

Puss. Walter de la Mare. OFC

Puss and the Boots, The, sels. Henry Duff Traill.
  "Put case I circumvent and kill him: good." BXAP

Puss came dancing out of a barn. Unknown. OxNR

Puss loves man's winter fire. Puss. Walter de la Mare. OFC

Pussicat, wussicat, with a white foot. Unknown. OxNR

Pussy and the Mice. Unknown. MoShBr

Pussy-Cat and Puppy-Dog. Lilian McCrea. BoTP

Pussy cat ate the dumplings. Pussycat. Mother Goose. OxNR; ReMoGo

Pussy-cat by [or beside] the fire. Mother Goose. See Pussy sits beside the fire.

Pussy-Cat Mew. Unknown. ReMoGo

Pussy Cat Mole. Unknown. OxNR

Pussy-Cat, Pussy-Cat,/ where have you been? Mother Goose. BoTP; FaBoBe; OxNR; ReMoGo; SoCa

Pussy, Pussy Baudrons. Unknown. CRH

Pussy sits beside the fire. By the Fire. Mother Goose. OxNR
  (Pussy-cat by [or beside] the fire.) ReMoGo

Pussycat. Mother Goose. OxNR; ReMoGo

Pussycat Sits on a Chair. Edward Newman Horn. OFC

Put a Finger Up My Arse, You Dear Old Man. Pietro Aretino, tr. fr. Italian by Alistair Elliot. FaBoBl

Put a sun in Sunday, Sunday. Yet Dish. Gertrude Stein. SOTW

Put a Woman into the Memory Box. Brigitte Frase. LoHo

Put aside the papers, your Honor. The Law. Aleksandar Ristovic, tr. fr. Serbo-Croatian by Charles Simic. HSix

Put case I circumvent and kill him: good. Henry Duff Traill. Fr. Puss and the Boots, The. BXAP

Put Down. Léon Damas, tr. fr. French by Seth L. Wolitz. TTY

Put-Down Come On, The. A. R. Ammons. NoP

Put down your weapons. Haka: The Blossoming. Pita Sharples, tr. fr. Maori by Pita Sharples. PeNZ

Put 'em up solid, they won't come down! Post-Rail Song. Unknown. AS

Put Forth, O God, Thy Spirit's Might. Howard Chandler Robbins. AH; TrPWD

Put forth thy leaf, thou lofty plane. Arthur Hugh Clough. EBEV; EnVR

Put forward your best foot! (LL) Respectability. Robert Browning. CBLP; EnLoPo

Put Hannibal i' th' scale. Hannibal ("Put Hannibal i' th' scale.") Juvenal, tr. by Henry Vaughan. Fr. Satires. OBVE

Put his head. Odiham. John Gray. FaBoCo

Put It Through. Edward Everett Hale. PAH

Put Me into the Breach. Yehuda Karni, tr. fr. Hebrew by Ruth Finer Mintz. MHP

Put me into the breach with every rolling stone. Put Me into the Breach. Yehuda Karni, tr. fr. Hebrew by Ruth Finer Mintz. MHP

Put Off Constricting Day. Mary Stanley. PeNZ

Put off the deference that this sea compels. Beach Talk. Norman MacCaig. PoA

Put off thy robe of purple, then go on. Good Friday: Rex Tragicus, or, Christ Going to His Cross. Robert Herrick. NOSC

Put on their youth and green. (LL) The Starre. Henry Vaughan. ESCV

Put on your silks, and piece by piece. To His Mistresses. Robert Herrick. CaPo

Put one-o. Spell Potatoes. Unknown. RoPo

Put out my eyes, and I can see you still. Rainer Maria Rilke, tr. fr. German by Babette Deutsch. UnAS

Put out to sea, if wine thou wouldest make. Sent from Egypt with a Fair Robe of Tissue to a Sicilian Vinedresser. T. Sturge Moore. OBEV

Put the rubber mouse away. For a Dead Kitten. Sara Henderson Hay. CRH

Put the sun a thought below his prime. Afternoon in the Garden. Ethel Anderson. NOBAu

Put the witches to their speed. (LL) Against Witches. Unknown. GBP

Put things in their place. The Sky Is Blue. David Ignatow. NNaP

Put this in your notebooks. The Last Class. Ellen Bryant Voigt. CrSp; MT

Put u red-eye in. Ron Welburn. NBV

Put up thy gold: go on, — here's gold, — go on. Shakespeare. Fr. Timon of Athens. OxAEP-1

Put up your wife, she's crosser than all four. (LL) Fool, to put up four crosses at your door. Swift. FaBoEE

Put your finger in Foxy's hole. *Unknown.* OxNR

Put your hand in the creel. Marriage. *Unknown.* GBP

Put your hand on my heart, say that you love me as. A Betrothal. E. J. Scovell. GBL

Put your head, darling, darling, darling. Dear Black Head. *Unknown, tr. by* Sir Samuel Ferguson. BIrV
(Cean Dubh Deelish.) GBL; PeIV

Put your/ self out. Chasm. A. R. Ammons. OBAL

Putta putta putt, A. Riding in a Motor Boat. Dorothy W. Baruch. FaPON

Putting away wedding gifts. The Quickness of Fear. Beverly Acuff Momoi. LoHo

Putting God in the nation's life. God in the Nation's Life. *Unknown.* BLRP; WBLP

Putting in the Seed. Robert Frost. ErPo; NoAM; OxBA

Putting It Somewhere. Richard Pflum. NGP

Putting On My Shoes I Hear the Floor Cry Out beneath Me. Michael Heffernan. BXAP

Putting On Nightgown. *Unknown.* OxNR

Putting out the candles. My Father after Work. Gary Gildner. Poetsp

Putting Out the Lamp. Yannis Ritsos, *tr. fr. Greek by* Paul Merchant. AnRep

Putting to Sea. Louise Bogan. LiTM; PoA

Putting up new curtains. Curtains. Ruth Stone. NAmP90

Puva, puva, puva. *Unknown, tr. fr. Hopi Indian by* Natalie Curtis. TTTS

Puzzle faces in the dying elms. "Mystery Boy' Looks for Kin in Nashville." Robert Hayden. LCAP; NoAM; PoE

Puzzled. Carolyn Wells. OBCA

Puzzled Centipede, The. *Unknown. See* Centipede was happy quite, A.

Pygmalion, *sels.* Hilda Doolittle ("H. D.").
"I made god upon god." WGRP

Pygmalion seeing these to spend their times. Ovid, *tr. fr. Latin. Fr.* Metamorphoses. OAEL-1, *tr. by* George Sandys

Pygmalion's Statue Comes to Life. Ovid, *tr. by* Arthur Golding. *Fr.* Metamorphoses. OAEL-1

Pygmies Are Pygmies Still, Though Percht on Alps. Gwendolyn Brooks. *Fr.* Notes from the Childhood and the Girlhood. LCAP; PoNe

Pygmy Elephant. Spike Milligan. ZA

Pygmy Elephant is made, The. Pygmy Elephant. Spike Milligan. ZA

Pylon for some incomplete gateway. The Monadnock. John Gould Fletcher. PoA

Pylons, The. Stephen Spender. AWP; NoAM

Pyramid of Supplications. Juan Felipe Herrera. AfAz

Pyramus and Thisbe, *sels.* Laurence Dakin.

Pyrargyrite Metal, 9. Cecília Meireles, *tr. fr. Portuguese by* James Merrill. PBWP

Pyrography. John Ashbery. PoM; VCAP

Pyrrha, what slender well-shap'd beau. Horace. *See* What slender youth bedewed with liquid odours.

Pyrrha! your smiles are gleams of sun. Walter Savage Landor. CBLP

Pythagoras planned it. Why did the people stare? The Statues. W. B. Yeats. NoAM; OAEL-2; PeIV; WeW

Pythagoric Letter, The. Thomas Stanley. NOSC

Pythagoric letter, two ways spread, The. The Pythagoric Letter. Thomas Stanley. NOSC

Python, The. Hilaire Belloc. OxBChV

Python. *Yoruba Oral Tradition, tr. by* Ulli Beier. WTO

Python I should not advise, A. The Python. Hilaire Belloc. OxBChV

Pythoness, The. Kathleen Raine. MoBrPo

Q

Q-Boat, The. H. E. Wilkes. NSI

Q:dwo. E. E. Cummings. OBAL

Qua Cursum Ventus. Arthur Hugh Clough. EBVVPR; OBEV

Quack, quack, quack! Dumpy Ducky. Lucy Larcom. OBCA

Quaco Sam. *Unknown.* FaBoVe

Quaco Sam. *Unknown.* PBCV

Quadratic function, ambitious, A. Leo Moser. PeLi

Quadrille. Carlos Drummond de Andrade, *tr. fr. Portuguese by* Mark Strand. AnRep

Quadroon mermaids, Afro angels, black saints. A Ballad of Remembrance. Robert Hayden. BPo; PoBA; PoNe

Quadrupedremian Song, A. Thomas Hood. FaBoNo

Quaerè. George Farewell. NOEC

Quail and rabbit hunters with tawny hounds. Hunters in the Snow: Brueghel. Joseph Langland. LiTM

Quail in Autumn. William Jay Smith. Poetsp

Quaint Mazes. Geoffrey Hill. *Fr.* Apology for the Revival of Christian Architecture in England, An. NoAM

Quaint medieval streets, where every house is new, The. (*LL*) One Tourist's Cologne. Hal Colebatch. NOBAu

Quake Theory. Sharon Olds. PBCAP

Quaker Graveyard in Nantucket, The. Robert Lowell. CMoP; HAP; LiTM; MoAB; MoP; NAAL-2; NoAM; NOBA; NoP; OxBA; PeECV; Poetr; TAP; UnPo; VCAP

Quaker Hill. Hart Crane. *Fr.* Bridge, The. LiTA; LiTM; NAAL-2

Quaker's Song, The. *Unknown.* CoMu

Quaker's stiffness, with a tradesman's grin, A. A Character. Clara Reeve. ECWP

Quaker's wife got up to bake, The. *Unknown.* OxNR

Quaker's Wooing, The. *Unknown.* AS

Qualities as they continue are the silk, The. Sketch for a Financial Theory of the Self. J. H. Prynne. VaA

Quality, The. Philip Schultz. NAmP90

Quality of mercy is not strained, The. Shakespeare. *Fr.* Merchant of Venice, The. EBEvV; ImPo; LiTB
(Mercy. TrGrPo; WBLP

Quality of these trees, green height, The. Robinson Jeffers. *See* Quality of these trees, green height; of the sky, shining, The.

Quality of these trees, green height; of the sky, shining, The. Shine, Republic. Robinson Jeffers. FaBoPV
(Quality of these trees, green height, The.) 09AmFN; GOA

Quangle Wangle's Hat, The. Edward Lear. OTCP

Quangle Wangle's Hat, The. Edward Lear. CBNP; EBEV; PeVV

Quantocks, The. Wordsworth. FaBoPP

Quantum. Martin Johnston. CBAP

Quantum Est Quod Desit. Thomas Moore. *See* 'Twas a new feeling — something more.

Quarrel, The. Conrad Aiken. MoAB; MoAmPo

Quarrel, The. Diane Di Prima. NMM

Quarrel, The. Eleanor Farjeon. FaPON

Quarrel, The. Josephine D. Henderson Heard. CBWP-4

Quarrel, The. Karen Swenson. GrPl

Quarrel. *Yoruba Oral Tradition, tr. by* Ulli Beier. WTO

Quarrel of the sparrows in the eaves, The. The Sorrow of Love. W. B. Yeats. MoAB; MoBrPo; NoAM; NOBVV; OAEL-2; PoEL-5; TEP

Quarrel with Fortune, A. Benjamin Colman. SCAP

Quarreling coons, The. (*LL*) Not Yet 40, My Beard is Already White. Lew Welch. PoBeRe

Quarrelling. Lyall Tao Tschung Yu. OBF

Quarrels have long been in vogue among sages. A Song from the Coptic. James Clarence Mangan. NOIV

Quarrelsome Bishop, A. Walter Savage Landor. FaBoEE

Quarrelsome Trio, The. "L. G." WBLP

Quarries in Syracuse. Louis Golding. TrJP

Quarrle, The. Mother Goose. *See* My little old man and I fell out.

Quarry, The. W. H. Auden. *See* O What Is That Sound.

Quarry, The. Vassar Miller. WPE

Quarry Pool, The. Denise Levertov. VGW

Quarry/Rock. Paul Mariah. GLP; PeHV

Quarter century ago, A. Wilberforce. Josephine D. Henderson Heard. CBWP-4

Quarter less four,/ Half twain. *Unknown.* AmFP

Quarter sounded from the steeple, The. (*LL*) Pan in Wall Street. Edmund Clarence Stedman. AnAmPo

Quartermaster of the spring, The. First Rondeau: After a French Poet of the Fourteenth Century. Johann Nikolaus Götz, *tr. fr. German by* George C. Schoolfield. GePo

Quarto Centennial, The. Josephine D. Henderson Heard. CBWP-4

Quartz Pebble, The, *sels.* Vasco [*or* Vasko] Popa, *tr. fr. Serbo-Croatian.*
Adventure of the Quartz Pebble, The. PoSu, *tr. by* Anne Pennington
Dream of the Quartz Pebble, The. PoSu, *tr. by* Anne Pennington
Heart of the Quartz Pebble, The. PoSu, *tr. by* Anne Pennington
Love of the Quartz Pebble, The. PoSu, *tr. by* Anne Pennington
Quartz Pebble, The. PoSu, *tr. by* Anne Pennington
Secret of the Quartz Pebble, The. PoSu, *tr. by* Anne Pennington
Two Quartz Pebbles. PoSu, *tr. by* Anne Pennington

Quartz Pebble, The. Vasco [*or* Vasko] Popa, *tr. fr. Serbo-Croatian. Fr.* Quartz Pebble, The. PoSu, *tr. by* Anne Pennington

Quasi Quasi . . . as If Repeated. Glenda George. NBrP

Quasimodo loomed. For Wilma. Don Johnson. GOYP

Quatorzain. Henry Timrod. AnAmPo

Quatrain. Jalal al-Din Rumi, *tr. fr. Persian by* John Moyne *and* Coleman Barks. ArLo

Quatrain 2: "How strange that grass should sing." Gwendolyn B. Bennett. ShDr

Quatrain: "Above the creek dallies a bright moon." Yuan Hao-wen, *tr. fr. Chinese by* Irving Y. Lo. SuSp

Quatrain: "Before you praise Spring's advent note." Tu Fu, *tr. fr. Chinese by* Robert Payne. TAL

Quatrain: "Beyond the gate the cormorant had gone and not returned." Tu Fu, *tr. fr. Chinese by* Jerome P. Seaton. SuSp

Quatrain: "Birds the more white, against green stream." Tu Fu, *tr. fr. Chinese by* Jerome P. Seaton. SuSp

Quatrain: "François am I, heavy my lot." Villon. OBD

Quatrain: "Golf links lie so near The mill." Sarah Norcliffe Cleghorn. *See* Golf Links, The.

Quatrain: "I cry:/ but you want comforting." Jalal al-Din Rumi, *tr. fr. Persian by* Omar S. Pound. ArPe

Quatrain: "I lounge on the jetty in the fragrance of catalpa." Tu Fu, *tr. fr. Chinese by* Jerome Seaton. SuSp

Quatrain: "Late sun, the stream and the hills; the beauty." Tu Fu, *tr. fr. Chinese by* Jerome Seaton. SuSp

Quatrain: "My bloodstream chokes on gall and spleen." Barend Toerien, *tr. fr. Afrikaans by the author.* PeSA

Quatrain: "Sarmèd, whom they intoxicated from the cup of love." Sarmèd the Yahud, *tr. fr. Persian by* David Shea. TrJP

Quatrain: "This existence has, without the azure sphere, no reality." Sarmèd the Yahud, *tr. fr. Persian by* David Shea. TrJP

Quatrain: "What is this day with two suns in the sky?" Jalal al-Din Rumi, *tr. fr. Persian by* John Moyne *and* Coleman Barks. ArLo

Quatrain: "With you away — despair!" Rudaki, *tr. fr. Persian by* Omar S. Pound. ArPe

Quatrain without Sparrows, Helpful Bells or Hope. Thomas McCarthy. PBCIP

Quatrains. Gwendolyn B. Bennett. CDC

Quatrains, *sels.* Emerson.
   Gardener. OxBA
   Orator. OxBA
   Poet. OxBA; OxBSP; Spl

Quatrains. Salah Jahin, *tr. fr. Arabic by* Samir M. Zoghby. TTY

Quatrains for Pegasus. James Merrill. BAP-90

Quatrains on Peking's Western Suburb, *sels.* Chu Yi-tsun, *tr. fr. Chinese by* Irving Lo.

Quatrains on Yung-chia, *sels.* Chu Yi-tsun, *tr. fr. Chinese by* Irving Lo.

Quatrina. Joseph Deericks Bennett. LiTA

Quavering cry, A. Screech-owl? Night, Death, Mississippi. Robert Hayden. CAPP; FF; LCAP; VCAP; VGW

"Quay recedes, The. Hurrah! Ahead we go!" The Colonel's Soliloquy. Thomas Hardy. OBWP

Quebec. H. Cordelia Ray. CBWP-3

Quebec Farmhouse. John Glassco. NOBC

Queen, The. Kenneth Pitchford. NYBP

Queen and huntress, chaste and fair. Hymn to Diana. Ben Jonson. *Fr.* Cynthia's Revels. AWP; CH; ChTr; EIL; GTBS; GTBS-P; HAP; NOBE; NoP; OAEL-1; OBEV; NoAM; NOBA; NoP; PoRA; SeCP; TFi; TrGrPo; WiR
   (Hesperus' Hymne[e] to Cynthia.) JCP; SeCV-1
   (Hesperus' Song.) GN
   (Hymn: "Queen and huntress, chaste, and fair.") EnRePo; InPS; PlP; PoEL-2
   (Hymn to Cynthia.) NOSC; PoE; PrIm; SCGP

Queen Anne. *Unknown.* ChTr

Queen Anne's Lace. June Jordan. TAP

Queen Anne's Lace. Mary Leslie Newton. FaPON; MoShBr

Queen Anne's Musicians. Thomas Hennell. FaBoTw

Queen-Ann's-Lace. William Carlos Williams. AmPP; BLPL; MeMAP; MoAB; MoAmPo; NAAL-2; NoAM; NOBA; NoP; PrIm; TAP

Queen Bee, The. Mary K. Robinson. BoTP

Queen Bess was Harry's daughter. Stand forward partners all! The Looking Glass. Kipling. FaBoEH; FaBoTw; NTP; OBMV

Queen Catharine; or, The Ruines of Love, *sels.* Catherine Trotter.
   "What Epilogues are made, for who can tell." KTR

Queen Catherine., *sels.* Mary Pix.
   "Work on my brain, help every faculty." KTR, *act I*

Queen Dido Rides Out Hunting. Virgil, *tr. by* Gavin Douglas. *Fr. Aeneid [or Eneados],* The. NAWM-1; OxBLMV

Queen Eleanor's Confession. *Unknown.* ESPB, A *and* B *vers.*; OBET; PrIm

Queen has lately lost a part, The. Verses Said to Be Written on the Union. Swift. APAS
   (On the Union.) FaBoEH

Queen is gone a-hunting in the royal wood, The. A-Hunting. Jennie Dunbar. BoTP

Queen is taking a drive today, The. The Queen's Last Ride. Ella Wheeler Wilcox. BLPA

Queen Jane sat at her window one day. The King's Dochter Lady Jean. *Unknown.* AmFP

Queen Jane was [*or* lay] in labor [*or* labour]. The Death of Queen Jane. *Unknown.* AmFP, 2 *vers.*; ESPB, A *and* B *vers.*; OBET
   (Queen Jeanie, Queen Jeanie, travel'd six weeks and more.) ESPB, B *vers.*

Queen Jeanie, Queen Jeanie, travel'd six weeks and more. *Unknown.* See Queen Jane was [*or* lay] in labor [*or* labour].

Queen Katherine to Owen Tudor. Michael Drayton. *Fr.* England's Heroical Epistles. NoSic

Queen Mab. Shakespeare. *See* O [*or* Oh], then, I see Queen Mab hath been with you.

Queen Mab, *sels.* Shelley.
   Magic Car Moved On, The. GN
   War Is the Statesman's Game. FF

Queen Mother to New Queen. Robert Graves. OBSV

Queen Nefertiti. *Unknown.* OTCP; TLR

Queen next morning fried, The. (*LL*) When good King Arthur ruled this [*or* the] land. Mother Goose. FaBoNo; OxNR

Queen of all Queens, oh! Wonder of the loveliness of women. Hymn to the Virgin Mary. Conor O'Riordan, *tr. fr. Irish by* Eleanor Hull. TIRV

Queen of Aragon, The, *sels.* William Habington.
   Fine Young Folly
   (Pretty Sport.) NOBE

Queen of black-earth Egypt, divine Isis. Philip of Thessalonica, *tr. fr. Greek by* Edwin Morgan. GrAn

Queen of Cheese. James McIntyre. FiBHP

Queen of Corinth, The, *sels.* John Fletcher *and others.*
   Weep No More. CH; EIL; OBEV; OxAEP-1
   (Mourn No More.) TrGrPo

Queen of Elfan's [*or* Elfland's] Nourice [*or* Nourrice], The. *Unknown.* ESPB
   Sels.
   "I heard a cow low, a bonnie cow low." FaBoCh

Queen of fragrance, lovely rose. The Rose-Bud. William Broome. OBEV

Queen of Hearts, The. Mother Goose. FaBoBe; OxNR
   (Tarts, The. ReMoGo

Queen of Hearts, The. Christina Rossetti. CBLP; PeVV

Queen of Hearts, The. *Unknown.* OBET

Queen of Heaven Mausoleum. Dennis Schmitz. LCAP

Queen of Lydia, The. C. H. Sisson. OxBC

Queen of martials, The. The Shield of Achilles. Homer, *tr. fr. Greek. Fr. Iliad,* The. NOSC, *tr. by* George Chapman

Queen of Night Walks Her Thin Dog, The. Diane Wakoski. SRLS

Queen of Paphos, Erycine, The. *Unknown.* EIL; GBL

Queen of Scotland, The. *Unknown.* ESPB

Queen of the Blues. Gwendolyn Brooks. NALW

Queen of the differentiated sites, administratrix of the. David Jones. *Fr.* Tutelar of the Place, The. AngWe

Queen of the Ebony Isles. Colleen J. McElroy. BCF

Queen of the Nile, The. William Jay Smith. GrPl

Queen of the River. Elizabeth Nannestad. PeNZ

Queen of the silver bow! — by thy pale beam. To the Moon. Charlotte Smith. Son

Queen of the world, and the child of the skies, The. (*LL*) Columbia. Timothy Dwight. PAH

Queen of Wands, The. Judy Grahn. SRLS

Queen, Queen Caroline. *Unknown.* TLR

Queen, Queen, Caroline. *Unknown.* ISE

Queen Sabbath. Hayyim Nahman Bialik, *tr. fr. Hebrew by* Jessie Sampter. TrJP

Queen she sent to look for me, The. Grenadier. A. E. Housman. OBMV; OBWP

Queen Victoria. *Unknown. See* Welcome now, Victoria.

Queen was beloved by a jester, A. The Cap and Bells. W. B. Yeats. ChTr; MoAB; MoBrPo; NoAM; NoP

Queen Yang-Se-Fu/ Has seventy great castles. Yang-Se-Fu. "Yehoash," *tr. fr. Yiddish by* Isidore Goldstick. TrJP

Queenie. Mary Weston Fordham. CBWP-2

Queens, The. Robert Fitzgerald. NYBP

Queens. J. M. Synge. ChTr; GBL; MoBrPo; OBMV; PeIV; PeVV

Queen's Dream, The. *Unknown.* PeVV

Queen's English, The. Tony Harrison. DiPo

Queen's Last Ride, The. Ella Wheeler Wilcox. BLPA

Queen's Marie, The. *Unknown.* OBEV; ScCV

Queens of Hell had lissome necks to crane, The. The Tall Girl. John Crowe Ransom. Son

Queen's Speech, The. Arthur Mainwaring. APAS

Queen's Wake, The, *sels.* James Hogg.

Kilmeny. OBEV; OxAEP-2
(When many a day had come and fled.) OtMeF
Queer, The. Henry Vaughan. PoEL-2
Queer are the ways of a man I know. The Phantom Horsewoman. Thomas Hardy. CMoP; FaBoPP; MeMBP; NOBE; PoEL-5
Queer Assayers of the Frontier, The. Peter Porter. Fr. Baroque Quatrains. AnAn
Queer sights we every day do find. The Dandy Horse. Unknown. OBET
Queer Thing, A. Nancy Keesing. NOBAu
Queer thing about those waters: there are no, A. Across the Bay. Donald Davie. NoAM
Queer's Song. Richard Howard. Fr. Gaiety. ErPo
Quenching water, The. (LL) Morning: The World in the Lake. Linda Hogan. SRLS
Quentin Durward., sels. Sir Walter Scott.
    Serenade. GTBS; GTBS-P
    (County Guy.) PFP
    (Song: "Ah! County Guy, the hour is nigh.") CH
Query. Ebon Dooley. PoBA
Query. Michael McTurk. PBCV
Query, a question, A. The Water of Kane. Unknown, tr. fr. Hawaiian by N. B. Emerson. WTO
Quesada, sels. C. K. Stead.
    "All over the plain of the world lovers are being hurt." PeNZ
    "Odysseus under wet snapping sheets." PeNZ
    "That the balls of the lover are not larger than the balls of the priest." PeNZ
Quest, The. W. H. Auden. Son
Sels.
    City, The.
    Door, The.
Quest. Anthony Barnett. VaA
Quest. Naomi Long Madgett. BPo
Quest, The. Sharon Olds. NAmP90
Quest, The. Eliza Scudder. TrPWD
Quest, The. Harold Vinal. GoYe
Quest, The. James Wright. NYBP
Quest of Silence, The, sels. Christopher John Brennan.
    Fire in the Heavens. CBAP; NOBAu
Quest of the Ideal, The. H. Cordelia Ray. AmWP; CBWP-3
Quest of the Sancgreall, The, sels. Thomas Westwood.
    Andromeda.
    "Motionless sat the shadow at the helm." PeVV
    "Whelming the dwellings of men, and the toils of the slow-/ footed oxen." PeVV
Quest of the Sangraal, The, sels. Robert Stephen Hawker.
    "Land is lonely now, The: Anathema." EBVV
Questing. Anne Spencer. CDC
Questing-for-Spring Arbor. Huang Ching-jen, tr. fr. Chinese by Chang Yin-nan and Lewis C. Walmsley. SuSp
Question, The. W. H. Auden. OxAEP-2
Question, The. James Beattie. FaBoCo
Question, The. Robert Duncan. NeAP
Question, The. Norman Gale. FiBHP
Question, The. W. W. Gibson. NSI; PAW
Question, The. Josephine D. Henderson Heard. CBWP-4
Question, The. David Ignatow. CAPP
Question, The. Karla Kuskin. NTCP; PDV
Question, The. Alexander McKee. PAW
Question, The. Wilhelm Müller, tr. fr. German by Philip L. Miller. Fr. Beautiful Maid of the Mill, The. RiWo
Question, The. F. T. Prince. BoLoP; GTBS-P; PeSA
Question, The. Muriel Rukeyser. IHMS; WPOW
Question, The. Shelley. CH; CoGr; EnRP; OBEV
Question. Martin Sorescu, tr. fr. Romanian by Michael Hamburger. CBNP
Question. May Swenson. LiTM; PrIm; SM; VGW
Question, A. Edna Livingston. GoYe
Question, A. J. M. Synge. MoBrPo; NoIV; OBMV; OxBTC; PeIV
Question, A. Unknown. NOSC
Question, A ("If I really, really trust him.") Unknown. BLRP
Question and Answer, The. Thomas Beedome. NOSC
Question and Answer. Samuel Hoffenstein. FiBHP
Question and Answer. Langston Hughes. BPo
Question and Answer. Kathleen Raine. MoBrPo
Question Answered [or A Question Answered], The. Blake. See What is it men in women do require?
Question, The ("I dream'd that, as I wander'd by the way.") Shelley. CH; EnRP; OBEV

Question in a Field. Louise Bogan. NYBP
Question is, The: how does one hold an apple. The Gesture. George Oppen. Fr. Five Poems about Poetry. NNaP
Question, lords and ladies, is, The. Percy Shelley. John Peale Bishop. ErPo
Question Mark, The. Gevorg Emin, tr. fr. Armenian by Diana Der Hovanessian. TSaS
Question me again. (LL) Casualty. Seamus Heaney. FaBoPV; IPY; NAEL-2; PBCIP; PoE
Question Not. Adam Lindsay Gordon. OtMeF; PoToHe
Question not, but live and labor. Question Not. Adam Lindsay Gordon. OtMeF; PoToHe
Question of Climate, A. Audre Lorde. NoAM
Question of Covenants, A. Gerald Dawe. PNI
Question of Form and Content, A. Jon Stallworthy. OxBC
Question of Libel, A. Pope. Fr. First Satire of the Second Book of Horace, The. OAEL-1; PPP; PrIm, abr
Question of Time, The. William Peskett. PNI
Question the beauty of the earth. Saint Augustine. Joseph Mary Plunkett. TIRV
Question then, to state it first, The. Samuel Butler. Fr. Hudibras. NOBL
Question Time. Jack Lindsay. NOBAu
Question Time. Thomas McCarthy. CIP; IB
Question to Life. Patrick Kavanagh. MoBrPo
Question to Lisetta. Matthew Prior. OBEV
Question was an academic one, The. Tomorrows. James Merrill. OBAL
Question, The ("Were the whole world good as you — not an atom better.") Unknown. WBLP
Question Whither, The. George Meredith. WGRP
Questioner Who Sits So Sly. W. H. Auden. OxAEP-2
Questioners, The. Edward Leslie Mayo. BCF
Questioning. H. Cordelia Ray. CBWP-3
Questioning Faces. Robert Frost. GrPl
Questionnaire. Susan Saxe. GLP
Questionnaire of Sleeplessness. Miodrag Pavlović, tr. fr. Serbo-Croatian by Charles Simic. HSix
Questions, The. Robert Pinsky. NAmP90; NoAM
Questions. Unknown. OtMeF
Questions at Night. Louis Untermeyer. FaPON
Questions My Son Asked Me, Answers I Never Gave Him. Nancy Willard. LCAP
Questions of Ethne Alba, The. Unknown, tr. fr. Irish by James Carney. PeIV; TIRV
Questions of Our Time. Kwesi Brew. PAW
Questions of Swimming, 1935. Peter Davison. DiPo
Questions of Travel. Elizabeth Bishop. NAAL-2; NOBA
Questions [1]. Donald Hall. FF
Questions [2]. Donald Hall. FF
Quetzalcoatl Looks down on Mexico. D. H. Lawrence. PeECV
Quha Is Perfyte. Alexander Scott. See Wha Is Perfyte.
Quhare in a lusty plane tuke I my way. James I, King of Scotland. Fr. Kingis Quair, The. ScCV
Quhen [or Qwhen or When] Alexander [or Alysandyr] our kynge [or King] was dede. The Death of Alexander. Unknown. OxBS
(When Alysandyr Our King Was Dede.) FaBoCh; ScCV
Quhen Flora Had O'erfret the Firth. Unknown. See When Flora Had Ourfret the Firth.
Quhen he wes yung, and cled in grene. Quhy Sowld Nocht Allane Honorit Be? Unknown. OxBS
Quhen [or When] Noy[e] had maid his Sacrifyce [or sacrifice]. After the Flood. Sir David Lindsay. Fr. Monarche, The. ChIV-1; OxBS
Quhen Tayis bank wes blumyt brycht. Tayis Bank. Unknown. FaBoVe
Quhen that I had oversene this regioun. Of the Realme of Scotland. Sir David Lindsay. Fr. Dreme, The. OxBS
Quhen thay war seruit and set to the Suppar. Unknown. Fr. Rauf Coilyear. ScCV
Quhen thou art careit to that cuntre. Virgil, tr. by Gavin Douglas. Fr. Aeneid [or Eneados], The. NAWM-1; OBVE
Quhom I luve, I dar nocht assay.' (LL) When Flora Had Ourfret the Firth. Unknown. NoP; ScCV
Quhy Sowld Nocht Allane Honorit Be? Unknown. OxBS
Quhy will ye, merchantis of renoun. To the Merchantis of Edinburgh. William Dunbar. FaBoPP; OxBS
Qui Bien Aime a Tard Oublie. Chaucer. See Now Welcom[e], Somer [or Summer].
Qui Laborat, Orat. Arthur Hugh Clough. EnVR; TrPWD
Quia amore langueo. (LL) Quia Amore Langueo. Unknown. ImPo; NOBE; NOCV; OBEV; PoEL-1

Quia Amore Langueo. *Unknown, tr.* by Helen Gardner. ImPo; NOBE; NOCV; OBEV; PoEL-1

Quia Amore Langueo. *Unknown, tr. fr. Middle English* by Helen Gardner. NOBE; NOCV; PoEL-1

Quick! a last poem before I go. On Rachmaninoff's Birthday. Frank O'Hara. PoM

Quick and Bitter. Yehuda Amichai, *tr. fr. Hebrew.* BoLoP, *tr.* by Assia Gutmann

Quick as lightning I saw a lizard. *(LL)* Lizard. Bundgaard Povlsen. TSaS

Quick-falling dew. Basho, *tr. fr. Japanese* by Curtis Hidden Page. AWP

Quick hands on spinning ropes. Dead Horse Bay. Robert Adamson. NOBAu

Quick! Hoist the jib and cast us off, my son. Over Bright Summer Seas. Robert Silliman Hillyer. NYBP

Quick in spite I said unkind. Brazen Tongue. William Rose Benét. MoAmPo

Quick lunch! quick lunch! the neon cries, and I. Essay on Lunch. Walker Gibson. NYBP

Quick on my feet in those Novembers of my loneliness. A Mad Fight Song for William S. Carpenter, 1966. James Wright. NoAM

Quick! quick!/The cat's been sick. *Unknown.* ISE

Quick, silver! Climb. Mercury. Naomi Segal. VBLP

Quick sparks on the gorse-bushes are leaping, The. The Wild Common. D. H. Lawrence. NoAM

Quick-Step. Robert Creeley. VGW

Quick, woman, in your net. The Net. W. R. Rodgers. BoLoP; CIP; ErPo; PeIV; PNI

Quicken. *(LL)* The Winds of Orisha. Audre Lorde. SRLS

Quickening, The. Stella Weston Tuttle. GoYe

Quicker/ than that can't. A Sight. Robert Creeley. NaP

Quicker in making drop biscuits, The. Recipe. Angela Greene. NWP

Quickly, love, be lyrical & let. La, La, La! Tom Disch. NBLV

Quickness. Thomas Stanley. ELP; GeHe; MeLP; NOBE; NOCV; NOSC; SeCP; SeCV-1

Quickness of Fear, The. Beverly Acuff Momoi. LoHo

Quickness which my God hath kissed, A. *(LL)* Quickness. Thomas Stanley. ELP; GeHe; MeLP; NOBE; NOCV; NOSC; SeCP; SeCV-1

Quicksands. William Zaranka. BXAP

Quid, omit, my simple friend. II, 11. To an Ambitious Friend ("Quid bellicosus.") Horace, *tr. fr. Latin* by Austin Dobson. *Fr.* Odes. AWP, *tr.* by Matthew Arnold

Quid Restat. Lucius Beebe. RFM

Quid Sit Futurum Cras Fuge Quaerere. Matthew Prior. FaBoEE

Quid the Cynic's Song. Blake. *See* When old corruption first begun.

Quidditie, The. George Herbert. GeHe; PoEL-2

Quiescent, a Person Sits Heart and Soul. Ring Lardner. OBAL

Quiet. Marjorie Pickthall. NOBC

Quiet. Brian Swann. AmPA

Quiet beyond recall, /Into irrelevance. *(LL)* To the Holy Spirit. Yvor Winters. MoAmPo; VGW

Quiet birds fly. John Riley. VaA

Quiet chamber kept for Thee, A. *(LL)* All Hail, Thou Noble Guest. Martin Luther. TrPWD

Quiet Days. Mildred T. Mey. PoToHe

Quiet deepens. You will not persuade, The. Farewell to Van Gogh. Charles Tomlinson. CMoP; GTBS-P; PoE

Quiet Desperation. Mike Frenkel. BTR

Quiet Desperation. Louis Simpson. SV

Quiet-eyed Cattle, The. Leslie Norris. PChr

Quiet Fog, The. Marge Piercy. UnPo

Quiet, fragrant, and relieved. *(LL)* The Dusk of Horses. James Dickey. LiTM; NYBP

Quiet from Fear of Evil. "S. C. McK." BLRP

Quiet Glades of Eden, The. Robert Graves. BoLoP; ErPo

Quiet Hour, The. Louise Hollingsworth Bowman. BLRP

Quiet House, The. Charlotte Mew. BrRo; EBEV; NALW

Quiet Kingdom, The. Carl Busse, *tr. fr. German* by Ludwig Lewisohn. AWP

Quiet Life, The. *At. to* William Byrd. ElL; NoSic

Quiet Life, The. Pope. *See* Happy the man whose wish and care.

Quiet moon, immaculate of face, The. William Baylebridge. *Fr.* Love Redeemed. CBAP

Quiet Neighbour, A. John Heywood. NoSic

Quiet Normal Life, A. Wallace Stevens. NAAL-2; NoAM

Quiet now, feel the kindly pressure of darkness. Winter Solstice Poem. Diana Scott. BrRo

Quiet of the Dead, The. Mary Morison Webster. PeSA

Quiet Pilgrim, The. Edith M. Thomas. AmWP

Quiet, purling spring! The Youth to the Spring. Johann Gaudenz von Salis-Seewis, *tr. fr. German* by Philip L. Miller. RiWo

Quiet room, the flowers, the perfumed calm, The. Schumann's Sonata in A Minor. Celia Laighton Thaxter. AiP

Quiet sands have run, The. *(LL)* Twilight Calm. Christina Rossetti. BoNaP; OBNC

Quiet season of flowering, the courtyard gate is shut. Palace Poem. Chu Ch'ing-yu, *tr. fr. Chinese* by Irving Y. Lo. SuSp

Quiet Soul, A. John Oldham. OBEV

Quiet Things. Grace Noll Crowell. PoLF

Quiet Tide near Ardossan, The. Charles Tennyson Turner. FaBoPP

Quiet Town. William Stafford. MAT

Quiet valley with no man's footprints, A. Sitting at Night. Om Ui-Gil, *tr. fr. Chinese* by Jong-gil Kim. OBF

Quiet Waters. Blanche Shoemaker Wagstaff. BLPA

Quiet, willows and primulas are growing. John Riley. VaA

Quiet Work. Matthew Arnold. FaBoBe; TrGrPo

Quietly. Kenneth Rexroth. ErPo

Quietly and while at rest on the trim grass I have gazed. The Air of June Sings. Edward Dorn. NeAP; PoM

Quietly at our side the dead. The Dead Men. Sophia de Mello Breyner Andresen, *tr. fr. Portuguese* by Allan Francovich. PBWP

Quietly I enter the closet. Communion. P. M. Snider. PoToHe

Quietly I sit on the side of the hill. In Spring. Ernst Konrad Friedrich Schulze, *tr. fr. German* by Philip L. Miller. RiWo

Quietly shining to the quiet moon. *(LL)* All Seasons Shall Be Sweet. Samuel Taylor Coleridge. BoTP

Quietly shining to the quiet Moon. *(LL)* Frost at Midnight. Samuel Taylor Coleridge. EBEV; EnRP; FHYEP; HAP; MeMBP; NAEL-2; NAs; NOBE; NoP; OAEL-2; OBNC; PFP; PoE; PoEL-4; Poetr; PPP; PrIm; TFi; TOF

Quietly step onto a land. Kayenta Times Yet Dreaming On. Nia Francisco. HATNAP

Quietly the world lay sleeping. The Birth of Jesus. Josephine D. Henderson Heard. CBWP-4

Quilled Quilt, a Needle Bed, A. Brad Leithauser. SM

Quilt, The. Mary Effie Lee Newsome. CDC

Quilt in the Bennington College Library, A. Dave Jeddie Smith. NAmP90

Quilt Song. Mark Vinz. GOYP

Quilts. Kathleen Peirce. PBCAP

Quilts sing on, The. *(LL)* My Mother Pieced Quilts. Teresa Palma Acosta. MDDM; WPOW

Quince. Nigel Wells. PWE

Quince Preserved through the Winter, Given to a Lady, A. Antiphilus, *tr. fr. Greek* by W. S. Merwin. GrAn

Quinn the Eskimo. Bob Dylan. RaBo

Quinnapoxet. Stanley Kunitz. AnAn

Quinquireme of Nineveh from distant Ophir. Cargoes. John Masefield. BLPL; CMoP; CoGr; EBEvV; FaBV; FaPON; FaPoR; GGP; InPK; LiTM; MoAB; MoBrPo; NOBE; OBEV; OBMV; OtMeF; PlP; PoRA; TEP; TFi

Quintana lay in the shallow grave of coral. Fox Hole. Karl Shapiro. ArOW

(Quintana Lay in the Shallow Grave of Coral.) VGW

Quintana Lay in the Shallow Grave of Coral. Karl Shapiro. *See* Quintana lay in the shallow grave of coral.

Quintets for Robert Morley, *sels.* Luis Cabalquinto. "It's like we also invented some of love." CBCK

Quintets for Robert Morley, *sels.* Les A. Murray. Achievements of the Fat. CBCK

Quintina of Crosses, A. Chad Walsh. TrCP

Quip, The. George Herbert. GeHe; JCP; LiTB; NOSC; OxAEP-1; SeCP; SeCV-1

Quirky old gent, name of Freud, A. Martin Fagg. PeLi

Quit now the town, and with a journeying dream. "George Eliot." *Fr.* Spanish Gypsy, The. OBTV

Quite Apart from the Holy Ghost. Adrian Mitchell. OBSV

Quite for no reason. I've Been to a Marvelous Party. Noël Coward. NBLV

Quite Forsaken. D. H. Lawrence. SCGP

Quite horfen, fer a lark, coves on a ship. The Helbatrawss. Kingsley Amis. NOBL

Quite like a Prayer. Briar Wood. NWP

Quite, quite./ Oh I agree. Restricted. Eve Merriam. TrJP

Quite rightly, we remained among the living. The Survivors. Adrienne Rich. NYBP

Quite spent with thoughts I left my cell, and lay. Vanity of Spirit. Henry Vaughan. ESCV; GeHe; NOSC; TOF

Quite the Cheese. H. C. Waring. BXAP

Quite unexpectedly as Vasserot. The End of the World. Archibald MacLeish. BLPL; CMoP; HoPM; ImPo; InPK; LiTM; MAT; MeMAP; MoAB; MoAmPo; NoAM; NOBA; OBAL; OxBA; Son; TAP; TFi; TrGrPo; VGW

Quits. Matthew Prior. *See* To John I ow'd great obligation.

Quitter, The. *Unknown.* BLPA; WBLP

Quivering fins. Cytherea. Mary Mackey. SRLS

Quivíra. Arthur Guiterman. PAH

Quo life, the warld is mine. The Flyting o' Life and Daith. Hamish Henderson. OxBS

Quo' the wee boy, and still he stude. (*LL*) The False Knight upon [*or* on] the Road. *Unknown.* AmFP; CH; EnSB; ESPB; GBP

Quod Dunbar to Kennedy. William Dunbar. OxBoLi

Quod skelton, laureat. (*LL*) Tell you I chyll. John Skelton. AAS; TrGrPo

Quoits. Mary Effie Lee Newsome. CDC

Quondam was I in my lady's grace. Sir Thomas Wyatt. GBL; NoSic; SiPSBD

Quoof. Paul Muldoon. CBNP; FaBoVe; PBCIP; PNI

Quotation from Shakespeare with Slight Improvements, A. "Lewis Carroll." FaBoNo

Quotations. George Oppen. NNaP

Quote from the Bureau of Information, from the Argus, August 27, 1986: "The Situation in Soweto Is Not Abnormal." Mavis Smallberg. WoWa

Quoth a cow in the marshes of Glynne. Conrad Aiken. PeLi

Quoth Cibber to Pope, tho' in verse you foreclose. Pope. FaBoEE

Quoth Dick to me, as once at College. The Madman and the Lethargist. Samuel Taylor Coleridge. CBNP

Quoth Elizabeth prisoner. (*LL*) Written with a Diamond on Her Window at Woodstock. Elizabeth I, Queen of England. PBWP; WPE

Quoth he, Miss Mouse, I'm come to thee. Kitty Alone. *Unknown.* CBNP

Quoth he, My faith as adamantine. Samuel Butler. *Fr.* Hudibras. OBSV

Quoth he, to bid me not to love. Samuel Butler. *Fr.* Hudibras. NOBL

Quoth John to Joan. *Unknown.* CH; OxBM

Quoth Satan to Arnold: "My worthy good fellow." *Unknown.* PAH

Quoth she, I wish I could prescribe your help. Rachel Speght. *Fr.* Dream, A. WPE

Quoth tongue of neither maid nor wife. Elena's Song. Sir Henry Taylor. *Fr.* Philip van Artevelde. OBEV

Qwhylum thair wes, as Esope can report. The Taill of the Wolf and the Wedder. Robert Henryson, *tr.* by Aesop. OxBLMV

R

R. Alcona to J. Brenzaida. Emily Brontë. *See* Cold in the earth, and the deep snow piled above thee!

R-and-R Centre: An Incident from the Vietnam War. D. J. Enright. OxBC

R-E-M-O-R-S-E. George Ade. FiBHP; NBLV; OBAL; PeLV

R is for ribbon. John Travers Moore *and* Margaret Moore *and* Margaret Moore. SiSoPo

R-P-O-P-H-E-S-S-A-G-R. E. E. Cummings. AmPP; NoP; PoE; PPP

R, the reviewer, reviewing my book. Hilaire Belloc. *Fr.* Moral Alphabet, A. NoAM

R. W. E. Lucy Larcom. AmWP

Rabbi, The. Christian Morgenstern, *tr. fr. German by* W. D. Snodgrass *and* Lore Segal. OBD

Rabbi Ben Ezra. Robert Browning. BLPL; FaBV; NAEL-2; OBNC; TEP; WGRP
Sels.
Rabbi Ben Ezra. MeMBP; PoToHe
(Grow Old Along With Me!) ImPo; LPA

Rabbi Ben Ezra. Robert Browning. *Fr.* Rabbi Ben Ezra. BLPL; FaBV; MeMBP; NAEL-2; OBNC; PoToHe; TEP; WGRP

Rabbi Yom-Tob of Mayence Petitions His God. A. M. Klein. TrJP

Rabbi Yussel Luksh of Chelm. Jacob Glatstein, *tr. fr. Yiddish by* Nathan Halper. TrJP

Rabbi's Song, The. Kipling. ChIV-1

Rabbit, The. Nina Cassian, *tr. fr. Romanian by* Christopher Hewitt. PoSu

Rabbit, The. Edith King. BoTP

Rabbit, The. Elizabeth Madox Roberts. OBCA

Rabbit. Tom Robinson. FaPON

Rabbit, The. *Unknown.* FaBoCo; FiBHP

Rabbit as King of the Ghosts, A. Wallace Stevens. NoAM; SoCa; SOTW; TTTS

Rabbit has a charming face, The. The Rabbit. *Unknown.* FaBoCo; FiBHP

Rabbit Story, The. Russell Edson. BAP-89

Rabbit's Advice, The. Elizabeth Jennings. PIP

Rabble of six arrived at my house, A. A Satire on the O'Haras. Tadhg Dall O'Huiginn. NOIV

Rabble Soldier. *Unknown.* AS

Rabid or dog-dull. Let me tell you how. A Professor's Song. John Berryman. HeIP; MoP; NAAL-2; NoAM; NOBA; OxBC

Rabinal-Achí, *sels. Unknown, tr. fr. Mayan by* Nathaniel Tarn. "Cala-Achí! Ha! Aha! Yeha! Ahau! Wow! Achí!" STP

Raccoon, The. Pyke Johnson, Jr.. ZA

Raccoon. Kenneth Rexroth. *Fr.* Bestiary, A. NNaP; OBAL; ZA

Raccoon on the Road. Joseph Payne Brennan. GoYe

Raccoon Poem. Miriam Palmer. NMM

Raccoon up a persimmon tree. *Unknown.* RoPo

Raccoon [*or* Racoon] wears a black mask, The. Raccoon. Kenneth Rexroth. *Fr.* Bestiary, A. NNaP; OBAL; ZA
(Racoon.) FiBHP

Raccoon wears a mask at night, The. The Raccoon. Pyke Johnson, Jr.. ZA

Raccoons. Aileen Fisher. PDV

Raccoons are selectively polygamous. Raccoon Poem. Miriam Palmer. NMM

Raccoons, quite a few of them. (*LL*) Inventory. Jacques Prévert. STV

Raccoon's tail is ring-around, The. *Unknown.* RoPo

Race, The. Nuala Ni Dhomhnaill, *tr. fr. Irish by* Michael Hartnett. CIP; PBCIP

Race, The. Sharon Olds. RaBo

Race and Battle. D. H. Lawrence. ChIV-1

Race is not to the swift, The. Race and Battle. D. H. Lawrence. ChIV-1

Race of the Kingfishers. Ray A. Young Bear. HATNAP

Race of the *Oregon*, The. John James Meehan. PAH

Race on Gathering Bites. Kojo Laing. HBAPE

Race Question, The. Naomi Long Madgett. BPo

Race round the track of the stadium pupil. (*LL*) The Stenographers. P. K. Page. HeIP; LiTM; NALW; NoAM; NoP

Racehorses assemble at the starting barrier, The. Flemington Racecourse. Kevin Hart. NOBAu

Racer's Widow, The. Louise Glück. AmPA; NYBP; SM

Rachel. Linda Pastan.

Rachel. Lizette Woodworth Reese. AmWP

Rachel (rā'chal), a Ewe. Linda Pastan. *See* We named you.

Racial Memories. Elizabeth Mische John. LoHo

Racing-Man, The. A. P. Herbert. FiBHP

Racing, reckoning fingers flick. Palladas, *tr. fr. Greek by* Tony Harrison. GrAn; OBVE

Racist Psychotherapy. Isaac J. Black. NBV

Racoon. Kenneth Rexroth. *See* Raccoon [*or* Racoon] wears a black mask, The.

Racoon up the 'simmon tree. The Persimmon Tree. *Unknown.* GBP

Radar. Alan Ross. FF

Raderus. John Donne. PeLV

Radiance of that star that leans on me, The. Delay. Elizabeth Jennings. NIP; OxBTC

Radiant blue grey. Driving Home. Richard Elman. Jaz

Radiant Ranks of Seraphim. Valery Yakovlevich Bryusov, *tr. fr. Russian by* Babette Deutsch *and* Avrahm Yarmolinsky. AWP

Radiant Silhouette I. John Yau. OpBo

Radiant Silhouette II. John Yau. OpBo

Radiant Silhouette III. John Yau. OpBo

Radiant Silhouette IV. John Yau. OpBo

Radiant Silhouette V. John Yau. OpBo

Radiation Victim. Colin Thiele. NOBAu

Radical, The. Waring Cuney. CDC

Radical Coherency. David Antin. UL

Radical Creed, A. Gelett Burgess. FaBoNo

Radical Song of 1786, A. St. John Honeywood. PAH

Radical War Song, A. Macaulay. OBSV

Radical Wife. (*LL*) Changes. Sally Cline. VBLP

Radio. Frank O'Hara. PoA

Radio Cradle-song. Eugène Marais, *tr. fr. Afrikaans by* Stephen Gray. PeSAV

Radio excuses our dawdling, The. Cameo. David Chaloner. VaA

Radio glimmers, The. Paper Cities. Gjertrud Schnackenberg. AnAn

Radio grovels from over the fence, A. Sydney. Robert Harris. NOBAu

Radio is teaching my goldfish Jujitsu, The. Heavy Water Blues. Bob Kaufman. NBV

Radio Religion, The. William Ludlum. WBLP

Radio Sky. Norman Dubie. NAmP90

Radio under the Bed, The. Reed Whittemore. NYBP

Radio Yerevan. Diana Der Hovanessian. LoHo

Radio's reality when. Monday, Monday. David Trinidad. UL

Radish. N. M. Bodecker. Spl

Radish is/ the only dish, The. Radish. N. M. Bodecker. Spl

R.A.F. (Aged Eighteen). Kipling. PoWW

Raft, The. Kathy Fagan. UTF

Raft drifted, The. John Heath-Stubbs. *Fr.* Artorius. EBEV; PeECV

Raftsmen on their floats. Buson, *tr. fr. Japanese* by Harold G. Henderson. TAL

Rag Doll and Summer Birds. Owen Dodson. PoNe

Ragas. David Meltzer. NeAP
   Sels.
   12th Raga: For John Wieners.
   15th Raga: For Bela Lugosi.

Rage, rage against the dying of the light. (*LL*) Do Not Go Gentle into That Good Night. Dylan Thomas. ClHu; CoGr; DL; EBEvV; FaPoB; FF; GGP; HAP; HeIL; HeIP; HoPM; InPK; InPS; LiTM; MeMBP; MoAB; MoBrPo; MoP; NAEL-2; NIP; NoAM; NOBE; NoP; OAEL-2; OBD; OxAEP-2; OxBTC; PeECV; PoE; Poetr; PrIm; RB; SCV; SoSe; TEP; TFi; TOF; TRP; TwCP; UnPo; UV; WeW

Rage through me, delightful. (*LL*) How Delightful, O My Queen. Georg Friedrich Daumer. RiWo

Ragged and Dirty. *Unknown.* AmFP

Ragged-and-Tough. Not Ragged-and-Tough. *Unknown.* ChTr; FaBoNo

Ragged Island. Edna St. Vincent Millay. NAAL-2; NoP

Ragged Robin. Elizabeth Godley. BoTP

Ragged Stocking, The. Frances E. W. Harper. AmWP

Ragged Wood, The. W. B. Yeats. CBLP; GBL

Raggedy Man, The. James Whitcomb Riley. FaPON; OBCA; OxBChV

Raggle, Taggle Gipsies, The. *Unknown. See* There were three gipsies a-come to my door.

Raging Canawl. *Unknown.* AS

Ragout. William Zaranka. BXAP

Ragoût Fin de Siècle (with Reference to Certain Cafés). Erich Kästner, *tr. fr. German* by Walter Kaufmann. ErPo; PeHV

Rags. Edmund Vance Cooke. BLPA

Rags and tatters. Ragged Robin. Elizabeth Godley. BoTP

Ragwort, The. John Clare. ChTr

Rahab. Diane Glancy. CRP

Raid, The. William Everson. ArOW; MoP; NoAM; PrIm

Raid of the Reidswire, The. *Unknown.* IBB

Raid on a Cheyenne Village. Diane Glancy. LoHo

Raider, The. W. R. Rodgers. MoBrPo

Raiders' Dawn. Alun Lewis. AngWe

Rail on, poor feeble scribbler, speak of me. The Author's Reply. Sir Carr Scroope. APAS

Railroad, The, *sels.* William Barnes.
   "An' while I went 'ithin a train." EnVR

Railroad, The. Thoreau. *See* What's the Railroad to Me?

Railroad Bill. *Unknown.* AS

Railroad Blues, The. *Unknown.* AmFP

Railroad bridge's, De. Homesick Blues. Langston Hughes. CDC; MoAmPo

Railroad Cars Are Coming, The. *Unknown.* AS; FaPON

Railroad Crossing — Look out for the cars! *Unknown.* ISE; RoPo

Railroad Happening, A. Daniil Kharms, *tr. fr. Russian* by Vladimir Markov and Merrill Sparks. CBNP

Railroad look so pretty. Two Hoboes. *Unknown.* WTO

Railroad track is miles away, The. Travel. Edna St. Vincent Millay. FaPON; MoShBr; OBCA; PDV

Railroad yard in San Jose. In Back of the Real. Allen Ginsberg. AmPP; HeIL; HeIP

Railroader for Me, A. *Unknown.* AmFP

Railroads and Freight Handler to the Nation. (*LL*) Chicago. Carl Sandburg. AiP; AmPP; AnAmPo; BLPL; CMoP; FaBV; LiTM; MoAB; MoAmPo; MoP; NAAL-2; NoAM; NOBA; NoP; OxBA; PoA; Poetr; TAP; TFi; TRP; UnPo; VGW

Rails pause barely to tie the horizons, The. The Depot. Lewis Turco. GrPl

Railway Junction, The. Walter de la Mare. OxBTC

Railway runs down the middle of the road, The. Mildmay Grove. Sue May. NBrP

Railway Stationery, The. Kenneth Koch. NoP

Railway Train, The. Emily Dickinson. *See* I like to see it lap the miles.

Rain. Vittoria Aganoor Pompilj, *tr. fr. Italian* by Philip L. Miller. RiWo

Rain, The, *sels.* John Ash.
   "We have to love the past." SCBI

Rain. David Chaloner. VaA

Rain. Martha Collins. FoLa

Rain, The. Robert Creeley. CAPP; CoAP; PoE; RaBo; TRP; VGW

Rain, The. W. H. Davies. BoTP; OxBTC

Rain. Emanuel diPasquale. InPK

Rain. Margiad Evans. OBWVE

Rain. Lance Henson. VoR

Rain. Anselm Hollo. PoM

Rain. Diana Der Hovanessian. VBLP

Rain. Donald Justice. *Fr.* Body and Soul. BAP-91

Rain. Vachel Lindsay. CMoP; RaBo

Rain. Myra Cohn Livingston. SiSoPo

Rain. Lilian McCrea. BoTP

Rain. Howard Moss. ErPo

Rain. Paul Murray. BIrV

Rain. Vladimir Nabokov. GrPl

Rain. Margaret Newlin. ArLo

Rain. Naomi Shihab Nye. NAmP90

Rain. James Whitcomb Riley. BoNaP

Rain, The. Solveig von Schoultz, *tr. fr. Finnish* by Anne Born. VBLP

Rain. Gary Soto. *Fr.* Elements of San Joaquin, The. NoAM; PBCAP

Rain. Robert Louis Stevenson. GoJo; NTCP; SiSoPo

Rain. Adrien Stoutenburg. PDV

Rain. Edward Thomas. NAEL-2; OBWP; OxBTC; PeFWW; PoWW

Rain, The. *Unknown.* BoTP; OxNR

Rain. James Wright. NaP

Rain. A heavy mane. Marina Tsvetayeva, *tr. fr. Russian* by Paul Schmidt. *Fr.* Daughter of Jairus, The. BoWoP

Rain after a Vaudeville Show. Stephen Vincent Benét. MoAmPo

Rain all over the cornfields. Butterfly Maidens. Lahpu, *tr. fr. Hopi Indian* by Natalie Curtis. WTO

Rain, and a flurry of wind shaking the pear's white blossom. C. K. Stead. *Fr.* Twenty-one Sonnets. PeNZ

Rain and sunlight and the boat between them. Leaving Inishmore. Michael Longley. IIP; PeIV

Rain and wind, the rain and wind, raved endlessly, The. Melancholy. Edward Thomas. NoP

Rain at Cold-Food Festival, *sels.* Su Shih, *tr. fr. Chinese.*
   "Since coming to Huang-chou." SuSp
   "Spring flood is coming up to my door." SuSp

Rain at Wildwood. May Swenson. NYBP

Rain beat upon my head, The. (*LL*) Rain. Vittoria Aganoor Pompilj. RiWo

Rain beats on trees south of the river. Tune: "Mountain Hawthorns." Wang An-shih, *tr. fr. Chinese* by James J. Y. Liu. SuSp

Rain before [*or* Raan afoor] seven. *Unknown.* FaBoBe; FaBoVe; OxNR; RoPo

Rain — Birdoswald. Frances Horovitz. NBrP; PWE

Rain brings me back, The. Patrizia Cavalli, *tr. fr. Italian* by Judith Baumel. NeIt

Rain came. Fog out of the slough and horses. Day after Chasing Porcupines. James Welch. NoAM

Rain carry us on spring and creek and river to the sea. (*LL*) This Room of Trees & Moving Earth/ This Room Where No One Knows How Sky Begins. Sister Mary Norbert Körte. SRLS

Rain Cleared and the Breeze and Sunshine Are Superb as I Stroll Outside the Gate, The. Lu Yu, *tr. fr. Chinese* by Burton Watson. SuSp

Rain comes and goes. The Green Refrain. Avraham Huss, *tr. fr. Hebrew* by Ruth Finer Mintz. MHP

Rain comes flapping through the yard, The. Gathering Mushrooms. Paul Muldoon. BiHa; CIP; PBCIP; PNI

Rain Down. Mary Ellen Solt. BoWoP

Rain Downriver. Philip Levine. VCAP

Rain drifts forever in this place. The Falls of Glomach. Andrew Young. OxBS

Rain falls like knives, The. Another Life. Derek Walcott. PBCV

Rain fell like grass growing, The. Rain at Wildwood. May Swenson. NYBP

Rain Forest. Eric Rolls. NOBAu

Rain Forest. Dave Jeddie Smith. HCAP; MT

Rain, Four Poems, *sels.* Tu Fu, *tr. fr. Chinese.*
   "Light rain doesn't slick the road." SuSp
   "This southern rain nourishes the mossy stones." SuSp

Rain frogs. James Whitcomb Riley. *See* It hain't no use to grumble and complane [*or* complain].

Rain gusts at the asphalt, The. Vincent Buckley. *Fr.* Golden Builders. FaBoMA

Rain had fallen, the Poet arose, The. The Poet's Song. Tennyson. EBVV; ELP; EPCY

Rain has beaded the panes. At the Office Early. Ted Kooser. PBCAP

Rain has passed, The. Birth. Amir Gilboa, *tr. fr. Hebrew by* Bernhard Frank. MHP, *tr. by* Ruth Finer Mintz

Rain hits over and over. Rain. Adrien Stoutenburg. PDV

Rain in its new edition of daily menace, The. Cambridge. John James. NBrP

Rain in my ears: impatiently there raps. Robert David Fitzgerald. *Fr.* Essay on Memory. CBAP

Rain in New York. Eva Salzman. NWP

Rain in Ohio. Mary Oliver. InPK

Rain in Summer. Longfellow. BoTP; GN

Rain in the hills. Lauris Edmond. PWE

Rain is chronic, The. Dido's Farewell. Linda Pastan. GOYP

Rain is due to fall, The. A Poet Thinks. Lui Chi, *tr. fr. Chinese by* E. Powys Mathers. AWP

Rain is Falling, The. Homero Aridjis, *tr. fr. Spanish by* John Frederick Nims. STV

Rain is over and gone!, The. (*LL*) Written in March. Wordsworth. BoNaP; BoTP; EnRP; FaPON; GoJo; NAEL-2; NTCP; PFP; PYC; SCGP; UnPo

Rain is raining all around, The. Rain. Robert Louis Stevenson. GoJo; NTCP; SiSoPo

Rain It Raineth, The. Lord Bowen. FiBHP; ISE; NBLV; NTCP

Rain it raineth every day, The. Pennsylvania Deutsch. Christopher Morley. NBLV

Rain, it streams on stone and hillock, The. A. E. Housman. CMoP

Rain Journal: London: June 65. Lee Harwood. PeHV

Rain Magic Song. *Unknown, tr. fr. Tewa Indian by* H. J. Spinden. WTO

Rain, midnight rain, nothing but the wild rain. Rain. Edward Thomas. NAEL-2; OBWP; OxBTC; PeFWW; PoWW

Rain Music. Joseph S. Cotter, Sr.. CDC

Rain of London pimples, The. London Rain. Louis MacNeice. NoP; Poetr

Rain of Rites, A. Jayanta Mahapatra. PoA

Rain of Tears. Wilhelm Müller, *tr. fr. German by* Philip L. Miller. *Fr.* Beautiful Maid of the Mill, The. RiWo

Rain on a Battlefield. Yehuda Amichai, *tr. fr. Hebrew by* Assia Gutmann. AnRep

Rain on a Grave. Thomas Hardy. OxAEP-2

Rain on Good Friday and Easter Day. *Unknown.* FaBoUs

Rain on the Cumberlands. James Still. GrPl

Rain on the Down. Arthur Symons. *Fr.* At Dieppe. OBNC

Rain on the far tip of the grove. Scattered Leaves. Lance Henson. VoR

Rain on the green grass. The Rain. *Unknown.* BoTP; OxNR

Rain on the River. Lu Yu, *tr. fr. Chinese by* Kenneth Rexroth. OHMPC

Rain on the West Side Highway. Adrienne Rich. *Fr.* Twenty-one Love Poems. GLP; NAAL-2

Rain over Munich, your plane's. Leaving a Country Behind. Carolyn Kreiter-Kurylo. BTR

Rain Poem. Elizabeth J. Coatsworth. SiSoPo

Rain, rain, and sun! a rainbow in the sky. Merlin's Riddling. Tennyson. *Fr.* Idylls of the King. FaBoRV

Rain, rain, go away. *Unknown.* ISE, diff. vers.; OxNR; ReMoGo; RoPo; SiSoPo

Rain, rain, go to Spain. Mother Goose. FaBoVe; OxNR; ReMoGo

Rain Rain on the Splintered Girl. Ishmael Reed. PoBA

Rain rains sair on Duriesdyke, The. Duriesdyke. Swinburne. OxBB

Rain rins doun through Mirry-land toune, The. Sir Hugh; or, The Jew's Daughter. *Unknown.* ESPB

(Hugh of Lincoln.) EnSB; OxBB

Rain, said the first, as it falls in Venice. Song Tournament: New Style. Louis Untermeyer. OBAL

Rain set early in to-night, The. Porphyria's Lover. Robert Browning. AWP; BeLS; CBLP; EnVR; FHYEP; HAP; MeMBP; NAEL-2; OBEV; TEP; TrGrPo

Rain shook its hair out carelessly over the streets, The. The Rain. Solveig von Schoultz, *tr. fr. Finnish by* Anne Born. VBLP

Rain smell comes with the wind. Leslie Silko. UnPo; VoR

Rain Song. Robert Loveman. *See* It isn't raining rain to me.

Rain Song of the Giant Society. *Unknown, tr. fr. Sia Indian by* Matilda Coxe Stevenson. AnAmPo

Rain stopped for one afternoon, The. Easter: Wahiawa, 1959. Cathy Song. OpBo

Rain stopped the clouds dissolved, The. Rain. David Chaloner. VaA

Rain-sunken roof, grown green and thin. The Barn. Edmund Blunden. MoBrPo

Rain That Fell upon the Height, The. Coventry Patmore. *See* Your love lacks joy, your letter says.

Rain, the welcome rain!, The. (*LL*) Rain in Summer. Longfellow. BoTP; GN

Rain thunderstorms over the Potomac, in Georgetown. Rainscapes, Hydrangeas, Roses, and Singing Birds. Richard Eberhart. MoAmPo

Rain to River to The Sea. Sister Mary Norbert Körte. SRLS

Rain to the Tribe. Al-Khansa, *tr. fr. Arabic by* Willis Barnstone *and* Tony Nawfal. BoWoP

Rain totally insistent drizzles. Andrew Crozier. VaA

Rain tries the one small foot and at length the other. Towards the Land of the Composer. Francis Webb. FaBoMA

Rain, The ("'twas in Koolau I met with the rain.") *Unknown, tr. fr. Hawaiian by* N. B. Emerson. WTO

Rain undoes the stone. Rain. Diana Der Hovanessian. VBLP

Rain unslanting, unceasing. Winter Afternoons in the V & A, Pre-W.W. II. Denise Levertov. CBCK

Rain walks all night across the greenhouse roof. The Scattering Layer. Martin Johnston. FaBoMA

Rain was full of the freshness, The. The Dark and Falling Summer. Delmore Schwartz. ImGa; NYBP

Rain was like a little mouse, The. Rain Poem. Elizabeth J. Coatsworth. SiSoPo

Rain was raining cheerfully, The. The Vulture and the Husbandman. Arthur Clement Hilton. FaBoCo

Rain, with a silver flail. Whale. William Rose Benét. MoAmPo

Rainbow, The. Walter de la Mare. NTP

Rainbow, The. Gerard Manley Hopkins. FaBoPP; OxBSP

Rainbow, The. D. H. Lawrence. NTP

Rainbow, The. David McCord. FaPON

Rainbow, The. Coventry Patmore. *Fr.* Angel in the House, The. GTBS-P

Rainbow, The. Christina Rossetti. *Fr.* Sing-Song. OxBChV

Rainbow, The. *Unknown, tr. fr. Hopi Indian by* Natalie Curtis. WTO

Rainbow, The. Henry Vaughan. GeHe

Rainbow, The. Wordsworth. *See* My heart leaps up [when I behold].

Rainbow arches in the sky, The. The Rainbow. David McCord. FaPON

Rainbow at night. *Unknown.* FaBoBe; RoPo

Rainbow faded, the animals dispersed, The. Return to Ararat. Martyn Halsall. TrCP

Rainbow Fairies, The. *Unknown.* BoTP

Rainbow is the shape of god's desire, The. Colour-Scheme. Edward Baugh. PBCV

Rainbow i'th'morning. *Unknown.* FaBoVe

Rainbow, The: or Curious Covenant. Robert Herrick. ChIV-1

Rainbow, rainbow. The Rainbow. *Unknown.* NTP

Rainbow stands red o'er the ocean, The. *Unknown, tr. fr. Hawaiian by* N. B. Emerson. WTO

Rainbow Writing. Eve Merriam. GrPl

Raindrops fall. To a Man Who is Rob Southland. Nia Francisco. HATNAP

Raindrops streak my window until morning. (*LL*) Farewell to Li. Nieh Sheng-ch'iung. WPC

Rainer,/ the man who was about to celebrate his 52nd birthday. The Death of Europe. Charles Olson. NeAP

Rainier. Jim Tollerud. VoR

Rainpoem. Michael Dransfield. CBAP

Rain's all right. The boys who physic. Biography of Southern Rain. Kenneth Patchen. VGW

Rains, already old, The. What She Said. Okkur Macatti, *tr. fr. Tamil by* A. K. Ramanujan. PBWP

Rains for the Harvest. *Unknown, tr. fr. Tewa Indian by* H. J. Spinden. WTO

Rains have come, The. It's Raining. Lucha Corpi, *tr. fr. Spanish by* Catherine Rodriguez-Nieto. AfAz

Rains in season. What He Said to His Charioteer, on His Way Back. Cittalai Cattanar, *tr. fr. Tamil by* A. K. Ramanujan. PLW

Rain's lovely gray daughter has lost her tall lover. Fog. Kenneth Patchen. NaP

Rain's Marriage, The. Marcia Southwick. NAmP90

Rainscapes, Hydrangeas, Roses, and Singing Birds. Richard Eberhart. MoAmPo

Rainstorm Has Dragged on for Ten Days Now, A, *sels.* T'ang Yin, *tr. fr. Chinese by* Jonathan Chaves.

Rainuv; a Romantic Ballad from the Early Basque. Margaret Widdemer. BXAP

Rainwalkers, The. Denise Levertov. PPP

Rainy Day, The. Longfellow. AWP; PoLF

Rainy Midnight. Ivor Gurney. FaBoPP

Rainy Mountain Cemetery. N. Scott Momaday. CDW; HATNAP

Rainy Night at the Writers' Colony. Josephine Jacobsen. TAP

Rainy Nights. Irene Thompson. BoTP

Rainy Pleiads Wester, The. A. E. Housman. BoLoP; CBLP

"Sol through white curtains shot a tim'rous ray." ECEV

"What dire offence from am'rous causes springs." EBNV; NOEC; Poetr

Rape of the Swan, The. Archibald MacLeish. AnAmPo

Rape Poem, The. Tommi Avicolli. GLP

Rape Poem. Marge Piercy. Poetsp

Raphael. H. Cordelia Ray. CBWP-3

Raphael. Priscilla Jane Thompson. CBWP-2

Raphael's Descent. Milton. *Fr.* Paradise Lost. EPCY; NOSC

Rapid day is gone; her banner swings the night, The. Evening. Andreas Gryphius, *tr. fr. German* by George C. Schoolfield. GePo

Rapid Transit. James Agee. MoAmPo

Rapidly cruising or lying on the air there is a bird. The Frigate Pelican. Marianne Moore. InvP

Rapier, lie there! and there, my hat and feather! The Poetaster. Samuel Rowlands. *Fr.* Melancholy Knight, The. EIL

Rapier of Treason, A. *Unknown, tr. fr. Arabic* by Willis Barnstone. BoWoP

Rapist, who reeked of cheap booze, A. *Unknown.* PeLi

Rapist's Villanelle, The. Tom Disch. SM

Rapparees. Richard Murphy. *Fr.* Battle of Aughrim, The. BIrV; NOIV; PBCIP

Rapping Along with Ronda Davis. James Cunningham. JB

Rapt. Irene McKinney. PBCAP

Rapture, The. Henry Baker. NOEC

Rapture. Stefan George, *tr. fr. German* by Ludwig Lewisohn. AWP

Rapture, The. Thomas Traherne. GeHe; NOSC

Rapture, A. Thomas Carew. BeJo; CaPo; ErPo; JCP; NAEL-1; OAEL-1; OxAEP-1; SeCP

Rapture Concerning His Lady, A. Cavalcanti, *tr. fr. Italian* by Dante Gabriel Rossetti. AWP

Rapunzel. Faye Kicknosway. UL

Rapunzel Rapunzel let down your hair. The After-Thought. Stevie Smith. OxBC

Rare are thy cheeks, Susanna, which do show. Upon Mistress Susanna Southwell, Her Cheeks. Robert Herrick. BeJo

Rare flower, leaf-fringed, or tender yellow gold. Yellow Sunflower of Szechwan. Chang Yü, *tr. fr. Chinese* by Irving Y. Lo. SuSp

Rare medieval Spirit! brooding seer! Dante. H. Cordelia Ray. CBWP-3

Rare music! I would rather hear cat-courtship. The Dancing Bear. Robert Southey. FM

Rare temples thou hast seen, I know. The Fairy Temple; or, Oberon's Chapel. Robert Herrick. CaPo

Rare Willie Drowned in Yarrow; or, The Water o Gamrie. *Unknown.* ESPB

Rare Willy Drowned in Yarrow. *Unknown. See* Willy's rare, and Willy's fair.

Rare Willy, *with music. Unknown. See* Willy's rare, and Willy's fair.

Raree Show, A. Stephen College. APAS

Rarely, rarely, comest thou. Rarely, Rarely, Comest Thou. Shelley. EnRP; OBNC; TrGrPo

(Barely, rarely, comest thou. CH; TEP

(Invocation: "Rarely, rarely, comest thou.") GTBS; GTBS-P

(Song: "Rarely, rarely comest thou.") FHYEP; Mes

Rarely, Rarely, Comest Thou. Shelley. EnRP; OBNC; TrGrPo

Rarest Thyme, The. Thomas McCarthy. IB

Rascal far gone in treachery, A. *Unknown.* PeLi

Raspberries. Laurence David Lerner. EBEV

Rastafarians in miami speak. Miami Rastas. Alurista. ETG

Rat, The. W. H. Davies. OBWVE; OxBTC

Rat-a-tat-tat, Rat-a-tat-tat. The Postman. Clive Sansom. BoTP

Rat and the Elephant, The. La Fontaine, *tr. fr. French* by Marianne Moore. OBVE

Rat-fink Baby. Brothers at the Bar. Naomi Long Madgett. NBV

Rat is in the trap, it is in the trap, The. Song of a Rat. Ted Hughes. CMoP; NoP

Rat Song. Margaret Atwood. NIP

Rat too has a skin (or tan), A. Sans Equity and sans Poise. Confucius, *tr. fr. Chinese* by Ezra Pound. *Fr.* Yung Wind. CTC

Rata blooms explode, the bow-legged tomcat, The. James K. Baxter. *Fr.* Autumn Testament. PeNZ

Ratatouille. Gina Berkeley. PeLi

Ratcatcher's Daughter, The. *Unknown.* ChTr; GBP; OxBoLi

Ratcliffe Highway. *Unknown.* OxBSS

Rath in front of the oak wood, The. *Unknown.* NOIV

"Rather dead than spotted"; and/ believe it. Then the Ermine. Marianne Moore. PoA

Rather extreme vegetarian, A. "Sagittarius." PeLi

(Reason, The.) IHNG

Rather notice, mon cher. To a Solitary Disciple. William Carlos Williams. VGW

Rather skinny beauty, you'll find,/ is Diocleia, A. Argentarius, *tr. fr. Greek* by Fleur Adcock. GrAn

Rather than Live in Snuff, will be put out. *(LL)* On the Snuff of a Candle. Sir Walter Ralegh. FaBoEE; OBD; SiPS

Rather than your fine hotels. Sightseers in a Courtyard. Nicolás Guillén, *tr. fr. Spanish* by Langston Hughes. TTY

Rather Too Good, Little Peggy! Adelaide O'Keeffe. FaBoUs

Rather unexpectedly, the lights went out. Brownout. Tony Perez. TSaS

Rathers. Mary Austin. FaPON

Ratio. Lillian Morrison. UnAS

Ration Card, The. Liz Sohappy Bahe. CDW; FaPON

Rats by night such mischief did, The. Fable XXI: The Rat-catcher and Cats. John Gay. OxAEP-1

Rats, Ducks, Dogs, Cats, Pigs. *Unknown. See* Three Young Rats.

Rat's Tight Schedule, The. Russell Edson. AnAn

Rattan bed, paper netting. I wake from morning sleep. Li Ch'ing-chao, *tr. fr. Chinese* by Willis Barnstone *and* Sun Chu-chin. BoWoP

Rattat! Rattat! Postman's Knock. Rodney Bennett. BoTP

Rattle. Peter Blue Cloud. HATNAP

Rattle Bag, The. Dafydd ap Gwilym, *tr. fr. Welsh* by Joseph Clancy. NBLV; RB

Rattle creak very white. Sheep's Skull. Lucy Jane Simpson. OBD

Rattler, Alert. Brewster Ghiselin. HAP; WeW

Rattlesnake. Brewster Ghiselin. FoLa

Rattlesnake, The. Alfred W. Purdy. OBAP

Rattlesnake Ceremony Song. *Unknown, tr. fr. Yokuts Indian* by A. L. Kroeber. OBAP

Rattlesnake Country. Robert Penn Warren. NAAL-2; VCAP

Rattlesnake Dance, Coronado Hills, El Paso, 1966. Ray Gonzáles. AfAz

Rattlesnakes have begun to come out, The. Snakes. Peter Wild. AmPA

Rattling little cart and patches of yellow dust at dusk. A Ballad of the Little Cart. Ch'en Tzu-lung, *tr. fr. Chinese* by Wu-chi Liu. SuSp

Rauf Coilyear, *sels. Unknown.*

"Coilyear, gudlie in feir, tuke him be the hand, The." OxBS

"Quhen thay war seruit and set to the Suppar." ScCV

Rav, The/ of Northern White Russia declined. Illustrious Ancestors. Denise Levertov. AmPP; MoP; NAAL-2; NOBA; VGW

Ravaged Villa, The. Herman Melville. CTC; NOBA; PoEL-5

Raven, The. Samuel Taylor Coleridge. WiR

Raven, The. Poe. AmPP; AnAmPo; BeLS; BLPA; CH; CoGr; EBEvV; EBNV; FaBoBe; FaBoCh; FaBV; GGP; GN; GoJo; HeIP; ImGa; LiTA; NAAL-1; NIP; NOBA; OBCA; OBNV; OxBA; PoRA; PWR; TAP; TFi; UV, abr.; VPP; WBLP

Raven, The. E. A. Robinson, *after* Nicarchus. AWP; FaBoEE; OBAL

Raven, The. Sarah Helen Whitman. AmWP

Raven croak'd as she sate at her meal, The. The Witch. Robert Southey. WiR

Raven Days, The. Sidney Lanier. AnAmPo; OxBA

Raven dies, The. *(LL)* The Raven. E. A. Robinson, *after* Nicarchus. AWP; FaBoEE; OBAL

Raven eyes blink. Raven is Two-Faced. Robert H. Davis. HATNAP

Raven, from the dim doninions. The Raven. Sarah Helen Whitman. AmWP

Raven, gather us to that dark breast. Raven Tells Stories. Robert H. Davis. HATNAP

Raven himself is hoarse, The. Shakespeare. *Fr.* Macbeth. EBEvV

Raven is Two-Faced. Robert H. Davis. HATNAP

Raven sat upon a tree, A. The Sycophantic Fox and the Gullible Raven. Guy Wetmore Carryl. BLPA; FiBHP; NBLV; OBCA

Raven Sweat. Rochelle Wallace. EaPr

Raven Tells Stories. Robert H. Davis. HATNAP

Ravenglass Railway Station, Cumberland. Norman Nicholson. NYBP

Ravening Coyote comes. Three Songs of Mad Coyote. *Unknown, tr. fr. Nez Percé Indian* by Herbert J. Spinden. STP

Raven/Moon. Anita Endrezze-Danielson. VoR

Ravenna. Louis MacNeice. OBTV

Ravenna Bridge. Leslie Norris. AngWe

Ravens. Ted Hughes. InPS; NAs

Ravens gnawing/ men's necks. Before the Last Battle. *Unknown, tr. fr. Irish* by Thomas Kinsella. *Fr.* Táin, The. NOIV

Raven's Monologue. Ivan V. Lalic, *tr. fr. Serbo-Croatian* by Charles Simic. HSix

Ravine on a Cold Evening. Li Ho, *tr. fr. Chinese* by Maureen Robertson. SuSp

Raving warre, begot. Thomas Campion. AAS

Ravings. Tom Hood. BXAP

Ravin's of Piute Poet Poe. C. L. Edson. BXAP

Ravished by all that to the eyes is fair. Michelangelo, *tr. fr. Italian by* George Santayana. *Fr.* Three Poems. AWP

Ravished in that fair *Via Lactea*. (*LL*) Upon Julia's Breasts. Robert Herrick. CaPo; NoP

Raw and overwhelming danger, The. The Unpredictable. Thomas Blackburn. OPOP

Raw Flesh, *sels*. Vasco [*or* Vasko] Popa, *tr. fr. Serbo-Croatian*. Be Seeing You. PoSu, *tr. by* Anne Pennington In the Village of My Forefathers. PoSu, *tr. by* Anne Pennington Time Swept Up. PoSu, *tr. by* Anne Pennington

Raw Honey. Lewis MacAdams. UL

Rawk o' the autumn, The. John Clare. SCGP

Rawk o' the autumn hangs over the woodlands, The. The Rawk o' the autumn. John Clare. SCGP

Ray Charles at Mississippi State. Tom Dent. NBV

Ray Charles is the black wind of Kilimanjaro. Blues Note. Bob Kaufman. PoBA

Rayle not to far. (*LL*) Gup, Scot! John Skelton. OxBoLi

Raynsford, a knight, fit to have served King Arthur. Sir John Raynsford's Confession. John Harington. NoSic

Rays of sunlight quietly fishing from tall trees. The Real World. Kevin Hart. FaBoMA

Rays of the low sun, The. To the Tune "The Bodhisattva's Barbaric Headdress." Lady Wei, *tr. fr. Chinese by* Kenneth Rexroth *and* Ling Chung. WPC

Rays of the sun, The. The Shepherd and His Flock. Mbuyiseni Oswald Mtshali. GrPl

Ray's third new car in half as many years. Family Reunion. Louise Erdrich. HATNAP; NoAM

Razón de Amor, *sels*. Pedro Salinas, *tr. fr. Spanish by* Linda Gutierrez *and* Lawrence Pitkethly.

Razors pain you. Résumé. Dorothy Parker. *Fr.* Some Beautiful Letters. AnAmPo; DL; HeIL; HeIP; IHNG; InPK; NAAL-2; NALW; NoP; OBAL; Poetr; TrJP; UV

Razzle Dazzle! Whiskers Meets Polly. Michael Stillman. TLR

Re-encounter. Joaquim Paço D'Arcos, *tr. fr. Portuguese by* Roy Campbell. PeSAV

Re-forming the Crystal. Adrienne Rich. TAP

Re-plyed, extorted, oft transposed, and fleeting. Sea Voyage. William Empson. CMoP

Re-reading Jane. Anne Stevenson. NALW

Re-registration of the duple name. (*LL*) Sea Side. Robert Graves. MeMBP

Re: Snow Jobs/ We Have Got. Robert Kelly. BCF

Re that winter cloak. Slow Giving. Ibn al-Rumi, *tr. fr. Arabic by* Omar S. Pound. ArPe

Re: the question of poems. Memo from the Desk of X. Donald Justice. TwCP

Rea(be)rran(com)gi(e)ngly/,Grasshopper. (*LL*) R-P-O-P-H-E-S-S-A-G-R. E. E. Cummings. AmPP; NoP; PoE; PPP

Reach for arrows of falling light. A man once sang. Falling Moon. Roberta Hill Whiteman. CDW

Reach like you never reached before past Night's somber robes. Tauhid. Askia Muhammad Touré. PoBA

Reach me down my Tycho Brahe, I would know him when we meet. The Old Astronomer to His Pupil. Sarah Williams. BLPA

Reach, with your whiter hands, to me. To the Water Nymphs, Drinking at the Fountain. Robert Herrick. BeJo; CaPo; NAEL-1

Reached no Alps: or, knows no Alps to reach. (*LL*) Pygmies Are Pygmies Still, Though Percht on Alps. Gwendolyn Brooks. LCAP; PoNe

Reaches as far as my little boat. (*LL*) Night at Anchor by Maple Bridge. Chang Chi. OHMPC

Reaching out into the sea, passing the waves its exhaust smoking. Mission Work-Boat. *Unknown, tr. fr. Aborigine by* Mungayana Nundhirribala. NOBAu

Reaching the Horizon. Robert Mezey. NaP

Reaching to light my cigarette your hand. Jumping into Joy. Marg Yeo. DT

Reaching Yellow River. Roberta Hill Whiteman. HATNAP

Re-act for Action ("Re-act to Animals.") Don L. Lee. BPo

Read a little Apollinaire and love it. French Desire. Keith Abbott. UL

Read about the Buddhist monk. Dilemma. Patricia Beer. OxBC

Read and committed to the flames, I call. On Not Being Milton. Tony Harrison. *Fr.* School of Eloquence, The. FaBoPV; NAEL-2; NoAM; SCBI

Read here the moral roundly writ. Boxing. Kipling. *Fr.* Verses on Games. OtMeF

Read here,/ This is the story of Evarraman. Evarra and His Gods. Kipling. MoBrPo

Read in My Face. Samuel Daniel. *Fr.* To Delia. EnRePo; ESo

Read in my face a volume of despairs. Read in My Face. Samuel Daniel. *Fr.* To Delia. EnRePo; ESo

Read it, and give it her to sing. (*LL*) The Ballad of Villon and Fat Madge. Villon. FaBoBl; OBVE

Read it not, noble lords. Shakespeare. *Fr.* Coriolanus. OxAEP-1

Read me Euripides. The Follies of Adam. Theodore Roethke. ChIV-1

Read Me, Please! Robert Graves. NYBP

Read my riddle, I pray. An Equal. *Unknown*. ReMoGo

Read no more of cantos Pisan. To a Young Poet. Harry M. Meacham. GoYe

Read not Milton, for he is dry; no Shakespeare. Proverbial Philosophy: Of Reading. Charles Stuart Calverley. FaBoCo

"Read out the names!" and Burke sat back. The Fighting Race. Joseph I. C. Clarke. AnAmPo; BLPA; BLPL; PAH

Read, sweet, how others strove. Emily Dickinson. AH; NOCV

Read the Bible, it will tell. The Bible. L. A. J. Moorer. CBWP-3

Read to shove up the privates of the world. (*LL*) Ego. Robert Siegel. PoA

Read up and down. *Unknown*. RoPo

Read yr/ exile. A Poem for a Poet. Don L. Lee. PoBA

Readen ov a Head-Stwone. William Barnes. CH

Reader, The. Thomas Merton. CRP

Reader, The. Wallace Stevens. SAmP

Reader, behold! this monster wild. Infant Innocence. A. E. Housman. FaBoNo; NOBL

Reader, beneath this turf I lie. Thomas Brown. FaBoEE

Reader! I am no poet: but I grieve! To the Reader. Urian Oakes. SCAP

Reader, I was born and cried. Epitaph on the Fart in the Parliament House. John Hoskyns. FaBoEE

Reader, I would not have thee mistake. His Own Epitaph, When He Was Sick. John Hoskyns. FaBoEE

Reader, listen ere we go. The Book's Creed. Joseph S. Cotter, Sr.. AAP

Reader over My Shoulder, The. Robert Graves. MeMBP; NAEL-2

Reader, pass on, nor idly waste [*or* don't waste] your time. In Peterborough Churchyard. Paulus Silentiarius, *tr. fr. Greek*. FaBoEE; NOBL

Reader, preserve thy peace: those busie eyes. An Elegie upon the Death of the Lord Hastings. Sir John Denham. SeCV-1

Reader, stay,/ And if I had no more to say. An Epitaph on Master Philip Gray. Ben Jonson. FaBoEE

Reader upon this field of Marble see. Inscription on Monument of Dorothy, Lady Hubert. Anne King. KTR

Reader, when these dumb stones have told. Another [On the Duke of Buckingham]. Thomas Carew. NOSC

Readers and the hearers like my books, The. The Critics. Martial, *tr. fr. Latin by* Sir John Harington. AWP

Readers of the *Boston Evening Transcript*, The. The *Boston Evening Transcript*. T. S. Eliot. InPK

Reading. Elizabeth Barrett Browning. *Fr.* Aurora Leigh. GN

Reading, The. David Dooley. BAP-89

Reading, The. Gabriel Gbadamosi. HBAPE

Reading. P'i Jih-hsiu, *tr. fr. Chinese by* William H. Nienhauser. SuSp

Reading. Jean-Joseph Rabéarivelo, *tr. fr. French by* Ellen Conroy Kennedy. NegPo

Reading a Medal. Terence Tiller. FaBoTw; GTBS-P

Reading a Story to My Child. Primus St. John. ETG

Reading Aquinas. Michael Heffernan. WeW

Reading beside Ox Tail River, *sels*. Cheng Chen, *tr. fr. Chinese by* William Schultz.

Reading Books, *sels*. Rai San'yo, *tr. fr. Chinese by* Burton Watson.

Reading Emerson. Cottonmouths are moving mildly. Lake Drummond Dream. Dave Jeddie Smith. VCAP

Reading Horace outside Sydney: 1970. David Malouf. FaBoMA

Reading how even the Swiss had thrown the sponge. Beyond the Alps. Robert Lowell. LCAP; NOBA

Reading in bed, full of sentiment. The Bat. Ellen Bryant Voigt. FoLa

Reading in Fall Rain. Robert Bly. GrPl

Reading in Li Po. After the Last Dynasty. Stanley Kunitz. TAP

Reading in my palanquin, I fall asleep and dream. Passing By Waterwheel Bay. Yang Wan-li, *tr. fr. Chinese by* Jonathan Chaves. SuSp

Reading in Place. Mark Strand. BAP-89

Reading in the Autumn. Shen Chou, *tr. fr. Chinese*. ImGa

Reading in the heat of noon. Summer Day. Yüan Mei, *tr. fr. Chinese by* Kenneth Rexroth. OHMPC

Reading in the Night. Roy Fuller. OxBC

Reading Indian Poetry. Ramona Wilson. VoR

Reading Lao Tzu Again in the New Year. Charles Wright. BAP-91

Reading Lesson, The. Richard Murphy. IPY; PBCIP

Reading Matter. Martin Sorescu, *tr. fr. Romanian.* CBNP

Reading Mother, The. Strickland W. Gillilan. BLPA

Reading my Verses, I like't them so well. The Poetresses Hasty Resolution. Margaret Cavendish, Duchess of Newcastle. KTR

Reading Myself. Robert Lowell. HCAP; NAAL-2; TAP; VCAP

Reading of the Rattlesnake. Lynn Lonidier. SRLS

Reading *Paradise Lost* in Protestant Ulster 1984. Seamus Deane. BiHa; PBCIP

Reading Pornography in Old Age. Howard Nemerov. NoAM

Reading Room, The New York Public Library. Richard Eberhart. GOYP

Reading some Russian novel. White Gloves. William Plomer. PeSAV

Reading the Bible Backwards. Eleanor Wilner. BAP-90

Reading the Book of Hills and Seas. T'ao Ch'ien, *tr. fr. Chinese by* Arthur Waley. ArNa

Reading the Books Our Children Have Written. Dave Jeddie Smith. HCAP

Reading the Brothers Grimm to Jenny. Lisel Mueller. NYBP

Reading the Collected Works of Li Po and Tu Fu: A Colophon. Po Chü-i, *tr. fr. Chinese by* Irving Y. Lo. SuSp

Reading the Facts about Frost in *The Norton Anthology.* George Starbuck. BAP-89

Reading the Greeks, negro statesmen divided. Government Quarters. Harry Clifton. IB

Reading the Newspaper. William Cowper. *Fr.* Task, The. ECEV

Reading the Parable of the Cave. Living in the Cave. Adrienne Rich. AnAn

Reading the Sky. Rebecca Gonzales. AfAz

Reading the Unpublished Manuscripts of Louis MacNeice at Kinsale Harbour. Desmond O'Grady. PBCIP

Reading through your work tonight. Negative Passage. Michael Newman. PoA

Reading Time: 1 Minute 26 Seconds. Muriel Rukeyser. PBWP

Reading Walt Whitman. Calvin Forbes. NBV; PoBA

Reading your poems I am aware. A Letter to Peter Levi. Elizabeth Jennings. OxAEP-2

Readings, Forecasts, Personal Guidance. Kenneth Fearing. MoAmPo

Ready. Phoebe Cary. PAH

Ready. Margaret Junkin Preston. PWR

Ready we stand in San Juan town. Rain Magic Song. *Unknown, tr. fr. Tewa Indian by* H. J. Spinden. WTO

Reagan, The, *parody.* Richard Quick. FaBoPa

Real dangers. gambles. and the edge of death. (*LL*) What You Should Know to Be a Poet. Gary Snyder. NNaP; PoM

Real duel of Apollo, The. Apollo and Marsyas. Zbigniew Herbert, *tr. fr. Polish by* Czeslaw Milosz. PoSu, *tr. by* John *and* Bogdana Capenter

Real horse of a man. McTaggart, A. Big Ned. Tom McGurk. PeIV

Real is a wilderness, The. To Frank O'Hara. Harold Brodkey. PRA

Real Life. Bob Arnold. ETG

Real Muse, The. Tom Scott. PoA

Real People Loves One Another, The. Rob Penny. PoBA

Real poems are being written in outports, The. Without Benefit of Tape. Dorothy Livesay. NOBC

Real Presence. Ivan Adair. WGRP

Real Property. Harold Monro. BoNaP

Real Question Calling for a Solution, A. Robert Penn Warren. PPP

Real Thing, The. Michael O'Loughlin. IB

Real was always something that came out of streets, The. The Epiphany. George A. Strong. GoYe

Real Work, The. Gary Snyder. FoLa

Real World, The. Kevin Hart. FaBoMA

Realist, The. Carl H. Greene. NBV

Realistic dreams with a whiff of terror. 29-77-02. Artur Miedzyrzecki, *tr. fr. Polish by* Stanislaw Barańczak *and* Clare Cavanagh. PoSu

Reality. Léon Damas, *tr. fr. French by* Ellen Conroy Kennedy. NegPo

Reality. Sir Aubrey De Vere. WGRP

Reality. Frances Ridley Havergal. WGRP

Reality. Angela Morgan. WGRP

Reality Is an Activity of the Most August Imagination. Wallace Stevens. NoAM

Reality of Autumn, The. Duane Niatum. HATNAP

Reality U.S.A. Mark Halliday. NAmP90

Realization. Ananda Acharya. WGRP

Really I do not know. (*LL*) To Winky. Amy Lowell. OFC; SoCa

Really, it is not the. In This Age of Hard Trying, Nonchalance Is Good and. Marianne Moore. MeMAP

Realm of Fancy, The. Keats. *Fr.* Fancy. EnRP; GTBS; GTBS-P; OBEV

Reaper, The. Wordsworth. *See* Behold her, single in the field.

Reapers. Mathilde Blind. WPE

Reapers. Jean Toomer. BPo; CDC; HAP; MoP; NoAM; PoBA; Poetr; PPP; SoSe; TRP; WeW

Rear Guard, The. Irene Fowler Brown. PAH

Rear-Guard, The. Siegfried Sassoon. MoBrPo; NAEL-2; NoAM; OBWP; PoWW

Rear half had been run over, The. Half a Hedgehog. Miroslav Holub, *tr. by* Ewald Osers. PWE

Rear Vision. William Jay Smith. NYBP

Rearmament. Robinson Jeffers. OxBA

Rearrange a wife's affection? Emily Dickinson. NALW; PoEL-5

Reason. Ralph Hodgson. *See* Reason Has Moons.

Reason. Josephine Miles. InPK; NALW; NoAM; NoP; Poetr; TAP

Reason, The. "Sagittarius." *See* Rather extreme vegetarian, A.

Reason. Elizabeth Oakes Smith. *Fr.* Atheism. AmWP

Reason, The. Chris Van Wyk. PeSAV

Reason, A. Robert Creeley. NaP

Reason and Imagination. Blake. *Fr.* Milton. EnRP

Reason and Revelation. Dryden. *See* Dim, as the borrow'd beams of moon and stars.

Reason for Poetry, The. Nancy Morejón, *tr. fr. Spanish by* Anita Whitney. WPOW

Reason for Refusal. Martin Bell. PAW; PWE

Reason for Skylarks, The. Kenneth Patchen. NaP

Reason for the Pelican, The. John Ciardi. PDV

Reason Has Moons. Ralph Hodgson. FaBoCh; OxBSP

Reason I Stay on Job So Long. *Unknown.* GBP

Reason, Reason is my middle name. (*LL*) Reason. Josephine Miles. InPK; NALW; NoAM; NoP; Poetr; TAP

Reason shall steer, and skill disarm the gale. (*LL*) Columbus to Ferdinand. Philip Freneau. OBCA; PAH

Reason, tell me thy mind, if here be reason. Love and Reason. Sir Philip Sidney. *Fr.* Arcadia. SiPS

Reason we're asked to endure, The. Bill Greenwell. PeLi

Reason Why, The. George Clinton Rowe. AAP

Reason why, The. The Reason. Chris Van Wyk. PeSAV

Reason why i do it, The. The Making of Poems. Lucille Clifton. CrSp

Reason with them. Speak softly. Hide your stick. 13 Ways of Eradicating Blackbirds. Mark DeFoe. BXAP

Reasonable Affliction, A. Matthew Prior. NOEC; NoP; TrGrPo

Reasons. Thomas James. PoA

Reasons for and against Marrying Widows. Henricus Selyns. SCAP

Reasons for Laughter and Crying. Friedrich Rückert, *tr. fr. German by* Philip L. Miller. RiWo

Reasons for Music. Archibald MacLeish. MeMAP

Reasons That Induced Dr. Swift to Write a Poem Called "The Lady's Dressing-Room," The. Lady Mary Wortley Montagu. FaBoBl

Reassurance, The. Thom Gunn. PFL

Reassurance. Julia Vinograd. SRLS

Rebeca in a Mirror. Judith Rodriguez. CBAP

Rebecca. Susan Griffin. MDDM

Rebecca Hill. Brendan Kennelly. PWE

Rebecca 1942. R. M. Cooper. BTR

Rebecca 1944. R. M. Cooper. BTR

Rebecca, sweet-one, little-one. Rebecca. Susan Griffin. MDDM

Rebecca, Who Slammed Doors for Fun and Perished Miserably. Hilaire Belloc. NOBL

Rebecca's Hymn. Sir Walter Scott. *Fr.* Ivanhoe. EnRP

Rebecca's maid: a girl come from afar. Jacob and Esau. Else Lasker-Schüler, *tr. fr. German by* Rosemarie Waldrop. BoWoP

Rebel, The. Mari Evans. CRP; IHMS; PoBA

Rebel, *sels.* Irene Rutherford McLeod.
   "Beyond the murk that swallows me." WGRP

Rebel, The. Padraic Pearse. PeIV

Rebel, The. Innes Randolph. NBLV; OBAL; OxBoLi

Rebel, A. John Gould Fletcher. MoAmPo

Rebel Camp in the Hindu Kush. Gu Cheng, *tr. fr. Chinese by* Donald Finkel *with* Chang Sheng-Tai. SpMi

Rebel General, The. Chris Wallace-Crabbe. CBAP

Rebel [*or* Rebell] Scot, The, *sels.* John Cleveland.
   "How? 'Providence,' and yet a Scottish crew?" NOSC
   "Lord! what a goodly thing is want of shirts." OBSV
   Nature herself doth Scotchmen beasts confess. OBSV

Rebel Soldier, The. *Unknown. See* One morning, one morning, one morning in May.

Rebellion against the North Side. Naomi Shihab Nye. WeW

Rebellion shook an ancient dust. April Mortality. Léonie Adams. MoAB; MoAmPo

Rebellion Suite/Straight. No Chaser. Askia Muhammad Touré. BCF

Rebellious fools that scorn to bow. The Bracelet. Thomas Stanley. BeJo

Rebels. Ernest Crosby. PAH

Rebel's Progress. Tom Earley. OBWVE

Rebirth. Margaret E. Bruner. PoToHe

Rebirth. Kipling. OBNC

Rebirth. Antonio Machado Ruiz, *tr. fr. Spanish by* Robert Bly. NU

Rebirth. Catriona Stamp. BrRo

Re-birth. *Unknown, tr. fr. Bushman by* W. H. I. Bleek *and* Jack Cope. PeSA

Rebolushinary X-mas. Carolyn M. Rodgers. JB

Reborn. Kingsley Amis. OxBC

Reborn may be as great as any. (*LL*) The Field of Glory. E. A. Robinson. AnAmPo; MoAmPo

Rebuke by the Bishop of London, A. Victor Gray. PeLi

Rebuke Me Not. John Addington Symonds. Son

Rebuke to Robert Southey, A. *Unknown.* ECWP

Rebuttal of "A Family of Plants." Tien Ch'ien, *tr. fr. Chinese.* LHF, *tr. by* Hualing Nieh

Rebuttal of Ai Ch'ing, A. Ting Mang, *tr. fr. Chinese.* LHF, *tr. by* Hualing Nieh

Rebuttal of Tung-p'o's Poem on "Bathing the Infant," A. Ch'ien Ch'ien-i, *tr. fr. Chinese by* Irving Y. Lo. SuSp

Rec Room in Paradise. Tom Clark. UL

Recall. Reed Whittemore. NYBP

Recall that memory. To the Personalities in the Works by José Montoya and the Chucos of the Future. Evangelina Vigil. BCF

Recalled. E. A. Robinson. MeMAP

Recalling Former Travels, *sels.* Tu Mu, *tr. fr. Chinese by* A. C. Graham.
"Caught in a storm outside Cloud Gate Abbey." PLT
"Li Po put it in a poem, this West-of-the-Waters Abbey." PLT
"Whirled ten years beyond all bounds." PLT

Recalling the past years, my heart is often bewildered. Tune: "Decorous and Pretty." Kung Tzu-chen, *tr. fr. Chinese by* An-yan Tang. SuSp

Recalling War. Robert Graves. CMoP; LiTM; MeMBP; NoAM; OAEL-2; OBWP; PeFWW; PoWW

Recalling When I Was Drunk. Yüan Chen, *tr. fr. Chinese by* Dell R. Hales. SuSp

Recantation. Minuchihri, *tr. fr. Persian by* Omar S. Pound. ArPe

Recapitulations, *sels.* Karl Shapiro.
"We waged a war within a war." PoNe

Receipt for Stewing Veal, A. *At. to* John Gay. FaBoUs

Receipt for the Vapours. Lady Mary Wortley Montagu. *See* Why will Delia thus retire.

Receipt for Writing a Novel, A. Mary Alcock. ECWP

Receipt to Cure a Love Fit, A. *Unknown.* NOEC

Receipt to Cure [*or for*] the Vapours, A. Lady Mary Wortley Montagu. ECWP; NOEC; PBWP

Receive before you write, and write before you pay. How to Keep Accounts. *Unknown.* FaBoUs

Receive, dear friend, the truths I teach. Receive, dear friend, the truths I teach" ("Rectius vives.") Horace, *tr. fr. Latin by* Austin Dobson. *Fr. Odes.* AWP, *tr. by* William Cowper; OBVE, *tr. by* William Cowper
(Of thy lyfe [life], Thomas, this compass well mark. OBVE, *tr. by* Henry Howard, Earl of Surrey; SiPSBD, *tr. by* Henry Howard, Earl of Surrey
(To Licinius.) AWP, *tr. by* William Cowper
(You better sure shall live, not evermore.) OBVE, *tr. by* Sir Philip Sidney

Receive, dear friend, the truths I teach" ("Rectius vives.") Horace, *tr. fr. Latin by* Austin Dobson. *Fr. Odes.* AWP, *tr. by* William Cowper; OBVE, *tr. by* William Cowper

Received on Freedom's field of honor! (*LL*) The Brave at Home. Thomas Buchanan Read. AnAmPo

Receivers its annual reply! (*LL*) Altered look about the hills, An. Emily Dickinson. OxBA; PPP; SoSe

Recent earthquake, A. Lucilius. *tr. fr. Greek by* Peter Porter. GrAn

Recently I read, "pain is a great incentive." Inspiration Is Just a Guy Called Art. David Chaloner. VaA

Reception, The. June Jordan. FaBoWP; NMM

Recessional. Georgia Douglas Johnson. CDC; PoNe

Recessional. Kipling. AWP; BLPA; BLPL; BLRP; CoGr; EBEvV; FaBoPV; FaBV; GN; LiTB; MoBrPo; NoAM; NOBE; NOBVV; NoP; OBEV; OBNC; OxAEP-2; PlP; PWR; SCGP; TFi; TrGrPo; UnPo; UV; WBLP; WGRP

Recessional. Thomas MacGreevy. CIP

Recessional. Isaac Watts. *See* O God, Our Help in Ages Past.

Recessional for the Class of 1959 of a School for Delinquent Negro Girls. Joseph R. Cowen. PoNe

Rechargeable Dry Cell Poem. Jim Wayne Miller. GOYP

Recipe. Angela Greene. NWP

Recipe for a Pleasant Dinner-Party. *Unknown.* FaBoUs

Recipe for an Ocean in the Absence of the Sea. Richard Howard. TAP

Recipe for Happiness Khabarovsk or Anyplace. Lawrence Ferlinghetti. ArLo

Recipe for Hell-Broth, The. Shakespeare. *See* Thrice the Brinded Cat Hath Mewed.

Recipe for Living. Alfred Grant Walton. PoToHe

Recipe: Gourds. Nicander, *tr. fr. Greek.* FaBoUs

Recipe: Hare. Archestratus, *tr. fr. Greek.* FaBoUs

Recipe: Onions. Philemon, *tr. fr. Greek.* FaBoUs

Recipe: Pastime for the Unemployed. Tom Pickard. NBrP

Recipe: Sausage. Axionicus, *tr. fr. Greek.* FaBoUs

Reciprocity. John Drinkwater. PoA

Reciprocity. Vassar Miller. IHMS; MT

Recital. John Updike. OBAL

Recitative. Hart Crane. FaBoMo

Recitative. Iwan Goll, *tr. fr. German by* Patrick Bridgwater. *Fr.* Requiem for the Dead of Europe. PeFWW

Recitative. Iwan Goll, *tr. fr. German by* Patrick Bridgwater. *Fr.* Requiem for the Dead of Europe. PeFWW

Recitative: "Farmer's son is good and mad," The. Ronald McCuaig. NOBAu

Recklessly/ I cast myself away. Lady Izumi Shikibu, *tr. fr. Japanese by* Edwin A. Cranston. PBWP

Reckoning, The. Theodore Roethke. PoA

Reckoning, The. Marie Syrkin. BTR

Reckoning. Fay Zwicky. NOBAu

Reckoning A.M. Thursday. Doris Turner. JB

Reclining Figure. Donald Hall. LCAP

Recluse, The, *sels.* Wordsworth.
"On Man, on Nature, and on Human Life." EPCY; OAEL-2 (Prospectus [*incl. in* The Excursion].) EnRP; NoP; PoE
Sunbeam Said, Be Happy, The. FaBoRV

Recluses, The. Stuart Z. Perkoff. NeAP

Recogitabo Tibi Omnes Annos Meos. William Habington. *See* Time! Where Didst Thou Those Years Inter.

Recognition, The. Denise Levertov. VGW

Recognition of Eve, The. Karl Shapiro. *Fr.* Adam and Eve. ChIV-1; MoAB

Recoil of his M-16, The. (*LL*) Boot Camp Incantation. Martín Espada. UTF

Recollection, A. John Peale Bishop. LiTA; Son

Recollection, A. Frances Cornford. FaBoWP; NTP

Recollection Long Ago: Sad Music. Robert Penn Warren. *See* In Tennessee once the [heart of the] campfire glowed.

Recollection of Bellagio. William Meredith. Poetr

Recollection of the Night of the Fourth, A, *sels.* Victor Hugo.
"Is it children we are killing now? My God." OBD

Recollection of the Stone Circle near Keswick, A. Keats. *Fr.* Hyperion; a Fragment. EnRP; FaBoPP; OAEL-2

Recollections. Yunna Petrovna Moritz, *tr. fr. Russian by* Thomas P. Whitney. WoWa

Recollections of a Day's Journey in Spain. Robert Southey. OBTV

Recollections of "Lalla Rookh." John Townsend Trowbridge. OBAL

Recollections of Love. Samuel Taylor Coleridge. NAEL-2

Recollections of the Sun. A. L. Hendricks. NBrP

Recompensed?. H. Cordelia Ray. CBWP-3

Reconcilement, The. John Sheffield, Duke of Buckingham and Normandy. OBEV

Reconciliation. "Æ." OBMV; TrCP

Reconciliation. C. Day Lewis. PoWW; TwCP

Reconciliation, *sels.* Elizabeth Doten.
"God of the Granite and the Rose!" TrPWD

Reconciliation. Goethe, *tr. fr. German by* John Frederick Nims. *Fr.* Trilogy of Passion. STV

Reconciliation. Else Lasker-Schüler, *tr. fr. German by* Robert Alter. PBWP

Reconciliation, The. Archibald MacLeish. MoAmPo

Reconciliation. Siegfried Sassoon. NSI

Reconciliation. *Unknown, tr. fr. Late Middle Irish by* Kenneth Jackson. PeIV, *tr. by* Brendan Kennelly

Reconciliation. Walt Whitman. HAP; MeMAP; MoAmPo; NAAL-1; NoP; OBWP; OxBA; OxBSP; PAW; TrGrPo; WeW

Reconciliation: A Modern Version, The. Horace. *See* While, Lydia, I was lov'd of thee.

Reconnaissance. Arna Bontemps. BPo

Record is nothing, and the hero great. Lord De Tabley. EBVV

Recorder, tax collector, landlord, friends. Ode for the Burial of a Citizen. John Ciardi. LiTM

Recorders Ages Hence. Walt Whitman. HeIP; MoAmPo; SAmP

Recording Angel, The. Carolyn Forché. BAP-91

Records all agree, The. Against Te Rauparaha. Alistair Campbell. *Fr.* Sanctuary of Spirits. PeNZ

Recounting of Gods, The. Carole Bergé. Jaz

Recovery, The. Edmund Blunden. MoBrPo

Recovery. Ron Schreiber. PFL

Recovery, The. Thomas Traherne. *Fr.* Third Century, The. ESCV

Recovery Room: Lying-in, The. Helen Chasin. IHMS

Recreation. Audre Lorde. NoP

Recreation. Jane Taylor. OxBoLi; WoRP

Recruit, The. A. E. Housman. FaPoR; PIP

Recruited Collier, The. *Unknown. See* Oh, what's the matter wi' [*or* with] you, my lass.

Recruiting Drive. Charles Causley. OxBTC; PrIm

Recruiting Officer of Shih-hao. Tu Fu, *tr. fr. Chinese by* Irving Y. Lo. SuSp

Recruiting Sergeant, The. *Unknown.* OBET

Recruiting Serjeant, The, *sels.* Isaac Bickerstaffe. "What a charming thing's a battle!" NOEC

Recruiting Song. Michael Foster. UV

Rectitude, and the terrible upstanding member. Washington in Love. John Berryman. LCAP

Rectitude of the earth. (*LL*) I swear the earth shall surely be complete to him or. Walt Whitman. EaPr

Rectors and parish priests complained to the bishop. William Langland. *Fr.* Vision of Piers Plowman, Prologue, The. FaBoPV

Rector's pallid neighbor at The Firs, The. The Villagers and Death. Robert Graves. OBD

Recuerdo. Edna St. Vincent Millay. ImPo; LiTA; LiTM; MeMAP; NAAL-2; NoAM; OxBA; PoA; Poetr; TAP

Reculver Bay. Vicki Raymond. NOBAu

Recuperating in Chang Villa. Huang Tsun-hsien, *tr. fr. Chinese by* Irving Y. Lo. SuSp

Recurrence, The. Edwin Muir. MeMBP

Red. Gerald William Barrax. *Fr.* Old Gory, The. NBV

Red and blue and delicate green. *Unknown.* GBP (Riddle.) RoPo

Red-and-green leather-helmeted. TV Room at the Children's Hospice. Michael Ryan. NAmP90

Red and green neon lights, the jazz hysteria. Nuit Blanche: North End. Conrad Aiken. OxBA

Red and the Green, The. Anne Wilkinson. MoCV

Red and White. Carl Sandburg. ArNa

Red Ant Way, *sels. Unknown, tr. fr. Navajo Indian by* Jerome K. Rothenberg. "Red young men under the ground, The." STP

Red ants in a bamboo — the passion. *Malay Oral Tradition, tr. by* R. J. Wilkinson *and* R. O. Winstedt. WTO

Red as his guide-book grows, moves on, and offers up a prayer for France. (*LL*) The Three Musicians. Aubrey Beardsley. NOBVV; OBTV; PeVV

Red as life? (*LL*) Raid on a Cheyenne Village. Diane Glancy. LoHo

Red as the guardroom lamp. Heartbreak Camp. Roy Campbell. OxBTC

Red August Letter. Colette Inez. ETG

Red beast, The. Tasting the Wild Grapes. Mary Oliver. CAPP

Red Beauty. *Unknown, tr. fr. Gond Oral Tradition by* V. Elwin *and* S. Hivale. WTO

Red Book of Hergest, The, *sels. Unknown, tr. fr. Middle Welsh by* Ernest Rhys. Lament for Urien, The. OBMV

Red Boots On. Kit Wright. PeLV

Red brick [*or* bricks] in the suburbs, white horse on the wall. Ballad to a Traditional Refrain. Maurice James Craig. BlrV; TIRV

Red brick monastery in, The/the suburbs. The Semblables. William Carlos Williams. FaBoMo; NOBA

Red-bud, the Kentucky tree, No. Christmas at Freelands. James Stephens. TIRV; TrCP

Red carpet-ing, The. While Cecil Snores: Mom Drinks Cold Milk. James Cunningham. JB

Red cliffs arise. And up them service lifts. NW5 and N6. Sir John Betjeman. SCV

Red cockatoo crests caught on coral-trees. Early Arrival: Sydney. Vivian Smith. NOBAu

Red comb on its head needs no adorning, The. Inscribed on a Painting of a Cock. T'ang Yin, *tr. fr. Chinese by* Chiang Yee. SuSp

Red Cotton Night-Cap Country. Robert Browning. EBVVPR

Sels.
"Accordingly, on weighty business bound."
"And now let pass a week. Once more behold."
"Thus I bestride the railing, leg o'er leg."

Red Cow Is Dead, The. E. B. White. NBLV; NYBP

Red Cuckatoo, The. Po Chü-i, *tr. fr. Chinese by* Arthur Waley. ChTr

Red dawn clouds coming up! the heavens proclaim you. Morning Light Song. Philip Lamantia. NeAP

Red dew on floral chamber, white honeycomb. Boudoir Feelings. Li Shang-yin, *tr. fr. Chinese by* Eugene Eoyang *and* Irving Y. Lo. SuSp

Red Dog, The. Laura Jensen. LCAP

Red Dust. Philip Levine. NNaP; NoAM

Red earth, The. What He Said ("The red earth.") Peyanar, *tr. fr. Tamil by* A. K. Ramanujan. *Fr.* Nine on Happy Reunion. PLW

Red Embankment. Tu Mu, *tr. fr. Chinese by* John M. Ortinau. SuSp

Red Embroidered Carpet. Po Chü-i, *tr. fr. Chinese by* Wu-chi Liu. SuSp

Red eyes of rabbits, The. The Springtime. Denise Levertov. CoAP

Red-faced and romping in the wind. The Fiend. Ted Berrigan. PRA

Red Flag, The. Jim Connell. SWP

Red Flag, The. Michael Jackson. PeNZ

Red flag is up, The. We Meet in the Lives of Animals. Peter Everwine. NNaP

Red flame flowers bloom and die, The. Crosbie Garstin. CH

Red fool, my laughing comrade. To a Comrade in Arms. Alun Lewis. FaBoTw; MoBrPo

Red for Santa's fur-lined cloak. All in Red. Eileen Mathias. BoTP

Red fox, the vixen, The. Abnegation. Adrienne Rich. WPE

Red Geranium and Godly Mignonette. D. H. Lawrence. GTBS-P; NoAM

Red Geraniums. Martha Haskell Clark. BLPA

Red globes of light, the liquor-green, The. William Street. Kenneth Slessor. CBAP

Red Glow in the Sky, A. Alexander Blok, *tr. fr. Russian by* Jon Stallworthy *and* Peter France. OBVE

Red-Gold Rain, The. Sacheverell Sitwell. MoBrPo

Red granite and black diorite, with the blue. The Skeleton of the Future. "Hugh MacDiarmid." MoBrPo; OBMV; OBTV

Red-haired Man's Wife, The. James Stephens. MoBrPo

Red Hanrahan's Song about Ireland. W. B. Yeats. CMoP; FaBoCh; IIP; NOIV

Red Harlaw. Sir Walter Scott. *Fr.* Antiquary, The. OxBB

Red head, red head. Blackbird's Song. *Unknown.* GBP

Red Herring, The. *Unknown.* FaBoNo

Red Hills of Home. Chenjerai Hove. HBAPE

Red hot needle, A. Hornet. Anne Sexton. AnAn

Red in Autumn. Elizabeth Gould. BoTP

Red Indian Corpse. Peter Redgrove. OxBC

Red Iron Ore,, with music. *Unknown.* AS

Red is the battlefield. Tipputtolar, *tr. fr. Tamil by* A. K. Ramanujan. PLW

Red is the down which is covering me. Ankotarinya. *Unknown, tr. fr. Aranda by* T. G. H. Strehlow. CBAP

Red Jacket. Fitz-Greene Halleck. AnAmPo

Red Journeys, *sels.* Nellie Wong. "I dream red dreams, an oasis of fire and light." MDDM

Red lantern calls the spring clouds from my sleep, A. Wang Chien, *tr. by* William H. Nienhauser. *Fr.* Palace Poems. SuSp

Red Leaf, The. Page Sullivan. ImGa

Red Light. Amiri Baraka. SOTW

Red light is stuck, A. Why We Are Late. Josephine Miles. NALW

Red Lilies. Barbara Guest. PoM

Red lips are not so red. Greater Love. Wilfred Owen. CMoP; EnLoPo; FaBoMo; FaBoRV; GTBS-P; ImPo; LiTB; LiTM; MeMBP; MoAB; MoBrPo; MoP; NoAM; TFi

Red lotus incense fades on/ the jewelled curtain. Li Ch'ing-chao, *tr. fr. Chinese by* Kenneth Rexroth. BoWoP; OHMPC

Red-Man, The. Frank Prewett. HATNAP

Red Monkey. *Unknown, tr. fr. Yoruba by* Ulli Beier. *Fr.* Hunter Poems of the Yoruba. RB

Red neon sign, The. Any Little Woman. Rod Jellema. *Fr.* Four Voices Ending on Some Lines from Old Jazz Records. Jaz

Red Oak. Jim Barnes. *Fr.* Ex-Deputy Sheriff Remembers the Eastern Oklahoma Murderers, An. NGP, *sect.* ii

Red oak leaves rustle in the wind. The Leaves of a Dream Are the Leaves of an Onion. Arthur Sze. OpBo

Red o'er the forest glows the setting sun. John Keble. *See* November.

Red of the dawn! The Dawn. Tennyson. NAEL-2

Red on sun sky sail. Six Eagles. Thomas Love Peacock. VoR

Red, orange, yellow, green, eternal blue, eternal violet. (*LL*) Homage to the Philosopher. Babette Deutsch. TrJP

Red, orange, yellow, green, turquoise, blue, violet. Tune: "Deva-like Barbarian" — Ta-po-ti. Mao Tse-tung, *tr. fr. Chinese by* Eugene Eoyang. SuSp

Red Palm, A. Gary Soto. AfAz

Red paths that wander through the gray, and cells. With God Conversing. Gene Derwood. ImPo; LiTA; LiTM

Red Peonies. Wang Wei, *tr. fr. Chinese by* Irving Y. Lo. SuSp

Red Poppy. Tess Gallagher. NAmP90

Red, Red Rose, A. Burns. ArLo; AWP; BoLoP; CBLP; ChTr; FaBV; FF; GBL; HAP; HeIP; ImPo; InvP; NAEL-2; NIP; NOBE; NOEC; NoP; NTP; OAEL-1; OBEV; OtMeF; OxAEP-2; OxBS; PlP; PoEL-4; Poetr; PoLF; PrIm; ScCV; SCGP; TEP; TFi

Red Ridinghood. Nathan Alterman, *tr. fr. Hebrew by* Ruth Finer Mintz. MHP

Red river, red river. Virginia. T. S. Eliot. *Fr.* Landscapes. InPK; RB

Red River Valley. *Unknown.* AS; FaBoBe

Red Rock Canyon, Summer 1977, *sels.* Kitty Tsui.

Red Rock Ceremonies. Anita Endrezze-Danielson. CDW; VoR

Red rock wilderness, The. Sidney Keyes. *Fr.* Wilderness, The. LiTB; OBWP; PoWW

Red Rose, proud Rose, sad Rose of all my days! To the Rose upon the Rood of Time. W. B. Yeats. NoAM; NoP; TEP

Red Rose, proud Rose, sad Rose of all my days. *(LL)* To the Rose upon the Rood of Time. W. B. Yeats. NoAM; NoP; TEP

Red rose whispers of passion, The. A White Rose. John Boyle O'Reilly. OBEV; PeIV

Red Roses. Gertrude Stein. *Fr.* Tender Buttons. TTTS

Red rowans in the rain. Ambulance Train. W. W. Gibson. NSI

Red Sandalwood Mouth. Chao Luan-luan, *tr. fr. Chinese by* Kenneth Rexroth *and* Ling Chung. WPC

Red Sea. James Agee. *Fr.* Two Songs on the Economy of Abundance. MoAmPo

Red Sea Place in Your Life, The. Annie Johnson Flint. *See* Have you come to the Red Sea place in your life.

Red Shift, *sels.* P. Inman.

Red silk lines the chamber curtains, their tassels fringed with gold. Ravine on a Cold Evening. Li Ho, *tr. fr. Chinese by* Maureen Robertson. SuSp

Red sky at night. *Unknown.* OxNR

Red sky in the morning. *Unknown.* FaBoUs

Red Slope, *sels.* Tu Mu, *tr. fr. Chinese by* A. C. Graham. "Milky in the spring grotto stone fattens, sprouts goose-quills." PLT

Red stockings, blue stockings. *Unknown.* OxNR

Red String. Minnie Bruce Pratt. ETG

Red sun fills the sky and the earth, The. Suffering from Heat. Wang Wei, *tr. fr. Chinese by* Hugh M. Stimson. SuSp

Red Suspenders, Boxes of Cigars. Joseph Hansen. PFL

Red Thread of Honour, The. Sir Francis Hastings Doyle. OtMeF

Red upon grey. Red upon grey. *(LL)* Decoration. Mary Ursula Bethell. PeNZ

Red walls of the old temple emerge from the blur of the blue-green mountain. Lieh Mountain. Wang Shih-chieng, *tr. fr. Chinese by* Richard John Lynn. SuSp

Red Wheelbarrow, The. William Carlos Williams. AnAmPo; BLPL; CMoP; GrPl; HeIP; HoPM; InPK; LiTA; LiTM; MoAB; MoAmPo; MoP; NAAL-2; NIP; NoAM; NOBA; NoP; PoE; Poetr; PrIm; SAmP; SoSe; SOTW; TAP; TFi; TRP; TTTS; UnPo; WeW

Red Whiskey. *Unknown.* AmFP

Red, White and Blue. *Unknown. See* O Columbia, the gem of the ocean.

Red, White and Red, The. *Unknown.* AmFP; ISE

Red Wig, The. *Unknown.* CoMu

Red-winged Lourie, The. Noëline Barry. OBAP

Red Wolf came, and Passenger Pigeon. Roll Call. Wendell Phillips Stafford. NGP

Red young men under the ground, The. *Unknown, tr. fr. Navajo Indian by* Jerome K. Rothenberg. *Fr.* Red Ant Way. STP

Redbreast, The. Anthony Rye. Spl

Redbreast, The, *sels.* Wordsworth.

Redbreast, Early in the Morning. Emily Brontë. OHCV

Redbreast smoulders in the waste of snow, The. The Redbreast. Anthony Rye. Spl

Redbummed Sweeney bolts the gate. Sweeney, Old and Phthisic, among the Hippopotami. David Cummings. BXAP

Redde pro victoria. (LL) The Agincourt Carol. *Unknown.* OAEL-1; OBET

Redé rose and the lilie-flowr, The. *(LL)* Maiden in the mor lay. *Unknown.* MiEL; PoEL-1

Redeem Time Past. William Drummond of Hawthornden. *See* More oft than once Death whispered in mine ear.

Redeem Zion! Edward Sanders. *Fr.* Poem From Jail. PoBeRe

Redeemer, The. "Fiona Macleod." WGRP

Redeemer, The. Siegfried Sassoon. WGRP

Redemption. George Herbert. *Fr.* Temple, The. ESCV; FF; GeHe; HAP; InPK; InPS; JCP; LiTB; MeLP; NAEL-1; NOBE; NOCV; NoP; NOSC; PeECV; PoE; Poetr; SCGP; SCV; SeCP; SeCV-1; Son; SoSe; TEP; TFi; TrCP; WeW

Redemption's problem unto thee well solved. *(LL)* Milton. H. Cordelia Ray. BlSi; CBWP-3

Redeployment. Howard Nemerov. ArOW; LiTM; OBWP; PoWW; TrJP

Redesdale and Wise William. *Unknown.* ESPB

Redingote and the Vamoose, The. Richard Kendall Munkittrick. OBCA

Rediscovery. Kofi Awoonor. TTY

Redlight. Jean Pedrick. ETG

Redondo. Ron Koertge. NGP

Redoubted knights, and honorable Dames. Spenser. *Fr.* Faerie Queene, The. NoP

Redshanks, The. Julian Bell. OBMV

Reductions, *sels.* Lamberto Pignotti, *tr. fr. Italian by* Lawrence R. Smith.

Redwings. James Wright. NNaP

Redwoods, The. Louis Simpson. CoAP

Reed, The. M. Y. Lermontov, *tr. fr. Russian by* J. J. Robbins. AWP

Reed: I sank roots first of all, stood. Unknown, formerly at. to Cynewulf, *tr. fr. Anglo-Saxon. Fr.* Riddles (Exeter Book). ASW, *tr. by* Kevin Crossley-Holland

Reed Pipe, The. Ai Ch'ing, *tr. fr. Chinese.* LHF, *tr. by* Hualing Nieh

Reeds give, The. Small Song. A. R. Ammons. NoAM; NoP

Reeds of Innocence. Blake. *See* Piping Down the Valleys Wild.

Reeds of Runnymede, The. Kipling. FaBoEH

Reeking of unsolved crimes, the cop. Two Hookers. A. K. Redwing. VoR

Reel o' Tullochgorum, The. *(LL)* Tullochgorum. John Skinner. OxBS

Reeling Silk. Fan Ch'eng-ta, *tr. by* Wu-chi Liu. *Fr.* Four Songs in Imitation of Wang Chien. SuSp

Reever ryves at the gullie, The. Wemen's Wather. T. S. Law. OxBS

Reeves Timber Yard. John Hall. VaA

Referred Back. Philip Larkin. PRA

Refined Man, The. Kipling. *Fr.* Epitaphs of the War, 1914–1918. FaBoEE; FaBoTw; NoP; OBWP; PeFWW

Refiner's Fire, The. *Unknown.* BLRP

Refiner's Gold, The. Frances E. W. Harper. PWR

Refining Fire. L. A. J. Moorer. CBWP-3

Reflected in the pensioner's eye. Karoo Town. Robert Dederick. PeSA

Reflecting on the Aging-Process. Robert Peters. BXAP

Reflection. Mona Elaine Adilman. WoWa

Reflection. Elisabeth Eybers, *tr. fr. Afrikaans by the author.* PeSAV

Reflection, The. Edith M. Thomas. AmWP

Reflection. W. J. Turner. OBMV

Reflection, A. Thomas Hood. FaBoEE

Reflection: After Visiting Old Friends. John Allison. GrPl

Reflection and Advice. Ezra Pound. OBSV

Reflection by a Mailbox. Stanley Kunitz. TrJP

Reflection from Rochester. William Empson. PoA

Reflection from Sea and Sky. Walter Savage Landor. FaBoEE

Reflection in a Green Arena. Gregory Corso. VGW

Reflection in Red. Oku Onuora. PBCV

Reflection Kiss, one given, The. Some Kisses from *The Kama Sutra.* Hugo Williams. BoLoP

Reflection on Babies. Ogden Nash. FaBoUs; NBLV

Reflection on Ingenuity. Ogden Nash. RB

Reflections. Anita Barrows. NMM

Reflections. Barbara Burford. DT

Reflections, *sels.* George Crabbe. Late Wisdom. OBEV; TrGrPo

Reflections. Antoinette Deshoulières, *tr. fr. French by* Yvor Winters. PBWP

Reflections. Janet Dubé. DT

Reflections. Carl Gardner. PoBA

Reflections. Vivian Smith. CBAP

Reflections at Dawn. Phyllis McGinley. FiBHP; NBLV; NOBL

Reflections by a Main Entrance, *sels.* N. A. Nekrasov, *tr. fr. Russian by* Alan Myers.

Reflections in a Slum. "Hugh MacDiarmid." FaBoTw

Reflections of a Proud Pedestrian. Oliver Wendell Holmes. AnAmPo

Reflections on a Visit to the Burke Museum, University of Washington, Seattle. Gail Tremblay. HATNAP

Reflections on a Womb Which Is Called "Vacant." Jeanine Hathaway. IHMS

Reflections on Having Left a Place of Retirement. Samuel Taylor Coleridge. EnRP

Reflections on Hillsborough in Memoriam. T. H. Naisby. NOBAu

Reflections on Ice-breaking. Ogden Nash. AiP; BLPL; FaBoCo; ImPo; LiTM; NBLV; NoP; OBAL; PeLV

Reflections on Mirrors. Elder Olson. CRP

Reflections on Sounds and Language. Christopher Smart. *Fr.* Jubilate Agno. FaBoVe

Reflections, Written on Visiting the Grave of a Venerated Friend. Ann Plato. BlSi

Reflections yet related light orange white to boom-boom. Prewar Late October Sea Breeze. Robert Grenier. UL

Reflective. A. R. Ammons. HCAP; VCAP

Reflexion, The. Edward Taylor. *See* Lord, art thou at the table head above.

Reflexions on suicide, & on my father, possess me. Of Suicide. John Berryman. NoAM

Reflexions on the Seizure of the Suez, and on a Proposal to Line the Banks of That Canal with Bill. Howard Nemerov. NBLV

Reforger. Miriam Offenberg. BTR

Reformation. The Countess of Winchilsea. ECWP

Reformation of Manners, *sels.* Daniel Defoe. London. NOEC
"Search all the Christian climes from pole to pole." OBSV
"Yet Ostia boasts of her regeneration." OBSV

Reformer to His Father, A. James Simmons. BIrV

Refracted Lights. Celia Parker Wooley. WGRP

[Refrain]. (*LL*) No More Booze. *Unknown.* OBAL

Refrain. Mary Jo Salter. EOEF

Refrain. (*LL*) The Erie Canal. William S. Allen. AS

Refrains. John Hollander. AnAn

Refreshing rest, ecstatic dream. In the Grass. Annette von Droste-Hülshoff, *tr. fr. German by* James Edward Tobin. PBWP

Refrigerium. Cardinal Newman. OBNC

Refuge. Mabel E. McCartney. BLRP

Refuge at the One Step Down. Belle Waring. PBCAP

Refugee. Naomi Long Madgett. PoNe

Refugee Blues. W. H. Auden. *See* Say this city has ten million souls.

Refugee in America. Langston Hughes. GOA

Refugees, The. Randall Jarrell. MoAB; MoAmPo

Refugees. Louis MacNeice. LiTB

Refugees, The. Edwin Muir. NoAM

Refugees at Cobh. Sean Dunne. BiHa

Refusal, A. Barnabe Googe. EnRePo; NoP

Refusal, A. Thomas Hardy. FaBoCo; LiTB; MeMBP

Refusal to Mourn, A. Derek Mahon. PNI

Refusal to Mourn the Death, by Fire, of a Child in London, A. Dylan Thomas. BLPL; CMoP; EBEV; FaBoMo; FF; GTBS-P; HeIP; HoPM; ImPo; LiTB; LiTM; MeMBP; MoAB; MoBrPo; MoP; NoAM; NOBE; NoP; OAEL-2; OBWVE; OxAEP-2; OxBTC; PAW; PoE; PoWW; TEP; TFi; TwCP; UnPo

Refuse of Our Teeming Shores. Cordelia Candelaria. AfAz

Refused admission! Baby, Baby. The Returned Picture. Mary O'Donovan Rossa. IIP

Regained my freedom with a sigh. (*LL*) The Prisoner of Chillon. Byron. BeLS; EnRP; PoLF

Regard her well — the austere face. Röntgen Photograph. Elisabeth Eybers, *tr. fr. Afrikaans by* Jack Cope, Uys Krige, *and* Ruth Miller. PeSA

Regard, O reader, how it is with me. Look, in the Labyrinth of Memory. Delmore Schwartz. TrJP

Regard the capture here, O Janus-faced. Recitative. Hart Crane. FaBoMo

Regard the little needle. The Needle. Grace Cornell Tall. GoYe

Regarding yours, dear Mrs Nightingale. Mrs Nightingale. Martin Fagg. UV

Regarding yours, dear Mrs Worthington. Noël Coward. *Fr.* Mrs Worthington. UV

Regement of Princes., *sels.* Thomas Hoccleve. Admirer's Lament of Chaucer, An. EPCY

Regeneration. Henry Vaughan. ChIV-1; ESCV; GeHe; JCP; MeLP; NAEL-1; NoP; PoE

Regent's Park Terrace. Bernard Spencer. FaBoPP

Reggae fi Dada. Linton Kwesi Johnson. NBrP; PBCV

Regina. Mary Elizabeth Coleridge. NALW

Reginald Pugh, The Man Who Came from the Army. Emma Lee Warrior. HATNAP

Region desolate and wild, A. Hayeswater. Matthew Arnold. *Fr.* Hayeswater Boat, The. FaBoPP

Region of life and light! The Life of the Blessed. Luís de León, *tr. fr. Spanish by* Bryant. AWP

Regions of Tyre are noted, The. Meleager, *tr. fr. Greek by* Peter Whigham. GrAn

Register of the Martyrs, The, *sels. Unknown.*
"When raging reign of tyrants stout." FaBoEH

Regnava nel silenzio. Aria. Briar Wood. NWP

Regrat. William Drummond of Hawthornden. PoEL-2

Regret. *Malay Oral Tradition, tr. by* R. J. Wilkinson. WTO

Regret, a bright meander on the nights. A Botanical Trope. William Meredith. Poetr

Regret and Refusal. *Unknown, tr. fr. Tewa Indian by* H. J. Spinden. WTO

Regretful Thoughts. Yü Hsüan-chi, *tr. fr. Chinese by* Geoffrey R. Waters. BoWoP

Regrets, *sels.* Joachim du Bellay, *tr. fr. French by* G. K. Chesterton. Hereux Qui, comme Ulysse, A Fait un Beau Voyage. AWP

Regrets, The, *sels.* C. H. Sisson.

Reguiem for a Friend, *sels.* Rainer Maria Rilke.
"Do not come back. Be, if you can bear it." OBF

Regular Bobbsey Twins./ That story. (*LL*) Cinderella. Anne Sexton. HeIP; InPS; NAAL-2

Rehearsal. Cyril Dabydeen. PBCV

Rehearsal, The. Horace Gregory. VGW

Reid at Fayal. John Williamson Palmer. PAH

Reid in the Loch Sayis, The. *Unknown.* OxBS

Reign of Peace, The. Mary Starck. WBLP

Reign over all. (*LL*) Curfew. Longfellow. AnAmPo; MeMAP; OxBA

Rein your sorry nags, boys, buckle the polished saddle. Dance on Pushback. James Still. GrPl

Reincarnating Pythagoras, say. Ausonius, *tr. fr. Latin.* PeHV

Reincarnation. Mae Jackson. PoBA

Reincarnation (I) ("Still, passed through the spokes of an old wheel.") James Dickey. HoPM

Reindeer and Engine. Josephine Jacobsen. GrPl; WPE

Reindeer Report. U. A. Fanthorpe. OBCP

Reinstate a black god low born of their thunder. (*LL*) Magic. Aimé Césaire. NegPo

Reivers they stole Fair Annie, The. Fair Annie. *Unknown.* CH

Rejected. Lord Alfred Bruce Douglas. OHCV; PeVV

Rejected, The. Louis Simpson. PRA

Rejected Lover, The. *Unknown.* AmFP

Rejected "National Hymns," The. "Orpheus C. Kerr." OBAL
Sels.
"Back in the years when Phlagstaff, the Dane, was monarch."
"Behold the flag! Is it not a flag?"
"Diagnosis of our hist'ry proves, A."
"In the days that tried our fathers."
"Little brown squirrel hops in the corn, The."
"My Native Land, thy Puritanic stock."
"One hue of our flag is taken."
"Pond'rous projectiles, hurl'd by heavy hands."
"Source immaterial of material naught."
"Sun sinks softly to his ev'ning post, The."

Rejected Wife, The. *Unknown. See* Entering the hall, she meets the new wife.

Rejection, The. Sir Robert Ayton. NOSC

Rejoice. Joaquin Miller. PAH

Rejoice bather between two waters. Milorad Pavic, *tr. fr. Serbo-Croatian by* Charles Simic. *Fr.* Holy Mass For Relja Krilatica. HSix

Rejoice eleventh finger reckoner of stars. Milorad Pavic, *tr. fr. Serbo-Croatian by* Charles Simic. *Fr.* Holy Mass For Relja Krilatica. HSix

Rejoice holy bundles, sacred bundles. They Went to the Moon Mother. *Unknown, tr. fr. Zuni Indian by* Barbara Tedlock. STP

Rejoice in God. Christopher Smart. *Fr.* Jubilate Agno. FaBoVe; PoE

Rejoice, Let Alleluias Ring. Sister M. Cherubim Schaefer. AH

Rejoice! let me dream of your felicity. (*LL*) You that in love find[e] luck[e] and abundaunce [*or* habundance]. Sir Thomas Wyatt. AAS; SiPS; SiPSBD

Rejoice mason of years. Milorad Pavic. *Fr.* Holy Mass For Relja Krilatica. HSix

Rejoice, O Bridegroom! *Unknown, tr. fr. Hebrew by* Israel Abrahams. TrJP

Rejoice, O youth, in the lovely hind. Moses ibn Ezra, *tr. fr. Hebrew by* Solomon Solis-Cohen. *Fr.* Wedding Song in honor of R. Solomon ben Matir. TrJP

Rejoice, rejoice, brave patriots, rejoice! Reparation or War. *Unknown.* PAH

Rejoice singer of songs for the deaf. Milorad Pavic. *Fr.* Holy Mass For Relja Krilatica. HSix

Rejoice you sots, your idol's come again. Upon the King's Return from Flanders. Henry Hall. APAS
(Upon the King's Return from Flanders, 1695.) NOSC

Rejoice you who sleep with a finger in your ear. Milorad Pavic. *Fr.* Holy Mass For Relja Krilatica. HSix

Rejoicing at the Arrival of Chi'en Hsiung. Po Chü-i, *tr. fr. Chinese by* Arthur Waley. AWP

Rejoicing/ because we had met again. The Good Dream. Denise Levertov. NNaP

Rejoicing That Attend the Murder of Famous Men, The. Robley Wilson, Jr. PBCAP

Rejoicing the Spirits. Fan Ch'eng-ta, *tr. by* Wu-chi Liu. *Fr.* Four Songs in Imitation of Wang Chien. SuSp

Relapse, The. Thomas Stanley. BeJo; NOSC; OBEV

Relapse, The. Henry Vaughan. ESCV; TrCP

Relating to Robinson. Weldon Kees. NaP

Relations. Orerulavanar, *tr. fr. Tamil by* A. K. Ramanujan. PLW

Relatives are leaning over, staring expectantly, The. "Dreadful Has Already Happened, The." Mark Strand. HCAP; NoAM; VCAP

Relativities. Louis Untermeyer. BXAP

Relativity. *At. to* Arthur Buller. *See* There was a young lady named [*or* called] Bright.

Relax. This won't last long. Poem for People Who Are Understandably Too Busy to Read Poetry. Stephen Dunn. GOYP

Relaxation. Dick Gallup. UL

Relaxed Abalone, The. Rosemarie Waldrop. InPK

Relaxed, nothing to do. Letting My Feelings Out. Yü Hsüan-chi, *tr. fr. Chinese by* Geoffrey R. Waters. BoWoP

Relaxing all day in this tropical atmosphere. Foreign Aid. Lionel Kearns. NOBC

Relearning the Alphabet. Denise Levertov. NOBA

Release. D. H. Lawrence. CMoP

Release, The. Adah Isaacs Menken. CBWP-1

Released. Richard Dehmel, *tr. fr. German by* Philip L. Miller. RiWo

Released [*or* Releas'd] from the noise of the butcher and baker. Jinny the Just. Matthew Prior. NOBE; NOEC; OBEV; PoEL-3

Released their own three men. (*LL*) Robin Hood Rescuing Three Squires. *Unknown.* ESPB

Relent, my dear yet unkind Coelia. William Percy. *Fr.* Coelia. AAS; Son

Relentless, black on white, the cable runs. T-Bar. P. K. Page. NoAM; NOBC

Relic, The. John Donne. EllL; EnRePo; FaPoB; FHYEP; GBL; HAP; HeIP; ImPo; LiTB; NOBE; NoP; NOSC; OAEL-1; PoEL-2; PPP; TFi

Relic, The. Robert Silliman Hillyer. GoYe

Relic. Ted Hughes. NAEL-2

Relief. Charles Vildrac, *tr. fr. French by* Christopher Middleton. PeFWW

Relief of Myopia, The. U. A. Fanthorpe. Spl

Relief of putting fingers on the keyboard, The. Thanking My Mother for Piano Lessons. Diane Wakoski. NoAM

Religio Laici. Dryden. SeCV-2
Sels.
"But if there be a power too just and strong." NOCV
"Dim, as the borrow'd beams of moon and stars." NOSC; OAEL-1
(Reason and Revelation.) 09OBS
"Thus man by his own strength to Heaven would soar." NOCV; WGRP

Religio Medici, *sels.* Sir Thomas Browne.

Religion. John Donne. *See* Kind pity [*or* Kinde pitty] chokes my spleen[e]; brave scorn forbids.

Religion. Henry Vaughan. ESCV; NOCV; OAEL-1; OxAEP-1; PeECV; TOF

Religion and Doctrine. John Milton Hay. WGRP

Religion and the Lower Classes. Evan Lloyd. *Fr.* Methodist, The. NOEC

Religion Back Home. William Stafford. OBAL

Religion is Revelation. Lew Welch. EaPr

Religion stands, the Church blocking the sun. (*LL*) The Landscape near an Aerodrome. Stephen Spender. LiTM; MoAB; MoBrPo; NoAM; OxBTC

Religious Musings, *sels.* Samuel Taylor Coleridge.
"Lovely was the death." EnRP
"There is one Mind, one omnipresent Mind." WGRP

Religious Use of [Taking] Tobacco. Robert Wisdome. EllL; SCGP

Religious wars of Europe have been numbered with the past, The. The Peonage System. L. A. J. Moorer. CBWP-3

Reliquary, The. Bruce Beasley. UTF

Reliquary. Hart Crane. PoA

Relique, The. John Donne. *See* When my grave is broke up again[e].

Reliques, *sels.* Edmund Blunden.

Relish. Miguel Algarin. BCF

Relish honey. If you please. To a Swallow. John Peale Bishop, *after* Euenus, *tr. fr. Greek.* GrAn; OBVE

Relishing this health, this singleness. The Night Skater. Frederick Morgan. ArNa

Reluctance. Robert Frost. CMoP; MoAB; MoAmPo; NOBA; OxBA

Relying on the disasters o' the war. March, 1941. Paul Goodman. LiTA

Remain, Ah Not in Youth Alone. Walter Savage Landor. *Fr.* Ianthe. HAP; OBNC

Remain, Rata. Te Puea Herangi, *tr. fr. Maori by* Margaret Orbell. PeNZ

Remain your only cause for tears. (*LL*) Epitaph for Erotion. Martial. FaBoEE

Remainder. Frederika Blankner. GoYe

Remains. Tony Harrison. FaBoVe

Remains, The. Mark Strand. NYBP; PPP

Remains of an Indian Village. Alfred W. Purdy. NOBC

Remains of blue bog children, The. Blue Bog Children. Roger Weingarten. AmPA

Remains the one thing that is new. (*LL*) The Egg. Jean Follain. AnRep

Remark. Charles Spear. PeNZ

Remarkable race are the Persians, A. *Unknown.* PeLi

Remarked a Tortoise to a Cat. The Vain Cat. Ambrose Bierce. SoCa

Remarked how ill we all dissembled. (*LL*) Merchant, to secure his treasure, The. Matthew Prior. AWP; EnLoPo; GTBS; GTBS-P; NOEC; NoP; PoRA

Remarks of Soul to Body. Robert Penn Warren. NAs

Rembrandt's Return of the Prodigal Son. Dick Davis. SCBI

Remedy Worse than the Disease, The. Matthew Prior. FaBoEE; TrGrPo

Remeidis of Luve. *Unknown.* OxBS

Remember. Joy Harjo. CrSp; SRLS

Remember! (*LL*) In Memoriam. Bernard Dadié. NegPo

Remember. Georgia Douglas Johnson. PoNe

Remember. *Unknown.* BXAP

Remember Dear Mary. John Clare. WeW

Remember, do you remember those solemn words. Thymocles, *tr. fr. Greek by* Peter Jay. GrAn

Remember Euboulos [*or* Eubolus], who lived and died sober? Leonidas of Tarentum, *tr. fr. Greek by* Fleur Adcock. GrAn; OBD

Remember Haiti, Cuba, Vietnam. Andrew Salkey. PBCV

Remember how unimportant. Milkweed. Philip Levine. LCAP

Remember I am a garnet woman. If I Am Too Brown or Too White for You. Wendy Rose. HATNAP

Remember it, although you're far away. Remember. *Unknown.* BXAP

Remember, it is forbidden to live in a town. Kiddushin 4:12. *Unknown.* EaPr

Remember last summer when God turned on the heat. The Honeymoon. James Simmons. PNI

Remember Me. Christina Rossetti. *See* Remember me when I am gone away.

"Remember me" implored the Thief! Emily Dickinson. ChIV-2

Remember me when I am dead. Simplify Me When I'm Dead. Keith Douglas. NoAM; OxBTC

Remember me when I am gone away. Remember [*or* Sonnet]. Christina Rossetti. AWP; BoLoP; CH; EBEvV; EnLoPo; FaBV; IMW; MeMBP; NOBE; NoP; OAEL-2; OBEV; OBNC; OxAEP-2; PlP; PoLF; PoRA; TFi; TrGrPo
(Remember Me.) OxBM

Remember me when you do pray. Anne Boleyn. FaBoEH

Remember Medusa? Eunice De Souza. AIW

Remember Not. Helene Johnson. PoNe

Remember now? Do you. Timocles, *tr. fr. Greek by* Kenneth Rexroth. PGA

Remember now, my Love, what piteous thing. A Carrion. Baudelaire, *tr. fr. French by* Allen Tate. AWP

Remember Now Thy Creator. Bible, *O.T. Fr.* Ecclesiastes. AWP; ChTr; OBVE

Remember [*or* Sonnet]. Christina Rossetti. AWP; BoLoP; CH; EBEvV; EnLoPo; FaBV; IMW; MeMBP; NOBE; NoP; OAEL-2; OBEV; OBNC; OxAEP-2; PlP; PoLF; PoRA; TFi; TrGrPo

Remember, Phyllis. Honeymoon. Samuel L. Albert. GoYe

Remember, remember the circle of the sky. *Unknown.* EaPr

Remember, remember!/ The fifth of November. The Gunpowder Plot. *Unknown.* FaBoUs
(Please to remember.) OxNR

Remember, Sinful Youth. *Unknown.* AH

Remember Stortford, Birthplace of Rhodes. Douglas Oliver. VaA

Remember Suez? Adrian Mitchell. OxBTC

Remember Tam o' Shanter's mare. (*LL*) Tam o' Shanter. Burns. BeLS; EBNV; EnRP; ImPo; NAEL-2; NoP; OAEL-1; OBNV; OxBS; PeLV; ScCV; TrGrPo, *sl. abr.*

Remember That Country. Jean Garrigue. VGW

Remember that night. *Unknown, tr. fr. Irish by* Thomas Kinsella. NOIV

Remember that old love song, Daphne? Delfica. Gérard de Nerval, *tr. fr. French by* Andrew Hoyem. NU

Remember the covenant of our youth. A Dying Wife to Her Husband. Moses ibn Ezra, *tr. fr. Hebrew.* TrJP

Remember the Day of Judgement. *Unknown.* MeEL

Remember the Day of Judgement. *Unknown.* MeEL

Remember the day the sea turned red. Plankton. Ruth Miller. PeSA

Remember the Last Things. *Unknown.* MeEL

Remember the loss is her own, if she loses it. *(LL)* Nonsense Verses. Charles Lamb. CBNP

Remember — the noise of moonlight. In the Lebanese Mountains. Nadia Tuéni. TSaS, *tr. by* Samuel Hazo

Remember the Poor. Matilda C. Edwards. PWR

Remember the sky that you were born under. Remember. Joy Harjo. CrSp; SRLS

Remember the sun in the autumn, its rays. The Secret Town. Abraham Sutzkever, *tr. fr. Yiddish by* Jacob Sonntag. TrJP

Remember the tree, Charlie? The Punishment. Susan Ludvigson. MT

Remember Thee! Remember Thee! Byron. BoLoP; IHNG; OxBSP

Remember then this lullaby! *(LL)* The Lullaby [*or* Lullabie] of a Lover. George Gascoigne. AAS; EBEV; EiL; EnRePo; HAP; NAEL-1; SCGP

Remember Then Thy Creator. Bible, *O.T. See* Remember Now Thy Creator.

Remember They Say. Lenrie Peters. PAW

Remember they say the dead. Remember They Say. Lenrie Peters. PAW

Remember those X-ray machines in shoe stores. On Hot Days. James Reiss. AmPA

Remember Thou Me. *Malay Oral Tradition, tr. by* R. J. Wilkinson *and* R. O. Winstedt. WTO

Remember Thy Creator Now. Peter Long. AH

Remember Times for Sandy. Carolyn M. Rodgers. JB

Remember us poor Mayers all. Song of the Mayers [*or* The Mayers' Song]. *Unknown.* CH; GBP

Remember? we were here once. love was a new cut. At the Jazz Club He Comes on a Ghost. Wanda Coleman. Jaz

Remember when. Among Strangers. William Stafford. NNaP

Remember when you are bemusing. Cyril Hughes. PeLi

Remember when you hear them beginning to say Freedom. Notes for My Son. Alex Comfort. *Fr.* Song of Lazarus, The. LiTM; MoBrPo

Remember when you were the first one awake, the first. Little Girl Wakes Early. Robert Penn Warren. PoE

Remember, while you are sleeping here, offshore. Evolution. John Blight. CBAP

Remembered City, The. Ken Smith. *Fr.* As It Happens. PWE

Remembered Morning. Janet Lewis. SoSe; WPE

Remembered Music. Sarah Helen Whitman. AmWP

Remembered on waking. *(LL)* I Love All Beauteous Things. Robert Bridges. BoTP; CMoP; EBEV; OxAEP-2; TrCP

Remembered them bareheaded round the altar. *(LL)* Chronicle. Aidan Carl Mathews. IB

Remembering. Akjartoq, *tr. fr. Eskimo.* WTO

Remembering. Xue Di, *tr. fr. Chinese.* TSaS, *tr. by* Iona Cook *and* Keith Waldrop

Remembering. Jill Maughan. NWP

Remembering. "Ping Hsin," *tr. fr. Chinese by* Kenneth Rexroth *and* Ling Chung. WPC

Remembering. Enid Shomer. BTR

Remembering Althea. William Stafford. NYBP

Remembering Carrigskeewaun. Michael Longley. PBCIP

Remembering Con Markievicz. C. Day Lewis. IIP

Remembering dark trees of home that keep. Pan in Battle. *Unknown.* PeNZ

Remembering Fannie Lou Hamer. Thadious M. Davis. BlSi

Remembering Golden Bells. Po Chü-i, *tr. fr. Chinese by* Arthur Waley. AWP

Remembering Lincoln. Frank Mundorf. GoYe

Remembering Lunch. Douglas Dunn. OxBC

Remembering Mexico, 1969. Barbara Lau. LoHo

Remembering Min Ch'e. Su Tung-p'o, *tr. fr. Chinese by* Kenneth Rexroth. OHMPC

Remembering Mykenai. Alfred Corn. SM

Remembering Nat Turner. Sterling A. Brown. PoBA; PoNe

Remembering. Pools. Remembering. Eyes. Remembering. Jimmy Woodsers. Randolph Stow. FaBoMA

Remembering Snow. Ralph Nixon Currey. PeSA

Remembering that war, I'd near believe. Night Operations, Coastal Command RAF. Howard Nemerov. ArOW

Remembering the descriptions by Wilson. Passenger Pigeons. Robert Morgan. MT

Remembering the past. What the Bones Know. Carolyn Kizer. VBLP

Remembering the Strait of Belle Isle or. Large Bad Picture. Elizabeth Bishop. NoP; NYBP; OxBC

Remembering the 'Thirties. Donald Davie. FaBoPV; OxBTC

Remembering what passed. Old Scent of the Plum Tree. Ietaka, *tr. fr. Japanese by* E. Powys Mathers. AWP

Remembering Yeats. Francis Stuart. BiHa

Remembers our meeting. Her eye moistens. *(LL)* I'm a strange creature, for I satisfy women. Unknown, formerly at. to Cynewulf. ASW

Remembrance. Emily Brontë. BLPL; BoLoP; BoWoP; CH; CoGr; EBEV; EnLoPo; GGP; HAP; IMW; LiTB; NAEL-2; NOBE; NOBVV; NoP; OBNC; OxAEP-2; PBWP; PoE; PoEL-5; Poetr; TEP; TFi; TrGrPo; WeW; WPE

Remembrance. Margaret E. Bruner. PoToHe

Remembrance. Joseph Freiherr von Eichendorff, *tr. fr. German by* Philip L. Miller. RiWo

Remembrance. Shakespeare. *See* When to the sessions of sweet silent thought.

Remembrance. Antoni Slonimski, *tr. fr. Polish by* Frances Notley. TrJP

Remembrance. Sir Thomas Wyatt. *See* They Flee [*or* Fle] from Me That Sometime Did Me Seek [*or* Seke].

Remembrance of a Color inside a Forest, A. Ray A. Young Bear. CDW

Remembrance of Beginnings of Things. Leah Goldberg, *tr. fr. Hebrew by* Ruth Finer Mintz. MHP

Remembrance of Collins, Composed upon the Thames near Richmond. Wordsworth. EPCY

Remembrance of My Friend Mr. Thomas Morley, A. John Davies of Hereford. OxBSP

Remembrancer of joys long passed away. To a Golden Heart, Worn round His Neck. Goethe, *tr. fr. German by* Margaret Fuller Ossoli. AWP

Remembrances, *sels.* John Clare.

Remembrances, *sels.* H. Leivick, *tr. fr. Yiddish by* Benjamin *and* Barbara Harshav.

Rememorised, Maurice Devane. Austin Clarke. *Fr.* Mnemosyne Lay in Dust. CMoP; 1970 ed.; IPY

Remind you, that there was darkness in my heart. Canticle of Darkness. Wilfred Watson. MoCV

Reminder, The. Thomas Hardy. CMoP; OBCP

Reminiscence. Vladimir Holan, *tr. fr. Czech by* George Theiner. PoSu

Reminiscence. Wallace Irwin. FiBHP; NOBL

Reminiscence, A. Anne Brontë. *See* Yes, thou art gone! and never more.

Reminiscence Forward. Molly Tenenbaum. BAP-91

Reminiscent Reflection. Ogden Nash. FaBoCo

Remittance Man. Judith Wright. NoAM

Remnant Ghosts at Dawn. Oliver La Grone. NBV

Remnant, hope, love — the unruined bird of Zimbabwe. *(LL)* My Birds. Solomon Mutswairo. PeSAV

Remnants and relics of a thousand years — here in a pit full of dust. The Book-burning Pit. Lo Yin, *tr. fr. Chinese by* Edward H. Schafer. SuSp

Remonstrance, A. John Gerrard. NOEC

Remonstrance, A. James Kenneth Stephen. NOBVV

Remonstrance in the Platonic Shade. Flourishing on an Height, *sels.* Ann Yearsley.
"These feeble sounds." ECWP

Remonstrance to the King. William Dunbar. OxBS; ScCV

Remorse. Sir John Betjeman. MoBrPo; OxBSP

Remorse, *sels.* Samuel Taylor Coleridge.
Voice Sings, A. CH
(Invocation, An.) PeECV

Remorse. Richmond Lattimore. PoA

Remorse. Shelley. *See* Away! the moor is dark beneath the moon.

Remorse Came Slowly. Nishi Junko, *tr. fr. Japanese by* Kenneth Rexroth *and* Ikuko Atsumi. WPJ

Remorse for Time, The. Howard Nemerov. Son

Remorse — is memory — awake. Remorse is memory awake. Emily Dickinson. NAAL-1; NOBA; NOCV; NoP; SAmP

Remote and ineffectual Don. Lines to a Don. Hilaire Belloc. FaBoCo; MoBrPo; OBSV; OtMeF

Remote music of his swans, their long. His Swans. Geoffrey Grigson. FaBoRV

Remote, unfriended, melancholy, slow. Goldsmith. *Fr.* Travel[l]er; or, A Prospect of Society, The. BIrV

Removal, The. *Unknown, tr. fr. Seminole Indian by* Frances Densmore. STP

Removal from Terry Street, A. Douglas Dunn. FaBoMo; FaBoVe; OxBC

Removal: Last Part. Carroll Arnett. VoR

Removal of Our Village, KwaBhanya, The. Mbuyiseni Oswald Mtshali, *tr. fr. Zulu by the author.* PeSAV

Remove me from this land of slaves. Ireland. Swift. FaBoPV

Remove my plate. *(LL)* When the Sun Shines More Years Than Fear. Janet Frame. PeNZ

Remove the Predicate. Clark Coolidge. UL

Removed!. *(LL)* Life in a Love. Robert Browning. FHYEP; OBNC; TrGrPo

Removed from Europe's feuds, a hateful scene. A Warning to America. Philip Freneau. TAP

Renaissance. Robert Avrett. GoYe

Renaissance Portrait of the Author, A. Frank O'Hara. PRA

Renaming, The. Valerie Sinason. BrRo

Renancing of Love, A. Sir Thomas Wyatt. *See* Farewell, love, and all thy laws [*or* lawes] for ever.

Renascence. Edna St. Vincent Millay. MoAB; MoAmPo

Sels.

    "All I could see from where I stood." PDV; PFP

Rencontre. Jessie Redmond Fauset. CDC

Rend America asunder. The Ship Canal from the Atlantic to the Pacific. Francis Lieber. PAH

Rendez-vous Manqué dans la Rue Racine. J. M. Synge. BIrV

Rendezvous. Mary Scott Fitzgerald. PoToHe

Rendezvous. Edna St. Vincent Millay. NALW

Rendezvous, The. Alan Seeger. *See* I Have a Rendezvous with Death.

Rendezvous. Alan Seeger. *See* I Have a Rendezvous with Death.

Rendezvous, The. Bernard Spencer. GTBS-P

Renegade Wants Words, The. James Welch. CDW

Renegado, The, *sels.* Philip Massinger.

René's Songs, *sels.* T. Carmi, *tr. fr. Hebrew by* Ruth Finer Mintz.

    First Song. MHP

    Second Song. MHP

    Third Song. MHP

Renewal. Steve Kowit. UL

Renewal, The, *sels.* George MacBeth.

Renewal, The. Theodore Roethke. VGW

Renewal, *sels.* Mustafa Zaidi, *tr. fr. Urdu by* Mahmood Jamal.

Renewal, A. James Merrill. OxBSP; SM; VCAP

Renewal by Her Element. Denis Devlin. CIP; IIP

Renewal of Strength. Frances E. W. Harper. PWR

Renouncement. Alice Meynell. BoLoP; MoBrPo; NOBE; OBEV; OBMV; OBNC; PlP; Son; WPE

Renowned as Black Geordie. Sporting the Plaid. Chris Wallace-Crabbe. NOBAu

Renowned Generations, The. W. B. Yeats. OxBoLi

Renowned Spenser [*or* Spencer] lye [*or* lie] a thought more nye [*or* nigh]. Elegy on Shakespeare. William Basse. ElL; FaBoRV

Rent. Jane Cooper. FYAP; TAP

Rent man knocked, The. Madam and the Rent Man. Langston Hughes. SAmP

Renunciation. Wathen Mark Wilks Call. WGRP

Renunciation. Emily Dickinson. *See* There came a day at summer's full.

Renunciation. Helen Hunt Jackson. AmWP

Renunciation. Padraic Pearse, *tr. fr. Irish by the author.* NOIV; PeIV

Renunciation. Lizette Woodworth Reese. AmWP

Renunciation, A. Edward de Vere, Earl of Oxford. *See* If women could be fair, and yet not fond.

Renunciation, A. Henry King. OBEV

Reparation or War. *Unknown.* PAH

Repartée. Charles Follen Adams. OBAL

Repast. Gertrude Tiemer-Wille. GoYe

Repeal of the Missouri Compromise Considered, The, *sels.* Elymas Payson Rogers.

    "Covetous Nebraskaites, The." AAP

Repeat that, repeat. Gerard Manley Hopkins. *See* Repeat that, repeat.

Repeat that, repeat. The Cuckoo. Gerard Manley Hopkins. MoAB; MoBrPo; OxBSP; RB; TTTS

    (Fragment, The "Repeat that, repeat".) FM

    (Repeat that, repeat.) NTP

Repeating fly, blueback, thumbthick — so gross, A. Harriet. Robert Lowell. NoP

Repentance. Brendan Behan, *tr. fr. Irish by* Ulick O'Conner. TIRV

Repentance. George Alexander Stevens. NOEC

Repentance. Louis Untermeyer. NBLV

Repetition. Anthony Rhodes. NSI

Repetition of Words and Weather. Ruth Stone. BoWoP

Repetitive Heart, The, *sels.* Delmore Schwartz.

    All Clowns Are Masked. LiTA; OxBA

    Calmly We Walk Through This April's Day. LiTM; PrIm

        (For Rhoda.) MoAB; MoAmPo; OxBA

        (Time Is the Fire.) LiTA

    "Heavy bear who goes with me, The." LiTA; LiTM; NoAM; NOBA; Poetr; TAP; TrJP; TwCP; UnPo

        (Heavy Bear, The.) ImPo

Replica, the. Vernon Watkins. AngWe

Reply. Reiner Kunze, *tr. fr. German by* Ewald Osers. PoSu

Reply, The. Philip Levine. PoA

Reply, The. Theodore Roethke. NoP; NYBP

Reply, A. *Unknown.* FaBoCo; NBLV; NOBL; PeLi

Reply from the Akond of Swat, A. Ethel Talbot Scheffauer. *See* Mr Lear, I'm the Akond of Swat.

Reply of Socrates, The. Edith M. Thomas. WGRP

Reply to a Creditor. George Harding. FaBoUs

Reply to a Marriage Proposal. Irihapeti Rangi Te Apakura, *tr. fr. Maori by* Roger Oppenheim *and* Allen Curnow. PBWP

Reply to Dipsychus. Arthur Hugh Clough. FaBoCo

Reply to "In Flanders Fields." John Mitchell. BLPA

Reply to Lines by Thomas Moore, A, *sels.* Walter Savage Landor.

    "Will you come to the bower I have shaded for you?" ChTr

Reply to Mr. Wordsworth, *sels.* Archibald MacLeish.

Reply to the Committed Intellectual. Francis Sparshott. NOBC

Reply to the Provinces. Galway Kinnell. NYBP

Replying to a Poem by a New Graduate Lamenting the Loss of His Wife. Yü Hsüan-chi, *tr. fr. Chinese by* Geoffrey R. Waters. SuSp

Replying to a Poem by Li T'ien-lin. Yang Wan-li, *tr. fr. Chinese by* Sherwin S. S. Fu. SuSp

Replying to a Poem by the Monk Ling-yi at the New Spring. Liu Ch'ang-ch'ing, *tr. fr. Chinese by* William H. Nienhauser. SuSp

Replying to Hsi-mei's "Thoughts in Early Autumn." Lu Kuei-meng, *tr. fr. Chinese by* Robin D. S. Yates. SuSp

Replying to "On the Occasion of Morning Audience after Snow" Poem by Assistant Secretary Wang of the Board of Sacrifices. Ts'en Shen, *tr. fr. Chinese by* Daniel Bryant. SuSp

Report, The. Jon Swan. NYBP

Report from a Far Place. William Stafford. CAPP

Report from a Planet. Richmond Lattimore. FYAP

Report from Another Country. Charlene Langfur. LoHo

Report from California. Lois Moyles. NYBP

Report from Paradise. Zbigniew Herbert, *tr. fr. Polish by* Czeslaw Milosz. OBD

Report from the Besieged City. Zbigniew Herbert, *tr. fr. Polish by* John Carpenter *and* Bogdana Carpenter. AnAn

Report from the Carolinas, *sels.* Helen Smith Bevington.

Report from the Correspondent They Fired. David McElroy. AmPA

Report from Vietnam for International Women's Day. Minerva Salado, *tr. fr. Spanish by* Daniela Gioseffi *with* Enildo Garcia. WoWa

Report on Experience. Edmund Blunden. CoGr; FaBoTw; GTBS-P; NOBE; OBMV; OBWP; PeFWW; PlP

Report on Her Remains. Daniel David Moses. HATNAP

Report Song [in a Dream], A. Nicholas Breton. GBL; NoSic

Report to Crazy Horse. William Stafford. AnAn; NoAM

Report to the Valley Camp. Jenny King. PAW

Reported Missing. John Clifford Bayliss. PoWW

Reporter of the courage of heroes. Antipater of Sidon, *tr. fr. Greek by* Peter Jay. GrAn

Reportless subjects, to the quick. Emily Dickinson. NOBA

Reports Come In, The. J. D. Reed. NYBP

Repose. Una Marson. PBCV

Repose. H. Cordelia Ray. CBWP-3

Repose of Rivers. Hart Crane. AWP; CMoP; LiTM; MeMAP; MoAB; MoAmPo; NOBA; OxBA; PoE

Repose they know in storefronts, The. The Village of the Presents. James McMichael. AmPA

Representing nothing on God's earth now. Lines on the Back of a Confederate Note. Samuel Alroy Jonas. BLPA

Repression of War Experience. Siegfried Sassoon. CMoP; NoAM; NSI; PeFWW; PoE

Reprieve, The. Hans Magnus Enzensberger. *Fr.* Sinking of the Titanic, The. PoSu

Reprieve on the Stoop. Belle Waring. PBCAP

Reprisal. Herbert Corby. PAW

Reprisal[1], The. George Herbert. ESCV; GeHe

Reprisals. W. B. Yeats. OBWP; PoWW

Reprise. Ogden Nash. OxBM

Resolution, *sels.* Josefa Masanés, *tr. fr. Spanish by* Robert L. Smith *and* Judith Candullo.

Resolution. W. S. Merwin. NYBP

Resolution. Charles L. O'Donnell. TrPWD

Resolution and Independence. (There was a roaring in the wind all night.) Wordsworth. BoNaP; EBEV; EnRP; FHYEP; HAP; InPS; LiTB; MAT; MeMBP; NOBE; NOCV; NoP; OAEL-2; OBNC; OxAEP-2; PoEL-4; PPP; TEP; TFi
Sels.
"Now, whether it were by peculiar grace." UV
We Poets in Our Youth. FaBoRV

Resolution in Four Sonnets, of a Poetical Question Put to Me by a Friend, Concerning Four Rural Sisters. Charles Cotton. PoEL-3; Prf; Son
Sels.
Alice. TrGrPo
(Two Rural Sisters.) BoLoP; EnLoPo
Marg'ret of Humbler Stature by the Head (Margaret.) TrGrPo
(Two Rural Sisters.) BoLoP; EnLoPo
Martha Is Not So Tall.
Mary Is Black.

Resolution of Dependence. George Barker. FaBoTw; LiTB; LiTM; MeMBP

Resolve, The. Alexander Brome. GGP; NOSC; OBEV

Resolve, The. Mary Lee, Lady Chudleigh. ECWP; WPE

Resolve. Charlotte Perkins Gilman. PoToHe; WGRP

Resolve, The. Denise Levertov. RFM

Resolve, The. Lady Mary Wortley Montagu. *See* Whilst thirst of praise, and vain desire of fame.

Resolve, The. Henry Vaughan *and* Thomas Stanley. ESCV

Resolve to make the best of life. Beyond the Beaten Way. George Sands Johnson. PWR

Resolved to dust, intombed here lieth Love. Here Lieth Love. Thomas Watson. *Fr.* Hecatompathia; or, Passionate Century of Love. EiL

Resolved to Love. Henry Constable. *Fr.* Diana. ESo; Son

Resolving Doubts. William Dickey. ErPo

Resonance. Christopher Gilbert. Jaz

Resort, *sels.* Patricia Hampl.

Resound my voyse [*or* voice], ye wodes [*or* woods] that here [*or* hear] me plain. Sir Thomas Wyatt. AAS; SiPS; SiPSBD

Respect all surfaces. The skater is. In Defense of Superficiality. Elder Olson. NYBP

Respect for Law and Order, A. John Hughes. PNI

Respect for the Dead. Laura Riding. LiTA

Respect the dreams of old men, said the cricket. Song for September. Robert Fitzgerald. VGW

Respectability. Robert Browning. CBLP; EnLoPo

Respectable Burgher, The. Thomas Hardy. ChIV-2; CMoP; NoAM

Respectable House. Anne Stevenson. NALW

Respectable People. Austin Clarke. CMoP

Respice Finem. Thomas Proctor. NoSic

Respite, The. Ingeborg Bachmann, *tr. fr. German by* Michael Hamburger. WPOW

Resplendent studs of heaven's frame. *Unknown.* SCAP

Respondez!. Walt Whitman. NoAM; PoEL-5

Responding to Yüan-ming's "Drinking Wine" Poems, *sels.* Cheng Chen, *tr. fr. Chinese by* Irving Lo.

Responds to love, don't call him or he will come. (*LL*) Unwanted. Edward Field. GLP; Poetsp

Response. Mary Ursula Bethell. ArLo; FaBoWP; PeNZ

Response. Linda Pastan. BTR

Response to Rimbaud's Later Manner. T. Sturge Moore. OBMV

Response to Wang Ssu-yüan's Poem on the Moon, A. Shen Yüeh, *tr. fr. Chinese by* Richard B. Mather. SuSp

Responses to Montale. Brian Turner. PeNZ

Responsibilities. Anthony Cronin. PBCIP

Responsibilities, *sels.* W. B. Yeats.
"Pardon, old fathers, if you still remain." PoEL-5
(Prologue to Responsibilities.) MeMBP

Responsibility. *Unknown.* FaBoUs

Responsive to the tune of lawns and trees. Dogs in the Morning Light. Bruce Dawe. NoAM

Responsory, 1948, A. Thomas Merton. VGW

Ressaif My Saul. R. Crombie Saunders. OxBS

resurrect me. (*LL*) If you really exist — show up. Nina Cassian. VBLP

Rest. Wilhelm Müller, *tr. fr. German by* Philip L. Miller. *Fr.* Winter's Journey, The. RiWo

Rest, The. Ezra Pound. *See* O helpless few in my country.

Rest. Christina Rossetti. MeMBP; NOBE; OAEL-2; OBEV; OBNC; TrGrPo

Rest. *Unknown.* PoToHe

Rest — anan., The. (*LL*) The Five Students. Thomas Hardy. CMoP; GTBS-P; PoEL-5

Rest, and be thankful! On the verge. Adam Lindsay Gordon. *Fr.* Hippodromania; or, Whiffs from the Pipe. CBAP

Rest, Christ! from tireless war. See, it's midsummer. Derek Walcott. *Fr.* Midsummer. TOF

Rest from Loving and Be Living. C. Day Lewis. MoBrPo; OBMV

Rest in Peace. Wilfred J. Funk. PoLF

Rest in peace, all souls. Litany for All Souls Day. Johann Georg Jacobi, *tr. fr. German by* Philip L. Miller. RiWo

Rest in peace, warriors of Soweto. Elegy for the Dead of Soweto. Thembinkosi Ndlovu, *tr. fr. Zulu by* Chris Mann. PeSAV

Rest is not quitting. True Rest. Goethe, *tr. fr. German by* John S. Dwight. WBLP

Rest is vanity of vanities, The. (*LL*) Ecclesiastes. G. K. Chesteron. ChIV-1; MoBrPo; OxBSP

Rest lightly O Earth upon this wretched Nearchos. Epitaph of Nearchos. Ammianus, *tr. fr. Greek by* Dudley Fitts. WeW

Rest, little guest. After Annunciation. Anna Wickham. MoBrPo

Rest, My Soul. Karl Henkell, *tr. fr. German by* Philip L. Miller. RiWo

Rest O Sun I Cannot. Joseph Tusiani. GoYe

Rest of the way will be only going down, The. (*LL*) The Long Hill. Sara Teasdale. LiTA; MoAmPo

Rest on me, dark eyes. Request. Nikolaus Lenau, *tr. fr. German by* Philip L. Miller. RiWo

Rest Only in the Grave. James Clarence Mangan. BIrV

"Rest, rest, and rest again." (*LL*) Nod. Walter de la Mare. BoTP; MoAB; MoBrPo; OxBTC; PFP

Rest thee aged pilgrim, now thy toils are o'er. Death of a Grandparent. Mrs. Jennette Bonneau. Mary Weston Fordham. CBWP-2

Rest thee with thy yellow nabob, spider-hearted Cousin Amy! (*LL*) The Lay of the Lovelorn. William Edmonstoune Aytoun *and* Sir Theodore Martin. FaBoCo

Rest! This little Fountain runs. For a Fountain. "Barry Cornwall." OBEV

Rest ye in peace, ye Flanders dead. America's Answer. R. W. Lilliard. BLPA

Restaurant. Maxine Hong Kingston. OpBo

Restaurant is empty, The. On Stopping Late in the Afternoon for Steamed Dumplings. Toi Derricotte. InPS

Restful place, reviver of my smart, The. Sir Thomas Wyatt. SiPS; SiPSBD

Resting. Josephine D. Henderson Heard. CBWP-4

Resting on the alien garden of your forehead. The Arrival. Lan Ling, *tr. fr. Chinese by* Kenneth Rexroth *and* Ling Chung. WPC

Restless and discontent. Agathias, *tr. fr. Greek by* Kenneth Rexroth. PGA

Restless and discontent/ I lie awake all night long. Agathias, *tr. fr. Greek by* Kenneth Rexroth. GrAn

Restless as a Wolf. Moyshe-Leyb Halpern, *tr. fr. Yiddish by* Jacob Sloan. TrJP

Restless at night and during storms. A Dream of France. Kevin Hart. FaBoMA

Restless he rolls about from whore to whore. The Earl of Rochester. *Fr.* Satire on Charles II, A. OBSV

Restless Heart, The. The Earl of Surrey. *See* Fancy, which that I have served long, The.

Restless Heart, The. *Unknown, tr. fr. Marathi.* WGRP

Restless Love. Goethe, *tr. fr. German by* Philip L. Miller. RiWo

Restless State of a Lover, The. The Earl of Surrey. *See* Sun hath twice brought forth[e] the tender green, The.

Restoration. Jeffrey Skinner. PBCAP

Restoration. Woodridge Spears. GoYe

Restoration of Enheduanna to Her Former Station, The. Enheduanna, *tr. fr. Sumerian.* BoWoP, *ad. by* Aliki *and* Willis Barnstone

Restorative broth of trouts learne to make. Methods of Cooking Trout. Thomas Barker. *Fr.* Art of Angling, The. FaBoUs

"Restore the lock!" she cries; and all around. Pope. *Fr.* Rape of the Lock, The. FHYEP; HAP; ImPo; NoP; OAEL-1; OBNV; OxAEP-1; PeLV; PoEL-3; TEP; TrGrPo

Restore us. (*LL*) Surround of Rainbows. Meridel LeSueur. SRLS

Restores the else-betrayed, too-human heart. (*LL*) At a Bach Concert. Adrienne Rich. NIP; SM

Restoring the Ancestral House. Katerina Te Hei Koko Mataira, *tr. fr. Maori by* Katerina Te Hei Koko Mataira. PeNZ

Restrain your tongue: it is a beast. (*LL*) When rage invades your burning breast. Sappho. InMo

Restricted. Eve Merriam. TrJP

Results of Stealing a Pin, The. *Unknown.* FaBoUs

Résumé. Dorothy Parker. *Fr.* Some Beautiful Letters. AnAmPo; DL; HeIL; HeIP; IHNG; InPK; NAAL-2; NALW; NBLV; NoP; OBAL; Poetr; TrJP; UV

Resurgam. W. Nelson Bitton. BLRP

Resurgam. Emily Dickinson. WGRP

Resurgam. Adah Isaacs Menken. CBWP-1

Resurgam. Marjorie Pickthall. TrCP

Resurgam. *Unknown.* WGRP

Resurge San Francisco. Joaquin Miller. PAH

Resurrection. Margaret Atwood. CrSp

Resurrection. R. P. Blackmur. PoA

Resurrection, The. Jonathan Henderson Brooks. CDC; PoNe

Resurrection, The. Abraham Cowley. ChIV-2

Resurrection. John Donne. *Fr. La Corona.* ChIV-2; ESCV; Son

Resurrection. Margiad Evans. OBWVE

Resurrection. Kenneth Fearing. CMoP; PoE

Resurrection. Joy Harjo. HATNAP

Resurrection. Vladimir Holan, *tr. fr. Czech by* George Theiner. PoSu

Resurrection. Frank Horne. PoBA

Resurrection. Marie Luise Kaschnitz, *tr. fr. German by* Michael Hamburger. WPOW

Resurrection. Sidney Lanier. PoEL-5

Resurrection, The, *sels.* W. B. Yeats.
　Two Songs from a Play. CMoP; FaBoTw; HAP; ImPo; LiTB; MeMBP; NOBE; NoP; OAEL-2; PoE; PPP; PrIm
　Two Songs from a Play. CMoP; FaBoTw; HAP; LiTB; NOBE; NoP; OAEL-2; PPP; PrIm

Resurrection. Yoshihara Sachiko, *tr. fr. Japanese by* Kenneth Rexroth *and* Ikuko Atsumi. WPJ

Resurrection: An Easter Sequence, *sels.* W. R. Rodgers.
　"It was a lovely night." PNI

Resurrection and Immortality. Henry Vaughan *and* Thomas Stanley. ESCV

Resurrection, Imperfect. John Donne. ChIV-2

Resurrection of Arp. A. J. M. Smith. MoCV; NOBC

Resurrection of Chirst, The. William Dunbar. *See* Done is a battell on the dragon blak.

Resurrection of the Right Side. Muriel Rukeyser. LCAP

Resurrection Song. Thomas Lovell Beddoes. FaBoEE

Resurrections. Benjamin Saenz. AfAz

Resuscitation Team. U. A. Fanthorpe. FaBoWP

Retaliation. Margaret E. Bruner. PoToHe

Retaliation. Goldsmith. OxBoLi
　Sels.
　David Garrick. IHNG; NOEC
　"Here lies our good Edmund, whose genius was such." FaBoEE; FaBoEH; FaBoPV
　(Edmund Burke.) InvP; NOEC
　"Of old, when Scarron his companions invited." NOIV
　Sir Joshua Reynolds. FaBoEE; FaBoEH; NOEC; OBD

Reticulations creep upon the slack stream's face. On Sturminster Foot-Bridge. Thomas Hardy. FaBoPP; OxBSP

Retinitis. John Harkness. UnDi

Retinue. Paul Verlaine, *tr. fr. French by* C. F. MacIntyre. ErPo

Retired Ballerinas, Central Park West. Lawrence Ferlinghetti. NoAM

Retired Cat, The. William Cowper. FM; OFC

Retired Civil Servant from Gateley, A. Ida Thurtle. PeLi

Retired Farmer. David Allan Evans. Poetsp

Retired gardener of solitudes. N.Y. to L.A. by Jet Plane. Sonya Dorman. GOA

Retired general is talking about restraint, The. Nightline: An Interview with the General. Ronald Wallace. PBCAP

Retired Lion by the Clothesline in the Cold Attic. Laura Jensen. AnAn

Retired Official Yüan's High Pavilion, The. Tu Mu, *tr. fr. Chinese by* A. C. Graham. PLT

Retired [Retyred] thoughts enjoy their own delights. Look [*or* Looke] Home. Robert Southwell. ESCV; NOCV; NoSic

Retired this hour from wondering crowds. Walter Savage Landor. GBL

Retirement, The. Charles Cotton. *Fr.* To Mr. Izaak Walton. FaBoPP

Retirement, *sels.* William Cowper.
　"How sweet, how passing sweet, is solitude!" OBF
　"I praise the Frenchman, his remark was shrewd." BLPA
　London Suburbs. FaBoPP

Retirement. *Unknown, tr. fr. Irish by* Frank O'Connor. ErPo

Retirement. Henry Vaughan. ChIV-1; GeHe

Retirement (I). Henry Vaughan. *See* Who on yon throne of Azure sits.

Retirement of the Elephant, The. Russell Edson. AmPA

Retort, The. George Pope Morris. AnAmPo

Retort to Jesus. D. H. Lawrence. PeECV

Retort to Whitman. D. H. Lawrence. MeMBP

Retreat. W. W. Gibson. NSI

Retreat[e], The. Henry Vaughan. AWP; BLPL; ClHu; ESCV; FF; GeHe; GTBS; GTBS-P; HAP; ImPo; InPK; InPS; InvP; JCP; LiTB; MeLP; NAEL-1; NIP; NOBE; NOCV; NoP; NOSC; OAEL-1; OBEV; OBWVE; PeECV; PoE; PoEL-2; PoRA; PPP; SCGP; SeCP; SeCV-1; TFi; TOF; TrGrPo

Retreat from Paradise, The. Milton. *See* He ended; and thus Adam last replied.

Retreat of Ita Cagney, The. Michael Hartnett. CIP; PBCIP

Retribution. Friedrich von Logau, *tr. fr. German by* Longfellow. BLPA; PoToHe

Retribution. L. A. J. Moorer. CBWP-3

Retrieval System, The. Maxine W. Kumin. FaBoWP; WeW

Retrieval System. Peter Porter. AnAn

Retrievers run through the meadow. Exercise in a Meadow. Jane Elliot. GoYe

Retro Me, Sathana. Dante Gabriel Rossetti. ChIV-2

Retrospect. Josephine D. Henderson Heard. CBWP-4

Retrospect. Wilhelm Müller, *tr. fr. German by* Philip L. Miller. *Fr.* Winter's Journey, The. RiWo

Retrospect — Love of Nature Leading to Love of Mankind. Wordsworth. *Fr.* Prelude [*or*, Growth of a Poet's Mind], The. EnRP; OAEL-2

Retrospection. H. Cordelia Ray. CBWP-3

Retrospection. Dunstan Shaw. NOBAu

Retrovir. Tim Dlugas. PFL

Return, The. Sebastian Barry. IB

Return, The. John Peale Bishop. ImPo; LiTA; OxBA

Return, The. Arna Bontemps. CDC; PoBA; PoNe

Return. Sterling A. Brown. CDC

Return, The. Alistair Campbell. PeNZ

Return. C. P. Cavafy, *tr. fr. Modern Greek by* John Mavrogordato. ErPo

Return. John Ciardi. ArOW

Return, The. Eleanor Rogers Cox. PAH

Return, The. Seamus Deane. BIrV; IIP; PBCIP; PNI

Return[, The]. Emily Dickinson. MoAmPo

Return. Mary Dorcey. AIW

Return, The. Jessie Redmond Fauset. CDC

Return. Robinson Jeffers. EaPr; GoYe

Return, The. Dori Katz. BTR

Return, The. Kipling. MoBrPo

Return, The, *sels.* Kipling.
　England. OtMeF

Return. Johari M. Kunjufu. BlSi

Return. John Robert Lee. PBCV

Return, The. George MacBeth. NYBP

Return, The. Pittendrigh Macgillivray. OxBS

Return, The. Thomas McGrath. FoLa

Return, The. Derek Mahon. SCBI

Return, The. Edna St. Vincent Millay. LiTA; MeMAP; MoAB; MoAmPo; MoP; NoAM; OxBA; Poetr

Return, The ("The doors flapped open in Ulysses' house.") Edwin Muir. CMoP

Return, The. Ezra Pound. AmPP; CMoP; HAP; MoAB; MoAmPo; MoP; NoAM; NOBA; OxBA; PoE; Poetr; RB; TRP; VGW; WeW

Return. The Earl of Rochester. *See* Absent from thee, I languish still.

Return, The. Theodore Roethke. *Fr.* Lost Son, The. HAP; HCAP; LiTM; NAAL-2; VGW

Return. Theodore Spencer. PoA

Return, The. Matthew Sweeney. IB

Return, The. Edward Taylor. *See* Inamoring Rayes, thy Sparkles, Pearle of Price.

Return, The. Evan J. Thomas. AngWe

Return, The. Thomas Traherne. GeHe

Return, The. Tu Fu, *tr. fr. Chinese by* Robert Payne. TAL

Return, The. Nika Turbina, *tr. fr. Russian by* Elaine Feinstein *and* Antonina Bouis. VBLP

Return. Mark Vinz. GOYP

Return, The, *sels.* Margaret L. Woods.
　"Father of Life, with songs of wonder." TrPWD

Return. Wordsworth. *Fr.* River Duddon, The. HAP

Return Alpheus, the dread voice is past. Milton. *Fr. Lycidas.* AWP; ChTr; ClHu; EBEV; EBEvV; FHYEP; GTBS; GTBS-P; HAP; ImPo; InPS; JCP; LiTB; NOBE; NoP; NOSC; OAEL-1; OBEV; OxAEP-1; PeECV; PoEL-3; Poetr; PPP; PrIm; SCGP; TFi; TrGrPo; UnPo; WGRP

Return, destroy, and create. What will be/ the sacred words? (*LL*) Ka 'Ba. Amiri Baraka. BPo; NBV; TAP

Return from Luluabourg. Michael Jackson. PeNZ

Return, my heart from wandering afar. Repose. Una Marson. PBCV

Return, my joys, and hither bring. Opposite to Melancholy. William Strode. NOSC

Return no more. (*LL*) The Far-Farers. Robert Louis Stevenson. BoTP

Return, o mysterious night! (*LL*) After a Dream. Romain Bussine. RiWo

Return of a Popular Statesman. Vincent Buckley. CBAP

Return of Aphrodite, The. May Sarton. SRLS

Return of Astraea, The. Ben Jonson. NOBE

Return of Robinson Jeffers, The. Robert Hass. AmPA; AnAn

Return of the Children, The. Kipling. OBD

Return of the Dead, The, *sels.* Samar Attar. "And you came back." PBWP

Return of the Goddess Artemis. Robert Graves. PoA

Return of the Greeks, The. Edwin Muir. *See* Veteran Greeks came home, The.

Return of the Native. Amiri Baraka. BPo

Return of the Proconsul, The. Zbigniew Herbert, *tr. fr. Polish by* Czeslaw Milosz. FaBoPV; PoSu

Return of the Prodigal Son, *sels.* Léopold Sédar Senghor, *tr. fr. French by* Ellen Conroy Kennedy. "Elephant of Moissel, hear my pious prayer." GrPl; NegPo

Return of the Wolves. Anita Endrezze-Danielson. HATNAP

Return often and take me. Return. C. P. Cavafy, *tr. fr. Modern Greek by* John Mavrogordato. ErPo

Return, return, my beloved! Absence. Théophile Gautier, *tr. fr. French by* Philip L. Miller. RiWo

Return, Return, O Shulammite. Bible, *O.T. Fr.* Song of Solomon, The. TrJP

Return, The ("The veteran Greeks came home.") Edwin Muir. CMoP

Return to Ararat. Martyn Halsall. TrCP

Return to Cardiff. Dannie Abse. AngWe

Return to Frankfurt., *sels.* Marie Luise Kaschnitz, *tr. fr. German by* Beatrice Cameron.

Return to Hinton. Charles Tomlinson. CMoP

Return to La Plata, Missouri. Jim Barnes. HATNAP

Return to Mankiller Flats, Oklahoma. Mary Crescenzo Simons. LoHo

Return to My Native Land. Aimé Césaire, *tr. fr. French by* Emile Snyders. NegPo

Sels. "I shall not regard my swelled head as a sign of real glory." TTY

Return to nestle here. (*LL*) Dream-Love. Christina Rossetti. CH; HAP; PoEL-5

Return to Sedgemoor. Patricia Beer. PAW

Return to Spring. Florence Ripley Mastin. GoYe

Return to the Native Land, A, *sels.* Aimé Césaire, *tr. fr. French by* Ellen Conroy Kennedy. "This flat city shortly after dawn." NegPo

Return to the Tree of Time, A. Vesna Parun, *tr. fr. Croatian by* Vasa D. Mihailovich *and* Ronald Morgan. WPOW

Return to the Womb/the Source. Blackbelt Rhapsody/ A Redemption Song. Askia Muhammad Touré. BCF

Return to Work, The. William Carlos Williams. NYBP

Return we to the dangers of the night. Juvenal, *tr. by* Dryden. *Fr.* Satires. OAEL-1

Return'd from the opera, as lately I sat. A Bon Mot. *Unknown.* ErPo

Returned, a wraith from her defrauded tomb. Transformation Scene. Constance Carrier. FYAP; GoYe

Returned American. Kathleen Cain. LoHo

Returned from California. Simon J. Ortiz. HATNAP

Returned from college R — — gets a wife. The Discontented Student. St. George Tucker. OBAL

Returned from Mehiko he'll grab. A Hex on the Mexican X. David McCord. FiBHP

Returned Heart, The. Sarah Dixon. ECWP

Returned Picture, The. Mary O'Donovan Rossa. IIP

Returned to Frisco, 1946. W. D. Snodgrass. ArOW

Returned to Say. William Stafford. NaP

Returning. Linda Pastan. WeW

Returning, *sels.* Peter Porter.

Returning after dark, I thought. Traditional Red. Robert Huff. HoPM

Returning at Night. James Harrison. VGW

Returning by Night to Lu-Men. Meng Hao Jan, *tr. fr. Chinese by* Kenneth Rexroth. OHMPC

Returning each morning from a timeless world. Autumn 1940. W. H. Auden. LiTA

Returning from court day after day, I pawn my spring clothes. Tu Fu, *tr. by* Irving Y. Lo. *Fr.* Meandering River. SuSp

Returning from Flower Law Mountain on a Winter Day. Wu Tsao, *tr. fr. Chinese by* Kenneth Rexroth *and* Ling Chung. WPC

Returning from Harvest. Vernon Watkins. NYBP

Returning from its daily quest, my Spirit. To Dante [*or* Sonnet: Guido Cavalcanti to Dante]. Cavalcanti, *tr. fr. Italian by* Shelley. AWP; OBVE

Returning from Kuang-ling. Ch'in Kuan, *tr. fr. Chinese by* Stephen West. SuSp

Returning Home. Tu Mu, *tr. fr. Chinese by* John M. Ortinau. SuSp

Returning Home at Dusk from Town, on the Fifteenth of the Seventh Month. Shen Chou, *tr. fr. Chinese by* Irving Y. Lo. SuSp

Returning, I find her just the same. Passing Visit to Helen. D. H. Lawrence. CMoP

Returning me, returning me. (*LL*) The Train Runs Late to Harlem. Conrad Kent Rivers. PoBA

Returning to Arizona. Maura Stanton. NGP

Returning to Earth., *sels.* James Harrison.

Returning to Goleufryn. Vernon Watkins. AngWe; OBWVE

Returning to Kilcoole. Aidan Carl Mathews. IB

Returning to my grandfather's house, after this exile. Returning to Goleufryn. Vernon Watkins. AngWe; OBWVE

Returning to Roots of First Feeling. Robert Duncan. PoA

Returning to Store Bay. Barbara Howes. Poetsp

Returning to the Alluvial Fields, *sels.* Wu Chia-chi, *tr. fr. Chinese by* Jonathan Chaves.

Returning to the Port of Authority: A Picaresque. Constance Urdang. PBCAP

Returning to the room. Margaret Atwood. *Fr.* Circle Game, The. MoCV

Returning to the Town Where We Used to Live. Susan Musgrave. NOBC

Returning to the valley. (*LL*) Sun. Gary Soto. TRP

Returning, We Hear the Larks. Isaac Rosenberg. FaBoMo; NAEL-2; NoAM; NSI; OAEL-2; OBWP; PeFWW; PoWW

Reuben Bright. E. A. Robinson. AnAmPo; MeMAP; MoAB; MoAmPo; NOBA; NoP; PFP; Son; TAP; TrGrPo

Reuben James. James Jeffrey Roche. PAH

Reuben Ranzo. *Unknown.* AmFP

Reuben, Reuben. Michael S. Harper. PoE

Reunion. Carolyn Forché. NoAM

Reunion. Judith Herzberg. *tr. fr. Dutch by* Shirley Kaufman. BoWoP

Reunion. E. A. Robinson. NOBA

Reunion. Cyril Tawney. OBET

Reunion. Charles Wright. CAPP

Reunited. Sir Gilbert Parker. OBEV

Reunited. H. Cordelia Ray. CBWP-3

Rev. Andrew Brown, over the Hill to Rest. Josephine D. Henderson Heard. CBWP-4

Rev. Homer Wilbur's "Festina Lente." James Russell Lowell. *Fr.* Biglow Papers, The. OBAL

Rev. Nicholas Noyes to the Rev. Cotton Mather, The. Nicholas Noyes. SCAP

Rev Owl. A. M. Klein. TrJP

Rev. Samuel Weston. Mary Weston Fordham. CBWP-2

Reve was a sclendre colerik man, The. Chaucer. *Fr.* Canterbury Tales, The. EnVB; FHYEP; NoP; OAEL-1; PPP, *abr.*

Reveal Thy Presence now, O Lord. A Grace. Thomas Tiplady. TrPWD

Reveille. John Godfrey. UL

Reveille, The. Bret Harte. GN; OHIP; OtMeF; PAH

Reveille. A. E. Housman. *Fr.* Shropshire Lad, A. CMoP; FaPoB; LiTB; LiTM; MeMBP; MoAB; MoBrPo; NoP; PoLF

Reveille. Ted Hughes. PPP

Réveille. Lola Ridge. WPE

Reveille Matin, or Good Morrow to a Friend. Mildmay Fane, 2d Earl of Westmorland. NOSC

Revel, The. Bartholomew Dowling. BLPA

Revel, The. Frances E. W. Harper. AmWP

Revel pauses and the room is still, The. Pannyra of the Golden Heel. Albert Samain, *tr. fr. French by* James Elroy Flecker. AWP

Revelation, *sels.* Bible, *N.T.*
    Four Horsemen, The. PAW
    New Jerusalem, The. TrGrPo
    There Shall Be No Night. TrGrPo

Revelation. Verne Bright. BLRP; WBLP

Revelation. Alice Brown. *Fr.* Road to Castaly, The. WGRP

Revelation. Warren F. Cook. BLRP

Revelation. Blanche Taylor Dickinson. CDC

Revelation. Robert Frost. ChIV-2

Revelation. Sir Edmund Gosse. OBEV

Revelation. Sir Edmund Gosse. OBEV

Revelation. Carole C. Gregory. BISi

Revelation. Edwin Markham. WGRP

Revelation, The. Coventry Patmore. *Fr.* Angel in the House, The. EnLoPo; GBL; GTBS-P; HAP; OBNC; OxBSP

Revelation. Edith Södergran, *tr. fr. Swedish by* David McDuff. VBLP

Revelation. Robert Penn Warren. LiTA; NoAM

Revelation, The. William Carlos Williams. SAmP

Revelation: The Movie. Elton Glaser. PBCAP

Revelations. David Meltzer. NeAP

Revelations — we've come to the lewd. *Unknown.* PeLi

Revenant, The. Walter de la Mare. GBL

Revenant, The. Rachel Hadas. UnDi

Revenge, The. Pierre de Ronsard, *tr. fr. French by* Thomas Stanley. AWP

Revenge, The. Tennyson. BeLS; EBVV; FaBoCh; FaPoR; PoRA Sels.
  "At Flores in the Azores Sir Richard Grenville lay." EBEvV; EBNV; FaBoEH; FaPoB; OBWP

Revenge. Mary E. Tucker. AmWP; CBWP-1

Revenge. Chase Twichell. BAP-91

Revenge, The, *sels.* Edward Young.
  "Life is the desert, life the solitude." OBD

Revenge of America, The. Joseph Warton. ECEV; OBTV

Revenge of Hamish, The. Sidney Lanier. EBNV; PoEL-5

Revenge of Rain-in-the-Face, The. Longfellow. PAH

Revenge of the Hunted. R. A. D. Ford. MoCV

Revenge to Come. Sextus Propertius, *tr. by* Kirby Flower Smith. *Fr.* Elegies. AWP

Revenger's Tragedy, The, *sels.* Cyril Tourneur.
  "Madame, his grace will not be absent long." PoEL-2
  "Thou sallow picture of my poison'd love." OBD

Reverberation. Maurice Kenny. HATNAP

Reverdure, *sels.* Wendell Berry.

Revere me for his sake, and love me for my own. *(LL)* Full Well I Know. Hartley Coleridge. Son

Reverend Butler came by. Madam and the Minister. Langston Hughes. NOBA

Reverend Ewing Sends Compasión Magazine. Julio Marzán. ETG

Reverend Henry Ward Beecher, The. Limerick [*or* An Eggstravagance *or* Henry Ward Beecher]. *At. to* Oliver Wendell Holmes. ChTr; FaBoNo; PeLi

Reverend Mr. Uprightly, The. *Unknown.* PeLi

Reverend Mr, The. Higginson. Edward Johnson. SCAP

Reverend William Winterbourne, The. Bishop Winterbourne. Walter de la Mare. FaBoNo

Reverie. Don Marquis. PoLF

Reverie. H. Cordelia Ray. CBWP-3

Reverie, A. Joanna Baillie. ECWP; WoRP

Reverie, A. Mary Weston Fordham. CBWP-2

Reverie at Dawn. Egan O'Rahilly. *See* One morning ere [*or* before] Titan had thought to stir [*or* thought of stirring] his feet.

Reverie of a Mum. Nancy Keesing. CBAP; NOBAu

Reverie of Poor Susan, The. Wordsworth. CoGr; EnRP; GTBS; GTBS-P; OxBoLi; WiR

Reversals. Janice Mirikitani. ETG

Reverse the flight of Lucifer. The Task. Ruth Pitter. MoBrPo

Reversion. Barry O. Higgs. PeSA

Reversionary. Stevie Smith. FaBoEE

Review from Staten Island. Gloria C. Oden. PoBA; PPP

Reviewing me without undue elation. A Choice of Weapons. Stanley Kunitz. LiTM; VGW

Reviewing Past Lives while Leaf-Burning. Anita Endrezze-Danielson. HATNAP

Reviews are gaudy shows — allowed. On the Frequent Review of the Troops. "M." NOEC

Revised Notes for a Sonnet. Edward Pygge. BXAP

Revisiting your marble-paved sea-perfumed town. Hardy's Plymouth. Geoffrey Grigson. FaBoPP

Revival. Steve Crow. HATNAP

Revival. George Garrett. MT

Revival, The. Henry Vaughan. NOCV; PoEL-2; TrGrPo

Revocation, A. Sir Thomas Wyatt. *See* What should [*or* shulde] I say[e].

Revolt of Islam, The, *sels.* Shelley.
  Child of Twelve, A. GN
  "Over the utmost hill at length I sped." OBWP
  "Soldiers, our brethren and our friends are slain." OBF

Revolution. A. E. Housman. MeMBP

Revolution, The, *sels.* George Meredith.
  "Not yet had History's Ætna smoked the skies." FaPoB, *sts.* I–V

Revolution. Nishi Junko, *tr. fr. Japanese by* Kenneth Rexroth *and* Ikuko Atsumi. WPJ

Revolution Is One Form of Social Change. Audre Lorde. Poetr

Revolution of the Aged, The. Njabulo S. Ndebele. PeSAV

Revolutionaries, The. R. P. Lister. NOBL

Revolutionaries, The. *Unknown.* NOBL

Revolutionary, The/ element remained. Mrs. Hamer. Jane Stembridge. NMM

Revolutionary Frescoes — the Ascension. Thomas McGrath. BCF

Revolutionary Letter #19. Diane Di Prima. IHMS

Revolutionary Petunias. Alice Walker. BlSi

Revolutionary Poets. Mutabaruka. PBCV

Revolutionary Revolution. George Buchanan. IIP

Revolutions. Shakespeare. *See* Like as the waves make towards the pebbled shore.

Revolving auger. *(LL)* Theris, whose hands were cunning. Leonidas. GrAn; PGA

Rev'rend Father stood inculcating, The. Camões, *tr. fr. Portuguese by* Sir Richard Fanshawe. *Fr.* Lusiads, The. OBVE; PeSAV

Revving Up la Rêve. Joel Dailey. UL

Reward. Shimon Halkin, *tr. fr. Hebrew by* Ruth Finer Mintz. MHP

Reward of Service. Elizabeth Barrett Browning. BLPA; FaBoBe

Rewarding Destiny! *(LL)* Anticipation. Emily Brontë. OBNC

Rewards and Fairies, *sels.* Kipling.
  Way through the Woods, The. CH; CoGr; EBEvV; FaBoCh; FaPON; NoAM; NOBE; NTP; OBEV; OBNC; OxAEP-2; OxBChV; OxBTC; PFP; PIP; RFM; SCGP; WHSW

Rewards and Fairies. Roger Woddis. UV

Rewrite. E. A. Markham. PBCV

Rex regum, for whom praise flows freely. Poem on His Death-Bed. Meilyr Brydydd, *tr. fr. Welsh by* Joseph P. Clancy. OBWVE

Reynard the Fox, *sels.* John Masefield.
  "Fox he was strong, he was full of running, The." CoGr
  "Fox knew well, that before they tore him, The." OBNV; OtMeF
  "Meet was at "The Cock and Pye," The." OxBTC
  "Ock Gurney and old Pete were there." CMoP
  Run to Mourne End Wood, The. EBNV
  "They were a lovely pack for looks." OtMeF
  "Tom Dansey was a famous whip." OtMeF

Rhaicos was born amid the hills wherefrom. The Hamadryad. Walter Savage Landor. *Fr.* Hellenics, The. EnRP

Rhapsody. Cynthia Huntington. NAmP90

Rhapsody. Frank O'Hara. NoAM

Rhapsody, A. Henry Vaughan. BeJo; NAEL-1

Rhapsody of Old Men, A, *sels.* Dimitris Tsaloumas, *tr. fr. Greek by* Margaret Carroll.
  "They brought him one morning." CBAP

Rhapsody on a Windy Night. T. S. Eliot. CMoP; HeIP; InPS; PoE

Rhapsody on Main Street. Patrick Williams. PNI

Rhapsody, Written at the Lakes in Westmorland, A. John Brown. NOEC

Rheia, submissive in love to Kronos. The Great Father Eating His Children. Hesiod, *tr. by* Richmond Lattimore. *Fr.* Theogony. RaBo

Rhenish Carol, A. Robert Finch. NAs, *ad. by* Bernard de la Mannoye

Rhetoric Leads to Cliché. Adrian C. Louis. NAmP90

Rhetoric of Langston Hughes, The. Margaret Danner. BlSi

Rhetorical Swing. Marilyn Kitchell. UL

Rhiannon. T. Harri Jones. AngWe

Rhine, the beautiful river, The. Heine. RiWo

Rhino is a homely beast, The. The Rhinoceros. Ogden Nash. FiBHP; MoAmPo; OBAL

Rhinoceros, The. Hilaire Belloc. ChTr; FaPON

Rhinoceros. Harold Farmer. OBAP

Rhinoceros, The. Ogden Nash. FiBHP; MoAmPo; OBAL

Rhinoceros, you are an ugly beast. *(LL)* The Rhinoceros. Hilaire Belloc. ChTr; FaPON

Rhinoceros, your hide looks all undone. The Rhinoceros. Hilaire Belloc. ChTr; FaPON

Rhoda Bok. Carolyn's Neighbor. Deborah S. Snyder. BTR

Rhodanthe. Agathias, *tr. fr. Greek by* Andrew Lang. AWP

Rhode Island. William Meredith. NGP; NoP

Rhodoclea, I send you this wreath which I wove with my own hands. Rufinus Domesticus, *tr. fr. Greek by* Barbara Hughes Fowler. *Fr.* Epigrams. HePo

Rhododendrons growing wild below a mountain. Under Creon. Tom Paulin. SCBI

Rhodope is so stuck up/ because of her beauty. Rufinus, *tr. fr. Greek by* Alan Marshfield. GrAn

Rhodope, Melite and Rhodoklea/ contested. Rufinus, *tr. fr. Greek by* Alan Marshfield. GrAn

Rhodora [On Being Asked Whence Is the Flower], The. Emerson. AmPP; AnAmPo; AWP; BoNaP; FaBV; GN; LiTA; MeMAP; NAAL-1; NOBA; NoP; OxBA; PFP; PoE; PWR; TAP; TFi; TrGrPo

Rhodri. R. S. Thomas. OxAEP-2

Rhodri Theophilus Owen. Rhodri. R. S. Thomas. OxAEP-2

Rhody. George Ella Lyon. ETG

Rhœcus, sels. James Russell Lowell.

Rhydcymerau. David Gwenallt Jones, tr. fr. Welsh by Anthony Conran. OBWVE

Rhyme. James Laughlin. WeW

Rhyme for ham? Jam, A. David McCord. Fr. Jamboree. SiSoPo

Rhyme for Night. Joan Aiken. TLR

Rhyme for Remembering How Many Nights There Are in the Month. Justin Richardson. FaBoUs

Rhyme for Remembering the Date of Easter. Justin Richardson. FaBoUs

Rhyme for the Child as a Wet Dog. Judith Johnson Sherwin. TAP

Rhyme for Washing Hands, A. Rodney Bennett. BoTP

Rhyme is after, The. For W.C.W. Robert Creeley. LCAP

Rhyme nor mars, nor makes, The. His Defence Against the Idle Critic. Michael Drayton. NOSC

Rhyme of Death's Inn, A. Lizette Woodworth Reese. AmWP

Rhyme of Joyous Garde, The, sels. Adam Lindsay Gordon.

Rhyme of My Inheritance. Joan Larkin. GLP

Rhyme of Rain. John Holmes. GrPl

Rhyme of the Antique Forest. H. Cordelia Ray. CBWP-3

Rhyme of the Dream-Maker Man, A. William Allen White. PoLF

Rhyme of the Fishermen's Children. Unknown. GBP

Rhyme of the poet, The. Merlin ("Rhyme of the poet, The.") Emerson. Fr. Merlin. AmPP; NOBA; PoEL-4

Rhyme of the Rail. John Godfrey Saxe. AnAmPo; MoShBr; PoLF

Rhyme of the Rain Machine, The. F. W. Clarke. BoNaP

Rhyme of the Sun-Dial, A. William Bell Scott. NOBVV

Rhyme of the Three Captains, The. Kipling. BeLS

Rhyme Sheet of Other Lands, A. Hugh Chesterman. BoTP

Rhyme, the rack of finest wits. Ben Jonson. See Rime, the rack of finest wits.

Rhymed Mnemonic of the Forty Counties of England. Donald Monat. FaBoUs

Rhymed Words Sent to My Eldest Son, sels. Yang Shih-ch'i, tr. fr. Chinese by Jonathan Chaves.

Rhymes. Charles Tomlinson. DiPo

Rhymes (?). Henry S. Leigh. NOBL

Rhymes for a Modern Nursery. Paul Dehn. FiBHP
Sels.
"Hey diddle diddle/ The physicists fiddle." FiBHP
"Jack and Jill went up the hill/ To fetch some heavy water." ReMoGo
"Two blind mice." FiBHP

Rhymes for the Times. "Hugh MacDiarmid." IHNG

Rhymes on the Road, sels. Thomas Moore.
"And is there then no earthly place." OBSV; OBTV

Rhyming a Friend's Poem. Yü Hsüan-chi, tr. by Geoffrey R. Waters. BoWoP

Rhyming Prophecy for a New Year. Leonard Cooper. FaBoCo

Rhyming Riddles, sels. Mary Austin.
Snow. BoNaP; GrPl

Rhyming with a Friend. Yü Hsüan-chi, tr. fr. Chinese by Geoffrey R. Waters. BoWoP

Rhyming with a Friend. Yü Hsüan-chi, tr. by Geoffrey R. Waters. BoWoP

Rhythm, The. Robert Creeley. LiTM

Rhythm and blues. The Blues Today. Mae Jackson. PoBA

Rhythm it is we. Spirits Unchained. Keorapetse Kgositsile. PoBA

Rhythm of the Tomtom, The. Antonio Jacinto, tr. fr. Bantu. TSaS, tr. by Donald Burness

Rhythm of the tomtom does not beat in my blood, The. The Rhythm of the Tomtom. Antonio Jacinto, tr. fr. Bantu. TSaS, tr. by Donald Burness

Ribald Romeos less and less berattle. Ribald Romeos Less and Less Berattle ("Parcius iunctas quatiunt fenestras.") Horace, tr. fr. Latin by Austin Dobson. Fr. Odes. I, 25. MAT, tr. by John Frederick Nims; STV, tr. by John Frederick Nims.
("Bloods and bucks of this lewd town, The.") OBVE, tr. by the Young Gentlemen of Mr. Rule's Academy at Islington.
(To Lydia.) OBVE, tr. by Philip Francis
("Young bloods come round less often now, The.") BoLoP, tr. by James Michie.

Ribbe ne rele ne spinne ich ne may. Unknown. MiEL

Ribbon-Fish, The. Robert Adamson. CBAP

Ribbons of iodine. Kelp. Nora Dauenhauer. HATNAP

Ribh Considers Christian Love Insufficient. W. B. Yeats. RaBo

Ribs and Terrors, The. Herman Melville. See Ribs and Terrors in the Whale, The.

Ribs and Terrors in the Whale, The. Herman Melville. Fr. Moby Dick. ch. 9.
(Whale, The) TrGrPo

Ribs of leaves lie in the dust, The. The Coming of the Cold. Theodore Roethke. OBCP

Rice. Carol Muske. AmPA

Rice Grass. Jeremy Hooker. SCBI

Rich and Poor; or, Saint and Sinner. Thomas Love Peacock. FaBoCo; NOBE; NOBL; OBSV; PeLV

Rich and secret odor of decay, The. (LL) The Reliquary. Bruce Beasley. UTF

Rich blood disturbed my thought. Arrival. John Wain. EBEV

Rich damask roses in fair cheeks do bide. Robert Tofte. Fr. Laura. EIL

Rich Days. W. H. Davies. BoNaP; BoTP

Rich earth has not pressed down. Epitaph for Mael Mhuru. Unknown. NOIV

Rich families ordered everything in crystal, The. Waterford. Medbh McGuckian. BiHa

Rich, flashy, puffy-faced. Cabaret. Sterling A. Brown. Jaz

Rich folks 'cided to take a trip, De. Titanic, De. Unknown. AS

Rich in the simple worship of a day. (LL) Fragment of an Ode to Maia Written on May Day, 1818. Keats. EnRP; OAEL-2; OBEV; PoEL-4

Rich in the waning light she sat. Waiting. John Freeman. CH

Rich Irish Lady, A. Unknown. AmFP

Rich king of a rainy country, The. The King in May. Michael Dennis Browne. NYBP

Rich Lazarus! richer in those gems, thy teares. Upon Lazarus His Teares. Richard Crashaw. GeHe; SeCV-1

Rich Man, The. Franklin P. Adams. FiBHP; NBLV; OBAL

Rich Man and the Poor Man, The. Unknown. SWP

Rich man bought a swan and goose, A. The Swan and the Goose. Aesop, tr. fr. Greek by William Ellery Leonard. AWP; FaPON

Rich man has his motorcar, The. The Rich Man. Franklin P. Adams. FiBHP; NBLV; OBAL

Rich man lay on his velvet couch, The. Mag's Song. Unknown. AS

Rich men, trust not in wealth. Thomas Nashe. Fr. Summer's Last Will and Testament. OBD; PIP

Rich nights in another climate. Emblems. Douglas Dunn. FaBoMo

Rich Old Miser, A. Unknown. AmFP

Rich, Rich,/ Fell in the ditch. Unknown. RoPo

Rich Statue, double-faced. To the New Yeere [or Year]. Michael Drayton. NOSC; PoEL-2

Rich tuft of ivy, A. Suibne Geilt. NOIV

Rich, voluptuous languor of dim pain, A. Vanitas Vanitatum. Israel Zangwill. TrJP

Rich Widow, The. Unknown. AmFP

Rich Words! HEAV'N, HEAV'N WILL MAKE AMENDS FOR ALL. (LL) Go then, my dove, but now no longer mine. Cotton Mather. AiP; SCAP

Richard II. Veronica Forrest-Thomson. VaA

Richard II, sels. Shakespeare.
"This royal throne of kings, this scepter'd isle." UV
"You may my glories and my state depose." IMW

Richard III's Speech. Sir John Beaumont. Fr. Bosworth Field. JCP

Richard Brought His Flute. Nancy Morejón, tr. fr. Spanish by Kathleen Weaver. AIW

Richard Cory. E. A. Robinson. AmPP; AnAmPo; CMoP; DL; EBEvV; FF; HAP; ImPo; InPK; LiTA; LiTM; MeMAP; MoAB; MoAmPo; NAAL-2; NOBA; NoP; NTP; OxBA; Poetr; PoLF; PoRA; PrIm; TAP; TFi; TrGrPo

Richard Cory. Paul Simon. InPK

Richard Davis. Dick Davis. SCBI

Richard Dick upon a stick. Unknown. OxNR

Richard, may I ask a question? What is an episteme? Richard Howard. Fr. Compulsive Qualifications. PoA

Richard Roe and John Doe ("Richard Roe wished himself Solomon.") Robert Graves. CMoP

Richard, thah thou be ever trichard. Against the Baron's Enemies. Unknown. MeEL

Richard, what will it be like when you ask the questions? Richard Howard. Fr. Compulsive Qualifications. PoA

Sir Richard's Confession. Richard William. AngWe

Sir Richard's Song. Kipling. OtMeF

Richer now the body's juices. Lyall Tao Tschung Yu. OBD

Riches. Blake. MeMBP; TrGrPo

Riches. Unknown. See Poor in my youth, and in life's later scenes.

"'Cuckoo: In former days my father and mother [*or* mother and father]." AnOE, *tr. by* Charles W. Kennedy; ASW, *tr. by* Kevin Crossley-Holland

"Fire: On earth there's a warrior of curious origin." ASW, *tr. by* Kevin Crossley-Holland

Fish in River: "My house is not quiet, I am not loud." AnOE

Honey-Mead: "I am valued by men, fetched from afar." AnOE

"Horn: I'm loved by my lord, and his shoulder." ASW, *tr. by* Kevin Crossley-Holland

Horn: "Time was when I was weapon and warrior." AnOE

"House Martins: This wind wafts little creatures." ASW, *tr. by* Kevin Crossley-Holland

"Ice: On the way a miracle: water become bone." ASW, *tr. by* Kevin Crossley-Holland

"Iceberg: Curious, fair creature came floating on the waves, A." ASW, *tr. by* Kevin Crossley-Holland

"I'm a strange creature, for I satisfy women." ASW (Onion (or Penis): "I'm a Strange Creature, for I Satisfy Women.") PeLV

"Jay: I've one mouth but many voices." ASW, *tr. by* Kevin Crossley-Holland

Key (or Penis): "Strange thing hangs by man's hip, A." PeLV, *tr. by* Kevin Crossley-Holland

"Leather: I travel by foot, trample the ground." ASW, *tr. by* Kevin Crossley-Holland

"Lot and his two daughters and their sons: Man sat sozzled with his two wives, A." ASW, *tr. by* Kevin Crossley-Holland

"One-Eyed Seller of Arrows: Creature came shuffling where there sat." ASW, *tr. by* Kevin Crossley-Holland

"Oyster: Deep sea suckled me, the waves sounded over me." ASW, *tr. by* Kevin Crossley-Holland

"Pen and four fingers: I watched four fair creatures." ASW, *tr. by* Kevin Crossley-Holland

"Plough: I keep my snout to the ground; I burrow." ASW, *tr. by* Kevin Crossley-Holland

Plow: "My beak is bent downward, I burrow below." AnOE

"Reed: I sank roots first of all, stood." ASW, *tr. by* Kevin Crossley-Holland

"Shield: I'm by nature solitary, scarred by spear." ASW, *tr. by* Kevin Crossley-Holland

Shield: "Lonely wanderer, wounded with iron, A." AnOE

"Soul and Body: I've heard tell of a noble guest." ASW, *tr. by* Kevin Crossley-Holland

"Storm at Sea: Sometimes I plunge through the press of waves." ASW, *tr. by* Kevin Crossley-Holland

"Sun and Moon: I saw a strange creature." ASW, *tr. by* Kevin Crossley-Holland

"Swan: Silent is my dress when I step across the earth." ASW, *tr. by* Kevin Crossley-Holland

(Swan, The: "Silent is my dress when I step across the earth.") OBAP, *tr. by* Kevin Crossley-Holland

Swan, The. ChTr; RB

Weathercock, The: "I puff my breast out, my neck swells." RB

(Weathercock: My breast is puffed up and my neck is swollen.) ASW, *tr. by* Kevin Crossley — Holland

Wild Swan: "My attire is noiseless when I tread the earth." AnOE, *tr. by* Charles W. Kennedy

Wind: "At times I resort, beyond man's discerning." AnOE

Riddles Wisely Expounded. *Unknown.* ESPB, 3 *vers.*; FaBoBa; GBP

Riddles Wisely Expounded. *Unknown.* ESPB

Riddles Wisely Expounded, A *vers. Unknown.* ESPB

Riddling Knight, The. *Unknown.* FaBoCh; PoEL-1

Riddling Letter, A. *Unknown.* CBNP

"Riddling world, A!" one cried. The Two Questions. Alice Meynell. WPE

Riddlum riddlum ranty pole. *Unknown.* FaBoVe

Riddym Ravings (The Mad Woman's Poem). Jean Binta Breeze. NBrP

Ride. Josephine Miles. FaBoWP

Ride a Cock Horse. Barry Pain. BXAP

Ride a cock-horse [*or* a-cock horse] to Banbury Cross,/ To see a fine lady upon a white horse. Mother Goose. BoTP; FaBoBe; OxBoLi; OxNR

Ride a cock-horse to Banbury Cross/ To buy little Johnny a galloping horse. *Unknown.* OxNR

Ride a cock-horse to Banbury Cross/ To see what Tommy can buy. *Unknown.* OxNR

Ride away, ride away/ Johnny shall ride. Mother Goose. OxNR; ReMoGo

Ride-by-Nights, The. Walter de la Mare. FaPON

Ride in a Blue Chevy from Alum Cave Trail to Newfound Gap, A. Jonathan Williams. ETG

Ride in the swing. Tune: Crimson Lips Adorned. Li Ch'ing-chao, *tr. fr. Chinese.* PBWP, *tr. by* C. H. Kwôck and Vincent McHugh

(After kicking on the swing.) BoWoP, *tr. by* Kenneth Rexroth and Ling Chung

Ride my horse to the Orchid Terrace, the wind-uprooted weed my likeness. (*LL*) Last night's stars, last night's winds. Li Shang-yin. PLT

Ride of Collins Graves, The. John Boyle O'Reilly. PAH

Ride, ride together, for ever ride. (*LL*) The Last Ride Together (from Her Point of View). James Kenneth Stephen. BXAP; FaBoCo; UnPo

Ride, ride together, forever ride? (*LL*) The Last Ride Together. Robert Browning. BoLoP; FHYEP; LiTB; NAEL-2; OBEV; PoEL-5; UnPo

Ride round the Parapet, The. Friedrich Rueckert, *tr. fr. German by* James Clarence Mangan. AWP

Sir Rider Haggard. W. H. Auden. FaBoCo

Rider, The/ is fat. Horse & Rider. Wey Robinson. BXAP

Rider Victory, The. Edwin Muir. CMoP; LiTM

Riders, The. Ann Stanford. WPE

Rides. Gene Derwood. LiTM

Rides, and earth rests as silently. (*LL*) Two Pewits. Edward Thomas. CH; FM

Ridge, The, *sels.* John Cowper Powys.
"Aye! What a thing is the passing of Cronos, the angular-minded." OBWVE

Ridge, The: 1919. W. W. Gibson. PAW

Riding. William Allingham. OxBChV

Riding a One-eyed Horse. Henry Taylor. HeIP; InPK

Riding across John Lee's Finger. Stanley Crouch. PoBA

Riding at anchor ships from the New World. The Disenchanted. Clive Wilmer. SCBI

Riding at dawn, riding alone. Gillespie. Sir Henry Newbolt. PeVV

Riding bicycles up hills. Everywhere Pregnant Women Appear. Eric Nelson. NGP

Riding by there every day. Dog Hospital. Peter Wild. AmPA

Riding Double. Peter Wild. AmPA

Riding Down from Bangor. Louis Shreve Osborne. BLPA

Riding from Coleraine. Peg of Limavaddy. Thackeray. OBTV

Riding Hood. Betsy Sholl. CrSp

Riding in a Motor Boat. Dorothy W. Baruch. FaPON

Riding in an Airplane. Dorothy W. Baruch. FaPON

Riding in the Rain. Maxine W. Kumin. RFM

Riding Lesson. Henry Taylor. NBLV

Riding on a Streetcar with My Father. Mary Ann Larkin. AiP

Riding out over the whine. Re: Snow Jobs/ We Have Got. Robert Kelly. BCF

Riding the blue sapphire mountains. Mahadevi, *tr. fr. Kannada by* A. K. Ramanujan. BoWoP; PBWP

Riding the North Point Ferry. Wing Tek Lum. OpBo

Riding through life. (*LL*) Poem of Alienation. Antonio Jacinto. PeSAV

Riding through Ruwu swamp, about sunrise. Bête Humaine. Francis Brett Young. CH

Riding Together. William Morris. EnVR; NOBE; OAEL-2

Riding with Kilpatrick. Clinton Scollard. PAH

Riesis the small. It Is a Lie. John Fowles. AnAn

Riffin'. Rod Jellema. *Fr.* Four Voices Ending on Some Lines from Old Jazz Records. Jaz

Rifle, The. Tymoteusz Karpowicz, *tr. fr. Polish by* Jan Darowski. PoSu

Rifled honeycomb, The. John Montague. *Fr.* Cave of Night, The. CIP (Cave.) IIP

Rifleman, shoot me a fancy shot. Civil War. Charles Dawson Shanly. PAH

Rifleman's Song at Bennington. Joseph Rodman Drake. PAH

Rifles, The. *Unknown.* OBET

Rig Veda, *sels. Unknown, tr. fr. Sanskrit by* Romesh Dutt. *Fr.* Vedic Hymns. EaPr

Rigadoon, rigadoon, now let him fly. *Unknown.* OxNR

Rigged poker-stiff on her back. All the Dead Dears. Sylvia Plath. IHMS

Right. (*LL*) Woman. Nikki Giovanni. HeIL

Right after her birth, they crowded in. Anaesthesia. Jean Valentine. TAP

Right Apprehension. Thomas Traherne. PoEL-2

Right Arm, The. Paul Muldoon. NoAM

"Right as a Ribstone Pippin!" But it lied. (*LL*) The False Heart. Hilaire Belloc. FaBoCh; FaBoEE; OxBSP

Right as the star [*or* stern] of day began [*or* begouth] to s[c]hine. The Poet's Dream. William Dunbar. *Fr.* Golden [*or* Goldyn] Targe, The. OxBS; PoEL-1

(Ryght as the stern of day begouth to schyne.) OxBLMV

Right down the shocked street with a siren-blast. A Fire-Truck. Richard Wilbur. AiP

Right fresshe flowr, whos I ben have and shal. The Sorrow of Troilus. Chaucer. *Fr.* Troilus and Criseyde [*or* Criseide]. EnVB; PoEL-1

Right from the ambiguous start. D-Zug. Julian Croft. NOBAu

Right from the start he is dressed in his best — his blacks and his whites. A March Calf. Ted Hughes. NoP

Right good is rest. (*LL*) Inscription for an Old Bed. William Morris. OBEV; WiR

Right Hand of a Mexican Farmworker in Somerset County, Maryland, The. Martín Espada. UTF

Right Heart in the Wrong Place, The. James Joyce. FaBoPV

Right here I was nearly killed one night in February. Solitude. Tomas Tranströmer, *tr. fr. Swedish by* Robert Bly. RB

Right Here the Other Night Something. E. E. Cummings. NoAM

Right Is Right. Frederick William Faber. WBLP

Right Kind of People, The. Edwin Markham. BLPA; PoToHe

Right Meaning, The. César Vallejo, *tr. fr. Spanish by* Robert Bly. RaBo

Right Must Win, The. Frederick William Faber. PWR

Right Now. William Stafford. NaP

Right now, even if a muscular woman wanted. Trying for Fire. Tim Seibles. NAmP90

Right now it's all I care about. Your Life. Ron Schreiber. PFL

Right of Way. Eugene McCarthy. IIP

Right-of-Way: 1865, A. William Plomer. PeLV

RIGHT ON / MOTHERS / MOTHER. (*LL*) A Grandson Is a Hoticeberg. Margaret Danner. BlSi

Right On: White America. Sonia Sanchez. PoBA

Right over old Marm Hackett's garden! (*LL*) The Alarmed Skipper. James Thomas Fields. AnAmPo; NBLV

Rt. Rev. Richard Allen. Josephine D. Henderson Heard. CBWP-4

Right Royal. John Masefield. OtMeF

Right so this river storms. The Course of the Tavy. William Browne. *Fr.* Britannia's Pastorals. FaBoPP

Right Thing, The. Theodore Roethke. PeECV

Right to make my dreams come true, the. Calling Dreams. Georgia Douglas Johnson. ShDr

Right to the end, that man, he was so hot. The Miracle. Thom Gunn. FaBoBl

Right True End, The. *Gond Oral Tradition, tr. by* V. Elwin *and* S. Hivale. WTO

Right under their noses, the green. The Dusk of Horses. James Dickey. LiTM; NYBP

Right Use of Prayer, The. Sir Aubrey De Vere. TIRV; WGRP

Right well declare his worthiness. (*LL*) An Epitaph of Sir Thomas Gravener [Knight]. Sir Thomas Wyatt. SiPS

Right well I wote [*or* wrote] most mighty Soueraine [*or* soverain]. Spenser. *Fr.* Faerie Queene, The. NoSic; OAEL-1

Righteous Anger. James Stephens. *See* Lanky hank of a she in the inn over there, The.

Righteous Man, The. Samuel Butler. OBSV

Rights of Woman, The. Anna Laetitia Barbauld. ECWP; NOEC; WoRP

Rigid Body Sings. James Clerk Maxwell. FaBoCo; FaBoPa; UV

Rigoletto. Newman Levy. OBAL

Rigor of beauty is the quest. But how will you find beauty when it is locked. William Carlos Williams. *Fr.* Paterson. NoAM

Rigorists. Marianne Moore. NU

Rigs o' Barley, The. Burns. LiTB

Rilke, my river, I know your locked look of a poet. Visions. Kathleen Spivack. AmPA

Rilloby-Rill. Sir Henry Newbolt. BXAP

Rillons, Rillettes. Richard Wilbur. NYBP

Rim of Red. Bernard Gutteridge. FaBoBl

Rimbaud and Verlaine, precious pair of poets. Conrad Aiken. *Fr.* Preludes for Memnon; or, Preludes to Attitude. FaBoMo; LiTA; LiTM; NoAM; TwCP

Rimbaud Fire Letter to Jim Applewhite. Fred Chappell. SM

Rime for the Christmas Baby. Anne Spencer. ShDr

Rime of the Ancient Feminist, The, *sels.* Stephanie Markman. "They lived out in a women's house." BrRo

Rime of the Ancient Mariner, The. ("It is an ancient mariner".) Samuel Taylor Coleridge. BeLS; CH; EBEV; EBNV; EnRP; FaBoBe; FaBoCh; FaBV; FaPoB; FHYEP; HAP; HeIP; HoPM; ImPo; InPS; LiTB; MeMBP; NOBE; NoP; OAEL-2; OBEV; OBNC; OBNV; OtMeF; OxAEP-2; PeECV; PoE; PoEL-4; PrIm; SCGP; TEP; TFi; TOF, *abr.*; TrGrPo
Sels.
"Farewell, farewell! but this I tell." PFP
He Prayeth Best. FaPON
(He Prayeth Well.) BoTP, *sl. longer sel.*
"This Hermit good lives in that wood." Poetr

Rime of the Auncient Waggonere, The. William Maginn. BXAP; ClHu

Rime of the Gentle Pacifist, The. "Pontiff." NSI

Rime, the rack of finest wits. A Fit of Rime against Rime. Ben Jonson. BeJo; InvP; MAT; OAEL-1; PoEL-2; SeCP; SeCV-1
(Fit of Rhyme against Rhyme, A.) TEP
(Rhyme, the rack of finest wits.) TEP

Rimmed in by cypresses, tin water flashed. White Lake. James Applewhite. MT

Rimrock, Where It Is. Hayden Carruth. NNaP

Rin and rout, rin and rout. The Deevil's Waltz. Sydney Goodsir Smith. FaBoTw

Rin Tin Tin swallowed a pin. *Unknown.* RoPo

Ring, The. Atsumi Ikuko, *tr. fr. Japanese by* Kenneth Rexroth *and* Ikuko Atsumi. WPJ

Ring, The. Diane Wakoski. PoA

Ring-a-Ring. Kate Greenaway. FaPON; MoShBr

Ring-a-ring o' roses. Mother Goose. FaBoEH, 2 *vers.*; OxNR, 2 *vers.*; ReMoGo, 2 *vers.*

Ring-a-ring of little boys. Ring-a-Ring. Kate Greenaway. FaPON; MoShBr

Ring and the Book, The, *sels.* Robert Browning.
"Beside, up to my marriage, thirteen years." EBVVPR
Browning Finds 'The Book' in the Piazza di San Lorenzo, on a Day of Buzzing and Blaze in June 1860. CBCK
"Do you see this square old yellow Book, I toss." FaBoVe
"First of the first,/ Such I pronounce Pompilia, then as snow." EBVVPR
"From dawn till now that it is growing dusk." EBVVPR
"If I, — instead of threatening, talking big." EBVVPR
"Thanks, Sir, but, should it please the reverend Court." EBVVPR

Ring around a rosey. Squat Down, Josey. *Unknown.* AmFP

Ring Cycle, The. James Merrill. BAP-91

Ring into golden bowls. (*LL*) An Opium Fantasy. Maria White Lowell. AmWP; AnAmPo; InPK

Ring Of, The. Charles Olson. NOBA; VGW

Ring of Irony, The. Diane Wakoski. NGP

Ring Out the Old, Ring In the New. Tennyson. *See* Ring out, Wild Bells (To the Wild Sky).

Ring out to the stars the glad chorus! Our Nation Forever. Wallace Bruce. OHIP

Ring out, Wild Bells (To the Wild Sky). Tennyson. *Fr.* In Memoriam A. H. H. BLPL; EBEvV; EBVV, *abr.*; FaPON, 2 *sts.*; FaPoR; FHYEP; LiTB; MeMBP; OAEL-2, *abr.*; OxAEP-2; PeECV, *abr.*; PIP, 7 *sts.*; TrGrPo; WiR, 7 *sts., incl.* 2 *sts. fr.* CV

Ring out your bells [*or* belles], let mourning shows [*or* shewes] be spread. Sir Philip Sidney. EIL; NoP; NoSic; SiPS; SiPSBD; TEP
(Dirge.) OxAEP-1
(Litany, A: "Ring out your bells.") EnRePo; GBL; UnPo
(Litany, A.) SCGP

Ring Presented to Julia, A. Robert Herrick. PeLV

Ring round her! children of her glorious skies. The Foe at the Gates. John Dickson Bruns. PAH

Ring, so worn as you behold, The. A Marriage Ring. George Crabbe. BoLoP; EnLoPo; OBEV; OxBM
(His Late Wife's Wedding-Ring.) NOBE
(His Mother's Wedding Ring.) OBNC; UnAS

Ring the bells, nor ring them slowly. Cedar Mountain. Annie Fields. PAH

Ring the bells, ring! The Dunce. *Unknown.* OxNR

Ring-ting! I wish I were a primrose. Wishing. William Allingham. BoTP; FaPON; OHIP; OxBChV

Ringed Plover by a Water's Edge. Norman MacCaig. OxBC

Ringers, The. John Peck, *tr. fr. Italian by* William Arrowsmith. AmPA; AnAn

Ringing in your innermost heart. (*LL*) Snow. Helge Rode. RiWo

Ringing the Bells. Anne Sexton. FF; HCAP; PoE; TAP; VGW

Ringing tire iron, A. Some Good Things to Be Said for the Iron Age. Gary Snyder. HoPM; TTTS

Ringless. Diane Wakoski. NALW; Prf

Ringleted Youth of My Love. *Unknown, tr. fr. Modern Irish by* Douglas Hyde. WTO

Ringneck Parrots. *Unknown.* OBAP

Ringneck parrots, in scattered flocks, The. Ringneck Parrots. *Unknown.* OBAP

Ringsend. Oliver St. John Gogarty. OBMV; OxBTC; PeIV

Rink Keeper's Sestina. George Draper. PrIm

Rino's Song. Lynne Lawner. IHMS

Rintrah roars & shakes his fires in the burden air. Blake. *Fr.* Marriage of Heaven and Hell, The. EnRP; NAEL-2; OAEL-2

Rio Bravo — a Mexican Lament. José de Saltillo, *tr. fr. Spanish by* Charles Fenno Hoffman. PAH

Rio Bravo! Rio Bravo! Rio Bravo — a Mexican Lament. José de Saltillo, *tr. fr. Spanish by* Charles Fenno Hoffman. PAH

Riot. Gwendolyn Brooks. BPo; NALW; NBV; PoBA; TAP

Riot, A. Mrs. Henry Linden. CBWP-4

Riot; or, Half a Loaf Is Better than No Bread, The. Hannah More. NOEC

Riots and Rituals. Richard W. Thomas. PoBA

Rioupéroux. James Elroy Flecker. OBEV; OBTV

Rip. James Wright. NaP

Ripe and Bearded Barley, The. *Unknown.* BoNaP; ChTr; GBP

Ripe apples were caught like red fish in the nets. The Great Scarf of Birds. John Updike. NYBP

Ripe, Being Plunged into Fire. Friedrich Hölderlin, *tr. fr. German by* James Blair Leishman. OBVE

Ripe cherries and ripe maidens. Cherries. Zalman Schneour, *tr. fr. Yiddish by* Joseph Leftwich. TrJP

Ripe cherries smiling, while that others blow. (*LL*) Upon Mistress Susanna Southwell, Her Cheeks. Robert Herrick. BeJo

Ripe fruit to follow. (*LL*) Rushes in a watery place. Christina Rossetti. ChTr; PDV

Ripe Plums. *Unknown, tr. fr. Chinese by* Robert Payne. TAL

Ripe plums are dropping. Ripe Plums. *Unknown, tr. fr. Chinese by* Robert Payne. TAL

Ripeness Is All. Peter Viereck. ArOW

Ripeness is all; her in her cooling planet. To an Old Lady. William Empson. FaBoTw; GTBS-P; MoAB; NoAM; NOBE; OxAEP-2

Ripening. Wendell Berry. EaPr; RaBo

Ripley or not. A Street in Kaufman-ville. James Cunningham. JB

Ripperty! Kye! Ahoo! Henry Lawson. CBAP

Ripples lap the sand on the beach of Parrot Isle. Tune: "Ripples Sifting Sand." Liu Yu Hsi, *tr. fr. Chinese by* Daniel Bryant. SuSp

Rippling in the ocean of that darkening room. Woman at the Piano. Marya Zaturenska. MoAmPo

Riprap. Gary Snyder. CAPP; HCAP; NAAL-2; NeAP; NoAM; NOBA; PoBeRe; PoM; VCAP

Rise and deride this sepulchre of crime. (*LL*) On Passing the New Menin Gate. Siegfried Sassoon. NAEL-2; NoAM; OBMV; PoWW; Son

Rise and hold up the curved glass. Pour Us Wine. Ibn Kolthum, *tr. by* E. Powys Mathers. *Fr.* Mu'allaqat, The. AWP

Rise and Shine. Richmond Lattimore. NYBP; Poetr

Rise! arise! arise! The Sunrise Call. *Unknown, tr. by* N. Barnes. WTO

Rise, Crowned with Light Imperial Salem Rise. Pope. *Fr.* Messiah. WGRP

Rise from these crimson seas of war. (*LL*) Ave Imperatrix! Oscar Wilde. PeVV

Rise from your virgin sheets, that be. Epithalamium: To Mistress M. A. Martin Lluellyn [*or* Lluelyn]. NOSC

Rise from the dead/ From. (*LL*) Three Sentences for a Dead Swan. James Wright. NaP; NOBA

Rise, hallowed Milton! rise, and say. William Mason. *Fr.* Ode to Memory. EPCY

Rise heart; thy Lord is risen. Sing his praise. Easter ("Rise, heart, thy Lord is risen.") George Herbert. ESCV; GeHe; NAEL-1; NOSC; PeECV; SeCV-1; TrCP

Rise, Lady Mistress, Rise! Nathaniel Field. *Fr.* Amends for Ladies. EIL

Rise, mighty nation, in thy strength. On the Expected General Rising of the French Nation. Anna Laetitia Barbauld. ECWP

Rise, O earth, from out thy slumber. Prayer for Rain. *Unknown, tr. fr. Finnish.* WGRP

Rise odors of ploughed field or flowery mead. (*LL*) Chaucer. Longfellow. AWP; HeIP; InvP; MeMAP; NOBA; NoP; OBEV; OxBA; PoE; PoRA; PrIm; Son; TAP; TFi; TrGrPo

Rise Oedipus, and if thou canst unfould. Thomas Morton. SCAP

Rise of capitalism parallels the advance of romanticism, The. Definition of Blue. John Ashbery. CAPP; NAAL-2

Rise of Shivaji, The. Zulfikar Ghose. MoBS

Rise, rise from sluggishness, fly fast my dear. The Verses of the Talkative Knight. Mary Sidney Wroth, Countess of Montgomery. *Fr.* Urania. WPE

Rise! Sleep no more! 'Tis a noble morn! The Hunter's Song. "Barry Cornwall." GN

Rise then, ere ruin swift surprize. John Trumbull. *Fr.* M'Fingal. GOA

Rise thou best and brightest morning. New Year's Day. Richard Crashaw. JCP

Rise to all eternity. (*LL*) Jesus, Lover of My Soul. Charles Wesley. WGRP

Rise to one brimming golden, spilling cry! (*LL*) The Road. Helene Johnson. BISi; CDC; PoNe; ShDr

Rise, underground sleepers, rise from the grave. Ode against St. Cecilia's Day. George Barker. PoA

Rise up and cry out: NO! (*LL*) Challenge. David Diop. NegPo

Rise up in their sweetness and dawdle the days past clocking. (*LL*) Elephant Languor. April Bernard. UTF

Rise up, my love, my fair one, and come away. Bible, *O.T. Fr.* Song of Solomon, The. EaPr

Rise Up, O Men of God. William Pierson Merrill. AH

Rise up, rise up,/ And, as the trumpet blowing. The Trumpet. Edward Thomas. MoBrPo; OHIP

Rise up, rise up, Jack Spratt. And you, his wife. Sonnet XIII. Winfield Townley Scott. ErPo

Rise up, rise up, my seven brave sons. Earl Brand (The Douglas Tragedy). *Unknown.* FaBoBa

("Rise up, rise up, now, Lord Douglas,") she says. NTP

"Rise up, rise up, now, Lord Douglas,' she says. *Unknown. See* "Rise up, rise up, my seven brave sons."

Rise up! rise up! Oh Israel. Deliverance. Frances E. W. Harper. AmWP

Rise up, thou monstrous ant-hill on the plain. Wordsworth. *Fr.* Prelude [*or,* Growth of a Poet's Mind], The. EnRP; HAP, *short sel.;* OAEL-2; PoEL-4, *sl. shorter*

Rise with the Lamb of Innocence. *Unknown.* MeEL

Rise, Ye Children. Justus Falckner, *tr. fr. German by* Emma Frances Bevan. AH

Rise You Up, My True Love. *Unknown.* AmFP

Risen above the uncertain. To Her. Robert Mezey. NaP

Risen from rented rooms, old ghosts. A Winter Ode to the Old Men of Lummus Park, Miami, Florida. Donald Justice. NGP; WeW

Risen in a/ welter of waters. The Birth of Venus. Muriel Rukeyser. NALW

Risen Matters. Clark Coolidge. UL

Rises a conflagration of peace, a bloody dawn. (*LL*) Apollo and Daphne. W. R. Rodgers. ErPo; LiTB

Rises at five, just when a late moon. The Insomniac Sleeps Well for Once and. Hayden Carruth. NNaP

Risest thou thus, dim dawn, again. Tennyson. *Fr.* In Memoriam A. H. H. EBVV, *abr.;* OAEL-2, *abr.;* OBNC; PeECV, *abr.;* PoEL-5

Rising, The. Jayne Cortez. NBV

Rising, The. Thomas Buchanan Read. *Fr.* Wagoner of the Alleghanies, The. PAH

Rising and falling back and rising. (*LL*) Delta Traveller. Charles Wright. AmPA; LCAP

Rising Early in the Morning. Chao Yi, *tr. fr. Chinese by* Chang Yin-nan *and* Lewis C. Walmsley. SuSp

Rising fondly before me. The Beloved's Image. *Unknown, tr. fr. Hawaiian.* WTO, *tr. by* M. W. Beckwith

Rising Glory of America, The. *sels.* Hugh Henry Brackenridge *and* Philip Freneau. AiP
 Eugenio. AiP
 Leander. AiP

Rising hills, the slopes, The. For the Children. Gary Snyder. NoP

Rising in lamplight dying at dawn. Voices Answering Back: The Vampires. Lawrence Raab. AmPA

Rising in the Morning. Hugh Rhodes. OxBChV

Rising in the North, The. *Unknown.* ESPB

Rising in Winter. Hsiao Kang, *tr. fr. Chinese by* Kenneth Rexroth. OHMPC

Rising, The/ Let me proceed by this way. Canoe-hauling Chant. *Unknown, tr. by* Apirana Ngata. WTO

Rising of the Moon A.D. 1798, The. John Keegan Casey. PeIV

Rising of the Session, The. Robert Fergusson. OxBS

Rising sun, The. (*LL*) On yonder hill there is a red deer. *Unknown.* ChTr; GBP

Rising to Meet It. Chana Bloch. CrSp

Rising Village, The, *sels.* Oliver Goldsmith, the Younger. (Lonely Settler, The.) NOBC

Rising without names today. The Survivor. Stephen Berg. *Fr.* Entering the Body. NaP

Risk, The. Anne Sexton. BoWoP

Risks of the Game, The. Adam Lindsay Gordon. *Fr.* Ye Wearie Wayfarer. OtMeF

Rite, The. Peter Dale. NAs

Rite, The. Dudley Randall. HoPM

Rite de Passage. Michele Roberts. NBrP

Rite of Passage. Audre Lorde. PoBA

Rite of Spring. Seamus Heaney. FaBoBl; OxBC

Rite of Spring!, The. Homard à Igor Stravinsky: Vernacular Variations. Hugh Haughton. CBNP

Rite of Spring, The. (*LL*) Homard à Igor Stravinsky: Vernacular Variations. Hugh Haughton. CBNP

Rites, *sels.* Edward Kamau Brathwaite.
 "Look wha' happen las' week at de Oval!" FaBoVe

Rites for Cousin Vit, The. Gwendolyn Brooks. *Fr.* Womanhood, The. BPo; HAP; WeW; WPE

Rites of Ancient Ripening. Meridel LeSueur. SRLS

Rites of Manhood, The. Alden Nowlan. RaBo

Rites of Passage., *sels.* Robert Duncan.
"Something is taking place." BCF; NoAM
"These are/ the passages of thought." BCF

Rites of the Eastern Star. Janine Pommy-Vega. UL

Ritual, The. E. J. Pratt. MoP

Ritual Girl. Frank Mkalawile Chipasula. HBAPE

Ritual Not Religious. *Unknown, tr. fr. Telugu.* WGRP

Ritual of Departure. Thomas Kinsella. CIP; CMoP

Ritual to Read to Each Other, A. William Stafford. RaBo

Ritualists, The. William Carlos Williams. NYBP

Rituals. Pat Mora. AfAz

Rituals along the Arkansas. William Mills. MT

Rival, The. Sylvia Plath. LPA

Rival, The. Sylvia Townsend Warner. MoAB; MoBrPo

Rival Curates, The. W. S. Gilbert. PeLV

Rivals, The, *sels.* Sir William Davenant.
"My lodging it is on the cold ground." JCP

Rivals, The. Daniel Mark Epstein. BAP-89

Rivals. *At. to* Sir George Etherege *and to* William Walsh. OBEV

Rivals, The. James Stephens. BoTP; FaPON; InvP; OBEV; OBMV

Rivals. *At. to* William Walsh *and* Sir George Etherege. OBEV

Riven Quarry, The. Gloria C. Oden. PoBA

River, The. Ethel M. Caution. ShDr

River, The. Sam Cornish. PoBA

River, The. Hart Crane. *Fr.* Bridge, The. AmPP; CMoP; GOA; LiTA; MoAB; MoAmPo; NAAL-2; NOBA; OxBA; PrIm

River. Ted Hughes. NAEL-2

River. Lawrence Locke. GrPl

River, The, *sels.* Pare Lorentz.

River, The. Roy Macnab. PeSA

River, The. Edwin Muir. MeMBP

River, The. Dabney Stuart. NYBP

River, The. *Unknown.* PWR

River Afram. Andrew Amankwa Opoku. PBA

River brought down, The. How We Heard the Name. Alan Dugan. CoAP; NoAM

River Compared to an Oratorical Sentence, The. Luis de Góngora y Argote, *tr. fr. Spanish by* Edward Meryon Wilson. *Fr.* First Solitude, The. OBVE

River Crossing, The. Denis Glover. *Fr.* Arawata Bill. PeNZ

River Dart, The. *Unknown.* GBP

River Don, The. *Unknown.* GBP

River Duddon, The, *sels.* Wordsworth.
"I thought of Thee, my partner and my guide." FaBoRV
(After-Thought.) EnRP; OBNC
(To the River Duddon: After-Thought.) FaBoPP
(Valediction to the River Duddon.) NOBE
(Valedictory Sonnet to the River Duddon.) OBEV
Return. HAP

River Fight, The. Henry Howard Brownell. PAH

River-Fog. Kiyowara Fukuyabu, *tr. fr. Japanese by* Arthur Waley. AWP; FaPON

River-Fog. Kiyowara Fukuyabu, *tr. fr. Japanese by* Arthur Waley. *Fr.* Shui Shu. AWP; FaPON

River God, The. John Fletcher. *Fr.* Faithful Shepherdess, The. TrGrPo

River God, The. Sacheverell Sitwell. MoBrPo

River God, The. Stevie Smith. BrRo; FaBoNo; FaBoTw; FaBoWP; PBWP

River[-]God's Song, The. John Fletcher. *Fr.* Faithful Shepherdess, The. FaPON; MoShBr; NOSC

River God's Song. Anne Ridler. NYBP

River Has No Hair to Hold Onto, The. Ralph Angel. NAmP90

River, I am passing. River Afram. Andrew Amankwa Opoku. PBA

River in its abundance, The. Eros at Temple Stream. Denise Levertov. NALW

River in March, The. Ted Hughes. OxBC

River in the Meadows, The. Léonie Adams. MoAB; MoAmPo

River irises, The. Grass. James Merrill. PRA

River is a decrepit old woman, the. The River. Ethel M. Caution. ShDr

River Is a Piece of Sky, The. John Ciardi. PDV

River is lined with the, The. At Ch'en Ch'u. Wang Shih-chieng, *tr. fr. Chinese by* Kenneth Rexroth. OHMPC

River is rising, *Ngoho,* the river, The. (*LL*) In a Storm. Antoine-Roger Bolamba. NegPo

River is rising, *Ngoho,* the river, The. In a Storm. Antoine-Roger Bolamba, *tr. fr. French by* Ellen Conroy Kennedy. NegPo

River is smooth and calm this evening, The. Spring River Flowers Moon Night. Emperor Yang of Sui, *tr. fr. Chinese by* Kenneth Rexroth. OHMPC

River is so much mica, The. The River; North of Guelph. Douglas G. Jones. NOBC

River Lynher, The. Richard Carew. *Fr.* Survey of Cornwall. FaBoPP

River-Mates. Padraic Colum. AWP

River Merchant's Wife, The; a Letter. Li Po, *tr. fr. Chinese.* AmPP; AWP; BoLoP; ClHu; FYAP; HAP; HeIP; InPK; InPS; LiTA; LPA, *tr. by* Ezra Pound; MeMAP; MoAB; MoAmPo; MoP; NAAL-2; NIP; NoAM; NOBA; NOBE; NoP; OBMV; OBVE; OxBA; Poetr; PPP; PrIm; RaBo; RB; SOTW; TAP; TFi; TRP; TTTS; TwCP; UnPo; WeW

River moans, The. River. Lawrence Locke. GrPl

River; North of Guelph, The. Douglas G. Jones. NOBC

River Now, The. Richard Hugo. VCAP

River of Bees, The. W. S. Merwin. HeIP; LCAP; VCAP

River of Dart, O river of Dart. The Dart. *Unknown.* GBP

River of Heaven, The. *Unknown, tr. by* Lafcadio Hearn. *Fr.* Manyo Shu, Part 3 of 4. AWP

River of Heaven turns in the night and floats the stars round, The. Up in Heaven. Li Ho, *tr. fr. Chinese by* A. C. Graham. PLT

River of Life, The. Thomas Campbell. GTBS; GTBS-P; ImPo; LiTB

River of Rivers in Connecticut, The. Wallace Stevens. HAP; HCAP; NOBA; VGW

River of sudden, The. Waterfall. Gareth Owen. Spl

River Rhyme. William Carlos Williams. PoA

River Road. Stanley Kunitz. MoP; NoAM

River Road Studio. Barbara Guest. PoM

River Roads. Carl Sandburg. VGW

River Roses. D. H. Lawrence. CMoP; GBL; OAEL-2

River Song. Weldon Kees. PPP

River Sound Remembered. W. S. Merwin. SM

River Stories. Dorothy Coffin Sussman. ArOW

River Swelleth More and More, The. Thoreau. NOBA

River takes the land, and leaves nothing, The. The Slip. Wendell Berry. NOCV

River that flows nowhere, like a sea, The. (*LL*) The River of Rivers in Connecticut. Wallace Stevens. HAP; HCAP; NOBA; VGW

River That Flows through Our Land, The. Jeremy Cronin. PeSAV

River That Is East, The. Galway Kinnell. Poetr

River that must turn full after I stop dying. "A 11" ("River that must turn full after I stop dying.") Louis Zukofsky. *Fr.* "A" (1–12). VGW

River, that rollest by the ancient walls. Stanzas to the Po. Byron. OAEL-2

River used to store up in its mouth, The. The River. Roy Macnab. PeSA

River Walk. John Stuart Williams. AngWe

River was announcing, The. The River Crossing. Denis Glover. *Fr.* Arawata Bill. PeNZ

River waters shiver in the west wind. On the Yangtze. Wang An-shih, *tr. fr. Chinese by* Jan W. Walls. SuSp

River, why in ceaseless flow. Maiden and River. Mary Weston Fordham. CBWP-2

River woods,/ dark made of owl hoots, in the crickets. The Wood House over the Wilia. Johannes Bobrowski, *tr. fr. German by* Don Bogen. AnAn

Riverbank, the long rigs. Broagh. Seamus Heaney. FaBoVe

Riverman, The. Elizabeth Bishop. NYBP

Riverrun where can you guess? *Unknown.* PeLi

Rivers. Czeslaw Milosz, *tr. fr. Polish by* Robert Hass *and* Renata Gorczynski. FoLa

Rivers. Thomas Storer. EIL; FaBoCh

Rivers. Giuseppe Ungaretti, *tr. fr. Italian by* Jon Silkin. PeFWW

Rivers and Mountains. John Ashbery. CoAP; NoAM; NOBA; TRP

Rivers Arise. Milton. *See* Rivers Arise; a Fragment.

Rivers Arise; a Fragment. Milton. ChTr

Rivers Come to the Hall of Proteus for the Marriage of the Thames and the Medway, The. Spenser. *Fr.* Faerie Queene, The. FaBoPP

River's Elegy, The. Aidan Carl Mathews. IB

River's End. Ralph Pomeroy. NGP

River's glint and mountain mist were floating in green. Composed on Horseback, Returning from Lakeview Pavilion at Hangchow, Presented to Yü-ju and Lo-tao. Wang An-shih, *tr. fr. Chinese by* Jan W. Walls. SuSp

River's just beyond that hill, The. Tugela River. William Plomer. PeSAV

Rivers level granite mountains. Sulpicius Lupercus Servasius the Younger, *tr. fr. Greek by* Kenneth Rexroth. PGA

Rivers of Ireland, The. Spenser. *Fr.* Faerie Queene, The. CBCK

Rivers rush into the sea, The. The Song of the Bird. Longfellow. BoTP

Rivers that flowed divided each from each. Chinese Poems: Arthur Waley. "C. A. Fair." PeSA

Riversongs of Arion, The. *sels.* Michael Anania. NoAM
"Adrift on an oil-drum raft." NoAM
"Among the provisions they carried." NoAM
"Which river is this." NoAM

Rivery field spread out below, A. Let All Things Pass Away. W. B. Yeats. ChTr

Rivulet crossing my ground. Tennyson. *Fr.* Maud: A Monodrama. EnVR

Rivulet-loving wanderer Abraham, The. Abraham. Edwin Muir. ChIV-1

Rizpah. Tennyson. PeVV; PoEL-5

R.M.S. *Titanic, sels.* Anthony Cronin.
"On the bog road the blackthorn flowers, the turf-stacks." BIrV
"Trembling with engines, gulping oil, the river." PBCIP

Roach, The. John Raven. BPo; HoPM

Roach, A/ came struttin. The Roach. John Raven. BPo; HoPM

Road, The. Conrad Aiken. MoAmPo

Road. D. C. Berry. MT

Road, The. Helene Johnson. BlSi; CDC; PoNe; ShDr

Road. Kevin Magee. BAP-90

Road, The. Herbert Morris. DiPo

Road, The. Edwin Muir. CMoP; ImPo; LiTB; LiTM; MeMBP; Mes

Road, The. Nikolay P. Ogarev, *tr. fr. Russian by* P. E. Matheson. AWP

Road, The. Zalman Schneour, *tr. fr. Yiddish by* Joseph Leftwich. TrJP

Road, The. James Stephens. PlP

Road ahead, The. Seamus Heaney. *Fr.* Sweeney Redivivus. TOF

Road at My Door, The. W. B. Yeats. *Fr.* Meditations in Time of Civil War. BIrV; LiTB; NOBE; PoE

Road at the top of the rise, The. The Middleness of the Road. Robert Frost. LiTA; NOBA

Road Back, The. Anne Sexton. NYBP

Road beneath the giant original trees, The. Sanctuary. Judith Wright. WPE

Road climbs steeply till it crests above the hills, The. Inner Mongolia — The Grasslands. Sibyl James. LoHo

Road climbs, villages, The. Going. Peter Everwine. NNaP

Road goes ever on and on, The. The Old Walking Song. J. R. R. Tolkien. RFM

Road he took was virgin territory, The. Theaitetos. Callimachus, *tr. fr. Greek by* Peter Jay. GrAn

Road is so rough Severn is walking, The. Posthumous Keats. Stanley Plumly. SV

Road is wide and the stars are out and the breath of the night is sweet, The. Roofs. Joyce Kilmer. BLPL; PoLF

Road might lead to anywhere, A. Roads. Rachel Field. FaPON; PDV

Road Not Taken, The. Robert Frost. AiP; AmPP; ChTr; CMoP; EBEvV; FaBoCh; FaPoB; HAP; HeIP; ImPo; LiTA; LiTM; MeMAP; MoAB; MoAmPo; MoP; NAAL-2; NIP; NoAM; NoP; NTP; OxBA; Poetr; PoLF; RFM; SAmP; SoSe; TAP; TFi; TRP; TwCP

Road of Life, The. William Morris. *Fr.* Earthly Paradise, The. OBNC

Road streams, to the moon, The. The sky. March Night. Alison Brackenbury. SCBI

Road to Bologna, The. Roy Macnab. PeSA

Road to Castaly, The, *sels.* Alice Brown.
Revelation. WGRP

Road to France, The. Daniel Henderson. PAH

Road to Hogan's Gap, The. Andrew Barton Paterson. CBAP

Road to Patmos, The. John Ennis. PBCIP

Road to Pengya, The. Tu Fu, *tr. fr. Chinese by* Rewi Alley *and* Edward Field. Prf

Road to Shu Is Hard, The. Li Po, *tr. fr. Chinese by* Irving Y. Lo. SuSp

Road to Town, The. H. M. Sarson. BoTP

Road to Vagabondia, The. Dana Burnet. PoLF

Road to Zoagli, The. Max Beerbohm. FaBoNo

Road turned out to be a cul-de-sac, The. Brother and Sisters. Judith Wright. FaBoWP

Road twisted through tongues of rock, The. The Vowels of Another Language. Tom Disch. PoA

Road where Ts'ao Chih watched the fighting cocks, The. Spending the Night in the Eastern Park. Shen Yüeh, *tr. fr. Chinese by* Richard B. Mather. SuSp

Road winds down through autumn hills, The. Tour 5. Robert Hayden. PPP

Roadmap, The. Thom Gunn. CBLP

Roadmenders' Song, The. *Gond Oral Tradition, tr. by* V. Elwin *and* S. Hivale. WTO

Roads. Rachel Field. FaPON; PDV

Roads. Peter Huchel, *tr. fr. German by* Michael Hamburger. PoSu

Roads. Antonio Machado Ruiz, *tr. fr. Spanish by* Willis Barnstone. *Fr.* Dream Below the Sun, The. IMW

Roads. Edward Thomas. PeFWW

Road's a wild stallion and he's riding bareback, The. Trucker. Robert Walton. AngWe

Roads Also, The. Wilfred Owen. EBEV; PlP

Roads are now impassable, The. Spring Season of Muddy Roads. Joseph Brodsky, *tr. fr. Russian by* George L. Kline. AnAn

Road's End. Rolf Jacobsen, *tr. fr. Norwegian by* Robert Bly. NU

Road's End, The. John Montague. *Fr.* Severed Head, A. IPY

Roads Go Ever On and On. J. R. R. Tolkien. FaPON

Roads have come to their end now, The. Road's End. Rolf Jacobsen, *tr. fr. Norwegian by* Robert Bly. NU

Roadside Attraction. Mark Vinz. NGP

Roadside forests here and there were touched with tawny gold, The. Mistress Hale of Beverly. Lucy Larcom. PAH

Roadside Fountain. Momcilo Nastasijevic, *tr. fr. Serbo-Croatian by* Charles Simic. HSix

Roadside Inn This Summer Saturday, A. Thomas Caulfield Irwin. PeIV

Roadside thistle, eager, The. Basho, *tr. fr. Japanese by* Curtis Hidden Page. AWP

Roadways. John Masefield. BoTP; OTCP

Roam not from pole to pole, but enter here. Swift. *Fr.* Inscription for the Sign of *The Jolly Barber,* with a Razor in One Hand, and a Pot of Beer in the Other. FaBoUS

Roaming Immortal. Ts'ao Chih, *tr. fr. Chinese by* Ronald C. Miao. SuSp

Roaming these/ Furry prairies. Fleas. Valerie Worth. OBAP

Roan Stallion. Robinson Jeffers. BeLS

Roar drowns the reproach, facing him. Edwin Denby. PRA

Roar of cannon, The/ Has died away. Between Battles. Zhimin Zhang. PAW

Roar of welcome though the welkin, A. The Elk, The Whelk. Robert Williams Wood. NBLV

Roaring alongside he takes for granted, The. Sandpiper. Elizabeth Bishop. AiP; HeIP; NYBP; RB; TOF

Roaring Frost, The. Alice Meynell. EBVV; WPE

Roaring Lad and the Ranting Lass, The; or, A Merry Couple Madly Met. *Unknown.* CoMu

Roaring Mad Tom. *Unknown. See* From the hag [or hagg] and hungry [or hungrie] goblin.

Roaring of the wheels has filled my ears, The. A Cry from the Ghetto. Morris Jacob Rosenfeld, *tr. fr. Yiddish by* Charles Weber Linn. TrJP

Roaring torrent. My Home. Ludwig Rellstab, *tr. fr. German by* Philip L. Miller. RiWo

Roaring waterfall, the. Su Tung-p'o, *tr. fr. Japanese by* Stephen Mitchell. EnIH

Roars of a million tongues, and none knows what they mean. *(LL)* Cataract, whirling to the precipice, The. John Clare. BoNaP

Roars to miraculous heat and turbulance. *(LL)* Golden Bough. Elinor Wylie. MoAmPo; PBWP

Roast chestnuts, a shilling. Walking against the Wind. Jon Stallworthy. OxBC

Roast Possum. Rita Dove. Poetr

Roasted Sucking Pig. *Unknown.* BXAP

Roasting alive of rabbits, The. In the Absence of Bliss. Maxine W. Kumin. NoAM

Rob me and maim me! Why, man, take such pains. To One Who Quotes and Detracts. Walter Savage Landor. FaBoEE

Rob Roy. *Unknown.* ESPB, A *and* B *vers.*

Robbed of our rights, and by such water-rats? In Defiance to the Dutch. *Unknown.* APAS

Robben Island. Robert Dederick. PeSA

Robben Island Sequence. Dennis Brutus. HBAPE

Robber, The. Hugh MacDiarmid. OBVE

Robber, The. W. J. Turner. MoBrPo

Robber Bridegroom, The. Margaret Atwood. LCAP

Robber Bridegroom, The. Allen Tate. CBLP

Robber of Kuan-shan, The, *sels.* Wang Chiu-ssu, *tr. fr. Chinese by* Jonathan Chaves.

Robbers came to our house, The. *Unknown.* GBP

Robby, git down wi'tha, wilt tha? Tennyson. *Fr.* Spinster's Sweet-Arts, The. FaBoVe

Robene and Makyne. Robert Henryson. *See* Robin [or Robene] sat on gude green [or gud grene] hill.

Robene sat on gud grene [or green] hill. Robert Henryson. *See* Robin [or Robene] sat on gude green [or gud grene] hill.

Robens' Promised Land. George Purdom. WTO

Robert. Wendy Rose. HATNAP

Robert Barnes, or [my] fellow fine. Mother Goose. OxNR; ReMoGo

Robert Bly Finds Something in New Jersey. Carol Poster. BXAP

Robert Bly Says Something Too. Henry Taylor. BXAP

Sir Robert Bolton had three sons. Sir Lionel. *Unknown.* ESPB

Robert Brackenbury. Alison Brackenbury. SCBI

Robert Bruce's March to Bannockburn. Burns. *See* Scots, wha hae wi' Wallace bled.

Robert Creeley Also Watches. D. C. Berry. BXAP

Robert Creeley Listens, Too. D. C. Berry. BXAP

Robert E. Lee. Julia Ward Howe. PAH

Robert Frost. David O'Bruadair. Robert Lowell. *Fr.* Writers. MoP; NAAL-2; NoAM; Poetr; Son

Robert Frost's Left-leaning *Trespassers Will Be Shot* Sign. William Zaranka. BXAP

Robert G. Shaw. H. Cordelia Ray. AAP; BlSi; CBWP-3; Son

Robert Gould Shaw. Paul Laurence Dunbar. Son

Robert Graves. Gavin Ewart. NoAM

Robert of Lincoln. Bryant. EAP; FaBoBe; FaPON; OBCA; WBLP, *abr*

Robert of Sicily, brother of Pope Urbane. King Robert of Sicily (The Sicilian's Tale). Longfellow. *Fr.* Tales of a Wayside Inn. BeLS; OHIP

Robert Rowley rolled a round roll round. Mother Goose. OxNR

Robert Sat. Tom Matthews. PNI

Robert, Second Duke of Normandy, *sels.* Thomas Lodge.
Pluck the Fruit and Taste the Pleasure. EiL; EnRePo; OxAEP-1

Robert Sheridan Lowell. Robert Lowell. *Fr.* Marriage. NAs

Robert the Bruce. Edwin Muir. OxBS

Robert Whitmore. Frank Marshall Davis. BPo; NoP; PoBA; PoNe

Robertin Tush. *Unknown.* GBP

Robes loosely flowing and aspect as free. Seeing Her Dancing. Robert Heath. NOSC; OxBSP

Robespierre and Mozart as Stage. Robert Lowell. FaBoMo

Robespierre could live with himself: "The Republic." Robespierre and Mozart as Stage. Robert Lowell. FaBoMo

Robin, The. Laurence Alma-Tadema. BoTP

Robin, The. O. M. Bent. BoTP

Robin, The. George Daniel. FaBoRV

Robin, The. William Bell Scott. FM

Robin, The. Jones Very. Son

Robin, A. Walter de la Mare. ChTr; CMoP; FaBoRV

Robin-a-Bobbin. *Unknown. See* Robin the Bobbin.

Robin-a-bobin. Mother Goose. OxNR

Robin; a Pastoral Elegy. John Dobson. NOEC

Robin and a robin's son, A. *Unknown.* OxNR

Robin and Gandelyn. *Unknown. See* I heard the carping [*or* herde a carpyng] of a clerk.

Robin [*or* Robene] and Makyne. Robert Henryson. OBEV; PeLV; PoEL-1

Robin and Richard. Mother Goose. OxBoLi; OxNR; ReMoGo

Robin and Richard/ Were two pretty men. Robin and Richard. Mother Goose. OxBoLi; OxNR; ReMoGo

Robin and the red-breast, The. Warning. The. *Unknown.* OxNR

Robin and the wren, The. Greed. *Unknown.* OxNR
(Four birds.) ChTr
(Robin, Wren, Martin, Swallow.) GBP

Robin cries: *rain!*, The. Rain in Ohio. Mary Oliver. InPK

Robin dwelt in greenë wood. The Death of Robin Hood. *Unknown.* EnSB

Robin Friend has gone to bed. Bed-Time. Laurence Alma-Tadema. BoTP

Robin Good-Fellow's Song: "Round about, little ones." *Unknown. Fr.* Robin Goodfellow. EiL

Robin Goodfellow, *sels. Unknown.*
Lily, Germander, and Sops-in-Wine. CBCK
(And Can the Physician.) ELP
(Song: "And can the physician make sick men well?") EiL
Robin Good-Fellow's Song: "Round about, little ones." EiL

Robin Goodfellow. *Unknown.* FaBoCh

Robin he's gane to the wast. The Wife Wrapt [*or* Wrapped] in Wether's Skin. *Unknown.* AmFP; ESPB

Robin Hode and the Munkee. *Unknown. See* In somer, when the shawes be sheyne.

Robin Hood. Keats. AWP; EnRP; SCGP

Robin Hood. Rachel MacAndrew. BoTP

Robin Hood. Phyllis McGinley. *Fr.* Speaking of Television. OBSV

Robin Hood. *Unknown.* FaBoCh

Robin Hood and Allen [*or* Allin] -a-Dale. *Unknown.* ESPB; FaBoBe; GBP; MoShBr; OxAEP-1

Robin Hood and Guy of Gisborne. *Unknown.* ESPB

Robin Hood and Little John. *Unknown.* AmFP; ESPB; ReMoGo

Robin Hood and Maid Marian. *Unknown.* ESPB

Robin Hood and Queen Katherine. *Unknown.* ESPB

Robin Hood and the Beggar, I. *Unknown.* ESPB

Robin Hood and the Beggar, II. *Unknown.* ESPB

Robin Hood and the Bishop. *Unknown.* ESPB

Robin Hood and the Bishop of Hereford. *Unknown.* ESPB

Robin Hood and the Butcher. *Unknown.* ESPB

Robin Hood and the Curtal Friar. *Unknown.* ESPB

Robin Hood and the Golden Arrow. *Unknown.* ESPB

Robin Hood and the Grey Friars. Thomas Love Peacock. *Fr.* Maid Marian. OxAEP-2

Robin Hood and the Monk. *Unknown.* ESPB; FaBoBa; OBNV, *abr.*

Robin Hood and the Pedlars. *Unknown.* ESPB

Robin Hood and the Potter. *Unknown.* ESPB

Robin Hood and the Prince of Aragon. *Unknown.* ESPB

Robin Hood and the Ranger. *Unknown.* ESPB

Robin Hood and the Scotchman. *Unknown.* ESPB

Robin Hood and the Shepherd. *Unknown.* ESPB

Robin Hood and the Tanner. *Unknown.* ESPB

Robin Hood and the Three Squires. *Unknown. See* There are twelve months in all the year.

Robin Hood and the Three Squires. *Unknown. See* In faith thou shalt haue mine.

Robin Hood and the Tinker. *Unknown.* ESPB

Robin Hood and the Valiant Knight. *Unknown.* ESPB

Robin Hood/ Has gone to the wood. Robin Hood. *Unknown.* OxNR

Robin Hood he was [*or* he was] and a tall young man. Robin Hood's Progress to Nottingham. *Unknown.* ESPB; OBET

Robin Hood Newly Revived. *Unknown.* ESPB

Robin Hood Rescuing Three Squires. *Unknown.* ESPB, A *and* B *vers.*

Robin Hood Rescuing Will Stutly. *Unknown.* ESPB

Robin Hood, Robin Hood,/ Is in the mickle wood. Mother Goose. BoTP; OxNR

Robin Hood, Robin Hood,/ Is in the mickle wood! Robin Hood and Little John. *Unknown.* ReMoGo

Robin Hood's Barn. John Ashbery. AnAn

Robin Hood's Birth, Breeding, Valor, and Marriage. *Unknown.* ESPB

Robin Hood's Chase. *Unknown.* ESPB

Robin Hood's Death, *diff. versions. Unknown.* ESPB, A *and* B *vers.*; FaBoBa; OBET; TrGrPo

Robin Hood's Delight. *Unknown.* ESPB

Robin Hood's Funeral. Anthony Munday. *See* Weep, weep, ye woodmen! wail.

Robin Hood's Golden Prize. *Unknown.* ESPB

Robin Hood's Progress to Nottingham. *Unknown.* ESPB; OBET

Robin is a lovely lad. The Dance. *At. to* Thomas Campion. EiL; FaBoCh

Robin is the one, The. Emily Dickinson. FaBV

Robin laughed in the orange tree, The. Tampa Robins. Sidney Lanier. AnAmPo

Robin once lunched with Herbert Read at his club. Robert Sheppard. *Fr.* Letter from the Blackstock Road. NBrP

Robin pipeth now, The. (*LL*) Feathers of the willow, The. Richard Watson Dixon. BoNaP; CH; FaBoCh; GTBS-P; NOBE; OBNC

Robin Red Breast. Lula Lowe Weeden. CDC

Robin Redbreast. William Allingham. FaBoBe; MoShBr; OxBChV

Robin Redbreast. Stanley Kunitz. Prf

Robin Redbreast in a cage, A. Blake. *Fr.* Auguries of Innocence. BLPL; EBEV; EnRP; FaBoCh; FaBV; FaPoR; FM; LiTB; OAEL-1; OBNC; OxBoLi, *sl. abr.*; PoEL-4; TrGrPo
(Three Things to Remember.) FaPON; MoShBr

Robin Redbreast's Testament. *Unknown.* GBP; NTP

Robin! Robin! call the Springtime. March. H. Cordelia Ray. CBWP-3

Robin sang sweetly. *Unknown.* BoTP

Robin [*or* Robene] sat on gude green [*or* gud grene] hill. Robin [*or* Robene] and Makyne. Robert Henryson. OBEV; PeLV; PoEL-1
(Robene and Makyne.) BoLoP; MiEL; OxBLMV; PoE
(Robene sat on gud grene [*or* green] hill.) BoLoP

Robin the Bobbin. *Unknown.* OxNR
(Robin-a-Bobbin.) ReMoGo

Robin, Wren, Martin, Swallow. *Unknown. See* Robin and the wren, The.

Robinets and Jenny Wrens. *Unknown.* OxNR

Robins in the treetop. Marjorie's Almanac. Thomas Bailey Aldrich. FaPON

Robins sang in England. Robin's Song. Rodney Bennett. BoTP

Robin's Song. Rodney Bennett. BoTP

Robin's Song, The. C. Lovat Fraser. BoTP; MoShBr

Robinson. Weldon Kees. MoP; NaP; NYBP

Robinson at cards at the Algonquin; a thin. Aspects of Robinson. Weldon Kees. CoAP; NaP; NYBP

Robinson at Home. Weldon Kees. CoAP; NYBP

Robinson Crusoe Daniel Defoe. Maurice Sagoff. NBLV

Robinson Crusoe's Story. Charles Edward Carryl. *See* Night was thick and hazy, The.

Robinson one,/ Robinson two. *Unknown.* ISE

Robot Camera. Robert Johnstone. PNI

Robyn, A/ Joly Robyn. Sir Thomas Wyatt. AAS

Robyn and Gandeleyn. *Unknown.* EnSB; ESPB; OxBB

Robyn lycœth in grene wode bowndyn. (*LL*) Robyn and Gandeleyn. *Unknown.* EnSB; ESPB; OxBB

Roc, The. Richard Eberhart. CMoP

Rochester Extempore. The Earl of Rochester. ChIV-1

Rock, The, *sels.* T. S. Eliot.
  Chorus from "The Rock." LiTB
  "Eagle soars in the summit of heaven, The." OBMV
  "I journeyed to the suburbs, and there I was told." UV
  "O Light Invisible, we praise Thee!" TrPWD

Rock, The. *Unknown, tr. fr. Welsh* by Geoffrey Grigson. ChTr; GBL

"Rock-a-by, baby, up in the tree-top!" In the Tree-Top. Lucy Larcom. OBCA

Rock-a-by Lady, The. Eugene Field. BoTP

Rock-a-bye, baby, thy cradle is green. Mother Goose. OxNR; ReMoGo

Rock, a leaf, mud, even the grass, A. The Concealment: Ishi, the Last Wild Indian. William Stafford. NaP

Rock and Hawk. Robinson Jeffers. NoAM; NOBA; OxBA; Poetr

Rock and precipice. Landscape. Octavio Paz, *tr. fr. Spanish.* OBVE, *tr. by Charles Tomlinson*

Rock, Ball, Fiddle. *Unknown. See* He that lies at the stock.

Rock Climbing. Jane Cooper. NMM

Rock Crumbles, The. Else Lasker-Schüler, *tr. fr. German.* TrJP, *tr. by Ralph Manheim*
  (My People.) WPOW, *tr. by Michael Hamburger*

Rock foundation of the fort was dread, The. Blockhouse. Olga Kirsch, *tr. fr. Afrikaans* by Jack Cope. PeSA

Rock grows brittle, The. My People. Else Lasker-Schüler, *tr. fr. German* by Michael Hamburger. WPOW

Rock Island Line, The. *Unknown.* AmFP

Rock-like the souls of men. Men Fade Like Rocks. W. J. Turner. OBMV

Rock Me to Sleep, [Mother]. Elizabeth Akers Allen. AnAmPo; BLPA; BLPL; FaBoBe; MDDM; OBCA; VPP; WBLP

Rock me to sleep, Mother — rock me to sleep! (*LL*) Rock Me to Sleep, [Mother]. Elizabeth Akers Allen. AnAmPo; BLPA; BLPL; FaBoBe; MDDM; OBCA; VPP; WBLP

Rock 'n' Roll. Lesley Frost. AiP

Rock 'n' roll Band. Shel Silverstein. ImGa

Rock of Ages. Augustus Montague Toplady. BLRP; FaPoR; NOCV; PlP; SCGP; WGRP

Rock of ages, cleft for me. Rock of Ages. Augustus Montague Toplady. BLRP; FaPoR; NOCV; PlP; SCGP; WGRP
  (Living and Dying Prayer for the Holiest Believer in the World, A.) NOEC
  (Prayer, Living and Dying, A.) ECEV

Rock of Cashel, The. Sir Aubrey De Vere. IIP; PeIV

Rock of My Salvation. Mordecai ben Isaac, *tr. fr. Hebrew* by Solomon Solis-Cohen. TrJP

Rock Painting. Carroll Arnett. VoR

Rock Painting. Jack Cope. PeSA

Rock Pilgrim. Herbert Edward Palmer. OxBTC

Rock, Rock, Sleep, My Baby. Clyde Watson. NTCP

Rock, Scissors, Paper. Deborah Digges. NAmP90

Rock-shores of the world and the secret waters. (*LL*) Birds. Robinson Jeffers. InPS; VGW

Rock that has broken and toppled across the track, The. Derelict Landscape. Robert Wells. SCBI

Rock Thrown into the Water Does Not Fear the Cold, A. Audre Lorde. NAAL-2

Rock video, and there you were, A. *Hot Club de France* Reprise on MTV. Vince Gotera. Jaz

Rockabye, baby, your cradle is hard. *Unknown.* RoPo

Rocked in the Cradle of the Deep. Emma Hart Willard. AnAmPo; BLPL; FaBoBe; PWR; WBLP; WGRP

Rocked in the cradle of the deep. (*LL*) Rocked in the Cradle of the Deep. Emma Hart Willard. AnAmPo; BLPL; FaBoBe; PWR; WBLP; WGRP

Rocked on this dreamy and indifferent tide. (*LL*) The Absinthe-Drinker. Arthur Symons. FaBoTw; NOBVV

Rocket and the car, The. (*LL*) Window Ledge in the Atom Age. E. B. White. NBLV; OBAL

Rockets bubble upward and explode, The. 14 July 1956. Laurence David Lerner. PeSA

Rockferns. Norman Nicholson. MoBrPo

Rocking Chair, The. A. M. Klein. HeIP; NoP

Rocking Hymn, A. George Wither. *See* Sweet baby sleep: What ail[e]s my dear?

Rocking My Child. Gabriela Mistral. ArLo, *tr. fr. Chilean* by Higman

Rockland. Julia Randall. WPE

Rocks. Florence Parry Heide. NTCP; SiSoPo

Rocks and Deals. Geoffrey Young. UL

Rocks flow and the mountain shapes flow, The. The Songs of the Birds. Edward Carpenter. WGRP

Rocks jagged in the morning mist. The Point. John Montague. IPY; PNI

Rocks turn to rivers, rivers turn to men. (*LL*) Dean-bourn, a Rude River in Devon, by Which Sometimes He Lived ("Dean-bourn, farewell; I never look to see.") Robert Herrick. BeJo; SeCV-1

Rocks with silver spray were wet, The. (*LL*) At the Cascade. H. Cordelia Ray. AmWP; CBWP-3

Rocky Acres. Robert Graves. LiTB; MeMBP; NoAM; UnPo

Rocky Island, The. *Unknown.* AmFP

Rocky Mountains, The. *Unknown.* AmFP

Rocky Road to Dublin, The. *Unknown.* FaBoBa

Rod full of wind and moon, A. Tune: "Immortal at the Magpie Bridge." Lu Yu, *tr. fr. Chinese* by James J. Y. Liu. SuSp

Rod light and taper, thy tackle fine, The. How to Catch Trout. Thomas Barker. *Fr.* Art of Angling, The. FaBoUs

Rod of Jesse, The. Bible, *O.T. Fr.* Isaiah. AWP; OBVE; TrJP

Rod was but a harmless wand, The. The Virtues of Sid Hamet, the Magician's Rod. Swift. APAS

Rodney's Ride. *Unknown.* PAH

Rodomontade on His Cruel Mistress, A. The Earl of Rochester. OxBSP

Roe (and my joy to name) th'art now, to go. To William Roe. Ben Jonson. BeJo; OAEL-1

Roe Deer. Ted Hughes. NoAM; OxAEP-2

Roethke Plain. John Malcolm Brinnin. TAP

Rogation Day: Portrush. James Simmons. PBCIP

Rogation Days. Kenneth Rexroth. NaP

Roger a doleful widower. The Widower's Courtship. Elizabeth Hands. WoRP

Roger and Dolly. Henry Carey. CBNP; CoMu; NOEC; OxNR, *sl. diff. vers.*

Roger Williams. Hezekiah Butterworth. PAH

Rogero's Song. George Canning , George Ellis, *and* John Hookham Frere. *Fr.* Rovers, The. NOEC

Róisín, have no sorrow for all that has happened you. Little Black Rose. *Unknown, tr. fr. Irish* by Thomas Kinsella. NOIV

Rokeby, *sels.* Sir Walter Scott.
  Allen-a-Dale. EnRP
  Brignall Banks. EnRP; OBEV
    (Edmund's Song.) PoRA
    (Outlaw, The.) GTBS; GTBS-P; OtMeF
    (Song: Brignall Banks.) OxAEP-2
  Man the Enemy of Man. WBLP
  Weary Lot Is Thine, A. CH
    (Rover, The.) GTBS; GTBS-P
    (Rover's Adieu [*or* Farewell], The.) NOBE; OBEV
    (Song: "Weary lot is thine, fair maid, A.") EnLoPo; OBNC

Rokeby Venus, The. Robert Conquest. MoP

Sir Roland; a Fragment. Robert Merry. NOEC

Roll, *Alabama*, Roll. *Unknown.* OxBSS

Roll back, you fabulous animal. Carnal Knowledge. Gwen Harwood. CBAP

Roll-Call. Nathaniel Graham Shepherd. OHIP

Roll Call. Wendell Phillips Stafford. NGP

Roll-Call In the Concentration Camp. Dan Pagis, *tr. fr. Hebrew* by Robert Friend. PoSu

Roll Call of Mirrors. Ivan V. Lalic, *tr. fr. Serbo-Croatian* by Charles Simic. HSix

Roll forth, my song, like the rushing river. The Nameless One. James Clarence Mangan. BIrV; EnRP; GGP; IIP; NOIV; OBEV; PeIV

Roll on the Ground. *Unknown.* AmFP

Roll on, thou ball, roll on! To the Terrestrial Globe. W. S. Gilbert. FaBoNo; NBLV; TrGrPo

Roll on, thou deep and dark blue ocean — roll! Byron. *Fr.* Childe Harold's Pilgrimage. PoEL-4; UV
  (Roll On, Thou Deep and Dark Blue Ocean.) FaPON
  (To the Ocean.) GN; WGRP

Roll out ye drums, peal organs' loudest thunder. Elegy on Albert Edward the Peacemaker. *Unknown.* CoMu

Roll the Chariot. *Unknown.* AS

Roll the Cotton Down. *Unknown.* AmFP

Roll the stone from its grave away! *(LL)* Maud Muller. Whittier. AnAmPo; BeLS; BLPL; FaBoBe; PoLF; TAP; WBLP

Roll the Union on. John Handcox *and* Lee Hays *and* Lee Hays. SWP

Rolled and teetered. *(LL)* The Henyard Round. Donald Hall. Poetsp

Rolled into one. *(LL)* Sundaysong. Liz Lochhead. VBLP

Rolled off a side of mountains or. Serpent Country. A. R. Ammons. EOEF

Rolled over on Europe: the sharp dew frozen to stars. Stephen Spender. CMoP

Rolled within coral-red clusters. *(LL)* Rondo for the Poet's Children. Jean-Joseph Rabéarivelo. NegPo

Roller perched upon the wire, The. Driving Cattle to Casas Buenas. Roy Campbell. PeSA

Roller, pitch, and stumps, and all, The. *(LL)* Brahma. Andrew Lang. BXAP; FaBoCo; NOBL; PeLV; UV

Roller Rink. Betty Adcock. MT

Roller Skates. John Farrar. FaPON

Rolling Chinese Wall, The. Roger Woddis. UV

Rolling English Road, The. G. K. Chesterton. CoGr; FaBoCh; NOBE; NOBL; OBEV; OBMV; OtMeF; OxAEP-2; OxBTC; PlP; UV

Rolling from St. Patrick's, The. Burial of An Irish President. Austin Clarke. BIrV

Rolling Home. *Unknown.* OxBSS

Rolling in Money. John Forbes. FaBoMA

Rolling John, *sels.* A. J. Wood.

Rolling mountains push toward the city. Lang Mountain Monastery. Yang Yi, *tr. fr. Chinese by* Jonathan Chaves. SuSp

Rolling Sailer, The. *Unknown.* OxBSS

Rolling the Lawn. William Empson. MoBrPo

Rollo says, "I can bring down rain." Rollo's Miracle. Paul Zimmer. GOYP

Rollo's Miracle. Paul Zimmer. GOYP

Rolly Trudum. *Unknown.* AmFP

Rom. Cap. 8 Ver. 19. Henry Vaughan. ESCV; GeHe; MeLP

Roma. Rutilius, *tr. fr. Latin by* Ezra Pound. CTC

Roman Calendar, The. Benjamin Hall Kennedy. FaBoUs

Roman Centurion's Song, The, *sels.* Kipling.
  "Legate, I had the news last night — my Cohort ordered home." FaBoEH

Roman Earl, The. *Unknown, tr. fr. Irish by* Douglas Hyde. OBVE

Roman Fountain. Louise Bogan. NoP; WPOW

Roman had an, A/ artist, a freedman. Marianne Moore. *Fr.* Jerboa, The. CMoP; FYAP; NALW

Roman History in Rhyme, *sels.* Edward B. Goodwin.
  "Aeneas built, in days of yore." FaBoUs

Roman miniature urchin, A. Seeking an Explanation. Richard Emil Braun. NoAM

Roman Numerals. *Unknown. See* X shall stand for playmates Ten.

Roman Officer Writes, A. Charles Montague Doughty. *Fr.* Dawn in Britain, The. FaBoTw

Roman Outposts. Derek Walcott. AnAn

Roman Presents. Martial, *tr. fr. Latin by* James Michie. OBCP

Roman Road, The. Thomas Hardy. FaBoPP; GoJo; MoBrPo; NOBE

Roman Road, The. *(LL)* The Roman Road. Thomas Hardy. FaBoPP; GoJo; MoBrPo; NOBE

Roman soldiers come riding in full speed. "Sin-Killer" Griffin. *Fr.* Man of Calvary, The. AmFP

Roman Stage, The. Lionel Johnson. NOBVV

Roman Thank-You Letter, A. Martial, *tr. fr. Latin by* James Michie. OBCP

Roman threw us a road, a road, The. History. G. K. Chesterton. *Fr.* Songs of Education. OBSV

Roman Virgil [*or* Vergil], thou that singest Ilion's lofty temples robed in fire. To Virgil [*or* Vergil]. Tennyson. AWP; ChTr; EBVVPR; GTBS-P; MeMBP; NoP; OAEL-2; PoEL-5

Roman Wall Blues. W. H. Auden. FaBoEH; NTP

Roman was the victor of the world., The. Petronius Arbiter, *tr. fr. Latin. Fr.* Satyricon. MLL, *tr. by* Helen Waddell.

Roman Women, *sels.* Thomas Edward Brown.
  "O Englishwoman on the Pincian." NOBVV; OBNC

Romance. Paul Charles Joseph Bourget, *tr. fr. French by* Philip L. Miller. RiWo

Romance. W. E. Henley. *Fr.* In Hospital. PAH

Romance. Poe. AmPP; AnAmPo; MeMAP; NAAL-1; OxBA

Romance. "Gabriel Setoun." BoTP

Romance. Gerald Stern. CAPP

Romance. Robert Louis Stevenson. BLPL; EBVV; MoBrPo; OBEV; OtMeF; TrGrPo

Romance. Richard Stull. EOEF

Romance. W. J. Turner. CH; CoGr; EBEvV; GoJo; MoBrPo; NOBAu; NOBE; NTP; OBMV; PlP; PoRA; TrGrPo

Romance, A. Chester Kallman. PoA

Romance of Citrus, The. Christy Sheffield Sanford. UL

Romance of Imprinting, The. Christy Sheffield Sanford. UL

Romance of police in their shiny cruisers washes, The. Have a Nice Day. Robert Long. NAmP90

Romance [*or* Romaunt] of the Rose, The, *sels.* Guillaume de Lorris *and* Jean de Meun, *tr. fr. French.*
  Garden of Amour, The. PoEL-1
  "Short space my feet had traversed ere." OAEL-1

Romance of the Swan's Nest. Elizabeth Barrett Browning. GN

Romance, who loves to nod and sing. Romance. Poe. AmPP; AnAmPo; MeMAP; NAAL-1; OxBA
  (Introduction: "Romance, who loves to nod and sing." NOBA

Romancero. Lex Banning. NOBAu

Romania, Romania. Gerald Stern. LCAP

Romans Angry about the Inner World. Robert Bly. NOBA

Romans in Dorset. Louise Imogen Guiney. AmWP

Romans in England awhile did sway, The. The Chapter of Kings. John Collins. FaBoUs

Romantic. George Garrett. HoPM

Romantic to Burlesque. Byron. *Fr.* Don Juan. EnRP; OAEL-2

Rome. Arthur Hugh Clough. *See* Rome disappoints me still; but I shrink and adapt myself to it.

Rome. J. V. Cunningham, *after the Latin of* Janus Vitalis Panormitanus. OBVE

Rome. Joachim du Bellay, *tr. fr. French by* Ezra Pound. AWP

Rome. Thomas Hardy. MoAB

Rome. Hildebert, *tr. fr. Latin by* Helen Waddell. MLL

Rome. Milton. *Fr.* Paradise Regained [*or* Regain'd]. NOSC

Rome Araieth Stilico in Vesture of the Consul. Claudian, *tr. fr. Latin by* Osborn Bokenham. *Fr.* De Consulatu Stilichonis. OxBLMV

Rome: Building a New Street in the Ancient Quarter. Thomas Hardy. Son FaBoPP

Rome by Metella's Tomb. Byron. *Fr.* Childe Harold's Pilgrimage. FaBoPP

Rome, Conqueror, Conquered. Joshua Sylvester. FaBoEE

Rome disappoints me much. — St. Peter's, perhaps, in especial. Rome ("Rome disappoints me much.") Arthur Hugh Clough. *Fr.* Amours de Voyage. FaBoPP; NOBVV

Rome disappoints me still; but I shrink and adapt myself to it. Arthur Hugh Clough. *Fr.* Amours de Voyage. EBVV; EBVVPR; NOBVV; OBTV; OxAEP-2

(Rome.) FaBoPP

Rome has a thousand fountains, and in May they sing. Maria Luisa Spaziani, *tr. fr. Italian by* Beverly Allen. NeIt

Rome never looks where she treads. A Pict Song. Kipling. *Fr.* Puck of Pook's Hill. NoAM

Rome Once Alone. Clark Coolidge. UL

Rome, queen of all, your fame will never die. Constantinople (New Rome). *Unknown, tr. fr. Greek by* Peter Jay. GrAn

Rome Remember. Sidney Keyes. MoAB

Rome ("Rome disappoints me much.") Arthur Hugh Clough. *Fr.* Amours de Voyage. FaBoPP; NOBVV

Rome Sunday June 1960. John Hewitt. TIRV

Rome will not suit me, Eustace; the priests and soldiers possess/ it; Arthur Hugh Clough. *Fr.* Amours de Voyage. EBVVPR, *canto* V, x; NOBVV

Romeo and Juliet. H. Phelps Putnam. ErPo

Romeo and Juliet, *sels.* Shakespeare.
  "Even or odd, of all days in the year." SCV
  "For here lies Juliet, and her beauty makes."
    (Thus with a Kiss I Die.) TrGrPo
  "How oft when men are at the point of death." DL; LPA
    Frost on the Flower. FaBoRV
  "Gallop apace, you fiery-footed steeds [*or* fierie footed steades]." CBLP; EBEvV; GBL
  "He jests at scars [that never felt a wound]." EBEvV; ImPo; LiTB
    (Living Juliet, The.) TrGrPo, II, i
  "If I profane with my unworthiest hand." OxAEP-1; Son; SoSe
    Music's Silver Sound. GN
  "O my love, my wife!" OBD; OxAEP-1
  "O [*or* Oh], then, I see Queen Mab hath been with you."
    (Mercutio's Queen Mab Speech.) LiTB
    (Queen Mab.) FaPON
  "She is the fairies' midwife, and she comes." RB
    (Mercutio Describes Queen Mab.) TrGrPo

Rome's guns are spiked; and they'll stay so. Of Rome. Herman Melville. *Fr.* Clarel. OxBA

Romira, stay. The Call. John Hall. MeLP; NOSC

Root-light, or the Lawyer's Daughter. James Dickey. NGP

Root of Our Evil, The. D. H. Lawrence. ChIV-2

Root of our present evil is that we buy and sell, The. The Root of Our Evil. D. H. Lawrence. ChIV-2

Rooted and blowing beyond sense or touch. (LL) This Measure. Léonie Adams. MoAB; MoAmPo

Roots. Lucille Clifton. CAPP

Roots. Seamus Deane. PNI

Roots. Louis Ginsberg. TrJP

Roots. Garrett Kaoru Hongo. Jaz

Roots. Seymour Mayne. NOBC

Roots and Branches. Robert Duncan. VGW

Roots around your soul and eyes, The. Sweating It Out on Winding Stair Mountain. Jim Barnes. CDW

Roots of Blue Bells. Nia Francisco. HATNAP

Roots of mankind are tangled in my hair, The. Epitaph. Wendy Rose. CDW

Rope, The. Tania van Zyl. PeSA

Rope for Harry Fat, A. James K. Baxter. MoBS

Rope of rushlight wavers, A. Cave Painter. Aidan Carl Mathews. IB

Ropero, so sad and so forlorn. El Ropero. Antonio di Montorio. TrJP

Ropes, pull them tight!, The. Fishermen's Song. Unknown, tr. fr. Maori by Margaret Orbell. PeNZ

Ropewalk, The. Longfellow. MeMAP

Ropley District. Sebastian Barry. IB

Rorate celi desuper. Of Christ's Nativity. William Dunbar. EnVB; ScCV (Unto Us a Child is Born.) ChIV-2

Rory and Liam are dead and gone. In Memoriam. Padraig de Brun. WTO

Rosa Luxembourg. Eileen Duggan. PeNZ

Rosabelle. Sir Walter Scott. Fr. Lay of the Last Minstrel, The. BeLS; GTBS; GTBS-P

Rosalind, in a negligee. Early Unfinished Sketch. Austin Clarke. ErPo

Rosalind [or Rosalynde]. Thomas Lodge. See Like to the clear [or cleere] in highest sphere [or sphaere].

Rosalind's [or Rosalynde's] Description. Thomas Lodge. See Like to the clear [or cleere] in highest sphere [or sphaere].

Rosalind's [or Rosalynd's] Madrigal[l]. Thomas Lodge. Fr. Rosalynde; or Euphues' Golden Legacy. CBLP; EIL; EnRePo; GGP; InvP; NOBE; NoP; NoSic; OBEV; PoEL-2; TrGrPo

Rosaline. Thomas Lodge. Fr. Rosalynde; or Euphues' Golden Legacy. GTBS; GTBS-P; LiTB; OBEV

Rosalynde; or Euphues' Golden Legacy, sels. Thomas Lodge.
Fancy, A. EIL
Montanus' Sonnet. PoEL-2
Rosalind's [or Rosalynd's] Madrigal[l]. CBLP; EIL; EnRePo; GGP; InvP; NOBE; NoP; NoSic; OBEV; PoEL-2; TrGrPo
(Love in My Bosom.) SCGP
Rosaline. GTBS; GTBS-P; LiTB; OBEV
(Rosalind [or Rosalynde].) EIL; TrGrPo
(Rosalind's [or Rosalynde's] Description.) OxAEP-1

Rosary. Rita Magdaleno. AfAz

Rosary, The. Robert Cameron Rogers. FaBoBe; WBLP

Rosary tattoo, A. The Right Hand of a Mexican Farmworker in Somerset County, Maryland. Martín Espada. UTF

Rosciad, The, sels. Charles Churchill. NOEC
Character of a Critic. NOEC

Rose, The. "Angelus Silesius," tr. fr. German. Fr. Cherubical Wanderer, The. GePo, tr. by George C. Schoolfield

Rose, The. William Browne. Fr. Visions. CH; OBEV

Rose, The. Goethe, tr. fr. German by James Clarence Mangan. AWP

Rose, The. George Herbert. LiTB; PoEL-2

Rose, The. Thomas Howell. EIL

Rose. Kathleen Raine. WPE

Rose, The. Theodore Roethke. NOBA; NYBP; TRP

Rose, The. Pierre de Ronsard, tr. fr. French by Andrew Lang. AWP

Rose, The. Novica Tadic, tr. fr. Serbo-Croatian by Charles Simic. HSix

Rose, The. Elizabeth Tollet. ECWP

Rose, The. William Carlos Williams. NOBA

Rose, A. Sir Richard Fanshawe, after the Italian of Giovanni Battista Guarini. Fr. Il Pastor Fido. OBEV; PoEL-2

Rose and Cushie. Charles Tennyson Turner. Mes

Rose and gold and violet, The. The Afterglow. H. Cordelia Ray. CBWP-3

Rose and grape, pear and bean. Unknown, tr. fr. Spanish by Willis Barnstone. BoWoP

Rose and the Gauntlet, The. "Christopher North." BeLS

Rose and the lily, the moon and the dove, The. Rose, die Lilie, die Taube, die Sonne, Die. Heine, tr. fr. German by Richard Garnett. AWP
(Love's Resume.) TrJP, tr. by "J. F. C."

(Rose and the lily, the moon and the dove, The.) NAWM-2, tr. by P. G. L. Webb

Rose and the Thorn, The. Paul Hamilton Hayne. FaBoBe

Rose and went a-roving, mother. Lass A-Laundering. Unknown, tr. fr. Spanish by John Frederick Nims. STV

Rose-apple is in fruit, The. Show Me the Way. Unknown, tr. fr. Burmese by U Win Pe. PBWP

Rose, as fair as ever saw the north, A. The Rose. William Browne. Fr. Visions. CH; OBEV
(Vision V.) NOSC

Rose Aylmer. Walter Savage Landor. AWP; BoLoP; CH; ELP; EnLoPo; EnRP; GBL; GGP; HAP; HoPM; LiTB; NAEL-2; NOBE; NoP; OAEL-2; OBEV; OBNC; OxAEP-2; PoEL-4; Poetr; SCGP; TEP; TFi; TrGrPo; UnPo; WeW

Rose-Bud, The. William Broome. OBEV

Rose, but one, none other rose had I, A. Tennyson. Fr. Idylls of the King. NAEL-2; PoEL-5

Rose-cheeked [or cheekt] Laura, Come. Thomas Campion. EnLoPo; InPK; InPS; InvP; NAEL-1; NoP; NOSC; OAEL-1; PoE; PoEL-2; TFi; TrGrPo; TRP
(Laura.) EIL; NOBE; OBEV
(Rose-cheecked Laura.) EnRePo
(Rose-cheekt Lawra, come.) AAS

Rose-cheekt Lawra, come. Thomas Campion. See Rose-cheeked Laura, come.

Rose Connoley. Unknown. AmFP

Rose, die Lilie, die Taube, die Sonne, Die. Heine, tr. fr. German by Richard Garnett. AWP

Rose Enthroned, The. Lucy Larcom. AmWP

Rose fades/ and is renewed again, The. William Carlos Williams. Poetr

Rose Family, The. Robert Frost. OBAL; OBCA

Rose-footed swan from snow, or girl from rose? (LL) The Swans. Edith Sitwell. CMoP; WPE

Rose for a young head, A. The Watcher. James Stephens. MoBrPo; OBEV

Rose from al-Mutanabbi's Blood, A, sels. Abd-Allah al-Baraduni, tr. fr. Arabic by Diana Der Hovanessian and Sharif Elmusa.

Rose-Geranium, The. Eiléan Ní Chuilleanáin sels.
"A l'usage de M. et Mme. van Gramberen." CIP
"Precious dry rose-geranium smell, The." CIP

Rose gives a tremulous glance, The. Anne Norris. PeLi

Rose Growing into the House, The. Gibbons Ruark. InPK

Rose, harsh rose. Sea Rose. Hilda Doolittle ("H. D."). FaBoMo; HeIP; NoAM; NoP; TRP

Rose has flushed red, the bud has burst, The. Hafiz, tr. by Gertrude Lowthian Bell. Fr. Odes. AWP; TAL

Rose in October, A. James Whitcomb Riley. OBAL

Rose in the Afternoon. Jenny Joseph. BrRo

Rose in the breast. On Waking. Alida Carey Gulick. GoYe

Rose in the Garden. Unknown. AmFP

Rose is a pink-yellow, The. Watching the Stolen Rose. Michael McClure. PoBeRe

Rose is a rose, The. The Rose Family. Robert Frost. OBAL; OBCA

Rose is not the rose unless thou see, The. Hafiz, tr. by Richard Le Gallienne. Fr. Odes. AWP

Rose is red, the grass is green, The. Unknown. OxNR

Rose is red, the rose is white, The. Unknown. OxNR

Rose is red, the violet's blue, The. Unknown. OxNR

Rose-Leaves. (Rose kissed me today). sels. Austin Dobson.
Urceus Exit. OBEV

Rose marie, The. (LL) The Two Sisters. Unknown. AmFP; MAT; PrIm; TrGrPo

Rose Mary, sels. Dante Gabriel Rossetti.
"And lo! on the ground Rose Mary lay" Poetr

Rose of Blue Flesh, The. Willis Barnstone. BTR

Rose of Eden, The. Susan K. Phillips. BeLS

Rose of England, The. Unknown. ESPB

Rose of Heaven, The. "Ping Hsin," tr. fr. Chinese by Kenneth Rexroth and Ling Chung. Fr. Multitudinous Stars. WPC

Rose of Life, The. Sir Richard Fanshawe, after the Italian of Giovanni Battista Guarini. See Blown[e] in the morning, thou shalt fade ere noon.

Rose of Sharon, The/ I lost in the tortured night. For the New Union Dead in Alabama. Edward Dorn. PoM

Rose of that Garland! fairest and sweetest. To the Most Beautiful Lady, the Lady Bridget Manners. Barnabe Barnes. EnLoPo

Rose of the World, The. John Masefield. PoRA

Rose of the World, The. W. B. Yeats. CMoP; MoAB; MoBrPo; NAEL-2

Rose, Oh Pure Contradiction. Rainer Maria Rilke, *tr. fr. German by* Stephen Mitchell. ArNa; TTTS

Rose, oh pure contradiction, joy. Rainer Maria Rilke, *tr. fr. German by* Stephen Mitchell. EnlH

Rose on My Cake, The. Karla Kuskin. TLR

Rose Red's hair is brown as fur. An Embroidery. Denise Levertov. NMM; NU

Rose, regarded here by your external eyes, The. The Rose. "Angelus Silesius," *tr. fr. German*. Cherubical Wanderer, The. GePo, *tr. by* George C. Schoolfield

Rose, Rose,/ Has big toes. *Unknown*. RoPo

Rose Solitude. Jayne Cortez. Jaz; VBLP

Rose Still Grows beyond the Wall, The. A. L. Frink. BLPA

Rose That Bore Jesu, The. *Unknown*. OxBLMV

Rose, the lily, the dove, the sun, The. Heine. RiWo

Rose the Red and White Lil[l]y. *Unknown*. ESPB; OxBB

Rose Thieves, The. Vasco [or Vasko] Popa, *tr. fr. Serbo-Croatian by* Anne Pennington. *Fr.* Games. RB

Rose to the living is more than, A. Nixon Waterman. PoToHe

Rose Tree, The. W. B. Yeats. CMoP; ELP; FaBoPV; OBMV

Rose, The/ was not searching for the sunrise. Casida of the Rose. Federico García Lorca, *tr. by* Robert Bly. ArNa; NU

Rose was sick and smiling died, The. The Funeral Rites of the Rose. Robert Herrick. CaPo; NOSC; OBEV

Rose, were you not extremely sick? (*LL*) A True Maid. Matthew Prior. ErPo; FaBoCo; FaBoEE; NAEL-1; NIP; NOEC; PeLV

Rose will cost you more, A. Bargain. Lizette Woodworth Reese. AmWP

Rose Wreaths, The. Friedrich Gottlieb Klopstock, *tr. fr. German by* J. W. Thomas. GePo

Roseberry to his lady says. Supper Is Na Ready. Burns. GBP

Rosebud in the Heather. Goethe, *tr. fr. German by* John Frederick Nims. STV

Rosebud in the heather. (*LL*) Rosebud in the Heather. Goethe. STV

Rosemary Lane. *Unknown*. OBET

Rosemary, Rosemary, let down your hair. A Nonsense Song. Stephen Vincent Benét. OBAL

Rosemary Spray, The. Luis de Góngora y Argote, *tr. fr. Spanish by* E. Churton. AWP

Roses. "George Eliot." BoTP

Roses. Pierre de Ronsard, *tr. fr. French by* Andrew Lang. AWP

Roses. Thomas Stanley, after the Greek of Anacreon. AWP

Roses and Revolutions. Dudley Randall. BPo; PoBA; TAP

Roses and the Grave. Vera Weislitz. BTR

Roses and tulips Flora gathers here. David Lloyd. *See* 'Twas well the wars were done before.

Roses are already here. Philodemus, *tr. fr. Greek by* Kenneth Rexroth. PGA

Roses are red. *Unknown*. OxNR; RoPo

Roses are red, diddle diddle, lavender's blue. The Lady's Song in Leap Year. *Unknown*. GBP

Roses at first were white. How Roses Came Red. Robert Herrick. BeJo; CaPo

Roses blossom, scatter, The. The Politics of Paradise. Alma Villanueva. SRLS

Roses every one were red, The. Spleen. John Gray. NOBVV

Roses first came red, The. (*LL*) How Roses Came Red. Robert Herrick. BeJo; CaPo

Roses hence, or lilies rather. (*LL*) Upon the Infant Martyrs. Richard Crashaw. GeHe; NoP; OAEL-1

Roses I gathered at night from the dark hedge. Sapphic Ode in Rhyme. Hans Schmidt, *tr. fr. German by* Philip L. Miller. RiWo

Roses in breathing forth their scent. Celia Singing. Thomas Stanley. BeJo; NOSC

Roses in December. G. A. Studdert-Kennedy. BLPA

Roses (Love's delight) let's join. Roses. Thomas Stanley, after the Greek of Anacreon. AWP

Roses of Ispahan, The. Charles Marie René Leconte de Lisle, *tr. fr. French by* Philip L. Miller. RiWo

Roses of Ispahan in their mossy sheaths, The. The Roses of Ispahan. Charles Marie René Leconte de Lisle, *tr. fr. French by* Philip L. Miller. RiWo

Roses of Sa'adi, The. Marceline Desbordes-Valmore, *tr. fr. French by* Barbara Howes. BoWoP

Roses of Saadi, The. Marceline Desbordes-Valmore, *tr. fr. French by* Deirdre Lashgari. WPOW

Roses Only. Marianne Moore. LiTM

Roses Red. Arno Holz, *tr. fr. German by* Jethro Bithell. AWP

Roses red upon my neighbor's vine, The. My Neighbor's Roses. Abraham L. Gruber. BLPA; PoToHe

Roses, rose-red and white, and green. Alleluya. Rubén Darío, *tr. fr. Spanish by* Lysander Kemp. TTY

Roses, roses, roses. June. H. Cordelia Ray. CBWP-3

Rose's Scent, The. *Unknown*. *See* All night by the rose, rose.

Roses, their sharp spines being gone. Bridal Song, A ("Roses, their sharp spines being gone.") John Fletcher *and* William Shakespeare. *Fr.* Two Noble Kinsmen, The. EIL; NOBE; NOSC; NoSic

Roses used to bloom in spring. Crinagoras, *tr. fr. Greek by* Alistair Elliot. GrAn

Roses with the scent bred out. In Lieu. Louis MacNeice. CMoP

Rosie Nell. *Unknown*. AS

Rosina Alcona to Julius Brenzaida. Judith Wright. NALW

Ross's Poems. *sels.* Geoffrey Lehmann. CBAP
  Auntie Bridge and Uncle Pat. CBAP
  "Driving through thick bush." FaBoMA; CBAP
  I Was Born at a Place of Pines. CBAP
  Music Is Unevenness. CBAP
  My Father's a Still Day. CBAP
  "Some musical intervals survive." FaBoMA; CBAP
  Some of Our Koorawatha Saints. CBAP
  There Are Some Lusty Voices Singing. CBAP
  "You can't hear it in the house." FaBoMA

Rostov. G. S. Fraser. PoWW

Rosy Apple, Lemon or Pear. *Unknown*. CH

Rosy Bosom'd Hours, The. Coventry Patmore. EnLoPo; NOBVV

Rosy Days Are Numbered, The. Moses ibn Ezra, *tr. fr. Hebrew by* Solomon Solis-Cohen. *Fr.* Wine-Songs. TrJP

Rosy Ear. Zbigniew Herbert, *tr. fr. Polish by* Czeslaw Milosz *and* Peter Dale Scott. AnRep

Rosy shield upon its back, A. The Dead Crab. Andrew Young. FaBoTw; FM; OBD; RB

Rot on the vine; in that land were we born. (*LL*) The Mediterranean. Allen Tate. FaBoMo; GOA; HAP; ImPo; LiTA; LiTM; MoAB; MoAmPo; VGW

Rotation. Julian Bond. FF

Rotogravure. Errol Francis. NBrP

Rotten borough of the human heart, The. (*LL*) Answer to —— 's Professions of Affection. Byron. OxBSP

Rotten wood is unfit for carving, so I slept at noon. For Guests after Their Visit. Liu Ya-tzu, *tr. fr. Chinese by* Wu-chi Liu. SuSp

Rotterdam — 1946. Thomas A. Goldman. BTR

Rottnest Island., *sels.* Nicholas Hasluck. CBAP
  "All day the bicycles come and go." NOBAu
  "Christmas Day. 1696." NOBAu

Rou-cou spoke the dove. Song of Fixed Accord. Wallace Stevens. InPS; SAmP

Rouen. May Wedderburn Cannan. NAEL-2; OBWP; OxBTC

Rouen, Place de la Pucelle. Maria White Lowell. AmWP

Rouge Bouquet. Joyce Kilmer. PAH

Rough. John James. VaA

Rough fir, hauled from the hills. The Making of the Cross. William Everson. VGW

Rough Sketch, The. Julia Ward Howe. AmWP

Rough Time in th' Barrio. José Montoya. ETG

Rough wind, that moanest loud. Shelley. ChTr; EnRP; NAEL-2; NOBE; PoRA; SCGP; TEP; TrGrPo; WiR

Rough Winds Do Shake. Louis Simpson. ErPo

Roughly estimated ones, who do not sort well, The. The Monuments of Hiroshima. D. J. Enright. OxBSP; PAW

Roughly figured, this man of moderate habits. Life Cycle of Common Man. Howard Nemerov. NBLV

Roughly-silvered leaves that are the snow. A Song from Armenia. Geoffrey Hill. FaBoMo

Round, A. *Unknown*. *See* Hey Nonny No!

Round a cleft in the cliffs to come upon. Venus of the Salty Shell. Denis Devlin. BIrV; NOIV

Round: "Out till 4 o'clock dancing, they're." Anne Rouse. NWP

Round: "Skunk cabbage, bloodroot." Philip Booth. BoNaP; GrPl

Round: " 'Wondrous life!' cried Marvell at Appleton House." Weldon Kees. CoAP; NaP

Round about in a fair ring-a. *Unknown*. BoTP

Round about, little ones. Robin Good-Fellow's Song: "Round about, little ones." *Unknown*. *Fr.* Robin Goodfellow. EIL

Round about Me. Sappho, *tr. fr. Greek by* William Ellery Leonard. AWP

Round about Midnight. Bob Kaufman. PoBeRe

Round about Midnight. (*LL*) Round about Midnight. Bob Kaufman. PoBeRe

Round about, round about,/ Catch a wee mouse. *Unknown*. OxNR

Round about, round about, here sits the hare. *Unknown*. OxNR

Round about, round about/ In a fair ring-a. The Elves' Dance. *At. to* John Lyly *and to* Thomas Ravenscroft. *Fr.* Mayde's Metamorphosis, The. CH; FaPON

Round about, round about,/ maggotty pie. *Unknown.* OxNR

Round about the cauldron go! Edward Abbott Parry. BXAP

Round about the rosebush. *Unknown.* OxNR

Round about there/ Sat a little hare. *Unknown.* OxNR

Round and round. Private Transport. Adrian Mitchell. FaBoEE

Round and round our lavatory. The Thinker. Anthony Delius. PeSA

Round and round the garden. *Unknown.* OxNR

Round and round the rugged rock. *Unknown.* OxNR

Round as a doughnut. *Unknown.* RoPo

Round blazing sun, The. What She Said, Thinking of Him Crossing the Wilderness Alone. Auvaiyar, *tr. fr.* Tamil *by* A. K. Ramanujan. PLW

Round-bottomed babe from Mobile, A. *Unknown.* PeLi

Round dance of day has gone. Sitting Alone in Tulsa Three A.M. Lance Henson. VoR

Round her red garland and her golden hair. Of His Last Sight of Fiammetta. Boccaccio, *tr. fr.* Italian *by* Dante Gabriel Rossetti. *Fr.* Sonnets. AWP

Round House, A. Matthew Sweeney. IB

Round moon hangs like a yellow lantern in the trees, The. The Ancient Thought. Watson Kerr. WGRP

Round — oblong — like jam. Contours. Noël Coward. UV

Round Quebec's embattled walls. Montgomery at Quebec. Clinton Scollard. PAH

Round Song, A. Rhyll McMaster. CBAP

Round table, holding eight, A. Recipe for a Pleasant Dinner-Party. *Unknown.* FaBoUs

'Round that little old sod shanty on the claim. (*LL*) Little Old Sod Shanty. *Unknown.* AmFP; AS

Round the cape of a sudden came the sea. Parting at Morning. Robert Browning. AWP; EBEvV; EnVR; FaBV; FF; FHYEP; HeIP; ImPo; InPS; NAEL-2; NOBE; OBEV; OBNC; OHCV; OxBSP; PFP; SCGP; SoSe; TFi; UnPo; WiR

Round the house and round the house/ and there lies a black glove in the window. *Unknown.* FaBoVe

Round the house and round the house/ and there lies a white glove in the window. *Unknown.* FaBoVe

Round the island of Zipangu. The Mimshi Maiden. Hugh McCrae. NOBAu

Round the margins invisible apertures and leaks. Fifth Variation. Andrew Crozier. VaA

Round the streets of this city I rode you. Farewell to My Scooter. Mbuyiseni Oswald Mtshali. PeSAV

Round the Year. Coventry Patmore. BoTP

Roundabout Turn, A. Robert E. Charles. MoShBr

Rounded Catalogue Divine Complete, The. Walt Whitman. NAAL-1

Roundel: "Now welcom[e], somer, with thy sunne [*or* sonne] softe." Chaucer. *See* Now Welcom[e], Somer [*or* Summer].

Roundel: "Syn I fro Love escaped am so fat." Chaucer. EnVB

Roundel in the Rain. *Unknown.* FiBHP

Roundelay, A: "It fell upon a holy eve." Spenser. *See* It Fell upon a Holy [*or* Holly] Eve.

Roundelay: "Tell me, thou skilful shepherd's swain." Michael Drayton. *Fr.* Shepherd's Garland, The. ElL

Roundhouse in Cheyenne is filled every night, The. The Dreary Black Hills. *Unknown.* AS

Roundhouse Voices, The. Dave Jeddie Smith. MT; NoAM; VCAP

Rounding a slip of the marsh, the boat skids. Looking for the Melungeon. Dave Jeddie Smith. HCAP

Rounding the Cape. Roy Campbell. PeSA

Rounding the Horn. John Masefield. *Fr.* Dauber. MoAB; MoBrPo

Rounding the Horn. *Unknown.* OxBSS

Rouse, Britons! at length. A New Ballad. *Unknown.* PAH

Rouse every generous, thoughtful mind. The Blasted Herb. Meshech Weare. PAH

Rouse for Stevens, The. Theodore Roethke. OBAL

Rousecastle. David Wright. MoBS

Roused by November seas, wrecked on Italian rocks. Theodoridas, *tr. fr.* Greek *by* W. G. Shepherd. GrAn

Rousseau in His Day. Donald Davie. DiPo

Rousseau — Voltaire — our Gibbon — and De Staël. Sonnet to Lake Leman. Byron. Son

Route March. Charles Hamilton Sorley. *See* All the Hills and Vales Along.

Route of evanescence, A. A Hummingbird. Emily Dickinson. HeIP; NAAL-1; NoP; PoEL-5

Route of the Táin, The. Thomas Kinsella. PBCIP

Routes. Peter Everwine. NNaP

Routine Things around the House, The. Stephen Dunn. NAmP90

Rover, The. Sir Walter Scott. *See* Weary Lot Is Thine, A.

Rover killed the goat. Brave Rover. Max Beerbohm. NBLV

Rovers, The, *sels.* George Canning , George Ellis, *and* John Hookham Frere.
  Rogero's Song. NOEC
  (Song by Rogero.) FaBoNo
  (Song of One Eleven Years in Prison.) FiBHP; PeLV

Rover's Adieu [*or* Farewell], The. Sir Walter Scott. *See* Weary Lot Is Thine, A.

Rover's Song, A. Bliss Carman. AnAmPo

Roving. Wilhelm Müller, *tr. fr.* German *by* Philip L. Miller. *Fr.* Beautiful Maid of the Mill, The. RiWo

Roving breezes come and go, the reed-beds sweep and sway, The. The Travelling Post Office. Andrew Barton Paterson. CBAP; NOBAu

Roving Gambler, The. *Unknown.* AS

Roving is the miller's delight. Roving. Wilhelm Müller, *tr. fr.* German *by* Philip L. Miller. *Fr.* Beautiful Maid of the Mill, The. RiWo

Roving Shanty Boy, The. *Unknown.* AmFP

Row. Anne Rouse. NWP

Row after row. The Mule. Boynton Merrill, Jr.. CRP

Row after row with strict impunity. Ode to the Confederate Dead. Allen Tate. AiP; FaBoMo; HeIP; LiTA; LiTM; MoAB; MoAmPo; MoP; NAAL-2; NoAM; NOBA; NoP; OBD, *ll.* 1–9; OBWP; OxBA; PrIm; TAP; TFi; UnPo

Row gently here, my gondolier; so softly wake the tide. Venetian Air. Thomas Moore. OxBSP

Row of Stalls, A, *sels.* Raymond Knister.
  Nell. Mes; NOBC

Row us out from Desenzano, to your Sirmione row! "Frater Ave atque Vale." Tennyson. ChTr; EBVV; FaBoPP; GTBS-P; HAP; InPS; NAEL-2; NoP; OBTV; OxBSP

Rowan County Crew, The. *At. to* James William Day. AmFP

Rowan like a lip-sticked girl, A. Seamus Heaney. IPY; TRP

Rowers, The. Laura Benét. GoYe

Rowing. Anne Sexton. BoWoP; CAPP; LCAP

Rowing Early. John Peck. SM

Rowing, I reach'd a rock — the sea was low. Gerard Manley Hopkins. *Fr.* Vision of the Mermaids, A. ChTr

Rowing in Familiar January. Milo De Angelis, *tr. fr.* Italian *by* Lawrence Venuti. NeIt

Rows of carriages, grooms at rest. Occasional Verse. Wang Ts'an, *tr. fr.* Chinese *by* Ronald C. Miao. SuSp

Rows of Cold Trees, The. Yvor Winters. NOBA

Roy Bean. *Unknown.* AnAmPo; BeLS; OBAL

Roy Kloof. Sydney Clouts. PeSAV

Royal Adventurer, The. Philip Freneau. PAH

Royal and saintly Cashel! I would gaze. The Rock of Cashel. Sir Aubrey De Vere. IIP; PeIV

Royal Angler, The, *sels. Unknown.*
  "Me thinks I see our mighty monarch stand." OBSV

Royal Charlie's now awa. Will He No Come Back Again? *Unknown.* OBEV

Royal Crown, The. (Wonderful are thy works, as my soul overwhelmingly knoweth.) Solomon ibn Gabirol, *tr. fr.* Hebrew. AWP, *tr. by* Israel Zangwill Sels.
  My God. TrJP

Royal Education. Winthrop Mackworth Praed. OBSV

Royal Fisherman, The. *Unknown.* GBP

Royal Fisherman, The. *Unknown.* ChTr; GBP

Royal George, The. William Cowper. *See* Toll for the brave!

Royal Guest, A. *Unknown. See* Yet if his majesty, our sovereign [*or* sovraign] Lord.

Royal Light Dragoon, The. *Unknown.* OBET

Royal Line, The. Leigh Hunt. FaBoUs

Royal loyal Lily O, The. (*LL*) The Orange Lily. *Unknown.* FaBoPV; GBP

Royal Mischief, The, *sels.* Delariviere Manley.
  "Criticks, ye are grown so much unkind of late." KTR
  "Our Poet tells me I am very pretty." KTR
  "What to conceal desire, when every." KTR

Royal Palm. Hart Crane. CMoP; MoAB; MoAmPo; MoP; NoAM; NoP; TrGrPo

Royal [*or* Royall] Presents, *sels.* Nathaniel Wanley.
  "Instead of Incense (Blessed Lord) if wee." TrPWD

Royal Princess, A. Christina Rossetti. BrRo

Royal Stag, The. "Hugh MacDiarmid." FaBoMo

Royal Tour, The, abr. "Peter Pindar." OxBoLi; PeLV

Royal Tour, and Weymouth Amusements, The. "Peter Pindar." OxBoLi
Sels.
   George III and the Sailor. NOEC
Royal Wedding Gifts. "Hugh MacDiarmid." IHNG
Royalties. D. J. Enright. NOBL; PeLV
Royalty. Rimbaud, tr. fr. French by Enid Rhodes Peschal. SOTW
Roye Robert the Bruss the rayke he avowit, The. Sir Richard Holland. Fr.
   Buke of the Howlat, The. OxBS
   (Douglas and the Bruce's Heart. OxBLMV
Rrrrrrrraaarghr/ We have paid you back. Fury against the Moslems at
   Uhud. Hind bint Utba, tr. fr. Arabic by Bridget Connelly and Deirdre
   Lashgari. WPOW
Ruaumoko — the Earthquake God. Mohi Turei, tr. fr. Maori by A.
   Armstrong. WTO
Rub, A. John Banister Tabb. OBAL
Rub a dub dub,/ Three men in a tub. Mother Goose. NOBL; OxNR;
   RoPo, diff. vers.
Rubaiyat. Mimi Khalvati. NWP
Rubaiyat for Sue Ella Tucker. Miller Williams. SM
Rubáiyát of Omar Khayyám of Naishápúr, The. (Awake! for Morning in the
   Bowl of Night.) Omar Khayyám, tr. fr. Persian by Edward Fitzgerald.
   AWP; EBVV, abr.; FaBoBe; FaBoRV, abr.; FaPoR, abr.; HAP, abr.;
   LiTB; NAEL-2; NoP; PoEL-5; PrIm, abr.; TrGrPo
Sels.
   "Ah Love! could you and I with Him conspire." GGP
   "Ah, with the grape my fading life provide." EBEvV; GTBS-P
   "And when like her, oh Sákí, you shall pass." GGP; TRP
   "Awake! for morning in the bowl of night." EBEvV; FaPoB; Mes;
      NOBVV; OxAEP-2, abr.; PeVV, sect. I–XII; PIP; TAL; UV
   "Book of verses underneath the bough, A." HoPM; NOBE; OBEV; TRP
   "Come, fill the cup, and in the fire of spring." FaBV; TEP; TRP; UV;
      WGRP
   "For some we loved, the loveliest and the best." TRP
   "Here with a Loaf of Bread beneath the Bough." UV
   'How sweet is mortal Sovranty!' — think some. UV
   "I sometimes think that never blows so red." TRP
   "Iram indeed is gone with all his rose." OBVE
   "Moving Finger writes; and, having writ, The." TRP
   "Myself when young did eagerly frequent." TRP; WGRP
   "Oh, come with old Khayyam and leave the Wise." PIP; UV
   "Some for the Glories of This World; and some." TRP
   "They say the lion and the lizard keep." EBEV
   "Think, in this batter'd caravanserai." ChTr; OBD
   "Wake! for the sun, who scattered [or scatter'd] into flight." EnVR; FF;
      ImPo; OBNC; OHCV; OtMeF; TRP
      (Wake!) FaPON
   "Would but some winged Angel ere too late." GGP
   "Would but the Desert of the Fountain yield." GGP
   "Yet Ah, that Spring should vanish with the Rose!" GGP
   "Yon rising Moon that looks for us again." GGP; TRP
Rubber penis, the wig, false breasts, The. Poggio. Lawrence Durrell.
   OxBTC
Rubbing sleep from her eyes, cradling. After the Impossible Dream. Tracey
   Herd. NWP
Rubens, de Vos, Memling — room after room. Antwerp: Musée Des
   Beaux-Arts. Alan Ross. NYBP
Rubin. Charles Cooper. PoBA
Ruby and amethyst eyes of anemones, The. Winter Anemones. Charles
   Brasch. Fr. Night Cries, Wakari Hospital. PeNZ
Ruby Tells All. Miller Williams. MT
Ruckled lips gaped slightly, but when, The. Six Belons. Chase Twichell.
   NAmP90
Ruddigore, sels. W. S. Gilbert.
   Darned Mounseer, The. NOBL
Ruddy fire-glow, like her sister's eyes, The. Lot and His Daughters I. A.
   D. Hope. ChIV-1
Rude Awakenings. Bob Rosenthal. UL
Rude Boreas. Unknown. OBET
Rude mass of earth, from which moilèd hands. On a Piece of Unwrought
   Pipeclay. John Frederick Bryant. NOEC
Rude unwelcome guest. Blackbird: Elegy for William Gordon Calvert.
   Barry MacSweeney. NBrP
Rudel to the Lady of Tripoli. Robert Browning. OtMeF
Rudely forced to drink tea, Massachusetts, in anger. Unknown. PAH
Rudolph Is Tired of the City. Gwendolyn Brooks. PDV
Rudolph Reed was oaken. The Ballad of Rudolph Reed. Gwendolyn
   Brooks. RB
Rueful Lamentation on the Death of Queen Elizabeth, A. Sir Thomas
   More. AAS; FaBoRV; LiTB
Ruffed blue-green garden, red blossoms. Tune: "Butterflies Lingering over
   Flowers." Ou-yang Hsiu, tr. fr. Chinese by Jerome P. Seaton. SuSp

"Rufinianus" was once just Rufus. Unknown, tr. fr. Greek by Peter Jay.
   GrAn
Rufty and Tufty. Isabell Hempseed. BoTP
Rufus Mitchell's Confession. Unknown. AmFP
Rufus Prays. L. A. G. Strong. MoBrPo
Rug, The. Michael McClure. NeAP
Rug of dead butterflies at my feet, A. Ghost. Nina Cassian, tr. fr.
   Romanian by Christopher Hewitt. PoSu
Rugby Chapel. Matthew Arnold. EBVVPR; EnVR; FaBoEH; PeECV;
   PoEL-5; WGRP
Rugged forhead that with grave foresight, The. Spenser. Fr. Faerie
   Queene, The. OAEL-1
Rugged up for winter snow. Greenham Women. Wendy Poussard. AIW
Ruhr-Gebiet, sels. Allen Ginsberg.
   "Too much industry." EaPr
Ruin, The. Dafydd ap Gwilym, tr. fr. Welsh by Rolfe Humphries.
   OBWVE
Ruin, The. Richard Hughes. OBMV
Ruin, The. Unknown, tr. fr. Anglo-Saxon by Charles W. Kennedy. AnOE;
   PrIm
Ruin, The. Unknown, tr. fr. Anglo-Saxon by Gavin Bone. EBEV
Ruin and death held sway. In Apia Bay. Sir Charles G. D. Roberts. PAH
Ruin, at least, was something; the yard, The. Late Return. E. A.
   Markham. PBCV
Ruin seize thee, ruthless King! Thomas Gray. Fr. Bard, The. EnRP;
   FaBoEH; GTBS; GTBS-P; NOBE; NOEC; OAEL-1 OxAEP-1
Ruined and ill, a man of two score. Remembering Golden Bells. Po Chü-i,
   tr. fr. Chinese by Arthur Waley. AWP
Ruined Cottage, The, diff. vers. Wordsworth. See 'Twas summer, and the
   sun had mounted high.
Ruined Maid, The. Thomas Hardy. BoLoP; CMoP; ErPo; FaBoBl;
   FaBoVe; FiBHP; HeLL; HeIP; LiTB; MeMBP; NAEL-2; NBLV; NOBL;
   NoP; OxBTC; PeLV; PeVV; SCV; TEP; TFi; TRP
Ruined, time ruined, all these once good things. Rimrock, Where It Is.
   Hayden Carruth. NNaP
Ruines of Time, The. Spenser. OxAEP-1
Ruins of a Great House. Derek Walcott. TwCP
Ruins of Corinth, The. Antipater of Sidon, tr. fr. Greek by Peter Jay.
   GrAn
Ruins of Rome, sels. Joachim du Bellay, tr. fr. French by Spenser.
   "He that has seen a great oak dry and dead." FaBoPP
   "Hope ye, my verses, that posterity." PoE
   "Thou stranger, which for Rome in Rome here seekest." FaBoPP; OBVE
   "Thou that at Rome astonished doth behold." FaBoPP
   "Who list the Romane greatnes forth to figure." OBVE
Ruins of the City of Hay. Randolph Stow. CBAP; FaBoMA
Ruins of Walsingham, The. Unknown. See In the wracks of Walsingham.
Ruins under the Stars. Galway Kinnell. LCAP; NaP
Sels.
   "Sometimes I see them." RFM
Rule, Britannia! James Thomson and David Mallet. Fr. Alfred, A
   Masque. EBEvV; FaPoR; GTBS; GTBS-P; NOEC; OBWP; PIP; ScCV;
   WBLP
Rule for Shooting, A. Unknown. FaBoUs
Rule of the Road, The. Unknown. FaBoUs
Rule well v, and come to hevyn. (LL) Kepe well X, and flee fro VII.
   Unknown. MiEL
Rulers: Philadelphia. Fenton Johnson. PoNe
Rules and Lessons. Henry Vaughan and Thomas Stanley. ESCV
Rules and Regulations. "Lewis Carroll." FaBoUs; NOBVV; PeVV
Rules break like a thermometer, The. Adrienne Rich. Fr. Twenty-one Love
   Poems. GLP
Rules of Sleep. Howard Moss. VCAP
Rules! they're a springboard only, and we're free!. (LL) Nature and Art.
   Goethe. STV
Rum Mort's Praise of Her Faithless Maunder, The. Unknown. CBNP
Rum Tum Tugger, The. T. S. Eliot. FaBoNo; FaBV; FaPON; NTP; PDV;
   PIP
Rum Tum Tugger is a Curious Cat:, The. The Rum Tum Tugger. T. S.
   Eliot. FaBoNo; FaBV; FaPON; NTP; PDV; PIP
Rumaucourt. Elizabeth Garrett. NWP
Rumba. José Zacarías Tallet, tr. fr. Spanish by Sangodare Akanji. TTY
Rumble on, machines of the gold mines. In the Gold Mines. B. W.
   Vilakazi. TTY
   (On the Gold Mines. PeSA
Rumble, rumble in the pot. Unknown. CBNP
Rumble, rumble, rumble, goes the gloomy "L." Roller Skates. John
   Farrar. FaPON
Rumbling sound of man. Buzz. Jim Tollerud. VoR

Rumbling under blackened girders, Midland, bound for Cricklewood. Parliament Hill Fields. Sir John Betjeman. FaBoTw; NOBE; OPOP

Ruminant pillows! Gregarious soft boulders! The Black Faced Sheep. Donald Hall. LCAP; SV

Rumination. Richard Eberhart. LiTA; LiTM

Rummaging inside yourself. The Death of Fathers. Theodore Weiss. SV

Rummle an' dunt o' watter. Sumburgh Heid. George Bruce. OxBS

Rumor Verified. Robert Penn Warren. AnAn

Rumoresque Senum Severiorum. Argentarius, tr. fr. Greek by Dudley Fitts. ErPo

Rumors of liberation. We could not believe it. Richard Eberhart. Fr. Brotherhood of Men. PoWW

Rumors open up. The Morning Star. Primus St. John. PoBA

Rumour. Owen Rutter. Fr. Song of Tiadatha, The. NSI

Rumours that you lodge in a mountain temple. Tu Fu, tr. fr. Chinese by A. C. Graham. Fr. To My Younger Brother. PLT

Rumpled river, The. River Rhyme. William Carlos Williams. PoA

Rumpled sheet, A/ of brown paper. The Term. William Carlos Williams. InvP; LiTA

Rumpty-iddity, row, row, row. Unknown. OxNR

Run down by fate's spite. Lament for Five Sons Lost in a Plague. Abu Dhu'ayb al-Hudhali, tr. fr. Arabic by Omar S. Pound. ArPe

Run from Manassas Junction, The. Unknown. PAH

Run in circles, scream and shout. (LL) Sound Advice. Unknown. FaBoUs; NBLV

Run like rats from the plague in you. Saint Coleman's Song for Flight/ An Ite Missa Est. Padraic Fiacc. PNI

Run, Nigger, Run! Unknown. BPo

Run of is Jessy Watson fair. On Jessy Watson's Elopement. Marjory Fleming. Mes

Run out the boat, my broken comrades. Thalassa. Louis MacNeice. BIrV; FaBoMo; FaBoRV; NOBE

Run, shepherds, run where Bethlehem [or Bethlem] blest appears. The Angels. William Drummond of Hawthornden. GN

Run to Mourne End Wood, The. John Masefield. Fr. Reynard the Fox. EBNV

Run toward the Nightland, sels. Unknown, tr. fr. Cherokee Indian. "Now! The Red Tobacco has come to strike your soul." STP

Run Upon the Bankers, The, sels. Swift. "No doubt he well invented, nobly felt." EPCY

Runagate Runagate. Robert Hayden. BPo; InPS; LCAP; PoBA; PoNe

Runaway. Linda France. NWP

Runaway, The. Robert Frost. AWP; CH; CoGr; FaBoCh; FaPON; GoJo; MoAB; MoAmPo; PDV; SAmP; TwCP; VGW

Runaway, The. Albery Allson Whitman. Fr. Not a Man and Yet a Man. AAP

Runaway Slave, The. Walt Whitman. Fr. Song of Myself. AmPP; LiTA; MoAmPo, abr.; NOBA; OxBA; PoNe; SOTW, much abr.

Runaway Slave at Pilgrim's Point, The. Elizabeth Barrett Browning. BrRo; NALW; PoNe

Runaways, The. Mark Van Doren. PoRA

Runaways Café I. Marilyn Hacker. NGP

Runaways Café II. Marilyn Hacker. NoAM

Rundown Church (Ballad of the First World War). Federico García Lorca. RaBo

Rune. Michael Longley. IIP

Rune. Muriel Rukeyser. SM

Rune for C, A. Barbara Howes. NYBP; SM

Rune of Hospitality. Unknown, tr. fr. Gaelic by Kenneth MacLeod. ScCV

Rune of Riches, A. Florence Converse. BoTP

Runes for an Old Believer. Rolfe Humphries. NYBP

Runes on Weland's Sword, The. Kipling. Fr. Puck of Pook's Hill. NoAM; PoEL-5

Rung from their marble caves 'Repent! Repent!' (LL) Saint John Baptist. William Drummond of Hawthornden. GTBS; GTBS-P; NOBE; OBEV; OxAEP-1; TrCP

Runnable Stag, A. John Davidson. CoGr; EBEvV; EBNV; FaPoR; FM; GGP; HAP; MeMBP; OBEV; OxBTC; PrIm; WiR

Runner, The. Gary Gildner. PRA; TAP

Runner, The. Walt Whitman. InPK; InPS; SAmP

Runner in the Skies, The. James Oppenheim. TrJP

Running. Leslie Ullman. PBCAP

Running. Richard Wilbur. CoAP

Running Battle, A. Brendan Kennelly. BiHa; PWE

Running downhill, spilling over, searching and spilling. Flood Water. Unknown, tr. fr. Aborigine by Mungayana Nundhirribala. NOBAu

Running Horse. Kathleen Iddings. NGP

Running Lightly over Spongy Ground. Theodore Roethke. RB

Running on Empty. Robert Phillips. InPK

Running on the shore. (LL) There Are Big Waves. Eleanor Farjeon. BoTP

Running over the fields. (LL) Days. Philip Larkin. EBEV; FaBoMo; Mes; NTP; OxAEP-2; OxBC; OxBSP; PeECV; RB; TOF

Running the Batteries. Herman Melville. PAH

Running the Blockade. Nora Perry. PAH

Running through Sleep. Kathleen Norris. IHMS

Running through the thick wiry grasses to the pond. Shore. Jean Garrigue. TAP

Running to Paradise. W. B. Yeats. NTP; OxBoLi

Running toward the dam, I was engulfed in a sea of man. Salute to the Construction of the Dam. Pien Chih-lin, tr. fr. Chinese. Fr. Poems Written at the Construction Site of the Ming Tombs Dam. LHF, tr. by Hualing Nieh

Running water never disappointed. Seamus Heaney. Fr. Crossings. BAP-90

Runoff. A. R. Ammons. PPP

Runoff. William Everson. NoAM

Runs falls rises stumbles on from darkness into darkness. Runagate Runagate. Robert Hayden. BPo; InPS; LCAP; PoBA; PoNe

Runs howling to his art. (LL) Journey to Iceland. W. H. Auden. OBTV; PoA

Runs the great bull, the dogs upon his heels. (LL) The Bull. Judith Wright. GrPl

Rupert Murdoch, with glee, shouted: "What." Frank Richards. PeLi

Rupert of the Rhine. E. C. Bentley. FaBoEH

Ruptured underbelly of a black horse flew overhead. The Apocrypha of Jacques Derrida. Norman Dubie. NAmP90

Rural Carrier Stops to Kill a Nine-Foot Cottonmouth, The. T. R. Hummer. Poetr; SM

Rural Colloquy with a Painter. Timothy Steele. CRP

Rural Dance about the Maypole, The. Unknown. GBP; OxBoLi

Rural Idyll. Margaret Toms. PAW

Rural Lass, The. Catherine Jemmat. ECWP; NOEC

Rural Life. George Crabbe. Fr. Village, The. NOBE

Rural Mail, The. John Glassco. MoCV

Rural Poesy. Sir Philip Sidney. See O words, which fall like summer dew on me!

Rural Rides: The Tractor Driver. Robert Maitre. FaBoBl

Rural Sights and Sounds. William Cowper. See For I have loved [or lov'd] the rural walk through lanes.

Rural Simplicity. Henry James Byron. NOBL

Rural Sports, sels. John Gay. "When a brisk gale against the current blows." FM

Rush from the heart, a crack, and that's that, A. (LL) The Backward Strut. Robert McDowell. UTF

Rush of the Oregon, The. Arthur Guiterman. PAH

Rush on glad stream, in thy power and pride. Meeting of the Susquehanna with the Lackawanna. Lydia Huntley Sigourney. AmWP

Rush to Ending, The. Kevin Jeffrey Clarke. PFL

Rushed through our veins. (LL) To the Tune "Glittering Sword Hilts." Liu Yu Hsi. OHMPC; UnAS

Rushes daily grow taller, The. Farm Routine. Ch'u Kuang-hsi, tr. fr. Chinese by Joseph J. Lee. SuSp

Rushes in a watery place. Christina Rossetti. ChTr; PDV

Rushing. Ray A. Young Bear. CDW

Rushing wind the Spirit came, A! A Prayer for Pentecost. Catherine Bernard Brown. BLRP

Rusia en 1931. Robert Hass. AnAn

Russia. Alexander Blok, tr. fr. Russian by Babette Deutsch and Avrahm Yarmolinsky. AWP

Russia. William Carlos Williams. VGW

Russia 1812. Victor Hugo, tr. fr. French by Robert Lowell. OBWP

Russia 1914/Bolinas 1988. Gail Shafarman. LoHo

Russia, 1927. Ai. NoAM

Russian Asylum. Marilyn Bowering. NOBC

Russian bear is huge and wild, The. Infant Innocence. A. E. Housman. MeMBP

Russian Cathedral. Claude McKay. See Bow down my soul in worship very low.

Russian Cradle Song, A. David Nomberg, tr. fr. Yiddish by Alter Brody. TrJP

Russian sailed over the blue Black Sea, A. "Soldier, Rest!" Robert J. Burdette. OBAL

Russian Soul II, The. John Hollander. NBLV

Russians. Keith Douglas. OxBTC

Russians Breathing. Philip Hammial. NOBAu

Russia's Resentment. L. A. J. Moorer. CBWP-3

Rust, a little pile of western color, lies, The. We Continue. W. S. Merwin. CAPP

Rust and silence fill the thatch. Wole Soyinka. HBAPE

Rust destroys the wheat. New Wife. *Gond Oral Tradition*, tr. by V. Elwin and S. Hivale. WTO

Rust moth fungus mildew. Worm. Bob Cobbing. NBrP

Rust spots his knives now: I never. Practice Board. Linda Saunders. NWP

Rustic Childhood. William Barnes. OBNC

Rustic Courtship. Robert Dodsley. *Fr.* Agriculture. ECEV

Rustic person like me seldom spends a night in a mountain home, A. Viewing Mr. Yü's Landscape Painting on the Wall. Wang Chi, tr. fr. *Chinese by* Joseph J. Lee. SuSp

Rustic Song, A. Anthony C. Deane. FiBHP

Rustic Temple Is Hidden, The. Chu Chen Po, tr. fr. *Chinese by* Kenneth Rexroth. OHMPC

Rustily creak the crickets: Jack Frost came down last night. Jack Frost. Celia Laighton Thaxter. OBCA

Rustle of each falling leaf, The. Love. Samuele Romanelli, tr. fr. *Hebrew by* A. B. Rhine. TrJP

Rustle of whispering wind over leaves, A. Kingfisher Flat. William Everson. PoM

Rustler. William Stroud. Spl

Rustling of leaves under the feet in woods and under hedges, The. Pleasant Sounds. John Clare. NTP

Rustling of the silk is discontinued, The. Liu Ch'e. Ezra Pound. OBVE; VGW

Rusty nail, went to jail. *Unknown.* RoPo

Ruth, *sels.* Bible, *O.T.*
    "And Ruth said, Intreat me not to leave." FF
    (Ruth to Naomi.) TrGrPo
    "And the name of the man was Elimelech." OBF
    Naomi and Ruth. TrJP

Ruth. Thomas Hood. BoLoP; ChIV-1; EnLoPo; EnRP; GN; NOBE; OBEV; OBNC; PlP

Ruth. Diane Q. Lewis. CrSp

Ruth. Colleen J. McElroy. BlSi

Ruth. Pauli Murray. NMM

Ruth; or, The Influences of Nature. Wordsworth. EnRP; GTBS; GTBS-P; PoEL-4

Ruth to Naomi. Bible, *O.T. See* And Ruth said, Intreat me not to leave.

Rutherford McDowell. Edgar Lee Masters. *Fr.* Spoon River Anthology. LiTA; OxBA

Ruthie, I'd like. Eve's Commentary. Michelene Wandor. NBrP

Ruthless unrest has urged slow feet. Rescue. Olive Tilford Dargan. GoYe

Ruth's Story, As Told to Lilith. Michelene Wandor. NBrP

Ruyter the while, that had our ocean curbed. The Dutch in the Medway. Andrew Marvell. *Fr.* Last Instructions to a Painter, The. APAS; FaBoEH

Rwose in the Dark, The. William Barnes. NOBVV

Ryan's Rebirth. Sean O'Brien. PWE

Rye Bread. William Stanley Braithwaite. CDC

Rye, flax, horses, platinum, timber, and fur." (*LL*) The Monkeys. Marianne Moore. CMoP; LiTA; MeMAP; NOBA; OxBA

Rye Whiskey. Rye Whiskey. *Unknown.* OxBoLi
    (Way Up on Clinch Mountain.) AS, A *and* B *vers.*

Rye Whiskey. *Unknown.* OxBoLi

Rye Whisky. *Unknown.* OxBoLi

Ryght as the stern of day begouth to schyne. William Dunbar. *See* Right as the star [*or* stern] of day began [*or* begouth] to s[c]hine.

Ryojin Hisho, *sels.* Emperor Go-Shirakawa, tr. fr. *Japanese.*

S

S. E. Celia Laighton Thaxter. AmWP

S M. Alice Walker. CrSp

S/ Rebuke boyne. Susan Howe. *Fr.* Formation of a Separatist. BCF

S sz sz SZ sz SZ sz ZS zs Zs zs zs z. Siesta of a Hungarian Snake. Edwin Morgan. InPK

S. T. Coleridge Dismisses a Caller from Porlock. Gerard Previn Meyer. GoYe

S — uche Is the Love I beare thy Honest Hart. Elizabeth Middleton. KTR

'S Wonderful. Ira Gershwin. CBLP

Sa-cá-ga-we-a. Edna Dean Proctor. PAH

"Sa lang as I may gear get to steal, I will never wirk." (*LL*) How the First Hielandman of God Was Made. *Unknown.* FaBoCo; GBP; OBSV

Saadi. Emerson. MeMAP; OxBA

Sabbath. John Berryman. *Fr.* Dream Songs. LCAP

Sabbath Bells. John Clare. FHYEP

Sabbath Bells. Josephine D. Henderson Heard. CBWP-4

Sabbath Day Was By, The. Howard Chandler Robbins. AH

Sabbath day was ending in a village by the sea, The. The Last Hymn. "Marianne Farningham." BLPA

Sabbath, My Love. Judah Halevi, tr. fr. *Hebrew by* Solomon Solis-Cohen. TrJP

Sabbath of Mutual Respect, The. Marge Piercy. CrSp; SRLS

Sabbath of Rest, A. Isaac Luria, tr. fr. *Hebrew by* Nina Davis Salaman. TrJP

Sabbath Sonnet. Felicia Dorothea Hemans. Son

Sabbath, the pious carry no money. A Voice out of the Sabbaths. Derek Walcott. WeW

Sable is my throat. Negro Spiritual. Perient Trott. PoNe

Saboteur autumn has riddled the pampered folds. Wild Honey. Francis Webb. NOBAu

Sabrina. Lucretia Davidson. AmWP

Sabrina. Milton. *See* Sabrina fair.

Sabrina Fair. Milton. *Fr.* Comus; a Masque Presented at Ludlow Castle. EBEV; ELP; FaBoCh, *much abr.*; FHYEP; GN; OAEL-1; PoEL-3

Sabrina fair. Sabrina Fair. Milton. *Fr.* Comus; a Masque Presented at Ludlow Castle. EBEV; ELP; FaBoCh, *much abr.*; FHYEP; GN; OAEL-1; PoEL-3
    (Sabrina.) CH, *abr.*; NOBE; OBEV
    (Song.) OxAEP-1

Sabrina's Song. Milton. *Fr.* Comus; a Masque Presented at Ludlow Castle. FHYEP; NOSC; OAEL-1

Sacheverell the learned. To the Tune of "Ye Commons and Peers Pray Lend Me Your Ears." *Unknown.* APAS

Sack of Deerfield, The. Thomas Dunn English. PAH

Sacrament of Sleep, The. John Oxenham. PoLF

Sacrament of the Altar, The. *Unknown.* MeEL

Sacramento. The Californian. *Unknown.* AmFP

Sacred. Gertrude Stein. OBAL

Sacred and Profane Love, or, There's Nothing New Under the Moon Either. Peter De Vries. NBLV

Sacred Book, The. *At.* to Zoroaster, tr. fr. *Persian by* A. V. Williams Jackson. AWP

Sacred Chant for the Return of Black Spirit and Power. Amiri Baraka. NBV

Sacred Formula to Attract Affection. *Unknown*, tr. fr. *Cherokee Indian by* James Mooney. LiTA

Sacred Formula to Destroy Life. *Unknown*, tr. by James Mooney. LiTA

Sacred Grove, A. Edward Cracroft Lefroy, *after the Greek of* Theocritus. *Fr.* Echoes from Theocritus. AWP

Sacred Grove, A. Fran Winant. BrRo

Sacred Hearth, The. David Gascoyne. FaBoTw

Sacred Heliconian spring, The. Clara Reeve. *Fr.* To My Friend Mrs. — -, on Her Holding an Argument in Favour of the Natural Equality of Both the Sexes. ECWP

Sacred mouthpiece of the Muses Pindar. The Nine Lyric Poets. *Unknown*, tr. fr. *Greek by* Peter Jay. GrAn

Sacred muse that first[e] made love divine [*or* devine]. Sir John Davies. *Fr.* Gulling[e] Sonnets, The. ESo; NoSic; Son

Sacred Objects. Louise Glück. *Fr.* Dedication to Hunger. AnAn

Sacred Objects. Louis Simpson. CAPP

Sacred Poetry. "Christopher North." WBLP

Sacred Religion, mother of form and fear. Samuel Daniel. *Fr.* Musophilus; or, Defence of All Learning. NoSic

Sacred Songs IV. Daniel Western. EaPr

Sacred to the Memory of Maria (To Say Nothing of Jane and Martha) Sparks. "Max Adeler." FaBoCo

Sacred tree midst the fair orchard grew, The. The Tree of Knowledge. Abraham Cowley. ChIV-1

Sacred wafer on the lip, The. (*LL*) Winter. Aubrey Thomas De Vere. PeIV

Sacrifice, The. Frank Bidart. GLP; VCAP

Sacrifice, The, *sels.* Chana Bloch.
    "In wings and starched." CrSp
    "Patriarch in black takes, The." CrSp

Sacrifice, *sels.* Emerson.
    Faith. OtMeF

Sacrifice, The. George Herbert. GeHe; PoEL-2

Sacrifice. Nana Issaia, tr. fr. *Modern Greek by* Helle Tzalopoulou Barnstone. BoWoP

Sacrifice. Maurice Kenny. ETG

Sacrifice. Thomas Kinsella. IPY

Sacrifice. Léon Laleau, tr. fr. *French by* Ellen Conroy Kennedy. *Fr.* Black Music. NegPo

Sagesse, *sels*. Hilda Doolittle ("H. D.").
"You look at me, a hut or cage contains." NOCV

Sagesse, *sels*. Paul Verlaine, *tr. fr. French*.
"Sky is up above the roof, The." AWP; FaPON
Sky Rises Above the Rooftop, The. ArNa, *tr. by* Kate Farrell
"Slumber dark and deep." AWP

Sagest of women, even of widows, she. Byron. *Fr.* Don Juan. NOBL; PeLV

Sagging Bough, The. Louis Untermeyer. BXAP

Sagimusume: The White Heron Maiden. Jonny Kyoko Sullivan. WPOW

Saginaw Song, The. Theodore Roethke. NBLV; RB

Sah gimme ah wuk nah. Wukhand. Paul Keens-Douglas. PBCV

Sahara. Coventry Patmore. *Fr.* Angel in the House, The. EBVV

Said. George Starbuck. OBAL

Said a boastful young student from Hayes. Frank Richards. PeLi

Said a diffident lady named Drood. *Unknown.* PeLi

Said a dreadfully literate cat. Conrad Aiken. PeLi

Said a fair-headed maiden of Klondike. Langford Reed. PeLi

Said a famous old writer called Fender. Victor Gray. PeLi

Said a fervent young lady of Hammels. Morris Bishop. PeLi

Said a foolish young lady of Wales. Langford Reed. PeLi

Said a frog on a log. *Unknown.* BoTP

Said a girl in green Mansfield Park. E. O. Parrott. PeLi

Said a gloomy young fellow called Fart. Victor Gray. PeLi

Said a God-fearing lady called Whitehouse. Roger Woddis. PeLi

Said a herring one day to a sole. Stanley J. Sharpless. PeLi

Said/ a hip/ lip-ful. Leg-acy of a Blue Capricorn. James Cunningham. JB

Said a luscious young lady called Wade. *Unknown.* PeLi

Said a maid: "I will marry for lucre." Limerick. *Unknown.* PeLi

Said a Marxist who stood on the pier. W. H. G. Price. PeLi

Said a medical student, unmanned. Allan M. Laing. PeLi

Said a parson, addressing his flock. W. J. Strachan. PeLi

Said a practical thinker: "One should." Frank Watson. PeLi

Said a pupil of Einstein: "It's rotten." C. F. Best. PeLi

Said a Tripper: "O joy, to have found." Thomas Thorneley. PeLi

Said a wife to her husband near Scole. Ida Thurtle. PeLi

Said active priest, "My work has increased." There Is None to Help. Chad Walsh. *Fr.* Psalm of Christ, The. TrCP

Said an ancient hermit, bending. The Olive Tree. Sabine Baring-Gould. GN

Said an ape as he swung by his tail. *Unknown.* PeLi

Said an elderly Bishop called Greville. Little Billee. *Unknown.* PeLi

Said an eminent, erudite ermine. *Unknown.* PeLi

Said an erudite sinologue: "How." R. J. P. Hewison. PeLi

Said Arnold to Arthur Hugh Clough. Victor Gray. PeLi

Said Burgoyne to his men, as they passed in review. The Progress of Sir Jack Brag. *Unknown.* PAH

Said Cap'n Morgan to Cap'n Kidd. Great Black-backed Gulls. John Heath-Stubbs. FaBoEH

Said Descartes, "I extol." Theological. Clifton Fadiman. FiBHP

Said Fading-leaf to Fallen-leaf. Fading-Leaf and Fallen-Leaf. Richard Garnett. EBVV

Said Freud: "I've discovered the Id." Frank Richards. PeLi

Said God, "You sisters, ere ye go." Hope and Despair. Lascelles Abercrombie. OBMV

Said Harry Fat to Holyoake. The Private Conference of Harry Fat. James K. Baxter. PeLV

Said, I, Oh, give me simplicity. Rural Simplicity. Henry James Byron. NOBL

Said Isolde to Tristan: "How curious!" Conrad Aiken. PeLi

Said Jeremy Jonathan Joseph Jones. The Rhyme of the Rain Machine. F. W. Clarke. BoNaP

Said Jerome K. Jerome to Ford Madox Ford. Mutual Problem. William Cole. OBAL

Said Jim X . . . . Ezra Pound. *Fr.* Cantos. NAs

Said Kelly and Burke and Shea. (*LL*) The Fighting Race. Joseph I. C. Clarke. AnAmPo; BLPA; BLPL; PAH

Said King Pompey. Edith Sitwell. UV

Said King Pompey, the emperor's ape. Said King Pompey. Edith Sitwell. UV

Said lady once to lover. The Three Bushes. W. B. Yeats. EBNV

Said Little Boy Blue. W. S. Brownlie. PeLi

Said Marlowe: "Bay City's a drag." Peter Alexander. PeLi

Said Mars when entangled with Venus. Mary Holtby. PeLi

Said Miss Farrow, on one of her larks. *Unknown.* PeLi

Said Mr. Smith, "I really cannot. Bones. Walter de la Mare. FiBHP

Said my landlord, white-headed Gil Gomez. Battle of the King's Mill. Thomas Dunn English. PAH

Said Nelson at his most la-di-da-di. A. Cinna. PeLi

Said Old Father William: "I'm humble." Conrad Aiken. PeLi

Said Old Gentleman Gay, "On a Thanksgiving Day." A Good Thanksgiving. "Marian Douglas." PoLF

Said Old Nick: "Mister Lewis and me." M. Cassell. PeLi

Said Opie Read to E. P. Roe. To Be Continued. Julian Street *and* James Montgomery Flagg. FiBHP

Said Orville to Wilbur "Hold tight!" Stanley J. Sharpless. PeLi

Said Paisley: "I've given up hope." Frank Richards. PeLi

Said Peter the Great to a Great Dane. Peterhof. Edmund Wilson. GoJo

Said philosopher-physicist Jeans. R. C. Owen. PeLi

Said Plato: "The things that we feel." Basil Ransome-Davies. PeLi

Said Powell: "Don't call me insane." Roger Woddis. PeLi

Said, Pull her up a bit will you, Mac, I want to unload there. Reason. Josephine Miles. InPK; NALW; NoAM; NoP; Poetr; TAP

Said Queen Isabella of Spain. *Unknown.* PeLi

Said Sally had a baby, and the baby had red hair. (*LL*) Joe Bowers. *Unknown.* AmFP

Said Tebbitt: "I don't understand 'em." Gerry Hamill. PeLi

Said Tennyson: "Yes, *Locksley Hall*'s." Victor Gray. PeLi

Said the boy driving home towards Clere. Ida Thurtle. PeLi

Said the Canoe. Isabella Valancy Crawford. NOBC

Said the Captain: "There was wire." Our Modest Doughboys. Albert Charlton Andrews. PAH

Said the chief of the marriage feast to the groom, The Wedding Feast. Edgar Lee Masters. ChIV-2

Said the Chinese philosopher, Lin. Len. PeLi

Said the Duchess of Alba to Goya. *Unknown.* PeLi

Said the Duck to the Kangaroo. The Duck and the Kangaroo. Edward Lear. OxBChV

Said the Eagle. The Eagle's Song. Mary Austin. GOA

Said the Englishman: "W'at's all this bloomin' wow?" Foreigners at the Fair. Fred Emerson Brooks. OBAL

Said the famous philosopher, Russell. Victor Gray. PeLi

Said the father to the daughter. Our Ship She Lies in Harbour. *Unknown.* OBET

Said the first little chicken. Five Little Chickens. *Unknown.* PDV (Chickens, The.) MoShBr; TLR (Wishes.) BoTP

Said the grave Dean of Westminster. A Refusal. Thomas Hardy. FaBoCo; LiTB; MeMBP

Said the Lion: "On music I dote." The Musical Lion. Oliver Herford. OBCA

Said the Lion to the Lioness — "When you are amber dust." Heart and Mind. Edith Sitwell. OxBTC; TwCP

Said the monkey to the donkey. *Unknown.* RoPo

Said the mythical King of Algiers. *Unknown.* PeLi

Said the newly-weds staying near Kitely. *Unknown.* PeLi

Said the Queen of the Nile. The Queen of the Nile. William Jay Smith. GrPl

Said the Queen to her favourite ghillie. A. Cinna. PeLi

Said the Robin to the Sparrow. Overheard in an Orchard. Elizabeth Cheney. BLRP

Said the Rose. George Henry Miles. BLPA

Said the shark to the flying fish over the phone. The Flattered Flying Fish. Emile Victor Rieu. PDV

Said the Stoic, tormented by gout. Thomas Thorneley. PeLi

Said the Sword to the Ax, 'twixt the whacks and the hacks. Ned Braddock. John Williamson Palmer. PAH

Said the trout to the fluke. Johnshaven. *Unknown.* GBP

Said the vet as he looked at my pet. Frank Richards. PeLi

Said the Wind to the Moon: "I will blow you out." The Wind and the Moon. George Macdonald. GoJo; MoShBr

Said Uncle Sam to Harry Fat. Harry Fat and Uncle Sam. James K. Baxter. PeLV

Said Wellington: "What's the location." Frank Richards. PeLi

Said Wilbur Wright, "Oh, this is grand." Frank Richards. PeLi

Said Wittgenstein: "Don't be misled!" Peter Alexander. PeLi

Said Zwingli to Muntzer. How to Start a War. Phyllis McGinley. OBSV

Saies, "Come here, cuzen Gawaine so gay." King Arthur and King Cornwall. *Unknown.* ESPB

Saigon Bar Girls, 1975. Yusef Komunyakaa. MT

Sail, A. M. Y. Lermontov, *tr. fr. Russian by* Max Eastman. AWP

"Sail, A! a sail! Oh, whence away." Heart's Content. *Unknown.* PoLF

Sail at the mast head dips from side to side, The. *Unknown, tr. fr. Aborigine by* C. H. Berndt. WTO

St. John, *sels.* Bible, *N.T.*
"As the Father hath loved me, so have I loved you." OBF
"I am the true vine, and my Father is the husbandman." OBVE
"In the beginnin o aa things the Wurd wis there ense." FaBoVe
Word, The. TrGrPo
St. John. Whittier. PAH
Saint John Baptist. William Drummond of Hawthornden. GTBS; GTBS-P; NOBE; OBEV; OxAEP-1; TrCP
Saint John did lean on Jesus's breast. For Saint John's Day. Luke Wadding. TIRV
Saint John divinely counsels us. The Praise of Godly Love Out of 1 John. 4. John Hall. ChIV-2
St. John of the Cross: Song of the Soul That Is Glad to Know God by Faith. Roy Campbell. PeECV
St. John of the Cross: Songs of the Soul in Rapture. Roy Campbell. PeECV
St. John of the Cross wore dark glasses. The Initiate. Charles Simic. BAP-90
Saint Judas. James Wright. LCAP; NOBA; SM
St. Julien's Eve. James Cunningham. JB
Saint-Just 1767-93 ("Saint-Just: his name seems stolen from the Missal.") Robert Lowell. FaBoMo
St. Kevin. *At.* to Samuel Lover. WTO
St Kilda-Wren, 1957. Colin Simms. NBrP
St. Lawrence and the Saguenay, *sels.* Charles Sangster.
Thousand Islands, The. NOBC
Saint Leger. Clinton Scollard. PAH
Saint-Lô. Samuel Beckett. NOIV
St. Louis Blues. William Christopher Handy. FF
St. Louis/ such a colored town/ a whiskey. Nappy Edges (A Cross Country Sojourn). Ntozake Shange. BlSi
St. Luke, *sels.* Bible, *N.T.*
"And it came to pass in those days, that there went out a decree from Caesar Augustus." NAWM-1
"And there were in the same country shepherds abiding in the field." PChr
"Feare not, litle flocke, for it is your fathers good pleasure to give you the kingdome." OBVE
Magnificat, The. BoWoP; WGRP
(And Marie said, My soule doth magnifie the Lord.) OBVE
Nunc Dimittis. WGRP
"Then drew near unto him all the publicans and sinners." NAWM-1
St. Malachy. Thomas Merton. VGW
Saint Malcolm. Jewel C. Latimore. BPo
St. Mark, *sels.* Bible, *N.T.*
"Aa this while, Peter wis doun ablò i the yaird." FaBoVe
"And as soon as it was morning the chief priests." DL
"And he said, So is the kingdome of God." OBVE
And he said, So soule doth magnifie the Lord. OBVE
"And Jesus saith unto them, All ye shall be offended." OBF, *abr.*
St. Martin and the Beggar. Thom Gunn. Mes; MoBS
Saint Mary Magdalene. Richard Crashaw. GeHe; MeLP; SeCV-1
Saint Mary Magdalene or the Weeper. Richard Crashaw. ChIV-2
St. Mary Virgine. A Cry to Mary. St. Godric. MeEL
St. Matthew, *sels.* Bible, *N.T.*
"And seeing the multitudes, he went up." NAWM-1
"Blessed are the poor[e] in spirit for theirs is the kingdom[e] of heaven." OBVE
God Provides. BLRP
"In the end the sabbath, as it began to dawn toward the first day of the week." NAWM-1
"No man can serve two masters." OBVE
"Our Father which [or who] art in heaven." PoLF; TrGrPo
(Father our, he-who is at-the-height, name Thy let-it-be.) PeSAV
(Prayer of-Lord, *Tswana vers.*.) PeSAV, *tr.* by Sol T. Plaatje
Parable of the Good Seed, The. InPK
"Then one of the twelve, called Judas Iscariot." NAWM-1; OBF, *abr.*
Treasures. TrGrPo
"When morning has come, all the chief priests and elders of the people." NAWM-1
Saint Nicholas. Marianne Moore. NYBP; WPE
Saint Patrick. Shane Leslie. TIRV
Saint Patrick, slave to Milcho of the herds. The Proclamation. Whittier. PAH
St. Patrick's Breastplate. *At.* to St. Patrick Saint Patrick, *tr. fr. Irish* by Frances Alexander. FaBoCh
Saint Patrick's Breastplate. *Unknown.* NOIV
Saint Patrick's Breastplate; or, The Deer's Cry. *At.* to St. Patrick Saint Patrick, *tr. fr. Irish.* TIRV, *tr.* by Kuno Meyer; WGRP
Saint Patrick's Day, 1973. Wendy Rose. CDW
St. Patrick's Dean, your country's pride. To Dr. Swift on His Birthday, 30th November 1721. Esther Johnson. EnLoPo

St. Patrick's Hymn before Tara. James Clarence Mangan. EnRP
St. Paul. Thomas Merton. ChIV-2
Saint Paul, *sels.* F.W.H. Myers.
Inner Light, The. WGRP
St. Peter. Christina Rossetti. ChIV-2; NOCV
St. Peter and the Angel. Denise Levertov. PWE
St. Peter at the Gate. Joseph Bert Smiley. BLPA
St. Peter Claver. Toi Derricotte. PBCAP
St. Peter once: "Lord, dost Thou wash my feet?" St. Peter. Christina Rossetti. ChIV-2; NOCV
Saint Peter sat by the celestial gate. Byron. *Fr.* Vision of Judgment, The. EnRP; FHYEP; OAEL-2; OBSV; OxBoLi; TEP
(Vision of Judgment, The.) OxAEP-2
St. Peter stood guard at the golden gate. St. Peter at the Gate. Joseph Bert Smiley. BLPA
Saint Peter's Complaint, *sels.* Robert Southwell.
Fear. CBCK
Sleep. CBCK
St. Peter's Day was celebrated by St. Brendan at sea. The Fish at Mass. *Unknown, tr. fr. Latin* by J. F. Webb. BIrV
St. Philip and St. James. Christopher Smart. *Fr.* Hymns and Spiritual Songs. NOCV; NOEC
Saint Pumpkin. Nancy Willard. LCAP
Saint Ras. Anthony McNeill. PBCV
St. Roach. Muriel Rukeyser. GLP
Saint Rose of Lima. Judith Ortiz Cofer. AfAz
St. Sava's Forge. Vasco [*or* Vasko] Popa, *tr. fr. Serbo-Croatian* by Anne Pennington. *Fr.* St Sava's Spring. PoSu
St. Sava's Journey. Vasco [*or* Vasko] Popa, *tr. fr. Serbo-Croatian* by Anne Pennington *Fr.* St Sava's Spring. PoSu
St. Sava's Spring, *sels.* Vasco [*or* Vasko] Popa, *tr. fr. Serbo-Croatian by* Anne Pennington
Life of St Sava, The. PoSu
St. Sava's Forge. PoSu
St. Sava's Journey. PoSu
St. Simeon Stylites. Tennyson. NOBVV; OAEL-2
St. Simon and Jude, on you I intrude. *Unknown.* FaBoUs
St. Sophia. John Fuller. DiPo
St. Stephen and King Herod. *Unknown.* ESPB, *Middle English vers.*; NoP, *mod. vers.*; OxBoLi, *Middle English vers.*; TrGrPo, *mod. vers.*
Saint Stephen had an angel's face. For Saint Stephen's Day. Luke Wadding. TIRV
St. Stephen's cloistered hall was proud. Columbus. Lydia Huntley Sigourney. PAH
St. Stephen's Day. Patric Dickinson. OBCP
St. Stephen's Day. John Hewitt. CIP
St. Stephen's is a stage. The Patriot's Progress. Horace Twiss. UV
Saint Steven Was a Clerk. *Unknown. See* Seynt Stevene was a clerk.
St. Theresa's Book-Mark. St. Theresa of Avila. *See* Let nothing disturb thee.
St. Thomas. Christopher Smart. ChIV-2
St. Thomas Aquinas thought. Vulture. Kenneth Rexroth. *Fr.* Bestiary, A. NNaP; OBAL
St. Thomas's Day is past and gone. *Unknown.* OxNR
St. Ursanne. Michael Roberts. LiTM
Saint Ursula of Llangwyryfon. Gwyn Williams. AngWe
St. Valentine. Marianne Moore. NYBP
St. Valentine's Day. Wilfrid Scawen Blunt. *Fr.* Love Sonnets of Proteus, The. EnLoPo
Saint Valentine's Day. Coventry Patmore. *Fr.* Unknown Eros, The. OBNC
Saint Valentine's Day. Shakespeare. *See* Tomorrow is saint valentine's day.
St. Vincent's. W. S. Merwin. VCAP
Saint Wears a Halo, The. "Peter." BoTP
Saint, who overlaps. John Logan. *Fr.* Cycle for Mother Cabrini, A. CRP
Saint with her halo, A. Paul Verlaine, *tr. fr. French* by Philip L. Miller. RiWo
Sainte Lucie, *sels.* Derek Walcott.
"Pomme arac." FaBoVe
Sainte Marye Virgine. A Cry to Mary. St. Godric. MeEL
Sainthood. Cristoir O'Flynn. TIRV
Saints, and Their Care. Alberto A. Ríos. AfAz; UL
Saints are gathering at the real, The. The Confirmers. A. R. Ammons. TAP
Saints are in such wise from God's own godhead drunk, The. The More Abandoned, The More Divine. "Angelus Silesius," *tr. fr. German.* *Fr.* Cherubical Wanderer, The. GePo, *tr.* by George C. Schoolfield
Saint's Bridge. Lola Ridge. WPE

Saints have adored the lofty soul of you. Charles Hamilton Sorley. *Fr.* Two Sonnets. MoBrPo; NSI; PeFWW

Saints, I give myself up to thee. Jack Kerouac. *Fr.* Mexico City Blues. NeAP

Saints in Glory, The. Dante, *tr. fr. Italian. Fr.* Divina Commedia. MeMAP; WGRP, *tr.* by Henry F. Cary

Saints in Glory, We Together. Nehemiah Adams. AH

Sair Fyel'd, Hinny. *Unknown.* GBP

Saith the poet of nonsense. Scraps of Lear. Edward Lear. FaBoNo

Sakhara. R. A. D. Ford. NOBC

Saki, for God's love, come and fill my glass. Hafiz, *tr.* by Richard Le Gallienne. *Fr.* Odes. AWP

Salaam Alaikum. *Unknown.* PoLF

Salad, *sels.* Mortimer Collins.
   (King Arthur Growing Very Tired Indeed.) FaBoCo

Salad, A. Sydney Goodsir Smith. FaBoUs; NBLV

Salad Days. Susan Musgrave. NoAM

Salad La Raza. Janet Campbell Hale. VoR

Salad of greens! Salad of greens! The Universal Favorite. Carolyn Wells. NBLV

Salamanca Doctor's Farewell, The. *Unknown.* APAS

Salami. Philip Levine. NNaP; NOBA; TAP; TRP

Salamis. Lawrence Durrell. NYBP

Salaziennes, Les, *sels.* Auguste Lacaussade, *tr. fr. French.*
   "My lips from this day forgot how to smile." TTY

Salcombe Seaman's Flaunt to the Proud Pirate, The. *Unknown.* ChTr

Sale. Josephine Miles. WPE

Sale began — young girls were there, The. The Slave Auction. Frances E. W. Harper. BPo; PoNe; TTY

Sale of Saint Thomas, The, *sels.* Lascelles Abercrombie.
   "They say the land is full of apes, which have." NSI

Sale of Smoke, A. Roberta Spear. AmPA

Sale of Souls. Adah Isaacs Menken. CBWP-1

Sale of the Pet Lamb, The. Mary Howitt. CH

Salem. Robert Lowell. AiP; Son

Salem. Edmund Clarence Stedman. PAH

Salem, Massachusetts. Edwin Muir. OBTV

Salem Witch, A. Ednah Proctor Clarke. PAH

Sales Talk for Annie. Morris Bishop. NBLV

Salesman, A. E. E. Cummings. *See* Salesman Is an It That Stinks Excuse, A.

Salesman Is an It That Stinks Excuse, A. E. E. Cummings. NoAM; OxBA; Poetr

Salesmen, disguised as befuddled policemen, waveringly, The. Condo Auction. Harry Mathews. BAP-89

Salient point, so first is call'd the heart, The. The Circulation of the Blood. Sir Richard Blackmore. *Fr.* Creation. FaBoUs

Salina sauntering in a shade. The Slattern. Sarah Dixon. ECWP

Salisbury Plain and Stonehenge. Wordsworth. *Fr.* Guilt and Sorrow. FaBoPP

Salisbury; the Cathedral Close. Coventry Patmore. *See* Once more I came to Sarum Close.

Sally Brown. Thomas Hood. *See* Young Ben he was a nice young man.

Sally Brown. *Unknown.* AmFP

Sally Brown. *Unknown.* AmFP

Sally bum-bally. *Unknown.* RoPo

Sally Free and Easy. Cyril Tawney. OBET

Sally go round the sun. *Unknown.* OxNR

Sally Goodin. *Unknown.* AmFP

Sally, having swallowed cheese. Cruel, Clever Cat. Geoffrey Taylor. ChTr; FaBoEE

Sally in Our Alley. Henry Carey. AnAmPo; AWP; BLPL; BoLoP; CoMu; FaBoBe; GGP; GTBS; GTBS-P; NOBE; OBEV; OxAEP-1

Sally is gone that was so kindly. Ha'nacker Mill. Hilaire Belloc. CoGr; FaPoR; MoBrPo; OxBTC; PlP; RB

Sally is the laundress, and every Saturday. The Dolls' Wash. Juliana Horatia Ewing. OxBChV

Sally Munro. *Unknown.* OxBSS

Sally over the water. *Unknown.* RoPo

Sally, Sally Waters. *Unknown.* OxNR

Sally Simpkin's Lament [or John Jones's Kit-Cat-astrophe]. Thomas Hood. CBNP; EnRP

Sally Sweetbread. Henry Carey. CoMu

Sally, tell my Mother I shall never come back. (*LL*) Gypsies in the Wood. *Unknown.* BoTP; CoGr; OxBoLi; OxBSP; OxNR

Sally: Twelfth Street. Naomi Long Madgett. NBV

Sally's Garden. *Unknown.* AmFP

Salmon. Jorie Graham. NAmP90

Salmon, The. Christian Morgenstern, *tr. fr. German* by Geoffrey Grigson. FaBoNo

Salmon Boy. David Wagoner. AnAn

Salmon Courage. Marlene Philip. PBCV

Salmon Drowns Eagle. Malcolm Lowry. MoCV

Salmon Eggs. Ted Hughes. NAs

Salmon lying in the depths of Llyn Llifon, The. The Ancients of the World. R. S. Thomas. RB

Salmon were just down there, The. Salmon Eggs. Ted Hughes. NAs

Salome. Ai. BCF; NoAM

Salome. Charles Lamb. ChIV-2

Salome was a dancer. *Unknown.* WTO

Salonika Campaign. Owen Rutter. *Fr.* Song of Tiadatha, The. NSI

Saloon is gone up the creek, The. Hemmed-in Males. William Carlos Williams. *Fr.* Folded Skyscraper, A. MAT; PoRA

Saloon is sometimes called a Bar, The. The Bar. *Unknown.* PoToHe

Salopian student of Greek, A. Martin Fagg. PeLi

Salsabíl. Jamil, *tr. fr. Arabic* by Omar S. Pound. ArPe

Salt. Monk Gibbon. PeIV

Salt. Anne Hartigan. CIP

Salt. Ruth Stone. NMM

Salt, The. May Swenson. *Fr.* Poet to Tiger. GLP

Salt and Memory. Zoltán Zelk, *tr. fr. Hungarian* by Barbara Howes. TSaS

Salt and oil purified the city just as well. The Murdered City. Anne Hébert, *tr. fr. French* by A. Poulin, Jr. WoWa

Salt brushed pelt of trees could hide them, The. Trencrom. Peter Scupham. SCBI

Salt creek mouths unflushed by the sea. The South Coast. William Everson. NeAP

Salt Peanuts. Louis McKee. NGP

Salt Pork, The. Robert Clayton Casto. HeIP

Salt sea-shore. (*LL*) Luscious and Sorrowful. Christina Rossetti. PoEL-5

Salt sprays deluge it, wild waves buffet it, hurricanes rave. Sir Lewis Morris. *Fr.* St. David's Head. AngWe

Salt Water Story. Richard Hugo. NAAL-2; NoAM; NoP

Salt wave sings, The. Fingernail Sunrise. Vernon Watkins. NYBP

Saltmarsh on the horizon, The. The Estuarial Republic. Douglas Dunn. FaBoMo

Saltpetre sucked up the cigarette with. Paul Brown. *Fr.* De Rebus. NBrP

Salutamus. Sterling A. Brown. CDC

Salutation. Robert Herrick. ChIV-2

Salutation. Ezra Pound. HeIP; MeMAP; MoAB; MoAmPo; NOBA; OxBA; TAP; VGW

Salutation of the Dawn, The. *Unknown.* PoLF

Salutation [or Salutations], The. Thomas Traherne. EnlH; ESCV; GeHe; InvP; NOCV; NoP; SeCP; SeCV-2

Salutation the Second. Ezra Pound. NOBA; OxBA

Salutation to Jesus Christ. John Calvin. WGRP

Salutation to the Dawn. Kalidasa, *tr. fr. Sanskrit.* PoToHe

Salutation to Walt Whitman. Fernando Pessoa, *tr. fr. Portuguese* by Edwin Honig. AnRep

Salute. Oliver Pitcher. PoBA

Salute. James Schuyler. FYAP; NeAP

Salute from the Fleet, A, *sels.* Alfred Noyes.
   Search-Lights, The. NSI

Salute the last and everlasting day. Ascension [or Ascention]. John Donne. *Fr.* La Corona. ChIV-2; ESCV; Son

Salute the stones that keep the limbs that held so good a mind. (*LL*) Epitaph on Sir Philip Sidney. *At.* to Fulke Greville *and* to Sir Edward Dyer. EnRePo; LiTB; Prf; SCGP

Salute to the Construction of the Dam. Pien Chih-lin, *tr. fr. Chinese. Fr.* Poems Written at the Construction Site of the Ming Tombs Dam. LHF, *tr.* by Hualing Nieh

Salute to the Elephant. Odeniyi Apolebieji, *tr. fr. Yoruba* by S. A. Babalola. WTO

Salute Your Partner. *Unknown.* AmFP

Salvador Dali. David Gascoyne. OxBTC

Salvation. George Ella Lyon. CrSp

Salvation Army lass, The. Lola Ridge. *Fr.* Ward X. WPE

Salvation comes by Christ alone. An Evening Thought. Jupiter Hammon. PoNe

Salvation lassie named Claire, A. *Unknown.* PeLi

Salvation to all that will is nigh. Annunciation. John Donne. *Fr.* La Corona. ChIV-2; ESCV; Son; TrCP

Salve!. Thomas Edward Brown. OBEV

Salve Deus Rex Judaeorum, *sels.* Emilia Lanier.
   Eves Apologie. BoWoP
   "Now Pontius Pilate is to judge the cause." NALW; NOSC

Satan's Soliloquy. Milton. *See* O thou that with surpassing glory crown'd.

Satan's Summons. Milton. *See* He scarce had ceas't [*or* ceased] when the superior fiend.

Satchmo. Melvin B. Tolson. BPo

Satellites. Gary Lenhart. UL

Sather Gate Illumination. Allen Ginsberg. NeAP

Satia Te Sanguine. Swinburne. PeVV

Satie, at the End of Term. Simon Curtis. NOBL; PeLV

Satin-clad. Stevie Smith. OxBC

Satin Doll. David Wojahn. Jaz; PBCAP

Satire, A, *sels*. John Oldham.
"On Butler who can think without rage." OBSV

Satire [*or* Satyre] against [Reason and] Mankind, A. (Were I, who to my cost already am.) The Earl of Rochester. NoP; NOSC; OAEL-1; OBSV; PoEL-3; SCV; SeCV-2
Sels.
"On Butler who can think without rage." OBSV
"Be Judge your self, I'll bring it to the test." PIP
(On Man.) IHNG
"Were I, who to my cost already am." LiTB

Satire on an Inconstant Lover, A. Swift. CBLP

Satire on Charles II, A. The Earl of Rochester. FaBoBl; NOSC, PeLV
Sels. "Restless he rolls about from whore to whore." OBSV

Satire on London, A. The Earl of Surrey. *See* London, hast thou [*or* thow] accused me.

Satire on Old Rowley. *Unknown*. APAS

Satire on the O'Haras, A. Tadhg Dall O'Huiginn. NOIV

Satire on the Town Ladies. Sir Richard Maitland. ScCV

Satire upon the French King, A. Thomas Brown. APAS

Satire upon the Heads. Thomas Gray. FaBoCo

Satire upon the Licentious Age of Charles II, *sels*. Samuel Butler.
"How silly were those sages heretofore." NOBL

Satires, *sels*. John Donne.
"Kind pity [*or* Kinde pitty] chokes my spleen[e]; brave scorn forbids." EBEV; ESCV; FHYEP; JCP; OAEL-1; PoEL-2; SeCV-1
(Religion.) NoP
(Satyre [*or* Satire] III.) MeLP; OxAEP-1
(Satyre III: On Religion.) NAEL-1; SeCP
(Satyre: Of Religion.) PoE
(Search for True Religion, The.) NoSic
London Street, A. NoSic
Seek True Religion! NOBE
"Seek true religion, O where? Mirreus." NOBE
"Sir: though (I thank God for it) I do hate." OBSV
"Thou shalt not laugh in this leaf, Muse, nor they." OBSV
"Well, I may now receive, and die: my sin." OBSV

Satires, *sels*. Horace.
"Thirsting Tantalus doth catch at streams that from him flee, The." SiPSBD, *tr. by* Sir Walter Ralegh

Satires, *sels*. Juvenal, *tr. fr. Latin*.
"But of all the plagues, the greatest is untold." OBSV
Celestial Wisdom. AWP
"Egyptians think it sin to root up, or to bite." SiPSBD
Faggots in Ancient Rome. PeHV
"Give store of days, good Jove, give length of years." OBSV
Hannibal ("Produce the urn that Hannibal contains"). OBVE
Hannibal ("Put Hannibal i' th' scale"). OBVE
Hannibal ("Throw Hannibal on the scales, how many pounds"). OBVE
"Hear what Claudius suffered: When his wife knew he was asleep." ErPo
"In Saturn's reign, at Nature's early birth." OAEL-1; OBSV; OBVE
"Life! length of life!" for this, with earnest cries. OBVE
On Fame. IHNG
On Old Age. IHNG
"Return we to the dangers of the night." OAEL-1
Sejanus ("How many men are killed by power, by power"). OBVE
Sejanus ("Some ask for envy'd pow'r; which publick hate"). OBVE
Sejanus ("What crowds by envied power, the wish of all"). OBVE
"What conscience has Venus drunk? Our inebriated beauties." PeHV
"When the last Flavius, drunk with fury, tore." OBVE
"Why do you look so gloomy, Naevolus?" PeHV

Satires, *sels*. John Marston.
Cynic Satire, A. NoSic
Humours. NoSic

Satires, *sels*. John Oldham, *after the French of* Boileau.
"Of all the creatures, in the world, that be." OBVE

Satires, *sels*. Persius, *tr. fr. Latin by* Dryden.
Prologue to the First Satire. AWP

Satires, *sels*. Sir Thomas Wyatt.
Mine Own John Poins [*or* Poyntz]. AAS; NoP; NoSic; OBSV; OBVE; PoEL-1; SCGP; SiPS; SiPSBD
"My mother's maids [*or* maydes], when they did sew and spin [*or* sowe and spynne]." AAS; NoSic; SiPS; SiPSBD

"Spending hand that alway poureth out [*or* powreth owte], A." AAS; NoSic; SiPSBD
(To Sir Francis Brian.) EnRePo; SiPS

Satires. *sels*. Edward Young. ECEV
On Women "Britannia's daughters" ECEV
On Women ("Lavinia is polite") ECEV

Satires of Circumstance, *sels*. Thomas Hardy.
At a Watering-Place. CMoP
At the Altar-Rail. MoAB; MoBrPo
At the Draper's. MoAB; MoBrPo; OBD; OxBM
By Her Aunt's Grave. MoAB; MoBrPo
In Church. IHNG; InPK; MoAB; MoBrPo; SCV
In the Cemetery. InPK; Son
In the Moonlight. NoAM
In the Nuptial Chamber. InPK
In the Restaurant. MoAB; MoBrPo
In the Room of the Bride-Elect. InPK

Satires [*or* Satyrs] upon the Jesuits, *sels*. John Oldham.
"For who can longer hold? when every Press." SeCV-2
"Satyr III: "When shaven Crown, and hallow'd Girdle's Power." SeCV-2

Satirical Elegy on the Death of a Late Famous General, A. Swift.
FaBoEH; FF; HoPM; NBLV; NoP; OBSV; PoE; PoEL-3; Poetr

Satirical Poem about Drink, A, *sels*. Chimedin Jigmed, *tr. fr. Mongol Oral Tradition by* C. R. Bawden.
"There is drink fermented." WTO

Satirical Romance, A. Sister Juana Inés de la Cruz, *tr. fr. Spanish by* Judith Thurman. PBWP
Sels.
"Critics: in your sight." VBLP
"Ignorant men, who disclaim" PBWP
"This evening, my love, even as I spoke vainly." VBLP
"What humour can be so rare" PBWP

Satirist, The. Louis MacNeice. IHNG

Satisfaction Coal Company, The. Rita Dove. LCAP

Satisfaction — is the agent. Emily Dickinson. NOBA

Satisfied. Samuel Valentine Cole. BLRP

Satisfied. Edgar Cooper Mason. BLRP

Satisfying Portion, The. *Unknown*. BLRP

Satori. Gayl Jones. BlSi

Saturday Afternoon at the Movies. John Logan. NNaP

Sat., Apr. 26, 1973. A Poem to Galway Kinnell. Etheridge Knight. NNaP

Saturday evening grows. Jasmine. Kyongjoo Hong Ryou, *tr. fr. Korean*. TSaS

Saturday in the '20s, A. Jean Earle. AngWe

Saturday Market. (Bury your heart in some deep green hollow.) Charlotte Mew. WPE
Sels.
Saturday Market "In Saturday Market, there's eggs a-plenty". FaPON

Saturday Morning. Richard Howard. ErPo

Saturday Morning Journal. Charles Wright. BAP-90

Saturday mornings, before. The Bait. Eric Chock. OpBo

Saturday Night. A. P. Herbert. NBLV

Saturday Night. Langston Hughes. MoAmPo

Saturday Night. Antigone Kefala. CBAP

Saturday Night. Martha Sansom. UnDi

Saturday night in August when, A. Last Meeting. Robert Penn Warren. DiPo

Saturday Night in the Village. Giacomo Leopardi, *tr. fr. Italian by* Robert Lowell. OBVE

Saturday night she comes in her little boat. Music on the Water. George Johnston. MoCV

Saturday Night Worship. Ann Carhart. CrSp

Saturday on Seventh Street. The Fields. W. S. Merwin. CAPP; HCAP

Saturday Review, The. Dora Greenwell. EBVV

Saturday, Sunday. Mother Goose. *See* On Saturday night shall be [all] my care.

Saturday: The Small-Pox. Lady Mary Wortley Montagu. *Fr.* Six Town Eclogues. ECWP; NOEC; WPE

Saturday, the sorrow's killing me. To My Dead Sister. Momcilo Nastasijevic, *tr. fr. Serbo-Croatian by* Charles Simic. HSix

Saturday Tub, The. Mary Gilmore. NOBAu

Saturday's Child. Countee Cullen. LiTM; NAs; PoBA

Saturday's Expedition, A, *sels*. Robert Fergusson.
"Ah that sweet period of revolving time." ScCV

Saturn. Keats. *See* Deep in the shady sadness of a vale.

Saturn. Sharon Olds. RaBo

Saturn's Three Sons. Robert Hayman. *Fr.* Owen's Epigrams. NOSC

Satyr. Charles Gullans. PoA

Satyr, The, *sels*. Ben Jonson.

Mab the Mistress-Fairy. EIL
(Mab.) WiR

Satyr III: "When shaven Crown, and hallow'd Girdle's Power." John Oldham. *Fr.* Satires [*or* Satyrs] upon the Jesuits. SeCV-2

Satyr, A, *sels.* John Oldham.
London. NOSC
"One night, as I was pondering of late." NOSC

Satyr, A. Elizabeth Tipper. *Fr.* Pilgrim's Viaticum; or, The Destitute, But Not Forlorn. KTR

Satyr Address'd to a Friend That Is About to Leave the University, and Come Abroad in the World, A, *sels.* John Oldham.
"If you're so out of love with happiness" OBSV

Satyr by Diodorus, A. Plato the Younger, *tr. fr. Greek by* G. R. H. Wright. GrAn

Satyr on Elysium lights, A. The Tenth Nimphall. Michael Drayton. *Fr.* Muses' Elysium [*or* Elizium]. JCP

Satyre III: On Religion. John Donne. *See* Kind pity [*or* Kinde pitty] chokes my spleen[e]; brave scorn forbids.

Satyre Entituled the Witch, A. *Unknown.* CoMu

Satyre: Of Religion. John Donne. *See* Kind pity [*or* Kinde pitty] chokes my spleen[e]; brave scorn forbids.

Satyre [*or* Satire] III. John Donne. *See* Kind pity [*or* Kinde pitty] chokes my spleen[e]; brave scorn forbids.

Satyretericall Charracter of a Proud Upstart, A. John Saffin. SCAP

Satyricon, *sels.* Petronius Arbiter, *tr. fr. Latin.*
"Fate brought three men to birth." MLL, *tr. by* Helen Waddell
"From the high Alpine pass." MLL, *tr. by* Helen Waddell
"Roman was the victor of the world., The." MLL, *tr. by* Helen Waddell
"Such flowers as Earth our Mother." MLL, *tr. by* Helen Waddell

Satyrs' Catch, The. Ben Jonson. *See* Buz[z], Quoth the Blue Fly.

Satyr's Song. John Fletcher. *Fr.* Faithful Shepherdess, The.

Satyr's Song, The ("Softly Gliding as I Go.") John Fletcher. *Fr.* Faithful Shepherdess, The. NOSC

Satyrs used to fall for nymphs. Love-Songs, at Once Tender and Informative. Samuel Hoffenstein. OBAL

Satyrus Peregrinans., *sels.* William Rankins.
"By this time long-gowned Lumen walked abroad." OBSV

Sauchs in the Reuch Heuch Hauch, The. "Hugh MacDiarmid." NoAM

Saucy Sailor, The. *Unknown.* OBET

Saul. Nathan Alterman, *tr. fr. Hebrew by* Dov Vardi. TrJP

Saul, *sels.* Robert Browning.
"Oh, our manhood's prime vigour! no spirit feels waste,." OtMeF
"Oh, the wild joys of living! the leaping from rock up to rock." BoTP; FaBV
(Youth.) BoTP
"Yea, my King." WGRP

Saul, Afterward, Riding East. John Malcolm Brinnin. Prf

Saul did much care and diligence express. Rowland Watkyns. FaBoEE

Sauntering home from church we lingered. Mary Ursula Bethell. *Fr.* By the River Ashley. PeNZ

Sauntering the pavement or riding the country by-road. Faces. Walt Whitman. PoEL-5

Sausage. Edgar A. Guest. OBAL

Sausalito,/ Little Willow. Lew Welch. EaPr

Savage lion in the zoo. Supper for a Lion. Dorothy Aldis. ZA

Savages, The. Josephine Miles. LiTM

Savage's romance, The. New York. Marianne Moore. NAAL-2

Savannah. Alethea S. Burroughs. PAH

Save all these shires. *Amen* say I. (*LL*) The Properties of the Shires of England. *Unknown.* FaBoPP; GBP

Save at the heels of some damned one eye'd whore. (*LL*) Epigram: To Lygdus. Martial. PeHV

Save by the Old Road none attain the new. Coventry Patmore. FaBoEE

Save desiring and a yearning heart. (*LL*) The Lark. Bernard de Ventadour. CTC, *tr. by* Ezra Pound

Save me from such as me assail. Bible, *O.T., paraphrased by* Sir Thomas Wyatt. *Fr.* Psalms. NoSic, *paraphrased by* the Countess of Pembroke

Save, O Save! (*LL*) Desire. Matthew Arnold. WGRP

Save of him who, desiring, honors her. (*LL*) Ballata: He Will Gaze upon Beatrice. Dante. AWP

Save, or we perish, Son of God! (*LL*) The Agony in the Garden. Felicia Dorothea Hemans. TrCP

Save that it sings in me. (*LL*) April. Sara Teasdale. FaPON; PDV

Save that one only — Lady, could'st thou know! (*LL*) Eyes, Calm beside Thee (Lady, Could'st Thou Know!). Robert Browning. Son

Save the Boys. Frances E. W. Harper. AAP; PWR

Save the Old South! Julia Ward Howe. AmWP

Save the squadron, honor France, love thy wife the Belle Aurore! (*LL*) Hervé Riel. Robert Browning. BeLS; FaBoBe; GN; OtMeF

Save what the living sun illumineth. (*LL*) Love, the Light-Giver [*or* To Tommaso de' Cavalieri]. Michelangelo. AWP; PeHV

Save yourself. Run and leave me. I must go back. C. S. Lewis. *Fr.* Epigrams and Epitaphs. EBEV

Saved. Maria Teresa Horta, *tr. fr. Portuguese by* Suzette Macedo. PBWP

Saved. Adah Isaacs Menken. CBWP-1

Saved. *Unknown.* FaBoUs

Saved a captive Englishman. (*LL*) Pocahontas. Thackeray. FaPON; GN; PAH

Saves us from our dreams. (*LL*) The World of Dreams. Philip Salom. NOBAu

Saville in Trouble. Albery Allson Whitman. *Fr.* Not a Man and Yet a Man. AAP

Saving My Skin from Burning. Gerald Stern. BAP-90

Saving the Children. Frieda Singer. BTR

Saving the Harvest. Geoffrey Lehmann. CBAP

Savior Is Abducted in Puerto Rico, The. Martín Espada. TRP

Savior [*or* Saviour]! I've no one else to tell. Emily Dickinson. TrCP; TrPWD

Savior looked on Peter, The. Ay, no word. The Look. Elizabeth Barrett Browning. TrCP

Saviour, Sprinkle Many Nations. Arthur Cleveland Coxe. AH

Saviour, Thy Dying Love. Sylvanus D. Phelps. AH

Saviour, Who Thy Flock Art Feeding. William Augustus Mühlenberg. AH

Saviour, Whose Love Is Like the Sun. Howard Chandler Robbins. TrPWD

Sâvitrî; or, Love and Death. *Unknown, tr. fr. Sanskrit by* Franklin Edgerton. *Fr.* Mahabharata, The. TAL, *tr. by* Sir Edwin Arnold

Savonarola. E. C. Bentley. *Fr.* Clerihews. CBNP

Savonarola ("Savonarola looks more grim today.") Max Beerbohm. BXAP

Savonarola ("Savonarola/Declined to wear a bowler.") E. C. Bentley. OxBoLi

Savor the hour as it comes. Preserve it in amber. V-Day. Phyllis McGinley. ArOW

Savouring the shade of our teacher's willow. Dog Day Lesson. John Hughes. PNI

Saw a girl in a food. Crystal Palace Market. James Laughlin. ArLo

Saw a lamb being born. Lamb. Michael Dennis Browne. NU; RaBo

Saw an iguana once. Iguana Memory. Grace Nichols. OBAP

Saw the Cloud Lynx. Samuel Makidemewabe, *tr. fr. Cree Indian by* Howard Norman. STP

Saw ye aught of my love a-coming from the market? My Love. *Unknown.* ReMoGo

Saw Ye Bonny Lesley. Burns. *See* O, saw ye bonny Lesley.

Saw ye owt o' ma' lad. The Waggoner. *Unknown.* GBP

Sawest thou not mine oxen, thou litill pretty boy. (*LL*) I Have Twelve Oxen. *Unknown.* ChTr; GBP

Sawyers lie outside the shed, The. The Boathouse. Robert Minhinnick. AngWe

Saxifrage is my flower that splits/ The rocks. (*LL*) A Sort of a Song. William Carlos Williams. HoPM; NAAL-2; NoP; OxBSP; TAP

Saxon Legend of Language, The. Mary Weston Fordham. AAP; AmWP; CBWP-2

Saxons of Flint, The. *Unknown, tr. fr. Welsh by* Mary C. Llewelyn. OBWVE

Saxophone. Christopher Gilbert. *Fr.* Horizontal Cosmology. Jaz

Saxophone turned into a dolphin, The. Albert Ayler: Eulogy for a Decomposed Saxophone Player. Stanley Crouch. PoBA

Saxophonetyx. Cyn Zarco. UL

Say, bud, ya got a cigarette? Refugee. Naomi Long Madgett. PoNe

Say, but did you love so long? Sir Toby Matthews. Sir John Suckling. SeCV-1

Say, crimson rose and dainty daffodil. A Nosegay. John Reynolds. OBEV

Say, darkeys hab you seen de massa. The Year of Jubilee. Henry Clay Work. PAH

Say, dear Maria! is the modish life. A Familiar Epistle. Ann Murry. WPE

Say, did you go to Mae's rent party? Mae's Rent Party. Ernest J. Wilson, Jr. PoNe

Say, dwarf, for it seems to me. *Unknown, tr. fr. Icelandic by* W. H. Auden *and* Paul B. Taylor. *Fr.* Words of the All-Wise, The. OBVE

Say, earth, why hast thou got thee new attire. Easter Morn. Giles Fletcher the Younger. *Fr.* Christ's Victory and Triumph. EIL; NOCV

Say father, say mother. Dove's Song in Winter. *Zulu Oral Tradition, tr. by* B. W. Vilakazi. WTO

Say, friend, if all is well still with the bowers. Vidya, *tr. fr. Sanskrit by* Daniel H. H. Ingalls. *Fr.* Wanton, The. PBWP

Say Girls in Shoe Ads: "I Go for a Man Who's Tall!" Robley Wilson, Jr.. PBCAP

Say good-by er howdy-do. Good-by er Howdy-do. James Whitcomb Riley. CTC

Say good night. (*LL*) Teddy Bear, Teddy Bear. *Unknown*. NTCP

Say goodbye. (*LL*) Death Certificate. Rui Knopfli. PeSAV

Say Goodbye to Big Daddy. Randall Jarrell. PoNe

Say goodbye to the help, the ranks. Dr. Joseph Goebbels. W. D. Snodgrass. *Fr.* Führer Bunker, The. CAPP

Say Hello to John. Sherley Anne Williams. BlSi

Say, how shall thoughtless, easy-natured youth. Stanzas Imitated From Psalm CXIX. Thomas, the Elder Warton. ChIV-1

Say, I come to-morrow. (*LL*) Westphalian Song. *Unknown*. AWP; OBVE

Say it and cry aloud. I Am a Negro. Muhammad al-Faituri, *tr. fr. Arabic by* Halim El-Dabh. TTY

Say It Now. *Unknown. See* If you have a friend worth loving.

Say it's an important event like this. Off to Patagonia. Theodore Weiss. AnAn; TAP

Say life is the one-way trip, the one-way flight. Watchmaker God. Robert Lowell. HCAP; SoSe

Say, light proceeding edgewise, like a sword. (*LL*) Gardens No Emblems. Donald Davie. LiTM; OAEL-2

Say, lovely Tory, why the jest. To Miss Eleanor Ambrose on the Occasion of Her Wearing an Orange Lily at a Ball in Dublin Castle on July the 12th. Earl of Chesterfield. EnLoPo

"Say me, wight in the brom [*or* broom]." *Unknown*. MiEL (Tell Me, Wight in the Broom.) NAEL-1

Say, mighty Love, and teach my song. Few Happy Matches. Isaac Watts. NOEC

Say Muses, say; who now in those rich fields. Phineas Fletcher. *Fr.* Locusts, or Appolyonists, The. ChIV-1

Say nay! say nay! (*LL*) And Wilt Thou Leave Me Thus? Sir Thomas Wyatt. EBEvV; ElL; EnLoPo; EnRePo; NAEL-1; NoSic; SCGP; SiPS; SiPSBD

Say Not. Arthur Hugh Clough. *See* Say not the struggle nought [*or* naught] availeth.

Say not, because no more you see. On the Death of Mr. Persall's Little Daughter, in the Beginning of the Spring, at Amsterdam. *Unknown*. NOSC

Say not of beauty she is good. Beauty. Elinor Wylie. NAAL-2; OxBA

Say not of me that weakly I declined. Robert Louis Stevenson. OBNC; PeVV

Say not the age is hard and cold. The Present Age. Frances E. W. Harper. AAP; PWR

Say not the mermaid is a myth. The Mermaid. Ogden Nash. Spl

Say Not the Struggle. Arthur Hugh Clough. *See* Say not the struggle nought [*or* naught] availeth.

Say Not the Struggle Nought Availeth. Arthur Hugh Clough. AWP; CoGr; EBEvV; EBVV; EnVR; FaBoRV; FaPoR; GGP; GTBS-P; LiTB; NAEL-2; NOBE; NOBVV; NTP; OAEL-2; OBEV; OBNC; OtMeF; PlP; SCGP; TEP; TFi; TrGrPo; WGRP
(Keeping On.) MoShBr
(Say Not.) FaBV
(Say Not the Struggle.) ImPo

Say over again, and yet once over again. Elizabeth Barrett Browning. *Fr.* Sonnets from the Portuguese. NAEL-2

Say, reverend man, why midst this stormy night. The Blind Man. Anne Batten Cristall. ECWP

Say, stranger, that this is the tomb of the mare Aethyia. Mnasalcas, *tr. fr. Greek by* Barbara Hughes Fowler. *Fr.* Epigrams. HePo

Say, sweet, my grief and I, we may not brook. Je ne veux de personne aupres de ma tristesse. Henri de Regnier, *tr. fr. French by* "Seumas O'Sullivan". AWP

Say (sweetest) whether thou didst use me well. To Cynthia on Her Being an Incendiary. Sir Francis Kynaston. HAP

Say that a ballad. Susan Howe. *Fr.* Speeches at the Barriers. UL

Say that I should say I love ye. An Assurance. Nicholas Breton. CBLP; SCGP

Say that the men of the old black tower. The Black Tower. W. B. Yeats. CMoP

Say that thou didst forsake me for some fault. Shakespeare. *Fr.* Sonnets. OxAEP-1

Say there! P'r'aps. "Jim." Bret Harte. AnAmPo

Say, there's a lamb in the daisies. (*LL*) For a Lamb. Richard Eberhart. CMoP; LiTM; OxBSP; RB; SoSe

Say this city has ten million souls. W. H. Auden. LiTM
(Refugee Blues.) LiTA; OxAEP-2
(Song: "Say this city has ten million souls!") NYBP

Say This of Horses. Minnie Hite Moody. PoLF

Say, tyrant Custom, why must we obey. The Emulation. Sarah Fyge Egerton. ECWP; NOEC

Say, Virgins, seated round the Throne Divine. The Catalogue of the Ships. Homer, *tr. fr. Greek by* Alexander Pope. *Fr.* Iliad, The. CBCK

Say well and do well. *Unknown*. OxNR

Say! what is life? 'Tis to be born. The Story of Life. John Godfrey Saxe. PoToHe

Say, what is the spell, when her fledglings are cheeping. A Song of Love. "Lewis Carroll." GN

Say what slim youth, with moist perfumes. Horace. *See* What slender youth bedewed with liquid odours.

Say what we will, at times it seems the rarest. Inspiration. Sherod Santos. NAmP90

Say what you did for me, too, only last Christmas Day. (*LL*) Christmas Day in the Workhouse. George R. Sims. BeLS; BLPA; EBNV

Say what you want about doctors or priests. The Lightning Rod Salesman. M. L. Hester. CRP

Say what you will in two. Air: Sentir avec Ardeur. Marie-Françoise-Catherine de, Marquise de Boufflers Beauveau, *tr. fr. French by* Ezra Pound. CTC; WPOW

Say, where is the maiden sweet. Sag', wo ist dein schönes Liebchen. Heine, *tr. fr. German by* James Thomson. AWP

Say why are beauties praised and honoured most. Pope. *Fr.* Rape of the Lock, The. ECEV; FHYEP; HAP; ImPo; NoP; OAEL-1; OBNV; PeLV; PoEL-3; TEP; TrGrPo

Say, why are you so sad today. Black Roses. Ernst Abraham Josephson, *tr. fr. Swedish by* Philip L. Miller. RiWo

Say, wilt thou go with me, sweet maid. Invitation to Eternity. John Clare. PoEL-4
(Invite to Eternity.) NAEL-1; NOBVV; OAEL-2; OBNC

Say, wilt thou more of scenes so sordid know? A Slum Dwelling. George Crabbe. *Fr.* Borough, The. OBNC

Say, wouldst thou guard thy son. Of Caution. Francesco da Barberini, *tr. fr. Italian by* Dante Gabriel Rossetti. AWP

Say Yes Quickly. Jalal al-Din Rumi, *tr. fr. Persian*. EnlH, *tr. by* Coleman Barks *and* A. J. Arberry; RaBo, *tr. by* Coleman Barks *and* John Moyne

Say You Love Me. Molly Peacock. NAmP90

Say you were the kid who could not sleep. The Actor. Thomas Snapp. NYBP

Sayes "Christ thee saue, good Child of Ell!" Earl Brand. *Unknown*. ESPB

Saying blackberry, blackberry, blackberry. (*LL*) Meditation at Lagunitas. Robert Hass. AnAn; NoP; VCAP

Saying Dante Aloud. James Wright. InPK

Saying Farewell to a Friend. Li Po, *tr. fr. Chinese by* Robert Payne. TAL

Saying Farewell to Magistrate Ch'en Ta-yu. Lin Hung, *tr. fr. Chinese by* Irving Y. Lo. SuSp

Saying Good-bye. Duo Duo, *tr. fr. Chinese by* Donald Finkel *with* Li Guohua. SpMi

Saying Goodby to the Monk Ling-ch'e. Liu Ch'ang-ch'ing, *tr. fr. Chinese by* Dell R. Hales. SuSp

Saying Goodbye. Suzanne Juhasz. IHMS

Saying One Thing. Robert Long. NAmP90

Saying, "There is no hope," he stepped. A Generous Creed. Elizabeth Stuart Phelps Ward. WGRP

Saying to himself. What Her Girl Friend Said ("Saying to himself.") Peyanar, *tr. fr. Tamil by* A. K. Ramanujan. *Fr.* Nine on Happy Reunion. PLW

Sayings from the Northern Ice. William Stafford. NU

Saylors for My Money. Martin Parker. CoMu

Sayre. Lynn Strongin. IHMS

Says A, give me a good large slice. A Curious Discourse That Passed between the Twenty-five Letters at Dinner-Time. *Unknown*. FaBoUs

Says Body to Mind, 'Tis amazing to see, A Dialogue. Elizabeth Carter. ECWP

Says far more than I am saying. (*LL*) The Penny Whistle. Edward Thomas. MoAB; MoBrPo

Says His Grace to Will Green, whom he found in his stall. Death and the Cobbler. *Unknown*. APAS

Says I, 'Old man, go diddle yourself, I'd rather bum.' (*LL*) Shovelling Iron Ore. *Unknown*. AS; GBP

Says I to Myself. Edward Lear. FiBHP

Says Jack: "There is very good news; there is peace both by land and sea." Distressed Men of War. *Unknown*. OxBSS

Says my Uncle, I pray you discover. Molly Mog; or, The Fair Maid of the Inn. John Gay. CoMu

Says the great bell of Bow. (*LL*) The Bells of London. *Unknown*. BoTP; OxNR; PoRA

Says the master to me, "Is it true, I am told." My Master and I. *Unknown*. CoMu; OBET

Says the Miner to the Mucker. *Unknown*. AmFP

Says the Pont to the Blyth. Pont and Blyth. *Unknown*. GBP

Says the Shan Van Vocht. (*LL*) The Shan Van Vocht. *Unknown*. FaBoPV; GBP; OxBoLi

Says the Shan Van Vocht. (*LL*) What Will We Do for Linen? *Unknown.* GBP; WTO

Says the window. Indoors. George Johnston. PoA

Says Tom to Jack, "'Tis very odd,' The Methodist. Thomas Chatterton. ECEV

Says Tweed tae Till. *Unknown. See* Says Tweed to [tae] Till.

Says Tweed to [tae] Till. Tweed and Till. *Unknown.* BoNaP; ChTr;
  FaBoCh; FaBoPP; GBP; OBEV; OxBSP
  (Says Tweed tae Till.) FaBoVe
  (Two Rivers, The.) ChTr; OBEV

Says William to Henry, "I cannot conceive." Henry's Secret. Dorothy Kilner. OxBChV

Says William to Phyllis, "How came you here so soon?" William and Phyllis. *Unknown.* OBET

Scabs Crawl in, The. *Unknown.* SWP

Scaffold in Winter. János Pilinszky, *tr. fr. Hungarian by* Peter Jay. PoSu

Scaffolding. Seamus Heaney. GOYP

Scala Coeli. Kathleen Raine. NYBP

Scald it and scour it like a doorstep. (*LL*) View of a Pig. Ted Hughes. LiTM; OxAEP-2; OxBTC; TwCP

Scalded cat. Night Letter. Marge Piercy. NMM

Scale of dragon, tooth of wolf. Shakespeare. *Fr.* Macbeth. UV

Scales, The. William Empson. CBLP; CMoP; FaBoMo; LiTM

Scales. Libby Houston. NBrP

Scales of pearly cloud inlay. Holiday at Hampton Court. John Davidson. EBVV; MeMBP

Scales of the Eyes, The. Howard Nemerov. CMoP

Scaling small rocks, exhaling smog. Central Park. Robert Lowell. LiTM

Scalp Dance Song. *Unknown, tr. fr. Tewa Indian by* H. J. Spinden. WTO

Scalp on either side, A. (*LL*) After the Camanches. Rose Terry Cooke. AmWP; PAH

Scandal among the Flowers, A. Charles S. Taylor. BLPA

Scandal or two, A. Tattle. Godfrey Turner. NOBL

Scandalous man, A. Mr. Tom Narrow. James Reeves. OBSP

Scant and straggling her yellow hair, from her lip. An Old Woman. David Gwenallt Jones, *tr. fr. Welsh by* H. Idris Bell. OBWVE

Scapegoat. W. R. Rodgers. CIP

Scapular of birds hung fast, A. Eclipses. Nancy Sullivan. TAP

Scar, The. John Hewitt. CIP; PNI

Scar — August, 1934, The. Hans Juergensen. BTR

Scaramouche and Pulcinella. Puppets. Paul Verlaine, *tr. fr. French by* Philip L. Miller. RiWo

Scaramouche waves a threatening hand. Fantoches. Paul Verlaine, *tr. by* Arthur Symons. AWP; OBMV

Scarborough Fair. *Unknown.* OxBoLi; PeLV

Scarce a breeze on the lake, with four oars to our boat. On Loch Leven. Christian Carstairs. ECWP

Scarce do I pass a day, but that I hear. Meditation 8. Philip Pain. NOBA; NOSC; OxBSP

Scarce I seen for the first time his eyes. To Luigi del Riccio, after the Death of Cecchino Bracci. Michelangelo, *tr. fr. Italian by* John Addington Symonds. PeHV

Scarce had I slept my wonted round. A Dream. Sir John Suckling. ChIV-2

Scarce had the morning star hid from the light. The Affectionate Shepherd. Richard Barnfield. NoSic

Scarce images of life, one here, one there. A Recollection of the Stone Circle near Keswick. Keats. *Fr.* Hyperion; a Fragment. EnRP; FaBoPP; OAEL-2

Scarce warms the surface of the deepest pool? (*LL*) August. Elinor Wylie. MoAB; MoAmPo

Scarcely believe things shameful to utter which yet I shall speak of. Bernard of Cluny, *tr. fr. Latin by* John Mason Neale. *Fr.* De Contemptu Mundi. PeHV

Scare-Fire, The. Robert Herrick. HAP; NoP

Scarecrow. Dermot Bolger. IB

Scarecrow, The. Walter de la Mare. MoBrPo; OxBTC

Scarecrow, The. Michael Franklin. BoTP

Scarecrow, The. Andrew Young. FaBoTw

Scarecrow stood in a field one day, A. The Scarecrow. Michael Franklin. BoTP

Scared?/ are responsible negros running. Concerning One Responsible Negro with Too Much Power. Nikki Giovanni. BPo

Scarf, The. Ivy O. Eastwick. BoTP

Scaring Crows. *Unknown.* BoTP; OxNR

Scarlet, warm and heavy in black velvet leaves. Leah Goldberg, *tr. fr. Hebrew by* Ruth Finer Mintz. *Fr.* On Blossoming. MHP

Scarlet Woman, The. Fenton Johnson. PoBA; PoNe

Scarred by flame, hollowed out by waves. To the Wooden Hermit. Han Yü, *tr. fr. Chinese by* Kenneth O. Hanson. SuSp

Scars Remaining, The. Samuel Taylor Coleridge. *Fr.* Christabel. CH, ll. 1-65; EnRP; FHYEP; OAEL-2; OBNC

Scatter Seeds of Kindness. May Riley Smith. WBLP

Scatter their snow around. (*LL*) Spring Goeth All in White. Robert Bridges. BoNaP; BoTP; ChTr

Scattered Congregation, The. Tomas Tranströmer, *tr. fr. Swedish by* Robert Bly. RaBo

Scattered Fog. Christy Sheffield Sanford. UL

Scattered Leaves. Lance Henson. VoR

Scattered petals gather on the road. Hatsui Shizue, *tr. fr. Japanese by* Kenneth Rexroth *and* Ikuko Atsumi. WPJ

Scattered pomp has fallen to the scented dust. Shih Ch'ung's 'Golden Valley' Garden. Tu Mu, *tr. fr. Chinese by* A. C. Graham. PLT

Scattering Ashes. David Scott. PWE

Scattering bloom, The. Buson, *tr. fr. Japanese by* Harold G. Henderson. TAL

Scattering Layer, The. Martin Johnston. FaBoMA

Scatters pears and apples. Cézanne. Angela Greene. NWP

Scazons. C. S. Lewis. EBEV

Scel Lem Duib. *Unknown. See* Here's a song.

Scene, The. Agnes Nemes Nagy, *tr. fr. Hungarian by* Bruce Berlind. PoSu

Scene, The: a public square in Ruritania. The Belle of the Balkans. Newman Levy. FiBHP

Scene after Hunting at Swallowfield in Berkshire, A. Sneyd Davies. NOEC

Scene changes, The. A Poem for Record Players. John Wieners. PoBeRe

Scene from a Play, Acted at Oxford, Called "Matriculation." Thomas Moore. OBSV

Scene from Shoah, A. Luada Sandler. BTR

Scene from the Movie *Giant*. Tino Villanueva. ETG

Scene in Paradise, A. Milton. *See* Adam the goodliest man of men since born.

Scene is different, and the place, The. Arthur Hugh Clough. *Fr.* Dipsychus. PeVV, *sc.* I

Scene is set now, The: in a silent room. Transfusion. Merrill Moore. PoA

Scene of a Summer Morning. Irving Feldman. BTR; NYBP

Scene of the Crime, A. David Groff. PFL

Scene on the Banks of the Hudson, A. Bryant. AnAmPo

Scene 6 The Boat Passage. Gabriel Gbadamosi. *Fr.* No Blacks, No Irish. NBrP

Scene with Figure. Babette Deutsch. TrJP

Scene within the paperweight is calm, The. The Paperweight. Gjertrud Schnackenberg. SM; VCAP

Scenery. Ted Joans. PoBA

Scènes de la Vie de Bohème, *sels.* Arthur Symons.
  Episode of a Night of May. OBTV; PeVV

Scenes from Carnac. Matthew Arnold. FaBoPP; OBTV

Scenes from the Life of the Peppertrees. Denise Levertov. LiTM; NeAP; NoP; PoM

Scenes of Childhood. James Merrill. CoAP

Scenes of Childhood. Carl Morse. GLP

Scenes of my childhood, The, how oft I recall! My Infundibuliform Hat. Charles Follen Adams. OBAL

Scent of ripeness from over a wall, A. Unharvested. Robert Frost. BoNaP; SAmP

Scent of rotted apples, The. Late October. Sara King Carleton. GoYe

Scent of unseen jasmine on the warm night beach, The. Malaga. Pearse Hutchinson. BIrV; PBCIP

Scented, cool, and marble dark. Lemons. Ted Walker. NYBP

Scented Herbage of My Breast. Walt Whitman. NAAL-1

Scentless laurel a broad leaf displays, The. Walter Savage Landor. FaBoEE

Schaft/ scaap/ scop. Ninth Matter: Shape. Robert Kelly. BCF

Scheherazade. Barbara Burford. DT

Scheme of a new Rotterdam humming in the vacancy, The. (*LL*) Vision of Rotterdam. Gregory Corso. PoBeRe

Schemmelfennig. Bret Harte. OBAL

Scherzo, A. Dora Greenwell. NOBVV

Schir, sen that God, of his preordinance. An Exhortation to His Grace the King. Sir David Lyndsay. ScCV

Schir William Wallace. Henry the Minstrel. *See* Wallace stature of greatness [*or* gretnes], and of hicht [*or* hycht].

Schir, ye have mony servitouris. Remonstrance to the King. William Dunbar. OxBS; ScCV

Schism, A/ Nurtured by foppery and barbarism. Keats. *Fr.* Sleep and Poetry. EnRP; EPCY

Schizophrenic. P. K. Page. HeIP

Schizophrenic, wrenched by two styles. Codicil. Derek Walcott. MoP; NoAM

Schizophrenics, The. Roy Fuller. AnAn

Schmaltztenor!. M. W. Branch. FiBHP

Schoenberg Op. 11. Thomas W. Shapcott. *Fr.* Piano Pieces. CBAP

Scholar, The. Austin Clarke. RB

Scholar, The. Frances Cornford. BrRo

Scholar I. Seamus Deane. NOIV

Scholar and the Cat, The. Frank O'Connor. OBF

Scholar Complains, The. *Unknown.* MeEL

Scholar first my love implored, A. Lady Dorothea Dubois. ECWP

Scholar Gi[y]psy, The. Matthew Arnold. ChTr; EBEV; EBVV; EBVVPR; EnVR; FaBoPP; FHYEP; HAP; ImPO; MeMBP; NAEL-2; NOBE; NOBVV; NoP; OAEL-2; OBEV; OBNC; OxAEP-2; PoE; PoEL-5; SCGP; TEP; TFi

Scholar in the Narrow Street, The. Tso Ssu, *tr. fr. Chinese* by Arthur Waley. AWP

Scholar of Oxford, while tipsy, A. A Tribute to Matthew Arnold in a Moment of Self-Abuse. Richard Shepherd. PeLi

Scholar II. Seamus Deane. CIP; NOIV

Scholars. Walter de la Mare. NoAM; Poetr

Scholars, The. W. B. Yeats. CMoP; NoP; OAEL-2; PoA

Scholars at the Orchid Pavilion. John Berryman. PoE

Scholar's Life, The. Samuel Johnson. *See* When first the college rolls receive his name.

Scholar's Life, The. *Unknown, tr. fr. Irish* by Thomas Kinsella. NOIV

Scholfield Huxley. Edgar Lee Masters. *Fr.* Spoon River Anthology. LiTA; TrPWD

School and Schoolfellows. Winthrop Mackworth Praed. OxAEP-2

School-Bell. Eleanor Farjeon. FaPON

School-bell rings, The. Nine o'Clock. Katharine Pyle. *Fr.* Wonder Clock, The. OBCA

School Boy, The. Blake. *Fr.* Songs of Experience. BoNaP; CH; FaBoCh; FHYEP; OxAEP-2

School Cadets. Anne Elder. CBAP

School Children, The. Louise Glück. AmPA; HCAP; Poetr; WeW

School Creed. *Unknown.* BoTP

School Days. Maltbie D. Babcock. PWR

School Days. William Stafford. LCAP

School Days in New Amsterdam. Arthur Guiterman. FaPON

School for Objects, The. Paul Hoover. UL

School for Satire, The. Lady Sophia Burrell. ECWP

School for Scandal, The, *sels.* Sheridan.
　Drinking Song. NOIV
　(Here's to the Maiden.) ELP
　(Song: "Here's to the maiden [*or* maid] of bashful fifteen.") NOEC; OxAEP-1; OxBoLi; PoRA
　(Song.) EBEvV; PeLV

School Globe, The. James Reaney. NOBC

School greets me like a series, The. Poet in Residence at a Country School. Don Welch. GOYP

School Hockey Team in Amsterdam, The. Frank Ormsby. OBTV

School is over. It is too hot. The Lonely Street. William Carlos Williams. PoA; TwCP

School-Master and the Truants, The. "John Brownjohn." OBCA

School-Mistress, The. William Shenstone. NOEC

School of Beauty's a tavern now, The. A Street in Bronzeville: Southeast Corner. Gwendolyn Brooks. VGW

School of Eloquence, The. *sels.* Tony Harrison.
　Book Ends. DiPo; NAEL-2; NoAM; SCBI
　Classics Society. SCBI
　Heredity. NAEL-2; NoAM
　History Classes. NoAM
　Lines to My Grandfathers. NoAM
　Long-Distance. NAEL-2
　Marked with D. NAEL-2; NoAM
　Me Tarzan. NoAM
　National Trust. NAEL-2; SCBI
　On Not Being Milton. FaBoPV; NoAM; SCBI
　Self Justification. NoAM
　Timer. NoAM; SCBI
　Turns. NAEL-2; NoAM

School of Music. Theodore Deppe. BTR

School Of Night, The. A. D. Hope. PoA

School of Sorrow, The. Harold Hamilton. BLRP

School Parted Us. "George Eliot." *Fr.* Brother and Sister. NALW; Son

School-Time. Wordsworth. *Fr.* Prelude [*or*, Growth of a Poet's Mind], The. EnRP; OAEL-2

Schoolbag, The. Seamus Heaney. BiHa

Schoolboys in Winter. John Clare. InvP; PoEL-4

Schoolboy's Lament, The. *Unknown. See* I wold fain be a clarke.

Schoolboys still their morning rambles take, The. Schoolboys in Winter. John Clare. InvP; PoEL-4

Schoolcraft's Diary Written on the Missouri: 1830. Robert Bly. ImGa

Schoolgirls Hastening. John Shaw Neilson. NOBAu

Schooling, A. Seamus Deane. CIP; PNI

Schoolmaster. George Rostrevor Hamilton. FaBoEE

Schoolmaster, The. Herodas, *tr. fr. Greek by* Barbara Hughes Fowler. HePo

Schoolmaster, The. *Unknown.* GBP

Schoolmaster Abroad, The. Sir Owen Seaman. OBTV

Schoolmaster Abroad with His Son, The. Charles Stuart Calverley. NOBL; PeLV

Schoolmaster once known as, The. History Teacher in the Warsaw Ghetto Rising. Evangeline Paterson. PAW

Schoolmaster's Admonition, A. *Unknown.* OxBChV

Schoolmaster's forgotten the present, The. A Snapshot. Debora Greger. *Fr.* Afterlife, The. BAP-91

Schoolmaster's Precepts, A. John Penkethman. OxBChV

Schoolroom: 158 – . James E. Warren, Jr.. GoYe

Schools. George Crabbe. *Fr.* Borough, The. CTC

Schools break up tonight, The. Lament for Fearghal Ruadh. Tadhg Og O'Huiginn. NOIV

School's Out. W. H. Davies. OBMV

Schoolyard in April. Kenneth Koch. PoA

Schooner. Edward Kamau Brathwaite. PBCV

Schooner *Fred Dunbar*, The. Amos Hanson. AmFP

Schooner *The Mother of Parliaments* has anchored in the bay, The. Tom Leonard. *Fr.* Situations Theoretical and Contemporary. NBrP

Schooners with their pale green lights, The. A Dream within a Song. H. Cordelia Ray. CBWP-3

Schreckhorn, The. Thomas Hardy. OAEL-2

Schubertiana. Tomas Tranströmer, *tr. fr. Swedish by* Robert Bly. NU

Schule Laddie's Lament on the Lateness o' the Season, A. James Logie Robertson. NOBVV

Schumann's Sonata in A Minor. Celia Laighton Thaxter. AiP

Schute, Bell, Badgery, Lumby. A Country Song. Douglas Stewart. NOBAu

Schwerner, Chaney, Goodman. Raymond R. Patterson. NBV

Science. Robinson Jeffers. NU; OxBA

Science. Sarah Helen Whitman. AmWP

Science as Art. Hugh Seidman. AmPA

Science Fiction. Kingsley Amis. NoAM

Science finds out ingenious ways to kill. The Modern World. Colin Ellis. FaBoEE

Science! meet daughter of old time thou art. Sonnet to Science. Poe. NAAL-1

Science of the Night, The. Stanley Kunitz. MoAmPo; TwCP

Science, the agile ape, may well. Coventry Patmore. FaBoEE

Science! thou fair effusive ray. Hymn to Science. Mark Akenside. ECEV; PoEL-3

Science! true daughter of Old Time thou art! Sonnet — Science. Poe. *Fr.* Al Aaraff. AmPP; MeMAP; NAAL-1; NoP; OxBA; TAP

Science, true daughter of old time thou art! To Science. Poe. AnAmPo; Son

Scientific Expedition in Siberia, 1913, A. Kelly Cherry. SM

Scientist has a test tube full of sheep, A. Counting Sheep. Russell Edson. LCAP

Scientist living at Staines, A. Genius. R. J. P. Hewison. PeLi

Scientists are in terror, The. Ezra Pound. *Fr.* Cantos. FaBoMo

"Scientists find universe awash in tiny diamonds." Pat Mayne Ellis. CrSp

Sicilian Muse, begin a loftier strain. The Messiah. Virgil, *tr. fr. Latin. Fr.* Eclogues. AWP, *tr.* by Dryden
　(Sicilian Muse, I Would Try Now a Somewhat Grander Theme. NAs, *tr.* by C. Day Lewis
　(Sicilian Muses, sing we greater things.) OBVE, *tr.* by Sir John Beaumont

Scilla's Metamorphosis, *sels.* Thomas Lodge.
　Earth, Late Choked with Showers, The. EIL

Scimitar for Brenda Lewis. Kenward Elmslie. UL

Scintilla. William Stanley Braithwaite. CDC

Scion of a noble stock! The Young American. Alexander Hill Everett. VPP

Scion of Boston society, A. Conrad Aiken. PeLi

"Sciplinin" Sister Brown. James Edwin Campbell. AAP

Scissor-Man. George MacBeth. FaBoMo

Scissor-Man, The. Madeleine Nightingale. BoTP

Scissors and string, scissors and string. *Unknown.* OxNR

Scissors cut the long-grown hair, The. Upon Shaving Off One's Beard. John Updike. OxBSP

Scissors cut you? What tender ears! On Words and Concepts and Things. Paul Ramsey. CRP

Scobble for whoredom[e] whips his wife, and cries [*or* cryes]. Upon Scobble [Epigram]. Robert Herrick. BeJo; CaPo; FaBoEE; NoP

Scoffers, The. Blake. *See* Mock On, Mock On, Voltaire, Rousseau.

Scolding Wives Vindication; or, An Answer to the Cuckold's Complaint, The. *Unknown.* CoMu

Scoops in the sea rock full of natural water. Bathtubs. Richmond Lattimore. NYBP

Scorching the known world, ripping the new world. (*LL*) Wars of Imperialism. John Foulcher. NOBAu

Score of years had come and gone, A. John Underhill. Whittier. PAH

Score rose from 99 to 105, The. (*LL*) Courage, a Tale. Thom Gunn. GLP

Scorn Not the Sonnet. Wordsworth. *See* Scorn not the sonnet; critic, you have frowned.

Scorn not the sonnet; critic, you have frowned. Wordsworth. EBEV; EPCY
(Scorn Not the Sonnet.) EnRP; HeIP; NoP; Son
(Sonnet: "Scorn not the sonnet; critic, you have frowned.") OBEV; TrGrPo

"Scorn not the sonnet," though its strength be sapped. On a Magazine Sonnet. Russell Hillard Loines. OBAL

Scorn the black regiment! (*LL*) The Black Regiment. George Henry Boker. AnAmPo; GN; PAH

Scorna Boy, the Barretts' bailiff, lewd and lame. The Vengeance of the Welshmen of Tirawley. Sir Samuel Ferguson. PeIV

Scorned, to be scorned by one that I scorn. Tennyson. *Fr.* Maud[: A Monodrama]. EnVR

Scorner, The. Félix TchiKaya U'Tamsi, *tr. fr. French by* Gerald Moore *and* Ulli Beier. TTY

Scorning religion all thy lifetime past. On Mr. Dryden, Renegade. Aphra Behn. FaBoVe

Scorpion. Linda Hogan. SRLS

Scorpion, The. William Plomer. OBMV; PeSAV

Scorpion. Stevie Smith. EBEV; FaBoWP; OxAEP-2; PeECV; PoE

Scorpions Fighting. Broughton Gingell. OBAP

Scot, a Welsh and an Irish Man, A. *Unknown.* GBP

Scotch Drink. Burns. ChIV-1

Scotch Rhapsody. Edith Sitwell. TwCP

Scotch Te Deum. Bible, *O.T., paraphrased by* Sir Thomas Wyatt. *See* Make a joyful noise unto the Lord, all ye lands.

Scotch Te Deum. William Kethe. *See* All people that on earth do dwell.

Scotland. Sir Alexander Gray. OxBS

Scotland. William Soutar. OxBS

Scotland 1941. Edwin Muir. OxBS

Scotland Small? "Hugh MacDiarmid." RB

Scotland the Ghost. Gerald Mangan. PWE

Scotland the Wee. Tom Buchan. IHNG

Scotland the wee, crèche of the soul. Scotland the Wee. Tom Buchan. IHNG

Scotland, when it is given to me. With a Lifting of the Head. "Hugh MacDiarmid." MoBrPo

Scotland Yet. *Unknown. See* From the lone shieling of the misty island.

Scotland's Winter. Edwin Muir. OxBS; OxBTC

Scots Pines. Vuyelwa Carlin. NWP

Scots steel tempered wi' Irish fire. The Weapon. "Hugh MacDiarmid." RB

Scots, wha hae wi' Wallace bled. Burns. EBEvV; EnRP; FaPoR; NAEL-2; OAEL-1; OxBS; PlP; ScCV; TEP
(Before Bannockburn.) FaBoCh
(Robert Bruce's March to Bannockburn.) FaBoEH

Scott, your last fragments I arrange tonight. On Editing Scott Fitzgerald's Papers. Edmund Wilson. NYBP

Scot[t]ish Field [*or* Feilde], *sels. Unknown.*
Battle of Flodden, The. NoSic; OxBLMV

Scottish Proverb, A. *Unknown.* FaBoUs

Scotts, Kerrs, and Murrays, and Deloraines all, The. A Border Ballad. Thomas Love Peacock. BXAP

Scottsboro. *Unknown.* InPK

Scottsboro, Too, Is Worth Its Song. Countee Cullen. PoBA

Scoundrel carries his baseness around like an ID card, The. Answer. Bei Dao, *tr. fr. Chinese by* Donald Finkel *with* Chen Xueliang. SpMi

Scourge deep, and quick be done. Martyr. Mary Elizabeth Fullerton. CBAP

Scourge of Folly, The, *sels.* John Davies of Hereford.
Author Loving These Homely Meats, The. CBLP; CBNP; EIl; FaBoNo; Son
(Buttered Pippin-Pies.) ChTr
(Homely Meats.) FaBoCh

Scourge of Villainy [*or* Villanie], The, *sels.* John Marston.
To Detraction I Present My Poesie. NoSic
To Everlasting Oblivion. NoSic; SCGP

Scouting. Philip Levine. BAP-90

Scrape no more your harmless Chins. Advice to the Old Beaux. Sir Charles Sedley. FaBoUs; SeCV-2

Scrape the bottom of the hole: gather up the stuff! The Digger's Song. Barcroft Henry Boake. NOBAu

Scraping in the cokehouse. One red car, A. 107 Poems. Roy Fisher. VaA

Scraping sound, A: The grasshopper. The Grasshopper's Song. Hayyim Nahman Bialik, *tr. fr. Hebrew by* Jessie Sampter. FaPON

Scraps of Lear. Edward Lear. FaBoNo

Scraps of Time. Mrs. Henry Linden. CBWP-4

Scratch a Jew and you'll find a Wailing Wall. The Wall. Eve Merriam. TrJP

Scratch Music. C. D. Wright. NAmP90

Scratching the door, an animal home. (*LL*) Sitting on Zero. Karen Murai. UTF

Scrawled in a rage by Dublin's poor. (*LL*) Inscription for a Headstone. Austin Clarke. BIrV; CIP; IIP

Scrawled in Pencil in a Sealed Car. Dan Pagis, *tr. fr. Hebrew by* Robert Friend. PoSu

Scream, The. May Miller. Poetr

Scream like a thousand tigers. The Tornado. Ts'ai Ch'i-chiao, *tr. fr. Chinese.* LHF, *tr. by* Hualing Nieh

Scream that climbs a candle, A. Screams in the Dark. Slavko Mihalic, *tr. by* Charles Simic. PoSu

Screamer Discusses Methods of Screaming, A. James Schevill. TAP

Screams in the Dark. Slavko Mihalic, *tr. by* Charles Simic. PoSu

Screams round the Arch-druid's brow the sea-mew — white. Trepidation of the Druids. Wordsworth. *Fr.* Ecclesiastical Sonnets. Son

Screen before which the defeated imagination sits. (*LL*) This Fast-Paced, Brutal Thriller. Vijay Seshadri. UTF

Screw Spring. William M. Hoffman. FF

Screw you. I don't give a rat's ass. The Zouave. Peter Cooley. NAmP90

Scribbled at a Cabinet Meeting. Sir Edward Carson. FaBoVe

Scribblers, The. Walter Savage Landor. FaBoEE; OBSV

Scribe, The. Walter de la Mare. CMoP; EBEvV; FaBoCh; OBMV; TrCP; TrPWD

Scribe, The. *Unknown, tr. fr. Irish.* TIRV, *tr. by* Robin Flower

Scribe, to the vulgar inclined, A. Douglas Catley. PeLi

Scribe's Prayer, The. Arthur Guiterman. TrPWD

Scribe's Prayer, The. Robert W. Service. TrPWD

Scripts for the Pageant, *sels.* James Merrill.
Samos. HCAP

Scripts I used to write for the young actor, The. Written, Directed by and Starring. James Simmons. PBCIP

Scripture bright in great woods now, A. (*LL*) The Scribe. *Unknown.* TIRV, *tr. by* Robin Flower

Scriptwriter's Discipline, A. Matthew Sweeney. IB

Scroobious Pip, The. Edward Lear. CBNP

Scrub woman for the old bank and jailhouse, The. Lamentations. Norman Dubie. NoAM

Scruffy one, The. Hyena. *Unknown, tr. fr. Yoruba by* Ulli Beier. *Fr.* Hunter Poems of the Yoruba. OBAP; RB

Scrutiny [*or* Scrutinie], The. Richard Lovelace. BeJo; BoLoP; CaPo; ELP; EnLoPo; GBL; MeLP; NoP; SeCP; TrGrPo

Scuba Diver Recovers the Body of a Drowned Child, The. Gerald William Barrax. NBV

Scudamor in the Temple of Venus. Spenser. *Fr.* Faerie Queene, The. PoE

Sculptor, The. *Unknown. See* I took a piece of plastic clay.

Sculptor first in breath and blood, A. With Metaphor. Sarah Wingate Taylor. GoYe

Sculptor musing sat one eve, A. The Sculptor's Vision. H. Cordelia Ray. AmWP; CBWP-3

Sculptor remarked: "I'm afraid," A. *Unknown.* PeLi

Sculptor's Vision, The. H. Cordelia Ray. AmWP; CBWP-3

Sculpture. *Unknown.* BLPL; PoLF

Sculpture in a bare white gallery, A. The Field. Jean Valentine. LCAP

Scunner. "Hugh MacDiarmid." FaBoTw

Scylla and Charybdis. Thomas Kinsella. OxBTC

Scylla's Lament. Thomas Hood. *Fr.* Hero and Leander. EnRP

Scyros. Karl Shapiro. HoPM; ImPo; LiTA; LiTM

Scythe, The. Henry Kanabus. UL

Scythe Song. Andrew Lang. GN

Sea Owl. Dave Jeddie Smith. HCAP

Sea pearl, western star. On Leaving. Gertrudis Gomez de Avellaneda, tr. fr. Spanish by Frederick Sweet. PBWP

Sea-perch over paddocks. Dunes. Salt light everywhere low down. The Greenhouse Vanity. Les A. Murray. FaBoVe

Sea Poem. John Robinson. FaBoBl

Sea Poppies. Hilda Doolittle ("H. D."). NALW

Sea Prayer. Unknown, tr. fr. Gaelic by Alexander Carmichael. ScCV

Sea-preserved, heaped with sea-spoils. Picture of a Nativity. Geoffrey Hill. NoAM; OxBC

Sea, The — quick pugilist. Training. Herrera S. Demetrio, tr. fr. Spanish by Dudley Fitts. TTY

Sea Replies to Byron, The. G. K. Chesteron. UV

Sea retreats as I advance, The. Sea Nocturne. Tchicaya U Tam'si, tr. fr. French by Ellen Conroy Kennedy. NegPo

Sea-Ritual, The. George Darley. Fr. Syren Songs. BIrV; OBNC; WiR

Sea Rose. Hilda Doolittle ("H. D."). FaBoMo; HeIP; NoAM; NoP; TRP

Sea-Sand and Sorrow. Christina Rossetti. See What Are Heavy?

Sea sang sweetly to the shore, The. Hymn Written for the Two Hundredth Anniversary of the Old South Church, Beverly, Massachusetts. Lucy Larcom. OHIP

Sea School. Barbara Howes. NYBP

Sea Serpent, The. Wallace Irwin. FiBHP

Sea-Shell, The. Robert Gray. FaBoMA

Sea Shell. Amy Lowell. BoTP; FaPON

Sea shone, The. During War, the Timeless Air. John Seed. VaA

Sea-Shore. Emerson. LiTA; OxBA

Sea Shroud, The. Jack Kerouac. PoM

Sea Side. Robert Graves. MeMBP

Sea Skater, The. Helen Dunmore. PWE

Sea-Song, A. Allan Cunningham. See Wet sheet and a flowing sea, A.

Sea Song, A. Digby Mackworth Dolben. EBVV

Sea Song, A. Shakespeare. See Master, the swabber, the boatswain and I, The.

Sea Song, A. Unknown. OxBSS

Sea Song, A: "Master, the swabber, the boatswain and I, The." Shakespeare. See Master, the swabber, the boatswain and I, The.

Sea-Song from the Shore, A. James Whitcomb Riley. BoTP

Sea Sonnet. Norma Lay. GoYe

Sea still plunges where as naked boys, The. The Grotto. Francis Scarfe. PoA

Sea sucks at its own, The. Landcrab. Margaret Atwood. NIP

Sea Surface Full of Clouds. Wallace Stevens. AmPP; CMoP; MoAB; MoAmPo; VGW

Sea, The! the sea! the open sea! The Sea. "Barry Cornwall." GN

Sea Things. Gwendolyn MacEwen. FaBoWP

Sea — turn yr Back on, The. Maximus from Dogtown-II. Charles Olson. Fr. Maximus Poems, The. PRA

Sea-Turtle and the Shark, The. Melvin B. Tolson. Fr. Harlem Gallery. PoBA

Sea Unicorns and Land Unicorns. Marianne Moore. NALW

Sea View, The. Charlotte Smith. ECWP

Sea Violet. Hilda Doolittle ("H. D."). NoP

Sea Voyage. William Empson. CMoP

Sea-Voyage from Tenby to Bristol, A. Katherine Philips. WPE

Sea voyagers talk about fairy islands. T'ien-mu Mountain Ascended in a Dream: A Farewell Song. Li Po, tr. fr. Chinese by Wu-chi Liu. SuSp

Sea-Wash. Carl Sandburg. OBCA

Sea waves are green and wet. Sand Dunes. Robert Frost. MoAB; MoAmPo; RFM

Sea-Weed. D. H. Lawrence. BoNaP; RB

Sea-weed sways and sways and swirls. Sea-Weed. D. H. Lawrence. BoNaP; RB

Sea-Wind. Stéphane Mallarmé, tr. fr. French by Arthur Symons. AWP

Sea Wind, The. Harry Edmund Martinson, tr. fr. Swedish by Robert Bly. NU

Sea-wind salts your head white. (LL) Watch the Lights Fade. Robinson Jeffers. CMoP; NOBA

Sea Without Poets. Branko Miljkovic, tr. fr. Serbo-Croatian by Charles Simic. HSix

Sea Wolf, The. Violet McDougal. FaPON

Sea would flow no longer, The. The Frozen Ocean. Viola Meynell. CH

Seacoast at Mera, The. Takada Toshiko, tr. fr. Japanese by Kenneth Rexroth and Ikuko Atsumi. WPJ

Seacoast late at night and a wheel of wind, A. On the Death of Her Mother. Muriel Rukeyser. SM

Seaconk or Rehoboths Fate. Benjamin Tompson. SCAP

Seaconk Plain Engagement. Benjamin Thompson. SCAP

Seadog and Seal. Philip Booth. PRA

Seafarer. Archibald MacLeish. NoP; Poetr

Seafarer, The. (May I for my own self song's truth reckon.) Unknown, tr. fr. Anglo-Saxon by Ezra Pound. CTC; FaBoTw; HeIL; HeIP; LiTA; NoP; OxBA

Sels.

"What does little birdie say?" BoTP; OxBChV

Miranda. NoAM

"I can sing of myself a true song." PoRA

(I can sing a true song about myself.) ASW, tr. by Kevin Crossley-Holland

"Song I sing of my sea adventure, A." AnOE

Seafarer, The. The Earl of Surrey. See O happy [or happie] dames, that may embrace.

Seafarer, The. Unknown, tr. fr. Anglo-Saxon by Charles W. Kennedy. AnOE

Seafarer, The. Unknown, tr. by Michael Alexander. OBVE

Seafarer. Unknown, tr. by Kemp Malone. PoE

Seafarer, The. Unknown, tr. by John Wain. EBEV

Seagull, The. Dafydd ap Gwilym, tr. fr. Welsh by Glyn Jones. OBWVE

Seagull, The. Siôn Phylip, tr. fr. Welsh by Joseph P. Clancy. OBWVE

Seagull flying from the sea. A Feather for My Cap. Ivy O. Eastwick. BoTP

Seagull, seagull, sit on the sand. Unknown. ISE

Seagull, spreadeagled, splayed on the wind, The. George Barker. Fr. Pacific Sonnets. LiTM

(Memorial for Two Young Seamen.) ImPo; MeMBP

Seagulls. Robert Francis. RFM

Seagulls. Patricia Hubbell. PDV

Seagulls. John Updike. Poetsp

Seal, The. Guillaume Apollinaire, tr. fr. French. CBNP

Seal. William Jay Smith. GrPl; RFM

Seal at Stinson Beach. Roberta Hill Whiteman. VoR

Seal Lullaby. Kipling. Fr. Jungle Book, The. FaPON; OBAP

Seal Mother's Song. Kipling. See Oh! hush thee, my baby, the night is behind us.

Seal Off Clogherhead, The. Angela Greene. NWP

Seal Run. Helen Dunmore. PWE

Seal up the book, all vision's at an end. On the Death of Mr. Pope. Unknown. NOEC

Sealed epistle submitted/ at dawn to Nine-fold Heaven, A. Demoted I Arrive at Lan-t'ien Pass and Show This Poem to My Brother's Grandson Han Hsiang. Han Yü, tr. fr. Chinese by Charles Hartman. SuSp

Sealed in rainlight one. The Magic Apple Tree. Elaine Feinstein. BrRo

Sealed Stillness, A. January. Frances Horovitz. PWE

Seals at High Island. Richard Murphy. BiHa; CIP; IPY; PBCIP

Seals at play off Western Isle, The. Seals, Terns, Time. Richard Eberhart. LiTM; MoAB; MoAmPo

Seals in Penobscot Bay, The. Daniel Hoffman. TwCP

Seals of Love. Shakespeare. See Take, O Take Those Lips Away.

Seals, Terns, Time. Richard Eberhart. LiTM; MoAB; MoAmPo

Seam. (LL) Alberta (Factory Poem/Variation 2). Brenda Marie Osbey. UTF

Seaman, 1941. Molly Holden. FaBoWP

Seaman's Compass, The. Laurence Price. OxBSS

Seaman's Confession of Faith, A. Harry Hibbard Kemp. TrPWD

Seamen and Soldiers' Last Farewell to Their Dearest Jewels, The. Unknown. OxBSS

Seamen Three. Thomas Love Peacock. See In a bowl to sea went wise men three.

Seamen's Distress, The. Unknown. OxBSS

Seamen's Mission. Gerald Dawe. PNI

Seamen's Wives' Vindication, The. Unknown. OxBSS

Seamstress, The. Harry Clifton. BiHa; IB

Seamstress at St. Léon. Gillian Clarke. Fr. Journal from France, A. OBTV

Seamus, Light-hearted and Loving Friend of My Brea, sels. Owen Roe O'Sullivan, tr. fr. Irish by Thomas Kinsella.

"Seamus, light-hearted and loving friend of my breast." NOIV

Séance. William Abrahams. NYBP

Séance. Francis King. PoA

Search. Claribel Alegría, tr. fr. Spanish by Aliki and Willis Barnstone. BoWoP

Search, The. Kwesi Brew. PBA

Search, The. Thomas Curtis Clark. WGRP

Search, The. George Herbert. ESCV; MiEL

Search, The. John Hewitt. PNI

Search, The. Nancy Peterson. LoHo

Search, The. Charles Shaw. NOBAu

Second Angel, The. Philip Levine. NaP

Second Ascension of Christ, The. John Wheelwright. *Fr.* Forty Days. NOCV

Second Attempt, A. Thomas Hardy. CBLP

Second Best. Rupert Brooke. MoBrPo

Second bounding snow, The. *(LL)* A Mill. William Allingham. FaBoEE; OxBSP

Second Brother, The, *sels.* Thomas Lovell Beddoes.
"Strew not earth with empty stars." OxBSP

Second Carolina Said-Song. A. R. Ammons. OBAL

Second-Class Citizen. Slavko Mihalic, *tr. by* Charles Simic. PoSu

Second class is the second grade, The. Primary Lesson: The Second Class Citizens. Sun-Ra. PoBA

Second Coming, The. Carl Clark. JB

Second Coming, The. John William Corrington. HoPM

Second Coming. Adam Small, *tr. fr. Afrikaans by* Carrol Lasker. PeSAV

Second Coming, The. W. B. Yeats. BIrV; BLPL; ChIV-2; ClHu; CMoP; CoGr; EBEvV; FaBoMo; FaBoPV; FaPoB; FF; GGP; GTBS-P; HAP; HeIP; HoPM; ImPo; InPK; InPS; LiTB; LiTM; MAT; MeMBP; MoAB; MoBrPo; MoP; NAEL-2; NAWM-2; NIP; NoAM; NOBE; NoP; OAEL-2; OxAEP-2; OxBTC; PAW; PoE; Poetr; PPP; PrIm; RaBo; SCV; SoSe; TEP; TFi; TRP; UnPo

Second coming, The. *(LL)* Yesterday. Gu Cheng. SpMi

Second crop of hay lies cut, A. Three Songs at the End of Summer. Jane Kenyon. BAP-89

Second Crucifixion, The. Richard Le Gallienne. WGRP

Second Cycle of Love Poems, *sels.* George Barker.
O Tender under Her Right Breast. MoAB; MoBrPo

Second Daughter: Li (Brightness), The. Diane Di Prima. *Fr.* Loba. SRLS

Second Dream, The. Jean Valentine. LCAP

Second Epistle of the Second Book of Horace Imitated, The, *sels.* Pope
"Bred up at home, full early I begun" TOF
"But grant I may relapse, for want of grace" TOF

Second Epistle to John Lapraik, *sels.* Burns.
"For thus the royal *Mandate* ran." OBF

Second Epitaph, A. *Unknown. See* All ye that passe be [*or* by] this holy place.

Second Fig. Edna St. Vincent Millay. NALW

Second Fragment. John Riley. VaA

Second Generation, The. Menachem Z. Rosensaft. BTR

Second Glance at a Jaguar. Ted Hughes. NoAM; NYBP; PrIm

Second-hand platitudes like antique watches. Catching One Clear Thought Alive. Paula Gunn Allen. WPOW

Second-hand sights, like crumpled. Newark, for Now (68). Carolyn M. Rodgers. PoBA

Second Honeymoon. *Unknown, tr. fr. Irish by* Augustus Young. BIrV

Second Hymn to Lenin. "Hugh MacDiarmid." OAEL-2

Second Hymn to the Night, The. "Novalis", *prose poem vers., tr. fr. German by* Robert Bly. *Fr.* Hymns to the Night. NU

Second Image Sequence. Umberto Piersanti, *tr. fr. Italian by* Stephen Sartarelli. NeIt

Second Jungle Book, The, *sels.* Kipling.
"Now this the Law of the Jungle — as old and as true as the sky." OBAP

Second Language. Christine Dumaine. LoHo

Second Law, The. Stephen Sandy. PFL

Second Life, The. Edwin Morgan. OxBS

Second Life of Lazarus, The. Gwen Harwood. CBAP

2nd Light Poem: For Diane Wakoski. Jackson MacLow. PoM

Second man I love, The. Spring. Carole Gregory Clemmons. PoBA

Second Marriage. Mei Yao Ch'en, *tr. fr. Chinese by* Jonathan Chaves. SuSp

Second Merseburg Spell. *Unknown, tr. fr. German by* Carroll Hightower. GePo

Second Nature. Ron Horning. BAP-91

Second Ode to Persephone. Robert Kelly. *Fr.* Book of Persephone, The. PoM

Second of August. *Unknown.* OxBSS

Second pageant the wrytyng was thus. *(LL)* Pageant Verses. Sir Thomas More. AAS; Mes

Second Pastoral; or, Alexis, The. Virgil, *tr. fr. Latin by* Dryden. PeHV

Second Poem. Peter Orlovsky. NeAP

Second Poem from Nicaragua Libre: War Zone. June Jordan. NoAM

Second Poem the Night-Walker Wrote, The. Goethe. *See* O'er all the hill-tops.

Second Prelude. Reality in Albuquerque: The Son. John Logan. *Fr.* Poem in Progress. CAPP

Second Rapture, The. Thomas Carew. CaPo; OPOP

Second Review of the Grand Army, A. Bret Harte. PAH

Second Rondeau. Johann Nikolaus Götz, *tr. fr. German by* George C. Schoolfield. GePo

Second Samuel, *sels.* Bible, *O.T.*
"And David lamented with this lamentation." OBF
"Beauty of Israel is slain [*or* slaine] upon thy high places, The." OBVE; OBWP
(David's Lament for Saul and Jonathan.) AWP
(David's Lament over Saul.) PAW
(David's Lament.) ChTr, I: 19–27; FF, I: 19–27; TrGrPo, I: 19–27; TrJP, I: 19–27

Second Satire of the First Book of Horace Imitated, The, *sels.* Pope.
"With all a woman's virtues but the pox." OBSV

Second Seeing. Louis Golding. WGRP

Second Sermon on the Warpland, The. Gwendolyn Brooks. BPo; NOBA; PoBA

Second Shadow. Theodore Roethke. PoA

Second Shaman Song. Gary Snyder. *Fr.* Myths and Texts. NeAP; NOBA; PoM

Second Shepherd's Play, The. (Lord, what these weders ar cold.)
Unknown. NAEL-1; PoEL-1
Sels.
"With all a woman's virtues but the pox." OBSV
Hail, Comly and Clene. NAs
(Haylle, Comly and Clene.) OBEV; OxBoLi
(Shepherds at Bethlehem, The.) ChTr

Second Skins — a Peyote Song. Joseph Bruchac. CDW

Second Song. T. Carmi, *tr. fr. Hebrew by* Ruth Finer Mintz. *Fr.* René's Songs. MHP

Second Song. Sir Philip Sidney. *Fr.* Astrophel and Stella. AAS; ESo, *sl. abr.*; GGP; HeIL, *Sonnets,* I–CVIII *and 11 Songs*; NoSic; Poetr; SCGP, *Sonnets,* I–CVIII *and 11 Songs*; SiPS, *Sonnets,* I–CVIII *and 11 Songs*; SiPSBD, *Sonnets,* I–CVIII *and 11 Songs*

Second Stanza for Dr. Johnson, A. Donald Hall. FiBHP

Second Venus rise, A. *(LL)* On Sight of a Gentlewoman's Face in the Water. Thomas Carew. CaPo; SeCV-1

Second Voyage, The. Eiléan Ní Chuilleanáin. PeIV

Second Wind. Fred Chappell. MT

Second Wisdom. Henry Morton Robinson. GoYe

Second Witness. Pattiann Rogers. FoLa

Second year of the emperor's reign, in autumn, The. Journey North. Tu Fu, *tr. fr. Chinese by* Hugh M. Stimson. SuSp

(Secondary experience, nouns). Zen Buddhism and Psychoanalysis/ Psychoanalysis and Zen Buddhism. Jackson MacLow. PoM

Secondhand Coat. Ruth Stone. NALW; NIP

Secrecy. Eduard Friedrich Mörike, *tr. fr. German by* Philip L. Miller. RiWo

Secrecy [*or* Secresie] Protested. Thomas Carew. CaPo; SeCP

Secret, The. "Æ." MoBrPo

Secret. Gwendolyn B. Bennett. BlSi; CDC; ShDr

Secret, The. Charles Bukowski. RaBo

Secret, The. John Clare. GBL

Secret, The. Elizabeth Fleming. BoTP

Secret. Goethe, *tr. fr. German by* Philip L. Miller. RiWo

Secret. Catherine Haydon Jacobs. GoYe

Secret. Mary Jenness. ShDr

Secret, The. Denise Levertov. CrSp; NaP; Poetr

Secret, The. Paul Armand Silvestre, *tr. fr. French by* Philip L. Miller. RiWo

Secret, The. Mary Morison Webster. PeSA

Secret behind locks and double bars, covered with green moss. First Month: at Ch'ung-jang House. Li Shang-yin, *tr. fr. Chinese by* A. C. Graham. PLT

Secret Cavern, The. Margaret Widdemer. FaPON

Secret Garden, The. Rita Dove. NoAM

Secret Garden, The. Thomas Kinsella. IPY; TwCP

Secret Garden, The. Robert Nichols. WGRP

Secret Gratitude, A. James Wright. NoAM

Secret Invitation. John Henry Mackay, *tr. fr. German by* Philip L. Miller. RiWo

Secret Joy, The. Mary Webb. BoTP

Secret Kept, A. Judah al-Harizi, *tr. fr. Hebrew by* Robert Mezey. UnAS

Secret Laughter. Christopher Morley. FaBV

Secret Love. John Clare. FaBV; OBNC; PoE; PoEL-4; SCGP; TrGrPo

Secret Love. Joseph Freiherr von Eichendorff, *tr. fr. German by* Philip L. Miller. RiWo

Secret Love. Isabel Stewart, *tr. fr. Gaelic by* Nigel MacNeill. ScCV

Secret Love; or, The Maiden Queen, *sels.* Dryden.
"I feed a flame within, which so torments me." AWP
(Hidden Flame.) OBEV

Prologue. PeLV; SeCV-2

Secret Love or Two I Must Confess[e], A. Thomas Campion. AAS; ErPo

Secret many years unseen, A. The Chess Play. Nicholas Breton. NoSic

SECRET murder hath been done of late. *Unknown.* NoSic

Secret Muse, The. Roy Campbell. PeSA

Secret of movement, The. The Time before You. Medbh McGuckian. CBLP

Secret of the Quartz Pebble, The. Vasco [*or* Vasko] Popa, *tr. fr. Serbo-Croatian. Fr.* Quartz Pebble, The. PoSu, *tr. by* Anne Pennington

Secret of these hills was stone, and cottages, The. The Pylons. Stephen Spender. AWP; NoAM

Secret People, The. G. K. Chesteron. CoGr; FaPoR; OtMeF; OxBTC

Secret People, The, *sels.* G. K. Chesteron.
    "Face of the King's servants grew greater than the King, The." FaBoEH

Secret Places. Irene Thompson. BoTP

Secret Rose, The. W. B. Yeats. MeMBP; NAEL-2

Secret Sits, The. Robert Frost. InPK

Secret Song, The. Margaret Wise Brown. OBCA; PDV

Secret they are, sealed, annealed, and brainless. Oystering. Richard Howard. NoAM

Secret Thoughts. Ella Wheeler Wilcox. PWR

Secret Town, The. Abraham Sutzkever, *tr. fr. Yiddish by* Jacob Sonntag. TrJP

Secret Virginity, The. "Angelus Silesius," *tr. fr. German. Fr.* Cherubical Wanderer, The. GePo, *tr. by* George C. Schoolfield

Secret was the garden. The Mistress of Vision. Francis Thompson. CH, *abr.*

Secretary. Ted Hughes. ErPo

Secretary, The. Peter Redgrove. OxBTC

Secretary moves around the room, checking, The. The Chairman's Widow. Thomas McCarthy. IB

Secrets. Richard Hovey. AnAmPo

Secrets of Angling, The, *sels.* John Dennys.
    Angler's Song, The. EIL

Secrets of the Earth, The. Blake. *Fr.* Book of Thel, The. EnRP; MeMBP; NAEL-2; NOBE; NoP; OAEL-2; OBNC; PoE; PoEL-4; TEP

Secretum, *sels.* Petrarch, *tr. fr. Latin by* W. H. Draper.
    Exchange between the Poet and St. Augustine, An. OxBLMV

Secular, The. Chris Wallace-Crabbe. NOBAu

Secular Elegies., *sels.* George Barker.
    O Golden Fleece ("O golden fleece she is where she lies tonight"). ErPo; LiTM; MoAB; MoBrPo
    (Secular Elegy V.) MeMBP
    Satan Is on Your Tongue. MoAB; MoBrPo

Secular Elegy V. George Barker. *See* O golden fleece she is where she lies tonight.

Secular Games. Richard Howard. PoA

Secular Masque, The. (Chronos, Chronos, mend thy ways.) Dryden. NAEL-1; PoE; PoEL-3; PrIm; SCGP; SeCV-2
    Sels.
    O Golden Fleece "O golden fleece she is where she lies tonight". ErPo; LiTM; MoAB; MoBrPo
    All, All of a Piece Throughout. ChTr; CoGr; ELP; HAP; ImPo; InPS
    (Chorus to the Gods.) OxBSP
    (Song: "All, all of a piece throughout.") WeW
    Diana's Hunting-Song. NOBE
    Momus' Song to Mars. OxBSP
    "Sound the trumpet, beat the drum." FaBoRV

Secured from conquest by captivity. (*LL*) The Bracelet. Thomas Stanley. BeJo

Securer lives the silly swain. (*LL*) Jack and Joan they think no ill. Thomas Campion. AAS

Security. Charles L. O'Donnell. TrPWD

Security. Margaret E. Sangster. BLRP

Seder-Night. Israel Zangwill. TrJP

Sediment. David Ignatow. NYBP

Sedley has that prevailing, gentle art. The Earl of Rochester. *Fr.* Allusion to Horace, An. EPCY

Seduced by Natassja Kinski. Ana Castillo. AfAz

Seduced Girl. Hedylos, *tr. fr. Greek by* Louis Untermeyer. BoLoP; ErPo

Seduction. Nikki Giovanni. NMM

Seduction. Jo Ann Hall-Evans. BlSi

Seduction. Suzanne Berger Rioff. NMM

Seduction of Engadu, The. *Unknown, tr. by* William Ellery Leonard. *Fr.* Epic of Gilgamesh, The. ErPo

See a man who so loves you as your fond S. T. COLERIDGE. (*LL*) Metrical Feet. Samuel Taylor Coleridge. FaBoUs; FHYEP; NIP; OxBChV; Poetr, *ll.* 1–6 *only*

See a man with sound eyes. Ingrown. James Berry. PBCV

See a pin and pick it up. *Unknown.* FaBoBe; RoPo
    (Pins.) ReMoGo

See a traveler in isorrow: deeper is his grief. Random Pleasures. Tu Fu, *tr. fr. Chinese by* Irving Y. Lo. SuSp

See all! say nought! hold thee content! (*LL*) Look or You Leap. Jasper Heywood. EIl

See an old unhappy bull. The Bull. Ralph Hodgson. LiTM; MoAB; MoBrPo; NSI, *abr.*; OBMV; OxBTC

See, and not see; and if thou chance t' espy. To the Generous Reader. Robert Herrick. CaPo

See, Ben, the water. To Ben, at the Lake. Cilla McQueen. PeNZ

See, Chloris, how the clouds. To Chloris. William Drummond of Hawthornden. OxBSP

See columns rang'd in proud Palladian style! *Unknown.* FaBoEE

See commons, peers, and ministers of state. Edward Young. *Fr.* Love of Fame, the Universal Passion. OBSV

See dear Pater with the bills. Christmas Bills. Joseph Hatton. OBCP

See erected. (*LL*) Anacreontic. Robert Herrick. CaPo

See Florio in his *vis-à-vis.* The Picture of a Fine Gentleman. Lady Sophia Burrell. ECWP

See! from the brake the whirring Pheasant springs. Pope. *Fr.* Windsor Forest. FHYEP; FM; PoEL-3
    (Hunting and Fishing.) ECEV

See, hear, and am silent. (*LL*) I Sit and Look Out. Walt Whitman. AnAmPo; MeMAP; NAAL-1; OxBA; SAmP; TAP

See her caught in the throb of a drum. Agbor Dancer. John Pepper Clark. PBA

See her come bearing down, a tidy craft! A Note on Wyatt. Kingsley Amis. WeW

See her there, Francie-the-Mad. Francie-the-Possessed. Oswald Durand, *tr. fr. French by* Ellen Conroy Kennedy. NegPo

See here an easy feast that knows no wound. On the Miracle of Multiplied Loaves. Richard Crashaw. OxBSP

See! Here, My Heart. *Unknown.* MeEL

See here, nice Death, to please his palate. Epitaph. *At. to* Pope Pope. FaBoEE

See, here's the grand approach. Verses on Blenheim. Martial, *tr. fr. Latin by* Swift. AWP

See, here's the workbox, little wife. The Workbox. Thomas Hardy. InPK; NAEL-2; UnPo

See him recall the day by moral trace, a squint. Of Movement towards a Natural Place. J. H. Prynne. VaA

See him ride the roaring air. At the Statue of William the Conqueror, Falaise. Charles Causley. FaBoEH

See His face, and sing His praise! (*LL*) A Cradle Hymn. Isaac Watts. OBEV; OxBChV; PoEL-3; SCGP

See how Flora smiles to see. On Clarastella walking in Her Garden. Robert Heath. NOSC

See how from far upon the eastern road. The Magi. Milton. *Fr.* On the Morning of Christ's Nativity. ChTr; MeLP; NAs; NOCV; NoP; PoEL-3; SCGP; WGRP

See how he dives. Seal. William Jay Smith. GrPl; RFM

See how He watches? He snatches the bad ones. (*LL*) Fräulein Reads Instructive Rhymes. Maxine W. Kumin. NYBP; Poetsp

See how it circles. *Ambo Oral Tradition. Fr.* Five Ghost Songs. TTTS

See how she strips her lily for the sun. The Double Looking Glass. A. D. Hope. CBAP

See how that pair of billing doves. Verses Written in a Garden. Lady Mary Wortley Montagu. ECWP

See how the brown kelp withers in air. Landed: A Valentine. Richard Howard. PoA

See how the flowers, as at parade. Andrew Marvell. *Fr.* Upon Appleton House, to My Lord Fairfax. SeCP; SeCV-1; TrGrPo
    (Garden, A.) OBEV

See, how the human animal is fed. The Digestive System. Sir Richard Blackmore. *Fr.* Creation. ECEV

See how the language listens up this spring. Poor Movies. Will Bennett. UL

See how the orient dew. On a Drop of Dew. Andrew Marvell. ESCV; GeHe; HAP; JCP; LiTB; MeLP; NOSC; PFP; SCGP; SeCP; SeCV-1; TEP

See how the rainbow in the sky. Justification. William Strode. NOSC

See How the Rising Sun. Elizabeth Scott. AH

See, — how the shining share. God Save the Plough. Lydia Huntley Sigourney. AnAmPo; OBAL

See how the sun has somewhat not of light. El Greco. Edward Leslie Mayo. HoPM

See how the willing earth gave way. The Fall. Edmund Waller. NOSC

See how they hurry. At Luca Signorelli's Resurrection of the Body. Jorie Graham. HCAP

See/ how they trace. Birds in Snow. Hilda Doolittle ("H. D."). PoA

See how this ivy strives to twine. Love's Innocence. Thomas Stanley. BeJo

See how this trim girl. Artemis. Peter Davison. ErPo

See how this violet which before. On a Violet in Her Breast. Thomas Stanley. NOSC

See! Hymen comes; how his torch blazes! Sir Charles Sedley. NOSC

See! I give myself to you, Beloved! A Gift. Amy Lowell. AnAmPo

See, I have climbed the mountain side. San Miniato. Oscar Wilde. TIRV

See in the Midst of Fair Leaves. Marianne Moore. MoAB

See, Lord,/ my coat hangs in tatters. The Prayer of the Old Horse. Carmen Bernos de Gasztold. PDV

See Lucifer Like Lightning Fall. John Keble. ChIV-2

See/ me. A Pair of Wings. Stephen Hawes. MeEL

See me safely home? (LL) Ode to Two Sisters in the Sun. Nellie Wong. SRLS

See me, the lord of deep-bosomed earth, who turned Acmonides upside down. Wings. Unknown, tr. fr. Greek by Barbara Hughes Fowler. HePo

See me with all the terrors on my roads. The Face. Edwin Muir. GTBS-P

See, Mignonne, hath not the Rose. The Rose. Pierre de Ronsard, tr. fr. French by Andrew Lang. AWP

See Mother Nature's bloomers here! Mother Nature's Bloomers. Leonard Barras. IHNG

See, my dear, what I bring. With a Waterlily. Ibsen, tr. fr. Norwegian by Philip L. Miller. RiWo

See my lov'd Britons, see your Shakespeare rise. Dryden. Fr. Troilus and Cressida. SeCV-2

"See, nothing has happened to her," said my guide. Seeing Oloalok. Marilyn Bowering. NOBC

See on one hand. The Rainbow. Gerard Manley Hopkins. FaBoPP; OxBSP

See on yon verdant lawn, the gathering crowd. On the Village Green. William Somervile. Fr. Hobbinol. ECEV

See, one physician, like a sculler, plies. Joseph Jekyll. FaBoEE

See-Saw, The. John Hollander. BAP-91

See-saw, down in my lap. Unknown. OxNR

See-saw, Margery Daw,/ Jack[y] shall have a new master. Mother Goose. OxNR; ReMoGo

See-saw, Margery Daw,/ Sold her bed and lay upon straw. Unknown. OxNR

See-saw, Margery Daw,/ The old hen flew over the malt house. Mother Goose. OxNR

See-saw, sacradown [or Sacaradown]. Mother Goose. CBNP; OxNR

See, see, mine own sweet jewel. Canzonet. Unknown. ElL

See, see, she wakes, Sabina wakes! Congreve. NOEC; OxBSP

See, see, what shall I see? Mother Goose. OxNR; ReMoGo

See sin, but through my tears. (LL) Drop, drop, slow tears. Phineas Fletcher. ElL; OxBSP

See that brave and trembling motorman. The Dying Mine Brakeman. Orville Jenks. AmFP

See that [or the] building which, when my mistress living. A Well-wishing to a Place of Pleasure. Unknown. GBL

See That One? Robert Bagg. ErPo

See the bunnies sitting there. Timid Bunnies. Jeannie Kirby. BoTP

See the chariot at hand here of Love. The Triumph of Charis. Ben Jonson. Fr. Celebration of Charis in Ten Lyric[k] Peeces [or pieces], A. BeJo; CTC; EBEV; ElL; ELP; InVP; JCP; LiTB; NOBE; NoP; OBEV; OPOP; PoEL-2; PrIm; SeCP; SeCV-1; TFi

(Her Triumph.) BeJo; CTC; EBEV; ElL; JCP; NOSC; OPOP; OxAEP-1; PoEL-2; PrIm; SeCV-1

See, the Day Begins to Break. John Fletcher. See See the day begins to break.

See the day begins to break. Satyr's Song. John Fletcher. Fr. Faithful Shepherdess, The.

(See, the Day Begins to Break.) SCGP

See the dazzled stripling stand. Goliath and David. Louis Untermeyer. TrJP

See the fountain opened wide. Zion's Sons and Daughters. Unknown. AmFP

See! the gleam. Chiyojo, tr. fr. Japanese by Kenneth Rexroth and Ikuko Atsumi. WPJ

See the golden Leopard with the spots! Leopard. Unknown, tr. fr. Sotho. OBAP

See the handsome hippopotamus. Hippopotamus. Joanna Cole. NTCP

See the headlands yonder stand. Dirge Sung at Death. Unknown, tr. fr. Maori by John White. WTO

See the House Took Flight. Daniil Kharms, tr. fr. Russian by Alice Stone Nakhamovsky. CBNP

See the kitten on the wall. The Kitten at Play. Wordsworth. Fr. Kitten and the Falling Leaves, The. FaPON; OFC; SoCa

See the land, her Easter keeping. Easter Week. Charles Kingsley. OHIP

See the little maunderer. A Love for Patsy. John Thompson, Jr.. LiTA

See the madly blowing dust. A Colorado Sand Storm. Eugene Fieldson, Jr. LiTA

See! the moon is smiling. Eliza in Uncle Tom's Cabin. Eloise Bibb. CBWP-4

See, the pretty planet! Blowing Bubbles. William Allingham. GN

See the scaffold it is mounted. Life of the Mannings. Unknown. FaBoBa

See, the see, the Bishop's see, The. The Bishop's See. Unknown. CoMu

See, the smelle of my sone is as the smell of a feld. Bible, O.T., tr. by William Tyndale. Fr. Genesis. OBVE

See! the smoking bowl before us. Burns. Fr. Jolly Beggars, The. EnRP, sl. diff. vers.; NBLV; PoEL-4

(Drinking Song.) TrGrPo

See the Spring herself discloses. Spring. Thomas Stanley, after the Greek of Anacreon. AWP

See the star-breasted villain. Village-Born Beauty. Unknown. VPP

See the yellow catkins cover. A Spring Song. Mary Howitt. BoTP

See the young man I've laid out. Funeral Lament (Kommos) from Epiros. Unknown, tr. fr. Modern Greek by Elene Margot Kolb. BoWoP

See them joined by strings to history. Puppets. P. K. Page. MoCV

See them sprawl with earth for bed. Angry Dusk. Jack Lindsay. NOBAu

See! there she goes. William Somervile. Fr. Chase, The. ECEV

See these happy youths, now made. Sung at Table by the Same Choir. Anne Penny. Fr. Odes Sung in Commemoration of the Marine Society. ECWP

See, they are clearing the sawdust course. Equestrienne. Rachel Field. Fr. Circus Garland, A. OBCA

See, they return; ah, see the tentative. The Return. Ezra Pound. AmPP; CMoP; HAP; MoAB; MoAmPo; MoP; NoAM; NOBA; OxBA; PoE; Poetr; RB; TRP; VGW; WeW

See this air, how empty it is of angels. Five for the Grace of Man. Winfield Townley Scott. VGW

See this finger? Unknown. RoPo

See those cherries, how they cover. The Cherries; a Parable. Thomas Moore. OBSV

See those resplendent creatures, as they glide. Fashion. Ada Cambridge. NOBAu

See through four blocks. Pretty Vomit. Bob Rosenthal. UL

See two passenger trains, Lawd. Dey Got Each and de Udder's Man. Unknown. WTO

See what a clouded majesty, and eyes. To My Worthy Friend Master [Mr] Peter Lely. Richard Lovelace. CaPo; NOSC

See What a Lovely Shell. Tennyson. Fr. Maud[: A Monodrama]. BoNaP; EnVR; GoJo; MeMBP; PoEL-5

See what a mass of gems the city wears. Impression de Nuit; London. Lord Alfred Bruce Douglas. OBEV

See what delights in sylvan scenes appear! Sylvan Delights. Pope. Fr. Pastorals. NOBE

See what happens so far. Venus on the Beach. Laura Rosenthal. UL

See where Capella with her golden kids. Edna St. Vincent Millay. Fr. Epitaph for the Race of Man. CMoP; MoAB; MoAmPo

See Where My Love a-Maying Goes. Unknown. ElL

See where she sits upon the grassie [or grassy] green[e]. Ditty, A: In Praise of Eliza, Queen of the Shepherds. Spenser. Fr. Shepheardes [or Shepeards or Shepherd's] Calender, The. NAEL-1; OBEV; PoEL-1

(Ditty, A: "See where she sits upon the grassy green.") FaBoCh

See where the falling day. Tomorrow. Anna Laetitia Barbauld. ECWP

See where the windows are boarded up. Where Are the Waters of Childhood? Mark Strand. HCAP; LCAP; VCAP; WeW

See where they blur, and die, and are outsoared. (LL) Camping Out. William Empson. CMoP; FaBoMo; OxBTC

See, Will, 'Ere's a Go. Unknown. ChTr; FaBoNo

See, Winter comes, to rule the varied year. Winter ("See, Winter comes, to rule the varied year.") James Thomson. Fr. Seasons, The. NOEC; TEP

See with what constant motion. Gratiana Dancing [or Dauncing] and Singing. Richard Lovelace. BeJo; CaPo; JCP; MeLP; OBEV, 2 sts.; SeCV-1, 2 sts.

See with what simplicity. The Picture of Little T. C. in a Prospect of Flowers. Andrew Marvell. ESCV; GeHe; JCP; LiTB; MeLP; NAEL-1; NOBE; NoP; OAEL-1; OBEV; OxAEP-1; PoE; PPP; PrIm; SCGP; SeCP; SeCV-1; TFi

See yonder hallow'd fane, the pious work. The Grave-yard on a Stormy Night. Robert Blair. Fr. Grave, The. OxAEP-1

Sees not my love how time resumes. To a Lady in a Garden. Edmund Waller. BeJo

Sees the man. The Carver. Lucille Clifton. CAPP

Seesaw, The. Oscar Williams. LiTA

See'st thou o'er my shoulders falling. Judah Halevi, *tr. fr. Hebrew by* Emma Lazarus. TrJP

Seest thou those diamonds which she wears. *Unknown.* NOSC

Seferis. Lawrence Durrell. EBEV

Seguidilla of Murcia. Manuel de Falla, *tr. fr. Spanish by* Philip L. Miller. RiWo

Sehnsucht. Anna Wickham. MoBrPo

Sehnsucht; or, What You Will. Korinna. FiBHP

Seicheprey. *Unknown.* PAH

Seil o'yer face! the send has come. The Fleggit Bride. "Hugh MacDiarmid." OxBS

16 heures/ L'Etoile. Two X. E. E. Cummings. FaBoMo

Seize, O seize the sounding lyre. The Hero of Bridgewater. Charles L. S. Jones. PAH

Seized with a fancy for fresh meat. Hymn to Mercury. *Unknown, tr. fr. Greek by* Shelley. *Fr.* Homeric Hymns. OBVE

Sejanus ("How many men are killed by power, by power.") Juvenal, *tr. by* Robert Lowell. *Fr.* Satires. OBVE

Sejanus ("Some ask for envy'd pow'r; which publick hate.") Juvenal, *tr. by* Dryden. *Fr.* Satires. OBVE

Sejanus ("What crowds by envied power, the wish of all.") Juvenal, *tr. by* William Gifford. *Fr.* Satires. OBVE

Selah. R. S. Thomas. FaBoMo

"Seldom we find," says Solomon Don Dunce. An Enigma. Poe. Son

Select fine arrows and call for falcons. Lu Lun, *tr. by* Ronald C. Miao. *Fr.* Frontier Songs. SuSp

Selected Epigrams. Kassia, *tr. fr. Byzantine Greek by* Patrick Diehl. PBWP

Selecting a loose vibration from the taut air. Soundwaves. Andrew Sant. NOBAu

Selecting a Reader. Ted Kooser. PBCAP

Selective Service. Carolyn Forché. Poetr

Selenologist, The. Bill Manhire. PeNZ

Self, The. Robin Morgan. *Fr.* Network of the Imaginary Mother, The. SRLS

Self. Norman Henry, II Pritchard. PoBA

Self. *(LL)* Sassy. Alma Villanueva. SRLS

Self. *(LL)* Winged Woman. Alma Villanueva. SRLS

Self-Acquaintance. William Cowper. NOCV

Self-Analysis. Anna Wickham. MoBrPo

Self and the Mulberry, The. Marvin Bell. FoLa

Self-centre. Cynthia Fuller. NWP

Self-Congratulatory Ode on Mr. Auden's Election to the Professorship of Poetry at Oxford. Ronald Mason. FaBoPa

Self-Consciousness Makes All Changes Happy; Ode. Jonathan Richardson. NOEC

Self-Criticism in February. Robinson Jeffers. AmPP

Self-Deceaver, The. Thomas Stanley. OBVE

Self-Defense. Santob de Carrion, *tr. fr. Spanish by* George Ticknor. TrJP

Self-Dependence. Matthew Arnold. MeMBP; OHCV; WGRP

Self Dirge. Wendy Rose. CDW

Self-Discipline. "Æ." MoBrPo

Self-educated William Blake. W. H. Auden. *Fr.* New Year Letter. EPCY

Self-employed. David Ignatow. NNaP

Self-Examination, The. *Unknown.* ECWP

Self-Examination. *Unknown.* FaBoUs

Self-Exposed, The. X. J. Kennedy. FaBoBl

Self-Hatred of Don L. Lee, The. Don L. Lee. BPo

Self, I want you now to be. The Thing is Violent. Gwendolyn MacEwen. MoCV; NOBC

Self in 1958. Anne Sexton. HCAP

Self Justification. Tony Harrison. *Fr.* School of Eloquence, The. NAEL-2; NoAM

Self-Mastery. H. Cordelia Ray. AmWP; CBWP-3

Self-mockery. Lu Hsun, *tr. fr. Chinese by* William R. Schultz. SuSp

Self-Pity. Philip Hodgins. NOBAu

Self-Pity. D. H. Lawrence. OxBTC; RB

Self-Pity Is a Kind of Lying, Too. James Schuyler. PoM

Self-Portrait. Frank Bidart. HCAP

Self-Portrait. Cecil Bodker, *tr. fr. Danish by* Nadia Christensen. BoWoP

Self-Portrait. Robert Creeley. NoAM

Self-Portrait. Moses Mendelssohn, *tr. fr. German.* TrJP

Self-Portrait. R. S. Thomas. NAs

Self-Portrait. William Carlos Williams. *Fr.* Pictures from Brueghel. LCAP

Self Portrait II. Tove Ditlevsen, *tr. fr. Danish by* Ann Freeman. IMW

Self-Portrait as Van Gogh. Peter Cooley. NAmP90

Self-Portrait at Thirty-Nine. Ted Kooser. PBCAP

Self Portrait 4. Tove Ditlevsen, *tr. fr. Danish by* Ann Freeman. WPOW

Self-Portrait in a Convex Mirror. John Ashbery. HCAP; NAAL-2

Self-Portrait of the Laureate of Nonsense. Edward Lear. *See* How Pleasant to Know Mr. Lear.

Self-Protection. D. H. Lawrence. NoP

Self-respecting and conscience free. *(LL)* Myself. Edgar A. Guest. BLPA; BLPL

Self-same Power that brought me there brought you, The. *(LL)* The Rhodora [On Being Asked Whence Is the Flower]. Emerson. AmPP; AnAmPo; AWP; BoNaP; FaBV; GN; LiTA; MeMAP; NAAL-1; NOBA; NoP; OxBA; PFP; PoE; PWR; TAP; TFi; TrGrPo

Self-same thing will be, The [or It's the self same thing to me]. *(LL)* As I Walked [*or* Walk'd] by Myself. *Unknown.* CBNP; ChTr; FaBoEE; FaBoEH; OxBSP; OxNR; ReMoGo

Self-slaved, The. Patrick Kavanagh. MoBrPo

Self-Storage. Alice Fulton. NAmP90

Self Unsatisfied Runs Everywhere, The. Delmore Schwartz. PoA

Self-Unseeing, The. Thomas Hardy. EBEV; HAP; MoBrPo; NOBE; NOBVV; OBNC; OxAEP-2; PrIm; RB; WeW

Self World. Clarence Major. NBV

Self[e] Accuser, A. John Donne. FaBoEE; PeLV

Selfishness. Margaret E. Bruner. PoToHe

Self's the Man. Philip Larkin. NOBL; PeLV

Selfsame Song, The. Thomas Hardy. CMoP

Selfsame surface that billowed once with, The. Skin Flick. Fred Chappell. InPK

Selfsame toothless voice for death or bridal, The. Bell Speech. Richard Wilbur. MoAB; MoAmPo

Sell in May. Stock Exchange Wisdom. *Unknown.* FaBoUs

Sell it, though it sleeps still at its mother's breast! Meleager, *tr. fr. Greek by* Barbara Hughes Fowler. *Fr.* Epigrams. HePo

Sell Out. Léon Damas, *tr. fr. French by* Ellen Conroy Kennedy. NegPo

Sell you of course, my dear, and you'll sell me. *(LL)* Varick Street. Elizabeth Bishop. VBLP

Sellin biscuit an salfish in de plantation shop at pie. Horse Weebles. Edward Kamau Brathwaite. PBCV

Selling Ruined Peonies. Yü Hsüan-chi, *tr. fr. Chinese by* Geoffrey R. Waters. BoWoP

Selling the feathers a penny a piece. *(LL)* Snow, snow faster. *Unknown.* ISE; OxNR

Selm . . . A Pot of Soup . . . A Bottle of Milk. Lodz, 1938. Kirtland Snyder. BTR

Selves eternal. *(LL)* Rose-cheeked [*or* cheekt] Laura, Come. Thomas Campion. EnLoPo; InPK; InPS; InvP; NAEL-1; NoP; NOSC; OAEL-1; PoE; PoEL-2; TFi; TrGrPo; TRP

Semantic. Robert Conquest. TEP

Semantic Limerick According to Dr. Johnson's Dictionary (Edition of 1765), The. Gavin Ewart. FaBoBl

Semantic Limerick According to the Shorter Oxford English Dictionary (1933), The. Gavin Ewart. FaBoBl

Semblables, The. William Carlos Williams. FaBoMo; NOBA

Semele. Rose Terry Cooke. AmWP

Semele. Dick Davis. SCBI

Semele Recycled. Carolyn Kizer. CAPP; InPS; NALW; Poetr; SRLS

Semen. Martha Paley Francescato, *tr. fr. Spanish by* Willis Barnstone. BoWoP

Semi-Revolution, A. Robert Frost. LiTM

Semiramis. Anne Bradstreet. *Fr.* Foure Monarchies, The. KTR

Semmes in the Garden. George Marion O'Donnell. NYBP

Semphill, his hat stuck full of hooks. Trout Fisher. George Mackay Brown. OxBC

Sempronius,/ Sends greeting, warden of this Roman shore. A Roman Officer Writes. Charles Montague Doughty. *Fr.* Dawn in Britain, The. FaBoTw

Sempstress's linnet sings, The. The Blind Linnet. Robert Williams Buchanan. FM

Sen Habbie's dead. *(LL)* The Life and Death of [Habbie Simson] the Piper of Kilbarchan. Robert Sempill. OxBS

Senator Smoot (Republican, Ut.). Ogden Nash. OBAL

Send down thy truth, O God! For the Gifts of the Spirit. Edward Rowland Sill. TrPWD

Send for Lord Timothy. John Heath-Stubbs. OxBC

Send Forth, O God, Thy Light and Truth. John Quincy Adams. AH

Send forth your songs like the doe and the fawn. Memento of Roads. Nathan Alterman, *tr. fr. Hebrew by* Ruth Finer Mintz. MHP

Send home my long-strayed [*or* strayd] eyes to me[e]. The Message. John Donne. EIL; MeLP

Send me no flowers, for they will die before they leave America. Junglegrave. S. E. Anderson. PoBA

Send me your pity bounteous Shepherdess. To Mrs. B. from a Lady Who Had a Desire to See Her. *Unknown*. KTR

Send-off, The. Wilfred Owen. LiTB; MoAB; MoBrPo; NSI; OBWP; OBWVE; OxBTC; PAW; PeFWW; PoWW; RB

Send Thy necessity. (*LL*) We who prayed and wept. Wendell Berry. EaPr

Send up our thanks to God! (*LL*) The Corn-Song. Whittier. GN; OHIP

Sending Off O.E. Who Brought an Orchid Home to Japan. Lu Hsun, *tr. fr. Chinese by* William R. Schultz. SuSp

Sending Spring Love to Tzu-an. Yü Hsüan-chi, *tr. fr. Chinese by* Kenneth Rexroth *and* Ling Chung. UnAS; WPC

Send'st *thou* no wondering thought to love and me? (*LL*) Where the red wine-cup floweth, there art thou! Caroline E. Norton. VBLP

Senec. Traged. ex Thyeste Chor. 2. Seneca. *See* Stand [*or* Stond] who so list upon the slipper top [*or* toppe].

Senex. Sir John Betjeman. RB

Senex to Matt. Prior. James Kenneth Stephen. *Fr.* Two Epigrams. FiBHP

Senful man, bethink and see. *Unknown*. MiEL

Senilio's Weather Saw. Martin Bell. PeLV

Senior Lady Sells Garden Eggs. Kojo Laing. HBAPE

Senior Members. Sean Lucy. CIP; PeIV

Senior Poet. Robert Pinsky. *Fr.* Three on Luck. AnAn

Senlin; a Biography, *sels*. Conrad Aiken.
 "It is morning, Senlin says, and in the morning." LiTM; NoAM
 (Morning Song of Senlin.) ImPo; LiTA; MoAmPo; OxBA
 (Morning Song.) CMoP; MoAB; TrGrPo

Sennacherib. Byron. *See* Assyrian came down like the wolf on the fold, The.

Señora, it is true the Greeks are dead. Invocation to the Social Muse. Archibald MacLeish. LiTM

Señora X No More. Pat Mora. AfAz

Señorita who strolled on the Corso, A. *Unknown*. PeLi

Senryu. Pat Nolan. UL

Sensation. Rimbaud, *tr. fr. French by* Kenneth Koch. SOTW; TTTS

Sensation. Rimbaud, *tr. fr. French*. AWP, *tr. by* Jethro Bithell

Sensation. Jon Stallworthy. IHNG

Sense and Spirit. George Meredith. WGRP

Sense of Coolness, A. Quincy Troupe. PoBA

Sense of danger must not disappear, The. Leap before You Look. W. H. Auden. NoAM

Sense of death is most in apprehension, The. Shakespeare. *Fr.* Measure for Measure. OBD

Sense of Smell, The. Louis MacNeice. NYBP

Sense of the Sleight-of-Hand Man, The. Wallace Stevens. HAP; ImPo; LiTM; MoAB; MoAmPo; NoAM; NOBA; PoA; TwCP; WeW

Sense of the world is short, The. Eros. Emerson. FaBoBe

Sense with keenest edge unused. Pater Filio. Robert Bridges. CMoP; OBEV

Senseless prof, A. *Unknown, tr. fr. French*. CBNP

Senseless school, where we must give, A. A Young Man's Epigram on Existence. Thomas Hardy. MoP

Senses loving Earth or well or ill, The. Sense and Spirit. George Meredith. WGRP

Sensibility; a Poetical Epistle, *sels*. Hannah More.
 "Sweet Sensibility! thou soothing power." ECWP

Sensible Girl's Reply to Moore's, A. Walter Savage Landor. FaBoEE

Sensible Is the Label. Eldon Grier. MoCV

Sensitive girl called O'Neill, A. *Unknown*. PeLi

Sensitive like hands. Madame. George McWhirter. UnAS

Sensitive Plant, The. (Sensitive Plant in a garden grew, A.) Shelley. EnRP; FHYEP
 Sels.
 "Whether the sensitive plant, or that." OAEL-2

Sensitive, Seldom and Sad. Mervyn Laurence Peake. OTCP

Sensitive Sydney. Wallace Irwin. FiBHP

Sensitiveness. Cardinal Newman. OHCV; TrCP

Sensualists, The. Theodore Roethke. ErPo

Sensuous during life. Lois Wickenhauser. EaPr

Sensuous Latin poet, now I will go off with a thermos, A. Lynn Strongin. *Fr.* First Aspen. IHMS

Sensuous/ sloe eyed. Seduction. Jo Ann Hall-Evans. BlSi

Sent as a present from Annam. The Red Cuckatoo. Po Chü-i, *tr. fr. Chinese by* Arthur Waley. ChTr

Sent from Egypt with a Fair Robe of Tissue to a Sicilian Vinedresser. T. Sturge Moore. OBEV

Sent from the Capital to Her Elder Daughter. Lady Otomo no Sakanoe, *tr. fr. Japanese by* Geoffrey Bownas *and* Anthony Thwaite. AIW; BoWoP; MDDM; WPOW

Sent in Lieu of a Letter to Shih-wu, Lan-ku, and Other Friends. Huang Tsun-hsien, *tr. fr. Chinese by* An-yan Tang. SuSp

Sent out of sight, somewhere becoming rain. (*LL*) The Whitsun Weddings. Philip Larkin. FaBoMo; FaPoB; HeIP; MoP; NoAM; NoP; OxAEP-2; OxBM; OxBTC

Sent to a Ch'an Master. Han Wo, *tr. fr. Chinese by* Irving Y. Lo. SuSp

Sent to a Lady, with a Seal. Robert Lloyd. FaBoUs

Sent to a Patient, with the Present of a Couple of Ducks. Edward Jenner. FaBoUs

Sent to All My Nephews and Nieces at Tung-ch'eng, *sels*. Yang Shih-ch'i, *tr. fr. Chinese by* Jonathan Chaves.

Sent to Chief Abbot of Tung-lin Monastery. Su Shih, *tr. fr. Chinese by* Chiang Yee. SuSp

Sent to Lo-t'ien for Thinking of Me after the Rainfall. Yüan Chen, *tr. fr. Chinese by* Angela Jung Palandri. SuSp

Sent to Miss Bell H—, with a Pair of Buckles. John Cunningham. FaBoUs

Sent to Recluse Ch'eng. Wang Chi, *tr. fr. Chinese by* Hellmut Wilhelm. SuSp

Sent to the Ch'an Master Wu-hsiang. Lo Yin, *tr. fr. Chinese by* Geoffrey R. Waters. SuSp

Sent to the Taoist of Dragon Mountain, Hsü Fa-leng. Liu Ch'ang-ch'ing, *tr. fr. Chinese by* William H. Nienhauser. SuSp

Sent to Wen T'ing-yün on a Winter Night. Yü Hsüan-chi, *tr. fr. Chinese by* Geoffrey R. Waters. BoWoP

Sent to Yü Te-fu upon His Receipt of an Official Commission, *sels*. Tsung Ch'en, *tr. fr. Chinese by* Jonathan Chaves.

Sentence, The. Martin Sorescu, *tr. fr. Romanian by* Paul Muldoon *and* Ioana Russell-Gebbett. PWE

Sentence — Life without a prison — struck, The. Divorcee. C. Webster Wheelock. SoSe

Sentence undulates, The. The End of the Parade. William Carlos Williams. NYBP

Sentences, *sels*. Tony Harrison.
 Brazil. OBTV

Sentences While Remembering Hiraethog. T. Glynne Davies, *tr. fr. Welsh by* R. Gerallt Jones. OBWVE

Sentience. Sandra McPherson. PoA

Sentiment. Thomas Chatterton. NOEC

Sentimental Bloke, The, *sels*. C. J. Dennis.

Sentimental Colloquy. Paul Verlaine, *tr. fr. French by* Philip L. Miller. RiWo

Sentimental Education. Jeffrey Wainwright. SCBI

Sentimental Lines to a Young Man Who Favors Pink Wallpaper While I Personally Lean to the Blue. Margaret Fishback. FiBHP

Sentimental Voyage Around My Room, A. Jovan Hristic, *tr. fr. Serbo-Croatian by* Charles Simic. HSix

Sentiments, The. *Unknown*. APAS

Sentiments are nice, "The Lonely Crowd." John Button Birthday. Frank O'Hara. NAs; OBF

Sentiments at Autumn. Han Yü, *tr. fr. Chinese by* Charles Hartman. SuSp

Sentiments on New Year's Eve in the Year Kuei-ssu. Huang Ching-jen, *tr. fr. Chinese by* Chang Yin-nan *and* Lewis C. Walmsley. SuSp

Sentinel, The. *Unknown*. BLRP

Sentinel of the grave who counts us all! (*LL*) Ode to the Confederate Dead. Allen Tate. AiP; FaBoMo; HeIP; LiTA; LiTM; MoAB; MoAmPo; MoP; NAAL-2; NoAM; NOBA; NoP; OBD, *ll.* 1–9; OBWP; OxBA; PrIm; TAP; TFi; UnPo

Sentinel's Song, A. Rarawa Kerehoma, *tr. by* Barry Mitcalfe. WTO

Sentry, The. Alun Lewis. AngWe; PoWW

Sentry, The. Wilfred Owen. EBNV; PeFWW; PoWW

Sentry and a ladder mark the wall, A. In Front of a Japanese Photograph. John Peck. SM

Sentry! What of the Night? *Unknown*. NSI

Senzangakhona. *Zulu Oral Tradition, tr. by* T. Cope. WTO

Separate Parties. Dabney Stuart. NYBP

Separated Lovers. *Unknown*. *See* My lefe is faren in a lond.

Separately I still recall. Portrait. Adèle Naudé. PeSA

Separating one by one. Island Waters. Tony Beyer. PeNZ

Separation, *sels*. Anne Bloch.
 Absent Friends. Mes

Separation. W. S. Merwin. HAP; NoP

Separation, A. William Johnson Cory. OBNC

Separation by Death. Ibn Hazm, *tr. fr. Arabic by* A. R. Nykel. RaBo, *ad. by* Robert Bly

Separation from the Torah. Solomon ibn Gabirol, *tr. fr. Hebrew by* David Goldstein. TOF

Separation on the River Kiang. Li Po, *tr. fr. Chinese by* Ezra Pound. InPS; SOTW; UnPo

Separations begin with placement. River Road Studio. Barbara Guest. PoM

Sephestia's Lullaby. Robert Greene. *See* Weep [*or* Weepe] not, my wanton, smile upon my knee.

Sephestia's Song. Robert Greene. *See* Weep [*or* Weepe] not, my wanton, smile upon my knee.

Sephestia's Song to Her Child[e]. Robert Greene. *Fr.* Menaphon. ELP; EnRePo; NoSic; OxAEP-1; PoEL-2; TrGrPo

Sepia Fashion Show. Maya Angelou. BlSi

September. Rachel Hadas. UnDi

September. Mary Howitt. BoTP

September. Ted Hughes. BoLoP

September. Aldous Huxley. EBEV

September. Joanne Kyger. UL

September. Robert Lowell. NaP

September. Linda Pastan. Poetsp

September. H. Cordelia Ray. CBWP-3

September. Folgore da San Geminiano, *tr. fr. Italian by* Dante Gabriel Rossetti. *Fr.* Sonnets of the Months. AWP

September, 1802: Near Dover. Wordsworth. *See* Inland, within a hollow Vale, I stood.

September 1957 summoned by my vision-agent. Vision of Rotterdam. Gregory Corso. PoBeRe

September Afternoon. Margaret Haley Carpenter. GoYe

September Afternoon at Four O'Clock. Marge Piercy. NIP

September Blue. Barbara Burford. DT

September [Days Are Here]. Helen Hunt Jackson. FaPON; GoJo; OBCA; PoLF

September Gale, The, *sels.* Oliver Wendell Holmes. "It chanced to be our washing day." FiBHP

September: Last Day at the Beach. Richard Tillinghast. GOYP

September; let us go. It is the time to migrate. The Shepherds. Gabriele D'Annunzio, *tr. fr. Italian by* Philip L. Miller. RiWo

September Midnight. Sara Teasdale. PoA

September Night, A. George Marion McClellan. AAP

September 1944. Charles Fishman. BTR

September 1913. W. B. Yeats. CMoP; FaBoPV; GTBS-P; HAP; MoP; NAEL-2; NoAM; PeIV; PoRA

September 1939, summer holiday over. The Loggia. Liz Cashdan. NWP

September 1, 1939. W. H. Auden. ArOW; CMoP; CoGr; FaBoEH, *abr.*; ImPo; LiTA; MoAB; MoBrPo; OxAEP-2; OxBA; PoE; PrIm

September rain falls on the house. Elizabeth Bishop. InPK; LCAP; NoP; PFP; PoE; Poetr; SM

September 7. Ellen Bass. NMM

September Song. Geoffrey Hill. NAEL-2; NoAM; NoP; OBWP

September, the First Day of School. Howard Nemerov. OxBC

September. The gypsy and the nightingale. Autumn. Itsik Manger, *tr. fr. Yiddish by* Ruth Whitman. TrJP

September Town. Anne Carson. *Fr.* Life of Towns, The. BAP-90

September twenty-second, Sir: today. After the Surprising Conversions. Robert Lowell. AmPP; HAP; NAAL-2; NoAM; NoP; PPP; TRP

September 2. Wendell Berry. PoA

September was when it began. The Coming of the Plague. Weldon Kees. ChIV-1; NaP; VGW

Sepulchre. George Herbert. ESCV; MiEL

Sepulchres, how thick they stand, The. Meditations on the Sepulchre in the Garden. Philip Doddridge. NOCV; NOEC

Sepulchrum Domus Mea Est. William Austin. NOSC

Sequaire. Godeschalk, *tr. fr. Latin by* Ezra Pound. CTC

Sequel, The. Theodore Roethke. NYBP

Sequel, The. Delmore Schwartz. LiTM

Sequel to the "Purple Cow." Gelett Burgess. *See* Ah, Yes, I Wrote the "Purple Cow."

Sequence. George Barker. PoA

Sequence. Edgar Daniel Kramer. BLRP

Sequence, A, *sels.* John Riley.
Story, A. VaA

Sequence for a Young Widow Passing. Deborah Munro. IHMS

Sequence for Saint Michael, A. Alcuin, *tr. fr. Irish by* Helen Waddell. TIRV

Sequence in Four Keys, A, *sels.* James Reaney.
Baby, The. NAs

Sequence/ 28 Separate Poems, A, *sels.* Robert Grenier.

Seravezza. Hoyt W. Fuller. PoBA

Sere of the sun exploded in the sea. (*LL*) O Carib Isle! Hart Crane. NoAM; PoA; VGW

Serenade, The. Count Arsenii Arkadyevich Golenishchev-Kutuzov, *tr. fr. Russian by* Philip L. Miller. *Fr.* Songs and Dances of Death. RiWo

Serenade: "Come now, and let us wake them: time." *Unknown, tr. fr. German by* Jethro Bithell. AWP

Serenade: "Did you know? — The surf makes a good wine." Kung Liu, *tr. fr. Chinese.* LHF, *tr. by* Hualing Nieh

Serenade: "Don't tell me love's kin is the forest." Kung Liu, *tr. fr. Chinese.* LHF, *tr. by* Hualing Nieh

Serenade: "Look out upon the stars, my love." Edward Coote Pinkney. AnAmPo

Serenade: "Lullaby, O lullaby" Thomas Hood. *Fr.* Domestic Poems. NBLV

Serenade: "Moon stands over the mountain, The." Franz Kugler, *tr. fr. German by* Philip L. Miller. RiWo

Serenade: "Open! Open! But softly, my child." Adolf Friedrich Graf von Schack, *tr. fr. German by* Philip L. Miller. RiWo

Serenade: "Sleep, love sleep." Mary Weston Fordham. CBWP-2

Serenade: "Softly, O midnight Hours!" Aubrey Thomas De Vere. OBEV

Serenade: "Softly pleading, my songs go." Ludwig Rellstab, *tr. fr. German by* Philip L. Miller. RiWo

Serenade: "Stars of the summer night!" Longfellow. *Fr.* Spanish Student, The. FaBoBe

Serenade. Sir Walter Scott. *Fr.* Quentin Durward. GTBS; GTBS-P

Serenade: Any Man to Any Woman. Edith Sitwell. NALW

Serenade at the Villa, A. Robert Browning. Mes

Serenade for Strings. Dorothy Livesay. NAs

Serenade in Vain, A. Anton Wilhelm Florentin von Zuccalmaglio, *tr. fr. German by* Philip L. Miller. RiWo

Serenade of a Loyal Martyr. George Darley. *See* Sweet in her green dell the flower of beauty slumbers.

Serenader, The. *Unknown, tr. fr. Greek by* Dudley Fitts. GrAn

Serene and outraged in a trenchcoat. Severances. Aidan Carl Mathews. CIP

Serene descent, as a red leaf's descending. Sara Teasdale. PoA

Serene, I fold my hands [*or* arms] and wait. Waiting. John Burroughs. AnAmPo; BLPA; FaBoBe; WGRP

Serene the silver fishes glide. At the Aquarium. Max Eastman. FaPON; WGRP

Serenely in the crystal jet. Ezra Pound. *Fr.* Cantos. PoE

Serenity in Stones, The. Simon J. Ortiz. CDW

Serenity of Faith, The. Bible, *O.T., paraphrased by* Sir Thomas Wyatt, *tr. by* McFayden. *Fr.* Psalms. BLRP

Serenity so arduously maintained, and at such, A. Ann Lee. Lynne McMahon. NAmP90

Serf, The. Roy Campbell. GTBS-P; LiTB; MoBrPo; OBMV

Sergeant Champe. *Unknown.* PAH

Sergeant, He Is the Worst of All, The. *Unknown.* AS

Sergeant-Major Money. Robert Graves. OBWP

Sergeant of the Lawe, war and wys, A. Chaucer. *Fr.* Canterbury Tales, The. CTC, *abr.*; EnVB; FHYEP; NoP; OAEL-1; PPP, *abr.*

Sergeant to Enyalios. Archilochus, *tr. fr. Greek by* Guy Davenport. GrAn

Sergeant's Weddin', The. Kipling. OxBTC

Sergei's a flower. Ruth Herschberger. FF

Serials are all wound up now, The. Where Are You Now Superman? Brian Patten. FF

Seriatim. Robert A. Frauenglas. BTR

Serious and a Curious Night-Meditation, A. Thomas Traherne. SeCP

Serious Merriment of Women, The. Patricia Goedicke. TAP

Serious over my cereals I broke one breakfast my fast. Breakfast with Gerard Manley Hopkins. Anthony Brode. BXAP; FaBoPa; FiBHP; NOBL

Serious Poem, A. Ernest Walsh. ErPo

Serious Readers. Peter Redgrove. OxBC

Serious young lady from Welwyn, A. C. Armstrong Gibbs. PeLi

Sermon, The. Richard Hughes. OBMV

Sermon, The. Ted Joans. PoBeRe

Sermon at Clevedon, A. Thomas Edward Brown. NOBVV

Sermon in a Stocking. Ellen A. Jewett. BLPA

Sermon on Swift, A. Austin Clarke. BlrV; IPY

Sermon on the Mount. Jeff Wright. UL

Sermon on the Warpland, The. Gwendolyn Brooks. BPo; LiTM; NOBA; PoBA

Sermon our Pastor, Rt. Rev., The. *Unknown.* PeLi

Sermonette. Ishmael Reed. PoBA

Serpent Country. A. R. Ammons. EOEF

"This is the last time." OBMV
"What is the meaning of this Ideal." OBMV
"What is this tempest." OBMV
Seven dead men, Brigit. The Celtic Lyric. J. C. Squire. BXAP
Seven Deadly Sins, The. Stephen Hawes. *Fr.* Pastime of Pleasure, The. PoEL-1
Seven dog-days we let pass. Queens. J. M. Synge. ChTr; GBL; MoBrPo; OBMV; PeIV; PeVV
Seven Evils. Bible, *O.T. Fr.* Proverbs. TrGrPo
Seven Fiddlers, The. Sebastian Evans. EBVV
7:v:60 (an interesting *lapsus calami*). For Kai Snyder. Philip Whalen. PoM
747 (London-Chicago). Robert Conquest. OxBC
Seven four seven slides sharply into the air, The. *(LL)* The Rank Harvest of Betrayal. Wilma Stockenström. PeSAV
Seven Hells of Jigoku Zoshi, The, *sels.* Jerome Rothenberg. NNaP
Fifth Hell, The. NNaP
Sixth Hell, The. NNaP
Seven Houses, The. George Mackay Brown. NAs
700 years ago. Slim Man Canyon. Leslie Silko. VoR
Seven in the Morning. Rhyll McMaster. FaBoMA
Seven Laments for the War — Dead, *sels.* Yehuda Amichai, *tr. fr. Hebrew* by Chana Bloch.
"Is this all there is?" CBCK
Seven lang years I hae served the King. The Whummil Bore. *Unknown.* CH; ESPB
Seven Little Pigs. *Unknown.* BoTP
Seven Long Years in State Prison. *Unknown.* AS
Seven lovely poplars. Poplars. Helen Leuty. BoTP
Seven Metal Mountains. Bible, Pseudepigrapha. *Fr.* Enoch. TrJP
Seven of Pentacles, The. Marge Piercy. CrSp
Seven of the Clock. Roy Macnab. PeSA
Seven Old Men, The. Baudelaire, *tr. fr. French* by Roy Campbell. OBVE
Seven Orange Tulips. Thomas McCarthy. IB
Seven orange tulips with their own glow. *(LL)* Seven Orange Tulips. Thomas McCarthy. IB
Seven pairs of leopard-skin underpants. Leopard Skin. Douglas Stewart. NOBAu
Seven plus thirty years are gone. Philodemus, *tr. fr. Greek* by William Moebius. GrAn
Seven Poems of Lament. Ts'ao Chih, *tr. fr. Chinese* by Ronald C. Miao. SuSp
Seven Poems of Lament, *sels.* Wang Ts'an, *tr. fr. Chinese.*
"Land of the Ching tribes is not my home, The." SuSp
"This frontier post brings me sorrow." SuSp
"Western Capital is in turmoil, The." SuSp
Seven Poems on Living in the Mountains: Seeing Off, *sels.* Chang Yü, *tr. fr. Chinese* by Jonathan Chaves.
Seven potato, MORE. *(LL)* One potato, two potato. *Unknown.* FaPON; ImGa; RoPo
Seven Rainy Months. William Plomer. OxBTC
Seven Sages, The. W. B. Yeats. NOIV
Seven Said by the Foster-Mother. Peyanar, *tr. fr. Tamil* by A. K. Ramanujan, *sels.*
"Embracing the young mother from behind." PLW
"Embracing this woman." PLW
"Evening in the yard." PLW
"His heart swells." PLW
"Like the red flame." PLW
"Minstrels sing the jasmine songs." PLW
"Way/ they lay together, The." PLW
Seven Seages, The, *sels.* John Rolland.
"In haist ga hy thee to sum hoill." OxBS
Seven Seas rose in the half-dark to make coffee. Omeros. Derek Walcott. BAP-91
Seven Sides and Seven Syllables. Edouard J. Maunick, *tr. fr. French* by Carolyn Kizer. NegPo
Seven Sleepers, The. Mark Van Doren. FYAP
Seven Songs Written During the Ch'ien-yüan Era, *sels.* Tu Fu, *tr. fr. Chinese* by Burton Watson.
Seven Songs Written while Living at T'ung-ku in 759. Tu Fu, *tr. fr. Chinese* by Goeffrey Waters. SuSp
Seven Sorrows, The. Ted Hughes. NAEL-2
Seven South African Poems,. *sels.* David Wright.
"My countryman, the poet, wears a Stetson." PeSA
"My grandfather was an elegant gentleman." PeSA
Seven Spiritual Ages of Mrs. Marmaduke Moore, The. Ogden Nash. MoAmPo
Seven Stanzas at Easter. John Updike. TrCP

Seven stars in the still water. The Dole of the King's Daughter. *Unknown, tr. fr. French* by Oscar Wilde. AWP
Seven sweet singing birds up in a tree. The Dream of a Girl Who Lived at Sevenoaks. William Brighty Rands. OxBChV
Seven thousand acres of grass have faded yellow. Farmer, Dying. Richard Hugo. CAPP
Seven threads make the shroud. Shroud. George Mackay Brown. RB 7 : 3, *sels.* Alta.
"Love is believable." CrSp
Seven times hath Janus ta'en new year by hand. Upon the Author's First Seven Years' Service. Thomas Tusser. EIL
Seven Times One — Exultation. Jean Ingelow. *Fr.* Songs of Seven. BLPA; FaPON; OBNC
Seven Times Three — Love. Jean Ingelow. *Fr.* Songs of Seven. PoLF
Seven Times Two — Romance. Jean Ingelow. *Fr.* Songs of Seven. GN
Seven Virgins, The. *Unknown.* CH; ChTr; GBP; OBET; OBEV
Seven wealthy towns contend for Homer dead. A Cure for Poetry. *Unknown, after the Latin of* George Buchanan. FaBoEE
Seven weeks of sea, and twice seven days of storm. Gibraltar. Wilfrid Scawen Blunt. OBEV
Seven white peacocks against the castle wall, The. What the Orderly Dog Saw. Ford Madox Ford. CTC
Seven Wonders of England, The, *sels.* Sir Philip Sidney.
Seven Wonders of England, The. SiPSBD
(Stonehenge.) FaBoPP
Seven Wonders of England, The. Sir Philip Sidney. *Fr.* Seven Wonders of England, The. SiPSBD
Seven Wonders of North Wales, The. *Unknown, tr. fr. Welsh.* OBWVE
Seven Woodland Crows. Gerald Vizenor. VoR
Seven Words, The. Jerzy Ficowski, *tr. fr. Polish* by Keith Bosley *and* Krystyna Wandycz. PoSu
Seven years ago, almost to the month and day. Ramon. E. A. Lacey. PeHV
Seven years ago/ at forty five. Now or Never. Astra. AIW; BrRo
7 Years from Somewhere. Philip Levine. AnAn
Seven years I have kept him, dead. The Corpse-Keeper. *Unknown, tr. fr. Catalan* by W. S. Merwin. BoWoP
Seven years lived in Italy leave me convinced. The Oak and the Olive. George Barker. FaBoMo; OBTV
Seven years ye shall be a stone. The Maid and the Palmer. *Unknown.* ESPB
Seventeen. Jonathan Holden. Poetsp
Seventeen Come Sunday. *Unknown.* OBET
17. IV. 71. Paul Blackburn. PoM
Seventeen hundred and thirty-nine. Ballad of 'Beau Brocade,' The. Austin Dobson. OxAEP-2
Seventeen Months. Carl Sandburg. ArLo
Seventeen Warnings in Search of a Feminist Poem. Erica Jong. AmPA
Seventeen years ago you said. À Quoi Bon Dire. Charlotte Mew. OxBTC
Seventeenth of May, The. Anthony Barnett. VaA
Seventeenth stanza, The. My heart aches, my tears fall. Ts'ai Yen, *tr. fr. Chinese* by Kenneth Rexroth *and* Ling Chung. *Fr.* Eighteen Verses Sung to a Tatar Reed Whistle. WPC; WPOW
Seventh, The. Attila József, *tr. fr. Hungarian* by John Batki. RB
Seventh Angel, The. Zbigniew Herbert, *tr. fr. Polish* by Czeslaw Milosz *and* Peter Dale Scott. AnRep
Seventh Avenue. Mark Halliday. NAmP90
Seventh Avenue. Muriel Rukeyser. NoAM
Seventh Birthday of the First Child. Sharon Olds. PBCAP
Seventh Day Seventh Month. Kuan Yun She, *tr. fr. Chinese* by Kenneth Rexroth. OHMPC
Seventh of July, the suith to say, The. The Raid of the Reidswire. *Unknown.* IBB
Seventh Property, The. Sir Thomas More. *Fr.* Twelve Weapons of Spiritual Battle, The. EnRePo
Seventh Son. Ed Roberson. PoBA
Seventh Street. Jean Toomer. NAAL-2
Seventies, The. Louis Johnson. PeNZ
Seventieth Year, The. Gary Soto. AfAz
Seventy-eight Tanka, *sels.* Princess Shikishi, *tr. fr. Japanese* by Hiroaki Sato.
Seventy Feet Down. Philip Larkin. *Fr.* Livings. RB
Seventy-five Are My Abyssed Forests. Shimon Halkin, *tr. fr. Hebrew* by Ruth Finer Mintz. MHP
Seventy-five feet hoed rows equals. Gary Snyder. *Fr.* Mountains and Rivers without End: The Market. NaP
Seventy-six. Bryant. PAH
Seventy-six Hokku., *sels.* Basho, *tr. fr. Japanese* by Burton Watson.
"Old pond,/ frog jumps in." EnlH, *tr. by* Michael Katz

Several months after we lost our way. The Natives. David Mura. ETG; WeW

Several Questions Answered, *sels*. Blake.
   Eternity ("He who binds [*or* bends] to himself a joy"). ArNa; AWP; EBEV; EnlH; FaBoEE; ImPo; MeMBP; NOBE; NoP; NTP; OBNC; OxBSP; PFP; Poetr; RB; SCGP; SoSe; Spl; TrGrPo
   "What is it men in women do require?" OAEL-2
   (Question Answered [*or* A Question Answered], The.) ErPo; FaBoEE; GBL; MeMBP; NoP; OxBM

Several things announced the fact to us. New Territory. Eavan Boland. PeIV

Several Voices out of a Cloud. Louise Bogan. NALW

Severances. Aidan Carl Mathews. CIP

Severed from the continental homeland? (*LL*) Black Island. Charles Pressoir. NegPo

Severed Head, A, *sels*. John Montague.
   Road's End, The. IPY

Severed Selves. Dante Gabriel Rossetti. *Fr*. House of Life, The. BoLoP

Severer Service of Myself. Emily Dickinson. TRP

Severn, The. Michael Drayton. *Fr*. Baron's War, The. ChTr

Severn and Vaga, each old Cambria's pride. Thoughts on Happiness. Francis Homfray. AngWe

Severn sweeping smooth and broad, The. At Arley. Andrew Young. FaBoPP

Sévignés, The. Anne Spencer. ShDr

Sew a Pocket. Jessie Welborn Smith. PWR

Sewing-Box, The. Gabriel Gbadamosi. NBrP

Sewing the long white seam. (*LL*) The Long White Seam. Jean Ingelow. GN; NOBVV

Sex. Jean Valentine. FaBoWP

Sex and the Over Forties. Peter Porter. CBLP

Sex, as they harshly call it. Adrienne Rich. *Fr*. Two Songs. NIP; NOBA; TAP

Sex Education. Jon Forrest Glade. NGP

Sex fingers toes. Dear John, Dear Coltrane. Michael S. Harper. AmPA; Jaz; NIP; VCAP

Sex floated like a moon. Circle, a Square, a Triangle and a Ripple of Water. Jane Cooper. TAP

Sex-life of Fish, The. William Diaper, *after the Greek of* Oppian. *See* Strange the formation of the eely race.

Sex, Politics, and Religion. Lavinia Greenlaw. NWP

Sex with Zsa Zsa and Eva Gabor. Brent Reiten. NGP

Sex without Love. Sharon Olds. HeIP; NIP; Poetr; TRP

Sexes waking, now separate and sore, The. The Martyrs. Jay Macpherson. MoCV

Sextain: "Sith gone is my delight and only pleasure." William Drummond of Hawthornden. NOSC

Sextain: "With elegies, sad songs, and mourning lays." William Drummond of Hawthornden. NOSC

Sexton is opening up the grave, The. The Third Light. Michael Longley. PNI

Sexton tolled the bell, The. (*LL*) Faithless Sally Brown. Thomas Hood. NOBL; OBNV

Sextus the Usurer. Martial, *tr. fr. Latin by* Kirby Flower Smith. AWP

Sexual Couplets. Craig Raine. FaBoBl

Sexual intercourse began. Annus Mirabilis. Philip Larkin. NBLV; NIP; NOBL; OBAL

Sexual Privacy of Women on Welfare. Pinkie Gordon Lane. BlSi

Sexual Sigh, The. Gavin Ewart. FaBoBl

Sexy Food Stamps. Jeffrey Miller. UL

Sexy young student once toyed, A. Richard Taylor. PeLi

Seynt Stevene was a clerk. St. Stephen and King Herod. *Unknown*. ESPB, *Middle English vers*.; NoP, (*mod. vers*.); OxBoLi, (*Middle English vers*.); TrGrPo, (*mod. vers*.)
   (Carol for St. Stephen's Day, A.) CH
   (Saint Steven Was a Clerk.) EnVB
   (Seynt Stevyn and Herowdes.) OxBB

Seynt Stevyn and Herowdes. *Unknown. See* Seynt Stevene was a clerk.

Seyton! — I am sick at heart. Shakespeare. *Fr*. Macbeth. OxAEP-1

Sez I: My Country Calls? Well, let it call. The Volunteer. Robert W. Service. NSI

S.F. Southward. Allen Ginsberg. *Fr*. Continuation of a Long Poem of These States. NAAL-2

Sgt. stands so fluently in leather, The. On a Photo of Sgt. Ciardi a Year Later. John Ciardi. AiP; ArOW

Sh-Ta-Ra-Dah-Dey. *Unknown*. AS

Sha-a-ame, sha-ame. *Unknown*. RoPo

Shabby Old Dad. Anne Campbell. PoToHe

Shack and a few trees, The. After Work. Gary Snyder. HoPM; NNaP

Shack Poem. Robert Bly. CAPP

Shackley-Hay. *Unknown*. GBP

Shad-Time. Richard Wilbur. NGP

Shadbush. Christina Rainsford. GoYe

Shade. Theodosia Garrison. OHIP

Shade-Catchers, The. Charlotte Mew. NTP

Shade of His hand shall cover us, The. His Hand Shall Cover Us. Isaac ben Samuel of Dampière, *tr. fr. Hebrew by* Nina Davis Salaman. TrJP

Shade of Night, A. Amos Neufeld. BTR

Shade once swept about your boughs, The. The Fallen Tree. Andrew Young. BoNaP

Shade-Seller, The. Josephine Jacobsen. TAP

Shade that was Elizabeth . . . immortal completeness! (*LL*) Life-long, Poor Browning. Anne Spencer. CDC; PoNe

Shaded lamp and a waving blind, A. An August Midnight. Thomas Hardy. NOBVV

Shades of Callimachus, Coan ghosts of Philetas. Ezra Pound. *Fr*. Homage to Sextus Propertius. CMoP; HAP; MoAB; NOBA; OBVE; OxBA

Shades of eve are quickly closing in, The. Night. Josephine D. Henderson Heard. CBWP-4

Shades of Grand Central, The. Chase Twichell. NAmP90

Shades of Night, The. A. E. Housman. BXAP; ChTr; FaBoNo; FiBHP; NBLV; UV

Shades of night were falling fast, The. Excelsior. Longfellow. EBEvV; FaPON; FaPoR; NAAL-1; OBCA; OBSP; PrIm; UV, sh. vers.; VPP; WBLP

Shades of Pharoah Sanders Blues for My Baby. John O'Neal. NBV

Shading porch, that's open to the west, A. Landscape with Self-Portrait. Howard Nemerov. NGP

Shadoof, The. Martin Sorescu, *tr. fr. Romanian by* Michael Longley *and* Ioana Russell-Gebbett. PWE

Shadow. Guillaume Apollinaire, *tr. fr. French by* Christopher Middleton. PeFWW

Shadow. Richard Bruce. CDC

Shadow. Anthony Delius. PeSA

Shadow, The. Ben Jonson. *See* Follow a shadow [*or* shaddow], it still flies you.

Shadow. Ann Mars. GoYe

Shadow, A. *At. to* Thomas Bateson. *See* I Heard a Noise and Wishèd for a Sight.

Shadow and Shade. Allen Tate. LiTA; VGW

Shadow and Substance. *At. to* Thomas Bateson. *See* I Heard a Noise and Wishèd for a Sight.

Shadow and Sunrise. H. Cordelia Ray. CBWP-3

Shadow and the Light, The, *sels*. Whittier.
   "All souls that struggle and aspire." TrPWD

Shadow bounces too, The. (*LL*) Kick a Little Stone. Dorothy Aldis. TLR

Shadow boxer, fighting. Father of Famine. Richard Ryan. PBCIP

Shadow does not leave my feet, The. David. Charles Reznikoff. ChIV-1

Shadow falls, the path I cannot trace, The. Satisfied. Samuel Valentine Cole. BLRP

Shadow for shadow, stripped for fight. The Search-Lights. Alfred Noyes. *Fr*. Salute from the Fleet, A. NSI

Shadow his father makes with joined hands, A. Alphabets. Seamus Heaney. NoAM

Shadow in Stone. Janice Mirikitani. OpBo

Shadow Inside Me, The. Tommy Olofsson, *tr. fr. Swedish. by* Jean Pearson. TSaS

Shadow is floating through the moonlight, A. The Bird of Night. Randall Jarrell. RFM

Shadow, killer of doves. Shadow. Anthony Delius. PeSA

Shadow-Love. Heine, *tr. fr. German by* Emma Lazarus. *Fr*. Songs to Seraphine. TrJP

Shadow of a Branch, The. Edith Marcombe Shiffert. WPE

Shadow of a fat man in the moonlight, The. Things to Come. James Reeves. OxBSP

Shadow of a summer tightly folded, The. Girls in the Plural. Medbh McGuckian. DT

Shadow of Cain, The. Edith Sitwell. OxBTC

Shadow of Darkness. Gladys May Casely Hayford. PBA

Shadow of her profile lay stringent, The. Woman, Gallup, N. M. Karen Swenson. NYBP

Shadow of Himself, The. William Renton. NOBVV

Shadow of Night, The, *sels*. George Chapman.
   Hymnus in Noctem. PoEL-2

Shadow of Night, The. Coventry Patmore. *See* How strange at night [*or* it is] to wake.

Shadow of the dwarf magnolia, The. The Magnolia's Shadow. Robert Lowell, *tr. fr. Italian by* Eugenio Montale. NaP

Shadow of the little fishing launch, The. The Parrot Fish. James Merrill. NOBA

Shadow of the night comes on, The. (*LL*) You, Andrew Marvell. Archibald MacLeish. AWP; CMoP; FaBV; FYAP; HAP; HeIP; HoPM; LiTA; LiTM; MeMAP; MoAB; MoAmPo; MoP; NAAL-2; NoAM; NOBA; NoP; OxBA; Poetr; PoRA; PPP; PrIm; SoSe; TFi; TrGrPo; TRP; TwCP

Shadow of the Trees, The. Paul Verlaine, *tr. fr. French by* Philip L. Miller. RiWo

Shadow of the trees in the misty river, The. The Shadow of the Trees. Paul Verlaine, *tr. fr. French by* Philip L. Miller. RiWo

Shadow of the Venetian blind on the painted wall, The. Forties Flick. John Ashbery. NoAM

Shadow of wings grew, The. Fight With An Angel. Tadeusz Różewicz, *tr. fr. Polish by* Victor Contoski. PoSu

Shadow on shadow his mind. Remembering Yeats. Francis Stuart. BiHa

Shadow people, projected on coffee-shop walls. Bagel Shop Jazz. Bob Kaufman. Jaz

Shadow Play. Ralph Angel. NAmP90

Shadow Songs. J. H. Prynne. VaA

Shadow streamed into the wall, The. Shadow and Shade. Allen Tate. LiTA; VGW

Shadow Train. John Ashbery. LCAP

Shadow Valley. Robert Morgan. AngWe

Shadowed by your dear hair, your dear kind eyes. The Sanctuary. Ford Madox Ford. PoA

Shadowgraphs, The. Richmond Lattimore. NYBP

Shadows. Samuel Daniel. *See* Are they shadows that we see?

Shadows. Patricia Hubbell. Spl

Shadows. D. H. Lawrence. OxBTC

Shadows. Victor Plarr. NOBVV

Shadows. *Unknown, tr. fr. Tewa Indian by* H. J. Spinden. WTO

Shadows. "Yehoash," *tr. fr. Yiddish by* Elias Lieberman. TrJP

Shadows are bodiless shapes, yet they have a song. (*LL*) Transaction. A. R. Ammons. HCAP; PoA

Shadows are descending, The. Outgoing Sabbath. *Unknown, tr. fr. Yiddish by* Joseph Leftwich. TrJP

Shadows become familiar. My Neighborhood. Stuart Dybek. PBCAP

Shadows blown from trees, The. Vain Advice at the Year's End. James Wright. NYBP

Shadows in Llanbadarn. Gillian Clarke. SCBI

Shadows in the Water. Thomas Traherne. GeHe; HAP; LiTB; NoP; OAEL-1; PoEL-2; SCGP; SeCP

Shadows lay along Broadway, The. Two Women. Nathaniel Parker Willis. BeLS

(Unseen Spirits.) AnAmPo

Shadows, like Navahoes, wear velvet. Tourist Country. William Stafford. NoAM

Shadows of His Lady. Jacques Tahureau, *tr. fr. French by* Andrew Lang. AWP

Shadows of night come like remembered sorrow, The. (*LL*) Evening Comes. Li Shang-yin. OHMPC

Shadows of night were a-comin' down swift, The. Higher. *Unknown*. FiBHP

Shadows of ringdoves chanting, but easing nothing, The. (*LL*) Winter Trees. Sylvia Plath. CAPP; HCAP; LCAP; NMM

Shadows of Taste., *sels*. John Clare. "In poesy's spells some all their raptures find." EPCY

Shadows of the cypresses, The. Wind Tossed Dragons. Hsieh Ngao, *tr. fr. Chinese by* Kenneth Rexroth. OHMPC

Shadows of the sails pass across his windows. Visiting the Garden at Monk Wen Ko's Home. Wu Wei-yeh, *tr. fr. Chinese by* Chang Yin-nan *and* Lewis C. Walmsley. SuSp

Shadows of the torn green, The. To the Tune "A Dream Song." Sun Tao-hsüan, *tr. fr. Chinese by* Kenneth Rexroth *and* Ling Chung. WPC

Shadows of the t'ung tree, glistening and clear. In a Dream. Lu Yu, *tr. fr. Chinese by* Irving Y. Lo. SuSp

Shadows, shadows,/ Hug me round. Escape. Georgia Douglas Johnson. PoBA; ShDr

Shadows whisper A new language of possibilities. Stardust Sequence. Dermot Bolger. IB

Shadrach, Meshach, Abednego. Warm Babies. Keith Preston. FiBHP

Shadrach/ Shake the bed. *Unknown*. FaBoNo

Shadwell Stair. Wilfred Owen. FaBoTw

Shady, Shady. T'ao Ch'ien, *tr. fr. Chinese by* Arthur Waley. AWP

Shady Woods. E. M. Adams. BoTP

Shaemus. Conrad Aiken. OxBA

Shaft, The. Charles Tomlinson. DiPo

Shaft we raise to them and thee, The. (*LL*) Concord Hymn. Emerson. AiP; AmPP; AWP; BLPA; BLPL; ClHu; FaBoBe; FaBoEH; FaPON; FaPoR; GN; GOA; HAP; HeIP; LiTA; MeMAP; NOBA; NoP; OBWP; OxBA; PAH; PAW; PeECV; PIP; TAP; TFi; TrGrPo

Shaft[e]sbury. Dryden. *See* Of these the false Achitophel was first.

Shag, The. Ellen Duggan. PeNZ

Shag Rock. "Paul Henderson." PeNZ

Shahnamah, The, *sels*. Firdausi, *tr. fr. Persian*. Birth of Sohráb, The. TAL, *tr. by* James Atkinson Death of Sohráb, The. TAL, *tr. by* James Atkinson

Shaka, King of the Zulus. (He is Shaka the unshakable.) *Unknown, tr. fr. Zulu by* A. C. Jordan. PBA; TTY

Sels. "Young viper grows as it sits, The." WTO

Shake hands, we shall never be friends, all's over. A. E. Housman. CBLP

Shake Hands with Your Bets, Friend. Lorenzo Thomas. UL

Shake, Mulleary, and Go-ethe. H. C. Bunner. FiBHP

Shake off this sadness, and recover your spirit. Throw Yourself Like Seed. Miguel De Unamuno, *tr. fr. Spanish by* Robert Bly. RaBo

Shake off your heavy trance! Francis Beaumont. *Fr.* Masque of the Inner Temple and Gray's Inne, The. NTP; TrGrPo
(Fit Only for Apollo.) ChTr
(Song for a Dance.) EIL; FaBoCh

Shaken already, I know. Goodbye, Sally. James Simmons. BIrV

Shake'nbake Ballad. Peter van Toorn. NOBC

Shakespeare. Matthew Arnold. EBVVPR; EPCY; FHYEP; HeIP; InvP; NoP; OBEV; OxAEP-2; SCGP; Son; TrGrPo

Shakespeare. Lucretia Davidson. AmWP

Shakespeare, *sels*. Walter Savage Landor. "He lighted with his golden lamp on high." EPCY

Shakespeare. Longfellow. AWP

Shakespeare. H. Cordelia Ray. CBWP-3

Shakespeare. Swinburne. EPCY; TrGrPo

Shakespeare; an Epistle to David Garrick, Esq, *sels*. Robert Lloyd. True Genius. NOEC

Shakespeare or I or anyone ever dreamed. (*LL*) Peripeteia. Anthony Hecht. VCAP

Shakespeare stand-ins, same string hair, gay, dirty. Ulysses. Robert Lowell. NAAL-2

Shakespeare: The Fairies' Advocate. Thomas Hood. *Fr.* Plea of the Midsummer Fairies, The. OBNC

Shakespeare (whom you and every playhouse bill). Pope. *Fr.* First Epistle of the Second Book of Horace, Imitation of. EPCY

Shakespeare, whose heartfelt scenes shall ever give. To Shakespeare. Thomas Edwards. Son

Shakespeare! with all thy faults (and few have more). Shakespeare. Lucretia Davidson. AmWP

Shakespearean fish swam the sea, far away from land. Three Movements. W. B. Yeats. CMoP; FaBoEE

Shaking ancient oaks. (*LL*) Eros seizes and shakes my very soul. Sappho. InMo

Shaking my head, I let the world of red dust. Tune: "Happy Events Approaching." Chu Tun-ju, *tr. fr. Chinese by* James J. Y. Liu. SuSp

Shako, The. Robert Lowell. Son

Shall a Frown. *At. to* William Corkine. EIL; EnRePo

Shall a frown or angry eye. Shall a Frown. *At. to* William Corkine. EIL; EnRePo

Shall ancient worth, or ancient fame. True Genius. Robert Lloyd. *Fr.* Shakespeare; an Epistle to David Garrick, Esq. NOEC

Shall at your feet for pardon cry. (*LL*) The Four Seasons of the Year. Anne Bradstreet. SCAP

Shall be a soldier's sepulchre. (*LL*) Hohenlinden. Thomas Campbell. BeLS; CH; ChTr; EnRP; FaBoCh; FaBoRV; FaPoR; GN; GTBS; GTBS-P; NOBE; OBNC; OBWP; PAW; TFi; WBLP

Shall be as fine as his is. (*LL*) The Death of Kin Chuen Louie. Michael McClure. PoBeRe

Shall be left standing face to face with God. (*LL*) Continued. Matthew Arnold. Son

Shall be lifted — nevermore! (*LL*) The Raven. Poe. AmPP; AnAmPo; BeLS; BLPA; CH; CoGr; EBEvV; EBNV; FaBoBe; FaBoCh; FaBV; GGP; GN; GoJo; HeIP; ImGa; LiTA; NAAL-1; NIP; NOBA; OBCA; OBNV; OxBA; PoRA; PWR; TAP; TFi; UV, *abr.*; VPP; WBLP

Shall be made friends in a left handed trance. (*LL*) Odd but True. *Unknown*. FaBoCo

Shall be thy doom. (*LL*) To a Mountain Daisy. Burns. EnRP; GN; PoLF; ScCV; WBLP

Shall be Yes for evermore. (*LL*) The Lady's "Yes." Elizabeth Barrett Browning. LPA

Shall bloom more sublimely after the rapture of the night. (*LL*) Open! Open! But softly, my child. Adolf Friedrich Graf von Schack. RiWo

Shall both rise with me. (*LL*) The Cherry-Tree Carol. *Unknown.* AmFP; ChTr, A *and* B *vers.*; EBEV, A *and* B *vers.*; ELP; EnSB. ESPB; FaBoBa. GBP; HeIL; HeIP; OAEL-1; OBCP; OBET; OxBB; OxBoLi; PeECV; SCGP; TFi; TrGrPo

Shall bring my boats ashore. (*LL*) Where Go the Boats? Robert Louis Stevenson. FaBoBe; FaBoCh; GoJo; Mes; NTCP; NTP; OxBChV; PYC; TLR; WHSW

Shall brithers be for a' that. (*LL*) For A' That [and A' That] ("Is there, for honest poverty.") Burns. EnRP; FaBoBe; FaBoPV; FaPoR; LiTB; NAEL-2; OAEL-1; OxAEP-2; TEP; TFi; UV; WBLP

Shall buffet the vexed forest in his rage. (*LL*) A Winter Piece. Bryant. AmPP; EAP; OxBA

Shall do it reverence. (*LL*) The City in the Sea *or* The Doomed City. Poe. AmPP; AnAmPo; LiTA; MAT; MeMAP; NAAL-1; NOBA; NoP; OxBA; PoE; PoEL-4; SCV; TAP; TFi; TrGrPo; TRP

Shall draw me safe to the land. (*LL*) The Widower. Kipling. CBLP; OxBM

Shall show the Thing as he sees It for the God of Things as They are! (*LL*) When Earth's last picture is painted, and the tubes are twisted and dried. Kipling. PWR; WGRP

Shall Dumpish Melancholy spoil my Joys. On Christmas-Day. Thomas Traherne. PoEL-2

Shall Earth No More Inspire Thee? Emily Brontë. ELP

Shall fear to seem untrue. The Rejection. Sir Robert Ayton. NOSC

Shall feast on the corpses that float by the ferry. (*LL*) Horsey Gap. *Unknown.* FaBoPP; GBP

Shall fill his mouth with mould. (*LL*) Ho, Everyone That Thirsteth. A. E. Housman. ChIV-1; OAEL-2

Shall find that sparing yields a goodly rent. (*LL*) Magnum Vectigal Parsimonia. George Gascoigne. NoSic

Shall find their fables true in us. (*LL*) To My Ingenuous Friend, R. W. Henry Vaughan. BeJo

Shall find wings waiting there. (*LL*) Going Down Hill on a Bicycle. Henry Charles Beeching. OBEV

Shall flock about thee, and keep time with kisses. (*LL*) On the Death of a Nightingale. Thomas Randolph. BeJo

Shall gentle Coleridge pass unnoticed here. Byron. *Fr.* Don Juan. EPCY

Shall have a [*or* the] gold fiddle. (*LL*) He that lies at the stock. *Unknown.* OxNR

Shall hearts that beat no base retreat. The Enthusiast. Herman Melville. ChIV-1; NAAL-1

Shall henceforth wash the river Rhine? (*LL*) Cologne. Samuel Taylor Coleridge. FaBoEE; NBLV; OBTV; PFP

Shall hog with holy child converse? Hog at the Manger. Norma Farber. PChr

Shall I abide this jesting? *Unknown.* GBL

Shall I ask the willow trees on the dike. Longing In My Heart. Wei Ying-wu, *tr. fr. Chinese by* Irving Y. Lo. SuSp

Shall I be one, of those obsequious Fools. The Liberty. Sarah Fyge. KTR

Shall I charge like a bull. Auvaiyar, *tr. fr. Tamil by* A. K. Ramanujan. WPOW

Shall I come, if I swim? wide are the waves, you see. Thomas Campion. EnLoPo

Shall I Come, Sweet Love. Thomas Campion. AAS; CBLP; EBEV; EIL; EnRePo; GBL; HAP; OxAEP-1; OxBoLi; PoEL-2

Shall I come, sweet love, to thee. Shall I Come, Sweet Love. Thomas Campion. AAS; CBLP; EBEV; EIL; EnRePo; GBL; HAP; OxAEP-1; OxBoLi; PoEL-2
(Lover's Plea, A.) NOBE

Shall I come there, or you here? Hafsa bint al-Hajj, *tr. fr. Arabic by* Michael Scott. WPOW

Shall I come to see. Lady Ise, *tr. fr. Japanese by* Kenneth Rexroth *and* Ikuko Atsumi. PRA; WPJ

Shall I compare her to a summer play? Sonnet on Famous and Familiar Sonnets and Experiences. Delmore Schwartz. Son; TRP

Shall I Compare Thee to a Summer's Day? Howard Moss. InPK

Shall I compare thee to a summer's day? Shakespeare. *Fr.* Sonnets. ArLo; BoLoP; ClHu; CTC; EIL; EnLoPo; FaBoBe; FaBV; FaPoB; GBL; HAP; HeIL; HeIP; ImPo; InPK; InPS; InvP; LiTB; LPA; MAT; NOBE; NoP; NoSic; OAEL-1; OBEV; PIP; PoE; PoEL-2; PoLF; PoRA; PrIm; SCGP; SCV; Son; TEP; TFi; TrGrPo; WeW
(To His Love.) GTBS; GTBS-P

Shall I Complain. Louise Chandler Moulton. PoToHe

Shall I complain because the feast is o'er. Shall I Complain. Louise Chandler Moulton. PoToHe

Shall I complain or not? Or shall I mask. Ovid, *tr. fr. Latin by* Henry Vaughan. *Fr.* De Ponto. OBVE

Shall I connect for this world's eyes. The Dumb World. W. H. Davies. OxBTC

Shall I Do This. Swami Purohit. OBMV

Shall I embrace my disease. Monologue of a Dying Beast. Mark Ameen. GLP

Shall I equate thee with a summer's day? New Improved Sonnet XVIII. Peter Titheradge. FaBoPa

Shall I ever see it, the Queen's River. Flyfisherman in Wartime. Leonard Bacon. FYAP

Shall I get drunk or cut myself a piece of cake. Cairo Jag. Keith Douglas. PoWW

"Shall I go with you?" "Aye, by-and-by." (*LL*) There was an old woman tossed up in a basket [*or* blanket]. Mother Goose. OxNR; PDV

Shall I have to spend the. Casablanca Time Again. Joy Howard. DT

Shall I, I wonder, ever find. Peace. Irwin Edman. TrJP

Shall I Look. Robert Jones. EnRePo

Shall I look to ease my grief? Shall I Look. Robert Jones. EnRePo

Shall I love God for causing me to be? The Proof. Richard Wilbur. CRP; OxBSP

Shall I Repine. Swift. *See* If neither brass, nor marble, can withstand.

Shall I say how it is in your clothes? How It Is. Maxine W. Kumin. CAPP; IMW; NALW; NoAM; Poetr

Shall I say that I love you. Of Disdainful Daphne. M. H. Nowell. EIL

Shall I sonnet-sing you about myself? House. Robert Browning. NAEL-2

Shall I strew on thee rose or rue or laurel. Ave atque Vale. Swinburne. NAEL-2; NOBE; OAEL-2; OBEV; OBNC

Shall I tell you the signs of a New Age coming? The New Age. Stevie Smith. NAEL-2

Shall I tell you who [*or* what] will come. Words from an Old Spanish Carol. *Unknown, tr. fr. Spanish by* Ruth Sawyer. PChr
(Christmas Morn.) OBCP
(On Christmas Morn.) FaPON; PDV

Shall I tell you whom I love? William Browne. *Fr.* Britannia's Pastorals. EIL; NOSC

Shall I then hope when faith is fled? Thomas Campion. AAS

Shall I then praise the heavens, the trees, the earth. Anne Bradstreet. *Fr.* Contemplations. AmPP; EAP; NOSC; PBWP; PoEL-3, *abr.*; SCAP; WPE, *abr.*

Shall I thus ever long, and be no whit the near? The Lady Prayeth the Return of Her Lover Abiding on the Seas. *Unknown.* EIL; GBL
(To Her Sea-faring Lover.) OBEV

Shall I wake him? Ah, no! (*LL*) In the Shadow of My Curls. Paul Johann Ludwig Heyse. RiWo

Shall I, Wasting in Despair, *also given in* Fidelia. George Wither. *Fr.* Fair Virtue, the Mistress of Philarete. EIL; LiTB; OxAEP-1; SCGP

Shall keep the blessed spirit that I praise. (*LL*) Canzone: He Beseeches Death for the Life of Beatrice. Dante. AWP

Shall last and shine when all of these are gone. (*LL*) Contemplations. Anne Bradstreet. AmPP; EAP; PoEL-3, *abr.*; SCAP; WPE, *abr.*

Shall lead the world the way to rest. (*LL*) Evening. Charles Cotton. PoEL-3; WiR

Shall, like a hallowed Lamp, for ever burn. (*LL*) Eternity of Love Protested. Thomas Carew. BeJo; MeLP

Shall live my Highland Mary. (*LL*) Highland Mary. Burns. AWP; EnRP; GTBS; GTBS-P; OBEV; TrGrPo; WBLP

Shall long keep his memory green in our souls. (*LL*) Oh, Breathe Not His Name! Thomas Moore. EnRP

Shall make. I place it in your hands: hold it in trust. (*LL*) And God saw everything that He had made, and found it very good. *Unknown.* EaPr

Shall Man, O God of Light. Timothy Dwight. AH

Shall mine eyes behold the glory, O my country? After Death. Fanny Parnell. IIP

Shall not be numbered with the dead. (*LL*) At a Friends' Meeting. Mary Elizabeth Coleridge. WPE

Shall one day mark the Port which ruled the Western seas. (*LL*) The Cotton Boll. Henry Timrod. AmPP

Shall place you living in your land. (*LL*) The New Ezekiel. Emma Lazarus. AmWP

Shall pour such splendour as your heart to me. (*LL*) Most Lovely Shade ("Most lovely dark, my Æthiopia born.") Edith Sitwell. FaBoTw; GTBS-P

Shall pride a heap of sculptur'd marble raise. Epitaph on Laurence Sterne. David Garrick. FaBoEE

Shall reach a judge who never can be bribed. (*LL*) Unhappy Boston. Paul Revere. AiP; PAH

Shall rise the glorious thought — I am with Thee. (*LL*) Still, Still, with Thee. Harriet Beecher Stowe. AH; BLRP

Shall royal praise be rhym'd by such a ribald. On the Candidates for the Laurel. Pope. FaBoEE

Shall silence shroud such sin. A Delcaration of the Death of John Lewes. Thomas Gilbart. NoSic

Shall sleep and sleep for ever. (*LL*) From the Antique. Christina Rossetti. EnLoPo

Shall still drink in the warmth and relish the light. (*LL*) In the Evening Glow. Franz Kugler. RiWo

Shall still revive and flourish in the dust. (*LL*) Childhood. Thomas Traherne. TrGrPo

Shall the Dead Praise Thee? George Macdonald. TrCP

Shall the voice of peace bring sweet release to the men behind the guns! (*LL*) The Men behind the Guns. John Jerome Rooney. BLPA; FaBoBe; PAH

Shall the water not remember Ember. Narcissus and Echo. Fred Chappell. MT

Shall Then Another. Kenneth Mackenzie. NOBAu

Shall then another do what I have done. Shall Then Another. Kenneth Mackenzie. NOBAu

Shall turn and welcome me at the door. (*LL*) The Wizard's Funeral. Richard Watson Dixon. ELP; NOBVV; PeVV

Shall we be there in time? Nursery Rhyme 1984. Paul Coltman. PAW

Shall we be thus for ever? (*LL*) Memory of Brother Michael. Patrick Kavanagh. MoAB

Shall we come out of it all, some day, as one does from a. Arthur Hugh Clough. *Fr.* Amours de Voyage. EBVVPR, *sect.* V, ix; NOBVV

Shall We Go A-Shearing? Mother Goose. *See* Old woman, old woman,/ Shall we go a-shearing?

Shall we go dance the hay? The hay? A Report Song [in a Dream]. Nicholas Breton. GBL; NoSic
(Country Song.) TrGrPo
(Wooing in a Dream.) NOBE

Shall we have a family born. For Walter Lowenfels. Wendy Rose. CDW

Shall we make love. *Unknown, tr. by* Arthur Waley. *Fr.* Manyo Shu, Part 3 of 4. AWP

Shall we not open the human heart. Give Way! Charlotte Perkins Gilman. WGRP

Shall we send back the Johnnies their bunting. Those Rebel Flags. John H. Jewett. PAH

Shall we sit here some more. August at the Lake. David Young. AmPA

Shall we win at love or shall we lose. Hôtel Transylvanie. Frank O'Hara. NeAP; PoM

Shall well appear and by my death be seen. (*LL*) Sun hath twice brought forth[e] the tender green, The. The Earl of Surrey. SiPSBD

Shall whet their knives, and think of you. (*LL*) What, still alive at twenty – two. Hugh Kingsmill. FaBoCo; NOBL; UV

Shall you complain who feed the world? To Labor. Charlotte Perkins Gilman. PoLF

Shallow Shallow Brown. (*LL*) Blow, Boys, Blow [*or* Blow, Bullies, Blow]. *Unknown.* FaBoVe

Shallow voice said, bitterly, "New friend!," A. My New Friend. Helen Hunt Jackson. AmWP

Shallows, brighter, The. The Pier: Under Pisces. James Merrill. LCAP; NoAM

Shalom Aleichem. *Unknown, tr. fr.* Hebrew. TrJP

Shaman. María Sabina, *tr. fr.* Spanish *by* Henry Munn. WPOW

Shaman Breaks. Gerald Vizenor. HATNAP

Shaman Song. Luswat, *tr. fr.* Tlingit Indian *by* James Koller. STP

Shamash of the glade, The. The Venerable Bee. A. M. Klein. TrJP

Shame. Richard Wilbur. FaBoMo; OxBC

Shame. C. K. Williams. PWE

Shame and ruin wait for you! (*LL*) Boadicea; an Ode. William Cowper. BeLS; FaBoEH; FaPoR

Shame checks our first attempts, but then 'tis proved. Sins Loathed, and Yet Loved. Robert Herrick. LiTB

Shame Kept My Tears Away. Mutanabbi, *tr. fr.* Arabic *by* Omar S. Pound. ArPe

Shame to all my thoughts now. On the Flightiness of Thought. *Unknown, tr. fr.* Irish *by* Brendan Kennelly. TIRV

Shame ye not that all things are gold but you. (*LL*) Ad Henricum Wottonem. Thomas Bastard. FaBoEE; FaBoPP

Shamed by the Creature. Mildmay Fane, 2d Earl of Westmorland. NOSC

Shameful Death. William Morris. ChTr; GTBS-P; PeVV

Shameful Impotence. Ovid. *See* Either she was foule, or her attire was bad.

Shampoo, The. Elizabeth Bishop. FaBoWP; OxBC; VCAP

Shan Van Vocht, The. *Unknown.* FaBoPV; GBP; OxBoLi

Shan Van Vocht, The. *Unknown.* OxBoLi

Shancoduff. Patrick Kavanagh. BIrV; CIP; FaBoTw; IIP; IPY; NoP; PeIV

Shandon Bells, The. Francis Sylvester Mahony. *See* With deep affection/ And recollection.

Shane O'Neill's Cairn. Robinson Jeffers. NoAM; NOBA

Shaneen and Maurya Prendergast. Patch-Shaneen. J. M. Synge. FaBoVe

Shang ya! Oath of Friendship. *Unknown, tr. fr.* Chinese. ArLo, *tr. by* Arthur Waley; OBF; TTTS, *tr. by* Arthur Waley

Shanghai Customs, The. The Clock Tower. Shanghai Serenade I. Kung Liu, *tr. fr.* Chinese. *Fr.* Shanghai Lyrics. LHF, *tr. by* Hualing Nieh

Shanghai Lyrics., sels. Kung Liu.
Shanghai Serenade I. LHF, *tr. by* Hualing Nieh
Shanghai Serenade II. LHF, *tr. by* Hualing Nieh
To a Black Sailor. LHF, *tr. by* Hualing Nieh
To the Huang-pu River. LHF, *tr. by* Hualing Nieh

Shanghai Serenade II. Kung Liu, *tr. fr.* Chinese. *Fr.* Shanghai Lyrics. LHF, *tr. by* Hualing Nieh

Shanghai Serenade I. Kung Liu, *tr. fr.* Chinese. *Fr.* Shanghai Lyrics. LHF, *tr. by* Hualing Nieh

Shango ("Shango is an animal like the gorilla.") *Unknown, tr. fr.* Yoruba *by* Gbadamosi *and* Ulli Beier. PBA, *st.* 1; TTY, (*st.* 1)

Shango ("Shango is the death who kills money with a big stick.") *Unknown, tr. fr.* Yoruba *by* Gbadamosi *and* Ulli Beier. TTY

Shannon and Chesapeake. *Unknown. See* Chesapeake and Shannon ("The Chesapeake so bold.")

Shannon and the *Chesapeake*, The. Thomas Tracy Bouvé. PAH

Shannon Estuary Welcoming the Fish, The. Nuala Ni Dhomhnaill, *tr. fr.* Irish *by the author.* CIP

Shantih shantih shantih. Edward Pygge. BXAP

Shanty Boys and the Pine, The. *Unknown.* AmFP

Shantyman's Life, A. *Unknown.* AmFP; AS

Shao and the South. Confucius, *tr. fr.* Chinese *by* Ezra Pound. CTC
Sels.
"Chkk! chkk!" hopper-grass
"Three stars, five stars rise over the hill"

Shapcot, to thee the Fairy [*or* faery] State. Oberon's Feast. Robert Herrick. BeJo; CaPo; NOSC; SeCV-1; TrGrPo

Shape-Changer, The. Chris Wallace-Crabbe. NOBAu

Shape, like folded light, embodied air, A. Aishah Schechinah. Robert Stephen Hawker. OBNC

Shape of a Roethke, The? Theodore Roethke Foots It. D. C. Berry. BXAP

Shape of Air. Robert Wells. SCBI

Shape of Autumn, The. Virginia Russ. GoYe

Shape of Death, The. May Swenson. TAP

Shape of the Fire, The. Theodore Roethke. CMoP; LCAP; LiTA; MoAB; VCAP

Shape of the summer has not changed at all, The. Landscape without Figures. Phyllis McGinley. ArOW

Shape the lips to an *o*, say *a*. Ö. Rita Dove. HCAP; WeW

Shaped and vacated. The Event. T. Sturge Moore. OBMV

Shaped new to your measure. Ark Articulate. Jay Macpherson. *Fr.* Ark, The. NOBC

Shaped tent to pick him up again. (*LL*) The New York City World's Fairs, 1939 and 1964. Judith Baumel. UTF

Shapes and Signs. James Clarence Mangan. PeIV

Shapes of Death, The. Stephen Spender. OBMV

Shards, The, sels. Michael O'Loughlin.
Boys of '69, The. IB
Bunkers, The. IB; PBCIP
Concert-Going in Vienna. IB
Frank Ryan Dead in Dresden. IB
From A Diary. IB
Heinrich Böll in Ireland. IB
Shards, the. IB

Shards, The. Michael O'Loughlin. *Fr.* Shards, The. IB

Share-Croppers. Langston Hughes. SAmP

Share my harvest and my home. (*LL*) Ruth. Thomas Hood. BoLoP; ChIV-1; EnLoPo; EnRP; GN; NOBE; OBEV; OBNC; PIP

Share wholly. The purist's God. Pride's mirror and island. (*LL*) Emily Dickinson's Mirror, Amherst. Donald Revell. UTF

Sharing Eve's Apple. Keats. *See* O Blush Not So! O Blush Not So!

Shark, The. E. J. Pratt. NOBC; OBAP

Sharks, The. Denise Levertov. NeAP

Sharks at the New York Aquarium. Charles Martin. SM

Sharks in Shallow Water. Fred Levinson. AmPA

Shark's Parlor, The. James Dickey. MT; NYBP

Sharks tooth is perfect for biting, The. Canticle. Michael McClure. NeAP; PoM

Sharon Will Be No/Where on Nobody's Best-selling List. Sharon Scott. JB

Sharp is the night, but stars with frost alive. Winter Heavens. George Meredith. NoP

Sharp Ridge, The. Robert Graves. FaBoEE

Sharpen the sword in the Sobbing Waters. Tu Fu, *tr. fr.* Chinese *by* Irving Y. Lo. *Fr.* Frontier Songs, First Series. SuSp

Sharpeville Inquiry. Anne Welsh. PeSA

Shash, The. *Unknown.* APAS

Shatterday nite aucung lau town. My Deery Honey. *Unknown.* PBCV

Shattered water made a misty din, The. Once by the Pacific. Robert Frost. CMoP; HAP; HeIP; LiTA; LiTM; MeMAP; MoAB; MoAmPo; NAAL-2; NOBA; PrIm; Son; TRP; VGW; WeW

Shattering of Love, The. *Gond Oral Tradition, tr. by* V. Elwin *and* S. Hivale. WTO

Shaving. Stephen Dobyns. NAmP90

Shaving cuts. The pallor of bad habits. Seamus Heaney. *Fr.* Crossings. BAP-90

Shavings, fall from the carved stick. Working Song. Buluguru, *tr. fr. Yaoro by* E. A. Worms. CBAP

She. Zinaida Nikolayevna Gippius, *tr. fr. Russian by* Dianne Levitin. WPOW

She. Theodore Roethke. BoLoP; ErPo

She. Mark Strand. AnAn

She. Richard Wilbur. AmPP

She, a beautician, came to see her friend. The Beautician. Thom Gunn. BAP-91

She always leaned to watch for us. The Watcher. Margaret Widdemer. OHIP

"She always seems so tied" is what friends say. Just to Be Needed. Mary Eversley. PoToHe

She always tries. Cat Bath. Aileen Fisher. ZA

She, and comparisons are odious. *(LL)* The Comparison. John Donne. PeLV

She and her parents escaped, but she still whispers. The Nightmare. Van K. Brock. BTR

She and I. Norman Cameron. OxBSP; RB

She and the Muse. Denise Levertov. CrSp

She answers the bothersome telephone, takes the message. Alzheimer's: The Wife. C. K. Williams. VCAP

She appears, present there. *(LL)* Autumn Garden. Dino Campana. STV

She, as a veil down to the slender waist. Milton. *Fr.* Paradise Lost. EPCY; ErPo

She asked brown eyes, "Burn me loose." Seal at Stinson Beach. Roberta Hill Whiteman. VoR

She asked me twice. Pity. William Mills. MT

She Attempts to Refute the Praises That Truth, Which She Calls Passion, Inscribed on a Portrait of the Poet. Sister Juana Inés de la Cruz, *tr. fr. Spanish.* BoWoP

She bade me follow to her garden, where. Snap-Dragon. D. H. Lawrence. ErPo

She Began to Wash His Feet with Tears and Wipe Them with the Hairs of Her Head. Richard Crashaw. NOSC

She Begining to Study Phisick, Takes Her Leave of Poetry. Jane Barker. KTR

She begins, and my grandmother joins her. I Ask My Mother to Sing. Li-Young Lee. OpBo

She begins to board the flight. White Bear. Joy Harjo. SRLS

She Being Brand. E. E. Cummings. ErPo; FaBoBl; MoP; NOBA; OxBA; PeLV

(New; and you.) PeLV

She Bewitched Me. Thomas Burbidge. EnLoPo

She beyond all others in deepest dreams comes. A Little Song. Charles O. Hartman. SM

She bites into the red skin. My Love Eats an Apple. Ralph Gustafson. MoCV

She Boasts of Her Constancy. Johann Rist, *tr. fr. German by* George C. Schoolfield. GePo

She bounded o'er the graves. Anna Playing in a Graveyard. Caroline Gilman. OBCA

She brings that breath, and music too. The Visitor. W. H. Davies. GBL; OBWVE

She brought a drinking-cup to him. Two. Hugo von Hofmannsthal, *tr. fr. German by* Jethro Bithell. TrJP

She brought us a month noisy with rain. Full Moon in Malta. "Asphodel." BrRo

She burnt like ho[ll]y gren. *(LL)* Young Hunting. *Unknown.* ESPB; OxBB

She Called Him Mr. *Unknown.* FaPON

She calved in the ravine, beside. November Calf. Jane Kenyon. InPS

She came among us from the South. Enrica, 1865. Christina Rossetti. NALW; TEP

She Came and Went. James Russell Lowell. AnAmPo

She came every morning to draw water. A Drink of Water. Seamus Heaney. OxBC; TRP

She came home, my Lord, and smashed-in the television. Wife Who Smashed Television Gets Jail. Paul Durcan. CIP

She came in from the snowing air. Ice. Stephen Spender. FaBoMo; GTBS-P

She came in reluctant. The dark shed. Teaching a Dumb Calf. Ted Hughes. AnAn

She came through the room like an answer in long division. A Victorian Idyll. David Wagoner. NoAM

She came to him in dreams — her ears. Cowper's Tame Hare. Norman Nicholson. RB

She came/ to hunt me down; carried down-ladder trussed. Dream: The Loba Reveals Herself. Diane Di Prima. *Fr.* Loba. SRLS

She came to the village church. Tennyson. *Fr.* Maud[: A Monodrama]. EBVV; EnVR; NAEL-2

She came up the hill carrying water. The Achill Woman. Eavan Boland. BiHa

She came walking. Parable. Bob Orr. PeNZ

She cannot love, and therefore thou must die! *(LL)* Corydon to His Phyllis. Sir Edward Dyer. EIL

She carefully regards her software. The amber. Nude Reclining at Word Processor, in Pastel. Carl Conover. GOYP

She carried a book, either to imply. Hilda Doolittle ("H. D."). *Fr.* Tribute to the Angels. NALW

She carries it unsteadily, warily. A Young Girl with a Pitcher Full of Water. David Wagoner. NoAM

She clasps the cup with both her hands. In a Café. Rosemary Dobson. CBAP

She cleaned house, and then lay down long. A Secret Gratitude. James Wright. NoAM

She climbs from the sea; moonlight. The Fish. Mary Oliver. CAPP

She closed her eyes when she made love. In Memory of Forgetting. Cyn Zarco. BCF

She coaxes her fat in front of her. New Day. Naomi Long Madgett. BlSi

She comes level with him at. Donahue's Sister. Thom Gunn. NoAM

She Comes Not When Noon Is on the Roses. Herbert Trench. OBEV

She comes on drenched in a perfume called Self Satisfaction. Mae West. Edward Field. FYAP

She comes! — the spirit of the dance! Celeste Dancing. Frances Sargent Osgood. AnAmPo

She could die laughing. Minnie and Mrs. Hoyne. Kenneth Fearing. PoRA

She could not have made it. Madame Orchidée. Sherod Santos. AnAn

She could not remember anything about the voyage. The Migrant. A. L. Hendricks. PBCV

She Cries. John Montague. BiHa

She danced, near nude, to tom-tom beat. Zalka Peetruza. Ray Garfield Dandridge. PoBA

She dealt her pretty words like blades. Emily Dickinson. HAP

She deserted you. Horse on the Wall. Marcia Southwick. NAmP90

"She did evil that good might come." May God be merciful. *(LL)* Angel Boley. Stevie Smith. EBNV

She did not climb the April Hill. The April Hill. Janet Lewis. CRP

She did not love to love, but hated him. The End of It. Francis Thompson. NOBVV; OxBSP

She didn't know he was so shook. California Crack, THe. Wanda Coleman. NGP

She didn't know she was beautiful. On Getting a Natural. Dudley Randall. PoBA

She died after the beautiful snow had melted. In Memorial. J. Gordon Coogler. OBAL

She died, as many travellers have died. Found Frozen. Helen Hunt Jackson. AmWP

"She died as she lived, sniffing cocaine." *(LL)* Cocaine Lil [and Morphine Sue]. *Unknown.* AS; CBNP; GBP; MAT; OxBoLi; RB

She died full long agone! *(LL)* Meg Merrilies [or Merrilees]. Keats. BoTP; ELP; FaBoCh; FaPON; OxBChV; PlP; TEP

She died in the upstairs bedroom. Death in Leamington. Sir John Betjeman. NoP; OxAEP-2; RB

She died, of course. *(LL)* Poor Old Lady. *Unknown.* OBCA

She died turning aside from the sink. Another Death. D. E. Borrell. FF

She does, always manages to make herself distinguished. *(LL)* Wife is like a blade of grass, A. Jean-Joseph Rabéarivelo. NegPo

She does not know. No Images. Waring Cuney. CDC; MAT; NIP; TTY

She doesn't say a word, concentrating on one thing only. Balgu Song. *Unknown, tr. fr. Balgu by* Clancy McKenna. CBAP

She don't have no sense. *(LL)* Admonitions. Lucille Clifton. BPo; CAPP; NALW; NMM

She dreamed they lived in Africa. Long History of the Short Poem. Paul Hoover. UL

She dressed his words in. Nuclear Unit. Valerie Sinason. DT

She drew an angel down. *(LL)* Alexander's Feast; or, The Power of Music [or Musique]. Dryden. FaPoR; GN; GTBS; GTBS-P; LiTB; NAEL-1; NOBE; OAEL-1; OtMeF, *ll.* 1–15; PeECV; SeCV-2; TFi; TrGrPo; WiR

She drew back; he was calm. The Subverted Flower. Robert Frost. CMoP; HAP; MeMAP; MoP; NoAM; NOBA; OxBA; PoE; Poetr

She dried her tears, and they did smile. Emily Brontë. NOBVV

She drinks of your soul; it flows — currents from finger and toe. *(LL)* A Kiss from Her. Rufinus Domesticus. STV

She Drives. Sophie Cabot Black. LoHo

She Dwelt among the Untrodden Ways. J. C. Squire. BXAP

She Dwelt among the Untrodden Ways. Wordsworth. *Fr.* Lucy. AWP; BLPA; BoLoP; EBEV; EBEvV; ELP; EnLoPo; EnRP; FaBV; FF; FHYEP; GBL; HAP; HeIL; HeIP; ImPo; IMW; LiTB; MeMBP; NIP; NOBE; NoP; OAEL-2; OBEV; OBNC; OxAEP-2; OxBSP; Poetr; PPP; PrIm; PWR; SCGP; TEP; TFi; TrGrPo; UnPo; UV; WeW

She enter into his Great House. Loveact. Grace Nichols. VBLP

She entertained his eyes. *(LL)* An Apologie for Having Loved Before. Edmund Waller. CBLP

She even thinks that up in heaven. For a Lady I Know. Countee Cullen. *Fr.* Four Epitaphs. CDC; HeIL; HeIP; InPK; NIP; OBAL; PoBA; PoNe; TAP; TRP
(Lady I Know, A.) MoAmPo

She ever since has kept her word. *(LL)* Meddlesome Matty. Ann Taylor. OxBChV

She examines her hand, fingers spread wide. My Daughter Considers Her Body. Floyd Skloot. SM

She fears him, and will always ask. Eros Turannos. E. A. Robinson. CMoP; GBL; HAP; HeIP; LiTA; LiTM; MeMAP; MoAB; MoAmPo; MoP; NAAL-2; NoAM; NOBA; NoP; OxBA; PoA; PoE; Poetr; TAP; TFi; TRP

She feels her presence as never. The Lost Carnival. Fred Chappell. GOYP

She fell asleep on Christmas Eve. My Sister's Sleep. Dante Gabriel Rossetti. EnVR; NAEL-2

She fell away in her first ages spring. Spenser. *Fr.* Daphnaïda. OBEV

She finds grief, her meat. Hyena. Carol Muske. AmPA

She finds the fountain where they wailed 'Mirage!' *(LL)* The Ancient Sage. Tennyson. WGRP

She flees, she flees through flat white lands, as patiently I take my aim. Song of the Initiate. Léopold Sédar Senghor, *tr. fr. French by* Ellen Conroy Kennedy. NegPo

She flourished in the Twenties, "hectic" days of peace. Mews Flat Mona. William Plomer. FaBoTw

She fluted with her mouth as when one sips. Beauty and the Bird. Dante Gabriel Rossetti. FM

She folds her wings about her sleeping child. *(LL)* Bats. Randall Jarrell. GrPl; NTCP; NU; OBCA; RFM

She followed him all afternoon. Looking for Camels. Selima Hill. NBrP

She found him drownd in Yarrow. *(LL)* Rare Willie Drowned in Yarrow; or, The Water o Gamrie. *Unknown.* ESPB

She Found Me Roots. R. W. Ransford. BXAP

She frowned and called him Mr. She Called Him Mr. *Unknown.* FaPON

She gambol'd on the greens. Olivia. Tennyson. *Fr.* Talking Oak, The. GN

She gave it out as if it were. The Aphrodisiac. Medbh McGuckian. PBCIP

She gave me childhood's flowers. Heirloom. Kathleen Raine. NALW

"She gives herself;" there's a poetic thought. Portrait in Black Paint, with a Very Sparing Use of Whitewash. Elinor Wylie. NALW

She glides along — the solitary-hearted. *(LL)* She Was a Queen. Hartley Coleridge. OxAEP-2

She goes but softly, but she goeth sure. Upon the [*or* a] Snail. Bunyan. ChTr; OxBSP

She goes down the steps and picks the cherry flowers. *(LL)* A Girl Combs Her Hair. Li Ho. PLT

She goes on with her story. Mother and Son. Alden Nowlan. RaBo

She goes out in the night again. The Wastrel-Woman Poem. Brenda Marie Osbey. MT

She goes with her pot for water. Who Can Tell? *Gond Oral Tradition*, *tr. by* V. Elwin *and* S. Hivale. WTO

She grew ninety years through sombre winter. Epitaph on a Fir-Tree. Richard Murphy. FaBoTw

She grew up in bedeviled southern wilderness. The Ballad of Sue Ellen Westerfield. Robert Hayden. AmPP; NoAM

She had a bad face, which did always molest her. *(LL)* Epitaph on Dr. Keene's Wife. Thomas Gray. FaBoEE

She had a little time to think. Leda Reconsidered. Mona Van Duyn. NMM

She Had a Name. Edward Thomas. *See* She had a name among the children.

She had a name among the children. A Cat. Edward Thomas.
(She Had a Name.) OxBSP

She had corn flowers in her ear. Gipsy Jane. William Brighty Rands. BoTP; FaPON

She had looked for his coming as warriors come. Love's Coming. Ella Wheeler Wilcox. AnAmPo

She had no business doin' it, but she come o' the East. The Peeler's Lament. *Unknown.* WTO

She had no saying dark enough. The Oft-Repeated Dream. Robert Frost. *Fr.* Hill Wife, The. CMoP; HAP; InPS; LiTM; NoP; Poetr

She had not died to-day. *(LL)* An Elegy on That [*or* the] Glory of Her Sex, Mrs. Mary Blaize. Goldsmith. FaBoNo; PIP

She had not held her secret long enough. The Visitation. Elizabeth Jennings. MoBS

She had raised the window. Destination: Tule Lake Relocation Center, May 20, 1942. Jim Mitsui. ETG; OpBo

She Had Some Horses. Joy Harjo. HATNAP

She had thought the studio would keep itself. Living in Sin. Adrienne Rich. FF; IHMS; NIP; NoP; NYBP; Poetr; SoSe; TAP; UnPo

She had to be Milked by a Man and his Wife. *(LL)* The Cow. Theodore Roethke. FiBHP; OBAL; OBCA

She has been condemned to death by hanging. Marrying the Hangman. Margaret Atwood. NOBC

She has begun to see men invite themselves. The Professional. David Ignatow. NNaP

She has calld to her her bower-maidens. Young Hunting. *Unknown.* ESPB

She has come next door to practice our piano. The "Wife Takes a Child." Ellen Bryant Voigt. CrSp; SM

She has decided that she no longer loves me. The Wind in the Tree. F. T. Prince. OxBSP

She has finished and sealed the letter. Parting, without a Sequel. John Crowe Ransom. MeMAP; MoAB; MoAmPo; OxBA; SoSe

She has gone, — she has left us in passion and pride. Brother Jonathan's Lament for Sister Caroline. Oliver Wendell Holmes. PAH

She has gone to the bottom! the wrath of the tide. The *Alabama*. Maurice Bell. PAH

She has had to bear. *(LL)* The Whipping. Robert Hayden. GrPl; PoBA; PoE; SoSe

She has kissed lips already grown inhuman. Cleopatra. "Anna Akhmatova," *tr. fr. Russian by* D. M. Thomas. AIW

She has laughed as softly as if she sighed. A Woman's Shortcomings. Elizabeth Barrett Browning. BLPA

She has left me, my pretty. Sylvia Townsend Warner. MoAB; MoBrPo

"She has no heart," they said, and turned away. In Time of Famine. Helen Hunt Jackson. AmWP

She has not come. Paulus Silentiarius, *tr. fr. Greek by* Andrew Miller. GrAn

She has not found herself a hard pillow. To Clarissa Scott Delany. Angelina Weld Grimké. ShDr

She has not put her face on. *(LL)* On a Painted Woman. Shelley. FaBoCo; NBLV

She has taken a woman lover. Carol, in the Park, Chewing on Straws. Judy Grahn. *Fr.* Common Woman, The. PeHV; WPOW

She has the votes; they know she does. The American Sonnet. Frederick Seidel. *Fr.* AIDS Days. BAP-90

She has withdrawn from us. Maude Meehan. *Fr.* Small Wings. MDDM

She hath an art to break them with her eyes. *(LL)* Thrice Toss [*or* Tosse] These Oaken Ashes in the Air [*or* Ayre]. Thomas Campion. CBLP; EBEV; EIL; EnLoPo; FaBoCh; HAP; MAT; OAEL-1; OxBSP; PoEL-2; PoRA; SCGP; TFi; WeW

She having gainèd both the wind and sun. *(LL)* The Fair Singer. Andrew Marvell. EnLoPo; MeLP; NOBE; NoP; PoEL-2; SCGP

She Hears the Storm. Thomas Hardy. NAEL-2

She hers, he his, pursuing. *(LL)* The Dalliance of the Eagles. Walt Whitman. AmPP; FM; HAP; HeIL; HeIP; NAAL-1; NoP; PPP; PrIm; SAmP; TAP; TRP

She hit her mother forty-one. *(LL)* Lizzie Borden took an axe. *Unknown.*

She/ holds th mirror to her eye. My Lai/ Remuera/ Ponsonby. David Mitchell. PeNZ

She holds the bird a minute to her lips. Poem. Steve Carey. UL

She holds things together, collects bail, Judy Grahn. *Fr.* Common Woman, The. NALW

She holds you by the hair. How She Operates. Grace Caroline Bridges. LoHo

She hopes to hear a word from her. Adoration of the Anchor. Laura Jensen. LCAP

She hovered hooded, blue-eyed. Catechism, 1958. W. M. Ransom. CDW

She Hugged Me and Kissed Me. *Unknown.* BPo

She hung away her years, her eyes grew young. Waiting for the Bus. D. J. Enright. OxBTC

She I loved so much will not appear again. Farewell and Good. Denis Devlin. IPY

She, in dowdy dress and dumpy. Still Life: Lady with Birds. Quandra Prettyman. PoBA

She in whose lipservice. The Goddess. Denise Levertov. LiTM; NALW; NeAP; NOBA; PoM; SRLS

She is a black crow being driven out of sight. Drinking the Wind. Tan Ying, *tr. fr. Chinese* by Kenneth Rexroth *and* Ling Chung. WPC; WPOW

She is a language I will never speak. Babel. Michael O'Loughlin. IB

She is a reed swaying in blue. Earle Thompson. HATNAP

She is a rich and rare land. This Native Land. Thomas Osborne Davis. BoTP

She is a writer. Where it all started? My daughter, *by a German Mother.* Christine McNeill. NWP

She is all so slight. After Two Years. Richard Aldington. MoBrPo

She is all there. For My Lover, Returning to His Wife. Anne Sexton. CBLP; HCAP; IHMS; LPA; NMM; Poetr; UnPo; WPE

She is as in a field a silken tent. The Silken Tent. Robert Frost. AmPP; BLPL; HeIL; ImPo; InPK; NOBA; Son; TAP; TRP; TwCP; WeW

She is coming towards me. Good Ghost, Gaunt Ghost. Peter Porter. FaBoMA

She is committed to the earth and the earth. Canaan. Muriel Spark. NYBP

She is dead. Birthdays. Hilde Domin, *tr. fr. German* by Tudor Morris. BoWoP

She is dead at twenty-seven. Vicente. Antionia Quintana Pigno. AfAz

"She is dead!" they said to him. "Come away." He and She. Sir Edwin Arnold. BLPA

She is facetious, of a gentle nature. Epigram VII: Winifred. Hugh Crompton. NOSC

She Is Far from the Land. Thomas Hood. FaBoNo; WiR

She Is Far from the Land. Thomas Moore. EnRP; FaBoNo; NOIV; OBNC; OxAEP-2; WiR

She is gathering lotos-seed in the river of Yueh. The Girl of Yueh. Li Po, *tr. fr. Chinese* by Robert Payne. TAL

She is gentil and al so wise. That Ever I Saw. *Unknown.* TrGrPo

She is gone, she is lost, she is found, she is ever fair. My Woe Must Ever Last. Sir Walter Ralegh. ElL

She is gone! The occasion for ever is past! Lines Written Immediately after Parting from a Lady. Sir Samuel Egerton Brydges. NOEC

She is in your painting the one you bought when the taxi. Framed. Claire Harris. PBCV

She is large and matronly. Lui et Elle. D. H. Lawrence. NoAM

She/ Is like/ A wrinkled apple. An Old Slave Woman. Joyce Sims Carrington. ShDr

She is like pearls, of course, and rubies, and other. Valentine. Hollis Spurgeon Summers. GoYe

She is like snow. My Youngest Daughter Getting Up in the Morning. Adèle Davide. Mes

She is long sword shining. Poplar. Liu Sha-ho, *tr. fr. Chinese. Fr. Family of Plants, A.* LHF, *tr. by* Hualing Nieh

She Is More to Be Pitied than Censured. William B. Gray. BeLS; BLPA

She is most fair. The Unknown. Edward Thomas. ArLo; GBL

She Is No Liar. Robert Graves. OxBSP

She is not dead, but sleepeth. Mrs. Rebecca Weston. Mary Weston Fordham. CBWP-2

She Is Not Fair. Hartley Coleridge. *See* She is not fair to outward view.

She Is Not Fair to Outward View. Hartley Coleridge. EnRP; OBEV

She is not fair to outward view. She Is Not Fair to Outward View. Hartley Coleridge. EnRP; OBEV
(She Is Not Fair.) FaBV
(Song.) OxAEP-2

She Is Not for Me. *Unknown, tr. by* V. Elwin *and* S. Hivale. WTO

She is not sure. An Old Thought for a New Couple. E. A. Markham. PBCV

She is now water and air. Sea Burial from the Cruiser "Reve." Richard Eberhart. NYBP

She is older than the rocks among which she sits. Mona Lisa. Walter Pater. OBMV

She is purposeless as a cyclone; she must move. Cubist Portrait. Marjorie Allen Seiffert. PoA

She is shameless, despicable, vile. She. Zinaida Nikolayevna Gippius, *tr. fr. Russian* by Dianne Levitin. WPOW

She is sixty. She lives. The Greatest Love. Anna Swirszczynska, *tr. fr. Polish* by Czeslaw Milosz *and* Leonard Nathan. PoSu

She is slim again. A Baby in the House. Patrick Williams. PNI

She is so proper and so pure. My Sweet Sweeting. *Unknown.* CH

She is so young, and never never before. Edward Davison. ErPo

She is standing on my lids. Lady Love. Paul Éluard, *tr. fr. French.* ArLo; OBVE, *tr. by* Samuel Beckett

She is teck'wi. The Taboo Woman. *Unknown, tr. fr. Zuni Indian by* K. Kennedy. WTO

She is that kind of a wife. She can see. Gertrude Stein. *Fr.* Sonatina Followed by Another, A. VBLP

She is the fairies' midwife, and she comes. Shakespeare. *Fr.* Romeo and Juliet. RB
(Mercutio Describes Queen Mab.) TrGrPo

She Is the Greatest Wealth. Georg Rudolph Weckherlin, *tr. fr. German* by George C. Schoolfield. GePo

She is the one you call sister. The Mirror in Which Two Are Seen as One. Adrienne Rich. NAAL-2; NNaP

She is the thing that she despises. (*LL*) A Hue and Cry after Fair Amoret. Congreve. NOEC; OBEV

She is the woman hanging from the 13th floor. The Woman Hanging from the Thirteenth Floor Window. Joy Harjo. GLP; HATNAP

She is touching the cycle — her tender tread. Tennessee. Virginia Fraser Boyle. PAH

She is tougher than me, harder. For My Mother. Iain Crichton Smith. OxBS

She is using. Persephone, 5, Outside. Keith Abbott. UL

She is washed by white-water, white if she looked up. Fish. Daniel Halpern. AmPA

She is yours! She is yours! (*LL*) Night in Spring. Joseph Freiherr von Eichendorff. RiWo

She issues radiant from her dressing-room. George Meredith. *Fr.* Modern Love. EnVR; NOBVV

She juliets him from a window in Soho. Short Time. Gavin Ewart. NoAM

She just hauls out and smacks him. Homeric. Richard Jackson. NAmP90

She keeps the memory-game. The Net. Fleur Adcock. PeNZ

She kept her secret well, oh, yes. My Angeline. Harry Bache Smith. NBLV

She kept her songs, they took so little space. Love Songs in Age. Philip Larkin. PPP

She kneads/ deep into the night. Don't Talk to Me about Bread. E. A. Markham. PBCV

She kneeled before me begging. Confession. Donald Jeffrey Hayes. CDC

She kneeled before the dead lamb weeping. Synekdechestai. Constance M. Schmid. GoYe

She knew how to use. Honey in the Flesh. David Trinidad. BAP-91

She knows. (*LL*) Splendid Moments. Alma Villanueva. SRLS

She knows them all. Urchins. Beggars. The Left Eye of Odin. Regina DeCormier-Shekejian. LoHo

She knows where to get cracked eggs, does Nelly. Old Nelly's Birthday. Ruth Pitter. NALW

She laid it where the sunbeams fall. Motherhood. Charles Stuart Calverley. FM

She laughs to see his bobbing dance. (*LL*) The Waltzer in the House. Stanley Kunitz. ErPo; GoJo; NYBP

She Lay All Naked in Her Bed. *Unknown.* BoLoP; ErPo

She lay all night beside me. Paulus Silentiarius, *tr. fr. Greek* by Andrew Miller. GrAn

She lay, and serving-men her lithe arms took. Abishag. Rainer Maria Rilke, *tr. fr. German* by Jethro Bithell. AWP

She lay as if at play. Emily Dickinson. LiTA

She lay beside me in the dawn. (*LL*) Alba. Ezra Pound. GBL; HAP; SOTW; WeW

She lay in her girlish sleep at ninety-six. Castoff Skin. Ruth Whitman. InPK

She Lay Wrapped. Gail Fox. NOBC

She Lays ("She lays each beautifully mooned finger.") Molly Peacock. EOEF

She leaned her back unto a thorn. The Cruel Mother. *Unknown.* ESPB

She leaned her head upon her hand. Vashti. Frances E. W. Harper. AAP; AIW; AmWP; BlSi; NALW

She leans across a golden table. For Amy Lowell. Countee Cullen. PoA

She learned early that in order to survive. The Survivor. John C. Pine. BTR

She leaves her soldier — *famine* and a *name!.* (*LL*) The American Soldier. Philip Freneau. TAP

She leaves the motor running. Shadow Play. Ralph Angel. NAmP90

She left me at the silent time. Lines Written in the Bay of Lerici. Shelley. OAEL-2

She let her golden ball fall down the well. The Frog and the Golden Ball. Robert Graves. NoP

She licked my salty nose. Old People. Michael Davitt, *tr. fr. Irish* by Michael Hartnett. PBCIP

She lies and watches the Weaver Girl meet the Herdboy Star. (*LL*) Autumn Evening. Tu Mu. PLT

She lies by the man her husband. The Wife of Winter's Tale. Michael Dennis Browne. SM

She lies far inland, and no stick nor stone of her. Inland City. John Crowe Ransom. CMoP

She lies on her left side her flank golden. Landscape as a Nude. Archibald MacLeish. *Fr.* Frescoes for Mr. Rockefeller's City. AmPP; CMoP; UnPo

She, like the morning, is still fresh and fair. Her Praises. Anthony Scoloker. EiL

She liked mornings the best — Thomas gone. Weathering Out. Rita Dove. LCAP; NoAM

She lived in storm and strife. That the Night Come. W. B. Yeats. PoEL-5

She lived long, till God gave her rest. (*LL*) A Cat. Edward Thomas.

She lives a prisoner within. The Shut-In. Nellie De Hearn. PoToHe

She lives in the porter's room; the plush is nicotined. Bitter Sanctuary. Harold Monro. FaBoMo; LiTB; OBMV

She Looked At the Sun. Tadeusz Rózewicz, *tr. fr. Polish by* Magnus F. Krynski. PoSu

She looked over his shoulder. The Shield of Achilles. W. H. Auden. EBEV; FaBoMo; FaBoPV; GTBS-P; HAP; NAEL-2; NoAM; NOBE; NOCV; NoP; OxAEP-2; PeECV; PoA; PoE; WeW

She looked to east, she looked to west. Mater Dei. Katharine Tynan. TIRV

She looks out in the blue morning. The Window. Conrad Aiken. CMoP

She looks out the window. The Journey Home. Irena Klepfisz. BTR

She Lost Her Sheep. J. Moyr Smith. FaBoNo

She Loves. Olga Broumas. GLP

She loves, and she confesses too. Honour. Abraham Cowley. BoLoP

She loves him . . . and what small child could deny. Americanized. Bruce Dawe. CBAP

She loves the wind. The Old One and the Wind. Clarice Short. IHMS

She made a little shadow-hidden grave. The Dead Faith. Fanny Heaslip Lea. WGRP

She made her crossing. Miss Geeta. Margaret Reckord. AIW

She may not accuse me. Friedrich von Hausen, *tr. fr. German by* Sylvia Stevens. GePo

She Mends an Ancient Wireless. Paul Durcan. PBCIP

She might have borne them had they come. Breaking Point. Sylvia Auxier. GoYe

She might, so noble from head. A Thought from Propertius. W. B. Yeats. OAEL-2; OxBSP

She mixes blue and mauve and green. The Patchwork Quilt. Elizabeth Fleming. BoTP

She mocks the bones in you, as if it had. In Lombardy. Donald Revell. SM

She mourn'd in silence, and was *Di-do-dum.* (*LL*) A Note on the Latin Gerunds. Richard Porson. FaBoCo; FaBoEE

She Moved through the Fair. Padraic Colum. BIrV; InvP; NOIV

She must be free, though I stand bounden still. (*LL*) On a Pair of Garters. Sir John Davies. OPOP; SiPS

She must have been kicked unseen or brushed by a car. Dog's Death. John Updike. Poetr; Poetsp

She never puts her toys away. Patty-Poem. Nick Kenny. PoToHe

She never told her love. Patience on a Monument. Shakespeare. *Fr.* Twelfth Night. TrGrPo

She never was quite one of us. Sleep-Walking Child. Elisabeth Eybers, *tr. fr. Afrikaans by* Jack Cope, Uys Krige, *and* Adèle Naudé. PeSA

She never will say no. (*LL*) I Care Not for These Ladies. Thomas Campion. AAS; ErPo; HAP; NAEL-1; NoP; NoSic; PoE; SCGP

She/ not to be confused with she, a dog. Lady Tactics. Anne Waldman. PoM

She now retraces her steps once more. December Portrait. Kathleen Tankersley Young. ShDr

She of the Impudent Face. Bible, *O.T. Fr.* Proverbs. TrJP

She only knew the birth and death. At Dawn. Arthur Symons. OBNC

She, only she, can please the taste! (*LL*) To an Author. Philip Freneau. AmPP; EAP; NOBA; OxBA

She paces mindlessly her shuttered room. Portrait. Timothy Brownlow. PeIV

She packs the flower beds with leaves. For Fran. Philip Levine. FF; SM

She passed away like morning dew. Early Death. Hartley Coleridge. OBEV

She Passed the Test. He Would Not Let Her Drive. Martin Stokes. PWE

She passes up and down life's various ways. S. E. Celia Laighton Thaxter. AmWP

She peeked out from under. The Missing Patriarch. Michael S. Weaver. PBCAP

She played me false, but that's not why. Our Photograph[s]. Frederick Locker-Lampson. NBLV; NOBL; PeLV

She plucked one thread. Paulus Silentiarius, *tr. fr. Greek by* Andrew Miller. GrAn

She practices a fugue, though it can matter. Suburban Sonnet. Gwen Harwood. CBAP

She practised strathspeying and hornpipes. (*LL*) There was a young lady of Ealing. Allan M. Laing. PeLi

She pricked herd and made her self to blede. (*LL*) Who hath he[a]rd of such[e] cruelty before: Sir Thomas Wyatt. AAS; SiPS; SiPSBD

She Promised She'd Meet Me. *Unknown.* AS

She Proves the Inconsistency of the Desires and Criticism of Men Who Accuse Women of What They Themselves Cause. Sister Juana Inés de la Cruz, *tr. fr. Spanish by* Aliki *and* Willis Barnstone. BoWoP

She put him on a snow-white shroud. The Little Shroud. Letitia Elizabeth Landon. VPP

She puts her face against the wall. She Cries. John Montague. BiHa

She puts on a silken blouse and comes down from the western chamber. Su Man-shu, *tr. by* Wu-chi Liu. *Fr.* Poems Written during My Sojourn in Japan. SuSp

She raises. The Loba Dances. Diane Di Prima. *Fr.* Loba. PoBeRe

She ran in. Love Town. Anne Carson. *Fr.* Life of Towns, The. BAP-90

She re-enters her life. Returning. Linda Pastan. WeW

"She reaped as she sowed, Lo! this is her son." (*LL*) To My Son. Margaret Johnston Grafflin. PoToHe

She recognizes miner's lettuce. Ellen Bass. MDDM

She returned from the clinic. Unhappy Diary Days. Gerald Vizenor. VoR

She roamed the meadows long in hope. Recompensed? H. Cordelia Ray. CBWP-3

"She rode a race on me," Jim chauffeur said. Rim of Red. Bernard Gutteridge. FaBoBl

She rose to His Requirement — dropt. Emily Dickinson. NALW

She Said . . . . Jonathan Henderson Brooks. PoNe

She Said. Walter de la Mare. ELP

She said, Creek Daughter. Beneath the Pole of Proud Raven. Jana Harris. SRLS

She said, "I was not born to mope at home in loneliness." The Ride round the Parapet. Friedrich Rueckert, *tr. fr. German by* James Clarence Mangan. AWP

She said, "I will come back again." She Said. Walter de la Mare. ELP

She said, if tomorrow my world were torn in two. The 5:32. Phyllis McGinley. *Fr.* I Know a Village. NMM; OxBM; WPE

She said: "I'm god and all." Against a Sickness: To the Female Double Principle God. Alan Dugan. NoAM

She said it was pear Robert, but non pear Jennet. (*LL*) I have a newe gardin. *Unknown.* MiEL

She said, "Not only music; brave men marching." She Said . . . . Jonathan Henderson Brooks. PoNe

She said, "Now give me flesh to eat." Cherry. Gene Baro. ErPo

She said she don't love me anymore because I drink whiskey. *Unknown, tr. fr. Kiowa Indian. Fr.* "49" Songs. STP

She said she don't want no man. Faith. Lorenzo Thomas. UL

She said she forgave me. Parted. Clara Ann Thompson. CBWP-2

She said the Jehovah Witness man. 3-31-70. Gayl Jones. *Fr.* Journal. BlSi

She said: the pitying audience melt in tears. Pope. *Fr.* Rape of the Lock, The. EBNV, *abr., canto* V; FHYEP; HAP; ImPo; NoP; OAEL-1; OBNV; PeLV; PoEL-3; TEP; TrGrPo

She Said the Same to Me. *Unknown.* AS

She said, "They gave me of their best." After Aughrim. Emily Lawless. OBEV; PeIV

She said to one: "How glows." Subalterns. Elizabeth Daryush. OBWP

She said, Wear my leather jacket, a looser. How to Dress like a Scary Dyke. Jane Barnes. GLP

She sang beyond the genius of the sea. The Idea of Order at Key West. Wallace Stevens. CMoP; FF; HAP; HCAP; HeIP; MeMAP; MoAB; MoAmPo; MoP; NAAL-2; NAWM-2; NIP; NoAM; NOBA; NoP; OxBA; PoE; Poetr; PPP; PrIm; SAmP; TAP; TFi

She sang the song of the Belgian refugees. The Song. Andrew Waterman. SCBI

She sang this "Song of the Shirt!" (*LL*) The Song of the Shirt. Thomas Hood. CoGr; EBEvV; EBVV; EnRP; FaPoR; GGP; OHCV; TEP; VPP; WBLP

She sat and looked at a picture. Her Son. Ebba M. Leaf. PWR

She sat and sang alway. Christina Rossetti. GBL; NAEL-2

She sat and sewed that hath done me the wrong. Sir Thomas Wyatt. SiPSBD

She sat and wept beside His feet; the weight. "Multum Dilexit." Hartley Coleridge. EnRP

She that but little patience knew. On a Political Prisoner. W. B. Yeats. FaBoPV; IIP; OAEL-2; OBMV

She That Denies Me I Would Have. Thomas Heywood. *Fr.* Rape of Lucrece, The. ErPo

She that holds me under the laws of love. Sir Arthur Gorges. GBL

She That Is Memory's Daughter. Vernon Watkins. NYBP

She that, oh, broke her faith, would soon break thee. (*LL*) A Jet Ring Sent. John Donne. CBLP; OxBSP

She, the mirror. Old Magic. Grace Nichols. PBCV

She, the sensual creature, the sweet singer. Slow Dancer That No One Hears but You. Duane Niatum. CDW

She thinks at first it is rain. 21 August 1984. Aleda Shirley. Jaz

She Thinks of Her Beloved. Lu Chi, *tr. fr. Chinese* by Kenneth Rexroth. OHMPC

She thus; when I had great desire to prove. Homer, *tr.* by George Chapman. *Fr.* Odyssey. NAWM-1; OBVE

She Tied Up Her Few Things. John Clare. HAP

She, to Him. (When you shall see me in the toils of time.) Thomas Hardy. EnVR; OBEV; OxBTC

Sels.

"This love puts all humanity from me." TOF

She told how they used to form for the country dances. One We Knew. Thomas Hardy. NAEL-2

She told the story, and the whole world wept. Harriet Beecher Stowe. Paul Laurence Dunbar. AAP; BPo

She, too, the voyaging in doors and Keys. This Alice. Herbert Morris. PoRA

She too went dark as dusk began, though rising. On the Death of Cleopatra-Selene. Crinagoras, *tr. fr. Greek* by Alistair Elliot. GrAn

She, too, would have been an old maid!, The. (*LL*) My Grandmother Green. *Unknown.* AmFP

She took a bus. (*LL*) Mary had a little lamb,/ Its fleece as white as snow. *Unknown.* RoPo

She took a last and simple meal when there were. The Lost Cat. Emile Victor Rieu. CRH

She took her name beneath according skies. The Ritual. E. J. Pratt. MoP

She took the dappled partridge flecked [*or* fleckt] with blood. Tennyson. FM; NAEL-2

She tosses and rumples alone on the double bed. Flying Fox. Thomas W. Shapcott. CBAP

She touches me. Her fingers nibble gently. In Love. David Wevill. MoCV

She transplanted each spruce, blue as the. Spruce. Phillip William George. VoR

She tripped and fell against a star. Innocence. Anne Spencer. CDC; ShDr

She trips across the meadows. April. H. Cordelia Ray. CBWP-3

She truly needs good character. Women. *Yoruba Oral Tradition, tr.* by Ulli Beier. WTO

She turned in the high pew, until her sight. A Church Romance. Thomas Hardy. FaBoTw; NOBE; OxAEP-2; OxBTC; PeECV

She turns and calls him by name. His Wife. Rachel, *tr. fr. Hebrew* by Sholom J. Kahn. WPOW

She turns them over in her slow hands. A Mongoloid Child Handling Shells on the Beach. Richard Snyder. InPK

She turns upon her other side. (*LL*) In Moncur Street. Dorothy Hewett. NOBAu

She Understands Me. Lucille Clifton. CAPP

She used to let her golden hair fly free. Petrarch, *tr. fr. Italian. Fr.* Sonnets to Laura. NAWM-1

She wadna bake, she wadna brew. The Wife Wrapt in Wether's Skin. *Unknown.* ESPB

She Waited. Tania van Zyl. PeSA

She waited eagerly on a park bench. The Poem in the Park. Peter Davison. GOYP

She waited on the 7th floor. Frank Albert and Viola Benzena Owens. Ntozake Shange. BlSi

She walked along the crowded street. Revelation. Blanche Taylor Dickinson. CDC

She Walked Unaware. Patrick MacDonogh. BoLoP; ErPo; FaBoTw

She walks down the road. Girl with the Green Skirt. Dana Naone. CDW

She Walks in Beauty. Byron. ArLo; AWP; BLPA; BoLoP; CBLP; EBEvV; ELP; EnRP; FaBoBe; FF; FHYEP; GTBS; GTBS-P; HeIP; ImPo; InPS; LiTB; MeMBP; NAEL-2; NOBE; NoP; OBEV; OBNC; OxAEP-2; PIP; PoE; PoEL-4; PrIm; SCGP; TFi; TrGrPo

She walks — the lady of my delight. The Shepherdess. Alice Meynell. AWP; MoBrPo; NOBVV; OBEV

(Lady of the Lambs, The.) OBEV

She wanted a little room for thinking. Daystar. Rita Dove. LCAP; NIP

She wanted rain. Dust. Kathleen Spivack. BoWoP

She wanted to be a blade. Woman. Nikki Giovanni. HeIL

She wants to hear. Sunday Greens. Rita Dove. LCAP

She Warns Him. Frances Cornford. EnLoPo

She was a high-class bitch and a dandy. Theodore Spencer. LiTA

She was a maid of high degree. He Took Her. Tom Masson. OBAL

She Was a Phantom of Delight. Wordsworth. ArLo; BLPL; EnRP; FaBoBe; FaBV; GTBS; GTBS-P; HeIP; ImPo; LiTB; MeMBP; NoP; OAEL-2; PIP; PoEL-4; PWR; SCGP; TFi; TrGrPo

She Was a Pretty Little Girl. Ramon Perez de Ayala, *tr. fr. Spanish by* Alida Malkus. FaPON

She Was a Queen. Hartley Coleridge. OxAEP-2

She was a queen of noble Nature's crowning. She Was a Queen. Hartley Coleridge. OxAEP-2

She was a small dog, neat and fluid. Praise of a Collie. Norman MacCaig. RB

She was a sweet country lassie. Blackpool Breezes. *Unknown.* CoMu

She was a year younger. Picture Bride. Cathy Song. AiP

She was able to kill herself. The Way Down. Ernest Sandeen. CRP

She was afraid of men. Chicken-Licken. Maya Angelou. FF

She was already lean when. Parting. A. R. Ammons. NoAM

She was at work on a poem about breath. Poem about Breath. David Wagoner. NoAM

She was beautiful that evening and so gay. An Escape. Abu Nuwas, *tr. fr. Arabic by* E. Powys Mathers. ErPo

She was best, but yet untrue. (*LL*) Change [Thy Mind since She Doth Change]. Earl of Essex. EIL

She was born in the midst of the black frock coats. Father and Daughter. Jean Follain, *tr. fr. French by* W. S. Merwin. AnRep

She was brought to church in summer. Old Gardens Are Not Relevant. Mary E. O'Donnell. NWP

She was careerish in a gentle way. Domestic: Climax. Merrill Moore. ErPo

She was caught, a young girl of Uttoxeter. Tim Hopkins. PeLi

She was cleaning — there is always. Black Silk. Tess Gallagher. FaBoWP

She was going on the bus he could see. Woman Looking Through a Viewmaster. C. D. Wright. LCAP

She was his instrument, and oh. Viola d'Amore. Joan Van Poznak. FaBoBl

She was in love with the same danger. Sandra McPherson. SM

She was in terrible pain the whole day. A Wedding. James Tate. NoAM

She was just a parson's daughter. It's the Syme the Whole World Over. *Unknown.* AS

(It's the Syme the Wide World Over.) BeLS

She was left with two sons. Ruth's Story, As Told to Lilith. Michelene Wandor. NBrP

She was lyin face down in her face. William Knott. MAT

She was my aunt, long dead when I was born. Sister Ev. Fiona Hall. NWP

She was my heir. Her severed head they say. Elizabeth Reflects on Hearing of Mary's Execution. John Loveridge. FaBoEH

She was my staff and I am blind. Jana Bai, *tr. fr. Marathi by* Willis Barnstone. BoWoP

She was not as pretty as women I know. My Kate. Elizabeth Barrett Browning. WBLP

She was older, say, thirty-five or so. His Slightly Longer Story Song. James Whitehead. NGP

She was playing with her cat. Woman and Cat. Paul Verlaine, *tr. fr. French* by C. F. MacIntyre. OFC; SoCa

She Was Poor but She Was Honest. *Unknown.* ErPo; FaBoCo; FiBHP; GBP; NOBL

She was pure and white, resembling the sun as it rises. Separation by Death. Iba Hazm, *tr. fr. Arabic by* A. R. Nykel. RaBo, *ad. by* Robert Bly

She was skilled in music and the dance. Alas! Poor Queen. Marion Angus. FaBoEH

She was so aesthetic and culchud. The Cultured Girl Again. Ben King. FiBHP; OBAL

She was the daughter of a fishmonger, she stood. Theatrical Venus. George Buchanan. PNI

She was the joke of the angels — a girl. Saint Rose of Lima. Judith Ortiz Cofer. AfAz

She was the one who lived up country. After Reading *Country of the Pointed Firs, The.* Jean Garrigue. VCAP

She was urgent to speak of the moon: she offered delight. An Old Woman Speaks of the Moon. Ruth Pitter. WPE

She was wearing the coral taffeta trousers. Full Moon. V. Sackville-West. MoShBr; NTP

She washed and washed the pity from her hands. (*LL*) The Intruder. Carolyn Kizer. BoWoP; InPK

She wears a colorful turban. Girl by the Han River. Ts'ai Ch'i-chiao, *tr. fr. Chinese.* Fr. Han River, The. LHF, *tr. by* Hualing Nieh

She wears her middle age like a cowled. From a Correct Address in a Suburb of a Major City. Helen Sorrells. WPE

She wears, my beloved, a rose upon her head. John Frederick Matheus. CDC

She wears the sailor suit — a blouse with anchors. Shore Leave. Lynda Hull. NAmP90

She welcomes him with pretty impatience. The Visit. Ogden Nash. FiBHP

She went along the road. Hagar. Francis Lauderdale Adams. OxBS

She Went to Stay. Robert Creeley. OBAL

She went to the local library, found. Digging. Frank Finale. BTR

She went up the hill to pick angelica. Old Poem. *Unknown, tr. fr. Chinese.* AWP, *tr. by* Arthur Waley

She went up the mountain to pluck wild herbs. Old and New ("She went up the mountain to pluck wild herbs.") *Unknown, tr. fr. Chinese by* Arthur Waley. AWP

She Wept, She Railed. Stanley Kunitz. ErPo; VGW

She who carries/ in her heart a love. Yosano Akiko, *tr. fr. Japanese by* Kenneth Rexroth *and* Ikuko Atsumi. WPJ

She, who could neither rest nor sleep. Alas! Sadi, *tr. by* L. Cranmer-Byng. *Fr.* Gulistan, The. AWP

She who had eyes but had not wherewithal. "If the Lord Would Make windows in Heaven." E. A. Robinson. MeMAP

She who has forgotten. Yr Iaith. Nigel Jenkins. AngWe

She who has no love for women. Calliope in the Labour Ward. Elaine Feinstein. BrRo

She who has power to call her man. An Unsaid Word. Adrienne Rich. NMM

She who hath felt a real pain. John Gay. EnLoPo

She who is always in my thoughts prefers. Bhartrihari, *tr. fr. Sanskrit by* John Brough. BoLoP

She who shook and swayed among the chorus. Macedonius, *tr. fr. Greek by* Adrian Wright. GrAn

She who to Heaven more Heaven doth annex. On a Virtuous Young Gentlewoman That Died Suddenly. William Cartwright. HAP; OBEV

She who usually feeds us. Teeth. Susan Griffin. CrSp

She who was burned more than half her body. The Praises. Charles Olson. VGW

She-Who-Watches . . . The Names are Prayer. Elizabeth Woody. BCF

She will be bound with garlands of her own. (*LL*) On the Sonnet. Keats. NIP; NoP; OAEL-2

She will not want this snake. (*LL*) Mother Doesn't Want a Dog. Judith Viorst. NBLV

She will run to you for love whoever. Children. Sandra McPherson. AnAn; FaBoWP

She Wolf, The. Muriel Spark. NYBP

She wonders how people get babies. The Facts of Life. Ronald Wallace. PBCAP

She won't woo her master with flowers. Cactus. Liu Sha-ho, *tr. fr. Chinese.* Fr. Family of Plants, A. LHF, *tr. by* Hualing Nieh

She wore a cloche hat. The Photo of Emily. Lawrence Ferlinghetti. CAPP

She wore a new "terra-cotta" dress. A Thunderstorm in Town. Thomas Hardy. BoLoP; CBLP; EnLoPo; GBL; OxBSP

She Wore a Wreath of Roses. Thomas Haynes Bayly. BeLS

She worked in the newsagent, redhaired. Graffiti. Julian Croft. NOBAu

She works and works against sadness. The Gardener. Robin Becker. CrSp

She would have one should mend it. (*LL*) Walking in a Meadowe Greene. *Unknown.* BoLoP; ErPo

She Would Have Roses. Nicholas Lloyd Ingraham. PWR

She would not see. (*LL*) A Leave-taking. Swinburne. CBLP; CH; CoGr; NOBE; NOBVV; OBNC; OPOP; PoEL-5; PoLF

She wreaks such havoc in my library. Minding Ruth. Aidan Carl Mathews. BiHa; CIP; IB; PBCIP

She writes to him again. Henri Michaux, *tr. fr. French by* Richard Ellmann. *Fr.* I Am Writing to You from a Far-Off Country. AnRep

Sheaf, The. Andrew Young. ChTr

Sheafe of snakes used heretofore to be, A. To Mr. George Herbert. John Donne. OBVE

Shealtiel, governor of Judah. Haggai. John Chagy. ChIV-1

Shear your sheep in May. *Unknown.* FaBoUs

Shearer man like toast and butter. Indian Bagman's Toast. *Unknown.* FaBoVe

Shearer's Wife, The. Louis Esson. NOBAu

Shearing, The. *Unknown, tr. fr. Welsh by* Glyn Jones. OBWVE

Shearing, as the gardener. That's All? Anna Hajnal, *tr. fr. Hungarian by* Jascha Kessler. PBWP

Sheath and Knife. *Unknown.* CH; ESPB

Sheaves, The. E. A. Robinson. AWP; CMoP; FaBV; HAP; ImGa; MoAB; MoAmPo; MoP; NoAM; NOBA; OxBA; Poetr; SoSe; TAP

Shed, The. Frank Flynn. OTCP

Shed a tear for the WREN named McGinnis. *Unknown.* PeLi

Shed all the blood, felt all the smart. (*LL*) Celia Bleeding, to the Surgeon. Thomas Carew. SeCP

She'd always been there. Interface. Gloria Anzaldúa. GLP

Shed no tear! O, shed no tear! Fairy Song. Keats. FaPON (Faery Song.) CH

She'd Say. Frank Davey. NOBC

She'd start the fires under the bed. The Split. Marie Howe. NAmP90

Sheding the saut, saut tear. (*LL*) Proud Margret. *Unknown.* OxBB

Shee brought her to her joyous paradize. The Garden of Adonis. Spenser. *Fr.* Faerie Queene, The. NOBE; PoEL-1

Shee is dead; and all which die. The Dissolution. John Donne. SeCV-1

Shee with whom troopes of Bustuary slaves. A Satyre Entituled the Witch. *Unknown.* CoMu

Sheen of the willows spreads ten thousand feet, The. "Song of Farewell" in the Tartar Mode. Chang Yü, *tr. fr. Chinese by* Irving Y. Lo. SuSp

Sheep. W. H. Davies. LiTM; MoBrPo; NTP; RB

Sheep. Robert Francis. LCAP

Sheep. Samuel Hoffenstein. TrJP

Sheep, *sels.* Ted Hughes.
"When we sat his mother on her tail, he mouthed her teat." OBD

Sheep. Rochelle Kraut. UL

Sheep, The. Ann Taylor. BoTP; OxBChV

Sheep. Mike Thaler. ZA

Sheep and a goat were going to the pasture, A. *Unknown.* RoPo

Sheep and Lambs. Katharine Tynan. BoTP; OBEV; TIRV

Sheep and the Goat, The. George Macdonald. EBVV

Sheep Child, The. James Dickey. CAPP; HCAP; MoP; MT; NoAM; NOBA; Prf; TAP; VCAP

Sheep Dipping. Norman MacCaig. OxBC

Sheep Fair, A. Thomas Hardy. Prf

Sheep-folds, holy spring of the Nymphs. Leonidas of Tarentum, *tr. fr. Greek by* Peter Levi. GrAn

Sheep in Fog. Sylvia Plath. FaBoWP; HCAP; LCAP; NaP

Sheep in the Sheade. William Barnes. FM

Sheep is blind, The; a passing owl. The Blind Sheep. Randall Jarrell. NYBP; OBAL

Sheep Meadow. Samuel Menashe. Mes

Sheep Shearing. *Unknown.* OBET

Sheep!/ Unhappy connotation. Bleat of Protest. Mildred Weston. FiBHP

Sheepdog Trials in Hyde Park. C. Day Lewis. MoP; NoAM; NoP; OxBTC

Sheepherder, The. Lew Sarett. FaPON

Sheep's in the meadow, The. Bonny at Morn. *Unknown.* GBP

Sheep's Skull. Lucy Jane Simpson. OBD

Sheet. Cole Swensen. UTF

Sheet of paper, placed, A. Lakshmi. Padraic Fallon. NOIV

Sheet of water turned over, A. Fog. J. D. McClatchy. PFL

Sheet of writing paper, The. The Alchemist. Richard Church. OxBTC

Sheeted in steel, embedded face to face. At a Low Mass for Two Hot-Rodders. X. J. Kennedy. NGP; Poetsp

Sheets, The. Timothy Steele. DiPo

Sheets of night mist travel a long valley, The. Mist Forms. Carl Sandburg. CMoP

Sheets were frozen hard, and they cut the naked hand, The. Christmas at Sea. Robert Louis Stevenson. BLPL; CH; EBVV; FaBoBe; FaBV; Mes; OBTV; PeVV

Sheffield Apprentice, The. *Unknown.* OBET

Sheffield grinder's a terrible blade, The. The Grinders; or, The Saddle on the Right Horse. *Unknown.* GBP

Sheffield 'Prentice, The. *Unknown.* AmFP

Sheffield 'Prentice, The, *diff. version. Unknown. See* When I was bound for London a lady met me there.

Shéhérazade. Wayne Koestenbaum. UTF

Sheila Na Gig at Kilpeck. Gillian Clarke. SCBI

Shekhinah. Karl Wolfskehl, *tr. fr. German.* TrJP, *tr. by* Carol North Valhope *and* Ernst Morwitz

Shell. Federico García Lorca, *tr. fr. Spanish.* CBNP

Shell, The. H. M. Sarson. NSI; PoWW

Shell, The. James Stephens. BoNaP; BoTP; CH; CMoP; MoAB; MoBrPo; MoShBr

Shell, The. Tennyson. *See* See What a Lovely Shell.

She'll be Comin' Round the Mountain. *Unknown.* AS, A *and* B *vers., with music*

Shell-less, on your slimey trail. After Tempest. Percy MacKaye. FYAP

Shell Secrets. *Unknown.* BoTP

Shepherd's Home, The. William Shenstone. *See* My banks they are furnished with bees.

Shepherd's House, The, *sels*. Alfred de Vigny, *tr. fr. French by* Robert Bly.
"Eva, I agree to love, among creation, all the creatures!" NU

Shephe[a]rd's Hunting, The, *sels*. George Wither.
Fourth Eclogue, The. SeCV-1, *abr*.
"I that erstwhile the world's sweet air did draw." NOSC

Shepherd's Hut, The. Andrew Young. GrPl; OxBTC

Shepherds' Hymn, The. Richard Crashaw. *Fr*. In the Holy Nativity of Our Lord God. GeHe; NOBE; PoEL-2; SeCV-1

Shepherd's Hymn, The ("We saw Thee in Thy balmy nest.") Richard Crashaw. *Fr*. In the Holy Nativity of Our Lord God. GeHe; PoEL-2; SeCV-1; TrGrPo, 3 *sts*.

Shepherd's Lament, The. Goethe, *tr. fr. German by* Bayard Taylor. AWP

Shepherd's Night Count. Jane Yolen. TLR

Shepherds on old hills, with robber. Gallery Shepherds. Patricia Beer. OxBC

Shepherd's Pipe, The, *sels*. William Browne.
Dawn of Day. EIL

Shepherd's Play (Townley cycle), *sels*. *Unknown*.
"It is sayde full ryfe." FaBoUs

Shepherd's Plea, The. Christopher Marlowe. *See* Come live with me[e] and be my love.

Shepherd's Praise of Diana, The. Sir Walter Ralegh. *See* Praised be Diana's fair and harmless light.

Shepherd's Sirena, The, *sels*. Michael Drayton.
Trent, The. FaBoPP; OBEV; PoEL-2
(Jovial Shepheard's Song, The.) PoEL-2
(Sirena.) OBEV

Shepherd's Song at Christmas. Langston Hughes. PChr

Shepherds' Song, Sung before Queen Anne, on the Wiltshire Downs, 11 June 1613, The, *sels*. George Ferebe.
Houseless Downs, The. FaBoPP

Shepherd's Sorrow, Being Disdained in Love, The. Thomas Lodge *and to* Robert Greene. NoSic

Shepherd's star with trembling glint, The. En Bateau. Paul Verlaine, *tr. fr. French by* Arthur Symons. AWP

Shepherd's Tale, The. James Kirkup, *after the French of* Raoul Ponchon. OBCP

Shepherd's Tale, A. Sir Philip Sidney. *Fr*. Arcadia. SiPS

Shepherds that on this mountain ridge abide. Cleitagoras. Leonidas of Tarentum, *tr. fr. Greek by* William M. Hardinge. AWP

Shepherd's Week, The, *sels*. John Gay.
Thursday; or, The Spell. PoEL-3
"Last May-day fair I search'd to find a snail" FaBoUs
Tuesday; or, the Ditty. NOEC
Wednesday; or, The Dumps. OAEL-1

Shepherd's Wife's Song, The. Robert Greene. *Fr*. Greene's Mourning Garment. EIL; HAP; NoSic

Sheridan at Cedar Creek. Herman Melville. LiTA; PAH

Sheridan's Ride. Thomas Buchanan Read. AnAmPo; BeLS; FaBoBe; FaBV; GN; OHIP; PAH; WBLP

Sherman Cyclone, The. *Unknown*. AmFP

Sherman's in Savannah. Oliver Wendell Holmes. PAH

Sherman's March to the Sea. Samuel H. M. Byers. PAH

Sherpa gasped out as they mounted the slope, The. Poem, Neither Hilláryous Norgay. Gardner E. Lewis. FiBHP

Sherwood. Alfred Noyes. *See* Sherwood in the twilight, is Robin Hood awake?

Sherwood in the twilight, is Robin Hood awake? A Song of Sherwood. Alfred Noyes. FaPON; MoBrPo
(Sherwood.) MoBrPo

She's a copperheaded waitress. Ella, in a Square Apron, along Highway 80. Judy Grahn. *Fr*. Common Woman, The. NALW; NMM

She's a young thing, and cannot leave her mother. (*LL*) Billy Boy. *Unknown*. AmFP; BLPA; HoPM; OBET

She's All My Fancy Painted Him. "Lewis Carroll." FaBoNo

She's combed his neckties out of her hair. A Widow. Ted Kooser. PBCAP

She's empty: hark, she sounds: there's nothing there. Nahum 2.10. Francis Quarles. ChIV-1

She's Free! Frances E. W. Harper. AIW; BlSi; Son

She's Gazing at You So Tenderly. Pushkin, *tr. fr. Russian by* D. M. Thomas. ArLo

She's gone! Call Rape! Call Robbers! Violence!. Meleager, *tr. fr. Greek by* Peter Whigham. GrAn

She's gone. She was my love, my moon or more. Complaint. James Wright. NOBA; TAP; VGW

She's Hoy'd Me Out o' Lauderdale. *Unknown*. CoMu

She's loveliest of the festal throng. The Rose and the Thorn. Paul Hamilton Hayne. FaBoBe

She's my wife. Ther' ain't none better than ole Filkin's daughter Nell. (*LL*) The Engineer's Story. Eugene J. Hall. VPP

She's not a faultless woman; no! James Kenneth Stephen. *Fr*. After the Golden Wedding. EBVV; NOBVV; OxBM

She's now yo' own. Salute yo' bride! (*LL*) Slave Marriage Ceremony Supplement. *Unknown*. BPo; TAP

She's somewhere in the sunlight strong. Richard Le Gallienne. OBEV

She's the camera. Judy-One. Don L. Lee. TAP

She's the plaything of the Navy, she's the nightmare of the Hun. The Q-Boat. H. E. Wilkes. NSI

Shet up dat noise, you chillen! Dar's some one at de do.' 'Sciplinin' Sister Brown. James Edwin Campbell. AAP

Shh. Shh. (*LL*) November. Linda Hogan. BCF; SRLS

Shi King, *sels*. *Unknown*, *tr. fr. Chinese*.
Chou and the South. CTC
How Goes the Night? AWP
I Wait My Lord. AWP
Maytime. AWP
Morning Glory, The. AWP
Pear-Tree, The. AWP
Under the Pondweed. AWP
Woman. AWP
You Will Die. AWP

Shibboleth. Paul Celan, *tr. fr. German by* Michael Hamburger. AnRep

Shickered As He Could Be. *Unknown*. NOBAu

Shield from every dart, The. What Christ Is to Us. *Unknown*. BLRP

Shield: I'm by nature solitary, scarred by spear. Unknown, formerly at. to Cynewulf, *tr. fr. Anglo-Saxon*. *Fr*. Riddles (Exeter Book). ASW, *tr. by* Kevin Crossley-Holland

Shield: "Lonely wanderer, wounded with iron, A." Unknown, formerly at. to Cynewulf, *tr. by* Charles W. Kennedy. *Fr*. Riddles (Exeter Book). AnOE

Shield of Achilles, The. W. H. Auden. EBEV; FaBoMo; FaBoPV; GTBS-P; HAP; NAEL-2; NoAM; NOBE; NOCV; NoP; OxAEP-2; PeECV; PoA; PoE; WeW

Shield of Achilles, The. Homer, *tr. fr. Greek*. *Fr*. Iliad, The. NOSC, *tr. by* George Chapman

Shield of War, The. Thomas Sackville. *Fr*. Induction to "A Mirror for Magistrates". AAS

Shift, here, in town, not meanest among squires. On Lieutenant Shift. Ben Jonson. OBSV

Shifting Colors. Robert Lowell. HCAP

Shiftless young fellow of Kent, A. *Unknown*. PeLi

Shifty limpet on his rocky shore, The. Every Earthly Creature. John Malcolm Brinnin. LiTA

Shih Ching, *sels*. *Unknown*, *tr. fr. Chinese by* Arthur Waley.
"Very handsome gentleman, A." BoWoP
Widow's Lament. BoWoP

Shih Ch'ung's "Golden Valley" Garden. Tu Mu, *tr. fr. Chinese by* A. C. Graham. PLT

Shillin' a Day. Kipling. NoAM

Shilling in the Armpit, The. Ieuan Gethyn. FaBoEH

Shilling life will give you all the facts, A. Who's Who. W. H. Auden. MeMAP; MoAB; MoBrPo; MoP; NoAM; Son

Shillong. Bernard Gutteridge. PoWW

Shiloh; a Requiem. Herman Melville. AnAmPo; FF; LiTA; NOBA; NoP; OBWP; OxBA; PAW; SCV; WiR

Shimmer. James Schuyler. VCAP

Shimmering Pediment. John Yau. UL

Shimmering water at its full — sunny day is best. Drinking at the Lake, First It's Sunny, Then It Rains. Su Shih, *tr. fr. Chinese by* Irving Y. Lo. SuSp

Shine. Léon Damas, *tr. fr. French by* Ellen Conroy Kennedy. NegPo

Shine alone, shine nakedly, shine like bronze. Nuances of a Theme by Williams. Wallace Stevens. CMoP; LiTA

Shine forth into the night, O flame. Give Our Conscience Light. Aline Badger Carter. TrPWD

Shine, O sun! tenderly on my skin. Love Dirge. *Unknown*, *tr. fr. Maori by* John White. WTO

Shine, O thou sacred shepherds' star. The Houseless Downs. George Ferebe. *Fr*. Shepherds' Song, Sung before Queen Anne, on the Wiltshire Downs, 11 June 1613, The. FaBoPP

Shine, "O world!" don't weary the gulping Pole. Frank O'Hara. *Fr*. Life on Earth. UnPo

Shine on me, moon. A Sentinel's Song. Rarawa Kerehoma, *tr. by* Barry Mitcalfe. WTO

Shine on Me, Secret Splendor. Edwin Markham. TrPWD

Shine Out, Fair Sun, with All Your Heat. *At. to* George Chapman. *Fr.* Masque of the Twelve Months, The. ChTr; ELP

Shine out, resplendent God of day. A Laplander's Song to His Mistress. Elizabeth Rowe. ECWP

Shine, Perishing Republic. Robinson Jeffers. CMoP; FF; LiTA; LiTM; MAT; MoAB; MoP; NAAL-2; NoAM; NOBA; NoP; OxBA; PrIm; TAP; TFi; UnPo; VGW

Shine, Poet! in thy place, and be content. (*LL*) If Thou Indeed Derive Thy Light from Heaven. Wordsworth. EnRP; TrCP

Shine, Republic. Robinson Jeffers. FaBoPV

Shine was up in Harlem damn near drunk. (*LL*) Dark Prophecy: I Sing of Shine. Etheridge Knight. BPo; PBCAP

Shines coldly away. Roy Fisher. *Fr.* Handsworth Liberties. VaA

Shingle roofs burgeon moss, green as tender acacia, The. Laguna Beach. Ruth Stone. FoLa

Shining black in the shining light. To a Black Greyhound. Julian Grenfell. OtMeF

Shining Eye of Horus cometh, The. He Kindleth a Fire. *Unknown, tr. fr. Egyptian by* Robert Hillyer. *Fr.* Book of the Dead. AWP

Shining fauna of that fire, The. (*LL*) Burning the Christmas Greens. William Carlos Williams. LiTM; MeMAP; MoP; NAAL-2; NoAM; NOBA

Shining in his stickiness and glistening with honey. The Friendly Cinnamon Bun. Russell Hoban. OTCP

Shining joy and jewel of all my kingdom, The. (*LL*) Although I Conquer All the Earth. *Unknown.* ArLo; TTTS

Shining like a star. Hunting Song. *Unknown, tr. fr. Chippewa Indian by* Jerome K. Rothenberg. STP

Shining neutral summer has no voice, The. In Memoriam: Ernst Toller. W. H. Auden. NYBP

Shining Night or Dick Daring, the Poacher, A. *Unknown.* CoMu

Shining Parlor, The. Anita Scott Coleman. ShDr

Shining pebble of the pond, The. (*LL*) Ode to Beauty. Emerson. AmPP; PoEL-4

Shining they stare! (*LL*) Lovely hill-torrents are. W. J. Turner. GoJo; MoBrPo

Shining Things. Elizabeth Gould. BoTP

Shining with time like any pilgrim? (*LL*) Spindrift. Galway Kinnell. NaP; NYBP

Shiny beings come down out of the sky. The Compound Eye. Sandra McPherson. AnAn

Shiny Little House, The. Nancy M. Hayes. BoTP

Shiny memory to take with me to travel around the world. (*LL*) Imagination. Dina Uahupirapi. LoHo

Shiny record albums scattered over. As You Leave Me. Etheridge Knight. FF; MT; NNaP

Ship, The. Charles MacKay. BLPA

Ship, The. J. C. Squire. CH

Ship, The. *Unknown.* PoLF

Ship, A/ A chain. I Sing This Song for Our Mothers: Ruise. Sherley Anne Williams. MDDM

Ship, an Isle, a Sickle Moon, A. James Elroy Flecker. FaBoRV

Ship Burning and a Comet All in One Day, A. Richard Eberhart. NYBP

Ship Canal from the Atlantic to the Pacific, The. Francis Lieber. PAH

Ship I have got in the North Country, A. The *Golden Vanity. Unknown.* FaBoCh

Ship in Distress, The. *Unknown.* OxBSS

Ship Is All Laden, The. *Unknown.* OxBSS

Ship Is Lost, The. William Falconer. *Fr.* Shipwreck, The. OxAEP-1

Ship, leaving or arriving, of my lover. After a Passage in Baudelaire. Robert Duncan. CMoP; PoA; PoE

Ship moves, The. 4th of July. William Carlos Williams. PoA

Ship of Death, The. D. H. Lawrence. CMoP; FaBoRV; FaBoTw; GTBS-P; LiTB; MeMBP; MoAB; MoBrPo; MoP; NAEL-2; NoAM; NoP; OAEL-2; OxAEP-2; PrIm

Ship of Fools, The, *sels.* Alexander Barclay. Of Glotons and Dronkardes. OxBLMV

Ship of Rio, The. Walter de la Mare. PDV

Ship of State, The ("O navis, referent.") Horace, *tr. fr. Latin by* Austin Dobson. *Fr.* Odes. AWP, *tr. by* William Ewart Gladstone

Ship of State, The. Longfellow. *See* Thou, too, sail on, O Ship of State!

Ship of the body, ship of the soul, voyaging, voyaging, voyaging. (*LL*) Aboard a Ship's Helm. Walt Whitman. NOBA; OxBA

Ship Sails Up to Bideford, A. Herbert Asquith. BoTP

Ship Sets out, the. William Falconer. *Fr.* Shipwreck, The. OxAEP-1

Ship sets sail, the ship is journeying, The. The Stoker. Shin Shalom, *tr. fr. Hebrew by* Ruth Finer Mintz. MHP

Ship That Never Returned, The. Henry Clay Work. BLPA

Ship That Sails, The. *Unknown.* PoToHe

Ship That Went Down, The. Adah Isaacs Menken. CBWP-1

Ship was large, The. Ode to a Lost Cargo in a Ship Called *Save.* José Craveirinha, *tr. fr. Portuguese by* Chris Searle. PeSAV

Ship with shields before the sun, A. Near Avalon. William Morris. OAEL-2

Ship you've boarded, The. Ark. Gu Cheng, *tr. fr. Chinese by* Donald Finkel *with* Li Guohua. SpMi

Shiperd-boy, what is yer trade? The Beggar-Laddie. *Unknown.* ESPB

Shipman, The. Chaucer. *Fr.* Canterbury Tales, The. EnVB; FHYEP; NoP; OAEL-1; PPP, *abr.*

Shipman was ther, woning [*or* wonynge] fer by weste, A. The Shipman. Chaucer. *Fr.* Canterbury Tales, The. EnVB; FHYEP; NoP; OAEL-1; PPP, *abr.*

Shipment to Maidanek. Ephim G. Fogel. BTR; OBWP; TrJP

Shiprock. Lucile Adler. FoLa

Ships, The. J. J. Bell. BoTP

Ship's Cook, a Captive Sings, The. Hugo von Hofmannsthal, *tr. fr. German by* Charles Wharton Stork. TrJP

Ship's master:/ before him, in the waist and before it. David Jones. *Fr.* Anathemata, The. FaBoTw

Ship's Nail, A. *Unknown.* ReMoGo

Ships of state, the. Australorp. Edith Speers. NOBAu

Ships That Pass in the Night. Paul Laurence Dunbar. AnAmPo; CDC

Ships that pass in the night, and speak each other in passing. Longfellow. *See* Ships That Pass in the Night (The Theologian's Tale).

Ships That Pass in the Night (The Theologian's Tale). Longfellow. *Fr.* Tales of a Wayside Inn.

Ship's Whistle, The. Tarapada Ray, *tr. fr. Hindi.* TSaS, *tr. by* Shyamasree Devi *and* P. Lal

Shipwreck, The, *sels.* William Falconer. "Amid this fearful trance, a thundering sound." ECEV "Fair Candia now no more beneath her lee." ScCV Ship Is Lost, The. OxAEP-1 Ship Sets out, the. OxAEP-1

Shipwreck. Mary Weston Fordham, *tr. by* Mary Ann Caws. CBWP-2

Shires, The. *Unknown.* CBCK

Shirt. Robert Pinsky. NAmP90

Shirt. Charles Simic. HCAP

Shirt of a Lad, The. *Unknown, tr. fr. Welsh by* Anthony Conran. OBWVE; VBLP

Shirt Poem, The. Gerald Stern. CAPP

Shirt races in the meadow, A. Storm. Agnes Nemes Nagy, *tr. fr. Hungarian by* Laura Schiff. PBWP

Shit. (*LL*) After / the Moratorium Reading. Nigel Roberts. NOBAu

Shitty. Kingsley Amis. OxBC

Shiva. Robinson Jeffers. NoAM; NOBA; Son

Shivering and hoping no one. Grandma's Bureau. Robert Morgan. EOEF; WeW

Shlup, shlup, the dog. Denise Levertov. *Fr.* Six Variations. AmPP; HeIL; HeIP; InPK; LCAP; Poetr

Sho Nuff. Nilene O. A. Foxworth. AIW

Sho-shó-ne Sa-cá-ga-we-a — captive and wife was she. Sa-cá-ga-we-a. Edna Dean Proctor. PAH

Shoah, The. Emily Borenstein. BTR

Shoal of idlers, from a merchant craft, A. Pelters of Pyramids. Richard Henry Horne. OBTV

Shoals of Herring, The. Ewan MacColl. OxBSS

Shocked that she missed the footbridge! The Suicide. V. R. Laing. PoA

Shocking Rape and Murder of Two Lovers. *Unknown.* CoMu

Shoe a little horse. *Unknown.* OxNR

Shoe Shop. Barton Sutter. SM; SoSe

Shoe the colt, shoe the colt. Mother Goose. OxNR (Shoeing.) ReMoGo

Shoe the steed with silver. Sheridan at Cedar Creek. Herman Melville. LiTA; PAH

Shoe-tying, The. Robert Herrick. CaPo

Shoe with legs, A. Lobster. Anne Sexton. AnAn

Shoebox, The. Mark Rudman. BAP-89

Shoeing. Mother Goose. *See* Shoe the colt, shoe the colt.

Shoemaker, The. *Unknown.* FaPON

Shoemaker makes shoes without leather, A. *Unknown.* OxNR

Shoemaker's Holiday, The, *sels.* Thomas Dekker *and others.* Drinking Song. TrGrPo (Troll the Bowl!) EIL "O the month of May, the merry month of May." NoSic (Maytime.) TrGrPo (O, the Month of May.) EIL

Shoemakker, The. *Unknown.* FaBoVe; OBET

Shoes. Victor Martinez. AfAz

Shoes are made to fit the feet. *Gond Oral Tradition*, tr. by V. Elwin *and* S. Hivale. WTO

Shoes, secret face of my inner life. My Shoes. Charles Simic. CoAP; HCAP; VCAP

Shoeshine man squats at the hotel door, The. Where the Disappeared Would Dance. Martín Espada. ETG

Shoichi brushed the black. Awakening. Lucien Stryk. CAPP; SV

Sholom Aleichem. Elias Lieberman. TrJP

Sholto Peach Harrison you are no son of mine. Correspondence between Mr. Harrison in Newcastle and Mr. Sholto Peach Harrison in Hull. Stevie Smith. FaBoNo; NBLV; OxBC

Shon a Morgan. *Unknown.* GBP; OxNR

Shona married a Ndebele, A. A Maze of Blood. N. C. G. Mathema. PeSAV

Shone through her body visibly. *(LL)* Phantom. *Unknown, sometimes at. to* Samuel Taylor Coleridge. MeMBP; NAEL-2; OAEL-2; OxBSP; PoEL-4

Shoni Onions. Sheenagh Pugh. AngWe

Shoofly, The. Felix O'Hare. AmFP

Shoot down the rebelsmen who dare. "Rebels." Ernest Crosby. PAH

Shoot from above. The Dart. "Eliza." KTR

Shoot me! *(LL)* Address to Mr. Cross, of Exeter 'Change, on the Death of the Elephant. Thomas Hood. FM

Shooter's Hill., *sels.* Robert Bloomfield. "Health! I seek thee; dost thou love." OBNC

Shooting a Farmhouse. Ted Kooser. PBCAP

Shooting Crows. David Huddle. GOYP

Shooting of Dan McGrew, The. Robert W. Service. BeLS; EBEvV; EBNV; FaBoBe; PoLF; PoRA; RB; UV, *sl. sh. vers.*

Shooting of His Dear. *Unknown.* OxBoLi

Shooting of John Dillinger outside the Biograph Theater July 22, 1934, The. David Wagoner. CoAP; FYAP; RB; SM

Shooting Script, *sels.* Adrienne Rich. "Mare's skeleton in the clearing: another sign of life, The." FaBoWP Newsreel. FaBoWP; HCAP "Of simple choice they are the villagers; their clothes come." HCAP "Old blanket. The crumbs of rubbed wool turning up, The." HCAP "They come to you with their descriptions of your soul." HCAP "We are driven to odd attempts; once it would not have occurred." HCAP "Whatever it was: the grains of the glacier caked in the." FaBoWP; HCAP

Shooting Song, A. William Brighty Rands. OxBChV

Shooting the Horses. Pamela Mordecai. PBCV

Shooting Whales. Mark Strand. CAPP

Shop and Freedom. *Unknown.* PAH

Shop o' Meat-Weare. William Barnes. NOBVV

Shop Talk. Roy Fuller. OxBC

Shop where leaves once glowed inside, The. *(LL)* Greenwood's. Michael Sharkey. NOBAu

Shopkeepers at the Party Meeting. Thomas McCarthy. BiHa; IB

Shoplifter, The. Matthew Sweeney. IB

Shoplifter has cut his hair, The. The Shoplifter. Matthew Sweeney. IB

Shopping for Meat in Winter. Oscar Williams. LiTA; LiTM

Shops, the streets are full of old men, The. Talk. Roo Borson. NIP; NOBC

Shore. Jean Garrigue. TAP

Shore, A. Timothy Steele. NGP

Shore Birds. Vi Gale. GoYe

Shore Leave. Lynda Hull. NAmP90

Shore looked wild, without a trace of man, The. Byron. *Fr.* Don Juan. HAP

Shore of Life, The. Robert Fitzgerald. VGW

Shore Scene. John Logan. SM

Shore Tullye. Robert Rendall. OxBS

Shore wind is cold on my travel clothes, The. Abutsu the Nun, tr. fr. *Japanese by* Edwin O. Reischauer. *Fr.* Diary of the Waning Moon, The. PBWP

Shoreham: Twilight Time. Samuel Palmer. OAEL-2

Shoreless breeze from heaven over an endless road. In a Dream I Traveled among Ten Thousand Acres of Lotuses. Lu Yu, tr. fr. *Chinese by* Irving Y. Lo. SuSp

Shoreline. Mary Barnard. PoA

Shores are crown'd with people, The. Camões, tr. fr. *Portuguese by* Sir Richard Fanshawe. *Fr.* Lusiads, The. OBVE

Shores of anguish. Magda Portal, tr. fr. *Spanish by* Allan Francovich *and* Kathleen Weaver. PBWP

Shores of my native land. Isaac Toussaint L'Ouverture, tr. fr. *French by* Edna Worthley Underwood. TTY

Shores of Styx are lone for evermore, The. Idle Charon. Eugene Lee-Hamilton. NOBVV

Shoriken. Charles Brasch. PeNZ

Shoring up the ocean. A railroad track. Blood-Sister. Adrienne Rich. NAAL-2; NoP

Shorn of landmarks, glued to a sere promontory. "No!" He Said. Wole Soyinka. HBAPE

Short, big-nosed men with nasty conical caps. The Hittites. Roy Fuller. OxBSP

Short Biography of a Washerwoman. Yolanda Ulloa. AIW

Short cut home lay through the cemetery, The. The Mistress. Joan Barton. OxBTC

Short dark passage to Eternal Light, A. *(LL)* The Christian's Reply to the Philosopher. Sir William Davenant. MeLP

Short day has grown, A. The Place of V. Ray A. Young Bear. VoR

Short Days, The. John Updike. AnAmPo

Short direction, A. Rules and Regulations. "Lewis Carroll." FaBoUs; NOBVV; PeVV

Short History of British India, A. Geoffrey Hill. OxBC

Short History of the New South, A. R. S. Gwynn. NGP

Short in measure, narrow in theme. Erinna's *Distaff.* Antipater of Sidon, tr. fr. *Greek by* Peter Jay. GrAn

Short Is My Rest. William Barley. EnRePo

Short is my rest, whose toil is over long. Short Is My Rest. William Barley. EnRePo

Short Lexicon of Torture in the Eighties, A. Edward Hirsch. VCAP

Short Life of the Hermit, A, *sels.* John Logan. "He told the crowd "The devils." CRP

Short on brains, long on stupidity, the mantis seizes the cicada. Huang T'ing-chien, tr. by Michael E. Workman. *Fr.* In My Study in Monastery, Rising after a Nap. SuSp

Short Order. Charles Bukowski. HoPM

Short Poem. William Carlos Williams. SAmP

Short Poem for Armistice Day, A. Sir Herbert Read. PeFWW

Short Prayer to Mary, A. *Unknown.* MeEL

Short service, to be sure, A. Lament for a Leg. John Ormond. AngWe; OBWVE

Short Song of Congratulation [*or* To a Young Heir], A. Samuel Johnson. EBEV; ELP; HAP; InPK; InPS; InvP; NOBE; NOEC; NoP; OBSV; OxAEP-1; PeLV; PlP; PoE; PoEL-3; TEP; TFi; UnPo

Short space my feet had traversed ere. Guillaume de Lorris *and* Jean de Meun, tr. by F. S. Ellis. *Fr.* Romance [*or* Romaunt] of the Rose, The. OAEL-1

Short Story, A. David Escobar Galindo, tr. fr. *Spanish.* TSaS, tr. by Jorge D. Piche

Short Story on a Painting of Gustav Klimt. Lawrence Ferlinghetti. PoBeRe

Short Time. Gavin Ewart. NoAM

Short Wave In Shanghai. Sibyl James. LoHo

Shortening the Road. Michael Davitt, tr. fr. *Irish by* Philip Casey. PBCIP

Shorter American Memory of the American Character According to Santayana. Rosemarie Waldrop. EOEF

Shorter hours and better pay. *(LL)* A Strike among the Poets. *Unknown.* FaBoCo; FiBHP

Shorter she grows, The. *(LL)* Little Nancy [*or* Nanny] Etticoat. Mother Goose. ChTr; OxNR

Shortest and Sweetest of Songs, The. George Macdonald. NOBVV

Shortest Day, The. William Dickey. IMW

Short/Excerpts. William Knott. PBCAP

Shortly after I Married, I Had to Go into Mourning, *sels.* Rai San'yo, tr. fr. *Chinese.*

Shortness and Misery of Life, The. Isaac Watts. NOCV

Shortness of Life. Thomas Fairfax, Baron Fairfax. NOSC

Shot at Random, A. D. B. Wyndham Lewis. FaBoCo; FiBHP; UV

Shot Deer, The. *Unknown, tr. fr. Hindi by* Denys Thompson. OBAP

Shot? So Quick, So Clean an Ending? A. E. Housman. *Fr.* Shropshire Lad, A. FaPoB; PeHV

Shot Who? Jim Lane! Merrill Moore. MoAmPo

Should all my life employ, and busy me. *(LL)* The Odour. George Herbert.

Should all our churchmen foam in spite. At Farringford. Tennyson. *Fr.* To the Rev. F. D. Maurice. FaBoPP; GTBS-P

Should all the world so wide to atoms fall. Our Insufficiency to Praise God Suitably for His Mercy. Edward Taylor. LiTA

Should also take the rod? *(LL)* Symbols. Christina Rossetti. NALW

Should any ask me on His form to dwell. He Hath No Parallel. Sadi, tr. by L. Cranmer-Byng. *Fr.* Gulistan, The. AWP

Should auld acquaintance be forgot. Auld Lang Syne. Burns. AWP; BLPL; EBEvV; EnRP; ImPo; LiTB; NAEL-2; NOBE; OBEV; OxAEP-2; OxBS; PoLF; SCGP; TEP

Should be clear: the darkness around us is deep. *(LL)* A Ritual to Read to Each Other. William Stafford. RaBo

Should blaze the path of thunder. *(LL)* Tableau. Countee Cullen. PoBA

Should come to nothing must be fairly faced. *(LL)* From a Milkweed Pod. Robert Frost.

Should Dennis print how once you robb'd your brother. On Dennis. Pope. FaBoEE

Should ever be forgot. *(LL)* Gunpowder Plot Day. *Unknown.* FaBoEH; FaBoPV; ISE, diff. vers.; OxNR

Should ever have tied up my garter for me! *(LL)* The Dark-eyed Gentleman. Thomas Hardy. MoAB; MoBrPo; NBLV; UnPo

Should find brief solace there, as I have found. *(LL)* Nuns Fret Not at Their Convent's Narrow Room. Wordsworth. EBEV; EnRP; NIP; NoP; Poetr; Son

Should fright us from the shore. *(LL)* There is a land of pure delight. Isaac Watts. TOF

Should Heaven send me any son. Alfred, Lord Tennyson. Dorothy Parker. *Fr.* Pig's-Eye View of Literature, A. NALW

Should help a man, not drag him in the mire. *(LL)* Ballade to His Mistress. Villon. WeW

Should I Be a Rabbi? Hayyim Nahman Bialik, *tr. fr. Hebrew by* Grace Goldin. TrJP

Should I be troubled when the purblind knight. The Earl of Rochester. *Fr.* Allusion to Horace, An. EPCY

Should I believe you, e'en my oaths are witty. *Unknown.* FaBoEE

Should I get married? Should I be good? Marriage. Gregory Corso. CBLP; CoAP; LiTM; MoP; NeAP; NoP; OBAL; PeLV; PoBeRe; PPP; PrIm; TAP; TRP

Should I give in to sleep? This fire's warm. Reading *Paradise Lost* in Protestant Ulster 1984. Seamus Deane. BiHa; PBCIP

Should I know this room. Locale. Penelope Shuttle. BrRo

Should I my steps turn to the rural seat. James Thomson. *Fr.* Seasons, The. FM; ScCV

Should I not be ashamed. The Ending. Paul Engle. NYBP

Should I say, my people? I turned stone. Maratea Porto: Saying Goodbye to the Vitolos. Richard Hugo. MAT

Should I tell what a miracle she was. *(LL)* The Relic. John Donne. ElL; EnRePo; FaPoB; FHYEP; GBL; HAP; HeIP; ImPo; LiTB; NOBE; NoP; NOSC; OAEL-1; PoEL-2; PPP; TFi

Should I then ranke with Radamanthus fell. A Satyretericall Charracter of a Proud Upstart. John Saffin. SCAP

(March 4th Anno 1698/9; a Charracteristicall Satyre, *diff. vers.*) SCAP

Should I with Silver Tooles Delve through the Hill. Edward Taylor. *Fr.* Preparatory Meditations Before My Approach to the Lord's Supper. ChIV-2, *sect.* II, lvi; EAP, *sect.* LVI; MeMAP; OxBA, *sect.* LVI; SCAP, *sect.* LVI

Should make men atheists and not women whores. *(LL)* A Rapture. Thomas Carew. BeJo; CaPo; ErPo; JCP; NAEL-1; OAEL-1; OxAEP-1; SeCP

Should old acquaintance be forgot. Old-Long-Syne. *Unknown.* (Auld Lang Syne.) NOSC

Should smile like you, and perish as they smile! *(LL)* Evening, as slow thy placid shades descend. William Lisle Bowles. NOEC

Should some ill painter, in a wild design. Horace, *tr. by* John Oldham. *Fr.* Art of Poetry, The. OBVE

Should the building totter, run for an archway! The Fallen Tower of Siloam. Robert Graves. ChIV-2

Should the cold Muscovit, whose furre and stove. To the Right Honourable the Countesse of C. William Habington. SeCP

Should the pillar sing, should salt. Lot. David Helwig. NIP

Should the shade of Plato. On Installing an American Kitchen in Lower Austria. W. H. Auden. NYBP

Should the wide world roll away. Stephen Crane. *Fr.* Black Riders, The. AmPP

Should Thy Love Die. George Meredith. ELP

Should we go now a-wand'ring, we should meet. London in 1646. Henry Vaughan. FaBoPP

Should wear all Time's destructions for a dress. *(LL)* The Poet Laments the Coming of Old Age. Edith Sitwell. NAEL-2; NoAM

Should you ask me, whence these stories. Longfellow. *Fr.* Song of Hiawatha, The. MeMAP; NOBA; PoE; Poetr

Should You Go First. Albert K. Rowswell. BLPL; PoLF; PoToHe

Should You, My Son, My Lord. Phillis Wheatley. *Fr.* To the Right Honourable William, Earl of Dartmouth. AmPP; BPo; ImGa; TTY

Should you, my lord, while you pursue my song. Should You, My Lord. Phillis Wheatley. *Fr.* To the Right Honourable William, Earl of Dartmouth. AmPP; BPo; ImGa; TTY

Should you revisit us. New Approach Needed. Kingsley Amis. NoAM; OxBTC

Shoulder-bag, cloak, unleavened barley-cake, stick. On Diogenes the Cynic. Antiphilus, *tr. fr. Greek by* W. S. Merwin. GrAn

Shoulder of rock, A. High Island. Richard Murphy. CIP; NOIV

Shoulder to shoulder. *(LL)* On your throne, a marvel of art, immortal. Sappho. STV

Shouldered box has nested deep, The. Farewell to a Jovial Friend. Gloria Escoffery. PBCV

Shouldering its way and shedding the earth crumbs. *(LL)* Putting in the Seed. Robert Frost. ErPo; NoAM; OxBA

Shouldering shapes of the skies of Broceliande. Taliessin's Song of the Unicorn. Charles Williams. FaBoTw

Shouldn't I pilfer wantonly this famed fragrance of a foreign land? Su Manshu, *tr. by* Wu-chi Liu. *Fr.* Poems Written during My Sojourn in Japan. SuSp

Shout came from the loquacious ones, A. A Welsh Ballad. Edmwnd Prys, *tr. fr. Welsh by* Gwyn Williams. OBWVE

Shout for Joy. *Unknown.* AmFP

Shout, Little Lulu. *Unknown.* AmFP

Shout, shout, up with your song! The March of the Women. Cicely Hamilton. BrRo

Shouting Song. *Unknown.* AmFP

Shouting the battle cry of Freedom. *(LL)* Battle-Cry of Freedom. George Frederick Root. AnAmPo; FaBoBe; PAH

Shouts rise again from the water. Again in the Black Cloud. J. H. Prynne. VaA

Shovel-gnats gnaw at the open wound, The. On the Edge of the Copper Pit. Pauline Henson. GoYe

Shovel Man, The. Carl Sandburg. HAP

Shovelling Iron Ore. *Unknown.* AS; GBP

Show, The. Wilfred Owen. ImPo; LiTB; LiTM; MoAB; MoBrPo; NSI; OBWVE; OxBTC; PeFWW

Show an affirming flame. *(LL)* September 1, 1939. W. H. Auden. ArOW; CMoP; CoGr; FaBoEH, *abr.*; ImPo; LiTA; MoAB; MoBrPo; OxAEP-2; OxBA; PoE; PrIm

Show from the mountainside of solitude. *(LL)* Compensation. Robinson Jeffers. MoAB; MoAmPo

Show is not the show, The. Emily Dickinson. AmPP

Show me again the time. Lines: To a Movement in Mozart's E-Flat Symphony. Thomas Hardy. ArLo; ELP; NoAM

Show me, dear Christ, Thy Spouse, so bright and clear. John Donne. *See* Show me dear[e] Christ, thy spouse, so bright and clear.

Show me dear Christ, thy spouse, so bright and clear. John Donne. *Fr.* Holy Sonnets. ESCV; MeLP; NAEL-1; NoP; NOSC; PoE; Son

(Show me, dear Christ, Thy Spouse, so bright and clear.) PeECV, *sect.* XVIII

Show me himself, himself (bright Sir) O show. Come See the Place Where the Lord Lay. Richard Crashaw. ChIV-2

Show me the flames you brag of, you that be. On the Great Frost (1634). William Cartwright. NOSC

Show Me the Way. *Unknown, tr. fr. Burmese by* U Win Pe. PBWP

Show me thy feet; show me thy legs, thy thighs. To Dianeme. Robert Herrick. CaPo; NOSC

Show Me Thyself. Margaret E. M. Sangster. TrPWD

"Show me your God!" the doubter cries. Blind. John Kendrick Bangs. PoToHe

Show the runner coming through the shadows. The Runner. Gary Gildner. PRA; TAP

Shower, *sels.* Les A. Murray.
Valet, a Pillar, a Cloudburst of Water, A. CBCK

Shower, The. Linda Smukler. GLP

Shower [or Showre], The. Henry Vaughan. BoNaP; ChTr; ESCV; FaBoPP; GeHe; LiTB; SeCP

Shower, The. Henry Vaughan. BoNaP; ChTr

Shower, a sprinkle, A. Summer Rain. Eve Merriam. PDV

Shower and Sunshine. Maud Morin. BoTP

Showers!. *(LL)* Dying in Your Garden of Death to Go Back into My Garden. *Unknown.* BAP-90

Showing. Liam Rector. TRP

Showing her child before it is born. *(LL)* The Beautiful. W. H. Davies. NTP

Showing Us the Fields. James McCorkle. BAP-89

Shown to My Son Yü. Lu Yu, *tr. fr. Chinese by* Irving Y. Lo. SuSp

Showre, The. Henry Vaughan. *See* Waters above! eternal springs!

Shrapnel lives in Morton's neck, so his head stays. Refuge at the One Step Down. Belle Waring. PBCAP

Shrew, The. Rowland Watkyns. AngWe

Shrewish, barren, bony, nosy servant, A. David O'Bruadair, *tr. fr. Irish by* Thomas Kinsella. NOIV

Shriek said the saw smile said the mice. To the Age's Insanities. Marie Ponsot. VGW

Shrieking its message the flying death. The Shell. H. M. Sarson. NSI; PoWW

Shrieks in dark leaves. The rumpled owl. Hunger and Thirst. John Peale Bishop. PoA

Shrill, glass-clear notes — "Titmouse!" I sighed, enchanted. Tat for Tit. Walter de la Mare. FM

Shrilling cicada, drunk on drops of dew, you sing. Meleager, tr. fr. Greek by Barbara Hughes Fowler. Fr. Epigrams. HePo

Shrilling locust slowly sheathes, The. James Whitcomb Riley. Fr. Beetle, The. FaPON

Shrimp, The, sels. Moses Browne.
  "Shrimp, A! Black thing as widow's crape." NOEC

Shrimp, The. Ogden Nash. CBNP

Shrimp, A! Black thing as widow's crape. Moses Browne. Fr. Shrimp, The. NOEC

Shrimp who sought his lady shrimp, A. The Shrimp. Ogden Nash. CBNP

Shrine and the Burning Wheel, The. Mark Jarman. NAmP90

"Shrink" is a misnomer. The religious. Some Terms. Robert Pinsky. Fr. Essay on Psychiatrists. HCAP

Shropshire Lad, A. Sir John Betjeman. MoBS

Shropshire Lad, A. A. E. Housman. FaPoB
Sels.
  Along the Field as We Came By. HAP; MoAB; MoBrPo; WeW
  "Be still, my soul, be still; the arms you bear are brittle." MoAB; MoBrPo; NOBVV; OAEL-2; OBNC; SCGP; TrGrPo
  Bredon Hill. EBVV; FaBoPP; MoAB; MoBrPo; NAEL-2; OxAEP-2; PlP; SoSe; UV
  Carpenter's Son, The. ChIV-2; MoAB; MoBrPo; OxAEP-2; UV
  1887. FaPoR; NIP; NOBVV; PlP; PrIm; SCGP; UnPo
  Far In a Western Brookland. AWP; PoEL-5
  Farewell to Barn and Stack and Tree. CMoP; MoAB; MoBrPo; UnPo
  From Far, from Eve and Morning. CMoP; HAP; MoBrPo; NoP; PoEL-5; PrIm
  Hughley Steeple. FaBoPP
  I Hoed and Trenched and Weeded. LiTM; MeMBP; MoBrPo; TrGrPo; UnPo; WeW
  "If it chance your eye offend you,." ChIV-2
  Immortal Part, The. MeMBP; MoBrPo; SCGP; SoSe; UnPo
  "In my own shire, if I was sad."
    (In My Own Shire.) PlP
  Into My Heart an Air That Kills. ChTr; CMoP; EBEV; LiTB; LiTM; MeMBP; Mes; MoAB; MoBrPo; NoAM; NOBE; NOBVV; NTP; OAEL-2; OxAEP-2; OxBTC; TFi
  Is My Team Ploughing [or Plowing]. CBLP; CMoP; EBEvV; EBVV; GGP; LiTM; MeMBP; MoAB; MoBrPo; NoAM; NoP; OBD; OBEV; Poetr; TrGrPo
  Isle of Portland, The. MoBrPo
  "It nods and curtseys and recovers." NOBVV
  Lads in Their Hundreds, The. MeMBP; MoBrPo; OxBTC
  Lent Lily, The. OHIP
  Loitering With a Vacant Eye. SoSe
  Look Not in My Eyes, for Fear. PeHV; PoEL-5
  Loveliest of Trees [the Cherry Now]. ArNa; AWP; BLPL; BoNaP; ChTr; ClHu; CMoP; ELP; FaBoBe; FaBV; FF; HAP; InPK; LiTB; LiTM; MeMBP; MoAB; MoBrPo; MoP; NAs; NoAM; NoP; OAEL-2; OHIP; OxBTC; PoE; Poetr; PoLF; PrIm; RB; SoSe; TEP; TFi; TrGrPo
    (Loveliest of Trees, the Cherry Now.) ImPo; NTP; WeW
    (Loveliest of trees, the cherry now.) EBEvV
  New Mistress, The. MoBrPo
  "Now hollow fires burn out to black." NOBVV
  Oh, See How Thick the Goldcup Flowers. FaBV; MeMBP; MoBrPo
  Oh, When I Was in Love with You. BoLoP; CBLP; FaBV; LiTB; MeMBP; MoBrPo; TTTS
  On Moonlit Heath and Lonesome Bank. CMoP; SCGP
  On the idle hill of summer. MoBrPo; NOBE; OAEL-2; OBNC; OBWP
  On Wenlock Edge the Wood's in Trouble. CoGr; GTBS-P; LiTB; MeMBP; Mes; MoAB; MoBrPo; NAEL-2; NOBE; NoP; OBNC; OxAEP-2; OxBTC; PlP; PoEL-5; PoRA; PrIm; RB; SCGP; TFi
  Others, I Am Not the First. CMoP; LiTB; MeMBP; MoBrPo; NOBVV; OxBTC; PoE; PPP
  Reveille. CMoP; LiTB; LiTM; MeMBP; MoAB; MoBrPo; NoP; PoLF
  Shot? So Quick, So Clean an Ending? PeHV
  Terence, This Is Stupid Stuff. CMoP; HeIP; InPK; LiTB; LiTM; MeMBP; MoP; NAEL-2; NoAM; NoP; Poetr; PrIm; TFi
    (Epilogue: "Terence, this is stupid stuff.") MoAB; MoBrPo; TrGrPo
  This Time of Year a Twelvemonth Past. PlP
  "'Tis spring; come out to ramble." OHIP
  To an Athlete Dying Young. BLPL; CMoP; DL; HAP; HeIP; ImPo; InPK; LiTB; LiTM; MeMBP; MoAB; MoBrPo; MoP; NAEL-2; NIP; NoAM; NoP; PoE; PoEL-5; Poetr; PoRA; PrIm; SCGP; SoSe; TEP; TFi; TrGrPo; TRP; UnPo; WeW
  True Lover, The. EBNV

Wenlock Edge (" 'Tis time, I think; by Wenlock town"). FaBoPP

When I was One-and-Twenty. ArLo; CBLP; CMoP; EBEvV; ELP; FaBV; HeIP; ImPo; InPK; LiTB; LiTM; MeMBP; MoAB; MoBrPo; NAEL-2; NoAM; OtMeF; PoE; PoLF; TFi; TrGrPo

When I Watch the Living Meet. CMoP; MoBrPo; NOBVV; NoP; SCGP; TrGrPo

When Smoke Stood up from Ludlow. MoBrPo; SCGP

When the Lad for Longing Sighs. MoBrPo

White in the Moon the Long Road Lies. AWP; CMoP; ELP; LiTB; MeMBP; NTP

With Rue My Heart Is Laden. AWP; BLPL; CMoP; HAP; HeIP; HoPM; ImPo; InPK; LiTB; LiTM; MeMBP; MoAB; MoBrPo; NAEL-2; NoAM; NoP; PoE; Poetr; PrIm; TFi; TrGrPo; UnPo

You Smile upon Your Friend To-day. MeMBP

Shropshire Lad, A. Unknown. ChTr

Shropshire Lad's Cousin, The. Samuel Hoffenstein. BXAP

Shroud. George Mackay Brown. RB

Shroud, The. Galway Kinnell. LCAP

Shrouded Stranger, The. Allen Ginsberg. NeAP

Shrouding of the Duchess of Malfi, The. John Webster. See Hark, Now Everything Is Still.

Shrovetide's Countenance. Rabelais, tr. fr. French by Sir Thomas Urquhart. FaBoNo

Shrub of tourists, A. Thoughts under the Giant Sequoia. Edmund Pennant. BTR

Shrubbery, The. William Cowper. FaBoRV; NOBE

Shu' Shu' of Delgo. Albert Brodrick. PeSAV

Shua-O! Shua-O! (LL) Scaring Crows. Unknown. BoTP; OxNR

Shubble, The. Walter de la Mare. FaBoNo

Shudder, The. Donald Hall. NYBP

Shuddring the Spectre howls, his howlings terrify the night. Blake. Fr. Jerusalem. OAEL-2

Shuffle and shudder of Autumn, The. Autumn Imagined. Donald Davie. PoA

Shui Shu., sels. Unknown, tr. fr. Japanese by Arthur Waley.
  "Deer which lives, The." AWP
  "If it were not for the voice." AWP
  River-Fog. AWP; FaPON
  "Time I went to see my Sister, The." AWP
  "When,/ Halting in front of it, I look." AWP
  "Winter has at last come." AWP

Shule, Shule, Shule, Agrah! "Fiona Macleod." OHCV

Shule, shule, shule, agrah! (LL) Shule, Shule, Shule, Agrah! "Fiona Macleod." OHCV

Shun delays, they breed remorse. Loss in Delay. Robert Southwell. NoSic

Shun my paws if you care to live. (LL) The Wolf and the Stork. La Fontaine. FM; OBVE

Shut fast again in Beauty's sheath. Monochrome. Louise Imogen Guiney. AmWP

Shut-In, The. Nellie De Hearn. PoToHe

Shut In. Robert B. Shaw. SoSe

Shut in from all the world without. Whittier. Fr. Snow-bound; a Winter Idyl [or Idyll]. AmPP; GN; NOBA; OBCP; OxBA; TAP; WiR

Shut not me alive away. The Commuted Sentence. Stevie Smith. OxAEP-2

Shut not so soon; the dull-eyed night. To Daisies, Not to Shut So Soon[e]. Robert Herrick. BeJo; CaPo; CH; ELP; GBL; OBEV; OxBSP; SeCV-1; TrGrPo

Shut Not Your Doors. Walt Whitman. NOBA; OxBA

Shut one eye then the other. Before the Game. Vasco [or Vasko] Popa, tr. fr. Serbo-Croatian. TSaS, tr. by Charles Simic

Shut Out. Christina Rossetti. NALW; PFP

Shut out/ of Masaccio's chapel where I'd tried. Sleeping in Santo Spirito. Bruce Beasley. UTF

Shut Out That Moon. Thomas Hardy. CMoP; NoAM; NOBE

Shut the gallery lock the door. Mouth. Dennis Scott. PBCV

Shut the Seven Seas against Us. George Barker. Fr. Third Cycle of Love Poems. MoAB; MoBrPo

Shut up! (LL) Why all the racket, you chattering birds? Unknown. GrAn; PeHV

Shut up. Shut up. There's nobody here. The Beast in the Space. W. S. Graham. FaBoTw; OxAEP-2; PoA

Shut-winged fish, brown as mushroom. Swifts. Glyn Jones. AngWe

Shut your trap, you. The question is, what about Karl Marx? (LL) Cultural Notes. Kenneth Fearing. CMoP; PoE

Shuts up her springs, and will no grace impart. (LL) If ever Sorrow spoke from soul that loves. Henry Constable. EiL; ESo

Shuts up the story of our days. (LL) Nature, That Washed [or Washt] Her Hands in Milk[e]. Sir Walter Ralegh. EnRePo; NoP

Shutter of time darkening ceaselessly, The. August. Louis MacNeice. LiTM

Shutting my gate, I walk away. All Souls. Ruth Bidgood. AngWe

Shuttles of trains going north, going south, drawing threads of blue. Morning Sun. Louis MacNeice. MoAB; MoBrPo; TwCP

Shy and timid, Gloom to me. The Outcast. James Stephens. MoBrPo

Shy Geordie. Helen B. Cruickshank. OxBS

Shy in their herding dwell the fallow deer. Deer. John Drinkwater. CH

Shy one, shy one. To an Isle in the Water. W. B. Yeats. AWP; TTTS

Shy speechless sound, The. Osip Mandelstam, tr. fr. Russian by Clarence Brown and W. S. Merwin. Spl

Shyly the silver-hatted mushrooms make. May. John Shaw Neilson. NOBAu

Shyness and modesty, they said. Disillusionment. Virginia Graham. NBLV

Si Hubbard. Unknown. AS

Si Monumentum Requiris. Daryl Hine. EOEF

Si, señor, is halligators here, your guidebook say it. Sinalóa. Earle Birney. MoCV; OxBC; PeLV

Siamese twins: one, maddened by. Twins. Robert Graves. FaBoEE

Siberia. James Clarence Mangan. BIrV; NOBVV; NOIV; PeIV

Sibilla's Dirge. Thomas Lovell Beddoes. See We Do Lie beneath the Grass.

Sibrandus Schafnaburgensis. Robert Browning. Fr. Garden Fancies. CTC; EBVV; TEP

Sibyl, The. Joan LaBombard. GoYe

Sibylla Palmifera. Dante Gabriel Rossetti. See Under the arch of life, where love and death.

Sibylline, yet benign. (LL) "Formerly a Slave." Herman Melville. PoNe; TAP

Sibyl's Song, The. Michele Roberts. BrRo

Sic a man was never seen. (LL) Wee man o' leather. Unknown. ChTr; GBP

Sic et Non. Sir Herbert Read. FaBoTw

Sic Itur. Arthur Hugh Clough. EBVV

Sic kindly kisses as he gae me. (LL) Kiss'd Yestreen. Unknown. ErPo; GBP; OtMeF

Sic Transit. At. to Thomas Proctor. See Ay me, ay me, I sigh to see the scythe afield.

Sic Transit Gloria Scotia. "Hugh MacDiarmid." CMoP

Sic Vita. At. to Henry King. CBCK; CoGr; ELP; FF; NOBE; NOSC; OxBSP; SCGP; SeCP

Sic Vita. Thoreau. See I Am a Parcel of Vain Strivings Tied.

Sicelides, sels. Phineas Fletcher.
Woman's Inconstancy. EIL

Sich a Nice Man Too! sels. Albert Chevalier.
"There's parties ad yer meets about." UV

Sicilian Cyclamens. D. H. Lawrence. NoAM

Sicilian Muse, I Would Try Now a Somewhat Grander Theme. Virgil. See Scilian Muse, begin a loftier strain.

Sicilian Muse, thy voice and subject raise. The Golden Age. Unknown. APAS

Sicilian Muses, sing we greater things. Virgil. See Scilian Muse, begin a loftier strain.

Sick . . . Sick . . . I will lie down and die. How. Isaac Rosenberg. Fr. Unicorn, The. PeFWW

Sick, am I sick of a jealous dread? Tennyson. Fr. Maud[: A Monodrama]. EnVR

Sick Birds, The, sels. H. Leivick, tr. fr. Yiddish.

Sick Child, The. Lydia Huntley Sigourney. AmWP

Sick Child, The. Robert Louis Stevenson. CH

Sick Child, A. Randall Jarrell. InPK; InvP; OxBC; VGW

Sick Cicada. Chia Tao, tr. fr. Chinese by Stephen Owen. SuSp

Sick cicada, unable now to fly, A. Sick Cicada. Chia Tao, tr. fr. Chinese by Stephen Owen. SuSp

Sick Image of My Father Fades, The. John Horder. RaBo; TEP

Sick Love. Robert Graves. BoLoP; CMoP; EBEV; GTBS-P; HAP; NOBE; OAEL-2; OxAEP-2

Sick Man, The. Wallace Stevens. Jaz

Sick Nought, The. Randall Jarrell. OxBA

Sick of all his women. Gambit. Tony Curtis. AngWe

Sick of the day's heat, of noise. The Underground Gardens. Robert Mezey. NaP

Sick of the piercing company of women. A Country Walk. Thomas Kinsella. CIP; CMoP

Sick of thy northern glooms, come, shepherd, seek. Philip Freneau. Fr. Beauties of Santa Cruz, The. AmPP; EAP

Sick person who does not suffer from chaotic respiration is taken care of, The. Henri Michaux, tr. fr. French. Fr. Emanglons, The. AnRep, tr. by Richard Ellmann

Sick-room, The. Maria White Lowell. AmWP

Sick-Room, The. R. A. Simpson. TSaS

Sick Rose, The. Blake. Fr. Songs of Experience. AWP; BoLoP; ChTr; ClHu; CoGr; EBEvV; ELP; EnLoPo; FHYEP; HAP; HeIP; InPK; InPS; MeMBP; NAEL-2; NAWM-2; NIP; NOBE; NOEC; NoP; OAEL-2; OBNC; OxAEP-2; OxBSP; PoE; PoEL-4; Poetr; PPP; PrIm; RB; SCGP; SoSe; TFi; TrGrPo; TRP; WeW

Sick Stockrider, The, sels. Adam Lindsay Gordon.
"I've had my share of pastime, and I've done my share of toil." OtMeF

Sick Stockrider, The. Adam Lindsay Gordon. CBAP

Sick unto Death of Love. Malay Oral Tradition, tr. by R. J. Wilkinson and R. O. Winstedt. WTO

Sickens my gut, Yellow Bittern. The Yellow Bittern. Unknown, tr. fr. Irish by Tom MacIntyre. CIP

Sickens my gut, Yellow Bittern. The Yellow Bittern. Tom MacIntyre. PBCIP

Sickles sound. Harvest Song. Ludwig Heinrich Christoph Hölty, tr. fr. German by Charles T. Brooks. AWP

Sickly taper/ By glimmering through thy low-browed misty vaults, The. Robert Blair. Fr. Grave, The. ECEV

Sickness, sels. William Thompson.
"Next, in a low-browed cave, a little hell." ECEV

Sickness and death, you are but sluggish things. A Winged Heart. Henry Vaughan. Fr. Of Life and Death. FaBoRV

Sickness, intending my love to betray. Sir John Davies. Fr. Sonnets to Philomel. SiPS

Sickness of Adam, The. Karl Shapiro. Fr. Adam and Eve. CRP; MoAB

Sickness of desire, that in dark days, The. Melancholia. Robert Bridges. CMoP

Sickness of Friends, The. Henri Coulette. NYBP

Sicknesses/ That are superficially and foolishly handled. Conversation with Rilke about Dragons. Rose Drachler. BCF

Sidanein, sels. Ludovic Lloyd.
"Flee, stately Juno, Samos fro." AngWe

Side by side after the meal. Valerio Magrelli, tr. fr. Italian by Dana Gioia. NeIt

Side by side in the crowded streets. The Cantelope. Bayard Taylor. AnAmPo

Side by side on the narrow bed. That Room. John Montague. CIP

Side by side, their faces blurred. An Arundel Tomb. Philip Larkin. FaBoEH; FaPoB; OxAEP-2; OxBM; PPP

Side Window. John James. ImPo; VaA

Sidera Cadentia. Ford Madox Ford. OxBSP

Sidewalk joins the concrete wall around the vacant lot, The. Where or When. Philip Whalen. PoM

Sidewalk Racer; or, On the Skateboard, The. Lillian Morrison. NTCP

Sidewalks of New York, The. James W. Blake. BLPA; FaBoBe

Sidonie. Jack Collom. UL

Sidrophel, the Rosicrucian Conjurer. Samuel Butler. Fr. Hudibras. OxBoLi

Sieg! Heil! Victory! Salvation!, The. Weltanschauung. Charles Fishman. BTR

Siege. Gillian Clarke. SCBI

Siege of Belgrade, The. At. to Alaric Alexander Watts. See Austrian Army, An.

Siege of Chapultepec, The. William Haines Lytle. PAH

Siege of Thebes, The, sels. John Lydgate.
"When brighte Phoebus passed was the Ram." EPCY

Siege of Valencia, sels. Felicia Dorothea Hemans.
"Calm on the bosom of thy God." OBEV
(Dirge, A ("Calm on the bosom of thy God").) WoRP

Siena Mi Fe'; Disfecemi Maremma. Ezra Pound. Fr. Hugh Selwyn Mauberly. (Life and Contacts). AmPP; CMoP; InPS; LiTA; LiTM; MoAmPo; NoAM; NOBA; NoP; TAP

Sierra. Alfonsina Storni, tr. fr. Spanish by Rachel Benson. PBWP

Sierra Kid, sels. Philip Levine.
He Faces the Second Winter. PoA

Siesta, The. Unknown, tr. fr. Spanish by Bryant. AWP

Siesta of a Hungarian Snake. Edwin Morgan. InPK

"Sieurs et dames!" and the door slams. A Day in France. David Holbrook. OBTV

Sieve, A. Mother Goose. See Riddle, a riddle, A/ As I suppose.

Sifting. Victor Emanuel Beck. GoYe

Sigh. Stéphane Mallarmé, tr. fr. French by Arthur Symons. AWP

Sigh. Sully-Prudhomme, tr. fr. French by Philip L. Miller. RiWo

Sigh, A. The Countess of Winchilsea. ECWP

Sigh, heart, and break not; rest, lark, and wake not! Nuptial Song. Lord De Tabley. GTBS-P; PeVV

Sigh, in the wind fall flowers, their petals dance. Selling Ruined Peonies. Yü Hsüan-chi, *tr. fr. Chinese by* Geoffrey R. Waters. BoWoP

Sigh, Louise, for you. (*LL*) The Youth to the Spring. Johann Gaudenz von Salis-Seewis. RiWo

Sigh no more, dealers, sigh no more. Much Ado about Nothing in the City. *Unknown.* FaBoPa; UV

Sigh no more, ladies [sigh no more]. Shakespeare. *Fr.* Much Ado about Nothing. AWP; CTC; EIL; ELP; FF; LiTB; NoSic; TrGrPo; UV (Song: "Sigh no more, ladies, sigh no more.") PoEL-2

Sigh, Sigh, Rushes. Gustaf Fröding, *tr. fr. Swedish by* Philip L. Miller. RiWo

Sigh sounds and a sough replies, A. The Ballad of Mulan. *Unknown, tr. fr. Chinese by* William H. Nienhauser. SuSp

Sigh that heaves the grasses, The. A. E. Housman. NOBVV

Sigh there thy last, and therewith break. (*LL*) Comfort thyself, my woeful [or woful] heart. Sir Thomas Wyatt. SiPS; SiPSBD

Sigh, wind in the pine. Douglas Stewart. *Fr.* Glencoe. CBAP; FaBoMA

Sighed a dear little shipboard divinity. Conrad Aiken. OBAL; PeLi

Sighing, and Sadly Sitting by My Love. Richard Barnfield. *Fr.* Cynthia. Son

Sighing, and sadly sitting by my Love. Richard Barnfield. *Fr.* Sonnets. PeHV

Sighing high and/ again a sigh! Weaving at the Window. Wang Chien, *tr. fr. Chinese by* William H. Nienhauser. SuSp

Sighing I murmur, *"O mihi pratteritos!"* (*LL*) Eheu Fugaces. "Thomas Ingoldsby." FaBoEE; OxBoLi

Sighing over Flowers. Tu Mu, *tr. fr. Chinese by* Eddie Tsang. SuSp

Sighing, sleeping alone all night. Mother of Michitsuna, *tr. fr. Japanese by* Kenneth Rexroth *and* Ikuko Atsumi. WPJ

Sighing that our years will soon be done? (*LL*) Evening: for Chang Chi and Chou K'uang. Han Yü. PLT

Sighs and Grones. George Herbert. PoEL-2

Sighs Are My Food. Sir Thomas Wyatt. *See* Sighs are my food, drink are my tears.

Sighs are my food, drink are my tears. Sir Thomas Wyatt. SiPS (Sighs Are My Food. NoSic; OxBSP)

Sighs of the Gunner from Dakar, The. Guillaume Apollinaire, *tr. fr. French by* Anne Hyde Greet. PeFWW

Sight. W. W. Gibson. MoBrPo

Sight, A. Robert Creeley. NaP

Sight and Insight. Eleanor Slater. TrPWD

Sight in Camp [in the Daybreak Gray and Dim], A. Walt Whitman. AmPP; MoP; NAAL-1; NoAM; OxBA; PoE; PoEL-5; SAmP; TAP

Sight of all these people in the street, The. Good People. Maura Stanton. SM

Sight of the coffee was good for sore eyes, The. Upon Receipt of a Pound of Coffee in 1863. Mary E. Tucker. AmWP; CBWP-1

Sight of the English is getting me down, The. Hiraeth in N.W.3. Wynford Vaughan-Thomas. NOBL

Sight Unseen. Kingsley Amis. ErPo; NoAM

Sighted a black tornado of. Comments. Peggy Susberry Kenner. JB

Sighted the shining waters and descended. (*LL*) The Spiritual Canticle. St. John of the Cross. STV

Sightings. Frances Horovitz. PWE

Sightseers, The. Paul Muldoon. BiHa; CIP

Sightseers in a Courtyard. Nicolás Guillén, *tr. fr. Spanish by* Langston Hughes. TTY

Sigil, *sels.* Hilda Doolittle ("H. D.").
"Are these ashes in my hand." AnAn
"Are we unfathomable night." AnAn
"But it won't be that way." AnAn
"I could say." AnAn
"I love you." AnAn
"If you take the moon in your hands." AnAn; FaBoWP (Moon in Your Hands, The.) BoWoP; NYBP
"Let me be." AnAn
"Now let the cycle sweep us here and there." AnAn; VGW
"So if you love me." AnAn
"There is no signpost to say." AnAn
"Time breaks the barrier." AnAn
"You'll go on, talking away." AnAn

Sigismonda and Guiscardo, *sels.* Dryden.

Sigismundo. Linda Gregg. AmPA

Sigmund Freud. Howard Nemerov. PoA

Sigmund Freud says that one who reflects. Peter Alexander. PeLi

Sign for father, The. (*LL*) Quinnapoxet. Stanley Kunitz. AnAn

Sign for My Father, Who Stressed the Bunt. David Bottoms. MT

Sign of Saturn, The. Sharon Olds. InPS

Sign of the Bonny Blue Bell, The. *Unknown.* OBET

Sign says Public Bridlepath but long ago the tracks through, The. Pavane for a Dead Cat. Tim Longville. VaA

Sign your name in the book. It's just ink. Sydney Bernard Smith. PeLi

Signal, The. David Ignatow. NNaP

Signal Fire, The. Aeschylus, *tr. by* Dallam Simpson. *Fr.* Agamemnon. CTC; NAWM-1

Signal flutters at the Flagship's fore, A. The Sailing of the Fleet. N.M.F. Corbett. NSI

Signal Gun, The. Mary E. Tucker. CBWP-1

Signal Hill. Sharon Doubiago. ETG; NGP

Signal; or, A Satire against Modesty, The, *sels.* Francis Hawling. Author Consults a Critic and Sells His Manuscript, The. NOEC

Signals. Jewel C. Latimore. PoBA

Signature. Hannah Kahn. IHMS

Signature for Tempo. Archibald MacLeish. CRP; VGW

Signature of All Things, The. (My head and my shoulders, and my book.) Kenneth Rexroth. NNaP; NU; TRP
Sels.
"When I dragged the rotten log." BoNaP

Signatures. Daniel Hoffman. VGW

Significance of a Water Animal, The. Ray A. Young Bear. HATNAP

Significant Fevers. Alison Fell. BrRo

Signpost. Robinson Jeffers. GoYe

Signs, *sels.* Ahmad al-Mushari al-Udwani, *tr. fr. Arabic.*

Signs. Jean Follain, *tr. fr. French by* W. S. Merwin. AnRep

Signs. Charles Martin. SM

Signs. Alejandra Pizarnik, *tr. by* Susan Bassnett. VBLP

Signs, The. Norman Henry, II Pritchard. NBV

Signs. Gjertrud Schnackenberg. InPK; PoA; VCAP

Signs of Christmas. Edwin Lees. OHIP

Signs of Love. Petrarch, *tr. fr. Italian.* *Fr.* Sonnets to Laura. AWP

Signs of Rain. Edward Jenner. BLPA; BoNaP; FaBoUs

Signs of Spring. Sir Thomas Browne. NOSC

Signs of the Times. Paul Laurence Dunbar. AnAmPo

Signs of the Zodiac, The. Ebenezer Cobham Brewer. FaBoUs

Signs of wear. Monogram 29. Martina Werner, *tr. fr. German by* Rosemarie Waldrop. BoWoP

Signs of Winter. John Clare. BoNaP; WiR
Sels.
"Cat runs races with her tail, The." OAEL-2

Sigurd of yore. The Lay [or Short Lay] of Sigurd. *Unknown, tr. by* William Morris *and* Eirikr Magnusson. *Fr.* Elder Edda, The. AWP

Sigurd Rideth to the Glittering Heath. William Morris. *Fr.* Story of Sigurd the Volsung, The. PoEL-5

Siilenboor. *Mongol Oral Tradition, tr. by* C. R. Bawden. WTO

Sila. Robert Penn Warren. NoP

Silence — . (*LL*) Twilight is a time for sharing — and a time for. Winston Abbott. EaPr

Silence. Bella Akhmadulina, *tr. fr. Russian by* Daniel Halpern. BoWoP

Silence. Alvin Aubert. MT

Silence. Robert Bly. NaP

Silence. E. E. Cummings. CMoP; PoE

Silence. Miroslav Holub, *tr. fr. Czech by* Ian Milner *and* Jarmila Milner. PoSu

Silence. Thomas Hood. CH; EBEV; EnRP; NOBE; OBEV; PoEL-4; Son

Silence. Tymoteusz Karpowicz, *tr. fr. Polish by* Jan Darowski. PoSu

Silence, The. Tomas Mac Siomoin, *tr. fr. Irish by the author.* TIRV

Silence. René Maran, *tr. fr. French by* Ellen Conroy Kennedy. NegPo

Silence. Edgar Lee Masters. MoAmPo; PoToHe

Silence. Marianne Moore. AnAmPo; CMoP; CoGr; FaBoMo; FaBoWP; InPS; LiTA; NALW; NOBA; TRP

Silence. Charles Hanson Towne. WGRP

Silence. W. J. Turner. MoBrPo

Silence. John Hall Wheelock. LiTM

Silence. William Carlos Williams. SAmP

Silence: A Sonnet. Henry King. NOSC

Silence all flesh, your selves prepare. A Judicious Observation of That Dreadful Comet. Ichabod Wiswall. SCAP

Silence, an Eloquent Applause. Leona Gregory. TrCP

Silence and aura. An ancient Yemenite woman gathers dry. Gleaning. David Shimoni, *tr. fr. Hebrew by* Ruth Finer Mintz. MHP

Silence, and on the wall the photographs. Government in Exile. Dick Davis. SCBI

Silence and poetry have their own reserves. T'ark. Tony Harrison. *Fr.* Art & Extinction. SCBI

Silence and solitude were vacancy? (*LL*) Mont Blanc. Shelley. EnRP; InPS; NAEL-2; NIP; NoP; OAEL-2; OBTV; TEP

Silence and Stealth of Day[e]s! Henry Vaughan. ESCV; JCP; NAEL-1; SeCV-1

Silence augmenteth grief, writing increaseth rage. Epitaph on Sir Philip Sidney. *At. to* Fulke Greville *and to* Sir Edward Dyer. EnRePo; LiTB; Prf; SCGP
  (Epitaph Upon the Right Honorable Sir Philip Sidney.) Prf

Silence brought by the dark night: Eryri's. Nightfall. Walter Davies, *tr. fr. Welsh by* Anthony Conran. OBWVE

Silence Concerning an Ancient Stone. Rosario Castellanos, *tr. fr. Spanish by* George D. Schade. PBWP

Silence in Court. "Lewis Carroll." *See* "They told me you had been to her."

Silence, in truth, would speak my sorrow best. Tears at the Grave of Sir Albertus Morton. Sir Henry Wotton. SeCP

Silence Invoked. Richard Flecknoe.

Silence is harder, Una said. The Cup. Judith Wright. FaBoWP

Silence is sucking the earth dry. Silence. Tymoteusz Karpowicz, *tr. fr. Polish by* Jan Darowski. PoSu

Silence of our watching, waiting springs, A. A View. Beverly Quint. NYBP

Silence on silence treads at each low morn. Philoctetes. Lord De Tabley. NOBVV

Silence. She Is Six Years Old. Lynn Emanuel. CrSp

Silence slipping around like death, A. A Winter Twilight. Angelina Weld Grimké. CDC; PoBA; PoNe; ShDr

Silence Spoke with Your Voice. Ryah Tumarkin Goodman. GoYe

Silence! "The best" (he said) "are silent now." On the Death of Lord Tennyson. Andrew Lang *and* Edward Burnett Tylor. EPCY

Silences. David Mitchell. PeNZ

Silences. Arthur O'Shaughnessy. OBNC

Silences. E. J. Pratt. NOBC

Silences. Linda Saunders. NWP

Silences; a Dream of Governments. Jean Valentine. LCAP

Silent, about-to-be-parted-from house. Denise Levertov. PoA

Silent alone, where none or saw, or heard. Anne Bradstreet. *Fr.* Contemplations. AmPP; EAP; PBWP; PoEL-3, *abr.*; SCAP; WPE, *abr.*

Silent are the woods, and the dim green boughs are. On Eastnor Knoll. John Masefield. CH

Silent as we, but crazed, crazed as the flame. (*LL*) The Lumberyard. Ruth Herschberger. LiTA; WPE

Silent bivouac of the dead, we say, A. Decorating the Soldiers' Graves. Minot Judson Savage. OHIP

Silent friend of many distances, feel. Rainer Maria Rilke, *tr. fr. German. Fr.* Sonnets to Orpheus. EnlH, *tr. by* Stephen Mitchell

Silent Girl, The. Joseph Freiherr von Eichendorff, *tr. fr. German by* Philip L. Miller. RiWo

Silent girl, The. In the Library. Ed Ochester. Poetsp

Silent hammers of decay. (*LL*) The Hammers. Ralph Hodgson. GoJo; MoBrPo; NOBE; OxBTC

Silent Hour. Rainer Maria Rilke, *tr. fr. German by* Jessie Lemont. AWP

Silent hush, the rusted hinges, The. Who Will Live in Our Houses When We Die? Michael C. Blumenthal. NoAM

Silent I gaze at the cataract. By the Waterfall. Friedrich Adler, *tr. fr. German by* Jethro Bithell. TrJP

Silent, I go up alone to the Western Pavilion. Tune: "Joy at Meeting." Li Yü, *tr. fr. Chinese by* Eugene Eoyang. SuSp

Silent Icicles, The. Samuel Taylor Coleridge. *Fr.* Frost at Midnight. BoTP; EBEV; EnRP; FaBoRV; FHYEP; HAP; MeMBP; NAEL-2; NAs; NOBE; NoP; OAEL-2; OBNC; PFP; PoE; PoEL-4; Poetr; PPP; PrIm; TFi; TOF

Silent in America. Philip Levine. NaP

Silent is the house: all are laid asleep. The Visionary. Emily Brontë. BrRo; CH; ELP; MeMBP; SCGP
  (Visionary, The.) BLPL; LiTB; NOBE; NOBVV; OBNC; PBWP; SCV

Silent Love. John Clare. EnRP

Silent Lover, The. Sir Walter Ralegh. ElL; OBEV, *abr. Sels.*
  "Passions are liken'd best to floods and streams." LiTB
  Wrong Not, Sweete Empress of My Heart.
    (Merit of True Passion, The.) LiTB

Silent Marriage. James Simmons. PWE

Silent Night, The. Mrs. Henry Linden. CBWP-4

Silent Night. Peter McDonald. PWE

Silent Noon. Dante Gabriel Rossetti. *Fr.* House of Life, The. EnVR; HAP; NAEL-2; NoP; OBNC; PFP; PoEL-5; TrGrPo; UnAS

Silent, O Moyle, be the roar of thy water. The Song of Fionnuala. Thomas Moore. BIrV

Silent on the subject of vengeance. Sappho, *tr. fr. Greek by* Sam Hamill. InMo

Silent One, The, *sels.* Ivor Gurney.

"Who died on the wires, and hung there, one of two." NAEL-2; OBD; OBWP; PeFWW; PoWW

Silent Piano, The. Louis Simpson. CAPP

Silent Poem. Robert Francis. CRP; LCAP

Silent Prophet, The. Norman Jordan. NBV

Silent Room, The. Kingsley Amis. OxBC

Silent room — gray with a dusty blight, A. Among His Books. E. Nesbit. NOBVV

Silent scream? The madrigal's top note?, A. Prague Spring. Tony Harrison. OBTV

Silent Slain, The. Archibald MacLeish. *See* We too, we too, descending once again.

Silent slain, The. (*LL*) The Too-late Born. Archibald MacLeish. GoJo; MeMAP; MoAB; MoAmPo; OxBA

Silent sliding silver waterfalls and stars. (*LL*) Fireworks. Valerie Worth. NTCP

Silent Snake, The. *Unknown.* BoTP; FaPON

Silent snakes goes creepy-creep!, The. (*LL*) The Silent Snake. *Unknown.* BoTP; FaPON

Silent stars. (*LL*) Happiness between Two People. Viggo Henrik Fog Stuckenberg. RiWo

Silent stream flows on and in its glass, The. The River. Edwin Muir. MeMBP

Silent the maid with the spindle spun. The Maid. Nathan Alterman, *tr. fr. Hebrew by* Ruth Finer Mintz. MHP

Silent Town, The. Richard Dehmel, *tr. fr. German by* Jethro Bithell. AWP

"Silent upon a peak in Darien." Darien. Sir Edwin Arnold. PAH

Silent, upon a peak in Darien. (*LL*) On First Looking into Chapman's Homer. Keats. BLPA; CH; ChTr; ClHu; CoGr; EBEvV; EnRP; EPCY; FaBoBe; FaBoCh; FaBV; FaPoB; FF; FHYEP; GN; GTBS; GTBS-P; HAP; HeIL; HeIP; HoPM; ImPo; InPK; LiTB; MeMBP; NAWM-2; NIP; NOBE; NoP; OAEL-2; OBAL; OBEV; OBNC; OxAEP-2; PIP; PoE; PoEL-4; Poetr; PPP; PrIm; SCGP; Son; SoSe; TEP; TFi; TrGrPo; TRP

Silent Woman, The, *sels.* Ben Jonson.
  "Still to be neat, still to be dressed [*or* drest]." BeJo; OxBSP; Poetr; TFi
    (Simplicity and Sweet Neglect.) OxAEP-1
  (Song.) EBEvV, *sect.* I, *pt.* i; PFP, *sect.* I, *pt.* i
    (Song: "Still to be neat, still to be dressed.") EnRePo

Silent Woman to the University of Oxford, The, *sels.* Dryden.
  "What Greece, when learning flourished, only knew." NOSC

Silent Wood, A. Elizabeth Siddal. NOBVV

Silent Words, The. Haim Guri, *tr. fr. Hebrew by* Ruth Finer Mintz. MHP

Silent, you say, I'm grown of late. Walter Savage Landor. GBL

Silently. Hatsui Shizue, *tr. fr. Japanese by* Kenneth Rexroth. PRA

Silently and very fast. (*LL*) The Fall of Rome. W. H. Auden. InPS; MAT; OAEL-2; OxBTC; UnPo

Silently my wife walks on the still wet furze. Berry Picking. Irving Layton. HeIP; MoCV; NIP; NoP

Silently, slowly falls the snow from an ashen sky. Snowfall. Giosuè Carducci, *tr. fr. Italian by* Romilda Rendel. AWP

Silently/ time passes. Hatsui Shizue, *tr. fr. Japanese by* Kenneth Rexroth *and* Ikuko Atsumi. WPJ

Silenus in Proteus. Thomas Lovell Beddoes. EnRP

Silet. Ezra Pound. MoAB; MoAmPo; Son

Silhouette. Marc Cohen. EOEF

Silhouette. Annette M'Baye, *tr. fr. French by* Kathleen Weaver. PBWP

Silhouette/ On the face of the moon. Shadow. Richard Bruce. CDC

Silhouettes, they lean against a ringed moon. Paiute Ponies. Jim Barnes. CDW

Silica Carbonate Rock. Fred Berry. NU

Silk Merchant's Daughter, The. *Unknown.* OxBSS

Silk Robe. Jeffrey Skinner. PBCAP

Silk,/ Satin. *Unknown.* OxNR

Silk Weaver's Daughter, The. *Unknown.* AmFP

Silken Snake, The. Robert Herrick. OxBSP

Silken Tent, The. Robert Frost. AmPP; BLPL; HeIL; ImPo; InPK; NOBA; Son; TAP; TRP; TwCP; WeW

Silkworms, The. Douglas Stewart. CBAP; FaBoMA

Siller Croun, The. Susanna Blamire. ECWP

Silly Boy. *Unknown.* NOSC

Silly boy, there is no cause. Thomas Pestel. EiL

Silly boy, 'tis full moon yet, thy night as day shines clearly. First Love. Thomas Campion. GBL; OxBoLi

Silly boy, wert you but wise. Silly Boy. *Unknown.* NOSC

Silly country maiden went, A. Leda in Stratford, Ont. Anne Wilkinson. MoCV

Silly Fool, The. W. H. Auden. OBMV

Silly girl! Yet morning lies. To a Pretty Girl. Israel Zangwill. TrJP

Silly Old Man, The. *Unknown.* CoMu

Silly Song. Federico García Lorca, *tr. fr. Spanish by* M. D. Herter Norton. TTTS

Silly swain whose love breeds discontent, The. Tityrus to His Fair Phyllis. John Dickenson. *Fr.* Shepherd's Complaint, The. ElL

Silly Sweetheart. *Unknown.* CH

Silos, The. Nancy Paddock. LoHo

Silver. A. R. Ammons. NoP

Silver. Walter de la Mare. BoNaP; BoTP; FaPON; MoAB; MoBrPo; PoRA; PYC; TTTS

Silver Age, The, *sels.* Thomas Heywood. Praise of Ceres. ElL

Silver bark of beech, and sallow. Counting-out Rhyme. Edna St. Vincent Millay. GoJo; InPK; MoShBr; Poetr; SoSe; TTTS

Silver Bells. Hamish Hendry. BoTP

Silver birch is a dainty lady, The. Child's Song in Spring. E. Nesbit. BoTP; OHIP; OxBChV

Silver Bowl, The, *sels.* Joseph Ezobi, *tr. fr. Spanish by* D. I. Friedmann. Barren Soul, A. TrJP

Silver Dagger, The. *Unknown.* AmFP

Silver dust. Pear Tree. Hilda Doolittle ("H. D."). BoWoP; CMoP; MoAmPo; NOBA; PoE; UnPo

Silver Eros the ankle bracelet, The. Leonidas of Tarentum, *tr. fr. Greek by* Peter Levi. GrAn

Silver Flask, The. John Montague. CIP; PNI

Silver-footed girl was bathing, letting the water, The. Rufinus Domesticus, *tr. fr. Greek by* Barbara Hughes Fowler. *Fr.* Epigrams. HePo

Silver herring throbbed thick in my seine, The. Kenneth Leslie. *Fr.* By Stubborn Stars. ErPo
(Sonnet: "Silver herring throbbed thick in my seine, The.") NOBC

Silver House, The. John Lea. BoTP

Silver Jubilee. Llewelyn Wyn Griffith. OBWVE

Silver Lake. Brigit Pegeen Kelly. NAmP90

Silver Love, an anklet, A. Leonidas of Tarentum, *tr. fr. Greek by* Kenneth Rexroth. PGA

Silver Lucifer, A. Lunar Baedeker. Mina Loy. VGW

Silver Mist, The. John Clare. FHYEP

Silver mist more lowly swims, The. The Silver Mist. John Clare. FHYEP

Silver Nakedness in Calumet City. Connie Deanovich. UTF

Silver Penny, The. Walter de la Mare. CMoP; NTP; OBMV

Silver rain, the shining sun, The. The Harvest. Alice Corbin. BoTP

Silver Road, The. Hamish Hendry. BoTP

Silver-scaled Dragon with jaws flaming red, A. The Toaster. William Jay Smith. GrPl; OTCP

Silver Ships. Mildred Plew Meigs. FaPON

Silver Swan, The. *At. to* Orlando Gibbons. ChTr; ElL; ELP; EnRePo; FaBoCh; HAP; HeIP; IMW; InPK; NAEL-1; NoP; OBD; OxBSP

Silver swan, who living had no note, The. The Silver Swan. *At. to* Orlando Gibbons. ChTr; ElL; ELP; EnRePo; FaBoCh; HAP; HeIP; IMW; InPK; NAEL-1; NoP; OBD; OxBSP
(Silver Swan[ne], Who Living Had No Note, The.) InPK; PoEL-2; RB

Silver Swan, Who Living Had No Note, The. *At. to* Orlando Gibbons. *See* Silver swan, who living had no note, The.

Silver Tassie, The. Burns. GTBS; GTBS-P; NOBE; OBEV; ScCV

Silver trumpets rang across the Dome, The. Easter Day. Oscar Wilde. OxAEP-2

Silver-vested monkey trips, A. Cortège. Paul Verlaine, *tr. fr. French by* Arthur Symons. AWP; OBVE

Silver wasp-nest hang like fruit., The. (*LL*) Escape. Elinor Wylie. LiTA; MoAmPo

Silver watch you've worn for years, A. Some Slippery Afternoon. Daniela Gioseffi. CrSp

Silver Wedding. Ralph Hodgson. CBLP; OxBTC; TrGrPo

Silverthorn Bush. Robert Finch. NOBC

Silvertoed virgin, A. Rufinus, *tr. fr. Greek by* Alan Marshfield. GrAn

Silvery autumn candlelight chills the painted screen. Autumn Evening. Tu Mu, *tr. fr. Chinese by* A. C. Graham. PLT

Silvery Fountain. Mary E. Tucker. CBWP-1

Silvery Tide, The. *Unknown.* AmFP

Silvia. Shakespeare. *See* Who is Silvia? what is she.

Silvia pretty nymph! within this shade. A Pastoral Dialogue between Two Shepherdesses. The Countess of Winchilsea. ECWP

Silvio's Complaint: A Song, to a Fine Scotch Tune. Aphra Behn. KTR

Sim Ines. Jane Stubbs. FiBHP

Simchas Torah. Morris Jacob Rosenfeld, *tr. fr. Yiddish.* TrJP

Simhat Torah. Judah Leib Gordon, *tr. fr. Hebrew by* Alice Lucas *and* Helena Frank. TrJP

Similar Cases. Charlotte Perkins Gilman. PoLF

Simile. N. Scott Momaday. CDW

Simile. Agnes Nemes Nagy, *tr. fr. Hungarian by* Frederic Will. PoSu

Simile, A. Matthew Prior. NOEC

Simile for Her Smile, A. Richard Wilbur. HoPM; InPK

Similes for Two Political Characters of 1819. Shelley. FaBoPV; RB

Simmer's a Pleasant Time. Burns. PoEL-4

Simon and Susan. *Unknown.* OxBoLi

Simon and the Tarantula. James Wright. AnAn; NNaP

Simon Danz has come home again. A Dutch Picture. Longfellow. MoShBr

Simon Gerty. Elinor Wylie. OBAL

Simon Judson. Lewis Turco. *Fr.* Bordello. SM

Simon Lee. Wordsworth. EnRP; NAEL-2

Simon Lee the Old Huntsman. Wordsworth. *See* In the sweet shire of Cardigan.

Simon Legree--a Negro Sermon. Vachel Lindsay. *Fr.* Booker Washington Trilogy, The. LiTA; MeMAP; TAP

Simon my son, son of my Nuptiall knot. A Lamentation on My Dear Son Simon. John Saffin. SCAP

Simon the Cyrenian Speaks. Countee Cullen. BPo; ChIV-2; HAP; MoAmPo; TrCP; TTY

Simoom, The. Martin Farquhar Tupper. OBTV

Simple. Naomi Long Madgett. PoBA

Simple Autumnal. Louise Bogan. MoAB; MoAmPo; Son

Simple child, A. Wordsworth. *Fr.* We Are Seven. BLPA; BLPL; EnRP; GN; NAEL-2; OBD; OxBChV; TEP; WBLP

Simple Faith. William Cowper. FHYEP

Simple life or death., A. (*LL*) Not in the Guide-Books. Elizabeth Jennings. LiTM

Simple living was clearly the nub. Joyce Johnson. PeLi

Simple lust is all my woe, A. Dennis Brutus. HBAPE

Simple Matter, A. Gloria Rawlinson. PeNZ

Simple nosegay, A! was that much to ask? The Troll's Nosegay. Robert Graves. Son

Simple Outlines, Human Shapes. Irving Feldman. *Fr.* All of Us Here. VCAP

Simple outlines, human shapes, daily acts, plain poses. Simple Outlines, Human Shapes. Irving Feldman. *Fr.* All of Us Here. VCAP

Simple Pastoral, A. George Alexander Stevens. NOEC

Simple Ploughboy, The. *Unknown.* FaBoCh

Simple Poem. Anthony Thwaite. DiPo

Simple pulse like a train is all we need, The. Peter Riley. VaA

Simple Purification, The. Kabir, *tr. fr. Hindi by* Robert Bly. EnlH; NU

Simple purity of your every morning, The. (*LL*) The Arrival. Lan Ling. WPC

Simple Rustic You Seemed, A. Shih Ching, *tr. fr. Chinese by* Wu-chi Liu. SuSp

Simple Simon. Mother Goose. *See* Simple Simon met a pieman.

Simple Simon met a pieman. Mother Goose. BoTP; FaBoBe; OxNR; ReMoGo

Simple Story, A. Gwen Harwood. FaBoWP; NOBAu

Simple thing, yet chancing as it did, A. An Incident. Elizabeth Oakes Smith. AmWP

Simple Truths. William Heyen. BTR

Simple Verses, José Martí, *tr. fr. Spanish by* Seymour Resnick. TTY *sels.*
"I am a sincere man."
"I grow a white rose."

Simpler Recipe for Hell-Broth, A. Lady Jane Cavendish *and* Lady Elizabeth Brackley. CBCK

Simplex Munditiis. Ben Jonson. *See* Still to Be Neat [Still to Be Drest (*or* Dressed)].

Simplicity. Louis Simpson. Prf

Simplicity. Valentine. Tom Pickard. NBrP

Simplicity Aims Circularly. Anna Walters. VoR

Simplicity and Sweet Neglect. Ben Jonson. *See* Still to be neat, still to be dressed [*or* drest].

Simplicity sings it and 'sperience doth prove. Simplicity's Song. Robert Wilson. *Fr.* Three Ladies of London, The. CTC

Simplicity so graven hurts the sense. So Graven. Josephine Miles. NoAM

Simplicity's Song. Robert Wilson. *Fr.* Three Ladies of London, The. CTC

Simplification, A. Richard Wilbur. CMoP

Simplify Me When I'm Dead. Keith Douglas. NoAM; OxBTC

Simply I would sing for the time being. Interlude. Keidrych Rhys. AngWe

Simply to breathe. An Emblem of Two Foxes. Barry Spacks. HoPM

Simply to leave him out of the scene forever. (*LL*) Anonymous Drawing. Donald Justice. CoAP; HeIP

Simultaneous Stories. Matthew Sweeney. IB

Simultaneously. David Ignatow. GrPl; TwCP

Simultaneously, as soundlessly. Prime. W. H. Auden. *Fr.* Horae Canonicae. CMoP; PoE

Simultaneously, five thousand miles apart. Simultaneously. David Ignatow. GrPl; TwCP

Sin. "Angelus Silesius," *Fr.* Cherubical Wanderer, The. GePo, *tr. fr. German.* by George C. Schoolfield

Sin. George Herbert. GeHe; NoP; OxAEP-1; OxBSP

Sin Adam's days begun. (*LL*) Sir Hugh; or, The Jew's Daughter. *Unknown.* CH; ESPB, A *and* C *vers.*; FaBoBa

Sin and Death. Milton. *See* Meanwhile the adversary of God and man.

Sin' auld lang syne. (*LL*) Auld Lang Syne. Burns. AWP; BLPL; EBEvV; EnRP; ImPo; LiTB; NAEL-2; NOBE; OBEV; OxAEP-2; OxBS; PoLF; SCGP; TEP

Sin!/ O only fatal Woe. Thomas Traherne. *Fr.* Third Century, The. ESCV

Sin of Omission, The. Margaret E. M. Sangster. *See* It isn't the thing you do, dear.

Sin [*or* Sinne] of self-love [*or* selfe-love] possesseth all mine eye [*or* eie]. Shakespeare. *Fr.* Sonnets. EBEV; EnRePo; OxAEP-1; PoEL-2

Sin that I have a nounparall maistress. A Mistress without Compare. *At. to* Charles, Duc d'Orléans Charles, Duc d' Orléans. MeEL

Sin' they nailed him to the tree. (*LL*) Ballad of the Goodly Fere. Ezra Pound. ChIV-2; CMoP; ImPo; LiTA; LiTM; MeMAP; MoAB; MoAmPo; MoBS; PoRA; TrCP; TrGrPo

Sin! wilt thou vanquish me! The Recovery. Thomas Traherne. *Fr.* Third Century, The. ESCV

Sinalóa. Earle Birney. MoCV; OxBC; PeLV

Since. W. H. Auden. CBLP; InPS

Since 1915/ the walled monastery. Radio Yerevan. Diana Der Hovanessian. LoHo

Since a harebrained Devil has changed the world. The Cats of Campagnatico. Peter Porter. OBTV

Since Adam's days begun. (*LL*) Sir Hugh; or, The Jew's Daughter. *Unknown.* ESPB

Since all our keys are lost or broken. An Art of Poetry. James McAuley. NOCV

Since all shall be nothing a hundred years hence. (*LL*) The Careless Gallant. Thomas Jordan. CoMu; HAP; OxBoLi

Since all that beat about in nature's range. Constancy to an Ideal Object. Samuel Taylor Coleridge. MeMBP; NAEL-2

Since all that I can ever do for thee. The Last Wish. "Owen Meredith." OxBSP

Since all the riches of this world. Blake. OAEL-2

Since apes are still able to learn. Shih Te, *tr. fr. Chinese by* James M. Hargett. SuSp

Since Bonny-Boots Was Dead. *Unknown.* PoEL-2

Since brass, nor stone, nor earth, nor boundless sea. Shakespeare. *Fr.* Sonnets. AWP; EnRePo; FF; HAP; InPS; LiTB; NAEL-1; NOBE; NoP; NoSic; OxAEP-1; PoRA; RaBo; SCGP; Son; TFi; UnPo
  (Since Brass, Nor Stone, Nor Earth.) ImPo
  (Time and Love, II.) GTBS; GTBS-P

Since Brunswick's smile has authoris'd my muse. Edward Young. *Fr.* Instalment, The. FaBoCo

Since bundling very much abounds. A New Bundling Song. *Unknown.* ErPo

Since buying this book more or less for nothing slightly over a year ago. Svensk Rapsodi. Frank Kuppner. SCBI

Since by just flames the guilty piece is lost. Advice to the Painter. Matthew Prior. APAS

Since Cassius first did whet me against Cæsar. Shakespeare. *Fr.* Julius Caesar. OxAEP-1

Since cast-iron has got all the rage. Humphrey Hardfeature's Descriptions of Cast-Iron Inventions. *Unknown.* OBET

Since certainly it is mine. (*LL*) Lilacs. Amy Lowell. BLPL; MoAmPo; OxBA; PoRA

Since Christmas they have lived with us. Balloons. Sylvia Plath. FaBoWP; PoE

Since clarity suggests simplicity. The Counterpart. Elizabeth Jennings. LiTM; TOF

Since coming to Huang-chou. Su Shih, *tr. by* Irving Y. Lo. *Fr.* Rain at Cold-Food Festival. SuSp

Since counterfeit plots have affected this age. A Ballad upon the Popish Plot. John Gadbury. CoMu

Since cruel seas and angry winds parted my love and me. (*LL*) The Lowlands o' [*or* of] Holland. *Unknown.* AmFP, *diff. vers.*; OxBB; ScCV, (*diff. vers.*)

Since earth has put you away, O sons of Barmak. Abu Nowas for the Barmacides. *Unknown, tr. fr. Arabic by* E. Powys Mathers. *Fr.* Thousand and One Nights, The. AWP

Since every quill is silent to relate. A Monumental Memorial of Marine Mercy. Richard Steere. SCAP

Since Feeling Is First. E. E. Cummings. MoAB; MoAmPo; NoP; PrIm

Since first break of dawn the fiend. The Tempter Disarmed. Milton. *Fr.* Paradise Lost. EPCY; NOSC

Since First I Saw Your Face. *Unknown.* ELP; LiTB; OBEV; OxBSP

Since first you knew my am'rous smart. Robert, Earl Nugent. NOEC

Since fortune's wrath envieth the wealth. The Earl of Surrey. SiPS; SiPSBD

Since gracious Heven, you have bestow'd on me. A Virgin Life. Jane Barker. KTR

Since Grandad broke the council's regulation in the park. (*LL*) West Paddocks. Arthur Davies. NOBAu

Since he kissed them and put them there. (*LL*) Little Boy Blue. Eugene Field. AnAmPo; BeLS; FaPON; OBAL; OBCA; PoLF; SoSe; VPP

Since honour from the honourer proceeds. Of Books. John Florio. EIL

Since I am coming [*or* comming] to that holy room[e]. Hymn[e] to God My God, In My Sickness[e]. John Donne. ChTr; EBEV; EnRePo; ESCV; HeIL; HeIP; ImPo; InPS; MeLP; NAEL-1; NoP; NOSC; OAEL-1; OBD; OxAEP-1; PoE; PoEL-2; PPP; SeCP; SeCV-1; SoSe; TFi; TOF; TrPWD

Since I am convinced. Saigyo, *tr. fr. Japanese by* Arthur Waley. AWP

Since I avail no more, O men! with you. Astræa. Louise Imogen Guiney. AmWP

Since I believe in God the Father Almighty. Johannes Milton, Senex. Robert Bridges. CMoP; LiTB; PeECV; PoEL-5

Since I care naught for what is pale and cold. To a Brown Girl. Ossie Davis. PoNe

Since I don't know my mother. Baba Akiko, *tr. fr. Japanese by* Kenneth Rexroth *and* Ikuko Atsumi. WPJ

Since I emerged that day from the labyrinth. The Labyrinth. Edwin Muir. CMoP; MeMBP; MoBrPo

Since I entered the inner rooms. Written on a Leaf. *Unknown, tr. fr. Chinese by* Geoffrey R. Waters. BoWoP

Since I find you will no longer love. Sway. Denis Johnson. SM

Since I Have Lacked the Comfort. Spenser. *Fr.* Amoretti. AAS; EnRePo; ESo, lacking epigrams I–IV; HeIL

Since I have lacked the comfort of that light. Since I Have Lacked the Comfort. Spenser. *Fr.* Amoretti. AAS; EnRePo; ESo, lacking epigrams I–IV; HeIL

Since I have learned to make balm from my voice. (*LL*) Communion II. Tchicaya U Tam'si. NegPo

Since I have seen a bird one day. The Truth. W. H. Davies. FaBoTw

Since I have seen him. Woman's Love and Life. Adelbert von Chamisso, *tr. fr. German by* Philip L. Miller. RiWo

Since I have set my lips to your full cup, my sweet. More Strong Than Time. Victor Hugo, *tr. fr. French by* Andrew Lang. AWP

Since I heard. Mitsune, *tr. by* Arthur Waley. *Fr.* Kokin Shu. AWP

Since I left you, mine eye is in my mind. Shakespeare. SCGP

Since I must love your north. To My Mountain. Kathleen Raine. OxBS

Since I must needs into thy school[e] return[e]. A Lady's Prayer to Cupid. Thomas Carew, *after* Giovanni Battista Guarini. CaPo
  (Ladies Prayer to Cupid, A.) OBVE

Since I no longer speak I. Silent in America. Philip Levine. NaP

Since I noo mwore do zee your feace. The Wife a-Lost. William Barnes. BoLoP; EBVV; ELP; EnLoPo; EnVR; HAP; OBEV; OxBM; SCGP

Since I was in Syracuse is a month ago. Quarries in Syracuse. Louis Golding. TrJP

Since I'm a girl. *Unknown, tr. fr. Spanish by* Willis Barnstone. BoWoP

Since I'm completely drunk. *Unknown, tr. fr. Greek by* Peter Jay. PeHV

Since in a land not barren still. Love and Discipline. Henry Vaughan. GeHe; TrPWD

Since in religion all men disagree. To Caelia. *Unknown.* FaBoEE

Since ista possum is a goner! (*LL*) Carmen Possum. *Unknown.* BLPA; NBLV

Since I've been in this colony I've written many a song. The Flash Colonial Barman. *At. to* William W. Coxon. NOBAu

Since I've felt this pain. Ono no Komachi, *tr. fr. Japanese by* Rob Swigart. WPOW

Since Just Disdain. Martin Peerson. EnRePo

Since just disdain began to rise. Since Just Disdain. Martin Peerson. EnRePo

Since last September I've been trying to describe. Edward Lear in February. Christopher Middleton. TwCP

Since last the tutelary hearth. Christmas Family Reunion. Peter De Vries. NBLV; NOBL

Since last we met, thou and thy horse, my dear. Henry Vaughan. *Fr.* Invitation to Brecknock, An. AngWe

Since laws were made for ev'ry degree. John Gay. *Fr.* Beggar's Opera, The. NOEC; OAEL-1

Since life is nothing in your philosophy. Nothing. Julia de Burgos, *tr. by* Aliki *and* Willis Barnstone. BoWoP

Since long ago, a child at home. To an Island Princess. Robert Louis Stevenson. OBTV

Since, Lord, to thee/ A narrow way and little gate. Holy Baptisme. George Herbert. PoEL-2
   (H. Baptism II.) ChIV-2
   (H. Baptisme.) SeCV-1

Since love and verse, as well as wine. A Letter to the Earl of Middleton. Sir George Etherege. OBTV

Since love is such that as ye wot. Sir Thomas Wyatt. SiPS

Since love will needs that I shall love. Sir Thomas Wyatt. SiPS; SiPSBD

Since lovers' joys then leave so sick a taste. Henry King. *Fr.* Paradox: That Fruition Destroys Love. ErPo

Since man has been articulate. Every Thing. Harold Monro. MoBrPo

Since man went out from the fields of paradise. On the Killing at Lindisfarne. Alcuin, *tr. fr. Latin by* Helen Waddell. MLL

Since Man's a little world, to make it great. An Epigram on Woman. Philip Ayres. FaBoEE

Since man's life is nothing but a bit of action at a distance. Piano Solo. Nicanor Parra, *tr. fr. Spanish by* William Carlos Williams. AnRep

Since men grow diffident at last. Youth Sings a Song of Rosebuds. Countee Cullen. PoLF; PoNe

Since more him none shall see. *(LL)* A Lamentation. Thomas Campion. CH; OHIP

Since mountains sink to vales, and valleys die. The Bathos. Richard Porson. FaBoEE

Since my father's death. Some Necessary Implements. Marmion Shakerley. CBCK

Since my life's been spent. Côte d'Azur. Katherine Hoskins. NYBP

Since my overdraft threatens to be. S. Tonkin. PeLi

Since my Vivian left me. The Barrel Organ. Daniel Mark Epstein. *Fr.* Homage to Mallarmé. DiPo

Since my wife was born. Notes for the Legend of Salad Woman. Michael Ondaatje. NoAM

Since naturally black is naturally beautiful. Naturally. Audre Lorde. BlSi

Since Nature's works be good, and death doth serve. Sir Philip Sidney. *Fr.* Arcadia. SiPSBD
   (Why Fear to Die?) SiPS

Since nought avails, let me arise and leave. Love's Last Resource. Sadi, *tr. by* L. Cranmer-Byng. *Fr.* Gulistan, The. AWP

Since now I dare not ask. The Sharp Ridge. Robert Graves. FaBoEE

Since now I have a mind to sing. William of Aquitaine, *tr. fr. Provençal by* Helen Waddell. MLL

Since now in every public place. The Sea Horse. Robert Graves. FaBoMo

Since now, once more beside this mound. Sing Again Together. William Barnes. SCGP

Since observed by Yours faithfully, God. *(LL)* A Reply. *Unknown.* FaBoCo; NBLV; NOBL; PeLi

Since of no creature living the last breath. Edna St. Vincent Millay. HeIP; VGW

Since one anthologist put in his book. Anthologistics. Arthur Guiterman. NBLV

Since our country, our God — Oh, my sire! Jephtha's Daughter. Byron. ChIV-1

Since our Lord was nail'd t' ye. *(LL)* The Elder, or Bourtree. *Unknown.* GBP

Since our relations/ are like the crumbling. Sei Shonagon, *tr. fr. Japanese by* Kenneth Rexroth *and* Ikuko Atsumi. WPJ

Since people like things to end in round numbers. The Poet, as Epilogue. Wilhelm Müller, *tr. fr. German by* Philip L. Miller. *Fr.* Beautiful Maid of the Mill, The. RiWo

Since Potiphar made you his overseer. Israel II. Charles Reznikoff. ChIV-1

Since Reverend doctors now declare. The Respectable Burgher. Thomas Hardy. ChIV-2; CMoP; NoAM

Since She Gives So Little Pay. Steinmar, *tr. fr. German by* J. W. Thomas. GePo

Since she must go, and I must mourn, come Night. His Parting from Her. John Donne. *Fr.* Elegies. EBEV

Since she was lovelier than any of you. *(LL)* Blue Girls. John Crowe Ransom. ChTr; CMoP; GBL; LiTA; MeMAP; MoAB; MoAmPo; NoAM; PrIm; RB; TAP; VGW; WeW

Since she whom I lov'd hath paid [*or* payd] her last debt. John Donne. *Fr.* Holy Sonnets. ESCV; JCP; NAEL-1; NOSC; Son

Since Shylock's book has walk'd the circles here. To a Noisy Politician. Philip Freneau. TAP

Since, Sir, you have made it your study to vex. The Lady's Receipt for a Beau's Dress. *Unknown.* CoMu

Since So Mine Eyes. Sir Philip Sidney. *Fr.* Arcadia. SiPS

Since so ye please to hear me plain. Sir Thomas Wyatt. SiPS

Since Sturdee cleared the Southern Seas. Off Coronel. Austin Threlfall Nankivell. NSI

Since that night/ I cannot know myself. Lady Izumi Shikibu, *tr. fr. Japanese by* Willis Barnstone. BoWoP

Since that our Deares wee cannot have. The 3 Sad Sheppards Sings This in Parts. Lady Jane Cavendish *and* Lady Elizabeth Brackley. *Fr.* Pastorall, A. KTR

Since That the Stormy Rage. Sir Philip Sidney. *Fr.* Arcadia. SiPSBD

Since that this thing we call the world. An Epicurean Ode. John Hall. CBLP; MeLP; NOSC

Since that to death is gone the shepherd high. Pastoral Elegy. Sir Philip Sidney. *Fr.* Arcadia. SiPSBD

Since the Conquest none of us. The Conquest. Oliver St. John Gogarty. OBMV

Since the good Bishop left his name. To Mr. Wren, My Valentine Six Year Old. Jane Holt. ECWP

Since the images you demand. Revolution. Nishi Junko, *tr. fr. Japanese by* Kenneth Rexroth *and* Ikuko Atsumi. WPJ

Since the night is dark. *Unknown, tr. fr. Spanish by* Willis Barnstone. BoWoP

Since the night your thin candle of youth ran out. *(LL)* Stardust Sequence. Dermot Bolger. IB

Since "the pillow knows all." Lady Ise, *tr. fr. Japanese by* Kenneth Rexroth *and* Ikuko Atsumi. WPJ

Since the rumor has been verified, you can, at least. Rumor Verified. Robert Penn Warren. AnAn

Since the storm two nights ago. The Recognition. Denise Levertov. VGW

Since the wise men have not spoken, I speak that am only a fool. The Fool. Padraic Pearse. PeIV; TIRV

Since Then. D. J. Enright. OBSV

Since, then, constrain'd, we must expel the flock. How to Build a Ha-ha. William Mason. *Fr.* English Garden, The. FaBoUs

Since then I was. The Significance of a Water Animal. Ray A. Young Bear. HATNAP

Since there your elements assemble. *(LL)* In Me, Past, Present, Future Meet. Siegfried Sassoon. OBEV; OxBSP

Since There's No Help. Michael Drayton. *See* Since There's No Help, Come Let Us Kiss and Part.

Since there's no help, come, let them kiss and part. The Limited. Robert Penn Warren. PoA

Since There's No Help, Come Let Us Kiss and Part. Michael Drayton. *Fr.* Idea. AAS; AWP; BoLoP; ClHu; ElL; EnLoPo; ESo; GBL; HAP; HeIP; InPS; JCP; NAEL-1; NOBE; NoP; OAEL-1; PoEL-2; PrIm; SCGP; Son; SoSe; TEP; TFi; TrGrPo

Since those bards. Ay: A Gift of Elephants. Mutamociyar, *tr. fr. Tamil by* A. K. Ramanujan. PLW

Since Those We Love and Those We Hate. W. E. Henley. OBMV

Since thou art gone, my friend, I seek in vain for peace. On Parting with Moses ibn Ezra. Judah Halevi, *tr. fr. Hebrew by* Solomon Solis-Cohen. TrJP

Since Thou Hast Given Me This Good Hope, O God. Robert Louis Stevenson. TrPWD

Since thou hast viewed [*or* view'd] some Gorgon, and art grown. The Double Rock. Henry King. CBLP; NOSC; SeCP

Since thou wou'dst [*or* wouldst] needs, bewitcht [*or* bewitched] with some ill charms. To One Married to an Old Man. Edmund Waller. FaBoEE; OxBSP; SeCP

Since thy third curing of the French infection. Against an Old Lecher. Sir John Harington. FaBoEE

Since Time began, such alphabets begin. From a Cheerful Alphabet. John Updike. FaBoCo

Since 'tis my doom, Love's undershrieve. To Julia to Expedite Her Promise. John Cleveland. CBLP

Since to obtaine thee, nothing me will sted. His Remedie for Love. Michael Drayton. *Fr.* Idea. AAS; ESo

Since tonight the wind is high. *Unknown. See* Fierce is the wind tonight.

Since we agreed to let the road between us. No Road. Philip Larkin. CBLP; EBEV; MoBrPo; OxAEP-2

Since we can die but once, what matters it. Sentiment. Thomas Chatterton. NOEC

Since we had changed. Message. Allen Ginsberg. NeAP; VGW

Since we halved the hairpin. Tune: "Slow Song of Chu Ying-t'ai" — Late Spring. Hsin Ch'i-chi, *tr. fr. Chinese by* Irving Y. Lo. SuSp

Since we must part, let's part as heroes do. *(LL)* Farewell in a Dream. Stephen Spender. MoAB; MoBrPo

Since we said politely thank you. Sun. Gill Vickers. VBLP

Since we were first married. On the Death of His Wife. Mei Yao Ch'en, *tr. fr. Chinese.* OxBM

Since we'd always sky about. Can. Lit. Earle Birney. NOBC

Since we're not young, weeks have to do time. Adrienne Rich. *Fr.* Twenty-one Love Poems. GLP; UnAS; VBLP

Since, when you die, delight. Modern Love Poems. *Somali Oral Tradition,* *tr. by* B. W. Andrzejewski *and* M. Laurence. WTO

Since without Thee we do no good. Elizabeth Barrett Browning. TrPWD

Since worms and dust must be your fate. Ausonius, *tr. fr. Latin by* Helen Waddell. MLL

Since ye delight to know. Sir Thomas Wyatt. SiPS

Since you all will have singing, and won't be said nay. The King's Own Regulars. *Unknown.* PAH

Since you are dead, Timon, tell me which. Callimachus, *tr. fr. Greek by* Peter Jay. GrAn

Since you ask, most days I cannot remember. Wanting to Die. Anne Sexton. IHMS; MoP; NoAM; TAP; TRP; VCAP

Since you have been. *(LL)* Birthday Poem for Thomas Hardy. C. Day Lewis. EBEvV; EPCY

Since you have turned unkind. To a Lady Friend. W. H. Davies. MoBrPo

Since You Left. Chang Chiu-ling, *tr. fr. Chinese by* Kenneth Rexroth. OHMPC

Since you left, my lover. Since You Left. Chang Chiu-ling, *tr. fr. Chinese by* Kenneth Rexroth. OHMPC

Since you lie buried in the hill. To Senna Hoy. Else Lasker-Schüler, *tr. fr. German by* Glauco Cambon. IMW

Since You Seem Intent. Gerald Locklin. GOYP

Since you walked out on me. Lady of Miracles. Nina Cassian, *tr. fr. Romanian by* Laura Schiff. AIW; WPOW

Since you went away. In Imitation of Hsü Kan ("Since You Went Away.") Liu Chun, *tr. fr. Chinese by* Jan W. Walls. SuSp

Since you will needs that I shall sing. Sir Thomas Wyatt. SiPS

Since you wrote a poem. What Color Is Lonely. Carolyn M. Rodgers. BPo

Since your marriage you have lost the look. Martial, *tr. fr. Greek by* Kenneth Rexroth. PGA

Since you're asking so many questions I'll be off to Tuia and seek ship. Song by a Woman Accused of Adultery. Kie Tapu, *tr. fr. Maori by* Margaret Orbell. PeNZ

Sincere Flattery of R. B. James Kenneth Stephen. FaBoPa; NOBL

Sincere Flattery of W. W. (Americanus). James Kenneth Stephen. FiBHP; NOBL

Sincere Man, The. Alfred Grant Walton. PoToHe

Sincere Praise, *sels.* Isaac Watts.
"Almighty Maker God!" TrPWD

Sindhi Woman. Jon Stallworthy. OxBC

Sinfonia Domestica. Jean Starr Untermeyer. MoAmPo

Sinful to Flirt. *Unknown.* AmFP

Sing a last song. The Locket. John Montague. BiHa; PBCIP

Sing a song of cobbler! Jeremy Hobbler. *Unknown.* BoTP

Sing a song of critics. Valentine. Ernest Hemingway. OBAL

Sing a song of hollow logs. Song of Summer Days. James William Foley. BoTP

Sing a song of laughter. The Giraffe and the Woman. Laura E. Richards. PDV

Sing a song of mincemeat. Mincemeat. Elizabeth Gould. BoTP

Sing a Song of People. Lois Lenski. OTCP

Sing a song of pop corn. A Pop Corn Song. Nancy Byrd Turner. FaPON; SiSoPo

Sing a song of Scissor-men. The Scissor-Man. Madeleine Nightingale. BoTP

Sing a song of sixpence. Mother Goose. FaBoBe; OxNR

Sing a Song of Sixpence. *Unknown. See* Sing a song o'[or of] sixpence.

Sing a song of washing-up. The Washing-Up Song. Elizabeth Gould. BoTP

Sing a song of winter. A Sledding Song. Norman C. Schlichter. FaPON

Sing a song o' sixpence. Song of Sixpence. *Unknown.* OxBoLi
(Sing a Song of Sixpence.) CBNP; ReMoGo

Sing again the great song. Peace. Mazisi Kunene, *tr. fr. Zulu.* PAW

Sing Again Together. William Barnes. SCGP

Sing agreeably, agreeably, agreeably of lvoe. *(LL)* Carry Her over the Water. W. H. Auden. FaBoTw; RB

Sing, bird, on green Missouri's plain. The Death of Lyon. Henry Peterson. PAH

Sing, Brothers, Sing! W. R. Rodgers. MoAB; MoBrPo

Sing, cuccu, nu! Sing, cuccu! *Unknown. See* Summer [*or* Sumer] is icumen [*or* y-comen] in.

Sing cuccu! Sing cuccu nu! *(LL)* Summer [*or* Sumer] is icumen [*or* y-comen] in. *Unknown.* EBEV; PeLV; TEP

Sing dum de whickerty, dum de way. *(LL)* The Factory Girl's Come-All-Ye. *Unknown.* AmFP; OBAL

Sing first the heroe in his goodly ship. *Unknown. Fr.* Pindarique Ode on the Arrival of His Excellency, A. PBCV

Sing goddamm, sing goddamm, DAMM. *(LL)* Ancient Music. Ezra Pound. BXAP; FaBoCo; FF; HeIL; HeIP; LiTM; NBLV; OBAL; OxBA; PeLV; UV

Sing!/ Great dark oak. Lines to the Black Oak. Oliver La Grone. NBV

Sing hey! for bold George Washington. George Washington. Rosemary *and* Stephen Vincent Benét *and* Stephen Vincent Benét. FaPON

Sing, hey! Sing, hey!/ For Christmas Day. *Unknown.* PChr
(Old Christmas Greeting, An. FaPON)

Sing his praises that doth keep. John Fletcher. *Fr.* Faithful Shepherdess, The.
(Hymn to Pan.) NOBE; OBEV

Sing ho! for a brave and a gallant ship. Ten Thousand Miles Away. *Unknown.* AS

Sing holly, go whistle and ivy! *(LL)* Sing Ivy. *Unknown.* BoTP; OxNR

Sing I for a brave and a gallant barque, and a stiff and a rattling breeze. Ten Thousand Miles Away. *Unknown.* AS

Sing Ivy. *Unknown.* BoTP; OxNR

Sing jigmijole the pudding-bowl. Kissing of My Dame. *Unknown.* GBP
(Sing jigmijole, the pudding bowl.) OxNR

Sing jigmijole, the pudding bowl. *Unknown. See* Sing jigmijole the pudding-bowl.

Sing little box. The Admirers of the Little Box. Vasco [*or* Vasko] Popa, *tr. fr. Serbo-Croatian by* Charles Simic. HSix

Sing Loud. Li Ho, *tr. fr. Chinese by* A. C. Graham. PLT

Sing loudly this my Lady-day. *(LL)* On a Birthday. J. M. Synge. ChTr; GBL; OBMV; PeIV

Sing lullaby [*or* lullabie] as women do[e]. The Lullaby [*or* Lullabie] of a Lover. George Gascoigne. AAS; EBEV; EiL; EnRePo; HAP; NAEL-1; SCGP
(Gascoigne's Lullaby [*or* Lullabie].) NoP; NoSic; PoEL-1; TrGrPo
(Lover's Lullaby, A.) OBEV
(Sing Lullaby, as Women Do.) InvP

Sing lullaby, mine only joy! *(LL)* Upon my lap my sovereign sits. Richard Verstegan. CH; EiL; OBEV; SCGP

Sing, magnarello, merrily. The Leaf-picking. Frédéric Mistral, *tr. fr. French by* Harriet Waters Preston. AWP

Sing me a hero! Quench my thirst. Tray. Robert Browning. FM

Sing Me a New Song. John Henrik Clarke. PoBA

Sing me a song of a lad that is gone. Robert Louis Stevenson. NOBE; NTP

Sing me a sweet, low song of night. Hildegarde Hawthorne. FaBoBe

Sing me the men ere this. He Would Have His Lady Sing. Digby Mackworth Dolben. EBEV

Sing me to sleep. *(LL)* Limpopo. Walter Battiss. PeSAV

Sing me "Woe," you glades and Dorian water. Moschus. *See* Ye mountain valleys, pitifully groan!

Sing, my golden cock, I'll give thee grain! Neidhart von Reuental, *tr. fr. German by* J. W. Thomas. GePo

Sing, My Soul. *Unknown.* AH

Sing, my tongue, the Saviour's glory. St. Thomas Aquinas, *tr. fr. Latin.* WGRP

Sing, O goddess, the wrath, the ontamable dander of Keitt. The Fight over the Body of Keitt. *Unknown.* PAH

Sing on a brittle sea of glass! The Summer. Morgan Llwyd. *Fr.* 1648. AngWe

Sing On, Blithe Bird. William Motherwell. GN

Sing on in the soul alway. *(LL)* The Human Touch. Spencer Michael Free. BLPA; FaBoBe; PoToHe

Sing out, my soul, thy songs of joy. Songs of Joy. W. H. Davies. MoBrPo

Sing out pent souls, sing cheerfully. The Vintage to the Dungeon. Richard Lovelace. BeJo; CaPo; SeCV-1

Sing, Sing for Christmas. J. H. Egar. OHIP

Sing, sing — Poet, sing! The Poet. Elizabeth Oakes Smith. AmWP

Sing, sing,/ What shall I sing? Mother Goose. OxNR; ReMoGo

Sing softly, Muse, the Reverend Henry White. B Flat. Douglas Stewart. FaBoMA

Sing-Song, *sels.* Christina Rossetti.
"Brown and furry." FaBoVe
(Caterpillar, The.) BoTP; FaPON; GoJo; OxBChV; SiSoPo
City Mouse and the Garden Mouse, The. BoTP; FaBoBe; FaPON; NTCP
Ferry Me across the Water. ChTr; GoJo; NTP; OxBChV; PDV; TLR
(Ferryman, The.) BoTP
Flint. OxBChV
"Horses of the sea, The." FaPON; GoJo; NTCP
Hurt No Living Thing. FaPON; FM; OTCP; PDV; SiSoPo
Let's Be Merry. FaPON; TLR
Minnie and Mattie. GoJo; InvP
Mix a Pancake. NTCP

(Pancake, The.)　BoTP
"O sailor, come ashore."　BoTP; FM
Oh, Fair to See.　FaPON; OHIP
Rainbow, The.　OxBChV
Sound of the Wind, The
　(Wind Has Such a Rainy Sound, The.)　TLR
What Do They Do?　FaPON
What Does the Bee Do?　OxBChV
What Is Pink?　GoJo; OxBChV; SiSoPo
"When fishes set umbrellas up."　FM
Who Has Seen the Wind?　ArNa; BoTP; FaPON; GoJo; NTCP; NTP;
　OHCV; PDV; SiSoPo; TLR; WHSW
　(Wind, The.)　BLPL; ChIV-2; FaBoBe; OxBChV
Sing-Song of Old Man Kangaroo, The.　Kipling.　FaPON
Sing them till the night expire!　*(LL)*　Christmas Carols.　Longfellow.
　BoTP
Sing to Apollo, God of Day.　John Lyly.　*Fr. Midas.*　NoSic
Sing to Ashtaroth and Bel.　To Ashtaroth and Bel.　Saul Tchernichowsky,
　tr. fr. Hebrew by L. V. Snowman.　TrJP
Sing to my God a grateful Song.　*(LL)*　An Evening Hymn.　Thomas Ken.
　OxBChV
Sing to the Lord, for what can better be.　Psalm CXLVII: "Praise ye the
　Lord."　The Countess of Pembroke.　NOCV
Sing to the Lord Most High.　Timothy Dwight.　AH
Sing unto Jehovah.　Bible, *O.T., paraphrased by* Sir Thomas Wyatt.　*See* O
　[*or* Oh] sing unto the Lord [*or* Jehovah] a new song.
Sing unto the Lord with thanksgiving.　Bible, *O.T., paraphrased by* Sir
　Thomas Wyatt.　*See* Praise ye the Lord!/ For it is good to sing praises
　unto our God.
Sing we all merrily.　A Catch by the Hearth.　*Unknown.*　OHIP
Sing We and Chant It.　*At. to* Thomas Morley.　EBEV; EnRePo; NoSic
Sing we for love and idleness.　An Immorality.　Ezra Pound.　CMoP; GoJo;
　GrPl; ImPo; LiTM; MoAB; MoAmPo; NOBA; OBAL
Sing We Yule.　*Unknown.*　MeEL
Sing while you may, O bird upon the tree!　Dark Wings.　James Stephens.
　PoA
Sing with Your Body.　Janice Mirikitani.　MDDM; WPOW
Sing your song, sing your song, bird in the net.　*(LL)*　The Green Refrain.
　Avraham Huss.　MHP
Singe we alle and say we thus.　My Purse.　*Unknown.*　EBEV
Singee a songee sick a pence.　Song.　*Unknown.*　BXAP
Singer, The.　Gerald William Barrax.　Jaz
Singer, The.　Dermot Bolger.　IB
Singer, The.　Colleen J. McElroy.　Jaz
Singer, The.　Diane Wakoski.　HeIP
Singer, The.　Anna Wickham.　MoBrPo
Singer Asleep, A (Algernon Charles Swinburne), *sels.*　Thomas Hardy.
　"Passionate pages of his earlier years, The."　EPCY
Singer in the Prison, The.　Walt Whitman.　BeLS
Singer of sweet Colonus, and its child.　*(LL)*　To a Friend.　Matthew
　Arnold.　NAEL-2; Son
Singers, The.　George Bruce.　OxBS
Singer's House, The.　Seamus Heaney.　EBEV; IIP
Singers in the Snow, The.　*Unknown.*　OHIP
Singers of Renown.　Anne Elder.　FaBoMA
Singers of serenades, The.　Mandoline.　Paul Verlaine, *tr. fr. French by*
　Arthur Symons.　AWP; OBMV
Singers, sing! The hoary world.　The Servants.　Richard Wightman.　WGRP
Singers to Come.　Alice Meynell.　WPE
Singing.　*(LL)*　Island.　Meredith Stricker.　LoHo
Singing & Doubling Together.　A. R. Ammons.　NAAL-2; NoAM
Singing & moaning in empty space.　*(LL)*　Makeup on Empty Space.　Anne
　Waldman.　SRLS
Singing, a friendliness, A.　*(LL)*　Sound arises out of the earth —, A.
　Cedric Wright.　EaPr
Singing about her head, as she rode by.　*(LL)*　Love without Hope.　Robert
　Graves.　BoLoP; ChTr; FaBoEE; GBL; GTBS-P; NAEL-2; NTP; OAEL-
　2; PlP; Spl
Singing Aloud.　Carolyn Kizer.　IHMS
Singing Bones, The.　Randolph Stow.　CBAP
Singing Cat, The.　Stevie Smith.　CRH; OFC; OxBTC
Singing Death.　Stan Rice.　FYAP; IMW
Singing Flower, The.　Shu Ting, *tr. fr. Chinese by* Carolyn Kizer *with* Y.H.
　Zhao.　SpMi
Singing Image of Fire.　Kukai, *tr. fr. Japanese by* Stephen Mitchell.　EnlH
Singing in the Dark.　Irma Wassall.　PoNe
Singing is sweet; but be sure of this.　James Thomson ("B.V.").　*Fr. Art.*
　NOBVV

Singing Leaves, The.　James Russell Lowell.　GN
Singing Lesson, The.　David Wagoner.　NoAM
Singing Maid, The.　*Unknown.*　MeEL
Singing Maid, The.　*Unknown.*　*See* Now springes the spray.
Singing my days.　Passage to India.　Walt Whitman.　AmPP; NAAL-1;
　PoEL-5
Singing nature when I need sing my nature nevermore.　*(LL)*　Singing &
　Doubling Together.　A. R. Ammons.　NAAL-2; NoAM
Singing School.　Seamus Heaney.　InPS
Singing School, *sels.*　Seamus Heaney.
　Constable Calls, A.　FaBoPV; IPY; NOIV
Singing the Internationale.　Alberto A. Ríos.　NGP
Singing the Reapers Homeward Come.　*Unknown.*　OHIP
Singing through the forests.　Rhyme of the Rail[s].　John Godfrey Saxe.
　AnAmPo; MoShBr; PoLF
Singing, today I married my white girl.　Dannie Abse.　OBWVE
Singing we ride over the field.　The Battle on the Blackbird's Field.　Vasco
　[*or* Vasko] Popa.　*Fr. Blackbird's Field, The.*　PoSu, *tr. fr. Serbo-
　Croatian. by* Anne Pennington
Singing with open mouths their strong melodious songs.　*(LL)*　I Hear
　America Singing.　Walt Whitman.　AiP, *ll.* 1–9; AnAmPo; AWP;
　FaBoBe; FaBV; FaPON; FF; HAP; LiTA; MoAmPo; PDV; SAmP; TFi;
　TrGrPo; WeW
Single clenched fist lifted and ready, The.　Choose.　Carl Sandburg.　Spl
Single ember in the fireplace, A.　In January.　Lance Henson.　ETG
Single evening can leave its wound in the soul, A.　*(LL)*　Impromptu.
　Meng Chiao.　PLT
Single-eyed to child and sunbeam.　Blue-eyed Mary.　Mary E. Wilkins
　Freeman.　OBCA
Single face follows me out of sleep, A.　Sitting Outside in Early Morning.
　Lance Henson.　ETG
Single fact is matter, The.　Chronic Meanings.　Bob Perelman.　BAP-91
Single flow'r he sent me, since we met, A.　One Perfect Rose.　Dorothy
　Parker.　FiBHP; NALW; NBLV; NIP; NoP; OBAL; Poetr; VBLP
Single Girl, The.　*Unknown.*　*See* When I was single [*or* a single girl].
Single Girl, The.　*Unknown.*　*See* Oh, when I was single, oh then, oh then!
Single-handed, and surrounded by Lecompton's black brigade.　Lecompton's
　Black Brigade.　Charles Graham Halpine.　PAH
Single leaf, A.　Dueteronomy.　Leaf From a French Bible (circa 1270).
　Peter Scupham.　*Fr. Marginalia.*　SCBI
Single man stands like a bird-watcher, A.　The Mouth of the Hudson.
　Robert Lowell.　AiP; NaP; VCAP
Single pavilion looms dark against clouds and forest, A.　Deepening-Green
　Pavilion.　Chu Yi-tsun, *tr. fr. Chinese by* Chang Yin-nan *and* Lewis C.
　Walmsley.　SuSp
Single pearl of dew suspended clear and chill, A.　Tune: "Lotus-leaf Cup."
　Wen T'ing-yün, *tr. fr. Chinese by* William R. Schultz.　SuSp
Single petal swirling diminishes the spring, A.　Tu Fu, *tr. by* Irving Y. Lo.
　Fr. Meandering River.　SuSp
Single post, a point of rusting, A.　Marina Tsvetayeva, *tr. fr. Russian by*
　Elaine Feinstein *and* Angela Livingstone.　*Fr. Poem of the End.*　BrRo
Single Principle of Forms, The.　Robert Gray.　FaBoMA
Single-Rhyme Alphabet, A.　*Unknown.*　FaBoUs
Single ripple starts from where he stood, A.　*(LL)*　The Heron.　Theodore
　Roethke.　OBAP; PDV; RFM
Single sleeper lying here, The.　Epitaph for the Poet.　George Barker.
　OxBSP
Single slender crescent brow before her dressing mirror, A.　Tune: "Echoing
　Heaven's Everlastingness."　Li Ching, *tr. fr. Chinese by* Daniel Bryant.
　SuSp
Single Sonnet.　Louise Bogan.　Son
Single soul that lacks a sweet crystalline cry., A.　*(LL)*　Paudeen.　W. B.
　Yeats.　HAP; OxBSP; PoEL-5
Single stench two winds have parted, A.　Nicarchus of Alexandria, *tr. fr.
　Greek by* Sam Hamill.　InMo
Single story two bedroom dwelling across from.　In the Orpheum Building.
　Kit Robinson.　UL
Single Vision.　Stanley Kunitz.　CAPP
Sings.　*(LL)*　Sistrum.　Lynn Lonidier.　SRLS
Sings for us two/ Especially.　*(LL)*　The Blackbird.　Humbert Wolfe.
　BoTP; FaPON; GoJo; GrPl
Sings Harry, *sels.*　Denis Glover.
　Once the Days.　PeNZ
　Song: "If everywhere in the street."　PeNZ
　Song: "These songs will not stand."　PeNZ
　Song: "When I am old."　PeNZ
　Thistledown.　PeNZ
Sings sweetest at the close of day.　*(LL)*　Dull Is My Verse.　Walter Savage
　Landor.　PoEL-4
Singular Indeed.　David McCord.　OBCA

Singular Singulars, Peculiar Plurals. Willard R. Espy. FaBoUs

Singularly and in pairs the decade has been ripped by bullets. Herbert Martin. PoBA

Sinister maryjane: the man sits. Funny Lotus Blues . . . Ray Bremser. PoBeRe

Sinister presence changed life in a twelvemonth, A. Mountain Convent. Laura Benét. GoYe

Sinkholes. Janet Reed McFatter. GrPl

Sinking. Lin Ling, tr. fr. Chinese by Kenneth Rexroth and Ling Chung. WPC

Sinking of the Graf Spee, The. Unknown. OxBSS

Sinking of the Mendi, The. S. E. K. Mqhayi, tr. fr. Xhosa by C. M. Mcanyangwa and Jack Cope. PeSA

Sinking of the Merrimac, The. Lucy Larcom. PAH

Sinking of the Titanic, The, sels. Hans Magnus Enzensberger.
Reprieve, The. PoSu
Sixteenth Canto. PoSu
Thirty-third Canto. PoSu
Twenty-ninth Canto. PoSu

Sinking of the Titanic proceeds according to plan, The. Sixteenth Canto. Hans Magnus Enzensberger. Fr. Sinking of the Titanic, The. PoSu

Sinks the fabrick of the world. (LL) The Descent of Odin. Thomas Gray. OxAEP-1

Sinks the sun below the desert. Cleopatra Dying. Thomas Stephens Collier. BLPA; BLPL; FaBoBe

Sinless Child, The, sels. Elizabeth Oakes Smith.

Sinn Fein: Ourselves Alone. Isobel Marchbank. NSI

Sinner, The. Margaret E. Bruner. PoToHe

Sinner, Is Thy Heart at Rest? Jared B. Waterbury. AH

Sinner man sat on the gates of hell, A. No Hiding Place Down There. Unknown. GBP

Sinners, abhor the Fiend. Charles Wesley. Fr. Horrible Decree, The. NOCV

Sinner's Lament, A. Lord Herbert of Cherbury. SeCP

Sinner's Rue. A. E. Housman. PeVV

Sinners, Will You Scorn the Message?. Jonathan Allen. AH

Sinnes Heavie Loade. Robert Southwell. ESCV

Sins Loathed, and Yet Loved. Robert Herrick. LiTB

Sins of Kalamazoo, The. Carl Sandburg. VGW

Sins' Round. George Herbert. MiEL; NOSC

Sion. George Herbert. ChIV-1; ESCV

Sion lies [or Syon lyes] waste, and thy Jerusalem. Fulke Greville. Fr. Caelica. EnRePo; NoP; NoSic; PeECV, sect. CX; PoEL-1 (Sion Lies Waste.) ChIV-1

Sion Lies Waste. Fulke Greville. See Sion lies [or Syon lyes] waste, and thy Jerusalem.

Sioux, The. Eugene Field. FiBHP

Sioux Indians. Unknown. AmFP

Sioux Metamorphoses. Unknown, tr. fr. Sioux Indian by James Koller. STP
Sels.
"He comes from the north."
"He was an old wolf, no teeth, his tail all but bare."
"I thought I saw buffalo."
"In wild flight."

Sip a little. Baby's Drinking Song. James Kirkup. NTCP; OTCP

Sip of Coors makes children be, A. Booze Turns Men into Women. Bernadette Mayer. UL

Sipping a Schlitz. Bullfrogs. David Allan Evans. Poetsp

Sipping judiciously, he saw come near. Narcissus in a Cocktail Glass. Frances Minturn Howard. GoYe

Sipping whiskey and gin. Analysands. Dudley Randall. BPo

Sipsop's Song. Blake. Fr. Island in the Moon, An. FaBoNo

Sir, after you have wip'd the eyes. A Consolatory Poem Dedicated unto Mr. Cotton Mather. Nicholas Noyes. SCAP

Sir Andrew Barton. Unknown. AmFP, 2 vers.; EnSB; ESPB; OxBB

Sir, as your mandate did request. The Inventory, in Answer to the Usual Mandate Sent by a Surveyor of the Taxes, Requiring a Return of the Number of Horses, Servants, Carriages, etc., Kept. Burns. FaBoUs

Sir — awaiting you. Waiting for the Emperor Tenji. Princess Nukada, tr. fr. Japanese. PBWP, tr. by Cid Corman and Susumu Kamaike

Sir,/ Ere you pass this threshold, stay. To the King, at His Entrance into Saxham: By Master John Crofts. Thomas Carew. CaPo

Sir George Prevost, with all his host. The Battle of Plattsburg. Unknown. PAH

Sir, God give you good-morrow! (LL) My lady went to Canterbury [or Caunterbury]. Unknown. FaBoCo; FaBoNo

Sir, God give you good morrow. (LL) Nonsense Song. Unknown. CBNP; OxBLMV

Sir Henry Clinton's Invitation to the Refugees. Philip Freneau. PAH

Sir, I admit your general [or gen'ral] rule, At. to Pope Pope, also at. to Matthew Prior and to Samuel Taylor Coleridge. FaBoEE; FiBHP; LiTB (Fool and the Poet, The.) NBLV

Sir, I was your pupil for five years. Elegy for Mr. Lewis (Welsh). Meic Stephens. AngWe

Sir Isaac Newton. Unknown. WeW

Sir John addressed the Snake-god in his temple. Robert Graves. Fr. Grotesques. CMoP; PeLV

Sir John Barleycorn. Unknown. FaBoBa

Sir, laugh no more at Pliny and the rest. Animal Weather-Forecasting. Thomas Lodge and to Robert Greene. NoSic

Sir Launfal and the Leper. James Russell Lowell. Fr. Vision of Sir Launfal, The. GN

Sir, more than kisses, letters mingle Souls. John Donne. Fr. To Sir Henry Wotton. OBF

Sir, more than kisses, letters mingle souls. To Sir Henry Wotton. John Donne. NoSic

Sir Nameless, once of Athelhall, declared. The Children and Sir Nameless. Thomas Hardy. NoP

Sir, no man's enemy, forgiving all. Petition. W. H. Auden. CMoP; LiTB; MeMAP; NAEL-2; Son

Sir, not that we did not hear the noise. What Her Girl Friend Said to Him. Kannan, tr. fr. Tamil by A. K. Ramanujan. PLW

Sir, now unravelled is the Golden Fleece. To Dr. F. B. on His Book of Chess. Richard Lovelace. CaPo

Sir Olaf. Johann Gottfried von Herder, tr. fr. German by Elizabeth Craigmyle. AWP

Sir Oluf he rideth over the plain. The Elected Knight. Unknown, tr. fr. Danish by Longfellow. AWP

Sir,/ Our times are much degenerate from those. To His Noble Friend, Mr Lovelace, upon His Poems. Andrew Marvell. EPCY

Sir Revel. Samuel Rowlands. NoSic

Sir, say no more. Dramatic Fragment. Trumbull Stickney. InPK; OxBA; OxBSP

Sir, so suspicious. Unknown, tr. fr. Irish by Thomas Kinsella. NOIV

Sir: though (I thank God for it) I do hate. John Donne. Fr. Satires. OBSV

Sir T. J.'s Speech to His Wife and Children. Unknown. CoMu
Sir, to be short, in this expensive town. London. John Oldham. Fr. Satyr, A. NOSC

Sir, We Would See Jesus. Frances E. W. Harper. AAP

Sir, whatsoever you are pleas'd to do. Dedications, II: To the Prince. Sir John Davies. Fr. Orchestra; or, A Poem[e] of Da[u]ncing. NoSic, abr.; SiPS; SiPSBD

Sir, whatsoever you are pleas'd to do. To the Prince. Sir John Davies. Fr. Dedications [of Orchestra]. SiPS

Sir! when I flew to seize the bird. Beau's Reply. William Cowper. FaBoCh

Sir, when you say. 15th Raga: For Bela Lugosi. David Meltzer. Fr. Ragas. NeAP

Sir/ Whether these lines do find you out. A Summons to Town. Sir John Suckling. NOSC

Sir William Dyer, Knight, sels. Lady Catherine Dyer.
Epitaph on the Monument of Sir William Dyer at Colmworth, 1641. BoLoP; EnLoPo; OxBM

Sir William Wallace, sels. Henry the Minstrel.
"Out off the south thai saw quhar at the queyn." ScCV

Sir, you are Sealed of the Tribe of Ben. (LL) An Epistle Answering to One That Asked to be Sealed of the Tribe of Ben. Ben Jonson. BeJo; SeCV-1

Sir,/ You need no Parian or Egyptian stone. To Sir Henry Newton, upon His Re-edifying the Church of Charleton in Kent. Thomas Philipott. NOSC

Sir, you should notice me: I am the Man. Lascelles Abercrombie. MoBrPo

Sir, you were a credit to whatever. To a Teacher of French. Donald Davie. OxBC

Sire. W. S. Merwin. CoAP; NaP; VGW

Siren Bird, The. H. Cordelia Ray. CBWP-3

Siren Chorus. George Darley. See Troop home to silent grots and caves.

Siren sang, and Europe turned away, A. To the Western World. Louis Simpson. CAPP; CoAP; GOA; LiTM; NOBA; SM; TAP; TRP

Siren Song. Margaret Atwood. Fr. Songs of the Transformed. HAP; NIP; PoA; WeW

Siren Song. Marg Yeo. DT

Siren waits thee, singing song for song, The. (LL) To Robert Browning. Walter Savage Landor. EnRP; EPCY; NoP

Sirena. Michael Drayton. See Near[e] to the silver Trent.

Sirens, The. Gordon Challis. PeNZ

Sirens, The. John Manifold. LiTB; LiTM; MoBrPo; Son

Sirens' Song, The. William Browne. Fr. Inner Temple Masque, The. NOBE; OBEV

Sitting in cold fear, boys, waiting for the end? (*LL*) Just a Smack at Auden. William Empson. FaBoCo; LiTM; MoBrPo; PeLV; UnPo; UV

Sitting in sunlight, the child. Eleven A.M. on My Day Off, My Sister Phones Desperate for a Babysitter. Sharon Hashimoto. OpBo

Sitting in the dusk, weeping. Circles. Celia Gilbert. MDDM

Sitting, legs crossed, copper-toned old man. My Song. King D. Kuka. VoR

Sitting naked together. Rain Journal: London: June 65. Lee Harwood. PeHV

Sitting on a Rock by Mountain Stream. Ch'en Yu Yi, *tr. fr. Chinese by* Irving Y. Lo. SuSp

Sitting on the divan. An Extravagant Lover's Note of Explanation. Dimitris Tsaloumas. FaBoMA

Sitting on Zero. Karen Murai. UTF

Sitting Outside in Early Morning. Lance Henson. ETG

Sitting Pretty. Margaret Fishback. PoLF

Sitting straightbacked, a modest Irish miss. A Lesson in Love. Philip Hobsbaum. OxBTC

Sitting there long after midnight. (*LL*) For the Dead. Adrienne Rich. AnAn; NAAL-2

Sitting This One Out. Steven Sher. BTR

Situation. Langston Hughes. OBAL

Situations Theoretical and Contemporary, *sels.* Tom Leonard.
"And their judges spoke with one dialect." NBrP
"Schooner *The Mother of Parliaments* has anchored in the bay, The." NBrP
"We have decided to make Scotland secure." NBrP

Siwashing It Out Once in Siuslaw Forest. Gary Snyder. *Fr.* Four Poems for Robin. MoP; NNaP; NoAM; NOBA; NoP; SOTW

Six Badgers, The. Robert Graves. GoJo; GrPl

Six beds in a square room: you give your name. Wait. Timothy Steele. PoA

Six Belons. Chase Twichell. NAmP90

Six days ago the water fell. A Peacock's Feather. Seamus Heaney. DiPo

Six Dukes Went a-Fishing. *Unknown.* FaBoBa; OBET

Six Eagles. Thomas Love Peacock. VoR

Six Epigrams, *sels.* Gerard Manley Hopkins.

Six Families of Puerto Ricans. Terence Winch. BCF

Six feet from my window the blackbirds. Amor Vacui. John Fowles. AnAn

Six Feet of Earth. *Unknown.* BLPA

Six Feet Under. Janet Campbell Hale. VoR

Six Filled the Woodshed with Soft Cries. Maura Dooley. PWE

Six-foot nest of the sea-hawk, The. Sea-Hawk. Richard Eberhart. OBAP; RB

Six-forty-two Farm Commune Struggle Poem. Jay Leifer. MAT

Six Haiku for Graham V. Phillips Who First Said the First One. Robert Phillips. GoJo; GrPl

Six Hermetic Songs, *sels.* Michael Palmer.
"At the fever of tongues." BAP-90
"Body in fog and the tongue, The." BAP-90
"How did we measure." BAP-90
"There were nine grand pianos in my father's house." BAP-90
"You can bring down a house with a sound." BAP-90

Six hundred dark feet from the cliffs. "But Still in Israel's Paths They Shine." Carter Revard. VoR

Six hundred stalwart warriors of England's pride the best. Balaclava. *Unknown.* OBET

Six Jolly Wee Miners. *Unknown.* CoMu

Six little mice sat down to spin. Mother Goose. BoTP; OxNR

Six long-headed jazzers play. (*LL*) Jazzonia. Langston Hughes. Jaz

Six men turned to smoke in the next square. The Parachutist's Wife. Sandra M. Gilbert. LoHo; WoWa

Six Million, The. Naomi Replansky. BTR

Six month child, The. Slippery. Carl Sandburg. FaPON

Six Movements on a Theme. David Ignatow. NNaP

Six Nations Museum Onchiota, New York — January. Wendy Rose. HATNAP

Six o'Clock. Owen Dodson. PoNe

Six o'Clock. Trumbull Stickney. AnAmPo; OxBA

Six o'clock and/ the sun rises . . . . Miller Williams. MAT

6 : o' clock our passageway. Travois of the Nameless. Sotère Torregian. NBV

Six o'clock: the kitchen bulbs which blister. Ode to Suburbia. Eavan Boland. PBCIP

Six of them, The. These Six. Sean Lucy. CIP

Six on the Desert Ways. Otalantaiyar, *tr. fr. Tamil by* A. K. Ramanujan. PLW

Six or seven rows of waves struggle landward. On the Oregon Coast. Galway Kinnell. NoAM

Six Periods of Creation. *Maori Oral Tradition, tr. by* Richard Taylor. WTO

Six Poems on Remembering, *sels.* Shen Yüeh, *tr. fr. Chinese by* Burton Watson.

Six Poets in Search of a Lawyer. Donald Hall. NYBP

Six-Quart Basket, The. Raymond Souster. MoCV

Six Reasons for Drinking. Vernon Scannell. OxBC

Six Religious Lyrics, *sels.* Karl Shapiro.
"I sing the simplest flower." CMoP

Six Said by the Concubines to Him. Ammuvanar, *tr. fr. Tamil by* A. K. Ramanujan. PLW

Six street-ends come together here. Blue Island Intersection. Carl Sandburg. MoAmPo

Six Strings, The. Federico García Lorca, *tr. fr. Spanish by* Donald Hall. RB

Six Ten Sixty-nine. Conyus. PoBA

Six Things for Christmas. John May. Mes

Six times faster than the fool can weep. The Peasant. Leonard Wolf. NYBP

Six to Six. *Unknown, tr. fr. Xhosa by* A. C. Jordan. PBA

Six Town Eclogues, *sels.* Lady Mary Wortley Montagu.
Saturday: The Small-Pox. ECWP; NOEC; WPE

Six Variations. (We have been shown.) Denise Levertov. AmPP; LCAP *Sels.*
"Shlup, shlup, the dog." HeIL; HeIP; InPK; Poetr

Six Winter Privacy Poems. Robert Bly. LCAP

Six wives I've had and they're all dead. The Fox and the Hare. *Unknown.* OBET

Six wounds of David's peeling star, The. (*LL*) The Dying Synagogue at South Terrace. Thomas McCarthy. BiHa; IB

Six Years. Alice Bloch. PeHV

Six Young Men. Ted Hughes. NSI; OBWP; PAW; PoWW

"Sixpence a week," says the girl to her lover. By Her Aunt's Grave. Thomas Hardy. *Fr.* Satires of Circumstance. MoAB; MoBrPo

Sixteen Dead Men. W. B. Yeats. FaBoPV; OBWP

1648, *sels.* Morgan Llwyd.
Excuse, The. AngWe
Harvest, The. AngWe
Spring, The. AngWe
Summer, The. AngWe
Winter, The. AngWe

Sixteen Hokku, *sels.* Kato Kyotai, *tr. fr. Japanese by* Burton Watson.

Sixteen Hokku, *sels.* Miura Chora, *tr. fr. Japanese by* Hiroaki Sato.

XVI. "One day as I unwarily did gaze." Spenser. *Fr.* Amoretti. AAS; ESo, lacking epigrams I–IV; HeIL; OAEL-1

16. ix. 65. James Merrill. NAs

Sixteen Sonnets, *sels.* Thomas A. Clark.
"As I walked out early." NBrP
"Each colour sits beside." NBrP
"Our boat touches the bank." NBrP
"Stag comes home at last, The." NBrP
"What the day weaves." NBrP

Sixteen Tons. Merle Travis. SWP

Sixteen years old and crooked. Meeting Mescalito at Oak Hill Cemetery. Lorna Dee Cervantes. BCF; PBCAP

Sixteenth Canto. Hans Magnus Enzensberger. *Fr.* Sinking of the Titanic, The. PoSu

Sixth and of creation last arose, The. Milton. *Fr.* Paradise Lost. ArNa; EPCY

Sixth Book of the Aeneis, The. Virgil, *tr. by* Dryden. *Fr.* Aeneid [*or* Eneados], The. NAWM-1; SeCV-2

Sixth Hell, The. Jerome Rothenberg. *Fr.* Seven Hells of Jigoku Zoshi, The. NNaP

Sixth-Month Song in the Foothills. Gary Snyder. HCAP

Sixth Pearle, The: Justice. Lady Diana Primrose. *Fr.* Chain of Pearl, A. KTR

Sixth Psalm. Anne Sexton. LCAP

Sixth was August, being rich arrayed, The. August. Spenser. *Fr.* Faerie Queene, The. GN

Sixties brought a clash of arms, The. Emancipation Day. L. A. J. Moorer. CBWP-3

Sixties, I think, were not a total loss, The. January 15 as a National Holiday. Carter Revard. VoR

Sixty-eighth Birthday. James Russell Lowell. OxBSP; PoEL-5

Sixty-four Caprices for a Long-Distance Swimmer: Notes on Swimming 100 Miles, *sels.* Janice M. Lynch.

Sixty-four Tanka, *sels.* Saigyo, *tr. fr. Japanese by* Burton Watson.

Sixty needles and sixty pins. Politics. *Unknown.* RoPo

Sixty-second spot, A. Watching My Old House Burn on the News. Jim Daniels. NGP

Sixty-Six Poems for a Blackfoot Bundle. *Unknown, tr. fr. Blackfoot Indian* by Jerome K. Rothenberg. STP

Sixty sun-decked years Charito has gotten to. Philodemus, *tr. fr. Greek by* William Moebius. GrAn

Size, The. George Herbert. GeHe

Size and Sheer Will. Sharon Olds. Poetr

Size of a cavern for men to crouch in, The. Dawn Hippo. Sydney Clouts. PeSA

Size of the human brain, The. Motorcycle Evolution. Peter Payack. PRA

Size of the Mother Superior, The. James Fenton *and* John Fuller. FaBoBl

Sizeline. Felix Mnthali. PeSAV

Skaian Gate, The, *sels.* Geoffrey Scott.
   "Hector, the captain bronzed, from simple fight." OBMV

Skara Brae. Michael Longley. PBCIP

Skate. Alan Brownjohn. OBAP

Skater, The. Sir Charles G. D. Roberts. NOBC

Skater comes to this blue pond, A. The Sea Skater. Helen Dunmore. PWE

Skaters, The. John Gould Fletcher. MoAmPo

Skating. Herbert Asquith. FaPON

Skating. Wordsworth. *Fr.* Prelude [or, Growth of a Poet's Mind], The. CH; EnRP; GN; HAP; NOBE; NoP; NU; OAEL-2; OBNC; OxAEP-2; PoE; SCV; TOF

Skein, The. Carolyn Kizer. PrIm; VGW

Skeleton, The. G. K. Chesteron. FaBoTw

Skeleton House. Laurence Smith. OTCP

Skeleton in Armor, The. Longfellow. AmPP; AnAmPo; AWP; BeLS; BLPL; FaBoBe; PAH

Skeleton is hiding in the closet as it should, The. Everything in Its Place. Arthur Guiterman. NBLV; OBAL

Skeleton Key. John Hollander. NoP

Skeleton of the Future, The. "Hugh MacDiarmid." MoBrPo; OBMV; OBTV

Skeleton of the Great Moa in the Canterbury Museum, Christchurch, The. Allen Curnow. PeNZ

Skeleton Parade. Jack Prelutsky. NTCP

Skeletons are out tonight, The. Skeleton Parade. Jack Prelutsky. NTCP

Skeltoniad, A. Michael Drayton. PoEL-2

Skeptic, The. Clara Ann Thompson. CBWP-2

Sketch. Robert Farnsworth. GOYP

Sketch, A. Christina Rossetti. GTBS-P

Sketch for a Financial Theory of the Self. J. H. Prynne. VaA

Sketch for a Job Application Blank. James Harrison. AmPA; MoP

Sketch for a Modern Love Poem, A. Tadeusz Rózewicz, *tr. fr. Polish by* Czeslaw Milosz.

Sketch from Private Life, A. Byron. OBNC

Sketch from the Campaign in the North, A. Vijay Seshadri. UTF

Sketch from the Great Bull Wall. Sebastian Barry. IB

Sketch in the background: pre-dawn. Petrol. Kathleen Jamie. PWE

Sketch of Lord Byron's Life. Julia A. Moore. FiBHP; OBAL

Sketch of Mount Chung, A. Wang An-shih, *tr. fr. Chinese by* Jan W. Walls. SuSp

Sketch of the Harbour. Robert Gray. FaBoMA

Sketch of the Zoo, The, *sels.* Ting Mang.
   Bat and the Owl, The. LHF, *tr. by* Hualing Nieh
   Crocodile, The. LHF, *tr. by* Hualing Nieh
   Lion, The. LHF, *tr. by* Hualing Nieh

Sketchbook, *sels.* Mihály Ladányi, *tr. fr. Hungarian by* Jascha Kessler.

Sketches from Berlin. Harry Clifton. IB

Sketches near Youngstown Ohio. Lance Henson. ETG

Sketches of Harlem. David Henderson. PoNe

Skier. Robert Francis. RFM

Skies and god's mystery look on, The. Another Alexandra. Mongane Wally Serote. PeSAV

Skies contain still groves of silver clouds, The. Spring 1943. Roy Fuller. LiTB; LiTM

Skies gan scowl, o'ercast with misty clouds, The. George Gascoigne. *Fr.* De Profundis. ChIV-1

Skies have sunk and hid the upper snow, The. Les Vaches. Arthur Hugh Clough. CBLP

Skies o'ercast and fierce winds blow, The. December. Josephine D. Henderson Heard. CBWP-4

Skies remind one of one of those mounds of custard, The. Lollipops of the Pomeranian Baroque. James Fenton. PeLV

Skies they were ashen and sober, The. The Willows. Bret Harte. BXAP

Skies they were ashen and sober, The. Ulalume. Poe. AmPP; AnAmPo; AWP; BLPL; ImPo; LiTA; MeMAP; NOBA; OxBA; TAP (Ulalume — a Ballad.) NAAL-1

Skiing on Russian Christmas. Nora Dauenhauer. HATNAP

Skilful Spearman! A. *Unknown, tr. fr. Hawaiian.* WTO

Skill'd to deceive our ears and eyes. The County Member. Winthrop Mackworth Praed. *Fr.* County Ball, The. OBNC

Skilled to pull wires, he baffles Nature's hope. The Boss. James Russell Lowell. OBAL

Skimbleshanks: The Railway Cat. T. S. Eliot. FaBoCo; NOBL

Skimmers. Ted Walker. NYBP

Skimming/ an asphalt sea. The Sidewalk Racer; or, On the Skateboard. Lillian Morrison. NTCP

Skimming lightly, wheeling still. Shiloh; a Requiem. Herman Melville. AnAmPo; FF; LiTA; NOBA; NoP; OBWP; OxBA; PAW; SCV; WiR

Skin. Sari Friedman. BTR

Skin-and-Bone Lady, The. *Unknown.* AmFP

Skin Divers, The. George Starbuck. NYBP

Skin Diving in the Virgins. John Malcolm Brinnin. NYBP; TAP

Skin Flick. Fred Chappell. InPK

Skin meeting skin, we want to think. Touching Each Other's Surfaces. Carol Jane Bangs. NIP

Skin of Her Neck, The. Bob Arnold. ETG

Skin of the sea, The. In Sylvia Plath Country. Erica Jong. IHMS

Skin/ practicing to be old. Rosario Morales. *Fr.* Old. ETG

Skin quickens to noises, The. One Eyed Black Man in Nebraska. Sam Cornish. PoBA

Skin ripples over my body like moon-wooed water, The. Prison Song. Alan Dugan. PoA

Skin Skin, Yuh Na Know Meh. John C. M. Lyons. NBrP

Skin-Teeth. Grace Nichols. AIW

Skin that is a closed curtain. Poll. Ed Roberson. PoBA

Skin the Goat's Curse on Carey. *Unknown.* BIrV

Skinfull of bowls, he bowls them. Second Glance at a Jaguar. Ted Hughes. NoAM; NYBP; PrIm

Skinny Girl, The. Anne Hébert, *tr. fr. French by* Willis Barnstone. BoWoP

Skinny Mrs. Snipkin. Mrs. Snipkin and Mrs. Wobblechin. Laura E. Richards. OxBChV

Skinny rocks — verdigris green. Crossing Ts'en River. Yang Wan-li, *tr. fr. Chinese by* Jonathan Chaves. SuSp

Skinny, Skinny, run for your life! *Unknown.* RoPo

Skinny waterfalls, footpaths, the. Lastness. Galway Kinnell. NNaP

Skinnydipping on the Molalla River. Walt Curtis. NGP

Skins. Charles Wright. HCAP
   Sels.
   "Under the rock, in the sand and the gravel run."
   "You've talked to the sun and moon."

Skip, The. James Fenton. SCBI

Skip-Scoop-Anellie. Tom Prideaux. FiBHP

Skip to My Lou. *Unknown.* AmFP

Skipper Ireson's Ride. Whittier. AnAmPo; BeLS; NOBA; OBAL; OBCA; OxBA; PAH; PoLF

Skippets, the Bad One. Christine E. Bradley. BoTP

Skirt Dance. Ishmael Reed. FF; UL

Skirting a scrub-pine forest there's a scent of snow in air. Patton. Lincoln Kirstein. ArOW

Skirting the river road, (my forenoon walk, my rest). The Dalliance of the Eagles. Walt Whitman. AmPP; FM; HAP; HeIL; HeIP; NAAL-1; NoP; PPP; PrIm; SAmP; TAP; TRP

Skreak and skritter of evening gone, The. Autumn Refrain. Wallace Stevens. LiTA

Skull Changed to Glass, A. Stephen Spender, *tr. by* Jeffrey Fiskin *and* Erik Vestville. AnAn

Skunk, The. Robert P. Tristram Coffin. FaPON

Skunk, The. Philip Dow. BXAP

Skunk, The. Seamus Heaney. NAEL-2; OxBC; PoE

Skunk. Ted Hughes. ZA

Skunk. Valerie Worth. OBAP

Skunk cabbage, bloodroot. Philip Booth. BoNaP; GrPl

Skunk Hour. Robert Lowell. AmPP; CAPP; CMoP; CoAP; FaBoMo; HAP; HCAP; HeIP; InPK; InPS; LCAP; MoAmPo; MoP; NAAL-2; NIP; NoAM; NOBA; NoP; OPOP; OxBC; PFP; PoE; Poetr; PPP; PrIm; SCV; TAP; TFi; TRP; VCAP

Skunks fight under the house and keep us. Bureau 2. Josephine Miles. NALW

Skunk's footfall plods padded. Skunk. Ted Hughes. ZA

Sky, The. Elizabeth Madox Roberts. MoAmPo

Sky, The. *Unknown, tr. fr. Ewe by* Ulli Beier. TTY

Sky a black sphere, The. Lighthouse in the Night. Alfonsina Storni, *tr. fr. Spanish by* Aliki *and* Willis Barnstone. BoWoP

Sky, above the Roofs, The. Paul Verlaine, *tr. fr. French by* Philip L. Miller. RiWo

Sky at night is like a big city, The. The Sky. *Unknown, tr. fr. Ewe by* Ulli Beier. TTY

Sky can't get in, The. Room. Shirley Kaufman. NMM

Sky ceases. There is only. Michael Dransfield. *Fr.* Geography. CBAP

Sky Clears, The. *Unknown, tr. by* Frances Densmore. OBVE

Sky Diving. Ishmael Reed. UL

Sky full of autumn. Autumn. Ngo Chi Lan, *tr. fr. Vietnamese by* M. S. Merwin and Nguyen Ngoh Bich. ArNa

Sky full of cymbals, of fiddles and lutes. Spring Joy Praising God. Catharina Regina von Greiffenberg, *tr. fr. German by* George C. Schoolfield. GePo

Sky glows one side black, three sides purple, The. The Northern Cold. Li Ho, *tr. fr. Chinese by* A. C. Graham. PLT

Sky grew darker with each minute, The. Before the Storm. Richard Dehmel, *tr. fr. German by* Ludwig Lewisohn. AWP

Sky hangs heavy tonight, The. Negro Woman. Lewis Alexander. CDC; PoBA

Sky has been dark, The. The Youngest Daughter. Cathy Song. NoAM

Sky in red mist. *Unknown.* FaBoUs

Sky is a dead fish, The. The Plaque in the Reading Room for My Classmates Killed in Korea. F. D. Reeve. GOA

Sky Is Blue, The. David Ignatow. NNaP

Sky is dark, and the hills are white, The. Norse Lullaby. Eugene Field. BoTP

Sky is dotted like th' unleavened bread, The. Haggadah. A. M. Klein. TrJP

Sky Is Full of Blue and Full of the Mind of God, The. Kathleen Norris. CrSp

Sky is gray with rain that will not fall, The. At the Zoo. Israel Zangwill. TrJP

Sky is Grey, The. Image. Gu Cheng, *tr. fr. Chinese by* Donald Finkel *with* Yi Jinsheng. SpMi

Sky is heavy, it is raining stars, The. The Cannibal Hymn. *Unknown, tr. fr. Egyptian by* Samuel A. B. Mercer. TTY

Sky is hot and yellow, filled, The. The Brides Come to Yuba City. Chitra Divakaruni. OpBo

Sky is low, the clouds are mean, The. Emily Dickinson. BoNaP; FaBV; MeMAP; MoAmPo; OxBA; PoEL-1.

Sky is overcast, The. A Night-Piece. Wordsworth. EnRP

Sky is pure, the clouds are light, The. The Yellow Fever. Lucretia Davidson. AmWP

Sky is strewn with stars, The. *Unknown, tr. fr. Serbo-Croatian by* Charles Simic. HSix

Sky is such a softness, is such dark. No Moon, No Star. Babette Deutsch. NYBP

Sky is up above the roof, The. Paul Verlaine, *tr. by* Ernest Dowson. *Fr.* Sagesse. AWP; FaPON

Sky Is Vast, The. Pramila Khadun, *tr. fr. French.* TSaS

Sky-lark hath perceived his prison-door, The. On a Picture by J. M. Wright, Esq. Robert Southey. FM

Sky, lazily disdaining to pursue, The. Georgia Dusk. Jean Toomer. BPo; CDC; NAAL-2; NoAM; NoP; PoBA; Poetr

Sky links cloud waves, links dawn fog. Li Ch'ing-chao, *tr. fr. Chinese by* Willis Barnstone *and* Sun Chu-chin. BoWoP

Sky low down in distant West, The. To Mary. Mary E. Tucker. CBWP-1

Sky lowers itself to my book, The. Blue Crêpe. Asa Benveniste. NBrP

Sky of Clouds. Susan Mitchell. BAP-91

Sky opening its abyss to the soul of the Argonaut, The. *(LL)* The Ascent of Vasco da Gama. Fernando Pessoa. PeSAV

Sky Pair, A, *sels.* Robert Frost.
Canis Major. MoAB; MoAmPo
Peaceful Shepherd, The. MoAB; MoAmPo

Sky People. Tato Laviera. BCF

Sky Picture. H. Cordelia Ray. CBWP-3

Sky Pictures. Mary Effie Lee Newsome. CDC

Sky Rises Above the Rooftop, The. Paul Verlaine, *tr. fr. French. Fr.* Sagesse. ArNa, *tr. by* Kate Farrell

Sky so pale, and the trees, such frail things, The. A la Promenade. Paul Verlaine, *tr. by* Arthur Symons. AWP; OBVE

Sky, stabbed by a rusty knife, bleeds midnight, The. Peru, 1955. Ai. *Fr.* He Kept On Burning. AnAn

Sky the color of a wren's [*or* wrens] breath, A. At Chadwicks Bar and Grill. Lance Henson. HATNAP

Sky was battened down, The. On Galveston Beach. Barbara Howes. MoAmPo

Sky was blue, so blue, that day, The. For the Candle Light. Angelina Weld Grimké. BlSi; CDC; PoNe

Sky was carpeted with Italian flak. Crump!, The. Malta. John Forbes. NOBAu

Sky was gold in those days, The. In the Beginning. Valerie Sinason. BrRo

Sky was low, the sounding rain was falling dense and dark, The. The Late Passenger. C. S. Lewis. TrCP

Sky was on the hill, The. When You Reach the Hilltop the Sky Is on Top of You. Etta Blum. GoYe

Sky where the white clouds stand in prayer. Easter. Mary Carolyn Davies. OHIP

Sky widens to Cornwall, The. A sense of sea. In Memoriam: A. C., R.J.O., K.S. Sir John Betjeman. NYBP

Sky will extinguish its stars, and the sun, The. Philip of Thessalonica, *tr. fr. Greek by* Edwin Morgan. GrAn

Sky, with all those eyes to stare at you!, The. *(LL)* Aster. Plato. PeHV

Sky with clouds was overcast, The. Washing Day. *Unknown.* CoMu

Skycoast. Samuel Hazo. GrPl

Skydiving. Jim Wayne Miller. ETG

Skye, *sels.* W. W. Gibson.

Skyhawks fly over my city. Friend and Foe. Karen Alkalay-Gut. WoWa

Skykomish River Running. Richard Hugo. PoA

Skylark, The. James Hogg. GN

Skylark, The. Frederick Tennyson. GN

Skylark, what prompts your silver song. Nature Poem. Adrian Mitchell. Spl

Skylarks. Ted Hughes. HAP

Skylarks are far behind that sang over the down, The. Good-Night. Edward Thomas. NoP

Skylark's nest among the grass, The. Birds' Nests. *Unknown.* BoTP

Skylike limpid eyes, The. Brennbaum. Ezra Pound. *Fr.* Hugh Selwyn Mauberly. (Life and Contacts). AmPP; CMoP; InPS; LiTA; LiTM; MoAmPo; NoAM; NOBA; NoP; TAP

Skyline of New York does not excite me, The. Review from Staten Island. Gloria C. Oden. PoBA; PPP

Skylines/ Are marking me in today. Bessie Mayle. ShDr

Sky's are a pitiful lot, The. Bob Scott. PeLi

Sky's as blue and black as ink, The. Calligram, 15 May 1915. Guillaume Apollinaire, *tr. fr. French by* O. Bernard. OBWP

Sky's blue lapels flap open, The. Flying Home. Gabriel Gbadamosi. NBrP

Sky's lip and the sea's lip shut in peace, The. Lines on the Sea. Dilys Bennett Laing. NYBP

Sky's unresting cloudland, that with varying play, The. Robert Bridges. *Fr.* Testament of Beauty, The. EBEV

Skyscraper. Carl Sandburg. ImGa

Skyscrapers. Rachel Field. FaPON

Skyscrapers are dancing by the river, The. The Skyscrapers of the Financial District Dance with Gasman. Marge Piercy. CAPP

Skyscrapers of the Financial District Dance with Gasman, The. Marge Piercy. CAPP

Skyward mazes. A Look Askance. James Merrill. AnAn

Slack your rope, hangs — a — man. The Maid Freed from the Gallows. *Unknown.* AS
(O good Lord Judge, and sweet Lord.) ESPB

Slade's Invective. Iain Sinclair. VaA

Slag. Charles David Wright. MT

Slain. T. W. H. Crosland. OBWP

Slain Lamb of God. Nikolaus Ludwig, Graf von Zinzendorf, *tr. fr. German by* Sheema Z. Buehne. AH

Slant of sun on dull brown walls, A. A Slant of Sun [on Dull Brown Walls]. Stephen Crane. *Fr.* War Is Kind. LiTM; MeMAP; NAAL-2

Slant of Sun [on Dull Brown Walls], A. Stephen Crane. *Fr.* War Is Kind. LiTM; MeMAP; NAAL-2

Slant sheen/ wrinkled silver. Ronald Johnson. *Fr.* Letters to Walt Whitman. VGW

Slant to the shore, and all their seamen land. *(LL)* There was an Indian, who had known no change. J. C. Squire. CH; FaPON

Slanted World. Rhyll McMaster. FaBoMA

Slanting rays shine on the hamlet. The Farms at Wei River. Wang Wei, *tr. fr. Chinese by* Paul W. Kroll. SuSp

Slap in the Face. Tien Ch'ien, *tr. fr. Chinese.* LHF, *tr. by* Hualing Nieh

Slap of spray on my left ear, A. Open Waters. Jack R. Clemo. PWE

Slate. Richard Murphy. *Fr.* Battle of Aughrim, The. PBCIP

Slate I picked from a nettlebed. Slate. Richard Murphy. *Fr.* Battle of Aughrim, The. PBCIP

Slate Quay: Felinheli. Peter Gruffydd. AngWe

Slated for demolition. The Cathedral Is. John Ashbery. InPK

Slattern, The. Sarah Dixon. ECWP

Slaughter-House, The. Alfred Hayes. ImPo; LiTA

Slaughter of the Laird of Mellerstain, The. *Unknown.* ESPB

Slaughterhouse. Takiguchi Masako, *tr. fr. Japanese by* Kenneth Rexroth *and* Ikuko Atsumi. WPJ

Slaughterhouse's heart is frost. Among the hung-up, The. Blue. Tim Longville. VaA

Slave. Langston Hughes. LiTM

Slave, The. James Oppenheim. TrJP

Slave, The. Jones Very. TAP

Slave and the Iron Lace, The. Margaret Danner. BPo

Slave Auction, The. Frances E. W. Harper. BPo; PoNe; TTY

Slave Chase, The. *Unknown.* CoMu

Slave Girl, The. Rufinus, *tr. fr. Greek by* Alan Marshfield. GrAn

Slave Girl's Song. *Unknown, tr. fr. Maori by* Margaret Orbell. PeNZ

Slave in his father's stead. *(LL)* Coronation. Helen Hunt Jackson. AmWP; BeLS; GN

Slave Marriage Ceremony Supplement. *Unknown.* BPo; TAP

Slave-mother, The. Maria White Lowell. AmWP

Slave Quarters. James Dickey. NYBP

Slave Singing at Midnight, The. Longfellow. GOA

Slave Song. David Dabydeen. PBCV

Slave Story. Hodding Carter. PoNe

Slavery. Hannah More. WoRP

Slavery, a Poem, *sels.* Hannah More.
    "Perish th' illiberal thought which would debase." ECWP

Slaves. James Grainger. *Fr.* Sugar Cane, The. NOEC

Slaves, *last st. James Russell Lowell. Fr.* Stanzas on Freedom. GN, 2 *sts.;* OHIP; PoNe

Slave's Complaint, The. George Moses Horton. AAP

Slave's Dream, The. Longfellow. FaPoR; NAAL-1; PoNe

Slaves/ Humming in the twilight by the shanty door. A. J. Seymour. PBCV

Slave's Lament, The. Massillon Coicou, *tr. fr. French by* Ellen Conroy Kennedy. NegPo

Slaves to London, I'll deceive you. A Song. Peter Anthony Motteux. NOSC

Slay fowl and beast; pluck clean the vine. Cavalier. Richard Bruce. CDC

Slayer of the winter, art thou here again? March. William Morris. *Fr.* Earthly Paradise, The. OtMeF

Sled Burial, Dream Ceremony. James Dickey. CAPP

Sledburn Fair. *Unknown.* CH

Sledding Song, A. Norman C. Schlichter. FaPON

Sleek, brown acrobat, he climbs, A. Harvest Mouse. Clive Sansom. OBAP

Sleep, The. Elizabeth Barrett Browning. ChIV-1; OxAEP-2; WGRP

Sleep. Abraham Cowley. ChTr

Sleep. Theophile de Viau, *tr. fr. French by* Sir Edmund Gosse. AWP

Sleep, *sels.* Robert Farren.
    "While now I lay me down to sleep." TIRV

Sleep. Dana Naone. CDW

Sleep. James Schuyler. GLP

Sleep. Sir Philip Sidney. *See* Lock up, fair lids, the treasure of my heart.

Sleep. Sir Philip Sidney. *See* Come sleepe, O sleepe, the certaine knot of peace.

Sleep. Charles Simic. CoAP

Sleep. Robert Southwell. *Fr.* Saint Peter's Complaint. CBCK

Sleep. Statius, *tr. fr. Latin by* W. H. Fyfe. AWP

Sleep. Randolph Stow. FaBoMA

Sleep, The. Mark Strand. CAPP

Sleep. Georg Trakl, *tr. fr. German by* Joachim Neugroschel. AnAn

Sleep, after Ray Charles Show and Hurricane Report. Heather McHugh. Jaz

Sleep after Toil. Spenser. *See* He there now does enjoy eternal rest.

Sleep: and between the closed eyelids of sleep. Conrad Aiken. *Fr.* Preludes for Memnon; or, Preludes to Attitude. LiTA

Sleep and death, the dusky eagles. Lament. Georg Trakl, *tr. fr. German by* Michael Hamburger. PeFWW

Sleep and Poetry. (What is more gentle than a wind in summer?) Keats. EnRP

Sels.
    "And can I ever bid these joys farewell?" TOF
    "O for ten years, that I may overwhelm." NAEL-2; OAEL-2
    "O Poesy! for thee I hold my pen." FHYEP
    "Schism, A/ Nurtured by foppery and barbarism." EPCY

Sleep, Angry Beauty. Thomas Campion. EnRePo; ErPo; OxBSP; TrGrPo

Sleep, Angry Beauty, Sleep. Thomas Campion. *See* Sleep, angry beauty, sleep, and fear not me.

"Sleep, angry beauty, sleep and fear me not!" Thomas Campion. *See* Sleep, angry beauty, sleep, and fear not me.

Sleep, angry beauty, sleep, and fear not me. Sleep, Angry Beauty. Thomas Campion. EnRePo; ErPo; OxBSP; TrGrPo
    (Sleep, Angry Beauty, Sleep.) FF
    ("Sleep, angry beauty, sleep and fear me not!") EIL

Sleep at noon. Window blind. Hurricane. Archibald MacLeish. ArNa

Sleep away, lad; wake no more. *(LL)* Wake Not for the World-heard Thunder. A. E. Housman. CMoP; NoAM

Sleep, Baby Boy. *Unknown.* FaPON

Sleep, Baby Mine, Desire. Sir Philip Sidney. OxBSP; SiPSBD

Sleep, baby mine, Desire; nurse Beauty singeth. Sleep, Baby Mine, Desire. Sir Philip Sidney. OxBSP; SiPSBD

Sleep, baby, sleep. *Unknown, tr. fr. Japanese by* Geoffrey Bownas *and* Anthony Thwaite. NOBE
    (Nurse's Song.) OTCP

Sleep, baby, sleep,/ Our cottage vale is deep. *Unknown.* ReMoGo

Sleep, Baby, Sleep ("Sleep baby sleep!/ Thy father watches the sheep.") *Unknown.* FaPON

Sleep Brings No Joy. Emily Brontë. MeMBP

Sleep brings no joy to me. Sleep Brings No Joy. Emily Brontë. MeMBP

Sleep Brought Me Vision. John Peale Bishop. Son

Sleep Bus, The. Paule Barton, *tr. fr. Creole by* Howard Norman. PRA

Sleep, calm winter sleep, the rides are woollen. Calm Winter Sleep. Hilary Corke. NYBP

Sleep, Christian warrior, sleep. To Rev. Thaddeus Saltus. Mary Weston Fordham. CBWP-2

Sleep Close to Me. Gabriela Mistral, *tr. fr. Spanish by* D. M. Pettinella. AIW; PBWP

Sleep cold at someone's. Callimachus, *tr. fr. Greek by* Edward Lucie-Smith. GrAn

Sleep, comrades, sleep and rest. Decoration Day. Longfellow. OHIP

Sleep, Darling. Sappho, *tr. by* Mary Barnard. VBLP

Sleep, Ellen Aubrey, sleep, and dream of me. Tennyson. *Fr.* Audley Court. CBLP

Sleep, Grandmother. Mark Van Doren. ImGa

Sleep, grandmother, sleep. Sleep, Grandmother. Mark Van Doren. ImGa

Sleep, grim Reproof; my jocund muse doth sing. Humours. John Marston. *Fr.* Satires. NoSic

Sleep in the Heat. Laura Jensen. AmPA; AnAn

Sleep in the Mojave Desert. Sylvia Plath. AiP; NoP

Sleep is a country of water. Country of Water. Bernice Ames. WPE

Sleep is a god too proud to wait in palaces. Sleep. Abraham Cowley. ChTr

Sleep Is a Reconciling. *Unknown. See* Weep [*or* Weepe] You No More [Sad Fountains].

Sleep is 20. 20. Barbara Guest. PoM

Sleep/ keeps me waiting. Night Treasures. Wilma Elizabeth McDaniel. ETG

Sleep, King Jesus. Mary's Song. Charles Causley. OBCP

Sleep late with your dream. Owen Dodson. *Fr.* Poems for My Brother Kenneth. PoBA; PoNe

Sleep-Learning. Ruth Fainlight. NMM

Sleep, little Baby, kip in peace through the night. Radio Cradle-song. Eugène Marais, *tr. fr. Afrikaans by* Stephen Gray. PeSAV

Sleep, little baby, sleep. Manuel de Falla, *tr. fr. Spanish by* Philip L. Miller. RiWo

Sleep, little pigeon, and fold your wings. Japanese Lullaby. Eugene Field. AnAmPo

Sleep, love sleep. Mary Weston Fordham. CBWP-2

Sleep, Mr. Speaker! it's surely fair. On Seeing the Speaker Asleep in His Chair. Winthrop Mackworth Praed. EnRP
    (Stanzas to the Speaker Asleep.) OBSV

Sleep, Mr Speaker — sleep, sleep while you may! *(LL)* On Seeing the Speaker Asleep in His Chair. Winthrop Mackworth Praed. EnRP

Sleep, my babe, lie still and slumber. All through the Night. *Unknown.* FaPON

Sleep, My Child. Sholom Aleichem, *tr. fr. Yiddish by* Alter Brody. TrJP

Sleep, my child, my little daughter. *Unknown, tr. fr. Yiddish by* Joseph Leftwich. TrJP

Sleep, my child, sleep. Lullaby. Elolongue Epanya Yondo, *tr. fr. French by* Ellen Conroy Kennedy. NegPo

Sleep, my little baby, sleep. Samuel Hoffenstein. TrJP

Sleep My Little Love. Breyten Breytenbach, *tr. fr. Afrikaans by* Stephen Gray *and* A. J. Coetzee. PeSAV

Sleep, my sweet girl! and all the sleep. La Promessa Sposa. Walter Savage Landor. NOBVV

Sleep now, O sleep now. James Joyce. GBL

Sleep/ Now the charge is won. Taps. Lizette Woodworth Reese. OHIP

Sleep of Adam, The. John Hejduk. ChIV-1

Sleep of My Lions, The. Douglas Livingstone. PeSAV

Sleep of the Painted Ladies, The. Nancy Willard. LCAP

Sleep of this night deepens, The. Under Stars. Tess Gallagher. InPK

Sleep on, and dream of Heaven awhile. The Sleeping Beauty. Samuel Rogers. GTBS; GTBS-P; OxAEP-2

Sleep on, beloved, sleep and take thy rest. The Christian's "Good-Night." Sarah Doudney. BLPA

Sleep on, I lie at heaven's high oriels. Nirvana. John Hall Wheelock. MoAmPo

Sleep on, my love, in thy cold bed. Henry King. Fr. Exequy, The. CH; CoGr; GBL; HAP; InvP; JCP; MeLP; NoP; OBD; OxBM; PoEL-2; PrIm; SCGP; SeCP; TEP; TrGrPo

Sleep on, sleep sound. (LL) Parta Quies. A. E. Housman. NOBE; TEP

Sleep on your breast to the airport. (LL) Wedding Day. Seamus Heaney. LPA; OxAEP-2

Sleep, our lord, and for thy peace. Night Song for a Child. Charles Williams. OBEV

Sleep, Silence' Child. William Drummond of Hawthornden. Son

Sleep, sleep, beauty bright. Blake. EnRP; OBEV; PoLF

Sleep sleep old sun, thou canst not have repast. Resurrection, Imperfect. John Donne. ChIV-2

Sleep softly . . . eagle forgotten . . . under the stone. The Eagle That Is Forgotten. Vachel Lindsay. AWP; CMoP; LiTA; MeMAP; MoAB; MoAmPo; NOBA; OxBA

Sleep Song. John Fletcher. See Care-charming Sleep [Thou Easer of All Woes].

Sleep Sweet. Ellen M. Huntington Gates. BLPA; BLRP; FaBoBe

Sleep Sweetly. Henry Timrod. See Sleep sweetly in your humble graves.

Sleep sweetly in your humble graves. Henry Timrod. GOA; NOBA; OxBA; TAP
  (At Magnolia Cemetery.) AnAmPo
  (Ode: "Sleep sweetly . . . .") GOA; NOBA; OxBA; TAP
  (Sleep Sweetly.) AH

Sleep, Thou little Child of Mary. Song of a Shepherd Boy at Bethlehem. Josephine Preston Peabody. OHIP

Sleep tried to split us apart. A Meeting with Vilakazi, the Great Zulu Poet. Raymond Mazisi Kunene, tr. fr. Zulu by the author. PeSAV

Sleep Upon the World. Alcman, tr. by Thomas Campbell. ChTr

Sleep-Walking Child. Elisabeth Eybers, tr. fr. Afrikaans by Jack Cope, Uys Krige, and Adèle Naudé. PeSA

Sleep-walking vapor, like a visitant ghost. Still Life. Anthony Hecht. AnAn

Sleep was only a dream. Chicago: Near West-Side Renewal. Dennis Schmitz. AmPA

Sleep Watch. Lance Henson. VoR

Sleep, Wayward Thoughts. Unknown. See Sleep, wayward thoughts, and rest you with my love.

Sleep, wayward thoughts, and rest you with my love. So Sleeps My Love. Unknown. TrGrPo
  (Sleep, Wayward Thoughts. EnRePo

Sleep well, my love, sleep well. Nightsong: City. Dennis Brutus. HBAPE

Sleep well, sleep well! The Brook's Lullaby. Wilhelm Müller, tr. fr. German by Philip L. Miller. Fr. Beautiful Maid of the Mill, The. RiWo

Sleep: you are my homestead, and my garden. Sleep. Randolph Stow. FaBoMA

Sleepe, Death's allye, oblivion of teares. Sleep. Robert Southwell. Fr. Saint Peter's Complaint. CBCK

Sleeper, The. Sydney Clouts. PeSA

Sleeper, The. Walter de la Mare. MoAB; MoBrPo

Sleeper, The. Poe. AmPP; AnAmPo; LiTA; MeMAP; NAAL-1; NOBA; OxBA; PoEL-4; TAP; TrGrPo

Sleeper, The. Unknown, tr. fr. Arabic by E. Powys Mathers. Fr. Thousand and One Nights, The. AWP

Sleeper in the Valley, The. Rimbaud. OBWP, tr. by Robert Lowell

Sleeper in the Valley, The. Rimbaud, tr. by Robert Lowell. Fr. Eighteen-Seventy. OBWP

Sleeper of the Valley, The. Rimbaud, tr. fr. French by Ludwig Lewisohn. AWP

Sleeper Rise. Gond Oral Tradition, tr. by V. Elwin and S. Hivale. WTO

Sleeper, the palm-trees drink the breathless noon. The Sleeper. Unknown, tr. fr. Arabic by E. Powys Mathers. Fr. Thousand and One Nights, The. AWP

Sleepers, The. Peter Kocan. CBAP

Sleepers. Branko Miljkovic, tr. fr. Serbo-Croatian by Charles Simic. HSix

Sleepers, The. Randolph Stow. Fr. Thailand Railway. CBAP

Sleepers, The. Walt Whitman. AmPP; NAAL-1

SLEEPERS AWAKE. Text for a Poster (2). Lee Harwood. NBrP

Sleepers humped down on the benches, The. Night Raid. Desmond Hawkins. PoWW

Sleepin' at the Foot o' the Bed. Luther Patrick. BLPA

Sleeping, The. Lynn Emanuel. AiP

Sleeping. Donald Hall. PRA

Sleeping. (LL) Weep [or Weepe] You No More [Sad Fountains]. Unknown. CH; EBEV; EiL; ELP; EnLoPo; GBL; HAP; NoP; NOSC; NoSic; NTP; PoE; PoEL-2; TFi; TrGrPo

Sleeping armies of the living God, The. The Death of Saul. Philip Levine. ChIV-1

Sleeping at Last. Christina Rossetti. NAEL-2; TrGrPo

Sleeping at last. (LL) Sleeping at Last. Christina Rossetti. NAEL-2; TrGrPo

Sleeping badly, he'd wake in a rage. Dreams. Fay Zwicky. FaBoMA

Sleeping Beauty. Olga Broumas. VBLP

Sleeping Beauty, The. Rachel Hadas. UnDi

Sleeping Beauty, The. Samuel Rogers. GTBS; GTBS-P; OxAEP-2

Sleeping Beauty, The, sels. Edith Sitwell.
  "In the great gardens, after bright spring rain." OxBTC
  (Innocent Spring, The.) NOBE
  "When we come to that dark house." OBMV

Sleeping Beauty; Variation of the Prince, The. Randall Jarrell. PoA

Sleeping beside you, I know a distance. 1985 — In a Small American Town. Judith Irwin. BTR

Sleeping Christchild. Eduard Friedrich Mörike, tr. fr. German by Philip L. Miller. RiWo

Sleeping Fury, The. Louise Bogan. IHMS; LiTM; NALW

Sleeping Giant, The. Donald Hall. GoJo; GrPl; NYBP; Poetsp; TwCP

Sleeping Heroes. Edward Shanks. OBMV

Sleeping House, The. Tennyson. Fr. Maud[: A Monodrama]. OBNC

Sleeping in Santo Spirito. Bruce Beasley. UTF

Sleeping in the Forest. Mary Oliver. CAPP; InPS; NU

Sleeping in their sheen.' (LL) Willie Macintosh. Unknown. ESPB, A and B vers.; OxBoLi

Sleeping Lord, The, sels. David Jones.
  "Tawny-black sky-scurries." OBWVE

Sleeping on the Ceiling. Elizabeth Bishop. TTTS

Sleeping on the Wing. Frank O'Hara. InPS; NAAL-2; SOTW

Sleeping or waking, thou sweet face. Unknown, tr. fr. Italian by John Addington Symonds. Fr. Popular Songs of Tuscany. AWP

Sleeping Out with My Father. Gibbons Ruark. ArOW; MT

Sleeping They Bear Me. Alfred Mombert, tr. fr. German by Jethro Bithell. AWP

Sleeping, turning in turn like planets. Adrienne Rich. Fr. Twenty-one Love Poems. GLP; PeHV; TRP

Sleeping with Foxes. Roberta Hill Whiteman. CDW

Sleeping with One Eye Open. Mark Strand. CAPP; NYBP; SM

Sleeping with Women. Kenneth Koch. PoM

Sleeping woman dreams she wakes, A. Nightmare. Isabella Gardner. CoAP

Sleepless. Al-Khansa, tr. fr. Arabic by Willis Barnstone. BoWoP

Sleepless as Prospero back in his bedroom. Darwin in 1881. Gjertrud Schnackenberg. NoAM; SM

Sleepless at Crown Point. Richard Wilbur. InPK; WeW

Sleepless ghost perpetually striving, The. Eros Out of the Sea. Dilys Bennett Laing. PoA

Sleepless hours who watch me as I lie, The. Hymn of Apollo. Shelley. EnRP; OAEL-2
  (Song of Apollo.) NAEL-2

Sleepless, I lie alone. (LL) Pleiades disappear, The. Sappho. InMo

Sleepless Night. Léon Damas, tr. fr. French by Ellen Conroy Kennedy. NegPo

Sleepless Night, A. Egan O'Rahilly, tr. fr. Modern Irish by Frank O'Connor. PeIV

Sleeplessness. Luigi Fontanella, tr. fr. Italian by W. S. Di Piero. NeIt

Sleepmask Dithyrambic. Thomas Lux. PRA

Sleep'ry Sim of the Lamb-kill. The Fray of Suport. Unknown. IBB

Sleeps as thy lover for a little while. (LL) Hymn to Earth. Elinor Wylie. LiTM; MoAB; MoAmPo

Sleeps here the sleep that must be slept by all. (LL) Crethis. Callimachus. AWP

Sleepwalkers. Bella Akhmadulina, tr. fr. Russian by Barbara Einzig. BoWoP

Sleepwalkers' Ballad. Federico García Lorca, tr. fr. Spanish by John Frederick Nims. STV; WeW

Sleepy Giant, The. Charles Edward Carryl. OTCP

Sleepy world of streams, A. *(LL)* The Garden of Proserpine. Swinburne. AWP; BLPA; BLPL; FaBoRV; FaBV; FaPoR; HAP; LiTB; NAEL-2; NOBE; NOBVV; NoP; OBNC; PoE; PoEL-5; PoRA; SCV; TrGrPo

Sleet. Norman MacCaig. OBCP

Sleet Storm on the Merritt Parkway. Robert Bly. NOBA

Slender bamboos grow by the window. After One of the 19 Famous Han Poems. Pao Ling-hui, *tr. fr. Chinese* by Kenneth Rexroth *and* Ling Chung. WPC

Slender Fingers ("Slender, delicate, soft jade.") Chao Luan-luan, *tr. fr. Chinese* by Kenneth Rexroth *and* Ling Chung. BoWoP; WPC

Slender Lad, The. *Unknown, tr. fr. Welsh* by Kenneth Hurlstone Jackson. OBWVE

Slender plank above a waterhole, A. The Founding of New Hampshire. Carl Rakosi. PRA

Slender, the grapevine comes down. The Vine. Sun Ching-hsuan, *tr. fr. Chinese.* LHF, *tr.* by Hualing Nieh

Slender young blackbird built in a thorn-tree, A. The Blackbird. Dinah Maria Mulock Craik. BoTP

Slepynge Long in Greet Quiete Is Eek a Greet Norice to Leccherie. John Hollander. ErPo

Sliab Cua, dark and broken, is full of wolf packs. *Unknown. Fr.* Toward Winter. NOIV

Slice of Wedding Cake, A. Robert Graves. BoLoP; NAEL-2; NOBE; OxBTC; PIP

Slicing my head off shaving I think of Charles I. Notes for a Revised Sonnet. Edward Pygge. BXAP

Slid on; and the lesser was gone. *(LL)* Turtles Hatching. Mark O'Connor. NOBAu

Slide soft, fair forth, and make a crystal plain. William Drummond of Hawthornden. NOSC

Slides. Jennifer Maiden. CBAP

Slides by on grease. *(LL)* For the Union Dead. Robert Lowell. AmPP; CoAP; FaBoPV; FYAP; HAP; HCAP; HeIP; InPS; LCAP; LiTM; MoP; NAAL-2; NaP; NoAM; NOBA; NoP; OBWP; PoE; Poetr; SCV; TFi; TRP; TwCP; UnPo; VCAP; WeW

Sliding. Sam Adams. AngWe

Sliding down the banisters. On the Banisters. Margaret E. Gibbs. BoTP

Slieve Gua. *Unknown, tr. fr. Old Irish.* ChTr

Slight accent, A. Emigrant/Immigrant. Rina Ferrarelli. LoHo

Slight as thou art, thou art enough to hide. To a Daisy. Alice Meynell. MoBrPo; Son; WGRP

Slight-boned animal, young, A. Small Colored Boy in the Subway. Babette Deutsch. PoNe

Slight Confusion, A. James Reiss. AmPA

Slight neglects of conversation, The. *(LL)* A Fib Detected. Catullus. AWP; OBVE

Slight person, yet you are, A. Rhetorical Swing. Marilyn Kitchell. UL

Slight unpremeditated words are borne. Love's Witness. Aphra Behn. BoWoP

Slighted Wife, The. Aaron Hodza, *tr. fr. Shona* by George Fortune. PeSAV

Slightly before the middle of Congressman Pudd. E. E. Cummings. FaBoEE; OBAL

Slightly Old. Bob Rosenthal. UL

Sligo and Mayo. Louis MacNeice. FaBoPP

Slim and singing copper girl, A. Early Copper. Carl Sandburg. HeIP

Slim Cunning Hands. Walter de la Mare. FaBoEE; NIP; WeW

Slim cunning hands at rest, and cozening eyes. Slim Cunning Hands. Walter de la Mare. FaBoEE; NIP; WeW

Slim dragonfly/ too rapid for the eye. Arthur Mitchell. Marianne Moore. PoNe

Slim in Hell ("Slim Greer went to heaven.") Sterling A. Brown. BPo

Slim Man Canyon. Leslie Silko. VoR

Slim sentinels. Trees at Night. Helene Johnson. BlSi; ShDr

Slim/ young fascist, A. On the Yard. Etheridge Knight. RaBo

Slime clung, The. Isaac Rosenberg. *Fr.* Amulet, The. PeFWW

Slimy obscene creatures, insane. The Nigga Section. Welton Smith. BPo

Slip, The. Wendell Berry. NOCV

Slip of loveliness, slim, seemly. In Praise of a Girl. Huw Morus, *tr. fr. Welsh* by Gwyn Williams. OBWVE

Slip off that gown. Paulus Silentiarius, *tr. fr. Greek* by Andrew Miller. GrAn

Slip useless away? *(LL)* To-Day. Thomas Carlyle. GN; WGRP

Slipped Quadrant. Nathaniel Mackey. BAP-90

Slippery. Carl Sandburg. FaPON

Slipping in blood, by his own hand, through pride. To an Artist, to Take Heart. Louise Bogan. GrPl; NYBP; TRP

Slips in a moment out of life. *(LL)* To H. C. Wordsworth. EnRP; MeMBP; PoEL-4

Slithergadee, The. Shel Silverstein. NBLV

Sloe Gin. Seamus Heaney. PNI

Sloe was lost in flower, The. A. E. Housman. CBLP

Slog brute streets with rebel tramping! Our March. Vladimir Mayakovsky, *tr. fr. Russian* by Babette Deutsch *and* Avrahm Yarmolinsky. AWP

Slogan, The. Paul Blackburn. PoM

Slogan Will Not Suffice, A. Kelvin Corcoran. NBrP

Sloops in the Bay. James Tate. AnAn

Sloth, The. Theodore Roethke. AnAmPo; FiBHP; OBAL; OBAP; OBCA; TRP

Sloth, The. George Romanes. FM; IHNG; PIP

Slouches towards Bethlehem to be born? *(LL)* The Second Coming. W. B. Yeats. BIrV; BLPL; ChIV-2; CIHu; CMoP; CoGr; EBEvV; FaBoMo; FaBoPV; FaPoB; FF; GGP; GTBS-P; HAP; HeIP; HoPM; ImPo; InPK; InPS; LiTB; LiTM; MAT; MeMBP; MoAB; MoBrPo; MoP; NAEL-2; NAWM-2; NIP; NoAM; NOBE; NoP; OAEL-2; OxAEP-2; OxBTC; PAW; PoE; Poetr; PPP; PrIm; RaBo; SCV; SoSe; TEP; TFi; TRP; UnPo

Slough. Sir John Betjeman. MoBrPo; NoAM; OxAEP-2

Slow bleak awakening from the morning dream. Living. Harold Monro. ImPo; LiTB

Slow burn, A. Pit Viper. George Starbuck. NYBP

Slow, cold breathing, The. The Marsh, New Year's Day. Peter Everwine. NNaP

Slow Dance. David St. John. AmPA; AnAn; LCAP

Slow Dancer That No One Hears but You. Duane Niatum. CDW

Slow-footed stockman called Beales, A. Cyril Mountjoy. PeLi

Slow freight wriggles along, The. The Freight Train. Rowena Bastin Bennett. PDV

Slow Giving. Ibn al-Rumi, *tr. fr. Arabic* by Omar S. Pound. ArPe

Slow, horses, slow. Night of Spring. Thomas Westwood. BoTP

Slow Movement. Louis MacNeice. CBLP

Slow Movement. William Carlos Williams. PoA

Slow moves the acid breath of noon. Field of Autumn. Laurie Lee. LiTM

Slow overture of rain, The. Mind. Jorie Graham. HCAP; Poetr

Slow Pacific Swell, The. Yvor Winters. NOBA

Slow pass the hours — ah, passing slow! Ballade Tragique à Double Refrain. Max Beerbohm. IHNG; OBSV

Slow Rain. Gabriela Mistral, *tr.* by Gunda Kaiser *and* James Tipton. PBWP

Slow Riff for Billy. James Cunningham. JB

Slow, rigid, is this masquerade. Spring 1916. Isaac Rosenberg. NSI

Slow sinks, more lovely ere his race be run. Sunset over the Aegean. Byron. *Fr.* Corsair, The. OBNC

Slow, Slow, Fresh Fount. Ben Jonson. *Fr.* Cynthia's Revels. BeJo; ChTr; EIL; ELP; InPS; NIP; NoP; OAEL-1; PrIm; SCGP; TFi

Slow, slow, fresh fount, keep time with my salt tears. Slow, Slow, Fresh Fount. Ben Jonson. *Fr.* Cynthia's Revels. BeJo; ChTr; EIL; ELP; InPS; NIP; NoP; OAEL-1; PrIm; SCGP; TFi
  (Echo's Lament for Narcissus.) CH; OxAEP-1
  (Echo's [or Eccho's] Song.) JCP; NOSC; SeCV-1; TrGrPo
  (Song: "Slow, slow fresh fount, keep time with my salt tears.") EnRePo; OxBSP; PoEL-2; SeCP

Slow — slow — slow — slow. *(LL)* A Swing Song. William Allingham. FaPON; MoShBr; OTCP; TLR

Slow Spring. Katharine Tynan. BoTP

Slow Summer Twilight. John Hall Wheelock. LiTM

Slow the Kansas sun was setting o'er the wheat fields far away. Towser Shall Be Tied Tonight. *Unknown.* BLPA

Slow to Come, Quick a-Gone. William Barnes. NOBVV

Slow wand'ring came the sightless seer and she. Antigone and Oedipus. H. Cordelia Ray. AAP; BlSi; CBWP-3

Slow-worm from my orchard seeking me, The. Jeffrey Wainwright. *Fr.* Mad Talk of George III, The. SCBI

Slowly. James Reeves. NTP

Slowly a hundred miles through the powerful rain. You Drive in a Circle. Ted Hughes. NYBP

Slowly, and flake by flake . . . At the drifted fond. Winter Night: Mount Royal. A. M. Klein. NoAM

Slowly, as one who bears a mortal hurt. La Mort d'Arthur. William Edmonstoune Aytoun. FaBoPa

Slowly, by God's hand unfurled. Evening Hymn. William Henry Furness. FaBoBe
  (Light of Stars, The.) TrPWD
  (Slowly, by God's Hand Unfurled.) AH

Slowly, by God's Hand Unfurled. William Henry Furness. *See* Slowly, by God's hand unfurled.

Slowly England's sun was setting o'er the hilltops far away. Curfew Must Not Ring Tonight. Rose Hartwick Thorpe. BeLS; BLPA; BLPL; FaBoBe; FaPON; VPP

Slowly flutters the snow from ash-coloured heavens in silence. Snowfall. Giosuè Carducci, *tr. fr. Italian*. AWP, *tr. by* Romilda Rendel

Slowly he spread his wings. The Red-winged Lourie. Noëline Barry. OBAP

Slowly he sways that head that cannot hear. Rattler, Alert. Brewster Ghiselin. HAP; WeW

Slowly he turns himself round and round. The Dancing Bear. Rachel Field. NTCP

Slowly I smoke and hug my knee. Ballade by the Fire. E. A. Robinson. AnAmPo

Slowly/ like a crippled cow. Jean-Joseph Rabéarivelo, *tr. fr. French by* Ellen Conroy Kennedy. NegPo

Slowly, O so slowly, longing rose up. Christ Walking on the Water. W. R. Rodgers. MoAB

Slowly, silently, now the moon. Silver. Walter de la Mare. BoNaP; BoTP; FaPON; MoAB; MoBrPo; PoRA; PYC; TTTS

Slowly, slowly, swinging low. Swinging. Irene Thompson. BoTP

Slowly, Slowly Wisdom Gathers. Mark Van Doren. PoA

Slowly the mist o'er the meadow was creeping. Lexington. Oliver Wendell Holmes. PAH

Slowly the Moon her banderoles of light. A Battle. Isabella Valancy Crawford. NOBC

Slowly the moon is rising out of the ruddy haze. Aware. D. H. Lawrence. BoNaP; MoBrPo; NoAM

Slowly the muddy pool becomes a river. Let the Dead Depart in Peace. *Yoruba Oral Tradition*, *tr. by* Ulli Beier. WTO

Slowly the night blooms, unfurling. Flowers of Darkness. Frank Marshall Davis. NoP; PoBA; PoNe

Slowly the poison on the whole blood stream fills. Missing Dates. William Empson. CMoP; HAP; LiTB; LiTM; MoAB; MoBrPo; MoP; NoAM; NOBE; NoP; OAEL-2; PoE; UnPo

Slowly the sugar dissolves in the tall glass of tea. Comfortable Words. Gillian Allnutt. NBrP

Slowly, the summer was ending with a shower. We were. A Sentimental Voyage Around My Room. Jovan Hristic, *tr. fr. Serbo-Croatian by* Charles Simic. HSix

Slowly the thing comes. Panic ("Slowly the thing comes.") Archibald MacLeish. *Fr.* Panic. MoAmPo

Slowly the tide creeps up the sand. Slowly. James Reeves. NTP

Slowly the vision grows. Lakeside Incident. Robin Skelton. NOBC

Slowly the women file to where he stands. Faith Healing. Philip Larkin. ChIV-2; NoAM

Slowly the world contracts about my ears. The Flagpole Sitter. Donald Finkel. CoAP

Slowly through the tomb-still streets I go. The Lover's Farewell. James Clarence Mangan. PeIV

Slowly thy flowing tide. The Ebb Tide. Robert Southey. OBNC

Slowly, till scissors of cockcrow snip the air. *(LL)* The Afterwake. Adrienne Rich. NOBA; Prf

Slowly up the cemetery steps. After School. Liz Cashdan. NWP

Slowly upwards past the girdles. The Escalator. Alex Glasgow. OBET

Slowly we learn; the oft repeated line. On National Vanity. J. E. Clare McFarlane. PBCV

Slowly we return to earth. *(LL)* Through the weeks of deep snow. Wendell Berry. EaPr

Slowly, with intention to tempt, she sidles out. Egyptian Dancer. Terence Tiller. OBTV

Slowness of gaze, the slowness behind fear. The Diagonal Is Diagonal. Douglas Oliver. VaA

Sludge of learning slides, A. The Dumps. Nigel Wells. PWE

Slug in Woods. Earle Birney. NOBC

Sluggard, The. W. H. Davies. OBMV

Sluggard, The. Isaac Watts. CH; EBEvV; ECEV; HAP; Mes; MoShBr; NOEC; OxBChV; OxBoLi; PoEL-3; UV, *sh. vers.*; VPP

Sluggardy-guise. *Unknown*. ISE

Sluggish morne as yet undrest, The. Upon Phillis Walking in a Morning before Sun-Rising. John Cleveland. MeLP

Sluggy and slowe, in spetinge muiche. *Unknown*. MiEL

Slum Dwelling, A. George Crabbe. *Fr.* Borough, The. OBNC

Slumber dark and deep. Paul Verlaine, *tr. by* Arthur Symons. *Fr.* Sagesse. AWP

Slumber Did My Spirit Seal, A. Wordsworth. *Fr.* Lucy. AWP; BLPL; EBEV; EBEvV; ELP; EnLoPo; EnRP; FaBoCh; FHYEP; GBL; GGP; GTBS; GTBS-P; HAP; HeIP; ImPo; InPK; InPS; InvP; MeMBP; NOBE; NoP; OAEL-2; OBEV; OBNC; PoEL-4; PoRA; PPP; PrIm; SCGP; SCV; TEP; TFi; TrGrPo; UnPo; WeW

Slumber in Spring. Elizabeth Gould. BoTP

Slumber pours down . . *(LL)* About the cool water. Sappho. ErPo; OBVE; PGA

Slumber Song. Louis V. Ledoux. FaPON

Slumber Song of the Gardens, A. John Runcie. PeSAV

Slumbering Passion. Josephine D. Henderson Heard. CBWP-4

Slump. Vassar Miller. BoWoP

Slumped on a chair, his body is an S. The Lavatory Attendant. Wendy Cope. UV

Slurped/ and waters moved. Lee-ers of Hew. James Cunningham. JB

Sly merchants plotted newer, greater gains. Renaissance. Robert Avrett. GoYe

Sly Mongoose. *Unknown* (add. *verses by* Knolly La Fortune). PBCV

Sly naked damsels nodding their downy plumes. *(LL)* Cranach. Sir Herbert Read. FaBoMo

Sma' was I, amang brether o' mine. David and Goliath. P. Hately Waddell. ChIV-1

Smacksman, The. Sam Larner. OxBSS

Small, The. Theodore Roethke. GrPl

Small Aircraft. Bella Akhmadulina, *tr. fr. Russian by* Daniel Halpern. BoWoP; PAW

Small and emptied woman you lie here a thousand years dead. In the Museum. Isabella Gardner. CAPP; NYBP; SoSe

Small Animal. Alberta Turner. FoLa

Small babe, tell me. The Baby. James Reaney. *Fr.* Sequence in Four Keys, A. NAs

Small bird/ tracks. Rain. Lance Henson. VoR

Small birds and turtle doves. Arise and Pick a Posy. *Unknown*. OBET

Small Bird's Nest Made of White Reed Fiber, A. Robert Bly. NNaP

Small birds swirl around, The. The Small. Theodore Roethke. GrPl

Small block of granite, A. A Child's Grave Marker. Ted Kooser. GOYP

Small Boy, Dreaming, A. Albert Herzing. NYBP

Small boy drove the shaggy ass, The. Turf Carrier on Aranmore. John Hewitt. PoRA

Small, busy flames play through the fresh laid coals. To My Brothers. Keats. NAs; Son; TEP

Small buttocks of men, that excite the women . . ., The. The Sexual Sigh. Gavin Ewart. FaBoBl

Small car distant, no life in it. Cross Divide. Tom Raworth. NBrP

Small change, when we're [*or* we are] to bodies gone. *(LL)* The Ecstasy. John Donne. BoLoP; EnRePo; FHYEP; HAP; ImPo; InPS; JCP; LiTB; NAEL-1; NOBE; NoP; OAEL-1; OBEV; PoE; PrIm; TEP; TFi; TOF; TrGrPo

Small cherries sip delicately. Red Sandalwood Mouth. Chao Luan-luan, *tr. fr. Chinese by* Kenneth Rexroth *and* Ling Chung. WPC

Small child of a wind, A. Requiem for Sonora. Richard Shelton. Poetsp

Small Colored Boy in the Subway. Babette Deutsch. PoNe

Small Comfort. Katha Pollitt. CrSp

Small Country. Claribel Alegría, *tr. fr. Spanish by* Aliki *and* Willis Barnstone. BoWoP

Small dawn, sailor, A. First light glints. Here, but Unable to Answer. Richard Hugo. CAPP

Small Death, A. Jill Maughan. NWP

Small Demand, A. Karen Murai. UTF

Small doses, effleurage will do. Sea or Sky? Medbh McGuckian. PBCIP

Small eyes water on the branch. Another Face. Ray A. Young Bear. CDW

Small fact and fingers and farthest one from me. A Poem for Emily. Miller Williams. MT; WeW

Small Faculty Stag for the Visiting Poet, A. Earle Birney. OxBC; PeLV

Small Farm, A. Michael Hartnett. CIP; PBCIP

Small Farmer. Jimmy Santiago Baca. ETG

Small Fat Boy Walking Backwards, A. Gerry Murphy. BiHa

Small Fig Tree, A. Donald Hall. ChIV-2

Small fists waving. The Baby Hilary, Sir Edmund. Kathleen Leland Baker. NBLV

Small foreign car full of farm ladies from Jones County, A. Double Semi-Sestina. George Starbuck. SM

Small Fountains. Lascelles Abercrombie. *Fr.* Emblems of Love. CH; MoBrPo

Small Frogs Killed on the Highway. James Wright. HCAP; NNaP; NoAM

Small Garden, The. Cheng Hsieh, *tr. fr. Chinese by* Wu-chi Liu. SuSp

Small girls hurried to the hill-top church, The. Whit Monday. John Hewitt. TIRV

Small girls on trikes. Christmas Day. Roy Fuller. OBCP

Small gnats that fly. Song: One Hard Look. Robert Graves. MoAB; MoBrPo

(One Hard Look.) PlP

Small grey cloudy louse that nests in my beard, The. James K. Baxter. *Fr.* Jerusalem Sonnets. NoP; PeNZ

Small householder now comes out warily, The. Spring Voices. Louis MacNeice. Son

Small ironic silence of his claws, The. *(LL)* Vicissitudes of the Creator. Archibald MacLeish. MeMAP

Small Lady, The. Stevie Smith. TEP

Small Light, A. Cathy Song. TRP

Small lights pirouette. Peterhead in May. Burns Singer. OxBS

Small men make love on stilts, and hold their poise. A Forked Radish. Jonathan Price. CBLP

Small moon. Prayer to the Young Moon. *Unknown, tr. fr. Bushman by* W. H. I. Bleek *and* Jack Cope. PeSA

Small-mouth bass breaks water, gorged with spawn. *(LL)* After the Surprising Conversions. Robert Lowell. AmPP; HAP; NAAL-2; NoAM; NoP; PPP; TRP

Small of the back has its answers. Cuba Night. Dave Jeddie Smith. NAmP90

Small ones wanted pieces of me, The. Volunteer Worker. Tony Perez. TSaS

Small Park in East Germany: 1969. Gerda Mayer. OBTV

Small Patch of Ice, A. Betsy Sholl. PBCAP

Small Paths. Henriëtte Roland-Holst, *tr. fr. Dutch by* Jonathan Crewe. WPOW

Small plot of ground, The. Belonging. Alla Renee Bozarth. EaPr

Small Prayer. Weldon Kees. IMW; PoA; VGW

Small Rains. N. M. Bodecker. Spl

Small Registry of Births and Deaths, A, *sels.* C. K. Stead. All Night It Bullied You. NAs

Small rivulets ran about her feet. Cythera. Suniti Namjoshi. AIW

Small Room with Large Windows, A. Allen Curnow. PeNZ *Sels.*
 "In the interim, how the children should be educated."
 "Kingfisher's naked arc alight, A."
 "Seven ageing pine tree hide."
 "What it would look like if really there were only."

Small room with one table and one chair, A. Poet in Winter. Edward Lucie-Smith. TwCP

Small sad man with a hat, A. At Last. John Montague. PBCIP

Small Sad Song. Alastair Reid. NYBP

Small-scale Reflections on a Great House. A. K. Ramanujan. OxBC

Small script take thy swift way across the sea. For His Friends. Alcuin, *tr. fr. Latin by* Helen Waddell. MLL

Small service is true service while it lasts. To a Child. Wordsworth. OxBSP
 (In a Child's Album.) GN
 (Written in an Album.) Spl
 (Written in the Album of a Child.) OxBChV

Small Song. A. R. Ammons. NoAM; NoP

Small space. Two Tile Beaks. Maria Amalia Fonte Boa, *tr. by* Willis Barnstone *and* Nelson Cerqueira. BoWoP

Small Splinters From My Cheek. Doina Uricariu, *tr. fr. Romanian by* Brenda Walker *and* Andrea Deletant. VBLP

Small splinters from my cheek hit me. *(LL)* Small Splinters From My Cheek. Doina Uricariu. VBLP

Small Square, The. Sophia de Mello Breyner Andresen, *tr. fr. Portuguese by* Alexis Levitin. WPOW

Small Talk in a Garden. O. B. Hardison, Jr. CRP

Small thing and moreover black is she, A. Philodemus, *tr. fr. Greek by* William Moebius. GrAn

Small things, like the turning of a key. Chimes. Michael Smith. PBCIP

Small thunder cut my autumn doze on the porch. Museum. Sydney Lea. NAmP90

Small Town with One Road. Gary Soto. SoSe

Small Towns of Ireland, The. Sir John Betjeman. OBTV

Small trees, smaller emotions; the small clear edge. The Verge of Speech. Tim Longville. VaA

Small type of great ones, that do hum. A Fly Caught in a Cobweb. Richard Lovelace. BeJo; CaPo; SeCP

Small, unimaginable, cold. *(LL)* Lint. Rita Dove. TRP

Small vampire, gorger at your mother's teat. Last Child. X. J. Kennedy. OxBSP

Small Wants. Bibhu Padhi, *tr. fr. Hindi.* TSaS

Small wax candles melt to light, The. Poor Women in a City Church. Seamus Heaney. TIRV

Small wheel, A. Watch Repair. Charles Simic. NoP

Small wind/ blows across the hedge/ into the yard, A. The Cat and the Wind. Thom Gunn. OFC

Small wind lightly, A. Count Carrots. Gerda Mayer. OBSP

Small window opened. I asked for the six-pack, The. Visionary Oklahoma Sunday Beer. James Whitehead. SM

Small Wings, *sels.* Maude Meehan.
 "She has withdrawn from us." MDDM

Small Woman on Swallow Street. W. S. Merwin. CoAP

Small Wonder. Brock. Paul Muldoon. NoAM

Small Words. Fiona Hall. NWP

Small worn street with side gulleys, A. A Synagogue in Samarkand. S. J. Litherland. NWP

Smaller and clearer as the years go by. *(LL)* Lines on a Young Lady's Photograph Album. Philip Larkin. EnLoPo; HAP; OAEL-2

Smallest bark on life's tumultuous ocean, The. Influence. Sarah Knowles Bolton. PWR

Smallest basil leaf was heard to whimper, The. *Unknown, tr. fr. Serbo-Croatian by* Charles Simic. HSix

Smalltown Dance. Judith Wright. FaBoMA

Smaragd the Emerald. Rose Drachler. BCF

Smart Alec Oration. *Unknown.* RoPo

Smart man was Bishop Colenso, A. Colenso Rhymes for Orthodox Children. Bret Harte. OBAL

Smart, solely of such songmen, pierced the screen. With Christopher Smart. Robert Browning. EPCY

Smarty, smarty, smarty. *Unknown.* RoPo

Smash and Scatteration. James McManus. BAP-91

Smash me looking-glass glass. Mirror's Song. Liz Lochhead. NBrP

Smashed into a likeness of the mad English king, George the Third. *(LL)* You Were Wearing. Kenneth Koch. AiP; CoAP; MoP; NIP; NNaP; NoP

Smear of blue peat smoke, The. The Shepherd's Hut. Andrew Young. GrPl; OxBTC

Smeared with the gold of the opulent sun. *(LL)* A Postcard from the Volcano. Wallace Stevens. HAP; HCAP; LiTA; MeMAP; NoAM; SAmP; WeW

Smell! William Carlos Williams. *See* Oh strong ridged and deeply hollowed.

Smell. William Carlos Williams. MoAB; MoAmPo; RaBo; TAP

Smell of Blue Grapes is Sweet, The. "Anna Akhmatova." ArNa

Smell of canyon rain storm. Eric Mottram. NBrP

Smell of cigar smoke, Sunday, after dinner. Cigar Smoke, Sunday, after Dinner. Louise Townsend Nicholl. FYAP

Smell of Coal Smoke, The. Les A. Murray. FaBoMA; NOBAu

Smell of death so powerful, The. Marguerite de Navarre, *tr. fr. French by* Aline Allard. PBWP

Smell of death was in the air, The. John Press. PoRA

Smell of him went soon, The. Four Years. Pamela Gillilan. PWE

Smell of Old Newspapers Is Always Stronger after Sleeping in the Sun, The. Mike Lowery. Poetsp

Smell of perfume still lingers in the air, The. *(LL)* A Sorrow in the Harem. Wang Ch'ang-ling. OHMPC

Smell of piss guides us down the halls. The Hospital State. Betsy Sholl. PBCAP

Smell of potatoes just taken out of the earth, The. Chilean Elegies: 5, The. The Interior. Tom Wayman. NOBC

Smell of sawdust, the zing and muffled, The. Declasse Memory. Michael O'Loughlin. IB

Smell of snow, stinging in nostrils as the wind lifts it from a beach, The. The Crystal Lithium. James Schuyler. PoM; VCAP

Smelling or feeling of the several holes. Dishonor. Edwin Denby. ErPo

Smells — how many. The Sense of Smell. Louis MacNeice. NYBP

Smelt! *(LL)* At the Zoo. Thackeray. NTCP; OxBChV

Smilax in our homes entwine, The. Christmas Eve. L. A. J. Moorer. CBWP-3

Smile, The. Blake. RB

Smile. ("Like a bread without the spreading") *Unknown.* BLPA; WBLP

Smile, A. ("A smile costs nothing but gives you much") *Unknown.* PoToHe

Smile, A. *Unknown.* BLPA; WBLP

Smile, and the world smiles with you. Hustle and Grin. *Unknown.* WBLP

Smile at us, pay us, pass us. But do not quite forget. *(LL)* The Secret People. G. K. Chesteron. CoGr; FaPoR; OtMeF; OxBTC

Smile at us, pay us, pass us; but do not quite forget. The Secret People. G. K. Chesteron. CoGr; FaPoR; OtMeF; OxBTC

Smile costs nothing but gives much —, A. A Smile. *Unknown.* PoToHe

Smile, Death. Charlotte Mew. WPE; WPOW

Smile fell in the grass, A. The Night Dances. Sylvia Plath. LCAP; LPA

Smile is quite a funny thing, A. Growing Smiles. *Unknown.* PoLF

Smile, Massachusetts, smile. *Unknown.* PAH

Smile of the Goat, The. Oliver Herford. FiBHP; PeLV

Smile of the Goat has a meaning that few, The. The Smile of the Goat. Oliver Herford. FiBHP; PeLV

Smile of the Walrus, The. Oliver Herford. FiBHP

Smile on the famed Mona Lisa, The. Stanley J. Sharpless. PeLi

Smile, smile/ Blest isle! A Lilliputian Ode on Their Majesties' Accession. Henry Carey. FaBoVe; NOEC

Smile, Smile, Smile. Wilfred Owen. PeFWW

Smile/ to see the lake. Lorine Niedecker. VGW

Smiles of the Bathers, The. Weldon Kees. NaP

Smiling and haunted, to a dark morning. (LL) To the Snake. Denise Levertov. AmPP; LiTM; NMM; PoA

Smiling Dawn, with diadem of dew, The. The Poet's Ministrants. H. Cordelia Ray. CBWP-3

Smiling girls, rosy boys. Mother Goose. OxNR

Smiling Mouth, The. Charles, Duc d'Orléans. See Smiling mouth and laughing eyn grey, The.

Smiling Mouth and Laughing Eyen Grey, The. Charles, Duc d'Orléans. See Smiling mouth and laughing eyn grey, The.

Smiling mouth and laughing eyn grey, The. Charles, Duc d'Orléans. MiEL (Smiling Mouth and Laughing Eyen Grey, The.) HAP (Smiling Mouth, The.) NoP

Smiling, sweet girl, this proffered toy approve. To a Lady, with a Present of a Fan. At. to Charles Brandling. FaBoUs; NOEC

Smiling the boy fell dead. (LL) Incident of the French Camp. Robert Browning. BeLS; CoGr; FaPoR; GN; OBWP; TrGrPo

Smith at the organ is like an anvil being. The Sound of Afroamerican History Chapt II. S. E. Anderson. PoBA

Smith makes me, a. The Runes on Weland's Sword. Kipling. Fr. Puck of Pook's Hill. NoAM; PoEL-5

Smith of Maudlin. George Walter Thornbury. PeVV

Smithereens. Dante Gabriel Rossetti. NOBVV

Smithfield Ham. Dave Jeddie Smith. HCAP

Smiths, The. E. G. Murphy. NOBAu

Smitty on the railroad, picking up sticks. Unknown. RoPo

Smog starts rolling in about 5 o'clock, The. Suburban Dream. Geraldine Kudaka. ETG

Smoke. Rubén Bonitaz Nuño, tr. fr. Spanish by John Frederick Nims. STV

Smoke. (LL) Dear. Erica Hunt. VBLP

Smoke. Thoreau. See Light-winged Smoke, Icarian Bird.

Smoke. Charles Wright. NYBP

Smoke and Steel, sels. Carl Sandburg.
  "Bar of steel — it is only, A." AiP
  "Smoke of the fields in spring is one." MoAmPo

Smoke Animals. Rowena Bastin Bennett. PDV

Smoke contending with smoke which will be maddest. Portrait of an Engine Driver. Bobi Jones, tr. fr. Welsh by Joseph P. Clancy. OBWVE

Smoke from Lisa's, The. Green Acres. David Trinidad. BAP-91

Smoke from the train-gulf hid by hoardings blunders upward. Birmingham. Louis MacNeice. CMoP; MoAB; MoBrPo; OxAEP-2

Smoke of the fields in spring is one. Carl Sandburg. Fr. Smoke and Steel. MoAmPo

Smoke of their foul dens, The. Wilfrid Scawen Blunt. Fr. Satan Absolved: a Victorian Mystery. FaBoEH

Smoke rises from the stones: no, it is mist. (LL) An Airstrip in Essex, 1960. Donald Hall. LCAP; LiTM; PAW

Smoke rises. Never before, The. The Achaian Invasion of Sparta. Unknown, tr. fr. Greek by Peter Jay. GrAn

Smoke snakes. Indian Camp. Janet Reed McFatter. GrPl

Smoke when the sun fell and when it rose. Peter Levi. Fr. Life Is a Platform. FaBoTw

Smoked Herring, The. Charles Cros, tr. fr. French by A. L. Lloyd. GrPl

Smokers for Celibacy. Fleur Adcock. FaBoBl; PWE

Smokey the Bear Sutra. Gary Snyder. MAT; PoBeRe

Smokey's Getting Old. Jessica Hagedorn. OpBo

Smoking bank and stood watching the boat disappear on the black waters of Lethe? (LL) A Supermarket in California. Allen Ginsberg. AmPP; BCF; CoAP; HAP; HCAP; HeIL; HeIP; InPK; InPS; LiTM; NAAL-2; NaP; NeAP; NoAM; NOBA; PoBeRe; PoM; PrIm; SOTW; TAP; TFi; TwCP; UnPo; WeW

Smoking in an Open Grave. David Bottoms. InPK

Smoking swamp before a cottage door, A. An Irish Picture. J. Stanyan Bigg. NOBVV

Smoky as peat your lank hair on my pillow. A Nest in a Wall. Richard Murphy. BiHa; CIP

Smoky bar in Matamoros. Blind date. Scattered Fog. Christy Sheffield Sanford. UL

Smoky rain riddles the ocean plains, A. My Father Paints the Summer. Richard Wilbur. NOBA

Smoky summer evening, The. The Window. Dino Campana, tr. fr. Italian by John Frederick Nims. STV

Smoky sunset. I dab my eyes, A. Required of You This Night. Peter Redgrove. PoE

Smoldering dry fern. And What of Me? Liz Sohappy Bahe. CDW

Smooth-bottomed fellow named Fritz, A. Unknown. PeHV

Smooth Divine, The. Timothy Dwight. Fr. Triumph of Infidelity, The. NOCV; WGRP

Smooth smell of Manhattan taxis, The. Dance of the Infidels. Al Young. NBV; PoBA

Smooth was the water, calm the air. Sir Charles Sedley. SeCV-2

Smoothness of onions infuriates him, The. Onion. Katha Pollitt. RaBo

Smothered Fires. Georgia Douglas Johnson. BlSi; ShDr

Smothering dark engulfs relentlessly, The. A Child's Winter Evening. Gwen John. CH

Smudging. Diane Wakoski. AmPA; PrIm

Smug in her Adriatic noon, Dubrovnik beams. Zudioska. Aaron Kramer. BTR

Smuggled human hair from Mexico. The Assassination of John Lennon as Depicted by the Madame Tussaud Wax Museum, Niagara Falls, Ontario, 1987. David Wojahn. Fr. Mystery Train: A Sequence. NAmP90; PBCAP

Smuggler's Song, A. Kipling. Fr. Puck of Pook's Hill. FaBoEH; NTP; OxBChV

Smuggler's Victory, The. Unknown. OxBSS

Snack, The. L. L. Zeigler. BXAP

Snail, The. Vincent Bourne, tr. fr. Latin by William Cowper. BoTP; OBVE

Snail, The. Vincent Bourne. See Frugal snail, with forecast of repose, The.

Snail. John Drinkwater. GoJo; SiSoPo

Snail. Elisabeth Eybers, tr. fr. Afrikaans by Elisabeth Eybers. PeSA; PeSAV

Snail. Langston Hughes. FaPON

Snail, The. Richard Lovelace. BeJo; CaPo; OAEL-1

Snail, The. Mother Goose. See Four and twenty tailors.

Snail ("The snail crawls over blackness.") Takahashi Shinkichi, tr. fr. Japanese by Lucien Stryk and Takashi Ikemoto. NU

Snail moves like a, The. Hedgehog. Paul Muldoon. BIrV; NoAM; PBCIP

Snail pushes through a green, The. Considering the Snail. Thom Gunn. GrPl; LiTM; NAEL-2; TwCP

Snail says, "Alas!," The. The Poor Snail. J. M. Westrup. BoTP

Snail, snail, come out of your hole. Unknown. ISE

Snail, snail, put out your horns. Unknown. OxNR

Snail upon the wall. Snail. John Drinkwater. GoJo; SiSoPo

Snails. E. D. Blodgett. NOBC

Snails. Liagarang, tr. fr. Dharlwangu dialect. CBAP, tr. by Ronald M. Berndt; WTO, tr. by Ronald M. Berndt

Snail's Derby, A. Eugene Lee-Hamilton. FM

Snails have made a garden of green lace, The. After Rain. P. K. Page. NOBC; PoE

Snails lead slow idyllic lives. The Widow's Yard. Isabella Gardner. CAPP; Poetr

Snail's Lesson, The. Priscilla Jane Thompson. CBWP-2

Snaith Marsh; a Yorkshire Pastoral. 'Ophelia'. ECWP

Snake. Dannie Abse. NoAM

Snake ("A Snake Came To My Water-trough). (Snake came to my water-trough, A.) D. H. Lawrence. CMoP; EBEvV; EBNV; FaBoMo; HeIP; HoPM; LiTB; LiTM; MeMBP; MoAB; NoAM; NOBE; NoP; NTP; NU; OAEL-2; Poetr; PoRA; PPP; PrIm; SOTW; TFi
Sels.
  "Snake came to my water-trough, A." UV

Snake, The. Kenneth Mackenzie. FaBoMA

Snake. Desanka Maksimovic, tr. fr. Serbo-Croatian by Charles Simic. HSix

Snake, The. Vance Palmer. NOBAu

Snake. Theodore Roethke. NOBA; NYBP; RFM

Snake, The. Andrew Suknaski. NOBC

Snake-Back Solo. Quincy Troupe. BCF

Snake came to my water-trough, A. D. H. Lawrence. Fr. Snake ("A Snake Came To My Water-trough). CMoP; EBEvV; EBNV; FaBoMo; HeIP; HoPM; LiTB; LiTM; MeMBP; MoAB; NoAM; NOBE; NoP; NTP; NU; OAEL-2; Poetr; PoRA; PPP; PrIm; SOTW; TFi; UV

Snake-Charmer, The. Sarojini Naidu [or Nayadu]. PBWP

Snake emptied itself into the grass, A. Monsoon. David Wevill. NYBP

Snake Eyes. Amiri Baraka. VGW

Snake is living yet, The. (LL) The Python. Hilaire Belloc. OxBChV

Snake on D. H. Lawrence, The. N. J. Warburton. UV

Snake Skins, The. Carol Frost. FoLa

Snake snatched, The. The Horned Snake. Louis Oliver. HATNAP

Snake Song, The. John S. Mbiti. OBAP

Snake to fear, A. Anaconda. Doug Macleod. ZA

Snake tooth pinches his own mail, The. Remorse. Richmond Lattimore. PoA

Snake Trying, The. W. W. Eustace Ross. MoCV; NOBC

Snakebite. Thomas James. SM

Snakes. Peter Wild. AmPA

Snakes in the mouth. Rattlesnake Dance, Coronado Hills, El Paso, 1966. Ray Gonzáles. AfAz

Snakes, Mongooses, Snake-Charmers and the Like. Marianne Moore. CMoP

Snakes of September, The. Stanley Kunitz. AnAn; FoLa

Snakeskin. Ray Gonzáles. AfAz

Snap-Dragon. D. H. Lawrence. ErPo

Snap his fingers. (LL) The Policeman's Ball. Martín Espada. UTF

Snapper, The. William Heyen. AmPA

Snapping gunshot cold. The Women in Old Parkas. Mary TallMountain. AIW

Snaps for Dinner, Snaps for Breakfast, and Snaps for Supper. George Moses Horton. OBAL

Snaps its twig-tethermounts. A Dove. Ted Hughes. OxBC

Snapshot, A. Debora Greger. Fr. Afterlife, The. BAP-91

Snapshot of a Crab-Picker among Barrels Spilling Over, Apparently at the End of Her Shift. Dave Jeddie Smith. NoAM

Snapshot of Adam. James Merrill. EOEF

Snapshots, sels. X. J. Kennedy.
  Birth Report. NAs

Snapshots of a Daughter-in-Law. Adrienne Rich. FaBoWP; HCAP; NAAL-2; NALW; NIP; NMM; NoAM; NoP; Poetr; VCAP

Snapshots of a Daughter-in-Law. Adrienne Rich. NMM; NoP

Snapshots of the Cotton South. Frank Marshall Davis. PoBA

Snare, The. James Stephens. BoTP; CH; CMoP; CoGr; PDV; SCGP

Snarleyyow; or, The Dog Fiend, sels. Frederick Marryat.
  Captain Stood on the Carronade, The.
  (Old Navy, The.) VPP

Snaw, snaw, coom faster. Snow. Unknown. GBP

Snayl, The. Richard Lovelace. See Wise emblem of our politic [or politick] world.

Sneaked about here. By the Road. Geoffrey Grigson. OxBTC

Sneer'd, "What a Transcendentalist!" (LL) The Flesh-Fly and the Bee. Coventry Patmore. FaBoEE

Sneeze on [a] Monday, [You] sneeze for danger. Unknown. NBLV; RoPo
  (Sneezing.) OTCP

Sneezing. Unknown. See Sneeze on [a] Monday, [You] sneeze for danger.

Sneezing. ("If you sneeze on Monday, you sneeze for danger") Unknown. ReMoGo

Snicketty Snacketty Sneeze. X. J. Kennedy. ZA

Sniff of the real, that's, The. Autobiography. Thom Gunn. NoAM

Sniffed, dilating my nostrils. Elvin's Blues. Michael S. Harper. BPo; Jaz

Sniper. Lucien Stryk. ArOW

Snobby Roberts' Message. Ken Smith. NBrP

Snodgrass is walking through the universe. (LL) These Trees Stand. W. D. Snodgrass. MoP; PPP

Snoopy, snippin'. Unknown. RoPo

Snore in the foam: the night is vast and blind. Tristan da Cunha. Roy Campbell. MoBrPo; PeSA

Snoring Bedmate, The. Unknown, tr. fr. Irish. BIrV, tr. by John V. Kelleher

Snorting his pleasure in the dying sun. Landscape, Deer Season. Barbara Howes. GoJo

Snot goes down. Pieces of Snot. Unknown, tr. fr. Bella Bella Indian by Franz Boas. STP

Snow. Mary Austin. Fr. Rhyming Riddles. BoNaP; GrPl

Snow. Margaret Avison. NOBC

Snow ("This meal-white snow.") Walter de la Mare. OxAEP-2

Snow, The. F. Ann Elliott. BoTP

Snow. Issa. SiSoPo

Snow, The. June Jordan. GLP

Snow. Longfellow. See Out of the bosom of the air.

Snow. Louis MacNeice. CIP; CMoP; FaBoMo; LiTM; MoP; NoAM; NOBE; OPOP; OxAEP-2; OxBSP; OxBTC; PNI

Snow. David Malouf. CBAP

Snow. Ralph Pomeroy. Poetsp

Snow. Helge Rode, tr. fr. Danish by Philip L. Miller. RiWo

Snow. W. R. Rodgers. LiTM

Snow. Ruth Stone. NYBP

Snow. Edward Thomas. FaBoTw; NTP

Snow. Unknown. GBP

Snow. David Wevill. MoCV

Snow. (LL) White bird floats down through the air, A. Unknown. ChTr; GBP

Snow. Charles Wright. CAPP; LCAP

Snow and then rain. The roads are wet. A car. Edgar Bowers. Fr. Autumn Shade. VCAP

Snow Anthology. Arthur S. Bourinot. GoYe

Snow-Ball, The. Soame Jenyns. OBVE

Snow-Ball, The. Thomas Stanley. CBLP

Snow-bound; a Winter Idyl [or Idyll]. Whittier. AmPP; GN; NOBA; OxBA; TAP; WiR
  Sels.
  Mother. OHIP
  "Shut in from all the world without." OBCP
  "Sun that brief December day, The." AiP; FaBV; NAAL-1; TFi; TrGrPo
    (Storm, The.) FaBV
    (Winter Day.) TrGrPo
    (Winter Idyl, A.) PFP
  "Unwarmed by any sunset light." AiP
  Winter Night. TrGrPo

Snow-bound in woodland, a mournful word. Postponement. Thomas Hardy. EnVR

Snow-bound mountains, snow-bound valleys. Carol of the Russian Children. Unknown, tr. fr. Russian. OHIP

Snow by Morning. May Swenson. NYBP

Snow came down last night like moths, The. First Snow in Alsace. Richard Wilbur. ArOW; NoP; OBWP

Snow cannot melt too soon for the birds left behind, The. Rag Doll and Summer Birds. Owen Dodson. PoNe

Snow, clothing sky & mountain. Apollonides, tr. fr. Greek by Peter Whigham. GrAn

Snow-cloud, a rainbow, blue sky, rain. Autumn in Hobart. James McAuley. FaBoMA

Snow Country Weavers. James Welch. CDW; HATNAP

Snow-covered and bleeding, he came home. Feeding Ground. Thomas McCarthy. CIP

Snow crept up overnight as we slept. The Vanishing Point. Peter Davison. DiPo

Snow Curlew, The. Vernon Watkins. NYBP

Snow curls in on the cold wind. Courtyard in Winter. John Montague. IPY

Snow dances and the frost flies, The. Plum Blossoms. Chu Shu-chen, tr. by Kenneth Rexroth and Ling Chung. PBWP; WPC

Snow dissolv'd no more is seen. IV, 7. ("Diffugere nives.") Horace, tr. fr. Latin by Samuel Johnson. Fr. Odes. NAEL-1; OBVE,
  (Diffugere Nives.) OBVE, tr. by A. E. Housman

Snow Falling. Gillian Hughes. NTP

Snow falling. Snowfall. Artis Bernard. NTCP

Snow falling and night falling fast, oh, fast. Desert Places. Robert Frost. AmPP; CMoP; InPK; MoAB; MoAmPo; MoP; NAAL-2; NoAM; NOBA; OxBA; PoE; PPP; RB; SoSe; TAP; TRP; UnPo

Snow falls deep, The; the forest lies alone. Gipsies ("The snow falls deep.") John Clare. CH; PoEL-4
  (Gipsy Camp, The.) ChTr
  (Gypsies.) NoP; PrIm

Snow falls on the cars in Doctors' Row and hoods the headlights. Doctors' Row. Conrad Aiken. HAP

Snow fell, and its power was multiplied, The. Russia 1812. Victor Hugo, tr. fr. French by Robert Lowell. OBWP

Snow-filled Nest, The. Rose Terry Cooke. OBCA

Snow-Flakes. Longfellow. ArNa; ChTr; FaBoRV; NOBA; NoP; PoEL-5; TAP; UnPo; WiR

Snow-Flakes, The. Priscilla Jane Thompson. CBWP-2

Snow had begun in the gloaming, The. James Russell Lowell. Fr. First Snowfall, The. AnAmPo; BLPA; BLPL; FaBoBe; FaPON; TAP; WBLP

Snow had begun in the gloaming, The. The First Snowfall [or Snow-Fall]. James Russell Lowell. AnAmPo; BLPA; BLPL; FaBoBe; FaPON; TAP; WBLP

Snow had fallen many nights and days, The. The End of the World. Gordon Bottomley. CH; MoBrPo

Snow, hail and smut the sky. Asclepiades, tr. fr. Greek by Alan Marshfield. GrAn

Snow! Hail! Lower! Lightning! Thunder! Asclepiades, tr. fr. Greek by Kenneth Rexroth. PGA

Snow Harvest. Andrew Young. BoNaP

Snow has covered the next line of tracks. Looking at New-fallen Snow from a Train. Robert Bly. NaP

Snow has fallen all night. The Snow Curlew. Vernon Watkins. NYBP

Snub nose, the guts of twenty mules are in your cylinders/ and transmission. New Farm Tractor. Carl Sandburg. FaPON

Snuff Movies. Dermot Bolger. IB

Snug at hearthside, while heart of the backlog. Heart of the Backlog. Robert Penn Warren. MT

Snug at the club two fathers sat. The Fathers. Siegfried Sassoon. MoP

Snuggles and lifts warm lips to kiss. (LL) Charm of my life, my dearest care. Martial. PeHV

Snugly you rest, sweet globes. Grapes: Still-Life. Anne Spencer. ShDr

So? Leonard Nathan. PBCAP

So Abram rose, and clave the wood, and went. The Parable of the Old Man and the Young. Wilfred Owen. ChIV-1; FaBoRV; OPOP

So active they seem passive, little sheep. Grace. Richard Wilbur. LiTA

So all day long the noise of battle rolled. Tennyson, incorporated in Idylls of the King with changes, as The Passing of Arthur. Fr. Morte d'Arthur. DL; EBNV; EBVVPR; EnVR; FaBoBe; FaBoRV; NIP; NOBVV; OAEL-2; OBNV; OxAEP-2; PoEL-5

So all day long the noise of battle rolled. The Passing of Arthur. J. C. Squire. BXAP

So all within be livelier than before. (LL) The Forerunners. George Herbert. AngWe; ESCV; GeHe; JCP; NAEL-1; NoP; TOF

So am I as the rich, whose blessed key. Shakespeare. Fr. Sonnets. OxAEP-1

So an age ended, and its last deliverer died. W. H. Auden. Fr. Sonnets from China. CMoP; PoE

So and no otherwise — so and no otherwise — hillmen desire their/ Hills. (LL) The Sea and the Hills. Kipling. FaBV; OtMeF; SCGP

So-and-So Reclining on Her Couch. Wallace Stevens. AmPP; LiTM; NOBA

So-and-So's, The. Sandra Cisneros. ETG

So anyway, I've taken a scunner. Out for the Elements. Andrew Waterman. SCBI

So Are You To My Thoughts As Food To Life. Shakespeare. Fr. Sonnets. PoEL-2

So as they travelled, the drouping night. Spenser. Fr. Faerie Queene, The. OAEL-1

So, back again? To a Dog. Josephine Preston Peabody. BLPA; WGRP

So bandit-eyed, so undovelike a bird. Blue Jay [or Bluejay]. Robert Francis. LCAP

So be it. I am. Hayden Carruth. VGW

So be merry, so be dead. (LL) All the Hills and Vales Along. Charles Hamilton Sorley. EBEV; FaBoCh; MoBrPo; NSI; OBWP; OxAEP-2; PeFWW; PoWW

So be within as fair, as good, as true. (LL) The Comparison. Thomas Carew. BeJo

So Beautiful. Indran Amirthanayagam. OpBo

So beautiful — God himself quailed. The Woman. R. S. Thomas. OxBC

So Beautiful Is the Tree of Night. Pauline Hanson. TAP

So beautiful it hurts. (LL) Cynthia in the Snow. Gwendolyn Brooks. TLR

So beautiful that couple. So Beautiful. Indran Amirthanayagam. OpBo

So, behind the heavy backyard orchard. We Wondered about the Mellow Peaches. Jack A. Mapanje. HBAPE

So blest are they who round a family board. The Family. Donna R. Lydston. PoToHe

So! Bonaparte's coming, as folks seem to say. The Berkshire Farmer's Thoughts on Invasion. Unknown. FaBoEH

So, bored with dragons, he lay down to sleep. Beowulf. Kingsley Amis. FaBoCo; OxBC

"So careful of the type?" but no. Tennyson. Fr. In Memoriam A. H. H. EBVV, abr.; EBVVPR; EnVR; FF; FHYEP; HAP; NoP; OAEL-2, abr.; OBNC; PeECV, abr.; TOF

So, circling about my head, a fly. For Mao Tse-tung; a Meditation on Flies and Kings. Irving Layton. NOBC

So Close Should Be Our Love. Gond Oral Tradition, tr. by V. Elwin and S. Hivale. WTO

So cold? (LL) The Warning. Adelaide Crapsey. Spl; WPE

So cold and lost for ever evermore. (LL) Dead before Death. Christina Rossetti. NAEL-2; NALW

So confortand his levis unto me bene. (LL) To a Lady[e]. William Dunbar. EBEV; GBL; MeEL; OBEV; OxBS; PeLV

So covetous Ballaam with fond intent. Abraham Cowley. Fr. Davideis. ChIV-1

So crossed in love as I? (LL) Abroad as I Was Walking. Unknown. OBET

So cruel [or cruell or crewell] prison how could betide [or howe coulde betyde], alas. The Earl of Surrey. AAS; NoSic; SiPS
(In Windsor Castle.) NOBE
(Prison in Windsor Castle.) SCGP
(So Cruel Prison.) EnRePo; HAP; NoP

So Cruel Prison. The Earl of Surrey. See So cruel [or cruell or crewell] prison how could betide [or howe coulde betyde], alas.

So cruel prison how could betide, alas. Prisoned in Windsor, He Recounteth His Pleasure There Passed. The Earl of Surrey. Fr. Windsor Castle. NAEL-1

So dance, my baby deary. (LL) Dance a baby diddy. Mother Goose. OxNR

So dark a mind within me dwells. Tennyson. Fr. Maud[: A Monodrama]. EnVR

So Davies wrote: "This leaves me in the pink." In the Pink." Siegfried Sassoon. CMoP

So delicate, so airy. Pink Almond. Katharine Tynan. BoTP

So delicate, so easily replaced. (LL) The People, No. Vicki Raymond. NOBAu

So detached and cool she is. The Mask. Clarissa Scott Delany. CDC; PoNe; ShDr

So died John So. On John So. Unknown. FaBoEE

So different, this man. Marriage. William Carlos Williams. PoA

So do I, Sir. (LL) I'd Have You, Quoth He. Unknown. ErPo; FF

So do I, so do I. (LL) Apple-pie, apple-pie. Unknown. OxNR

So does the sun withdraw his beam[e]s. On His Mistress Going from Home [Song]. Unknown. NOSC

So dream thy sails, O phantom bark. The Phantom Bark. Hart Crane. CMoP

So drink them all! so drink them all! (LL) To Ladies' Eyes. Thomas Moore. OxBoLi; PoEL-4

So earnest with thy God, can no new care. Of His Majesties Receiving the News of the Duke of Buckingham's Death. Edmund Waller. SeCV-1

So earth's inclined toward the one invisible. Winter Scene. Marguerite Young. NU; WPE

So ended Saturn; and the God of the Sea. Keats. Fr. Hyperion; a Fragment. EnRP; FHYEP; OAEL-2

So, even with a severed tongue, Philomela recounted her tribulations. Philomela. Yannis Ritsos, tr. fr. Greek by Edmund Keeley. AnAn

So every day we live a day we die. (LL) Come, Cheerful Day! Thomas Campion. AAS; EIL

So Fair, So Sweet, Withal So Sensitive. Wordsworth. EnRP; NoP; PFP

So faith is strong. The Tide of Faith. "George Eliot." Fr. Minor Prophet, A. WGRP

So fallen! so lost! the light withdrawn. Ichabod. Whittier. AnAmPo; LiTA; NAAL-1; NOBA; OxBA; PAH; PoEL-4; TAP

So far as I can see. Meditations of a Tortoise Dozing under a Rosetree Near a Beehive at Noon While a Dog Scampers About and a Cuckoo Calls from a Distant Wood. Emile Victor Rieu. FiBHP

So far as our story approaches the end. A Light Woman. Robert Browning. OBF

So Far, So Near. Christopher Pearse Cranch. TrPWD

So Fast Entangled. Unknown. TrGrPo

So feeble is the thread that doth the burden stay. Petrarch, tr. fr. Italian by Sir Thomas Wyatt. SiPSBD

So few birds house! (LL) A Fallen Yew. Francis Thompson. MoAB; MoBrPo

So few, really. What Her Friend Said to Her, within the Lover's Hearing. Paranar, tr. fr. Tamil by A. K. Ramanujan. PLW

So firm, so burdened, on such light gay feet. (LL) The Beautiful Train. William Empson. OxAEP-2

So flies love's meteor to her shroud of winds. The Dead Words. Vernon Watkins. LiTM

So, forth issued [or issew'd] the Seasons of the year(e). The Mask of Mutability. Spenser. Fr. Faerie Queene, The.
(Pageant of the Seasons and the Months, The.) OxAEP-1
(Seasons, The.) GN

So forth she comes, and to her coche does clyme. Spenser. Fr. Faerie Queene, The. NAEL-1; OAEL-1

So, friends, every day do something. Wendell Berry. EaPr

So frisky and fit. Simchas Torah. Morris Jacob Rosenfeld, tr. fr. Yiddish. TrJP

So from the ground we felt that virtue branch. The Transfiguration. Edwin Muir. ChIV-2; OxBS

So from the years their gifts were showered: each. W. H. Auden. Fr. Sonnets from China. CMoP

So from this life, male in its first motion. Vittoria Colonna. Roy Marz. PoA

So full of courtly reverence. Dudley North. OxBSP

So gay on your lovely head. Relaxation. Dick Gallup. UL

So gentle and so beautiful, should perish with the flowers. (LL) The Death of the Flowers. Bryant. AnAmPo; BLPL; BoNaP; EAP; GN; OBCA; PoLF; WBLP

So go to your grave, you silly old man (LL) The Silly Old Man. Unknown. CoMu

So God send to my foes all they have thought. (*LL*) Oh fortune, [how] thy wresting wavering state. Elizabeth I, Queen of England. FaBoEH

So God spoke to her. Ann Griffith. R. S. Thomas. PeECV

So good luck came, and on my roof did light. The Coming of Good Luck. Robert Herrick. FaBoEE; JCP; OxBSP; Spl

So goodbye, Mrs. Brown. To-Day I Leave Mrs. Brown's Lodgings. Sir Walter Scott. FaBoEE

So Graven. Josephine Miles. NoAM

So hard for women to believe each other. Apron Strings. Marge Piercy. TAP

So hath been dawning another blue day. Today. Thomas Carlyle. PWR

So have I seen a little silly fly. A Quarrel with Fortune. Benjamin Colman. SCAP

So Have I Spent on the Banks of Ysca Many a Serious Hour. Thomas Vaughan. FaBoPP

So having ended, silence long ensewed. Nature's Reply to Mutability. Spenser. *Fr*. Faerie Queene, The. NOBE

So he came to write again. Burning Hills. Michael Ondaatje. NoAM; NOBC; NoP

So he that saileth in this world of pleasure. Anne Bradstreet. *Fr*. Contemplations. AmPP; EAP; PoEL-3, *abr*.; SCAP; WPE, *abr*.; WPOW

So he was exiled from rome. Ovid Twice Exiled. Jerzy Ficowski, *tr. fr. Polish* by Frank J. Corliss, Jr., *and* Grazyna Sandel. PoSu

So he won't talk to me when we meet? Confucius, *tr. fr. Chinese* by Ezra Pound. *Fr*. Songs of Cheng. CTC

So Hector Protector was sent back again. (*LL*) Hector Protector was dressed all in green. Mother Goose. MoShBr; OxNR; ReMoGo

So Help Me God. Catullus, *tr. fr. Latin* by James Michie. FaBoBl

So help me God, I couldn't choose between. So Help Me God. Catullus, *tr. fr. Latin* by James Michie. FaBoBl

So here hath been dawning. To-Day. Thomas Carlyle. GN; WGRP

So here I sit behind my nasty desk. Any Man to His Secretary. Hilary Corke. ErPo

So hot the sun in our hearts. (*LL*) Harlem. Maureen Seaton. LoHo

So how is life with your new bloke? An Attempt at Jealousy. Craig Raine. NoAM

So, how was I to know, when he invited. Helen. James Harrison. NBLV

So Hrothgar's men lived happy in his hall. *Unknown*, *tr*. by Burton Raffel. *Fr*. Beowulf. ASW, *tr*. by Kevin Crossley-Holland; PoE

So humble things thou hast borne for us, O God. Veni Creator. Alice Meynell. WPE

So I came down the steps to Lenin. Dorothy Wellesley. *Fr*. Lenin. OBMV

So I cut my hair; so I'm shorn. Song of the Strange Young Duckling. Deborah Munro. IHMS

So I did sit and eat. (*LL*) Love. George Herbert. AWP; CH; ChTr; ClHu; EBEV; EnlH; FaBV; FHYEP; GeHe; GGP; HeIL; HeIP; ImPo; InPK; JCP; LiTB; MAT; MeLP; NAEL-1; NOBE; NOCV; NoP; OAEL-1; OBEV; OBWVE; OtMeF; PFP; PlP; PoEL-2; PoLF; PPP; Prf; SCV; SeCP; SeCV-1; TEP; TOF; TrCP; TrGrPo; WeW

So, I have seen a man killed! Arthur Hugh Clough. *Fr*. Amours de Voyage. EBVV; NOBVV; PeVV

So I left it laying in the same position. (*LL*) As I Was Laying on the Green. *Unknown*. FiBHP

So I Let Her Go. *Unknown*. AmFP

So I rode homeward, free of doubt. (*LL*) The Traveller. C. J. Dennis. NOBAu

So I Said I Am Ezra. A. R. Ammons. NAAL-2; NoAM; NOBA; NoP

So, I shall see her in three days. In Three Days. Robert Browning. CBLP

So I took her to the riverside. The Unfaithful Wife. Federico García Lorca. OxBM

So I wait — bereft of 2,000 years and the bath of life. (*LL*) Marriage. Gregory Corso. CBLP; CoAP; LiTM; MoP; NeAP; NoP; OBAL; PeLV; PoBeRe; PPP; PrIm; TAP; TRP

So I walked her down to the river. The Unfaithful Wife. Federico García Lorca, *tr. fr. Spanish* by John Frederick Nims. STV

So I will teach you as though you were a schoolboy. (*LL*) An Old Poem to Yän ChÅF/. Hsüeh T'ao. WPC

So I would hear out those lungs. Buckdancer's Choice. James Dickey. HeIP; NoAM; NOBA; NoP; NYBP; PoNe

So if you love me. Hilda Doolittle ("H. D."). *Fr*. Sigil. AnAn

So I'm "crazy," in loving a man of three-score. The Old Man's Darling. Phoebe Cary. AmWP

So in Pieria, from the wedded bliss. In Memory of Bryan Lathrop. Edgar Lee Masters. PoA

So, in the evening, to the simple cloister. Conrad Aiken. *Fr*. Preludes for Memnon; or, Preludes to Attitude. LiTA

(Cloister.) MoAB; MoAmPo

So in the eye of Nature let him die! (*LL*) The Old Cumberland Beggar. Wordsworth. EnRP

So, in the midst of Neptune's angry tide. The Halcyon's Nest. Giles Fletcher the Younger. *Fr*. Christ's Victory and Triumph. FaBoPP

So inward force my heart doth all to-break. (*LL*) The Furious Gun. Sir Thomas Wyatt. PoE

So Is It Not With Me As With That Muse. Shakespeare. *Fr*. Sonnets. HeIP, *sect*. XXI; InvP, *sect*. XXI

So it begins. Adam is in his earth. James Agee. *Fr*. Sonnets. MoAmPo; OPOP

So it is. Coleman Barks. *Fr*. New Words. CRP

So it is, my dear. Even So. Dante Gabriel Rossetti. NOBE; NOBVV; OBNC

So it's hullo now. Rufinus, *tr. fr. Greek* by Alan Marshfield. GrAn

So I've thought the matter over and think I'll marry Bill. (*LL*) Common Bill. *Unknown*. AmFP; AS

So joyful he to Alma Mater went. The Student. James Hurdis. *Fr*. Adriano; or, The First of June. ECEV

So Kings and Chiefs and Bards, in Eman of the Kings. The Fate of the Sons of Usna. John Todhunter. *Fr*. First Duan: The Coming of Deidre, The. PeIV

So late in the 20th century. Au Bout du Temps. Andrei Codrescu. UL

So late, so late, so haunting. On the Threshold. Karl Kraus, *tr. fr. German* by Albert Bloch. TrJP

So lay the youth with Mary in his arms. J. C. Squire. *Fr*. Country Wooing. BXAP

So learned men in controversies spend. Learning ("So Learned Men in Controversies Spend"). George Chapman. *Fr*. Euthymiae Raptus; or, The Teares of Peace. NOSC

So leave her, and cast care from thy heart. His Camel. Alqamah, *tr. fr. Arabic* by Sir Charles Lyall. *Fr*. Mufaddaliyat, The. AWP

So Let's Live — Really Live! Catullus. *See* So let's live — really live! — for love and loving.

So let's live — really live! — for love and loving. Catullus, *tr. fr. Latin* by John Frederick Nims. STV

(So Let's Live — Really Live! ArLo

So light no one noticed. Edward Dorn. VGW

So like a harrow pin. Iron Spike. Seamus Heaney. TRP

So like a ship the dead man comes to shore. (*LL*) One whom I knew, a student and a poet. Alex Comfort. MoBrPo

So like the smaller stars we rowed among. (*LL*) The Lotus Flowers. Ellen Bryant Voigt. MT

So Little and So Much. John Oxenham. BLRP

So, little Master Wagtail, I'll bid you a good-bye. (*LL*) Little Trotty Wagtail. John Clare. BoTP; FaPON; NTP; RB; SCGP; UnPo

So Live. Bryant. *See* To him who in the love of Nature holds.

So live, so love, so use that fragile hour. Robert Louis Stevenson. NOBVV

So lonely am I. Ono no Komachi, *tr. fr. Japanese* by David Keene. BoWoP; PBWP

So Long. Jayne Cortez. BoWoP

So long. James Dickey. *Fr*. For the First Manned Moon Orbit. AiP

So Long Ago. Morris Jacob Rosenfeld, *tr. fr. Yiddish* by Elbert Aidline. TrJP

So long as I loved shadows, the shadows of vain gods. Christian Rome. Hildebert, *tr. fr. Latin* by Helen Waddell. MLL

So Long As There's Weather. Tamara Kitt. SiSoPo

So long as you live and move. Teach Us to Mark This, God. Franz Werfel, *tr. fr. German* by Jacob Sloan. TrJP

So Long, It's Been Good to Know You. Woody Guthrie. SWP

So Long Solon. Jack Myers. AmPA

So Long? Stevens. John Berryman. *Fr*. Dream Songs. HAP; HCAP; NOBA

So long you stay on shore. (*LL*) The Wreck of the *Julie Plante* [*or* The *Julie Plante*]. William Henry Drummond. BeLS; BLPA; FaBoBe; FaPON

So long you wandered on the dusky plain. To His Friend in Elysium. Joachim du Bellay, *tr. fr. French* by Andrew Lang. AWP

So Look the Mornings. Robert Herrick. ELP

So looks Anthea, when in bed she lyes. To Anthea Lying in Bed. Robert Herrick. BeJo; SeCP

So lost a thing as thou hadst been. (*LL*) Upon My Lady Carlisle's Walking in Hampton Court Garden. Sir John Suckling. BeJo; CaPo; NoP

So Love and Folly were in hell. (*LL*) A Barley-Break. Sir John Suckling. CaPo; SeCV-1

So lovely . . . / so tender. Alcaeus, *tr. fr. Greek* by Sam Hamill. InMo

So low it used to seem almost. Full Moon, Rising. Jonathan Holden. GOYP

So luminous around them lay the air. Oystercatchers. Christopher Middleton. FaBoTw

So many cloisters closed. John Skelton. *Fr.* Manner of the World Nowadays, The. PeECV

So many convolutions and not enough simplicity! To Marina. Kenneth Koch. NoAM

So many crutches. Now even the daylight. A Landscape with Crutches. Charles Simic. FoLa

So Many Feathers. Jayne Cortez. BlSi

So many goblins you shall see. (*LL*) Ceremony upon Candlemas Eve. Robert Herrick. OBCP

So many little flowers. Cycle. Langston Hughes. FaPON

So many new crimes since then! Since Then. D. J. Enright. OBSV

So many nights the solitary light had burned. Rousseau in His Day. Donald Davie. DiPo

So many people lie in this alley. The Neighborhood House. Jay Wright. NBV

So many pigeons at Columbus. Arthur Gregor. VGW

So many poems about the deaths of animals. Essay. Hayden Carruth. FoLa

So many things happen. The War of the Worlds. Vern Rutsala. Poetsp

So many thousands for a house! On a Certain Lord Giving Some Thousand Pounds for a House. David Garrick. FaBoEE

So many want to be lifted by song and dancing. A Dark Thing Inside the Day. Linda Gregg. BAP-89

So many women are murdered because some man. Body Count. Leonard Nathan. PBCAP

So many years have passed. Disillusion with the French Revolution. Charlotte Smith. *Fr.* Emigrants, The; a Poem. ECWP

So many years I've seen the sun. The Mystery of Life. John Gambold. NOEC

So may God send you luck! (*LL*) The Bells of Würzburg. Thor Lange. RiWo

So may the auspicious Queen of Love. I, 3. To the Ship on Which Virgil Sailed to Athens ("Sic te diva potens Cyri.") Horace, *tr. fr. Latin by* Austin Dobson. *Fr.* Odes. AWP, *tr. by* Dryden

So me saary. Men and Women. David Dabydeen. PBCV

So mean I. (*LL*) Waiting Both. Thomas Hardy. MoAB; MoBrPo; OxBoLi; TTTS

So merrily march the merchant men. (*LL*) Hey diddle dinkety, poppety, pet. Mother Goose. OxNR

So merrily we'll run around. (*LL*) Fool's Song. Thomas Holcroft. CBNP; NOEC

So, midst the withered waste of life, those tears would flow to me. (*LL*) There's not a joy the world can give like that it takes away. Byron. EnRP; GTBS; HAP

So Might is Right, you say; I fight in vain. Might Is Right. Israel Zangwill. TrJP

So Might It Be. John Galsworthy. BLPL; PoLF

So mine be your eyes! (*LL*) To Morfydd. Lionel Johnson. MoBrPo; OAEL-2; OBMV

So Miss Myrtle is going to marry? The Charming Woman. Helen Selina Sheridan. WPE

So, Mister Moneybags, you're loaded? So? Palladas, *tr. fr. Greek by* Tony Harrison. GrAn

So moping flat and low our valleys lie. Winter in the Fens. John Clare. BoNaP; EnVR

So much could stay a moment in so little. (*LL*) On a Child Who Lived One Minute. X. J. Kennedy. HoPM; NYBP; Poetr

So much depends. The Red Wheelbarrow. William Carlos Williams. AnAmPo; BLPL; CMoP; GrPl; HeIP; HoPM; InPK; LiTA; LiTM; MoAB; MoAmPo; MoP; NAAL-2; NIP; NoAM; NOBA; NoP; PoE; Poetr; PrIm; SAmP; SoSe; SOTW; TAP; TFi; TRP; TTTS; UnPo; WeW

So much for the elves' wergild, the true governance. Geoffrey Hill. *Fr.* Mercian Hymns. NoAM

So much have I forgotten in ten years. Flame-Heart. Claude McKay. CDC; PoNe

So much is parchment where I gloom. The Black Mesa. James Merrill. PoA

So much the thirst of honour fires the blood. On Fame. Juvenal, *tr. by* John Dryden. *Fr.* Satires. IHNG

So much to tell you. 2 Variations: All About Love. Philip Whalen. NeAP

So — Murray to Byron in Italy. Kaleidoscope. G. K. Page. NoAM

So my soul can sing. (*LL*) Feeling Fucked Up. Etheridge Knight. NNaP; PBCAP; RaBo

So Near and Yet So Near. Lemn Sissay. NBrP

So neck to stubborn neck, and obstinate knee to knee. Antaeus; a Fragment. Wilfred Owen. PeHV

So nigh is grandeur to our dust. Duty. Emerson. *Fr.* Voluntaries. GN

So nothing is left of your agony. Talking to Jim. Walta Borawski. PFL

So now I have confess'd that he is thine. Shakespeare. *Fr.* Sonnets. HeIP; InVP; OxAEP-1

So now I'm brooding moodily upon. A Simple Matter. Gloria Rawlinson. PeNZ

So now is come our joyful'st feast. George Wither. (Our Joyful Feast.) OHIP

So now it's your turn. Instructions to the Double. Tess Gallagher. FaBoWP

So now just suppose that someone wanted to know. Surgery. Kenneth Pitchford. GLP

So now my summer task is ended, Mary. To Mary. Shelley. EnRP

So now the very bones of you are gone. Doricha. Poseidippus, *tr. fr. Greek by* E. A. Robinson. AWP; FaBoEE; OBVE

So now the Victorians are all in heaven. After Mr. Mayhew's Visit. Ken Smith. PWE

So now, this poet, who forsakes the stage. Prologue to "Love Triumphant." Dryden. *Fr.* Love Triumphant. OxBoLi

So now you know how blood tricks life. Positive. Michael Klein. PFL

So obese is my cousin from Hendon. A. H. Baynes. PeLi

So oft as I with state of present time. Spenser. *Fr.* Faerie Queene, The. OAEL-1

So Often. Léon Damas, *tr. fr. French by* Ellen Conroy Kennedy. NegPo

So often artists have painted a woman. January 18, 1979. John Yau. UL

So often it appears like an escape. Works of Art. Elizabeth Jennings. PeECV

So often my feeling of race. So Often. Léon Damas, *tr. fr. French by* Ellen Conroy Kennedy. NegPo

So often we hear of the vacant chair. The Chair That Is Filled. Carrie Biggs. PWR

So on a night when a heavy full moon was low. On the Eve of a Birthday. Geoffrey Grigson. NAs

So on he pricked, and loe, he gan espy. Ride a Cock Horse. Barry Pain. BXAP

So on his Nightmare through the evening fog. Nightmare. Erasmus Darwin. *Fr.* Botanic Garden, The. NOEC

So on she goes, and in her idle flight. Christopher Marlowe. *Fr.* Hero and Leander. AAS; NoP; PoE

So, on the bloody sand, Sohrab lay dead. Matthew Arnold. *Fr.* Sohrab and Rustum. EBEvV; EBNV; GTBS-P; OBNV; PeVV (Sohrab Dead.) NOBE

So once again, hearing the tired aunts. In the House of the Dying. Jane Cooper. CrSp; NMM

So once again, poor much-lamented shadow. To Werther. Goethe, *tr. fr. German by* John Frederick Nims. *Fr.* Trilogy of Passion. STV

So once again the trouble's o'er. The Matron-Cat's Song. Ruth Pitter. OFC

So open was his mind, so wide. The Independent. Phyllis McGinley. FaBoEE

So Paradise was brightened, so 'twas blest. To Philomela. Benjamin Colman. SCAP

So passed they naked on, nor shunned the sight. Milton. *Fr.* Paradise Lost. EPCY; PeECV, *ll.* 319–334

So poor I've nothing to lose, I must gamble. (*LL*) He is almost a god, a man beside you. Sappho. InMo

So prayis me as ye think caus quhy. Remeidis of Luve. Unknown. OxBS

So proud in his furry robe. Baboon. Unknown, *tr. fr. Yoruba by* Ulli Beier. *Fr.* Hunter Poems of the Yoruba. RB

So proud she was to die. Emily Dickinson. NOBA; OBD

So prudent and so young a wife! To Geron. Hildebrand Jacob. NOEC

So, pure and dutiful, she sought that place. Unknown, *tr. fr. Sanskrit by* Franklin Edgerton. *Fr.* Mahabharata, The. DL

So Quick, So Hot, So Mad is Thy Fond Sute. Thomas Campion. PoEL-2

So Quietly. Leslie Pinckney Hill. PoBA

So rare, so mere. Presence of Snow. Melville Cane. GoYe

So runed on a rune-stick, and the rune-stick put. Gudveig. Francis Berry. OBTV

So runs the round of life from hour to hour. (*LL*) Circumstance. Tennyson. CBLP

So sang he: and as meeting rose and rose. Willowwood ("So sang he: and as meeting rose and rose.") Dante Gabriel Rossetti. *Fr.* House of Life, The. NAEL-2; OAEL-2

So Sat the Muses. William Browne. *Fr.* Caelia. Son

So Satan spake, and him Beëlzebub. Milton. *Fr.* Paradise Lost. EPCY (Council of Satan, The.) PoEL-3

So saying, light-foot Iris passed away. Homer, *tr. by* Tennyson. *Fr.* Iliad, The. OBVE

So serious. Why don't you smile? Handful of Pebbles, Mouthful of Stones. Pegatha Hughes. LoHo

So several factions from this first ferment. Achitophel: The Earl of Shaftsbury. Dryden. *Fr.* Absalom and Achitophel, Pt. I. NOBE; NoP; OAEL-1; SeCV-2

So shaken as we are, so wan with care. Shakespeare. *Fr.* King Henry IV, Pt. I. NAEL-1; OxAEP-1

So Shall I Live, Supposing Thou Art True. Shakespeare. *Fr.* Sonnets. InvP, *sect.* XCIII

So shall it ever be. As Thy Days. Grant Colfax Tullar. BLRP

So shall we smoothly pass away in sleep. (*LL*) A Dialogue between Thyrsis and Dorinda. Andrew Marvell. SeCP

So shall ye waste to dust. (*LL*) The Aged Lover Renounceth Love. Thomas, Lord Vaux. EiL; EnRePo; NoSic; OAEL-1; PoEL-1; SCGP

So she became a bird and bird-like danced. Procne. Peter Quennell. LiTB; LiTM; MoBrPo

So she came back into his house again. Sonnets from an Ungrafted Tree. Edna St. Vincent Millay. NALW

So she must have been pleased with us, Hilda Doolittle ("H. D."). *Fr.* Tribute to the Angels. NALW

So she sat down. For P—Celtic: found text from Machen. Bill Griffiths. NBrP

So she went into the garden. The Great Panjandrum [Himself]. Samuel Foote. CBNP; FaBoCh; FaBoCo; MoShBr; PoLF

So shines the Earth in certain mornings' light. Yes to the Earth. "Sibilla Aleramo," *tr. fr. Italian by* Muriel Kittel. WoWa

So shoots a star as doth my mistress glide. John Davies of Hereford. CBLP; EIL

So-shu dreamed. Ancient Wisdom, Rather Cosmic. Ezra Pound. NOBA

So shuts the marigold her leaves. William Browne. *Fr.* Britannia's Pastorals. ChTr

(Memory.) OBEV

So Shy Shy Shy(and with a. E. E. Cummings. MeMAP

So silly as a silly laugh? (*LL*) Egnatius has fine teeth, and those. Catullus. OBVE

So, since your heart is set on those sweet fields. To Colman Returning. *Unknown, tr. by* Helen Waddell. BIrV

So Sleeps My Love. *Unknown.* TrGrPo

"So small and young" the silver moon with its spoons hung. Donagh MacDonagh. James Liddy. BiHa

So small are the flowers of Seamu. *Unknown, tr. fr. Egyptian hieroglyphics into Italian by* Boris de Rachewiltz; *English vers. by* Ezra Pound *and* Noel Stock. BoWoP; PBWP

So small I could cup her in my hands. (*LL*) Jackson Hotel. Lynda Hull. UTF

So smell those odours that do rise. To the Most Fair and Lovely Mistress Anne Soame, Now Lady Abdie [*or* Abdy]. Robert Herrick. CaPo; NOBE; NOSC

So smiles the spring, and so smiles lovely May. (*LL*) To the Lady May. Aurelian Townshend. GBL

So smooth, so sweet, so silv'ry is thy voice. Upon Julia's Voice. Robert Herrick. InPK; JCP; NOBE; SeCP; SoSe

So, So. William Clerke. ELP

So, so, break[e] off this last lamenting kiss[e]. The Expiration. John Donne. CBLP; EiL; MeLP; OxBSP; SeCP

So soft in the hemlock wood. Robert Silliman Hillyer. MoAmPo

So soft streams meet, so springs with gladder smiles. The Welcome to Sack. Robert Herrick. BeJo; CaPo; SeCP; SeCV-1

So soon grown old! Hast thou been six years dead. The Anniverse; an Elegy. Henry King. JCP

So soon my body will have gone. Immortal. Sara Teasdale. WGRP

So spake our morning star then in his rise. Milton. *Fr.* Paradise Regained [*or* Regain'd]. PeECV, *ll.* 294–320

So spake our Mother Eve, and Adam heard. Milton. *Fr.* Paradise Lost. EPCY

(Banishment, The.) NOBE

(Exile.) NOSC, *ll.* 624–49

(Exit from Eden, The.) FaBoRV

So spake th' archangel Michael; then paused. Milton. *Fr.* Paradise Lost. EPCY; FaBoPV, *ll.* 466–551; NAEL-1; OAEL-1

So spake the enemy of mankind, enclosed. Milton. *Fr.* Paradise Lost. EPCY; FM

So spake the godlike power, and thus our sire. Milton. *Fr.* Paradise Lost. EPCY; NAEL-1

So spends a summer's jasper century. (*LL*) Slug in Woods. Earle Birney. NOBC

So Spring. Nigel Wells. PWE

So squeezed, wince you I scream? I love you & hate. John Berryman. *Fr.* Homage to Mistress Bradstreet. FF

So stretched out huge in length the Arch-Fiend lay. Milton. *Fr.* Paradise Lost. EPCY; TEP

So strong you thump, O terrible drums — so loud you bugles blow. (*LL*) Beat! Beat! Drums! Walt Whitman. AnAmPo; FaBV; HeIP; InPK; InPS; NAAL-1; NoP; OBWP; PAW; PoLF

So suete a kis yistrene fra thee I reft. To His Mistress. Alexander Montgomerie. ScCV

So summer comes in the end to these few stains. The Beginning. Wallace Stevens. VGW

So Sweet a Kiss. Shakespeare. *Fr.* Love's Labour's Lost. EiL; InvP

So Sweet Is She. Ben Jonson. *See* Have you seen but a bright lily grow.

So Sweet Love Seemed. Robert Bridges. FaBV

So sweet, so golden. Christian Hofmann von Hofmannswaldau, *tr. fr. German by* Alexander Gode. GePo

So sweet the plum trees smell! Plum Trees. Ranko, *tr. fr. Japanese.* FaPON

So swete a kis yistrene fra thee I reft. To His Maistrês [*or* Mistress]. Alexander Montgomerie. GBL; OxBS

So take a happy view. A Happy View. C. Day Lewis. CMoP

So tell me what you have. Tell Me. Pamela Mordecai. PBCV

So thank Mum for the book of poetry. 1916. R. S. Gwynn. MT

So that all be fulfilled in me: those ultimate mysteries. (*LL*) Hecuba's Testament. Rosario Castellanos. STV

So that each person may quickly find that. Johann Joachim Quantz's Five Lessons. W. S. Graham. FaBoMo

So that I can't refuse. (*LL*) My Garden, My Daylight. Jorie Graham. HCAP; Poetr

So that I could mark it; the continuance of. Concerning Quality, Again. J. H. Prynne. VaA

So that I count me blest a certain while. (*LL*) Of His Lady's Face. Jacopo da Lentino

So that life can be guarded. (*LL*) I hear a voice. W. S. Rendra. EaPr

So that soldierly legend is still on its journey. Kearny at Seven Pines. Edmund Clarence Stedman. AnAmPo; PAH

So that the vines burst from my fingers. Ezra Pound. *Fr.* Cantos. InPS; MeMAP; NAAL-2; OBMV

So that you always have a home. (*LL*) Long time I have lived with you, A. Nancy Wood. EaPr

So That's Who I Remind Me Of. Ogden Nash. BLPL; PoLF

So the committee met again, and again. The Committee. C. Day Lewis. CMoP

So. The curtain has come. In Memoriam the Master — Noel Coward (1900-1973). E. J. Thribb. PeLV

So the distances are Galatea. The Distances. Charles Olson. NAAL-2; NeAP; NoP

So the jungle/ was pard and barred. A Glimpse of Shere Khan. Chris Wallace-Crabbe. OBAP

So the last day's come at last, the close of my fifteen year. The Old Place. B. E. Baughan. PeNZ

So the little children sing. (*LL*) Christmas Song. *At. to* Eugene Field. BoTP; OHIP

So the man spread his blanket on the field. A Tall Man Executes a Jig. Irving Layton. MoCV; NoAM; NOBC

So the next parson stubbed and burnt it. (*LL*) Baucis and Philemon; Imitated from the Eighth Book of Ovid. Swift. GN; NOEC; OAEL-1

So the seeds are cut, loose and like. J. H. Prynne. VaA

So the sky wounded you, jagged at the heart. Daylights. Rosanna Warren. NoAM

So the soldier replied to the poet. The Volunteer's Reply to the Poet. Roy Campbell. IHNG

So the struck eagle, stretch'd upon the plain. Byron. OBD

So the villa, having learned its many skills. Madrid. Jay Wright. BAP-89

So, the year's done with! Love. Robert Browning. ArLo; EnLoPo

So! then be their masters your son and mine. (*LL*) Grace before Meat. Robert David Fitzgerald. NOBAu

So then came his word here. Beginnings. *Unknown, tr. fr. Mayan by* Munro Edmonson. *Fr.* Popol Vuh, The. STP

So Then, I Feel Not Deeply! Walter Savage Landor. EnRP

So then naturally/ This Count Rainuv I speak of. Rainuv; a Romantic Ballad from the Early Basque. Margaret Widdemer. BXAP

So then you won't fight? Dooley Is a Traitor. James Michie. OxBTC

So there stood Matthew Arnold and this girl. The Dover Bitch. Anthony Hecht. BXAP; MAT; NBLV; NIP; NOBA; NOBL; OBAL; PeLV; PPP; UnPo; VGW

(Dover Bitch, The: A Criticism of Life.) Poetr; TRP

So there was no one left but me. (*LL*) A Good Play. Robert Louis Stevenson. FaPON; MoShBr; OTCP; PWR

So there we were stuck. The Life of . . . . Theodore Weiss. NYBP

So, there, when sunset made the downs look new. Charles Hamilton Sorley. *Fr.* Marlborough. WGRP

So there you are, in wispy veil and hat. Tea Party. Nancy Vieira Couto. PBCAP

So these then are the deeds of Alligator in turn. Alligator's Struggles with the 400 sons. *Unknown, tr. fr. Mayan by* Munro Edmonson. *Fr.* Popol Vuh, The. STP

So these two faced each other there. A Portrait in the Guards. Laurence Whistler. GTBS-P

So. They and I are back from the outside. Carl Bode. IMW

So they are satisfied with our Brigade. After the Battle. A. P. Herbert. NSI

So they begin. With two years gone. Boris Pasternak, *tr. fr. Russian by* C. M. Bowra. TrJP

So they came. The Animals' Arrival. Elizabeth Jennings. PBWP

So they have got you down at last, omera. Omera. Marjorie Oludhe Macgoye. HBAPE

So they in Heav'n their odes and vigils tun'd. Milton. *Fr.* Paradise Regained [*or* Regain'd]. PeECV, *bk.* I, *ll.* 182–195

So they smashed that old man of Whitehaven. (*LL*) There was an old man of Whitehaven. Edward Lear. CBNP; EBEV; OxAEP-2

So They Went Deeper into the Forest. Roy Daniells. Mes

So they went, leaving a picnic-litter of talk. The Party. W. R. Rodgers. BIrV; PNI

So, they will have it! Sumter. Henry Howard Brownell. PAH

So this bird comes, and under his wing is a crutch. The Bird. Moyshe-Leyb Halpern, *tr. fr. Yiddish by* John Hollander. PPP

So this is, Jimmy, where we live. An Urgent Letter. Hugh Maxton. PBCIP

So this is the dust that passes through porcelain. The Iron Lung. Stanley Plumly. AmPA; LCAP

So this is the man you dreamt I had betrayed. Gwyneth Lewis. *Fr.* Welsh Espionage. NWP

So Thomas Edison. Lines to Be Embroidered on a Bib; or, The Child Is Father of the Man, but Not for Quite a While. Ogden Nash. FaBoUs

So thou art come again, old black-winged night. To Night. Thomas Lovell Beddoes. Son

So through that unripe day you bore your head. Philip Larkin. NoAM

So through the darkness and the cold we flew. Wordsworth. *Fr.* Prelude [*or*, Growth of a Poet's Mind], The. CH; EnRP; GN; HAP; NOBE; NoP; NU; OAEL-2; OBNC; OxAEP-2; PoE; SCV

So thus he sorrowed till it was day. David Jones. *Fr.* In Parenthesis. NoAM; OAEL-2

So tired! so weary. Catharine of Arragon. Eloise Bibb. CBWP-4

So, 'tis enough. (*LL*) Kissing. Lord Herbert of Cherbury. EnLoPo; NOSC

So, to begin with, ghosts of rain arise. The Dance of Dust. Louis Untermeyer. BXAP

So to Tell the Truth. Janet Dubé. BrRo

So to the sea we came; the sea, that is. Her Heards Be Thousand Fishes. Spenser. *Fr.* Colin Clout's Come Home Again. ChTr

So to the sylvan lodge. Milton. *Fr.* Paradise Lost. EPCY; NAEL-1

So Touch Our Hearts with Loveliness. Gail Brook Burket. AH

So understood, not trying to understand. (*LL*) Seeing St. James's. Ray Mathew. NOBAu

So unwarely was never no man caught. Sir Thomas Wyatt. SiPS; SiPSBD

So, up the steep side of the rugged hill. Jack and Jill. A. E. Housman. UV

So vile was poor Wat, such a miscreant slave. Burns. FaBoEE

So warm I may melt. Sunday Morning. Christina Jenkins. BrRo

So was it even then. So soundlessly. A Trysting. Richard Dehmel, *tr. fr. German by* Jethro Bithell. AWP

So we are taking off our masks, are we, and keeping. Homosexuality. Frank O'Hara. LCAP; PeHV; PoA; TAP

So we came at last to meet, after the lights were out. John Hollander. *Fr.* Powers of Thirteen. VCAP

"So we diverted the river," he said. Requiem for a River. Kim Williams. RFM

So we meet as of old where the rosevine. Person to Person. Gwen Harwood. FaBoMA

So we must part, my body, you and I. Any Soul to Any Body. Cosmo Monkhouse. NOBVV

So we must say goodbye, my darling. Goodbye. Alun Lewis. AngWe; BoLoP; NAEL-2; OBWP; OxBM; OxBTC; PoWW

So we ride, and ride through milked heaven. Rides. Gene Derwood. LiTM

So we sat there all afternoon. (*LL*) On the Lawn at the Villa. Louis Simpson. CoAP; GOA; OBAL; OxBC; PPP

So we were together. Hilda Doolittle ("H. D."). *Fr.* Winter Love. FaBoWP

So we, who've supped the self-same cup. After the Quarrel. Paul Laurence Dunbar. AnAmPo; CDC

So, We'll Go No More a-Roving. Byron. AWP; BLPL; BoLoP; CBLP; ClHu; CoGr; EBEvV; ELP; EnRP; FaPoB; FF; FHYEP; HAP; HeIP; ImPo; LiTB; MeMBP; NAEL-2; NOBE; NoP; OAEL-2; OtMeF; OxBS; OxBSP; PlP; PoE; PoELL-4; Poetr; PoRA; PrIm; SCGP; TFi; TTTS

So Well I Love Thee. Michael Drayton. *See* So well I love thee, as without thee I.

So well I love thee, as without thee I. Michael Drayton. GBL (So Well I Love Thee.) EnRePo (Verses Made the Night before He Died.) NOBE

So well is me begone. Unknown. MiEL

So/ Went this little pig from the mainland to the market. Archibald MacLeish Suspends the Five Little Pigs. Louis Untermeyer. *Fr.* Mother Goose Up-to-Date. MoAmPo

So, we're estranged again — how it goes on! Drought. David Holbrook. OxBTC

So We've Come at Last to Freud. Alice Walker. IHMS

So What. Philip Appleman. BXAP

So what I would, and yet for all I could not. (*LL*) A Little Pretty Bonny Lass. Unknown. CBLP; EIL

So what if clowns and gnomes. The Golden Age. Artur Miedzyrzecki, *tr. fr. Polish by* Stanislaw Barańczak *and* Clare Cavanagh. PoSu

So what if Lowry got spooked by sea-birds and volcanoes crossing. Imperfect Sestina. Phyllis Webb. NOBC

So what is the use of poetry these days. Uses of Poetry. Lawrence Ferlinghetti. PoBeRe

So what said the others and the sun went down. Mrs. Alfred Uruguay. Wallace Stevens. TwCP

So what shall we do about this angel. Lord, Forgive a Spirit. Gerald Stern. CAPP

So what would you do? (*LL*) What? Langston Hughes. NBLV; OBAL

So what's love? I'd watch my 2 older sisters. My Sisters. Bill Kushner. UL

So when he calls me, Death shall find me ready. (*LL*) To My Ninth Decade I Have Tottered On. Walter Savage Landor. EnRP; NAs

So When the Hammers of the Witnesses of Heaven Are Raised All Together. Edward Kamau Brathwaite. *Fr.* Cherries. NAs

So whether it is that the King, unknown. Unknown. *Fr.* Song of Lewes, The. FaBoEH

So while it seems we're beginning to get somewhere. Peter Riley. VaA

So White, So Soft, So Sweet. Ben Jonson. *See* Have you seen but a bright lily grow.

So wild it was when first we settled here. (*LL*) Domicilium. Thomas Hardy. FaBoPP

So wild yet candle-calm. The Grave's Cherub. Sydney Clouts. PeSA

So will I, said Goody Fry. (*LL*) Fire. Langston Hughes. NOBA

So winter closed its fist. Rite of Spring. Seamus Heaney. FaBoBl; OxBC

So write, before I die, "'E liked it all!" (*LL*) Sestina of the Tramp-Royal. Kipling. ImPo; LiTB; MoBrPo; OtMeF; PrIm

So ye're runnin' fer Congress, mister? Le' me tell ye 'bout my son. Whisperin' Bill. Irving Bacheller. PoLF

So, yet even so. (*LL*) World of dew is, The. Issa. OBD

So you are married, girl. It makes me sad. Roy McFadden. PNI

So you aren't Tolstoy or Saint Francis. So? Leonard Nathan. PBCAP

So you beg for a story, my darling, my brown-eyed Leopold. How He Saved St. Michael's. Mary A. P. Stansbury. BLPA

So, you be'n to ole Kentucky. Answer to Dunbar's "After a Visit." Joseph S. Cotter, Sr. AAP

So, you have gone my erstwhile glad boy. Ballygrand Widow. Deborah Randell. VBLP

So you have swept me back. Hilda Doolittle ("H. D."). *Fr.* Eurydice. NALW; VBLP; VGW

So you met him in a magic place? Tam Lin's Lady. Liz Lochhead. VBLP

So you said you'd go home to work on your father's farm. To a Young Poet Who Fled. John Logan. CAPP; SM

So you travel, Parraruru. (*LL*) The Witch Doctor's Magic Flight. Smiler Narautjarri. NOBAu

So you want to be hip little girls. The Sermon. Ted Joans. PoBeRe

So. You were. Lines on the Hundredth Anniversary of the Birth of W. Somerset Maugham. E. J. Thribb. PeLV

So you were David's father. In Memoriam[, Private D. Sutherland]. E.A. Mackintosh. PoWW

So you will presently my loving hands abjure. To This Book. Martin Opitz, *tr. fr. German by* George C. Schoolfield. GePo

So you're back, your face. Old Business: The Drowned Bride. Ken Smith. PWE

So you're twenty-five, three kids, on welfare and getting fat. Fat Blues. Charmaine Crowell. AIW

So, you've come to the tropics, heard all you had to do. Down and Out. Clarence Leonard Hay. BeLS; BLPA

So you've reached your thirty-eighth birthday. My Husband's Birthday. Josephine D. Henderson Heard. CBWP-4

So zestfully canst thou sing? The Blinded Bird. Thomas Hardy. CMoP; LiTM

Soaked to the skin I peer through the drizzle, and I perceice. Thirty-third Canto. Hans Magnus Enzensberger. *Fr.* Sinking of the Titanic, The. PoSu

Soaked with dew at noon. (*LL*) All Morning. Gregory Orr. TRP

Soap. Gerald Stern. BTR

Soap (II). Jerome Rothenberg. NNaP

Soap-Pig, The. Paul Muldoon. PBCIP

Soap Suds. Louis MacNeice. FaBoMo; NAEL-2; NOIV; NoP; NTP; SCV

Soap, the Oppressor. Burges Johnson. PoLF

Soar up, my soul, unto thy rest. Seek Flowers of Heaven. Robert Southwell. TrCP

Soaring hawk from fist that flies, The. The Lover Compareth Himself to the Painful Falconer. *Unknown.* NoSic

Soaring into the distant sky, a lone bird disappears. Climbing Up to the Lo-yu Plain. Tu Mu, *tr. fr. Chinese by* Irving Y. Lo. SuSp

Sober, he thinks of her; so he gets drunk. Man and Woman. Robert Conquest. OxBTC

Sober man, I'll take the wine, A. Paulus Silentiarius, *tr. fr. Greek by* Sam Hamill. InMo

Sobering Up. Yüan Chen, *tr. fr. Chinese by* Dell R. Hales. SuSp

Social Glass, The. L. A. J. Moorer. CBWP-3

Social Life, The. L. A. J. Moorer. CBWP-3

Social Note. Dorothy Parker. *Fr.* Some Beautiful Letters. AnAmPo; FaBoUs

Social Realists, The. Brian Higgins. IHNG

Social Revolution in England. Dannie Abse. AngWe

Social Virtue's liberal plan. Sung by a Choir of Boys Marching Round the Room. Anne Penny. *Fr.* Odes Sung in Commemoration of the Marine Society. ECWP

Society, gregarious dame! An Ode to Society. Hester Lynch Thrale. ECWP

Society has quite forsaken all her wicked courses. Utopia Anglicized. W. S. Gilbert. *Fr.* Utopia Limited. OBSV

Society has to organize. (*LL*) Kyrielle: Party Politics. Frederick Macartney. NOBAu

Society upon the Stanislaus, The. Bret Harte. AnAmPo; BeLS; OBAL

Socrates' Death. Michael Jackson. PeNZ

Socrates' Ghost Must Haunt Me Now. Delmore Schwartz. LiTM

Socrates Snooks. Fitz Hugh Ludlow. BLPA

Socratic. Hilda Doolittle ("H. D."). HoPM

Sod lifted, turned, slapped back again with spade. (*LL*) A Whim of Time. Stephen Spender. MoAB; MoBrPo

Sodden moss sinks underfoot, The. Ales Debeljak, *tr. fr. Slovene.* TSaS, *tr. by* Christopher Merrill

Sodden with drink. Known. Joel Dailey. UL

Sodger laddie's socht a hoose, A. Under the Greenwood Tree. "Hugh MacDiarmid,"
after the Cretan. OBVE

Sodom. Chaim Grade, *tr. fr. Yiddish by* Joseph Leftwich. TrJP

Sodom. Herman Melville. *Fr.* Clarel. AmPP

Sodom; or The Quintessence of Debauchery, *sels. At. to* The Earl of Rochester John Wilmot, 2d Earl of Rochester.
"To Love and Nature all their rights restore." PeHV

Soe, Mistress Anne, faire neighbour myne. Salem. Edmund Clarence Stedman. PAH

Sofa, The. William Cowper. *Fr.* Task, The. EnRP

Sofa, The. Medbh McGuckian. PBCIP; PNI

Sofa Book, The, *sels.* Paul Evans.
"Blair Peach died with a broken head." NBrP
"City is a crowded lift, The." NBrP
"Hail, Garcia, hammer of pigeons." NBrP
"Man points with his umbrella, A." NBrP
"Poets detained by Thought Police." NBrP

Soft answer turneth away wrath, A. The Lips of the Wise. Bible, *O.T. Fr.* Proverbs. TrGrPo

Soft Answers. Robert Bagg. FF

Soft are Sappho's kisses. Paulus Silentiarius, *tr. fr. Greek by* Andrew Miller. GrAn

Soft Black Eyes. Priscilla Jane Thompson. CBWP-2

Soft colored clouds obscured by the sun. Tune: "Song of the Southern Country" – Spring Thoughts at Pearl River. Chu Yi-tsun, *tr. fr. Chinese by* Irving Y. Lo. SuSp

Soft Days After Snow. Jeremy Hooker. SCBI

Soft falls the night. Evening Song. Edith King. BoTP

Soft falls the sweet evening. John Clare. NOBVV

Soft grass tempts us to sleep under the fresh poplars, The. Phidylé. Charles Marie René Leconte de Lisle, *tr. fr. French by* Philip L. Miller. RiWo

Soft gray hands of sleep, The. Forgotten Dreams. Edward S. Silvera. PoNe

Soft hangs the opiate in the brain. An Opium Fantasy. Maria White Lowell. AmWP; AnAmPo; InPK

Soft haze upon the mountain and a haze upon the sea. A Slumber Song of the Gardens. John Runcie. PeSAV

Soft lamp shinin. Any Woman's Blues. Sherley Anne Williams. Jaz

Soft, lovely, rose-like lips, conjoined with mine. Barnabe Barnes. *Fr.* Parthenophil and Parthenophe. EnLoPo

Soft misty rain and a drop of thirty degrees. Bruce Beaver. *Fr.* Letters to Live Poets. CBAP; FaBoMA

Soft new grass is creeping o'er the graves, The. By the Potomac. Thomas Bailey Aldrich. PAH; Son

Soft on the wave the oars at distance sound. Netley Abbey; Midnight. William Sotheby. NOEC

Soft *quem quam* will be Scops the Owl, The. Acropolis. Lawrence Durrell. OxAEP-2

Soft Sea washed around the House, A. Emily Dickinson. SAmP

Soft Snow. Blake. FF; SoSe; TEP

Soft sound of his steps on the pier, The. Photograph of a Child, Japanese-American Evacuation, Bainbridge Island, Washington, March 30, 1942. Jim Mitsui. OpBo

Soft sounds and odours brim up through the night. Guided Missiles Experimental Range. Robert Conquest. OxBC

Soft spread the southern summer night. Saint Cloud. Sir Walter Scott. OBTV

Soft, To Your Places. Thomas Kinsella. LPA

Soft, to your places, animals. Soft, To Your Places. Thomas Kinsella. LPA

Soft toys that make to seem girls. Strip-tease. Lawrence Durrell. OxAEP-2

Soft whoosh, the sunset blaze, A. Leavings. Seamus Heaney. PRA

Soft wind will blow me home, The. (*LL*) Living in the Summer Mountains. Yü Hsüan-chi. WPC

Soft Wood. Robert Lowell. LiTM

Soft you; a word or two before you go. Shakespeare. *Fr.* Othello. OxAEP-1

Softened by time's consummate plush. Emily Dickinson. NOBA

Softening of her face which comes, The. At Only That Moment. Alan Ross. ErPo

Softer than silence, stiller than still air. The Snowing of the Pines. Thomas Wentworth Higginson. GN

Softly. John White. ArLo

Softly along the road of evening. Nod. Walter de la Mare. BoTP; MoAB; MoBrPo; OxBTC; PFP

Softly and humbly to the Gulf of Arabs. Beach Burial. Kenneth Slessor. CBAP; FaBoMA; PAW

Softly Baby I'll stop having a thing for you. Softly. John White. ArLo

Softly blow lightly. Donald Jeffrey Hayes. CDC

Softly croons the radiogram, loudly hoot the owls. Invasion Exercise on the Poultry Farm. Sir John Betjeman. NOBL

Softly Fades the Twilight Ray. Samuel Francis Smith. AH

Softly gliding I go. Satyr's Song, The ("Softly Gliding as I Go.") John Fletcher. *Fr.* Faithful Shepherdess, The. NOSC

Softly, in the dusk, a woman is singing to me. Piano. D. H. Lawrence. BLPL; CMoP; FaPoB; GrPl; GTBS-P; HAP; HeIL; HeIP; InPK; InvP; LiTB; MoAB; MoBrPo; MoP; NAEL-2; NoAM; NOBE; NoP; OAEL-2; OxBSP; PoE; Poetr; PPP; RB; SCGP; TFi; TRP; UnPo; WeW

Softly now the day is dawning. The Signal Gun. Mary E. Tucker. CBWP-1

Softly now the light of day. Evening Contemplation. George Washington Doane. AH; BLPA; BLPL; FaBoBe

Softly, O midnight Hours! Aubrey Thomas De Vere. OBEV

Softly pleading, my songs go. Ludwig Rellstab, *tr. fr. German by* Philip L. Miller. RiWo

Softly rustled the oaks, whispered low in my ear. The Graveyard. Hayyim Nahman Bialik, *tr. fr. Hebrew by* Bertha Beinkinstadt. TrJP

Softly sailing emerald lights. Fireflies. "Fiona Macleod." *Fr.* Transcripts from Nature. FM

Softly sighs the April air. Bel m'es quan lo vens m'alena. Arnaut Daniel, *tr. fr. French by* Harriet Waters Preston. AWP

Softly, softly, through the darkness. Christmas Night. B. E. Milner. BoTP

Softly stroke the stiffened wing. (*LL*) The Death of Lesbia's Bird. Catullus. AWP

Softly the civilized. Raiders' Dawn. Alun Lewis. AngWe

Softly the Evening. William Hurrell Mallock. BXAP

Softly the Night. *Unknown.* OBET

Softly the waters ripple. Ares. Albert Ehrenstein, *tr. fr. German by* Babette Deutsch *and* Avrahm Yarmolinsky. TrJP

Softly through the Mellow Starlight. *Unknown.* OHIP

Softly, you open your door. After the Night. Mang Ke, *tr. fr. Chinese by* Donald Finkel *with* Li Guohua. SpMi

Soggarth Aroon. John Banim. TIRV

Soho. Edwin Morgan. FaBoBl

Sohrab and Rustum. (And the first grey of morning filled the east.) Matthew Arnold. EBNV; OBNV

Sels.
"So, on the bloody sand, Sohrab lay dead." EBEvV; GTBS-P; PeVV
(Sohrab Dead.) NOBE
"Then Sohrab with his sword smote Rustum's helm." OBWP

Sohrab Dead. Matthew Arnold. *See* So, on the bloody sand, Sohrab lay dead.

Soil for legs. Nanao Sakaki. EaPr

Soil glistens, the furrow rolls, sleet shifts, brightens. (*LL*) Boy Remembers in the Field. Raymond Knister. NOBC

Soil is freshly dug, the half-faded wreaths of leaves, The. Heraclitus of Halicarnassus, *tr. fr. Greek by* Edwin Morgan. GrAn

Soil now gets a rumpling soft and damp, The. The Strong Are Saying Nothing. Robert Frost. CMoP

Soil of man's escape, The. Suburbia. Maurice Martinez. PoNe

Soil was deep and the field well-sited, The. A Failure. C. Day Lewis. NOBE

Soiled light, A. Manchester. Pamela Gillilan. PWE

Sois sage o ma douleur. Baudelaire. *See* Peace, Be at Peace, O Thou My Heaviness.

Sois sage, ô ma doleur . . . I don't. Michael Foley. *Fr.* True Life Love Stories. PNI

Soissons. Keith Douglas. NoAM

Sojourn in the Whale. Marianne Moore. NALW

Sojourner Truth. Sojourner Truth. WoWa

Sokoya, I said, looking through. There Is No Word for Goodbye. Mary TallMountain. HATNAP

Sokrates to Agathon. Plato, *tr. fr. Greek by* Peter Jay. GrAn

Sokrates to Xanthippé. Plato, *tr. fr. Greek by* Peter Jay. GrAn

Sol through white curtains shot a tim'rous ray. Pope. *Fr.* Rape of the Lock, The. ECEV; FHYEP; HAP; ImPo; NoP; OAEL-1; OBNV; PeLV; PoEL-3; TEP; TrGrPo

Sol took his nightcap off and gazed. After the Storm. H. Cordelia Ray. AmWP; CBWP-3

Solace. Clarissa Scott Delany. *See* My window opens out into the trees.

Solace. Josephine D. Henderson Heard. CBWP-4

Solace in Age. Sir Richard Maitland. OxBS

Solar Creation. Charles Madge. FaBoMo; OBMV; OxBTC

Solar Myth. Genevieve Taggard. MoAmPo

Solar Years. David Rokeah, *tr. fr. Hebrew by* Ruth Finer Mintz. MHP

Solarium, The. Rachel Hadas. UnDi

Sold for salad. (*LL*) Voodoo Cucumbers. Martín Espada. UTF

Soldier, The, *sels.* Conrad Aiken.

Soldier, The. Rupert Brooke. *Fr.* 1914. CoGr; EBEvV; FaBoEH; FaBV; FaPoB; FaPoR; FF; HeIP; LiTB; LiTM; MoBrPo; NAEL-2; NOBE; NoP; NSI; OBEV; OBWP; OxBTC; PAW; PeFWW; PlP; PoA; PoLF; PoRA; PoWW; Son; TEP; TFi; TrGrPo; UV

Soldier, The. Adelbert von Chamisso, *tr. fr. German by* Philip L. Miller. RiWo

Soldier, The. Gerard Manley Hopkins. MeMBP

Soldier, The. Uys Krige, *tr. fr. Afrikaans by the author.* PeSA

Soldier, A. Sir John Suckling. PoE; SeCV-1

Soldier, The. J. Y. Watson. BXAP

Soldier Addresses his Body, The. Edgell Rickword. PeFWW; PoWW

Soldier and a Sailor, A. Congreve. *Fr.* Love for Love. CoMu

Soldier and a Sailor, A. John Gay. *See* Fox may steal your hens, sir, A.

Soldier and statesman, rarest unison. Washington. James Russell Lowell. *Fr.* Under the Old Elm. GN; OHIP

Soldier Asleep. Phyllis McGinley. ArOW

Soldier asleep, and stirring in your sleep. Soldier Asleep. Phyllis McGinley. ArOW

Soldier Bathing. Frank Ormsby. *Fr.* Northern Spring, A. PNI

Soldier Boy for Me. *Unknown.* AmFP

Soldier Boy's Dream, The. Mary E. Tucker. CBWP-1

Soldier brave, sailor true. *Unknown.* OxNR

Soldier from the Wars Returning. A. E. Housman. LiTB; OBMV

Soldier Going to the Field, The. Sir William Davenant. NOBE; OBWP

Soldier in the Park, The. Elizabeth Riddell. CBAP

Soldier Is Home, The. John Shaw Neilson. CBAP

Soldier Loves His Rifle, The. W. H. Auden. TEP

Soldier maimed and in the beggars' list, A. The Pluralist and Old Soldier. John Collier. NOEC

Soldier of the Legion lay dying in Algiers, A. Bingen on the Rhine. Caroline E. Norton. BeLS; BLPA; WBLP

Soldier passed me in the freshly fallen snow, A. To a Conscript of 1940. Sir Herbert Read. LiTB; LiTM; NSI; OBWP; PoWW

Soldier, Rest! Robert J. Burdette. OBAL

Soldier Rest! [Thy Warfare O'er]. Sir Walter Scott. *Fr.* Lady of the Lake, The. AWP; GN; MoShBr; NOBE; PoRA; TrGrPo

Soldier That Has Seen Service, The. *Unknown.* NOEC

Soldier, think before you marry. John Gay. *Fr.* Achilles. PeLV

Soldier: Twentieth Century. Isaac Rosenberg. PoWW

Soldier Walks under the Trees of the University, The. Randall Jarrell. OxBA

Soldier, Won't You Marry Me? *Unknown.* AmFP; OxBoLi; PeLV

Soldier, There Is a War between the Mind. Wallace Stevens. *Fr.* Notes toward a Supreme Fiction. LiTM; NoAM

Soldiers. Padraic Fiacc. PNI

Soldiers. *Unknown.* FaBoEE; GBP

Soldiers and poor, unable to rejoice. (*LL*) The Owl. Edward Thomas. ChTr; EBEV; FaBoRV; FaBoTw; FF; GTBS-P; LiTB; MoP; NAEL-2; NIP; NoAM; NOBE; NoP; OAEL-2; OBWVE; OxAEP-2; PeFWW; PlP; PoE; Poetr; RB; SCGP; TFi; TRP; UnPo

Soldiers are citizens of death's grey land. Dreamers. Siegfried Sassoon. MoBrPo; NoAM; Son

Soldiers Bathing. F. T. Prince. GTBS-P; ImPo; LiTB; LiTM; MoBrPo; NOCV; OBWP; OxBTC; PeSA

Soldier's Bride, The. Aleksei Nikolayevich Pleshcheyev, *tr. fr. Russian by* Philip L. Miller. RiWo

Soldiers came, brewed tea in Snoddy's field, The. After the War. Douglas Dunn. OxBC

Soldiers' Chorus from Faust. *Unknown.* NOBAu

Soldier's Cigarette, The. Harold Beckh. NSI

Soldier's Death, The. Anne Finch. OtMeF

Soldier's Dream, The. Thomas Campbell. BeLS; EnRP; FaPoR; GTBS; GTBS-P; OxAEP-2; PlP

Soldier's Farewell to Manchester, The. *Unknown.* CoMu

Soldier's Grave, The. Henry D. Muir. OHIP

Soldiers have to fight and swear. Unequal Distribution. Samuel Hoffenstein. TrJP

Soldiers in a Small Camp. W. J. Turner. NSI

Soldiers never do die well. Champs d'Honneur. Ernest Hemingway. AiP; PoA

Soldiers of Christ, arise. The Whole Armour of God. Charles Wesley. NOCV

Soldiers, our brethren and our friends are slain. Shelley. *Fr.* Revolt of Islam, The. OBF

Soldier's Prayer, A. Robert Freeman. TrPWD

Soldiers Returning, The. Richard Shelton. GOYP

Soldier's Song. Goethe, *tr. by* Bayard Taylor. *Fr.* Faust. AWP

Soldier's Song. *Unknown.* WiR

Soldier's Tale, The. *Unknown.* PeLV

Soldiers who wish to be a hero. Soldiers. *Unknown.* FaBoEE; GBP

Soldier's Wife, The. Robert Southey. OxBSP

Soldier's Wooing, The. *Unknown.* AmFP

Sole heir of virtue, and of beauty both. Sir John Davies. *Fr.* Orchestra; or, A Poem[e] of Da[u]ncing. NAEL-1; NoSic, *abr.*; SiPS; SiPSBD

Sole positive of night. Ne Plus Ultra. Samuel Taylor Coleridge. OAEL-2

Sole true something — This! In Limbo's den, The. Limbo. Samuel Taylor Coleridge. OAEL-2

Sole watchman of the flying stars, guard me. John Berryman. *Fr.* Eleven Addresses to the Lord. OxBC; UnPo

Soledad. Robert Hayden. CAPP; Jaz

Solemn Hour. Rainer Maria Rilke, *tr. fr. German by* C. F. MacIntyre. TrJP

Solemn Meditation, A. William Shenstone. NOEC

Solemn plain-faced child stands gazing there, A. A Portrait. Walter de la Mare. NoAM

Solemn thing — it was — I said, A. Emily Dickinson. NALW

Solemn whip-poor-will, The. The Queens. Robert Fitzgerald. NYBP

Solemnly, mournfully,/ Dealing its dole. Curfew. Longfellow. AnAmPo; MeMAP; OxBA

Soles of my feet are burning, The. Retrospect. Wilhelm Müller, *tr. fr. German by* Philip L. Miller. *Fr.* Winter's Journey, The. RiWo

Solicitors' World, A. Evan Jones (b. 1927). FaBoMA

Solicitudes canine, four-footed amities. (*LL*) Sonnet: To Tartar, a Terrier Beauty. Thomas Lovell Beddoes. FM; NOBVV; OBNC

Solid citizens, The. Undertow. Langston Hughes. LiTM

Solid man and the coxcomb., The. (*LL*) Crazy Jane and the Bishop. W. B. Yeats. CMoP; LiTM

Some are nights the others ashes. Vasco [*or* Vasko] Popa. *See* Some are nights others stars.

Some are plain lucky we ourselves among them. A Lost Soul. Jay Macpherson. NOBC

Some are teethed on a silver spoon. Saturday's Child. Countee Cullen. LiTM; NAs; PoBA

Some ask for envy'd pow'r; which publick hate. Sejanus ("Some ask for envy'd pow'r; which publick hate.") Juvenal, *tr.* by Dryden. *Fr.* Satires. OBVE

Some Atheist or vile Infidel in love. Michael Drayton. BOEP

Some autumn leaves a painter took. The Sumach Leaves. Jones Very. NOBA

Some beauties yet no precepts can declare. Pope. *Fr.* Essay on Criticism. HAP; PoEL-3

Some Beautiful Letters, sels. Dorothy Parker.
     Comment. AnAmPo; NBLV; NIP; OBAL; VBLP
     News Item. FaBoUs; NALW; OBAL
     Observation. FiBHP
     Résumé. AnAmPo; DL; HeIL; HeIP; IHNG; InPK; NAAL-2; NALW; NBLV; NoP; OBAL; Poetr; TrJP; UV
     Social Note. AnAmPo; FaBoUs

Some bite off the others'/ Arm. He. Vasco [*or* Vasko] Popa, *tr. fr.* Serbo-Croatian by Anne Pennington. *Fr.* Games. CBNP; PoSu; RB

Some Blaze the Precious Beauties of Their Loves. John Davies of Hereford. *Fr.* Wit's Pilgrimage. Son

Some Blesseds. John Oxenham. WGRP

Some bloodied sea-bird's hovering decay. The Lie. Howard Moss. LiTM; MoAB

Some books are lies frae end to end. Death and Doctor Hornbook. Burns. OxBS

Some Boys. Chuck Ortleb. GLP; PeHV

Some Boys. John Penkethman. OxBChV

Some bright umbrella, suddenly blowing free. Rain. Donald Justice. *Fr.* Body and Soul. BAP-91

Some broken. A State of Nature. John Hollander. AiP

Some by their friends, more by themselves thought wise. Dryden. *Fr.* Absalom and Achitophel, Pt. I. ChIV-1; NoP; OAEL-1; OBSV; SeCV-2

Some call Experience. (*LL*) I stepped from plank to plank. Emily Dickinson. CMoP; NOBA; NOCV; OxBSP; SAmP

Some call that deep-deep bell. Hilda Doolittle ("H. D."). *Fr.* Tribute to the Angels. NALW

Some can gaze and not be sick. A. E. Housman. FaBoEE; NOBVV; OBSV

Some can leave the truth unspoken. Truth. Eileen Duggan. PeNZ

Some candle clear burns somewhere I come by. The Candle Indoors. Gerard Manley Hopkins. ChIV-2; ImPo; LiTB; LiTM; OxAEP-2; PoEL-5

Some cawing Crows, a hooting Owl. Ella Wheeler Wilcox. AmWP

Some celebration./ One by one they all left me. On the Carpet, Staring at Myself. Slavko Mihalic, *tr.* by Peter Kastmiler. PoSu

Some change in the wording of the charm. Last Days of Prospero. Donald Justice. PRA

Some consommé? Les Plaisirs. Tommy McClennan. UnDi

Some Contemplations of the Poor, and Desolate State of the Church at Deerfield. John Williams. SCAP

Some Cook. John Ciardi. PDV

Some creep came to my water trough. The Snake on D. H. Lawrence. N. J. Warburton. UV

Some cry up Haydn, some Mozart. Free Thoughts on Several Eminent Composers. Charles Lamb. FaBoCo; OxBoLi; PeLV

Some curse that traitor Judas life and limb. On Judas Iscariot. Francis Quarles. FaBoEE

Some day. — Alas, alas! (*LL*) Near Lanivet, 1872. Thomas Hardy. AWP; CMoP; NoAM

Some day, all unawares, alone in the deep forest. My Death. Carl Zuckmayer, *tr. fr. German* by E. B. Ashton. TrJP

Some day I will go to Aarhus. The Tollund Man. Seamus Heaney. BIrV; CIP; EBEV; FaBoMo; IPY; NoP; PBCIP; PNI; TEP

Some Day, Some Day. Cristóbal de Castillejo, *tr. fr. Spanish by* Longfellow. AWP

Some day, some happy day. The Reign of Peace. Mary Starck. WBLP

Some day the fields will be always green. Song of Hope. Daisy Zamora, *tr. fr. Spanish by* Jane Glazer *and* Elizabeth Linder. WoWa

Some day, when trees have shed their leaves. After the Winter. Claude McKay. PoBA; PoNe

Some day will be wondrous fair. (*LL*) Life and the Weaver. A. W. Dewar. BLRP; WBLP

"Some Days," Dorothy Parker Said, "It's Better Than Digging Ditches." Maureen Owen. UL

Some days go by "like elevators," while others do not. Elephant Languor. April Bernard. UTF

Some days he would wander around his attic-room. The Wisdom of Æ. Thomas McCarthy. PBCIP

Some days, I'm sorely tempted to throw out the baby. Lamentations of an Au Pair Girl. Susan Feldman. AmPA

Some days must be dark and dreary. (*LL*) The Rainy Day. Longfellow. AWP; PoLF

Some Days/ Out Walking Above. De Leon Harrison. PoBA

Some days, you say, are good days. Warp and Woof. Harry Halbisch. BLRP

Some define the happening. (*LL*) Native's Letter. Arthur Nortje. HBAPE; PeSAV

Some die too late and some too soon. The Lost Occasion. Whittier. BLPL; NOBA

Some Dreams They Forgot. Elizabeth Bishop. NoAM

Some Eyes Condemn. Edward Thomas. NoAM

Some Flowers o' the Spring. Shakespeare. *Fr.* Winter's Tale, The. ChTr; GBL

Some folk like the chaffinch. The Robin. O. M. Bent. BoTP

Some folks are drunk, yet do not know it. An English Ballad, on the Taking of Namur by the King of Great Britain, 1695. Matthew Prior. PoEL-3

Some folks as can afford. Under a Wiltshire Apple Tree. Anna Bunston de Bary. CH

Some folks in looks take so much pride. *Unknown.* PoToHe

Some for everyone. Snow by Morning. May Swenson. NYBP

Some for the Glories of This World; and some. Omar Khayyám, *tr. fr. Persian by* Edward Fitzgerald. *Fr.* Rubáiyát of Omar Khayyám of Naishápúr, The. AWP; EBVV, *abr.;* FaBoBe; FaBoRV, *abr.;* FaPoR, *abr.;* HAP, *abr.;* LiTB; NAEL-2; NoP; PoEL-5; PrIm, *abr.;* TrGrPo; TRP

Some Foreign Letters. Anne Sexton. MoAmPo

Some Fowls There Be. Petrarch. *See* Some fowls there be that have so perfect sight.

Some fowls there be that have so perfect sight. How the Lover Perisheth in His Delight, As the Fly in the Fire. Petrarch, *tr. fr. Italian by* Sir Thomas Wyatt. *Fr.* Sonnets to Laura. Son
     (Some Fowls There Be.) SCGP

Some Frenchmen. John Updike. FaBoCo; NBLV

Some Friends. Arthur Yap. OBF

Some Geese. Oliver Herford. *Fr.* Child's Natural History. FiBHP

Some generous painter now assist my pen. The True Effigies of a Certain Squire: Inscribed to Clemena. Elizabeth Thomas. ECWP

Some glowing in the common blood./ Some specialness within. (*LL*) Of Robert Frost. Gwendolyn Brooks. MoP; NoAM; NOBA

Some gold lies veiled behind each evening cloud. Hidden Essence. H. Cordelia Ray. CBWP-3

Some golden-haired light lady. (*LL*) The Student. *Unknown.* OBMV

Some good people, daring and subtle voices. John Berryman. *Fr.* Dream Songs. HCAP

Some Good Things to Be Said for the Iron Age. Gary Snyder. HoPM; TTTS

Some Grand River Blues. Daniel David Moses. HATNAP

Some hae [*or* have] meat and [*or* that] canna [*or* cannot] eat. *At. to* Burns Burns. *Fr.* Two Graces. FaBoCh
     (Child's Grace, A.) FaPON; MoShBr
     (Grace at Kirkudbright.) NTP; OxBSP

Some hand, that never meant to do thee hurt. On Finding a Small Fly Crushed in a Book. Charles Tennyson Turner. FM

Some Hands Are Lovelier. Mae V. Cowdery. ShDr

Some Harvard men, stalwart and hairy. Edward Gorey. OBAL

Some hearts go hungering thro' the world. Hungering Hearts. *Unknown.* PoToHe

Some in the Godspeed, the Susan C. Enough. Marianne Moore. NOBA

Some in the Town go betimes to the Downs. The Hunt. *Unknown.* CoMu

Some in their harts their mistris colours bears. William Smith. *Fr.* Chloris [or the Complaint of the Passionate Despised Shepheard]. AAS

Some Indian Uses of History on a Rainy Day. A. K. Ramanujan. OxBC

Some innocent girlish kisses by a charm. Wild Rose. William Allingham. GN

Some ither day. (*LL*) The Holy Fair. Burns. EnRP; OBSV

Some keep the Sabbath [*or* Sunday] going to church. Emily Dickinson. HeIP; MoAB; MoAmPo; WGRP

Some kinds of trees seem ever eager. The Mast Year. Medbh McGuckian. CIP

Some Kisses from *The Kama Sutra.* Hugo Williams. BoLoP

Some lasses are nice and strange. The Innocent Country-Maid's Delight; or, A Description of the Lives of the Lasses of London. *Unknown.* CoMu

Some Last Questions. W. S. Merwin. CAPP; HCAP; VCAP

Some leaders lead too far ahead. Leaders. *Unknown.* WBLP

Some like cats, and some like dogs. Cats and Dogs. N. M. Bodecker. TLR

Some like drink. Not I. Robert Louis Stevenson. NOBL

Some like them gentle and sweet. I Like Them Fluffy. A. P. Herbert. NBLV

Some Litanies. Michael Benedikt. CoAP; TwCP

Some Little Bug. Roy Atwell. PoLF

Some lives are so odd — you agree? *Unknown.* PeLi

Some Loss. Roy Fisher. VaA

Some lovers speak, when they their muses entertain. Sir Philip Sidney. *Fr.* Astrophel and Stella. AAS; ESo, *sl. abr.*; GGP; HeIL; NAEL-1; NoSic; Poetr; SCGP; SiPS; SiPSBD; Son

Some lucky day each November great waves awake and are drawn. November Surf. Robinson Jeffers. NAAL-2; OxBA

Some Magic. James Koller. PoM

Some Magnetism in the Sea. Rodney Hall. *Fr.* Owner of My Face, The. CBAP

Some make potteries. Womanwork. Paula Gunn Allen. SRLS

Some may occasion snatch to carp, The Harp. Ralph Knevet. ChIV-2

Some may wish for city streets, jewels or silken gown. Wishes. A. C. Child. PoToHe

Some Men. Dazzly Anderson. AIW

Some men break your heart in two. Experience. Dorothy Parker. NAAL-2

Some men deem. Ideals. Robert Greene. PoToHe

Some men marriage do commend. De Se. John Weever. FaBoEE

Some men say there is a God. God? Cristoir O'Flynn. TIRV

Some men, some men. Chant for Dark Hours. Dorothy Parker. VBLP

Some men, 'tis said, prefer a woman fat. Nathaniel Parker Willis. *Fr.* Lady Jane, The; a Humorous Novel in Rhyme. OBAL

Some, Milton-mad (an affectation). Robert Lloyd. *Fr.* On Rhyme. EPCY

Some moments. Broken Gauges. David St. John. BAP-89

Some moralist or mythological poet. W. B. Yeats. *Fr.* Nineteen Hundred and Nineteen. PoE

Some More Cases of Love with Solutions, *sels. At. to* Pietro Aretino, *tr. fr. Italian by* Alistair Elliot.
"At the Jesuits' church, the sexton father's racked." FaBoBl

Some morning, while you and I are dozing. Intruder. Susan Feldman. AmPA

Some musical intervals survive. Geoffrey Lehmann. *Fr.* Ross's Poems. CBAP; FaBoMA

Some must employ the scythe. The Dedicated. Philip Larkin. OxBC

Some names are ominous, wherein wise fate. Of St Stephen. Francis Quarles. NOSC

Some names there are of telling sound. The *Cumberland.* Herman Melville. PAH

Some names there are that win the best applause. William Lloyd Garrison. H. Cordelia Ray. CBWP-3

Some Necessary Implements. Marmion Shakerley. CBCK

Some ne'er advance a judgment of their own. Pope. *Fr.* Essay on Criticism. OBSV; PoEL-3

Some newness of the heart I would discern. Mid Winter. Hubert Witheford, *tr. fr. Maori by* Sam Karetu. PeNZ

Some nieces won't, some nieces can't. Aunts and Nieces or Time and Space. A. E. Housman. CBNP

Some Night Again. William Stafford. GOYP

Some nights it's bound to be your best way out. Insomnia I. Howard Nemerov. DiPo

Some nights/ the rat with pointed teeth. Hello. Naomi Shihab Nye. MT; NAmP90

Some nights you need to get into the car and drive. We Never Close. David Clewell. NAmP90

Some nine hundred fifty circlings of my moon. Birthday. Earle Birney. NAs

Some nineteen German planes, they say. Reprisals. W. B. Yeats. OBWP; PoWW

Some Notes on Courage. Susan Ludvigson. MT

Some of my best friends are white boys. Friends. Ray Durem. PoBA

Some of our dead are famous, but they would not care. W. H. Auden. *Fr.* In Time of War. GLP

Some of Our Koorawatha Saints. Geoffrey Lehmann. *Fr.* Ross's Poems. CBAP

Some of the cats I know about. My Cat Mrs. Lick-a-Chin. John Ciardi. CRH; SiSoPo

Some of the girls are playing jacks. Narcissa. Gwendolyn Brooks. GrPl; NTCP

Some of the time. Working with Mother. Myra Cohn Livingston. TLR

Some of their chiefs were princes of the land. Dryden. *Fr.* Absalom and Achitophel, Pt. I. EBEV; NoP; OAEL-1; SCV; SeCV-2
(On the Duke of Buckingham.) IHNG
(Zimri: "Some of their chiefs were princes of the land.") AWP

Some of them evil, most good. Seen Out. Anne Elder. FaBoMA

Some of them with staves. Basho, *tr. fr. Japanese by* Harold G. Henderson. TAL

Some of us are a little tired of hearing that cigarettes kill. Smokers for Celibacy. Fleur Adcock. FaBoBl; PWE

Some of us barefoot. (*LL*) Group Photo from Pretoria Local on the Occasion of a Fourth Anniversary (Never Taken). Jeremy Cronin. PeSAV

Some of us stayed forever, under the lough. Frank Ormsby. *Fr.* Northern Spring, A. CIP

Some of us/ these days. Resurrection. Frank Horne. PoBA

Some of Wordsworth. Walter Savage Landor. ChTr

Some "old Robin Down" they call me. Ibby Damsel. *Unknown.* AmFP

Some One. Walter de la Mare. PYC; TLR

Some One Liked Me when I Was Twelve. Peter Orlovsky. GLP

Some one prepared this mighty show. Emily Dickinson. SAmP

Some one started the whole day wrong — was it you? Was It You? Stewart I. Long. WBLP

Some Opposites. Richard Wilbur. OBCA

Some pages have eyes, some mouths. They desire. The Family Album. Lisa Ress. BTR

Some People. Wendy Cope. FaBoBl

Some People. Rachel Field. FaPON; NTCP; PDV

Some people admire the work of a fool. Blake. OAEL-2

Some people are good at. Calendars. Wilma Elizabeth McDaniel. ETG

Some people are incurably gentle. Portrait of a Lady. Elizabeth Nannestad. PeNZ

Some people cannot endure. Going the Rounds; a Sort of Love Poem. Anthony Hecht. BoLoP

Some people hang portraits up. A Likeness. Robert Browning. CTC

Some people have names like pitchforks, some people have names. Nomenclature. Stephen Vincent Benét. AnAmPo

Some people in the sky. Song for a Scalp Dance. *Unknown, tr. fr. Chippewa Indian by* Jerome K. Rothenberg. STP

Some people know how to love. Poem of Explanations. Dahlia Ravikovitch, *tr. fr. Hebrew by* Chana Bloch. BoWoP

Some people like each other and are therefore like each other. My Esmeralda. Vijay Seshadri. UTF

Some people like sex more than others. Some People. Wendy Cope. FaBoBl

Some people may think I'm a bit la-di. C. Vita-Finzi. PeLi

Some people,/ no matter what you give them. Adam's Complaint. Denise Levertov. BoWoP; NNaP

Some people say a teacher's made out of steel. The Teacher's Lament. Merle Travis. SWP

Some people say the world's all a stage. The Gate at the End of Things. *Unknown.* BLPA

Some people see only you. The Couple. Ana Blandiana, *tr. fr. Romanian by the author* and William M. Murray. WPOW

Some people think I think I'm good. Oh, If They Only Knew! Edith L. Mapes. BLRP; WBLP

Some people understand all about machinery. Up from the Wheelbarrow. Ogden Nash. FaBoBe

Some People's Dreams Pay All Their Bills. Irina Ratushinskaya. PWE

Some pimps wear summer hats. What? Langston Hughes. NBLV; OBAL

Some pleasure for our punishment! (*LL*) An Argument. Thomas Moore. BoLoP; EnLoPo; OxBSP

Some prefer a glory of horsemen; warships. Sappho, *tr. fr. Greek by* John Frederick Nims. STV

Some primal termite knocked on wood. The Termite. Ogden Nash. NBLV; OBCA

Some prowl sea-beds, some hurtle to a star. X-Ray. Dannie Abse. AngWe

Some Question You Might Ask. Mary Oliver. BAP-89

Some Questions to Be Asked of a Rajah, Perhaps by the Associated Press. Preston Newman. FiBHP

Some 're lovely N nawu nnnn but some 're & are at my hawuz nawu wnn. The 13th Horse Song of Frank Mitchell (White). Frank Mitchell, *tr. fr. Navajo Indian by* Jerome K. Rothenberg *and* David P. McAllester. STP

Some Reflections. The Countess of Winchilsea. ChIV-1

Some rhythms must remain unbroken. Grande Jetée. Mary Mackey. *Fr.* Arabesque: Five Poems for Women without Children. AIW

Some Ruthless Rhymes, *sels.* Harry Graham.
Compensation. CBNP; PeLV
Englishman's Home, The. CBNP; PeLV

Some years of late, in 'eighty-eight, as I do well remember-a. Sir Francis Drake; or, Eighty-eight. *Unknown.* GBP
(Some years of late, in eighty-eight.) FaBoCh
Some young and saucy dandelions. The Dandelions. *Unknown.* BoTP
Somebodies walked the woods. The North. Barry McKinnon. NOBC
Somebody. Tennyson. FaBoEE; NOBL
Somebody. *Unknown.* OxBS
Somebody almost walked off wid alla my stuff. Ntozake Shange. WPOW
Somebody being a nobody. Somebody. Tennyson. FaBoEE; NOBL
(Somebody Being a Nobody.) OxBSP
Somebody Being a Nobody. Tennyson. *See* Somebody being a nobody.
Somebody Call. Carolyn M. Rodgers. JB
Somebody,/ Cut his hair. Young Poet. Myron O'Higgins. PoBA; PoNe
Somebody Died. Robert Creeley. LCAP
Somebody has given my. Proust's Madeleine. Kenneth Rexroth. NoAM; TRP
Somebody is hanging. A Wreath for the Suicide Heart. Anthony McNeill. PBCV
Somebody is shooting at something in our town. The Swarm. Sylvia Plath. NALW
Somebody loses whenever somebody wins. Crapshooters. Carl Sandburg. VGW
Somebody loves us all. (*LL*) Filling Station. Elizabeth Bishop. FaBoMo; HAP; HCAP; InPK; NoP; NYBP; VCAP; WeW
Somebody must have. A Gift Horse. Alamgir Hashmi, *tr. fr. Urdu.* TSaS
Somebody said that it couldn't be done. It Couldn't Be Done. Edgar A. Guest. BLPA; FaBoBe; WBLP
Somebody Said That It Couldn't Be Done, *parody. Unknown.* FiBHP
Somebody said wrecks. The Drowned. Norman MacCaig. OxBC
Somebody ("Somebody's tall and handsome."). *Unknown.* AS
Somebody threw a baby. Crossing Over. Demetria Martinez. AfAz
Somebody threw away a piano. Street Music. Barbara Angell. AiP
Somebody told me I didn't exist even though he was. The Warmth of Hot Chocolate. Thylias Moss. BAP-89
Somebody told me I wouldn't know how to choose. Song: Paper. Keith Waldrop. MAT
Somebody told me you were dead. Callimachus, *tr. fr. Greek by* Kenneth Rexroth. PGA
Somebody treat her real bad. Lady on a Bus. Jeanne Lohmann. CrSp
Somebody up in the rocky pasture. The Ant Village. Marion Edey *and* Dorothy Grider. FaPON
Somebody, when I was young, stole my toy horse. The Toy Horse. Valentin Iremonger. NOIV
Somebody who should have been born. The Abortion. Anne Sexton. CAPP; IHMS; LCAP; MAT; NMM; Poetr; SM; VGW
Somebody's Darling. Marie La Coste. BLPA; UnPo; WBLP
Somebody's done for. (*LL*) Death and Co. Sylvia Plath. CMoP; FF; LCAP; PrIm
Somebody's in there. Saint Pumpkin. Nancy Willard. LCAP
Somebody's knockin' at th' door. The Collier's Wife. D. H. Lawrence. FaBoVe; OxBTC
Somebody's Mother. Mary Dow Brine. BeLS; BLPA; WBLP
Somebody's tall and handsome. Somebody. *Unknown.* AS
Someday I'd like to climb the Puig. Balearic Idyll. Frederick Packard. FiBHP
Someday you will be dead. Sappho, *tr. fr. Greek by* Sam Hamill. InMo
Somedays now/ I can squash a cockroach. Wendy G. Rickert. NMM
Somehow began the/ measured rise. (*LL*) The Diver. Robert Hayden. AmPP; BPo
Somehow he's become a friendly uncle: bachelor. G.I. Joe from Kokomo. William Trowbridge. ArOW
Somehow it should have been. Masks. Elizabeth Fenton. NMM
Somehow the tutorial takes an unplanned direction. How Come the Truck-Loads? Judith Rodriguez. FaBoWP
Somehow, the two of us sit in a café. Still Life. Patricia Storace. PRA
Someone [*or* Some One]. Walter de la Mare. FaPON; MoBrPo; PDV; SiSoPo
Someone approaches to say his life is ruined. The Dream. David Ignatow. CoAP; MAT; NNaP
Someone Asked the Publisher. J. B. Morton. *Fr.* When We Were Very Silly. FaBoPa; UV
Someone at Least. David Constantine. SCBI
Someone at least reading about beauty in a room. Someone at Least. David Constantine. SCBI
Someone be a rose tree. The Rose Thieves. Vasco [*or* Vasko] Popa, *tr. fr. Serbo-Croatian by* Anne Pennington. *Fr.* Games. RB
(Someone is a rose bush.) HSix
Someone before him to see and to know. (*LL*) Bouquet of Belle Scavoir. Wallace Stevens. MoAB; MoAmPo

Someone came knocking. Someone [*or* Some One]. Walter de la Mare. FaPON; MoBrPo; PDV; SiSoPo
Someone dancing inside us. Advice. Bill Holm. RaBo
Someone Digging in the Ground. Jalal al-Din Rumi, *tr. fr. Persian by* Coleman Barks. RaBo
Someone dropped me on my head? (*LL*) Theory. Dorothy Parker. VBLP
Someone drove a two-by-four. Child's Grave, Hale County, Alabama. Jim Simmerman. WeW
Someone Else. Sophie Behrens. NBrP
Someone else cut off my head. Bread. Brendan Kennelly. PBCIP
Someone else/ looked at the sky. Lady Izumi Shikibu, *tr. fr. Japanese by* Willis Barnstone. BoWoP
Someone enters without knocking. Hunter. Vasco [*or* Vasko] Popa, *tr. fr. Serbo-Croatian by* Anne Pennington. *Fr.* Games. HSix, *tr. by* Charles Simic; RB
Someone fits a flute to his lips, and. Deception. Alfred Corn. PoA
Someone has lived here where twin chimneys. The Grapevine. Zoe Kincaid Brockman. GoYe
Someone has opened and undone. Beyond the Tapestries. Norma Farber. GoYe
Someone has remembered to dry the dishes. Red Lilies. Barbara Guest. PoM
Someone has shut the shining eyes, straightened and folded. Beside the Bed. Charlotte Mew. MoAB; MoBrPo; OxBSP; TrGrPo; WPE
Someone hides from someone. Hide-and-Seek. Vasco [*or* Vasko] Popa, *tr. by* Charles Simic. *Fr.* Games. HSix; RB
Someone, I tell you,/ will remember us. Sappho, *tr. fr. Greek by* Willis Barnstone. BoWoP
Someone in Quaker meeting talks about greed and aggression. Greed and Aggression. Sharon Olds. RaBo
Someone in the next apartment. Room. Ruth Stone. BoWoP
Someone is a rose bush. Vasco [*or* Vasko] Popa. *See* Someone be a rose tree.
Someone is breathing in the room. Waking. Hugh Maxton. BIrV; CIP; PeIV
Someone is coming home. (*LL*) Snow on Lotus Mountain. Liu Ch'ang-ch'ing. OHMPC
Someone is dead. Anne Sexton. WPE
Someone is glad that I, Theodorus, am dead. Simonides, *tr. fr. Greek by* Peter Jay. OBD
(On Theodoros.) GrAn
Someone is locking out the stars and the yellow flowers. Old Man in a Moon Loft. T. Glynne Davies, *tr. fr. Welsh by the author.* OBWVE
Someone is walking through the snow. Hearing Steps. Charles Simic. HCAP
Someone/ just climbed to the top of the cliff. Man Cursing the Sea. Miroslav Holub, *tr. fr. Czech by* Ian Milner *and* George Theiner. AnRep
Someone Knocks. Peter Everwine. NNaP
Someone later may hear these playthings, thinking. Strato, *tr. fr. Greek by* Teddy Hogge. GrAn
Someone Lies On A Path. Allen Grossman. *Fr.* Ether Dome (an Entertainment), The. BAP-91
Someone lies on a path in the Public Garden. Someone Lies On A Path. Allen Grossman. *Fr.* Ether Dome (an Entertainment), The. BAP-91
Someone like No One Else. Forugh Farrokhzad, *tr. fr. Farsi by* Deirdre Lashgari. WPOW
Someone passes. Murasaki Shikibu, *tr. fr. Japanese by* Kenneth Rexroth *and* Ikuko Atsomi. BoWoP
Someone, perhaps a friend. Roses and the Grave. Vera Weislitz. BTR
Someone pouring light. The Open Shutter. Karl Krolow, *tr. fr. German.* TSaS, *tr. by* Kevin Perryman
Someone runs about. Bullfight. Miroslav Holub, *tr. fr. Czech by* Ian Milner *and* Jarmila Milner. RB
Someone said dead men make islands in the sea. Fishermen, Drowned beyond the West Coast. Vivian Smith. CBAP
Someone said, I remember the first hard crack. After the Last Practice. Edward Hirsch. NAmP90
Someone said this was the ugliest cat. The Cat. Sister Mary Norbert Körte. SRLS
Someone sows someone. The Seed. Vasco [*or* Vasko] Popa, *tr. fr. Serbo-Croatian by* Anne Pennington. *Fr.* Games. PoSu; RB
Someone spoke of your death, Herakleitos. It brought me. Callimachus, *tr. fr. Greek by* Peter Jay. GrAn
Someone told me. Patrizia Cavalli, *tr. fr. Italian by* Judith Baumel. NeIt
Someone told me, Heraclitus. Callimachus, *tr. fr. Greek.* *Fr.* Epigrams. HePo
Someone touches my shoulder and *bang* this. Peter Riley. VaA
Someone who well knew how she'd toss her chin. Loose Woman. X. J. Kennedy. WeW

Someone with skill juggles. Juggler. Lucien Stryk. CAPP

Someone would like to have you for her child. *Unknown.* TTTS

Somer is comen and winter gon. *Unknown.* MiEL

Somer is comen with love to toune. *Unknown.* MiEL

Somersby, Lincolnshire; after Leaving the Refectory. Tennyson. *See* Unwatch'd [*or* unwatched], the garden bough shall sway.

Somerset Dam for Supper, The. John Holmes. NYBP

Somerset Wassail. *Unknown. See* Wassail! wassail! all round [*or* over] the town.

Somethin' Else and/ Kind of Blue. Cannon Arrested. Michael S. Harper. Jaz

Something. Robert Creeley. NaP

Something about pumpkins caused. What Brings Us Out. Naomi Shihab Nye. NAmP90

Something about the idea. Abandonment of Autos. Bruce Dawe. CBAP

Something befell. At the Bottom of the Well. Louis Untermeyer. GoJo

Something broken something. Nightbreak. Adrienne Rich. IHMS

Something cracks every moment because. Brief Thoughts on Cracks. Miroslav Holub, tr. fr. *Czech* by Ian Milner *and* Jarmila Milner. PoSu

Something else that went before. (*LL*) The Presence. Maxine W. Kumin. RFM; WPE

Something for Jesus. Sylvanus D. Phelps. *See* Saviour, Thy Dying Love.

Something for My Russian Friends. Edmund Wilson. OBAL

Something for Supper. Carroll Arnett. VoR

Something forgotten for twenty years: though my fathers. A Map of the Western Part of the County of Essex in England. Denise Levertov. CoAP; NAAL-2

Something from the first in the way. Couple. Fiona Hall. NWP

Something gnaws inside my head. Kirilov on a Skyscraper. Randall Jarrell. CAPP

Something hangs in back of me. The Wings. Denise Levertov. CAPP; NALW

Something happened I couldn't have told you then. Blackout Sonnets. Joan Larkin. ETG

Something happened the other day that never happened before. Shovelling Iron Ore. *Unknown.* AS; GBP

Something has ceased to come along with me. Death of a Son. Jon Silkin. FF; GTBS-P; MoP; OxBTC

Something has happened to me. Kofi Awoonor. HBAPE

Something/ holds up two or three leaves. In One Place. Robert Wallace. Poetsp

Something I saw or thought I saw. On the Heart's Beginning to Cloud the Mind. Robert Frost. CMoP

Something I should like to know is, which. Visitors Laugh at Locksmiths or, Hospital Doors Haven't Got Locks Anyhow. Ogden Nash. PFP

Something important about love, and about love's grace. (*LL*) Revelation. Robert Penn Warren. LiTA; NoAM

Something in my soul. Meleager, tr. fr. *Greek* by Sam Hamill. InMo

Something in the climate of a hammer. Because Going Nowhere Takes a Long Time. Kenneth Patchen. NaP

Something in us is angry at the rain. This Room of Trees & Moving Earth/ This Room Where No One Knows How Sky Begins. Sister Mary Norbert Körte. SRLS

Something inspires the only cow of late. The Cow in Apple Time. Robert Frost. MoAB; MoAmPo; OxBSP; PoLF

Something is pushing against my blood. Posthumous. Michael O'Loughlin. IB; PBCIP

Something is shattering high in the frozen. A Heart Attack in the Country. Terry Hummer. NAmP90

Something is taking place. Robert Duncan. *Fr.* Rites of Passage. BCF; NoAM

Something is very gently. The Thread. Denise Levertov. CrSp

Something muffled/ barely audible. The String. Momcilo Nastasijevic, tr. fr. *Serbo-Croatian* by Charles Simic. HSix

Something must be done right away. Song for Those Who Know. Hans Magnus Enzensberger. PoSu

Something occurred after the operation. Surgical Ward: Men. Robert Graves. FaBoMo

Something of a Departure. Paul Muldoon. PBCIP

Something of glass about her, of dead water. Circe. Louis MacNeice. OBMV

Something old and tyrannical burning there. A Coal Fire in Winter. Thomas McGrath. NU; RaBo

Something Old, Something New. Carl H. Greene. NBV

Something out of it, I think. (*LL*) The Best. Elizabeth Barrett Browning. ArNa; CBCK; OxBSP

Something shook itself out of the ash./ Wings. Perhaps. (*LL*) For the Last Time, Fire. Dennis Scott. PBCV

Something startles me where I thought I was safest. This Compost. Walt Whitman. AWP; LiTA; MoAmPo; NAAL-1

Something strange is creeping across me. A Hollywood Everything. John Ashbery. *Fr.* Daffy Duck in Hollywood. CBCK

Something That Has to Do With. Joanne Townsend. NGP

Something there is that doesn't love a wall. Mending Wall. Robert Frost. AmPP; AnAmPo; ClHu; CMoP; CoGr; EBEvV; FaBoPV; FaBV; HAP; HeIP; HoPM; ImGa; InPS; LiTA; LiTM; MeMAP; MoAB; MoAmPo; MoP; NAAL-2; NoAM; NOBA; NoP; OtMeF; OxBA; PoE; Poetr; PrIm; SAmP; SCV; SoSe; TAP; TFi; VGW; WeW

Something this foggy day, a something which. Christina Rossetti. *Fr.* Later Life. NAEL-2

Something to be tinkered with at their leisure. (*LL*) Talk. Roo Borson. NIP; NOBC

Something to Remember Me By. Inge Auerbacher. BTR

Something Told the Wild Geese. Rachel Field. NTCP; OBAP; OBCA; PDV

Something turning slowly green, and holy. (*LL*) This Spring. Regina DeCormier-Shekejian. LoHo

Something under the bones is calling. The Voices. Janine Pommy-Vega. UL

Something was whispered. Accusation. Utahania, tr. fr. *Eskimo.* WTO

Something went crabwise. The Presence. Maxine W. Kumin. RFM; WPE

Something Whispered in the *Shakuhachi.* Garrett Kaoru Hongo. InPS

Something you said — I found it written down. A Postcard to Send to Sumer. William Bronk. VGW

Something's nested/ In his tomb. Hat-Tomb. Guillaume Apollinaire, tr. fr. *French.* CBNP

Something's there, by Pan there's something hidden — . Callimachus, tr. fr. *Greek* by Peter Jay. GrAn

Sometime. May Riley Smith. BLPA

Sometime ago there was a rich old codger, *mod. vers.* by Nevill Coghill. Chaucer. *See* Whylom [*or* Whilom] Ther was dwellinge at Oxenford [*or* Oxenforde].

Sometime during eternity. Lawrence Ferlinghetti. *Fr.* Coney Island of the Mind, A. CAPP; Jaz; NoAM; Poetr

Sometime I fled the fire that me brent. Sir Thomas Wyatt. NoSic; SiPSBD

Sometime I sigh, sometime I sing. Sir Thomas Wyatt. SiPS; SiPSBD

Sometime I sit and wonder long. Dis Time No Stan' Like befo' Time. James Martinez. PBCV

Sometime in the night I stir, rain. Loft. Michael Dransfield. CBAP

Sometime let gorgeous Tragedy. Poetry and the Melancholy Man. Milton. *Fr.* Il Penseroso. AWP; EPCY; FHYEP; GTBS; GTBS-P; HAP; HoPM; ImPo; JCP; LiTB; NoP; NOSC; OAEL-1; OBEV; PPP; TEP; TFi; TrGrPo

Sometime shortly after the rain began. Honeymoon, South Coast. Evan Jones (b. 1927). FaBoMA

Sometime, Somewhere. Ophelia Guyon Browning. *See* Unanswered yet the prayer your lips have pleaded.

Sometime the world seems sad and lonely. Lonely World. Mrs. Henry Linden. CBWP-4

Sometime this winter if you go. Snowflakes. David McCord. SiSoPo

Sometime, when all life's lessons have been learned. Sometime. May Riley Smith. BLPA

Sometimes. Hermann Hesse, tr. fr. *German* by Robert Bly. EaPr; NU

Sometimes. Maggie Pogue Johnson. CBWP-4

Sometimes. Greg Kuzma. Poetsp

Sometimes. Lilian Moore. TLR

Sometimes . . . Injustice. Maurice Kenny. BCF

Sometimes a crumb falls. Luck. Langston Hughes. SAmP

Sometimes a lantern moves along the night. The Lantern out of Doors. Gerard Manley Hopkins. CMoP; LiTB; MeMBP; TrCP

Sometimes a light surprises. Joy and Peace in Believing. William Cowper. NOCV

Sometimes a Man Stands Up During Supper. Rainer Maria Rilke, tr. fr. *German* by Robert Bly. RaBo

Sometimes a mesh of ideas. Dennis Brutus. HBAPE

Sometimes a rain comes. A Rain of Rites. Jayanta Mahapatra. PoA

Sometimes a right white mountain. Sky Pictures. Mary Effie Lee Newsome. CDC

Sometimes after hours of wine I can almost see. Jackson Hotel. Lynda Hull. UTF

Sometimes alone at night. Vanderdecken. Douglas Livingstone. PeSAV

Sometimes, apart in sleep, by chance. The Trance. Stephen Spender. OxBM

Sometimes, around/ Moonrise, a wraith. Skunk. Valerie Worth. OBAP

Sometimes at night when the heart stumbles and stops. Caesura. Kenneth Mackenzie. CBAP; FaBoMA; NOBAu

Sometimes before great events a person will try. Things That Happen. William Stafford. NNaP

Sometimes, childishly watching a beetle, thrush or trout. Clarence Mangan. Thomas Kinsella. CIP

Sometimes goldfinches one by one will drop. Keats. *Fr.* I Stood Tiptoe [upon a Little Hill]. EnRP; FaPON (Goldfinches.) GN

Sometimes he was cool like an eternal. Lester Young. Ted Joans. Jaz

Sometimes I. Song of the Thunders. *Unknown, tr. fr. Chippewa Indian by Frances Densmore.* OBVE

Sometimes I am a Tapster new. The Jolly Trades-Men. *Unknown.* CoMu

Sometimes I am an unseen. Cat. Alan Brownjohn. CRH

Sometimes I catch a glimpse of it. The Presence. Dana Naone. CDW

Sometimes/ I cool out. Spacin. Ronda Davis. JB

Sometimes I dont understand you, sometimes i sit helpless in. Lorelei. Alta. CrSp

Sometimes I dress, with women sit. Matthew Green. *Fr.* Spleen, The. ECEV

Sometimes I feel like I will never stop. To Satch. Samuel Allen. PoBA; PoNe; TTY

Sometimes I feel so passionate a yearning. As by Fire. Ella Wheeler Wilcox. AmWP; AnAmPo

Sometimes I fly at dawn above the sea. The Dawn Patrol. Paul Bewsher. NSI

Sometimes I get the feeling that I have been here before. Reincarnation. Mae Jackson. PoBA

Sometimes/ I go about pitying myself. *Unknown, tr. fr. Chippewa Indian by Frances Densmore.* EaPr; RaBo, *sl. diff. vers.*

Sometimes I Go to Camarillo and Sit in the Lounge. K. Curtis Lyle. NBV; PoBA

Sometimes I have supposed seals. Soft Wood. Robert Lowell. LiTM

Sometimes I have to cross the road. Bobby Blue. John Drinkwater. FaPON

Sometimes/ I help my dad. Automobile Mechanics. Dorothy W. Baruch. FaPON

Sometimes, I know not why, nor how, nor whence. Inspirations. William James Dawson. WGRP

Sometimes I know the way. Absence. Charlotte Mew. MoAB; MoBrPo

Sometimes I like to go. Memorandum. Rudy Bee Graham. PoNe

Sometimes I pause and sadly think. It Might Have Been Worse. G. J. Russell. PoToHe

Sometimes I recall how, in the early eighteen-eighties. Stars in Sand. Francis Carey Slater. PeSAV

Sometimes I see churches. Winter Walking. Alfred W. Purdy. NoAM

Sometimes I see them. Galway Kinnell. *Fr.* Ruins under the Stars. LCAP; NaP; RFM

Sometimes I stare into an awning of spirit. Sometimes I Go to Camarillo and Sit in the Lounge. K. Curtis Lyle. NBV; PoBA

Sometimes I think. Last Flash. Erica Jong. WoWa

Sometimes I think that nothing. Small-scale Reflections on a Great House. A. K. Ramanujan. OxBC

Sometimes I think we're like. Boarded Up. Al Masarik. NGP

Sometimes I walk in the shadow. Walking with God. *Unknown.* BLRP

Sometimes I walk where the deep water dips. Frederick Goddard Tuckerman. *Fr.* Sonnets. NOBA

Sometimes I want to die because of this. (*LL*) The Holes. Stephen Berg. NaP; NYBP

Sometimes I watch the moon at night. The Moon and a Cloud. W. H. Davies. RB

Sometimes I wish that I his pillow were. Richard Barnfield. *Fr.* Sonnets. PeHV

Sometimes I wish that I might do. Patience. G. A. Studdert-Kennedy. TrPWD

Sometimes I wish that I were Helen-fair. Lesbia Harford. NOBAu

Sometimes in bonnet that she. Heart-summoned. Jesse Stuart. GoYe

Sometimes, in morning sunlights by the river. Resurrection. Sidney Lanier. PoEL-5

Sometimes in summer months, the gestate earth. Summer Idyll. George Barker. FaBoMo

Sometimes, in the middle of the lesson. Music Lessons. Mary Oliver. CAPP

Sometimes in the over-heated house, but not for long. Fame. Charlotte Mew. BrRo; InPK; PBWP

Sometimes/ in the tangled boughs. A Dream of Paradise in the Shadow of War. Munir Niazi, *tr. fr. Arabic.* TSaS, *tr. by Daud Kamal*

Sometimes in weariness I stop. Years. Jon Anderson. AmPA

Sometimes it happens. The Porch. Gary Gildner. NGP

Sometimes it seems. The Children. Susan MacDonald. IHMS

Sometimes it seems as though some puppet player. The Puppet Player. Angelina Weld Grimké. CDC

Sometimes I've seen. A Little Bird's Song. Margaret Rose. BoTP

Sometimes my daughter looks at me with an. The Sign of Saturn. Sharon Olds. InPS

Sometimes, old pal, in the morning. Is It Really Worth the While? *Unknown.* BLPA

Sometimes, riding in a car, in Wisconsin. Three Kinds of Pleasures. Robert Bly. AiP

Sometimes she is a child within mine arms. Heart's Haven. Dante Gabriel Rossetti. *Fr.* House of Life, The. Son

Sometimes she is like sherry, like the sun through a vessel of glass. Polarities. Kenneth Slessor. CBAP

Sometimes, she remembers, a chipped flint. Imago. Amy Clampitt. VCAP

Sometimes she wished they were travelling again. Wedding in the Port. Sophie Behrens. NBrP

Sometimes the celestial syrup slows. Terminations. A. R. Ammons. AnAn

Sometimes the frugal matron seems in haste. William King. *Fr.* Art of Making Puddings, The. FaBoUs

Sometimes the lake water writes and writes and gets. To a Girl Writing Her Father's Death. Beckian Fritz Goldberg. NAmP90

Sometimes the light falls here too as at Florence. The Old Age of Michelangelo. F. T. Prince. PeSA

Sometimes the night echoes to prideless wailing. John Berryman. NoAM

Sometimes the night is not enough. I rise remembering. The Biplane. Steve Orlen. GOYP

Sometimes the pencil, in cool airy halls. James Thomson. *Fr.* Castle of Indolence, The. PoEL-3, I

Sometimes/ the poems. Sharon Scott. JB

Sometimes the sea lays. Dragging in Winter. David McElroy. AmPA

Sometimes the weather goes on for days. The Mystery of Emily Dickinson. Marvin Bell. CAPP

Sometimes there are airs grave and gentle. *Unknown.* PeLi

Sometimes there is a man. John Clare. Mark Halperin. SM

Sometimes they cross an avenue at dusk. Survivors. Frank Ormsby. CIP

Sometimes they smear the evening on the air. Bat Angels. Larry Levis. AmPA

Sometimes they thought he might be only shewn. Milton. *Fr.* Paradise Regained [*or* Regain'd]. PeECV, *bk.* II, *ll.* 13–29

Sometimes this quiet settles in like a stone. A Letter from a Friend. Carolyn Maisel. IHMS

Sometimes to think about age. Age. Rae Desmond Jones. CBAP

Sometimes up out of this land. Bifocal. William Stafford. RB

Sometimes waking, sometimes sleeping. Nestus Gurley. Randall Jarrell. HeIP; TwCP

Sometimes walking late at night. Butcher Shop. Charles Simic. AmPA; InPK; LCAP; NNaP

Sometimes want makes touch too much. Warmth. Barton Sutter. GOYP

Sometimes we get up. Resurrection. Marie Luise Kaschnitz, *tr. fr. German by Michael Hamburger.* WPOW

Sometimes we go our way carefree. Rebirth. Margaret E. Bruner. PoToHe

Sometimes we sit in Phil's. My Care. Peter Fallon. CIP

Sometimes, when a bird cries out. Sometimes. Hermann Hesse, *tr. fr. German by Robert Bly.* EaPr; NU

Sometimes when a customer in a shadowy restaurant. Signs. Jean Follain, *tr. fr. French by W. S. Merwin.* AnRep

Sometimes when alone. Outcast[, The]. "Æ." OxBSP

Sometimes when clouds float. At the Edge of Town. William Stafford. NNaP

Sometimes when I feel hurried or dismayed. For One Who Is Serene. Margaret E. Bruner. PoToHe

Sometimes when I have dropped to sleep. The Room beneath the Rafters. Ella Wheeler Wilcox. PWR

Sometimes when I hold. The School Globe. James Reaney. NOBC

Sometimes when I see the bare arms of trees in the evening. The Bare Arms of Trees. John Tagliabue. Poetsp

Sometimes when I'm lonely. Hope. Langston Hughes. OBAL; OBCA; TRP

Sometimes when my eyes are red. My Sad Self. Allen Ginsberg. Poetr; UnPo; VCAP

Sometimes When Night. V. Sackville-West. WPE

Sometimes when the boy was troubled he would go. The Cave. Glenn Ward Dresbach. RFM

Sometimes when you are gone. Suite from Catullus. Vincent McHugh. ErPo

Sometimes when you couldn't sleep it off. Cows. Stanley Plumly. AnAn

Sometimes, when you're away from home. Away from Home. *Unknown*. PWR

Sometimes, when you're called a bastard. When Something Happens. James A. Randall, Jr. BPo

Sometimes while I sleep. 1925. Edwin Honig. *Fr.* To Restore a Dead Child. NoAM

Sometimes with One I Love. Walt Whitman. ArLo; GBL; OxBSP; SAmP

Sometimes with one I love I fill myself with rage for fear. Sometimes with One I Love. Walt Whitman. ArLo; GBL; OxBSP; SAmP

Sometimes you brought invective down. On Dublin. Oliver St. John Gogarty. *Fr.* Elegy on the Archpoet William Butler Yeats Lately Dead. IHNG

Sometimes you come on a whole. Driving through Coal Country in Pennsylvania. Jonathan Holden. GOYP

Sometimes/ you feel/ like/ a/ bottle. No Deposit. Earle Thompson. HATNAP

Somewhat back from the village street. The Old Clock on the Stairs. Longfellow. PWR; WBLP

Somewhat more splendid in dress, in a waistcoat work of a lady. Arthur Hugh Clough. *Fr.* Bothie of Tober-na-Vuolich, The [A Long-Vacation Pastoral]. FaBoVe; OBF

Somewhere. Sir Edwin Arnold. *See* Somewhere there waiteth in this world of ours.

Somewhere. Robert Creeley. NoAM

Somewhere. Walter de la Mare. FaPON

Somewhere, a cup tinkles in its saucer. The English Earthquake. Eva Salzman. NWP

Somewhere a forest, every. These Leaves. William Stafford. NNaP

Somewhere a man puts on his shorts. Andrei Voznesensky, *tr. fr. Russian by* William Jay Smith *and* Vera Dunham. CBNP

Somewhere/ a niche. Wish. Lance Henson. CDW

Somewhere afield here something lies. Shelley's Skylark. Thomas Hardy. FaBV

Somewhere along the Way. Henry Taylor. Poetr

Somewhere beneath that piano's superb sleek black. The Piano. D. H. Lawrence. WeW

Somewhere East of Suez. H. W. Berry. NSI

Somewhere his number must have been betrayed. The Common Man. A. J. M. Smith. NOBC

Somewhere I Have Never Travelled[, Gladly Beyond]. E. E. Cummings. ArLo; BoLoP; InPS; LiTA; LiTM; LPA; MoAB; MoAmPo; NAAL-2; NoP; Poetr; SOTW; TrGrPo; TwCP; UnAS; VGW

Somewhere I read that high and loe notes. Comfort. Maura Stanton. SoSe

Somewhere, I think in Dakota. A Sound from the Earth. William Stafford. NNaP; RFM

Somewhere in. Ifé: A Bronze Lament. Askia Muhammad Touré. BCF

Somewhere in Africa. Anne Sexton. NALW

Somewhere in Chelsea, early summer. Relating to Robinson. Weldon Kees. NaP

Somewhere, in deeps. Sport. Hamlin Garland. AnAmPo

"Somewhere in France," upon a brown hillside. The First Three. Clinton Scollard. PAH

Somewhere in his body a blood-clot is moving. Little Death. Gwyn Thomas, *tr. fr. Welsh by* Joseph P. Clancy. OBWVE

Somewhere in India, upon a time. An Oriental Apologue. James Russell Lowell. PoEL-5

Somewhere in Mauriac a girl. F. T. Prince. *Fr.* Memoirs in Oxford. PeSAV

Somewhere in the next block. Early Sunday Morning. John Stone. MT

Somewhere in the night. At Midnight. Ted Kooser. GOYP

Somewhere inside me. Coming Back Home. Ray A. Young Bear. CDW

Somewhere Is Such a Kingdom. John Crowe Ransom. CMoP; LiTA

Somewhere it being yesterday. A Song of Mary. Lucille Clifton. NALW

Somewhere it is about to snow. Weather Forecast. Linda Pastan. AnAn

Somewhere near here a new-loosed creek sloughs down. A Walk in March. Tim Reynolds. MAT

Somewhere near the end of a snowshoe trail. A Baby Ten Months Old Looks at the Public Domain. William Stafford. NYBP

Somewhere now she takes off the dress I am putting. Palindrome. Lisel Mueller. IHMS; WeW

Somewhere nowhere in Utah, a boy by the roadside. Utah. Anne Stevenson. FaBoVe

Somewhere on his travels the strange child. Santa Claus. Howard Nemerov. HAP

Somewhere or Other. Christina Rossetti. FaBoVe; NOBE; NOBVV

Somewhere or other there must surely be. Somewhere or Other. Christina Rossetti. FaBoVe; NOBE; NOBVV

Somewhere outside your window. A Sense of Coolness. Quincy Troupe. PoBA

Somewhere overseas England are struggling. Homing In. U. A. Fanthorpe. VBLP

Somewhere she waits to make you win, your soul in her firm, white hands. The Woman Who Understands. Everard Jack Appleton. PoLF

Somewhere she was certain, but the sensation. Special Pleading. Charles Bernstein. UL

Somewhere someone is traveling furiously toward you. At North Farm. John Ashbery. HCAP; PoE; Poetr

Somewhere, sometime, in an April twilight. Willa Cather. WPE

Somewhere, somewhen I've seen. The Parrots. W. W. Gibson. CH

Somewhere the Equation Breaks Down. Daniel Berrigan. NYBP

Somewhere there figures a man. In uniform. Kings' Daughters, Home for Unwed Mothers, 1948. C. D. Wright. NAmP90

Somewhere there is Grace, Lord. Latter Day Psalms. Cliff Ashby. NOCV

Somewhere there waiteth in this world of ours. Destiny. Sir Edwin Arnold. PoLF

(Somewhere.) PoToHe

Somewhere you are always going home. The Sums. Lauris Edmond. FaBoWP

Somewhile before the dawn I rose, and stept. A Memory. Rupert Brooke. PFP

Somnolence of star-stones, ice-tears, The. Laurentia. Medbh McGuckian. BiHa

Somnolent through landscapes and by trees. The Permanent Tourists. P. K. Page. LiTM; NOBC

Somnour was ther with us in that place, A. Chaucer. *Fr.* Canterbury Tales, The. EnVB; FHYEP; NoP; OAEL-1; PPP, *abr.*

Somnus, the humble god, that dwells. Sir John Denham. BeJo

Somtyme the world was so stedfast and stable. Chaucer. MiEL

Son, The. John Donne. *Fr.* Litanie, The. NOCV; PoEL-2

Son. James A. Emanuel. PoNe

Son, The. George Herbert. *Fr.* Temple, The. GeHe; Son

Son, The. Denise Levertov. NALW

Son, The. R. S. Thomas. NAs

Son, The. Ridgely Torrence. InvP

Son, A. Kipling. *Fr.* Epitaphs of the War, 1914–1918. FaBoEE; NoP; OBWP; PeFWW

Son and Surf. Julia Hurd Strong. GoYe

"Son, come tell me 'bout the meetin." The Old and the New. Clara Ann Thompson. CBWP-2

Son Cotton! these light idle brooks. Izaac Walton, Cotton, and William Oldways. Walter Savage Landor. PoEL-4

Son David. *Unknown*. OxBB; OxBS

Son-Days [dayes]. Henry Vaughan. CBCK; GeHe; NOSC; SeCP

Son, my son! Lament of a Man for His Son. *Unknown, tr. fr. Paiute Indian by* Mary Austin. AWP; IMW

(Lament of a Young Man for His Son.) DL

Son of a Gambolier, The. *Unknown*. AS

Son of a mystic race, he came. Heinrich Heine. Ludwig Lewisohn. TrJP

Son of Enops, Thestor next he smote, The. Homer, *tr. by* William Cowper. *Fr.* Iliad, The. OBVE

Son of God Goes Forth to War, The. Who Follows in His Train? Reginald Heber. WGRP

Son, of great fortune have I none. Christine to Her Son. Christine de Pisan, *tr. fr. French by* Barbara Howes. BoWoP

Son of the King of Moy, The. *Unknown, tr. fr. Old Irish by* Myles Dillon. PeIV

Son of the righteous one, he who thunders on the ground. Praises of the King Tshaka. *Unknown, tr. fr. Zulu*. PeSA

Son of the Romanovs, A. Louis Simpson. OxBC

Son of the Thundercloud. Song of the Thunder. *Unknown, tr. fr. Hottentot*. PeSA

Son of the virgin, Heavenly Child! On the ground. Sleeping Christchild. Eduard Friedrich Mörike, *tr. fr. German by* Philip L. Miller. RiWo

Son replied, The, "For all your good advice." To His Father on Praising the Honest Life of the Peasant. Parvin E'tesami, *tr. fr. Persian by* Deirdre Lashgari. WPOW

Son who came forth on a winter's morning. Song for Te Hauapu. Noho-mai-te-Rangi, *tr. fr. Maori by* Margaret Orbell. PeNZ

Son'ahchi. The Boy and the Deer. Andrew Peynetsa, *tr. by* Dennis Tedlock. STP

Sonata. John Fuller. DiPo

Sonatina Followed by Another, A, *sels.* Gertrude Stein. "She is that kind of a wife. She can see." VBLP

Sonatina in Yellow. Donald Justice. CAPP; LCAP

Sondayes. Henry Vaughan. *See* Bright shadows of true Rest! some shoots of bliss[e].

Sonet: "Fra bank [*or* banc] to bank [*or* banc], fra wood [*or* wod] to wood [*or* wod] I rin." Mark Alexander Boyd. *See* Fra banc to banc, fra wod to wod, I rin.

Sonet to Sleepe. William Drummond of Hawthornden. *See* Sleep, Silence' Child.

Sonet Written in Prayse of the Browne Beautie, A. George Gascoigne. AAS

Sonetto XXXV: To Guido Orlando. Cavalcanti, *tr. fr. Italian by* Ezra Pound. CTC

Song. Dryden. *See* Sylvia the fair, in the bloom of fifteen.

Song. Ebenezer Elliot. *See* When working blackguards come to blows.

Song. Thomas Hood. *See* He dreamt that he saw the buffalant.

Song. Ben Jonson. *See* Still to be neat, still to be dressed [*or* drest].

Song. Charles Kingsley. *See* I once had a sweet little doll, dears.

Song. Philip Massinger. *See* Why art thou slow, thou rest of trouble, Death.

Song. Milton. *See* Sabrina fair.

Song. Shakespeare. *See* Tell Me Where Is Fancy [*or* Fancie] Bred.

Song. Shakespeare. *See* Who is Silvia? what is she.

Song. William Shenstone. GGP

Song. Sheridan. *See* Here's to the maiden of bashful fifteen.

Song. James Shirley. *See* Victorious Men of Earth.

Song. *Unknown.* BXAP

Song. *Unknown.* EIl

Song, [A]: "Ask [*or* Aske] me no more where Jove bestows." Thomas Carew. *See* Ask [*or* Aske] Me No More Where Jove Bestows [*or* Bestowes].

Song: "Absent from thee, I languish still." The Earl of Rochester. BoLoP; ELP; EnLoPo; GBL; SeCV-2
(Return.) NOBE; OBEV

Song: "Adieu, farewell earth's blisse." Thomas Nashe. *See* Adieu, Farewell, Earth's Bliss[e].

Song: "Ae fond kiss, and then we sever." Burns. *See* Ae fond kiss, and then we sever.

Song: "Afternoon cooking in the fall sun." Robert Hass. AmPA

Song: "Again rejoicing Nature sees." Burns. BoNaP

Song: "Ah! County Guy, the hour is nigh." Sir Walter Scott. *See* Ah! County Guy, the hour is nigh.

Song: "Ah Dangerous Swain, tell me no more." Delariviere Manley. *Fr.* Lost Lover, The. KTR

Song: "Ah fading joy, how quickly art thou past!" Dryden. *See* Ah, Fading Joy.

Song: "Ah false Amyntas, can that hour." Aphra Behn. *Fr.* Dutch Lover, The. WPE

Song: "Ah, vale of woe, of gloom and darkness moulded." Rachel Morpurgo, *tr. fr. Hebrew by* Nina Davis Salaman. TrJP

Song: "All, all of a piece throughout." Dryden. *See* All, all of a piece throughout.

Song: "All joy to mortals, joy and mirth." Aphra Behn. *Fr.* Emperor of the Moon. WPE

Song: "All night I weep, all day I cry, ay me." Mary Sidney Wroth, Countess of Montgomery. *Fr.* Urania. NOSC; WPE

Song: "And can the physician make sick men well?" *Unknown. See* And can the physician make sick men well?

Song: "April, April,/ Laugh thy girlish laughter." Sir William Watson. OBEV; TrGrPo
(April.) BoTP; FaBV
(Song to April.) GN

Song: "Are they shadowes that we see?" Samuel Daniel. *See* Are they shadows that we see?

Song: "As Chloris [*or* Cloris] full of harmless thoughts." The Earl of Rochester. ErPo; TEP

Song: "As I walked out one evening." W. H. Auden. *See* As I Walked Out One Evening.

Song III: "As Phyllis the gay, at the break of the day." Edward Moore. ECEV

Song: "At the center of the earth." *Unknown, tr. fr. Chippewa Indian by* Jerome K. Rothenberg. STP

Song: "Balkis was in her marble town." Lascelles Abercrombie. *Fr.* Judith. MoBrPo

Song: "Barefaced baby with the three minute dream." Thomas McGrath. BCF

Song: "Beauty no more the subject be." Thomas Nabbes. NOSC

Song: "Because I know deep in my own heart." Pauli Murray. BlSi

Song: "Because they are traitors, your eyes." Manuel de Falla, *tr. fr. Spanish by* Philip L. Miller. RiWo

Song: "Before the barn-door crowing." John Gay. *Fr.* Beggar's Opera, The. ErPo; OAEL-1; OxBSP; PoEL-3

Song: "Before we shall again behold." Sir William Davenant. *See* Before we shall again behold.

Song: "Blow, blow, thou winter wind." Shakespeare. *Fr.* As You Like It. AWP; CH; ChTr; EiL; ELP; EnRePo; GBL; GTBS; GTBS-P; ImPo; InPS; LiTB; NAEL-1; NOBE; NoP; NoSic; OAEL-1; OBEV; PrIm; SCGP; TrGrPo; WiR
(Blow, Thou Winter Wind.) 09FaFP; 08TreF
(Song: "Blow, blow, thou winter wind.") CTC; EBEvV; OxAEP-1; PoEL-2
(Songs of the Greenwood: "Blow, blow, thou winter wind.") TrGrPo

Song: "Boat is chafing at our long delay, The." John Davidson. OBEV

Song: "Bone-aged is my white horse." Brenda Chamberlain. (Talysarn.) OBWVE

Song: Brignall Banks. Sir Walter Scott. *See* O [*or* Oh], Brignal[l] banks are wild and fair.

Song: "But I'm the one from whom they stole a button from his trouser leg." Milorad Pavic. *Fr.* Holy Mass For Relja Krilatica. HSix

Song: "But I'm the one to whom others spit in the hand when he works." Milorad Pavic. *Fr.* Holy Mass For Relja Krilatica. HSix

Song: "But I'm the one who carries a garlic clove in the ear." Milorad Pavic. *Fr.* Holy Mass For Relja Krilatica. HSix

Song: "Caesar's back, and they've built him a throne to sit on." Christiania Whitehead. NWP

Song: "Calm was the even, and clear [*or* cleer] was the sky." Dryden. *Fr.* Evening's Love, An. FF; SeCV-2

Song: "Can life be a blessing." Dryden. *See* Can Life Be a Blessing.

Song: "Can love be controlled by advice?" John Gay. *Fr.* Beggar's Opera, The. OAEL-1; OxBSP

Song: "Care-charming sleep, thou easer of all woes." John Fletcher. *See* Care-charming Sleep [Thou Easer of All Woes].

Song: "Child, is thy father dead?" Ebenezer Elliot. FaBoEH

Song: "Chloris, forbear a while." Henry Bold. GBL; NOSC

Song: "Chloris, it is not thy disdaine." Sidney Godolphin. *See* Cloris, it is not thy disdaine.

Song: "Choose now among this fairest number." William Browne. GBL

Song: "Christ keep the Hollow Land." William Morris. *See* Christ keep the Hollow Land.

Song: "Cloris misfortunes that can be exprest." Elizabeth Wilmot, Countess of Rochester. KTR

Song: "Come away, come away, death." Shakespeare. *See* Come away, come away, death.

Song: "Come, cheer up, my lads, like a true British band." *Unknown.* PAH

Song: "Come into the garden, Maud." Tennyson. *See* Come into the garden, Maud.

Song: "Come, live with me and be my love." C. Day Lewis. *See* Come, live with me and be my love.

Song: "Come on, come on! and where you go." Ben Jonson. *Fr.* Pleasure Reconciled to Virtue. NAEL-1; OAEL-1

Song: "Come unto these yellow sands." Shakespeare. *Fr.* Tempest, The. BoTP; CH; EiL; NOSC; NoSic; OAEL-1; OBEV; SCGP; SoSe; TFi; TTTS
(Ariel's Song: "Come unto these yellow sands.") CTC; FaBoCh; GN; GoJo; NOBE; TEP
(Song: "Come unto these yellow sands.") EBEvV; PoEL-2

Song: "Curse upon that faithless maid, A." Aphra Behn. *Fr.* Emperor of the Moon. WPE

Song: "Day will rise and the sun from eastward." George Campbell Hay. OxBS

Song: "Deftly, admiral, cast your fly." W. H. Auden. GTBS-P

Song: "Delicious beauty that doth lie." John Marston. EiL

Song: "Did you see me walking by the Buick Repairs?" Frank O'Hara. TTTS

Song: "Distil not poison in mine ears." John Hall. OxBSP

Song: "Do not fear to put thy feet." John Fletcher. *See* Do not fear to put thy feet.

Song: "Do your balls hang low?" *Unknown.* NSI

Song: "Does the policeman sleep with his boots on." Gerda Mayer. FaBoBl; PeLV

Song: "Donought would have everything." Ebenezer Elliot. NOBVV

Song: "Don't Tell Me What You Dreamt Last Night." Franklin P. Adams. FiBHP

Song: "Dorinda's sparkling wit, and eyes." Charles Sackville. *See* Dorinda's sparkling wit, and eyes.

Song: "Dressed up in my melancholy." M. Carl Holman. PoNe

Song: "Drinke and be merry, merry, merry boyes." Thomas Morton. SCAP

Song: "Each night I sleep more lightly." Herman von Lingg, *tr. fr. German* by Philip L. Miller. RiWo

Song: "Endimion Porter and Olivia." Sir William Davenant. *See* Before we shall again behold.

Song: Eternity of Love Protested. Thomas Carew. *See* How ill doth he deserve a lovers [*or* lover's] name.

Song: "Eye of looking back were well, An." Ben Jonson. *Fr.* Pleasure Reconciled to Virtue. NAEL-1; OAEL-1

Song: "Fair Chloris in a pigsty lay." The Earl of Rochester. *See* Fair Cloris in a pig-stye lay.

Song: "Fair Iris I love, and hourly I die." Dryden. *Fr.* Amphitryon. AWP (Mercury's Song [to Phaedra].) NOSC; OxBSP; PoEL-3; SeCV-2

Song: "Fairest Nymph that ever bless'd our Shore." Mary Pix. *Fr.* Spanish Wives, The. KTR

Song: "False though she be to me and love." Congreve. *See* False Though She Be.

Song: "Fame let thy trumpet sound." Joel Barlow. AmPP

Song: "Farewell, adieu, that court-like life!" John Pickering. *See* Farewell, adieu, that courtly life.

Song: "Farewell my Betty, and farewell my Annie." Christian Carstairs. ECWP

Song: "Farewell ungrateful[l] traytor [*or* traitor]." Dryden. *See* Farewell, Ungrateful Traitor.

Song: "Fear no more the heat o' the Sun." Shakespeare. *Fr.* Cymbeline. AWP; CH; ChTr; ClHu; CoGr; EBEV; EiL; ELP; EnRePo; FaPoB; FF; GBL; HAP; ImPo; InPS; LiTB; Mes; NAEL-1; NoP; NoSic; OBD; OxAEP-1; PoRA; PrIm; RB; SCGP; SCV; SoSe; TFi; TrGrPo
(Dirge: "Fear no more the heat o' the sun.") OAEL-1
(Dirge for Fidele.) NOBE
(Fidele.) GTBS; GTBS-P; OBEV
(Fidele's Dirge.) FaBoCh
(Song: "Fear[e] no more the heat[e] o' the sun.") CTC; EBEvV; NOSC; PoE; PoEL-2

Song: "Feathers of the willow, The." Richard Watson Dixon. BoNaP; CH; FaBoCh; GTBS-P; NOBE; OBNC
(Willow.) OBEV

Song: Fie My Fum. Allen Ginsberg. ErPo

Song: "Fire, fire." Henry Bold. GBL

Song: "First month of his absence, The." Alun Lewis. LiTM; NAEL-2; OBWP

Song: "Fish in the unruffled lakes." W. H. Auden. BoLoP; CBLP; CMoP; MoAB; MoBrPo; MoP

Song: "Flowers that in thy garden rise, The." Sir Henry Newbolt. FaBoTw

Song: "Fond affection, hence, and leave me!" Robert Parry. *Fr.* Mirror of Knighthood, The. EiL

Song: "Fond men! whose wretched care the life soon ending." Phineas Fletcher. *Fr.* Brittain's Ida. EiL

Song: "Fool, take up thy shaft again." Thomas Stanley. EnLoPo

Song: "Foolish eyes, thy streams give over." Martha Sansom. ECWP

Song: "For her gait, if she be walking." William Browne. OBEV
(Sonnet.) NOSC

Song: "For mercy, courage, kindness, mirth." Laurence Binyon. BoTP; MoBrPo

Song: "For the tender beech and the sapling oak." Thomas Love Peacock. *See* For the Slender Beech and the Sapling Oak.

Song: "Four arms, two necks, one wreathing." *Unknown.* CBLP; EiL

Song: "Fresh from the dewy hill, the merry year." Blake. EnRP; PeECV

Song: "Full fathom [*or* fadom] five thy father lies." Shakespeare. *See* Full fathom [*or* fadom] five thy father lies.

Song: "Give Isaac the nymph who no beauty can boast." Sheridan. *Fr.* Duenna, The. NOIV

Song: "Give me leave to rail at you." The Earl of Rochester. NOSC

Song: "Give me more love, or more disdain." Thomas Carew. BeJo; PFP

Song: "Go and catch a falling star." John Donne. AWP; ClHu; CoGr; EBEV; EiL; ELP; EnRePo; FaBV; FHYEP; HAP; HeiP; ImPo; InPK; InPS; JCP; LiTB; NAEL-1; NAWM-1; NIP; NOBE; NoP; OBEV; OxAEP-1; SoSe; TFi; TrGrPo
(Goe and catche a falling starre.) CBNP; ESCV; FaPoB; HoPM; MeLP; NBLV; PoEL-2; SeCP; SeCV-1
(Song: Go and Catch a Falling Star.) ArLo; EBEvV; GGP; NOSC; PoE

Song: "Go [*or* Goe] lovely rose." Edmund Waller. *See* Go [*or* goe], lovely rose.

Song: Good Counsel to a Young Maid. Thomas Carew. *See* When you the sunburnt pilgrim see.

Song: Good Counsel to a Young Maid. Thomas Carew. *See* Gaze not on thy beauties pride.

Song: "Great friend and servant of the good." Ben Jonson. *Fr.* Pleasure Reconciled to Virtue. NAEL-1; OAEL-1

Song: Green Grow the Rashes. Burns. *See* Green Grow the Rashes, O.

Song: "Hang sorrow, cast away care." *Unknown.* NOSC

Song: "Hark! hark! the lark at heaven's gate sings." Shakespeare. *Fr.* Cymbeline. AWP; BoTP; CH; ChTr; EnRePo; FaBoCh; FaBV; FaPON; ImPo; LiTB; NIP; NoP; NoSic; PFP; PrIm; TFi; TrGrPo; UV
(Aubade: "Hark! hark! the lark at heaven's gate sings.") OBEV
(Morning Song, A.) GN
(Song: "Hark! hark! the lark at heaven's gate sings.") NOSC; EBEvV; EiL; 09FiP

Song: "Hark! 'tis freedom that calls, come, patriots, awake!" *Unknown.* PAH

Song: "Hast thou seen the down i' th' air." Sir John Suckling. *See* Hast thou seen the down i' th' air.

Song: "He that will court a wench that is coy." *Unknown.* ErPo

Song: "Heap cassia, sandal-buds and stripes." Robert Browning. *Fr.* Paracelsus. OBEV

Song: "Hear me, ye smokeless skies and grass-green earth." Charles Mair. *Fr.* Last Bison, The. NOBC

Song: "Heare ye Ladies that despise." John Fletcher. *See* Hear, Ye Ladies [That Despise].

Song: "Hears not my Phillis how the birds." Sir Charles Sedley. EnLoPo; SeCV-2

Song: "Hence all you vaine delights." John Fletcher. *See* Hence all you vain delights.

Song: "Here's to the maiden of bashful fifteen." Sheridan. *Fr.* School for Scandal, The. NOIV
(Here's to the Maiden.) ELP
(Song: "Here's to the maiden [*or* maid] of bashful fifteen.") NOEC; OxAEP-1; OxBoLi; PoRA
(Song.) EBEvV; PeLV

Song: "Hold back thy hours, dark night, till we have done." Francis Beaumont *and* John Fletcher. *See* Hold back thy hours.

Song: How Can I Care? Robert Graves. GBL

Song: "How many times do I love thee, dear?" Thomas Lovell Beddoes. *Fr.* Torrismond. LiTB; PoEL-4; TrGrPo
(How Many Times?) ELP
(How Many Times Do I Love Thee, Dear?) EnRP; NAEL-2
(Song.) ImPo

Song: "How pleasant it is that always." Florence Smith. BLPA

Song: "How should I your true love know." Shakespeare. *See* How should I your true love know.

Song: "How strongly does my passion flow." Aphra Behn. OxAEP-1

Song: "How sweet I roamed from field to field." Blake. CH; ChTr; EnLoPo; EnRP; LiTB; MeMBP; NAEL-2; NOEC; NoP; OAEL-2; OBNC; PoEL-4; TFi; TrGrPo
(Prince of Love, The.) NOBE
(Song.) ImPo; Poetr

Song: "I am weaving a song of waters." Gwendolyn B. Bennett. BlSi; ShDr

Song: "I can't be talkin' of love, dear." Esther Mathews. ImPo

Song: "I feed a flame within, which so torments me." Dryden. *Fr.* Secret Love; or, The Maiden Queen. AWP
(Hidden Flame.) OBEV

Song: "I had a bicycle called 'Splendid.'" Arthur Waley. Mes

Song: "I had a dove, and the sweet dove died." Keats. *Fr.* I Had a Dove [and the Sweet Dove Died]. CH; FaPON; OBEV

Song: "I hid my love when young while I." John Clare. *See* I hid my love when young while I.

Song: "I keep running around." *Unknown, tr. fr. Chippewa Indian by* Jerome K. Rothenberg. STP

Song: "I know that any weed can tell." Louis Ginsberg. TrJP

Song: "I made another garden, yea." Arthur O'Shaughnessy. OBEV

Song: "I peeled bits of straw and I got switches too." John Clare. NAEL-2
(Bits of Straw.) WiR

Song: "I placed my dream in a boat." Cecília Meireles, *tr. fr. Portuguese by* Eloah F. Giacomelli. TSaS; WPOW

Song: "I prithee let my heart alone." Thomas Stanley. BeJo

Song: "I prithee send me back my heart." *At. to* Henry Hughes Suckling *and also to* Sir John Suckling. JCP

Song: "I prithee spare me, gentle boy." Sir John Suckling. BeJo

Song: "I sing a song of sorrow." J. L. Kubíček. BTR

Song: "I thought no more was needed." W. B. Yeats. CBLP

Song: "I walk'd in the lonesome evening." William Allingham. EnLoPo

Song: "I was so chill, and overworn, and sad." Anna Wickham. MoBrPo

Song: "I went my Sunday mornings round." John Clare. NOBVV

Song: "I went to her who loveth me no more." Arthur O'Shaughnessy. OBNC

Song: "I wish I was where I would be." John Clare. NOBVV

Song: "I Work with the shape." Michael McClure. PoBeRe

Song: "I would not feign a single sigh." John Clare. GBL

Song: "If any wench Venus's girdle wear." John Gay. *Fr.* Beggar's Opera, The. OAEL-1; PeLV; PoEL-3

Song: "If everywhere in the street." Denis Glover. *Fr.* Sings Harry. PeNZ

Song: "If I freely may discover." Ben Jonson. *Fr.* Poetaster, The. BeJo; EIL

Song: "If she be not as kind as fair." Sir George Etherege *and to* William Walsh. NOSC

Song: "If the scorn of your bright eyne." Shakespeare. *Fr.* As You Like It. CTC

Song: "If thou art sleeping, maiden." Gil Vicente, *tr. fr. Spanish by* Longfellow. AWP; CTC

Song: "If you love God, take your mirror between your hands and look." Mahmud Djellaladin Pasha, *tr. fr. Turkish by* E. Powys Mathers. ErPo

Song: "I'm about to go shopping." James Schuyler. TTTS

Song: "I'm living in a cave." *Unknown, tr. fr. Chippewa Indian by* Jerome K. Rothenberg. STP

Song: "In a maiden-time professed." Thomas Middleton. *Fr.* Witch, The. OxBSP

Song: "In mine own [or one] monument I lie [or lye]." Richard Lovelace. CBLP; OxBSP

Song: "In the middle of the sea." *Unknown, tr. fr. Chippewa Indian by* Jerome K. Rothenberg. STP

Song: "Isle!/ Island of the syllables of flame!" Jacques Rabémanganjara, *tr. fr. French by* Ellen Conroy Kennedy. NegPo

Song: "It follows now you are to prove." Ben Jonson. *Fr.* Pleasure Reconciled to Virtue. NAEL-1; OAEL-1

Song, A: "It is not beauty I demand." George Darley. *See* It is not Beauty I demand.

Song: "It was a lover and his lass." Shakespeare. *Fr.* As You Like It. AWP; CBLP; CH; EIL; ELP; GBL; GTBS; GTBS-P; HeIL; ImPo; InPS; LiTB; NAEL-1; NOBE; NoP; NoSic; OBEV; RB; SCGP; TFi; TTTS (Country Song.) TrGrPo

(Song: "It was a lover and his lass.") OxAEP-1; EBEvV; CTC; 09FiP

Song 2: "Keep the dream alive and growing always." Edwin Rolfe. TrJP

Song: "It was upon a Lammas night." Burns. *See* It was upon a Lammas night.

Song: "Jog on, jog on, the footpath way." Shakespeare. *See* Jog On, jog on, the footpath way.

Song: "Kind lovers, love on." John Crowne. *Fr.* Calisto. InvP; OxBSP

Song: "Know then, my brethren, heaven is clear." *Unknown. Fr.* Song of Anarchus, The. FaBoCo

Song: "Know what I'll promise you?" *Unknown, tr. fr. Chippewa Indian by* Jerome K. Rothenberg. STP

Song: "Ladies, though to your conquering eyes." Sir George Etherege. *Fr.* Comical Revenge, The. OxBSP

Song: "Lady, you are with beauties so enriched." Francis Davison. EIL

Song XI: "Lay your sleeping head, my love." W. H. Auden. *See* Lay your sleeping head, my love.

Song: "Lark now leaves his wat'ry [or watery] nest, The." Sir William Davenant. *See* Lark Now Leaves His Watery [or Wat'ry] Nest.

Song — Last Day. John Clare. EnVR

Song: "Leave this gaudy gilded stage." The Earl of Rochester. OxBSP

Song: "Leave this gaudy gilded stage." The Earl Rochester. OxBSP

Song: "Let it be forgotten, as a flower is forgotten." Sara Teasdale. AnAmPo; MoAmPo; PoA; TrGrPo

Song: "Let me tell you the story of how I began." Robert Graves. NTP; OxAEP-2

Song: "Let not the sluggish sleep." *Unknown.* OxBSP

Song: "Let school-masters puzzle their brain." Goldsmith. *Fr.* She Stoops to Conquer. BIrV; NOIV

(Three Jolly Pigeons, The.) PoRA

(Three Pigeons, The.) ELP

Song: "Linnet in the rocky dells, The." Emily Brontë. HAP; OBNC

(My Lady's Grave.) OxAEP-2

Song: "Little Black Rose shall be red at last!, The." Aubrey Thomas De Vere. BIrV

(Song.) PeIV

Song: "Lo! here we come a-reaping, a-reaping." George Peele. *Fr.* Old Wives' [or Wife's] Tale, The. TrGrPo

Song: "Lord, when the sense of Thy sweet grace." Richard Crashaw. TrPWD

(Ecstasy, An.) OxAEP-1

Song: "Love a child is ever criing [or crying]." Mary Sidney Wroth, Countess of Montgomery. *Fr.* Urania. KTR; NOSC; WPE

Song: "Love a woman? You're [or Y'are] an ass." The Earl of Rochester. FaBoBl; GBL; NBLV; NOBL; NOSC; PeHV; PeLV; TEP

Song: "Love and harmony combine." Blake. ArLo; EnRP

Song: Love Armed. Aphra Behn. *See* Love in fantastic [or fantastique] triumph sat [or sate or satt].

Song: "Love for such a cherry lip." Thomas Middleton. *Fr.* Blurt, Master Constable. EIL

Song: "Love in fantastic triumph sate." Aphra Behn. *See* Love in fantastic [or fantastique] triumph sat [or sate or satt].

Song: "Love is a green girl." Michael Stillman. TLR

Song: "Love laid his sleepless head." Swinburne. TrGrPo

Song: "Love, love today, my dear." Charlotte Mew. MoBrPo

Song: "Love still has something of the sea." Sir Charles Sedley. GBL; NOBE; OxAEP-1; SeCV-2

Song: "Love that is hoarded, moulds at last." Harold C. Sandall. PoToHe

Song: "Lovely hill-torrents are." W. J. Turner. GoJo; MoBrPo

Song: "Lovers in ladies' magazines." Thomas McGrath. VGW

Song: "Lying is an occupation." Laetitia Pilkington. WPE

Song: "Maid of Athens, ere we part." Byron. EBEV; EnRP; FaBV; PrIm (Song.) FHYEP

Song: "Man's a poor deluded bubble." Robert Dodsley. OxBSP

Song: "Master, the swabber, the boatswain and I, The." Shakespeare. *See* Master, the swabber, the boatswain and I, The.

Song: "Memory, hither come." Blake. MeMBP; NAEL-2; PoEL-4

Song: "Men of England," A. Shelley. *See* Men of England, wherefore plough.

Song: "Merchant, to secure his treasure, The." Matthew Prior. *See* Merchant, to secure his treasure, The.

Song: "Methinks the poor town has been troubled too long." Charles Sackville. SeCV-2

Song: "Might have known it." *Unknown, tr. fr. Chippewa Indian by* Jerome K. Rothenberg. STP

Song: "Mist rauk is hanging, The." John Clare. NOBVV

Song: "Misty and dim, a bush in the wilds of Kapa'a." Kaiama, *tr. fr. Hawaiian by* N. B. Emerson. WTO

Song — Molly Magee. John Clare. EnVR

Song: Montrose. Charles Cotton. NOSC

Song: "Morpheus, the humble god, that dwells." Sir John Denham. NOSC

Song: "Mother Mother shave me." *Unknown, tr. fr. Nyasa by* Ulli Beier. BoWoP

Song: "Moth's kiss, first, The!" Robert Browning. *See* Moth's kiss, first, The!

Song: Murdring Beautie. Thomas Carew. SeCP

Song: "Music, thou queen of souls, get up and string." Thomas Randolph. OxBSP

Song: "My cabinets are oyster-shells." Margaret Cavendish, Duchess of Newcastle. *See* My Cabinets Are Oyster-Shells.

Song: "My dear mistress has a heart." The Earl of Rochester. SeCV-2

Song: "My head on moss reclining." *Unknown.* NOEC

Song: "My luve's [or luve is] like a red, red rose." Burns. EBEvV; EnRP; FaBoBe; HoPM

Song: "My silks and fine array." Blake. EnRP; OBNC; SCGP; TrGrPo (My Silks and Fine Array.) ChTr; ELP; GBL; TEP; UnPo

Song: "My straying thoughts, reduced stay." Anne Collins. WPE

Song: "Nay but you, who do not love her." Robert Browning. MeMBP; TrGrPo

Song: "No, no, fair heretic[k], it needs must be." Sir John Suckling. *Fr.* Aglaura. BeJo; CaPo; PrIm

Song: "No, no, no, no, I cannot hate my foe." Sir Philip Sidney. SiPS

Song: "No, no, poor suff'ring Heart no Change endeavour." Dryden. *See* No, No, Poor Suffering Heart.

Song: "No riches from his scanty store." Helen Maria Williams. WoRP

Song: "Noe more unto my thoughts appeare." Sidney Godolphin. MeLP

Song: "Nothing ades to Loves fond fire." Elizabeth Wilmot, Countess of Rochester. KTR

Song: "Now and then there will arise." *Unknown, tr. fr. Chippewa Indian by* Frances Densmore. OBVE

Song: "Now sleeps the crimson petal, now the white." Tennyson. *See* Now Sleeps the Crimson Petal, Now the White.

Song: "Now that Fate is dead and gone." Edith Sitwell. MoAB; MoBrPo

Song: "Now this bloody war is over." George Barker. PeLV

Song: "Nymph in vain bestows her pains, The." The Countess of Winchilsea. OxBSP

Song: "O fair! O sweet! when I do look on thee." Sir Philip Sidney. SiPS

Song: "O for doors to be open and an invite with gilded edges." W. H. Auden. PeLV

Song: "O harmless feast." Barten Holyday. *Fr.* Technogamia. EIL

Song: "O, let us howl some heavy note." John Webster. *See* Oh, let us howl some heavy note.

Song: "O Love, how strangely sweet." John Marston. EIL

Song: "O lovely April, rich and bright." Gustave Kahn, *tr. fr. French by* Ludwig Lewisohn. TrJP

Song: "O Mary sing thy songs to me." John Clare. CBLP

Song: "O more, and more! this was so well." Ben Jonson. *Fr.* Pleasure Reconciled to Virtue. NAEL-1; OAEL-1

Song: "O ruddier than the cherry." John Gay. *See* O ruddier than the cherry!

Song: "O sing into my roundelay." Thomas Chatterton. *See* Oh! sing unto my roundelay [*or* O! Synge untoe mie roundelaie].

Song: "O sweet, sad, singing river." H. Cordelia Ray. CBWP-3

Song: " 'O Where Are You Going?' said reader to rider." W. H. Auden. *See* O where are you going? said reader to rider.

Song: "O'er the smooth enamelled green." Milton. *See* O'er [*or* O're] the smooth enameled green.

Song: "O'er the waste of waters cruising." Philip Freneau. PAH

Song: "Oh, baby, baby, baby dear." E. Nesbit. NOBVV

Song: "Oh do[e] not wanton with those eyes." Ben Jonson. CBLP; SeCP; TEP

Song: "Oh [*or* O] fair[e] sweet face, oh [*or* O] eyes celestial[l] bright." John Fletcher. *Fr.* Women Pleased. PoEL-2

(To His Sleeping Mistress.) NOSC

Song: "Oh, foully slighted Ethiope maid!" Priscilla Jane Thompson. CBWP-2

Song: "Oh! Love, that stronger art than wine." Aphra Behn. *Fr.* Lucky Chance, The. WPE; WPOW

Song: " 'Oh! Love,' they said, "is King of Kings.' " Rupert Brooke. ArLo; PFP

Song: "Oh me, the time is come to part." Mary Sidney Wroth, Countess of Montgomery. *Fr.* Urania. NOSC; WPE

Song: "Oh no more, no more, no more, too late." John Ford. *See* Oh [*or* O], no more, no more, too late.

Song: "Oh roses for the flush of youth." Christina Rossetti. ELP; GTBS-P; NOBVV

Song: "Oh say not that my heart is cold." Charles Wolfe. OxAEP-2

Song: "Oh the charming month of May!" Joseph Addison. NOEC

Song: "Oh, you powerful Gods, if I must be." Frances Boothby. *Fr.* Marcelia; or, Treacherous Friend, The. KTR

Song: "Old England is eaten by Knaves." Alexander McLachlan. *Fr.* Emigrant, The. NOBC

Song: "Old Farmer Oats and his son Ned." John Jay Chapman. PoEL-5

Song: Old Rowley the King. *Unknown.* APAS

Song, A: On His Mistress. Sir Robert Ayton. NOSC

Song: "One day the god of fond desire." James Thomson. EnLoPo

Song: One Hard Look. Robert Graves. MoAB; MoBrPo

Song: "Only the wanderer." Ivor Gurney. FaBoPP

Song: "Ope, aged Atlas, open then thy lap." Ben Jonson. *Fr.* Pleasure Reconciled to Virtue. NAEL-1; OAEL-1

Song: "Or love me less, or love me more." Sidney Godolphin. *See* Or love me [*or* mee] less [*or* lesse], or love me [*or* mee] more.

Song: "Orpheus with his Lute made Trees." John Fletcher *and* William Shakespeare. *See* Orpheus with his lute made trees.

Song: "Over hill, over dale." Shakespeare. *See* Over Hill, over Dale.

Song — Owl, The. Tennyson. *See* When cats run home and light is come.

Song: Paper. Keith Waldrop. MAT

Song: "Pardon, goddess of the night." Shakespeare. *See* Claudio's Lament: "Pardon, goddess of the night."

Song: Persuasions [*or* Persuasions] to Enjoy. Thomas Carew. *See* If the quick spirits in your eye.

Song: "Phillis for shame let us improve." Charles Sackville. *See* Phillis for Shame Let Us Improve.

Song: "Phillis is my only joy." Sir Charles Sedley. EnLoPo; SeCV-2

Song: "Phillis, let's shun the common fate." Sir Charles Sedley. SeCV-2

Song: "Pious Selinda goes to prayers." Congreve. BoLoP; ECEV; ELP; ErPo; FaBoCo; NBLV; NOBE; NOEC; OxBSP

Song: "Place in thy memory, dearest, A." Gerald Griffin. BLPA

Song: "Plucke the fruite and tast the pleasure." Thomas Lodge. *Fr.* Robert, Second Duke of Normandy. ElL; EnRePo; OxAEP-1

Song: "Pursuing beauty, men descry." Thomas Southerne. NOSC

Song: Railway Train, The. *Unknown, tr. by* George Taplin. NOBAu

Song: "Rarely, rarely, comest thou." Shelley. EnRP; OBNC; TrGrPo

(Barely, rarely, comest thou.) CH; TEP

(Invocation: "Rarely, rarely, comest thou.") GTBS; GTBS-P

(Song: "Rarely, rarely, comest thou.") FHYEP; Mes

Song: "Red young men under the ground, The." *Unknown, tr. fr. Navajo Indian by* Jerome K. Rothenberg. *Fr.* Red Ant Way. STP

Song: "Rejoice bather between two waters." Milorad Pavic, *tr. fr. Serbo-Croatian by* Charles Simic. *Fr.* Holy Mass For Relja Krilatica. HSix

Song: "Rejoice eleventh finger reckoner of stars." Milorad Pavic, *tr. fr. Serbo-Croatian by* Charles Simic. *Fr.* Holy Mass For Relja Krilatica. HSix

Song: "Rejoice mason of years." Milorad Pavic. *Fr.* Holy Mass For Relja Krilatica. HSix

Song: "Rejoice singer of songs for the deaf." Milorad Pavic. *Fr.* Holy Mass For Relja Krilatica. HSix

Song: "Rejoice you who sleep with a finger in your ear." Milorad Pavic. *Fr.* Holy Mass For Relja Krilatica. HSix

Song: "Rowan like a lip-sticked girl, A." Seamus Heaney. IPY; TRP

Song: "Sabrina fair." Milton. *Fr.* Comus; a Masque Presented at Ludlow Castle. EBEV; ELP; FaBoCh, *much abr.*; FHYEP; GN; OAEL-1; PoEL-3

(Sabrina.) CH, *abr.*) NOBE; OBEV

(Song.) OxAEP-1

Song: "Say this city has ten million souls!" W. H. Auden. *See* Say this city has ten million souls.

Song: "Scholar first my love implored, A." Lady Dorothea Dubois. ECWP

Song: Scrutiny, The. Richard Lovelace. *See* Why should you [*or* shouldst thou] swear I am forsworn.

Song: "See, see, she wakes, Sabina wakes!" Congreve. NOEC; OxBSP

Song: "Seeke not to know my love, for shee." Thomas Carew. SeCP

Song: "Sergei's a flower." Ruth Herschberger. FF

Song: "She has left me, my pretty." Sylvia Townsend Warner. MoAB; MoBrPo

Song: "She is not fair to outward view." Hartley Coleridge. EnRP; OBEV

(She Is Not Fair.) FaBV

(Song.) OxAEP-1

Song: "She sang the song of the Belgian refugees." Andrew Waterman. SCBI

Song: "She sat and sang alway." Christina Rossetti. GBL; NAEL-2

Song: "She was lyin face down in her face." William Knott. MAT

Song: "Shephard loveth thow me vell?" Jean Passerat, *tr. fr. French by* William Drummond of Hawthornden. OBVE

Song: "Shepherd, who can pass such wrong." Jorge de Montemayor, *tr. fr. Spanish by* Bartholomew Young. *Fr.* Diana. ElL

Song: "She's somewhere in the sunlight strong." Richard Le Gallienne. OBEV

Song: "Shine out, fair sun, with all your heat." *At. to* George Chapman. *See* Shine Out, Fair Sun, with All Your Heat.

Song: "Shining like a star." *Unknown, tr. fr. Chippewa Indian by* Jerome K. Rothenberg. STP

Song: "Sigh no more, ladies, sigh no more." Shakespeare. *See* Sigh no more, ladies [sigh no more].

Song: "Silly boy, there is no cause." Thomas Pestel. ElL

Song: "Sing me a sweet, low song of night." Hildegarde Hawthorne. FaBoBe

Song: "Slaves to London, I'll deceive you." Peter Anthony Motteux. NOSC

Song: "Slow, slow fresh fount, keep time with my salt tears." Ben Jonson. *See* Slow, slow, fresh fount, keep time with my salt tears.

Song: "Smile, Massachusetts, smile." *Unknown.* PAH

Song: "Smooth was the water, calm the air." Sir Charles Sedley. SeCV-2

Song: "So light no one noticed." Edward Dorn. VGW

Song: "Soft falls the sweet evening." John Clare. NOBVV

Song: "Soldier rest! thy warfare o'er." Sir Walter Scott. *See* Soldier Rest! [Thy Warfare O'er.]

Song: "Some people in the sky." *Unknown, tr. fr. Chippewa Indian by* Jerome K. Rothenberg. STP

Song: "Somnus, the humble god, that dwells." Sir John Denham. BeJo

Song: "Song of grass, A,/ A song of earth." "Yehoash," *tr. fr. Yiddish by* Isidore Goldstick. TrJP

Song: "Soules joy, now I am gone." *At. to* The Earl of Pembroke William Herbert, Earl of Pembroke. ESCV

Song: "Sound is fading out." *Unknown, tr. fr. Chippewa Indian by* Jerome K. Rothenberg. STP

Song: "Spirit haunts the last year's hours, A." Tennyson. *See* Spirit haunts the year's last hours, A.

Song: "Stay Phoebus, stay." Edmund Waller. BeJo; SeCP

Song: "Still to be neat, still to be dressed [*or* drest]." Ben Jonson, *of Jean Bonnefons. Fr.* Silent Woman, The. BeJo; OxBSP; Poetr; TFi

(Simplicity and Sweet Neglect.) OxAEP-1

(Song.) EBEvV, *sect.* I, *pt.* i; PFP, *sect.* I, *pt.* i

(Song: "Still to be neat, still to be dressed.") EnRePo

Song: Stop All the Clocks. W. H. Auden. *See* Stop All the Clocks, Cut Off the Telephone.

Song: "Stranger, you who hide my love." Stephen Spender. FaBoTw

Song: "Strephon has fashion, wit and youth." Elizabeth Taylor. KTR

Song: "Strew not earth with empty stars." Thomas Lovell Beddoes. *Fr.* Second Brother, The. OxBSP

Song IV: Sudden Light. Dante Gabriel Rossetti. *See* I have been here before.

Song for Healing. Roberta Hill Whiteman. CDW

Song for Ireland. Phil *and* June Colclough. OBET

Song for Ishtar. Denise Levertov. MoP; NALW; NaP; NMM; NoAM; PoM

Song for Jeannie. William Tremblay. Jaz

Song for Joseph. *Unknown, tr. fr. Maori by* Margaret Orbell. PeNZ

Song for Memorial Day. Clinton Scollard. OHIP

Song for My Lady. A. Godwin. *See* Now wolde I fayne sum merthis [*or* faine some merthes] mak[e].

Song for My Mother, A: Her Hands. Anna Hempstead Branch. *Fr.* Songs for My Mother. OHIP

Song for My Mother, A: Her Stories. Anna Hempstead Branch. *Fr.* Songs for My Mother. OHIP

Song for My Mother, A: Her Words. Anna Hempstead Branch. *Fr.* Songs for My Mother. FaPON; OHIP

Song for Occupations, A, *sels.* Walt Whitman.
 "Will you seek afar off? you surely come back at last." ChIV-1

Song for Past Midnight. Geoffrey Lehmann. CBAP

Song for Ranelagh. William Whitehead. ECEV

Song for St. Cecilia's Day. W. H. Auden. FaBoTw; TwCP

Song for St. Cecilia's Day, 1687, A. (From harmony, from heavenly harmony.) Dryden. AWP; FaBoTw; FHYEP; GGP; GTBS; GTBS-P; HAP; InPS; LiTB; NOSC; OAEL-1; OBEV; OPOP; PoEL-3; PPP; SCGP; SeCV-2; TEP; TFi; TrGrPo
Sels.
 Compensation. CBNP; PeLV
 Fife and Drum. GN, 8 *ll.*

Song for September. Robert Fitzgerald. VGW

Song for Simeon, A. T. S. Eliot. ChIV-2; LiTB; NAs; NOCV

Song for Straphangers. George Buchanan. PNI

Song for Te Hauapu. Noho-mai-te-Rangi, *tr. fr. Maori by* Margaret Orbell. PeNZ

Song for the Bureaucrat. Li Pai-feng, *tr. fr. Chinese.* LHF, *tr. by* Hualing Nieh

Song for the Cattle. David Campbell. NOBAu

Song for the Clatter-Bones. F. R. Higgins. ChIV-1; ImPo; LiTB; OBMV

Song for the Dead, III. *Unknown, tr. by* Frances S. Herskovits. TTY

Song for the Greenwood Fawn. I. L. Salomon. GoYe

Song for the Head. George Peele. *See* Gently dip: but not too deepe.

Song for the Heroes. Alex Comfort. MoBrPo

Song for the Infant Judas. Thomas Blackburn. NAs

Song for the Last Act. Louise Bogan. GoJo; NoP; NYBP; UnPo; WPE

Song for the Middle of the Night, A. James Wright. SM; WeW

Song for the Newborn. *Unknown. See* Newborn, on the naked sand.

Song for the Passing of a Beautiful Woman. *Unknown, tr. fr. Paiute Indian by* Mary Austin. LiTA

Song for the Richest Woman in Wrangell. Guxnawu, *tr. fr. Tlingit Indian by* James Koller. STP

Song for the Single Table on New Year's Day, A. Elizabeth Frances Amherst. ECWP

Song for the Squeeze-Box. Theodore Roethke. NBLV

Song for the Subjectivist. Li Pai-feng, *tr. fr. Chinese. Fr.* Pearls and Earth. LHF, *tr. by* Hualing Nieh

Song for the Sun That Disappeared behind the Rainclouds. *Hottentot Oral Tradition, tr. by* Ulli Beier. TTTS; TTY

Song for the unsung heroes who rose in the country's need, A. The Unsung Heroes. Paul Laurence Dunbar. BPo

Song for the Yesman. Li Pai-feng, *tr. fr. Chinese. Fr.* Pearls and Earth. LHF, *tr. by* Hualing Nieh

Song for Those Who Know. Hans Magnus Enzensberger. PoSu

Song for Unbound Hair. Genevieve Taggard. PoRA

Song for .Wei City, A. Wang Wei, *tr. fr. Chinese by* Robert Payne. TAL

Song Form. Amiri Baraka. SOTW; TTTS

Song from a Country Fair. Léonie Adams. GoJo; GrPl

Song from a Two-Desk Office. Byron Buck. NYBP

Song from "Al Aaraaf." Poe. *Fr.* Al Aaraaf. AmPP; AnAmPo; OxBA

Song from Armenia, A. Geoffrey Hill. FaBoMo

Song from "Chartivel." Marie de France. *See* Hath any loved you well, down there.

Song from Sylvan, A. *At. to* Elizabeth Barrett Browning *and to* Louise Imogen Guiney. *See* Little cares that fretted me, The.

Song from the Bride of Smithfield. Sylvia Townsend Warner. MoBrPo

Song from the Coptic, A. James Clarence Mangan. NOIV

Song from the Italian, A. Dryden. *Fr.* Kind Keeper, The. SeCV-2

Song from the Waters. Thomas Lovell Beddoes. *See* Swallow leaves her nest, The.

Song gives birth to . . . The woman with white hair. The Song of Ancient Ways. William Oandasan. HATNAP

Song, *Hamlet.* John F. Poole. BXAP

Song I sing of my sea-adventure, A. The Seafarer. *Unknown, tr. fr. Anglo-Saxon by* Charles W. Kennedy. AnOE

Song I sing of my sea adventure, A. *Unknown, tr. by* Charles W. Kennedy. *Fr.* Seafarer, The. AnOE; CTC; FaBoTw; HeIL; HeIP; LiTA; NoP; OxBA

Song I sing of sorrow unceasing, A. The Wife's Lament. *Unknown.* AnOE, *tr. by* Charles W. Kennedy
 (Wife's Complaint, The. BoLoP, *tr. by* Michael Alexander

Song I sing of sorrow unceasing, A. *Unknown. See* I make this song about me full sadly.

Song: I Want a Witness. Michael S. Harper. CAPP

Song in His Lady's Absence, A. A. Godwin. *See* Now wolde I fayne sum merthis [*or* faine some merthes] mak[e].

Song in Making of the Arrows, The. John Lyly. *See* My shag-hair Cyclops, come, lets ply.

Song in Passing, A. Yvor Winters. CRP; VGW

Song in Praise of a Favourite Humming-Top, A. Hone Tuwhare. PeNZ

Song in Praise of Gowfing. Andrew Duncan. FaBoEH

Song in Praise of Paella. C. W. V. Wordsworth. FiBHP

Song in the Cold Season. Samuel French Morse. PoA

Song in the Front Yard, A. Gwendolyn Brooks. *Fr.* Street in Bronzeville, A. BlSi; BPo; CAPP; FaBoWP; NAAL-2; NMM; NoAM; NOBA; PoBA

Song: In the Name of a Lover, to His Mistress; Who Said, She Hated Him for His Grey Hairs, Which He Had at Thirty, A. William Wycherley. SeCV-2

Song in the valley of Nemea, A. Nemea. Lawrence Durrell. FaBoTw; GTBS-P

Song in the Wood. John Fletcher, *sometimes at. to* Francis Beaumont. *Fr.* Little French Lawyer, The. EIL; NOSC

Song in Time of Plague. Thomas Nashe. *See* Adieu, Farewell, Earth's Bliss[e].

Song is gone; the dance, The. Bora Ring. Judith Wright. NoAM

Song-Maker. Anita Endrezze-Danielson. HATNAP

Song-Maker, The. Anna Wickham. MoBrPo

Song Making. Sara Teasdale. WGRP

Song: Mary Morison. Burns. *See* O [*or* Oh] Mary, at the window be.

Song My. Susan Griffin. NMM; WPOW

Song My Paddle Sings, The. Emily Pauline Johnson. FaPON

Song (October 1969). Kath Fraser. PeHV

Song of a Bear. *Unknown, tr. fr. Navajo Indian.* OBAP

Song of a Common Lover. Flavien Ranaivo, *tr. fr. French by* Alan Ryder. TTY

Song of a Farmer. P'i Jih-hsiu, *tr. fr. Chinese by* William H. Nienhauser. SuSp

Song of a Heathen, The. Richard Watson Gilder. AnAmPo; WGRP

Song of a Hebrew. Dannie Abse. *See* Working is another way of praying.

Song of a Jewish Boy. "M. J.," *tr. fr. Polish by* A. Glanz-Leyeles. TrJP

Song of a Man about to Die in a Strange Land. *Unknown, tr. fr. Chippewa Indian by* Mary Austin. DL

Song of a Man Who Has Come Through, *sels.* D. H. Lawrence.
 "Not I, not I, but the wind that blows through me!" CMoP; FaBoMo; GTBS-P; InPS; LiTM; MeMBP; OxBTC; PeFWW; PoE; RaBo; TRP

Song of a Man Who Is Loved. D. H. Lawrence. OxBM

Song of a Rat. Ted Hughes. CMoP; NoP

Song of a Second April. Edna St. Vincent Millay. CMoP; OxBA

Song of a Shepherd Boy at Bethlehem. Josephine Preston Peabody. OHIP

Song of a Sick Child. *Malay Oral Tradition, tr. by* R. J. Wilkinson *and* R. O. Winstedt. DL

Song of a Spirit. Ann Radcliffe. ECWP

Song of a Traveller, The. Robert Louis Stevenson. *See* I will make you brooches and toys for your delight.

Song of a Woman Abandoned by the Tribe. *Unknown, tr. fr. Shoshone Indian by* Mary Austin. AIW; WPE

Song of a Young Lady to Her Ancient Lover, A. The Earl of Rochester. BoLoP; EBEV; ErPo; FaBoBl; GBL; NOSC; OPOP; OxAEP-1

Song of Absinthe Granny, The. Ruth Stone. NALW

Song of Abuse. *Yoruba Oral Tradition, tr. by* Ulli Beier *and* B. Gbadamosi. WTO

Song of Albert Graeme. Sir Walter Scott. *Fr.* Lay of the Last Minstrel, The. EnRP

Song of Ale, A. *At. to* William Stevenson *and also to* John Still. *See* Back and Side Go Bare, Go Bare.

Song of Anarchus, The, *sels. Unknown.*
 "Know then, my brethren, heaven is clear." FaBoCo

Song of Ancient Ways, The. William Oandasan. HATNAP

Song of Apollo. Shelley. *See* Sleepless hours who watch me as I lie, The.

Song of Autumn Night. Wang Yu, *tr. fr. Chinese* by Irving Y. Lo. SuSp

Song of Battle. Bertrans de Born. *See* Well Pleaseth Me the Sweet Time of Easter.

Song of Bekotsidi, The. *Unknown, tr. fr. Navajo Indian* by Washington Matthews. OBVE

Song of Black Cubans. Federico García Lorca, *tr. fr. Spanish* by William B. Logan. SOTW

Song of Bliss. Spenser. *See* Whiles someone did chant this lovely lay, The.

Song of Blood, A. Sidney Walter Powell. *Fr.* Gallipoli. NSI

Song of Blue and Red, A. Amir Gilboa, *tr. fr. Hebrew* by Ruth Finer Mintz. MHP

Song of Braddock's Men, The. Stephen Tilden. PAH

Song of Bread. Diana Der Hovanessian. WoWa

Song of Breath. Peire Vidal, *tr. fr. French* by Ezra Pound. AWP

Song of Bullets, The. Jessica Hagedorn. ETG

Song of Callicles, The ("Through the black, rushing smoke-burst.") Matthew Arnold. *Fr.* Empedocles on Etna. NOBE; OAEL-2; OBEV

Song of canaries, The. The Canary. Ogden Nash. FiBHP; PeLV

Song of Caribou, Musk Oxen, Women, and Men Who Would Be Manly. (Glorious it is to see/ The caribou flocking down from the forests.) *Unknown, tr. fr. Eskimo.* WTO
Sels.
   "Glorious it is/ to see long-haired winter caribou." RFM

Song of Catching Tigers, *sels.* Hsü Chung-hsing, *tr. fr. Chinese* by Jonathan Chaves.

Song of Chang Ching-yüan Picking Lotus Flowers, A. Wen T'ing-yün, *tr. fr. Chinese* by William R. Schultz. SuSp

Song of Chess, The. *At. to* Abraham ibn Ezra Abraham Ibn Ezra, *tr. fr. Hebrew* by Nina Davis Salaman. TrJP

Song of Chiang-nan, *sels.* Tsung Ch'en, *tr. fr. Chinese* by Jonathan Chaves.

Song of Chiang-nan, *sels.* Wei Yüan, *tr. fr. Chinese* by Irving Lo.

Song of Childbirth, The. *Unknown, tr. fr. Irish* by Eleanor Hull. TIRV

Song of Chin Men District, A. Hsueh Ch'iung, *tr. fr. Chinese* by Kenneth Rexroth *and* Ling Chung. WPC

Song of Choyong, The, *sels.* Kim Chun-soo, *tr. fr. Korean* by Koh Chang-soo.

Song of Clover, A. Helen Hunt Jackson. GN

Song of Cove Creek Dam, The. *Unknown.* AmFP

Song of Crede, The. *Unknown, tr. fr. Middle Irish* by Alfred Perceval Graves. BIrV

Song of Dalliance, A. William Cartwright. ErPo; JCP; NOSC

Song of Deborah, The. Bible, *O.T. Fr.* Judges. AWP; BoWoP; PBWP

Song of Dejection. W. H. Auden. *Fr.* Man of La Mancha. AnAn

Song of Derivations, A. Alice Meynell. OHCV; WGRP

Song of Despair. Rangiaho, *tr. fr. Maori* by Barry Mitcalfe. WTO

Song of Diego Valdez, The. Kipling. OtMeF

Song of Distant Waters, A. Wen T'ing-yün, *tr. fr. Chinese* by William R. Schultz. SuSp

Song of Doubt, A. Josiah Gilbert Holland. WGRP

Song of Duke William. Hilaire Belloc. FaBoNo

Song of Dust, A. Lord De Tabley. EnLoPo

Song of Ecstasy, *sels.* Abu al-Qasim al-Shabbi, *tr. fr. Arabic* by Sargon Boulus *and* Christopher Middleton.

Song of Emptiness to Fill up the Empty Pages Following, A. Michael Wigglesworth. SCAP

Song of Enitharmon. Blake. *Fr.* Vala; or The Four Zoas. OAEL-2

Song of Esechia, The. John Hall. ChIV-1

Song of Exile, *sels.* Antônio Gonçalves Dias, *tr. fr. Portuguese* by Frances Ellen Buckland.
   "There are palm trees in my homeland." TTY

Song of Exile, A. Bible, *O.T., par.* by Sir Thomas Wyatt. *Fr.* Psalms. AWP; NAWM-1; OAEL-1; OBVE; TrGrPo; TrJP

Song of Faith, A. Josiah Gilbert Holland. WGRP

Song of Faith Forsworn, A. Lord De Tabley. PeVV

"Song of Farewell" in the Tartar Mode. Chang Yü, *tr. fr. Chinese* by Irving Y. Lo. SuSp

Song of Finis, The. Walter de la Mare. MoBrPo

Song of Fionnuala, The. Thomas Moore. BIrV

Song of Fixed Accord. Wallace Stevens. InPS; SAmP

Song of Foxes, A. Duncan Ban MacIntyre, *tr. fr. Gaelic* by John Stuart Blackie. ScCV

Song of grass, A,/ A song of earth. "Yehoash," *tr. fr. Yiddish* by Isidore Goldstick. TrJP

Song of Greatness, A. *Unknown, tr. fr. Chippewa Indian.* FaPON; ImGa, *tr. by* Mary Austin

Song of Grief, A. Pan Chieh-yû, *tr. fr. Chinese* by Kenneth Rexroth *and* Ling Chung. WPC

Song of "Hand-in-Hand," A. Ou-yang Hsiu, *tr. fr. Chinese* by Irving Y. Lo. SuSp

Song of Hannah, The. Bible, *O.T. See* My heart doth in the Lord rejoice [or rejoiceth in the Lord], that living Lord of might.

Song of Hate. Jacob ben David Frances, *tr. fr. Hebrew* by A. B. Rhine. TrJP

Song of Hate for Eels. Arthur Guiterman. OBAL

Song of Heavenly Ascent. Ts'ao Chih, *tr. fr. Chinese* by Ronald C. Miao. SuSp

Song of Hiawatha, The, *sels.* Longfellow.
   "By the shores of Gitche [*or* Gitchee] Gumee." EBEvV; FaPON; WBLP
   (At the door on summer evenings.) BoTP
   (Downward through the evening twilight.) FaBV
   (Hiawatha's Childhood.) FaPoB; PFP
   "From his wanderings far to eastward." GOA
   "Give me of your bark, O Birch-tree!" Mes
   (Hiawatha's Canoe.) OHIP
   Hiawatha's Brothers. BoTP
   Hiawatha's Wooing. BeLS; EBNV
   "Honour be to Mudjekeewis!" UV
   "Should you ask me, whence these stories." MeMAP; NOBA; PoE; Poetr
   When He Heard the Owls at Midnight. ArNa; FM

Song of Honor [*or* Honour], The. Ralph Hodgson. LiTB; MoBrPo; OtMeF

Song of Hope. Mary Artemisia Lathbury. BLPA

Song of Hope. Daisy Yamora, *tr. fr. Spanish* by James Black *and* Bernardo Garcia-Pandavenes. AIW

Song of Hope. Daisy Yamora, *tr. fr. Spanish* by Jane Glazer *and* Elizabeth Linder. WoWa

Song of Hsi-ling Lake, A. Su Hsiao-hsiao, *tr. fr. Chinese* by Kenneth Rexroth *and* Ling Chung. WPC

Song of Hsiang-yang. Li Po, *tr. fr. Chinese* by Joseph J. Lee. SuSp

Song of Hungarrda, The. Ngunaitponi (David Unaipon). NOBAu

Song of Instruction, A. Te Kooti Rikirangi, *tr. fr. Maori* by Margaret Orbell. PeNZ

Song of Jed Smith, The, *sels.* John G. Neihardt.
   "One more rendezvous." FYAP

Song of Jehane du Castel Beau, The. William Morris. *Fr.* Golden Wings. ChTr; OBNC

Song of Jonah in the Whale's Belly, The. Michael Drayton. ChIV-1

Song of Joy. *Unknown. See* Great Sea, The.

Song of Kai-hsia. Hsiang Chi, *tr. fr. Chinese* by Ronald C. Miao. SuSp

Song of Kuk-ook, the Bad Boy, The. *Eskimo Oral Tradition.* TTTS

Song of Labour, A, *sels.* Alexander Anderson.

Song of Lament, A. Ts'ao Chih, *tr. fr. Chinese* by Hans H. Frankel. SuSp

Song of Lazarus, The, *sels.* Alex Comfort.
   Notes for My Son. LiTM; MoBrPo

Song of Lewes, The. *Unknown.* OxBoLi

Song of Lewes, The, *sels. Unknown.*
   "So whether it is that the King, misled." FaBoEH

Song of Liberty, A. Blake. EnRP

Song of Lies, The. *Unknown, tr. fr. Irish* by Donal O'Sullivan. CBNP

Song of Lies on Sabbath Eve, A. Yehuda Amichai, *tr. fr. Hebrew* by Chana Bloch. PoSu

Song of Life, A. Franz Werfel, *tr. fr. German* by Edith Abercrombie Snow. TrJP

Song of Lo-fu, The. *Unknown, tr. fr. Chinese* by Arthur Waley. AWP

Song of Loneliness. Judah Halevi, *tr. fr. Hebrew* by Nina Davis Salaman. TrJP

Song of Longing. *Gond Oral Tradition, tr.* by V. Elwin *and* S. Hivale. WTO

Song of Longing. *Unknown, tr. fr. Maori* by John White. WTO

Song of Love, A. The. Rainer Maria Rilke, *tr. fr. German* by Ludwig Lewisohn. AWP

Song of Love, A. "Lewis Carroll." GN

Song of Love and Death, The. Tennyson. *Fr.* Idylls of the King. OBNC

Song of Love for Jesus, A. Richard Rolle. MeEL

Song of Magpies, A. Lady Ho, *tr. fr. Chinese* by Kenneth Rexroth *and* Ling Chung. WPC

Song of Man Chipping an Arrowhead. W. S. Merwin. InPK

Song of Marion's Men. Bryant. AnAmPo; PAH

Song of Mary, A. Lucille Clifton. NALW

Song of Mehitabel, The. Don Marquis. *Fr.* Archy and Mehitabel. FiBHP; OFC; SoCa

Song of Milkanwatha, The, *sels.* George A. Strong.
   Modern Hiawatha, The. FaBoCo; FaBoPa; FaPON; FiBHP; MoShBr; PeLV; UV
   (Hiawatha Revisited.) BXAP
   (When he killed the Mudjokivis.) EBEvV

Song of Mr. Toad, The. Kenneth Grahame. *Fr.* Wind in the Willows, The. CoGr; FaPON; FiBHP; GoJo; NOBL; ZA

Song of My Song, in Three Parts, A. *Unknown, tr. fr. Seneca Indian by Jerome K.* Rothenberg *and Richard Johnny John.* STP

Song of My Soul. Ralph Chubb. PeHV

Song of Myself. Walt Whitman. AmPP; LiTA; MoAmPo, *abr.*; NOBA; OxBA; SOTW, *much abr.*
Sels.
"All goes onward and outward, nothing collapses." IMW
"Alone far in the wilds and mountains I hunt." SAmP
"Child said *What is the grass?*, A." NoP; SAmP
(Grass.) BLPL; ImPo
Drayman, The. PoNe
"Oxen that rattle the yoke and chain or halt in the leafy shade." FM
"Flaunt of the sunshine I need not your bask." TrGrPo
Gigantic Beauty of a Stallion, A. ImGa; PDV
Has Any One Supposed It Lucky to Be Born? NAs
"Houses and rooms are full of perfumes." EBEvV; TrGrPo; UnPo
I Am of Old and Young. ImGa, XVI, *sl. shorter*
"I am the poet of the Body and I am the poet of the Soul." WeW
I Am He That Walks with the Tender and Growing Night. ChTr
"I believe a leaf of grass is no less than the journey-work of the stars." EaPr; PDV; SAmP
"I believe in the flesh and the appetites." Prf
"I believe in you my soul." Prf
Swiftly Arose
"I celebrate myself, and sing myself." FaBoVe; MeMAP; NAWM-2; NoAM; NoP; NTP; PoE; RaBo; SAmP
(I celebrate myself,/ And what I assume you shall assume.) HeIP, *earlier vers.*
(Myself.) BLPL; FaBoBe
"I have said that the soul is not more than the body." EnlH, *longer sel*
(Hub of the Universe, The.) ImPo
"I hear and behold God in every object, yet understand God not in the least." WGRP
"I think I could turn and live awhile with animals." EaPr; HAP; NU; PDV; PFP; SAmP/ TrGrPo; WeW; WGRP
(Animals.) ImPo
"I understand the large hearts of heroes." SAmP
"Little one sleeps in its cradle, The." SAmP; TrGrPo
"My signs are a rain-proof coat, good shoes, a staff cut from the woods." Prf
"Now I will do nothing but listen." HoPM; SAmP
"Pure contralto sings in the organloft, The." TTTS
Runaway Slave, The. PoNe
"Spotted hawk swoops by and accuses me, The." NoP; SAmP
"Trippers and askers surround me." EnlH; UnPo
"Twenty-eight young men bathe by the shore." HAP; LPA; NoP; SAmP
Walt Whitman. NoAM
"Walt Whitman, a kosmos, of Manhattan the son." NoP; SAmP; SCV
"Who goes there? hankering, gross, mystical, nude." TrGrPo
"With music strong I come, with my cornets and my drums." TrGrPo
Would You Hear of an Old-Time [*or* Old-Fashioned] Sea fight? ImGa, *sect.* XXXV–XXXVI; SAmP, *sect.* XXXV
(Battle of the *Bonhomme Richard* and the *Serapis*.) RB, *sect.* XXXV–XXXVI; UnPo, *sect.* XXXV–XXXVI
Wounded Person, The. PoNe

Song of Nezahualcoyotl. *Unknown.* DL

Song of "Night After Night," A. Ou-yang Hsiu, *tr. fr. Chinese by Irving Y. Lo.* SuSp

Song of Nu-Numma-Kwiten, The. *Unknown, tr. fr. Bushman.* PeSA

Song of One Eleven Years in Prison. George Canning , George Ellis, *and John Hookham Frere. See* Whene'er with haggard eyes I view.

Song of One of the Girls. Dorothy Parker. NALW

Song of Pajaro. Jeff Tagami. OpBo

Song of Panama, A. Damon Runyon. PAH

Song of Parable, A. *Unknown, tr. fr. Chinese by Jan W. Walls.* SuSp

Song of Parents Who Want to Wake Up Their Son. *Unknown, tr. fr. Kwakiutl Indian.* TTTS

Song of Poverty. *Gond Oral Tradition, tr. by V. Elwin and S. Hivale.* WTO

Song of Praise, A. Bible, *O.T., paraphrased by Sir Thomas Wyatt. See* Praise ye the Lord/ Praise ye the Lord.

Song of Quoodle, The. G. K. Chesterton. GoJo

Song of Reasons. Robert Pinsky. AnAn; HCAP

Song of Resignation. Yehuda Amichai, *tr. fr. Hebrew by Assia Gutmann.* NYBP

Song of Right and Wrong, The. G. K. Chesterton. OtMeF

Song of Roland, The. (Charles the King, our Emperor, the Great.) *Unknown, tr. fr. Old French.* NAWM-1, *tr. by Frederick Goldin, abr.*
Sels.
"In wrath and grief away the Paynims fly." OBWP

Song of Rubber. Shao Yen-hsiang, *tr. fr. Chinese.* LHF, *tr. by Hualing Nieh*

Song of Samuel Sweet, The. Charles Causley. OBNV

Song of Saul Before His Last Battle. Byron. ChIV-1

Song of Seyd Nimetollah of Kuhistan. Emerson. NOBA

Song of shadows: never glory was, A. Shadows. Victor Plarr. NOBVV

Song of Shem. James McAuley. *Fr.* Family of Love, The. ChIV-1

Song of Sherman's Army, The. Charles Graham Halpine. PAH

Song of Sherwood, A. Alfred Noyes. FaPON; MoBrPo

Song of Sickness, A. Hine Tangikuku, *tr. fr. Maori by Barry Mitcalfe.* WTO

Song of Sitting Bull. *Unknown.* GOA

Song of Sixpence. *Unknown.* OxBoLi

Song of Slaves in the Desert. Whittier. OxBA

Song of Snow-white Heads. Chuo Wen-chün, *tr. by Arthur Waley.* BoWoP

Song of Solomon, The. (Let him kiss me with the kisses of his mouth.) *sels.* Bible, *O.T.*
"Arjuna said:/ How shall I in battle against Bhisma." DL
As a Seal upon Thy Heart. TrJP
(Set me as a seal on your heart.) BoWoP, *ad. by Willis Barnstone*
Awake! FaPON
"Behold, thou art fair." OxBM; TrJP
"For, lo, the winter is past." PDV
(Lo, the Winter Is Past.) FaPON; SiSoPo
Hark! My Beloved! TrJP
(Voice of my darling, The.) BoWoP, *ad. by Willis Barnstone,* 8–14
"I am come into my garden, my sister, my spouse." OBVE; TOF
I Am My Beloved's. TrJP
(I am my lover's and he desires me.) ArLo, *tr. by Willis Barnstone*
(I am my lover's and he desires me.) BoWoP, *ad. by Willis Barnstone*
"I am the rose of Sharon, and the lily of the valleys." BoLoP; FF; GBL; OBVE
(I Am the Rose of Sharon.) ChTr
I Sleep, but My Heart Waketh. TrJP
(I sleep but my heart is awake.) BoWoP, *ad. by Willis Barnstone,* 2–18
"My love has gone down to his garden." BoWoP, *ad. by Willis Barnstone*
"My love is white and ruddy." BoWoP, *ad. by Willis Barnstone*
On My Bed I Sought Him. TrJP; VBLP
(In my bed at night.) BoWoP, *ad. by Willis Barnstone*
Return, Return, O Shulammite. TrJP
"Rise up, my love, my fair one, and come away." EaPr
Song of Songs. ArNa
"Song of songs, which is Solomon's, The." OBVE
"Turning to him, who meets me with desire." PBWP
"Under the quince tree." PBWP
"Yes, I am black! and radiant." PBWP

Song of Songs. Bible, *O.T. Fr.* Song of Solomon, The. ArNa

Song of songs, which is Solomon's, The. Bible, *O.T. Fr.* Song of Solomon, The. OBVE

Song of Spring. Keats. BoTP

Song of Spring at West Lake, A, Sent to Circuit Officer Hsieh. Ou-yang Hsiu, *tr. fr. Chinese by* Irving Y. Lo. SuSp

Song of Spring Journeying. Wang Yu, *tr. fr. Chinese by* Irving Y. Lo. SuSp

Song of Spring Replying to a Poem by Po Chü-yi, A. Liu Yu Hsi, *tr. fr. Chinese by* Daniel Bryant *and* Ronald C. Miao. SuSp

Song of Starvation. *Unknown, tr. fr. Chippewa Indian by Jerome K.* Rothenberg. STP

Song of Sukkaartik, the Assistant Spirit. Ajukutooq, *tr. fr. Eskimo.* WTO

Song of Summer Days. James William Foley. BoTP

Song of sunshine through the rain, A. Calvary and Easter. "Susan Coolidge." WBLP
(Easter Song, An. BLRP

Song of Supplication, A. Bible, *O.T., par. by* Sir Thomas Wyatt. *See* Out of the depths [*or* deep] have I cried [*or* called] (unto) Thee, O Lord.

Song of Texas. William Henry Cuyler Hosmer. PAH

Song of the Air, A. Gordon Alchin. NSI

Song of the Angels. L. A. J. Moorer. CBWP-3

Song of the Bald Eagle. *Unknown, tr. fr. Crow Indian by* Lewis Henry Morgan. STP

Song of the Ballet. J. B. Morton. FiBHP

Song of the Banana Man, The. Evan Jones. PBCV

Song of the Banjo, The. Kipling. FaBoCh; OtMeF; PrIm

Song of the Barber. W. H. Auden. *Fr.* Man of La Mancha. AnAn

Song of the Bath, The. Margaret E. Gibbs. BoTP

Song of the Bay Steed of Governor Wei, A. Ts'en Shen, *tr. fr. Chinese by* Daniel Bryant. SuSp

Song of the Bird, The. Longfellow. BoTP

Song on the South Sea, A. The Countess of Winchilsea. ECWP; NOEC

Song on the Water. Thomas Lovell Beddoes. *Fr.* Death's Jest Book. FaBoCh

Song on the Way to Jail. Kakayek, *tr. fr. Tlingit Indian* by James Koller. STP

Song Sequence, *sels.* Ben-Zion Tomer, *tr. fr. Hebrew* by Bernhard Frank.

Song Set by John Farmer. *Unknown.* CTC; NoSic

Song Set by Nicholas Yonge. *Unknown. See* Brown Is My Love.

Song Sung by Egistus and Clytemnestra. John Pickering. *Fr.* Horestes. NoSic

Song that I'm going to sing, The. The Crafty Farmer. *Unknown.* ESPB

Song that she sang was all written, The. The Moon of Mobile. Thomas Holley Chivers. OBAL

Song That Sounds Like This, The. James Fenton. SCBI

Song thumbed down a cruiser for a ride, A. James Cunningham. *Fr.* Narrator's Trance, The. JB

Song, 'tis my will that thou do seek out Love. Dante, *tr. fr. Italian* by Dante Gabriel Rossetti. *Fr.* Vita Nuova, La. AWP

Song to a Fair Young Lady, Going Out of the Town in the Spring. Dryden. OBEV

Song to a Lover. *Unknown*, *tr. fr. Amharic* by Willis Barnstone. BoWoP

Song to a Lute, A. Sir John Suckling. BeJo; CaPo; TrGrPo

Song to a Tree. Edwin Markham. FaPON

Song: To Amarantha, That She Would Dishevel Her Hair. Richard Lovelace. *See* Amarantha sweet and fair.

Song to April. Sir William Watson. *See* April, April,/ Laugh thy girlish laughter.

Song to be Sung by the Father of Infant Female Children. Ogden Nash. MoAmPo

Song to be Sung on the Water, A. Friedrich Leopold Graf zu Stolberg, *tr. fr. German* by Philip L. Miller. RiWo

Song to Be Written on a Wave. José Emilio Pacheco, *tr. fr. Spanish* by John Frederick Nims. STV

Song to Celia. Ben Jonson. *See* Come, my Celia, let us prove.

Song: To Celia. Ben Jonson. *See* Come, my Celia, let us prove.

Song: To Celia. Ben Jonson. *See* Drink[e] to me only [*or* onely] with thine eyes.

Song to Cloris, A. The Earl of Rochester. ErPo

Song to David, A. Christopher Smart. ChTr; EBEV; NAEL-1; NOBE, *abr.*; OAEL-1; PoEL-3; TrGrPo, *abr.*
Sels.
"Glorious the sun in mid career." FaBoCh
"O David, highest in the list." NOEC
"O thou, that sitst [*or* sit'st] upon a throne." OBWVE; OxAEP-1, 25 *sts.*; PoE
(Song to David, A.) ImPo
"Strong is the horse upon his speed." UV
(Man of Prayer, The.) LiTB; OtMeF
"Strong is the lion — like a coal." HAP
"Sublime — invention ever young." OBEV
"Tell them, I AM, Jehovah said." WGRP

Song to David, A. Christopher Smart. *See* O thou, that sitst [*or* sit'st] upon a throne.

Song to Erin. Mary Weston Fordham. CBWP-2

Song to His Purse for the King, A. Chaucer. *See* To you [*or* yow], my purse [*or* purs], and to non [*or* no *or* noon] other wight.

Song to Hymen: 1942. Anthony Richardson. PoWW

Song to Imogen [in Basic English]. Richard Leighton Greene. BXAP

Song to John, Christ's Friend, A. *Unknown.* MeEL

Song to John, Christ's Friend, A. *Unknown.* MeEL

Song to Mary, A. *At. to* William of Shoreham. *See* Marye, maide, milde and fre.

Song to Mithras, A. Kipling. *Fr.* Puck of Pook's Hill. NoAM

Song to Promote Growth. *Unknown, tr. by* Washington Matthews. OBVE

Song to Sleep. John Fletcher. *See* Care-charming Sleep [Thou Easer of All Woes].

Song to the Brandy. Duncan Ban MacIntyre. ScCV

Song to the Lamb. Novica Tadic, *tr. fr. Serbo-Croatian* by Charles Simic. HSix

Song to the Masquers. James Shirley. *Fr.* Triumph of Peace, The. OxBSP

Song to the Men of England. Shelley. EnRP; InPS; TrGrPo

Song to the Mountains. *Unknown, tr. fr. Pawnee Indian* by Alice C. Fletcher. AWP

Song To the New Day, *sels.* Giaconda Belli, *tr. fr. Spanish* by Angel Flores.

Song to the oak, the brave old oak, A. The Brave Old Oak. Henry Fothergill Chorley. FaBoBe

Song to the Runaway Slave. *Unknown.* BPo

Song to the Wife of His Youth, The. Nathan Alterman, *tr. fr. Hebrew* by Ruth Finer Mintz. *Fr.* Joy of the Poor, The. MHP

Song to the Wind, A. Taliesin, *tr. fr. Welsh* by A. P. Graves. FaBoCh

Song Tournament: New Style. Louis Untermeyer. OBAL

Song Turning Back into Itself, The, *sels.* Al Young.

Song unto liberty's brave buccaneer, A. Paul Jones. *Unknown.* PAH

Song went to the garden, The. Where the Song Went She Went & What Happened When They Met. *Unknown, tr. fr. Seneca Indian* by Jerome K. Rothenberg *and* Richard Johnny John. STP

Song will deceive you, the scent will incite you to sing, The. You Cannot Go Down to the Spring. John Shaw Neilson. CBAP

Song with Words. James Agee. ChIV-1; MoAmPo

Song without a lute. (LL) Without You I Am. Diana Der Hovanessian. LoHo

Song Without End. *Unknown.* RoPo

Song Written at Sea in the First Dutch War (1665), the Night before an Engagement. Charles Sackville. CoMu; EnLoPo; NOBE; OBEV; OBWP; OxAEP-1

Song Yet Song. Amir Gilboa, *tr. fr. Hebrew* by Ruth Finer Mintz. MHP

Songbirds in the public boughs, The. (LL) After the Last Bulletins. Richard Wilbur. CoAP; MoAB; MoAmPo; NYBP; TrGrPo

Songe betwene the Quenes Majestie and Englande, A. William Birche. CoMu

Songless Land, The. Francis Carey Slater. PeSAV

Songs, The. Martin Bell. FF

Songs, *sels.* Steve Crow.
"They say a man dies." HATNAP

Songs. *Unknown.* PBCV
Sels.
"New-come buckra/ He get sick"
"One, two, tree/ All de same"

Songs, The. *Unknown, tr. fr. Zuni Indian* by K. Kennedy. WTO

Songs about Life and Brighter Things Yet. Samuel Hoffenstein. NBLV
Sels.
"Nothing from a straight line swerves"
"Of all the birds that sing and fly"

Songs and Dances of Death. Count Arsenii Arkadyevich Golenishchev-Kutuzov, *tr. fr. Russian* by Philip L. Miller. RiWo
Sels.
"Child is moaning. The candle burning low, The".
Commander, The.
Forgotten One A Ballad, The.
Serenade, The.
Trepak.

Songs Anthome. Lady Jane Cavendish *and* Lady Elizabeth Brackley. *Fr.* Pastorall, A. KTR

Songs Composed in Prison, *sels.* Sung Wan, *tr. fr. Chinese* by William Schultz.

Song's Eternity. John Clare. FaBoCh

Songs for a Colored Singer. Elizabeth Bishop. PoNe; RB
Sels.
"Washing hangs upon the line, A." FaBoVe; FaBoWP

Songs for a Three-String Guitar. Léopold Sédar-Senghor, *tr. fr. French* by Miriam Koshland. PBA

Songs for My Mother. Anna Hempstead Branch. OHIP
Sels.
Song for My Mother, A: Her Hands.
Song for My Mother, A: Her Stories.
Song for My Mother, A: Her Words. FaPON

Songs for Signare, *sels.* Léopold Sédar Senghor, *tr. fr. French* by Ellen Conroy Kennedy.
"I walked you to the village where the granaries are at the threshold of Night." NegPo
"Long, long between your hands you held the warrior's black face." NegPo
"We shall bathe, my love, in an African presence." NegPo
"Your face, the beauty of a time long past evokes the perfumed robes in faded hues." NegPo

Songs for the Cisco Kid; or, Singing for the Face. K. Curtis Lyle. PoBA

Songs for the Cisco Kid; or, Singing: Song #2. K. Curtis Lyle. PoBA

Songs for the Four Parts of the Night. Owl Woman, *tr. fr. Papago Indian* by Frances Densmore. PBWP

Songs for the People. Frances E. W. Harper. AAP; PWR

Songs from Cyprus. Hilda Doolittle ("H. D."). MoAmPo
Sels.
"Gather for festival."
"Where is the nightingale."

Songs from Living in the Mountains, *sels.* Huang Tsung-hsi, *tr. fr. Chinese* by Lynn Struve.

Songs I Had, The. Ivor Gurney. NTP

Songs of Maximus. Charles Olson. *Fr.* Maximus Poems, The. NeAP

Songs of Satsuma, *sels.* Rai San'yo, *tr. fr. Chinese by* Burton Watson.

Songs of Seven, *sels.* Jean Ingelow.
    Longing for Home. WGRP
    Maternity. OHIP
    Seven Times One — Exultation. BLPA; FaPON; OBNC
    Seven Times Three — Love. PoLF
    Seven Times Two — Romance. GN

Songs of shepherds and rustical roundelays. The Hunting of the Gods. *Unknown.* OxBoLi

Songs of Sorrow. Kofi Awoonor. HBAPE

Songs of Sorrow (Spring 1918), *sels.* Viljo Kajava, *tr. fr. Finnish by* Aili Jarvenpa.

Songs of T'ang, *sels.* Confucius, *tr. fr. Chinese by* Ezra Pound.
    Alba. CTC

Songs of the Birds, The. Edward Carpenter. WGRP

Songs of the Common Day, *sels.* Sir Charles G. D. Roberts.
    Herring Weir, The. NOBC
    Pea-Fields, The. NOBC

Songs of the Frontier, *sels.* Li K'ai-hsien, *tr. fr. Chinese by* Jonathan Chaves.

Songs of the Greenwood. Shakespeare. *See* Under the greenwood tree.

Songs of the Greenwood: "Blow, blow, thou winter wind." Shakespeare. *See* Blow, blow, thou winter wind.

Songs of the Harp Player. Goethe, *tr. fr. German by* Philip L. Miller. RiWo

Songs of the Land of Zion Jerusalem, *sels.* Yehuda Amichai, *tr. fr. Hebrew by* Warren Bargod *and* Stanley F. Chyet.

Songs of the People. Hayyim Nahman Bialik, *tr. fr. Hebrew by* Maurice Samuel. AWP
    Sels.
    "On a hill there blooms a palm."
    "Two steps from my garden rail."

Songs of the Psyche, *sels.* Thomas Kinsella.
    "Character, indistinct, entered, A." NoAM

Songs of the PWD Man, The. Tony Harrison. FaBoBl

Songs of the Sea-Children, *sels.* Bliss Carman.

Songs of the Squatters. Robert Lowe. NOBAu

Songs of the Squatters, *sels.* Robert Lowe.
    "Commissioner bet me a pony, The — I won, The." NOBAu
    "Gum has no shade, The." NOBAu

Songs of the Stream, *sels.* Leah Goldberg, *tr. fr. Hebrew by* Ruth Finer Mintz.
    Blade of Grass Sings to the River, The. TrJP
    Blade of Grass Sings to the Stream, The. MHP
    Girl Sings to the Stream, The. MHP
    Moon Sings to the Stream, The. MHP
    Stream Sings to the Stone, The. MHP
    Tree Sings to the Stream, The. MHP

Songs of the Transformed, *sels.* Margaret Atwood.
    Siren Song. HAP; NIP; PoA; WeW

Songs of Travel. Robert Louis Stevenson. OBNC
    Sels.
    "Bright is the ring of words." TrGrPo
    If This Were Faith. TrPWD; WGRP
    To S. R. Crockett. CoGr
    (Blows the Wind To-Day.) SCGP

Songs of Yen-ching, *sels.* Hsü Wei, *tr. fr. Chinese by* Jonathan Chaves.

Songs on Accompanying the Governor-General, *sels.* Shih Jun-chang, *tr. fr. Chinese by* William Schultz.

Songs on the Death of Children, *sels.* Friedrich Rückert.
    "Sun is soon to rise as bright, The." OBD

Songs on the Voices of Birds, *sels.* Jean Ingelow.
    Child and Boatman. FM

Songs, so old and bitter, The. The Coffin. Heine, *tr. fr. German by* Louis Untermeyer. AWP

Songs to Seraphine. Heine, *tr. fr. German by* Emma Lazarus. TrJP
    Sels.
    Shadow-Love
    Waves Gleam in the Sunshine, The.

Songs to Survive the Summer. Robert Hass. AmPA

Songs to Welcome the Society of the Mystic Animals. *Unknown, tr. fr. Seneca Indian by* Jerome K. Rothenberg *and* Richard Johnny John. STP

Songs without Words. John Ashbery. NAAL-2

Songs you sent me I have read, The. Hildebert, *tr. fr. Latin by* Helen Waddell. MLL

Sonia at 32. Morrie Warshawski. BTR

Sonja Henie, the young girl. Theodore Weiss. VGW

Sonne, The. George Herbert. PeECV; SeCP

Sonne, with his bemes of brightnesse, The. Balade and Roundel to Master Somer. Thomas Hoccleve. OxBLMV

Sonnet. William Browne. *See* For her gait, if she be walking.

Sonnet. Hartley Coleridge. *See* Long Time a Child.

Sonnet IV. E. E. Cummings. *See* This Is the Garden.

Sonnet. William Drummond of Hawthornden. *See* Sweet Spring, thou turn'st with all thy goodly train.

Sonnet. Milton. *See* When I consider how my light is spent.

Sonnet. Milton. *See* Cyriack, this three years' day these eyes, though clear.

Sonnet. Milton. *See* Lawrence, of virtuous father virtuous son.

Sonnet 129. Shakespeare. *See* Expense of spirit in a waste of shame, The [*or* Th'].

Sonnet. Charles Hamilton Sorley. *See* When You See Millions of the Mouthless Dead.

Sonnet, A. James Kenneth Stephen. *See* Two voices are there: one is of the deep.

Sonnet. Richard Chenevix Trench. *See* Lord, what a change within us one short hour.

Sonnet XVI: "After an age when thunderbolts and hail." Louise Labé, *tr. fr. French by* Willis Barnstone. BoWoP

Sonnet XIX: "After having slain very many beasts." Louise Labé, *tr. fr. French by* Willis Barnstone. BoWoP

Sonnet: "After dark vapours have oppress'd our plains." Keats. *See* After Dark Vapours.

Sonnet: "Afterwards there are dogends in." Maureen Duffy. PeHV

Sonnet: "Ah, sweet Content! where is thy mild abode." Barnabe Barnes. *See* Ah, sweet Content! where is thy mylde abode?

Sonnet: "Alas for me, who loved a falcon well!" *Unknown, tr. fr. Italian by* Dante Gabriel Rossetti. AWP

Sonnet: "Alexis, here she stayed; among these pines." William Drummond of Hawthornden. EIL; NOSC
    (Spring Bereaved.) OBEV

Sonnet: "All my senses, like beacon's flame." Fulke Greville. *See* All my senses, like beacon's flame.

Sonnet: "All we were going strong last night this time." John Berryman. FaBoMo

Sonnet: At Ostend. William Lisle Bowles. *See* How sweet the tuneful bells' responsive peal!

Sonnet: "Am I thus conquered? Have I lost the powers." Mary Sidney Wroth, Countess of Montgomery. *See* Am I thus conquered? Have I lost the powers.

Sonnet: "Amazing thing happened to me, An." Daniil Kharms, *tr. fr. Russian by* George Gibian. FaBoNo

Sonnet: "And on the porch, across the upturned chair." Donald Justice. MT; WeW

Sonnet: "And then I sat me down, and gave the rein." Gustav Rosenhane, *tr. fr. Swedish by* Sir Edmund Gosse. AWP

Sonnet: "As in a duskie [*or* dusky] and tempestuous night." William Drummond of Hawthornden. NOSC; OxAEP-1

Sonnet: "As long as I continue weeping." Louise Labé, *tr. fr. French by* Joan Keefe *and* Richard Terdiman. PBWP

Sonnet IX: "As soon as I lie down in my soft bed." Louise Labé, *tr. fr. French by* Willis Barnstone. BoWoP

Sonnet: "As when, to one who long hath watched, the morn." John Codrington Bampfylde. NOEC

Sonnet: At Ostend. William Lisle Bowles. *See* How sweet the tuneful bells' responsive peal!

Sonnet: "Avenge, O Lord, thy slaughtered saints, whose bones." Milton. *See* Avenge, O Lord, thy slaughtered [*or* slaughter'd] saints, whose bones.

Sonnet: "Avising the bright beams of these fair eyes." Sir Thomas Wyatt. SiPSBD

Sonnet: "Azured [*or* Azur'd] vault, the crystal circles bright, The." James I, King of England. EIL
    (All These the Lord Did Frame.) CBCK
    (Heaven and Earth.) ChTr

Sonnet: "Be you all pleased? Your pleasures grieve me not." Mary Sidney Wroth, Countess of Montgomery. *Fr.* Urania. NOSC; WPE

Sonnet: "Beauty, sweet love, is like the morning dew." Samuel Daniel. *See* Beauty, sweet love, is like the morning dew.

Sonnet: "Because my grief seems quiet and apart." Robert Nathan. TrJP

Sonnet: "Beckie, my luve! — What is't, ye twa-faced tod?" George Campbell Hay. OxBS

Sonnet: "Bible says Sennacherib's campaign was spoiled, The." C. S. Lewis. TrCP

Sonnet: "Brilliant stills of food, the cozy, The." Sandra M. Gilbert. NIP

Sonnet: "Caesar, when that the traitor of Egypt." Sir Thomas Wyatt. SiPSBD

Sonnet: "Caelica, I overnight was finely used." Fulke Greville. *See* Caelica, I overnight was finely used.

Sonnet: "Captain or colonel, or knight in arms." Milton. GTBS; GTBS-P; NoP; SCGP; Son

  (Sonnet: "Captain or colonel or knight in arms.") OAEL-1; OxAEP-1

Sonnet: "Care-charmer sleep[e], son[ne] of the sable night." Samuel Daniel. *See* Care-charmer sleep[e], son[ne] of the sable night.

Sonnet: "Cleare moving cristall, pure as the Sunne beames." William Alexander, Earl of Stirling. Fr. Aurora. OxBS

Sonnet: "Come, darkest night, becoming sorrow best." Mary Sidney Wroth, Countess of Montgomery. *Fr.* Urania. NOSC; WPE

Sonnet VI: "Coming of that limpid star is twice, The." Louise Labé, *tr. fr. French* by Willis Barnstone. BoWoP

Sonnet: Content and Resolute. William Drummond of Hawthornden. JCP

Sonnet: "Crumbled rock of London is dripping under, The." Roy Fuller. PoA

Sonnet: "Cry, crow." Hayden Carruth. NNaP; Son

Sonnet: "Cyriack, this three years' day these eyes, though clear." Milton. NOSC; PeECV; Son

  (Sonnet.) OxAEP-1

  (To Cyriack Skinner ("Cyriack, this three years' day").) TrGrPo

Sonnet: "Cyriack, whose grandsire, on the royal bench." Milton. *See* Cyriack, whose grandsire, on the royal bench.

Sonnet: Dante Alighieri to Guido Cavalcanti. Dante. *See* Guido, I would that Lapo, thou, and I.

Sonnet: "Dark, puckered hole: a purple carnation." Paul Verlaine, *tr. fr. French* by J. Murat *and* W. Gunn. PeHV

  (Crumpled like a carnation, mauve and dim.) FaBoBl, *tr.* by Alistair Elliot

  (Lines on the Arsehole.) FaBoBl, *tr.* by Alistair Elliot

Sonnet: "Dear [*or* Deere], why should you command me to my rest." Michael Drayton. *See* Deare [*or* Dear], why should you command [*or* commaund] me to my rest.

Sonnet: "Dear to my soul! then leave me not forsaken!" Henry Constable. *See* Dear to my soul! then leave me not forsaken!

Sonnet: Death Is Not without but within Him. Cino da Pistoia, *tr. fr. Italian* by Dante Gabriel Rossetti. AWP

Sonnet: Death Warnings. Francisco de Quevedo y Villegas, *tr. fr. Spanish* by John Masefield. AWP

Sonnet: Death Will Find Me. Rupert Brooke. *See* Oh! Death will find me, long before I tire.

Sonnet: Death's Last Will. William Drummond of Hawthornden. JCP

Sonnet: "Deep in a vale where rocks on every side." Gustav Rosenhane, *tr. fr. Swedish* by Sir Edmund Gosse. AWP

Sonnet: Dolce Stil Novo. Gavin Ewart. GrPl

Sonnet XXIV: "Don't blame me, ladies, if I've loved. No sneers." Louise Labé, *tr. fr. French.* BoWoP, *tr.* by Willis Barnstone

  ("Don't scold me, ladies, if I have loved.") PBWP, *tr.* by Carol Cosman

Sonnet: "Dost see how unregarded now." Sir John Suckling. BeJo; CaPo; ELP; NOSC

Sonnet: "Down[e] in the depth of mine iniquity." Fulke Greville. *See* Down in the depth of mine iniquity.

Sonnet: "Each man me telleth I change most my devise." Sir Thomas Wyatt. SiPS

Sonnet: "Earth with thunder torn, with fire blasted, The." Fulke Greville. *See* Earth with thunder torn[e], with fire blasted, The.

Sonnet: England in 1819. Shelley. *See* Old, mad, blind, despised, and dying king, An.

Sonnet: "England! the time is come when thou shouldst wean." Wordsworth. Son

Sonnet: Equality of the Sexes. Gavin Ewart. Son

Sonnet: "Evening, as slow thy placid shades descend." William Lisle Bowles. NOEC

Sonnet: "Everyone makes love to their bereft & go." Bernadette Mayer. VBLP

Sonnet: "Fair is my love, and cruel as she's fair." Samuel Daniel. *See* Fair is my love, and cruel as she's fair.

Sonnet: "Fair is my love that feeds among the lilies." Bartholomew Griffin. *See* Faire Is My Love.

Sonnet: "Farewell, love, and all thy laws [*or* lawes] for ever." Sir Thomas Wyatt. AAS; CBLP; LiTB; NAEL-1; NoSic; OAEL-1; SCGP; SiPS; SiPSBD

  (Lover Renounceth Love, The.) TrGrPo

  (Renancing of Love, A.) GBL; Son

Sonnet: "Fie, tedious hope, why do you still rebel?" Mary Sidney Wroth, Countess of Montgomery. *Fr.* Urania. NOSC; WPE

Sonnet: "First *loue*, as greatest God *aboue* the rest." James I, King of England. ScCV

Sonnet: "Franklin sailed a key-hung kite." James Facos. NBLV

Sonnet: "From a rived tree, that stands beside the grave." Anna Seward. ECWP

Sonnet IV: "From that first flash when awful Love took flame." Louise Labé, *tr. fr. French* by Willis Barnstone. BoWoP

Sonnet: "Glory to God and to God's Mother chaste." Giovanni Quirino, *tr. fr. Italian* by Dante Gabriel Rossetti. AWP

Sonnet: "Go, thou that vainly dost mine eyes invite." Henry King. OxBSP

Sonnet: "Go you, O winds that blow from north to south." Alexander Craig. EIL

  (To Pandora.) Son

Sonnet: "Guido, I wish that you and Lapo and I." Dante, *tr. fr. Italian* by Kenneth Koch. ArLo; RB; TTTS

Sonnet: He Argues His Case with Death. Cecco Angiolieri, da Siena, *tr. fr. Italian* by Dante Gabriel Rossetti. AWP

Sonnet: "He came in silvern armor, trimmed with black." Gwendolyn B. Bennett. CDC; PoBA; PoNe

Sonnet: He Compares All Things with His Lady, and Finds Them Wanting. Cavalcanti, *tr. fr. Italian* by Dante Gabriel Rossetti. AWP

Sonnet: He Craves Interpreting of a Dream of His. Dante da Maiano, *tr. fr. Italian* by Dante Gabriel Rossetti. AWP

Sonnet: "He is like a cloud that for an instant." Jacqueline Osherow. UTF 30

Sonnet: He Is Past All Help. Cecco Angiolieri, da Siena, *tr. fr. Italian* by Dante Gabriel Rossetti. AWP

Sonnet: He Jests Concerning His Poverty. Bartolomeo di Sant' Angelo, *tr. fr. Italian* by Dante Gabriel Rossetti. AWP

Sonnet: He Rails against Dante, Who Had Censured His Homage to Becchina. Cecco Angiolieri, da Siena, *tr. fr. Italian* by Dante Gabriel Rossetti. AWP

Sonnet: He Speaks of a Third Love of His. Cavalcanti, *tr. fr. Italian* by Dante Gabriel Rossetti. AWP

Sonnet: He Will Not Be Too Deeply in Love. Cecco Angiolieri, da Siena, *tr. fr. Italian* by Dante Gabriel Rossetti. AWP

Sonnet: He Will Praise His Lady. Guido Guinicelli, *tr. fr. Italian* by Dante Gabriel Rossetti. AWP

Sonnet: "Her face has made my life most proud and glad." Jacopo da Lentino, *tr. fr. Italian* by Dante Gabriel Rossetti.

  (Sonnet: Of His Lady's Face.) AWP

Sonnet: "Here in the self is all that men can know." John Masefield. *Fr.* Lollingdon Downs. AWP; LiTB, I–XV

Sonnet: "High on the wall that holds Jerusalem." G. K. Chesteron. OBTV MM

Sonnet, A: "His golden locks time hath to silver turned." George Peele. *See* His golden locks time hath to siluer turn'd.

Sonnet: "Honora, should that cruel time arrive." Anna Seward. ECWP

Sonnet: "How do I hate you? Let me count the ways." Stanley J. Sharpless. UV

Sonnet: "How fast thou fliest, O time, on love's swift wings." Mary Sidney Wroth, Countess of Montgomery. *Fr.* Urania. NOSC; WPE

Sonnet: "How like a fire doth love increase in me." Mary Sidney Wroth, Countess of Montgomery. *Fr.* Urania. NOSC; WPE

Sonnet: "How many faults you might accuse me of." Elinor Wylie. NAAL-2

Sonnet: He Will Praise His Lady. Guido Guinicelli, *tr. fr. Italian* by Dante Gabriel Rossetti. AWP

Sonnet: "How shall I work that she may not forget." Owen Barfield. ArLo

Sonnet: "How soon hath time the subtle thief of youth." Milton. *See* How Soon Hath Time [the Subtle Thief of Youth].

Sonnet: "How sweet the tuneful bells' responsive peal!" William Lisle Bowles. OBTV

  (Bells of Ostend, The.) EnRP

  (Sonnet: At Ostend.) NOEC

Sonnet: "How that vast heaven intitled First is rolled." William Drummond of Hawthornden. EIL

Sonnet: "I abide and abide and better abide." Sir Thomas Wyatt. BoLoP; EnLoPo; SiPS; SiPSBD

Sonnet: "I am in need of music that would flow." Elizabeth Bishop. LPA

Sonnet: "I, being born a woman and distressed." Edna St. Vincent Millay. *See* I, being born a woman and distressed.

Sonnet: "I dreamed the nymph that o'er my fancy reigns." William Alexander, Earl of Stirling. *Fr.* Aurora. NOSC

Sonnet: "I envy not Endymion now no more." William Alexander, Earl of Stirling. *See* I Envy Not Endymion.

Sonnet: "I feel I am; — I only know I am." John Clare. *See* I Feel I Am.

Sonnet XVII: "I flee the city, temples, and each place." Louise Labé, *tr. fr. French* by Willis Barnstone. BoWoP

Sonnet: "I had no thought of violets of late." Alice Dunbar Nelson. BlSi; CDC; PoBA; PoNe; Son

Sonnet: "I hate the Spring in parti-coloured vest." Mary Locke. ECWP

Sonnet: "I have it in my heart to serve God so." Jacopo da Lentino, *tr. fr. Italian* by Dante Gabriel Rossetti. AWP

Sonnet: "I have not spent the April of my time." Bartholomew Griffin. *See* I have not spent the April of my time.

Sonnet: "I hereby swear that to uphold your house." Elinor Wylie. *Fr.* One Person. LiTA; MoAB; NAAL-2; OxBA; Son
  (I Hereby Swear.) ImPo
  (Sonnet from "One Person.") LiTA; MoAmPo

Sonnet: "I know that all beneath the moon decays." William Drummond of Hawthornden. JCP; Son

Sonnet VIII: "I live, I die, I burn myself and drown." Louise Labé, *tr. fr. French* by Willis Barnstone. BoWoP

Sonnet: "I love to rise ere gleams the tardy light." Anna Seward. ECWP

Sonnet: "I must not grieve my love, whose eyes would read." Samuel Daniel. *See* I must not grieve my love, whose eyes would read.

Sonnet XII: "I saw an ugly beast come from the sea." Spenser. ChIV-2

Sonnet XIII: "I saw a woman sitting on a beast." Spenser. ChIV-2

Sonnet: "I saw magic on a green country road." Michael Hartnett. BIrV; PBCIP

Sonnet: "I that erstwhile the world's sweet air did draw." George Wither. *Fr.* Shephe[a]rd's Hunting, The. NOSC

Sonnet: "I wandered out a while agone." George Wither. *Fr.* Fair Virtue, the Mistress of Philarete. NOSC

Sonnet: "Ice over time." David Shapiro. UL

Sonnet: "Idly she yawned, and threw her heavy hair." George Moore. ErPo

Sonnet: "If amorous faith in heart unfeigned." Sir Thomas Wyatt. SiPSBD

Sonnet: "If any man would know the very cause." Guerzo di Montecanti, *tr. fr. Italian* by Dante Gabriel Rossetti. AWP

Sonnet: "If ever Sorrow spoke from soul that loves." Henry Constable. *Fr.* Diana. EiL; ESo

Sonnet XIII: "If I could linger on his lovely chest." Louise Labé, *tr. fr. French* by Aliki *and* Willis Barnstone. BoWoP

Sonnet I: "If it must be; if it must be, O God!" David Gray. *Fr.* In the Shadows. OxBS

Sonnet: "If love is chaste, what bears adultery?" Sibylla Schwarz, *tr. fr. German* by George C. Schoolfield. GePo

Sonnet: "Ile give thee leave my love, in beauties field." William Alexander, Earl of Stirling. *Fr.* Aurora. OxBS

Sonnet 63: "In a distant field, small animals prepare." John Tranter. *Fr.* Crying in Early Infancy. FaBoMA

Sonnet: In Absence from Becchina. Cecco Angiolieri, da Siena, *tr. fr. Italian* by Dante Gabriel Rossetti. AWP

Sonnet: "In Cyprus springs, whereas dame Venus dwelt." The Earl of Surrey. SiPSBD

Sonnet: "In every dream thy lovely features rise." William Barnes. BoLoP

Sonnet: "Ingratitude, how deadly is the smart." Anna Seward. ECWP; NOEC

Sonnet: "Innumerable Beauties, thou white haire." Lord Herbert of Cherbury. PoEL-2

Sonnet: "Is there a solitary wretch who hies." Charlotte Smith. ECWP; WoRP

Sonnet XI: "Is God invisible? This very room." Adele Greeff. GoYe

Sonnet: "It is as true as strange, else trial feigns." John Davies of Hereford. EiL

Sonnet: "It is not death, that sometime in a sigh." Thomas Hood. OBNC

Sonnet: "It shall be said [or sayd] I died [or dy'de] for Coelia." William Percy. *Fr.* Coelia. EiL

Sonnet: Kamikaze. Bernadette Mayer. UL

Sonnet: Lady, That in the Prime. Milton. *See* Lady that in the prime of earliest youth.

Sonnet 7: "I've found out why, that day, that suicide." John Berryman. PoE

Sonnet XVIII: "Kiss me again, re-kiss and kiss me whole." Louise Labé, *tr. fr. French.* WPOW, *tr.* by Raymond Oliver
  (Sonnet XVIII: "Kiss me again, rekiss and kiss me more.") BoWoP, *tr.* by Willis Barnstone

Sonnet XVIII: "Kiss me again, rekiss, kiss me more." Louise Labé. *See* Kiss me again, re-kiss and kiss me whole.

Sonnet: "Lamp of heaven's crystal hall that brings the hours." William Drummond of Hawthornden. JCP

Sonnet: "Lawrence, of virtuous father virtuous son." Milton. *See* Lawrence, of virtuous father virtuous son.

Sonnet: "Leave me, all sweet refrains my lip hath made." Camões, *tr. fr. Spanish* by Richard Garnett. AWP

Sonnet: "Leave me, O love which reachest but to dust." Sir Philip Sidney. ESo

Sonnet: Leaves. William Barnes. BoNaP; ChTr; FaBoRV; OBNC
  (Leave Me, O Love.) EnRePo; SiPSBD

Sonnet: "Let others of the world's decaying tell." William Alexander, Earl of Stirling. *Fr.* Aurora. EiL

Sonnet: "Let others sing of knights and paladin[e]s." Samuel Daniel. *See* Let others sing of knights and paladins [or palladines].

Sonnet: "Let us leave talking of angelic hosts." Elinor Wylie. *Fr.* One Person. OxBA

Sonnet: "Lift not the painted veil which those who live." Shelley. EnRP; OBNC, *sl. diff. vers.*; Son
  (Lift not the veil which those who live.) FHYEP
  (Sonnet: "Lift Not the Veil Which Those Who Live.") FHYEP

Sonnet: "Lights in daytime indoors make outside." Ron Padgett. NGP

Sonnet: "Like to an hermit poor, in place obscure." *At. to* Sir Walter Ralegh. EiL
  (Like to a Hermit Poor. GBL; SiPSBD

Sonnet: "Like to the Indians, scorched with the sun." Mary Sidney Wroth, Countess of Montgomery. *Fr.* Urania. NOSC; WPE

Sonnet: "Like Memnon's rock, touched with the rising sun." Giles Fletcher the Elder. *See* Like [or Lyke] Memnons rock, touched [or rocke toucht] with the rising sun[ne].

Sonnet: "Lock up, fair lids, the treasure of my heart." Sir Philip Sidney. *See* Lock up, fair lids, the treasure of my heart.

Sonnet: "Look, Delia, how we esteem the half-blown rose." Samuel Daniel. *See* Look, Delia, how we [e]steem the half-blown rose.

Sonnet: "Love is the peace, whereto all thoughts do strive." Fulke Greville. *See* Love is the peace, whereto all thoughts do[e] strive.

Sonnet XII: "Lute, companion of my calamity." Louise Labé, *tr. fr. French* by Aliki *and* Willis Barnstone. BoWoP

Sonnet: "Madam, 'tis true, your beauties move." Sidney Godolphin. JCP

Sonnet: "Man, dream[e] no more of curious mysteries." Fulke Greville. *See* Man, dream[e] no more of curious mysteries.

Sonnet: "Men call you fair, and you do credit it." Spenser. *See* LXXIX. "Men call you fair [or fayre], and you do[e] credit it."

Sonnet: "Methought I saw my late espoused saint." Milton. *See* Methought I saw my late espoused saint.

Sonnet: "Month of January has flown Past, The." Joseph Brodsky, *tr. fr. Russian* by George L. Kline. AnAn

Sonnet: "My dream a drink with Lonnie Johnson." Ted Berrigan. NoAM

Sonnet: "My duchess was the werst she laffed she bitte." Ernest Walsh. ErPo

Sonnet 63: "In a distant field, small animals prepare." John Tranter. *Fr.*

Sonnet: "My God, where is that ancient heat towards Thee." George Herbert. ESCV; GeHe; NOSC; OAEL-1

Sonnet: "My heart I gave thee not to do it pain." Sir Thomas Wyatt. SiPSBD

Sonnet: "My lady's presence makes the roses red." Henry Constable. *Fr.* Diana. EiL; ESo; NIP

Sonnet: "My love and I for kisses played [or play'd]." William Strode. FaBoEE; NOSC

Sonnet: "My Love, I cannot thy rare beauties place." William Smith. *Fr.* Chloris [or the Complaint of the Passionate Despised Shepheard]. EiL; ESo; InvP

Sonnet: "My love, if I write a song for you." Veronica Forrest-Thomson. VBLP

Sonnet: "My love took scorn my service to retain." Sir Thomas Wyatt. SiPS

Sonnet: "My lute, be as thou wast [or wert] when thou didst grow." William Drummond of Hawthornden. EiL; NOSC; SCGP; Son
  (To His Lute. GTBS; GTBS-P

Sonnet: "My pain, still smothered in my grieved breast." Mary Sidney Wroth, Countess of Montgomery. *Fr.* Urania. NOSC; WPE

Sonnet: "My soul surcharged with grief now loud complains." Rachel Morpurgo, *tr. fr. Hebrew* by Nina Davis Salaman. TrJP

Sonnet: "My true love hath my heart." Sir Philip Sidney. *See* My true love hath my heart, and I have his.

Sonnet: "No worst, there is none." Gerard Manley Hopkins. *See* No worst, there is none. Pitched past pitch of grief.

Sonnet: Not, I'll not, carrion comfort, Despair, not feast on thee. Gerard Manley Hopkins. *See* Not, I'll not, carrion comfort, Despair, not feast on thee.

Sonnet I: "Not Ulysses, no, nor any other man." Louise Labé, *tr. fr. Italian* by Willis Barnstone. BoWoP

Sonnet: "Not wrongly moved by this dismaying scene." William Empson. LiTM

Sonnet: "Now the bat circles on the breeze of eve." Ann Radcliffe. WPE

Sonnet: "Nuns fret not at their convent's narrow room." Wordsworth. *See* Nuns Fret Not at Their Convent's Narrow Room.

Sonnet: "Nurse-life wheat within his green husk growing, The." Fulke Greville. *See* Nurse-life wheat, within his greene huske growing, The.

Sonnet: "O shady vales, O fair enriched meads." Thomas Lodge. *Fr.* Margarite of America, A. EiL
  DD

Sonnet XXII: "O blazing Sun, how happy you are there." Louise Labé, *tr. fr. French* by Willis Barnstone. BoWoP
106

Sonnet: To Certain Ladies; When Beatrice Was Lamenting Her Father's Death. Dante, *tr. fr. Italian by* Dante Gabriel Rossetti. AWP

Sonnet XI: "O eyes clear with beauty, O tender gaze." Louise Labé, *tr. fr. French by* Willis Barnstone. BoWoP

Sonnet II: "O handsome chestnut eyes, evasive gaze." Louise Labé, *tr. fr. French by* Willis Barnstone. BoWoP

Sonnet III: "O interminable desires, O futile hope." Louise Labé, *tr. fr. French by* Willis Barnstone. BoWoP

Sonnet, A: "O lovely O most charming pug." Marjory Fleming. *See* O lovely O most charming pug.

Sonnet: "O thou who never harbored fear." Eloise Bibb. CBWP-4

Sonnet: "October's gold is dim — the forests rot." David Gray. OxAEP-2

Sonnet: Of All He Would Do. Cecco Angiolieri, da Siena, *tr. fr. Italian by* Dante Gabriel Rossetti. AWP

Sonnet: Of an Ill-Favored Lady. Cavalcanti, *tr. fr. Italian by* Dante Gabriel Rossetti. AWP

Sonnet: Of Beatrice de' Portinari, on All Saints' Day. Dante, *tr. fr. Italian by* Dante Gabriel Rossetti. AWP

Sonnet: Of Beauty and Duty. Dante, *tr. fr. Italian by* Dante Gabriel Rossetti. AWP

Sonnet: Of Becchina in a Rage. Cecco Angiolieri, da Siena, *tr. fr. Italian by* Dante Gabriel Rossetti. AWP

Sonnet: Of Becchina, the Shoemaker's Daughter. Cecco Angiolieri, da Siena, *tr. fr. Italian by* Dante Gabriel Rossetti. AWP

Sonnet: Of His Lady's Face. Jacopo da Lentino. *See* Her face has made my life most proud and glad.

Sonnet: Of His Pain from a New Love. Cavalcanti, *tr. fr. Italian by* Dante Gabriel Rossetti. AWP

Sonnet: Of Love, in Honor of His Mistress Becchina. Cecco Angiolieri, da Siena, *tr. fr. Italian by* Dante Gabriel Rossetti. AWP

Sonnet: Of Love in Men and Devils. Cecco Angiolieri, da Siena, *tr. fr. Italian by* Dante Gabriel Rossetti. AWP

Sonnet: Of Moderation and Tolerance. Guido Guinicelli, *tr. fr. Italian by* Dante Gabriel Rossetti. AWP

Sonnet: Of the Eyes of a Certain Mandetta. Cavalcanti, *tr. fr. Italian by* Dante Gabriel Rossetti. AWP

Sonnet: Of the Grave of Selvaggia, on the Monte della Sambuca. Cino da Pistoia, *tr. fr. Italian by* Dante Gabriel Rossetti. AWP

Sonnet: Of the Making of Master Messerin. Rustico di Filippo, *tr. fr. Italian by* Dante Gabriel Rossetti. AWP

Sonnet: Of the 20th of June 1291. Cecco Angiolieri, da Siena, *tr. fr. Italian by* Dante Gabriel Rossetti. AWP

Sonnet: "Of thee (kind boy) I ask no red and white." Sir John Suckling. BeJo; CaPo; MeLP; NoP; NOSC; OxBoLi; SeCP; SeCV-1

Sonnet: Of Virtue. Folgore da San Geminiano, *tr. fr. Italian by* Dante Gabriel Rossetti. AWP

Sonnet: Of Why He Is Unchanged. Cecco Angiolieri, da Siena. *See* Whoever without money is in love.

Sonnet: Of Why He Would Be a Scullion. Cecco Angiolieri, da Siena, *tr. fr. Italian by* Dante Gabriel Rossetti. AWP

Sonnet: "Oh! Death will find me, long before I tire." Rupert Brooke. PoRA

(Sonnet: Death Will Find Me.) MoBrPo; Son

Sonnet: "Oh for a poet — for a beacon bright." E. A. Robinson. OxBA

Sonnet: "Oh! [*or* O!] for some honest lover's ghost." Sir John Suckling. BeJo; BXAP; JCP; MeLP; PoEL-3; SeCP; SeCV-1

(Doubt of Martyrdom, A.) BoLoP; CaPo; NOBE; OBEV

Sonnet: "Oh, if thou knew'st how thou thyself dost harm." William Alexander, Earl of Stirling. *See* Oh, If Thou Knew'st How Thou Thyself Dost Harm.

Sonnet: "Oh strive not still to heap didain on me." Mary Sidney Wroth, Countess of Montgomery. *Fr.* Urania. NOSC; WPE

Sonnet: "Oh, to vex me, contraries [*or* contraryes] meet in one." John Donne. *Fr.* Holy Sonnets. ESCV; NOSC; OAEL-1; PoEL-2; Son

(Oh, to vex me, two contraries meet in one.) ChIV-2
82

Sonnet: On a Picture of Leander. Keats. EnRP
83

Sonnet: on Loss. Sir Robert Ayton. NOSC
84

Sonnet: On the Detection of a False Friend. Cavalcanti, *tr. fr. Italian by* Dante Gabriel Rossetti. AWP
85

Sonnet: On the Late Massacre in Piedmont. Milton. *See* Avenge, O Lord, thy slaughtered [*or* slaughter'd] saints, whose bones.
86

Sonnet: On the Religious Memorie of Mrs. Catherine Thomason My Christian Freind Deceas'd Decem. 1646. Milton. ChIV-2
87

Sonnet: On the River Tweed. Sir Robert Ayton. NOSC

Sonnet: "Open wound which has been healed anew, An." Richard Chenevix Trench. TrPWD

Sonnet: "Orgasm completely, The." Tom Clark. CoAP

Sonnet: "Oxford, since late I left thy peaceful shore." Thomas Russell. Son

Sonnet: "Patience, hard thing! the hard thing but to pray." Gerard Manley Hopkins. NOBVV; OBNC

(Patience, Hard Thing!) EnVR; MeMBP; Prf; Son

Sonnet: "Ponder thy cares, and sum them all in one." Sir David Murray. *Fr.* Caelia. EIL

Sonnet: "Record is nothing, and the hero great." Lord De Tabley. EBVV

Sonnet: "Remember me when I am gone away." Christina Rossetti. AWP; BoLoP; CH; EBEvV; EnLoPo; FaBV; IMW; MeMBP; NOBE; NoP; OAEL-2; OBEV; OBNC; OxAEP-2; PlP; PoLF; PoRA; TFi; TrGrPo

(Remember Me.) OxBM

Sonnet: "Roar drowns the reproach, facing him." Edwin Denby. PRA

Sonnet: "Say, wouldst thou guard thy son." Francesco da Barberini, *tr. fr. Italian by* Dante Gabriel Rossetti. AWP

Sonnet: "Seer foretold that I would love one day, A." Louise Labé, *tr. fr. French by* Judith Thurman. PBWP

Sonnet — Science. Poe. *Fr.* Al Aaraff. AmPP; MeMAP; NAAL-1; NoP; OxBA; TAP

Sonnet: "Scorn not the sonnet; critic, you have frowned." Wordsworth. *See* Scorn not the sonnet; critic, you have frowned.

Sonnet: "Seer foretold that I would love one day, A." Louise Labé. *See* I was foretold that on a certain day.

Sonnet: "Shall I, wasting in despair." George Wither. *See* Shall I, Wasting in Despair.

Sonnet: "She is so young, and never never before." Edward Davison. ErPo

Sonnet: "She took the dappled partridge flecked [*or* fleckt] with blood." Tennyson. FM; NAEL-2

Sonnet: "Since thou hast viewed [*or* view'd] some Gorgon, and art grown." Henry King. CBLP; NOSC; SeCP

Sonnet: Silence. Thomas Hood. *See* There is a silence where hath been no sound.

Sonnet — Silence. Poe. MeMAP; NOBA

Sonnet: "Silver herring throbbed thick in my seine, The." Kenneth Leslie. *See* Silver herring throbbed thick in my seine, The.

Sonnet: "Sits by a fireplace, the seducer talks." Leonard Wolf. ErPo

Sonnet: "Sleep, silence' child, sweet father of soft rest." William Drummond of Hawthornden. *See* Sleep, Silence' Child.

Sonnet: "Slide soft, fair forth, and make a crystal plain." William Drummond of Hawthornden. NOSC

Sonnet: "So shoots a star as doth my mistress glide." John Davies of Hereford. CBLP; EIL

Sonnet: "Sometimes the night echoes to prideless wailing." John Berryman. NoAM

Sonnet: "Sonnet is a moment's monument, A." Dante Gabriel Rossetti. *Fr.* House of Life, The. EnVR; NAEL-2; NoP; Son

Sonnet: Supernatural Beings. Gavin Ewart. Son

Sonnet: Suppos'd to Be Written at Lemnos. Thomas Russell. NOEC

Sonnet: "Sure, Lord, there is enough in Thee to dry." George Herbert. NOSC

Sonnet: "Sweet semi-circled Cynthia played at maw." John Taylor. *Fr.* Odcomb's Complaint. EIL

(Mockado, Fustian, and Motley.) FaBoNo

(Sonnet in Praise of Mr. Thomas the Deceased.) CBNP

Sonnet: "Sweet soul, which in the April of thy years." William Drummond of Hawthornden. JCP

Sonnet: "Tell me[e] no more how fair[e] she[e] is." Henry King. EnLoPo; MeLP; SeCP

(That Distant Bliss.) TrGrPo

Sonnet XIV: "Then might I see upon a white horse set." Spenser. ChIV-2

Sonnet: "There, on the darkened deathbed, dies the brain." John Masefield. EBEV

(There, on the Darkened Deathbed.) DL; LiTB

Sonnet: "There was an Indian, who had known no change." J. C. Squire. CH; FaPON

(There Was An Indian.) 09AmFN

Sonnet: "There was never file half so well filed." Sir Thomas Wyatt. SiPSBD

Sonnet: "They may suppose, because I would not cloy your ear." John Berryman. NoP

Sonnet: "They say that shadow[e]s of deceased ghosts." Joshua Sylvester. EIL

(They Say that Shadows of Deceased Ghosts.) Son

Sonnet: "This is the garden: colours come and go." E. E. Cummings. *See* This Is the Garden.

Sonnet: "This world is too much with us: late and soon." Wordsworth. *See* World is too much with us; late and soon, The.

Sels.
August. CTC
February.
July.
June.
March.
November.
September.
"Unto the blithe and lordly fellowship."
Sonnets of the Months: Conclusion. Folgore da San Geminiano, *tr. by* Dante Gabriel Rossetti. AWP
Sonnets of the Months: September. Folgore da San Geminiano, *tr. fr. Italian by* Dante Gabriel Rossetti. AWP
Sonnets of the Triple-headed Manichee, *sels.* George Barker.
"Keelhauled across the star-wrecked death of God." PoA
Sonnets to Aurelia. Robert Nichols. OBMV
Sels.
"But piteous things we are — when I am gone."
"Come, let us sigh a requiem over love."
"Though to your life apparent stain attach."
"When the proud World does most my world despise."
Sonnets to his Mystresse Diana, *sels.* K. Soowthern.
"Thou find'st not heere, neither the furious alarmes." ESo
Sonnets to Karl Theodore German. August, Graf von Platen. PeHV
Sels.
"How shall I still mankind's good will retrieve."
"When shall I master this anxiety."
Sonnets to Laura, *sels.* Petrarch, *tr. fr. Italian.*
Alas! So All Things Now Do Hold Their Peace. NAEL-1; NoP; OAEL-1; OBVE
(Alas, so all things now do hold their peace.) NoSic, *tr. by* the Earl of Surrey, *sect.* CIX
(Alas, So All Things Now.) EnRePo
(Lover for Shamefastnesse Hideth His Desire within His Faithfull Hart, The.) AAS, (2 *ver.*)
"Blest be the day, and blest the month and year." NAWM-1, *tr. by* Joseph Auslander
(Father in heaven, after each lost day.) NAWM-1, *tr. by* Bernard Bergonzi
"Eyes that drew from me such fervent praise, The." NAWM-1
"First day she passed up and down through the Heavens, The." OBMV
"Go, grieving rimes of mine, to that hard stone." NAWM-1
"Great is my envy of you, earth, in your greed." NAWM-1, *tr. by* Edwin Morgan
Heart on the Hill, The. AWP
How the Lover Perisheth in His Delight, As the Fly in the Fire. Son
(Some Fowls There Be.) SCGP
"I find no peace and all my war[r] is done." AAS; LiTB; OAEL-1; OBVE; Poetr; SiPS; SiPSBD
(Description of the Contrarious Passions in a Lover.) FF; Son; TrGrPo
I saw a Phoenix in the Wood Alone. AWP, *tr. by* Spenser; ChTr, *tr. by* Helen Lee Peabody
If It Be Destined. AWP, *tr. by* Edward FitzGerald; SiPS, *tr. by* Edward FitzGerald
"In the years of her age the most beautiful." OBMV
"It was the morning of that blessed day." NAWM-1
"Love, That Doth Reign [*or* Raine] and Live Within My Thought." AAS; HeIP; NAEL-1; NoP; OAEL-1; OBVE; SiPSBD
(Complaint of a Lover Rebuked.) AWP; Son; TrGrPo
(Love that liveth and reigneth in my thought.) SiPS
"My flowery and green age was passing away." OBMV, *tr. by* J. M. Synge
(He Understands the Great Cruelty of Death.) BIrV
My Galley ("My galley charged with forgetfulness"). AAS; HAP; NoP; OAEL-1; OBVE; PPP; SCGP; SiPS; SiPSBD; Son; WeW
(Lover Comparath His State to a Ship in Perilous Storm Tossed on the Sea, The.) EIL; GBL; 09HeIP; PoEL-1
"Set me whereas the sun doth parch the green [*or* sonne dothe perche the grene]." AAS; HAP; NoSic; SiPS; SiPSBD
(Love's Fidelity.) AWP
(Vow to Love Faithfully, Howsoever He Be Rewarded, A.) TrGrPo
"She used to let her golden hair fly free." NAWM-1
Signs of Love. AWP
To Laura in Life
"I saw the tracks of angels in the earth." ArLo, *tr. by* Nicholas Kilmer
Visions, The. AWP
"What a grudge I am bearing the earth"
(Translation from Petrarch, A.) MoBrPo, *tr. by* J. M. Synge
Sonnets to Miranda., *sels.* Sir William Watson.
"If I had never known your face at all." FaBoBe
Sonnets to Orpheus, *sels.* Rainer Maria Rilke, *tr. fr. German.*
"As once the winged energy of delight." EnlH, *tr. by* Stephen Mitchell
"Be ahead of all parting, as though it already were." EnlH
"Call me to the one among your moments." EnlH, *tr. by* Stephen Mitchell

"Full, ripe apple, a pear and banana." SOTW
"Mirrors, no one yet has really described." SOTW
"O you lovers that are so gentle, step occasionally." RaBo
"Silent friend of many distances, feel." EnlH, *tr. by* Stephen Mitchell
"Spring has come again. The earth." SOTW
"This is the creature there has never been." OBVE
"Tree ascending there. O pure transcension, A." TOF
"Wait . . . that tastes good . . . already it is on the wing." SOTW
"We are the driving ones." EnlH, *tr. by* Stephen Mitchell
"Where in what ever-blissfully watered gardens." OBVE
(Where, in whatever happily watered garden, on what trees.) SOTW, *tr. by* Christopher Hawthorne
"Where praise already is is the only place Grief." RaBo
Sonnets to Philomel. Sir John Davies. SiPS
Sels.
If you would know the love which I you bear
"Oft did I hear our eyes the passage were"
"Once did my Philomel reflect on me"
"Sickness, intending my love to betray"
Sonnets to the Seasons. Hartley Coleridge. PIP
Sels.
November. OBNC
Sonnets Written in the Fall of 1914. George Edward Woodberry. PAH
Sonnets Written in the Orillia Woods, *sels.* Charles Sangster.
"Our life is like a forest, where the sun." NOBC
Sonny. Ku K'uang, *tr. fr. Chinese by* Irving Y. Lo. SuSp
Sonny Greer. Howard Hart. Jaz
Sonny grows up in Fukien. Sonny. Ku K'uang, *tr. fr. Chinese by* Irving Y. Lo. SuSp
Sonora for Sale. Richard Shelton. FoLa
Sonrisas. Pat Mora. NIP
Sons. Jack Cope. PeSA
Sons and Fathers. Larry Mitchell. GLP
Sons, my sons. Black Star Line. Henry Dumas. PoBA
Sons of freedom, listen to me, and ye daughters, too, give ear. James Bird. *Unknown.* AmFP
Sons of Levi, The. *Unknown.* AmFP
Sons of Levi; Gershon, Kohath, and Merari, The. The Begats. Bible, *O.T. Fr.* First Chronicles. CBCK
Sons of Martha, The. Kipling. ChIV-2; WGRP
Sons of Mary seldom bother, for they have inherited that good part, The. The Sons of Martha. Kipling. ChIV-2; WGRP
Sons of New England, in the fray. Treason's Last Device. Edmund Clarence Stedman. PAH
Sons of Our Sons, The. Ilya Ehrenburg, *tr. fr. Russian by* Babette Deutsch. TrJP
Sons of Promise. Thomas Curtis Clark. PoToHe
Sons of Saint Crispin, 'tis in vain! "Peter Pindar." *Fr.* Resignation; an Ode to the Journeyman Shoemakers. NOEC
Sons of the King. Joan Agnew. BoTP
Sons of the prophet are hardy and bold, The. Abdul, the Bulbul Ameer. *Unknown.* AS
Sons of valor, taste the glories. Off from Boston. *Unknown.* PAH
Sons of War sometimes are known, The. Evan Lloyd. *Fr.* Methodist, The. OBSV
"Sooeep!" Walter de la Mare. BoTP
Soon after, he a crystal stream espying. Ariosto, *tr. fr. Italian by* Sir John Harington. *Fr.* Orlando Furioso. NoSic
Soon as the Azure-colored Gates. Richard Lynche. *Fr.* Diella. Son
Soon as the harvest hath laid bare the plains. Stephen Duck. *Fr.* Thresher's Labour, The. NOEC
Soon as the sun forsook the eastern main. An Hymn to the Evening. Phillis Wheatley. WPE
Soon as/ you stop. Cleavage. A. R. Ammons. OBAL
Soon at Last My Sighs and Moans. Louis Ginsberg. TrJP
Soon for you too. (*LL*) Song of the Traveler at Evening. Goethe. STV
Soon I shall be in tears this birthday morning. A Birthday in Hospital. Elizabeth Jennings. NAs
Soon I will climb the hill to the sunlight. From the Rain Forest. Desirée Flynn. BrRo
Soon it will be thirty-five years. Glen Canyon on the Colorado. Richard Shelton. FoLa
Soon kindled and soon spent, we that were the pick of many. (*LL*) An Old Woman's Lamentations. Villon. MoBrPo; OBMV
Soon now that day is coming. Two Worlds. Matija Beckovic, *tr. fr. Serbo-Croatian by* Charles Simic. HSix
Soon over Meles' grave the wild flower dropt. Death of Altheëtor. Maria Gowen Brooks. *Fr.* Zophiël. AmWP

Soon ripe, soon rot, Young Saint, Old Divell. Loe. First Satans Assault Against Those That First Came up to Mercys Terms. Edward Taylor. *Fr.* God's Determinations [touching his Elect]. EAP

Soon soured his nature, which was never sweet. (*LL*) The Villagers and Death. Robert Graves. OBD

Soon, summer's drum will shake the earth no longer. Fall of Leaves. D. S. Savage. PoA

Soon the night in mantle dark. The Ploughboy. John Clare. PoEL-4

Soon we entered in the woods. The Arrival. Alexander McLachlan. *Fr.* Emigrant, The. NOBC

Soon we will hear its cracking. (*LL*) On the Melting Lake. Chung Ling. WPC

Sooner I may some fixed statue be. On the Duke of Buckingham, Slain by Felton, the 23rd August, 1628. Owen Felltham [*or* Feltham]. JCP; NOSC

Sooner tears than sleep this midnight. The Wind's Lament. John Morris-Jones, *tr. fr. Welsh by* Anthony Conran. OBWVE

Sooner, the better for Roger and me!, The. (*LL*) The Vagabonds. John Townsend Trowbridge. AnAmPo; BeLS; BLPA

Soonest Mended. John Ashbery. HCAP; NAAL-2; Prf; VCAP

Soote Season, The. The Earl of Surrey, *after* Petrarch. AAS; EnRePo; InPS; NAEL-1; NoP; NoSic; SiPSBD; Son

Soote season, that bud and bloom forth brings, The. The Soote Season. The Earl of Surrey, *after* Petrarch. AAS; EnRePo; InPS; NAEL-1; NoP; NoSic; SiPSBD; Son

(Description of Spring, Wherein Each Thing Renews Save Only the Lover. ElL; OBEV

(Description of Spring.) SCGP

Sooth-Sayer, The. Sadi, *tr. by* Sir Edwin Arnold. *Fr.* Gulistan, The. AWP

Soothed by the murmurs on the sea-boat shore. To the Curlew. Helen Maria Williams. WoRP

Sooty, swart smiths, smattered with smoke. The Blacksmiths. *Unknown.* (Swarte-smeked Smithes.) HAP

Sophia, her age between. Wisdom of the Gazelle. George P. Solomos. GoYe

Sophocles. *Unknown, tr. fr. Greek by* Lee T. Pearcy. GrAn

Sopolis. Callimachus, *tr. fr. Greek by* William M. Hardinge. AWP

Soraidh Slan Don Oidhche Areir. Niall Mor MacMuireadach, *tr. fr. Irish.* BIrV, *tr. by* Maire Cruise O'Brien

Sorcerer, Mr. Wells, The, *sels.* W. S. Gilbert.

Sorcerers, they've turned. Living with Children. Jim Wayne Miller. GOYP

Sorceress, The! Vachel Lindsay. PDV

Sorceress, The. Eugène Marais, *tr. fr. Afrikaans by* Jack Cope *and* Uys Krige. PeSA

Sordello, *sels.* Robert Browning.
"In Mantua-territory half is slough." EBVVPR

Sore this dere strykyn ys. Blow Thy Horn, Hunter. *Unknown.* OxBLMV

Sorrow. Chu Shu-chen, *tr. fr. Chinese by* Kenneth Rexroth. BoWoP; OHMPC

Sorrow. Aubrey Thomas De Vere. BLPA; WGRP; WiR

Sorrow. Emily Dickinson. WGRP

Sorrow. T. R. Hummer. MT

Sorrow. D. H. Lawrence. CMoP; GTBS-P; OBD; OBMV

Sorrow. Josephine Miles. IMW

Sorrow. Marie Tello Phillips. GoYe

Sorrow. Laetitia Pilkington. ECWP

Sorrow. George Santayana. WGRP

Sorrow. *Unknown, tr. fr. Russian by* W. R. S. Ralston. AWP

Sorrow and mourn and fast. (*LL*) Merry It Is. *Unknown.* HAP

Sorrow Garden, The. Thomas McCarthy. BiHa; IB

Sorrow has a harp of seven strings. The Harp of Sorrow. Ethel Clifford. WGRP

Sorrow heaped on sorrow, ruin on disaster. On My Sorrowful Life. Moses ibn Ezra, *tr. fr. Hebrew by* Solomon Solis-Cohen. TrJP

Sorrow how high it is. Dark Song. A. R. Ammons. MAT

Sorrow Humanize Our Race. Jean Ingelow. WGRP

Sorrow in the Harem, A. Wang Ch'ang-ling, *tr. fr. Chinese by* Kenneth Rexroth. OHMPC

Sorrow is my own yard. The Widow's Lament in Springtime. William Carlos Williams. CMoP; HAP; IMW; LiTM; MoP; NAAL-2; NoAM; NOBA; PFP; PoE; SAmP; SoSe; TAP

Sorrow is my stock in trade. Reunion. Cyril Tawney. OBET

Sorrow lay upon my breast more heavily than winter clay. "Desolation Is a Delicate Thing." Elinor Wylie. MoAmPo

Sorrow of Departure, The. Li Ch'ing-chao, *tr. fr. Chinese by* Kenneth Rexroth *and* Ling Chung. WPC

Sorrow of Kodio, The. *Unknown, tr. fr. Baule by* Miriam Koshland. PBA

Sorrow of Love, The. W. B. Yeats. MeMBP; MoAB; MoBrPo; NAEL-2; NoAM; NOBVV; OAEL-2; PeVV; PoEL-5; TEP

Sorrow of Mydath. John Masefield. CoGr; MoBrPo

Sorrow of Troilus, The. Chaucer. *Fr.* Troilus and Criseyde [*or* Criseide]. EnVB; PoEL-1

Sorrow of your great playthings, The. (*LL*) Moon. Nathan Alterman. MHP

Sorrowful Song. Henri Cazalis, *tr. fr. French by* Philip L. Miller. RiWo

Sorrowing for the Past at Western Pass Mountain. Liu Yu Hsi, *tr. fr. Chinese by* Daniel Bryant. SuSp

Sorrowing nymph, oh why display. On a Statue of Sir Arthur Sullivan. George Rostrevor Hamilton. FaBoCo

Sorrows. Mang Ke, *tr. fr. Chinese by* Donald Finkel *with* Chang Sheng-Tai. SpMi

Sorrows of my heart enlarged are, The. Some Contemplations of the Poor, and Desolate State of the Church at Deerfield. John Williams. SCAP

Sorrows of Sunday; an Elegy, The, *sels.* "Peter Pindar."
"Susan, the constant slave to mop and broom." NOEC

Sorrows of Werther, The. Thackeray. BLPA; FaBoCo; FiBHP; NBLV; NOBL; NOBVV; OBD; PeLV

Sorrows play at the edge of these willow leaf curves. Willow Eyebrows. Chao Luan-luan, *tr. fr. Chinese by* Kenneth Rexroth *and* Ling Chung. WPC

Sorry I am, my God, sorry I am. (*LL*) Sins' Round. George Herbert. MiEL; NOSC

Sorry I am, my God, sorry I am. Sins' Round. George Herbert. MiEL; NOSC

Sort of a Song, A. William Carlos Williams. HoPM; NAAL-2; NoP; OxBSP; TAP

Sort of extra hunger, A. Poet Wondering What He Is Up To. D. J. Enright. OxBC

Sort of girl I like to see, The. The Olympic Girl. Sir John Betjeman. ArLo

Sorting Laundry. Elisavietta Ritchie. SoSe

Sorting out letters and piles of my old. Mementos, I. W. D. Snodgrass. FF; MoAmPo; UnPo; VCAP

Sory beverech [*or* beverech] it is, and sore it is abought [*or* abouth], A. *Unknown.* MiEL

SOS. Amiri Baraka. BPo; PoBA

Sosicles the farmer dedicated these sheaves. Philip of Thessalonica, *tr. fr. Greek by* Edwin Morgan. GrAn

Sōsos the cattleman slew the lion. Leonidas of Tarentum, *tr. fr. Greek by* W. G. Shepherd. GrAn

Sospetto d'Herode. Giovanni Battista Marino, *tr. fr. Italian by* Richard Crashaw. *Fr.* Strage degli innocenti, La. SeCV-1

Sot-Weed Factor, The. Ebenezer Cook. EAP

Soto, a Character. Mary Leapor. ECWP

Soucouyant, Soucouyant. "Skin Skin, Yuh Na Know Meh." John C. M. Lyons. NBrP

Soufrière. Andrew Salkey. PBCV

Soufrière (79). Ellsworth McGranaham Keane. *Fr.* Volcanoe Suite. PBCV

Sought by the world, and hath the world disdained. *Unknown.* NoSic

Soul, The. Peter Cooley. NAmP90

Soul, The. Richard Henry Dana. AnAmPo

Soul. D. L. Graham. PoBA

Soul, A. Randall Jarrell. CMoP

Soul, A. Christina Rossetti. NALW; WPOW

Soul a crystal is, the Godhead is its shine, The. Body, Soul, And Godhead. "Angelus Silesius," *tr. fr. German by* George C. Schoolfield. *Fr.* Cherubical Wanderer, The. GePo

Soul and Body. Friedrich von Logau, *tr. fr. German by* George C. Schoolfield. GePo

Soul and Body. Margaret Cavendish, Duchess of Newcastle. OxBSP

Soul and Body. Shakespeare. *See* Poor[e] soul[e], the centre of my sinful[l] earth.

Soul and Body: I've heard tell of a noble guest. Unknown, *formerly at. to* Cynewulf, *tr. fr. Anglo-Saxon. Fr.* Riddles (Exeter Book). ASW, *tr. by* Kevin Crossley-Holland

Soul and Body of John Brown, The. Muriel Rukeyser. MoAmPo

Soul and race. Here Where Coltrane Is. Michael S. Harper. CAPP; Jaz; PoBA

Soul and the Body, The. Sir John Davies. *See* But how shall we this union well expresse?

Soul-animating strains — alas, too few! (*LL*) Scorn not the sonnet; critic, you have frowned. Wordsworth. EBEV; EPCY

Soul, be your own. The Outcast. John Davidson. MeMBP

Soul counsels flight. Meleager, *tr. fr. Greek by* Peter Whigham. GrAn

Soul Food. Janice Mirikitani. OpBo

Soul has bandaged moments — , The. Emily Dickinson. NALW; TRP

Soul-hunter, The. Julia Ward Howe. AmWP

Soul Incense. H. Cordelia Ray. CBWP-3

Soul is a prisoner, and body is its jail. Soul and Body. Friedrich von Logau, tr. fr. German by George C. Schoolfield. GePo

Soul is a region without definite boundaries, The. Terrain. A. R. Ammons. VCAP

Soul is kissed by God, The. Hildegard von Bingen, tr. fr. Latin. CrSp

Soul is lonely, The. La Selva. Cid Corman. VGW

Soul lies buried in the ink that writes, The. (LL) Language has not the power to speak what love indites. John Clare. FaBoEE; OAEL-2; OBNC; OxBSP; PoEL-4

Soul lies buried in the ink that writes, The. (LL) To Stella. Plato. EnLoPo; FaBoEE; OBVE

Soul lonely comes and goes; for each our theme. Lachesis. Kathleen Raine. NYBP

Soul Longs to Return Whence It Came, The. Richard Eberhart. CMoP

Soul Music: The Derry Air. Eamon Grennan. BiHa; PBCIP

Soul of Earth, sanctify me. Unknown. Fr. Anima Christi. EaPr, ad. by Jane Pellowski

Soul of Jesus Is Restless, The. Cyprus R. Mitchell. TrCP

Soul of man is cast, The. (LL) A Creed. Edwin Markham. BLPA; BLPL; FaBoBe

Soul of Man is larger than the sky, The. To Shakespeare. Hartley Coleridge. EPCY

Soul of my child, Princess Splendid! Invocation before the Rice Harvest. Malay Oral Tradition, tr. by R. O. Winstedt. WTO

Soul of the Black Land, The. Guy Tirolien, tr. fr. French by Ellen Conroy Kennedy. NegPo

Soul of the sea, The. (LL) Variations on [or of] an Air: After [Algernon Charles] Swinburne. G. K. Chesterson. FaBoPa; NOBL

Soul of Things, The. Edith M. Thomas. AmWP

Soul of Time, The. Trumbull Stickney. LiTA

Soul, Remember This! Eduard Friedrich Mörike. OBD

Soul Remembers, The. Richard Burdick Eldridge. GoYe

Soul selects her own society, The. Emily Dickinson. AmPP; AWP; BLPL; BoWoP; CMoP; HeIP; ImPo; InPK; InPS; MeMAP; MoAB; MoAmPo; NAAL-1; NALW; NAWM-2; NoAM; NOBA; NoP; OxBA; PoE; PoEL-5; Poetr; SAmP; TAP; TFi; TrGrPo; UnPo; WPE

Soul-Severance. St. John Hankin. FaBoPa

Soul-soothing drug! your virtues let me laud. A Sonnet to Opium; Celebrating Its Virtues. "Orestes." NOEC

Soul that knew it well, A. (LL) The Happiest Day, the Happiest Hour. Poe. AmPP; LiTA; MeMAP; OxBA

Soul that must endure it, The. (LL) All Is Vanity, Saith the Preacher. Byron. ChIV-1; TrCP

Soul that's fed on Nature is content, The. Nature's Uplifting. H. Cordelia Ray. CBWP-3

Soul, thou must seek thyself in Me. St. Theresa of Avila, tr. fr. Spanish by E. Allison Peers. TOF

Soul wherein God dwells, The. The Cherubic Pilgrim. "Angelus Silesius," tr. fr. German. Fr. Cherubical Wanderer, The. WGRP

Soul which doth with God unite, The. Cupio Dissolvi. William Habington. ChIV-2

Soldiers Farewell to His Love, The. Unknown. CoMu

Soule, by prayer it lives, The. (LL) Ensamples of Our Savior. Robert Southwell. PoEL-2

Soul[e] of my soul[e]! my Joy, my crown, my friend! L'Amitie: To Mrs. M. Awbrey. Katherine Philips. KTR; NOSC

Soules joy, now I am gone. At. to The Earl of Pembroke William Herbert, Earl of Pembroke. ESCV

Soulfolk, think a minute. To Soulfolk. Margaret Goss Burroughs. BlSi

Souls. Paul Wertheimer, tr. fr. German by Jethro Bithell. TrJP

Soul's Beauty. Dante Gabriel Rossetti. Fr. House of Life, The. OBEV

Soul's Bitter Cry, The. Unknown, tr. fr. Tamil. WGRP

Soul's Calm Sunshine, The. Pope. Fr. Essay on Man, An. FaBoRV

Soul's Courts, The. H. Cordelia Ray. CBWP-3

Soul's Dark Cottage, The. Edmund Waller. Fr. Of The Last Verses in the Book. BeJo; ChTr; EBEV; FaBoRV; HAP; NoP; NOSC; OBD; PeECV; SCGP; SeCP; SeCV-1

Soul's Desire, The. Unknown, tr. fr. Irish by Eleanor Hull. TIRV

Soul's distinct connection, The. Emily Dickinson. SAmP

Soul's Errand, The. Sir Walter Ralegh. See Go, Soul [or Goe soule], the body's guest.

Soul's Garment, The. Margaret Cavendish, Duchess of Newcastle. WPE

Soul's Groan to Christ for Succo[u]r, The. Edward Taylor. Fr. God's Determinations [touching his Elect]. NAAL-1; PoEL-3

Souls joy, when thou art gone. A Parodie. George Herbert. (Parodie, A.) ESCV

Soul's Kiss. Samuel Greenberg. LiTA

Souls Lake. Robert Fitzgerald. TwCP

Soul's Liberty. Anna Wickham. MoBrPo; OxBSP

Souls of men! why will ye scatter. God Our Father. Frederick William Faber. WGRP

Souls of poets dead and gone. Lines on the Mermaid Tavern. At. to Keats EnRP; FaBoEH, st. 1 only; FHYEP; PoRA; SCGP (Mermaid Tavern, The.) BLPL; FaBoBe; GTBS; GTBS-P

Souls of the patriot dead. The Kidnapping of Sims. John Pierpont. PAH

Souls of the Slain, The. Thomas Hardy. CMoP; LiTB; MeMBP; PoEL-5

Souls of Women at Night, The. Wallace Stevens. CMoP

Soul's Soliloquy, A. Wenonah Stevens Abbott. BLPA

Soul's Superior instants, The. Emily Dickinson. EnlH

Sound. James Harrison. VGW

Sound, The. Robert Kelly. PoM

Sound, A. Gertrude Stein. Fr. Tender Buttons. TTTS

Sound Advice. Unknown. FaBoUs; NBLV

Sound and Sense. Pope. See True ease in writing comes from art, not chance.

Sound arises out of the earth — , A. Cedric Wright. EaPr

Sound Country Lass, The. Unknown. CoMu; ErPo

Sound from the Earth, A. William Stafford. NNaP; RFM

Sound grates on the river tower, one blast of the horn, The. The Gate Tower of Ch'i-an City. Tu Mu, tr. fr. Chinese by A. C. Graham. PLT

Sound in your mind, The. Jack Kerouac. Fr. Mexico City Blues. PoBeRe

Sound is fading out. Unknown, tr. fr. Chippewa Indian by Jerome K. Rothenberg. STP

Sound is forced, the notes are few!, The. (LL) To the Muses. Blake. ChTr; EnRP; EPCY; HAP; HeIP; ImPo; LiTB; MeMBP; NAEL-2; NOBE; NOEC; NoP; OAEL-2; OBEV; SCGP; TrGrPo

Sound is in the Pyrenees!, A. Murder of a Spanish Lady by a Pirate. Richard Henry Dana. AnAmPo

Sound like a great big crowd. (LL) Morning After. Langston Hughes. Jaz; MoP; NAAL-2; NBLV; NoAM

Sound of Afroamerican History Chapt I, The. S. E. Anderson. PoBA

Sound of Afroamerican History Chapt II, The. S. E. Anderson. PoBA

Sound of autumn from a stretch of reed flowers, The. "Song of Plucking Cassia." Ch'iao Chi, tr. fr. Chinese by Sherwin S. S. Fu. SuSp

Sound of Breaking. Conrad Aiken. AWP

Sound of Drums, The. Karen Randlev. NGP

Sound of happy laughter leap with shadows on the walls. Taos Winter. Patty L. Harjo. VoR

Sound of its thump at dawn hurries the circling sun, The. The Watchman's Drum in the Streets of Officials. Li Ho, tr. fr. Chinese by A. C. Graham. PLT

Sound of me watching, if I had been a bird, The. (LL) The Bird's Nest. John Drinkwater. PDV

Sound of Mexican music in, The. The Flagrant Mala Puta. Alma Villanueva. ETG

Sound of My Sneezing Nose, The. Te Whetu, tr. fr. Maori by Margaret Orbell. PeNZ

Sound of Night, The. Maxine W. Kumin. BoNaP; SoSe; WPE

Sound of Rain, The. Bella Akhmadulina, tr. fr. Russian by Daniel Halpern and Albert Todd. BoWoP

Sound of Rain, The. David Allan Evans. GOYP

Sound of snails — crying. Snails. Liagarang, tr. fr. Dharlwangu dialect. CBAP, tr. by Ronald M. Berndt; WTO, tr. by Ronald M. Berndt

Sound of tears the moment when, A. (LL) Dream, A [or The]. William Allingham. BIrV; NOBVV

Sound of the Drum, The. Unknown. OBET

Sound of the Horn, The. Alfred de Vigny, tr. fr. French by Wilfred Thorley. AWP

Sound of the Trees, The. Robert Frost. See I wonder about the trees.

Sound of the Wind, The. Christina Rossetti. Fr. Sing-Song.

Sound of the Wind That Is Blowing, The, sels. J. Kitchener Davies, tr. fr. Welsh by Joseph P. Clancy.
   "Today,/ there came a breeze thin as the needle of a syringe." OBWVE

Sound of thy sweet name, my dearest treasure, The. Francis Davison. EIL

Sound of Trees, The. Robert Frost. NoAM

Sound of Water. Mary O'Neill. NTCP

Sound out, sound over Hirta sound rare. St Kilda-Wren, 1957. Colin Simms. NBrP

Sound, Sound the Clarion. At. to Thomas Osbert Mordaunt. Fr. Verses Written during the War, 1756 – 1763. EBEV; FaBoEE; FaPoR; NOBE; OxAEP-2

Sound the flute! Spring. Blake. *Fr.* Songs of Innocence. BoTP; FaBoCh; FaPON; FHYEP; MoShBr; NTP; TTTS

Sound the Loud Timbrel. Thomas Moore. ChIV-1

Sound the trumpet, beat the drum. Dryden. *Fr.* Secular Masque, The. FaBoRV; NAEL-1; PoE; PoEL-3; PrIm; SCGP; SeCV-2

Sound variegated through beneath lit. Gyre's Galax. Norman Henry, II Pritchard. PoBA

Sounding, The. Conrad Aiken. AnAmPo

Sounding cataract, The/ Haunted me like a passion. Wordsworth. *Fr.* Lines Composed a Few Miles above Tintern Abbey [on Revisiting the Banks of the Wye during a Tour, July 13, 1798]. BLPL; EBEvV; EnRP; FaBoPP; FF; FHYEP; HeIP; InPS; LiTB; MeMBP; NoP; OAEL-2; OBNC; OxAEP-2; PoEL-4; Poetr; PPP; PrIm; SCGP; TEP; TFi; TrGrPo; WGRP

Sounding down this world. (*LL*) We Dance Like Ella Riffs. Carolyn M. Rodgers. PoBA

Sounding Fog, The. Susan Nichols Pulsifer. PDV

Soundings. Paula Gunn Allen. HATNAP

Soundless as dots — on a Disc of Snow. (*LL*) Safe in their alabaster chambers. Emily Dickinson. AmPP; NAAL-1; NAWM-2; NOBA; NoP, 2 *vers.*; OxBA; RaBo; WPE

Sounds are heard too high for ears. Watching Television. Robert Bly. CoAP

Sounds Begin Again, The. Dennis Brutus. HBAPE

Sounds in the dim washed room. Learning to Count. Sara Berkeley. BiHa

Sounds like big. Waking from a Nap on the Beach. May Swenson. NTCP; RFM

Sounds make the song, not sense,/ Thus I inhibit! (*LL*) Psycholophon. Gelett Burgess. CBNP

Sounds of Autumn. Lu Yu, *tr. fr. Chinese by* Irving Y. Lo. SuSp

Sounds of Ireland, The. Windharp. John Montague. CIP; IIP; PNI

Sounds of joy once heard, and heard no more, The. (*LL*) How sweet the tuneful bells' responsive peal! William Lisle Bowles. OBTV

Sounds of love are needles in my ears, The. Meleager, *tr. fr. Greek by* Sam Hamill. InMo

Sounds of the African cicada, The. The Room of Rhetoric. Sebastian Barry. IB

Sounds of the Day. Norman MacCaig. RB

Sounds That Arrived, The. Milo De Angelis, *tr. fr. Italian by* Lawrence Venuti. NeIt

Sounds that shapes make in the air, The. Death of a Ceiling. Medbh McGuckian. DT

Soundwaves. Andrew Sant. NOBAu

Soup. Carl Sandburg. NOBA; NOBE; OBCA

Soup, The. Charles Simic. AnAn

Soup Jar, The. Dabney Stuart. MT

Soup Kitchen. Betsy Sholl. PBCAP

Soup Kitchen Song. *Unknown.* NOBAu

Soup of Venus, The. James Tate. AmPA

Soup Song. Joseph Glazer. SWP

Sour daylight cracks through my sleep-caked lids, The. The Distant Winter. Philip Levine. VGW

Sour fiend, go home and tell the Pit. Ghoul Care. Ralph Hodgson. MoBrPo

Sour smell, The. Getting in the Wood. Gary Snyder. NoAM

Source, The. Andrew Crozier. VaA

Source, The. Jon Stallworthy. CBLP; NoP

Source, The. David Wagoner. VCAP

Source immaterial of material naught. "Orpheus C. Kerr." *Fr.* Rejected "National Hymns," The. OBAL

Sources of Good Counsel. Peter Idley. OxBChV

Sources of My Being, The. Moses ibn Ezra, *tr. fr. Hebrew by* David Goldstein. TOF

Sourdough mountain called a fire in. Gary Snyder. *Fr.* Myths and Texts. NAAL-2; NaP; NeAP; NoP; PoM

Sourdough Mountain Lookout. Philip Whalen. NeAP; PoBeRe; PoM

Sourwood Mountain. *Unknown.* AS; GBP

Sourwood Mountain. *Unknown.* AmFP

Sous-Entendu. Anne Stevenson. OxBSP

South, The. Wang Chien, *tr. fr. Chinese by* Arthur Waley. AWP

South African Broadsheets, *sels.* David Wright.
"Under the African lintel, Table Mountain." PeSA

South African Exhibition, 1907. Kingsley Fairbridge. PeSAV

South America. Tom Raworth. NBrP

South America Mi Hija, *sels.* Sharon Doubiago.
"Out the window, Colombia, out the window." PBCAP

South Carolina, The. *Unknown.* PAH

South Carolina to the States of the North. Paul Hamilton Hayne. PAH

South Coast, The. William Everson. NeAP

South-coast sun, the play of light and air, The. A Line from Keats. Evan Jones (b. 1927). FaBoMA

South Country, The. Hilaire Belloc. MoBrPo; OxAEP-2

South Country. Kenneth Slessor. CBAP; FaBoMA

South End. Conrad Aiken. CMoP; HoPM; OxBA

South-Folk in Cold Country. Ezra Pound, *after the Chinese.* OBVE

South is green with coming spring, The. The Trial. Muriel Rukeyser. PoNe

South is mistress of his grave, The. (*LL*) Scenes from Carnac. Matthew Arnold. FaBoPP; OBTV

South Mount Soaring High. Shih Ching, *tr. fr. Chinese by* C. H. Wang. SuSp

South Mountain! So full of sorrows! In Protest. Li Ho, *tr. fr. Chinese by* Maureen Robertson. SuSp

South Mountain stuffs all heaven and earth. Wandering on Mount Chung-nan. Meng Chiao, *tr. fr. Chinese by* A. C. Graham. PLT

South Mountains, The, *sels.* Han Yü, *tr. fr. Chinese by* A. C. Graham.
"Fine weather since yesterday." PLT
"Gazing as I climbed a high peak." PLT
"North of the great lake of K'un-ming." PLT

South of Boston, south of Washington. Robert Lowell. *Fr.* Mexico. HCAP

South of My Days. Judith Wright. FaBoWP; WPE

South of success and east of gloss and glass are. The Wall. Gwendolyn Brooks. *Fr.* Two Dedications. PoBA; PoNe

South of the fabled pillars of Hercules. Volubilis, North Africa. Ralph Nixon Currey. PeSA

South of the Line, inland from far Durban. A Christmas Ghost-Story. Thomas Hardy. OBWP

South Parks Road. James Fenton. PeLV

South Seas. Cesare Pavese, *tr. fr. Italian by* William Arrowsmith. AnAn

South Street. Edward S. Silvera. CDC

South Texas Summer Rain. Rebecca Gonzales. AiP

South-west wind is blowing, The. Autumn Morning. Adeline White. BoTP

South Wind. Siegfried Sassoon. BoTP

South wind brings wet weather, The. *Unknown.* FaBoUs

South wind does not shed so great a cast, The. Callimachus, *tr. fr. Greek by* Barbara Hughes Fowler. *Fr.* Hecale. HePo

South-wind strengthens to a gale, The. Low Barometer. Robert Bridges. CMoP; LiTB; MoP; NoAM; NOCV; OBNC; Poetr; SCGP

South wind's gust against the hill will make it flat land, The. Sing Loud. Li Ho, *tr. fr. Chinese by* A. C. Graham. PLT

South wind's molded by a spine of hill, The. Another Kind of Burning. Ruth Fox. NYBP

Southbound. Betty Adcock. MT

Southbound on the Freeway. May Swenson. GoJo; ImGa; NTCP; NYBP

Southeast, and storm, and every weathervane. Hatteras Calling. Conrad Aiken. BoNaP; NOBA; TAP

Southeast at low tide. Skiing on Russian Christmas. Nora Dauenhauer. HATNAP

Souther, wind, souther! Rhyme of the Fishermen's Children. *Unknown.* GBP

Southern Africa. Nguno Wakolele. PeSAV

Southern Cop. Sterling A. Brown. SoSe

Southern Cross. Hart Crane. *Fr.* Bridge, The. LiTA; NAAL-2

Southern Cross. Herman Melville. LiTA

Southern hill-billy named Hollis, A. *Unknown.* PeLi

Southern hills, how mournful!, The. Li Ho, *tr. fr. Chinese by* A. C. Graham. *Fr.* Criticisms. PLT

Southern Mansion. Arna Bontemps. AiP; FF; LiTM; PoBA; PoNe; TTY

Southern Mountains. Han Yü, *tr. fr. Chinese by* Charles Hartman. SuSp

Southern Pacific. Carl Sandburg. AnAmPo

Southern Pines. John Peale Bishop. GOA

Southern Press, The. L. A. J. Moorer. CBWP-3

Southern Pulpit, The. L. A. J. Moorer. CBWP-3

Southern Road. Sterling A. Brown. BPo; PoBA

Southern Road, The. Dudley Randall. PoBA; SM

Southern Scene, A. Priscilla Jane Thompson. CBWP-2

Southern Work of Dr. and Mrs. L. M. Dunton. L. A. J. Moorer. CBWP-3

Southerner, The. Karl Shapiro. NYBP; PoNe

Southey and Wordsworth. Byron. *See* Bob Southey! You're a poet — poet-laureate.

Southey Looks out of the Window at Greta Hill. Robert Southey. *Fr.* Vision of Judgement, A. FaBoPP

Southrons, hear your country call you! Dixie. Albert Pike. PAH

Spared by a car- or airplane-crash or. Accidents of Birth. William Meredith. NoP

Sparhawk [or Sparrow-hawk] proud did hold in wicked jail, A. A Sparrow-Hawk. Unknown. CH; EBEV

Spark, The. Joseph Mary Plunkett. AWP

Sparkle like a swarm of fireflies. (LL) Evening Lights on the River. Chiang Shih-ch'üan. OHMPC

Sparkled, and ran into the shade. (LL) Defiance. Walter Savage Landor. CBLP

Sparkled to the zun a-zettèn. (LL) Between the Traveller and the Setting Sun. Thoreau. PoEL-4

Sparkles from the wheel. (LL) Sparkles from the Wheel. Walt Whitman. InPS; NAAL-1; SAmP

Sparkles from the Wheel. Walt Whitman. InPS; NAAL-1; SAmP

Sparkling eyes of diamond jet. To E.J.J. Ethel M. Caution. ShDr

Spark's Farewell to Its Clay, The. R. A. K. Mason. PeNZ

Sparrow, The. Bible, O.T., paraphrased by Sir Thomas Wyatt. Fr. Psalms. FaPON; TrJP

Sparrow. Unknown. TSaS

Sparrow, The. William Carlos Williams. InPS; LCAP; Poetr; PrIm; VGW

Sparrow and Diamond, The. Matthew Green. FM

Sparrow dips in his wheel-rut bath, The. The Five Students. Thomas Hardy. CMoP; GTBS-P; PoEL-5

Sparrow-Hawk, A. Unknown. CH; EBEV

Sparrow Hills. Robert Lowell, tr. fr. Russian by Boris Pasternak. NaP

Sparrow Hills. Robley Wilson, Jr.. PBCAP

Sparrow in the Dust, A. Ruth Domino, tr. fr. Italian by Daniel Hoffman and Jerre Mangione. BoWoP

Sparrow in the Zoo, The. Howard Nemerov. MoP

Sparrow in Winter. Takahashi Shinkichi, tr. fr. Japanese by Lucien Stryk and Takashi Ikemoto. NU

Sparrow of Espanola. Michael Pettit. NAmP90

Sparrow sits and sings, and sings, The. Submission. Celia Laighton Thaxter. AmWP

Sparrows. Christopher Buckley. FoLa

Sparrows among Dry Leaves ("The sparrows/ by the iron fence post.") William Carlos Williams. NYBP

Sparrows' Chorus, The. Elizabeth Jennings. PlP

Sparrow's Dirge, The. John Skelton. See When I remember again.

Sparrow's Fall, The. Frances E. W. Harper. PWR

Sparrow's Feather, A. George Barker. NYBP

Sparrow's Nest, The. Wordsworth. EnRP

Sparrows pitch at the wooden walls. Birds. Ralph Hawkins. NBrP

Sparrows quarreled outside our window. Waking an Angel. Philip Levine. NaP

Sparrow's Skull, The. Ruth Pitter. FaBoWP

Sparrows were feeding in a freezing drizzle. Because You Asked about the Line between Prose and Poetry. Howard Nemerov. VCAP; WeW

Sparse fence, winding path, a small farmhouse. Chou Pang-yen, tr. by Irving Y. Lo. Fr. "Beautiful Lady Yü, The". SuSp

Spate in Winter Midnight. Norman MacCaig. GTBS-P

Spatial depths of being survive. The Lost Dancer. Jean Toomer. PoBA

Spawn. Jean Hanff Korelitz. PWE

Spawn of fantasies. Love Songs. Mina Loy. VBLP; VGW; WPE, abr

Spawn of Fantasies. Mina Loy. Fr. Love Songs to Joannes. VBLP

Spawn of Slums, The. James W. Thompson. BPo

Spawning in Northern Minnesota. David McElroy. AmPA

S.P.C.A. Sermon. Stuart Hemsley. FiBHP

Speak! Wordsworth. OBEV

Speak. James Wright. HAP; SM; TAP

Speak and tell us, our Ximena, looking northward far away. The Angels of Buena Vista. Whittier. BeLS; PAH

Speak earth and bless me with what is richest. Audre Lorde. GLP; NoAM

Speak! fairy Moon, interpret this! (LL) The Dawn of Love. H. Cordelia Ray. BISi; CBWP-3

"Speak, gentlemen, what shall we do today?" Sir Revel. Samuel Rowlands. NoSic

Speak Gently. David Bates. PWR; VPP

Speak Gently. G. W. Langford. PoToHe; UV

Speak gently, Spring, and make no sudden sound. Four Little Foxes. Lew Sarett. FaPON; PDV; RFM

Speak, Gracious Lord, oh speak; thy Servant hears. Pope. Fr. Paraphrase on Thomas à Kempis, A. TrPWD

Speak no evil today, for we honour Cornutus' birth. Dicamus Bona Verba. Tibullus, tr. fr. Latin by Constance Carrier. NAs

Speak not ill of womankind. (LL) Against Blame of Woman. Gerald Fitzgerald, Earl of Desmond, tr. by the Earl of Longford. BIrV

Speak not ill of womankind. Against Blame of Woman. Gerald Fitzgerald, Earl of Desmond, tr. by the Earl of Longford. BIrV

Speak not of Death: it is a merry morn. The Sun Is Up. John Shaw Neilson. FaBoMA

Speak not of niceness, when there's chance of wreck. Sir Walter Scott. Fr. Peveril of the Peak. FaBoEE

Speak Out. Unknown. See If you have a friend worth loving.

Speak [or Speke], Parrot, sels. John Skelton.
"My name is Parrot, a bird [or byrd] of paradise." NoSic; OxBoLi (Parrot's Soliloquy.) PoEL-1
"Now, Parrot, my sweet bird, speak our yet once again." NoSic

Speak roughly to your little boy. "Lewis Carroll." Fr. Alice's Adventures in Wonderland. FaBoCh; FaBoCo; NBLV; UV (Duchess's Lullaby, The.) CBNP; FaBoNo

Speak softly; sun going down. Fall of the Evening Star. Kenneth Patchen. ArLo

Speak! speak! thou fearful guest! The Skeleton in Armor. Longfellow. AmPP; AnAmPo; AWP; BeLS; BLPL; FaBoBe; PAH

Speak Thou and Speed. Sir Thomas Wyatt. EnRePo

Speak to dead walls: but those hear not my moan. (LL) My Body in the Walls Captived. Sir Walter Ralegh. SiPS; SiPSBD

Speak to Her Tenderly. Mary E. Tucker. CBWP-1

Speak to me. Take my hand. What are you now? Effort at Speech between Two People. Muriel Rukeyser. FYAP; MoAB; MoAmPo; Poetr; TrGrPo; TrJP; TwCP

Speak to the Sun. Dedie Huffman Wilson. GoYe

Speak to us who/ are also split. Tiresias. George Garrett. SM

Speak when I have nothing to say. (LL) Lady Love. Paul Éluard. ArLo; OBVE, tr. by Samuel Beckett

Speak when you're spoken to,/ Come for one call. Mother Goose. OxNR

Speake gentle heart, where is thy dwelling place? Thomas Watson. Fr. Hecatompathia; or, Passionate Century of Love. AAS

Speaker, The. Charles G. Ballard. VoR

Speaker in the Square, A. George Buchanan. PNI

Speakin' in general, I 'ave tried 'em all. Sestina of the Tramp-Royal. Kipling. ImPo; LiTB; MoBrPo; OtMeF; PrIm

Speaking. Michael Ryan. AmPA; SoSe

Speaking and Kissing. Thomas Stanley. BeJo

Speaking like wind. Swimmer. Gladys Cardiff. CDW

Speaking of Gethsemane in Yoruba Land. Edouard J. Maunick, tr. fr. French by Ellen Conroy Kennedy. Fr. As Far as Yoruba Land. NegPo

Speaking of Loss. Lucille Clifton. CAPP

Speaking of marvels, I am alive. Alive Together. Lisel Mueller. IHMS

Speaking of Poetry. John Peale Bishop. LiTA; OxBA

Speaking of Television, sels. Phyllis McGinley.
Robin Hood. OBSV

Speaking Tree, The. Muriel Rukeyser. VGW

Speaks a new scene; the last act crowns the play. (LL) My soul, sit thou a patient looker-on. Francis Quarles. NOBE; PoToHe

Speaks Bito's tomb to whomsoever reads. Nicaenetus, tr. fr. Greek by Peter Whigham. GrAn

Speaks the Whispering Grass. Jesse Stuart. FYAP

Spear is his alone. Nobody else, The. The Wound. David R. Slavitt. BAP-91

Speargrass crackles under the billy and overhead is the winter sun, The. While the Billy Boils. David McKee Wright, tr. fr. Maori by Margaret Orbell. PeNZ

Spearmen heard the bugle sound, The. Beth Gêlert. William Robert Spencer. BeLS
(Beth Gêlert; or, The Grave of the Greyhound.) BLPA; EBNV; OBNV

Spearo's Blues (or: Ode to a Grecian Yearn). Eugene B. Redmond. NBV

Special Bulletin. Langston Hughes. PoBA

Special Delivery. John Montague. IPY

Special Jurymen of England! who admire your country's laws. Damages, Two Hundred Pounds. Thackeray. OBSV

Special Pleading. Charles Bernstein. UL

Special Rider Blues. Unknown. AmFP

Special Theory of Relativity, A. Alan Bold. FaBoBl

Specifications for a Perfect Lover. Richard Crashaw. Fr. Wishes. To His (Supposed) Mistresse. CBCK

Specimen of an Induction to a Poem. Alan Bernheimer. UL

Speck of protoplasm in a finch's egg, The. Birdsong. Burns Singer. FaBoTw

Speck Speaks, A. Adrian Mitchell. OBSP

Speck that would have been beneath my sight, A. A Considerable Speck. Robert Frost. MoAB; MoAmPo; OBAL; PPP; SAmP

Speckle-black Toad and freckle-green Frog. George Darley. Fr. Thomas à Becket, a Dramatic Comedy. FM

Speckled bird sings in the tree, The. The Nightingale. Katharine Tynan. BoTP

Speckled cat and a tame hare, A. Two Songs of a Fool. W. B. Yeats. CMoP; RB

Speckled horse is bucking, The. *Mongol Oral Tradition, tr. by* C. R. Bawden. WTO

Speckled sky is dim with snow, The. Midwinter. John Townsend Trowbridge. AnAmPo; GN

Specks on the fingers. *Unknown.* RoPo

Spectacular Blossom. Allen Curnow. PeNZ

Spectator, The. Evan J. Thomas. AngWe

Spectator ab Extra. ("As I Sat at the Café I said to myself.") Arthur Hugh Clough. FaBoCo; OxBoLi; PeLV; PeVV
Sels.
As I Sat at the Café. ELP; FiBHP; GTBS-P, 3 *sts.*; NBLV
(How Pleasant It Is to Have Money.) NOBE; OAEL-2
"Come along, 'tis the time, ten or more minutes past." OBSV

Spectator's Guide to Contemporary Art, *sels.* Phyllis McGinley.
On the Farther Wall, Marc Chagall. OBSV
Squeeze Play. FaBoEE; OBSV

Spectators only on this bustling stage. Charles Churchill. *Fr.* Night; an Epistle to Robert Lloyd. OBSV

Specter, The. Ernst Hardt, *tr. fr. German by* Jethro Bithell. AWP

Spectral Lovers. John Crowe Ransom. GBL; HeIP

Spectre is haunting America — the spectre of hoodooism, A. Black Power Poem. Ishmael Reed. BPo

Spectrum. Mari Evans. BPo

Spectrum. Aidan Carl Mathews. IB; PBCIP

Spectrum Trench. Autumn. Nineteen-Sixteen. The Dead Soldiers. Max Plowman. PoWW

Speculation. Howard Nemerov. TAP

Speculative Evening. Marguerite Young. LiTA

Speculators, The. Thackeray. OBSV

Speech. Chief Mothibi. PeSAV

Speech. Leopold Staff, *tr. fr. Polish by* Adam Czerniawski. PoSu

Speech. Henry Taylor. MAT; NBLV

Speech after long silence; it is right. After Long Silence. W. B. Yeats. BoLoP; CMoP; EnLoPo; HeIP; HoPM; LiTM; NAEL-2; OAEL-2; OBMV; PPP; PrIm; UnPo

Speech and Silence. Richard Hovey. AnAmPo

Speech for the Clown, A. James Simmons. PWE

Speech for the Repeal of the McCarran Act. Richard Wilbur. CMoP; GOA

Speech Former Mayor Bob Wagner Made, A. Terence Winch. BCF

Speech of Emer, The. William Larminie. *Fr.* Fand. PeIV

Speech to a Crowd. Archibald MacLeish. MoAB; MoAmPo

Speech to Those Who Say Comrade. Archibald MacLeish. OxBA

Speech Warts. Myra Sklarew. CRP

Speeches at the Barriers, *sels.* Susan Howe.
"Say that a ballad." UL

Speechless, innept, and totally unmanned. (*LL*) Double Sonnet. Anthony Hecht. SM; Son

Speechless tree and animal and bird. A Lesson from Van Gogh. Howard Moss. MoAB

Speechless [upon the Marriage of Two Deaf and Dumb Persons]. Philip Bourke Marston. EBVV

Speechlesse still, and never crie[y]. (*LL*) Epitaph on the Earl of Strafford. John Cleveland. FaBoEE; FaBoEH; FaBoPV; JCP; NOBE; NOSC; OtMeF; PeECV; TrGrPo

Speed had not served, strength had not flowed amain. Losses. Edith M. Thomas. AmWP

Speed of Darkness, The. Muriel Rukeyser. GLP; LCAP

Speed Track, The. "Peter." BoTP

Speeding carriage climbs through eastern gate, A. *Unknown, tr. fr. Chinese by* Charles Hartman. SuSp

Speeding flowers along the shores mirror my boat red. Journeying to Hsiang-yi. Ch'en Yu Yi, *tr. fr. Chinese by* Irving Y. Lo. SuSp

Speir ye for Maggie Lauder. (*LL*) Maggie Lauder. *At. to* Francis Sempill. OxBS

Spell, The. Robert Herrick. CaPo

Spell, A. Dryden. *See* Choose the darkest part o' the grove.

Spell, A. George Peele. *Fr.* Old Wives' [*or* Wife's] Tale, The. ChTr

Spell against Sorrow. Kathleen Raine. PBWP

Spell against Spelling, The. George Starbuck. FYAP

Spell before Winter, A. Howard Nemerov. LiTM

Spell for Making the First Man. *Unknown, tr. fr. Maori by* Margaret Orbell. PeNZ

Spell for Sleeping, A. Alastair Reid. NTP

Spell me that in four letters. (*LL*) Pease porridge [*or* pudding] hot. Mother Goose. ISE; OxNR, 2 *vers.*; ReMoGo

Spell of Creation. Kathleen Raine. FaBoCh; OxBS

Spell of Invisibility, A. *At. to* Christopher Marlowe. ChTr

Spell of the Yukon, The. Robert W. Service. BLPA; BLPL; FaBoBe

Spell Potatoes. *Unknown.* RoPo

Spell, treasure-bearing spell, prop up the sky standing above. *Unknown, tr. fr. Maori by* Margaret Orbell. PeNZ

Spellbound. Emily Brontë. *See* Night Is Darkening round Me.

Spellbound: An Alphabet. Maurya Simon. FoLa
Sels.
"It is February in the mountains"

Spelling. Margaret Atwood. NALW; NoAM; NoP

Spelling It Out. Robert Maitre. FaBoBl

Spelling of Elliot, The. *Unknown.* FaBoUs

Spelling reformer indicted, A. Ambrose Bierce. *Fr.* Devil's Dictionary, The. OBAL; PeLi

Spells. James Reeves. NTP

Spelt from Sibyl's Leaves. Gerard Manley Hopkins. CMoP; EnVR; FaBoMo; LiTM; MeMBP; NOBVV; OAEL-2; PrIm; TOF

Spencer the Rover. *Unknown.* OBET

Spend the years of learning squandering. Gnome. Samuel Beckett. BIrV; OxBSP

Spende and god schall sende. Penny. *Unknown.* EnVB; FaBoVe; MiEL

Spending beyond their income on gifts for Christmas. Christmas Shopping. Louis MacNeice. OBCP

Spending hand that alway poureth out [*or* powreth owte], A. Sir Thomas Wyatt. *Fr.* Satires. AAS; NoSic; SiPSBD
(To Sir Francis Brian.) EnRePo; SiPS

Spending the Night. Maxine W. Kumin. CAPP

Spending the Night at a Mountain Temple. Chia Tao, *tr. fr. Chinese by* Stephen Owen. SuSp

Spending the Night at the Hillside Lodge of Master Yeh and Waiting for My Friend Ting. Meng Hao Jan, *tr. fr. Chinese by* Daniel Bryant. SuSp

Spending the Night in an Inn at Swatow and Writing about My Feelings, Sent to Liang Shih-wu. Huang Tsun-hsien, *tr. fr. Chinese by* An-yan Tang. SuSp

Spending the Night in the Eastern Park. Shen Yüeh, *tr. fr. Chinese by* Richard B. Mather. SuSp

Spending the Night on Stone Gate Mountain. Hsieh Ling-yün, *tr. fr. Chinese by* Francis Westbrook. SuSp

Spendthrift, disinherited and graceless, The. Remittance Man. Judith Wright. NoAM

Spendthrifts. Lotte Moos. NBrP

Spenser! a jealous honourer of thine. Keats. EPCY

Spenser's Ireland. Marianne Moore. FaBoWP; IIP; LiTA; LiTM; MeMAP; NoAM; NOBA; OxBA; TAP

Spent purpose of a perfectly marvellous, The. In Favor of One's Time. Frank O'Hara. NeAP; PoA

Sperrins surround it, the Faughan flows by, The. Claudy. James Simmons. BiHa; CIP; PBCIP; PWE

Sphere, *sels.* A. R. Ammons.
"I don't know about you,/ but I'm sick of good poems." HCAP
"I was pulling Veronica out of the lawn when this hornet came." NoAM
"There is a faculty or knack, smallish, in the mind that can turn." NoAM

Sphincter. Allen Ginsberg. PFL

Sphinx, The. Emerson. AmPP; NOBA; OxBA

Sphinx. Robert Hayden. HCAP

Sphinx, The, *sels.* Oscar Wilde.
"How subtle-secret is your smile! Did you love none then? Nay, I know." MoBrPo

Sphinxes Inclined to Be. Olga Orozco, *tr. fr. Spanish by* Leslie Keffer. WPOW

Spicewood. Lizette Woodworth Reese. MoAmPo

Spider. Basho, *tr. fr. Japanese.* TTTS

Spider. Thomas Cole. PoA

Spider, The. Richard Eberhart. NoAM; PoA

Spider, The. Norma Farber. PChr

Spider, The. Hannah Flagg Gould. OBCA

Spider. Judy Grahn. BCF

Spider, The. Edward Littleton. NOEC

Spider. Duane Niatum. ETG

Spider, The. César Vallejo, *tr. fr. Spanish by* Robert Bly. RaBo

Spider, The. Robert Penn Warren. MT

Spider and the Fly, The. Mary Howitt. BeLS; FaPON; OTCP; OxBChV; PWR; UV; WBLP

Spider and the Ghost of the Fly, The. Vachel Lindsay. VGW

Spider bite the size of a dinner plate, A. Into the Dark. Paul Monette. AmPA

Spider crouching on the ledge above the sink, The. James K. Baxter. *Fr.* Autumn Testament. PeNZ

Spider Crystal Ascension. Charles Wright. HCAP; LCAP; VCAP

Spider, dropping down from twig, The. Natural History. E. B. White. ArLo

Spider expects the cold of winter, The. The Spider. Richard Eberhart. NoAM; PoA

Spider holds a silver ball, The. Emily Dickinson. FM; WPOW

Spider in the bath, A. The image noted. The Image. Roy Fuller. GTBS-P; OxBTC

Spider, juiced crystal and Milky Way, drifts on his web through the night sky, The. Spider Crystal Ascension. Charles Wright. HCAP; LCAP; VCAP

Spider Reeves. Henry Carlile. Poetsp

Spider sewed at night, A. Emily Dickinson. NAAL-1; NALW

Spider! thou need'st not run in fear about. To a Spider. Robert Southey. FM

Spider weaves his silver wire, The. Of a Spider. Wilfred Thornley. FaPON; PDV

Spiders. David Wevill. MoCV

Spiders started out to go with the wind on its pilgrimage, The. The Broken. W. S. Merwin. LCAP

Spider's web, The. Special Delivery. John Montague. IPY

Spiderwebs on the casement. Old Times. Daniel Mark Epstein. DiPo

Spiel of the Three Mountebanks. John Crowe Ransom. MoAB; MoAmPo

Spies, you are lights in state, but of base stuff. On Spies. Ben Jonson. BeJo; FaBoVe; NoP; OxBSP

Spiked cadillacs with silver teeth. N. J. Loftis. Jaz

Spikenard. Laurence Housman. TrPWD

Spikes of new smell driven up nostrils. Gary Snyder. *Fr.* Myths and Texts. NaP; NeAP; PoM

Spilled into the cup. Bubbling Wine. Abu Zakariya, *tr. fr. Arabic by* A. J. Arberry. TTY

Spilling out/ into the world. *(LL)* Where Mountain Lion Lay [*or* Laid] Down with Deer. Leslie Silko. ImGa; Poetr; TRP; VoR; WPOW

Spilling their dreams like salt. *(LL)* Shopkeepers at the Party Meeting. Thomas McCarthy. BiHa; IB

Spilt Milk. W. B. Yeats. OxBSP

Spin a coin, spin a coin. Queen Nefertiti. *Unknown.* OTCP; TLR

Spin, a hardy spin, and here's the globe, A. A Small Boy, Dreaming. Albert Herzing. NYBP

Spin cheerfully. Leave the Thread with God. *Unknown.* BLRP

Spin, Dame, spin. *Unknown.* OxNR

Spin the ball! I reel, I burn. Song of Seyd Nimetollah of Kuhistan. Emerson. NOBA

Spindrift. Galway Kinnell. NaP; NYBP

Spine has been tingled; the horn has been swoggled, The. Woolly Words. Robert N. Feinstein. NBLV

Spinning. Alfred W. Purdy. NoAM; NOBC

Spinning away from the center. Dream of the Burning Longhouse. Duane Niatum. ETG

Spinning Song. Edith Sitwell. MoAB; MoBrPo

Spinning-Wheel, The. John Francis Waller. ChTr

Spinning Woman, The. Leonidas of Tarentum, *tr. by* Andrew Lang. *Fr.* Epigrams. AWP

Spinoza/ Collected curiosa. *Unknown.* NOBL

Spinoza Was a Bee. Jaroslaw Marek Rymkiewicz, *tr. fr. Polish by* Czeslaw Milosz. CBNP

Spinster. Sylvia Plath. FaBoWP; SoSe

Spinster with a mouth like a dam and a heart, A. Lizzie. Nancy Vieira Couto. PBCAP

Spinster's Lullaby. Vassar Miller. BoWoP; NMM

Spinster's Sweet-Arts, The, *sels.* Tennyson.
 "Robby, git down wi'tha, wilt tha?" FaBoVe

Spiralwise it spins. Time. Ralph Hodgson. GTBS-P

Spire, The. Ellen Bryant Voigt. NoAM

Spire cranes, The. Its statue is an aviary. Dylan Thomas. PoA

Spires, firm on their monster feet rose light and thin, The. Denis Devlin. *Fr.* Heavenly Foreigner, The. CIP

Spires of Oxford, The. Winifred M. Letts. PoLF; PoRA; WGRP

Spirit Appeared to Me, A. Herman Melville. ChIV-1

Spirit Craft, The. Charles G. Ballard. VoR

Spirit cries *Be strong!* and cries *Be still!*, A. *(LL)* Dead. Lionel Johnson. OBNC; PoEL-5

Spirit Epiloguizes, The. Milton. *See* To the ocean now I fly.

Spirit Flowers. Della Burt. BlSi

Spirit from Perfecter Ages. Arthur Hugh Clough. *See* Is it illusion? or does there a spirit from perfecter ages.

Spirit from Whom Our Lives Proceed. Howard Chandler Robbins. TrPWD

Spirit Haunts the Year's Last Hours, A. Tennyson. *Fr.* Princess, The. InvP; MeMBP
 (Song: "Spirit haunts the last year's hours, A.") GTBS-P; HeIP; OBNC

Spirit in Our Hearts, The. Henry Ustic Onderdonk. AH

Spirit is treading the earth, A. The Sick-room. Maria White Lowell. AmWP

Spirit Land, The. Jones Very. HAP

Spirit Levels. Iain Sinclair. VaA

Spirit moves, The. A Light Breather. Theodore Roethke. NoP

Spirit of Gama! round the stormy Cape. The Cape of Storms. John Wheatley. PeSAV

Spirit of God in the clear running water. *Unknown.* EaPr

Spirit of Life, in This New Dawn. Earl Bowman Marlatt. AH

Spirit of light divine! Semele. Rose Terry Cooke. AmWP

Spirit of Love. Barbara Deming. EaPr

Spirit of Night, The. Thomas Rogers. EIL

Spirit of Plato. *Unknown, tr. fr. Greek by* Shelley. AWP; OBVE

Spirit of Poetry, The. Ai Ch'ing, *tr. fr. Chinese.* LHF, *tr. by* Hualing Nieh

Spirit of power. *(LL)* Come, Thou Almighty King. Charles Wesley. WGRP

Spirit of romance dies not to those, The. Pictures of the Rhine. George Meredith. OBTV

Spirit of the, *Maine*, The. Tudor Jenks. PAH

Spirit of the Birch, The. Arthur Ketchum. OHIP

Spirit of the Maine!, The. *(LL)* Spirit of the *Maine*, The. Tudor Jenks. PAH

Spirit of the Place, The. Tony Curtis. AngWe

Spirit of the wolf returns, The. *(LL)* You are the last whale. Gary Lawless. EaPr

Spirit of Wrath, The. William Heyen. AmPA

Spirit Passed Before Me, A. Byron. ChIV-1

Spirit seems to pass, A. Lausanne. Thomas Hardy. FaBoRV; FaBoTw; OBTV

Spirit, Silken Thread. Margot Ruddock. OBMV

Spirit Song. *Unknown, tr. fr. Eskimo.* WTO

Spirit that walked upon the face of the waters, The. Passage. Denise Levertov. CAPP

Spirit to thee. *(LL)* Overlord. Bliss Carman.

Spirit Voice, The; or Liberty Call to the Disfranchised (State of New York). Charles Lewis Reason. AAP

Spirit! What art thou erecting. The Poet's Ideal. H. Cordelia Ray. CBWP-3

Spirit who sweepest the wild Harp of Time! Ode to the Departing Year. Samuel Taylor Coleridge. EnRP

Spirit Whose Work Is Done. Walt Whitman. NAAL-1

Spirits. Robert Bridges. *See* Angel Spirits of Sleep.

Spirits. Victor Hernandez Cruz. PoBA

Spirits. Birago Diop, *tr. fr. French by* Ellen Conroy Kennedy. NegPo

Spirits and illusions have died. Life from the Lifeless. Robinson Jeffers. CMoP

Spirits, Dancing. Arthur Gregor. NYBP; VGW

Spirit's Epilogue, The. Milton. *See* To the ocean now I fly.

Spirit's Epochs, The. Coventry Patmore. *Fr.* Angel in the House, The. EBEV; GBL; OxBSP

Spirits Everywhere. Ludwig Uhland, *tr. fr. German by* James Clarence Mangan. AWP

Spirit's Odyssey, The. M. Krishnamurti. InPK

Spirits of Movement. James Berry. NBrP

Spirits of old that bore me. The Knight Errant. Louise Imogen Guiney. AmWP

Spirits/ of the abnormally born. October. Audre Lorde. SRLS

Spirits of well-shot woodcock, partridge, snipe. "New King Arrives in His Capital by Air . . . " — Daily Newspaper. Sir John Betjeman. OxBoLi
 (Death of King George V. FaBoEH; NOBE

Spirit's Song. Louise Bogan. NYBP

Spirits Unchained. Keorapetse Kgositsile. PoBA

Spirits walking everywhere. W. J. Turner. *Fr.* Seven Days of the Sun, The. OBMV

Spiritual, A. Paul Laurence Dunbar. BPo

Spiritual Alchemy, The. "Angelus Silesius," *tr. fr. German.* *Fr.* Cherubical Wanderer, The. GePo, *tr. by* George C. Schoolfield

Spur the others to fey elation; no mad dogs in the house for me. (*LL*) Attis. Catullus. STV

Spurs upon a chamber-pot I never saw before. (*LL*) Shickered As He Could Be. *Unknown.* NOBAu

Spy bears his bald intent like a maniac, The. John Tranter. *Fr.* Crying in Early Infancy. CBAP

Spyglass Conversations. *Unknown, tr. fr. Tule Indian by* Frances Densmore. STP

Squalid, empty-headed hen, A. Hen under Bay-Tree. Ruth Pitter. OxBTC

Squalid Things. Sei Shonagon, *tr. fr. Japanese by* Ivan Morris. CBCK

Squalid village set in wintry mud, A. Born without a Chance. Edmund Vance Cooke. BLPA

Squalid with wounds, and many a gaping sore. The Wounded Man and the Swarm of Flies. William Somervile. FM

Squall. Stanley Moss. CoAP

Squander for me no scent of myrrh. Epitaph on a Tomb near Rome. *Unknown, tr. fr. Greek by* Frank Kuenstler. GrAn

Square along the couch, and stark. George Meredith. *Fr.* Nuptials of Attila, The. PeVV

Square as a seed-box, in their attic stands. The Handloom. Judith Rodriguez. FaBoWP

Square Dance, A. Roger McGough. NSI

Square figures climb off and on. On the "Sievering" Tram. Bernard Spencer. NAs

Square-heeled boat sets off for the Statue, The. To the Statue. May Swenson. GOA

Square sheets — they saw the marble into. Island Quarry. Hart Crane. PPP

Square, squat room (a cellar on promotion), A. Waiting. W. E. Henley. *Fr.* In Hospital. NAEL-2; NOBVV

Squares. Michael Hamburger. FF

Squaring the Circle. Louis O. Coxe. NYBP

Squash in Blossom. Robert Francis. FYAP

Squat Down, Josey. *Unknown.* AmFP

Squat in swamp shadows. Second Shaman Song. Gary Snyder. *Fr.* Myths and Texts. NeAP; NOBA; PoM

Squats on a toad-stool under a tree. Thomas Lovell Beddoes. *Fr.* Death's Jest Book. InvP; OBD

(Song by Isbrand.) InvP; NOBVV; OBNC; PrIm

Squatter in the Foreground. Kenward Elmslie. UL

Squatter's Children. Elizabeth Bishop. NoP

Squatting a day in the sun. Fire in the Hole. Gary Snyder. NAAL-2

Squeak the fife, and beat the drum. Independence Day. Royall Tyler. PAH

Squeal. Louis Simpson. BXAP; FiBHP; UnPo

Squealing under city stone. Rapid Transit. James Agee. MoAmPo

Squeeze Play. Phyllis McGinley. *Fr.* Spectator's Guide to Contemporary Art. FaBoEE; OBSV

Squeezes. Brian Patten. OTCP; Spl

Squinting against neon signs. Eclipse. Anita Endrezze-Danielson. CDW

Squire, a squire, he lived in the woods, A. The Broomfield Wager. *Unknown.* OBET

Squire and Milkmaid; or, Blackberry Fold. *Unknown.* CoMu; OBET; OxBB

Squire he had whose name was Ralph, A. Independent Squire. Samuel Butler. *Fr.* Hudibras. NOBE

Squire is in his library, The. He is rather worried. Send for Lord Timothy. John Heath-Stubbs. OxBC

Squire Meldrum at Carrickfergus. Sir David Lindsay. *Fr.* Historie of Squyer William Meldrum, The. OxBS

Squire nagged and bullied till I went to fight. Memorial Tablet. Siegfried Sassoon. IHNG; PoWW

Squire sat alone beside the board, The. Little Fay's Thanksgiving. H. Cordelia Ray. CBWP-3

Squire Squint, shooting at a pheasant. G. J. Blundell. UV

Squire's Boar Hunt, The. Rose Terry Cooke. AmWP

Squirrel. Lucile Adler. FoLa

Squirrel, The. Saleem Barakat, *tr. fr. Arabic by* Lena Jayyusi *and* Naomi Shihab Nye. TSaS

Squirrel, The. Mary Howitt. BoTP

Squirrel, The. *Unknown.* FaPON; PDV

Squirrel, The. *Unknown.* BoTP; OxNR

Squirrel in his shirt, The. Ground-Squirrel Song. *Navajo Indian Oral Tradition.* TTTS

Squirrel is the curliest thing, The. The Curliest Thing. *Unknown.* BoTP

Squirrel near Library. Genevieve Taggard. WPE

Squirrel Stand. Jim Wayne Miller. MT

Squirrels. John Mole. OBAP

Sri Rama's Raiment. *Malay Oral Tradition, tr. by* R. O. Winstedt. WTO

Ssŭ-ma Hsiang-ju pondered Leafy Mound. Li Ho, *tr. fr. Chinese by* A. C. Graham. *Fr.* Musing. PLT

Stab me with sword, or poison strong. Sextus Propertius, *tr. fr. Latin by* Robert Burton. *Fr.* Elegies. AWP; OBF

Stabat Mater [*or* Stabat Mater Dolorosa]. *At. to* Jacopone da Todi, *tr. fr. Latin by* Abraham Coles. WGRP

Stable Cat, The. Leslie Norris. PChr

Stable-lamp is lighted, A. A Christmas Hymn. Richard Wilbur. ChIV-2; OBCP; PChr; TrCP

Stable Straw. Robert Farren. TIRV

Stable yields a stercoraceous heap, The. How to Grow Cucumbers. William Cowper. *Fr.* Task, The. FaBoUs

Stack Arms! Joseph Blynth Alston. PAH

Stacking the Straw. Amy Clampitt. VCAP

Staff. John Engman. NAmP90

Staff and slippers hang here, Kypris, A. Leonidas, *tr. fr. Greek by* Kenneth Rexroth. PGA

Staff is now greased, The. The Hag. Robert Herrick. CaPo

Staff of Aesculapias, The. Marianne Moore. ImOP

Staff Officer. Shakespeare. *Fr.* King Henry IV, Pt. I. NAEL-1; OtMeF

Staff slips from the hand, The. Outward. Louis Simpson. NYBP

Stafford in Kansas. James Baker Hall. BXAP

Stag comes home at last, The. Thomas A. Clark. *Fr.* Sixteen Sonnets. NBrP

Stag, the runnable stag, The. (*LL*) A Runnable Stag. John Davidson. CoGr; EBEvV; EBNV; FaPoR; FM; GGP; HAP; MeMBP; OBEV; OxBTC; PrIm; WiR

Stage-Driver's Story, The. Bret Harte. EBNV

Stage is about to be swept of corpses, The. Horatian Epode to the Duchess of Malfi. Allen Tate. FaBoMo

Stage-lit streets. S.F. Southward. Allen Ginsberg. *Fr.* Continuation of a Long Poem of These States. NAAL-2

Stage Love. Swinburne. PoEL-5

Stage was set, the house was packed, The. Concert Party: Busseboom. Edmund Blunden. NSI

Stages on a Journey Westward. James Wright. LCAP; NaP

Staggering down the road at midnite. The Encounter. Paul Blackburn. NeAP

Stagnant, and green, and full of slimy things. (*LL*) October Journey. Margaret Walker. PoBA; PoNe

Stagolee. *Unknown.* MAT; OxBoLi; TTY

Staid schizophrenic named Struther, A. Limerick. *Unknown.* NIP

Stains. Theodosia Garrison. WGRP

Staircase, The. Samuel Allen. PoBA

Stairs. Oliver Herford. FiBHP

Stairs mount to his eternity, The. The Staircase. Samuel Allen. PoBA

Stairway is not, The. The Jacob's Ladder. Denise Levertov. AmPP; CAPP; ChIV-1; PoM; PPP

Stalagmites and Stalactites. *Unknown.* FaBoUs

Stalagmites in spring caves rise to more stalactites. Red Embankment. Tu Mu, *tr. fr. Chinese by* John M. Ortinau. SuSp

Stalin. Robert Lowell. HCAP

Stalin Epigram, The. Osip Mandelstam, *tr. fr. Russian by* W. S. Merwin *and* Clarence Brown. FaBoPV

Stalin stood committed to peasant hunger. Reply to the Committed Intellectual. Francis Sparshott. NOBC

Stalks of Wild Hay. H.L. Davis. PoA

Stalky Jack. William Brighty Rands. BoTP

Stalled before my metal shaving mirror. Notes for a Sonnet. Edward Pygge. BXAP

Stallion, The. Tudur Aled, *tr. fr. Welsh by* Joseph P. Clancy. OBWVE

Stamps. (*LL*) What a Proud Dreamhorse. E. E. Cummings. InvP; VGW

Stand back, Tom Devil, I'm gonna rule Hell by myself. (*LL*) Stagolee. *Unknown.* MAT; OxBoLi; TTY

Stand back, ye sleeping jacks at home. The Vice's Song. John Pickering. *Fr.* Horestes. NoSic

Stand by me, Death, lest these dark days. Three Pleas. Henry Treece. PoWW

Stand by the Flag. John Nichols Wilder. GN

Stand close around, ye Stygian set. Dirce. Walter Savage Landor. *Fr.* Pericles and Aspasia. AWP; CTC; EBEV; EnRP; FaBoEE; GBL; HAP; LiTB; NOBE; NoP; OAEL-2; OBEV; OBNC; OxAEP-2; OxBSP; PoEL-4; PoRA; SCGP; TFi; TrGrPo; WeW

(Stand Close Around.) ChTr

Stand fast, my child, and after all. Fortitude. Christopher Smart. ChIV-2

Stand here, you can see the hill. A Memory of the Hill. Kapilar, *tr. fr. Tamil by* A. K. Ramanujan. PLW

Stand in a row and learn. (*LL*) The Drunk in the Furnace. W. S. Merwin. CAPP; LiTM; MAT; MoP; NAAL-2; NoAM; NoP; PoE; Poetr; SM; TwCP

Stand in their sylvan bowers. (*LL*) To the Maiden in the East. Thoreau. AnAmPo; OxBA

Stand not uttering sedately. Epitaphium Citharistriae. Victor Plarr. EnLoPo; NBLV

  (Stand Not Uttering Sedately.) PoRA

Stand off, daughter of the dusk, Gwendolyn Brooks. *Fr.* Womanhood, The. NALW

Stand off, physician! Let me frolic. On Melancholy. *Unknown.* NOSC

Stand on the highest pavement of the stair. La Figlia Che Piange. T. S. Eliot. CBLP; FaBoTw; FaPoB; GBL; HeIP; LiTA; MAT; OPOP; OxBTC; PlP; PoA; UnPo; VGW

Stand [*or* Stond] who so list upon the slipper top [*or* toppe]. Seneca, *tr. by* Sir Thomas Wyatt. *Fr.* Thyestes. AAS; NoP; NoSic; OBVE; PoEL-1; SiPS

  "Climb at court for me that will." OBVE, *tr. by* Andrew Marvell

  "Let him that will, ascend the tottering seat." OBVE, *tr. by* Sir Matthew Hale

  "Let who so lyst with might mace to raygne." OBVE, *tr. by* Jasper Heywood

  "Senec. Traged. ex Thyeste Chor. 2." SeCV-1, *tr. by* Andrew Marvell

  "Upon the slippery tops of humane state." OBVE, *tr. by* Abraham Cowley

Stand out, maids, and look on the land of Cynddylan. *Unknown, tr. fr. Welsh by* Kenneth Hurlstone Jackson. *Fr.* Elegy on Cynddylan, The. OBWVE

Stand, Stately Tavie. *Unknown.* ErPo

Stand still. In the Fog. Lilian Moore. TLR

Stand still, and I will read to thee. A Lecture upon the Shadow. John Donne. AWP; EnRePo; ESCV; ImPo; NAEL-1; NoSic; SCGP; SeCP; TEP; UnPo

Stand still. The trees ahead and bushes beside you. Lost. David Wagoner. ArNa; FoLa; PoA

Stand still, true poet that you are! Popularity. Robert Browning. OAEL-2

Stand still, yet we will make him run. (*LL*) To His Coy Mistress. Andrew Marvell. ArLo; AWP; BoLP; CBLP; ClHu; CoGr; EBEV; EBEvV; ELP; EnLoPo; ErPo; ESCV; FaBV; FaPoB; FF; FHYEP; GBL; GeHe; HAP; HeIL; HeIP; HoPM; ImPo; InPK; InPS; InvP; JCP; LiTB; MAT; MeLP; NAEL-1; NIP; NOBE; NoP; NOSC; OAEL-1; OBD; OBEV; OPOP; OtMeF; OxAEP-1; PlP; PoE; PoEL-2; Poetr; PoLF; PPP; PrIm; SCGP; SCV; SeCP; TFi; TRP; UV

Stand still, you floods, do[e] not deface. On Sight of a Gentlewoman's Face in the Water. Thomas Carew. CaPo; SeCV-1

Stand! the ground's your own, my braves! Warren's Address at Bunker Hill [*or* to the American Soldiers]. John Pierpont. AnAmPo; FaBoBe; GN; GOA; PAH; WBLP

Stand-to, The. C. Day Lewis. OBWP

Stand-to: Good Friday Morning. Siegfried Sassoon. FaBoTw

Stand to one side. No, over here with me. Venetian Interior, 1889. Richard Howard. VCAP

"Stand to your guns, men!" Morris cried. On Board the *Cumberland*. George Henry Boker. PAH

Stand Up! D. H. Lawrence. OxBTC

Stand Up! Stand Up for Jesus. George Duffield, Jr. AH

Stand! Who goes there? John Lyly. *Fr.* Endimion. NoSic

Stand whoso list upon the slipper top. Sir Thomas Wyatt. SiPSBD

Stand with thy nose against. Of One That Had a Great Nose. George Turbeville, *after the Greek of* Trajan. FaBoEE

Stand with Your Lover on the Ending Earth. E. E. Cummings. MeMAP

Stand you here, murdering shaft, no longer. Dedication: A Spear. Anyte, *tr. fr. Greek by* John Heath-Stubbs *and* Carol A. Whiteside. GrAn

Standards in Hopeful Anticipation of the Bicentenery of the National Emblem of the United States of America. Tony Harrison. *Fr.* Art & Extinction. SCBI

Standards of the King go forth, The. Saint Venantius Fortunatus, *tr. fr. Latin by* Helen Waddell. MLL

Standin' on the Walls of Zion. *Unknown.* AS

Standing all day on Lake View Tower. Written on Lake View Tower. P'an Lang, *tr. fr. Chinese by* Jonathan Chaves. SuSp

Standing aloof in giant ignorance. To Homer. Keats. EBEV; NAEL-2; NoP; Son

Standing at the portal. At the Portal. Frances Ridley Havergal. BLRP

Standing beside you, fiddler. *Unknown, tr. fr. Greek by* Peter Jay. GrAn

Standing corn is green, the wild in flower, The. Nunc Viridant Segetes. Sedulius Scottus, *tr. fr. Medieval Latin by* Helen Waddell. BIrV; NAWM-1

Standing guests, a grotesque glade, The. The Party. Margaret Avison. PoA

Standing high on the shoulders of all things, all things. The Place at Albert Bay. Muriel Rukeyser. PoA

Standing high to see tidal dawn. Cockcrow. Ted Hughes. AnAn

Standing in a stillness that now is yours. (*LL*) Water Island. Howard Moss. CoAP; NYBP; Prf

Standing in ribbons, over our heads, for an hour. (*LL*) End of the Picnic. Francis Webb. NOBAu

Standing in the Doorway, I Watch the Young Child Sleep. Sharon Hashimoto. OpBo

Standing in the garden. Listen. Linda Lancione Moyer. CrSp

Standing in the hall against the/ wall. Listening to Grownups Quarreling. Ruth Whitman. NTCP

Standing just outside the brass linings of Paris . . . Paris . . . Clark Coolidge. BAP-89

Standing on a stepladder. Soy Sauce. Gary Snyder. CAPP

Standing on Earth ("Standing on Earth, not rapt above the Pole.") Milton. *Fr.* Paradise Lost. ChTr; EPCY

Standing on the Corner. Philip Levine. NNaP

Standing on the mountaintop. Lost Silvertip. J. D. Reed. NYBP

Standing on top of the hay. The Farm. Donald Hall. LiTM

Standing sentry for the avalanche. (*LL*) Strength through Joy. Kenneth Rexroth. FYAP; VGW

Standing Stone. Ruth Bidgood. AngWe

Standing tall, the legions of the hungry! (*LL*) New Negro Sermon. Jacques Roumain. NegPo

Standing there they began to grow skins. Pilgrims. Jean Valentine. LCAP; TAP

Standing under the greengrocer's awning. The Hailstone. Peter Didsbury. PWE

Standing under the shower. A Dream of Washed Hair. Rhyll McMaster. FaBoMA

Standing Up, *sels.* Tomas Tranströmer, *tr. fr. Swedish.*

  "It's been a hard winter, but summer is here and the fields." RaBo

Standing up on lifted, folded rock. By Frazier Creek Falls. Gary Snyder. EaPr; GOA; InPS

Standing upon a hill of fancies high. A Landscape. Margaret Cavendish, Duchess of Newcastle. NOSC

Stands beside her smoking gun. (*LL*) Captain Molly. William Collins. ImGa

Stands, face to the wall. The Man with the Lepidoptera on His Ass. Albert Stainton. PRA

Stands for Gnu, whose weapons of Defense. G. Hilaire Belloc. FiBHP

Stands forever the camp of that dead brigade. (*LL*) The Centenarian's Story. Walt Whitman. CTC

Stands open to the stars. (*LL*) By these, by these same chains, O Rome. Alcuin. MLL

Stands/ outside my door this morning. A New Refugee. Marisella Veiga. LoHo

Stane-chack!. Malison of the Stone-chat. *Unknown.* GBP

Stanley Matthews. Alan Ross. OxBTC

Stanley Meets Mutesa. James David Rubadiri. PBA

Stanza Put on Westminster Hall Gate, A. *Unknown.* APAS

Stanza Written in Jest. Yang Wan-li, *tr. fr. Chinese by* Sherwin S. S. Fu. SuSp

Stanzas: "Black absence hides upon the past." John Clare. EnLoPo; NOBVV

Stanzas: "Childhood's glad smile was on my lip, life's sunshine on my brow." Emma Catherine Embury. AmWP

Stanzas: "How smooth that lake expands its ample breast!" Ann Radcliffe. WPE

Stanzas: "I don't want to pay down the last penny of my soul." Osip Mandelstam, *tr. fr. Russian by* W. S. Merwin *and* Clarence Brown. AnAn

Stanzas: "I thought I woke: the midnight sun." Paul Goodman. PoA

Stanzas: "I'll not weep that thou art going to leave me." Emily Brontë. WPE

Stanzas: "In a drear-nighted December." Keats. *See* In a Drear-nighted December.

Stanzas: "In this vain, busy world, where the good and the gay." Mary Robinson. ECWP; WoRP

Stanzas: "Mighty thought of an old world, The." Thomas Lovell Beddoes. *See* Mighty Thoughts of an Old World, The.

Stanzas: "No voice but that of gladness." Emma Catherine Embury. AmWP

Stanzas: "Often rebuked, yet always back returning." *At. to* Emily Brontë, *also at. to* Charlotte Brontë. LiTB; MeMBP; NOBVV; OAEL-2; OBNC; OHCV; PBWP; SCGP

  (Stanza. OBEV

  (Stanzas.) NALW; PFP

Stanzas: "Passing of a dream, The." John Clare. NOBVV
Stanzas: "Princes and kings decay and die." Philip Freneau. GOA
Stanzas: "Sleep, Mr. Speaker! it's surely fair." Winthrop Mackworth Praed. EnRP
  (Stanzas to the Speaker Asleep. OBSV
Stanzas: "When a man hath no freedom to fight for at home." Byron. EnRP; FaBoEE; NAEL-2; NBLV; OxAEP-2; PAW; PFP; Poetr; PoLF; TrGrPo; TRP
Stanzas: "With tears thy grief thou dost bemoan." Solomon ibn Gabirol, tr. fr. Hebrew by Emma Lazarus. TrJP
Stanzas: "You ask me how to pray to someone who is not." Czeslaw Milosz, tr. fr. Polish by Robert Hass. AnAn
Stanzas, sels. Charles Newton. NOEC
  Wild Nature. NOEC
Stanzas — April, 1814. Shelley. EnRP; OBNC; SCGP
Stanzas Concerning an Ecstasy Experienced in High Contemplation. St. John of the Cross, tr. fr. Spanish by K. Kavanaugh and O. Rodrigues. TOF
Stanzas Concerning Love. Stefan George, tr. fr. German by Ludwig Lewisohn. AWP
Stanzas for Music., sels. Byron.
  "There be none of Beauty's daughters." AWP; CBLP; ELP; EnRP; GTBS; GTBS-P; HAP; LiTB; NAEL-2; NoP; OAEL-2; PFP; PoRA; TrGrPo
  (There Be None of Beauty's Daughters.) MeMBP
  "There's not a joy the world can give like that it takes away." EnRP; GTBS; HAP
  (There's Not a Joy.) MeMBP
  (Youth and Age.) GTBS; GTBS-P
  "They say that hope is happiness." NAEL-2; OxBSP
Stanzas for the Harp. Unknown, tr. fr. Welsh by Tony Conran. VBLP
Stanzas from "Child Harold." John Clare. Fr. Child Harold. OBNC
Stanzas from the Grande Chartreuse, sels. Matthew Arnold. EBVV; EnVR; NAEL-2; OAEL-2; PoE; PoEL-5; TEP
  "For rigorous teachers seized my youth." FHYEP
Stanzas from "The Ivory Gate." Thomas Lovell Beddoes. See Mighty Thoughts of an Old World, The.
Stanzas Imitated From Psalm CXIX. Thomas, the Elder Warton. ChIV-1
Stanzas in Meditation., sels. Gertrude Stein.
  "Full well I know that she is there." PoA
  "How I wish I were able to say what I think." PBWP
Stanzas Occasioned by the Ruins of a Country Inn or On the Ruins of a Country Inn. Philip Freneau. AnAmPo; OxBA
Stanzas of the Graves, The, sels. Unknown, tr. fr. Welsh by Gwyn Jones.
  "Graves the rain makes wet and sleek, The." OBWVE
Stanzas of the Soul that Suffers with Longing to See God. St. John of the Cross, tr. fr. Spanish by K. Kavanaugh and O. Rodrigues. TOF
Stanzas on Charles Armitage Brown. Keats. See He is to weet a melancholy carle.
Stanzas on Freedom, sels. James Russell Lowell. GN, 2 sts.; OHIP; PoNe Slaves
  (On Freedom.) ImGa
Stanzas on Mutability. Hugo von Hofmannsthal, tr. fr. German by Jethro Bithell. AWP; TrJP
Stanzas on the Psalms. Thomas, the Elder Warton. ChIV-1
Stanzas on the Taking of Quebec, sels. Goldsmith.
  "Alive, the foe thy dreadful vigour fled." FaBoEH
Stanzas: On Woman. Goldsmith. See When lovely woman stoops to folly.
Stanzas Subjoined to the Yearly Bill of Mortality of the Parish of All Saints, Northampton; for the Year 1787. William Cowper. NOCV
Stanzas to ———. Emily Brontë. WPE
Stanzas to a Lady, with the Poems of Camoëns. Byron. FaBoUs
Stanzas to Augusta. Byron. EnRP
Stanzas to Edward Williams. Shelley. OBNC
Stanzas to Mr. Bentley. Thomas Gray. NoP
Stanzas to the Po. Byron. OAEL-2
Stanzas to the Speaker Asleep. Winthrop Mackworth Praed. See Sleep, Mr. Speaker! it's surely fair.
Stanzas Written between Dover and Calais, in July, 1792. Martha Robinson. ECWP
Stanzas Written in Dejection [December 1818], near Naples. Shelley. EnRP; FaBV; GTBS; GTBS-P; NAEL-2; NAWM-2; NoP; PoRA; TEP
Stanzas Written in London in 1773, sels. Edward Williams.
  "Why, Cambria did I quit thy shore." AngWe
Stanzas Written in My Pocket Copy of Thomson's "Castle of Indolence." Wordsworth. EnRP
Stanzas Written on the Road between Florence and Pisa. Byron. EnRP; NAEL-2; PFP
Star, A. George MacBeth. NYBP
Star, A. (LL) I have a little sister, they call her Peep-Peep. Mother Goose. BoTP; OxNR

Star. Iain Sinclair. NBrP
Star, The. Marion Couthouy Smith. PAH
Star, The. Jane Taylor. BoTP; FaBoBe; FaPON; ImGa; NTCP; OTCP; OxBChV; OxNR; PYC; UV, st. 1 only
Star & Garter Theater. Dennis Schmitz. LCAP
Star and Sea. William Peskett. PNI
Star Blanket. Ray A. Young Bear. CDW
Star-breath descends. line. Star. Iain Sinclair. NBrP
Star crashes in a small plaza and a bird loses its eyes, A. The Things I Say Are True. Blanca Varela, tr. fr. Spanish by Donald Yates. BoWoP
Star-crowned solitude of thine oblivious hours!, The. (LL) To One in Bedlam. Ernest Dowson. MoBrPo; OBMV; Son
Star een an' honey mou'? (LL) Think Lang. Marion Angus. VBLP
Star Field, The. Mei-Mei Berssenbrugge. VBLP
Star-filled seas are smooth tonight, The. The Isle of Portland. A. E. Housman. Fr. Shropshire Lad, A. FaPoB; MoBrPo
Star-fix. Marilyn Nelson Waniek. NAmP90
Star frightens the steeple cross, A. Guard-Duty. August Stramm, tr. fr. German by Patrick Bridgwater. PeFWW
Star-Gazer. Louis MacNeice. NAEL-2; NoP
Star-Gazers. Wordsworth. Poetr
  Sels.
  "What crowd is this? what have we here! we must not pass it by."
Star-Gazing. Ptolemy, tr. fr. Greek by Dudley Fitts. ArNa; GrAn
Star,/ If you are. A Christmas Tree. William Burford. SoSe
Star is gone, A! a star is gone! The Fallen Star. George Darley. OBEV
Star Journey. Naomi Long Madgett. BPo
Star light, star bright. Wishing Poem. Unknown. NTCP; OxNR; RoPo
  (Star Wish. OTCP
Star looks down at me, A. Waiting Both. Thomas Hardy. MoAB; MoBrPo; OxBoLi; TTTS
Star Morals. Friedrich Wilhelm Nietzsche, tr. fr. German by Ludwig Lewisohn. AWP
Star Motel. Bill Berkson. UL
Star Obscure, The. Gueni Zaimof. WoWa
Star of Free Will, The, sels. Maria Luisa Spaziani, tr. fr. Italian by Beverly Allen.
  "I shall find in paradise that emaciated rose shoot." NeIt
  "Sunday in the provinces, a plaintive Norman bell-peal." NeIt
  "Traveling with too much baggage is not a good idea." NeIt
Star of the Evening. James M. Sayles. UV, sl. sh. vers.
Star of the sea, surest point of brightness. Stella Maris. O. B. Hardison, Jr. CRP
Star over all. Christmas Tree. Laurence Smith. OBCP
Star Quilt. Roberta Hill Whiteman. CDW; NoAM
Star-Shell, The. Patrick MacGill. NSI
Star Song. H. Cordelia Ray. CBWP-3
Star-Song; a Carol to the King; Sung at White-Hall, The. Robert Herrick. GN
Star Song of the Bushman Women. Unknown, tr. fr. Bushman by W. H. I. Bleek. PeSA
Star-spangled Banner, The. Francis Scott Key. AiP; AnAmPo; BLPA; EBEvV; FaBoBe; FaPON; PAH; TAP; UV, abr.; WBLP
Star System, The. Richard Wilbur. NBLV
Star-Talk. Robert Graves. BoNaP; GoJo; MoBrPo; OxBTC
Star that bids the shepherd fold, The. Milton. Fr. Comus; a Masque Presented at Ludlow Castle. FaBoCh; FHYEP; OAEL-1; OBEV
  (Comus' Invocation to His Readers. TrGrPo
  (Comus Speaks.) NOBE
  (Comus' Summons.) NOSC
  (Mask, A.) 09FiP
Star that bringest home the bee. To the Evening Star. Thomas Campbell. GTBS; GTBS-P
Star Trek III. Richard Harteis. GLP
Star-Tribes, The. Aborigine Oral Tradition, tr. by Fred Biggs. NOBAu
Star Watcher, The. Peter Davison. TwCP
Star Wish. Unknown. See Star light, star bright.
Stardust Sequence, The, sels. Dermot Bolger. IB
  "Last night in swirling colour we daced again." BiHa
Stare at the monster: remark. Famous Poet. Ted Hughes. LiTM
Stare at the stars, the stars. Look at me. Ego. Norman MacCaig. GTBS-P
Stare into my toilet table mirror. (LL) Playing All a Summer's Day by the Lake. Chu Shu-chen. WPC
Stared, astonied all. È, the Feasting Florentines. Daniel Hoffman. VGW
Stared Story, A. William Stafford. Son
Stare's Nest by My Window, The. W. B. Yeats. Fr. Meditations in Time of Civil War. BIrV; GTBS-P; InPS; LiTB; NOBE

Startled/ By a single scream. Saigyo, *tr. fr. Japanese* by Arthur Waley. AWP

Startled stag, the blue-grey night, A. The Dark Stag. Isabella Valancy Crawford. NOBC

Startles me. (*LL*) Creation. Alma Villanueva. SRLS

Startles the desert over Africa! (*LL*) At Gibraltar. George Edward Woodberry. GN

Starvation and Blues. Edward Kamau Brathwaite. PBCV

Starvation Camp near Jaslo. Wislawa Szymborska, *tr. fr. Polish* by Jan Darowski. WPOW

Starved children begging chocolate on the tracks. (*LL*) Between the Wars. Robert Hass. VCAP

Starved Lovers. Archibald MacLeish. MeMAP

Starved old gelding, blind and lamed, A. An Irish Marriage Night. Brian Merriman, *tr.* by Frank O'Connor. *Fr.* Midnight Court, The. BIrV; NOIV, *tr.* by Thomas Kinsella

Starved to death. In Memoriam. Bernard Dadié, *tr. fr. French* by Ellen Conroy Kennedy. NegPo

Starving to Death on a Government Claim. *Unknown.* AmFP; OBAL

Stasis in darkness. Ariel. Sylvia Plath. CMoP; HCAP; HeIP; LCAP; MoP; NAAL-2; NALW; NoAM; NOBA; NoP; PBWP; PoE; Poetr; VCAP

State, The. Randall Jarrell. LiTM

State, a state, oh! dungeon state indeed, A. Edward Taylor. *Fr.* Preparatory Meditations Before My Approach to the Lord's Supper. ChIV-1, Division II, *sect.* LXXVII; EAP

State and 32nd, Cold Morning Blues. Kenneth Rexroth. *Fr.* Written to Music. Jaz

State, as if to stamp the final seal. Wordsworth. *Fr.* Prelude [or, Growth of a Poet's Mind], The. EnRP; FaBoPV; OAEL-2

State Funeral. Thomas McCarthy, *tr. fr. Irish.* CIP; IB; PeIV

State of Innocence, The. Dryden. NOCV
Sels.
   Death the Consequence of the Fall
   Predestination and Free Will

State of Nature, A. John Hollander. AiP

State of the Nation, The. *Unknown.* CBCK

State of the Union. Aimé Césaire, *tr. fr. French* by Denis Kelly. NegPo

State Poetry Day. Ronald Wallace. PBCAP

State Street is lonely today. Aunt Jane Allen. Fenton Johnson. PoBA; PoNe

State with the prettiest name, The. Florida. Elizabeth Bishop. TwCP

Stately Homes of England, The. Noël Coward. UV

Stately homes of England, The. The Homes of England. Felicia Dorothea Hemans. FaPoR; UV, abr.; VPP; WPE

Stately, kindly, lordly friend. To a Cat. Swinburne. OFC; SoCa

Stately Lady, The. Flora Sandstrom. BoTP

Stately palace in which the queen dwells, The. Her Descending Down. Margaret Cavendish, Duchess of Newcastle. NOSC

Stately rainbow came and stood, A. The Rainbow. Coventry Patmore. *Fr.* Angel in the House, The. GTBS-P

Stately Southerner, The. *Unknown. See* 'Tis of a gallant Yankee ship that flew the stripes and stars.

Stately Southerner, The. *Unknown.* AmFP

Stately state that wise men count their good, The. Barmenissa's Song. Robert Greene. FaBoRV

Stately Structure of This Earth, The. Martha Brewster. AH

Stately the feast, and high the cheer. The Grave of King Arthur. Thomas Warton the Younger. EnRP

Stately Verse. *Unknown.* FaPON

Statement on Our Higher Education. W. M. Ransom. CDW

States when they black out and lie there rolling, The. Falling. James Dickey. LCAP; MT; NoAM; NYBP

Statesman, The. Hilaire Belloc. NOBE

Statesman's Holiday, The. W. B. Yeats. CMoP; OxBTC

Statesmen bicker about the non-essential, The. Vital Statistics. William Rose Benét. AnAmPo

Static. Judith Kazantzis. DT

Static Autumn. Yvor Winters. PoA

Station. Sharon Olds. PBCAP

Station is empty and desolate, The. Goods Train at Night. Kenneth H. Ashley. PIP

Station Island., *sels.* Seamus Heaney.
   "Black water. White waves. Furrows snowcapped." NoAM
   "I had come to the edge of the water." NoAM
   "Like a convalescent, I took the hand." FaBoPV; NAEL-2; NoAM; TOF
   "My brain dried like spread turf, my stomach." CIP

Stationmaster is garrulous in, The. Daphne Stillorgan. Denis Devlin. CIP

Stations. Ted Hughes. NoAM

Statistics. Stephen Spender. MoBrPo

Statuary. John Ashbery. NoAM

Statue, The. Hilaire Belloc. OxAEP-2

Statue, The. Robert Creeley. LCAP

Statue, The. John Fuller. NOBE

Statue, The. Edith Roseveare. Mes

Statue, The. Matthew Sweeney. IB

Statue and Birds. Louise Bogan. MoAB; MoAmPo

Statue and the Bust, The, *sels.* Robert Browning.
   "There's a palace in Florence, the world knows well." Mes

Statue in Stocks-Market, The, *sels.* Andrew Marvell.
   "But with all his faults restore us our King." FaBoEH

Statue of Bereniké, A. Callimachus, *tr. fr. Greek* by Peter Jay. GrAn

Statue of Eros, A. Zenodotus, *tr. fr. Greek* by Peter Jay. GrAn

Statue of Liberty, The. Thomas Hardy. LiTB

Statue of Nemesis at Rhamnus, The. Parmenion of Macedon, *tr. fr. Greek* by Alistair Elliot. GrAn

Statue of Shadow, The. John Peale Bishop. LiTA

Statue to Pygmalion, The. Frances Sargent Osgood. AmWP

Statues, The. Laurence Binyon. OBEV

Statues. Kathleen Raine. NYBP

Statues, The. W. B. Yeats. NoAM; OAEL-2; PeIV; WeW

Statues with exposed hearts and barbed-wire crowns. The Mud Vision. Seamus Heaney. PBCIP

Status Quo. Binga Dismond. PoNe

Stavro's dead. A truant vine. Lawrence Durrell. FaBoCo

Stay . . . I can wait a little yet. (*LL*) Reproof of Thanks. Walter Savage Landor. CBLP

Stay All Night, Stay a Little Longer. *Unknown.* AmFP

Stay Beautiful. Jeff Wright. UL

Stay beautiful/ but dont stay down underground too long. For Poets. Al Young. PoBA; RFM

Stay Behind, The. Andrew Elliott. PNI

Stay! Beneath your feet is a wonder of women. On a Woman. Robert Williams, *tr. fr. Welsh* by H. Idris Bell. OBWVE

Stay, fairest Chari[e]ssa, stay and mark. The Glowworm. Thomas Stanley. BeJo; NOSC

Stay, gentle Child of Taste! who'er thou art. A Prefatory Epistle. Maria Falconar. ECWP

Stay here, fond youth, and ask no more, be wise. Against Fruition Sir John Suckling. BeJo; CaPo; NOSC

Stay, lady, stay, for mercy's sake. The Orphan Boy's Tale. Amelia Alderson Opie. VPP

Stay mad, stay mad. *Unknown.* RoPo

Stay My Steps in Thy Paths, That My Feet Do Not Slide. Francis Quarles. *Fr.* Emblems. *Fr.*

Stay, my tendrils, where hung. Asclepiades, *tr. fr. Greek* by Alan Marshfield. GrAn

Stay near me — do not take thy flight! To a Butterfly. Wordsworth. EnRP; FM

Stay near me. Speak my name. Oh, do not wander. Midcentury Love Letter. Phyllis McGinley. OxBM

Stay now with me, and listen to my sighs. Dante, *tr. fr. Italian* by Dante Gabriel Rossetti. *Fr.* Vita Nuova, La. AWP

Stay, Nymph. Francis Pilkington. EnRePo

Stay, O sweet, and do not rise! Break of Day. *Unknown, at.* to John Donne. EIL; TrGrPo
   (Aubade. BoLoP; NOBE
   (Daybreak.) OBEV

Stay off from me, wild sea. A Tomb on the Shore. Asclepiades, *tr. fr. Greek* by Alan Marshfield. GrAn

Stay, passenger, and lend a tear. On a Hopeful Youth. Owen Felltham [*or* Feltham]. NOSC

Stay Phoebus, stay. Edmund Waller. BeJo; SeCP

Stay, shade of my shy treasure! Oh, remain. Sister Juana Inés de la Cruz, *tr. fr. Spanish* by Alice Stone Blackwell. WPOW

Stay, should I answer, Lady, then. To Mrs K. T. (Who Asked Him Why He Was Dumb). John Cleveland. CBLP

Stay silent/ keep away from sharks. Anticipation of Sharks. Diane Wakoski. MAT

Stay, Speedy Time. Michael Drayton. *Fr.* Idea. EnRePo; ESo

Stay, Spring. Andrew Young. FaBoTw

Stay, stay at home, my heart, and rest. Home Song. Longfellow. GN

Stay, stay, sweet Time; behold, or ere thou pass. Michael Drayton. BOEP

Stay, Thames, to heare my Song, thou great and famous Flood. Michael Drayton. *Fr.* Third Eclogue, The. PoEL-2

Stay weary traveler, stay! The Fountain at the Tomb. Nicias, *tr. fr. Greek* by Charles Merivale. AWP

Stay yet, pale flower, though coming storms will tear thee. On a Rose in December. Ebenezer Elliot. FaBoEE

Stay your rude steps, or e'er your feet invade. John Hookham Frere. *Fr.* Loves of the Triangles, The. FaBoNo

Stayed by what was, and pulled by what would be. (*LL*) She. Theodore Roethke. BoLoP; ErPo

Staying Alive. David Wagoner. BoNaP; CoAP; InPK; NYBP; RFM; SM

Staying at Ed's Place. May Swenson. VCAP

Staying in the Mountains in Summer. Yü Hsüan-chi, *tr. fr. Chinese by* Geoffrey R. Waters. BoWoP

Staying Overnight at the Temple of the Holy Vulture. Yang Wan-li, *tr. fr. Chinese by* Sherwin S. S. Fu. SuSp

Steadfast a lamp burns sheltered from the wind. *Unknown, tr. by* Sir Edwin Arnold. *Fr.* Bhagavad-Gita, The. TOF

Steadfastness. Sir Thomas Wyatt. *See* Forget [*or* Fforget] not yet the tried intent.

Steady cedars levelling the shade, The. Effacements. Peter Scupham. SCBI

Steady drift of rain curtaining her, The. Encounter. Cynthia Fuller. NWP

Steady heart, which in its steadiness, The. Angina Pectoris. W. R. Moses. LiTA

Steady in the darkness. Put a Woman into the Memory Box. Brigitte Frase. LoHo

Steady time of being unknown, The. Consider a Move. Michael Ryan. SM

Steady world pursued its common way, The. Tenants at Will. William Allingham. *Fr.* Lawrence Bloomfield in Ireland. PeIV

Steal Away to Jesus. *Unknown.* BPo

Steal not this book for fear of shame. *Unknown.* FaBoUs; ISE

Stealer of beef, A. (*LL*) Laird, a lord, A. *Unknown.* OxNR

Stealing along in this eyelighter city. Rome Once Alone. Clark Coolidge. UL

Stealing Trout. Ted Hughes. NYBP

Steam digger, The. The Steam Shovel. Rowena Bastin Bennett. SiSoPo

Steam Engine; or, The Power of the Flame, The, *sels.* Thomas Baker.
    Electric Telegraph, The. FaBoUs
    "I dream'd I walk'd in raptures high." BXAP
    Means of Propulsion for Steam-Ships. FaBoUs
    Watt's Improvements to the Steam Engine. FaBoUs

Steam in Sacrifice. Robert Herrick. CaPo

Steam Power. Erasmus Darwin. *Fr.* Botanic Garden, The. NOEC

Steam Shovel, The. Rowena Bastin Bennett. SiSoPo

Steam Shovel. Charles Malam. NTCP; PYC

Steam Threshing-Machine, The. Charles Tennyson Turner. OBNC

Steamboat Whistle, The. Archibald MacLeish. MeMAP

Steamboats, Viaducts, and Railways. Wordsworth. NAEL-2

Steamer left he black and oozy wharves, The. Alexander Smith. *Fr.* Boy's Poem, A. PeVV

Steaming and silent and standing straight,/ sprouting leaves. (*LL*) Simultaneously. David Ignatow. GrPl; TwCP

Steaming hunk of meat, A. Hero's Portion. John Montague. NOIV

Steaming past Breaksea and Michaelmas. (*LL*) The Gathering Place. Alan Alexander. NOBAu

Stedefast [*or* Steddefast *or* Steadfast] cross[e], inmong [*or* among] alle [*or* all] other. Venantius Fortunatus. MiEL
    (Hymm to the Cross, A.) MeEL

Stedes ther stumbelyd in that stownde. *Unknown.* OxBLMV

Steed, a steed of matchlessespeed, A! The Cavalier's Song. William Motherwell. GN

Steed bit his master, The. On a Clergyman's Horse Biting Him. *Unknown.* FaBoCo; FaBoEE; NBLV; OxBoLi
    (Steed Bit His Master, The.) ChIV-1

Steekit, consecrat, fou o fire but fuel. Douglas Young, *after the French of* Paul Valéry. *Fr.* Kirkyaird by the Sea, The. OBVE

Steel doors — guillotine gates. The Prisoners. Robert Hayden. CAPP

Steel fibrous slant & ribboned glint, The. The Turncoat. Amiri Baraka. NeAP; PoE

Steel mind. (*LL*) Out the You of Yesterday. Liliane Lijn. VBLP

Steel Usurps the Forests; Silence Dethrones Dialogue. Bible, Apocrypha. HBAPE

Steel voice of a steel god. Pans at Carnival. Henry Beissel. PBCV

Steel worker on the girder, The. The Building of the Skyscraper. George Oppen. GOA

Steele Glas, The. George Gascoigne. AAS

Steely train in the stupid green, The. Train: Abstraction. Genevieve Taggard. WPE

Steelyards, the long lines of workers, The. Meditation at Pearl Street. Bruce Weigl. NAmP90

Steep cliffs pierce the sky. Mount T'ai P'ing. Ch'ien Ch'i, *tr. fr. Chinese by* Kenneth Rexroth. OHMPC

Steep, steep the lofty mountain peak. Hsü Kan, *tr. by* Ronald C. Miao. *Fr.* Boudoir Thoughts. SuSp

Steep valley overhung by trees, A. Plea for Peace. Frank Prewett. HATNAP

Steeped in ecstasies of perfume. Spring Nocturne. Abraham Liessin, *tr. fr. Yiddish.* TrJP

Steepies for the bairnie. Supper. William Soutar. OxBS

Steeple-Jack, The. Marianne Moore. *Fr.* Part of a Novel, Part of a Poem, Part of a Play. BoWoP; CMoP; FaBoMo; FaBoWP; HAP; InPS; NoAM; NOBA; NoP; OxBA; PBWP; Poetr; WPE

Steer, Bold Mariner, On! Schiller, *tr. fr. German.* PAH

Steer hither, steer your wingéd pines. The Sirens' Song. William Browne. *Fr.* Inner Temple Masque, The. NOBE; OBEV
    (Song of the Sirens.) EiL
    (Song of the Syrens.) ChTr
    (Syrens' Song, The.) GBL

Steer me safely in the dark. (*LL*) Captain of a Space Ship. Dermot Bolger. IB

Steered straight into this century I see narrowboats. Homage to the Canal People. Andrew Sant. NOBAu

Stefansson Island. Philip Booth. SoSe

Stele and my Sirens and mournful pitcher that hold. Erinna, *tr. fr. Greek by* Barbara Hughes Fowler. *Fr.* Epigrams. HePo

Stella, *sels.* James McAuley.
    "Cassiopei stirs." PeIV

Stella and Flavia. Mary Barber. ECWP

Stella at Wood-Park. Swift. BIrV

Stella Maris. O. B. Hardison, Jr. CRP

Stella oft sees the very face of woe. Sir Philip Sidney. *Fr.* Astrophel and Stella. AAS; ESo, *sl. abr.*; GGP; HeIL, *Sonnets, I–CVIII and 11 Songs*; InPS; NAEL-1; NoSic; PoE; Poetr; SCGP, *Sonnets, I–CVIII and 11 Songs*; SiPS, *Sonnets, I–CVIII and 11 Songs*; SiPSBD, *Sonnets, I–CVIII and 11 Songs*

Stella since thou so right a Princess art. Sir Philip Sidney. *Fr.* Astrophel and Stella. AAS; ESo, *sl. abr.*; GGP; HeIL, *Sonnets, I–CVIII and 11 Songs*; NoP; OxAEP-1; Poetr; SCGP, *Sonnets, I–CVIII and 11 Songs*; SiPS, *Sonnets, I–CVIII and 11 Songs*; SiPSBD, *Sonnets, I–CVIII and 11 Songs*

Stella, think not that I by verse seek fame. Sir Philip Sidney. *Fr.* Astrophel and Stella. AAS; ESo, *sl. abr.*; GGP; HeIL, *Sonnets, I–CVIII and 11 Songs*; NoSic; Poetr; SCGP, *Sonnets, I–CVIII and 11 Songs*; SiPS, *Sonnets, I–CVIII and 11 Songs*; SiPSBD, *Sonnets, I–CVIII and 11 Songs*

Stella's Birth-day, 1718/19. Swift. NAs
    (On Stella's Birthday, [1718] 1719. IIP; InPK; NIP; NOIV; OAEL-1
    (Stella's Birthday.) CBLP

Stella's Birthday; March 13, 1726/27. Swift. NAs; NoP; OAEL-1; PoE; PoEL-3; SCGP

Stella's Birthday 1720. Swift. *See* All travelers [*or* travellers] at first incline.

Stella's Birthday, 1725. Swift. NOEC

Stella's Birthday, 1721 ("All travelers at first incline.") Swift. NAEL-1; PeIV; PoEL-3

Stella's Epitaph. Mary Jones. ECWP

Stella's Kiss. Sir Philip Sidney. *Fr.* Astrophel and Stella. AAS; CBCK; ESo, *sl. abr.*; GGP; HeIL, *Sonnets, I–CVIII and 11 Songs*; NoSic; Poetr; SCGP, *Sonnets, I–CVIII and 11 Songs*; SiPS, *Sonnets, I–CVIII and 11 Songs*; SiPSBD, *Sonnets, I–CVIII and 11 Songs*

Stellenbosch. Kipling. OBTV; PeSAV

Stem heaped up, heaped, heaped up. Spell for Making the First Man. *Unknown, tr. fr. Maori by* Margaret Orbell. PeNZ

Stenographers, The. P. K. Page. HeIP; LiTM; NALW; NoAM; NoP

Step aside, you ornery tenderfeet. I'm an Old Cowhand. Johnny Mercer. OBAL

Step Away from Them, A. Frank O'Hara. HCAP; InPS; NAAL-2; VCAP; VGW

Step in a ditch. *Unknown.* RoPo

Step in the dirt. *Unknown.* RoPo

Step in, young man, I know your face. The Gaol Song. *Unknown.* GBP

Step into my room tonight. People Trying to Love. Stephen Berg. NaP

Step is on the stairs, A. (*LL*) Hope. Randall Jarrell. MoAB; MoAmPo

Step on a crack. *Unknown.* RoPo

Step on His Head. James Laughlin. VGW

"Step on it," said Aunt Alice, "for God's sake." The Ascension: 1925. John Malcolm Brinnin. InPK

Step out into the dark I know knows me. (*LL*) Galaxies. Alan Gould. NOBAu

Step out onto the Planet. Lew Welch. EaPr

Step to the garden from the cool-roomed house. Weekend Stroll. Frances Cornford. BoNaP

Stepfathers. David Donnell. NOBC

Stephano Remembers. James Simmons. PBCIP; PNI; PWE

Stephen Smith, University of Iowa sophomore, burned what he said was his draft card. Of Late. George Starbuck. VGW

Stephen to Lazarus. C. S. Lewis. ChIV-2

Stepping deftly to the jetty. Newport, 1930. Herbert Morris. PRA

Stepping gingerly. Cat in the Snow. Aileen Fisher. NTCP

Stepping in the Same River. Karen Chamberlain. FoLa

Stepping out through the west-wall gate. Leaving West Archery Hall at Dusk. Hsieh Ling-yün, tr. fr. Chinese by Francis Westbrook. SuSp

Stepping Outside. Tess Gallagher. AmPA

Stepping through the morning dew. White Birch. Unknown, tr. fr. Chinese by Hualing Nieh. LHF

Stepping Westward. Denise Levertov. CAPP; CrSp; NALW; NMM; Poetr; VGW

Stepping Westward. Wordsworth. CH; EnRP; PoEL-4; SCGP

Steps. Frank O'Hara. CAPP

Steps. Roberta Hill Whiteman. VoR

Steps out/ from a lily. Woman. Carl Rakosi. TAP

Sterile vision-and a great / wind we ride. (LL) A Gift of Great Value. Robert Creeley. LCAP; NaP

Sterkfontein. Ruth Miller. PeSA; PeSAV

Stern Brow, The. Walter Savage Landor. CBLP

Stern daughter of the voice of God! Ode to Duty. Wordsworth. AWP; EnRP; FHYEP; GTBS; GTBS-P; ImPo; NAEL-2; NoP; OAEL-2; OBEV; WGRP

Stern eagle of the far north-west. The Song of the Reim-Kennar. Sir Walter Scott. Fr. Pirate, The. OAEL-2; OBNC

Stern Master Munchem, rod in hand, stole out of school one day. The School-Master and the Truants. "John Brownjohn." OBCA

Stern Miss Frugle always said. What Happened to Miss Frugle. Brian Patten. OBSP

Stern parent, The. Harry Graham. Fr. Some Ruthless Rhymes. CBNP; ChTr; PeLV

Stern truth will never write, "By hands unknown." (LL) So Quietly. Leslie Pinckney Hill. PoBA

Stethoscope tells what everyone fears, The. Academic. Theodore Roethke. FaBoEE; OBAL

Steve Biko is Dead. Jack A. Mapanje. PeSAV

Steveston, sels. Daphne Marlatt. Imagine: A Town. NOBC

Sthenelais. Unknown, tr. fr. Greek by Guy Davenport. GrAn

Sticheron for Matins, Wednesday of Holy Week. Kassia, tr. fr. Greek by Patrick Diehl. WPOW

Stick he used to tap out feet, The. Phanias, tr. fr. Greek by Peter Porter. GrAn

Stick in the Forest, The. William Stafford. CAPP

Stick of Incense, A. W. B. Yeats. ChIV-2; MeMBP

Stick one in the old man's crown. (LL) Tit, tat, toe. Unknown. OxNR

Stick, the fan, the basket, the morning paper, The. Visiting. Rosemary Dobson. Fr. Daily Living. FaBoMA

Stick the finger inside. Black Mail. Alice Walker. AmPA

Stick your patent name on a signboard. The River. Hart Crane. Fr. Bridge, The. AmPP; CMoP; GOA; LiTA; MoAB; MoAmPo; NAAL-2; NOBA; OxBA; PrIm

Sticks and stones/ May break my bones. Unknown. ISE

Sticks and stone may break my bones. Unknown. RoPo

Sticks and stones may break my bones. Truth. Barrie Wade. OTCP

Sticks-in-a-drowse droop over sugary loam. Cuttings. Theodore Roethke. HCAP; LCAP; MoP; NAAL-2; NoAM; NOBA; TAP; UnPo

Sticky inside their winter suits. Thaw. Margaret Avison. FaBoWP; NOBC

Stiff in a white coat. A Child's Visit to the Biology Lab. Kathleen Spivack. AmPA

Stiff old Philly saints dripped gold. Can I Tell You This Story, Or Will You Send Me through All Kinds of Changes? Larry Neal. BCF

Stiff spokes of this wheel, The. July in Washington. Robert Lowell. LCAP; NAAL-2; NaP; Prf

Stiff standing on the bed. Unknown. GBL

Stiff wind off the channel, A. Wet Thursday. Weldon Kees. NaP; NYBP

Stiff with weapons, fighting back over the same ground. (LL) Thistles. Ted Hughes. FaBoVe; NoAM; OxBSP; OxBTC; SoSe

Stigmata. Patrick Lane. NOBC

Stigmata. Charles Warren Stoddard. TrPWD

Stil'd but the shaddowes of us men? (LL) That Women Are but Men's Shadows. Ben Jonson. ElL

Stiles. John Pudney. NYBP

Still. Lucille Clifton. InPS

Still. Andrew Greig. PWE

Still. Tony Harrison. OBD

Still. Aila Meriluoto, tr. fr. Finnish by Jaakko A. Ahokas. PBWP

Still. Lisa Zeidner. SM

Still a bit dazed. Saul, Afterward, Riding East. John Malcolm Brinnin. Prf

Still, after all, the kelp remain. At the Western Shore. Sarah Youngblood. IHMS

Still Alive. Ron Schreiber. PFL

Still am I haunting. Come Down. George Macdonald. TrPWD

Still amorous, and fond, and billing. Samuel Butler. FaBoEH

Still and All. Burns Singer. OxBS

Still and dark along the sea. Twilight on Sumter. Richard Henry Stoddard. PAH

Still are there wonders of the dark and day. To Keep the Memory of Charlotte Forten Grimké. Angelina Weld Grimké. BlSi; ShDr

Still be renownëd. (LL) A Prayer to the Holy Trinity. Richard Stanyhurst. ElL; PoEL-2

Still-born silence, thou that art. Invocation of Silence. Richard Flecknoe. OxBSP

Still Century. Tom Paulin. BiHa

Still, Citizen Sparrow. Richard Wilbur. AmPP; CMoP; HoPM; LiTM; MoAB; MoP; NoAM; TRP

Still clear, that morning his family moved. After a Friendship. Robert Minhinnick. AngWe

Still clinging to your shirt. (LL) My Papa's Waltz. Theodore Roethke. AnAmPo; CAPP; ClHu; CMoP; FF; HAP; HCAP; HeIL; HeIP; HoPM; InPK; InPS; LCAP; LiTM; MoAB; MoP; NAAL-2; NBLV; NIP; NoAM; NOBA; NoP; NTP; PoE; Poetr; PPP; PrIm; RaBo; SM; TAP; TFi; TRP; VGW

Still cramped and wet from the journey. (LL) May 10th. Maxine W. Kumin. BoNaP; NYBP; RFM

Still, Dear, it is incredible to me. Her Second Husband Hears Her Story. Thomas Hardy. OBD

Still Do I Keep My Look, My Identity . . . . Gwendolyn Brooks. PoA

Still do I love, still shed my innocent light, my Blood, for thee. (LL) Still Falls the Rain. Edith Sitwell. BoWoP; LiTM; MoAB; MoBrPo; MoP; NAEL-2; NoAM; NOBE; OBWP; PeECV; TEP; TFi; TrGrPo; TwCP

Still do the stars impart their light. Falsehood. William Cartwright. OBEV

Still drifting together. The Unpossessed. Adèle Naudé. PeSA

Still explosions on the rocks, The. The Shampoo. Elizabeth Bishop. FaBoWP; OxBC; VCAP

Still fainter as the dewdrops settle on the flowers. (LL) Stars and Moon on the Yangtse. Tu Fu. PLT

Still Falls the Rain. Edith Sitwell. BoWoP; LiTM; MoAB; MoBrPo; MoP; NAEL-2; NoAM; NOBE; OBWP; PeECV; TEP; TFi; TrGrPo; TwCP

Still fettered, still unconquered, still in pain. Prometheus Unbound. A. D. Hope. OxBC

Still for the world he lives, and lives in bliss. Written on the Anniversary of Our Father's Death. Hartley Coleridge. Son

Still green on the limbs o' the woak wer the leaves. Which Road? William Barnes. NOBVV

Still green with bays each ancient altar stands. Pope. Fr. Essay on Criticism. EPCY; PoEL-3

Still Growing. Unknown. See Trees They Do Grow High, The.

Still He Sings. Allan Taylor. OBET

Still hearing the Hawk in his region. Homage to Coleman Hawkins. Ken Irby. Jaz

Still-Heart. Frank Pearce Sturm. OBMV

Still Here. Langston Hughes. BPo

Still holding and feeding the stem of the contained flower. (LL) The Shape of the Fire. Theodore Roethke. CMoP; LCAP; LiTA; MoAB; VCAP

Still I complain; I am complaining still. Edward Taylor. Fr. Preparatory Meditations Before My Approach to the Lord's Supper. MeMAP; OxBA; PoEL-3

(Was Ever Heart Like Mine? CBCK

Still I Rise. Maya Angelou. BlSi

Still I see them. Infirm, creeping. The Ghetto. Gloria Glickstein. BTR

Still,/ I would love too. Small Frogs Killed on the Highway. James Wright. HCAP; NNaP; NoAM

Still in an amorphous world she moves. The Idiot. Adèle Naudé. PeSA

Still in her purity. (LL) Ballata: In Exile at Sarzana. Cavalcanti. AWP

Still in his mother's lap the baby Love played. Meleager, tr. fr. Greek by Barbara Hughes Fowler. Fr. Epigrams. HePo

Still in October, the woodcock. On the Mountain. Ruth Stone. BoWoP

Still in sleeping bags, the promised delivery. Bats. Dave Jeddie Smith. NoAM

Still, in some hidden towns of our Dispersion. The Talmud Student. Hayyim Nahman Bialik, *tr. fr. Hebrew* by Helena Frank. TrJP

Still in the cool and silent shades of sleep. (*LL*) To Perilla. Robert Herrick. CaPO; SCGP; SeCP; SeCV-1

Still in the countryside among the lowly. Graveyard in Norfolk. Sylvia Townsend Warner, *tr. fr. Greek* by Edmund Keeley *and* Philip Sherrard. OBD

Still is the night, the streets are asleep. My Double. Heine, *tr. fr. German* by Philip L. Miller. RiWo

Still it is raining lightly. A Love Medicine. Louise Erdrich. HATNAP

Still/ it was nice. Still. Lucille Clifton. InPS

Still let me pierce into the midnight depth. James Thomson. *Fr.* Seasons, The. EnRP

Still, let my tyrants know, I am not doomed to wear. Emily Brontë. *Fr.* Prisoner, The. NOBE; NoP; OBEV; OBNC

Still let us go the way of beauty; go. A Prayer for the Old Courage. Charles Hanson Towne. TrPWD

Still Life. Diane Ackerman. PRA

Still-Life. Elizabeth Daryush. FaBoWP; WPE

Still Life. Raymond Garlick. AngWe

Still Life. Thom Gunn. PFL

Still Life. Anthony Hecht. AnAn

Still-Life. Ted Hughes. NYBP

Still Life. Patricia Storace. PRA

Still Life. Francis Sullivan. CRP

Still Life. Reed Whittemore. CoAP

Still Life: In the Epidemic. Jean Valentine. PFL

Still Life: Lady with Birds. Quandra Prettyman. PoBA

Still myself, still the Fugitive. (*LL*) The Fugitive. Michael O'Loughlin. IB

Still night. The old clock ticks. Last Night in Calcutta. Allen Ginsberg. NoAM

Still Night Thoughts. Li Po, *tr. fr. Chinese* by Burton Watson. TTTS

Still no sleep cools my eyes. Early Morning. Eduard Friedrich Mörike, *tr. fr. German* by Philip L. Miller. RiWo

Still on my cheeks I feel their fondling breath. Stanzas on Mutability. Hugo von Hofmannsthal, *tr. fr. German* by Jethro Bithell. AWP; TrJP

Still on the spot Lord Marmion stay'd. Edinburgh from the Pentland Hills. Sir Walter Scott. *Fr.* Marmion. FaBoPP

Still, passed through the spokes of an old wheel. Reincarnation (I) James Dickey. HoPM

Still Poem 9. Philip Lamantia. *See* There is this distance between me and what I see.

Still Pond, No More Moving. Howard Moss. NYBP

Still Pool, The. Kathleen Raine. MoAB

Still pressing through these weeping solitudes. Frederick Goddard Tuckerman. *Fr.* Sonnets. NOBA

Still round the world triumphant Discord flies. A Picture of the Times. Philip Freneau. EAP

Still round thy towers descend the fertile rain! Cordova. Ibn Zaydun, *tr. fr. Arabic* by H. A. R. Gibb. AWP

Still salt pool locked in with bars of sand. A. Lincolnshire Shores. Tennyson. *Fr.* Palace of Art, The. FaBoPP

Still seems to need. (*LL*) Memories of a Lost War. Louis Simpson. ArOW; OBWP; VGW

Still shall the tyrant scourge of Gaul. Ode to the Inhabitants of Pennsylvania. Longfellow. PAH

Still Shines When You Think of It. Vincent O'Sullivan. PeNZ

Still sits the school-house by the road. In School-Days. Whittier. AnAmPo; BLPA; FaBoBe; FaPON; OBCA; OxBChV

Still small voice spake unto me, A. The Two Voices. Tennyson. MeMBP

Still small voice unto, The. A Successful Summer. David Schubert. ChIV-1

Still smells to me of pine shavings. (*LL*) And there is nothing at all — neither fear. Natalya Gorbanevskaya. BoWoP

Still south I went and west and south again. J. M. Synge. AWP; BoNaP; ChTr; FaBoPP; IIP; MoBrPo; OBMV; PeIV

Still spanning a rainbow cinnabar-red. (*LL*) The Stones Where the Haft Rotted. Meng Chiao. PLT

Still sparkles here the glory of the west. M. J. Chapman. *Fr.* Barbadoes. PBCV

Still, still my eye will gaze long fixed on thee. The Columbine. Jones Very. NOBA

Still, Still, with Thee. Harriet Beecher Stowe. AH; BLRP

Still such an Ethiope be. (*LL*) A Mask for Lydia. Thomas Randolph. BeJo

Still, that doesn't quite explain the money. (*LL*) The Usual Immigrant Uncle Poem. Askold Melnyczuk. UTF

Still the ghost of Joseph Alston. Theodosia Burr. Myra Burnham Terrell. GoYe

Still the mighty mountains stand. Epilogue to Alun Mabon. John Ceiriog Hughes, *tr. fr. Welsh* by H. Idris Bell. OBWVE

Still the Mind Smiles. Robinson Jeffers. CMoP

Still the season's changes can stir the heart. (*LL*) Moon is full, the autumn nights grow longer, The. Wei Ying-wu. EaPr

Still the world is wondrous large, — seven seas from marge to marge. The Wide, Wide World. Kipling. *Fr.* In the Neolithic Age. NOBVV; OtMeF

Still There's No Trace. Zim Mnotoza. PeSAV

Still this, still that I would! all I surmise. William Lithgow. OBTV

Still to Be Neat [Still to Be Drest (*or* Dressed)]. Ben Jonson, *tr. fr. Latin* by Jean Bonnefons. *Fr.* Epicoene; or, The Silent Woman. BeJo; ElL; FF; GBL; HAP; JCP; NoP; OxBSP; Poetr; PrIm; TEP; TFi; WeW (Simplicity and Sweet Neglect. OxAEP-1 (Song.) EBEvV, *sect.* I, *pt.* i; PFP, *sect.* I, *pt.* i (Song: "Still to be neat, still to be dressed.") EnRePo

Still to one end they both so justly drew. David and Jonathan. Abraham Cowley. *Fr.* Davideis. PeHV

Still Trees. Momcilo Nastasijevic, *tr. fr. Serbo-Croatian* by Charles Simic. HSix

Still unable to pronounce the months. Ice Cream. Peter Wild. Poetsp

Still visioning the stars! (*LL*) Oriflamme. Jessie Redmond Fauset. BlSi; PoBA; ShDr

Still Voice of Harlem, The. Conrad Kent Rivers. PoBA

Still — Volcano — Life, A. Emily Dickinson. TRP

Still Water Tread. Jennifer Rankin. FaBoMA

Still young and fine! but what is still in view. The Rainbow. Henry Vaughan. GeHe

Still your people and mine were tearing each other to pieces when we. Letter to the Actor Charles Laughton concerning the Work on the Play "The Life of Galileo." Bertolt Brecht, *tr. fr. German* by Michael Hamburger. AnAn; PoSu

Stillborn (Domesticity # three), The. William Knott.

Stillborn [*or* Still-born] Silence! thou that art. Silence Invoked. Richard Flecknoe. (Invocation of Silence.) NOSC

Stilled room to which I am called, A. The Call. Dennis Haskell. NOBAu

Stillness. James Elroy Flecker. CH; GoJo; MoBrPo

Stillness and moonlight, with. Loneliness. Hayden Carruth. SM

Stillness of morning. (*LL*) Woman sits on her porch. Earle Thompson. HATNAP

Stillness of the Austral noon, The. The Bell-Bird. "Fiona Macleod." *Fr.* Australian Transcripts. FM

Stillness of the jungle, The. The Stillness of the Poem. Ron Loewinsohn. NeAP; PoM

Stillness of the Poem, The. Ron Loewinsohn. NeAP; PoM

Stillness of the rose, The. The Rose. William Carlos Williams. NOBA

Stillness, The/ of the wood. The Figures. Robert Creeley. UnPo

Stillness, the Dancing, The. Linda Bierds. NAmP90

Stimulus beyond the Grave, The. Emily Dickinson. OxBSP

Stingier your suppers, The. Karl Marx. Alfred M. Lee. AmPA

Stinging/ gold swarms. Sunset. E. E. Cummings. MoAmPo

Stingo! to thy bar-room skip. Anacreontic to Flip. Royall Tyler. OBAL

Stings. Sylvia Plath. AnAn; NALW; NaP

Stink, and are thrown away. End fair enough. (*LL*) On Spies. Ben Jonson. BeJo; FaBoVe; NoP; OxBSP

Stir not the sand too much, for there lies Stuyvesant. Epitaph for Peter Stuyvesant. Henricus Selyns. SCAP

Stir of the world, the music of the mountain, The. (*LL*) Fawn's Foster-Mother. Robinson Jeffers. MoP; NoAM; NOBA

Stir the Wallaby Stew. *Unknown.* FaBoBa

Stirling's Hotel. *Unknown.* AmFP

Stirring as among, A/ cattle. Snow. David Malouf. CBAP

Stirring of a feathering cloud, The. Nature's Minor Chords. H. Cordelia Ray. CBWP-3

Stirring suddenly from long hibernation. Mid-Winter Waking. Robert Graves. MoAB

Stirring the red; a single boat. "Charm of Nien-nu." Chiang K'uei, *tr. fr. Chinese* by James J. Y. Liu. SuSp

Stirrup-Cup, The. Sidney Lanier. AmPP; AnAmPo

Stirs in his heart who plants a tree. (*LL*) The Heart of the Tree. H. C. Bunner. OHIP

Stirs its ashes and embers, its burnt sticks. Old Age Gets Up. Ted Hughes. NoAM

Stirs the Culprit-Life! (*LL*) Surgeons must be very careful. Emily Dickinson. MeMAP; SAmP; TAP

Stitch in the side. Want of %&$ Want of — +. Anne Szumigalski. FaBoWP

Stitchwort has done well for itself, clinging, The. On Miles Platting Station. Simon Armitage. PWE

Stock Exchange Wisdom. *Unknown.* FaBoUs

Stocking Fairy. Winifred Welles. FaPON

Stocking Song on Christmas Eve. Mary Mapes Dodge. OHIP

Stockpiling. Jayne Cortez. WoWa

Stockpiling of frozen trees, The. Stockpiling. Jayne Cortez. WoWa

Stocky, cocky little man, A. Instamatic. · Edwin Morgan. FF

Stocky woman at the door, The. The Last Day and the First. Theodore Weiss. TwCP; VGW

Stockyard, The. J. C. Squire. OxBTC

Stoic. Lawrence Durrell. NYBP

Stoic: for Laura von Courten, The. Edgar Bowers. ArOW; CoAP; MT

Stoker, The. Shin Shalom, *tr. fr. Hebrew by* Ruth Finer Mintz. MHP

Stoklewath; or, The Cumbrian Village, *sels.* Susanna Blamire.
  "From where dark clouds of curling smoke arise." ECWP; NOEC

Stolen Branch, The. Pablo Neruda, *tr. fr. Spanish by* Donald Devenish Walsh. ArNa

Stolen Child, The. W. B. Yeats. CMoP; NAEL-2; NoP; OHCV

Stolen Kiss, The. Robert Dodsley. ECEV

Stolen kisses, wary eyes. Strato, *tr. fr. Greek by* Sydney Oswald. PeHV

Stolen Pleasure. William Drummond of Hawthornden. EnLoPo

Stomach. Kathleen Norris. OBAL

Stomach of goat, crushed. Salami. Philip Levine. NNaP; NOBA; TAP; TRP

Stond well, moder, under Rode. *Unknown.* MiEL
  (Mother and Her Son on the Cross, The. MeEL

Stone, The. Paul Blackburn. NYBP

Stone, The. Walter de la Mare. WeW

Stone. (*LL*) Desire. Shushanig Gourghenian. VBLP

Stone, The. W. W. Gibson. MoBrPo

Stone. Donald Justice. *Fr.* Things. CRP

Stone. Charles Simic. InPS; NU

Stone, The. Henry Vaughan. ChIV-1

Stone, The. Thomas Vaughan. OBWVE

Stone, A. Richard Wilbur. *Fr.* Two Voices in a Meadow. CRP

Stone Age. Pat Nolan. UL

Stone and Fern. Leslie Norris. AngWe

Stone at dawn, A. Easter Morning. Amy Clampitt. ChIV-2

Stone, bronze, stone, steel, stone, oakleaves, horses' heels. Triumphal March. T. S. Eliot. *Fr.* Coriolan. OBWP

Stone Canyon Nocturne. Charles Wright. HCAP; LCAP; VCAP

Stone/ cold/ daylight. Poem for Etheridge. Sonia Sanchez. BPo

Stone cries from the wall, The. *Unknown.* TrJP

Stone-cutters fighting time with marble, you foredefeated. To the Stone-Cutters. Robinson Jeffers. AmPP; MoAB; MoAmPo; NAAL-2; NOBA; NoP; OxBA; PoRA; PrIm; TrGrPo

Stone Diary, A. Pat Lowther. NOBC

Stone Face, The. Harri Webb. AngWe

Stone-flake and salmon. Gary Snyder. *Fr.* Myths and Texts. NaP; NeAP; PoM

Stone for the sake of the souls of the slain birds sailing. (*LL*) Over Sir John's Hill. Dylan Thomas. AngWe; LiTB; MoAB; TOF

Stone found me in bright sunlight, The. The Stone. Paul Blackburn. NYBP

Stone from the Gods. Irma Wassall. GoYe

Stone from the mouth of the well?, The. (*LL*) Here on Earth. Rachel. MHP

Stone Gentleman, The. James Reeves. OxBSP

Stone Giant. Joseph Bruchac. CDW

Stone goes straight, The. Washington Monument by Night. Carl Sandburg. CMoP; FaPON; ImGa; OHIP

Stone Gullets. May Swenson. VCAP

Stone Hammer Poem. Robert Kroetsch. NOBC

Stone-Hitter, The. Medbh McGuckian. DT

Stone Horse Shoals. Malcolm Cowley. NYBP

Stone of Megakles who's dead, The. Simonides, *tr. fr. Greek by* Peter Jay. GrAn

Stone Ruck a place tired pinnacle? Stump Cross — The Long Wait. Geraldine Monk. VBLP

Stone says that it covers here the white dog, The. Tymnes, *tr. fr. Greek by* Barbara Hughes Fowler. *Fr.* Epigrams. HePo

Stone, Scissors, Paper. Jennifer Strauss. FaBoMA

Stone stands among new firs, The. Standing Stone. Ruth Bidgood. AngWe

Stone-story. The story of stone, brokenbricks. Eugene B. Redmond. *Fr.* Epigrams for My Father. ETG

Stone Trees. John Freeman. BoNaP

Stone Wall and Celebration. János Pilinszky, *tr. fr. Hungarian by* Peter Jay. PoSu

Stone went out, dressed as a man, The. Concerning the Stone. Gregory Orr. AnAn

Stone, which is incapable?, The. (*LL*) To Kyris. Strato. GrAn; PeHV

Stone, who was his father that lies beneath you? Hektor of Troy. Archias of Macedon, *tr. fr. Greek by* Dudley Fitts. GrAn

Stone, The/ would like to be. Evolution. May Swenson. TrGrPo

Stoned cheek turned again. March. Roy McFadden. TIRV

Stoned dogs crawl back through the blood, The. The Contours of Fixation. Weldon Kees. NaP

Stonehenge. Michael Drayton. *Fr.* Polyolbion. FaBoPP

Stonehenge. Sir Philip Sidney. *See* Near Wilton sweet huge heaps of stone are found.

Stones. William Jeffrey. OxBS

Stones. Maxine W. Kumin. CAPP

Stones, The. Sylvia Plath. SM

Stones. Charles Hamilton Sorley. NSI

Stones (a miracle to mortal view), The. Ovid, *tr. by* Dryden. *Fr.* Metamorphoses. OBVE

Stones: Avesbury. Daisy Aldan. PoA

Stones in Jordan's stream, The. Stones. William Jeffrey. OxBS

Stones must form a circle first not a wall. First Rule. Maurice Kenny. HATNAP

Stones of Gallows Hill shall tread, The. (*LL*) Salem. Edmund Clarence Stedman. PAH

Stones of Rome to rise and mutiny, The. (*LL*) Friends, Romans, countrymen, lend me your ears. Shakespeare. EBEvV

Stones of Time, The. Kenneth Koch. *Fr.* Days and Nights. NoAM

Stones only, the *disjecta membra* of this Great House. Ruins of a Great House. Derek Walcott. TwCP

Stones Where the Haft Rotted, The. Meng Chiao, *tr. fr. Chinese by* A. C. Graham. PLT

Stonewall Jackson. Henry Lynden Flash. PAH

Stonewall Jackson's Way. John Williamson Palmer. PAH

Stoney Ridge Dance Hall. Alden Nowlan. MoCV

Stony Grey Soil. Patrick Kavanagh. CIP

Stony Lonesome. Langston Hughes. NOBA; SAmP

Stony rock of death's insensibility, The. Tired Memory. Coventry Patmore. *Fr.* Unknown Eros, The. EnVR

Stony Town. John Shaw Neilson. FaBoMA

Stood, at the closed door. Conrad Aiken. *Fr.* Preludes for Memnon; or, Preludes to Attitude. LiTM

Stood for years in the square. (*LL*) The Statue. Matthew Sweeney. IB

Stood like the closed gate of your own backyard. (*LL*) Returned to Frisco, 1946. W. D. Snodgrass. ArOW

Stood on the top of a spur once. Still Shines When You Think of It. Vincent O'Sullivan. PeNZ

Stood straight/ holding the choker high. Gary Snyder. *Fr.* Myths and Texts. NaP; NOBA

Stood the Giraffe beside a Tree. (*LL*) Giraffe and Tree. W. J. Turner. CH; GrPl

Stool Ball. *Unknown.* CH

Stoop, and begin the ancient croaking. (*LL*) The Poets Agree to Be Quiet by the Swamp. David Wagoner. CoAP; VGW

Stoop on the log-house is brown with sweet rain-rot, The. Joan Finnigan. *Fr.* May Day Rounds: Renfrew County. WPE

Stooped down and whipt a bit beneath his nose. (*LL*) Field Path. John Clare. OxBSP

Stop. Richard Wilbur. LCAP

Stop All the Clocks, Cut Off the Telephone. W. H. Auden. RB

Stop bleeding said the knife. Bleeding. May Swenson. NALW

Stop, Christian passer-by! — Stop, child of God. Samuel Taylor Coleridge. EnRP; NAEL-2; NOCV; NoP; OAEL-2
  (Epitaph: "Stop, Christian Passer-by!") PFP
  (Epitaph: "Stop, Christian Passer-by! — Stop, Child of God.") PeECV
  (Epitaph.) MeMBP
  (O, Lift One Thought.) CH

"Stop!" cried the knight. "No more of this good sir!" Chaucer. *See* "Ho!" quod the knight, "Good sir, namore of this."

Stop! Don't touch me. *Unknown, tr. fr. Spanish by* Willis Barnstone. BoWoP

Stop! for thy tread is on an empire's dust! Byron. *Fr.* Childe Harold's Pilgrimage. InPS

Stop, friends, spin with me past. Spider. Duane Niatum. ETG

Story, A. Rose Terry Cooke. AmWP

Story, A. Li-Young Lee. RaBo

Story. Jo McDougall. NGP

Story, The. Dan Pagis, *tr. fr. Hebrew by* Stephen Mitchell. PoSu

Story, The. Charles Simic. NNaP

Story, The. Mark Strand. AnAn

Story, A. John Riley. *Fr.* Sequence, A. VaA

Story, A. William Stafford. NNaP; RFM

Story, a story, A! Rowing. Anne Sexton. BoWoP; CAPP; LCAP

Story, a story, a story anon, A. The Bishop of Canterbury. *Unknown.* AmFP

Story, a story to you I will tell, A. The Cunning Cobbler Done Over. *Unknown.* CoMu

Story about Chicken Soup, A. Louis Simpson. BTR; NNaP; PoE; PoWW; TAP

Story about Indians, A. The Climate of Paradise. Louis Simpson. NOBA

Story about the Body, A. Robert Hass. NAmP90; RaBo

Story Books on a Kitchen Table, *sels.* Audre Lorde.
  "Out of her womb of pain my mother spat me." MDDM

Story I Can't Tell, The. P. H. Liotta. ArOW

Story I Like to Tell, The. Robin Becker. PBCAP

Story I shall tell today, The. The Nightingale. Marie de France, *tr. fr. French by* Patricia Terry. BoWoP

Story is/ that whole families of fruitpickers, The. Federico's Ghost. Martín Espada. AfAz

Story is wrong, The; Lies. Blake or Yeats Slept with You. Anthony Barnett. VaA

Story of a Hotel Room. Rosemary Tonks. AIW; OxBTC

Story of a Story, The. Vasco [*or* Vasko] Popa, *tr. fr. Serbo-Croatian by* Anne Pennington. CBNP

Story of a Stowaway, The. Clement Scott. VPP

Story of a Well-made Shield, The. N. Scott Momaday. CDW; GrPl; HATNAP

Story of Augustus, Who Would Not Have Any Soup, The. Heinrich Hoffmann, *tr. fr. German.* FaBoUs; GoJo; MoShBr; NBLV; OxBChV

Story of Canobie Dick, The. Libby Houston. OBSP

Story of Fidgety Philip, The. Heinrich Hoffmann, *tr. fr. German.* OxBChV

Story of Good, The. Phyllis Janik. IHMS

Story of How a Wall Stands, A. Simon J. Ortiz. HATNAP

Story of Inkle and Yarico, The. Frances, Countess of Hertford Seymour. ECWP

Story of Johnny Head-in-Air, The. Heinrich Hoffmann, *tr. fr. German.* OxBChV

Story of Joshua. Alicia Ostriker. ChIV-1

Story of Lava, The. David Allan Evans. Poetsp

Story of Life, The. John Godfrey Saxe. PoToHe

Story of Lovers Leap, The. Maggie Pogue Johnson. CBWP-4

Story of My Life, The. Carroll Arnett. VoR

Story of My Life, The. Liz Rosenberg. PBCAP

Story of Our Lives, The. Mark Strand. VCAP

Story of Phoebus and Daphne Applied, [etc.], The. Edmund Waller. InvP; NAEL-1; NOSC

Story of Ponce de Leon, A. The Fountain of Youth. Hezekiah Butterworth. PAH

Story of Prince Agib, The. W. S. Gilbert. CBNP; FaBoCo

Story of Rimini, The, *sels.* Leigh Hunt.
  "Noble range it was, of many a rood, A." EnRP

Story of Sigurd the Volsung, The, *sels.* William Morris.
  Sigurd Rideth to the Glittering Heath. PoEL-5

Story of the Ashes and the Flame, The. E. A. Robinson. AnAmPo; MeMAP

Story of the Corn. K. Fisher. BoTP

Story of the Eaters, A. Santiago Mendes Zapata, *tr. fr. Tzeltal Indian by* W. S. Merwin. STP

Story of the Gadsbys, The, *sels.* Kipling.
  Winners, The. BLPA; FaPoR
  (L'Envoi: "What is the moral? Who rides may read.") MoBrPo; TrGrPo

Story of the Pot and the Kettle, The. Charles Montagu. APAS

Story of the Shepherd, The. *Unknown, tr. fr. Spanish.* OHIP

Story of the Zeros, The. Victor Hernandez Cruz. PoBA

Story of Uriah, The. Kipling. NOBVV; PeVV; SCV

Story of Vinland, The. Sidney Lanier. *Fr.* Psalm of the West. PAH

Story So Far, The. John Clarke. UV

Story That Could Be True, A. William Stafford. GOYP; NTCP; RaBo

Story to you I'll tell of little Omie Wise, A. Poor Omie. *Unknown.* PrIm

Story usually goes like this, The. War Story. Roger Vincent Small. PAW

Story We Know, The. Martha Collins. *See* Way to begin is always the same, The.

Storys to rede ar delitabill. John Barbour. *Fr.* Bruce, The. OxBS

Storytime. Judith Nicholls. OBSP

Stout seamen, come away, never be daunted. The Boatswain's Call. *Unknown.* OxBSS

Stove. Philip Booth. FYAP

Stove was grey, the coal was gone, The. Into Laddery Street. Laura Riding. *Fr.* Forgotten Girlhood. RB

Stow, birde, stow, stow! John Skelton. *Fr.* Magnificence. NoSic

Stowaway in a fold. The Witnesses. X. J. Kennedy. PChr

Stowed away in a Montreal lumber room. O God! O Montreal! Samuel Butler. FaBoCo; OBSV; OxBoLi; PeLV
  (Psalm of Montreal, A.) OBTV

Strage degli innocenti, La, *sels.* Giovanni Battista Marino, *tr. fr. Italian by* Richard Crashaw.
  Sospetto d'Herode. SeCV-1

Stragglers. Pietro Aretino, *tr. fr. Italian by* Samuel Putnam. ErPo

Strahan, Tonson, Lintot of the times. To Mr. Murray. Byron. FaBoCo; UV

Straight as a nun I sit. Señora X No More. Pat Mora. AfAz

Straight flagged road, laid on the rough earth, A. Field Ambulance in Retreat. May Sinclair. OBTV

Straight-jacketing sprang to every lock. Austin Clarke. *Fr.* Mnemosyne Lay in Dust. CMoP; IPY

Straight up away from this road. Achieving Perspective. Pattiann Rogers. MT

Strained daybreak breaks in past the blinds. Lorenzo Thomas. UL

Strains of Sight. Robert Duncan. CMoP; PoE

Strand, The. Michael Longley. IIP

Strand at Lough Beg, The. Seamus Heaney. AnAn; CIP; NoAM; NoP; OBWP

Strand Hotel, Rosslare, The. James Liddy. CIP

Strand on the Green. *Unknown.* GBP

Strand-Thistle. Gustav Falke, *tr. fr. German by* Jethro Bithell. AWP

Stranded in My Ontario. Ronald G. Everson. NOBC

Stranded on the moon. Moon-Man. Dorothy Hewett. CBAP

Stranded Whales, The. Geoffrey Dutton. CBAP

Strange. Stanley Burnshaw. TrJP

Strange. Kirby Doyle. NeAP

Strange Adventure. Rossana Ombres, *tr. fr. Italian by* Ruth Feldman. NeIt

Strange, All-absorbing Love. Digby Mackworth Dolben. TrPWD

Strange and slow work: they dig in turn. The Well. Philip Salom. NOBAu

Strange and unnatural! lets stay and see. Destinie. Abraham Cowley. MeLP

Strange and wonderful are too much with us, The. Nothing Stays Put. Amy Clampitt. FoLa

Strange are the feelings arising within me. The Love of Hell. Abraham Burstein. TrJP

Strange — as I sat brooding here. Lucy. Walter de la Mare. CMoP

Strange, beautiful girl, A. By T'ing Yang Waterfall. Hsieh Ling-yün, *tr. fr. Chinese by* Kenneth Rexroth. OHMPC

Strange beauty, eight-limbed and eight-handed. Octopus. Arthur Clement Hilton. BXAP; FaBoCo; FaBoPa; UV

Strange bed, whose recurrent dream we are, The. Hotel de l'Univers et Portugal. James Merrill. MoAB; PoA

Strange bird/ His song remains secret. Youth. James Wright. NaP; NoP

Strange, bright dancers, The. Poppies. P. A. Ropes. BoTP

Strange but true is the story. The Sea-Turtle and the Shark. Melvin B. Tolson. *Fr.* Harlem Gallery. PoBA

Strange Case of Mr. Ormantude's Bride, The. Ogden Nash. OxBM

Strange church smelled a bit 'high,' of censers, The. Geoffrey Hill. *Fr.* Mercian Hymns. PoE

Strange Dolls. Vuyelwa Carlin. NWP

Strange Filth. Harry Clifton. IB

Strange Fits of Passion Have I Known. Wordsworth. EBEV; EnRP; GBL; LiTB; NAEL-2; NOBE; OAEL-2; OBEV; OBNC; PoE; PPP; TEP; TrGrPo

Strange Fortunes of Two Excellent Princes, The, *sels.* Nicholas Breton.
  "I would thou wert not fair, or I were wise." EIL; InvP

Strange Fruit. Cyrus Cassells. Jaz

Strange grows the river on the sunless evenings! Vesperal. Ernest Dowson. OBMV

Strange he seemed to her dark. Stranger, Husband. Thomas McCarthy. IB

Strange Hells. Ivor Gurney. OxBTC; PeFWW

Strange how the mind will stand outside. Chopping Wood. Dave Jeddie Smith. SM

Strange Legacies. Sterling A. Brown. PoBA; TTY

Strange Love. Moses ibn Ezra, *tr. fr. Hebrew* by Solomon Solis-Cohen. TrJP

Strange Man, The. *Unknown.* FaPON

Strange Meeting. Wilfred Owen. CMoP; EBEvV; FaBoMo; FaBoRV; FaPoB; GGP; GTBS-P; HeIP; HoPM; ImPo; LiTB; MeMBP; MoAB; MoBrPo; MoP; NAEL-2; NoAM; NOBE; NoP; OAEL-2; OBF; OBWP; OxAEP-2; PeFWW; PoE; PoWW; RB; SCV; TFi; TrGrPo

Strange Meetings., *sels.* Harold Monro.
Birth. PoA
Flower Is Looking, A. MoBrPo
If Suddenly a Clod of Earth. MoBrPo
You Live There; I Live Here. Mes

Strange Monsters. Rowland Watkyns. FaBoEE

Strange Music, The. G. K. Chesterton. OtMeF

Strange news! a cittie full? will none give way. Upon Christ His Birth. Sir John Suckling.
(Strange news! a city full? will none give way.) ChIV-2

Strange now to think of you, gone without corsets & eyes. Kaddish. Allen Ginsberg. HCAP; NAAL-2; NeAP; NOBA; PoBeRe; PoM

Strange Old Woman, A. Mother Goose. *See* There was an old woman, and what do you think?

Strange particularity, A. The Revenant. Rachel Hadas. UnDi

Strange people, we who trust — . To a Despondent Evening. Iftiqar Arif. NBrP

Strange pie that is almost a passion. A Melton Mowbray Pork Pie. Richard Le Gallienne. BXAP

Strange Power! I trust thy might; trust thou my constancy. (*LL*) The Visionary. Emily Brontë. BrRo; CH; ELP; MeMBP; SCGP

Strange race of critics, A. Antiphanes, *tr. fr. Greek* by Sam Hamill. InMo

Strange sea: sudden sea: no thing can be the same. Alison Brackenbury. SCBI

Strange spirit with inky hair. The Lion. W. J. Turner. MoBrPo

Strange Talk. L. E. Yates. BoTP

Strange Tears. Liu Ya-tzu, *tr. fr. Chinese* by Wu-chi Liu. SuSp

Strange Thanksgiving. Tess Gallagher. NAmP90

Strange that I did not know him then. An Old Story. E. A. Robinson. AnAmPo; MoAmPo; OxBSP

Strange, that I felt so gay. Tennyson. *Fr.* Maud[: A Monodrama]. EnVR

Strange that in "crimes of passion" what results. Love and Murder. Roy Fuller. CBLP

Strange,/ That in this nigger place. Esthete in Harlem. Langston Hughes. BPo

Strange, that such horror and such grace. To a Fair Lady Playing with a Snake. Edmund Waller. CBLP; EBEV; HoPM; NOSC; PoE
(Of a Fair Lady Playing with a Snake.) PoEL-3

Strange that your image should occur to me. The Grudge. Dimitris Tsaloumas. FaBoMA

Strange the formation of the eely race. William Diaper, *after the Greek of* Oppian. *Fr.* Halieutica. OBVE
(Eels and Tortoises.) NOEC
(Sex-life of Fish, The.) ECEV

Strange things hangs by man's hip, A. Key (or Penis): "Strange thing hangs by man's hip, A." *Unknown, formerly at. to* Cynewulf, *tr. fr. Anglo-Saxon* by Kevin Crossley-Holland. *Fr.* Riddles (Exeter Book). PeLV

Strange to be torn away from your embrace. Strange. Stanley Burnshaw. TrJP

Strange to step straight into the beautiful dawn. Miraculous Dawn. R. Williams Parry, *tr. fr. Welsh* by Joseph P. Clancy. OBWVE

Strange Tree. Elizabeth Madox Roberts. BoNaP; FaPON; GrPl

Strange tropic warmth and hints of summer seas. (*LL*) Ethnogenesis. Henry Timrod. AmPP; AnAmPo; NOBA; OxBA

Strange Visitor, The. *Unknown.* ChTr; FaBoCh; GBP

Strange Western town at the round edge of night. Western Town. Karl Shapiro. NYBP

Strangely assorted, the shape of song and the bloody man. The Military Harpist. Ruth Pitter. FaBoTw; NALW

Strangeness in me, A. Virus. Christine McNeill. NWP

Strangeness of Heart. Siegfried Sassoon. TrJP

Stranger, The. Walter de la Mare. OxBTC

Stranger, The. William Everson. FF

Stranger, The. Jean Garrigue. LiTA; LiTM; NOBA; TwCP

Stranger, A. Lionel Johnson. NOBVV

Stranger, The. Adrienne Rich. NNaP

Stranger. Elizabeth Madox Roberts. MoAmPo

Stranger! Approach this spot with gravity! A Dentist. *Unknown.* FaBoCo; FaBoEE
(Epitaph on a Dentist.) OxBoLi

Stranger arrives at her door, A. The Widow. Susan Ludvigson. MT

Stranger, beware! This terrible tomb. Philip of Thessalonica, *tr. fr. Greek* by Edwin Morgan. GrAn

Stranger by the roadside, do not smile. Epitaph of a Dog. *Unknown, tr. fr. Greek* by Dudley Fitts. GrAn

Stranger came one night to Yussouf's tent, A. Yussouf. James Russell Lowell. BeLS; BLPA; BLPL; BoTP; FaBoBe

Stranger came to the door at eve, A. Love and a Question. Robert Frost. MoBS

Stranger here, as all my fathers were, A. John Amner. OxBSP

Stranger, Husband. Thomas McCarthy. IB

Stranger I came, A. Good Night. Wilhelm Müller, *tr. fr. German* by Philip L. Miller. *Fr.* Winter's Journey, The. RiWo

Stranger, if I can save thee, wilt thou bear. Euripides, *tr. fr. Greek* by Gilbert Murray. *Fr.* Iphigenia in Tauris. OBF

Stranger, if thou hast learned a truth which needs. Inscription for the Entrance to a Wood. Bryant. AmPP; EAP; OxBA; TAP

Stranger in his own element. Penguin on the Beach. Ruth Miller. PeSA

Stranger in my gates, The — lo! that am I. Omnia Exeunt in Mysterium. George Sterling. WGRP

Stranger in the Corridor, The. John Ash. SCBI

Stranger in the Pumpkin, The. John Ciardi. NTCP

Stranger in This Land, A. Cliff Ashby. NOCV

Stranger it was never meant for, A. Mine. Frank Polite. NYBP

Stranger Not Ourselves, The. William Stafford. NNaP

Stranger, pause and drop a tear. Sacred to the Memory of Maria (To Say Nothing of Jane and Martha) Sparks. "Max Adeler." FaBoCo

Stranger! Tell the people of Spoon River two things. Unknown Soldiers. Edgar Lee Masters. *Fr.* New Spoon River, The. NoAM; TAP

Stranger, tell the Spartans how we die. On the Tomb of the Spartan Dead at Thermopylae. *Unknown.* PAW

Stranger than the Worst. Babette Deutsch. WPE

Stranger, the bark you see before you says. The Yacht. Catullus, *tr. fr. Latin* by John Hookham Frere. AWP; OBVE

Stranger to Europe. Guy Butler. PeSAV

Stranger walls, that shell no violent presence. Zimbabwe. F. D. Sinclair. PeSA

Stranger was short: let my verse be such, The. Callimachus, *tr. fr. Greek* by Peter Jay. GrAn

Stranger, when you come to/ Lakedaimon. Simonides, *tr. fr. Greek* by Kenneth Rexroth. OBVE; PGA

Stranger, whoe'er thou art, whose ling'ring feet. Sonnet Written in Tintern Abbey, Monmouthshire. Edmund Gardner. NOEC

Stranger, wond'ring, stalks, and stares upon, The. Rome, Conqueror, Conquered. Joshua Sylvester. FaBoEE

Stranger, you who hide my love. Stephen Spender. FaBoTw

Strangers. William Stafford. NNaP

Strangers, The. Jones Very. AnAmPo; OxBA

Strangers are people we haven't seen before. Conversations with Strangers. George Buchanan. PNI

Strangers Are We All upon the Earth. Franz Werfel, *tr. fr. German* by Edith Abercrombie Snow. TrJP

Strangers are we and pilgrims here! At a Friends' Meeting. Mary Elizabeth Coleridge. WPE

Strangers' eyes don't see. Memorial Poem. Jacob Glatstein, *tr. fr. Yiddish* by Ruth Whitman.
(Nightsong.) BTR

Strangers on a train. Travels with the Band-Aid Army. Lance Henson. VoR

Strangers to meek compassion's tender touch. Mary Latter. *Fr.* Soliloquies on Temporal Indigence. ECWP

Strangers! your eyes are on that valley fixed. The Field of the Grounded Arms. Fitz-Greene Halleck. PoEL-4

Strangling women in the suburban bush. Das Kapital. Amiri Baraka. PoM

Strappado for the Devil, A, *sels.* Richard Brathwaite [*or* Brathwait].
Of Maids' Inconstancy. EIL

Strapped at the center of the blazing wheel. A Pilot from the Carrier. Randall Jarrell. PoWW

Strapped helpless, monarchs and prelates, round they swung. The Wheel of Fortune. Thom Gunn. OxBC

Strapped to my seat, I turn. Above It All. Philip Levine. NOBA

Strategic Air Command. Gary Snyder. BCF

Strategies. Welton Smith. PoBA

Stratton Water. Dante Gabriel Rossetti. OxBB

Straunge [*or* Strange] Passion of a Lover, A. George Gascoigne. AAS; EnRePo

Straus Park. Gerald Stern. PRA

Straw, The. Robert Graves. OxBTC

Straw, and figures of moulded clay. Stable Straw. Robert Farren. TIRV

Straw rustling everywhere. Clearing-Station. Wilhelm Klemm, *tr. fr.*
German by Patrick Bridgwater. PeFWW
Strawberries. Edwin Morgan. BoLoP
Strawberries that in gardens grow. Wild Strawberries. Robert Graves.
FaBoCh
Strawberry, The. Maggie Pogue Johnson. CBWP-4
Strawberry Fair. *Unknown.* OBET
Strawberry Jam. May Justus. FaPON
Strawberry Moon. Mary Oliver. InPS
Strawberry shortcake, cream on top. *Unknown.* RoPo
Strawberry Shrub, The. Edna St. Vincent Millay. CMoP; FaBoWP
Strawberrying. Maurice Kenny. HATNAP
Strawberrying. May Swenson. VCAP
Straws like tame lightnings lie about the grass. Summer Farm. Norman
MacCaig. OxBTC
Stray, The. Barbara Euphan Todd. CRH
Stray Animals. James Tate. NoAM
Stray Cat, The. Eve Merriam. OFC
Stray Dog. Charlotte Mish. PoLF
Stray Dog, near Ecully. Margaret Avison. PoA
Strayed Reveller, The. (Faster, Faster/ O Circe, Godess.) Matthew
Arnold. EBVVPR; OAEL-2
Sels.
Strayed Reveller to Ulysses, The. OBEV
Strayed Reveller to Ulysses, The. Matthew Arnold. *Fr.* Strayed Reveller,
The. EBVVPR; OAEL-2; OBEV
Straying Student, The. Austin Clarke. BIrV; CIP; IPY; MoAB; NOIV;
PeIV
Streak of Sappho, it is said, A. Mould of Castile. Jack R. Clemo. NOCV
Stream, The. Mona Van Duyn. VCAP
Stream, The. Lula Lowe Weeden. CDC
Stream, a god, another autumn, A. *(LL)* Two Brothers Up. Sebastian
Barry. IB
Stream flowing steadily over a stone does not wet its core, A. An Elder's
Reproof to his Wife. 'Abdillaahi Muuse, *tr. fr. Somali by* B. W.
Andrzejewski *and* I. M. Lewis. TTY; WTO
Stream of Faith, The. William Channing Gannett. *See* From Heart to
Heart.
Stream, The/ piles out of the pile. The Crossing. Paul Blackburn. NYBP
Stream ripples pure, The. By a Stream on Mount T'ien-t'ung. Wang An-
shih, *tr. fr. Chinese by* Jan W. Walls. SuSp
Stream Sings to the Stone, The. Leah Goldberg, *tr. fr. Hebrew by* Ruth
Finer Mintz. *Fr.* Songs of the Stream. MHP
Stream sorrow, eyes. Elegy for Her Brother Sakhr. Al-Khansa, *tr. fr.*
Arabic. BoWoP, *tr. by* Willis Barnstone; WPOW, *tr. by* Bridget
Connelly
Stream swirls, The. The wind moans in. Jade Flower Palace. Tu Fu, *tr. fr.*
Chinese by Kenneth Rexroth. VCAP
Stream to mingle with your favorite Dee, A. To Lady Eleanor Butler and
the Honourable Miss Ponsonby, Composed in the Grounds of Plas-
Newydd, Llangollen. Wordsworth. PeHV
Stream was swift, and so cold, The. Captivity. Louise Erdrich. HATNAP;
NoAM
Streamers. Sandra McPherson. VCAP
Streamers choking the main arteries, The. Victims of the Latest Dance
Craze. Cornelius Eady. UTF
Streams are fettered, and with us as rare, The. Thomas Shipman. *Fr.*
Frost, 1654, The: To Mr. W.L. NOSC
Streams fall down and through the darkness bear, The. Spate in Winter
Midnight. Norman MacCaig. GTBS-P
Streams of Bunclody, The. *Unknown.* BIrV
Streams of Lovely Nancy, The. *Unknown.* FaBoBa; OBET; OxBoLi
Stream's Song, The. Lascelles Abercrombie. OBMV
Street, The. Gene Baro. NYBP
Street, The. James Russell Lowell. AnAmPo; Son
Street, The. Octavio Paz, *tr. fr. Spanish by* Willis Knapp Jones. FF
Street climbs upward steeply, The. The Street. Gene Baro. NYBP
Street Corner College. Kenneth Patchen. MoAmPo
Street Cries. Marjorie Welish. EOEF
Street Demonstration. Margaret Walker. BPo
Street Fight. Harold Monro. FaBoTw
Street Fire. Daniel Halpern. AmPA
Street in Bronzeville, A. Gwendolyn Brooks. BlSi; BPo; CAPP; FaBoWP;
NMM
Sels.
Kitchenette Building. FF; NAAL-2; NoP; PoE; Poetr; PoNe; UnPo
Mother, The. CrSp; MDDM; NALW
Of De Witt Williams on His Way to Lincoln Cemetery. NoAM; NOBA

Song in the Front Yard, A. NAAL-2; NoAM; NOBA; PoBA
Street in Bronzeville: Southeast Corner, A. Gwendolyn Brooks. VGW
Street in Kaufman-ville, A. James Cunningham. JB
Street in our town, A. The Watchmaker's Shop. *Unknown.* BoTP
Street in Shadow, The. Antonio Machado Ruiz, *tr. fr. Spanish by* Willis
Barnstone. ArLo
Street is a void in the sequence of man, The. The Common Gain,
Reverted. J. H. Prynne. VaA
Street is soon there, The. To Ride. Paul Éluard, *tr. fr. French by* Kenneth
Koch. TTTS
Street is very long and filled with silence, The. The Street. Octavio Paz,
tr. fr. Spanish by Willis Knapp Jones. FF
Street Lamps in Early Spring. Gwendolyn B. Bennett. ShDr
Street Lanterns. Mary Elizabeth Coleridge. BoTP; PoRA
Street lights reflected in the wet. Winter Intimacies. Andrew Crozier.
VaA
Street Music. Barbara Angell. AiP
Street Music. Greg Pape. PBCAP
Street Musician. Donald Justice. *Fr.* Body and Soul. BAP-91
Street Musicians. John Ashbery. CAPP; HCAP
Street of Named Houses, The. Robert David Cohen. NYBP
Street of Nectar, Street of Contingency. Address. Bruce Smith. *Fr.* In My
Father's House. Son
Street Performers, 1851. Terence Tiller. GTBS-P
Street Scene. W. E. Henley. BoTP
Street Scene. Robert Mezey. LiTM
Street Scene, A. Lizette Woodworth Reese. OBCA
Street Scene — 1946. Kenneth Porter. PoNe
Street Song. Thom Gunn. HeIP; NoP; OxBC
Street Song. Edith Sitwell. CMoP
Street Sounds to the Soldiers' Tread, The. A. E. Housman. PPP
Street threatened, The. The Aerial. Reiner Kunze, *tr. fr. German by* Ewald
Osers. PoSu
Streetcar clanks by outside, The. *(LL)* Tōji. Gary Snyder. PoBeRe
Streets. Naomi Shihab Nye. NAmP90
Streets of Air, The. Malcolm Cowley. *Fr.* Blue Juniata. PoA
Streets of Baltimore. *Unknown.* BLPA
Streets of Forbes, The. Jack McGuire. CBAP; NOBAu
Streets of Laredo, The. Louis MacNeice. ChTr; MoBS; OBWP
Streets of Laredo, The. *Unknown. See* As I Walked Out in the Streets of
Laredo.
Streets of the roaring town. On a Soldier Fallen in the Philippines. William
Vaughn Moody. AnAmPo; NOBA; PAH
Streets of your glances, The. Vasco [or Vasko] Popa, *tr. fr. Serbo-Croatian*
by Anne Pennington. *Fr.* Far Within Us. PoSu
Strength for To-Day. *Unknown.* PWR
Strength from the Hills. Elizabeth Oakes Smith. AmWP
Strength I had to uproot hills. Song of Kai-hsia. Hsiang Chi, *tr. fr.*
Chinese by Ronald C. Miao. SuSp
Strength leaves the hand I lay on this beech bole. The Beech. Andrew
Young. BoNaP
Strength, Love, Light. Robert II, King of France. WGRP
Strength of Fate, The. Euripides, *tr. fr. Greek by* A. E. Housman. *Fr.*
Alcestis. AWP
Strength of Fields, The. James Dickey. VCAP
Strength through Joy. Kenneth Rexroth. FYAP; VGW
Strength to the spoiler thine? *(LL)* Clerical Oppressors. Whittier. NAAL-
1; PAH
Strength to the spoiler thine? *(LL)* Just God! and these are they. Frederick
Douglass. NAAL-1
Strengthen, my Love, this castle of my heart. Charles, Duc d'Orléans, *tr.*
fr. French by Andrew Lang. AWP
Strengthened to live, strengthened to die for. In Distrust of Merits.
Marianne Moore. ArOW; LiTA; LiTM; MeMAP; MoAB; MoAmPo;
NAAL-2; OBWP; OxBA; TrGrPo
Strephon has fashion, wit and youth. Elizabeth Taylor. KTR
Strephon I saw, and started at the sight. Love's First Approach.
"Ephelia." KTR
Strephon to Celia; a Modern Love-Letter. Mary Leapor. ECWP
Stress of Gijón are wider in the dark, The. Three or Four Shades of Blues.
Dionisio D. Martinez. Jaz
Stretch of wall, The. The Volga Towns. Johannes Bobrowski, *tr. fr.*
German by Ruth Mead *and* Matthew Mead. PoSu
Stretched in the shadow of the broad beech. The Shepherd's Gratitude.
Virgil, *tr. by* Charles Stuart Calverley. *Fr.* Eclogues. AWP
Stretcher Case. Siegfried Sassoon. NSI
Stretching. Robert Morgan. WeW

Stretching across the miles that severe you from me. *(LL)* In Death Divided. Thomas Hardy. SCGP

Strew lightly o'er the soldier's grave. The Soldier's Grave. Henry D. Muir. OHIP

Strew me with blossoms when I die. *Unknown, tr. fr. Italian by* John Addington Symonds. *Fr.* Popular Songs of Tuscany. AWP

Strew not earth with empty stars. Thomas Lovell Beddoes. *Fr.* Second Brother, The. OxBSP

Strew on her roses, roses. Requiescat. Matthew Arnold. AWP; EBEvV; ELP; FHYEP; InvP; LiTB; MeMBP; NOBE; OBD; OBEV; PoRA; TrGrPo

Stricken Average, The. William Rose Benét. AnAmPo

Stricken South to the North, The. Paul Hamilton Hayne. PAH

Stricken with fists. *(LL)* The Drunk Man. *Unknown.* NOBAu

Strict and Particular Old Lady. Tim Longville. VaA

Strict hairshirt of circumstance tears the flesh. The Veterans. Donagh MacDonagh. CIP

Strictly Bucolic. Charles Simic. FoLa

Strictly for Posterity. Charles Simic. NNaP

Strictly Germ-proof. Arthur Guiterman. BLPA; TrJP

Strictures on the Economy of Nature. George Outram. FaBoCo

Strike, The. *Unknown.* OBET

Strike among the Poets, A. *Unknown.* FaBoCo; FiBHP

Strike, churl; hurl, cheerless wind, then; heltering hail. Hailstorm in May. Gerard Manley Hopkins. Spl

Strike down into my breast, O sun, and cleanse my soul. Hymn to the Sun. William A. Percy. TrPWD

Strike! for tge brave revere the brave! *(LL)* The Banner of the Jew. Emma Lazarus. AmWP; TrJP

Strike his wakening, slap his eyes ajar. Dub Eleven. Jeff Nuttall. NBrP

Strike the Bell. *Unknown.* OxBSS

Strike the Blow. *Unknown.* PAH

Strike the concertina's melancholy string! The Story of Prince Agib. W. S. Gilbert. CBNP; FaBoCo

Strike up, you lusty gallants, with music [*or* musick] and sound of drum. Captain Ward and the *Rainbow. Unknown.* ESPB; OBET; OxBSS

Striking Times. *Unknown.* OBET

String, The. Momcilo Nastasijevic, *tr. fr. Serbo-Croatian by* Charles Simic. HSix

String. Dennis Schmitz. LCAP

String-chewing bass players. Mingus. Bob Kaufman. PoBA

Stringer's Field. Roy McFadden. PNI

Stringfive. Richard Kostelanetz. Jaz

Stringfour. Richard Kostelanetz. Jaz

Strings' Excitement, The. W. H. Auden. MoAB; MoBrPo

Strings lay all about. The Disconnection. Rita Mae Brown. IHMS

Stringybark Cockatoo, The. *Unknown.* NOBAu

"Strip," Leofric said, "and you'll find." Harry Thomas. PeLi

Strip Me Naked, or Royal Gin for Ever; a Picture. *Unknown.* NOEC

Strip of Blue, A. Lucy Larcom. WGRP

Strip off your clothes and give them to a man. The Visiting Hour. David Wagoner. HoPM

Strip-tease. Lawrence Durrell. OxAEP-2

Striped blouse in a clearing by Bazille, A. Ceremony. Richard Wilbur. CoAP; MoP; NAAL-2; NoAM

Striped suit. The New Suit. Nidia Sanabria de Romero, *tr. fr. Spanish by* Arnaldo D. Larrosa Morán *with* Naomi Shihab Nye. TSaS

Stripped almond of the plane is gone, The. Between Two Worlds. Rosemary Thomas. NYBP

Stripped of his crown. The Bombax Tree. Fily-Dabo Sissoko, *tr. fr. French by* Ellen Conroy Kennedy. NegPo

Stripped of its leaves. Trees on a Frosty Night. Mairtin O Direain, *tr. fr. Irish by the author.* TIRV

Stripped/ you're beginning to float free. November 1968. Adrienne Rich. CAPP; NMM

Stripper, The. Anita Endrezze-Danielson. CDW

Strippers. Dick King-Smith. OBAP

Stripping and Putting on. May Swenson. WeW

Strive in this, and love the strife. *(LL)* The Banquet. George Herbert. ESCV; GeHe

Strive not with Love; for if ye do, it will ye thus befall. *(LL)* When summer took in hand the winter to assail. The Earl of Surrey. SiPSBD

Striving to save the whole, by parcells dye. *(LL)* Distraction. Henry Vaughan. GeHe; SeCP

Stroke. Mike Lowery. Poetsp

Stroll-Joy. Johann Klaj, *tr. fr. German by* George C. Schoolfield. GePo

Stroll on, thou dark not deep "blue" dandy, stroll. The Sea Replies to Byron. G. K. Chesteron. UV

Strolling along the Riverbank, Looking for Flowers, *sels.* Tu Fu, *tr. fr. Chinese.*
"Masses of flowers and plants envelop the riverbanks." SuSp
"'Tis not I pity the flowers are about to die." SuSp

Strolling in the Countryside. Chao Yi, *tr. fr. Chinese by* Chang Yin-nan *and* Lewis C. Walmsley. SuSp

Strolling Player, The. Rimbaud, *tr. fr. French by* William Jay Smith. GrPl

Strolling vaguely after luncheon through the streets of Amsterdam. Belle de Jour. George Melly. FaBoPa

Strong and slippery,/ built for the midnight grass-party/ confronted by four cats. Peter. Marianne Moore. CMoP; NAAL-2; NoP; OxBA; SoCa (Strong and Slippery.) OFC

Strong ankled, sun burned, almost naked. Vitamins and Roughage. Kenneth Rexroth. NoAM

Strong Are Saying Nothing, The. Robert Frost. CMoP

Strong Bond, The. Juana de Ibarbourou, *tr. fr. Spanish by* Linda Scheer. PBWP

Strong demand, contend, prevail; the beggar is a fool!, The. *(LL)* The Suppliant. Georgia Douglas Johnson. CDC; PoBA; PoNe; ShDr

Strong drink, hundred-year-old, A. Soul Music: The Derry Air. Eamon Grennan. BiHa; PBCIP

Strong extreme speed, that the brain burries with. Boulogne to Amiens and Paris. Dante Gabriel Rossetti. *Fr.* Trip to Paris and Belgium, A. PeVV

Strong hot breath of the land is lashing, The. A Night in the Red Sea. Sir Alfred Comyn Lyall. OBTV

Strong in a dream of perfect bloom. To the Brave Soul. Wilbur Underwood. WGRP

Strong is the horse upon his speed. Christopher Smart. *Fr.* Song to David, A. ChTr; EBEV; NAEL-1; NOBE, *abr.*; OAEL-1; PoEL-3; TrGrPo, *abr.*; UV

(Man of Prayer, The.) LiTB; OtMeF

Strong is the lion — like a coal. Christopher Smart. *Fr.* Song to David, A. ChTr; EBEV; HAP; NAEL-1; NOBE, *abr.*; OAEL-1; PoEL-3; TrGrPo, *abr.*

Strong is your hold O love. *(LL)* The Last Invocation. Walt Whitman. GGP; MoAmPo; OBD; OxBA; PoEL-5; TrGrPo; TrPWD

Strong Love. A. E. Housman. OtMeF

Strong Men. Sterling A. Brown. BPo; PoBA; TTY

Strong men git stronger, The. *(LL)* Strong Men. Sterling A. Brown. BPo; PoBA; TTY

Strong men keep coming on, The. Upstream. Carl Sandburg. MoAB; MoAmPo

Strong Men, Riding Horses. Gwendolyn Brooks. PoBA

Strong now / you really gotta hold on me. *(LL)* Motown/ Smokey Robinson. Jessica Hagedorn. UL

Strong rods for scepters to bear sway. On the Decease of the Religious and Honourable Jno Haynes Esqr. John James. SCAP

Strong-shouldered mole. A Dead Mole. Andrew Young. FM; GTBS-P; OxBSP

Strong sob of the chafing stream, The. Orara. Henry Clarence Kendall. CBAP

Strong Son of God (Immortal Love). Tennyson. *Fr.* In Memoriam A. H. H. EBVV, *abr.*; EBVVPR; EnVR; HAP; LiTB; MeMBP; NAWM-2; OAEL-2, *abr.*; PeECV, *abr.*; TrCP; TrGrPo; TrPWD; WGRP

Strong song tows, A. Coda. Basil Bunting. *Fr.* Briggflatts [An Autobiography]. OAEL-2

Strong sun across the sod can make. Song for the Passing of a Beautiful Woman. *Unknown, tr. fr. Paiute Indian by* Mary Austin. LiTA

Strong Swimmer, The. William Rose Benét. PoNe

Strong Thighs astride My Chest. Caroline Griffin. DT

Strong Wind, A. Austin Clarke. BoNaP; RB

Strong women told the faggots that there are two important, The. Women Wisdom. Larry Mitchell. GLP

Strongest, The. "Yehoash," *tr. fr. Yiddish by* Marie Syrkin. TrJP

Strongest and the noblest argument, The. Sir John Davies. *Fr.* Nosce Teipsum. NoSic, *abr.*; SiPS

Strongest August sun, The. Whole Lives Missing. Michael Klein. PFL

Strongest creature for his size, The. Weary Will. Andrew Barton Paterson. OBAP

Strongly it bears us along in swelling and limitless billows. The Homeric Hexameter. Samuel Taylor Coleridge. OxAEP-2

Strongly worded to say on the subject. *(LL)* Seascape. Elizabeth Bishop. FaBoWP; MoAB; OxBC; PPP

Struck with huge Love, of what is to be possest. Prefatory Poem, on . . . *Magnalia Christi Americana.* Nicholas Noyes. SCAP

Structural Study of Myth, The. Jerome Rothenberg. PoM

Structure of process, The. Process. John Montague. CIP

Struggle, The. Toi Derricotte. PBCAP

Struggle. Sidney Lanier. LiTA; OxBA

Struggle, The. Sully-Prudhomme, tr. fr. French by Arthur O'Shaughnessy. AWP

Struggle to preserve once spoken words, The. The Birds of America: John James Audubon. Tony Harrison. Fr. Art & Extinction. SCBI

Strugnell's Bargain. Wendy Cope. UV

Strugnell's Rubáiyát. Wendy Cope. UV

Strugnell's Sonnets., sels. Wendy Cope.
"Expense of spirits is a crying shame, The." FaBoBl

Struma, The/ It lay in the harbor at Istanbul. The Death Ship. Ruth Whitman. BTR

Strumming and patter/ the meaningful glances, The. Philodemus, tr. fr. Greek by William Moebius. GrAn

Strut for Roethke, A. John Berryman. NOBA

Stuck in a bottle on the window-sill. Geraniums. W. W. Gibson. NSI

Stuck in a club with a group that calls itself. Death Jazz: A Review. Jack Mueller. Jaz

Stuck on the fridge, our favorite pin-up girl. Heather McHugh. See On the refrigerator a gash.

Stud. Michael Lassell. Fr. Times Square Poems. GLP

Stud, The. Fred Voss. NGP

Student. Cheng Min, tr. by Kenneth Rexroth and Ling Chung. PBWP; WPC

Student, The. James Hurdis. Fr. Adriano; or, The First of June. ECEV

Student. Josephine Miles. NoP

Student, The. Marianne Moore. NAAL-2; TwCP

Student, The. Unknown, tr. fr. Early Modern Irish by Frank O'Connor. OBMV

Student came from Oxford town also, A, mod. vers. by Louis Untermeyer. Chaucer. See Clerk ther was of Oxenford also, A.

Student, do the simple purification. The Simple Purification. Kabir, tr. fr. Hindi by Robert Bly. EnlH; NU

Student from Pembroke once said, A. Andrew Stoker. PeLi

Student of nuclear fission, A. W. Bernard Wake. PeLi

Student's life is pleasant, The. The Student. Unknown, tr. fr. Early Modern Irish by Frank O'Connor. OBMV

Students, like students, form and fly. When the Students Resisted, a Minor Clash Ensued. David Knight. MoCV

Students of Justice, The. W. S. Merwin. NaP

Student's Serenade, The. Anne Brontë. OHCV

Student's Tale, The. Longfellow. Fr. Tales of a Wayside Inn. AmPP

Studies at Delhi, 1876. Sir Alfred Comyn Lyall. OBTV
Sels.
Badminton. PeVV

Studies which they shall renew, The. (LL) Aesop at Play. Phaedrus. AWP

Studio Poem. Cilla McQueen. PeNZ

Study in Aesthetics, A. Robert Peters. BXAP

Study in Aesthetics, The. Ezra Pound. CMoP; NOBA; NoP

Study in Blue. Evan Jones (b. 1927). NOBAu

Study of a Spider, The. Lord De Tabley. NOBVV

Study of Reading Habits, A. Philip Larkin. InPK; NOBL; PPP

Study of the Object. Zbigniew Herbert, tr. fr. Polish by Czeslaw Milosz and Peter Dale Scott. AnRep

Study of Two Pears. Wallace Stevens. InPS; NAAL-2; NoAM; NU; OxBA

Study Peace. Amiri Baraka. PoBA

Studying Physics with My Daughter. Jeanne Murray Walker. WeW

Studying the ancient manuscript crumbly with age. Following the Rhymes of Chang Hsün, in My Study in Late Spring. Huang T'ing-chien, tr. fr. Chinese by Michael E. Workman. SuSp

Stuff, naked, without a name, A. (LL) The Death of the Craneman. Alfred Hayes. LiTA

Stuff of Dreams, The. Shakespeare. See Our revels now are ended. These our actors.

Stuff of the moon. Nocturne in a Deserted Brickyard. Carl Sandburg. MoAmPo

Stuff'd chavender, or chub. (LL) A False Gallop of Analogies. Warham St. Leger. FaBoCo; FiBHP

Stuffed owls drum in my heart. Fear. Thomas Love Peacock. VoR

Stuffy chill of clouded Summer, crowdsmell, booksmell. Supervising Examinations. Sean Lucy. OLIr

Stump Cross — The Long Wait. Geraldine Monk. VBLP

Stumpfoot on 42nd Street. Louis Simpson. NNaP; UnPo; VGW

Stun. James Schuyler. MAT

Stuntman. Lionel Kearns. MoCV

Stupendious love! all saints astonishment. Edward Taylor. Fr. Preparatory Meditations Before My Approach to the Lord's Supper. EAP; MeMAP; OxBA

Stupid and abiding jelly, The. (LL) Bacchanal. Peter De Vries. BXAP; NBLV; NOBL; OBAL

Stupid Catullus! Stubborn soul, endure. (LL) O poor Catullus, stupid long enough! Catullus. STV

Stupid Old Body, The. Edward Carpenter. WGRP

Stupidity. Mary Elizabeth Fullerton. CBAP

Stupidity achieves the crime. Martyr. Mary Elizabeth Fullerton. CBAP

Stupidity Street. Ralph Hodgson. CH; IHNG; LiTM; MoAB; MoBrPo; OBD; OxBTC; PDV

Stupor on the heath, A. Romans in Dorset. Louise Imogen Guiney. AmWP

Sturdiest of forest trees, The. The Holly. Walter de la Mare. CMoP

Sturdy Conq'ror, politic, severe, The. The Royal Line. Leigh Hunt. FaBoUs

Sturdy ploughman doth the soldier see, The. Joseph Hall. Fr. Virgidemiarum. OBSV

Stutterer. Alan Dugan. NYBP

Stuttering rain at the window. Sister Midnight. John James. NBrP; VaA

Stwonen Steps, The. William Barnes. NOBVV

Stwuns that built Gaarge Ridler's oven, The. George Ridler's Oven. Unknown. OBET

Stygian council thus dissolved; and forth, The. Milton. Fr. Paradise Lost. EPCY; OAEL-1

Style. Charles Bukowski. HoPM

Style. Howard Nemerov. NoAM

Style thee a most great fool, but no great man. (LL) On Don Surly. Ben Jonson. FaBoEE; NAEL-1

Styx. Robert Duncan. VCAP

Suave and paltry man, my enemy, A. In the Tail of the Scorpion. Genevieve Taggard. VGW

Suave Mari Magno. Lucretius, tr. by W. H. Mallock. Fr. De Rerum Natura (On the Nature of Things). AWP

Sub-average Time Reader, The. Ernest Wittenberg. FiBHP

Sub Rosa. Susan Prospere. AnAn

Sub Specie Aeternitatis. Robert Hayden. AmPP

Subalterns. Elizabeth Daryush. OBWP

Subalterns, The. Thomas Hardy. CMoP; MeMBP; MoAB; MoBrPo; MoP; NoAM; NOBVV; OAEL-2; Poetr; PPP; TEP

Subaltern's Love-Song, A. Sir John Betjeman. BoLoP; EBeVV; HAP; NoAM; NOBL; OxAEP-2; OxBTC; TwCP

Subject. Marie Ponsot. VGW

Subject chosen for tonight's discussion, The. An Evening of Russian Poetry. Vladimir Nabokov. NYBP

Subject to All Pain. Unknown. MeEL

Subject to ev'ry mounter's bended knee. (LL) The H. Scriptures. George Herbert. ChIV-1; ESCV; MiEL

Subject was put to bed at midnight, The. Operative No. 174 Resigns. Kenneth Fearing. NYBP

Subjection of Women, The. Austin Clarke. CIP

Subjectivist has a thousand faceted eyes, The. Song for the Subjectivist. Li Pai-feng, tr. fr. Chinese by Hualing Nieh. Fr. Pearls and Earth. LHF

Subjectivity at Sestos. P. M. Hubbard. NYBP

Sublimation. Alex Comfort. ErPo

Sublime — invention ever young. Christopher Smart. Fr. Song to David, A. ChTr; EBEV; NAEL-1; NOBE, abr.; OAEL-1; OBEV; PoEL-3; TrGrPo, abr.

Submarine Bed, The. John Peale Bishop. LiTA

Submarines. "Klaxon." NSI

Submerged Door, The. Matthew Sweeney. IB

Submerged, silent, rooted in water. Foetus. Phyllis Haring. PeSA

Submission. George Herbert. JCP

Submission. Celia Laighton Thaxter. AmWP

Submission. Clara Ann Thompson. CBWP-2

Submission. Unknown, tr. fr. Siamese by E. Powys Mathers. ErPo

Submission and Rest. Anna Temple Whitney. See Camel at the close of day, The.

Submission to Afflictive Providences. Isaac Watts. NOCV

Submitting to a sentry's fate. Common Dawn. Guy Butler. PeSA

Subplot. Jack Butler. MT

Subscribe myself your servant/ Francis Ben. (LL) A Messe of Nonsense. Unknown. CBNP; NOSC

Substance and Shadow. John Hewitt. PNI

Substance, Shadow, and Spirit, sels. T'ao Ch'ien, tr. fr. Chinese by Burton Watson.

Substantiations, *sels.* Vidya, *tr. fr. Sanskrit* by Daniel H. H. Ingalls. "One born to hardship in his place and station." PBWP

Substitute Bassist, The. C. D. Wright. Jaz

Substitute for Time, The. John Koethe. EOEF

Substitution. Elizabeth Barrett Browning. WGRP

Substitution. Anne Spencer. BlSi; CDC; ShDr

Subtle almost beyond thought are these dim colours. Dun-Colour [*or* Dun-Color]. Ruth Pitter. FM; PoRA

Subtle capering on a simple thought. Fleadh Cheoil. Pearse Hutchinson. PBCIP

Subtle chain of countless rings, A. Nature. Emerson. AWP

Subtlest strain a great musician weaves, The. Limitations. H. Cordelia Ray. CBWP-3

Subtlety. Bruce St. John. PBCV

Subtract the size of the world. To the Newlyweds in the Barrio. Rebecca Gonzales. AfAz

Suburb, The. Anne Stevenson. NMM

Suburb Hilltop. Richard Moore. NYBP

Suburban. John Ciardi. NBLV

Suburban. H. R. Coursen. GOYP

Suburban Childhood, A. Liz Rosenberg. PBCAP

Suburban Dream. Geraldine Kudaka. ETG

Suburban Dreams. Edwin Muir. OxBTC

Suburban Lovers. Bruce Dawe. NOBAu

Suburban Song. Elizabeth Riddell. CBAP; NOBAu

Suburban Sonnet. Gwen Harwood. CBAP

Suburban villas, highway-side retreats. London Suburbs. William Cowper. *Fr.* Retirement. FaBoPP

Suburban Wife's Song. Robert Hutchinson. NYBP

Suburbia. Maurice Martinez. PoNe

Suburbs is a Fine Place, The. *Unknown.* CoMu

Suburbs on a Hazy Day. D. H. Lawrence. OBMV

Subverted Flower, The. Robert Frost. CMoP; HAP; MeMAP; MoP; NoAM; NOBA; OxBA; PoE; Poetr

Subway. Susan Fawcett. CrSp

Subway, The. Allen Tate. NOBA

Subway Rush Hour. Langston Hughes. InPK

Subway Singer, The. Amy Clampitt. NGP

Subway Vespers. Molly Peacock. NGP

Subway Wind. Claude McKay. PBCV

Subway Witnesses, The. Lorenzo Thomas. PoBA

Success! Berton Braley. WBLP

Success ("If you want a thing bad enough."). Berton Braley. PoToHe

Success. Rupert Brooke. OxBTC

Success, *sels.* C. C. Cameron. Don't Give Up. PoToHe

Success. William Empson. OxBTC

Success. *Unknown.* PoToHe

Success is counted sweetest. Emily Dickinson. CMoP; EBEvV; GoJo; HelP; ImPo; InPS; LiTA; LiTM; MeMAP; MoAB; MoAmPo; NAAL-1; NOBA; OxBA; PoRA; SAmP; TAP; TFi; WPE (Success. AnAmPo; AWP

Success is like some horrible disaster. After Publication of Under the Volcano. Malcolm Lowry. FaBoTw

Success is speaking words of praise. Success. *Unknown.* PoToHe

Success Story. Terence Winch. UL

Successful Summer, A. David Schubert. ChIV-1

Succubus, The. Robert Graves. OAEL-2

Succubus, The. Harriet Rose. BrRo

Succulence by implication pinks the eye with condensation, A. Cris Cheek. *Fr.* Drawing on the Traditions. NBrP

Succulent flower bleeds molasses, The. Sugar Cane. Faustin Charles. PBCV

Succumbing. Paul Eaton Reeve. ErPo

Such a Blustery Day! Elizabeth Gould. BoTP

Such a dangerous thing. Reading of the Rattlesnake. Lynn Lonidier. SRLS

Such a fool as I am you had better ignore. The Usk. C. H. Sisson. NOCV

Such a heart! A Love-Song. *Unknown, tr. fr. Irish* by Brendan Kennelly. PeIV

Such a hubbub in the nests. Freaks of Fashion. Christina Rossetti. FM

Such a King Harry? (*LL*) Fair [*or* Faire] stood the wind for France. Michael Drayton. EBEvV; EBNV

"Such a little king's eye," said my mother. Roy Kloof. Sydney Clouts. PeSAV

Such a morning it is when love. Day of These Days. Laurie Lee. BoNaP; PAW

Such a Parcel of Rogues in a Nation. Burns. OxBS

Such a peculiar lot. Fantasy of an African Boy. James Berry. NTP; PBCV

Such a prelate, I trow. John Skelton. *Fr.* Why Come Ye Not to Court. OBSV

Such a result so soon — and from such a beginning! (*LL*) A Hand-Mirror. Walt Whitman. NAAL-1; OxBA

Such a ship as nevermore will be. (*LL*) The Brave Old Ship, the *Orient.* Robert Traill Spence Lowell. FaBoBe

Such a strange girl!. Chiqui and Terra Nova. Jessica Hagedorn. UL

Such a strong color on the late chrysanthemums. José Juan Tablada. *Fr.* Two Drinking Songs. NU

Such a time of it they had. Stanley Meets Mutesa. James David Rubadiri. PBA

Such a very lovely name? (*LL*) The Concert. *Unknown.* PeSAV

Such a wide, still landscape, all cold and white! A Greenland Winter. Lucy Diamond. BoTP

Such a wizened creature. Old Age. E. Keary. NOBVV

Such an itch and tickle of slow. Stretching. Robert Morgan. WeW

Such are the little memories of you. To Theodore. George Marion McClellan. AAP

Such as in God the Lord Do Trust. William Kethe. AH

Such as, retired from sight of men, like thee. To Saint Mary Magdalen. Henry Constable. Son

Such as she was, such as she would become. (*LL*) The Gift Outright. Robert Frost. AiP; AmPP; CMoP; GOA; LiTM; MeMAP; MoAB; MoAmPo; MoP; NAAL-2; NoAM; NOBA; NoP; OxBA; Poetr; PPP; TFi; TRP

Such as these have lived and died! (*LL*) Footsteps of Angels. Longfellow. AnAmPo

Such as thou art, some time was I. Richard Barber. FaBoEH

Such be the dog, I charge, thou mean'st to train. Thomas Tickell. *Fr.* Fragment of a Poem on Hunting, A. ECEV

Such brazen slatterns. Dandelions. Gerda Mayer. Spl

Such cats are useful to calm the horses. Throwing the Racetrack Cats at Saratoga. David Ray. SM

Such Cloe is, and common as the air. (*LL*) Cloe ("Bright as the day, and like the morning fair.") George Granville. FaBoCo; FaBoEE; NIP

Such closets to search, such alcoves to importune! (*LL*) Love in a Life. Robert Browning. CBLP; EBVVPR; FHYEP; InvP; NOBE; NOBVV; OBNC

Such counsels ye gave to me, O! (*LL*) Edward [*or* Edward, Edward]. *Unknown.* AmFP; CH; ClHu; EBEV; EBEvV; ELP; EnRP; ESPB; FaBoBa; FaPoR; GGP; HAP; HoPM; InPK; InPS; LiTB; Mes; NAEL-1; NOBE; NoP; OBEV; OxBB; OxBS; PoEL-1; PoRA; PrIm; SCGP; SoSe; TFi; TrGrPo; TRP

Such darkness as when Jesus died! San Francisco. Joaquin Miller. PAH

Such Different Wants. Robert Bly. ArLo

Such dissonance can e'er be sweet, and low. (*LL*) Incompleteness. H. Cordelia Ray. AmWP; CBWP-3

Such easy, easy hours. Moon as Medusa. Vinnie-Marie D'Ambrosio. IHMS

Such eyes, such hair, such wit, and such a hand? (*LL*) Those eyes that [*or* which] set my fancy on a fire. Philippe Desportes. NoSic

Such fame as I have drops from me in a flash. The Perturbations of Uranus. Roy Fuller. ErPo

Such flowers as Earth our Mother. Petronius Arbiter, *tr. fr. Latin* by Helen Waddell. *Fr.* Satyricon. MLL

Such foolish, foolish men.' (*LL*) Art Thou That She. *Unknown.* OxBSP

Such gaudy Tulips rais'd from Dung. (*LL*) The Lady's Dressing Room. Swift. ErPo; FaBoBl; IHNG; NoP; TEP

Such grace, so self-contained, was the best escape to know. (*LL*) The Ballet of the Fifth Year. Delmore Schwartz. MoAB; OxBA; TwCP

Such hap as I am happed in. Sir Thomas Wyatt. SiPS; SiPSBD

Such happiness as I have known to-day. (*LL*) 'Tis Said That Some Have Died for Love. Wordsworth. EnRP

Such haukes, such hounds, and such a leman. (*LL*) The Three Ravens. *Unknown.* ChTr; ESPB; FaBoBa; GBP; HelP; InPK; Mes; NAEL-1; NoP; OAEL-1; OBD; OBET; OBEV; OxBB; PoE; PoEL-1; SCGP; TFi; TrGrPo; UnPo

Such heate they cast as lifts the Spirit high. (*LL*) To Music Bent Is My Retired Mind. Thomas Campion. AAS; EnRePo; NOCV; PeECV

Such icy kisses, anchorites that live. The Cold Kiss. Thomas Stanley. CBLP

Such ills attend. Advice to Lovers. John Armstrong. *Fr.* Oeconomy of Love; a Poetical Essay, The. NOEC

Suddenly they came flying, like a long scarf of smoke. The Thing. Theodore Roethke. CMoP

Suddenly this voice is calling. The Backyard. Christopher Gilbert. *Fr.* Horizontal Cosmology. Jaz

Suddenly to become John Benbow. *(LL)* Metempsychosis. Kenneth Slessor. NOBAu

Suddenly to become John Benbow, walking down William Street. Metempsychosis. Kenneth Slessor. NOBAu

Suddenly We Will Wake. Shin Shalom, *tr. fr. Hebrew* by Ruth Finer Mintz. MHP

Suddenly you feel a touch. Henri Michaux, *tr. fr. French. Fr.* In the Land of Magic. AnRep

Sue asked, why is there a line. Spring. Patricia Cumming. MDDM

Sue Ella Tucker was barely in her teens. Rubaiyat for Sue Ella Tucker. Miller Williams. SM

Suelick is the greatest Indian power. The Origin of the Skagit Indians. Lucy Williams, *tr. fr. Skagit Indian* by Carl Cary. STP

Suet Dumpling, The. *Unknown.* BXAP

Suez Crisis. *Somali Oral Tradition, tr.* by B. W. Andrzejewski. WTO

Suffenus, whom so well you know [*or* whom you know]. Catullus, *tr. fr. Latin. Fr.* Carmina. AWP, *tr.* by Walter Savage Landor; OBVE, *tr.* by Matthew Prior
(To Varus.) AWP, *tr.* by Walter Savage Landor

Suffer, Poor Negro! David Diop, *tr. fr. French* by Langston Hughes. PBA

Suffer the Children. Audre Lorde. PoBA

Sufferance of her race is shown, The. Formerly a Slave. Herman Melville. PoNe; TAP

Suffering. Albert Ehrenstein, *tr. fr. German* by Babette Deutsch. TrJP

Suffering. Miroslav Holub, *tr. fr. Czech* by Ian Milner *and* George Theiner. AnRep; PoSu

Suffering. P. K. Page. NoAM

Suffering from Heat. Wang Wei, *tr. fr. Chinese* by Hugh M. Stimson. SuSp

Suffering has settled like a sly disguise. A Korean Woman Seated by a Wall. William Meredith. Poetr

Sufficed not, madame, that you did tear. Sir Thomas Wyatt. SiPS; SiPSBD

Sufficeth it to you [*or* yow] my joys [*or* joyes] interred. Sir Walter Ralegh. *Fr.* Ocean's Love to Cynthia, The. SiPS, *sl. abr.*
(Vith and Last Book of the Ocean to Cynthia.) SiPSBD
(Ocean to Cynthia, The.) NoSic

Suffolk. Swinburne. *Fr.* By the North Sea. FaBoPP

Suffolk Miracle, The. *Unknown.* ESPB

Suffolk Miracle, The. *Unknown.* AmFP

Suffolk Shore, The. George Crabbe. *Fr.* Borough, The. FaBoPP

Sufi Quatrain. Rabi'a bint Isma'il of Syria, *tr. fr. Arabic* by Deirdre Lashgari. WPOW

Sugar and cream. *(LL)* Curly Locks! Curly Locks! wilt thou be mine? Mother Goose. OxNR; ReMoGo

Sugar Cane. Faustin Charles. PBCV

Sugar Cane, The, *sels.* James Grainger.
Compost. NOEC
(How to Fertilize Soil.) FaBoUs
How to Exterminate Rats. FaBoUs
"On festal days; or when their work is done." PBCV
Slaves. NOEC
"Then earthquakes, nature's agonizing pangs." PBCV

Sugar-cane is just a cubit high, The. Love Songs (Dadaria). *Gond Oral Tradition, tr.* by V. Elwin *and* S. Hivale. WTO

Sugar in the Cane. Tennessee Williams. OBAL

Sugar Loaf. David Campbell. FaBoMA

Sugar-Plum Tree, The. Eugene Field. NBLV; OTCP; OxBChV

Sugarfields. Barbara Mahone. PoBA

Suggestion Made by the Posters of the *Globe*, A. J. E. Thorold Rogers. FaBoEE

Suicide, The. V. R. Laing. PoA

Suicide. Robert Lowell. PoE

Suicide, The. Joyce Carol Oates. Poetsp

Suicide. Anne Stevenson. FaBoWP

Suicide. Alice Walker. FF

Suicide applicant, A. Ant Dodger. William Knott. PBCAP

Suicide in [the] Trenches. Siegfried Sassoon. PAW; PoWW

Suicide is such a bore. one wishes one's friends would stop it. 3 : 1. Alta. CrSp

Suicide off Egg Rock. Sylvia Plath. PPP

Suicide on Pentwyn Bridge. Gillian Clarke. AngWe

Suicide Pond. Kathy McLaughlin. PoA

Suicides, The. Donald Justice. Poetr

Suicide's Note. Langston Hughes. CDC

Suilven. Andrew Young. OxBS

Suilven and the Eagle, *sels.* Gordon Bottomley.
Eagle Song. MoBrPo

Suit of Nettles, A, *sels.* James Reaney.
Branwell's Sestina. MoCV

Suitable for a gentleman with medals. War Lord in the Early Evening. P. K. Page. NoAM

Suite for Celery and Blind Date. Philip Dow. BXAP

Suite for Marriage, A. David Ignatow. NNaP

Suite from Catullus. Vincent McHugh. ErPo

Suite to Fathers. James Harrison. AmPA

Suitor, The. Jane Kenyon. InPK

Sukey [*or* Suky], you shall be my wife. *Unknown.* OxBM; OxNR; TLR

Sukla Yajur Veda. *Unknown, tr. fr. Sanskrit* by Romesh Dutt. *Fr.* Vedic Hymns. EaPr

Sulkily the sticks burn, and though they crackle. Under the Pot. Robert Graves. FaBoEE

Sulky old gray brute!, The. The Bristol Channel. Thomas Edward Brown. NOBVV

Sulky Sue. Mother Goose. *See* Here's Sulky Sue.

Sullen and dark [*or* dull], in the September day. The Last Reservation. Walter Learned. PAH

Sullivan arrived at the very lowest Heaven. John L. Sullivan Enters Heaven. Robert Frost. BXAP

Sulphur-yellow chord of the eleventh, A. On Hearing Prokofieff's Grotesque for Two Bassoons, Concertina and Snare-Drums. Louis Untermeyer. BXAP

Sultry air, the smoke of shavings. A Night in a Village. Ivan Savvich Nikitin, *tr. fr. Russian* by P. E. Matheson. AWP

Sum, A. "Lewis Carroll." Spl

Sum — / I am a gentleman. *Unknown.* ISE

Sum, Es, Est ("Sum — I am a gentleman.") *Unknown.* ChTr

Sum of Life, The, *abr.* Ben King. CTC

Sum speiks of lords, sum speiks of lairds. Johnie Armstrang. *Unknown.* ESPB; IBB; OxBB

Sum the History. *(LL)* How the waters closed above him. Emily Dickinson. DL; PoEL-5

Sum tyme an Englis schip we had. *Unknown.* FaBoEH

Sum wyfis of the burrows-toun. Satire on the Town Ladies. Sir Richard Maitland. ScCV

Sumac showing faint traces of red. Autumn Thoughts. Lu Yu, *tr. fr. Chinese* by Burton Watson. SuSp

Sumach Leaves, The. Jones Very. NOBA

Sumburgh Heid. George Bruce. OxBS

Sumer is comen and winter gon. An Easter Song. *Unknown.*
(Sumer Is Icumen In.) ImPo

Sumer Is Icumen In. *Unknown. See* Summer [*or* Sumer] is icumen [*or* y-comen] in.

Sumer is icumen in. *Unknown.* MiEL
(Sing! cuccu, nu. Sing! cuccu. UV

Summa is i-cumen in. Baccalaureate. David McCord. BXAP; HeIL; NBLV; OBAL

Summary. Sonia Sanchez. BPo

Summe men sayen that I am blac. *Unknown.* MiEL

Summer. Conrad Aiken. NoAM; Poetr

Summer. Frank Asch. NTCP

Summer. John Ashbery. NAAL-2

Summer. Sir John Betjeman. PeLi

Summer. John Clare. BoNaP

Summer. Douglas Crase. NoP

Summer. John Davidson. BoNaP

Summer. Duo Duo, *tr. fr. Chinese* by Donald Finkel *with* Li Guohua. SpMi

Summer. Fan Ch'eng-ta, *tr.* by Irving Y. Lo. *Fr.* Seasonal Poems on Fields and Gardens. SuSp

Summer, The. Morgan Llwyd. *Fr.* 1648. AngWe

Summer. Jayanta Mahapatra, *tr. fr. Hindi.* TSaS

Summer. Tom Marshall. NOBC

Summer. Josephine Miles. FaBoWP; WPE

Summer. Christina Rossetti. BoNaP; ELP; PlP

Summer. Spenser. *Fr.* Faerie Queene, The. GN

Summer. Lucien Stryk. CAPP

Summer. James Thomson. *Fr.* Seasons, The. FM

Summer. *Unknown, tr. fr. Chinese. Fr.* Tzu-yeh Songs of the Four Seasons. SuSp

Summer. Diane Wakoski. VGW

Summer Solstice. George Seferis, *tr. fr. Greek by* Edmund Keeley *and* Philip Sherrard. AnAn

Summer Solstice, New York City. Sharon Olds. NAmP90; NGP

Summer Song, A. George Peele. *See* Whenas [*or* When as] the Rye [Reach to the Chin].

Summer Song. W. W. Watt. FiBHP

Summer, splendid summer, nourishing the poet on the milk of your light. Midnight Elegy. Léopold Sédar Senghor, *tr. fr. French by* Ellen Conroy Kennedy. NegPo

Summer Stars. Carl Sandburg. RFM

Summer still plays across the street. Dying: An Introduction. L. E. Sissman. NYBP

Summer Storm. John Montague. IPY

Summer Storm. Louis Simpson. ErPo; OxBC

Summer Sun. Robert Louis Stevenson. MoBrPo; PWR

Summer sun is sinking low, The. Sunset. Longfellow. BoTP

Summer Sunday morning, A. A Battle Ballad. Francis Orrery Ticknor. PAH

Summer Term had just begun, The. Mamzelle. Mary Wilson. AIW

Summer that I was ten, The. The Centaur. May Swenson. FaBoWP; GrPl; NMM; NTP; TwCP

Summer!/ the painting is organized. The Corn Harvest. William Carlos Williams. *Fr.* Pictures from Brueghel. ArNa; PPP

Summer, this is our flesh. Seasons of the Soul. Allen Tate. OxBA

Summer Time on Bredon. Hugh Kingsmill. *See* 'Tis summer time on Bredon.

Summer Vacation. Wordsworth. *Fr.* Prelude [or, Growth of a Poet's Mind], The. EnRP; OAEL-2; PoEL-4

Summer was dry, dry the garden. On the Debt My Mother Owed to Sears Roebuck. Edward Dorn. TRP

Summer was over, the season unkind, The. The Colliers' March. John Freeth. OBET

Summer was sauntering by. Austin Clarke. *Fr.* Mnemosyne Lay in Dust. IPY

Summer when our life was fair, The. (*LL*) Musings. William Barnes. HAP; NOBE; OBNC

Summer Wind. Bryant. PoEL-4

Summer wind, The. What Her Girl Friend Said before the Elopement. Kutavayir Kirattanar, *tr. fr. Tamil by* A. K. Ramanujan. PLW

Summer Wish, A. Christina Rossetti. OBNC

Summer Words of [*or* for] a Sistuh [*or* Sister] Addict. Sonia Sanchez. BlSi; BPo; UnPo

Summerfield. Jim Barnes. *Fr.* Ex-Deputy Sheriff Remembers the Eastern Oklahoma Murderers, An. HATNAP, *sect.* i; NGP, *sect.* i

Summer's Afternoon, A. (*LL*) Not any higher stands the Grave. Emily Dickinson. AnAmPo; SAmP

Summers Ago. Isabella Gardner. CAPP

Summers and summers have come, and gone with the flight of the swallow. The Tantramar Revisited. Sir Charles G. D. Roberts. NOBC

Summer's Day, A. Joanna Baillie. WoRP

Summer's Day, A. Alexander Hume. CH

Summer's Day, A. Tom Leonard. NBrP

Summer's Day, A. James Whitcomb Riley. AnAmPo

Summer's Dream, A. Elizabeth Bishop. OxBC

Summer's Early End at Hudson Bay. Hayden Carruth. NYBP

Summer's Farewell. Thomas Nashe. *Fr.* Summer's Last Will and Testament. PlP; PoEL-2

Summer's gone brown, and, with it. Me to You. Alastair Reid. NYBP

Summer's last half moon waning high. 16. ix. 65. James Merrill. NAs

Summer's Last Will and Testament. Thomas Nashe. PlP
Sels.
    Adieu, Farewell, Earth's Bliss[e]. CH; CoGr; EBEV; EIl; ELP; HAP; HeIP; InvP; NoSic; TEP; TFi; TRP
    (Adieu, farewell earth's bliss.) PeECV
    (In a Time of Pestilence.) HoPM; OBEV; OtMeF; TrGrPo
    (In Plague Time.) FaBoCh; FaPoR
    (In Time of Pestilence.) NOBE
    (In Time of Pestilence.) PeECV
    (In Time of Plague.) EnRePo
    (Litany in Time of Plague, A.) ClHu; DL; NAEL-1; NIP; NoP; OAEL-1; PoRA; PPP; PrIm
    (Lord, Have Mercy on Us.) ChTr
    (Song: "Adieu, farewell earth's blisse.") GGP; PoEL-2
    (Song in Time of Plague.) SCV
    Autumn. EIl; NoSic; OAEL-1; SCGP; TrGrPo
    (Autumn Hath All the Summer's Fruitful Treasure.) EnRePo
    "Fair summer droops, droop men and beasts therefore." NoSic
    (Baning Summer.) OxBSP; SCGP
    (Fair Summer Droops.) EIl

"Rich men, trust not in wealth." OBD

Spring, the Sweet Spring. ArNa; CH; ImPo; LiTB; NAEL-1; NoP; NoSic; TFi

(Spring.) BoNaP; EIl; GTBS; GTBS-P; NOBE; OBEV; SCGP; TrGrPo; WiR

Summer's Farewell. PoEL-2

Summer's morning sun creeps up the blue, The. Sunrise in Summer. John Clare. FaBoPP

Summer's put the idy in, The. A Summer's Day. James Whitcomb Riley. AnAmPo

Summer's sun is warm and bright. Pleasant Changes. Jane Euphemia Browne. OxBChV

Summer's sun was beaming hot, The. Mother's Songs. Frank Barbour Coffin. AAP

Summer's the time for fun. (*LL*) Grasshopper Green. Nancy Dingman Watson. BoTP; FaPON

Summertime. Su Shun-ch'in, *tr. fr. Chinese by* Michael E. Workman. SuSp

Summertime and the Living. Robert Hayden. PoBA; PPP; TwCP

Summing-up, The. Stanley Kunitz. OBAL

Summit, The. Kathleen Raine. *Fr.* Beinn Naomh. OxBS

Summit gain'd how glorious the reward, The. Robert Dunbar. *Fr.* Cruise, The. PBCV

Summit Temple, The. Li Po, *tr. fr. Chinese by* Robert Payne. TAL

Summon the Earth (the fair Astrea's gone,). An Elegy upon the Death of Mrs. A. Behn, the Incomparable Astrea. *Unknown.* KTR

Summoned by Bells, *sels.* Sir John Betjeman.
    "Afternoons/ Brought coconut smell of gorse." FaBoPP
    Back Again for the Holidays. FaBoPP
    "My dear deaf father, how I loved him then." OxBTC

Summoned by conscious recollection, she. Misery and Splendor. Robert Hass. VCAP

Summonee's Tale, The. Stanley J. Sharpless. BXAP; FaBoPa

Summons, The. James Laughlin. LiTA

Summons. David Rivard. NAmP90

Summons to Love. William Drummond of Hawthornden. *See* Phoebus, Arise.

Summons to Town, A. Sir John Suckling. NOSC

Summum Bonum. Robert Browning. OHCV; PFP

Sumo Wrestlers. James Kirkup. OBTV

Sums, The. Lauris Edmond. FaBoWP

Sumter. Henry Howard Brownell. PAH

Sumter. Edmund Clarence Stedman. PAH

Sumter — a Ballad of 1861. *Unknown.* PAH

Sumter's Band. J. W. Simmons. PAH

Sun, The. John Drinkwater. FaPON; NTCP

Sun. Omer Hillel, *tr. fr. Hebrew by* Ruth Finer Mintz. MHP

Sun, The. Charlie Mehrhoff. EaPr

Sun. Branko Miljkovic, *tr. fr. Serbo-Croatian by* Charles Simic. HSix

Sun, The. Andrew Oerke. PoA

Sun. Michael Palmer. BAP-89

Sun. Henry Rowe. OBEV

Sun, The. Anne Sexton. NYBP; PBWP

Sun. Gary Soto. TRP

Sun. (*LL*) The Horse Cursed by the Sun. *Unknown.* PeSAV

Sun, The. Francis Thompson. *Fr.* Ode to the Setting Sun. MoAB; MoBrPo

Sun, The. W. J. Turner. MoBrPo

Sun. Gill Vickers. VBLP

Sun, The, *sels.* Vidya, *tr. fr. Sanskrit by* Daniel H. H. Ingalls.
    "I praise the disk of the rising sun." PBWP; WPOW

Sun, The. William Carlos Williams. *Fr.* Paterson. MeMAP

Sun a shine but tings noh bright. Dutty Tough. Louise Bennett. PBCV

Sun above the hills raged in the height, The. Lot and His Daughters II. A. D. Hope. ChIV-1

Sun and Fog contested, The. Emily Dickinson. NTP; Spl

Sun and Fun. Sir John Betjeman. PlP

Sun and Moon. Charlotte Druitt Cole. BoTP

Sun and Moon: I saw a strange creature. *Unknown, formerly at. to* Cynewulf, *tr. fr. Anglo-Saxon by* Kevin Crossley-Holland. *Fr.* Riddles (Exeter Book). ASW

Sun and Moon So High and Bright, The. *Unknown.* AH

Sun and moon, that ceaselessly sing. Immortal Israel. Judah Halevi, *tr. fr. Hebrew by* Solomon Solis-Cohen. TrJP

Sun and Rain and Dew from Heaven. Adam Lindsay Gordon. *Fr.* Ye Wearie Wayfarer. PoLF

Sun and rain at work together. The Red-Gold Rain. Sacheverell Sitwell. MoBrPo

Sun and Shadow. Oliver Wendell Holmes. AnAmPo

Sun and the Moon and Fear of Loneliness, The. *Unknown, tr. fr. Eskimo.* WTO

Sun appearing, The: a pendant. Plainview: 3. N. Scott Momaday. CDW

Sun at noon to higher air, The. March. A. E. Housman. FaBoCh

Sun-beames in the East are spred, The. Epithalamion Made at Lincolnes Inne. John Donne. SeCP

Sun, beholding so as he does pass, The. On a Fair Lady, Looking in the Glass. Richard Leigh. NOSC

Sun blazed while the thunder yet, The. The Mill-Pond. Edward Thomas, *tr. fr. German.* RB

Sun blazing slowly in its last hour, The. An Evening. Robert Mezey. NaP

Sun blooms in our bodies. Summer. Tom Marshall. NOBC

Sun brightly beam'd, the birds sweetly sang, The. (*LL*) Who Was It, Tell Me. Heine. TrJP

Sun Came, The. Etheridge Knight. PoBA

Sun Came Out in April, The. C. Day Lewis. MoBS

Sun came up, The. Rain Rain on the Splintered Girl. Ishmael Reed. PoBA

Sun cheers us for a pin-point, flicks, then westers. Mating Answer. Ronald Bottrall. PoA

Sun Children. Leslie Silko. VoR

Sun climbs down, The. November. Linda Hogan. BCF; SRLS

Sun-Day Hymn. Oliver Wendell Holmes. *See* Lord of All Being, Throned Afar.

Sun dazzle and black shadow. Mending the Adobe. Hayden Carruth. Poetsp

Sun descending in the west, The. Night. Blake. *Fr.* Songs of Innocence. BLPL; BoNaP; BoTP; CH; EnRP; FaBoBe; FaPON; FHYEP; MeMBP; OBEV; OxBChV; PoLF; WiR

Sun-Dial, The. Thomas Love Peacock. *Fr.* Melincourt. OBNC

Sun did not shine, The. "Dr. Seuss." *Fr.* Cat in the Hat, The. OFC

Sun dissolves, The. Mindoro. Ramon C. Sunico, *tr. fr. Spanish.* TSaS, *tr. by* Sunico Ramon C.

Sun does what it does because the earth tilts, The. (*LL*) Made in the Tropics. Vijay Seshadri. UTF

Sun doth [*or* does] arise, The. The Echoing [*or* Ecchoing] Green. Blake. *Fr.* Songs of Innocence. BoTP; CH; FHYEP; NAEL-2; NTP; OxAEP-2; PoE; UnPo; WiR

Sun drew off at last his piercing fires, The. Witchcraft: New Style. Lascelles Abercrombie. MoBrPo

Sun drops below the elms. Routes. Peter Everwine. NNaP

Sun drops luridly into the west, The. Augusta Webster. *Fr.* Circe. PeVV

Sun-Flower, The. Dora Greenwell. WPE

Sun frets, a fat wafer falling like a trap of failed mesh, The. Hole, Where Once in Passion We Swam. Dave Jeddie Smith. NoAM

Sun from the east tips the mountains with gold, The. Hunting Song. Paul Whitehead. *Fr.* Apollo and Daphne. OxBoLi

Sun God, The. Aubrey Thomas De Vere. OHCV

Sun-god was reclining on a couch of rosy shells, The. Sunset Picture. H. Cordelia Ray. CBWP-3

Sun goes down', The. Midsummer Night. Elizabeth Gould. BoTP

Sun goes down, and over all, The. Low Tide on Grand Pré. Bliss Carman. NOBC

Sun goes down for hours, taking more of her along, The. The Lady in the Pink Mustang. Louise Erdrich. HATNAP

Sun goes down in the dusty April night, The. An Evening When the Full Moon Rose as the Sun Set. Robert Bly. ArNa

Sun Going Down upon Our Wrath, The. Denise Levertov, *tr. fr. Japanese.* AIW

Sun had clos'd the winter-day, The. The Vision. Burns. OxBS

Sun had grown on lessening day, The. Ballad: The Sun Had Grown on Lessening Day. John Clare. EnVR

Sun had set, The;/ The leaves with dew. Keenan's Charge. George Parsons Lathrop. PAH

Sun had sunk beneath the west, The. The Ocean-Fight. *Unknown.* PAH

Sun had wheeled from Grey's to Dammer's Crest, The. The Burghers. Thomas Hardy. EBNV

Sun has climbed the hill, the day is on the downward slope, The. D. H. Lawrence. EaPr

Sun has come, I know, The. The Sun. W. J. Turner. MoBrPo

Sun has disappeared, The. *Unknown, tr. fr. Ghanaian.* EaPr

Sun has gone from the shining skies, The. A Summer Lullaby. Eudora S. Bumstead. BoTP

Sun has long been set, The. A Night in June. Wordsworth. BoTP

Sun has risen on the eastern brim of the world, The. The Song of Lo-fu. *Unknown, tr. fr. Chinese by* Arthur Waley. AWP

Sun Has Set, The. Emily Brontë. MeMBP; UnPo

Sun has set, the moon is in darkness, The. Swarming Mosquitoes. Mei Yao Ch'en, *tr. fr. Chinese by* Jonathan Chaves. SuSp

Sun has sunk 'neath yonder distant hill, The. Belshazzer's Feast. Eloise Bibb. CBWP-4

Sun hath twice brought forth[e] the tender green, The. The Earl of Surrey. SiPSBD

(Restless State of a Lover, The.) AAS; SiPS

Sun Heals, A. Jewel C. Latimore. JB

Sun, hung by a string, The. Diptych. Birago Diop, *tr. fr. French by* Ellen Conroy Kennedy. NegPo

Sun-Hunters, The. Mark O'Connor. NOBAu

Sun in Capricorn, The. Joyce Mansour, *tr. fr. French.* PBWP, *tr. by* Carol Cosman

Sun, in clownish yellow, but not a clown, The. Wallace Stevens. *Fr.* Esthétique du Mal. LiTM; NOBA

Sun in the mouth of the day. Envoi. Robley Wilson, Jr.. PBCAP

Sun is a huntress young, The. An Indian Summer Day on the Prairie. Vachel Lindsay. RFM

Sun is about to set when I board the boat, The. Sailing at Night on Flowing-sand River. Lin Hung, *tr. fr. Chinese by* Irving Y. Lo. SuSp

Sun is aloft!, The. (*LL*) Minnie and Winnie. Tennyson. OxBChV; TTTS

Sun is blazing and the sky is blue, The. Pink Dog. Elizabeth Bishop. NALW

Sun is blue and scarlet on my page, The. Falling Asleep over the Aeneid. Robert Lowell. MoAmPo; OxBA

Sun is bright, — the air is clear, The. It Is Not Always May. Longfellow. PWR

Sun is down, The. What the Passersby Said to the Lover Eloping with the Girl. Uraiyur Mutukorran, *tr. fr. Tamil by* A. K. Ramanujan. PLW

Sun is folding, cars stall and rise, The. The New World. Amiri Baraka. NoAM; NoP

Sun is going down, The. Aranda Song. *Unknown, tr. fr. Aranda by* T. G. H. Strehlow. CBAP

Sun is just appearing, The. Lyn Hejinian. UL

Sun is lord and god, sublime, serene, The. The Lake of Gaube. Swinburne. NAEL-2; OAEL-2

Sun is low, to say the least, The. The Sunset. Gelett Burgess. FaBoNo

Sun is nigh the verge, The. Soon we must part. A Walk. Hedwig Lachmann, *tr. fr. German by* Jethro Bithell. TrJP

Sun is not abed, when I, The. The Sun's Travels. Robert Louis Stevenson. FaPON

Sun is not in love with us, The. The Isles of Greece. Demetrios Capetanakis. GTBS-P

Sun is rising, The. Healing Song. *Unknown, tr. by* Frances Densmore. OBVE

Sun is set, and masked night, The. Robert Sidney. NoSic

Sun is shining in my backdoor, The. Myself When I Am Real. Al Young. PoBA

Sun is soon to rise as bright, The. Friedrich Rückert. *Fr.* Songs on the Death of Children. OBD

Sun is the blind eyes of statues gilded, The. The Sun. Andrew Oerke. PoA

Sun Is Up, The. John Shaw Neilson. FaBoMA

Sun is warm, the sky is clear, The. Stanzas Written in Dejection [December 1818], near Naples. Shelley. EnRP; FaBV; GTBS; GTBS-P; NAEL-2; NAWM-2; NoP; PoRA; TEP

Sun just up on the century's earliest equinox. Marches. Philip Booth. PFL

Sun leaves a virgin spot/ of joy., The. (*LL*) Making Chicago. Dennis Schmitz. LCAP

Sun like a sleepy giant, The. Narcolepsy. Maureen Owen. TTTS

Sun like an orange mousse through the trees. Dog Day Vespers. Charles Wright. LCAP

Sun makes music as of old, The. Prologue in Heaven [*or* The Chorus of the Archangels]. Goethe, *tr. by* Shelley. *Fr.* Faust. AWP; OBVE

Sun [*or* Sunne] may set and rise, The. Sir Walter Ralegh, *after the Latin of* Catullus. FaBoEE; NoSic; OBVE

(Lines from Catullus.) EnRePo; SiPS

(Sun May Set, The.) FaBoRV

Sun moon stars rain. (*LL*) Anyone Lived in a Pretty How Town. E. E. Cummings. CMoP; EBEvV; HAP; InPK; LiTA; LiTM; MeMAP; MoAB; MoAmPo; NAAL-2; NOBA; NoP; PoA; Poetr; PrIm; RB; TAP; TFi; TwCP; VGW

Sun now darts his fervid rays, The. Lines Written in the Dog-Days. William Woty. NOEC

Sun Now Risen, The. Johann Conrad Beissel. AH

Sun of Our Existence, The. Mrs. Henry Linden. CBWP-4

Sun, of whose terrain we creatures are, The. Solar Creation. Charles Madge. FaBoMo; OBMV; OxBTC

Sun on hillsides, wind on seas. Desolation. *Unknown, tr. fr. Welsh by* Aneirin Talfan Davies. OBWVE

Sun on the tree-tops no longer is seen, The. Queen Sabbath. Hayyim Nahman Bialik, *tr. fr. Hebrew by* Jessie Sampter. TrJP

Sun plants a foot in the pasture, The. Goree. Niyi Osundare. HBAPE

Sun/ proud Bessemer. World Winter. Earle Birney. GrPl

Sun revolving on his axis turns, The. The Copernican System. Thomas Chatterton. FaBoUs

Sun rises, The. In Fields of Summer. Galway Kinnell. BoNaP; RFM; VGW

Sun rises at the southeastern corner, The. Mulberry by the Path. *Unknown, tr. fr. Chinese by* Hans H. Frankel. SuSp

Sun [or Sunne] Rising, The. John Donne. BoLoP; CBLP; ClHu; EBEvV; EnRePo; ESCV; FF; FHYEP; GBL; HAP; HeIL; HeIP; InPS; InvP; JCP; LiTB; MeLP; NAEL-1; NIP; NOBE; NoP; NOSC; OAEL-1; PFP; PoE; PoEL-2; Poetr; PPP; SCV; SeCP; SeCV-1; TEP; TFi; TrGrPo; WeW

Sun rushed up the sky, The; the taxi flew. Parting as Descent. John Berryman. LiTA; MoAmPo

Sun sank in the thunderous sky of the town, The. Marriage. W. J. Turner. NOBAu

Sun scanned the river with its lidless, The. The Breakdown. Sherod Santos. SM

Sun set, but set not his hope, The. Character. Emerson. LiTA; OxBSP

Sun sets in night, and the stars shun the day, The. North American Death Song. Anne Hunter. ECWP

Sun sets in the cold without friends, The. Dusk in Winter. W. S. Merwin. NaP

Sun sets on the dike where I walk. A Song of "Hand-in-Hand." Ou-yang Hsiu, *tr. fr. Chinese by* Irving Y. Lo. SuSp

Sun sets, The. The wind moans. Ts'ai Yen, *tr. fr. Chinese by* Kenneth Rexroth *and* Ling Chung. *Fr.* Eighteen Verses Sung to a Tatar Reed Whistle. BoWoP; WPC; WPOW

Sun shines, The. Tommies in the Train. D. H. Lawrence. PoWW

Sun shines bright, but sadly, The. Autumn   Priscilla Jane Thompson. CBWP-2

Sun shines bright in the old Kentucky home, The. My Old Kentucky Home, [Good Night]. Stephen Collins Foster. AnAmPo; FaBoBe; FaBV; PoLF; TrGrPo

Sun shines high on yonder hill, The. The False Lover Won Back. *Unknown.* ESPB; OxBB

Sun Shines over the Mountain, The. *Unknown.* AmFP

Sun shone in my hut, The. He Who Has Lost All. David Diop, *tr. fr. French by* Anne Atik. TTY

Sun sinks softly to his ev'ning post, The. "Orpheus C. Kerr." *Fr.* Rejected "National Hymns," The. OBAL

Sun-son. Stonebone. Blackblitz. Eugene B. Redmond. *Fr.* Epigrams for My Father. ETG

Sun sought thy dim bed and brought forth light, The. Africa. Claude McKay. Son

Sun Spirit, The, *sels.* Ralph Chubb.
"At the time of puberty I had obsessions." PeHV

Sun still proud, the shadow still disdained, The. *(LL)* Follow Thy Fair Sun [Unhappy Shadow]. Thomas Campion. ElL; ELP; EnLoPo; EnRePo; LiTB; NOBE; NoP; NOSC; NoSic; PoEL-2; SCGP; UnPo

Sun stood still, The. The Day They Came for Our House. Don Mattera. PeSAV

Sun strikes gold the dirty street, The. Brest Left Behind. John Farrar. PAH

Sun struts over the asphalt world, The. Noon of the Sunbather. Marge Piercy. NMM

Sun-tanned men and women, toiling there together. Reapers. Mathilde Blind. WPE

Sun, that brave man, The. The Brave Man. Wallace Stevens. PFP; SAmP; SOTW

Sun that brief December day, The. Whittier. *Fr.* Snow-bound; a Winter Idyl [or Idyll]. AiP; AmPP; FaBV; GN; NAAL-1; NOBA; OxBA; TAP; TFi; TrGrPo; WiR
(Storm, The.) FaBV
(Winter Day.) TrGrPo
(Winter Idyl, A.) PFP

Sun that shines all day so bright, The. Night. *Unknown.* BoTP

Sun, the moon, the stars, the seas, the hills and the plains, The. The Higher Pantheism. Tennyson. EnVR; OHCV; WGRP

Sun, the rose, the lily, the dove, The. Love's Résumé. Heine, *tr. by* J. F. C. TrJP

Sun, the sun is King! *(LL)* Dawn. Joseph Kumbirai. PeSAV

Sun throat cut. *(LL)* Zone. Guillaume Apollinaire. SOTW

Sun through the window, The. The Mullins Farm. Richard H. W. Dillard. MT

Sun-treader, life and light be thine for ever! Robert Browning. *Fr.* Pauline. EPCY

Sun upon the lake is low, The. Datur Hora Quieti. Sir Walter Scott. GTBS; GTBS-P

Sun upon the Weirdlaw Hill, The. The Dreary Change. Sir Walter Scott. FaBoPP; NAEL-2; OAEL-2; OBNC

Sun Used to Shine, The. Edward Thomas. FaBoTw; OBF

Sun was black with judgment, and the moon, The. Femina Contra Mundum. G. K. Chesteron. OxAEP-2

Sun was bright when we went in, The. At the Theater. Rachel Field. FaPON

Sun was down, and twilight grey, The. In the Room. James Thomson ("B.V."). NOBVV; PeVV

Sun was now withdrawn, The. Damon and Cupid. John Gay. EnLoPo

Sun was shining on the sea, The. The Walrus and the Carpenter. "Lewis Carroll." *Fr.* Through the Looking-Glass. BeLS; BLPA; CBNP; EBEvV; FaBoBe; FaBoCo; FaBoNo; FaBV; FaPoB; FaPON; FiBHP; GN; LiTB; NAEL-2; NoAM; NOBL; NOBVV; OBSP; OHCV; OTCP; OxAEP-2; OxBChV; PeLV; PoRA; TEP; TFi

Sun was slow in arriving that morning, The. Creation. Trinity Site, New Mexico. 5:30 A.M., July 16th, 1945. Benjamin Saenz. AfAz

Sun Was Slumbering in the West, The. Thomas Hood. FiBHP

Sun went down behind yon hill, The. The Farmer's Boy. *Unknown.* OBET

Sun Went down in Beauty, The. George Marion McClellan. AAP

Sun went out just like that, The. Jackie Kay. *Fr.* Generations. NWP

Sun, when he enamels day, The. Praise of a Yellow Skin, The, or An Elizabeth in Gold. John Collop. NOSC

Sun, which doth the greatest comfort bring, The. A Letter to Ben Jonson. Beaumont *and* John Fletcher. BeJo

Sun which doth the greatest comfort bring[e], The. Mr. Francis Beaumont's Letter to Ben Johnson. Francis Beaumont.
(Francis Beaumont's Letter from the Country to Jonson.) SeCP

Sun whirls an axle on fire, The. Leonidas of Tarentum, *tr. fr. Greek by* Peter Levi. GrAn

Sun Wields Mercy, The. Charles Bukowski. MAT

Sun will never see you, The. On a Pet Grasshopper. Aristodicus of Rhodes, *tr. fr. Greek by* Kenneth Rexroth. PGA

Sun-Witch to the Sun, The. George Howe. NYBP

Sun, with his great eye, The. Daisy's Song. Keats. BoNaP

Sun Witness, The. Nurunnessa Choudhury, *tr. fr. Bengali by* Nurunnessa Choudhury *and* Paul Joseph Thompson. AIW

Sun woke me this morning loud, The. A True Account of Talking to the Sun at Fire Island. Frank O'Hara. HCAP; NNaP; PRA; RB; SOTW; TTTS

Sun Yat Sen Comes to Lodi. Alan Chong Lau. BCF

Sunbeam and zephyr were playing about, A. The Daisy's Mistake. Frances Sargent Osgood. AmWP

Sunbeam Said, Be Happy, The. Wordsworth. *Fr.* Recluse, The. FaBoRV

Sunbeams. Avner Trainin, *tr. fr. Hebrew by* Ruth Finer Mintz. MHP

Sunbeams stream forward, dawn boys, The. *Unknown, tr. fr. Apache Indian.* EaPr

Sunbeams streamed without, The. In the Morgue. Israel Zangwill. TrJP

Sunburned, with lustre of her own. *(LL)* To the State of Love; or, The Senses' Festival. John Cleveland. CBLP

Suncoming. Oliver La Grone. NBV

Sunday. George Herbert. GeHe; PeECV; SeCV-1; TrCP

Sunday. Josephine Miles. PoA

Sunday. James Schuyler. TTTS

Sunday. Ludwig Uhland, *tr. fr. German by* Philip L. Miller. RiWo

Sunday: A Fragment Transcribed from a Ms. in Chatterton's Handwriting. Thomas Chatterton. ECEV

Sunday Afternoon. Denise Levertov. IHMS

Sunday Afternoon. Philip Levine. NaP

Sunday afternoon and the water. Fording the River. Seamus Deane. PBCIP; PNI

Sunday Afternoon at Fulham Palace. Elizabeth Spires. BAP-89; NAmP90

Sunday Afternoon at the State Hospital. Marilyn J. Boe. LoHo

Sunday afternoon in late September, one of the last, A. Sunday Afternoon at Fulham Palace. Elizabeth Spires. BAP-89; NAmP90

Sunday Afternoon Service in St. Enodoc Church, Cornwall. Sir John Betjeman. NOCV

Sunday Afternoons. Yusef Komunyakaa. NAmP90

Sunday Afternoons. Anthony Thwaite. OxBTC

Sunday and sunlight ashen on the Square. The Self Unsatisfied Runs Everywhere. Delmore Schwartz. PoA

Sunday and the Cigarette Salesman. Barbara Helfgott Hyett. ETG

Sunday at Hampstead., *sels.* James Thomson ("B.V.").

Sunny Prestatyn. Philip Larkin. NoAM

Sunny shaft did I behold, A. Glycine's Song. Samuel Taylor Coleridge. *Fr. Zapolya.* CH; OBEV

(Song: "Sunny shaft did I behold, A.") MeMBP

Sunrise. Ben King. AnAmPo

Sunrise. Sidney Lanier. *Fr.* Hymns of the Marshes. PoEL-5

Sunrise. Mary Oliver. CrSp

Sunrise. H. Cordelia Ray. *Fr.* Idyl. BlSi; CBWP-3

Sunrise. Jim Tollerud. VoR

Sunrise Call, The. *Unknown, tr. by N. Barnes.* WTO

Sunrise Comes to Second Avenue. Thylias Moss. TRP

Sunrise in Summer. John Clare. FaBoPP

Sunrise on Rydal Water. John Drinkwater. LiTM

Sunrise on the Sea. Shakespeare. *Fr.* Midsummer Night's Dream, A. ChTr

Sunrise Sequence. *Unknown, tr. fr. Aborigine by Ronald M. Berndt. Fr.* Dulngulg Song Cycle, The. NOBAu

Sunrise Thought. H. Cordelia Ray. *Fr.* Group of Musings, A. CBWP-3

Sunrise . . . & toward the sunrise stands the village of the Bow People. Muu's Way; or Pictures from the Uterine World. *Unknown, tr. fr. Cuna Indian by Jerome K. Rothenberg.* STP

Sunrise Trumpets. Joseph Auslander. TrJP

Sunrise weather news, I kissed him & filled my pen and wept, The. *(LL)* White Shroud. Allen Ginsberg. PoBeRe

Sun's accomplice, the tree./ Maurice. *(LL)* Dusting. Rita Dove. HCAP; HeIP; LCAP; Poetr

Sun's bright orb, declining all serene, The. Ship Sets out, the. William Falconer. *Fr.* Shipwreck, The. OxAEP-1

Sun's Darling, The, *sels.* Thomas Dekker *and others.* Haymakers, Rakers. ELP

(Song.) NOSC

Sun's going down. Which is nothing new, The. "Heaven in Ordinarie." Daniel Wolff. SM

Suns have set and suns will rise. Keep Cool. Marcus Garvey. PBCV

Suns in a skein, the uncut stones of night. Roy Fuller. *Fr.* Mythological Sonnets. GTBS-P

Sun's low light splinters in a plastic gleam, The. On a Scooter. Desmond A. Greig. PeSA

Sun's Perpendicular Rays, The. William Lort Mansel. ChTr; FaBoEE

Sun's rays that shoot up, stretched out, The. An Old Song of Rejoicing. *Unknown, tr. fr. Maori by Margaret Orbell.* PeNZ

Sun's snow, conversing, lowly slides from limbs. To a Young Lady Swinging Upside Down on a Birch Limb over a Winter-swollen Creek. James H. Koch. GoYe

Sun's Travels, The. Robert Louis Stevenson. FaPON

Sunset. Hayyim Nahman Bialik, *tr. fr. Hebrew by Helena Frank.* TrJP

Sunset, The. Gelett Burgess. FaBoNo

Sunset, A. Samuel Taylor Coleridge. OxBSP

Sunset. E. E. Cummings. MoAmPo

Sunset, A. Mary Weston Fordham. CBWP-2

Sunset, A. Victor Hugo, *tr. fr. French by Francis Thompson. Fr.* Feuilles d'Automne. AWP

Sunset. Longfellow. BoTP

Sunset. Edwin Muir. ArNa

Sunset. H. Cordelia Ray. *Fr.* Idyl. BlSi; CBWP-3

Sunset. Lizette Woodworth Reese. AmWP

Sunset. Ella Wheeler Wilcox. AnAmPo

Sunset, a huge flower, wilts on the horizon, The. Flowers. Roo Borson. NOBC

Sunset after Rain. W. S. Merwin. PoA

Sunset and evening star. Crossing the Bar. Tennyson. BLRP; ChIV-2; ClHu; CoGr; DL; EBVV; EBVVPR; FaBoRV; FaBV; FaPoR; FF; HeIP; ImPo; LiTB; NAEL-2; NOBE; NOBVV; NoP; OAEL-2; OBEV; OBNC; PeECV; PlP; PoLF; PoRA; PWR; SoSe; TEP; TFi; TrCP; TrGrPo; WBLP; WGRP

Sunset and silence! A man: around him earth savage, earth broken. The Plower. Padraic Colum. MoBrPo

(Plougher.) PeIV

Sunset at Twin Lake. Anita Endrezze-Danielson. HATNAP

Sunset. Blue peaks vanish in dusk. Snow on Lotus Mountain. Liu Ch'ang-ch'ing, *tr. fr. Chinese by Kenneth Rexroth.* OHMPC

Sunset Frisko hilly tincan evening sitdown vision. *(LL)* Sunflower Sutra. Allen Ginsberg. AmPP; BCF; CoAP; HCAP; InPS; MAT; NAAL-2; NeAP; NOBA; PoBeRe; VCAP

Sunset from Omaha Hotel Window. Carl Sandburg. AiP

Sunset — God's face from which grief radiates. Sodom. Chaim Grade, *tr. fr. Yiddish by Joseph Leftwich.* TrJP

Sunset Horn. Myron O'Higgins. PoNe

Sunset in the Sea. Tom Hood. FaBoNo

Sunset is always disturbing. Afterglow. Jorge Luis Borges, *tr. fr. Spanish by Norman Thomas di Giovanni.* NYBP

Sunset/ molten bronze. Endless Union. Li Ch'ing-chao, *tr. fr. Chinese by C. H. Kwôck and Vincent McHugh.* PBWP

Sunset of the City, A. Gwendolyn Brooks. FaBoWP; LCAP; LPA; PBWP

Sunset on Calvary. *Unknown. See* Now Goeth [*or* goth *or* goothe] Sun [*or* Sonne *or* Sunne] under Wood.

Sunset over the Aegean. Byron. *Fr.* Corsair, The. OBNC

Sunset Picture. H. Cordelia Ray. CBWP-3

Sunset Song. *Unknown, tr. fr. Pueblo Indian by N. Barnes.* WTO

Sunset: the blaze of evening burns. Hospital Evening. Gwen Harwood. FaBoWP

Sunset, the cheapest of all picture-shows. Frederiksted, Dusk. Derek Walcott. NoAM

Sunset Thought. H. Cordelia Ray. *Fr.* Group of Musings, A. CBWP-3

Sunset Wings. Dante Gabriel Rossetti. FM

Sunsets. Carl Sandburg. MoAmPo

Sunset's mounded cloud, A. An Evening. William Allingham. EnLoPo; NOBVV

Sunshade, The. Thomas Hardy. OxBTC

Sunshine. Mother Goose. *See* Hick-a-more, Hack-a-more.

Sunshine after Cloud. Josephine D. Henderson Heard. CBWP-4

Sunshine and Music. *Unknown.* PoToHe

Sunshine and shadow play amid the trees. July. H. Cordelia Ray. CBWP-3

Sunshine, come softly here. Prayer for a Play House. Elinor Lennen. TrPWD

Sunshine let it be or frost. After St. Augustine. Mary Elizabeth Coleridge. TrPWD

Sunshine not yet through. *(LL)* Poem for Ben Barney. Leslie Silko. CDW; VoR

Sunshine of the Gods, The, *sels.* Bayard Taylor.

Sunshiny shower, A. *Unknown.* FaBoBe; OxNR; ReMoGo; RoPo

Sunstrike. Douglas Livingstone. PeSA

Sunt Leones. Stevie Smith. NoAM

Sunthin' in the Pastoral Line. James Russell Lowell. *Fr.* Biglow Papers, The.

Sunup until night. *(LL)* Little Lion Face. May Swenson. VBLP

Super-Brave. Teresa Whitman. LoHo

Super-cool/ ultrablack. But He Was Cool; or, He Even Stopped for Green Lights. Don L. Lee. BPo; MoP; PoBA

Super Flumina Babylonis. Swinburne. PoEL-5

Super-suburbia of the Southern Seas. Farewell to New Zealand. Wynford Vaughan-Thomas. NOBL; OBTV

Superb Lily, The. Robert Pinsky. AnAn

Superballs. Tom Clark. PRA

Supercilious nabob of the East, A. A Modest Wit. Selleck Osborn. BLPA

Supererogatory divinations one is. The Unknown. Denise Levertov. NAAL-2

Superfluous Were the Sun. Emily Dickinson. AnAmPo

Superintindint wuz Flannigan. Finnigin to Flannigan. Strickland W. Gillilan. FaBoBe

Superliminare. George Herbert. ESCV; NOSC; SeCP

Supermarket. Felice Holman. OTCP

Supermarket. Peter Meinke. PBCAP

Supermarket in California, A. Allen Ginsberg. AmPP; BCF; CoAP; HAP; HCAP; HeIL; HeIP; InPK; InPS; LiTM; NAAL-2; NaP; NeAP; NoAM; NOBA; PoBeRe; PoM; PrIm; SOTW; TAP; TFi; TwCP; UnPo; WeW

Supernatural Love. Gjertrud Schnackenberg. DiPo; NoAM; VCAP

Superscription, A. Dante Gabriel Rossetti. *Fr.* House of Life, The. EBVV; GTBS-P; NAEL-2; NoP; OAEL-2; OBNC; PoEL-5

Supersensual. Evelyn Underhill. WGRP

Superstition. Rebecca Gonzales. AfAz

Superstition. Minji Karibo. WPOW

Superstition. Martin Sorescu, *tr. fr. Romanian by Michael Hamburger.* PWE

Superstitions. Maggie Pogue Johnson. CBWP-4

Supervising Examinations. Sean Lucy. CIP

Supine in the rough grass. Exposure. Esther Cameron. BTR

Supper. Walter de la Mare. NYBP

Supper ("Her pinched grey body.") Walter de la Mare. OFC

Supper. Alison Fell. VBLP

Supper. William Soutar. OxBS

Supper after the Last, The. Galway Kinnell. NOBA

Supper at Apelles'/ was a garden-butcher's work. Ammianus, *tr. fr. Greek by Peter Jay.* GrAn

Supper for a Lion. Dorothy Aldis. ZA

Supper Is Na Ready. Burns. GBP

Supper is over, the hearth is swept, The. Sermon in a Stocking. Ellen A. Jewett. BLPA

Supplement, A. Benjamin Tompson. SCAP

Suppliant. Florence Earle Coates. TrPWD

Suppliant, The. Georgia Douglas Johnson. CDC; PoBA; PoNe; ShDr

Supplication. Joseph S. Cotter, Sr.. CDC; PoNe

Supplication, A. Abraham Cowley. *Fr.* Davideis. GTBS, III; GTBS-P, III

Supplication. Josephine Johnson. TrPWD

Supplication. Edgar Lee Masters. TrCP; TrPWD

Supplication. Edith Lovejoy Pierce. TrPWD

Supplication, A. Sir Thomas Wyatt. *See* Forget [*or* Fforget] not yet the tried intent.

Supplication of the Black Aberdeen. Kipling. BLPA

Supplied the epithalamy. (*LL*) Upon a Maid That Died [*or* Dyed] the Day She Was Married [*or* Marryed]. Meleager. AWP; OBD; OBVE

Support the green entablature of boys and dogs and grass. (*LL*) Manly Ferry. John Philip. NOBAu

Support Your Local Police Dog. Carter Revard. VoR

Supported by the ivy-covered wall. To An Aeolian Harp. Eduard Friedrich Mörike, *tr. fr. German by* Philip L. Miller. RiWo

Suppose. Phoebe Cary. BLPA; BLPL

Suppose a man were dying and this sound. Clive Wilmer. *Fr.* Antiphonal Sonnets. SCBI

Suppose he had been tabled at thy teats. Luke XI: Blessed Be the Paps Which Thou Hast Sucked. Richard Crashaw. BXAP; JCP
  (Blessed Be The Paps which Thou Hast Sucked.) NOSC
  (Blessed Be The Paps.) ChIV-2

Suppose his body was the meticulous layering. Suppose Your Father Was a Redbird. Pattiann Rogers. MT

Suppose I can convince myself this world. Summons. David Rivard. NAmP90

Suppose it, for the last time, in that moment. The Coming of the White Man. Patrick Anderson. *Fr.* Poem on Canada. MoCV

Suppose it is nothing but the hive. Davis Matlock. Edgar Lee Masters. *Fr.* Spoon River Anthology. LiTA; LiTM

Suppose me dead; and then suppose. Swift. *Fr.* Verses on the Death of Doctor Swift [D.S.P.D., Occasioned by Reading a Maxim in Rochefoucauld]. NOBE; NOEC; OxBoLi, *abr.; PeLV; PoEL-3; TEP

Suppose, my little lady. Suppose. Phoebe Cary. BLPA; BLPL

Suppose one thing. For Those Who Always Fear the Worst. *Unknown.* NBLV

Suppose the dead could crown their wit. A Responsory, 1948. Thomas Merton. VGW

Suppose they had cheated me out of my. Remember Times for Sandy. Carolyn M. Rodgers. JB

Suppose This Moment Some Stupendous Question. Alden Nowlan. NOBC

Suppose we are standing together a minute. April. Jean Valentine. TAP

Suppose you screeve? or go cheap-jack? Villon's Straight Tip to All Cross Coves. W. E. Henley, *after* Villon. AWP; CBNP; FaBoCo; InvP; OxAEP-2

Suppose you were dreaming about your family. Benign Neglect/ Mississippi, 1970. Primus St. John. PoBA

Suppose Your Father Was a Redbird. Pattiann Rogers. MT

Suppose your parents had called you Dirk. A Name. Maxine Chernoff. UL

Suppose your whole life. An Everlasting Once. Theodore Weiss. AnAn

Suppose you're a solo native here. Solo Native. Thomas Lux. LCAP

Supposing all the things on the playground. On a Cold Autumn Day. Bonnie Nims. TLR

Supposing we could just go on and on as two. Sunflower Sonnet Number Two. June Jordan. SM; Son

Suppression. Jayne Cortez. NBV

Supremacy. E. A. Robinson. NoAM

Supreme Death. Douglas Dunn. FaBoMo

Supreme Fortune Falls Soonest. Robert Herrick. CaPo

Supreme my holdings, greater yet my need. John Berryman. *Fr.* Dream Songs. CRP

Supreme Sacrifice, The. John S. Arkwright. WGRP

Supremer Sacrifice, The. Suzanne Gardinier. CBAP

Supremes done gone, The. Memorial. Sonia Sanchez. BlSi

Sure. Naomi Shihab Nye. MT

Sure. Hugo Williams. CBLP

Sure a Poor Man. *Unknown, tr. fr. Hawaiian by* M. K. Pukui *and* A. L. Korn. WTO

Sure an' twas a/ fine st. patrick's day. Saint Patrick's Day, 1973. Wendy Rose. CDW

Sure, if those Babel-builders had thought good. On the Babel-Builders. Francis Quarles. ChIV-1

Sure, It was so. Man in those early days. Corruption. Henry Vaughan. ESCV; GeHe; JCP; NAEL-1; NOCV; NOSC; OAEL-1; Prf; SeCP; SeCV-1

Sure John and I are more than quit. (*LL*) To John I ow'd great obligation. Matthew Prior. FaBoCo; FaBoEE; OBVE

Sure Lord, there is enough in thee to dry. Sonnet. George Herbert. GeHe; NOSC

Sure never was picture drawn more to the life. The Virginia Song. *Unknown.* PAH

Sure, Saul as little looked to be a king. On Saul and David. Francis Quarles. ChIV-1

Sure some malignant star diffused its ray. The Power of Destiny. Mary Whateley. ECWP

Sure Test, A. *Unknown. See* If you are a gentleman.

Sure the last end. Peace the End of the Good Man. Robert Blair. *Fr.* Grave, The. OxAEP-1

Sure there's a lethargy in mighty woe. Dryden. *Fr.* Threnodia Augustalis. IMW

Sure, there's a tie of bodies! and as they. Henry Vaughan. GeHe

Sure thing/ I'm a spirit! *Unknown, tr. fr. Chippewa Indian by* Jerome K. Rothenberg. STP

Sure, this world is full of trouble. Ain't It [*or* It's] Fine Today. Douglas Malloch. BLPA; WBLP

Sure thou didst flourish once! and many springs. The Timber. Henry Vaughan. FaBoRV, *abr.;* GeHe, *abr.;* NoP; OBEV; SeCP; SeCV-1

Sure to catch you sooner or later. Who's the next? (*LL*) The Undertaker's Horse. Kipling. FaBoNo; FM

Surely a mouse! (*LL*) The Old Woman. Beatrix Potter. GoJo; NTCP; PDV

Surely among a rich man's flowering lawns. Ancestral Houses. W. B. Yeats. *Fr.* Meditations in Time of Civil War. LiTB; OAEL-2

Surely in my eyes that light is now lost. The Photograph of Myself. Jon Anderson. AmPA

Surely is death to come here. Tlanusi' Yi, the Leech Place. Gladys Cardiff. CDW

Surely My Soul . . . . Jacob Cohen, *tr. fr. Hebrew by* I. M. Lask. TrJP

Surely now I'm out of danger. To the Tune — "But I Fancy Lovely Nancy." Patrick Carey. CBLP

Surely one of my finest days, I'd just. Extract from Memoirs. Howard Nemerov. OxBC

Surely, so alike, airborne wind gave birth. Spirits of Movement. James Berry. NBrP

Surely there is a mine for silver. Bible, *O.T. Fr.* Job. NAWM-1, *abr.* (Price of Wisdom.) TrGrPo

Surely They're Just So Large. Irving Feldman. *Fr.* All of Us Here. VCAP

Surely those eyes are of marble. Icon. Ephim G. Fogel. BTR

Surely you paused at this roadside oasis. A Garage in Co. Cork. Derek Mahon. DiPo; PBCIP

Surely you stay my certain own, you stay. Love Note. Gwendolyn Brooks. VBLP

Surely you would not ask me to have known. Question to Life. Patrick Kavanagh. MoBrPo

Surf. Lillian Morrison. NTCP

Surf-casting. W. S. Merwin. NOBA

Surf is a partial deafness islanders. Polynesia. Allen Curnow. PeNZ

Surface of the pond was mostly green, The. The Lotus Flowers. Ellen Bryant Voigt. MT

Surfer, The. Judith Wright. WPE

Surfers at Santa Cruz. Paul Goodman. FF

Surge, The. Molly Peacock. NAmP90

Surge and thunder of the Odyssey, The. (*LL*) The Odyssey. Andrew Lang. OBEV; OBNC; OtMeF; PoLF; PoRA

Surge of spirit that goes with using an axe, The. Felling a Tree. Ivor Gurney. FaBoVe

Surgeons must be very careful. Emily Dickinson. MeMAP; SAmP; TAP

Surgery. Kenneth Pitchford. GLP

Surgical Ward: Men. Robert Graves. FaBoMo

Surging sea of human life forever onward rolls, The. A Hundred Years from Now. Mary A. Ford. BLPA

Surnames to Be Avoided in Marriage. *Unknown.* FaBoUs

Surplice, The. David Scott. PWE

Surprise. Bible, Apocrypha, *tr. fr. Spanish.* TSaS, *tr. by* Aurelio Major

Surprise at Ticonderoga, The. Mary A. P. Stansbury. PAH

Surprised by Evening. Robert Bly. CAPP; NaP; VGW

Swallows over the Camp. Uys Krige, *tr. fr. Afrikaans by the author* and Jack Cope. PeSA

Swallows travel to and fro. Robert Louis Stevenson. EBVV

Swam too far out: the swell took him. Elegy for a School-Friend. Augustus Young. BIrV

Swamp. Roberta Hill Whiteman. VoR

Swamp Fox, The. William Gilmore Simms. BeLS; FaBoBe; PAH

Swamp reeds murmur the song, The. Marsh Leaf. David Wagoner. PoA

Swampstrife and spatterdock. The Marsh. W. D. Snodgrass. BoNaP

Swampy State of Illinois, The. Excelsior. *Unknown.* BXAP

Swan, The. Mei-Mei Berssenbrugge. OpBo

Swan, A. Ibsen, *tr. fr. Norwegian by* Philip L. Miller. RiWo

Swan. D. H. Lawrence. CMoP; PoE

Swan. Edward Lowbury. GTBS-P

Swan. Leslie Norris. OBAP

Swan, The. W. R. Rodgers. PNI

Swan, The. Theodore Roethke. VGW

Swan, The. *Unknown. See* Swan swam [or swan] over the sea.

Swan, The. *Unknown, formerly at. to* Cynewulf, tr. by Geoffrey Grigson. *Fr.* Riddles (Exeter Book). PoE

Swan and Shadow. John Hollander. InPK; NoP; PoA; VCAP

Swan and the Goose, The. Aesop, *tr. fr. Greek by* William Ellery Leonard. AWP; FaPON

Swan Bathing, The. Ruth Pitter. MoBrPo

Swan has a neck that is curly and long, The. Necks. Rowena Bastin Bennett. SiSoPo

Swan has sung his dying lay, The. (*LL*) Es fällt ein Stern herunter. Heine. AWP

Swan saith, The. (*LL*) The Bereaved Swan. Stevie Smith. FaBoNo; FaBoTw

Swan: Silent is my dress when I step across the earth. *Unknown, formerly at. to* Cynewulf, *tr. fr. Anglo-Saxon. Fr.* Riddles (Exeter Book). ASW, *tr. by* Kevin Crossley-Holland
(Swan, The: "Silent is my dress when I step across the earth.") OBAP, *tr. by* Kevin Crossley-Holland

Swan Song. Swinburne. *Fr.* Garden of Proserpine, The. AWP; BLPA; BLPL; FaBoRV; FaBV; FaPoR; HAP; LiTB; NAEL-2; NOBE; NOBVV; NoP; OBNC; OtMeF; PoE; PoEL-5; PoRA; SCV; TrGrPo

Swan swam [or swan] over the sea. *Unknown.* OxNR
(Swan, The.) ChTr; FaPON; ReMoGo

Swan swims So Bonny, The. *Unknown.* OBET

Swan, tell my your old story. Kabir, *tr. fr. Hindi by* Czeslaw Milosz and Robert Hass. EnlH

Swan, unbelievable bird, a cloud floating. Swan. Leslie Norris. OBAP

Swank luncheon thrown in Union Square by San Francisco, A. The Chronicle. Robert Glück. ETG; NGP

Swann had gone to the estate that afternoon to tell his. Norman Dubie. *Fr.* Duchess' Red Shoes, The. AnAn

Swann has visited the Duc and Duchess de Guermantes. Norman Dubie. *Fr.* Duchess' Red Shoes, The. AnAn

Swans. Lawrence Durrell. MoBrPo

Swans, The. Edith Sitwell. CMoP; WPE

Swans. Leonora Speyer. FYAP

Swan's Feet, The. E. J. Scovell. FaBoWP; OxBTC

Swans in Flight. Miroslav Holub, *tr. fr. Czech by* Ewald Osers. FaBoPV

Swans Mating. Michael Longley. IIP; PNI

Swans of Vadstena, The. Ralph Gustafson. MoCV

Swans Sing before They Die. Samuel Taylor Coleridge. FaBoCo

Swansea Bay. Julia Ann Hatton. AngWe

Swansong. Carol Muske. AmPA

Swarm, The. Sylvia Plath. NALW

Swarm of Bees. (*LL*) As I went owre the Hill o' Hoos. *Unknown.* GBP

Swarm of bees in May, A. Proverb. *Unknown.* FaBoBe; OxNR; ReMoGo
(Swarm of bees in May, A.) FaBoBe; OxNR

Swarming Bees, The. James Laughlin. VGW

Swarming Mosquitoes. Mei Yao Ch'en, *tr. fr. Chinese by* Jonathan Chaves. SuSp

Swarming over the damp ground with pocket lenses. Sweet Everlasting. Ellen Bryant Voigt. AnAn; MT

Swarms of flies crowd my sick horse. Ballad of Ching Mountain. Meng Chiao, *tr. fr. Chinese by* Stephen Owen. SuSp

Swart Italian with his breast of fur, The. Public Beach (Long Island Sound). Christopher Morley. NBLV

Swart swarthy smiths besmattered with smoke. The Blacksmiths. *Unknown.* RB; WiR
(Swarte smeked smethes smatered with smoke.) FaBoVe; MiEL

Swarte-smeked Smithes. *Unknown. See* Sooty, swart smiths, smattered with smoke.

Swarthy bee is a buccaneer, The. A More Ancient Mariner. Bliss Carman. AnAmPo; OBAL

Swarthy little statue, The. Naked War. Michael Heffernan. BXAP

Swarthy youth rambled, A. Pushkin. "Anna Akhmatova," *tr. fr. Russian by* Stanley Kunitz *with* Max Hayward. AnAn

Swawk swawk. (*LL*) The Cutting Prow. Edward Sanders. PoBeRe

Sway. Steve Carey. UL

Sway. Denis Johnson. SM

Sway. Louis Simpson. NoAM

Sway song. Eye of God. Jim Tollerud. VoR

Swearest thou, ungracious boy, henceforth ne'er look on me. Villanious and Abominable Falstaff. Shakespeare. *Fr.* King Henry IV, Pt. I. CBCK; NAEL-1

Swearing an oath to Demeter. Asclepiades, *tr. fr. Greek by* Sam Hamill. InMo

Sweat. Richard Hoffman. ETG

Sweat begins to ooze from Compass's forehead. Get Angry, Compass. Inoue Michiko, *tr. fr. Japanese by* Kenneth Rexroth *and* Ikuko Atsumi. WPJ

Sweat-House Ritual No. 1. *Unknown, tr. fr. Omaha Indian by* Jerome K. Rothenberg *from* Alia Fletcher *and* Francis La Flesche. STP

Sweat is a style of the body. John Tranter. *Fr.* Crying in Early Infancy. NoAM

Sweat like drops of blood run down, The. Dark Was the Night. *Unknown.* AmFP

Sweat-lodge. Hilton Obenzinger. BCF

Sweat Song. Peter Blue Cloud. VoR

Sweater, The. Gregory Orr. TRP

Sweating It Out on Winding Stair Mountain. Jim Barnes. CDW

Swedenborg's Skull. Vernon Watkins. FaBoTw

Swedes. Edward Thomas. OAEL-2; RB

Swedish Angel. Winfield Townley Scott. LiTM

Swedish Lesson. Barton Sutter. SM

Sweeet silver trumpets,/ Jesus! (*LL*) When Sue Wears Red. Langston Hughes. TTY

Sweeney Agonistes. T. S. Eliot. UnPo
Sels.
"Under the bamboo."
"Well here again that don't apply." FaBoVe
"You'll be my little seven stone missionary!"

Sweeney among the Nightingales. T. S. Eliot. AmPP; AnAmPo; CMoP; FaBoMo; HAP; HeIP; InvP; LiTA; LiTM; MoP; NAAL-2; NAEL-2; NoAM; NOBA; NOBE; NoP; OBMV; OxBA; Poetr; PPP; TFi; WeW

Sweeney Astray., *sels.* Seamus Heaney.

Sweeney Erect. T. S. Eliot. OxBTC; VGW

Sweeney in Articulo. "Myra Buttle." *See* Sunday is the dullest day, treating.

Sweeney, Old and Phthisic, among the Hippopotami. David Cummings. BXAP

Sweeney Praises the Trees. *Unknown, tr. fr. Irish by* Seamus Heaney. RB

Sweeney Redivivus., *sels.* Seamus Heaney.
"I stirred wet sand and gathered myself." NoAM
"Road ahead, The." TOF

Sweeney to Mrs. Porter in the Spring. L. E. Sissman. NYBP

Sweeniad, The, *sels.* "Myra Buttle."
"Sunday is the dullest day, treating." FaBoPa
(Sweeney in Articulo.) BXAP

Sweep. Rodney Jones. MT

Sweep Me through Your Many-Chambered Heart. Diane Ackerman. NIP

Sweep the house. The Dead Baby. William Carlos Williams. NAAL-2

Sweep the house clean. William Carlos Williams. MoAB; MoAmPo; SAmP

Sweep thy faint strings, Musician. The Song of the Shadows. Walter de la Mare. CMoP; MoBrPo; TrGrPo

Sweeper collects dry leaves with his broom, The. Time Swept Up. Vasco [or Vasko] Popa, *tr. fr. Serbo-Croatian by* Anne Pennington. *Fr.* Raw Flesh. PoSu

Sweeper of Ways, The. Howard Nemerov. HCAP

Sweepers, The. William Whitehead. ECEV, *ll.* 1–38, *sl. diff. vers.*; NOEC

Sweeping Gesture, The. John Ash. BAP-90

Sweeping up confessions. (*LL*) Sunrise Comes to Second Avenue. Thylias Moss. TRP

Sweet, a delicate white mouse, A. The Waltzer in the House. Stanley Kunitz. ErPo; GoJo; NYBP

Sweet, acidulous, down-reaching thrill, A. Ode on [*or* to] a Jar of Pickles. Bayard Taylor. BXAP; FaBoPa

Sweet after showers, ambrosial air. Tennyson. *Fr.* In Memoriam A. H. H. EBVV, *abr.*; OAEL-2, *abr.*; PeECV, *abr.*

Sweet Afton. Burns. *See* Flow Gently, Sweet Afton.

Sweet age of blest illusion! blooming boys. Written on Seeing Her Two Sons at Play. Henrietta O'Neill. ECWP

Sweet Amarillis, by a spring's. Upon Mistress Elizabeth Wheeler under the Name of Amarillis. Robert Herrick. CaPo

Sweet Amoret in all her prime. *(LL)* Amoret. Mark Akenside. OBEV

Sweet and calm the breezes stealing. Sabbath Bells. Josephine D. Henderson Heard. CBWP-4

Sweet and Low [Sweet and Low]. Tennyson. *Fr.* Princess, The. BLPL; BoTP; FaBoBe; FaPON; FHYEP; NAEL-2; OxBChV; PlP; SCGP; TrGrPo
 (Lullaby: "Sweet and low, sweet and low.") PoLF

Sweet and sad/ like love overwhelmed. Yosano Akiko, *tr. fr. Japanese by* Kenneth Rexroth *and* Ikuko Atsumi. WPJ

Sweet-and-Twenty. Shakespeare. *See* Oh [*or* O] mistress mine, where are you roaming?

Sweet anecdotes of love —. *(LL)* An Anecdote of Love. John Clare. NOBVV

Sweet Angels come, and sing the Rest. *(LL)* On the Glorious Assumption of Our Blessed Lady. Richard Crashaw.

Sweet antidote to sorrow, toil and strife. To a Segar. Samuel Low. OBAL

Sweet Apple. James Stephens. CMoP

Sweet Are the Days. George Santayana. *Fr.* Sonnets. AnAmPo

Sweet are the thoughts that savo[u]r of content. Maesia's Song. Robert Greene. *Fr.* Farewell to Folly. CTC; PoToHe; UnPo
 (Mind Content, A.) CBCK; EiL
 (Poor Estate, The.) TrGrPo
 (Song: "Sweet are the thoughts that savour of content.") PoEL-2

Sweet are the ways of death to weary feet. Lord De Tabley. *Fr.* Medea. OBEV

Sweet are the whispers of yon pine that makes. The Death of Daphnis. Theocritus [*or* Theokritus], *tr. by* Charles Stuart Calverley. *Fr.* Idylls. AWP
 (Sweet is the whispering of that pine tree, goatherd. HePo, *tr. by* Barbara Hughes Fowler

Sweet are thy strains, celestial bard. To Cowper. Anne Brontë. EPCY

Sweet Armida tooke this charge on hand, The. Tasso, *tr. fr. Italian by* Edward Fairfax. *Fr.* Godfrey of Bulloigne; or, The Recoverie of Jerusalem. OBVE

Sweet, at this morn I chanced. Buen Matina. Sir John Salusbury. EiL

Sweet Auburn, loveliest village of the plain. The Deserted Village. Goldsmith. *Fr.* Deserted Village, The. BeLS; ECEV; EnRP; FHYEP; ImPo; LiTB; NOBE; NOEC; NoP; OAEL-1; OxAEP-1; PoEL-3; TEP; TFi
 (Village, The.) TrGrPo

Sweet Auburn! parent of the blissful hour. Goldsmith. *Fr.* Deserted Village, The. BeLS; EBEV; EnRP; NOEC; NoP; OAEL-1; PoEL-3; TEP

Sweet baby sleep: What ail[e]s my dear? A Hymn L: Rocking Hymn. George Wither. *Fr.* Hallelujah; or, Britain's Second Remembrancer. SeCV-1
 (Rocking Hymn, A.) OxBChV

Sweet baked apple dappled cinnamon speckled sin of mine. Love Child — a Black Aesthetic. Everett Hoagland. BPo

Sweet basil. Having Replaced Love with Food and Drink. Diane Wakoski. NAs

Sweet, be not proud of those two eyes. To Dianeme. Robert Herrick. BeJo; CaPo; GTBS; GTBS-P; JCP; NOBE; NOSC; OBEV; SeCV-1; TrGrPo

Sweet beast, I have gone prowling. W. D. Snodgrass. MoAmPo; NYBP; SM

Sweet beats of jazz impaled on slivers of wind. Walking Parker Home. Bob Kaufman. Jaz; PoBA

Sweet beguilings. The Cheat. Joseph Beaumont. NOSC

Sweet Be'mi'ster, that bist a-bound. Be'mi'ster. William Barnes. EBVV

Sweet Benedict, whilst thou art young. To His Little Son Benedict from the Tower of London. John Hoskyns. OxBChV
 (To His Son Benedict Hoskyns.) NOSC

Sweet Betsey from Pike. *Unknown.* AmFP; AS; FaBoBa; OBAL; OxBoLi

Sweet bird that shunn'st the noise of folly. Milton. *Fr.* Il Penseroso. AWP; CH; FHYEP; GTBS; GTBS-P; HAP; HoPM; ImPo; JCP; LiTB; NoP; NOSC; OAEL-1; OBEV; PPP; TEP; TFi; TrGrPo

Sweet birds! that sit and sing amid the shady valleys. Phyllis. Nicholas Breton. TrGrPo
 (Pastoral, A: "Sweet Bird! that sit and sing amid the shady valleys.") EiL

Sweet blackbird is silenced with chaffinch and thrush. Winter. Christina Rossetti. BoTP

Sweet boy, gentle boy. Pushkin, *tr. fr. Russian by* Valery Pereleshin. PeHV

"Sweet boy," she says, "this night I'll waste in sorrow." Shakespeare. *Fr.* Venus and Adonis. BeLS; ErPo

Sweet candle-smoke wreathed. After Mass. Tony Flynn. PWE

Sweet Catullus's all-but-island, olive-silvery Sirmio! *(LL)* Frater Ave atque Vale. Tennyson. ChTr; EBVV; FaBoPP; GTBS-P; HAP; InPS; NAEL-2; NoP; OBTV; OxBSP

Sweet Chance, that led my steps abroad. A Great Time. W. H. Davies. AngWe; ImPo; LiTB; MoBrPo

Sweet cheat gone, The. *(LL)* The Ghost. Walter de la Mare. CBLP; CMoP; ELP; EnLoPo; LiTM; MoAB; MoBrPo; NOBE; OAEL-2; OxBTC

Sweet Chestnut. John Greening. PWE

Sweet children amid the apple boughs. On the Picture of a Child. H. Cordelia Ray. CBWP-3

Sweet Content. Thomas Dekker *and others*. *See* Art thou poor, yet hast thou golden slumbers?

Sweet corrall lips, where Nature's treasure lies. Richard Barnfield. *Fr.* Sonnets. PeHV

Sweet Country Life, A. *Unknown.* OBET

Sweet country life, to such unknown. The Country Life, to the Honored Mr. Endymion Porter. Robert Herrick. BeJo

Sweet Cupid, Ripen Her Desire. *At. to* William Corkine. EnRePo; OxBSP

Sweet cyder is a great thing. Great Things. Thomas Hardy. GTBS-P; NOBE

Sweet Cynthia, take the book away. To Cynthia, Not to Let Him Read the Ladies' Magazines. P. M. Hubbard. FiBHP

Sweet daughter of a rough and stormy sire. Ode to Spring. Anna Laetitia Barbauld. OxAEP-1

Sweet day, so cool, so calm, so bright. Virtue. George Herbert. AWP; CH; ClHu; ELP; GeHe; HAP; HeiP; InPS; InvP; JCP; NAEL-1; NOBE; NOCV; NoP; NOSC; OAEL-1; OBD; OBEV; PoE; PoRA; PPP; SCGP; SoSe; TEP; TFi; TrGrPo; WGRP
 (Vertue.) FaBoRV; MeLP; PeECV; SeCP; SeCV-1

Sweet, deep sense of mystery filled the wood, A. In Cool, Green Haunts. Mahlon Leonard Fisher. WeW

Sweet disorder in the dress, A. Delight in Disorder. Robert Herrick. BeJo; CaPo; ClHu; BEEv; EBEvV; EnLoPo; ErPo; FaBV; FF; GGP; GTBS; GTBS-P; HAP; HeiP; InPK; InPS; JCP; LiTB; NAEL-1; NIP; NOBE; NoP; NOSC; OAEL-1; OBEV; OxAEP-1; PeLV; PoE; Poetr; PoRA; PPP; PrIm; SCGP; SeCP; SeCV-1; TEP; TFi; TrGrPo; TRP; WeW
 (Sweet Disorder.) AWP; BLPL; ImPo
 (Sweet disorder in the dresse, A.) FaPoB

Sweet Disorder in the Dress, A. Harry Hooton. NOBAu

Sweet Dreams. Ogden Nash. OTCP

Sweet dreams, form a shade. Blake. *Fr.* Songs of Innocence. EnRP; FHYEP; OBCP

Sweet dreams, sweet memories, sweet taste of earth. Cemetery Nights. Stephen Dobyns. SV

Sweet earth, he ran and changed his shoes to go. Arrangements with Earth for Three Dead Friends. James Wright. NIP

Sweet Echo, sweetest Nymph, that livest unseen. Echo. Milton. *Fr.* Comus; a Masque Presented at Ludlow Castle. ELP; FHYEP; OAEL-1; OBEV
 (Lady Sings, The.) NOBE
 (Lady's Song.) TrGrPo

Sweet elfin music comes to me. A Dream of Elfland. H. Cordelia Ray. CBWP-3

Sweet especial rural scene. *(LL)* Binsey Poplars (Felled 1879). Gerard Manley Hopkins. BoNaP; EBVV; ELP; EnVR; FaBoPP; InPS; Mes; NAEL-2; NoAM; NoP; RB

Sweet Ethel. Linda Piper. BlSi

Sweet Eva! shall I send thee forth. Elizabeth Oakes Smith. AmWP

Sweet Everlasting. Ellen Bryant Voigt. AnAn; MT

Sweet father I have shrunk a bit. Father Father Son and Son. Jon Swan. NYBP

Sweet fever of wind-troubled flowers. Shepherd's Flute. Branko Miljkovic, *tr. fr. Serbo-Croatian by* Charles Simic. HSix

Sweet flocks, whose soft enamel's wing. Flying Fowl, and Creeping Things, Praise Ye the Lord. Isaac Watts. ChIV-1

Sweet flower, that art so fair and gay. *Unknown, tr. fr. French by* John Addington Symonds. *Fr.* Medieval Norman Song. AWP

Sweet floweret, pledge o' meikle love. On the Birth of a Posthumous Child, Born in Peculiar Circumstances of Family Distress. Burns. NAs

Sweet for a little even to fear, and sweet. Erotion. Swinburne. PoEL-5

Sweet fore-warning?, A. *(LL)* Hester. Charles Lamb. EnRP; GTBS; GTBS-P; OBEV

Sweet friend, when you and I are gone. Patience with the Living. Margaret E. M. Sangster. PoToHe

Sweet gem of infant fairy-flowers! To an Infant Daughter. John Clare. NAs

Sweet gentle angel, not that I aspire. To Miss M ———, Written by Moonlight, July 18, 1782. Sir Samuel Egerton Brydges. Son

Sweet girl graduate, lean as a fawn, A. Nancy Hanks, Mother of Abraham Lincoln. Vachel Lindsay. CMoP

Sweet, harmles[s] livers [or lives]! (on whose holy leisure). The Shepherds [or Shepheards]. Henry Vaughan. ChIV-2; ESCV

Sweet heart,/ A morning, climbing in its brass. Letter from an Island. John Malcolm Brinnin. TAP

Sweet Highland Girl, a very shower. To the [or a] Highland Girl of Inversneyde. Wordsworth. EnRP; GTBS; GTBS-P

Sweet homes wherein to live and die. (LL) My Love. James Russell Lowell. BLPL; FaBoBe

Sweet Hour of Prayer. William W. Walford. BLRP; WBLP

Sweet if thou wilt be. Come Turn to Mee, Thou Pretty Little One. Unknown. CoMu

Sweet, if you like and love me still. His Farewell to His Unkind and Unconstant Mistress. Francis Davison. ElL

Sweet in goodly fellowship. There's No Lust like to Poetry. Unknown, tr. by John Addington Symonds. AWP

Sweet in her green dell the flower of beauty slumbers. George Darley. OBEV

(Serenade of a Loyal Martyr.) NOBE; OBNC

(Song.) OxAEP-2

Sweet in your antique body, not yet young. To a Child. Wilfred Owen. Son

Sweet in your sight the fiery stride. Unknown, tr. fr. Irish by Thomas Kinsella. Fr. Exile of the Sons of Uisliu. NOIV

Sweet infancy! The Rapture. Thomas Traherne. GeHe; NOSC

Sweet Innisfallen. Thomas Moore. OBNC

Sweet is the breath of Morn, her rising sweet. Milton. Fr. Paradise Lost. EPCY

(World Beautiful, The.) GN

Sweet is the evening twilight; but, alas! Bridal of Helon. Maria Gowen Brooks. Fr. Zophiël. AmWP

"Sweet is the fruit," say. Cillactor, tr. fr. Greek by Edward Lucie-Smith. GrAn

"Sweet is the holiness of youth," so felt. Edward VI. Wordsworth. Fr. Ecclesiastical Sonnets. EPCY

Sweet is the scholar's life. The Scholar's Life. Unknown, tr. fr. Irish by Thomas Kinsella. NOIV

Sweet is the time for joyous folk. Hora Christi. Alice Brown. TrPWD; WGRP

Sweet is the whispering of that pine tree, goatherd. Theocritus [or Theokritus]. See Sweet are the whispers of yon pine that makes.

Sweet is true love tho' given in vain, in vain. The Song of Love and Death. Tennyson. Fr. Idylls of the King. OBNC

Sweet it is to be a child. Tabitha. FaBoVe

Sweet it is to see the sun. Every Day Thanksgiving Day. Harriet Prescott Spofford. OHIP

Sweet Jane. Unknown. AmFP

Sweet Killen Hill. Tom MacIntyre. See Flower of the flock.

Sweet kiss, thy sweets I fain would sweetly indite. Stella's Kiss. Sir Philip Sidney. Fr. Astrophel and Stella. AAS; CBCK; ESo, sl. abr.; GGP; HeIL, Sonnets, I-CVIII and 11 Songs; NoSic; Poetr; SCGP, Sonnets, I-CVIII and 11 Songs; SiPS, Sonnets, I-CVIII and 11 Songs; SiPSBD, Sonnets, I-CVIII and 11 Songs

Sweet land of song, thy harp doth hang. The War Ship of Peace. Samuel Lover. PAH

Sweet, Let Me Go! Unknown. ElL; InvP; OxBSP; TrGrPo

Sweet, let us love enjoy. Love Play. William Cavendish. ErPo

Sweet Levinsky. Allen Ginsberg. NBLV

Sweet Like a Crow. Michael Ondaatje. CBCK; TSaS

Sweet little bell. Unknown, tr. fr. Old Irish. NOIV

Sweet little bird in russet coat. The Autumn Robin. John Clare. BoTP

Sweet Love dead. (LL) An Evening. William Allingham. EnLoPo; NOBVV

Sweet Love, mine only treasure. Where His Lady Keeps His Heart. "A. W." CTC; EiL

Sweet Love, Renew Thy Force, Be It Not Said. Shakespeare. Fr. Sonnets. PoLF; SCGP

Sweet lovely infant, innocently gay. Oh My Own Little Daughter, Four Years Old. Unknown. ECWP

Sweet Loving Friendship. Peter Bellamy. OBET

Sweet Lullaby, A. Nicholas Breton. See Come, little babe, come, silly soul.

Sweet Lydia, take this mask, and shroud. A Mask for Lydia. Thomas Randolph. BeJo

Sweet maid, if thou wouldst charm my sight. A Persian Song of Hafiz. Hafiz, tr. fr. Persian by Sir William Jones. AWP

Sweet Mary was a servant girl. Edwin in the Lowlands Low. Unknown. AmFP

Sweet Meat Has Sour Sauce; or, The Slave-Trader in the Dumps. William Cowper. ECEV; NOEC; OBSV

Sweet mermaid of the incomparable eyes. The Mermaid. Ben King. AnAmPo; OBAL

Sweet Mother! rare in gifts of tenderness! To My Mother. H. Cordelia Ray. CBWP-3

Sweet Mountains — Ye tell Me no lie. Emily Dickinson. NALW

Sweet mouth, that send'st a musky-rosed breath. Joshua Sylvester. EnLoPo

Sweet Muse, Descend. Isaac Watts. NOBE

Sweet Music's Power. John Fletcher and William Shakespeare. See Orpheus with his lute made trees.

Sweet my musings used to be. Mot eran dous miei cossir. Arnaut Daniel, tr. by Harriet Waters Preston. AWP

Sweet nature, give me holy dreams. At Nature's Shrine. H. Cordelia Ray. CBWP-3

Sweet Nicarete, who served Athene's shuttle. Nicarchos, tr. fr. Greek by Peter Porter. GrAn

Sweet "No! no!" with a sweet smile beneath, A. A Love-Lesson. Clément Marot, tr. fr. French by Leigh Hunt. AWP

Sweet Nosegay, A, or Pleasant Posy. Isabella Whitney. WPE

Sels.

"Do not account that for thine own."

"Gold savours well, though it be got."

"In loving, each one hath free choice."

"Little gold in law will make, A."

"Present day we cannot spend, The."

"Seek not man to please, for that."

"Such poor folk as to law do go."

Sweet nymph, come to thy lover. Unknown. NoSic

Sweet o' the Year, The. George Meredith. BoNaP

Sweet peace, where dost thou dwell? I humbly crave. Peace. George Herbert. AWP; ChTr; ELP; ESCV; GeHe; NOCV; NOSC; TEP

Sweet Peas. Keats. Fr. I Stood Tiptoe [upon a Little Hill]. EnRP; FaPON; FHYEP; GN

Sweet Peril. George Macdonald. BLPA; FaBoBe

Sweet Phosphor tricks to a smile the brow of heaven. All's Right with the World. Gerald Massey. EBVV

Sweet Pity, Wake. Unknown. EiL

Sweet poet of the woods, a long adieu! On the Departure of the Nightingale. Charlotte Smith. WoRP

Sweet Rain. Tony Hoagland. NAmP90

Sweet Rivers of Redeeming Love. John A. Granade. AH

Sweet Robinette. Unknown. CoMu

Sweet Rose, Fair Flower. At. to Shakespeare. Fr. Passionate Pilgrim, The. EiL

Sweet rose [or Sweit rois] of virtue [or vertew] and of gentleness [or gentilnes]. To a Lady[e]. William Dunbar. EBEV; GBL; MeEL; OBEV; OxBS; PeLV

Sweet, sacred hill! on whose fair brow. Mount of Olives. Henry Vaughan. GeHe

Sweet Saints grant I live not long, The. (LL) Riding Together. William Morris. EnVR; NOBE; OAEL-2

Sweet semi-circled Cynthia played at maw. John Taylor. Fr. Odcomb's Complaint. EiL

(Mockado, Fustian, and Motley.) FaBoNo

(Sonnet in Praise of Mr. Thomas the Deceased.) CBNP

Sweet Sensibility! thou soothing power. Hannah More. Fr. Sensibility; a Poetical Epistle. ECWP

Sweet September. George Arnold. GN

Sweet serene sky-like Flower. To Lucasta: The Rose. Richard Lovelace. BeJo; SeCV-1

Sweet she was, as kind a love. She Smiled like a Holiday. Unknown. OxBoLi

Sweet Silence after Bells! Christopher John Brennan. NOBAu

Sweet silence after bells. (LL) Sweet Silence after Bells! Christopher John Brennan. NOBAu

Sweet sleep, that makes more short the night. (LL) The Country Life, to the Honored Mr. Endymion Porter. Robert Herrick. BeJo

Sweet Slug-a-Bed. Unknown. FaBoCo

Sweet smell of earth and easy rain on. Sleeping Out with My Father. Gibbons Ruark. ArOW; MT

Sweet smiling, and sweet spoken. (LL) To Sally. John Quincy Adams, after Horace. AWP; OBAL

Sweet smiling village, loveliest of the lawn. Goldsmith. *Fr.* Deserted Village, The. BeLS; EnRP; FaBoEH; NOEC; NOIV; NoP; OAEL-1; PoEL-3; TEP

Sweet Solitude, thou placid queen. Solitude. Hannah More. *Fr.* Search after Happiness, The. WBLP

Sweet soul, which in the April of thy years. William Drummond of Hawthornden. JCP

Sweet soul, which now with heavenly songs dost tell. To the Marquess of Piscat's Soul. Henry Constable. NoSic

Sweet sounds, oh, beautiful music, do not cease! On Hearing a Symphony of Beethoven. Harry M. Meacham. LiTA; LiTM; MoAB; MoAmPo; TrGrPo

Sweet Spenser, sweetest bard; yet not more sweet. Robert Southey. EPCY

Sweet Spirit, comfort me! (*LL*) His Litany to the Holy Spirit. Robert Herrick. BeJo; BLPL; ELP; JCP; NOSC; PeECV; PoLF; TEP

Sweet Spirit of Sleep, who brings peace and rest. *Unknown.* EaPr

Sweet spouse, you must presently troop and be gone. Imitation of Martial, Book II Ep, An 105. "Captain H––." NOEC

Sweet Spring, thou turn'st with all thy goodly train. Spring Bereaved 2. William Drummond of Hawthornden. OBEV
(Sonnet.) EiL
(Sweet Spring.) Son

Sweet Stay-at-Home. W. H. Davies. CH

Sweet stream, that dost with equal pace. On His Mistress Drown'd. Thomas Spratt. EnLoPo

Sweet stream, that winds through [or thro'] yonder glade. To a Young Lady. William Cowper. GTBS; GTBS-P
(Addressed to a Young Lady.) EnRP

Sweet Suffolk Owl. At. to Thomas Vautor. CH; ChTr; EBEV; EiL; EnRePo; FaBoRV

Sweet Surprises. Sarah Doudney. BoTP

Sweet Swan of Avon! what a sight it were. Ben Jonson. *Fr.* To the Memory of My Beloved Master William Shakespeare [and What He Hath Left Us]. BeJo; ChTr; EnRePo; EPCY; JCP; LiTB; NoP; NOSC; OAEL-1; OxAEP-1; TrGrPo

Sweet sweet Robinette all the shepherds do declare. Sweet Robinette. *Unknown.* CoMu

Sweet, sweet, sweet, let me go. *Unknown.* GBL

Sweet sweet sweet sweet tea. (*LL*) Susie Asado. Gertrude Stein. NoAM; SOTW; TAP

Sweet sweet sweet sweet sweet tea. Susie Asado. Gertrude Stein. NoAM; SOTW; TAP

Sweet Teviot! on thy silver tide. A Father's Notes of Woe. Sir Walter Scott. *Fr.* Lay of the Last Minstrel, The. OBNC

Sweet Thames I honour thee, not for thou art. Richard Barnfield. *Fr.* Sonnets. PeHV

Sweet then the ploughman's slumbers, hale and young. The Ploughman's Horse. Robert Bloomfield. *Fr.* Winter. ECEV

Sweet Thing Is Marriage, A. Christine de Pisan, *tr. fr.* French by Helen R. Lane. VBLP

Sweet, thou art pale. The Three Enemies. Christina Rossetti. TrCP

Sweet, though short, our. The Silver Flask. John Montague. CIP; PNI

Sweet-tied-tight-in-the-middle. His Praises. Swidi-Nonkamfela Mhlongo, *tr. fr.* Zulu by Elizabeth Gunner. PeSAV

Sweet timber land. Homing. Arna Bontemps. CDC

Sweet to the morning traveller. The Traveller's Return. *Unknown.* BoTP

Sweet trees who shade this mould. *Unknown, tr. fr. Spanish* by James Mabbe. GBL

Sweet Trinity, The. *Unknown.* AmFP

Sweet Trinity; or, The Golden Vanity, The. *Unknown.* OBET

Sweet Trinity (The Golden Vanity), The. *Unknown.* See There was a gallant ship, and a gallant ship was she.

Sweet Unsure. Sir Walter Ralegh. SiPS

Sweet upland, to whose walks, with fond repair. To Hampstead. Leigh Hunt. EnRP

Sweet Violets. *Unknown.* NoP

Sweet Violets, Love's Paradise. *Unknown. See* Sweet Violets.

Sweet voice of the Garb. Suibne Geilt. NOIV

Sweet waft their rounds those tuneful brothers five. Balsham Bells. Kenrick Prescot. NOEC

Sweet Was the Song. *Unknown.* NOCV

Sweet was the sound, when oft at evening's close. The Village. Goldsmith. *Fr.* Deserted Village, The. BeLS; EnRP; IIP; NOEC; NoP; OAEL-1; PeIV; PIP; PoEL-3; TEP

Sweet were the day [or dayes], when thou didst lodge with Lot. Decay. George Herbert. ESCV; SCGP; SeCP; SeCV-1

Sweet were the joys that both might like and last. Sweet Unsure. Sir Walter Ralegh. SiPS

Sweet [*or* Swete] were the sauce would please e[a]ch kind of tast[e]. In Commendation of George Gascoigne's Steel Glass. Sir Walter Ralegh. SiPS

(Walter Rawley [*or* Ralegh] of the Middle Temple, in Commendation of the Steel[e] Glass[e].) AAS; SiPSBD

Sweet western wind, whose luck it is. To the Western Wind. Robert Herrick. CaPo; OBEV; SeCV-1

Sweet Will. Philip Levine. LCAP; VCAP

Sweet William. *Unknown. See* Sailor's Life, A.

Sweet William ("A sailor's life is a merry life.") *Unknown.* OBET

Sweet William and May Margaret. *Unknown. See* Whan bells war rung, an mass was sung.

Sweet William he married [him] a wife. The Wife Wrapt in Wether's Skin. *Unknown.* AmFP; ESPB, F *vers.*

Sweet William he would a-wooing ride. Fair Margaret and Sweet William *Unknown.* ESPB; (B *vers*); OBET

Sweet William rode up to the old man's gate. Earl Brand. *Unknown.* AmFP

Sweet william, silverweed, sally-my-handsome. A Spell for Sleeping. Alastair Reid. NTP

Sweet William's Farewell to Black-eyed [or ey'd] Susan. John Gay. AmFP, *folk vers.*; BeLS; BoLoP; CBLP; NOEC

Sweet William's Ghost *or* Sweet William and May Margaret. *Unknown.* AWP; CH; ESPB

Sweet William's Ghost. *Unknown.* ScCV

Sweet William's Ghost. *Unknown.* AWP; ESPB, A, B, F, *and* G *vers.*

Sweet William's gone over seas. Lord William; or, Lord Lundy. *Unknown.* ESPB

Sweet Willie. *Unknown.* OxBB

Sweet Willie was a widow's son. Willie and Lady Margerie [*or* Maisry]. *Unknown.* ESPB; OxBB

Sweet, winsome May, coy, pensive fay. May. H. Cordelia Ray. CBWP-3

Sweeter Far than the Harp, More Gold than Gold. "Michael Field." OBMV; PeVV

Sweeter Saint I Serve, A. Sir Philip Sidney. *See* Phoebus farewell, a sweeter saint I serve.

Sweetest heresy received, The. Emily Dickinson. CBLP

Sweetest lives are those to duty wed, The. Reward of Service. Elizabeth Barrett Browning. BLPA; FaBoBe

Sweetest Love, I Do Not Go. John Donne. AWP; BoLoP; EiL; ELP; EnRePo; ESCV; FHYEP; HeiP; InPS; InvP; JCP; MeLP; NOBE; NoP; NoSic; OAEL-1; PFP; PoEL-2; SeCP; SeCV-1; TEP; TFi; TrGrPo

Sweetest of all childlike dreams. The Vanishers. Whittier. AnAmPo

Sweetest of sweets, I thank you: when displeasure. Church-Music[k]. George Herbert. ESCV; GeHe; OxBSP; SeCV-1

Sweetest Saviour, if my soul. A Dialogue. George Herbert. GeHe; OBEV; SeCV-1
(Dialogue.) NOSC

Sweetest Thing, The. *Unknown, tr. fr. Susu* by Ulli Beier. TTY

Sweetest time of all my life to deem in thinking spent, The. (*LL*) Of a Contented Mind. Thomas, Lord Vaux. EiL; EnRePo

Sweetgrass. Maurice Kenny. HATNAP

Sweetheart. Phil Hey. GOYP

Sweetheart/ when you break thru. Song for Baby-O, Unborn. Diane Di Prima. PoBeRe

Sweetly Empty Woods. Sir Philip Sidney. *Fr.* Arcadia. CBCK; NoSic; SiPSBD

Sweetly-favored face, The. Canzonetta: Of His Lady in Absence. Giacomino Pugliesi, *tr. fr. Italian* by Dante Gabriel Rossetti. AWP

Sweetly hath Dorcas of Lycaenis learnt. Meleager, *tr. fr. Greek* by Peter Whigham. GrAn

Sweetly (my Dearest) I left thee asleep. John Saffin. SCAP

Sweetness. *Unknown, tr. fr. Irish* by John Montague. BIrV

Sweetness and wit, they're but *Mummy*, possessed. (*LL*) Love's Alchemy [*or* Alchemie]. John Donne. ESCV; NAEL-1; NoP; OAEL-1; PoE; SeCP

Sweetness of England, The. Elizabeth Barrett Browning. *Fr.* Aurora Leigh. OxAEP-2

Sweetness of Nature, The. *Unknown, tr. fr. Irish* by Frank O'Connor. IIP; PeIV; TIRV

Sweetness of poverty like this, The. Aspiration. Mário de Andrade, *tr. fr. Portuguese* by John Nist. TTY

Sweet'st in the close! (*LL*) Come, virgin tapers of pure wax. Richard Crashaw. NOCV

Swell foams where they float and crawl, The. Girls Bathing, Galway 1965. Seamus Heaney. InPS

Swell Idea, A. Steve Kowit. UL

Swell me a bowl with lusty wine. Ben Jonson. *Fr.* Poetaster, The. BeJo

Swell My Net Full. *Unknown.* OxBSS

Swell the Anthem, Raise the Song. Nathan Strong. AH

Swell'd with our late successes on the foe. Dryden. *Fr.* Annus Mirabilis. EBEV

Swelling with boundless happiness. *(LL)* Evening in the Garden Clear after Rain. Ch'u Ch'uang I. OHMPC

Swell's Soliloquy. *Unknown.* FiBHP

Swept all my pride away, and trembling I forgave! *(LL)* Forgiveness. Whittier. TrCP

Swerve, The. William Stafford. SM

"Swerve to the left, son Roger," he said. The Judgement of God. William Morris. PeVV

Swerving east, from rich industrial shadows. Here. Philip Larkin. CMoP; PoE

Swet Jesus. Friar Michael of Kildare. NOIV

Swet Jesus/ Is cum to us. Welcome! Our Messiah. *Unknown.* MeEL

Swete Jesu, king of blisse. *Unknown.* MiEL

Swete sone, reu on me. *Unknown.* MiEL

Swetnam, the Woman-Hater, *sels. Unknown.* Ding Dong. EIL

Swich fyn hath, lo, this Troilus for love! Chaucer. *Fr.* Troilus and Criseyde [*or* Criseide]. EnVB; NOCV

Swift, *sels.* Thomas Caulfield Irwin. "It was a dim October day." BIrV

Swift. Delmore Schwartz. PoA

Swift as a spirit hastening to his task. The Triumph of Life. Shelley. NAEL-2; OAEL-2; PoEL-4

Swift cold and deep. *(LL)* Charon's Cosmology. Charles Simic. HCAP; NoP

Swift fleet the billowy clouds along the sky. Charlotte Smith. *Fr.* Montalbert. BoWoP; WPE

Swift Floods. Kata Szidónia Petröczi, *tr. fr. Hungarian by* Laura Schiff. WPOW

Swift had pains in his head. January 1940. Roy Fuller. LiTM (War Poet.) HoPM

Swift had sailed into his rest. Swift's Epitaph. W. B. Yeats. CMoP; OBVE

Swift is't in pace, light poiz'd, to look in clear. Description of a New England Spring. John Josselyn. SCAP

Swift Love, Sweet Motor. Hildegarde Flanner. WPE

Swift red flash, a winter king, The. The Dance. Hart Crane. *Fr.* Bridge, The. LiTA; LiTM; MoAB; MoAmPo; NAAL-2; OxBA

Swift shot the curlew 'thwart the rising blast. Ode on Lord Macartney's Embassy to China. William Shepherd. NOEC

Swift stream in the high mountains, dropping dental, lateral, A. The River That Flows through Our Land. Jeremy Cronin. PeSAV

Swift through the yielding air I glide. The Lark. *Unknown.* NOSC

Swift to the western bounds of this wide land. On the Completion of the Pacific Telegraph. Jones Very. TAP

Swiftly and out of sight is borne the brave corpse. *(LL)* The Beautiful Swimmer. Walt Whitman. PeHV

Swiftly Arose. Walt Whitman. *Fr.* Song of Myself. AmPP; LiTA; MoAmPo, *abr.*; NOBA; OxBA; Prf; SOTW, *much abr.*; TrCP, *abr.*

Swiftly re-light the flame, Hilda Doolittle ("H. D."). *Fr.* Tribute to the Angels. NALW

Swiftly walk o'er the western wave. To Night. Shelley. AWP; EnRP; FHYEP; MeMBP; NAEL-2; NoP; OAEL-2; OBNC; PlP; PoLF; PoRA; TEP; TFi; TrGrPo; WiR
(Night.) OBEV
(To the Night.) CH; GTBS; GTBS-P

Swifts. Glyn Jones. AngWe

Swift's Epitaph. W. B. Yeats. CMoP; OBVE

Swim staring at a night-mare doom. *(LL)* Cold-blooded Creatures. Elinor Wylie. OxBSP

Swimmer. Gladys Cardiff. CDW

Swimmer. Robert Francis. WeW

Swimmer, The. Brendan Kennelly. PBCIP

Swimmers, The. Allen Tate. InPS; MoAmPo; NoAM; NOBA

Swimmer's Moment, The. Margaret Avison. NOBC

Swimming. Byron. *Fr.* Two Foscari, The. GN

Swimming. Clinton Scollard. FaPON

Swimming. Swinburne. *Fr.* Tristram of Lyonesse. GN

Swimming by Night. James Merrill. NYBP; SM; VGW

Swimming Chenango Lake. Charles Tomlinson. FaBoMo; MoP; NoAM

Swimming Lady; or, A Wanton Discovery, The. *Unknown.* ErPo

Swimming Lesson, The. Mary Oliver. CAPP

Swimming Pool. Maria Teresa Horta, *tr. fr. Portuguese by* Suzette Macedo. PBWP

Swinburne, old Swinburne, silly old Swinburne. Sister Swallow to Swinburne. Mary Holtby. UV

Swine com jingling doun Pelton lonin, The. Pigs o' Pelton. *Unknown.* GBP

Swine gobble dead men's flesh. Han-shan, *tr. fr. Chinese by* Edward H. Schafer. SuSp

Swineherd. Eiléan Ní Chuilleanáin. BIrV; CIP; FaBoWP; WPOW

Swing, The. Mary I. Osborn. BoTP

Swing, The. Robert Louis Stevenson. FaBoBe; GoJo; NTCP; PDV; SiSoPo; TEP; TLR

Swing dat hammer — hunh. Southern Road. Sterling A. Brown. BPo; PoBA

Swing Low, Sweet Chariot. *Unknown.* GBP

Swing Low, Sweet Chariot. *Unknown.* FaPON; UnPo

Swing Low, Sweet Chariot. *Unknown.* AnAmPo

Swing over the Calm Source of Our Names, The. Milorad Pavic, *tr. fr. Serbo-Croatian by* Charles Simic. HSix

Swing Song, A. William Allingham. FaPON; MoShBr; OTCP; TLR

Swinging. Irene Thompson. BoTP

Swinging. *Unknown.* OxNR

Swinging Goddess — / Sally Ride; First American Woman Astronaut, The. Lynn Lonidier. SRLS

Swinging on a swing. *(LL)* Silver Nakedness in Calumet City. Connie Deanovich. UTF

Swinging swinging the, The, The, The. The Swinging Goddess — / Sally Ride; First American Woman Astronaut. Lynn Lonidier. SRLS

Swirl and smash of waves against the legs. Mutoscope. Elizabeth Spires. NAmP90

Swirl of water dominated the plain, The. The Blue-Hole. Charles G. Bell. GrPl

Swirl sleeping in the waterfall! Chomei at Toyama. Basil Bunting. OxBTC

Swirling spring. Young Girl. Ricarda Huch, *tr. fr. German by* Janine Canan *and* Deidre Lashgari. WPOW

Swirling, swirling — aloeswood-scented smoke. Young Noble at Night's End; a Song. Li Ho, *tr. fr. Chinese by* Maureen Robertson. SuSp

Switch Blade; or, John's Other Wife, The. Jonathan Williams. NeAP

Switch on lights yellow as the sun. City Midnight Junk Strains. Allen Ginsberg. PRA

Switch on the Night. Ray Bradbury. OBSP

Switchback. Edith Sitwell. PBWP

Switchblade. Michael Ryan. BAP-90; NAmP90

Switzerland, *sels.* Matthew Arnold.
Absence. EnVR
Dream, A. EnVR; GBL; GTBS-P; OBTV
Farewell. EnVR; MeMBP
Lake, The. EnVR
Parting. EnVR
Solution: To Marguerite
(To Marguerite.) EnVR
Terrace at Berne, The. EnVR; OBTV
To Marguerite — Continued. SoSe
(To Marguerite, in Returning a Volume of the Letter of Ortis.) EnVR
To My Friends, Who Ridiculed a Tender Leave-Taking. EnVR

Switzerland. Alfred Denis Godley. OBTV

Switzerland. Anthony Thwaite. OBTV

Swollen river sang through the green hole, The. The Sleeper in the Valley. Rimbaud, *tr. by* Robert Lowell. *Fr.* Eighteen-Seventy. OBWP
(There's a green hollow where a river sings.) AWP, *tr. by* Ludwig Lewisohn

Someone is vigilant like a serpent. First Idiom. Reed Bye. UL

Swoon. Andrew Crozier. VaA

Sword, The. Abu Bakr, *tr. fr. Arabic by* A. J. Arberry. TTY

Sword, A. Karin Boye, *tr. fr. Swedish by* Joanna Bankier. WPOW

Sword and the Sickle, The. Blake. *See* Sword sang on the barren heath, The.

Sword in length a reaping-hook amain. King Harald's Trance. George Meredith. EBNV; PeVV

Sword is a cold bride. Yuk!, The. Michael Foley. *Fr.* True Life Love Stories. PNI

Sword of Surprise, The. G. K. Chesteron. MoBrPo

Sword of Tethra, The. William Larminie. *Fr.* Moytura. PeIV

Sword sang on the barren heath, The. Blake. *Fr.* Gnomic Verses. FaBoEE; TrGrPo
(Sword and the Sickle, The.) ChTr

Sword Swallower. Sean Murphy. PeIV

Sword was sheathed, The: in April's sun. The Vow of Washington. Whittier. PAH

Swordfish Tooth, The. Cynthia Zarin. UTF

Swordscape, tombscape, flame ploughed. After the Fall. Gloria Escoffery. PBCV

Swore, but too late, he shouldn't catch him twice. (*LL*) The Crow and the Fox. La Fontaine. AWP

Sycamore Tree, The. *Unknown*. AmFP

Sycophantic Fox and the Gullible Raven, The. Guy Wetmore Carryl. BLPA; FiBHP; NBLV; OBCA

Sydney. Robert Harris. NOBAu

Sydney and the Bush. Les A. Murray. DiPo

Sydney Cove, 1788. Peter Porter. NoAM

Syllables disintegrate ingrate alphabets. Phyllis Webb. *Fr.* Kropotkin Poems, The. NOBC

Sylphs! on each oak-bud wound the wormy galls. The Protection of Plants. Erasmus Darwin. *Fr.* Economy of Vegetation, The. FaBoUs

Sylva, *sels*. Abraham Cowley.
To His Mistress. NOSC; OxAEP-1

Sylvae, *sels*. Statius, *tr. fr. Latin*.
"Too harsh the man who setting bounds to grief." PeHV

Sylvan Delights. Pope. *Fr.* Pastorals. NOBE

Sylvan Revel, A. Edward Cracroft Lefroy, *after the Greek of* Theocritus. *Fr.* Echoes from Theocritus. AWP

Sylvester's Dying Bed. Langston Hughes. NoAM; Poetr; SAmP; UnPo

Sylvia. Samuel Croxall. NOEC

Sylvia. Robert Lowell. NaP

Sylvia the fair, in the bloom of fifteen. Dryden. EBEV; ErPo
(Song.) OxAEP-1

Sylvia Town. Anne Carson. *Fr.* Life of Towns, The. BAP-90

Sylvia's Death. Anne Sexton. LCAP; NAAL-2; NALW

Sylvie and Bruno., *sels*. "Lewis Carroll."
Mad Gardener's Song, The. BLPL; CBNP; FaBoCo; FaBoNo; FiBHP, 6 sts.; OxBChV; WiR

Sylvie and Bruno Concluded, *sels*. "Lewis Carroll."
King-Fisher [*or* King-Fisher's] Song, The. CBNP; FaBoNo
Little Birds ("Little birds are playing"). FaBoNo; OxBoLi; PeLV
Pig-Tale, A. WiR
(Melancholy Pig, The.) FaPON

Sylvius, your hands near my mouth are heady flowers. Marguerite Burnat-Provins, *tr. fr. French by* Cassia Berman. BoWoP

Sym of Lyntoun, be the ramis horn. King Berdok. *Unknown*. OxBS

Symbol of life, me with such faith endow! (*LL*) Ode to a Butterfly. Thomas Wentworth Higginson. FaBoBe

Symbols. Christina Rossetti. NALW

Symbols. W. B. Yeats. OBMV

Symbols of Gross Experience. C. Day Lewis. *Fr.* Oh Dreams, Oh Destinations. Son

Symbolum. Goethe, *tr. fr. German by* Tom Paulin. FaBoPV

Symmetry of alleyways and courtyard. Entrance to the Old Cracow Ghetto. David Zucker. BTR

Symon's Lesson of Wisdom for All Manner of Children. *Unknown*. OxBChV

Sympathy. Paul Laurence Dunbar. AAP; CDC; PoBA; PoNe

Sympathy. Reginald Heber. BeLS

Sympathy. L. A. J. Moorer. CBWP-3

Sympathy, a Welcome, A. John Berryman. GrPl; NYBP

Symphony, The. Sidney Lanier. AmPP; LiTA

Symphony in Yellow. Oscar Wilde. EBVV; FaBoPP; MoBrPo; NoAM; NOBVV; OxBSP

Symphony No. 3, in D Minor. Jonathan Williams. *Fr.* Mahler. VGW

Symposium, The, *sels*. Leah Goldberg, *tr. fr. Hebrew by* Robert Alter.
"Outside the cats are wailing." PBWP

Symptoms of Love. Robert Graves. BoLoP

Syn I fro Love. Chaucer. EnVB

Synagogue, The, *sels*. Christopher Harvey.
"What Church is this? Christ's Church. Who builds it?" EPCY

Synagogue in Samarkand, A. S. J. Litherland. NWP

Syndrome. Robert Louthan. PFL

Synekdechestai. Constance M. Schmid. GoYe

Syng a song of Saxons. Old-Saxon Fragment. *Unknown*. CBNP

Synopsis of the Great Welsh Novel. Harri Webb. AngWe

Syntax of the Mind Grips, The. Quincy Troupe. NBV

Synthesizing Several Abstruse Concepts with an Experience. Carol Poster. BXAP

Syphilis surge and crack use raise AIDS fears. Less Than Kind. Rachel Hadas. UnDi

Syren Songs, *sels*. George Darley.
Mermaidens' Vesper-Hymn, The. GBL; NAEL-2; OBNC; PoEL-4
(Siren Chorus.) BIrV; FaBoRV
Sea-Ritual, The. BIrV; OBNC; WiR

(Deadman's Dirge.) CH

Syrens' Song, The. William Browne. *See* Steer hither, steer your wingéd pines.

Syringa. John Ashbery. HCAP; NoAM; VCAP

Syringe cloud of aspiration, The. Arthur Hugh Clough. EnVR

Syrinx. John Lyly. *See* Pan's Syrinx was a girl[e] indeed.

Syrinx. James Merrill. HCAP

System, The. Charles Simic. PRA

System. Robert Louis Stevenson. PWR; TEP

Systems Alert. Marael Johnson. NGP

Szechuan Boatman's Song. Ts'ai Ch'i-chiao, *tr. fr. Chinese by* Hualing Nieh. LHF

T

T-Bar. P. K. Page. NoAM; NOBC

T' devil tak t' pynot an' God save me. (*LL*) Against the Magpie. *Unknown*. GBP

T. E. Lawrence Poems, The. Gwendolyn MacEwen. NOBC
Sels.
There Is No Place to Hide
Void, The

T. H. Blake. *See* Thy [*or* Your] friendship oft has made my heart to ache [*or* ake].

'T is he alone that lives and reigns! (*LL*) Guilielmus Rex. Thomas Bailey Aldrich. AnAmPo

T. R. Donald Hall. PoA

T. S. Eliot. W. H. Auden. OBAL

T. S. Eliot. Robert Lowell. NoAM; NOBA

T. S. Eliot is quite at a loss. W. H. Auden. PeLi

T' snow is witherin' off'n th' gress. The Drained Cup. D. H. Lawrence. CBLP

T, U, turkey, T, U, ti. *Unknown*. RoPo

T.V. (1). Anselm Hollo. UL

'T were folly still to hope for higher Heaven. (*LL*) Oh! that my young life were a lasting dream! Poe. AmPP; MeMAP; OxBA; Poetr, *ll*. 1–12; TAP

Tabernacle. D. H. Lawrence. ChIV-1

Tabernacle Thought, A. Israel Zangwill. TrJP

Table, The. Michael Heffernan. PoA

Table-Birds. Kenneth Mackenzie. NOBAu

Table is spread, the lamp glitters and sighs, The. The Expected Guest. Sidney Keyes. PoWW

Table Manners. Gelett Burgess. OBCA

Table Manners. *Unknown*. OxBLMV

Table of Contents. Henry Lawes, *tr. fr. Italian by* Peggy Forsyth. CBNP

Table Richly Spread, A. Milton. *Fr.* Paradise Regained [*or* Regain'd]. FaBoCh

Table Rules for Little Folk[s]. *Unknown*. FaBoUs; OxBChV

Table Talk, *sels*. William Cowper.
"Contemporaries all surpassed, see one." EPCY
"Then Pope, as harmony itself exact." EPCY
"When Cromwell fought for power, and while he reigned." EPCY

Table Talk. Derek Mahon. DiPo

Table Talk. Donald Mattam. FiBHP

Table Talk. Wallace Stevens. NoP

Tableau. Countee Cullen. PoBA

Tableau. Judith Wright. CBAP

Tableau at Twilight. Ogden Nash. FiBHP

Table's long and gleaming, The. The Board Meets. John Gloag. FiBHP

Tables Turned, The. Wordsworth. ArNa; EnRP; FHYEP; NAEL-2; OAEL-2; PIP; TOF

Tablets, The. Nicanor Parra, *tr. fr. Spanish by* W. S. Merwin. AnRep

Taboo to Boot. Ogden Nash. FiBHP; RB

Taboo Woman, The. *Unknown, tr. fr. Zuni Indian by* K. Kennedy. WTO

Taborer beat/ Your little drum. Jig for Sackbuts. D. B. Wyndham Lewis. ErPo

Taches Jaunes, Les, *sels*. Théophile Gautier, *tr. fr. French by* Lafcadio Hearn.
Clarimonde. AWP

Tacking Ship Off Shore. Walter Mitchell. FaBoBe; GN

Tact. Emerson. AnAmPo

Tact. Paul Pascal. WeW

Tact. E. A. Robinson. NoAM

Tadhg sat up on his hills. Senior Members. Sean Lucy. CIP; PeIV

Tadlow. Abel Evans. FaBoCo

Tadoussac. Charles Bancroft. BLPA

Tadpole, The. E. E. Gould. BoTP

Tae be wan o them Kings. Stars. George Mackay Brown. OxBS

Tae titly. *Unknown.* FaBoVe; OxNR

Taffy, the topaz-coloured cat. In Honour of Taffy Topaz. Christopher Morley. CRH; WHSW

Taffy was a Welshman, Taffy was a thief. Mother Goose. GBP; OxNR; RB; ReMoGo

Taffy was born. *Unknown.* OxNR

Tagus farewell, that westward with thy streams. Sir Thomas Wyatt. EnRePo; NoSic; SCGP
(Epigram! 'Tagus farewell, that westward with thy streams.") SiPSBD
(Tagus, fare well, that westward with thy stremes [*or* streams].) AAS; OBTV

Tahiti. Louis Johnson. PeNZ

Tahiti, Tahiti. Vor a Gauguin Picture zu Singen. Kurt M. Stein. FiBHP

Taiaha Haka Poem. Apirana Taylor. PeNZ

Taid's Funeral. Gillian Clarke. SCBI

Tail behind, a trunk in front, A. The Elephant, or the Force of Habit. A. E. Housman. NOBL
(Elephant, The.) FaBV

Tail of the See, A. Elizabeth T. Corbett. OBCA

Tail toddle, tail toddle. Tommie Makes My Tail Toddle. Burns. ErPo

Taill of the Foxe, That Begylit the Wolf, in the Schadow of the Mone, The. Robert Henryson. OxBS

Taill of the Wolf and the Wedder, The. Robert Henryson, *tr. by* Aesop. OxBLMV

Taille of the Sone and Air of the Foxe, The, *sels.* Robert Henryson. Lion Calls All the Beasts to His Parliment. CBCK

Tailor, The. "S. Ansky," *tr. fr. Yiddish by* Joseph Leftwich. TrJP

Tailor. Eleanor Farjeon. OTCP; OxBChV

Tailor, The. Patricia Garfinkel. BTR

Tailor, The. Joseph Leftwich. TrJP

Tailor Called Sorrow, A. Betti Alver, *tr. fr. Estonian by* Willis Barnstone *and* Felix Oinas. BoWoP

Tailor of Bicester. *Unknown.* OxNR

Tailor's goose will never fly, A. (*LL*) Hyder Iddle. *Unknown.* OxNR

Tailor's Wedding, The. Louis Simpson. NNaP

Tailor, Sailor, Poor man, Thief. (*LL*) Tinker,/ Tailor. *Unknown.* OxNR

Tailpiece. Max Fatchen. OTCP

Tails. Rowena Bastin Bennett. SiSoPo

Tails and Heads. Suzanne Knowles. RB

Tails like dandelion clocks. Squirrels. John Mole. OBAP

Tailspin, The. Edward Field. ETG

Táin, The. *Unknown, tr. fr. Irish by* Thomas Kinsella. NOIV
Sels.
Armies Enter Cuailnge, The.
Before the Last Battle.

Taisigh Agat Fein Do Phog. *Unknown, tr. fr. Irish by* Maire Cruise O'Brien. BIrV

Taj, The. H. G. Keene. OBTV

Tajo, tajo, tajo! tajo, my mackey massa! *Unknown. Fr.* Dancing Songs. PBCV

Tak for Sidst. Babette Deutsch. PoA

Tak tyme in tym, or tym will not be tane. A Description of Tyme. Alexander Montgomerie. OxBS

Tak' Your Auld Cloak about Ye. *Unknown.* OxBS

Take a father's admonition, from a heart disturbed. A Father's Testament. Judah ibn Tibbon, *tr. fr. Hebrew by* Israel Abrahams. TrJP

Take a harp. Song of the Harlot. Bible, O.T. *Fr.* Isaiah. TrJP

Take a knuckle of veal. A Receipt for Stewing Veal. *At. to* John Gay. FaBoUs

Take a large olive, stone it and then stuff it. A Dish for a Poet. *Unknown.* OBCP

Take a little back-ache. The Soup. Charles Simic. AnAn

Take a long view from Mynydd Bach. Jeremy Hooker. AngWe

Take a model of the world so big. The Rescued Year. William Stafford. LCAP

Take a pen in your uncertain fingers. The Pen. Muhammad al-Ghuzzi, *tr. fr. Arabic by* May Jayyusi *and* John Heath-Stubbs. TSaS

Take a statement: the same as yesterday's dictation. Vowel Movements. Daryl Hine. PoA

Take a Whiff on Me. *Unknown.* NOBA

Take all my loves, my Love, yea, take them all. Shakespeare. *Fr.* Sonnets. HeIP; InvP; OxAEP-1; SCGP

Take all the rest the sun goes round! (*LL*) On a Girdle. Edmund Waller. AWP; BeJo; BLPL; FF; GTBS; GTBS-P; ImPo; InPK; LiTB; NAEL-1; NoP; NOSC; OBEV; PoE; PoRA; SCGP; SeCV-1; TFi; TrGrPo

Take as a sign of the rising wind the swelling sea. Weather Signs. Aratus, *tr. fr. Greek by* Barbara Hughes Fowler. *Fr.* Phaenomena. HePo

Take Away. Margot Ruddock. OBMV

Take away the stuff! Dry. Samuel Hoffenstein. BXAP

Take Back the Virgin Page. Thomas Moore. OBNC

Take back your suit. A Song of Faith Forsworn. Lord De Tabley. PeVV

Take care of that face! That Face. Mairtin O Direain. BiHa

Take charge of me, and of my End. (*LL*) Dies Irae. Thomas of Celano. AWP; TIRV

Take Down the Fiddle, Karl! John Shaw Neilson. CBAP; FaBoMA

Take down your dress and rock in my arms. The Woman's Daughter. Dermot Bolger. IB

Take for the sake of example. Credo. Jean Lipkin. AIW

Take fortune as it falls, as one adviseth. The Author, of His Own Fortune. Sir John Harington. FaBoEE

Take Frankincense, O God. Charles Fitz-Geffry. *Fr.* Holy Transportations. ChTr

Take, friend, Orthon of Syracuse' advice. Theocritus [*or* Theokritus], *tr. fr. Greek by* Anthony Holden. GrAn

Take fright in his bewildering bower, and die. (*LL*) The Heaving Roses of the Hedge Are Stirred. Richard Watson Dixon. CH

Take from my palms, to soothe your heart. Osip Mandelstam, *tr. fr. Russian by* Clarence Brown *and* W. S. Merwin. UnAS

Take from the earth its tragic hunger, Lord. Hazel J. Fowler. TrPWD

Take, gentle marble, to thy trust. An Elegy upon His Tomb in Herndon-Hill Church, Erected by His Wife, Who Speaks. James Howell. OBWVE

Take heart, monsieur, four-fifths of this province. For Jean Vincent d'Abbadie, Baron St.-Castin. Alden Nowlan. NOBC

Take heart, Prytherch. Aside. R. S. Thomas. OxBC

Take heart, the journey's ended. In the Town. *Unknown, tr. fr. French by* Eleanor Farjeon. OBCP; PChr

Take heed betime, lest ye be spied. Sir Thomas Wyatt. SiPS

Take Heed of Gazing Overmuch. Thomas Richardson. *Fr.* Proper New Song, A. EII

Take heed of loving me[e]. The Prohibition. John Donne. EII; GBL; MeLP; NOSC

Take heed of this small child of earth. The Poor Children. Victor Hugo, *tr. fr. French by* Swinburne. AWP

Take hence this tuneful trifler's lays! Ode: Written After Reading Some Modern Love-Verses. John Scott of Amwell. ECEV

Take Him away, he's dead as they die. Obituary. Kenneth Fearing. VGW

Take him to the Gulley! Take him to the Gulley! A Popular Negro Song. *Unknown.* PBCV

Take him up tendahly. Parody on Thomas Hood's "The Bridge of Sighs." *Unknown.* FiBHP

Take home Thy prodigal child, O Lord of Hosts! Birthday Sonnet. Elinor Wylie. MoAB; MoAmPo

Take in hand the cup of delusion. Drink On. Mary E. Tucker. CBWP-1

Take it as earnest of a faith renewed. Nathaniel Lee. *Fr.* To the Unkown Author of *Absalom and Achitophel.* EPCY

Take It from Me. Kenneth O. Hanson. CoAP

Take it from me kiddo. Poem, or Beauty Hurts Mr. Vinal. E. E. Cummings. InPS; MoAB; MoAmPo; NAAL-2; OBAL; OxBA; PeLV; TRP

Take it not back! the priceless gift. Invocation to the Muse. H. Cordelia Ray. CBWP-3

Take, Lord, this soul of furred unblemished worth. Epitaph for a Good Mouser. Anne Stevenson. Spl

Take me as I drive alone. White Blossoms. Robert Mezey. NaP

Take Me Out to the Ball Game. Jack Norworth. OBAL

Take my hand. There are two of us in this cave. The Blind Leading the Blind. Lisel Mueller. IHMS

Take My Life and Let It Be. Frances Ridley Havergal. BLRP

Take my song of love to heart. *Unknown, tr. fr. Irish by* Thomas Kinsella. NOIV

Take my thanks. (*LL*) Thanks. Herman von Gilm zu Rosenegg. RiWo

Take my tunic, woman. Goll Mac Morna Parts from His Wife. *Unknown.* NOIV

Take note, passers-by, of the sharp erosions. The Circuit Judge. Edgar Lee Masters. *Fr.* Spoon River Anthology. FaBoEE

Take note who stoop. Nicarchus of Alexandria, *tr. fr. Greek by* Peter Porter. GrAn

Take, O take the cream away. Breakfast Song in Time of Diet. Stoddard King. OBAL

Take, O Take Those Lips Away, (*also given, with add. st., in* The Bloody Brother *by* John Fletcher *and others*). Shakespeare. *Fr.* Measure for Measure. AWP; EBEV; EII; ELP; EnLoPo; EnRePo; FaBV; GBL; ImPo; InPS; LiTB; NoP; NoSic; OAEL-1; OBEV; SCGP; TFi

Take of English earth as much. A Charm. Kipling. OtMeF

Take of me what is not my own. Kathleen Raine. NOBE

Take of my feders but not of my toe. (LL) The False Fox. Unknown. ChTr; GBP

Take off his hide and feed him to the crows. (LL) On Buying a Horse. Unknown. NBLV; RB

Take off those flimsy nets, Lysidice. Argentarius, tr. fr. Greek by Fleur Adcock. GrAn

Take off your clothes, love. Old Song. Robert Creeley. ArLo

Take off your clothes, my love! Paulus Silentiarius, tr. fr. Greek by Sam Hamill. InMo

Take off your hat. Pass Office Song. Unknown, tr. fr. Afrikaans. PBA, tr. by Peggy Rutherford; TTY, tr. by Peggy Rutherford; WTO, tr. by H. Tracey

Take, Oh, Take Those Lips Away. John Fletcher and others. Fr. Bloody Brother, The. NoP

Take I, 4:11:58. Philip Whalen. NeAP

Take 1 green pepper and 2 tomatoes. Pour Commencer. Jon Stallworthy. NoAM

Take One Home for the Kiddies. Philip Larkin. OBD; OxBTC

Take Physic, Pomp. Shakespeare. Fr. King Lear. TrGrPo

Take quantum sufficit of meadows and trees. To Make a Pastoral; a Receipt. Unknown. FaBoUs

Take Temperance to thy breast. A Talisman. Louise Imogen Guiney. AmWP

Take that, damn you; and that! Mezzo Forte. William Carlos Williams. SAmP

Take the back off the watch. Time Piece. William Cole. GrPl

Take the cloak from his face, and at first. After. Robert Browning. TrGrPo

Take the cloak of all my love. Song for a Jewess. Iwan Goll, tr. fr. French by Joseph T. Shipley. TrJP

Take the Crust. Sadi, tr. by L. Cranmer-Byng. Fr. Gulistan, The. AWP

Take the thanks of a boy. (LL) Prayers. Henry Charles Beeching. BoTP; OBEV

Take the Toys from the Boys. Ulli Freer. NBrP

Take the World As It Is, sels. Charles Swain.
    "Take the world as it is! — with its smiles and its sorrow." PoToHe

Take the world as it is! — with its smiles and its sorrow. Charles Swain. Fr. Take the World As It Is. PoToHe

Take them, then, beloved, these songs. Alois Jeitteles, tr. by Philip L. Miller. RiWo

Take, then your paltry Christ. To the Christians. Francis Lauderdale Adams. ChIV-2; OxBS; WGRP

Take Therefore That You May Have. "Angelus Silesius," tr. fr. German. Fr. Cherubical Wanderer, The. GePo, tr. by George C. Schoolfield

Take these who will as may be: I. Permit Me Voyage. James Agee. MoAmPo

Take This Hammer. Unknown. SWP

Take this news to the Lakedaimonians, friend. Simonides. See Go tell at Sparta, traveler passing by.

Take this old man with the soldierly straight back. Louis MacNeice. Fr. Kingdom, The. LiTM

Take Thou Our Minds, Dear Lord. William H. Foulkes. AH

Take thou the world and all that will. (LL) The Flesh and the Spirit. Anne Bradstreet. AmPP; AnAmPo; ChIV-2; LiTA; NAAL-1; NOBA; OxBA; SCAP; TAP

Take Thy Bliss, O Man. Blake. Fr. Visions of the Daughters of Albion. EnRP; OAEL-2

Take time, my dear, ere Time takes wing. Fading Beauty. Unknown. FaBoEE

Take Time to Be Holy. W. D. Longstaff. BLRP

Take Time to Live. Thomas Curtis Clark. PoToHe

Take time while time doth last. Song Set by John Farmer. Unknown. CTC; NoSic

Take up the pen and write a text. Malay Oral Tradition, tr. by R. J. Wilkinson and R. O. Winstedt. WTO

Take up the pen: fall into the net of law. Call to Arms. Lu Hsun, tr. fr. Chinese by William R. Schultz. SuSp

Take up the White Man's burden. The White Man's Burden. Kipling. FaBoPV

Take Ye Heed, Watch and Pray. Jones Very. ChIV-2

Take yesterday's worries and sort them all out. Worries. Unknown. PoToHe

Take Your Accusation Back! Kittaararter, tr. fr. Eskimo. WTO

Take your bucket, and take your spade. The Sea. E. M. Adams. BoTP

Taken away from her language. Island. Meredith Stricker. LoHo

Taken By Each Thing. Linda Gregg. FoLa; PRA

Taken by surprise. Meeting Bida. Fily-Dabo Sissoko, tr. fr. French by Ellen Conroy Kennedy. NegPo

Taken from the. The Primitive. Don L. Lee. BPo

Takes a taste of green. The Moon. Wendy Mulford. NBrP

Takes a young lettuce for a sallet. (LL) Epitaph. At. to Pope. FaBoEE

Takes longer now: whole pharmacies of pain. Waiting to Die. Paul Monette. PFL

Takes one long slow step nearer. (LL) Golden Calf. Norman MacCaig. ChIV-1; OxBS

Taking a Captive/ 1984. Barney Bush. HATNAP

Taking between them/ A specially straight willow tree. Eulogy to the Bow and Arrow. Mongol Oral Tradition, tr. by C. R. Bawden. WTO

Taking Ford's dictation on Samuel Butler. Ford Madox Ford. Robert Lowell. OxBC

Taking, giving back their lives. The Field Hospital. Paul Muldoon. CIP; PNI

Taking Leave. Carol Ganzer. BTR

Taking Leave of a Friend. Li Po, tr. fr. Chinese by Ezra Pound. RB; SOTW

Taking me into your body. The Source. Jon Stallworthy. CBLP; NoP

Taking Notice, sels. Marilyn Hacker.
    "And I shout at Iva, whine at you. Easily." VCAP
    "If we talk, we're too tired to make love; if we." VCAP
    "In the Public Theater lobby, I wait for Marie." VCAP
    "We work, play, don't cross-reference calendars." VCAP

Taking of the Koppie. The. Uys Krige. PeSAV

Taking Off My Clothes. Carolyn Forché. AmPA; AnAn; NoAM

Taking picture after picture after picture. (LL) Desperate Message #3 (Desire). Mark Svenvold. UTF

Taking root in windy sand. Dunes. A. R. Ammons. FoLa

Taking Sides. Rachel Hadas. UnDi

Taking the air rifle from my son's hand. Cain. Irving Layton. MoCV

Taking the Census. Charles Robert Thatcher. NOBAu

Taking the Ferry at Ta-kao at Dawn. Yang Wei-chen, tr. fr. Chinese by Jonathan Chaves. SuSp

Taking the Hands of Someone You Love. Robert Bly. TRP

Taking the last of it down with us. (LL) You Know. Jean Garrigue. NYBP; UnPo

Taking this train / to visit miriam. (LL) Going Uptown to Visit Miriam. Victor Hernandez Cruz. FF; MAT

Taking to the Woods. Henry Taylor. MT

Taking Turns. Norma Farber. TLR

Taking us by and large, we're a queer lot. The Sisters. Amy Lowell. NALW

Taku Skanskan. Paula Gunn Allen. ETG; HATNAP

Talbingo. Kenneth Slessor. FaBoMA

Tale, A. Edward Thomas. ChTr

Tale About a Tale, The. Vasco [or Vasko] Popa, tr. fr. Serbo-Croatian. Fr. Yawn of Yawns, The. AnRep, tr. by Charles Simic; HSix

Tale for Husbands, A. Sir Philip Sidney. See Neighbour mine not long ago there was, A.

Tale I frame shall be found to tally, The. The Seafarer. Unknown, tr. by Michael Alexander. OBVE

Tale is told of long ago, A. A Song of the Yellow Cedar Face. George Clutesi. HATNAP

Tale of a Dog, The. James H. Lambert, Jr. ZA

Tale of a Dog and a Bee, The. Unknown. BoTP

Tale of a Friar and A Shoemaker's Wife, A. Thomas Churchyard. NoSic

Tale of a Pony, The. Bret Harte. OBNV

Tale of Custard the Dragon, The. Ogden Nash. FaPON; OBCA; OTCP; PoRA; PYC

Tale of Drury Lane, A. Horace Smith. FaBoCo

Tale of Genji, The, sels. Murasaki Shikibu, tr. fr. Japanese by Kenneth Rexroth and Ikuko Atsumi.
    "Lady Murasaki says." BoWoP; WPJ
    "Troubled waters, The/ are frozen fast." WPJ; WPOW

Tale of Genji. Hugh Seidman. AmPA

Tale of Italy, A. Eloise Bibb. CBWP-4

Tale of Jorkyns and Gertie; or, Vice Rewarded, The. R. P. Lister. NYBP

Tale of Lord Lovell, The. Unknown. NOBL; PeLV

Tale of Lord Lovell, The. Unknown. See Lord Lovel he stands at his stable-door.

Tale of Sigemund, The. Unknown, tr. by Charles W. Kennedy. Fr. Beowulf. AnOE; ASW, tr. by Kevin Crossley-Holland

Tale of Sunlight, The. Gary Soto. NoAM

Tale of the Airly Days, A. James Whitcomb Riley. AnAmPo

Tale of the Beginning of Friars and Cloisterers, A. William Warner. Fr. Albion's England. NoSic

Teevo cheevo cheevio chee. The Woodlark. Gerard Manley Hopkins. RB

Teh. has six claims to fame: its numerous hotsprings. Sestina for the Ladies of Tehuántepec. Earle Birney. PeLV

Teisa, a Descriptive Poem of the River Tees, Its Towns and Antiquities, *sels.* Anne Wilson.
In Praise of Drainage. ECWP

Telegram. Milo De Angelis, *tr. fr. Italian by* Lawrence Venuti. NeIt

Telegrams, The. Julia Ward Howe. AmWP

Telegrams of Tenderness for Sanaa, *sels.* Abd al-Aziz al-Maqalih, *tr. fr. Arabic by* Lena Jayyusi *and* Christopher Middleton.

Telemachus with a Transistor. Ruth Dallas. PeNZ

Teleology. May Swenson. VCAP

Telephone, The. Robert Frost. ArLo; ImGa

Telephone Conversation. Wole Soyinka. TTY

Telephone-installer was interested, The. Moving In. Josephine Miles. NoP

Telephone line goes cold, A. The Farm on the Great Plains. William Stafford. HAP; VGW

Telephone Message, A (To Whom it May Concern). John Oxenham. NSI

Telephone poles, The. Crossing Kansas by Train. Donald Justice. AiP; NYBP

Telephone Poles. John Updike. FYAP; Poetsp

Telephoning God. Gary Soto. PBCAP

Telephoning Home. Carol Ann Duffy. NBrP

Telephonist. Janet Frame. WPE

Tele/vision. Amiri Baraka. PRA

Television. Anne Stevenson. PRA

Television aerials, Chinese characters. On Roofs of Terry Street. Douglas Dunn. OxBTC

Television/ radio sunday benevolent sunday. They Are Killing All the Young Men. David Henderson. PoBA

Tell a wise person, or else keep silent. The Holy Longing. Goethe, *tr. fr. German by* Robert Bly. NU; RaBo

Tell all my mourners. Wake. Langston Hughes. OBAL

Tell all the truth but tell it slant. Emily Dickinson. AmPP; HeIL; HeIP; LiTA; NAAL-1; NALW; NAWM-2; NoAM; NOBA; NoP; PFP; Poetr; PPP; TAP; UnPo; WeW

Tell, dear Aminta, now 'tis over. Close to Aminta, on the Loss of Her Lover. Sarah Dixon. ECWP

Tell Freedom, *sels.* Peter Abrahams.
Me, Colored. PBA

Tell her I love. Poems for My Daughter. Horace Gregory. MoAmPo

Tell her! smell her! *Unknown.* ISE

Tell Her So. Mrs. Henry Linden. CBWP-4

Tell Her So. *Unknown.* PoToHe

Tell her we still expose our bottoms. Messages. Jack A. Mapanje. HBAPE

Tell Him, O Night. *Unknown, tr. fr. Arabic by* E. Powys Mathers. *Fr.* Thousand and One Nights, The. AWP

Tell Him So. J. A. Egerton. PWR

Tell Him So. *Unknown.* BLPA; BLPL; WBLP

Tell him the tale is a lie! A Learned Mistress. *Unknown. tr. fr. Irish by* Frank O'Connor. OBMV

Tell it to the locked up trees. Cuckoo Song. Kipling. NTP

Tell Me. Langston Hughes. SAmP

Tell Me. Pamela Mordecai. PBCV

Tell Me. Edith M. Thomas. *Fr.* Inverted Torch, The.

Tell me. What She Said Her Lover within Earshot. Kapilar, *tr. fr. Tamil by* A. K. Ramanujan. PLW

Tell me a story. Bedtime Story. Lilian Moore. NTCP

Tell Me a Story. Robert Penn Warren. *Fr.* Audubon. MT

Tell me a story, father, please. The Natives of America. Ann Plato. BlSi

Tell me a story, Father, please do. Request Number. G. N. Sprod. AAP; FiBHP

Tell me, abandoned miscreant, prithee tell. Upon the Author of a Play Called Sodom. John Oldham. FaBoBl

Tell me about that harvest field. Real Property. Harold Monro. BoNaP

Tell me about yourself they. A Word in Edgeways. Charles Tomlinson. NOBL

Tell Me Again. Nigâr Hanim, *tr. fr. Turkish by* Tâlat S. Halman. PBWP

Tell Me Again. Paul Keens-Douglas. PBCV

Tell Me Dearest, What is Love? Beaumont *and* Fletcher. *Fr.* Captain, The. EIL

Tell me, good dog, whose tomb you guard so well. The Tomb of Diogenes. *Unknown, tr. fr. Greek by* John Addington Symonds. AWP

Tell me good Hobbinoll, what garres thee greete? Aprill. Spenser. *Fr.* Shepheardes [*or* Shepeards *or* Shepherd's] Calender, The. NAEL-1; PoEL-1

(Tell me, good Hobbinoll, what garres thee greete?) OBEV; PoEL-1

Tell me/ Have you ever seen woods so. Town on the Way Through God's Woods. Anne Carson. *Fr.* Life of Towns, The. BAP-90

Tell me herdsman for the sake of Pan. Erucius, *tr. fr. Greek by* Peter Levi. GrAn

Tell me if I am not glad! (*LL*) Lines for an Old Man. T. S. Eliot. FaBoTw; RaBo; RB

Tell me if it is too far for you. Elegy for N. N. Czeslaw Milosz, *tr. fr. Polish by* Larence Davis. AnRep; SV

Tell me is there anything lovelier. Greenness. Angelina Weld Grimké. CDC

Tell me, is there sovereign cure. Tell Me. Edith M. Thomas. *Fr.* Inverted Torch, The.
(Cure-All.) AmWP

Tell Me, Love. Ingeborg Bachmann, *tr. fr. German by* Mark Anderson. VBLP

Tell me, lovely, loving pair! On the Friendship betwixt Two Ladies. Edmund Waller. PeHV

Tell me, mamma, if I must die. Jane Taylor. VPP

Tell me, men with wisdom gifted. Hiraeth. *Unknown, tr. fr. Welsh by* Aneirin Talfan Davies. OBWVE

Tell me more about that long street. Of Dreams and Dreaming. John Ashbery. BAP-91

Tell me, my heart, how wilt thou do. Sir Arthur Gorges. *Fr.* Desportes. NoSic

Tell me (my love) since Hymen ty'de. An Hymeneall Dialogue. Thomas Carew. SeCP

Tell me, my patient friends, awaiters of messages. Speech to a Crowd. Archibald MacLeish. MoAB; MoAmPo

Tell Me No More. William Drummond of Hawthornden. TrGrPo

Tell me[e] no more how fair[e] she[e] is. Henry King. EnLoPo; MeLP; SeCP
(That Distant Bliss.) TrGrPo

Tell me no more of constancy. Against Constancy. The Earl of Rochester. GBL; NOSC; OxAEP-1

Tell me no more of minds embracing minds. No Platonic [*or* Platonique] Love. William Cartwright. BeJo; ErPo; GBL; ImPo; InvP; JCP; LiTB; NOSC; OAEL-1; PoEL-2

Tell me no secret, friend. The Burden. Francesca Yetunde Pereira. PBA

Tell me not, friend, you are unkind. Lucasta Replies to Lovelace. G. K. Chesteron. UV

Tell Me Not Here [It Needs Not Saying]. A. E. Housman. CoGr; ELP; GTBS-P; LiTM; NoAM; NOBE; OAEL-2; OBNC; OxBTC; PlP; SCV

Tell me not in idle jingle. Psalm of Marriage. Phoebe Cary. PWR

Tell me not in joyous numbers. Stephen Crane. OBAL

Tell me not, in mournful numbers. A Psalm of Life. Longfellow. AH; AnAmPo; EBEvV; FaBoBe; NAAL-1; OBCA; PlP; PoLF; PrIm; PWR; TAP; WBLP

Tell Me Not in Mournful Numbers. Longfellow. *Fr.* Psalm of Life, A. AH; FaBoBe; OBCA; PoLF; PrIm; TAP; VPP; WBLP

Tell me not of a face that's fair. The Resolve. Alexander Brome. GGP; NOSC; OBEV

Tell me not of joy; there's none. The Dead Sparrow. William Cartwright. CH

Tell me not, Sweet, I am unkind. Lines Where Beauty Lingers. Franklin P. Adams. OBAL

Tell me not, Sweet, I am unkind. To Lucasta, Going to the Wars [*or* Warres]. Richard Lovelace. AWP; BeJo; CaPo; CBLP; ClHu; CoGr; EBEvV; ELP; EnLoPo; FaBoEH; FaBV; FF; GBL; GTBS; GTBS-P; HAP; HoPM; ImPo; InPS; JCP; LiTB; MeLP; NAEL-1; NIP; NOBE; NoP; OAEL-1; OBEV; OBWP; OxAEP-1; OxBSP; PAW; PoEL-3; Poetr; PoRA; SCV; SeCP; SeCV-1; TFi; TrGrPo; UV; WeW
(Going to the Wars.) SCGP
(Song: To Lucasta, Going to the Wars.) NOSC; PoE
(To Lucasta.) InPK

Tell me not what too well I know. On Catullus. Walter Savage Landor. OBEV

Tell Me Now. Wang Chi, *tr. fr. Chinese by* Arthur Waley. FaBoCh

Tell me now in what hidden way is. Ballad[e] of Dead Ladies. Villon, *tr. fr. French by* Dante Gabriel Rossetti. AWP; CTC; HeIL; OBVE; PoRA; PrIm
(Snows of Yester-year, The.) WiR

Tell me now, what should a man want. Tell Me Now. Wang Chi, *tr. fr. Chinese by* Arthur Waley. FaBoCh

Tell me, O Muse of the shifty, the man who wandered afar. Jubilee before Revolution. Andrew Lang. BXAP

Tell me, O Octopus, I begs. The Octopus. Ogden Nash. RB

Tell me, O Swan, your ancient tale. Songs of Kabir. Kabir, *tr. fr. Hindi by* Rabindranath Tagore. WGRP

Tell me of thy heart's devotion. Whisper Words of Love to Me. L. A. J. Moorer. CBWP-3

Tell Me, Oh Fate. James Ephriam McGirt. AAP

Tell me, oh fate, is it decreed. Tell Me, Oh Fate. James Ephriam McGirt. AAP

Tell me, O[h] Muse (for thou, or none canst tell. The Power of Numbers. Abraham Cowley. *Fr.* Davideis.
(Number, Weight, and Measure.) NOSC

Tell me, O[h] tell, what kind[e] of thing is wit. Ode: Of Wit. Abraham Cowley. BeJo; MeLP; NAEL-1; NOSC; OAEL-1; SeCP; SeCV-1
(Ode to Wit.) OxAEP-1
(Poetic wit.) EPCY

Tell me once, dear, how it does prove. To the Unconstant Cynthia. Sir Robert Howard *and* John Dryden.
(To the Unconstant Cynthia: a Song.) NOSC

Tell me, Perigot, what shalbe the game. August. Spenser. *Fr.* Shepheardes [*or* Shepeards *or* Shepherd's] Calender, The.

Tell me, pray, if you may, how to make a sailor's pie? How to Make a Sailor's Pie. Joan Aiken. NTP

Tell me, Pyrrha, what fine youth. Horace. *See* What slender youth bedewed with liquid odours.

Tell me, shepherd, tell me, pray. Country Gods. Cometas, *tr. fr. Greek by* T. F. Higham. FaBoCh

Tell Me, Tell Me. Marianne Moore. LiTM; NYBP

Tell me, tell me, gentle Robin. The Cat and the Bird. George Canning. ChTr

Tell me, tell me, smiling child. Emily Brontë. NALW; TEP

Tell me, tell me,/ Unknown stranger. The Galliass. Walter de la Mare. FaBoTw

Tell me the auld, auld story. The Parrot Cry. "Hugh MacDiarmid." OxBS

Tell me the truths which you hear of our constant young lady. Difference of Opinion with Lygdamus. Ezra Pound. *Fr.* Homage to Sextus Propertius. MeMAP

Tell me, thou skilful shepherd's swain. Michael Drayton. *Fr.* Shepherd's Garland, The. EIL

Tell me, thou Star, whose wings of light. The World's Wanderers. Shelley. TTTS

Tell me thou safest end of all our woe. On Death. Anne Killigrew. BoWoP; ChIV-1; KTR

Tell me today, when all my tides are gone. Sea Sonnet. Norma Lay. GoYe

Tell me,/ Was Venus more beautiful. Venus Transiens. Amy Lowell. NALW; PoA

Tell me what sail the seas. Under the Stars. Wallace Rice. OHIP

Tell me what you're doing over here, John Gorham. John Gorham. E. A. Robinson. MoAB; MoAmPo

Tell me whaur, in whit countrie. Ballat o the Leddies o Langsyne. Villon, *tr. fr. French by* Tom Scott. OBVE

Tell me, where doth Whiteness grow. Whiteness, or Chastity. Joseph Beaumont. NOSC

Tell me where, in what country, where. Villon, *tr. fr. French by* John Frederick Nims. STV

Tell Me Where Is Fancy [*or* Fancie] Bred. Shakespeare. *Fr.* Merchant of Venice, The. CH; EIL; ELP; EnRePo; LiTB; NAEL-1; NoSic; OAEL-1; SCGP; TFi
(Fancy.) FaPON; 08TreFS; TrGrPo
(Love.) OBEV
(Madrigal: "Tell me where is fancy bred.") GTBS; GTBS-P
(Song: "Tell me where is fancy bred.") CTC; PoEL-2
(Song.) EBEvV

Tell me where thy lovely love is. Heine, *tr. fr. German by* Ezra Pound. *Fr.* Heimkehr, Die. AWP

Tell me, why such a foul mood? Demon in Paradise. Minuchihri, *tr. fr. Persian by* Omar S. Pound. ArPe

Tell Me, Wight in the Broom. Unknown. *See* Say me, wight in the brom [*or* broom].

Tell me, woman, your parents, your name, your land. B. Calliteles. Antipater of Sidon, *tr. fr. Greek by* Barbara Hughes Fowler. *Fr.* Epigrams. HePo

Tell me, you anti-saints, why glass. Upon Fairford Windows. Richard Corbett [*or* Corbet]. BeJo; NOSC

Tell me you Hate; and Flatter me no more. To J. G. "Ephelia." KTR; NOSC

Tell me your secrets, pretty shell. Shell Secrets. Unknown. BoTP

Tell of smashed holly, pokeweed, smilax, prickly pear? (*LL*) The Uccello. Valerie Wohlfeld. UTF

Tell Our Daughters. Besmilr Brigham. CrSp; IHMS

Tell tale tit. Unknown. ISE

Tell the story to your sons. The Fight of the *Armstrong* Privateer. James Jeffrey Roche. PAH

Tell them, I AM, Jehovah said. Christopher Smart. *Fr.* Song to David, A. ChTr; EBEV; NAEL-1; NOBE, *abr.*; OAEL-1; PoEL-3; TrGrPo, *abr.*; WGRP

Tell them in Lacedaemon [*or* Lakedaimon], passer-by. At Thermopylae. Simonides.
(On the Army of Spartans, Who Died at Thermopylae.) ChTr; FaBoEE

Tell them ye smile, for your eyes know To-morrow. (*LL*) Go, songs, for ended is our brief, sweet play. Francis Thompson. MoBrPo

Tell this to ladies: how a hero man. Man without Sense of Direction. John Crowe Ransom. LiTM; MeMAP; OxBA

Tell us, streaming lady. History. James Liddy, *tr. fr. Irish.* CIP

Tell us, thou clear and heavenly tongue. The Star-Song; a Carol to the King; Sung at White-Hall. Robert Herrick. GN

Tell us! ye dead! Will none of you in pity. Robert Blair. *Fr.* Grave, The. OBD

Tell Us, Ye Servants of the Lord. William Staughton. AH

Tell where I lie. (*LL*) Ode on [*or* to] Solitude. Pope. AWP; EBEvV; FHYEP; GGP; HeIL; HeIP; InVP; NAEL-1; NOSC; PoRA; Prf; SCGP; TEP

Tell you? ha! who. Maximus, to Gloucester, Letter 2. Charles Olson. *Fr.* Maximus Poems, The. NoAM

Tell you I chyll. John Skelton. *Fr.* Tunnyng [*or* Tunning] of Elynour [*or* Elinor] Rummyng [*or* Rumming], The. AAS; TrGrPo

Tell you what I like the best. Knee-deep in June. James Whitcomb Riley. PFP

Tell your son, my son. Message. Renata Pallottini, *tr. fr. Portuguese by* Monique *and* Carlos Altschul. WPOW

Tellers will be Jews and their speech Hebrew, The. (*LL*) Let other people come as streams. Charles Reznikoff. VGW

Telling about Coyote. Simon J. Ortiz. STP

Telling It. Nancy Sullivan. TAP

Telling My Feelings. Yü Hsüan-chi, *tr. by* Geoffrey R. Waters. BoWoP

Telling Part, The. Jackie Kay. NWP

Telling the Bees. Lizette Woodworth Reese. AmWP

Telling the bees. (*LL*) Telling the Bees. Lizette Woodworth Reese. AmWP

Telling the Bees. Whittier. AnAmPo; AWP; BLPL; NOBA; TAP

Tells me what I unto my God should be. (*LL*) Bishop Doane on His Dog. George Washington Doane. BLPA; FaBoBe

Telltale tit. You Worthless. Unknown. FaBoVe

Tèma con Variazióni. "Lewis Carroll." FaBoNo

Temper. Rose Fyleman. OxBChV

Temper. Unknown. PoToHe

Temper, The. ("How should I praise Thee, Lord"). George Herbert. ESCV; GeHe; NOCV; NoP; PFP; PoEL-2

Temper, The. ("It cannot be. Where is that mighty joy."). George Herbert. GeHe

Temper my spirit, O Lord. The Passionate Sword. Jean Starr Untermeyer. TrJP; TrPWD

Temperament. Robert Frost. *See* With anyone to death, comes so far short.

Temperament. Martial, *tr. fr. Latin by* Joseph Addison. AWP; OBF

Temperaments, The. Ezra Pound. BoLoP; ErPo; FaBoBl; MeMAP; NoAM; NOBA

Temperance Billiards Rooms, The. P. J. Kavanagh. OxBTC

Temperance Note: and Weather Prophecy. James Agee. *Fr.* Two Songs on the Economy of Abundance. MoAmPo

Temperance or the Cheap Physitian upon the Translation of Lessius. Richard Crashaw. SeCV-1

Temperance Song. Unknown. FaBoUs

Temperature. Gerard Malanga. NYBP

Temperature/ Cruises down, slides, The. Storm. Mary Oliver. CAPP

Tempered, annealed, the hard essence of autumn metals. Needle and Thread. Pan Chao, *tr. fr. Chinese by* Richard Mather *and* Rob Swigart. WPOW

Tempest, The. (Boatswain!) Shakespeare. OAEL-1
Sels.
"Be cheerful, sir:" EnlH
"Be not afeard: the isle is full of noises." OxAEP-1; RB
(To Dream Again. TrGrPo
Brave New World. TrGrPo
"Come unto these yellow sands." BoTP; CH; EIL; NOSC; NoSic; OBEV; SCGP; SoSe; TFi; TTTS
(Ariel's Song: "Come unto these yellow sands.") CTC; FaBoCh; GN; GoJo; NOBE; TEP
(Song: "Come unto these yellow sands.") EBEvV; PoEL-2
"Dost thou forget." OxAEP-1
"Earth's increase, foison plenty"
Full Fathom Five. AWP; ChTr; ClHu; EBEV; EIL; ELP; FaBoCh; HAP; HoPM; ImPo; InPK; InPS; LiTB; NAEL-1; NoP; NoSic; OBEV; OxBSP; PoE; PoRA; TEP; TFi

Ten Thousand Miles Away. *Unknown.* AS

Ten thousand rivers of tears. Licymnios, *tr. fr. Greek by* Sam Hamill. InMo

Ten thousand things are heard when born. On Sound. Wei Ying-wu, *tr. fr. Chinese by* Irving Y. Lo. SuSp

Ten thousand thousand fathoms down. Thomas Love Peacock. *Fr.* Sir Proteus, a Satirical Ballad. CBNP

Ten thousand years. *(LL)* Above Pate Valley. Gary Snyder. CoAP; LCAP; NaP; NoP; TRP

Ten Types of Hospital Visitor. Charles Causley. OxBC

Ten Years Ago. Eileen Moeller. CrSp

Ten years ago it seemed impossible. In Progress. Christina Rossetti. BoWoP; NAEL-2; WPE

Ten Years and More. Miriam Waddington. NOBC

Ten years! and to my waking eye. The Terrace at Berne. Matthew Arnold. *Fr.* Switzerland. EnVR; OBTV

Ten years/ and will you be/ a footnote. Return to Hinton. Charles Tomlinson. CMoP

Ten years old with my father. Trails. Patrick Williams. PNI

Ten years older in an hour. In the Ward. Robert Lowell. NAAL-2

Ten years the world upon him falsely smiled. Sir Richard Fanshawe. FaBoEH

Ten years together without yet a cloud. Firelight. E. A. Robinson. NoAM

Tenancy, The. Mary Gilmore. CBAP

Tenant at Number 9. John Blight. CBAP

Tenants at Will. William Allingham. *Fr.* Lawrence Bloomfield in Ireland. PeIV

Tenants of the Little Box, The. Vasco [*or* Vasko] Popa, *tr. fr. Serbo-Croatian by* Charles Simic. AnRep; HSix

Tend me my birds, and bring again. Norman Gale. TrPWD

Tended by Faustina. Faustina, or Rock Roses. Elizabeth Bishop. FaBoMo

Tender Buttons, *sels.* Gertrude Stein.
  Blue Coat, A. PBWP
  Colored Hats. TTTS
  Dog, A. TTTS
  More. PBWP
  New Cup and Saucer, A. TTTS
  Nothing Elegant. PBWP
  Petticoat, A. TTTS
  Piano, A. PBWP
  Red Roses. TTTS
  Sound, A. TTTS
  Umbrella, An. TTTS
  Water Raining. PBWP

Tender each to the other, gentle. Imperialists in Retirement. Edward Lucie-Smith. PBCV

Tender fingers ran up my ankle. "Can I Tempt You to a Pond Walk?" James Schuyler. PoA

Tender-handed stroke a nettle. Written on a Window. Aaron Hill. OxBSP

Tender heart, hairy muscle. Maria Luisa Spaziani, *tr. fr. Italian by* Beverly Allen. NeIt

Tender-Heartedness. Harry Graham. *Fr.* Some Ruthless Rhymes. CBNP; NBLV; PeLV

Tender Infant, Meek and Mild, The. Samuel Johnson. CBNP; OxAEP-1

Tender mulberry leaves picked so clean. Walking in the Countryside. Wang An-shih, *tr. fr. Chinese by* Jan W. Walls. SuSp

Tender, semi-/ articulate flickers. For My Mother: Genevieve Jules Creeley. Robert Creeley. PoM; TRP

Tender, Slow. *Unknown, tr. fr. Greek by* Wallace Rice. ErPo

Tender Snow, of Granis Soft & Quyht, The. Alexander Montgomerie. ScCV

Tender softness, infant mild. To an Infant Expiring the Second Day of Its Birth. Mehetabel Wright. ECWP; NOEC

Tender speeches, until they feed us to the truth. *(LL)* Never Seek to Tell Thy Love. John Ashbery. HCAP; InPS

Tender, the young auburn woman. Spring. Paul Verlaine, *tr. fr. French by* Roland Grant *and* Paul Archer. ErPo; PeHV

Tendered by Professor Ames, tidings from. What Word Did the Greeks have for It? Richard Howard. BAP-91

Tenderfoot, The. D. J. O'Malley. AS

Tenderly, day that I have loved, I close your eyes. Day That I Have Loved. Rupert Brooke. PoLF

Tenderness. Stephen P. Dunn. NIP

Tenderness, ache on me, and lay your neck. James Dickey. *Fr.* Zodiac, The. TAP

Tenderness and resolution! Reliquary. Hart Crane. PoA

Tenderness of dignity of souls, The. Peter Viereck. *Fr.* Crass Times Redeemed by Dignity of Souls. HoPM

Tending the Graves. Jennifer Strauss. NOBAu

Tendons sewn together and the small bones, The. Safe. Linda Gregerson. BAP-91

Tendril in the Mesh, *sels.* William Everson.
  "Daughter of earth and child of the wave be appeased." NoAM

Tenebrae. Paul Celan, *tr. fr. German by* Michael Hamburger. PoSu, *tr. by* Michael Hamburger

Tenebrae. Austin Clarke. BIrV; CIP; IPY; NOIV

Tenebrae. David Gascoyne. PeECV

Tenebrae. Denise Levertov. NoP

Tenebris. Angelina Weld Grimké. CDC; PoBA; PoNe; ShDr

Tenebris Interlucentem. James Elroy Flecker. MoBrPo

Tennessee. Virginia Fraser Boyle. PAH

Tennessee. *Unknown.* AmFP

Tennis. Margaret Avison. MoP

Tennis Court Oath, The. John Ashbery. NoAM; TAP

Tennyson. Alan Ansen. CoAP

Tennyson. Karl Shapiro. BAP-89

Tennyson's Poems. Josephine D. Henderson Heard. CBWP-4

Tenor of your madness, The. Up Early. Kit Robinson. UL

Tenson. Carenza *and* Iselda, *tr. fr. Provençal by* Bridget Connelly *and* Doris Earnshaw. WPOW

Tent-mates. Lincoln Kirstein. ArOW

Tent stitch is repeated in the blue and red, The. Oh, Nothing. John Ashbery. NAAL-2

Tent tethered among jackpine and blue-/ bells. Robert Maclean. EaPr

Tent that is pitched at the base, A. War. Edgar Wallace. OBWP

Tentacled for food. In the Sea of Tears. Naomi Replansky. BrRo

Tentacles, the brazen phiz whose glare, The. Medusa. Amy Clampitt. VCAP

Tenth Eclogue, The. Michael Drayton. *Fr.* Shepherd's Garland, The. JCP

Tenth Elegy. Elegy in Joy, *sels.* Muriel Rukeyser.
  Now Green, Now Burning. LPA

Tenth Matter: Story. Robert Kelly. BCF

Tenth Nimphall, The. Michael Drayton. *Fr.* Muses' Elysium [*or* Elizium]. JCP

Tenth Reunion. Edward Steese. GoYe

Tenth Symphony. John Ashbery. NOBA

Tenuous and Precarious. Stevie Smith. FaBoNo; OxBTC

Tenzone. Ezra Pound. *Fr.* Contemporania. MeMAP; PoA

Tepehua Thought-Songs. *Unknown, tr. fr. Tepehua Indian by* Charles Boilès. STP
Sels.
  "Knowing that the music knows."
  "Thought was/ & though it had been."
  "When they play like that where everyone is."

Tequila & chicken. In a Motel on Lake Erie. James Tate. LCAP

Teratology. Melinda Mueller. BAP-90

Terce. James McMichael. PoA

Terence, if I could return. To Myself, after Forty Years. T. H. White. NYBP

Terence McDiddler. *Unknown.* OxNR

Terence MacSwiney. Anne Spencer. ShDr

Terence, This Is Stupid Stuff. A. E. Housman. *Fr.* Shropshire Lad, A. CMoP; FaPoB; HeIP; InPK; LiTB; LiTM; MeMBP; MoP; NAEL-2; NoAM; NoP; Poetr; PrIm; TFi

Terentius Neo and wife. Their oval eyes. Portrait of a Married Couple. Margaret Scott. NOBAu

Teresa. Richard Wilbur. NoAM

Teresa of Avila. Elizabeth Jennings. PeECV; TOF

Tergvinder's Stone. W. S. Merwin. CAPP

Term, The. William Carlos Williams. InvP; LiTA

Terminal. Thom Gunn. PFL

Terminal hotel, the world shuddering with trains. *(LL)* Black Mare. Lynda Hull. UTF

Terminal Moraine, A. James Fenton. SCBI

Terminally Ill. Anna Swirszczynska, *tr. fr. Polish by* Czeslaw Milosz *and* Leonard Nathan. PoSu

Terminations. A. R. Ammons. AnAn

Terminus. Emerson. AmPP; AWP; MeMAP; NOBA; OxBA; PoEL-4; PoLF; TAP

Termite, The. Ogden Nash. NBLV; OBCA

Terms of all kinds mellow with time, growing. Their Speech, Compared with Wisdom and Poetry. Robert Pinsky. *Fr.* Essay on Psychiatrists. NoAM; PoA

Terms of Appointment. A. R. D. Fairburn. PeNZ

Ternarie of Littles, upon a Pipkin of Jellie [*or* Jelly] Sent to a Lady, A. Robert Herrick. BeJo; FaBoCh; FaBoUs; GoJo; PoEL-3

Ternissa. Walter Savage Landor. *See* Ternissa! You Are Fled.

Ternissa! You Are Fled. Walter Savage Landor. *Fr.* Hellenics, The. PoEL-4

Terpander. Tryphon, *tr. fr. Greek by* Peter Jay. GrAn

Terpês died among the Spartans, playing. Terpander. Tryphon, *tr. fr. Greek by* Peter Jay. GrAn

Terpsichore looks kindly on me. Korinna, *tr. fr. Greek by* John Dillon. PBWP

Terra Australis. James McAuley. NOBAu

Terra Australis. Douglas Stewart. NOBAu

Terra Australis. Chris Wallace-Crabbe. PAW

Terra cotta girl, The. In the Counselor's Waiting Room. Bettie M. Sellers. InPK

Terra Incognita. Sherod Santos. AnAn

Terra Nova. Sean O'Brien. PeSAV

Terrace and pool of the Prince of Liang stand up in mid-sky. The Liang Terrace. Li Ho, *tr. fr. Chinese by* A. C. Graham. PLT

Terrace at Berne, The. Matthew Arnold. *Fr.* Switzerland. EnVR; OBTV

Terrace in the Snow, The. Su Tung-p'o, *tr. fr. Chinese by* Kenneth Rexroth. NaP

Terrace is empty, which shows how flat it is, The. Heron Weather. Douglas Crase. NoP

Terraces of Rain. David St. John. NAmP90

Terrain. A. R. Ammons. VCAP

Terrapin, The. Elizabeth Smither. PeNZ

Terrapin War. *Unknown.* PAH

Terre, A. Wilfred Owen. LiTM; NSI; OxBTC; PeFWW; PoWW

Terre Promise. Ernest Dowson. NOBVV

Terrestrial Cuckoo, A. Frank O'Hara. CBNP; SOTW

Terribilis Est Locus Iste. John Engels. AnAn

Terrible/ a horse at night. Lawrence Ferlinghetti. HoPM

Terrible Beauty. Kingsley Amis. *See* Hearing how tourists, dazed with reverence.

Terrible beauty is born, A. (*LL*) Easter, 1916. W. B. Yeats. CMoP; FaBoMo; FaBoPV; FaPoR; HAP; HeIP; IIP; InPS; LiTM; MoAB; MoP; NAEL-2; NAWM-2; NIP; NoAM; NOBE; NOIV; NoP; OAEL-2; OBWP; OxAEP-2; OxBTC; PoE; PPP; TFi

Terrible child-bed hast thou had, my dear, A. Shakespeare. *Fr.* Pericles. EBEV; OxAEP-1

Terrible Door, The. Harold Monro. BoLoP; EnLoPo; FaBoTw

Terrible Infant, A. Frederick Locker-Lampson. FiBHP

Terrible is my plight this night. Wolves for Company. *Unknown, tr. fr. Irish.* BIrV

Terrible is the price. The Price. John Davidson. EBVV

Terrible Path, The. Brian Patten. OTCP

Terrible slowness/ overtaking haste. (*LL*) The Tortoise. Cid Corman. InPK; SM; VGW

Terrible Sons, The. Eleazar ben Kalir, *tr. fr. Hebrew by* Israel Zangwill. TrJP

Terrible sons of the mighty race, The. The Terrible Sons. Eleazar ben Kalir, *tr. fr. Hebrew by* Israel Zangwill. TrJP

Terrible Thought, A. Eliezer Steinbarg, *tr. fr. Yiddish by* Joseph Leftwich. TrJP

Terribly for mystery or glory my dawns have arisen. Dawns I Have Seen. Ivor Gurney. FaBoPP

Terrified Meadows, The. William Pillen. BTR

Terrifying are the attent sleek thrushes on the lawn. Thrushes. Ted Hughes. FaBoMo; GoYe; TRP

Territory. Jean Chapman. CRH

Territory is Not the Map, The. Jack Spicer. CBNP

Terror. Denise Levertov. PoE

Terror. Robert Penn Warren. PoA

Terror. "Yehoash," *tr. fr. Yiddish by* Isidore Goldstick. TrJP

Terror and stillness and ebon-hued horror, night in its iciness. Midnight. Andreas Gryphius, *tr. fr. German by* George C. Schoolfield. GePo

Terror Conduction. Philip Lamantia. NeAP

Terror does not belong to open day. Counterpoint. Owen Dodson. PoNe

Terror for fat burghers on far plains below. (*LL*) Rocky Acres. Robert Graves. LiTB; MeMBP; NoAM; UnPo

Terror is, all promises are kept., The / even happiness.y. (*LL*) Treasure Hunt. Robert Penn Warren. NoP

Terror strikes lightly your stillness. Spider. Thomas Cole. PoA

Terrorist. Paul Hyland. PWE

Terrorist, He Watches, The. Wislawa Szymborska, *tr. fr. Polish by* Adam Czerniawski. PoSu

Terrorist Smiles, The. Anselm Hollo. UL

Terrorist's Wife. Angela Greene. NWP

Terry. Albert Rowe. CRH

Terse Elegy for J.V. Cunningham. X. J. Kennedy. DiPo

Terzetto: Brixton. Bill Griffiths. NBrP

Tess's Lament. Thomas Hardy. FaBoTw; FaBoVe; TEP

Test, The. Emerson. OBAL

Test of Manhood, The, *sels.* George Meredith.
"In fellowship Religion has its founts." WGRP

Test of Men, The. Bible, Apocrypha. *Fr.* Ecclesiasticus. TrJP

Testament. Bei Dao, *tr. fr. Chinese by* Donald Finkel *with* Chen Xueliang. SpMi

Testament. Roland Mathias. AngWe

Testament, *sels.* James Weigel, Jr..

Testament. Bill Zavatsky. UL

Testament of a Rebel. Breyten Breytenbach, *tr. fr. Afrikaans by* André P. Brink. PeSAV

Testament of a Vivisector, The. John Davidson. MeMBP

Testament of Beauty, The, *sels.* Robert Bridges.
Ethick. OxBTC
"Sky's unresting cloudland, that with varying play, The." EBEV

Testament of Cresseid, The. Robert Henryson. OxBLMV; OxBS
Sels.
Assembly of the Gods, The. PoEL-1
Cresseid's Complaint against Fortune. MeEL
"I mend the fyre and beikit me about." EBEV; PoE
"Lipper folk to Cresseid than can draw, The." ScCV

Testament of John Davidson, The, *sels.* John Davidson.

Testament of Mr. Andro Kennedy, The. William Dunbar. OxBS

Testament of Perpetual Change, The. William Carlos Williams. GOA

Testaments, *sels.* James Weigel, Jr..

Teste Moanial. Anne MacNaughton. BAP-89

Testimony. Jane Flanders. CrSp

Testimony. Dan Pagis, *tr. fr. Hebrew by* Stephen Mitchell. PoSu

Testimony, A. Carolyn M. Rodgers. BPo

Testimony, A. George Ella Lyon. GOYP

Testimony in trials that never got heard. A Woman Is Talking to Death. Judy Grahn. GLP

Testing-Tree, The. Stanley Kunitz. FYAP; MAT; UnPo

Testubicles spill blood across the page. Crossedroads. Martin Staples Shockley. FF

Tête-à-Tête. Edwin Honig. NoAM

Tête à Tête; or, Fashionable has its Eclogue, The. Ann Murry. ECWP

Tetélestai. Conrad Aiken. LiTA; LiTM; MoAB; MoAmPo; PrIm

Tethy's Festival., *sels.* Samuel Daniel.
"Are they shadows that we see?" NOSC
(Are They Shadows [That We See]?) CH; EIL; InvP; NoP
(Shadows.) NOBE
(Song: "Are they shadowes that we see?") PoEL-2

Tewksbury Road. John Masefield. BoTP

Texan Rhodes Scholar named Fred, A. Lyndon T. Mole. PeLi

Texas. Mei-Mei Berssenbrugge. UL

Texas. Whittier. PAH

Texas Cowboy, The. *Unknown.* AmFP

Texas Cowboy [lay down] on a barroom floor, A. The Hell-bound Train. *Unknown.* BeLS; BLPA

Texas Ranger, The. Margie B. Boswell. AiP

Text. Audrey Wurdemann. FYAP

Text for a Poster (2). Lee Harwood. NBrP

Text for These Distracted Times, A. Rodney Hall. CBAP

Text, Silk. Novica Tadic, *tr. fr. Serbo-Croatian by* Charles Simic. HSix

Th Wundrfulness uv th Mountees Our Secret Police. Bill Bissett. NOBC

Thaba Bosio. S. D. R. Sutu, *tr. fr. Sotho by* Dan Kunene *and* Jack Cope. PeSA

Thack church and a wooden steeple, A. Legsby, Lincolnshire. *Unknown.* GBP

Thaddeus Stevens. Phoebe Cary. PAH

Thai passit in thare pilgramage. *Unknown. Fr.* Golagros and Gawane. OxBS

Thailand Railway. Randolph Stow. CBAP
Sels.
Jungle, The.
Sleepers, The.

Thair is nocht ane Winche. *Unknown.* OxBS

Thaïs. Newman Levy. FiBHP; PeLV

Thais, why do you call me old. Martial, *tr. fr. Greek by* Kenneth Rexroth. PGA

Thalaba the Destroyer., *sels.* Robert Southey.

Thalamos. Peter Kane Dufault. ErPo

Thalassa. Louis MacNeice. BIrV; FaBoMo; FaBoRV; NOBE

Thames, The. Sir John Denham. *See* Here should my wonder dwell, and here my praise.

Thames, The. M. M. Hutchinson. BoTP

Thames Head Wassailers' Song. *Unknown.* OBET

Thames nocturne of blue and gold, The. Impression du Matin. Oscar Wilde. EBVV; MoBrPo; NAEL-2; NoAM

Thamuris Marching. Robert Browning. OAEL-2

Than all men else, than thy self only less. (*LL*) To Ben Jonson. Thomas Carew. BeJo; CaPo; EPCY; NAEL-1; NOSC

Than all the eastern sages knew. (*LL*) On the Emigration to America [and Peopling the Western Country]. Philip Freneau. NAAL-1; PAH; TAP

Than all the flour'shing wreaths by laureates worn. (*LL*) To My Worthy Friend Master George Sands [or Sandys], on His Translation of the Psalms. Thomas Carew. BeJo; CaPo; EPCY; JCP; MeLP; SeCV-1

Than all the gold that leaden minds can frame. (*LL*) To the Lady Margaret, Countess [or Countesse] of Cumberland. Samuel Daniel. NOSC

Than any memory its walls and domes. (*LL*) The Yiddish Muses. Jacqueline Osherow. UTF

Than any other thing! (*LL*) Wishing. William Allingham. BoTP; FaPON; OHIP; OxBChV

Than anywhere else on earth. (*LL*) The Lord God Planted a Garden. Dorothy Frances Gurney. BLPA; EBEvV; FaBoBe; WGRP

Than at the diggins-oh. (*LL*) The Diggins-Oh. *Unknown.* NOBAu

Than aught, except its living years. (*LL*) And Thou Art Dead. Byron. MeMBP; PoEL-4

Than by my threatenings rest still innocent. (*LL*) The Apparition. John Donne. EnLoPo; EnRePo; ESCV; GBL; HeIP; NAEL-1; NAWM-1; NOBE; NOBL; NoSic; OAEL-1; OBD; OBEV; PoE; SCGP; SCV; SeCP; SeCV-1; SoSe; TFi

Than by one to hazard all. (*LL*) The Scare-Fire. Robert Herrick. HAP; NoP

Than (By Yon Sunset's Wintry Glow). E. E. Cummings. VGW

Than calm in waters, seen. (*LL*) To Jane: The Recollection. Shelley. OBNC

Than can be now, when plentie makes me poore. (*LL*) An Elegy on Ben Jonson. John Cleveland. MeLP

Than could whole seas of craw-fish soup. (*LL*) To a Young Lady, with Some Lampreys. John Gay. CBLP; ECEV; FaBoUs; NOEC

Than did his quartos upon us! (*LL*) Epitaph on Robert Southey. Thomas Moore. FaBoCo; FaBoEE

Than even Oxford town. (*LL*) The Spires of Oxford. Winifred M. Letts. PoLF; PoRA; WGRP

Than ever did th' adviser! (*LL*) Epistle to a Young Friend. Burns. EBEV

Than for a pardon that he dares admire. (*LL*) At Penshurst [Another]. Edmund Waller. BeJo; OAEL-1; SeCV-1

Than go to church with oily Sue and afterwards to bed. (*LL*) Correspondence between Mr. Harrison in Newcastle and Mr. Sholto Peach Harrison in Hull. Stevie Smith. FaBoNo; NBLV; OxBC

Than he could do in seven. (*LL*) Father Grumble. *Unknown.* AmFP

Than he is, or I am. (*LL*) Youth. James Wright. NaP; NoP

Than him that said, "Rejoice! rejoice!" (*LL*) The Two Voices. Tennyson. MeMBP

Than I may fruitful be. (*LL*) Deliverance from a Fit of Fainting. Anne Bradstreet. TAP

Than in foreign lands to follow you again. (*LL*) Adieu, to Fortune. Henry Francis Fynn. PeSAV

Than in your mynde Dydo ye shall espy. The Letter of Dydo to Eneas. Chaucer. OxBLMV

Than loafin' around The Throne. (*LL*) Little Breeches. John Milton Hay. AnAmPo; BeLS; FaBoBe; VPP

Than meet with a wicked woman! (*LL*) Sweet little bell. *Unknown.* NOIV

Than mind a child/ That yelps like this/ I'd all day work. *Unknown, tr. fr. Japanese* by Geoffrey Bownas *and* Anthony Thwaite. Mes

Than none at all. Provide, provide! (*LL*) Provide, Provide. Robert Frost. AmPP; ChIV-1; CMoP; HAP; MoAB; MoP; NAAL-2; NoAM; NOBA; NoP; OPOP; PoE; Poetr; PPP; TAP; TFi; TwCP; UnPo; WeW

Than not have been at Monterey? (*LL*) Monterey. Charles Fenno Hoffman. AnAmPo; FaBoBe; PAH

Than passion's death! (*LL*) Dead Fires. Jessie Redmond Fauset. PoNe

Than Robene Roy begouth to revell. *At.* to James V, King of Scotland. *Fr.* Christ's Kirk on the Grene. OxBS; ScCV

Than rule yon isle and be a slave. (*LL*) Holyhead, Sept. 25th, 1727. Swift. BIrV

Than sav'd in vulgar company. (*LL*) Epitaph on Tuft-Hunter. Thomas Moore. FaBoCo; FaBoEE

Than share the city's year forlorn. (*LL*) Nature. Thoreau. AiP; BLPL; FaBoBe

Than she fled through the broom. (*LL*) The Broomfield Hill. *Unknown.* ESPB; OxBB

Than smiles of other maidens are. (*LL*) She Is Not Fair to Outward View. Hartley Coleridge. EnRP; OBEV

Than stockit mailins. (*LL*) A Poet's Welcome to His Love-begotten Daughter. Burns. LiTB; NAs; NOEC; OxBoLi; PoEL-4

Than teach ten thousand stars how not to dance. (*LL*) You Shall above All Things Be Glad and Young. E. E. Cummings. NoAM; NOBA; OxBA

Than that it lived at all. Farewell. (*LL*) Epitaph on Elizabeth, L. H. Ben Jonson. BeJo; EIL; ELP; EnRePo; FaBoEE; HAP; NAEL-1; NIP; NoP; NOSC; OBEV; PoE; Poetr; SCGP; SeCP; SeCV-1

Than that the quick should die? (*LL*) Apparitions. Thomas Bailey Aldrich. AnAmPo

Than that you should remember and be sad. (*LL*) Remember [or Sonnet]. Christina Rossetti. AWP; BoLoP; CH; EBEvV; EnLoPo; FaBV; IMW; MeMBP; NOBE; NoP; OAEL-2; OBEV; OBNC; OxAEP-2; PlP; PoLF; PoRA; TFi; TrGrPo

Than the screens around your bed. (*LL*) Shitty. Kingsley Amis. OxBC

Than the strong man in his wrath. (*LL*) The Cry of the Children. Elizabeth Barrett Browning. CoGr; EBVV; FaBoEH; OxAEP-2

Than the wind goin' over my hand. (*LL*) Sea Love. Charlotte Mew. MoAB; MoBrPo; OxAEP-2; OxBTC; TrGrPo

Than this smart Misery. (*LL*) Of course I prayed. Emily Dickinson. BoWoP; MoAmPo

Than this, the Fairies' once, now thine. (*LL*) The Fairy Temple; or, Oberon's Chapel. Robert Herrick. CaPo

Than those that to the earth with many tears they give. (*LL*) The Dead. Jones Very. AnAmPo; HAP; NOBA; OxBA; TAP

Than to live not perfected. (*LL*) His Request to Julia. Robert Herrick. BeJo; CaPo; NOSC

Than to say "abide" and yet not obtain. (*LL*) I abide and abide and better abide. Sir Thomas Wyatt. BoLoP; EnLoPo; SiPS; SiPSBD

Than to see you. (*LL*) Spring Joy. Chu Shu-chen. WPC

Than when I was a boy. (*LL*) I Remember, I Remember. Thomas Hood. BLPA; CoGr; EBEvV; ELP; EnRP; FaBoPo; FaPoR; ImPo; LiTB; NOBE; NTP; OxAEP-2; PlP; PoEL-4; TFi

Than where I loathed so much. (*LL*) Discontents in Devon. Robert Herrick. BeJo; CaPo; OxBSP; SeCV-1

Than where it scatters light. (*LL*) Claim to Love. Giovanni Battista Guarini. AWP

Than with these horrid moods be left i' the lurch. (*LL*) Epistle to John Hamilton Reynolds. Keats. OBNC

Than write such hopeless rubbish as thy worst. (*LL*) Two voices are there: one is of the deep. James Kenneth Stephen. BXAP; EPCY; FaBoCo; FaBoPa; FiBHP; NOBL; UV

Than you are now. (*LL*) I Shall Not Care. Sara Teasdale. MoAmPo; TrGrPo; UnPo

Than you touch with decay. (*LL*) To Death. Oliver St. John Gogarty. FaBoEE; OBD; OBMV; OtMeF

Thanam o'n dhoul, do ye think I'm dead? (*LL*) Finnegan's Wake. *Unknown.* CBNP; FaBoBa; NBLV

Thanatopsis. Bryant. AmPP; AnAmPo; AWP; BLPL; BoNaP; DL; FaBoBe; GGP; LiTA; NAAL-1; NOBA; OBEV; OxBA; PWR; TAP; TFi; TrGrPo; WBLP; WGRP

Thank God. Joseph Rolnik, *tr. fr. Yiddish by* Joseph Leftwich. TrJP

Thank God! *Unknown.* PoToHe

Thank God, bless God, all ye who suffer not. Tears. Elizabeth Barrett Browning. WPE

Thank God for life! Thank God! *Unknown.* PoToHe

Thank God for Little Children. Frances E. W. Harper. PWR

Thank God for peace! Thank God for peace, when the great gray ships come in! (*LL*) When the Great Gray Ships Come In. Guy Wetmore Carryl. AnAmPo; FaBoBe

Thank God for sleep! The Sacrament of Sleep. John Oxenham. PoLF

Thank God for sleep in the long quiet night. Morning Thanksgiving. John Drinkwater. BoTP

Thank God for the Country! Irene Arnold. WBLP

Thank God my brain is not inclined to cut. The Menagerie. William Vaughn Moody. AnAmPo

Thank God our liberating lance. The Road to France. Daniel Henderson. PAH

Thank God, thank God, we do believe. Christina Rossetti. PChr

Thank God they're all gone. Nazis. Ira Sadoff. NAmP90

Thank Goodness, the moving is over. "When the World Was in Building." Ford Madox Ford. CTC

Thank Heaven! the crisis. For Annie. Poe. AmPP; AnAmPo; BLPL; LiTA; MeMAP; NOBA; OBEV; OxBA

Thank heav'n! I'm safely landed frae Ostend. To the Memory of Gavin Wilson (Boot, Leg and Arm Maker). George Galloway. NOEC

Thank her. *(LL)* Womanwork. Paula Gunn Allen. SRLS

Thank Thee, O Giver of life, O God! Thanksgiving. Angela Morgan. TrPWD

Thank You. Kenneth Koch. NeAP; PoM

Thank You: A Poem in Seventeen Parts. *Unknown, tr. fr. Seneca Indian by* Richard Johnny John *and* Jerome Rothenberg. STP

Thank you Father for your free gift of fire. *Unknown, tr. fr. Masai.* EaPr

Thank You for Friends, A. Rodney Bennett. BoTP

Thank you for leaving the bar of soap. Note to the Previous Tenants. John Updike. GOYP

Thank you for some ventilation and free hands. Subway Vespers. Molly Peacock. NGP

Thank you for the introduction, headmaster. Prize giving Speech. James K. Baxter. IHNG

Thank You for the Valentine. Diane Wakoski. HoPM

Thank You, God. Nina Stiles. PoToHe

Thank You, Lord, *sels.* Maya Angelou.
"I see You." CrSp

Thank you, my dear. Sappho, *tr. fr. Greek by* Mary Barnard. UnAS

Thank you, pretty cow, that made. The Cow. Ann Taylor. OxBChV

Thank you. You are too. *(LL)* My Erotic Double. John Ashbery. LCAP; PoE; VCAP

Thanked it, and let it go. *(LL)* A Fairy Went a-Marketing. Rose Fyleman. BoTP; OxBChV

Thankful Acknowledgment of God's Providence, A. John Cotton. SCAP

Thankful Country Lass, The; or, The Jolly Batchelor Kindly Entertained. *Unknown.* CoMu

Thankful Heart, A. Robert Herrick. *See* Lord, Thou hast given me a cell.

Thankful soil manured and winter dressed, The. Shamed by the Creature. Mildmay Fane, 2d Earl of Westmorland. NOSC

Thankfulness. Adelaide Anne Procter. TrPWD

Thanking My Mother for Piano Lessons. Diane Wakoski. NoAM

Thanking Prince Chen-chi, *sels.* Hsü Chung-hsing, *tr. fr. Chinese by* Jonathan Chaves.

Thankless for favours from on high. On a Similar Occasion for the Year 1792. William Cowper. NOCV

Thanks. Nina Cassian, *tr. fr. Romanian by* Laura Schiff. AIW

Thanks. Herman von Gilm zu Rosenegg, *tr. fr. German by* Philip L. Miller. RiWo

Thanks! *(LL)* Make the Earth Bright and Thanks. Meridel LeSueur. SRLS

Thanks a million, oh revolving stars. Horoscope. Eva Salzman. NWP

Thanks and a Plea to Mary. *Unknown. See* Levedy, ic thonke thee.

Thanks Be to God. Janie Alford. PoToHe

Thanks, fair Urania; to your scorn. The Indifference. Sir Charles Sedley. SeCV-2

Thanks for Everything. Helen Isabella Tupper. *See* For all that God in mercy sends.

Thanks for the haggis. Could you really spare. Palladas, *tr. fr. Greek by* Tony Harrison. GrAn

Thanks from Earth to Heaven, *sels.* John Hall Wheelock.
"Holy Poet, I have heard." TrPWD

Thanks in Old Age. Walt Whitman. SAmP

Thanks in old age — thanks ere I go. Thanks in Old Age. Walt Whitman. SAmP

Thanks in Winter. Harri Webb. AngWe

Thanks Just the Same. *Unknown.* PoLF

Thanks, Sir, but, should it please the reverend Court. Robert Browning. *Fr.* Ring and the Book, The. EBVVPR

Thanks to Flowers. Kate Farrell. ArNa

Thanks to Industrial Essex. Donald Davie. OxBTC

Thanks to Saint Matthew, who had been. Comrade Jesus. Sarah Norcliffe Cleghorn. WGRP

Thanks to Spring. Mary Anderson. BoTP

Thanks to the Brook. Wilhelm Müller, *tr. fr. German by* Philip L. Miller. *Fr.* Beautiful Maid of the Mill, The. RiWo

Thanks to the morning light. The World-Soul. Emerson. PFP

Thanksgibin' day am now at han'. Day befo' Thanksgibin', De. Maggie Pogue Johnson. CBWP-4

Thanksgiving. Susie Montgomery Best. TrPWD

Thanksgiving. Florence Earle Coates. TrPWD

Thanksgiving. Louise Glück. FoLa

Thanksgiving, The. George Herbert. ESCV; GeHe

Thanksgiving. Robert Herrick. LiTB

Thanksgiving. Kenneth Koch. VGW

Thanksgiving. David Abenatar Melo, *tr. fr. Spanish by* Henry Hart Milman. TrJP

Thanksgiving. L. A. J. Moorer. CBWP-3

Thanksgiving. Angela Morgan. TrPWD

Thanksgiving. John Oxenham. BLRP; WBLP

Thanksgiving. Liz Rosenberg. PBCAP

Thanksgiving. Margaret E. M. Sangster. BLRP

Thanksgiving. "Yehoash," *tr. fr. Yiddish by* Isidore Goldstick. TrJP

Thanksgiving, A. William Dean Howells. TrPWD
Sels.
"Lord, for the erring thought." WGRP

Thanksgiving, A. Lucy Larcom. OHIP
Sels.
"For the rosebud's break of beauty." TrPWD

Thanksgiving, A. Cardinal Newman. TrPWD

Thanksgiving after Communion. *Unknown, tr. fr. Gaelic by* Douglas Hyde. WTO

Thanksgiving at Snake Butte. James Welch. AiP

Thanksgiving Day. John Kendrick Bangs. TrPWD

Thanksgiving Day. Robert Bridges. OHIP

Thanksgiving Day. Lydia Maria Child. FaPON; ImGa; NTCP; OHIP; WHSW

Thanksgiving Day. Annette Wynne. OHIP

Thanksgiving for a former, doth invite. Thanksgiving. Robert Herrick. LiTB

Thanksgiving for a Habitat. W. H. Auden. NYBP
Sels.

Thanksgiving for America, The. Hezekiah Butterworth. PAH

Thanksgiving Hymn. *Unknown.* PAH

Thanksgiving in Boston Harbor, The. Hezekiah Butterworth. OHIP; PAH

Thanksgiving (1956). E. E. Cummings. FaBoPV; IHNG

Thanksgiving [or Father in Heaven]. At. to Emerson Emerson.

Thanksgiving to God for His House, A. Robert Herrick. BeJo; BLPL; ChTr; FaBoBe; HAP; NOSC; OHIP; PeECV; PoRA; SeCP; SeCV-1; TrCP; TrPWD; WGRP

Thanksgivings for the Beauty of His Providence. Thomas Traherne. FaBoCh

Thar's More in the Man than Thar Is in the Land. Sidney Lanier. NOBA

Thass a funny title, Mr. Bones. April Fool's Day, or St. Mary Egypt. John Berryman. *Fr.* Dream Songs. ChIV-2; NaP

Thassyryans king, in peas with fowle desyre. The Earl of Surrey. *See* Assyrian [*or* Assyrians'] King in peace, with foul desire, The [*or* Th'].

That a pile of paradoxes are expected to result! *(LL)* Federation. W. T. Goodge. NOBAu

That a woman not ask a man to leave meaningful work to. Prayer for Revolutionary Love. Denise Levertov. CrSp

That all my trust and travaill is but wast. *(LL)* Ever myn happe is slack and slo in commyng. Petrarch. OBVE

That all these dyings may be life in death. *(LL)* Mortification. George Herbert. ESCV; GeHe; NOSC; SeCP

That all things should be mine. Amendment. Thomas Traherne. SeCV-2

That all we love is born again. *(LL)* Christmas at Freelands. James Stephens. TIRV; TrCP

That amusing old man with a beard. *(LL)* There was an old man with a beard. John Clarke. UV

That any just to long for. Root-light, or the Lawyer's Daughter. James Dickey. NGP

That aquatic old personn of Grange. *(LL)* There was an old person of Grange. Edward Lear. CBNP; FaBoNo

That are impossible. *(LL)* To cause accord or to agree [*or* aggre]. Sir Thomas Wyatt. AAS; SCGP; SiPS; SiPSBD

That are so wondrous sweet and fair. *(LL)* Go, Lovely Rose. Edmund Waller. AWP; BeJo; BoLoP; ClHu; CTC; EBEvV; EnLoPo; FF; GGP; GTBS; GTBS-P; HAP; HeIP; InPK; NAEL-1; NOBE; OBEV; OPOP; PoE; PoRA; TEP; TFi; TrGrPo; UnPo; WeW

That are the holy spaces of my life. *(LL)* Ghosts, Places, Stories, Questions. Vincent Buckley. NOBAu

That Asia had its future in my pocket. *(LL)* Einstein's Bathrobe. Howard Moss. VCAP

That Asiatic striptease girl/ who goes in for those. Automedon, *tr. fr. Greek by* Alan Marshfield. GrAn

That August afternoon the family. State Funeral. Thomas McCarthy, *tr. fr. Irish.* CIP; IB; PeIV

That August the birds kept away from the village, afraid. For the Last Time, Fire. Dennis Scott. PBCV

That axe that I hear. Buson, *tr. fr. Japanese by* Harold G. Henderson. TAL

That balmy eve, within a trellised bower. The Marriage of Pocahontas. Mary Morison Webster. PAH

That bears the Human soul. *(LL)* There is no frigate like a book. Emily Dickinson. GoJo; MoAmPo; OBCA; PoLF; SAmP; SoSe; TAP; TrGrPo

That bears the zodiac. *(LL)* The Goose Fish. Howard Nemerov. CMoP; HeIP; LiTM; NIP; NoAM; NoP; PoE; Poetr; SM

That beautiful color on the leaf. The Red Leaf. Page Sullivan. ImGa

That black forest and the fire in earnest. *(LL)* Gretel in Darkness. Louise Glück. AmPA; NoAM

That blessed day. *(LL)* I Thank Thee, Lord. *Unknown.* BLRP; WBLP

That board — you'd rave and rend them with your teeth. *(LL)* A Question. J. M. Synge. MoBrPo; NOIV; OBMV; OxBTC; PeIV

That boatman am I. *(LL)* In the Past. Trumbull Stickney. AnAmPo; NOBA; OxBA

That bony potbellied arrow, wing-pumping along. The Cormorant in His Element. Amy Clampitt. InPK

That bounds the dim perpective of our days. *(LL)* Playing the Game. *Unknown.* PWR

That boy was hungry. His mother gave him Dog Salmon. Salmon Boy. David Wagoner. AnAn

That breathed the living breath of spring. *(LL)* The Resurrection. Jonathan Henderson Brooks. CDC; PoNe

That breathes on earth the air of paradise. *(LL)* Yes! hope may with my strong desire keep pace. Michelangelo. OBVE

That brekis thair hairt and nocht the bettir. *(LL)* To Luve Unluvit. Alexander Scott. OxBS

That briar patch looks uninhabitable. Thorny. William Cole. ZA

That bridge from the city, that was Waimakariri. Mary Ursula Bethell. *Fr.* By the River Ashley. PeNZ

That broke up our society upon the Stanislow. *(LL)* The Society upon the Stanislaus. Bret Harte. AnAmPo; BeLS; OBAL

That broken star. David McCord. *Fr.* Christmas Package, A. PChr

That buttoned down before. *(LL)* Abram Brown. *Unknown.* OxNR

That by snow were set on fire. *(LL)* The Snow-Ball. Thomas Stanley. CBLP

That by the flame of mine 'twill melted be. *(LL)* The Cold Kiss. Thomas Stanley. CBLP

That calm above those trees in the gray spaces. A Colloquy of Silences. Michael Heffernan. SM

That can arise from aught beside. *(LL)* Called Proud. Walter Savage Landor. GBL

That can count all they have and more. *(LL)* To His Love When He Had Obtained Her. *At.* to Sir Walter Ralegh. NoSic

That can only mean someone is watching. *(LL)* Back in the Twilight Zone. Martha Hollander. UTF

That "cannot be done," and you'll do it. *(LL)* It Couldn't Be Done. Edgar A. Guest. BLPA; FaBoBe; WBLP

That Cat. Ben King. AnAmPo; CRH; FiBHP; OFC

That cat gits out. *(LL)* That Cat. Ben King. AnAmPo; CRH; FiBHP; OFC

That cat who comes during sleep, quiet. Without Violence. Pattiann Rogers. SoCa

That cautious old person of Dean. *(LL)* There was an old person of Dean. Edward Lear. MoShBr

That cheers the heart! *(LL)* I will sing of the well-founded Earth. *Unknown.* EaPr, *ad.* by Elizabeth Roberts

That child will never lie in me, and you. The Unknown Child. Elizabeth Jennings. PBWP

That childish thoughts such joys inspire. Thomas Traherne. *Fr.* Third Century, The. ESCV

That Chinese restaurant was a joke. The Will to Change. Adrienne Rich. NMM

That circles between the mother and her young. *(LL)* The Circle of Weeping. Amir Gilboa. MHP

That civilisation may not sink. Long-legged Fly. W. B. Yeats. CMoP; FaBoMo; FaBoTw; InPS; LiTM; MoP; NAEL-2; NoAM; NOBE; NoP; OPOP; PoE; TEP

That clock is ticking. Marie Lucille. Gwendolyn Brooks. TLR

That comes into and steadies my soul. *(LL)* The Pangolin. Marianne Moore. HAP; NoAM; NOBA; PBWP; Poetr

That conversation we were always on the edge. Adrienne Rich. *Fr.* Twenty-one Love Poems. BoWoP; GLP; NoAM

That converse bone to bone? *(LL)* Sixteen Dead Men. W. B. Yeats. FaBoPV; OBWP

That cop was powerful mean. The Idiot. Dudley Randall. BPo

That corner of the earth. Aware Aware. Tram Combs. TwCP

That cost some dear, if thou may'st ha't for nought. *(LL)* A Counterlove. *Unknown.* NoSic

That crackle is well worth hearing. Mr. T. S. Eliot Cooking Pasta. József Tornai, *tr. fr. Hungarian by* Richard Wilbur. GrPl

That crafty cat, a buff-black Siamese. Double Dutch. Walter de la Mare. CRH

That "Craning of the Neck." Isabella Gardner. WPE

That crazed girl improvising her music. The Crazed Girl. W. B. Yeats. InPS; Son

That creepycrawly traversing the stone. Close-ups of Summer. Norman MacCaig. OxBC

That creye, "How! how!" *(LL)* Holly and Ivy ("Holly stand in the hall.") *Unknown.* MeEL

That cries, "All souls are mine." *(LL)* The Prince of Peace His Banner Spreads. Harry Emerson Fosdick. AH

That cross my gaze with such terrible speed. *(LL)* This Day. Lawrence Raab. NoP

That dandy black-and-white gentleman doodling notes. Magpie and Pines. Louis Johnson. PeNZ

That dared attack my Chesterton. *(LL)* Lines to a Don. Hilaire Belloc. FaBoCo; MoBrPo; OBSV; OtMeF

That dared attack my Chesterton. *(LL)* The Lion. Hilaire Belloc. MoBrPo; NBLV; WHSW

That dares nor write things false, nor hide things true. *(LL)* To Sir Henrie Savile upon His Translation of Tacitus. Ben Jonson. SeCV-1

That dark brown rabbit, lightness in his ears. John Berryman. *Fr.* Dream Songs. TwCP

That Dark Other Mountain. Robert Francis. CRP

That Day, *sels.* Kipling.
"It got beyond all orders an' it got beyond all 'ope." PIP
"There was thirty dead an' wounded on the ground we wouldn't keep." PIP

That Day. John Leax. TrCP

That Day. Anne Sexton. BoWoP

That day all the slaves were freed. Brazilian Fazenda. P. K. Page. FaBoWP

That day began with a shower. The Day Duke Raised; May 24th, 1974. Quincy Troupe. Jaz

That day, blue-white shirted. Terzetto: Brixton. Bill Griffiths. NBrP

That day everything went wrong. Poetry Defined. John Holmes. GrPl

That day I died. *(LL)* Here We have No Firm Dwelling-Place. Eugène Marais. PeSAV

That day in the Interpreter's house, in one of his Significant Rooms. Christiana. Peter Redgrove. OxBC

That day, in the slipping of torsos and straining flanks. Lola Ridge. WPE

That day she threw the goose over the roof. Grandma's Man. James Welch. NoAM

That day, so innocent appeared. Picnic Remembered. Robert Penn Warren. NAAL-2

That day the eggshell of appearance split. Transfigured Bird. James Merrill. MoAB

That day the huge water drowned all voices until. River Sound Remembered. W. S. Merwin. SM

That day, the last of my youth, on the last of our mountains. *(LL)* David. Earle Birney. NOBC

That day the sails of the ship were torn. Lament for Tadhg Cronin's Children. Michael Hartnett. PBCIP; RB

That day the sunlight lay on the farms. On Heaven. Ford Madox Ford. CTC

That day the/ words. That Day. John Leax. TrCP

That day when oats were reaped, and wheat was ripe. When Oats Were Reaped. Thomas Hardy. OxBTC

That days drone elsewhere. *(LL)* Summer. Christina Rossetti. BoNaP; ELP; PIP

That death in his windows would rise. Leah Goldberg, *tr. fr. Hebrew by* Ruth Finer Mintz. *Fr.* On Blossoming. MHP

That death might not be casual. Burns Singer. FaBoTw

That death should spare perfection so complete? *(LL)* The Doom of Beauty. Michelangelo. AWP

That Death should thus from hence our Butler catch. In Obitum Promi. Henry Parrot. FaBoCo

That decade with Rimbaud I don't regret. Rimbaud Fire Letter to Jim Applewhite. Fred Chappell. SM

That desire is quite over. Thinking of Love. Elizabeth Jennings. GOYP

That did invite, but seek another place. *(LL)* I prithee spare me, gentle boy. Sir John Suckling. BeJo

That did invite, but seek another place. *(LL)* Loves Feast. Sir John Suckling. CBLP

That didn't misconduct itself. *(LL)* 'Twas Ever Thus. *Unknown.* BXAP

That dignified old woman. Mothers. Maturaipputan Ilanakanar, *tr. fr. Tamil by* A. K. Ramanujan. PLW

That dirty no-good man treats me just like I'm a dog. *(LL)* Dirty No Gooder Blues. Bessie Smith. VBLP

That Distance Apart. Jackie Kay. NBrP

That Distant Bliss. Henry King. *See* Tell me[e] no more how fair[e] she[e] is.

That does not ask my sins. (LL) No camellia. Yosano Akiko. PBWP

That dolphin-torn, that gong-tormented face. The Death of Yeats. George Barker. LiTB; MeMBP

That dolphin-torn, that gong-tormented sea. (LL) Byzantium. W. B. Yeats. CMoP; EBEV; FaBoMo; HAP; InPS; LiTM; MeMBP; MoAB; MoBrPo; MoP; NAEL-2; NAWM-2; NIP; NoAM; NOBE; NoP; OAEL-2; OxBTC; PoE; Poetr; PPP; TEP

That doubtful hope, that certain woe, and sure despair of health. (LL) Such[e] wayward[e] ways [or wais] hath love, that most[e] part[e] in discord[e]. The Earl of Surrey. AAS; SiPS; SiPSBD

That dried-up arse, Lykainis. Antipater of Thessalonica, tr. fr. Greek by Alistair Elliot. GrAn

That Each Thing Is Hurt of Itself. Unknown. EIL

That earth shall be forgiven. (LL) Hesperus. John Clare. EBVV; FaBoRV; GTBS-P; NOBVV; OAEL-2

That equal love knows no disparity. (LL) To One That Pleaded Her Own Want of Merit. Thomas Stanley.

That eternal spring is hidden. Song of the Soul that Rejoices in Knowing God through Faith. St. John of the Cross, tr. fr. Spanish by K. Kavanaugh and O. Rodrigues. TOF

That Eureka of Archimedes out of his bath. Voluptuaries and Others. Margaret Avison. MoCV

That evening all in fond discourse was spent. The Sad Lover. George Crabbe. Fr. Tales of the Hall. OBNC

That evening Sinda thought she heard the drums. The Dream. Robert Hayden. NBV

That Ever I Saw. Unknown. TrGrPo

That ever went on Tipple Tyne. (LL) As I went over Tipple Tyne. Unknown. ChTr

That ever went over Tipple Tine. (LL) As I was going o'er Tipple Tine. Unknown. OxNR

That ever your eyes did see. (LL) The Laily Worm and the Machrel of the Sea. Unknown. ChTr; ESPB; InvP; OxBB; PoEL-1; SCGP

That every county in this developed state. Manifest Destiny. Pearse Hutchinson. CIP

That every fool is not a poet. (LL) Sir, I admit your general [or gen'ral] rule, At. to Pope Pope, also at. to Matthew Prior and to Samuel Taylor Coleridge. FaBoEE; FiBHP; LiTB

That every man in arms should wish to be. (LL) Character of the Happy Warrior. Wordsworth. EnRP; FaBoBe; LiTB; MeMBP

That everything he'd ever done was straw. (LL) Stacking the Straw. Amy Clampitt. VCAP

That Everything Moves Its Bowels. David R. Slavitt. BXAP

That evil ended. So also may this! (LL) Deor's Lament. Unknown. AnOE; OAEL-1

That expensive young lady of Corsica. (LL) There was a young lady of Corsica. Edward Lear. ChTr; FaBoNo

That Exploit of Yours. Ford Madox Ford. PeFWW; PoWW

That Face. Mairtin O Direain. BiHa

That fall and clothe my body with dream. (LL) Thinking of Someone. Hsiung-hung. WPC

That falls through the clear ether silently. (LL) To one who has been long in city pent. Keats. BLPA; EnRP; FaBoBe; FHYEP; ImPo; LiTB; MeMBP; TrGrPo

That Fame's immortal wreath has crowned his brow. (LL) In Memoriam Paul Laurence Dunbar. H. Cordelia Ray. CBWP-3

That famous old pederast, Wilde. Unknown. PeHV

That feels each pain and knows no joy at all. (LL) No Pleasure without Some Pain. Thomas, Lord Vaux. EIL; EnRePo

That fellow rides a big horse. Wang Fun-chih, tr. fr. Chinese by Eugene Eoyang. SuSp

That final newsreel of the war. A Welcoming Party. John Montague. IPY; PNI

That finds no object worth its constancy? (LL) The Waning Moon. Shelley. CH; FHYEP; OxBSP; TrGrPo

That fine English poet, John Donne. Wendy Cope. PeLi

That first September day was blue and warm. The Artist on Penmaenmawr. Charles Tennyson Turner. FaBoPP; OBNC

That flattering glass whose smooth face wears. A Looking-Glass. Thomas Carew. CaPo

That Flesh and Blood can't bear it. (LL) On Two Monopolists. John Byrom. FaBoCo; FaBoEE

That floats through many olden days. (LL) The Sculptor's Vision. H. Cordelia Ray. AmWP; CBWP-3

That flower unseen, that gem of purest ray. In a Churchyard. Richard Wilbur. HeIP

That fluttering thingas have so distinct a shade. (LL) Le Monocle de Mon Oncle. Wallace Stevens. LiTM; MeMAP; MoAB

That for a loved one must wait in longing. (LL) The Wife's Lament. Unknown. WPE

That for seven lustres [or lusters] I did never come. To the Reverend Shade of His Religious Father. Robert Herrick. CaPo; JCP; SeCV-1

That force is lost. Snake Eyes. Amiri Baraka. VGW

That frantic error I adore. The Apostasy of One and But One Lady. Richard Lovelace. CaPo

That from which it sprung — Eternity. (LL) Death. Emily Brontë. EBVV; OBNC

That from which these things are born. Carolyn Forché. Fr. Burning the Tomato Worms. MDDM

That ga' me a' my will. (LL) King Henry. Unknown. ESPB; OxBB

That gallant lady, gloriously bright. Petrarch, tr. fr. Italian by Mary Sidney Herbert, Countess of Pembroke. Fr. Triumph of Death. SiPSBD

That Gentle Man from Boston Town. Joaquin Miller. AnAmPo

That gilds your glorious tomb. (LL) The Bivouac of the Dead. Theodore O'Hara. AnAmPo; BLPA; PAH

That girl from the sun is bathing in the creek. The Dosser in Springtime. Douglas Stewart. ErPo

That glitter a cold span above the sea. (LL) The Laureate. Robert Graves. BIrV; FaBoTw; OBSV

That Glove. Mary E. Tucker. CBWP-1

That God is All, His shadow shows. (LL) Plaint. Ebenezer Elliot. OBD; OBEV

That God marked out for you. (LL) Get Somebody Else. Paul Laurence Dunbar. BLRP

That God of ours, the Great Geometer. Grace to Be Said at the Supermarket. Howard Nemerov. SoSe

That good, my sire, I dedicate to thee. (LL) Dedicatory Sonnet to S. T. Colerige. Hartley Coleridge. OAEL-2; Son

That grand and noble woman dear. Harriet Beecher Stowe's Works. Frank Barbour Coffin. AAP

That grows, at the first touch of day,/ Unendurable. (LL) First Light. Thomas Kinsella. BIrV; CMoP; PoE

That grows to him, rubbed silver tipped with flame. (LL) A Pilot from the Carrier. Randall Jarrell. PoWW

That had thee here obscure. (LL) Phoebus with Admetus. George Meredith. NOBE; OBEV

That happily you may always live. (LL) Beseeching the breath of the divine one. Unknown. EaPr

That Harp You Play So Well. Marianne Moore. MoAB; MoAmPo; PoA

That has no outward sign. (LL) Love Is a Wound Within the Body. Marie de France. VBLP

That has not been rent. (LL) Crazy Jane Talks with the Bishop. W. B. Yeats. BoLoP; CMoP; EBEV; ErPo; InPK; MeMBP; MoP; NAEL-2; NoAM; NoP; OAEL-2; OxAEP-2; PoE; PPP; TOF; TRP

That has sunk many islands in its good time. (LL) Nigger's Leap, New England. Judith Wright. NOBAu

That haughty tyranny of thine. Luís de León, tr. fr. Spanish by Thomas Walsh. TrJP

That He Findeth Others as Fair, but Not So Faithful as His Friend. George Turberville. EIL

That he may sleep upon his hill again? (LL) Abraham Lincoln Walks at Midnight. Vachel Lindsay. AmPP; CMoP; FaBV; FaPON; GOA; LiTA; MeMAP; MoAmPo; NOBA; OHIP; OxBA; PAH; TAP; TFi; VGW

That he us to him take. (LL) The Annunciation. Unknown. MeEL

That he was born it cannot be denied. On a Certain Alderman. John Cunningham, after the Greek of Simonides. FaBoEE

That he was ugly we have no doubt. Socrates' Death. Michael Jackson. PeNZ

That heartless chase. Wordsworth. Fr. Prelude [or, Growth of a Poet's Mind], The. EnRP; OAEL-2; PoEL-4; TOF

That heeds no call to die. (LL) Heredity. Thomas Hardy. CTC; EBEV; RB

That her serene influence should spread. Two Loves. Richard Eberhart. CMoP

That here, obedient to their laws, we lie. (LL) Thermopylae. Simonides. AWP; OBVE; OBWP

That he's another. (LL) Contentment. Charles Stuart Calverley. NOBVV

That hid the shyest grape. (LL) Monody. Herman Melville. LiTA; NAAL-1; OxBSP; PoE; PoEL-5

That Hill. Blanche Taylor Dickinson. CDC

That his cloak's much less worn than the hole in his rump. (LL) Epigram: On Hedylus. Martial. PeHV

That history is an event. Taku Skanskan. Paula Gunn Allen. ETG; HATNAP

That hobnailed goblin, the bobtailed Hob. Country Dance. Edith Sitwell. MoP; NoAM

That Holy Thing. George Macdonald. *Fr.* Paul Faber, Surgeon. OBEV; TrPWD; WGRP

That horrid dream of marble walls! *(LL)* The Palace of humbug. "Lewis Carroll." CBNP; FaBoNo

That hour-glass, which there ye see. The Hour-Glass. Robert Herrick. BeJo; CaPo

That houses forme within was rude and strong. The House of Richesse. Spenser. *Fr.* Faerie Queene, The. CH

That hump of a man bunching chrysanthemums. Old Florist. Theodore Roethke. OxBSP

That hungry face. A Kangaroo. Robert Gray. FaBoMA

That Hypocrite. *Unknown.* BPo

That I am clothed in holy robes for glory. *(LL)* Huswifery. Edward Taylor. EAP; FaBV; LiTA; MeMAP; NAAL-1; NIP; NOBA; NOBE; NoP; OxBA; SCAP; TAP; TFi

That I am mortal I know and do confess/ My span of day. Star-Gazing. Ptolemy, *tr. fr. Greek by* Dudley Fitts. ArNa; GrAn

That I am Thine. *(LL)* Endure Hardness. Christina Rossetti. NOBVV

That I belong to. *(LL)* Grant me the ability to be alone. Nachman of Bratslav. EaPr

That I bought for a halfpenny, yesterday. *(LL)* A Maudle-in Ballad. *Unknown.* BXAP; FaBoPa

That I ensconce Swinburne! *(LL)* A Refusal. Thomas Hardy. FaBoCo; LiTB; MeMBP

That I gae maiden hame!' *(LL)* Fair Annie. *Unknown.* ESPB; FaBoBa

That I had alighted there! *(LL)* Faintheart in a Railway Train. Thomas Hardy. CBLP; CTC; EnLoPo

That I have felt the rushing wind of Thee. The Poet's Prayer. Stephen Philipps. WGRP

That I have lakt so long. *(LL)* Now must I learn to live [*or* lerne to lyve] at rest. Sir Thomas Wyatt. AAS; SiPS

That I have often been in love, deep love. "Peter Pindar." NOEC

That I loved them, & that meant. Primavera. David Miller. NBrP

That I may fold it round me and in comfort lie. *(LL)* The Embankment [*or* Fantasia of a Fallen Gentleman]. T. E. Hulme. EBEV; FaBoMo; GTBS-P; OxBSP; OxBTC

That I may know that in myself, in me, all is not yet snuffed out. *(LL)* Guard Me, Oh God. Shin Shalom. MHP

That I may lose my way/ And myself. *(LL)* Lights Out. Edward Thomas. Mes; NOBE; OBD; OxAEP-2; PoWW

That I might give way to that lowly mistress of yours. *(LL)* It Is Pleasing. Sulpicia. VBLP

That I might ithere present it! — Oh! to whomm? *(LL)* The Question. Shelley. CH; CoGr; EnRP; OBEV

That I might there present it — O! to Whom? *(LL)* Question, The ("I dream'd that, as I wander'd by the way.") Shelley. CH; EnRP; OBEV

That I must journey on. *(LL)* Supplication. Joseph S. Cotter, Sr.. CDC; PoNe

That I Not Be a Restless Ghost. Margaret Mead. MDDM
Sels.

That I say: "Lady, I am wholly thine." *(LL)* Ballata: Of a Continual Death in Love. Cavalcanti. AWP

That I see around or about me. *(LL)* Ringleted Youth of My Love. *Unknown.* WTO

That I shall never find him. *(LL)* The Mad Maid's Song. Robert Herrick. AWP; CaPo; CH; EnLoPo; OAEL-1; OBEV; SeCV-1; TrGrPo; WiR

That I shall never find my home. *(LL)* The Mower to the Glow-Worms [*or* Glowworms]. Andrew Marvell. AWP; ELP; FHYEP; GeHe; InvP; NAEL-1; NOBE; NoP; OAEL-1; OxBoLi; PeLV; PPP; SCGP; TFi; TrGrPo

That I should love, and he should be ingrate. *(LL)* To One That Asked Me Why I Loved J. G. "Ephelia." KTR; NOSC; VBLP

That I was never blest. *(LL)* The Repulse. Thomas Stanley. BeJo; MeLP

That I went to warm my self in Lady Betty's Chamber. To Their Excellencies the Lords Justices of Ireland, the Humble Petition of Frances Harris, Who Must Starve, and Die a Maid if It Miscarries. Swift. NOEC; PoEL-3

That I would not persuaded be. Service Is No Heritage. Nicholas Breton. NoSic

That I would wish me thus to dream and die. *(LL)* The Ivory, Coral, Gold. William Drummond of Hawthornden. ELP

That if I dipped my hand the spawn would clutch it. *(LL)* Death of a Naturalist. Seamus Heaney. HAP; NoAM; OxBC; WeW

That if I stepped out of my body I would break/ Into blossom. *(LL)* A Blessing. James Wright. ArNa; CAPP; GoJo; GrPl; InPK; InPS; NAAL-2; NaP; NoAM; NOBA; NoP; PoE; Poetr; PPP; RaBo; TRP; TwCP; VCAP

That I'm alive to tell you so. *(LL)* Stella's Birthday; March 13, 1726/27. Swift. NAs; NoP; OAEL-1; PoE; PoEL-3; SCGP

That insect, without antennae, over its. The Crane. Charles Tomlinson. MoBrPo

That is, a quality of man and his becoming. Frost and Snow, Falling. J. H. Prynne. VaA

That Is All I Heard. "Yehoash," *tr. fr. Yiddish by* Isidore Goldstick. TrJP

That is fit home for Thee! *(LL)* To the Cuckoo. Wordsworth. BoTP; EBEvV; ELP; EnRP; GTBS; GTBS-P; PoLF; TrGrPo; UV, *st.* 1 *only*

That is fluent in even the wintriest bronze. *(LL)* The Sense of the Sleight-of-Hand Man. Wallace Stevens. HAP; ImPo; LiTM; MoAB; MoAmPo; NoAM; NOBA; PoA; TwCP; WeW

That is her lover lying there. Illumination. Jeffrey Wainwright. DiPo

That is most difficult. *(LL)* To a Friend Whose Work Has Come to Nothing. W. B. Yeats. AWP; InPK; LiTM; MoAB; MoBrPo; OAEL-2; OBMV; OxAEP-2; PoA

That is no country for old men. The young. Sailing to Byzantium. W. B. Yeats. ClHu; CMoP; FaPoB; FF; GTBS-P; HAP; HeIP; HoPM; IIP; ImPo; InPK; InPS; InvP; LiTB; LiTM; MoAB; MoBrPo; MoP; NAEL-2; NAWM-2; NIP; NoAM; NOBE; NoP; OAEL-2; OBMV; OxBTC; PIP; PoE; PoRA; PPP; PrIm; RaBo; SCGP; SoSe; TEP; TFi; TIRV; TOF; UnPo; WeW

That is the glebe and this is the glissando. The future is nothing. Codex. Stephen Rodefer. UL

That is the only truly great happiness on earth. *(LL)* Eros. Otto Benzon. RiWo

That is the truth in five words. *(LL)* You Loved Me. Marina Tsvetayeva. VBLP

That is what they say, who were broken off from love. Children's Elegy. Muriel Rukeyser. *Fr.* Eighth Elegy. LCAP

That is why I say "cold!" *(LL)* A Song of Winter. *Unknown.* CH

That isn't looking at you. You must change your life. *(LL)* Archaic Torso of Apollo. Rainer Maria Rilke. NU

That it come, my heart, await! *(LL)* Afternoon Light. Jacob Fichman. MHP

That it should end in an Albert Pick hotel. At the End of the Affair. Maxine W. Kumin. TAP

That it will never come again. Emily Dickinson. NOBA

That Journeys Are Good. Jalal al-Din Rumi, *tr. fr. Persian by* Robert Bly. RaBo

That joys so ripe so little keep. *(LL)* To Amarantha, That She Would Dishevel Her Hair. Richard Lovelace. BeJo; HoPM; NoP; OBEV; SeCP; SeCV-1; TrGrPo

That June before the judge gave. Seventeen. Jonathan Holden. Poetsp

That Justice is a blind goddess. Justice. Langston Hughes. BPo

That kill, that kill, that kill. *(LL)* Elm. Sylvia Plath. NoAM; NOBA; NoP; Poetr

That kindles my mother's fire! *(LL)* The Wife of Usher's Well. *Unknown.* AmFP; AWP; CH; ChTr; EBEV; EnRP; EnSB; ESPB, A, B, C, *and* D *vers.*; FaBoBa; ImPo, A *vers.*; LiTB; NAEL-1; NOBE; NoP; OAEL-1; OBEV; OxAEP-1; OxBB; OxBS; PoEL-1; Poetr; PrIm; RB; ScCV; SCGP; TFi; TrGrPo

That kings for such a tomb would wish to die. *(LL)* On Shakespeare. Milton. EPCY; HeIL; InvP; MeLP; NAEL-1; NoP; NOSC; PoE; PoRA; SCGP; TrGrPo

That knot in the wood if wood. The Man with the Hollow Breast. Tania van Zyl. PeSA

That knows-it cannot see. *(LL)* Difference between despair, The. Emily Dickinson. NAAL-1; NoP

That labor/ a face to remember in wonder. Sappho, *tr. fr. Greek by* Guy Davenport. OBVE

That lady of all gentle memories. Dante, *tr. fr. Italian by* Dante Gabriel Rossetti. *Fr.* Vita Nuova, La. AWP

That lamb it came a-trottin'. *(LL)* Mary had a little lamb,/ Its coat was white as cotton. *Unknown.* RoPo

That lately kissed thee. *(LL)* To Electra. Robert Herrick. BLPL; CaPo; HoPM; OBEV; SeCV-1

That lay in the house that Jack built. *(LL)* The House That Jack Built. Mother Goose. BoTP; FaBoBe; OxBoLi; OxNR; ReMoGo

That lay in the house that Jack built. *(LL)* The House That Jack Built. *Unknown.* NBLV; OxBoLi

That leader clamouring at dawngate. *(LL)* Copernicus. Robert David Fitzgerald. NOBAu

That leads me to the Lamb. *(LL)* Walking with God. William Cowper. ECEV; EnRP; NOCV; NOEC; PeECV; PoEL-3; TEP; TOF

That led back from nature into history. *(LL)* MacDuff. Charles Tomlinson. NAs; OxBC

That lies in the house of Bedlam. *(LL)* Visits to St. Elizabeths. Elizabeth Bishop. CBNP; CoAP; VGW

That life may be more comfortable yet. John Pomfret. *Fr.* Choice, The. OBF

That lifted blade transformed our jangling clans. James Russell Lowell. *Fr.* Under the Old Elm. GOA

That light, reflected, but makes darkness plain. (*LL*) In Dispraise of the Moon. Mary Elizabeth Coleridge. BoNaP; CH

That lightens o'er the heart. (*LL*) I Saw Thee Weep. Byron. CBLP

That linkage of warnings sent a tremor through June. Red Poppy. Tess Gallagher. NAmP90

That literature breeds distress. (*LL*) Sarah Byng Who Could Not Read and Was Tossed into a Thorny Hedge by a Bull. A Cautionary Tale. Hilaire Belloc. GoJo

That Little Black Cat. D'Arcy Wentworth Thompson. OFC; OxBChV

That little care. (*LL*) Place where soon I think to lie, The. Walter Savage Landor. CBLP

That little grey-haired lady. The Little Old Lady. Rodney Bennett. BoTP

That Little Lump of Coal. *Unknown.* AmFP

That little pretty bleeding part. To His Savior. The New Years Gift. Robert Herrick. ChIV-2

(That liv'd so sweetly) dead, so sweet a Grave! (*LL*) Music[k]'s Duel[l]. Richard Crashaw. GeHe; OAEL-1; SeCP; SeCV-1

That live to weep and sing their fall. (*LL*) The Death of Hoel. Thomas Gray. NOEC

That lone heath and its melancholly pond. (*LL*) The Sand Martin. John Clare. TEP

That long have watched for light, and wept in vain. (*LL*) As when, to one who long hath watched, the morn. John Codrington Bampfylde. NOEC

That look you had, Agnes, was a temporary fact. Temporary Facts. William Stafford. CAPP

That love is all there is. Emily Dickinson. NOBA

That Love is ever nigh. (*LL*) God the Omniscient. James Cowden Wallace. BLRP

That love of mine for him had waxen wings. The Comet. Maria Luisa Spaziani, *tr. fr. Italian by* Beverly Allen. NeIt

That love to her, I cast away. (*LL*) Disdain Returned. Thomas Carew. BeJo; PFP

That love which once was nearest to my heart. Vetus Flamma. Robert Mezey. PoA

That Love, — whose power and sovranty we own. The Creation of My Lady. Francesco Redi, *tr. fr. Italian by* Sir Edmund Gosse. AWP

That lovely spot which thou dost see. Upon a Mole in Celia's Bosom. Thomas Carew. CaPo; CBLP

That lover of a night. Crazy Jane on God. W. B. Yeats. CMoP; EBEV; MoAB; OxBTC

That made the woods of April bright. (*LL*) The Yellow Violet. Bryant. BLPL; EAP; NAAL-1; PoLF; TAP

That made them what they were! (*LL*) Transformations. Thomas Hardy. PPP; RB; TEP; TRP

That maids make not half such a tumult, as wives. (*LL*) Another True Maid. Matthew Prior. FaBoEE

That make them live — in dreams. (*LL*) "Tropicals." René Maran. NegPo

That makes her so divine. (*LL*) Chloe Divine. Thomas D'Urfey. OBEV

That man. Night Song for Two Mystics. Paul Blackburn. NeAP

That man entered through my eyes. Dream of the Forgotten Lover. Lucia Fox, *tr. fr. Spanish by* R. Maghan. BoWoP

That man over there say. Ain't I a Woman? Sojourner Truth. AIW; BlSi

That mans most Noble Passion is to Love. (*LL*) The Call. John Hall. MeLP; NOSC

That many friends had opened long ago. (*LL*) Mr. Flood's Party. E. A. Robinson. AmPP; AWP; BLPL; ClHu; CMoP; EBNV; FF; GGP; HAP; HeIL; HeIP; HoPM; LiTA; LiTM; MAT; MeMAP; MoAB; MoAmPo; MoP; NAAL-2; NIP; NoAM; NOBA; NoP; OBF; OxBA; PoE; Poetr; PoRA; PPP; PrIm; SoSe; TAP; TFi; TrGrPo; TRP; UnPo; WeW

That many years. (*LL*) To learn how to die cut down a tree. "Antler." EaPr

That matter of the murder is hushed up. The Cenci. Shelley. EnRP

That may be so, but you don't come in. (*LL*) Six little mice sat down to spin. Mother Goose. BoTP; OxNR

That me alone you lov'd, you once did say. Catullus, *tr. by* Richard Lovelace. *Fr.* Carmina. FMP; OBVE

That Men Should Fear. Shakespeare. *See* Cowards die many times before their deaths.

That mendacious Old Person of Gretna. (*LL*) There was an old person of Gretna. Edward Lear. ChTr; OxBChV

That mirror/ Which makes of men a transparency. Moments of Vision. Thomas Hardy. OAEL-2

That Moment. Ted Hughes. *Fr.* Crow. FF; PoE; UV

That Moment. Sharon Olds. Poetr

That moment on my mind. For Comrade Katharine. John Manifold. FaBoMA

That monk the bold baron. (*LL*) The Eve of Saint John. Sir Walter Scott. EnRP; PoEL-4

That Month. The daughter of Pari, *tr. fr. Tamil by* A. K. Ramanujan. PLW

That morn which saw me made a bride. Upon a Maid That Died [*or* Dyed] the Day She Was Married [*or* Married]. Meleager, *tr. fr. Greek by* Robert Herrick. AWP; OBD; OBVE

That morning, after the storm. After the Storm. Elizabeth Bartlett. GoYe

That most ancient Briton of English beasts. (*LL*) The Combe. Edward Thomas. FM; GTBS-P; RB

That mountain there. Pilgrimage Song. *Unknown, tr. fr. Pueblo Indian by* Mary Austin. WPE

That mourns a man like thee. (*LL*) On the Death of Joseph Rodman Drake. Fitz-Greene Halleck. AnAmPo; BLPA; PAH; PoEL-4

That moves about their feet. (*LL*) Ad Infinitum. Joan Aronsten. NOBAu

That music, remote, forlorn. (*LL*) The Old Summerhouse. Walter de la Mare. CMoP; FaBoPP; FaBoRV; GTBS-P

That must escape the knife. (*LL*) Autobiography of a Lungworm. Roy Fuller. MoP; NoAM; NoP; OxBC

That my flesh felt the carillon. (*LL*) Antwerp and Bruges. Dante Gabriel Rossetti. OBTV

That my old bitter heart was pierced in this black doom. A Grey Eye Weeping. Egan O'Rahilly, *tr. fr. Irish by* Frank O'Connor. FaBoPV; OBMV; PeIV

That Nature Is a Heraclitean Fire and of the Comfort of the Resurrection. Gerard Manley Hopkins. EnlH; EnVR; FaBoMo; FaBoVe; GTBS-P; LiTB; MeMBP; MoAB; NoP; OAEL-2; PoE; PoEL-5; TEP

That ne'er did wrong to thine or thee. (*LL*) The Lovely Lass o' Inverness. Burns.

That neither fame nor love might wanting be. To Sir Henry Cary. Ben Jonson. NoP; NOSC

That never were, nor are, nor e'er shall be. (*LL*) Against Fruition. Sir John Suckling. BeJo

That never were, nor are, nor e'er shall be. (*LL*) Against Fruition. Sir John Suckling. CaPo; ErPo

That never yet drowned me. (*LL*) Our Bog is Dood. Stevie Smith. CBNP; FaBoNo; NAEL-2; NBLV; PoE; WeW

That night I think that no one slept. The Last Fight. Lewis Frank Tooker. FaBoBe

That night my angel stooped and strained. My Angel. Jonathan Henderson Brooks. PoNe

That night she felt those searching hands. Mary, Mother of Christ. Countee Cullen. PChr

That night the moon drifted over the pond. The Prediction. Mark Strand. LCAP; VCAP

That night the whole world mingled. A Certain Evening. G. K. Chesterton. OxAEP-2

That Night They All Gathered on the Highest Tower. Jovan Hristic, *tr. fr. Serbo-Croatian by* Charles Simic. HSix

That night we blew our guns. We placed a shell. B. G. Bonallack. FaBoEH

That night, when I woke suddenly, was sweet. Conversation with Rain. Louise D. Gunn. GoYe

That Night When Joy Began. W. H. Auden. OxBTC; SoSe

That night, when storms were spent and tranquil heaven. John Addington Symonds. *Fr.* Ithocles. PeHV

That night, when through the mooring-chains. The Ballad of Fisher's Boardinghouse. Kipling. PoRA

That night which did the dreadful hap ensue. Petrarch, *tr. fr. Italian by* Mary Sidney Herbert, Countess of Pembroke. *Fr.* Triumph of Death. SiPSBD

That night will long delight us, Nealce. Petronius Arbiter, *tr. fr. Greek by* Kenneth Rexroth. PGA

That night your great guns, unawares. Channel Firing. Thomas Hardy. CMoP; EBEV; HAP; HeIP; ImPo; LiTB; MeMBP; MoP; NAEL-2; NIP; NoAM; NoP; OAEL-2; OxBTC; PeECV; PeFWW; PoE; PoEL-5; Poetr; PoRA; PoWW; PrIm; RB; SoSe; TFi; UnPo

That no fair woman will, wonder not why. Catullus, *tr. fr. Latin. Fr.* Carmina. OBVE, *tr. by* Richard Lovelace

That noble Chaucer, in those former times. Michael Drayton. *Fr.* To Henry Reynolds, of Poets and Poesy. EPCY

That nobody roweth or steereth. (*LL*) Erith, on the Thames. *Unknown.* ChTr; FaBoPP; GBP

That none are fair but who are kind. (*LL*) The Deposition. Thomas Stanley. CBLP

That None Beguiled Be. Sir John Suckling. PoEL-3

That none beguiled be by time's quick flowing. That None Beguiled Be. Sir John Suckling. PoEL-3
(Love's Clock. CaPo; NOSC

That nose is out of drawing. With a gasp. Sonnet for a Picture. Swinburne. *Fr.* Heptalogia, The. BXAP; FaBoNo; OAEL-2; UV

That note comes clear, like water running clear. The Piano Tuner's Wife. Karl Shapiro. NoAM

That note you hold, narrowing and rising, shakes. For Sidney Bechet. Philip Larkin. Jaz

That Nova was a moderate star like our good sun. Nova. Robinson Jeffers. CMoP; HAP

That now maken cheer. (*LL*) A Lullaby of the Nativity. *Unknown.* MeEL

That now to them dost all thy substance give. (*LL*) The Lost. Jones Very. NOBA

That o night were hire guest. (*LL*) With longing I am lad. *Unknown.* MiEL

That ocean you of late surveyed. To Mr. Newton on His Return from Ramsgate. William Cowper. NOEC

That odyssey? We three left Amherst late. To My Fellow-Mariners, March, '53. Thomas Whitbread. NYBP

That of heuen they may neuer mysse! (*LL*) Adam Bel [*or* Bell], Clym [*or* Clim] of the Clough[e], and Wyllyam [*or* William] of Cloudesle [*or* Cloudesly]. *Unknown.* ESPB; OxBB

That of heuen they may neuer mysse! (*LL*) Adam Bell, Clim of the Clough, and William of Cloudesly. *Unknown.* ESPB

That often change doth please a woman's mind. (*LL*) Divers Doth Use. Sir Thomas Wyatt. NAEL-1; SiPS; Son

That old crow-beaked hag. Agathias, *tr. fr. Greek by* Sam Hamill. InMo

That 'old last act'! Adrienne Rich. *Fr.* Two Songs. NIP; NOBA; TAP

That Old Mulemba. Geraldo Bessa Victor, *tr. fr. Portuguese by* Donald Burness. PeSAV

That Old Sauna High. Anselm Hollo. PoM

That on her lap she casts her humble eye. On the Blessed Virgin's Bashfulness. Richard Crashaw. HAP; OxBSP

That on the seventh he can nor preach or pray. (*LL*) Upon Parson Beanes. Robert Herrick. BeJo

That once this life was really mine. A Song of Life. Franz Werfel, *tr. fr. German by* Edith Abercrombie Snow. TrJP

That once which pained to think of. The Forgiven Past. Laura Riding. PBWP

That one poor Blossome. (*LL*) Praise. Henry Vaughan *and* Thomas Stanley. ESCV

That one small boy with a face like pallid cheese. Incendiary. Vernon Scannell. OxBC

That only thine, thine is the saving name. (*LL*) Eternal mover, whose diffused glory. Sir Henry Wotton. TrPWD

That opens and bends closed those leaves. (*LL*) The Swan's Feet. E. J. Scovell. FaBoWP; OxBTC

That Orpheus Calliops sonne who stayde the running brooke. Seneca, *tr. fr. Latin by* John Studley. *Fr.* Medea. OBVE

That other arrow veered towards your heart. (*LL*) Memoriter. Charles Spear. PeNZ

That our earth mother may wrap herself. Our Earth Mother. *Unknown, tr. fr. Zuni Indian by* R. Bunzel. WTO

That our thought may take her immediate in its embrace. (*LL*) Sonnet [*or* Sonetto] VII. Cavalcanti. CTC; OBVE

That pay their Homage to my Eyes. (*LL*) Song by the Wavering Nymph. Aphra Behn. VBLP

That perhaps I shall be healed. (*LL*) Sorrowful Song. Henri Cazalis. RiWo

That perishes at the heart. (*LL*) The Bitter Withy. *Unknown.* FaBoBa; NOCV; NoP

That Pobbles are happier without their toes. (*LL*) The Pobble Who Has No Toes. Edward Lear. CBNP; FaBoCh; FaBoCo; FaBoNo; MoShBr; OTCP; OxBChV

That poet is best. Lucilius, *tr. fr. Greek by* Sam Hamill. InMo

That poets are far rarer births than kings. To Elizabeth, Countess of Rutland. Ben Jonson. BeJo; OxBSP

That poets should each other eat. (*LL*) To a Swallow. John Peale Bishop, *after* Euenus. GrAn; OBVE

That poor men pay for all. (*LL*) The Poore [*or* Poor] Man Payes [*or* Pays] for All. *Unknown.* CoMu; OBET

That portrait of physics buried in the transparent. (*LL*) Glass. Vickie Karp. UTF

That Priapus with his big divining rod. To Bellinus. *Unknown, tr. fr. Latin.* PeHV

That Pull from the Left. Louise Erdrich. NoAM

That quiet man with the hoe is a beast. An Inmate. Peter Kocan. NOBAu

That raddled old queen. Tom Donnelly. PeLi

That ragged/ leaking raft held. Ireland. Richard Ryan. CIP

That ragged vagabond, snow, brings. Intruder. Alison Bielski. AngWe

That Rama whom the Indian sung. Of Rama. Herman Melville. LiTA

That rather had to die in troth than live forsaken so. (*LL*) The Lady Prayeth the Return of Her Lover Abiding on the Seas. *Unknown.* EIL; GBL

That rebellious rodent called Jerry. Bill Greenwell. PeLi

That Reminds Me. Ogden Nash. FiBHP

That resigned look! Here I am. Self-Portrait. R. S. Thomas. NAs

That river is full of mushrooms. Mushroom River. Xue Di, *tr. fr. Chinese.* TSaS, *tr. by* Ping Wang *and* Gale Nelson

That Room. John Montague. CIP

That rose slowly toward me, watching. (*LL*) Pike. Ted Hughes. CMoP; FaBoMo; HAP; HeIL; HeIP; InPS; LiTM; MAT; NAEL-2; OxBTC; PoE

That row of icicles along the gutter. Beyond Words. Robert Frost. Spl; WeW

That runs around the street. (*LL*) My father owns the butcher shop. *Unknown.* RoPo

That runs his link full in your face. (*LL*) Dorinda's sparkling wit, and eyes. Charles Sackville. OBEV; SeCV-2

That sail in cloudless light. Sea Grapes. Derek Walcott. TRP

That Saturday at eventide. (*LL*) The High Tide on the Coast of Lincolnshire (1571). Jean Ingelow. BeLS; EBVV; FaBoPP; GN; Mes, *abr.*; OtMeF; OxAEP-2; VPP

That savage trinity warily watching. (*LL*) Patrolling Barnegat. Walt Whitman. NoP

That scalps your naked soul. (*LL*) He fumbles at your soul. Emily Dickinson. NAAL-1; NOCV; TRP

That scorched earth can still be used. (*LL*) Nearer. Judith Herzberg. BoWoP

That sculptor we know, the passionate-eyed son of a quarryman. An Artist. Robinson Jeffers. VGW

That scything wind has cut the rich corn down. John Knox. Iain Crichton Smith. OxBS

That sea was greater than we knew. The Voyage. Edwin Muir. LiTM; MeMBP

That season when the leaf deserts the bole. October 1. Karl Shapiro. MoAB; MoAmPo; PoA

That seat of Science, Athens. Free America. Joseph Warren. PAH

That second time they hunted me. The Italian in England. Robert Browning. FaBoPV; OBNV

That selfish, callous woman whom the English call "the Queen." (*LL*) The English Queen. Henry Lawson. NOBAu

That selfsame tongue which first did thee entreat. The Constancy of a Lover. George Gascoigne. EnRePo

That servile path thou nobly dost decline. Sir John Denham. *Fr.* To Sir Richard Fanshawe, Upon His Translation of Pastor Fido. EPCY

That shaman, owl man. The Deadly Dance. *Unknown, tr. fr. Aztec Indian by* Edward Kissam. STP

That she adored me as the most. Elegy on Any Lady by George Moore. Max Beerbohm. FaBoEE

That she could die, or that she could live here. (*LL*) On a Virtuous Young Gentlewoman That Died Suddenly. William Cartwright. HAP

That she hath gone to Heaven suddenly. Dante, *tr. fr. Italian by* Dante Gabriel Rossetti. *Fr.* Vita Nuova, La. CTC

That she in peace may wake and pity me. (*LL*) Sleep, Angry Beauty. Thomas Campion. EnRePo; ErPo; OxBSP; TrGrPo

That she will move from mourning into morning. (*LL*) Sonnet to My Mother. George Barker. ImPo; LiTB; MoAB; RaBo

That Sheba led a dance. (*LL*) On Woman. W. B. Yeats. ChIV-1; CMoP

That shot Jesse James on the sly. (*LL*) Jesse James. *Unknown.* AS; BeLS; FaBoBe; UnPo; WiR

That silent publicizer of unheard-of news. Philodemus, *tr. fr. Greek by* William Moebius. GrAn

That simple duty hath no place for fear. (*LL*) Abraham Davenport. Whittier. AmPP; NoP

That since you would save none of me, I bury some of you. (*LL*) The Funeral[l]. John Donne. AWP; BoLoP; EBEV; EnLoPo; EnRePo; ESCV; HeIP; ImPo; MeLP; NAEL-1; NAWM-1; NoP; OAEL-1; OBEV; PoEL-2; PoRA; SCGP; SeCP; SeCV-1; TFi

That sit on tombstone for your mats. (*LL*) My Cats. Stevie Smith. CBNP; FaBoNo

That skin wasn't made for this weather. North. Lavinia Greenlaw. NWP

That sleeps, a mimic echo, in the shell. (*LL*) My Voice. Oscar Wilde. EBVV

That smasher of shams, Bernard Shaw. Frank Buckland. PeLi

That smudge of mascara by your mouth. Steve Kowit. UL

That soldier with a machinegun bolted. Two Summers in Moravia. Roger McDonald. CBAP

That somebody, my own special one. Shadows. *Unknown, tr. fr. Tewa Indian by* H. J. Spinden. WTO

That son of Italy who tried to blow. Austerity of Poetry [*or* Jacopone da Todi]. Matthew Arnold. EPCY

That song there I borrow. Take Your Accusation Back! Kittaararter, *tr. fr. Eskimo.* WTO

That sort of place where you stop. Colville 1964. Kendrick Smithyman. PeNZ

That sound like the scratch. One, The Other, And. Wendy Wieber. NMM

That Spring I was twelve. Walking in the Lambing Paddock. Christine Churches. FaBoMA

That Spring Night I Spent. Lady Suo, *tr. fr. Japanese* by Kenneth Rexroth. VBLP

That springs, and perisheth in one short hour. (*LL*) A Description of Beauty. Samuel Daniel, *after the Italian of* Giambattista Marini.

That stad is in perplexytie. (*LL*) The Death of Alexander. *Unknown.* OxBS

That star I now see. Star and Sea. William Peskett. PNI

That still pool of the air. Variation. Federico García Lorca, *tr. fr. Spanish* by Carlos Bauer. ArLo

That stone called *Kiph!* (*LL*) Kiph. Walter de la Mare. CBNP

That story which the bold Sir Bedivere. The Passing of Arthur. Tennyson. *Fr.* Idylls of the King. FHYEP; NAEL-2; OBNC (Morte d'Arthur.) DL; OAEL-2

That strange flower, the sun. Gubbinal. Wallace Stevens. NAAL-2; SOTW

That Strangest is of all; yet brought to pass. (*LL*) The Salutation [*or* Salutations]. Thomas Traherne. EnlH; ESCV; GeHe; InvP; NOCV; NoP; SeCP; SeCV-2

That sultry afternoon the world went strange. One Tuesday in Summer. James McAuley. FaBoMA

That Summer. Henry Treece. NYBP

That summer day. (*LL*) The Waking ("I strolled across/ An open field.") Theodore Roethke. RFM; TTTS

That Summer I did not go crazy. To the Bone. Dorothy Allison. GLP

That summer it just appeared. Roller Rink. Betty Adcock. MT

That summer, the red may and the white may made. That Summer. Henry Treece. NYBP

That summer we rode giant white Frisbees. Three Men Speak to Me. Felice Picano. ETG; PFL

That Summer's Shore. John Ciardi. ErPo

That sun that breathed love's fire into my youth. Dante, *tr. fr. Italian. Fr.* Divina Commedia. MeMAP; NAWM-1, *tr. by* John Ciardi

That Sunday morning, at half past ten. The Ballad of Longwood Glen. Vladimir Nabokov. NYBP

That Sunday was like an unfinished dream. A Sunday in Cambridge. Eddie Linden. PeHV

That surrounds Montecito like the echo of a scream. (*LL*) In Montecito. Randall Jarrell. CoAP; MAT; NoP; NYBP; VGW

That sway from mood to mood the willing mind! (*LL*) The Poet. Bryant. EAP; NAAL-1; TAP

That sweet accord is seldom seen. (*LL*) Throughout the World, If It Were Sought. Sir Thomas Wyatt. MAT; NoSic; OxBSP

That swell'd so sorrowful beneath its sheath. (*LL*) Magwere, Who Waits Wondering. Kingsley Fairbridge. PeSAV

That swollen paunch you are doomed to bear. Heredity. William Dean Howells. AnAmPo

That taunts her bayonet. (*LL*) My country need not change her gown. Emily Dickinson. GOA

That tea is not the most benign of Latter-day beverages. Peter Titheradge. *Fr.* Teatime Variations. FaBoPa

That teacher gave me a new name . . . again. Name Giveaway. Phillip William George. VoR

That teenage boy. Into Fish. Sheryl L. Nelms. GOYP

That terra-cotta waitress. The Villa Restaurant. Derek Walcott. WeW

That Texan Cattle Man. Joaquin Miller. AnAmPo

That/ that / whose/ track is it like? *Unknown, tr. fr. Chippewa Indian* by Frances Densmore. *Fr.* Poems for the Game of Silence. STP

That! that! there I was told. The Bible. Thomas Traherne. PeECV

That that which stands not, stands thee in so much. (*LL*) Against an Old Lecher. Sir John Harington. FaBoEE

That the balls of the lover are not larger than the balls of the priest. C. K. Stead. *Fr.* Quesada. PeNZ

That the buldozer's due to return. (*LL*) Split Level. Matthew Sweeney. IB

That the Female of Her Species is more deadly than the Male. (*LL*) The Female of the Species. Kipling. BLPA; FaBoEH, Abr.; OtMeF

That the glass would melt in heat. The Glass of Water. Wallace Stevens. MeMAP; MoAB; MoAmPo; OxBA; TAP

That the heart grows old? (*LL*) I thought no more was needed. W. B. Yeats. CBLP

That the high sheen of death could blot. Midsummer. James Scully. NYBP; TwCP

That the king enjoys his own again. (*LL*) The King Enjoys His Own Again. Martin Parker. FaBoCh; OxBoLi

That the Lord He was born in a dark and cold byre./ Mhuire as truagh! (*LL*) The Feast o' Saint [*or* St.] Stephen. Ruth Sawyer. OBCP; OHIP

That the neighborhood might be covered. Larry Eigner. PoM

That the Night Come. W. B. Yeats. PoEL-5

That the poet "does not number the streaks of the tulip." To Hugh MacDiarmid. Edwin Morgan. FaBoTw

That the right man lay in the dust. (*LL*) After Goliath. Kingsley Amis. NOBL; OxBTC

That the Traylee's the best cigarette. A Prize-winning Limerick. R. Rhodes. FaBoUs

That the war would be over before they got to you. When You Have Forgotten Sunday: The Love Story. Gwendolyn Brooks. WPOW

That the world will never be quite—what a cliché—the same again. Tam Cari Capitis. Louis MacNeice. OBD; OBF

That there are powers above us I admit. Arthur Hugh Clough. EnVR

That there is falsehood in his looks. The Parson's Looks. Burns. OxBoLi

That these may be thy Praise, and my Joy too. (*LL*) Mount of Olives. Henry Vaughan *and* Thomas Stanley. ESCV; GeHe

That these we take for granted. Hitchcock Blue. Lucie Brock-Broido. EOEF

That they are brown, no man will dare to say. Her Eyes. Helen Hunt Jackson. AmWP

That they may water the earth. (*LL*) White floating clouds. *Unknown.* EaPr

That Things Are No Worse, Sire. Helen Hunt Jackson. OHIP

That things inanimate lack buddhahood? (*LL*) Man whose mind is rounded out to perfection, The. Chan-Jan. EaPr

That thinks it worth the pain. (*LL*) Full well it may be seen. Sir Thomas Wyatt. SiPS

That this land has. (*LL*) This Land. Ian Mudie. NOBAu

That thou art blam'd shall not be thy defect. Shakespeare. *Fr.* Sonnets. OxAEP-1; SCGP

That Thou Art Nowhere to Be Found. George Macdonald. *Fr.* Diary of an Old Soul. TrCP

That thou hast her, it is not all my grief[e]. Shakespeare. *Fr.* Sonnets. CBLP; HeIP; InvP; OxAEP-1

That thou mayst fit thyself against thy fall. (*LL*) Church Monuments. George Herbert. GeHe; HAP; JCP; NAEL-1; NOCV; NoP; NOSC; OAEL-1; PoE; TRP

That thou mayst injure no man, dove-like be. Prudent Simplicity. William Cowper. FaBoEE

That thou mayst know me, and I'll turn my face. (*LL*) Good Friday [*or* Goodfriday], 1613. Riding Westward. John Donne. ChIV-2; EnRePo; ESCV; InPS; JCP; MeLP; NAEL-1; NOCV; NoP; NOSC; OAEL-1; PeECV; PoE; PoEL-2; PPP; SeCP; SeCV-1; TEP; TFi

That Time in Tangier. Marvin Bell. AnAn

That time/ in the sun. When Sun Came to Riverwoman. Leslie Silko. VoR

That time of drought the embered air. Drought Year. Judith Wright. NoAM

That time of evening, weightless and disparate. Blackwater Mountain. Charles Wright. CAPP

That time of year thou may'st [*or* maist] in me behold. Shakespeare. *Fr.* Sonnets. ArNa; AWP; BoLoP; ChTr; ClHu; CTC; EBEV; EIL; EnRePo; FaPoB; GTBS; GTBS-P; HAP; HeIP; HoPM; ImPo; InPK; InPS; InvP; LiTB; NAEL-1; NIP; NOBE; NoP; NoSic; OAEL-1; OBD; OBEV; PlP; PoE; PoEL-2; PoRA; PPP; Prlm; SCGP; Son; SoSe; TEP; TFi; TrGrPo; UnPo; WeW

That time of year you may in me behold. The Winter Twilight, Glowing Black and Gold. Delmore Schwartz. NoAM

That time that mirth did steer my ship. Sir Thomas Wyatt. SiPS; SiPSBD

That time/ we all heard it. Paul Robeson. Gwendolyn Brooks. PoBA

That time without contentment brings. (*LL*) What Shall I Give? Edward Thomas. FaBoCh; OxBChV

That tomorrow a new walk is a new walk. (*LL*) Corsons Inlet. A. R. Ammons. CoAP; FoLa; MoP; NAAL-2; NoAM; NOBA; NoP; PoE; PPP; VCAP

That touched your glass intrude on my writing-desk. (*LL*) Particulars. Thomas McCarthy. IB

That town seemed comfortless once. Border Town. Mary E. O'Donnell. NWP

That trumpet tongue which taught a nation. The Demagogue. Phyllis McGinley. FaBoEE

That tumbled meaning into wind. (*LL*) Snow Country Weavers. James Welch. CDW; HATNAP

That your substance never may decay. *(LL)* The Maunding Soldier; or, The Fruits of Warre Is Beggery. Martin Parker. CoMu

That you're not. *(LL)* From an Island You Cannot Name. Martín Espada. UTF

That zephyr every year. Spring Bereaved. William Drummond of Hawthornden. OBEV

Thatcher. Seamus Heaney. IPY

Thatcher, The. Brendan Kennelly. CIP

Thatcher of Thatchwood went to Thatchet a-thatching, A. *Unknown.* OxNR

That's a rich man coming. *Unknown, tr. fr. Tlingit Indian by* James Koller. STP

That's All? Anna Hajnal, *tr. fr. Hungarian by* Jascha Kessler. PBWP

That's All. Lawrence Joseph. EOEF; PBCAP

That's all right. *(LL)* Xylophone Luncheonette. Connie Deanovich. UTF

That's all that I remember. *(LL)* Incident. Countee Cullen. BPo; CDC; FF; NAAL-2; NoAM; NTCP; OBCA; PoBA; Poetr; PoNe; VGW

(That's all the Spanish i know). *(LL)* Skirt Dance. Ishmael Reed. FF; UL

"That's certainly the case," said he. *(LL)* Crazy Jane on the Day of Judgment. W. B. Yeats. CMoP; SOTW

That's enough of that, Mr Bones. Some lady you make. John Berryman. *Fr.* Dream Songs. NAAL-2; VCAP

That's Ethan Allen on the monument. Green Mountain Boy. Florida Watts Smyth. GoYe

That's flat. *(LL)* The Cat and the Bird. George Canning. ChTr

That's Jack. Jack. Charles Henry Ross. OxBChV; Spl

That's just the way with asses, just the way. *(LL)* Ass in the Lion's Skin, The ("An ass put on a lion's skin and went.") Aesop. AWP

That's known as Lou. *(LL)* The Shooting of Dan McGrew. Robert W. Service. BeLS; EBEvV; EBNV; FaBoBe; PoLF; PoRA; RB; UV, *sl. sh. vers.*

That's Life? Alan Bold. FF

That's me, second from the left. Perpetuum Immobile. Bruce Dawe. CBAP

That's my last duchess painted on the wall. My Last Duchess. Robert Browning. AWP; BeLS; ClHu; EBNV; EBVV; FaBoPV; FF; FHYEP; GGP; GTBS-P; HAP; HeIL; HeIP; HoPM; ImPo; InPK; InPS; LiTB; MAT; MeMBP; NAEL-2; NIP; NOBE; NOBVV; NoP; OAEL-2; OBNC; OHCV; OtMeF; PeVV; PoE; PoEL-5; Poetr; PoLF; PPP; PrIm; SCGP; SCV; SoSe; TEP; TFi; TrGrPo; ZPW
(My Last Duchess: Ferrara.) EBVVPR; EnVR

That's my topic. How complex, Alhambran arabesques of weather. How the World Works: An Essay. Albert Goldbarth. NAmP90

That's not a man in pain. A Short Lexicon of Torture in the Eighties. Edward Hirsch. VCAP

That's not my point, and where are we at. *(LL)* Liberal, or Innocent by Definition. James McAuley. NOBAu

That's right: keep on singing, "Carry Me Back to Old Virginny." Carry Me Back to Old Virginny. Elma Ehrlich Levinger. ShDr

That's slowish work, Bob. What'st a-been about? Sam and Bob. William Barnes. *Fr.* Best Man in the Vield, The. PeVV, *tr. by* Hualing Nieh, *Eclogue*

That's some joy in misery. *(LL)* To the Tune — "But I Fancy Lovely Nancy." Patrick Carey. CBLP

That's Success! Berton Braley. *See* It's doing your job the best you can.

"That's the Cape of Cats ahead," the captain said to me. The Cats of Saint Nicholas. George Seferis, *tr. fr. Greek by* Edmund Keeley. SoCa

That's the cuckoo, you say. I cannot hear it. The Cuckoo. Edward Thomas, *tr. fr. Spanish.* OBD

That's the life for a man! *(LL)* Young Washington. Arthur Guiterman. FaPON; OHIP

That's the only image. A Wall. Charles Simic. HCAP

That's the queer life said the chair. Chair, Dog, and Clock. Hilary Corke. NYBP

That's the tid i fa la truth. *(LL)* The Derby Ram. *Unknown.* CBNP; FaBoNo; GBP; NTP; OxNR; ReMoGo

That's the way for Billy and me. *(LL)* A Boy's Song. James Hogg. BoTP; CH; CoGr; FaPON; FaPoR; MoShBr; OBEV; OTCP; OxAEP-2; OxBChV; PlP; WiR

That's the way it was. *(LL)* Magic Words. *Unknown.* ImGa, *tr. by* Edward Field; NU; RaBo; STP

That's to lay me. *(LL)* Cauld Lad of Hilton, The *or* The Wandering Spectre. *Unknown.* CoGr; OxBoLi

That's what I said. *(LL)* The Song of the Mad Prince. Walter de la Mare. EBEV; FaBoCh; GoJo; MoP; NoAM; NOBE; NTP; OxAEP-2; OxBChV

That's what I've been saying. The Hardest. Ron Schreiber. PFL

That's what love is like. The whole river. Crossing Over. William Meredith. NoAM

That's what misery is. Poetry Is a Destructive Force. Wallace Stevens. AnAmPo; MeMAP; OxBA; RaBo

That's what they ordered. Abishag. Shirley Kaufman. CrSp

That's what we went for, Holly and I. Carnies. Debra Allbery. PBCAP

That's What We'd Do. Mary Mapes Dodge. OBCA

That's what young women are made of. *(LL)* What are little boys made of, made of? Mother Goose. CBCK, *shorter, diff. vers.*; ReMoGo, *(shorter, diff. vers.)*; UV, *(sts. 1–2)*

That's/ your son? the brother. A Man's Song, about His Daughter. *Unknown, tr. fr. Eskimo by* Armand Schwerner. STP

That's your third sneeze now, my good lamp. Argentarius, *tr. fr. Greek by* Fleur Adcock. GrAn

Thaw. Margaret Avison. FaBoWP; NOBC

Thaw. Edward Thomas. ArNa; EBEV; FaBoTw; FM; GTBS-P; MoAB; MoBrPo; NTP; OxAEP-2; OxBSP; OxBTC; Spl

Thaw in the City. Lou Lipsitz. MAT

Thaw to the hedgerows. Dragons in the Snow. Jeremy Hooker. SCBI

The dachs-hound, Geist, their little friend. *(LL)* Geist's Grave. Matthew Arnold. FM; NOBVV; TEP

The end. *(LL)* The Cenci. Shelley. EnRP

The falcon hath stol'n my mate away. *(LL)* Corpus Christi Carol, The ("Heron flew east, the heron flew west, The.") *Unknown.* GBP

The falling out of faithful friends is the renewing of love. *(LL)* Amantium Irae Amoris Redintegratio. Richard Edwards. EiL; OBEV

The Flowers of the Forest are a' wede away. *(LL)* The Flowers of the Forest. Jane *(or* Jean) Elliot. CH; CoGr; ECWP; FaBoCh; FaBoRV; OxBS; ScCV; SCGP; WPE

The grave no conquest gets, Death hath no sting. *(LL)* Death be not proud, thy hand gave not this blow. Lucy Harington, Countess of Bedford. PeECV; WPE

The/ Quick Gold, Slant Blue, Sharp Scarlet. Peyton Houston. *Fr.* Sonnet Variations. Son

The reign of terror is no more. *(LL)* Jefferson and Liberty. *Unknown.* SWP

The rest is lost. *(LL)* Epistle to Elizabeth, Countess of Rutland. Ben Jonson. BeJo

The state is your conservator; the prairie will be your life! *(LL)* The Administrator. Marilyn Chin. LoHo

The waters hurtle through the flooded night. *(LL)* A Country Walk. Thomas Kinsella. CIP; CMoP

(The web is wove. The work is done). *(LL)* The Curse upon Edward. Thomas Gray. OBEV

The wind shall blow my topknot off. *(LL)* Tom, He Was a Piper's Son. *Unknown.* GBP; OxNR

Theaitetos. Callimachus, *tr. fr. Greek by* Peter Jay. GrAn

Thealma and Clearchus, *sels.* John Chalkhill.

Thease stwonen steps a-zet so true. The Stwonen Steps. William Barnes. NOBVV

Theatre Hour. Ogden Nash. ImGa

Theatrical Venus. George Buchanan. PNI

Thebes. Honestus, *tr. fr. Greek by* Peter Jay. GrAn

Thee for my recitative. To a Locomotive in Winter. Walt Whitman. AmPP; FaBV; InPK; MoAmPo; MoP; NAAL-1; NoAM; NoP; PoEL-5; Poetr; TAP

Thee never made sway enormous. Sway. Steve Carey. UL

Thee Pompey thy past deeds by turns infest. Lucan, *tr. by* Nicholas Rowe. *Fr.* Pharsalia. OBVE

Thee sets a bell to swinging in my soul. Hildegarde Flanner. *Fr.* Sonnets in Quaker Language. WPE

Thee, Sovereign God, our grateful accents praise. The Te Deum. *Unknown, tr. fr. Latin by* Dryden. AWP

Thee thyself we could not lose. *(LL)* After St. Augustine. Mary Elizabeth Coleridge. TrPWD

Thee to adore thy God, the first of all. *(LL)* God to Be First Served. Robert Herrick. OxBChV

Thee too, enamoured of the life I loved. William Cowper. *Fr.* Task, The. EPCY

Thee too, modest tressèd maid. Moon. Henry Rowe. OBEV

Thee with all mine eyes. *(LL)* The Lover to His Lady. *At. to* Plato. CTC; FaBoEE; FF; NoSic

Thee, Thee, Only Thee. Thomas Moore. GBL; OBNC

Theft. Esther Popel. ShDr

Theft of fire, The. Man's worst bargain yet. Palladas, *tr. fr. Greek by* Tony Harrison. GrAn

Theft's hour — the bus. Late Bus (After a Series of Hold-Ups). Russell Atkins. ETG

Theh Thet Hi Can Wittes Fule-Wis. *Unknown.* HAP

Thei I singe and murthes make. *Unknown.* MiEL

Their adornment for the evening finished now, their bright skin like snow. Tune: "Spring in Jade Pavilion." Li Yü, *tr. fr. Chinese by* Daniel Bryant. SuSp

Their ancient, glittering eyes, are gay. *(LL)* Lapis Lazuli. W. B. Yeats. CMoP; EnlH; FaBoMo; FaBoTw; FF; HeIP; InPS; LiTB; LiTM; MAT; MeMBP; MoP; NAEL-2; NAWM-2; NoAM; NOBE; NoP; OAEL-2; TEP; TFi

Their ardour kindless all the Grecian pow'rs. Homer, *tr. by* Pope. *Fr.* Iliad, The. OBVE

Their attendant nuns spare the tourists well. Bathing the Aged. Paul Monette. AmPA

Their barbarism did not assuage the grief. The Retreat of Ita Cagney. Michael Hartnett. CIP; PBCIP

Their Beginning. C. P. Cavafy, *tr. fr. Greek.* AnAn, *tr. by* Edmund Keeley *and* Philip Sherrard; PeHV, *tr. by* John Mavrogordato

Their Beginning. C. P. Cavafy, *tr. fr. Greek by* John Mavrogordato. PeHV

Their Behaviour. Dennis Brutus. HBAPE

Their black truck rattled up the dusty hill. The Diviners. Mary Oliver. WPE

Their bodies lined up against the walls. Waiting for Truth. Susan Griffin. GLP

Their Book of Stella. Susan Howe. BCF

Their breath smells as sweet as the good old moonshine. *(LL)* Kentucky Moonshiner. *Unknown.* AS; OBAL

Their calendars are based on rice. Rice. Carol Muske. AmPA

Their children eat out of our hands. Philanthropist. Tony Flynn. PWE

Their children's children shall say they have lied. *(LL)* Aedh Thinks of Those Who Have Spoken Evil of His Beloved. W. B. Yeats. NoAM

Their Cone-like Cabins. Charles G. Ballard. VoR

Their crowns bare and dripped from their feet. *(LL)* November. Ted Hughes. CMoP; GTBS-P; NoP

Their deepest selves dragged up to life. *(LL)* The Poet's Progress. Chris Mann. PeSAV

Their departures hence and die. *(LL)* Upon the Loss[e] of His Mistresses. Robert Herrick. BeJo; CaPo; NAEL-1; NOSC; PoE; SeCV-1

Their early blessings on his name. *(LL)* Jesus Shall Reign Where'er the Sun. Isaac Watts. WGRP

Their eyelids are drooping, no tears lie beneath. Weavers. Heine. TrJP

Their eyes had known the quiet color blue. Prisoner of War. Gertrude May Lutz. GoYe

Their eyes shining, grave with a perfect pleasure. *(LL)* The Little Dancers. Laurence Binyon. BoTP; CH; MoBrPo; OxBTC

Their faces I thought were knives. Town of the Sound of a Twig Breaking. Anne Carson. *Fr.* Life of Towns, The. BAP-90

Their faces, safe as an interior. The Middle-aged. Adrienne Rich. HCAP

Their Fate; likewise his Garden Quail. *(LL)* Dingle Bank. Edward Lear. FaBoNo

Their feathers were like white silk. The Birds from the Mountains. Chang Chi, *tr. fr. Chinese by* Kenneth Rexroth. OHMPC

Their feet on London, their heads in the grey clouds. Whit Monday. Louis MacNeice. ChIV-1; NYBP; OAEL-2; PeECV

Their fingernails and hair continue to grow. The Old. Franz Wright. LCAP

Their graven semblance in the eternal stone. *(LL)* Eagle, stooping from yon snow-blown peaks, The. Whittier. GOA

Their ground they stil made good. Homer, *tr. by* George Chapman. *Fr.* Iliad, The. OBVE

Their guilt/ is not so very different from ours. Their Behaviour. Dennis Brutus. HBAPE

Their hair, pomaded, faces jaded. Sepia Fashion Show. Maya Angelou. BlSi

Their hands have found in each other. Desperate Message #3 (Desire). Mark Svenvold. UTF

Their heart's desire. *(LL)* How Far Is It to Bethlehem? Frances Chesterton. BoTP; PChr

Their heels slapped their bumping mules. Merchants from Cathay. William Rose Benét. MoAmPo

Their high pitched baying. Denise Levertov. EaPr

Their home was the endless. Lament for the Gypsies. Julius Balbin. BTR

Their house faces east, is protected by trees. A Storm from the East. Reed Whittemore. NYBP

Their illicit pleasure has been fulfilled. Their Beginning. C. P. Cavafy, *tr. fr. Greek.* AnAn, *tr. by* Edmund Keeley *and* Philip Sherrard; PeHV, *tr. by* John Mavrogordato

Their inescapable, empty mark. *(LL)* The Detective Examines the Body. Martha Hollander. UTF

Their life, and ours, the evidence. *(LL)* Profil Perdu. Elizabeth Spires. VBLP

Their lips upon each other's lips are laid. Speechless [upon the Marriage of Two Deaf and Dumb Persons]. Philip Bourke Marston. EBVV

Their little room grew light with cries. Proper Clay. Mark Van Doren. PoRA; TrGrPo

Their Lonely Betters. W. H. Auden. ArNa; GoJo; NAEL-2; NoAM

Their looks are incidental, monumental, sweeping. *(LL)* Gargoyle. Thomas Rabbitt. MT

Their mockery brought him double force. Blind Samson. William Plomer. PeSA

Their mouths, to take her back to another silence. *(LL)* The Excursion of the Speech and Hearing Class. David Wagoner. VCAP

Their new landlord was a handsome man. On his rounds to collect rent she became. A Deserter. Charles Reznikoff. TRP

Their noblest monuments. *(LL)* The Field of the Grounded Arms. Fitz-Greene Halleck. PoEL-4

Their ordeal over now, and all of time before them. *(LL)* Flemington Racecourse. Kevin Hart. NOBAu

Their own poor Little Jim. *(LL)* Little Jim. Edward Farmer. VPP

Their Party, Our House. Jon Swan. NYBP

Their Patients. Robert Pinsky. *Fr.* Essay on Psychiatrists. NoAM

Their pensive light from a departed sun! *(LL)* Decay of Piety. Wordsworth. TrCP

Their Philistinism Considered. Robert Pinsky. *Fr.* Essay on Psychiatrists. NoAM

Their ránsom, théir rescue, ánd first, fást, last friénd. *(LL)* The Lantern out of Doors. Gerard Manley Hopkins. CMoP; LiTB; MeMBP; TrCP

Their ravish'd spirits did possess. *(LL)* Ode, upon a Question Moved, Whether Love Should Continue Forever? An. Lord Herbert of Cherbury. JCP; MeLP; NOBE; OxAEP-1; SeCP

Their rugs are sodden, their heads are down. Gun Teams. Gilbert Frankau. OxBTC; PAW

Their scrape and clink together of musical coin. Some Small Shells from the Windward Islands. May Swenson. FYAP

Their sense is with their senses all mixed in. George Meredith. *Fr.* Modern Love. NAEL-2; NoP; OAEL-2; SCGP

Their Seriousness, with Further Comparisons. Robert Pinsky. *Fr.* Essay on Psychiatrists. NoAM

Their shoulders you shook. The Preacher. Al-Mahdi, *tr. fr. Arabic by* A. J. Arberry. TTY

Their skin like the frills on overfried eggs. *(LL)* Mutton Bird Man. Rhyll McMaster. NOBAu

Their small pink mouths were opened. Drowning Puppies. James Simmons. PWE

Their souls froze into jade. *(LL)* Bound Feet. Cyrus Cassells. UTF

Their spades grafted through the variably-resistant. Geoffrey Hill. *Fr.* Mercian Hymns. PoE

Their spare, fanatic sentry comes. Ants and Others. Adrien Stoutenburg. FYAP; NYBP

Their Speech, Compared with Wisdom and Poetry. Robert Pinsky. *Fr.* Essay on Psychiatrists. NoAM; PoA

Their squints and stammers disappeared. The Children. Robert Minhinnick. AngWe

Their Thing. Léon Damas, *tr. fr. French by* Ellen Conroy Kennedy. NegPo

Their thoughts are night gulls. Old People Dozing. Denise Levertov. AIW

Their Thoughts Cling to Everything They See on the Way. Allen Afterman. NOBAu

Their throats glittering like blue sapphire. What Her Girl Friend Said to Her. Maturai Marutan Ilanakanar, *tr. fr. Tamil by* A. K. Ramanujan. PLW

Their time past, pulled down. Burning the Christmas Greens. William Carlos Williams. LiTM; MeMAP; MoP; NAAL-2; NoAM; NOBA

Their tongues are knives, their forks are hands and feet. Adrian Mitchell. FaBoEE; GBL; OxBSP

Their trunks are raising a city. *(LL)* Concrete Mixers. Patricia Hubbell. PDV

Their verdure dare not show. Louis MacNeice. PeIV

Their voices heard, I stumble suddenly. One More New Botched Beginning. Stephen Spender. CMoP; NoAM; NYBP

Their war-boots said big shots to the plank floor. Behold, One of Several Little Christs. Kenneth Patchen. NaP

Theirs is a gesture of sorrow, infinite and taut. Snails. E. D. Blodgett. NOBC

Theirs is the house whose windows — every pane. On the Asylum Road. Charlotte Mew. MoBrPo

Theirs is yon house that holds the parish poor. The Poor-House. George Crabbe. *Fr.* Village, The. ECEV

(Parish Work-House, The. PlP

Thekla's Song. Schiller, *tr. fr. German by* Samuel Taylor Coleridge. *Fr.* Piccolomini, The. AWP

Theld the man for nothing in my arms. *(LL)* Saint Judas. James Wright. LCAP; NOBA; SM

Thel's Motto. Blake. *Fr.* Book of Thel, The. ChTr, 4 *ll.*; EnRP; MeMBP; NAEL-2; NoP; OAEL-2; OBNC; PoE; PoEL-4; TEP

Them both. *(LL)* To Our Blessed Lord upon the Choice of His Sepulchre. Richard Crashaw. GeHe; NOSC

Them Decade, The. Terence Winch. UL

Them ez wants, must choose. A Baker's Duzzen uv Wize Sawz. Edward Rowland Sill. FaBoBe

Them ez will, kin. *(LL)* A Baker's Duzzen uv Wize Sawz. Edward Rowland Sill. FaBoBe

Them Gar'n Town People. *Unknown.* PBCV

Them only with/ spring). *(LL)* O Sweet Spontaneous. E. E. Cummings. MoP; NAAL-2; NoAM; NoP; PFP; Poetr; PrIm; RaBo

Theme. James Stephens. ArNa

Theme and Variation. Peter De Vries. NYBP

Theme and Variations, *sels.* Edna St. Vincent Millay. "Not even my pride will suffer much." VBLP

Theme for a Tapestry. Julio Cortázar, *tr. by* Paul Blackburn. AnRep

Theme for English B. Langston Hughes. HCAP; MoP; NIP; NoAM; NOBA; NoP; Poetr

Theme no poet gladly sung. Prudence. Emerson. OBAL

Theme One: The Variations. August Wilson. PoBA

Theme tune occurs again, The! Das Liebesleben. Thom Gunn. ErPo

Then. Diane Glancy. LoHo

Then. Lawrence Joseph. PBCAP

Then. Edwin Muir. CMoP; PoA; PoE

Then. Muriel Rukeyser. GLP; LCAP

Then a partridge-shaped cloud over dust storm. Ezra Pound. *Fr.* Cantos. NYBP

Then a ploughman said, Speak to us of Work. On Work. Kahlil Gibran. *Fr.* Prophet, The. PoToHe, *abr.*

Then after Eden. New World. Derek Walcott. OxBC

Then all the evidence we have of who is. The Plague. Marvin Bell. PFL

Then all the nations of birds lifted together. The Season of Phantasmal Peace. Derek Walcott. NoP

Then Almitra spoke, saying, We would ask now of Death. Kahlil Gibran. *Fr.* Prophet, The. DL

Then and Now. Frances E. W. Harper. PWR

Then and Now. Kapilar, *tr. fr. Tamil by* A. K. Ramanujan. PLW

Then and Now. Kath Walker. IHMS

Then, at 3 A.M. I see her bend. Intensive Care. Carol Muske. PBCAP

Then ay it is full weet. *(LL)* Clerk Saunders. *Unknown.* ESPB, A, B, *and* F *vers.*; FaBoBa; OBEV; OxBS

Then be blessed with light, more light. *(LL)* Let the Light Enter. Frances E. W. Harper. AmWP; PoNe

Then birds of ill omen, and women no more. *(LL)* An Ape, Lion, Fox and Ass. *Unknown.* OBET

Then bold Robin Hood to the north he would go. Robin Hood and the Scotchman. *Unknown.* ESPB

Then both ourselves and seed at once to free. Milton. *Fr.* Paradise Lost. EPCY; OBD

Then by a sunne-beam I will climbe to thee. *(LL)* Mattens. George Herbert. ESCV; TrPWD

Then call me traitor if you must. To Certain Critics. Countee Cullen. BPo

Then call your neighbours in. *(LL)* Cross Patch/ Draw the latch. Mother Goose. ChTr; GBP; OxNR; ReMoGo

Then came fair May, the fairest maid on ground. May. Spenser. *Fr.* Faerie Queene, The. GN

Then came I to the shoreless shore of silence. Conrad Aiken. *Fr.* Preludes for Memnon; or, Preludes to Attitude. LiTA; OxBA

Then came jolly Summer, being dight. Summer. Spenser. *Fr.* Faerie Queene, The. GN

Then came the Autumn all in yellow clad. Autumn. Spenser. *Fr.* Faerie Queene, The. GN

Then came the cry of "Call all hands on deck!" Rounding the Horn. John Masefield. *Fr.* Dauber. MoAB; MoBrPo

Then ceased like these. *(LL)* This quiet dust was gentlemen and ladies. Emily Dickinson. CMoP; DL; OxBA

Then chiefly lives. *(LL)* Virtue. George Herbert. AWP; CH; ClHu; ELP; GeHe; HAP; HeIP; InPS; InvP; JCP; NAEL-1; NOBE; NOCV; NoP; NOSC; OAEL-1; OBD; OBEV; PoE; PoRA; PPP; SCGP; SoSe; TEP; TFi; TrGrPo; WGRP

Then — close the Valves of her attention/ Like Stone. *(LL)* Soul selects her own society, The. Emily Dickinson. AmPP; AWP; BLPL; BoWoP;

CMoP; HeIP; ImPo; InPK; InPS; MeMAP; MoAB; MoAmPo; NAAL-1; NALW; NAWM-2; NoAM; NOBA; NoP; OxBA; PoE; PoEL-5; Poetr; SAmP; TAP; TFi; TrGrPo; UnPo; WPE

Then Come, deare bridgrome, Come away! *(LL)* As Weary Pilgrim, Now at Rest. Anne Bradstreet. NAAL-1; PoEL-3; SCAP

Then Constantine, mindful of the Holy Cross. Helena Embarks for Palestine. Cynewulf, *tr. fr. Anglo-Saxon by* Charles W. Kennedy. *Fr.* Elene. AnOE

Then count that day as worse than lost. *(LL)* Count That Day Lost. "George Eliot."

Then, crushed by rules, and weakened as refined. Samuel Johnson. *Fr.* Prologue Spoken by Mr. Garrick at the Opening of the Theatre in Drury Lane. EPCY

Then dainty Sandys, that hath to English done. Michael Drayton. *Fr.* To Henry Reynolds, of Poets and Poesy. EPCY

Then, day by day, her broidered gown. The Earth in Spring. Judah Halevi, *tr. fr. Hebrew by* Edward G. King. TrJP

Then did he to the throng around. The Kingdom of Heaven Compared to a Grain of Mustard-Seed. Henry Vaughan. ChIV-2

Then draw your curtains, and begin the dawn. *(LL)* Lark Now Leaves His Watery [*or* Wat'ry] Nest. Sir William Davenant. CH; ChTr; InvP; OxBSP; PoRA; TFi

Then drew near unto him all the publicans and sinners. Bible, *N.T. Fr.* St. Luke. NAWM-1

Then earthquakes, nature's agonizing pangs. James Grainger. *Fr.* Sugar Cane, The. PBCV

Then, far away, the thudding of the guns. *(LL)* The Death-Bed. Siegfried Sassoon. LiTM; NSI; PeFWW

Then fears not the eye to show her heart. *(LL)* And if an eye may save or slay. Sir Thomas Wyatt. SiPS

Then, finally, we cried. *(LL)* The Wedding. Maria Banus. VBLP

Then fire burned my body to a clear shell. A Clear Shell. Frances Bellerby. FaBoWP

Then first he form'd th' immense and solid shield. Homer, *tr. by* Pope. *Fr.* Iliad, The. OBVE

Then first with locks dishevelled and bare. Barnabe Barnes. *Fr.* Parthenophil and Parthenophe. NoSic

Then fled, O brethren, the wicked juba. The Ballad of Nat Turner. Robert Hayden. BPo; SM; VGW

Then flit not from this heavenly boy. *(LL)* New Heaven, New War[re]. Robert Southwell. ChIV-2; ESCV; NOBE; NoP

Then for God's sake match word with deed always. *(LL)* If. Sipho Sepamla. PeSAV

Then for/ twelve years. Low Volume. Reiner Kunze, *tr. fr. German by* Michael Hamburger. AnRep

Then forth issewed (great goddesse) great Dame Nature. Dame Nature. Spenser. *Fr.* Faerie Queene, The. PoEL-1

Then from her Eyes, with fresh supplies, down trickles many a brinish Tear. *(LL)* The Dutchess of Monmouth's Lamentation for the Loss of Her Duke. *Unknown.* CoMu; FaBoBa

Then from the bore I was forced to go. *(LL)* The Whummil Bore. *Unknown.* CH; ESPB

Then from their poverty they rose. The Ordinary Women. Wallace Stevens. OxBA

Then Frome (a nobler flood) the Muses doth implore. Michael Drayton. *Fr.* Polyolbion. NOSC

Then froze, listening for her steps. *(LL)* Grandma's Bureau. Robert Morgan. EOEF; WeW

Then gan this crafty couple to devise. The Fox and the Ape Go to Court. Spenser. *Fr.* Mother Hubbard's Tale. NoSic

Then hasten to old age! *(LL)* The Ebb Tide. Robert Southey. OBNC

Then hate me when thou wilt; if ever, now. Shakespeare. *Fr.* Sonnets. AWP; EBEV; ElL; NOBE; NoSic; OBEV; OxAEP-1; PoEL-2

Then hatred is in head. *(LL)* Of Drunkenness. George Turberville. NBLV; NoP

Then he began again. *(LL)* Cock Robin got up early. *Unknown.* BoTP; OxNR

Then her retort comes in it! *(LL)* Joe's Luck. Albert Brodrick. PeSAV

Then how much greater mischief as a king? *(LL)* Charles II. *Unknown.* FaBoEE

Then Hrothgar's minstrel rehearsed the lay. The Lay of Finn. *Unknown, tr. by* Charles W. Kennedy. *Fr.* Beowulf. AnOE; ASW, *tr. by* Kevin Crossley-Holland

Then I cried out upon him: Cease. Despised and Rejected. Christina Rossetti. PeVV

Then I loved/ the oriole. Childhood. Johannes Bobrowski, *tr. fr. German by* Ruth Mead *and* Matthew Mead. AnRep

Then I said to the elegant ladies. Sappho, *tr. fr. Greek by* Willis Barnstone. BoWoP

Then the brave warrior raised his spear. The Battle of Maldon. *Unknown, tr. fr. Anglo-Saxon by* Kevin Crossley-Holland. FaBoEH

Then the Brother of the Wind. C. K. Williams. CAPP

Then the dreadful night shall break. *(LL)* Sleep, sleep, beauty bright. Blake. EnRP; OBEV; PoLF

Then, the drops were freezing on black branches of ancient ash trees. Rade Drainac, *tr. fr. Serbo-Croatian by* Charles Simic. *Fr.* When the Poet Without Lying Verses in His Heart Returns to His Native Country. HSix

Then the Ermine. Marianne Moore. PoA

Then the gods with a myriad outriders go back to the blue mountains. *(LL)* Magic Strings. Li Ho. PLT

Then the golden hour. Length of Moon. Arna Bontemps. CDC; LiTM; PoNe

Then the knee of the wave. Reclining Figure. Donald Hall. LCAP

Then the leader of the people. A Man without Food. Mari Evans. ETG

Then the little Hiawatha. Hiawatha's Brothers. Longfellow. *Fr.* Song of Hiawatha, The. BoTP

Then the long sunlight lying on the sea. The Insusceptibles. Adrienne Rich. HeIP; SM; Son

Then the Lord answered Job out of the whirlewind, and sayd. Bible, *O.T. Fr.* Job. AWP; NAWM-1, *abr.*; OBVE

Then the Lord Answered ("Who is this that darkeneth counsel by words without knowledge?") Bible, *O.T. Fr.* Job. AWP; NAWM-1, *abr.*

Then the Lord God spoke and said unto Noah. Noah's Flood. Caedmon, *tr. by* C. W. Kennedy. *Fr.* Genesis. AnOE

Then the Master. Longfellow. *Fr.* Building of the Ship, The. NAAL-1

Then the mighty Lord Maxfield over the mountains fleeth. The Battle of Flodden. *Unknown. Fr.* Scot[t]ish Field [*or/*RO/ Feilde*]. NoSic

Then the Provost he uprose. William Edmonstoune Aytoun. *Fr.* Edinburgh after Flodden. OBWP

Then the son of Weohstan, stalwart in war. The Funeral Pyre. *Unknown, tr. by* Charles W. Kennedy. *Fr.* Beowulf. AnOE; ASW, *tr. by* Kevin Crossley-Holland

Then the sun full soone shott under the clouds. The Battle of Flodden. *Unknown. Fr.* Scot[t]ish Field [*or/*RO/ Feilde*]. OxBLMV

Then there is this civilising love of death, by which. Ignorance of Death. William Empson. CMoP; LiTM; NoAM; OBD

Then there shall be signs in Heaven. The Fifteen Days of Judgment. Sebastian Evans. NOBVV

Then there was cool dispersion everywhere. The Aftermath: Yorkshire 1644. Chris Wallace-Crabbe. FaBoMA

Then they paraded Pompey's urn. Jenny Mastoraki, *tr. fr. Modern Greek by* Nikos Germanakos. BoWoP; PBWP

Then they will die. *(LL)* Cut thistles in May. *Unknown.* FaBoUs; OxNR

Then thick as locusts black'ning all the ground. Carnations and Butterflies. Pope. *Fr.* Dunciad, The. NOEC

Then this great Mystery to admire. *(LL)* For Christmas Day. Luke Wadding. TIRV

Then those ill-favour'd Ones, whom none. George Crabbe. *Fr.* Sir Eustace Grey. ELP

Then, though we do not know, we love. *(LL)* Lord, when the wise men came from far[r]. Sidney Godolphin. BeJo; HAP; JCP; MeLP; NOCV; PeECV

Then thou'st come a maiden home. *(LL)* The Maid and the Palmer. *Unknown.* ESPB

Then thus the sire of gods, with look serene. Ovid, *tr. by* Dryden. *Fr.* Metamorphoses. OBD

Then 'tis at the very best. *(LL)* When the wind is in the east. Mother Goose. BoTP; CTSV; FaBoUs; FaBoVe; OxNR

Then, to conclude these pleasant acts. Andrew Marvell. *Fr.* Upon Appleton House, to My Lord Fairfax. CBNP; SeCP; SeCV-1

Then to the bar, all they drew near. Michael Wigglesworth. *Fr.* Day of Doom, The. NAAL-1, *abr.*; OBCA; SCAP

Then to the poor she freely gives the milk. *(LL)* Upon Sybilla. Robert Herrick. CaPo

Then to the well-trod stage amon. Mirth and Poetry. Milton. *Fr.* L'Allegro. AWP; EPCY; FaPoB; FHYEP; GTBS; GTBS-P; HAP; HoPM; ImPo; JCP; LiTB; NoP; NOSC; OAEL-1; OBEV; PPP; TEP; TFi; TrGrPo

Then trust on Mon, whose yerde can talke. *(LL)* Imitation of Chaucer. Pope. FaBoPa

Then Trystan and Gwalchmai went to Arthur. Trystan and Esyllt. *Unknown, tr. fr. Welsh by* Gwyn Jones. OBWVE

Then turn on the music, Marcia. Rock 'n' Roll. Lesley Frost. AiP

Then two juncoes trapped in the house this morning. The Phase after History. Jorie Graham. BAP-91

Then up I rose, and made no more delay. Elizabeth Melvill, Lady Culross. *Fr.* Godly Dream, A. WPE

Then vanishes. *(LL)* A Crack. Gu Cheng. SpMi

Then was I cast from out my state. Frenzy. George Crabbe. *Fr.* Sir Eustace Grey. NOBE

Then was the dinner served, and the Minister prayed for a blessing. Arthur Hugh Clough. *Fr.* Bothie of Tober-na-Vuolich, The [A Long-Vacation Pastoral]. OBF; PeLV

Then was there heard a most celestial sound. The Rivers Come to the Hall of Proteus for the Marriage of the Thames and the Medway. Spenser. *Fr.* Faerie Queene, The. FaBoPP

Then watch and labour while time is. *(LL)* Awake, Awake! [Thou Heavy Sprite]. Thomas Campion. ChIV-1; ELP

Then watching the unposed beggars pose. Et Quid Amabo Nisi Quod Aenigma Est. Stephen Sandy. NYBP

Then we weep for ourselves, and wish thee good-bye. *(LL)* Dirge Written for a Drama. Thomas Lovell Beddoes. EnRP

Then wear the gold hat, if that will move her. Epitaph from *The Great Gatsby.* F. Scott Fitzgerald. *Fr.* Great Gatsby, The. OxBM

Then, we'll go through with the journey. Jansenist Journey. Denis Devlin. IPY

Then we'll sing of Lydia Pinkham. Lydia Pinkham. *Unknown.* AS

Then what is? I ask. What is? *(LL)* Consider a Move. Michael Ryan. SM

Then, what is life? I cried. *(LL)* The Triumph of Life. Shelley. NAEL-2; OAEL-2; PoEL-4

Then what is the answer? — Not to be deluded by dreams. The Answer. Robinson Jeffers. CMoP; GoYe

Then, when I'd seen them leave the bay. And Back. Rodney Bennett. BoTP

Then, when the child was gone. The Empty House. Stephen Spender. NYBP

Then why do they sneer at me? *(LL)* The Jew. Isaac Rosenberg. ChIV-1; MoBrPo

Then will a quiet gather round the door. Beyond Wars. David Morton. PAH

Then will no more such sport be found. *(LL)* Sweet Cupid, Ripen Her Desire. *At. to* William Corkine. EnRePo; OxBSP

Then will thou go and leave me here? Valediction. Sir Robert Ayton. NOSC

Then wonder not to see this Soul extend. John Dryden *and* Nahum Tate. *Fr.* Eleonora: A Panegyrical Poem, Dedicated to the Memory of the Late Countless of Abingon. OBF

Then/ You/ Died. *(LL)* Fall Down. Calvin C. Hernton. PoBA

Thence forward by that painfull way they pas. Spenser. *Fr.* Faerie Queene, The. OAEL-1

Thence is it, as we all believe. At Cock-crow. Prudentius, *tr. fr. Latin by* Helen Waddell. MLL

Thenk, man, of min harde stundes. *Unknown.* MiEL

Thenmy of liff decayer of all kynde. Sir Thomas Wyatt. FaBoVe

Thenne wax I wounder wroth, as I well might. *Unknown. Fr.* Mum and the Sothsegger. EnVB

Theobald James. J. B. Morton. *Fr.* When We Were Very Silly. FaBoPa

Theocritus. Oscar Wilde. NOBE

Theodor Herzl. Israel Zangwill. TrJP

Theodore and Honoria, From Boccace, *sels.* Dryden. Disdain Punished. EBNV; NOSC

Theodore Roethke Foots It. D. C. Berry. BXAP

Theodosia Burr. Myra Burnham Terrell. GoYe

Theodosia Burr: The Wrecker's Story. John Williamson Palmer. PAH

Theogenes sent us for Piso's pleasure. Antipater of Thessalonica, *tr. fr. Greek by* Alistair Elliot. GrAn

Theogony, *sels.* Hesiod, *tr. fr. Greek.* Great Father Eating His Children, The. RaBo

Theological. Clifton Fadiman. FiBHP

Theological Limerick. T. Lindsay. FaBoCo

Theology. Ted Hughes. FaBoMo; NAEL-2; NoAM

Theology and a Patchwork Absolute. Heather McPherson. PeNZ

Theology of Bongwi, the Baboon, The. Roy Campbell. OBAP; PeSA

Theology of Jonathan Edwards, The. Phyllis McGinley. MoAmPo

Theophany. Evelyn Underhill. WGRP

Theophia, *sels.* Edward Benlowes. Pleasures of Retirement, The. NOSC

Theophilus Thistledown, the successful thistle sifter. *Unknown.* OxNR

Theory. David Chaloner. VaA

Theory. Dorothy Parker. VBLP

Theory, A. Charles Simic, *tr. fr. Czech by* Jeffrey Fiskin *and* Erik Vestville. AnAn

Ther is no rose of swych vertu. The Rose That Bore Jesu. *Unknown.* OxBLMV

Ther once was this ladye from Tyre. Tim Hopkins. PeLi

Ther was a frier of order gray. The Friar and the Nun. *Unknown.* OxBLMV

Ther was a knight, a worthy for the chaffre. Portrait of the Pornographer. G. W. Jones. BXAP

Ther was a lady fair an rear. The Kitchie-Boy. *Unknown.* ESPB

Ther was also a povre closet queane. Lost Lines from Chaucer's Prologue to "The Canterbury Tales." *Unknown.* PeHV

There. Rodney Bennett. BoTP

There. Robert Mezey. NaP

There. (LL) You Are There. Nikki Giovanni. HeIL

There, — my blessing with you [or thee]! Polonius' Advice to Laertes. Shakespeare. *Fr.* Hamlet. NAWM-1
   (Polonius to Laertes.) GN
   (This Above All.) TrGrPo
   (To Thine Own Self Be True.) ImPo; LiTB

There Actually Stood. Roy Fuller. *Fr.* Mythological Sonnets. Son

There ain' no liars there. In My Father's House. *Unknown.* AS

There all the golden codgers lay. News for the Delphic Oracle. W. B. Yeats. CMoP; FaBoMo; LiTB; LiTM; MeMBP; NoAM

There also was a nun, a Prioress, *mod. vers. by* Louis Untermeyer. Chaucer. *See* There [or Ther] was also a nun [or Nonne], a Prioress[e].

There alway, alway something sings. (LL) Music. Emerson. FaBV; WGRP

There always is a noise when it is dark! In the Night. James Stephens. OBMV

There ance was a may, and she lo'ed na men. Werena My Heart Licht I Wad Dee. Lady Grisel Baillie. OBEV; ScCV
   (Werena My Heart Licht.) VBLP

There are abandoned corners of our Exile. The Mathmid. Hayyim Nahman Bialik, *tr. fr. Hebrew by* Maurice Samuel. AWP

There are about fifty of them. Galahs. William Hart-Smith. OBAP

There are all kinds of men. A Thank You for Friends. Rodney Bennett. BoTP

There are always the poor. Soliloquy at Potsdam. Peter Porter. NOBAu

There Are Bad Times Just around the Corner. Noël Coward. NOBL

There Are Big Waves. Eleanor Farjeon. BoTP

There Are Black. Jimmy Santiago Baca. InPS

There!/ are/ Black men in the south. On Seeing the Black Male as #1 Sex Object in America. Etheridge Knight. BCF

There are blind eyes. A Prayer in Time of Blindness. Clement Wood. TrPWD

There are blows in life so violent — Don't ask em! The Black Riders. César Vallejo, *tr. fr. Spanish by* Robert Bly. RaBo

There are brightest apples on those trees. The Fertile Muck. Irving Layton. NoAM; NOBC

There are caverns/ under our feet. Shirley Kaufman. BoWoP

There are certain brisk people among us today. Profiteers. Jessie Pope. NSI

There are certain ladies in our land. To L. R-M. Noël Coward. ArLo

There are constantly, she told him further, lions in the village. Henri Michaux, *tr. fr. French by* Richard Ellmann. *Fr.* I Am Writing to You from a Far-Off Country. AnRep

There are days when the dead will have nothing to do with us. Tending the Graves. Jennifer Strauss. NOBAu

There are dealers in pictures named Agnew. Tom Agnew, Bill Agnew. Dante Gabriel Rossetti. ChTr; FaBoEE

There Are Delicacies. Earle Birney. NoP

There are depths even in a household. The Whale in the Blue Washing Machine. John Haines. AnAn

There Are Different Gardens. Carl Sandburg. ImGa

There are different ways of dying without. After the Revolution. Marilyn Hacker. AmPA

There are dreams that need rest. Okay. Sharon Scott. JB

There are exact arrangements. Mimikòs. Luigi Fontanella, *tr. fr. Italian by* Michael Palma. NeIt

There are fairies at the bottom of our garden! Fairies. Rose Fyleman. FaPON; OxBChV

There are few of us now, soon. For Eli Jacobson. Kenneth Rexroth. RaBo

There are flowers of Zait in the garden. *Unknown, tr. fr. Egyptian hieroglyphics into Italian by* Boris de Rachewiltz; *English vers. by* Ezra Pound *and* Noel Stock. BoWoP; PBWP

There are four Graces. Beside the original three. A Statue of Bereniké. Callimachus, *tr. fr. Greek by* Peter Jay. GrAn

There are four Graces, two Aphrodites, ten Muses. *Unknown, tr. fr. Greek by* Peter Jay. GrAn

There are four men mowing down by the Isar. A Youth Mowing. D. H. Lawrence. InPK; MoAB; MoBrPo; NoAM; TrGrPo

There are four officers, this message says. Escape. Edmund Blunden. NSI

There are four vibrators, the world's exactest clocks. Four Quartz Crystal Clocks. Marianne Moore. AmPP; TwCP

There Are Gains for All Our Losses. Richard Henry Stoddard. AnAmPo

There are gold ships. *Unknown.* RoPo

There are hermit souls that live withdrawn. The House by the Side of the Road. Sam Walter Foss. AnAmPo; BLPA; BLPL; FaBoBe; WBLP; WGRP

There are in our existence spots of time. Imagination and Taste, How Impaired and Restored. Wordsworth. *Fr.* Prelude [or, Growth of a Poet's Mind], The. EnRP; OAEL-2; PoE; PoEL-4, XII, *abr.*; TOF

There are in Paradise. The Shepherd Who Stayed. Theodosia Garrison. OHIP; PChr

There are just so many years. Turning Pro. Ishmael Reed. SoSe

There are lilies in the lake, the lilies of still water. Castle. Alison Brackenbury. SCBI

There are limits to imagination. (LL) Heroic Simile. Robert Hass. VCAP

There are lions and roaring tigers, and enormous camels and things. At the Zoo. A. A. Milne. FaPON

There are lonely hearts to cherish. While the Days Are Going By. George Cooper. BLRP; WBLP

There are loved ones who are missing. The Blessings That Remain. Annie Johnson Flint. BLRP

There are loyal hearts, there are spirits brave. Life's Mirror. "Madeline Bridges." BLPA; FaBoBe; PoToHe; PWR; WBLP

There are magpies on the South hill. A Song of Magpies. Lady Ho, *tr. fr. Chinese by* Kenneth Rexroth *and* Ling Chung. WPC

There are many cumbersome ways to kill a man. Five Ways to Kill a Man. Edwin Brock. DL

There are many dead in the brutish desert. First Elegy for the Dead in Cyrenaica. Hamish Henderson. OxBS

There are many dead in the brutish desert, who lie uneasy. End of a Campaign. Hamish Henderson. PoWW

There Are Many Languages in the World. Reed Bye. UL

There are many like him there — unsymbolled heap. A Grave in Ukraine. Saul Tchernichowsky, *tr. fr. Hebrew by* L. V. Snowman. TrJP
   (Grave, The.) VWA, *tr. by* Robert Mezey *and* Shula Starkman.

There are many monsters that a glassen surface. The Octopus. James Merrill. CAPP; CoAP

There are many sounds which are neither music nor voice. The Ear. Louis MacNeice. OxBSP

There Are Many Things I Want to Tell You. Indran Amirthanayagam. OpBo

There are many things in the world and you. Love Recognized. Robert Penn Warren. ArLo

There are many Washingtons. Which Washington? Eve Merriam. NTCP

There are many ways to die. History among the Rocks. Robert Penn Warren. *Fr.* Kentucky Mountain Farm. GOA; MoAmPo

There are many who say that a dog has his day. The Song of the Mischievous Dog. Dylan Thomas. GrPl

There are men in the village of Erith. Erith, on the Thames. *Unknown.* ChTr; FaBoPP; GBP
   ("There are men in the village of Erith".) CoGr

There are men in the village of Erith. *Unknown. See* There are men in the village of Erith.

There are men making death together in the wood. The Delta. Michael Dennis Browne. NYBP

There Are Nights. Léon Damas, *tr. fr. French by* Ellen Conroy Kennedy. NegPo

There are nights with no name. There Are Nights. Léon Damas, *tr. fr. French by* Ellen Conroy Kennedy. NegPo

There are no accidents, or so. What Could Hold Us. Heather McHugh. NIP

There are no angels yet. Gabriel. Adrienne Rich. VGW

There are no bolts that do not exactly. Kirkwall Auction Mart. David Scott. PWE

There are no crosses. A Death in the Desert. Charles Tomlinson. FF

There are no handholds up that wall of light. (LL) A Sketch from the Campaign in the North. Vijay Seshadri. UTF

There are no more shopping days to Christmas. Eve. Howard Nemerov. CRP

There are no nightmares now. Only when memory settles. Seravezza. Hoyt W. Fuller. NNaP

There Are No People Song. *Navajo Indian Oral Tradition.* TTTS

There are no rent days on the sea. (LL) The Fisher's Life. *Unknown.* ChTr; GBP

There are no roads but the frost. Old Age Compensation. James Wright. NNaP

There are no signs. The sky is entirely bland. Augury. W. H. Oliver. PeNZ

There are no stars to-night. My Grandmother's Love Letters. Hart Crane. BLPL; CMoP; FaBoBe; InPK; MoAB; NoAM; NOBA; NoP; Poetr

There are no trenches dug in the park, not yet. Nightmare at Noon. Stephen Vincent Benét. OxBA

There are no upper hands in love. After You, Madam. Alex Comfort. ErPo

There are notes to lightning in my bedroom. Star Quilt. Roberta Hill Whiteman. CDW; NoAM

There are of course tho' we don't see them. Postscripts 2. Dennis Brutus. HBAPE

There are only two things now. New Year's Eve. D. H. Lawrence. BoLoP; ErPo

There are palm trees in my homeland. Antônio Gonçalves Dias, *tr. fr. Portuguese* by Frances Ellen Buckland. *Fr. Song of Exile.* TTY

There are people, I know, to be found. Drinking Song. James Kenneth Stephen. NOBL; PeLV

"There are people so dumb," my father said. Plain Talk. William Jay Smith. FiBHP; MoAmPo

There are, perhaps, whom passion gives a grace. The Aged Lover Discourses in the Flat Style. J. V. Cunningham. NoAM; SM

There are pines that are tall enough. An Elegy Is Preparing Itself. Donald Justice. CRP; HoPM

There are places in Wales I don't go. Reservoirs. R. S. Thomas. AngWe; PWE

There are portraits and still-lifes. Paring the Apple. Charles Tomlinson. CMoP; OxBTC; PoE; TRP

There are questions that must be asked. Incidents in Playfair House. Nicholas Moore. ErPo

There are records. Do not. Buying a Record. Robert Peters. BXAP

There are rock-rooted ranges to dominate. Rex Ingamells. *Fr. Memory of Hills.* CBAP

There Are Roughly Zones. Robert Frost. CMoP; PPP

There are seagulls inland, extensive flooding. Fürth I. Wald. Michael Hofmann. SCBI

There are seeds within the tide. City. Joseph Bruchac. CDW

There are seven steps to heaven. Roots. Garrett Kaoru Hongo. Jaz

There are seventy-five post-stations from here to home. (*LL*) The Gate Tower of Ch'i-an City. Tu Mu. PLT

There are seventy times seven kinds of loving. Veterans. George Johnston. NOBC

"There are sixteen lang miles, I'm sure." The Bent Sae Brown. *Unknown.* ESPB

There are so many lies in nature. Degas. Paul Monette. AmPA

There are so many things to do to-day. Every Day. Mary I. Osborn. BoTP

There Are So Many Ways of Going Places. Leslie Thompson. FaPON

There are some birds in these valleys. The Decoys. W. H. Auden. CMoP; PoE

There are some days the happy ocean lies. Seascape. Stephen Spender. NoP

There are some heights in Wessex, shaped as if by a kindly hand. Wessex Heights. Thomas Hardy. CMoP; EBVV; FaBoPP; MeMBP; OAEL-2; OBNC; PoEL-5; SCGP

There Are Some Lusty Voices Singing. Geoffrey Lehmann. *Fr. Ross's Poems.* CBAP

There are some qualities — some incorporate things. Sonnet — Silence. Poe. MeMAP; NOBA

There are some questions one should know by heart. Postscript. Henri Coulette. DiPo

There are some quiet crossings in his city. Water Color. Stephen Mooney. NYBP

There are some/ secrets. July 31. Norman Jordan. PoBA

There are songs too wide for sound. There are quiet. Answerers. William Stafford. CAPP

There are spaces. Old Maps and New. Norman MacCaig. OxBC

There are spaces we cannot reach. Valentine. Wendy Mulford. NBrP

There are stars above Japan. Stars at Night. Takenaka Iku, *tr. fr. Japanese.* TSaS, *tr.* by Edith Marcombe Shiffert *and* Yuki Sawa

There are strange hells within the minds war made. Strange Hells. Ivor Gurney. OxBTC; PeFWW

There are strange things done in the midnight sun. The Cremation of Sam McGee. Robert W. Service. BLPL; NOBC; OBNV; PoLF

There are strange trees in that pale field. The Forest of the Dead. J. Griffyth Fairfax. NSI; PoWW

There are sunsets who whisper a good-by. Sunsets. Carl Sandburg. MoAmPo

There Are Sweet Flowers. Walter Savage Landor. EnRP

There are the Alps. What is there to say about them? On the Fly-Leaf of Pound's Cantos. Basil Bunting. FaBoTw; NoAM; OxBTC

There are the fair-limbed nymphs o' the woods. Leigh Hunt. *Fr. Nymphs, The.* OBNC

There are the local orchard boughs. Hart Crane. AnAn

There are things best not set down in books. The Road to Patmos. John Ennis. PBCIP

There are things to be said. No doubt. Cid Corman. VGW

There are things you have words for. Two Words; a Wedding. B. P. Nichol. NOBC

There are thirteen months in all the year. Robin Hood and the Three Squires. *Unknown.* EnSB

There are those fish that swim ever in the dim. Pearl Perch. John Blight. CBAP

There are those to whom place is unimportant. The Rose. Theodore Roethke. NOBA; NYBP; TRP

There are those who think. Prologue from "Legacy." Patricia Parker. GLP

There are those who grow. A Knocker. Zbigniew Herbert, *tr. fr. Polish* by Czeslaw Milosz. PoSu

There are three names. National Security. Archibald MacLeish. GOA

There are three plenties. The Fort of Ard Ruide. *Unknown.* NOIV

There are three preachers, ever preaching. The Three Preachers. Charles MacKay. EBVV

There are three things which are too wonderful for me. Too Wonderful. Bible, *O.T. Fr.* Proverbs. TrJP

There are three valleys where the warm sun lingers. The Long Harbour. Mary Ursula Bethell. PeNZ

There are three who await my death. *Unknown, tr. fr. Irish* by Thomas Kinsella. NOIV

There are times for dreaming. The Hours. David Diop, *tr. fr. French* by Ellen Conroy Kennedy. NegPo

There are times in life when one does the right thing. . Ellen Bass. MDDM

There Are Times In Life When One Does the Right Thing. Ellen Bass. MDDM

There are times in one's life which one cannot forget. Mr. Billings of Louisville. Eugene Field. NBLV

There are times when. May Sarton. *Fr. Invocation to Kali, The.* SRLS

There are times when I can't move. Roberto Juarroz, *tr. fr. Spanish.* TSaS, *tr.* by W. S. Merwin

There are too many waterfalls here. Questions of Travel. Elizabeth Bishop. NAAL-2; NOBA

There are trails that a lad may follow. Silver Ships. Mildred Plew Meigs. FaPON

There are truths you Americans need to be told. James Russell Lowell. *Fr. Fable for Critics, A.* OBSV

There are twelve months in all the year. Robin Hood Rescuing Three Squires. *Unknown.* ESPB
(Robin Hood and the Three Squires.) NAEL-1

There are twelve months throughout the year. September. Mary Howitt. BoTP

There are twenty dead who're sleeping near the slopes of Bud Dajo. The Fight at Dajo. Alfred E. Wood. PAH

There are two angels, messengers of light. Peace and Love. Ella Wheeler Wilcox. PWR

There are two bends in the road, and an unexpected dip. Pont y Caniedydd. Alun Llywelyn-Williams, *tr. fr. Welsh* by Joseph R. Clancy. OBWVE

There are two births: The one when light. William Cartwright. *See* Chloe, why wish you that your years.

There are two births; the one when light. William Cartwright. *Fr. To Chloe Who for His Sake Wished Herself Younger.* GGP

There are two kinds of people on earth today. Lifting and Leaning. Ella Wheeler Wilcox. BLPA; WBLP
(Two Kinds of People.) PoToHe

There are two Mays. Emily Dickinson. NOBA

There are two men. Two Men. Andrew Lansdown. NOBAu

There are/ two members. In the Case of Lobsters. Petra von Morstein, *tr. fr. German* by Rosemarie Waldrop. BoWoP

There are two miseries in human life. Walter Savage Landor. FaBoEE

There are two women; one I love, and one. Twins. "Owen Meredith." ErPo

There are voices, voices. Light's dying. Birds have quit. John Berryman. *Fr. Dream Songs.* CAPP

There are, who, to my person pay their court. Pope. *Fr.* Epistle to Dr. Arbuthnot. FHYEP; InPS; NoP; OAEL-1; OBF; OxAEP-1; PoE; PoEL-3; TFi

There are wolves in the next room waiting. The Wolves. Allen Tate. LiTA; LiTM; NOBA; OxBA; PoA

There are words like freedom. Refugee in America. Langston Hughes. GOA
(Words Like Freedom.) BPo

There are words that can only be said on paper. Words. Robert Finch. PoA

There are wrongs done in the fair face of heaven. The Deeds That Might Have Been. Wilfrid Scawen Blunt. *Fr.* In Vinculis. TrGrPo

There are youngsters now. Furniture. Phyllis Beauvais. LPA; NYBP

There arent. Untitled Requiem for Tomorrow. Conyus. PoBA

There at the watershed I turned. Ba Cottage. Andrew Young. OxBSP

There Be None of Beauty's Daughters. Byron. *See* There be none of Beauty's daughters.

There be none of Beauty's daughters. Byron. *Fr.* Stanzas for Music. AWP; CBLP; ELP; EnRP; GTBS; GTBS-P; HAP; LiTB; NAEL-2; NoP; OAEL-2; PFP; PoRA; TrGrPo
(There Be None of Beauty's Daughters.) MeMBP

There be three badgers on a mossy stone. The Three Badgers. "Lewis Carroll." CBNP; FaBoNo

There be three hundred different ways and more. Tears. "Owen Meredith." *Fr.* Glenaveril. EBVV

There be three things seeking my death. Prayer for the Speedy End of Three Great Misfortunes. *Unknown, tr. fr. Irish by* Frank O'Connor. OBMV

There be who say, in these enlightened days. Byron. *Fr.* English Bards and Scotch Reviewers. EPCY

There between the riverbank. Angel. Brad Leithauser. DiPo; FYAP

There Blooms No Bud in May. Walter de la Mare. MoAB; MoBrPo

There blows a cold wind today, today. *Unknown.* MiEL

There, breathless, with his digging nails he clung. Byron. *Fr.* Don Juan. OxAEP-2

There by some wrinkled stones round a leafless tree. The Twelve. Allen Tate. ChIV-2

There calleth me ever a marvelous horn. Home-Sickness. Justinus Kerner, *tr. fr. German by* James Clarence Mangan. AWP

There cam' seven Egyptians on a day. The Gypsy Countess. *Unknown.* OBET

There came a bird out o' a bush. Lady Isabel and the Elf-Knight. *Unknown.* ESPB

There came a day at summer's full. Emily Dickinson. NAAL-1; NOBA
(Renunciation. MoAmPo

There came a dove, an Easter dove. My Easter Dove. H. Cordelia Ray. CBWP-3

There came a ghost to Margret's door. Sweet William's Ghost *or* Sweet William and May Margaret. *Unknown.* AWP; CH; ESPB

There came a knocking at the front door. A Person from Porlock. R. S. Thomas. TOF

There came a whisper from the night to me. God's Remembrance. Francis Ledwidge. TIRV

There came a wind like a bugle. Emily Dickinson. CMoP; MeMAP; MoAB; NAAL-1; NAWM-2; NOBA; OPOP; OxBA; RB; SAmP

There came an earl a-riding by. The Gypsy Countess. *Unknown.* OBET

There came an old woman from France. The Old Woman from France. *Unknown.* ReMoGo

There came from Normandy an old. The Two Lovers. Marie de France, *tr. by* Patricia Terry. BoWoP

There came this bright young thing. As for the Quince. Nuala Ni Dhomhnaill, *tr. fr. Irish by* Paul Muldoon. BiHa; CIP; PBCIP

There came three men from out of the west. Sir John Barleycorn. *Unknown.* FaBoBa

There can be no songs for dead children. Kindertotenlieder. Michael Longley. CIP

There chanced to be a pedlar bold. The Bold Pedlar and Robin Hood. *Unknown.* AmFP; ESPB

There chanced to meet together in an inn. John Taylor. NOSC

There Charon stands, who rules the dreary coast. Virgil, *tr. by* Dryden. *Fr.* Aeneid [*or* Eneados], The. NAWM-1; OBVE

There come to me. Pause. Octavio Paz, *tr. fr. Spanish by* John Frederick Nims. STV

There comes a moment when to believe is not enough. Action. James Oppenheim. TrJP

There Comes a Time. Ella Wheeler Wilcox. PWR

There comes a wail of anguish. A Cry for Light. *Unknown.* BLRP

There comes Emerson first, whose rich words, every one. James Russell Lowell. *Fr.* Fable for Critics, A. NAAL-1
(Emerson. AmPP; NOBA; OxBA; TAP

There comes Poe, with his raven, like Barnaby Rudge. Poe and Longfellow. James Russell Lowell. *Fr.* Fable for Critics, A. AmPP; NOBA; OxBA; TAP
(Poe. TAP

There comes the time. Moving. Darrell Gray. UL

There died a myriad. Ezra Pound. *Fr.* Hugh Selwyn Mauberly. (Life and Contacts). AmPP; CMoP; FaBoEH; FF; InPS; LiTA; LiTM; MoAmPo; NoAM; NOBA; NOBE; NoP; PoE; TAP; TRP

There died last night. Field Observation. Padraic Fallon. PeIV

[There Douglas] landed Lord Percye. (*LL*) Northumberland Betray[e]d by Douglas [*or* Dowglas]. *Unknown.* ESPB; OxBB

There dwelt a fair maid in the West. James Harris (The Daemon Lover). *Unknown.* ESPB

There dwelt a man in fair[e] Westmoreland [*or* Westmerland]. Johnie Armstrong. *Unknown.* ESPB, A *vers.*; FaBoBa; HoPM; NoP, A *vers.*; TrGrPo

There dwelt a miller, hale and bold. The Miller of Dee. *Unknown.* GBP

There dwelt an old woman at Exeter. The Woman of Exeter. *Unknown.* ReMoGo

There dwelt the Man, the flower of human kind. Mount Vernon, the Home of Washington. William Day. OHIP

There exifted a person, not a woman or a boy, being in the firft part of life. The Semantic Limerick According to Dr. Johnson's Dictionary (Edition of 1765). Gavin Ewart. FaBoBl

There existed an adult male person who had lived a relatively short time. The Semantic Limerick According to the Shorter Oxford English Dictionary (1933). Gavin Ewart. FaBoBl

There exists no proof as. E. C. Bentley. *Fr.* Clerihews. NOBL

There fared a mother driven forth. The House of Christmas. G. K. Chesterton. MoBrPo

There Faunus and Sylvanus keep their courts. Sir John Denham. *Fr.* Cooper's Hill. BeJo; JCP; SeCP; SeCV-1

There fell red rain of spears athwart the sky. Last Judgment. John Gould Fletcher. AWP

There, figured and pre-figured in the nothing-transfiguri wheel. (*LL*) The Figured Wheel. Robert Pinsky. NoAM

There flourished once a potentate. The King of Yvetot. Pierre Jean de Béranger, *tr. fr. French by* William Toynbee. AWP

There God himself gives light. (*LL*) Jerusalem, My Happy Home. *Unknown.* PoE

There goes the dog of the mind. Soliloquy by the Shore. Martin Scholten. GoYe

There goes the grandson, run off to the beach! The Grandson. James Scully. NYBP

There goes the Wapiti. The Wapiti. Ogden Nash. MoShBr; TLR

There Gowans Are Gay. *Unknown.* GBP

There grateful to heaven, with trasport shall bring. (*LL*) As Down a Lone Valley. Timothy Dwight. AH

There grew a goodly tree him faire beside. Balme. Spenser. *Fr.* Faerie Queene, The. CH

There grew two olives, closest of the grove. Homer, *tr. by* Pope. *Fr.* Odyssey. NAWM-1; OBVE

There grows no rootless flower. The First Reader. Winfield Townley Scott. PoA

There had been rain in the morning and a chaffinch. All Possession Is Theft. Lauris Edmond. PeNZ

There had been years of passion — scorching, cold. And There Was a Great Calm. Thomas Hardy. ChTr; CMoP; FaBoRV; LiTM; OAEL-2

There had to be a context, a route. Caption Block. David Chaloner. VaA

There hartes ware so roted in the popes lawes. Fragment of an Anti-Papist Ballad. *Unknown.* CoMu

There has been. To W. C. W. M. D. Alfred Kreymborg. PoA

There has been a death in the street. Community. Sally Roberts Jones. AngWe

There has been a light snow. In a Train. Robert Bly. CAPP; NaP; TTTS

There has been a play on T.V. Lesbian Play on T.V. Caroline Gilfillan. PeHV

There has been no change. Autumn. Princess Shikishi, *tr. fr. Japanese by* Hiroaki Sato. PBWP

There Has to Be a Jail for Ladies. Thomas Merton. VGW

There have been plates but no appetite. The Museum. Wislawa Szymborska, *tr. fr. Polish by* Magnus F. Krynski. PoSu

There have been poets that in verse display. To Wordsworth. Hartley Coleridge. Son

There have been times when I have looked at life. Vision. Elizabeth N. Hauer. PoToHe

There have been times when I well might have passed and the ending have come. Thomas Hardy. *Fr.* In Tenebris. LiTB; MeMBP; NOBE; NoP; OAEL-2; PrIm

There have been times when on a city street. On City Streets. Margaret E. Bruner. PoToHe

There he goes, went, catch him. Losses and Recoveries. Chris Wallace-Crabbe. FaBoMA

There he is, Mars rising, a purulent red dot. For Thomas Stearns Eliot on the Occasion of His One Hundredth Birthday. Thomas Rabbitt. NAmP90

There he is, woman! The Seduction of Engadu. *Unknown, tr. by* William Ellery Leonard. *Fr.* Epic of Gilgamesh, The. ErPo

There he moved, cropping the grass at the purple canyon's lip. The Horse Thief. William Rose Benét. MoAmPo

There he was — having spent. "Yes, But . . . ." Theodore Weiss. TAP

There I could never be a boy. Frank O'Hara. NNaP

There I learned how faces fall apart. "Anna Akhmatova," *tr. by* D. M. Thomas. *Fr.* Requiem 1935-1940. AIW; BoWoP

There. I set you free. Manumission. Barbara Burford. DT

There I sit afloat in. Ohnedaruth's Day Begun. Nathaniel Mackey. Jaz

There, I was so interested to hear about it. *(LL)* The Horse Show. William Carlos Williams. CMoP; NOBA; TAP; VGW

There in Fiesole it was always fresh. Basil. Gibbons Ruark. MT

There, in his club, hard by: *(LL)* Where the Dead Men Lie. Barcroft Henry Boake. CBAP

There in the bracken was the ominous spoor mark. The Tantanoola Tiger. Max Harris. MoBS

There, in the corner, staring at his drink. Docker. Seamus Heaney. HeIL; HeIP; IIP; MoP; NOIV; Poetr

There, in the earliest and chary spring, the dogwood flowers. Sunday: Outskirts of Knoxville, Tennessee. James Agee. ErPo

There in the flower garden. *Unknown, tr. fr. Spanish by* Willis Barnstone. BoWoP

There in the hard light. An Irish Lake. W. R. Rodgers. BIrV

There, in the market, with Mrs. Peters. Journal of the Storm. Greg Kuzma. AmPA

There, in the very middle. Mothers. Auvaiyar, *tr. fr. Tamil by* A. K. Ramanujan. PLW

There is a bareness in the images. Substance and Shadow. John Hewitt. PNI

There is a big artist named Val. Dante Gabriel Rossetti. FaBoEE; PeLi

There is a bird bath on our grass. The Bird Bath. Florence Hoatson. BoTP

There is a bird in the poplars. Metric Figure. William Carlos Williams. MoAB; MoAmPo

There is a blue star, Janet. Baby Toes. Carl Sandburg. FaPON

There is a boat on the lake to float on. Blarney castle. Francis Sylvester Mahony. IIP

There is a brook in the mountains. A Mountain Spring. Ch'u Ch'uang I, *tr. fr. Chinese by* Kenneth Rexroth. OHMPC

There is a camp upon a rounded hill. Soldiers in a Small Camp. W. J. Turner. NSI

There is a change — and I am poor. A Complaint. Wordsworth. NOBE; PoEL-4

There is a charm in solitude that cheers. John Clare. NOBVV (Solitude.) EnRP; OxBSP

There Is a Charming Land. Adam Oehlenschläger, *tr. fr. Danish by* Robert Hillyer. AWP; FaPON

There Is a City. "The Jewish Sibyl," *tr. fr. Greek by* Bohn. *Fr.* Fourth Book of Sibylline Oracles, The. TrJP

There is a club for boys where they. To G. R. Samuel Elsworth Cottam. PeHV

There is a coarseness. Jungle Taste. Edward S. Silvera. CDC

There is a Coke bottle on the roof. Kissing Game. Bob Rosenthal. UL

There is a connection between us. Connection. Caroline Halliday. DT

There is a country Lost. Ice, Eden. Paul Celan, *tr. fr. German by* Michael Hamburger. OBD

There is a creator named God. On the Painter Val Prinsep. Dante Gabriel Rossetti. FaBoEE

There is a creature called God. Dante Gabriel Rossetti. PeLi

There is a crying in the world. End of the World. Else Lasker-Schüler, *tr. fr. German by* Willis Barnstone *and* Michael Gillespie. BoWoP

There is a dark planet striking against us. Invisible. The Dark Planet. John Heath-Stubbs. OAEL-2

There is a darkness, dark. Lost Moments. Glover Davis. SM

There is a day, a dreadful day. Song — Last Day. John Clare. EnVR

There is a dead part of the day. Late Naps. Marvin Bell. AnAn

There is a dear and lonely tract of hell. Supremacy. E. A. Robinson. NoAM

There is a deep brooding. My Arkansas. Maya Angelou. BlSi

There is a destiny that makes us brothers. A Creed. Edwin Markham. BLPA; BLPL; FaBoBe

There is a dish to hold the sea. Imagination. John Davidson. *Fr.* New Year's Eve. ArNa; MeMBP; MoBrPo

There is a dotty woman. Her Friend Flo. Gerda Mayer. OBF

There is a drunk on Main Avenue, slumped. Song-Maker. Anita Endrezze-Danielson. HATNAP

There is a faculty or knack, smallish, in the mind that can turn. A. R. Ammons. *Fr.* Sphere. NoAM

There is a fair one. The Lute Song. Kung Tzu-chen, *tr. fr. Chinese by* An-yan Tang. SuSp

There is a fashion in this land. The Knight's Ghost. *Unknown.* ESPB

There is a feast in your father's house. Leesome Brand. *Unknown.* ESPB

There is a fever of the spirit. Song by Mr. Cypress. Thomas Love Peacock. *Fr.* Nightmare Abbey. OAEL-2; OBNC

There is a fine stuffed chavender. A False Gallop of Analogies. Warham St. Leger. FaBoCo; FiBHP

There is a flower, a little flower. A Field Flower. James Montgomery. *Fr.* Daisy, The. BoTP

There is a flower blossoming out of season. Flower Ensnarer of Psalms. Rossana Ombres, *tr. fr. Italian by* I. L. Salomon. BoWoP

There is a flower I wish to wear. Hearts-Ease. Walter Savage Landor. EnRP

There is a flower that bees prefer. Purple Clover. Emily Dickinson. MoAmPo

There is a flower that blooms out of season. Ensnaring Flower of Psalms. Rossana Ombres, *tr. fr. Italian by* Ruth Feldman. NeIt

There is a flower, the Lesser Celandine. A Lesson. Wordsworth. GTBS; GTBS-P

There is a fountain filled with blood. Praise for the Fountain Opened. William Cowper. InPK
(Fountain, The.) ChIV-1

There is a friendship that exists between. A Dog's Vigil. Margaret E. Bruner. PoToHe

There Is a Garden. Thomas Campion. *See* There Is a Garden in Her Face.

There Is a Garden in Her Face. Thomas Campion. AAS; EBEvV; ElL; EnRePo; GoJo; HeIP; ImPo; InPK; NAEL-1; NoP; NOSC; OAEL-1; OPOP; PoE; PoEL-2; Poetr; PrIm; SCGP; TFi; TrGrPo

There is a garden where lilies. Eutopia. Francis Turner Palgrave. EBVV; OHCV

There is a girl dragging heavy. Ritual Girl. Frank Mkalawile Chipasula. HBAPE

There Is a Girl Inside. Lucille Clifton. CAPP

There is a girl you like so you tell her. Courtship. Mark Strand. HCAP

There is a glow in the kitchen window now. Les A. Murray. *Fr.* Evening Alone at Bunyah. FaBoMA

There is a goddess and I know her. Her hands are not clean. Apotheosis of the Kitchen Goddess II. Teresa Noelle Roberts. CrSp

There is a golden rule in life. Do As You Would Be Done By. Matilda C. Edwards. PWR

There is a grape vine threatening my house. Anticipation. Sheila Richter. LoHo

There is a great amount of poetry in unconscious/ fastidiousness. Critics and Connoisseurs. Marianne Moore. AmPP; CMoP; FaBoWP; MeMAP; NoAM; NOBA; OxBA; Poetr

There is a great river this side of Stygia. The River of Rivers in Connecticut. Wallace Stevens. HAP; HCAP; NOBA; VGW

There Is a Green Hill Far Away. Cecil Frances Alexander. BLRP; OxBChV; TIRV; WGRP

There is a green ruin where they gather. How Words Meet to Make a Poem. Aidan Carl Mathews. IB

There is a green spell stolen from Birmingham. A Death at Winson Green. Francis Webb. FaBoMA

There is a growth that hurts the child. An Age. Laura Jensen. LCAP

There is a halo around the moon. Debt. Gond Oral Tradition, *tr. by* V. Elwin *and* S. Hivale. WTO

There is a hawk there is picking the birds out of our sky. Shiva. Robinson Jeffers. NoAM; NOBA; Son

There is a heigh-ho in these glowing coals. Heigh-ho on a Winter Afternoon. Donald Davie. OxBTC

There Is a High Place. Edwin Markham. AH

There is a hill and on that hill is a stone. The Heart of the World. Rabbi Nahman of Bratzlav, *tr. fr. Yiddish by* Joseph Leftwich. TrJP

There is a hill in England. Three Hills. Everard Owen. NSI

There is a hornet in the room. Buried at Springs. James Schuyler. CoAP; PoM; PRA

There is a hush this golden afternoon. Classroom in October. Elias Lieberman. GoYe

There is a joyful night in which we lose. When the Dumb Speak. Robert Bly. NOBA

There is a kind of lace laid over the city, a lightness. The Serious Merriment of Women. Patricia Goedicke. TAP

There is a lady conquering with glances. There Is a Lady ("There is a lady conquering with glances.") Walther von der Vogelweide, *tr. fr. German by* Jethro Bithell. AWP

There is a way of seeing that is not seeing. Trompe L'Œil. Daryl Hine. MoCV

There is/ A welcome at the door to which no one comes? Angel Surrounded by Paysans. Wallace Stevens. HCAP; LCAP; PPP

There is a white mare that my love keeps. Alex Comfort. *Fr.* Postures of Love, The. ErPo

There is a willow grows aslant a brook. Shakespeare. *Fr.* Hamlet. NAWM-1; OxAEP-1; RB (Ophelia's Death.) ChTr

There is a wind where the rose was. Autumn. Walter de la Mare. OxBTC

There is a window stuffed with hay. The Hay Hotel. Oliver St. John Gogarty. BIrV

There is a wine shop by the shore of West Lake. To the Tune "A Branch of Bamboo." Chu Chung-hsien, *tr. fr. Chinese by* Kenneth Rexroth *and* Ling Chung. WPC

There is a wolf in me . . . fangs pointed for tearing gashes. Wilderness. Carl Sandburg. RaBo

There is a woman climbing a glass hill. Two Women. Naomi Replansky. NMM

There is a woman in our town. William Carlos Williams. *Fr.* Paterson. CMoP; PoE

There Is a Woman in This Town. Patricia Parker. BlSi

There is a word at heart for the next of death. Written in Exile. Kathleen Raine. TrCP; WPE

There is a wordless tomorrow. Wordless Day. Chang Shiang-Lua, *tr. fr. Chinese.* TSaS, *tr. by* Stephen L. Smith *with* Naomi Shihab Nye

There is a yew tree, pride of Lorton Vale. Yew Trees. Wordsworth. EnRP; UnPo

There is a young lady, whose nose. Edward Lear. OxBChV

There is a young Muslim Chinese. Taunt. *Malay Oral Tradition, tr. by* R. J. Wilkinson *and* R. O. Winstedt. WTO

There is always a first flinging. Variations on a Theme. Anne Wilkinson. MoCV

There Is Always a Place for You. Anne Campbell. PoToHe

There is always a place for you at my table. There Is Always a Place for You. Anne Campbell. PoToHe

There is always a wicked secret, a private reason for this. (*LL*) At Last the Secret Is Out. W. H. Auden. InPS

There is an aggression of fact. After Jericho. R. S. Thomas. OxBC

There is an air for which I would disown. An Old Tune. Gérard de Nerval, *tr. fr. French by* Andrew Lang. AWP

There is an amazing bird. The Tin Bird. Ramon C. Sunico, *tr. fr. Spanish.* TSaS, *tr. by* Sunico Ramon C.

There is an ancient forest, its giant trees. The Flower Pot. David Shimoni, *tr. fr. Hebrew by* Ruth Finer Mintz. MHP

There is an ancient story. My Father's Story. Priscilla Jane Thompson. CBWP-2

There is an archipelago rising. Sow. W. S. Merwin. PRA

There is an embalmer who operates. Embalmer. Rossana Ombres, *tr. fr. Italian by* Ruth Feldman. NeIt

There is an end of joy and sorrow. Ilicet. Swinburne. NOBVV

There is an evening coming in. Going. Philip Larkin. CMoP

There is an Eye that never sleeps. God the Omniscient. James Cowden Wallace. BLRP (God.) WGRP

There is an eye, there was a slit. Sabbath. John Berryman. *Fr.* Dream Songs. LCAP

There Is an Hour of Peaceful Rest. William Bingham Tappan. *See* Hour of Peaceful Rest, The.

There is an inevitability. Norman Harris. NYBP

There is an inn, a merry old inn. The Man in the Moon Stayed up To Late. J. R. R. Tolkien. OBSP

There is an island in a far-off sea. Where the Single Men Go in Summer. Nina Bourne. FiBHP

There is an old and very cruel god. Vicarious Atonement. Richard Aldington. MoBrPo; WGRP

There Is an Old City. Karl Bulcke, *tr. fr. German by* Ludwig Lewisohn. AWP

There is an old he-wolf named Gambart. Dante Gabriel Rossetti. FaBoEE; PeLi

There is an olden story. The Flowers' Ball. Ben King. AnAmPo

There is, at times, an evening sky. Vincent Ogé. George Boyer Vashon. AAP

There is blood on thy desolate shore. Apostrophe to the Island of Cuba. James Gates Percival. PAH

There is Bryant, as quiet, as cool, and as dignified. Bryant. James Russell Lowell. *Fr.* Fable for Critics, A. NOBA; TAP

There is but one, and that one ever. (*LL*) Easter ("I got me flowers to straw Thy Way.") George Herbert. BoTP; CH; FaBoCh; FHYEP; NAEL-1; NOBE; OBEV; OHIP; TrGrPo

There is but one May in the year. May-Time. *Unknown.* BoTP

There is Celilo. She-Who-Watches . . . The Names are Prayer. Elizabeth Woody. BCF

There is comfort in old houses. Old Houses. Homer D'Lettuso. PoToHe

There is danger where I move my feet. Song of a Bear. *Unknown, tr. fr. Navajo Indian.* OBAP

There is death enough in Europe without these. Dead Ponies. Brenda Chamberlain. OBWVE; WPE

There is delight in singing, though none hear. To Robert Browning. Walter Savage Landor. EnRP; EPCY; NoP

There is downpour, always. Diesel to Yesterday. John Tripp. AngWe

There is drink fermented. Chimedin Jigmed, *tr. fr. Mongol Oral Tradition by* C. R. Bawden. *Fr.* Satirical Poem about Drink, A. WTO

There is enough. What We Know. Raymond R. Patterson. NBV

There is enough for us all. David Chaloner. VaA

There is ever a song somewhere, my dear. James Whitcomb Riley. AnAmPo

There is fear in/ Turning the mind away. The Sun and the Moon and Fear of Loneliness. *Unknown, tr. fr. Eskimo.* WTO

There is flight around me. (*LL*) I part the out thrusting branches. Wendell Berry. EaPr

There is frost in the air. Schoenberg Op. 11. Thomas W. Shapcott. *Fr.* Piano Pieces. CBAP

There is good news that spring's in the air. Spring Sentiments. Chao Yi, *tr. fr. Chinese by* Chang Yin-nan *and* Lewis C. Walmsley. SuSp

There is great mystery, Simone. Hair. Remy de Gourmont, *tr. fr. French by* Jethro Bithell. AWP; ErPo

There is "great rejoicing at the nation's capital." War and Hell. Ernest Crosby. PAW

There is Hawthorne, with genius so shrinking and rare. Hawthorne. James Russell Lowell. *Fr.* Fable for Critics, A. AmPP; NOBA; OxBA; TAP

There is health in thy gray wing. To a Marsh Hawk in Spring. Thoreau. PoEL-4

There is in each body something splendid, I think. The Quality. Philip Schultz. NAmP90

There is in human closeness a sacred boundary. "Anna Akhmatova," *tr. fr. Russian by* Dianne Levitin. WPOW

There is in the human voice. Caught. Rodney Jones. NAmP90

There is in this world something. The Sweetest Thing. *Unknown, tr. fr. Susu by* Ulli Beier. TTY

There is joy. Welcome Morning. Anne Sexton. CrSp; HeIL

There is joy in/ Feeling the warmth. Eskimo Chant. *Unknown, tr. fr. Eskimo by* Knud Rasmussen. RFM

There is Law for Fire. The Seasons of Fire. Billy Marshall-Stoneking. NOBAu

There is little in afternoon tea. On Drawing-Room Amenities. Gelett Burgess. FaBoNo

There is Lowell, who's striving Parnassus to climb. Lowell. James Russell Lowell. *Fr.* Fable for Critics, A. AmPP; NOBA; OxBA; TAP

There is more than glass between the snow and the huge roses. (*LL*) Snow. Louis MacNeice. CIP; CMoP; FaBoMo; LiTM; MoP; NoAM; NOBE; OPOP; OxAEP-2; OxBSP; OxBTC; PNI

There is much to be said for the portrait painted in winter. Portrait in Winter. Katherine Garrison Chapin. GoYe

There is music in me, the music of a peasant people. The Banjo Player. Fenton Johnson. PoNe

There is my country under glass. At the Tourist Center in Boston. Margaret Atwood. NoP; Poetr

There is naught for thee by thy haste to gain. The Created. Jones Very. NOCV

There Is Never a Day So Dreary. Lilla M. Alexander. BLRP

There is never an open door to the wild beasts' home. The Uninvited. William D. Mundell. NYBP

There is never enough time to become a man. Maturity. Stephen Knight. UnDi

There is no answer. We do here what we will. The Usurpers. Edwin Muir. CMoP

There is no balm on earth. Gilbert Thomas. TrPWD

There is no bountie to be shew'd to such. Ben Jonson. *Fr.* Poetaster, The. PoEL-2

There is no chance, no destiny, no fate. Will. Ella Wheeler Wilcox. BLPA; PoToHe

There is no chapel on the day. Oscar Wilde. *Fr.* Ballad of Reading Gaol, The. BeLS; EBVV; NoAM; OBNV; OxAEP-2; TIRV

There Is No Country. Julian Tuwim, *tr. fr. Polish by* Watson Kirkconnell. TrJP

There Is No Death. John Luckey McCreery. BLPA; FaBoBe; PWR; WBLP

There Is No Death. *Unknown.* BLPA

There is no death, O child divine. The Great Victory. R. V. Gilbert. BLRP

There is no death! The stars go down. There Is No Death. John Luckey McCreery. BLPA; FaBoBe; PWR; WBLP

There is no death — there's immortality. (LL) There Is No Death. Unknown. BLPA

There is no debauchery worse than thought. A Contribution on Pornography. Wislawa Szymborska, tr. fr. Polish by Adam Czerniawski. PoSu

There is no difference between being raped. Rape Poem. Marge Piercy. Poetsp

There is no faith in claret, and it shall. Two Gentlemen That Broke Their Promise of a Meeting. James Shirley. BeJo

There is no fire of the crackling boughs. Glenaradale. Walter Chalmers Smith. OBEV; PeVV

There is no frigate like a book. Emily Dickinson. GoJo; MoAmPo; OBCA; PoLF; SAmP; SoSe; TAP; TrGrPo
(Book, A "There is no frigate like a book".) FaPON

"There is no God!" (LL) A Common Inference. Charlotte Perkins Gilman. WGRP

There Is No God. Arthur Hugh Clough. See "There is no God," the wicked saith.

There is no God, as I was taught in youth. John Masefield. Fr. Sonnets. CMoP; WGRP

"There is no God," the foolish saith. Convinced by Sorrow. Elizabeth Barrett Browning. Fr. Cry of the Human, The. BLRP; WBLP

"There is no God," the wicked saith. Arthur Hugh Clough. Fr. Dipsychus. NAEL-2; NOBVV
(There Is No God.) BLPL; NOBE

There is no great and no small. The Informing Spirit. Emerson. AWP

There is no happy life. Love's Matrimony. William Cavendish. NOSC

There is no Job but cries to God and hopes. A Copy of Verses. John Wilson. SCAP

There is no joy in water apart from the sun. Ralph Nixon Currey. PeSA

There Is No Land Yet. Laura Riding. ChIV-1

There is no limit to the number of times. From Father to Son. Emyr Humphreys. AngWe; OBWVE

There is no Lover hee or shee. A Paradox. Aurelian Townshend. SeCP

There is no music now in all Arkansas. Variations for Two Pianos. Donald Justice. GoJo; NYBP

There is no mystery in it so far. Entering the Kingdom of the Moray Eel. James Wright. PRA

There Is No Name So Sweet on Earth. George Washington Bethune. AH

There is no needle without piercing point. Death. Unknown. RaBo

There is no night/ when the lightning does not flash. Lady Sagami, tr. fr. Japanese by Kenneth Rexroth and Ikuko Atsumi. WPJ

There is no one among men that has not a special failing. Madly Singing in the Mountains. Po Chü-i, tr. fr. Chinese by Arthur Waley. Mes

There Is No Opera like "Lohengrin." John Wheelwright. NYBP

There is no other happiness. (LL) The Second Rapture. Thomas Carew. CaPo; OPOP

There is no other hope. (LL) Tomorrow the Heroes. Alfred B. Spellman. PoBA

There is no other life. (LL) Why Log Truck Drivers Rise Earlier than Students of Zen. Gary Snyder. NNaP; SOTW

There is no page or servant, most or least. The Seventh Property. Sir Thomas More. Fr. Twelve Weapons of Spiritual Battle, The. EnRePo

There is no peace with you. Enigma. Jessie Redmond Fauset. PoNe

"There is no permanence," you sagely said. Samuel A. DeWitt. Fr. Two Sonnets for a Lost Love. GoYe

There is no person lonelier . . . Than he who lies in bed. Visit the Sick. James J. Metcalfe. PoToHe

There is no place in this dark. Radiant Silhouette II. John Yau. OpBo

There is no place like home. Here and There. Ralph Meredith. Mes

There Is No Place to Hide. Gwendolyn MacEwen. Fr. T. E. Lawrence Poems, The. NOBC

"There is no place to turn," she said. The Sensualists. Theodore Roethke. ErPo

There is no point in work. Work. D. H. Lawrence. OBMV

There is no portrait. Robert Creeley Listens, Too. D. C. Berry. BXAP

There is no quenching of the other thirst. Hagar. Elisabeth Eybers, tr. fr. Afrikaans by the author. PeSA

There is no race of men. Boethius, tr. fr. Latin. Fr. Consolation of Philosophy, The. MLL, tr. by Helen Waddell

There is no reason for amazement: surely one always knew that cultures decay, and life's end is death. (LL) The Purse-Seine. Robinson Jeffers. CMoP; HAP; NoAM; NOBA; NoP; OxBA; Poetr; PrIm; WeW

There is no remedy. (LL) O Death, Rock Me Asleep. At. to George Boleyn. EIL; FaBoRV; FF; TrGrPo; WPE

There is no rest for her, and sleep has left her bed. Gond Oral Tradition, tr. by V. Elwin and S. Hivale. WTO

There is no rhyme that is half so sweet. Madison Cawein. BoNaP

There Is No Riot. Martin Carter. PBCV

There is no salvation for mankind. Ballad of a Little Lamp. René Depestre, tr. fr. French by Ellen Conroy Kennedy. NegPo

There is no sense that I should write a line. To Cynthia. Sir Francis Kynaston. NOSC

There is no signpost to say. Hilda Doolittle ("H. D."). Fr. Sigil. AnAn

There is no silence in the earth — so silent. Emily Dickinson. FaBoEE

There is no silence upon the earth or under the earth like the silence under the sea. Silences. E. J. Pratt. NOBC

There is no sky today. Echoes of birds. Counterparts. Stephen Dobyns. PoA

There is no sorrow. Away. Walter de la Mare. NoP

There is no story behind it. The Butterfly. Arun Kolatkar. OBAP

There is no sun today. A Half-Life. Henri Cole. PFL

There is no thing in all the world but love. The Camel-Rider. Unknown, tr. fr. Arabic by Wilfrid Scawen Blunt. AWP

There Is No Unbelief. Elizabeth York Case. WBLP; WGRP

There is no whispering of any friend. No Friend Like Music. Daniel Whitehead Hicky. PoToHe

There Is No Word for goodbye. Mary TallMountain. HATNAP

There is no word for goodbye. (LL) There Is No Word for Goodbye. Mary TallMountain. HATNAP

There is no worldly pleasure here below. The Exercise of Affection. Sir Robert Ayton.
(Upon Love.) NOSC

There is nobody anywhere near him. Day-Dream. Samarendra Sengupta. TSaS, tr. by Lila Ray

There Is None like Her. Tennyson. Fr. Maud[: A Monodrama]. OBNC

There is none like the Boy that sold Broom, green Broom. (LL) Broom, Green Broom. Unknown. LiTB; OxBoLi; PoRA

There is none, no none but I. Sir Robert Ayton. NOSC

There Is None, O None but You. Thomas Campion. EIL

There Is None to Help. Chad Walsh. Fr. Psalm of Christ, The. TrCP

There is not half so warm a fire. Against Fulfillment of Desire. Unknown. TrGrPo

There is not in the wide world a valley so sweet. The Meeting of the Waters. Thomas Moore. ArLo; IIP; NOIV; OxBoLi; PoEL-4

There Is Nothin' like a Dame. Oscar Hammerstein II. OBAL

There is nothing as sweet as independence. Independence. Adebayo Faleti, tr. fr. Yoruba by Bakare Gbadamosi and Ulli Beier. PBA

There is nothing between us. (LL) Medusa. Sylvia Plath. NALW

There is nothing but water in the holy pools. How Much Is Not True. Kabir. RaBo

There is nothing in the world so still as snow. Snow. Helge Rode, tr. fr. Danish by Philip L. Miller. RiWo

There is nothing like the cool. The Wind From Mt. Fuji. Tagami Kikusha-Ni, tr. fr. Japanese by Kenneth Rexroth and Ikuko Atsumi. WPJ

There is nothing more to say. (LL) The House on the Hill. E. A. Robinson. FaPON; GoJo; MoAmPo; NAAL-2; PrIm; TrGrPo

There is nothing Orphic, nothing foreign. A Setting. Donald Revell. UTF

There is nothing to save, now all is lost. Nothing to Save. D. H. Lawrence. SOTW

There is/ One great society alone on earth. The Noble. Wordsworth. Fr. Prelude [or, Growth of a Poet's Mind], The. ChTr; EnRP; OAEL-2

There is one grief worse than any other. Daughter. Ellen Bryant Voigt. MT

There is one Mind, one omnipresent Mind. Samuel Taylor Coleridge. Fr. Religious Musings. WGRP

There is one sin: to call a green leaf grey. Ecclesiastes. G. K. Chesteron. ChIV-1; MoBrPo; OxBSP

There is one story and one story only. To Juan at the Winter Solstice. Robert Graves. CMoP; EBEV; FaBoMo; ImPo; LiTB; LiTM; MeMBP; MoBrPo; MoP; NAAL-2; NoAM; OAEL-2; PoE; RaBo; TwCP

There Is One Synagogue Extant in Kiev. Yaacov Luria. BTR

There is one that has a head without an eye. Christina Rossetti. OxBChV

There is one word. My Favorite Word. Lucia M. and James L. Hymes, Jr. and James L. Hymes. SiSoPo

There Is Only One of Everything. Margaret Atwood. NOBC

There is only the grass to fight! (LL) Dandelion. Hilda Conkling. FaPON; PDV

There is pain in my heart. Neidhart von Reuental, tr. fr. German by Frederick Goldin. GePo

There is playing of flutes and fiddles. Heine. RiWo

There is pleasure in the wet, wet clay. The Lie. Kipling. NOBL

There is red/ on the clown-lady's lips. Toulouse Lautrec. Melvin B. Tolson, *tr. fr. Norwegian* by Nadia Christensen. PBWP

There is religion in everything around us. John Ruskin. EaPr

There is so little that is close and warm. Debris of Life and Mind. Wallace Stevens. SAmP

There is so much blossom and naked dawn. Mountain Girl. Rafaela Chacón Nardi, *tr. fr. Spanish* by Margaret Randall. AIW

There is so much good in the worst of us. Charity. *Unknown.* BLPA

There is so much of loneliness. *Unknown.* PoToHe

There is some beauty in sorrow. Placing a $2 Bet for a Man Who Will Never Go to the Horse Races Any More. Diane Wakoski. UnPo

There is some demon turning me into an old man. The Banjo. Robert Winner. FF

There is some will talk of lords and knights. Robin Hood's Delight. *Unknown.* ESPB

There/ is someone I can bear. W. S. Landor. Marianne Moore. OBAL

There is something banal about evil. Aleister Crowley Slept Here. Elaine Equi. UTF

There is something between us. Breasts. Donald Hall. OBAL

There is something in all of this. The heat. With the Conchero Dancers, Mission Espada, July. Rosemary Catacalos. AfAz

There is something in the autumn that is native to my blood. A Vagabond Song. Bliss Carman. AnAmPo; FaPON; GN

There is somewhere a Secret Garden, which none hath seen. The Secret Garden. Robert Nichols. WGRP

There is sorrow enough in the natural way. The Power of the Dog. Kipling. BLPA; BLPL

There Is Strength in the Soil. Arthur Stringer. OHIP

There Is Sweet Music Here. Tennyson. *Fr.* Lotus-Eaters, The. ChTr, 5 *sts.*; EnVR; FaBV; LiTB; MeMBP; NAEL-2; NoP; OAEL-2; PoEL-5; SCGP; TEP

There is sweet music here that softer falls. There Is Sweet Music Here. Tennyson. *Fr.* Lotus-Eaters, The. ChTr, 5 *sts.*; EnVR; FaBV; LiTB; MeMBP; NAEL-2; NoP; OAEL-2; PoEL-5; SCGP; TEP (Choric Song of the Lotos-Eaters.) ImPo (Choric Song: "There is sweet music here that softer falls.") HeIP; OBNC (Song of the Lotus-Eaters.) GGP; NOBE; OBEV

There is that sound like the wind. Summer. John Ashbery. NAAL-2

There is the caw of a crow. Jonathan Houghton. Edgar Lee Masters. *Fr.* Spoon River Anthology. OxBA

There is the city of glass and money. From a Front Window. Richard Hoffman. ETG

There is the curdling sky. Supper. Alison Fell. VBLP

There is the morning shuffle of traffic confined. City Walk-up, Winter 1969. Carolyn Forché. Poetr

There is the one who turns. Chiapas. Gary Soto. NoAM

There is the sleep of my tongue. The Sleep. Mark Strand. CAPP

There is the sound of hail washed over a porthole, but. Off the Aleutian Chain. Linda Bierds. NAmP90

There is the sound of trumpets brilliant off the brick. Bell & Capitol. Daniel Halpern. BAP-90

There is the star bloom of the moss. Forest. Jean Garrigue. LiTM; NOBA

There is the weight of the word. Letter to Ellen Conroy Kennedy. Edouard J. Maunick, *tr. fr. French* by Ellen Conroy Kennedy. NegPo

There is the western gate, Luke Havergal/ Luke Havergal. *(LL)* Luke Havergal. E. A. Robinson. AmPP; AWP; GBL; LiTA; LiTM; MeMAP; MoAB; MoAmPo; NAAL-2; NoAM; NOBA; PoEL-5; TFi; UnPo

There is this cave. The Jewel. James Wright. CAPP; CoAP; NAAL-2

There Is This Distance between Me and What I See. Philip Lamantia. PoBeRe

There is this distance between me and what I see. There Is This Distance between Me and What I See. Philip Lamantia. PoBeRe (Still Poem 9.) NeAP

There is unfeminine, (but oh, so Female). Questionnaire. Susan Saxe. GLP

There is unknown dust that is near us. Surprised by Evening. Robert Bly. CAPP; NaP; VGW

There is war. *(LL)* Poem for the Young White Man Who Asked Me How I, an Intelligent, Well-read Person, Could Believe in the War between Races. Lorna Dee Cervantes. BCF; PBCAP; WPOW

There Is Weeping in My Heart. Paul Verlaine, *tr. fr. French* by Philip L. Miller. RiWo

There is Whittier, whose swelling and vehement heart. Whittier. James Russell Lowell. *Fr.* Fable for Critics, A. AmPP; NOBA; OxBA

There Is Wind, There Are Matches. Gerald Stern. LCAP

There is your "dream" and its "approximation." The Blue Taj. Mei-Mei Berssenbrugge. UL

There isn't a shadow of doubt. *Unknown.* PeLi

There isn't a word for what I want from you. This Song Is Dedicated to the One Eye Love. Nick Totton. VaA

There Isn't Time. Eleanor Farjeon. BoTP; FaPON

There it is!/ You play beside a death-bed like a child. Elizabeth Barrett Browning. *Fr.* Aurora Leigh. BrRo

There it was, word for word. The Poem That Took the Place of a Mountain. Wallace Stevens. LCAP

There Lackethe Somethynge Style. Thomas Chatterton. *See* Budding floweret blushes at the light [*or* Boddynge flourettes bloshes atte the lyghte], The.

There lay she all her length and kiss'd his feet. Tennyson. *Fr.* Idylls of the King. EBVVPR

There lays a ship in the harbour. Our Ship She Lies in Harbour. *Unknown.* NTP

There left a may, an a weel-far'd may. Katharine Jaffray. *Unknown.* ESPB

There leeved a wee man at the fit o yon hill. Get Up and Bar the Door. *Unknown.* ESPB

There lies a cold corpse upon the sands. Death Song. Robert Stephen Hawker. OBNC

There lies a somnolent lake. In the Past. Trumbull Stickney. AnAmPo; NOBA; OxBA

There lies afar behind a western hill. The Town without a Market. James Elroy Flecker. MoBrPo

There! little girl, don't cry! *(LL)* A Life-Lesson. James Whitcomb Riley. PoLF

There! little girl, don't cry! A Life-Lesson. James Whitcomb Riley. PoLF

There liv'd a lady in Lauderdale. She's Hoy'd Me Out o' Lauderdale. *Unknown.* CoMu

There livd a laird down into Fife. The Wife Wrapt in Wether's Skin. *Unknown.* ESPB

There liv'd a lass in yonder dale. Katharine Jaffray. *Unknown.* ESPB

There liv'd a lord on yon sea-side. Fair Annie. *Unknown.* ESPB

There liv'd a man in yonder glen. Johnie Blunt. *Unknown.* OxBB

There liv'd a wife in Whistle Cockpen. Will Ye Na Can Ye Na Let Me Be. *Unknown.* FaBoVe

There liv'd, as authors tell, in days of yore. Chaucer. *See* Poore [*or* Povre] widwe [*or* widow], somdeel [*or* somedeal *or* somedel] stape in age, A.

There liv'd of late in Luteners Lane. A Westminster Wedding; or, Like unto Like, Quoth the Devil to the Collier. *Unknown.* CoMu

There lived a carl in Kellyburnbraes. Kellyburnbraes. *Unknown.* OxBB

There lived a fat old lady, in London she did dwell. The Old Lady of London. *Unknown.* AmFP

There Lived a King. W. S. Gilbert. *Fr.* Gondoliers, The. FiBHP

There lived a king in Thule. The King in Thule. Goethe, *tr. fr. German by* John Frederick Nims. STV

There lived a man at the foot of a hill. Get Up and Bar the Door. *Unknown.* EnSB

There lived a Puddy in a well. The Puddy and the Mouse. *Unknown.* GBP

There lived a sage in days of yore. A Tragic Story. Adelbert von Chamisso, *tr. fr. German by* Thackeray. BoTP; FaPON; MoShBr

There lived a small hermaphrodite beside the silver Brent. The Waif. Walter de la Mare. FaBoNo

There lived a wife at Usher's Well. The Wife of Usher's Well. *Unknown.* AmFP; AWP; CH; ChTr; EBEV; EnRP; EnSB; ESPB, A, B, C, and D *vers.*; FaBoBa; ImPo, A *vers.*; LiTB; NAEL-1; NOBE; NoP; OAEL-1; OBEV; OxAEP-1; OxBB; OxBS; PoEL-1; Poetr; PrIm; RB; ScCV; SCGP; TFi; TrGrPo

There Lived among the Untrodden Ways. Hartley Coleridge. BXAP

There lived an old man in the Kingdom of Tess. The New Vestments. Edward Lear. NOBVV

There lived an old woman at Lynn. *Unknown.* OxBChV

There lived in a laburnum tree. The Yellow Fairy. Charlotte Druitt Cole. BoTP

There lived in ancient Scribbletown a wise old writer-man. Puzzled. Carolyn Wells. OBCA

There lived in Gothic days, as legends tell. Edwin, The Minstrel. James Beattie. OxAEP-1

There lives a good-for-nothing cat. The Lazy Pussy. Palmer Cox. OBCA

There lives a land beside the western sea. On the South Coast of Cornwall. John Gray. NOBVV

There lives a maid down under yon brae. Katherine Jaffray. *Unknown.* OxBB

There lives a man in Rynie's land. Lang Johnny More. *Unknown.* ESPB

There lives in/ my childhood street. Self Portrait 4. Tove Ditlevsen, *tr. fr. Danish by* Ann Freeman. WPOW

There Love in very presence seemed to be. *(LL)* Ballata: Concerning a Shepherd-Maid. Cavalcanti. AWP

There lyes all this great erles gold. *(LL)* Young [or Younge] Andrew. *Unknown.* ESPB; OxBB

There May Be Chaos Still. George Santayana. *Fr.* Sonnets. AnAmPo

There may be chaos still around the world. There May Be Chaos Still. George Santayana. *Fr.* Sonnets. AnAmPo

There might be found the flowing grace. My Welsh Home. John Morgan. AngWe

There mounts in squalls a sort of rusty mire. The Exile's Return. Robert Lowell. AmPP; OxBA

There mournful cypress grew in greatest store. The Garden of Proserpina. Spenser. *Fr.* Faerie Queene, The. ChTr

There must be a place in this world. Mariana. Lucha Corpi. AfAz

There must be fairy miners. Buttercups. Wilfrid Thorley. FaPON

There must be hundreds like us now. Gateshead Grammar. George Charlton. PWE

There must be somewhere work to do. *(LL)* Habeas Corpus. Helen Hunt Jackson. WGRP

There, my lad, lie the Articles. Scene from a Play, Acted at Oxford, Called "Matriculation." Thomas Moore. OBSV

There never yet was honest man. Loving and Beloved. Sir John Suckling. BeJo; CaPo; NAEL-1

There never yet was woman made. Woman's Constancy. Sir John Suckling. CaPo

There, O there, where'er I go I'll leave my heart behind me! *(LL)* Since First I Saw Your Face. *Unknown.* ELP; LiTB; OBEV; OxBSP

There, on the Darkened Deathbed. John Masefield. *See* There, on the darkened deathbed, dies the brain.

There, on the darkened deathbed, dies the brain. John Masefield. EBEV (There, on the Darkened Deathbed.) DL; LiTB

"There, on the left!" said the colonel. Marthy Virginia's Hand. George Parsons Lathrop. PAH

There on the sea sails wandered. The Names of Georgian Women. Bella Akhmadulina, *tr. fr. Russian.* BoWoP, *tr. by* Stanley Noyes *and* Olga Carlisle

There on the top of the down. June Bracken and Heather. Tennyson. EnLoPo

There once the walls. A Tale. Edward Thomas. ChTr

There once was a bull named the Duke of Buccleuch. The Duke Of Buccleuch. J. A. Phelp. NOBAu

There once was a child who said: "How." A Postscript to Orwell's *Animal Farm.* Miadesnia. PeLi

There once was a cobbler. The Kind Mousie. Natalie Joan. BoTP

There once was a couple named Mound. *Unknown.* PeLi

There once was a cow with a double udder. The Cow. Theodore Roethke. FiBHP; OBAL; OBCA

There once was a doctor who said. Towanbucket. PeLi

There once was a fellow called Hyde. E. J. Jackson. PeLi

There once was a Fellow of Trinity. *Unknown.* PeLi

There once was a Fellow of Wadham/ Who approved of the doings of Sodom. *Unknown.* PeLi

There once was a flock of wild geese. B. Semeonoff *and* C. Semeonoff. PeLi

There once was a girl from St. Paul. *Unknown.* NIP

There once was a girl from the Congo. George Seferis, *tr. fr. Greek by* Hugh Haughton. CBNP

There once was a judge of Assize. *Unknown.* PeLi

There once was a lady called Lily. *Unknown.* PeLi

There once was a lass of Shalott. Mary Holtby. PeLi

There once was a man [or There was a young man] who said, "Damn!" Maurice Evan Hare. NOBL; OxBoLi; PeLi
(Determinism.) FaBoCo
(Limerick.) PeLV

There once was a man who said, "God." Idealism. Ronald Arbuthnott Knox. FaBoCo; NBLV
(Limerick: "There once was a man who said "God.") NOBL; PeLi

There once was a Marquis de Sade. De Sade. John Fuller. NBLV; PeLV

There once was a monarch of Spain. *Unknown.* PeLi

There once was a painter named Scott. Dante Gabriel Rossetti. PeLi

There once was a person of Chiswick. J. M. Ross. PeLi

There once was a plesiosaurus. *Unknown.* PeLi

There Once Was a Puffin. Florence Page Jaques. NTCP

There once was a Renaissance man. *Unknown.* PeHV

There once was a Scot who said: "Evil." H. M. PeLi

There once was a sculptor named Phidias. *Unknown.* PeLi

There Once Was a Spinster of Ealing. *Unknown.* NIP

There once was a time. *Unknown.* NOIV

There once was a union maid. Union Maid. Woody Guthrie. SWP

There once was a vicar of Ryhill. *Unknown.* PeLi

There once was a warden of Wadham. *Unknown.* PeHV

There once was a wicked young minister. Conrad Aiken. OBAL; PeLi

There once was a Willow, and he was very old. The Willow-Man. Juliana Horatia Ewing. OxBChV

There once was a wise politician. A. M. Sayers. PeLi

There once was a witch of Willowby Wood. Rowena Bastin Bennett. *Fr.* Witch of Willowby Wood, The. SiSoPo

There once was a wonderful wizard. Conrad Aiken. FaBoNo

There once was a writer called James. R. K. R. Thornton. PeLi

There once was an artist called Pat. Margaret Galbreath. PeLi

There once was an eccentric of Metz. Leslie Johnson. PeLi

There once was an eccentric old boffin. *Unknown.* PeLi

There once was monarch called Harry. Mary Holtby. PeLi

There once were some people called Sioux. The American Indian. *Unknown.* FaBoCo; FiBHP; NBLV

There once were three brothers from merry Scotland. Sir Andrew Barton. *Unknown.* AmFP

There once were two Babes in the Wood. Roger Woddis. PeLi

There ought to be capital punishment for cars. Thoughts on Capital Punishment. Rod McKuen. InPK

There our murdered brother lies. The Wake of William Orr. William Drennan. PeIV; TIRV

There out of hell the Old One bellows. Lamentations of the Fallen Angels. *Unknown, tr. fr. Anglo-Saxon by* Charles W. Kennedy. *Fr.* Christ and Satan. AnOE

There piped a piper in the wood. The Magic Piper. E. L. Marsh. BoTP

There pipes the wood-lark, and the song thrush there. Thomas Gray. FM

There Rolls the Deep. Tennyson. *Fr.* In Memoriam A. H. H. EBVV, *abr.*; FaBoRV; HAP; NOBE; OAEL-2, *abr.*; PeECV, *abr.*

There sat a happy fisherman. The Reed. M. Y. Lermontov, *tr. fr. Russian by* J. J. Robbins. AWP

There sat an old man on a rock. Too Late. Fitz Hugh Ludlow. PoLF

There sat down, once, a thing on Henry's heart. John Berryman. *Fr.* Dream Songs. CAPP; HAP; HCAP; NoP; PeV; VCAP

There sat two glasses filled to the brim. The Two Glasses. Ella Wheeler Wilcox. BLPA; BLPL

There sate the seniors of the Trojan Race. Homer, *tr. by* Pope. *Fr.* Iliad, The. OBVE

There, sea and sky are at a mortal war. Petronius Arbiter, *tr. fr. Latin by* Helen Waddell. MLL

There set out, slowly, for a different world. A War. Randall Jarrell. ArOW; OxBSP

There shall be no more of you. *(LL)* The Still Voice of Harlem. Conrad Kent Rivers. PoBA

There shall be no more songs. Black Power. Alvin Saxon. PoBA

There Shall Be No Night. Bible, *N.T. Fr.* Revelation. TrGrPo

There she goes! There she goes! *Unknown.* RoPo

There she sits a'-smokin.' Motorcycle Irene. Skip Spence. MAT

There She Stands a Lovely Creature. *Unknown.* AmFP

There should be two words, dearest, one made up. Alone. Carolyn Wells. PoToHe

There Should Have Been. Sydney Lea. SM

There sits a fair couple courting. The Jealous Brothers. *Unknown.* AmFP

There smiled the smooth Divine, unused to wound. The Smooth Divine. Timothy Dwight. *Fr.* Triumph of Infidelity, The. NOCV; WGRP

There smoke, sooty smoke. *Unknown, tr. fr. Serbo-Croatian by* Charles Simic. HSix

There souls of men are bought and sold. London ("There souls of men are bought and sold.") Blake. *Fr.* Human Image, The. ChTr

There, spring lambs jam the sheepfold. In air. Watercolor of Grantchester Meadows. Sylvia Plath. LCAP; NYBP; SM

There squats amid these pyramids. Clay-Land Moods. Jack R. Clemo. PWE

There stand three mills on Manor Water. Manor Water. *Unknown.* GBP

There stands a lady on a mountain. Kiss in the Ring. *Unknown.* OxBoLi

There stands a lonely pine-tree. Heine, *tr. fr. German by* Emma Lazarus. TrJP

There stood a hill not far whose grisly top. Milton. *Fr.* Paradise Lost. EPCY; OAEL-1

There the ash-tree leaves do vall. Leaves a-Vallen. William Barnes. NOBVV

There the black river, boundary to hell. The Southern Road. Dudley Randall. PoBA; SM

There the companions of his fall, o'erwhelmed. Milton. *Fr.* Paradise Lost. EPCY
(Immortal Hate. NOBE)

There the most daintie Paradise on ground. Spenser. *Fr.* Faerie Queene, The. EBEV

There the Parthenon, & there. Slides. Jennifer Maiden. CBAP

There the true Silence is, self-conscious and alone. (*LL*) Silence. Thomas Hood. CH; EBEV; EnRP; NOBE; OBEV; PoEL-4; Son

There then shalt find[e] my faults are thine. (*LL*) Judgement. George Herbert. ESCV; GeHe; SeCP

There, there is no mountain within miles. Nebraska. Jon Swan. RFM

There, there, O there lies Cupid's fire. (*LL*) Beauty, Since You So Much Desire. Thomas Campion. ErPo; OAEL-1

There, there where those black spruces crowd. Ragged Island. Edna St. Vincent Millay. NAAL-2; NoP

There they are. The Blackstone Rangers. Gwendolyn Brooks. NoAM; PoBA

There they are. The Fury of Cocks. Anne Sexton. CAPP

There they are again. It's after dark. The Black Riviera. Mark Jarman. NAmP90

There they are now. Three Sentences for a Dead Swan. James Wright. NaP; NOBA

There they go. Seed Journey. Gregory Corso. VGW

There they go, down to the fatal ship. Cythera. David Ferry. DiPo

There they stand, on their ends, the fifty faggots. Fifty Faggots. Edward Thomas. MoAB; MoBrPo; PeFWW; PoWW

There 'tis the shepherd's task the winter long. Retrospect — Love of Nature Leading to Love of Mankind. Wordsworth. *Fr*. Prelude [or, Growth of a Poet's Mind], The. EnRP; OAEL-2

There to lead my life. (*LL*) I Have Been a Foster. *Unknown*. EBEV; FaBoRV; GBP; OxBSP

There, truly they said in this house. The Hidden People and the Star People. *Unknown, tr. fr. Osage Indian by* Barbara Tedlock. *Fr*. Ceremony of Sending. STP

There .XX. thousande met in fere. Capystranus. *Unknown*. OxBLMV

There used to be a picket fence. The Picket Fence. Christian Morgenstern, *tr. fr. German by* Max Knight. GrPl

There used to be a rich old oaf who made, *mod. vers. by* Theodore Morrison. Chaucer. *See* Whylom [*or* Whilom] Ther was dwellinge at Oxenford [*or* Oxenforde].

There used to be gods in everything, and now they're gone. The Companions. Howard Nemerov. NYBP

There waits the peace thy spirit dwelleth in. (*LL*) Vain Questioning. Walter de la Mare. OtMeF

There walked on Plover's shady banks. Driving Saw-Logs on the Plover. *Unknown*. AS

There wanders many a lighted star. The North Star. John Morris-Jones, *tr. fr. Welsh by* Anthony Conran. OBWVE

There wanders through the world, a knee. The Knee. Christian Morgenstern, *tr. fr. German by* W. D. Snodgrass *and* Lore Segal. CBNP; RB

There wanst was [*or* once were] two cats of [*or* in] Kilkenny. The Kilkenny Cats. *Unknown*. CRH

There was a bad poet named Clough. On Arthur Hugh Clough. Swinburne. FaBoEE

There was a battle fought of late. To His Mother. John Harington. NoSic

There was a battle in the north. Geordie. *Unknown*. ESPB; FaBoBa; OxBB

There was a big bear. Honey Bear. Elizabeth Lang. BoTP

There was a black girl from Pretoria. George Seferis, *tr. fr. Greek by* Hugh Haughton. CBNP

There was a blacksmith in my breast. The Dead Sheep. Andrew Young. FM

There was a boy bedded in bracken. John Short. FaBoCh; FaBoTw

There was a boy in a village who made. Saw the Cloud Lynx. Samuel Makidemewabe, *tr. fr. Cree Indian by* Howard Norman. STP

There was a boy of other days. Lincoln. Nancy Byrd Turner. FaPON

There Was a Boy ("There was a boy, ye knew him well.") Wordsworth. *Fr*. Prelude [or, Growth of a Poet's Mind], The. EnRP; FaBoCh; FaBoRV; FHYEP; MeMBP; OAEL-2; OBNC; PoE; PoEL-4; RB

There was a boy whose name was Jim. Jim, Who Ran Away from His Nurse, and Was Eaten by a Lion. Hilaire Belloc. ChTr; EBNV; OBSP; OxAEP-2; OxBChV
(Jim.) ChTr; FaPoB; NoAM; PeLV

There was a brave girl of Connecticut. Benjamin. Ogden Nash. PeLi

There was a bridge that Rozinante would not cross. The Bridge of Heraclitus. George Reavey. BIrV

There was a bright and happy tree. The Happy Tree. Gerald Gould. WGRP

There was a chap — I forget his name. The Gemlike Flame. R. P. Lister. FiBHP

There was a child. Courage, a Tale. Thom Gunn. GLP

There Was a Child Went Forth. Walt Whitman. *Fr*. Autumn Rivulets. ImPo; NAAL-1; NTP; SAmP

There Was a Child Went Forth. Walt Whitman. AmPP; AWP; InPS; OxBA; SAmP; TAP
Sels.
"There was a child went forth every day." RFM

There was a child went forth every day. There Was a Child Went Forth. Walt Whitman. *Fr*. Autumn Rivulets. ImPo; NAAL-1; NTP; SAmP

There was a child went forth every day. *Fr*. There Was a Child Went Forth. AmPP; AWP; InPS; OxBA; RFM; SAmP; TAP

There was a clever skipper, in Akron he did dwell. The Clever Skipper. *Unknown*. AmFP

There was a collection of schemers. Basil Ransome-Davies. PeLi

There was a company of young folk living, *mod. vers. by* Theodore Morrison. Chaucer. *See* In Flaundres [*or* Flandres] whylom [*or* whilom] was a companye [*or* compaignye].

There was a contest. Peaches. Siv Cedering Fox. PBCAP; PRA

There Was a Crimson Clash of War. Stephen Crane. UnPo

There Was a Crooked Man. Mother Goose. BoTP; CBNP; FaBoBe; OxBoLi; OxNR; PeLV; PYC; SiSoPo

There was a crooked man, and he went [*or* walked] a crooked mile. There Was a Crooked Man. Mother Goose. BoTP; CBNP; FaBoBe; OxBoLi; OxNR; PeLV; PYC; SiSoPo
(Crooked Sixpence, The.) ReMoGo

There was a crusader of Parma. *Unknown*. PeLi

There was a dark and awful wood. Wood. Thomas Hornsby Ferril. PoRA

There was a dining-room, called a drawing room. Mr. Gradgrind's Country. Sylvia Townsend Warner. FaBoEH

There was a duck egg as green as the evening sky. Ulinda. David Campbell. CBAP

There was a duke's daughter lived in York. The Cruel Mother. *Unknown*. ESPB

There was a fair maiden who lived on the shore. The Fair Maid by the Shore. *Unknown*. AmFP

There was a fair young creature who lived by the seaside. The Silvery Tide. *Unknown*. AmFP

There was a faith-healer of Deal. *Unknown*. PeLi
(Mind and Matter.) FaBoCo

There was a farmer's son kept sheep upon a hill. Blow Away the Morning Dew. *Unknown*. OBET

There was a fat lady of Clyde. *Unknown*. PeLi

There was a fat man of Bombay. The Man of Bombay. *Unknown*. ReMoGo

There was a French bard who said: "Hell!" Towanbucket. PeLi

There was a French writer named Sartre. Weldon Kees. Poetr

There was a friend of mine. The Night Whispers. Ken Smith. NBrP

There was a frozen tree that I wanted to paint. Vegas. Charles Bukowski. NoP

There was a gallant lady all in her tender youth. Canada-I-O ("There was a gallant lady all in her tender youth.") *Unknown*. AmFP

There was a gallant ship, and a gallant ship was she. The Golden Vanity. *Unknown*. CH; ELP; FaBoCh; OBET; WiR
(Sweet Trinity The Golden Vanity, The.) ESPB, B *vers*.

There was a giant in times of old. The Dorchester Giant. Oliver Wendell Holmes. FaPON

There was a girl in our town. *Unknown*. OxNR

There was a gloomy lady. Not a Very Cheerful Song, I'm Afraid. Adrian Mitchell. OTCP

There was a good Canon of Durham. William Ralph Inge. PeLi

There was a graveyard once — or cemetery. Evening Hour. Robert Penn Warren. MT

There was a great battle Saturday morning. The Battle of Argoed Llwyfain. Taliesin, *tr. fr. Welsh by* Anthony Conran. OBWVE

There was a great German Grammarian. Thomas Thorneley. PeLi

There was a great Marxist called Lenin. Ted Pauker. PeLi

There was a great swimmer named Jack. On Being Much Better Than Most and Yet Not Quite Good Enough. John Ciardi. GOYP

There was a great white wallbare, bare, bare. The Smoked Herring. Charles Cros, *tr. fr. French by* A. L. Lloyd. GrPl

There was a hag who kept two chambermaids. The Hag and the Slavies. La Fontaine, *tr. fr. French by* Edward Marsh. AWP; OBVE

There was a hardware shop in Main Street sold. Didn't He Ramble. James Simmons. PNI

There was a hole in the ground once; there was a manhole. Saving My Skin from Burning. Gerald Stern. BAP-90

There was a jolly beggar, and a begging he was born. The Jolly Beggar. *At. to* James V, King of Scotland. CoMu; OxBB

There was a jolly fat frog that did in the river swim O. The Frog and the Crow. *Unknown*. GBP

There was a jolly miller once. Isaac Bickerstaffe. *Fr*. Love in a Village. EBEvV; OxNR

There was a jovial beggar. The Jovial Beggar. *Unknown.* BoTP

There was a jury sat at Perth. The Earl of Errol. *Unknown.* ESPB

There was a kind lady called Gregory. James Joyce. FaBoEE; PeLi

There was a kind of drooping bronze head. The Founder. Gerald Stern. NAmP90

There Was a King. *Unknown.* CBNP; NBLV; OxBoLi

There was a king, and a very great king. Lady Diamond. *Unknown.* ESPB

There was a King in Brentford, — of whom no legends tell. The King of Brentford. Thackeray. OtMeF

There was a king met a king. *Unknown.* OxNR

There was a knicht riding frae the east. Riddles Wisely Expounded. *Unknown.* ESPB, 3 *vers.*; FaBoBa; GBP
(Jennifer Gentle and Rosemary.) OxBoLi
(There Was a Knight.) CH; Mes

There Was a Knight. *Unknown.* *See* There was a knicht riding frae the east.

There was a knight, an he had a daughter. Erlinton. *Unknown.* ESPB

There was a knight and a lady bright. The Broomfield Hill. *Unknown.* ESPB; OxBB

There Was a Knight [and He Was Young]. *Unknown.* *See* Yonder comes a courteous Knight.

There was a knight, in a summer's night. The Bonny Birdy. *Unknown.* ESPB

There was a Knight of Bethlehem. Henry Neville Maughan. *Fr.* Husband of Poverty, The. BoTP

There was a lad was born in Kyle. Rantin, Rovin Robin. Burns. OxBS

There was a lady all skin and bone. The Skin-and-Bone Lady. *Unknown.* AmFP

There was a lady fair and gay. The Wife of Usher's Well. *Unknown.* ESPB

There was a lady fine and gay. Willie o [*or* of] Winsbury. *Unknown.* AmFP; ESPB, A *and* D *vers.*

There was a lady in this land. The Tinker. *Unknown.* CoMu

There was a lady lived in a hall. Two Red Roses across the Moon. William Morris. EBVV; UV

There was a lady lived in York. The Cruel Mother. *Unknown.* AmFP; OBET

There Was a Lady Loved a Swine. *Unknown.* GBP; OxNR

There was a lady of beauty rare. The Wife of Usher's Well. *Unknown.* AmFP

There was a lady of the North Country. Riddles Wisely Expounded. *Unknown.* ESPB

There was a Lass of Islington. The Lass of Islington. *Unknown.* CoMu
(Fair Lass of Islington, The.) OxBB

There was a little baby. *Unknown.* RoPo

There was a little Baby once. A Child's Christmas Carol. Christine Chaundler. BoTP

There was a little boy and a little girl. Mother Goose. OxNR
(Boy and Girl.) ReMoGo

There was a little boy went into a barn. *Unknown.* OxNR

There was a little dog, and he had a little tail. *Unknown.* BoTP

There was a little, Elvish man. The Man Who Hid His Own Front Door. Elizabeth MacKinstry. FaPON

There Was a Little Girl. *At.* to Mother Goose, *st.* 1; *sts.* 2 *and* 3, *Unknown, at.* to Longfellow. BLPA, *st.* 1; OxBChV, *st.* 1; OxNR; ReMoGo, *st.* 1

There was a little girl/ Dressed in blue. *Unknown.* RoPo

There was a little guinea-pig. The Guinea-Pig. *Unknown.*
(Guinea-Pig Song, A.) OxBChV

There was a little maid, and she was afraid. *Unknown.* OxNR

There was a little man and he had a little can. No More Booze. *Unknown.* OBAL
(Fireman Save My Child.) AS

There was a little man,/ And he had a little gun. Mother Goose. OxNR; ReMoGo

There was a little man,/ and he wooed a little maid. Mother Goose. OxNR; ReMoGo

There was a little one-eyed gunner. *Unknown.* OxNR

There was a little pig. *Unknown.* RoPo

There was a little rabbit sprig. *Unknown.* BoTP

There was a little rill of water, near the den. The Coyote. Carter Revard. VoR

There was a little ship in South Amerikee. The Sweet Trinity. *Unknown.* AmFP

There was a little turtle. The Little Turtle. Vachel Lindsay. FaPON; GoJo; NTCP; OBAL; OBCA; OBSP; PDV; SiSoPo

There was a little woman, as I've been told. Hot Codlins. *Unknown.* ReMoGo

There was a little woman, as I've heard tell. Mother Goose. *See* There was an old [*or* little woman], as I've heard tell.

There was a lord of worthy fame. The Lady Isabella's Tragedy. *Unknown.* GBP

There Was a Mad Man. *Unknown.* CBNP

There Was a Maid. *Unknown.* *See* There was a maid come out of Kent.

There was a maid come out of Kent. A Maid of Kent. *Unknown.* CBLP; OxBoLi
(There Was a Maid.) ElL

There was a maid, richly arrayd. Blancheflour and Jellyflorice. *Unknown.* ESPB

There Was a Maid Went to the Mill. *Unknown.* GBP

There was a man a-coming from the south. Trooper and Maid. *Unknown.* AmFP

There was a man and he had nought. Mother Goose. OxNR; ReMoGo

There Was a Man and He Was Mad. *Unknown.* GBP; RB

There was a man,/ And his name was Dob. *Unknown.* OxNR

There was a man from Singapore. Some Sound Advice from Singapore. John Ciardi. GrPl

There was a man, he went mad. *Unknown.* OxNR

There was a man here, Samian born, but he. Ovid, *tr.* by Rolfe Humphries. *Fr.* Metamorphoses. NAWM-1

There was a man in Arkansaw. Tuscaloosa Sam. "Orpheus C. Kerr." OBAL

There was a man in olden times. Dives and Lazarus ("There was a man in olden times.") *Unknown.* AmFP

There was a man in our town. Man in Our Town. *Unknown.* ReMoGo

There was a man in the land of Ur. Services. Carl Rakosi. ChIV-1

There was a man lived in the moon. Aiken Drum. *Unknown.* FaBoCh; FaBoNo; OxNR

There was a man made a thing. *Unknown.* GBP

There was a man named Johnny Sands, who married Betty Hague. Johnny Sands ("There was a man named Johnny Sands, who married Betty Hague.") *Unknown.* AmFP

There was a man, now please take note. The Goat. *Unknown.* BLPL; PoLF

There was a man of double deed. *Unknown.* CoGr; GBP; OxNR; RB

There was a man of Thessaly. The Man of Thessaly. *Unknown.* CBNP; FaBoCo; FaBoNo; OxNR

There was a man rode through our town. *Unknown.* OxNR

There Was a Man So Wise. *Unknown.* CBNP

There was a man who always wore. *Unknown.* ISE

There was a man who found two leaves. The Fall. Russell Edson. LCAP

There was a man who had no eyes. *Unknown.* OxNR

There was a man who married a maid. She laughed as he led her home. I Love My Love. Helen Adam. NeAP; NMM; WPOW

There was a man who wanted to be an amateur animal. He could. The Amateur. Russell Edson. LCAP

There was a man who would marry his mother. The Having to Love Something Else. Russell Edson. AnAn

There was a man/ Whose name was Pete. The Tragedy of Pete. Joseph S. Cotter, Sr. CDC

There Was a Man with a Tongue of Wood. Stephen Crane. *Fr.* War Is Kind. LiTA; MeMAP; MoAmPo

There was a man within our tenement. The Spritely Dead. Oscar Williams. *Fr.* Variations on a Theme. LiTA; Son

There was a marriage in Cana of Galilee . . . And both. The Bridegroom of Cana. Marjorie Pickthall. TrCP

There was a monkey climbed a tree. *Unknown.* OxNR

There was a most Monstrous Whale. The Whale. Theodore Roethke. ZA

There Was a Naughty Boy. Keats. *Fr.* Song about Myself, A. BoTP, *sts.* 1 *and* 2; CBNP; FaBoCh; FaBoCo, *st.* 4; FHYEP, *sts.* 1 *and* 4; LiTB; MoShBr; OxBChV, *sts.* 1 *and* 4

There was a pattering in the rafters, mother. Dialogue. James McAuley. FaBoMA

There was a Pig that sat alone. A Pig-Tale. "Lewis Carroll." *Fr.* Sylvie and Bruno Concluded. WiR
(Melancholy Pig, The.) FaPON

There was a piper had a cow. Mother Goose. OxNR
(Piper and His Cow, The.) ReMoGo

There was a place. Place. Robert Creeley. LCAP

There was a poet whose untimely tomb. Shelley. *Fr.* Alastor; or, The Spirit of Solitude. EnRP; FHYEP; OAEL-2; TOF

There was a Presbyterian cat. *Unknown.* FaBoCh
(Auld Seceder Cat, The.) FaBoCo

There was a professor of Beaulieu. Materialism. C. E. M. Joad. FaBoCo; PeLi

There was a queen that fell in love with a jolly sailor. The Sailor and the Shark. Paul Fort, *tr. fr. French by* Frederick York Powell. OBMV

There was a rabbit. *Unknown.* RoPo

There was a Raja, pious-minded, just. Sâvitrî; or, Love and Death. *Unknown, tr. fr. Sanskrit by* Franklin Edgerton. Fr. Mahabharata, The. TAL, *tr. by* Sir Edwin Arnold

There was a rash fellow called Weir. *Unknown.* PeLi

There was a rat, for want of stairs. *Unknown.* OxNR

There was a rich lady, from London she came. A Rich Irish Lady. *Unknown.* AmFP

There was a rich lord, and lived in Forfar. Bonnie Annie. *Unknown.* ESPB

There was a rich man and he lived in Jerusalem. The Rich Man and the Poor Man. *Unknown.* SWP

There was a rich merchant in London did right. The Silk Merchant's Daughter. *Unknown.* OxBSS

There was a river overhung with trees. In a Notebook. James Fenton *and* John Fuller. PIP; SCBI

There was a road ran past our house. The Unexplorer. Edna St. Vincent Millay. MoShBr; PoA

There Was a Roof over Our Heads. Alberto A. Ríos. *Fr.* Lost on Septemter Trail, 1967. AfAz; FYAP; ImGa

There was a row in the pub. After the Massacre. Musaemura Bonus Zimunya. PeSAV

There Was a Saviour. Dylan Thomas. ChIV-2; NAEL-2

There was a shepherd's dochter [*or* daughter]. The Knight and Shepherd's Daughter. *Unknown.* ESPB
(Shepherd's Dochter, The.) OxBB

There was a shepherd's son. Blow the Winds, I-Ho. *Unknown.* GBP; OxBoLi

There was a ship and a ship of fame. Captain Glen's Unhappy Voyage to New Barbary. *Unknown.* OxBSS

There was a ship called The *Golden Vanitie*. The *Golden Vanitie*. *Unknown.* EnSB

There was a ship of Rio. The Ship of Rio. Walter de la Mare. PDV

There was a ship sailed from the North Countree. The *Golden Vanity*. *Unknown.* WiR

There was a sick man of Tobago. *Unknown.* OxBChV; PeLi

There was a sixties hitch. America's Wailing Wall. Naomi Quinonez. AfAz

There was a small boy of Quebec. At. to Kipling Kipling. PeLi

There was a sound of grouse from the field. Solstice. Kathy Fagan. UTF

There was a sound of hunting in the mountains. Incident on a Front Not Far from Castel di Sangro. Harry Brown. NYBP

There Was a Sound of Revelry by Night. Byron. *See* There was a sound of revelry by night.

There was a sound of revelry by night. Byron. *Fr.* Childe Harold's Pilgrimage. EBEV; FaBoEH; OBWP; OxAEP-2
(Eve of Waterloo, The.) EBEvV; OtMeF; BeLS; FaBoBe; FaBoCh; 08FaBoEn; FaBV; 08HBV 1-2; NOBE; OBNC
(Night before the Battle of Waterloo, The.) WBLP
(Night before Waterloo, The.) GN
(There Was a Sound of Revelry by Night.) TFi
(Waterloo.) TrGrPo

There was a stange student from Yale. *Unknown.* PeLi

There was a stunted handpost just on the crest. Near Lanivet, 1872. Thomas Hardy. AWP; CMoP; NoAM

There was a sudden croon of lilies. The Martyrdom of St. Theresa. A. D. Hope. CBAP

There was a sunlit absence. Mossbawn Sunlight. Seamus Heaney. *Fr.* Mossbawn: Two Poems in Dedication. BIrV; CIP; PNI
(Sunlight.) NoP

There was a taut dryness all that summer. A Lyric Afterwards. Tom Paulin. PNI; SCBI

There was a thing a full month old. *Unknown.* OxNR

There was a thorn in your foot. Sword Swallower. Sean Murphy. PeIV

There was a time for discoveries. Voyage West. Archibald MacLeish. VGW

There was a time in former years. She Hears the Storm. Thomas Hardy. NAEL-2

There was a time on this fair continent. Charles Mair. *Fr.* Tecumseh. NOBC

There was a time (such songs begin this way). Inflation. Charles O. Hartman. PoA

There was a time! that time the muse bewails. Verses on Hearing That an Airy and Pleasant Situation, near a Populous and Commercial Town, Was Surrounded with New Buildings. Maria Logan. ECWP

There was a time when death was terror. New Fashions. George Moses Horton. OBAL

There was a time when Eucritus and I were going. Theocritus [*or* Theokritus]. *See* Once on a time did Eucritus and I.

There was a time when fanfares. Decampment. Ernst Stadler, *tr. fr. German by* David McDuff. PeFWW

There was a time, when I could feel. Palinodia. Winthrop Mackworth Praed. CBLP

There was a time when I thought sweeter than the quiet. The Wild Man Comes to the Monastery. *Unknown.* RaBo

There was a time when I was very small. Childhood. Jens Baggesen, *tr. fr. Danish by* Longfellow. AWP

There was a time when meadow, grove and stream. Wordsworth. *Fr.* Ode: Intimations of Immortality from Recollections of Early Childhood. AWP; BLPL; EnRP; FaBoRV; FHYEP; HAP; HeIL; HeIP; ImPo; InvP; LiTB; MeMBP; NAEL-2; NAs; NOBE; NoP; OAEL-2; OBEV; OBNC; PoE; PoEL-4; PPP; PrIm; SCGP; TEP; TFi; TOF; TrGrPo; TRP

There was a time when meadow, grove, and stream. Wordsworth. *Fr.* Ode: Intimations of Immortality from Recollections of Early Childhood. AWP; BLPL; EnRP; FaBoRV; FaPoB; FHYEP; HAP; HeIP; InvP; LiTB; MeMBP; NAs; NOBE; NoP; OAEL-2; OBEV; OBNC; PoE; PoEL-4; PPP; PrIm; TEP; TrGrPo

There was a tinker liv'd of late. The Jovial Tinker; or, The Willing Couple. *Unknown.* CoMu

There was a tree stood in the ground. The Green Grass Growing All Around. *Unknown.* MoShBr

There was a trombonist called Herb. Ron Rubin. PeLi

There was a troop of merry gentlemen. The Broom of Cowdenknows. *Unknown.* ESPB

There was a tumult in the city. Independence Bell — July 4, 1776. *Unknown.* BLPA; FaBoBe

There was a water dump there and regimental. Crucifix Corner. Ivor Gurney. NSI

There was a wealthy merchant/ in London still did dwell. The Wars of Santa Fe. *Unknown.* AmFP

There was a weasel lived in the sun. The Gallows. Edward Thomas. FM; InPS; LiTB; MoAB; MoBrPo; MoP; NoAM; SCGP; UnPo

There was a wee bit mousikie. *Unknown.* MoShBr; SoCa
(Cheetie-Poussie-Cattie, O.) FaBoCh

There was a wee bit wifie. *Unknown.* OxNR

There was a wee lassie of Ulva. David Fisher. PeLi

There was a whispering in my hearth. Miners. Wilfred Owen. MeMBP; MoAB; MoBrPo; NAEL-2; NOBE; NSI; OBWVE; OxAEP-2; PeFWW

There was a wicked woman called Malady Festing. Angel Boley. Stevie Smith. EBNV

There was a widow-woman lived in far Scotland. The Wife of Usher's Well. *Unknown.* ESPB

There was a Wife from Bath, a well-appearing, *mod. vers. by* Louis Untermeyer. Chaucer. *See* Good Wif [*or* Wyf] was ther of biside [*or* bisyde] Bathe, A.

There was a witch. Two Witches. Charles Reznikoff. OTCP

There was a witch who knitted things. Karla Kuskin. *Fr.* Knitted Things. SiSoPo

There was a woman of Ming snow. Bound Feet. Cyrus Cassells. UTF

There was a wood, a witches' wood. The Witches' Wood. Mary Elizabeth Coleridge. PBWP

There Was a Wyly Ladde. *Unknown.* ErPo

There was a young artist called Saint. *Unknown.* PeLi

There was a young belle of old Natchez. Ogden Nash. NoP

There was a young boy, Jack Horner. Fiona Pitt-Kethley. PeLi

There was a young boy [*or* man] of Quebec. At. to Kipling Kipling. FaBoCo
(Boy of Quebec, The.) FaBoNo

There was a young bride named McWing. *Unknown.* PeLi

There was a young critic of King's. Arthur Clement Hilton. PeLi

There was a young curate called Lloyd. At. to Duncan Campbell McGregor. PeLi

There was a young curate of Hants. E. V. Knox. PeLi

There was a young curate of Kew. *Unknown.* PeLi

There was a young curate of Salisbury. *Unknown.* FaBoCo; PeLi

There was a young doctor, from London he came. The Fair Damsel from London. *Unknown.* AmFP

There was a young faggot called Willy. Kenneth Petchenik. PeLi

There was a young farmer of Leeds. A Young Farmer of Leeds. *Unknown.* SiSoPo

There was a young fellow called Baker. *Unknown.* PeLi

There was a young fellow called Bliss. *Unknown.* PeLi

There was a young fellow called Cager. *Unknown.* PeLi

There was a young fellow called Chubb. *Unknown.* PeLi

There was a young fellow called Clyde. *Unknown.* PeLi
There was a young fellow called Crouch. Victor Gray. NOBL; PeLi
There was a young fellow called Hall. *Unknown.* PeLi
There was a young fellow called Lancelot. *Unknown.* PeLi
There was a young fellow called Price. *Unknown.* PeLi
There was a young fellow called Shit. Victor Gray. PeLi
There was a young fellow called Wyatt. *Unknown.* PeLi
There was a young fellow from Tyne. *Unknown.* PeLi
There was a young fellow named Fisher. *Unknown.* PeLi
There was a young fellow named Fonda. Ogden Nash. PeLi
There was a young fellow named Menzies. *Unknown.* PeLi
There was a young fellow named Nutz. *Unknown.* PeHV
There was a young fellow named Skinner. Norman Douglas. PeLi
There was a young fellow named Sydney. Don Marquis. PeLi
There was a young Fellow of Burma. Aldous Huxley. PeLi
There was a young fellow of Caius. *Unknown.* NOBL
There was a young fellow of Ceuta. *Unknown.* NOBL
There was a young Fellow of King's. *Unknown.* NOBL
  (Young Fellow of King's, The.) FaBoBl
There was a young fellow of Lyme. *Unknown.* PeLi
There was a young fellow of Perth. *Unknown.* PeLi
There was a young fellow of Trinity. *Unknown.* PeLi
There was a young Fellow of Wadham. *Unknown.* NOBL
  (Young Fellow of Wadham, The.) FaBoBl
There was a young Fellow of Wadham/ Who asked for a ticket to Sodom. *Unknown.* PeLi
There was a young fellow went by. Trinity Brethren Attend. I. A. Richards. CRP
There was a young fir-tree of Bosnia. The Fir-Tree of Bosnia. Dante Gabriel Rossetti. FaBoNo
There was a young genius of Queens. Arthur Clement Hilton. PeLi
There was a young girl called Bianca. *Unknown.* PeLi
There was a young girl from a Mission. A. H. Baynes. PeLi
There was a young girl from Uttoxeter/ Who kept hens, but refused to have cocks. It a. Alastair Chambre. PeLi
There was a young girl from Uttoxeter/ Who made passing oarsmen gape through locks at her. L. W. Bailey. PeLi
There was a young girl from Uttoxeter/ Who one dreary night had a fox at her. George Cowley. PeLi
There was a young girl from Uttoxeter/ Who out on a date with two Jocks at a. Bob Scott. PeLi
There was a young girl from Uttoxeter/ Who sported a tight-fitting baroque sweater. Stanley J. Sharpless. PeLi
There was a young girl of Aberystwyth. Swinburne. PeLi
There was a young girl of Australia. *Unknown.* PeLi
There was a young girl of Bahari. R. P. M. Lehmann. PeLi
There was a young girl of Cape Cod. *Unknown.* PeLi
There was a young girl of Darjeeling. *Unknown.* PeLi
There was a young girl of East Anglia. Aldous Huxley. PeLi
There was a young girl of La Plata. *Unknown.* PeLi
There was a Young Girl of Majorca. Edward Lear. PeLi
There was a young girl of Mauritius. Victor Gray. PeLi
There was a young girl of old Natchez. Ogden Nash. PeLi
There was a young girl of Penzance. *Unknown.* PeLi
There was a young girl of St. Cyr. *Unknown.* PeLi
There was a young girl of Shanghai. Bertrand Russell. PeLi
There was a young girl of Siam. *Unknown.* PeLi
There was a Young Girl of Siberia. T. S. Eliot. FaBoBl
There was a young girl of Tralee. *Unknown.* PeLi
There was a young girl of Trebarwith. R. J. P. Hewison. PeLi
There was a young girl of Uttoxeter/ Who noticed that men waved their cocks at her. D. Kartun. PeLi
There was a young girl of Uttoxeter/ Who worked nine to five as a choc-setter. Stanley J. Sharpless. PeLi
There was a young girl whose frigidity. *Unknown.* PeLi
There was a young girl with a hernia. Mopev. PeLi
There was a young gourmand of John's. Arthur Clement Hilton. PeLi
There was a young Jap on a syndicate. *Unknown.* PeLi
There was a young Japanese geisha. Ron Rubin. PeLi
There was a young lady . . . tut, tut! Stanley J. Sharpless. PeLi
There was a young lady at court. D. H. Cudmore. PeLi
There was a young lady called Alice. *Unknown.* PeLi
There was a young lady called Clarice. H. A. C. Evans. PeLi
There was a young lady called Dawes. *Unknown.* PeLi
There was a young lady called Etta. *Unknown.* PeLi
There was a young lady called Flynn. *Unknown.* PeLi

There was a young lady called Gloria. *Unknown.* PeLi
There was a young lady called Harris. Ogden Nash. PeLi
There was a young lady called Hilda. *Unknown.* PeLi
There was a young lady called Kate. *Unknown.* PeLi
There was a young lady called Maud. *Unknown.* PeLi
There was a young lady called Muffet. *Unknown.* PeLi
There was a young lady called Smith. *Unknown.* PeLi
There was a young lady called Starky. *Unknown.* PeLi
There was a young lady from Glitch. A Young Lady From Glitch. Tamara Kitt. SiSoPo
There was a young lady from Pecking. *Unknown.* PeLi
There was a young lady from Ulva. Russell Lucas. PeLi
There was a Young Lady in White. Limerick. Edward Lear. PeLi
There was a young lady named Kent. *Unknown.* PeLi
There was a young lady named Miller. Austen Baker. PeLi
There was a young lady named [*or* called] Bright. *At.* to Arthur Buller. NOBL; OxBoLi; PeLi; PeLV
  (Relativity.) FaBoCo
  (Young Lady Named Bright, A.) FaPON
There was a young lady of Aenos. *Unknown.* PeLi
There was a young lady of Brabant. *Unknown.* PeLi
There was a young lady of Chichester. *Unknown.* PeLi
There was a young lady of Chiswick. *Unknown.* PeLi
There was a young lady of Corsica. Edward Lear. ChTr; FaBoNo
There was a young lady of Ealing. Allan M. Laing. PeLi
There was a young lady of Ealing. *Unknown.* PeLi
There was a young lady of Ealing/ And her lover before her was kneeling. Isaac Asimov. PeLi
There was a young lady of Exeter. The Young Lady of Exeter. *Unknown.* FaBoBl
There was a young lady of fashion. *Unknown.* PeLi
There was a young lady of Florence. *Unknown.* PeLi
There was a young lady of Graz. George Seferis, *tr. fr. Greek by* Peter Levi. CBNP
There was a young lady of Hull. Edward Lear. MoShBr
There was a young lady of Joppa. *Unknown.* PeLi
There was a young lady of Kew. *Unknown.* PeLV
There was a young lady of Leicester. Alan Clark. PeLi
There was a young lady of Limerick. Andrew Lang. PeLi
There was a young lady of Louth. Norman Douglas. PeLi
There was a Young Lady of Lucca. *Unknown.* CBNP
There was a young lady of Lundy. W. F. N. Watson. PeLi
There was a young lady of Nantes. S. Littman. PeLi
There Was a Young Lady of Niger. *At.* to Cosmo Monkhouse. FaPON; InvP; NBLV; PDV; TLR
There was a young lady of Nîmes. Little Billee. PeLi
There Was a Young Lady of Norway. Edward Lear. *See* There was a Young Lady of Norway,/ Who casually sat in a doorway.
There was a young lady of Norway,/ Who casually sat in a doorway. Edward Lear. PeLi
  (There Was a Young Lady of Norway.) EBEV
  (Young Lady of Norway, A.) FaPON
There was a young lady of Norway/ Who hung by her toes in a doorway. Swinburne. PeLi
There was a young lady of Portugal. Edward Lear. OxBoLi; PeLi; PeLV
There was a young lady of Rheims. Moonshine. Walter de la Mare. FiBHP
There was a young lady of Riga. Cosmo Monkhouse. FaBoCo; PeLi
There was a young lady of Russia. Edward Lear. MoShBr
There was a young lady of Ryde,/ Who ate some green apples and died. *Unknown.* PeLi
There was a young lady of Ryde/ Who was carried too far by the tide. *Unknown.* PeLi
There was a young lady of Ryde/ Whose shoe-strings were seldom untied. Edward Lear. OxBoLi; PeLi; PeLV
There was a young lady of Rye. *Unknown.* PeLi
There was a young lady of Slough. *Unknown.* PeLi
There was a young lady of Spain. *Unknown.* FaBoCo; PeLi
There Was a Young Lady of Station. "Lewis Carroll." FaBoNo; PeLi
There was a young lady of Sweden. Edward Lear. CBNP; EBEV; PeVV
There was a young lady of Tottenham. *Unknown.* PeLi; WeW
There was a young lady of Trent. *Unknown.* PeLi
There was a young lady of Ulva/ Who drunkenly said: "What a hulva." Bill Greenwell. PeLi
There was a young lady of Ulva/ Who kept a pet bee in her hand-bag. T. Johnston. PeLi

There was a young lady of Ulva/ Who said: "I have granted a culver." T. Griffiths. PeLi

There was a young lady of Ulva/ Who was famed far and wide for her vulva. Gavin Ewart. PeLi

There was a young lady of Ulva/ Whose boy-friend said: "Look, I will pulver." Stanley J. Sharpless. PeLi

There was a young lady of Ulva/ Whose sexual feelings were null. Va. Barbara E. Goff. PeLi

There was a young lady of Wantage. *Unknown.* PeLi

There was a young lady of Where? *Unknown.* PeLi

There was a young lady of Whitby. "Lewis Carroll." PeLi

There was a young lady whose bonnet. Edward Lear. EBEV

There was a Young Lady whose chin. Edward Lear. PeLi

There was a young lady whose eyes. Edward Lear. EBEV; NOBVV

There Was a Young Lady Whose Nose. Edward Lear. EBEV; FaPON

There was a young lass of Pitlochry. *Unknown.* PeLi

There was a young lawyer called Rex. *Unknown.* PeLi

There was a young maid of Peru. Isaac Asimov. PeLi

There was a young maid who said, "Why." *Unknown.* SoSe

There was a young maiden from Multerry. *Unknown.* PeLi

There was a young maiden of Devon. *Unknown.* PeLi

There was a young man from Darjeeling. *Unknown.* PeLi

There was a young man in Iowa. Limerick. Edward Lear. PFP

There was a young man named Racine. *Unknown.* PeLi

There was a young man of Australia. *Unknown.* PeLi

There was a young man of Belgrade. Isaac Asimov. PeLi

There was a young man of Bengal. *Unknown.* OxBoLi

There was a young man of Calcutta. *Unknown.* PeLi

There was a young man of Cape Horn. Swinburne. PeLi

There was a young man of Cape Race. *Unknown.* PeLi

There was a young man of Devizes. *At.* to Archibald Marshall. PeLi

There was a young man of Dumfries. *Unknown.* PeLi

There was a young man of Ghent. *Unknown.* PeLi

There was a young man of Japan. *Unknown.* FaBoCo; PeLi

There was a young man of Madras. *Unknown.* PeLi

There was a young man of Mauritius. Theological Limerick. T. Lindsay. FaBoCo

There was a young man of Montrose. Arnold Bennett. FaBoNo; OxBoLi; PeLi

There was a young man of Nepal. *Unknown.* PeLi

There was a young man of Newcastle. Terence Melican. PeLi

There was a young man of Ostend. E. O. Parrott. PeLi

There was a young man of Porthcawl. A. G. Prys-Jones. PeLi

There was a young man of St. Bees. *Unknown.* FaBoCo

There was a young man of St John's. *Unknown.* PeLV

There was a young man of Wood's Hole. *Unknown.* PeLi

There was a young man so benighted. Frances Parkinson Keyes. PeLi

There was a young man who said: "Ayer." *Unknown.* PeLi

There was a young monarch called Ed. *Unknown.* PeLi

There was a young monk from Siberia. *Unknown.* PeLi

There was a young outlaw named Hood. E. O. Parrott. PeLi

There was a young peasant named Gorse. *Unknown.* PeLi

There was a young person called Tate. Carolyn Wells. PeLi

There was a Young Person of Crete. Edward Lear. FaBoNo

There was a Young Person of Kew. Edward Lear. CBNP

There was a young person of Leigh. Basil Ransome-Davies. PeLi

There was a young person of Smyrna. Edward Lear. OxBoLi; PeLV; TEP

There was a young plumber of Leigh. *Unknown.* PeLi

There was a young poet of Kew. *Unknown.* PeLi

There was a young poet of Thusis. *Unknown.* OxBoLi; PeLi

There was a young priest of Dun Laoghaire. *Unknown.* PeLi

There was a young princess, Snow-White. Gerard Benson. PeLi

There was a young student called Fred. V. R. Ormerod. PeLi

There was a young student called Jones. *Unknown.* PeLi

There was a young student of John's. *Unknown.* PeLi

There was a young woman, as I've heard tell. Ripperty! Kye! Ahoo! Henry Lawson. CBAP

There was a young woman called Myrtle. *Unknown.* PeLi

There was a young woman called Starkie [*or* Starky]. Mendelian Theory. *Unknown.* FaBoCo; NOBL

There was a young woman from Aenos. The Young Woman from Aenos. *Unknown.* OBAL

There was a young woman named Plunnery. Edward Gorey. OBAL

There was a young woman of Dee. *Unknown.* PeLi

There was a young woman who said. Frances Cornford. PeLi

There was a youth[e], and a well belovd [*or* well-belovéd] youth[e]. The Bailiff's Daughter of Islington. *Unknown.* ESPB; FaBoBa; GN; OBET; OxBB; OxBoLi

There was airy music and sport at the fair. The Fair at Windgap. Austin Clarke. OxBTC

There [*or* Ther] was also a nun [*or* Nonne], a Prioress[e]. The Prioress. Chaucer. *Fr.* Canterbury Tales, The. CTC, *abr.*; EnVB; FHYEP; NoP; OAEL-1; PPP, *abr.*

(Madam Eglantine.) NOBE

(There also was a nun, a Prioress, *mod. vers. by* Louis Untermeyer.) TrGrPo

There was always the river or the train. Grandmother Watching at Her Window. W. S. Merwin. PrIm; VGW

There was an a May and she lo'ed na men. Were Ne My Hearts Light I Wad Dye. Lady Grisel Baillie. KTR

There was an ancient Grecian boy. A Tiger Tale. John Bennett. OBCA

There was an ancient sage philosopher. Arms and the Man. Samuel Butler. *Fr.* Hudibras. NOSC

There was an ancient spring inside the glacier. Found. Carol Muske. AmPA

There was an archbishop named Tait. Archbishop Tait. *Unknown.* ChTr; FaBoNo

There was an archdeacon who said. *Unknown.* OxBoLi

There was an Auchtergaven mouse. A Whigmaleerie. William Soutar. OxBS

There was an earthquake. The Earthquake. *Unknown, tr. fr. Zuni Indian by* K. Kennedy. WTO

There was an end to hearts and rhymes. John Hollander. EOEF

There Was An Indian. J. C. Squire. *See* There was an Indian, who had known no change.

There was an Indian, who had known no change. J. C. Squire. CH; FaPON

(There Was An Indian.) AmFN

There was an old bear that lived near a wood. The Bear and the Squirrels. Christopher Pearse Cranch. OBCA

There was an old Begum of Frome. Walter de la Mare. PeLi

There was an old Bey of Calcutta. *Unknown.* PeLi

There was an old chap who said: "Well." W. Stewart. PeLi

There was an old crow. *Unknown.* OxNR

There was an old cynic who said. Allan M. Laing. PeLi

There was an old dame from Jerusalem. George Seferis, *tr. fr. Greek by* Hugh Haughton. CBNP

There was an old dame of Toulouse. A. M. Sayers. PeLi

There was an old decan-/ ter. Song of the Decanter. Alfred Gibbs Campbell. AAP

There was an old Doctor called Coué. Bob Scott. PeLi

There was an old drunk called Hieronymus. Ron Rubin. PeLi

There was an old drunkard of Devon. Ron Rubin. PeLi

There was an old farmer in Sussex did dwell. The Farmer's Curst Wife. *Unknown.* ESPB

There was an old farmer of Readall. Melodies. "Lewis Carroll." CBNP

There was an old fellow called Hugger. Arnold Hyde. PeLi

There was an old fellow named Hewing. *Unknown.* PeLi

There was an old fellow of Fife. *Unknown.* PeLi

There was an old fellow of Trinity. *At.* to Arthur Clement Hilton. PeLi

There was an old Fox. The Owl and the Fox. *Unknown.* BLPA

There was an old gossip called Baird. Ogden Nash. PeLi

There was an old grocer of Goring. Green. Walter de la Mare. FaBoNo

There was an old housewife of Staines. E. O. Parrott. PeLi

There was an old lady of Chertsey. Edward Lear. OxBChV

There was an old lady of Harrow. An Old Lady of Harrow. *Unknown.* PeLi

There was an old lady of Leicester. Ian T. MacKenzie. PeLi

There was an Old Lady whose folly. Edward Lear. OHCV

There was an old madam called Rainey. *Unknown.* PeLi

There was an old maid of Duluth. *Unknown.* PeLi

There was an old-man and a jolly old-man. The Old Man and Young Wife. *Unknown.* CoMu

There was an old man,/ And he had a calf. *Unknown.* OxNR

There was an old man and he lived [out] in a wood. Broom, Green Broom. *Unknown.* LiTB; OxBoLi; PoRA

(Green Broom.) CH, *diff. vers.*

There was an old man at the bank today. Fourth Street, San Rafael. Bill Berkson. UL

There was an old man at the foot of the hill. The Farmer's Curst Wife. *Unknown.* AmFP

There was an old man called Dupree. R. I. PeLi

There was an old man from Darjeeling. Old Man from Darjeeling. *Unknown.* NTCP

There was an old man in a Barge. Edward Lear. EBEV

There was an old man in a boat. Edward Lear. CBNP; EBEV; FaBoNo (Floating Old Man, The.) WiR

There was an old man in a pew. Edward Lear. MoShBr

There Was an Old Man in a Tree. Edward Lear. *See* There was an old man in a tree.

There was an old man in a tree. Edward Lear. CBNP; FaBoNo; MoShBr; OxBChV; PeLi; Poetr; TEP (There Was an Old Man in a Tree.) InvP; NoP

There was an old man in a trunk. Ogden Nash. PeLi (Ultimate Reality.) FaBoCo

There was an old man in a velvet coat. Mother Goose. OxNR; ReMoGo

There was an old man in the North Countrie. The Two Sisters. *Unknown.* PrIm

There Was an Old Man Named Michael Finnigin. *Unknown.* CBNP

There was an old man of Bengal. "F. Anstey." PeLi

There was an old man of Blackheath. *Unknown.* PDV

There Was an Old Man of Boulogne. *Unknown. See* There was an old man of Boulogne.

There was an old man of Boulogne. *Unknown.* FaBoCo; PeLi; PeLV; OxBoLi

There was an old man of Calcutta. Arthur. Ogden Nash. FiBHP; NoP; PeLi

There was an old man of Cape Horn. Edward Lear. CBNP; EBEV; PeLi

There was an old man of Cape Race. *Unknown.* FaBoCo

There Was an Old Man of Dumbree. Edward Lear. OxBChV

There was an old man of Dunblane. Edward Lear. EBEV

There was an old man of Dundee. Edward Lear. FaBoNo

There was an old man of Dundee. *Unknown.* PeLi

There was an old man of El Hums. Edward Lear. FaBoNo

There was an old man of Girgenti. Edward Lear. FaBoNo

There was an old man of Hong Kong. Edward Lear. FaBoCo

There was an old man of Ibreem. Edward Lear. EBEV

There was an old man of Kamschatka. Edward Lear. NOBL

There Was an Old Man of Khartoum. *At. to* William Ralph Inge. NOBL; OxBoLi; PeLi

There was an old man of Lugano. Victor Gray. PeLi

There was an old man of Madras. Edward Lear. FaBoNo

There was an Old Man of Nantucket. The Old Man of Nantucket. *Unknown.* PeLi

There was an old man of [*or* from] Peru/ Who dreamt [*or* dreamed] he was eating his shoe. *Unknown.* PDV; SiSoPo; SoSe (Old Man from Peru, An.) NTCP

There was an old man of Peru/ Who never knew what he should do. Edward Lear. EBEV

There was an old man of Peru/ Who watched his wife making a stew. Edward Lear. EBEV

There was an old man of St. Bees. W. S. Gilbert. InvP; PeLi; PeLV

There was an old man of Spithead. Edward Lear. FaBoNo

There was an old man of the Cape. Robert Louis Stevenson. PeLi

There was an old man of the coast. Edward Lear. MoShBr; OHCV; PeLi

There was an old man of the Dargle. Edward Lear. ChTr

There was an old man of the Dee. Edward Lear. FaBoNo

There was an old man of the East. Edward Lear. EBEV

There was an old man of the West. Edward Lear. EBEV

There was an old man of Thermopylae. Edward Lear. EBEV; FaBoNo; NOBL; OxAEP-2; PeLi

There was an old man of Three Bridges. Edward Lear. FaBoNo

There was an old man of Tobago. *Unknown.* CBNP; ReMoGo

There was an old man of Vesuvius. Edward Lear. FaBoNo

There was an old man of West Dumpet. Edward Lear. EBEV

There was an old man of Whitehaven. Edward Lear. CBNP; EBEV; OxAEP-2

There was an old man on some rocks. Edward Lear. NOBVV; PeLi

There was an old man on the Border. Edward Lear. EBEV

There was an Old Man on whose nose. Edward Lear. PeLi

There was an old man said, "I fear." The Shubble. Walter de la Mare. FaBoNo

There was an old man who averred. *Unknown.* PeLi

There was an old man who had a kite for a son. An Old Man's Son. Russell Edson. LCAP

There was an old man who lived [*or* liv'd] in Middle Row. The Five Hens. *Unknown.* GBP; OxNR

There was an old man who [*or* that] lived in the [*or* a] wood [*or* woods]. Father Grumble. *Unknown.* AmFP (Old Man Who Lived in a Wood, The.) MoShBr

There was an old man who made his will. The Dishonest Miller. *Unknown.* AmFP

There Was an Old Man Who Said, "Do." *Unknown.* FaPON

There was an old man who said: "How." Edward Lear. OxBChV; PeLi (Old Man and the Cow.) SiSoPo

There was an old man who said, "Hush!" Edward Lear. FaBoCo; GoJo; NOBL; OxBChV; PeLi; PeLV; TEP

There was an Old Man who said: "Well!" Edward Lear. PeLi

There was an old man who screamed out. Edward Lear. CBNP; EBEV; NOBVV; OxAEP-2

There was an Old Man Who Supposed. Edward Lear. NAEL-2; NOBVV; PeLi; Poetr

There was an old man whose despair. Edward Lear. CBNP; FaBoNo

There was an Old Man whose giardino. Edward Lear. OHCV

There was an old man with a beard. John Clarke. UV

There Was an Old Man with a Beard. Edward Lear. CBNP; ChTr; FaBoCo; FaBoNo; NOBL; OHCV; OxBChV; PDV; PeLi; PeLV; PFP; Poetr; PYC; TEP; TLR

There was an Old Man with a Beard/ Who said: "I demand to be feared." Roger Woddis. PeLi

There was an old man with a gong. Edward Lear. GoJo

There was an old man with a gun. Miss Pheasant. Walter de la Mare. FaBoNo

There was an old man with a ribbon. Edward Lear. FaBoNo

There was an old Member called Bevan. Barbara Leigh. PeLi

There was an old mickey called Cassidy. Conrad Aiken. PeLi

There was an old miser at [*or* of] Reading. *Unknown.* OxBChV; PeLi

There was an old Monk of great renown. The Monk of Great Renown. *Unknown.* CoMu

There was an old owl. The Owl and the Crow. Ben King. AnAmPo

There was an old party called Pennycomequick. Mr. Pennycomequick. Phyllis M. Stone. BoTP

There was an old party of lyme. *At. to* Edward Lear. FaBoCo; FF; OxBoLi

There was an old person of Anerley. Edward Lear. FaBoCo

There was an old person of Bar. Edward Lear. FaBoNo

There was an old person of Basing. Edward Lear. CBNP; EBEV; OxAEP-2; PeLi

There was an old person of Blythe. Edward Lear. EBEV

There was an old person of Bow. Edward Lear. CBNP; EBEV; OxAEP-2

There was an Old Person of Bree. *Unknown.* CBNP

There was an Old Person of Brigg. Edward Lear. CBNP

There was an old person of Brussels. Edward Lear. FaBoNo

There was an old person of Burton. Edward Lear. EBEV

There was an Old Person of Cadiz. *Unknown.* CBNP

There was an old person of Cassel. Edward Lear. EBEV

There was an Old Person of Cromer. Edward Lear. PeLi

There was an old person of Crowle. Edward Lear. FaBoNo

There was an old person of Dean. Edward Lear. MoShBr

There was an old person of Diss. Edward Lear. GoJo

There was an old person of Dover. Edward Lear. FaBoNo

There was an old person of Dutton. Edward Lear. EBEV

There was an Old Person of Ems. *Unknown.* CBNP

There was an old person of Fratton. *Unknown.* PeLi

There was an old person of Grange. Edward Lear. CBNP; FaBoNo

There was an old person of Gretna. Edward Lear. ChTr; OxBChV

There was an old person of Harrow. Edward Lear. FaBoNo

There was an old person of Hove. Edward Lear. FaBoNo

There was an Old Person of Hurst. Edward Lear. PeLi

There was an old person of Persia. William Plomer. PeLi

There was an old person of Philae. Edward Lear. CBNP; FaBoNo

There was an old person of Prague. Edward Lear. EBEV

There was an old person of Rhodes. Edward Lear. EBEV

There was an old person of Skye. Edward Lear. ChTr

There was an old person of Slough. George Robey. PeLi

There was an Old Person of Slough. *Unknown.* CBNP

There was an old person of Twickenham. Edward Lear. FaBoNo

There was an old person of Wick. Edward Lear. FaBoNo

There was an old person whose habits. Edward Lear. FaBoNo

There was an old pros. Zelda Chevette. PeLi

There was an old sage of New Delhi. Joyce Parr. PeLi

There was an old Scot called McTavish. *Unknown.* PeLi

There was an old skinflint of Hitching. Buttons. Walter de la Mare. FaBoNo; PeLi

There Was an Old Soldier. *Unknown.* AS

There was an old soldier of Bicester. *Unknown.* FaBoNo; OxBChV

There was an old vicar of Sinder. J. J. Walter de la Mare. FaBoNo

There was an old Welshman called Morgan. Ron Rubin. PeLi

There was an old wife and she lived all alone. The Old Wife and the Ghost. James Reeves. OTCP; PDV; SiSoPo

There Was an Old Woman. *Unknown.* CBNP; ReMoGo

There was an old woman/ And nothing she had. *Unknown.* OxNR

There was an old woman and she lived in a shoe. Mother Goose. *See* There Was An Old Woman Who Lived in a Shoe.

There was an old woman, and what do you think? Mother Goose. FaBoCh (Strange Old Woman, A. ReMoGo

There was an old [or little woman], as I've heard tell. Mother Goose. MoShBr
(Old Woman and the Pedlar, The.) ReMoGo
(There was a little woman, as I've heard tell.) InvP; OxNR

There was an old woman as ugly as sin. An Old Woman. Charles Henry Ross. OxBChV

There was an old woman called Nothing-at-all. Mother Goose. OxNR

There was an old woman had three cows. *Unknown.* OxNR

There was an old woman had three sons. The Three Sons. *Unknown.* ReMoGo

There was an old woman, her name was Peg. *Unknown.* OxNR

There was an old woman in Surrey. Mother Goose. OxBChV
(Old Woman of Surrey.) ReMoGo

There was an old woman/ Lived down in a dell. Was She a Witch? Laura E. Richards. PDV

There was an old woman lived on the seashore. The Two Sisters. *Unknown.* AmFP
(Cruel Sister, The.) OxBB

There was an old woman/ Lived under a hill/ And if she's not gone. *Unknown.* OxNR

There was an old woman/ Lived under a hill/ She put a mouse in a bag. Mother Goose. OxNR

There was an old woman lived under the hill. The Trooper's Horse. *Unknown.* OBET

There Was an Old Woman Named Piper. William Jay Smith. TLR

There was an old woman named Towl. Mistress Towl. *Unknown.* FaBoNo; OxBChV

There was an Old Woman of Gloster. *Unknown.* PeLi

There was an old woman of Gloucester. The Old Woman of Gloucester. *Unknown.* ReMoGo

There was an old woman of Harrow. Old Woman of Harrow. *Unknown.* FaBoNo; ReMoGo

There was an old woman of Leeds. The Old Woman of Leeds. *Unknown.* ReMoGo

There was an Old Woman of Lynn. *Unknown.* PeLi

There was an old woman of Wales. George Seferis, *tr. fr. Greek by* Peter Levi. CBNP

There was an old woman sat spinning. Mother Goose. OxNR
(That's All.) ReMoGo

There was an old woman/ Sold puddings and pies. *Unknown.* OxNR

There was an old woman tossed up in a basket [or blanket]. Mother Goose. OxNR; PDV

There was an old woman tossed [up] in a basket. Old woman, old woman. Mother Goose. ReMoGo

There was an old woman/ Went blackberry picking. Berries. Walter de la Mare. MoBrPo

There Was An Old Woman Who Lived in a Shoe. Mother Goose. FaBoBe; ImGa; OxNR; ReMoGo

There was an old woman/ Who lived in Dundee. *Unknown.* OxNR

There was an old woman who never was wed. Ballad of an Old Woman. Frank A. Collymore. NTP; PBCV

There was an Orchestra. F. Scott Fitzgerald. *See* There'd be an orchestra.

There was an orchestra — Bingo-Bango. F. Scott Fitzgerald. *See* There'd be an orchestra.

There was an owd yowe wi' only one horn. The One-horned Ewe. *Unknown.* GBP

There was an owl lived in an oak. *Unknown.* OxNR

There was an owl lived in an oak,*sl. diff. vers..* *Unknown.* See In an oak there liv'd an owl.

There was an unwanted child. End, Middle, Beginning. Anne Sexton. PoE

There was Dai Puw. He was no good. On the Farm. R. S. Thomas. OxBTC; PWE

There was distant thunder that was its. Town Gone to Sleep. Anne Carson. *Fr.* Life of Towns, The. BAP-90

There was earth inside them, and. Paul Celan, *tr. fr. German by* Michael Hamburger. PoSu

There was fire & the people were yelling. running crazy. Urban Dream. Victor Hernandez Cruz. NBV

There was great beauty by the Tree. Eve. Arthur J. Bull. UnPo

There was in Asia, in a great city. The Prioress's Tale. Chaucer. *Fr.* Canterbury Tales, The. EnVB
(O lord, oure lord, thy name how merveilous.) EnVB

There was in danger desperate delight. The Aging Poet, on a Reading Trip to Dayton, Visits the Air Force Museum and Discovers There a Plane He Once Flew. Richard Snyder. Poetsp

There was just no time. A Fire Story. Joseph Bruchac. ETG

There was little important. An American Boyhood. Jonathan Holden. Poetsp

There was little more that summer. Harlem. Maureen Seaton. LoHo

There was monie a braw noble. Glenlogie. *Unknown.* GN

There was movement at the station, for the word had passed around. The Man from Snowy River. Andrew Barton Paterson. CBAP

There was music in the air. Music in the Air. Ronald McCuaig. ErPo

There was never a leaf on bush or tree. A Winter Morning. James Russell Lowell. *Fr.* Vision of Sir Launfal, The. GN

There was never a sound beside the wood but one. Mowing. Robert Frost. AnAmPo; BLPL; CMoP; HoPM; LiTA; NAAL-2; NOBA; OxBA; PPP; TRP; VGW

There was never file laid so well filed. Sir Thomas Wyatt. SiPSBD

There was never nothing more me pained [or payned]. Sir Thomas Wyatt. AAS; GBL; SiPS; SiPSBD

There was no beauty on thy brow. Madame de Staël. Emma Catherine Embury. AmWP

There was no change in the summer wind. In the Flowering Season. Michael Roberts. FaBoTw

There was no hole in the universe to fit him. Suicide. Anne Stevenson. FaBoWP

There was no malady. (*LL*) Sorrow. Emily Dickinson. WGRP

There was no one like 'im, 'Orse or Foot. Follow Me 'ome. Kipling. CoGr

There was no road at all to that high place. The Grove. Edwin Muir. LiTM

There was no song nor shout of joy. The Ship. J. C. Squire. CH

There was no union in the land. Gettysburg. James Jeffrey Roche. PAH

There was not a man amongst them. (*LL*) The Emperor Asks Why My Husband Surrendered. Lady Hua Jui. WPC

There was not one who did not think of home. (*LL*) Conquerors. Henry Treece. GOYP; OBWVE

There was once a boat on a billow. Longing for Home. Jean Ingelow. *Fr.* Songs of Seven. WGRP

There was once a considerate crocodile. The Considerate Crocodile. Amos R. Wells. OBCA

There was once a Filipino hombre. A Filipino Hombre. *Unknown.* AS

There was once a hog theater where hogs performed. A Performance at Hog Theater. Russell Edson. AmPA

There was once a little animal. Similar Cases. Charlotte Perkins Gilman. PoLF

There was once a maiden who loved a cheese. Quite the Cheese. H. C. Waring. BXAP

There was once a swing in a walnut tree. The Walnut Tree. David McCord. OBCA

There was once a woman whose father over the years had become an ox. The Ox. Russell Edson. RaBo

There was once a young lady of Ryde. Limerick. *Unknown.* PDV

There was once a young man of Oporta. "Lewis Carroll." FaBoNo; PeLi

There was once two Irish labouring men; to England they came over. How Paddy Stole the Rope. *Unknown.* BLPA

There was once upon a time a man who lost the. Doctor Bill Williams. Ernest Walsh. InvP

There was one among us who rose. Death of a Friend. Pauli Murray. PoBA

There Was One I Met [upon the Road]. Stephen Crane. MeMAP

There was one I recognised in a train. Just a Product of a Certain Situation. Steve Griffiths. AngWe

There Was Set Before Me a Mighty Hill. Stephen Crane. MeMAP

There was six jovial tradesmen, they all sat down to drinking. When Jones's Ale Was New. *Unknown.* AmFP

There was something cozy. Mystic Craze. Paul Trachtenberg. NGP

There was such speed in her little body. Bells for John Whiteside's Daughter. John Crowe Ransom. CMoP; FF; HAP; HeIP; HoPM; IMW; InPK; InPS; LiTA; LiTM; MeMAP; MoAB; MoAmPo; MoP; NAAL-2; NIP; NoAM; NOBA; NoP; OxBA; PoE; Poetr; PPP; PrIm; RB; TAP; TFi; UnPo; VGW; WeW

There was that business in Siberia, in '19. The Soviet Union. John Berryman. FaBoPV

There was that fall the fall of desire. Two. Winfield Townley Scott. NYBP

There was the buffalo blowing. Composition. Peter Blue Cloud. VoR

There was the chiropodist. Plain Song. Craig Raine. TOF

There was the Dog Man again today. One Man's Family. Rosemary Catacalos. AfAz

There was the solitary palm, or scattered clumps. In Times and Places. Umberto Piersanti, *tr. fr. Italian by* Stephen Sartarelli. NeIt

There was the sonne of Ampycus of great forecasting wit. Meleager. Ovid, *tr. by* Arthur Golding. *Fr.* Metamorphoses. CTC

There was the story of a power station. Simultaneous Stories. Matthew Sweeney. IB

There was thirty dead an' wounded on the ground we wouldn't keep. Kipling. *Fr.* That Day. PlP

There was this empty bird cage in the garden. A Sparrow's Feather. George Barker. NYBP

There was this gym-teacher. Strato, *tr. fr. Greek by* Teddy Hogge. GrAn; PeHV

There was this head had this mouth he kept shooting off. The Mouth. Ciaran Carson. PNI

There was this road. The Legs. Robert Graves. ImPo; LiTB; LiTM; MeMBP; PeLV; RB

There was this time in Boston. The Wedding Night. Anne Sexton. PoA

There was three kings into the east. Burns. *See* There was three kings into the east.

There was three kings into the east. John Barleycorn. Burns. FaBoCh
(There was three kings into the east.) RB

There was three ladies play'd at the ba'. The Cruel Brother. *Unknown.* AmFP; ESPB; OxBB

There was three worms on yonder hill. Died of Love. *Unknown.* OBET

There was, 'tis said, and I believe, a time. Burials. George Crabbe. *Fr.* Parish Register, The. OAEL-1, *abr.*

There was twa sisters in a bow'r [*or* bower]. The Twa Sisters. *Unknown.* ESPB; FaBoBa; NoP; OxBS

There was two little boys going to the school. The Twa Brothers. *Unknown.* CH; EBEV; ESPB, A *and* B *vers.*; OxBB

There we two, content, happy in being together, speaking little, perhaps not a word. (*LL*) A Glimpse. Walt Whitman. AmPP; AnAmPo; OxBA; PeHV; PPP; RaBo

There we was, and wanting our tea. P. E. A. PeLi

There went most passionately to life, impellance. Life and Impellance. William Frederick Stevenson. NOBVV

There went out in the dawning light. *Unknown, tr. fr. Latin by* John Addington Symonds. AWP

There went three children down to the shore. The Black Pebble. James Reeves. OTCP; PDV

There Were an Old and Wealthy Man. *Unknown.* AmFP

There were bees about. From the start I thought. Shore Scene. John Logan. SM

There were bizarre beginnings in old lands for the making of me. Dark Blood. Margaret Walker. NALW

There were blood spots on the skirt. James Cunningham. *Fr.* Narrator's Trance, The. JB

There were bonfires on the hillsides. Ohakune Fires. Lauris Edmond, *tr. fr. Maori by* Margaret Orbell. PeNZ

There were fifteen men in green. David Campbell. *See* Oh, there were fifteen men in green.

There were five of us within the room. I Come to Bury Caesar. Sydney Justin Harris. PoA

There were four of us about that [*or* the] bed. Shameful Death. William Morris. ChTr; GTBS-P; PeVV

There were four red apples on the bough. August. Swinburne. WiR

There were ghosts that returned to earth to hear his phrases. Large Red Man Reading. Wallace Stevens. HAP; LCAP

There were ladies, they lived in a bower. Mary [*or* Marie] Hamilton. *Unknown.* ESPB, B *vers.*

There were miners from Bisbee. Tramp Miner's Song. *Unknown.* AmFP

There were never strawberries. Strawberries. Edwin Morgan. BoLoP

There were nine grand pianos in my father's house. Michael Palmer. *Fr.* Six Hermetic Songs. BAP-90

There Were Ninety and Nine. Elizabeth C. Clephane. WGRP

There were no antelope on the balcony. Midnight Special. Kenneth Patchen. VGW

There were no hidden motives to his life. David Ignatow. CAPP

There were no men and women then at all. Then. Edwin Muir. CMoP; PoA; PoE

There were no poems that year. For Imelda. James Simmons. PNI

There were no undesirables or girls in my set. Commander Lowell. Robert Lowell. VGW

There were once two cats of Kilkenny. The Cats of Kilkenny. *Unknown.* OFC; PeLi; ReMoGo

There were once two young people of taste. Monica Curtis. PeLi

There were other forms. Other Forms of Slaughter. Catherine Obianuju Acholonu. HBAPE

There were saddened hearts in Mudville for a week or even more. Casey's Revenge. James Wilson. BLPA

There were some dirty plates. The Last Words of My English Grandmother. William Carlos Williams. RaBo; RB; SAmP; SOTW

There were some pines, a canal, a piece of sky. Landscape with Little Figures. Donald Justice. CAPP; LCAP

There Were Some Summers. Thomas Lux. LCAP

There were the roses, in the rain. The Act. William Carlos Williams. ArNa; SAmP; SOTW; VGW

There were the whales, six of them. The Stranded Whales. Geoffrey Dutton. CBAP

There Were Those. Susan Dambroff. BTR

There were three brethren come from Spain. Three Knights from Spain. *Unknown.* CH
(We Are Three Brethren Come from Spain.) GBP
(We are three brethren out of Spain.) OxNR

There were three cherry trees once. The Three Cherry Trees. Walter de la Mare. CMoP

There were three cooks of Colebrook. *Unknown.* OxNR

There were three crows sat on a tree. *Unknown. See* There were three ravens [*or* rauens *or* crows] sat on a tree.

There were three ghostesses. *Unknown.* ISE

There were three gipsies a-come to my door. The Wraggle Taggle Gipsies. *Unknown.* BoTP; CH; FaPON; WiR
(Black Jack Davey.) MAT
(Raggle, Taggle Gipsies, The.) FaPON
(Three gipsies stood at the Castle gate.) OtMeF, *diff. vers.*

There were three in the meadow by the brook. The Code. Robert Frost. OBNV; PoA; UnPo

There were three jovial Welshmen. There Were Three Jovial Welshmen. *Unknown.* AngWe; CBNP
(Three Welshman, The.) MoShBr

There Were Three Jovial Welshmen. *Unknown.* AngWe; CBNP

There were three ladies [*or* maids] lived in a bower [*or* barn]. Babylon; or, The Bonnie Banks o' Fordie. *Unknown.* AmFP; ESPB; OxBB

There were three little owls in a wood. *Unknown.* PeLi

There were three maidens who loved a king. Three Loves. Lucy H. Hooper. BeLS

There were three men came out of the west. John Barleycorn. *Unknown.* OBET

There were three men of Gotham. The Three Wise Men of Gotham. *Unknown.* FaBoNo

There were three ravens [*or* rauens *or* crows] sat on a tree. The Three Ravens. *Unknown.* ChTr; ESPB; FaBoBa; GBP; HeIP; InPK; Mes; NAEL-1; NoP; OAEL-1; OBD; OBET; OBEV; OxBB; PoE; PoEL-1; SCGP; TFi; TrGrPo; UnPo
(There were three crows sat on a tree.) AmFP

There were three sailors of Bristol city. Little Billee. Thackeray. FaBoCh; FaBoCo; NOBL; OHCV; OxAEP-2; PlP
(Three Sailors, The.) OxBB

There were three sisters fair and bright. The Riddling Knight. *Unknown.* FaBoCh; PoEL-1

There were three sisters in a hall. *Unknown.* OxNR

There were trains that went in the tunnels. Cipriana. Ernesto Trejo. AfAz

There were twa brethren in the North. The Twa Brothers. *Unknown.* CH; EBEV; ESPB, A *vers.*; OxBB

There were twa knights in fair Scotland. The Twa Knights. *Unknown.* ESPB

There were twa sisters [sat] in a bower [*or* bour *or* bowr]. Binnorie; or, The Two Sisters. *Unknown.* OBEV; PoE; TrGrPo
(Twa Sisters of Binnorie.) CH; EnSB

There were two birds sat on a stone. Mother Goose. OxNR
(Aristotle's Story.) CBNP; ReMoGo

There were two blackbirds, sitting on a hill. *Unknown.* RoPo

There were two royal children. *Unknown, tr. fr. German by* Ingrid Waløe-Engel. GePo

There were two sisters sat in a bour. The Cruel Sister. *Unknown.* OxBB

There were two sisters, they went playing. The Twa Sisters. *Unknown.* ESPB

There were two surprises for us. At Ynysddu. Graham Thomas. AngWe

There were two wrens upon a tree. *Unknown.* OxNR

There were years when I knew. The Falcons. W. S. Merwin. CAPP

There where he sits, in the cold, in the gloom. The Hidden Weaver. Odell Shepard. WGRP

There, where it was, we never noticed how. The Sagging Bough. Louis Untermeyer. BXAP

There where the course is. At Galway Races. W. B. Yeats. IIP

There, where the rusty iron lies. Rooks. Charles Hamilton Sorley. MoBrPo; NSI

There, where the sun shines first. The Azalea. Coventry Patmore. *Fr.* Unknown Eros, The. ELP; GBL

There, where we still stand talking in the quad. *(LL)* One More New Botched Beginning. Stephen Spender. CMoP; NoAM; NYBP

There will be a rusty gun on the wall, sweetheart. A. E. F. Carl Sandburg. CMoP; MoAB; MoAmPo

There will be a Talking. Michael Hartnett. PBCIP

There will be a talking of lovely things. There will be a Talking. Michael Hartnett. PBCIP

There Will Be Animals. Thylias Moss. BAP-90

There will be animals to teach us. There Will Be Animals. Thylias Moss. BAP-90

There will be bluebells growing under the big trees. Bluebells for Love. Patrick Kavanagh. IPY

There will be bridge and booze 'till after three. Hilaire Belloc. FaBoEH

There will be many other nights like. Listening to Sonny Rollins at the Five-Spot. Paul Blackburn. Jaz

There will be no deluge again. *(LL)* Cat in the Dovecote. Avner Trainin. MHP

There will be no Holyman crying out this year. Jitterbugging in the Streets. Calvin C. Hernton. PoBA

There will be no monograms on our skulls. Rebellion against the North Side. Naomi Shihab Nye. WeW

There will be no more cats. Mort aux Chats. Peter Porter. OxBC

There will be no speech from. No Speech from the Scaffold. Thom Gunn. OxBTC

There will be rose and rhododendron. Elegy before Death. Edna St. Vincent Millay. CMoP; LiTA; LiTM; MeMAP

There Will Come Soft Rains. Sara Teasdale. LiTA; PAW

There, with ten Rembrandts. Ten Little Rembrandts. Theodore Weiss. NoAM

There, wrapped in his own roars, the lone airman. The Raider. W. R. Rodgers. MoBrPo

There you are. Jean-Joseph Rabéarivelo, *tr. fr. French by* Ellen Conroy Kennedy. NegPo

There you are again. To Marie Osmond. Jack Skelley. UL; UTF

There you are dancing with your child. Tsena Tsena (Second Generation). Marilyn Mohr. BTR

There you were in my dreams last night. Stepfathers. David Donnell. NOBC

There'd be an orchestra. F. Scott Fitzgerald. *Fr.* Thousand-and-First Ship. AiP; GoJo

(There was an Orchestra.) OTCP, *sl. diff.*

(There was an orchestra — Bingo-Bango.) OTCP, *sl. diff.*

There'd be no work for tinker's hands. *(LL)* Proverb. Unknown. FaBoBe; ISE

There'd ha'e to be nae warnin'. Times ha'e changed. Prayer for a Second Flood. "Hugh MacDiarmid." EBEV

Therefore all seasons shall be sweet to thee. All Seasons Shall Be Sweet. Samuel Taylor Coleridge. BoTP

Therefore I Must Tell the Truth. Torlino, *tr. fr. Navajo Indian by* Washington Matthews. STP

Therefore John read how that thou wouldst. Anna Trapnell. *Fr.* Cry of a Stone, A. ChIV-2; KTR

Therefore let pass, as they are transitory. Milton. *Fr.* Paradise Regained [*or* Regain'd]. OAEL-1

Therefore release me and depart on your way. *(LL)* Whoever You Are Holding Me Now in Hand. Walt Whitman. InvP; NAAL-1; PoEL-5

Therefore that he may raise the Lord throws down. *(LL)* Hymn[e] to God My God, In My Sickness[e]. John Donne. ChTr; EBEV; EnRePo; ESCV; HeIL; HeIP; ImPo; InPS; MeLP; NAEL-1; NoP; NOSC; OAEL-1; OBD; OxAEP-1; PoE; PoEL-2; PPP; SeCP; SeCV-1; SoSe; TFi; TOF; TrPWD

Therefore the sound of the whistle I cut seemed to weep. *(LL)* Spring. Aasmund Olavsen Vinje. RiWo

Therefore We Preserve Life. Shen Ch'üan, *tr. fr. Chinese by* William C. White. TrJP

Therefore, We Thank Thee, God. Reuben Grossman, *tr. fr. Hebrew by* L. V. Snowman. TrJP

Therefore, when thou wouldst pray, or dost thine alms. The Right Use of Prayer. Sir Aubrey De Vere. TIRV; WGRP

Therefore, who doeth work rightful to do. *Unknown, tr. by* Sir Edward Arnold. *Fr.* Bhagavad-Gita, The. TAL

Therein is sunlight, and sweet sound. Withheld. Ina Coolbrith. AmWP

There'll be a day when dust flies at the bottom of the sea. Po Chü-i, *tr. by* Irving Y. Lo. *Fr.* Tune: "Ripples Sifting Sand". SuSp

There'll Be No Better. Gerda Mayer. DT

There'll be no more. Finished. Kate Llewellyn. NOBAu

There'll be no time for kicking. *(LL)* Horse Sense. *Unknown.* BLPA; PWR; WBLP

There'll be no war. No War. Judith Kazantzis. AIW

There'll come a time when brother speaks with brother. Alcuin, *tr. fr. Latin by* Helen Waddell. MLL

There's a barrel of porter at Tammany Hall. Fitz-Greene Halleck. OBAL

There's a barrel-organ caroling across a golden street. The Barrel-Organ. Alfred Noyes. BLPL; FaBV; MoBrPo; PoRA

There's a beautiful island away in the West. The Land of the Evening Mirage. *Unknown, tr. fr. Sioux Indian by* A. M. Bede. WGRP

There's a bird perched on my shoulder. Bird. Agnes Nemes Nagy, *tr. fr. Hungarian by* Bruce Berlind. BoWoP; PoSu

There's a bit of sky across the street. My "Patch of Blue." Mary Newland Carson. BLPA

There's a black fog hiding London. Promise. Florence Lacey. BoTP

There's a Breathless Hush. Noel Petty. UV

There's a breathless hush in the Close tonight. There's a Breathless Hush. Noel Petty. UV

There's a breathless hush in the Close tonight. Vitaï Lampada. Sir Henry Newbolt. BLPA; EBEvV; FaBoEH; FaPoR; NSI; OBWP; PlP; UV; VPP

(Play Up! Play Up!) CoGr

There's a Breathless Hush on the Centre Court. Stanley J. Sharpless. UV

There's a brief spring in all of us and when it finishes. To S. T. C. on His 179th Birthday, October 12th, 1951. Maurice Carpenter. FaBoTw

There's a buzz in my ears crying: "Is there a point in these." Song of Dejection. W. H. Auden. *Fr.* Man of La Mancha. AnAn

There's a certain slant of light. Emily Dickinson. AmPP; BLPL; BoWoP; CMoP; HAP; HeIL; HeIP; ImGa; ImPo; LiTM; MeMAP; MoAB; MoAmPo; MoP; NAAL-1; NALW; NAWM-2; NoAM; NOBA; NoP; NTP; OxBA; PoE; PoEL-5; Poetr; PPP; RB; SAmP; SoSe; TFi; TOF; WPE

(Certain Slant of Light, A.) LiTA

There's a certain young lady. A Certain Young Lady. Washington Irving. FaBoBe

There's a class of men (and women) who are always on their guard. The Men Who Come Behind. Henry Lawson. NOBAu

There's a combative artist named Whistler. Dante Gabriel Rossetti. FaBoEE; PeLi

There's a comforting thought at the close of the day. Touching Shoulders. *Unknown.* BLPA

There's a craze among us mortals that is cruel hard to name. The Other Fellow's Job. Strickland W. Gillilan. WBLP

There's a cut-price whore. Pascoe Polglaze. PeLi

There's a deep murmer unravelled. Cuernavaca. Aline Pettersson, *tr. fr. Spanish.* TSaS, *tr. by* Judith Infante

There's a fabulous story. The Place Where the Rainbow Ends. Paul Laurence Dunbar. PWR

There's a faerie at the bottom of my garden. My Garden. Janice Appleby Succorsa. HoPM

There's a fairmer up in Cairnie. Drumdelgie. *Unknown.* GBP

There's a family nobody likes to meet. The Grumble Family. *Unknown.* PWR; WBLP

There's a famous seaside place called Blackpool. The Lion and Albert. Marriott Edgar. OBNV

There's a feeling that comes with the daze of joy. Undertones. George R. Sims. NOBVV

There's a fortunate priest of St. Paul's. Douglas Catley. PeLi

There's a fortune to be made in just about everything. My Great Great etc. Uncle Patrick Henry. James Tate. OBAL

There's a Friend for little children. Albert Midlane. *Fr.* Above the Bright Blue Sky. OxBChV

There's a game much in fashion — I think it's called Euchre. The Game of Life. John Godfrey Saxe. BLPA; BLPL

There's a gathering in the village, that has never been outdone. The Country Doctor. Will M. Carleton. BLPA

There's a glade in Aghadoe, Aghadoe, Aghadoe. Aghadoe. John Todhunter. PeIV

There's a goblin as green. The Goblin. Jack Prelutsky. TLR

There's a good old war-cry sounding, it hangs on every lip. Waitekauri Every Time! Edwin Edwards. PeNZ

There's a good time coming, boys. The Good Time Coming. Charles Mackey. VPP

There's a Grandfather's Clock in the Hall. Robert Penn Warren. NoAM; NoP

There's a graveyard near the White House. The Unknown Soldier. Billy Rose. BLPA

There's a gray cat who's not allowed into the house. Sisterhood. Daniel Halpern. SoCa

There's a great big mystery. Diddie Wa Diddie. Blind Blake. CBNP

There's a great divinity. For Windows. Robert Grenier. UL

There's a green hollow where a river sings. Rimbaud. *See* Swollen river sang through the green hole, The.

There's a green hollow where a river sings. The Sleeper of the Valley. Rimbaud, *tr. fr. French by* Ludwig Lewisohn. AWP

There's a grey wind wails on the clover. Numerous Celts. J. C. Squire. BXAP

There's a grim one-horse hearse in a jolly round trot. The Pauper's Drive. Thomas Noel. VPP

There's a half hour towards dusk when flies. In the Attic. Donald Justice. SM

There's a haven of sure rest. Forgetfulness. James Russell Lowell. AnAmPo

There's a heap o' love in the human heart. The Human Heart. Frank Carleton Nelson. PoToHe

There's a Hole in the Middle of the Sea. *Unknown.* RoPo

There's a hole, there's a hole, there's a hole in the middle of the sea. There's a Hole in the Middle of the Sea. *Unknown.* RoPo

There's a kite stuck on the misted glass. Letter From My Son. Shihab Sarkar. TSaS

There's a knack in living with you. Living with You. Angela Langfield. FF

There's a land bears a well-known name. The Englishman. Eliza Cook. VPP

There's a latent queer. Tim Hopkins. PeLi

There's a little black train a-coming. The Little Black Train. *Unknown.* AmFP

There's/ A/ Little/ Light. Little Light. Jim Brodey. UL

There's a little wet home in the trench. Canadian Song. *Unknown.* NSI

There's a long-legged girl. Pickin Em Up and Layin Em Down. Maya Angelou. CBLP; NBLV

There's a lot of music in 'em — the hymns of long ago. The Old Hymns. Frank Lebby Stanton. BLRP

There's a man at Crewe. E. O. Parrott. PeLi

There's a man goin' 'round takin' names. The Angel of Death. *Unknown.* AmFP

There's a man going 'round taking names. (*LL*) The Angel of Death. *Unknown.* AmFP

There's a man, I really believe, compares with. Sappho, *tr. fr. Greek by* John Frederick Nims. STV

There's a man I really believe's in heaven. Sappho, *tr. fr. Greek by* John Frederick Nims. WeW

There's a man who lives in a London apartment. So Near and Yet So Near. Lemn Sissay. NBrP

There's a man with a nose. Ambrose Bierce. *Fr.* Devil's Dictionary, The. OBAL

There's a memory keeps a-runnin. The Old Apple-Tree. Paul Laurence Dunbar. AnAmPo

There's a merry brown thrush sitting up in the [*or* a] tree. The Brown Thrush. Lucy Larcom. BoTP; FaPON; OBCA

There's a mob of rumours from s. of the river. Hurricane Drummers! Self-Aid in Haggerston. Iain Sinclair. NBrP

There's a mouse house. I Wouldn't. John Ciardi. TLR

There's a neat little clock. The Clock. Mother Goose. ReMoGo

There's a notable family named Stein. *Unknown.* NOBL

There's a one-eyed yellow idol to the north of Khatmandu. The Green Eye of the Yellow God. J. Milton Hayes. BLPA; EBEvV; EBNV; VPP

There's a palace in Florence, the world knows well. Robert Browning. *Fr.* Statue and the Bust, The. Mes

There's a part o' the sun in an apple. Each a Part of All. Augustus Wright Bamberger. WBLP

There's a patch of old snow in a corner. A Patch of Old Snow. Robert Frost. CMoP; OxBSP; WeW

There's a path that leads to Nowhere. The Path that Leads to Nowhere. Corinne Roosevelt Robinson. BLPA

There's a place the man always say. Where? Kenneth Patchen. LiTM

There's a Portuguese person named Howell. *At. to* Dante Gabriel Rossetti. PeLi

There's a pretty fuss and bother both in country and in town. A New Song on the Birth of the Prince of Wales. *At. to* John Harkness. CoMu; FaBoBa; FaBoEH; NOBVV

There's a publishing party named Ellis. Dante Gabriel Rossetti. PeLi

There's a puckle lairds in the auld house. The Auld House. William Soutar. OxBS

There's a puff — and so good night! (*LL*) Good Night. Thomas Hood. OTCP; Spl

There's a quaint little place they call Lullaby Town. Lullaby Town. John Irving Diller. BLPA

There's a race of men that don't fit in. The Men That Don't Fit In. Robert W. Service. BLPA; BLPL

There's a ragged old man in the garden to-day. Mr. Scarecrow. Sheila Braine. BoTP

There's a red light on the track for Bolsum Brown. Bolsum Brown. *Unknown.* AS

There's a reid lowe in yer cheek. Sang. Robert MacLellan. OxBS

There's a Sampson lying, sleeping in the land. The Black Sampson. Josephine D. Henderson Heard. CBWP-4

There's a saucy, wild packet and a packet of fame. The *Dreadnought.* *Unknown.* AmFP

There's a sensitive type in Tom's River. *Unknown.* PeLi

There's a serpent, namely, drinking. The Social Glass. L. A. J. Moorer. CBWP-3

There's a shed at the bottom of our garden. The Shed. Frank Flynn. OTCP

There's a silver house in the lovely sky. The Silver House. John Lea. BoTP

There's a Silvery Lining to Every Cloud. Matilda C. Edwards. PWR

There's a slow tolling bell in the dark. Gavin Ewart. PeLi

There's a small café off the avenue. Wardour Street. Humbert Wolfe. OxBTC

There's a song in the air! Josiah Gilbert Holland. GN; OHIP

There's a sorry little scrub that is servant unto me. To Samuel, Bishop of Sens In Time of Dearth. Alcuin, *tr. fr. Latin by* Helen Waddell. MLL

There's a stir among the trees. The Christmas Trees. Mary Frances Butts. OHIP

There's a strange frenzy in my head. Jalal al-Din Rumi, *tr fr. Persian by* John Moyne *and* Coleman Barks. UnAS

There's a sweet old story translated for man. The Gospel According to You. *Unknown.* BLRP

There's a three-penny Lunch on Dover Street. Eat and Walk. James Norman Hall. BLPA

There's a tiresome young man of Bay Shore. Morris Bishop. PeLi

There's a town called Don't-You-Worry. The Town of Don't-You-Worry. I. J. Barlett. BLPA; WBLP

There's a trade you all know well. The Overlander. *Unknown.* NOBAu

There's a train that runs through Hawthorn. The Late Express. Barbara Giles. OTCP

There's a tramping of hoofs in the busy street. The Troop of the Guard. Hermann Hagedorn. OHIP

"There's a tree in father's garden, lovelye William," says she. Lovelye William. *Unknown.* AmFP

There's a tree out in our garden which is very nice to climb. The Tree in the Garden. Christine Chandler. BoTP; OTCP

There's a very prim girl called McDrood. *Unknown.* PeLi

There's a vile old man. Limeraiku. Ted Pauker. NOBL; PeLi

There's a wanderer, there's a wanderer, his name is Tzu-mei. Seven Songs Written while Living at T'ung-ku in 759. Tu Fu, *tr. fr. Chinese by* Goeffrey Waters. SuSp

There's a whisper down the field where the year has shot her yield. Kipling. OBEV; OtMeF

(Long Trail, The.) FaBV

There's a whisper down the line at 11:39. Skimbleshanks: The Railway Cat. T. S. Eliot. FaBoCo; NOBL

There's a wicked wind tonight. *Unknown. See* Fierce is the wind tonight.

There's a Wideness. Frederick William Faber. *See* There's a wideness in God's mercy.

There's a Wideness. Frederick William Faber. WBLP

There's a wideness in God's mercy. The All-embracing. Frederick William Faber. BLRP

(There's a Wideness.) WBLP

There's a woman called Faithless. A Woman Called Faithless. Linda France. NWP

There's a woman like a dew-drop, she's so purer than the purest. Earl Mertoun's Song. Robert Browning. *Fr.* Blot in the 'Scutcheon, A. OBEV

There's a wonderful family called Stein. *Unknown.* PeLi

There's a wonderful story. The Angel's Message. Clara Ann Thompson. CBWP-2

There's a zone. No-Man's-Land. H. d'A. B. NSI

There's all of pleasure and all of peace. A Friend of Two. Wilbur D. Nesbit. PoLF

There's all sorts of fowl and fish. An Invitation to Lubberland. *Unknown.* FaBoNo; GBP

There's always a headscart stooped. Glasgow 1956. Gerald Mangan. PWE

There's always a killer with a name like Tony. This Fast-Paced, Brutal Thriller. Vijay Seshadri. UTF

There's an ancient party. Old Brown's Daughter. *Unknown.* OBET

There's an early memory that I carry around. My Father's Back. Edward Hirsch. VCAP

There's an emerald frog down the loo. Ruth Silcock. PeLi

There's an end to all Misery. (*LL*) The Smile. Blake. RB

There's an enormous comfort knowing. Under This Sky. Zia Hyder, *tr. fr. Bengali.* TSaS, *tr.* by Bhabani Sengupta *with* Naomi Shihab Nye

There's an Irishman, Arthur O'Shaughnessy. Dante Gabriel Rossetti. PeLi

There's an Orange Tree Out There. Alfonso Quijada Urias, *tr. fr. Spanish.* TSaS, *tr.* by Darwin J. Flakoll

There's an orange tree out there, behind that old. There's an Orange Tree Out There. Alfonso Quijada Urias, *tr. fr. Spanish.* TSaS, *tr.* by Darwin J. Flakoll

There's an ordinary woman whom the English call the "the Queen." The English Queen. Henry Lawson. NOBAu

There's antimony, arsenic, aluminium, selenium. The Elements. Tom Lehrer. FaBoUs; UV

There's beauty in the azure skies. The World Is Full of Beauty. Matilda C. Edwards. PWR

There's been a death in the opposite house. Emily Dickinson. CoGr; InPS; MeMAP; SAmP; SoSe

"There's been an accident," they said. Harry Graham. UV
(Common Sense.) FiBHP; OtMeF
(Mr. Jones.) FaBoCo

"There's been an accident!" they said. Harry Graham. *Fr.* Some Ruthless Rhymes.
(Mr Jones.) PeLV

There's blood between us, love, my love. The Convent Threshold. Christina Rossetti. MeMBP; NALW; NoP; PFP

There's dust on Mr Dinneen's boots! Where has. The President's Men. Thomas McCarthy. IB

There's enough wind. From an English Sensibility. Roy Fisher. VaA

There's fortune in't, we'll have a drink. Song to the Brandy. Duncan Ban MacIntyre. ScCV

There's four square miles of timber, mostly oak. Wild Pigs. Ted Kooser. SM

There's heaven above, and night by night. Johannes Agricola in Meditation. Robert Browning. TOF

There's Holmes, who is matchless among you for wit. Holmes. James Russell Lowell. *Fr.* Fable for Critics, A. NOBA

There's holy holy people. Capel Calvin. Idris Davies. AngWe

There's in my mind a woman. In Mind. Denise Levertov. NALW; NMM

"There's just one Book!" cried the dying sage. Just One Book. *Unknown.* BLRP

There's Life in a Mussel; a Meditation. George Farewell. NOEC

"There's light ahead!" Hope ever cries. Hope Deferred. Clara Ann Thompson. CBWP-2

There's light upon it still. (*LL*) Lincoln. Nancy Byrd Turner. FaPON

There's little coin and less devotion. (*LL*) The Bounty of Our Age. Henry Farley. FaBoCh; FaBoEE; NOSC

There's little joy in life for me. On the Death of Anne Brontë. Charlotte Brontë. IMW; WPE

There's loss in the Atlantic sky. Atlantic. Peter Scupham. SCBI

There's lots of things I'd like to be. The Hurdy-Gurdy Man. Elizabeth Fleming. BoTP

There's machinery in the butterfly. The Horrid Voice of Science. Vachel Lindsay. PoA

There's Many a Man Killed on the Railroad. *Unknown.* AS

There's moaning somewhere in the dark. Voice in Darkness. Richard Dehmel, *tr. fr. German by* Margarete Münsterberg. AWP

There's Money in Mother and Father. Morris Bishop. FiBHP

There's more in words than I can teach. Loving and Liking [Irregular Verses Addressed to A Child]. Dorothy Wordsworth. OxBChV; WoRP

There's More Pretty Girls than One. *Unknown.* AmFP

There's much afoot in heaven and earth this year. The Rainy Summer. Alice Meynell. GoJo; OxBSP; OxBTC

There's music in a hammer. *Unknown.* RoPo

There's music in the old bones yet. (*LL*) Song for the Clatter-Bones. F. R. Higgins. ChIV-1; ImPo; LiTB; OBMV

There's my war club. Hunting Song ("There's my war club.") *Unknown, tr. fr. Chippewa Indian by* Jerome K. Rothenberg. STP

There's Nae Luck about the House. *At. to* William Julius Mickle, *also at. to* Jean Adam. *See* And are ye sure the news is true?

There's nane again sae bonnie. (*LL*) Bonnie Lesley. Burns. CTC; GTBS; GTBS-P; NOBE; OBEV

There's naught (thou say'st) but one eternal flux. The Infidel Reclaimed. Edward Young. *Fr.* Night Thoughts. NOEC

There's never enough whiskey or rain. Wishing Africa. Marilyn Bowering. NOBC

There's no a bird in a' this foreste. Johnie Cock. *Unknown.* ESPB, B *vers.*

There's no carousing. (*LL*) Anacreontic. Robert Herrick. CaPo; OxBoLi

There's no comfort inside me, only a small. Beehive Cell. Richard Murphy. CIP

There's no dew left on the daisies and clover. Seven Times One — Exultation. Jean Ingelow. *Fr.* Songs of Seven. BLPA; FaPON; OBNC

There's No First Class to Heaven. Pennethorne Hughes. IHNG

There's No Lust like to Poetry. *Unknown, tr.* by John Addington Symonds. AWP

There's no more to be said. (*LL*) On Prince Frederick. *Unknown.* CoGr; FaBoCo; FaBoEE; NOBL; NTP

There's no salvation in elsewhere. Tangier. Stephen Dunn. SM

There's no smoke in the chimney. The Deserted House. Mary Elizabeth Coleridge. BoTP; CH

There's no such thing as death everybody. Then the Brother of the Wind. C. K. Williams. CAPP

There's no way out. In the Suburbs. Louis Simpson. CAPP; MAT; TRP

There's not a chance now that I might recover. The Scar. John Hewitt. CIP; PNI

There's not a husband whom storms don't benight. *Unknown, tr. fr. Greek by* Peter Jay. GrAn

There's Not a Joy. Byron. *See* There's not a joy the world can give like that it takes away.

There's not a joy the world can give like that it takes away. Byron. *Fr.* Stanzas for Music. EnRP; GTBS; HAP
(There's Not a Joy.) MeMBP
(Youth and Age.) GTBS; GTBS-P

There's not a nook within this solemn Pass. The Trosachs. Wordsworth. OBEV

There's nothing grieves me, but that age should haste. Michael Drayton. *Fr.* Idea. AAS; ESo; NOSC; OAEL-1

There's nothing happening that you hate. Leave Them Alone. Patrick Kavanagh. OxBSP

There's nothing in this gardenous world more delightful. Gerald Stern. CAPP

There's nothing left. When Hope Comes Back. Gu Cheng, *tr. fr. Chinese by* Donald Finkel *with* Chang Sheng-Tai. SpMi

There's Nothing like the Sun. Edward Thomas. ArNa; FaBV

There's nothing makes a Greenland Whale. It Makes a Change. Mervyn Laurence Peake. OTCP

There's nothing very beautiful and nothing very gay. Little Things. John Orrick. PoToHe

There's old Molly Hogan who cooks from a book. Stirling's Hotel. *Unknown.* AmFP

There's one Grammarian I know. Lucilius, *tr. fr. Greek by* Peter Porter. GrAn

There's one rides very sagely on the road. Upon the Horse and His Rider. Bunyan. OxBChV

There's order and law in a battleship's might. The Mystery Ships. R. A. Hopwood. NSI

There's parties ad yer meets about. Albert Chevalier. *Fr.* Sich a Nice Man Too! UV

There's pleasure, sure, in being clad in green. A Scene after Hunting at Swallowfield in Berkshire. Sneyd Davies. NOEC

There's quite enough to. Invisibility Poem: Lesbian. Ilze Mueller. LoHo

There's raw meat for the tiger cub. Song for the Infant Judas. Thomas Blackburn. NAs

There's recompense to balm your spirit's ire. Da Silva Gives the Cue. Walter Hart Blumenthal. TrJP

There's silence between one page and another. Valerio Magrelli, *tr. fr. Italian by* Jonathan Galassi. NeIt

There's snakes on the mountain. Wanderin'. *Unknown.* AS, B *vers.*

There's snow in every street. Winter. J. M. Synge. NOIV; OBMV; OxBTC

There's Snow on the Fields. Christina Rossetti. BoTP

There's some are fat, and some are lean. Alicia D'Anvers. *Fr.* Academia; or The Humours of the University of Oxford. KTR

There's some magic influential. Song of the Barber. W. H. Auden. *Fr.* Man of La Mancha. AnAn

There's some really good work. The Cream Song. Apirana Ngata, *tr. fr. Maori by* Margaret Orbell. PeNZ

There's some who say she put death up her dress. Ellie Mae Leaves in a Hurry. Peter Klappert. SM

There's somebody who's dying. They Warned Him Then They Threw Him Away. C. K. Williams. CAPP

"There's someone at the door," said gold candlestick. Green Candles. Humbert Wolfe. MoBrPo

There's Someone I Know. Jack Prelutsky. SiSoPo

There's Somethin'. Adam Small, *tr. fr. Afrikaans.* PeSA; PeSAV

There's something I want to tell you. (*LL*) It's Going to Rain. Martin Sorescu. PWE

There's something in a noble tree. The Trees. Samuel Valentine Cole. OHIP

There's something in the air. The Coming of Spring. Nora Perry. PWR

"There's something in the air," he said. Two Voices. Edmund Blunden. OBWP; PeFWW

There's somewhat on my breast, father. The Confession. "Thomas Ingoldsby." FiBHP

There's such a tiny little mouse. The Mouse. Thirza Wakley. BoTP

There's talk of a New Dawn for Blacks. The New Dawn. Mafika Pascal Gwala. PeSAV

There's teuch sauchs growin' i' the Reuch Heuch Hauch. The Sauchs in the Reuch Heuch Hauch. "Hugh MacDiarmid." NoAM

There's the field. I can see it. The Word. Neil Weiss. NYBP

There's the Irishman Arthur O'Shaughnessy. On the Poet O'Shaughnessy. Dante Gabriel Rossetti. ChTr

There's the story of me sitting in the grass in the dark. In the Dead of the Night. Norman Dubie. AmPA

There's the wonderful love of a beautiful maid. Love. *Unknown.* SoSe

There's three fair maids went to play at ball. The Cruel Brother. *Unknown.* AmFP

There's time the grass turns pink, the seed is setting. Weather. David Campbell. *Fr.* Works and Days. FaBoMA

There's trampling of hoofs in the busy street. A Troop of the Guard. Hermann Hagedorn. OHIP

There's wheat at home where you didn't leave it? Callicteros, *tr. fr. Greek by* Sam Hamill. InMo

There's where we'll meet and we'll never part no more. (*LL*) Carry Me Back to Old Virginny. James A. Bland. FaBoBe

Therese. Gottfried Keller, *tr. fr. German by* Philip L. Miller. RiWo

Theresienstadt Poems, *sels.* Robert Mezey. Theresienstadt Poemm. BTR; NaP

Thereupon dreamed that I dreamed. (*LL*) Yesterday, dreamed He was near me. Antonio Machado Ruiz. STV

Theris, the old man who lived by his fish traps. Leonidas, *tr. fr. Greek by* Kenneth Rexroth. GrAn; PGA

Theris the old, the waves that harvested. The Fisherman. Leonidas of Tarentum, *tr. by* Andrew Lang. *Fr.* Epigrams. AWP

Theris, thrice-old, who got his living from. Leonidas of Tarentum, *tr. fr. Greek by* Barbara Hughes Fowler. *Fr.* Epigrams. HePo

Theris, whose hands were cunning. Leonidas, *tr. fr. Greek by* Kenneth Rexroth. GrAn; PGA

Thermal Stair, The. W. S. Graham. FaBoMo

Thermopylae. Simonides, *tr. fr. Greek by* William Lisle Bowles. AWP; OBVE; OBWP

Thermopylai. Hegemon, *tr. fr. Greek by* Peter Jay. GrAn

Thermopylai. Parmenion of Macedon, *tr. fr. Greek by* Peter Jay. GrAn

Theromachos of Crete came to hang up. Leonidas of Tarentum, *tr. fr. Greek by* Peter Levi. GrAn

These. William Carlos Williams. MoAB; MoAmPo; MoP; NOBA; NoP; OxBA

These accents seem their own defence. (*LL*) Some Trees. John Ashbery. HCAP; NAAL-2; SM

These acres, always again lost. Lost Acres. Robert Graves. MeMBP; NoAM

These all their care expend on outward show. Edward Young. *Fr.* Love of Fame, the Universal Passion. OBSV

These alternate nights and days, these seasons. Archibald MacLeish. MoAmPo

These are amazing: each. Some Trees. John Ashbery. HCAP; NAAL-2; SM

These are Aristophanes' marvellous plays. Antipater of Thessalonica, *tr. fr. Greek by* Alistair Elliot. GrAn

These are his due. (*LL*) The Relapse. Henry Vaughan. ESCV; TrCP

These are men! the gaunt, unforesold, the vocal. Ol' Bunk's Band. William Carlos Williams. Jaz; NOBA

These are my legs. I don't have to tell them, legs. Walter Jenks' Bath. William Meredith. HoPM

These are my murmur-laden shells that keep. On Some Shells Found Inland. Trumbull Stickney. LiTA; Son

These are my thoughts on realising. Anniversary. John Wain. TwCP

These, are not brayed of Tongue. (*LL*) The Soul Has Bandaged Moments. Emily Dickinson. NALW; TRP

These Are Not Lost. Richard Metcalf. PoToHe

These are not words set down for the rejected. A Communication to Nancy Cunard. Kay Boyle. PoNe

These are notes to lightning in my bedroom. Star Quilt. Roberta Hill Whiteman. CDW

These are the arrows that kill sleep. Créide's Lament for Dínertech. *Unknown.* NOIV

These are the arrows that murder sleep. The Song of Crede. *Unknown, tr. fr. Middle Irish by* Alfred Perceval Graves. BIrV

These Are the Chosen People. Robert Nathan. TrJP

These are the damned circles Dante trod. Grotesque. Frederic Manning. PeFWW

These are the days of our youth, our days of glory and honor. The Days of Our Youth. *Unknown, tr. fr. Arabic by* Wilfrid Scawen Blunt. AWP

These are the days when birds come back. Emily Dickinson. FF; NAAL-1 (Indian Summer.) MoAmPo

These are the days whose fingers. Ninth of Av. Myra Sklarew. CRP

These are the desolate, dark weeks. These. William Carlos Williams. MoAB; MoAmPo; MoP; NOBA; NoP; OxBA

These/ are the desolate, dark weeks. William Carlos Williams. *See* Are the desolate, dark weeks.

These are the dog days. Songs to Survive the Summer. Robert Hass. AmPA

These are the dream machines. The Nightmare Factory. Maxine W. Kumin. WoWa

These are the facts. The uncle, the elder brother, the squire. Arthur Hugh Clough. *Fr.* Amours de Voyage. FaBoVe; NOBVV

These are the fields of light, and laughing air. The Pea-Fields. Sir Charles G. D. Roberts. *Fr.* Songs of the Common Day. NOBC

These are the first citizens of contingency. Proposition. Robert Pinsky. *Fr.* Essay on Psychiatrists. HCAP; NoAM

These are the gardens of the Desert, these. The Prairies. Bryant. AmPP; EAP; NAAL-1; NOBA; OxBA; PoEL-4; TAP

These are the ghosts of the unwilling dead. Ghosts, Fire, Water. James Kirkup. PAW

These Are the Gifts I Ask. Henry van Dyke. FaBoBe

These are the green paths trodden by patience. The Rural Mail. John Glassco. MoCV

These are the little shoes that died. The Little Shoes That Died. Mary Gilmore. NOBAu

These are the middle years. The Middle Years. Anthony Cronin. CIP

These are the original monies of the earth. A Cabinet of Seeds Displayed. Howard Nemerov. CRP

These are/ the passages of thought. Robert Duncan. *Fr.* Rites of Passage. BCF

These are the poems of Eliot. Sage Homme. Ezra Pound *and* Noel Stock. OBF

These are the richest weeks. Midsummer. Kevin Hart. FaBoMA

These are the signs in which my days endure. Museum Piece. Lawrence P. Spingarn. GoYe

These are the small hours when. Michael Longley. CIP

These are the things men seek at dusk. Dusk. Helen Welshimer. PoToHe

These are the things which once possessed. True Happiness. Morris Talpalar. PoToHe

These are the voices of the pastors calling. The Old Lutheran Bells at Home. Wallace Stevens. NoAM

These are the words. Stone from the Gods. Irma Wassall. GoYe

These are thy glorious works, Parent of good. Milton. *Fr.* Paradise Lost. EPCY
  (Adam's Morning Hymn.) WGRP
  (Morning Hymn of Adam.) TrPWD

These are times when their faith in gods. *From* Florrie Abraham Witness, December 1972. Jack A. Mapanje. HBAPE

These are your lips. Vasco [*or* Vasko] Popa, *tr. fr. Serbo-Croatian.* *Fr.* Far Within Us. PoSu, *tr. by* Anne Pennington

These, as they change, Almighty Father, these. A Hymn on the Seasons. James Thomson. *Fr.* Seasons, The. EnRP

These as they clack in the wind. In the Pea Patch. Maxine W. Kumin. CAPP

These barrows of the century-darkened dead. Prehistoric Burials. Siegfried Sassoon. MoBrPo

These be great cities, new roofs mounting up. Alcuin, *tr. fr. Latin by* Helen Waddell. MLL

These be/ Three silent things. Triad. Adelaide Crapsey. IMW; WPE

These beauties make me die. (*LL*) White and Red. Edward de Vere, Earl of Oxford.

These beds of bracken, climax of the summer's growth. Bracken Hills in Autumn. "Hugh MacDiarmid." NoP

These being the haunts of those. The Death of Friends. Adele Levi. GoYe

These birds were born singing for joy. Another Song of the Same Woman, to Some Partridges, Sent to Her Alive. Florencia del Pinar, *tr. fr. Spanish by* Julie Allen. BoWoP

These Bones. T. H. Parry-Williams, *tr. fr. Welsh by* H. Idris Bell. OBWVE

These bottle-washer trees that give no shade. Palm Trees. Rex Warner. OBTV

These buildings are too close to me. Rudolph Is Tired of the City. Gwendolyn Brooks. PDV

These caverns yield. The Bats. Robert Silliman Hillyer. GoYe

These cherries are not wine-filled bowls for thirsty birds. The Flowering Cherry. Janet Frame. PeNZ

These chill pillars of fluted stone. Winter Homily on the Calton Hill. Douglas Young. OxBS

These clouds above. Alois Jeitteles, *tr. by* Philip L. Miller. RiWo

These coastal mountains are as sharp as swords. Viewing Mountains with His Reverence Hao Ch'u: To My Friends and Relatives in the Capital. Liu Tsung-yüan, *tr. fr. Chinese by* Jan W. Walls. SuSp

These conquered kings pass furiously away. End of a Year. Robert Lowell. HCAP

These country folk dancing a schottische. Country Dance. Edward Baugh. PBCV

These creatures of the languid Orient. Albery Allson Whitman. *Fr.* Octoroon, The. AAP

These Damned Trees Crouch. Jim Barnes. CDW

These daughters are bone. God's Mood. Lucille Clifton. CAPP

These Days. Mang Ke, *tr. fr. Chinese by* Donald Finkel *with* Chang Sheng-Tai. SpMi

These Days. Andrew Motion. DiPo

These Days. Charles Olson. RaBo

These Days. William Stafford. NNaP

These days are abject and craven. These Days. Mang Ke, *tr. fr. Chinese by* Donald Finkel *with* Chang Sheng-Tai. SpMi

These days are too full fraught with diverse dangers. Alcuin, *tr. fr. Latin by* Helen Waddell. MLL

These days I get up with the birches. Days in White. Ingeborg Bachmann, *tr. fr. German.* BoWoP, *tr. by* Daniel Huws.

These days in Europe no one is safe. Three or Four Shades of Blues. Dionisio D. Martinez. Jaz

These days of disinheritance, we feast. Cuisine Bourgeoise. Wallace Stevens. LiTA; MeMAP

These Days the Papers in the Street. Charles Reznikoff. VGW

These days, the ubiquitous db. A. P. Cox. PeLi

These days you keep on meeting. The Seventies. Louis Johnson. PeNZ

These dried-out paint brushes which fell from my lips have been removed. Sestina from the Home Gardener. Diane Wakoski. MoP

These emotional dive-bombers. Nervous Miracles. Jim Gustafson. UL

These errors loved no less than the saint loves arrows. Elegy V: [Separation of Man from God]. George Barker. FaBoTw; LiTB; MeMBP

These eyes, [deare Lord], once brandons of desire. For the Magdalene. William Drummond of Hawthornden. ChIV-2; PoEL-2

These faces are true. Back to Hometown Kingston. James Berry. PBCV

These fat cassia trees. What Her Girl Friend Said to Her. Kovatattan, *tr. fr. Tamil by* A. K. Ramanujan. PLW

These feeble sounds. Ann Yearsley. *Fr.* Remonstrance in the Platonic Shade. Flourishing on an Height. ECWP

These fell miasmic rings of mist, with ghoulish menace bound. Prejudice. Georgia Douglas Johnson. PoBA; ShDr

These flames are made to measure. Flames. Jill Maughan. NWP

These flowers are I, poor Fanny Hurd. Voices from Things Growing in a Churchyard. Thomas Hardy. FaBoVe; OBD; OxBTC

These foreign laws of God and man. (*LL*) The Laws of God, the Laws of Man. A. E. Housman. MeMBP; MoAB; MoBrPo; NOBVV; NTP; OBSV; PeHV

These forty years past, our house and our domain. Tune: "Dance of the Cavalry." Li Yü, *tr. fr. Chinese by* Daniel Bryant. SuSp

These fought in any case. Ezra Pound. *Fr.* Hugh Selwyn Mauberly. (Life and Contacts). AmPP; CMoP; FaBoEH; FF; HeIL; HeIP; InPS; LiTA;

LiTM; MoAmPo; NoAM; NOBA; NOBE; NoP; OBWP; PoE; PoWW; TAP; TRP; VGW

These fragmented verses. "Ping Hsin," *tr. fr. Chinese by* Kenneth Rexroth *and* Ling Chung. *Fr.* Multitudinous Stars. WPC

These fresh beauties, we can prove. Why Flowers Change Color. Robert Herrick. HAP

These gifts to Aphrodite. Callimachus, *tr. fr. Greek. Fr.* Epigrams. HePo

These going home at dusk. French Peasants. Monk Gibbon. TIRV

These Gothic windows, how they wear me out. The Young Glass-Stainer. Thomas Hardy. CTC

These grand and fatal movements toward death. Rearmament. Robinson Jeffers. OxBA

These great brown hills move in herds, humped like bison. Among the Finger Lakes. Robert Wallace. GrPl

These Green-going-to-Yellow. Marvin Bell. CAPP; FYAP

These green painted park benches are. In a Season of Unemployment. Margaret Avison. MoCV; NOBC

These had been together from the first. Leolin and Edith. Tennyson. *Fr.* Aylmer's Field. GN

These hearts were woven of human joys and cares. Dead, The ("These hearts were woven.") Rupert Brooke. *Fr.* 1914. CH; LiTB; OtMeF; PeFWW; PoA; SoSe

These hips are big hips. Homage to My Hips. Lucille Clifton. CAPP; Poetr

These honours, Homer, had been just to thee. (*LL*) Mr. Pope's Welcome from Greece. John Gay. EBEV, *abr.*; OxAEP-1; OxBoLi, *abr.*; PoEL-3

These Horses Came. Ray A. Young Bear. CDW

These I Have Loved. Rupert Brooke. *Fr.* Great Lover, The. CBCK

These I have loved with passion, loved them long. Quiet Things. Grace Noll Crowell. PoLF

These, in the day when heaven was falling. Epitaph on an Army of Mercenaries. A. E. Housman. *Fr.* Last Poems. CoGr; EBEvV; NSI; OtMeF; PAW; SCGP; SoSe

These Indians once imitated life. The Only Bar in Dixon. James Welch. AmPA; FF

These insects, golden. Insect Heads. Robert Bly. CAPP

These is money. (*LL*) On Money. George Orwell. IHNG

These jagged passions trample. Mr and Mrs. Wendy Mulford. NBrP

These labor days, when shirking hardly looks like working. Back to Town. John Hollander. NoAM

These laboratories and those picnics. In Hospital. Frank O'Hara. LCAP

These labouring wits, like paviours, mend our ways. Edward Young. *Fr.* Epistles to Mr. Pope. OBSV

These Lacustrine Cities. John Ashbery. HCAP; PoM; UnPo

These layers of piled-up skulls. The Tower of Skulls. Isaac Rosenberg. PeFWW

These Leaves. William Stafford. NNaP

These light-footed, celebrated cats, created. The Tigers of Nanzen-ji. Brad Leithauser. DiPo

These little firs to-day are things. A Young Fir-Wood. Dante Gabriel Rossetti. GN

These little limbs [*or* limmes]. The Salutation [*or* Salutations]. Thomas Traherne. EnlH; ESCV; GeHe; InvP; NOCV; NoP; SeCP; SeCV-2

These locks on doors have brought me happiness. Locks. Kenneth Koch. CoAP

These locusts by day, these crickets by night. Wallace Stevens. PoA

These lodge in London in Lent and at other times too. The Civil Service. William Langland. *Fr.* Vision of Piers Plowman, The. NOCV

These London wenches are so stout. The Sound Country Lass. *Unknown.* CoMu; ErPo

These lovely groves of fountain-trees that shake. Golden Bough. Elinor Wylie. MoAmPo; PBWP

These lover's inklings which our loves enmesh. Counsel to Unreason. Léonie Adams. PoA

These lusty plants, complete with blaring sex. Marrows. Louis Johnson. PeNZ

These market-dames, mid-aged, with lips thin-drawn. Former Beauties. Thomas Hardy. *Fr.* At Casterbridge Fair. CBLP; NoAM; OBMV; OBNC

These meetings in dreams. Yakamochi, *tr. fr. Japanese by* Arthur Waley. TAL

These men clothed their land with incorruptible. For the Spartan Dead at Plataia. Simonides, *tr. fr. Greek by* Peter Jay. GrAn

These men? In their dented felt hats. The Colors of Desire. David Mura. NAmP90

These men were kings, albeit they were black. Black Majesty. Countee Cullen. PoBA; VGW

These messages are secret, the initials. Personal Column. Tom Paulin. PNI

They all took one, and left four in. (*LL*) Elizabeth, Elspeth, Betsy, and Bess. Mother Goose. OxNR; ReMoGo

They All Want to Play Hamlet. Carl Sandburg. NOBA

They all were looking for a king. That Holy Thing. George Macdonald. Fr. Paul Faber, Surgeon. OBEV; TrPWD; WGRP

They also serve who only stand and wait. (*LL*) On His Blindness. Milton. FaPoB; HeIL; InPK; NAEL-1; PoE; Poetr

They always put a large crimson sheet. Parakeet. Leonard Clark. Mes

They amputated/ Your thighs off my hips. A Pity; We Were Such a Good Invention. Yehuda Amichai, *tr. fr. Hebrew*. AnRep; BoLoP; LPA, *tr. by* Assia Gutmann; OxBM

They and I are civilized. (*LL*) Heritage. Countee Cullen. BPo; FaBV, *abr.*; HeIP; MoAmPo; NAAL-2; NoAM; NoP; PoBA; Poetr; TTY

They Answer Back. "Francis." FiBHP

They answer one's questions. People's Surroundings. Marianne Moore. CBCK

They are a gift I have wanted again. Horses in Snow. Roberta Hill Whiteman. NoAM

They are able, with science, to measure. C Stands for Civilization. Kenneth Fearing. TrJP

They are all dying. Death as History. Jay Wright. PoBA

They Are All Gone. Henry Vaughan. *See* They Are All Gone into the World of Light.

They are all gone away. The House on the Hill. E. A. Robinson. FaPON; GoJo; MoAmPo; NAAL-2; PrIm; TrGrPo

They Are All Gone into the World of Light. Henry Vaughan. ChTr; ESCV; FaBoRV; GeHe; InPS; JCP; NAEL-1; NOBE; NoP; NOSC; OAEL-1; PeECV; PoEL-2; SCGP; SeCP; SeCV-1; TFi

They are all outline, uniformly gray. Those before Us. Robert Lowell. LCAP

They are as light as upper air! (*LL*) The Garden Seat. Thomas Hardy. GoJo; HAP; Mes; RB

They are at rest. Refrigerium. Cardinal Newman. OBNC

They are by nature lonely things. Ideal Angels. John Robert Colombo. MoCV

They are chanting now the service of All the Dead. All Souls. D. H. Lawrence. FaBoRV

They Are Coming? Josephine D. Henderson Heard. AAP; CBWP-4

They are cutting down the great plane-trees at the end of the gardens. The Trees Are Down. Charlotte Mew. BoNaP; BrRo; ChIV-2; MoAB; MoBrPo; NTP; OxAEP-2; TrCP; WPE; WPOW

They are dreaming of children. Torrential. Nocturne in the Women's Prison. Maria Beneyto, *tr. fr. Spanish by* Catherine Rodriguez-Nieto. WPOW

They are 18 inches long. Trees at the Arctic Circle. Alfred W. Purdy. NoP

They are ever Free and Common. (*LL*) The Merchant and the Fidler's Wife. *Unknown*. CoMu; OxBB

They are extremely rare. (*LL*) The Frog. Hilaire Belloc. FaBoBe; FaBV; FaPON; FiBHP; GoJo; MoShBr; NTCP; OxBChV

They are formidable under any feather. The Murmurers. Josephine Jacobsen. GrPl

They are fruit. Advent. Kathleen Norris. CrSp

They are gathering round. Concert Party. Siegfried Sassoon. NSI

They are heard as a choir of swan. The Pleiades. Mary Barnard. NYBP

They are immortal, voyagers like these. Flight. Harold Vinal. FaPON

They are in the forest. In the Forest. George Bowering. NOBC

They are incontrovertible, the evidences. In the Garden. Lynne McMahon. FoLa

They are inspecting hearts again. A Glimpse of the Body Shop. Stephen Berg. NaP

They Are Killing All the Young Men. David Henderson. PoBA

They are kneeling upright on a flowered bed. Short Story on a Painting of Gustav Klimt. Lawrence Ferlinghetti. PoBeRe

They are lang deid, folk that I used to ken. Robert Garioch. OxBS

They are left alone in the dear old home. They Two. Mrs. Frank A. Breck. WBLP

They are light as flakes of dandruff with scrawny legs. Crabs. Marge Piercy. NBLV

They are like figures held in some glass ball. Children Walking Home from School through Good Neighborhood. Donald Justice. DiPo; NIP

They are making a crèche at the Saturday morning classes. The Crib. Robert Finch. OBCP

They are murdering all the young men. Thou Shalt Not Kill: A Memorial for Dylan Thomas. Kenneth Rexroth. PoBeRe

They are my secret food. The Children's Letters. Dorothy Livesay. NALW; NOBC

They are no trophies of the sun. (*LL*) Praise for an Urn. Hart Crane. AWP; CMoP; HAP; LiTM; MeMAP; MoAB; MoAmPo; NoAM; NOBA; OxBA; PPP; WeW

They are not dead, they are not dead! The Argonauts. D. H. Lawrence. NoAM

They are not here. And we, we are the Others. The Absent. Edwin Muir. MeMBP; NoAM

They Are Not Long. Ernest Dowson. *See* They are not long, the weeping and the laughter.

They are not long, the weeping and the laughter. Vitae Summa Brevis Spem Nos Vetat Incohare Longam. Ernest Dowson. AWP; ChTr; EBVV; FaBoRV; HAP; NOBE; NoP; OBEV; OHCV; OxBSP; PeVV; TFi; TrGrPo; WGRP

(Envoy: "They are not long, the weeping and the laughter.") MoBrPo; NOBVV

(They Are Not Long.) NAEL-2; PoRA

They are our creatures, clover, and they love us. Veronica Forrest-Thomson. VaA

They Are Ours. A. B. Magil. PoNe

They are pounded into the earth. It Is This Way with Men. C. K. Williams. CAPP; RaBo; VCAP

They are rattling breakfast plates in basement kitchens. Morning at the Window. T. S. Eliot. AWP; PoA

They are rebuilding/ the old bridge, the Nagara. Lady Ise, *tr. fr. Japanese by* Etsuko Terasaki *and* Irma Brandeis. BoWoP

They are rhymes rudely strung with intent less. Adam Lindsay Gordon. CBAP

They are 7 in number, just 7. The Seven. *Unknown, tr. fr. Sumerian by* Jerome K. Rothenberg. RB

They are sitting down, they are opening wounds. (*LL*) The Wars. Howard Moss. VCAP

They are slaves who fear to speak. Slaves. James Russell Lowell. *Fr.* Stanzas on Freedom. GN, 2 *sts.*; OHIP; PoNe

(On Freedom.) ImGa

They are so like. Dolls. David St. John. LCAP

They are so moving in. The Love of Older Men. James Kirkup. PeHV

They are such dear familiar feet that go. Be Patient. "George Klingle." PoToHe

They are taking us beyond Miami. The Removal. *Unknown, tr. fr. Seminole Indian by* Frances Densmore. STP

They are talking about how we are Dotito's people. (*LL*) Dotito is Our Brother. Charles Mungoshi. PeSAV

They are taller than their cars. (*LL*) Do It Yrself. Larry Eigner. NeAP; PoM

They are terribly white. Cyclamens. "Michael Field." NOBVV

They are the flesh we feed upon come from the depths. The Ribbon-Fish. Robert Adamson. CBAP

They are the last romantics, these candles. Candles. Sylvia Plath. NMM

They are the oldest living captive race. Ginkgoes in Fall. Howard Nemerov. HCAP

They Are the Same. Priscilla Jane Thompson. CBWP-2

They are the spit of virtue now. Austin Clarke. *Fr.* Civil War. NOIV

They are too much for me. Dioscorides, *tr. fr. Greek by* Sam Hamill. InMo

They are very small, my neighbors. The Minotaur Next Door. Greg Pape. PBCAP

They are waiting for me somewhere beyond Eden Rock. Eden Rock. Charles Causley. NTP

They are weighing the babies again on color television. Video Cuisine. Maxine W. Kumin. NoAM

They Are Wicked. Ernest Sandeen. CRP

They arrive, always, unexpected. The Yiddish Muses. Jacqueline Osherow. UTF

They bade me cast the thing away. Doubt. Helen Hunt Jackson. WGRP

They bear no laurels on their sunless brows. Failures. Arthur W. Upson. WGRP

They belong here in their own quenched country. By the Boat House, Oxford. Anne Stevenson. FaBoWP

They bide their time off serpentine. Ancient Monuments. John Ormond. AngWe; OBWVE

They borrowed a bed to lay His head. The Cross Was His Own. *Unknown*. BLPA

(Borrowed.) BLRP

They bowed to him: "O man of God." The Prophet. "Yehoash," *tr. fr. Yiddish by* Isidore Goldstick. TrJP

They breakfast; hardly speak. (*LL*) A Winter Story. Matthew Sweeney. IB

They bring me gifts, they honour me. If They Honoured Me, Giving Me Their Gifts. "Michael Field." OBMV

They brought a bouquet of thistles. Thistle. Nikolai Alekseevich Zabolotsky, *tr. fr. Russian by* Daniel Weissbort. RB

They brought him in on a stretcher from the world. Grandfather. Derek Mahon. OxBC

They brought him one morning. Dimitris Tsaloumas, *tr. fr. Greek by* Margaret Carroll. *Fr.* Rhapsody of Old Men, A. CBAP

They brought in the brine-crusted drift-wood. Drift-Wood. Clara Ann Thompson. CBWP-2

They brought me ambrotypes. Rutherford McDowell. Edgar Lee Masters. *Fr.* Spoon River Anthology. LiTA; OxBA

They brought thy body back to me quite dead. Luca Signorelli to His Son. Eugene Lee-Hamilton. PeVV

They brought up some tale about white fox. J. H. Prynne. VaA

They built the front, upon my word. The Building of a New Church. *Unknown.*
(On the Building of a New Church.) FaBoEE

They bulldozed the upper meadow at Squaw Valley. Name as the Shadow of the Predator's Wing. Robert Hass. NGP

They buried him today. My Father Today. Sam Hunt. PeNZ

They burn the radio and listen to the blues. John Tranter. *Fr.* Crying in Early Infancy. NoAM

They burn you. The Hitchhikers. Diane Wakoski. NoAM

They call all experience of the senses, when the experience is considered. Mystic. D. H. Lawrence. HeIL

They call it regional, this relevance. Lake Chelan. William Stafford. NaP

They call me and I go. Complaint. William Carlos Williams. SAmP

They call me cruel. Do I know if mouse or songbird feels? The Cat. Charles Stuart Calverley. *Fr.* Sad Memories. ChTr; FM; SoCa

They call me Hanging Johnny. Hanging Johnny. *Unknown.* GBP

They call thee rich; I deem thee poor. Treasure. Lucilius, *tr. fr. Greek by* William Cowper. AWP

They call this "Black North." Names. Gerald Dawe. IIP; PNI

They call us aliens, we are told. On Behalf of Some Irishmen Not Followers of Tradition. "Æ." IIP; PeIV

They call your mama girl. Brown Lullaby. Adam Small. PeSAV

They called her a cat. What They Said. Tanure Ojaide. HBAPE

They called him Bill, the hired man. William Brown of Oregon. Joaquin Miller. AnAmPo

They called it Annandale — and I was there. How Annandale Went Out. E. A. Robinson. MoAB; MoAmPo; NoAM; NOBA; SoSe

They called my love a poor blind maid. On a Blind Girl. Baha Ad-din Zuhayr, *tr. fr. Arabic by* E. H. Palmer. AWP

They called the place Lookout Farm. Memoirs of a Spinach-Picker. Sylvia Plath. GrPl

They Called Them RAF 2C's. *Unknown.* NSI

They came back from the bush-haunts. Arrivants. Musaemura Bonus Zimunya. HBAPE

They came from Persia to the sacred way. Peacocks. Walter Adolphe Roberts. PBCV

They came hurrying across the mountain highway. Monkeys on Mt. Hiei. Edith Marcombe Shiffert. WPE

They came in to the little town. We Are Going. Kath Walker. CBAP; NOBAu

They came on to fish-hook Gettysburg in this way, after this fashion. The Battle of Gettysburg. Stephen Vincent Benét. *Fr.* John Brown's Body. BeLS

They came out of the sun undetected. The Raid. William Everson. ArOW; MoP; NoAM; PrIm

They came running over the perilous sands. 1945. Sir Herbert Read. OxBTC

They Came That Night. Léon Damas, *tr. fr. French by* Ellen Conroy Kennedy. NegPo

They came that night as the. They Came That Night. Léon Damas, *tr. fr. French by* Ellen Conroy Kennedy. NegPo

They Came This Evening. Léon Damas, *tr. fr. French by* Seth L. Wolitz. TTY

They Came to Me and Said, "There Is a Child." Muriel Rukeyser. *Fr.* Nine Poems for the Unborn Child. Son

They came to the lodge door. Wolf "Aunt." Maurice Kenny. HATNAP

They came when the Czar banned the Yiddish. Yiddish Speaking Socialists of the Lower East Side. Edward Sanders. UL

They can enter the window and they will. Alien. Nancy Paddock. LoHo

They cannot speak who have no words to say. Green Hammock, White Magnolia Tree. Ruth Gilbert. PeNZ

They cannot spread nets where a harvest yields. (*LL*) O Lapwing! Blake. ChTr; FaBoEE

They cannot steal, thou giv'st so much. (*LL*) To Saxham. Thomas Carew. CaPo; JCP; NoP

They Can't Do That. *Unknown.* WTO

They can't plow and harvest. Poverty on the Bank. Mei Yao Ch'en, *tr. fr. Chinese by* Jonathan Chaves. SuSp

They cared for nothing but the days and hours. The Disinherited. Charles Spear. PeNZ

They Carried Their Truth to the Ditch where They Were Thrown. Christian Santos, *tr. fr. Spanish by* Anna Kirwan Vogel *and* Isabella Halsted. WoWa

They carry on. Floodtide. Askia Muhammad Touré. PoBA; PoNe

They Cast Their Nets in Galilee. William A. Percy. AH

They changed her name. Nechama. Shirley Kaufman. LCAP

They choose paths. Let Them Choose Paths. Odia Ofeimun. HBAPE

They Clapped. Nikki Giovanni. WPOW

They climbed on sketchy ladders towards God. Cathedral Builders. John Ormond. PeECV

They Closed Her Eyes. Gustavo Adolfo Bécquer, *tr. fr. Spanish by* John Masefield. AWP

They come as a boon and a blessing to men. The Waverley Pen. *Unknown.* FaBoUs

They come from beds of lichen green. The Assembling of the Fays. Joseph Rodman Drake. *Fr.* Culprit Fay, The. GN

They come from the white barrier of noon. The Diatribe of the Kite. Norman Dubie. NAmP90

They come into. Feeding the Lions. Norman Jordan. PoBA

They come into this room while the quail are crying to huddle up. Reading the Books Our Children Have Written. Dave Jeddie Smith. HCAP

They come like the ghosts of horses, shyly. The Pit Ponies. Leslie Norris. TSaS

They come not within the tall woods. To One Elect. S. I. Hayakawa. PoA

They come! — they come! — the heroes come. Evacuation of New York by the British. *Unknown.* PAH

They come, they come, with fife and drum. The Palace. Charles Stuart Calverley. EBVV

They come to you with their descriptions of your soul. Adrienne Rich. *Fr.* Shooting Script. HCAP

They come with, ah, fell footfall. Fêtes, Fates. John Malcolm Brinnin. LiTA

They couldn't understand why the drover cried. The Drover's Boy. Ted Egan. NOBAu

They crawled out slowly. Work-in-progress. Mahmood Jamal. NBrP

They cross from Glasgow to a black city. Settlers. Tom Paulin. IIP; PNI

They cross the frontier as their names cross your pages. The New Emigration. Kay Boyle. WPE

They cross the yard. From the Suburbs. Louise Glück. *Fr.* Dedication to Hunger. AnAn; FaBoWP; NALW

They crucified my Lord, an' He never said a mumbalin' word. Crucifixion. *Unknown.* BPo; TAP; TrGrPo

They cut it in squares. Socratic. Hilda Doolittle ("H. D."). HoPM

They danced by the light of the moon. (*LL*) The Owl and the Pussy-Cat. Edward Lear. BeLS; BoTP; CBNP; EBEvV; FaBoBe; FaBoCh; FaBoNo; FaPON; GoJo; GTBS-P; MoShBr; NBLV; NOBE; NoP; NTCP; NTP; OBSP, *St.* 1 *only*; OFC; OHCV; OTCP; OtMeF; OxBChV; OxBM, *St.* 1 *only*; OxBoLi; PDV; PeLV; PlP, *St.* 1 *only*; PoLF; PoRA; PYC; SoCa; TFi; TLR; TrGrPo; TTTS

They Dared Him. Kevin Myhill. PAW

They descended into hell after injustice. Miners. Branko Miljkovic, *tr. fr. Serbo-Croatian by* Charles Simic. HSix

They did not come to claim you back. Helen Todd: My Birthname. Sandra McPherson. LCAP

They did not know this face. Job. Elizabeth Sewell. ChIV-1

They did the deed of darkness. You and I Saw Hawks Exchanging the Prey. James Wright. NAAL-2; NoAM

They did their thing so well. Their Thing. Léon Damas, *tr. fr. French by* Ellen Conroy Kennedy. NegPo

They Didn't Hire Him. Gary Snyder. *Fr.* Hitch Haiku. LCAP; Poetr, *st.* 1 *only*; SM

They dither softly at her bedroom door. Cover Her Face. Thomas Kinsella. CIP; IPY

They do it with knives. Alistair Paterson. *Fr.* Toledo Room, The. PeNZ

They do me wrong who say I come no more. Opportunity. Walter Malone. BLPA; BLPL; FaBoBe; PWR; WBLP

They do move with grace. Dressed to Kill. Clarence Major. UL

They do not care, the dying, whether it be dawn or dusk or daylight full and clear. Illi Morituri. Mary Morison Webster. PeSA

They do not come with furred caps. Barbarians. John Fowles. AnAn

They do not live in the world. The Animals. Edwin Muir. ChIV-1; CMoP; CRP; EBEV; HeIP; MoBrPo; NoP

They do not love the earth. (*LL*) Those Who Want Out. Denise Levertov. LoHo

They do not talk of loss at Babi Yar. There Is One Synagogue Extant in Kiev. Yaacov Luria. BTR

They do not talk of Myrddin on the bridge at Beddgelert. Dinas Emrys. Brian Morris. AngWe

They do zay that a travellen chap. The Leane. William Barnes. EBVV

They dogged him all one afternoon. On the Way to the Mission. Duncan Campbell Scott. NOBC

They done took Cordelia. Stony Lonesome. Langston Hughes. NOBA; SAmP

They don't build houses like that any more. Verandahs. R. F. Brissenden. CBAP; NOBAu

They don't get anywhere. The Couple Overheard. William Meredith. HoPM

They don't hold grudges. First Monday Scottsboro Alabama. Tom Weatherly. PoBA

They don't know, do you? (LL) Emigrant/Immigrant. Rina Ferrarelli. LoHo

They don't like strangers. Stoney Ridge Dance Hall. Alden Nowlan. MoCV

They Don't Speak English in Paris. Ogden Nash. OBAL

They dragged you from [the] homeland. Strong Men. Sterling A. Brown. BPo; PoBA; TTY

They Dream Only of America. John Ashbery. CAPP

They dressed us up in black. The Funeral. Walter de la Mare. CMoP

They drift down the dusk. Flying Foxes. Lydia Pender. OBAP

They drive me mad, those rosy lips, forever prattling. Dioscorides, tr. fr. Greek by Barbara Hughes Fowler. Fr. Epigrams. HePo

They dropped like flakes, they dropped like stars. Emily Dickinson. OHIP

They dug his grave by lantern light. The Grave. Kipling. NSI

They eat beans mostly, this old yellow pair. The Bean Eaters. Gwendolyn Brooks. AIW; BlSi; GrPl; HAP; HeIL; HeIP; LCAP; MAT; NALW; NoP; PoBA; PoE; Poetr; PrIm; TAP; TRP; TTY; WeW

They Eat Out. Margaret Atwood. NoAM; NoP

They ended parle, and both addressed for fight. Milton. Fr. Paradise Lost. EPCY; OBWP

They enter the bare wood, drawn. The Novices. Denise Levertov. NaP

They entered the fiery furnace. The Six Million. Naomi Replansky. BTR

They expanded. McDonald's, New Hartford, NY. Valerie Worth. AiP

They faded away; and they never came back! (LL) The Nutcrackers and the Sugar-Tongs. Edward Lear. BLPL; Mes; PoLF

They faltered when we came there and I knew very well. Christ to Lazarus. David Constantine. PWE

They fastened a people to merchant ships. Edouard Glissant, tr. fr. French by Ellen Conroy Kennedy. Fr. Indies, The. NegPo

They fastened a poor man here on a rope's end. Eldon Hole. David Constantine. PWE

They Feed They Lion. Philip Levine. CAPP; LCAP; MAT; MoP; NNaP; NoAM; NOBA; Prf; VCAP

They feed they Lion and he comes. (LL) They Feed They Lion. Philip Levine. CAPP; LCAP; MAT; MoP; NNaP; NoAM; NOBA; Prf; VCAP

They feel the calm delight, and thus proceed. The Suffolk Shore. George Crabbe. Fr. Borough, The. FaBoPP

They fell asleep but not for long, for soon. Callimachus, tr. fr. Greek by Barbara Hughes Fowler. Fr. Epigrams. HePo

They fished and they fished. The Fish with the Deep Smile. Margaret Wise Brown. PDV

They Flee from Me. Sir Thomas Wyatt. See They Flee [or Fle] from Me That Sometime Did Me Seek [or Seke].

They Flee from Me That Sometime Did Me Seek. Gavin Ewart. OxBC

They Flee [or Fle] from Me That Sometime Did Me Seek [or Seke]. Sir Thomas Wyatt. BLPL; CBLP; ClHu; EnLoPo; EnRePo; FaBoPV; FF; GGP; HAP; HeIL; HeIP; ImPo; imPK; LiTB; LPA; NAEL-1; NoP; NoSic; OAEL-1; OPOP; OxBC; PoE; PPP; PrIm; SCV; SiPS; SiPSBD; TEP; TFi; TRP

They fling their flags upon the morn. Spain's Last Armada. Wallace Rice. PAH

They flourish at home in my own country. (LL) The Oak and the Ash. Unknown. FaBoCh

They fluttered off like withered souls of men. (LL) The Pity of the Leaves. E. A. Robinson. AnAmPo; MoAmPo

They Followed Us into the Night. Michele Najlis, tr. fr. Spanish by Amina Muñoz-Ali. WoWa

They formed the ritual circle. A Local Man Goes to the Killing Ground. James Whitehead. MT

They fought south of the Castle. Fighting South of the Castle. Unknown, tr. fr. Chinese by Arthur Waley. AWP

They fought south of the ramparts. Fighting South of the Ramparts. Unknown, tr. fr. Chinese by Arthur Waley. OBD; PAW

They Fought South of the Walls. Li Po, tr. fr. Chinese by Joseph J. Lee. SuSp

They Fought South of the Walls. Unknown, tr. fr. Chinese by Hans H. Frankel. SuSp

They found a man. Survivor, The: Anishinabe Man. Carlos Cumpian. AfAz

They found a taxi. He took her home. The Moral Taxi Ride. Erich Kästner, tr. fr. German by Jerome K. Rothenberg. ErPo

They Found Him Sitting in a Chair. Horace Gregory. MoAmPo

They found the path and I found the puddle. J. M. Synge. CBNP

They fuck you up, your mum and dad. This Be the Verse. Philip Larkin. NoAM

They gained a better peace than ours. (LL) Peace. Phoebe Cary. AmWP; PAH

They gathered around and told him not to do it. Noah. Roy Daniells. Mes

They gave him a finger, but he took the whole hand. King Saul and I. Yehuda Amichai, tr. fr. Hebrew by Assia Gutmann. PoSu

They Gave Him Vinegar and Gall (Matt. 27) and Wine Mingled with Myrrh (Mark 15). Francis Quarles. NOSC

They gave it back to me/ life. The Black Man's Lament. Léon Damas, tr. fr. French by ELlen Conroy Kennedy. NegPo

They gave me a big plate of soup. (LL) Soup Kitchen Song. Unknown. NOBAu

They gave me in my kindergarten year. Now or Never. Judith Moffett. SM; Son

They gave me the wrong name, in the first place. Her Story. Naomi Long Madgett. IHMS; PoBA

They gave my father a television. Death. Howard Byatt. FF

They gave us the mysterious deep warehouse. The Ajax Samples. Laura Jensen. LCAP

They get so thick on the ground. Walking on Frogs. John Cassidy. PWE

They give a man a taste for death. (LL) Some can gaze and not be sick. A. E. Housman. FaBoEE; NOBVV; OBSV

They give me a bad. Crows. Marge Piercy. CAPP

They go by, go by, love, the days and the hours. Teresa de Jesús, tr. fr. Spanish by Maria A. Proser, Arlene Scully and James Scully. WPOW

They got to stop kickin' my dog around. (LL) Every time I come to town. Unknown. RoPo

They grabbed fast, they grabbed big. Verses to Chekhia, 1938. Marina Tsvetayeva, tr. fr. Russian by Daniela Gioseffi with Sophia Buzevska. WoWa

They grew in beauty side by side. The Graves of a Household. Felicia Dorothea Hemans. FaPoR; PlP; WBLP; WPE

They grow over the Yangtze, the plum rains. Nisei: Second Generation Japanese-American. Jim Mitsui. OpBo

They guided birds and came to hear their story. Of History More Like Myth. Jean Garrigue. NYBP

They had agreed, walking into the delicatessen on 6th Avenue. Vintage. Robert Hass. AnAn; NAmP90

They had been there a month; the water had begun to tear them apart. A Negro Soldier's Viet Nam Diary. Herbert Martin. PoBA

They had changed their throats and had the throats of birds. (LL) Cuchulain Comforted. W. B. Yeats. CMoP; LiTM; OAEL-2; TOF

They had come to see the salmon lunging and leaping. The Excursion of the Speech and Hearing Class. David Wagoner. VCAP

They had dragged for hours. These Trees Are No Forest of Mourners. Douglas G. Jones. NOBC

They had forgotten. The Harvest. Alma Villanueva. ETG

They had hot scent across the spumy sea. Destroyers Off Jutland. Reginald McIntosh Cleveland. NSI

They had long met o' Zundays — her true love and she. The Bride-Night, Fire. Thomas Hardy. EnVR

They had made love early in the high bed. The Honeycomb. Pauline Stainer. PWE

They had never had one in the house before. Bronzeville Woman in a Red Hat. Gwendolyn Brooks. NALW

They had questioned him for hours. Campaign. Ciaran Carson. BiHa; CIP; PNI; PWE

They had secured their beauty to the dock. The Crowd. John Masefield. OxBTC

They had stolen my soul away! (LL) Romance. W. J. Turner. CH; CoGr; EBEvV; GoJo; MoBrPo; NOBAu; NOBE; NTP; OBMV; PlP; PoRA; TrGrPo

They had taken away. Saving the Children. Frieda Singer. BTR

They had the nerve to name you Constance. Macedonius, tr. fr. Greek by Sam Hamill. InMo

They hanged him on a clement morning, swung. Dennis Scott. PBCV

They hanged Jeff Buckner from a sycamore tree. Jeff Buckner. Frank Beddo. WTO

They hanged the King of Ai at eventide. The King of Ai. Hyam Plutzik. LiTM

They have been with us a long time. Telephone Poles. John Updike. FYAP; Poetsp

They have brought me a shell. Shell. Federico García Lorca, *tr. fr. Spanish*. CBNP

They have carried the mahogany chair and the cane rocker. Mourning Picture. Adrienne Rich. CoAP

They have chiseled on my stone the words. Cassius Hueffer. Edgar Lee Masters. *Fr. Spoon River Anthology*. OxBA

They have come again to graze the orchard. Thanksgiving. Louise Glück. FoLa

They have come by carloads. Surfers at Santa Cruz. Paul Goodman. FF

They have come from a factory. Nightshift Workers. George Charlton. PWE

They have connived at those jewelled fascinations. Auspice of Jewels. Laura Riding. LiTA

They have crucified their Lord afresh. *Unknown, tr. fr. Latin. Fr. Carmina Burana*. MLL, *tr.* by Helen Waddell

They have dreamed as young men dream. Old Black Men. Georgia Douglas Johnson. CDC; PoBA; PoNe

They have emptied the heart of Westport. Westport House, Portrush. James Simmons. PBCIP

They have fenced in the dirt road. Burial. Alice Walker. AmPA; LoHo; PrIm

They have gone into the gray hills quilled with birches. Mined Country. Richard Wilbur. ArOW

They have gone/ into the green hill. Apples. Donald Hall. LCAP

They have him squeezed into the square room. Internment. Vincent Buckley. FaBoMA

They have laid the penthouse scenes away. Elegy in a Theatrical Warehouse. Kenneth Fearing. NYBP

They have left bread on the table. Bread. Gabriela Mistral, *tr. fr. Spanish* by Allan Francovich *and* Kathleen Weaver. WPOW

They have lived in each other so long. The Demolition. Anne Stevenson. OxBSP

They have met at last — as storm-clouds. Manassas. Catherine Anne Warfield. PAH

They have no graves as yet. (*LL*) Elegy in a Country Churchyard. G. K. Chesterton. CoGr; FaBoEH; FaPoR; MoBrPo; NSI; OBWP; OxBSP; TrGrPo

They have no word for conscience. Carrier Indians. Ken Belford. NOBC

They have not gone from us. O no! they are. Our Dead. Robert Nichols. WGRP

They have not sown, and feed on bitter fruit. (*LL*) A Black Man Talks of Reaping. Arna Bontemps. BPo; CDC; PoBA; PoNe

They have [*or* They've *or* Th' have] left Thee naked, Lord, O[h] that they had! Upon the Body of Our Blessed Lord, Naked and Bloody. Richard Crashaw. InvP; NOSC; SeCP

(On Our Crucified Lord, Naked and Bloody.) HoPM; OAEL-1; OxBSP; SeCV-1; TrCP

They have put my bed beside the unpainted screen. Last Poem. Po Chü-i, *tr. fr. Chinese* by Arthur Waley. OBD

They have said evil of my dear. *Unknown, tr. fr. French* by John Addington Symonds. *Fr. Medieval Norman Song*. AWP

They have sed. Hospital/Poem. Sonia Sanchez. BPo; PoBA

They Have Taken. Gael Turnbull. NBrP

They have taken my father. They Have Taken. Gael Turnbull. NBrP

They have taken the gable from the roof of clay. Swedes. Edward Thomas. OAEL-2; RB

They have taken the maps and spread them out. Still Pond, No More Moving. Howard Moss. NYBP

They have the faces of/ no-one. (*LL*) The Animals in That Country. Margaret Atwood. NALW; NoAM; NoP

They have turned, and say that I am dying. That. I Substitute for the Dead Lecturer. Amiri Baraka. PoE

They Have Turned the Church Where I Ate God. Gary Gildner. PBCAP

They have used the bodies. For Victims. David Shapiro. BTR

They have yarns. Carl Sandburg. *Fr. People, Yes, The*. LiTA; MoAmPo

They haven't got no noses. The Song of Quoodle. G. K. Chesterton. GoJo

They hear and see, and sigh, and then they break. (*LL*) The Lowest Trees Have Tops. Sir Edward Dyer. EnRePo; FaPoB; NoSic; OPOP; OxBSP; RB

They hear Thee not, O God! nor see. Ezekiel. Whittier. ChIV-1

They heard the south wind sighing. The Crocuses. Frances E. W. Harper. BlSi

They heaved the stone; they heaped the cairn. Aideen's Grave. Sir Samuel Ferguson. NOIV

They held her south to Magellan's mouth. The Rush of the *Oregon*. Arthur Guiterman. PAH

They held up a stone. Amir Gilboa, *tr. fr. Hebrew* by Dannie Abse. PAW

They hire you for the silk to line their budgets. Advice from Euterpe. Carter Revard. VoR

They hold their hands over their mouths. The Poets Agree to Be Quiet by the Swamp. David Wagoner. CoAP; VGW

They hunt chameleon worlds with cameras. Adina. Harold Milton Telemaque. TTY

They hunt, the velvet tigers in the jungle. (*LL*) India. W. J. Turner. MoBrPo; OBAP; PDV

They hunt, the velvet tigers in the jungle. India. W. J. Turner. MoBrPo; OBAP; PDV

They hurt no one. They rove the North. In Fur. William Stafford. RFM

They in the sea being burnt, they in the burnt ship drown'd. (*LL*) A Burnt Ship. John Donne. EBEV; InPK; OBWP

They invented a kind of glass which let flies through. Progress and Retrogression. Julio Cortázar, *tr.* by Paul Blackburn. AnRep

They journeyed,/ When the darkness of night. Ibn al-Arabi, *tr. fr. Arabic* by R. A. Nicholson. AWP

They kept it all level. And low. Even. The Early Ones. William Stafford. CAPP

They Kill Us. Ron Schreiber. ETG

They killed my brothers, my children, my uncles. Obsidian Butterfly. Octavio Paz, *tr. fr. Spanish* by Eliot Weinberger. AnRep

They kneel on the slanting floor. The Foot-Washing. George Ella Lyon. CrSp; ETG

They knew the conjugations of the flesh. Emeritus, n. Henri Coulette. FF

They knew they were fighting our war. As the months grew to years. Pershing at the Tomb of Lafayette. Amelia Josephine Burr. PAH

They knew what was coming to Radom, to all the Jews. The Blue Parakeet. Julie N. Heifetz. BTR

They know how to spin a gossamer web in the void. (*LL*) Song of the Weaving Woman. Yüan Chen. SuSp

They know not of their mission from above. Cowper's Three Hares. Charles Tennyson Turner. FM

They know the time to go! Time to Go. "Susan Coolidge." GN

They laid this stone trap. The Empty Church. R. S. Thomas. AngWe

They laughed at one I loved. Innocence. Patrick Kavanagh. RB

They Lay Dying Side by Side. Anna Swirszczynska, *tr. fr. Polish* by Magnus J. Krynski *and* Robert A. Maguire. PoSu

They lean against the cooling car, backs pressed. The Discovery of the Pacific. Thom Gunn. HeIP

They lean over the path. Orchids. Theodore Roethke. CMoP; TRP

They leave us — artists, singers, all. When London Calls. Victor James Daley. CBAP

They leave us so to the way we took. In Neglect. Robert Frost. OxBSP; VGW

They left my hands like a printer's. Blackberries. Yusef Komunyakaa. NAmP90

They left the primrose glistening in its dew. Spring, and the Blind Children. Alfred Noyes. OxBTC

They left their Babylon bare. The Destruction of Jerusalem by the Babylonian Hordes. Isaac Rosenberg. PeFWW

They licked the platter clean. (*LL*) Jack Sprat could eat no fat. Mother Goose. FaBoBe; OxNR; ReMoGo

They lie at rest, our blessed dead. Christina Rossetti. NOBVV

They lie in the Sunday street. The Dead. C. Day Lewis. TwCP

They lie, the men who tell for reasons of their own. Faces in the Street. Henry Lawson. CBAP

They lied, those lying traitors all. *Unknown, tr. fr. French* by John Addington Symonds. *Fr. Medieval Norman Song*. AWP

They like to come here. Pleasant sidestreets pave. The Visitors. Richard Moore. DiPo

They live alone. Neighbors. David Allan Evans. Poetsp

They live as well as they can — the irony. The Austrians After Sadowa (1866). Michael Hofmann. SCBI

They live by the Lakes, an appropriate quarter. On the Lake Poets. Charles Townsend. FaBoEE

They live 'neath the curtain. Puk-Wudjies. Patrick R. Chalmers. BoTP

They lived out in a women's house. Stephanie Markman. *Fr.* Rime of the Ancient Feminist, The. BrRo

They locked us out without a cause. The Glorious Strike of the Builders. *Unknown*. FaBoVe

They look at each other dully. Two Quartz Pebbles. Vasco [*or* Vasko] Popa, *tr. fr. Serbo-Croatian. Fr.* Quartz Pebble, The. PoSu, *tr.* by Anne Pennington

They look like big dogs badly drawn, drawn wrong. Wolves in the Zoo. Howard Nemerov. NoAM

They look/ like newlyweds. Ryota, *tr. fr. Japanese*. TTTS

They look like shepherds moving on a plain. *(LL)* The Inca Tupac Upanqui. William Hart-Smith. NOBAu

They look up with their pale and sunken faces. Elizabeth Barrett Browning. *Fr.* Cry of the Children, The. CoGr; EBVV; FaBoEH; OBD; OxAEP-2

They looked at me all ghosts. Mellisandra. Harriet Rose. BrRo

They looked so good. The Young Fenians. Padraic Fallon. BIrV

They made her a grave too cold and damp. The Lake of the Dismal Swamp. Thomas Moore. BLPA

They made impudent inspection of our coast. Rex Ingamells. *Fr.* Great South Land, The. CBAP

They made love under bridges, lacking beds. Vagabond Love. William Plomer. IHNG

They Made Me Erect and Lone. Thoreau. OxBSP

They made packages of the human presence. Exhumation. Zoé Karélli, *tr. fr. Greek by* Rae Dalven. WoWa

They made the back part shabby. *(LL)* The Building of a New Church. *Unknown.*

They made their grim, sad faces and went out. Death of the Polar Explorers. Gabriel Gbadamosi. HBAPE

They made them idols in the elder days. Idols. Richard Burton. TrPWD

They make in the twining tide the motions of birds. The Bathers. W. S. Merwin. PoE

They make it sound easy: some disjointed. Fradel Schtok. Irena Klepfisz. ETG

They married us when they put. Drafted. Su Wu, *tr. fr. Chinese by* Kenneth Rexroth. OHMPC

They May Rail at This Life. Thomas Moore. PoEL-4

They may suppose, because I would not cloy your ear. John Berryman. NoP

They meet but with unwholesome Springs. Against Them Who Lay Unchastity to the Sex of Women. William Habington. *Fr.* Castara. BeJo; JCP; SeCP

They met in passion; Satyrs of the glade. Once. George Ives. PeHV

They might not need me; but they might. Emily Dickinson. PoToHe; Spl

They more than we are what we are. Statues. Kathleen Raine. NYBP

They mount the lonely street. *(LL)* The Lonely Street. William Carlos Williams. PoA; TwCP

They mouth love's language. Gnash. A Memory of the Players in a Mirror at Midnight. James Joyce. InvP

They move on tracks of never-ending light. The Master Singers. Rhys Carpenter. WGRP

They moved like rivers in their mended stockings. The Grandmothers. Mary Oliver. WPE

They must be muzzled in the dog days for fear they might go mad. *(LL)* Alphabetical Song on the Corn Law Bill. *Unknown.* OxBoLi

They must be shown as about to taste of the tree. Adam and Eve. C. H. Sisson. FaBoTw

They must to keep their certainty accuse. The Leaders of the Crowd. W. B. Yeats. EBEV; MoAB; MoBrPo; OxAEP-2

They Name Heaven. Bruce Weigl. NAmP90

They named it Aultgraat — Ugly Burn. Black Rock of Kiltearn. Andrew Young. FaBoTw; RB

They named the huge one Grendel. Grendel. *Unknown, tr. by* Burton Raffel. *Fr.* Beowulf. ASW, *tr. by* Kevin Crossley-Holland; NU

They never came back to me! *(LL)* Calico Pie. Edward Lear. FaBoCh; FaPON; NTP; PYC; TrGrPo

They never let him any deeper in. *(LL)* You ask me how Contempt who claims to sleep. J. V. Cunningham. ErPo; VCAP

They Never Quite Leave Us. Margaret E. M. Sangster. WBLP

They never seem to be far away. Within the Veil. Margaret E. M. Sangster. BLRP

They never wept . . . nor would. *(LL)* Listen, mad girl! for giving ear. Walter Savage Landor. CBLP

They nicknamed me Mririda. Mririda. Mririda n'Ait Attik, *tr. fr. Berber into French by* René Euloge; *English vers. by* Daniel Halpern *and* Paula Paley. AIW; WPOW

They nod at me and I at stems. Open. Larry Eigner. NeAP

They often haunt me, these substantial ghosts. The Hymn Tunes. Edward Lucie-Smith. PBCV

They only find a medicine for the itch. *(LL)* No Platonic *[or* Platonique*]* Love. William Cartwright. BeJo; ErPo; GBL; ImPo; InvP; JCP; LiTB; NOSC; OAEL-1; PoEL-2

They opn our mail petulantly. Th Wundrfulness uv th Mountees Our Secret Police. Bill Bissett. NOBC

They paddled the street as fast as rowboats can. The Flood Viewed by the Tourist from Iowa. James Whitehead. SM

They paper the walls of their world. The Recluses. Stuart Z. Perkoff. NeAP

They pass factories and pits and poverty. The Decadent Voyeurs. Tom Pickard. IHNG

They pass like a warning of snow. The Insects. Nancy Willard. LCAP

They pass me by like shadows, crowds on crowds. The Street. James Russell Lowell. AnAmPo; Son

They pass too fast. Ships, and there's time for sighing. Earth Has Shrunk in the Wash. William Empson. CMoP

They pity me./ "Look at him, see." Lonely. André Spire, *tr. fr. French by* Jethro Bithell. AWP; TrJP

They played with the pebble. The Heart of the Quartz Pebble. Vasco [*or* Vasko] Popa, *tr. fr. Serbo-Croatian. Fr.* Quartz Pebble, The. PoSu, *tr. by* Anne Pennington

They plunged — and were knocked back at the world's rim. *(LL)* Transmarine. Carol Moldaw. UTF

They pointed me out on the highway, and they said. The Traveller. John Berryman. PoA; VGW

They possessed nothing. The Inheritors. Gary Geddes. NOBC

"They pray for children? Let them!" cried Polyxo. Antipater of Thessalonica, *tr. fr. Greek by* Alistair Elliot. GrAn

They Pray the Best Who Pray and Watch. Edward Hopper. AH

They Pu'd down the steeple, and drunkit the bell. *(LL)* Ech, Sic a Pairish. *Unknown.* FaBoCo; FiBHP

They purge the air[e] without, within the breast. *(LL)* The Storm. George Herbert. ESCV; MiEL

They pursue space. Egypt. Wendy Mulford. NBrP

They pushed him straight against the wall. At Sunrise. Rosa Zagnoni Marinoni. PoToHe

They put him here because God came at night. Dementia Praecox. Morris Bishop. PoA

They put up big wooden gods. Manufactured Gods. Carl Sandburg. WGRP

They quite forgot their quarrel. *(LL)* Tweedledum and Tweedledee. Mother Goose. NOBL; OxNR; PeLV; ReMoGo

They ran through the streets of the seaport town. A Greyport Legend. Bret Harte. AnAmPo; GN

They rejected life to seek the Way. Their footprints are before us. Written on a Monastery Wall. Li Shang-yin, *tr. fr. Chinese by* A. C. Graham. PLT

They Return. Jay Macpherson. *Fr.* Way Down, The. NOBC; PoA

They rise, they walk again. *(LL)* The Heaven of Animals. James Dickey. CAPP; CoAP; EaPr; FoLa; HeIP; LiTM; MT; NAAL-2; NoAM; NOBA; PoE; TAP; TRP; VCAP

They rode north. Blackie Thinks of His Brothers. Stanley Crouch. PoBA

They roused him with muffins — they roused him with ice. The Baker's Tale. "Lewis Carroll." *Fr.* Hunting of the Snark, The. CBNP; EBEV; EBEvV, *Pt. 1 only;* FaBoNo; FiBHP, *much abr.;* NAEL-2; OBNC; OBNV; OxAEP-2; PoEL-5

They run and throb a black tattoo. Scorpions Fighting. Broughton Gingell. OBAP

They sadly travelled thus, until they came. Arthur's Fight with Orgoglio and Duessa. Spenser. *Fr.* Faerie Queene, The. EBNV

They Said. Lucy Larcom. AmWP

They said a while ago that the fuzz were coming to take us away. Moment of Truth. Rowley Habib. PeNZ

They said I got away in a boat. Bruce Ismay's Soliloquy. Derek Mahon. PNI

They said, "The Master is coming." Unawares. Emma A. Lent. PoLF

They said the moon wasn't going to rise no no. August 18. Joanne Kyger. PoM

They said there was a woman in the hills. Women Are Not Gentlemen. Harley Matthews. NOBAu

They said there were those who dig and those who blow. Snowmelt from Yesteryears. Jim Montgomery. Jaz

They said this mystery shall never cease. Blake. *Fr.* Gnomic Verses. TrGrPo

They said, "Wait." Well, I waited. Alabama Centennial. Naomi Long Madgett. BPo

They said (when they had dined at Ciro's). G. K. Chesterton. FaBoEH

They said, "You are no longer a lad." Battle Won Is Lost. Phillip William George. GrPl

They sate to meat, and Satyrane his chaunce. Spenser. *Fr.* Faerie Queene, The. OAEL-1

They saw the young girls twisting their strings, Goulburn Island. *Unknown, tr. fr. Aborigine by* Ronald M. Berndt. *Fr.* Goulburn Island Song Cycle. NOBAu

They saw you behind your muzzle much more clearly. To a Farmer Who Hung Five Hawks on His Barbed Wire. David Wagoner. NoAM

They Say. Ella Wheeler Wilcox. WBLP

They say a maiden conceived. Christmas Carols. Patricia Beer. OxBC

They say a man dies. Steve Crow. *Fr.* Songs. HATNAP

They say a wife and husband, bit by bit. A Bridge instead of a Wall. *Unknown.* PoToHe

They say dogs killed you. No, Euripides. Adaios of Macedon, *tr. fr. Greek by* Alistair Elliot. GrAn

They say, God wot! On the Death of the Giraffe. Thomas Hood. FaBoEE; OBD

They say he became deaf — but it isn't true. Beethoven. Zbigniew Herbert, *tr. fr. Polish by* John Carpenter *and* Bogdana Carpenter. AnAn

They say: He lives with colours. Sons. Jack Cope. PeSA

They say, his strange, large eyes. Father. Margit Kaffka, *tr. fr. Hungarian by* Laura Schiff. PBWP

They say I am excitable! How could. The King of Owls. Louise Erdrich. NoAM

They say I am harsh and haughty. Uncle Sam's Soliloquy. George Sands Johnson. PWR

They say I should feed you. Survivor. Barbara Goldberg. BTR

They say ideal beauty cannot enter. Hiram Powers' "Greek Slave." Elizabeth Barrett Browning. NALW

They say, in other days. John Gray. NOBVV

They say it is waiting for more, the snow. Snow Signs. Charles Tomlinson. NoAM

They say La Jac Brite Pink Skin Bleach avails not. Government Injunction. Josephine Miles. PoNe

They say Monk. Humphf. John Sinclair. Jaz

They say my majo is ugly. The Discreet Majo. Fernando Periquet Y Zuaznabar, *tr. fr. Spanish by* Philip L. Miller. RiWo

They Say My Verse Is Sad: No Wonder. A. E. Housman. NoAM

They say, old man, your horse will die. The Dead Horse. *Unknown.* AS

They say Revis found a flatrock. Mountain Bride. Robert Morgan. MT

They Say She Is Veiled. Judy Grahn. BCF; CrSp; UL

They say "Son." Old Black Men Say. James A. Emanuel. PoBA

They say that Byron, though lame. Anacreontic. Austin Clarke. NOIV

They say that every idle word. Idle Words. Walter Savage Landor. OBSV

They say that God lives very high! A Child's Thought of God. Elizabeth Barrett Browning. FaPON

They say that hope is happiness. Byron. *Fr.* Stanzas for Music. NAEL-2; OxBSP

They say that I was in my youth. *Unknown.* PeLi

They say that in some Gower glen. The Bone Prison. E. Howard Harries. AngWe

They Say That in the Unchanging Place. Hilaire Belloc. *Fr.* Dedicatory Ode. PoLF

They say that man is mighty. What Rules the World. William Ross Wallace. OHIP

They say that my music is angelic. The Master. Czeslaw Milosz, *tr. fr. Polish by the author.* AnRep

They say that plants don't talk, nor do. Rosalía de Castro, *tr. fr. Spanish by* Aliki *and* Willis Barnstone. BoWoP

They say that Richard Cory owns. Richard Cory. Paul Simon. InPK

They say that shadow[e]s of deceased ghosts. Joshua Sylvester. EIL (They Say that Shadows of Deceased Ghosts.) Son

They Say that Shadows of Deceased Ghosts. Joshua Sylvester. *See* They say that shadow[e]s of deceased ghosts.

They say that the barn owl. The Barn Owl. Jean Follain, *tr. fr. French by* W. S. Merwin. AnRep

They say that "Time assuages." Sorrow. Emily Dickinson. WGRP (They Say That Time Assuages.) OxBSP

They say that when they burned young Shelley's corpse. The Fishes and the Poet's Hands. Frank Yerby. PoNe

They say the experimental. Nothing. Burns Singer. OxBS

They say the land is full of apes, which have. Lascelles Abercrombie. *Fr.* Sale of Saint Thomas, The. NSI

They say "the lighthouse keeper's world is round." Sam Hunt. PeNZ

They say the lion and the lizard keep. Omar Khayyám, *tr. fr. Persian by* Edward Fitzgerald. *Fr.* Rubáiyát of Omar Khayyám of Naishápúr, The. AWP; EBEV; EBVV, *abr.;* FaBoBe; FaBoRV, *abr.;* FaPoR, *abr.;* HAP, *abr.;* LiTB; NAEL-2; NoP; PoEL-5; PrIm, *abr.;* TrGrPo

They say the men are. Men Are Coming Back! The. Barry Cole. OxBTC

They say the Phoenix is dying, some say dead. News of the Phoenix. A. J. M. Smith. MoCV

They say the sea is cold, but the sea contains. Whales Weep Not! D. H. Lawrence. CMoP; MeMBP; NoAM; NU

They say the Spanish ships are out. The Dragon of the Seas. Thomas Nelson Page. PAH

They say the war is over. But water still. Redeployment. Howard Nemerov. ArOW; LiTM; OBWP; PoWW; TrJP

They say the woman with the black hair. Babi Yar. Carole Glasser Langille. BTR

They say the world is round, and yet. Life's Scars. Ella Wheeler Wilcox. BLPA

They say there is. *Unknown, tr. fr. Japanese by* Arthur Waley. TAL

They Say There Is a Country. Saul Tchernichowsky, *tr. fr. Hebrew by* Ruth Finer Mintz. MHP

They say there is a land. Idaho. *Unknown.* GBP

They say there is a sweeter air. A Carriage from Sweden. Marianne Moore. HAP; LiTA; LiTM; MoAB; TwCP

They say there is no hope. Sea Gods. Hilda Doolittle ("H. D."). LiTA

They say 'tis sinful to flirt. Sinful to Flirt. *Unknown.* AmFP

They say we don't love each other. Jota. Manuel de Falla, *tr. fr. Spanish by* Philip L. Miller. RiWo

They say you have the face. Girl by the River. Federico García Lorca, *tr. fr. Spanish.* CBNP

They/ say/ you/ went/ abroad. Incidental Pieces to a Walk. James Cunningham. JB

They Say You're Staying in a Mountain Temple. Tu Fu, *tr. fr. Chinese by* Burton Watson. TTTS

They see Gods wonders that are call'd. Roger Williams. SCAP

They seem hundreds of years away. Breughel. The Seed Cutters. Seamus Heaney. *Fr.* Mossbawn: Two Poems in Dedication. CIP; PNI

They seize the young girls of the western tribes, with their swaying. *Unknown, tr. fr. Aborigine by* Ronald M. Berndt. *Fr.* Goulburn Island Song Cycle. NOBAu

They sell good beer at Haslemere. West Sussex Drinking Song. Hilaire Belloc. MoBrPo

They sent him back to her. The letter came. Not to Keep. Robert Frost. CMoP; OxBA; Poetr

They serve revolving saucer eyes. The Ex-Queen among the Astronomers. Fleur Adcock. FaBoWP; NALW

They served tea in the sandpile, together with. The Party. Reed Whittemore. CoAP

They set out to bring Beethoven. The Bringers of Beethoven. Reiner Kunze, *tr. fr. German by* Gordon Brotherston *and* Gisela Brotherston. PoSu

They set the fish upon the table. Pesci Misti. Leonard Aaronson. FaBoTw

They set the slave free, striking off his chains. The Slave. James Oppenheim. TrJP

They shall all be here one day. At the Ferry. Vijaya Mukhopadhyay, *tr. fr. Hindi.* TSaS, *tr. by* Mukhopadhyay Vijaya

They shall be thick and cloudy to my breast. (*LL*) Confession. George Herbert. ESCV; JCP

They shall bee upon one day. (*LL*) Child Waters. *Unknown.* ESPB; FaBoBa; OxBB

They shall bee upon one day. (*LL*) Child Waters. *Unknown.* ESPB, A *and* B *vers.;* FaBoBa; OBET; OxBB

They shall find him ware an' wakin', as they found him long ago! (*LL*) Drake's Drum. Sir Henry Newbolt. EBEvV; FaBoCh; FaBoEH; FaPoR; OBMV; OxBA; PoRA; UV; VPP

They shall go down unto life's borderland. Sonnet to Negro Soldiers. Joseph S. Cotter, Sr.. PoBA

They shall lie there, together. (*LL*) The Old Churchyard of Bonchurch. Philip Bourke Marston. EBVV; OBNC

They shall never sound in slavery. (*LL*) The Minstrel Boy. Thomas Moore. FaBoBe; GN; OxAEP-2; PrIm

They shall not return to us, the resolute, the young. Mesopotamia. Kipling. PoWW

They shall see Him in the crimson flush. The Pure in Heart Shall See God. Frances E. W. Harper. PWR

They shall sink under water. The Cities. "Æ." OBMV

They shook the green leaves down. Magic Fox. James Welch. CDW; HATNAP; NoAM

They shorten tedious nights. (*LL*) Now Winter Nights Enlarge. Thomas Campion. AAS; EBEV; EIL; ELP; EnRePo; NoP; NTP; OxAEP-1; TEP

They shot him on the Nine-Stane Rig. Barthram's Dirge. *Unknown.* FaBoRV

They should let it go by. (*LL*) Women. Louise Bogan. LiTA; MoAB; MoAmPo; NALW; NoAM; TwCP; VGW; WPE

They shout no stranger, troublous news. Waifs. Vivian Virtue. PBCV

They showed up for awhile and they died. Showing. Liam Rector. TRP

They shut me up in prose. Emily Dickinson. FaBoVe; InPS; NALW; NOBA

They shut the road through the woods. The Way through the Woods. Kipling. *Fr.* Rewards and Fairies. CH; CoGr; EBEvV; FaBoCh; FaPON; NoAM; NOBE; NTP; OBEV; OBNC; OxAEP-2; OxBChV; OxBTC; PFP; PlP; RFM; SCGP; WHSW

They Warned Him Then They Threw Him Away. C. K. Williams. CAPP

They was twenty men on the Cabbage Rose. The Fate of the Cabbage Rose. Wallace Irwin. FiBHP

They watched her glide across the stage. A Dark Actress — Somewhere. Blanche Taylor Dickinson. ShDr

They wear air. Naked in Borneo. May Swenson. NYBP

They wear white scarves and shawls. The Madwomen of the Plaza de Mayo. Eli W. Mandel. NOBC

They Went Forth to Battle but They Always Fell. Shaemas O'Sheel. WGRP

They Went Home. Maya Angelou. AIW; IHMS

They went to sea in a Sieve, the did. Eat Your Heart Out, Edward Lear! Roger Woddis. UV

They went to sea in a sieve, they did. The Jumblies. Edward Lear. BLPL; CBNP; ChTr; EBEV; EBEvV; FaBoBe; FaBoNo; GoJo; ImPo; LiTB; NAEL-2; OtMeF; OxBChV; OxBoLi; PeLV; PeVV; PoRA; SiSoPo; TEP; TFi; UV, sh. vers.; WiR

They Went to the Moon Mother. *Unknown, tr. fr. Zuni Indian by* Barbara Tedlock. STP

They went with axe and rifle, when the trail was still to blaze. Western Wagons. Rosemary *and* Stephen Vincent Benét *and* Stephen Vincent Benét. AiP; ImGa

They wept upon the stock exchange. (*LL*) Headlined in Heaven. Paul Grano. NOBAu

They were a lovely pack for looks. John Masefield. *Fr.* Reynard the Fox. OtMeF

They were a man's words, a ballad of an old time. James Still. MT

They Were All like Geniuses. Horace Gregory. *Fr.* Passion of M'Phail, The. NYBP

They were alone once more; for them to be. Byron. *Fr.* Don Juan. EBEV

They were at play, she and her cat. Femme et Chatte. Paul Verlaine, *tr. fr. French by* Arthur Symons. AWP; OBVE

They were beautiful, the old books, beautiful I tell you. The Old Books. Vernon Scannell. OxBC

They were both still. Lamentations. Louise Glück. BoWoP; HCAP; VCAP

They were burnt in tanks, my comrades. My Comrades. Boris Slutsky, *tr. fr. Russian by* George Reavey. PAW

They were coming across the prairie, they were galloping hard and fast. The Cattle Thief. Emily Pauline Johnson. WPOW

They were dancing as if. Glass. Takako Uchino Lento, *tr. fr. Japanese by the author.* BoWoP

They were hopeful of a curtain raiser. Because in This Sorrowing Statue of Flesh. Kenneth Patchen. NaP

They were human, they suffered. Founding Fathers, Nineteenth-Century Style. Robert Penn Warren. *Fr.* Promises. NoAM

They were, I cannot say. (*LL*) At Ballyshannon, Co. Donegal. William Allingham. FaBoPP; NOBVV

They were introduced in a grave glade. Louis MacNeice. PNI

They were just meant as covers. My Mother Pieced Quilts. Teresa Palma Acosta. MDDM; WPOW

They were like fish meal. Lead. Jayne Cortez. PoBA

They were looking for. (*LL*) Petrified Echoes. Vasco [*or* Vasko] Popa. PoSu, *tr. by* Anne Pennington

They were neither up nor down. (*LL*) The Noble [*or* Brave Old] Duke of York. *Unknown.* GBP

They were parted then at last? Winter Song. George Macdonald. NOBVV

They were sitting on the thin mattress. Wavelength. David St. John. NAmP90

They were so bad I cried. (*LL*) My Father, My Son. John Malcolm Brinnin. NYBP

They were so exceptionally well got-up for an ordinary Sunday. Love: Intimacy. C. K. Williams. CAPP

They were still young, younger than I am now. I Remember the Room Was Filled with Light. Judith Hemschemeyer. SM

They were the local Ohio palm, tropic in the heat of trains. Tree Ferns. Stanley Plumly. SM

They were the people, those who. The Broken String. *Unknown, tr. fr. Bushman by* W. H. I. Bleek. PeSA
(People were those who.) PeSAV, *sl. diff. vers.*

They were there falling. Hart Crane. AnAn

They were trying to put their poodles. Sex with Zsa Zsa and Eva Gabor. Brent Reiten. NGP

They were twa lovers dear. (*LL*) Prince Robert. *Unknown.* AmFP; ESPB, A *and* B *vers.*; OxBB

They were women then. Women. Alice Walker. GOA; WPOW

They whisper of you, Nicole. Lucilius, *tr. fr. Greek by* Sam Hamill. InMo

They whispered when she passed — gave knowing looks. The Sinner. Margaret E. Bruner. PoToHe

They who create rob death of half its stings. The Sovereigns. Lloyd Mifflin.
(Sovereign Poets.) WGRP

They who have best succeeded on the stage. Dryden. *Fr.* Conquest of Granada, The. SeCV-2

They who have the ocean as their eldest. *Unknown, tr. fr. Sanskrit.* EaPr

They who in folly or mere greed. Where Are the War Poets? C. Day Lewis. FaBoMo; OBWP; OxBSP; OxBTC; PAW

They will be telling you soon who you are. Arsenic. Howard Moss. CoAP; NYBP

They will be without arms like God. Hummingbirds. Norman Dubie. LCAP

They will blow from your mouth one morning. For the Mute. Lucille Clifton. CAPP

They will bury that fair body and cover you. Epitaph on a Young Child. Ivor Gurney. FaBoEE

They will catch me. On Hearing the Airlines Will Use a Psychological Profile to Catch Potential Skyjackers. Stephen Dunn. AmPA

They will come for you in morning. Whispers. Roberta Hill Whiteman. CDW

They will come no more. Ezra Pound *and* Noel Stock. *Fr.* Mœurs Contemporaines. UV

They will fit, she thinks. The Marriage. Anne Stevenson. NALW

They will have it. Coming to the Salt Lick. John Woods. FoLa

They will never die on that battlefield. Uccello. Gregory Corso. FF; NeAP; PoM

They will not blame me for anything. (*LL*) Sleep in the Heat. Laura Jensen. AmPA; AnAn

They will soon be down. For the Last Wolverine. James Dickey. FoLa

They will tell the spider: Go on, you're doing good work. (*LL*) A. E. F. Carl Sandburg. CMoP; MoAB; MoAmPo

They will tumble down from the rooftops. Judgement Day. Odia Ofeimun. HBAPE

They will wash all my kisses and fingerprints off you. Poem Ended by a Death. Fleur Adcock. PeNZ

They will win, I thought once. Politics. Tom Marshall. NOBC

They wished [*or* whisted] all, with fixèd face attent. Virgil, *tr. by* Henry Howard, Earl of Surrey. *Fr.* Aeneid [*or* Eneados], The. LiTB; NAWM-1; SiPS; SiPSBD

They without message, having read. Typists. P. K. Page. NALW

They Wondered Why. W. H. Auden. *Fr.* In Time of War. Son

They wondered why the fruit had been forbidden. W. H. Auden. *Fr.* Sonnets from China. ChIV-1; CMoP

They won't like that. We only have our words. (*LL*) All Friends Together. R. A. Simpson. NOBAu

They wore it walking Sunday, three small men. Spanish Blue. Herbert Morris. NYBP

They wore light dresses and their arms were bare. A Pride of Ladies. Anne Halley. NMM

They work in garages. Decoys. Leslie Norris. FoLa

They worked all night with cardboard and with wood. Reprisal. Herbert Corby. PAW

They would be as miserable as men. (*LL*) To an Old Tune. Lu Kuei Meng. OHMPC

They would have mourned him, dead. Survivor. Ruth Feldman. BTR

They would like doves and sparrows do. (*LL*) The Chaste Arabian Bird. The Earl of Rochester. ErPo

They would say that she of the neck like a duiker's. On Reading an Archeological Article. Molara Ogundipe-Leslie. HBAPE

They wouldn't bring me the food. Isolation. Martha Sansom. UnDi

They'd latch the screen doors. Sunday Afternoons. Yusef Komunyakaa. NAmP90

They'd learn more playing stickball in the street. Ghetto Summer School. Douglas Worth. FF

They'd ploughed them every one! (*LL*) The Vulture and the Husbandman. Arthur Clement Hilton. FaBoCo

They'd run like hell from in the slums. (*LL*) An Old Woman, Outside the Abbey Theater. L. A. G. Strong. FiBHP; MoBrPo

They'd spend one night, or two or three,/ But. (*LL*) They Went Home. Maya Angelou. AIW; IHMS

They'll be damned like the sinners in hell. (*LL*) The Gresford Disaster. *Unknown.* GBP; OBET

They'll be priestin' him the morra. The Priestin' of Father John. John D. Sheridan. TIRV

They'll make their boasts and brag, Sir. (*LL*) The Battle of the Kegs. Francis Hopkinson. AnAmPo; OBAL

They'll None of 'Em Be Missed. W. S. Gilbert. *See* As some day it may happen that a victim must be found.

They'll put you on the chain gang if you don't pay it all. (*LL*) Down on Penny's Farm. *Unknown.* SWP

They'll yet regret they sent Jim Jones in chains to Botany Bay. (*LL*) Jim Jones. *Unknown.* CBAP

They're all growing green in the old countrie. (*LL*) Home *or* Falmouth. W. E. Henley. GN; MoBrPo; PoLF

They're altogether otherworldly now. Grandparents. Robert Lowell. LiTM

They're at it again. Storm. Roger McGough. OTCP

They're changing guard at Buckingham Palace. Buckingham Palace. A. A. Milne. OxBChV; PDV

They're dealing in twos and threes. The Cardplayers. Peter Fallon. PeIV

They're doing a "Ring" cycle at the Met. The "Ring" Cycle. James Merrill. BAP-91

They're Dying Just the Same in Station Homesteads. Rodney Hall. *Fr.* Black Bagatelles. CBAP

They're dying off, the kerchiefed. Elegy for Bella, Sarah, Rosie, and All the Others. Sonya Dorman. GOA

They're gonna throw you, get off. (*LL*) Riding Lesson. Henry Taylor. NBLV

They're here tonight as they always are. Beasts from the Heart. Lonny Kaneko. ETG

They're hiding by the pebbles. Sea Fairies. Eileen Mathias. BoTP

They're in the hardware store. At Anfinson's in Hettinger, North Dakota. Kathleen Norris. NGP

They're more beautiful than the angels of heaven. Lennox Island. David McFadden. NOBC

They're nice — one would never dream of going over. A Healthy Spot. W. H. Auden. AiP

They're out of sorts in Sunderland. There Are Bad Times Just around the Corner. Noël Coward. NOBL

They're richer who diminish their desires. The Truly Rich. T. Urchard. PWR

They're Shifting Father's Grave. *Unknown.* CoMu

They're taking down a tree at the front door. Learning by Doing. Howard Nemerov. HAP; Poetr; TwCP; WeW

They're taking me to the gallows, mother——they mean to hang me high. Death-Doomed. Will M. Carleton. VPP

They're waiting to be murdered. Old Couple. Charles Simic. HCAP

They're with O'Leary in the grave. (*LL*) September 1913. W. B. Yeats. CMoP; FaBoPV; GTBS-P; HAP; MoP; NAEL-2; NoAM; PeIV; PoRA

They's a predjudice allus twixt country and town. Town and Country. James Whitcomb Riley. AnAmPo

They've advertised for whalermen, five hundred brave and true. Blow Ye Winds. *Unknown.* OxBSS

They've all grown up ugly, and nobody cares. (*LL*) John, Tom, and James. Charles Henry Ross. NBLV; OxBChV

They've brains the size of a man's and they like music. Dolphins. Jonathan Griffin. OBAP

They've Come. Alfonsina Storni, *tr. fr. Spanish.* BoWoP, *tr. by* Aliki *and* Willis Barnstone; WPOW, *tr. by* Marti Moody

They've found the body. After Forty Years. Carolyne Wright. BTR

They've got a brand-new organ, Sue. The New Church Organ. Will M. Carleton. PoLF

They've got a voice, with which to pay the debt. (*LL*) Bury the Great Horse. Douglas Garman. FaBoEH; UV

They've killed you. Martyrdom. Richard W. Thomas. PoBA

They've lost it, lost it. Aaron Kramer. EaPr

They've opened up a road in the jungle and found. 2976. Julia Uceda, *tr. fr. Spanish by* Willis Barnstone. BoWoP

They've paid the last respects in sad tobacco. Padraic O'Conaire — Gaelic Storyteller. F. R. Higgins. OBMV

They've put their songbird next to the window. They. Laura Mullen. BAP-90

They've putten her into prison strang. Sir Aldingar. *Unknown.* ESPB

They've turned at last! Good-by, King George. Haarlem Heights. Arthur Guiterman. PAH

Thick condensation gathers on the glass. White Launch. Andrew Crozier. VaA

Thick darkness broodeth o'er the world. The Past. Sarah Helen Whitman. AmWP

Thick dust on Paddy's lucerne, burr. Robert David Fitzgerald. *Fr.* Eleven Compositions: Roadside. FaBoMA

Thick lids of night closed upon me, The. The Souls of the Slain. Thomas Hardy. CMoP; LiTB; MeMBP; PoEL-5

Thicket of deadly nightshade, The. The Latvian Autumn. Johannes Bobrowski, *tr. fr. German by* Ruth Mead *and* Matthew Mead. PoSu

Thief, The. Abraham Cowley. *Fr.* Mistress, The. JCP

Thief, The. Josephine Jacobsen. WPE

Thief, The. Stanley Kunitz. MoAmPo; VGW

Thief, The. Abraham Linik. BTR

Thief, The. Alden Nowlan. RaBo

Thief, The. Irene F. Pawsey. BoTP

Thief. Novica Tadic, *tr. fr. Serbo-Croatian by* Charles Simic. HSix

Thief, and triply so! A. Diophanes of Myrina, *tr. fr. Greek by* Edward Lucie-Smith. GrAn

Thief became the rabbi, The. The Structural Study of Myth. Jerome Rothenberg. PoM

Thief in me is running a, The/ round in circles. Zapata & the Landlord. Alfred B. Spellman. PoBA

Thier daily bread. (*LL*) Mother. Theresa Helburn. FaPON; OHIP

Thieves, The. Robert Graves. BoLoP; CMoP; GTBS-P; LiTM; OAEL-2

Thieves, The. Martin Sorescu, *tr. fr. Romanian by* Michael Hamburger. PWE

Thieves and Whores. John Gay. *See* Who can the various city frauds recite.

Thieves' Anthology, The, *sels.* Theodore Martin.
    "I met a cracksman coming down the Strand." FaBoPa

Thieves, find some other house, worthy of robbing. An Unguarded House. Julianus of Egypt, *tr. fr. Greek by* W. S. Merwin. GrAn

Thigh-deep in sedge and marigolds. The Other Side. Seamus Heaney. CIP; PNI

Thin brown house waits with me, The. Williamstown. Jennifer Rankin. FaBoMA

Thin Façade for Edith Sitwell, A. John Malcolm Brinnin. FiBHP; NYBP

Thin fox, A/ sidled by with his stingy shadow. Dead Center. Ruth Whitman. NYBP

Thin gray banner., A. (*LL*) The Sun. Anne Sexton. NYBP; PBWP

Thin ill-natured ghost that haunts the king, A. The Nine. John Sheffield, Duke of Buckingham and Normandy. APAS

Thin in beard, and thick in purse. On Tom-o-Combe. *Unknown.* FaBoEE

Thin leaves wave on the *wu-t'ung* tree beside the well. Lonely Night in Early Autumn. Po Chü-i, *tr. fr. Chinese by* Robert Payne. TAL

Thin-legged, thin chested, slight unspeakably. Apparition. W. E. Henley. *Fr.* In Hospital. TrGrPo

Thin little leaves of wood fern, ribbed and toothed. Frederick Goddard Tuckerman. *Fr.* Sonnets. TAP

Thin Man, The. Donald Justice. SM

Thin Mary sits there. Winter Angel. Agnes Nemes Nagy, *tr. fr. Hungarian by* Hugh Maxton. PoSu

Thin mists — thick clouds — sad all day long. Tune: "Tipsy in the Flower's Shade." Li Ch'ing-chao, *tr. fr. Chinese by* Eugene Eoyang. SuSp

Thin neon light spills on the hands in the tubs, The. Night Shift at the Fruit Cannery. Ilze Mueller. LoHo

Thin Prison, The. Leslie Norris. OTCP

Thin steel in paired lines, forever mated, cuts. North Philadelphia, Trenton, and New York. Richmond Lattimore. NYBP

Thin wet sky, that yellows at the rim, A. Marshlands. Emily Pauline Johnson. NOBC

Thin wind winds off the water. Touch of Spring. John Updike. SoCa

Thin women woo each other, The. C.M. Donald. AIW

Thine be those motions strong and sanative. To Coleridge in Sicily. Wordsworth. *Fr.* Prelude [or, Growth of a Poet's Mind], The. EnRP; OAEL-2; OBNC

Thine elder that I am, thou must not cling. Sweeter Far than the Harp, More Gold than Gold. "Michael Field." OBMV; PeVV

Thine elders ask, and they will tell it thee. (*LL*) Give Ear, O Heavens, to That Which I Declare. Henry Ainsworth. AH; ChIV-1

Thine eyes I love, and they, as pitying me. Shakespeare. *Fr.* Sonnets. OxAEP-1

Thine eyes shall see the light of distant skies. To Cole, the Painter, Departing for Europe. Bryant. AiP; AmPP; EAP; TAP
(Sonnet: To an American Painter Departing for Europe.) NAAL-1

Thine Eyes Still Shined. Emerson. NOBA

Thine eyes were light; thy lips were life. (*LL*) Another for the Briar Rose. William Morris. NOBVV

Thine is a strain to read amongst the hills. To the Poet Wordsworth. Felicia Dorothea Hemans. BrRo

Thine Own. Josephine D. Henderson Heard. CBWP-4

Thine own reflection in Eternity! (*LL*) Aspiration. Adah Isaacs Menken. AAP; AmWP; CBWP-1

Thine was a brain of nature's finest mould. Charles Sumner. H. Cordelia Ray. CBWP-3

Thing, The. Theodore Roethke. CMoP

Thing about a shark is — teeth, The. About the Teeth of Sharks. John Ciardi. OBCA; ZA

Thing About Cats, The. John L'Heureux. SoCa

"Sin!/ O only fatal Woe." ESCV

"That childish thoughts such joys inspire." ESCV

Third Cycle of Love Poems, *sels.* George Barker.
  Shut the Seven Seas against Us. MoAB; MoBrPo

Third Day. Thomas Traherne. *Fr.* Meditations on the Six Days of the
  Creation. ChIV-1

Third Degree. Langston Hughes. BPo

Third Dimension, The. Denise Levertov. NeAP

Third Eclogue, The, *sels.* Michael Drayton.
  "Stay, Thames, to heare my Song, thou great and famous Flood." PoEL-2

Third Eye, The. Jay Macpherson. MoCV

Third Generation, The. Katherine Janowitz. BTR

Third House, The, *sels.* Amy Károlyi, *tr. fr. Hungarian.*

Third Jungle Book, The. Ogden Nash. OxBM

Third Light, The. Michael Longley. PNI

Third Limick. Ogden Nash. PeLi

Third Month, Night of the Seventeenth, Written While Drunk. Lu Yu, *tr.
  fr. Chinese* by Burton Watson. SuSp

Third Ode to Persephone. Robert Kelly. *Fr.* Book of Persephone, The.
  PoM

Third Person Neuter. Heather McHugh. NAmP90; PFL

Third Psalm. Anne Sexton. *Fr.* O Ye Tongues. NALW

Third Sermon on the Warpland, The. Gwendolyn Brooks. BPo

3d Sheppard Speakes This to the Rest, The. Lady Jane Cavendish *and* Lady
  Elizabeth Brackley. *Fr.* Pastorall, A. KTR

Third Song. T. Carmi, *tr. fr. Hebrew* by Ruth Finer Mintz. *Fr.* René's
  Songs. MHP

Third Song. Sir Philip Sidney. *Fr.* Astrophel and Stella. AAS; ESo, *sl.
  abr.*; GGP; HeIL, *Sonnets,* I–CVIII *and 11 Songs*; PoEL-1; Poetr;
  SCGP, *Sonnets,* I–CVIII *and 11 Songs*; SiPS, *Sonnets,* I–CVIII *and 11
  Songs*; SiPSBD, *Sonnets,* I–CVIII *and 11 Songs*

Third Wonder, The. Edwin Markham. FYAP

Third World Snapshots. John Robert Lee. PBCV

Third Ypres. Edmund Blunden. PeFWW

Thirst. Emily Dickinson. *See* We thirst at first — 'tis nature's act.

Thirst for green, because too long deprived, A. Vega. Lawrence Durrell.
  OxAEP-2

Thirst is no thing and yet it cruel can torment you. Sin. "Angelus
  Silesius," *tr. fr. German. Fr.* Cherubical Wanderer, The. GePo, *tr. by*
  George C. Schoolfield

Thirsting Tantalus doth catch at streams that from him flee, The. Horace.
  Fr. Satires. SiPSBD, *tr. by* Sir Walter Ralegh

Thirsty Earth, The. Abraham Cowley, after the Greek of Anacreon. *See*
  Thirsty earth soaks up the rain, The.

Thirsty earth soaks up the rain, The. Drinking. Abraham Cowley, after the
  Greek of Anacreon. BeJo; BLPL; FF; GGP; NOBE; OBEV; OBVE;
  OtMeF; OxAEP-1; SeCP; SeCV-1; TrGrPo
  (Anacreontic: Drinking.) 09HeIP
  (Thirsty Earth, The.) WiR

Thirsty Island. Jim Tollerud. VoR

Thirteen. Ronald Wallace. PBCAP

Thirteen Hokku, *sels.* Kaai Chigetsu, *tr. fr. Japanese* by Hiroaki Sato.

Thirteen Hokku, *sels.* Raizan, *tr. fr. Japanese* by Hiroaki Sato.

XIII. "In That proud port, which her so goodly graceth." Spenser. *Fr.*
  Amoretti. AAS; ESo, lacking epigrams I–IV; HeIL; Son

Thirteen Things about A Catheter. Edward Kleinschmidt. UnDi

Thirteen Ways of Being Looked at by a Possum. Everette Maddox. PRA

13 Ways of Eradicating Blackbirds. Mark DeFoe. BXAP

Thirteen Ways of Looking at a Blackbird. Wallace Stevens. BLPL; CMoP;
  HCAP; HeIL; HeIP; InPK; InPS; LiTM; MoP; NAAL-2; NoAM; NOBA;
  NoP; PoE; Poetr; RB; SAmP; SOTW; TAP; TFi

Thirteen Ways to Look at a Son. Stephen Knight. UnDi

Thirteen years. Wordsworth. *Fr.* Prelude [or, Growth of a Poet's Mind],
  The. EnRP; OAEL-2; OxAEP-2

13th Horse Song of Frank Mitchell (White), The. Frank Mitchell, *tr. fr.
  Navajo Indian* by Jerome K. Rothenberg *and* David P. McAllester. STP

Thirti dayes hath Novembir. The Months. *Unknown.* OxBLMV

Thirtieth Anniversary Report of the Class of '41. Howard Nemerov. HCAP

Thirtieth of November, The. Toward the Solstice. Adrienne Rich. NAAL-
  2; NoP

Thirtieth of November last, eighteen hundred and thirty, The. The
  Owslebury Lads. *Unknown.* OBET

Thirty Bob a Week. John Davidson. EBEV; EBVV; FaBoPV; FaBoTw;
  ImPo; LiTB; MeMBP; NOBE; NOBVV; OAEL-2; OBNC; OxBS;
  OxBTC

Thirty candles and one. The Birthday. Philip Dacey. AmPA

Thirty days hath November. Richard Grafton. MiEL
  (Months of the Year, The.) FaBoUs

Thirty days hath September. Mother Goose. FaBoBe; FaBoUs; OxNR;
  ReMoGo

Thirty-eight. Charlotte Smith. ECWP; NALW; WPOW

.38, The. Ted Joans. WeW

Thirty eighth year, The. Lucille Clifton. AmPA

35/10. Sharon Olds. CrSp; MDDM

34 Blues. Charlie Patton. FaBoPV

XXXIV. "Like as a ship, that through the ocean wide." Spenser. *Fr.*
  Amoretti. AAS; ESo, lacking epigrams I–IV; HeIL; NAEL-1; PoE

34. Chapter of the Prophet Isaiah, The. Abraham Cowley. ChIV-1

Thirty-nine Haiku., *sels.* Masaoka Shiki, *tr. fr. Japanese* by Burton Watson.

Thirty-nine Tanka., *sels.* Yosano Akiko, *tr. fr. Japanese* by Hiroaki Sato.

Thirty-one nights hath December. Rhyme for Remembering How Many
  Nights There Are in the Month. Justin Richardson. FaBoUs

Thirty Poems of Longing for People, *sels.* Chin Nung, *tr. fr. Chinese* by
  Jonathan Chaves.

XXXVII. "What guile [or guyle] is this, that those her golden tresses."
  Spenser. *Fr.* Amoretti. AAS; ESo, lacking epigrams I–IV; HeIL;
  NAEL-1; NoP; Son; TrGrPo

Thirty Tanka, *sels.* Shunzei, *tr. fr. Japanese* by Burton Watson.

Thirty Tanka, *sels.* Tachibana Akemi, *tr. fr. Japanese* by Burton Watson.

"Thirty," the doctor said, "three grains, each one." Felo de Se. Thomas
  Blackburn. OxBTC

Thirty-third Canto. Hans Magnus Enzensberger. *Fr.* Sinking of the Titanic,
  The. PoSu

33. Julia Alvarez. Son
  Sels.
  33 Is the Year That Jesus Christ
  He: Age Doesn't Matter When You're Both in Love
  Mother Asks What I'm Put To

Thirty-three, goodbye. Happy Birthday. Frank Bidart. HCAP; VCAP

Thirty-three Hokku, *sels.* Takarai Kikaku, *tr. fr. Japanese* by Hiroaki Sato.

33 Is the Year That Jesus Christ. Julia Alvarez. *Fr.* 33. Son

Thirty today, I saw. A Birthday Candle. Donald Justice. NYBP

Thirty-two times I went forth to my life. On My Birthday. Yehuda
  Amichai, *tr. fr. Hebrew* by Ruth Finer Mintz. MHP

Thirty-two years since, up against the sun. Zermatt: To the Matterhorn.
  Thomas Hardy. OBNC

Thirty white horses upon a red hill. Mother Goose. NTCP; OxNR
  (Riddle.) RoPo
  (Teeth and Gums.) ReMoGo

Thirty years after. A Second Attempt. Thomas Hardy. CBLP

Thirty years ago. From an Island You Cannot Name. Martín Espada. UTF

Thirty years ago: gulls keen in the blue. A Woman. Robert Pinsky. WeW

Thirty years ago we stood in rows. Invitation to a Dance. Susan
  Wallbank. AIW

Thirtyish, Irish, red-nosed carpenter, The. And the Scream. Stephen Berg.
  NAmP90

33⅓ RPM. George Economou. Jaz

This Above All. Shakespeare. *See* There, — my blessing with you [*or*
  thee]!

This above All Is Precious and Remarkable. John Wain. LiTM

This act reminds me, ge'men, under favour. John Byrom. *Fr.* Four
  Epigrams on the Naturalization Bill. NOBL

This admirable gadget, when it is. Gyroscope. Howard Nemerov. NoAM

This ae nighte [*or* ean night], this ae nighte. Lyke-Wake Dirge, The [*or*
  A]. *Unknown.* CH; ChTr; CoGr; EBEvV; FaBoCh; FaBoRV; GBP;
  HAP; HoPM; NOBE; NoP; NTP; OBEV; OtMeF; PeECV; PoEL-1;
  ScCV; TFi; WeW
  (Cleveland Lyke Wake Dirge, The.) EnSB

This afternoon as I sat. Elegy for Jack Bowman. Joseph Bruchac. CDW

This afternoon I have taken the irises. The Irises. Jeanne Foster. CrSp

This afternoon I stood on the corner. Salt Peanuts. Louis McKee. NGP

This afternoon I swam with a school of fish. Sea School. Barbara Howes.
  NYBP

This afternoon, my love, speaking to you. In Which She Satisfies a Fear
  with the Rhetoric of Tears. Sister Juana Inés de la Cruz, *tr. by* Aliki
  and Willis Barnstone. BoWoP

This Age. Raymond R. Patterson. NBV

This aimless drifting will conclude. Sun. Branko Miljkovic, *tr. fr. Serbo-
  Croatian* by Charles Simic. HSix

This Alice. Herbert Morris. PoRA

This all took place in Chinese. (*LL*) Chronicle. Mei-Mei Berssenbrugge.
  OpBo

This almost bare tree is racing. November through a Giant Copper Beech.
  Edwin Honig. NoAM; NYBP

This altar for the Gods. *Unknown, tr. fr. Greek* by Sam Hamill. InMo

This Amber Sunstream. Mark Van Doren. GoYe; LiTA

This and That. Florence Boyce Davis. FaPON

This and That. Gareth Owen. OTCP

This angel, who mediates between us. The Angel. Galway Kinnell. LCAP; NoAM

This animal, this sleek and beautiful ox ambling along the pleasant road. The Ox. Mary Morison Webster. PeSA

This antique dome the insatiate tooth of time. The Deserted Farm-House. Philip Freneau. EAP

This apartment full of books could crack open. Adrienne Rich. *Fr.* Twenty-one Love Poems. GLP

This apple tree, that once was green. The Birds of Steel. W. H. Davies. NSI

This autumn scene is worthy of the brush. Kuan Han-ch'ing, *tr. by* Jerome P. Seaton. *Fr.* Tune: "Green Jade Flute". SuSp

This autumn the days have been hot. Sitting at Night on the Moon-viewing Terrace. Yang Wan-li, *tr. fr. Chinese by* Jonathan Chaves. SuSp

This bank makes welcome citizen and foreigner. Theocritus [*or* Theokritus], *tr. fr. Greek by* Anthony Holden. GrAn

This Be Our Revenge. Saul Tchernichowsky, *tr. fr. Hebrew by* Shalom Spiegel. TrJP

This Be the Verse. Philip Larkin. NoAM

This Beast That Rends Me. Edna St. Vincent Millay. PrIm

This beast which preyed on sheep. Leonidas, *tr. fr. Greek by* Kenneth Rexroth. GrAn; PGA

This beauty that I see. James Schuyler. PoA

This bed thy center is, these walls, thy sphere [or spheare]. (*LL*) The Sun [*or* Sunne] Rising. John Donne. BoLoP; CBLP; ClHu; EBEvV; EnRePo; ESCV; FF; FHYEP; GBL; HAP; HeIL; HeIP; InPS; InvP; JCP; LiTB; MeLP; NAEL-1; NIP; NOBE; NoP; NOSC; OAEL-1; PFP; PoE; PoEL-2; Poetr; PPP; SCV; SeCP; SeCV-1; TEP; TFi; TrGrPo; WeW

This beggar maid shall be my queen! (*LL*) The Beggar Maid. Tennyson. BeLS; BoTP

This beginning of miracles did. Cana. Thomas Merton. TrCP (Once when our eyes were clean as noon, our rooms.) ChIV-2

This being a fair and peaceful day. Benediction for the Tent. *Mongol Oral Tradition, tr. by* C. R. Bawden. WTO

This biplane is the shape of human flight. The Wrights' Biplane. Robert Frost. WeW

This bird that a cat sprang loose in the house. More Joy in Heaven. Howard Nemerov. NoAM

This bird was happy once in the high trees. Boethius, *tr. fr. Latin. Fr.* Consolation of Philosophy, The. MLL, *tr. by* Helen Waddell

This birthday card. Poem for the Birthday of Huey P. Newton. Sotère Torregian. NBV

This black life. Spring Rain. William Hawkins. MoCV

This black scrap from Viet Nam. Nocturn at the Institute. David McElroy. Poetsp

This Blatant Beast was finally overcome. Saint. Robert Graves. CMoP

This bleak world alone? (*LL*) 'Tis the Last Rose of Summer. Thomas Moore. BLPA; BoNaP; ELP; NOIV; PoEL-4; WBLP

This Blessed Plot . . . This England. Shakespeare. *See* This royal throne of kings, this sceptred isle.

This blessing love gives again into our arms. (*LL*) After Making Love We Hear Footsteps. Galway Kinnell. InPS; NIP; NoAM; RaBo; VCAP

This blue-washed, old, thatched summerhouse. The Old Summerhouse. Walter de la Mare. CMoP; FaBoPP; FaBoRV; GTBS-P

This Body That You Love So Much. Barbara Angell. LPA

This bond of the prelates I pray you revoke. Now God Stand Up for Bastards. Brian Merriman, *tr. by* Arland Ussher. *Fr.* Midnight Court, The. BIrV; NOIV, *tr. by* Thomas Kinsella.

This Book Belongs to Susan Someone. David Clewell. NAmP90

This book by any yet unread. Anne Bradstreet. MDDM

This book is all that's left me now. My Mother's Bible. George Pope Morris. AnAmPo; BLRP; VPP; WBLP

This book is mine. *Unknown.* FaBoUs

This book is one thing. *Unknown.* FaBoUs; ISE, *diff. vers.*

This book, — precisely on that palace step. Browning Finds 'The Book' in the Piazza di San Lorenzo, on a Day of Buzzing and Blaze in June 1860. Robert Browning. *Fr.* Ring and the Book, The. CBCK

This book was written in order to change the world. Foreword to New Numbers. Christopher Logue. OxBTC

This Bouillabaisse a noble dish is. Thackeray. *Fr.* Ballad of Bouillabaisse, The. FaBoUs; OBEV; OBTV; OHCV; OxAEP-2

This brand of soap has the same smell as once in the big. Soap Suds. Louis MacNeice. FaBoMo; NAEL-2; NOIV; NoP; NTP; SCV

This Bread I Break. Dylan Thomas. ChIV-2; FaBoTw; TRP

This bread I break was once the oat. This Bread I Break. Dylan Thomas. ChIV-2; FaBoTw; TRP

This Bridge of Wonders is the paramount. (*LL*) Of London Bridge, and the Stupendous Sight, and Structure Thereof. James Howell. ChTr; FaBoPP

This bright burning pyre. Auvaiyar, *tr. fr. Tamil by* A. K. Ramanujan. PLW

This brilliant boy was stupidly drowned. In Memoriam, J.A.R., Drowned, East London. Guy Butler. PeSAV

This burly son of a bitch. Not Just Yet. Carter Revard. VoR

This calls for a toast. She hates. Jane Seagrim's Party. Leonard Nathan. GOYP

This came from my counsel. On the Statue of Epaminondas in Thebes. *Unknown, tr. fr. Greek by* Peter Levi. GrAn

This cankered earth, this murrain'd patch of land. King Ethelred the Unready. Bill Greenwell. BXAP

This cat was bought upon the day. The Family Cat. Roy Fuller. OxBC; TEP

This cattle shed is Heaven now. *Unknown, tr. fr. Greek by* Robin Skelton. GrAn

This Cave Is Dark. Sir Philip Sidney. *Fr.* Arcadia. SiPSBD

This cave is dark, but it had never light. This Cave Is Dark. Sir Philip Sidney. *Fr.* Arcadia. SiPSBD

This celestial seascape, with white herons got up as angels. Seascape. Elizabeth Bishop. FaBoWP; MoAB; OxBC; PPP

This child is an angel. Angel. Maxine Scates. PBCAP

This Child Is the Mother. Gloria C. Oden. BlSi

This Child ("This child, exile of hope.") Norman Rosten. TrJP

This Christmas Day you pray me sing. For Christmas Day. Luke Wadding, *tr. by* Thomas Kinsella. TIRV

This city and this country has brought forth many mayors. Good English Hospitality. Blake. *Fr.* Island in the Moon, An. CoMu (Mayors, The.) CH; CoGr

This city is made of stone, of blood, and fish. Anchorage. Joy Harjo. HATNAP

This city is the child of France and Spain. Vieux Carré. Walter Adolphe Roberts. PoNe

This clerk-work, this first January chore. A New Diary. Dannie Abse. AngWe; NoAM

This cloak of purple, Leonidas, Xerxês gives you. Imaginary Dialogue. Antiphilus, *tr. fr. Greek by* Dudley Fitts. GrAn

This clock. Clock. Valerie Worth. TLR

This coloured counterfeit that thou beholdest. Sister Juana Inés de la Cruz, *tr. fr. Spanish by* Samuel Beckett. PBWP

This Compost. Walt Whitman. AWP; LiTA; MoAmPo; NAAL-1

This concord tempers then the elements. Boethius, *tr. fr. Latin. Fr.* Consolation of Philosophy, The. MLL, *tr. by* Helen Waddell

This Configuration. John Ashbery. PRA

This consciousness that is aware. Emily Dickinson. NAAL-1

This cool night is strange. Gwendolyn B. Bennett. ShDr

This Corruptible. Elinor Wylie. MoAB; MoAmPo

This country might have. Right On: White America. Sonia Sanchez. PoBA

This Country's Needs ("This country needs more noble men.") Mrs. Henry Linden. CBWP-4

This courageous Young Lady of Norway. (*LL*) There was a Young Lady of Norway,/ Who casually sat in a doorway. Edward Lear. PeLi

This creature kneeling. November. Margaret Atwood. NOBC

This Cristial Exhibition. (*LL*) Mr. Molony's Account of the Crystal Palace. Thackeray. PeVV

This Cross-Tree Here. Robert Herrick. ChIV-2

This crowded night my people's kindling pride. The Hour. Vivian Virtue. PBCV

This Cruel Age Has Deflected Me. "Anna Akhmatova," *tr. fr. Russian by* Stanley Kunitz *with* Max Hayward. AnAn

This Dai adjusts his slipping shoulder-straps. David Jones. *Fr.* In Parenthesis. AngWe

This Dark Apartment. James Schuyler. NGP

This Dark Longing. Sylvia Kantaris. PWE

This darksome burn, horseback brown. Inversnaid. Gerard Manley Hopkins. BLPL; CMoP; EnVR; FaBoPP; FaBoVe; GTBS-P; ImPo; LiTB; LiTM; MeMBP; MoAB; MoBrPo; NoAM; OAEL-2; PeVV; PoRA; RB; SCGP; TFi; UnPo

This dawn he rose early again. Shooting the Horses. Pamela Mordecai. PBCV

This Day. Hildegarde Flanner. WPE

This Day. Kevin Hart. FaBoMA

This Day. Lawrence Raab. NoP

This Day Be with Me. George Macdonald. *Fr.* Diary of an Old Soul. TrCP

This day beginning to a creature gave. On Her Own Birthday. Judith Madan. ECWP

This day day dawes. The Lily-white Rose. *Unknown.* MeEL

This day for our new navigation. The New Navigation. John Freeth. OBET

This day, I think, will be a common day. Help Me Today. Elsie Robinson. PoToHe

This day is called the Feast of Crispian. Shakespeare. *Fr.* King Henry V. EBEvV; FaBoEH
  (Henry V before Agincourt.) FaPoR
  (St. Crispin's Day.) FF

This day is for Israel light and rejoicing. A Sabbath of Rest. Isaac Luria, *tr. fr. Hebrew* by Nina Davis Salaman. TrJP

This day is our last! (*LL*) Jamaican Bus Ride. A. S. J. Tessimond. OBTV; OxBTC

This Day is Thine. Verna Whinery. BLRP

This day of all our days has done. Byron. FaBoEE

This day the children of Speakthunder. In My Lifetime. James Welch. CDW

This day, twice as long as the same day in Sheffield, Vermont. December Day in Honolulu. Galway Kinnell. AnAn

This Day, under My Hand. David Malouf. CBAP

This day, whate'er the Fates decree. Stella's Birthday; March 13, 1726/27. Swift. NAs; NoP; OAEL-1; PoE; PoEL-3; SCGP

This day when I lay my hope aside. This Day. Hildegarde Flanner. WPE

This day/ Whenever I pause. Death Town. Anne Carson. *Fr.* Life of Towns, The. BAP-90

This day will be remembered by America's noble sons. The Battle of Bull Run. *Unknown.* AmFP

This day winding down now. Prologue. Dylan Thomas. AngWe; MeMBP
  (Author's Prologue.) ChIV-1

This day writhes with what? The Ultimate Poem Is Abstract. Wallace Stevens. PoA

This day's a riddle; for the God that made. Upon the Day of Our Saviour's Nativity. Francis Quarles. NOSC

This dead street never stops! (*LL*) Crossing the Atlantic. Anne Sexton. NoAM

This Decoration. Hayden Carruth. NNaP

This definition poetry doth fit. Thomas Randolph. FaBoEE

This delightful young man. Heine, *tr. fr. German* by Ezra Pound. *Fr.* Heimkehr, Die. AWP

This desert is a plateau of light. The Language of Fossils. Anita Endrezze-Danielson. HATNAP

This despicable earth. (*LL*) No, Love Is Not Dead. Robert Desnos. UnAS

This Dim and Ptolemaic Man. John Peale Bishop. LiTA; LiTM

"This dining table will be great," she says. Moving to Her New House. Nellie Wong. ETG

This dirty little heart. Emily Dickinson. PoEL-5

This divine October afternoon I would like. Pain. Alfonsina Storni, *tr. fr. Spanish* by Merrilee Antrim. WPOW

This Do in Remembrance of Me, *sels.* Horatius Bonar.
  "Here, O my Lord, I see Thee face to face." TrPWD

This downhill path is easy, but there's no turning back. (*LL*) Amor Mundi. Christina Rossetti. MeMBP; NoP; PoEL-5; Poetr

This drawing/ came/ from subtle hands. On the Portrait of a Girl. Erinna, *tr. fr. Greek* by Lenore Mayhew. GrAn

This dread is like a calm. Winter Holding off the Coast of North America. N. Scott Momaday. CDW

This dreadful, dark and dismal day. Frankie Silvers. Frances Silvers. AmFP

This dream the world is having about itself. Vocation. William Stafford. CAPP

This dry night unusual. The War Horse. Eavan Boland. BIrV; CIP; PBCIP

This dust was Timas. The Dust of Timas. Sappho, *tr. fr. Greek* by E. A. Robinson. AWP

This early May morn when there is none to wed. (*LL*) The Cherry Trees. Edward Thomas. NAEL-2; OBWP; PeFWW; Spl

This earth is not the steadfast place. William Vaughn Moody. *Fr.* Gloucester Moors. AnAmPo; NOBA; OxBA; WGRP

This earth Pythonax and his brother hides. On Two Brothers. Simonides, *tr. fr. Greek* by W. H. D. Rouse. AWP

This Earthen Body. *Gond Oral Tradition, tr.* by V. Elwin *and* S. Hivale. WTO

This Easter, Arthur Winslow, less than dead. Death from Cancer. Robert Lowell. *Fr.* In Memory of Arthur Winslow. TwCP

This Edward in the April· of his age. Michael Drayton. *Fr.* Piers Gaveston. PeHV

This endless gray-roofed city, and each heart. London Despair. Frances Cornford. OBMV

This Endris Night. *Unknown.* EBEV; NOCV

This endsaying — moon pried loose. The Goodbye. Myra Sklarew. GOYP

This England. Shakespeare. *Fr.* King Richard II. BoTP; TrGrPo

This England never did, nor never shall. Shakespeare. *Fr.* King John. OxAEP-1

This Englishwoman. Stevie Smith. *See* This Englishwoman is so refined.

This Englishwoman is so refined. Stevie Smith. FaBoEE
  (This Englishwoman.) NALW

This evening holds her breath. Winter Night. C. Day Lewis. PoA

This evening I prepared Wardance Soup. Wardance Soup. Phillip William George. VoR

This evening, my love, even as I spoke vainly. Sister Juana Inés de la Cruz, *tr. fr. Spanish* by Judith Thurman. *Fr.* Satirical Romance, A. PBWP; VBLP

This evening the cuckoo and the corncrake. Seamus Heaney. *Fr.* Glanmore Sonnets. IPY

This evening with the breeze. My Mother at Evening. Harry Humes. NGP

This Excellent Machine. John Lehmann. OxBTC

This existence has, without the azure sphere, no reality. Sarmèd the Yahud, *tr. fr. Persian* by David Shea. TrJP

This expanse that spreads its nostrils wide. Shepherd. Avraham Shlonsky, *tr. fr. Hebrew* by Ruth Finer Mintz. MHP

This fabulous shadow only the sea keeps. (*LL*) At Melville's Tomb. Hart Crane. HAP; MoAmPo; MoP; NAAL-2; NoAM; NoP; PoA; TAP; UnPo; VGW

This face had no use for light, took none of it. Made Shine. Josephine Miles. NoAM

This fairest lady, who, as well I wot. Sonnet: Death Is Not without but within Him. Cino da Pistoia, *tr. fr. Italian* by Dante Gabriel Rossetti. AWP

This fairest one of all the stars, whose flame. Ballata: One Speaks of the Beginning of His Love. *Unknown, tr. fr. Italian* by Dante Gabriel Rossetti. AWP

This fall you will taste carrots. Digging In. Marge Piercy. CAPP

This far out in the country no one is talking. Starting a Pasture. Walter McDonald. MT

This Fast-Paced, Brutal Thriller. Vijay Seshadri. UTF

This feast-day of the sun, his alter there. The Hill Summit. Dante Gabriel Rossetti. *Fr.* House of Life, The. NoP; PFP

This Feast of the Law. *Unknown, tr. fr. Hebrew* by Israel Zangwill. TrJP

This fellow grazed his woolly goats. The Damned. A. R. Ammons. BAP-90

This field-grass brushed our legs. In the Field. Richard Wilbur. NAAL-2; NYBP

This field is almost white with stones. Stones. Charles Hamilton Sorley. NSI

This field of stones, he said. In a Christian Churchyard. James Thomson ("B.V."). NOBVV

This final drouth of penitential tears? (*LL*) John Sutter. Yvor Winters. MoAmPo; MoP; NoAM; NOBA

This first day of the year. On the Circumcision: New Year's Day. Luke Wadding. NOIV

This fisher, netted like a fish. On Naucratius, Brother of St. Basil. Gregory of Nazianzus, Saint, *tr. fr. Greek* by Robin Skelton. GrAn

This flat city shortly after dawn. Aimé Césaire, *tr. fr. French* by Ellen Conroy Kennedy. *Fr.* Return to the Native Land, A. NegPo

This flattering glass, whose smooth face wears. On His Mistress Looking in a Glass. Thomas Carew. CaPo

This flickering at night. Little Testament. Eugenio Montale, *tr. fr. Italian* by William Arrowsmith. AnAn

This Flock So Small. Anna Nitschmann, *tr. fr. German* by Sheema Z. Buehne. AH

This flying angel's torrent cry. Eastern Tempest. Edmund Blunden. MoBrPo

This, for my soul's peace, have I heard from Thee. *Unknown, tr. by* Sir Edward Arnold. *Fr.* Bhagavad-Gita, The. TAL

This Form of Life Needs Sex. Allen Ginsberg. NNaP

This formula for drawing comic rabbits made. (*LL*) Epitaph on an Unfortunate Artist. Robert Graves. FaBoEE; NOBL

This from that soul incorrupt whom Athens had doomed to the death. The Reply of Socrates. Edith M. Thomas. WGRP

This frontier post brings me sorrow. Wang Ts'an, *tr. by* Ronald C. Miao. *Fr.* Seven Poems of Lament. SuSp

This fugitive between the Earth and Sky. Tu Fu, *tr. fr. Chinese* by Robert Payne. TAL

This fugue must be hummed, found. Dumb Dick. Leslie A. Fiedler. ErPo

This furnish't Ark presents the greedy view. Francis Quarles. *Fr.* Emblems. ESCV

This garden does not take my eyes. The Garden. James Shirley. BeJo; NOSC

This garden is outlandish. The Women's Jail. Miriam Waddington. NOBC

This ghoul-haunted woodland of Weir. (LL) Ulalume. Poe. AmPP; AnAmPo; AWP; BLPL; ImPo; LiTA; MeMAP; NOBA; OxBA; TAP

This gift, her gold-hemmed saffron gown. Phalaicus, tr. fr. Greek by Peter Jay. GrAn

This girl all in white is my crystal of light. Francis Warner. OxBM

This girl child speaks five words. Seventeen Months. Carl Sandburg. ArLo

This girl/ Waits at the corner for. Girl, Boy, Flower, Bicycle. M. K. Joseph. PeNZ

This girlchild was born as usual. Barbie Doll. Marge Piercy. CAPP; NIP; Poetr

This golden head has wit in it. I live. George Meredith. Fr. Modern Love. NOBVV

This Golden Summer. Robert Lowell. NoP

This grandson of fishes holds inside him. Evolution from the Fish. Robert Bly. MoP; NoAM; NOBA

This great Grandmother of all creatures bred. Mutability Claims to Rule the World. Spenser. Fr. Faerie Queene, The. NoSic

This great oppressing Ninus dead, and gone. Semiramis. Anne Bradstreet. Fr. Foure Monarchies, The. KTR

This grove is too secret: one thinks of murder. The Grove beyond the Barley. Alden Nowlan. MoCV

This guy on t.v. The Electric Cop. Victor Hernandez Cruz. PoBA

This hand? Poquito Allá. Carmen Tafolla. AfAz

This handless clock stares blindly from its tower. A Clock in the Square. Adrienne Rich. HeIP

This handwriting wears itself away. Valerio Magrelli, tr. fr. Italian by Dana Gioia. NeIt

This happy place with all delights abounds. James Thomson and David Mallet. Fr. On Beauety. UV

This harpie with dry red curls. Red Dust. Philip Levine. NNaP; NoAM

This has nothing to do with eating. The Meal. Martha Sansom. UnDi

This haunted heart doesn't fit. Betrayal. Léon Laleau, tr. fr. French by Ellen Conroy Kennedy. Fr. Black Music. NegPo

This having learnt, thou hast attaind the summe. Milton. Fr. Paradise Lost. EPCY; SCV

This He was then. The Carpenter. Mary Brent Whiteside. TrCP

This heavenly harbor at last? (LL) In Harbor. Paul Hamilton Hayne. AnAmPo

This helmet, I suppose. Arac's Song. W. S. Gilbert. Fr. Princess Ida. FiBHP

This Hermit good lives in that wood. Samuel Taylor Coleridge. Fr. Rime of the Ancient Mariner, The. BeLS; CH; EBEV; EBNV; EnRP; FaBoBe; FaBoCh; FaBV; FaPoB; FHYEP; HAP; HeIP; HoPM; ImPo; InPS; LiTB; MeMBP; NOBE; NoP; OAEL-2; OBEV; OBNV; OtMeF; OxAEP-2; PeECV; PoE; PoEL-4; Poetr; PrIm; SCGP; TEP; TFi; TOF, abr.; TrGrPo

This high-caught hooded Reason broods upon my wrist. The Falcon and the Dove. Sir Herbert Read. FaBoMo

This high-way. March of the Three Kings. Unknown. OHIP

This highest scholar in the school of sin. Sir Francis Hubert. Fr. Life and Death of Edward II, The. NOSC

This holy night in open forum. Office Party. Phyllis McGinley. OBSV

This home of Thine, have we called for it? (LL) Great Hymm. Ntsikana Gaba. PeSAV

This honest wife, challenged at dusk. With Her Lips Only. Robert Graves. OxBM

This horrible but superb painting. The Parable of the Blind. William Carlos Williams. LCAP; SAmP

This Hour. Oliver La Grone. PoNe

This hour was set the time for heaven's descent. Twilit Revelation. Léonie Adams. MoAB; MoAmPo

This Houre Her Vigill. Valentin Iremonger. CIP; NOIV; OxBTC

This House. Ray A. Young Bear. CDW

This house cannot be handed down. Usufruct. Austin Clarke. IPY

This house has been far out at sea all night. Wind. Ted Hughes. NAEL-2; Poetr

This house is a wreck said the children. The Sad Children's Song. Grace Paley. SoSe

This house is haunted, this house is haunted. Calliope. Unknown. AS

This Humanist Whom No Beliefs Constrained. J. V. Cunningham. InPK

This I admit, Death is terrible to me. Pure Death. Robert Graves. AWP; GTBS-P; MoAB

This I ask Thee — tell it to me truly, Lord! The Sacred Book. At. to Zoroaster, tr. fr. Persian by A. V. Williams Jackson. AWP (Zoroaster Devoutly Questions Ormazd.) WGRP

This I beheld, or dreamed it in a dream. Opportunity. Edward Rowland Sill. AnAmPo; BLPL; GN; WGRP

(Broken Sword, The.) PoToHe

This I know, how love begins to be. Albrecht von Johannsdorf, tr. fr. German by M. L. Richey. GePo

This I know to be my way. Azimuth. Unknown. NBrP

This I would like to be — braver and bolder. Lord, Make a Regular Man out of Me. Edgar A. Guest. BLPA; BLPL

This idiotic me is left alone to enjoy this solitude. Questing-for-Spring Arbor. Huang Ching-jen, tr. fr. Chinese by Chang Yin-nan and Lewis C. Walmsley. SuSp

This, if Japanese. Thyme Flowering among Rocks. Richard Wilbur. EOEF; LCAP

This ignorance upon my tongue. On Reading Aloud My Early Poems. John Williams. WeW

This impartial dog's nose. The Passport Officer. Basil Bunting. IHNG

This Imperial city. Vienna. Peter Porter. OBTV

This Indian weed, that once did grow. Tobacco. Philip Freneau. TAP

This institution,/ perhaps one should say enterprise. Marriage. Marianne Moore. NALW; NOBA

This introspective exile here today. Desmond O'Grady. Fr. Lines in a Roman Schoolbook. PBCIP

This iridescent coal. (LL) Long Time Coming. Daphne Marlatt. VBLP

This is a beautiful way). (LL) Who Are You, Little I. E. E. Cummings. LPA; NYBP

This is a brave night to cool a courtesan. The Fool's prophecy. Shakespeare. Fr. King Lear. CBNP

This is a busy corner. Near Roscoe and Coldwater. Amy Uyematsu. OpBo

This is a common plantain, the simple weed. Ground Hog Lock. Gerald Stern. AnAn

This is a corner of heaven here. In Carpenter's Woods. Gerald Stern. CAPP

This is a country where there are no mountains. Morning on the St. John's. Jane Cooper. NYBP

This is a damned inhuman sort of war. Unseen Fire. Ralph Nixon Currey. OBWP; OxBTC; PoWW

This is a day to celebrate can-openers. The Cast Off. Marge Piercy. NoAM

This is a dream of Winter, sweet as Spring. (LL) Swedes. Edward Thomas. OAEL-2; RB

This Is a Fatherland to Me. Joseph Cephas Holly. AAP

This is a fearful thing to bear. Horror. Peter Baum, tr. fr. German by Jethro Bithell. AWP

This is a hard life you are living. Album. Josephine Miles. FaBoWP

This is a journey to Egypt. Loba as Kore in the Labyrinth of Her Beauty/ The Loba Seeks the Mother, in the Infinite Reaches of Night. Diane Di Prima. Fr. Loba. SRLS

This is a morning to say something. Morning to Remember, A; or, E Pluribus Unum. Edward Dorn. NoAM

This is a new sort of poem. Buy One Now. D. J. Enright. NOBL

This is a nice vase that's so very Greek. Ode on a Grecian Urn. Edward Abbott Parry. BXAP

This Is a Photograph of Me. Margaret Atwood. NALW; NoAM; NoP; Poetr

This is a place of ease. Marion Strobel. PoA

This is a place where a door might be. A Door. W. S. Merwin. CAPP

This Is a Poem for the Dead. Michael Ryan. AmPA

This Is a Poem for the Fathers and for Michael Ryan. Thomas Lux. AmPA

This is a poem like a suitcase. Wedding Preparations in the Country. David St. John. LCAP

This is a poem. Take it. Pack it up. Notes to the Reader. Robert Bringhurst. NOBC

This is a poem to my son Peter. Peter Meinke. PBCAP

This is a pool which bears deep looking into. A Pool. Thomas Whitbread. NYBP

This is a quiet sector of a quiet front. A Letter from Aragon. John Cornford. OBWP

This is a sailor's grave, while opposite. Unknown, tr. fr. Greek by Peter Jay. GrAn

This is a silence. Arabesque. Fred Johnson. PoBA

This is a 16mm film of 7 minutes in which no words are spoken. Treatment. C. D. Wright. Jaz

This is a small boy. Reading a Story to My Child. Primus St. John. ETG

This is a song for you about you. Song for Jeannie. William Tremblay. Jaz

This is a song to celebrate banks. Bankers Are Just like Anybody Else, except Richer. Ogden Nash. IHNG; LiTA

This is a spray the bird clung to. Misconceptions. Robert Browning. EnVR; OBEV

This is a story Jung would understand. Candelaria and the Sea Turtle. Gladys Cardiff. HATNAP

This is a story my father told to me. *Tsa'lagi* Council Tree. Gladys Cardiff. HATNAP

This is a strange museum. In one square yard see. In a Country Museum. Patricia Beer. FaBoWP

This is a symbol of beauty (you continue), Hilda Doolittle ("H. D."). *Fr.* Tribute to the Angels. NALW

This is a tomb, no corpse within. On Lot's Wife Turned to Salt. Agathias, *tr. fr. Greek by* Dudley Fitts. GrAn

This is a white. Imperial Thumbprint. Tom Weatherly. PoBA

This is a wild land, country of my choice. Rocky Acres. Robert Graves. LiTB; MeMBP; NoAM; UnPo

This is a word we use to plug. Variations on the Word *Love*. Margaret Atwood. NoAM

This is about the summer and the wheels of sleep. The Salt Pork. Robert Clayton Casto. HeIP

This Is about the Way It Should Be. Luis Omar Salinas. AfAz

This is about the women of that country. The Women in Vietnam. Grace Paley. NMM

This is all the life there is. Palladas, *tr. fr. Greek by* Kenneth Rexroth. PGA

This Is an African Worm. Margaret Danner. BPo

This is an ancient pattern on these hills. American Vineyard. Mildred Cousens. GoYe

This is an animal without shape, the strongest of all, three-fourths of him muscles. The Enanglom. Henri Michaux, *tr. fr. French by* Richard Ellmann. AnRep

This is an old and very cruel god. Vicarious Atonement. Richard Aldington. MoBrPo

This is an old fiction of reliability. Affections Must Not. Denise Riley. NBrP; VBLP

This is Anacreon's grave. Here lie. Antipater of Sidon, *tr. fr. Greek by* Robin Skelton. GrAn; OBD

This is Ancona, yonder is the sea. *(LL)* The Guardian-Angel. Robert Browning. PeECV

This is Avram the cello-mender. A Son of the Romanovs. Louis Simpson. OxBC

This is awkward I apologise. Bird-Woman. Rachel McAlpine. PeNZ

This is before electricity. Game after Supper. Margaret Atwood. FaBoWP; LCAP

This is before I'd read Nietzsche. Before Kant or Kierkegaard, even before. The Gas Station. C. K. Williams. CAPP; VCAP

This is Callaeschrus' empty tomb. Argentarius, *tr. fr. Greek by* Fleur Adcock. GrAn

This is Campidojo, whaur Titus ran. Campidoglio. Robert Garioch, *after* Giuseppe Belli. OBVE

This is Charing Cross. Ford Madox Ford. *Fr.* Antwerp. PeFWW

This is dedicated to Merry Clayton, Cissy Houston, Vonetta Washington. The Black Back-Ups. Kate Rushin. Jaz

This Is Disgraceful and Abominable. Stevie Smith. IHNG

This is earthquake. Today. Langston Hughes. GLP; VGW

This Is England. Laurence Binyon. BoTP

This is Erinna's sweet *oeuvre*, but small. Colophon to a Roll of Erinna's Poems. Asclepiades, *tr. fr. Greek by* Lee T. Pearcy. GrAn

This is eternity. *(LL)* What Are Years? Marianne Moore. BLPL; CMoP; LiTA; MeMAP; MoAB; MoAmPo; MoP; NoAM; NOBA; OxBA; SoSe; TrGrPo

This is for the woman with one black wing. Sonnet in Primary Colors. Rita Dove. NAmP90

This is genuine coin of the realm. Bogart in the Dumb Waiter. Ken Smith. PWE

This is God's will, for you and me. *(LL)* God's Will for Us. *Unknown.* BLRP; WBLP

This is hard to say. The Old Words. David Wagoner. ArLo

This is he — Arion — / the Grecian Caruso. Arion. Zbigniew Herbert, *tr. fr. Polish by* Czeslaw Milosz *and* Peter Dale Scott. AnRep

This is her picture as she was. The Portrait. Christina Rossetti. OHCV

This is Hill 49, an arena for bad dreams. The Tin Woodsman. Paulette Jiles. NOBC

This is how death. Testimony. Jane Flanders. CrSp

This is how it was. At the Movie: Virginia, 1956. Ellen Bryant Voigt. NoAM

This is how snowflakes play about. A Finger Play for a Snowy Day. *Unknown.* BoTP

This is idle fyno. *(LL)* Fara Diddle Dyno. *At. to* Thomas Weelkes. CBNP; EiL; FaBoCh; FaBoCo; FaBoNo

This is idle idle fyno. *(LL)* Idle Fyno. *Unknown.* ChTr; PoEL-2

This is it and so: so long. P.O.E. Lincoln Kirstein. PoWW

This is Izieu during the war, Izieu and the neighboring. Carolyn Forché. *Fr.* Angel of History, The. BTR

This is joye, this is true pleasure. Verses by the Princess Elizabeth, Given to Lord Harington, of Exton, Her Preceptor. Elizabeth, Queen of Bohemia. KTR

This Is Just to Say. William Carlos Williams. FF; GoJo; HeIP; HoPM; InPK; InPS; NAAL-2; NIP; NoAM; NOBA; NoP; NTP; PFP; Poetr; SOTW; TAP; TRP

This is Mab, the mistress-fairy. Mab the Mistress-Fairy. Ben Jonson. *Fr.* Satyr, The. EiL
(Mab.) WiR

This is Mister Beers. Mister Beers. Hugh Lofting. FaPON

This is Morgan's country: now steady, Bill. Morgan's Country. Francis Webb. FaBoMA

This is my creed: To do some good. My Creed. Samuel Ellsworth Kiser. PoToHe

This is my curse, Pompous, I pray. J. V. Cunningham. HAP

This is my father. My Wicked Wicked Ways. Sandra Cisneros. ETG

This Is My Father's World. Maltbie D. Babcock. AH; BLRP

This is my home. *(LL)* My Home. Ludwig Rellstab. RiWo

This is my last affair. *(LL)* Last Affair: Bessie's Blues Song. Michael S. Harper. HCAP; LCAP

This is my last cry. For Stephen Dixon. Zack Gilbert. PoBA

This is my letter to the world. Emily Dickinson. AmPP; HeIP; MeMAP; MoP; NAAL-1; NALW; NoAM; NOBA; OxBA; Poetr; SAmP; SCV; TAP; WPE

This is my mule, a poor long-suffering hack. Palladas, *tr. fr. Greek by* Tony Harrison. GrAn

This is my page for English B. *(LL)* Theme for English B. Langston Hughes. HCAP; MoP; NIP; NoAM; NOBA; NoP; Poetr

This is my play's [*or* plays] last scene, here heavens appoint. John Donne. *Fr.* Holy Sonnets. EBEV; ESCV; FaBoVe; JCP; MeLP; SeCP; Son; TEP

This is my portrait of Joanna — since the split. The Seed-Picture. Medbh McGuckian. PNI

This Is My Rock. David McCord. FaPON; NTCP; PDV; TLR

This is my task: to move five cocoons. The Sleep of the Painted Ladies. Nancy Willard. LCAP

This is my wolf. He sits. The Appointment. Maxine W. Kumin. NMM

This is my work so. Ann Bell. FaBoVe

This is newness: every little tawdry. New Year on Dartmoor. Sylvia Plath. FaBoWP

This Is No Case of Petty Right or Wrong. Edward Thomas. NSI; PeFWW; PoWW

This is no lif, alas, that I do lede. *Unknown.* MiEL

This is no poet's heaven. Colophon for Lan-t'ing Hsiu-hsi. John Peck. AmPA

This is no proper route for middle-age. Stringer's Field. Roy McFadden. PNI

This is no rune nor riddle. Hilda Doolittle ("H. D."). *Fr.* Tribute to the Angels. InPS
(This is no rune nor symbol.) NALW, *sl. diff.*

This is no rune nor symbol. Hilda Doolittle ("H. D."). *See* This is no rune nor riddle.

This is no white man lan.' Starvation and Blues. Edward Kamau Brathwaite. PBCV

This is no wood for me to walk. Forest. Harriet Gray Blackwell. GoYe

This is none of I! *(LL)* There was an old [*or* little woman], as I've heard tell. Mother Goose. MoShBr

This is Not a Poem but a Proem. Edward Vincent Swart. PeSAV

This is not a poem but a proem. I want to be in the wide. This is Not a Poem but a Proem. Edward Vincent Swart. PeSAV

This is not all I would have said. Arlington Cemetery Looking toward the Capitol. Winthrop Palmer. GoYe

This Is Not Death. Humbert Wolfe. MoBrPo

This is not I. I had no body once. Naked Girl and Mirror. Judith Wright. NALW

This is not poetry, he said. Some Tips on Watching Birds. Deatt Hudson. NYBP

This is not real: this is the shape of a dream spun. Grant Wood's American Landscape. Winfield Townley Scott. GOA

This is not sorrow, this is work: I build. The Tomb of Lt. John Learmonth, A.I.F. John Manifold. CBAP; FaBoMA; PAW

This is not the language of reconciliation. Row. Anne Rouse. NWP

This is not the man that women choose. Act of Love. Vernon Scannell. ErPo

This is not what I meant to keep. Souvenir. Naomi Long Madgett. NBV

This is not yet my poem. Poem of Alienation. Antonio Jacinto, *tr. fr. Portuguese by* Michael Wolfers. PeSAV

This is the light of the mind, cold and planetary. The Moon and the Yew Tree. Sylvia Plath. CoAP; FaBoMo; FaBoWP; NaP; NYBP; PlP; PPP; VGW; WPE; WPOW

This is the light we dream in. Negatives. Charles Wright. PoA

This is *The Making of America in Five Panels. Empire Builders.* Archibald MacLeish. OxBA

This is the man — all shaven and shorn. *Unknown. Fr.* Political House that Jack Built, The. FaBoEH

This is the meadow of the mind. A Way of Keeping. Nancy Willard. IHMS

This is the metre Colombian. The Metre Colombian. *Unknown.* BXAP; UV

This is the midnight — let no star. The Storm Cone. Kipling. NoAM; OxBTC

This is the month the nightingale, clod-brown. The Nightingale. John Clare. EBVV

This is the most audacious landscape. The gangster's. Alloy. Muriel Rukeyser. NoAM

This is the most ridiculous womb! Womb Song. Susan Fromberg Schaeffer. IHMS

This is the mouth-filling song of the race/ that was run by a Boomer. The Sing-Song of Old Man Kangaroo. Kipling. FaPON

This is the needle that we give. Magda Goebbels. W. D. Snodgrass. ArOW

This is the night I come to my room. The Anniversary. David Bottoms. ArOW

This is the night mail crossing the border. The Night Mail. W. H. Auden. ChTr; GrPl; OxBTC

This is the night of Halloween. *Unknown.* ISE

This is the one song everyone. Siren Song. Margaret Atwood. *Fr.* Songs of the Transformed. HAP; NIP; PoA; WeW

This is the only thing that clarifies my life. Days of 1978. Gerald Stern. CAPP

This is the part where after a few minutes. Rapt. Irene McKinney. PBCAP

This is the place: be still for a while, my high-pressure steamboat! Nauvoo. Bayard Taylor. OBAL

This is the place. Even here that dauntless soul. William Blake (To Frederick Shields, on His Sketch of Blake's Work-room and Death-room, 3 Fountain Court, Strand). Dante Gabriel Rossetti. EPCY

This is the place I love. Here I belong. Mountain Creed. Medora C. Addison. GoYe

This is the place, I was told. Certainty. John B. Keane. PeIV

This Is the Place to Wait. Horace Gregory. *Fr.* Passion of M'Phail, The. MoAmPo

This is the place/ Where far from the unholy populace. In a Meadow. John Swinnerton Phillimore. OBEV

This is the place/ you would rather not know about. Notes towards a Poem That Can Never Be Written. Margaret Atwood. NOBC

This Is the Poem I Never Meant to Write. Colleen J. McElroy. BCF

This is the poetry reading. Before the Poetry Reading. Louis Simpson. OxBC

This is the point when we are innocent. In Perfect Time. Dinah Livingstone. DT

This is the prettiest motion. To a Lady That Desired Me I Would Bear My Part with Her in a Song. Richard Lovelace. CaPo

This is the profession that never will alter. (*LL*) The Careless Good Fellow. John Oldham. APAS; SeCV-2

This is the realm no man dares. The World Looks On. Louis I. Newman. PoNe

This is the repugnant part, where now. Lasting Influence. Susan Wheeler. BAP-91

This is the river that flows through this land. (*LL*) The River That FLows through Our Land. Jeremy Cronin. PeSAV

This is the river that had to be dammed. Pentagonia. G. E. Bates. NYBP

This is the road I tread today. The Death of Moses. *Unknown, tr. fr. Hebrew* by Alice Lucas. TrJP

This Is the Shape of the Leaf. Conrad Aiken. *Fr.* Priapus and the Pool. CMoP; NOBA; OxBA; TrGrPo

This is the ship of pearl, which, poets feign. The Chambered Nautilus. Oliver Wendell Holmes. *Fr.* Autocrat of the Breakfast Table, The. AmPP; FaBoBe; GN; HoPM; ImPo; LiTA; NOBA; NoP; PoEL-5; PoLF; PrIm; TFi; WGRP

This is the silence known, a place. Twentieth Anniversary. Betty Adcock. MT

This is the sin against the Holy Ghost. The Unpardonable Sin. Vachel Lindsay. ChIV-2; CMoP; MeMAP

This is the skull of a hard-working man. Serapion of Alexandria, *tr. fr. Greek* by Peter Jay. GrAn

This is the solid-looking quagmire. Liberal, or Innocent by Definition. James McAuley. NOBAu

This is the song I rested with. Mammy Hums. Carl Sandburg. PoNe

This is the song of Kuk-ook, the bad boy. The Song of Kuk-ook, the Bad Boy. *Eskimo Oral Tradition.* TTTS

This is the song of Mehitabel. The Song of Mehitabel. Don Marquis. *Fr.* Archy and Mehitabel. FiBHP; OFC; SoCa

This is the song of the blooming trench. From the Front: The Song of the Trench, December, 1914. C. W. Blackall. NSI

This is the song of the Plane. A Song of the Air. Gordon Alchin. NSI

This is the song of those who live alone. William Justema. NYBP

This is the song the poilus sing. Madelon. Peter Scupham. *Fr.* Notes from a War Diary, H.J.B. 1914–19. SCBI

This is the sorrowful story. The Legends of Evil, I. Kipling. MoShBr

This is the sort of place you might arrive at after a long journey. Ferns and the Night. John Ash. SCBI

This is the south. I look for evidence. New Orleans. Joy Harjo. HATNAP

This is the State above the Law. A Death-bed. Kipling. IHNG; PoWW

This is the surest death. Mortality. Naomi Long Madgett. PoBA; PoNe

This is the sweet work of Erinna, not much, of course. Asclepiades, *tr. fr. Greek* by Barbara Hughes Fowler. *Fr.* Epigrams. HePo

This is the tale. To My Mother Who Endured. Liliane Richman. BTR

This is the tale of the man. Ticonderoga; a Legend of the West Highlands. Robert Louis Stevenson. EBNV; OBNV

This is the tale that Cassidy told. The Mornin's Mornin. Gerald Brennan. BLPA

This is the terminal: the light. At the San Francisco Airport. Yvor Winters. AiP; HeIP; InPK; NIP; NOBA

This is the time. (*LL*) The Advice. *Unknown.* APAS

This is the time lean woods shall spend. Sundown. Léonie Adams. MoAB; MoAmPo; TrGrPo

This is the time of year. The Armadillo[— Brazil]. Elizabeth Bishop. CAPP; HCAP; MoP; NAAL-2; NoAM; NOBA; NoP; NYBP; Poetr; SM; TAP; VCAP; VGW

This is the time of year. William Carlos Williams. SAmP

This is the tomb of great Megistias. On His Friend Megistias, Who Died at Thermopylai. Simonides, *tr. fr. Greek* by Peter Jay. GrAn

This is the true end of desire. The Ballad of the Frozen Field. Dabney Stuart. MT

This is the truth sent from above. The Truth from Above. *Unknown.* OBET

This is the truth what I now tell you. The Miramichi Fire. *Unknown.* AmFP

This is the twentieth century. A First on TV. David Ignatow. RaBo

This is the urgency: Live! The Second Sermon on the Warpland. Gwendolyn Brooks. BPo; NOBA; PoBA

This is the voice of high midsummer's heat. The Mowing. Sir Charles G. D. Roberts. NOBC

This is the way a tree: from the rain down. From the Rain Down. Rhina P. Espaillat. GoYe

This is the way it is. We see. Ingmar Bergman's "Seventh Seal." Robert Duncan. CAPP; PoE

This is the way the ladies ride. Mother Goose. OxNR; ReMoGo

This is the way we come. Riding in the Rain. Maxine W. Kumin. RFM

This is the way we do it dear. The Old Whore Speaks to a Young Poet. Dave Jeddie Smith. SM

This is the way we make our hay. Haymaking. A. P. Graves. BoTP

This is the way we say it in our time. Winfield Townley Scott. ErPo

This is the way we wash our clothes. Wash-Day. Lilian McCrea. BoTP

This is the weather the cuckoo likes. Weather[s]. Thomas Hardy. BoTP; CH; EBEvV; FaBoCh; FaBV; MoAB; MoBrPo; NTP; OBMV; OtMeF; RB

This is the week when Christmas comes. (*LL*) In the Week When Christmas Comes. Eleanor Farjeon. PChr; PDV

This is the Wheel of Dreams. Carriers of the Dream Wheel. N. Scott Momaday. CDW

This is the Wiggledywasticus/ Very remarkable beast. After a Visit to the Natural History Museum. Laura E. Richards. ImGa

This is the wind, the wind in a field of corn. Wind. James Fenton. NAEL-2; SCBI

This is the wisdom of the ape. The Theology of Bongwi, the Baboon. Roy Campbell. OBAP; PeSA

This is the world we wanted. Gretel in Darkness. Louise Glück. AmPA; NoAM

This is the young man, two cars ahead. The Accident. Liz Rosenberg. PBCAP

This is thi. Tom Leonard. *Fr.* Unrelated Incidents. NBrP

This is Thomas Jones's book. Thomas Samuel Jones, Jr.. FaBoUs

This is thy hour O Soul, thy free flight into the wordless. A Clear Midnight. Walt Whitman. HAP; NTP; OxBSP; SAmP; Spl

This is thy province, this thy wonderous way. Dryden. *Fr.* MacFlecknoe; or, A Satire [*or* Satyr] upon the True-Blue [*or* -Blew] Protestant Poet T. S. CBNP, *sl. abr.*; EPCY; FHYEP; HAP, *abr.*; NoP; OAEL-1; OBSV; OxBoLi; PeLV; Poetr; TEP; TFi

This is to be my symphony. (*LL*) To live content with small means. William Ellery Channing. EaPr

This is to say, my dear Augusta. King William's Dispatch to Queen Augusta. Coventry Patmore. FaBoEE

This is to say we remember. Not that remembering saves us. For Victor Jara. Miller Williams. SM

This is to walk squinting into a sun. Defining an Absence. John Cassidy. PWE

This is too good for words. I lie here naked. Fritz. Gerald Stern. AnAn

This is true Love, by that true Cupid got. The Dance of Love. Sir John Davies. *Fr.* Orchestra; or, A Poem[e] of Da[u]ncing. EiL; NoSic, *abr.*; SiPS; SiPSBD

This is what comes of snapshots. Of talkinig in bed. (*LL*) A Family Man. Maxine W. Kumin. IHMS; TAP

This is what I want to happen. Offering. *Unknown*, *Tr. fr. Zuni Indian by* Ruth Bunzel; *ad. by* Robert Bly. EaPr; NU

This is what it was like? God on a donkey. The Palms. David Knight. MoCV

This Is What the Watchbird Sings, Who Perches in the Lovetree. Bruce Boyd. NeAP

This is what we have. Tiny Histories. Mark Svenvold. UTF

This is what we really want. By Fiat of Adoration. Oscar Williams. LiTM

This is what you changed me to. Pig Song. Margaret Atwood. NoP

This is where all the stars bow down. (*LL*) Pibroch. Ted Hughes. FaBoMo; OAEL-2

This is where he sought God. Llanrhaeadr Ym Mochnant. R. S. Thomas. AngWe

This is where I once saw a deaf girl playing in a field. Deaf Girl Playing. James Tate. LCAP

This is where the People take tea. In a Chain-Store Cafeteria. Paul Grano. NOBAu

This is where the serpent lives, the bodiless. Wallace Stevens. *Fr.* Auroras of Autumn, The. CMoP; PoE

This is where the warrior from Ibokun came. Edouard J. Maunick, *tr. fr. French by* Ellen Conroy Kennedy. *Fr.* As Far as Yoruba Land. NegPo

This is where we're at the gate. Photograph at the Cloisters: April 1972. Helen Chasin. NMM

This is Willy Walker, and that's Tam Sim. *Unknown.* OxNR

This Is Your Hour. Herbert Kaufman. PoToHe

This is your hour — creep upon it! This Is Your Hour. Herbert Kaufman. PoToHe

This island, garlanded with wild woods. Archilochus, *tr. fr. Latin by* Guy Davenport. OBVE

This Island Mopsy. Victor Questel. PBCV

This isn't about unrequited love. Open Windows. Marilyn Hacker. Poetr

This Italian square. Dancers at the Moy. Paul Muldoon. BIrV

This itch of scribbling has no end, no ease. The Author's Quietus. Henry Carey. FaBoVe

This? it's my Lounge Lizard look, very. Up. Bill Kushner. GLP; UL

This jar of roses and carnations on the window-sill. Decoration. Mary Ursula Bethell. PeNZ

This Journey. Ingrid Jonker, *tr. fr. Afrikaans by* Jack Cope *and* William Plomer. BoWoP

This journey through another world, beyond bad dreams. Sacristans. Elizabeth Cook-Lynn. *Fr.* Journey. HATNAP

This keeps my hands. Bracelets. William Strode. NOSC

This kind o' sogerin' ain't a mite like our October trainin.' Letter, A ("This kind o' sogerin' ain't a mite like our October trainin' .") James Russell Lowell. *Fr.* Biglow Papers, The. OxBA

This kiss. Mary. Lucille Clifton. CrSp

This kiss, father, from him who was your son. (*LL*) The Gardener. John Hall Wheelock. NYBP

This kissing princess. Fractured Fairy Tale. David Trinidad. BAP-91

This knot I knit. To Know Whom One Shall Marry. *Unknown.* GBP

This kyng lay at Camylot upon Krystmasse. *Unknown*, *tr. fr. Middle English by* Brian Stone. *Fr.* Sir Gawain and the Green Knight. OAEL-1; PoE

This labour passed, by Bridewell all descend. Pope. *Fr.* Dunciad, The. OxAEP-1

This laconic old person of Wick. (*LL*) There was an old person of Wick. Edward Lear. FaBoNo

This lady of the West Country? (*LL*) Here lies a most beautiful lady. Walter de la Mare. ImPo; LiTB; LiTM; MoAB; MoBrPo; OBEV; RB

This Lady She Wears a Dark Green Shawl. *Unknown.* AmFP

This Land. Ian Mudie. NOBAu

This land like a mirror turns you inward. Dark Pines under Water. Gwendolyn MacEwen. NOBC

This land will not always be foreign. The Winds of Orisha. Audre Lorde. SRLS

This landscape demands: open vowels. Campi Flegrei. Barend Toerien, *tr. fr. Afrikaans by the author.* PeSA

This last disguise, himself. (*LL*) The Missing Person. Donald Justice. CAPP; NYBP; Poetr

This Last Pain. William Empson. CMoP; EBEV; FaBoMo; GTBS-P; LiTM; MoAB; MoBrPo; NoAM; OAEL-2

This late in our century. Sheltering the Same Needs. Alex Kuo. UL

This lay, a favorite of mine. Honeysuckle (Chevrefoil). Marie de France, *tr. by* Patricia Terry. BoWoP

This lazy prince of tennis balls and lutes. Navigator. May Sarton. ArOW

This legend is told of me. Actaeon. Rayner Heppenstall. FaBoTw

This legendary house, this dear enchanted tomb. Monticello. May Sarton. GOA

This let me further add, that nature knows. Ovid, *tr. by* Dryden. *Fr.* Metamorphoses. OBVE

This Life. Rita Dove. AmPA; VBLP

This Life. *Unknown.* FaBoRV

This life a Dream and Shadow. Sir Thomas More. *Fr.* Twelve Weapons of Spiritual Battle, The. EnRePo

This Life a Theater. Palladas, *tr. fr. Greek by* Robert Bland. NIP

This life a theatre we well may call. This Life a Theater. Palladas, *tr. fr. Greek by* Robert Bland. NIP

This Life Is All Chequer'd with Pleasures and Woes. Thomas Moore. ELP

This life is but a game of cards. Life's a Game. *Unknown.* BLPA

This Life Is Full of Numbness. Christina Rossetti. *Fr.* Later Life. Son

This life is not a circus where. Lawrence Ferlinghetti. *Fr.* Coney Island of the Mind, A. PPP

This life like no other. Gregory Orr. AmPA

This life of ours would not cause you sorrow. Murasaki Shikibu, *tr. fr. Japanese by* Kenneth Rexroth *and* Ikuko Atsumi. WPJ

This life, which seems so fair. William Drummond of Hawthornden. CH; NOSC; TrGrPo

(Madrigal: "This life which seems so fair.") EiL; GTBS; GTBS-P; OAEL-1

This life's a hollow bubble. Fin de Siècle. Edmund Vance Cooke. BLPA

This Lime-Tree Bower My Prison. Samuel Taylor Coleridge. EnRP; FaBoPP; FHYEP; HeIP; MeMBP; NAEL-2; OxAEP-2; PoE; PoEL-4; TOF

This Little Bride and Groom Are. E. E. Cummings. AmPP

This little bunny said, "Let's play." Finger Play. *Unknown.* BoTP

This little flag to us so dear. The Union Jack. Jeannie Kirby. BoTP

This little flower from afar. With a Pressed Flower. James Russell Lowell. AnAmPo

This Little House Is Sugar. Langston Hughes. NTCP

This little house swallows. Ray A. Young Bear. STP

This little pig had a rub-a-dub. *Unknown.* OxNR

This Little Pig Went to Market. Mother Goose. ImGa; OxNR; ReMoGo; RoPo

This little Pipkin fits this little Jelly. (*LL*) A Ternarie of Littles, upon a Pipkin of Jellie [*or* Jelly] Sent to a Lady. Robert Herrick. BeJo; FaBoCh; FaBoUs; GoJo; PoEL-3

This Little Red Riding Hood. One of the Gang. Tracey Herd. NWP

This little, silent, gloomy monument. Epitaph on the Tombstone of a Child, the Last of Seven That Died Before. Aphra Behn. KTR; NOSC

This little stone, dear Sabinos. *Unknown*, *tr. fr. Greek by* Kenneth Rexroth. PGA

This little vault, this narrow room. An Epitaph on the Lady Mary Villiers. Thomas Carew. SeCP

(Another [Epitaph on Lady Mary Villiers].) BeJo; CaPo

(Epitaph, An.) OBEV

(Other, An.) SeCV-2

This Living Hand, Now Warm and Capable. Keats. BoLoP; InPK; InPS; NoP; OAEL-1; TRP

This lonely following in the old town. Lines for a Young Wanderer in Mexico. John Logan. PoA

This longed-for morning here is our sacrifice/ to Zeus the finisher, and Artemis goddess of childbirth. Crinagoras, *tr. fr. Greek by* Alistair Elliot. GrAn

This, Lord, was an anxious brother, and. Funeral Oration for a Mouse. Alan Dugan. HAP; OBD, *st.* 1; Poetr; PPP

This prophecy came by mail. Requiem for "Bird" Parker. Gregory Corso. PoNe

This purple cloud of grief within my heart. Old Love Butchered (Colorado Springs and Huachuca). Lance Jeffers. NBV

This queen of prey (now prey to you). A Lady with a Falcon on Her Fist. Richard Lovelace. CaPo

This *quidam* gives that *quidam* for *one* round. Philodemus, *tr. fr. Greek by* William Moebius. GrAn

This Quiet Dust. John Hall Wheelock. MoAmPo

This quiet dust was gentlemen and ladies. Emily Dickinson. CMoP; DL; OxBA
  (Cemetery, A.) MoAB; MoAmPo

This quiet morning light. To Mark Anthony in Heaven. William Carlos Williams. NOBA; SAmP

This quiet mound beneath. Corporal Pym. Walter de la Mare. FaBoEE

This quiet roof, bestirred with pigeon plumes. The Graveyard by the Sea. Paul Valéry, *tr. fr. French by* John Frederick Nims. STV

This quiet roof where jabbed the fo'c'sle flocks. (*LL*) The Graveyard by the Sea. Paul Valéry. STV

This Quintus, Corydon, for whom you lust. "Panormitanus," *tr. fr. Latin.* PeHV

This, quoth the Eskimo master. Latter-day Geography Lesson. R. A. K. Mason. PeNZ

This racer of the watry plain. Catullus, *tr. fr. Latin.* OBVE

This Railway Station. Allan M. Laing. UV

This ration card, once shocking pink. The Ration Card. Liz Sohappy Bahe. CDW; FaPON

This red/ Italian hand. For My Daughter. John Logan. CRP

This region, surely, is not of the earth. Naples. Samuel Rogers. OBTV

This rehabilitation system! (*LL*) Solitary Confinement. Robert Walker. NOBAu

This reverend shadow cast that setting sun. Upon Bishop Andrewes's [*or* Andrewes His] Picture before His Sermons. Richard Crashaw. NOSC

This rich room how you dropped the mask! (*LL*) Appearances. Robert Browning. OxBSP

This road I'm taking is long and bright. Artemis. Rita Boumi-Pappas, *tr. fr. Greek by* Eleni Fourtouni. AIW

This road is so fuzzy. Cinéma Vérité. Dorothy Walters. IHMS

This Room and Everything in It. Li-Young Lee. OpBo

This room is not for staying. Demon-Lover. Sylvia Paskin. DT

This Room of Trees & Moving Earth/ This Room Where No One Knows How Sky Begins. Sister Mary Norbert Körte. SRLS

This root of bog-oak the sea dug up she found. Trouvaille. Richard Murphy. IPY

This rose tree is not made to bear. Envy. Charles Lamb *and* Mary Lamb. OxBChV; WoRP

This Royal Infant. John Fletcher *and* William Shakespeare. *Fr.* King Henry VIII. NAs

This royal throne of kings, this scepter'd isle. Shakespeare. *Fr.* Richard II. UV

This royal throne of kings, this sceptred isle. John of Gaunt Speaks. Shakespeare. *Fr.* King Richard II. EBEvV; FaBoEH; FaBoPP; FaPoR (This Blessed Plot . . . This England.) FaBV

This rudely sculptured porter-pot. Undying Thirst. Antipater of Sidon, *tr. fr. Greek by* Robert Bland. AWP

This rule in gardening ne'er forget. *Unknown.* FaBoUs

This Runner. Francis Webb. CBAP

This sad world we inhabit. *Unknown. Fr.* Calendar of Oengus, The. NOIV

This said, he reacht to take his sonne. Homer, *tr. by* George Chapman. *Fr.* Iliad, The. OBVE

This said, he turned about his steed. Sidrophel, the Rosicrucian Conjurer. Samuel Butler. *Fr.* Hudibras. OxBoLi

This sailor knows of wondrous lands afar. The Child and the Mariner. W. H. Davies. CH

This Sampler will declare! (*LL*) With cheerful mind we yield to men. Frances Gray. FaBoVe

This savage wish on certain days. Cannibal. Léon Laleau, *tr. fr. French by* Ellen Conroy Kennedy. *Fr.* Black Music. NegPo

This saying good-by on the edge of the dark. Good-by and Keep Cold. Robert Frost. CMoP

This scorn one day, one day by endless love. (*LL*) Chloris, It Is Not Thy Disdain. Sidney Godolphin. BeJo

This sea like shot-silk, every day such light. At the Sea's Edge. Andrew Waterman. SCBI

This sea will never die, neither will it ever grow old. Middle of the World. D. H. Lawrence. HAP; NoAM

This seems, in a world where love must take its chances. Mona Van Duyn. *Fr.* Footnotes to "The Autobiography of Bertrand Russell." HAP

This sentence have I left behind. A Nameless Epitaph. Matthew Arnold. FaBoEE

This shade-bestowing pear-tree, thou. The Pear-Tree. *Unknown, tr. by* Allen Upward. *Fr.* Shi King. AWP

This shadow at my shoulder doesn't shed. Climbing. Jennifer Maiden. CBAP

This shall be called the laying on of hands. A Necessary Miracle. Eda Lou Walton. NYBP

This she? no, this is Diomed's Cressida. Shakespeare. *Fr.* Troilus and Cressida. OxAEP-1

This Sheet that brought thee in shall lay thee out. (*LL*) Ad Librum. Samuel Danforth, Jr. SCAP

This ship is the ship of butchery and increase. Songs for the Cisco Kid; or, Singing: Song #2. K. Curtis Lyle. PoBA

This short straight sword. R. A. K. Mason. PeNZ

This Side of the Truth. Dylan Thomas. MeMBP

This silken wreath, which circles in mine arm. Upon a Ribband [*or* Ribbon]. Thomas Carew. BeJo; CaPo; NOSC; OAEL-1; PoE

This silver thing I send you for your birthday. Crinagoras, *tr. fr. Greek by* Alistair Elliot. GrAn

This silver was not carved but mesmerized. A Satyr by Diodorus. Plato the Younger, *tr. fr. Greek by* G. R. H. Wright. GrAn

This sky is to be opened. Hermetic Bird. Philip Lamantia. VGW

This slow one. (*LL*) Tortoise-Shell. D. H. Lawrence. CMoP; FaBoVe; FM; MeMBP; NAEL-2; OAEL-2; OxAEP-2

This small lodge is now. Old Man, the Sweat Lodge. Phillip William George. GrPI

This Smoking World. Graham Lee Hemminger. *See* Tobacco ("Tobacco is a dirty weed.")

This Solitude of Cataracts. Wallace Stevens. LCAP

This Song Is Dedicated to the One Eye Love. Nick Totton. VaA

This song of late autumn. Autumn. Itsik Manger, *tr. fr. Yiddish.* TrJP, *tr. by* Ruth Whitman *and* Joseph Leftwich.

This song of mine sets my soul free. Vusumzi's Song. L. T. Manyase, *tr. fr. Xhosa by* C. M. Mcanyangwa *and* Jack Cope. PeSA

This song of mine will wind its music around. My Song. Rabindranath Tagore. OHIP

This song shall be our parting hymn. (*LL*) The Red Flag. Jim Connell. SWP

This song that springs only from love. (*LL*) For My Mother. David Diop. NegPo

This soup is cold. The Soup of Venus. James Tate. AmPA

This southern rain nourishes the mossy stones. Tu Fu, *tr. by* William H. Nienhauser. *Fr.* Rain, Four Poems. SuSp

This sparrow/ who comes to sit at my window. The Sparrow. William Carlos Williams. InPS; LCAP; Poetr; PrIm; VGW

This speech all Trojans did applaud; who from their traces loos'd. The Trojans Outside the Walls. Homer, *tr. by* George Chapman. *Fr.* Iliad, The. OBVE

This spoke, a huge wave tooke him by the head. Homer, *tr. by* George Chapman. *Fr.* Odyssey. NAWM-1; OBVE

This spoonful of chocolate tapioca. Thinking of the Lost World. Randall Jarrell. NoAM; NOBA

This spot is the sweetest I've seen in my life. *Unknown.* FiBHP

This Spring. Regina DeCormier-Shekejian. LoHo

This spring as it comes bursts up in bonfires green. The Enkindled Spring. D. H. Lawrence. NoAM

This Spring of Love. Shakespeare. *Fr.* Two Gentlemen of Verona, The. ChTr

This spring, you'd swear it actually gets dark earlier. Turning Thirty. Katha Pollitt. InPS

This squalid dome of soot-obscuréd glass. This Railway Station. Allan M. Laing. UV

This star is only an augury of the morning. And in the 51st Year of That Century, While My Brother Cried in the Trench, While My Enemy Glared from the Cave. Hyam Plutzik. RB

This starry world, and I in it. Death. James Oppenheim. WGRP

This statue of Liberty, busy man. The Statue of Liberty. Thomas Hardy. LiTB

This stone. Stone Hammer Poem. Robert Kroetsch. NOBC

This Stone. *Unknown, tr. fr. Greek by* Goldwin Smith. AWP

This stone commemorates his name. Epitaph on a Dwarf. Emmanuel ben David Frances, *tr. fr. Hebrew by* Hyam Maccoby. OBD

This stone I set at your feet. Penguin. Michael Richards. OBAP

This stone incorporates three gods:/ the head is unmistakably goat-horned Pan's. Philodemus, *tr. fr. Greek by* William Moebius. GrAn

This story ends with me still rowing. (*LL*) Rowing. Anne Sexton. BoWoP; CAPP; LCAP

This story's strange, but altogether true. "R. B." SCAP

This Strange Calculation of Roots. Edouard J. Maunick, *tr. fr. French by* Teo Savory. NegPo

This strange thing must have crept. Fork. Charles Simic. AmPA; HCAP; LCAP; TRP; WeW

This string upon my harp was best beloved. Harmonics. William Vaughn Moody. AnAmPo

This sudden cockerel who stood. Cock-Crow. Ralph Nixon Currey. PeSA

This summer. *(LL)* Burning Island. Gary Snyder. VCAP

This Summer and Last. Thomas Hardy. OxBTC

This summer is your perfect summer. Never will the skies. To a Child before Birth. Norman Nicholson. NAs

This Summer's Sky. Bertolt Brecht, *tr. fr. German by* Michael Hamburger. PoSu

This Sun Is Hot. *Unknown.* BPo

This sunlight shames November where he grieves. Autumn Idleness. Dante Gabriel Rossetti. *Fr.* House of Life, The. GBL; OAEL-2

This that I give you now. Bread. Stanley Burnshaw. TrJP

This that is washed with weed and pebblestone. The Figurehead. Léonie Adams. WPE

This the house of Circe, queen of charms. Circe. Lord De Tabley. NOBVV

This the house that Jack built. The House That Jack Built. *Unknown.* FaBoBe

This, the last ornament among the peers. Hilaire Belloc. OBSV

This, the twentieth day of March. A Letter to Three Irish Poets. Michael Longley. BIrV

This then is love — deep joy that you should be. Farewell to a Trappist. Lucy Boston. VBLP

This, then, is the grave of my son. The Nettles. Thomas Hardy. OxBSP

This, then, the river he had to swim. Thomas at the Wheel. Rita Dove. Poetr

This they know well: the Goddess yet abides. In Her Praise. Robert Graves. BIrV

This thin-lipped king with his helmeted head. To President bush at the Start of the Gulf War. Robert Bly. RaBo

This thin, white mist that soon will disappear. *(LL)* He is like a cloud that for an instant. Jacqueline Osherow. UTF

This, this is he; softly a while. Milton. *Fr.* Samson Agonistes. FHYEP; OAEL-1; PoEL-3; UnPo

This time, I mean it. A Little Tumescence. Jonathan Williams. ErPo; NeAP; PoM

This time I won't permit the blue, glimpsed. Patrizia Cavalli, *tr. fr. Italian by* Judith Baumel. NeIt

This time I'll show up. Hunting Song ("This time I'll show up.") *Unknown, tr. fr. Chippewa Indian by* Jerome K. Rothenberg. STP

This time/ in the darkness. Stuntman. Lionel Kearns. MoCV

This time of pause is as though. Shag Rock. "Paul Henderson." PeNZ

This Time of Year a Twelvemonth Past. A. E. Housman. *Fr.* Shropshire Lad, A. FaPoB; PlP

This time the tomb. *(LL)* A Great Time. W. H. Davies. AngWe; ImPo; LiTB; MoBrPo

This time tomorrow, where shall I be? *Unknown.* ISE

This time, unless I feed you with my heart? *(LL)* The Grey Wolf. Arthur Symons. FaBoTw

This to be done. John James. VaA

This to the crown and blessing of my life. A Letter to Daphnis. The Countess of Winchilsea. EnLoPo; NALW; VBLP (Letter to Daphnis, April 2, 1685, A.) NOSC

This Tokyo. Gary Snyder. NeAP

This tomb Damis built for his courageous horse. Anyte, *tr. fr. Greek by* Barbara Hughes Fowler. *Fr.* Epigrams. HePo

This tomb, inscribed to gentle Parnell's name. Goldsmith. EPCY

This tombstone heavy with grief announces. Philetas, *tr. fr. Greek by* Peter Jay. GrAn

This, too, I want you to know, my dear Phaedrus. To Phaedrus. Jovan Hristic, *tr. fr. Serbo-Croatian by* Charles Simic. HSix

This too is an experience of the soul. Isis Wanderer. Kathleen Raine. NALW; OxBS

This, Too, Shall Pass Away. A. L. Alexander. PoToHe

This, Too, Shall [*or* Will] Pass Away. Lanta Wilson Smith. BLPA

This Tooth. Lee Bennett Hopkins. TLR

This torch, still burning in my hand. From the Greek Anthology. Crinagoras, *tr. fr. Greek by* Kenneth Rexroth. PGA

This town has docks where channel boats come sidling. Arrivals, Departures. Philip Larkin. MoBrPo

This town, now, yes, Mother. Euripides, *tr. fr. Greek by* Edith Hamilton. *Fr.* Trojan Women, The. PAW

This trade-wind idleness between two harbours. *(LL)* Pearls. Alan Gould. NOBAu

This Train Don't Carry No Gamblers. *Unknown. See* This Train ("This train is bound for glory, this train.")

This Train ("This train is bound for glory, this train.") *Unknown.* OxBoLi (This Train Don't Carry No Gamblers.) AmFP

This treasure is the best, of all those gifts the grain. Upon the Birth of a Young and Highly Desired Son. Christian Weise, *tr. fr. German by* George C. Schoolfield. GePo

This tree outside my window here. On Not Saying Everything. C. Day Lewis. NoP

This tribute from a grateful heir. *(LL)* For My Ancestors. Rolfe Humphries. PoRA

This Troilus [*or* Troylus], with blisse [*or* Blysse] of that supprysed [*or* supprised]. Chaucer. *Fr.* Troilus and Criseyde [*or* Criseide]. EBEV; EnVB; PoE

This truly wonderful steed. Title of a Swift Horse. *Mongol Oral Tradition, tr. by* C. R. Bawden. WTO

This truth-telling is well enough. Visited. Fleur Adcock. PeNZ

This tuft that thrives on saline nothingness. The Air Plant. Hart Crane. MoAB; MoAmPo; NoP

This Unimportant Morning. Lawrence Durrell. BoLoP; OxBTC

This unphilosophic sight. To a Lady's Countenance. Elinor Wylie. NALW

This urge, wrestle, resurrection of dry sticks. Cuttings ("This urge, wrestle, resurrection of dry sticks.") Theodore Roethke. CAPP; HCAP; LCAP; MoP; NAAL-2; NoAM; NOBA; TAP; TRP; UnPo; VCAP

This used to be a dam. Damside. Margaret Atwood. LCAP

This vale of teargas. Unlawful Assembly. D. J. Enright. OxBTC

This valley wood is hedged. An English Wood. Robert Graves. PlP

This Version of Love. Dorothy Hewett. CBAP

This very day, a little while ago, you lived. Dead on the War Path. *Unknown, tr. fr. Tewa Indian by* H. J. Spinden. OBD; WTO

This voice an older friend has kept. Isaiah by Kerosene Lantern Light. Robert Harris. ChIV-1; NOBAu

This votive pledge of fond esteem. Stanzas to a Lady, with the Poems of Camoëns. Byron. FaBoUs

This wall-paper has lines that rise. Missing My Daughter. Stephen Spender. GTBS-P

This warning, Gallus, for thy love I send. Hylas. Sextus Propertius, *tr. by* F. A. Wright. *Fr.* Elegies. AWP

This was a city once, that's now a copse. Lament for Troy. Hugh Primas of Orleans, *tr. fr. Latin by* Helen Waddell. MLL

This was a dream. *(LL)* In winter in my room. Emily Dickinson. AmPP; ErPo; LiTA; MoP; NAAL-1; NALW; NoAM; NOBA; OxBA; Poetr

This was a love in which there was always. Brief Farewell. Anthony Delius. PeSA

This was a man of mighty mould. On a Bust of Lincoln. Clinton Scollard. OHIP

This was a poet — It is that. Emily Dickinson. AmPP; NAAL-1; NOBA

This was as far as I had got. David Wright. *Fr.* Peripatetic Letter to Isabella Fey, A. PeSAV

This was Mr. Bleaney's room. He stayed. Mr. Bleaney. Philip Larkin. HoPM; InPS; OxBC; PoE; TRP; UV

"This was Mr. Strugnell's room," she'll say. Mr. Strugnell. Wendy Cope. FaBoPa; UV

This was my dream! I saw a forest. Robert Browning. *Fr.* Bad Dreams. OAEL-2

This was my dream: Nature stood nigh me. A View from Middle-Earth. William Langland. *Fr.* Vision of Piers Plowman, The. Mes

This was not to be expected. Seaman, 1941. Molly Holden. FaBoWP

This was our first line of defense. It held. Ferniehirst Castle. Richard Hugo. NoAM

This was that mystery of clearest light. The Statue of Shadow. John Peale Bishop. LiTA

This was the brown bull of Cuailnge. The Two Bulls. *Unknown, tr. fr. Irish by* Thomas Kinsella. *Fr.* How the Bulls Were Begotten. NOIV

This was the color of coolness. Spring Cellar. Gladys McKee. GoYe

This was the crucifixion on the mountain. Dylan Thomas. *Fr.* Altarwise by Owl-Light. CMoP; LiTM

This was the first world, where the wild dove cries. Creation. Louise Townsend Nicholl. GoYe

This was the hawk's way. This was the hawk. Hawk's Way. Ted Olson. HoPM

This was the man God gave us when the hour. George Washington. John Hall Ingham. OHIP; PAH

This was the moment when Before. BC:AD. U. A. Fanthorpe. OBCP

This was the noblest Roman of them all. Portrait of Brutus. Shakespeare. *Fr.* Julius Caesar. TrGrPo

This was the summer when the tired girls. Now Kindness. Peter Viereck. LiTA

This was the surplus childhood, held as cheap! The Sunderland Children. Alice Meynell. NALW

This was the table. Its surface, its legs. The Ghost. Agnes Nemes Nagy, *tr. fr. Hungarian by* Bruce Berlind. PoSu

This was the woman; what now of the man? George Meredith. *Fr.* Modern Love. EnVR; OHCV; Son

This water droplet, charity of the air. Man Seeking Experience Enquires His Way of a Drop of Water. Ted Hughes. OxAEP-2

This water, sad and fearful. Slow Rain. Gabriela Mistral, *tr. by* Gunda Kaiser *and* James Tipton. PBWP

This way from the north. Corn-grinding Song. *Unknown, tr. fr. Tewa Indian by* N. Barnes. WTO

This way, this way, come and hear. Song in the Wood. John Fletcher, *Sometimes at.* to Francis Beaumont. *Fr.* Little French Lawyer, The. ElL; NOSC

This wet sack, wavering slackness. MacDuff. Charles Tomlinson. NAs; OxBC

This while we are abroad. An Ode Written in the Peak[e]. Michael Drayton. FaBoPP; NOSC

This wight all mercenary projects tries. Sir Samuel Garth. *Fr.* Dispensary, The. OBSV

This wild night, gathering the washing as if it were flowers. From the Roof. Denise Levertov. NoP

This will be the last ditch to fall. Capital. John Tripp. AngWe

This will go too, this curve of shore. Slate Quay: Felinheli. Peter Gruffydd. AngWe

This will really try you. Mamma! Frank Horne. BPo

This wine-press is call'd war on earth. Blake. *Fr.* Milton. EBEV (Wine-Press of Los, The.) EnRP

This wingtip feather from a hook-beaked eagle. Crinagoras, *tr. fr. Greek by* Alistair Elliot. GrAn

This winter's morning, turning the other way. Turning. Robert Finch. MoCV

This Winter's Weather It Waxeth Cold. *Unknown.* InvP

This wit was with experience bought. A Mirror for Detractors. Esther Lewis. ECWP

This woman had a number of beautiful lovers. Disfigurement. Yannis Ritsos, *tr. fr. Greek by* Edmund Keeley. AnAn

This woman is getting on her last bus. Poem for Jacqueline Hill. *Unknown.* BrRo

This woman vomiten [*or* vomiting] her. Present. Sonia Sanchez. WPOW

This woman with a dead face. A Cold Front. William Carlos Williams. NAs

This word is all too wide for thee. (*LL*) On Fanny Godwin. Shelley. OBNC

This world a hunting is. William Drummond of Hawthornden. OxBSP

This world a vale of soul-making. In Cemeteries. D. J. Enright. OxBC

This world and this life are so scattered, they try me. Zu fragmentarisch ist Welt und Leben. Heine, *tr. fr. German by* Charles Godfrey Leland. AWP

This World Fares as a Fancy. *Unknown. See* I wolde witen of sum [*or* som] wis wight.

This world/ is amazingly flat. Natalya Gorbanevskaya, *tr. fr. Russian by* Barbara Einzig. BoWoP

This world is gradually becoming a place. John Berryman. *Fr.* Dream Songs. MoP; NoAM; NOBA

This world is not conclusion. Emily Dickinson. NAAL-1

This world is the abode of God. Angad. EaPr

This world is very odd we see. Reply to Dipsychus. Arthur Hugh Clough. FaBoCo

This World Lives Because. Ilam Peruvaluti, *tr. fr. Tamil by* A. K. Ramanujan. PLW

This worlde is full of variaunce. The Duplicity of Women. John Lydgate. MeEL

This worthy lymytour, this noble Frere. The Friar's Prologue. Chaucer. *Fr.* Canterbury Tales, The. EnVB; PoE

This would not be the war we fought in. See, the foliage. Newsreel. Adrienne Rich. *Fr.* Shooting Script. FaBoWP; HCAP

This wretched life, the trust and confidence. This life a Dream and Shadow. Sir Thomas More. *Fr.* Twelve Weapons of Spiritual Battle, The. EnRePo

This year again the bruise-colored oak. Seeing the Bones. Maxine W. Kumin. NoAM

This Year, before It Ends. Eve Langley. NOBAu

This year, before it ends, holds out time as a weight to us. This Year, before It Ends. Eve Langley. NOBAu

This year,/ I'm raising the emotional ante. These Green-going-to-Yellow. Marvin Bell. CAPP; FYAP

This year King Athelstan, ring-giver, lord. Battle of Brunanburh. *Unknown, tr. fr. Anglo-Saxon by* Harold Massingham. FaBoEH

This year,/ Next year. *Unknown.* OxNR

"This year she has changed greatly" — meaning you. Change. Robert Graves. OxBTC

This year, till late in April, the snow fell thick and light. The Nineteenth of April. Lucy Larcom. PAH

This Yonder Night I Sawe a Sighte. *Unknown.* MiEL; NAs

This yonge fresshe wenche, wel loking honey-swete. The Hicche-Hykeres Tale. W. F. N. Watson. BXAP

This, you were sure, whatever happened. A Pair of Shoes. Theodore Weiss. NoAM

This young boy on my hands at middle age. Teasing Hsiao-te, My Son. Huang T'ing-chien, *tr. fr. Chinese by* Michael E. Workman. SuSp

This young girl was good-looking and worked hard. Coyote Man and the Young Lady. Peter Blue Cloud. BCF

This young mandarin had undoubted genius. Lament for Hsieh T'iao. Shen Yüeh, *tr. fr. Chinese by* Lenore Mayhew *and* William McNaughton. SuSp

This Zone, this Breastband & girlish frock. Artemis. Perses, *tr. fr. Greek by* Peter Whigham. GrAn

Thise olde gentil Britons in hir dayes. The Franklin's Prologue. Chaucer. *Fr.* Canterbury Tales, The. EnVB; NAEL-1; OAEL-1

Thistle. Nikolai Alekseevich Zabolotsky, *tr. fr. Russian by* Daniel Weissbort. RB

Thistle and darnel and dock grew there. Nicholas Nye. Walter de la Mare. BoTP

Thistledown. Denis Glover. *Fr.* Sings Harry. PeNZ

Thistledown. James Merrill. UnPo

Thistledown. Harold Monro. OxBTC

Thistledown blows over the poisoned fields. The Martyred Earth. Ewart Milne. BIrV

Thistledown's flying/ Though the winds are all still, The. Autumn ("Thistledown's flying, The.") John Clare. BoNaP; EnVR; HAP; NU; PoEL-4; WeW

Thistles. Ted Hughes. FaBoVe; NoAM; OxBSP; OxBTC; SoSe

Tho' [*or* Though] grief and fondness in my breast rebel. London. Samuel Johnson. PoEL-3; TEP

Tho' I can not your cruelty constrain. Sir Thomas Wyatt. SiPS

Tho' I my party long have chose. Moderation. Christopher Smart. *Fr.* Hymns for the Amusement of Children. NOCV

Tho' ill at ease, a stranger and alone. Thoughts on Pausing at a Cottage near the Paukataug River. Sarah Kemble Knight. SCAP

Tho' I'm no Catholic. The Catholic Bells. William Carlos Williams. CMoP; NOBA; OxBSP; SAmP

Tho' it were ten thousand mile! (*LL*) My luve is like a red, red rose. Burns. EBEvV; EnRP; FaBoBe; HoPM

Tho' men say thou bring'st the Spring. (*LL*) The Swallow. Abraham Cowley. EBEV; FM; OBEV; OxAEP-1

Tho' my verse is exact. Hence These Rimes. Bert Leston Taylor. FiBHP

Tho' ne'er another trow me. (*LL*) If Doughty Deeds ("If daughty deeds my lady pleases.") Robert Graham. GTBS; GTBS-P; OBEV

Tho' the same death you should die. (*LL*) Fair Mary of Wallington. *Unknown.* ESPB

Tho when as chearelesse night ycovered had. Spenser. *Fr.* Faerie Queene, The. OAEL-1

Thocht raging stormes movis us to schaik. The Reid in the Loch Sayis. *Unknown.* OxBS

Thocht that this warld be verie strange. Solace in Age. Sir Richard Maitland. OxBS

Th'o'erflowing of unbounded Wit. &c. (*LL*) Enquiry after Peace. A Fragment. The Countess of Winchilsea. ECWP; PoE

Thole a Little. *Unknown. See* Loverd, thou clepedest me.

Thomalin, since Thirsil nothing has to leave thee. To Thomalin. Phineas Fletcher. NOSC

Thomas à Becket, a Dramatic Comedy, *sels.* George Darley. "Speckle-black Toad and freckle-green Frog." FM

Thomas a Didymus, hard of belief. *Unknown.* ISE

Thomas and Charlie. Peter Wild. AmPA

Sir Thomas Armstrong's Last Farewell to the World. *Unknown.* APAS

Thomas at Chickamauga. Kate Brownlee Sherwood. PAH

Thomas at the Wheel. Rita Dove. Poetr

Thomas Campey and the Copernican System. Tony Harrison. SCBI

Thomas Carlyle. Dorothy Parker. *Fr.* Pig's-Eye View of Literature, A. FiBHP; NALW

Thomas Cromwell. *Unknown.* ESPB

Thomas Dudley, Ah! Old Must Dye. *Unknown.* SCAP

Thomas Gray's View of Nature. William Mason. *Fr.* English Garden, The. EPCY; NOEC

Thomas Hardy. Walter de la Mare. NoAM

Thomas Hardy. Norman Dubie. LCAP

Thomas Hardy and A. E. Housman. Max Beerbohm. NBLV

Thomas hit and hit. The Human Tyrants. Alison Murdoch. PAW

Thomas Hobbes of Malmesbury thought. Peter Alexander. PeLi

Thomas in the Fields. Lois Moyles. NYBP

Thomas Iron-Eyes. Marnie Walsh. WPOW

Thomas Jefferson [1743-1826]. Rosemary *and* Stephen Vincent Benét *and* Stephen Vincent Benét. FaPON

Thomas lay on the Huntlie bank. Thomas the Rhymer [*or* Rimer]. *Unknown.* ELP; EnSB; FaBoCh; InPS; LiTB; NOBE; OAEL-1; OBEV; OxBB; Prf
   (Thomas Rymer.) ESPB
   (True Thomas.) OxBS; TrGrPo

Thomas Logge. Walter de la Mare. FaBoEE

Thomas MacDonagh. Francis Ledwidge. *See* He shall not hear the bittern cry.

Sir Thomas More. Robert Lowell. FaBoEH

Thomas Müntzer. Jeffrey Wainwright. SCBI

Thomas o Yonderdale. *Unknown.* ESPB

Thomas Rhymer [and the Queen of Elfland]. *Unknown. See* True Thomas lay o'er yond grassy [*or* on Huntlie] bank.

Thomas Rymer. *Unknown. See* Thomas lay on the Huntlie bank.

Thomas Sackevyll in Commendation of the Worke to the Reader. Thomas Sackville. AAS

Thomas Shadwell the Poet. John Dryden *and* Nahum Tate. *Fr.* Absalom and Achitophel, Pt. II. ChTr

Thomas speech beyond. Cobalt. Tom Weatherly. UL

Thomas Stuart was a lord. Lord Thomas Stuart. *Unknown.* ESPB

Thomas the Rhymer [*or* Rimer]. *Unknown.* ELP; EnSB; FaBoCh; InPS; LiTB; NOBE; OAEL-1; OBEV; OxBB; Prf

Thomas the Rhymer. *Unknown.* ELP; FaBoCh; InPS; LiTB; NOBE; OAEL-1; OBEV; OxBB; OxBS; PoE; Prf; RB; ScCV; TFi

Thomas the Rimer. *Unknown. See* True Thomas lay o'er yond grassy [*or* on Huntlie] bank.

Thomas, the vagrant piper's son. John Masefield Relates the Story of Tom, Tom, the Piper's Son. Louis Untermeyer. *Fr.* Mother Goose Up-to-Date. MoAmPo

Sir Thopas. Chaucer. *Fr.* Canterbury Tales, The. EnVB

Sir Thopas's Tale. Chaucer. *See* Listeth, lordes, in good entent [*or* intent].

Thoreau,/ grabbing on, hard. The Distances to the Friend. Jonathan Williams. NeAP

Thorn, The. Wordsworth. EnRP
Sels.

Thorn, A. *Unknown.* ReMoGo

Thorn has pierced her heart, The. (*LL*) The Rose and the Thorn. Paul Hamilton Hayne. FaBoBe

Thorn Leaves in March. W. S. Merwin. TwCP

Thorn Piece. Amy Lowell. PeHV

Thorny. William Cole. ZA

Thorough their own delay. (*LL*) Do Not, Oh, Do Not Prize. *Unknown.* EIl

Those aeroplanes. Timetable. Gunter Eich, *tr. fr. German by* Michael Hamburger. CBNP

Those animals that follow us in dream. Lupus in Fabula. Malcolm Lowry. (Xochitepec.) NOBC

Those are the features, those the smiles. Lines Written on Seeing My Husband's Picture, Painted When He Was Young. Anna Sawyer. ECWP

Those autumns my parents slept. A Dream of Glass Bangles. Agha Shahid Ali. OpBo

Those awful words "Till death do part." Early Thoughts of Marriage. Nathaniel Cotton. OxBChV
   (Marriage.) FaBoUs

Those Beauteous Maids. Moses ibn Ezra, *tr. fr. Hebrew by* Solomon Solis-Cohen. TrJP

Those before Us. Robert Lowell. LCAP

Those Being Eaten by America. Robert Bly. CoAP; NaP

Those blessed structures, plot and rhyme. Robert Lowell. CAPP; HCAP; NAAL-2; VCAP
   (Those blessèd structures, plot and rhyme.) NoAM; NoP

Those blessèd structures, plot and rhyme. Robert Lowell. *See* Those blessed structures, plot and rhyme.

Those boy-scouts practicing again! (*LL*) Solo for Ear-Trumpet. Edith Sitwell. MoAB; MoBrPo

Those boy-scouts practicing again! (*LL*) The King of China's Daughter. Edith Sitwell. BoTP; FaBoMo; MoBrPo

Those Boys That Ran Together. Lucille Clifton. PoBA

Those calm swamp-green eyes. Pisces Child. Sandra McPherson. NMM

Those Cambridge generations, Russell's, Keynes. On Bertrand Russell's "Portraits from Memory." Donald Davie. FaBoTw

Those charming eyes within whose starry sphere. On the Death of Catarina de Attayda. Camões, *tr. fr. Spanish by* R. F. Burton. AWP

Those dabbing hens I ferociously love. Cock before Dawn. Norman MacCaig. OxBC

Those dark mountains face to face. Dark Mountains. Milton Lockyer, *tr. fr. Yindjibarndi by* Frank Wordick. CBAP

Those days are now. Wordsworth. *Fr.* Prelude [or, Growth of a Poet's Mind], The. EnRP; HAP, *short sel.*; OAEL-2; OxAEP-2; PoEL-4, *sl. shorter*

Those days when it was all right. Letter to E. Franklin Frazier. Amiri Baraka. BPo; PoBA

Those dew-moist roses and that bushy thyme. Theocritus [*or* Theokritus], *tr. fr. Greek by* Anthony Holden. GrAn

Those dreams that on the silent night intrude. On Dreams. Swift. BIrV

Those — dying then. Emily Dickinson. NoP; OBD

Those eyes (dear Lord) once brandons of desire. On Mary Magdalene. William Drummond of Hawthornden. OAEL-1

Those eyes that [*or* which] set my fancy on a fire. Philippe Desportes. NoSic
   (Conquest [*or* His Lady's Might].) AWP

Those famous men of old, the Ogres. Ogres and Pygmies. Robert Graves. CMoP; FaBoMo; LiTB; LiTM; MeMBP; MoP; NoAM

Those fantastic forms, fang-sharp. City without Walls. W. H. Auden. NYBP

Those Flapjacks of Brown's. Bert Leston Taylor. OBAL

Those flaxen locks, those eyes of blue. To My Son. Byron. NAs

Those former loves wherein our lives have run. James Agee. *Fr.* Sonnets. MoAmPo

Those four black girls blown up. American History. Michael S. Harper. BPo; HCAP; NoAM

Those Gambler's Blues. *Unknown.* AS

Those Game Animals. *Unknown, tr. by* Denys Thompson. OBAP

Those game animals, those long-haired caribou. Those Game Animals. *Unknown, tr. by* Denys Thompson. OBAP

Those goldnails and their gaylinks that hang along a lime. (*LL*) By Magdalen Bridge, Oxford. Gerard Manley Hopkins. FaBoPP

Those great rough ranters, Branns. A Simplification. Richard Wilbur. CMoP

Those great sweeps of snow that stop suddenly six feet from the house. Snowbanks North of the House. Robert Bly. AiP; LCAP; RaBo

Those groans men use. The Mutes. Denise Levertov. IHMS; NALW; NaP; NOBA; PWE

Those hands, which heav'n like to a curtain spread. Crucified. Francis Quarles. NOSC

Those hands which you so clapt [*or* clapped], go now and wring. Upon the Lines and Life of the Famous Scenic Poet, Master William Shakespeare. Hugh Holland. OBWVE
   (O William Shakespeare.) AngWe

Those Hours, That With Gentle Work Did Frame. Shakespeare. *Fr.* Sonnets. TEP

Those Hours When Happy Hours Were My Estate. Edna St. Vincent Millay. PrIm

Those Images. W. B. Yeats. CMoP

Those in the vegetable rain retain. Stories of Snow. P. K. Page. NOBC; NoP; PoA

Those laden lilacs. The Lilacs. Richard Wilbur. FoLa

Those Last, Late Hours of Christmas Eve. Lou Ann Welte. PChr

Those Lips That Love's Own Hand Did Make. Shakespeare. *Fr.* Sonnets. Son

Those little girls sound. Distant Children. Cole Swenson. UTF

Those long days measured by my little feet. "George Eliot." *Fr.* Brother and Sister. NALW; NOBVV

Those long uneven lines. MCMXIV. Philip Larkin. EBEV; FaBoEH; NAEL-2; NoAM; NSI; OBWP; OxAEP-2

Those lumbering horses in the steady plough. Horses. Edwin Muir. CMoP; FaBoCh; OAEL-2

Those men who love the *crwth* and harp. Song and Poetry. *Unknown, tr. fr. Welsh by* Gwyn Jones. OBWVE

Those men whom the gods wish. Rec Room in Paradise. Tom Clark. UL

Those men with dollars on the mind. Gamble. Linda Hogan. HATNAP

Those mighty whisperers/ Missouri Mississippi. (*LL*) Like Ghosts of Eagles. Robert Francis. GOA; LCAP

Those mindes that wholy dote upon delight. Lady Elizabeth Carey. *Fr.* Mariam. KTR; WPE

Those moon-gilded dancers. The Gay. "Æ." OBMV

Those most assailed trees. Macrocarpas. Michael Jackson. PeNZ

Those mothers down there off the hill. Seventh Son. Ed Roberson. PoBA

Those my friendships most obtain. Contentment. Nathaniel Cotton. OxBChV

Those occasions involving the veering of axles. [Munich] Elegy No. 1. George Barker. MeMBP

Those of flowers I give to you. (*LL*) Lord, What Will the Earth Bring Forth. Paul Johann Ludwig Heyse. RiWo

Those of Pure Origin. Roy Fuller. FaBoMo

Those old tunes take me back. I used to go. Her Dancing Days. Anna Adams. BrRo

Those old Winnebago men. Beautiful Ohio. James Wright. CAPP

Those other clouds only Jews. (*LL*) On Clouds. Douglas Livingstone. PeSAV

Those Others. Ian Wedde. PeNZ

Those paths on the mountainside. Circumambulation of Mt. Tamalpais. Andrew Hoyem. PoA

Those petty [*or* pretty] wrongs that liberty commits. Shakespeare. *Fr.* Sonnets. InvP; OxAEP-1

Those picnics covered with sand. The North Coast. Gary Snyder. ArLo

Those quaint old worn-out words! Antiques. Walter de la Mare. PoA

Those Rainy Mornings. Frank Mkalawile Chipasula. HBAPE

Those ravens black that rested. Heavy-hearted. Judah al-Harizi, *tr. fr. Hebrew.* TrJP

Those Rebel Flags. John H. Jewett. PAH

Those reckless hosts rush to the wells. Baruch of Worms, *tr. fr. Hebrew.* TrJP

Those red men you offended were my brothers. In My First Hard Springtime. James Welch. AmPA; CDW

Those rivers run from that land. Robert Creeley. VGW

Those rocket gentlemen. (*LL*) A Projection. Reed Whittemore. AiP

Those screams that freeze your spine. (*LL*) From Death's Point of View. Duo Duo. SpMi

Those ships which left. Saigyo, *tr. fr. Japanese by* Arthur Waley. AWP

Those snooty boys in all their purple drag! Strato, *tr. fr. Greek by* Tony Harrison. GrAn; PeHV

Those speckled trout we glimpsed in a pool last year. Two Fish. Katha Pollitt. DiPo; NIP

Those summer children long since safely dead. (*LL*) 1904. Frederick Morgan. WeW

Those that can give, open their hands this day. A New Year's Sacrifice: To Lucinda. Thomas Carew. CaPo

Those that go searching for love. Search for Love. D. H. Lawrence. CBLP

Those times I have you when my flesh. For Eyes to Bless You. Pamela Mordecai. PBCV

Those Troublesome Disguises. Jonathan Williams. NeAP

Those trumpeting/ petals. (*LL*) Iris. William Carlos Williams. InPS; LCAP; WeW

Those Two Boys. Franklin P. Adams. FiBHP; TrJP

Those two eyes there, which dazzle me. (*LL*) The Moon Has Complained. Paul Johann Ludwig Heyse. RiWo

Those two young men, dancing quietly together in a corner. Gay Boys. James Kirkup. PeHV

Those upon whom Almighty doth intend. The Frowardness of the Elect in the Work of Conversion. Edward Taylor. *Fr.* God's Determinations [touching his Elect]. EAP; SCAP

Those Upright Men. Judith Kazantzis. FaBoBl

Those Various Scalpels. Marianne Moore. CBCK

Those/ various sounds consistently indistinct. Those Various Scalpels. Marianne Moore. CBCK

Those verses surfaced thirty years ago. Postscript, 1984. John Hewitt. BiHa

Those we have loved the dearest. The Fallen. Duncan Campbell Scott. TrPWD

Those We Love the Best. Ella Wheeler Wilcox. PoToHe

Those we love truly never die. Forever. John Boyle O'Reilly. WGRP

Those were countries simple to observe, difficult. Report from a Planet. Richmond Lattimore. FYAP

Those were fluid days. And the wind that met us. The New Reforms. Jack Roberts. BAP-91

Those were the conquered, still too proud to yield. The Battle-Field. Lloyd Mifflin. PAH

Those Were the Days. *Zulu Oral Tradition, tr. by* H. Tracey. WTO

Those who are dead are never gone. Birago Diop. EaPr

Those who arrive at Thekla can see little of the city. Italo Calvino, *tr. fr. Italian. Fr.* Cities and the Sky. AnRep, *tr. by* William Weaver

Those who await him, wound his limbs with stones. (*LL*) Here Is Much Burning Anger. Shimon Halkin. MHP

Those who cannot love the heavens or the earth. The Chaff. W. S. Merwin. PPP

Those who can't find anything to live for. The Basic Con. Lew Welch. PoBeRe

Those who favor our plan to alter the river. Plans for Altering the River. Richard Hugo. FYAP

Those who fling off, toss head. Meeting Together of Poles & Latitudes: In Prospect. Margaret Avison. NOBC

Those who have chosen to pass the night. Violent Storm. Mark Strand. NYBP

Those who have descended to the nethermost deeps. Bathymeter. William Hart-Smith. FaBoMA

Those who have laid the harp aside. To Wordsworth. Walter Savage Landor. OAEL-2

Those Who Lost Everything. David Diop, *tr. fr. French by* Langston Hughes. PBA

Those who love Thee may they find. George F. Chawner. BLRP

Those who realize true wisdom. *Unknown, tr. fr. Sanskrit. Fr.* Bhagavad-Gita, The. EnlH, *vers. by* Stephen Mitchell

Those who turn their face to the wall. Jenny Joseph. *Fr.* Persephone. PWE

Those Who Want Out. Denise Levertov. LoHo

Those who win Heaven, blest are they! (*LL*) One Way of Love. Robert Browning. OtMeF

Those Who Wrestle with the Angel for Us. Brigit Pegeen Kelly. NAmP90

Those Winter Sundays. Robert Hayden. CAPP; FF; GoJo; GrPl; HAP; HCAP; HeIL; InPK; LCAP; MoP; NIP; NoAM; NoP; PoBA; Poetr; PPP; RaBo; SoSe; TFi; UnPo; WeW

Those with experience look for a special kind. Going for Peaches, Fredericksburg, Texas. Naomi Shihab Nye. MT

Thou art alone, fond lover. (*LL*) The Evening Darkens Over. Robert Bridges. CMoP; HAP; NOBVV; PoEL-5; SCGP

Thou art avenged, my first-born, sleep in peace! (*LL*) Yussouf. James Russell Lowell. BeLS; BLPA; BLPL; BoTP; FaBoBe

Thou Art Coming! Frances Ridley Havergal. WGRP

Thou art gone to thine island home. To My Wife. John Willis Menard. AAP

Thou Art Indeed Just, Lord, If I Contend. Gerard Manley Hopkins. AWP; ChIV-1; CMoP; EBVV; GTBS-P; HAP; HoPM; InPK; LiTM; MoAB; MoBrPo; NAEL-2; NoAM; NOBE; NOBVV; NoP; OAEL-2; PeECV; SCGP; TOF; TrPWD; UnPo

Thou art King of Israel and of Davides kunne. A Palm-Sunday Hymn. William Herebert. MeEL

Thou art like to a flower. The Translated Way. Franklin P. Adams. FiBHP

Thou art love's victim; and must die. Richard Crashaw. *Fr.* Hymn to the Name and Honour [*or* Honor] of the Admirable Saint[e] T[h]eresa, A. JCP; NOBE; NoP; OBD; OBEV; PoEL-2; SeCV-1, *abr.*

Thou art my God, sole object of my love. Prayer of St. Francis Xavier. Pope. TrPWD
(Hymn: "Thou art my God, sole object of my love.") ChIV-2

Thou art not dead, although the spoiler's hand. Africa. Lewis Alexander. CDC

Thou art not dead, my Prote! thou art flown. To Prote. Simmias of Thebes, *tr. fr. Greek by* John Addington Symonds. AWP

Thou Art Not Fair. Thomas Campion. EiL; EnRePo; InvP

Thou art not fair for all thy red and white. Thomas Campion. *See* Thou Art Not Fair.

Thou art not near me, but I see Thine eyes. I Love Thee. Josephine D. Henderson Heard. CBWP-4

Thou art not so black as my heart. A Jet Ring Sent. John Donne. CBLP; OxBSP
(Jeat Ring Sent, A.) PoEL-2

Thou Art, O God, *abr.* Thomas Moore. *See* Thou art, O God, the life and light.

Thou Art, O God, the God of Might. Emily Swan Perkins. AH

Thou art, O God, the life and light. The Glory of God in Creation. Thomas Moore. OHIP
(Thou Art, O God, *abr.*) PWR; TrPWD

Thou Art of All Created Things. Pedro Calderón de la Barca, *tr. fr. Spanish.* WGRP

Thou art Orplid, my land. Weyla's Song. Eduard Friedrich Mörike, *tr. fr. German by* Philip L. Miller. RiWo

Thou art so fair, and young [*or* yong] withal [*or* withall]. Youth and Beauty. Aurelian Townshend. GBL; SeCP

Thou art the essence of all created things. Thou Art of All Created Things. Pedro Calderón de la Barca, *tr. fr. Spanish.* WGRP

Thou Art the Sky. Rabindranath Tagore. *Fr. Gitanjali.* OBMV

Thou Art the Tree of Life. Edward Taylor. AH

Thou Art the Way. George Washington Doane. AH

Thou art the Way. "I Am the Way." Alice Meynell. NOBVV; OBMV; OxBSP

Thou art the worn memorial, Baker Street. *(LL)* The Metropolitan Railway. Sir John Betjeman. EBEV; OxAEP-2; OxBTC

Thou art to all lost love the best. To the Willow-Tree. Robert Herrick. CaPo; OBEV; SCGP

Thou art too hard for me in Love. Love. George Herbert. PeECV

Thou, att whose feete I waste mie soule in sighes. To Mie Tirante. George Darley. Son

Thou barren waste; unprofitable strand. Winter in Lower Canada. Standish O'Grady. *Fr. Emigrant, The.* NOBC

Thou bearst the bottle, I the bag (oh Lord). The Bottle. Ralph Knevet. ChIV-2

Thou beauteous off-spring of a syre as fair. On a Sunbeam. Thomas Heyrick. NOSC

Thou Beautiful Sabbath. *Unknown, tr. fr. Yiddish by* Isidore Myers. TrJP

Thou best of men and friends! we will create. Richard Lovelace. *Fr. Grasshopper, The.* OBF

Thou bidest wall nor floor, Lord! *(LL)* The Hurricane. Hart Crane. CMoP; MoAB; MoAmPo; OxBA; TrCP

Thou bid'st me come away. To Death. Robert Herrick. BeJo

Thou bleedest, my poor heart! and thy distress. On a Discovery Made Too Late. Samuel Taylor Coleridge. EnRP; Son

Thou Blind Man's Mark. Sir Philip Sidney, Sometimes considered Sonnet CIX of Astrophel and Stella *and also in* Certain Sonnets. EnRePo; ErPo; ESo; HeIP; NAEL-1; PPP; SCGP; SiPSBD; Son

Thou blind man's mark, thou fool's self-chosen snare. Thou Blind Man's Mark. Sir Philip Sidney, Sometimes considered Sonnet CIX of Astrophel and Stella *and also in* Certain Sonnets. EnRePo; ErPo; ESo; HeIP; NAEL-1; PPP; SCGP; SiPSBD; Son
(Desire.) ImPo; LiTB; NOBE; SiPS; TrGrPo

Thou blossom bright with autumn dew. To the Fringed Gentian. Bryant. AnAmPo; AWP; FaBoBe; GN; NoP; PoLF; TAP

Thou, born to sip the lake or spring. On a Honey Bee *[or* To a Honey Bee]. Philip Freneau. TAP
(To a Honey Bee.) AnAmPo

Thou breath of things unseen! *(LL)* Lord of My Heart's Elation. Bliss Carman. AH; NOBC; TrPWD

Thou call'st me madman, but I call thee blockhead. *(LL)* To Flaxman. Blake. FaBoEE; OxBoLi

Thou canst not die whilst any zeal abound. Samuel Daniel. *Fr.* To Delia. ESo; NoSic; Son

Thou canst not prove that thou art body alone. The Ancient Sage. Tennyson. WGRP

Thou Christ, my soul is hurt and bruised! The Doubter. Richard Watson Gilder. TrPWD

Thou comest, much wept for: such a breeze. Tennyson. *Fr.* In Memoriam A. H. H. EBVV, *abr.*; OAEL-2, *abr.*; PeECV, *abr.*

Thou com'st and dost relieve. *(LL)* A Parodie. George Herbert.

Thou cursed cock, with thy perpetual noise. On a Cock at Rochester. Sir Charles Sedley. FaBoEE; NOSC; OPOP

Thou darling of the sire! *(LL)* Inhuman Henry. A. E. Housman. FiBHP; NBLV

Thou daughter of the royal line. The Ninth Canticle. George Wither. ChIV-1

Thou dear and mystic semblance. Lines to the Blessed Sacrament. *Unknown, tr. fr. Irish by* Jeremiah J. Callanan. TIRV

Thou Didst Delight My Eyes. Robert Bridges. ELP; MoAB; MoBrPo

Thou dost loth me, — I love thee, though cause of my death. *(LL)* The Green Willow. *Unknown.* EBEvV; SCGP

Thou dravest love from thee, who dravest Me. *(LL)* The Hound of Heaven. Francis Thompson. BLPL; ChIV-2; EBEvV, *ll.* 1–15; EnVR; FaBV; GGP, *ll.* 1–15; ImPo; LiTB; LiTM; MoAB; MoBrPo; NAEL-2; OBMV; OtMeF; PoEL-5; TFi; TrGrPo; WGRP

Thou dread'st and hop'st Thou know'st not what. *(LL)* Adriani Morientis ad Animam Suam. Emperor Hadrian. OBVE; OxBSP

Thou dreamest still which way my life to wast. *(LL)* Thou Sleepest Fast. *Unknown.* ElL; OxBSP

Thou, Earth, calm empire of a happy soul. Shelley. *Fr.* Prometheus Unbound. EnRP; FaBoRV; OAEL-2; PeECV

Thou fair-hair'd *[or* fair-haired] angel of the evening. To the Evening Star. Blake. BoNaP; CH; ChTr; EnRP; FaBoRV; FaBV; NAEL-2; NOEC; NoP; OAEL-2; PoE; PoLF; TEP; TFi; TrGrPo; WiR

Thou find'st not heere, neither the furious alarmes. K. Soowthern. *Fr.* Sonnets to his Mystresse Diana. ESo

Thou first and worst disturber of man's rest. *(LL)* On a Cock at Rochester. Sir Charles Sedley. FaBoEE; NOSC; OPOP

Thou fool profane, be silent! *Unknown, tr. fr. Hebrew. Fr.* Duel with Verses over a Great Man. TrJP

Thou gallant Chief whose glorious name. Washington. Denis O'Crowley. OHIP

Thou gav'st me leave to kiss. Chop-Cherry. Robert Herrick. EnLoPo

Thou God of all, whose presence dwells. John Haynes Holmes. TrPWD

Thou God of This Great Vast, Rebuke These Surges. Shakespeare. *Fr.* Pericles. NAs

Thou God, whose high, eternal Love. Wedding-Hymn. Sidney Lanier. TrPWD

Thou Grace Divine, Encircling All. Eliza Scudder. AH

Thou graunte me amendinge! *(LL)* Marye, maide, milde and fre. At. to William of Shoreham. MiEL

Thou Great God. *Unknown, tr. fr. Xhosa by* A. C. Jordan. PBA

Thou great Lord God. *(LL)* An Easter Canticle. Charles Hanson Towne. OHIP; TrPWD

Thou great Supreme, whom angel choirs adore. Unseen. Fanny Crosby. TrPWD

Thou green and blooming, cool and shaded hill. The Heart on the Hill. Petrarch, *tr. fr. Italian. Fr.* Sonnets to Laura. AWP

Thou grimmest far o grusome tykes. To a Hedgehog. Samuel Thompson. BIrV

Thou Guide to doubt, be silent evermore. *Unknown, tr. fr. Hebrew. Fr.* Duel with Verses over a Great Man. TrJP

Thou hadst all passion's splendour. Emily Brontë: Du hast Diamanten. Robert Bridges. EPCY

Thou hadst the peace and I the undying pain. *(LL)* Not Thou but I. Philip Bourke Marston. BLPA; BLPL

Thou happy, happy elf! *A* Parental Ode to My Son, Aged Three Years and Five Months. Thomas Hood. FiBHP, *abr.*; PoLF
(To My Son, Aged Three Years and Five Months.) FaPON, *abr.*

Thou has come from the old city. The Old City. Ruth Manning-Sanders. CH

Thou Has Wounded the Spirit That Loved Thee. Mrs. David Porter. BLPA

Thou hast a sister by the mother's side. Shakespeare. *Fr.* Antony and Cleopatra. OxAEP-1

Thou hast brought him a pardon from good King John. *(LL)* King John and the Abbot of Canterbury. *Unknown.* BoTP; EnSB; GN; TrGrPo

Thou hast come safe to port. Lament for Hathimoda, Abbess of Gandesheim. *Unknown, tr. fr. Latin by* Helen Waddell. MLL

Thou Hast Diamonds. Heine, *tr. by* Emma Lazarus. *Fr.* Homeward Bound. TrJP

Thou hast made me, and shall thy work[e] decay? John Donne. *Fr.* Holy Sonnets. EBEV; EnRePo; ESCV; MeLP; NAEL-1; NOBE; NOCV; NoP; NOSC; OxAEP-1; PoEL-2; SCGP; SeCP; Son; TEP

Thou hast not drooped thy stately head. Savannah. Alethea S. Burroughs. PAH

Thou hast not left the rough-barked tree to grow. I Was Sick and in Prison. Jones Very. NOBA

Thou hast not rais'd, Ianthe, such desire. Walter Savage Landor. *Fr.* Ianthe. GBL

Thou hast on earth a Trinity. To the Christ. John Banister Tabb. TrPWD

Thou hast thy calling to some palace floor. Elizabeth Barrett Browning. *Fr.* Sonnets from the Portuguese. OxAEP-2; Son

Thou hearest the nightingale begin the song of spring. Blake. *Fr.* Milton.
(Choir of Day, The.) EnRP
(Lark's Song, The.) WiR
(Vision of Beulah, The ("Thou hearest the nightingale begin the song of spring").) NOBE
(Vision of the Lamentation of Beulah, A.) OBNC

Thou heaven-threat'ning Rock, gentler then she! Echo to a Rock. Lord Herbert of Cherbury. PoEL-2

Thou heavenly quivering beneath the deathlike above! To a Lark in War-Time. Franz Werfel, *tr. fr. German by* Edith Abercrombie Snow. TrJP

Thou hermit, haunter of the lonely glen. The Sand Martin. John Clare. TEP

Thou hidden love of God, whose height. John Wesley. NOEC
(Hymn.) ECEV

Thou hide thy face? *(LL)* Speak. James Wright. HAP; SM; TAP

Thou ill-formed offspring of my feeble brain. The Author to Her Book. Anne Bradstreet. AmPP; AnAmPo; EAP; InPK; NAAL-1; NALW; NOBA; NoP; OxBA; PoE; Poetr; SCAP; TAP

Thou inmost, ultimate. To the Body. Alice Meynell. PeVV

Thou jestedst when thou swor'st that thou betrothedst. Tudor Aspersions. R. A. Piddington. FiBHP

Thou king of terrors with thy gastly eyes. A Fig for Thee, Oh! Death. Edward Taylor. NAAL-1

Thou king of wele and blisse. William Herebert. MiEL

Thou Knowest. Katharine Lee Bates. TrPWD

Thou knowest, love, I know that thou dost know. Michelangelo, *tr. fr. Italian by* John Addington Symonds. PeHV
(Love's Entreaty.) AWP

Thou knowest my praise of nature most sincere. William Cowper. *Fr.* Task, The. NAEL-1

Thou knowest my years entire, my life. Walt Whitman. *Fr.* Prayer of Columbus. AmPP; TrPWD; WGRP

Thou knowest that toads and snakes and loathly worms. Shelley. *Fr.* Prometheus Unbound. EnRP; OAEL-2; PoE

Thou knowest, Thou who art the soul of all. Thou Knowest. Katharine Lee Bates. TrPWD

Thou knowest what is best. Trust and Obedience. *Unknown.* BLRP

Thou know'st, my Julia, that it is thy turn. To Julia, the Flaminica Dialis, or Queen-Priest. Robert Herrick. CaPo

Thou large-brained woman and large-hearted man. To George Sand: A Desire. Elizabeth Barrett Browning. BoWoP; NAEL-2; NALW; TEP

Thou leadest, O God! All's well with Thy troopers that follow. *(LL)* The Wild Ride. Louise Imogen Guiney. AmWP

Thou leanest to the shell of night. James Joyce. EBEV

Thou Light of Ages. Rolland W. Schloerb. TrPWD

Thou Ling'ring Star. Burns. EnRP

Thou little bird, thou dweller by the sea. The Little Beach-Bird. Richard Henry Dana. AnAmPo

Thou, little sandpiper, and I? *(LL)* The Sandpiper. Celia Laighton Thaxter. FaBoBe; FaPON; GN; OBCA; OxBChV; PWR; WBLP

Thou Long Disowned, Reviled, Oppressed. Eliza Scudder. AH

Thou, Lord, and I. *(LL)* The Scribe. Walter de la Mare. CMoP; EBEvV; FaBoCh; OBMV; TrCP; TrPWD

Thou, Lord, Hast Been Our Sure Defense. John Hopkins. AH

Thou Lord of Hosts, Whose Guiding Hand. Octavius Brooks Frothingham. AH

Thou lovedst life, but not to brand it thine (O rich in all forborne felicities!). Pascal. Louise Imogen Guiney. AmWP

Thou lovely and belovèd, thou my love. Mid-Rapture. Dante Gabriel Rossetti. *Fr.* House of Life, The. BLPL; FaBoBe

Thou Lovest Me. Josephine D. Henderson Heard. CBWP-4

Thou mak'st the heaven thou hop'st indeed thy home. *(LL)* East London. Matthew Arnold. SCGP; WGRP

Thou mercenary renagade, thou slave. To Mr. Bays. Charles Sackville. APAS

Thou mighty gulf, insatiate cormorant. To Everlasting Oblivion. John Marston. *Fr.* Scourge of Villainy [*or* Villanie], The. NoSic; SCGP

Thou mighty Mars, the god of soldiers brave. An Epitaph on Sir Philip Sidney. James I, King of England. Son

Thou monstrous gilt and rainbow-tinted thing. The New Organ. Josephine D. Henderson Heard. CBWP-4

Thou Moon, that aidest us with thy magic might. A Charm. Dryden. ChTr

Thou more than most sweet glove. The Glove. Ben Jonson. *Fr.* Cynthia's Revels. EIL; GBL

Thou most absurd of all absurdities. The Sloth. George Romanes. FM; IHNG; PIP

Thou mother dear and thou my father's shade. For Erotion's Grave. Martial, *tr. fr. Latin by* F. A. Wright. OBD

Thou *Murth'rer* which hast *kill'd,* and *Devil* which wouldst *Damn me. (LL)* Beauty. Abraham Cowley. ImPo; LiTB; PoEL-2; TrGrPo

Thou must be true thyself. Be True [*or* Be True Thyself]. Horatius Bonar. FaBoBe; GN; PWR

Thou need'st not flutter from thy half-built nest. The Robin. Jones Very. Son

Thou ne're wutt [*or* nere wilt] riddle, neighbour Jan [*or* John]. A Devonshire Song. *At. to* William Strode. PoEL-2, *sl. diff. vers.*

Thou noblest monument of Albion's isle! Written at Stonehenge. Thomas Warton the Younger. Son

Thou, of the living lyre. Female Education. Lydia Huntley Sigourney. AmWP

Thou One in All, Thou All in One. Seth Curtis Beach. AH

Thou our health, our glory Thou. In Honour of the Holy Spirit. Hildebert, *tr. fr. Latin by* Helen Waddell. MLL

Thou, paw-paw-paw; thou, glurd; thou, spotted. Adam's Task. John Hollander. NIP; NoP; PPP

Thou perceivest the flowers put forth their precious odors. The Wild Thyme. Blake. *Fr.* Milton. WiR

Thou pleasant island, whose rich garden-shores. Corfou. Richard Monckton Milnes. *Fr.* Ionian Islands, The. OBTV

Thou Pleiad of the lyric world. Adelina Patti. Adah Isaacs Menken. CBWP-1

Thou priest that art behind the screen. Ipsissimus. Eugene Lee-Hamilton. PeVV

Thou, proud man, look upon yon starry vault. Man's Littleness in Presence of the Stars. Henry Kirke White. WBLP

Thou Remainest. Annie Johnson Flint. BLRP

Thou retir'st to endless Rest. *(LL)* The Grasshopper. Abraham Cowley, *after the Greek of* Anacreon. AWP; BeJo; FM; NOSC; OAEL-1; OBVE; OxAEP-1; SeCV-1; WiR

Thou rob'st [*or* robb'st] my days of bus'ness [*or* business] and delights. The Thief. Abraham Cowley. *Fr.* Mistress, The. JCP

Thou saidst that I alone thy heart cou'd move. Catullus, *tr. fr. Latin by* William Walsh. OBVE
(To His False Mistress.) OxBSP

Thou sai'st I swore I lov'd thee best. The Variety. John Dancer. NOSC

Thou saist Love's dart. To Oenone. Robert Herrick. CaPo

Thou saist my lines are hard. To My Ill Reader. Robert Herrick. CaPo

Thou sallow picture of my poison'd love. Cyril Tourneur. *Fr.* Revenger's Tragedy, The. OBD

Thou Seemest Like a flower. Heine. *See* E'en as a lovely flower.

Thou seest me, Lucia, this year droop. Crutches. Robert Herrick. CaPo

Thou seest the under side of every leaf. Omniscience. Blanche Mary Kelly. TrPWD

Thou seest this world is but a thoroughfare. Eternal Reward, Eternal Pain. Sir Thomas More. *Fr.* Twelve Weapons of Spiritual Battle, The. EnRePo

Thou sent to me [*or* mee] a heart was crowned [*or* crown'd]. Upon a Diamond Cut in Form[e] of a Heart . . . Sent in a New Year's [*or* New-yeares] Gift. Sir Robert Ayton. EIL

Thou shalt die. *Unknown, tr. fr. Latin by* Helen Waddell. MLL

Thou shalt eat curds and cream, all the year lasting. The Shepherd's Enticements. *Unknown. Fr.* Phyllida Flouts Me. CBCK

Thou shalt have no other gods before me. The Ten Commandments. Bible, *O.T. Fr.* Exodus. WBLP

Thou shalt have one God only; who. The Latest Decalogue. Arthur Hugh Clough. ChIV-1; ChTr; CoGr; EBEV; EBVV; EBVVPR; EnVR; FaBoCo; FaBoEE; FF; GTBS-P; HAP; HeIL; HoPM; IHNG; NAEL-2; NOBE; NOBVV; OAEL-2; OBNC; OBSV; OPOP; OtMeF; PeECV; PIP; PPP; SCGP; TFi; WeW; WGRP

Thou shalt hear the Master calling. *(LL)* Christmas Eve. Eugene Field. OHIP

Thou Shalt Not. Malka Heifetz-Tussman, *tr. fr. Yiddish by* Marcia Falk. AWP

Thou Shalt Not Kill: A Memorial for Dylan Thomas. Kenneth Rexroth. PoBeRe

Thou shalt not laugh in this leaf, Muse, nor they. John Donne. *Fr.* Satires. OBSV

Thou shalt not laugh, thou shalt not romp. A Fleeting Passion. W. H. Davies. NSI

Thou shalt seek the beach of sand. The Fay's Sentence. Joseph Rodman Drake. *Fr.* Culprit Fay, The. GN

Thou silver deity of secret night. Hymn to the Moon. Lady Mary Wortley Montagu. ECWP

Thou simple bird what mak'st thou here to play? Upon the Lark and the Fowler. Bunyan. CH

Thou Sleepest Fast. *Unknown.* EIL; OxBSP

Thou sleepest where the lilies fade. Buried. Christina Rossetti. CBLP

Thou snowy farm with thy five tenements! Elinda's [*or* Ellinda's] Glove. Richard Lovelace. CaPo; CBLP; NOSC

Thou, so far, we grope to grasp thee. So Far, So Near. Christopher Pearse Cranch. TrPWD

Thou sorrow, venom elfe. Upon a Spider Catching a Fly. Edward Taylor. AmPP; EAP; MeMAP; NOBA; NoP; OxBA; PeECV; PoEL-3; SCAP; TAP

Thou spark of life that wavest wings of gold. Ode to a Butterfly. Thomas Wentworth Higginson. FaBoBe

Thou stately stream that with the swelling tide. The Lover to the Thames of London, to Favour [*or* Favor] His Lady Passing Thereon. George Turberville. ChTr; EIL; NoP

Thou still unravish'd bride of quietness. Keats. *See* Thou still unravished bride of quietness.

Thou still unravished bride of quietness. Ode on a Grecian Urn. Keats. AWP; ClHu; EBEV; EnRP; FaBoBe; FF; HAP; HeIP; HoPM; ImPo; InPS; LiTB; NAEL-2; NAWM-2; NIP; NOBE; NoP; OAEL-2; OBEV; OBNC; PoE; PoEL-4; PPP; PrIm; SCGP; TEP; TFi; TOF; TrGrPo; UnPo
(Thou still unravish'd bride of quietness.) FaPoB

Thou strainest through the mountain fern. Robert Louis Stevenson. NOBVV

Thou stranger, which for Rome in Rome here seekest. Joachim du Bellay, *tr. fr. French by* Spenser. *Fr.* Ruins of Rome. FaBoPP; OBVE

Thou swear'st thou'lt drink no more; kind Heaven send. To Julius. Martial, *tr. by* Sir Charles Sedley. FaBoEE

Thou sweetly-smelling fresh red rose. Dialogue: Lover and Lady. Ciullo d'Alcamo, *tr. fr. Italian by* Dante Gabriel Rossetti. AWP

Thou that art by Fates degree. New Canaans Genius; Epilogus. Thomas Morton. SCAP

Thou that art wise, let wisdom minister. Sonnet: He Craves Interpreting of a Dream of His. Dante da Maiano, *tr. fr. Italian by* Dante Gabriel Rossetti. AWP

Thou that at Rome astonished doth behold. Joachim du Bellay, *tr. fr. French by* Spenser. *Fr.* Ruins of Rome. FaBoPP

Thou that canst sing so high, canst reach as low. (LL) An Answer to Mr. Ben Jonson's Ode, to Persuade Him Not to Leave the Stage. Thomas Randolph. BeJo

Thou that comest from heaven. Wanderer's Night Song. Goethe, *tr. fr. German by* Philip L. Miller. RiWo

Thou that didst leave the ninety and the nine. Missing. John Banister Tabb. TrPWD

Thou that from the heavens art. Goethe, *tr. fr. German. Fr.* Wanderer's Night-Songs. AWP

Thou that in prayeres hes bene lent. Rise with the Lamb of Innocence. *Unknown.* MeEL

Thou that loved once now loves no more. The Answer. Sir Robert Ayton. NOSC

Thou the faint beams of reason's scattered light. Solitude and Reason, in the Village. Abraham Cowley. *Fr.* Of Solitude. FaBoPP

Thou to their teeth hast proved Thy Deity. (LL) On the Miracle of Loaves. Richard Crashaw. OxBSP

Thou, to whom my name bears witness. Be Not Silent. David ben Meshullam, *tr. fr. Hebrew.* TrJP

Thou, to whom the World unknown. Ode to Fear. William Collins. NOEC; SCGP; TrGrPo, *abr.*

Thou too art gone, thou loved and lovely one! To Eddleston. Byron. *Fr.* Childe Harold's Pilgrimage. PeHV

Thou, too, sail on, O Ship of State! Longfellow. *Fr.* Building of the Ship, The. PWR
(Republic, The.) 09AA; PAH; WGRP; 09OPP
(Sail On, O Ship of State.) FaPON
(Ship of State, The.) FaBoBe; OHIP

Thou tool of faction, mercenary scribe. Upon the Anonymous Author of Legion's Humble Address to the Lords. Thomas Brown. APAS

Thou tryant, whom I will not name. Wedlock; a Satire. Hetty Wright. NOEC

Thou two-faced year, Mother of Change and Fate. 1492. Emma Lazarus. WPE

Thou tyrant, whom I will not name. Wedlock, a Satire. Mehetabel Wright. ECWP

Thou vague dumb crawler with the groping head. To My Tortoise Chronos. Eugene Lee-Hamilton. FM

Thou visitest the earth, and waterest it. Bible, *O.T., paraphrased by* Sir Thomas Wyatt. *Fr.* Psalms. OHIP, *abr.*

Thou visor'd, vast, unspeakable show and lesson! (LL) Broadway. Walt Whitman. NAAL-1

Thou wast all that [*or* that all] to me, love. To One in Paradise. Poe. *Fr.* Assignation, The. AmPP; AnAmPo; BLPL; BoLoP; LiTA; OBEV; OxBA; PoLF; TAP; TrGrPo

Thou wast not born for death, immortal Bird! Magic Casements. Keats. *Fr.* Ode to a Nightingale. AWP; BLRP; ClHu; EBEV; EnRP; FaBoBe; FaBV; FaPoB; GTBS; GTBS-P; HAP; HeIP; ImPo; InPS; LiTB; NAEL-2; NAWM-2; NOBE; NoP; OAEL-2; OBEV; OBNC; OPOP; PoE; PoLF-4; PoRA; PPP; PrIm; RB; SCGP; SoSe; TEP; TFi; TOF; TrGrPo; UnPo

Thou water turn'st to Wine (faire friend of Life). To Our Lord, upon the Water Made Wine. Richard Crashaw. GeHe

Thou wert the morning star among the living. To Stella. Plato, *tr. fr. Greek by* Shelley. EnLoPo; FaBoEE; OBVE
(Morning and Evening Star.) AWP

Thou who art clothed in silk, who drawest on. Man Is a Weaver. Moses ibn Ezra, *tr. fr. Hebrew by* Emma Lazarus. TrJP

Thou who art Lord of the wind and rain. A Hymn of Thanksgiving. Wilbur D. Nesbit. OHIP

Thou who art thrown at by the great (shepherd) boys. The Zebra. *Unknown, tr. fr. Hottentot by* W. H. I. Bleek. PeSAV

Thou Who Createdst Everything. *Unknown, tr. fr. Middle English by* Donald Davie. NOCV

Thou who descendest river by river. *Unknown. See* You who descend river by river.

Thou who didst hang upon a barren tree. Long Barren. Christina Rossetti. PBWP; TrCP

Thou who dost all my worldly thoughts employ. Verses Written on Her Death-bed at Bath to Her Husband in London. Mary Monck. ECWP

Thou, who dost dwell alone. Desire. Matthew Arnold. WGRP

Thou, who dost feel Life's vessel strand. Edmund Clarence Stedman. *Fr.* Ordeal by Fire, The. WGRP

Thou, who dost flow and fourish here below. The Garland. Henry Vaughan. BOEP

Thou who hast slept all night upon the storm. To the Man-of-War-Bird. Walt Whitman. AmPP; FaBoBe; FM

Thou who makest thy escape from the tumult! *Unknown. See* You who make your escape from the tumult.

Thou who, when fears attack. Ode to Tobacco. Charles Stuart Calverley. FaBoCo; FiBHP

Thou who wilt not love, do [*or* doe] this. Upon Some Women. Robert Herrick. BeJo; CaPo; CBCK

Thou wouldst see the lovely and the wild. Monument Mountain. Bryant. BeLS; EAP

Thou, who wouldst wear the name. The Poet. Bryant. EAP; NAAL-1; TAP

Thou, Whom rich and poor adore. An Offer. Arthur Guiterman. TrJP

Thou, whom the former precepts have. Superliminare. George Herbert. ESCV; NOSC; SeCP

Thou whose birth on earth. Swinburne. *Fr.* Christmas Antiphones. TrPWD

Thou whose chaste song simplicity inspires. To Mrs. Smith, Occasioned by the First of Her Sonnets. William Hayley. Son

Thou, whose diviner soul hath caus'd thee now. To Mr. Tilman after He Had Taken Orders. John Donne. EBEV

Thou, whose sad heart, and weeping head lyes low. Easter-Day. Henry Vaughan. ESCV; PeECV

Thou, whose sweet youth and early hopes inhance. The Church-porch. George Herbert. ESCV

Thou, whose unmeasured temple stands. Bryant. BLRP
(How Amiable Are Thy Tabernacles!) TrPWD

Thou wilt forget me. "Love has no such word." Spring and Autumn. William James Linton. EBVV

Thou wilt remember. Thou art not more dear. Robert Browning. *Fr.* Pauline. OAEL-2

Thou wingèd bloom! Thou blossom-butterfly. (LL) The Mariposa Lily. Ina Coolbrith. AmWP

Thou, with thy looks, on whom I look full oft. The Looks of a Lover Enamoured. George Gascoigne. EIL

Thou with thy Savior art in endless bliss. (LL) In Memory of My Dear Grandchild [Anne Bradstreet]. Anne Bradstreet. BoWoP; NAAL-1; TrCP

Thou wommon boute fere. William Herebert. MiEL
(Devout Man Prays to His Relations, The.) MeEL

Thou wonder of the Atlantic shore. To Aaron Burr, under Trial for High Treason. Sarah Wentworth Morton. PAH

Thou worshipest the shadow upon earth. (LL) A Sonnet to Heavenly Beauty. Joachim du Bellay. AWP; CTC

Thou wouldst be scorched and drowned again! (LL) A Fly about a Glass of Burnt Claret. Richard Lovelace. CaPo

Thou wouldst not part thy spoil. To "A Certain Rich Man." Alice Meynell. ChIV-2

Thou wretched man, whom I discover, born. Peace Discovers the Poet. George Chapman. *Fr.* Euthymiae Raptus; or, The Teares of Peace. NOSC

Thou youngest virgin-daughter of the skies. To the Pious Memory of the Accomplished [*or* Accomplisht] Young Lady, Mrs. Anne Killigrew, [Excellent in the Two Sister-Arts of Poesie and Painting]. Dryden. NAEL-1; OAEL-1; PoEL-3; SeCV-2
(Ode to the Pious Memory of the Accomplished Young Lady, Mrs. Anne Killigrew.) OBEV

Thou, Zion, old and suffering. David Levi, *tr. fr. Italian by* Mary A. Craig. *Fr.* Bible, The. TrJP

Though a seeker since my birth. A Garland of Precepts. Phyllis McGinley. NBLV

Though ain't no vision visited my cell. (LL) The Sun Came. Etheridge Knight. PoBA

Though all of you consort now underground. (LL) In Memoriam Francis Ledwidge. Seamus Heaney. CIP; NoAM

Though All the Fates Should Prove Unkind. Thoreau. HAP

Though all the force to hold the parts together. Being Human. Ruth Stone. IMW

Though all thy gestures and discourses be. The Innocent Ill. Abraham Cowley. OPOP

Though Amaryllis Dance in Green. *Unknown.* EiL; NAEL-1

Though at night there is the smell of morning. *(LL)* Neither Here nor There. W. R. Rodgers. ImPo; LiTB; LiTM; MoAB; MoBrPo

Though authors are a dreadful clan. I Missed His Book, I Read His Name. John Updike. OBAL

Though aware of our rank and alert to obey orders. Ode: To My Pupils. W. H. Auden. MoBrPo

Though beauty be the mark of praise. Ben Jonson. BeJo; EnRePo; NoP; OBEV

(Elegie, An: "Though beautie be the marke of praise.") SeCV-1

Though between sullen hills. Shad-Time. Richard Wilbur. NGP

Though Bodies Are Apart. C. Day Lewis. *Fr.* From Feathers to Iron. NAs

Though buds still speak in hints. Field-Glasses. Andrew Young. GTBS-P; RB

Though by a sodaine and unfeard surprise. Under Mr. Hales Picture. Anne King. KTR

Though clasp'd and cradled in his nurse's arms. William Cowper. *Fr.* Hope. PoEL-3

Though clerical errors are fun. *Unknown.* PeLi

Though clock,/ To tell how night drawes hence, I've none. His Grange, or Private Wealth. Robert Herrick. BeJo; CaPo; FM; GoJo; SeCV-1

Though conscience void of all offence. Praise. Christopher Smart. OxBChV

Though countless as the grains of sand. Boethius, *tr.* by Samuel Johnson. *Fr.* Consolation of Philosophy, The. OBVE

"Though cowards flinch," the Labour Party trolled. "Sagittarius." *Fr.* Lest Cowards Flinch. FaBoEH

Though critics may bow to art, and I am its own true lover. Art and Heart. Ella Wheeler Wilcox. AnAmPo

Though days do gain upon the night. The Vierzide Chairs. William Barnes. NOBVV

Though Earth has full many a beautiful spot. The Land Which No Mortal May Know. Bernard Barton. PWR

Though every thing we see or hear may raise. My Observation at Sea. Mildmay Fane, 2d Earl of Westmorland. BeJo

Though faction's scorn at first did shun. John Clare. *Fr.* To John Keats, from His Honored Friend, William Davenant. EPCY

Though far off it be. *(LL)* Spring Quiet. Christina Rossetti. ArNa; BoNaP; BoTP; CH; GTBS-P; InPS; MeMBP; PoE; PoEL-5; WPE

Though fast youth's glorious fable flies. Lone Founts. Herman Melville. LiTA

Though Fatherland Be Vast. Allen Eastman Cross. AH

Though forts of adamant shall ring you round. The Enemy in the Fortress. Marbod of Rennnes, *tr. fr. Latin* by Helen Waddell. MLL

Though frost and snow locked [*or* lock'd] from mine eyes. To Saxham. Thomas Carew. BeJo; JCP; NoP

Though good things answer many good intents. Crosses. Robert Herrick. CaPo

Though 'half the convex globe intrudes between.' *(LL)* The Emigrant's Cabin. Thomas Pringle. PeSAV

Though handsome, rich and clever you may be. Vita Edwardi Secundi. *Unknown, tr. fr. Latin* by N. Denholm-Young. FaBoEH

Though he hung dumb upon her wall. And One Shall Live in Two. Jonathan Henderson Brooks. PoNe

Though he lives in the same town. What She Said. Palaipatiya Perunkatunko, *tr. fr. Tamil* by A. K. Ramanujan. PLW

Though he that, ever kind and true. Verses Written in 1872. Robert Louis Stevenson. BLPA; BLPL

Though he was but a bully.' *(LL)* The Day We Buried Our Bully. Mbuyiseni Oswald Mtshali. PeSAV

Though heart grows faint and spirits sink. The Word of God. Annie Johnson Flint. BLRP

Though her mother told her/ Not to go a-bathing. Leda and the Swan. Oliver St. John Gogarty. EBNV; HAP

Though his plan, when he gave her a buzz. *Unknown.* PeLi

Though humid summer's unfit for excursions. *Unknown, tr.* by Michael E. Workman. *Fr.* Tzu-yeh Songs of the Four Seasons. SuSp

Though I am dark. *Unknown, tr. fr. Spanish* by Willis Barnstone. BoWoP

Though I am Laila of the Persian romance. Princess Zeb-un-Nissa, *tr. fr. Persian* by Willis Barnstone. BoWoP; VBLP

Though I Am Young and Cannot Tell. Ben Jonson. *Fr.* Sad Shepherd, The. BeJo; ELP; NoP; TEP

Though I be foul, ugly, lean, and mis-shape. Death. Sir Thomas More. *Fr.* Pageant Verses. EnRePo

Though I be strange, sweet friend, be thou not so. A Court lady Addresses Her Lover. Edward de Vere, Earl of Oxford. NoSic

Though I be wooden Priapus (as thou see'st). Epigrams on Priapus. *Unknown.* ErPo

Though I get home how late, how late! The Return. Emily Dickinson. MoAmPo

Though I had one already and the other came. *(LL)* The Evil Eye. John Ciardi. MoBS; NAs

Though I had [*or* have] been at the doors [*or* doores] of death. To Sir William Alexander. William Drummond of Hawthornden. (To Sir W. A.) PoEL-2

Though I have an admiration for your charming resignation. Not Tonight, Josephine. Colin Curzon. ErPo

Though I have given. Lines Written in a Mausoleum. Lillian Grant. GoYe

Though I must live here, and by force. To My Mistress[e] in My Absence. Thomas Carew. CaPo; NOSC

Though I regarded not. The Earl of Surrey. AAS; SiPS

Though I sang in my chains like the sea. *(LL)* Fern Hill. Dylan Thomas. AngWe; ClHu; CMoP; FaBoPP; FaBV; FaPoB; GoJo; GTBS-P; HAP; HeIL; HeIP; ImPo; InPK; InPS; LiTB; LiTM; MeMBP; MoAB; MoBrPo; MoP; NAEL-2; NIP; NoAM; NOBE; NoP; NTP; OAEL-2; OBWVE; OxBTC; PoE; Poetr; PoLF; PoRA; PPP; SoSe; TFi; TrGrPo; TRP; TwCP

Though I should be maligned by those. Prayer for Strength. Margaret E. Bruner. PoToHe

Though I Should Seek. Henry Ustic Onderdonk. AH

Though I Speak with the Tongues of Men and Angels. Bible, *N.T. Fr.* First Corinthians. OAEL-1

Though I speak with the tongues of men and of angels. On Money. George Orwell. IHNG

Though I Thy Mithridates Were. James Joyce. MoP; NoAM; Poetr

Though I with strange desire. Kisses Desired. William Drummond of Hawthornden. EnLoPo

Though I would take comfort against sorrow. The Cry of the Daughter of My People. Bible, *O.T. Fr.* Jeremiah. TrJP

Though I'm in Kyoto. Basho, *tr. fr. Japanese* by John Tarrant. EnlH

Though it can take no more to the long road. *(LL)* Yangtse and Han. Tu Fu. PLT

Though it may look like (*Write* it!) like disaster. *(LL)* One Art. Elizabeth Bishop. CAPP; DiPo; HAP; NAAL-2; NALW; NoAM; PFP; PoE; SM; SoSe; VCAP

Though it were ten thousand mile. *(LL)* My Luve's like a Red, Red Rose. Burns. EnRP; FaBoBe; HoPM

Though it were ten thousand mile. *(LL)* Oh, My Love Is Like a Red, Red Rose. Burns. InPK; LiTB

Though it will die soon. Basho, *tr. fr. Japanese* by Anne Pennington. OBD

Though it's not so sure they will rise to high command. *(LL)* The Autumn Wastes. Tu Fu. PLT

Though it's true we were young girls when we met. For Jan, in Bar Maria. Carolyn Kizer. VGW

Though I've a Clever Head. *Unknown.* HAP

Though Sir James (God's-a-Formula) Jeans. R. J. P. Hewison. PeLi

Though joy is better than sorrow, joy is not great. Joy. Robinson Jeffers. CMoP

Though knowledge must be got with pain. For Scholars and Pupils. George Wither. OxBChV

Though leaves are many, the root is one. The Coming of Wisdom with Time. W. B. Yeats. FaBoEE; SoSe

Though life be dead, and my joys gone. *(LL)* As Time One Day by Me Did Pass. Henry Vaughan. ESCV; GeHe; MeLP; SeCV-1

Though loath to grieve. Ode Inscribed to W. H. Channing. Emerson. AmPP; HAP; MeMAP; NAAL-1; NOBA; NoP; OxBA; TAP

Though logic-choppers rule the town. Tom O'Roughley. W. B. Yeats. CMoP

Though love repine, and reason chafe. Faith. Emerson. *Fr.* Sacrifice. OtMeF

Though loves languish and sour. Prospect. Louis MacNeice. IIP

Though love's my daily and my nightly theme. To Emma, Extempore; Hyaena, off Gambia, June 4, 1779. Edward Thompson. NOEC

Though marriage by some folks. My Three Wives. *Unknown, after* Etienne Pasquier. FaBoEE

Though Mine Eye Sleep Not. *Unknown, tr.* by Theodor H. Gaster. *Fr.* Dead Sea Scrolls, The. TrJP

Though most of the crewmen are whites. On Board Starship *Enterprise.* *Unknown.* PeLi

Though much a little map unfolds, more still. The River Compared to an Oratorical Sentence. Luis de Góngora y Argote, *tr. fr. Spanish* by Edward Meryon Wilson. *Fr.* First Solitude, The. OBVE

Though my eyes are dim. *(LL)* An Old Song Ended. Dante Gabriel Rossetti. BoLoP; EBVV

Though My Thoughts. Francis Daniel Pastorius, *tr. fr. German by* Sheema Z. Buehne. AH

Though my wanderings are many. Suibne Geilt. NOIV

Though naked trees seem dead to sight. Hopeless Desire Soon Withers and Dies. "A. W." NoSic

Though naughty flesh will multiply. No Mean City. Patrick MacDonogh. BIrV; OxBSP

Though never claimed by us within my hearing. (*LL*) The Swimmers. Allen Tate. InPS; MoAmPo; NoAM; NOBA

Though never in the wards of the hospital for/ Disabled servicemen at Erskine. Warriors. Douglas Dunn. OxBC

Though no blossoms cluster. Mrs. Mary Furman Weston Byrd. Mary Weston Fordham. CBWP-2

Though now you are bereft and ways seem black. For One Lately Bereft. Margaret E. Bruner. PoToHe

Though of white marble and dressed straight. Crinagoras, *tr. fr. Greek by* Alistair Elliot. GrAn

Though on the day your hard blue eyes met mine. Heritage. Dorothea MacKellar. NOBAu

Though once a puppy, and though Fop by name. Epitaph on Fop. William Cowper. OBD

Though one with all that sense or soul can see. Transcendence. Richard Hovey. WGRP

Though only wind hears it. (*LL*) Song-Maker. Anita Endrezze-Danielson. HATNAP

Though [or thogh] ye to me ne do no daliaunce. (*LL*) To Rosamond. Chaucer. NoP

Though pleasures still can touch my soul. How Singular. Tom Hood. FaBoNo

Though prejudice perhaps my mind befogs. I Think I Know No Finer Things than Dogs. Hally Carrington Brent. BLPA

Though proud once as Juno! (*LL*) Going or Gone. Charles Lamb. BXAP

Though regions far [*or* farr] divided. Aurelian Townshend. JCP; NOSC; PoEL-2

Though riders be thrown in black disgrace. *Unknown, tr. fr. Irish by* Douglas Hyde. BIrV

Though rudely blows the wintry blast. The Charcoalman. John Townsend Trowbridge. AnAmPo

Though set like dough, they shall be drawn like bread. (*LL*) Like to a baker's oven is the grave. Francis Jeffrey. FaBoEE

Though seven times, or seventy times seven. The Women of Jericho. Phyllis McGinley. ChIV-1

Though Shakespeare asks us, "What's in a name?" Her Christening. Thomas Hood. *Fr.* Miss Kilmansegg and Her Precious Leg. NOBVV

Though she would neither wife nor widow be. (*LL*) A Contention betwixt a Wife, a Widow, and a Maid. Sir John Davies. SiPS

Though short her strain nor sung with mighty boast. Erinna. Antipater of Sidon, *tr. fr. Greek by* A. J. Butler. AWP

Though silent your tongue, you can speak with your pen. (*LL*) How to Write a Letter. Elizabeth Turner. MoShBr; OxBChV

Though since thy first sad entrance by Just Abel's blood. Death. Henry Vaughan. AngWe

Though skilled in Latin and in Greek. To a New England Poet. Philip Freneau. NAAL-1

Though somewhat large, exuberant, and truculent. Byron. *Fr.* Don Juan. OAEL-2

Though Tennyson,the poet king. James Madison Bell. *Fr.* Poem Entitled the Day and the War, A. AAP

Though the bee. In Him. James Vila Blake. WGRP

Though the cover is worn. My Old Bible. *Unknown.* BLRP

Though the cunning of the Indian and the Zulu's thirst for blood. Claflin's Alumni. L. A. J. Moorer. CBWP-3

Though the day of my destiny's over. Stanzas to Augusta. Byron. EnRP

Though the Earth Be Removed. Bible, *O.T., paraphrased by* Sir Thomas Wyatt. *See* God is our refuge and strength, a very present help in trouble.

Though the great song return no more. The Nineteenth Century and After. W. B. Yeats. FaBoEE

Though the limerick can not be deaded. *Unknown.* PeLi

Though the little clouds ran southward still, the. Autumn Evening. Robinson Jeffers. ArNa

Though the mills of God grind slowly, yet they grind exceeding small. Retribution. Friedrich von Logau, *tr. fr. German by* Longfellow. BLPA; PoToHe

Though the moon beaming matronly and bland. To Lucia at Birth. Robert Graves. NAs

Though the music of love is Schubérty. *Unknown.* PeHV

Though the New Teacher Is a Trifle Odd. Richard Moore. *Fr.* Word from the Hills. Son

Though the road turn at last. Prisoners. Denise Levertov. NoAM; VCAP

Though the rough, bitter-sweet haw of pioneering. American History. W. R. Moses. LiTA

Though the tough cough and hiccough plough me through. Ways of Pronouncing "Ough." *Unknown.* FaBoUs

Though the willows bent down to shelter us where we played. Doll. Josephine Miles. BCF; NALW

Though the world fall apart, surely ye shall prevail. (*LL*) Carthusians. Ernest Dowson. NAEL-2

Though the world fills with sorrow and rage. Original Mind. Nancy Paddock. LoHo

Though the world has slipped and gone. Edith Sitwell. CMoP; LiTM; NALW

Though the worst cold's to come. (*LL*) New Year's [*or* Year] Song. Ted Hughes. OBCP

Though then I smile, and speak no words at all. (*LL*) To His Lovely Mistresses. Robert Herrick. CaPo; CTC; SeCP

Though there are distances between us. Desert Warfare. Michael Longley. CIP

Though there are wild dogs. Orpheus and Eurydice. Geoffrey Hill. TRP

Though they are accounted good talkers. Ballade of the Women of Paris. Villon, *tr. fr. French by* Philip L. Miller. RiWo

Though this the [or thy] port and I thy servant true. Sir Thomas Wyatt. SiPS; SiPSBD

Though [Tho'] it were ten thousand mile. (*LL*) A Red, Red Rose. Burns. ArLo; AWP; BoLoP; CBLP; ChTr; FaBV; FF; GBL; HAP; HeIP; ImPo; InvP; NAEL-2; NIP; NOBE; NOEC; NoP; NTP; OAEL-1; OBEV; OtMeF; OxAEP-2; OxBS; PlP; PoEL-4; Poetr; PoLF; PrIm; ScCV; SCGP; TEP; TFi

Though thou hast passed thy summer standing, stay. Epithalamion, or a Song Celebrating the Nuptials of That Noble Gentleman, Mr. Jerome Weston. Ben Jonson. BeJo

Though thou, indeed, hast quite forgotten ruth. Ballata: Of a Continual Death in Love. Cavalcanti, *tr. fr. Italian by* Dante Gabriel Rossetti. AWP

Though thou, my ring, be small. To His Ring, Given to His Lady, Wherein Was Graven This Verse, "My Heart Is Yours." George Turberville. EIL

Though thou well dost wish me ill. Na Audiart. Ezra Pound. MeMAP

Though thousands traipse round Wordsworth's Lakeland shrine. Remains. Tony Harrison. FaBoVe

Though three men dwell on Flannan Isle. Flannan Isle. W. W. Gibson. CH; PoRA

Though to good breeding she made no pretence. On a Gentleman Marrying His Cook. Colin Ellis. FaBoEE

Though to strangers' approach. Paired Lives. W. R. Rodgers. CIP; IIP

Though to think/ Rejoiceth me. Margot Ruddock. OBMV

Though to your life apparent stain attach. Robert Nichols. *Fr.* Sonnets to Aurelia. OBMV

Though Truth and Falsehood be. Seek True Religion! John Donne. *Fr.* Satires. NOBE

Though truth be gold in any mould, and talents all for use. The Excuse. Morgan Llwyd. *Fr.* 1648. AngWe

Though we lived in the same lane. Answering Li Ying Who Showed Me His Poems about Summer Fishing. Yü Hsüan-chi, *tr. fr. Chinese*. BoWoP, *tr. by* Geoffrey R. Waters.

Though we may waver, he remaineth steadfast. The Everlasting Love. Annie Johnson Flint. BLRP

Though we thought it, Doña Carolina did not die. A Dream of Husbands. Alberto A. Ríos. NoAM

Though when I lov'd thee thou wert fair. The Deposition. Thomas Stanley. CBLP

Though with no lily, stay with me! (*LL*) Cock-crowing. Henry Vaughan. ESCV; GeHe; OAEL-1; SeCV-1

Though with the North we sympathize. Shop and Freedom. *Unknown.* PAH

Though wolves against the silver moon do bark. To the Detracted. John Andrews. *Fr.* Anatomy of Baseness, The. EIL

Though ye destroy their dust. (*LL*) Indian Names. Lydia Huntley Sigourney. FaPON; GOA; OBCA ; PAH; PoLF

Though Ye Suppose. John Skelton. OxBSP

Though you are a continent and two seasons away. Cape Coast Castle Revisited. Jo Ann Hall-Evans. BlSi

Though you are in your shining days. The Lover Pleads with his Friend for Old Friends. W. B. Yeats. OBF

Though you are sedentary always, though. Crinagoras, *tr. fr. Greek by* Alistair Elliot. GrAn

Though You Are Young. Thomas Campion. EnRePo

Haroun Al-Rachid for Heart's-Life. AWP
Haroun's Favorite Song. AWP
Her Rival for Aziza. AWP
Inscription on a Chemise. ErPo
Inscriptions at the City of Brass. AWP
Love ("Love was before the light began"). AWP
"O sons of men." OBD
Of Women. ErPo
Poems of the Arabic. ErPo
Psalm of Battle. AWP
Sleeper, The. AWP
Song of the Narcissus, The. AWP
Tell Him, O Night. AWP
To Lighten My Darkness. AWP
Tumadir al-Khansa for Her Brother. AWP
  (For Her Brother.) PBWP
Wazir Dandan for Prince Sharkan, The. AWP
Thousand and Second Night, The. James Merrill. NYBP
Thousand and Three, A. Paul Verlaine, *tr. fr. French* by Alistair Elliot. FaBoBl
Thousand Chinese Dinners, A, *sels.* Robert Mezey.
  "From a thousand Chinese dinners, one cookie." RaBo
Thousand days great Beelzebub and Pope his son and fool, A. The Winter. Morgan Llwyd. *Fr.* 1648. AngWe
Thousand goblets at the farewell feast, A. To Tzu-an. Yü Hsüan-chi, *tr. fr. Chinese* by Jan W. Walls. SuSp
Thousand great resolves, as great, A. To Mutius. Elizabeth Singer. KTR
Thousand guileless sheep have bled, A. Song from the Bride of Smithfield. Sylvia Townsend Warner. MoBrPo
Thousand Hairy Savages, A. Spike Milligan. NBLV
Thousand Islands, The. Charles Sangster. *Fr.* St. Lawrence and the Saguenay. NOBC
Thousand Killed, A. Bernard Spencer. OBWP
Thousand knights have rein'd their steeds, A. Calais Sands. Matthew Arnold. EBVVPR
Thousand Martyrs I Have Made, A. Aphra Behn. OPOP
Thousand men then came thronging together, A. Saint Called "Truth," A. William Langland. *Fr.* Vision of Piers Plowman, The. NOCV
Thousand people stand in the sunlight, The. My Fear in the Crowd. Josephine Miles. BCF
Thousand pricks. *(LL)* Epitaph on a Willing Girl. *At. to* Thomas Rowlandson. FaBoEE
Thousand score. *(LL)* To Dianeme. Robert Herrick. CaPo; FaBoBe
Thousand silent years ago, A. Praxiteles and Phryne. William Wetmore Story. BeLS
Thousand sounds, and each a joyful sound, A. Omnipresence. Edward Everett Hale. WGRP
Thousand strands of willow at spring river's bend, A. Willow Branches. Liu Yu Hsi, *tr. fr. Chinese* by Dell R. Hales. SuSp
Thousand streets of London gray, The. The Sheep and the Goat. George Macdonald. EBVV
Thousand times a day, A. *(LL)* Of the Birth and Bringing Up of Desire. Edward de Vere, Earl of Oxford. FaBoEE; NoSic; SCGP
Thousand times I have sat in resaurant windows, A. There Is Wind, There Are Matches. Gerald Stern. LCAP
Thousand times you've seen that scene, A. Country Burying (1919). Robert Penn Warren. LiTM
Thousand years from now, A. The Extermination of the Jews. Marvin Bell. BTR; CAPP
Thousand Years Have Come, A. Thomas T. Lynch. BLRP
Thousand years have passed away, A. A Call to Action. Charles Hamilton Sorley. NSI
Thousand years I was sick with darkness, A. Sun. Omer Hillel, *tr. fr. Hebrew* by Ruth Finer Mintz. MHP
Thousand years now had his breed, A. E. J. Pratt. *Fr.* Cachalot, The. MoCV
Thousand years shall come and go, A. The Iconoclast. Rose Terry Cooke. AmWP
Thousand years, with God (the Scriptures say), A. On the Life of Man. Francis Quarles. ChIV-2
Thousand years, you said, A. Lady Heguri, *tr.* by Geoffrey Bownas *and* Anthony Thwaite. *Fr.* Manyo Shu, Part 4 of 4. BoLoP
Thousands and Three. Paul Verlaine, *tr. fr. French* by François Pirou. PeHV
Thousands have lived without love, not one without water. *(LL)* First Things First. W. H. Auden. CBLP; NYBP
Thousands of new-born loves with your chaste eyes. *(LL)* An Anniversary on the Hymeneals of My Noble Kinsman, Thomas Stanley, Esquire. Richard Lovelace. CaPo
Thousandth Man, The. Kipling. ArLo; FaPoB

Thow art pretty but unconstant. Lines in the Corner of a Manuscript. *Unknown.* FaBoVe
Thracian page-boy/ mastered, A. Dioscorides, *tr. fr. Greek* by Peter Whigham. GrAn
Thracian Wonder, The, *sels. At. to* John Webster *and* William Rowley.
  Art Thou Gone in Haste? EiL; ELP; OxBoLi
  (Chase, The.) CH
  (Love Pursued.) GBL
  (Pursuit of Love.) ChTr
  Love Is a Law. EiL; GBL
  "Whither shall I go." GBL
Thraldome, The. Abraham Cowley. *Fr.* Mistress, The. SeCV-1
Thrash away, you'll hev to rattle. Letter, A ("Thrash away, you'll hev to rattle.") James Russell Lowell. *Fr.* Biglow Papers, The. AmPP; OxBA
  (Mr. Hosea Biglow Speaks.) PAH
Thraso. Samuel Rowlands. NoSic
Thraw oot your shaddaws. Moonlight among the Pines. "Hugh MacDiarmid." OAEL-1
Thrawn water? Aye, owre thrawn to be aye thrawn! By Wauchopeside. "Hugh MacDiarmid." EBEV; OxAEP-2
Thre Prestis of Peblis, The, *sels. At. to* John Reid of Stobo.
  "In Peblis town sum tyme, as I heard tell." OxBS
Thread, The. Denise Levertov. CrSp
Thread in the hand of a kind mother, The. Wanderer's Song. Meng Chiao, *tr. fr. Chinese* by A. C. Graham. PLT
Thread of Life, The, *sels.* Christina Rossetti.
  "Irresponsive silence of the land, The." NOBE; OBNC
  (Aloof.) OBEV, I; TrGrPo, I
Thread of red ants, A. Ants. Yusuf al-Sa'igh, *tr. fr. Arabic* by Diana Der Hovanessian *with* Salma Khadra Jayyusi. TSaS
Thread of silver marks along the sand, A. The Lost Continent. Jenny Joseph. BrRo
Thread Suns. Paul Celan. *See* Thread suns/ above the gray-black [*or* grey-black] wasteland [*or* wilderness].
Thread suns/ above the gray-black [*or* grey-black] wasteland [*or* wilderness]. Paul Celan, *tr. fr. German* by Beth Bjorklund.
  (Thread Suns.) OBVE, *tr.* by Michael Hamburger
Thread the Needle. *Unknown.* FaBoVe
Thread the needle   thread the needle. Thread the Needle. *Unknown.* FaBoVe
Thread the nerves through the right holes. Resurrection Song. Thomas Lovell Beddoes. FaBoEE
Threading the Miles. Alfred Encarnacion. OpBo
Threading the palm, a web of little lines. Signs. Gjertrud Schnackenberg. InPK; PoA; VCAP
Threat, The. Andrei Codrescu. UL
Threat'ning clouds of yesternight, The. While the Choir Sang. Priscilla Jane Thompson. CBWP-2
Three, The. Martin Steingesser. BTR
3 : 6, *sels.* Alta.
  "One hesitates to bring a child into this world without fixing." CrSp
Three Aldis, not one of them dim. Joyce Johnson. PeLi
3 A.M. John Updike. AnAmPo
Three a.m. — a far bell. December. Gary Snyder. InPS
Three Amphigouris. Jean-Joseph Vade, *tr. fr. French.* CBNP
Three ancient men in Bethlehem's cave. The Mystic Magi. Robert Stephen Hawker. ChTr; OBCP
Three and away. *(LL)* Bell horses, bell horses, what time of day? Mother Goose. BoTP; OxNR; ReMoGo
Three Angels. Bob Dylan. RaBo
Three angels came to the red red clay. From the Coptic. Stevie Smith. Mes
Three angels up above the street. Three Angels. Bob Dylan. RaBo
Three Animals. Ron Padgett. TTTS
  Sels.
  Butterfly, The.
  Electric Eel, The.
  Giraffe, The.
Three anti-depressants and one diuretic a day. Bruce Beaver. *Fr.* Letters to Live Poets. CBAP
Three Badgers, The. "Lewis Carroll." CBNP; FaBoNo
Three Ballate. A. Poliziano, *tr. fr. Italian* by John Addington Symonds. AWP
  Sels.
  "He who knows not what thing is Paradise."
  "I found myself one day all, all alone."
  "I went a roaming, maidens, one bright day."
Three Best Things, The, *sels.* Henry van Dyke.
  Zest of Life, The. WBLP

Three black boys. Panther. Sam Cornish. PoBA
Three blind mice, see how they run! Mother Goose. OxNR; ReMoGo
Three blind mice, three blind mice,/ Dame Julian, Dame Julian. *Unknown.* FaBoNo
Three bold brothers of merrie Scotland. Henry Martyn. *Unknown.* ESPB
Three boys, American, in dungarees. February 22. John Updike. GOA
Three Bushes, The. W. B. Yeats. EBNV
Three Bushes, The, *sels.* W. B. Yeats.
 Lady's Third Song, The. FaBoTw
Three Butchers, The. *Unknown.* PeVV
Three Captains, The. *Unknown, tr. fr. French by* Andrew Lang. AWP
Three Cars. Nichola Manning. NGP
Three cars covered three, The. Three Cars. Nichola Manning. NGP
Three Cheers for the Black, White and Blue. Ruth Pitter. OFC
Three Cherry Trees, The. Walter de la Mare. CMoP
Three chestnuts for morning, four at night. Tune: "Sheep on Mountain Slope." Ch'iao Chi, *tr. fr. Chinese by* Wayne Schlepp. SuSp
Three Children. At. to John Gay. *See* Three children sliding on the ice.
Three children dash in the dim dooryard. Tree Tag. Mary E. Caragher. GoYe
Three children sliding on the ice. At. to John Gay. OxNR; ReMoGo
 (Three Children.) NOBL
Three Christmas Carols, *sels.* *Unknown.*
Three City Cantos. Charles Wagner. GoYe
Three college sophs, and three pert templars came. Pope. *Fr.* Dunciad, The. FHYEP
Three-Coloured Banner. János Pilinszky, *tr. fr. Hungarian by* Peter Jay. PoSu
Three 'coons come at his garbage. He be cross. John Berryman. *Fr.* Dream Songs. LCAP
Three crests against the saffron sky. Twilight on Tweed. Andrew Lang. EBVV
Three crooked cripples went through Cripplegate. Mother Goose. OxNR
Three cups of wine a prudent man may take. The Benefits and Abuse of Alcohol. Eubulus, *tr. fr. Greek by* Richard Cumberland. FaBoUs; NBLV
Three dark maids, I loved them when. Villancico. *Unknown, tr. fr. Spanish by* Thomas Walsh. AWP
Three Darks Come Down Together. Robert Francis. CRP
Three Dawns. Jean-Joseph Rabéarivelo, *tr. fr. French by* Ellen Conroy Kennedy. NegPo
Three days before he died the hospital called me. Tongues. Philip Martin. NOBAu
Three days of rain: indoors. Rainpoem. Michael Dransfield. CBAP
Three days of rest. The Sun in Capricorn. Joyce Mansour, *tr. fr. French.* PBWP, *tr. by* Carol Cosman
Three days through sapphire seas we sailed. The Bay Fight. Henry Howard Brownell. PAH
Three Dead and the Three Living, The. George Barker. LiTB
Three dead men have I loved, and thou art last of the three. (*LL*) In the Garden at Swainston. Tennyson. OBEV; OBNC
Three Dispositions Regarding One Woman, *sels.* Sa'di Yusuf, *tr. fr. Arabic by* Sargon Boulus *and* Naomi Shihab Nye.
Three Dogs. E. C. Brereton. BoTP
Three Dreams at Chiang-ling. Yüan Chen, *tr. fr. Chinese by* William H. Nienhauser. SuSp
Three drunks, a leg on one quite gone, bereft. My Iambic Pentameter Lines. Robert Crawford. InPK
Three Easters. Alberta Turner. LCAP
Three Emily's, The. Dorothy Livesay. NALW
Three Enemies, The. Christina Rossetti. TrCP
Three Epigrams. Paul Ramsey. CRP
 Sels.
 Consolations.
 Exiles, The.
 Modern Theologian, A.
Three Epigrams. Theodore Roethke. NBLV
 Sels.
 Mistake, The.
Three Epitaphs on John Hewet and Sarah Drew. Pope. NIP
 Sels.
 Epitaph on the Stanton-Harcourt Lovers. FaBoEE; OBD
 "Think not by rigorous judgment seized"
 "When Eastern lovers feed the fun'ral fire"
Three excellent qualities in narration. Triads ("Three excellent qualities in narration.") *Unknown, tr. by* Thomas Kinsella. *Fr.* Triads of Ireland, The. BIrV
Three-faced, The. Robert Graves. FaBoEE

Three faces . . . /mirrored in the muddy streams of living. For Andy Goodman — Michael Schwerner — and James Chaney. Margaret Walker. BPo
Three Fates, The. Rosemary Dobson. BoWoP
Three fellows were marching over the Rhine. The Hostess' Daughter. Ludwig Uhland, *tr. fr. German by* Margarete Münsterberg. AWP
Three Fishers [Went Sailing], The. Charles Kingsley. BeLS; EBVV; FaPoR; GGP; OHCV; OtMeF; PlP; PoLF; PWR; WBLP
Three Floors. Stanley Kunitz. SM
Three floors up, I fall. Living Near the Plaza of Thieves. Leslie Ullman. PBCAP
Three flutes, two oboes, English horn, violins. Guide to the Symphony. Weldon Kees. VGW
Three folds in cloth, yet there is but the one cloth. To the Holy Trinity. *Unknown, tr. fr. Irish by* Thomas Kinsella. NOIV
Three Found Poems. George Hitchcock. OBAL
Three Foxes, The. A. A. Milne. GoJo; GrPl; MoShBr; OxBChV
Three Friends. *Unknown, tr. fr. Yoruba by* Ulli Beier. BoWoP; PBA
Three Gates. Beth Day. BLPA
Three Gates of Gold. Beth Day. *See* If you are tempted to reveal.
Three Ghostesses. *Unknown.* OxNR
Three ghosts on the lonesome road, The. Stains. Theodosia Garrison. WGRP
Three gipsies stood at the Castle gate. *Unknown. See* There were three gipsies a-come to my door.
Three Graves, The, *sels.* Samuel Taylor Coleridge.
Three Green Windows. Anne Sexton. NYBP
Three grey boys tracked us to an old house. In One Battle. Amiri Baraka. BPo
Three grey geese in a green field grazing. *Unknown.* OxNR
Three-handed Fugue. Phyllis Gotlieb. NOBC
Three Hermits, The. W. B. Yeats. CMoP
Three Hills. Everard Owen. NSI
Three Holy Kings from Morgenland. Heine, *tr. fr. German by* Herman Eichenthal. PChr
Three hours ago he blundered up the trench. A Working Party. Siegfried Sassoon. CMoP; PeFWW
Three hours of peace and soothing rest of brain. (*LL*) An Evening Lull. Walt Whitman. NAAL-1
Three hugest dinosaurs do not outweigh. The Blue Whale. Robert Watson. MAT
300,000,000. What Happened Here Before. Gary Snyder. NNaP
Three Hundred Thousand More. James Sloan Gibbons. PAH
Three-hundred-year-old ash tree, A. The Ash Tree on Ching Hill. Liu Sha-ho, *tr. fr. Chinese. Fr.* Two Poems of Peking. LHF, *tr. by* Hualing Nieh
Three images of dying stick in my mind like morbid transfers. Bruce Beaver. *Fr.* Letters to Live Poets. CBAP; NOBAu
Three Jolly Fishermen. *Unknown.* OxBSS
Three Jolly Pigeons, The. Goldsmith. *See* Let school-masters puzzle their brain.
Three Jovial Gentlemen. Daniel Hoffman. MoBS
Three kinds of enemy walk. Of The Enemy. W. H. Auden. *Fr.* Orators, The. CBCK
Three Kinds of Pleasures. Robert Bly. AiP
Three Kingdoms of Nature, The. Gotthold Ephraim Lessing, *tr. fr. German.* NU, *tr. by* Alfred Baskerville
Three Kings, The. Rubén Darío, *tr. fr. Spanish by* Lysander Kemp. PChr
Three Kings, The. Eugene Field. GN
Three Kings, The. Longfellow. ChIV-2; GN
Three Kings. James P. Vaughn. PoNe
Three Kings came riding from far away. The Three Kings. Longfellow. ChIV-2; GN
Three kings embark on a long journey. Starlight. Freda Downie. FaBoWP
Three kings stood before the manger. The Gifts. John Heath-Stubbs. OxBC
Three kings went down to the soul of the sea. Three Kings. James P. Vaughn. PoNe
Three Knights from Spain. *Unknown.* CH
Three Ladies, The. Robert Creeley. NeAP
Three Ladies of London, The, *sels.* Robert Wilson.
 New Brooms. EIL
 Simplicity's Song. CTC
Three Laments. Diane Di Prima. PoBeRe
Three limbs, three seasons smashed; well, one to go. John Berryman. *Fr.* Dream Songs. HCAP
Three little chickens. A Tug-of-War. M. M. Hutchinson. BoTP

Three scribblers whose names end in Bert. C. Vita-Finzi. PeLi

Three Seamstresses, The. Isaac Leibush Peretz, tr. fr. Yiddish by Joseph Leftwick. TrJP

Three Seasons. Francis Sparshott. NOBC

Three Secret Poems, sels. George Seferis, tr. fr. Greek by Edmund Keeley and Philip Sherrard.

Three secrets that never were said. Secrets. Richard Hovey. AnAmPo

Three Sentences for a Dead Swan. James Wright. NaP; NOBA

Three Sermons to the Dead. Laura Riding. LiTA
  Sels.
  Nor Is It Written
  Not All Immaculate
  Way of the Air, The

III, 7. Dear Molly, why so oft in tears? ("Quid fles, Asterie.") Horace, tr. fr. Latin by Austin Dobson. Fr. Odes. OBVE, tr. by George Stepney.

Three ships of war had Preble when he left the Naples shore. Reuben James. James Jeffrey Roche. PAH

Three silences made him a single word. R. P. Blackmur. PoA

Three Singing Birds, The. James Reeves. PDV

Three Sisters. Walter de la Mare. FaBoEE

Three slender things that best support the. Unknown, tr. fr. Irish by Kuno Meyer. Fr. Triads of Ireland, The. IIP

Three Small Songs for the Muse. Kathleen Norris. CrSp

Three Snakes, Strawberry Canyon, Berkeley. Ray Gonzáles. AfAz

Three Songs. Hart Crane. Fr. Bridge, The. LiTA; NAAL-2

Three Songs. Thom Gunn. AnAn
  Sels.
  Baby Song. NAs; RB
  Encolpius
  Hitching into Frisco

Three Songs at the End of Summer. Jane Kenyon. BAP-89

Three Songs from the Haida, sels. Unknown, tr. by Constance Lindsay Skinner.
  Bear's Song, The. AWP
  Love Song. AWP
  Song for Fine Weather. AWP

Three Songs from the Temple. Don Domanski. NOBC

Three Songs of Mad Coyote. Unknown, tr. fr. Nez Percé Indian by Herbert J. Spinden. STP

Three Songs of Mary, sels. Madeleine L'Engle.
  O Simplicitas. OBCP; PChr

Three Sonnets for Iva. Marilyn Hacker. GLP

Three Sons, The. Unknown. ReMoGo

Three sortes of teares doe from myne eies distraine. William Alabaster. Fr. Divine Meditations. ESCV; Son

Three Sorts of Serpents Do Resemble Thee. Michael Drayton. Fr. Idea. EnRePo; ESo

III. Soverayne beauty which I doo admire, The. Spenser. Fr. Amoretti. AAS; ESo, lacking epigrams I–IV; HeIL; PoEL-1

Three spirits came to me. April. Ezra Pound. CMoP

Three Spring Notations on Bipeds. Carl Sandburg. AWP

3 Stanzas about a Tree. Marvin Bell. Prf

Three Star Final. Conrad Aiken. OxBA

Three stars, five stars rise over the hill. Confucius, tr. fr. Chinese by Ezra Pound. Fr. Shao and the South. CTC

Three strange men came to the inn. A Lady Comes to an Inn. Elizabeth J. Coatsworth. MoAmPo

Three Straws. Unknown. ReMoGo

Three strings, a neck of almond, and the heart. Balalaika. Norman Dubie. AmPA

Three students once tarried over the Rhine. From the German of Uhland. James Weldon Johnson. CDC

Three summers since I chose a maid. The Farmer's Bride. Charlotte Mew. BoLoP; CBLP; EBNV; ErPo; FaBoWP; MoAB; MoBrPo; NALW; OxBM; OxBTC; TrGrPo; WPE

Three Sweatshop Women. Nanying Stella Wong. CrSp

Three Tall Men, The. Unknown. OBET

III, 10. Extremum Tanain. Horace, tr. fr. Latin by Austin Dobson. Fr. Odes. AWP, tr. by Austin Dobson.

Three then came forward out of darkness, one. The Road. Conrad Aiken. MoAmPo

Three Things. Joseph Auslander. TrJP

Three Things. W. B. Yeats. OBMV

Three Things Enchanted Him. "Anna Akhmatova," tr. fr. Russian by Stanley Kunitz with Max Hayward. AiP

Three things filled this day for me. Three Things. Joseph Auslander. TrJP

Three Things Jeame Lacks. Unknown. MeEL

Three things make earth unquiet. A Servant When He Reigneth. Kipling. ChIV-1

Three Things [or Thinges] There Be[e] That Prosper All [or Up] Apace. Sir Walter Ralegh. NoP; PoEL-2

Three things the Master hath to do. Pray — Give — Go. Annie Johnson Flint. BLRP

Three things there are more beautiful. The Beautiful. W. H. Davies. NTP

Three things there be in man's opinion dear[e]. Fulke Greville. Fr. Caelica. LiTB; NOCV; NoSic; PoEL-1
  (Sonnet: "Three things there be in mans opinion dear[e].") NOSC

Three Things there be that prosper up apace. Three Things [or Thinges] There Be[e] That Prosper All [or Up] Apace. Sir Walter Ralegh. NoP; PoEL-2
  (Sir Walter Ralegh to His Son.) EnRePo; NAEL-1; NoSic; RB; SiPSBD; Son
  (To His Son.) InPS; OxBSP; SCGP
  (Wood, the Weed, the Wag, The.) SiPS

Three Things to Remember. Blake. See Robin Redbreast in a cage, A.

III, 13. To the Fountain[s] of Bandusia ("O fons Bandusiae.") Horace, tr. by Eugene Field. Fr. Odes. AWP

III, 30. This Monument Will Outlast ("Exegi momumentum aere perennius," Horace, tr. fr. Latin by Austin Dobson. Fr. Odes. CTC, tr. by Ezra Pound

Three times! four times! Then leave us now! (LL) Dead on the War Path. Unknown. OBD; WTO

Three times he crossed our way where with me went. Old Man Pondered. John Crowe Ransom. MoAmPo

Three times round the cuckoo waltz. Cuckoo Waltz. Unknown. AS

Three times the carline grain'd and rifted. Lucky Spence's Last Advice. Allan Ramsay. FaBoBl

Three times to the world's end I went. The Edge. Rosemary Dobson. NOBAu

Three Tiny Songs., sels. Cid Corman.
  "I have come far to have found nothing." VGW
  3 : 1. Alta. CrSp

Three translated Poems for October, sels. Ray A. Young Bear.
  "Although there is yet." ETG
  "Now that the autumn season." ETG
  "Old woman, I hope that at least." ETG

Three Trees. Charles Henry Crandall. OHIP

Three Troopers, The. George Walter Thornbury. BeLS

Three turkeys fair their last have breathed. A Melancholy Lay. Marjory Fleming. FaBoCh; FiBHP; NBLV

III, 28. Holiday ("Festo quid potius die.") Horace, tr. fr. Latin by Austin Dobson. Fr. Odes. AWP, tr. by Louis Untermeyer

III, 29. Descended of an ancient line ("Tyrrhena regum progenies."), paraphrased by Dryden. Horace, tr. fr. Latin by Austin Dobson. Fr. Odes. OBVE

III, 23. To Phidyle ("Caelo supinas si tuleris.") Horace, tr. fr. Latin by Austin Dobson. Fr. Odes. AWP, tr. by Austin Dobson

III, 22. Pine Tree for Diana, The ("Montium custos nemorumque.") Horace, tr. fr. Latin by Austin Dobson. Fr. Odes. AWP, tr. by Louis Untermeyer

III, 2. Let the youth hardened by a sharp soldier's life ("Angustam amice.") Horace, tr. fr. Latin by Austin Dobson. Fr. Odes.

Three Variations. Boris Pasternak, tr. fr. Russian by Babette Deutsch. TrJP

Three viands in three different courses served. Oyster-Crabs. Carolyn Wells. BXAP

Three Voices, The. "Lewis Carroll." BXAP

Three Warnings, The. Hester Lynch Thrale. BeLS

Three Ways to Screw Up on Your Way to The Doings Three Ways. Unknown, tr. fr. Seneca Indian by Jerome K. Rothenberg and Richard Johnny John. STP

Three wee bit puddocks. The Three Puddocks. William Soutar. FaBoVe

Three weeks, and now I hear! My Olson Elegy. Irving Feldman. Prf

Three weeks gone and the combatants gone. Vergissmeinnicht. Keith Douglas. FaBoEH; FaBoMo; GTBS-P; InPS; NAEL-2; NoAM; OBD; OBWP; OxBTC; PoWW; RB; SoSe
  (Elegy for an 88 Gunner.) PAW

Three Welshman, The. Unknown. See There were three jovial Welshmen.

Three Wise Couples, The. Elizabeth T. Corbett. BLPA

Three wise men looked equivocally, The. The Magi. Ramon Guthrie. PoE

Three wise men of Gotham. Mother Goose. CBNP; FaBoBe; FaBoNo; OxNR; ReMoGo; Spl

Three Wise Men of Gotham, The. Unknown. FaBoNo

Three Wise Monkeys, The. Florence Boyce Davis. WBLP

Three Wise Old Women. Elizabeth T. Corbett. BLPA; OBCA; OBSP; OxBChV

Three wise old women were they, were they. Three Wise Old Women. Elizabeth T. Corbett. BLPA; OBCA; OBSP; OxBChV

Three Women. Alan Dienstag. ErPo

Three Women. (I am slow as the world. I am very patient.) Sylvia Plath. NAs

Sels.

Three women laugh aloud. Pommes de Terre. Kathleen Norris. NGP

Three wonderful people called Ley. Tim Hopkins. PeLi

Three wonderful people called Wick. A. M. Sayers. PeLi

Three Woodchoppers. Robert Francis. TRP

Three woodchoppers walk up the road. Three Woodchoppers. Robert Francis. TRP

Three words fall sweetly on my soul. Mother, Home, Heaven. William Goldsmith Brown. FaBoBe

Three-year-old Archianax. Poseidippus, *tr. fr. Greek by* Edward Lucie-Smith. GrAn

Three years accounts from gamekeepers' records, an estate. Three Years in Glen Garry. Colin Simms. NBrP

Three Years in Glen Garry. Colin Simms. NBrP

Three Years She Grew in Sun and Shower. Wordsworth. *Fr.* Lucy. EBEV; EnRP; FHYEP; GBL; GN; HAP; NOBE; NoP; OAEL-2; OBEV; OBNC; PoEL-4; SCGP; TFi; TrGrPo

Three Young Rats. *Unknown.* ChTr; FaBoNo; InvP; OxBoLi; OxNR

Three youths went a-fishing. The Banished Duke of Grantham. *Unknown.* EnSB

Threefold terror of love, The; a fallen flare. The Mother of God. W. B. Yeats. ChIV-2

Threes. Carl Sandburg. AnAmPo; CMoP; OxBA; PoLF

Threissa, someone's knocking at the door. The Procuress. Herodas, *tr. fr. Greek by* Barbara Hughes Fowler. HePo

Threnodia Augustalis, *sels.* Dryden.
   "Sure there's a lethargy in mighty woe." IMW

Threnody. Thomas Lovell Beddoes. EnRP

Threnody, *sels.* Emerson.
   "Was there no star that could be sent." IMW

Threnody: "Truth is a golden sunset far away." I. O. Scherzo. HoPM

Threnody: "What, what, what/ What's the news from Swat?" George Thomas Lanigan. FiBHP; NBLV
   (Ahkoond of Swat, The.) AnAmPo

Threshed corn lay piled like grit of ivory. The Barn. Seamus Heaney. HAP

Thresher's Labour, The, *sels.* Stephen Duck.
   "Soon as the harvest hath laid bare the plains." NOEC

Threshing Machine, The. Alice Meynell. WPE

Threshold. Dean Young. NAmP90

Thresholds of Identity. Lionel Abrahams. PeSAV

Thrice, and above, blest, my soul's half [*or* my soules halfe], art thou. A Country Life: To His Brother, Master Thomas Herrick. Robert Herrick. CaPo; SeCP; SeCV-1

Thrice Blest the Man. John Barnard. AH

Thrice-cruel maid, may Heaven frown on thee. The Elusive Maid. Abraham ibn Chasdai, *tr. fr. Hebrew by* J. Chotzner. TrJP

Thrice fairer e'en would Diocles have seemed. (*LL*) But yesterday, when from the bath he stept. Strato. PeHV

Thrice hail! proud land, whose genius boasts a Clay! The Runaway. Albery Allson Whitman. *Fr.* Not a Man and Yet a Man. AAP

Thrice happy authors, who with little skill. A Soliloquy in the Suburbs. Charles Jenner. *Fr.* Eclogue IV: The Poet. AWP; NOEC

Thrice Happy He. William Drummond of Hawthornden. BoNaP

Thrice he came. Malacoda. Samuel Beckett. CIP

Thrice Holy. Reginald Heber. *See* Holy, Holy, Holy.

Thrice the age of a deer is that of an eagle. (*LL*) The Age of Animals. *Unknown.* FaBoUs

Thrice the age of a dog is that of a horse. The Age of Animals. *Unknown.* FaBoUs

Thrice the Brinded Cat Hath Mewed. Shakespeare. *Fr.* Macbeth. InvP; RB

Thrice-threefold walled with emerald from our mortal mornings grey. (*LL*) The Mistress of Vision. Francis Thompson. CH, *abr.*

Thrice Toss [*or* Tosse] These Oaken Ashes in the Air [*or* Ayre]. Thomas Campion. CBLP; EBEV; EiL; EnLoPo; FaBoCh; HAP; MAT; OAEL-1; OxBSP; PoEL-2; PoRA; SCGP; TFi; WeW

Thrice Welcome First and Best of Days. Isaac Chanler. AH

Thrifties thred which pampred beauty spinnes, The. A Sonet Written in Prayse of the Browne Beautie. George Gascoigne. AAS

Thrifty Elephant, The. John Holmes. NYBP

Thrippsy pillivinx. A Letter to Evelyn Baring. Edward Lear. FaBoNo

Thro elm and maple and syringa branches. Commencement. Constance Carrier. WPE

Thro' the night of doubt and sorrow. Pilgrim's Song. Bernard S. Ingemann, *tr. fr. Danish by* Sabine Baring-Gould. WGRP

Thro' the night Thy angels kept. A Child's Prayer. William Canton. BoTP

Throat Song: The Whirling Earth. Wendy Rose. HATNAP

Throbbing? (*LL*) French Garden. Léopold Sédar Senghor. NegPo

Throbs the Night with Mystic Silence. Hayyim Nahman Bialik, *tr. fr. Hebrew by* Bertha Beinkinstadt. TrJP

Throne of the Lily-King, The. Joseph Rodman Drake. *Fr.* Culprit Fay, The. GN

Throne was reared upon the grass, The. The Throne of the Lily-King. Joseph Rodman Drake. *Fr.* Culprit Fay, The. GN

Throned, yet adoring! (*LL*) The Day of Judgement [*or* Judgment]; an Ode. Isaac Watts. ECEV; HAP; NOBE; NOEC; NoP; OBEV

Thronging the heart. Residues: Thronging the Heart. Gael Turnbull. NBrP

Throstle, The. Tennyson. BoNaP; FaPON

Through a crack on the right. Outhouse. Aleksandar Ristovic, *tr. fr. Serbo-Croatian by* Charles Simic. HSix

Through a dull tract of woe, of dread. My Birthday. George Crabbe. OxBSP

Through a Glass Eye, Lightly. Carolyn Kizer. BoWoP

Through a red prairie. (*LL*) The Last Quatrain of the Ballad of Emmett Till. Gwendolyn Brooks. LCAP; PoBA; WPE

Through a second youth of a hundred years. (*LL*) Dorothy Q. Oliver Wendell Holmes. NOBA

Through a straw. (*LL*) Sucking Cider through a Straw. *Unknown.* AS; GBP

Through a wild midnight all my mountainous past. The Monster. Henry Rago. PoA

Through a window in the attic. Burglar Bill. "F. Anstey." FiBHP

Through all the city's streets there poured a flood. The Gathering of the Grand Army. Charlotte L. Forten Grimke. AAP

Through all the employments of life. The Employments of Life. John Gay. *Fr.* Beggar's Opera, The. OAEL-1; PeLV

Through all the evening. Borderlands. Louise Imogen Guiney. AmWP

Through all the pomp of kingdoms still he shines. Homer's Gift of Fame. Homer, *tr. fr. Greek. Fr.* Iliad, The. NOSC, *tr. by* George Chapman.

Through all thy various *Winter, full are found.* David Mallet. *Fr.* To Mr. Thomson, on His Publishing the Second Edition of His Poem Called Winter. EPCY

Through All Your Abstract Reasoning. Brian Patten. FaBoTw

Through Alpine meadows soft-suffused. Stanzas from the Grande Chartreuse. Matthew Arnold. EBVV; EnVR; NAEL-2; OAEL-2; PoE; PoEL-5; TEP

Through an amber dazzle of aspen. Aspen Oktoberfest. Reg Saner. BTR

Through and through the inspired leaves. The Book-Worms. Burns. ChTr; FaBoEE; FiBHP

Through Baltimore. Bayard Taylor. PAH

Through Binoculars. Charles Tomlinson. OAEL-2

Through black, cannot but be divine. (*LL*) To Her Eyes. Lord Herbert of Cherbury. JCP

Through bushes and through briars I lately took my way. Bushes and Briars. *Unknown.* OBET

Through calm and storm the years have led. Centennial Hymn. Bryant. PAH

Through centuries he lived in poverty. The Good Man Has No Shape. Wallace Stevens. MeMAP

Through clouds of fire and clouds of blood. At Day's End. Hayyim Nahman Bialik, *tr. fr. Hebrew by* Ruth Finer Mintz. MHP

Through darkening pines the cavaliers. The Legend of Waukulla. Hezekiah Butterworth. PAH

Through every age, eternal God. Isaac Watts. AmFP

Through every land, by every tongue. (*LL*) From all that dwells below the skies. *Unknown.* EaPr

Through every minute of this day. John Oxenham. BLRP

Through every night we hate. Mothers, Daughters. Shirley Kaufman. BoWoP; CrSp; NMM

Through Eyes. Cole Swenson. UTF

Through Fire in Mobile Bay. *Unknown.* PAH

Through frost and snow locked from mine eyes. To Saxham. Thomas Carew. CaPo; JCP; NoP

Through glades and glooms! Oh fair! Oh, sad! Collins. Lionel Johnson. OxAEP-2

Through gladness of this lusty May. (*LL*) Lusty May. *Unknown.* OBEV

Through glass while their bodies remain outside. (*LL*) The Black Bird's Golden House. Valerie Wohlfeld. UTF

Through grass, through amber'd cornfields, our slow Stream. Meadowsweet. William Allingham. OBNC

Through grief and through danger thy smile hath cheered my way. The Irish Peasant to His Mistress. Thomas Moore. TIRV

Through hallowed death are reunited. *(LL)* Although Tormented. Kalonymos ben Judah. TrJP

Through high defiles of warehouses that dwarf. Memories of Cochin. Dick Davis. SCBI

Through high still air. *(LL)* Mid-August at Sourdough Mountain Lookout. Gary Snyder. HAP; InPK; MAT; NaP; NoP; PoBeRe; TAP; VCAP

Through infinite immensity. *(LL)* I'm happiest when most away. Emily Brontë. EnVR; NAEL-2

Through Jesus Christ our Lord. *(LL)* O God, I thank thee. George Appleton. EaPr

Through lane or black archway. The Young Woman of Beare. Austin Clarke. MoP; NoAM

Through lenses the world opens. Microscope. Gwyn Thomas, *tr. fr. Welsh by* Joseph P. Clancy. OBWVE

Through life's dull road, so dim and dirty. On My Thirty-third Birthday. Byron. FaBoEE; NAs

Through love to light! O, wonderful the way. After-Song. Richard Watson Gilder. TrPWD

Through me you enter the city of lament. Dante, *tr. by* Ronald Bottrall. *Fr. Divina Commedia.* MeMAP; NAWM-1, *tr. by* John Ciardi; OBD

Through moonlight's milk. White Cat in Moonlight. Douglas Gibson. CRH

Through my lips, and say her prayer. *(LL)* Earth ("Grasshopper, your fairy song.") John Hall Wheelock. EaPr; LiTA; MoAmPo

Through New Mexico. *(LL)* The Railroad Cars Are Coming. *Unknown.* AS; FaPON

Through nights of slanting rain. Ripeness Is All. Peter Viereck. ArOW

Through Nurseryland. *Unknown.* BoTP; OTCP

Through pearly deeps of sky, cloud-mountains rose. Sky Picture. H. Cordelia Ray. CBWP-3

Through pleasures and palaces. Nostalgia. Amy Lowell. AnAmPo

Through rain falling on us no faster. Goodbye to Serpents. James Dickey. NYBP

Through random doors we wandered. Exits and Entrances. Naomi Long Madgett. BlSi

Through reedy banks. The Nima. Jorge Isaacs, *tr. fr. Spanish by* Alice Jane McVan. TrJP

Through Ruddy Orchards. Mary Oliver. SoSe; WPE

Through salt marsh, grassy channel where the shark's. Tide Turning. John Frederick Nims. DiPo; FYAP

Through springtime walks, with flowers perfumed. Anne Batten Cristall. ECWP

Through storm and fire and gloom, I see it stand. The Celtic Cross. Thomas D'Arcy Magee. TIRV

Through storm and wind. *Unknown.* OxNR

Through storms you reach them and from storms are free. The Enviable Isles. Herman Melville. FaBoBe

Through swamps and alligators I wend my weary way. On the Lakes of Ponchartrain. *Unknown.* AmFP

Through that window — all else being extinct. The Room. Conrad Aiken. LiTM; MoAmPo; NOBA

Through the ample open door of the peaceful country barn. A Farm Picture. Walt Whitman. InPS; TRP

Through the black, rushing smoke-burst. Song of Callicles, The ("Through the black, rushing smoke-burst.") Matthew Arnold. *Fr.* Empedocles on Etna. NOBE; OAEL-2; OBEV
(Callicles' Song.) ChTr
(Not Here, O Apollo.) FaBoRV
(Song of the Muses, The.) WiR

Through the blinds, it must have been the streetlamp I saw. The Landing. J. D. McClatchy. PFL

Through the bound cable strands, the arching path. Atlantis. Hart Crane. *Fr.* Bridge, The. LiTA; LiTM; NAAL-2

Through the broad bright land.y. *(LL)* The Song of the Ungirt Runners. Charles Hamilton Sorley. MoBrPo; OBEV

Through the clangor of the cannon. Defeat and Victory. Wallace Rice. PAH

Through the cracks. Ray A. Young Bear. STP

Through the dark city. *(LL)* The Great Figure. William Carlos Williams. AiP; HeIP; InPK; MoP; NoAM; SAmP; TTTS

Through the dark night. Destroyers. "Klaxon." NSI

Through the Dark Sod — as Education. Emily Dickinson. NALW

Through the Dark the Dreamers Came. Earl Bowman Marlatt. AH

Through the deep night a magic mist led me. A Magic Mist. Owen Roe O'Sullivan, *tr. fr. Irish by* Thomas Kinsella. NOIV

Through the dull wear of commonplace. *(LL)* Vision. James Devaney. NOBAu

Through the dusky purple glimmer. Anita and Giovanni. H. Cordelia Ray. CBWP-3

Through the Eternal Love. *(LL)* Eternal Light! Thomas Binney. NOCV; WGRP

Through the Forest Have I Gone. Shakespeare. *Fr.* Midsummer Night's Dream, A. CTC

Through the forest the boy wends all day long. The Boy and the Flute. BjØornstjerne BjØornson, *tr. fr. Norwegian by* Sir Edmund Gosse. AWP

Through the great sinful streets of Naples as I past. Easter Day, Naples, 1849. Arthur Hugh Clough. EBVVPR

Through the green tassels of the weeper tree. Triumphal Ode MCMXXXIX. George Barker. LiTB

Through the House. Shakespeare. *Fr.* Midsummer Night's Dream, A. CTC

Through the house what busy joy. The First Tooth. Charles Lamb *and* Mary Lamb. OxBChV; WoRP

Through the imperfect glass of windows. Imperfect Air. Ralph Hawkins. NBrP

Through the light rain I think I see them going. The Burial in Flanders. Robert Nichols. PeHV

Through the lit crystal of the cup. *(LL)* Autumn. Roy Campbell. GTBS-P; MoBrPo; OBMV; OxBTC

Through the long death of the moon. The Death of the Moon. David Wagoner. PoA

Through the Long Night. Edward Carpenter. *Fr.* Towards Democracy. PeHV

Through the Looking-Glass, *sels.* "Lewis Carroll."
"I'll tell thee everything I can." InvP; TFi; UV
(A-Sitting on a Gate.) PoRA
(Aged, Aged Man, The.) BXAP; FaBoPa; OxBChV
(Ways and Means.) FiBHP
(White Knight's Ballad, The.) FaBoNo; HAP
(White Knight's Song, The.) CBNP; FaBoCh; FaBoCo; InPS; NAEL-2; NoAM; NOBE; NOBL; NoP; OAEL-2; PeLV
"In winter, when the fields are white." EBEV; NOBVV
(Humpty Dumpty's Poem.) Mes
(Humpty Dumpty's Poetic Recitation.) CBNP
(Humpty Dumpty's Recitation.) ChTr; FaBoCo; FaBoNo; FiBHP; OBSP; PeVV
(Humpty Dumpty's Song.) GTBS-P; OxBChV; OxBoLi; PeLV
Jabberwocky. CBNP; ClHu; CoGr; EBEV; EBEvV; EBVvV; FaBoBe; FaBoCo; FaBoNo; FaBV; FaPON; FF; FiBHP; GoJo; HeIP; HoPM; ImPo; InPK; InPS; LiTB; NAEL-2; NBLV; NoAM; NOBE; NOBL; NOBVV; NoP; NTCP; OAEL-2; OBSP; OHCV; OPOP; OxAEP-2; OxBChV; PeLV; PeVV; Poetr; PoRA; PPP; RB; TEP; TFi; TRP; TTTS; UV
"To the Looking-Glass world it was Alice that said." UV
Walrus and the Carpenter, The. BeLS; BLPA; CBNP; EBEvV; FaBoBe; FaBoCo; FaBoNo; FaBV; FaPoB; FaPON; FiBHP; GN; LiTB; NAEL-2; NoAM; NOBL; NOBVV; OBSP; OHCV; OTCP; OxAEP-2; OxBChV; PeLV; PoRA; TEP; TFi

Through the lush marsh grass. *(LL)* Snow Line. Bei Dao. SpMi

Through the Maze. *Unknown.* BLRP

Through the misty trees. *(LL)* Starting at Dawn. Sun Yün-feng. PBWP; WPC

Through the narrow aisles of pain. *(LL)* Solitude. Ella Wheeler Wilcox. AnAmPo; EBEvV; PoLF; PWR; VPP

Through the night on fire with my blood. She Speaks the Morning's Filigree. Philip Lamantia. VGW

Through the open french window the warm sun. Still-Life. Elizabeth Daryush. FaBoWP; WPE

Through the pain of sick wards. Sunday Evening. Elsa Morante, *tr. fr. Italian by* Ruth Feldman *and* Brian Swann. WoWa

Through the Parklands, through the Parklands. The Parklands. Stevie Smith. MoBS

Through the Porthole. Marjorie Wilson. BoTP

Through the pregnant universe rumbles life's terrific thunder. Exhortation: Summer, 1919. Claude McKay. CDC

Through the rain forests, up a long river. The Deceptive Grin of the Gravel Porters. Gavin Ewart. FaBoMo

Through the sea's crust of prisms looking up. Sea Burial. John Ciardi. ArOW

Through the shrubs as I can crack[e]. Doron's Jigge. Robert Greene. *Fr.* Menaphon. PoEL-2
(Jig, A.) ElL

Through the shuttered light of the blinking trees we race. Bluebells for Grainne. Dermot Bolger. IB

Through the small door of a hut. The Collector of the Sun. Dave Jeddie Smith. SM

Through the steamed-up windows it says. One Way at Any Time. J. H. Prynne. VaA

Through the strait gate of passion. Paradise Re-entered. D. H. Lawrence. ChIV-2

Through the strait pass of suffering. Emily Dickinson. TOF

Through the stricken air, through the buttonwood balls. Rain on the Cumberlands. James Still. GrPl

Through the sunny garden. Chillingham. Mary Elizabeth Coleridge. BoTP

Through the teeth. *Unknown.* RoPo

Through the throng of courtiers, to his home. (*LL*) Zito the Magician. Miroslav Holub. AnRep; PoSu

Through the vague morning, the heart preoccupied. Bombers. C. Day Lewis. CMoP; MoAB

Through the Valley. Ella Wheeler Wilcox. AnAmPo

Through the viridian (and black of the burnt match). Virgo Descending. Charles Wright. LCAP; TRP

Through the voice barrier, and formulaic atrophy. Not Slipping into Something More Comfortable. Nick Totton. VaA

Through the weeks of deep snow. Wendell Berry. EaPr

Through the white thin bone of a hare. (*LL*) The Collarbone [Collar-Bone] of a Hare. W. B. Yeats. CBNP; NTP; OxAEP-2; OxBTC; RB

Through the window I see you running. To a Child. Aidan Carl Mathews. IB

Through the window of the school. Asia. Jean Follain, *tr. fr. French by* Richard Ellmann. AnRep

Through the window the sky clears. Treatment in the Field. J. H. Prynne. VaA

Through the wood covered with hoar frost I walked. The Tomb of the Naiads. Pierre Louÿs, *tr. fr. French by* Philip L. Miller. RiWo

Through the Year. Julian S. Cutler. BLPA

Through These Pale Cold Days. Isaac Rosenberg. TrJP

Through this toilsome world, alas! I Shall Not Pass This Way Again. *Unknown.* BLPA

Through throats where many rivers meet, the curlews cry. In the White Giant's Thigh. Dylan Thomas. LiTB

Through thy Increase grow new, and quick. (*LL*) The Match. Henry Vaughan *and* Thomas Stanley. ESCV

Through torrid entrances, past icy poles. To Shakespeare. Hart Crane. Son

Through tranquil years they watched the changes. Clearing for the Plough. Ernest G. Moll. NOBAu

Through Unknown Paths. Frederick L. Hosmer. TrPWD

Through verdant banks where Thames's branches glide. The Assault on the Fortress. Timothy Dwight. PAH

Through Warmth and Light of Summer Skies. Austin Faricy. AH

Through water, his own waterfall. Cold Fire. George Starbuck. NYBP

Through what long heaviness, assayed in what strange fire. Carthusians. Ernest Dowson. NAEL-2

Through what obscure, half-comprehending night. Candlemas Day. Sister Mary Madeleva. CRP

Through which we go/ Is I. (*LL*) Napoleon. Walter de la Mare. FaBoCh; FaBoTw; NOBE; OtMeF; RB; Spl

Through Willing Heart and Helping Hand. Frederick L. Hosmer. AH

Through winter-time we call on spring. The Wheel. W. B. Yeats. GTBS-P; Poetr

Through woods, Mme Une Telle, a trifle ill. Autumn Chapter in a Novel. Thom Gunn. FaBoMo; OxBTC

Through years and years. The Day We Buried Our Bully. Mbuyiseni Oswald Mtshali. PeSAV

Through years of Irish history. Mr. Gunman. Vin Garbutt. OBET

Through You. Edwin Honig. TAP

Through you, I entered heaven and hell. Afterglow. Georgia Douglas Johnson. ShDr

Through your love words became clear. The Word "Silk." Thomas McCarthy. CIP

Through your pocket glass you have let disease expand. Florence Nightingale. Michael Longley. FaBoEH

Throughe a forest as I can ryde. Crow and Pie. *Unknown.* ESPB

Throughout a garden greene and gay. The Rose of England. *Unknown.* ESPB

Throughout Australian history no tongue or pen can tell. The Death of Morgan. *Unknown.* FaBoBa

Throughout my book. 'Troth, put out *woman* too. (*LL*) To a Friend. Ben Jonson. BeJo

Throughout Our Lands, *sels.* Czeslaw Milosz, *tr. fr. Polish by the author* and Peter Dale Scott.

Throughout the day our sweet bells chime. Bluebells. P. A. Ropes. BoTP

Throughout the day we are able to ban the voices. Henriëtte Roland-Holst, *tr. fr. Dutch by* Manfred Wolf. PBWP

Throughout the field I find no grain. Winter in Durnover Field. Thomas Hardy. MoBrPo

Throughout the whole wide earth. (*LL*) All One in Christ. John Oxenham. BLRP

Throughout the whole world, experts say. *Unknown.* PeLi

Throughout the World, If It Were Sought. Sir Thomas Wyatt. MAT; NoSic; OxBSP

Throw Away the Flowers. Elizabeth Daryush. PBWP

Throw away Thy rod. Discipline. George Herbert. FHYEP; GeHe; LiTB; MeLP; NAEL-1; NOBE; NOCV; NoP; OBEV; OxAEP-1; PoLF; TrGrPo

Throw away thy wrath. (*LL*) Discipline. George Herbert. FHYEP; GeHe; LiTB; MeLP; NAEL-1; NOBE; NOCV; NoP; OBEV; OxAEP-1; PoLF; TrGrPo

Throw Hannibal on the scales, how many pounds. Hannibal ("Throw Hannibal on the scales, how many pounds.") Juvenal, *tr. by* Robert Lowell. *Fr.* Satires. OBVE

Throw him into the river. Kasenduaxtc, *tr. fr. Tlingit Indian by* James Koller. STP

Throw into the little box/ A stone. The Tenants of the Little Box. Vasco [*or* Vasko] Popa, *tr. fr. Serbo-Croatian by* Charles Simic. AnRep; HSix

Throw Yourself Like Seed. Miguel De Unamuno, *tr. fr. Spanish by* Robert Bly. RaBo

Throwing a bomb is bad. Ethics for Everyman. Roger Woddis. NOBL

Throwing her arms around her father. Anyte, *tr. fr. Greek by* Sally Purcell. GrAn

Throwing Out the Flowers. Gwendolyn Brooks. *Fr.* Notes from the Childhood and the Girlhood. LCAP

Throwing the Beads. Sean Dunne. BiHa

Throwing the Racetrack Cats at Saratoga. David Ray. SM

Thrown in, for her. (*LL*) Sleep, Darling. Sappho. VBLP

Thrush, The. Alfred Austin. TEP

Thrush before Dawn, A. Alice Meynell. MoBrPo; WPE

Thrush in February, The. George Meredith. OBNC

Thrush In the Trenches, A. Humbert Wolfe. NSI

Thrush is tapping a stone, A. Dawn. Gordon Bottomley. BoTP; MoBrPo

Thrush, linnet, stare and wren. In Glencullen. J. M. Synge. FM; OBMV

Thrushes. Ted Hughes. FaBoMo; GoYe; TRP

Thrushes sing as the sun is going, The. Proud Songsters. Thomas Hardy. MoP

Thrush's Nest, The. John Clare. BoTP; GoJo

Thrush's Song, The. *Unknown, tr. fr. Gaelic by* William MacGillivray. CH

Thrust & Parry. Greg Delanty. BiHa

Thrust and Riposte. Eugenio Montale, *tr. fr. Italian by* Gavin Ewart. PeFWW

Thrust of the dragon's tight bone, The. The Dream Feast (Three Poems). Anita Endrezze-Danielson. VoR

Thrusting its armoury of hot delight. Descartes and the Stove. Charles Tomlinson. FaBoMo

Thu sikest sore. Christ's Tear Breaks My Heart. *Unknown.* MeEL

Thula! Thula! Thula! my child. (*LL*) But who killed Johannes, mama . . .? Jeremy Cronin. PeSAV

Thumb, The. Dennis Saleh. MAT

Thumb bold. *Unknown.* OxNR

Thumb, for a summer's promise, The. The Sand Painters. Ben Belitt. GOA

Thumb he. *Unknown.* OxNR

Thumb, loose tooth of a horse. Bestiary for the Fingers of My Right Hand. Charles Simic. AmPA; LCAP

Thumbikin, Thumbikin, broke the barn. *Unknown.* OxNR

Thumbing Old Magazines. Gerald Vizenor. VoR

Thumbkin says, I'll dance. *Unknown.* OxNR

Thumbprint. Celeste Turner Wright. Poetsp

Thumbs in the thumb-place. The Mitten Song. Marie Louise Allen. NTCP

Thumping gavel the Otterburn Ranges behind and never unravel. Otter, Redewetter. Colin Simms. NBrP

Thumping old tunes give a voice to its whereabouts. Fairground. W. H. Auden. NYBP

Thunder. Walter de la Mare. BoNaP

Thunder. Fu Hsüan, *tr. fr. Chinese by* Kenneth Rexroth. OHMPC

Thunder & the flaw of their great quarrel, The. John Berryman. *Fr.* Dream Songs. VCAP

Thunder Can Break. Christopher Okigbo. HBAPE

Thunder clouds are sweeping, shrouding. A Russian Cradle Song. David Nomberg, *tr. fr. Yiddish by* Alter Brody. TrJP

Thunder mutters louder and more loud, The. John Clare. EnVR; NOBVV

Thunder. My heart trembles. Thunder. Fu Hsüan, *tr. fr. Chinese by* Kenneth Rexroth. OHMPC

Thus queth Alvred:/ 'Ne schaltu nevere thi wif by hire wlyte cheose.' *At. to* Alfred, King of England. *Fr.* Proverbs of Alfred, The. PoE

Thus queth Alvred:/ 'Ne würth thu never so wod ne so wyn-drunke.' *At. to* Alfred, King of England. *Fr.* Proverbs of Alfred, The. PoE

Thus queth Alvred:/ 'Nevre thu, bi thine lyve, the word of thine wyve.' *At. to* Alfred, King of England. *Fr.* Proverbs of Alfred, The. PoE

Thus reader, by our astrologick art. Almanac Verse. *Unknown.* SCAP

Thus said The Lord in the Vault above the Cherubim. The Last Chantey. Kipling. FaBoCh; MoBrPo; OtMeF

Thus said the rushing raven. A Croon on Hennacliff. Robert Stephen Hawker. NOBVV

Thus saith my Chloris bright. Giovanni Battista Guarini, *tr. fr. Italian.* GBL

Thus saith the great god Thoth. He Is Declared True of Word. *Unknown, tr. fr. Egyptian* by Robert Hillyer. *Fr.* Book of the Dead. AWP

Thus saith the Ruler of the Skies. The Passion and Exaltation of Christ. Isaac Watts. NOCV

Thus, San Augustine's church and prison joined. Albery Allson Whitman. *Fr.* Twasinta's Seminoles; Or Rape of Florida. AAP

Thus saying, from her husband's hand her hand. Milton. *Fr.* Paradise Lost. EPCY
(Fall, The.) PoEL-3
(No more talk where God or angel guest.) FHYEP, *bk.* IX

Thus saying, from her side the fatal key. Milton. *Fr.* Paradise Lost. EBEV; EPCY

Thus saying rose. Occupations of Hell. Milton. *Fr.* Paradise Lost. EPCY; NOSC

Thus shall I use me. (*LL*) Pastime with good company. Henry VIII, King of England. NoSic

Thus she had lain. Africa. Maya Angelou. NIP; WoWa

Thus should have been our travels. Over 2000 Illustrations and a Complete Concordance. Elizabeth Bishop. HCAP; LCAP; NAAL-2; NoAM; VCAP

Thus, some tall tree that long hath stood. On the Death of Benjamin Franklin. Philip Freneau. PAH

Thus spake an old Chinese mandarin. *Unknown.* PeLi

Thus spake the Lord. The Word of the Lord from Havana. Richard Hovey. PAH

Thus Spake the Saviour. Jeremy Belknap. AH

Thus spoke the lady underneath the tree. Colonel Fantock. Edith Sitwell. MoAB; MoBrPo; OBMV

Thus Sung Orpheus to His Strings. *Unknown.* GBL

Thus talking hand in hand alone they pass'd. Milton. *Fr.* Paradise Lost. EBEV; EPCY

Thus the Mayne Glideth. Robert Browning. *Fr.* Paracelsus. OBEV

Thus the tale ended. (*LL*) The Skeleton in Armor. Longfellow. AmPP; AnAmPo; AWP; BeLS; BLPL; FaBoBe; PAH

Thus they in Heav'n, above the starry sphear. Milton. *Fr.* Paradise Lost. EBEV; EPCY

Thus to Glaucus spake/ Divine Sarpedon. Homer, *tr. by* Sir John Denham. *Fr.* Iliad, The. OBVE

Thus, up to manhood he arose. His Manhood. George Clinton Rowe. *Fr.* Toussaint L'Overture. AAP

Thus was my love, thus was my Ganymed. Richard Barnfield. *Fr.* Sonnets. PeHV

Thus was this place. Milton. *Fr.* Paradise Lost. EPCY; PeECV, *ll.* 246– 275

Thus when the swallow, seeking prey. John Gay. *Fr.* Beggar's Opera, The. OAEL-1; PoEL-3

Thus while my joyless hours I lingring spend. John Phillips. *Fr.* Splendid Shilling, The. BXAP; FaBoPa; OAEL-1, *abr.*

Thus will despair/ In ecstasy of nightmare. The Succubus. Robert Graves. OAEL-2

Thus with a Kiss I Die. Shakespeare. *See* For here lies Juliet, and her beauty makes.

Thus with Hermetic art the adept combines. The Action of Invisible Ink. Erasmus Darwin. *Fr.* Economy of Vegetation, The. FaBoUs

Thus with imagin'd wing our swift scene flies. Shakespeare. *Fr.* King Henry V. EBEV; OxAEP-1

Thus with the year/ Seasons return. Milton. *Fr.* Paradise Lost. EPCY; PIP, *ll.* 40–55

Thus without death how sweet it is to die. (*LL*) Come, gentle sleep, death's image though thou art. Thomas Warton the Younger. OBVE

Thus writeth Meer Djafrit. To the Ingleezee Khafir, Calling Himself Djan Bool Djenkinzun. James Clarence Mangan. PeIV

Thwarted. Priscilla Jane Thompson. CBWP-2

Thy after shock, Manassas, share. (*LL*) The March into Virginia. Herman Melville. BLPL; HAP; ImPo; LiTA; NAAL-1; NoP; PoE; TAP; TrGrPo

Thy arms with bracelets I will deck. Homage. Gustave Kahn, *tr. fr. French by* Jethro Bithell. TrJP

Thy ax shall harm it not. (*LL*) Woodman, Spare That Tree. George Pope Morris. AnAmPo; BLPA; FaBoBe; FaPON; OHIP; PWR; VPP; WBLP

Thy azure robe, I did behold. Julia's Petticoat. Robert Herrick. BeJo; CaPo

Thy banks, O Barrow, sure must be. Written by the Barrow Side, Where She Was Sent to Wash Linen. Ellen Taylor. ECWP

Thy beauty haunts me heart and soul. The Moon. W. H. Davies. MoBrPo

Thy benediction still. (*LL*) Eternal God, How They're Increased. Cotton Mather. AH

Thy Best. Henry Cole. *See* Before God's footstool to confess.

Thy best its best, Please God, thy best its best. (*LL*) Cardinal Newman. Christina Rossetti. NAEL-2

Thy blessing on the boys — for time has come. Haim Guri, *tr. fr. Hebrew by* Ruth H. Lask. TrJP

Thy blue waves, Patapsco, flow'd soft and serene. Fort McHenry. *Unknown.* PAH

Thy body as it is. (*LL*) Blest, Blest and Happy He. *Unknown.* GBL

Thy Bosom Is Endeared With All Hearts. Shakespeare. *Fr.* Sonnets. NOBE, *sect.* XXXI; OBEV, *sect.* XXXI; PoEL-2, *sect.* XXXI

Thy braes were bonny, Yarrow stream. The Braes of Yarrow. John Logan. GTBS; GTBS-P; SCGP

Thy breath is far sweeter than honey. Far Sweeter than Honey. Abraham ibn Ezra, *tr. fr. Hebrew by* Israel Abrahams. TrJP

Thy byrth, thy beautie, nor thy brave attyre. Farewell with a Mischeife. George Gascoigne. AAS

Thy copp's, too, nam'd of Gamage, thou hast there. Ben Jonson. *Fr.* To Penshurst. AWP; BeJo; FaBoPP; FM; JCP; NoP; NOSC; OAEL-1; PoEL-2; PPP; SeCP; SeCV-1; TEP; TFi

Thy country, Wilberforce, with just disdain. To William Wilberforce, Esq. William Cowper. Son

Thy curate's place, thy fruitful wife. Swift. *Fr.* Parson's Case, The. UV

Thy dawn, O Master of the world, thy dawn. James Elroy Flecker. *Fr.* Hassan. OtMeF

Thy dawn, O Ra, opens the new horizon. Adoration of the Disk by King Akhnaten and Princess Nefer Neferiu Aten. *Unknown, tr. fr. Egyptian by* Robert Hillyer. *Fr.* Book of the Dead. AWP

Thy error, Frémont, simply was to act. To John C. Frémont. Whittier. PAH

Thy eyes and eyebrows I could spare. *Unknown.* FaBoEE

Thy eyes are sparks, Lycines, god-like made. Strato, *tr. fr. Greek by* Sydney Oswald. PeHV

Thy fabulous provinces belong. (*LL*) Philomela. John Crowe Ransom. ChTr; CMoP; FaBoPP; NAAL-2; NoAM; NOBA; OBAL; OBSV; OxBA

Thy fair smoothe words? no, no, thy fair smoothe haunches. (*LL*) The Author to His Wife, of a Woman's Eloquence. Sir John Harington. BoLoP; ErPo; LPA; OxBM

Thy faith is all the knowledge that thou hast. (*LL*) To My Mere English Censurer. Ben Jonson. BeJo

Thy Faithful Sons. Eleazar, *tr. fr. Hebrew.* TrJP

Thy Father's call of love! (*LL*) The Call of the Christian. Whittier. NOCV

Thy fever'd arms around me. The Sick Child. Lydia Huntley Sigourney. AmWP

Thy fingers make early flowers of all things. E. E. Cummings. MoAmPo; NAAL-2

Thy flattering picture, Phryne, is like thee. Phryne. John Donne. FaBoEE

Thy flow'r afloat, goolden zummer clote! (*LL*) The Clote (Water-Lily). William Barnes. ELP; FaBoVe; PoEL-4

Thy forests, Windsor! and thy green retreats. Pope. *Fr.* Windsor Forest. NOEC; OxAEP-1

Thy friend, whom thy deserts to thee enchaine. To Mr. C.B. John Donne. ESCV

Thy [*or* Your] friendship oft has made my heart to ache [*or* ake]. To William Hayley. Blake. FaBoCo
(T. H.) FF
(To Hayley.) FaBoEE; TrGrPo

Thy Garden. Don Johnson, *tr. fr. Arabic by* Dulcie L. Smith. AWP

Thy garden, orchard, fields. Francis Daniel Pastorius. SCAP

Thy Genius, Colebrooke, faithless to his charge. To Colebrooke Dale. Anna Seward. ECWP

Thy glass will show thee how thy beauties wear. Shakespeare. *Fr.* Sonnets. EnRePo; HeIP

Thy God, thy life, thy Cure. (*LL*) Peace. Henry Vaughan. AWP; ChTr; EBEV; ELP; ESCV; FaBoCh; GeHe; GN; HAP; NOBE; NOCV; OBD; OBEV; OxAEP-1; PIP; PoE; SCGP; SeCV-1; TEP; TFi; TOF; TrCP; WeW; WGRP

Thy grace, dear Lord's my golden wrack I find. Edward Taylor. *Fr.* Preparatory Meditations Before My Approach to the Lord's Supper. EAP; NoP; SCAP.

Thy Heaven. Thomas Moore. TIRV

Thy hue, dear pledge, is pure and bright. To a Lock of Hair. Sir Walter Scott. GTBS; GTBS-P

Thy human frame, my glorious Lord, I spy. Edward Taylor. *Fr.* Preparatory Meditations Before My Approach to the Lord's Supper. ChIV-1, *Division* I; LiTA; MeMAP

Thy husband to a banquet goes with me. Ovid, *tr. fr. Latin by* Christopher Marlowe. *Fr.* Amores. NoSic

Thy Kingdom Come, O Lord. Frederick L. Hosmer. WGRP

Thy Kingdom Come ("Thy kingdom come — on bended knee."). Frederick L. Hosmer. WGRP

Thy kingdom come: yea, bid it come. Holy Family. Katharine Tynan. TIRV

Thy Kingdom, Lord, We Long For. Vida Scudder. WGRP

Thy lady hath forgotten to be kind. (*LL*) Benedicite, What Dreamed I This Night? *Unknown.* HAP; PoEL-1

Thy leopard legs and python thighs. The Zoo of You. Arthur Freeman. ErPo

Thy life be written, and not read. (*LL*) An Elegy Upon the Death of His Own Father. Richard Corbett [*or* Corbet]. BeJo; NOSC

Thy life has touched the edges of my life. My Spirit's Complement. H. Cordelia Ray. AAP; CBWP-3

Thy looks are wan, thine eyes are wet. (*LL*) O [*or* Oh] snatch'd away in beauty's bloom! Byron. EnRP; GTBS; GTBS-P

Thy Loving Kindness, Lord, I Sing. George Barrell Cheever. AH

Thy mansion is the christian's heart. The House of Prayer. William Cowper. ChIV-2

Thy Mercies, Lord, to Heaven Reach. William Kethe. AH

Thy mercy on Thy People, Lord! (*LL*) Recessional. Kipling. AWP; BLPA; BLPL; BLRP; CoGr; EBEvV; FaBoPV; FaBV; GN; LiTB; MoBrPo; NoAM; NOBE; NOBVV; NoP; OBEV; OBNC; OxAEP-2; PlP; PWR; SCGP; TFi; TrGrPo; UnPo; UV; WBLP; WGRP

Thy merits, Wolfe, transcend all human praise. The Death of Wolfe. *Unknown.* PAH

Thy Mother Was like a Vine. Bible, *O.T. Fr.* Ezekiel. TrJP

Thy nags (the leanest things alive). Matthew Prior. FaBoEE

Thy name, thy fame, thy passions, and thy throne. (*LL*) Red Jacket. Fitz-Greene Halleck. AnAmPo

Thy Name We Bless and Magnify. John Power. BLRP

Thy nature, and Thy name is Love. (*LL*) Wrestling Jacob. Charles Wesley. NOBE; NOCV; NOEC; OBEV; OxAEP-1; PeECV; PoEL-3; TOF

Thy nature, immortality! who knows? Edward Young. *Fr.* Night Thoughts. OBD

Thy nights moan into my days. Psalms of Love. Peter Baum, *tr. fr. German by* Jethro Bithell. AWP

Thy own, to find them colder, fill. (*LL*) The Perfidious. Walter Savage Landor. CBLP

Thy Praise, O God, in Zion Waits. Jacob Kimball. AH

Thy praise, O Lord, will I proclaim. Palms and Myrtles. Eleazar ben Kalir, *tr. fr. Hebrew by* Alice Lucas. TrJP

Thy praise or dispraise is to me alike. To Fool, or Knave. Ben Jonson. FaBoEE; NoP

Thy prayer was "Light — more Light — while Time shall last!" Fiat Lux. Tennyson. FaBoEH

Thy restless feet now cannot go. Christ Crucified. Richard Crashaw. OBEV

Thy Rising Is Beautiful. Akhenaton, *tr. fr. Egyptian.* LPA, *tr. by* Anne and Christopher Freemantle.

Thy rising is beautiful, O living Aton, lord of Eternity. Thy Rising Is Beautiful. Akhenaton, *tr. fr. Egyptian.* LPA, *tr. by* Anne and Christopher Freemantle.

Thy sacred dew: protect them with thine influence. (*LL*) To the Evening Star. Blake. BoNaP; CH; ChTr; EnRP; FaBoRV; FaBV; NAEL-2; NOEC; NoP; OAEL-2; PoE; PoLF; TEP; TFi; TrGrPo; WiR

Thy sacred law, O God. On God's Law. Francis Quarles. ChIV-1

Thy said, "To die is glorious." They lied. (*LL*) Battle Won Is Lost. Phillip William George. GrPl

Thy satire point, and animate thy page. (*LL*) London. Samuel Johnson. PoEL-3; TEP

Thy Sea So Great ("Thy sea, O God, so great."). Winfred Ernest Garrison. TrPWD

Thy sheep with thee. (*LL*) Rom. Cap. 8 Ver. 19. Henry Vaughan. ESCV; GeHe; MeLP

Thy sinnes and haires may no man equall call. A Licentious Person. John Donne. PeLV

Thy sleep makes ridiculous. (*LL*) The Humble-Bee. Emerson. AnAmPo; FaPON; FM; GN; MeMAP; NOBA; OxBA

Thy sooty godhead I desire. To Vulcan. Robert Herrick. CaPo

Thy soul/ Grown delicate with satieties. O Atthis. Ezra Pound. PoA

Thy soul within such silent pomp did keep. A Quiet Soul. John Oldham. OBEV

Thy spirit's wings unfolded in the light. (*LL*) Mignon. H. Cordelia Ray. AmWP; CBWP-3

Thy stricken daughter, now, O Lord, prepares. Hymn for the Eve of the New Year. Abraham Gerondi, *tr. fr. Hebrew by* Solomon Solis-Cohen. TrJP

Thy summer voice, Musketaquit. Two Rivers. Emerson. AmPP; NOBA; OxBA; PoE; TrGrPo

Thy sword within the scabbard keep. Momus' Song to Mars. Dryden. *Fr.* Secular Masque, The. NAEL-1; OxBSP; PoE; PoEL-3; PrIm; SCGP; SeCV-2

Thy temple face is chiselled from within. (*LL*) Everymaid. John Oxenham. TrCP

Thy thoughts, dear Keats, are like fresh-gathered leaves. To Keats: On Reading His Sonnet Written in Chaucer. John Hamilton Reynolds. Son

Thy trivial harp will never please. Merlin ("Thy trivial harp will never please."). Emerson. *Fr.* Merlin. AmPP; NAAL-2; NOBA; OxBA

Thy various works, imperial queen, we see. On Imagination. Phillis Wheatley. AmPP; BlSi; PoNe

Thy voice, as tender as the light. To a Friend. James Fenimore Cooper. PeHV

Thy voice is heard through rolling drums. Tennyson. *Fr.* Princess, The. TrGrPo

Thy voice is hovering o'er my soulit lingers. To Constantia Singing. Shelley. EnRP

Thy voice is on the rolling air. Tennyson. *Fr.* In Memoriam A. H. H. EBVV, *abr.*; EBVVPR; FHYEP; HeIP; NoP; OAEL-2, *abr.*; PeECV, *abr.*; PeHV

Thy Way, Not Mine. Horatius Bonar. TrPWD

Thy weary feet have pressed once more thy native soil. Welcome Home. Josephine D. Henderson Heard. CBWP-4

Thy Will Be Done. John Milton Hay. *See* Not in Dumb Resignation.

Thy Will Be Done. Hugh Thomson Kerr. BLRP

Thy Will is best for me. God's Will Is Best. *Unknown.* BLRP

Thy will, O God, is best. Thy Will Be Done. Hugh Thomson Kerr. BLRP

Thy wisdom speaks in me, and bids me dare. Shelley. *Fr.* Epipsychidion. EnRP; OAEL-2

Thy words are compounded of sweet-smelling myrrh. Words Wherein Stinging Bees Lurk. Judah Halevi, *tr. fr. Hebrew by* Nina Davis Salaman. TrJP

Thy worldly hopes and fears have passed away. To the Memory of John Keats. John Clare. EPCY

Thyestes, *sels.* Seneca, *tr. fr. Latin.*
"O yee, whome lorde of lande and waters wyde." OBVE
"Stand [*or* Stond] who so list upon the slipper top [*or* toppe]." AAS; NoP; NoSic; OBVE; PoEL-1; SiPS
(Climb at court for me that will.) OBVE, *tr. by* Andrew Marvell
(Let him that will, ascend the tottering seat.) OBVE, *tr. by* Sir Matthew Hale
(Let who so lyst with might mace to raygne.) OBVE, *tr. by* Jasper Heywood
(Senec. Traged. ex Thyeste Chor. 2.) SeCV-1, *tr. by* Andrew Marvell
(Upon the slippery tops of humane state.) OBVE, *tr. by* Abraham Cowley

Thyme. *Unknown.* AmFP

Thyme Flowering among Rocks. Richard Wilbur. EOEF; LCAP

Thyrsis. Matthew Arnold. NAEL-2; NOBE; NoP; OBEV; OBNC
Sels.
Thyrsis. EnVR; FaBoPP; FHYEP; Mes
"What though the music of thy rustic flute." EPCY

Thyrsis. Matthew Arnold. *Fr.* Thyrsis. EnVR; FaBoPP; FHYEP; Mes; NAEL-2; NOBE; NoP; OBEV; OBNC

Thyrsis. Edward Cracroft Lefroy, *after the Greek of* Theocritus. *Fr.* Echoes from Theocritus. AWP

Thyrsis, a youth of the inspired train. The Story of Phoebus and Daphne Applied, [etc.]. Edmund Waller. InvP; NAEL-1; NOSC

Thyrsis and Milla, arm in arm together. *Unknown.* GBL

Thyrsis, Sleep'st Thou? *Unknown.* InvP; NoSic; OxBSP

Thyrsis, sleep'st thou? Holla! Let not sorrow stay us. Thyrsis, Sleep'st Thou? *Unknown.* InvP; NoSic; OxBSP

Thys ender nyght. *Unknown.* TrGrPo, *abr.*

Tiara. Mark Doty. PFL

Tibby has a Store of Charms. Genty Tibby and Sonsy Nelly. Allan Ramsay. ScCV

Till I think the Milky Way has tumbled from the ninth height of Heaven. *(LL)* Viewing the Waterfall at Mount Lu. Li Po. TTTS

Till I too bloom and dance with the fulness of Your life. *(LL)* Sandhya. Ishpriya. EaPr

Till I too blossom and rejoice and sing. *(LL)* The First Spring Day. Christina Rossetti. FaBoVe; WiR

Till it could come no more. *(LL)* At the Seaside. Robert Louis Stevenson. NTCP; OxBChV; TLR; WHSW

Till it's caught by the tail. *(LL)* As round as an apple, as deep as a pail. *Unknown.* OxNR

Till life became a Legend of the Dead. *(LL)* The Jewish Cemetery at Newport. Longfellow. AmPP; ChIV-1; HAP; HeIP; HoPM; MeMAP; NOBA; NoP; OxBA; TAP

Till love's put off and pain and wish and death. *(LL)* My Naked Aunt. Archibald MacLeish. MeMAP

Till May be out. *(LL)* Button to chin. *Unknown.* FaBoUs; OxNR

Till now the doubtful dusk reveal'd. Tennyson. *Fr.* In Memoriam A. H. H. EBVV, *abr.*; GTBS-P; OAEL-2, *abr.*; PeECV, *abr.*

Till now your indiscretion sets us free. Eves Apologie. Emilia Lanier. *Fr.* Salve Deus Rex Judaeorum. BoWoP

Till St. Mungo come o'er the sea. *(LL)* Kemp Owyne. *Unknown.* EnSB; ESPB, A *and* B *vers.*

Till sunset in the living flesh. *(LL)* She Sleeps. T. Carmi. MHP

Till that we meet again. *(LL)* Whereto should I express. Henry VIII, King of England. NoSic

Till the April sun set. *(LL)* Allie ("Allie, call the birds in.") Robert Graves. FaPON; GoJo; NTP; PeLV

Till the day-spring breaks forth again from high. *(LL)* The Bird. Henry Vaughan. ESCV; FM; GeHe; OBEV; PoE; PoEL-2; SeCV-1

Till the good morning star. *Unknown, tr. fr. Greek by* Peter Jay. GrAn

Till the gossamer thread you fling catch somewhere, O, my soul. *(LL)* A Noiseless Patient Spider. Walt Whitman. AmPP; AnAMPo; AWP; BLPL; FF; HAP; HeIL; HeIP; ImPo; InPK; InPS; LiTA; MoAMPo; NAAL-1; NOBA; NoP; NTP; OxBA; OxBSP; PoE; Poetr; SAmP; SCV; TAP; TFi; TrGrPo; WiR

Till the gunpowder ran out at the heels of their boots. *(LL)* The Great Panjandrum [Himself]. Samuel Foote. CBNP; FaBoCh; FaBoCo; MoShBr; PoLF

Till the Sea Runs Dry. *Malay Oral Tradition, tr. by* R. J. Wilkinson. WTO

Till the slow daylight pale. The Sun-Flower. Dora Greenwell. WPE

Till the white winged Reapers come! *(LL)* The Seed Growing Secretly. Henry Vaughan. ChIV-2; ESCV; GeHe; SeCV-1

Till the young brood come chirping to the door. *(LL)* Hen's Nest. John Clare. Soe

Till they be hid o'er with a wood of darts. *(LL)* Good Christians. Robert Herrick. LiTB

Till they touch in flood. *(LL)* The Elephant Is Slow to Mate. D. H. Lawrence. ArNa; LiTB; LiTM; MeMBP; PPP; TEP

Till thinking had worn out my enterprise. Spring Mountain Climb. Richard Eberhart. GoYe

Till Time present her with the Universe. *(LL)* An Elegie upon the Death of the Lord Hastings. Sir John Denham. SeCV-1

Till twelve years' age, how Christ His childhood spent. Christ's Childhood. Robert Southwell. ChIV-2

Till you've earned. Mahadevi, *tr. fr. Kannada by* A. K. Ramanujan. PBWP

Tiller of the Soil. Avraham Shlonsky, *tr. fr. Hebrew by* Ruth Finer Mintz. MHP

Tilly. James Joyce. RB

Tilt. Wilt. Snow. Ralph Pomeroy. Poetsp

Tilth. Robert Graves. FaBoEE; OBSV

Tim Finnegan [or Finnigin or Finigan] liv'd in Walkin [or lived in Walker] Street. Finnegan's Wake. *Unknown.* CBNP; FaBoBa; NBLV (Finigan's Wake.) BLPA

Tim looks at his watch, reaches into his. Driving Back from New Haven. David Trinidad. NGP; PFL

Tim tryeth truth convicting all that strive. T. Street. SCAP

Tim Turpin. Thomas Hood. WiR

Timarista and Krito. Rosanna Warren. *Fr.* Funerary Portraits. NoAM

Timber. *Unknown.* AS

Timber, The. Henry Vaughan. FaBoRV, *abr.*; GeHe, *abr.*; NoP; OBEV; SeCP; SeCV-1

Time. Mary Ursula Bethell. FaBoWP

Time. Bhartrihari, *tr. fr. Sanskrit by* Paul Elmer More. AWP

Time. Robert Creeley. LCAP

Time. Giles Fletcher the Elder. *See* In Time the Strong and Stately Turrets Fall.

Time. Robert Graves. LiTM

Time. George Herbert. NAEL-1; TEP

Time. Ralph Hodgson. GTBS-P

Time. Thomas Lux. BAP-90

Time. Jasper Mayne. OBEV

Time. Sir Thomas More. *Fr.* Pageant Verses. EnRePo

Time. Shelley. FaBoRV; PoLF

Time. William Stafford. Son

Time. Allan Taylor. OBET

Time. Thomas Watson. *Fr.* Hecatompathia; or, Passionate Century of Love. CBCK; FaBoRV

Time. John Huddlestone Wynne. OxBChV

Time & time again the laughter after the footsteps. The Jungle. Diane Di Prima. PoM

Time again subdues her. *(LL)* Wives in the Sere. Thomas Hardy. NOBE; NOBVV

Time allowed for sleep at length elapsed, The. Thomas Cole. *Fr.* Life of Hubert, The. NOEC

Time and again. Theology and a Patchwork Absolute. Heather McPherson. PeNZ

Time and Eternity. Bunyan. WiR

Time and Eternity. Stephen Hawes. *Fr.* Pastime of Pleasure, The. PoEL-1

Time and Grief. William Lisle Bowles. OBEV

Time and Love, I. Shakespeare. *See* When I have seen by Time's fell hand defac'd.

Time and Love, II. Shakespeare. *See* Since brass, nor stone, nor earth, nor boundless sea.

Time & prayer fitting, I, the god. Perses, *tr. fr. Greek by* Peter Whigham. GrAn

Time and the changing passions played them tricks. The Early Rebels. Mervyn Morris. PBCV

Time and the Garden. Yvor Winters. MoAMPo; NoAM; VGW

Time and the mortal will stand never fast. Camões, *tr. fr. Spanish by* Richard Garnett. AWP

Time and the weather wear away. Houses. Donald Justice. (Poem: "Time and the weather wear away.") PoA

Time and the World, whose magnitude and weight. Robert Southey. OBNC

Time and Tide. Hazel Washington Lamarre. PoNe

Time before You, The. Medbh McGuckian. CBLP

Time breaks the barrier. Hilda Doolittle ("H. D."). *Fr.* Sigil. AnAn

Time can [or will] say nothing but I told you so. W. H. Auden. LiTA; MoAB; MoBrPo

Time cannot break the bird's wing from the bird. To a Young Poet. Edna St. Vincent Millay. OxBSP

Time comes when you no longer can say: my God, A. Your Shoulders Hold Up the World. Carlos Drummond de Andrade, *tr. fr. Portuguese by* Mark Strand. AnRep

Time, cruel time, come and subdue that brow. Samuel Daniel. *Fr.* To Delia. ESo; SCGP

Time Does Not Bring Relief. Edna St. Vincent Millay. FaBV; HeIP

Time does not matter to Jerusalem. Costumes of Jerusalem. Julia Vinograd. BCF

Time drawes neere. Anne Waldman. UL

Time draws near the birth of Christ, The. Tennyson. *Fr.* In Memoriam A. H. H. EBVV, *abr.*; EBVVPR, *sect.* XXVIII; FaBoRV, *sect.* XXVIII; FHYEP, *sect.* XXVIII; NOCV, *sect.* XXVIII; OAEL-2, *abr.*; PChr, *sect.* XXVIII; PeECV, *abr.*; SoSe, *sect.* XXVIII

Time drops in decay. W. B. Yeats. CTC; EBVVPR

Time ends when vision sees its lapse in/ liberty. Beata l'Alma. Sir Herbert Read. FaBoMo

Time Exposures. Muriel Rukeyser. PoA

Time flits away, time flits away, lady. Variation on Ronsard. T. Sturge Moore. OBMV

Time for Building, A. Myra Cohn Livingston. PDV

Time for Everything, A. Bible, *O.T. See* To Everything There Is a Season.

Time for rain! for your long hot dry autumn. Piano di Sorrento. Robert Browning. *Fr.* Englishman in Italy, The. FaBoPP; PoEL-5

Time for summer clothes and wine-tasting. Tune: "Six Toughies" — Written after the Roses Have Faded. Chou Pang-yen, *tr. fr. Chinese by* James J. Y. Liu. SuSp

Time for trembling's past, I've Titus' love, The. Bérénice Enumerates the Triumph of Titus. Jean Racine, *tr. fr. French by* John Cairncross. *Fr.* Bérénice. CBCK

Time for tremblin's past, I've Titus' love, The. Jean Racine, *tr. fr. French by* John Cairncross. *Fr.* Berenice Enumerates the Triumph of Titus. CBCK

Time goes, you say? Ah, no! The Paradox of Time. Pierre de Ronsard, *tr. fr. French by* Austin Dobson. AWP

Time gone. Blue Mason Jars. Keith Abbott. UL

Time has an end, they say. Hilda Doolittle ("H. D."). *Fr.* Good Frend. NOBA; VGW

Time has been that these wild solitudes, The. A Winter Piece. Bryant. AmPP; EAP; OxBA

Time has been, when yet the muse was young, The. Byron. *Fr.* English Bards and Scotch Reviewers. FHYEP

Time has brought about great changes. Scraps of Time. Mrs. Henry Linden. CBWP-4

Time has come for us to part, The. I'm Through with You. *Unknown.* WTO

Time has come, the clock says time has come, The. Conrad Aiken. *Fr.* Preludes for Memnon; or, Preludes to Attitude. LiTA; OxBA

Time has not quenched your beauty. Much of your bygone prime. Rufinus Domesticus, *tr. fr. Greek by* Barbara Hughes Fowler. *Fr.* Epigrams. HePo

Time has pulled up a chair, dashed. Ron Mason. Hone Tuwhare. PeNZ

Time has triumphed, the wind has scattered all. Hope. *Unknown, tr. fr. Irish by* Brendan Kennelly. PeIV

Time has wrinkled your face. Voodoo. Léon Laleau, *tr. fr. French by* Ellen Conroy Kennedy. *Fr.* Black Music. NegPo

Time hath, my Lord, a wallet at his back. Ulysses Advises Achilles. Shakespeare. *Fr.* Troilus and Cressida. ImPo; LiTB

Time heals not: it extends a sorrow's scope. J. V. Cunningham. IMW; VGW

Time I dropped your almost body down, The. The Lost Baby Poem. Lucille Clifton. BlSi; CAPP; WPE

Time I went to church I sat, The. Mr. Rockefeller's Hat. Helen Smith Bevington. OBAL

Time I went to see my Sister, The. Tsurayuki, *tr. fr. Japanese by* Arthur Waley. *Fr.* Shui Shu. AWP

Time in the Rock [or, Preludes to Definition]. Conrad Aiken. VGW *Sels.*
"Bird flying past my head said previous previous, The."
"But no, the familiar symbol, as that the."
"Mysticism, but let us have no words."
"What face she put on it, we will not discuss."
"Where we were walking in the day's light, seeing."

Time is, The. Anger. Robert Creeley. NaP

Time is a fox on quick, velvet feet. Earthly Illusion. Louise Leighton. GoYe

Time is a thief who leaves his tools behind him. The Angel-Thief. Oliver Wendell Holmes. AnAmPo

Time is a thing. Stephen Spender. MoBrPo

Time is a treasure. New Time. *Unknown.* BLRP

Time is after dinner, The. Cigarettes. The Boarder. Louis Simpson. InPK; SM

Time is at the end, The. Ox-Bow. Donald Davie. DiPo

Time is divided into. Time Is the Mercy of Eternity. Kenneth Rexroth. VGW

Time is engraved on the pale green faces. Written in the Sunset. Hsiung-hung, *tr. fr. Chinese by* Kenneth Rexroth *and* Ling Chung. WPC

Time is mainly a fiction here. There are. New Guinea Time. Louis Johnson. PeNZ

Time is my debtor for my years untold. *(LL)* Long Time a Child. Hartley Coleridge. EnRP; PoEL-4; Son

Time is never wasted, listening to the trees. The Trees. Lucy Larcom. OHIP

Time is not remote when I, The. Swift. *Fr.* Verses on the Death of Doctor Swift [D.S.P.D., Occasioned by Reading a Maxim in Rochefoucauld]. EBEV; Mes; NOBE; NOBL; NOIV; PeLV
(On the Death of Dean Swift.) OxAEP-1

Time is of the essence. This is a highly skilled. Polo Grounds. Rolfe Humphries. HoPM

Time is peculiar. Lengths of Time. Phyllis McGinley. SiSoPo

Time is ripe and I repent, The. Oengus Céile Dé. NOIV

Time Is Swiftly Rolling On, The. Berryman Hicks. AH

Time is the feather'd thing. Time. Jasper Mayne. OBEV

Time Is the Fire. Delmore Schwartz. *See* Calmly We Walk Through This April's Day.

Time Is the Mercy of Eternity. Kenneth Rexroth. VGW

Time is the root of all this earth. Time. Bhartrihari, *tr. fr. Sanskrit by* Paul Elmer More. AWP

Time Is Today, The. John Farrar. GoYe

Time Is What You Make of It. Leo Romero. AfAz

Time it took he could have, The. The Invention of the Telephone. Peter Klappert. AmPA

Time I've Lost in Wooing, The. Thomas Moore. EnRP; HoPM; NAEL-2; PeLV

Time like an Ever-rolling Stream. P. G. Wodehouse. FiBHP

Time like the receptions of a child's piano. The Reconciliation. Archibald MacLeish. MoAmPo

Time Machine, The. Jon Anderson. AnAn

Time of Burning, The. May Sarton. *Fr.* Invocation to Kali, The. SRLS

Time of Change, A. Egan O'Rahilly, *tr. fr. Irish by* Eavan Boland. BIrV; FaBoPV

Time of Creation Has Come, The. *Yoruba Oral Tradition, tr. by* Ulli Beier. WTO

Time of Day. Selden Rodman. PoA

Time of Fish Dying. Gabriela Melinescu, *tr. fr. Romanian by* Stavros Deligiorgis. BoWoP

Time of fools is coming. Aleksandar Ristovic, *tr. fr. Serbo-Croatian by* Charles Simic. HSix

Time of grease beginneth at Midsummer day. Julians Barnes. *Fr.* Book of Hunting. WPE

Time of great fatigue comes. The morning dazzling, The. Putting Out the Lamp. Yannis Ritsos, *tr. fr. Greek by* Paul Merchant. AnRep

Time of lamentation and curses is passing, The. Audre Lorde. *Fr.* Prologue. CrSp

Time of Man, The. Phyllis Webb. MoCV

Time of Martyrdom, The. David Diop, *tr. fr. French by* Ellen Conroy Kennedy. NegPo

Time of naked spears, A. Death Certificate. Rui Knopfli, *tr. fr. Portuguese by the author.* PeSAV

Time of Roses. Thomas Hood. *See* It Was Not in the Winter.

Time of the Barmecides, The. James Clarence Mangan. EnRP; PeIV

Time of Turtles. Grace Perry. NOBAu

Time of Waiting. Geoffrey Dutton. CBAP

Time of Waiting in Amsterdam. Ingrid Jonker, *tr. fr. Afrikaans by* Jack Cope *and* William Plomer. BoWoP

Time of white violets; and on the slopes. The Convent in '45. Maria Luisa Spaziani, *tr. fr. Italian by* Beverly Allen. NeIt

Time; or, How the Line about Chagall's Lovers Disappears. Jane Miller. SM

Time Out. Frances Westgate Butterfield. GoYe

Time Out. Donald Finkel. HoPM

Time Out. Oliver Jenkins. GoYe

Time Out. Eva Salzman. NWP

Time parts the hearts of men. *(LL)* Come, walk with me. Emily Brontë. NOBVV

Time Passes. R. P. Lister. NYBP

Time Passing, Beloved ("Time passing, and the memories of love.") Donald Davie. BoLoP

Time Past, A. Denise Levertov. NoAM

Time Piece. William Cole. GrPl

Time-Piece, The. William Cowper. *Fr.* Task, The. EnRP

Time pleats dark flesh. Faces and Skulls. Jan Carew. PBCV

Time present and time past. Burnt Norton. T. S. Eliot. *Fr.* Four Quartets. CMoP; LiTM; MoAB; MoAmPo; NAAL-2; PoE

Time quietly compiling us like sheaves. Seferis. Lawrence Durrell. EBEV

Time, Real and Imaginary. Samuel Taylor Coleridge. EnRP; MeMBP; NOBE; OBEV; OxBSP; PFP

Time Recover'd. Thomas Stanley, *after the Italian of* Girolamo Casone. OBVE

Time Reminded Me. Julia Uceda, *tr. fr. Spanish by* Willis Barnstone. BoWoP

Time rolls his ceaseless course. The race of yore. The Gathering. Sir Walter Scott. *Fr.* Lady of the Lake, The. OBNC

Time-Servers. Judah Halevi, *tr. fr. Hebrew by* Solomon Solis-Cohen. TrJP

Time shall come, when free as seas or wind, The. Progress. Pope. *Fr.* Windsor Forest. ECEV

Time sitting on the throne of Memory. October XXIX, 1795. William Stanley Braithwaite. CDC

Time Speaks. Shao Yen-hsiang, *tr. fr. Chinese.* LHF, *tr. by* Hualing Nieh.

Time spirals upright this unflowing river. The Well. A. J. Seymour. PBCV

Time stands still. The Unbeseechable. Frances Cornford. MoBrPo

Time stands still, with gazing on her face! *Unknown.* EnLoPo

Time Swept Up. Vasco [*or* Vasko] Popa, *tr. fr. Serbo-Croatian. Fr.* Raw Flesh. PoSu, *tr. by* Anne Pennington.

Time that brings [*or* bringes] all things to light. Thomas Morton. NOSC; SCAP

Time that is moved by little fidget wheels. Five Bells. Kenneth Slessor. CBAP; FaBoMA; NOBAu; PoRA

Timon, for you exist no more. Callimachus, *tr. fr. Greek. Fr.* Epigrams. HePo

Timon of Athens, *sels.* Shakespeare.
"My worthy friends, will you draw near?" OBF
"O blessed breeding sun! draw from the earth." OxAEP-1
"O you gods, think I, what need we have any friends." OBF
"Put up thy gold: go on, — here's gold, — go on." OxAEP-1
Timon's Epitaph. AWP
"Warr'st thou 'gainst Athens?" EBEV

Timon's Epitaph. Shakespeare. *Fr.* Timon of Athens. AWP

Timon's Villa. Pope. *Fr.* Epistles to Several Persons, to Richard Boyle, Earl of Burlington: Of the Use of Riches. PoE

Timon's Villa. Pope. *See* At Timon's villa let us pass a day.

Timor Mortis. *Unknown.* FF; NoP

Timor Mortis Conturbat Me. William Dunbar. *See* I that in heill wes [*or* health was] and gladnes[s] [*or* gladiness].

Timor Mortis conturbat me. (*LL*) Lament for the Makaris. William Dunbar. ChTr; EBEV; HAP; NoP; OxBS; ScCV

Timor mortis conturbat me. (*LL*) Timor Mortis. *Unknown.* FF; NoP

Timoshenko. Sidney Keyes. OBWP

Timothy. Timothy Steele. InPK

Timothy Titus took two ties. *Unknown.* OxNR

Timothy Winters. Charles Causley. PeECV; RB

Tin Bird, The. Ramon C. Sunico, *tr. fr. Spanish.* TSaS, *tr. by* Sunico Ramon C.

Tin Frog, The. Russell Hoban.

Tin-Ore. *Malay Oral Tradition, tr. by* W. W. Skeat. WTO

Tin Roof Blues. Robert Sargent. Jaz

Tin shack, where my baby sleeps on his back. Everything: Eloy, Arizona, 1956. Ai. AmPA; FF

Tin Woodsman, The. Paulette Jiles. NOBC

Tina and Seth met in the midst of an overcrowded militarism. Histoire. Harry Mathews. NIP

Tinder, The. Thomas Carew. CaPo

Tinder. Seamus Heaney. OxAEP-2

Tiniest of turtles! Ladybird. Clive Sansom. GrPl

Tink dere is a God in a top. *Unknown. Fr.* Work-Songs. PBCV

Tinker, The. *Unknown.* CoMu

Tinker,/ Tailor. *Unknown.* OxNR

Tinker, The ("There was a lady in this land.") *Unknown.* CoMu

Tinker's Wife. Patrick Kavanagh. CIP; InPS; MoP; NoAM

"Tinkle, tinkle, tinkle": 'tis the muffin-man you see. The Muffin-Man's Bell. Ann Hawkshawe. BoTP

Tint I cannot take is best, The. Emily Dickinson. MoAmPo

Tintern Abbey. Edward Davies. *Fr.* Chepstow: A Poem. OBWVE

Tintock. *Unknown.* GBP

Tiny ant at night you would be seeking, The. The Disdainful Mistress. *Malay Oral Tradition, tr. by* R. J. Wilkinson *and* R. O. Winstedt. WTO

Tiny baby, you're ugly. King D. Kuka. VoR

Tiny Catullus. Steve Levine. UL

Tiny children. Yityangu Ejong, *tr. fr. Yindjibarndi by* Frank Wordick. CBAP

Tiny creature moves, A. The Milk Bottle. Galway Kinnell. Poetr; PRA

Tiny Erotion, borne away/ By a gnat had this to say. Lucilius, *tr. fr. Greek by* Peter Porter. GrAn

Tiny fish enjoy themselves, The. Little Fish. D. H. Lawrence. OxBTC; RB; SOTW; Spl; TTTS

Tiny Histories. Mark Svenvold. UTF

Tiny Montgomery. Bob Dylan. CBNP

Tiny moon as small and white as a single jasmine flower, A. A White Blossom. D. H. Lawrence. MoBrPo

Tiny nut, a bit of tasteless betel, A. Carved on an Areca Nut. Ho Xuan Huong, *tr. fr. Vietnamese by* Nguyen Ngoc Bich *and* Burton Raffel. PBWP

Tiny pools of water glisten on the street. (*LL*) My Father's Back. Edward Hirsch. VCAP

Tiny shoes so trim and neat. The Fairy Shoemaker. Phyllis L. Garlick. BoTP

Tiny slippers of gold and green. To a Pair of Egyptian Slippers. Sir Edwin Arnold. OBTV

Tiny snow of the stunningly cold black day. In the Snowfall. Gwerfyl Mechain, *tr. fr. Welsh by* Willis Barnstone. BoWoP

Tío-Vivo, or the Merry-go-round. Federico García Lorca, *tr. fr. Spanish.* CBNP

Tion — this is life; to do less would be nothing but/ Dishonesty. (*LL*) Peter. Marianne Moore. CMoP; NAAL-2; NoP; OxBA; SoCa

Tip, The. Albert Goldbarth. HCAP

Tip, The. Belle Waring. PBCAP

Tip-of-the-Single-Feather. Velema, *tr. fr. Fijian by* B. H. Quain. WTO

Tip the Light Fantastic. Ira Cohen. NGP

Tip-Toe Tail. Dixie Willson. NTCP

Tippecanoe and Tyler Too. Alexander Coffman Ross. AnAmPo

Tipperary. Desmond O'Grady. BiHa

Tipperty-toes, the smallest elf. Red in Autumn. Elizabeth Gould. BoTP

Tips Tongueless. Robert Herrick. CaPo

Tiptoe. Karla Kuskin. PDV

Tire Hangs in the Woods, The. Dave Jeddie Smith. NGP

Tired. Fenton Johnson. PoBA; PoLF; PoNe; TTY

Tired and thirsty, weary of the way. After the Hunt. Detlev von Liliencron, *tr. fr. German by* Ludwig Lewisohn. AWP

Tired and Unhappy, You Think of Houses. Delmore Schwartz. LiTM; MoAB; MoAmPo

Tired as I Can Be. *Unknown.* FaBoVe

Tired Memory. Coventry Patmore. *Fr.* Unknown Eros, The. EnVR

Tired nature's sweet restorer, balmy Sleep! Edward Young. *Fr.* Night Thoughts. EnRP; NOEC
(Night Thoughts.) OxAEP-1

Tired new trooper scans the beach, A. Vet. Lincoln Kirstein. ArOW

Tired Night, A. Tu Fu, *tr. fr. Chinese by* Jan W. Walls. SuSp

Tired of all who come with words, words but no language. Tomas Tranströmer. EaPr

Tired of Eating Kisses. Edward Vincent Swart. PeSA

Tired of Towns. Andrew Lang. EBVV; OHCV

Tired [*or* Tyr'd, *or* Tir'd] with all these, for restful death I cry. Shakespeare. *Fr.* Sonnets. AWP; CoGr; CTC; EBEV; FaBoPV; HAP; InPS; LiTB; NOBE; NoSic; OAEL-1; OxAEP-1; PoEL-2; TFi; TrGrPo; WeW
(Tired With All These.) CBCK; ImPo
(World's Way, The.) GTBS; GTBS-P

Tired Petitioner, The, *sels.* George Wither.
"It may be 'tis observ'd, I want relations." SeCV-1

Tired Tim. Walter de la Mare. BoTP; FaPON; MoShBr; NTCP

Tired With All These. Shakespeare. *See* Tired [*or* Tyr'd, *or* Tir'd] with all these, for restful death I cry.

Tired with books and rolling on the bed. The New River Head, a Fragment. E. Dower. NOEC

Tired with dull grief, grown old before my day. 1916 Seen from 1921. Edmund Blunden. PeFWW

Tired with its dogs and doves. Summer Band Concert. Vivian Smith. CBAP

Tired with the noisome follies of the age. The Earl of Rochester. *Fr.* Farewell to the Court. TrGrPo

Tired with too long a chase, though stout. On the Death of Squire Christopher. John Wigson. OxBSP

Tired Woman, The. Anna Wickham. MoBrPo

Tired Worker, The. Claude McKay. BPo

Tireles Sculptor, The. H. Cordelia Ray. CBWP-3

Tiresias, *sels.* Austin Clarke.
"My mother wept loudly." CIP

Tiresias. George Garrett. SM

Tirocinium; or, A Review of Schools. William Cowper. OBSV
Sels.
"Father, who designs his babe a priest, The."
"To you, then, tenants of life's middle state."
"Would you your son should be a sot or dunce."

Tiros II. Fred Chappell. PRA

Tirumal. Katuvan Ilaveyinanar, *tr. fr. Tamil by* A. K. Ramanujan. PLW

Tirzah. Jacob Cohen, *tr. fr. Hebrew by* Ruth Finer Mintz. MHP

'Tis a dull sight. Old Song. Edward Fitzgerald. GN; OBEV; OxAEP-2

'Tis a favorite project of mine. Harvey L. Carter. Poetr

'Tis a lesson you should heed. Try, Try Again. At. to T. H. Palmer. FaPON; ImGa

'Tis a Little Journey. *Unknown.* PoToHe

'Tis a little thing. A Friend. Sir Thomas N. Talfourd. PoToHe

'Tis a moon-tinted primrose, with a well. Another. Thomas Lovell Beddoes. Son

'Tis a new life; — thoughts move not as they did. The New Birth. Jones Very. NOBA

'Tis a noble gift to be brown, all brown. The Bronze Legacy. Mary Effie Lee Newsome. ShDr

'Tis a sad land, that in one day. Death. Henry Vaughan. ChIV-1

'Tis a soft Rogue, this Lycias. Lycias. The Earl of Rochester. ErPo

'Tis a stern and startling thing to think. Her Death. Thomas Hood. *Fr.* Miss Kilmansegg and Her Precious Leg. NOBVV

'Tis a time for much rejoicing. Emancipation. Priscilla Jane Thompson. CBWP-2

'Tis a world of silences. I gave a cry. Silences. Arthur O'Shaughnessy. OBNC

'Tis advertised in Boston, New York and Buffalo. Blow Ye Winds in the Morning. *Unknown.* AmFP; SWP

'Tis affection but dissembled. Sidney Godolphin. BeJo; JCP

'Tis all a myth that Autumn grieves. Autumn's Mirth. Samuel Minturn Peck. GN

'Tis all that Heav'n allows. *(LL)* Love and Life. The Earl of Rochester. BoLoP; ELP; EnLoPo; FF; GBL; HAP; NOBE; OBEV; PoEL-3; SeCV-2; TrGrPo

'Tis all the way to Toe-town. Foot Soldiers. John Banister Tabb. OBAL

'Tis an act of the priest to give patience a test. Matrimony. John Williams. NOEC

'Tis bad enough in man or woman. On Inclosures. *Unknown.* FaBoCo
(Epigram: On Inclosures.) OxBoLi
(On Enclosures.) FaBoEE

'Tis beauty truly blent, whose red and white. Olivia's Face. Shakespeare. *Fr.* Twelfth Night. CBCK

'Tis better to be vile than vile esteem'd. Shakespeare. *Fr.* Sonnets. InVP; NoSic; OAEL-1; OxAEP-1; PoEL-2; SCGP

'Tis bitter, yet 'tis sweet. Troubled with the Itch and Rubbing with Sulphur. George Moses Horton. AAP

Tis braul I cudgel, ranters, Quakers braul. Claudius Gilbert. John Wilson. SCAP

'Tis but a phantom of the weary brain. Life for a Life. Mary E. Tucker. CBWP-1

'Tis Christmas weather, and a country house. George Meredith. *Fr.* Modern Love. NAEL-2; NOBVV

Tis clear, Great Dane, thy barque's worse than thy bite. King Canute. Stanley J. Sharpless. BXAP

'Tis colour, not merit, that pays! *(LL)* Prejudice against Colour. Langham Dale. PeSAV

'Tis day, my crystal Usk: now the sad night. "So Have I Spent on the Banks of Ysca Many a Serious Hour." Thomas Vaughan. FaBoPP

'Tis daylight still, but now the golden cross. The Plaça Santiago. "George Eliot." *Fr.* Spanish Gypsy, The. OBTV

'Tis dead night round about: Horror [*or* Horrour] doth creep[e]. The Lamp[e]. Henry Vaughan. ChIV-2; ESCV

'Tis dead of night; storms rend the troubled air. Mary Locke. ECWP

'Tis death! and peace, indeed, is here. Youth and Calm. Matthew Arnold. FHYEP; MeMBP

'Tis done! Dread Winter spreads his latest glooms. James Thomson. *Fr.* Seasons, The. OxAEP-1

'Tis "Done" — the wondrous thoroughfare. The Pacific Railway. C. R. Ballard. PAH

'Tis down in the valley my father does dwell. The Only Daughter. *Unknown.* OBET

'Tis dreadful! The Aisle of a Temple. Congreve. OxAEP-1

'Tis drinking Sally Birkett's ale. *(LL)* O mortal man, that lives by bread. *At. to* Julius Caeser Ibbetson. ChTr; FaBoEE

'Tis easy enough to be twenty-one. Responsibility. *Unknown.* FaBoUs

'Tis easy to be true! *(LL)* Not, Celia, that I juster am. Sir Charles Sedley. GTBS; GTBS-P

'Tis eight o'clock — a clear March night. The Idiot Boy. Wordsworth. OBNV

'Tis evening, the black snail has got on his track. Evening. John Clare. NOBVV

'Tis fine to see the Old World, and travel up and down. America for Me. Henry van Dyke. BLPA; BLPL; WBLP

'Tis folly to be wise. *(LL)* Ode on a Distant Prospect of Eton College. Thomas Gray. BLPL; GTBS; GTBS-P; ImPo; LiTB; NAEL-1; NOBE; NOEC; NoP; OAEL-1; OxAEP-1; PoE; PoEL-3; PrIm; SCGP

'Tis God that girds our armor on. The American Soldier's Hymn. *Unknown.* PAH

'Tis gone, that bright and orbèd blaze. Evening. John Keble. TrPWD

'Tis goodbye then to last night. Soraidh Slan Don Oidhche Areir. Niall Mor MacMuireadach, *tr. fr. Irish.* BIrV, *tr. by* Maire Cruise O'Brien.

'Tis grown almost a danger to speak true. Epistle to Katharine, Lady Aubigny. Ben Jonson. BeJo

'Tis Hard to Find God. Robert Herrick. LiTB

'Tis hard to find in life. True Friendship. *Unknown, tr. fr. Sanskrit by* Arthur Ryder. *Fr.* Panchatantra, The. AWP

'Tis hard to say, if greater want of skill. Pope. *Fr.* Essay on Criticism. HAP; NAEL-1; OAEL-1; OxAEP-1; PoEL-3; TFi

'Tis hard we should be by the men despised. Mary Lee, Lady Chudleigh. ECWP

'Tis I, — dear Caledonians, blythsome *TONY.* Prologue Spoken by Mr. Anthony Alston, 1726. Allan Ramsay. ScCV

'Tis I must learn to die. *(LL)* Verses Written in a Lady's Sherlock "Upon Death." Earl of Chesterfield. EBEV

'Tis idle! we exhaust and squander. The One Mystery. James Clarence Mangan. PeIV

'Tis, in good truth, a most wonderful thing. Sir William Davenant. NOSC

'Tis in the spirit that attire. Elegance. Christopher Smart. *Fr.* Hymns for the Amusement of Children. NOCV

'Tis late and cold; stir up the fire. The Dead Host's Welcome. John Fletcher. *Fr.* Lover's Progress, The. OxAEP-1; TrGrPo

'Tis Lent, the holy time of fast and prayer. The Easter Light. Clara Ann Thompson. CBWP-2

'Tis like stirring living embers when, at eighty, one remembers. Grandmother's Story of Bunker-Hill Battle. Oliver Wendell Holmes. PAH

'Tis Love That Moveth the Celestial Spheres. George Santayana. AnAmPo

'Tis love that moveth the celestial spheres. George Santayana. *Fr.* Sonnets. AnAmPo

'Tis madness to give physic to the dead. Upon Castara's Absence. William Habington. *Fr.* Castara. BeJo

'Tis Martinmass, from rig to rig. John Clare. EnVR

'Tis May, and yet the skies are overcast. Lines Written on a Very Boisterous Day in May, 1844. John Clare. OxBSP

Tis Merry in Greenwood. Sir Walter Scott. *Fr.* Harold the Dauntless. FaPON; OHIP

'Tis Midnight. *Unknown.* NTCP

'Tis Midnight, and the setting sun. 'Tis Midnight. *Unknown.* NTCP

'Tis mirth that fills the veins with blood. Mirth. Beaumont *and* Fletcher. *Fr.* Knight of the Burning Pestle, The. ElL
(Laugh and Sing.) TrGrPo

Tis morning; and the sun with ruddy orb. William Cowper. *Fr.* Task, The. PoEL-3
(Frosty Morning, A.) NOEC

'Tis mute, the word they went to hear on high Dodona mountain. The Oracles. A. E. Housman. HAP

'Tis Nancy's birth-day raise your strains. On My Wife's Birth-Day. Christopher Smart. NAs

'Tis never or but seldom known. Power and Peace. Robert Herrick. CaPo

'Tis nigh two thousand years. Sir Lewis Morris. *Fr.* Christmas 1898. TrPWD

'Tis no sin for a man to labour in his vocation. The Ballad of Villon and Fat Madge. Villon, *tr. fr. French by* Swinburne. FaBoBl; OBVE

'Tis noonday by the buttonwood, with slender-shadowed bud. The Minute-Men of Northboro'. Wallace Rice. PAH

'Tis not a coat of gray or shepherd's life. To John Donne. Sir Henry Wotton. NoSic
(To John Donne from Mr Henry Wotton.) NOSC

'Tis not by brooding on delight. Marcus Curtius. Oliver St. John Gogarty. OBMV

'Tis not by guilt the onward sweep. Edward Rowland Sill. *Fr.* Fool's Prayer, The. BeLS; FaBoBe; PoLF; TrPWD; WBLP; WGRP

'Tis not enough for one that is a wife. Lady Elizabeth Carey. *Fr.* Mariam. WPE

'Tis not ev'ry day that I. Not Every Day Fit for Verse. Robert Herrick. BeJo; PoRA

'Tis not for the unfeeling, the falsely refined. The Farmer of Tilsbury Vale. Wordsworth. EBEV

'Tis not his Face; I've sence enough to see. Why Do I Love? "Ephelia." *Fr.* To One That Ask'd Me Why I Lov'd J. G. CBCK

'Tis not how witty, nor how free. Upon Kind[e] and True Love. Aurelian Townshend. MeLP; NOSC; PlP

'Tis not I pity the flowers are about to die. Tu Fu, *tr. by* Irving Y. Lo. *Fr.* Strolling along the Riverbank, Looking for Flowers. SuSp

'Tis not on the face displayed. The Bedlamite. Thomas Mozeen. NOEC

'Tis not that both my eyes are black. The Penalties of Baldness. Sir Owen Seaman. FiBHP

'Tis not that dying hurts us so. Emily Dickinson. BoWoP

'Tis not that I am weary grown. Upon [His] Leaving His Mistress. The Earl of Rochester. EnLoPo; GBL; NBLV; NOSC; TEP; TrGrPo

'Tis not the gaudy stream of rosy flame. Self-Consciousness Makes All Changes Happy; Ode. Jonathan Richardson. NOEC

'Tis not the President alone. McKinley. *Unknown.* PAH

'Tis not to be improved. *(LL)* Eros. Emerson. FaBoBe

'Tis not your faire out-side (though famous Greece. To the Queenes Most Excellent Majestie. Elizabeth Cary, Viscountess Falkland. KTR

'Tis now clear day: I see a rose. The Search. Henry Vaughan. ChIV-2; ESCV; GeHe; SeCP

'Tis now since I began to dy. Upon Absence. Katherine Philips. PBWP

(To Mrs. M. A. upon Absence.) CBLP

'Tis Now, Since I Sat[e] Down Before. Sir John Suckling. PoEL-3; SeCV-1

'Tis of a blind beggar who a long time was blind. The Blind Beggar. *Unknown.* AmFP

'Tis of a brisk young Farmer, in — — shire did dwel. The Frolicsome Farmer. *Unknown.* CoMu

'Tis of a gallant Yankee ship that flew the stripes and stars. The Yankee Man-of-War. *Unknown.* FaBoBe; OxBSS; PAH; VPP
(Stately Southerner, The.) AmFP

'Tis of a jolly soldier that lately came from war. The Jolly Soldier. *Unknown.* AmFP

'Tis of a lady both fair and handsome. The Servant Man. *Unknown.* AmFP

'Tis of a little drummer. The Little Drummer. Richard Henry Stoddard. AmFP; PAH

'Tis of a pedlar, a pedlar trim. The Bold Pedlar and Robin Hood. *Unknown.* AmFP

'Tis of a sad and dismal story that happened off the fatal rock. The Loss of the *New Columbia. Unknown.* AmFP

'Tis of a wild Colonial boy, Jack Doolan was his name. The Wild Colonial Boy. *Unknown.* FaBoBa

'Tis of just a cabin home. Whispering Wind. Catherine Braan Layne. PWR

'Tis of my country that I would endite. Ezra Pound. *Fr.* L'Homme Moyen Sensuel. OBSV

'Tis oft I'm tired of an old man. An Old Man He Courted Me. *Unknown.* OBET

'Tis on October thirty-first. Hallowe'en. L. A. J. Moorer. CBWP-3

'Tis one thing to be tempted, Escalus. Shakespeare. *Fr.* Measure for Measure. OxBM

'Tis only a half truth the poet has sung. Crowded Ways of Life. Walter S. Gresham. BLPA

'Tis Pity She's a Whore, *sels.* John Ford.
"There is a place,/ List, daughter! in a black and hollow vault." OBD

'Tis queer, it is, the ways o' men. The Ways o' Men. Angelina Weld Grimké. CDC

'Tis raging noon; and vertical, the sun. James Thomson. *Fr.* Seasons, The. EBEV; OAEL-1

'Tis religion that can give. The Satisfying Portion. *Unknown.* BLRP

'Tis said, as Cupid danced among. How Roses Came Red. Robert Herrick. CaPo; ChTr; SoSe

'Tis said but a name is friendship. Lines to Mrs. Isabel Peace. Mary Weston Fordham. CBWP-2

'Tis said that faith declines; believe it not; Faith, Hope, and Charity Are the Prospects of Manhood. Leigh Hunt. ChIV-2

'Tis Said That Some Have Died for Love. Wordsworth. EnRP

'Tis said the Gods lower down that chain above. George Alsop. SCAP

'Tis said there were no thought of hell. Heaven and Hell. Francis Thompson. OxBSP

'Tis so appalling — it exhilirates. Emily Dickinson. PoE

'Tis so much joy! 'tis so much joy! Emily Dickinson. NOCV

'Tis sometimes difficult to discriminate. (*LL*) The Songless Land. Francis Carey Slater. PeSAV

'Tis Sorrow Builds the Shining Ladder Up. James Russell Lowell. WGRP

'Tis spring; come out to ramble. A. E. Housman. *Fr.* Shropshire Lad, A. FaPoB; OHIP

'Tis spring, warm glows the south. Birds' Nests. John Clare. OAEL-2; OxBSP

'Tis still observ'd, that Fame ne'er sings. Fame. Robert Herrick. FaBoEE

'Tis strange how my head runs on! 'tis a puzzle to understand. The City Clerk. Thomas Ashe. EBVV

'Tis strange how the newspapers honour. Eugene Field. PeLi

'Tis strange indeed to hear us plead. Dr. Booker T. Washington to the National Negro Business League. Joseph S. Cotter, Sr. AAP

'Tis strange, the miser should his cares employ. To Richard Boyle, Earl of Burlington: Of the Uses of Riches. Pope. *Fr.* Moral Essays. NOEC; OAEL-1; OBSV; PoEL-3; PPP

'Tis summer time on Bredon. Hugh Kingsmill. FaBoCo; NOBL
(Summer Time on Bredon.) UV

'Tis Sweet. Wordsworth. *Fr.* Prelude [or, Growth of a Poet's Mind], The. EnRP; MeMBP; OAEL-1

'Tis Sweet to Rest in Lively Hope. *Unknown.* AmFP

'Tis sweet to see the evening star appear. 'Tis Sweet. Wordsworth. *Fr.* Prelude [or, Growth of a Poet's Mind], The. EnRP; MeMBP; OAEL-2

'Tis sweeter to forgive. (*LL*) Revenge. Mary E. Tucker. AmWP; CBWP-1

'Tis ten to one he'll ne'er come back. (*LL*) Epitaph on G — —. Pope. OBD

'Tis the Arabian bird alone. The Chaste Arabian Bird. The Earl of Rochester. ErPo

'Tis the Chameleon you see. (*LL*) How To Tell the Wild Animals. Carolyn Wells. FaPON; FiBHP; NBLV; ZA

T'is the Cur dog of Britain and spaniel of Spain. (*LL*) The Character of Sir Robert Walpole. Swift. FaBoEE; PoE

'Tis the Gift To Be Simple. *Unknown.* AH

'Tis the great art of life to manage well. Madness. John Armstrong. *Fr.* Art of Preserving Health, The. NOEC

'Tis the hour of fairy ban and spell. Fairy Dawn. Joseph Rodman Drake. *Fr.* Culprit Fay, The. GN

'Tis the hour when white-horsed Day. Morning. Charles Stuart Calverley. FiBHP

'Tis the human touch in this world that counts. The Human Touch. Spencer Michael Free. BLPA; FaBoBe; PoToHe

'Tis the Last Rose of Summer. Thomas Moore. BLPA; BoNaP; ELP; NOIV; PoEL-4; WBLP

'Tis the middle of night by the castle clock. Samuel Taylor Coleridge. *Fr.* Christabel. CH, ll. 1-65; EnRP; FaBoVe; FHYEP; MeMBP; NAEL-2; OAEL-2

'Tis the middle watch of a summer's night. The Culprit Fay. Joseph Rodman Drake. AnAmPo

'Tis the Octoroon ball! And the halls are alight! Ballade des Belles Milatraisses. Rosalie Jonas. BlSi

'Tis the season when Nature awakes from her sleep. Easter; or, Spring-Time. L. A. J. Moorer. CBWP-3

'Tis the Voice of the Lobster. "Lewis Carroll." *See* 'Tis the voice of the Lobster: I heard him declare.

'Tis the voice of the Lobster: I heard him declare. Alice's Recitation. "Lewis Carroll." *Fr.* Alice's Adventures in Wonderland. FaBoCo; FaBoNo; NOBL; UV
(Lobster, The,) *sl. diff. vers..* OxBChV
('Tis the Voice of the Lobster.) CBNP; PeLV

'Tis the voice of the [*or* a] sluggard; I heard him complain. The Sluggard. Isaac Watts. CH; EBEvV; ECEV; HAP; Mes; MoShBr; NOEC; OxBChV; OxBoLi; PoEL-3; UV, *sh. vers.*; VPP

'Tis the week before Christmas and every night. For the Children or the Grown-ups? *Unknown.* OBCP

'Tis the white anemone, fashioned so. "Owen Meredith." *Fr.* White Anemone, The. GN

'Tis the witching hour of night. Keats. TEP

'Tis the year's [*or* yeares] midnight, and it is the day's [*or* dayes]. A Nocturnal[l] upon Saint Lucy's [*or* S. Lucies] Day, Being the Shortest Day. John Donne. EBEV; EnRePo; ESCV; FHYEP; GBL; JCP; LiTB; MeLP; NAEL-1; NOBE; NoP; NOSC; OAEL-1; OxAEP-1; PoE; PoEL-2; PPP; SCGP; SeCP; SeCV-1; TEP; TFi

'Tis then broad day throughout the east. (*LL*) Upon Electra. Robert Herrick. BeJo

'Tis these that free the small entangled fly. Shakespeare: The Fairies' Advocate. Thomas Hood. *Fr.* Plea of the Midsummer Fairies, The. OBNC

'Tis thus with people in an open boat. Byron. *Fr.* Don Juan. FaBoPV

'Tis Timarion. Meleager. *tr. fr. Greek by* Peter Whigham. GrAn

'Tis time, I think; by Wenlock town. Wenlock Edge (" 'Tis time, I think; by Wenlock town.") A. E. Housman. *Fr.* Shropshire Lad, A. FaBoPP; FaPoB

'Tis time this heart should be unmoved. On This Day I Complete My Thirty-sixth Year. Byron. EnRP; FHYEP; MeMBP; NAs; NoP; OAEL-2; OBWP; PoE

'Tis time to conclude, for I make it a rule. Conclusion of a Letter to the Rev. Mr. C — —. Mary Barber. ECWP

'Tis to pen anthems for an angels' choir. (*LL*) A Gratulatory to Mr. Ben Johnson for His Adopting of Him to Be His Son. Thomas Randolph. BeJo; JCP

'Tis to yourself I speak; you cannot know. Yourself. Jones Very. NOBA; OxBA; PoEL-4; Son

'Tis true, dear[e] Ben, thy just chastising [*or* chastizing] hand. To Ben Jonson. Thomas Carew. BeJo; CaPo; EPCY; NAEL-1; NOSC

'Tis true no human eye can penetrate. Eugenio. Hugh Henry Brackenridge *and* Philip Freneau. *Fr.* Rising Glory of America, The. AiP

'Tis true our life is but a long dis-ease. Katherine Philips. OxBSP

'Tis true — then why should I repine. In Sickness Written Soon after the Author's Coming to Live in Ireland, upon the Queen's Death, October 1714. Swift. NOEC

'Tis true, 'tis day; what though it be? Break[e] of Day. John Donne. EnRePo; ErPo; LiTB; NAEL-1; SoSe

'Tis true what famed Pythagoras maintained. Christopher Pitt. *Fr.* To Mr. Pope, on His Translation of Homer's Iliad. EPCY

'Tis very sure God walks in mine. (*LL*) My Garden. Thomas Edward Brown. BLPL; EBEvV; FaBV; InPK; OBEV; PoLF; UV; WBLP; WGRP

To Aberdeen. William Dunbar. FaBoPP

To Adam, His Scribe. Chaucer. OAEL-1

To Adelhard, Archbishop of Canterbury ("Brief is our life."). Alcuin, tr. fr. Latin by Helen Waddell. MLL

To Adelhard, Archbishop of Canterbury ("Prince-Archbishop."). Alcuin, tr. fr. Latin by Helen Waddell. MLL

To Adhiambo. Gabriel Okara. PBA

To admit the beauty of a snake. Mediterranean Snake Admitter. Lynn Lonidier. SRLS

To after times thy wit. (LL) To the Virginian Voyage. Michael Drayton. AiP, sl. abr.; EnRePo; FaBoEH, sl. abr.; HAP; NAEL-1; NOBE; NOSC; OBEV; PAH; PoEL-2; SCGP, sl. abr.; TEP

To Age. Walter Savage Landor. EnRP

To Ailsa Rock. Keats. EnRP; OBNC

To Alexander Meiklejohn, sels. John Beecher. "I read your testimony and I thought." GOA

To Alexander Neville. Barnabe Googe. EnRePo; NoP

To Alexis in Answer to his Poem against Fruition. Aphra Behn. KTR

To Alexis in Answer to His Poem against Fruition: Ode. Aphra Behn. See Ah hapless sex! who bear no charms.

To Algebra God is inclined. J. C. B. Date. PeLi

To All Angels and Saints. George Herbert. SeCV-1

To All Brothers. Sonia Sanchez. BPo

To all my length. (LL) To Earthward. Robert Frost. BLPL; ImPo; LiTA; MeMAP; MoAB; MoAmPo; MoP; NoAM; NOBA; NoP; OxBA; RaBo; TAP; TRP

To All Sisters. Sonia Sanchez. PoBA

To all that is brief and fragile. A Furtive Glass. Maria Eugenia Baz Ferreira. EaPr

To all that live. (LL) Grandfather Great Spirit. Unknown. EaPr

To all the fat dogs in Kamschatka. (LL) There was an old man of Kamschatka. Edward Lear. NOBL

To all the humble beasts there be. Prayer for Gentleness to All Creatures. John Galsworthy. BoTP

To all the lists of Clay! (LL) Of all the souls that stand create. Emily Dickinson. AmPP; NAAL-1; TrGrPo

To All the Princes of Europe. Sir John Davies. Fr. Hymns of Astræa [in Acrostic Verse]. SiPSBD

To all things light gives force; God dwells Himself in light. The Light Exists In The Fire. "Angelus Silesius," tr. fr. German. Fr. Cherubical Wanderer, The. GePo, tr. by George C. Schoolfield

To all who carve their love on a picnic table. Open Letter from a Constant Reader. Mona Van Duyn. PoA

To all you ladies now at Bath. Farewell to Bath. Lady Mary Wortley Montagu. WPE

To all you ladies now at land. Charles Sackville. See To all you ladies now at land.

To all you ladies now at land. Song Written at Sea in the First Dutch War (1665), the Night before an Engagement. Charles Sackville. CoMu; EnLoPo; NOBE; OBWP; OxAEP-1
("To all you ladies now at land.") SeCV-2
(Written at Sea, in the First Dutch War.) NOSC

To all young men that love to wooe. To Chuse a Friend, but Never Marry. At. to The Earl of Rochester John Wilmot, 2d Earl of Rochester. CoMu

To Allegra Florence in Heaven, sels. Thomas Holley Chivers. "As an egg, when broken, never." BXAP

To allow himself to be properly held. The Man Who Closed Shop. Stephen P. Dunn. NIP

To Almystrea, on her Divine Works. Elizabeth Thomas. ECWP

To Althea, from Prison. Richard Lovelace. AWP; BeJo; BLPA; CaPo; EBEvV; FaBoBe; GBL; GGP; GTBS; GTBS-P; HAP; ImPo; InPS; JCP; LiTB; MeLP; NAEL-1; NOBE; NoP; NOSC; OBEV; PoE; PoRA; SCGP; SeCP; SeCV-1; TEP; TFi; TrGrPo

To Amanda Walking in the Garden. N. Hookes. NOSC

To Amarantha, That She Would Dishevel Her Hair. Richard Lovelace. BeJo; HoPM; NoP; OBEV; SeCP; SeCV-1; TrGrPo

To America. Alfred Austin. GN

To America, on Her First Sons Fallen in the Great War. E. M. Walker. PAH

To Amine. James Clarence Mangan. OBEV

To Amoret. Henry Vaughan. SeCP; EnLoPo

To Amoret. Edmund Waller. SeCV-1

To Amoret Gone from Him. Henry Vaughan. BeJo; EnLoPo; MeLP; SeCP

To Amoret, of the Difference 'twixt Him and Other Lovers, and What True Love Is. Henry Vaughan. BeJo

To Amoret, Walking in a Starry Evening. Henry Vaughan. BeJo

To amuse His Royal Majesty he will change water into wine. Zito the Magician. Miroslav Holub, tr. fr. Czech by Ian Milner and George Theiner. AnRep; PoSu

To Amuse Myself. Li Po, tr. fr. Chinese by Joseph J. Lee. SuSp

To Amy. J. Gordon. OBAL

To an admiring bog. (LL) I'm Nobody! Who are you? Emily Dickinson. AmPP; AnAmPo; BoWoP; CBNP; HeIP; MeMAP; NALW; NBLV; NOBA; NTP; OBCA; OTCP; OxBSP; PDV; PFP; SAmP; TAP; WPE

To An Aeolian Harp. Eduard Friedrich Mörike, tr. fr. German by Philip L. Miller. RiWo

To an American Poet Just Dead. Richard Wilbur. HCAP; NBLV; NoP

To an Angry God. X. J. Kennedy. CRP

To an Army Wife in Sardis. Sappho, tr. fr. Greek by Daniela Gioseffi. WoWa

To an Artful Theatre Manager. Lorenzo da Ponte, tr. fr. Italian by John Mazzinghi. Fr. Capriccio Dramatico, Il. TrJP

To an Artist, to Take Heart. Louise Bogan. GrPl; NYBP; TRP

To an Astronomer. Anne Lynch Botta. AmWP

To an Athlete Dying Young. A. E. Housman. Fr. Shropshire Lad, A. BLPL; CMoP; DL; FaPoB; HAP; HeIP; ImPo; InPK; LiTB; LiTM; MeMBP; MoAB; MoBrPo; MoP; NAEL-2; NIP; NoAM; NoP; PoE; PoEL-5; Poetr; PoRA; PrIm; SCGP; SoSe; TEP; TFi; TrGrPo; TRP; UnPo; WeW

To an Author. Philip Freneau. AmPP; EAP; NOBA; OxBA

To an Avenue Sport. Helen Johnson Collins. PoNe

To an Early Primrose. Henry Kirke White. OBNC

To an Elder Poet. William Carlos Williams. PoA

To an Elderly Virgin. Mael Isu O Brolchain, tr. fr. Old Irish by Thomas Kinsella. NOIV

To an Enemy. Maxwell Bodenheim. TrJP

To an eternal fire. (LL) The Second Generation. Menachem Z. Rosensaft. BTR

To an Expatriate Friend. Mervyn Morris. PBCV

To an Icicle. Blanche Taylor Dickinson. CDC; ShDr

To an Imaginary Father. Wendy Rose. CDW

To an impervious nothingness they're thinned. Paul Valéry, tr. fr. French by C. Day Lewis. Fr. Graveyard by the Sea, The. OBD

To an Inconstant One. Sir Robert Ayton. See I loved thee once, I'll love no more.

To an Indian Poet. Patty L. Harjo. VoR

To an Indian Skull, sels. Alexander McLachlan.

To an Infant. Mary Weston Fordham. CBWP-2

To an Infant Daughter. John Clare. NAs

To an Infant Expiring the Second Day of Its Birth. Mehetabel Wright. ECWP; NOEC

To an Insect. Oliver Wendell Holmes. AnAmPo

To an Island Princess. Robert Louis Stevenson. OBTV

To an Isle in the Water. W. B. Yeats. AWP; TTTS

To an Oak Tree. Sir Walter Scott. Fr. Waverley. OBNC

To an Old Gentlewoman That Painted Her Face. George Turberville. EnRePo; OxBSP

To an Old Lady. William Empson. FaBoTw; GTBS-P; MoAB; NoAM; NOBE; OxAEP-2

To an Old Philosopher in Rome. Wallace Stevens. EnlH; MeMAP; MoP; NoAM; NOBA; Poetr

To an Old San Francisco Poet. Keith Abbott. UL

To an Old Tune. Hsin Ch'i-chi, tr. fr. Chinese by Kenneth Rexroth. OHMPC

To an Old Tune. Lu Kuei Meng, tr. fr. Chinese by Kenneth Rexroth. OHMPC

To an open house in the evening. Home at Last. G. K. Chesteron. WGRP

To an Unborn Infant. Isabella Kelly. ECWP

To an Unborn Pauper Child. Thomas Hardy. FaBoRV; GTBS-P; LiTB; MeMBP; NAs

To and fro in the city I go. A City Flower. Austin Dobson. TEP

To Angélique, sels. Heine, tr. fr. German by Emma Lazarus. "This mad carnival of loving." TrJP

To Ann Lear. Edward Lear. CBNP

To Annie. Mary E. Tucker. CBWP-1

To another as I did to you! (LL) First Love. Charles Stuart Calverley. FiBHP

To Another Housewife. Judith Wright. FaBoMA; NALW

To Anthea. Robert Herrick. CaPo; PoEL-3

To Anthea Lying in Bed. Robert Herrick. BeJo; SeCP

To Anthea, Who May Command Him Anything. Robert Herrick. CaPo; GTBS; GTBS-P; JCP; NOBE; NOSC; OAEL-1; OBEV; SeCP; SeCV-1; TrGrPo

To Any Dead Officer. Siegfried Sassoon. NSI

To any dream deserving the sensible world. (LL) Always Begin Where You Are. Thomas Hornsby Ferril. PrIm; VGW

To Any Member of My Generation. George Barker. LiTM; MeMBP; Son

To any port may trade. (LL) Ye Parliament of England. Unknown. AmFP; PAH

To any watch they keep? (LL) Neither Out Far nor In Deep. Robert Frost. AmPP; ChTr; HAP; LiTA; MeMAP; MoAB; MoP; NAAL-2; NoAM; NOBA; NoP; Poetr; TAP; TRP; WeW

To Aphrodite these wreaths. Kallirrhoê: A Dedication. Agathias, tr. fr. Greek by Dudley Fitts. GrAn

To Ararat; all men are Noah's sons. (LL) Still, Citizen Sparrow. Richard Wilbur. AmPP; CMoP; HoPM; LiTM; MoAB; MoP; NoAM; TRP

To Archaeanassa, on whose furrow'd brow. On Archaeanassa. Plato, tr. fr. Greek by Thomas Stanley. AWP

To Archinus. Callimachus, tr. fr. Greek by F. A. Wright. AWP

To Ariake Kambara. Norman Rosten. NYBP

To Aristius Fuscus. Horace. See Virtue, dear friends, needs no 'defense.'

To Arms. Park Benjamin. PAH

To arms, to arms! my jolly grenadiers. The Song of Braddock's Men. Stephen Tilden. PAH

To Arno of Salzburg. Alcuin, tr. fr. Latin by Helen Waddell. MLL

To arrive in front of large video screen. Manifest Destiny. Anselm Hollo. UL

To Arthur's court, when men began. A Scot, a Welsh and an Irish Man. Unknown. GBP

To Ashtaroth and Bel. Saul Tchernichowsky, tr. fr. Hebrew by L. V. Snowman. TrJP

To Ask for All Thy Love. Unknown. ElL

To ask that allotment of darkness always. The Indian River. Sebastian Barry. IB

To ask the hard question is simple. The Question. W. H. Auden. OxAEP-2

To assassinate the Chase Manhattan Bank. The Plot to Assassinate the Chase Manhattan Bank. Carl Larsen. FF

To Astarte. Unknown, tr. fr. Greek by Guy Davenport. GrAn

To Astræa. Sir John Davies. Fr. Hymns of Astræa [in Acrostic Verse]. SiPSBD

To Auden on His Fiftieth. Richard Eberhart. NAs

To Aunt Rose. Allen Ginsberg. LiTM; NAAL-2; NoAM; NoP; PoE; VGW

To Aurora. William Alexander, Earl of Stirling. See Oh, If Thou Knew'st How Thou Thyself Dost Harm.

To Ausonius. Paulinus of Nola, tr. fr. Latin by Helen Waddell. PeHV

To Autumn. Blake. BoNaP; NAEL-2; WiR

To Autumn. Keats. ArNa; AWP; BoNaP; BoTP; CH; ClHu; CoGr; EBEV; EBEvV; EnRP; FaBoRV; FaPoB; FF; FHYEP; GTBS; HAP; HeIP; ImPo; InPK; InPS; InvP; LiTB; MeMBP; Mes; NAEL-2; NAWM-2; NIP; NOBE; NoP; NTP; NU; OAEL-2; OBEV; OBNC; OxAEP-2; PIP; PoE; PoEL-4; Poetr; PoLF; PPP; Prf; PrIm; RaBo; RB; SCGP; SCV; SoSe; TEP; TFi; TRP; UnPo; WeW

To 'ave a garden in fettle. Michael Hyde. BXAP

To Avisa. Henry Willoby. Fr. Willobie His Avisa. CBLP; ElL

To avoid matrimonial disasters. Martin Fagg. PeLi

To B. C. Sir John Suckling. CaPo

To Babylon. Mother Goose. See 'How Many Miles to Babylon?'

To banish the less, I find my chief relief. (LL) So cruel [or cruell or crewell] prison have could betide [or howe coulde betyde], alas. The Earl of Surrey. AAS; NoSic; SiPS

To Barba. Edward May. FaBoEE

To Bary Jade. Charles Follen Adams. OBAL

To battered footpaths crossing o'er the fields. (LL) The Beanfield. John Clare. BoTP

To be a birth there must be a begetting. Begetting. Dorothea Spears. PeSA

To be a giant and keep quiet about it. Trees. Howard Nemerov. BoNaP; Poetsp

To be a Jew in the twentieth century. Muriel Rukeyser. Fr. Letter to the Front. NALW; TrJP

To be a mistress. Kiyoko Tsuda, tr. fr. Japanese by Edith Marcombe Shiffert and Yuki Sawa. BoWoP

To Be A Nurse. A. H. Lawrence. PoToHe

To be a nurse is. To Be A Nurse. A. H. Lawrence. PoToHe

To Be a Pilgrim. Robert Conquest. OxBC

To be a Pilgrim. sl. diff. vers. Bunyan. See Who would true valour see.

To be a poet and not know the trade. Sanctity. Patrick Kavanagh. BIrV; NOIV

To be a poet is to be vanquished. Ars Poetica. Victor van Vriesland, tr. fr. Dutch by Adriaan J. Barnouw. TrJP

To Be a Slave of Intensity. Kabir, tr. fr. Hindi by Robert Bly. RaBo

To be a stranger in a strange land. Thinking of My Brother in Shantung on the Ninth Day of the Ninth Moon. Wang Wei, tr. fr. Chinese by Robert Payne. TAL

To be a whore, despite of grace. Madrigal. Charles Cotton. FaBoEE

To be a writer and write things. John Ashbery. CAPP

To be able/ and not to do it. To an Elder Poet. William Carlos Williams. PoA

To be able to see every side of every question. Editor Whedon. Edgar Lee Masters. Fr. Spoon River Anthology. CMoP; FaBoEE; NOBA; OBSV; OxBA; PoE

To be alive in such an age! Today. Angela Morgan. BLPA

To be an orphan. The Orphan. Unknown, tr. fr. Chinese by Arthur Waley. PoA

To be Aphrodite today. Above Drudgery. Carlos Cumpian. AfAz

To be at once together alone. (LL) The Aged Lover Discourses in the Flat Style. J. V. Cunningham. NoAM; SM

2 B BLK. Val Ferdinand. NBV

To be black Is/ To be/ Very-hot. (LL) But He Was Cool; or, He Even Stopped for Green Lights. Don L. Lee. BPo; MoP; PoBA

To Be Black, to Be Lost. Hannah Kahn. GoYe

To be Carved on a Stone at Thoor Ballylee. W. B. Yeats. FaBoEE; IIP; NoAM; NoP

To be chosen. Jeanne d'Arc. Susan Ludvigson. MT

To Be Closely Written on a Small Piece of Paper Which Folded into a Tight Lozenge Will Fit Any Girl's Locket. William Carlos Williams. ArNa

To Be Continued. Julian Street and James Montgomery Flagg. FiBHP

To be dead, and never again behold my city! (LL) My City. James Weldon Johnson. CDC; PoNe

To Be Engraven on a Dial. Samuel Sewall. SCAP

To-Be-Forgotten, The. Thomas Hardy. MeMBP

To be full. Conversations among Poems. Tim Longville. VaA

To be grumpy, grouchy, petulant, paranoid, and mean: to hit out. If I Ever Grow Old: Grim and Gleeful Resolutions. Elinor Nauen. UL

To be homeless is a pride. A Jealous Man. Robert Graves. CMoP

To Be Honest, to Be Kind. Robert Louis Stevenson. Fr. Christmas Sermon, A. PoLF

To be in a place for spring and not have lived its winter. Vincent O'Sullivan. Fr. Brother Jonathan, Brother Kafka. PeNZ

To Be in Love. Gwendolyn Brooks. IHMS

To Be in love is like going outside. The Business. Robert Creeley. CAPP

To be like God, up in the sky! (LL) A Child's Thought. Bertha Moore. VPP

To be like the water. "Transients Welcome." Gregory Orr. AnAn

To be long silent was my thought. Unknown, tr. fr. German by Frederick Goldin. GePo

To be male, always. Eros. Louise Glück. Fr. Dedication to Hunger. AnAn

To be moved comes of want, though want be complete. 1892-1941. Louis Zukofsky. PoA

To be my own Messiah to the. The Rows of Cold Trees. Yvor Winters. NOBA

To be of the Earth is to know. John Soos. EaPr

To Be of Use. Marge Piercy. CAPP; CrSp

To Be or Not to Be, parody. William H. Edmunds. FaBoPa

To Be or Not to Be. Unknown. FaBoCo; MoShBr

To Be or Not to Be ("I sometimes think I'd rather crow.") Unknown. FaBoCo; MoShBr

To be or not to be, that is the question. Arthur's Anthology of English Poetry. Laurence David Lerner. PeLV

To be, or not to be, that is the question. Shakespeare. Fr. Hamlet. EBEvV; FF; HoPM; ImPo; LiTB; NAWM-1; OBD; OxAEP-1; PlP; TrGrPo; UV

(Hamlet's Soliloquy.) WBLP

To be, or not to be, that is the question./ Whether to suffer with mental anguish. Plantation Bitters. Unknown. FaBoUs

To be put on the train and kissed and given my ticket. Observation Car. A. D. Hope. MoP; NoAM

To Be Quicker. Don L. Lee. JB

To Be Read above the Castle-Gate, When His Princely Highness Rode in to His Marriage Bed. Simon Dach, tr. fr. German by George C. Schoolfield. GePo

To Be Recited to Flossie on Her Birthday. William Carlos Williams. VGW

To Be Said at the Seder. Karl Wolfskehl, tr. fr. German by Carol North Valhope and Ernst Morowitz. TrJP

To Be Sung. Peter Viereck. FaBV

To Be Sung on the Water. Louise Bogan. PrIm; VGW

To be ten and skinny. Exodus. Anita Endrezze-Danielson. CDW

To be the Victim for Mankind. (LL) Song to a Fair Young Lady, Going Out of the Town in the Spring. Dryden. OBEV

To be their haunting and their earthly home. (LL) The Disinherited. Charles Spear. PeNZ

To be undone! (*LL*) With Serving Still. Sir Thomas Wyatt. ElL; InPK; NoSic; SiPS

To be unraveling. (*LL*) The Rhetoric of Langston Hughes. Margaret Danner. BlSi

To be untangled from these mother's bones. (*LL*) With Child. Genevieve Taggard. AIW; MoAmPo

To be up high. (*LL*) Get Up, Blues. James A. Emanuel. PoBA

To be without a comforting light to shine through the shadows of my life. (*LL*) Love and Hate. Fernando Periquet Y Zuaznabar. RiWo

To beat real iron out, to work the bellows. (*LL*) The Forge. Seamus Heaney. NAEL-2; OxAEP-2

To bed. (*LL*) Changed. Charles Stuart Calverley. FiBHP; NOBVV

"To bed! To bed!"/ Says Sleepy-head. Come, Let's to Bed. *Unknown*. ReMoGo

To Begin. Fran Winant. BrRo

To Begin the Day. *Unknown*. BLRP

To begin with she wouldn't have fallen in. Our Silly Little Sister. Dorothy Aldis. FaPON

To Belinda. Goethe, *tr. fr. German by* John Frederick Nims. STV

To Bellinus. *Unknown, tr. fr. Latin*. PeHV

To Belshazzar. Byron. ChIV-1

To Ben, at the Lake. Cilla McQueen. PeNZ

To Ben Jonson. Thomas Carew. BeJo; CaPo; EPCY; NAEL-1; NOSC

To Bethlem did they go, the shepherds three. Masters, in This Hall. William Morris. ChTr

To better the condition of humanity. Our Club Work. Mrs. Henry Linden. CBWP-4

To blend once more in gentle wantonness? (*LL*) Reflection. Elisabeth Eybers. PeSAV

To blink behind bars at the zoo. (*LL*) Famous Poet. Ted Hughes. LiTM

To Blossoms. Robert Herrick. BeJo; BoNaP; CaPo; GTBS; GTBS-P; JCP; NAEL-1; NOSC; OBEV; SCGP; SeCP; SeCV-1

To Bobby Seale. Lucille Clifton. PoBA

To Borglum's Seated Statue of Abraham Lincoln. Charlotte Brewster Jordan. OHIP

To brave and to know the unknown. The Unknown. John Davidson. MeMBP; MoBrPo

To break earth's sleep at all? (*LL*) Futility. Wilfred Owen. CMoP; FaBoMo; GTBS-P; MeMBP; MoAB; MoBrPo; NAEL-2; NoAM; NoP; NSI; OBWP; PAW; PeFWW; RB; TrGrPo

To break off in the middle. (*LL*) Sally Simpkin's Lament, [or John Jones's Kit-Cat-astrophe]. Thomas Hood. CBNP; EnRP

To Breisach, Taken by That Supremely Celebrated Hero, Bernhard, Duke of Saxony. Georg Rudolph Weckherlin, *tr. fr. German by* George C. Schoolfield. GePo

To bring forth and rear a son is my duty. A Mother's List of Duties. Ponmutiyar, *tr. fr. Tamil by* A. K. Ramanujan. PLW

To bring my overcoat to me. (*LL*) The Angel's Visit. Eugene Field. PWR

To Bring the Dead to Life. Robert Graves. MoBrPo

To bring them to my brother King Iamye. (*LL*) Sir Andrew Bart[t]on. *Unknown*. AmFP, 2 *vers.*; EnSB; ESPB; OxBB

To Brooklyn Bridge. Hart Crane. *Fr.* Bridge, The. AiP; AmPP; BLPL; ChIV-1; ClHu; CMoP; HAP; HeIP; ImPo; InPS; LiTA; LiTM; MeMAP; MoAB; MoAmPo; NAEL-2; NoAM; NOBA; NoP; OxBA; PoE; PrIm; TAP; TFi; TRP; WeW

To Build a Poem. Christine E. Hemp. GOYP

To Bülow. August, Graf von Platen, *tr. fr. German by* Reginald Bancroft Cooke. PeHV

To burst into fulfillment's desolate attic. (*LL*) Deceptions. Philip Larkin. CMoP; ErPo; GTBS-P; OxAEP-2

To buy the bairn a bell. (*LL*) Dingle dingle doosey. *Unknown*. OxNR

To C. F. H. on Her Christening-Day. Thomas Hardy. NAs

To C —— her lover. Love-Letter One ("To C —— her lover.") *Unknown*. PeHV

To Caelia. Richard Duke. NOSC

To Caelia. *Unknown*. FaBoEE

To Calliope. Robert Graves. CMoP

To Carrey Clavel. Thomas Hardy. CBLP

To Carry All of Us. Maggie Anderson. ETG

To Carry the Child. Stevie Smith. MoP; NoAM; NYBP

To carry you home. (*LL*) Ancestral Messengers/Composition 11. Ntozake Shange. SRLS

To Castara, Being to Take a Journey. William Habington. NOSC

To Castara ("Do[e] not Their profane orgies hear[e].") William Habington. *Fr.* Castara. BeJo

To Castara ("Give me a heart where no impure.") William Habington. *Fr.* Castara. BeJo

To Castara, upon an Embrace. William Habington. *Fr.* Castara. BeJo

To Castara, upon Beautie. William Habington. *Fr.* Castara. BeJo; SeCP

To catch the spirit in its wayward flight. Self-Mastery. H. Cordelia Ray. AmWP; CBWP-3

To Cattraeth's vale in glitt'ring row. Aneirin, *tr. by* Thomas Gray. *Fr.* Gododdin, The. OBVE

To Catulinus That He Cannot Write Him an Epithalamium Because of the Enemy Hosts. Sidonius Apollinaris, *tr. fr. Latin by* Helen Waddell. MLL

To cause accord or to agree [*or* aggre]. Sir Thomas Wyatt. AAS; SCGP; SiPS; SiPSBD

To celebrate the need of comrades. (*LL*) In Paths Untrodden. Walt Whitman. NOBA; OxBA

To Celia. Ben Jonson. *See* Come, my Celia, let us prove.

To Celia. Sir Charles Sedley. *See* Not, Celia, that I juster am.

To Celia ("Drink to me only with thine eyes.") Ben Jonson. BoLoP; CBLP; EBEvV; EnLoPo; FaBoBe; FaBV; GGP; GTBS; GTBS-P; ImPo; InPK; LiTB; NOBE; OBEV; OBVE; PlP; PoLF; SCGP; TEP; TrGrPo

To Celia Pleading Want of Merit. Thomas Stanley. *See* Dear urge no more that killing cause.

To Censorious Courtling. Ben Jonson. NOSC

To Certain Critics. Countee Cullen. BPo

To change the name, and not the letter. Surnames to Be Avoided in Marriage. *Unknown*. FaBoUs

To Charles Burney. Frances Burney. ECWP

To Charles Cowden Clarke. Keats. EnRP

To Charlotte von Stein. Goethe, *tr. fr. German by* John Frederick Nims. STV

To charm our souls, as thou enchant'st our ears. (*LL*) To Music: A Song. Robert Herrick. CaPo

To Chatterton. Keats. EPCY

To Cheer Our Minds. William Ronksley. OxBChV

To Cherry-Blossomes. Robert Herrick. SeCV-1

To "Chick." Frank Horne. *Fr.* Letters [*or* Notes] Found near a Suicide. BPo; CDC; PoBA; PoNe

To Children. Lawrence McGaugh. PoBA

To Chloe. William Cartwright. *See* Chloe, why wish you that your years.

To Chloë ("Vitas hinnuleo.") Horace, *tr. fr. Latin by* Austin Dobson. *Fr.* Odes. AWP; OBVE

To Chloe Who for His Sake Wished Herself Younger, *sels.* William Cartwright.
    "There are two births; the one when light." GGP

To Chloe, who for His Sake Wished Herself Younger. William Cartwright. *See* Chloe, why wish you that your years.

To Chloe, Who Wished Herself Young Enough for Me. William Cartwright. BeJo; JCP; LiTB; NOSC; OxAEP-1

To Chloris. William Drummond of Hawthornden. OxBSP

To Chloris. Sir Charles Sedley. *See* Child and Maiden.

To Chloris, upon a Favour Received. Edmund Waller. OxBSP

To Christ. William Alabaster. NoSic

To Christ Our Lord. Galway Kinnell. HeIP; PrIm; RFM; SM; TwCP

To Christian Montpelier, *sels.* George Jonas.

To Christopher North. Tennyson. FaBoEE; FiBHP; PeLV

To church! I heard a sermon once in spring. God. Harold Monro. *Fr.* Dawn. WGRP

To Chuse a Friend, but Never Marry. *At. to* The Earl of Rochester John Wilmot, 2d Earl of Rochester. CoMu

To civilize with graver notes our wits again. (*LL*) An Ode to Mr. Anthony Stafford to Hasten Him into the Country. Thomas Randolph. BeJo; NOSC

To civilize with graver notes our wits again. (*LL*) An Ode to Mr. [*or* Master] Anthony Stafford to Hasten Him into the Country. Thomas Randolph. NOBE; OBEV

To clack their beaks. (*LL*) The Bombax Tree. Fily-Dabo Sissoko. NegPo

To claim, at a dead party, to have spotted a grackle. Lying. Richard Wilbur. DiPo; HCAP; PeVV; Poetr; SV

To Clarissa. Robert, Earl Nugent. NOEC

To Clarissa Scott Delany. Angelina Weld Grimké. ShDr

To cleave a running stream with a sword. Written in Behalf of My Wife. Li Po, *tr. fr. Chinese by* Joseph J. Lee. SuSp

To cleave the soul back to the spine. (*LL*) The Swordfish Tooth. Cynthia Zarin. UTF

To Clement Edmonds, on His *Caesar's Commentaries* Observed, and Translated. Ben Jonson. NOSC

To Clements' Ferry. Josephine D. Henderson Heard. CBWP-4

To Cleon's Eyes. Martha Sansom. ECWP

To climb a hill that hungers for the sky. Fulfillment. Helene Johnson. CDC; PoNe; ShDr

To climbe to thee. (LL) The Pearl. George Herbert. EBEV; FHYEP; GeHe; HAP; JCP; NOCV; OAEL-1; PoEL-2; SeCP

To Clio, from Rome. John Dyer. NOEC

To Cloe. George Granville. FaBoEE; NBLV

To Cloe. Hildebrand Jacob. NOEC

To Cloe. Martial, tr. fr. Latin by Thomas Moore. AWP; NBLV

To Cloris. Sir Charles Sedley. BoLoP

To Close. William Carlos Williams. SAmP

To clothe the fiery thought. Poet. Emerson. Fr. Quatrains. OxBA; OxBSP; Spl

To Coelia. Charles Cotton. OBEV

To Cole, the Painter, Departing for Europe. Bryant. AiP; AmPP; EAP; TAP

To Colebrooke Dale. Anna Seward. ECWP

To Coleridge in Sicily. Wordsworth. Fr. Prelude [or, Growth of a Poet's Mind], The. EnRP; OAEL-2; OBNC

To Colman Returning. Unknown, tr. by Helen Waddell. BIrV

To Columbus. Rubén Darío, tr. fr. Spanish by Lysander Kemp. TTY

To come back from the sweet South, to the North. Italia, Io Ti Saluto. Christina Rossetti. CoGr; OBTV; WPE

To come to the river. The Resolve. Denise Levertov. RFM

To come vor evermwore. (LL) The Wife a-Lost. William Barnes. BoLoP; EBVV; ELP; EnLoPo; EnVR; HAP; OBEV; OxBM; SCGP

To Conquer Variety. Hart Crane. AnAn

To consecrate the flicker, not the flame. (LL) George Crabbe. E. A. Robinson. BLPL; CMoP; LiTA; LiTM; MeMAP; MoAB; MoAmPo; NAAL-2; NOBA; NoP; OxBA; PoEL-5; TAP

To Constantia Singing. Shelley. EnRP

To contemplate darkness again. (LL) Accomplices. Bei Dao. SpMi

To Cordelia. Joseph Stansbury. NOBC

To Cowper. Anne Brontë. EPCY

To Critics. Robert Herrick. CaPo

To crown her head, and bosom fill. (LL) The Gallery. Andrew Marvell. ESCV; MeLP; NoP; PoE

To Crown It. Robert Herrick. CaPo

To Cupid. Michael Drayton. EIL

To cure a wart. (LL) Washrags. Vern Rutsala. ETG

To cure the mind's wrong bias, Spleen. Matthew Green. Fr. Spleen, The. ECEV

To cure the spital world of maladies. (LL) To Julia to Expedite Her Promise. John Cleveland. CBLP

To Cynthia. Sir Francis Kynaston. CBLP

To Cynthia. Sir Francis Kynaston. NOSC

To Cynthia, Not to Let Him Read the Ladies' Magazines. P. M. Hubbard. FiBHP

To Cynthia, on Concealment of Her Beauty. Sir Francis Kynaston. MeLP; NOBE

To Cynthia on Her Being an Incendiary. Sir Francis Kynaston. HAP

To Cynthia, on Her Embraces. Sir Francis Kynaston. GBL

To Cyriack Skinner ("Cyriack, this three years' day.") Milton. See Cyriack, this three years' day these eyes, though clear.

To Cyriack Skinner ("Cyriack, whose grandsire.") Milton. GTBS; GTBS-P; NoP; OBEV; Son

To D — — , Dead by Her Own Hand. Howard Nemerov. PoA

To Daffodils [or Daffadills]. Robert Herrick. AWP; BeJo; BoNaP; CaPo; EBEvV; ELP; FaBoCh; GN; GoJo; GTBS; GTBS-P; InPS; JCP; LiTB; NOBE; NoP; NOSC; NTP; OBEV; OxAEP-1; PlP; PoEL-3; PoRA; PPP; SCGP; SeCP; SeCV-1; TFi; TrGrPo; TTTS; UnPo

To Daisies, Not to Shut So Soon[e]. Robert Herrick. BeJo; CaPo; CH; ELP; GBL; OBEV; OxBSP; SeCV-1; TrGrPo

To dance — / In the light of moon. Longings. Mae V. Cowdery. ShDr

To D'Annunzio: Lines from the Sea. Robert Nichols. OBMV

To Dante. Vittorio Alfieri, tr. fr. Italian by Lorna De' Lucchi. AWP

To Dante [or Sonnet: Guido Cavalcanti to Dante]. Cavalcanti, tr. fr. Italian by Shelley. AWP; OBVE

To Dante Alighieri. Cavalcanti, tr. fr. Italian by Dante Gabriel Rossetti. AWP

To Dante Alighieri (He Commends the Work of Dante's Life). Giovanni Quirino, tr. fr. Italian by Dante Gabriel Rossetti. AWP

To Dante Alighieri: He Conceives of Some Compensation in Death. Cino da Pistoia, tr. fr. Italian by Dante Gabriel Rossetti. AWP

To Dante Alighieri: He Interprets Dante Alighieri's Dream. Dante da Maiano, tr. fr. Italian by Dante Gabriel Rossetti. AWP

To Dante Alighieri: He Interprets Dante's Dream. Cino da Pistoia, tr. fr. Italian by Dante Gabriel Rossetti. AWP

To Dante Alighieri: He Mistrusts the Love of Lapo Gianni. Cavalcanti, tr. fr. Italian by Dante Gabriel Rossetti. AWP

To Dante Alighieri: He Reports, in a Feigned Vision, the Successful Issue of Lapo Gianni's Love. Cavalcanti, tr. fr. Italian by Dante Gabriel Rossetti. AWP

To Dante in Paradise, after Fiammetta's Death. Boccaccio, tr. fr. Italian by Dante Gabriel Rossetti. Fr. Sonnets. AWP

To David, about His Education. Howard Nemerov. HCAP

To-Day. Thomas Carlyle. GN; WGRP

To-Day. Lessie M. Drown. PWR

To-day a rude brief recitative. Song for All Seas, All Ships. Walt Whitman. CH; FaBoBe

To-Day a Shepherd. St. Theresa of Avila, tr. fr. Spanish by Arthur Symons. AWP

To-day, all day, I rode upon the Down. St. Valentine's Day. Wilfrid Scawen Blunt. Fr. Love Sonnets of Proteus, The. EnLoPo

To-day as I went out to play. The Brown Frog. Mary K. Robinson. BoTP

To-day at Deadman's Bar. (LL) A Health at the Ford. Robert Cameron Rogers. FaBoBe

To-Day I Leave Mrs. Brown's Lodgings. Sir Walter Scott. FaBoEE

To-day, I saw the catkins blow. February. Dorothy Una Ratcliffe. BoTP

To-day/ Is the feast day of Saint Anne. The Madwoman of Cork. Patrick Galvin. BiHa

To Day it self's too late, the Wise liv'd Yesterday. (LL) Procrastination. Martial. AWP; FaBoEE; OBVE

To day old Janus opens the new yeare. A New-Yeares-Gift Sung to King Charles, 1635. Ben Jonson. SeCP

To-day the lot caved in upon me. Page from a Diary. Desmond O'Grady. NoAM

To-day they laid him in the earth's cold colour. For Angus MacLeod. Iain Crichton Smith. OxBS

To-day we have naming of parts. Yesterday. Naming of Parts. Henry Reed. Fr. Lessons of the War. CoGr; EBEvV; FaBoEH; FF; GoJo; HeIP; HoPM; ImPo; InPS; LiTB; MoAB; MoBrPo; NOBE; NoP; OBWP; OxBTC; PAW; Poetr; PoRA; PrIm; RaBo; SoSe; TFi; TrGrPo; UnPo; UV

To-day's house makes to-morrow's road. The Survival. Edmund Blunden. OBEV; OBMV

To dazzle your night! (LL) Nocturne Varial. Lewis Alexander. PoBA; PoNe

To Dean-bourn, a Rude River in Devon, by which Sometimes He Lived. Robert Herrick. See Dean-bourn, a Rude River in Devon, by Which Sometimes He Lived ("Dean-bourn, farewell; I never look to see.")

To Dear Daniel. Samuel Greenberg. LiTA

To Death. Johann Wilhelm Ludwig Gleim, tr. fr. German by George C. Schoolfield. GePo

To Death. Oliver St. John Gogarty. FaBoEE; OBD; OBMV; OtMeF

To Death. Robert Herrick. BeJo

To Death, of His Lady. Villon, tr. fr. French by Dante Gabriel Rossetti. AWP

To deck her, froze into a gem. (LL) On Chloris Walking in the Snow. William Strode. ELP; JCP; OAEL-1

To deities of gauds and gold. Ad Patriam. Clinton Scollard. PAH

To Delia. Samuel Daniel. ESo
Sels.
"And yet I cannot reprehend the flight." OBEV
"Beauty, sweet love, is like the morning dew." EnRePo; NOBE; NoSic; OBEV
(Sonnet: "Beauty, sweet love, is like the morning dew.") EIL
"But love whilst that thou mayst be loved again." EIL; NoP; NoSic
"Care-charmer sleep[e], son[ne] of the sable night." AAS; EnRePo; GTBS; GTBS-P; InPS; NAEL-1; NOBE; NoP; NoSic; SCGP; TFi; TrGrPo
(Care-Charmer Sleep.) ImPo; LiTB; NIP; OAEL-1; OxAEP-1; Son
(Sonnet: "Care-charmer sleep[e], son[ne] of the sable night.") EIL; PoEL-2
"Fair is my love, and cruel as she's fair." AAS; NOBE; NoP; TEP; TrGrPo
(Beauty, Time and Love.) OBEV
(Fair Is My Love.) EnRePo; LiTB
(Sonnet: "Fair is my love, and cruel as she's fair.") EIL; HoPM
"I must not grieve my love, whose eyes would read." OBEV
(Sonnet: "I must not grieve my love, whose eyes would read.") EIL
"I once may see when yeares shall wreck my wrong." AAS
"If so it hap, this of-spring of my care." AAS
"If this be love, to draw [or drawe] a weary [or wearie] breath." AAS; GBL; TrGrPo
"Let others sing of knights and paladins [or palladines]." AAS; NOBE; NoP; NoSic; OBEV; SCGP
(Sonnet: "Let others sing of knights and paladin[e]s.") EIL
"Look, Delia, how we [e]steem the half-blown rose." NoP; NoSic; SCGP

(Sonnet: "Look, Delia, how we esteem the half-blown rose.") EIL
"My spotless love hovers, with purest wings." OBEV
"None other fame mine unambitious muse." AAS
Read in My Face. EnRePo
"These plaintive verse, the posts [or postes] of my desire." AAS
"Thou canst not die whilst any zeal abound." NoSic; Son
"Time, cruel time, come and subdue that brow." SCGP
"When men shall find thy flower [or flow'r], thy glory, pass." NAEL-1;
    NOBE; NoP; NoSic; OBEV; SCGP; Son; TrGrPo
(Sonnet: "When men shall find thy flower, thy glory, pass.") EIL
"When winter snows upon thy sable hairs." CTC; EnRePo; NoSic; Son;
    TEP
Why Should I Sing in Verse. Son
To demolish it. All Splendor on Earth. Karin Kiwus, tr. fr. German by
    Almut McAuley. BoWoP
To Dennis Brutus. Kofi Awoonor. HBAPE
To dethe hathe brouth my spouse and me. (LL) Alas, that ever that speche
    was spoken. Unknown. EnLoPo
To Detraction I Present My Poesie. John Marston. Fr. Scourge of Villainy
    [or Villanie], The. NoSic
To Dian, Queen of Earth, and Heaven, and Hell. (LL) To Homer.
    Keats. EBEV; NAEL-2; NoP; Son
To Dianeme. Robert Herrick. BeJo; CaPo; GTBS; GTBS-P; JCP; NOBE;
    NOSC; OBEV; SeCV-1; TrGrPo
To Dianeme. Robert Herrick. CaPo; FaBoBe
To Dianeme ("Dear, though to part it be a hell.") Robert Herrick. CaPo
To die and know it. This is the Black Widow, death. (LL) Mr. Edwards
    and the Spider. Robert Lowell. CAPP; CMoP; CoAP; FaBoMo; HeIP;
    InPS; LiTM; MoAB; NAAL-2; NOBA; NoP; SM; TFi; TwCP
To die for Man's Redemption. (LL) For Innocents' Day. Luke Wadding.
    NOIV; TIRV
To die like thirsting larks. Agony. Giuseppe Ungaretti, tr. fr. Italian by
    Charles Tomlinson. PeFWW
To die with a forlorn hope, but soon to be raised. The Survivor. Robert
    Graves. CMoP
To Dinah Washington. Etheridge Knight. PoBA
To dip, alas, into some unseemlier world. (LL) Old Mansion. John Crowe
    Ransom. HeIP; MeMAP; NOBA; OxBA
To Disgrace of Price. (LL) Publication — is the auction. Emily
    Dickinson. AmPP; NAAL-1; NALW; NoP
To Dispel the Cold: Two Poems on Spring, sels. Hung Liang-chi, tr. fr.
    Chinese by Irving Lo.
To Disraeli. Shirley Brooks. NOBL
To distant men, who must go there, or die. (LL) Sea-Shore. Emerson.
    LiTA; OxBA
To dive for the nimbus on the sea-floor. Nimbus. Douglas Le Pan.
    MoCV
To Dives. Hilaire Belloc. ChIV-2; OBSV
To do his will, whose glory shines in thame. (LL) Azured [or Azur'd]
    vault, the crystal circles bright, The. James I, King of England. EIL
To do the best you can? (LL) Suppose. Phoebe Cary. BLPA; BLPL
To do the wrong'd Corinna right for thee. (LL) The Imperfect Enjoyment.
    The Earl of Rochester. BoLoP; ErPo
To do us good. (LL) Consider. Christina Rossetti. GN
To do without what blood remained these wounds. (LL) A Terre. Wilfred
    Owen. LiTM; NSI; OxBTC; PeFWW; PoWW
To — do without you altogether. (LL) To Chloe. Martial. AWP; NBLV
To doat upon me ever. (LL) Love Not Me. Unknown. BLPL; CH; EIL;
    ELP; ImPo; LiTB; PoLF
To Doctor Bale. Barnabe Googe. NoSic
To Doctor Empiric. Ben Jonson. FaBoEE; NoP; SeCP
To Dr. F. B. on His Book of Chess. Richard Lovelace. CaPo
To Dr. Jonathan Swift. Pope. See Mighty mother, and her son who brings,
    The.
To Dr. Kipling. Richard Porson. FaBoCo
To Dr. Moore, in Anser to a Poetical Epistle Written by Him in Wales.
    Helen Maria Williams. ECWP; WoRP
To doggerel now I turn my pen. Letter to Miss E.B. at Bath. Mary
    Savage. ECWP
To Don at Salaam. Gwendolyn Brooks. CAPP
To Don Juan Baz. Mary E. Tucker. CBWP-1
To Dorothy. Marvin Bell. CAPP; VCAP
To Dorothy on Her Exclusion from the Guinness Book of World Records.
    X. J. Kennedy. Poetsp
To Dr. Swift on His Birthday, 30th November 1721. Esther Johnson.
    EnLoPo
To draw the unwilling bolts and set us free. (LL) 'Tis Sorrow Builds the
    Shining Ladder Up. James Russell Lowell. WGRP
To Dream Again. Shakespeare. See Be not afeard: the isle is full of noises.

To dream of love, and, waking, to remember you. Dreams. Arthur
    Symons. PoA
To drift with every passion till my soul. Hélas! Oscar Wilde. MoBrPo;
    NAEL-2; Son; TEP; TIRV
To Drink. Jane Hirshfield. CrSp
To Drink. Gabriela Mistral, tr. fr. Spanish by Gunda Kaiser. NU
To drink in moderation, and to smoke. Party Knee. John Updike. FiBHP
To drive away all heaviness. (LL) Dear Son, Leave Thy Weeping.
    Unknown. CTC
To drive Paul out of any lumber camp. Paul's Wife. Robert Frost. EBNV
To drive the kine one summer's morn. The Cow-Chace. John André.
    PAH
To drive us made. (LL) Madhouse. Calvin C. Hernton. ETG; PoNe
To drum-beat and heart-beat. Nathan Hale. Francis Miles Finch. PAH
To dry those tears and to blow out those fires? (LL) Tears, Flow No
    More. Lord Herbert of Cherbury. EIL; SeCP
To dwell a weeping hermit there! (LL) How Sleep the Brave. William
    Collins. GN; NOBE; OBEV; OtMeF; OxAEP-1; TFi
To Dwell Together in Unity. Bible, O.T., paraphrased by Sir Thomas
    Wyatt. See Behold, how good and how pleasant it is.
To E. Fitzgerald. Tennyson. NOBVV; OBF; PoEL-5
To E. O. S. Sarah Helen Whitman. AmWP
To each one is given a marble to carve for the wall. The Task That Is
    Given to You. Edwin Markham. WBLP
To Earth. James Applewhite. PoA
To Earthward. Robert Frost. BLPL; ImPo; LiTA; MeMAP; MoAB;
    MoAmPo; MoP; NoAM; NOBA; NoP; OxBA; RaBo; TAP; TRP
To ease his rumbling stomach our Kriton sniffs. On Kriton the Miser.
    Lucilius, tr. fr. Greek by Dudley Fitts. GrAn
To eastward ringing, to westward winging, o'er mapless miles of. When the
    Great Gray Ships Come In. Guy Wetmore Carryl. AnAmPo; FaBoBe;
    PAH
To eat pain like bread is a condition. Ruth Miller. Fr. Cycle. PeSA
To Eddleston. Byron. Fr. Childe Harold's Pilgrimage. PeHV
To Edom. Heine, tr. fr. German. TrJP
To Edward Allen (Alleyne). Ben Jonson.
To Edward Alleyn. Ben Jonson. See If Rome so great, and in her wisest
    age.
To Edward Fitzgerald. Robert Browning. NAEL-2; OxBSP
To Sir Edward Herbert at Julyers. John Donne. SeCV-1
To Edward Thomas. Alun Lewis. PoWW
To E.J.J. Ethel M. Caution. ShDr
To Electra. Robert Herrick. BLPL; CaPo; HoPM; OBEV; SeCV-1
To Electra ("More white than whitest Lillies far.") Robert Herrick. CBCK
To Eliza, Duchess of Dorset. Joseph Deericks Bennett. LiTA
To Elizabeth Barrett Browning. Anne Lynch Botta. AmWP
To Elizabeth, Countess of Rutland. Ben Jonson. BeJo; NoP
To Elsie. William Carlos Williams. CMoP; InPS; MeMAP; NAAL-2;
    NOBA; OxBA; PoE
To embrace me. (LL) Who/ took the dream. Charlie Mehrhoff. EaPr
To Emily Dickinson. Hart Crane. CMoP; NIP; NoAM; NOBA; NoP; Son;
    TAP
To Emily Dickinson. Yvor Winters. Son
To Emma, Extempore; Hyaena, off Gambia, June 4, 1779. Edward
    Thompson. NOEC
To End Her Fear. John Freeman. OBMV
To end in madness — both in misery. (LL) The Dream. Byron. BeLS;
    TEP
To end it all, the people elected a thumb. The Thumb. Dennis Saleh.
    MAT
To English Connoisseurs. Blake. OxBoLi
To Entertain Divine Zenocrate. Christopher Marlowe. Fr. Tamburlaine the
    Great. ChTr
To Envy. Sir John Davies. Fr. Hymns of Astræa [in Acrostic Verse].
    SiPSBD
To Epicles. Antipater of Thessalonica, tr. fr. Greek by Tony Harrison.
    GrAn
To Evening. William Collins. See If aught [or ought] of oaten stop, or
    pastoral song.
To everlasting life. (LL) Victory. Unknown. CoMu; WGRP
To Everlasting Oblivion. John Marston. Fr. Scourge of Villainy [or
    Villanie], The. NoSic; SCGP
To every Form of being is assigned. Discourse of the Wanderer, and an
    Evening Visit to the Lake. Wordsworth. Fr. Excursion, The. EnRP
To every heart which the sweet pain doth move. Dante, tr. fr. Italian by
    Dante Gabriel Rossetti. Fr. Vita Nuova, La. AWP
To every hearth a little fire. A Christmas Wish. Rose Fyleman. BoTP

To every man. The Treehouse. James A. Emanuel. BPo; PoBA

To every man there openeth. The Ways. John Oxenham. PoLF

To Everything There Is a Season. Bible, *O.T. Fr.* Ecclesiastes. EaPr; FF; NAWM-1; OBVE

To explain the nature of fishes in craft of verse. The Whale. *Unknown, tr. by* Gavin Bone. *Fr.* Physiologus. AnOE, *tr. by* Charles Kennedy; EBEV

To eye, and they fail at my closet of glass. *(LL)* The Sheep Child. James Dickey. CAPP; HCAP; MoP; MT; NoAM; NOBA; Prf; TAP; VCAP

To F. C. Mortimer Collins. NOBVV

To fail — is infidel. *(LL)* Sweetest heresy received, The. Emily Dickinson. CBLP

To fair Fidele's grassy tomb. A Fidele. William Collins. EnRP; NOEC (Dirge in "Cymbeline.") ELP; Mes; NOBE; SCGP (Fidele.) OBEV

To fall in love, though classically human. Advice to Colonel Valentine. Robert Graves. NYBP

To fall into your lap. *(LL)* Neocolonialism. Felix Mnthali. PeSAV

To fall, like an apple, no mind. In the Emptied Rest Home. Bella Akhmadulina, *tr. fr. Russian by* Jean Valentine *and* Olga Carlisle. BoWoP

To Fannie. Mary E. Tucker. CBWP-1

To Fanny. Keats. BoLoP; EBEV; EnRP; PPP; Son; TrGrPo

To Fanny Brawne. Keats. *See* This Living Hand, Now Warm and Capable.

To Father. Mary E. Tucker. CBWP-1

To Father Gerard Manley Hopkins, S.J. George Barker. MeMBP

To fear himself, and love all human kind. *(LL)* Hymn to Intellectual Beauty. Shelley. BLPL; EnRP; FHYEP; HAP; HeIP; ImPo; MeMBP; NAEL-2; NoP; OAEL-2; OBNC; PoE; TOF

To feed thy needy neighbours. *(LL)* Advice from Poor Robin's Almanack. *Unknown.* OBCP

To feed you: they do what they can. *(LL)* Brass Furnace Going Out: Song, after an Abortion. Diane Di Prima. PoBeRe

To feel and speak the astonishing beauty of things. The Beauty of Things. Robinson Jeffers. PoA

To fetch her the Drake! *(LL)* The Manlet. "Lewis Carroll." BXAP

To fight aloud is very brave. Emily Dickinson. LiTA; WPE

To fill the catalogue of human woes. *(LL)* I hate that drum's discordant sound. John Scott of Amwell. NIP; NOEC; OxAEP-1

To fill the paste that's a-kneading. *(LL)* Ceremonies for Christmas[se]. Robert Herrick. BeJo; GN; OBCP; OHIP; TEP

To fill the world with light. *(LL)* As Shadows Cast by Cloud and Sun. Bryant. AH

To find beyond death/ Bridgeport, Ohio. *(LL)* In Response to a Rumor That the Oldest Whorehouse in Wheeling, West Virginia, Has Been Condemned. James Wright. CAPP; CoAP; NNaP; NoAM; VCAP

To find in Art no fellow but the wind. *(LL)* The Wind at Penistone. Donald Davie. LiTM

To Find My Tom of Bedlam. *Unknown.* CBNP

To find my Tom of Bedlam, ten thousand years I'll travel. To Find My Tom of Bedlam. *Unknown.* CBNP

To find out death, but missest life at hand. *(LL)* Vanity [*or* Vanitie]. George Herbert. GeHe; NoP; NOSC; SeCV-1

To find the Western path. Morning. Blake. FaBoCh; OAEL-2

To find they have flown away? *(LL)* Trees are in their autumn beauty, The. W. B. Yeats. ArNa; ChTr; CMoP; FaBoPP; FaBoRV; FM; HeIP; InPS; MoAB; MoBrPo; MoP; NAEL-2; NoAM; NoP; PFP; Poetr; PPP; SCGP; SoSe; SOTW; TEP; TFi; UnPo

To find words for this. In Western Massachusetts, Sixteen Months Sober. Joan Larkin. LoHo

To finde God. Robert Herrick. BeJo; WGRP

To Fine Grand. Ben Jonson. JCP

To Fine Lady Would-Be. Ben Jonson. FaBoEE; JCP; NoP; NOSC; OxBSP

To finish what's begun, was my intent. An Apology. Anne Bradstreet. KTR

To Flaxman. Blake. FaBoEE; OxBoLi

To flee from memory. Emily Dickinson. FaBoEE

To fleece the Fleece from golden sheep. The Scales of the Eyes. Howard Nemerov. CMoP

To fling my arms wide. Dream Variation [*or* Variations]. · Langston Hughes. CDC; HAP; NAAL-2; NOBA; PoBA; PoNe (Dream Variations.) SAmP

To float. — The swimmer floats, the lover sleeps. *(LL)* Swimmer. Robert Francis. WeW

To float in the space between. *(LL)* The Idea of Ancestry. Etheridge Knight. BPo; NIP; NNaP; PBCAP; PoBA; RaBo; SV

To Flood Stage Again. James Wright. NOBA; Prf

To Flora. Sir John Davies. *Fr.* Hymns of Astræa [in Acrostic Verse]. SiPSBD

To Flossie. William Carlos Williams. SAmP

To fly. *(LL)* Tent tethered among jackpine and blue-/ bells. *Unknown.* EaPr

To fly high hardly fills the belly. Cicada. Li Shang-yin, *tr. fr. Chinese by* Eugene Eoyang *and* Irving Y. Lo. SuSp

To fly off, a ripe pear in a storm. Definition of the Soul. Boris Pasternak, *tr. fr. Russian by* Babette Deutsch. TrJP

To fold up silks, may wrap up wit. *(LL)* A Fancy. Thomas Carew. BeJo; NOSC

To follow, to seek, to be with her dear dead son. *(LL)* Come Up from the Fields Father. Walt Whitman. AnAmPo; MoAmPo; OBWP; OxBA; PPP; SAmP; UnPo

To Fool, or Knave. Ben Jonson. FaBoEE; NoP

To Ford Madox Ford in Heaven. William Carlos Williams. AmPP; NOBA

To Forget Me. Theodore Weiss. CoAP

To forgive enemies Hayley [*or* H.] does pretend. Blake. FaBoEE; OBF

To fork out his penny and pocket your shilling. *(LL)* What is a communist? One who hath yearnings. Ebenezer Elliot. NOBVV

To Form a Just and Finish'd Piece. Swift. *Fr.* Directions for Making a Birth-Day Song. NAs

To forsake a good thing when 'tis to be had. *(LL)* An Amorous Dialogue between John and His Mistress. *Unknown.* CoMu

To Fortune. Robert Herrick. OxBSP; SeCV-1

To frame her cloudy prison for the soul! *(LL)* Autumn. Thomas Hood. BLPL; ImPo; LiTB; OBEV; OxAEP-2

To France were returning two grenadiers. The Grenadiers. Heine, *tr. fr. German by* Philip L. Miller. RiWo

To Francis Beaumont. Ben Jonson. BeJo

To Sir Francis Brian. Sir Thomas Wyatt. *See* Spending hand that alway poureth out [*or* powreth owte], A.

To Frank O'Hara. Harold Brodkey. PRA

To Frankfort I on *Schobbas* came. The Best Religion. Heine, *tr. fr. German by* Emma Lazarus. *Fr.* Tannhäuser. TrJP

To free me from domestic strife. At Hadleigh, Suffolk. *Unknown.* FaBoCo

To free the ball the chief now turns his mind. Victory on the Last Green. Thomas Mathison. *Fr.* Goff; an Heroi-comical Poem, The. NOEC

To Freedom. Agnes Nemes Nagy, *tr. fr. Hungarian by* Bruce Berlind. PoSu

To freight cars in the air. The Descent of Winter (Section 10/30). William Carlos Williams. InPK

To Friend and to Foe. *Unknown.* CoMu

To Friends Who Have Also Considered Suicide. Phyllis Webb. NOBC

To Frighten a Storm. Gladys Cardiff. CDW

To Fuscus Arustus. Horace, *tr. fr. Latin by* Abraham Cowley. *Fr.* Epistles. AWP

To future Times without an Epitaph. *(LL)* Advertising Epitaph: On One Lockyer, Inventor of a Patent Medicine. *Unknown.* FaBoUs

To G. H. B. James Bayard Taylor. Son

To G, her one and only rose. Love-Letter Two. *Unknown.* PeHV

To G. R. Samuel Elsworth Cottam. PeHV

To gallop off to town post-haste. Friar Lubin. Clément Marot, *tr. fr. French by* Longfellow. AWP

To gather flowers Sappha went. The Apron of Flowers. Robert Herrick. CaPo; SeCV-1

To gaze at the river made of time and water. Ars Poetica. Jorge Luis Borges, *tr. fr. Spanish by* Harold Morland. ArNa

To gaze with envy on their gloomy rest. *(LL)* Pressed by the Moon, Mute Arbitress of Tides. Charlotte Smith. NALW

To GB from Tuscany. Paul Monette. PFL

To George Pulling Buds. Adelaide O'Keeffe. FaBoUs

To George Sand: A Desire. Elizabeth Barrett Browning. BoWoP; NAEL-2; NALW; TEP

To George Sand: A Recognition. Elizabeth Barrett Browning. BoWoP; NAEL-2; NALW; TEP

To Germany. Charles Hamilton Sorley. MoBrPo; NSI

To Germany. Georg Rudolph Weckherlin, *tr. fr. German by* George C. Schoolfield. GePo

To Geron. Hildebrand Jacob. NOEC

To get a fix on it. What Is Happening Now? Hubert Witheford. PeNZ

To get back to st. louis/the dirt there didnt crawl. *(LL)* Sechita Had Heard These Things. Ntozake Shange. SRLS

To get betimes in Boston town I rose this morning early. A Boston Ballad. Walt Whitman. OBAL

To Get Clear. J. P. Ward. AngWe

To get into it/ As it lies. Shirt. Charles Simic. HCAP

To get recruits for Pain, I use. Cupid. Bernard O'Dowd. NOBAu

To get to know the flight of birds, blossoming. Czargrad. John Riley. VaA

To Gild Refinèd Gold. Shakespeare. *Fr.* King John. ImPo; LiTB

To Gisi Fleischmann, Rescuer of Her People. Joan Campion. BTR

To give employment to the artisan. *(LL)* Lord Finchley. Hilaire Belloc. FaBoCo; FaBoEE; FiBHP; NBLV; NoAM; NOBL; OxAEP-2; OxBoLi; PeLV

To give everything away. *(LL)* The Way We Live Now. April Bernard. UTF

To give One's Life. Mary Carolyn Davies. PoToHe

To give one's life through eighty years is harder. To Give One's Life. Mary Carolyn Davies. PoToHe

To give the square distance of a dream. *(LL)* The February Town. Sebastian Barry. IB

To give up everything. Huck Finn at Ninety, Dying in a Chicago Boarding House Room. James Schevill. TAP

To given us strokes grete. *(LL)* Wenest thou, usher, with thyn cointise. *Unknown.* MiEL

To glad the heart and save from harm. *(LL)* The Lament of the Flowers. Jones Very. AnAmPo; NOBA; OxBA

To Glaukos, and to Nereus. Lucianus, *tr. fr. Greek by* Peter Jay. GrAn

To Gluttony and Guzzling, that fastidious gourmet. Leonidas of Tarentum, *tr. fr. Greek by* Barbara Hughes Fowler. *Fr.* Epigrams. HePo

To go along dying and singing. And to baptize the darkness. Pagan Woman. César Vallejo, *tr. fr. Spanish by* Robert Bly. AnAn

To go back where we came from. *(LL)* Belle Isle, 1949. Philip Levine. VCAP

To go three journeys ere your letter came. *(LL)* Country Letter. John Clare. EnVR

To go upon my winter's task again. *(LL)* Winter Memories. Thoreau. AmPP; AnAmPo; OxBA

To God. Blake. OAEL-2

To God. Robert Herrick. ChIV-2; TrPWD; WGRP

To God alone, the only donour. Francis Daniel Pastorius. SCAP

To God: An Anthem, Sung In The Chapel at White-Hall, Before the King. Robert Herrick. ChIV-1

To God Our Strength Shout Joyfully. Henry Ainsworth. AH

To God, the Architect. Harry Hibbard Kemp. *See* Who Thou art I know not.

To God, the everlasting, who abides. John Addington Symonds. WGRP

To God the highest glory. Song of the Angels. L. A. J. Moorer. CBWP-3

To God the Holy Ghost. Henry Constable. NoSic

To God: to illuminate all men. Beginning with Skid Road. Psalm III. Allen Ginsberg. CAPP; ChIV-1

To Graham and Anna: from the Arctic Gate. Letter to Graham and Anna. Louis MacNeice. OBTV

To Grandmother on Her Going. Gail Tremblay. HATNAP

To grass, or leaf, or fruit, or wall. The Snail. Vincent Bourne, *tr. fr. Latin by* William Cowper. BoTP; OBVE

To Greet a Letter-Carrier. William Carlos Williams. OBAL; SAmP

To greet you. You will understand. *(LL)* To a Poet a Thousand Years Hence. James Elroy Flecker. ChTr; FaBoRV; MoBrPo; PoRA

To Grosphus. Godfrey the Satirist, *tr. fr. Latin.* PeHV

To Groves. Robert Herrick. CaPo

To grow more loving every day. *(LL)* A Child's Prayer. *Unknown.* BLRP; BoTP

To grow unguided at a time when none. A Tough Generation. David Gascoyne. LiTM

To Guillaume Apollinaire. Jim Brodey. UL

To H. C. Wordsworth. EnRP; MeMBP; PoEL-4

To Sir H. W. at His Going Ambassador to Venice. John Donne. MeLP

To hail the King of Glory. *(LL)* Before the Paling of the Stars. Christina Rossetti. TrCP

To Hampstead. Leigh Hunt. EnRP

To hang all old strange things, let his wife beware. *(LL)* Antiquary. John Donne. EBEV; FF; NOSC

To hang his pants on while he slept. *(LL)* Museum Piece. Richard Wilbur. FaBoMo; FaBoMo; InPK; NIP; NoP; TAP; TRP

To happiest end address. *(LL)* In Pilgrim Life Our Rest. Edwin Sandys. AH; ChIV-1

To haste me hence to find my fortune's fold. *(LL)* Farewell to the Court. Sir Walter Ralegh. EnRePo; NoSic; SiPS; SiPSBD

To have been a little ill. Convalescence. Noël Coward. TTTS

To have been gone so long. Granizo. Leroy V. Quintana. AfAz

To have been loved once by someone — surely. When the Sun Went Down. John Ashbery. NAAL-2

To have been one. Aspects of Eve. Linda Pastan. CRP

To have it out or not? that is the question. "C. A. W." BXAP; UV

To have known him, to have loved him. Monody. Herman Melville. LiTA; NAAL-1; OxBSP; PoE; PoEL-5

To have liv'd eminent in a degree. Upon the Death of My Ever Desired Friend Doctor Donne Dean of Pauls. Henry King. SeCP

To have/ red mouth and green shanks. Moorhen. William Logan. DiPo

To have to go to bed by day? *(LL)* Bed in Summer. Robert Louis Stevenson. GoJo; NBLV; OTCP; OxBChV; PFP

To Have without Holding. Marge Piercy. CrSp; NIP

To Haydn. Thomas Holcroft. NOEC

To Hayley. Blake. *See* Thy [*or* Your] friendship oft has made my heart to ache [*or* ake].

To heal the impossible wounds. *(LL)* The Wounds. Sebastian Barry. IB

To heal you Hieronymus I had brought you. Bear's Blood. Ileana Malancioui, *tr. fr. Romanian by* Stavros Deligiorgis. BoWoP

To hear a cart go jolting down the street. *(LL)* The Shell. James Stephens. BoNaP; BoTP; CH; CMoP; MoAB; MoBrPo; MoShBr

To hear an oriole sing. Emily Dickinson. PoEL-5

To Heaven. Robert Herrick. ChIV-2

To Heaven. Ben Jonson. BeJo; ChIV-2; EnRePo; HAP; JCP; LiTB; NAEL-1; NOCV; NOSC; SCGP; SeCP; TRP; TrPWD; UnPo

To Heaven or to Guinea? *(LL)* Country Graveyard. Charles Pressoir. NegPo

To Helen. Poe. AmPP; AnAmPo; AWP; BoLoP; CH; ChTr; ClHu; FaBoBe; FaBV; GBL; HAP; HeIP; HoPM; ImPo; InPS; InvP; LiTA; MeMAP; NAAL-1; NIP; NOBA; NOBE; NoP; OBEV; OtMeF; OxBA; PoE; PoEL-4; PoLF; PoRA; PrIm; TAP; TFi; TrGrPo; WeW

To Helen. Winthrop Mackworth Praed. NOBVV

To Helen in a Huff. Nathaniel Parker Willis. AnAmPo; OBAL

To Helen of Troy (N.Y.). Peter Viereck. WeW

To Helen, with Crabbe's Poems: a Birthday Present. Winthrop Mackworth Praed. EPCY

To Hell with Commonsense. Patrick Kavanagh. FaBoTw

To Hell with It. Frank O'Hara. NeAP

To Hell with Your Fertility Cult. Gary Snyder. NAs

To Sir Henrie Savile upon His Translation of Tacitus. Ben Jonson. SeCV-1

To Henrietta, on Her Departure for Calais. Thomas Hood. OBTV; OxBChV

To Sir Henry Cary. Ben Jonson. NoP; NOSC

To Sir Henry Goodyere. Ben Jonson. NOSC

To Sir Henry Newton, upon His Re-edifying the Church of Charleton in Kent. Thomas Philipott. NOSC

To Henry Reynolds, of Poets and Poesy, sels. Michael Drayton.
"And be it said of thee." EPCY
Chapman the Translator. EPCY
Christopher Marlowe. ChTr
"Grave moral Spenser after these came on." EPCY
"Neat Marlowe, bathed in the Thepian springs." EPCY
"Noble Sidney with this last arose, The." EPCY
"That noble Chaucer, in those former times." EPCY
"Then dainty Sandys, that hath to English done." EPCY
"When after those, four ages very near." EPCY

To Sir Henry Vane the Younger. Milton. Son

To Sir Henry Wotton. John Donne. NoSic; OxAEP-1

To Sir Henry Wotton, sels. John Donne.
"Sir, more than kisses, letters mingle Souls." OBF

To Henry Wright of Mobberley, Esq. on Buying the Picture of Father Malebranche. John Byrom. NOEC

To Her. Robert Mezey. NaP

To her are echoes sending. *(LL)* Awake, mine eyes, see Phoebus bright arising. *Unknown.* EiL

To Her Dead Mate: Montana, 1966. Elizabeth Libbey. AmPA

To Her Eyes. Lord Herbert of Cherbury. JCP

To Her Father with Some Verses. Anne Bradstreet. NALW

To her friends, said the Bright one, in chatter. Arthur Buller. PeLi

To her gardener, a lady named Liliom. *Unknown.* PeLi

To Her in Absence; a Ship. Thomas Carew. CaPo

To Her Love. Edward May. FaBoEE

To Her Lover's Complaint. Jane Barker. OxBSP

To her nest back again. *(LL)* The Pretty Ploughboy. *Unknown.* GBP

To Her Picture. Sir John Davies. *Fr.* Hymns of Astræa [in Acrostic Verse]. SiPSBD

To Her Questioning His Estate. William Hammond. JCP

To her royall highnesse the Dutchesse of Yorke. Katherine Philips. KTR

To Her Sea-faring Lover. *Unknown. See* Shall I thus ever long, and be no whit the near?

To herald in another year. January. H. Cordelia Ray. CBWP-3

To His Ring, Given to His Lady, Wherein Was Graven This Verse, "My Heart Is Yours." George Turberville. ElL

To His Sacred Majesty, a Panegyrick on His Coronation, 1661, *sels.* Dryden.

To His Savior. The New Years Gift. Robert Herrick. ChIV-2

To His Saviour, a Child; a Present, by a Child. Robert Herrick. BeJo; ChIV-2; OHIP; PeECV; SeCP; TrCP

To His Scornful Mistress. William Hammond. CBLP

To His Scribe Adam. Chaucer. *See* Adam scrivein [*or* scrivain], if ever it thee bifalle.

To His Sleeping Mistress. John Fletcher. *See* Oh [*or* O] fair[e] sweet face, oh [*or* O] eyes celestial[l] bright.

To His Son. Sir Walter Ralegh. *See* Three Things there be that prosper up apace.

To His Son Benedict Hoskyns. John Hoskyns. *See* Sweet Benedict, whilst thou art young.

To His Son Bennet. John Hoskyns. FaBoEE

To His Son [*or* Sonne], Vincent Corbet[t]. Richard Corbett [*or* Corbet]. BeJo; FaBoCh; NOSC; OxAEP-1; OxBChV; TrGrPo

To His Soul. Pierre de Ronsard, *tr. fr. French by* Philip L. Miller. RiWo

To His Tomb-Maker. Robert Herrick. SeCV-1

To His Valentine. Michael Drayton. PoEL-2

To His Very Friend, Master Richard Martin. Sir John Davies. *Fr.* Dedications [*of* Orchestra]. SiPS

To His Watch. Gerard Manley Hopkins. MoAB; MoBrPo

To His Watch, When He Could Not Sleep. Lord Herbert of Cherbury. JCP; NOBE; PoEL-2

To His Wife. Ausonius, *tr. fr. Latin by* Terrot Reaveley Glover. AWP

To His Wife. Ausonius, *tr. fr. Latin by* Helen Waddell. OxBM

To His Wife, for Striking Her Dog. Sir John Harington. OxBSP

To his wife said the lynx-eyed detective. Langford Reed. PeLi

To His Young Mistress. Pierre de Ronsard, *tr. fr. French by* Andrew Lang. AWP

To Homer. Keats. EBEV; NAEL-2; NoP; Son

To honor the return of sparkling sun. Louise Labé, *tr. fr. French by* Willis Barnstone. BoWoP

To honor thy immortal name! (*LL*) Washington's Monument. *Unknown.* OHIP; PAH

To Honora Sneyd. Anna Seward. ECWP

To Sir Horace Vere. Ben Jonson. BeJo

To house the hag, you must do this. Another to Bring In the Witch. Robert Herrick. BeJo

To Houston at Gonzales town, ride, Ranger, for your life. The Men of the Alamo. James Jeffrey Roche. PAH

To Sir Hudson Lowe. Thomas Moore. OBSV

To Hugh MacDiarmid. Edwin Morgan. FaBoTw

To Sir Humphry Mackworth, *sels.* Thomas Yalden. "Miner thus through perils digs his way, The." ECEV

To Hunt. Blake. OxBoLi

To hunt rode fierce King Rufus. The Death of Rufus. Menella Bute Smedley. FaBoEH

To hunt the waterfalls. (*LL*) Louisa. Wordsworth. EnRP; GBL

To hurt the Negro and avoid the Jew. University. Karl Shapiro. LiTA; OxBA

To I. Lavrentevaya. Natalya Gorbanevskaya, *tr. fr. Russian by* Daniel Weissbort. BoWoP

To Ianthe. John Lyle Donaghy. *See* Past ploughed and fallow, at the top.

To Ianthe. Walter Savage Landor. *See* Past ruin'd [*or* ruined] Ilion Helen lives.

To Ibn Zaidun. Wallāda, *tr. fr. Arabic by* James Monroe *and* Deirdre Lashgari. WPOW

To Imagination. Emily Brontë. EnVR

To Inez Milholland. Edna St. Vincent Millay. AiP; NALW; WPE

To infancy, O Lord, again I come. The Return. Thomas Traherne. GeHe

To insure courageous chocolate dwells there. (*LL*) The Chocolate Soldiers. Calvin Forbes. MAT

To Insure Survival. Simon J. Ortiz. CDW

To interpose them oft, is not unwise. (*LL*) To Mr. Lawrence. Milton. AWP; GTBS; GTBS-P; OBEV; PoE

To Ioan Madog, Poet, Ancestor. John Idris Jones. AngWe

To Ireland in the Coming Times. W. B. Yeats. NoAM; NOIV; PeIV

To Iron-Founders and Others. Gordon Bottomley. OBEV; OBMV

To it, O jazzmen. (*LL*) Jazz Fantasia. Carl Sandburg. AiP; Jaz; MoAB; MoAmPo; Poetr; PoNe

To Italy. Giacomo Leopardi, *tr. fr. Italian by* Romilda Rendel. AWP

To J. G. "Ephelia." KTR; NOSC

To James. Frank Horne. *Fr.* Letters [*or* Notes] Found near a Suicide. BPo; CDC; PoBA; PoNe

To James Smith. Burns. HoPM

To Jane. Shelley. FHYEP; Mes; NoP

To Jane: The Invitation. Shelley. *See* Best and brightest, come away.

To Jane: The Keen Stars Were Twinkling. Shelley. *See* Keen stars were twinkling, The.

To Jane: The Recollection. (Now the last day of many days.) Shelley. OBNC

Sels.
"Come then! and while the slow icicle hangs." FaBoRV
"We wandered to the pine forest." CH

To Janet. Ralph Pomeroy. NYBP

To Jann, in Her Absence. C. J. Driver. PeSA

To Jesus of Nazareth. Frederic Lawrence Knowles. TrPWD

To Jesus on His Birthday. Edna St. Vincent Millay. ChIV-2; HeIP; TrCP; TrGrPo

To Joan. Lucille Clifton. CrSp

To John Ashbery. Frank O'Hara. CAPP

To John C. Frémont. Whittier. PAH

To John Clare. John Clare. Son

To John Donne. Sir Henry Wotton. NoSic

To John Donne ("Donne, the delight of Phoebus, and each Muse.") Ben Jonson. BeJo; EPCY; NAEL-1; SeCV-1

To John Donne from Mr Henry Wotton. Sir Henry Wotton. *See* 'Tis not a coat of gray or shepherd's life.

To John Donne ("Who shall doubt, Donne, whe'er I a poet be.") Ben Jonson. BeJo; EPCY; JCP; NoP; SeCP; SeCV-1

To John Garfield, for Whom the Postman Only Rang Once. Charles B. Stetler. NGP

To John I ow'd great obligation. Matthew Prior. FaBoCo; FaBoEE; OBVE (Quits.) AWP

To John Keats. Leigh Hunt. Son

To John Keats. Amy Lowell. Son

To John Keats, from His Honored Friend, William Davenant, *sels.* John Clare.
"Though faction's scorn at first did shun." EPCY

To John Keats, Poet, at Springtime. Countee Cullen. CDC

To John Lamb, Esq.: Of the South-Sea House. Charles Lamb. Son

To join with them, who here confer. His Offering, With the Rest, At the Sepulcher. Robert Herrick. ChIV-2

To Joseph. Elizabeth Sullam. PFL

To Joseph Brenan. James Clarence Mangan. PeIV

To Joshua. Alice Thomas Ellis. OBD

To joy, annoy, friends, foes; but 'twill not be. (*LL*) Of the Great and Famous . . . Sir Francis Drake, and of My Little-Little Selfe. Robert Hayman. CH; FaBoCh; NoP

To Juan at the Winter Solstice. Robert Graves. CMoP; EBEV; FaBoMo; ImPo; LiTB; LiTM; MeMBP; MoBrPo; MoP; NAEL-2; NoAM; OAEL-2; PoE; RaBo; TwCP

To Judge Han Ch'o at Yang-chou. Tu Mu, *tr. fr. Chinese by* A. C. Graham. PLT

To Judith Asleep. John Ciardi. LiTM; LPA

To Julia. Robert Herrick. CaPo

To Julia. Robert Herrick. CaPo; NOSC

To Julia de Burgos. Julia de Burgos, *tr. fr. Spanish by* Grace Schulman. BoWoP; PBWP

To Julia in Shooting Togs. Sir Owen Seaman. BXAP

To Julia, the Flaminica Dialis, or Queen-Priest. Robert Herrick. CaPo

To Julia to Expedite Her Promise. John Cleveland. CBLP

To Julia under Lock and Key. Sir Owen Seaman. BXAP; FaBoPa

To Julius. Martial, *tr. by* Sir Charles Sedley. FaBoEE

To jump, but we don't. (*LL*) Doppelgänger. Jason Shinder. UTF

To jump his mortal coil. (*LL*) Elegy on Thomas Hood. Martin Fagg. FaBoPa; NOBL; UV

To jump off in the midst of the sea, rise again, nod to me, shout, and laughingly dash with your hair. (*LL*) Walt Whitman. Walt Whitman. AmPP; LiTA; MoAmPo, *abr.*; NoAM; NOBA; OxBA; SOTW, *much abr.*

To justify-Despair. (*LL*) It was not death, for I stood up. Emily Dickinson. MeMAP; NAAL-1; NOBA; NoP; SAmP

To justify the dream. (*LL*) I reckon — when I count at All. *At.* to Emily Dickinson. MoAmPo; NIP

To justify your coming back here. (*LL*) Pure Valentine. Connie Deanovich. UTF

To K. H. Thomas Edward Brown. OBNC

To Kalon. Ezra Pound. PoA

To Kate, Skating Better than Her Date. David Daiches. FiBHP; NYBP

To Kattos. Robert Louis Stevenson. OBNC

To Keats: On Reading His Sonnet Written in Chaucer. John Hamilton Reynolds. Son

To Keep a True Lent. Robert Herrick. TrCP

To keep my health! Resolve. Charlotte Perkins Gilman. PoToHe; WGRP

To keep no beauty to himself. (*LL*) For Raftery. Alan Alexander. NOBAu

To keep our metaphysics warm. (*LL*) Whispers of Immortality. T. S. Eliot. CMoP; CTC; LiTA; NoAM; NOBA; NoP; OBMV; OxAEP-2

To Keep the Memory of Charlotte Forten Grimké. Angelina Weld Grimké. BlSi; ShDr

To keep things whole. (*LL*) Keeping Things Whole. Mark Strand. CoAP; HCAP; HeIP; LCAP; PPP; TAP; VCAP

To kepe the cold wind awaye. (*LL*) There blows a cold wind today, today. *Unknown*. MiEL

To kill a bat is easy. Easy as a Bat. *Gond Oral Tradition*, tr. by V. Elwin and S. Hivale. WTO

To Kill a Deer. Carol Frost. FoLa

To kill a language is to kill a people. The Frost is All Over. Pearse Hutchinson. PBCIP

To kill its enemies and cheat its friends. International Conference. Colin Ellis. FaBoEE

To kill love so as not to commit suicide. Resurrection. Yoshihara Sachiko, tr. fr. *Japanese by* Kenneth Rexroth and Ikuko Atsumi. WPJ

To Kiss God's Rod; Occasioned upon a Child's Sickness. Mildmay Fane, 2d Earl of Westmorland. BeJo

To kiss the cross. (*LL*) The Rosary. Robert Cameron Rogers. FaBoBe; WBLP

To kiss upon thy lips a stainless fame. (*LL*) To George Sand: A Desire. Elizabeth Barrett Browning. BoWoP; NAEL-2; NALW; TEP

To know (*LL*) Heirloom. Cinda Thompson. LoHo

To Know All Is to Forgive All. Nixon Waterman. BLPA

To know he still is warm tho' I am cold. (*LL*) After Death. Christina Rossetti. GBL; NAEL-2; NALW; TEP

To know just how He suffered would be dear. Emily Dickinson. InvP

To know my self, thy will, and Thee. (*LL*) For Scholars and Pupils. George Wither. OxBChV

To know that love lodged in a woman's breast Is but a guest. (*LL*) A Poem Written by Sir Henry Wotton, in His Youth. Sir Henry Wotton. NoSic

To know there are rhododendrons on the slopes of the Himalayas. Nearer. Judith Herzberg, tr. fr. *Dutch by* Shirley Kaufman. BoWoP

To Know Whom One Shall Marry. *Unknown*. GBP

To know you by the signs of this world! (*LL*) Ripening. Wendell Berry. EaPr; RaBo

To Krishna Haunting the Hills. Andal, tr. fr. *Tamil by* Willis Barnstone. BoWoP

To Kuvos. Theognis, tr. fr. *Greek by* G. Lowes Dickinson. PeHV

To Kyris. Strato, tr. fr. *Greek by* Teddy Hogge. GrAn; PeHV

To L. Julianne Perry. PoBA

To L. R-M. Noël Coward. ArLo

To Labienus. Martial, tr. fr. *Latin*. PeHV

To Labor. Charlotte Perkins Gilman. PoLF

To Ladies' Eyes. Thomas Moore. OxBoLi; PoEL-4

To Lady Anne Fitzpatrick, When about Five Years Old, with a Present of Shells, 1772. Horace Walpole. NOEC

To Lady Eleanor Butler and the Honourable Miss Ponsonby, Composed in the Grounds of Plas-Newydd, Llangollen. Wordsworth. PeHV

To Lady Wyatt. Edward Lear. CBNP

To Lake Aghmoogenegamook. The American Traveller. "Orpheus C. Kerr." FaBoCo; OBAL

To Larr [or Lar]. Robert Herrick. CaPo; SeCV-1

To Laura. H. Cordelia Ray. CBWP-3

To Laura in Life. Petrarch, tr. fr. *Italian*. Fr. Sonnets to Laura.

To Laura, on the French Fleet Parading before Plymouth. Ann Thomas. ECWP

To Laura Phelan: 1880-1906. Leon Stokesbury. MT

To Laurels. Robert Herrick. CaPo; SeCV-1

To lay a cornerstone at earth's extremest end! (*LL*) The First Stone of the New Castle. *Unknown*. PeSAV

To lazy to be ambitious. Ryokan, tr. fr. *Japanese by* Stephen Mitchell. EnlH

To learn experience at the last, than never. (*LL*) Brainsick race that wanton youth ensues, The. *Unknown*. NoSic

To learn how to die cut down a tree. "Antler." EaPr

To Learn How to Speak. Jeremy Cronin. PeSAV

To learn the transport by the pain. Emily Dickinson. NOCV

To leave a light for them when they should come. (*LL*) The Insusceptibles. Adrienne Rich. HeIP; SM; Son

To leave me. (*LL*) The Quickness of Fear. Beverly Acuff Momoi. LoHo

To leave my boots. (*LL*) Our Photograph[s]. Frederick Locker-Lampson. NBLV; NOBL; PeLV

To leave the Krauts in peace! (*LL*) Et Cetera. Léon Damas. NegPo

To leave the world and serve God. Compiuta Donzella, tr. fr. *Italian by* Laura Stortoni. WPOW

To Leigh Hunt, Esq. Keats. EnRP; Son

To Let. D. Newey-Johnson. BoTP

To let a thousand such enjoy their quiet. (*LL*) A Sparrow-Hawk. *Unknown*. CH; EBEV

To let in death when Love and fortune will. (*LL*) Like to an Hermit Poor. At. to Sir Walter Ralegh. EIL

To let mee live, O love and hate mee too. (*LL*) The Prohibition. John Donne. EIL; GBL; MeLP; NOSC

To let the warm Love in! (*LL*) Ode to Psyche. Keats. EnRP; FHYEP; InPS; LiTB; MeMBP; NAEL-2; NOBE; NoP; OAEL-2; OBEV; OBNC; OxAEP-2; PFP; PoE; PoEL-4; PPP; TFi; TOF

To Leven Water. Tobias Smollett. OBEV

To Li Chien. Po Chü-i, tr. fr. *Chinese by* Arthur Waley. AWP

To Li Po. 'Aisha bint Ahmad al-Qurtubiyya, tr. fr. *Chinese by* Eugene Eoyang. SuSp

To Li Po. Wing Tek Lum. BCF

To Li Po. Tu Fu, tr. fr. *Chinese by* Robert Payne. TAL

To Li Po on a Spring Day. Tu Fu, tr. fr. *Chinese by* Robert Payne. TAL

To liberty without. (*LL*) The Faithful Friend. William Cowper. FM; OBF

To Licinius. Horace. *See* Receive, dear friend, the truths I teach.

To lie down and sleep than to quarrel and fight. (*LL*) Two Little Kittens. *Unknown*. OBCA; OFC; OxBChV

To Liebig. August, Graf von Platen, tr. fr. *German by* Reginald Bancroft Cooke. PeHV

To Life. Lizette Woodworth Reese. AmWP

To Life I Said Yes. Chaim Grade, tr. fr. *Yiddish by* Joseph Leftwich. TrJP

To life upon these shores. (*LL*) Middle Passage. Robert Hayden. BPo; InPS; NoAM; PoBA; TRP; VCAP

To lift a leg and play the baptist. (*LL*) The Scribblers. Walter Savage Landor. FaBoEE; OBSV

To lift Her Brows on You. (*LL*) Sweet Mountains — Ye tell Me no lie. Emily Dickinson. NALW

To lift her over the threshold, and let her in at the door! (*LL*) The Witch. Mary Elizabeth Coleridge. BrRo; NALW; OHCV; WPE

To lift their silken lashes. (*LL*) The Maid of Neidpath. Thomas Campbell. GTBS; GTBS-P

To Light. Linda Hogan. HATNAP

To light young poets' hearts. Cephalus, tr. fr. *Greek by* W. G. Shepherd. GrAn

To Lighten My Darkness. *Unknown*, tr. fr. *Arabic by* E. Powys Mathers. Fr. Thousand and One Nights, The. AWP

To Like, to Love. Anne Sexton. AnAn

To like, to love, to choose alike. (*LL*) Conceit Begotten by the Eyes. Sir Walter Ralegh. EnRePo; NoSic; SiPS

To linger till ninety, like Landor. (*LL*) Obit on Parnassus. F. Scott Fitzgerald. NBLV; NYBP; PrIm

To listen to her son's one and only poem. (*LL*) Mr. Nabokov's Memory. Thomas McCarthy. IB

To Little Sister From No. 16. *Unknown*. NSI

To live always as on the brink of leaving — but Goethe said. John Riley. VaA

To live and die for thee. (*LL*) To Anthea, Who May Command Him Anything. Robert Herrick. CaPo; GTBS; GTBS-P; JCP; NOBE; NOSC; OAEL-1; OBEV; SeCP; SeCV-1; TrGrPo

To live and lack the thing should rid my pain. (*LL*) Alas, so all things now do hold [or thinges nowe doe holde] their peace. The Earl of Surrey, after Petrarch. SiPSBD

To live and not to be thine own. Thine Own. Josephine D. Henderson Heard. CBWP-4

To live by, in sunlight and moolight, until they died. (*LL*) Patriotic Tour and Postulate of Joy. Robert Penn Warren. AiP; NYBP

To live content with small means. William Ellery Channing. EaPr

To live, I think of these! (*LL*) Ballade Made in the Hot Weather. W. E. Henley. MoBrPo

To live in court among the crew is care. To His Friend P. of Courting, Traveling, Dicing, and Tennis. George Turberville. NoSic

To live in hell, and heaven to behold. Henry Constable. Fr. Diana. AAS; ESo; Son

(If Love In These Be Founded.) CBCK

To live in mankind, far, far more . . . than to live in a name. (*LL*) The Eagle That Is Forgotten. Vachel Lindsay. AWP; CMoP; LiTA; MeMAP; MoAB; MoAmPo; NOBA; OxBA

To Mr. Murray. Byron. FaBoCo; UV

To Mr. Newton on His Return from Ramsgate. William Cowper. NOEC

To Mr. Pope, *sels.* Thomas Parnell.
"How flame the glories of Belinda's hair." EPCY

To Mr. Pope, on His Translation of Homer's Iliad, *sels.* Christopher Pitt.
"'Tis true what famed Pythagoras maintained." EPCY

To Mr. Punchinello. *Unknown.* OxNR

To Mr. R.W. John Donne. ESCV

To Mr. Rowland Woodward. John Donne. ESCV

To Mr. S. T. Coleridge. Anna Laetitia Barbauld. NOEC; WoRP

To Mr. Thomson, on His Publishing the Second Edition of His Poem Called Winter, *sels.* David Mallet.
"Through all thy various Winter, full are found." EPCY

To Mr. Tilman after He Had Taken Orders. John Donne. EBEV

To Mr. W. B., at the Birth of His First Child. William Cartwright. BeJo

To Mr. William Long, On His Recovery from a Dangerous Illness, 1785. William Hayley. Son

To Mr. Wren, My Valentine Six Year Old. Jane Holt. ECWP

To Mistress Anne. John Skelton. EnRePo

To Mistress Anne Cecil, upon Making Her a New Year's Gift, January 1, 1567-8. William Cecil, 1st Baron Burghley. EIL; FaBoEH

To Mrs. B. from a Lady Who Had a Desire to See Her. *Unknown.* KTR

To Mrs. Francis-Arabella Kelly. Mary Barber. ECWP

To Mrs. K ———, On Her Sending Me an English Christmas Plum-Cake at Paris. Helen Maria Williams. WoRP

To Mistress Katherine Bradshaw, the Lovely, That Crowned Him with Laurel. Robert Herrick. CaPo

To Mrs. M. A. at Parting. Katherine Philips. OBF

To Mrs. M. A. upon Absence. Katherine Philips. *See* 'Tis now since I began to dy.

To Mrs. M. B. on Her Birthday. Pope. EnLoPo

To Mrs. Manley. Catherine Trotter. KTR

To Mrs. Manley, upon Her Tragedy Call'd The Royal Mischief. Mary Pix. KTR

To Mistress Margaret Tilney. John Skelton. *Fr.* Garland [*or* Garlande *or* Garlands] of Laurel[l], The. MeEL

To Mistress Margery Wentworth. John Skelton. *Fr.* Garland [*or* Garlande *or* Garlands] of Laurel[l], The. EBEV; EnLoPo; EnRePo; NOBE; OAEL-1; OBEV; TrGrPo

To Mrs. ———, on the Death of Her Husband. Hannah Wallis. ECWP

To Mistress [*or* Maystres] Isabell Pennell. John Skelton. *Fr.* Garland [*or* Garlande *or* Garlands] of Laurel[l], The. AAS; InPS; NAs; NOBE; NoSic; OBEV; OxBoLi; PoEL-1; SCGP; TrGrPo; TTTS

To Mistress [*or* Maystres] Margaret Hussey. John Skelton. *Fr.* Garland [*or* Garlande *or* Garlands] of Laurel[l], The. AAS; EBEV; EnLoPo; GGP; GN; GoJo; HoPM; InPS; NAEL-1; NBLV; NOBE; NoP; NoSic; NTP; OAEL-1; OBEV; OPOP; PeLV; PIP; PoE; PoEL-1; PoRA; PPP; SCGP; SCV; TFi; TrGrPo

To Mrs. Smith, Occasioned by the First of Her Sonnets. William Hayley. Son

To Mrs. Thrale [on Her Thirty-fifth Birthday]. Samuel Johnson. FaBoEE; NAs

To Mrs. W. on Her Excellent Verses. Aphra Behn. KTR

To Mrs. Will H. Low. Robert Louis Stevenson. NOBVV

To mock the riddle corpses round Bapaume. (*LL*) Blighters. Siegfried Sassoon. CMoP; FaBoTw; MoP; NoAM; OxBSP; PoWW

To Modigliani to Prove to Him That I Am a Poet. Max Jacob, *tr. fr. French by* Wallace Fowlie. TrJP

To Monsieur de la Mothe le Vayer. Molière, *tr. fr. French by* Austin Dobson. AWP

To Morfydd. Lionel Johnson. MoBrPo; OAEL-2; OBMV

To Morning. Blake. Fr. Milton. EnRP; OxAEP-2

To-Morrow. Lope de Vega, *tr. fr. Spanish by* Longfellow. AWP; TrPWD

To-morrow. John Masefield. MoBrPo; OtMeF; TrGrPo

To-morrow, and to-morrow, and to-morrow. Shakespeare. *Fr.* Macbeth. EBEvV; ImPo
(Hang out our banners on the outward walls. EBEV; OxAEP-1

To-morrow shall be my dancing day. My Dancing Day. *Unknown.* OxBoLi
(Tomorrow shall be my dancing day.) PoEL-1

To-morrow we're starting for Florence. Arthur Hugh Clough. *Fr.* Amours de Voyage. EBVVPR, *canto* II, xv; NOBVV

To mortal men Peace giveth these good things. Peace on Earth. Bacchylides, *tr. fr. Greek by* John Addington Symonds. AWP

To Mother. Lessie M. Drown. PWR

To Mother. Frank Horne. *Fr.* Letters [*or* Notes] Found near a Suicide. BPo; CDC; PoBA; PoNe

To Mother and Steve. Mari Evans. BPo; PoBA

To Mother Fairie. Alice Cary. OBCA

To mount the earth in my black people's time! (*LL*) Trellie. Lance Jeffers. NBV

To move over shifting borders. Eeva-Liisa Manner, *tr. fr. Finnish by* Jaakko A. Ahokas. *Fr.* Cambrian. PBWP

To move with the grace. Ode to Tennis. Paul Evans. NBrP

To Mr. Henry Lawes, Who Had Then Newly Set a Song of Mine in the Year 1635. Edmund Waller. BeJo; CTC; SeCP; SeCV-1

To Mr Thomas Griffith at the University of Glasgow, *sels.* Jane Brereton.
"You, friend, who whilom tossed the ball." ECWP

To Mrs K. T. (Who Asked Him Why He Was Dumb). John Cleveland. CBLP

To Music. Robert Herrick. CaPo

To Music. Franz von Schober, *tr. fr. German by* Philip L. Miller. RiWo

To Music: A Song. Robert Herrick. CaPo

To Music Bent Is My Retired Mind. Thomas Campion. AAS; EnRePo; NOCV; PeECV

To Music, to Becalm a Sweet-sick Youth. Robert Herrick. CaPo

To Music, to Becalm His Fever. Robert Herrick. CaPo; OBEV
Sels.
"Charm me asleep, and melt me so." BeJo; GoJo; SeCV-1

To Musicke Bent. Thomas Campion. *See* To Music Bent Is My Retired Mind.

To mute and to material things. Nelson, Pitt, Fox. Sir Walter Scott. *Fr.* Marmion. OBEV

To Mutius. Elizabeth Singer. KTR

To My Antenor, March 16, 1661/2. Katherine Philips. KTR

To My Body. Nancy Sullivan. TAP

To My Book. Ben Jonson. BeJo; FaBoVe; NAEL-1; SeCV-1

To My Brother. Louise Bogan. AiP; NYBP

To My Brother at St. John's College in Cambridge. Elizabeth Tollet. ECWP

To My Brother George. Keats. EnRP

To My Brother Hanson. W. S. Merwin. NAAL-2

To My Brothers. Keats. NAs; Son; TEP

To My Cat. Rosamund Marriott Watson. OFC

To My Child Carlino. Walter Savage Landor. NoP

To My Children Unknown, Produced by Artificial Insemination. James Kirkup. NAs

To My Cosen Mrs. Ellinor Evins. George Alsop. SCAP

To My Country. Rachel, *tr. fr. Hebrew by* Diane Mintz. PBWP

To My Cousin (C.R.) Marrying My Lady (A.). Thomas Carew. SeCP

To My Cousin Mary, for Mending My Tobacco Pouch. Francis Scott Key. OBAL

To My Daughter. James Michie. OxBSP

To My Daughter Betty. Thomas Michael Kettle. TIRV

To My Daughter Riding in the Circus Parade. Joan LaBombard. GOYP

To My Dead Brother. Clara Ann Thompson. CBWP-2

To My Dead Father. Frank O'Hara. CAPP

To My Dead Friend Ben: Johnson. Henry King. SeCP

To My Dead Sister. Momcilo Nastasijevic, *tr. fr. Serbo-Croatian by* Charles Simic. HSix

To My Dear and Loving Husband. Anne Bradstreet. AmPP; AnAmPo; ArLo; BLPL; BoWoP; EAP; FF; HAP; HeIP; KTR; LPA; NAAL-1; NIP; NOBA; NOCV; NOSC; OPOP; OxBA; OxBM; OxBSP; PoE; PoEL-3; PoLF; PrIm; SCAP; TAP; TFi; VBLP; WeW; WPE

To My Dear Friend Mr. Congreve [on His Comedy Called "The Double-Dealer"]. Dryden. EBEV; OAEL-1; OxAEP-1; PoEL-3; SeCV-2

To my dear wife. A Last Will and Testament. John Winstanley. FaBoVe; OBSV

To My Distant Beloved. Alois Jeitteles, *tr. fr. German by* the Reverend Dr. Troutbeck. TrJP

To My Dog "Blanco." Josiah Gilbert Holland. PoLF

To My Elder Brother. Liz Cashdan. NWP

To My Ever-honoured Cousin W. R. Esquire, *sels.* Phineas Fletcher. Lines Written at Cambridge, to W. R., Esquire. EIL

To My Excellent Lucasia, on Our Friendship. Katherine Philips. MeLP; NALW; NOSC; PeHV; VBLP; WPE; WPOW

To My Father. Dinah Butler. AIW

To My Father. Tony Curtis. AngWe

To My Father. W. S. Graham. FaBoTw

To My Father. Wing Tek Lum. BCF

To My Father. H. Cordelia Ray. AAP; BlSi; CBWP-3; Son

To My Father Norman Alone in the Blue Mountains. Jack Lindsay. NOBAu

To My Fellow-Mariners, March, '53. Thomas Whitbread. NYBP

To My First Born. Emma Catherine Embury. AmWP

To My First Love, My Mother. Christina Rossetti. OHIP

To my firstborn land, in the south. The Firstborn Land. Ingeborg Bachmann, *tr. fr. German by* Daniel Huws. BoWoP

To My Friend. Anne Campbell. PoToHe

To My Friend. Francis Thompson. PoA

To My Friend and Patron, M —— K ——, Esq. Lucretia Davidson. AmWP

To My Friend Butts I Write. Blake. EnRP

To My Friend, Dr. Charleton, on His Learned and Useful Works; and More Particularly This of Stone-Heng, by Him Restored to the True Founders. Dryden. SeCV-2

To my Friend G.N. from Wrest. Thomas Carew. BeJo; CaPo

To My Friend Mrs. ——, on Her Holding an Argument in Favour of the Natural Equality of Both the Sexes, *sels.* Clara Reeve. "Sacred Heliconian spring, The." ECWP

To My Friends. Stephen Berg. NaP; NYBP

To My Friends. Peter De Vries. FiBHP

To My Friends. Schiller, *tr. fr. German by* James Clarence Mangan. AWP

To My Friends, Who Ridiculed a Tender Leave-Taking. Matthew Arnold. *Fr.* Switzerland. EnVR

To My Generation. Benyamin Galai, *tr. fr. Hebrew by* Jacob Sonntag. TrJP

To My God. George Macdonald. TrPWD

To My God in His Sickness. Philip Levine. NNaP

To My Honour'd Kinsman, John Driden, of Chesterton, *sels.* Dryden. "No porter guards the passage of your door." EBEV

To My Honoured Patron Humphery Davie. Benjamin Tompson. SCAP

To My Husband. "Eliza." KTR

To My Ill Reader. Robert Herrick. CaPo

To My Inconstant Mistress [*or* Mistris]. Thomas Carew. BeJo; EnLoPo; MeLP; NOBE; SeCV-1; TFi; TrGrPo

To My Infant Daughter. Yvor Winters. VGW

To My Ingenious and Worthy Friend William Lowndes, Esq. John Gay. OBSV

To My Ingenuous Friend, R. W. Henry Vaughan. BeJo

To My Lady. E. S. Miller. Son

To My Lord Colrane, in Answer to His Complemental Verses Sent Me under the Name of Cleanor. Anne Killigrew. KTR

To My Lord Fairfax. Andrew Marvell. *Fr.* Upon Appleton House, to My Lord Fairfax. NOSC; SeCP; SeCV-1

To My Love. Amorous Lady, The. ECWP

To My Lucasia, in Defence of Declared Friendship. Katherine Philips. MeLP

To My Mere English Censurer. Ben Jonson. BeJo

To My Mistress Sitting by a River's Side; an Eddy. Thomas Carew. BeJo; CaPo

To My Mistress in My Absence. Thomas Carew. CaPo; NOSC

To My Mistris, I Burning in Love. Thomas Carew. SeCP

To My More Than Meritorious Wife. The Earl of Rochester. OxBSP

To My Most Dearly-loved Friend, Henry Reynolds, Esquire, of Poets and Poesy. Michael Drayton.

To My Mother. George Barker. *See* Most near, most dear, most loved and most far.

To My Mother. Mary Weston Fordham. CBWP-2

To My Mother. Heine, *tr. fr. German by* Matilda Dickson. AWP

To My Mother. W. E. Henley. OHCV

To My Mother. Thomas Moore. OHIP

To My Mother. Poe. OxBA; PFP

To My Mother. H. Cordelia Ray. CBWP-3

To My Mother. Hannah Senesh, *tr. fr. Yiddish by* Ruth Finer Mintz. MDDM

To My Mother. R. A. Simpson. FaBoMA

To My Mother — 1916. Donald S. Cox. NSI

To My Mother at 73. Elizabeth Jennings. NAs

To My Mother Who Endured. Liliane Richman. BTR

To My Mountain. Kathleen Raine. OxBS

To My Mouse-colored Mare. Tristan Corbière, *tr. fr. French by* C. F. MacIntyre. ErPo

To My Much Esteemed Friend on Her Play Call'd Fatal-Friendship. Lady Sarah Piers. KTR

To My Nephew, J. B. Clement Barksdale. OxBSP

To My Niece, A.M., with a New Pair of Shoes. *Unknown.* ECWP

To My Ninth Decade I Have Tottered On. Walter Savage Landor. EnRP; NAs

To My Noble Kinsman, Thomas Stanley, Esquire, on His Lyric Poems Composed by Master John Gamble. Richard Lovelace. CaPo

To My Nose. Alfred A. Forrester. BLPA

To My Old Schoolmaster. Whittier. NOBA

To My People. Edwin Seaver. TrJP

To my people it's as though he gave them a sacrifice. Eadwacer. *Unknown, tr. fr. Anglo-Saxon.* PBWP, *tr. by* Kemp Malone; WPE; Wulf and Eadwacer. BoWoP, *tr. by* Willis Barnstone *and* Elene Kolb; CIP, *ad. by* Richard Ryan; TrGrPo

To my poore reed. (*LL*) Employment ("If as a flowre doth spread and die.") George Herbert. GeHe; SeCV-1

To my prowd foe thus, sister, humblie saye. Virgil, *tr. by* the Earl of Surrey. *Fr.* Aeneid [*or* Eneados], The. NAWM-1; OBVE

To my revenge and to her desperate fears. The Bubble; a Song. Robert Herrick. CaPo

To My Reverend Dear Brother, M. Samuel Stone. John Cotton. SCAP

To My Setter, Scout. Frank H. Seldon. BLPA

To My Sister. Olga Berggolts, *tr. fr. Russian.* BoWoP, *tr. by* Daniel Weissbort

To My Sister. Wordsworth. ArLo; EnRP; OAEL-2

To My Son, *sels.* George Barker. "My darkling child the stars have obeyed." TwCP

To My Son. Byron. NAs

To My Son. Margaret Johnston Grafflin. PoToHe

To My Son. *Unknown.* PoLF

To My Son, Aged Three Years and Five Months. Thomas Hood. *See* Thou happy, happy elf!

To My Son Parker, Asleep in the Next Room. Bob Kaufman. PoBA; TwCP; VGW

To My Tortoise Chronos. Eugene Lee-Hamilton. FM

To my true king I offered free from stain. A Jacobite's Epitaph. Macaulay. FaBoEH; FaPoR; NOBE; OBEV; OBNC (Epitaph on a Jacobite. EBEV; NOBVV; OxAEP-2; PAW

To My Truly Valiant, Learned Friend, Who in His Book Resolved the Art Gladiatory into the Mathematics. Richard Lovelace. CaPo; PoEL-3

To my twin who lives in a cruel country. The Dual Site. Michael Hamburger. TwCP

To My Unborn Son. Cyril Morton Thorne. BLPA

To My Unknown Friend. Irina Ratushinskaya, *tr. fr. Russian by* David McDuff. AIW

To my village fair no lass can compare. The Lovely Village Fair; or, I Dont Mean to Tell You Her Name. *Unknown.* CoMu

To My Wife. J. V. Cunningham. VCAP

To My Wife. Clarence Day. OxBM

To My Wife. John Willis Menard. AAP

To My Worthy and Honoured Friend, Mr George Chapman, On His Translation of Hesiod's *Works and Days.* Ben Jonson. EPCY

To My Worthy Friend Master George Sands [*or* Sandys], on His Translation of the Psalms. Thomas Carew. BeJo; CaPo; EPCY; JCP; MeLP; SeCV-1

To My Worthy Friend Master [Mr] Peter Lely. Richard Lovelace. CaPo; NOSC

To My Worthy Friend, Mr. James Bayley. Nicholas Noyes. SCAP

To My Younger Brother, *sels.* Tu Fu, *tr. fr. Chinese by* A. C. Graham. "Rumours that you lodge in a mountain temple." PLT

To My Youngest Kinsman, R. L. Abraham Chear. OxBChV

To Myra. Fulke Greville. *See* I, with whose colors [*or* colours] Myra dressed [*or* dress'd] her head.

To Myself, after Forty Years. T. H. White. NYBP

To Naso. Catullus, *tr. fr. Latin by* Jack Lindsay. ErPo

To Nature. Samuel Taylor Coleridge. ArNa; OAEL-2

To Nature, in her shop one day, at work compounding simples. Filling an Order. John Townsend Trowbridge. AnAmPo; OBAL

To Nature Seekers. Robert W. Chambers. MoShBr

To Ned. Herman Melville. NAAL-1; NOBA; PoEL-5

To New York. Léopold Sédar-Senghor, *tr. fr. French by* Ulli Beier. PBA

To Night. Thomas Lovell Beddoes. Son

To Night. Shelley. AWP; EnRP; FHYEP; MeMBP; NAEL-2; NoP; OAEL-2; OBNC; PlP; PoLF; PoRA; TEP; TFi; TrGrPo; WiR

To Night. Joseph Blanco White. EBEV; OBEV; OxAEP-2; Son; WGRP

To-night I do not come to conquer thee. Anguish. Stéphane Mallarmé, *tr. fr. French by* Arthur Symons. AWP

To-night I saw three maidens on the beach. Ibant Obscuræ. Thomas Edward Brown. OBNC

To-night is a midnight meeting, and the Earl is in the chair. George R. Sims. *Fr.* Two Women. UV

To night puts on perfection, and a womans name. (*LL*) Epithalamion Made at Lincolnes Inne. John Donne. SeCP

To-night retir'd the queen of heaven. Ode to the Evening Star. Mark Akenside.

(Nightingale, The.) OBEV

(To the Evening Star.) PoEL-3

To Night, the Mother of Sleep and Death. John Addington Symonds. Son

To-night the very horses springing by. Winter Evening. Archibald Lampman. NOBC

To-night the Winds Begin. Tennyson. *Fr.* In Memoriam A. H. H. EBVV, *abr.*; GTBS-P; ImPo; LiTB; NOBE; OAEL-2, *abr.*; OBNC; PeECV, *abr.*; PoEL-5

To-night the winds begin to rise. To-night the Winds Begin. Tennyson. *Fr.* In Memoriam A. H. H. EBVV, *abr.*; GTBS-P; ImPo; LiTB; NOBE; OAEL-2, *abr.*; OBNC; PeECV, *abr.*; PoEL-5

(Tonight the winds begin to rise.) PeECV, *sect.* XV

To-night this sunset spreads two golden wings. Sunset Wings. Dante Gabriel Rossetti. FM

To-night we strive to read, as we may best. Longfellow. *Fr.* John Endicott. PAH

To no delta at sea-level. (*LL*) The River's Elegy. Aidan Carl Mathews. IB

To no one Muse does she her glance confine. On a Squinting Poetess. Thomas Moore. FaBoCo

To Nobodaddy. Blake. OAEL-2

To Noel. Gabriela Mistral, *tr. fr. Spanish by* Doris Dana. PChr

To Noël Coward. Noël Coward. FaBoPa

To nothing fitter can I thee compare. Michael Drayton. *Fr.* Idea. EIL; ESo; SCGP; Son; TrGrPo

To Nye Bevan Despite His Change of Heart. Adrian Mitchell. IHNG

To Nysus. Sir Charles Sedley. FaBoEE; OBSV

To O. E. A. Claude McKay. BPo

To Odelia. James Shirley. BeJo

To Oenone. Robert Herrick. CaPo; OBEV

To Old Age. Walt Whitman. Spl

To Olive. Lord Alfred Bruce Douglas. OBEV

To Olivia. Francis Thompson. MoBrPo

To One Black, and Not Very Handsome, Who Expected Commendation. Lord Herbert of Cherbury. NOSC

To One Elect. S. I. Hayakawa. PoA

To one fair Lady out of Court. The Challenge. Pope. PoEL-3

To One in Bedlam. Ernest Dowson. MoBrPo; OBMV; Son

To One in Beirut. Karen Alkalay-Gut. WoWa

To one in love with solitude and song. (*LL*) Echoes. Emma Lazarus. AmWP

To One in Paradise. Poe. *Fr.* Assignation, The. AmPP; AnAmPo; BLPL; BoLoP; LiTA; OBEV; OxBA; PoLF; TAP; TrGrPo

To one kneeling down no word came. In a Country Church. R. S. Thomas. FaBoMo; TOF

To One Married to an Old Man. Edmund Waller. FaBoEE; OxBSP; SeCP

To One Persuading a Lady to Marriage. Katherine Philips. *See* Forbear, bold youth, all's heaven here.

To One That Ask'd Me Why I Lov'd J. G. sels. "Ephelia." Why Do I Love? CBCK

To One That Asked Me Why I Loved J. G. "Ephelia." KTR; NOSC; VBLP

To One That Desired To Know My Mistris. Thomas Carew. SeCP

To One That Pleaded Her Own Want of Merit. Thomas Stanley.

To One Unequally Matched. Walter Savage Landor. CBLP

To One Who Died in a Garret in Cardiff. Huw Menai. AngWe

To One Who Had Censured His Public Exposition of Dante. Boccaccio, *tr. fr. Italian by* Dante Gabriel Rossetti. *Fr.* Sonnets. AWP

To one who has been long in city pent. Keats. BLPA; EnRP; FaBoBe; FHYEP; ImPo; LiTB; MeMBP; TrGrPo

To One Who Has Been Long in City Pent. To one who has been long in city pent. Keats. BLPA; EnRP; FaBoBe; FHYEP; ImPo; LiTB; MeMBP; TrGrPo

To One Who Quotes and Detracts. Walter Savage Landor. FaBoEE

To One Who Said I Must Not Love. Sarah Fyge Egerton. ECWP

To One Who Sleepeth. Mary E. Tucker. CBWP-1

To One Who Was with Me in the War. Siegfried Sassoon. NSI

To onpreise women it were a shame. A Woman Is a Worthy Thing. *Unknown.* FaBoCo; GBP

(Women Are Worthy.) MeEL

To orisons, the midnight bell. William Beckford. OBTV

To other eyes and ears you are a great. Bernard O'Dowd. *Fr.* Bush, The. CBAP

To Others Than You. Dylan Thomas. MeMBP

To Our Blessed Lady. Henry Constable. NoSic

To Our Blessed Lord upon the Choice of His Sepulchre. Richard Crashaw. GeHe; NOSC

To Our Daughter. Jennifer Armitage. BrRo

To our homes, to our labours. We Must Return. Agostinho Neto, *tr. fr. Portuguese by* Michael Wolfers. PeSAV

To Our House-Dog Captain. Walter Savage Landor. PoEL-4

To Our Lord, upon the Water Made Wine. Richard Crashaw. GeHe

To our mother, maimed. American Rain. Marilyn Chin. OpBo

To our ruined vineyards come. Love Song for the Future. Vassar Miller. PRA

To our theme. — The man who has stood on the Acropolis. Byron. *Fr.* Don Juan. InPS; OBSV

To own nothing, but to be. Words Spoken Alone. Dannie Abse. NYBP

To Oxford. Gerard Manley Hopkins. FaBoPP

To Oxford. Thomas Russell. Son

To Paint the [or a] Portrait of a Bird. Jacques Prévert, *tr. fr. French by* Michael Benedikt.

To Pallas, three girls, all of an age, skilled as the spider. Antipater of Sidon, *tr. fr. Greek by* Barbara Hughes Fowler. *Fr.* Epigrams. HePo

To Pallas, Theris, cunning of hand, dedicated. Leonidas of Tarentum, *tr. fr. Greek by* Barbara Hughes Fowler. *Fr.* Epigrams. HePo

To Pan. John Fletcher. *See* All ye woods, and trees, and bowers.

To Pan the forest-ranger, Gelo the hunter. Philip of Thessalonica, *tr. fr. Greek by* Edwin Morgan. GrAn

To Pan three brothers hung up these tools of the trade. Antipater of Sidon, *tr. fr. Greek by* Barbara Hughes Fowler. *Fr.* Epigrams. HePo

To Pandora. Alexander Craig. *See* Go you, O winds that blow from north to south.

To Paris that was once her owne though now it be not so. Ovid, *tr. fr. Latin by* George Turberville. *Fr.* Heroides. OBVE

To Parker. George Turberville. OBTV

To pass all men's believing. (*LL*) An Immorality. Ezra Pound. CMoP; GoJo; GrPl; ImPo; LiTM; MoAB; MoAmPo; NOBA; OBAL

To Pass the Place Where Pleasure Is. *Unknown.* CoMu

To pay their taxes. (*LL*) The Old Cowboy. Kao Ch'i. OHMPC

To Peace. Richard Watson Dixon. OxAEP-2

To Penshurst. (Thou art not, Penshurst, built to envious show.) Ben Jonson. AWP; BeJo; FaBoPP; JCP; NAEL; NIP; NoP; NOSC; OAEL-1; PoEL-2; PPP; SeCP; SeCV-1; TEP; TFi

Sels.

"Thy copp's, too, nam'd of Gamage, thou hast there." FM

To people who allege that we. The Uses of Ocean. Sir Owen Seaman. FiBHP

To Percy Shelley: On the Degrading Notions of Deity. Leigh Hunt. Son

To Perilla. Robert Herrick. BeJo; CaPo; NOSC; SCGP; SeCP; SeCV-1

To perish, or to live? (*LL*) 'Twas like a maelstrom, with a notch. Emily Dickinson. CMoP; LiTM; PoE

To Pertinax Cob. Ben Jonson. BeJo; JCP

To Pete Atkin: A Letter from Paris, sels. Clive James.

"Weather's cleared, The. We're filming at Versailles." OBSV

To Peter, Bishop of Poitiers, Who Withstood William of Aquitaine and Died in Exile. Hildebert, *tr. fr. Latin by* Helen Waddell. MLL

To Petronius Arbiter. Oliver St. John Gogarty. OBMV

To Phaedrus. Jovan Hristic, *tr. fr. Serbo-Croatian by* Charles Simic. HSix

To Philaster. Sarah Fyge Egerton. ECWP

To Sir Philip Sidney's Soul. Henry Constable. *See* Give pardon, blessèd soul, to my bold cries.

To Phillis. Edmund Waller. SeCP

To Philomela. Benjamin Colman. SCAP

To Phoebus. Martial, *tr. fr. Latin.* PeHV

To Phryne. Owen Felltham [*or* Feltham]. NOSC

To Phyllis. Edmund Waller. BeJo; TrGrPo

To Phyllis, to Love and Live with Him. Robert Herrick. CaPo

To Phylocles, Inviting Him to Friendship. "Ephelia." KTR; NOSC; WPE

To pink your flesh. (*LL*) The Search. Nancy Peterson. LoHo

To Piso, on Epicurus' Birthday. Philodemus, *tr. fr. Greek by* William Moebius. GrAn

To place one's little boy — just so. Archery. Walter de la Mare. FaBoNo

To plant three roses for you each one only a dollar. Third Ode to Persephone. Robert Kelly. *Fr.* Book of Persephone, The. PoM

To play on the fiddle and dance. (*LL*) The Weasel. *Unknown.* ChTr; CoGr

To play with fools, O what a fool was I! (*LL*) If Women Could Be Fair. Edward de Vere, Earl of Oxford. EIL; NoSic

To please the gray-haired boys. (*LL*) The Old Man Dreams. Oliver Wendell Holmes. AnAmPo; BLPL; PoLF

To Poet Edmund Waller, Occasioned for His Writing a Panegyric on Oliver Cromwell. Charles Cotton. EPCY

To Poets. George Darley. Son

To Poets. Walter Savage Landor. FaBoEE

To poll their tops that seek such change and gape for joy. (LL) The Doubt of Future Foes. Elizabeth I, Queen of England. CTC; NAEL-1; NALW; NoSic; PBWP; WPE

To popularize the mule, its neat exterior. The Labors of Hercules. Marianne Moore. MeMAP; OxBA

To Pose a Chicken. Judith C. Root. PRA

To practice for Eternity. (LL) Bearded Oaks. Robert Penn Warren. LiTM; MoAmPo; MoP; NAAL-2; NoAM; NOBA; PoA; PoE; TAP; TwCP

To Praise. Ellen Bass. CrSp

To praise the blue whale's crystal jet. The Whale, His Bulwark. Derek Walcott. OxBC; TTY

To praise thy life or wail thy worthy death. Epitaph on Sir Philip Sidney. At. to Sir Walter Ralegh. SiPS
(Epitaph upon the right Honourable Sir Philip Sidney Knight, Lord Governor of Flushing, An.) SiPSBD

To pray you open your whole self. Eagle Poem. Joy Harjo. CrSp; HATNAP; WeW

To preserve our precious planet. (LL) Water flows over these hands. Thich Nhat Hanh. EaPr

To President Bush at the Start of the Gulf War. Robert Bly. RaBo

To Priapos. Unknown, tr. fr. Greek by Guy Davenport. GrAn

To Primroses Filled with Morning Dew. Robert Herrick. SeCV-1

To Prince Charles. Sir William Alexander. ScCV

To princke me up, and make me higher plaste. (LL) And every yeare a worlde my will did deeme. George Gascoigne. AAS

To prink me up and make me higher placed. George Gascoigne. Fr. Gascoigne's Memories. EnRePo; Son

To prinke me up and make me higher plaste. George Gascoigne. AAS

To print, or not to print — that is the question. Hamlet's Soliloquy Imitated. Richard Jago. BXAP; FaBoCo; FaBoPa

To print our poems the propulsive cause. Fame Makes Us Forward. Robert Herrick. CaPo

To Professor Byrd Prillerman. Maggie Pogue Johnson. CBWP-4

To promise, pause, prepare, postpone. Winthrop Mackworth Praed. FaBoEH

To Prote. Simmias of Thebes, tr. fr. Greek by John Addington Symonds. AWP

To prove himself no plagiary, Moore. On J. M. S. Gent. Pope. FaBoEE

To prove thy days but dream and slumber. (LL) Omnia Somnia. Joshua Sylvester. FaBoEE

To pull the metal splinter from my palm. The Gift. Li-Young Lee. OpBo; RaBo

To Purity and Truth. Unknown, tr. fr. Chinese by William C. White. TrJP

To put off a decision. No Easy Harbour. Anne Hartigan. CIP

To put out the word, whore, thou dost me woo. To a Friend. Ben Jonson. BeJo

To Pyrrha. Horace. See What slender youth bedewed with liquid odours.

To Queen Anne on a New Year's Day 1604. Sir Robert Ayton. ScCV

To quench their lewd fire. On George I. Unknown. IHNG

To quicklime and to clay. (LL) The Man from Strathbogie. Olive Mary Finnin. NOBAu

To R. B. Gerard Manley Hopkins. CMoP; EnVR; EPCY; GTBS-P; InvP; OAEL-2; OxAEP-2

To R. Hudson. Alexander Montgomerie. OxBS

To R. K. James Kenneth Stephen. BXAP; FaBoCo; FaBoEE; FaBoPa; NBLV; NOBL; OtMeF; PeLV; UV

To rack and torture thy unmeaning brain. On the Supposed Author of a Late Poem "In Defense of Satire." The Earl of Rochester. APAS

To rail or jest, ye know I use it not. Sir Thomas Wyatt. SiPS

To Raja Rao. Czeslaw Milosz. TOF

To ramble through field and forest. The Poet. Goethe, tr. fr. German by Philip L. Miller. RiWo

To reach it. Waterfall. Anne Welsh. PeSA

To reach it, a ladder has to be set up. Inventory. Jorge Luis Borges, tr. fr. Spanish by Alastair Reid. CBCK

To read it well: that is, to understand. (LL) To the Reader. Ben Jonson. BeJo; NoP; PoE; SeCV-1

To read my book[e], the virgin shy [or shie]. To His Book[e]. Martial, tr. fr. Latin by Robert Herrick. AWP; OBVE

To read our few poets. Ode. Hugh Maxton. PBCIP

To Redouté. John Ashbery. PoA

To Remain. C. P. Cavafy, tr. fr. Modern Greek by John Mavrogordato. ErPo

To Remain. C. P. Cavafy, tr. fr. Modern Greek by Nikos Stangos and Stephen Spender. BoLoP

To remember is not always to go back to what was. Time Reminded Me. Julia Uceda, tr. fr. Spanish by Willis Barnstone. BoWoP

To remember that, so far, you've returned. (LL) Off to Patagonia. Theodore Weiss. AnAn; TAP

To remember with tears! (LL) Four Ducks on a Pond. William Allingham. EBEvV; NOBVV; NOIV; OxAEP-2

To reply, in face of a bad season. The Ill Wind. Jay Macpherson. MoCV

To resemble these horses is no cause for pride. (LL) The Blinkered Mind. Amy Witting. NOBAu

To Rest! Justinus Kerner, tr. fr. German by Philip L. Miller. RiWo

To rest, to rest. To REST!. Justinus Kerner, tr. fr. German by Philip L. Miller. RiWo

To Restore a Dead Child, sels. Edwin Honig.
1925. NoAM

To Retiredness. Mildmay Fane, 2d Earl of Westmorland. BeJo; NOSC

To Retirement. Luis de León, tr. fr. Spanish by Thomas Walsh. TrJP

To Rev. Thaddeus Saltus. Mary Weston Fordham. CBWP-2

To Richard Boyle, Earl of Burlington: Of the Uses of Riches. Pope. Fr. Moral Essays. NOEC; OAEL-1; OBSV; PoEL-3; PPP

To Sir Richard Fanshawe, Upon His Translation of Pastor Fido, sels. Sir John Denham.
"That servile path thou nobly dost decline." EPCY

To Richard Wright. Conrad Kent Rivers. PoBA

To riddle me that. (LL) Land was white, The. Unknown. ChTr; FaBoVe; ISE; OxNR

To Ride. Paul Éluard, tr. fr. French by Kenneth Koch. TTTS

To ride piggy-back. Slave. Langston Hughes. LiTM

To robbers furious, and to lovers tame. Samuel Johnson, after the Latin of Joachim du Bellay. FaBoEE

To Robert Browning. Walter Savage Landor. EnRP; EPCY; NoP

To Robert Louis Stevenson. W. E. Henley. MoBrPo

To Robert Nichols. Robert Graves. PeFWW

To Sir Robert Wroth. Ben Jonson. BeJo; SeCV-1

To Robin Redbreast. Robert Herrick. PoE; TrGrPo

To Robinson Jeffers. Czeslaw Milosz, tr. fr. Polish by the author and Richard Lourie. AnRep

To Rosamond. Chaucer. NoP

To Rosamound. Chaucer. See Madame, ye been [or ben] of alle [or all or al] beautee [or beaute] shrine [or shryne].

To Rosemounde, sels. Chaucer.
"Ma dame, ye ben of all beauté shrine." EnVB

To Roses in the Bosom[e] of Castara. Fr. Castara. BeJo; EnLoPo; MeLP; NOSC; OBEV; SCGP; SeCP

To Rotenham. August, Graf von Platen, tr. fr. German by Reginald Bancroft Cooke. PeHV

To row you on the tide. (LL) The Royal Fisherman. Unknown. ChTr; GBP

To S. A. Thomas Edward Lawrence. PeHV

To S. C. Robert Louis Stevenson. PeVV

To S. R. Crockett. Robert Louis Stevenson. Fr. Songs of Travel. CoGr; OBNC

To S. R. Crockett. Robert Louis Stevenson. See Blows the Wind Today.

To S. T. C. on His 179th Birthday, October 12th, 1951. Maurice Carpenter. FaBoTw

To safeguard man from wrongs, there nothing must. Distrust. Robert Herrick. CaPo

To Saffold's Customers. At. to John Case. FaBoUs

To St. Augustine. "Angelus Silesius," tr. fr. German. Fr. Cherubical Wanderer, The. GePo, tr. by George C. Schoolfield

To Saint Margaret. Henry Constable. NoSic

To Saint Mary Magdalen ("Blessed Offendour: who thyself haist try'd.") Henry Constable. NoSic; PoEL-2; Son

To St. Michael the Archangel. Henry Constable. ChIV-2

To St. Peter and St. Paul. Henry Constable. NoSic; Son

To Sally. John Quincy Adams, after Horace. AWP; OBAL

To Sally. Horace. See Virtue, dear friends, needs no 'defense.'

To Samuel, Bishop of Sens In Time of Dearth. Alcuin, tr. fr. Latin by Helen Waddell. MLL

To San Francisco. S. J. Alexander. PAH

To Satch. Samuel Allen. PoBA; PoNe; TTY

To save the Athenian walls from ruin bare. (LL) When the Assault Was Intended to the City. Milton. GTBS; GTBS-P; NoP; SCGP; Son

To save your world, you asked this man to die. Epitaph for the Unknown Soldier. W. H. Auden. FaBoCo

To Saxham. Thomas Carew. BeJo; CaPo; JCP; NoP

To say I failed, that is walked out. Brass Furnace Going Out: Song, after an Abortion. Diane Di Prima. PoBeRe

To say it once held daisies and bluebells. The Broken Bowl. James Merrill. PoA

To scare myself with my own desert places. (*LL*) Desert Places. Robert Frost. AmPP; CMoP; InPK; MoAB; MoAmPo; MoP; NAAL-2; NoAM; NOBA; OxBA; PoE; PPP; RB; SoSe; TAP; TRP; UnPo

To Schmidlein. August, Graf von Platen, *tr. fr. German* by Reginald Bancroft Cooke. PeHV

To School! Stevie Smith. FaBoEE

To Science. Poe. AnAmPo; Son

To Scilla. Sir Charles Sedley. FaBoEE

To Scott. Winifred M. Letts. PoLF

To scratch for their own bread. (*LL*) The Old Gray Goose. *Unknown.* AmFP; GBP

To scrutinize the future like a sunset! Half in Love. Rachel Hadas. UnDi

To scug his deadly sin. (*LL*) Young Benjie. *Unknown.* ESPB; OxBB

To Sea. Thomas Lovell Beddoes. *Fr.* Death's Jest Book. CH

To sea, to sea! The calm is o'er. To Sea. Thomas Lovell Beddoes. *Fr.* Death's Jest Book. CH
(Sailors' Song.) OxAEP-2

To Secretary Lu Ch'ien of Jen City. Li Po, *tr. fr. Chinese* by Joseph J. Lee. SuSp

To see a strange [*or* quaint] outlandish fowl. The Bounty of Our Age. Henry Farley. FaBoCh; FaBoEE; NOSC

To See a world in a grain of sand. Auguries of Innocence. Blake. *Fr.* Auguries of Innocence. BLPL; CoGr, *ll.* 1–58; EBEV; EBEvV, *ll.* 1–58; EnlH, *ll.* 1–58; EnRP; FaBoCh; FaBV; FaPoR; FM; ImPo; InPK; LiTB; MeMBP; NTP; OAEL-1; OBNC; OtMeF; OxAEP-2; OxBoLi; PeECV, *ll.* 1–58; PlP; PoEL-4; TFi; TrGrPo; WGRP

To see both blended in one flood. Upon the Infant Martyrs. Richard Crashaw. GeHe; NoP; OAEL-1

To see her is a picture. Emily Dickinson. PeHV

To see her red coats marching from the hill. (*LL*) Gibraltar. Wilfrid Scawen Blunt. OBEV

To see if I could be consoled. Asturiana. Manuel de Falla, *tr. fr. Spanish* by Philip L. Miller. RiWo

To see may lady joyful in her place. (*LL*) Of His Lady in Heaven. Jacopo da Lentino. AWP

To see my father. Golden State. Frank Bidart. NoAM

To See Ol' Booker T. Maggie Pogue Johnson. CBWP-4

To see such dainty ghosts as you appear. On Meeting a Gentlewoman in the Dark. *Unknown.* FaBoEE

To see that fair lady. (*LL*) Edom o' Gordon. *Unknown.* OxBB

To see the abysses of the human heart. (*LL*) The Heart's Abysses. Walter Savage Landor. FaBoEE; OBSV

To see the cherry hung with snow. (*LL*) Loveliest of Trees [the Cherry Now]. A. E. Housman. ArNa; AWP; BLPL; BoNaP; ChTr; ClHu; CMoP; ELP; FaBoBe; FaBV; FaPoB; FF; HAP; InPK; LiTB; LiTM; MeMBP; MoAB; MoBrPo; MoP; NAs; NoAM; NoP; OAEL-2; OHIP; OxBTC; PoE; Poetr; PoLF; PrIm; RB; SoSe; TEP; TFi; TrGrPo

To See the Cross at Christmas. Roger Cooper. TrCP

To see the greatness of a mountain, one must keep one's distance. Lama Govinda. EaPr

To see the land I love. (*LL*) Night Journey. Theodore Roethke. GOA; NYBP

To see the lark, delighted, dare. Bernard de Ventadour, *tr. fr. French* by John Frederick Nims. STV

To see the lizard there. Jerome in Solitude. James Wright. AnAn

To see the Moscow-bound express withdraw. The Poetry of Motion. Raymond Garlick. AngWe

To see the parliament soldiers go by. (*LL*) The Parliament Soldiers. *Unknown.* GBP

To see them coming headstrong. In Love with the Bears. Greg Kuzma. NYBP

To see them go by drowning in the river. Eli, Eli. Judith Wright. CBAP

To see them so; fleshed, fair, erected indivisible. (*LL*) The Imaginary Iceberg. Elizabeth Bishop. FaBoWP; ImPo; LiTM; MoAB; MoAmPo

To see these lines writ for his epitaph. (*LL*) Like to the Thundering Tone. Richard Corbett [*or* Corbet]. OxBB

To see what my black hen doth lay. (*LL*) Higgledy, piggledy, my black hen. Mother Goose. FaBoBe

To see who made those ringing noises in the summer bay. (*LL*) Glen Lough. Geoffrey Grigson. FaBoPP; OBTV

To see you, is more than food or drink. (*LL*) So small are the flowers of Seamu. *Unknown.* BoWoP; PBWP

To seek each where where man doth live. Sir Thomas Wyatt. SiPS

To seek new lechery in Death. (*LL*) An Epitaph on M. H. Charles Cotton. EBEV; FaBoEE; OPOP

To Seem the Stranger. Gerard Manley Hopkins. *See* To Seem the Stranger Lies My Lot (My Life).

To Seem the Stranger Lies My Lot (My Life). Gerard Manley Hopkins. MeMBP

To Senaca Lake. James Gates Percival. BoTP

To Send Away Melancholy. Huang Tsun-hsien, *tr. fr. Chinese* by An-yan Tang. SuSp

To Senna Hoy. Else Lasker-Schüler, *tr. fr. German* by Glauco Cambon. IMW

To Sergius. Sir Charles Sedley. FaBoEE

To serve Thee is to reign. (*LL*) Put Forth, O God, Thy Spirit's Might. Howard Chandler Robbins. AH; TrPWD

To set before the king? (*LL*) Sing a song of sixpence. Mother Goose. FaBoBe; OxNR

To Sextus. Martial, *tr. fr. Latin* by Sir Charles Sedley. FaBoEE

To Shades of Underground. Thomas Campion, *after the Latin of* Propertius. *See* When thou must home to shades of underground.

To shadow from shine. (*LL*) Romancero. Lex Banning. NOBAu

To shadows and delusions here. (*LL*) The Indian Burying Ground. Philip Freneau. AmPP; AnAmPo; EAP; HAP; LiTA; NAAL-1; NOBA; NoP; OBD, *abr.;* OxBA; PoEL-4; PoLF; TAP; TFi

To shaggy Pan, and all the Wood-Nymphs fair. A Shepherd's Gift. Anyte, *tr. fr. Greek* by John William Burgon. AWP

To Shakespeare. Hartley Coleridge. EPCY

To Shakespeare. Hart Crane. Son

To Shakespeare. Thomas Edwards. Son

To Shakespeare. Fanny Kemble. Son

To sharpen others when themselves are blunt. (*LL*) Ad Tusserum. *Unknown.* FaBoUs

To shave, or not to shave? that is the question. T. F. Dillon Crocker. BXAP

To shock-haired Pan and the nymphs who protect the cow-byres. Anyte, *tr. fr. Greek* by John Heath-Stubbs *and* Carol A. Whiteside. GrAn

To shoot, to shoot, would be my delight. A Shooting Song. William Brighty Rands. OxBChV

To SHOUT/ RAVE/ RANT/ and RAGE is being militant. A Few Blue Words to the Wise. Ted Joans. PoBeRe

To Show How Humble. *Unknown.* AH

To show that still she lives. (*LL*) The Harp That Once through Tara's Halls. Thomas Moore. BLPL; EnRP; FaPoR; GN; NAEL-2; OBNC; PoLF

To show the laboring [*or* lab'ring] bosom's deep intent. To S.M., a Young African Painter, on Seeing His Works. Phillis Wheatley. BlSi; NAAL-1

To show the unchanging shamelessness of bone. (*LL*) Love and Murder. Roy Fuller. CBLP

To shred them: a narrow labor, and simply toss. Destruction of Letters. Babette Deutsch. WPE

To shut one human soul from hope. (*LL*) God of the strong, God of the weak. Richard Watson Gilder. TrPWD

To Sickness. Ben Jonson. BeJo

To Sidmouth and Castlereagh. Shelley. *See* As from an [*or* their] ancestral oak.

To sigh and mone. (*LL*) My Lute and I. Sir Thomas Wyatt. MeEL; SiPS

To Silence. Thomas Lovell Beddoes. Son

To Simplicity. Samuel Taylor Coleridge. *Fr.* Sonnets Attempted in the Manner of Contemporary Writers. FaBoPa; Son

To simulate the burning of the heart, the humiliation. Patrizia Cavalli, *tr. fr. Italian* by Judith Baumel. NeIt

To sin, unshamed, to lose, unthinking. Russia. Alexander Blok, *tr. fr. Russian* by Babette Deutsch *and* Avrahm Yarmolinsky. AWP

To sing of wars, of captain[e]s, and of kings. Anne Bradstreet. BoWoP; EAP; NAAL-1; NALW; NOBA; OxBA; PoE; SCAP; TAP; WPE

To sing some pleasant song. (*LL*) Marvel [*or* Marvaill] no more although [*or* all tho]. Sir Thomas Wyatt. SiPSBD

To sin's a vice in nature, and we find. Daniel Defoe. *Fr.* More Reformation. OBSV

To sit composing like a sunlit ghost. The Table. Michael Heffernan. PoA

To Sit in Solemn Silence. W. S. Gilbert. *Fr.* Mikado, The. FiBHP

To sit on a shelf in the cabin across the lake. What Good Poems Are For. Tom Wayman. NoP

To sit people on gas-stove jets. The Mother-in-Law of the Marquis de Sade. Jennifer Maiden. NOBAu

To sit silent. Otomo No Tabito, *tr. fr. Japanese* by Arthur Waley. TAL

To skedaddle on up the promontory. (*LL*) Simultaneous Stories. Matthew Sweeney. IB

To Sleep. Giovanni della Casa, *tr. fr. Italian* by John Addington Symonds. AWP

To Sleep. John Fletcher. *See* Care-charming Sleep [Thou Easer of All Woes].

To Sleep. Keats. ChTr; EBEvV; EnRP; FaBoRV; MeMBP; NIP; OBEV; PlP; PoEL-4; PrIm; Son; TEP

To Sleep. Sir Philip Sidney. *See* Come sleepe, O sleepe, the certaine knot of peace.

To Sleep. Charlotte Smith. Son; WPE

To Sleep. Wordsworth. EnRP; GTBS; GTBS-P; TrGrPo

To sleep easy all night. *Unknown.* OxNR

To sleep ("Fond words have oft been spoken to thee, sleep!") Wordsworth. Son

To sleep here, I play dead. Ia Drang Valley. Yusef Komunyakaa. MT

To sleep I give my powers away. Tennyson. *Fr.* In Memoriam A. H. H. EBVV, *abr.*; EnVR; OAEL-2, *abr.*; PeECV, *abr.*

To Sleep ("O gentle sleep! do they belong to thee"). Wordsworth. Son

To S.M., a Young African Painter, on Seeing His Works. Phillis Wheatley. BlSi; NAAL-1

To sniff at a green plum. (*LL*) Tune: Crimson Lips Adorned. Li Ch'ing-chao. PBWP, *tr.* by C. H. Kwôck *and* Vincent McHugh

To So-kin of Rakuyo, ancient friend, Chancellor of Gen. Exile's Letter. Li Po, *tr. fr. Chinese by* Ezra Pound. CTC; FaBoMo; OxBA

To Soar in Freedom and in Fullness of Power. Walt Whitman. RFM

To Softness. Laurie Sheck. CrSp

To Solitude. Alice Cary. AmWP

To Solitude. Keats. *See* O Solitude! if I must with thee dwell.

To Some Millions Who Survive Joseph E. Mander, Sr. Sarah E. Wright. PoBA

To Some Supposed Brothers. Essex Hemphill. GLP

To Song. Olga Berggolts, *tr. fr. Russian by* Daniel Weissbort. BoWoP

To soothe my lady's dreams. (*LL*) Linnet in the rocky dells, The. Emily Brontë. HAP; OBNC

To Soulfolk. Margaret Goss Burroughs. BlSi

To Spain — a Last Word. Edith M. Thomas. PAH

To spare my sack of coals. (*LL*) Winter. J. M. Synge. NOIV; OBMV; OxBTC

To speak in a flat voice. Speak. James Wright. HAP; SM; TAP

To speak in summer in a lecture hall. Lecture Hall. Patrick Kavanagh. FaBoTw

To Speak of Woe That Is in Marriage. Robert Lowell. CAPP; MoP; NAAL-2; NoAM

To speak out clean. Telling It. Nancy Sullivan. TAP

To Spencer. George Turberville. NoSic; OBTV

To spend uncounted years of pain. Arthur Hugh Clough. EnVR; NOBVV; OBNC; OxBSP

To Spenser. John Hamilton Reynolds. Son

To spider in our dirt-filled eyes. (*LL*) Osip Mandelstam. Seamus Deane. BiHa; PBCIP

To split my worship too in twain. (*LL*) Stella's Birth-day, 1718/19. Swift. EnLoPo; NAs

To spoil the first impression. (*LL*) To His Saviour, a Child; a Present, by a Child. Robert Herrick. BeJo; ChIV-2; OHIP; PeECV; SeCP; TrCP

To Spring. Blake. BLPL; BoNaP; BoTP; EnRP; MeMBP; NAEL-2; NOEC; OAEL-2; OBEV; PoEL-4; PoLF; PPP; SCGP; WiR

To Spring. Charlotte Smith. WPE

To St John Baptist. Henry Constable. ChIV-2; NoSic

To St Mary Magdalen. Henry Constable. ChIV-2; NoSic

To stain the stiff dishonored shroud. (*LL*) Sweeney among the Nightingales. T. S. Eliot. AmPP; AnAmPo; CMoP; FaBoMo; HAP; HeIP; InvP; LiTA; LiTM; MoP; NAAL-2; NAEL-2; NoAM; NOBA; NOBE; NoP; OBMV; OxBA; Poetr; PPP; TFi; WeW

To stand hushed an hour or so. Bruce Beaver. *Fr.* Lauds and Plaints. FaBoMA

To stand on common ground. A Common Ground. Denise Levertov. PoM

To stand — to advance — and after all to stand! (*LL*) Autumnal Ode. Aubrey Thomas De Vere. OBNC

To Stand Up Straight. A. E. Housman. OAEL-2

To stars on a clear night. (*LL*) Don't Grieve. Jalal al-Din Rumi. EaPr

To start again with something beautiful. Cedar Waxwing on Scarlet Firethorn. Stanley Plumly. NAmP90

To start, I have to draw blood. Un Poco Loco. Clarence Major. Jaz

To starve, or not to starve? that is the question. W. H. Ireland. BXAP

To state each horror. From the Monkey House and Other Cages: Monkey II. Irena Klepfisz. GLP

To stave off disaster, or bring the devil to heel. Tapu. A. R. D. Fairburn. PeNZ

To steal my Basil-pot away from me! (*LL*) Isabella; or, The Pot of Basil. Keats. EnRP

To Stella. Hester Mulso. ECWP

To Stella. Plato, *tr. fr. Greek by* Shelley. EnLoPo; FaBoEE; OBVE

To Stella. Sir Philip Sidney. *See* Doubt you to whom my Muse these notes intendeth [*or* entendeth].

To Stella. Swift. NOEC

To step over the low wall that divides. To the Sea. Philip Larkin. AnAn

To Stew a Rump-Steak. *Unknown.* FaBoUs

To stop the collectors. (*LL*) I Expected My Skin and My Blood to Ripen. Wendy Rose. WPOW

To Strephon. Sarah Dixon. ECWP

To strive, to seek, to find, and not to yield. (*LL*) Ulysses. Tennyson. AWP; ClHu; EBEV; EBVVPR; EnVR; FaPoB; FaPoR; FF; FHYEP; HAP; HeIL; HeIP; HoPM; ImPo; InPK; InPS; LiTB; MeMBP; NAEL-2; NAWM-2; NIP; NOBE; NOBVV; NoP; OAEL-2; OxAEP-2; PoE; Poetr; PoRA; PPP; PrIm; SCGP; SCV; SoSe; TEP; TFi; TrGrPo; TRP; UnPo; WeW

To strongly, wrongly, vainly love thee still. (*LL*) Love and Death. Byron. EBEV; NOBE

To Stygian Forty-seventh Street below. (*LL*) The West Forties: Morning, Noon, and Night. L. E. Sissman. CoAP; NYBP

To subdue me, I would not know what to do. (*LL*) Close by, to the north, there were two oranges. Jean-Joseph Rabéarivelo. NegPo

To Subprefect Chang. Wang Wei, *tr. fr. Chinese by* Irving Y. Lo. SuSp

To Sultan Murad II. James Clarence Mangan, *tr. fr. Turkish.* NOIV

To Summer. Blake. WiR

To sup with thee thou didst me home invite. The Invitation. Robert Herrick. CaPo

To survive the pardon of Assisi. (*LL*) The Pardon of Assisi. Sebastian Barry. IB

To Switzerland, right up the Rhine. The Salmon. Christian Morgenstern, *tr. fr. German by* Geoffrey Grigson. FaBoNo

To Sycamores. Robert Herrick. CaPo

To T. A. R. H. Stephen Spender. PeHV

To T. H., a Lady Resembling My Mistress. Thomas Carew. CaPo

To-ta Ti-om. Peter Blue Cloud. HATNAP

To take on something new, something that was always there. (*LL*) The Members of the Orchestra. Kevin Hart. NOBAu

To take the Cat from me. (*LL*) May Colven. *Unknown.* OxBB; TrGrPo

To take the only way to be forgiven. (*LL*) On the Benefactions in the Late Frost. Pope. NOEC; OxBSP

To take the wrong road. Little Infinite Poem. Federico García Lorca, *tr. fr. Spanish by* Robert Bly. RaBo

To take us sick, that sound would not take thee? (*LL*) The Pursuit[e]. Henry Vaughan. AngWe; GeHe; NOSC; SeCP; TrCP; TrPWD

To talk to each other. (*LL*) Little. Dorothy Aldis. FaPON; NTCP; WHSW

To tame the rudeness of his native land. (*LL*) For a Statue of Chaucer at Woodstock. Mark Akenside. EPCY

To Tan Ch'iu. Li Po, *tr. fr. Chinese by* Robert Payne. TAL

To Tan Ch'iu. Li Po, *tr. fr. Chinese by* Arthur Waley. AWP

To tangled grass I cling. Spring. Marjorie Frost Fraser. ImGa

To Tarshish. Shimon Halkin, *tr. fr. Hebrew by* Ruth Finer Mintz. MHP

To Ted Hughes. Steve Ellis. PWE

To Telembrotos. Antipater of Thessalonica, *tr. fr. Greek by* Alistair Elliot. GrAn

To tell him so. (*LL*) Did This Happen to Your Mother? Alice Walker. VBLP

To tell it in. (*LL*) Ash Wednesday. Christina Rossetti. TrCP

To tell of great tidings, strange and true. (*LL*) From Far Away. William Morris. OHIP

To tell strange feats of deamons, here I am. To the Much Honoured R. F. Esq. Richard Chamberlain. SCAP

To tell the truth, each piece he read. On Hearing James W. Riley Read. Joseph S. Cotter, Sr.. AAP

To tell the truth, I really am. The All-Night Waitress. Maura Stanton. AmPA

To tell the truth plainly. John Skelton. *Fr.* Why Come Ye Not to Court. FaBoEH

To tell this truth, it kills him unforgiven. (*LL*) The People. Tomasso Campanella. AWP

To tell what others were, came down? (*LL*) An Epicurean Ode. John Hall. CBLP; MeLP; NOSC

To tell you from the start, I have lost him whose hand and eye are gentle. He Whose Hand and Eye Are Gentle. *Unknown, tr. fr. Welsh by* Kenneth Hurlstone Jackson. OBWVE

To tend a small coal with the brass tongs. (*LL*) Passages. Aidan Carl Mathews. IB

To tender love. (*LL*) I Heard a Linnet Courting. Robert Bridges. LiTB; LiTM; OBMV

To Terraughty, on His Birth-Day. Burns. NAs

To Thaliarchus ("Behold yon mountains.") I, 9. "Behold yon mountain's hoary height." ("Vides ut alta.") Horace, *tr. fr. Latin by* Austin Dobson. *Fr.* Odes. OBVE, *tr. by* Dryden

(To Thaliarchus "Thou seest the hills".) OBVE, *tr. by* Sir Richard Fanshawe

(You see how, white with snows to the north of us.) STV, *tr. by* John Frederick Nims

To Thaliarchus ("Thou seest the hills.") Horace. *See* To Thaliarchus ("Behold yon mountains.")

To that deliberate progress. (*LL*) Considering the Snail. Thom Gunn. GrPl; LiTM; NAEL-2; TwCP

To that, friend? (*LL*) A Dream of Maps. Matthew Sweeney. IB

To that lov'd bowl my spoon by instinct flies. (*LL*) The Hasty Pudding. Joel Barlow. AmPP; EAP; NOBA; OBAL, *abr.*; OxBA; TAP

To That Most Senseless Scoundrel, the Author of Legion's Humble Address to the Lords. Thomas Brown. APAS

To that sole Being, merciful and just. (*LL*) An Answer to a Lady Advising Me to Retirement. Lady Mary Wortley Montagu. TEP

To the Accuser Who Is the God of This World. Blake. *See* Truly, my Satan, thou art but a dunce.

To the Age's Insanities. Marie Ponsot. VGW

To the Almighty on his radiant throne. The Countess of Winchilsea. *Fr.* Pindaric Poem, A. ChIV-1

To the Ancestors. *Unknown.* TSaS

To the Anxious Mother. Valente Malangatana, *tr. fr. Portuguese by* Dorothy Guedes *and* Philippa Rumsey. PBA

To the Archbishop of Tuam. *Unknown.* FaBoEE

To the Archdeacon. George Farewell. NOEC

To the Asshole. Paul Verlaine, *tr. fr. French by* J. Murat *and* W. Gunn. PeHV

To the Author of Agnes de Castro. Delariviere Manley. KTR

To the Author of Clarissa. Thomas Edwards. Son

To the Avon River above Stratford, Canada. James Reaney. MoCV

To the banks of the Moldau River. How They Made the Golem. John Robert Colombo. MoCV

To the Banquet of the Earth. Martial Sinda, *tr. fr. French by* Ellen Conroy Kennedy. NegPo

To the Bat. Edith King. BoTP

To the Best, and Most Accomplished Couple. Henry Vaughan. PeECV

To the Blacksmith with a Spade. Owen Roe O'Sullivan. IIP

To the Blessed Sacrament. Henry Constable. NoSic

To the Blessed Virgin. William Alabaster. NoSic

To the Blessed Virgin Mary. Gerald Griffin. TIRV

To the Body. Alice Meynell. PeVV

To the Body. Coventry Patmore. *Fr.* Unknown Eros, The. EnVR; OAEL-2; PoEL-5

To the bog. (*LL*) The Peatbog Soldiers. *Unknown.* SWP

To the Bone. Dorothy Allison. GLP

To the Borrower of This Book. Samuel Showell, Jr.. FaBoUs

To the Boston Women. *Unknown.* PAH

To the boy who comes in summer the country. The Goat God. Cesare Pavese, *tr. fr. Italian by* William Arrowsmith. AnAn

To the Brave Soul. Wilbur Underwood. WGRP

To the Canary Bird. Jones Very. AnAmPo

To the Child Jesus. Henry van Dyke. TrPWD

To the Children of Prison Warden Akimkina. Irina Ratushinskaya, *tr. fr. Russian by* Carol Rumens. PWE

To the chimney a bull's horns. Ljubomir Simovic, *tr. fr. Serbo-Croatian by* Charles Simic. HSix

To the Christ. John Banister Tabb. TrPWD

To the Christians. Francis Lauderdale Adams. ChIV-2; OxBS; WGRP

To the Christians. Blake. *See* I give you the end of a golden string.

To the City of London [*or* In Honour of the City of London]. William Dunbar. ChTr; EBEV; FaBoPP; OBEV

To the Conference. Mrs. Henry Linden. CBWP-4

To the Countess Dowager of Huntingdon. Bathsua Pell Makin. KTR

To the Countess of Bedford ('Madam,/ Reason is Our Soul's Left Hand, Faith Her Right. John Donne. NOSC

To the Countess of Salisbury. John Donne. PeECV

To the Countesse of Bedford. John Donne. MeLP

To the Countesse of Salisbury. Aurelian Townshend. SeCP

To the Cowpens riding proudly, boasting loudly, rebels scorning. The Battle of the Cowpens. Thomas Dunn English. PAH

To the Critic. Michael Drayton. *See* Methinks I See Some Crooked Mimic Jeer.

To the Critics, *sels.* Priscilla Pointon.
   On Her Blindness. ECWP

To the cross of a rifle sight. (*LL*) Down in Dallas. X. J. Kennedy. FF

To the Cuckoo. Michael Bruce, *rev. by* John Logan. OBEV

To the Cuckoo. F. H. Townsend. *See* O Cuckoo! shall I call thee Bird.

To the Cuckoo. Wordsworth. BoTP; EBEvV; ELP; EnRP; GTBS; GTBS-P; PoLF; TrGrPo; UV, *st.* 1 *only*

To the Curlew. Helen Maria Williams. WoRP

To the Daisy ("With little here to do or see.") Wordsworth. EnRP; GTBS; GTBS-P

To the Dandelion, *sels.* James Russell Lowell.
   "Dear common flower, that grow'st beside the way." AnAmPo; FaPON, 2 *sts.*; GN; NAAL-1

To the dawn. (*LL*) The Gull's Flight. Nigel Roberts. NOBAu

To the Dead. Frank Bidart. EOEF

To the Dead Cardinal of Westminster. Francis Thompson. PeVV

To the Dead Owner of a Gym. Thom Gunn. PFL

To the Defenders of New Orleans. Joseph Rodman Drake. PAH

To the Detracted. John Andrews. *Fr.* Anatomy of Baseness, The. EIL

To the dim light and the large circle of shade. Of the Lady Pietra degli Scrovigni. Dante, *tr. fr. Italian by* Dante Gabriel Rossetti. AWP; OAEL-2; OBVE

To the distant Beloved. Alois Jeitteles, *tr. fr. German by* Philip L. Miller. RiWo

To the Distant One. Po Chü-i, *tr. fr. Chinese by* Robert Payne. TAL

To the Driving Cloud. Longfellow. ChTr; FaBoRV; PoEL-5

To the Eagle. Mary Weston Fordham. CBWP-2

To the Earl of Oxford, Late Lord Treasurer. Swift, *after the Latin of* Horace. OBVE

To the Earl of Roscommon, on His Excellent Essay on Translated Verse, *sels.* John Dryden *and* Nahum Tate.
   "Whether the fruitful Nile, or Tyrian shore." EPCY

To the Earl of Warwick, on the Death of Mr. Addison. Thomas Tickell. NOEC; OxAEP-1

To the Earle of Somerge. Homer, *tr. fr. Greek by* Robert Fitzgerald. *Fr.* Odyssey. NAWM-1

To the eastern grove where a spring rises. Replying to a Poem by the Monk Ling-yi at the New Spring. Liu Ch'ang-ch'ing, *tr. fr. Chinese by* William H. Nienhauser. SuSp

To the Editor of Mr. Pope's Works. Thomas Edwards. Son

To the Eminent Scholar and Meddler. Kofi Awoonor. HBAPE

To the empty air. (*LL*) I cannot sleep. Tzu Yeh. WPC

To the End. John E. Bode. BLRP

To the End. Jeffrey A. Z. Zable. BTR

To the end, to the end, they remain. (*LL*) For the Fallen. Laurence Binyon. CoGr; EBEvV; FaBoEH; NOBE; OBEV; OBWP; OxBTC; PIP

To the Eternal Feminine. Tristan Corbière, *tr. fr. French by* C. F. MacIntyre. ErPo

To the Etruscan Poets. Richard Wilbur. OxBC

To the Evening. John Codrington Bampfylde. NOEC

To the Evening Star. Mark Akenside. *See* To-night retir'd the queen of heaven.

To the Evening Star. Blake. BoNaP; CH; ChTr; EnRP; FaBoRV; FaBV; NAEL-2; NOEC; NoP; OAEL-2; PoE; PoLF; TEP; TFi; TrGrPo; WiR

To the Evening Star. Thomas Campbell. GTBS; GTBS-P; OBNC

To the Evening Star: Central Minnesota. James Wright. NaP

To the Excellent Mrs. Anne Owen. Katherine Philips. *See* We are complete [compleat]; and fate hath now.

To the Excellent Mrs A. O. upon her receiving the name of Lucasia. Katherine Philips. KTR

To the Excellent Orinda. "Philo-Philippa." KTR

To the Excellent Pattern of Beauty and Virtue, Lady Elizabeth, Countess of Ormonde. James Shirley. BeJo

To the Fair Clarinda, Who Made Love to Me, Imagin'd More than Woman. Aphra Behn. NALW; VBLP

To the fallen heart that does not cease to fall. (*LL*) Wild Bees. James K. Baxter. NoP

To the Fates. Friedrich Hölderlin, *tr. fr. German by* Michael Hamburger. OBD

To the Father through the features of men's faces. (*LL*) As Kingfishers Catch Fire [Dragonflies Draw Flame]. Gerard Manley Hopkins. CMoP; EBEV; EBVV; EnlH; FaBoMo; LiTM; NAEL-2; NOBVV; NOCV; NoP; PoE; PrIm; RB

To the Federal Convention. Timothy Dwight. PAH

To the fence posts leaning. Go Home. Janet Reed McFatter. GrPl

To the Film Industry in Crisis. Frank O'Hara. NOBA; OBAL; SOTW

To the First of August. Ann Plato. BlSi

To the first of my lovers. The First of My Lovers. Sydney Carter. OBET

To the First Slave Ship. Lydia Huntley Sigourney. AmWP

To the fishers of Gjendin the bold Skipper spoke. Ode to the Last Pot of Marmalade. "John." OBTV

To the Foot from Its Child. Pablo Neruda, *tr. fr. Spanish by* Alastair Reid. RB

To the Queen, Entertain[e]d at Night by the Countess[e] of Anglesey. Sir William Davenant. MeLP; NOSC

To the Queenes Most Excellent Majestie. Elizabeth Cary, Viscountess Falkland. KTR

To the Quick. Heather McHugh. PRA

To the Rats. E.J.L.. NSI

To the Reader. Ben Jonson. BeJo; NoP; PoE; SeCV-1

To the Reader. Denise Levertov. AmPP; PoM; VGW

To the Reader. Urian Oakes. SCAP

To the Reader of Master William Davenant's Play, The Wits. Thomas Carew. CaPo

To the Reader of These Sonnets. Michael Drayton. *See* Into these loves, who but for passion look[e]s.

To the Reader ("This figure, that thou here seest put.") Ben Jonson. EnRePo

To the real work, to/ "What is to be done." (*LL*) I Went into the Maverick Bar. Gary Snyder. CAPP; HCAP; MAT; NAAL-2; PoBeRe; PoE; VCAP

To the Red Lory. John Shaw Neilson. NOBAu

To the Redbreast. John Codrington Bampfylde. Son

To the Republic. James Galvin. BAP-90

To the Respective Judges. *Unknown.* APAS

To the Returning Brave. Robert Underwood Johnson. PAH

To the Rev. F. D. Maurice. Tennyson. GTBS-P; NOBVV; OBF; PeECV *Sels.*
    At Farringford. FaBoPP

To the Rev. Mr. Powell. Christopher Smart. OBWVE

To the Revd. Mr. —— on His Drinking Sea-Water. John Winstanley. NOEC

To the Rev'd Mr. Jno. Sparhawk on the Birth of his Son. Samuel Sewall. SCAP

To the Reverend Shade of His Religious Father. Robert Herrick. CaPo; JCP; SeCV-1

To the Reverend W. L. Bowles. Samuel Taylor Coleridge. EnRP; Son

To the Right Hon. Henry Pelham. Edward Moore. OBSV

To the Right Honorable Mildmay, Earl of Westmorland. Robert Herrick. BeJo

To the Right Honorable the Lord Windsor. Perdam Sapientiam Sapientum. William Habington. ChIV-2

To The Right Honourable Lord Byron, *sels.* James Hogg.
    "Nor for the crabbed state-creed, wayward wight." EPCY

To the Right Honourable the Countesse of C. William Habington. SeCP

To the Right Honourable William, Earl of Dartmouth. (Hail happy day, when smiling like the morn.) Phillis Wheatley. AmPP; NALW *Sels.*
    "No more, America, in mournful strain." WPOW
    Should You, My Lord. BPo; ImGa; TTY

To the Right Worshipful My Singular Good Friend, Mater Gabriel Harvey, Doctor of the Laws. Spenser. NoSic

To the River Duddon: After-Thought. Wordsworth. *See* I thought of Thee, my partner and my guide.

To the River Isca. Henry Vaughan. FaBoPP

To the River Itchin, near Winton. William Lisle Bowles. OAEL-2

To the River Otter. Samuel Taylor Coleridge. *See* Dear native brook! wild streamlet of the west!

To the Rose. Sir John Davies. *Fr.* Hymns of Astræa [in Acrostic Verse]. SiPSBD

To the Rose; a Song. Robert Herrick. SeCP

To the Rose of England I will give free. (*LL*) King Henry Fifth's Conquest of France. *Unknown.* ESPB

To the Rose upon the Rood of Time. W. B. Yeats. NoAM; NoP; TEP

To the roughness of the cement rubbing their palms. (*LL*) Their Thoughts Cling to Everything They See on the Way. Allen Afterman. NOBAu

To the Royal Society, *sels.* Abraham Cowley.
    "Philosophy, the great and only heir." BeJo; JCP

To the Rulers. Howard Nemerov. OxBC

To the Rural Muse, *sels.* John Clare.
    "Muse of the fields, oft have I said farewell." EPCY

To the Sad Moon. Sir Philip Sidney. *See* With how sad steps, O Moone, thou climb'st the skies!

To the sagging wharf. A Summer's Dream. Elizabeth Bishop. OxBC

To the Same. William Cowper. *See* Twentieth year is well-nigh past, The.

To the Same. Ben Jonson. *Fr.* Volpone. AWP; BeJo; EiL; JCP; NOSC; OAEL-1; OBVE; SeCP; SeCV-1

To the Same Flower. Wordsworth. EnRP

To the Same Flower. Wordsworth. *See* With little here to do or see.

To the Same [My Dear Sister, Mrs S.]: The Tears. William Hammond. NOSC

To the Same Purpos. Thomas Traherne. NoP; SeCV-2

To the Same [Robert, Earl of Salisbury] Upon the Accension of the Treasurship to Him. Ben Jonson. NOSC

To the scullery, and down to the back room. (*LL*) Ancestor. Thomas Kinsella. BIrV; NOIV; PBCIP; PoE

To the Sea. Philip Larkin. AnAn

To the Second Person, *sels.* John Skelton.
    "O benign Jesu, my sovereign Lord and King." SCGP

To the Senegalese veterans of war. Et Cetera. Léon Damas, *tr. fr. French by* Ellen Conroy Kennedy. NegPo

To the ship I carried statues. I Carried Statues. Agnes Nemes Nagy, *tr. fr. Hungarian.* BoWoP, *tr. by* Bruce Berlind; PoSu, *tr. by* Bruce Berlind

To the Short Tune "The Magnolias." Li Ch'ing-chao, *tr. fr. Chinese by* Kenneth Rexroth *and* Ling Chung. WPC

To the side of the road. (*LL*) The Old Flame. Robert Lowell. BoLoP; CBLP; HeIL; NoAM; NOBA

To the Skylark. Wordsworth. *See* Ethereal minstrel! pilgrim of the sky!

To the Small Celandine. Wordsworth. EnRP

To the Snake. Denise Levertov. AmPP; LiTM; NMM; PoA

To the Snipe. John Clare. FaBoPV; OBNC

To the Soldiers of El Salvador Who from 1931 to 1980 Have Ruled the Country through a Military Dictatorship. Lillian Jimenéz, *tr. by* Mary McAnally. WoWa

To the Soul. John Collop. TrGrPo

To the Sour Reader. Robert Herrick. NBLV; NoP; SeCP

To the South. Brewster Ghiselin. LiTA

To the Sphinx. Silvia Dobson. VBLP

To the Spider. Thomas Russell. Son

To the Spider in the Crevice behind the Toilet Door. Janet Sutherland. DT; VBLP

To the Spirit Great and Good. Leigh Hunt. TrPWD

To the Spirit of Keats. James Russell Lowell. Son

To the Spring. Sir John Davies. *Fr.* Hymns of Astræa [in Acrostic Verse]. SiPSBD

To the Stars. Andreas Gryphius, *tr. fr. German by* George C. Schoolfield. GePo

To the State of Love; or, The Senses' Festival. John Cleveland. CBLP

To the state of West Virginia. The Story of Lovers Leap. Maggie Pogue Johnson. CBWP-4

To the States. Walt Whitman. CTC; NAAL-1; RaBo

To the statistical Sparta of the champs. (*LL*) On Hurricane Jackson. Alan Dugan. CoAP; TRP

To the Statue. May Swenson. GOA

To the still dwelling. (*LL*) In valleys green and still. A. E. Housman. FaBoTw; OAEL-2; SCV

To the Stone-Cutters. Robinson Jeffers. AmPP; MoAB; MoAmPo; NAAL-2; NOBA; NoP; OxBA; PoRA; PrIm; TrGrPo

To the Street Piano, *sels.* John Davidson.
    Labourer's Wife, A. EBVV

To the Sun. Ingeborg Bachmann, *tr. fr. German.* BoNaP, *tr. by* Michael Hamburger

To the Sun. Sir John Davies. *Fr.* Hymns of Astræa [in Acrostic Verse]. SiPSBD

To the Sun, *sels.* Saul Tchernichowsky, *tr. fr. Hebrew by* Ruth Finer Mintz.
    "I have been to my God like the iris and the anemone." MHP
    "Images of a faded world possessed me, I cannot flee!" MHP
    "Or the image-kingdom's idol of the past generation." MHP

To the Sun from a Flower. Guido Gezelle, *tr. fr. Flemish by* Jethro Bithell. FaPON

To the Sun/ Who has shone. Last Song. James Guthrie. PDV

To the Superhuman Adelmund, When She Would Undo the Kiss Already Done. Philipp von Zesen, *tr. fr. German by* George C. Schoolfield. GePo

To the Supreme Being. Michelangelo. *See* Prayers I make will then be sweet indeed, The.

To the Swallow. William Cowper, *after the Greek of* Euenus. OBVE

To the Swallow. Pamphilus, *tr. fr. Greek by* Dennis Schmitz. GrAn

To the Swallows of Viterbo. Gibbons Ruark. SM

To the temple, singing. (*LL*) In the Suburbs. Louis Simpson. CAPP; MAT; TRP

To the Terrestrial Globe. W. S. Gilbert. FaBoNo; NBLV; TrGrPo

To the Thawing Wind. Robert Frost. OxBA

To the Thirty-ninth Congress. Whittier. PAH

To the thorn'd brow that makes the heavens pale. (*LL*) From the small life that loves with tooth and nail. Coventry Patmore. FaBoEE

To the Thoughtful Reader. William Meredith. NoAM

To the Thrice-Sacred Queen Elizabeth. The Countess of Pembroke. NALW

To the thunder of bells a voice calls for blood! The Bells. Saul Tchernichowsky, *tr. fr. Hebrew by* Ruth Finer Mintz. MHP

To the Translator of Lucan [*or* Lucan's Pharsalia, 1614]. Sir Walter Ralegh. SiPS; SiPSBD

To the triple goddess of Amarynthus. Theodoridas, *tr. fr. Greek by* John Heath-Stubbs *and* Carol A. Whiteside. GrAn

To the Tune "A Branch of Bamboo." Chu Chung-hsien, *tr. fr. Chinese by* Kenneth Rexroth *and* Ling Chung. WPC

To the Tune "A Dream Song." Sun Tao-hsüan, *tr. fr. Chinese by* Kenneth Rexroth *and* Ling Chung. WPC

To the Tune "A Dream Song." Wu Tsao, *tr. fr. Chinese by* Kenneth Rexroth *and* Ling Chung. WPC

To the Tune "A Floating Cloud Crosses Enchanted Mountain." Huang O, *tr. fr. Chinese by* Kenneth Rexroth *and* Ling Chung. AIW; BoWoP; WPC

To the Tune "A Hilly Garden." Li Ch'ing-chao, *tr. fr. Chinese by* Kenneth Rexroth *and* Ling Chung. WPC

To the Tune "A Watered Silk Dress." Ho Shuang-ch'ing, *tr. fr. Chinese by* Kenneth Rexroth *and* Ling Chung. WPC

To the Tune — "But I Fancy Lovely Nancy." Patrick Carey. CBLP

To The Tune "Eternal Happiness." Li Ch'ing-chao, *tr. fr. Chinese by* Kenneth Rexroth *and* Ling Chung. AIW; WPC

To the Tune "Flowers Along the Path through the Field." Wu Tsao, *tr. fr. Chinese by* Kenneth Rexroth *and* Ling Chung. WPC

To the Tune "Glittering Sword Hilts." Liu Yu Hsi, *tr. fr. Chinese by* Kenneth Rexroth. OHMPC; UnAS

To the Tune "Honor of a Fisherman." Li Ch'ing-chao, *tr. fr. Chinese by* Kenneth Rexroth *and* Ling Chung. WPC

To the Tune "I Paint My Lips Red." Li Ch'ing-chao. *See* After kicking on the swing.

To the Tune "Intoxicated with Shadows of Flowers." Yü Ch'ing-tseng, *tr. fr. Chinese by* Kenneth Rexroth *and* Ling Chung. WPC

To the Tune of, In Fayth I Cannot Keepe My Father's Sheepe. Sidney Godolphin.

To the Tune of the Coventry Carol. Stevie Smith. FaBoTw; OPOP

To the Tune of "Ye Commons and Peers Pray Lend Me Your Ears." *Unknown.* APAS

To the Tune — "Once I Lov'd a Maiden Fair." Patrick Carey. CBLP

To the Tune "Picking Mulberries." Li Ch'ing-chao, *tr. fr. Chinese by* Kenneth Rexroth *and* Ling Chung. WPC

To the Tune "Plucking a Cinnamon Branch." Huang O, *tr. fr. Chinese by* Kenneth Rexroth *and* Ling Chung. WPC

To the Tune "Red Embroidered Shoes." Huang O, *tr. fr. Chinese by* Kenneth Rexroth *and* Ling Chung. PBWP; VBLP; WPC; WPOW

To the Tune "Soaring Clouds." Huang O, *tr. fr. Chinese by* Kenneth Rexroth *and* Ling Chung. BoWoP; PBWP; WPC; WPOW

To the Tune "Spring at Wu Ling." Li Ch'ing-chao, *tr. fr. Chinese by* Kenneth Rexroth. OHMPC

To the Tune "The Bodhisattva's Barbaric Headdress." Lady Wei, *tr. fr. Chinese by* Kenneth Rexroth *and* Ling Chung. WPC

To the Tune "The Fair Maid of Yu." Chiang Chieh, *tr. fr. Chinese by* Kenneth Rexroth. OHMPC

To the Tune "The Fall of a Little Wild Goose." Huang O, *tr. fr. Chinese by* Kenneth Rexroth *and* Ling Chung. AIW; WPC; WPOW

To the Tune "The Joy of Peace and Brightness." Wu Tsao. *See* Bitter rain in my courtyard.

To the Tune "The Pain of Lovesickness." Wu Tsao, *tr. fr. Chinese by* Kenneth Rexroth *and* Ling Chung. WPC

To the Tune "The Phoenix Hairpin." T'ang Wan, *tr. fr. Chinese by* Kenneth Rexroth *and* Ling Chung. WPC; WPOW

To the Tune "The River Is Red." Ch'iu Chin, *tr. fr. Chinese by* Kenneth Rexroth *and* Ling Chung. AiP; BoWoP; PBWP; WPC

To the Tune "The River Is Red." Wang Ch'ing-hui. *See* Now the lotuses in the imperial lake.

To the Tune "T'ien ching sha," *sels.* Ma Chih-yüan, *tr. fr. Chinese by* Jonathan Chaves.

To the Tune "Washing Silk in the Stream." Ho Shuang-ch'ing, *tr. fr. Chinese by* Kenneth Rexroth *and* Ling Chung. WPC

To the Unborn and Waiting Children. Lucille Clifton. InPK

To the Unconstant Cynthia. Sir Robert Howard *and* John Dryden.

To the Unconstant Cynthia: a Song. Sir Robert Howard *and* John Dryden. *See* Tell me once, dear, how it does prove.

To the Undeceived. Clive Wilmer. SCBI

To the Union Savers of Cleveland. Frances E. W. Harper. AAP

To the United States of America. Robert Bridges. PAH

To the University. Alicia D'Anvers. *Fr.* Academia; or The Humours of the University of Oxford. KTR; NOSC

To the University of Cambridge, in New-England. Phillis Wheatley. AmPP; NAAL-1; TAP

To the Unknown Eros. Coventry Patmore. *Fr.* Unknown Eros, The. PoEL-5

To the Unknown Light. Edward Shanks. TrPWD

To the Unknown Warrior. G. K. Chesterton. NSI

To the Unkown Author of *Absalom and Achitophel, sels.* Nathaniel Lee. "Take it as earnest of a faith renewed." EPCY

To the Unseeable Animal. Wendell Berry. ArNa

To the Vermont Cadets. Lucretia Davidson. AmWP

To the Virginian Voyage. Michael Drayton. AiP, *sl. abr.*; EnRePo; FaBoEH, *sl. abr.*; HAP; NAEL-1; NOBE; NOSC; OBEV; PAH; PoEL-2; SCGP, *sl. abr.*; TEP

To [the] Virgins, to Make Much of Time. Robert Herrick. AWP; BeJo; BLPA; BoLoP; CaPo; ChTr; ClHu; CoGr; EBEvV; ELP; EnLoPo; ErPo; FaBV; FF; GBL; HAP; HeIP; ImPo; InPK; InPS; JCP; LiTB; NAEL-1; NBLV; NIP; NOBE; NoP; NOSC; OAEL-1; OBEV; OxAEP-1; PoE; PoEL-3; Poetr; PrIm; SCGP; SCV; SeCP; SeCV-1; SoSe; TEP; TFi; TrGrPo; UV

To the Virtuosos. William Shenstone. ECEV

To the Water Nymphs, Drinking at the Fountain. Robert Herrick. BeJo; CaPo; NAEL-1

To the Waters of the Chia-ling. Yüan Chen, *tr. fr. Chinese by* William H. Nienhauser. SuSp

To the Western Wind. Judah Halevi, *tr. fr. Hebrew by* Solomon Solis-Cohen. TrJP

To the Western Wind. Robert Herrick. CaPo; OBEV; SeCV-1

To the Western World. Louis Simpson. CAPP; CoAP; GOA; LiTM; NOBA; SM; TAP; TRP

To the Wheel of Progress. Mrs. Henry Linden. CBWP-4

To the white clouds at the end of the east I'll look for you! (*LL*) They Say You're Staying in a Mountain Temple. Tu Fu. TTTS

To the White Fiends. Claude McKay. PoBA

To the white-mantled maidens. Korinna, *tr. fr. Greek by* Richmond Lattimore. WPOW

To the White People of America. Joshua McCarter Simpson. AAP

To the wild wild beat of a tom tom tom. Reversion. Barry O. Higgs. PeSA

To the Willow-Tree. Robert Herrick. CaPo; OBEV; SCGP

To the winds give our banner! St. John. Whittier. PAH

To the Wine Treasurer of the Circuit Mess. Horace Smith *and* James Smith. UV

To the Woman in Bond Street Station. Edward Weismiller. LiTA

To the Woman in the Office. "Kim." DT

To the Wooden Hermit. Han Yü, *tr. fr. Chinese by* Kenneth O. Hanson. SuSp

To the Woodville Depot. D. C. Berry. MT

To the workers, to your family and to us all. (*LL*) This Poem Is Dedicated to Brother Andries Raditsela. Nise Malange. PeSAV

To the World; a Farewell for a Gentlewoman, Virtuous and Noble. Ben Jonson. BeJo; EnRePo; JCP; SeCP

To the World: the Perfection of Love. William Habington. *Fr.* Castara. BeJo; JCP

To the Writers' Worship in Zomba. Felix Mnthali. PeSAV

To the young man I would say. I'm Older than You, Please Listen. A. R. D. Fairburn. PeNZ

To thee, dear Henry Morison. Fynes Moryson. OBTV

To Thee, Eternal Soul, Be Praise. Richard Watson Gilder. AH

To thee, fair freedom! I retire. Written at [*or* in] an Inn at Henley. William Shenstone. AWP; NOBE; NOEC; OBEV; OxAEP-1

To thee, my way in epigrams seems new. To My Mere English Censurer. Ben Jonson. BeJo

To thee now, Christes dere derling. A Song to John, Christ's Friend. *Unknown.* MeEL

To Thee, O God. Abiel Holmes. AH

To Thee, O God, the Shepherd Kings. John G. C. Brainard. AH

To thee obeyeth all the East as far as Ganges goes. Ovid, *tr. by* Arthur Golding. *Fr.* Metamorphoses. OBVE

To thee, pure sprite, to thee alone's addressed. Dedicatory poem: To the Angel Spirit of the Most Excellent Sir Philip Sidney. The Countess of Pembroke. *Fr.* Psalms of David, The. SiPSBD

To thee — rude warrior, who, we once admired. Susanna Centlivre. *Fr.* Epistle to the King of Sweden, An. ECWP

To thee, sweet Fop, these lines I send. Bounce to Fop; an Heroick Epistle from a Dog at Twickenham to a Dog at Court. Pope. FM

To Thee the Tuneful Anthem Soars. Mather Byles. AH

To thee, whose cautious step and specious air. Annabella Plumptre. *Fr.* Ode to Moderation. ECWP; NOEC

To Thee, Then, Let All Beings Bend. Nathaniel Evans. AH

To Their Excellencies the Lords Justices of Ireland, the Humble Petition of Frances Harris, Who Must Starve, and Die a Maid if It Miscarries. Swift. NOEC; PoEL-3

To their long home the greatest princes go. Upon a Funeral. Sir John Beaumont. FaBoRV; NOSC

To them who crossed the flood. Inscription for Marye's Heights, Fredericksburg. Herman Melville. UnPo

To Theodora. *Unknown.* OxBChV

To Theodore. George Marion McClellan. AAP

To these, whom death again did wed. An Epitaph upon Husband and Wife Who Died and Were Buried Together. Richard Crashaw. EBEV; NOBE; OBEV; OxAEP-1; OxBM; TrGrPo

(Epitaph upon a Young Married Couple Dead and Buried Together, An. ELP; FaBoEE; SeCP)

To Thine Eternal Arms, O God. Thomas Wentworth Higginson. AH

To Thine Own Self Be True. Shakespeare. *See* There, — my blessing with you [*or* thee]!

To think how to unthink that thought again. (*LL*) Confusion. Christopher Hervey. BXAP; UV

To think of it! He knows me. And Yet. Arthur B. Rhinow. BLRP

To Think of Time. Walt Whitman. BLPL; ImPo; LiTA; MeMAP

To think of you surcharged with. Loneliness. Kenneth Rexroth. ArLo

To think so many battles have been fought. The Surplice. David Scott. PWE

To think that these are so much and so nigh to other drivers, and he there takes no interest in them. (*LL*) To Think of Time. Walt Whitman. BLPL; ImPo; LiTA; MeMAP

To think that this meaningless thing was ever a rose. Summer Is Ended. Christina Rossetti. NOBVV

To think the face we love shall ever die. Etruscan Tombs. Agnes Mary Frances Robinson. PeVV

To think to know the country and not know. A Hillside Thaw. Robert Frost. CMoP

To This Book. Martin Opitz, *tr. fr. German by* George C. Schoolfield. GePo

To this dear Benefactor of the race. (*LL*) Abraham Lincoln. Richard Henry Stoddard. GN; OHIP

To this long pelt over the back of a chair. (*LL*) An Otter. Ted Hughes. CMoP; MoP; NoAM

To this the Panther, with a scornful smile. Dryden. *Fr.* Hind and the Panther, The. SeCV-2

To this world, farewell. Chikamatsu Monzaemon, *tr. by* Geoffrey Bownas *and* Anthony Thwaite. *Fr.* Love Suicides at Sonezaki, The.

(Farewell to the world, and to the night farewell.) DL

To Thomalin. Phineas Fletcher. NOSC

To Thomas Moore. Byron. EnRP

To Thomas Palmer, on His Book "The Sprite of Trees and Herbs." Ben Jonson. NoSic

To Thoreau on Rereading Walden. Isabella Gardner. CAPP

To those fair isles where crimson sunsets burn. Toussaint L'Ouverture. H. Cordelia Ray. CBWP-3

To Those of My Sisters Who Kept Their Naturals. Gwendolyn Brooks. ETG

To those who have seen spirit. Seamus Heaney. *Fr.* Crossings. BAP-90

To those who have tried and seemingly have failed. Courage to Live. Grace Noll Crowell. PoToHe

To those who kiss in fear that they shall never kiss again. Cordelia. Veronica Forrest-Thomson. VaA

To thrill with all the sweets of life — is living. (*LL*) Living. *Unknown.* BLPA; FaBoBe

To throw away the key and walk away. The Walking Tour. W. H. Auden. *Fr.* Paid on Both Sides. CMoP

(Chorus: "To throw away the key and walk away." MoBrPo)

To thrust aside half-truths and grasp the whole. (*LL*) Progress. Ella Wheeler Wilcox. BLPA

To Thy continual Presence, in me wrought. William Ellery Channing. TrPWD

To Thy great service dedicate. (*LL*) Expectans Expectavi. Charles Hamilton Sorley. FaBoCh; WGRP

To thy lover. Out of the Italian; a Song. Richard Crashaw. SeCV-1

To thy renown, I paint what 'longs thereto. (*LL*) And Who Has Seen a Fair Alluring Face. George Peele. ErPo

To Time. Mary Tighe. IMW

To Time. "A. W." ElL

To Tirzah. Blake. *Fr.* Songs of Experience. EnRP; FHYEP; NAEL-2; NOBE; OAEL-2

To Sir Toby. Philip Freneau. NAAL-1; NoP; TAP

To toil. (*LL*) Toil. Avraham Shlonsky. MHP

To Tom Saunders on His Imprisonment. Bill Griffiths. NBrP

To Tommaso de' Cavalieri. Michelangelo, *tr. fr. Italian by* John Addington Symonds. PeHV

To touch all points in the past. Reflection: After Visiting Old Friends. John Allison. GrPl

To touch the cup with eager lips and taste, not drain it. Living. *Unknown.* BLPA; FaBoBe

To Toussaint L'Ouverture. Wordsworth. EnRP; FaBoPV; InPK; NOBE; OBNC; PoNe; PoRA; PPP; TrGrPo

To travel like a bird, lightly to view. C. Day Lewis. *Fr.* O Dreams, O Destinations. GTBS-P

To treat the thing directly, Ezra Pound. A High-toned Old Fascist Gentleman. William Zaranka. BXAP

To true roses uplifted on the bilious tide of evening. To Redouté. John Ashbery. PoA

To Trust. Antonia Pozzi, *tr. fr. Italian by* Lynne Lawner. PBWP

To trust in God and Heaven securely. (*LL*) Four Things. Henry van Dyke. PoLF; PoToHe

To Truth. *Unknown, tr. fr. Greek by* J. Rendel Harris. *Fr.* Solomon. WGRP

To Try to Find. Wang Kuo-wei, *tr. fr. Chinese by* Irving Y. Lo. SuSp

To try to find my heart, it's hard enough. To Try to Find. Wang Kuo-wei, *tr. fr. Chinese by* Irving Y. Lo. SuSp

To Tu Fu. Li Po, *tr. fr. Chinese by* Robert Payne. TAL

To Turn Back. John Haines. BoNaP; TRP

To Turn from Love. Sarah Webster Fabio. BlSi

To turn my volume o'er nor find. How to Read Me. Walter Savage Landor. NOBVV

To Two Bereaved. Thomas Ashe. NOBVV

To type this bitter little poem. (*LL*) On Saint-Urbain Street. Milton Acorn. NOBC

To Tzu-an. Yü Hsüan-chi, *tr. by* Geoffrey R. Waters. BoWoP

To Tzu-an. Yü Hsüan-chi, *tr. fr. Chinese by* Jan W. Walls. SuSp

To Tzŭ-chih: among the "Flowers." Li Shang-yin, *tr. fr. Chinese by* A. C. Graham. PLT

To unknown lands to fight an unknown foe. (*LL*) Troopship: Mid-Atlantic. W. W. Gibson. NSI

To uplift their bleeding brothers rescued from the dust. (*LL*) The Way, the Truth, and the Life. Theodore Parker. TrPWD; WGRP

To Urania. Joseph Brodsky. PRA

To Urania. Benjamin Colman. SCAP

To uses, arts, and charities. (*LL*) Opposition. Sidney Lanier. AnAmPo; LiTA

To Usward. Gwendolyn B. Bennett. BlSi; ShDr

To Vanity. Darwin T. Turner. PoNe

To Varus. Catullus. *See* Suffenus, whom so well you know [*or* whom you know].

To Verse Let Kings Give Place. Ovid, *tr. by* Christopher Marlowe. *Fr.* Elegies. ChTr

To very few, or else to none. (*LL*) His Content in the Country. Robert Herrick. CaPo; SeCV-1; TEP

To Victor Hugo of My Crow Pluto. Marianne Moore. CBNP

To Vietnam. Charlie Cobb. PoBA

To Vineyarders in cold Korea. Pinkletinks. Grace Elisabeth Allen. GoYe

To Violet [with Prewar Poems]. Basil Bunting. FaBoMo; PoA

To Violets. Robert Herrick. CaPo; JCP; OBEV; PFP; SeCP; TrGrPo

To Virgil [*or* Vergil]. Tennyson. AWP; ChTr; EBVVPR; GTBS-P; MeMBP; NoP; OAEL-2; PoEL-5

To Virgins. Robert Herrick. CaPo

To Vittoria Colonna. Michelangelo, *tr. fr. Italian by* Longfellow. AWP

To Vulcan. Robert Herrick. CaPo

To Sir W. A. William Drummond of Hawthornden. *See* Though I had [*or* have] been at the doors [*or* doores] of death.

To W. C. W. M. D. Alfred Kreymborg. PoA

To W. J. M. "G. G." PeHV

To W. L. G. on Reading His "Chosen Queen." Charlotte Forten. BlSi

To W. P, *sels.* George Santayana.

"With you a part of me hath passed away." TrGrPo

To W. R. W. E. Henley. *See* Madam Life's a Piece in Bloom.

To wade the sea mist, then to wade the sea. Stone Horse Shoals. Malcolm Cowley. NYBP

To Wait and Hart. Harold Norse. ETG

To wait for that great gittin' up morning — Amem. (*LL*) Listen, Lord — [a Prayer]. James Weldon Johnson. BPo

To wake and find you sitting up in bed. Possibly. Lesléa Newman. VBLP

To wake in thee. (*LL*) Come, come, what doe I here? Henry Vaughan. ESCV; SeCV-1

To wake up and discover. The Well-beloved. John Montague. BiHa

To wake us. (*LL*) How Gentle. Joyce Carol Oates. VBLP

To Waken a Small Person. Donald Justice. NYBP

To Waken an Old Lady. William Carlos Williams. HAP; InPK; NoP; SoSe; WeW

To Walk Abroad. Thomas Traherne. ELP

To walk amid the springing green. (LL) Christ hath a garden walled around. Isaac Watts. FaBoCh

To wander far from you, the centre. (LL) An Excuse of Absence. Thomas Carew. CaPo; SeCP

To Waning Day, To the Wide Round of Shadow. Dante, tr. fr. Italian by John Frederick Nims. STV

To wash the stain ingrain and to make me clean again. (LL) What Would I Give? Christina Rossetti. OPOP; OxBSP

To watch it. (LL) Christmas Eve — Another Ceremony. Robert Herrick. OHIP

To watch the tipsy cripples on the beach. After Tennyson. Edward Lear. FaBoNo

To water His flowers again. (LL) For the Master's Use. Unknown. BLPA

To wear the arctic fox. The Arctic Ox. Marianne Moore. NYBP

To weary hearts, to mourning homes. The Angel of Patience. Whittier. WGRP

To weaving. (LL) Poem to Lee Forest. Brenda Frazer. PoBeRe

To Wed or Not to Wed. Una Marson. PBCV

To wed, or not to wed? That is the question. Unknown. BXAP

To weep thine ashes am I come. Lament for Aquileia Destroyed, and Never to be Built Again. Paulinus of Aquileia, tr. fr. Latin by Helen Waddell. MLL

To weep, to sing, thy Death, my Life. (LL) The Passion. Henry Vaughan and Thomas Stanley. ESCV

To welcome the New-livery'd year. (LL) On a Bank [or Banck] as I Sate [or Sat] a-Fishing; a Description of the Spring. Sir Henry Wotton. NOSC; SeCP

To Werther. Goethe, tr. fr. German by John Frederick Nims. Fr. Trilogy of Passion. STV

To western woods and lonely plains. On the Emigration to America [and Peopling the Western Country]. Philip Freneau. NAAL-1; PAH; TAP

To wet your eye withouten tear. Sir Thomas Wyatt. SiPS

To what intent or purpose was Man made. As Concerning Man. Alexander Radcliffe. CBCK; NOSC; OBSV

To what new fates, my country, far. Unmanifest Destiny. Richard Hovey. WGRP

To what purpose, April, do you return again? Spring. Edna St. Vincent Millay. BoWoP; MeMAP; MoAB; MoAmPo; NoP

To What Serves Mortal Beauty? Gerard Manley Hopkins. MeMBP

To What Strangers, What Welcome. J. V. Cunningham. NoAM
Sels.
Miramar Beach. PoA

To which they can't admit they can never be admitted. (LL) Misery and Splendor. Robert Hass. VCAP

To which this Work so Wonderfull doth tend. (LL) Amendment. Thomas Traherne. SeCV-2

To Whistler, American. Ezra Pound. AiP; NAAL-2; PoA

To Whitbread now deign'd Majesty to say. On George III. "Peter Pindar." IHNG

To Whittier. Josephine D. Henderson Heard. AAP; CBWP-4

To Whom Else? Robert Graves. FaBoMo

To whom I owe the leaping delight. A Dedication to My Wife. T. S. Eliot. ArLo; BoLoP; FF; LPA; OxBM

To Whom It May Concern. J. V. Cunningham. FYAP

To Whom It May Concern. Adrian Mitchell. IHNG; OBWP

To Whom It May Concern. Jon Stallworthy. CBLP

To whom now, Pyrrha, art thou kind? Horace. See What slender youth bedewed with liquid odours.

To whom our Saviour calmly thus reply'd. True and False Glory ("To whom our Saviour calmly thus reply'd.") Milton. Fr. Paradise Regained [or Regain'd]. LiTB

To whom shall I this dancing poem send. Dedications, I: To His Very Friend, Master Richard Martin. Sir John Davies. Fr. Orchestra; or, A Poem[e] of Da[u]ncing. NoSic, abr.; SiPS; SiPSBD

To Whom Shall the World Henceforth Belong? John Oxenham. WBLP

To whom should I speak today? A Dispute over Suicide. Unknown, tr. fr. Egyptian by T. Eric Peet. TTY

To whom the Father, without cloud, serene. Milton. Fr. Paradise Lost. EPCY; PeECV, ll. 45–66

To whom the fiend with fear abasht repli'd. Milton. Fr. Paradise Regained [or Regain'd]. PeECV, bk. IV, ll. 195–203

To whom the Tempter impudent replied. Milton. Fr. Paradise Regained [or Regain'd]. ChIV-2, ll. 155-232, 285-352

To whom the winged hierarch replied. Ascent of Species. Milton. Fr. Paradise Lost. EPCY; NOSC

To whom thus also th' angel last replied. Milton. Fr. Paradise Lost. EPCY; OxAEP-1; PeECV

To whom thus Michael. Justly thou abhorr'st. Milton. Fr. Paradise Lost. EPCY; FaBoPV

To whom thus Michael. Those whom last thou saw'st. Milton. Fr. Paradise Lost. EPCY; FaBoPV

To whom with healing words Adam replied. Uncloistered Virtue. Milton. Fr. Paradise Lost. EPCY; NOSC

To whomsoever lust for to proffer most. (LL) Alas the grief, and deadly woful smart! Sir Thomas Wyatt. SiPS

To Sir William Alexander. William Drummond of Hawthornden.

To William Camden. Ben Jonson. AWP; BeJo; JCP; NAEL-1; NOSC; SeCV-1

To William Carlos Williams. Galway Kinnell. NoAM; Poetr; SM

To Sir William Davenant, Upon His Two First Books of Gondibert. Abraham Cowley. SeCV-1

To William Drummond of Hawthornden. Mary, of Morpeth Oxlie. KTR

To William Earle of Pembroke. Ben Jonson. SeCP

To William Hayley. Blake. FaBoCo

To William Hayley, Esq.: In Reply to His Solicitation to Write with Him in a Literary Work. William Cowper. Son

To William Lloyd Garrison. Whittier. PAH

To William Roe. Ben Jonson. BeJo; NOSC; OAEL-1; SeCV-1

To William Simpson, Ochiltree. Burns. OxBS

To William (Whom We Have Missed). P. G. Wodehouse. NOBL

To William Wilberforce, Esq. William Cowper. Son

To William Wordsworth. Samuel Taylor Coleridge. EnRP; EPCY; FHYEP; NAEL-2; OAEL-2

To William Wordsworth from Virginia. Julia Randall. NMM; WPE

To William Wordsworth on His Seventy-Fifth Birthday. Hartley Coleridge. EPCY

To win the love of women one should first discover. Kenneth Koch. Fr. Art of Love, The. NNaP

To windward midnight glowed, iridium sheen. Ice. Alan Gould. NOBAu

To Winky. Amy Lowell. OFC; SoCa

To Winter. Blake. WiR

To wipe his pretty nose. (LL) I had a little husband. Unknown. BoTP; OxNR; ReMoGo

To wish and want and not obtain. Sir Thomas Wyatt. SiPS; SiPSBD

To wish/ for the moon. You Can't Go to the Moon There's No Trains. Joy Howard. DT

To wish to climb a ladder to the loft. James K. Baxter. Fr. Autumn Testament. PeNZ

To ———, with an Ivory Hand-Glass. Lord Alfred Bruce Douglas. FaBoUs

To wither, envy, pine, and fade? (LL) The Poet and the Rose. John Gay. PeLV; TEP

To witness agony. (LL) Open House. Theodore Roethke. NoAM; NOBA; NoP

To Women. Richard Hugo. NIP

To Women, as Far as I'm Concerned. D. H. Lawrence. InPS; OxBSP; RaBo

To women in contemporary voice and dislocation. Re-reading Jane. Anne Stevenson. NALW

To Women, to Hide Their Teeth, if They Be Rotten or Rusty. Robert Herrick. FaBoUs

To wood and field. (LL) Snow-Flakes. Longfellow. ArNa; ChTr; FaBoRV; NOBA; NoP; PoEL-5; TAP; UnPo; WiR

To Wordsworth. John Clare. OAEL-2; Son

To Wordsworth. Hartley Coleridge. Son

To Wordsworth. Walter Savage Landor. OAEL-2

To Wordsworth, sels. Walter Savage Landor. "Chatting on deck was Dryden too." EPCY

To Wordsworth. Shelley. EnRP; EPCY; FHYEP; NoP; PFP; Son

To work away in art's traditional measure. Goethe, tr. fr. German by John Frederick Nims. STV

To work upon the railway. (LL) Pat Works on the Railway. Unknown. SWP

To wrestle with the angel — Art. (LL) Art. Herman Melville. AmPP; NAAL-1; NOBA

To write a poem in the endless night. (LL) She Thinks of Her Beloved. Lu Chi. OHMPC

To write of Sol in his exaltation. Robert Copland. Fr. High Way to the Spital House, The. NoSic

To write threescore: this is the second of our reign [or raigne]. (LL) The Anniversary [or Anniversarie]. John Donne. BoLoP; ESCV; FHYEP;

HAP; HoPM; JCP; LiTB; MeLP; NOBE; NoP; NoSic; OAEL-1; OxBM; SCGP; SeCP; SeCV-1; TFi; WeW

To Wystan Auden. Geoffrey Grigson. NAs

To yet more boastful visions of despair. *(LL)* Recalling War. Robert Graves. CMoP; LiTM; MeMBP; NoAM; OAEL-2; OBWP; PeFWW; PoWW

To yon fause stream that, by the sea. The Mermaid. *Unknown.* CH

To You. Frank Horne. *Fr.* Letters [*or* Notes] Found near a Suicide. BPo; CDC; PoBA; PoNe

To You. Kenneth Koch. ArLo

To You, *sels.* Huda Na mani, *tr. fr. Arabic* by Lena Jayyusi.

To You. Elolongue Epanya Yondo, *tr. fr. French* by Ellen Conroy Kennedy. NegPo

To you, dere herte, variant and mutable. *Unknown.* MiEL

To you I dedicate this work of grace. Emilia Lanier. *Fr.* To the Lady Anne, Countess of Dorset. NOSC

To you, Kypris, Lysidike. Asclepiades, *tr. fr. Greek* by Alan Marshfield. GrAn

To you [*or* yow], my purse [*or* purs], and to non [*or* no *or* noon] other wight. The Complaint of Chaucer to His Empty Purse. Chaucer. MiEL; MIS; NAEL-1; SCGP
   (Complaint of Chaucer to His Purse, The.) ImPo; OAEL-1
   (Complaint to His Purse.) NoP
   (Compleinte of Chauser to His Empty Purs, The, [*or*] Chaucer's Complaint to His Empty Purse.) TrGrPo, 2 *vers.*
   (Song to His Purse for the King, A.) MeEL

To you, then, tenants of life's middle state. William Cowper. *Fr.* Tirocinium; or, A Review of Schools. OBSV

To you this fragrant oil, sweets to the sweet. A Gift. *Unknown, tr. fr. Greek* by Guy Davenport. GrAn

To you this little village is dear as the moon. Dear as the Moon. *Gond Oral Tradition, tr. by* V. Elwin *and* S. Hivale. WTO

To you, troop so fleet. Hymn to the Winds. Joachim du Bellay, *tr. fr. French by* Andrew Lang. AWP

To you, whose dignitie strikes us with awe. To her royall highnesse the Dutchesse of Yorke. Katherine Philips. KTR

To your children. *(LL)* Point Lobos: Animism. Michael McClure. PoBeRe

To your Cream here's Strawberries. *(LL)* Fresh Cheese and Cream. Robert Herrick. CBLP

To your owne bents dispose you: you'le be found. Shakespeare. *Fr.* Winter's Tale, The. FaBoVe

To Your Question. Duane Niatum. CDW

To Youth. Josephine D. Henderson Heard. CBWP-4

To Youth. Walter Savage Landor. EnRP

To youths, who hurry thus away. On a Painted Woman. Shelley. FaBoCo; NBLV

To Yvor Winters, 1955. Thom Gunn. GTBS-P

To zig-zag with the ant. Summer Afternoon. Raymond Souster. BoNaP

To Zion. Judah Halevi, *tr. fr. Hebrew by* Maurice Samuel. AWP

Toad, A. Elizabeth Akers Allen. OBCA

Toad beneath the harrow knows, The. Pagett, M. P. Kipling.
   (Toad Beneath the Harrow, The.) CoGr

Toad Beneath the Harrow, The. Kipling. *See* Toad beneath the harrow knows, The.

Toad that lived on Albury Heath, A. A Roundabout Turn. Robert E. Charles. MoShBr

Toad the power mower caught, A. The Death of a Toad. Richard Wilbur. CMoP; LiTM; MoP; NAAL-2; NoAM; NoP; PoA; Poetr

Toad the Tailor. Norah E. Hussey. BoTP

Toads. Philip Larkin. CMoP; NoAM; NOBL; OxAEP-2; OxBTC; PoE; Poetr; SoSe

Toads Revisited. Philip Larkin. CMoP; NOBL; OxAEP-2

Toadstools. Elizabeth Fleming. BoTP

Toady toady min yoself. A Digging Sing. *Unknown.* FaBoVe

Toast. Frank Horne. PoNe

Toast. Thomas McCarthy. PBCIP

Toast to Our Native Land, A. Robert Bridges. PAH

Toast to the Flag, A. John Jay Daly. PoLF

Toaster, The. William Jay Smith. GrPl; OTCP

Tobacco. Philip Freneau. TAP

Tobacco crumbs, vases and fringes. *(LL)* The Bean Eaters. Gwendolyn Brooks. AIW; BlSi; GrPl; HAP; HeIL; HeIP; LCAP; MAT; NALW; NoP; PoBA; PoE; Poetr; PrIm; TAP; TRP; TTY; WeW

Tobacco is a filthy weed. *Unknown.* FaBoEE

Tobacco Plant. Ivor Gurney. OBTV

Tobacco Shop. Fernando Pessoa, *tr. fr. Portuguese by* Edwin Honig. AnRep

Tobacco ("Tobacco is a dirty weed.") Graham Lee Hemminger. PoLF

Tobera. Jeff Tagami. OpBo

Tobias and the Angel. John Gray. NOBVV

Tobias, journeying to Ecbatane. Tobias and the Angel. John Gray. NOBVV

Tobit, *sels.* Bible, Apocrypha, *tr. fr. Greek* by D. C. Simpson. Blessed Is God. TrJP

Tobroken ben the statuts hye in hevene. Envoy to Scogan. Chaucer. EnVB

Sir Toby Matthews. Sir John Suckling. SeCV-1

Toccata of Galuppi's, A. Robert Browning. EBVV; EBVVPR; EnVR; FaBoVe; FaPoB; GTBS-P; HAP; LiTB; Mes; NAEL-2; NOBE; NOBVV; NoP; OAEL-2; OtMeF; TEP; UV

Today. John Kendrick Bangs. PoToHe

Today. Thomas Carlyle. PWR

Today. Ethel Romig Fuller. PoToHe

Today. Langston Hughes. GLP; VGW

Today. Angela Morgan. BLPA

Today. Frank O'Hara. TTTS

Today. Jones Very. TAP

Today above the gull's call. Louise Glück. AnAn

Today, as at my glass I stood. To Mrs. Francis-Arabella Kelly. Mary Barber. ECWP

Today as I hang out the wash I see them again, a code. The Geese. Jorie Graham. HCAP

Today as in the past, who is the master of these rivers and mountains? Tune: "Butterflies Lingering over Flowers" — Leaving the Border. Nalan Hsing-te, *tr. fr. Chinese by* An-yan Tang. SuSp

Today as the news from Selma and Saigon. Monet's "Waterlilies." Robert Hayden. CAPP; Poetr

Today Backwards. David Chaloner. VaA

Today before a goblet of wine I was shamed. Drunk Too Soon. Yüan Chen, *tr. fr. Chinese by* Dell R. Hales. SuSp

Today beneath Benignant Skies. Denis Wortman. AH

Today, catorce de julio. 14 de Julio. Sandra Cisneros. ETG

Today, dear heart, but just today. Her Answer. John Bennett. BLPA

Today ees com' from Eetaly. Boy from Rome, Da. T. A. Daly. FaPON

Today:/ Hark! Heaven sings! On Christmas Day to My Heart. Clement Paman. NOSC

Today has it all, sunshine. Gwyn Williams. *Fr.* Aspects of Now. OBWVE

"Today," he said to the mirror, "the person I am inside of." Not Thinking of Himself. Jack Myers. NAmP90

Today I am at home. A Few Sirens. Alice Walker. CrSp

Today/ I am 24. January 3, 1970. Mae Jackson. PoBA

Today I am walking alone in a bare place. Late November in a Field. James Wright. CAPP; NAAL-2; NNaP

Today I bring you cold chrysanthemums. Between Seasons. Li-Young Lee. TRP

Today I cleared out the kitchen with Dougie so Hedley could sand the kitchen floor. A Day in the Life. Stef Pixner. BrRo

Today I failed to see you. Self-centre. Cynthia Fuller. NWP

Today I feel altogether unbuttoned. Aurora Borealis and the Body Louse. Sidney Wade. BAP-90

Today I found the right fruit for my prime. A Kumquat for John Keats. Tony Harrison. SCBI

Today I have grown taller from walking with the trees. Good Company. Karle Wilson Baker. FaPON; WGRP

Today I learn "tamarisk." On Returning. Brigitte Frase. LoHo

Today/ I lost my temper. For Witches. Susan Sutheim. NMM

Today I put on. Saint Patrick's Breastplate. *Unknown.* NOIV

Today I saw a picture of the cancer cells. The Cancer Cells. Richard Eberhart. HAP; LiTM

Today I saw a place no one has seen. Iron Heaven. Betti Alver, *tr. by* Willis Barnstone *and* Felix Oinas. BoWoP

Today I saw a thing of arresting poignant beauty. Snow in October. Alice Dunbar Nelson. BlSi; CDC; ShDr

Today I saw a woman plowing a furrow. Sister. Gabriela Mistral, *tr. fr. Spanish by* Langston Hughes. BoWoP

Today I saw a woman wrapped in rags. At the Slackening of the Tide. James Wright. UnPo; VGW

Today I think. Digging. Edward Thomas. MoAB; MoBrPo; OxBTC

Today I think of a boy in the Transvaal. Remembering Snow. Ralph Nixon Currey. PeSA

Today I trade my last unwise. How It Goes On. Maxine W. Kumin. FoLa

Today I watched a woman by the water. Levee, The: Letter to No One. Lorna Dee Cervantes. AfAz

Today I wished without mercy. All Day the Light Is Clear. Tess Gallagher. VBLP

Today I woke up missing. Rising to Meet It. Chana Bloch. CrSp

Today I wrote the ending of all poems. Discreet. Maria Flook. EOEF

Today I'm a hill. Magic. Dahlia Ravikovitch, tr. fr. Hebrew. TSaS, tr. by Chana Bloch and Ariel Bloch

Today in a horse landscape. The Horse Landscape. Helen Dunmore. PWE

Today in Peru, this first day of summer. Lawrence Raab. AmPA

Today in the field I saw. Sacred Objects. Louise Glück. Fr. Dedication to Hunger. AnAn

Today Is a Day of Great Joy. Victor Hernandez Cruz. TTY

Today is a holiday in the Western heart. Today Is Armistice, a Holiday. Delmore Schwartz. TrJP

Today is a thought, a fear is tomorrow. Dirge Written for a Drama. Thomas Lovell Beddoes. EnRP

Today Is Armistice, a Holiday. Delmore Schwartz. TrJP

Today Is Friday. Ramon Guthrie. PoE

Today Is Not Like They Said. Kirk Hall. NBV

Today Is Ours. Abraham Cowley. See Fill the bowl with rosie [or rosy] wine.

Today is the anniversary of our parting. Ise Tayu, tr. fr. Japanese by Kenneth Rexroth and Ikuko Atsumi. WPJ

Today is your. April Fool Birthday Poem for Grandpa. Diane Di Prima. PoBeRe

Today it rained vengefully and hard. Barquisimeto, Venezuela, October 27, 1561. Ai. Fr. Gilded Man, The. AnAn

Today it's going to cost us twenty dollars. How Things Work. Gary Soto. NoAM

Today it's schoolgirl shots. Male Order. Robert Maitre. FaBoBl

Today lacks the conviction of my feelings. Hotel Zingo. David Chaloner. VaA

Today, lonely for my father, I saw. My Father's Wedding. Robert Bly. CAPP; InPS; NoAM; RaBo

Today my mother and sisters. They've Come. Alfonsina Storni, tr. fr. Spanish. BoWoP, tr. by Aliki and Willis Barnstone; WPOW, tr. by Marti Moody

Today on a sandy road. On a Recollected Road. Amir Gilboa, tr. fr. Hebrew by Ruth Finer Mintz. MHP

Today on the lip of a bowl in the backyard. The Caterpillar. Miller Williams. MT

Today ready ripe, tomorrow all too shaken. (LL) Brittle beauty [or beautie], that nature made so frail[e]. The Earl of Surrey. AAS; EnLoPo; SiPS; SiPSBD; TrGrPo

"Today" said Hassan — through a mouthful of honey. Medine in Turkey. Alison Brackenbury. SCBI

Today she parades her shape like swellings of song. Portrait of a Pregnant Woman. Bobi Jones, tr. fr. Welsh by Joseph P. Clancy. OBWVE

Today, should you let fall a glass it would. Tramontana at Lerici. Charles Tomlinson. GTBS-P

Today six slender fruit trees stand. Planting Trees. Violet Helen Friedlaender. BoNaP

Today snow sparks the air like mica — the sun's. Margaret Gibson. Fr. Unborn Child Elegy. CrSp

Today, ten thousand people will die. Choosing to Think of It. Stephen Dunn. AnAn

Today, the angels are all writing postcards. Saying One Thing. Robert Long. NAmP90

Today, the first dead leaf in the hall. A Dead Leaf. Howard Moss. NYBP

Today the jailbird maple in the yard. For My Son on the Highways of His Mind. Maxine W. Kumin. MAT

Today the journey is ended. A Soul's Soliloquy. Wenonah Stevens Abbott. BLPA

Today the leaves cry, hanging on branches swept by wind. The Course of a Particular. Wallace Stevens. HCAP

Today the peace of autumn pervades the world. Autumn. Rabindranath Tagore. WGRP

Today the self-destroying anger. Bruce Beaver. Fr. Letters to Live Poets. CBAP

Today the sixth of june. Nigeria in the Year 1999. Catherine Obianuju Acholonu. HBAPE

Today the skies are clear and blue. Now. Unknown. PWR

Today the sky hangs just above my brows. Reflections. Barbara Burford. DT

Today, the Twenty-sixth of February. George Barker. Fr. True Confession of George Barker, The. MeMBP; NAs

Today/ the west/ burns down. The Coup-clock Clicks. Brian Meeks. PBCV

Today,/ there came a breeze thin as the needle of a syringe. J. Kitchener Davies, tr. fr. Welsh by Joseph P. Clancy. Fr. Sound of the Wind That Is Blowing, The. OBWVE

Today Was Not. Michael Rosen. PYC

Today we have marking of folders. Yesterday. Marking of Folders. Anne Anderton. UV

Today, whatever may annoy. Today. John Kendrick Bangs. PoToHe

Today will be the day of what we both said. (LL) West-running Brook. Robert Frost. BLPL; MoAB; MoAmPo; NOBA; NoP

Today Will Pass. Lemn Sissay. NBrP

Today you grasped. Fire Roses. Cynthia Fuller. VBLP

Today you rain on me from every corner of the sky. Sure. Naomi Shihab Nye. MT

Today's American car. Emergency Poem 1973. Cyn Zarco. UL

Today's News. Ted Berrigan. UL

Today's poetry should be a bold thrust of the democratic spirit. The Spirit of Poetry. Ai Ch'ing, tr. fr. Chinese. LHF, tr. by Hualing Nieh

Today's the case. Unknown. ISE

Tod's Hole, The. Unknown. GBP

Toe sticking out from under the hem, The. On a Fifteenth-Century Flemish Angel. David Ray. CRP

Toe tipe. Unknown. OxNR

Toe, trip and go. Unknown. OxNR

Toe upon [or after] toe, a snowing flesh. Nude Descending a Staircase. X. J. Kennedy. CoAP; HoPM; NIP; OxBSP; PoA; SM

Toe'osh; a Laguna Coyote Story. Leslie Silko. CDW; NoAM; VoR

Together. Maxine W. Kumin. BoWoP; NMM

Together. Ludwig Lewisohn. PoToHe; TrJP

Together eternity and death threaten me. Patrizia Cavalli, tr. fr. Italian by Judith Baumel. NeIt

Together, fourteen years older. In the Cathedral. Patricia Beer. OxBC

Together how many hours. Tant' Amare. Unknown, tr. fr. Mozarabe by Paul Blackburn. ErPo

Together in infinite shade. Too Much Coffee. E. A. Robinson. MoAmPo

Together twists their threads, and yet draws hers the longer. (LL) A Dialogue betwixt Time and a Pilgrime [or Pilgrim]. Aurelian Townshend. NOBE; OAEL-1; PoEL-2; SeCP

Together with my stones. Shibboleth. Paul Celan, tr. fr. German by Michael Hamburger. AnRep

Together with the day which comes. (LL) Day arises. Unknown. EaPr

To help me eat up her money. (LL) Song for the Squeeze-Box. Theodore Roethke. NBLV

Toil. Avraham Shlonsky, tr. fr. Hebrew by Ruth Finer Mintz. MHP

Toil! toil! toil! The Wandering Jew. Eloise Bibb. CBWP-4

Toilet. The. Pope. See And now, unveiled, the toilet stands displayed.

Toilet. Hugo Williams. FaBoBl

Toilette, The. John Gay and Alexander Pope. ECEV

Toiling fisher here is tewing of his net, The. The Fen-Men of Lincolnshire's Holland. Michael Drayton. Fr. Polyolbion. FaBoPP

Toiling of Felix, The, sels. Henry van Dyke.
  Angler's Reveille, The. GN
  "Legend of Felix is ended, the toiling of Felix is done, The." BLPA

Toils Are Pitched, The. Sir Walter Scott. Fr. Lady of the Lake, The. EnRP

To'invent, and practise this one way, to'annihilate all three. (LL) The Will. John Donne. CBCK; EBEV; ImPo; LiTB; NoSic

Tōji. Gary Snyder. PoBeRe

Token. Alison Bielski. AngWe

Token, The. F. T. Prince. FaBoTw; OxBTC

Token, A. Robert Creeley. VGW

Token Woman, The. Marge Piercy. NALW

Token woman gleams like a gold molar in a toothless mouth, The. The Token Woman. Marge Piercy. NALW

Tokens. William Barnes. PoEL-4

Tokens, The. Francis Thompson. Fr. Daisy. OtMeF

Tokens of Love, The. Unknown. GBP

Told us that she would never die. (LL) Women Are Not Gentlemen. Harley Matthews. NOBAu

Toledo. Roy Campbell. MoBrPo

Toledo Room, The, sels. Alistair Paterson.
  "They do it with knives." PeNZ

Tolerance of Crows, The. Charles Donnelly. CIP

Toleration. John Barford. PeHV

Toll for the brave! On the Loss of the Royal George. William Cowper. EBEV; GN; NOBE; TrGrPo
  (Royal George, The. FaPoR; PlP
  (Loss of the "Royal George".) GTBS; GTBS-P; OxAEP-1

Toll no bell for me, dear Father, dear Mother. The Changeling. Charlotte Mew. CH; CoGr

Toll! Roland, toll! The Great Bell Roland. Theodore Tilton. PAH

Toll the bell, fellow. The Red Cow Is Dead. E. B. White. NBLV; NYBP

Tolling. Lucy Larcom. OHIP

Tolling from St. Patrick's, The. Burial of an Irish President. Austin Clarke. BIrV; IPY

Tollund Man, The. Seamus Heaney. BIrV; CIP; EBEV; FaBoMo; IPY; NoP; PBCIP; PNI; TEP

Tolquhon Castle. Margaret Toms. PAW

Tom. Victor Questel. PBCV

Tom. James Schuyler. GLP

Tom Agnew, Bill Agnew. Dante Gabriel Rossetti. ChTr; FaBoEE

Tom Bowling. Charles Dibdin. See Here, a sheer hulk, lies poor Tom Bowling.

Tom Brainless as Student and Preacher at College. John Trumbull. Fr. Progress of Dulness, The. AmPP

Tom Brainless, at the close of last year. An Amorous Temper. John Trumbull. Fr. Progress of Dulness, The. AmPP

Tom Brown's two little Indian boys. Unknown. OxNR

Tom-Cat, The. Don Marquis. PoRA

Tom Child had often painted Death. This Morning Tom Child, the Painter, Died. Samuel Sewall. SCAP

Tom Dansey was a famous whip. John Masefield. Fr. Reynard the Fox. OtMeF

Tom Dooley. Unknown. AmFP

Tom Farley. Colin Thiele. NOBAu

Tom Fool at Jamaica. Marianne Moore. NYBP

Tom Gage's Proclamation. Unknown. PAH

Tom — garlanded with squat and surely steel. Tom's Garland: Upon the Unemployed. Gerard Manley Hopkins. EnVR; FaBoPV; Son

Tom, He Was a Piper's Son. Unknown. GBP; OxNR

Tom Joanides. Lloyd Schwartz. EOEF

Tom Jones's Plum Tree. Unknown. AmFP

Tom o' Bedlam. Unknown. CH; CoGr; FaBoCh; PoRA

Tom o' Bedlam's Song. Unknown. ChTr; GGP; ImPo; InvP; LiTB; Mes; OtMeF; PoEL-2; TFi; TrGrPo

Tom o'Bedlam. Unknown. See From the hag [or hagg] and hungry [or hungrie] goblin.

Tom O'Roughley. W. B. Yeats. CMoP

Tom Pearse, Tom Pearse, lend me your gray mare. Widdecombe [or Widdicombe] Fair. Unknown. CH; MoShBr

Tom Potts. Unknown. ESPB

Tom Southerne's Birth-Day Dinner at LD. Orrery's. Pope. NAs

Tom Sucklebat, in dressing-gown, without his teeth. An Administrator. Geoffrey Grigson. FaBoEE

Tom Teeple ate a steeple. Unknown. RoPo

Tom Tell-Truth. Unknown. CBNP

Tom the Porter. John Byrom. NOEC

Tom Thumbkin. Unknown. OxNR

Tom tied a kettle to the tail of a cat. Unknown. ISE

Tom Tiler; or, The Nurse. Unknown. APAS

Tom-tom, c'est moi. The blue guitar. Wallace Stevens. Fr. Man with the Blue Guitar, The. CMoP; LiTA; RaBo

Tom, Tom, the piper's son. Mother Goose. OxNR

Tom Tyler and His Wife, sels. Unknown.
"Proverb reporteth, no man can deny, The." EII

Tom Wedgwood Tells. Brian W. Aldiss. NOBL

Tomarata. Kendrick Smithyman. PeNZ

Tomato Ketchup. Unknown. See If you do not shake the bottle.

Tomatoes. Stephen Dobyns. NAmP90

Tomatoes, The. Teresa Moszkowicz-Syrop. BTR

Tomatoes. Luis J. Rodriguez. AfAz

Tomb — just a canal-bank seat for the passer-by. (LL) Lines Written on a Seat on the Grand Canal, Dublin. Patrick Kavanagh. BIrV; CMoP; InPS; IPY; NOIV

Tomb of an Ancestor, sels. Allen Curnow.
"Oldest of us burst into tears and cried, The." PeNZ

Tomb of Crethon, The. Leonidas of Tarentum, tr. fr. Greek by John Hermann Merivale. AWP

Tomb of Diogenes, The. Unknown, tr. fr. Greek by John Addington Symonds. AWP

Tomb of Heracles, The. James McAuley. Fr. Hero and the Hydra, The. FaBoMA

Tomb of Ibykos, The. Unknown, tr. fr. Greek by Peter Jay. GrAn

Tomb of Lt. John Learmonth, A.I.F., The. John Manifold. CBAP; FaBoMA; PAW

Tomb of the Brave, The. Joseph Hutton. PAH

Tomb of the Kings, The. Anne Hébert, tr. by Kathleen Weaver. PBWP

Tomb of the Kings, The. Anne Hébert, tr. by Aliki and Willis Barnstone. BoWoP

Tomb of the Naiads, The. Pierre Louÿs, tr. fr. French by Philip L. Miller. RiWo

Tomb on the Shore, A. Asclepiades, tr. fr. Greek by Alan Marshfield. GrAn

Tomb on the Thracian approaches of Olympus holds, A. On the Tomb of Orpheus. Damagetus, tr. fr. Greek by John Heath-Stubbs and Carol A. Whiteside. GrAn

Tombstone told when she died, The. Dylan Thomas. OxBTC

Tomcat born on railroad. Autobiography. Tom Weatherly. NBV

Tomlinson. Kipling. BeLS; OtMeF

Tommie Makes My Tail Toddle. Burns. ErPo

Tommies in the Train. D. H. Lawrence. PoWW

Tommy. Kipling. EBEV; FaBoEH; FaBV; FaPoR; MoBrPo; NoP; OBWP; OHCV; OxAEP-2; OxBTC; PAW; PeVV; PFP; PlP; UV, ll. 1–18

Tommy Again, Finally. David Budbill. ETG

Tommy has dropped his atom bomb. They Dared Him. Kevin Myhill. PAW

Tommy Johnson is no good. Unknown. ISE

Tommy kept a chandler's shop. Unknown. OxNR

Tommy O'Linn was a Scotsman born. Unknown. OxNR

Tommy Tibule. Unknown. OxNR

Tommy Tittlemouse. Mother Goose. See Little Tommy Tittlemouse/ Lived in a little house.

Tommy Trot, a man of law. Unknown. OxNR

Tommy Tucker. Mother Goose. OxNR; ReMoGo

Tommy's Dead. Sydney Thompson Dobell. PeVV

Tommy's tears and Mary's fears. Fears and Tears. Unknown. ReMoGo

Tomorrow. Anna Laetitia Barbauld. ECWP

Tomorrow. John Collins. GTBS; GTBS-P

Tomorrow. Kenneth Fearing. CMoP

Tomorrow. John Henry Mackay, tr. fr. German by Philip L. Miller. RiWo

Tomorrow. William Olsen. NAmP90

Tomorrow. Mark Strand. GOYP

Tomorrow, and Tomorrow, and Tomorrow. Shakespeare. See She should have died hereafter.

Tomorrow come never. Unknown. ISE

Tomorrow, friend, will be another day. Faith for Tomorrow. Thomas Curtis Clark. PoToHe

Tomorrow, half past nine? Yes, I'll be here. (LL) Monologue in a Rand Hospital. William Elijah Hunter. PeSAV

Tomorrow Is a Birthday. Gwendolen Haste. GoYe

Tomorrow Is My Birthday, sels. Edgar Lee Masters.
Thing Is Sex, Ben, The. NAs

Tomorrow is saint valentine's day. Shakespeare. Fr. Hamlet. EnLoPo; NAWM-1; NoSic
(Saint Valentine's Day.) CH; LiTB
(Song: "Tomorrow is Saint Valentine's Day.") EBEvV; FaPON; NTCP

Tomorrow, Julia, I betimes must rise. The Perfume. Robert Herrick. CaPo

Tomorrow let loveless, let lover tomorrow make love. The Vigil of Venus. Unknown, tr. fr. Latin by Allen Tate. GBL

Tomorrow morn I'll be sixteen, and Billy Grimes the rover. Billy Grimes. Unknown. AmFP

Tomorrow Morning. John Harkness. UnDi

Tomorrow morning I will take a shower. Valerio Magrelli, tr. fr. Italian by Dana Gioia. NeIt

Tomorrow morning, some poet will wake up. Modern Poetry. Anita Skeen. IHMS

Tomorrow shall be my dancing day. Unknown. See To-morrow shall be my dancing day.

Tomorrow, since I have so few. Rooster. James Tate. LCAP, tr. by Dreamy cars graze on the dewy boulevard

Tomorrow storm shall carry you away. (LL) Prophet, Go, Flee! Hayyim Nahman Bialik. MHP

Tomorrow the Heroes. Alfred B. Spellman. PoBA

Tomorrow, the twentieth, we celebrate. To Piso, on Epicurus' Birthday. Philodemus, tr. fr. Greek by William Moebius. GrAn

Tomorrow the wind will have fallen. Epitaph of a Sailor. Antiphilus, tr. fr. Greek by Dudley Fitts. GrAn

Tomorrow to fresh woods and pastures new. (LL) Lycidas. Milton. AWP; ChTr; EBEV; EBEvV; FHYEP; HAP; ImPo; InPS; JCP; LiTB; NOBE; NoP; NOSC; OAEL-1; OBEV; OxAEP-1; PoEL-3; Poetr; PPP; PrIm; SCGP; TFi; TrGrPo; UnPo; WGRP

Tomorrow we part. Tune: "Song of the Southern Country." Chu Yi-tsun, tr. fr. Chinese by Irving Y. Lo. SuSp

Tomorrow we'll be good. Bad Blood. Tchicaya U Tam'si, *tr. fr. French* by Ellen Conroy Kennedy. NegPo

Tomorrow when the farm boys find this. The Two-headed Calf. Laura Gilpin. FYAP

Tomorrow will be Monday. (*LL*) As Tommy Snooks and Bessy Brooks. Mother Goose. OxNR; ReMoGo

Tomorrow with the maple grow old. (*LL*) High Dike. Li Ho. PLT

Tomorrow you will live, you always cry. Procrastination. Martial, *tr. by* Abraham Cowley. AWP; FaBoEE; OBVE

Tomorrows. James Merrill. OBAL

Tomorrows reactivate somnolence. Of Promises and Prophecy. Steve Chimombo. HBAPE

Tomorrow's the Fair. *Unknown.* GBP

Tom's Angel. Walter de la Mare. Mes

Tom's Garland: Upon the Unemployed. Gerard Manley Hopkins. EnVR; FaBoPV; Son

Tom's sickness did his morals mend. Matthew Prior. FaBoEE

Tomtit, The. Walter de la Mare. FM

Ton of white rain will overflow my self-shaped sleeping-bag of earth, A. Exultation. John James. VaA

Tone-deaf old person of Tring, A. *Unknown.* PeLi

Tone of Voice, The. *Unknown.* PoToHe

Tones on the mind. I pick them and they sing. (*LL*) Music by the Waters. John Hay. FoLa

Tongs. Mother Goose. *See* Long legs, crooked thighs.

Tongue, The. Phillips Burrows Strong. PoToHe; WBLP

Tongue, The. Pia Tafdrup. TSaS, *tr. by* Monique M. Kennedy *and* Thomas E. Kennedy

Tongue (De First Instrument), De. Levi Tafari. NBrP

Tongue-Doughty Pedant. Thomas Edwards. Son

Tongue, never cease to sing Fidessae's praise. Bartholomew Griffin. *Fr.* Fidessa, More Chaste than Kind[e]. ESo

Tongue of the waves tolled in the earth's bell, The. The Want Bone. Robert Pinsky. EOEF

Tongue shapes and molds sound. Speech, The. Not Sense. Gail Tremblay. WeW

Tongue that mothered such a metaphor, The. Hogwash. Robert Francis. LCAP; NIP; TRP

Tongue-tied in Black and White. Michael S. Harper. HCAP

Tongues. Philip Martin. NOBAu

Tongues of Dying Men, The. Shakespeare. *See* O, but they say the tongues of dying men.

Tongues we use for talking. Tailpiece. Max Fatchen. OTCP

Tonight. Franklin P. Adams. FiBHP

Tonight. Julius Balbin. BTR

Tonight. (*LL*) Distress. Flavien Ranaivo. NegPo

Tonight a blackout. Twenty years ago. Christmas Eve under Hooker's Statue. Robert Lowell. CAPP; FF; OxBA

Tonight, after a rain. The Longing for Eternal Life. Liz Rosenberg. PBCAP

Tonight and forever I shall be yours so says the oleo king. Some Stories of the Beauty Wapiti. Ebbe Borregaard. NeAP

Tonight as I sleep alone. *Unknown, tr. fr. Japanese by* Kenneth Rexroth *and* Ikuko Atsumi. WPJ

Tonight, at Least, My Sinner. Gond Oral Tradition, *tr. by* V. Elwin *and* S. Hivale. WTO

Tonight, at Least, My Sinner. *Unknown, tr. by* V. Elwin *and* S. Hivale. WTO

Tonight, at the bar. The Leather Bar. Ralph Pomeroy. PeHV

Tonight, because her hand. The Skin of Her Neck. Bob Arnold. ETG

Tonight, grave sir, both my poor[e] house and I. Inviting a Friend to Supper. Ben Jonson, *after* Martial. AWP; BeJo; EnRePo; JCP; LiTB; NOBE; NoP; NOSC; OAEL-1; OBF; OxBoLi; PeLV; PoEL-2; PPP; SeCP; SeCV-1

Tonight/ he is understanding Canada. Understanding Canada. Peter Sirr. PBCIP

Tonight I am told. Juan Rulfo Moved Away. Alberto A. Ríos. UL

Tonight I Can Write the Saddest Lines. Pablo Neruda, *tr. fr. Spanish.* BoLoP; LPA, *tr. by* W. S. Merwin

Tonight I could die as easily as the grass. In the Soul Hour. Robert Mezey. AmPA; NaP

Tonight I disentangle. Wakepick I. Kristjana Gunnars. NOBC

Tonight I looked at it; I don't adore. The Poet Holds His Future in His Hand. B. S. Johnson. FaBoBl

Tonight I looked at the pale northern sky. Back. Robert Mezey. AmPA

Tonight I think about your flat in Sundays Well. Particulars. Thomas McCarthy. IB

Tonight I thought of you as I smoked a cigar. Havana Blues. Henry Carlile. SM

Tonight I want to say something wonderful. For the Sleepwalkers. Edward Hirsch. FYAP

Tonight I watch my father's hair. Two Postures beside a Fire. James Wright. HCAP; HeIP

Tonight I will remember the model. When Father Decided He Did Not Love Her Anymore. Lynn Emanuel. NAmP90

Tonight, I'll pull your limbs through. The Mulatta as Penelope. Lorna Goodison. PBCV

Tonight I'll walk the razor along your throat. Punk Pantoum. Pamela Stewart. SM

Tonight in our secret town. Right Now. William Stafford. NaP

Tonight in the cold I know most of the living are waiting. Elegy for the Nightbound. Anthony Cronin. PBCIP

Tonight in the hills there was a light. Hawktree. Dave Jeddie Smith. HCAP

Tonight is the night. Hallowe'en. Harry Behn. FaPON; PDV

Tonight it is raining ice, no thunder, no light-. Night Gives Us the Next Day. Minnie Bruce Pratt. ETG

Tonight let reeds be growing. Beyond Silence. Lan Ling, *tr. fr. Chinese by* Kenneth Rexroth *and* Ling Chung. WPC

Tonight my children hunch. It Out-Herods Herod. Pray You, Avoid It. Anthony Hecht. CoAP; NIP; NoAM; NOBA; OxBC

Tonight my mother was born. Toys, Dream. Novica Tadic, *tr. fr. Serbo-Croatian by* Charles Simic. HSix

Tonight no one takes fish. Tattered pennants. Sailing the Back River. Dave Jeddie Smith. MT

Tonight, on the deck, the lights. Two Stories. Charles Wright. FYAP; LCAP

Tonight on the stormy mountain. (*LL*) When Will I Be Home? Li Shang-yin. OHMPC

Tonight our cat, Tahi, who lately lost. The Buried Stream. James K. Baxter. OxBC

Tonight our heaven is an estuary. Pearls. Alan Gould. NOBAu

Tonight she comes for me. (*LL*) On the Morning of the Third Night above Nisqually. W. M. Ransom. CDW; NU

Tonight the Famous Psychiatrist. Louis Simpson. OxBC

Tonight, the first snow. November Song. Mark Vinz. Poetsp

Tonight the moon is high, to summon all. William Bell. FaBoTw

Tonight the moths. Tyranny of Moths. Gerald Vizenor. VoR

Tonight the wind gnaws. Christmas Landscape. Laurie Lee. OBCP

Tonight the winds begin to rise. Tennyson. *See* To-night the winds begin to rise.

Tonight there's a mirror on the sidewalk. Heaven. Mark Doty. NAmP90

Tonight they need to be both host and stranger. Familiar Story. Alan Shapiro. DiPo; NIP

Tonight, tonight, the pillow fight. *Unknown.* RoPo

Tonight ungathered let us leave. Tennyson. *Fr.* In Memoriam A. H. H. EBVV, *abr.*; FHYEP; OAEL-2, *abr.*; PeECV, *abr.*

Tonight when I knelt down next to our cat, Zooey. Wild Gratitude. Edward Hirsch. SoCa

Tonight when the hoar frost falls on the wood. Christmas in the Wood. Frances Frost. TrCP

Tonight/ when the moon comes out. Proposition. Nicolás Guillén, *tr. fr. Spanish by* Langston Hughes. FaPON; TTY

Tonight with the blade's weight. Before the Wall. Roberta Hill Whiteman. ETG

Tonight with wine being poured. Jalal al-Din Rumi, *tr. fr. Persian by* Coleman Barks *and* John Moyne. *Fr.* Four Quatrains. RaBo

Tonight, within my heart. (*LL*) My Little Dreams. Georgia Douglas Johnson. BlSi; CDC; PoNe

Tonight words fall away from me like shed clothing. Last Poem. Margaret Atwood. LCAP

Tonight you broke into my dreams. For Anne, Who Doesn't Know. Gail Fox. IHMS

Tonio told me at catechism. The Purpose of Altar Boys. Alberto A. Ríos. AfAz

Tonite I walked out of my red apartment door on East tenth street's dusk. Allen Ginsberg. *Fr.* Mugging. HCAP; NoAM; PoBeRe

Tonite, thriller was. Beware: Do Not Read This Poem. Ishmael Reed. BPo; NIP; NoP; PoBA

Tonopah's/ the only place. Driving to Vegas. Kirk Robertson. NGP

Tonversation with Baby, A. Morris Bishop. FiBHP

Tony Get the Boys. D. L. Graham. PoBA

Tony O! Colin Francis. CH; CoGr; FaBoCo

Tony/ To be casual and have the wish to heal. The Book of Gawain. Jack Spicer. *Fr.* Holy Grail, The. PoM

(How Many Times?) ELP
(How Many Times Do I Love Thee, Dear?) EnRP; NAEL-2
(Song.) ImPo
Torso: Passages 18, The. Robert Duncan. CAPP
Tortoise, The. Cid Corman. InPK; SM; VGW
Tortoise Gallantry. D. H. Lawrence. CMoP; MoP
Tortoise in Eternity, The. Elinor Wylie. FaPON
Tortoise-Shell. D. H. Lawrence. CMoP; FaBoVe; FM; MeMBP; NAEL-2; OAEL-2; OxAEP-2
Tortoise Shout. D. H. Lawrence. LiTM; NAEL-2
Torture. Margaret Atwood. PoE
Torture. Wislawa Szymborska. WoWa
Torture chamber is not like anything, The. Footnote to the Amnesty Report on Torture. Margaret Atwood. NoAM
Torture scene developed under a glass bell, The. Heirloom. Leonard Cohen. NOBC
Torture, that we pray it may be mild. The Beanstalk, Meditated Later. Judith Wright. NoAM
Tortured body, lie at rest alone. Unknown Man in the Morgue. Merrill Moore. MoAmPo
Tortured Heart, The. Rimbaud, tr. fr. French. PeHV
Tortured mullet served the Roman's pride, The. On a Vase of Gold-Fish. Charles Tennyson Turner. NOBVV
Tortured, sick, and hungry. Auschwitz #6. Alfred Van Loen. BTR
Tory Pledges. Thomas Moore. FaBoCo; OBSV
Toss and turn on bamboo mat. Unknown, tr. by Michael E. Workman. Fr. Tzu-yeh Songs of the Four Seasons. SuSp
Toss not my soul, O Love, 'twixt hope and fear. Unknown. NoSic
Toss your gay heads. At April. Angelina Weld Grimké. BlSi; VBLP
Tossed in a troubled sea of griefs, I float. To Her in Absence; a Ship. Thomas Carew. CaPo
Tossed night between us, A. Schooner. Edward Kamau Brathwaite. PBCV
Tossed on the stormy waves of time. I Was a Stranger and Ye Took Me In. Mary E. Tucker. CBWP-1
Tossing his mane of snows in wildest eddies and tangles. Earliest Spring. William Dean Howells. OBEV
(In Earliest Spring.) FaBoBe
Total Eclipse. Michael J. Rosen. DiPo
Total Influence or Outcome of the Matter: The Sun, The. Marge Piercy. WPOW
Total inventory of one wife's general store, The. (LL) One Man's Wife. Philip Booth. VGW
Totalled. Peter McDonald. PNI
Totally conscious, and apropos of nothing, he comes to see me. Jalal al-Din Rumi, tr. fr. Persian by Coleman Barks with A. J. Arberry. EnlH
Totem, The. Léopold Sédar Senghor, tr. fr. French by Ellen Conroy Kennedy. NegPo
T'other eb'ning eb'ryting was still, Oh! babe. Mister Johnson. Ben Harney. OBAL
Totting up the takings, quick Death can/ reckon much faster than the businessman. Palladas, tr. fr. Greek by Tony Harrison. GrAn
Toucan, The. Pyke Johnson, Jr. NTCP; ZA
Touch. Thom Gunn. CMoP
Touch, The. James Graham, Marquess of Montrose. Fr. My Dear and Only Love. BeJo; JCP; OtMeF
Touch. Octavio Paz, tr. fr. Spanish. BoLoP; LPA, tr. by Charles Tomlinson
Touch black, touch black! Unknown. RoPo
Touch but thy lyre, my Harry, and I hear. To Master Henry Lawes, the Excellent Composer, of His Lyrics. Robert Herrick. CaPo
Touch, cup/ the lips. Leontios, tr. fr. Greek by Peter Jay. GrAn
Touch — for there is a spirit in the woods. (LL) Nutting. Wordsworth. EnRP; NAEL-2; NU; OAEL-2; PFP; Poetr; RB
Touch/ is what the eyes do, sometimes. From a Brother Dreaming in the Rye. James Cunningham. JB
Touch It. Robert Mezey. NaP
Touch it: it won't shrink like an eyeball. A Life. Sylvia Plath. NOBA
Touch me, touch me. Grass Fingers. Angelina Weld Grimké. CDC; ShDr
Touch my hand as though it were an old coin. Sailing in Crosslight. Anita Skeen. IHMS
Touch of cold in the autumn night, A. Autumn. T. E. Hulme. FaBoMo; NTP
Touch of Human Hands, The. Thomas Curtis Clark. PoToHe
Touch of Impatience, A. Fleur Adcock. PWE
Touch of Spring. John Updike. SoCa
Touch of the Master's Hand, The. Myra Brooks Welch. BLPA; PoToHe

Touch pages picturing snakes. (LL) Reading of the Rattlesnake. Lynn Lonidier. SRLS
Touch some gray ruin on the hill. (LL) From Sorrow Sorrow Yet Is Born. Tennyson. OxBSP
Touch Thou Mine Eyes. Marion Franklin Ham. AH
Touché. Jessie Redmond Fauset. BlSi; CDC; ShDr; VBLP
Touching Each Other's Surfaces. Carol Jane Bangs. NIP
Touching Ezekiel his workman's hand. Jesus. James McAuley. CBAP; ChIV-2; FaBoMA
Touching Heartsease. Janet Sutherland. DT; NBrP
Touching Shoulders. Unknown. BLPA
Touching the Past. Robert Sargent. Jaz
Touching the tulips was a shyness. Tulips. Medbh McGuckian. PNI
Touching Up. Janet Fisher. NWP
Touching your goodness, I am like a man. The Illiterate. William Meredith. NoP; VCAP
Touchstone, The. Kalonymos ben Kalonymos, tr. fr. Hebrew by J. Chotzner. TrJP
Sels.
  Hypocrite, The.
  Unfortunate Male, The.
  Yoke, The.
Tough Captain Spud and his First Mate, Spade. Captain Spud and His First Mate, Spade. John Ciardi. OBCA
Tough Generation, A. David Gascoyne. LiTM
Tough hand closes gently on the load, The. Man Carrying Bale. Harold Monro. MoBrPo
Tough traveller with your Celtic view. Pelagius. Gwyn Williams. AngWe
Toughest gal I ever did see. Kissie Lee. Margaret Walker. BlSi; NALW; NMM
Toujours la Politesse. Ezra Pound, after the Chinese. OBVE
Toulouse Lautrec. Melvin B. Tolson, tr. fr. Norwegian by Nadia Christensen. PBWP
Tour de Force. Peter Kane Dufault. ErPo
Tour 5. Robert Hayden. PPP
Tour Guide: La Maison des Esclaves. Melvin Dixon. ETG
Tour of Duty. David Huddle. Son
Sels.
  Nerves.
  Words.
Tour to the Glaciers of Savoy, A, sels. "Eliza." Epistle to John Walker, Esq., An. ECWP
Touring. David Morton. TrPWD
Touring the old miles again. Baldpate Pond. E. F. Weisslitz. NYBP
Touris, white man, wipin his face. The Song of the Banana Man. Evan Jones (b. 1927). PBCV
Tourist. Yehuda Amichai, tr. fr. Hebrew by Assia Gutmann. AnRep
Tourist, as he views the place, The. Taliesin Williams. Fr. Cardiff Castle. AngWe
Tourist came in from Orbitville, A. Southbound on the Freeway. May Swenson. GoJo; ImGa; NTCP; NYBP
Tourist Country. William Stafford. NoAM
Tourist dame, A. Miss Tourist. "Lord Kitchener." PBCV
Tourist Death. Archibald MacLeish. NAAL-2
Tourist from Syracuse, The. Donald Justice. CAPP; NoAM; TwCP; VCAP
Tourist in Seat 29, The, sels. M. K. Joseph.
Tourist, spare the avid glance. The Attic Landscape. Herman Melville. AnAmPo; NOBA; OBAL
Tourists. Yehuda Amichai, tr. fr. Hebrew by Glenda Abramson and Tudor Parfitt. PoSu
Tourists, The. C. Day Lewis. OBTV
Tourists. Howard Moss. FiBHP; NYBP; PeLV
Tournament of Tottenham, The. Unknown. OxBoLi
Tours. Charles David Wright. MT
Toussaint L'Ouverture. H. Cordelia Ray. CBWP-3
Toussaint L'Ouverture. E. A. Robinson. PoNe
Toussaint L'Overture., sels. George Clinton Rowe.
  His Ancestry. AAP
  His Boyhood. AAP
  His Manhood. AAP
  His Prime. AAP
Toussaint, the most unhappy man of men! To Toussaint L'Ouverture. Wordsworth. EnRP; FaBoPV; InPK; NOBE; OBNC; PoNe; PoRA; PPP; TrGrPo
Toward Lesbos. Renée Vivien, tr. fr. French by Sandia Belgrade. PeHV
Toward lifting them above their crippling storm. (LL) The Elevator Man Adheres to Form. Margaret Danner. PoBA; PoNe

Toward morning the sun strolled in the forest. Isaac. Amir Gilboa, *tr. fr. Hebrew* by Ruth Finer Mintz. MHP

Toward my own face. (*LL*) Fog and the Fire-Hose. Nina Solomon. VBLP

Toward the dawn. B. E. Baughan. *Fr.* Maui's Fish. PeNZ

Toward the end of her life she said that the. Berthe Morisot. Anne Waldman. UL

Toward the end of my. A Girl My Age. Lizbeth Parker. NGP

Toward the Messiah's advent. (*LL*) Put Me into the Breach. Yehuda Karni. MHP

Toward the person who has died. Dying Away. William Meredith. NoAM

Toward the river ferry taking sounding after sounding. (*LL*) Lost Letter to James Wright, with Thanks for a Map of Fano. Gibbons Ruark. MT

Toward the sea turning my troubled eye. The Huge Leviathan. Spenser. *Fr.* Visions of the World's Vanity. ChTr

Toward the Solstice. Adrienne Rich. NAAL-2; NoP

Toward the Verrazano. Stephen Dunn, *tr.* by Joachim Neugroschel. AnAn

Toward Umbria. Stanley Plumly. NAmP90

Toward which all hungers leap, all pleasures pass. (*LL*) A Baroque Wall-Fountain in the Villa Sciarra. Richard Wilbur. AmPP; CAPP; NAAL-2; NoP; NYBP; Poetr; TwCP; VCAP

Toward which you lend no part! (*LL*) El Hombre. William Carlos Williams. CMoP; LiTA; SAmP

Toward Winter. *Unknown.* NOIV
Sels.
"Night is cold on the Great Bog, The."
"Sliab Cua, dark and broken, is full of wolf packs."
"Want and winter are upon us."
"We are shattered and battered, engulfed."

Toward world's end, through the bare. The Magi. Louise Glück. PoA

Towards Democracy, *sels.* Edward Carpenter.
Through the Long Night. PeHV

Towards Evening. Andreas Grimelund Jynge, *tr. fr. Norwegian* by Philip L. Miller. RiWo

Towards Lillers. Ivor Gurney. NAEL-2

Towards nightfall when the wind. Winter Mask. Allen Tate. OxBA; Prf

Towards the altar sober-paced I went. Keats. *Fr.* Fall of Hyperion, The. TOF

Towards the end he sailed into an extraordinary mildness. Herman Melville. W. H. Auden. LiTA; MeMAP; OxBA

Towards the End of a Century. E. A. Markham. NBrP

Towards the end the fortunes of the king. Of Kings and Dukes. Roy Fuller. AnAn

Towards the Land of the Composer. Francis Webb. FaBoMA

Towards the Last Spike, *sels.* E. J. Pratt.
Gathering, The. MoCV
Precambrian [*or* Pre-Cambrian] Shield, The. MoCV; NOBC

Towards the songs' pretended sea. (*LL*) Legacy. Amiri Baraka. MoP; NoAM; NOBA; PoBA

Towards the Source., *sels.* Christopher John Brennan.

Towards the starry sky. Hashimoto Takako, *tr. fr. Japanese* by Kenneth Rexroth *and* Ikuko Atsumi. WPJ

Towards the sun, towards the south-west. D. H. Lawrence. *Fr.* Eagle in New Mexico. RB

Towards the Vanishing Point. David Lehman. SM

T'owd pig's got mezzles an' she's deead, poor thing. The Dead Pig. *Unknown.* FaBoNo

Tower, The. (What shall I do with this absurdity.) W. B. Yeats. CMoP; LiTB; LiTM; MeMBP; NoAM; PoE; SCGP
Sels.
"Now shall I make my soul." OBD

Tower, no ivy, I. The wind was powerless, A. Hecuba's Testament. Rosario Castellanos, *tr. fr. Spanish* by John Frederick Nims. STV

Tower of Babel, The. Nathaniel Crouch. OxBChV

Tower of Babel, The. Joshua Sylvester. *Fr.* Divine Weeks and Works of Guillaume de Saluste Sieur Du Bartas, The. NoSic

Tower of Babel, The. Laurance Wieder. ChIV-1

Tower of Famine, The. Shelley. Poetr

Tower of Refuge is our God, A! Ein feste Burg ist unser Gott. Martin Luther, *tr.* by M. Woolsey Stryker. CTC

Tower of Skulls, The. Isaac Rosenberg. PeFWW

Tower of the Dream, The, *sels.* Charles Harpur.

Towering, thick, its straight trunk soars. An Old Pine. Wang An-shih, *tr. fr. Chinese* by Jan W. Walls. SuSp

Towery city and branchy between towers. Duns Scotus's Oxford. Gerard Manley Hopkins. EBEV; FaBoPP; GTBS-P; MeMBP; NAEL-2; NoAM; OBMV; OxAEP-2; PeECV; PoEL-5

Town again, trailing your legs and crying! The. (*LL*) Wild Swans. Edna St. Vincent Millay. CMoP; MoAmPo; PBWP; UnPo

Town and Country. James Whitcomb Riley. AnAmPo

Town Betrayed, The. Edwin Muir. CMoP

Town,/ branches over the river. Kaunas 1941. Johannes Bobrowski, *tr. fr. German* by Ruth Mead *and* Matthew Mead. AnRep

Town Called Providence, Its Fate, The. Benjamin Tompson. SCAP

Town Child, The. Irene Thompson. BoTP

Town Clerk's Views, The. Sir John Betjeman. CMoP

Town does not exist, The. The Starry Night. Anne Sexton. NoAM; PoE; VCAP

Town Dump, The. Howard Nemerov. CMoP; MAT

Town Eclogues. Lady Mary Wortley Montagu. ECEV
Sels.
"Ill fates pursue me, may I never find"

Town Gone to Sleep. Anne Carson. *Fr.* Life of Towns, The. BAP-90

Town History, 1917. David Huddle. PBCAP

Town I Have Heard of, A. Anne Carson. *Fr.* Life of Towns, The. BAP-90

Town I Left. Helen Sorrells. CrSp; IHMS

Town I was born in was destroyed by shells, The. Yehuda Amichai, *tr. fr. Hebrew. Fr.* Patriotic Songs. PoSu, *tr.* by Yehuda Amichai *and* Ted Hughes

Town is burning somewhere, The. (*LL*) The Fire Station's Delight. Susan Hampton. NOBAu

Town is tilted toward the stream, The. A Sunday Dreamer's Guide to Yarrow, Missouri. Jim Barnes. HATNAP

Town Just Before the Lightning Flash. Anne Carson. *Fr.* Life of Towns, The. BAP-90

Town lies in the valley, A. The Silent Town. Richard Dehmel, *tr. fr. German* by Jethro Bithell. AWP

Town might abort, A. How the Death of a City Is Never More than the Sum of the Deaths of Those Who Inhabit Its Spaces. Victor Coleman. NOBC

Town Mouse and the Country Mouse, The. Matthew Prior. BXAP

Town of Bathsheba's Crossing. Anne Carson. *Fr.* Life of Towns, The. BAP-90

Town of Don't-You-Worry, The. I. J. Barlett. BLPA; WBLP

Town of Finding Out about the Love of God. Anne Carson. *Fr.* Life of Towns, The. BAP-90

Town of Hill, The. Donald Hall. CAPP; TAP

Town of My Farewell to You. Anne Carson. *Fr.* Life of Towns, The. BAP-90

Town of Nogood, The. W. E. Penny. BLPA

Town of Passage, The. *Unknown.* OxBoLi

Town of Passage is both large and spacious, The. The Attractions of a Fashionable Irish Watering-Place. Francis Sylvester Mahony. FaBoPP

Town of Spring Once Again. Anne Carson. *Fr.* Life of Towns, The. BAP-90

Town of the Death of Sin. Anne Carson. *Fr.* Life of Towns, The. BAP-90

Town of the Dragon Vein. Anne Carson. *Fr.* Life of Towns, The. BAP-90

Town of the Little Mouthful. Anne Carson. *Fr.* Life of Towns, The. BAP-90

Town of the Man in the Mind at Night. Anne Carson. *Fr.* Life of Towns, The. BAP-90

Town of the Sound of a Twig Breaking. Anne Carson. *Fr.* Life of Towns, The. BAP-90

Town of the Wrong Questions. Anne Carson. *Fr.* Life of Towns, The. BAP-90

Town on the Way Through God's Woods. Anne Carson. *Fr.* Life of Towns, The. BAP-90

Town or poem, I don't care how it looks. Old woman. White Center. Richard Hugo. NAAL-2; NoP

Town-Rakes, The. *At. to* Peter Anthony Motteux. CoMu

Town remembers no such plenty, The. Lancashire Winter. Tony Connor. OxBTC

Town Window, A. John Drinkwater. BoTP

Town without a Market, The. James Elroy Flecker. MoBrPo

Townspeople peer out of their windows, The. The Wind Carol. Lewis Turco. SM

Tow'rds the lofty walls of Balbi, lo! Durand of Blonden hies. Durand of Blonden. Ludwig Uhland, *tr. fr. German* by James Clarence Mangan. AWP

Towser Shall Be Tied Tonight. *Unknown.* BLPA

Toy Band, The. Sir Henry Newbolt. BoTP

Toy Bone, The. Donald Hall. CAPP

Toy Horse, The. Valentin Iremonger. NOIV

Toy Instruments: A Song. Peter Riley. VaA

Toy of the Titans. Ebenezer Elliot. *Fr.* Year of Seeds, The. Son

Toys, The. Coventry Patmore. *Fr.* Unknown Eros, The. BeLS; EBEV; EBVV; NOBVV; OBEV; OHCV; OxAEP-2; PlP; PoToHe, *sl. diff.*; SoSe; TrGrPo; TrPWD

Toys, Dream. Novica Tadic, *tr. fr. Serbo-Croatian* by Charles Simic. HSix

Toys Talk of the World, The. Katharine Pyle. OBCA

Tra la la la / See me dance the polka. Polka. Edith Sitwell. CBNP

Tra la la la — See me dance the polka. Neptune — Polka. Edith Sitwell. NOBE

Trace, The. Roy Fisher. VaA

Traces, Fine Bird Prints. Lillian Mohin. VBLP

Track. Tomas Tranströmer, *tr. fr. Swedish* by Robert Bly. RB

Track-lining Song. *Unknown.* AmFP

Track of a broad rattler, dragged over dust at dawn, The. The Catch. Brewster Ghiselin. FoLa; HAP

Tracking Rabbits: Night. Jim Barnes. CDW

Tracking the Siuslaw Man. Jim Barnes. HATNAP

Trackless near sea relating to sea. Their Book of Stella. Susan Howe. BCF

Tracks. John Montague. CIP

Tract. William Carlos Williams. BLPL; DL; FF; LiTA; LiTM; MeMAP; MoAB; MoAmPo; MoP; NoAM; NOBA; SAmP; TAP; TrGrPo; TwCP; VGW

Tractatus. Derek Mahon. *See* World Is Everything That Is the Case, The.

Tractor. Ted Hughes. OxAEP-2

Tractor now is an essential, A. Horatian Variation. Leonard Bacon. NYBP

Tractor stands frozen — an agony, The. Tractor. Ted Hughes. OxAEP-2

Trade. Egbert Martin. PBCV

Trade Winds. John Masefield. FaBoCh; OBMV

Trader I am to the African shore, A. Sweet Meat Has Sour Sauce; or, The Slave-Trader in the Dumps. William Cowper. ECEV; NOEC; OBSV

Trader, untie the long stern-cables. Argentarius, *tr. fr. Greek* by Fleur Adcock. GrAn

Traders in Beauty and Delight. Abu Dolama, *tr. fr. Arabic* by Omar S. Pound. ArPe

Trading Cities, *sels.* Italo Calvino, *tr. fr. Italian.* "Proceeding eighty miles into the northwest wind." AnRep, *tr. by* William Weaver

Tradition, Thou Art for Suckling Children. Stephen Crane. MeMAP

Traditional Funeral Songs. *Unknown, tr. fr. Modern Greek* by Willis Barnstone *and* Elene Kolb. BoWoP

Traditional Red. Robert Huff. HoPM

Traditional Women's Song of Algeria. *Unknown. See* Be happy for me, girls,/ my mother-in-law is dead!

Traditions. Seamus Heaney. FaBoMo

Trafalgar. Thomas Hardy. *See* In the wild October night-time, when the wind raved round the land.

Trafalgar. Francis Turner Palgrave. BeLS; FaBoBe

Traffic eyes went blank with cataracts, The. Power Games. Eva Salzman. NWP

Traffic Lights. Lina Kasdaglis, *tr. fr. Modern Greek* by Edmund *and* Mary Keeley. BoWoP

Trafique Is Earth's Great Atlas. George Alsop. SCAP

Tragedie of Philotas, The, *sels.* Samuel Daniel.

Tragedy. "Æ." MoBrPo

Tragedy. Jill Spargur. BLPA

Tragedy, A. Tom Masson. OBAL

Tragedy is Over, The. Jovan Hristic, *tr. fr. Serbo-Croatian* by Charles Simic. HSix

Tragedy is over. Blind Oedipus exits, The. The Tragedy is Over. Jovan Hristic, *tr. fr. Serbo-Croatian* by Charles Simic. HSix

Tragedy of a face in pain, The. Commands of Love. Molly Peacock. PFL

Tragedy of a Shepherd. Mark Akenside. *See* Whoe'er thou art whose path, in summer lies.

Tragedy of Charles Duke of Byron, The. George Chapman. OBD

Tragedy of Dido, The, *sels.* Christopher Marlowe. I Have an Orchard. ChTr

Tragedy of Leaves, The. Charles Bukowski. HoPM

Tragedy of Pete, The. Joseph S. Cotter, Sr. CDC

Tragedy of Pompey the Great, The, *sels.* John Masefield. "Man is a sacred city built of marvelous earth." WGRP

Tragedy of Valentinian, The, *sels.* John Fletcher. Care-charming Sleep [Thou Easer of All Woes]. ELP; FaBoRV; OxBSP; SCGP; TrGrPo (Sleep Song.) NOSC (Song: "Care-charming sleep, thou easer of all woes.") PoEL-2 (Song to Sleep.) OxBoLi

(To Sleep.) PoRA

God Lyaeus, Ever Young. OBEV

Hear, Ye Ladies [That Despise]. CBLP; ElL; ELP; NOBE; OBEV (Mighty Love.) TrGrPo (Song: "Heare ye Ladies that despise.") PoEL-2

Now the Lusty Spring [Is Seen]. ELP; ErPo; FF (Love's Emblems.) BoLoP; ElL; NOBE; NOSC

Tragi-Comedy of Titus Oates, The. *Unknown.* APAS

Tragic Condition of the Statue of Liberty, The. Bernadette Mayer. UL

Tragic Love. W. J. Turner. OBMV

Tragic Mary Queen of Scots, The. "Michael Field." EnLoPo; OBMV

Tragic Mary Queen of Scots, The, II. "Michael Field." OBMV

Tragic, said I. Oh, Tragicker, says she. Noël Tragique. Ramon Guthrie. ErPo

Tragic Story, A. Adelbert von Chamisso, *tr. fr. German* by Thackeray. BoTP; FaPON; MoShBr

Tragic Verses. *Unknown.* CoMu

Tragiques, Les, *sels.* Théodore Agrippa d' Aubigné, *tr. fr. French.* Portrait of Henri III, A. PeHV

Trail All Your Pikes. The Countess of Winchilsea. WPE

Trail all your pikes, dispirit every drum. The Soldier's Death. Anne Finch. OtMeF

Trail among the Pines, A. Lin Pu, *tr. fr. Chinese* by Irving Y. Lo. SuSp

Trail beside the River Platte, The. William Heyen. GOA

Trail climbing/ you have to watch your footing. Finding a Poem. Eve Merriam. RFM

Trail climbs in zig-zags, The. The Trail up Wu Gorge. Sun Yün-feng, *tr. fr. Chinese* by Kenneth Rexroth *and* Ling Chung. BoWoP; PBWP; WPC

Trail Crew Camp at Bear Valley. 9000 Feet. Gary Snyder. HCAP

Trail into Kansas, The. W. S. Merwin. GOA

Trail to Mexico, The. *Unknown.* AmFP

Trail to Mexico, The. *Unknown.* AS

Trail up Wu Gorge, The. Sun Yün-feng, *tr. fr. Chinese* by Kenneth Rexroth *and* Ling Chung. BoWoP; PBWP; WPC

Trailing Consequence: A Triptych, The. Tino Villanueva. AfAz

Trailing her father, bearing his hand axe. Goose. Richard Emil Braun. NoAM

Trailing her silk skirts in the grass. (LL) The Cuckoo Calls from the Bamboo Grove. *Unknown.* OHMPC

Trailing my stick I go down to the garden edge. Poem without a Category. Gensei, *tr. fr. Japanese* by Burton Watson. EnlH

Trails. Patrick Williams. PNI

Train, The. Alan Brownjohn. OxBTC

Train, The. Mary Elizabeth Coleridge. BoTP

Train. Helen Mackay. NSI

Train. Tuo Ssu, *tr. fr. Chinese* by Kenneth Rexroth *and* Ling Chung. WPC

Train, The. *Unknown, tr. by* D. F. van der Merwe. TTY

Train: Abstraction. Genevieve Taggard. WPE

Train at night, A. Night Train. Adrien Stoutenburg. PDV

Train Butcher, The. Thomas Hornsby Ferril. GoYe

Train has come to rest and ceased its creaking, The. La Máquina a Houston. Edward Dorn. PoM

Train has stopped for no apparent reason, The. En Route. Duncan Campbell Scott. NOBC

Train is a dragon that roars through the dark, A. A Modern Dragon. Rowena Bastin Bennett. PDV

Train Is Off the Track, The. *Unknown.* AmFP

Train is Passing, A. Poul Borum, *tr. fr. Danish.* TSaS

Train Journey. Judith Wright. FaBoMA; PBWP

Train of Religion, The, *sels.* Martin Farquhar Tupper. "How beautiful their feet." FaBoCo

Train Ride. John Wheelwright. VGW

Train Runs Late to Harlem, The. Conrad Kent Rivers. PoBA

Train she rides is sixteen coaches long. Mystery Train: Janis Joplin Leaves Port Arthur for Points West, 1964. David Wojahn. *Fr.* Mystery Train: A Sequence. PBCAP

Train shot through the dark, The. Return. Seamus Deane. BIrV; IIP; PBCIP; PNI

Train Song. Fiona Kidman. PeNZ

Train started to take off, The. Exile. Marta Fenyves. LoHo

Train, The! The twelve o'clock for paradise. Week-End. Harold Monro. *Fr.* Week-End. MoBrPo

Train was going downwards very slowly, The. A Dream. Evan Jones (b. 1927). NOBAu

Train will come tomorrow year, The. The Train. Alan Brownjohn. OxBTC

Training. Herrera S. Demetrio, *tr. fr. Spanish* by Dudley Fitts. TTY

Training for the Apocalypse. Gloria Frym. UL

Training I received did not apply because. Nerves. David Huddle. *Fr.* Tour of Duty. Son

Trainride, Vienna — Bonn. Margaret Atwood. LCAP

Trains, The. "Seumas O'Sullivan." BoTP

Trains. Hope Shepherd. BoTP

Trains. James S. Tippett. FaPON

Train's french horn sighs, sheds a few tears, The. To I. Lavrentevaya. Natalya Gorbanevskaya, *tr. fr. Russian by* Daniel Weissbort. BoWoP

Trains Made of Stone. Ray A. Young Bear. CDW

Trains ran through the eleven, The. The Dance of the Elephants. Michael S. Harper. LCAP

Trainyard at Night. Russell Atkins. ETG

Traipsing from school, I used mouth them. Passages. Aidan Carl Mathews. IB

Trakl. Norman Dubie. NAmP90

Tram Driver's Song. R. A. Simpson. FaBoMA

Tramontana at Lerici. Charles Tomlinson. GTBS-P

Tramp. Frank Mkalawile Chipasula. PeSAV

Tramp. Frank Mkalawile Chipasula. HBAPE

Tramp. Richard Hughes. MoBrPo

Tramp, The. Ben King. AnAmPo

Tramp Miner's Song. *Unknown.* AmFP

Tramp, Tramp, Tramp, Keep on a-Tramping. *Unknown.* AS

Tramping. Eduard Friedrich Mörike, *tr. fr. German by* Philip L. Miller. RiWo

Trample her glass. *(LL)* Reckoning. Fay Zwicky. NOBAu

Trample! trample! went the roan. The Cavalier's Escape. George Walter Thornbury. FaBoBe; GN

Trampwoman's Tragedy, A. Thomas Hardy. BeLS; NAEL-2; OBNC; OBNV

Tramway climbs from Merthyr to Dowlais, The. The Deluge 1939. Saunders Lewis, *tr. fr. Welsh by* Gwyn Morgan. OBWVE

Trance, The. Stephen Spender. OxBM

Trane. Edward Kamau Brathwaite. Jaz

Trane/ must have. The Silent Prophet. Norman Jordan. NBV

Trane,/ Trane. Am/Trak. Amiri Baraka. Jaz

Tranquil above the rapids, rocks, and shoals. Richard Monckton Milnes. *Fr.* Burden of Egypt, The. OBTV

Tranquil, vacant is the river, girdled by the setting sun. A Crossing South of Li-chou. Wen T'ing-yün, *tr. fr. Chinese by* William R. Schultz. SuSp

Tranquil waters slept 'neath nature's smile, The. Noonday Thought. H. Cordelia Ray. *Fr.* Group of Musings, A. CBWP-3

Tranquility as his breath, his eye a camera. Observation Car and Cigar. William Stafford. LCAP

Tranquilized, she speaks or does not speak. Marie Ponsot. *Fr.* Nursing: Mother. MDDM

Transaction. A. R. Ammons. HCAP; PoA

Transcendence. Richard Hovey. WGRP

Transcendental Vision: Indigo. Askia Muhammad Touré. BCF

Transcripts from Nature. "Fiona Macleod." FM
Sels.
Eagle, The.
Fireflies.
Rookery at Sunrise, The.
Wasp, The.

Transfiguration, The. Robert Herrick. CaPo

Transfiguration, The. Edwin Muir. ChIV-2; OxBS

Transfiguration of Beauty, The. Michelangelo, *tr. fr. Italian by* John Addington Symonds. AWP

Transfigured Bird. James Merrill. MoAB

Transfigured Night. Ralph Gustafson. MoCV

Transformation. Lewis Alexander. CDC; PoNe

Transformation Scene. Constance Carrier. FYAP; GoYe

Transformations. Rachel Blake. NWP

Transformations. Thomas Hardy. PPP; RB; TEP; TRP

Transformations. Joy Harjo. HATNAP

Transformations. Tadeusz Rózewicz, *tr. fr. Polish by* Czeslaw Milosz. TSaS

Transfusing life, health, comfort, and happiness too. *(LL)* The Song of Hungarrda. Ngunaitponi (David Unaipon). NOBAu

Transfusion. Merrill Moore. PoA

Transience. John Armstrong. *Fr.* Art of Preserving Health, The. NOEC

Transient Americans. Gifts. Karen Snow. FYAP

Transient as a Rose. John Lydgate. MeEL

Transient city, marvellously fair, A. Buffalo. Florence Earle Coates. PAH

Transients Welcome. Gregory Orr. AnAn

Transit. Margaret Avison. FaBoWP

Transit. John Berryman. AnAn

Transit. Adrienne Rich. NoP

Transit. Richard Wilbur. DiPo; LCAP; NGP

Transition — S.M., The. Alfred Islay Walden. AAP

Transitional Objects. Rachel Hadas. UnDi

Transitions, *sels.* Kay Keeshan Hamod. "Your mother's often gone." MDDM

Translate thy proud speech of the sunlight — O lory, come down! *(LL)* To the Red Lory. John Shaw Neilson. NOBAu

Translated Way, The. Franklin P. Adams. FiBHP

Translation. Roy Fuller. NOBE; OxBTC

Translation. Rika Lesser. PoA

Translation. Howard Nemerov. CRP

Translation From, A. Fred Levinson. AmPA

Translation from a Lost Source. Richard Caddel. NBrP

Translation from Petrarch. Petrarch. *See* Mine old dear enemy, my froward master.

Translation from Petrarch, A. Petrarch. *See* What a grudge I am bearing the earth.

Translation from Walter von der Vogelweide, A. Walther von der Vogelweide, *tr. by* J. M. Synge. MoBrPo

Translation is man's deep, continual task. Required Course. Frances Stoakley Lankford. GoYe

Translation of a South American Ode. Goldsmith. NOIV

Translation of Lines by Benserade. Samuel Johnson, *after the French of* Isaac Benserade. FaBoEE

Translation of the Death of a Sparrow, out of Passerat. William Drummond of Hawthornden. ScCV

Translations. Adrienne Rich. WPOW

Translations from the English. George Starbuck. VGW

Translator to Translated. Ezra Pound. FaBoEE

Translucent green on the wall, a dance of leaves. The Green Afternoon. Henry Rago. VGW

Translucent Night, The. Ai Ch'ing, *tr. fr. Chinese.* LHF, *tr. by* Hualing Nieh

Transmarine. Carol Moldaw. UTF

Transmutation. Antoinette Adam. EaPr

Transparence a virtue, as in prose or water. Pears Soap. Cynthia Zarin. UTF

Transparent Grief. Bei Dao, *tr. fr. Chinese by* Donald Finkel *with* Chen Xueliang. SpMi

Transparent Itineraries: 1984. Gustaf Subin. BAP-90

Transparent Life, The. Luigi Fontanella, *tr. fr. Italian by* W. S. Di Piero. NeIt

Transparent Man, The. Anthony Hecht. FYAP

Transplanting. Theodore Roethke. ArNa

Transport of the Bird, The. *(LL)* The Wind Took Up the Northern Things. Emily Dickinson. ArNa; SOTW; TTTS

Transubstantiation. Gary Geddes. NOBC

Trap setter in a steel dawn, The. Once Bitten, Twice Bitten; Once Shy, Twice Shy. Peter Porter. FaBoMA

Trapped me in ice. No, not one chink is gaping. Ennui. Peter Viereck. NYBP

Trapping fairies in West Virginia. Gelett Burgess. FaBoNo

Trappings. Lynda Schramfragel. BAP-89

Tras Os Montes, *sels.* L. E. Sissman. NoP

Trash Men, The. Charles Bukowski. NoP

Trashmen Shaking Hands with Hubert Humphrey at the Opening of Apache Plaza Shopping Center, Suburban Minneapolis, August 1963, The. David Wojahn. *Fr.* Mystery Train: A Sequence. PBCAP

Traubel, Traubel, boil and bubble. I Like to Sing Also. John Updike. FiBHP

Trauma. Brad Leithauser. InPK

Travail of Passion, The. W. B. Yeats. TrCP

Travel. Edna St. Vincent Millay. FaPON; MoShBr; OBCA; PDV

Travel. Robert Louis Stevenson. FaBoCh; FaPON; MoShBr; OHCV; OTCP

Travel Plans. Mary Kathryn Stillwell. PRA

Travel Song. Hugo von Hofmannsthal, *tr. fr. German by* Charles Wharton Stork. TrJP

Travel was homespun, The. Distance of a City. James Berry. PBCV

Traveler, The. Ho Hsun, *tr. fr. Chinese by* Kenneth Rexroth. OHMPC

Traveler, The. Vachel Lindsay. MoAmPo

Traveler, The. Duane Niatum. HATNAP

Traveler, The. *Unknown.* AmFP

Traveler, don't ridicule this farming house as too small. A Farming Family Invites the Guest to Stay Overnight. Fan Ch'eng-ta, *tr. by* Wu-chi Liu. *Fr.* Four Songs in Imitation of Wang Chien. SuSp

Traveler in the wilds, do not. Leonidas, *tr. fr. Greek by* Kenneth Rexroth. PGA

Traveler on a dusty road, A. Little and Great. Charles MacKay. PoLF

Traveler tires of nights on the water, A. Entering the Mouth of P'eng-li Lake. Hsieh Ling-yün, *tr. fr. Chinese by* Francis Westbrook. SuSp

Traveler with his heavy heart, The. The Traveler. Ho Hsun, *tr. fr. Chinese by* Kenneth Rexroth. OHMPC

Traveler's Moon, A. Po Chü-i, *tr. fr. Chinese by* Chiang Yee. SuSp

Travelers return from the city of Zirma with distinct memories. Italo Calvino, *tr. fr. Italian. Fr.* Cities and Signs. AnRep, *tr. by* William Weaver

Traveler's thoughts stretch on forever, A. Climbing Stone Drum Mountain Above the Shores of Shang-shu. Hsieh Ling-yün, *tr. fr. Chinese by* Francis Westbrook. SuSp

Travelers who came that day to Pisa's Baptistry. Echo. Elizabeth Stanton Hardy. GoYe

Travelers who come along the road, The. *(LL)* Crossing Han River. Li P'in. OHMPC

Traveling at Break of Day. Huang Ching-jen, *tr. fr. Chinese by* Chang Yin-nan *and* Lewis C. Walmsley. SuSp

Traveling Back. Sara Hunter. LoHo

Traveling by Boat., *sels.* Wang T'ing-hsiang, *tr. fr. Chinese by* Jonathan Chaves.

Traveling fair pitched by our pasture gate, A. One-Night Fair. Nancy Price. GOYP

Traveling for days to reach you. Journey. Diane Wakoski. IHMS

Traveling for the last time. Traveling Back. Sara Hunter. LoHo

Traveling in the City, *sels.* David Avidan, *tr. fr. Hebrew by* Warren Bargad *and* Stanley F. Chyet.

Traveling merchant west of the river, A. Tune: "Eternal Longing." Unknown, *tr. fr. Chinese by* Hellmut Wilhelm. SuSp

Traveling Onion, The. Naomi Shihab Nye. MT

Traveling sky goes landward, the blind mass, The. Headland. Brewster Ghiselin. PoA

Traveling Star. Ljubomir Simovic, *tr. fr. Serbo-Croatian by* Charles Simic. HSix

Traveling through Ports That Begin with "M." Christy Sheffield Sanford. UL

Traveling through the Dark. William Stafford. CAPP; CoAP; GrPl; HAP; HeIP; InPK; LCAP; LiTM; NoAM; NoP; Poetr; SM; SoSe; TRP; WeW

Traveling to Town. Duane Big Eagle. AiP

Traveling with too much baggage is not a good idea. Maria Luisa Spaziani, *tr. fr. Italian by* Beverly Allen. *Fr.* Star of Free Will, The. NeIt

Traveller, The. John Berryman. PoA; VGW

Traveller, The. C. J. Dennis. NOBAu

Traveller, The. Allen Tate. LiTM

Traveller, A. J. R. Rowland. CBAP

Traveller, A. *Unknown.* WGRP

Traveller for many long years I have been, A. The Widow That Keeps the Cock Inn. *Unknown.* CoMu

Traveller Has Regrets, The. G. S. Fraser. OBTV

Traveller on the skirt of Sarum's Plain, A. Salisbury Plain and Stonehenge. Wordsworth. *Fr.* Guilt and Sorrow. FaBoPP

Traveller, on this ridge a leafless, barkless tree. Philip V, King of Macedon, *tr. fr. Greek by* Edwin Morgan. GrAn

Travel[l]er; or, A Prospect of Society, The, *sels.* Goldsmith.
  Britain. NOEC
  First, Best Country, The. GN
  "My soul . . . turn we to survey." FHYEP
  On Freedom and Ambition. NOIV
  "Remote, unfriended, melancholy, slow." BIrV
  "Turn we to survey." OBTV

Travel[l]er take heed for journeys undertaken in the dark of the year. October Journey. Margaret Walker. PoBA; PoNe

Traveller to Timbuktu, A. *Unknown.* PeLi

Traveller who walks a temperate zone, A. Against Romanticism. Kingsley Amis. NoAM

Travellers. Arthur St. John Adcock. BoTP

Travellers came, after the long day's ride, The. The Blinkered Mind. Amy Witting. NOBAu

Travel[l]er's Curse after Misdirection, The. Robert Graves. CMoP; FiBHP; HoPM; LiTM; MeMBP; MoAB; MoBrPo; NBLV

Traveller's Guide to Antarctica. Adrien Stoutenburg. NYBP

Travellers have seen it, uncovered. Lost City. Harold Farmer. PeSAV

Traveller's Return, The. *Unknown.* BoTP

Travellers Turning Over Borders. Basil Ransome-Davies. BXAP

Travelling. David Chaloner. VaA

Travelling. Dick Davis. SCBI

Travelling. Dorothy Graddon. BoTP

Travelling, a man met a tiger, so . . . Good Taste. Christopher Logue. OBSP

Travelling Backward. Gene Baro. NYBP

Travelling Companions. Richard Armour. GrPl

Travelling eye has seen its many birds, The. Many Birds. Anne Welsh. PeSA

Travelling homesick with the West wind. Travelling in the Mountains. Sun Yün-feng, *tr. fr. Chinese by* Kenneth Rexroth *and* Ling Chung. WPC

Travelling in the Mountains. Sun Yün-feng, *tr. fr. Chinese by* Kenneth Rexroth *and* Ling Chung. WPC

Travelling in the Mountains. Tu Mu, *tr. fr. Chinese by* A. C. Graham. PLT

Travelling Out, The. Lucile Adler. IHMS; NYBP

Travelling Post Office, The. Andrew Barton Paterson. CBAP; NOBAu

Travelling south, leaves overflow the farms. The Puritan on His Honeymoon. Robert Bly. FF

Travelling,/ where darkness hauls the world. Tanks. Rhyll McMaster. CBAP; NOBAu

Travelogue, *sels.* Peter Reading.

Travelogue for Exiles. Karl Shapiro. MoAmPo; TrJP

Travels in Clouds, seekes Manna, where none is. *(LL)* The Search. Henry Vaughan. ChIV-2; ESCV; GeHe; SeCP

Travels of a Latter-Day Benjamin of Tudela, *sels.* Yehuda Amichai, *tr. fr. Hebrew.*
  "I am a solitary man, not a democracy." PoSu, *tr. by* Ruth Nevo

Travels with the Band-Aid Army. Lance Henson. VoR

Travis, the Kid Was All Heart. Terry Stokes. AmPA

Travois of the Nameless. Sotère Torregian. NBV

Tray. Robert Browning. FM

Treacherous rain and perilous bridge made me fear for my life. Sent to Lo-t'ien for Thinking of Me after the Rainfall. Yüan Chen, *tr. fr. Chinese by* Angela Jung Palandri. SuSp

Treacherous sea, The. *(LL)* Fife Tune. John Manifold. CBAP; FaBoMA; GoJo; ImPo; InPS; LiTB; LiTM; Mes; NBLV; NOBAu

Treacherous words, — tearing my thought across. Nowhere. John Berryman. AnAn

Treachery. Karl von Lemcke, *tr. fr. German by* Philip L. Miller. RiWo

Tread back — and back, the lewd and lay. III, 1. "Tread back — and back, the lewd and lay!" ("Odi profanum vulgus.") Horace, *tr. fr. Latin by* Austin Dobson. *Fr.* Odes. OBVE, *tr. by* Gerard Manley Hopkins
  (Hence ye prophane; I hate ye all.) OBVE, *tr. by* Abraham Cowley, 2 *sts.*
  (Profane, The.) AWP, *tr. by* Abraham Cowley

Tread lightly here, for here, 'tis said. An Epitaph on a Robin Redbreast. Samuel Rogers. FaBoEE; FM

Tread lightly, she is near. Requiescat. Oscar Wilde. EBVV; InVP; MoBrPo; OBNC; OHCV; PeVV; TrGrPo

Tread lightly, Stranger! Meleager, *tr. fr. Greek by* Peter Whigham. GrAn

Tread not the earth where lies her youthful form. Mrs. E. Cohrs Brown. Mary Weston Fordham. CBWP-2

Tread soft, for if you wake this knight alone. Epitaph on the Monument of Sir William Strode. William Strode. NOSC

Tread softly because you tread on my dreams. *(LL)* He Wishes for the Cloths of Heaven. W. B. Yeats. ArLo; FaPoB; MoBrPo; NoAM; OBEV

Tread softly; bid a solemn music sound. Epitaph. J. B. Morton. FaBoEE

Treading a field I saw afar. Death on a Live Wire. Michael Baldwin. MoBS

Treading pigeon arcs his wings, The. The Ivory Bed. Winfield Townley Scott. ErPo

Treading Water. Tracey Herd. NWP

Treadmill prisoner of that century, The. Scene with Figure. Babette Deutsch. TrJP

Treason. Sir John Harington. *See* Treason doth never prosper [*or* Treason never prospers]; what's the reason?

Treason doth never prosper [*or* Treason never prospers]; what's the reason? Of Treason. Sir John Harington. FaBoEE; FF; InPK; NoSic; OxBoLi; SoSe
  (Epigram IV.v: Of Treason.) NOSC
  (Epigram.) OtMeF
  (On Treason.) FiBHP
  (Treason.) FaBoCo
  (Treason never prospers; what's the reason?) InvP

Treason never prospers; what's the reason? Sir John Harington. *See* Treason doth never prosper [*or* Treason never prospers]; what's the reason?

Treason? yes, make it treason, if ye will. Warning. Alfred Gibbs Campbell. AAP

Treason's Last Device. Edmund Clarence Stedman. PAH

Treasure. Lucilius, *tr. fr. Greek by* William Cowper. AWP

Treasure Hunt. Robert Penn Warren. NoP

Treasure Island, *sels.* Robert Louis Stevenson.
Pirate Ditty. NOBVV

Treasure Lies In the Cornerstone, The. "Angelus Silesius," *tr. fr. German. Fr.* Cherubical Wanderer, The. GePo, *tr. by* George C. Schoolfield

Treasure-like, I found her in a field. The Meeting. Pierre Louÿs, *tr. fr. French. Fr.* Chansons de Bilitis. PeHV

Treasures. Bible, *N.T. Fr.* St. Matthew. TrGrPo

Treasures. Claire Richcreek Thomas. PoToHe

Treaties. A. R. Ammons. HCAP

Treating Sheep Ailments. John Dyer. *Fr.* Fleece, The. ECEV

Treatise of Monarchy, A, *sels.* Fulke Greville.
Of Nobility
"For as the harmony which sense admires." NOSC
Of Peace
"Peace is the next in order, first in end." NOSC

Treatise of the Subtle Body, A. Salamis. Lawrence Durrell. NYBP

Treatment. C. D. Wright. Jaz

Treatment by old Mr. Mears, The. *Unknown.* PeHV

Treatment in the Field. J. H. Prynne. VaA

Treaty of Human Learning, A, *sels.* Fulke Greville.
"Mind of man is this world's true dimension, The." NOSC

Trebetherick. Sir John Betjeman. CMoP

Tree, The. Dorothy Auchterlonie. NOBAu

Tree, The. Bjøornstjerne Bjøornson, *tr. fr. Norwegian.* FaPON; OHIP

Tree, The. Ilya Ehrenburg, *tr. fr. Russian by* Babette Deutsch. TrJP

Tree, The. John Freeman. BoTP

Tree, The. Ezra Pound. CMoP

Tree, The. Joel Sloman. VGW

Tree, The. Cinda Thompson. CrSp

Tree, The. Jones Very. GN; OHIP

Tree, A. Klara Koettner-Benign, *tr. fr. German.* TSaS, *tr. by* Herbert Kuhner

Tree and the Chaff, The. Bible, *O.T., paraphrased by* Sir Thomas Wyatt. *See* Blessed is the man that walketh not in the counsel of the ungodly [or wicked].

Tree and the Lady, The. Thomas Hardy. MoAB; MoBrPo

Tree as dream as family, The. Mother Glacier. Iain Sinclair. VaA

Tree ascending there. O pure transcension, A. Rainer Maria Rilke, *tr. by* James Blair Leishman. *Fr.* Sonnets to Orpheus. TOF

Tree at My Window. Robert Frost. BLPL; BoNaP; FaBoBe; MeMAP; MoAB; MoAmPo; NoAM; OxBA; TAP; TrGrPo

Tree Birthdays. Mary Carolyn Davies. OHIP

Tree Design, A. Arna Bontemps. CDC

Tree enters and says with a bow, A. Lesson, THe. Miroslav Holub, *tr. fr. Czech by* Ian Milner *and* Jarmila Milner. PoSu

Tree Ferns. Stanley Plumly. SM

Tree grew inside my head, A. A Tree Within. Octavio Paz, *tr. fr. Spanish.* TSaS, *tr. by* Eliot Weinberger

Tree grew under your hand one day, The. Lines for a Painter. Anthony Cronin. PBCIP

Tree has entered my hands, The. A Girl. Ezra Pound. MoAB; MoAmPo

Tree House. Shel Silverstein. SiSoPo

Tree house, a free house. Tree House. Shel Silverstein. SiSoPo

Tree I know where a love-bird's lighted, A. Open the Door. *Malay Oral Tradition, tr. by* R. J. Wilkinson *and* R. O. Winstedt. WTO

Tree in December. Melville Cane. MoAmPo

Tree in the courtyard turns color suddenly, The. Thoughts on the First Day of Autumn, Sent to Su Tzu-mei. Ou-yang Hsiu, *tr. fr. Chinese by* Irving Y. Lo. SuSp

Tree in the Garden, The. Christine Chandler. BoTP; OTCP

Tree in the wind remembered like a letter. Ivan V. Lalic, *tr. fr. Serbo-Croatian by* Charles Simic. *Fr.* Spring Liturgy for Branko Miljkovic. HSix

Tree in the Wood, The. *Unknown.* AmFP

Tree is all alone, The. A Thought. Linda Hogan. CrSp

Tree is more than a shadow, A. A Tree Design. Arna Bontemps. CDC

Tree let your arms fall. No Ordinary Sun. Hone Tuwhare. PeNZ

Tree Marriage. William Meredith. GLP

Tree moth in the garage was an omen, The. Superstition. Rebecca Gonzales. AfAz

Tree of deepest root is found, The. The Three Warnings. Hester Lynch Thrale. BeLS

Tree of Faith its bare dry boughs must shed, The. Adjustment. Whittier. WGRP

Tree of intense, The. Ode to the Watermelon. Pablo Neruda, *tr. fr. Spanish by* Robert Bly. NU

Tree of Knowledge, The. Abraham Cowley. ChIV-1

Tree of Knowledge, The. L. A. J. Moorer. CBWP-3

Tree of Liberty, The. Burns. FaBoPV

Tree of roses. The water crashed headlong. Peter Levi. TOF

Tree Old Woman. Samuel Makidemewabe, *tr. fr. Cree Indian by* Howard Norman. STP

Tree Party. Louis MacNeice. OxBTC

Tree-planting. Samuel Francis Smith. OHIP

Tree Planting. *Unknown.* OHIP

Tree, says good Swedenborg, is a close relative of man, The. Into the Tree. Czeslaw Milosz, *tr. fr. Polish by* Robert Hass. AnAn

Tree Sings to the Stream, The. Leah Goldberg, *tr. fr. Hebrew by* Ruth Finer Mintz. *Fr.* Songs of the Stream. MHP

Tree still bends over the lake, The. Winter. Sheila Wingfield. EnLoPo

Tree Tag. Mary E. Caragher. GoYe

Tree, the close willow, swayed, The. *(LL)* The Visitant. Theodore Roethke. CMoP; PoE; RB; TRP; UnPo

Tree the tempest with a crash of wood, The. On a Tree Fallen across the Road. Robert Frost. RB

Tree Toad ("A tree toad loved a she-toad.") *Unknown.* NTCP, *ad. by* Stephanie Calmenson

Tree Toad, The ("The tree Toad is a creature neat.") Monica Shannon. FaPON

"Tree toad loved a she-toad, A." Tree Toad ("A tree toad loved a she-toad.") *Unknown.* NTCP, *ad. by* Stephanie Calmenson

Tree, too, wants to bend over, The. 3 Stanzas about a Tree. Marvin Bell. Prf

Tree-topped Hill. *Unknown.* NOEC

Tree Within, A. Octavio Paz, *tr. fr. Spanish.* TSaS, *tr. by* Eliot Weinberger

Treefrog winks without springing. Drawings of the Song Animals. Duane Niatum. HATNAP

Treehouse, The. James A. Emanuel. BPo; PoBA

Trees. Alison Brackenbury. SCBI

Trees, The. Vuyelwa Carlin. NWP

Trees. Bliss Carman. OHIP

Trees, The. Samuel Valentine Cole. OHIP

Trees. Sara Coleridge. BoTP; OHIP; OxBChV

Trees. Walter de la Mare. OHIP

Trees. Ted Hughes. NYBP

Trees. Joyce Kilmer. BLPA; EBEvV; FaBoBe; FaPON; UV; WBLP; WGRP

Trees, The. Lucy Larcom. OHIP

Trees, The. Philip Larkin. AnAn; Mes; NoAM

Trees, The. Bill Manhire. PeNZ

Trees, The. Christopher Morley. OHIP

Trees. Agnes Nemes Nagy, *tr. fr. Hungarian by* Bruce Berlind. PoSu

Trees. Howard Nemerov. BoNaP; Poetsp

Trees, The. Adrienne Rich. CoAP; NOBA; WPE

Trees along this city street, The. City Trees. Edna St. Vincent Millay. FaPON

Trees and Evening Sky. N. Scott Momaday. CDW

Trees/ and the wind. The Hand. Brian Fawcett. NOBC

Trees are afraid to put forth buds, The. A Backward Spring. Thomas Hardy. PPP

Trees are a'ivied, the leaves they are green, The. The Bonnie Laddie's Lang a-Grouwin'. *Unknown.* OxBS

Trees are all bare not a leaf to be seen, The. Christmas Song. *Unknown.* NTP

Trees are cages for them: water holds its breath. Stars and Planets. Norman MacCaig. OxBSP

Trees are coming into leaf, The. The Trees. Philip Larkin. AnAn; Mes; NoAM

Trees Are Down, The. Charlotte Mew. BoNaP; BrRo; ChIV-2; MoAB; MoBrPo; NTP; OxAEP-2; TrCP; WPE; WPOW

Trees are God's great alphabet, The. A B C's in Green. Leonora Speyer. OHIP

Trees are in their autumn beauty, The. W. B. Yeats. *Fr.* Wild Swans at Coole, The. ArNa; ChTr; CMoP; FaBoPP; FaBoRV; FM; HeIP; InPS; MoAB; MoBrPo; MoP; NAEL-2; NoAM; NoP; PFP; Poetr; PPP; SCGP; SoSe; SOTW; TEP; TFi; UnPo

Trees are never the same, The. The Return. Thomas McGrath. FoLa

Trees are rustling outside the open window, The. Sophie Behrens. NBrP

"Bitter, bitter jewel." NALW
"But nearer than Guardian Angel." NALW
"Every hour, every moment." NALW; NoAM
"Hermes Trismegistus." NALW
"I can not invent it." NALW
"I had been thinking of Gabriel." NALW
"I John saw. I testify." NALW
"Invisible, indivisible Spirit." BoWoP
"Not in our time, O Lord." NOBA
"Now polish the crucible." NALW
"O swiftly, re-light the flame." NALW
"O yes — you understand, I say." NALW
"Of the no need." NALW
"One of us said, how odd." NALW
"She carried a book, either to imply." NALW
"So she must have been pleased with us." NALW
"Some call that deep-deep bell." NALW
"Swiftly re-light the flame." NALW
"This is a symbol of beauty (you continue)." NALW
"This is no rune nor riddle." InPS
   (This is no rune nor symbol.) NALW, (*sl. diff.*)
"We have seen her/ the world over." CRP; NALW; Poetr; VGW
'What is the jewel colour?'. NALW
"Your walls do not fall, he said." NALW
Tribute to the Bride and Groom, A. Priscilla Jane Thompson. CBWP-2
Tribute to the Founder, A. Kingsley Amis. IHNG
Tribute to the Memory of the Same Dog. Wordsworth. FM
Tribute to Washington. *Unknown.* OHIP
Tribute to Wyatt. The Earl of Surrey. *See* Wyatt Resteth Here.
Tricchen shalt thou neuermore. (*LL*) The Song of Lewes. *Unknown.* OxBoLi
Trick for Tyburn A.; or, A Prison Rant, *Unknown.* APAS
Trick is, to live your days, The. Advice to My Son. Peter Meinke. Poetsp
Trick that everyone abhors, A. Rebecca, Who Slammed Doors for Fun and Perished Miserably. Hilaire Belloc. NOBL
Trickle Drops. Walt Whitman. NAAL-1
Trickle of sand on the grave's edge, A. Ad Infinitum. Joan Aronsten. NOBAu
Trickling, trickling/ drop by tiny drop in welcome. Roadside Fountain. Momcilo Nastasijevic, *tr. fr. Serbo-Croatian by* Charles Simic. HSix
Tricks With Mirrors. Margaret Atwood. NIP
Trico's Song. John Lyly. *Fr.* Alexander and Campaspe. EIl; NoSic; TrGrPo
Tries a nosedive, kamikaze. Baby Random. Belle Waring. NAmP90; PBCAP
Trifle for Trafalgar Day, A. Ted Pauker. NOBL
Trifling Women. *Unknown.* AmFP
Trilby, *sels.* George Du Maurier.
   Little Work, A. FaBoBe; PoLF
Trilogy. Cecile Hamermesh. BTR
Trilogy for X, *sels.* Louis MacNeice.
   "And love hung still as crystal over the bed." CIP; GBL
   (And Love Hung Still.) MoBrPo
   "When clerks and navvies fondle." ErPo
   (For X.) BoLoP; EnLoPo
Trilogy of Passion. Goethe, *tr. fr. German by* John Frederick Nims. STV
Sels.
   Elegy.
   Reconciliation.
   To Werther.
Trim the lamp; polish the lens; draw, one by one, rare coins. Geoffrey Hill. *Fr.* Mercian Hymns. FaBoMo
Trim, Tran. *Unknown.* ISE
Trimdon Grange Explosion, The. Thomas Armstrong. OBET
Trimming the lamp flower's smoking wick. (*LL*) The Sorrow of Departure. Li Ch'ing-chao. WPC
Trimming the Sails. Vassar Miller. NMM
Trim's Song: The Fair Kitchen-Maid. Sir Richard Steele. *Fr.* Funeral, The. OxBSP
Trinity. Amen, The. (*LL*) Upon a Dead Man's Head. John Skelton. EnRePo; HAP; SCGP
Trinity [*or* Trinitee] blessed, deity [*or* deitee] coequal. A Prayer to the Holy Trinity. Richard Stanyhurst. EIl; PoEL-2
   (Prayer to the Trinity [*or* Trinitie], A.) EIl; TIRV
Trinity Brethren Attend. I. A. Richards. CRP
Trinity Place. Phyllis McGinley. MoAmPo; OxBSP; SoSe
Trinity Sunday. George Herbert. OxBSP
Trinket. Marvin Bell. AnAn

Trio for Two Cats and a Trombone. Edith Sitwell. *Fr.* Façade. NAEL-2; PBWP
Triolet. Gerard Manley Hopkins. *See* Child Is Father to the Man, The.
Triolet: "She was in love with the same danger." Sandra McPherson. SM
Triolet: "When first we met we did not guess." Robert Bridges. OxBSP
Triolet against Sisters. Phyllis McGinley. OBCA
Trip to Four or Five Towns, A. John Logan. CoAP; NNaP
Trip to Paris and Belgium, A, *sels.* Dante Gabriel Rossetti.
   Antwerp to Ghent. OBTV; PeVV, *sect.* V
   Boulogne to Amiens and Paris. PeVV
   "Constant keeping-past of shaken trees." PeVV, *pt.* I
   (Constant keeping-past of shaken trees.) EnVR
Trip to Stone Man Peak, A. Yang Wan-li, *tr. fr. Chinese by* Jonathan Chaves. SuSp
Trip to the Grand Banks, A. Amos Hanson. AmFP
Trip trap in a gap. *Unknown.* GBP
Trip upon trenchers, and dance upon dishes. Mother Goose. NOBL; OxNR; ReMoGo
Tripart. Gayl Jones. BlSi
Triphammer Bridge. A. R. Ammons. NAAL-2; NOBA
Triple Benison, The. H. Cordelia Ray. CBWP-3
Triple Feature. Denise Levertov. FF; NoP
Triple Fool, The. John Donne. GBL; NOSC; SoSe
Triple League to Mrs. Susan Dove, The. Elizabeth Thomas. KTR
Triple Mirror, The. Gloria C. Oden. IHMS
Triple Trouble. Assotto Saint. GLP
Triplets. Michael Brownstein. UL
Trippers and askers surround me. Walt Whitman. *Fr.* Song of Myself. AmPP; EnlH; LiTA; MoAmPo, *abr.*; NOBA; OxBA; SOTW, *much abr.*; UnPo
Triptych. Frank A. Collymore. PBCV
Tristan Crazy, *sels.* Ken Smith.
   Four, Being a Prayer to the Western Wind. PWE
Tristan da Cunha. Roy Campbell. MoBrPo; PeSA
Tristan da Cunha. Ian D. Colvin. PeSAV
Tristan had no choice. Heinrich von Veldeke, *tr. fr. German by* Frederick Goldin. GePo
Tristan und Isolt. Gottfried von Strassburg, *tr. fr. German.* OBD
Tristium, *sels.* Ovid, *tr. fr. Latin.*
   "And here I wish my soul died with my breath." OBVE
   "And on this day, which poets unto thee." OBVE
   "Look, he is superfluous — for of what use was it to be born?" NAs
Tristram lies sick to death. Tristram's End. Laurence Binyon. OBMV
Tristram of Lyonesse, *sels.* Swinburne.
   King Mark, Tristram, and Palamede. EBNV
   Swimming. GN
Tristram's End. Laurence Binyon. OBMV
Tristram's Song. Tennyson. *Fr.* Idylls of the King. FaBoRV
Sir Tristrem, *sels. At. to* Thomas of Erceldoune.
   Tristrem and the Hunters. OxBS
Tristrem and the Hunters. *At. to* Thomas of Erceldoune. *Fr.* Sir Tristrem. OxBS
Trit trot to market to buy a penny doll. *Unknown.* OxNR
Triumph, The. Sidney Lanier. *Fr.* Psalm of the West. PAH
Triumph, The. William Gilmore Simms. Son
Triumph. L. D. Stearns. BLRP
Triumph! How strange, how strong had triumph come. Third Ypres. Edmund Blunden. PeFWW
Triumph! My Jesus has! Triumph! His empire gained! The 15th Kühl-Psalm. Quirinus Kuhlmann, *tr. fr. German by* George C. Schoolfield. GePo
Triumph of Bacchus and Ariadne. Lorenzo de' Medici, *tr. fr. Italian by* Richard Aldington. *Fr.* Carnival Songs. CTC
Triumph of Beautie Song, The, *sels.* James Shirley.
   "Heigh-ho, what shall a shepheard doe." ErPo
Triumph of Charis, The. Ben Jonson. *Fr.* Celebration of Charis in Ten Lyric[k] Peeces [*or* pieces], A. BeJo; CTC; EBEV; EIl; ELP; InvP; JCP; LiTB; NOBE; NoP; OBEV; OPOP; PoEL-2; PrIm; SeCP; SeCV-1; TFi
Triumph of Death., *sels.* Petrarch, *tr. fr. Italian by* Mary Sidney Herbert, Countess of Pembroke.
   "That gallant lady, gloriously bright." SiPSBD
   "That night which did the dreadful hap ensue." SiPSBD
Triumph of Death, The. Shakespeare. *See* No longer mourn for me when I am dead.
Triumph of Dullness [*or* Dulness], The. Pope. *Fr.* Dunciad, The. EBEV; FaBoPV; NOBE; NOEC; NoP; SCV
Triumph of Infidelity, The, *sels.* Timothy Dwight.

"And now the morn arase, when o'er the plain." EAP
"Here stood Hypocrisy, in sober brown." NOCV
  Smooth Divine, The.
Triumph of Life, The. Shelley. NAEL-2; OAEL-2; PoEL-4
Triumph of Love. John Hall Wheelock. MoAmPo
Triumph of Peace, The, *sels.* James Shirley.
  Song to the Masquers. OxBSP
Triumph of Sensibility. Sylvia Townsend Warner. MoAB; MoBrPo
Triumph of the Muses over Love, The, *sels.* Pernette de Guillet, *tr. fr.
  French by* Dorothy Backer.
Triumph of the Whale, The, *sels.* Charles Lamb.
  "Io! Paean! Io! sing." OxAEP-2
Triumph of Time, The, *sels.* Swinburne.
  I Will Go Back to the Great Sweet Mother. NAEL-2
  (Sea, The.) TrGrPo
Triumph of Vice, The. Pope. *See* Virtue may choose the high or low
  degree.
Triumph or the tomb., The. (*LL*) Charleston. Henry Timrod. AmPP;
  AnAmPo; NOBA; OxBA; PAH; TAP
Triumphal Chant. Bible, *O.T. See* I will sing unto the Lord, for he hath
  triumphed gloriously.
Triumphal March. T. S. Eliot. *Fr.* Coriolan. OBWP
Triumphal Ode MCMXXXIX. George Barker. LiTB
Triumphant. (*LL*) Be praised my lord with all your creatures. St. Francis
  of Assisi. EaPr
Triumphant Demons stand, and Angels start. The Heart's Abysses. Walter
  Savage Landor. FaBoEE; OBSV
Triumphing chariots, statues, crowns of bay. William Drummond of
  Hawthornden. *Fr.* Urania, or Spiritual Poems. NOSC
Triumphing over Death, and Chance, and thee O Time. (*LL*) On Time.
  Milton. BLPL; ImPo; LiTB; OBEV; SCGP
Triumphs. Petrarch, *tr. fr. Italian by* Morris Bishop. OBD
Triumphs of Death, *sels.* Anna Hume.
  Arguement, The. KTR
Triumphs of Owen, The. Thomas Gray. EnRP; PoEL-3
Triumphs of the Gout, The, *sels.* Gilbert West.
  "Lives there on Earth to whom I am unknown." ECEV
Triumvirate, The. Elizabeth Thomas. ECWP
Trivia; or, The Art of Walking the Streets of London, *sels.* John Gay.
  About in London. FaBoPP
  "Experienced men, inured to city ways." OAEL-1
  "If clothed in black you tread the busy town." ECEV
  "Let due civilities be strictly paid." OAEL-1
  London at Night. FaBoPP
  "Thoughtless wits shall frequent forfeits pay, The." ECEV
  "Where Lincoln's Inn, wide space, is railed around." ECEV
  "Where the mob gathers, swiftly shoot along." OAEL-1
  (Pickpockets.) ECEV
  "Who can the various city frauds recite." OAEL-1
  (Thieves and Whores.) ECEV
  "Winter my theme confines; whose nitry wind." NOEC
  (Winter Sports.) ECEV
Triviality, A. Waring Cuney. CDC
Troades, *sels.* Seneca, *tr. fr. Latin by* the Earl of Rochester.
  "After death nothing is, and nothing, death." EBEV; OBD; OBVE
Trochee trips from long to short. Metrical Feet. Samuel Taylor Coleridge.
  FaBoUs; FHYEP; NIP; OxBChV; Poetr, *ll.* 1–6 *only*
Troika, The. Louis Simpson. NOBA
Troilus and Cressida., *sels.* Dryden.
  Can Life Be a Blessing
  (Song: "Can life be a blessing.") NoP; SeCV-2
  "See my lov'd Britons, see your Shakespeare rise." SeCV-2
Troilus and Cressida., *sels.* Shakespeare.
  "And is it true that I must go from Troy?" OxAEP-1
  "Have you seen my cousin?" OxAEP-1
  "Heavens themselves, the planets and this center, The." FaBoEH
  "Peace, you ungracious clamours! peace, rude sounds!" OxAEP-1
  Portrait of Cressida. TrGrPo
  Portrait of Helen. TrGrPo
  "This she? no, this is Diomed's Cressida." OxAEP-1
  Ulysses Advises Achilles. ImPo; LiTB
  "What! are my deeds forgot?" OxAEP-1
  "You are for dreams and slumbers, brother priest." OxAEP-1
Troilus and Criseyde [*or* Criseide]. Chaucer. EnVB
  Sels.
  Complaint of Troilus, The. NOBE; OBEV
  Go, Little Book "Go, litel book, go litel myn tragedye". OAEL-1
  (Chaucer's Wishes for his 'Troilus'.) EPCY
  "If no love is, O God, what fele I so." FF; OAEL-1
  (Song of Troylus, The.) AWP
  "In May, that moder is of monthes glade"

Love Unfeigned. NOBE; OBEV
Sorrow of Troilus, The. PoEL-1
"Swich fyn hath, lo, this Troilus for love!" NOCV
"This Troilus [*or* Troylus], with blisse [*or* Blysse] of that supprysed [*or*
  supprised]." EBEV; PoE
"Whan they unto the paleys were yoemen." PoE
Wooing of Criseide, The, III. PoEL-1
Trojan Women, The. Euripides, *tr. fr. Greek by* Edith Hamilton. PAW
  Sels.
  "This town, now, yes, Mother"
Trojans Outside the Walls, The. Homer, *tr. by* George Chapman. *Fr.* Iliad,
  The. OBVE
Troll the Bowl! Thomas Dekker *and others. See* Cold's the wind, and
  wet's the rain.
Troll to her Children, The. Jane Yolen. OTCP
Troll's Nosegay, The. Robert Graves. Son
Trombone Solo. Stoddard King. NBLV
Trompe L'Œil. Daryl Hine. MoCV
Tromping down soft summer grass. (*LL*) At last, on delicate feet.
  Sappho. InMo
Troop home to silent grots and caves. The Mermaidens' Vesper-Hymn.
  George Darley. *Fr.* Syren Songs. GBL; NAEL-2; OBNC; PoEL-4
  (Siren Chorus. BIrV; FaBoRV
Troop of camels, A. In the North. Kung Liu, *tr. fr. Chinese.* LHF, *tr. by*
  Hualing Nieh
Troop of the Guard, The [*or* A]. Hermann Hagedorn. OHIP
Troop ship, The. Isaac Rosenberg. NSI; PoWW
Troop Train. Karl Shapiro. ArOW; OxBA
Trooper and Maid. *Unknown.* AmFP
Trooper's Horse, The. *Unknown.* OBET
Troops. The. Siegfried Sassoon. CMoP
Troops exulting sate in order round, The. Homer, *tr. by* Pope. *Fr.* Iliad,
  The. OBVE
Troopship, The. Lionel Johnson. EBVV
Troopship: Mid-Atlantic. W. W. Gibson. NSI
Trophy, The. Edwin Muir. LiTM
Tropic of ice. Cape Ann; a View. John Malcolm Brinnin. NYBP
Tropic Rain. Robert Louis Stevenson. OBTV
Tropic tonight, burning, filled with fast trains. At the Band Concert. John
  Malcolm Brinnin. PoA
Tropicals. René Maran, *tr. fr. French by* Ellen Conroy Kennedy. NegPo
Tropics. Ellen Bryant Voigt. SM
Tropics in New York, The. Claude McKay. ArNa; NoAM; PoBA; PoNe;
  TTY
Tropics vanish, and meseems that I, The. Robert Louis Stevenson. PeVV
Tropisms on John Berryman. Gerald Vizenor. VoR
Trossachs, The. Wordsworth. OBEV
Trot, and a canter, a gallop, and over, A. *Unknown.* OxNR
Troubadour. Peter Sirr. BiHa
Troubadour of God, The. Charles Wharton Stork. WGRP
Trouble. David Keppel. PoLF; WBLP
Trouble. James Wright. FF
Trouble at the Farm. Ivy O. Eastwick. BoTP
Trouble has done her good. Charity. Connie Bensley. FaBoWP
Trouble in the "Amen Corner." Thomas Chalmers Harbaugh. BLPA
Trouble is, it's getting harder. Wild West. Mark Vinz. Poetsp
Trouble, not of clouds, or weeping rain, A. On the Departure of Sir Walter
  Scott from Abbotsford, for Naples. Wordsworth. EBEV; EnRP
Trouble Oh. *Unknown.* PBCV
Trouble was too much, The. Indian Love Song. Lew Blockcolski. VoR
Trouble with a kitten is, The. The Kitten. Ogden Nash. CRH; FaPON;
  MoShBr; OFC
Trouble with General Sherman, The. Basil Ransome-Davies. PeLi
Trouble with you is, The. Denunciation; or, Unfrock'd Again. Philip
  Whalen. NeAP
Trouble with you is, The. Love in a Warm Room in Winter. James
  Wright. OBAL
Troubled midnight and the noon's repose, The. (*LL*) La Figlia Che
  Piange. T. S. Eliot. CBLP; FaBoTw; FaPoB; GBL; HeIP; LiTA;
  MAT; OPOP; OxBTC; PlP; PoA; UnPo; VGW
Troubled Soldier, The. *Unknown.* AS
Troubled was a house in Ealing. The Widow's Plot; or, She Got What Was
  Coming to Her. William Plomer. MoP
Troubled waters, The/ are frozen fast. Murasaki Shikibu, *tr. fr. Japanese by*
  Kenneth Rexroth *and* Ikuko Atsumi. *Fr.* Tale of Genji, The. WPJ;
  WPOW
Troubled with the Itch and Rubbing with Sulphur. George Moses Horton.
  AAP

Troubles of the Day. William Barnes. GTBS-P

Trousers first of ancient fabric. Sri Rama's Raiment. *Malay Oral Tradition, tr. by* R. O. Winstedt. WTO

Trousers of Wind. *Unknown, tr. fr. Amharic by* Sylvia Pankhurst. PBA; TTY

Trout, The. Daryl Hine. CoAP

Trout, The. John Montague. IIP; IPY; PBCIP; PeIV; PNI; PoE

Trout, The. Christian David Schubart, *tr. fr. German by* Philip L. Miller. RiWo

Trout Fisher. George Mackay Brown. OxBC

Trouvaille. Richard Murphy. IPY

Troy. Agathias, *tr. fr. Greek by* Ezra Pound. GrAn

Troy. Paul Coltman. PAW

Troy. Edwin Muir. CMoP

Troynovant ("Troynovant is now no more a city.") Thomas Dekker *and others. Fr.* Entertainment to James. ChTr

Truant, The. E. J. Pratt. NOBC; NoP

Truants, The. Walter de la Mare. MoBrPo

Truce. Paul Muldoon. PBCIP; PNI

Truce, gentle love, a parley now I crave. Michael Drayton. *Fr.* Idea. ESo; NoP; NoSic

Truck put me off on Fell. Hitching into Frisco. Thom Gunn. *Fr.* Three Songs. AnAn

Trucker, The. Will Dyson. NOBAu

Trucker. Robert Walton. AngWe

Trucks. James S. Tippett. FaPON

Trudge, Body. Robert Graves. MoAB

True Account of Talking to the Sun at Fire Island, A. Frank O'Hara. HCAP; NNaP; PRA; RB; SOTW; TTTS

True American, The. Georgia Douglas Johnson. ShDr

True and Faithful Inventory of the Goods Belonging to Dr. Swift, Vicar of Laracor, A; upon Lending His House to the Bishop of Meath, till His Palace Was Rebuilt. Swift. FaBoUs

True and False Glory ("To whom our Saviour calmly thus reply'd.") Milton. *Fr.* Paradise Regained [*or* Regain'd]. LiTB

True and Joyful News. *Unknown.* APAS

True Apostolate, The. Ruby Weyburn Tobias. BLRP

True Arab knows how to catch a fly in his hands, A. Blood. Naomi Shihab Nye. NGP

True Aristocrat, The. W. Stewart. WBLP

True Ballad of the Great Race to Gilmore City, The. Phil Hey. Poetsp

True Beauty. Francis Beaumont. EIL

True-blue the salmon — from his sally. No Place Like Home. Llawdden, *tr. fr. Welsh by* Gwyn Jones. OBWVE

True-Born Englishman, The. Daniel Defoe. *Fr.* True-born Englishman, The. APAS; FaBoEH

True-born Englishman, The. (Speak, Satire, for there's none can tell like thee.) Daniel Defoe. APAS
Sels.
  "Breed's described, The: Now, Satire, if you can." OBSV
  "He rais'd no Money, for he paid in land." FaBoEH
  "In their religion they are so unev'n." OBSV
  "Labouring poor, in spite of double pay, The." NOBL
  On Lord Mayors. IHNG
  "Then let us boast of ancestors no more." OBSV
  True-Born Englishman, The. FaBoEH
  Well-Extracted Blood of Englishmen, The. IHNG
  "Wherever God erects a house of prayer." NOBL; OBSV

True Brahmin, in the morning meadows wet. Gardener. Emerson. *Fr.* Quatrains. OxBA

True Brotherhood. Ella Wheeler Wilcox. WBLP

True Confession of George Barker, The. (Today, recovering from influenza.) George Barker. MeMBP
Sels.
  "I see the young bride move among." ErPo
  "I sent a letter to my love." FaBoTw
  "Today, the Twenty-sixth of February." NAs

True Confessional. Lawrence Ferlinghetti. NAs

True Dream, A. Elizabeth Barrett Browning. NALW

True ease in writing comes from art, not chance. Pope. *Fr.* Essay on Criticism. HAP; InPK; PoEL-3; PrIm; TrGrPo
  (Sound and Sense.) SoSe; UnPo

True Effigies of a Certain Squire: Inscribed to Clemena, The. Elizabeth Thomas. ECWP

True Encounter, The. Edna St. Vincent Millay. OxBSP

True Englishman, A. *Unknown.* FaBoEH

True Englishmen, drink a good health to the miter. A New Catch in Praise of the Reverend Bishops. *Unknown.* APAS; FaBoEH

True Facts of the Case, The. Anthony Euwer. OBAL; PeLi

True faith discovered was, The. Wisdom. W. B. Yeats. TrCP

True faith, he claims, has the most doubt. A Modern Theologian. Paul Ramsey. *Fr.* Three Epigrams. CRP

True Friendship. *Unknown, tr. fr. Sanskrit by* Arthur Ryder. *Fr.* Panchatantra, The. AWP

True friendship unfeigned. Of Perfect Friendship. Henry Cheke. EIL

True Genius. Robert Lloyd. *Fr.* Shakespeare; an Epistle to David Garrick, Esq. NOEC

True genius, but true woman! dost deny. To George Sand: A Recognition. Elizabeth Barrett Browning. BoWoP; NAEL-2; NALW; TEP

True gut-funky blues to make her really dance, A. *(LL)* The Reception. June Jordan. FaBoWP; NMM

True Happiness. Morris Talpalar. PoToHe

True Heaven, The. Paul Hamilton Hayne. WGRP

True Hymn, A. George Herbert. GeHe; InvP; NOCV

True Import of Present Dialogue, Black vs, The Negro. Nikki Giovanni. BPo; PoBA

True Knight [*or* True Knighthood], The. Stephen Hawes. *Fr.* Pastime of Pleasure, The. OBEV; TrGrPo

True knight, worthy of the name, A. Don Quixote's Credo. W. H. Auden. *Fr.* Man of La Mancha. AnAn

True Knowledge. Panatattu, *tr. fr. Sanskrit.* WGRP

True Knowledge. William Wilkie. *Fr.* Grasshopper and the Glowworm, The. ECEV

True Lent, A. Robert Herrick. *See* Is this a fast, to keep.

True Life Love Stories, *sels.* Michael Foley.
  "Ah no, ah no, they weren't all gross and slow." PNI
  "Sois sage, ô ma doleur . . . I don't." PNI
  "Sword is a cold bride, The. Yuk!" PNI

True life, natural breath; not this phantasma. *(LL)* The Pier-Glass. Robert Graves. CMoP; MoAB; NoAM

True Life Romance. Lindsay MacRae. DT

True Love. Phoebe Cary. PoToHe

True Love. Waring Cuney. CDC

True Love. Shakespeare. *See* Let Me Not to the Marriage of True Minds.

True Love. Sir Philip Sidney. *See* My true love hath my heart, and I have his.

True Love. *Unknown, tr. fr. German by* Jethro Bithell. AWP

True Love, A. Nicholas Grimald. EIL; OBEV

True love, come O come to me. True Love. *Unknown, tr. fr. German by* Jethro Bithell. AWP

True Love Ditty, A. Thomas Middleton. *Fr.* Blurt, Master Constable. EIL

True love doth pass away! *(LL)* My silks and fine array. Blake. EnRP; OBNC; SCGP; TrGrPo

True Love in this differs from gold and clay. Shelley. *Fr.* Epipsychidion. EnRP; FHYEP; OBNC

True love is sweet and true love is pleasant. William Hall. *Unknown.* AmFP

True love, true love, what have I done. In the Pines. *Unknown.* AmFP

True Lover, The. A. E. Housman. *Fr.* Shropshire Lad, A. EBNV; FaPoB

True Lovers Bold, The. *Unknown.* AmFP

True Lover's Farewell, The. *Unknown.* AS

True Maid, A. Matthew Prior. ErPo; FaBoCo; FaBoEE; NAEL-1; NIP; NOEC; PeLV

True Marriage Is True Love. William Ellery Leonard. *Fr.* Two Lives. Son

True Meaning. Anthony Barnett. VaA

True mirth resides not in the smiling skin. Mirth. Robert Herrick. LiTB

True or False. Catullus, *tr. fr. Latin by* Walter Savage Landor. AWP; OBVE

True poesy is not in words. Pastoral Poesy. John Clare. OAEL-2, *abr.* (Pastoral Poetry.) FHYEP, *sl. abr.*

True Protocol of Poets, The. Kapilar, *tr. fr. Tamil by* A. K. Ramanujan. PLW

True Rest. Goethe, *tr. fr. German by* John S. Dwight. WBLP

True shape of death and power. *(LL)* To a Military Rifle, 1942. Yvor Winters. MoAmPo

True Solar Holiday. Douglas Crase. BAP-89

True Son of God, Eternal Light. P. J. Cormican. AH

True Story, A. Marvin Bell. SV

True Story Ending in False Hope, A. Pearse Hutchinson. PBCIP

True Story of Snow White, The. Bruce Bennett. SM

True Story of the Pins. Alberto A. Ríos. NAmP90

True Tale, A. Mary Chandler. ECWP

True Tale of Robin Hood, A. *Unknown.* ESPB

True Thomas. *Unknown. See* Thomas lay on the Huntlie bank.

True Thomas. *Unknown. See* True Thomas lay o'er yond grassy [*or* on Huntlie] bank.

True Thomas lay o'er yond grassy [or on Huntlie] bank. Thomas the Rhymer. *Unknown.* ELP; FaBoCh; InPS; LiTB; NOBE; OAEL-1; OBEV; OxBB; OxBS; PoE; Prf; RB; ScCV; TFi
    Thomas Rhymer [and the Queen of Elfland]. CH; ChTr; ESPB, A *and* C vers.; FaBoBa; HAP
    (Thomas the Rimer.) EnSB; InPK
    (True Thomas.) OtMeF; OxBS; TrGrPo
True Thomas on earth was never seen. (*LL*) Thomas the Rhymer. *Unknown.* ELP; FaBoCh; InPS; LiTB; NOBE; OAEL-1; OBEV; OxBB; OxBS; PoE; Prf; RB; ScCV; TFi
True to our native land. (*LL*) Lift Every Voice and Sing. James Weldon Johnson. FaBV; PoNe
True to the Best. Benjamin Keech. PoToHe
True to the kindred points of Heaven and Home! (*LL*) To a Skylark ("Ethereal minstrel! pilgrim of the sky.") Wordsworth. EnRP; TrGrPo
True to your might [or Truth to your mighty] winds on dusky shores. On the Death of William Edward Burghardt Du Bois by African Moonlight and Forgotten Shores. Conrad Kent Rivers. PoBA
True Vine. Elinor Wylie. LiTA
True, we are the children. The Second Generation. Menachem Z. Rosensaft. BTR
True, we must tame our rebel will. Courage. Matthew Arnold. OAEL-2
True Witness, The. Lucy Larcom. AmWP
True worth is in being, not seeming. Nobility. Alice Cary. WBLP
Truest Poetry Is the Most Feigning; or, Ars Poetica for Hard Times, The. W. H. Auden. NYBP
Truganinny. Wendy Rose. HATNAP
Truisms, The. Louis MacNeice. IIP; NOBE; OBSV; PNI
Truly. Ingeborg Bachmann, *tr. fr. German by* Susan L. Cocalis. PoSu, *tr. by* Mark Anderson
Truly alone mulely. Times. Tom Weatherly. UL
Truly buzzards/ Around my sky are circling! Glyph. *Unknown, tr. fr. Washoe-Paiute Indian by* Mary Austin. LiTA
Truly do we live on earth? *Unknown, tr. fr. Nahuatl Indian by* Jack Emory Davis. OBD
Truly Great. W. H. Davies. OBMV
Truly in the East. Songs in the Garden of the House God. *Unknown, tr. fr. Navajo Indian by* Washington Matthews. AnAmPo
Truly in the east/ The white bean. Song to Promote Growth. *Unknown, tr. by* Washington Matthews. OBVE
Truly it was morning, and few to equal it. Levivot. Saul Tchernichowsky, *tr. fr. Hebrew by* Ruth Finer Mintz. MHP
Truly, my Satan, thou art but a dunce. Blake. *Fr.* For the Sexes; the Gates of Paradise. HAP; ImPo; LITB; OAEL-2; OBNC; PoE; PoEL-4; WeW; (Epilogue.) PeECV
    (To the Accuser Who is the God of This World.) FHYEP; NoP; OxBSP; SCGP; TrGrPo
Truly my soul waiteth upon God. Bible, *O.T., paraphrased by* Sir Thomas Wyatt. *Fr.* Psalms.
    (Psalm LXII: "Yet shall my soule in silence still," *paraphrased by* the Countess of Pembroke.) PBWP
Truly Rich, The. T. Urchard. PWR
Truly the light is sweet. The Light Is Sweet. Bible, *O.T. Fr.* Ecclesiastes. FaPON
Trumpet, The. Ilya Ehrenburg, *tr. fr. Russian by* Y. Hornstein. TrJP
Trumpet, The, *sels.* Robinson Jeffers.
    Grass on the Cliff. PoA
Trumpet, The. Edward Thomas. MoBrPo; OHIP
Trumpet, A/ A trumpet. Lewis Has a Trumpet. Karla Kuskin. PDV
Trumpet call and grand white stars. Christ. *Unknown, tr. fr. Greek by* Guy Davenport. GrAn
Trumpet of Liberty, The. John Taylor. NOEC
Trumpet Player. Langston Hughes. NAAL-2; TTY
Trumpet Voluntary. Paul Hoover. UL
Trumpeter, The. *Unknown.* CoMu
Trumpeter of Fyvie, The. *Unknown.* OxBB
Trumpets. Georg Trakl, *tr. fr. German by* David McDuff *and* Jon Silkin. PeFWW
Trumpets from the Islands of Their Eviction. Martín Espada. NGP
Trumpet's loud clangor, The. Fife and Drum. Dryden. *Fr.* Song for St. Cecilia's Day, 1687, A. AWP; FaBoTw; FHYEP; GGP; GN, 8 *ll.*; GTBS; GTBS-P; HAP; InPS; LiTB; NOSC; OAEL-1; OBEV; OPOP; PoEL-3; PPP; SCGP; SeCV-2; TEP; TFi; TrGrPo
Trumpets sound and steeples ring. A Trick for Tyburn; or, A Prison Rant. *Unknown.* APAS
Trundled from/ the strangeness of the sea. The Sea-Elephant. William Carlos Williams. LiTA; MeMAP; NU; SAmP

Trunk of cherry-tree without bark or flowers. Materia Nupcial. Pablo Neruda, *tr. fr. Spanish by* Clayton Eshleman. ErPo
Trus' an' Smile. B.Y. Williams. BLRP
Trust and Obedience. *Unknown.* BLRP
Trust him not to breathe a word. (*LL*) Under the Lindens [or Lime Tree]. Walther von der Vogelweide. CTC, *tr. by* Ford Madox Ford
Trust in God. Norman Macleod. *Fr.* Trust in God and Do the Right. BLRP
Trust in God and Do the Right. Norman Macleod. BLRP; VPP
Trust in God and Do the Right, *sels.* Norman Macleod.
    Trust in God. BLRP
Trust in Me. *Unknown.* AH
Trust in the Lord, *paraphrased by* Charles Frederic Sheldon. Bible, *O.T., paraphrased by* Sir Thomas Wyatt. *See* Fret not thyself because of evildoers.
Trust in Women (When nettles in winter bring forth roses red), *sels. Unknown.*
Trust is a meadow, the light in my eyes. A Hat Thrown in the Air, a Leg That's Lost. Iain Sinclair. VaA
Trust Man a Little Bit More. Chang Ming-ch'uan, *tr. fr. Chinese.* LHF, *tr. by* Hualing Nieh
Trust man a little bit more! What to Trust? Shao Yen-hsiang, *tr. fr. Chinese.* LHF, *tr. by* Hualing Nieh
Trust Me. Jean Valentine. BAP-89
Trust me. The world is run on a shoestring. Hard Times. John Ashbery. NoAM
Trust not his wanton tears. Aeliana's Ditty. Henry Chettle. *Fr.* Piers Plainness' Seven Years' Prenticeship.
    (Of Cupid.) EIL
Trust not that thing called woman: she is worse. A Rodomontade on His Cruel Mistress. The Earl of Rochester. OxBSP
Trust not the treason of those smiling looks. Spenser. *Fr.* Amoretti, XLVII. AAS; *F* So, lacking epigrams I-IV; TrGrPo
Trust not too much, fair youth, unto thy feature. White Primit Falls. *Unknown.* ChTr
Trust Only Yourself. *Unknown.* MeEL
Trust-Song, A. Eben E. Rexford. BLRP
Trust the Great Artist. Thomas Curtis Clark. WBLP
Trust Thou Thy Love. John Ruskin. OBEV
"Trust us," the Voices said. (*LL*) The Lovely Shall Be Choosers. Robert Frost. MoAB; MoAmPo; NOBA; OxBA; PoE
Trusted the servile womb to breed free men? (*LL*) Advice to Young Ladies. A. D. Hope. FaBoMA; NoAM; NoP
Trustful curator has left me alone, The. Museum of Man. Earle Birney. OxBC
Trusts in God, that as well as he was, he shall be. (*LL*) Epitaph on Himself. Pope. FaBoEE
Truth. "Æ." MoBrPo
Truth. Chaucer. *See* Flee from [or Fle fro] the press [or prees or pres] and dwelle with soothfastnesse [or sothefastnesse or sothfastnesse].
Truth, *sels.* William Cowper.
    "Man on the dubious waves of error toss'd." NOCV
Truth, The. W. H. Davies. FaBoTw
Truth. Eileen Duggan. PeNZ
Truth. Josephine D. Henderson Heard. CBWP-4
Truth, The. Randall Jarrell. OxBC
Truth, The. Ted Joans. TTY
Truth. Claude McKay. BPo
Truth. John Masefield. WGRP
Truth. Howard Nemerov. HoPM; LiTM
Truth, The. Frankie Paino. NAmP90
Truth. Coventry Patmore. *See* Here, in This Little Bay.
Truth. Lizette Woodworth Reese. AmWP
Truth. Susan Fromberg Schaeffer. IHMS
Truth. Barrie Wade. OTCP
Truth? A pebble of quartz? For once, then, something. (*LL*) For Once, Then, Something. Robert Frost. NoAM; NOBA
Truth about Horace, The. Eugene Field. AnAmPo
Truth about My Sister and Me, The. Anita Endrezze-Danielson. CDW
Truth about truth is elusive, The. *Unknown.* PeLi
Truth and Consequences. Edward Baugh. PBCV
Truth, be more precious to me than the eyes. Max Eastman. WGRP
Truth Brought to Light, or Murder Will Out. Stephen College. APAS
Truth from Above, The. *Unknown.* OBET
Truth Has Perished. Ulma Seligman, *tr. fr. Yiddish by* Joseph Leftwich. TrJP
Truth I do not stretch or shove, The. The Dog. Ogden Nash. Spl

Truth I pursued, as Fancy sketch'd the way. Samuel Taylor Coleridge. FaBoEE

Truth in Poetry. George Crabbe. *Fr.* Village, The. EPCY; FHYEP

Truth Is, The. Linda Hogan. ETG; HATNAP

Truth is a golden sunset far away. I. O. Scherzo. HoPM

Truth is a native, naked beauty; but. Roger Williams. SCAP

Truth is as old as God. Emily Dickinson. MoAmPo

Truth is love and love is truth. Mendacity. A. E. Coppard. OBMV

Truth is that there comes a time, The. Sad Strains of a Gay Waltz. Wallace Stevens. OxBA

Truth like the Belly of a Woman Turning, The. Gary Snyder. NNaP

Truth-loving Persians do not dwell upon. The Persian Version. Robert Graves. CMoP; FaBoCo; LiTB; LiTM; MoP; NoAM; NOBL; OBWP; WeW

Truth Made Breakfast, The. Jeffrey Miller. UL

Truth Never Dies. *Unknown.* WBLP

Truth Shall Set You Free. Chaucer. *See* Flee from [*or* Fle fro] the press [*or* prees *or* pres] and dwelle with soothfastnesse [*or* sothefastnesse *or* sothfastnesse].

Truth, so far, in my book; the truth which draws. Elizabeth Barrett Browning. *Fr.* Aurora Leigh. WGRP

Truth Suppressed, The. L. A. J. Moorer. CBWP-3

Truth that's told with bad intent, A. Blake. *Fr.* Auguries of Innocence. BLPL; EBEV; EnRP; FaBoCh; FaBV; FaPoR; FM; LiTB; OAEL-1; OBNC; OxBoLi; PlP; PoEL-4; TrGrPo

Truth the Dead Know, The. Anne Sexton. IMW; LCAP; MoAmPo; NoAM; PBWP; TAP; VCAP

Truth, Truth, nobody's daughter. *Unknown.* ISE

Truth's the Best. Elizabeth Turner. OxBChV

Truxton's Victory. *Unknown.* PAH

Try. Philip Appleman. BXAP

Try Again. Eliza Cook. BoTP

Try first this figure 2. A Lesson in Handwriting. Alastair Reid. NYBP

Try our Rubber Girl-Friend (air-inflatable). *Unknown.* PeLi

Try Smiling. *Unknown.* BLPA; PWR; WBLP

Try the Uplook. *Unknown.* BLRP

Try This Once. *Unknown.* WBLP

Try to avoid inhaling the laden air. (*LL*) The Lovers of the Poor. Gwendolyn Brooks. CAPP; LCAP; MoP; NAAL-2; NoAM; NOBA; Poetr

Try to see them as Monet would. The Hackeysack Players. Cynthia Huntington. NAmP90

Try Topic. Genevieve Taggard. MoAmPo

Try, Try Again. *At. to* T. H. Palmer. FaPON; ImGa

Try, try again. (*LL*) Try, Try Again. *At. to* T. H. Palmer. FaPON; ImGa

Try wading in sand. Try. Philip Appleman. BXAP

Trying for Fire. Tim Seibles. NAmP90

Trying On for Size. Mary Dorcey. AIW

Trying out edifices. (*LL*) What Idiots Lovers Are. Judith Kazantzis. VBLP

Trying to chop mother down is like. She Went to Stay. Robert Creeley. OBAL

Trying to establish a beachhead. (*LL*) Wire. Rod Moran. NOBAu

Trying to fall asleep. Night Thought. Gerald Jonas. NYBP

Trying to make/ Trouble. (*LL*) The Rebel. Mari Evans. CRP; IHMS; PoBA

Trying to open locked doors with a sword, threading. Sojourn in the Whale. Marianne Moore. NALW

Trying to reason, trying to rhyme. Ammon Wrigley. *Fr.* Fall Sonnets. UnDi

Trying to Talk with a Man. Adrienne Rich. HCAP

Tryst. John Hewitt. BiHa

Tryst. Eve Merriam. NMM

Tryst. Peter Reading. FaBoBl

Tryst [*or* Trysting Place], The. William Soutar. EBEV; ErPo; OxBS

Tryst, The. John Banister Tabb. OBAL

Tryst, The. Mary E. Tucker. CBWP-1

Tryst, The. *Unknown, tr. fr.* Welsh by Joseph P. Clancy. OBWVE

Tryst in Brobdingnag, A. Adrienne Rich. NYBP

Trystan and Esyllt. *Unknown, tr. fr.* Welsh by Gwyn Jones. OBWVE

Trysting, A. Richard Dehmel, *tr. fr.* German by Jethro Bithell. AWP

Trysting Bush, The. Joanna Baillie. WPE

Trysting Place, The. William Soutar. *See* O luely, luely, cam she in.

Ts'ai Chi'h. Ezra Pound. NoP

Tsa'lagi Council Tree. Gladys Cardiff. HATNAP

Tsena Tsena (Second Generation). Marilyn Mohr. BTR

Tu/ cson's of blackmens. Ron Welburn. NBV

Tu Non Se' in Terra, Si Come Tu Credi. Kathleen Raine. WPE

Tu-Whit To-Who. Shakespeare. *See* When icicles hang by the wall.

Tu-whitt, Tu-whitt, Tu-whoo, Tu-whoo. "Good Night," Says the Owl. Lady Erskine Crum. BoTP

Tua Mariit Wemen and the Wedo, The, *sels.* William Dunbar. Widow Has Buried Her Second Husband, The. OxBLMV

Tubal Cain. Charles MacKay. WBLP

Tubby or not tubby — there's the rub. F. C. Burnand. BXAP

Tube Time. Eve Merriam. TLR

Tubes. Donald Hall. BAP-91

Tuckett. Bill Tuckett. Telegraph operator, Hall's Creek. Morse. Les A. Murray. NTP

Tucking in yellow curls, she poises, set. The Diver. Leonard Nathan. ErPo

Tudor Aspersions. R. A. Piddington. FiBHP

Tudor indeed is gone and every rose. Ezra Pound. *Fr.* Cantos. FaBoTw

Tuesday in Holy Week, 1990, Dark Grey Day in Peekskill, NY. Stephen Knight. UnDi

Tuesday; or, the Ditty. John Gay. *Fr.* Shepherd's Week, The. NOEC

Tuft of Flowers, The. Robert Frost. AWP; GoYe; LiTA; MoAB; MoAmPo; NAAL-2; OxBA; PAW

Tuft of Kelp, The. Herman Melville. ChTr; FaBoEE; FaBoRV

Tug-of-War, A. M. M. Hutchinson. BoTP

Tug with bright streets at lonely lights like his. (*LL*) Flying at Night. Ted Kooser. InPK; PBCAP

Tugela River. William Plomer. PeSAV

Tugging my forelock fathoming Xenophon. Still. Tony Harrison. OBD

Tugs. James S. Tippett. FaPON

Tulip. Humbert Wolfe. MoBrPo

Tulip Tree. Sacheverell Sitwell. MoBrPo

Tulips. Medbh McGuckian. PNI

Tulips. Sylvia Plath. HAP; NaP; NoP; NYBP; PPP; WeW; WPE

Tulips & Chimneys, *sels.* E. E. Cummings. "Spring omnipotent goddess thou dost." NBLV; OxBA

Tulips: A Selected History. Vickie Karp. UTF

Tulips and Addresses. Edward Field. NYBP; Poetsp

Tulips are too excitable, it is winter here, The. Tulips. Sylvia Plath. HAP; NaP; NoP; NYBP; PPP; WeW; WPE

Tulips charge the grazing dikes, and I walk. Dutch April. Daniel Halpern. GrPI

Tullie's Love, *sels.* Robert Greene.

Tullochgorum. John Skinner. OxBS

Tully, the queen of beauty's boast. Molly Moor. George Farewell. NOEC

Tumadir al-Khansa for Her Brother. *Unknown, tr. fr.* Arabic by E. Powys Mathers. *Fr.* Thousand and One Nights, The. AWP

Tumble me down, and I will sit. To Fortune. Robert Herrick. OxBSP; SeCV-1

Tumble shall heaven, and so down wil. (*LL*) To God. Robert Herrick. TrPWD; WGRP

Tumbled out of heaven. The Blue Day Journey. Gwyn Jones. OBWVE

Tumbleweed. Jonathan Holden. NAmP90

Tumbleweed. David Wagoner. BoNaP

Tumbling. *Unknown.* OxBChV

Tumbling, pausing, leaping, knocking together. Metaphysic of Snow. Donald Finkel. PoA

Tumult. Charles Enoch Wheeler. PoNe

Tumult in a Syrian town had place, A. The Great Physician. Sadi, *tr. fr.* Persian by Sir Edwin Arnold. *Fr.* Bustan, The. AWP

Tumult in the street! A. *Unknown, tr. fr.* Greek by Edward Lucie-Smith. GrAn

Tumult of death, dizziness hath seized me, The. Elegy (for Himself). Moses Rimos of Majorca, *tr. fr.* Hebrew by Israel Abrahams. TrJP

Tumult of my fretted mind, The. Self-Analysis. Anna Wickham. MoBrPo

Tumult, weeping, many new ghosts. Snow Storm. Kenneth Rexroth. NaP

Tumultuous sea, whose wrath and foam are spent. Eumares. Asclepiades, *tr. fr.* Greek by Richard Garnett. AWP

Tunbridge Wells. The Earl of Rochester. FaBoPP; OBSV

T'undo, or be undone. (*LL*) Ulysses and the Siren [*or* Syren]. Samuel Daniel. EIL; EnRePo; HAP; NAEL-1; NOBE; NoP; OBEV; OxAEP-1; PoE; PoEL-2; TEP

Tundra, The. John Haines. FoLa

Tundra is a living, The. The Tundra. John Haines. FoLa

Tune: "Alone I stand in autumn cold." Mao Tse-tung, *tr. fr. Chinese by* Eugene Eoyang. SuSp

Tune: "As in a Dream; a Song," Li Ch'ing-chao, *tr. fr. Chinese by* Eugene Eoyang. BoWoP; SuSp

Tune: "Song of the Lunar Palace." Lu Chih, *tr. fr. Chinese by* Hellmut Wilhelm. SuSp

Tune: "Song of the Lunar Palace" — Sending Off Spring. Kuan Yun-shih, *tr. fr. Chinese by* Richard John Lynn. SuSp

Tune: "Song of the Southern Country." — Spring Thoughts at Pearl River. Chu Yi-tsun, *tr. fr. Chinese by* Irving Y. Lo. SuSp

Tune: "Song of the Southern Country." Li Hsün, *tr. fr. Chinese by* Edward Schafer. SuSp

Tune: "Song of the Southern Country" — Presented to a Courtesan. Hsin Ch'i-chi, *tr. fr. Chinese by* Irving Y. Lo. SuSp

Tune: "Song of the Wine Spring." P'an Lang, *tr. fr. Chinese by* James J. Y. Liu. SuSp

Tune: "Song of Tzu-yeh." Li Yü, *tr. fr. Chinese by* Daniel Bryant. SuSp

Tune: "Southern Song, A." Li Ch'ing-chao, *tr. fr. Chinese by* Eugene Eoyang. SuSp

Tune: "Southern Song, A." Wen T'ing-yün, *tr. fr. Chinese by* William R. Schultz. SuSp

Tune: "Sparse Shadows" — Plum Blossoms. Chiang K'uei, *tr. fr. Chinese by* An-yan Tang. SuSp

Tune: "Sprig of Flowers, A" — Not Bowing to Old Age. Kuan Han-ch'ing, *tr. fr. Chinese by* Jerome P. Seaton. SuSp

Tune: "Sprig of Flowers, A" — Written for My "Ugly Studio." Chung Ssu-ch'eng, *tr. fr. Chinese by* Sherwin S. S. Fu. SuSp

Tune: "Spring at Wu-ling." Li Ch'ing-chao, *tr. fr. Chinese by* Eugene Eoyang. SuSp

Tune: "Spring in Ch'in's Garden." Hsin Ch'i-chi, *tr. fr. Chinese by* Irving Y. Lo. SuSp

Tune: "Spring in Ch'in's Garden" ("Northern landscape.") Mao Tse-tung, *tr. fr. Chinese by* Eugene Eoyang. SuSp

Tune: "Spring in Jade Pavilion." Li Yü, *tr. fr. Chinese by* Daniel Bryant. SuSp

Tune: "Spring in Jade Pavilion." Yen Shu, *tr. fr. Chinese by* An-yan Tang. SuSp

Tune: "Squabbling Quails." Kuan Yun-shih, *tr. by* Richard John Lynn. *Fr.* Medley of Southern and Northern Tunes — Scenic Tour of West Lake. SuSp

Tune: "Stretch of Cloud over Mount Wu, A." Li Hsün, *tr. fr. Chinese by* Hellmut Wilhelm. SuSp

Tune: "Tartar Tune of Eighteen Beats." *Unknown, tr. fr. Chinese by* Sherwin S. S. Fu. SuSp

Tune: "Telling of Innermost Feelings." Ku Hsiung, *tr. fr. Chinese by* James J. Y. Liu. SuSp

Tune: "Telling of Innermost Feelings." Li Ch'ing-chao, *tr. fr. Chinese by* Eugene Eoyang. SuSp

Tune: "Telling of Innermost Feelings." Lu Yu, *tr. fr. Chinese by* James J. Y. Liu. SuSp

Tune: "Telling of Innermost Feelings." Wen T'ing-yün, *tr. fr. Chinese by* William R. Schultz. SuSp

Tune: "Telling of Innermost Feelings" — Wandering in Spring. Ch'en Tzu-lung, *tr. fr. Chinese by* Bruce Carpenter. SuSp

Tune: "Tipsy in the Flower's Shade." Li Ch'ing-chao, *tr. fr. Chinese by* Eugene Eoyang. SuSp

Tune: "Treading on Grass." Ou-yang Hsiu, *tr. fr. Chinese by* An-yan Tang. SuSp

Tune: "Treading on Grass." Yen Shu, *tr. fr. Chinese by* James J. Y. Liu. SuSp

Tune: "Wanderings of a Youth." Liu Yung, *tr. fr. Chinese by* Jerome P. Seaton. SuSp

Tune: "Water Dragon's Chang" After Chang Chi-fu's Lyric on the Willow Catkin. Su Shih, *tr. fr. Chinese by* James J. Y. Liu. SuSp

Tune: "Water Dragon's Chant" — Loathsome Spring. Ch'en Liang, *tr. fr. Chinese by* Hellmut Wilhelm. SuSp

Tune: "Wild Geese Have Come Down; Song of Victory." *Unknown, tr. fr. Chinese by* Sherwin S. S. Fu. SuSp

Tune: "Wild Geese Have Come Down; Song of Victory" — Idle Leisure. Teng Yu-ein, *tr. fr. Chinese by* Hellmut Wilhelm. SuSp

Tune: "Willow Branches." *Unknown, tr. fr. Chinese by* Hellmut Wilhelm. SuSp

Tune: "Wu-t'ung Leaves" — Written in Jest at a Banquet. Lu Chih, *tr. fr. Chinese by* Hellmut Wilhelm. SuSp

Tune, A. Arthur Symons. BoLoP; OBNC

Tune for a Lonesome Fife. Donald Justice. *See* Merry the green, the green hill shall be merry.

Tune is cowboy, The; the words, sentimental crap. D-Y Bar. James Welch. CDW

Tune me for life again, oh, quiet Musician. A Prayer after Illness. Violet Alleyn Storey. TrPWD

Tune Me, O Lord, into One Harmony. Christina Rossetti. TrPWD

Tune of Seven Towers, The. William Morris. EnVR

Tune on my pipe the praises of my Love. In Praise of His Daphnis. Sir John Wotton. EIL

Tune on my pipe the praises of my Love. Of His Mistress. Robert Greene. *Fr.* Menaphon. EIL

Tune thy music[ke] to thy heart [*or* hart]. Heart's Music. *At. to* Thomas Campion. AAS; OBEV

Tune to the Devonshire Cant, The. *Unknown.* APAS

Tuneful Hipponax rests him here. Epitaph of Hipponax. Theocritus [*or* Theokritus], *tr. fr. Greek by* Charles Stuart Calverley. FaBoEE

Tuneful poet, Britain's glory. The Mutual Congratulations of the Poets Anna Seward and Hayley. Richard Porson. FaBoEE; OBSV

Tunes fainter on winds waywarder than others. Graves Are Made to Waltz On. Peter Viereck. PoA

Tunes for Bears to Dance To. Ronald Wallace. GOYP

Tungeei, that was her native name. Captain Cook. *Aborigine Oral Tradition, tr. by* Percy Mumbulla. NOBAu

Tunnel, The. Hart Crane. *Fr.* Bridge, The. CMoP; LiTA; MAT; MoAB; MoAmPo; NAAL-2; OxBA

Tunnel, The. Nicanor Parra, *tr. fr. Spanish by* W. S. Merwin. AnRep

Tunnel, The. Mark Strand. HeIP; TwCP

Tunnel through the earth, A. (*LL*) The Longest Night. Marge Piercy. SRLS

Tunnel Visions, *sels*. Felix Pollak.

Tunny girls are lounging on its suckers, The. (*LL*) This Octopus Exploits Women. James Fenton. CBNP; NoAM

Tunnyng [*or* Tunning] of Elynour [*or* Elinor] Rummyng [*or* Rumming], The. John Skelton. AAS

Sels.

"Tell you I chyll." TrGrPo

"Then Margery [*or* Marjorie] Milkduck." EBEV; OAEL-1; PoE

Tupelo Destruction, The. *Unknown.* AmFP

Turbulent Water, The. *Unknown, tr. fr. Chinese by* Robert Payne. TAL

Turf Carrier on Aranmore. John Hewitt. PoRA

Turf-Stacks. Louis MacNeice. *See* Among These Turf-Stacks.

Turkey in the Straw. *Unknown.* AS; GBP

Turkey in the straw, *etc.* (*LL*) Turkey in the Straw. *Unknown.* AS; GBP

Turkey is dancing near the rocks, A. *Unknown, tr. fr. Navajo Indian by* Jerome K. Rothenberg *after* David McAllester. STP

Turkeys. John Clare. FaBoVe

Turkeys wade the close to catch bees, The. Turkeys. John Clare. FaBoVe

Turkish Bakery, The. *Unknown, tr. fr. Korean by* Peter H. Lee. PBWP; VBLP

Turkish Carpet, The. Paul Durcan. CIP

Turkish government allows no law, The. Fulke Greville. FaBoPV

Turkish Legend, A. Thomas Bailey Aldrich. GN

Turkish Love Songs. *Unknown, tr. by* Reza Baraheni *and* Zahra-Soltan Shokoohtaezeh. BoWoP

Turkish Trench Dog, The. Geoffrey Dearmer. Mes; NSI

Turkish war both far and near, The. Lovely Albert. *Unknown.* IHNG

Turn, The. Robert Creeley. LCAP

Turn (a Poem in 4 Parts). Ken Belford. NOBC

Turn again, maiden, twice slain and rotten. Hilaire Kirkland. *Fr.* Observations. PeNZ

Turn Again to Life. Mary Lee Hall. BLPL; PoLF

Turn again, turn again, turn once again. Carrousel Tune. Tennessee Williams. NBLV; OBAL

Turn Back, O Man. Clifford Bax. NOCV

Turn/ back oh man. Retrovir. Tim Dlugas. PFL

Turn back to their day, their grieving and staying. (*LL*) Grief. Wendell Berry. MT

Turn back. Turn, young lady dear. The Robber Bridegroom. Allen Tate. CBLP

Turn from Self. George Macdonald. PWR

Turn from that girl. I Shall Laugh Purely. Robinson Jeffers. LiTA; LiTM

Turn him, and see his threads; look if he be. Ben Jonson. *Fr.* Epistle to Master Arthur Squib, An. OBF

Turn inward on the brain. What the Emanation of Casey Jones Said to the Medium. A. J. M. Smith. MoCV

Turn like a top, spin on your dusty axis. Instead of a Journey. Michael Hamburger. NYBP

Turn me like a waterwheel turning a millstone. After Being in Love, the Next Responsibility. Jalal al-Din Rumi, *tr. fr. Persian by* John Moyne *and* Coleman Barks. UnAS

Turn my pages, — never mind. Oliver Wendell Holmes. *Fr.* Programme. OBF

Twa Travellers, as they were wa'king. The Chamaeleon. Allan Ramsay. ScCV

Twain that were foes, while Mary lived, are fled. His Lady's Death. Pierre de Ronsard, tr. fr. French by Andrew Lang. AWP

'Twas well the wars were done before. David Lloyd. Fr. Legend of Captain Jones, The. AngWe
(Roses and tulips Flora gathers here.) AngWe

'Twas a balmy summer evening, and a goodly crowd was there. The Face upon [or on] the Floor. Hugh Antoine D'Arcy. BeLS; BLPA; FaBoBe; VPP

'Twas a busy day in the courtroom, and a curious crowd was there. The Bank Thief. J. R. Farrell. BeLS; BLPA

'Twas a cloudless morning and the sun shone bright. The Cherokee. Mary Weston Fordham. AmWP; CBWP-2

'Twas a comical sight that I saw by the roadside. The Song of Lies. Unknown, tr. fr. Irish by Donal O'Sullivan. CBNP

'Twas a dangerous cliff, as they freely confessed. A Fence or an Ambulance. Joseph Malins. BLPA

'Twas a grand display was the prince's ball. Baron Renfrew's Ball. Charles Graham Halpine. PAH

'Twas a new feeling — something more. Did Not. Thomas Moore. BoLoP; ErPo; PeLV
(Quantum Est Quod Desit.) EnLoPo

Twas a night of dreadful horror. The Night of Death. Frances E. W. Harper. PWR

'Twas a stylish congregation, that of Theophrastus Brown. Trouble in the "Amen Corner." Thomas Chalmers Harbaugh. BLPA

'Twas a summer evening. Robert Southey. Fr. Battle of Blenheim, The. FaBoEH

'Twas a Sunday morning, quite serene the air. City Eclogue. "W. J." NOEC

'Twas a tough task, believe it, thus to tame. Upon Dr. Davies's British Grammar. James Howell. AngWe; OBWVE

'Twas a wonderful brave fight! The Fight at Sumter. Unknown. PAH

'Twas after dread Pultowa's day. Mazeppa. Byron. EnRP
(Mazeppa's Ride.) CoGr

'Twas all along the Binder Line. Sensitive Sydney. Wallace Irwin. FiBHP

'Twas all on board a ship down in a southern sea. The Golden Vanity. Unknown. CH; ELP; FaBoCh; OBET; WiR

'Twas at that sober hour when the light of the day is receding. Southey Looks out of the Window at Greta Hill. Robert Southey. Fr. Vision of Judgement, A. FaBoPP

'Twas at the Matin Hour. Unknown. OHIP

'Twas at the royal feast, for Persia won. Alexander's Feast; or, The Power of Music [or Musique]. Dryden. FaPoR; GN; GTBS; GTBS-P; LiTB; NAEL-1; NOBE; OAEL-1; OtMeF, ll. 1–15; PeECV; SeCV-2; TFi; TrGrPo; WiR

'Twas at the silent, solemn hour. William and Margaret. David Mallet. NOEC; OxAEP-1

'Twas at the solemn hour of night. Dr. Johnson's Ghost. Elizabeth Moody. ECWP

'Twas August, and the fierce sun overhead. East London. Matthew Arnold. SCGP; WGRP

'Twas autumn and 'round me the leaves were descending. The Banks of Champlain. Unknown. AmFP

'Twas battered and scarred, and the auctioneer. The Touch of the Master's Hand. Myra Brooks Welch. BLPA; PoToHe

'Twas brillig, and the slithy toves. Jabberwocky. "Lewis Carroll." Fr. Through the Looking-Glass. CBNP; ClHu; CoGr; EBEV; EBEvV; EBVV; FaBoBe; FaBoCo; FaBoNo; FaBV; FaPON; FF; FiBHP; GoJo; HeIP; HoPM; ImPo; InPK; InPS; LiTB; NAEL-2; NBLV; NoAM; NOBE; NOBL; NOBVV; NoP; NTCP; OAEL-2; OBSP; OHCV; OPOP; OxAEP-2; OxBChV; PeLV; PeVV; Poetr; PoRA; PPP; RB; TEP; TFi; TRP; TTTS; UV

'Twas but a single Rose. Upon a Virgin Kissing a Rose. Robert Herrick. SeCP; SeCV-1

'Twas Captain Church, bescarred and brown. King Philip's Last Stand. Clinton Scollard. PAH

'Twas Christmas Eve, the month was May. A Tragedy. Tom Masson. OBAL

'Twas Christmas Eve, the snow lay deep. When the Christ Child Came. Frederic E. Weatherly. OHIP

'Twas Christmas on the Spanish Main. T. S. Eliot. FaBoBl

'Twas early in 'eighty-two, and I think on March the twentieth day. Tiger Bay. Unknown. OxBSS

'Twas early in the month of May. Barbara Allen ("Twas early in the month of May.") Unknown. OBET

'Twas early in the springtime of the year. Early in the Springtime. Unknown. OBET

'Twas early on a May morning. Lady Isabel. Unknown. ESPB

'Twas early one morning a fair maid arose. A Kiss in the Morning Early. Unknown. GBP

'Twas early one morning by the break of the day. All Jolly Fellows That Follow the Plough. Unknown. OBET

'Twas earlye, earlye in the spring. Earlye, Earlye, in the Spring. Unknown. AmFP

'Twas enough to make a man stare. (LL) Rub a dub dub,/ Three men in a tub. Mother Goose. NOBL; OxNR; RoPo, diff. vers.

'Twas eve in sunny Italy. A Tale of Italy. Eloise Bibb. CBWP-4

'Twas evening, though not sun-set, and spring-tide. Tamar's Wrestling. Walter Savage Landor. Fr. Gebir. EnRP
(Shepherd and the Nymph, The.) OBNC

'Twas Ever Thus. Henry S. Leigh. FaBoCo; FaBoPa

'Twas Ever Thus. Unknown. BXAP

'Twas ever thus from childhood's hour! Disaster. Charles Stuart Calverley. FM; NBLV

'Twas fancy first made Celia fair. Fancy. Jonathan Smedley. OxBSP

'Twas Friday morn: the train drew near. Through Baltimore. Bayard Taylor. PAH

'Twas going to snow — 'twas snowing! Curse his luck! The Drove-Road. W. W. Gibson. OxBTC

'Twas hurry and scurry at Monmouth town. Molly Pitcher. Kate Brownlee Sherwood. PAH

'Twas in a basement tobble d'hote. Reverie. Don Marquis. PoLF

'Twas in eighteen eleven those bards came to dine; Leigh Hunt. Fr. Feast of the Poets, The. EPCY

'Twas in heaven pronounced, and 'twas muttered in hell. Catherine Fanshawe. ChTr
('Twas whispered in Heaven, 'twas muttered in hell.) GN

'Twas in Koolau I met with the rain. Rain, The ("'twas in Koolau I met with the rain.") Unknown, tr. fr. Hawaiian by N. B. Emerson. WTO

'Twas in Rosemary Lane, sirs. Neddy Nibble'm and Biddy Finn. Unknown. GBP

'Twas in that island summer where. He Loves and He Rides Away. Sydney Thompson Dobell. OBNC

'Twas in that place o' Scotland's isle. Burns. Fr. Twa Dogs, The. OBF

'Twas in the days of the Revolution. Emily Geiger. Unknown. BLPL; PoLF

'Twas in the middle of the night. Mary's Ghost. Thomas Hood. FiBHP

'Twas in the month of August, or the middle of July. She Said the Same to Me. Unknown. AS

'Twas in the month of December, and in the year 1883. The Famous Tay Whale. William McGonagall. PeVV

'Twas in the moon of winter time when all the birds had fled. Jesous Ahatonhia. Jesse Edgar Middleton. OBCP
(Huron Carol, The.) OBCP

'Twas in the prime of summer time. The Dream of Eugene Aram [the Murderer]. Thomas Hood. BeLS; EnRP

'Twas in the reign of George the Third. A New Song Called the Gaspee. Unknown. PAH

'Twas in the spring of '72. The April Fool. Eugene Field. PWR

'Twas in the town of Jacksboro in the spring [or year] of seventy-three. The Buffalo Skinners. Unknown. AmFP; AS; GBP; RB; SWP

'Twas in the year of 1898, and on the 21st of June. The Albion Battleship Calamity. William McGonagall. BXAP

'Twas in the year of forty-nine. The Whale. Unknown. ChTr
(Greenland Whale, The.) GBP

'Twas Jolly, Jolly Wat. C. W. Stubbs. OHIP

'Twas Juet spoke — the Half Moon's mate. The Death of Colman. Thomas Frost. PAH

'Twas June on the face of the earth, June with the rose's breath. The Eve of Bunker Hill. Clinton Scollard. PAH

'Twas just this time, last year, I died. Emily Dickinson. PoE

'Twas late, and the gay company was gone. The Declaration. Nathaniel Parker Willis. AnAmPo; OBAL

'Twas laurel'd Martial roaring murther. (LL) On Elphinston's Translation of Martial. Burns. FaBoCo; FaBoEE

'Twas like a maelstrom, with a notch. Emily Dickinson. CMoP; LiTM; PoE
(Final Inch, The.) LiTA

'Twas May upon the mountains, and on the airy wing. The Surprise at Ticonderoga. Mary A. P. Stansbury. PAH

'Twas mercy brought me from my pagan land. On Being Brought from Africa to America. Phillis Wheatley. FF; GOA; NAAL-1; NALW; NOBA; NOEC; TAP; TTY; WPE

'Twas midnight — every mortal eye was closed. The Helmets; a Fragment. Thomas Penrose. NOEC

'Twas midsummer: cooling breezes all the languid forests fanned. The Death of Jefferson. Hezekiah Butterworth. PAH

'Twas more significant, she's dead. (LL) Enough; and leave the rest to fame. Andrew Marvell. OBEV

'Twas night; and Flavia, to her room retired. Soliloquy of a Beauty in the Country. George Lyttelton. ECEV

'Twas night upon the Darro. The Thanksgiving for America. Hezekiah Butterworth. PAH

'Twas not as lonesome as it might have been. The Cricket Kept the House. Edith M. Thomas. OBCA

" 'Twas not so in my time," surly Grumio exclaims. Samuel Bishop. NOEC

'Twas not the brown of chestnut boughs. Gwendoline. Bayard Taylor. BXAP

'Twas November the fourth, in the year of ninety-one. Sainclaire's Defeat. Unknown. PAH

'Twas of a brisk young sailor, as I have heard it said. Johnny German. Unknown. AmFP

'Twas of a lovely creature who dwelled by the seaside. Mary in the Silvery Tide. Unknown. OBET

'Twas of a nobleman's daughter. Caroline and Her Young Sailor Bold. Unknown. AmFP

'Twas of a shepherd's son. Blow Away the Morning Dew. Unknown. OBET

'Twas of a young brickster a-going from his work. The Brickster. Unknown. OBET

'Twas on a dark and stormy night well southward of the Cape. The Flying Dutchman. Unknown. OxBSS

'Twas on a glorious summer eve. The Angel's Visit. Charlotte L. Forten Grimke. AAP

'Twas on a Holy Thursday, their innocent faces clean. Holy Thursday (" 'Twas on a Holy Thursday, their innocent faces clean.") Blake. Fr. Songs of Innocence. CH; EnRP; FHYEP; InPS; MeMBP; NAEL-2; NAWM-2; NOBE; NOEC; NoP; OAEL-2; PeECV; PoE; SCV; TEP; TFi; TrCP

'Twas on a lofty vase's side. Ode on [or On] the Death of a Favourite [or Favorite] Cat, Drowned in a Tub [or Bowl] of Gold Fishes. Thomas Gray. ClHu; EBEV; ECEV; FaBoBe; FHYEP; FM; HoPM; NAEL-1; NBLV; NOBE; NOBL; NOEC; NoP; OAEL-1; OFC; PeLV; PoE; PoEL-3; PPP; SoCa; TEP; TFi
(Cat and the Fish, The.) WiR
(On a Favorite Cat Drowned in a Tub of Gold Fishes.) BeLS; EBEvV; EBNV; FaBoCo; GN; GTBS; GTBS-P; InvP; LiTB; OxAEP-1
(On the Death of a Favorite Cat, Drowned in a Tub of Gold Fishes.) InPS; PoLF; PoRA

'Twas on a Monday morning. Charlie, He's My Darling. Burns. CH; FaBoPV

'Twas on a Monday morning, just at the break of day. Maggie Mac. Unknown. AmFP

'Twas on a Monday morning, the first I saw my darling. Hanging Out the Linen Clothes. Unknown. AS

'Twas on a night, an evening bright. Proud Lady Margaret. Unknown. ESPB

'Twas on a pleasant mountain. The Battle of King's Mountain. Unknown. PAH

'Twas on a summer noon, in Stainsford mead. My Ox Duke. John Dyer. NOEC

'Twas on a summer's day — the sixth of June. Byron. Fr. Don Juan. PPP

'Twas on an evening fair I went to take the air. Willie's Fatal Visit. Unknown. ESPB

'Twas on board the sloop of war Wasp, boys. The Wasp's Frolic. Unknown. PAH

'Twas on Lake Erie's broad expanse. John Maynard. Horatio Alger, Jr.. BeLS; BLPA; FaBoBe

'Twas on the eighth of January, just at the dawn of day. The Battle of New Orleans. Unknown. AmFP

'Twas on the field of Antietam where many's the soldier fell. The Battle of Antietam Creek. Unknown. AmFP

'Twas on the glorious day. The Death of General Pike. Laughton Osborn. PAH

'Twas on The [or the] Longstone Lighthouse there dwelt an English maid. Grace Darling. Unknown. OBET; OxBSS

'Twas on the shores that round our coast. The Yarn of the Nancy Bell. W. S. Gilbert. BeLS; BLPA; EBEvV; EBNV; FaBoBe; FaBoCh; FaBoCo; FaBV; HoPM; MoShBr; NOBL; TFi; TrGrPo; UV, sh. vers.

'Twas on the twelfth of April. Sumter — a Ballad of 1861. Unknown. PAH

'Twas once look up, 'tis now look down to Heaven. (LL) On the Blessed Virgin's Bashfulness. Richard Crashaw. HAP; OxBSP

'Twas once upon a time, when Jenny Wren was young. When Jenny Wren Was Young. Unknown. ReMoGo

'Twas one October mornin'. Bigerlow. Unknown. AS

'Twas only a passing thought, my love. Only a Thought. Charles MacKay. Poetr

'Twas [or It was] a summer [or summer's] evening. The Battle of Blenheim. Robert Southey. BeLS; CoGr; EnRP; FaBoPV; FaBV; FaPoR; GN; OBNC; OBWP; PoLF; TFi; TrGrPo; VPP; WBLP
(After Blenheim.) GTBS; GTBS-P; OxAEP-2; PAW; UV, Abr.

'Twas out upon mid ocean that the San Jacinto hailed. Death of the Lincoln Despotism. Unknown. PAH

'Twas over hills and over dales. Locks and Bolts. Unknown. OBET

'Twas Rollog, and the Minim Potes. Unknown. UV

'Twas said of Greece two thousand years ago. Colonial Nomenclature. John Dunmore Lang. NOBAu

'Twas so, I saw thy birth: that drowsy [or drowsie] lake. The Shower [or Showre]. Henry Vaughan. BoNaP; ChTr; ESCV; FaBoPP; GeHe; LiTB; SeCP

'Twas spring, and dawn returning breathed new-born. Idyll of the Rose. Ausonius, tr. fr. Latin by John Addington Symonds. AWP

'Twas summer, and the sun had mounted high. The Wanderer. Wordsworth. Fr. Excursion, The. EnRP, abr.
(Ruined Cottage, The, diff. vers.). NoP; OAEL-2

'Twas Sunday morning, quite serene the air. A City Eclogue. "W. J." NOEC

'Twas sung of old in hut and hall. Birthday Verses Written in a Child's Album. James Russell Lowell. OxBChV

'Twas sunset's hour, the glorious day. The Exile's Reverie. Mary Weston Fordham. CBWP-2

'Twas sure a luckless planet. Out of Luck. Abraham ibn Ezra, tr. fr. Hebrew by Solomon Solis-Cohen. TrJP

'Twas the angel of death that to us downward flew. In Memoriam of E. B. Clark. L. A. J. Moorer. CBWP-3

'Twas the angel of Eden, to Adam he said. Dedication Day Poem. L. A. J. Moorer. CBWP-3

'Twas the dead of the night. By the pine-knot's red light. New England's Chevy Chase. Edward Everett Hale. PAH

'Twas the dream of a God. Ireland. Dora Sigerson Shorter. IIP; OBEV; TIRV

'Twas the eve before Christmas. "Good night," had been said. Annie and Willie's Prayer. Sophia P. Snow. BeLS; BLPA

'Twas the gray of early morning when the dreadful cry of "Fire! The Milwaukee Fire. Unknown. AmFP

'Twas the heart of the murky night, and the lowest ebb of the tide. Wayne at Stony Point. Clinton Scollard. PAH

'Twas the horse thief, Andy Regan, that was hunted like a dog. Father Riley's Horse. Andrew Barton Paterson. NOBAu

'Twas the night before Christmas, when all through the house. A Visit from St. Nicholas. Clement Clarke Moore. AiP; AnAmPo; BeLS; BLPA; FaBoBe; FaBV; FaPON; NTCP; OBAL; OBCA; OBCP; OxBChV; PChr; TFi; VPP
(Night before Christmas, The.) OHIP; PWR; WBLP

'Twas the old flute still whistling 'The Protestant Boys'. (LL) The Old [or Ould] Orange Flute. Unknown. FaBoBa; GBP; OxBoLi; WTO

'Twas the proud Sir Peter Parker came sailing in from the sea. The Boasting of Sir Peter Parker. Clinton Scollard. PAH

'Twas the very verge of May. Dewey at Manila. Robert Underwood Johnson. PAH

Twas the voice of the Wanderer, I heard her exclaim. The Wanderer. Stevie Smith. NALW

'Twas the year of the famine in Plymouth of old. Five Kernels of Corn. Hezekiah Butterworth. PAH

'Twas warm — at first — like us. Emily Dickinson. CMoP; LiTA; NAWM-2; SoSe

'Twas when bright Cynthia with her silver car. A Night-Piece; or, Modern Philosophy. Christopher Smart. NOEC

'Twas when Tacita hushed the noisy world. The Dream. "Brian Bendo." NOEC

'Twas when the friendly shade of night. To Clarissa. Robert, Earl Nugent. NOEC

'Twas when the Proclamation came. Bartow Black. Timothy Thomas Fortune. AAP

'Twas When the Seas Were Roaring. John Gay. Fr. What D'Ye-Call-It, The. HAP

'Twas When the Spousal Time of May. Coventry Patmore. Fr. Angel in the House, The. GBL; OxAEP-2

'Twas when the spousal time of May. 'Twas When the Spousal Time of May. Coventry Patmore. Fr. Angel in the House, The. GBL; OxAEP-2

'Twas whispered in Heaven, 'twas muttered in hell. Catherine Fanshawe. See 'Twas in heaven pronounced, and 'twas muttered in hell.

'Twas wond'rous, then, a bardling should be found. The Tribulations of an Uneducated Poet in the 1760's. James Woodhouse. Fr. Life and Lucubrations of Crispinus Scriblerus, The. NOEC

Twasinta's Seminoles; Or Rape of Florida, *sels.* Albery Allson Whitman.
　"Come now, my love, the moon is on the lake." AAP
　"Dark rose the walls, a church and prison joined." AAP
　"Hail! home of exiles and of Seminoles!" AAP
　"I never was a slave — a robber took." AAP
　"Is manhood less because man's face is black?" AAP
　"Poet hath a realm within, and throne, The." AAP
　"Thus ends my lay: Reluctantly I leave." AAP
　"Thus, San Augustine's church and prison joined." AAP
　"Upon the shells by Carribea's wave." AAP
　"We leave thee with thy guests, thou sunny maid!" AAP
Tweed and Till. *Unknown.* BoNaP; ChTr; FaBoCh; FaBoPP; GBP; OBEV; OxBSP
Tweed Visited, The. William Lisle Bowles. Son
Tweedledum and Tweedledee. Mother Goose. NOBL; OxNR; PeLV; ReMoGo
"Tweet" pipes the robin as the cat creeps by. The Firetail's Nest. John Clare. EnRP
Twelfth day of Christmas, The. The Twelve Days of Christmas. *Unknown.* OxBoLi
12th Horse Song of Frank Mitchell (Blue), The. Frank Mitchell, *tr. fr. Navajo Indian by* Jerome K. Rothenberg *and* David P. McAllester. STP
Twelfth Morning; or What You Will. Elizabeth Bishop. CBNP
Twelfth Night. Peter Scupham. OBCP
Twelfth Night, *sels.* Shakespeare.
　"Come away, come away, death." ElL; ELP; GBL; NOBE; NoP; NoSic; TFi
　(Clown's Song, The.) CTC
　(Come Away, Death.) PoRA
　(Dirge: "Come away, come away, death.") OBEV
　(Dirge of Love.) GTBS; GTBS-P
　(Love's Despair.) TrGrPo
　(Song: "Come away, come away, death.") PoEL-2
　"I see you what you are: you are too proud." OxAEP-1
　"If Music be the food of love, play on." EBEvV
　(Food of Love, The.) TrGrPo
O Mistress Mine. AWP; BoLoP; ClHu; CoGr; CTC; ElL; ELP; FaBV; GBL; GoJo; HAP; ImPo; InPS; LiTB; NAEL-1; NBLV; NOBE; NoP; NoSic; OAEL-1; OxBoLi; OxBSP; PFP; PoRA; SCGP; TFi; TrGrPo
　(Carpe Diem.) GTBS; GTBS-P
　(Sweet-and-Twenty.) OBEV; PoE
Olivia's Face. CBCK
　"Once more, Cesario." SCV
Patience on a Monument. TrGrPo
　"When that I was and a little tiny boy." CH; EBEV; ElL; EnRePo; FaBoCh; ImPo; LiTB; NOBE; NoP; NoSic; OAEL-1; PoRA; SCGP; TFi
　(Clown's Song.) FaBoBl
　(Feste's Song ("When that I was and a little tiny boy").) CBNP; NBLV; OxBoLi
　(Song: "When that I was and a little tiny boy.") EBEvV; OxAEP-1; PoEL-2
　(Wind and the Rain, The.) WiR
12th Raga: For John Wieners. David Meltzer. *Fr. Ragas.* NeAP
Twelve, The, *sels.* Alexander Blok, *tr. fr. Russian by* Babette Deutsch *and* Avrahm Yarmolinsky.
　"Black Night./ White snow." AWP
Twelve. Rossana Ombres, *tr. fr. Italian by* Ruth Feldman. NeIt
Twelve, The. Allen Tate. ChIV-2
Twelve and ugly. Dresses. Kathleen Fraser. NMM
Twelve Articles. Swift. NBLV
Twelve Bells/ Benny's on the ropes. The Memory of Boxer Benny (Kid) Paret. Frank Lima. PoNe
Twelve children, twelve gray geese in starched. The Handbell Choir. Jane Flanders. PBCAP
Twelve Days of Christmas, The. *Unknown.* AmFP; OxBoLi; OxNR; PChr
12 Gates to the City. Nikki Giovanni. IHMS; PoBA
Twelve good friends. Peter and John. Elinor Wylie. MoAB; MoAmPo; MoBS
Twelve herds of oxen, no less flockes of sheepe. Homer, *tr. by* George Chapman. *Fr. Odyssey.* CTC; NAWM-1
Twelve hours after the Allies arrive. Women Bathing at Bergen-Belsen. Enid Shomer. BTR
Twelve Minutes. J. C. Hall. OBD
Twelve Miscellaneous Poems on the Fang Garden, *sels.* Chang Yü, *tr. fr. Chinese by* Jonathan Chaves.
Twelve o'clock./ Along the reaches of the street. Rhapsody on a Windy Night. T. S. Eliot. CMoP; HeIP; InPS; PoE
12 o'Clock News. Elizabeth Bishop. OxBC
12 October. Myra Cohn Livingston. NTCP
Twelve Oxen, The. *Unknown. See* I Have Twelve Oxen.
Twelve pears hanging high. Mother Goose. OxNR; ReMoGo

Twelve-Thousand-Day Honeymoon, The. Anne Sexton. AnAn
Twelve turns of the rail on walls of emerald. The Walls of Emerald. Li Shang-yin, *tr. fr. Chinese by* A. C. Graham. PLT
Twelve typographical typographers typically translating types. *(LL)* One Old Oxford Ox. *Unknown.* CBNP
Twelve Weapons of Spiritual Battle, The, *sels.* Sir Thomas More.
　Eleventh Property, The. EnRePo
　Eternal Reward, Eternal Pain. EnRePo
　First Property, The. EnRePo
　Peace of a Good Mind, The. EnRePo; FaBoRV
　Seventh Property, The. EnRePo
　This life a Dream and Shadow. EnRePo
Twelve years ago I came here. The Burn. Galway Kinnell. Poetr
Twelve years ago I made a mock. School and Schoolfellows. Winthrop Mackworth Praed. OxAEP-2
Twelve years old, my father put. Harvest Time. G. A. Watermeyer, *tr. fr. Afrikaans by* Guy Butler, Uys Krige, *and* Jack Cope. PeSA
Twentieth Anniversary. Betty Adcock. MT
Twentieth-Century Alphabet. *Unknown.* ISE
Twentieth-Century Blues. Kenneth Fearing. CMoP
20th Century, The. Darrell Gray. UL
Twentieth year is well-nigh past, The. To Mary. William Cowper. EnLoPo; EnRP; NOEC; UV, *sl. sh. vers.*
　(My Mary.) OBEV
　(To the Same.) GTBS; GTBS-P
20. Barbara Guest. PoM
Twenty Below. R. A. D. Ford. NOBC
28 VIII 69. Laura Chester. IHMS
Twenty-Eight Poems Inscribed on T'ien-kuan Mountain, *sels.* Chao Meng-fu, *tr. fr. Chinese by* Jonathan Chaves.
Twenty-eight young men bathe by the shore. Walt Whitman. *Fr.* Song of Myself. AmPP; HAP; LiTA; LPA; MoAmPo, *abr.*; NOBA; NoP; OxBA; SAmP; SOTW, *(much abr.)*
Twenty-fifth Year of His Life, The. C. P. Cavafy, *tr. fr. Greek by* Edmund Keeley *and* Philip Sherrard. PeHV
Twenty-First. Night. Monday. "Anna Akhmatova," *tr. fr. Russian by* Jane Kenyon. RaBo
Twenty-Five. Paul Hoover. *Fr.* Novel, The. BAP-89
25 December 1960. Ingrid Jonker, *tr. fr. Afrikaans by* Jack Cope *and* Uys Krige. PeSA
25:I:68. Philip Whalen. PoM
Twenty-five/ to four blackness no. Town of the Man in the Mind at Night. Anne Carson. *Fr.* Life of Towns, The. BAP-90
Twenty-four Hokku., *sels.* Kito, *tr. fr. Japanese by* Hiroaki Sato.
Twenty-four Poems of Living in the Mountains, *sels.* Zengetsu, *tr. fr. Chinese by* Lucien Stryk *and* Takashi Ikemoto.
Twenty-four Tanka., *sels.* Sanetomo, *tr. fr. Japanese by* Burton Watson.
Twenty-four Years. Dylan Thomas. CMoP; MAT; MoAB; NAs; OxBSP
Twenty Golden Years Ago. James Clarence Mangan. NOBVV; PeIV
Twenty Grand (Saturday Night on the Block), The. Naomi Long Madgett. NBV
Twenty Hokku, *sels.* Mukai Kyorai, *tr. fr. Japanese by* Burton Watson.
Twenty lost years have stol'n their hours away. Alone in an Inn at Southampton, April the 25th, 1737. Aaron Hill. NOEC
Twenty men crossing a bridge. Metaphors of a Magnifico. Wallace Stevens. SOTW
20 minutes later. Charles Bukowski. *Fr.* Horsemeat. NGP
Twenty months out of the womb. Standing in the Doorway, I Watch the Young Child Sleep. Sharon Hashimoto. OpBo
29. Alta. CrSp
Twenty-nine Hokku., *sels.* Taigi, *tr. fr. Japanese by* Hiroaki Sato.
29 Poems. Louis Zukofsky. PoE
Sels.
　"Blue light is the night harbor-slip"
　"Not much more than being"
29-77-02. Artur Miedzyrzecki, *tr. fr. Polish by* Stanisław Barańczak *and* Clare Cavanagh. PoSu
Twenty-ninth Canto. Hans Magnus Enzensberger. *Fr.* Sinking of the Titanic, The. PoSu
Twenty of those, and two of these. *(LL)* Pyrrha! your smiles are gleams of sun. Walter Savage Landor. CBLP
Twenty one are gone. *(LL)* To the Tune "Flowers Along the Path through the Field." Wu Tsao. WPC
21 August 1984. Aleda Shirley. Jaz
Twenty-one Hokku., *sels.* Boncho, *tr. fr. Japanese by* Hiroaki Sato.
Twenty-one Hokku., *sels.* Kaya Shairo, *tr. fr. Japanese by* Hiroaki Sato.
Twenty-one Love Poems, *sels.* Adrienne Rich.
　"Across a city from you, I'm with you." GLP; PeHV
　"Can it be growing colder when I begin." GLP; NAAL-2
　"Dark lintels, the blue and foreign stones, The." GLP; NALW; NoAM

Twilight's Last Gleaming. Arthur W. Monks. NIP

Twilit Revelation. Léonie Adams. MoAB; MoAmPo

'Twill be alovely sight. (LL) The Rain. W. H. Davies. BoTP; OxBTC

'Twill learn of things *Divine*, and first of *Thee* to sing. (LL) On the Death of Mr. Crashaw. Abraham Cowley. BeJo; EPCY; MeLP; SeCP; SeCV-1

"'Twill take some getting." "Sir, I think 'twill so." Man and Dog. Edward Thomas. FM; PeFWW

Twin. Phyllis Haring. PeSA

Twin Aces. Keith Wilson. Poetsp

Twin-born. Ella Wheeler Wilcox. AmWP

Twin stars through my purpling pane. Dusk. Angelina Weld Grimké. CDC; ShDr

Twin streaks twice higher than cumulus. Vapor Trails. Gary Snyder. CAPP; NAAL-2

Twine then the rays. Psycholophon. Gelett Burgess. CBNP

Twined together and, as is customary. Never Such Love. Robert Graves. BoLoP

Twinings Orange Pekoe. Judith Moffett. PoA; SM

Twink Drives Back, in a Bad Mood, from a Party in Massachusetts. George Amabile. NYBP

Twinkle, twinkle, little bat! "Lewis Carroll." *Fr.* Alice's Adventures in Wonderland. UV
(Mad Hatter's Concert Song, The. CBNP
(Mad Hatter's Song, The.) FaBoNo; NOBL

Twinkle, twinkle, little star. (LL) The Star. Jane Taylor. BoTP; FaBoBe; FaPON; ImGa; NTCP; OTCP; OxBChV; OxNR; PYC; UV, *st.* 1 only

Twinkle, twinkle, little star. The Star. Jane Taylor. BoTP; FaBoBe; FaPON; ImGa; NTCP; OTCP; OxBChV; OxNR; PYC; UV, *st.* 1 only

Twins, The. Robert Browning. FaBoVe; Mes

Twins. Gloria Escoffery. PBCV

Twins. Robert Graves. FaBoEE

Twins, The. Henry S. Leigh. FaPON

Twins. "Owen Meredith." ErPo

Twins, The. Karl Shapiro. MoAmPo; TrJP

Twins, The. James Stephens. RaBo

Twins, The. Mona Van Duyn. VCAP

Twins of a Gazelle Which Feed Among the Lilies. Catherine Bowman. BAP-89

Twirling. Jane Flanders. PBCAP

Twirling your blue skirts, travel[l]ing the sward. Blue Girls. John Crowe Ransom. ChTr; CMoP; GBL; LiTA; MeMAP; MoAB; MoAmPo; NoAM; PrIm; RB; TAP; VGW; WeW

Twist about, turn about. *Unknown.* OxNR

Twist me a crown of windflowers. A Crown of Windflowers. Christina Rossetti. OxBChV

Twist of cloth on the flat stones, A. Desmond O'Grady. *Fr.* Dark Edge of Europe, The. PBCIP

Twist thou and twine! in light and gloom. Featherstone's Doom. Robert Stephen Hawker. OBNC

Twist Ye, Twine Ye! Even So. Sir Walter Scott. *Fr.* Guy Mannering. EnRP

Twisted rhombs ceased their clamour of accompaniment, The. Ezra Pound. *Fr.* Homage to Sextus Propertius. MeMAP

Twister Twisting Twine. John Wallis. *See* When a twister a-twisting will twist him a twist.

Twisting words into slow shape. I Wonder What Went of Him. Christine Churches. FaBoMA

Twitched strings, the clang of metal, beaten drums. Javanese Dancers. Arthur Symons. OHCV

Twitching in the cactus. Deathwatch. Michael S. Harper. AmPA; PoBA

Twittingpan seized my arm, though I'd have gone. The Encounter. Edgell Rickword. OxBTC

'Twixt Carrowbrough Edge and Settlingstones. Old Skinflint. W. W. Gibson. OBMV

'Twixt clouded heights Spain hurls to doom. The *Brooklyn* at Santiago. Wallace Rice. PAH

'Twixt Cup and Lip. Mark Hollis. FiBHP; NBLV

Twixt devil and deep sea, man hacks his caves. Arachne. William Empson. InvP; OBMV

'Twixt East and West a giant shape she grew. Sonnet on the Crimean War. William Forster. CBAP

'Twixt failure and success the point's so fine. Don't Give Up. C. C. Cameron. *Fr.* Success. PoToHe

'Twixt handkerchief and nose. A Rub. John Banister Tabb. OBAL

Twixt nature and Pygmalion there might appear great strife. *Unknown.* OAEL-1

Twixt noble men may ceaze! (LL) Chevy Chase. *Unknown.* FaBoBa; GN; OBET

Twixt the Girthhead and Langwoodend. The Lads of Wamphray. *Unknown.* ESPB; IBB

Twixt those twin worlds — the world of sleep, which gave. Percy Bysshe Shelley: Inscription for the Couch, Still Preserved, on which He Passed the Last NIght of His Life. Dante Gabriel Rossetti. EPCY

'Twixt Tweedledum and Tweedledee! (LL) Epigram on the Feuds between Handel and Bononcini. John Byrom. FaBoEE; NOBL; NOEC

'Twixt womens love, and mens will ever bee. (LL) Air[e] and Angels. John Donne. CBLP; EnRePo; ESCV; JCP; MeLP; NAEL-1; OAEL-1; Prf; SeCP; SeCV-1

Two. Robert Canzoneri. HoPM

Two. Hugo von Hofmannsthal, *tr. fr. German* by Jethro Bithell. TrJP

Two, The. Hugo von Hofmannsthal, *tr. fr. German* by Ludwig Lewisohn. AWP

Two. Winfield Townley Scott. NYBP

Two alabaster pillars stand, (LL) A Description. Lord Herbert of Cherbury. OPOP; SeCP

Two aldermen, three lawyers, five physicians. Of a Zealous Lady. Sir John Harington, *after the Latin of* Martial. FaBoEE

2 a.m.: moonlight. The train has stopped. Track. Tomas Tranströmer, *tr. fr. Swedish* by Robert Bly. RB

Two Anchors, The. Richard Henry Stoddard. BeLS

Two and One Are a Problem. Ogden Nash. FiBHP

Two and two is four. Why are Fire Engines Red? *Unknown.* CBNP

Two angels from the North. Charm: Burns. *Unknown.* FaBoUs

2 Antemasque, The: Two Countrye Wives, the Songe. Lady Jane Cavendish *and* Lady Elizabeth Brackley. *Fr.* Pastorall, A. KTR

Two Appeals to John Harralson, Agent. *Unknown.* OBAL

Two April Mornings, The. Wordsworth. EBEV; EnRP; GTBS; GTBS-P; NAEL-2

Two are better than one; because they have a good reward for their labour. Bible, *O.T. Fr.* Ecclesiastes. OBF

Two Are Together. Geoffrey Grigson. GBL

Two Armies. Stephen Spender. OBWP; OxBTC

Two armies covered hill and plain. Music in Camp. John R. Thompson. BLPA

Two beers screw my head up. Hustlers. Dennis Cooper. ETG; UL

Two bees within a chrystal flowerbell rockèd. Dualisms. Tennyson. EnVR

Two birds, one of them mortal, the other immortal. *Unknown, tr. fr. Hindi. Fr.* Upanishads, The. EnlH, *vers.* by Stephen Mitchell

Two Birth Poems, *sels.* Lauris Edmond.

Two blind mice. Paul Dehn. *Fr.* Rhymes for a Modern Nursery. FiBHP

Two bloated bodies in rotted rags. War. Sulamith Ish-Kishor. GoYe

Two bodies have I. *Unknown.* OxNR

Two-boots in the forest walks. The Intruder. James Reeves. PDV

Two Boys, The. Mary Lamb. WoRP

Two boys uncoached are tossing a poem together. Catch. Robert Francis. InPK; RaBo

Two boys, whose birth beyond all question springs. Charles Churchill. *Fr.* Prophecy of Famine, The. OBSV

Two Brothers, The. *Unknown.* AmFP

Two Brothers in a Field of Absence. Cynthia MacDonald. NIP

Two Brothers Up. Sebastian Barry. IB

Two brothers we are. *Unknown.* OxNR

Two brown heads with tossing curls. Katie Lee and Willy [*or* Willie] Grey. *At. to* Josie R. Hunt *and to* J. H. Pixley. BeLS; BLPA

Two Bulls, The. *Unknown, tr. fr. Irish by* Thomas Kinsella. *Fr.* How the Bulls Were Begotten. NOIV

Two Campers in Cloud Country. Sylvia Plath. NYBP

Two campers (King Lear and his clown?). Outward Bound. James Simmons. CIP; PWE

Two Captains, The. William Johnson Cory. *See* When George the Third was reigning a hundred years ago.

Two cars, three loos, a swimming pool. The Whiteman Blues. Lionel Abrahams. PeSAV

Two caterpillars crawling on a leaf. Immortality. Joseph Jefferson. BLPA

Two Cats/ One up a tree. Diamond Cut Diamond. Ewart Milne. FaBoCh

Two cats together. This and That. Gareth Owen. OTCP

Two-Cent Coal. *Unknown.* AmFP

Two Centos. William Empson. CBNP

Two Character Studies. Swift. *See* With favour and fortune fastidiously blest.

Two Chartist Songs., *sels.* Thomas Cooper.

Two Children, The. Emily Brontë. MeMBP; PoEL-5

Two children, dressed in court costume. An Old Picture. Howard Nemerov. OxBSP

Two children in two neighbour villages. Circumstance. Tennyson. CBLP

Two Choral Stanzas. Robert Bly. PRA

Two Chorale-Preludes. Geoffrey Hill. OxBC

Two Christs were at Golgotha. Early Lynching. Carl Sandburg. ChIV-2; MoAmPo

Two coffees in the Español, the last. Conrad Aiken. *Fr.* Preludes for Memnon; or, Preludes to Attitude. FYAP; LiTA; NoAM

Two Coffins, The. Eugene Field. AnAmPo

Two college sophs of Cambridge growth. Cassinus and Peter. Swift. OAEL-1; PPP

Two Comical Folk. Mother Goose. OxNR; ReMoGo

Two converging from. The Paths. Richard Caddel. NBrP

Two Countries. José Martí, *tr. fr. Spanish* by Mona Hinton. TTY

Two crows sew themselves onto the lace flag. The Process. Tom Clark. UL

Two dayes now in that sea he sayled has. Guyon's Voyage to the Bower of Bliss. Spenser. *Fr.* Faerie Queene, The. NoSic

Two days ago the sky was. Autumn Rain. Kenneth Rexroth. NU

Two days she miss'd her dove, and then alas! Minnie and Her Dove. Charles Tennyson Turner. FM

Two dead divers hauled up in their bell, The. Alison Brackenbury. DiPo

Two Decisions. Vernon Watkins. OxBTC

Two Dedications., *sels.* Gwendolyn Brooks.
Chicago Picasso, The. BPo; LiTM
Wall, The. PoBA
Wall, The. PoNe

Two Deserts, The. Coventry Patmore. BoNaP

Two dictators, seated cheek by jowl, The. Colloque Imaginaire. "Sagittarius." IHNG

Two disciples/ went on their way after. U.F.W. Pickets on Old Highway 99. Wilma Elizabeth McDaniel. ETG

Two Dogs. John Davidson. FM

Two doves upon the selfsame branch. Christina Rossetti. CBLP

Two dreams came down to earth one night. The Dreams. Eugene Field. AnAmPo

Two Drinking Songs., *sels.* José Juan Tablada.
"I built my hut near where people live." NU
(I Built My Hut.) AWP, *tr.* by Arthur Waley
"Such a strong color on the late chrysanthemums." NU

Two Drops. Zbigniew Herbert, *tr. fr. Polish* by Czeslaw Milosz. RB

Two dykes went their separate routes. *Unknown.* PeHV

Two earnest young fellows named Wright. Basil Ransome-Davies. PeLi

Two empires by the sea. International Hymn. George Huntington. PoLF

Two Englishmen. Douglas Stewart. CBAP

Two Epigrams, *sels.* James Kenneth Stephen.
Senex to Matt. Prior. FiBHP

Two Epigrams. Sir William Watson. TrGrPo
Sels.
Love.
Poet, The.

Two events have a spacelike separation. Proper Distance and Proper Time. Judith Baumel. UTF

Two evils, monstrous either one apart. Winter Remembered. John Crowe Ransom. CBLP; HAP; MeMAP; MoAB; NOBA; OxBA; PrIm; UnPo; VGW

Two eyes, the cathedral's spires look black. One Tourist's Cologne. Hal Colebatch. NOBAu

Two-Faced Too. *Unknown, tr. fr. Welsh* by Glyn Jones. OBWVE

Two Families, The. Joyce L. Brisley. BoTP

Two Fawns That Didn't See the Light This Spring. Gary Snyder. HCAP

Two figures in deep water. Walking to Bellrock. Michael Ondaatje. NOBC

Two Figures in Dense Violet Light. Wallace Stevens. MoAB; MoAmPo

Two Figures on Canvas. Gerald William Barrax. MT

Two figures there beneath the dome, walking with similar pace. St. Sophia. John Fuller. DiPo

Two Fires, The. Judith Wright. MoBrPo

Two Fish. Katha Pollitt. DiPo; NIP

Two Fishermen. Stanley Moss. CoAP

Two fleets have sailed from Spain. The one would seek. The Sailing of the Fleet. *Unknown.* PAH

Two floods I read of; water, and of wine. On the Two Great Floods. Francis Quarles. ChIV-1

Two foot-companions once in deep discourse —. The Nimmers. John Byrom. OxAEP-1

Two forms move among the dead, high sleep. The Owl in the Sarcophagus. Wallace Stevens. FaBoMo

Two forms of darkness are there. One is Night. Doubt. Mary Elizabeth Coleridge. NALW

Two Foscari, The, *sels.* Byron.
Swimming. GN

Two, four, six, eight. *Unknown.* RoPo

Two Friends. Norman MacCaig. OBF

Two friends at the close of summer. Why She Says No. Ellen Bryant Voigt. FaBoWP

Two friends took a trip together to Stone Man Peak. A Trip to Stone Man Peak. Yang Wan-li, *tr. fr. Chinese* by Jonathan Chaves. SuSp

2 f's/ in giraffe, The. The Giraffe. Ron Padgett. *Fr.* Three Animals. TTTS

Two Garnett brothers who run the Shell station here, The. Sweep. Rodney Jones. MT

Two gates unto the road of life there are. The Road of Life. William Morris. *Fr.* Earthly Paradise, The. OBNC

Two Generations. L. A. G. Strong. OBMV

Two Gentlemen of Verona, The, *sels.* Shakespeare.
My Thoughts Do Harbour. CTC
This Spring of Love. ChTr
"Thus have I shunned the fire for fear of burning." GBL
Who Is Silvia [or Sylvia]? BLPL; EiL; EnRePo; FaBoBe; GN; ImPo; LiTB; NoSic; OAEL-1; SCGP; TrGrPo
(Silvia.) OBEV
(Song.) EBEvV

Two Gentlemen That Broke Their Promise of a Meeting. James Shirley. BeJo

Two German officers crossed the Rhine, parlee-voo. Hinky Dinky, Parlee-Voo. *Unknown.* AS

Two Gifts. *Unknown, tr. fr. Catalan by* Willis Barnstone. BoWoP

Two Girls. Sallie Bingham. NGP

Two girls discover. The Secret. Denise Levertov. CrSp; NaP; Poetr

Two Glasses, The. Ella Wheeler Wilcox. BLPA; BLPL

Two Graces, *sels. Unknown.*
"Hurly, hurly, roon the table." FaBoCh
"Some hae meat that canna eat." FaBoCh
(Child's Grace, A.) FaPON; MoShBr

Two Gray Kits. *Unknown.* ReMoGo

Two green-webbed chairs. Children Playing Checkers at the Edge of the Forest. Adrienne Rich. LCAP; WeW

Two Gretels, The. Robin Morgan. CrSp; SRLS

Two Gretels were exploring the forest, The. The Two Gretels. Robin Morgan. CrSp; SRLS

Two Guitars. Víctor Hernández Cruz. AfAz

Two Guitars, *sels.* Gloria A. Maxson.

Two guitars were left in a room all alone. Two Guitars. Víctor Hernández Cruz. AfAz

Two halfgrown girls hailing hallowed Easter. William Carlos Williams. *Fr.* Paterson. MeMAP

Two Hands. Anne Sexton. CAPP; PRA

Two hands lie still, the hairy and the white. Love for a Hand. Karl Shapiro. CoAP; NYBP

Two hands the God of Nature gave. Save the Old South! Julia Ward Howe. AmWP

Two hands upon the breast. Now and Afterwards. Dinah Maria Mulock Craik. PoLF; WGRP

Two Hangovers. James Wright. LCAP

Two-headed Calf, The. Laura Gilpin. FYAP

Two Hearts Divided. R. Williams Parry, *tr. fr. Welsh* by Joseph P. Clancy. OBWVE

Two hearts: two blades of grass I braid together. Weaving Love-Knots 2. Hsüeh T'ao, *tr.* by Carolyn Kizer. BoWoP

Two Heavens. Leigh Hunt. GN

Two heavy trestles, and a board. My Table. W. B. Yeats. *Fr.* Meditations in Time of Civil War. LiTB

Two Heroes. Harriet Monroe. *See* When dreaming [or foolish] kings, at odds with swift-paced time.

Two Hoboes. *Unknown.* WTO

Two Hookers. A. K. Redwing. VoR

Two horses in yellow light. August. Adrienne Rich. CAPP; NNaP; PBWP

Two hours have I walked the streets. A Walk. Fernando Periquet Y Zuaznabar, *tr. fr. Spanish* by Philip L. Miller. RiWo

Two hours, or more, beyond the prime of a blithe April day. The Battle of Charleston Harbor. Paul Hamilton Hayne. PAH

Two Houses. Edward Thomas. FaBoCh

Two hummingbirds as evanescent as. Vision. Richard Eberhart. NYBP

Two hundred men and eighteen killed. James Henry. NOBVV

209 Canal. Richard Howard. TAP

225 days under grass. For Jane. Charles Bukowski. HoPM

Two hundred wagons, rolling out to Oregon. The Oregon Trail. Arthur Guiterman. FaPON

Two in August. John Crowe Ransom. AWP; MeMAP; OxBA; PPP

Two in Bed. Abram Bunn Ross. FaPON; NTCP

Two in Search of Dawn. Andrew Taylor. FaBoMA

Two in the afternoon. The restlessness. Down the Nile. Robert Lowell. HCAP

Two in the bush. (LL) Concerning My Neighbors, the Hittites. Charles Simic. VCAP

Two in the Campagna. Robert Browning. EBEV; EBVV; ELP; EnVR; FHYEP; GTBS-P; MeMBP; NAEL-2; NOBE; NOBVV; NoP; OAEL-2; OBNC; OxAEP-2; OxBM; PFP; PoE; PoEL-5; SCGP; TFi; TOF; TrGrPo

Two in Twilight. Eugenio Montale, tr. fr. Italian by William Arrowsmith. AnAn

Two infants vis-à-vis. Bleecker Street. Jean Garrigue. TAP

Two ink-blue butterflies. In the Garden. Rupendra Guha Majumdar. OBAP

Two Invocations of Death, sels. Kathleen Raine.
  "Death, I repent." OxBTC
  (Invocation of Death.) MoAB
  "From a place I came." OxBTC

Two Irish yews, prickly green, poisonous. Gate Lodge. Richard Murphy. PBCIP

Two Japanese Poems., sels. Gust Gils.

Two Kinds of People. Ella Wheeler Wilcox. See There are two kinds of people on earth today.

Two Kitchen Songs. Edith Sitwell. CMoP

Two Kitchen Songs. Edith Sitwell. CMoP

Two ladies sit in the spotless driveway. Garage Sale. Karl Shapiro. Poetsp

Two ladies to the summit of my mind. Sonnet: Of Beauty and Duty. Dante, tr. fr. Italian by Dante Gabriel Rossetti. AWP

Two Lean Cats. Myron O'Higgins. PoBA; PoNe

Two leaps the water from its race. A Mill. William Allingham. FaBoEE; OxBSP

Two Legends. Ted Hughes. Fr. Crow. FF; PoE

Two-legs sat on Three-legs by Four-legs. Unknown. RoPo

Two legs sat upon three legs. Mother Goose. OxNR
  (Riddle: "Two legs sat upon three legs.") NTCP

Two liddle niggers all dressed in white. Raise a "Rucus" To-Night. Unknown. BPo; TAP

Two, like two ripe shocks of corn. (LL) An Epithalamy to Sir Thomas Southwell and His Lady. Robert Herrick. CaPo

Two Limericks after Lear, sels. John Updike.

Two-line epigram is perfect, A. Step. Cyrillus, tr. fr. Greek by Peter Jay. GrAn

Two Lines from the Brothers Grimm. Gregory Orr. AmPA

Two Lips. Thomas Hardy. BoLoP

Two arabs adult and arabesque. Hans Arp, tr. fr. French by Harriet Watts. FaBoNo

Two little beaks went tap! tap! tap! To Let. D. Newey-Johnson. BoTP

Two little birdies, one wintry day. The Birdies' Breakfast. Unknown. BoTP

Two Little Blackbirds. Unknown. BoTP

Two little clouds, one summer's day. The Rainbow Fairies. Unknown. BoTP

Two little creatures. Monkeys. Padraic Colum. Mes; OxBTC

Two little dicky-birds. Dicky-Birds. Natalie Joan. BoTP

Two little dicky birds. Unknown. OxNR

Two little dogs/ Sat by the fire. Unknown. OxNR

Two little elves/ Were lost one night. A Fairy Dream. Dorothy Graddon. BoTP

Two little girls, one fair, one dark. The Lost Children. Randall Jarrell. CoAP; PrIm; TAP

Two Little Kittens. Jane Taylor. BoTP

Two Little Kittens. Unknown. OBCA; OFC; OxBChV

Two Little Miss Lloyds, The. Elizabeth Turner. OxBChV

Two little ships were sailing by. Upon a Christmas Morning. Unknown. AmFP

Two Lives. William Ellery Leonard. Son
Sels.
  Love's Primal Want
  True Marriage Is True Love

Two lofty ships of Eng-e-land set sail. The Wild Barbaree. Unknown. AmFP

Two Look at Two. Robert Frost. MoAB; MoAmPo; NU

Two Lovers, The. Marie de France, tr. by Patricia Terry. BoWoP

Two lovers to a midnight meadow came. The Amateurs of Heaven. Howard Nemerov. SoSe

Two Loves. Lord Alfred Bruce Douglas. PeHV

Two Loves. Richard Eberhart. CMoP

Two Loves I Have. Shakespeare. See Two Loves I Have of Comfort and Despair.

Two Loves I Have of Comfort and Despair. Shakespeare. Fr. Sonnets. EBEV; HeIP; InvP; NAEL-1; NIP; OAEL-1; PeHV; PoEL-2; Son

Two low whistles, quaint and clear. Guild's Signal. Bret Harte. VPP

Two Lyrics. Lorenzo de' Medici, tr. fr. Italian by John Addington Symonds. AWP
Sels.
  "How can I sing light-souled and fancy-free."
  "Into a little close of mine I went."

Two Magicians, The. Unknown. See Lady stands in her bower door, The.

Two Magicians, The. Unknown. ChTr; OAEL-1; OxBoLi

Two Magpies Sat on a Garden Rail. D'Arcy Wentworth Thompson. MoShBr

Two magpies under the cypresses, The. What Birds Were There. William Everson. NoAM

Two Man a Road. Unknown. PBCV

Two Meetings, The. Eugene Field. PWR

Two Men. Andrew Lansdown. NOBAu

Two men appear on a tractor. Poem about the Future. Hans Magnus Enzensberger. PoSu

Two Mexicanos Lynched in Santa Cruz, California, May 3, 1877. Martín Espada. AfAz

Two middle-aged ladies from Fordham. Unknown. PeLi

Two Months Married. Aidan Carl Mathews. IB; PBCIP

Two More about a Crow, in the Manner of Zukofsky. Unknown, tr. fr. Seneca Indian by Jerome K. Rothenberg and Richard Johnny John. STP

Two Mornings. Lawrence McGaugh. PoBA

Two Mornings and Two Evenings. Elizabeth Bishop. PoA

Two Mountains Men Have Climbed. Pauline Starkweather. GoYe

Two Movements Which Begin at the Head and End at the Feet. Richard Caddel. NBrP

Two moving figures flow together: see. Reflection. Elisabeth Eybers, tr. fr. Afrikaans by the author. PeSAV

Two mules stand in front of the brick wall of a warehouse. Mule Team and Poster. Donald Justice. AnAn; VCAP

Two murders this month. October. Greg Pape. AmPA

Two Musicians, The. H. Cordelia Ray. CBWP-3

Two Mysteries, The. Mary Mapes Dodge. PWR; TrCP; WGRP

Two nails, The. (LL) The Mirror. Michael Davitt. BiHa; CIP; PBCIP

Two Neighbours, The. George Campbell Hay. OxBS

Two never-ever-will-be lovers each. Mathematics of Encounter. Isabella Gardner. ErPo

Two Nights, The. Nicki Jackowska. DT

Two nights in Manchester: nothing much to do. Mr. Cooper. Anthony Thwaite. OxBTC

Two nights running I was out there. The Mummies. Maxine W. Kumin. Poetsp

Two Noble Kinsmen, The, sels. John Fletcher and William Shakespeare.
  Bridal Song, A ("Roses, their sharp spines being gone"). EIL; NOBE; NOSC; NoSic
  "Hail Sovereign Queen of secrets, who hast power." PoEL-2
  Urns and Odours Bring Away! EIL
  (Dirge of the Three Queens.) OBEV
  (Funeral Song.) ChTr

Two nudists of Dover. Third Limick. Ogden Nash. PeLi

Two o'Clock. Katharine Pyle. Fr. Wonder Clock, The. OBCA

2 o'clock: strong moonlight, few stars. (LL) Track. Tomas Tranströmer. RB

Two, of course there are two. Death and Co. Sylvia Plath. CMoP; FF; LCAP; PrIm

Two of far nobler shape erect and tall. Milton. Fr. Paradise Lost. EPCY; PeECV, ll. 288–299

Two of Them, The. Hugo von Hofmannsthal, tr. fr. German by John Frederick Nims. STV

Two of Thy children one summer day worked in their garden, Lord. The Garden. Rose Parkwood. WGRP

Two Old Bachelors, The. Edward Lear. BeLS; FiBHP

Two Old Crows. Vachel Lindsay. FaBoNo; OBAL

Two old dancing shoes my grandfather. Genius. Philip Levine. NoAM

Two Old Kings, The. Lord De Tabley. OBEV

Two Old Ladies. Siegfried Sassoon. OxBTC

Two Old Lenten Rhymes, sels. Unknown.

Two or Three; a Recipe [or Receipt] to Make a Cuckold. Pope. BoLoP; FaBoEE

Two or three minutes — two or three hours. Minutes of Gold. *Unknown*. PoToHe

Two or three posies. Keats. CBNP

Two or three visits, and two or three bows. Two or Three; a Recipe [or Receipt] to Make a Cuckold. Pope. BoLoP; FaBoEE

Two Orgasms, sels. Nancy Sullivan.

Two Paintings by Gustav Klimt. Jorie Graham. SV

Two pairs of hands go round. Korf's Clock. Christian Morgenstern, *tr. fr. German* by Geoffrey Grigson.
  (Korf a kind of clock invents.) CBNP, *tr.* by Max Knight

Two pairs of mallards, tandem. Nearing Winter. Ernest Sandeen. NYBP

Two Parents, The. "Hugh MacDiarmid." FaBoTw; OxBTC

Two passive and two active — you'd imagine. Two Plus Two. Strato, *tr. fr. Greek* by Teddy Hogge. GrAn

Two people in a room, speaking harshly. Novella. Adrienne Rich. PPP

Two people meet. The sky turns winter. Glances. William Stafford. SM

Two Performing Elephants. D. H. Lawrence. RB

Two petals from that wild-rose tree. *(LL)* Memory. Thomas Bailey Aldrich. AnAmPo; BoNaP; GGP; PoLF

Two Pewits. Edward Thomas. CH; FM

Two Pictures. *Unknown*. BeLS; BLPA; FaBoBe

Two Pieces for Suetonius. Robert Penn Warren. NOBA

Two Pigeons. *Unknown*. *See* I had two pigeons bright and gay.

Two pilgrims, broiling in the sun. Beware of Dogmas. Ebenezer Elliot. FaBoEE

Two playwrights called Beaumont and Fletcher. Fiona Pitt-Kethley. PeLi

Two Plus Two. Strato, *tr. fr. Greek* by Teddy Hogge. GrAn

Two Poems about President Harding. James Wright. CoAP; MoP

2 Poems for Black Relocation Centers. Etheridge Knight. NNaP

Two Poems of Peking., sels. Liu Sha-ho.
  Ash Tree on Ching Hill, The. LHF, *tr.* by Hualing Nieh
  Evening View at the Western Palace. LHF, *tr.* by Hualing Nieh

Two Poems on Insect Painting by Candidate Yin, sels. Su Shih, *tr. fr. Chinese.*
  On a Snail. SuSp
  On a Toad. SuSp

Two Poems on Night. Tu Fu, *tr. fr. Chinese* by Jan Walls. SuSp

Two Poems on the Catholic Bavarians. Edgar Bowers. CRP
  Sels.
  "Fierce and brooding holocaust of faith, The."
  "I know a wasted place high in the Alps."

Two Poems on the Eretrians Taken Prisoner by the Persians, sels. Plato, *tr. fr. Greek* by Peter Jay.
  "Leaving behind for ever the thundering Aegean." GrAn
  "We are Eretrians from Euboia." GrAn

Two Poems Presented to the Gentlemen in the Office of Palace Writers Ku Yen-hsien, sels. Lu Chi, *tr. fr. Chinese* by Burton Watson.

Two Poems to the Tune "Chin-tzu ching," sels. Ma Chih-yüan, *tr. fr. Chinese* by Jonathan Chaves.

Two Poems to the Tune "Hsiao-t'iao hung," sels. Ni Tsan, *tr. fr. Chinese* by Jonathan Chaves.

Two Poems to the Tune "Jen-yüeh yüan," sels. Ni Tsan, *tr. fr. Chinese* by Jonathan Chaves.

Two Poems to the Tune "Po pu tuan," sels. Ma Chih-yüan, *tr. fr. Chinese* by Jonathan Chaves.

Two Poems to the Tune "The Narcissus by the River," sels. Ch'iu Chin, *tr. fr. Chinese* by Kenneth Rexroth *and* Ling Chung.
  "Lady T'ao Ch'ui-tse gave a farewell party in T'ao Jan." WPC
  "We have drunk wine and discussed literature." WPC

Two Portraits, sels. Tanikawa Shuntaro, *tr. fr. Japanese* by Hiroaki Sato.

Two Postures beside a Fire. James Wright. HCAP; HeIP

Two Prayers, The. Andrew Gillies. BLRP

Two Prayers. Andrew Gillies. *See* Last night my boy [or little boy] confessed to me.

Two Prayers. Charlotte Perkins Gilman. WGRP

Two purple pigeons circle a London square. The Exiled Heart. Maurice Lindsay. OxBS

Two Pursuits. Christina Rossetti. WPE

Two-quart virgin in my lap, A. The Aged Wino's Counsel to a Young Man on the Brink of Marriage. X. J. Kennedy. FF

Two Quartz Pebbles. Vasco [or Vasko] Popa, *tr. fr. Serbo-Croatian.* Fr. Quartz Pebble, The. PoSu, *tr.* by Anne Pennington

Two Quatrains on the "Awash-in-Springtime Garden," sels. Ch'ien Ch'ien-i, *tr. fr. Chinese.*

Two Questions, The. Alice Meynell. WPE

Two Ravens, The. *Unknown*. *See* As I was walking all alane [or alone].

Two Red Roses across the Moon. William Morris. EBVV; UV

Two Rivers. Emerson. AmPP; NOBA; OxBA; PoE; TrGrPo

Two Rivers, The. *Unknown*. *See* Says Tweed to [tae] Till.

Two Roads, The. SCBI

Two roads diverged in a yellow wood. The Road Not Taken. Robert Frost. AiP; AmPP; ChTr; CMoP; EBEvV; FaBoCh; FaPoB; HAP; HeIP; ImPo; LiTA; LiTM; MeMAP; MoAB; MoAmPo; MoP; NAAL-2; NIP; NoAM; NoP; NTP; OxBA; Poetr; PoLF; RFM; SAmP; SoSe; TAP; TFi; TRP; TwCP

Two Roads, Etc. Dorothy Walters. IHMS

Two Robin Croft. Andrew Crozier. VaA

Two rooms, rather, one flight up, half seen. A Room at the Heart of Things. James Merrill. BAP-89

Two rows of foolish faces blent. Bored. Horatio Brown. PeHV

Two Rural Sisters. Charles Cotton. *See* Alice is tall and upright as a pine.

Two Rural Sisters. Charles Cotton. *See* Marg'ret of Humbler Stature by the Head.

Two Selves, The. Margaret Avison. MoP

Two separate divided silences. Severed Selves. Dante Gabriel Rossetti. *Fr.* House of Life, The. BoLoP

2 : 7, sels. Alta.
  "Loving your neighbor is all very fine when you have nice." CrSp

Two Shadows. Elizabeth Spires. DiPo

Two shall be born, the whole wide world apart. Fate. Susan Marr Spalding. BLPA; PoToHe

Two Shapes. Arthur Gregor. TAP

Two she-camels spied on a goat. *Unknown*. PeLi

Two Sisters, The. *Aborigine Oral Tradition*, *tr.* by Manoowa. NOBAu

Two Sisters, The. *Unknown*. PrIm

Two Sisters, The. *Unknown*. AmFP

Two Sisters, The. *Unknown*. AmFP; MAT; PrIm; TrGrPo

Two sisters who had no brother. Brotherless Sisters. *Unknown*, *tr. fr. Serbo-Croatian* by Charles Simic. HSix

Two Solitudes. Evelyn Ames. GoYe

Two Songs. C. Day Lewis. HAP; NoAM

Two Songs, sels. Adrienne Rich.
  "Sex, as they harshly call it." NIP; NOBA; TAP
  "That 'old last act'!" NIP; NOBA; TAP

Two Songs about Flowers & Where I Was Walking. *Unknown*, *tr. fr. Seneca Indian* by Jerome K. Rothenberg *and* Johnny John. STP

Two Songs from a Play. W. B. Yeats. *Fr.* Resurrection. The. CMoP; FaBoTw; HAP; ImPo; LiTB; MeMBP; NOBE; NoP; OAEL-2; PoE; PPP; PrIm

Two Songs from a Play. W. B. Yeats. *Fr.* Resurrection. The. CMoP; FaBoTw; HAP; LiTB; NOBE; NoP; OAEL-2; PPP; PrIm

Two Songs of a Fool. W. B. Yeats. CMoP; RB

Two Songs on the Economy of Abundance. James Agee. MoAmPo
  Sels.
  Red Sea.
  Temperance Note: and Weather Prophecy

Two Songs with Spanish Burdens, sels. David Campbell.
  Spring Lambs. FaBoMA

Two Sonnets. John Ashbery. VGW
  Sels.
  Dido.
  Idiot, The.

Two Sonnets, sels. Paul Evans.
  "Mixed with age, we could foresee the future." NBrP
  "Professor stood still, tall, thin, with stains, The." NBrP

Two Sonnets. Charles Hamilton Sorley. MoBrPo
  Sels.
  "Saints have adored the lofty soul of you." NSI; PeFWW
  "Such, such is Death: no triumph: no defeat." NSI; PeFWW

Two Sonnets for a Lost Love. Samuel A. DeWitt. GoYe
  Sels.
  "If I were less the man, I might have kept."
  'There is no permanence,' you sagely said.

Two Sonnets on Fame. Keats. EnRP
  Sels.
  "Fame, like a wayward girl, will still be coy."
  "How fever'd is the man who cannot look."

Two Sons. Laoiseach Mac an Bhaird. NOIV

Two Souls. Marjorie Pickthall. NOBC

Two spheres on meeting may so softly collide. Divided. Walter de la Mare. CBLP

Two Spirits [an Allegory], The. Shelley. CH; OAEL-2; Prf; WiR

Two spoons of sherry. The Witch's Work Song. T. H. White. FaBoNo

Two Springs. Li Ch'ing-chao, *tr. fr. Chinese* by Kenneth Rexroth. BoWoP

Two standing women are watchtowers. A House. Libby Houston. NBrP

Two Stars, The. W. H. Davies. MoBrPo

Two stars there are in one faire firmament. Richard Barnfield. *Fr.* Sonnets. PeHV

Two statesmen met by moonlight. What the Moon Saw. Vachel Lindsay. FaBoEE; OxBSP

Two steps from my garden rail. Hayyim Nahman Bialik, *tr. fr. Hebrew by* Maurice Samuel. *Fr.* Songs of the People. AWP

Two Stories. Charles Wright. FYAP; LCAP

Two stories high above Saturn St. For My Mother. Doris Brett. NOBAu

Two Strange Worlds. Francesca Yetunde Pereira. PBA

Two strong impulses: One. Jalal al-Din Rumi, *tr. fr. Persian by* Coleman Barks *and* John Moyne. *Fr.* Four Quatrains. RaBo

Two summers ago this hot spring turned cold. On Mayon Volcano. Gwyneth Lewis. NWP

Two Summers in Moravia. Roger McDonald. CBAP

Two Surprises. R. W. McAlpine. PoLF

Two swallows in the rafters hear the long sigh. *(LL)* Where is it, the sad lyre which follows the quick flute? Li Shang-yin. PLT

Two Swans, The. Thomas Hood. CH

Two sweeter babes you nare did see. *Unknown.* FaBoEE

Two Tales of Clumsy., *sels.* Gjertrud Schnackenberg. "When Clumsy harks the gladsome ting-a-lings." NoAM

Two tapsters traded on Thames's side. Ballad of the Two Tapsters. Vernon Watkins. MoBS

Two telephones all morning giving each other hell. Cash Positive. Peter McDonald. PNI

Two Temples. Hattie Vose Hall. BLPA

Two that could not have lived their single lives. Two in August. John Crowe Ransom. AWP; MeMAP; OxBA; PPP

Two that through windy nights kept company. The Two Neighbours. George Campbell Hay. OxBS

Two thimblefuls of wine, and slightly later. The Stone-Hitter. Medbh McGuckian. DT

Two things I have asked of Thee. Neither Poverty nor Riches. Bible, *O.T. Fr.* Proverbs. TrJP

Two Things of Opposite Natures Seem to Depend. Wallace Stevens. *Fr.* Notes toward a Supreme Fiction. MeMAP

"Two things," said Kant, "fill me with breathless awe." The Third Wonder. Edwin Markham. FYAP

Two thousand feet beneath our wheels. Cockpit in the Clouds. Dick Dorrance. FaPON

2976. Julia Uceda, *tr. fr. Spanish by* Willis Barnstone. BoWoP

2001: The Tennyson/ Hardy Poem. Gavin Ewart. FaBoCo

MMDCCXIII½. Lorenzo Thomas. UL

Two Tile Beaks. Maria Amalia Fonte Boa, *tr. by* Willis Barnstone *and* Nelson Cerqueira. BoWoP

Two-toned Olds swinging sideways out of, The. Infidelity. Stanley Plumly. NAmP90

Two Tongue-Pointing (Satirical) Songs. *Unknown, tr. fr. Aborigine.* NOBAu

Two Tramps in Mud Time. Robert Frost. BLPL; CMoP; HeIL; ImPo; LiTA; LiTM; MeMAP; MoAB; MoAmPo; MoP; NAAL-2; NoAM; PrIm; SAmP; TrGrPo

Two Translations from Kabir, *sels.* Robert Bly.
Breath, The. PRA
Doors Are Closed, The. PRA

Two Trees, The. W. B. Yeats. OAEL-2

Two trees breathe. Some Hands Are Lovelier. Mae V. Cowdery. ShDr

Two Trinities. Kenneth Mackenzie. CBAP; FaBoMA

Two Uses, The. Robert Francis. ArLo

Two Variations. Denise Levertov. NaP

2 Variations: All About Love. Philip Whalen. NeAP

Two vases stood on the Shelf of Life. Vases. Nan Terrell Reed. BLPA

Two Veterans. Walt Whitman. *See* Last sunbeam, The.

Two Vietnam Poems: (1966). William Knott. PBCAP

Two Views of a Cadaver Room. Sylvia Plath. CMoP; GoYe

Two Views of Two Ghost Towns. Charles Tomlinson. NoAM

Two vipers tangled into one. *(LL)* Similes for Two Political Characters of 1819. Shelley. FaBoPV; RB

Two virtues ride, by stallion, by nag. The Death of Myth-making. Sylvia Plath. PoA

Two Voices. Edmund Blunden. OBWP; PeFWW

Two Voices, The. Tennyson. MeMBP

Two voices are there: one is of the deep. James Kenneth Stephen. BXAP; EPCY; FaBoCo; FaBoPa; FiBHP; NOBL; UV
(Sonnet, A.) PeLV

Two voices are there; one is of the Sea. Thought [*or* Thoughts] of a Briton on the Subjugation of Switzerland. Wordsworth. EnRP; UV (England and Switzerland 1802.) GTBS; GTBS-P

Two Voices in a Meadow. Richard Wilbur. CRP
Sels.
Milkweed, A.
Stone, A.

Two ways I love Thee, selfishly. Rabi'a al-Adawiyya, *tr. fr. Persian by* A. J. Arberry. TOF

Two webfoot brothers loved a fair. That Gentle Man from Boston Town. Joaquin Miller. AnAmPo

Two Wedding Songs. John Heath-Stubbs. NTP
Sels.
"Hang flags in the airs of July."
London Birds: a Lollipop.

Two weeks across a strange sea. Katori Maru, October 1920. Jim Mitsui. OpBo

Two went to pray? o rather say. Two Went Up into the Temple to Pray. Richard Crashaw. ChIV-2; HAP

Two Went Up into the Temple to Pray. Richard Crashaw. ChIV-2; HAP

Two were silent in a sunless church, The. Her Dilemma. Thomas Hardy. EnVR; NOBVV

Two White Horses. *Unknown.* AS

Two wild duck of the upland spaces. Duck. John Lyle Donaghy. BIrV

Two Wise Generals. Ted Hughes. MoBS

Two Witches. Robert Frost. CMoP
Sels.
Witch of Coös, The. InPS; LiTM; MeMAP; MoAB; MoP; NoAM; NOBA; PoE

Two Witches. Charles Reznikoff. OTCP

Two Women, *sels.* Michael O'Loughlin.
Lotte Lenya. IB
Nadezhda Mandelstam. IB

Two Women. Naomi Replansky. NMM

Two Women, *sels.* George R. Sims.
"To-night is a midnight meeting, and the Earl is in the chair." UV

Two Women. Tania van Zyl. PeSA

Two Women. Nathaniel Parker Willis. BeLS

Two women find the square-root of a sheet. Smalltown Dance. Judith Wright. FaBoMA

Two women on the lone wet strand. The Watchers. William Stanley Braithwaite. PoNe

Two women sit at a table by a window. Light breaks. After Twenty Years. Adrienne Rich. TRP

Two Words; a Wedding. B. P. Nichol. NOBC

Two words from China: "Ku li" — bitter strength. Ku Li. "Robin Hyde." PeNZ

Two workmen were carrying a sheet of asbestos. Christo's. Paul Muldoon. CIP

Two Worlds. Matija Beckovic, *tr. fr. Serbo-Croatian by* Charles Simic. HSix

Two Worlds, The. Alfred Noyes. PFP

Two worlds there are. One you think. Cleaning the Well. Fred Chappell. MT

2 Wren Street. Christian McEwen. VBLP

Two X. E. E. Cummings. FaBoMo

Two-Year-Old Has Had a Motherless Week, The. Karl Shapiro. WeW

Two Years. Pamela Gillilan. PWE

Two years I've been in the Eastern Capital. For Li Po. Tu Fu, *tr. fr. Chinese by* Eugene Eoyang. SuSp

Two Years Later. John Wieners. PoM; RaBo

Two years now since my second marriage. Year Wu-tzu [1048], The, First Month, Night of the Twenty-sixth: A Dream. Mei Yao Ch'en, *tr. fr. Chinese by* Jonathan Chaves. SuSp

Two years thus spent in gathering knowledge. Tom Brainless as Student and Preacher at College. John Trumbull. *Fr.* Progress of Dulness, The. AmPP

Two years we spent. The Woods. Derek Mahon. NOIV; PBCIP; SCBI

Two young maids in a beauty fair. *Malay Oral Tradition, tr. by* R. O. Winstedt. WTO

Two Young Men, 23 to 24 Years Old. C. P. Cavafy, *tr. fr. Greek by* Edmund Keeley *and* Philip Sherrard. FaBoBl; PeHV

Two's company,/ Three's a crowd. *Unknown.* RoPo

'Twould ring the bells of Heaven. The Bells of Heaven. Ralph Hodgson. BoTP; CoGr; GoJo; LiTM; MoAB; MoBrPo; NOBE; OBEV; OtMeF; OxBSP

Ty. *(LL)* Reality. Léon Damas. NegPo

Tycoon, Poet, Saint. Abdur-Rahman Slade Hopkinson. PBCV

Tyler scuffs oak leaves to frisk. Nothing Happened. Belle Waring. PBCAP

Tyndarus attempting too kis a fayre lasse with a long nose. Of Tyndarus, That Frumped a Gentlewoman. *Unknown, tr. fr. Latin.* BIrV, *tr. by* Richard Stanyhurst

Type of the antique Rome! Rich reliquary. The Coliseum. Poe. AmPP; NOBA

Types and Symbols of Eternity. Wordsworth. *Fr.* Prelude [or, Growth of a Poet's Mind], The. CBCK; EnRP; OAEL-2; PoEL-4

Typewriter Revolution, The. D. J. Enright. NoP

Typhoon. Cyrus Cassells. UTF

Typists. P. K. Page. NALW

Tyrannic Love, *sels.* Dryden.
    Ah, How Sweet It Is to Love! HoPM
    Epilogue to "Tyrannick Love." SeCV-2

Tyrannous and bloody act is done, The. Shakespeare. *Fr.* King Richard III. FaBoEH

Tyranny of Moths. Gerald Vizenor. VoR

Tyrant in Sleep, Naught Differeth from a Common Man, A. Timothy Kendall. NoSic

Tyrant, why swell'st thou thus. Bible, *O.T., paraphrased by* Sir Thomas Wyatt. *See* Why boastest thou thyself in mischief, O mighty man?

Tyre brought me up, who born in thee had been. Of Himself. Meleager, *tr. fr. Greek by* Richard Garnett. AWP

Tyrian dye why do you wear. To His Mistress. Abraham Cowley. *Fr.* Sylva. NOSC; OxAEP-1

Tyson's Corner. Primus St. John. PoBA

Tywater. Richard Wilbur. ArOW; CMoP; LiTA; LiTM; MoAB; TRP

Tzar Dusan/ I ask pardon. For Maria Magdalenes. Desanka Maksimovic, *tr. fr. Serbo-Croatian by* Charles Simic. HSix

Tzu Yeh Songs, *sels. Unknown, tr. fr. Chinese.*
    "All night I could not sleep." BoWoP, *tr. by* Arthur Waley
    "At the time when blossoms." BoWoP
    "I heard my love was going to Yang-chou." BoWoP
    "I will carry my coat and not put on my belt." BoWoP

Tzu-yeh Songs of the Four Seasons, *sels. Unknown, tr. fr. Chinese.*
    Spring. SuSp
        "Before jade pavilions the new moon dims."
        "Bewwitching the blossoms of the spring grove."
        "Luminous winds flicker in the moonrise."
        "Plum flowers all fallen and gone."
        "Spring breeze stirs a springtime heart."
        "Young swallows trill their new tune."
    Summer. SuSp
        "All winds died this hot day."
        "At dawn I stand on cool roof garden."
        "Green lotus leaves, a canopy on the pond."
        "These scanty clothes too drab."
        "Though humid summer's unfit for excursions."
        "Toss and turn on bamboo mat."

U

U. Douglas Oliver. VaA

U. A. W.-C. I. O. Bess *and* Baldwin Hawes *and* Baldwin Hawes. SWP

U bet u wer. To a Poet I Knew. Jewel C. Latimore. PoBA

U feel that way sometimes. Mixed Sketches. Don L. Lee. BPo; TAP

U Name This One. Carolyn M. Rodgers. BlSi; NMM; PoBA

U. S. 1946 King's X. Robert Frost. NIP

U. S. Sailor with the Japanese Skull, The. Winfield Townley Scott. ArOW; LiTM

U-24 Anchors off New Orleans. Turner Cassity. ArOW; MT

Ubi Sunt? *Unknown.* PoE

Ubi Sunt Qui ante Nos Fuerunt? [*or* Contempt of the World]. *Unknown.* NoP

Ubi Sunt Qui ante Nos Fuerunt? *Unknown, tr. fr. Latin by* George Perkins. NoP; PrIm; WeW

Ubique. *At. to* Joshua Sylvester. *See* Were I as Base as Is the Lowly Plain.

Ubu Cocu, *sels. Unknown.*
    Chanson du Décervelage, La. CBNP

Uccello. Gregory Corso. FF; NeAP; PoM

Uccello, The. Valerie Wohlfeld. UTF

U.F.W. Pickets on Old Highway 99. Wilma Elizabeth McDaniel. ETG

Ugliest little boy. The Life of Lincoln West. Gwendolyn Brooks. NoAM

Ugly Black Dog Named Goya, An. Ana Castillo. AfAz

Ugly creatures, ugly grunting creatures. Suffering. Miroslav Holub, *tr. fr. Czech by* Ian Milner *and* George Theiner. AnRep; PoSu

Ugly old man, An. No Great Matter. David Lawson. VGW

Ugly Things. Teresita Fernández, *tr. fr. Spanish by* Margaret Randall. AIW

Ugolino. Dante, *tr. by* Seamus Heaney. *Fr.* Divina Commedia. AnAn; FaBoPV; MeMAP; NAWM-1, *tr. by* John Ciardi

Uh nebah cross dese courts agen ess uh live un hundred yares. Lizzie and Joe in Court. Edward Cordle. PBCV

Ula Masondo's Dream. William Plomer. MoBS

Ulalume. Poe. AmPP; AnAmPo; AWP; BLPL; ImPo; LiTA; MeMAP; NOBA; OxBA; TAP

Ulalume — a Ballad. Poe. *See* Skies they were ashen and sober, The.

Ulcerated tooth keeps me awake, there is. Letters from a Father. Mona Van Duyn. FYAP

Ulezalka, Ulezalka. The Tailor. Patricia Garfinkel. BTR

Ulinda. David Campbell. CBAP

Ulric Dahlgren. Kate Brownlee Sherwood. PAH

Ulrich von Hutten's Song. Ulrich von Hutten, *tr. fr. German by* Catherine Winkworth. GePo

Ulster. Kipling. FaBoPV; IIP

Ulster Names. John Hewitt. BiHa

Ulster Twilight, An. Seamus Heaney. CIP; PBCIP

Ulster Unionist Walks the Streets of London, An. Tom Paulin. PNI

Ulsterman, An. "Lynn Doyle." TIRV

Ulstir fur fucks sake. Tom Leonard. *Fr.* Ghostie Men. NBrP

Ultima Ratio Regum. Stephen Spender. CMoP; ImPo; LiTB; LiTM; OAEL-2; OBWP; PAW; PoWW

Ultimate Antientropy, The. Theodore Weiss. NoAM

Ultimate Equality. Ray Durem. PoNe

Ultimate Exile IV. Ralph Nixon Currey. PeSA

Ultimate Poem Is Abstract, The. Wallace Stevens. PoA

Ultimate Problems. William Stafford. NU

Ultimate Reality. Ogden Nash. *See* There was an old man in a trunk.

Ultimately, only the moment counts. Perspectives. Aidan Carl Mathews. IB

Ultimatum, The. Ben King. AnAmPo

Ulysses. Robert Graves. CBLP; CMoP; FaBoTw; MoP; NoAM; PrIm

Ulysses, *sels.* James Joyce.
    Yes. FF

Ulysses. Robert Lowell. NAAL-2

Ulysses. Tennyson. AWP; ClHu; EBEV; EBVVPR; EnVR; FaPoB; FaPoR; FF; FHYEP; HAP; HeIL; HeIP; HoPM; ImPo; InPK; InPS; LiTB; MeMBP; NAEL-2; NAWM-2; NIP; NOBE; NOBVV; NoP; OAEL-2; OxAEP-2; PoE; Poetr; PoRA; PPP; PrIm; SCGP; SCV; SoSe; TEP; TFi; TrGrPo; TRP; UnPo; WeW

Ulysses Advises Achilles. Shakespeare. *Fr.* Troilus and Cressida. ImPo; LiTB

Ulysses and the Siren [*or* Syren]. Samuel Daniel. ElL; EnRePo; HAP; NAEL-1; NOBE; NoP; OBEV; OxAEP-1; PoE; PoEL-2; TEP

Ulysses Insults over the Cyclops. Homer, *tr. fr. Greek by* Robert Fitzgerald. *Fr.* Odyssey. NAWM-1; NOSC, *tr. by* George Chapman

Ulysses Invokes the Dead. Homer, *tr. fr. Greek by* Robert Fitzgerald. *Fr.* Odyssey. NAWM-1; NOSC, *tr. by* George Chapman

Ulysses Leaves the Nymph Calypso. Homer, *tr. by* George Chapman. *Fr.* Odyssey. JCP; NAWM-1

Ulysses Leaves the Nymph Calypso. Homer, *tr. by* George Chapman. *Fr.* Odyssey. JCP; NAWM-1

Ulysses' Library. David Daiches. PoA

Ulysses Reunited with Penelope. Homer. *See* And now Eurynome had bath'd the king.

Umber slant lands under the Apennines, The. To the South. Brewster Ghiselin. LiTA

Umber was painting of a lion fierce. Upon Umber: Epigram. Robert Herrick. CaPo

Umbrella, The. Ann Stanford. NYBP

Umbrella, An. Gertrude Stein. *Fr.* Tender Buttons. TTTS

Umbrella, An/ And a raincoat. Conversation. Buson, *tr. fr. Japanese.* NTCP; SiSoPo

Umbrellas for the Wind. John Harkness. UnDi

Un-American Investigators. Langston Hughes. BPo

U.N. Environmental Sabbath Program, *sels. Unknown.*
    "Great Spirit." FHYEP
    "Great Spirit, whose dry lands thirst, help us to find." FHYEP
    "We have forgotten who we are." FHYEP
    "We join with the earth and with each other." FHYEP

Un Poco Loco. Clayton Eshleman. Jaz

Un Poco Loco. Clarence Major. Jaz

Una Bhan. *At. to* Tomas Mac Coisdealbhaigh, *tr. fr. Irish by* Thomas Kinsella. NOIV

Una fair, my flower of the amber tresses. Una Bhan. *At. to* Tomas Mac Coisdealbhaigh, *tr. fr. Irish by* Thomas Kinsella. NOIV

Una pluma volando siempre jamás. *(LL)* The Lake. Alma Villanueva. SRLS

Unable by Long and Hard Travel to Banish Love, Returns Her Friend. George Turberville. OBTV

Unable, Father, Still, to Disavow. Richard Moore. *Fr.* Word from the Hills. Son

Unable to distinguish between flying and falling. Fear and Trembling. David Lehman. PRA

Unable to mortgage my life to the future. *(LL)* In the Suburbs. Michael O'Loughlin. IB

Unable to sleep/ I gaze at the flowers of the bush clover. Ise Tayu, *tr. fr. Japanese by* Kenneth Rexroth *and* Ikuko Atsumi. WPJ

Unaccompanied. Harvey Andrews. OBET

Unalterables. Arthur Gregor. NYBP

Unanimal mankind (and not until). *(LL)* When Serpents Bargain for the Right to Squirm. E. E. Cummings. MeMAP; PrIm; TwCP

Unanswerable Apology for the Rich, An. Mary Barber. ECWP

Unanswerable Questions. Reva Sharon. BTR

Unanswered Prayers. Ella Wheeler Wilcox. WGRP

Unanswered yet the prayer your lips have pleaded. Pray without Ceasing. Ophelia Guyon Browning. BLPA; BLPL

(Sometime, Somewhere. BLRP

Unarmed Combat. Henry Reed. *Fr.* Lessons of the War. HeIP; LiTB; OBWP

Unanswered Letter. Tess Gallagher. NIP

Unattained, The. Elizabeth Oakes Smith. AmWP

Unavoidable/ Said Edwards — that and pain, The. The Bracelet. John Peck. AnAn

Unawakened, sweet/ women. *(LL)* Belly Dancer. Diane Wakoski. NALW; NoAM

Unawares. Emma A. Lent. PoLF

Unbeliever, The. Elizabeth Bishop. LiTA; NAAL-2; NoAM

Unbeliever, An. Anna Hempstead Branch. WGRP

Unbeseechable, The. Frances Cornford. MoBrPo

Unbiased at least he was when he arrived on his mission. Partition. W. H. Auden. FaBoEH

Unbind Your Angered Tresses, sels. Petronilla Paolini Massimi, *tr. fr. Italian by* Muriel Kittel.

Unblinding, The. Laurence Lieberman. NYBP

Unborn. John Le Gay Brereton. NOBAu

Unborn, The. John Daniel. FoLa

Unborn, The. Thomas Hardy. CMoP

Unborn Child, An. Derek Mahon. PNI

Unborn Child Elegy, sels. Margaret Gibson. "Today snow sparks the air like mica — the sun's." CrSp

Unborn children are rowing out to the far edge of the sky, The. Cloud River. Charles Wright. MT

Unbounded is thy range; with varied style. The Stormy Hebrides. William Collins. *Fr.* Ode on the Popular Superstitions of the Highlands of Scotland, An. EnRP; NOBE; NOEC; OAEL-1; OxAEP-1

Unbowel the meaning. Paul Brown. *Fr.* De Rebus. NBrP

Unbridled licentiousness with no holds barred. Reading Pornography in Old Age. Howard Nemerov. NoAM

Unbridled Now. Laura Lourene LeGear. GoYe

Uncapturable, the indefinable thing, the unlearned, The. *(LL)* Whenever I Have. "Furnley Maurice." NOBAu

Uncarved Block professes no activity, The. Inscribed on the Painting "Pleasures of the Lute by the River." Lin Hung, *tr. fr. Chinese by* Irving Y. Lo. SuSp

Uncertain-aged Miss Thereabouts. Smithereens. Dante Gabriel Rossetti. NOBVV

Uncertain Battle, The. David Gascoyne. PoWW

Uncertain State of a Lover, The. *Unknown.* EIL

Uncertain Steps. Richard Caddel. NBrP

Uncessant minutes, whil'st you move you tell. To His Watch, When He Could Not Sleep. Lord Herbert of Cherbury. JCP; NOBE; PoEL-2

Unchangeable, The. Shakespeare. *See* O [*or* Oh]! Never say that I was false of heart.

Unchanged from what they were when I was young. *(LL)* I Shall Go Back. Edna St. Vincent Millay. MeMAP; MoAmPo; UnPo

Unchanging Jesus. Karl Johann Philipp Spitta, *tr. fr. German by* R. Massie. BLRP

Uncharted. Mary E. O'Donnell. NWP

Unchristian Jacobin whoever. Ode to a Jacobin. *Unknown.* UV

Uncle. Julia Kasdorf. PBCAP

Uncle. Philip Levine. NNaP

Uncle Alfred's Long Jump. Gareth Owen. OBSP

Uncle an' Aunt. William Barnes. NOBVV

Uncle Ananias. E. A. Robinson. MoAmPo; NIP

Uncle Bill had been there. Almost Going. David Huddle. PBCAP

Uncle Bull-Boy. June Jordan. PoBA

Uncle Dog; the Poet at 9. Robert Sward. CoAP; PrIm; VGW

Uncle Henry. W. H. Auden. NOBL; PeHV; PeLV

Uncle Ike's Holiday. Priscilla Jane Thompson. CBWP-2

Uncle Iv Surveys His Domain from His Rocker. Jonathan Williams. NBLV; OBAL

Uncle Jim. Countee Cullen. NAAL-2

Uncle Jimmie's Yarn. Priscilla Jane Thompson. CBWP-2

Uncle Remus and His Friends, sels. Joel Chandler Harris. My Honey, My Love. FaBoBe

Uncle Rube on the Race Problem. Clara Ann Thompson. CBWP-2

Uncle Rube to the Young People. Clara Ann Thompson. CBWP-2

Uncle Rube's Defense. Clara Ann Thompson. CBWP-2

Uncle Sam's Soliloquy. George Sands Johnson. PWR

Uncle sent for O. T. told him we have to fight. O. T.'s Blues. Waring Cuney. MAT

Uncle Time. Dennis Scott. PBCV

Uncle Tom. Langston Hughes. SAmP

Unclean spirits cry out in the body, The. The Guest Ellen at the Supper for Street People. David Ferry. NIP

Unclean, unclean: my Lord, undone, all vile. Edward Taylor. *Fr.* Preparatory Meditations Before My Approach to the Lord's Supper. NAAL-1

Uncle's First Rabbit. Lorna Dee Cervantes. ETG; NoAM

Uncloistered Virtue. Milton. *Fr.* Paradise Lost. EPCY; NOSC

Uncomfortable facts of verisimilitude, The. Pact and Impact. David Chaloner. VaA

Unconcerned, The. Thomas Flatman. FaBoCh

Unconcerned, The: Song. Thomas Flatman. *See* Now that the world is all in a maze.

Unconquer'd Canaanite, An. *(LL)* A Farewell to Tobacco. Charles Lamb. OxBoLi

Unconquer'd captive! — close thine eye. Virginia Capta. Margaret Junkin Preston. PAH

Unconscious Came a Beauty. May Swenson. VCAP

Uncontrollable mystery on the bestial floor, The. *(LL)* The Magi. W. B. Yeats. ChIV-2; CMoP; FaBoRV; HAP; InPK; NoAM; OAEL-2; OxAEP-2; PChr; PoA; PoE; TrCP; TRP

Uncontrollable night, An. Fist Fight. Doug Cockrell. Poetsp

Uncurls and flutters; it will never fall. *(LL)* Mother and Son. Allen Tate. LiTA; MoAB; MoAmPo

Und now Ladies und Gentlemun, *Der Peedles!*. Fab Four Tour Deutschland: Hamburg, 1961. David Wojahn. *Fr.* Mystery Train: A Sequence. PBCAP

Undated dreams: the sea at Heringsdorf. Dreams in German. "David Martin." NOBAu

Undead, The. Richard Wilbur. CoAP; OxBC

Undefined Tenderness, An. Joel Oppenheimer. VGW

Undeodorized and radiant in rags. The First of the Month. Adrian C. Louis. NAmP90

Under. J. C. Squire. FaBoTw

Under a bent when the night was deep. William Morris. *Fr.* Earthly Paradise, The. PChr

Under a dung-cake. D. J. Opperman, *tr. fr. Afrikaans by* Jack Cope. PeSA; PeSAV

Under a full moon. Thomas A. Clark. *Fr.* Twenty Poems. NBrP

Under a futile Torah. Both Your Mothers. Jerzy Ficowski. PoSu

Under a gable: Here lived Francis Jammes. *(LL)* Amsterdam. Francis Jammes. AWP; FaPON, *ll.* 1–20

Under a Hat Rim. Carl Sandburg. AnAmPo

Under a hill. *Unknown.* OxNR

Under a Lady's Picture. Edmund Waller. EnLoPo

Under a lawne, than skyes more cleare. Upon Roses. Robert Herrick. SeCP

Under a low sky. Silence. William Carlos Williams. SAmP

Under a night sky growing bright with stars. *(LL)* Lufthansa. John Tranter. NOBAu

Under a sky studded with asterisks. On the Night in Question. Patricia Goedicke. TAP

Under a sky the color of pea soup. The Seven of Pentacles. Marge Piercy. CrSp

Under a splintered mast. A Talisman. Marianne Moore. GoJo; MoAB; MoAmPo

Under a spreading chestnut-tree. The Village Blacksmith. Longfellow. AiP; AnAmPo; BLPL; EBEvV; FaBoBe; FaPON; FaPoR; OBAL; OBCA; PWR; UV, sh. vers.; VPP; WBLP

Under a spreading gooseberry bush the village burglar lies. The Village Blacksmith. *Unknown.* FiBHP

Under a swaying. El Dorado. Richard Ryan. BIrV

Under a throne I saw a virgin sit. Fulke Greville. FaBoPV

Under a toadstool. The Elf and the Dormouse. Oliver Herford. FaBoBe; FaPON

Under a tree. Mary Is with Child. *Unknown.* MeEL

Under a white coverlet of snow. January. John Heath-Stubbs. OBCP

Under a Wiltshire Apple Tree. Anna Bunston de Bary. CH

Under an ominous sky trees uprooted themselves. The Shoah. Emily Borenstein. BTR

Under an overwashed, stiff, gray. In the Missouri Ozarks. Mona Van Duyn. NGP

Under Attack. Margaret Randall. AIW

Under bare Ben Bulben's head. W. B. Yeats. *Fr.* Under Ben Bulben. CMoP; FaBoRV; HAP; IIP; LiTM; MoP; NAEL-2; NoAM; NoP; OxBTC; WeW

Under Ben Bulben. (Swear by what the sages spoke.) W. B. Yeats. CMoP; HAP; IIP; LiTM; MoP; NAEL-2; NoAM; NoP; OxBTC *Sels.*
"Cast a cold eye." FaBoEE
"Irish poets, learn your trade." OxAEP-2
"Under bare Ben Bulben's head." FaBoRV; WeW

Under Cancer. John Hollander. CoAP

Under clouds, at the tag end of August. Lighting the Night Sky. Kenneth O. Hanson. FYAP

Under cracking pieces of the moon, eelpout. Spawning in Northern Minnesota. David McElroy. AmPA

Under Creon. Tom Paulin. SCBI

Under every cathedral. The Invention of Fire. Andrew Taylor. CBAP

Under 500 kings three kingdoms groan. The Parliament Dissolved at Oxford. *Unknown.* APAS

Under glass: glass dishes which changed. The Fundamental Project of Technology. Galway Kinnell. CAPP; SM; SV

Under God's violent unsleeping eye. Difference. T. Harri Jones. OBWVE

Under great yellow flags and banners of the ancient cold. The Shadow of Cain. Edith Sitwell. OxBTC

Under her deep plush roof. "Vierge Ouvrante." Miriam Palmer. NMM

Under her solemn fillet saw the scorn. (LL) Days. Emerson. AmPP; AnAmPo; HAP; HeIL; HeIP; LiTA; MeMAP; NAAL-1; NOBA; NoP; OxBA; OxBSP; PoE; PoEL-4; TAP; TFi; TrGrPo

Under his Crosse. (LL) A Hymn to God the Father. Ben Jonson. BeJo; EnRePo; NoP; NOSC; OxAEP-1; Poetr; SeCP; SeCV-1; TrCP; TrPWD

Under his view the wind. The View. Howard Nemerov. NYBP

Under it a puddle of blood. Pocket Watch. Novica Tadic, *tr. fr. Serbo-Croatian* by Charles Simic. HSix

Under it out toward the island. (LL) Henry's Understanding. John Berryman. CAPP; MoP; NoAM; NOBA

Under its spreading bankruptcy. The Splendid Bankrupt. Arthur A. Sykes. UV

Under junk heaps and stripped and burning cars. To Softness. Laurie Sheck. CrSp

Under Leafy Bowers. Judah al-Harizi, *tr. fr. Hebrew.* TrJP

Under mercury light the little pup strives. A sinister shadow. Reveille. John Godfrey. UL

Under Milk Wood., *sels.* Dylan Thomas.
"In the blind-drawn dark dining-room of School." FaPoB
Johnnie Crack and Flossie Snail. FaPON; FiBHP; GoJo; OTCP; PDV

Under Mr. Hales Picture. Anne King. KTR

Under my thoughts may I God-thoughts find. Thoughts of God. *Unknown,* *tr. fr. Gaelic by* Douglas Hyde. WTO

Under my window. Letter in Winter. Raymond R. Patterson. PoBA

Under my window-ledge the waters race. Coole Park and Ballylee, 1931. W. B. Yeats. CMoP; GTBS-P; NoAM; NOIV; OBMV; PPP

Under silver wing. Crossing Nation. Allen Ginsberg. AiP

Under Sirius. W. H. Auden. FaBoMo

Under Sorrow's Sign. Gofraidh Fionn O'Dalaigh, *tr. fr. Irish by* John Montague. BIrV

Under Stars. Tess Gallagher. InPK

Under stress the great hawk circles. No Greener Pastures. Brenda Hillman. BAP-90

Under thatched eaves people are quiet. Tune: "Immortal at the Magpie Bridge" — On Hearing the Cuckoo at Night. Lu Yu, *tr. fr. Chinese by* James J. Y. Liu. SuSp

Under the African lintel, Table Mountain. David Wright. *Fr.* South African Broadsheets. PeSA

Under the after-sunset sky. Two Pewits. Edward Thomas. CH; FM

Under the almond tree. In Kensington Gardens. Arthur Symons. EnLoPo

Under the Anheuser Bush. Andrew B. Sterling. OBAL

Under the Arc de Triomphe: October 17. Marilyn Hacker. PoA

Under the arch of life, where love and death. Soul's Beauty. Dante Gabriel Rossetti. *Fr.* House of Life, The. OBEV
(Sibylla Palmifera.) OxAEP-2

Under the Baby Blanket. May Swenson. AnAn

Under the bamboo. T. S. Eliot. *Fr.* Sweeney Agonistes. UnPo

Under the bed. Under Which Heading Does All This Information Go? Mira Teru Kurka. UL

Under the big 500-watted lamps, in the huge sawdusted government inspected slaughter-house. The Slaughter-House. Alfred Hayes. ImPo; LiTA

Under the Boathouse. David Bottoms. MT

Under the Boughs. Gene Baro. BoNaP

Under the Bram Bush. *Unknown.* FaBoVe

Under the bronze crown. A Baroque Wall-Fountain in the Villa Sciarra. Richard Wilbur. AmPP; CAPP; NAAL-2; NoP; NYBP; Poetr; TwCP; VCAP

Under the calm ferocity of the immense geranium our sun. (LL) Mississippi. Aimé Césaire. NegPo

Under the concrete benches. Weed Puller. Theodore Roethke. AmPP; HCAP; NAAL-2

Under the cone of flurried light. The Underworld. Garrett Kaoru Hongo. NAmP90

Under the cover of night. Cities and Seas. Norman Jordan. PoNe

Under the Drooping Willow Tree. *Unknown.* OxBoLi

Under the dry swath. Snake. Desanka Maksimovic, *tr. fr. Serbo-Croatian* by Charles Simic. HSix

Under the dusty print of hobnailed boot. Country Press. Rosemary Dobson. FaBoWP; NOBAu

Under the eaves, their back burned by the sun as hot as fire. Winter. Fan Ch'eng-ta, *tr.* by Irving Y. Lo. *Fr.* Seasonal Poems on Fields and Gardens. SuSp

Under the Edge of February. Jayne Cortez. BISi

Under the Eildon Tree, *sels.* Sydney Goodsir Smith.
"Here I ligg, Sydney Slugabed Godless Smith." OxBS

Under the El on Sunday afternoon. Aside. Alan Dugan. PoA

Under the Eyes. Tom Paulin. CIP; PNI

Under the falling snow flakes. (LL) The Bamboo by Li Ch'e Yun's Window. Po Chü-i. OHMPC

Under the far far harking of the crows. (LL) My Wish for My Land. Randolph Stow. NOBAu

Under the financier's. The Jersey Marsh. David Galler. NYBP

Under the fire escape, crouched, one knee in cinders. The Desk. David Bottoms. MT; WeW

Under the forest, where the day is dark. The Manzanita. Yvor Winters. VGW

Under the Frontier Post. Wang Ch'ang-ling, *tr. fr. Chinese by* Rewi Alley. ChTr

Under the great hill sloping bare. The King's Missive. Whittier. PAH

Under the green hedges, after the snow. Violets. John Moultrie. BoTP

Under the green lamp-light her letter there. Letter of a Mother. Robert Penn Warren. MoAmPo

Under the Greenwood Tree. "Hugh MacDiarmid", *after the Cretan.* OBVE

Under the greenwood tree. Shakespeare. *Fr.* As You Like It. AWP; BoNaP; BoTP; CH; EIL; ELP; EnRePo; FaBoBe; FaPON; GN; GTBS; GTBS-P; HoPM; ImPo; InPS; LiTB; NAEL-1; NoP; NoSic; OAEL-1; OBEV; OHIP; PFP; SCGP; TTTS; UnPo; WiR
(Song: "Under the greenwood tree.") EBEvV; CTC; 09FiP
(Songs of the Greenwood.) TrGrPo

Under the Greenwood Tree. *Unknown.* GBP

Under the hemlocks Fancy came. On the Concord River. H. Cordelia Ray. CBWP-3

Under the Hill. Richard Eberhart. PoA

Under the Hill. Daryl Hine. MoCV

Under the hills and veins of water. Last Letter to Pablo. Pat Lowther. NOBC

Under the hive-like dome the stooping haunted readers. The British Museum Reading Room. Louis MacNeice. LiTM; MoAB; MoBrPo; NOBE

Under the house, between the road the sea-cliff. Grass on the Cliff. Robinson Jeffers. *Fr.* Trumpet, The. PoA

Under the Ice. Stewart Conn. PWE

Under the ice with its bouldery death's faces. The Bread Hot from the Oven. John Thompson. NOBC

Under the Ladder to Heaven. Elizabeth Fenton. NMM

Under the Leaves. Albert Laighton. OHIP

Under the Leaves Green. *Unknown. See* Who shall have my fair [*or* faire *or* fayre] lady?

Under the levys grene. (*LL*) My Fair Lady. *Unknown.* EnLoPo; PoEL-1

Under the Light, yet under. Emily Dickinson. FaBoVe

Under the Lime Tree. Walther von der Vogelweide. *See* Under the Lindens [*or* Lime Tree].

Under the lime-tree, on the daisied ground. Walther von der Vogelweide. *See* Under the Lindens [*or* Lime Tree].

Under the linden in Sands. Wolf-Ancestry. Vasco [*or* Vasko] Popa, *tr. fr. Serbo-Croatian.* TSaS, *tr. by* Charles Simic.

Under the Lindens [*or* Lime Tree]. Walther von der Vogelweide, *tr. fr. German.* CTC, *tr. by* Ford Madox Ford.

Under the Locust Blossoms. Frederick Goddard Tuckerman. NOBA

Under the long dark boughs, like jewels red. Cherry Robbers. D. H. Lawrence. MoAB; MoBrPo

Under the longleaf pines. A Quilled Quilt, a Needle Bed. Brad Leithauser. SM

Under the low-slung pearl. The Exile. Vuyelwa Carlin. NWP

Under the lucent glass. In the Egyptian Museum. Janet Lewis. NYBP

Under the mattress was a day-old newspaper rolled into a scroll. Spontaneous Combustion. David Lehman. NAmP90

Under the Maud Moon. Galway Kinnell. CAPP; NNaP

Under the Microscope. Slavko Mihalic, *tr. by* Charles Simic. PoSu

Under the Mirabeau Bridge the Seine/ Flows and [*or* with] our love[s]. The Mirabeau Bridge. RHTwFp Guillaume Apollinaire, *tr. fr. French.* BoLoP, *tr. by* Quentin Stevenson; LPA; OBVE, *tr. by* W. S. Merwin.

Under the Mirabeau Bridge there flows the Seine. Mirabeau Bridge. RHTwFp Guillaume Apollinaire, *tr. fr. French by* Richard Wilbur. ArLo; PRA

Under the Mistletoe. Countee Cullen. PChr

Under the mountain, as when first I knew. Frederick Goddard Tuckerman. *Fr.* Sonnets. HAP; TAP

Under the new pond-dam. Looking Before and After. Carter Revard. HATNAP

Under the oak tree, oak tree. *Unknown, tr. fr. Spanish by* Willis Barnstone. BoWoP

Under the Old Elm, *sels.* James Russell Lowell.
"Never to see a nation born." GOA
New-come Chief, The. PAH
"That lifted blade transformed our jangling clans." GOA
Washington. GN; OHIP

Under the orchards, under. Rogation Days. Kenneth Rexroth. NaP

Under the parabola of a ball. How to Kill. Keith Douglas. FaBoMo; NOBE; PoWW; RB

Under the pines and hemlocks. The Deer. Mary Austin. FaPON

Under the pink quilted covers. The Fortress. Anne Sexton. LiTM

Under the plum-blossoms are nightingales. Desolation. Amy Lowell. PoA

Under the plum moon, he sits. The Haiku Master. Elizabeth Spires. BAP-91

Under the pond, among rocks. The Dragonfly. Howard Nemerov. GoJo; PoA

Under the Pondweed. *Unknown, tr. by* Helen Waddell. *Fr.* Shi King. AWP

Under the Pot. Robert Graves. FaBoEE

Under the quince tree. Bible, *O.T., tr. by* Marcia Falk. *Fr.* Song of Solomon, The. PBWP

Under the Range. Irene Gough. OBAP

Under the red-and-white striped awning. The Luncheon of the Boating Party. Leon Stokesbury. MT

Under the red Korean banner. The Inupiat Christmas Pageant. Peggy Shumaker. PBCAP

Under the rock, in the sand and the gravel run. Charles Wright. *Fr.* Skins. HCAP

Under the roof and the roof's shadow turns. The Merry-go-round. Rainer Maria Rilke, *tr. fr. German by* C. F. MacIntyre. WeW

Under the roofs of their mouth. (*LL*) A Poem for Tea Heads. John Wieners. PoBeRe

Under the Rose. *Unknown.* OBET

Under the running tap that are not the hands of a child. (*LL*) Soap Suds. Louis MacNeice. FaBoMo; NAEL-2; NOIV; NoP; NTP; SCV

Under the sagging clotheslines of crepe paper. The Best Slow Dancer. David Wagoner. NoAM; VCAP

Under the scarlet-licking leaves. My Many-Coated Man. Laurie Lee. NYBP

Under the September Peach. Robert Wallace. Son

Under the Shade of the Trees. Margaret Junkin Preston. PAH

Under the shadow of the gloomy night. Samuel Rowlands. NOSC

Under the sheet of transparent wool. Penumbra. Pierre Louÿs, *tr. fr. French. Fr.* Chansons de Bilitis. PeHV

Under the silver, and home again. (*LL*) The Ride-by-Nights. Walter de la Mare. FaPON

Under the sloped snow. As Children Together. Carolyn Forché. NoAM

Under the slumber and winter of a silent night. In Lord Carpenter's Country. Barry O. Higgs. PeSA

Under the snow. (*LL*) I Never Shall Love the Snow Again. Robert Bridges. CH; CMoP; FaBV

Under the sovereign crests of dead volcanoes. On a Bougainvillaea Vine at the Summer Palace [*or* in Haiti]. Barbara Howes. MoAmPo; NYBP

Under the Stairs. Frank Ormsby. PBCIP

Under the Stars. Wallace Rice. OHIP

Under the Sudden Blue. Sylvia Townsend Warner. VBLP

Under the sudden blue, under the embrace. Under the Sudden Blue. Sylvia Townsend Warner. VBLP

Under the sun is nothing new? To the Archdeacon. George Farewell. NOEC

Under the surface of flux and of fear there is an underground movement. Louis MacNeice. *Fr.* Kingdom, The. LiTM

Under the Table Manners. *Unknown.* CRH

Under the tall black sky you look out of your body. Endless. Muriel Rukeyser. NYBP

Under the too white marmoreal Lincoln Memorial. The March 1. Robert Lowell. HCAP; NoP

Under the urination of astronauts. Everything Is Wonderful. Jayne Cortez. AIW

Under the Vulture-Tree. David Bottoms. MT

Under the walls of Monterey. Victor Galbraith. Longfellow. PAH

Under the waning moon. Starting at Dawn. Sun Yün-feng, *tr. fr. Chinese by* Kenneth Rexroth *and* Ling Chung. PBWP; WPC

Under the water tower at the edge of town. To the Evening Star: Central Minnesota. James Wright. NaP

Under the Waterfall. Thomas Hardy. BoLoP; CTC; LiTB; NAEL-2

Under the wave it is altogether still. The Return of Aphrodite. May Sarton. SRLS

Under the white silence of the great gumtree avenue. A Finished Gentleman. Geoffrey Dutton. NOBAu

Under the wide and starry sky. Robert Louis Stevenson. CoGr; DL; EBVV; FaBV; FaPoR; MoBrPo; NBLV; NOBE; NOBVV; OBD; OBEV; OBNC; OHCV; PoLF; PoRA; TrGrPo; WGRP
(Requiem.) EBEvV; GGP; NTP; OtMeF; SCGP; TFi

Under the Willow Shades. Sir William Davenant. BoLoP; ELP

Under the willow the willow. Recruiting Drive. Charles Causley. OxBTC; PrIm

Under the Window: Ouro Preto. Elizabeth Bishop. NYBP; VCAP

Under the Woods. Edward Thomas. CH

Under the words you are my silence. (*LL*) When a Woman Feels Alone. May Sarton. SRLS

Under the yew-tree's heavy weight. Les Hiboux. Baudelaire, *tr. by* Arthur Symons. AWP

Under these words. Bi-lingual. Maria Jastrzebska. NBrP

Under this heap of stones interred lies. Upon Stephen Stoned. Sir John Suckling. ChIV-2

Under this marble, or under this sill. Epitaph on Himself. Pope. FaBoEE

Under this plaque I lie, the famous woman. *Unknown, tr. fr. Greek by* Peter Jay. GrAn

Under this real estate — squared street on street. Asphodel. David Malouf. CBAP

Under This Sky. Zia Hyder, *tr. fr. Bengali.* TSaS, *tr. by* Bhabani Sengupta *with* Naomi Shihab Nye.

Under this stone doth lie. An Epitaph upon Thomas, Lord Fairfax. George Villiers. NOSC

Under this stone/ Lies a Reverend Drone. An Epitaph upon That Profound and Learned Casuist, the Late Ordinary of Newgate. Thomas Brown. OBSV

Under this stone, reader, survey. On Sir John Vanbrugh [Architect]. Abel Evans. FaBoCo; FaBoEE; FaBoEH; FiBHP; IHNG

Under this stone there lieth at rest. An Epitaph of Sir Thomas Gravener [Knight]. Sir Thomas Wyatt. SiPS

Under this sun voices on the radio run down. The Complete Birth if the Cool. C. D. Wright. LCAP

Under various names, I have praised only you, rivers! Rivers. Czeslaw Milosz, *tr. fr. Polish by* Robert Hass *and* Renata Gorczynski. FoLa

Under Which Heading Does All This Information Go? Mira Teru Kurka. UL

Under Which Lyre, a Reactionary Tract for the Times. W. H. Auden. MoAB; MoBrPo; NOBL; PeLV

Under yonder beech-tree single [or standing] on the green-sward. Love in the Valley. George Meredith. AWP; EBVV; EnVR; ErPo; LiTB; NOBE; OAEL-2; OBEV, abr.; TrGrPo

Under your Milky Way. Return of the Goddess Artemis. Robert Graves. PoA

Under Your Voice, among Legends. Phyllis Beauvais. NMM

Underdeveloped Country, An. D. J. Enright. NOBL

Underfoot rotten boards, forest rubble, bones. Remains of an Indian Village. Alfred W. Purdy. NOBC

Undergraduate. Merrill Moore. ErPo

Underground Gardens, The. Robert Mezey. NaP

Underground grower, blind and a common brown, An. Potato. Richard Wilbur. CAPP; LiTA; MoAB; TrGrPo

Underground Stream, The. James Dickey. NOBA

Undergrowth's a conveyance of butterflies, The. Hope's Okay. A. R. Ammons. HCAP

Underlife, The. Sharon Olds. FoLa

Underneath a cypress shade, the Queen of Love sat mourning. Unknown. GBL

Underneath a light straw boater. Henley Regatta, 1902. Sir John Betjeman. FaBoEH

Underneath an old oak tree. The Raven. Samuel Taylor Coleridge. WiR

Underneath my lids another eye has opened. From the Prison House. Adrienne Rich. NNaP

Underneath the Archers or What's All This about Walter's Willy? Kit Wright. FaBoBl

Underneath the boardwalk, way, way back. The Secret Cavern. Margaret Widdemer. FaPON

Underneath the broad hat is the face of the Ambassador. The Ambassador. Stevie Smith. Mes

Underneath the growing grass. The Bourne. Christina Rossetti. ELP; OBNC

Underneath the water-weeds. The Tadpole. E. E. Gould. BoTP

Underneath this marble stone/ Lie two beauties join'd in one. Epitaph of Pyramus and Thisbe. Abraham Cowley. EnLoPo; FaBoEE (Epitaph: "Underneath this marble stone.") EnLoPo

Underneath this myrtle shade. The Epicure. Abraham Cowley. OxAEP-1

Underneath this sable hearse [or herse]. On the Countess Dowager of Pembroke. At. to William Browne. AWP; HAP; InvP; JCP; NoP; OAEL-1; PoEL-2; PoRA; TFi (Epitaph on the Countess[e] Dowager of Pembroke.) FaBoEE; NOBE; OBEV; SCGP (On the Death of Marie, Countess[e] of Pembroke.) NOSC; OAEL-1

Undersea Fever. William Cole. FiBHP

Undersong of terrible holy joy, An. (LL) The Old Women. George Mackay Brown. OxBS

Understand. (LL) Earth Song. Thomas Love Peacock. VoR

Understand, he is naked in the sea. The Loved One. Joseph Hansen. NYBP

Understand me: I am a mediocre being. Words to My Friend. Renée Vivien, tr. fr. French by Sandia Belgrade. PeHV

Understand too late? Of course we can. Poem for Gerard. Edward Leslie Mayo. BCF

Understanding. H. W. Bliss. PoToHe

Understanding. Pauline E. Soroka. PoLF

Understanding. Sara Teasdale. AnAmPo

Understanding. Unknown. PoToHe

Understanding Canada. Peter Sirr. PBCIP

Understands. (LL) I Work with the shape. Michael McClure. PoBeRe

Undertakers. Robert Johnstone. PNI

Undertakers' Club, The. Unknown. GBP

Undertaker's Horse, The. Kipling. FaBoNo; FM

Undertaking, The. John Donne. NAEL-1; NOBE

Undertaking, The. Louise Glück. FaBoWP

Undertone. William Bedell Stanford. PeIV

Undertones. George R. Sims. NOBVV

Undertow. Langston Hughes. LiTM

Underwater eyes, an eel's. An Otter. Ted Hughes. CMoP; MoP; NoAM

Underwear. Lawrence Ferlinghetti. OBAL

Underwood. Howard Moss. TwCP

Underworld, The. Garrett Kaoru Hongo. NAmP90

Underworld of children becomes the overworld, The. Blue Glass. Fleur Adcock. FaBoWP

Undesirable you may have been, untouchable. September Song. Geoffrey Hill. NAEL-2; NoAM; NoP; OBWP

Undine. Irving Layton. ErPo

Undo! Unknown. NOCV

Undo thy dore, my spuse dere! Unknown. MiEL

Undo Your Heart. Unknown. See I am Jesu that cum to fight.

Undoing the straps. The Sewing-Box. Gabriel Gbadamosi. NBrP

Undone, undone the lawyers are. The Downfall of Charing Cross. Unknown. FaBoCo

Undressing a maiden called Sue. Brian Allgar. PeLi

Undressing Aunt Frieda. Richard Michelson. BTR

Undressing Aunt Frieda, I think of how. Undressing Aunt Frieda. Richard Michelson. BTR

Undressing, her fingers find the zip. The New Dress. Tony Flynn. PWE

Undue significance a starving man attaches. Emily Dickinson. LiTA; LiTM

Unduly elected body of our elders, An. Elegy for Yards, Pounds, and Gallons. David Wagoner. PoA

Undying Thirst. Antipater of Sidon, tr. fr. Greek by Robert Bland. AWP

Unemployed. Stephen Spender. FaBoEH; NOBE

Unemployment. William Mills. HoPM

Unemployment in our bones, The. Derry. Seamus Deane. CIP; IIP; PeIV

Unemployment/Monologue. June Jordan. WPOW

Unending Love. Rabindranath Tagore, tr. fr. Bengali by Rabindranath Tagore. ArLo

Unending search in endless quest. P'u-Shen Sheng Man. Li Ch'ing-chao, tr. fr. Chinese by Duncan Mackintosh. IMW

Unequal Distribution. Samuel Hoffenstein. TrJP

Unequal Fetters, The. The Countess of Winchilsea. VBLP

Unerring Guide, The. Anna Shipton. BLRP

Unexpected Pleasure, An. Unknown. FaBoCo; UV

Unexpected Sunflowers. Paul Goodman. ArNa

Unexplorer, The. Edna St. Vincent Millay. MoShBr; PoA

Unfading, The. "Marie Madelaine," tr. fr. German by Ferdinand E. Kappey. PeHV

Unfailing Friend, The. Joseph Scriven. BLRP

Unfailing One, The. Phillips Brooks. BLRP

Unfailing sympathy,/ Undying Love. (LL) What God Hath [or Has] Promised! Annie Johnson Flint. BLRP; WBLP

Unfair to Men. Unknown, tr. fr. Welsh by Gwyn Jones. OBWVE

Unfair to Women. Unknown, tr. fr. Welsh by Gwyn Jones. OBWVE

Unfaithful [or Faithless] Shepherdess or Philon the Shepherd or Adieu Love, Untrue Love, The. Unknown. GTBS; GTBS-P

Unfaithful Wife, The. Federico García Lorca, tr. fr. Spanish by John Frederick Nims. STV

Unfaithful Wife, The. Federico García Lorca. OxBM

Unfallen Love. Milton. See Hail wedded love, mysterious law, true source.

Unfalling, trailing white foam, white fire. (LL) Skier. Robert Francis. RFM

Unfamiliar Quartet. Stephen Vincent Benét. AnAmPo

Unfamiliar Shore. Bei Dao, tr. fr. Chinese by Donald Finkel with Chen Xueliang. SpMi

Unfashionably diverse dreams, needing laddered stockings. (LL) Is he painting with tips. Grace Lake. VBLP

Unfathomable Sea? (LL) Time. Shelley. FaBoRV; PoLF

Unfathomable Sea! whose waves are years. Time. Shelley. FaBoRV; PoLF

Unfinished Exile. Fabio Doplicher, tr. fr. Italian by Stephen Sartarelli. NeIt

Unfinished History, An. Archibald MacLeish. NYBP; VGW

Unfinished Poem. Jiang He, tr. fr. Chinese by Donald Finkel with Yi Jinsheng. SpMi

Unfinished Race, The. Norman Cameron. OxBS

Unflushed Urinals. Donald Justice. AnAn

Unfold, Unfold. Henry Vaughan. See Unfold, unfold! take in his light.

Unfold, unfold! take in his light. The Revival. Henry Vaughan. NOCV; PoEL-2; TrGrPo (Unfold, Unfold.) ELP

Unforgettable. Mark Pawlak. BTR

Unforgiven, The. E. A. Robinson. CMoP

Unfortunate admiral! Your poor America. To Columbus. Rubén Darío, tr. fr. Spanish by Lysander Kemp. TTY

Unfortunate Coincidence. Dorothy Parker. BXAP; FaBoUs; NoP

Unfortunate lad from Madrid, An. Unknown. PeLi

Unfortunate Male, The. Kalonymos ben Kalonymos, tr. fr. Hebrew by J. Chotzner. Fr. Touchstone, The. TrJP

Unfortunate Miller, The. A. E. Coppard. FaBoTw

Unfortunate Miller; or, The Country Lasses Witty Invention, The. Unknown. CoMu; OxBB

Unfortunate Miss Bailey. George Colman the Younger. FiBHP; GBP

Unfortunate Mole, The. Mary Kennedy. GoYe

Unfortunate Occurrence at Cwm-Cadno. A. G. Prys-Jones. AngWe

Unfriendly Fortune. John Skelton. MeEL

Unfriendly friendly universe. The Child Dying. Edwin Muir. FaBoTw; GTBS-P; MeMBP; PoWW; RB

Unfulfilled Love. Ljiljana Djurdjic, *tr. fr. Serbo-Croatian by* Charles Simic. HSix

Unfurled gull on the tide, and over the skerry, The. December Day, Hoy Sound. George Mackay Brown. OxBS

Unfurls in rain. The Newest Banana Plant Leaf. Ingrid Wendt. NMM

Ungar and Rolfe. Herman Melville. *Fr.* Clarel. OxBA

Ungathered Apples, The. James Wright. ErPo

Ungathered Love. Philip Bourke Marston. OBNC

Ungrateful Garden, The. Carolyn Kizer. CAPP

Ungrateful Jenny. Mother Goose. OxNR

Ungreeted, and shall give its light embrace. *(LL)* Inscription for the Entrance to a Wood. Bryant. AmPP; EAP; OxBA; TAP

Unguarded Gates. Thomas Bailey Aldrich. AnAmPo; PAH

Unguarded House, An. Julianus of Egypt, *tr. fr. Greek by* W. S. Merwin. GrAn

Unhand me nurse! thou saucy quean! Maternal Despotism; or, The Rights of Infants. Richard Graves. NOEC

Unhappie [*or* Unhappy] Light. William Drummond of Hawthornden. NOSC

Unhappy about some far off things. The Stars Go over the Lonely Ocean. Robinson Jeffers. LiTA; LiTM

Unhappy and at home. *(LL)* The Tollund Man. Seamus Heaney. BIrV; CIP; EBEV; FaBoMo; IPY; NoP; PBCIP; PNI; TEP

Unhappy Bella. *Unknown.* ErPo

Unhappy Boston. Paul Revere. AiP; PAH

Unhappy country, what wings you have! Even here. Eagle Valor, Chicken Mind. Robinson Jeffers. LiTA; OxBA; OxBSP

Unhappy Diary Days. Gerald Vizenor. VoR

Unhappy dreamer, who outwinged in flight. On the Death of a Metaphysician. George Santayana. *Fr.* Sonnets. AnAmPo

Unhappy fate: that you have died. Song at Graveside. Ewald von Kleist, *tr. fr. German by* George C. Schoolfield. GePo

Unhappy Lover, The. Judah al-Harizi, *tr. fr. Hebrew by* J. Chotzner. TrJP

Unhappy man! *Whose every breath.* On Sin. Francis Quarles. *Fr.* Divine Fancies, The. CBCK

Unhappy men, why do we travel so. Crinagoras, *tr. fr. Greek by* Alistair Elliot. GrAn

Unhappy merchant, Thus t'expose thy Lord. Elizabeth Middleton. *Fr.* Death and Passion of Our Lord Jesus Christ, The. KTR

Unhappy people in a happy world, An. Wallace Stevens. *Fr.* Auroras of Autumn, The. CMoP

Unhappy Phaeton's splendidious sire. Virgo, August. John Taylor. NOSC

Unhappy Returns. Daryl Hine. PFL

Unhappy Revenge, The, *sels.* Swinburne.

Unhappy Schoolboy, The. *Unknown.* OxBChV

Unhappy sex! how hard's our fate. On Sir J — — S — — Saying in a Sarcastic Manner, My Books Would Make Me Mad; an Ode. Elizabeth Thomas. ECWP

Unhappy summer you. This Summer and Last. Thomas Hardy. OxBTC

Unhappy Verse. Spenser. *See* Unhappy [*or* Unhappie] Verse, the witness[e] of my unhappy state.

Unhappy [*or* Unhappie] Verse, the witness[e] of my unhappy state. Iambicum Trimetrum. Spenser. BoLoP; EBEV; EiL; OBEV; OPOP; PoEL-1
(Iambica.) OxBoLi
(Unhappy Verse.) GGP

Unhappy wit, like most mistaken things. Pope. *Fr.* Essay on Criticism. EPCY; PoEL-3

Unharvested. Robert Frost. BoNaP; SAmP

Unholy Missions. Bob Kaufman. TTY

Unhurried as a snake I saw Time glide. On Time. Richard Hughes. MoBrPo

Unhurt, like him, your Charms I'll hear. *(LL)* Farewell to Worldly Joyes, A ("Farewel to unsubstantial joyes.") Anne Killigrew. BoWoP

Unicorn, The. George Darley. *Fr.* Nepenthe. ChTr; OBNC; PoEL-4

Unicorn, The. Ruth Pitter. MoBrPo

Unicorn, The. Emile Victor Rieu. OBSP

Unicorn, The, *sels.* Rainer Maria Rilke, *tr. fr. German by* Stephen Mitchell. "Oh this is the animal that never was." TTTS

Unicorn, The, *sels.* Isaac Rosenberg. "Sick . . . Sick . . . I will lie down and die. How." PeFWW

Unicorn, The. Ella Young. FaPON

Unicorn and the Lady, The. Jean Garrigue. NYBP

Unicorn Is a Symbol of Virginity, The. Christiania Whitehead. NWP

Unicorn stood, like a king in a dream, The. The Unicorn. Emile Victor Rieu. OBSP

Unicorn Tapestries, The. William Olsen. NAmP90

Unicorn to hand, A. Haste to the Wedding. Alex Comfort. ErPo

Unicornis Tale, The. *Unknown. Fr.* Talis of the Fyve Bestis, The. OxBLMV

Unicorn's hoofs, The! Dance Song. *Unknown, tr. fr. Chinese by* Arthur Waley. FaBoCh

Unifying Principle, The. A. R. Ammons. CAPP; NOBA

Unintelligible Terms. Charles Simic. NoP

Uninvited, The. Dorothy Livesay. NOBC

Uninvited, The. William D. Mundell. NYBP

Union and Liberty. Oliver Wendell Holmes. OHIP

Union is behind us, The. We Shall Not Be Moved. *Unknown.* SWP

Union is the place for me, The. On the Line. *Unknown.* SWP

Union Jack, The. Jeannie Kirby. BoTP

Union Maid. Woody Guthrie. SWP

Union Man. Albert Morgan. AmFP; SWP

Union Pier Michigan. We called it Shapiro. That Was Then. Isabella Gardner. CAPP

Union Train. *Unknown.* SWP

Unique among Girls. *Malay Oral Tradition, tr. by* R. J. Wilkinson *and* R. O. Winstedt. WTO

Unison, A. William Carlos Williams. NOBA

Unit. Mary Elizabeth Fullerton. NOBAu,

Unit unperceived, A. The Crowd in the Crystal Palace. *Unknown. Fr.* Lily and the Bee, The. CBCK

Unite, ne'er more (rapt thought) to say "farewell!" *(LL)* On Parting with a Friend. Mary Weston Fordham. AmWP; CBWP-2

Unite, unite, let us all unite. The Padstow Night Song. *Unknown.* ChTr; GBP

United. Paulus Silentiarius, *tr. fr. Greek by* W. H. D. Rouse. AWP

United Fruit Co, The. Pablo Neruda, *tr. fr. Spanish by* Robert Bly. FaBoPV

United keeps for ever. *(LL)* The Knot. Henry Vaughan. MiEL

United States, The. Goethe, *tr. fr. German by* Robert Bly. AiP

United States and *Macedonian*, The. *Unknown.* PAH

United States Constitution, The. Peter Alexander. PeLi

United States is giving the Suez Canal back to Panama, The. "Some Days," Dorothy Parker Said, "It's Better Than Digging Ditches." Maureen Owen. UL

United States of America We, The. Sam Abrams. UL

United Steelworkers Are We. M. T. Montgomery. SWP

Unity. Fazil Hüsnü Daglarca, *tr. fr. Turkish by* Tâlat S. Halman. RaBo

Unity. Alfred Noyes. PFP

Unity of God, The. Panatattu, *tr. fr. Sanskrit.* WGRP

Univac to Univac. Louis B. Salomon. FF

Universal Beauty., *sels.* Henry Brooke. "While ocean thus the latent store bequeaths." ECEV

Universal Favorite, The. Carolyn Wells. NBLV

Universal Prayer, The. Pope. BLPA; FaBoBe; NoP; WGRP

University. Karl Shapiro. LiTA; OxBA

University Curriculum. William Price Turner. OxBS

University Examinations in Egypt. D. J. Enright. OxBTC; TwCP

University Hospital, Boston. Mary Oliver. CAPP

University of Hunger. Martin Carter. PBCV

Unjust steals [*or* stole] the just's umbrella, The. *(LL)* The Rain It Raineth. Lord Bowen. FiBHP; ISE; NBLV; NTCP

Unjustly Punished Child. Sharon Olds. PBCAP

Unkindness. George Herbert. NOSC; OBF

Unkindness Has Killed Me. *Unknown.* MeEL

Unknown, The. John Davidson. MeMBP; MoBrPo

Unknown, The. Elmer Osborn Laughlin. BLPA

Unknown, The. Denise Levertov. NAAL-2

Unknown, The. Edward Thomas. ArLo; GBL

Unknown Bird, The. Edward Thomas. RB

Unknown Child, The. Elizabeth Jennings. PBWP

Unknown Citizen, The. W. H. Auden. FF; HeIL; HeIP; InPK; LiTA; LiTM; MeMAP; MoAB; NBLV; NIP; NOBL; NYBP; OBSV; Poetr; PoRA; SoSe; TRP; UnPo

Unknown Color, The. Countee Cullen. FaPON; OBCA

Unknown Eros, The, *sels.* Coventry Patmore.
  Arbor Vitae. OBNC; PeVV
  Azalea, The. ELP; GBL
  Departure. NOBE; OBEV; OBNC
  Here, in This Little Bay. BoNaP; CoGr
  (Magna Est Veritas.) ArNa; GTBS-P; HAP; NOBE; NOBVV; OBEV; OBNC; OxBSP
  (Truth.) TrGrPo
  Legem Tuam Dilexi. PoEL-5

Saint Valentine's Day. OBNC

Tired Memory. EnVR

To the Body. EnVR; OAEL-2; PoEL-5

To the Unknown Eros. PoEL-5

Toys, The. BeLS; EBEV; EBVV; NOBVV; OBEV; OHCV; OxAEP-2; PIP; PoToHe, *sl. diff.*; SoSe; TrGrPo; TrPWD

"With all my will, but much against my heart." BoLoP; EnLoPo; GTBS-P; NOBE; OBEV; OBNC; PoEL-5; TrGrPo

Unknown faces in the street. The Turning. Philip Levine. PRA; VGW

Unknown Female Corpse. Kipling. PoWW

Unknown Girl in the Maternity Ward. Anne Sexton. MoP; NAs; NoAM

Unknown God, The. "Æ." MoBrPo; WGRP

Unknown God, The. Sir William Watson. WGRP

Unknown Ideal. Dora Sigerson. IIP

Unknown Land, *sels.* Rex Ingamells.

"We who are called Australians have no country." NOBAu

Unknown love/ Is as bitter a thing. Lady Otomo no Sakanoe. *Fr.* Manyo Shu, Part 4 of 4. AWP, *tr. by* Arthur Waley; PBWP, *tr. by* Arthur Waley

(Unknown love/ is bitter.) BoWoP, *tr. by* Willis Barnstone

Unknown love/ is bitter. Lady Otomo no Sakanoe. *See* Unknown love/ Is as bitter a thing.

Unknown Man in the Morgue. Merrill Moore. MoAmPo

Unknown Master of Moulins, The. The Cardinal's Dog. John Glassco. MoCV

Unknown road still marching, The. (*LL*) A March in the Ranks Hard-Prest, and the Road Unknown. Walt Whitman. AmPP; NAAL-1; OxBA

Unknown Shepherd's Complaint, The. Richard Barnfield. ElL

Unknown Soldier, The. Alun Lewis. MoBrPo

Unknown Soldier, The. Billy Rose. BLPA

Unknown Soldiers. Edgar Lee Masters. *Fr.* New Spoon River, The. NoAM; TAP

Unknown unwanted life, The. (*LL*) The Orient Express. Randall Jarrell. CMoP; CoAP; NOBA; PoE

Unknown Wind, The. "Fiona Macleod." BoTP

Unlawful Assembly. D. J. Enright. OxBTC

Unlearning to Not Speak. Marge Piercy. CrSp

Unless I walk outside these whitethorn hedges. (*LL*) Innocence. Patrick Kavanagh. RB

Unless it trembled with the strings. (*LL*) Romance. Poe. AmPP; AnAmPo; MeMAP; NAAL-1; OxBA

Unless one keep the affectionate spirit firm. (*LL*) Much as a man who takes delight in dreaming. Ausiàs March. STV

Unless they hold. (*LL*) For Friendship. Robert Creeley. VCAP

Unless we organize. (*LL*) Which Side Are You on? Florence Reese. SWP

Unless we're as good as can be. (*LL*) The Brown Thrush. Lucy Larcom. BoTP; FaPON; OBCA

Unless you can dance through a common bar. Mahsati, *tr. fr. Farsi by* Deirdre Lashgari. AIW; WPOW

Unless you can muse in a crowd all day. Elizabeth Barrett Browning. *Fr.* Woman's Shortcommings, A. PFP

Unless you come of the gipsy stock. Gipsy Vans. Kipling. OtMeF

Unless you remind me. Pavlov. Naomi Long Madgett. BPo

Unlike are we, unlike, O princely heart! Elizabeth Barrett Browning. *Fr.* Sonnets from the Portuguese. EnVR; OBEV; OxAEP-2; TrGrPo

Unlike flying or astral projection, walking through walls is a. Walking through a Wall. Louis Jenkins. RaBo

Unlike my subject now shall be my song. Earl of Chesterfield. FaBoEE

Unlike the hawk he has no dream of height. Sea Owl. Dave Jeddie Smith. HCAP

Unloading hell behind him step by step. (*LL*) The Rear-Guard. Siegfried Sassoon. MoBrPo; NAEL-2; NoAM; OBWP; PoWW

Unloading Rails. *Unknown.* AmFP

Unlocking the Doors. Jill Breckenridge. LoHo

Unlucky Nicanor, quenched by the grey and deep. Antipater of Thessalonica, *tr. fr. Greek by* Alistair Elliot. GrAn

Unmanifest Destiny. Richard Hovey. WGRP

Unmarked Ceiling, The. Mary Michaels. DT

Unmarked faces/ fierce with grief. Falls Funeral. John Montague. CIP

Unmitigated England. Great Central Railway, Sheffield Victoria to Banbury. Sir John Betjeman. NYBP

Unmoved by cricket song of thee or me. (*LL*) The Cricket. Frederick Goddard Tuckerman. FM; NOBA

Unmoved by what the wine does. Sleeping with One Eye Open. Mark Strand. CAPP; NYBP; SM

Unmuzzle the broad joke. Catullus, *tr. fr. Latin by* James Michie. *Fr.* Hymeneal. PeHV

Unnamable God, you are fathomless. Bible, *O.T., paraphrased by* Sir Thomas Wyatt. *See* Bless the Lord, O my soul/ O Lord my God.

Unnamed Lake, The. Frederick George Scott. NOBC

Unnoticed the first of autumn as nights grow longer. The First of Autumn. Meng Hao Jan, *tr. fr. Chinese by* Paul W. Kroll. SuSp

Unnumbered suppliants crowd preferment's gate. Samuel Johnson. *Fr.* Vanity of Human Wishes, The: The Tenth Satire of Juvenal Imitated. EBEV; ECEV; NOEC; NoP; OAEL-1; OBSV; OxAEP-1; PoEL-3; PrIm; TEP; TFi

Unpardonable Sin, The. Vachel Lindsay. ChIV-2; CMoP; MeMAP

Unperson from West Oceania, An. C. Vita-Finzi. PeLi

Unpetal the flower of me. To Life. Lizette Woodworth Reese. AmWP

Unpopular man of Cologne, An. *Unknown.* PeLi

Unportrayable on the light silk of a small fan. Tune: "Butterflies." Kuan Yun-shih, *tr. by* Richard John Lynn. *Fr.* Medley of Southern and Northern Tunes — Scenic Tour of West Lake. SuSp

Unpossessed, The. Adèle Naudé. PeSA

Unposted Birthday Card. Norman MacCaig. NAs

Unprayed-for,/ And final. (*LL*) What Can I Tell My Bones? Theodore Roethke. AmPP; NOBA

Unpredictable, The. Thomas Blackburn. OPOP

Unpredicted, The. John Heath-Stubbs. BoLoP; OxBC

Unprofitablenes. Henry Vaughan. ESCV; GeHe; NOSC; SeCV-1

Unpublished Poems by Thomas Wyatt and His Circle, *sels.* Sir Thomas Wyatt.

"In mourning wise since daily I increase." NoSic; PeECV

Unpurged images of day recede, The. Byzantium. W. B. Yeats. CMoP; EBEV; FaBoMo; HAP; InPS; LiTM; MeMBP; MoAB; MoBrPo; MoP; NAEL-2; NAWM-2; NIP; NoAM; NOBE; NoP; OAEL-2; OxBTC; PoE; Poetr; PPP; TEP

Unquiet Grave, The. *Unknown.* CH; ELP; ESPB; GBP; HAP; HeIP; IMW; NoP; OAEL-1; OBD; OxBB; PoEL-1; RB; TFi; WeW

Unquiet Grave, The. *Unknown.* FaBoBa; OBET

Unquiet Grave, The. *Unknown.* EnSB

Unquiet Grave, The. *Unknown.* AmFP

Unquiet Ones, The. Stanley Kunitz. CAPP

Unreal Dwelling: My Years in Volcano, The. Garrett Kaoru Hongo. OpBo

Unreal silence, An. Swallows over the Camp. Uys Krige, *tr. fr. Afrikaans by the author and* Jack Cope. PeSA

Unreal Song of the Old, The. James Koller. PoM

Unreal tall as a myth. The Bear on the Delhi Road. Earle Birney. HeIP; MoCV; NoAM; NOBC; NoP; NYBP; PrIm

Unreal the Buffalo Is Standing. *Unknown.* GOA

Unrealities, The. Schiller, *tr. fr. German by* James Clarence Mangan. AWP

Unrecorded Speech. Anna Adams. BrRo

Unrelated Incidents., *sels.* Tom Leonard.

"This is thi." NBrP

Unrelenting Flood. William Matthews. Jaz

Unremarkable Year, The. Roy Fuller. OxBC

Unreproached, unforgiven; our feet heavy with life. (*LL*) Tending the Graves. Jennifer Strauss. NOBAu

Unrest. Richard Watson Dixon. OBNC

Unrestricted/unrestrained/uncomprimising. Freedom Hair. Raymond Washington. NBV

Unreturning, The. Wilfred Owen. MoBrPo

Unreturning, The. Clinton Scollard. PAH

Unreturning Spring, The. Laurence Binyon. NSI

Unreturning voyage, my friends to me, The. (*LL*) Godspeed. Whittier. Son

Unrhymed, unrhythmical, the chatter goes. At the Party. W. H. Auden. OxBSP

Unrighteous Lord of love, what law is this. Spenser. *Fr.* Amoretti. AAS; ESO, lacking epigrams I-IV; HeIL; NoP; OxBSP

Unroll the chill precision of moving feet. (*LL*) Death of Little Boys. Allen Tate. LiTA; MoAB

Unromantic Awakening, An. Priscilla Jane Thompson. CBWP-2

Unromantic Song. Anthony Brode. FiBHP

Unsagacious Animal, An. David Gascoyne. PeLV

Unsaid. A. R. Ammons. NOBA

Unsaid Word, An. Adrienne Rich. NMM

Unsatisfied. (*LL*) To the Tune "Red Embroidered Shoes." Huang O. PBWP; VBLP; WPC; WPOW

Unseals her earth, and lifts love in its shower. (*LL*) The Broken Tower. Hart Crane. AmPP; CMoP; LiTM; MeMAP; MoAB; MoAmPo; NoAM; NOBA; NoP; OxBA; Poetr; TrGrPo

Unseaworthy Ship, The. J. Smith. OxBSS

Unseemly as a marvellous and astral renegade. Queen Anne's Lace. June Jordan. TAP

Unseen. Fanny Crosby. TrPWD

Unseen Buds. Walt Whitman. ArNa

Unseen buds, infinite, hidden well. Unseen Buds. Walt Whitman. ArNa

Unseen Deer, An. John Tagliabue. Poetsp

Unseen deer through seen shadows leaps through my heart, An. An Unseen Deer. John Tagliabue. Poetsp

Unseen Fire. Ralph Nixon Currey. OBWP; OxBTC; PoWW

Unseen Playmate, The. Robert Louis Stevenson. OBF

Unseen, snow slides from over-laden boughs. Fire-Queen. Ruth Fainlight. PoA

Unseen Spirits. Nathaniel Parker Willis. See Shadows lay along Broadway, The.

Unsettled, a bird lost from the flock. T'ao Ch'ien, tr. by Wu-chi Liu. Fr. Drinking Wine. SuSp

Unsettled again and hearing Russian spoken. Hearing Russian Spoken. Donald Davie. GTBS-P

Unsettled Motorcyclist's Vision of His Death, The. Thom Gunn. PoA

Unsettled, unhappy, near the end of April. Lamentations of the Bronze Camels. Li Ho, tr. fr. Chinese by Irving Y. Lo. SuSp

Unsexed by the cold sea, prone out of it on the beach. Watch Hill. Winfield Townley Scott. ErPo

Unshoed the armchair. (LL) Battle of India and Europe. Aleksei Kruchenykh. CBNP

Unshrinking Faith. W. H. Balhurst. BLRP

Unshunnable is grief; we should not fear. Grief and God. Stephen Phillips. WGRP

Unsolicited Letters to Five Artists. Clive James. FaBoPa

Unspeakable. Margaret Avison. NOBC

Unspeakable! His Gift! (LL) Thanks Be to God. Janie Alford. PoToHe

Unspoken. Judith Ortiz Cofer. CrSp

Unspoken World. Helen Ruggieri. LoHo

Unstable dream [or dreame], accordyng [or according] to the place. The Lover Having Dreamed Enjoying of His Love, Complaineth That the Dreame Is Not either Longer or Truer. Sir Thomas Wyatt. AAS; SiPSBD

Unsubdued. Samuel Ellsworth Kiser. PoToHe

Unsung Heroes, The. Paul Laurence Dunbar. BPo

Until he comes in sight. (LL) The Ostrich is a Silly Bird. Mary E. Wilkins Freeman. FaPON; OBCA

Until he died. (LL) An Old Story. E. A. Robinson. AnAmPo; MoAmPo; OxBSP

Until I find the Holy Grail. (LL) Sir Galahad [or The Purple Heart]. Tennyson. OHCV

Until I lose my soul and lie. Sara Teasdale. TrPWD

Until I rest by thee. (LL) The Churchyard on the Sands. Lord De Tabley. CH, abr.; FaBoPP; GBL; OBNC

Until I Saw the Sea. Lilian Moore. NTCP; SiSoPo

Until I was in heaven! (LL) The Silent Girl. Joseph Freiherr von Eichendorff. RiWo

Until it comes to seem a boring hanger-on. (LL) As Much as You Can. C. P. Cavafy. RB

Until it is settled right. (LL) An Inspiration. Ella Wheeler Wilcox. AnAmPo; WGRP

Until Tatum passed. Standing on the Corner. Philip Levine. NNaP

Until that sun, which keeps. Trains Made of Stone. Ray A. Young Bear. CDW

Until the basket overflows with light. (LL) Song for the Sun That Disappeared behind the Rainclouds. Hottentot Oral Tradition. TTTS; TTY

Until the debt I owe for this is paid. (LL) Fear. Anna Hajnal. BoWoP

Until the desert knows. Emily Dickinson. NOBA

Until the destruction of language. (LL) Permanently. Kenneth Koch. CoAP; GoJo; NoP; PoA; PoM; PPP

Until the roof turn round. (LL) A Frolic. Robert Herrick. FaBoEE

Until they have made themselves warm, poor things! (LL) North wind doth blow, The. Mother Goose. OxNR; ReMoGo; SiSoPo

Until They Have Stopped. Sarah E. Wright. PoBA

Until thine hands clasp girdlewise the waist of the Belov'd. Sadi, tr. fr. Persian by R. A. Nicholson. AWP

Until we are pure spirit at the end. (LL) Infirmity. Theodore Roethke. CoAP; NAAL-2; NYBP

Until we cross the border into sleep. (LL) There you are. Jean-Joseph Rabéarivelo. NegPo

Until ye start, as if the sea-nymphs quired! (LL) On the Sea. Keats. EnRP; FF; LiTB; MeMBP; NoP; OAEL-2; TEP; TrGrPo

Until yesterday I was polite and peaceful. Opinions of the New Student. Regino Pedroso, tr. fr. Spanish by Langston Hughes. TTY

Until you burn again, burn again. (LL) On the Lord Mayor and Court of Aldermen, Presenting the Late King and Duke of York Each with a Copy of Their Freedoms. Andrew Marvell. CoMu; FaBoBa

Until you have looked at something so long. The Makings of Happiness. Ronald Wallace. PBCAP

Until your laughter. Tumult. Charles Enoch Wheeler. PoNe

Untill the grave increase our cold. (LL) Employment ("He that is weary, let him sit.") George Herbert. FaBoVe; GeHe; JCP; SeCP; TEP

Untimely Thought, An. Thomas Bailey Aldrich. PWR

Untitled. Franz Wright. LCAP

Untitled Poem. Alan Dugan. CAPP

Untitled Requiem for Tomorrow. Conyus. PoBA

Unto a heavenly course decreed. Star Morals. Friedrich Wilhelm Nietzsche, tr. fr. German by Ludwig Lewisohn. AWP

Unto Adam, His Own Scriveyn. Chaucer. See Adam scrivein [or scrivain], if ever it thee bifalle.

Unto all life of mine may die. (LL) The Flaming Heart. Richard Crashaw. LiTB; NAEL-1; OAEL-1, abr; PoEL-2; SeCV-1; TEP

Unto empty pockets. (LL) I Am Raftery [or Raferty]. Anthony Raftery. AWP, tr. by Douglas Hyde.

Unto God let praise be brought. And It Came to Pass at Midnight. Yannai, tr. fr. Hebrew. TrJP

Unto Jehovah Sing Will I. Henry Ainsworth. AH

Unto me hearken, O Elders, to me, aye, me shall ye listen. Unknown, tr. by R. Campbell Thompson. Fr. Epic of Gilgamesh, The. OBF

Unto my faith as to a spar, I bind. Adrift. Elizabeth Dickinson Dowden. WGRP

Unto my thinking, thou beheld'st all worth. To Dante Alighieri. Cavalcanti, tr. fr. Italian by Dante Gabriel Rossetti. AWP

Unto no body my woman saith she had rather a wife be. Catullus, tr. fr. Latin by Sir Philip Sidney. OBVE

Unto Our God Most High We Sing. John Vance Cheney. AH

Unto the blithe and lordly fellowship. Folgore da San Geminiano, tr. fr. Italian by Dante Gabriel Rossetti. Fr. Sonnets of the Months. AWP

Unto the Breach. A. Poliziano, tr. fr. Latin by John Addington Symonds. PeHV

Unto the deep the deep heart goes. The Place of Rest. "Æ." WGRP

Unto the gates of hell. The Song of Esechia. John Hall. ChIV-1

Unto the Person Kind there came. Mother Doorstep. Victor James Daley. NOBAu

Unto the silver night. Revelation. Sir Edmund Gosse. OBEV

Unto the Upright Praise, sels. Moses Hayyim Luzzatto, tr. fr. Hebrew by Nina Davis Salaman.
"All ye that handle harp and viol." TrJP

Unto this place when as the Elfin Knight. The Hill of the Graces. Spenser. Fr. Faerie Queene, The. NOBE

Unto this process briefly compiled. John Skelton. Fr. Magnificence. NoSic

Unto Thy Favor. Robert Tofte. Fr. Laura. Son

Unto Us a Child is Born. William Dunbar. See Rorate celi desuper.

Unto you, most froward, this letter I write. A Grotesque Love-Letter. Unknown. MeEL

Untold Truth about Hank, The. Charles Ghigna. NGP

Untold Want, The. Walt Whitman. MoAmPo

Untouched grandeur in the hinterlands. Life in the Boondocks. A. R. Ammons. HAP

Untrammelled giant of the West. The Parting of the Ways. Joseph B. Gilder. PAH

Untranslatable Factual Items. E. L. T. Mesens, tr. fr. French. CBNP

Unusual View of the Town, A. J. P. Ward. AngWe

Unutterable Beauty, The. G. A. Studdert-Kennedy. TrPWD

Unutterable void of Hell is stirred, The. The Lesbian Hell. Aleister Crowley. PeHV

Unuttered Prayer. Josephine D. Henderson Heard. CBWP-4

Unveiling. Hilary Sametz Lloyd. MDDM

Unwanted. Edward Field. GLP; Poetsp

Unwanted, The. Mary Gordon. IHMS

Unwanted and went out? (LL) Dear, Though the Night Is Gone. W. H. Auden. BoLoP; CBLP; InvP

Unwarmed by any sunset light. Whittier. Fr. Snow-bound; a Winter Idyl [or Idyll]. AiP; AmPP; GN; NOBA; OxBA; TAP; WiR

Unwatch'd [or unwatched], the garden bough shall sway. Tennyson. Fr. In Memoriam A. H. H. EBVV, abr.; ELP; FHYEP; GTBS-P; OAEL-2, abr.; OBNC; PeECV, abr.; PoEL-5; SCV
(Somersby, Lincolnshire; after Leaving the Refectory. FaBoPP
(Unwatched, the garden bough shall sway.) PeECV, sect. CI

Up to thy summit, Lewesdon, to the brow. William Crowe. *Fr.* Lewesdon Hill. NOEC

Up, Up, Home & Away. John Forbes. NOBAu

Up! up! let us a voyage take. The Northern Seas. *At.* to Mary Howitt, *and to* William Howitt. GN

Up! Up! my friend, and quit your books. The Tables Turned. Wordsworth. ArNa; EnRP; FHYEP; NAEL-2; OAEL-2; PlP; TOF

Up! Up! the time for sleep is past! The Expensive Wife. Judah ibn Sabbatai. *Fr.* Gift of Judah the Woman-Hater, The. TrJP

Up, Up! Ye Dames and Lasses Gay. Samuel Taylor Coleridge. BoTP

Up! Up! You brothers, now be strong. Song of the Cape of Good Hope. Christian David Schubart, *tr. fr. German by* Alfred Baskerville. NU, *ad. by* Robert Bly

Up where the world grows cold. A North Pole Story. Menella Bute Smedley. OxBChV

Up with me! up with me into the clouds! Wordsworth. *Fr.* To a Skylark. TTTS

Up yonder hill, behold how sadly slow. Thomas Parnell. *Fr.* Night Piece on Death. NOEC; OBD

Up yonder on the mountain. The Shepherd's Lament. Goethe, *tr. fr. German by* Bayard Taylor. AWP

Upanishads, The, *sels. Unknown, tr. fr. Hindi.*
  Brihadaranyaka Upanishad
    "Golden God, the Self, the immortal Swan, The." EnlH, (*vers. by* Stephen Mitchell)
  Mundaka Upanishad
    "Two birds, one of them mortal, the other immortal." EnlH, (*vers. by* Stephen Mitchell)

Upbraiding, An. Thomas Hardy. OPOP

Upended, it crouches on broken limbs. Charles Tomlinson. CMoP

Upgrade, past snow-tangled bramble, past. Sila. Robert Penn Warren. NoP

Uphill [*or* Up-Hill]. Christina Rossetti. BLPA; CH; CoGr; EBEvV; EBVV; FaBoBe; FaBoRV; HAP; InPK; MeMBP; NAEL-2; NALW; NOBE; NoP; NTP; OAEL-2; OBD; OBEV; OBNC; OtMeF; PoE; Poetr; PoRA; PPP; TFi; TrCP; TrGrPo; WeW; WGRP; WiR; WPE

Upland. A. R. Ammons. NOBA

Upland flocks grew starved and thinned, The. The Lambs of Grasmere, 1860. Christina Rossetti. FM

Upland shepherd, as reclined he lies. The Sea View. Charlotte Smith. ECWP

Upn the reedy bosom of the water. (*LL*) A Flight of Wild Ducks. Charles Harpur. NOBAu

Upon a bed of humble clay. Thomas Parnell. ECEV

Upon a Black Twist, Rounding the Arm of the Countess of Carlisle. Robert Herrick. CaPo

Upon a Braid of Hair in a Heart. Henry King. EnLoPo

Upon a Brook. Ku K'uang, *tr. fr. Chinese by* Irving Y. Lo. SuSp

Upon a Child. Robert Herrick. *See* Here a pretty baby lies.

Upon a Child That Died. Robert Herrick. BeJo; CaPo; CH; CoGr; InPK; NoP; OBEV; Poetr; SeCV-1

Upon a Christmas Morning. *Unknown.* AmFP

Upon A Cloke Lent Him, *sels.* Henry Vaughan.
  "Here, take again thy sackcloth! and thank heaven." AngWe

Upon a cock-horse to market I'll trot. *Unknown.* OxNR

Upon a dark ball spun in time. Giraffe and Tree. W. J. Turner. CH; GrPl

Upon a dark, light, gloomy, sunshine day. A Messe of Nonsense. *Unknown.* CBNP; NOSC

Upon a darksome night. St. John of the Cross, *tr. fr. Spanish by* E. Allison Peers. ErPo

Upon a day, came sorrow in to me. Sonnet: On the 9th of June 1290. Dante, *tr. fr. Italian by* Dante Gabriel Rossetti. AWP

Upon a Dead Man's Head. John Skelton. EnRePo; HAP; SCGP

Upon a Diamond Cut in Form[e] of a Heart . . . Sent in a New Year's [*or* New-yeares] Gift. Sir Robert Ayton. EIL

Upon a Dying Lady. W. B. Yeats. LiTB; UnPo

Upon a fibry fern-tree bough. Mid-Noon in January. "Fiona Macleod." *Fr.* Australian Transcripts. FM

Upon a Flie. Robert Herrick. FM

Upon a Fool. John Hoskyns. FaBoEE

Upon a Friend's Pet Cat, Being Sick. John Winstanley. OFC

Upon a Funeral. Sir John Beaumont. FaBoRV; NOSC

Upon a Girl of Seven Years Old. Pope. OxBSP

Upon a gloomy night. St John of the Cross: Songs of the Soul in Rapture. Roy Campbell. PeECV

Upon a grassie hillock He was laid. Giles Fletcher the Younger. *Fr.* Christ's Victory and Triumph. PeECV

Upon a Great Shower of Snow That Fell on May-Day, 1654. Thomas Washbourne. NOCV

Upon a House Shaken by the Land Agitation. W. B. Yeats. CMoP

Upon a lady my love is lente. *Unknown.* MiEL

Upon a lonely desert beach. The Haunted Beach. Mary Robinson. ECWP

Upon A. M. Sir John Suckling. ErPo

Upon a Maid. Robert Herrick. CaPo; ChTr; FaBoCh; FaBoEE; OxBoLi

Upon a Maid That Died [*or* Dyed] the Day She Was Married [*or* Marryed]. Meleager, *tr. fr. Greek by* Robert Herrick. AWP; OBD; OBVE

Upon a Mole in Celia's Bosom. Thomas Carew. BeJo; CaPo; CBLP

Upon a night an aungell bright. Now the Most High Is Born. James Ryman. MeEL

Upon a Notorious Shrew. *Unknown.* FaBoEE

Upon a Passing Bell. Thomas Washbourne. FaBoRV

Upon a Rare Voice. Owen Felltham [*or* Feltham]. NOSC

Upon a Ribband [*or* Ribbon]. Thomas Carew. BeJo; CaPo; NOSC; OAEL-1; PoE

Upon a Rich Country Gentleman. *Unknown.* FaBoEE

Upon a Ring of Bells. Bunyan. CH

Upon a Row of Old Books and Shoes in a Pawnbroker's Window. Suzanne Gardinier. CBAP

Upon a Sabbath-day it fell. The Eve of Saint Mark. Keats. CH; EnRP

Upon a sacrament. (*LL*) Light exists in spring, A. Emily Dickinson. BoWoP; EaPr; LiTA; NOBA; OxBA

Upon a Second Marriage. James Merrill. *See* Orchards, we linger here because.

Upon a simmer Sunday morn. The Holy Fair. Burns. EnRP; OBSV

Upon a Spider Catching a Fly. Edward Taylor. AmPP; EAP; MeMAP; NOBA; NoP; OxBA; PeECV; PoEL-3; SCAP; TAP

Upon a sudden, as I gazing stood. Rachel Speght. *Fr.* Dream, A. WPE

Upon a summer Sunday: sweet the sound. The Runaways. Mark Van Doren. PoRA

Upon a summer's time. A Pleasant New Court Song. *Unknown.* CoMu

Upon a time a neighing steed. The Council of Horses. John Gay. GN

Upon a tree there mounted guard. The Cock and the Fox. La Fontaine, *tr. fr. French by* Elizur Wright. AWP

Upon a tuffet of most soft and verdant moss. Little Miss Muffet. *Unknown.* BXAP; FaBoPa

Upon a Virgin Kissing a Rose. Robert Herrick. SeCP; SeCV-1

Upon a Wasp Chilled [*or* Child] with Cold. Edward Taylor. EAP; GGP; NAAL-1; NOBA; NOCV; PoEL-3

Upon a Young Mother of Many Children. Robert Herrick. CaPo

Upon Absence. Katherine Philips. PBWP

Upon an Ingenious Friend, Over-Vain. Thomas Fitzgerald. OxBSP

Upon an obscure night. The Obscure Night of the Soul. St. John of the Cross, *tr. by* Arthur Symons. AWP; OBMV

Upon an old estate from ancient sires descended. The Portraits. Anna Maria Lenngren, *tr. fr. Swedish by* C. W. Stork. WPOW

Upon ane day as I did mourne full soir. Ane Godlie Dreame. Elizabeth Melvill, Lady Culross. KTR

Upon Apennine Slope. Arthur Hugh Clough. *See* Yet to the wondrous St. Peter's, and yet to the solemn Rotonda.

Upon Appleton House, to My Lord Fairfax. Andrew Marvell. SeCP; SeCV-1
  Sels.
  After Floods on the Wharfe. FaBoPP
  "And now to the abyss I pass." OAEL-1
  Carrying Their Coracles. ChTr
  "From that blest bed the hero came." JCP
  Garden of Appleton House, The. "When in the east the morning ray". NOBE
  Hewel, or Woodpecker, The. ChTr
  Kingfisher, The. ChTr
  "Oh thou, that dear and happy isle." OxBoLi
  "See how the flowers, as at parade." TrGrPo
  (Garden, A.) OBEV
  "Then, to conclude these pleasant acts." CBNP
  To My Lord Fairfax. NOSC

Upon Batt. Robert Herrick. FaBoEE

Upon Ben Johnson [*or* Jonson]. Edmund Waller. BeJo; EPCY; NOSC; SeCV-1

Upon Ben Jonson. Robert Herrick. BeJo; CaPo; FaBoEE; NoP; SeCV-1

Upon Bishop Andrewes's [*or* Andrewes His] Picture before His Sermons. Richard Crashaw. NOSC

Upon Boys Diverting Themselves in the River. Thomas Foxton. OxBChV

Upon Bunce: Epigram. Robert Herrick. CaPo

Upon Castara's Absence. William Habington. *Fr.* Castara. BeJo

Upon Castara's Departure. William Habington. NOSC

Upon Christ His Birth. Sir John Suckling. NOSC

Upon Christ's Nativity or Christmas. Rowland Watkyns. OBWVE

Upon the Curtain of Lucasta's Picture It Was Thus Wrought. Richard Lovelace. CaPo

Upon the Day of Our Saviour's Nativity. Francis Quarles. NOSC

Upon the Death of Sir Albert [or us] Morton's Wife. Sir Henry Wotton. BoLoP; CoGr; EnLoPo; FaBoEE; GGP; NoP; OBD; OBEV; OxBM; SeCP; TrGrPo; WeW

Upon the Death of G. B. John Cotton. SCAP

Upon the Death of Her Husband. Elizabeth Rowe. ECWP

Upon the Death of His Much Esteemed Friend Mr. Jno Saffin Junr. Grindall Rawson. SCAP

Upon the Death of His Sparrow; an Elegie. Robert Herrick. FM

Upon the Death of Mr. King Drowned in the Irish Seas. John Cleveland. *See* I like not tears in tune, nor will [or do] I prize.

Upon the Death of My Ever Desired Friend Doctor Donne Dean of Pauls. Henry King. SeCP

Upon the Death of the Lord Hastings. Dryden. SeCV-2

Upon the Decease of Mrs. Anne Griffin. John Fiske. SCAP

Upon the earth there are so many treasures. Earth Felicities, Heavens Allowances. Richard Steere. SCAP

Upon the Eastern shore of Windermere. On Windermere; Bowness Bay and Belle Isle. Wordsworth. *Fr.* Prelude [or, Growth of a Poet's Mind], The. CH; EnRP; FaBoPP; GN; HAP; NOBE; NoP; NU; OAEL-2; OBNC; OxAEP-2; PoE; SCV

Upon the ecstatic diving board the diver. Lone Bather. A. M. Klein. HeIP

Upon the eighteenth day of June. Bonny John Seton. *Unknown.* ESPB

Upon the Ensigns of Christ's Crucifying. William Alabaster. NoSic

Upon the eyes, the lips, the feet. Extreme Unction. Ernest Dowson. MoBrPo; OAEL-2; OBMV; PeECV; PeVV

Upon the fantastic garden. Night. Ada Negri, *tr. fr. Italian by* Philip L. Miller. RiWo

Upon the fifth day of November. On Mr. Pricke. *Unknown.* FaBoEE

Upon the future life we build. Timothy Thomas Fortune. *Fr.* Dreams of Life. AAP

Upon the gale she stooped her side. The Gallant Ship. Sir Walter Scott. BoTP

Upon the grass. Noontide. H. Cordelia Ray. *Fr.* Idyl. CBWP-3

Upon the grass no longer hangs the dew. Hay making. Joanna Baillie. OxAEP-2

Upon the Grave of a Beggar. Timothy Kendall. NoSic

Upon the Heavenly Scarp. A. M. Klein. *Fr.* Psalter of Avram Haktani, The. PoA

Upon the Hill before Centreville. George Henry Boker. PAH

Upon the hill my lover stands. The House o' the Mirror. Helen Adam. MAT; NMM

Upon the hill there is a yellow house. *Unknown.* RoPo

Upon the Holy Sepulchre. Richard Crashaw. FaBoEE

Upon the Horse and His Rider. Bunyan. OxBChV

Upon the house a crooked sign. For Sale or Rent. *Unknown.* PoToHe

Upon the Image of Death. Robert Southwell. CH; EIL; NOBE Sels.
"Before my face the picture hangs." NoSic; OBD

Upon the Infant Martyrs. Richard Crashaw. GeHe; NoP; OAEL-1

Upon the King's Return from Flanders. Henry Hall. APAS

Upon the King's Return from Flanders, 1695. Henry Hall. *See* Rejoice you sots, your idol's come again.

Upon the King's Voyage to Chatham to Make Bulwarks against the Dutch. *Unknown.* APAS

Upon the Lark and the Fowler. Bunyan. CH

Upon the level field behold. Baseball. Frank Dempster Sherman. OBCA

Upon the Lines and Life of the Famous Scenic Poet, Master William Shakespeare. Hugh Holland. OBWVE

Upon the Loss of His Little Finger. Thomas Randolph. BeJo; NOSC

Upon the Loss of His Mistresses. Robert Herrick. BeJo; CaPo; NAEL-1; NOSC; PoE; SeCV-1

Upon the man who's buried here. J. E. Thorold Rogers. FaBoEE

Upon the Most Useful Knowledge, Craft or Cunning, Which Is More Wisdom, as 'Tis Less Wit. William Wycherley. SeCV-2

Upon the mountain's edge with light touch resting. A Sunset. Samuel Taylor Coleridge. OxBSP

Upon the mounts of spices. (*LL*) The British [or Brittish] Church. Henry Vaughan. ESCV; PeECV

Upon the Much Lamented Death of the Right Honourable, the Lady Elizabeth Langham. Bathsua Pell Makin. KTR

Upon the Much-to Be Lamented Decease of the Reverend Mr. John Cotton. John Fiske. SCAP

Upon the New Building at Appleton. Thomas Fairfax, Baron Fairfax. NOSC

Upon the Nipples of Julia's Breast. Robert Herrick. CaPo; ErPo; NAEL-1; NOSC; PeLV

Upon the [or a] Snail. Bunyan. ChTr; OxBSP

Upon the patch of earth that clings. Public Aid for Niagara Falls. Morris Bishop. NBLV

Upon the Poet of His Time, Ben Jonson: His Honoured Friend and Father. James Howell. NOSC

Upon the Priory Grove, His Usual Retirement. Henry Vaughan. BeJo; FaBoPP

Upon the Professor we'll waste not a glance. To an Astronomer. Anne Lynch Botta. AmWP

Upon the Same (Detractor). Robert Herrick. CaPo

Upon the Sand. Ella Wheeler Wilcox. AnAmPo

Upon the Saying That My Verses Were Made by Another. Anne Killigrew. KTR; NALW; WPE

Upon the shells by Carribea's wave. Albery Allson Whitman. *Fr.* Twasinta's Seminoles; Or Rape of Florida. AAP

Upon the slippery tops of humane state. Seneca. *See* Stand [or Stond] who so list upon the slipper top [or toppe].

Upon the soft brown pillow of thy shore. Apostrophe to the Parret. E. H. Burrington. FaBoPP

Upon the Springs Issuing out from the Foot of Plimouth Beach. Samuel Sewall. SCAP

Upon the street they lie. The Children. William Soutar. PAW

Upon the Sudden Restraint of the Earl[e] of Somerset, Then Falling from Favor [or Favour]. Sir Henry Wotton. ELP; FaBoEH; JCP; NOBE; NoP; NOSC; SeCP

Upon the Swallow. Bunyan. OxBChV

Upon the threshold of the year we stand. The New Year. Homera Homer-Dixon. BLRP

Upon the Times. Mildmay Fane, 2d Earl of Westmorland. BeJo

Upon the Tomb of the Most Reverend Mr. John Cotton. Benjamin Woodbridge. SCAP

Upon the topmost branches dies. Doubt. Fernand Gregh, *tr. fr. French by* Ludwig Lewisohn. WGRP

Upon the Translation of the Psalms by Sir Philip Sidney, and the countess of Pembroke His Sister. John Donne. EPCY

Upon the tree of time. A Harvest to Seduce. Melville Cane. NYBP

Upon the Troublesome Time. Robert Herrick. CaPo

Upon the utmost corners of the warld. In Orknay. William Fowler. OxBS; ScCV

Upon the Weathercock. Bunyan. OxBChV

Upon the work of Walter Landor. Walter Savage Landor. Dorothy Parker. *Fr.* Pig's-Eye View of Literature, A. NALW

Upon the Works of Ben Jonson, *sels.* John Oldham.
"Plain Humour, shown with her whole various face." EPCY

Upon thee many a benison. (*LL*) Crutches. Robert Herrick. CaPo

Upon their quivering wings. (*LL*) Fairyland. Poe. NAAL-1

Upon this leafy bush. The Linnet. Walter de la Mare. LiTB

Upon this marble bust that is not I. To Inez Milholland. Edna St. Vincent Millay. AiP; NALW; WPE

Upon this place the great Gustavus died. On Gustavus Adolphus, King of Sweden. Sir Thomas Roe. FaBoEE

Upon this primrose hill. The Primrose, Being at Montgomery Castle, upon the Hill, on Which It Is Situate. John Donne. FaBoPP; GBL

Upon This Rock. Ruthven Todd. PoA

Upon thy tender limbs! and so good night. (*LL*) To One Married to an Old Man. Edmund Waller. FaBoEE; OxBSP; SeCP

Upon Time. Robert Herrick. BeJo

Upon Umber: Epigram. Robert Herrick. CaPo

Upon Venus Putting on Mars His Armes. Richard Crashaw. SeCP

Upon Visiting His Lady by Moonlight. "A. W." CTC

Upon Wedlock and Death of Children. Edward Taylor. AmPP; EAP; NAAL-1; NoP

Upon Westminster Bridge. Wordsworth. *See* Earth has not anything to show more fair.

Upon ye Sight of My Abortive Birth. Mary Carey. KTR

Upon Your Leaving. Etheridge Knight. NNaP

Upon your sunken cheek a hectic stain! Moriturus. "Marie Madelaine," *tr. fr. French by* Ferdinand E. Kappey. PeHV

Upone Tabacco. Sir Robert Ayton. OxBS

Upper Broadway. Adrienne Rich. HCAP; InPS

Upper Canadian, The. James Reaney. NOBC

Upper Chamber, An. Frances Bannerman. OBEV

Upper chamber in a darkened house, An. Frederick Goddard Tuckerman. *Fr.* Sonnets. NOBA; NoP; TAP

Upper Family. Maxwell Bodenheim. OBAL

Upper Lambourne. Sir John Betjeman. FaBoTw

Upper Skies, The. Robert Bridges. BoTP

Upper slopes are busy with the cricket, The. Elegy on the Dust. Thom Gunn. NoAM

Uppon a Deedmans Hed. John Skelton. *See* Your ugly token.

Uppon the First Sight of New England, June 29, 1638. Thomas Tillam. GOA; SCAP

Uprear their motionless statuary. (*LL*) The Rider Victory. Edwin Muir. CMoP; LiTM

Upright and glorious. Do So. Denise Riley. NBrP

Uprightness. Camouflaged Troop-Ship. Amy Lowell. AiP

Uprooted tree leaves, An. Group Photo from Pretoria Local on the Occasion of a Fourth Anniversary (Never Taken). Jeremy Cronin. PeSAV

Uprose the King of Men with speed. The Descent of Odin. Thomas Gray. OxAEP-1

Upside Down. Aileen Fisher. OTCP

Upside-Down World, The. Hamish Hendry. BoTP

Upstairs, a man is writing a screenplay about assassins. Goodbye. Vickie Karp. UTF

Upstairs Child. Harry Clifton. IB

Upstairs Downstairs. Hervey Allen. PoA; PoNe

Upstairs on the third floor. Bottled [New York]. Helene Johnson. BlSi; CDC; PoBA; ShDr

Upstood upstaffed passing sinuously away over an airy arch. Christophe. Russell Atkins. PoNe

Upstream. Carl Sandburg. MoAB; MoAmPo

Uptown. Allen Ginsberg. FF; TwCP

Uptown New Orleans, 1940. Touching the Past. Robert Sargent. Jaz

Uptown on Lenox Avenue. Prime. Langston Hughes. PoBA

Upward, and rarefy the air. (*LL*) The Snail. Richard Lovelace. BeJo; CaPo; OAEL-1

Upward in motion with wet wind. (*LL*) Wales Visitation. Allen Ginsberg. CAPP; NNaP; NOBA; NYBP; Prf; VCAP

Upward through crystal in a kümmel bottle. Dreamscape in Kümmel. Harold Witt. NYBP

Ur ol' Hyar lib in ur house on de hill. Ol' Doc' Hyar. James Edwin Campbell. AAP

Urania. Robert Andrews. NOEC

Urania. Mary Sidney Wroth, Countess of Montgomery. WPE
Sels.
  "All night I weep, all day I cry, ay me." NOSC
  "Be you all pleased? Your pleasures grieve me not." NOSC
  "Come, darkest night, becoming sorrow best." NOSC
  Duke's Song, The
  "Fie, tedious hope, why do you still rebel?" NOSC
  "How fast thou fliest, O time, on love's swift wings." NOSC
  "How like a fire doth love increase in me." NOSC
  "Like to the Indians, scorched with the sun." NOSC
  Lindamira's Complaint
  Love Leave to Urge. Son
  Morea's Sonnet
  "My pain, still smothered in my grieved breast." NOSC
  "Oh me, the time is come to part." NOSC
  "Oh strive not still to heap didain on me." NOSC
  Pamphilia to Amphilanthus
    "After long trouble in a taedious way." KTR
    "Am I thus conquered? Have I lost the powers" NAEL-1
    (Sonnet "Am I thus conquered? Have I lost the powers." NOSC
    "False hope which feeds but to destroy, and spill" NAEL-1
    "Faulce hope which feeds butt to destroy, and spill" KTR
    "Fly hence O! joy noe longer heere abide" KTR
    "Griefe, killing griefe: have nott my torments binn" KTR
    "I, that ame of all most crost" KTR
    "Late in the Forest I did Cupid see" KTR
    "Love a child is ever criing [*or* crying]" KTR; NOSC
    "You blessed shades, which give mee silent rest" KTR
  Pamphilia's Sonnet
  Verses of the Talkative Knight, The
  When Night's Black Mantle. Son

Urania, or Spiritual Poems, *sels.* William Drummond of Hawthornden.
  "Astrea in this time." NOSC
  Too Long I Followed. Son
  "Triumphing chariots, statues, crowns of bay." NOSC

Urania takes her morning flight. The Adventurous Muse. Isaac Watts. NOEC

Urania: The Divine Muse. On the Death of John Dryden, Esq. Lady Sarah Piers. KTR

Uranium, with which we know. What It Could Be. Denise Levertov. WoWa

Uranne. Mary Weston Fordham. CBWP-2

Urban. Oliver Davies. AngWe

Urban Convalescence, An. James Merrill. CoAP; NAAL-2; NOBA

Urban Dream. Victor Hernandez Cruz. NBV

Urban Experience: Part One, The. Lew Blockcolski. VoR

Urban Experience: Part Two, The. Lew Blockcolski. VoR

Urban Guerrilla, An. Allen Curnow. *Fr.* Moro Assassinato. PeNZ

Urban Love Songs. Wing Tek Lum. OpBo

Urban, or Sylvan, or whatever name. The Passive Participle's Petition. John Byrom. ECEV

Urban Pollution. John Armstrong. *Fr.* Art of Preserving Health, The. ECEV; NOEC

Urban Progress. John Dyer. *See* Thus all is here in motion, all is life.

Urban Renewal, Baltimore. David Bergman. NGP

Urbane man, composed, aware, An. Like Father. Herbert Williams. AngWe

Urceus Exit. Austin Dobson. *Fr.* Rose-Leaves. OBEV

Urchin saw a rose — a dear. Rosebud in the Heather. Goethe, *tr. fr. German by* John Frederick Nims. STV

Urchin's Dance, The. *At. to* John Lyly *and to* Thomas Ravenscroft. *See* By the Moon ("By the moon we sport and play.")

Urgency. Sarah E. Wright. PoNe

Urgent Letter, An. Hugh Maxton. PBCIP

Urging Her of a Promise. Ben Jonson. *Fr.* Celebration of Charis in Ten Lyric[k] Peeces [*or* pieces], A. BeJo; OxAEP-1; SeCP

Uriel. Emerson. LiTA; NAAL-1; NOBA; OxBA

Uriel, *sels.* William Force Stead.
  "I thought the night without a sound was falling." TrPWD
  (How Infinite Are Thy Ways.) OBMV

Uriel to his charge/ Returned on that bright beam. Milton. *Fr.* Paradise Lost. EPCY
(Now Came Still Evening On. FaBoRV

Urn I: Silent for Twenty-five Years, the Father of My Mother Advises Me, *sels.* Walter Lew.

Urn Burial. Ted Hughes. EBEV

Urn for Burial, An. Unknown, *tr. fr. Tamil by* A. K. Ramanujan. PLW

Urn/ that my aunt carried through Brazil. Wandering. Carlos Drummond de Andrade, *tr. fr. Portuguese by* Mark Strand. AnRep

Urns and Odours Bring Away! John Fletcher *and* William Shakespeare. *Fr.* Two Noble Kinsmen, The. ElL

Ursula. David Ray. VGW

Uru-tu-sendo's Song. Unknown, *tr. fr. Tewa Indian by* H. J. Spinden. WTO

Urumbula Song, The. Unknown, *tr. fr. Aranda by* T. G. H. Strehlow. CBAP

Us. Julius Lester. PoBA

Us. Anne Sexton. CAPP

U.S. Army Holds Dance for Camp Survivors. Germany 1945. Lisa Ress. BTR

Us can matter. (*LL*) Valentine. Donald Hall. GrPl; NTCP

Us from fleas. (*LL*) Dover to Munich. Charles Stuart Calverley. NOBL, *abr.*; OBTV

Us men to overreach. (*LL*) A Woman's Looks. *Unknown*. TrGrPo

Us raunsound on the rude. (*LL*) Ballad of Our Lady. William Dunbar.

Us the grace to labour for. (*LL*) Things, good Lord, that we pray for, give, The. Sir Thomas More. EaPr

Us Two. Nina Cassian, *tr. fr. Romanian by* Nina Cassian. PoSu

Us Two. A. A. Milne. OxBChV

Use all your hidden forces. Do not miss. Attainment. Ella Wheeler Wilcox. WGRP

Use maketh maistry [*or* mast'ry], this hath been said alway. Of Use. John Heywood. FaBoEE

Use the muscle/ in yr heart. (*LL*) Young Soul. Amiri Baraka. BPo

Use, then, my lust for whisky and for thee. The Light of Life. "Hugh MacDiarmid." CMoP

Use three physicians still [*or* physicians' skill] : first Doctor Quiet. Health Counsel. Sir John Harington. FaBoUs

Use words to describe feelings? 4/13/79. Lewis Warsh. UL

Used. Rita Dove. NAmP90

Used to hang and brush their bosoms? — I feel chilly and grown old. (*LL*) A Toccata of Galuppi's. Robert Browning. EBVV; EBVVPR; EnVR; FaBoVe; FaPoB; GTBS-P; HAP; LiTB; Mes; NAEL-2; NOBE; NOBVV; NoP; OAEL-2; OtMeF; TEP; UV

Used to long nights, springtime is past. In Remembrance of the Forgotten. Lu Hsun, *tr. fr. Chinese by* William R. Schultz. SuSp

Useful for Avoiding Collisions at Sea. *Unknown*. FaBoUs

Useless Day. Rosario Castellanos, *tr. by* Maureen Ahern. WPOW

Useless except to a collector, a rich man. (*LL*) Behaviour of Fish in an Egyptian Tea Garden. Keith Douglas. FaBoMo; OBTV; RB

Useless, they lingered on the edge of fat. The Social Realists. Brian Higgins. IHNG
Uselessness. Ella Wheeler Wilcox. TrPWD
Uses of Ocean, The. Sir Owen Seaman. FiBHP
Uses of Poetry. Lawrence Ferlinghetti. PoBeRe
Uses of Poetry. Winfield Townley Scott. PoA
Ushers in a drearier day. (*LL*) Fall, Leaves, Fall. Emily Brontë. ArNa; CH; ELP; FaBoCh; FaBoRV; FaBV; OxBSP; PoEL-5; TrGrPo
Using carbon-based ink. The Gardener's Preface. Allen Fisher. NBrP
Usk. T. S. Eliot. *Fr.* Landscapes. FaBoCh; NOCV; PeECV; RB
Usk, The. C. H. Sisson. NOCV
Usquebaugh. Wendy Cope. UV
Usual exquisite boredom of patrols, The. Hugh Popham. OxBTC
Usual Immigrant Uncle Poem, The. Askold Melnyczuk. UTF
Usufruct. Austin Clarke. IPY
Usurpers, The. Edwin Muir. CMoP
Ut, re, mi, fa, sol, la. *Unknown.* FaBoNo
Utah. Anne Stevenson. FaBoVe
Utah Iron Horse, The. *Unknown.* AmFP
Utamaro Variations. Andrew Crozier. VaA
Ute Mountain. Charles Tomlinson. RB
Utilitarian View of the *Monitor's* Fight, A. Herman Melville. AmPP; NAAL-1; UnPo
Utmost grace the Greeks could show, The. Grecian Kindness. The Earl of Rochester. OxBSP
Utopia. Jewel C. Latimore. BPo
Utopia Anglicized. W. S. Gilbert. *Fr.* Utopia Limited. OBSV
Utopia Limited, *sels.* W. S. Gilbert.
    Utopia Anglicized. OBSV
Utopia TV Store. Maxine Chernoff. UL
Utter moorland, high, and wide, and flat, An. The Fork of the Road. William Renton. NOBVV
Utter Passion Uttered Utterly, An. John Todhunter. BXAP
Utter Zoo Alphabet, The. Edward Gorey. CBNP
Utterance: any continuous stretch. You Must Change Your Life. Ken Edwards. NBrP
Uttering cries that are almost human. (*LL*) American Poetry. Louis Simpson. CAPP; MoP; NoAM; NOBA; TAP
Uuuuuuuuuu. Dope. Amiri Baraka. BCF
Uvavnuk. *Unknown, tr. fr. Eskimo by* Knud Rasmussen. NU

V

Five. Tony Harrison. PWE
V. B. Nimble, V. B. Quick ("V. B. Wigglesworth wakes at noon.") John Updike. NYBP
V-Day. Phyllis McGinley. ArOW
V. Innocentia Veritas Viat Fides Circumdederunt Me Inimici Mei. Sir Thomas Wyatt. AAS
V. Innocentia/ Veritas Viat Fides/ Circumdederunt me inimici mei. Sir Thomas Wyatt. *See* Who lyst his welthe and eas retayne.
V-J Day. John Ciardi. ArOW
V-Letter. Karl Shapiro. NoAM; TrJP
V. N. and C. I, The. Maggie Pogue Johnson. CBWP-4
V-Winged and Hoary. Henri Cole. UTF
Vacancy in the Park. Wallace Stevens. ArNa; LCAP; SAmP
Vacancy in which, apparently, A. All is Emptiness, and I Must Spin. Thomas Kinsella. PBCIP
Vacant Cage, The. Charles Tennyson Turner. FM
Vacant Lot, The. Gwendolyn Brooks. NAAL-2; NoAM; NOBA
Vacant Lot. Dudley Randall. NoAM
Vacant shuttles/ Weave the wind. I have no ghosts. T. S. Eliot. *Fr.* Gerontion. UV
Vacation. William Stafford. Poetsp
Vacation. Nixon Waterman. *See* It seems to me I'd like to go.
Vacation is over. Leavetaking. Eve Merriam. PDV
Vacation Time. Frank Hutt. BoTP
Vacations. Lyn Lifshin. NGP
Vacillation. (Between extremities.) W. B. Yeats. NoAM
    Sels.
    "Must we part, Von Hügel, though much alike." OBMV
    "My fiftieth year had come and gone." RaBo
Vacuum, The. Howard Nemerov. NIP; RB
Vacuum cleaner held over my head, A. In a Dream. David Ignatow. PoA
Vadoga, my middle-aged brother. The Dying Chair. Randolph Stow. FaBoMA

Vagabond. John Masefield. OtMeF
Vagabond, The. Robert Louis Stevenson. OxAEP-2
Vagabond, A. James Tate. NoAM
Vagabond House. Don Blanding. BLPA
Vagabond Love. William Plomer. IHNG
Vagabond Song, A. Bliss Carman. AnAmPo; FaPON; GN
Vagabondia. Richard Hovey. AnAmPo
Vagabonds. Langston Hughes. SAmP
Vagabonds. "Marie Madelaine," *tr. fr. German by* Ferdinand E. Kappey. PeHV
Vagabonds, The. John Townsend Trowbridge. AnAmPo; BeLS; BLPA
Vague Apprehension. Lin Ling, *tr. fr. Chinese by* Kenneth Rexroth *and* Ling Chung. WPC
Vague Lyric by G. M. Max Beerbohm. FaBoEE
Vague sea thuds against the marble cliffs, The. Time. Robert Graves. LiTM
Vaguely I hear the purple roar of the torn-down Third Avenue El. You Are Gorgeous and I'm Coming. Frank O'Hara. NeAP; SM
Vaices That Be Gone, The. William Barnes. NOBVV
Vain Advice at the Year's End. James Wright. NYBP
Vain and Careless. Robert Graves. NTP
Vain and not to trust. Woman. Irving Layton. ErPo
Vain are those joys that erring man provides. The World Not Our Rest. Maria Frances Cecelia Cowper. ECWP
Vain Britons, boast no longer with proud indignity. War and Washington. Jonathan Mitchell Sewall. PAH
Vain Cat, The. Ambrose Bierce. SoCa
Vain excess of flattering fortune's gifts, The. George Gascoigne. *Fr.* Gascoigne's Memories. EnRePo
Vain, frail, short liv'd, and miserable Man. A Song of Emptiness to Fill up the Empty Pages Following. Michael Wigglesworth. SCAP
Vain Hope, Adieu. John Attey. EnRePo
Vain Hope, adieu! thou life-consuming moth. Vain Hope, Adieu. John Attey. EnRePo
Vain is the chiming of forgotten bells. Poets. Joyce Kilmer. WGRP
Vain old Professor of Greek, A. Ron Rubin. PeLi
Vain Questioning. Walter de la Mare. OtMeF
Vain World Adieu. *Unknown.* AmFP
Vainly mourns for them that play. (*LL*) Anacreontic, on Parting with a Little Child. Samuel Wesley. NOEC
Vainly my heart had with thy sorceries striven: To ———. Sarah Helen Whitman. AmWP
Vainly ("Vainly/the epistles burn.") Nelly Sachs, *tr. fr. German by* Michael Roloff. NYBP
Vala, Night the Ninth Being the Last Judgment. Blake. *Fr.* Vala; or The Four Zoas. OAEL-2
Vala; or The Four Zoas, *sels.* Blake.
    Enion Replies from the Caverns of the Grave. OBNC
    Enitharmon Revives with Los. OBNC
    (Enitharmon's Song.) ChTr
    Lamentation of Enion, The. OBNC
    Night VIII (The Eternal Man). PoE
    Price of Experience, The. EnRP; Prf
    (Night II (Enion's Lament).) PoE
    Song of Enitharmon. OAEL-2
    Vala, Night the Ninth Being the Last Judgment. OAEL-2
Vale from Carthage. Peter Viereck. ArOW; LiTM; MoAmPo
Vale of Tears, A. Robert Southwell. NoSic
Vale there is enwrapped with dreadful shades, A. A Vale of Tears. Robert Southwell. NoSic
Valediction. Sir Robert Ayton. NOSC
Valediction, A. Ernest Dowson. BoLoP
Valediction, A: Forbidding Mourning. John Donne. BLPL; CBLP; EnRePo; ESCV; FaPoB; FF; FHYEP; HAP; HeIP; HoPM; ImPo; InPS; JCP; LiTB; MeLP; NAEL-1; NOBE; NoP; NOSC; OAEL-1; PoE; PoEL-2; Poetr; PPP; PrIm; SCGP; SeCP; SeCV-1; SoSe; TEP; TFi; UnPo; WeW
Valediction: "Before the seas again divide." Walter Adolphe Roberts. PBCV
Valediction: "Bid me not go where neither suns nor showers [show'rs]." William Cartwright. BeJo
Valediction: "Their verdure dare not show." Louis MacNeice. PeIV
Valediction: Forbidding Mourning, A, *sels.* John Donne.
    "Our two soules therefore, which are one." UV
Valediction Forbidding Mourning, A. Adrienne Rich. NAAL-2; NoAM; NoP
Valediction (Liverpool Docks), A. John Masefield. OBMV
Valediction: Of My Name in the Window, A. John Donne. EnRePo

Verses Made the Night before He Died. Michael Drayton. *See* So well I love thee, as without thee I.

Verses Made the Night before He Died [*or* Dyed]. Sir Walter Ralegh. *See* Even such is time, that takes in trust.

Verses, my love! As soon could I. On the Author's Husband Desiring Her to Write Some Verses. Mary Whateley. ECWP

Verses Occasioned by the Sudden Drying Up of St. Patrick's Well, *sels.* Swift.
"Wretched Ierne! with what grief I see." OBSV

Verses of the Talkative Knight, The. Mary Sidney Wroth, Countess of Montgomery. *Fr.* Urania. WPE

Verses on a Cat. Shelley. OFC; SoCa

Verses on Blenheim. Martial, *tr. fr. Latin by* Swift. AWP

Verses on Daniel Good. *Unknown.* CoMu; OxBB

Verses on Games, *sels.* Kipling.
Boxing. OtMeF

Verses on Hearing That an Airy and Pleasant Situation, near a Populous and Commercial Town, Was Surrounded with New Buildings. Maria Logan. ECWP

Verses on Sir Joshua Reynolds's Painted Window at New College, Oxford. Thomas Warton the Younger. NOEC; PoEL-3

Verses on the Death of Doctor Swift [D.S.P.D., Occasioned by Reading a Maxim in Rochefoucauld], *sels.* Swift.
"Behold the fatal day arrive!" PeLV; SCV
"Doctors tender of their fame, The." NOBL
"Here shift the scene, to represent." OBD
"My female friends, whose tender hearts." NOBL
"Now Curll his shop from rubbish drains." PeLV
"Perhaps I may allow, the Dean." EPCY; NOBE; PeLV
"Suppose me dead; and then suppose." NOBE; NOEC; OxBoLi, *abr.;* PeLV; PoEL-3; TEP
"Time is not remote when I, The." EBEV; Mes; NOBE; NOBL; NOIV; PeLV
(On the Death of Dean Swift.) OxAEP-1

Verses on the Death of Dr. Swift, D.S.P.D., Occasioned by Reading a Maxim in Rochefoucauld. Swift. NOEC; OBF, *abr.;* PoEL-3; TEP

Verses Put into a Lady's Prayer-Book. The Earl of Rochester. *See* Fling this useless book away.

Verses Said to Be Written on the Union. Swift. APAS

Verses Supposed to Be Written by Alexander Selkirk during His Solitary Abode on the Island of Juan Fernandez. William Cowper. EBEvV; NOEC; PoEL-3; PoLF

Verses to a Lady, on Her Saying She Preferred Commonalty to an Irish Peerage, *sels.* Lady Sophia Burrell.
"Clock strikes five — the watchman goes, The." ECWP

Verses to Be Repeated by an Attorney Leaving His Lodging to Wait upon Judges Riding the Circuits from One County to Another, Least He Forget Some Necessary Thing. John Willis. FaBoUs

Verses to Chekhia, 1938. Marina Tsvetayeva, *tr. fr. Russian by* Daniela Gioseffi *with* Sophia Buzevska. WoWa

Verses to Miss ———. J. Wilde. NOEC

Verses to Mr. Richardson on his History of Sir Charles Grandison. Anna Williams. ECWP

Verses to my Heart's-Sister. H. Cordelia Ray. AAP; CBWP-3

Verses Written at Montauban in France, 1750. Joseph Warton. ECEV; OBTV

Verses Written at The Hague. Anno 1696. Matthew Prior. OBTV

Verses Written by Mrs. Hutchinson. Lucy Hutchinson. KTR; NOSC

Verses Written during the War, 1756–1763, *sels. At. to* Thomas Osbert Mordaunt.
Sound, Sound the Clarion. EBEV; FaBoEE; FaPoR; NOBE
(Call, The.) OBEV
(One Crowded Hour.) TrGrPo
(To a Lady on Reading Sherlock "Upon Death.") NOEC

Verses Written in 1872. Robert Louis Stevenson. BLPA; BLPL

Verses Written in a Garden. Lady Mary Wortley Montagu. ECWP

Verses Written in a Lady's Sherlock "Upon Death." Earl of Chesterfield. EBEV

Verses Written in a London Churchyard. Christopher Smart. CBNP

Verses Written in the Chiosk [of the British Palace], at Pera, Overlooking [the City of] Constantinople. Lady Mary Wortley Montagu. ECEV; ECWP; OBTV

Verses Written on a Pane of Glass, on the Occasion of a National Thanksgiving for a Naval Victory. Burns. IHNG

Verses Written on Her Death-bed at Bath to Her Husband in London. Mary Monck. ECWP

Verses Written the Night before His Execution. Sir Walter Ralegh. *See* Even such is time, that takes in trust.

Verses Written upon Windows. Swift. IHNG

Version. Dennis Scott. PBCV

Versions. Robert Kelly. *Fr.* Book of Persephone, The. PoM

Versions of Love. Roy Fuller. CBLP; LiTM

Versos de Montalgo. *Unknown, tr. by* Frank J. Dobie. AS

Vertigo is my territory. Eagle. Robin Skelton. NOBC

Vertue. George Herbert. *See* Sweet day, so cool, so calm, so bright.

Very acme of my woe, The. Little Son. Georgia Douglas Johnson. CDC

Very apt question struck me, A. Sydney Bernard Smith. PeLi

Very bitter weeping that ye made, The. Dante, *tr. fr. Italian by* Dante Gabriel Rossetti. *Fr.* Vita Nuova, La. AWP

Very day one son was drowned, The. Honestus, *tr. fr. Greek by* Robin Skelton. GrAn

Very Early. Karla Kuskin. PDV

Very Fair My Lot. Jacob David Kamzon, *tr. fr. Hebrew by* Sholom J. Kahn. TrJP

Very few can. The Pecan, The Toucan. Robert Williams Wood. NBLV

Very fine conga of sweat, A. I See Chano Pozo. Jayne Cortez. ETG

Very fine is my valentine. A Very Valentine. Gertrude Stein. ArLo

Very first joy that Mary had, The. The Joys of Mary. *Unknown.* AmFP

Very fownder and begynner of owr fyrst creacyon, The. *Unknown. Fr.* Mankind. OxBLMV

Very friendly, A/ prison. Tripart. Gayl Jones. BlSi

Very grandiloquent goat, A. The Grandiloquent Goat. Carolyn Wells. MoShBr

Very handsome gentleman, A. *Unknown, tr. fr. Chinese by* Arthur Waley. *Fr.* Shih Ching. BoWoP

Very Heroical Epistle in Answer to Ephelia, A. The Earl of Rochester. APAS

Very language of the poem, The. (*LL*) Midnight Elegy. Léopold Sédar Senghor. NegPo

Very like a Whale. Ogden Nash. BLPL; HAP; InPK; InPS; PoLF; TrGrPo

Very Minor Poet Speaks, A. Isabel Valle. BLPA

Very Nearly. Queenie Scott-Hopper. FaPON

Very Odd Fish, A. D'Arcy Wentworth Thompson. OxBChV

Very often when you are striving. The Would-be Critic. Mrs. Henry Linden. CBWP-4

Very Old, The. Ted Kooser. PBCAP

Very old are forever, The. The Very Old. Ted Kooser. PBCAP

Very old are the woods. All That's Past. Walter de la Mare. ArNa; GoJo; MoAB; NOBE; OAEL-2; OBMV; OtMeF; OxBTC; TrGrPo

Very Old Man. James Henry. NOBVV

Very Old Woman, A. Clayton Eshleman. MAT

Very pitiful lady, very young, A. Dante, *tr. fr. Italian by* Dante Gabriel Rossetti. *Fr.* Vita Nuova, La. AWP; CTC, *shorter sel.*

Very Pretty Maid of This Town, and the Amorous 'Squire Not One Hundred Miles from the Place, The. *Unknown.* CoMu

Very Sad Conversation at Night, A. Anna Swirszczynska, *tr. fr. Polish by* Czeslaw Milosz *and* Leonard Nathan. PoSu

Very Shocking Poem Found among the Papers of an Eminent Victorian Divine, A. Gavin Ewart. FaBoBl

Very Simply Topping Up the Brake Fluid. Simon Armitage. PWE

Very small chickens in tattered feathers. The. A Study in Aesthetics. Robert Peters. BXAP

Very small children in patched clothing, The. The Study in Aesthetics. Ezra Pound. CMoP; NOBA; NoP

Very soon the Yankee teachers. Learning to Read. Frances E. W. Harper. AAP; BlSi; NALW

Very True, the Linnets Sing. Walter Savage Landor. TrGrPo

Very Valentine, A. Gertrude Stein. ArLo

Vesi, the black one, the leaper who sprang. Praises of the King Dingana (Vesi). *Unknown, tr. fr. Zulu.* PeSA

Vesperal. Ernest Dowson. OBMV

Vespers. W. H. Auden. *Fr.* Horae Canonicae. FaBoMo

Vespers. Thomas Edward Brown. BoTP

Vespers, *sels.* A. A. Milne.
"Hush! Hush! Whisper who dares!" UV

Vespers. A. A. Milne. OxBChV

Vespers. Silas Weir Mitchell. WGRP

Vespers. Odell Shepard. TrPWD

Vesta. Whittier. TrPWD

Vestal, The. Nathalia Crane. TrJP

Vestal, The. Pope. *Fr.* Eloisa to Abelard. NAEL-1; PoEL-3; TEP

Vestal Lady on Brattle, The. Gregory Corso. Poetr

Vestal Virgin, The. Eloise Bibb. CBWP-4

Vestal Virgin, The, *sels.* John Plummer Derwent Llwyd.

Vesta's Father. Julia Kasdorf. PBCAP

Vestigia. Bliss Carman. WGRP

Vet. Lincoln Kirstein. ArOW

Veteran, The. Frank S. Brown. NSI

Veteran, The. Edward Field. PFL

Veteran, The. Margaret Isabel Postgate. NSI

Veteran. Lola Ridge. WPE

Veteran Greeks came home, The. Return, The ("The veteran Greeks came home.") Edwin Muir. CMoP
  (Return of the Greeks, The. NoP; PoE

Veteran Sirens. E. A. Robinson. NOBA

Veteran smiled and let us pass through, A. Thomas Kinsella. *Fr.* Technical Supplement, A. BiHa

Veterans. George Johnston. NOBC

Veterans, The. Donagh MacDonagh. CIP

Vet's Rehabilitation. Ray Durem. PoBA

Vetus Flamma. Robert Mezey. PoA

Vex no man's secret soul — if that can be. Help. Sadi, *tr.* by Sir Edwin Arnold. *Fr.* Gulistan, The. AWP

Vex th'ill-natur'd fools we cannot please. (*LL*) To Nysus. Sir Charles Sedley. FaBoEE; OBSV

Vexation of mind. Hi De Buckras Hi! Grace Nichols. AIW

Via Margutta. Maria Luisa Spaziani, *tr. fr. Italian* by Beverly Allen. NeIt

Via, Veritas, et Vita. Alice Meynell. WGRP

Viable. A. R. Ammons. TAP

Viaticum. Birago Diop, *tr. fr. French* by Ellen Conroy Kennedy. NegPo

Viaticum. Pao Yu, *tr. fr. Chinese* by Kenneth Rexroth. OHMPC

Viaticum. Tchicaya U Tam'si, *tr. fr. French* by Ellen Conroy Kennedy. NegPo

Vibrant naive Naabeeho women. Modern on the Surface. Nia Francisco. HATNAP

Vibration in the summer air. (*LL*) Midsummer. James Scully. NYBP; TwCP

Vicar, The. George Crabbe. *Fr.* Borough, The. OBSV

Vicar, The. Winthrop Mackworth Praed. *Fr.* Every-Day Characters. EnRP; GGP; OBEV; OBNC; OxAEP-2; PoEL-4

Vicar of Bray, The. *Unknown.* FaBoPV; GBP; GGP; NOBE; NOBL; OBSV; OxBoLi

Vicar of Wakefield, The, *sels.* Goldsmith.
  Elegy on the Death of a Mad Dog, An. BeLS; BLPA; CoGr; FaBoBe; FaBoCh; FaBoCo; GN; NBLV; NOEC; NOIV; OBNV; OxAEP-1; TEP; TFi
  (On the Death of a Mad Dog.) NTP
  "When lovely woman stoops to folly." CoGr; GTBS; GTBS-P; HAP; NoP; PrIm; UnPo
  (Song: "When lovely woman stoops to folly.") AWP; BoLoP; EBEvV; FHYEP; NOBE; NOEC; OxAEP-1; TrGrPo
  (Stanzas: On Woman.) ELP; PeIV
  (When Lovely Woman Stoops to Folly.) SCGP; TFi
  (Woman.) ImPo; LiTB; OBEV

Vicarious Atonement. Richard Aldington. MoBrPo; WGRP

Vice. Anthony Hecht. OBAL

Vice most obscene and unsavoury, A. *Unknown.* NOBL; PeLV

Vice now may lift aloft her speckled head. Spoken Extempore on the Death of Mr. Pope. *Unknown.* NOEC

Vice-regal walls dominate the back street. Gym. Richard Murphy. BiHa

Vicente. Antonia Quintana Pigno. AfAz

Vice's Song, The. John Pickering. *Fr.* Horestes. NoSic

Vicious Circle. Marsha Prescod. VBLP

Vicious winter finally yields, The. W. D. Snodgrass. *Fr.* Heart's Needle. SM

Vicissitudes of the Creator. Archibald MacLeish. MeMAP

Vicissitudes of the world, O Olaad, are like the clouds of the seasons, The. To a Dictatorial Sultan. *Somali Oral Tradition*, *tr.* by B. W. Andrzejewski. WTO

Vickery's Mountain. E. A. Robinson. MoAmPo

Vicksburg. Paul Hamilton Hayne. PAH

Victim, The. Ellen Bryant Voigt. CrSp

Victim of Himself. Marvin Bell. BAP-90

Victims, The. Sharon Olds. InPS; SoSe

Victims of the Latest Dance Craze. Cornelius Eady. UTF

Victims of the Little Box, The. Vasco [or Vasko] Popa, *tr. fr. Serbo-Croatian* by Charles Simic. AnRep; HSix

Victor, The. C. W. Longenecker. PWR

Victor Dog, The. James Merrill. NoAM; NoP

Victor Galbraith. Longfellow. PAH

Victor is he who can go it alone!, The. (*LL*) The Game of Life. John Godfrey Saxe. BLPA; BLPL

Victor of Antietam, The. Herman Melville. PAH

Victor or vanquished, thou the slave of friend or foe. (*LL*) Italy. Vincenzo da Filicaia. AWP

Victor Vanquished, The. Richard Howard. BAP-90

Victoria Market. Francis Brabazon. NOBAu

Victoria Markets Recollected in Tranquility, The. "Furnley Maurice." NOBAu

Victoria Markets Recollected in Tranquillity, The, *sels.* Suzanne Gardinier.

Victoria said: "We've no quarrel." Frank Richards. PeLi

Victoria Station. Luigi Fontanella, *tr. fr. Italian by* Michael Palma. NeIt

Victoria was bitterly short. Cyril Mountjoy. PeLi

Victorian gent said: "This dance," A. Frank Richards. PeLi

Victorian Grandmother. Margo Lockwood. Poetsp

Victorian Guitar. Seamus Heaney. FaBoBl

Victorian Hangman Tells His Love, A. Bruce Dawe. NoAM

Victorian Idyll, A. David Wagoner. NoAM

Victorian Paraphrase, A. Horace. *See* Boy, I have their empty shouts.

Victorian Song. John Farrar. GoYe

Victorian Trains, *sels.* Patricia Beer.
  "Whistle blows, The train moves, The." FaBoEH

Victories of Love, The, *sels.* Coventry Patmore.
  Lonely Cloud of Care, The. FaBoRV
  Music of Forefended Spheres, The. FaBoRV
  "Your love lacks joy, your letter says." GBL
  (Rain That Fell upon the Height, The.) FaBoRV

Victorious beauty, though your eyes. To the Countesse of Salisbury. Aurelian Townshend. SeCP
  (Loves Victory. MeLP

Victorious knights without reproach or fear. To the Returning Brave. Robert Underwood Johnson. PAH

Victorious Men of Earth. James Shirley. *Fr.* Cupid and Death. TrGrPo

Victors, The. Denise Levertov. NoP

Victors, The. Anthony McNeill. PBCV

Victory. Lionel Johnson. NOBVV

Victory, The. Anne Stevenson. VBLP

Victory. *Unknown.* CoMu; WGRP

Victory. *Unknown. See* I am a youthful lady, my troubles they are great.

Victory and praise in their own right belong. (*LL*) Hymn of Apollo. Shelley. EnRP; OAEL-2

Victory Calypso, Lord's 1950. Egbert Moore, ("Lord Beginner.") PeLV

Victory comes. The New Victory. Margaret Widdemer. WGRP

Victory comes late. Emily Dickinson. InPK

Victory Dance, A. Alfred Noyes. NSI; PoLF

Victory Drive, near Fort Benning, Georgia. Bin Ramke. MT

Victory in Defeat. Edwin Markham. BLPL; PoLF

Victory on the Last Green. Thomas Mathison. *Fr.* Goff; an Heroi-comical Poem, The. NOEC

Victory-Wreck, The. Will M. Carleton. PAH

Vida. Judith Ortiz Cofer. AfAz

Video Cuisine. Maxine W. Kumin. NoAM

Vield Path, The. William Barnes. NOBVV

Vienna. Peter Porter. OBTV

Viennese Remembrance. Christine McNeill. NWP

Vierge Ouvrante. Miriam Palmer. NMM

Vierzide Chairs, The. William Barnes. NOBVV

Viet Minh. Tran Thi Nga *and* Wendy Wilder Larsen. WoWa

Vietnam. Clarence Major. PoBA

Vietnam #4. Clarence Major. FF; NBV; PoBA

Vietnamese Fisherman on Tampa Bay, The. Peter Meinke. NGP

Vieux Carré. Walter Adolphe Roberts. PoNe

View, The. Howard Nemerov. NYBP

View, A. Beverly Quint. NYBP

View, A. Mona Van Duyn. VCAP

View, all ye eyes above, this sight which flings. Edward Taylor. *Fr.* Preparatory Meditations Before My Approach to the Lord's Supper. NOSC

View from a Cab, The. Henry Taylor. NBLV

View from an Apartment. Michael Palmer. UL

View from an Attic Window, The. Howard Nemerov. CoAP

View from Here, The. William Stafford. RFM

View from Middle-Earth, A, *mod. vers. by* Naomi Lewis. William Langland. *Fr.* Vision of Piers Plowman, The. Mes

View from the Cliffs. Tu Mu, *tr. fr. Chinese by* Kenneth Rexroth. OHMPC

View from the Ghetto, A. Helen Degan Cohen. BTR

View from the Gorge. Ben Belitt. NYBP

View From the Ming Tombs, The. Pien Chih-lin, *tr. fr. Chinese.* *Fr.* Poems Written at the Construction Site of the Ming Tombs Dam. LHF, *tr. by* Hualing Nieh

View from the Window. Christine McNeill. NWP

Virtues of the cane must now be sung, The. Nathaniel Weekes. *Fr.* Barbados. PBCV

Virtuoso, A. Austin Dobson. PeVV

Virtuous Wife, The. Süsskind von Trimberg, *tr. fr. Middle High German.* TrJP

Virtuous Woman, The. Bible, *O.T. See* Who can find a virtuous woman? for her price is far above rubies.

Virus. Christine McNeill. NWP

Viruses, when the lens is right. First Photos of Flu Virus. Harold Witt. SM

Visage becomes armed, The: within. Armed Vision. N. P. van Wyk Louw, *tr. fr. Afrikaans by* Jack Cope *and* Uys Krige. PeSA

Viscount Demos. William Kean Seymour. IHNG

Viscount Stansgate, or Wedgwood, or Benn. Tim Hopkins. PeLi

Viscous air, wheres' ere she fly, The. The Kingfisher. Andrew Marvell. *Fr.* Upon Appleton House, to My Lord Fairfax. ChTr; SeCP; SeCV-1

Visibility. Maura Stanton. VBLP

Visibility Zero. John Ciardi. ArOW

Visible Baby, The. Peter Redgrove. NAs

Visible, invisible. A Jellyfish. Marianne Moore. OxBSP

Visibly here the tide. Wellfleet Harbor. Paul Goodman. CoAP

Vision. Delmira Augustini, *tr. fr. Spanish by* Marti Moody. WPOW

Vision, The. Burns. OxBS

Vision, The. Daniel Defoe. APAS

Vision. James Devaney. NOBAu

Vision. Richard Eberhart. NYBP

Vision. Elizabeth N. Hauer. PoToHe

Vision, The. Robert Herrick. CaPo; ErPo; JCP; SCGP; SeCP

Vision. Louis Johnson. PeNZ

Vision, The. Egan O'Rahilly, *tr. fr. Irish by* Thomas Kinsella. NOIV

Vision. Francis Reginald. MoCV

Vision, The. William Taylor. NOEC

Vision, The. Katharine Tynan. NSI

Vision. Israel Zangwill. TrJP

Vision V. William Browne. *See* Rose, as fair as ever saw the north, A.

Vision, A. John Clare. ChTr; EBVV; FaBoRV; GTBS-P; NAEL-2; NOBVV; NTP; OAEL-2; OBNC; OPOP; PoE; PPP

Vision, A. Lord Herbert of Cherbury. SeCP

Vision, A. Hugo von Hofmannsthal, *tr. fr. German by* Charles Wharton Stork. TrJP

Vision, A. Maria Konopnicka, *tr. fr. Polish by* Jerzy Peterkiewicz *and* Burns Singer. WPOW

Vision, A, *sels.* W. B. Yeats.
   All Souls' Night. OxAEP-2

Vision and Prayer. Dylan Thomas. LiTM

Vision as of crowded city streets, A. Shakespeare. Longfellow. AWP

Vision at Knock. Gerry Murphy. BiHa

Vision by Sweetwater. John Crowe Ransom. CMoP; FaBoMo; MeMAP; MoAB; NOBA; OxBA; RB

Vision Clear, The. J. M. Westrup. BoTP

Vision from the Ghetto. Raymond Washington. NBV

Vision in long filaments flows. Vision. Francis Reginald. MoCV

Vision of Beasts, A. John Heath-Stubbs. ChIV-1

Vision of Beauty. Ben Jonson. *See* It Was a Beauty That I Saw.

Vision of Belshazzar, The. Byron. GN

Vision of Beulah, The ("There is a place where contrarieties are equally true.") Blake. *Fr.* Milton. OAEL-2

Vision of Beulah, The ("Thou hearest the nightingale begin the song of spring.") Blake. *See* Thou hearest the nightingale begin the song of spring.

Vision of Children, A. Thomas Ashe. EBVV

Vision of Christ that thou dost see, The. Blake. *Fr.* Everlasting Gospel, The. ChIV-2

Vision of Connaught in the Thirteenth Century, A. James Clarence Mangan. NOIV; PeIV

Vision of Delight, The. Ben Jonson. PoEL-2

Vision of Delight Presented at Court in Christmas, 1617, The. Ben Jonson. SeCV-1

Vision of Eve, The. H. Cordelia Ray. CBWP-3

Vision of Judgement, A, *sels.* Robert Southey.
   Absolvers, The. EnRP
   Southey Looks out of the Window at Greta Hill. FaBoPP

Vision of Judgment, The. Byron. EnRP; OAEL-2; TEP
   Sels.
   "At length with jostling, elbowing, and the aid." OBSV
   "He said — I only give the heads — he said." EPCY
   "Saint Peter sat by the celestial gate." FHYEP; OBSV; OxBoLi

   (Vision of Judgment, The.) OxAEP-2

Vision of Judgment, The. Byron. *See* Saint Peter sat by the celestial gate.

Vision of Sir Launfal, The, *sels.* James Russell Lowell.
   Brook in Winter, The. GN
   Day in June, A ("And what is so rare as a day in June?"). FaPON
   "For a cap and bells our lives we pay."
   (June Weather.) GN
   "For Christ's sweet sake, I beg an alms." WGRP
   Not Only around Our Infancy. ImPo
   "Over his keys the musing organist." LiTA
   Sir Launfal and the Leper. GN
   What [*or* And what] Is So Rare as a Day in June? BLPL; FaBoBe; FaPON; ImGa
   (Day in June, A ("And what is so fair as a day in June?").) FaPON
   (June ("What is so rare as a day in June?").) FaBV
   Winter Morning, A. GN

Vision of Lazarus, The, *sels.* Fenton Johnson.

Vision of MacConglinne, The. MacConglinne, *tr. fr. Middle Irish.* BIrV, *tr. by* John Montagu; CH, *tr. by* Kuno Meyer; FaBoNo, *tr. by* Kuno Meyer.

Vision of Moonlight, A. H. Cordelia Ray. CBWP-3

Vision of Nature, A. William Langland. *See* And I bowed [*or* ich bowede] my body and beheld all about [*or* bihelde al aboute].

Vision of Piers Plowman, The, *sels.* William Langland.
   Age of Reason, The. NOCV
   "And I bowed [*or* ich bowede] my body and beheld all about [*or* bihelde al aboute]." CTC
   (Vision of Nature, A.) PoEL-1
   "Barones an burgeises and bondemen als." FaBoVe
   Civil Service, The. NOCV
   Descent into Hell, The. PoEL-1
   Entertainment Industry, The. NOCV
   "Envy with heavy heart asked for shrift." NAEL-1
   Et Incarnatus Est. NOBE, Passus II (C *text*)
   Glutton [*or* Glutton in the Tavern], The. PoE
   God's Mercy. NOCV
   Good Works. NOCV
   "In a summer [*or* somer] season, when soft[e] was the sun [*or* sunne *or* sonne]"
   (Field Full of Folk, The.) PoE
   (Field of Folk, The.) PoEL-1
   (In a summer season when the sun was mild.) NAEL-1
   (On Malverne Hilles, the Place of Piers Plowman's Vision.) FaBoPP
   (Prologue: "In a summer season, when soft was the sun," *mod. by* J. B. Trapp (B *text*).) EBVV; OAEL-1
   (Prologue, The: "In a summer season when the sun was mild," *mod. by* E. T. Donaldson.) NAEL-1
   Incarnation, The. OBEV
   (Incarnation, The.) PoEL-1
   Poor, The. PoEL-1
   (Poor, The.) FaBoEH
   Prologue. FaBoPV
   Saint Called "Truth," A. NOCV
   View from Middle-Earth, A. Mes
   "What for feere of this ferly and of the false Jewes." EBEV
   "What this mountain means, and the murky dale." OAEL-1
   "Wolleward and wete-shoed went I forth after." EnVB, *Passus XVIII*
   "Wool-chafed and wet-shoed I went forth after." NAEL-1
   "Yet I courbed on my knees and cried hire of grace." EBEV

Vision of Piers Plowman, Prologue, The, *sels.* William Langland.
   "Barones and burgieses and bandemen als." FaBoVe
   "Rectors and parish priests complained to the bishop." FaBoPV

Vision of Rotterdam. Gregory Corso. PoBeRe

Vision of Sin, The. (I had a vision when the night was late.) Tennyson. EBVVPR; OAEL-2
   Sels.
   Song at the Ruin'd Inn. PoEL-5

Vision of Sunday in Heaven, A. Victor James Daley. ChIV-2

Vision of the Day of Judgment. Bible, *O.T. Fr.* Isaiah. WGRP

Vision of the Graces, The. Spenser. *Fr.* Faerie Queene, The. NoSic

Vision of the Lamentation of Beulah, A. Blake. *See* Thou hearest the nightingale begin the song of spring.

Vision of the Mermaids, A, *sels.* Gerard Manley Hopkins.
   "Rowing, I reach'd a rock — the sea was low." ChTr

Vision of the Night, The. Philip Freneau. EAP

Vision of the world burgeons at its head, The. (*LL*) Midnight. Jacob Fichman. MHP

Vision of the World's Instability, A. Richard Verstegan. ElL

Vision of Truth, A. J. C. Squire. NOBL

Vision that appeared to me, A [*or* The]. The Vision of MacConglinne. MacConglinne, *tr. fr. Middle Irish.* BIrV, *tr. by* John Montagu; CH, *tr. by* Kuno Meyer; FaBoNo, *tr. by* Kuno Meyer.

"Where icy and bright dungeons lift." HAP; MoAB; MoAmPo; UnPo

Voyages of Captain Cock, The. William Jay Smith. ErPo

Voyeur. John Edward Hardy. ErPo

Voyeur's Dream. Barney Bush. HATNAP

Voyvodina. Ivan Gadjanski, *tr. fr. Serbo-Croatian* by Charles Simic. HSix

Vrindaban. Octavio Paz, *tr. fr. Spanish* by Lysander Kemp. AnRep

Vuillard: "The Mother and Sister of the Artist." W. D. Snodgrass. CoAP

Vulcan, contrive me such a cup. Upon Drinking in a Bowl. The Earl of Rochester. OxBoLi; SeCV-2
(Bowl, The.) OxAEP-1

Vulcan's Song. John Lyly. *Fr.* Sapho and Phao. EBEV; EIL

Vulgar Error, A. J. E. Thorold Rogers. FaBoEE

Vulgar of manner, overfed. Owed to New York. Byron Rufus Newton. BLPA; NBLV

Vulgar race of men, like herds that graze, The. Sage Philosophy. Richard Jago. *Fr.* Edge-Hill; or, The Rural Prospect Delineated and Moralised. ECEV

Vulnerary, A. Jonathan Williams. PoM

Vulture, The. Samuel Beckett. *Fr.* Echo's Bones. NoAM

Vulture, The. Hilaire Belloc. OxBChV

Vulture. Robinson Jeffers. NAAL-2; NoAM; NOBA; NoP

Vulture. Douglas Livingstone. OBAP

Vulture. Kenneth Rexroth. *Fr.* Bestiary, A. NNaP; OBAL

Vulture and the Husbandman, The. Arthur Clement Hilton. FaBoCo

Vulture eats between his meals, The. The Vulture. Hilaire Belloc. OxBChV

Vultures. Margaret Atwood. LCAP

Vultures, The. David Diop, *tr. fr. French* by Ulli Beier. PBA; TTY

Vultures waft circles. Remnant Ghosts at Dawn. Oliver La Grone. NBV

Vusumzi's Song. L. T. Manyase, *tr. fr. Xhosa* by C. M. Mcanyangwa *and* Jack Cope. PeSA

W

W. W. James Reeves. ChTr; NTCP; SiSoPo

W. H. Louise Imogen Guiney. AmWP

W. H. *Eheu!* Samuel Taylor Coleridge. FaBoEE

W. L. M. K. F. R. Scott. NOBC

Sir W. Ralegh, on the Snuff of a Candle the Night Before He Died. Sir Walter Ralegh. *See* Cowards fear to die, but courage stout.

W. resteth here, that quick could never rest. The Earl of Surrey. SiPSBD

W. S. Landor. Marianne Moore. OBAL

W. W. Amiri Baraka. HeIL; HeIP; NOBA; PoBA

Waäit till our Sally cooms in, fur thou mun a' sights to tell. The Northern Cobbler. Tennyson. EBEV

Wad be my queen, wad be my queen. (*LL*) O Wert Thou in the Cauld Blast. Burns. FaBoVe; OxAEP-2

Wad be my queen, wad be my queen. (*LL*) O [*or* Oh], Wert Thou in the Cauld Blast. Burns. EBEV; ELP; EnRP; HAP; NOBE; NoP; OxBS; ScCV; SCGP; TrGrPo

Wadasa Nakamoon, Vietnam Memorial. Ray A. Young Bear. HATNAP

Wade in the Water. Robert Adamson. FaBoMA

Wade/ through black jade. The Fish. Marianne Moore. AmPP; FaBoWP; MeMAP; MoAB; MoAmPo; MoP; NAAL-2; NoAM; OxBA; Poetr

Waement the deid. Coronach. Alexander Scott. OxBS

Waes-hael for [the] knight and [the] dame! King Arthur's Waes-hael. Robert Stephen Hawker. OBEV

Wae's me, wae's me. Cauld Lad of Hilton, The *or* The Wandering Spectre. *Unknown.* CoGr; OxBoLi
(Cauld Lad's Song, The.) ChTr
(Ghost's Song, The.) FaBoCh
(Song of the Cauld Lad of Hylton.) GBP
(Wandering Spectre, The.) CH

Wafer; thin and hard and bitter pill I. To His Book. Leon Stokesbury. Poetr; SM

Wafting your Charge to soft Parthenope! (*LL*) On the Departure of Sir Walter Scott from Abbotsford, for Naples. Wordsworth. EBEV; EnRP

Wafts of old incense mixed with Cuban coffee. Dance Lessons of the Thirties. Donald Justice. BAP-89

Wag a leg, wag a leg. *Unknown.* OxNR

Wag ballock wag. *Unknown.* FaBoVe

Wages of sin is death. These words run, The. AIDS, Among Other Things. Peter Kocan. ChIV-2

Wagging their tails behind them. (*LL*) Little Bo-Peep has lost her sheep. Mother Goose. FaBoBe; OxNR; ReMoGo

Waggon-Maker, The. John Masefield. EBEV

Waggoner, The. *Unknown.* GBP

Wagner. Rupert Brooke. FaBoTw; NOBL; PeLV

Wagon Full of Thunder. Louis Oliver. HATNAP

Wagon-Whip. (*LL*) A Song of the Wagon-whip. Samuel Cron Cronwright. PeSAV

Wagoner of the Alleghanies, The, *sels.* Thomas Buchanan Read.
Rising, The. PAH
Valley Forge. PAH

Wagoner's Lad, The. *Unknown.* AmFP

Wagtail and Baby. Thomas Hardy. PeLV

Wah and dry. Airing Linen. Henry Taylor. GoJo

Wahiawa is still. Leaving. Cathy Song. NoAM

Waif, The. Walter de la Mare. FaBoNo

Waifs. Vivian Virtue. PBCV

Waiheke 1972 — Rocky Bay. Christina Beer. PeNZ

Waikato-Taniwha-Rau. Vincent O'Sullivan. PeNZ

Waikiki. Rupert Brooke. OBTV

Wail, for the world's wrong. (*LL*) Rough wind, that moanest loud. Shelley. ChTr; EnRP; NAEL-2; NOBE; PoRA; SCGP; TEP; TrGrPo; WiR

Wail of Archy, The. Don Marquis. *Fr.* Archy and Mehitabel. FiBHP

Wail of Prometheus Bound, The. Aeschylus, *tr. fr. Greek* by Elizabeth Barrett Browning. *Fr.* Prometheus Bound. WGRP

Wail of the Divorced. Mary E. Tucker. AmWP; CBWP-1

Wail of the Waiter, The. Marcus Clarke. NOBAu

Wail, wail, Ah for Adonis! Lament for Adonis. Bion, *tr. fr. Greek* by John Addington Symonds. AWP
(I weep for Adonis, "The lovely Adonis is dead.") HePo, *tr.* by Barbara Hughes Fowler

Waile whit ase whalles bon, A. The White Beauty. *Unknown.* MeEL

Wailing of a clarinet, The. Strange Fruit. Cyrus Cassells. Jaz

Wailing, wailing, wailing, the wind over land and sea. Rizpah. Tennyson. PeVV; PoEL-5

Wailing wind doth not enough despair, The. Awake. Mary Elizabeth Coleridge. OBNC

Wailings of a maiden I recite, The. Wednesday; or, The Dumps. John Gay. *Fr.* Shepherd's Week, The. OAEL-1

Waillie, waillie! *Unknown. See* When cockle shells turn silver bells.

Wain upon the northern steep, The. Astronomy. A. E. Housman. OBWP

Waist thin as the purslane creeper. Peace Poem. Maturai Velacan, *tr. fr. Tamil* by A. K. Ramanujan. PLW

Wait. Timothy Steele. PoA

Wait a Little! *Unknown.* NOCV

Wait a little longer. (*LL*) The Good Time Coming. Charles Mackey. VPP

Wait for Me. Robert Creeley. NOBA; PPP

Wait for the Wagon. *At. to* R. Bishop Buckley. PAH

Wait for the Wagon. *Unknown.* PAH

Wait here, and I'll be back, though the hours divide. Three Star Final. Conrad Aiken. OxBA

Wait, Kate! You skate at such a rate. To Kate, Skating Better than Her Date. David Daiches. FiBHP; NYBP

Wait Mister. Which way is home? Music Swims Back to Me. Anne Sexton. VCAP

Wait; the great horned owls. Owls. W. D. Snodgrass. Poetsp

Wait till the darkness is deep. Wallāda, *tr. fr. Arabic* by James Monroe *and* Deirdre Lashgari. WPOW

Waitekauri Every Time! Edwin Edwards. PeNZ

Waiter, Please. *Unknown. See* Epicure, Dining at Crewe, An.

Waiting. John Burroughs. AnAmPo; BLPA; FaBoBe; WGRP

Waiting. Jane Cooper. CrSp; TAP

Waiting. Hilary Corke. ErPo

Waiting. Robert Creeley. VGW

Waiting. John Freeman. CH

Waiting. W. E. Henley. *Fr.* In Hospital. NAEL-2; NOBVV

Waiting. Arthur Nortje. HBAPE

Waiting. Robert Pack. GOYP

Waiting. James Reeves. OTCP

Waiting, The. Whittier. WGRP

Waiting. William Carlos Williams. SAmP

Waiting. Yevgeny Yevtushenko, *tr. fr. Russian* by Robin Milner-Gulland *and* Peter Levi. UnAS

Waiting Both. Thomas Hardy. MoAB; MoBrPo; OxBoLi; TTTS

Waiting by your door. (*LL*) Evening Rendezvous. Cheng Min. WPC

Waiting For Breakfast, While She Brushed Her Hair. Philip Larkin. NoAM

Waiting for Death. Mordecai Gebirtig, *tr. fr. Yiddish* by Joseph Leftwich. TrJP

Waiting for Fidel. John Agard. PBCV

Waiting for Godot, *sels.* Samuel Beckett.
Vladimir's Song. CBNP

Waiting for Icarus. Muriel Rukeyser. LCAP; NNaP

Waiting for Robinson. Roberta Hill Whiteman. HATNAP

Waiting for the Barbarians. C. P. Cavafy, *tr. fr. Greek by* Edmund Keeley
and Philip Sherrard.

Waiting for the Bus. D. J. Enright. OxBTC

Waiting for the Dawning. *Unknown.* BLRP

Waiting for the Doctor. Colette Inez. IHMS

Waiting for the Emperor Tenji. Princess Nukada, *tr. fr. Japanese.* PBWP,
tr. by Cid Corman *and* Susumu Kamaike.

Waiting for the end, boys, waiting for the end. Just a Smack at Auden.
William Empson. FaBoCo; LiTM; MoBrPo; PeLV; UnPo; UV

Waiting for the flesh that dies. *(LL)* The Bull. Ralph Hodgson. LiTM;
MoAB; MoBrPo; NSI, *abr.*; OBMV; OxBTC

Waiting for the Post. Dorothy Auchterlonie. CBAP

Waiting for the Storm. Gerald Mangan. PWE

Waiting for the subway, bad station, no one near me, the. The Underlife.
Sharon Olds. FoLa

Waiting for Truth. Susan Griffin. GLP

Waiting for weeks till the last one is ready to run, they. Turtles Hatching.
Mark O'Connor. NOBAu

Waiting for when the sun an hour or less. In Santa Maria del Popolo.
Thom Gunn. CMoP; FaBoMo; GTBS-P; OxBC; PoE

Waiting for You to Come By. Simon J. Ortiz. CDW

Waiting in Front of the Columnar High School. Karl Shapiro. HAP

Waiting, in their dark clothes, apart. *(LL)* An Elegy Is Preparing Itself.
Donald Justice. CRP; HoPM

Waiting Inside. David Ignatow. CAPP

Waiting is the poem of waiting. On Arrival. Richard Howard. TAP

Waiting like a trap-door spider for a rookie sell-out. Baseball or the name
game? Four Poems for *The St. Louis Sporting News.* Jack Spicer.
PoM

Waiting on the silent shelf. *(LL)* You, Doctor Martin. Anne Sexton.
MoAmPo; NAAL-2

Waiting Out Rain, Sheltered by Overhang. Reg Saner. FoLa

Waiting-Room, The. Robin Fulton. PoA

Waiting Rooms. Howard Nemerov. PoA

Waiting to Be Fed. Ray A. Young Bear. CDW

Waiting to Die. Paul Monette. PFL

Waiting to melt, and become real again. *(LL)* Winter and Summer.
Stephen Spender. MoAB; MoBrPo

Waiting, waiting, waiting. Waiting. James Reeves. OTCP

Waitnig for something immense and unspeakable to uncover its face. *(LL)*
Cloud River. Charles Wright. MT

Waitress's Kid, The. Peggy Shumaker. PBCAP

Waits, The. John Freeman. BoTP

Waits on a stile. *(LL)* Verses Written in 1872. Robert Louis Stevenson.
BLPA; BLPL

Wait . . . that tastes good . . . already it is on the wing. Rainer Maria
Rilke, *tr. by* Christopher Hawthorne. *Fr.* Sonnets to Orpheus. SOTW

Wake. Langston Hughes. OBAL

Wake, The. S. J. Litherland. NWP

Wake! Omar Khayyám. *See* Wake! for the sun, who scattered [*or* scatter'd]
into flight.

Wake All the Dead. Sir William Davenant. *Fr.* Law against Lovers, The.
CoGr; ELP; FaBoCh; HAP; SCGP

Wake all the dead! What ho! What ho! Wake All the Dead. Sir William
Davenant. *Fr.* Law against Lovers, The. CoGr; ELP; FaBoCh; HAP;
SCGP

(Viola's Song.) NOSC

Wake. And my eyes stun. I Wake, My Friend, I. Faye Kicknosway.
IHMS

Wake as you will, but wake in me. To Song. Olga Berggolts, *tr. fr.
Russian by* Daniel Weissbort. BoWoP

Wake at the Well, The. *Unknown. See* I have forsworn[e] it whil[e] I live
[*or* life].

Wake, child with the flute. Mirabai, *tr. fr. Hindi by* Willis Barnstone *and*
Usha Nilsson. BoWoP

Wake! for the sun has driven in equal flight. The Golfer's Rubaiyat. H.
W. Boynton. BXAP

Wake! for the sun, who scattered [*or* scatter'd] into flight. Omar Khayyám,
tr. fr. Persian by Edward Fitzgerald. *Fr.* Rubáiyát of Omar Khayyám
of Naishápúr, The. AWP; EBVV, *abr.*; EnVR; FaBoBe; FaBoRV,
abr.; FaPoR, *abr.*; FF; HAP, *abr.*; ImPo; LiTM; NAEL-2; NoP; OBNC;
OHCV; OtMeF; PoEL-5; PrIm, *abr.*; TrGrPo; TRP

(Wake!) FaPON

Wake, Hercules, awake: but heave up thy black eye. Ben Jonson. *Fr.*
Pleasure Reconciled to Virtue. NAEL-1; OAEL-1

Wake I, or sleep? The pickle-jar is void. *(LL)* Ode on [*or* to] a Jar of
Pickles. Bayard Taylor. BXAP; FaBoPa

Wake, Israel, wake! Recall to-day. The Banner of the Jew. Emma
Lazarus. AmWP; TrJP

Wake not again the cannon's thundrous voice. Alfred Gibbs Campbell.
AAP

Wake Not for the World-heard Thunder. A. E. Housman. CMoP; NoAM

Wake, now my love, awake; for it is time. Spenser. *Fr.* Epithalamion.
AAS; BoLoP; EIL; EnRePo; FHYEP; GBL; InPS; NOBE; NoP; NoSic;
OAEL-1; OBEV; OxAEP-1; PoEL-1; TEP

Wake, O my soul; awake, and raise. Phineas Fletcher. NOSC

Wake of William Orr, The. William Drennan. PeIV; TIRV

Wake, Sleepy Thyrsis. Francis Pilkington. EnRePo

Wake, sleepy Thyrsis, wake. Wake, Sleepy Thyrsis. Francis Pilkington.
EnRePo

Wake the serpent not — lest he. Fragment: Wake the Serpent Not.
Shelley. SCGP

Wake: the silver dusk returning. Reveille. A. E. Housman. *Fr.* Shropshire
Lad, A. CMoP; FaPoB; LiTB; LiTM; MeMBP; MoAB; MoBrPo; NoP;
PoLF

Wake the Song of Jubilee. Leonard Bacon. AH

Wake Up. Raymond Carver. BAP-90

Wake up a few quarts lighter. *(LL)* Father and Mother. X. J. Kennedy.
GrPI

Wake up, dear boy that holds the flute! Mirabai, *tr. fr. Hindi by* Usha
Nilsson. WPOW

Wake up, Jacob. *Unknown.* RoPo

Wake up Lord. Caribbean Woman Prayer. Grace Nichols. NBrP

Wake up, my heart, get out of bed. A Priest in the Sabbath Dawn
Addresses His Somnolent Mistress. Peter Didsbury. PWE

Wake-up Niggers. Don L. Lee. PoBA

Wake up, wake up, darlin' Cory. Darling Cory. *Unknown.* AmFP

Waked by the breeze, and, as they mourn, expire! *(LL)* At Tynemouth
Priory, after a Tempestuous Voyage. William Lisle Bowles. Son

Waked by the Gospel's Powerful Sound. Samson Occom. AH

Waked by the pale pink. The Genius. Archibald MacLeish. MeMAP

Wakeful all night I lay and thought of God. Renunciation. Wathen Mark
Wilks Call. WGRP

Wakeful in the Township. Elizabeth Riddell. NOBAu

Wakeful they lie. *(LL)* Counting the Beats. Robert Graves. ELP; GBL;
GTBS-P; HAP; LPA; OxAEP-2; OxBTC; WeW

Wakeful, vagrant, restless thing. The Power of Fancy. Philip Freneau.
AmPP

(Ode to Fancy.) EAP

Waken each morning to the exact value of what you did and said./ which
remains. *(LL)* Definition of Blue. John Ashbery. CAPP; NAAL-2

Waken into falling light. *(LL)* Listen. Put on Morning. W. S. Graham.
FaBoTw; LiTM

Waken, lords and ladies gay. Hunting Song. Sir Walter Scott. *Fr.* Lay of
the Last Minstrel, The. EnRP; GN; GTBS; GTBS-P; SCGP; TrGrPo;
WiR

Wakening, The. *Unknown. See* On a Time the Amorous Silvy.

Wakepick I. Kristjana Gunnars. NOBC

Wakes that boats make, The. The Ways. Louis Zukofsky. PoE

Waking. Hugh Maxton. BIrV; CIP; PeIV

Waking. Katharine Pyle. OBCA

Waking, The. Theodore Roethke. AmPP; CAPP; CoAP; CRP; HAP;
HCAP; HeIP; InPK; InPS; LiTM; MoAmPo; MoP; NAAL-2; NIP;
NoAM; NOBA; NoP; OPOP; PFP; Poetr; PPP; PrIm; RaBo; SM; TAP;
TFi; TwCP; VCAP; WeW

Waking Alone. *Unknown.* MeEL

Waking [*or* Walking] alone in a multitude of loves when morning's light.
On the Marriage of a Virgin. Dylan Thomas. EnLoPo; MeMBP;
OxBM

(Marriage of a Virgin, The.) ErPo

Waking an Angel. Philip Levine. NaP

Waking at Dusk from a Nap. William Matthews. AnAn

Waking at morn, with the accustomed sigh. On the Death of His Son
Vincent. Leigh Hunt. NOBVV

Waking, Child, While You Slept. Ethel Anderson. *Fr.* Bucolic Eclogues.
WPE

Waking Early Sunday Morning. Robert Lowell. FaBoMo; HCAP; NOBA;
OxBC; VCAP

Waking from a bad dream, and thrashing out. Dream Time. Anthony
Thwaite. DiPo

Waking from a Nap on the Beach. May Swenson. NTCP; RFM

Waking from Sleep. Robert Bly. CAPP; NOBA; NoP; Poetr

Waking, he found himself in a train, andante. Slow Movement. Louis MacNeice. CBLP

Waking ("I strolled across/ An open field"), The. Theodore Roethke. RFM; TTTS

Waking in the Blue. Robert Lowell. CoAP; HCAP; MoAmPo; UnPo

Waking in the Dark. Dorothy Livesay. NOBC

Waking in the Dark. Adrienne Rich. FaBoWP

Waking is this easy. Aubade. Marilyn Chin. NIP

Waking Jesus sudden riding a scream like a/ train. I Scream You Scream. Don McKay. NOBC

Waking, my eyes, and in the night. Petronius Arbiter, *tr. fr. Greek by* Kenneth Rexroth. PGA

Waking, the Love Poem Sighs. Jim Hall. GOYP

Waking this morning. This Morning. Muriel Rukeyser. BoWoP; CrSp; NMM

Waking to drizzle and the inevitable. Exmatriate. Jacqueline Lapidus. LoHo

Waking to the clatter of hot-plate kettle. The Years. John Ennis. CIP

Waking Up. *Unknown.* BoTP

Waking up this morning, I see the blue sky. Thich Nhat Hanh. EaPr

Waking up this morning, I smile. Thich Nhat Hanh. EaPr

Wakinyan. Adrian C. Louis. NAmP90

Wakonda! Talako! deathonic turkey gobbling in the soft-footpatch night! Spontaneous Requiem for the American Indian. Gregory Corso. MAT; PoM

Walam [or Wallum] Olum; or, Red Score, *sels. Unknown, tr. fr. Delaware (Lenape) Indian.*
"After the Seizer there were ten chiefs, and there was much warfare south and east." OBVE
Deluge, The. LiTA
On the Creation and Ontogony. LiTA

Waldeinsamkeit. Emerson. NOBA; WGRP

Walden, *sels.* Thoreau.
Light-winged Smoke, Icarian Bird. NOBA; TAP
(Smoke.) AWP; NoP; OxBA

Walden in July. Donald Junkins. NYBP

Walden Pond/ All those noxious gases rising from it. Jack Spicer. *Fr.* Graphemics. VGW

Waldere 1. *Unknown, tr. fr. Anglo-Saxon by* Charles W. Kennedy. AnOE

Waldere 1 (". . . Hildegund eagerly urged him.") *Unknown, tr. fr. Anglo-Saxon by* Kevin Crossley-Holland. ASW

Waldere 2. *Unknown, tr. fr. Anglo-Saxon by* Charles W. Kennedy. AnOE

Waldere 2 (". . . a blade better.") *Unknown, tr. fr. Anglo-Saxon by* Kevin Crossley-Holland. ASW

Waldere addressed him, the warrior brave. Waldere 2. *Unknown, tr. fr. Anglo-Saxon by* Charles W. Kennedy. AnOE

Wales England Wed. Ernest Rhys. AngWe

Wales England wed; so I was bred. Wales England Wed. Ernest Rhys. AngWe
(Autobiography, An.) OBEV; OBWVE

Wales, full of gentlemen. (*LL*) The Shires. *Unknown.* CBCK

Wales Visitation. Allen Ginsberg. CAPP; NNaP; NOBA; NYBP; Prf; VCAP

Wales, which I have never seen. For My Ancestors. Rolfe Humphries. PoRA

Walk, The. Sebastian Barry. IB

Walk, The. Thomas Hardy. CMoP; NAEL-2; PoE; PoEL-5; PrIm

Walk. Frank Horne. BPo

Walk. Brian Merriman, *tr. by* Brendan Behan. *Fr.* Midnight Court, The. BIrV; NOIV, *tr. by* Thomas Kinsella

Walk, A. Hedwig Lachmann, *tr. fr. German by* Jethro Bithell. TrJP

Walk, A. Fernando Periquet Y Zuaznabar, *tr. fr. Spanish by* Philip L. Miller. RiWo

Walk, A. Rainer Maria Rilke, *tr. fr. German by* Robert Bly. RaBo

Walk, A. Gary Snyder. NOBA

Walk, A. Nikolai Alekseevich Zabolotsky, *tr. fr. Russian by* Daniel Weissbort. RB

Walk by the Charles, A. Adrienne Rich. NYBP

Walk, Damn You, Walk! William De Vere. PoLF

Walk east. Dawn polishes the sky. Direction. Roberta Hill Whiteman. CDW

Walk fast in snow, in frost walk slow. Winter Wise. *Unknown.* Spl

Walk in Central Park, A. Central Park. Julian Symons. PeLV

Walk in Kyoto, A. Earle Birney. GoYe

Walk in March, A. Tim Reynolds. MAT

Walk in Spring, A. K. C. Lart. BoTP

Walk in the Country, A. T'ang Yen-ch'ien, *tr. fr. Chinese by* Edward H. Schafer. SuSp

Walk in the Precepts. Moses ibn Ezra, *tr. fr. Hebrew by* Solomon Solis-Cohen. TrJP

Walk in Würzburg, A. William Plomer. NYBP

Walk in your sleep beyond Yeppoon. Assignation with a Somnambulist. John Manifold. CBAP

Walk into the prison, that domed citadel. My Lessons in the Jail. Miriam Waddington. MoCV

Walk on the Moon. N. Scott Momaday. CRP

Walk on the Water. Olga Broumas. PFL

Walk onto the dark stage dressed for a funeral. The Members of the Orchestra. Kevin Hart. NOBAu

Walk out into your country. Who Shall Die. James A. Randall, Jr. BPo

Walk Slowly. Adelaide Love. BLPA

Walk Together Children. *Unknown.* BPo

Walk with de Mayor of Harlem. David Henderson. PoBA

Walk with the sun. Dream Song. Lewis Alexander. PoBA; PoNe; WHSW

Walk with thy fellow-creatures: note the hush. Henry Vaughan. WGRP

Walked in, envying his Brando face. (*LL*) The Night Post. Matthew Sweeney. IB

Walked in his garden in the cool of the evening, waited. (*LL*) Intimate Supper. Peter Redgrove. FaBoMo; OxBC

Walked J. Cooke. (*LL*) The Ballad of Mr. Cooke. Bret Harte. AnAmPo

Walken Hwomme at Night. William Barnes. NOBVV

Walker, a large two-hundred-fifty pound blackman. Christmas 1962. Paul Mariah. GLP

Walking. James Harrison. FoLa

Walking. Thomas Traherne. *See* To Walk Abroad.

Walking a cliff with a lamb. Three Easters. Alberta Turner. LCAP

Walking against the Wind. Jon Stallworthy. OxBC

Walking all the day. Song for Ireland. Phil *and* June Colclough. OBET

Walking alone in a multitude of loves when morning's light. The Marriage of a Virgin. Dylan Thomas. ChIV-2; ErPo

Walking along the Hudson. Donald Petersen. CoAP

Walking among my own windy morning. The Spring Vacation. Derek Mahon. PNI

Walking among sceptre-headed. Walking-Sticks and Paperweights and Watermarks. Marianne Moore. PoA

Walking Around. Pablo Neruda, *tr. fr. Spanish by* Robert Bly. RaBo

Walking around in the park. Toads Revisited. Philip Larkin. CMoP; NOBL; OxAEP-2

Walking at last by the tame little edge of the sea. Evening before Rain. L. A. G. Strong. OxBTC

Walking at Leisure. Wang Wei, *tr. fr. Chinese by* Robert Payne. TAL

Walking at leisure we watch laurel flowers falling. Walking at Leisure. Wang Wei, *tr. fr. Chinese by* Robert Payne. TAL

Walking at Night. Amory Hare. PoLF

Walking at night on asphalt campus. Death News. Allen Ginsberg. MoP

Walking back on a chill morning past Kilmer's Lake. Walking. James Harrison. FoLa

Walking back to the office after lunch. Clothes. Edgar Bowers. ArOW

Walking by map, I chose unwonted ground. On the Hall at Stowey. Charles Tomlinson. CMoP; PoE

Walking by the river, the morning cold. River Walk. John Stuart Williams. AngWe

Walking down Jalan Thamrin. R. F. Brissenden. CBAP

Walking Down the Road. Adrienne Rich. NIP

Walking east on 3rd street. Pharoah Sanders, in the Flesh. George Bowering. Jaz

Walking east towards no-more-home. Blackshaw 289: the Replies. Peter Riley. VaA

Walking eight hundred. Removal: Last Part. Carroll Arnett. VoR

Walking for the first time. Echo. Leonard Clark. Mes

Walking Home. Gjertrud Schnackenberg. WeW

Walking home from school one afternoon. Walking Home. Gjertrud Schnackenberg. WeW

Walking, I heard the water dripping, running in the gutter. Partly to My Cat. Ellen Bass. NMM

Walking in a Meadowe Greene. *Unknown.* BoLoP; ErPo

Walking in a Swamp. David Wagoner. HAP

Walking in darkness. Into What Depth Thou Seest from What Height Fallen. John Seed. VaA

Walking in late afternoon. Bruce Beaver. *Fr.* Letters to Live Poets. CBAP; FaBoMA

Walking in the Countryside. Wang An-shih, *tr. fr. Chinese by* Jan W. Walls. SuSp

Wanderlust. Justinus Kerner, *tr. fr. German by* Philip L. Miller. RiWo

Wanders in the night. *(LL)* To the Moon. Goethe. STV

Wand'ring in this place as a wilderness. *Unknown.* GBL

Wandsworth Common. David Bromwich. PoA

Wang Chao-chün. Li Shang-yin, *tr. fr. Chinese by* Irving Y. Lo. SuSp

Wang Chao-chün. Tai Shu-lun, *tr. fr. Chinese by* William H. Nienhauser. SuSp

Waning Moon, The. Shelley. CH; FHYEP; OxBSP; TrGrPo

Waning moon looks upward, this grey night, The. Nostalgia. D. H. Lawrence. PoA

Waning of Love, The. "Arthur Lyon Raile." PeHV

Wanna hear something really funny? A Woman like Me. Eileen Myles. GLP

Wanne mine eyhnen misten. How Death Comes. *Unknown.* MeEL

Want. Mae V. Cowdery. ShDr

Want a penny? *Unknown.* RoPo

Want and ache not yet appeased, A. *(LL)* Give Me My Infant Now. Te-whaka-io-roa. NAs; WTO

Want and winter are upon us. *Unknown. Fr.* Toward Winter. NOIV

Want Bone, The. Robert Pinsky. EOEF

Want decides, let it be me. *(LL)* For My Unborn and Wretched Children. Alfred B. Spellman. PoBA

Want of %&$ Want of — +. Anne Szumigalski. FaBoWP

Want of You, The. Angelina Weld Grimké. ShDr

Want of You, The. Ivan Leonard Wright. BLPA; FaBoBe; SoSe

Want quickens wit: Want's pupils needs must work. The Fishermen. Theocritus [*or* Theokritus], *tr. by* Charles Stuart Calverley. *Fr.* Idylls. AWP; OBVE

Wanted. Josiah Gilbert Holland. *See* God, Give Us Men!

Wanted — A Man. Edmund Clarence Stedman. AnAmPo; PAH

Wanted, a Minister's Wife. *Unknown.* BLPA

Wanted — a Witch's Cat. Shelagh McGee. CRH

Wanted: Men. Ad. Kenneth Fearing. BTR

Wanted/ to give away pride. A Defeat. Denise Levertov. PBWP

Wanting a Child. Jorie Graham. FoLa

Wanting a Mummy. Sandra McPherson. AmPA; LCAP

Wanting children a couple once sat. G. W. Hanney. PeLi

Wanting for their young limbs praise. To the Girls of My Graduating Class. Irving Layton. ErPo

Wanting leads to worse than oddity. Where I'll Be Good. Michael Ryan. SM

Wanting to Die. Anne Sexton. IHMS; MoP; NoAM; TAP; TRP; VCAP

Wanting to hide my passion. *(LL)* Light of My Life. Sulpicia. VBLP

Wanting to Move. Vijaya Mukhopadhyay, *tr. fr. Hindi.* TSaS, *tr. by* Mukhopadhyay Vijaya.

Wanting to say things. My Father's Song. Simon J. Ortiz. HATNAP

Wanting to swim in touch with soft-mouthed life. *(LL)* The Guttural Muse. Seamus Heaney. NOIV; NoP

Wanting to welcome the emperor. Wang Chien, *tr. by* William H. Nienhauser. *Fr.* Palace Poems. SuSp

Wanton, *sels.* Silabhattarika, *tr. fr. Sanskrit.*
"My husband is the same who took my maidenhead." PBWP
(My husband is the same man who first pierced me.) BoWoP, *tr. by* Willis Barnstone.

Wanton, The, *sels.* Vidya, *tr. fr. Sanskrit by* Daniel H. H. Ingalls.
"Say, friend, if all is well still with the bowers." PBWP

Wanton droll, whose harmless play. The Kitten. Joanna Baillie. OFC

Wanton Eye. Charles, Duc d'Orléans. OxBLMV

Wanton laird of Young Logie, The. *(LL)* The Laird o' Logie. *Unknown.* CH; ESPB

Wanton Seed, The. *Unknown.* OBET

Wanton Trick, The. *Unknown.* CoMu

Wanton troopers riding by, The. The Nymph Complaining for the Death of Her Fawn. Andrew Marvell. CH; ESCV; FM; GeHe; NAEL-1; OAEL-1; OBF, *abr.;* PoEL-2; SeCP; SeCV-1

Wanton with long delay the gay spring leaping cometh. April, 1885. Robert Bridges. OxBSP; OxBTC

Wanton young lady of Wimley, A. *Unknown.* PeLi

Wants. Philip Larkin. GTBS-P; NoP

Wants of Man, The. John Quincy Adams. OBAL, *abr.;* PoLF

Wants to be admired. The Horse in the Drugstore. Tess Gallagher. AmPA; AnAn

Wants to be finished waiting in the car. He ate his pear. The Alcoholic's Son at Ten. Kathleen Peirce. PBCAP

Wapentake. Longfellow. EPCY

Wapiti, The. Ogden Nash. MoShBr; TLR

War, The. Linda Gregg. BAP-90

War. Miguel Hernández, *tr. fr. Spanish by* Hardie St. Martin. RaBo

War. Georg Heym, *tr. fr. German by* Patrick Bridgwater. PeFWW

War. S. S. Hunt. NSI

War. Sulamith Ish-Kishor. GoYe

War. Joseph Langland. AiP; FF

War! James Gilchrist Lawson. WBLP

War. Li Po, *tr. fr. Chinese by* Rewi Alley. ChTr

War, The. Vesna Parun, *tr. fr. Yugoslavian by* Ivana Spalatin *and* Daniela Gioseffi. WoWa

War. Andrei Voznesensky, *tr. fr. Russian by* William Jay Smith *and* Vera Dunham. RB

War. Edgar Wallace. OBWP

War (?) in the Desert, A. *Unknown.* PeSAV

War, A. Randall Jarrell. ArOW; OxBSP

War against the Jews, The. Gerald Stern. CAPP

War against the Trees, The. Stanley Kunitz. CAPP; HAP

War and Hell. Ernest Crosby. PAW

War-and-Peace. George Buchanan. PNI

War and Washington. Jonathan Mitchell Sewall. PAH

War-Baby. D. H. Lawrence. NAs

War Baby. William Trowbridge. ArOW

War between the French and the Viet Minh, The. Viet Minh. Tran Thi Nga *and* Wendy Wilder Larsen. WoWa

War Bird's Burlesque, A. *Unknown.* AS

War Blinded. Douglas Dunn. DiPo; OBWP

War Books. Ivor Gurney. PeFWW

War Bride. Douglas Worth. FF

War broke out in autumn at the empty border, The. Yehuda Amichai, *tr. fr. Hebrew. Fr.* Patriotic Songs. PoSu, *tr. by* Yehuda Amichai *and* Ted Hughes.

War canoes were ready. Thirsty Island. Jim Tollerud. VoR

War chief danced the old way, The. At the Klamath Berry Festival. William Stafford. InPK

War Comes. Zalman Schneour, *tr. fr. Yiddish by* Joseph Leftwich. TrJP

War Dance. Miidhu, *tr. fr. Aborigine by* Georg von Brandenstein. NOBAu

War Down a Monkland. *Unknown.* PBCV

War drum is beating, prepare for the fight, The. "We Conquer or Die." James S. Pierpont. PAH

War Film, A. Teresa Hooley. PAW

War God wakened drowsily, The. The Awakened War God. Margaret Widdemer. WGRP

War God's Horse Song, The. *Unknown, tr. fr. Navajo Indian.* LiTA, *tr. by* Dane Coolidge *and* Mary Roberts Coolidge; RB, *tr. by* Louis Watchman; TTTS

War Has Been Given a Bad Name. Bertolt Brecht, *tr. fr. German by* John Willett. PoSu

War Hope. William Hathaway. NAmP90

War Horse, The. Eavan Boland. BIrV; CIP; PBCIP

War in Spain has ended long ago, The/ Aunt Rose. *(LL)* To Aunt Rose. Allen Ginsberg. LiTM; NAAL-2; NoAM; NoP; PoE; VGW

War in the Air, The. Howard Nemerov. ArOW; DiPo; VCAP

War Is Kind, *sels.* Stephen Crane.
Candid Man, The. MoAmPo
"Do not weep maiden, for war is kind." AmPP; LiTA; LiTM; MeMAP; NAAL-2; NOBA; OBWP; PAW; PoLF; RaBo; TAP
"Fast rode the knight." MeMAP; NAAL-2
Man Said to the Universe, A. AmPP; FaBoEE; FF; LiTM; NAAL-2; OBAL; OBSV; PrIm; TAP; WeW
Newspaper [Is a Collection of Half-Injustices], A. AmPP; MeMAP; NAAL-2
On the Desert. LiTM
Peaks, The. WGRP
Peaks, The. WGRP
Slant of Sun [on Dull Brown Walls], A. LiTM; MeMAP; NAAL-2
There Was a Man with a Tongue of Wood. LiTM; MeMAP; MoAmPo
Trees in the Garden Rained Flowers, The. LiTM; PrIm
"Wayfarer, perceiving the pathway to birth, The." AmPP; LiTA; MeMAP; MoAmPo
(Wayfarer, The.) AnAmPo

War is no longer declared. Every Day. Ingeborg Bachmann, *tr. fr. German.* PBWP, *tr. by* Michael Hamburger.
(War is not declared any more.) BoWoP, *tr. by* Christopher Middleton; PoSu

War is not declared any more. Ingeborg Bachmann. *See* War is no longer declared.

War is over, The; A survivor. On Hearing Peace Has Been Declared. Argentina Daley, *tr. fr. Spanish by* Susana Stettri. WoWa

War is the angry man waving his desperate. War-and-Peace. George Buchanan. PNI

War Is the Statesman's Game. Shelley. *Fr.* Queen Mab. FF

War Lord in the Early Evening. P. K. Page. NoAM

War Memento (Somewhere in France 1915). Roger Hecht. CRP

War Memoir. Bob Kaufman. Jaz

War Memoir: Jazz, Don't Listen to It at Your Own Risk. Bob Kaufman. Jaz

War movie last leave nineteen forty four. Patricia Storace. BAP-91

War of the Secret Agents, The, *sels.* Henri Coulette.

War of the Worlds, The. Vern Rutsala. Poetsp

War of words is done, The. Battle. John Davidson. MeMBP

War on the Periphery. George Johnston. NOBC

War Party. Eddy Grant. PBCV

War-path is true and straight, The. Just One Signal. *Unknown.* PAH

War Photographers, The. Frank Ormsby. PNI

War Poet. Donald Bain. PAW

War Poet. Roy Fuller. *See* Swift had pains in his head.

War Poet. Sidney Keyes. PAW; PoWW

War Poetry. John Philips. *Fr.* Blenheim. NOEC

War separated, The. The Friends. Bertolt Brecht, *tr. fr. German by* Michael Hamburger. OBF; PoSu

War Ship of Peace, The. Samuel Lover. PAH

War shook the land where Levi dwelt. The Field of Glory. E. A. Robinson. AnAmPo; MoAmPo

War shows what each man's country is to him. Invasion. Ellen Duggan. PeNZ

War Song. John Davidson. MeMBP; OBNC

War Song. Zulu Oral Tradition, *tr. by* D. K. Rycroft. WTO

War Song, A. Bertrans de Born. *See* Well Pleaseth Me the Sweet Time of Easter.

War Song, A. Blake. *See* Prepare, prepare the iron helm of war.

War Song of Dinas Vawr, The. Thomas Love Peacock. *Fr.* Misfortunes of Elphin, The. AWP; CoGr; EBEvV; EnRP; FaBoCh; FaPoR; GGP; HAP; InvP; NAEL-2; NOBE; NTP; OAEL-2; OxAEP-2; PrIm; WiR

War Song of the Basotho, A. *Unknown, tr. by* Daniel P. Kunene. PeSAV

War Song of the Saracens. James Elroy Flecker. *Fr.* Hassan. CoGr; FaBV; MoBrPo; OtMeF

War Song to Englishmen, A. Blake. *Fr.* King Edward the Third. CH

War Story. Roger Vincent Small. PAW

War Story. Jon Stallworthy. OxBC

War that we have carefully for years provoked, The. Black-out. Robinson Jeffers. LiTA; LiTM

War-Time. W. R. Rodgers. OxBSP

War-time picnic, A. Mimi Khalvati. NWP

War to end them all, The. Firebell for Peace. Joyce Lee. NOBAu

War-Token, The. Longfellow. *Fr.* Courtship of Miles Standish, The. AiP, *st.* 1; BeLS; PAH

War Walking Near. Ray A. Young Bear. CDW

War was her life, with want and the wild air. Yorkshire Wife's Saga. Ruth Pitter. NALW

War Widow. Kathleen Jamie. PWE

Warble for Lilac Time. Walt Whitman. ArNa

Warble me now for joy of lilac-time (returning in reminiscence,). Warble for Lilac Time. Walt Whitman. ArNa

Ward X, *sels.* Lola Ridge. "Salvation Army lass, The." WPE

Ward, and still in bonds, one day, A. Regeneration. Henry Vaughan. ChIV-1; ESCV; GeHe; JCP; MeLP; NAEL-1; NoP; PoE

Ward has no heart, they say, but I deny it. On J. W. Ward. Samuel Rogers. FaBoEE

Ward 130 in the passage on the right. 25 December 1960. Ingrid Jonker, *tr. fr. Afrikaans by* Jack Cope *and* Uys Krige. PeSA

Ward 6. Tanure Ojaide. HBAPE

Ward Two. Francis Webb. CBAP

Wardance. Phillip William George. VoR

Wardance Soup. Phillip William George. VoR

Warden at ocean's gate. Liberty Enlightening the World. Edmund Clarence Stedman. PAH

Warden Said to Me the Other Day, The. Etheridge Knight. FF; MT; NBV; PBCAP; SoSe

Wardour Street. Humbert Wolfe. OxBTC

Waring. Robert Browning. OtMeF; PoEL-5

Warlike of the Isles, The. *Unknown.* OBTV

Warm ashes of the word, The. Cuncta Semper. Rodolfo Di Biasio, *tr. fr. Italian by* Stephen Sartarelli. NeIt

Warm Babies. Keith Preston. FiBHP

Warm Heart Contains Life. Evangelina Vigil. BCF

Warm perfumes like a breath from wine and tree. Waikiki. Rupert Brooke. OBTV

Warm rain and pure wind, The. The Sorrow of Departure. Li Ch'ing-chao, *tr. fr. Chinese by* Kenneth Rexroth *and* Ling Chung. WPC

Warm rain falls unfeeling, The. To the Tune "Washing Silk in the Stream." Ho Shuang-ch'ing, *tr. fr. Chinese by* Kenneth Rexroth *and* Ling Chung. WPC

Warm rain, sunny wind start to break the chill. Li Ch'ing-chao, *tr. fr. Chinese by* Willis Barnstone *and* Sua Chu-chin. BoWoP

Warm shone the sun, the wind as warmly blew. Hay-Time; or, The Constant Lovers. A Pastoral. Josiah Relph. NOEC

Warm summer sun. Epitaph Placed on His Daughter's Tomb. "Mark Twain." PoLF, *ad. by* Robert Richardson.

Warm sun is failing, The; the bleak wind is wailing. Autumn; a Dirge. Shelley. CH

Warm them worms waitin' undergroun'. (*LL*) The Yellow Bittern. Tom MacIntyre. PBCIP

Warm walnut seats crisscross braces. Powwow remnants. Lew Blockcolski. VoR

Warm winds crossed from the eastern coast, The. The Boss's Wife. *Unknown.* CBAP

Warm Winter Day, A. Julian Cooper. BoNaP

Warme by a glit'ring chimnie all the yeare. (*LL*) To Larr [*or* Lar]. Robert Herrick. CaPo; SeCV-1

Warmest welcome, at an inn, The. (*LL*) Written at [*or* in] an Inn at Henley. William Shenstone. AWP; NOBE; NOEC; OBEV; OxAEP-1

Warming Up. Anne Waldman. PRA

Warmth. Barton Sutter. GOYP

Warmth of Hot Chocolate, The. Thylias Moss. BAP-89

Warn all the other fishes. (*LL*) The Fish Weeps. *Unknown.* OHMPC

Warning. Alfred Gibbs Campbell. AAP

Warning. John Ciardi. PDV

Warning, The. Adelaide Crapsey. Spl; WPE

Warning, The. Robert Creeley. NeAP; TAP; VGW

Warning. Robert Frost. AnAmPo

Warning. Langston Hughes. BPo

Warning. Jenny Joseph. AlW; FaBoWP; GOYP; OxBTC; PWE

Warning, The. Longfellow. ChIV-1

Warning. Tadeusz Różewicz, *tr. fr. Polish by* Magnus F. Krynski. PoSu

Warning. *Unknown.* OxNR

Warning, A. Coventry Patmore. EnLoPo

Warning against the Gypsies, A. John Langhorne. *Fr.* Country Justice, The. ECEV

Warning and Reply. Emily Brontë. WPE

Warning of Winter. Mary Ursula Bethell. FaBoWP; PeNZ

Warning to America, A. Philip Freneau. TAP

Warning to Children. Robert Graves. CBNP; FaBoCh; MeMBP; NoP; NTP; OAEL-2

Warning to Conquerors, A. Donagh MacDonagh. IIP

Warning to One. Merrill Moore. MoAmPo; TrGrPo

Warning to Those Who Serve Lords, A. *Unknown.* MeEL

Warning to Travailers Seeking Accomodations at Mr. Devills Inn. Sarah Kemble Knight. SCAP

Warp and Woof. Harry Halbisch. BLRP

Warping bandstand reminds you of the hard rage, The. Return to La Plata, Missouri. Jim Barnes. HATNAP

Warren Phinney. Bernadette Mayer. UL

Warren's Address at Bunker Hill [*or* to the American Soldiers]. John Pierpont. AnAmPo; FaBoBe; GN; GOA; PAH; WBLP

Warring sighs and groans I'll wage thee. (*LL*) Ae fond kiss, and then we sever. Burns. EBEvV; ELP; EnRP; NAEL-2; OAEL-1; OBEV; PoEL-4; PPP

Warrior. Frank Mkalawile Chipasula. PeSAV

Warrior, A/ I have been. Song of Sitting Bull. *Unknown.* GOA

Warrior Artists of the Southern Plains, *sels.* Duane Niatum. Howling Wolf (1850-1927) Cheyenne. NGP, *sect.* III Prisoners at Fort Marion: 1875-1878. NGP, *sect.* I

Warrior is going a journey, The. Incantation. Alistair Paterson. *Fr.* Incantations for Warriors. PeNZ

Warrior Nation Trilogy. Lance Henson. ImGa; VoR

Warriors. Douglas Dunn. OxBC

Warriors and chiefs! should the shaft or the sword. Song of Saul Before His Last Battle. Byron. ChIV-1

Warrior's Lament, The. Sir Owen Seaman. FiBHP

Warr'st thou 'gainst Athens? Shakespeare. *Fr.* Timon of Athens. EBEV

Wars, The. Howard Moss. VCAP

Wars. Ammon Wrigley. UnDi

War's dust-bin charior drawing near. *(LL)* Sing, Brothers, Sing! W. R. Rodgers. MoAB; MoBrPo

Wars of Imperialism. John Foulcher. NOBAu

Wars of Santa Fe, The. *Unknown.* AmFP

Wars of the Roses, The. *Unknown.* GBP

Warszava, the plaintive flute of the East. Copenhagen Dreaming of Leningrad. Michael O'Loughlin. IB

Wartime Dawn, A. David Gascoyne. LiTM

Warty Bliggens, the Toad. Don Marquis. *Fr.* Archy and Mehitabel. FiBHP

Warum sind denn die Rosen so blass. Heine, *tr. fr. German by* Richard Garnett. AWP

Wary of time O it seizes the soul tonight. Easter Eve. Muriel Rukeyser. VGW

Was a bird; and the song was wordless; the singing/ Will never be done. *(LL)* Everyone Sang. Siegfried Sassoon. EBEvV; FaBV; GGP; GTBS-P; InvP; MoBrPo; NAEL-2; NoAM; NOBE; NSI; OBEV; OBWP; OxBSP; OxBTC; PAW; TrJP

Was a lying son of a bitch. *(LL)* The Derby Ram. *Unknown.* AmFP

Was a Man. Philip Booth. VGW

Was anything else possible. *(LL)* Proud Error. Vasco [or Vasko] Popa. AnRep, *tr. by* Charles Simic; HSix, *tr. by* Charles Simic.

Was, at all hazards, to try to copy the Celt! *(LL)* The Cult of the Celtic. Anthony C. Deane. BXAP; NOBL; PeLV

Was blest with such an evening-shower! *(LL)* The Shower. Henry Vaughan. BoNaP; ChTr

Was born on Christmas Day. *(LL)* God Rest You [or ye] Merry, Gentlemen. Dinah Maria Mulock Craik. GN, *sl. diff. vers.*; LiTB

Was breathing His love by a cut-away bog. *(LL)* The One. Patrick Kavanagh. MoBrPo; TIRV

Was brimming o'er and floated o'er the top. *(LL)* Deluge. John Clare. BoNaP

Was broken./ He bade a warrior abandon his horse. The Battle of Maldon. *Unknown, tr. fr. Anglo-Saxon by* Charles W. Kennedy. AnOE, *tr. by* Kevin Crossley-Holland; OAEL-1, *tr. by* Kevin Crossley-Holland; OBWP, *tr. by* Kevin Crossley-Holland.

Was captured, was perverted by their Christianity. *(LL)* Myris: Alexandria, A.D. 340. C. P. Cavafy. AnAn; OBF

Was 'Carry me safe to Dover.' *(LL)* As I was going up the hill. *Unknown.* OxNR

Was clapped fast under board, A. *(LL)* John Dory. *Unknown.* ESPB; OxBSS

Was Eat-it-all Elaine. *(LL)* Eat-It-All Elaine. Kaye Starbird. PDV

Was Ever Heart Like Mine? Edward Taylor. *See* Still I complain; I am complaining still.

Was faithful unto death, and shamed the Devil. *(LL)* Lying. Richard Wilbur. DiPo; HCAP; PeVV; Poetr; SV

Was for 300 or maybe 400 years. *(LL)* Toe'osh; a Laguna Coyote Story. Leslie Silko. CDW; NoAM; VoR

Was *From Charybdis into Scylla.* *(LL)* The Hag and the Slavies. La Fontaine. AWP; OBVE

Was Fun Running 'Round Descalza. Evangelina Vigil. BCF

Was gazing where she'll never know. *(LL)* Girl. Octavio Paz. STV

Was he a mining on the flat. He Done His Level Best. "Mark Twain." AiP

Was He Henpecked? Phoebe Cary. AmWP

Was He Married? Stevie Smith. MoP; NoAM; Poetr

Was he then Adam of the Burning Way? Such Is the Sickness of Many a Good Thing. Robert Duncan. CAPP

Was heaven sent. *(LL)* Little Lyric (of Great Importance). Langston Hughes. NBLV; OBAL

Was how she spent her wedding night. *(LL)* Moggy's Wedding. Charles Robert Thatcher. NOBAu

Was I never yet of your love grieved. Sir Thomas Wyatt. SiPSBD

Was I Not a Blade of Grass. Ivan Zakharovich Surikov, *tr. fr. Russian by* Philip L. Miller. RiWo

Was I not a blade of grass in the field? Was I Not a Blade of Grass. Ivan Zakharovich Surikov, *tr. fr. Russian by* Philip L. Miller. RiWo

Was I too glib about eternal things. The Sequel. Theodore Roethke. NYBP

Was, Is, and Yet-To-Be. Ella Wheeler Wilcox. PoToHe

Was it a blast to the balls dear brother. A Black Poet Leaps to His Death. Etheridge Knight. ETG

"Was it a dream, or did I see it plain?" Spenser. *Fr.* Amoretti. AAS; CBLP; ESo, lacking epigrams I-IV; HeIL; NIP

Was it a dream? The Books were men. The Wounded. Louise Louis. GoYe

Was it a dream? We sailed, I thought we sailed. A Dream. Matthew Arnold. *Fr.* Switzerland. EnVR; GBL; GTBS-P; OBTV

Was it a little baby. A Tonversation with Baby. Morris Bishop. FiBHP

Was it a "please urge" or "a police purge" or some combination. The Kiss. John Yau. UL

Was it a vision, or a waking dream? I heard her voice before I saw. The Irish for No. Ciaran Carson. PNI

Was It All Worth While? *Zulu Oral Tradition, tr. by* H. Tracey. WTO

Was it D + 10 or D + 12 we caught. Apples, Normandy, 1944. Frank Ormsby. *Fr.* Northern Spring, A. PNI

Was it fancy, sweet nurse. Don Marquis. *Fr.* Grotesques. FiBHP

Was It for This. Wordsworth. *Fr.* Prelude [or, Growth of a Poet's Mind], The. CH; EnRP; GN; HAP; NOBE; NoP; NU; OAEL-2; OBNC; OxAEP-2; PoE; RB; SCV

Was it for this I uttered prayers. Grown-up. Edna St. Vincent Millay. NoAM

Was it hundreds of years ago, my love. James Thomson ("B.V."). *Fr.* Sunday at Hampstead. EnVR

Was It Not Curious? Stevie Smith. IHNG

Was it not curious of Aúgustin. Was It Not Curious? Stevie Smith. IHNG

Was it really you all the time? Dream Sequence, Part 9. Naomi Long Madgett. BPo

Was it the proud full sail of his great verse. Shakespeare. *Fr.* Sonnets. InvP; NoSic; OAEL-1; OxAEP-1; SCGP; Son; TEP

Was it wind off the dumps. Summer Home. Seamus Heaney. IPY; PBCIP

Was It You? Stewart I. Long. WBLP

Was Jesus Chaste? or did he. Blake. *Fr.* Everlasting Gospel, The. ChIV-2

Was just that I was leaving home and my folks were growing old. *(LL)* Christmas at Sea. Robert Louis Stevenson. BLPL; CH; EBVV; FaBoBe; FaBV; Mes; OBTV; PeVV

Was left all alone/ Fa, le, la, la, lal, de. *(LL)* There were two birds sat on a stone. Mother Goose. OxNR

Was made steward in king Henerys hall. *(LL)* Sir Aldingar. *Unknown.* ESPB, *A, B, and C vers.*; OxBB

Was made the Lady of the May. *(LL)* In the merry month of May. Nicholas Breton. EBEvV; NoSic

Was Nature angry when she formed my clay? On Viewing Herself in a Glass. Elizabeth Teft. ECWP

Was never day came on my head. George Turberville. *Fr.* Lover Abused Renounceth Love, The. EIL

Was never said in rhyme. *(LL)* In a Drear-nighted December. Keats. CH; ELP; EnRP; NOBE; TEP

Was never seen again. *(LL)* The Fisherman. Goethe. STV

Was no more than his due who brought good news from Ghent. *(LL)* How They Brought the Good News from Ghent to Aix. Robert Browning. BeLS; BLPL; EBEvV; EBNV; FaBoBe; FaPoR; FHYEP; GN; HoPM; NAEL-2; OBSP, *sh. vers.*; PeVV; UV, *sh. vers.*; VPP

Was not to be expected. *(LL)* Seaman, 1941. Molly Holden. FaBoWP

Was nothing else but secret love. *(LL)* Secret Love. John Clare. FaBV; OBNC; PoE; PoEL-4; SCGP; TrGrPo

Was one that kept his word. *(LL)* Because I liked you better. A. E. Housman. CBLP; GBL; NOBVV; OxBTC; PeHV; PeVV

Was out on the street, the word. Garland. Gavin Selerie. NBrP

Was quenched by death, and broken the bruised reed. *(LL)* Keats. Longfellow. Son; TAP

Was She a Witch? Laura E. Richards. PDV

Was, she thought, a good woman. But the difference. Janet Fisher. NWP

Was she wae, &c. *(LL)* The Twa Magicians. *Unknown.* ESPB; GBP; OAEL-1; OxBB

Was sitting by the shed. *(LL)* As little Jenny Wren/ Was sitting by the shed. Mother Goose. OxNR

Was slain for thee. *(LL)* A Poem to Be Said on Hearing the Birds Sing. Biddy Crummy. AWP; WTO

Was slipped once more in place. *(LL)* The Mask. Clarissa Scott Delany. CDC; PoNe; ShDr

Was sure to split, and sink, and damn. *(LL)* An Epistle to My Friend J. B. Robert Dodsley. NOEC

Was taken and carried to Canada. *(LL)* Bar's Fight, August 28, 1746. Lucy Terry. BlSi; BPo; PoNe

Was that sticky infusion, that rank flavor of blood, that poetry, by which I lived? *(LL)* The Bear. Galway Kinnell. CAPP; CoAP; InPS; NNaP; RFM; TAP; TRP; VCAP; VGW

Was that the wind? she said. A Moment. John Todhunter. PeIV

Was that young, faithful heart. *(LL)* Casabianca. Felicia Dorothea Hemans. BeLS; BLPA; EBEvV; FaBoBe; FaBoPa; FaPON; VPP; WBLP

Was the arrangement made between the two couples legal? Some Litanies. Michael Benedikt. CoAP; TwCP

Was the *child* that played in the streets of Rome. *(LL)* Two Pictures. *Unknown.* BeLS; BLPA; FaBoBe

Was the forgetful kingdom of death. *(LL)* Janet Waking. John Crowe Ransom. CMoP; InPK; MeMAP; MoAB; MoAmPo; MoP; NAAL-2; NoAM; NoP; OBD; PoE; Poetr; RB; TAP

Was the founder! *(LL)* A Fit of Rime against Rime. Ben Jonson. BeJo; InVP; MAT; OAEL-1; PoEL-2; SeCP; SeCV-1

Was the love between them. His Lunch Bucket. Doug Cockrell. Poetsp

Was the only thing I had. *(LL)* Homecoming. Langston Hughes. SAmP; TRP

Was the silkiest day of the young year. The Day He Died. Ted Hughes. OxAEP-2

Was there another Troy for her to burn? *(LL)* No Second Troy. W. B. Yeats. CMoP; EnLoPo; GTBS-P; MoP; NAEL-2; NoAM; NOBE; OAEL-2; OxAEP-2; OxBTC; PoEL-5; PPP; TFi; WeW

Was there ere sic a parish, a parish, a parish. Little Dunkeld. *Unknown.* GBP

Was there ever message sweeter. A Message. Elizabeth Stuart Phelps Ward. PAH

Was there no star that could be sent. Emerson. *Fr.* Threnody. IMW

Was this His coming! I had hoped to see. Ave Maria, Gratia Plena. Oscar Wilde. ChIV-2

Was This the Face. Christopher Marlowe. *Fr.* Doctor Faustus. EBEV; EBEvV; GBL; LPA; NAEL-1; OAEL-1; TrGrPo

Was this the face that launched a thousand ships? Was This the Face. Christopher Marlowe. *Fr.* Doctor Faustus. EBEV; EBEvV; GBL; LPA; NAEL-1; OAEL-1; TrGrPo
(Face of Helen, The.) FaBV
(Helen of Troy.) FF
(Helen.) BLPL; ImPo; LiTB

Was this what was intended. Thanks to the Brook. Wilhelm Müller, *tr. fr. German* by Philip L. Miller. *Fr.* Beautiful Maid of the Mill, The. RiWo

Was told the mystic name of Love. *(LL)* Natura Naturans. Arthur Hugh Clough. CBLP; EnVR; HAP; NOBVV

Was two sisters loved one man. The Two Sisters. *Unknown.* AmFP; MAT; PrIm; TrGrPo

Was, 'Wae to my sister, fair Ellen.' *(LL)* The Twa Sisters. *Unknown.* ESPB; FaBoBa; NoP; OxBS

Was you at de hall las' night. Leap Yeah Party, De. Maggie Pogue Johnson. CBWP-4

Was your/ love. *(LL)* To Mother and Steve. Mari Evans. BPo; PoBA

Wash. Eiléan Ní Chuilleanáin. BIrV; WPOW

Wash and wipe together. *Unknown.* RoPo

Wash-Day. Lilian McCrea. BoTP

Wash Days. Beverlyjean Smith. ETG

Wash, hands, wash. A Rhyme for Washing Hands. Rodney Bennett. BoTP

Wash it well, and season it hot. To Stew a Rump-Steak. *Unknown.* FaBoUs

Wash man out of the earth, shear off. Wash. Eiléan Ní Chuilleanáin. BIrV; WPOW

Wash the dishes, wipe the dishes. Mother Goose. OxNR

Wash your hands clean of guilt, and scour. Robert David Fitzgerald. *Fr.* Eleven Compositions: Roadside. FaBoMA

Wash your hands, or else the fire. Another to the Maids. Robert Herrick. OHIP

Washed ashore. Repulse Bay. Marilyn Chin. OpBo

Washed by the rain, dust and grime are laid. Starting Early from the Ch'u-ch'êng Inn. Po Chü-i, *tr. fr. Chinese* by Arthur Waley. OBVE

Washers of the Shroud, The. James Russell Lowell. PAH

Washerwoman, The. Alice Cary. AmWP

Washerwoman, The. Mary Collier. *Fr.* Woman's Labour; an Epistle to Mr. Stephen Duck, The. ECWP; NOEC

Washerwoman, The. Mary Weston Fordham. AmWP; CBWP-2

Washing. John Drinkwater. FaPON

Washing and Dressing. Ann Taylor. FaBoUs

Washing-Day. Anna Laetitia Barbauld. ECWP; WoRP

Washing Day. *Unknown.* CoMu

Washing hanging from the lemon tree, The. The Five-Day Rain. Denise Levertov. NeAP

Washing hangs upon the line, A. Elizabeth Bishop. *Fr.* Songs for a Colored Singer. FaBoVe; FaBoWP; PoNe; RB

Washing Kai in the sauna. The Bath. Gary Snyder. CAPP; NNaP; PoBeRe; TAP; VCAP

Washing the Coins. Douglas Dunn. FaBoPV

Washing the Dishes. Christopher Morley. PoLF

Washing the Money. Rhyll McMaster. FaBoMA

Washing-Up Song, The. Elizabeth Gould. BoTP

Washington. Byron. *Fr.* Ode to Napoleon Buonaparte. OHIP; PAH

Washington. Lorna Dee Cervantes. *Fr.* Visions of Mexico While at a Writing Symposium in Port Townsend, Washington. NoAM

Washington. James Russell Lowell. *Fr.* Under the Old Elm. GN; OHIP

Washington. Geraldine Meyrich. OHIP

Washington. Harriet Monroe. *Fr.* Commemoration Ode. FaBoBe

Washington. Denis O'Crowley. OHIP

Washington. John A. Prentice. OHIP

Washington. James Jeffrey Roche. PAH

Washington. Nancy Byrd Turner. FaPON

Washington. Mary Wingate. OHIP

Washington and Jefferson made many a joke. Presidents of the United States. *Unknown.* FaBoUs

Washington by the Delaware. Joaquin Miller. AnAmPo

Washington Heights, 1959. Michael C. Blumenthal. HCAP

Washington in Love. John Berryman. LCAP

Washington Monument by Night. Carl Sandburg. CMoP; FaPON; ImGa; OHIP

Washington Sequoia, The, *sels.* Milicent Washburn Shinn.

Washington, the brave, the wise, the good. Inscription at Mount Vernon. *Unknown.* OHIP

Washington's Birthday. Arthur J. Burdick. OHIP

Washington's Monument. *Unknown.* OHIP; PAH

Washington's Tomb. Ruth Lawrence. OHIP

Washington's Vow. Whittier. OHIP

Washrags. Vern Rutsala. ETG

Wasn't it pleasant, O brother mine. Out to Old Aunt Mary's. James Whitcomb Riley. PFP

Wasn't That a Mighty Storm? *Unknown.* AmFP

Wasn't this a queer thing? I stood with your mother. A Queer Thing. Nancy Keesing. NOBAu

Wasn't this the site, asked the historian. House and Land. Allen Curnow. PeNZ

Wasn't your mother a woman? Hennamma, *tr. fr. Kannada* by Willis Barnstone. BoWoP

Wasp, The. John Davidson. FM

Wasp, The. Daryl Hine. NYBP

Wasp, The. "Fiona Macleod." BoTP; FaPON

Wasp, The. "Fiona Macleod." *Fr.* Transcripts from Nature. FM

Wasp arouses the flower with terrible thrusts, The. The Window in the Cliff. Bei Dao, *tr. fr. Chinese* by Donald Finkel *with* Chen Xueliang. SpMi

Wasp, climbing the window pane. Epigrams, I-IX. Howard Nemerov. OBAL

Wasp Sex Myth (One). Anselm Hollo. PoM

Wasp Sex Myth (Two). Anselm Hollo. PoM

WASP Woman Visits a Black Junkie in Prison, A. Etheridge Knight. NBV

Wasp's Frolic, The. *Unknown.* PAH

Wasps' Nest, The. George MacBeth. OxBTC

Wasp's Song, The. "Lewis Carroll." FaBoNo

Wassail Song. *Unknown.* GBP; OHIP

Wassail Song ("Wassail! wassail! all round the town.") *Unknown.* OHIP

Wassail Song: "We have been a-walking," *diff. vers. Unknown. See* Wassail! wassail! all round [or over] the town.

Wassail the trees, that they may bear. Robert Herrick. *Fr.* Ceremonies for Christmas[se]. BeJo; GN; OBCP; OHIP; PChr; TEP

Wassail, Wassail. John Bale. ChTr

Wassail, wassail, all over the town! Gloucestershire Wassail. *Unknown.* OBET

Wassail, wassail, all over the town. Thames Head Wassailers' Song. *Unknown.* OBET

Wassail! Wassail! all over the town. Wassailer's Song. Robert Southwell. OHIP

Wassail! wassail! all round [or over] the town. Wassail Song ("Wassail! wassail! all round the town.") *Unknown.* OHIP
(Somerset Wassail.) OBET
(Wassail Song: "We have been a-walking," *diff. vers.*) GBP

Wassail, wassail, out of the milk pail. Wassail, Wassail. John Bale. ChTr

Wassailer's Song. Robert Southwell. OHIP

Wassailing Song. *Unknown.* OBCP

Waste Land, The. (April is the cruelest month.) T. S. Eliot. AmPP; CMoP; FaBoMo; HAP; LiTA; LiTM; MoAB; MoAmPo; NAWM-2; NoAM; NOBA; NOBE; NoP; OAEL-2; OxBA; OxBTC; TAP; UnPo *Sels.*
Death by Water. OBVE
Game of Chess, A. SCV

Waters of Waiapu, The. Paraire Henare Tomoana, *tr. fr. Maori by* Margaret Orbell. PeNZ

Waters rippled, gleamed and fell, The. At the Cascade. H. Cordelia Ray. AmWP; CBWP-3

Waters, you are the ones who bring us the life force. *Unknown, tr. fr. Sanskrit.* EaPr

Watershed, The. W. H. Auden. OAEL-2

Watershed. Robert Penn Warren. PoA

Waterspout. James Merrill. CAPP

Waterwings. Cathy Song. NoAM

Watt Tyler, *sels.* Ebenezer Elliot.
  "Too seldom, if the righteous fight is won." FaBoEH

Watteau was slightly silly to equip. L'Embarquement pour Cythère. John Manifold. CBAP

Watts, *sels.* Shirley Kaufman.
  "He's learning to shoot." CrSp

Watts. Shirley Kaufman. NMM

Watts. Conrad Kent Rivers. PoBA

Watts. Alvin Saxon. PoBA

Watt's dream was the cream of steam engines. Bill Greenwell. PeLi

Watt's Improvements to the Steam Engine. Thomas Baker. *Fr.* Steam Engine; or, The Power of the Flame, The. FaBoUs

Waulking Song: Two. Minnie Bruce Pratt. GLP

Wave, The. Daryl Hine. Prf

Wave approaching and the wave returning, The. Sequence. George Barker. PoA

Wave it, save it, evermore. (*LL*) Our National Banner. Dexter Smith. PAH

Wave of coldness, A. Yosano Akiko, *tr. fr. Japanese by* Glenn Hughes *and* Yozan T. Iwasaki. WPOW

Wave Symphony, The. Arthur Davison Ficke. *Fr.* Four Japanese Paintings. PoA

Wave, wave your glorious battle-flags, brave soldiers of the North. Gettysburg. Edmund Clarence Stedman. PAH

Wave withdrawing, The. "Dover Beach" — a Note to That Poem. Archibald MacLeish. FF

Wavelength. David St. John. NAmP90

Waverley, *sels.* Sir Walter Scott.
  Hie Away, Hie Away. EnRP; MoShBr; OxAEP-2
  To an Oak Tree. OBNC

Waverley Pen, The. *Unknown.* FaBoUs

Wavers, a candle's shadow, at the end. (*LL*) Legal Fiction. William Empson. CMoP; FaBoMo; ImPo; LiTB; LiTM; MoP; NoAM; NoP

Waves. Emerson. *See* All day the waves assailed the rock.

Waves. *Unknown, tr. fr. Arabic by* Omar S. Pound. ArPe

Waves are erasing the footprints, The. At the Beach. Kemal Ozer, *tr. fr. Turkish.* TSaS, *tr. by* O. Yalim, W. Fielder, *and* Dionis Riggs.

Waves bluster up the bay and through the throat. A Family Photograph 1939. James K. Baxter. OxBC

Waves claw, The. On The Beach. John Corben. Spl

Waves gather differently off the shore of Crete, The. The Gathering of Waves. Thomas McCarthy. IB

Waves Gleam in the Sunshine, The. Heine, *tr. fr. German by* Emma Lazarus. *Fr.* Songs to Seraphine. TrJP

Waves lap against rock. John Riley. VaA

Waves surge higher still, The. Elegy: Ise Lamenting the Death of Empress Onshi. Lady Ise, *tr. fr. Japanese by* Etsuko Terasaki *and* Irma Brandeis. BoWoP; IMW

Waves, the rough surf, swept me on the shore, The. Antipater of Thessalonica, *tr. fr. Greek by* Alistair Elliot. GrAn

Waves, the strides, the feet on which I go?, The. (*LL*) Tristan da Cunha. Roy Campbell. MoBrPo; PeSA

Waves want/ to be wheels. Surf. Lillian Morrison. NTCP

Waves which have kept me from reaching you, The. (*LL*) To the Harbormaster. Frank O'Hara. CoAP; CRP; NAAL-2; PoM; VCAP

Waving a Bough. Boris Pasternak, *tr. fr. Russian by* Babette Deutsch. TrJP

Waving of a Hand, The. W. S. Merwin. CAPP

Wawking of the Fauld, The. Allan Ramsay. *See* My Peggy is a young thing.

Wax. Winfield Townley Scott. ErPo

Wax-contoured, in your face a Muse. Philodemus, *tr. fr. Greek by* William Moebius. GrAn

Waxwings. Robert Francis. LCAP; NU; RaBo

Way, The. Robert Creeley. BoLoP; LiTM; NeAP; PPP

Way a crow, The. Dust of Snow. Robert Frost. CMoP; MoShBr; OxBA; OxBSP; PDV; PrIm; SAmP; SoSe; TAP; UnPo; WeW

Way a Ghost Dissolves, The. Richard Hugo. NAAL-2; NoAM; NoP; SM

Way a tired Chippewa woman, The. Hush. David St. John. LCAP

Way back in eighty-two or three. The Dreadful Fate of Naughty Nate. John Kendrick Bangs. OBCA

Way back in the days of depression. Soup Song. Joseph Glazer. SWP

Way Djanbun went across the mountain range, The. (*LL*) The Platypus. *Aborigine Oral Tradition.* NOBAu

Way Down, The. Philip Levine. NOBA

Way Down, The, *sels.* Jay Macpherson.
  They Return. NOBC; PoA

Way Down, The. Ernest Sandeen. CRP

Way down Geneva. Red Boots On. Kit Wright. PeLV

Way down in the bottom. Poor Little Johnny. *Unknown.* AmFP

Way down in yonders low valley, in some lonesome place. Pretty Saro. *Unknown.* AmFP

Way down Souf whar de lillies grow. To See Ol' Booker T. Maggie Pogue Johnson. CBWP-4

Way Down South. *Unknown.* RoPo

Way down south in Dixie. Song for a Dark Girl. Langston Hughes. AmPP; CDC; NAAL-2; PoBA; SAmP

Way down South in Grandma's lot. *Unknown.* RoPo

Way down South in the land of cotton. Crazy Song to the Air of "Dixie." "Andy Lee." AS

Way down South where bananas grow. Way Down South. *Unknown.* RoPo

Way down South where I was born. A Long Time Ago. *Unknown.* AmFP

Way down upon the [*or* de] Swanee River [*or* ribber]. The Old Folks at Home. Stephen Collins Foster. AnAmPo; FaBoBe; WBLP

Way down upon the Wabash. El-a-noy. *Unknown.* AS

Way down yonder on the Piankatank. *Unknown.* RoPo

Way enchased with glass and beads, A. The Temple. Robert Herrick. CaPo

Way feare with thy projectes, noe false fyre, A. William Alabaster. *Fr.* Divine Meditations. ESCV; Son

Way her breasts meet is hidden from me, The. Old Fellow. Ernest Walsh. ErPo

Way home is close, The. Tune: "Song of the Southern Country." Li Hsün, *tr. fr. Chinese by* Edward Schafer. SuSp

Way I hear tell Aunt Jennie, The. Caledonia. Colleen J. McElroy. BlSi

Way I mix up Death and Life — a bridge of sweetness links them, The. (*LL*) I Know Not When It Was. Léopold Sédar Senghor. NegPo

Way I read a letter's — this, The. Emily Dickinson. CBLP; InPS; WPE

Way in is only hinted at, The. Garlic. Jeanne Foster. CrSp

Way It Is, The. Gloria C. Oden. IHMS

Way It Sometimes Is, The. Henry Taylor. MT; Poetr

Way It Was, The. Lucille Clifton. WPE

Way Lorene and I went back, The. Need Increasing Itself by Rounds. Kathleen Peirce. PBCAP

Way of Keeping, A. Nancy Willard. IHMS

Way of Life, A. Howard Nemerov. NIP

Way of peace, The. (*LL*) O our Mother the Earth, blessed is our name. Helen Weaver. EaPr

Way of the Air, The. Laura Riding. *Fr.* Three Sermons to the Dead. LiTA

Way of the World, The. Congreve. NAEL-1
  Sels.
  "After our Epilogue this crowd dismisses."
  "Of those few fools, who with ill stars are cursed."

Way of the World, The. Ella Wheeler Wilcox. *See* Laugh, and the world laughs with you.

Way out in California. The Santa Barbara Earthquake. *Unknown.* AmFP

Way Out in Idaho. *Unknown.* AmFP

Way Out in Idaho ("Come all you jolly railroad men.") *Unknown.* AmFP

Way Out West. Amiri Baraka. NeAP; PoBA; PoBeRe

Way Over in the New Buryin' Groun'. *Unknown.* AS

Way-Side Well, The. Joseph S. Cotter, Sr. CDC; PoNe

Way the Bird Sat, The. Ray A. Young Bear. CDW; VoR

Way the buildings curve (as if a thought, The.) Central Park South. Donald Revell. UTF

Way, the Truth, and the Life, The. Theodore Parker. TrPWD; WGRP

Way; the Truth; the Life, The. Samuel Judson Porter. BLRP

Way the world is not, The. Sonnet. William Knott. PBCAP

Way they do, The. Loo-wit. Wendy Rose. HATNAP

Way/ they lay together, The. Peyanar, *tr. fr. Tamil by* A. K. Ramanujan. *Fr.* Seven Said by the Foster-Mother. PLW

Way Through, The. Denise Levertov. NeAP; PoM

Way through the Woods, The. Kipling. *Fr.* Rewards and Fairies. CH; CoGr; EBEvV; FaBoCh; FaPON; NoAM; NOBE; NTP; OBEV; OBNC; OxAEP-2; OxBChV; OxBTC; PFP; PlP; RFM; SCGP; WHSW

We artists have strange nerves! In a Hotel Writing-Room. John Cowper Powys. OxBTC

We ask for peace. We, at the bound. Surrender. Angelina Weld Grimké. CDC

We ask not that the slave should lie. The Abolitionist Hymn. *Unknown.* SWP

We Assume: On the Death of Our Son, Reuben Masai Harper. Michael S. Harper. AmPA; LCAP

We ate no flesh in Eden, but afterwards. Jean Pearson. *Fr.* Daily Prayer, A. EaPr

We ate our breakfast lying on our backs. Breakfast. W. W. Gibson. OBMV; OxBTC

We athletes who, with sternest discipline. The Golden Road to Barcelona: 1992. Martin Fagg. UV

We awaken in Christ's body. Symeon, *tr. fr. Greek by* Stephen Mitchell. EnlH

We banter/ back and forth. Perfecto Flores. Jimmy Santiago Baca. TRP

We Be Soldiers Three. *Unknown.* ChTr; CoGr; GBP

We be the King's men, hale and hearty. Men Who March Away. Thomas Hardy. *Fr.* Dynasts, The. CH; OBWP (What of the faith and fire within us.) PoWW

We Become New. Marge Piercy. TAP

We began to dance. Xylophone Luncheonette. Connie Deanovich. UTF

We begin with the osprey who cries, "Clang, clang!" Marriage Song. Carolyn Kizer. BAP-91

We ben chapmen lyght of fote. *Unknown.* MiEL (Chapmen.) FaBoVe

We bend our beer cans like dummies, and sit. (*LL*) Meeting My Best Friend from the Eighth Grade. Gary Gildner. SM

We bend over my old flower-press. The Flower-Press. Penelope Shuttle. AIW

We bless you, cicada. Cicada. *Unknown, tr. fr. Greek by* Willis Barnstone. EaPr

We blk blues singers. For Walter Washington. Tom Dent. NBV

We blossom by. (*LL*) Only the winds of spring. Walt Franklin. EaPr

We borrowed the loan of Kerr's big ass. Kerr's Ass. Patrick Kavanagh. NOIV; RB

We both have voices inside. The Poet and the Schizophrenic. Andrew Duncan. NBrP

We bought from Laotian refugees a cloth. Absorption of Rock. Maxine Hong Kingston. OpBo

We break off a branch of poplar catkins. All Year Long. *Unknown, tr. fr. Chinese by* Kenneth Rexroth. OHMPC

We Bring No Glittering Treasures. Harriet C. Phillips. AH

We broke out of our dream into a clearing. Stephano Remembers. James Simmons. PBCIP; PNI; PWE

We brought him home, I was so pleased. My New Rabbit. Elizabeth Gould. BoTP; OTCP

We brushed our hair back and our. The Last Refuge. Augustus Young. BIrV

We built a palace for them, made of bedrooms. R-and-R Centre: An Incident from the Vietnam War. D. J. Enright. OxBC

We built a ship upon the stairs. A Good Play. Robert Louis Stevenson. FaPON; MoShBr; OTCP; PWR

We Bumped Off Your Friend the Poet. Harold Norse. GLP

We burrowed night and day with tools of lead. Barbury Camp. Charles Hamilton Sorley. NSI

We bury ourselves to get high. Smoking in an Open Grave. David Bottoms. InPK

We busse our Wantons, but our Wives we kisse. (*LL*) Kissing and Bussing. Robert Herrick. BeJo; CBLP

We but begin to hope to know, having known. Subject. Marie Ponsot. VGW

We call it the permanent city. The Permanent City. Matthew Sweeney. IB

We Call Them Greasers. Gloria Anzaldúa. GLP

We called him "Rags." He was just a cur. Rags. Edmund Vance Cooke. BLPA

We called the statue. Niyi Osundare. *Fr.* Moonsongs. HBAPE

We came down above the houses. Deaths and Engines. Eiléan Ní Chuilleanáin. PWE

We came home to the stranger. Deadly Weapon. Beatrix Gates. GLP

We came of age, and were made man and wife. Mourning for My Wife. Mei Yao Ch'en, *tr. fr. Chinese by* Jonathan Chaves. SuSP

We came to the edge. A Pretty Woman. Simon J. Ortiz. CDW

We came to the high cliffs of Bonaventure. Long-billed Gannets. Frances D. Emery. GoYe

We came to the islands. We came saying. The Quest. Harold Vinal. GoYe

We came to the outer light down a ramp in the dark. Westland Row. Thomas Kinsella. MoP

We came to visit the cow. Freedom, New Hampshire. Galway Kinnell. LCAP; NaP

We came upon him sitting in the sun. The Veteran. Margaret Isabel Postgate. NSI

We can always be found. Elegy: Breece D'J Pancake. Franz Wright. NAmP90

We can but say, 'Farewell, good sense.' (*LL*) The Lion in Love. Marianne Moore. VBLP

We can only see a little of the ocean. God's Love. *Unknown.* BLRP

We can supply you with a cradle, too. (*LL*) Under the Willow Shades. Sir William Davenant. BoLoP; ELP

We can tell already. Two Months Married. Aidan Carl Mathews. IB; PBCIP

We Can Try Again Another Day. Judith Kazantzis. DT

We cannot bear to roast a book. The Parental Critic. Keith Preston. NBLV

We cannot get. By Faith Not Sight. Heather McHugh. PFL

We cannot go to the country. Raleigh Was Right. William Carlos Williams. NIP; NoAM; Poetr; RB

We cannot know his legendary head. Archaic Torso of Apollo. Rainer Maria Rilke, *tr. fr. German.* NAWM-2, *tr. by* Stephen Mitchell; RaBo

We cannot stay their death nor stay our death. Pause. Witter Bynner. IMW

We cannot trap them in our zoos, oh, no! Dinosaurs. Carolyn Stoloff. NYBP

We cannot walk like Byron among Ayasoluk's ruined. The Pleasure of Ruins. J. D. McClatchy. PoA

We Can't Be Too Careful. D. H. Lawrence. IHNG

We can't give them up, though. Avant Garde. Louis Dudek. *Fr.* Provincetown. MoCV

We can't tonight! We're overworked and busy. Tonight. Franklin P. Adams. FiBHP

We Cared for Each Other. Heine, *tr. fr. German by* John Todhunter. AWP

We caroused. I Met This Guy Who Died. Gregory Corso. NAs; Poetsp

We caught the tread of dancing feet. The Harlot's House. Oscar Wilde. EBVV; GGP; MoBrPo; NAEL-2; NoAM; OHCV

We chanced in passing by that afternoon. The Black Cottage. Robert Frost. VGW

We change our cars and eat our meat. Song of the South. Sean O'Brien. PWE

We chant and enchant. Velimir Khlebnikov, *tr. fr. Russian by* Paul Schmidt. CBNP

We charge through the skies of disillusion. Song at the African Middle Class. Molara Ogundipe-Leslie. HBAPE

We choose to say goodbye against our will. Departing Words to a Son. Robert Pack. GOYP

We climb the slopes of life with throbbing heart. Aspiration. H. Cordelia Ray. AmWP; CBWP-3

We climbed the dark. We. The Island. George Woodcock. MoCV

We climbed the hill to look over our land. Our Land. Yannis Ritsos, *tr. fr. Greek by* Edmund Keeley. AnAn

We climbed through a broken window. An Old Whorehouse. Mary Oliver. CAPP

We clung together an hour. Waterloo Station. Rosemary Norman. DT

We come from a long line. For My Mother, Who Lives. Lorraine Duggin. LoHo

We come in peace from the third planet. The First Men on Mercury. Edwin Morgan. CBNP; PeLV

We come to uncrate the newness of this world. First Things. Lucienne Desnoues, *tr. fr. French by* Miller Williams. WPOW

We come together once more, we four, in the center. Head Couples. William H. Matchett. NYBP

We Conquer or Die. James S. Pierpont. PAH

We conquered France, but felt our captive's charms. Pope. *Fr.* First Epistle of the Second Book of Horace, Imitation of. (?) EPCY

We Continue. W. S. Merwin. CAPP

We could be going home. The Second Angel. Philip Levine. NaP

We could be here. This is the valley. Small Town with One Road. Gary Soto. SoSe

We could count the times we went for a walk. The End of the Affair. James Simmons. PBCIP

We could have become a silence. (*LL*) Quick and Bitter. Yehuda Amichai. BoLoP, *tr. by* Assia Gutmann.

We could have crossed the road but hesitated. The Interrogation. Edwin Muir. CMoP; LiTB; PoWW

We could not live there. (*LL*) Honesty-Stones. J. S. Harry. NOBAu

We could not pause, while yet the noontide air. Obsequies of Stuart. John Randolph Thompson. PAH

We could not yet describe ourselves. (*LL*) There Was a Roof over Our Heads. Alberto A. Ríos. AfAz; FYAP; ImGa

We could swing all the way from March to August. (*LL*) A Appointment. Chang Shiang-Lua. TSaS, *tr. by* Stephen L. Smith *with* Naomi Shihab Nye.

We could wipe away a fly. The Jungle Café. Gary Soto. NoAM

We couple in the grace/ of that mysterious race. (*LL*) At night Chinamen jump. Frank O'Hara. CBNP; NoAM; NOBA; SM

We cover the hole in the ground. Grandmother's Ninetieth Birthday. Christine Churches. FaBoMA

We crawled and cried and laughed. Autobiography. Mbella Sonne Dipoko. TTY

We cross a stream and my horse. Under the Frontier Post. Wang Ch'ang-ling, *tr. fr. Chinese by* Rewi Alley. ChTr

We cross many rivers, but here is no anguish; our. Arawak Prologue. Basil McFarlane. PBCV

We cross the prairie as of old. The Kansas Emigrants. Whittier. PAH

We cross the river over dark waves. Rain on the River. Lu Yu, *tr. fr. Chinese by* Kenneth Rexroth. OHMPC

We crossed the broad Pecos, we forded the Nueces. The Brazos River. *Unknown*. PrIm

We curl into your eyes. The Female God. Isaac Rosenberg. FaBoTw

We Dance Like Ella Riffs. Carolyn M. Rodgers. PoBA

We dance round in a ring and suppose. The Secret Sits. Robert Frost. InPK

We Delighted, My Friend. Léopold Sédar Senghor, *tr. fr. French by* Miriam Koshland. PBA; TTY

We descended the first night from Europe. Coming Back to America. James Dickey. NYBP

WE. DID. BEGINNE. TO. BE. VNDONE. (*LL*) As soone as wee to bee begvnne. *Unknown*. OBD

We Did It. Yehuda Amichai, *tr. fr. Hebrew by* Harold Schimmel. AnRep; BoLoP

We did it in front of the mirror. We Did It. Yehuda Amichai, *tr. fr. Hebrew by* Harold Schimmel. AnRep; BoLoP

We did kowtow to a blazing sun. Letter to the Immigration Officer. Jan Kemp. PeNZ

We did not expect this; we were not ready for this. Early March. Norman Nicholson. PAW

We did not flinch but gave our lives to save. Cenotaph at the Isthmos. Simonides, *tr. fr. Greek by* Peter Jay. GrAn

We did not know the first thing about. Thinking about Bill, Dead of AIDS. Miller Williams. NGP; PFL

We did sums at school, Mummy. Halfway Street, Sidcup. Fleur Adcock. Spl

We didn't think/ nuthin. Poems about Playmates. Ronda Davis. JB

We didn't want to be white — or did we? The Struggle. Toi Derricotte. PBCAP

We died in Zortman on a Sunday. The Renegade Wants Words. James Welch. CDW

We do accept thee, heavenly Peace! Acceptation. Margaret Junkin Preston. PAH

We do assemble that a funeral. An Elegy in Memory of the Worshipful Major Thomas Leonard Esq. Samuel Danforth, Jr. SCAP

We Do Lie beneath the Grass. Thomas Lovell Beddoes. *Fr.* Death's Jest Book. ELP

We do lie beneath the grass. Thomas Lovell Beddoes. *See* Swallow leaves her nest, The.

We do not fear thhe verdict of posterity. Bronxville Darby And Joan. Noël Coward. *Fr.* Sail Away.
(?) IHNG

We do not know who made them. Negro Spirituals. Rosemary *and* Stephen Vincent Benét. FaPON

We do not play on graves. Emily Dickinson. NIP; PoEL-5

We do not see them come. Scala Coeli. Kathleen Raine. NYBP

We do not wish anything to happen. T. S. Eliot. *Fr.* Murder in the Cathedral. OxBTC

We do: the present desperate stage. The Miners' Response. Dugald Sutherland MacColl. NSI

We do to ourselves. (*LL*) Teach your children. Chief Seattle. EaPr

We don't have much language for tragedy. Autumn. Thomas W. Shapcott. CBAP

We don't have seasons, we just repeat. Kathleen Jamie. *Fr.* Katie's Poems. PWE

We don't know the ins and outs. The Wall. David Jones. PoA

We don't lack people here on the Northern coast. Amusing Our Daughters. Carolyn Kizer. VCAP; VGW

We don't like that girl from Tooting Bec. *Unknown*. FaBoUs

We don't want to fight, but, by Jingo, if we do. G. W. Hunt. FaBoEH

We don't; we take things as they are. (*LL*) Lying Awake. W. D. Snodgrass. HoPM; MoAmPo; NYBP

We drank from the bought bottle. The Visions. Sebastian Barry. IB

We draw our lives after ourselves in streams. The Lynx. Charles Edward Eaton. DiPo

We dream — it is good we are dreaming. Emily Dickinson. BoWoP

We dressed each other. Empress Eifuku, *tr. fr. Japanese by* Kenneth Rexroth. WPOW

We Drink Farewell. Tu Mu, *tr. fr. Chinese by* Kenneth Rexroth. OHMPC

We drive all day from mildly picturesque Coumbes-sur-Seine. Hijack. Lincoln Kirstein. ArOW

We drive between lakes just turning green. Driving through Minnesota during the Hanoi Bombings. Robert Bly. NoP; Poetr

We dwell in Him, oh, everlasting Home. In Him. Annie Johnson Flint. BLRP

We eat and drink and laugh and energize. Death's Transfiguration. Israel Zangwill. TrJP

We embrace, and when I look in the mirror. Reflection. Mona Elaine Adilman. WoWa

We embrace the world! (*LL*) Suddenly We Will Wake. Shin Shalom. MHP

We enter. Climbing the Chagrin River. Mary Oliver. Poetr

We entered the city at noon! High bells. The radio on. One Night Stand. Amiri Baraka. NeAP

We fail, and white men call us faggots till the end of the earth. (*LL*) A Poem for Black Hearts. Amiri Baraka. PoBA; PoM; SOTW

We fancied he'd share in our cause. Instead. What's In It for Me? Edgar A. Guest. PoToHe

We feed the chickens every day. Off We Go to Market. Gwen A. Smith. BoTP

We fell in love at "Journey for Margaret." First Love. Judith Hemschemeyer. Poetsp

We fell on the chair. Hilbert's Program. Milo De Angelis, *tr. fr. Italian by* Lawrence Venuti. NeIt

We few, we happy few, we band of brothers. Shakespeare. *Fr.* King Henry V. UnPo

We find in the East Indies stars there be. Of Stars. Margaret Cavendish, Duchess of Newcastle. NOSC

We finished clearing the last. Above Pate Valley. Gary Snyder. CoAP; LCAP; NaP; NoP; TRP

We Fish. Herman Melville. WHSW

We Fish Our Lives Out. Jana Harris. NGP

We fish, we fish, we merrily swim. We Fish. Herman Melville. WHSW

We fished up the Atlantic Cable one day between the Barbadoes. The Cable Ship. Harry Edmund Martinson, *tr. fr. Swedish by* Robert Bly. RB

We five looked out over the moor. The Last Day of Leave (1916). Robert Graves. PAW

We five owls were once alive. From a Printed Bill, Fixed in the Beak of One in a Group of Five Stuffed Owls in the Shop Window of a Bird Stuffer, at Richmond, Yorkshire. *Unknown*. FaBoUs

We fix the ages of the irises at flower. To the Quick. Heather McHugh. PRA

We fled from the sight inland and that night. Columbus Reaches Juana, 1492. Ralph Gustafson. NOBC

We floating Islands, living *Hebrides*. (*LL*) On the Memory of Mr. Edward King, Drowned in the Irish Seas. John Cleveland. OAEL-1; SeCP

We flung gravel out in arcs then cut. Before Breakup on the Chena outside Fairbanks. David McElroy. Poetsp

We follow where the Swamp Fox guides. The Swamp Fox. William Gilmore Simms. BeLS; FaBoBe; PAH

We followed her unto the chamber-door. The Palace of Pleasant Regard. Lady of the Assembly. *Fr.* Assembly of Ladies, The. WPE

We followed the river to Fortune's Wheel. Douglas Oliver. *Fr.* Infant and the Pearl, The. NBrP

We forget where we came from. Our Jewish. Jews in the Land of Israel. Yehuda Amichai, *tr. fr. Hebrew by* Warren Bargad *and* Stanley F. Chyet. PoSu

We found dead animals in our sagebrush hills. Dobbin. George Bowering. NOBC

We frolic while 'tis May. (*LL*) Ode on the Spring. Thomas Gray. GTBS; GTBS-P; NOEC

We from the black sun of fear. Chorus of the Dead. Nelly Sachs, *tr. fr. German by* Ruth Mead *and* Matthew Mead. WoWa

We gather our bones from many places, look for. Corn Children. Carol Lee Sanchez. SRLS

We gather where the weeping willow waves. Decoration Day. Josephine D. Henderson Heard. CBWP-4

We gave a helping hand to grass. A Helping Hand. Miroslav Holub, *tr. fr. Czech by* George Theiner. PoSu; PWE

We gave away our futures long ago. (*LL*) Letter to Breyten Breytenbach from Hong Kong. C. J. Driver. PeSAV

We get no good/ By being ungenerous. Reading. Elizabeth Barrett Browning. *Fr.* Aurora Leigh. GN

We give-away our thanks to the earth. Dolores La Chapelle. EaPr

We give thanks. Elk Song. Linda Hogan. FoLa

We give Thee thanks, O Lord! Thanksgiving Day. Robert Bridges. OHIP

We Go. Karl Wolfskehl, *tr. fr. German.* TrJP, *tr. by* Carol North Valhope *and* Ernst Morwitz

We Go as American Tourists. Nellie Wong. ETG

We go back. Proclamation/ From Sleep, Arise. Carolyn M. Rodgers. JB

We go no more to Calverly's. Calverly's. E. A. Robinson. NoAM

We go out in the stony midnight. Thomas McGrath. *Fr.* Letter to an Imaginary Friend, Part One. NNaP

We Go Out Together. Kenneth Patchen. MoAmPo

We go to sleep like anybody else. Good Old Harry. John James. VaA

We gon have/ mo room! (*LL*) An Inconvenience. John Raven. BPo; CRP

We got a mountain on the horizon. "What Have We Got." Lemn Sissay. NBrP

We got away — for just two nights. To Be a Pilgrim. Robert Conquest. OxBC

We Got Everything We Needed Here and Aint It Something. *Unknown, tr. fr. Seneca Indian by* Jerome K. Rothenberg *and* Richard Johnny John. STP

We got ready and showed our home. The Scattered Congregation. Tomas Tranströmer, *tr. fr. Swedish by* Robert Bly. RaBo

We got sunlight on the sand. There Is Nothin' like a Dame. Oscar Hammerstein II. OBAL

We got this idea. Our Hands in the Garden. Anne Hébert, *tr. fr. French by* A. Poulin, Jr. BoWoP

We Greeks have fallen on evil. Palladas, *tr. fr. Greek by* Kenneth Rexroth. PGA

We Greet Each Other in the Side. *Unknown.* BXAP

We greet thee now open this festal morn. Greeting. H. Cordelia Ray. CBWP-3

We greet them in the sky over the opening of the kiva. (*LL*) It is our quiet time. Nancy Wood. EaPr

We greet you rarest White Heron of One Flight. A Greeting to Queen Elizabeth, the Rare White Heron of Single Flight. Wiremu Kingi Kerekere, *tr. fr. Maori by* Wiremu Kingi Kerekere. PeNZ

We grow accustomed to the Dark. Emily Dickinson. SAmP

We grow to the sound of the wind. Dates. *Unknown, tr. fr. Arabic by* E. Powys Mathers. *Fr.* Thousand and One Nights, The. AWP; FaPON

We had a drinking party. Drinking with Friends amongst the Blooming Peonies. Liu Yu Hsi, *tr. fr. Chinese by* Kenneth Rexroth. OHMPC

We had a motorbike all through the war. A Motorbike. Ted Hughes. InPS

We had a Rabbi which was named the Kozienicer Rabbi. Harry Lenga. Julie N. Heifetz. BTR

We had already left him. Ugolino. Dante, *tr. by* Seamus Heaney. *Fr.* Divina Commedia. AnAn; FaBoPV; MeMAP; NAWM-1, *tr. by* John Ciardi

We had been in the tall grass for hours. At Midsummer. Norman Dubie. NoAM

We had been school-mates, — she and I. Imogene. Eloise Bibb. CBWP-4

We had exchanged our hearts indeed. (*LL*) The Exchange. Samuel Taylor Coleridge. FiBHP

We had expected everything but revolt. Nightmare Number Three. Stephen Vincent Benét. MoAmPo

We had forgotten You, or very nearly. Christ in Flanders. Lucy Whitmell. NSI

We had gathered for the love-feast on the time appointed. Who Is My Neighbor? Josephine D. Henderson Heard. CBWP-4

We had many problems set us when Coolgardie was a camp. The Smiths. E. G. Murphy. NOBAu

We had more than. Words. Vern Rutsala. ETG; WeW

We had no petnames, no diminutives for you. Mary Gravely Jones. Adrienne Rich. *Fr.* Grandmothers. HCAP; MDDM; NAAL-2; NoAM

We had red earth once to smear on our cheeks. Arrowy Dreams. Witter Bynner. GOA

We had the selfsame world enlarged for each. "George Eliot." *Fr.* Brother and Sister. GN; NALW

We had this stuff that Wayne found in the shed. Cro-Kill. Anthony Lawrence. NOBAu

We had to enter. Yad Vashem. Hans Juergensen. BTR

We had to stop. River's End. Ralph Pomeroy. NGP

We halted in a town the host. A Halt. Zbigniew Herbert, *tr. fr. Polish by* Czeslaw Milosz *and* Peter Dale Scott. AnRep

We harden like trees, and like rivers are cold. (*LL*) Lover, The; a Ballad. Lady Mary Wortley Montagu. ECWP; GGP; NAEL-1; NoP

We have a bed, and a baby too. The Laborer. Richard Dehmel, *tr. fr. German by* Jethro Bithell. AWP

We have a dog named "Here." Birthday. William Stafford. NAs

We have a fiction that we live by: it is the river. Waikato-Taniwha-Rau. Vincent O'Sullivan. PeNZ

We have/ a map of the universe. Wings. Miroslav Holub, *tr. fr. Czech by* Ian Milner *and* George Theiner. PoSu

We have a pritty witty king. The Earl of Rochester. *See* God bless our good and gracious King.

We have a small hand with five fingers. Toil. Avraham Shlonsky, *tr. fr. Hebrew by* Ruth Finer Mintz. MHP

We have all been in rooms. Adultery. James Dickey. CAPP; MT; TAP

We have all, one time or another, met a famous figure. Back Room Joys. Justin Richardson. FiBHP

We have all seen them circling pastures. Under the Vulture-Tree. David Bottoms. MT

We have an old mother that peevish is grown. The Mother Country. Benjamin Franklin. AiP; PAH

We have ascended to this paradise. The Attic. Henri Coulette. PoRA

We have bathed, where none have seen us. Bridal Song to Amala. Thomas Lovell Beddoes. *Fr.* Death's Jest Book. GBL; OBNC (Epithalamia.) PoEL-4
(Song: "We have bathed, where none have seen us.") NOBVV; OBNC

We have become one in thought. (*LL*) The Fire in the Stone. Tuvia Rivner. MHP

We have been a walking. Wassail Song. *Unknown.* GBP

We Have Been Believers. Margaret Walker. PoBA; PoNe

We have been helping with the cake. Day before Christmas. Marchette Chute. NTCP; SiSoPo

We Have Been Here Before. Morris Bishop. FiBHP; NYBP

We have been sailing in a certain small fountain. About This Course. David Shapiro. PoA

We have borne good sons to broken men. Miners' Wives. Joe Corrie. OxBS

We have climbed the mountain. Sestina: Here in Katmandu. Donald Justice. SM
(Here in Katmandu.) CoAP; HeIP; RFM

We have come in the winter. Song for a Country Wedding. William Jay Smith. GrPl

We have come to the edge of the woods. Jacklight. Louise Erdrich. HATNAP; WeW

We have come to the end of a dream. The Cities Have Fallen. Fragano Ledgister. PBCV

We have come to the jungle. Jungle. Phyllis Haring. PeSA

We have come to your shrine to worship. A Plea for Mercy. Kwesi Brew. PBA

We have cried in our despair. When Helen Lived. W. B. Yeats. CMoP

We have decided to make Scotland secure. Tom Leonard. *Fr.* Situations Theoretical and Contemporary. NBrP

We have done what we wanted. Coming to This. Mark Strand. HCAP; VCAP

We have done with dogma and divinity. After Trinity. John Meade Falkner. OxBTC

We have drunk wine and discussed literature. Ch'iu Chin, *tr. fr. Chinese by* Kenneth Rexroth *and* Ling Chung. *Fr.* Two Poems to the Tune "The Narcissus by the River". WPC

We have faith in old proverbs full surely. Where There's a Will There's a Way. Eliza Cook. BLPA

We have for many years been bored. The Pen-guin. The Sword-fish. Robert Williams Wood. NBLV

We have forgotten who we are. *Unknown. Fr.* U.N. Environmental Sabbath Program. FHYEP

We have gathered just one stalk. (*LL*) This Morning Our Boat Left. *Unknown.* OHMPC

We have gone out in boats upon the sea at night. Passage over Water. Robert Duncan. NoAM; NOBA

We have grown a tree of knowledge, "Worthy Claflin" is the name. The Tree of Knowledge. L. A. J. Moorer. CBWP-3

We have had too much consecration. Hilda Doolittle ("H. D."). *Fr.* Walls Do Not Fall, The. NAAL-2

We have heard no nightingales singing. Working Class. Bertram J. Warr. NOBC

We have here, she said, only one sun in the month, and for only a little while. Henri Michaux, *tr. fr. French by* Richard Ellmann. *Fr.* I Am Writing to You from a Far-Off Country. AnRep

We have kept the miracle. I will not be here. *(LL)* In the Deep Museum. Anne Sexton. MoAmPo; Prf

We Have Lived and Loved Together. Charles Jefferys. BLPA; FaBoBe; PoToHe

We have lived like civilized people. The Silent Piano. Louis Simpson. CAPP

We Have Lost Our Little Hanner. "Max Adeler." FiBHP

We have lost the old tongue, and with it. The Old Tongue. Herbert Williams. AngWe

We have loved each other in this time twenty years. An Unfinished History. Archibald MacLeish. NYBP; VGW

We have met. To a Butterfly. W. H. Davies. FM

We have met late — it is too late to meet. A Denial. Elizabeth Barrett Browning. GBL; OBNC

We have moving over us, over head and spire. Sunday. Josephine Miles. PoA

We have no heart for the fishing, we have no hand for the oar. The Dykes. Kipling. CoGr; OBWP

We have no idea what his fantastic head. Archaic Torso of Apollo. Rainer Maria Rilke, *tr. fr. German by* Robert Bly. NU

We have no prairies. Bogland. Seamus Heaney. HeIP; IPY; NoAM; NOIV; NoP; PBCIP; PNI

We have no time for bridges. Seagulls. Patricia Hubbell. PDV

We have no time to stand and stare. *(LL)* Leisure. W. H. Davies. AngWe; ArNa; AWP; BoNaP; BoTP; CH; CoGr; EBEvV; FaBoBe; FaPON; GGP; LiTB; LiTM; MoBrPo; MoShBr; NOBE; NTP; OBEV; OBMV; OtMeF; PoRA; TFi; TrGrPo

We have not been happy, my Lord, we have not been too happy. T. S. Eliot. *Fr.* Murder in the Cathedral. OxBTC

We have one foe and one alone — England! *(LL)* A Chant of Hate against England. Ernst Lissauer. OtMeF

We have opened the door. The Dead Feast of the Kol-Folk. Whittier. PoEL-4

We have plenty of matches in our house. Love Poem. Ron Padgett. UL

We have reached the end of pastime, for always. End of Play. Robert Graves. EBEV

We have scarcely time to tell thee. Shelly. James McIntyre. FiBHP

We have seen her/ the world over. Hilda Doolittle ("H. D."). *Fr.* Tribute to the Angels. CRP; NALW; Poetr; VGW

We have seen how the most amiable. Hilda Doolittle ("H. D."). *Fr.* Walls Do Not Fall, The. BoWoP; PBWP

We have seen thee, queen of cheese. Queen of Cheese. James McIntyre. FiBHP

We have sent him seeds of the melon's core. Ku Klux. Madison Cawein. PAH

We have shared beauty and have shared grief, too. A Prayer for a Marriage. Mary Carolyn Davies. TrPWD

We have slept in. The Message on Cape Cod. Michael S. Weaver. PBCAP

We have struck the regions wherein we are keel or reef. Zone. Louise Bogan. IMW; WPE

We have survived. Survival. Robin Morgan. VBLP

We have tangled together. Growing Together. Joyce Carol Oates. CrSp; IHMS

We have tested and tasted too much, lover. Advent. Patrick Kavanagh. IIP; TIRV

We have the mauve or the cerise. Shop Talk. Roy Fuller. OxBC

We have the statue for it — Liberty. Address to the Refugees. John Malcolm Brinnin. GOA

We have to love the past. John Ash. *Fr.* Rain, The. SCBI

We have tried words before — always in vain. The Knife. Milton Kaplan. TrJP

We have voided all but freedom and all but our own joy. *(LL)* We are nature, long have we been absent, but now we return. Walt Whitman. EaPr

We have watched again. Among Hawks. Lance Henson. VoR

We have welded the towbar. The Meadow. Peter Fallon. PBCIP

We hear all past and future in one stroke of the temple bell. *(LL)* Written on a Monastery Wall. Li Shang-yin. PLT

We hear her in the square. At two o'clock. A Speaker in the Square. George Buchanan. PNI

We hear you want to die. The Seventieth Year. Gary Soto. AfAz

We heard the stories big-screen like. Singing the Internationale. Alberto A. Ríos. NGP

We heard the thrushes by the shore and sea. In Kerry. J. M. Synge. FaBoPP; GBL; MoBrPo; PeIV

We, Hermia. Helena and Hermia. Shakespeare. *Fr.* Midsummer Night's Dream, A. GN; OBF

We hesitate along. A Graveyard in Queens. John Montague. IPY

We hold our flat shields, we wear our jerkins of hide. Hymn to the Fallen. *Unknown, tr. fr. Chinese by* Arthur Waley. OBWP

We hold these truths to be self-evident. Decoy. John Ashbery. PoM

We hunted the wren for Robin the Bobbin. Hunting the Wren. *Unknown.* FaBoVe

We hurry on, nor passing note. Digby Mackworth Dolben. OBNC

We in our haste can only see the small components of the scene. War Poet. Donald Bain. PAW

We in our wandering. A Song of the Open Road. *Unknown, tr. fr. Latin by* John Addington Symonds. AWP

We inherit everything. *(LL)* Voices Answering Back: The Vampires. Lawrence Raab. AmPA

We inherited dreams. History Teaches, But It Has No Pupils. John Seed. VaA

We invite him to die. Colobus Monkey. *Unknown, tr. fr. Yoruba by* Ulli Beier. *Fr.* Hunter Poems of the Yoruba. RB

We Irish pride ourselves as patriots. Ireland. John Hewitt. CIP; FaBoPP; IIP

We is gathahed hyeah, my brothahs. An Ante-Bellum Sermon. Paul Laurence Dunbar. AAP; BPo

We issue from the meat of Pineapple Street. On the Island. L. E. Sissman. NYBP

We join with the earth and with each other. *Unknown. Fr.* U.N. Environmental Sabbath Program. FHYEP

We keep our quilts in closets and do not dance. Mennonites. Julia Kasdorf. LoHo; PBCAP

We kept him an hour in the/ bottom. A Cocker of Snooks. Phyllis Gotlieb. NOBC

We kept the Spartan code, and here we lie. *(LL)* At Thermopylae. Simonides.

We Kiss'd Again with Tears. Tennyson. *See* As through the land at eve we went.

We kissed at the barrier; and passing through. On the Departure Platform. Thomas Hardy. CBLP; NOBE; OBNC; OxBTC

We knew it was the end. Molly Brant, Iroquois Matron, Speaks. Paula Gunn Allen. ETG

We knew it would rain, for all the morn. Before the Rain. Thomas Bailey Aldrich. GN

We knew so much; when her beautiful eyes could lighten. Sagacity. William Rose Benét. MoAmPo

We know as we grow older. Ella Wheeler Wilcox. *See* I know, as my life grows older.

We know it doesn't rhyme much anymore. What Is Poetry. James Scully. FYAP

We know not what it is, dear, this sleep so deep and still. The Two Mysteries. Mary Mapes Dodge. PWR; TrCP; WGRP

We know that hereabouts. Wonders of Obligation. Roy Fisher. VaA

We know that our master has left us for the day. *(LL)* Waking from Sleep. Robert Bly. CAPP; NOBA; NoP; Poetr

We know the cities by their stones. A Postcard from Berlin. Derek Mahon. BiHa

We know/ the winter earth. November Twenty-sixth Nineteen Hundred and Sixty-three. Wendell Berry. LiTM

We know this story: how his daddy died of drink. Custom Job: Hank Williams, Jr., and the Death Car, 1958. David Wojahn. *Fr.* Mystery Train: A Sequence. PBCAP

We know who her father is. Dan's Shoe Repair: 1959. Christine Lahey. BTR

We ladies sense it is the cuckoo builds no nest. Liberation. Ruth Stone. BoWoP

We Laughed. Rochelle Kraut. UL

We lay in the trenches we'd dug in the ground. The Ballad of Bunker Hill. Edward Everett Hale. PAH

We lay red roses on his grave. Paul Laurence Dunbar. Robert Hayden. NoP

We lean across the kitchen table. Arm Wrestling with My Father. Jack Driscoll , Jack Driscoll *and* Bill Meissner. GOYP

We learn from Horace, Homer sometimes sleep. Byron. *Fr.* Don Juan. EPCY

We learned that you don't shoot. Statement on Our Higher Education. W. M. Ransom. CDW

We learned to laugh. Although the flying bombs. Coman Leavenworth. *Fr.* Norfolk Memorials. LiTA

We leave the well-beloved place. Tennyson. *Fr.* In Memoriam A. H. H. EBVV, *abr.*; FHYEP; OAEL-2, *abr.*; PeECV, *abr.*; PoEL-5

We leave thee with thy guests, thou sunny maid! Albery Allson Whitman. *Fr.* Twasinta's Seminoles; Or Rape of Florida. AAP

We leave thy courts to-day. Farewell to Allen University. Josephine D. Henderson Heard. CBWP-4

We left the horses in the draw. A Season of Loss. Jim Barnes. HATNAP

We left the western island to live among strangers. The Search. John Hewitt. PNI

We left them there and went our way. (LL) Desire. William Cornish. Mes

We let fire rip, we blacken the pale-gold acres. Burning Off. Geoffrey Dutton. NOBAu

We lie back to back. Curtains. The Suitor. Jane Kenyon. InPK

We lie, day creatures, overhearing night. (LL) The Sound of Night. Maxine W. Kumin. BoNaP; SoSe; WPE

We lie on love's breath. (LL) Puriri moth's wing, A. Jan Kemp. PeNZ

We lie one against the other. Seventh Day Seventh Month. Kuan Yun She, tr. fr. Chinese by Kenneth Rexroth. OHMPC

We lift the curtain of the past to-day. Lincoln. H. Cordelia Ray. AmWP; CBWP-3

We like March — his shoes are purple. Emily Dickinson. SOTW; TTTS

We, like shades that were first conjured up. And through the Caribbean Sea. Margaret Danner. BPo

We/ little children in our shifts. Clap Your Hands for Herod. Josef Hanzlik, tr. fr. Czech by Ian Milner. OBCP

We live as best we can. (LL) Half Past Four, October. Anna Hajnal. BoWoP

We live by the sun. Stephanie Kaza. EaPr

We live: — dishonoured, in the shit. So what? it had to be. Iambes VIII. André de Chénier, tr. fr. French by Tom Paulin. FaBoPV

We live here to eat. Biological Light. Primus St. John. ETG

We Live in a Cage. William J. Harris. PoBA

We Live in a Rickety House. Alexander McLachlan. NOBC

We live in deeds, not years; in thoughts, not breaths. Philip James Bailey. Fr. Country Town, A. PoToHe

We live in history, says one. Talk in the Dark. Denise Levertov. PWE

We live in houses of ample weight. Edvard Munch. Charles Wright. HCAP

We live, while we see the sun. Pedro Calderón de la Barca, tr. fr. Spanish by Arthur Symons. Fr. Life Is a Dream. AWP; NAWM-1

We lived deep in a land of optative moods. From the Canton of Expectation. Seamus Heaney. CIP

We lived one and twenty year. Upon a Notorious Shrew. Unknown. FaBoEE

We looked, we loved, and therewith instantly. Pure Death. Robert Graves. GTBS-P; MeMBP; MoAB

We lose — because we win. Emily Dickinson. HeIP

We lose our jewels, but we break our chains. (LL) The Angel-Thief. Oliver Wendell Holmes. AnAmPo

We Love the Venerable House. Emerson. AH

We love thee, Ann Maria Smith. The Editor's Wooing. "Orpheus C. Kerr." OBAL

We love to squeeze bananas. Squeezes. Brian Patten. OTCP; Spl

We love with great difficulty. Sing with Your Body. Janice Mirikitani. MDDM; WPOW

We loved as friends now twenty years and more: The Change. Henry King. NOSC

We loved each other and were ignorant. (LL) After Long Silence. W. B. Yeats. BoLoP; CMoP; EnLoPo; HeIP; HoPM; LiTM; NAEL-2; OAEL-2; OBMV; PPP; PrIm; UnPo

We loved our nightjar, but she would not stay with us. The Nightjar. Sir Henry Newbolt. Mes; PlP

We loved the wild clamor of battle. The Song of the Flags. Silas Weir Mitchell. PAH

We Lying by Seasand. Dylan Thomas. PoA

We made a mistake in this song. Unknown, tr. fr. Seneca Indian by Jerome K. Rothenberg and Richard Johnny John. STP

We made castles of grass, green halls, enormous stem-lined rooms. The Riders. Ann Stanford. WPE

We make both mead and garden gay. Daffodils. P. A. Ropes. BoTP

We make our meek adjustments. Chaplinesque. Hart Crane. CMoP; HeIP; LiTM; MoP; NAAL-2; NoAM; NOBA; OxBA; SoCa; VGW

We make ourselves a place apart. Revelation. Robert Frost. ChIV-2

We make the world in which we live. The World We Make. Alfred Grant Walton. PoToHe

We Manage Most When We Manage Small. Linda Gregg. AmPA

We many men from Mauritania see. The Blackamoors. Rowland Watkyns. AngWe

We marched, and saw a company of Canadians. Canadians. Ivor Gurney. FaBoTw

We marry our grandfathers. Extensions of Linear Mobility. Jeanine Hathaway. IHMS

We May Be Learning How to Tell the Truth. Marilyn Hacker. Fr. La Fontaine de Vaucluse. Son

We may live without poetry, music and art. "Owen Meredith." PoToHe

We may no longer stay on shore. The Greenland Whale Fishery. Unknown. OBET

We may not climb the heavenly steeps. Our Master. Whittier. BLRP; WBLP

We may shut our eyes. Joys. James Russell Lowell. BoTP

We may sigh o'er the heavy burdens. The Burdens of All. Frances E. W. Harper. PWR

We may well wonder at those froward hermits. The Eremites. Robert Graves. LiTB

We mean to thrash these Prussian Pups. Unknown. NSI; PoWW

We meet in a cheap diner and I think, God. The Last Bohemians. Edward Field. NGP

We Meet in the Lives of Animals. Peter Everwine. NNaP

We meet 'neath the sounding rafter. The Revel. Bartholomew Dowling. BLPA

We meet/ on the dot. Meeting You at an Underground Station. Gillian Allnutt. VBLP

We meet upon the Level and we part upon the Square. The Level and the Square. Robert Morris. BLPA

We Met. Mary E. Tucker. CBWP-1

We met, a hundred of us met. The Vision. William Taylor. NOEC

We met but in one giddy dance. To ——. Winthrop Mackworth Praed. CBLP

We met for supper in your flat-bottomed boat. Dream Barker. Jean Valentine. PrIm; VGW

We met hand to hand. Twilight Night. Christina Rossetti. CBLP

We met on Charles Bridge, it was snowing. The Old Priest. Vladimir Holan, tr. fr. Czech by George Theiner. PoSu

We Met on Roads of Laughter. Charles Divine. FaBoBe

We met the British in the dead of winter. Meeting the British. Paul Muldoon. BiHa; CIP; FaBoPV; NoAM; PNI

We met upon a crowded street one day. Casual Meeting. Margaret E. Bruner. PoToHe

We might have known it always: music. An Die Musik. David Malouf. CBAP

We mind not now the merits of our kind. Marriage and Money. Sir Charles Sedley. Fr. Happy Pair, The. OBSV

We miss a kinsman more. Emily Dickinson. OxBSP

We more than others have the perfect right. Song of the Moderns. John Gould Fletcher. AWP

We Mothers. Nelly Sachs, tr. fr. German by Ruth Mead and Matthew Mead. MDDM

We mourn to-day o'er our sister dead. Resting. Josephine D. Henderson Heard. CBWP-4

We move from one. The River. Sam Cornish. PoBA

We move in elephantine row. Express. William Allingham. NOBVV

We moved like fingers. San Francisco Poem. John Logan. NNaP

We Must Be Free or Die. Wordsworth. See It Is Not to Be Thought Of [That the Flood].

We Must Be Polite. Carl Sandburg. SiSoPo

We must bear witness to something. The Cats of Balthus. Bin Ramke. SoCa

We must buy a filter. (LL) Aunt Eliza. Harry Graham. ChTr

We Must Die Because We Have Known Them. Rainer Maria Rilke, tr. fr. German by Stephen Mitchell. RaBo

We must fight, or lose our cattle! (LL) Speech. Chief Mothibi. PeSAV

We must kill our gods before they kill us. Black Trumpeter. Henry Dumas. PoBA

We must leave the handrails and the Ariadne-threads. À l'Ange Avantgardien. Francis Reginald. MoCV

We Must Look at the Harebell. "Hugh MacDiarmid." Fr. In Memoriam James Joyce. NAEL-2

We must meet today in freedom's cause. Hold the Fort. Unknown. SWP

We must not sever, you and I. Brotherhood. "J. J. W." PeHV

We must pass like smoke or live within the spirit's fire. Immortality. "Æ." AWP; OBMV; TIRV; WGRP

We Must Return. Agostinho Neto, tr. fr. Portuguese by Michael Wolfers. PeSAV

We must sit down. Councils. Marge Piercy. CrSp

We mustered at midnight, in darkness we formed. Bethel. A. J. H. Duganne. PAH

We named you. Rachel. Linda Pastan.
(Rachel (rā'chal), a Ewe.) BTR

We need him now — his rugged faith that held. Abraham Lincoln, the Master. Thomas Curtis Clark. OHIP

We need no runners here. Booze is law. Harlem, Montana; Just Off the Reservation. James Welch. CDW; HATNAP

We Never Close. David Clewell. NAmP90

We never half believed the stuff. James Wetherell. E. A. Robinson. MoAmPo

We Never Know. Yusef Komunyakaa. MT

We never know how high we are. Emily Dickinson. AnAmPo

We never know we go. Emily Dickinson. AnAmPo

We never laughed much. Cartwheels. Mary Lonnberg Smith. AIW

We Never Said Farewell. Mary Elizabeth Coleridge. OxBSP; WPE

We never spent time in the mountains. Interlude. Welton Smith. PoBA

We no longer control could drag us back. (LL) July in Washington. Robert Lowell. LCAP; NAAL-2; NaP; Prf

We now lament not, but congratulate. John Donne. Fr. Of the Progres[se] of the Soule; the Second Anniversarie. ESCV; NOSC; SeCP

We Object. Unknown, tr. fr. Maori by A. Armstrong. WTO

We of Sparta fought the Argives — equal in number and arms. Chairemon, tr. fr. Greek by Richard Evans. GrAn

We offer you, Lord, in our strong, our sensitive hands. Offertory. John F. Deane. TIRV

We only know that here it lies. (LL) Epitaph on the World. Thoreau. FF

We only know that in the sultry weather. England and America, 1863. Richard Monckton Milnes. EBVV; OHCV

We only live between. For Sheridan. Robert Lowell. HCAP

We open the street door. The Same Month They Bombed Cambodia. Amy Uyematsu. OpBo

We ought to be together, you and I. (LL) You and I. Henry Alford. BLPA; FaBoBe

We oughtta take somma these college perfessers. What the Sixties Were Really Like. Sam Abrams. UL

We outgrow love, like other things. Emily Dickinson. NOBA; SoSe

We overcome this wind. A Litany for Rain. John S. Mbiti. EaPr

We owe the ancients something. You have read. Fitz-Greene Halleck. Fr. Fanny. OBAL

We own the love that calls us back to Thee! (LL) Father of all! in Death's relentless claim. Oliver Wendell Holmes. TrPWD

We Own the Night. Amiri Baraka. PoBA

We oxen are not only good. Leonidas of Alexandria, tr. fr. Greek by Robin Skelton. GrAn

We paid six francs to see Droseraceae, dead flies. Summer at the Jardin d'Hiver. Richard McCann. PFL

We park and stare. A full sky of the stars. The Death of the Sheriff. Robert Lowell. MoAB; MoAmPo

We parked the car in a dusty village. Waterfall. Gillian Clarke. SCBI

We part not with thee at this meeting day. (LL) Three Things [or Thinges] There Be[e] That Prosper All [or Up] Apace. Sir Walter Ralegh. NoP; PoEL-2

We pass a stranger. He glances. The Stranger Not Ourselves. William Stafford. NNaP

We pass the flayed carcass of a cow. The Man from Changi. Graeme Hetherington. NOBAu

We Passed by Green Closes. John Clare. EnVR

We passed each other, turned and stopped for half an hour, then went our way. On the Road to the Sea. Charlotte Mew. BrRo; FaBoWP; PeHV; VBLP

We passed the ice of pain. The Moment. Theodore Roethke. NYBP

We passed the Northern Sea! (LL) A Ballad of Sir John Franklin. George Henry Boker. AnAmPo

We passed their graves. Peace. Langston Hughes. BPo

We photographed everything. The 20th Century. Darrell Gray. UL

We pick/ the bittersweet grapes. Napa, California. Ana Castillo. WPOW

We picked flints. Tinder. Seamus Heaney. OxAEP-2

We planned to shake the world together, you and I. Lamplight. May Wedderburn Cannan. NSI

We planted a garden/ Of all kinds of flowers. Flowers. Harry Behn. FaPON

We pledged our hearts, my love and I. The Exchange. Samuel Taylor Coleridge. FiBHP

We plough and sow — we're so very, very low. The Song of the Lower Classes. Ernest Charles Jones. CoGr; CoMu

We plucked them as we passed! (LL) It Was Not in the Winter. Thomas Hood. ELP, longer vers.

We Poets in Our Youth. Wordsworth. Fr. Resolution and Independence. BoNaP; EBEV; EnRP; FaBoRV; FHYEP; HAP; InPS; LiTB; MAT; MeMBP; NOBE; NOCV; NoP; OAEL-2; OBNC; OxAEP-2; PoEL-4; PPP; TEP; TFi

We Poets Speak. Francis Thompson. Fr. Sister Songs. FaBV

We pointed it out to his bed-ridden eyes. Hospital. Geoffrey C. Millard. PeSA

We poor Agawams. Mr. Ward of Anagrams Thus. Nathaniel Ward. SCAP

We practice our scales. Fish Story: How Language Carries Us into the Unknown. Brigitte Frase. LoHo

We praise Love the limiter. (LL) Je T'Adore. Thomas Kinsella. MoP; NoAM

We Praise Thee, God, for Harvests Earned. John Coleman Adams. AH

We Praise Thee, If One Rescued Soul. Lydia Huntley Sigourney. AH

We praise thee, O God; we acknowledge thee to be the Lord. Te Deum Laudamus. Unknown, tr. fr. Latin. WGRP

We pray. (LL) Sun, The. Charlie Mehrhoff. EaPr

We pray Thee, have mercy on Zion! Prayer for Redemption. Unknown. TrJP

We pray to life's source, Mary. The Virgin Mary. Unknown, tr. fr. Welsh by Joseph P. Clancy. OBWVE

We prepare/ the meal together. Soul Food. Janice Mirikitani. OpBo

We promise letters and send postcards. Letter Following. Aidan Carl Mathews. IB; PBCIP

We pulled for you when the wind was against us and the sails were low. Song of the Galley-slaves. Kipling. ChTr; GTBS-P; HAP; NTP; PoEL-5; SCGP

We put more coal on the big red fire. Father's Story. Elizabeth Madox Roberts. FaPON; ImGa

We put out our hands on the window — cold. In Time of Need. William Stafford. UnPo

We put the shoe on him the first time this morning. The First Shoe. Máire Mhac an tSaoi, tr. fr. Gaelic by Brendan O Hehir. TSaS, tr. by Brendan O Hehir

We Rainclouds. Marvin Wyche, Jr.. EaPr

We raise de wheat. Unknown. BPo; TAP

We rake the past, down to an ounce of wants. Squatter in the Foreground. Kenward Elmslie. UL

We ran across the meadow scabbed with the cow-dung. Geoffrey Hill. Fr. Mercian Hymns. HAP

We reach the promised land. Story of Joshua. Alicia Ostriker. ChIV-1

We Reached Out Far. Perets Markish, tr. fr. Yiddish by Jacob Sonntag. TrJP

We read and hear about you every day. To the Rulers. Howard Nemerov. OxBC

We Read of a People. Unknown. AH

We Real Cool. Gwendolyn Brooks. CAPP; FF; HAP; HeIL; HeIP; HoPM; InPK; NALW; NoP; PoA; PoBA; PoE; PrIm; RaBo; SM; SoSe; TAP; TRP; TTY; WeW

We Real Cool. We. Gwendolyn Brooks. See Pool players, The.

We really didn't see it. Three Snakes, Strawberry Canyon, Berkeley. Ray Gonzáles. AfAz

We received the Torah on Sinai. Dead Men Don't Praise God. Jacob Glatstein, tr. fr. Yiddish by Ruth Whitman. BTR

We recognize each other, neighbors before the war. U.S. Army Holds Dance for Camp Survivors. Germany 1945. Lisa Ress. BTR

We reconstruct lives in the intensive. Clan Meeting: Births and Nations: A Blood Song. Michael S. Harper. NoAM

We reden ofte and finde ywrite. Sir Orfeo. Unknown. EnVB

We remember you/ calling America. Poetry Concert. Michael S. Harper. TAP

We return thanks to our mother, the earth. Unknown, tr. fr. Iroquois Indian. EaPr

We ride down the coast hwy through the rain. The Great Santa Barbara Oil Disaster OR. Conyus. AmPA; NBV

We rise from the snow where we've. Selective Service. Carolyn Forché. Poetr

We rise to Sion Mount from Herndon-Hill. (LL) An Elegy upon His Tomb in Herndon-Hill Church, Erected by His Wife, Who Speaks. James Howell. OBWVE

We rise up early and. Anna Speaks of the Childhood of Mary Her Daughter. Lucille Clifton. NALW

We rock and grunt, grunt and/ Shine. (LL) Song for Ishtar. Denise Levertov. MoP; NALW; NaP; NMM; NoAM; PoM

We rode the canals. Boxing the Fox. Pearse Hutchinson. CIP

We rode the tawny Texan hills. That Texan Cattle Man. Joaquin Miller. AnAmPo

We row along the shore on the bay side. Crabbing for Blue-claws. James Ulmer. UTF

We run the dangercourse. We Walk the Way of the New World. Don L. Lee. BPo; PoBA

We said: there will surely be hawthorn out. Spring Snow and Tui. Mary Ursula Bethell. PeNZ

We sail out of season into an oyster-gray wind. Crossing the Atlantic. Anne Sexton. NoAM

We sailed to and fro in Erie's broad lake. Perry's Victory. *Unknown.* PAH

We sang the great anthems of the uLundi mountains. *(LL)* A Meeting with Vilakazi, the Great Zulu Poet. Raymond Mazisi Kunene. PeSAV

We sat across from each other in the dusk. The Last Time I Saw Jack. Carolyn Lau. BCF

We sat across the table. The Friend. Marge Piercy. CAPP; CrSp; NALW; NMM; Poetr

We sat at the hut of the fisher. Twilight. Heine, *tr. fr. German by* Louis Untermeyer. AWP

We sat before an October fire. The Necessity of Falling. William Mills. MT

We sat down and wept by the waters. By the Rivers of Babylon We Sat Down and Wept. Byron. ChIV-1

We sat in the courtyard. Merida, 1969. William Matthews. EOEF

We sat so intimately together. Rain of Tears. Wilhelm Müller, *tr. fr. German by* Philip L. Miller. *Fr.* Beautiful Maid of the Mill, The. RiWo

We sat together at one summer's end. Adam's Curse. W. B. Yeats. BIrV; CMoP; NAEL-2; NoAM; NoP; OAEL-2; PFP; SOTW; TEP; WeW

We sat together in the trench. Trench Idyll. Richard Aldington. PeFWW

We sat, two children, warm against the wall. The Gate. Edwin Muir. CMoP; LiTM

We sat within the farm-house old. The Fire of Drift-wood. Longfellow. AmPP; BLPL; MeMAP; NAAL-1; NOBA; NoP; OxBA; TAP

We saw a bloody sunset over Courtland. Remembering Nat Turner. Sterling A. Brown. PoBA; PoNe

We saw a town by the track in Colorado. Holding the Sky. William Stafford. RFM

We saw anchored worlds in a shallow stream. Lying on a Bridge. Van K. Brock. MT; SM

We saw it all. We saw the souvenir shops, and sitting. Niagara Falls. Alan Dugan. PoA

We saw reindeer. Rigorists. Marianne Moore. NU

We saw that sky. Blackness. Place of Fire. Johannes Bobrowski, *tr. fr. German by* Ruth Mead *and* Matthew Mead. PoSu

We saw the light shine out a-far. The Golden Carol. *Unknown.* OHIP

We Saw the Swallows. George Meredith. *See* We saw the swallows gathering in the sky.

We saw the swallows gathering in the sky. George Meredith. *Fr.* Modern Love. EnLoPo; GTBS-P; Mes; NOBE; NOBVV; OAEL-2; OBNC (We Saw the Swallows.) ELP

We saw Thee in Thy balmy nest. The Shepherd's Hymn. Richard Crashaw. *Fr.* In the Holy Nativity of Our Lord God. GeHe; PoEL-2; SeCV-1; TrGrPo, 3 *sts.*
(Verses from the Shepherd's Hymn.) OBEV

We say he is dead; ah, the word is too somber. Not Dead, but Sleeping. Clara Ann Thompson. CBWP-2

We say it for an hour, or for years. Good-By. Grace Denio Litchfield. PoToHe

We say, "It rains." An unbelievable age! Hath the Rain a Father? Jones Very. ChIV-1

We say that a loon, most graceful and dark. A Woman Gave Me a Red Star to Wear on My Headband. Jimmie Durham. HATNAP

We say the blood rose, meaning it came to the surface. Pityriasis Rosea. Stanley Plumly. PFL

We say the sea is lonely; better say. The Open Sea. William Meredith. CoAP; GoJo; GrPl; TAP; UnPo

We seamen are the bonny boys. A Song of the Seamen and Land Soldiers. *Unknown.* OxBSS

We search the world for truth; we cull. The Book Our Mothers Read. Whittier. *Fr.* Miriam. BLRP
(Knowledge.) PoToHe

We search, yet find it not o'er widest lands. *(LL)* Lost Opportunities. H. Cordelia Ray. AmWP; CBWP-3

We see death coming into our midst like black smoke. The Shilling in the Armpit. Ieuan Gethyn. FaBoEH

We see each living thing finally die. Louise Labé, *tr. fr. French by* Willis Barnstone. BoWoP

We see God clear and high above the town. *(LL)* Soul's Liberty. Anna Wickham. MoBrPo; OxBSP

We see her now (and again). Lucille. Steve Carey. UL

We see in authors, too stiff to recant. John Donne. *Fr.* Of the Progres[se] of the Soule; the Second Anniversarie. ESCV; NOSC; SeCP

We See Jesus. Annie Johnson Flint. BLRP

We see lots of people at the party. The Party. Jerome Sala. UL

We see them not — we cannot hear. Are They Not All Ministering Spirits? Robert Stephen Hawker. ArNa; OxAEP-2

We seek a renewed stirring of life for the earth. Nancy Newhall. EaPr

We Seek You, One and Only God. Luba Krugman Gurdus. BTR

We seem to exist in a hazardous time. Evolution. Ben King. AnAmPo

We sent him to one-with. The Psychonaut Sonnets: Jones. Albert Goldbarth. SM

We set our sights on living, and on that alone. Ghazal. Iftiqar Arif. NBrP

We set out yesterday upon a winter drive. Alexandre Dumas, *tr. fr. French by* Gerard Manley Hopkins. *Fr.* Lady of the Pearls, The. TTY

We Settled by the Lake. F. D. Reeve. NYBP

We shall bathe, my love, in an African presence. Léopold Sédar Senghor, *tr. fr. French by* Ellen Conroy Kennedy. *Fr.* Songs for Signare. NegPo

We shall be called harsh names by men unborn. Contemporary. Hortense Flexner. PoA

We shall cede with a brotherly embrace. The Rise of Shivaji. Zulfikar Ghose. MoBS

We shall certainly find ourselves in Hell! *(LL)* We Shall Not Escape Hell. Marina Tsvetayeva. BoWoP

We shall come tomorrow morning, who were not to have her love. Emily Hardcastle, Spinster. John Crowe Ransom. CMoP; MeMAP; OxBSP

We shall die easily who loved this dying first. *(LL)* Marriage and Death. E. J. Scovell. VBLP

We shall die in transparent Petropolis. Petropolis. Osip Mandelstam, *tr. fr. Russian by* David McDuff. PeFWW

We shall do much in the years to come. What Have We Done Today? Nixon Waterman. WBLP

We Shall Drink to Them That Sleep. Alexander Robertson. NSI

We shall go mad no doubt and die that way. *(LL)* The Cool Web. Robert Graves. AWP; GTBS-P; MoP; NAEL-2; NoAM; NoP; OxBTC; PoA; Poetr; PrIm; SCV

We shall have beds round which light scents are wafted. The Death of Lovers. Baudelaire, *tr. fr. French by* Roy Campbell. OBD

We shall have everything we want and there'll be no more dying. Ode to Joy. Frank O'Hara. GLP; NeAP; PPP

We shall hew our fill! *(LL)* Biterolf. Joseph Victor von Scheffel. RiWo

We Shall Know. *Unknown.* PWR

We shall live again. *Unknown, tr. fr. Sioux Indian by* James Mooney. *Fr.* Ghost Dance Songs. STP

We shall not always plant while others reap. From the Dark Tower. Countee Cullen. BPo; CDC; LiTM; NAAL-2; PoBA; PoNe; Son

We Shall Not Escape Hell. Marina Tsvetayeva, *tr. fr. Russian by* Elaine Feinstein. BoWoP

We shall not ever meet them bearded in heaven. On the Death of Friends in Childhood. Donald Justice. InPK; LCAP

We shall not go up against you. This Be Our Revenge. Saul Tchernichowsky, *tr. fr. Hebrew by* Shalom Spiegel. TrJP

We shall not want to use again/ Until Eternity. *(LL)* Bustle in a house, The. Emily Dickinson. FaBV; HAP; HeIL; HeIP; NAAL-1; NoP; OBD; OxBA; PoEL-5; PoLF; SAmP; WGRP

We Shall Overcome. Breyten Breytenbach, *tr. fr. Afrikaans by* Ernst van Heerden. PeSAV

We Shall Overcome. *Unknown.* AH

We shall remember him. John Butler Yeats. Jeanne Robert Foster. GoYe

We shall remember the wheat stalk in the greenness of her youth. Remembrance of Beginnings of Things. Leah Goldberg, *tr. fr. Hebrew by* Ruth Finer Mintz. MHP

We Shall Say. Miriam Allen DeFord. GoYe

We shall share our courage. *(LL)* Fear. Thomas Love Peacock. VoR

We shall walk in the snow. *(LL)* Velvet Shoes. Elinor Wylie. CH; FaPON; GoJo; HeIL; MoAB; MoAmPo; TrGrPo; WHSW

We shan't see Willy any more, Mamie. To a Bull-Dog. J. C. Squire. FM; NSI

We share this: that vanishing figure. Illusions. Sally Roberts Jones. AngWe

We shared not one idea in thirty years. A Reformer to His Father. James Simmons. BIrV

We shipped him at the Sandwich Isles. The Whaler's Pig. Edwin James Brady. NOBAu

We shot the Choctaw way back in '94. Red Oak. Jim Barnes. *Fr.* Ex-Deputy Sheriff Remembers the Eastern Oklahoma Murderers, An. NGP, *sect.* ii

We should cultivate our different tastes. Cultivation. Mrs. Henry Linden. CBWP-4

We should try not to look away. At a Mass Grave. M. Truman Cooper. BTR

We shouldered like pigs along the rail to try. Returned to Frisco, 1946. W. D. Snodgrass. ArOW

We Show You That Death as a Dancer. Hamish Henderson. PoWW

We shut them out, the houses. Time Out. Oliver Jenkins. GoYe

We sing a hymn to Artemis, for it is. Hymn to Artemis. Callimachus, *tr. fr. Greek by* Barbara Hughes Fowler. *Fr.* Hymns. HePo

We sirens, since we rigged up stereophonic sound. The Sirens. Gordon Challis. PeNZ

We sit at a sidewalk table. The Firebreathers at the Café Deux Magots. Miller Williams. MT

We sit at our kitchen table. The Day Before They Bombed Nagasaki. Rebecca Baggett. CrSp

We sit at the table and that is grace. November and Aunt Jemima. Thylias Moss. TRP

We sit, crookbacked, at the bar. At the Telephone Club. Henri Coulette. CoAP

We sit here, talking of Barea and Lorca. Conversation in Gibraltar 1943. Charles Causley. PoWW

We sit in someone else's house. Winter Quarters. Gwen Harwood. FaBoMA

We sit indoors and talk of the cold outside. There Are Roughly Zones. Robert Frost. CMoP; PPP

We sit late, watching the dark slowly unfold. September. Ted Hughes. BoLoP

We sit like drunkards and inhale the swans. (*LL*) Swans. Lawrence Durrell. MoBrPo

We sit on a green bench in Harrison Railroad Park. Dreams in Harrison Railroad Park. Nellie Wong. OpBo

We sit outside. Death of Dr. King. Sam Cornish. PoBA

We Sit Solitary. *Unknown.* TrJP

We sit watching the afternoon summer smell ripely. James Powell on Imagination. Larry Neal. BPo

We six pile in, the engine churning ink. Nigger Song: An Odyssey. Rita Dove. AmPA

We slept through it. A stray bomber. Heinrich Böll in Ireland. Michael O'Loughlin. *Fr.* Shards, The. IB

We slip into a dream. Dream Garden. Gu Cheng, *tr. fr. Chinese by* Donald Finkel *with* Li Guohua. SpMi

We smell a rat close by. (*LL*) The Three Little Kittens. *At. to* Eliza Lee Follen *and to* Eliza Cook. BoTP; FaPON; OBCA; OFC; OxNR

We smell their minds like silver hammers. (*LL*) Jacklight. Louise Erdrich. HATNAP; WeW

We sometimes ride, and sometimes walk. Life at Richkings. Frances, Countess of Hertford Seymour. ECWP

We sound like crying bullheads. Voices. Nora Dauenhauer. HATNAP

We sow the fertile seed and then we reap it. Evening Hymn in the Hovels. Francis Lauderdale Adams. OxBS

We speak or will never hear. (*LL*) Bee Mother. Meredith Stricker. LoHo

We speed through tunnels under the frozen ground. Subway. Susan Fawcett. CrSp

We spend our lives trying to construct sentences. Paris 1912. Gavin Selevie. NBrP

We spend our morning. The Memory of Elena. Carolyn Forché. NoAM

We spent all day fishing and talking. Late at Night During a Visit of Friends. Robert Bly. InPS

We spoke/ At all. (*LL*) The Night-blooming Cereus. Robert Hayden. CAPP; NoP; NU

We stand amazed but take the blow, transfigured, idiot. (*LL*) The Beating. T. R. Hummer. MT

We stand at the edge of the cliff and in the depths beneath us. Molokai. Tomas Tranströmer, *tr. fr. Swedish by* Samuel Charters. AnAn

We stand before the long building. Wild Light. Lonny Kaneko. ETG

We stand facing each other, our. Stars. Sara Boyes. DT

We stand naked behind the line. On the Death of Sylvia Plath. Judith Herzberg, *tr. fr. Dutch.* WPOW, *tr. by* Manfred Wolf

We stand on the edge of wounds, hugging canned meat. Dream of Rebirth. Roberta Hill Whiteman. CDW

We stand pinned. Zocalo. Michael S. Harper. NBV

We stand together. Last Journey. John Montague. CIP; PBCIP; PNI

We stare and say, 'Well, we have come this far.' (*LL*) Cirque d'Hiver. Elizabeth Bishop. InPS; LiTA

We started our house midway through the Cultural Revolution. Building. Gary Snyder. BAP-89

We stayed the night in the pathless gorge. Oh, Lovely Rock. Robinson Jeffers. NU

We still have bards who, with aspiring head. *Unknown. Fr.* Common Sense: A Poem. EPCY

We still want to say the one true thing. Still. Lisa Zeidner. SM

We stole a glass and hung the canopy. Rebecca 1942. R. M. Cooper. BTR

We stood at Gardiner's Corner. October 1936. Milly Harris. FaBoEH

We stood at the edge. The Jews Speak in Heaven. Gary Catalano. NOBAu

We stood by a pond that winter day. Neutral Tones. Thomas Hardy. CMoP; EBVV; EnVR; HAP; HeIP; InPK; InPS; MeMBP; MoBrPo; MoP; NAEL-2; NoAM; NOBVV; OAEL-2; PPP; TEP; TFi; UnPo

We stood up before day. In the Dordogne. John Peale Bishop. OBWP; PeFWW; PoWW; VGW

We stripped in the first warm spring night. Belle Isle, 1949. Philip Levine. VCAP

We Survive! Hirsch Glick, *tr. fr. Yiddish by* Ruth Rubin. TrJP

We swing ungirded hips. The Song of the Ungirt Runners. Charles Hamilton Sorley. MoBrPo; OBEV

We take it with us, the cry. Departure. Carolyn Forché. AnAn; PAW

We take place in what we believe. Elephant Rock. Primus St. John. PoBA

We take up with the black branch. A Dream of Retained Colour. J. H. Prynne. VaA

We talk about God. Saturday Night Worship. Ann Carhart. CrSp

We talk of old men who have forgotten their/ thoughts. Errore. Pier Giorgio di Cicco. NOBC

We talk upward. Loop. Kate Ruse-Glason. VBLP

We talked of things but all the time we wanted each other. And What with the Blunders. Kenneth Patchen. NaP

We talked [*or* talk'd] with open heart, and tongue. The Fountain. Wordsworth. EnRP; GTBS; GTBS-P; OxAEP-2

We tend tall hedges till they hide our garden. (*LL*) Process. Aidan Carl Mathews. IB

We test our lives by thine. (*LL*) Immortal Love, Forever Full. Whittier. AH

We test our lives by Thine! (*LL*) Our Master. Whittier. BLRP; WBLP

We Thank Thee. John Oxenham. BLRP

We Thank Thee. *Unknown.* FaPON

We thank Thee for the joy of common things. A Prayer for Thanksgiving. Joseph Auslander. TrPWD

We thank Thee for the morning light. *Unknown.* BLRP

We thank Thee, Heavenly Father. Thanks to Spring. Mary Anderson. BoTP

We Thank Thee, Lord. Calvin W. Laufer. AH

We Thank Thee, Lord. John Oxenham. *Fr.* Little Te Deum of the Commonplace, A. WBLP

We thank Thee, Lord, for quiet upland lawns. Grace and Thanksgiving. Elizabeth Gould. BoTP

We thank Thee, Lord, for this our food. *Unknown.* BLRP

We thank Thee, now, O Father. The Most Acceptable Gift. Matthias Claudius, *tr. fr. German by* J. M. Campbell. BLRP

We Thank You! L. E. Cox. BoTP

We, that did nothing study but the way. A Renunciation. Henry King. OBEV

We that have done and thought. Spilt Milk. W. B. Yeats. OxBSP

We that with like hearts love, we lovers twain. A Vow to Heavenly Venus. Joachim du Bellay, *tr. fr. French by* Andrew Lang. AWP

We, the Ancient Ones. Rain Song of the Giant Society. *Unknown, tr. fr. Sia Indian by* Matilda Coxe Stevenson. AnAmPo

We, the boys of Sanpete County, in obedience to the cause. The Boys of Sanpete County. *Unknown.* AmFP

We, the captives of a thousand skies. Farewell to Europe. William Pillen. BTR

We, the mystic N O W. (*LL*) Manifesto. D. H. Lawrence. CBLP

We, the rescued. Chorus of the Rescued. Nelly Sachs, *tr. fr. German.* PoSu; WPOW, *tr. by* Ruth Mead *and* Matthew Mead

We, the symmetrians, seek justice here. N. B., Symmetrians. Gene Derwood. LiTA

We, the unborn. Chorus of the Unborn. Nelly Sachs, *tr. fr. German by* Ruth Mead *and* Matthew Mead. NYBP

We the White Witches are, that free. Masque of the Virtues against Love. Mary Monck. ECWP; NOEC

We think our loved ones pull us under. On the Waterfront. Michael Foley. PNI

We think to create festivals. Antonio Machado Ruiz, *tr. fr. Spanish by* John Dos Passos. AWP

We think we've all heard quite enough of this your sad disaster! (*LL*) Alphabet. Edward Lear. FaBoNo

We thirst at first — 'tis nature's act. Emily Dickinson. NOCV (Thirst.) WGRP

We thirst for in dreams we dread. (*LL*) Styx. Robert Duncan. VCAP

We thought at first, this man is a king for sure. Blue Blood. James Stephens, *after the Irish of* David O'Bruaidar. IHNG; MoAB; MoBrPo; OBMV

We thought the grass. Photographs: A Vision of Massacre. Michael S. Harper. PoBA

We three are on the cedar-shadowed lawn. George Meredith. *Fr.* Modern Love. NOBVV

We Three Kings. John Henry Hopkins, Jr. *See* We Three Kings of Orient Are.

We three kings all orient are. We Three Kings. *Unknown.* FaBoVe

We Three Kings of Orient Are. John Henry Hopkins, Jr. AH; PChr

We Three Kings ("We three kings all orient are.") *Unknown.* FaBoVe

We to our beds; you to Broceliande Wood. (*LL*) Visitation. John Dronsfield. PeSAV

We too, we too, descending once again. The Too-late Born. Archibald MacLeish. GoJo; MeMAP; MoAB; MoAmPo; OxBA (Silent Slain, The.) CMoP; LiTM; PeFWW

We took our work, and went, you see. Recreation. Jane Taylor. OxBoLi; WoRP

We took turns at laying. Tremors. Stewart Conn. PWE

We tore the green tree down. Verifying the Dead. James Welch. CDW

We touched land. Not That Far. May Miller. BISi

We trudge on together, my good man and I. Getting Along. Lucy Larcom. AmWP

We turn aside from everything. Birthday Wishes to a Minister of the Gospel. L. A. J. Moorer. CBWP-3

We two are lain in hell: what may we fear. Barley-Break; or, Last in Hell. Robert Herrick. CaPo

We Two Boys Together Clinging. Walt Whitman. OBF; PeHV

We two stood simply friend-like side by side. Inapprehensiveness. Robert Browning. CBLP; NOBVV

We unlock the door. We Are Welcome. Sue Sanders. DT

We used to gather at the high window. When Mahalia Sings. Quandra Prettyman. PoBA

We used to picnic where the thrift. Trebetherick. Sir John Betjeman. CMoP

We Used to Play. Don Welch. Poetsp

We used to shadow-box on the shining grass. Dimidium Animae Meae. Charles A. Brady. GoYe

We used to spend the spring together. The Most Beautiful Girl in the World. Lorenz Hart. OBAL

We used to talk of so many things. Before and After Marriage. Anne Campbell. PoToHe

We venerate the Three Treasures. *Unknown.* EaPr

We visited the World's Fair. The New York City World's Fairs, 1939 and 1964. Judith Baumel. UTF

We vow to not abuse the great truth of the Three Treasures. (*LL*) Knowing how deeply our lives intertwine. Stephanie Kaza. EaPr

We waged a war within a war. Karl Shapiro. *Fr.* Recapitulations. PoNe

We waited for an omnibus. Walking Song. William E. Hickson. OxBChV

We waited in silence for our children. Death of the Miners or, The Widows of the Earth. Mazisi Kunene, *tr. fr. Zulu by the author.* PeSAV

We wake and watch the sun make bright. Another Sunday Morning. Derek Mahon. CIP

We wake to hear the storm come down. The Storm. Edward Shanks. BoNaP

We wake; we wake the day. Indian Singing in 20th Century America. Gail Tremblay. HATNAP

We walk across the snow. On Frozen Fields. Galway Kinnell. CAPP

We walk, as all around walks on creation. In the Shadow of the Valley of Death. Abu al-Qasim al-Shabbi. DL

We walk in under the empty tower, snow. KZ. Carolyne Wright. BTR

We walk round this acre of old garden. The Walk. Sebastian Barry. IB

We Walk the Way of the New World. Don L. Lee. BPo; PoBA

We walked across a frozen river in Manchuria. Expatriates. David Woo. OpBo

We walked along, while bright and red. The Two April Mornings. Wordsworth. EBEV; EnRP; GTBS; GTBS-P; NAEL-2

We walked the bar. The Life: Hoodoo Hollerin' Bebop Ghosts. Larry Neal. BCF

We Walked Together. Georg Friedrich Daumer, *tr. fr. German by* Philip L. Miller. RiWo

We walked, we two together. We Walked Together. Georg Friedrich Daumer, *tr. fr. German by* Philip L. Miller. RiWo

We wander in the stifling heat. Shadow in Stone. Janice Mirikitani. OpBo

We wander now who marched before. Old Soldier. Padraic Colum. OBMV

We wandered to the pine forest. Shelley. *Fr.* To Jane: The Recollection. CH; OBNC

We want our fevers. A Small Demand. Karen Murai. UTF

We want what is real. Song of the Bald Eagle. *Unknown, tr. fr. Crow Indian by* Lewis Henry Morgan. STP

We wanted Li Wing. Lapsus Linguae. Keith Preston. NBLV; OBAL

We was in the 'Blue Dragon', Sid 'Awkins and me. Homœopathy. J. C. Squire. NSI

We watch the heavy-odoured beast. Port of Call: Brazil. Alun Lewis. OBTV

We watched from the house. I Was Sleeping Where the Black Oaks Move. Louise Erdrich. FoLa; HATNAP

We watched [*or* watch'd] her breathing thro' the night. The Death-Bed. Thomas Hood. CoGr; EnRP; GTBS; GTBS-P; NOBE; OBD; OBEV; OBNC

We watched our love burn with the lumberyard. The Lumberyard. Ruth Herschberger. LiTA; WPE

We watched the condors winging towards the moon. Condors. Padraic Colum. GoJo

We watched you waving as we pulled away, the ground swept. Showing Us the Fields. James McCorkle. BAP-89

We Wear the Mask. Paul Laurence Dunbar. AAP; CDC; FF; NIP; NoP; PoBA; TTY; UnPo

We wear the mask! (*LL*) We Wear the Mask. Paul Laurence Dunbar. AAP; CDC; FF; NIP; NoP; PoBA; TTY; UnPo

We weave up a switchback gully & out to sloping pasture. Naive Invocation. David Rivard. NAmP90

We went along a way we'd gone before. Wells River. J. D. McClatchy. ETG

We went north/ to escape winter. Indian Song: Survival. Leslie Silko. CDW; VoR

We went off to the wake of the "whelpish youngster." Harvest of the Sea. Máire Mhac an tSaoi. PBWP

We went out, early one morning. Out Fishing. Barbara Howes. WPE

We went there on the train. Protocols. Randall Jarrell. LCAP; OxBC; VGW

We went there to confer. Detroit Conference of Unity and Art. Nikki Giovanni. HoPM

We went to reconnoitre. Report to the Valley Camp. Jenny King. PAW

We were a people taut for war; the hills. Welsh History. R. S. Thomas. AngWe; OBWVE

We were a tribe, a family, a people. Scotland 1941. Edwin Muir. OxBS

We were all drunk, and Acindynus was determined to keep sober. Lucianus, *tr. fr. Greek by* Edwin Morgan. GrAn

We were all sitting round the table. Christmas Dinner. Michael Rosen. OBCP

We were alone and did your life. To Children. Lawrence McGaugh. PoBA

We were apart; yet, day by day. Solution: To Marguerite. Matthew Arnold. *Fr.* Switzerland. (To Marguerite.) EnVR

We were as limmp as the guidebooks. The Surrealists' Summer Convention Came to Our City. Jo Shapcott. PWE

We were as tough as our glasses. Tyson's Corner. Primus St. John. PoBA

We were at the border and they were checking. The War. Linda Gregg. BAP-90

We were brought up to believe. Brief Thoughts on Floods. Miroslav Holub, *tr. fr. Czech by* Ian Milner *and* Jarmila Milner. PoSu

We were carrying our dance shoes. Kathleen Jamie. *Fr.* Katie's Poems. PWE

We were challenged by The Dingoes — they're the pride of Squatter's Gap. A Friendly Game of Football. Edward Dyson. CBAP

We were closed, each to each, yet dear. Each to Each. Melville Cane. GoYe

We were consigned. Continuous Time. Milo De Angelis, *tr. fr. Italian by* Lawrence Venuti. NeIt

We were crowded in the cabin. Ballad of the Canal. Phoebe Cary. AnAmPo

We were crowded in the cabin. Ballad of the Tempest. James Thomas Fields. AnAmPo; BeLS; BLPL; FaBoBe; PoLF

We were dauntless then. Remembering Mexico, 1969. Barbara Lau. LoHo

We were discussing Siva. Evasion. Claribel Alegría, *tr. fr. Spanish by* Lynne Beyer. WoWa

We were drinking buddies in high old time town. Mommy's Hubby. Leo Connellan. Jaz

We were driving the down express. The Engine Driver's Story. William Wilkins. BeLS

We were forty miles from Albany. The E-ri-e. *Unknown.* AS

We were halfway through July. Handsome afternoon! On the Banks of the Duero. Antonio Machado Ruiz, *tr. fr. Spanish by* John Frederick Nims. STV

We were in love and his uncle had a farm. Geese. Mark Cox. NAmP90

We were laying in Surrey Dock one day. Stormy Weather, Boys. *Unknown*. OxBSS

We were married near the base. Happiness. Ruth Stone. NAmP90

We were nearly. Above the Pool. John Montague. NOIV

We were nine lives, cat claws plunged in. A las Gatas. Lorna Dee Cervantes. AfAz

We were nine to leave the lake in the north. Complaint of the Wild Goose. *Unknown, tr. fr. Mongolian* by Willard R. Trask. OBAP

We were not even moving. No one was moving. On the Eve of Our Mutually Assured Destruction. C. D. Wright. LCAP

We were not ever of their feline race. Frightened Men. Robert Graves. OFC; SoCa

We were not here. Plato was a spider. Spinoza Was a Bee. Jaroslaw Marek Rymkiewicz, *tr. fr. Polish* by Czeslaw Milosz. CBNP

We Were Not Likened to Dogs among the Gentiles. Uri Zvi Greenberg, *tr. fr. Hebrew* by Ruth Finer Mintz. MHP

We were not many — we who stood. Monterey. Charles Fenno Hoffman. AnAmPo; FaBoBe; PAH

We were ordered to Samoa from the coast of Panama. An International Episode. Caroline Duer. PAH

We were out in Arizona, on the Painted Desert ground. Arizona. *Unknown*. AmFP

We were playing on the green together. "Is It Nothing to You?" May Probyn. OBEV

We were rumbling o'er Trumpington stones. (*LL*) The Country Clergyman's Trip to Cambridge. Macaulay. OBSV; OxBoLi; PeLV

We were sick of seeing the liners leave. Refugees at Cobh. Sean Dunne. BiHa

We Were Sisters Weren't We. Katie Donovan. BiHa

We were smoking some of this knockout weed when. Operation Memory. David Lehman. NAmP90

We were so poor I had to take the place of the. Charles Simic. *Fr.* World Doesn't End, The. VCAP

We were starving. We had nothing. Reminiscence Forward. Molly Tenenbaum. BAP-91

We were talking about the great things. Great Things Have Happened. Alden Nowlan. GOYP

We were the wrecked elect. The Fiction-Makers. Anne Stevenson. DiPo

We were three women, three men. The Sorrow of Kodio. *Unknown, tr. fr. Baule* by Miriam Koshland. PBA

We were together. Yakamochi, *tr. fr. Japanese* by Kenneth Rexroth. UnAS

We were together since the War began. A Servant. Kipling. *Fr.* Epitaphs of the War, 1914–1918. NoP; OBWP; PeFWW

We were two daughters of one race. The Sisters. Tennyson. InvP

We were two pretty babes, the youngest she. Childhood Fled. Charles Lamb. EnRP

We were very tired, we were very merry. Recuerdo. Edna St. Vincent Millay. ImPo; LiTA; LiTM; MeMAP; NAAL-2; NoAM; OxBA; PoA; Poetr; TAP

We were waiting at the station. The Parting Kiss. Josephine D. Henderson Heard. CBWP-4

We were walking and talking on the roof of the world. End of the Seers' Convention. Kenneth Fearing. LiTA

We were warned about frost, yet all day the summer. Early Frost. Leslie Norris. AngWe

We were young, we were merry, we were very very wise. Unwelcome. Mary Elizabeth Coleridge. CH; CoGr; GGP; OBEV; OBNC; WPE

We whisper in her ear, "You are not true." (*LL*) Epistemology. Richard Wilbur. CRP; NoAM; NOBA; OxBSP

We who also linger near the border of insanities. Near the Border of Insanities. Dannie Abse. PoA

We who are called Australians have no country. Rex Ingamells. *Fr.* Unknown Land. NOBAu

We who are left, how shall we look again. W. W. Gibson. NSI; OxBTC

We who devour our unclean dead are now arisen. Letter to Robert. Mary Fabilli. IHMS

We who find no joy in celebrity. Rufinus Domesticus, *tr. fr. Greek* by Sam Hamill. InMo

We who had known the desert's grit and granite. Exodus. Charles Reznikoff. ChIV-1

We who have bridged the river. Appalachia in Cincinnati. Turner Cassity. NGP

We who must act as handmaidens. A Muse of Water. Carolyn Kizer. NMM; VCAP

We who play under the pines. The Song of the Rabbits outside the Tavern. Elizabeth J. Coatsworth. OBCA; SoSe

We who prayed and wept. Wendell Berry. EaPr

We who survived the war and took to wife. Thirtieth Anniversary Report of the Class of '41. Howard Nemerov. HCAP

We Who Were Born. Eiluned Lewis. FaPON (Birthright, The.) AngWe

We who with songs beguile your pilgrimage. James Elroy Flecker. *Fr.* Golden Journey to Samarkand, The. FaBoRV; FaPoR; GoJo; OBMV; OxBTC; PlP; UV (Prologue: "We Who with Songs Beguile Your Pilgrimage.) CoGr

We will . . . the north wind blows. (*LL*) Come tip a few with me. Alcaeus. InMo

We will drive our point — home. Contracts. Marilyn Kitchell. UL

We will gather up the fragments that remain. (*LL*) Hallelujah! A. E. Housman. CBNP; FaBoNo; FiBHP; PeLV

We will go no more to Shaemus, at the Nip. Shaemus. Conrad Aiken. OxBA

We will go to the wood, says Robin to Bobbin. *Unknown*. OxNR

We will grow old, and older. Robin Morgan. *Fr.* Ceremony, A. CrSp

We will kill our love. We Are Going to Shoot at the Heart. Anna Swirszczynska, *tr. fr. Polish* by Czeslaw Milosz *and* Leonard Nathan. PoSu

We will long to feel pain, suffering, anything of life. (*LL*) Scarecrow. Dermot Bolger. IB

We will meet again. (*LL*) The Animals. W. S. Merwin. VCAP

We will never meet again face to face. Yosami, *tr. fr. Japanese* by Kenneth Rexroth *and* Ikuko Atsumi. WPJ

We Will Not Fear. David Diamond. AH

We will not whisper, we have found the place. Hilaire Belloc. MoBrPo

We Will Overcome. *Unknown*. SWP

We will overcome, we will overcome. We Will Overcome. *Unknown*. SWP

We will pull, we will haul, hearty, healthy, and gay. Blow the Man Down ("I'll put on my boots and I'll blow the man down.") *Unknown*. AmFP

We will return to life. Comanche Ghost Dance: An Impression. Lance Henson. VoR

We will take it seriously as we open our morning paper. Sonnet to Be Written from Prison. Robert Adamson. CBAP

We will take our spears and fight for our lands. (*LL*) The Removal of Our Village, KwaBhanya. Mbuyiseni Oswald Mtshali. PeSAV

We will watch the Northern Lights. *Unknown, tr. fr. Abanaki Indian*. RFM

We wish not the mechanic arts to scan. Power of Women, The. Matilda Betham-Edwards. ECWP

We with our Fair pitched among the feathery clover. The Individualist Speaks. Louis MacNeice. OBMV

We woke early. Names in Monterchi: To Rachel. James Wright. AnAn; NNaP

We Women. Edith Södergran, *tr. fr. Swedish* by Samuel Charters. WPOW

We women here all live with tightened throats. Henri Michaux, *tr. fr. French* by Richard Ellmann. *Fr.* I Am Writing to You from a Far-Off Country. AnRep

We wonder what the horoscope did show. Shakespeare. H. Cordelia Ray. CBWP-3

We wonder whether the dream of American liberty. Archibald MacLeish. *Fr.* Land of the Free. MoAB

We Wondered about the Mellow Peaches. Jack A. Mapanje. HBAPE

We wondered at the tobacco plants there in France. Tobacco Plant. Ivor Gurney. OBTV

We wondered what our walk should mean. Peace Walk. William Stafford. Poetsp

We won't forget the padre in a hurry. The Padre. Frank Ormsby. BiHa

We work here together. The Pine Planters. Thomas Hardy. FaBoVe

We work, play, don't cross-reference calendars. Marilyn Hacker. *Fr.* Taking Notice. VCAP

We worked in the kitchen. The Function Room. Patrice Phillips. MAT

We would climb the highest dune. With Kit, Age 7, at the Beach. William Stafford. RaBo; RFM

We would learn and know! (*LL*) Night of Spring. Thomas Westwood. BoTP

We would live merrily, merrily. (*LL*) The Merman. Tennyson. BoTP, *ll.* 1–20; FaPON; GN; UV, (*ll.* 1–20)

We would march forth to meet with destiny. (*LL*) 1966. Dermot Bolger. IB

We Would See Jesus. Anna B. Warner. AH

We would see Jesus; earth is grand. Sir, We Would See Jesus. Frances E. W. Harper. AAP

We wreathed about our darling's head the morning-glory bright. The Morning-Glory. Maria White Lowell. AmWP

We zealots, made up of stiff clay. Let Us All Be Unhappy on Sunday. Lord Neaves. FaBoCo

Weak flame zone. The Furnaces. Douglas Oliver. VaA

Weak is the assurance that weak flesh reposeth. By Her That Is Most Assured to Her Self. Spenser. *Fr.* Amoretti. AAS; EnRePo; ESo, lacking epigrams I–IV; HeIL

Weak Is the Will of Man, His Judgment Blind. Wordsworth. EnRP

Weak man is like a broken jug, A. Lucianus, *tr. fr. Greek by* Sam Hamill. InMo

Weak Monk, The. Stevie Smith. BoWoP; FaBoTw

Weak-winged is song. James Russell Lowell. *Fr.* Ode Recited at the Harvard Commemoration. NOBA; OBWP; PAH

Wealth. Sadi, *tr. by* Sir Edwin Arnold. *Fr.* Gulistan, The. AWP

Wealth came by water to this farmless island. Delos. Bernard Spencer. NoAM

Wealth covers sin — the poor. Kassia, *tr. fr. Greek by* Patrick Diehl. WPOW

Wealth-move, or earth-hewn. (*LL*) The Echo-Elf Answers. Thomas Hardy. CBLP

Wealth, my lad, was made to wander. Samuel Johnson. *Fr.* One-And-Twenty. OtMeF

Wealth unto every man, I see. Worldly Wealth. Rowland Watkyns. FaBoEE

Wealthy Cit, grown old in trade, The. The Cit's Country Box. Robert Lloyd. NOEC

Weapon, The. "Hugh MacDiarmid." RB

Weapon shapely, naked, wan. The Broad-Ax. Walt Whitman. *Fr.* Song of the Broad-Ax [*or* Broad-Axe]. MoAmPo

Weapon that you fought with was a word, The. "He Knoweth Not That the Dead Are Thine." Mary Elizabeth Coleridge. OBNC

Weapons. Anna Wickham. MoBrPo

Weapons alone. One Flight Up. Bob Holman. UL

Weapons Training. Bruce Dawe. FaBoMA

Wear a dress. An Answer to a Man's Question, "What Can I Do about Women's Liberation?" Susan Griffin. GLP

Wear it as a bangle on your arm. Fame. Eleanor Hollister Cantus. GoYe

Wear your colors. Look Not to Memories. Angela de Hoyos. AfAz

Weare all his beard, and none upon his chinn. (*LL*) A Lady's Prayer to Cupid. Thomas Carew, *after* Giovanni Battista Guarini. CaPo

Wearied arm and broken sword. Pocahontas. Thackeray. FaPON; GN; PAH

Wearied arm, and broken sword. Thackeray. *Fr.* Pocahontas. AiP

Wearied of its own turning. The Burning Wheel. Aldous Huxley. ChIV-1

Wearily, drearily. In Prison. William Morris. OHCV; PeVV

Wearily, still in her dressing gown. Eliza Telefair. Jocelyn Macy Sloan. GoYe

Wearin' o' the Green, The. *Unknown.* NOIV

Weariness. Mary E. Tucker. CBWP-1

Weariness of life that has no will, The. Everyman. Siegfried Sassoon. MoBrPo

Wearing an overcoat in August heat. Bag Woman. Dudley Randall. NoAM

Wearing her yellow rubber slicker. Myrtle. Ted Kooser. GOYP

Wearing my yellow straw hat. My Yellow Straw Hat. Lessie Jones Little. TLR

Wearing of [*or* Wearin' o'] the Green, The. *Unknown.* AWP; FaPoR; GBP; IIP; OxBoLi; WTO

Wearing the Collar. Charles Bukowski. ArLo

Wearing worry about money like a hair shirt. Worry about Money. Kathleen Raine. FaBoTw

Weary already, weary miles to-night. A Match with the Moon. Dante Gabriel Rossetti. NOBVV

Weary are at rest. (*LL*) The May Queen. Tennyson. PFP

Weary Blues, The. Langston Hughes. FaBV; Jaz; MoP; NoAM; NOBA; NoP; PoNe; SAmP

Weary, I open wide the antique pane. Poetry and the Poet. H. C. Bunner. OBAL

Weary I was, and thought to sit at rest. Elizabeth Melvill, Lady Culross. *Fr.* Godly Dream, A. WPE

Weary in Well-doing. Christina Rossetti. TrPWD

Weary is he, and sick of the sorrow of war. The Soldier Is Home. John Shaw Neilson. CBAP

Weary Lot Is Thine, A. Sir Walter Scott. *Fr.* Rokeby. CH

Weary men, what reap ye? — "Golden corn for the stranger." The Famine Year. Lady Wilde. IIP; TIRV

Weary of all who come with words, words but no language. From March 1979. Tomas Tranströmer, *tr. fr. Swedish by* Robin Fulton. PWE

Weary of battle and burned by the sun. Biterolf. Joseph Victor von Scheffel, *tr. fr. German by* Philip L. Miller. RiWo

Weary of myself, and sick of asking. Self-Dependence. Matthew Arnold. MeMBP; OHCV; WGRP

Weary on ye, sad waves! On an Island. "Ethna Carbery." WPE

Weary one had rest, the sad had joy that day, The. Because We Do Not See. *Unknown.* BLRP

Weary Road, The. Lu Chao-lin, *tr. fr. Chinese by* Robin D. S. Yates. SuSp

Weary Road, The, *sels.* Pao Chao, *tr. fr. Chinese.*
"Have you not seen the grasses on the riverbank?" SuSp
"Water spilled on level ground." SuSp

Weary Song to a Slow Sad Tune, A. Li Ch'ing-chao, *tr. fr. Chinese by* Kenneth Rexroth. BoWoP; OHMPC

Weary teacher sat alone, The. The Teacher's Dream. William Henry Venable. BeLS

Weary the cry of the wind is, weary the sea. Sorrow of Mydath. John Masefield. CoGr; MoBrPo

Weary was when coming on a stream. Aswelay. Norman Henry, II Pritchard. PoBA

Weary way-wanderer, languid and sick at heart. The Soldier's Wife. Robert Southey. OxBSP

Weary Will. Andrew Barton Paterson. OBAP

Weary with reading and with meditation. The Storm and Calm: Sent from Embden to M. Edw. Ma. and M. Tho. Ly. Nicholas Murford. NOSC

Weary with toil, I haste me to my bed. Shakespeare. *Fr.* Sonnets. HeIP; NoSic; PlP; SCGP

Weary, worn, and sorrow-laden. Storm-Beaten. Clara Ann Thompson. CBWP-2

Wearyin' for You. Frank Lebby Stanton. AnAmPo

Weasel, The. *Unknown.* ChTr; CoGr

Weasel, by a person caught, A. The Man and the Weasel. Phaedrus, *tr. fr. Latin by* Christopher Smart. AWP

Weasel (or a stoat), A. The Aesthete Weasel. Christian Morgenstern, *tr. fr. German by* Geoffrey Grigson. FaBoNo

Weather. David Campbell. *Fr.* Works and Days. FaBoMA

Weather. Marchette Chute. SiSoPo

Weather, The. Gavin Ewart. OTCP

Weather. Archibald MacLeish. MoAmPo

Weather. William Meredith. NYBP; Poetr

Weather. Eve Merriam. SiSoPo; TLR

Weather. *Unknown.* ImGa; OTCP

Weather buffets our houses in armour all night. Gales. Anne Stevenson. Spl

Weather-Cock Points South, The. Amy Lowell. NALW

Weather Ear. Norman Nicholson. OxBSP

Weather Forecast. Linda Pastan. AnAn

Weather/ if it has a poetry, The. Peter Philpott. VaA

Weather isn't news unless extreme, The. No News at All. Jack Butler. MT

Weather-leech of the topsail shivers, The. Tacking Ship Off Shore. Walter Mitchell. FaBoBe; GN

Weather Markings. Siri Hustvedt. PRA

Weather Nose. Steve Fisher. NGP

Weather of Olympus, The. Robert Graves. FaBoEE

Weather of Six Mornings, The. Jane Cooper. IHMS; NYBP

Weather Signs. Aratus, *tr. fr. Greek by* Barbara Hughes Fowler. *Fr.* Phaenomena. HePo

Weather-vanes clatter. (*LL*) Half of Life. Friedrich Hölderlin. ChTr; OBVE

Weather was fine, The. They took away his teeth. John Berryman. *Fr.* Dream Songs. CAPP

Weathercock, The. Rose Fyleman. BoTP

Weathercock, The: "I puff my breast out, my neck swells." Unknown, formerly at. to Cynewulf, *tr. by* Geoffrey Grigson. *Fr.* Riddles (Exeter Book). RB

Weathercock: My breast is puffed up and my neck is swollen. Unknown, formerly at. to Cynewulf. *See* I puff my breast out, my neck swells.

Weathercock once again heading south, The. This Morning. Jon Stallworthy. NoP

Weathering. Fleur Adcock. DiPo

Weathering Out. Rita Dove. LCAP; NoAM

Weathering the Depths. Alfred M. Lee. AmPA

Weather[s]. Thomas Hardy. BoTP; CH; EBEvV; FaBoCh; FaBV; MoAB; MoBrPo; NTP; OBMV; OtMeF; RB

Weather's cleared, The. We're filming at Versailles. Clive James. *Fr.* To Pete Atkin: A Letter from Paris. OBSV

Weather's hot — the cabin's free! The Bath. William Hone. FaBoEH

Weathervane, The. Wilhelm Müller, *tr. fr. German by* Philip L. Miller. *Fr.* Winter's Journey, The. RiWo

Weave garlands of roses for our hair. Anacreon, *tr. fr. Greek by* Sam Hamill. InMo

Weave the warp, and weave the woof. The Curse upon Edward. Thomas Gray. OBEV

Weaver, The. William Henry Burleigh. BLPA

Weaver, The. "Fanny Forester." BLPA

Weaver and the Factory Maid, The. *Unknown.* OBET

Weaver Bird, The. Kofi Awoonor. HBAPE

Weaver bird built in our house, The. The Weaver Bird. Kofi Awoonor. HBAPE

Weaver-Girl, The. Medbh McGuckian. VBLP

Weaver, The ("I sat at my loom in silence.") *Unknown.* BLRP

Weaver, The ("I was a bachelor, I lived by myself.") *Unknown.* AS

Weaver of Snow, The. "Fiona Macleod." OHCV

Weaver sat by the side of his loom, A. The Weaver. "Fanny Forester." BLPA

Weavers. Heine. TrJP

Weaving. Lucy Larcom. AmWP

Weaving a garland long ago. Anacreon, *tr. fr. Greek by* Sam Hamill. InMo

Weaving at the Window. Wang Chien, *tr. fr. Chinese by* William H. Nienhauser. SuSp

Weaving Love-Knots. Hsüeh T'ao, *tr. by* Carolyn Kizer. BoWoP

Weaving Love-Knots 2. Hsüeh T'ao, *tr. by* Carolyn Kizer. BoWoP

Web, The. Gregory O'Donoghue. BIrV

Web, The. Theodore Weiss. CoAP

Web, the self-true mind, the trusty reflex. (LL) Speech for the Repeal of the McCarran Act. Richard Wilbur. CMoP; GOA

Webern. Thomas W. Shapcott. *Fr.* Piano Pieces. CBAP

Webster; an Ode, *sels.* William Cleaver Wilkinson.

Webster was much possessed by death. Whispers of Immortality. T. S. Eliot. CMoP; CTC; LiTA; NoAM; NOBA; NoP; OBMV; OxAEP-2

We'd ask her to start over. (LL) Elegies for Etsuko. Mary Jo Salter. UTF

"We'd better leave him in the sump," he said. (LL) Mending Sump. Kenneth Koch. BXAP; InPK; MoP; NeAP; NoAM

We'd ever so many kinds of cake. The Pirates' Tea-Party. Dorothy Una Ratcliffe. BoTP

We'd found an old Boche dug-out, and he knew. The Sentry. Wilfred Owen. EBNV; PeFWW; PoWW

We'd gained our first objective hours before. Counter-Attack. Siegfried Sassoon. MoBrPo; OxAEP-2; PeFWW; PoWW

We'd launch out, but a spiral failure binds so close. John Wilkinson. NBrP

We'd left the cameras in the Hertz. Daytrip. Anne Rouse. NWP

We'd rather have the iceberg than the ship. The Imaginary Iceberg. Elizabeth Bishop. FaBoWP; ImPo; LiTM; MoAB; MoAmPo

Weddin' a woo a clog an' a shoe, A. Weddings. *Unknown.* FaBoVe

Wedding, The. Conrad Aiken. CMoP; TAP

Wedding, The. Maria Banus, *tr. fr. Romanian by* Brenda Walker *and* Andrea Deletant. VBLP

Wedding, The. Julia Ward Howe. AmWP

Wedding, A. James Tate. NoAM

Wedding and Funeral. *Unknown.* GBP

Wedding Anniversary. Margaret E. Bruner. PoToHe

Wedding at Aughrim, Galway 1900. Catherine Byron. VBLP

Wedding-cake face in a paper frill, A. Sylvia Plath. *Fr.* Berck-Plage. OBD

Wedding Coat, The. Harriet Rose. BrRo

Wedding Day. Seamus Heaney. LPA; OxAEP-2

Wedding Day at Nagasaki. Rodney Hall. CBAP

Wedding Feast, The. Luis de Góngora y Argote, *tr. fr. Spanish by* Edward Meryon Wilson. *Fr.* First Solitude, The. OBVE

Wedding Feast, The. Edgar Lee Masters. ChIV-2

Wedding Gift, The. Minna Irving. BLPA

Wedding-Hymn. Sidney Lanier. TrPWD

Wedding in the Courthouse, The. Kathleen Norris. CrSp

Wedding in the Port. Sophie Behrens. NBrP

Wedding Morn. D. H. Lawrence. MoAB; MoBrPo

Wedding Night, The. Anne Sexton. PoA

Wedding night/ Graciela bled lightly. Graciela. Gary Soto. NoAM

Wedding Party. Donald Hall. LCAP

Wedding Preparations in the Country. David St. John. LCAP

Wedding procession moved along the mountain, A. In the Woods. Joseph Freiherr von Eichendorff, *tr. fr. German by* Philip L. Miller. RiWo

Wedding Reception. Melinda Goodman. GLP

Wedding-Ring. Denise Levertov. CAPP

Wedding Song. *Unknown.* OBET

Wedding Song in honor of R. Solomon ben Matir, *sels.* Moses ibn Ezra, *tr. fr. Hebrew by* Solomon Solis-Cohen.
 "Rejoice, O youth, in the lovely hind." TrJP

Wedding-Wind. Philip Larkin. MAT

Weddings. *Unknown.* FaBoVe

Wedlock, a Satire. Mehetabel Wright. ECWP

Wedlock; a Satire. Hetty Wright. NOEC

Wednesbury Cocking, The. *Unknown.* EnSB; FaBoBa

Wednesday. Marvin Bell. VCAP

Wednesday at North Hatley. Ralph Gustafson. NOBC

Wednesday in Holy Week. Christina Rossetti. TrCP

Wednesday, January 1, 1701. Samuel Sewall. *See* Once More, Our God, Vouchsafe to Shine!

Wednesday Night Prayer Meeting. Jay Wright. PoBA

Wednesday of Holy Week, 1940. Kenneth Rexroth. ChIV-1

Wednesday; or, The Dumps. John Gay. *Fr.* Shepherd's Week, The. OAEL-1

Wednesdays at the bone orchard deliveries. Memo. Charles Lynch. PoBA

Wee Davie Daylicht. Robert Tennant. OxBChV

Wee Falorie Man, The. *Unknown.* FaBoVe

Wee Jamie, a canny young Scot. Joyce Johnson. PeLi

Wee Jenny Wren, The. *Unknown.* FaBoVe

Wee jenny wren she lays sixteen, The. The Wee Jenny Wren. *Unknown.* FaBoVe

Wee leave Creete Country; and our sayls unwrapped uphoysing. Virgil, *tr. by* Richard Stanyhurst. *Fr.* Aeneid [*or* Eneados], The. NAWM-1; OBVE

Wee little nut lay deep in its nest, A. Among the Nuts. *Unknown.* BoTP

Wee Little Worm, A. James Whitcomb Riley. PDV

Wee man o' leather. *Unknown.* ChTr; GBP

Wee, modest, crimson-tippèd flow'r. To a Mountain Daisy. Burns. EnRP; GN; PoLF; ScCV; WBLP
 (Daisy, The.) BoNaP

Wee nah look no quarrel wi dem. Some Men. Dazzly Anderson. AIW

Wee, sleeket [*or* sleekit], cow'rin' [*or* cowran], tim'rous beastie. To a Mouse[, on Turning Her Up in Her Nest with the Plough]. Burns. EBEvV; EnRP; FaBoVe; FF; FM; HAP; HeIP; InPS; NAEL-2; NOEC; NoP; OAEL-1; OxAEP-2; OxBS; PoE; PoLF; PPP; PrIm; ScCV; SCGP; TEP; TFi; TrGrPo; UV
 (To a Field Mouse.) GTBS; GTBS-P
 (To a Mouse.) ImPo

Wee Tammy Tyrie. *Unknown.* OxNR

Wee, Wee German Lairdie, The. Allan Cunningham. FaBoEH

Wee Wee Man, The. *Unknown.* CH; EBEV; ELP; ESPB; FaBoCh; GBP; OAEL-1; OxBB

Wee, wee tailor. (LL) The Oviparous Tailor. Thomas Lovell Beddoes. CBNP; WiR

Wee, wee tailor. The Oviparous Tailor. Thomas Lovell Beddoes. CBNP; WiR

Wee Willie Gray. Burns. OxBChV

Wee Willie Winkie rins [*or* runs] through the town. William Miller. NOBVV; OxNR; ReMoGo
 (Willie Winkie.) OxBChV

Weed from Catholic Europe, it took root, A. Macao. W. H. Auden. MeMAP

Weed-mobbed terrace; plinths, A. The Site of the Crystal Palace. Philip Gross. FaBoEH

Weed Puller. Theodore Roethke. AmPP; HCAP; NAAL-2

Weeds. Ann Stanford. GrPl

Weeds grow shamelessly/ on my tongue. Self-Portrait. Cecil Bodker, *tr. fr. Danish by* Nadia Christensen. BoWoP

Weedy creek, A. Making a Door. Dennis Schmitz. LCAP

Weedy light through the uncurtained glass, The. Hiatus. Margaret Avison. HAP

Week after our child was born, A. New Mother. Sharon Olds. CrSp

Week after week, month after month, in pain. Memorial Poem. Roy Fuller. OxBSP

Week ago I had a fire, A. All in June. W. H. Davies. OxBSP

Week-End, *sels.* Harold Monro.
 "Train, The! The twelve o'clock for paradise." MoBrPo

Week-End by the Sea. Edgar Lee Masters. MoAmPo

Week-End Indian, The. Anita Endrezze-Danielson. VoR

Week-End of Dermot and Grace, The, *sels. Unknown.*
 "It is late, late." PeIV

Week in August you come home, The. Family Reunion. Maxine W. Kumin. CAPP

Week is dealt out like a hand, The. Hope. Randall Jarrell. MoAB; MoAmPo

Week of Birthdays, A. Mother Goose. *See* Monday's child is fair of face.

Week of Che Guevara, hunted, hurt. October and November. Robert Lowell. MAT

Week on the Concord and Merrimack Rivers, A, *sels*. Thoreau. Low-anchored Cloud. ArNa; NoP
(Mist.) AmPP; AnAmPo; AWP; OxBA
Woof of the Sun (Ethereal Gauze). TAP
(Haze.) NoP; PFP

Week one: our expedition slowed. A Scientific Expedition in Siberia, 1913. Kelly Cherry. SM

Week-Seek. Jim Tollerud. VoR

Week to Christmas, A. Louis MacNeice. *Fr*. Autumn Journal. TIRV

Weekend at Home. John Pook. AngWe

Weekend Evening. Shu Ting, *tr. fr. Chinese by* Carolyn Kizer *with* Y.H. Zhao. SpMi

Weekend Stroll. Frances Cornford. BoNaP

Weekly at the start. The Face. Lucien Stryk. ArOW

Weeks, maybe months, have passed and just. Sherod Santos. BAP-91

Weeksville Women. Elouise Loftin. PoBA

Weep again, come another year. *(LL)* Lament for Adonis. Bion. AWP

Weep, ah weep love's losing, love's with its dwelling place. Imr el Kais, *tr. fr. Arabic by* Lady Anne Blunt *and* Wilfrid Scawen Blunt. *Fr*. Mu'allaqat, The. AWP; TAL

Weep, and weep long, but do not weep for me. To a Troubled Friend. James Wright. Son

Weep, Children of Israel. Thomas Moore. ChIV-1

Weep eyes, break heart! Parting. Thomas Middleton. *Fr*. Chaste Maid in Cheapside, A. EIL

Weep for me, friends, for now that I am hence. Tears of the World. Mu'tamid, King of Seville, *tr. fr. Arabic by* Dulcie L. Smith. AWP

Weep for the dead, for they have lost this light. Robert Herrick. *Fr*. On Himself[e]. FaBoEE
(On Himself.) NOSC

Weep, Israel! your tardy meed outpour. Bar Kochba. Emma Lazarus. TrJP

Weep, Lovers, with Love's very self doth weep. Dante, *tr. fr. Italian by* Dante Gabriel Rossetti. *Fr*. Vita Nuova, La. AWP

Weep No More. *At. to* John Fletcher. *Fr*. Queen of Corinth, The. CH; EIL; OBEV; OxAEP-1

Weep no more for what is past. What Is Past. Sir William Davenant. TrGrPo

Weep no more, woful shepherds weep no more. Milton. *Fr*. Lycidas. AWP; ChTr; ClHu; EBEV; EBEvV; FaBoRV; FHYEP; GTBS; GTBS-P; HAP; ImPo; InPS; JCP; LiTB; NOBE; NoP; NOSC; OAEL-1; OBEV; OxAEP-1; PoEL-3; Poetr; PPP; PrIm; SCGP; TFi; TrGrPo; UnPo; WGRP

Weep not because this child hath died so young. On the Death of Mistress Mary Prideaux. William Strode. JCP; NOSC

Weep not for little Leonie. Compensation. Harry Graham. *Fr*. Some Ruthless Rhymes. CBNP; PeLV

Weep Not My Wanton. Robert Greene. *See* Weep [or Weepe] not, my wanton, smile upon my knee.

Weep not, nor backward turn your beams. A Lover, upon an Accident Necessitating His Departure, Consults with Reason. Thomas Carew. CaPo
(Lover Consults with Reason, The.) TrGrPo

Weep not that you no longer feel the tide. Lost Youth. Sir Roger Casement. TIRV

Weep Not To-Day. Robert Bridges. OBMV

Weep not, weep not. Go Down Death. James Weldon Johnson. DL; PoBA

Weep o'er the mis'ries of a wretched maid. Dying Prostitute, The; an Elegy. Thomas Holcroft. NOEC

Weep [or Weepe] not, my wanton, smile upon my knee. Sephestia's Song to Her Child[e]. Robert Greene. *Fr*. Menaphon. ELP; EnRePo; NoSic; OxAEP-1; PoEL-2; TrGrPo
(Sephestia's Lullaby.) NOBE; OBEV
(Sephestia's Song.) NTP
(Weep Not My Wanton.) EIL; SCGP

Weep [or Weepe] with me, all you that read. Epitaph on S. P. [Salomon *or* Salathiel Pavy], a Child of Q[ueen] El[izabeth's] Chapel. Ben Jonson. BeJo; EIL; EnRePo; HoPM; JCP; Mes; NAEL-1; NoP; NOSC; OAEL-1; OBD; OBEV; PoEL-2; PPP; SCGP; SeCP; SeCV-1; TrGrPo; UnPo
(Epitaph on S. P.) TFi
(On Solomon Pavy, a Child of Queen Elizabeth's Chapel.) NOBE

Weep [or Weepe] You No More [Sad Fountains]. Unknown. CH; EBEV; EIL; ELP; EnLoPo; GBL; HAP; NoP; NOSC; NoSic; NTP; PoE; PoEL-2; TFi; TrGrPo

Weep thy golden tears! *(LL)* April, April,/ Laugh thy girlish laughter. Sir William Watson. OBEV; TrGrPo

Weep, weep for him, the Man of God. Weep, Children of Israel. Thomas Moore. ChIV-1

Weep! Weep! Weep! Tumadir al-Khansa for Her Brother. *Unknown, tr. fr. Arabic by* E. Powys Mathers. *Fr*. Thousand and One Nights, The. AWP
(For Her Brother.) PBWP

Weep, weep, ye dwellers in the delvèd earth. Elegy on the Death of Bingo Our Trench Dog. Sir Edward de Stein. NSI

Weep, weep, ye woodmen! wail. Anthony Munday. *Fr*. Death of Robert, Earl of Huntingdon. CH
(Dirge: "Weep, weep, ye woodmen, wail.") CTC
(Robin Hood's Funeral.) WiR
(Song: "Weep, weep, ye woodmen, wail.") EIL

Weep, you may weep, for you may touch them not. *(LL)* Greater Love. Wilfred Owen. CMoP; EnLoPo; FaBoMo; FaBoRV; GTBS-P; ImPo; LiTB; LiTM; MeMBP; MoAB; MoBrPo; MoP; NoAM; TFi

Weepe O mine eyes. Unknown. PoEL-2

Weeper, The. Richard Crashaw. *See* Hail[e], sister springs!

Weepers, The. Rodney Jones. NAmP90

Weepers Tower in Amsterdam, The. Paul Goodman. VGW

Weepies, The. Paul Muldoon. NoAM; PNI

Weeping and Kissing. Sir Edward Sherburne. NOSC

Weeping and lamenting. Chipmunk. Irina Ratushinskaya. OBAP

Weeping and Wailing. Gerald Stern. CAPP

Weeping and wakeful all the night I lie. Rhodanthe. Agathias, *tr. fr. Greek by* Andrew Lang. AWP

Weeping for the Zen Master Po-yen. Chia Tao, *tr. fr. Chinese by* Stephen Owen. SuSp

Weeping Headstones of the Isaac Becketts, The. Paul Durcan. PBCIP

Weeping Melpomene assist my lays. The Fatal Dream; or, The Unhappy Favourite. Emanuel Collins. NOEC

Weeping, murmuring, complaining. Goldsmith. NOIV

Weeping o'er the sacred urn. Ambrose Philips. *Fr*. To the Memory of Lord Halifax. FaBoCo

Weeping rose in her dark night of leaves, The. A Song at Morning. Edith Sitwell. CMoP

Weeping Sinner, Dry Your Tears. Oliver Holden. AH

Weeping Willow, The. Unknown. AmFP

Weeps for us all through the night. *(LL)* We Drink Farewell. Tu Mu. OHMPC

Weeps out of western country something new. The Birth in a Narrow Room. Gwendolyn Brooks. BlSi; NAs; PoNe

Weepy drunk, Christmas Eve, 1988, my father in his steamy kitchen. River Stories. Dorothy Coffin Sussman. ArOW

Weevily Wheat. Unknown. AmFP; AS

Wei Wind, *sels*. Confucius, *tr. fr. Chinese by* Ezra Pound. Pedlar. CTC; OBVE

Weigh me the fire; or canst thou find. To Finde God. Robert Herrick. BeJo; WGRP

Weighing-In, The. Ibn al-Rumi, *tr. fr. Arabic by* Omar S. Pound. ArPe

Weighing the Baby. Ethel Lynn Beers. PoToHe

Weighing the stedfastness and state. Man. Henry Vaughan. ESCV; GeHe; MeLP; NOBE; NOCV; OBEV; PoEL-2; SCGP; SeCV-1

Weight of Sweetness, The. Li-Young Lee. RaBo

Weight of the Sheets, The. Jon Forrest Glade. NGP

Weight of the world, The. Allen Ginsberg. BCF; PoBeRe

Weightless and/ "smiling." *(LL)* In a Season of Unemployment. Margaret Avison. MoCV; NOBC

Weights. Les A. Murray. TSaS

Weingarten Travel Blessing, The. *Unknown, tr. fr. German by* Carroll Hightower. GePo

Weir Bridge. Padraic Fallon. CIP

Weird Sister. In Salem. Lucille Clifton. AmPA

We'l begin with a Tallen, a Brimmer to the KING! *(LL)* The Courtier's Health; or, Merry Boys of the Times. *Unknown*. CoMu

Wel mended tinker! sans dispute. Of John Bunyan's Life. John James. SCAP

Wel, wanton ey, but must ye nedis pley. Wanton Eye. Charles, Duc d'Orléans. OxBLMV

Weland knew fully affliction and woe. Deor's Lament. *Unknown, tr. fr. Anglo-Saxon by* Charles W. Kennedy. AnOE; OAEL-1

Weland, that dauntless man, well learned to bear [or well knew about exile]. Deor. *Unknown, tr. fr. Anglo-Saxon*. ASW, *tr. by* Kevin Crossley-Holland; TEP, *tr. by* Walter Kendrick
(Among snake-patterned swords Weland tasted sorrow.) EBEV, *tr. by* John Wain
(Wayland knew the wanderer's fate.) EEP, *tr. by* Michael Alexander

Welcome, The. Abraham Cowley. *Fr.* Mistress, The. BoLoP; SeCV-1

Welcome among my pleasant smart. *(LL)* Farewell the reign of cruelty. Sir Thomas Wyatt. SiPS

Wel/come back, brother. Huey. Etheridge Knight. NNaP

Welcome back, Mr. K: Love of My Life —. Welcome Back, Mr. Knight: Love of My Life. Etheridge Knight. PBCAP; RaBo

Welcome Back, Mr. Knight: Love of My Life. Etheridge Knight. PBCAP; RaBo

Welcome be ye when ye go. *Unknown.* MiEL

Welcome, brave gallant, with those locks so fair. A Periwig. Rowland Watkyns. NOSC

Welcome! but yet no entrance, till we bless. The Entertainment, or Porch-Verse, at the Marriage of Master Henry Northleigh and the Most Witty Mistress Lettice Yard. Robert Herrick. CaPo

Welcome Christmas! heel and toe. Stocking Song on Christmas Eve. Mary Mapes Dodge. OHIP

Welcome dear book, souls Joy, and food! The feast. H. Scriptures. Henry Vaughan. ChIV-2; ESCV

Welcome, dear dawn of summer's rising sway. May-Day. Aaron Hill. NOEC

Welcome, dear wanderer, once more! Upon Her Play Being Returned to Her, Stained with Claret. Mary Leapor. ECWP

Welcome Eumenides. Eleanor Ross Taylor. NALW

Welcome, fayre chylde, what is thy name? Dalyaunce. *Unknown.* CH

Welcome for Etheridge, A. James Cunningham. JB

Welcome freshness over the garden lay, A. Suspended Moment. Mariana B. Davenport. GoYe

Welcome, friend. Newton to Einstein. Jeannette Chappell. GoYe

Welcome, great Caesar, welcome now you are. To the King, Upon His Welcome to Hampton Court. Robert Herrick. BeJo

Welcome, grinned Henry, welcome fifty-one! John Berryman. *Fr.* Dream Songs. TAP

Welcome, happy Easter day! Easter Praise. Rodney Bennett. BoTP

Welcome Home. Josephine D. Henderson Heard. CBWP-4

Welcome home, driving downhill. Lament City. Thomas Lux. AmPA

Welcome home from the exhausting voyage. Sea Legs. Susan Feldman. AmPA

Welcome House, The. Mary E. O'Donnell. NWP

Welcome, kind Death: my long tired spirit bear. Algernon Sidney's Farewell. *Unknown.* APAS

Welcome, little Robin. *Unknown.* BoTP

Welcome, maids of honor. To Violets. Robert Herrick. CaPo; JCP; OBEV; PFP; SeCP; TrGrPo

Welcome me, if you will. For James Dean. Frank O'Hara. NeAP; NNaP

Welcome Morning. Anne Sexton. CrSp; HeIL

Welcome, most welcome, to our vows and us. To the King, upon His Coming with His Army into the West. Robert Herrick. BeJo; CaPo

Welcome my dearest. *(LL)* The [Valiant] Seaman's Happy Return [to His Love]. *Unknown.* ChTr; GBP

Welcome now, Victoria. *Unknown.* FaBoEH
(Queen Victoria.) CoMu

Welcome O Great Mary. Alice O'Gallagher, *tr. fr. Gaelic by* Douglas Hyde. WTO

Welcome, old friend, long-necked bottle. Argentarius, *tr. fr. Greek by* Fleur Adcock. GrAn

Welcome, old friend! These many years. To Age. Walter Savage Landor. EnRP

Welcome! Our Messiah. *Unknown.* MeEL

Welcome over the Door of an Old Inn. *Unknown. See* Hail, guest! We ask not what thou art.

Welcome, precious stone of the night. Welcome to the Moon. *Unknown, tr. fr. Gaelic.* BoNaP; ChTr

Welcome, Queen Sabbath. Zalman Schneour, *tr. fr. Hebrew by* Harry H. Fein. TrJP

Welcome, red and roundy sun. The Wood-Cutter's Night Song. John Clare. EnRP

Welcome, stranger! glad I greet thee. To Don Juan Baz. Mary E. Tucker. CBWP-1

Welcome, Summer. Chaucer. *See* Now Welcom[e], Somer [*or* Summer].

Welcome sweet and sacred cheer. The Banquet. George Herbert. ESCV; GeHe

Welcome sweet, and sacred feast; welcome life! The Holy Communion. Henry Vaughan *and* Thomas Stanley. ESCV

Welcome, Sweet Rest. Michael Wigglesworth. AH

Welcome the dawn. *(LL)* Nightingales. Robert Bridges. CMoP; GGP; ImPo; LiTB; LiTM; MoAB; MoBrPo; NOBE; OAEL-2; OBEV; OBMV; OBNC; SCGP; TFi; TrGrPo; UnPo

Welcome the Wrath. Stanley Kunitz. VGW

Welcome them and dance with them. *(LL)* The Fairies Are Dancing All Over the World. Michael Rumaker. GLP; PeHV

Welcome thou of high estate. Welcome O Great Mary. Alice O'Gallagher, *tr. fr. Gaelic by* Douglas Hyde. WTO

Welcome thou safe retreat! Solum Mihi Superest Sepulchrum. William Habington. ChIV-1; NOSC

Welcome, thrice welcome to thy native place! Mary Gulliver to Captain Lemuel Gulliver. John Gay *and* Alexander Pope. OAEL-1

Welcome to Freedom's birth-place — and a den! Ode to the Cameleopard. Thomas Hood. FaBoNo

Welcome to Hiroshima. Mary Jo Salter. ArOW; DiPo; NIP

Welcome to Hon. Frederick Douglass. Josephine D. Henderson Heard. CBWP-4

Welcome to Sack, The. Robert Herrick. BeJo; CaPo; SeCP; SeCV-1

Welcome to Spring. John Lyly. *See* What bird so sings, yet so does wail?

Welcome to Spring. Irene Thompson. BoTP

Welcome to the Moon. *Unknown, tr. fr. Gaelic.* BoNaP; ChTr

Welcome to the Nations. Oliver Wendell Holmes. PAH

Welcome to this my college, and thought late. To His Kinsman, Master Thomas Herrick, Who Desired to Be in His Book. Robert Herrick. CaPo

Welcome to Wales. John Tripp. AngWe

Welcome to you, rich Autumn days. Rich Days. W. H. Davies. BoNaP; BoTP

Welcome, welcome with one voice! Opening of the Indian and Colonial Exhibition by the Queen. Tennyson. EBVVPR

Welcome, wild Northeaster! Ode to the Northeast Wind. Charles Kingsley. FaPoR; GN; OxAEP-2; PlP

Welcome, Ye Hopeful Heirs of Heaven. Phoebe Hinsdale Brown. AH

Welcome Yule. *Unknown.* CH

Welcomed to islands over the long water. Islanders, Inlanders. Michael Mott. PoA

Welcoming Party, A. John Montague. IPY; PNI

Welcum, illustrat Ladye, and oure Quene! A New Year Gift to the Queen Mary When She First Came Home, 1562. Alexander Scott. ScCV

Wele, herying and worshipe be to Crist [*or* Christ] that dere us [*or* ous] boughte. William Herebert. MiEL
(Palm-Sunday Hymn, A.) MeEL

Wele, thu art a waried thing. *Unknown.* MiEL

Welford Wedding, The. Elizabeth Frances Amherst. ECWP

Welkin's wind, way unhindered. The Wind. Dafydd ap Gwilym, *tr. fr. Welsh by* Joseph P. Clancy. OBWVE

Well, The. Thomas Edward Brown. NOBVV

Well, The. Mother Goose. *See* As round as an apple, as deep as a cup.

Well, The. Philip Salom. NOBAu

Well, The. A. J. Seymour. PBCV

Well — it's Me! *(LL)* Fairies. Rose Fyleman. FaPON; OxBChV

We'll all drop anchor in the same final harbour. *(LL)* Remember Euboulos [*or* Eubulus], who lived and died sober? Leonidas of Tarentum. GrAn; OBD

We'll All Go a-Hunting Today. *Unknown.* OBET

Well, all these seamen — sailors and skippers — they. Tristan Corbière, *tr. fr. French by* C. F. MacIntyre. *Fr.* End, The. OBD

Well, alter ego, Time has trudged. Why Do We Live? Israel Zangwill. TrJP

Well, as Kavanagh said, we have lived. Singing School. Seamus Heaney. InPS

We'll begin with a box, and the plural is boxes. Why English Is So Hard. *Unknown.* FaBoUs

Well-beloved, The. John Montague. BiHa

Well boss did it/ ever strike you. The Hen and the Oriole. Don Marquis. *Fr.* Archy and Mehitabel. FiBHP

Well boss I met. Cheerio My Deario. Don Marquis. *Fr.* Archy and Mehitabel. FaBoCo

Well boss/ mehitabel the cat. Mehitabel and Her Kittens. Don Marquis. *Fr.* Archy and Mehitabel. SoCa

Well, boy, you're off to war. The Veteran. Frank S. Brown. NSI

Well-bred young girl of Gomorrah, A. *Unknown.* PeHV

Well-buggered boy named Delpasse, A. *Unknown.* PeHV; PeLi

Well — but you mean Lord — ? Hush! we mean the same. *(LL)* On a Lord. Samuel Taylor Coleridge. FaBoCo; FiBHP

Well clay it's strange at last we've come to it. The Spark's Farewell to Its Clay. R. A. K. Mason. PeNZ

Well, dear Mr. Wright, I must send you a line. To Henry Wright of Mobberley, Esq. on Buying the Picture of Father Malebranche. John Byrom. NOEC

Well, Did You Evah? Cole Porter. OBAL

Well died, my old cat. *(LL)* My Old Cat. Hal Summers. CRH; OBD; OFC; OxBTC

Well dost thou, Love, thy solemn feast to hold. Saint Valentine's Day. Coventry Patmore. *Fr.* Unknown Eros, The. OBNC

Well-dressed couple haggle, The. Knowingness. John Hughes. PNI

Well, endure is all I can do, reduced to. *(LL)* There's a man, I really believe, compares with. Sappho. STV

Well-Extracted Blood of Englishmen, The. Daniel Defoe. *Fr.* True-born Englishman, The. APAS; IHNG

Well formed is the child, well formed now. The Dawn of Day. Keaulumoku, *tr. fr. Hawaiian by* M. W. Beckwith. *Fr.* Kumulipo, The; a Creation Chant. WTO

Well, Froggie went a-courting and he did ride. Froggie Went a-Courting. *Unknown.* AmFP

We'll frolic with sweet Dolly. *(LL)* Jog On, Jog On. *Unknown.* ChTr; GBP

We'll from our own add far more years to his. *(LL)* To the King, Upon His Welcome to Hampton Court. Robert Herrick. BeJo

Well, General Grant, have you heard the news? Lee's Parole. Marion Manville. PAH

We'll give them to the poor, says John the Red Nose. *(LL)* The Cutty Wren. *Unknown.* GBP; OxBoLi; SWP; UV, abr.; WiR

We'll give to idleness. *(LL)* To My Sister. Wordsworth. ArLo; EnRP; OAEL-2

"We'll go home by the water," says Brian O'Linn. *(LL)* Brian O'Linn. *Unknown.* CBNP; FaBoBa; FaBoNo; NBLV; RB

We'll Go No More a-Roving. Byron. *See* So, We'll Go No More a-Roving.

We'll Go No More a-Roving. W. E. Henley. *Fr.* Echoes. MoBrPo

We'll go our ways, the world is wide. *(LL)* After the Quarrel. Paul Laurence Dunbar. AnAmPo; CDC

We'll go to Sea No More. *Unknown.* ChTr; GBP

We'll go to sea no more. *(LL)* We'll Go to Sea No More. *Unknown.* ChTr; GBP

We'll go to the meadows, where cowslips do grow. The Meadows. Ann Taylor. BoTP

Well, God is/ love. Puerto Rico Song. William Carlos Williams. NYBP

Well, Heaven be thanked my first-love failed. The County Ball. Coventry Patmore. *Fr.* Angel in the House, The. EBVV

Well here again that don't apply. T. S. Eliot. *Fr.* Sweeney Agonistes. FaBoVe; UnPo

Well here we are! — and don't you think we're looking quite. Address. Andrew Geddes Bain. PeSAV

Well, honest John, how fare you now at home? To John Clare. John Clare. Son

Well, how are things in Heaven? I wish you'd say. To Any Dead Officer. Siegfried Sassoon. NSI

Well, how do they look, the hills of Vermont. No News from the Old Country. Andrew Motion. SCBI

Well, how d'ye do, Private William McBride. No Man's Land. Eric Bogle. OBET

Well, I drink to you, David Campbell, but I drop a curse in the cup. A Letter to David Campbell on the Birthday of W. B. Yeats, 1965. A. D. Hope. NAs

Well, I forget the rest. *(LL)* Memorabilia. Robert Browning. FHYEP; NAEL-2; NOBVV; NoP; OAEL-2; OBNC; PoE; RB

Well, I guess you won, Virge. Martin Kirby. *Fr.* Afterlife of a Troll. NGP

Well, I may now receive, and die: my sin. John Donne. *Fr.* Satires. OBSV

Well, I never did see it before. *(LL)* Our Goodman. *Unknown.* AmFP

Well I never, did you ever. *Unknown.* FaBoCh

Well I Remember [How You Smiled]. Walter Savage Landor. *Fr.* Ianthe. HAP; OBNC; TrGrPo

Well I remember in my boyish hours. Thoughts of Boyhood. John Lloyd. AngWe

Well, I swanee! Martin Kirby. *Fr.* Afterlife of a Troll. NGP

"Well, I took your advice, Doc," said Knopp. *Unknown.* PeLi

Well, I was at the dresser. Just How It Happened. Priscilla Jane Thompson. CBWP-2

Well, I was camped out on the draw at the head of Cimarron. The Zebra Dun. *Unknown.* AmFP

Well, I went to California in the year of Seventy-six. Root Hog or Die. *Unknown.* AmFP

Well I woke up this mornin' it was Christmas Day. Adrian Henri's Talking after Christmas Blues. Adrian Henri. PeLV

Well, I would have it so. I should have known. André de Chénier, *tr. fr. French by* Arthur Symons. *Fr.* Elegies. AWP

Well, if a King's a lion, at the least. Pope. *Fr.* First Epistle of the First Book of Horace Imitated, The. OBSV (Profiteers.) ECEV

Well; if ever I saw such another Man since my Mother bound my Head. Mary the Cook-Maid's Letter to Dr. Sheridan. Swift. OxBoLi; PeLV

Well, if it's a sin to like Guinness. Cyril Ray. PeLi

Well! If the Bard was weather-wise, who made. Dejection; an Ode. Samuel Taylor Coleridge. EnRP; FHYEP; HeIP; LiTB; MeMBP; NAEL-2; NAWM-2; NOBE; NoP; OAEL-2; OBNC; OxAEP-2; PoE; PoEL-4; PPP; TFi; TOF

Well, if you must know all the facts. A Visitor. "Lewis Carroll." FaBoNo

Well, Ignorance, the cause is yet unknown. On Learning. Elizabeth Teft. ECWP

Well! I'm goin' home. Special Rider Blues. *Unknown.* AmFP

Well, I'm in love with a feller, a feller you have seen. Common Bill. *Unknown.* AmFP; AS

Well, it isn't the King, after all, my dear creature! From Miss Biddy Fudge to Miss Dorothy ———. Thomas Moore. *Fr.* Fudge Family in Paris, The. PeLV

Well, it was never mine. This Day, under My Hand. David Malouf. CBAP

Well, it's partly the shape of the thing. *Unknown.* SoSe

Well, Jesus died to save me in all of my sin. The Rock Island Line. *Unknown.* AmFP

We'll kiss, and smile, and walk again. *(LL)* Upon the Priory Grove, His Usual Retirement. Henry Vaughan. BeJo

Well Langston. A Message for Langston. "Kush." NBV

Well, let's go. Basho, *tr. fr. Japanese by* Kenneth Koch *and* Harold Henderson. TTTS

Well look a-here, honey. Depot Blues. *Unknown.* AmFP

We'll make a warm quilt for the ground. *(LL)* The Leaves in a Frolic. *Unknown.*

Well may I weene, faire ladies, all this while. Spenser. *Fr.* Faerie Queene, The. OAEL-1

Well may that kisse be sweet that's giv'n t' a sleek. Sir Richard Fanshawe, *after the Italian of* Giovanni Battista Guarini. *Fr.* Il Pastor Fido. OBVE

Well may they write, that sit in parlours fine. On His Writing Verses. John Hawthorn. NOEC

"We'll meet no more as wont!" she said. Not as Wont. Joseph Skipsey. NOBVV

Well, Menestratus, you ask me what I think. Lucilius, *tr. fr. Greek by* Peter Porter. GrAn

Well met, well met, my friend, all on the highway riding. The Husbandman and Serving-Man. *Unknown.* OBET

Well met, well met, my own true love. The Carpenter's Wife. *Unknown.* OAEL-1, *diff.vers.*; OBET; OxBB
(Demon *[or* Daemon] Lover.) EnSB; HAP; LiTB; MAT; Mes; UnPo; WeW
(House Carpenter, The.) AmFP
(James Harris.) AmFP; ESPB; FaBoBa
(Well Met, Well Met, My Old True Love.) AmFP

We'll move away still further into now. *(LL)* All Ignorance Toboggans into Know. E. E. Cummings. MeMAP; NAAL-2; NOBA; OxBA

We'll never belong to the family of Grumble! *(LL)* The Grumble Family. *Unknown.* PWR; WBLP

Well, never mind that now. Good night! Good night! *(LL)* The Sisters. Amy Lowell. NALW

Well Now, the Virgin. Roy Fuller. *Fr.* Mythological Sonnets. Son

We'll o'er the water and o'er the sea. O'er the Water to Charlie. Burns. FaBoCh

Well of freshness, A. Juxta. Grover Jacoby. GoYe

Well of St. Keyne, The. Robert Southey. BeLS; FaBoBe

Well of Vertew and Flour of Womanheid, The. *Unknown.* OxBS

Well-oiled spring pleasantly confirms. *(LL)* The Pleasures of the Door. Francis Ponge. AnRep

Well O.K., he was wrong. David Guest. Martin Bell. OBF

Well, old spy. Award. Ray Durem. BPo; PoBA; TTY

Well, on the day I was born. Have You Anything to Say in Your Defense? César Vallejo. RaBo

We'll, placed in Love's triumphant chariot high. William Cavendish. *Fr.* Humorous Lovers, The. OxBSP

Well Pleaseth Me the Sweet Time of Easter. Bertrans de Born, *tr. by* Ezra Pound. InvP

Well pleasing 'tis to me. Goat's-Leaf. Marie de France, *tr. by* Aline Allard. PBWP

Well, remember to do it by doing rather than by not doing. *(LL)* Portrait of the Artist as a Prematurely Old Man. Ogden Nash. BLPL; ImPo; InPS; LiTA; LiTM

We'll return to the little box. The Benefactors of the Little Box. Vasco [*or* Vasko] Popa, *tr. fr. Serbo-Croatian by* Charles Simic. HSix

Well Rising, The. William Stafford. NaP; RB

We'll roll, we'll roll the chariot along. Roll the Chariot. *Unknown.* AS

"We'll see if it is," said Rivera. (*LL*) I Paint What I See. E. B. White. NBLV; NYBP

Well-shadowed landscape, fare ye well! Farewell to Love. Sir John Suckling. CaPo

Well, she's gone, and. At a Queen's Funeral. Arnie Kantrowitz. PFL

Well, since in spight of all that Love can do. A Farewel to Love. Elizabeth Singer. KTR

Well, Sir, 'tis granted, I said D[ryden's] rhimes [*or* rhymes]. An Allusion to Horace; the Tenth Satire of the First Book. The Earl of Rochester. APAS

Well, So That Is That. W. H. Auden. *Fr.* For the Time Being; a Christmas Oratorio. LiTA; OAEL-2; OBCP

Well so that is that. Now we must dismantle the tree. Well, So That Is That. W. H. Auden. *Fr.* For the Time Being; a Christmas Oratorio. LiTA; OAEL-2; OBCP

(After Christmas.) MoAB; MoBrPo

(Flight into Egypt, The.) OxBA

(Narrator.) MeMAP

Well, some may hate, and some may scorn. Stanzas to ———. Emily Brontë. WPE

Well, sometimes it's Heaven, and sometimes it's Hell. Heaven and Hell. Willie Nelson. InPK

Well, son de story of my life. The Favorite Slave's Story. Priscilla Jane Thompson. AAP; CBWP-2

Well, son, I'll tell you. Mother to Son. Langston Hughes. CDC; HeIL; NAAL-2; NTCP; OBCA; PoNe; SAmP; TTY

Well swam, swan. (*LL*) Swan swam [*or* swan] over the sea. *Unknown.* OxNR

Well-tam'd Heart, A. Specifications for a Perfect Lover. Richard Crashaw. *Fr.* Wishes. To His (Supposed) Mistresse. CBCK

Well, Teddy, I have found you. The Lost Teddy Bear. Maggie Pogue Johnson. CBWP-4

We'll tell the hive, you died afloat. (*LL*) On a Honey Bee [*or* To a Honey Bee]. Philip Freneau. TAP

Well, the day of slavery back again! The Yankees Back. "The Mighty Sparrow." PBCV

Well, the grass is a pleasant thing. Latesummer Blues. Kenneth Patchen. Jaz

Well the sunset rays are shining. The Wild Mushroom. Gary Snyder. NoP

Well then. Dirty Niggers. Jacques Roumain, *tr. fr. French by* Ellen Conroy Kennedy. NegPo

Well then; I now do plainly see. The Wish. Abraham Cowley. *Fr.* Mistress, The. LiTB; NOBE; NoP; NOSC; OBEV; OxAEP-1; SeCV-1; TrGrPo

Well, then, poor G — — lies under ground! Epitaph on G — —. Pope. OBD

Well, then, the last day the sharks appeared. The Sharks. Denise Levertov. NeAP

Well then, the promis'd [*or* promised] hour is come at last. To My Dear Friend Mr. Congreve [on His Comedy Called "The Double-Dealer"]. Dryden. EBEV; OAEL-1; OxAEP-1; PoEL-3; SeCV-2

Well then, tomorrow! the wood exalts under the mild. Finally. Vittoria Aganoor Pompili, *tr. fr. Italian by* Brenda Webster. PBWP

Well there is in the west country, A. The Well of St. Keyne. Robert Southey. BeLS; FaBoBe

Well, they are gone, and here must I remain. This Lime-Tree Bower My Prison. Samuel Taylor Coleridge. EnRP; FaBoPP; FHYEP; HeIP; MeMBP; NAEL-2; OxAEP-2; PoE; PoEL-4; TOF

(Seen from the Quantocks.) FaBoPP

Well they knew/ Both warriors, that the fortunes of that day. The Combat at the Ford. Aubrey Thomas De Vere. *Fr.* Foray of Queen Meave, The. PeIV

Well they'd made up their minds to be everywhere because why not. The Last One. W. S. Merwin. FoLa; LCAP; NoAM; VGW

Well, they're quite dead, Rambuncto; thoroughly dead. Rambuncto. Margaret Widdemer. BXAP

Well, this bird comes, and under his wing is a crutch. The Bird. Moyshe-Leyb Halpern, *tr. fr. Yiddish by* John Hollander. PPP

Well, this is where I go down to the river. Heat. Kenneth Mackenzie. CBAP

Well, though it seems. Liddell and Scott; on the Completion of Their Lexicon. Thomas Hardy. OxBoLi; PeLV

Well, thrill. That's their story. (*LL*) Freely Espousing. James Schuyler. NeAP; NoP

Well, to start with. Jonah and the Whale. Gareth Owen. OBSP

Well, to the matter then, there's grown of late. Old England. Anne Bradstreet. *Fr.* Dialogue between Old England and New, A. KTR

We'll to the woods and gather may. (*LL*) Alons au bois le may cueillir. Charles, Duc d'Orléans. AWP

We'll to the woods and gather may. Alons au bois le may cueillir. Charles, Duc d'Orléans, *tr. fr. French by* W. E. Henley. AWP

We'll to the Woods No More. A. E. Housman. OAEL-2; PoRA

Well: Two Songs, The. *Gond Oral Tradition, tr. by* V. Elwin *and* S. Hivale. WTO

Well-uh Bird, Bird, Bird, Bird is the Word. The Trashmen Shaking Hands with Hubert Humphrey at the Opening of Apache Plaza Shopping Center, Suburban Minneapolis, August 1963. David Wojahn. *Fr.* Mystery Train: A Sequence. PBCAP

Well Uncle Ike! This beats me. Uncle Ike's Holiday. Priscilla Jane Thompson. CBWP-2

Well, Wanton Eye. Charles, Duc d'Orléans. HAP

Well water. Eight Sandbars on the Takano River. Gary Snyder. NOBA; NoP; VGW

Well Water. Randall Jarrell. InPK; NAAL-2; NOBA; NoP; OxBSP; VCAP; VGW

Well — we have reached the precipice at last. On the Masquerades. Christopher Pitt. ECEV; NOEC

Well, we went down town a-shopping. The Christmas Rush. Clara Ann Thompson. CBWP-2

Well, we will do that rigid thing. Parting with Lucasia; a Song. Katherine Philips. CBLP; PeHV

Well, well, I know the wise ones talk and talk. Augusta Webster. *Fr.* Castaway, A. BrRo

Well, well, 'tis true. Plain Dealing. Alexander Brome. NOSC

Well, well, you's cum at las'. People's Literary, De. Maggie Pogue Johnson. CBWP-4

Well, when all is said and done. "Æ." MoBrPo

Well, wife, I've found the model church! I worshipped there to-day. The Model Church. John H. Yates. PWR

We'll wish in hell we had been last and first! (*LL*) Barley-Break; or, Last in Hell. Robert Herrick. CaPo

Well-wishing to a Place of Pleasure, A. *Unknown.* GBL

Well, World, you have kept faith with me. He Never Expected Much. Thomas Hardy. NAEL-2; NAs; NoAM; OxBTC; SCV

Well worthy to be magnified are they. The Pilgrim Fathers. Wordsworth. AiP, *abr.*; PAH

Well, yes, I've lived in Texas since the spring of '61. A Spool of Thread. Sophie E. Eastman. PAH

Well you can tell ev'rybody. Tiny Montgomery. Bob Dylan. CBNP

Well, you have gone now, comrades. E.A. Mackintosh. NSI

Well, you know the sun is going down. Lowdown Dirty Blues. *Unknown.* AmFP

Welladay, welladay, poor Colin, thou art going to the ground. George Peele. *Fr.* Arraignment of Paris, The. EIL

Wellcome, to the Caves of Artá! Robert Graves. MeMBP; NBLV; NOBL; NYBP; PeLV

Wellfleet Harbor. Paul Goodman. CoAP

Wellfleet Sabbath. Marge Piercy. SRLS

Wellfleet Whale, The. Stanley Kunitz. CAPP; DiPo; FoLa; NoAM

Welling water — to which I add these tears, The. (*LL*) The Stream. Mona Van Duyn. VCAP

Wellington. Charles Harpur. NOBAu

Wells of Jesus Wounds, The. *Unknown.* MeEL

Wells River. J. D. McClatchy. ETG

Wellspring, The. Sharon Olds. BAP-89

Welsh Ballad, A. Edmwnd Prys, *tr. fr. Welsh by* Gwyn Williams. OBWVE

Welsh Espionage, *sels.* Gwyneth Lewis.
Advice on Adultery. NWP
"From Craig y Foelallt I can see it all." NWP
"So this is the man you dreamt I had betrayed." NWP
"Welsh was the mother tongue, English was his." NWP

Welsh Hill Country, The. R. S. Thomas. AngWe

Welsh History. R. S. Thomas. AngWe; OBWVE

Welsh Homer. Cliff James. AngWe

Welsh Incident. Robert Graves. CBNP; CMoP; EBEvV; MeMBP; NOBE; OBSP; OxBTC

Welsh Landscape. R. S. Thomas. FaBoMo; PWE

Welsh Marches, The. A. E. Housman. FaBoTw; SCGP

Welsh was the mother tongue, English was his. Gwyneth Lewis. *Fr.* Welsh Espionage. NWP

Welsh Wordscape, A. Peter Finch. AngWe

Welshman at St. James' Park, A. R. S. Thomas. AngWe

Welshman in Exile Speaks, The. T. Harri Jones. AngWe; OBWVE

Welshman to Any Tourist, A. R. S. Thomas. OxBC

Welt ist dumm, die Welt ist blind, Die. Heine, *tr. fr. German by* James Thomson. AWP

Weltanschauung. Charles Fishman. BTR

Weltering London ways where children weep, The. John Keats. Dante Gabriel Rossetti. EPCY

Women's Wather. T. S. Law. OxBS

Wen, wen, little wen. Against a Wen. *Unknown, tr. fr. Anglo-Saxon by* Kevin Crossley-Holland. ASW

We'n you see a man in woe. "Hullo!" Sam Walter Foss. VPP

Wenberi's Song. Wenberi, *tr. fr. Woiworung by* A. W. Howitt. CBAP

Wendell Phillips. H. Cordelia Ray. CBWP-3

Wendling. Coman Leavenworth. *Fr. Norfolk Memorials.* LiTA

Wendy Yoshimura. Biographical Notes. Al Robles. ETG

Wenest thou, usher, with thyn cointise. *Unknown.* MiEL

Wenlock Edge (" 'Tis time, I think; by Wenlock town.") A. E. Housman. *Fr. Shropshire Lad, A.* FaBoPP; FaPoB

Wensleydale Lad, The. *Unknown.* FaBoPP

Went by; but all my grief ageàn awoke. (*LL*) The Wind at the Door. William Barnes. ELP; EnVR; GBL; GTBS-P; OxAEP-2; PoEL-4

Went down to St. Joe's infirmary. Those Gambler's Blues. *Unknown.* AS

Went forth to fight, with murderous faces. (*LL*) A London Fete. Coventry Patmore. EBVV; EnVR; FaBoEH; HAP; PeVV

Went home and put a bullet through his head. (*LL*) Richard Cory. E. A. Robinson. AmPP; AnAmPo; CMoP; DL; EBEvV; FF; HAP; ImPo; InPK; LiTA; LiTM; MeMAP; MoAB; MoAmPo; NAAL-2; NOBA; NoP; NTP; OxBA; Poetr; PoLF; PoRA; PrIm; TAP; TFi; TrGrPo

Went home, and was cudgell'd again by his wife. (*LL*) As Thomas was cudgell'd [*or* cudgel'd] one day by his wife. Swift. FaBoEE

Went into a shoestore to buy a pair of shoes. Sale. Josephine Miles. WPE

Went on cutting bread and butter. (*LL*) The Sorrows of Werther. Thackeray. BLPA; FaBoCo; FiBHP; NBLV; NOBL; NOBVV; OBD; PeLV

Went to dinner with her Thursday. Pubescence at 39. Vickie Sears. GLP

Went to the garden to pick a posy. Stanzas for the Harp. *Unknown, tr. fr. Welsh by* Tony Conran. VBLP

Went up a year this evening. Emily Dickinson. HAP; WeW

Went weeping away. (*LL*) Six Dukes Went a-Fishing. *Unknown.* FaBoBa; OBET

Weping haveth min wonges wet. *Unknown.* MiEL

Wept at the way they gave of theirselves. Olden Scrapple Sonnet. Kenward Elmslie. UL

Wer ther outher in this toun. *Unknown.* MiEL

We're A' Dry wi' the Drinkin' O't. *Unknown.* ErPo

Were a tadpole and I was a fish. (*LL*) Evolution. Langdon Smith. BeLS; BLPA; FaBoBe

Were able to pipe, in Pluto's house I'd sing. (*LL*) Lament for Bion. Moschus. AWP

We're all Americans, except the Doc. A Mad Negro Soldier Confined at Munich. Robert Lowell. FaBoMo; OxBC

We're all at home. Having Eaten Breakfast. D. C. Berry. BXAP

We're All Dry. *Unknown. See* We're A' Dry wi' the Drinkin' O't.

We're all in the dumps. In the Dumps. *Unknown.* CBNP

Were all our sins so empty of enjoyment. The Muted Screen of Graham Greene. Phyllis McGinley. FaBoEE

We're at the Bath-house. Martial, *tr. fr. Latin by* Fergus Pickering. FaBoBl

Were barren as this moorland hill. (*LL*) The Dreary Change. Sir Walter Scott. FaBoPP; NAEL-2; OAEL-2; OBNC

Were [*or* Where] beth [*or* beeth] they [that] biforen us weren. Ubi Sunt Qui ante Nos Fuerunt? [*or* Contempt of the World]. *Unknown.* NoP
  (Contempt of the World.) MeEL
  (Were beth they biforen us weren.) PrIm
  (Where beeth they biforen us weren.) EBEV
  (Where beth they beforen us weren.) WeW
  (Where beth they, beforen us weren.) MeEL
  (Where beth they biforen us weren.) HAP

We're boy and girl, and lass and lad, and man and wife together. (*LL*) Ballad of Human Life. Thomas Lovell Beddoes. BeLS

We're brave and gallant miner boys who work down underground. The Eight Hour Day. *Unknown.* SWP

Were bright and fearful presences to me. (*LL*) Horses. Edwin Muir. CMoP; FaBoCh; OAEL-2

We're connecting. Poems for the New. Kathleen Fraser. CrSp; IHMS; NMM

We're crossing the bar of another year. I Am with Thee. Ernest Bourner Allen. BLRP

We're 'er Majesty's bold troubleshooter; wherever they send us we goes. Bold Troubleshooters. Peter Veale. NOBL

Were ever able to dispatch, by fear. (*LL*) Far greater numbers have been lost by hopes. Samuel Butler. FaBoEE

Were fading and all wars were done. (*LL*) The Dark Hills. E. A. Robinson. AiP; GoJo; HAP; ImPo; LiTA; LiTM; MoAB; MoAmPo; NoAM

We're flattered they come so close. Animal Song. Heather McHugh. AnAn

Were flooded over with eddying song. (*LL*) The Dying Swan. Tennyson. WiR

We're foot — slog — slog — slog — sloggin' over Africa. Boots. Kipling. BLPA; FaPoR; MoBrPo

We're going to build our union strong. (*LL*) Great Day. *Unknown.* SWP

We're going to have a party. The Christmas Party. Adeline White. BoTP

We're Going to Miss Our Chance to go to Jail. (*LL*) Street Demonstration. Margaret Walker. BPo

We're going to the fair at Holstenwall. Holstenwall. Sidney Keyes. FaBoTw

We're gonna roll, we're gonna roll. Roll the Union on. John Handcox *and* Lee Hays. SWP

Were half the power that fills the world with terror. A Message of Peace. Longfellow. *Fr.* Arsenal at Springfield, The. AmPP; WBLP

Were he composer, he would surely write. Portrait of the Boy as Artist. Barbara Howes. MoAmPo

We're hoping to be arrested. Street Demonstration. Margaret Walker. BPo

Were I a king, I could command content. Edward de Vere, Earl of Oxford. NoSic
  (Doubtful Choice, A.) ElL
  (Epigram: "Were I a king, I could command content.") FaBoEE; OxBSP
  (Epigram.) GGP
  (Were I a King.) NTP

Were I as Base as Is the Lowly Plain. *At. to* Joshua Sylvester. NoSic; Son

Were I in Trouble. Robert Frost. OxBSP

Were I invited to a nectar feast. Sylvia. Samuel Croxall. NOEC

Were I laid on Greenland's coast. John Gay. *Fr.* Beggar's Opera, The. CBLP; EBEvV, *sect.* I, *pt.* i; EnLoPo; NAEL-1; OAEL-1; OxBoLi; PeLV; PoEL-3
  (Macheath and Polly.) NOEC
  (Over the Hills and Far Away.) NOBE; PrIm

Were I that wandering citizen whose city is the world. The English Graves. G. K. Chesterton. NSI

Were I the palm tree which your love returning. E Questo il Nido in Che la Mia Fenice? A. D. Hope. OxBC

Were I the red-brushed fox, I should go warier. November Fugitive. Henry Morton Robinson. GoYe

Were I to leave no more than a good friend. The Departure; an Elegy. Henry King. SeCP

Were I to take an iron gun. Facts. "Lewis Carroll." FaBoUs

Were I, who to my cost already am. The Earl of Rochester. *Fr.* Satire [*or* Satyre] against [Reason and] Mankind, A. LiTB; NoP; NOSC; OAEL-1; OBSV; PoEL-3; SCV; SeCV-2

Were it but to pleasure you. (*LL*) To His Mistresses. Robert Herrick. CaPo; ErPo; SeCP

Were it undo that is ido [*or* y-do]. *Unknown.* MiEL
  (He Is Far.) OAEL-1

Were just three days apart. (*LL*) Calvary and Easter. "Susan Coolidge." WBLP

We're launched into the darkness. Night Ferry. Mark Doty. NAmP90

Were left in loneliness behind. (*LL*) A Winter Night. William Barnes. ChTr; FaBoRV; NOBE; OBNC

Were lost, if that were enable. (*LL*) The Fairies' Farewell. Richard Corbett [*or* Corbet]. BeJo; CoGr; NOSC; OxAEP-1

We're low, we're low, etc. (*LL*) The Song of the Low. Ernest Charles Jones. NOBVV

We're low — we're low — we're very, very low. The Song of the Low. Ernest Charles Jones. NOBVV

We're marching 'round the levee. Marching 'round the Levee. *Unknown.* AmFP

We're married, they say, and you think you have won me, — . The Bridal Veil. Alice Cary. AmWP

Were My Hart as Some Men's Are. Thomas Campion. AAS

Were Ne My Hearts Light I Wad Dye. Lady Grisel Baillie. KTR

"We're not amused," said Victoria. Stanley J. Sharpless. PeLi

Were not the one dead, turned to their affairs. (*LL*) Out, Out. Robert Frost. DL; FF; HAP; HeIP; NAAL-2; OxBA; Poetr; RB; SoSe; TRP; UnPo; VGW

We're OK. Gloria Fuertes, *tr. fr. Spanish by* Philip Levine. WPOW

We're on our way. Night Highway Ninety-Nine. Gary Snyder. PoBeRe

Were one, two, three. *(LL)* As I went up the garden. *Unknown.* BoTP

We're patient, prayerful, meek, resigned. *(LL)* Another to Urania. Benjamin Colman. ChIV-1; SCAP

Were spellbound on the moon. *(LL)* The Hunter's Song at Nightfall. Goethe. STV

Were that woman's postcoital charms. Rufinus Domesticus, *tr. fr. Greek by* Sam Hamill. InMo

We're the D-Day Dodgers, out in Italy. Ballad of the D-Day Dodgers. *Unknown.* WTO

We're the hardrock men. Dynamite Song. *Unknown.* AmFP

Were the whole world good as you — not an atom better. Question, The *Unknown.* WBLP

Were there no crowns on earth. The Dead President. Edward Rowland Sill. PAH

Were there no limits to my lust. To His Importunate Mistress. Paul Griffin. UV

Were there too many revolving mirrors? Air Circus. Carl Sandburg. AnAmPo

Were thrilling in his heart. *(LL)* Young Johnstone ("Young Johnstone and the young Colnel.") *Unknown.* ESPB; OxBB

Were toward Eternity. *(LL)* Because I Could not Stop for Death. Emily Dickinson. AmPP; AWP; BoWoP; ClHu; CMoP; DL; EBEvV; FF; HAP; HeIL; HeIP; ImPo; InPK; LiTA; LiTM; MeMAP; Mes; MoAB; MoAmPo; MoP; NAAL-1; NALW; NAWM-2; NIP; NoAM; NoP; OBD; OxBA; PBWP; PoE; PoEL-5; Poetr; SAmP; SCV; SoSe; SOTW; TAP; TFi; TRP; UnPo; WeW; WGRP; WPE

Were we now to fall. The Mechanic. Robert Creeley. NaP

We're wed to one eternity. *(LL)* An Invite to Eternity. John Clare. NAEL-2; NOBVV; OAEL-2; OBNC

Were you a leper bathed in wounds. Proving. Georgia Douglas Johnson. CDC

Were You There When They Crucified My Lord? *Unknown.* AH; BPo

Were you there when they laid him in the tomb? *(LL)* Were You There When They Crucified My Lord? *Unknown.* AH; BPo

Were yu normal today did yu screw society. Christ I Wudint Know Normal if I Saw It When. Bill Bissett. NOBC

Werena My Heart Licht. Lady Grisel Baillie. *See* There ance was a may, and she lo'ed na men.

Werena My Heart Licht I Wad Dee. Lady Grisel Baillie. OBEV; ScCV

Were't aught to me I bore the canopy. Shakespeare. *Fr.* Sonnets. NoSic

Were't not enclos'd within a pale of gold. *(LL)* On a Seal. Plato. AWP; FaBoEE

Werther had a love for Charlotte. The Sorrows of Werther. Thackeray. BLPA; FaBoCo; FiBHP; NBLV; NOBL; NOBVV; OBD; PeLV

We's invited down to brudder Browns. Krismas Dinnah. Maggie Pogue Johnson. CBWP-4

Wesley in Heaven. Thomas Edward Brown. OBNC

Wessex Heights. Thomas Hardy. CMoP; EBVV; FaBoPP; MeMBP; OAEL-2; OBNC; PoEL-5; SCGP

West, The. Michael Longley. BiHa; PBCIP

West and away the wheels of darkness roll. Revolution. A. E. Housman. MeMBP

West Ch'Ang-an Street. Pien Chih-lin, *tr. fr. Chinese.* LHF, *tr. by* Hualing Nieh

West Cliff. Chu Yi-tsun, *tr. fr. Chinese by* Chang Yin-nan *and* Lewis C. Walmsley. SuSp

West Coast Indian. George Clutesi. HATNAP

West Country, The. Alice Cary. AmWP

West-Country Damosel's Complaint, The. *Unknown.* ESPB

West-Easterly Divan. Goethe, *tr. fr. German by* John Weiss. PeHV
Sels.
  Cupbearer Speaks, The.
  "Market square's admiring throngs, The."

West Forties: Morning, Noon, and Night, The. L. E. Sissman. CoAP; NYBP

West Indian Primer. Elizabeth Alexander. NGP

West Indies, The. James Montgomery. PBCV
Sels.
  Inspiration, The. PAH
  Lust of Gold, The. PAH

West Kansas full moon. Directions in Our Blood. Barney Bush. HATNAP

West Lake. Kenneth O. Hanson. CoAP

West London. Matthew Arnold. FF; OBF; OHCV; SCGP; Son

West of Alice. W. E. Harney. NOBAu

West of Chicago. John Dimoff. RFM

West of the Sierras where. The California Phrasebook. Dennis Schmitz. AmPA

West of Your City. William Stafford. LiTM

West of your door, Blue Mountain dreams of melting. Blue Mountain. Roberta Hill Whiteman. VoR

West Paddocks. Arthur Davies. NOBAu

West Palm Beach Storm, The. *Unknown.* AmFP

West Ridge Is Menthol-Cool, The. D. L. Graham. PoBA

West River's watershed sounds beyond the sky, The. The Retired Official Yüan's High Pavilion. Tu Mu, *tr. fr. Chinese by* A. C. Graham. PLT

West-running Brook. Robert Frost. BLPL; MoAB; MoAmPo; NOBA; NoP

West Strand Visions. James Simmons. PBCIP

West Sussex Drinking Song. Hilaire Belloc. MoBrPo

West Virginia Hills. Walter Seacrist. SWP

West Wall. W. S. Merwin. RaBo

West Wind, The. John Masefield. LiTB; LiTM; MoAB; MoBrPo; PlP

West wind, blow from your prairie nest. The Song My Paddle Sings. Emily Pauline Johnson. FaPON

West wind sets the dragon rippling over the flag. Dragon. Ruth Bidgood. AngWe

Westering. Douglas V. Kane. GoYe

Western Approaches, The. Howard Nemerov. HCAP; TAP

Western Capital is in turmoil, The. Wang Ts'an, *tr. by* Ronald C. Miao. *Fr.* Seven Poems of Lament. SuSp

Western Town. David Wadsworth Cannon, Jr. PoNe

Western Town. Karl Shapiro. NYBP

Western Wagons. Rosemary *and* Stephen Vincent Benét. AiP; ImGa

Western Waves of Ebbing Day, The. Sir Walter Scott. *Fr.* Lady of the Lake, The. PoEL-4

Western Wind. *Unknown.* ArLo; BoLoP; ClHu; CTC; EBEV; EnLoPo; FaBoCh; FF; GBP; GGP; HAP; HeIL; HeIP; InPK; MAT; MeEL; NOBE; NoP; NoSic; OAEL-1; OxBLMV; OxBSP; Poetr; PPP; PrIm; SCGP; SoSe; TEP; TFi; UnPo; WeW
  (Lover in Winter Plaineth for the Spring, The.) OBEV
  (Westron Wind[e], When Will Thou Blow.) InvP; MeEL; NAEL-1; NIP; OBTV; PoE; PoEL-1
  (Westron wynde when wyll thou blow.) FaBoVe; GBL

Western wind has blown but a few days, The. The Cranes. Po Chü-i, *tr. fr. Chinese by* Arthur Waley. OBVE

Westgate-on-Sea. Sir John Betjeman. OxBoLi

Westland Row. Thomas Kinsella. MoP

Westminster Synagogue. Aaron Kramer. BTR

Westminster Wedding; or, Like unto Like, Quoth the Devil to the Collier, A. *Unknown.* CoMu

Westphalian Song. *Unknown, tr. fr. German by* Samuel Taylor Coleridge. AWP; OBVE

Westport House, Portrush. James Simmons. PBCIP

Westron Wind, When Will Thou Blow. *Unknown. See* Wester[n] wind, when will thou blow.

Westward, hit a low note, for a roarer lost. A Strut for Roethke. John Berryman. NOBA

Westward Ho! Joaquin Miller. AnAmPo; FaBoBe

Westward the field of the cloth of gold. A Visit. Sherwood Anderson. PoA

Wet almond-trees, in the rain. Bare Almond-Trees. D. H. Lawrence. FaBoPP; FaBoVe; OBTV

Wet August, A. Thomas Hardy. PPP

Wet Casements. John Ashbery. NAAL-2; PoM

Wet centre is bottomless, The. *(LL)* Bogland. Seamus Heaney. HeIP; IPY; NoAM; NOIV; NoP; PBCIP; PNI

Wet dawn inks are doing their blue dissolve, The. Winter Trees. Sylvia Plath. CAPP; HCAP; LCAP; NMM

Wet dog is the lovingest, A. *(LL)* The Dog. Ogden Nash. Spl

Wet gray day, A — rain falling slowly. Morels. William Jay Smith. BoNaP; MAT; NYBP; RFM

Wet Hair: If Now His Mother Should Come. Robert Penn Warren. *Fr.* Penological Study: Southern Exposure. NoAM

Wet leaf that clings to the threshold, A. *(LL)* Liu Ch'e. Ezra Pound. OBVE; VGW

Wet Night, A. Richard Ryan. CIP

Wet oats at the windows of our flat. *(LL)* Windows. Thomas McCarthy. IB

Wet sheet and a flowing sea, A. Allan Cunningham. EnRP; GTBS; GTBS-P; OxAEP-2; VPP
  (Sea-Song, A.) BoTP; FaBoBe; FaPoR; GN; PlP

Wet, sickly/ smells of cattle yard silage fill the prairie air. Dream. Elizabeth Cook-Lynn. *Fr.* Journey. HATNAP

Wet snow falling on no snow. Drysdale and Mantle Whitey Ford and to You. Steve Carey. UL

Wet streets. It has rained drops big as silver coins. Eighteen. Maria Banus, *tr. fr. Romanian by* Willis Barnstone *and* Matei Calinescu. BoWoP

Wet Summer. May Williams Ward. GoYe

Wet Thursday. Weldon Kees. NaP; NYBP

Wet Weather. Patricia Low. VGW

Wet Weather at Cannes. Edward Lear. FaBoNo

Wet-Weather Talk. James Whitcomb Riley. AnAmPo

Wetting the ground to form our roots. (*LL*) Rehearsal. Cyril Dabydeen. PBCV

We've all been invited up to Killisnoo. *Unknown, tr. fr. Tlingit Indian by* James Koller. STP

We've been taught for two thousand years. A Late Twentieth-Century Prayer. Ernest Sandeen. WeW

We've come intil a gey queer time. Epistle to John Guthrie. Sydney Goodsir Smith. OxBS

We've drunk the boys who rushed the hills. Abdul. *Unknown.* NSI

We've formed our band and are well manned. The Californian. *Unknown.* AmFP

We've fought before, but this is worse than rape! Baobab Fruit Picking; or, Development in Monkey Bay. Jack A. Mapanje. PeSAV

We've fought with many men acrost the seas. Fuzzy-Wuzzy. Kipling. MoBrPo; TrGrPo

We've found this Scott Fitzgerald chap. Effervescence and Evanescence. Keith Preston. OBAL

We've got a new maid called Chrysanthemum. *Unknown.* PeLi

We've got as far as poison-gas. (*LL*) Christmas: 1924. Thomas Hardy. FaBoEE; OBCP

We've heard and heard, and finally believe. The Diary. Goethe, *tr. fr. German by* John Frederick Nims. STV

We've hung David's *La Vierge et Les Saintes.* The Living Room. Gjertrud Schnackenberg. FYAP

We've lived for forty years, dear wife. The Ideal Husband to His Wife. Sam Walter Foss. AnAmPo

We've made a great mess of love. The Mess of Love. D. H. Lawrence. ArLo; CBLP; OAEL-2

We've nothing vast to offer you, no deserts. A Welshman to Any Tourist. R. S. Thomas. OxBC

We've our business to attend Day's duties. Bending the Bow. Robert Duncan. CAPP

We've possums in our roof — how very sweet! Possums. Ann Coleridge. OBAP

We've put a fine addition on the good old church at home. The Ladies' Aid. *Unknown.* PoLF

We've reached the land of desert sweet. Dakota Land. *Unknown.* AS

We've seen him before. A Charmer Turned Ascetic. Marippittiyar, *tr. fr. Tamil by* A. K. Ramanujan. PLW

We've socially-conscious biography. *Unknown.* PeLi

We've sworn off nostalgia. Little Elegy for the Age. Lynne McMahon. NAmP90

We've taken our burlap sacks and entered. The Killigrew Wood. Norman Dubie. AmPA

We've traveled long together. Verses to my Heart's-Sister. H. Cordelia Ray. AAP; CBWP-3

We've trod the maze of error round. Late Wisdom. George Crabbe. *Fr.* Reflections. OBEV; TrGrPo

Wexford Girl, The. *Unknown.* AmFP

Wey, Ned, Man! Susanna Blamire. ECWP

Weyla's Song. Eduard Friedrich Mörike, *tr. fr. German by* Philip L. Miller. RiWo

Wha daur meddle wi' me? Little Jock Elliot. *Unknown.* IBB

Wha ebah Joe an me duz lib we likes to hab um neat. Lizzie and Joe Catch a Thief. Edward Cordle. PBCV

Wha Fe Call I'. Valerie Bloom. AIW; FaBoVe

Wha Hes Gud Malt. *Unknown.* ScCV

Wha Is Perfyte. Alexander Scott.

Wha Is That at My Bower-Door? Burns. ErPo; InvP

Wha kens on whatna Bethlehems. The Innumerable Christ. "Hugh MacDiarmid." EBEV; NoP; OxAEP-2; OxBS

Wha learns my carol and carries it away? (*LL*) The Yule Days. *Unknown.* ChTr; GBP; NTP

Wha lies here? Johnny Dow [*or* Doo]. *Unknown.* FaBoCo; FaBoEE; FiBHP

Wha the deil hae we gotten for a king. The Wee, Wee German Lairdie. Allan Cunningham. FaBoEH

Wha wadna be in love. Maggie Lauder. *At. to* Francis Sempill. OxBS

Whack Fol the Diddle. Peadar Kearney. FiBHP

Whale. William Rose Benét. MoAmPo

Whale. Geoffrey Dearmer. BoTP

Whale, The. John Donne. *Fr.* Progress[e] of the Soul[e], The. ChTr

Whale, The. Herman Melville. *See* Ribs and Terrors in the Whale, The.

Whale, The. Theodore Roethke. ZA

Whale, The. *Unknown.* ChTr

Whale, The. *Unknown, tr. by* Richard Wilbur. *Fr.* Bestiary, The. CRP

Whale, The. *Unknown, tr. fr. Anglo-Saxon. Fr.* Physiologus. AnOE, *tr. by* Charles Kennedy. EBEV, *tr. by* Gavin Bone

Whale, His Bulwark, The. Derek Walcott. OxBC; TTY

Whale in the Blue Washing Machine, The. John Haines. AnAn

Whale, The/ is a room. In a Blind Garden. David Shapiro. ChIV-1

Whale is the greatest beast in all the ocean waste. The Whale. *Unknown, tr. by* Richard Wilbur. *Fr.* Bestiary, The. CRP

Whale Wisdom Peace Illumination. Jeff Poniewaz. EaPr

Whalefeathers. Paul Violi. UL

Whaler's Pig, The. Edwin James Brady. NOBAu

Whaler's Rhyme. *Unknown.* NOBAu

Whales, The. Marguerite Young. WPE

Whales off Wales, The. X. J. Kennedy. OBCA

Whales Weep Not! D. H. Lawrence. CMoP; MeMBP; NoAM; NU

Whalesong. Judith Nicholls. OBAP

Wha'll buy [my] caller herrin? Caller Herrin'. Lady Nairne. OxBS; ScCV; WoRP

Whan bells war rung, an mass was sung. Sweet William's Ghost. *Unknown.* ESPB

(Sweet William and May Margaret.) CH

Whan Cnut Cyng the Witan wold enfeoff. The Beoleopard; or, Witan's Whail. *Unknown.* CBNP

Whan he of the apple ete and Eve it him betoght. (*LL*) Lollay, Lollay, Littel Child. *Unknown.* EnVB

Whan netilles in winter bere roses rede. Impossible to Trust Women. *Unknown.* MeEL; MiEL

Whan said was al this miracle, every man. Chaucer. *See* When seyd was al this miracle, every man.

Whan that Aprill with his shoures [*or* shower] soote. Chaucer. *Fr.* Canterbury Tales, The. ChTr; CTC, *abr.*; EBEvV; EnVB; FHYEP; InPS; NAEL-1; NIP; NoP; OAEL-1; PoE; PPP, *abr.*; SCV; TrGrPo; TRP

(As soon as April pierces to the root, *mod. vers. by* Theodore Robinson.) NAWM-1

(When April with its sweet showers.) TFi, *mod. vers. by* William Harmon

(When April with Its Sweet Showers.) PrIm

(When in April the Sweet Showers Fall, *mod. vers. by* Nevill Coghill.) TEP

(When the Sweet Showers of April Follow March, *mod. vers. by* Louis Untermeyer.) TrGrPo

Whan that Aprille with hise shoures soote. Aprilly. Bert Leston Taylor. OBAL

Whan that the knight had [*or* hadde] thus his tale ytold. Chaucer. *See* Miller's Prologue, The.

Whan they cam' first to Yarrow. (*LL*) The Dowie Houms o' Yarrow. *Unknown.* OBEV; OxBS

Whan they unto the paleys were yoemen. Chaucer. *Fr.* Troilus and Criseyde [*or* Criseide]. EnVB; PoE

Whane lordes wol leefe theire olde lawes. Prophecia Merlini Doctoris Perfecti. *Unknown.* OxBLMV

Whan'll we be marry'd. *Unknown.* CBLP

Whanne I this Supplicacioun. The Parting of Venus and Old Age. John Gower. *Fr.* Confessio Amantis. PoEL-1

Whanne ic se on Rode. I Ought to Weep. *Unknown.* MeEL

Whanne mine eyhnen misten. *Unknown.* MiEL

Whar hae ye been a' day, my boy Tammy? My Boy Tammy. Hector MacNeill. CH

Whare the braid planes in dowy murmurs wave. The Ghaists; a Kirk-yard Eclogue. Robert Fergusson. OxBS

Whare'er your sinfu' pintle be. (*LL*) Godly Girzie. Burns. CoMu; ErPo; FaBoBl

Wharrupede thrimmered, the glottal stopped, The. Bollam's Replover, The: Farewell to Jabberwocky. Hugh Haughton. CBNP

Wharton ("Wharton! the scorn and wonder of our days.") Pope. *Fr.* Epistle to Sir Richard Temple. AWP

What? Langston Hughes. NBLV; OBAL

What a 16 years it's been. Columbia U Poesy Reading — 1975. Gregory Corso. PoBeRe

What a bullet is. (*LL*) The Ballot and the Bullet. Chris Van Wyk. PeSAV

What a calamity! What dreadful loss! Honesty at a Fire. J. C. Squire. FiBHP

What a charming thing's a battle! Isaac Bickerstaffe. *Fr.* Recruiting Serjeant, The. NOEC

What a Circus. Alan Dugan. AnAn

What a commanding power. Thomas Washbourne. WGRP

What a cost to be pure! did e'er strike your mind. Refining Fire. L. A. J. Moorer. CBWP-3

What a dainty life the milkmaid leads! Thomas Nabbes. NOSC

What a delight it is/ When a guest you cannot stand. Tachibana Akemi, tr. fr. Japanese by Geoffrey Bownas and Anthony Thwaite. Fr. Poems of Solitary Delights. Mes

What a delight it is/ When, after a hundred days. Tachibana Akemi, tr. fr. Japanese by Geoffrey Bownas and Anthony Thwaite. Fr. Poems of Solitary Delights. Mes

What a delight it is/ when, borrowing. Tachibana Akemi, tr. fr. Japanese by Geoffrey Bownas and Anthony Thwaite. Fr. Poems of Solitary Delights. Mes

What a delight it is/ When everyone admits. Tachibana Akemi, tr. fr. Japanese by Geoffrey Bownas and Anthony Thwaite. Fr. Poems of Solitary Delights. Mes

What a delight it is/ When I blow away the ash. Tachibana Akemi, tr. fr. Japanese by Geoffrey Bownas and Anthony Thwaite. Fr. Poems of Solitary Delights. Mes

What a delight it is/ When I find a good brush. Tachibana Akemi, tr. fr. Japanese by Geoffrey Bownas and Anthony Thwaite. Fr. Poems of Solitary Delights. Mes

What a delight it is/ When, of a morning. Tachibana Akemi, tr. fr. Japanese by Geoffrey Bownas and Anthony Thwaite. Fr. Poems of Solitary Delights. Mes

What a delight it is/ When on the bamboo matting. Tachibana Akemi, tr. fr. Japanese by Geoffrey Bownas and Anthony Thwaite. Fr. Poems of Solitary Delights. Mes

What a delight it is/ When, skimming through the pages. Tachibana Akemi, tr. fr. Japanese by Geoffrey Bownas and Anthony Thwaite. Fr. Poems of Solitary Delights. Mes

What a delight it is/ When, spreading paper. Tachibana Akemi, tr. fr. Japanese by Geoffrey Bownas and Anthony Thwaite. Fr. Poems of Solitary Delights. Mes

What a fine cow your predecessor was! To a Sacred Cow. Unknown, tr. fr. Toda by W. E. Mashiel. WGRP

What a fine evening is this. Song of the Boatswain of Yüeh. Unknown, tr. fr. Chinese by Irving Y. Lo. SuSp

What a fine hostess! "Song of the Southern Country" — Presented to a Courtesan. Hsin Ch'i-chi, tr. fr. Chinese by Irving Y. Lo. SuSp

What a fine hunting day, it's as balmy as May. We'll All Go a-Hunting Today. Unknown. OBET

What a Friend We Have in Cheeses! William Cole. OBAL

What a friend we have in Jesus. The Unfailing Friend. Joseph Scriven. BLRP

What a girl called "the dailiness of life." Well Water. Randall Jarrell. InPK; NAAL-2; NOBA; NoP; OxBSP; VCAP; VGW

What a grand time was the war! World War II. Langston Hughes. HCAP

What a great battle you and I have fought. The Marriage. Anna Wickham, tr. fr. Hungarian. AIW

What a grudge I am bearing the earth. Petrarch, tr. fr. Italian. Fr. Sonnets to Laura.

(Translation from Petrarch, A.) MoBrPo, tr. by J. M. Synge

What a host you are, Mancinus. Martial, tr. fr. Latin by Peter Porter. OBVE

What a hot day it is! A Terrestrial Cuckoo. Frank O'Hara. CBNP; SOTW

What a Little Girl Had on Her Mind. Ibaragi Noriko, tr. fr. Japanese by Kenneth Rexroth and Ikuko Atsumi. WPJ

What a lovely being is a mother! Mother. Hettye Rayburn Ramsey. PWR

"What a lovely world," said the baby chick. An Easter Chick. Thirza Wakley. BoTP

What a Man Needs. Vikram Seth. CBCK

What a mess they leave. (LL) Middle Age. Paula Rankin. MT

What a moment of strange dreaming! Mind Flying Afar. Edgar Lee Masters. PoA

What a night! The wind howls, hisses, and but stops. Snowstorm. John Clare. BoNaP; WiR

What a pox do you mean with your pride and ill-nature. A Solitary Canto to Chloris the Disdainful. John Smith. NOEC

What a Proud Dreamhorse. E. E. Cummings. InvP; VGW

What?/ a rhythm. Paul Niger, tr. fr. French by Ellen Conroy Kennedy. Fr. Initiations. NegPo

What a splish-splash that would be! (LL) If all the seas were one sea. Mother Goose. BoTP; OxNR; ReMoGo

What a sublime end of one's body, what an enskyment; what a life after death. (LL) Vulture. Robinson Jeffers. NAAL-2; NoAM; NOBA; NoP

What a thing it is to sit absolutely alone. Thomas Merton. EaPr

What a thrill. Cut. Sylvia Plath. CAPP; TAP

What a trick. Ragout. William Zaranka. BXAP

What a way to go! (LL) In Passing. Gerald Jonas. GrPl

What a wonderful bird the frog are. The Frog. Unknown. MoShBr; NBLV; NTCP; RB

What a wonderful pursuit. Marvelous Pursuits. Julio Cortázar, tr. by Paul Blackburn. AnRep

What a word and I thought it would be. Alone. Richard Shelton. NYBP

What abou' de Law? Adam Small, tr. fr. Afrikaans by Carrol Lasker. PeSAV

What abou' de law? (LL) What abou' de Law? Adam Small. PeSAV

What about each Great Canadian Lake? The Great Lakes of Canada. Gordon Perry. FaBoUs

What about that bad short you saw last week. Black People! Amiri Baraka. BPo

What about the people who came to my father's office. The Questions. Robert Pinsky. NAmP90; NoAM

What about You? Edward Pygge. BXAP; FaBoPa

What above reason is, or beneath sense. (LL) Love's Innocence. Thomas Stanley. BeJo

What age is this? What times are now? Time's Whirligig, Or, The Blue-New-Made-Gentleman Mounted. Humphrey Willis. NOSC

What ailes Pigmalion? Is it lunacy. Thomas Morton. SCAP

What am I glad will stay when I have passed. The Things that Will Not Die. Edward Rowland Sill. AnAmPo

What am I? how produced? and for what end? Know Yourself. John Arbuthnot. ECEV

What am I in the place of nourishment. A Curse on Uruk. Enheduanna, tr. fr. Sumerian by Aliki and Willis Barnstone. BoWoP

What am I? Nosing here, turning leaves over. Wodwo. Ted Hughes. CBNP; MoP; NoAM

What am I to do with my sister? Prince Yuhara, tr. by Arthur Waley. Fr. Manyo Shu, Part 4 of 4. AWP

What Am I Who Dare. William Habington. TrPWD

What an anxious existence I led. Anna Town. Anne Carson. Fr. Life of Towns, The. BAP-90

What an elusive target. The Fights. Milton Acorn. MoCV; NOBC

What? an English sparrow sing? Did You Ever Hear an English Sparrow Sing? Bertha Johnston. BLPA

What an intolerable deal of history! The Compound Eye. Peter Davison. SM

What angel fit? (LL) Dulnesse. George Herbert. ESCV; MiEL

What Any Lover Learns. Archibald MacLeish. MeMAP

What are all the hillmen wanting. The Keeper of the Midnight Gate. George Mackay Brown. OxBC

What are all those fish that lie gasping on the strand? (LL) Three Movements. W. B. Yeats. CMoP; FaBoEE

What are days for? Days. Philip Larkin. EBEV; FaBoMo; Mes; NTP; OxAEP-2; OxBC; OxBSP; PeECV; RB; TOF

What are deep? The ocean and truth. (LL) What Are Heavy? Christina Rossetti. FaBoRV; NTP; OxBChV; Spl

What are friends? A Friend in Need Will Be Around in Five Minutes. Ogden Nash. OBF

What Are Heavy? Christina Rossetti. FaBoRV; NTP; OxBChV; Spl

What are little boys made of, made of? Mother Goose. CBCK, shorter, diff. vers.; ReMoGo, shorter, diff. vers.; UV, sts. 1–2
(Natural History, diff. vers..) OxNR

What! are my deeds forgot? Shakespeare. Fr. Troilus and Cressida. OxAEP-1

What are our light afflictions here. Our Light Afflictions. Unknown. BLRP

What are ruins to us. At Lindos. May Sarton. WPE

What are the bugles blowin' for? said Files-on-Parade. Danny Deever. Kipling. CoGr; EBEvV; EBVV; FaBoBa; FaPoR; GTBS-P; InPS; LiTB; MoBrPo; NAEL-2; NoAM; NOBE; NOBVV; OHCV; OxBoLi; OxBTC; PeVV; PlP; PoLF; SCGP; SCV; TEP; TFi; TrGrPo; UnPo

What are the islands to me. The Islands. Hilda Doolittle ("H. D."). MoAmPo

What are the Signs of Zodiac. Zodiac. Eleanor Farjeon. OTCP

What are the suburbs made of? Nursery Rhyme. Gavin Ewart. UV

What are the thoughts that are stirring his breast? Under the Shade of the Trees. Margaret Junkin Preston. PAH

What are these women up to? They've gone and strung. The Deodand. Anthony Hecht. DiPo; NoAM

What are they doing now? I imagine Oliver. A Running Battle. Brendan Kennelly. BiHa; PWE

What are we first? First, animals; and next. George Meredith. Fr. Modern Love. GBL; HAP; NoP; PoEL-5

What are we men indeed? Grim torment's habitation. Human Misery. Andreas Gryphius, tr. fr. German by George C. Schoolfield. GePo

What Are We Playing At? Andrée Chedid, *tr. fr. French by* Samuel Hazo *and* Mirène Ghossem. BoWoP

What are we to do with a heaven. Three Songs from the Temple. Don Domanski. NOBC

What are we waiting for, assembled in the forum? Waiting for the Barbarians. C. P. Cavafy, *tr. fr. Greek by* Edmund Keeley *and* Philip Sherrard.
(What are we waiting for, gathered in the market-place?) PAW

What Are Years? Marianne Moore. BLPL; CMoP; LiTA; MeMAP; MoAB; MoAmPo; MoP; NoAM; NOBA; OxBA; SoSe; TrGrPo

What are you able to build with your blocks? Block City. Robert Louis Stevenson. FaPON; NTCP

What Are You Doing? Edmund Vance Cooke. PWR

What are you doing? "Plus Ça Change . . ." Philip Whalen. PoBeRe

What are you doing away up there. Night Walk. Max Fatchen. OTCP

What are you doing here. A Dialogue at the Ground-Breaking Ceremony. Pien Chih-lin, *tr. fr. Chinese.* Fr. Poems Written at the Construction Site of the Ming Tombs Dam. LHF, *tr. by* Hualing Nieh

What are you doing here, ghost, among these urns. Father in the Railway Buffet. U. A. Fanthorpe. FaBoWP

What are you doing here in this strange world that goes on and off. Traffic Lights. Lina Kasdaglis, *tr. fr. Modern Greek by* Edmund *and* Mary Keeley. BoWoP

What are you doing, my lady, my lady. *Unknown.* OxNR

What, are you drop't? John Webster. Fr. White Devil, The. PoEL-2

What are you going to do with us, who have. The Pleaders. Peter Davison. NYBP

What are you, Lady? — naught is here. Portrait of a Lady in the Exhibition of the Royal Academy. Winthrop Mackworth Praed. *Fr.* Every-Day Characters. NOBL; PeLV; PoEL-4

What are you looking at? Looking. Binoculars. Fleur Adcock. PWE

What are you saving it for? Asclepiades, *tr. fr. Greek by* Kenneth Rexroth. PGA

What are you, then, my love, my friend, my father. The Quarry. Vassar Miller. WPE

What are you . . . ? they ask, in wonder. Cold Colloquy. Patrick Anderson. *Fr.* Poem on Canada. NOBC

What are you waiting for, George, I pray? Tardy George. *Unknown.* PAH

What art thou, frost? and whence are thy keen stores. Winter. James Thomson. *Fr.* Seasons, The. OxBS

What art thou, love? Whence are those charms. Jacob Allestry. NOSC

What art thou, Mignon, child of mystery? Mignon. H. Cordelia Ray. AmWP; CBWP-3

What art thou, Spleen, which ev'ry thing dost ape. The Spleen. The Countess of Winchilsea. NALW; NOSC

What asks the Bard? He prays for naught. After Horace. Alfred Denis Godley. NOBL

What authors lose, their booksellers have won. On Authors and Booksellers [*or* Publishers]. Pope. FaBoEE; IHNG

What availeth it me though I say, nay? (*LL*) The Scholar Complains. *Unknown.* MeEL

"What bait do you use," said a Saint to the Devil. The Lure. John Boyle O'Reilly. TIRV

What beasts and angels practice I ignore. Little Ode. Paul Goodman. PoA

What Became of Them? *Unknown.* BoTP; OBCA; OxBChV

What becomes of the girl who lives always alone? The Sorceress. Eugène Marais, *tr. fr. Afrikaans by* Jack Cope *and* Uys Krige. PeSA

What began that bustle in the village. The Birth of Moshesh. David Granmer T. Bereng, *tr. fr. Sotho by* Dan Kunene *and* Jack Cope. PeSA; TTY

What bird so sings, yet so does wail? Trico's Song. John Lyly. *Fr.* Alexander and Campaspe. EIL; NoSic; TrGrPo
(Spring, The.) CH
(Spring's Welcome.) OBEV
(Welcome to Spring.) NOBE
(What Bird So Sings.) SCGP

What Birds Were There. William Everson. NoAM

What birth is this; a poore despissed creature? Upon ye Sight of My Abortive Birth. Mary Carey. KTR

What Blood redeemeth you and me! (*LL*) Bethlehem Town. Eugene Field. WBLP

What bluid's that on thy coat lap. Edward. *Unknown.* ESPB

What blust'ring noise now interrupts my sleep. William Drummond of Hawthornden. *Fr.* Forth Feasting. NOSC

What bones? What bones? Stones instead. Georgia. Bin Ramke. MT

What Booker can prognosticate. The King Enjoys His Own Again. Martin Parker. FaBoCh; OxBoLi
(Upon Defacing of Whitehall.) NOSC

What boots it, thy virtue. Tact. Emerson. AnAmPo

What booty gave the German War? Booty from the German War. Friedrich von Logau, *tr. fr. German.* GePo, *tr. by* George C. Schoolfield

What Bright Pushbutton? Samuel Allen. PoNe

What bright soft thing is this? The Tear [*or* The Teare]. Richard Crashaw. ImPo; LiTB; SeCP

What Brings Us Out. Naomi Shihab Nye. NAmP90

What bring you, sailor, home from the sea. Luck. W. W. Gibson. MoShBr; OBMV

What bullet killed him? Dead Soldier. Nicolás Guillén, *tr. fr. Spanish by* Langston Hughes. TTY

What burlesque could, was by that genius done. Walter Harte. EPCY

What business, or what hope brings thee to town. To Sextus. Martial, *tr. fr. Latin by* Sir Charles Sedley. FaBoEE

What calendar do you consult for an explosion of the sun? Sestina to the Common Glass of Beer: I Do Not Drink Beer. Diane Wakoski. SM

What calls itself Crane. Agreeable Monsters. Amy Clampitt. AnAn

What can a man do that. Of the Confident Stranger. Clark Coolidge. UL

What can be the matter. The Wind. Dorothy Graddon. BoTP

What can be wrong. Housewife. Susan Fromberg Schaeffer. CrSp; IHMS

What Can I Do? Horace L. Traubel. *Fr.* Chants Communal. TrJP

What can I do in Poetry. The Departure of the Good Daemon. Robert Herrick. CoG; FaBoRV

What can I do to drive away. Keats. OAEL-2

What can I give Him. My Gift. Christina Rossetti. *Fr.* Christmas Carol, A. ChTr; FaPON; InPS; NOBVV; OHIP; PChr

What can I give thee back, O liberal. Elizabeth Barrett Browning. *Fr.* Sonnets from the Portuguese. OxAEP-2

What can I say, but that it's not easy? Rosalie Sorrels. *Fr.* Apple of My Eye. MDDM

What can I say to you? How can I now retract. Protocols. Vikram Seth. OBF

What can I send you under the earth. Traditional Funeral Songs. *Unknown, tr. fr. Modern Greek by* Willis Barnstone *and* Elene Kolb. BoWoP

What Can I Tell My Bones? Theodore Roethke. AmPP; NOBA

What can it mean? Is it aught to Him. God Cares. "Marianne Farningham." BLRP; WBLP
(He Careth.) WBLP

What can lambkins do. A Chill. Christina Rossetti. BoTP

What can melt a traveler's grief? Rhyming a Friend's Poem. Yü Hsüan-chi, *tr. by* Geoffrey R. Waters. BoWoP

What can she be/ Looking at? (*LL*) In the Mirror. Elizabeth Fleming. BoTP

What can the cause be, when the K. have given. An Epigram, to the Household, 1630. Ben Jonson. BeJo; Son

What, can these dead bones live, whose sap is dried. The New Ezekiel. Emma Lazarus. AmWP

What can they do. The Low Road. Marge Piercy. CrSp

What can Tommy Onslow [*or* little T. O.] do? On Thomas, Second Earl of Onslow. *Unknown.* FaBoCo
(On Tom Onslow, Earl of Onslow.) FaBoEE

What can you expect. Maryam bint Abi Ya'qub al-Ansari, *tr. fr. Arabic by* Elene Margot Kolb. WPOW

What can you say better than carcinoma? Some Things Left Unsaid. Victor Martinez. AfAz

What can you see in yonder bay. Thomas Jeffrey Llewelyn Prichard. *Fr.* Land Beneath the Sea, The. AngWe

What cannot be committed to memory, this can save. Photograph. Quandra Prettyman. PoBA

What Care I. George Wither. *See* Shall I, Wasting in Despair.

What care I for the leagues o sand. The Mither's Lament. Sydney Goodsir Smith. OxBS

What care I how black I be? *Unknown.* OxNR

What care I if good God be. Egocentric. Stevie Smith. FaBoNo

What care I, so they stand the same. Merops. Emerson. OxBA

What care I, what cares he. The Cowboy. John Antrobus. FaBoBe; FaPON

What Care I Though the World Reprove. *Unknown.* NOSC

What celebration showed there be? III, 28. Holiday ("Festo quid potius die."). Horace, *tr. fr. Latin by* Austin Dobson. *Fr.* Odes. AWP, *tr. by* Louis Untermeyer

What ceremony can we fit. For a Child Born Dead. Elizabeth Jennings. AIW

What ceremony else? Shakespeare. *Fr.* Hamlet. EBEV; NAWM-1

What changes take place in the course of a year. The Course of a Year. George Sands Johnson. PWR

What cher? Gud cher; gud cher, gud cher. Cheerful Welcome. *Unknown.* MeEL

What Christ Is to Us. *Unknown.* BLRP

What Church is this? Christ's Church. Who builds it? Christopher Harvey. *Fr.* Synagogue, The. EPCY

What Color Is Lonely. Carolyn M. Rodgers. BPo

What comes out of the harp? Music! The Doors Are Closed. Robert Bly. *Fr.* Two Translations from Kabir. PRA

What cometh here from west to east a-wending? A Death Song. William Morris. NAEL-2

What composes a life? Mine comes, too much, from books. The Muse of Distance. Alan Williamson. BAP-89

What conscience has Venus drunk? Our inebriated beauties. Juvenal, *tr. by* Peter Green. *Fr.* Satires. PeHV

What conscience, say, is it in thee. To Oenone. Robert Herrick. OBEV

What Constitutes a State? Sir William Jones. BLPA

What could anyone want from the water poppies. Water Gardening. Lee Upton. FoLa

What could be done? The house was full of folks! The Inn That Missed Its Chance. Amos R. Wells. TrCP

What could be nicer than the spring. A Walk in Spring. K. C. Lart. BoTP

What could he do but claw that. *(LL)* For A' That an' A' That. *At. to* Burns. CoMu

What could he know of sky and stars, or heaven's all-hidden life. The Sooth-Sayer. Sadi, *tr. by* Sir Edwin Arnold. *Fr.* Gulistan, The. AWP

What Could Hold Us. Heather McHugh. NIP

"What could I make," Socrates might have asked. The Makers. David Galler. NYBP

What could make me more morose. The Ovibos. Robert Beverly Hale. FiBHP

What could my father do? My Father Went to Funerals. Howard Nelson. RaBo

What creature's this with his short hairs. The Character of a Roundhead. *Unknown.* FaBoPV; NOSC

What cross impetuous Planets govern me. On My Leaving London, June the 29. Sarah Fyge. KTR

What crowd is this? what have we here! we must not pass it by. Wordsworth. *Fr.* Star-Gazers. Poetr

What crowding thoughts around me wake. To Mrs. K———, On Her Sending Me an English Christmas Plum-Cake at Paris. Helen Maria Williams. WoRP

What crowds by envied power, the wish of all. Sejanus. Juvenal, *tr. by* William Gifford. *Fr.* Satires. OBVE

What cruel laws depress the female kind. Elizabeth Tollet. *Fr.* Hypatia. ECWP; NOEC

What cry was that. Encounter. Geraldine Hammond. IHMS

What cunning can express. White and Red. Edward de Vere, Earl of Oxford.
(What Cunning Can Express.) EIL; NoSic

What danger is the pilgrim in. Bunyan. *Fr.* Pilgrim's Progress, The. EBEV

What dark and terrible shadow is swaying in the wind? Easter in Christmas. Alun Lewis. PoWW

What dawn is it? Karl Shapiro. VGW

What day is it today? The way I live. Extract from a Diary. János Pilinszky, *tr. fr. Hungarian by* Peter Jay. PoSu

What day was it she slid. Birth of Venus. Constance Urdang. PoA

What death? John Webster. *Fr.* Duchess of Malfi, The. NAEL-1; OBD

What death is worse than this. Sir Thomas Wyatt. SiPS

What demented malice, my silly Ravidus. Catullus, *tr. fr. Latin by* Celia *and* Louis Zukofsky. OBVE

What demons moved thee, what malicious fiends. To That Most Senseless Scoundrel, the Author of Legion's Humble Address to the Lords. Thomas Brown. APAS

What desperate nightmare rapts me to this land. Legacy: My South. Dudley Randall. PoBA; PoNe

What dexterous thousands just within the goal. Causes of Old Age. John Armstrong. *Fr.* Art of Preserving Health, The. ECEV

What did he do except lie. Banneker. Rita Dove. LCAP; NoAM

What did I do on my blooming vacation? The Jokesmith's Vacation. Don Marquis. FiBHP

What Did I Lose? Sun Yü-tang. Mes

What did I study in your School of Night? The School Of Night. A. D. Hope. PoA

What did that purr reflect? The tender. Vikram Seth. *Fr.* Golden Gate, The. OFC

What did the day bring? Letter from a Coward to a Hero. Robert Penn Warren. MoAmPo

What did the Indians call you? To the Avon River above Stratford, Canada. James Reaney. MoCV

What did they expect of our toil and extreme. War Books. Ivor Gurney. PeFWW

What did those girls say when you walked the strip. Words. David Huddle. *Fr.* Tour of Duty. Son

What did we say to each other. Simile. N. Scott Momaday. CDW

What did you hear? Advent; a Carol. Patric Dickinson. OBCP

What did you see out there, my lad. Face to Face with Reality. John Oxenham. WBLP

What did you think when first. The Triple Mirror. Gloria C. Oden. IHMS

What difference does it make. *Unknown, tr. fr. Japanese by* Kenneth Rexroth *and* Ikuko Atsumi. WPJ

What Different Dooms Our Birthdays Bring! Thomas Hood. *Fr.* Miss Kilmansegg and Her Precious Leg. NAs

What dire offence from am'rous causes springs. Pope. *Fr.* Rape of the Lock, The. EBNV; FHYEP; HAP; ImPo; NOEC; NoP; OAEL-1; OBNV; PeLV; PoEL-3; Poetr; TEP; TrGrPo

What distant thunders rend the skies. On the Death of Captain Nicholas Biddle. Philip Freneau. PAH

What do caterpillars do? Caterpillars. Aileen Fisher. TLR

What do I care. Pursuit. Hilda Doolittle ("H. D."). WPE

What Do I Care. Sara Teasdale. VGW

What Do I Care for Morning. Helene Johnson. CDC; ShDr

What do I gain by that I have undone? *(LL)* What Shall it Profit? William Dean Howells.

What Do I Love? Allen Grossman. *Fr.* Ether Dome (an Entertainment), The. BAP-91

What do I remember of my visit to Ravenna? Firstly. Ravenna. Louis MacNeice. OBTV

What do I stare at — not the colt. The White Horse. W. H. Davies. OxBTC

What do I wish? No more than what I have. Out of Horace. James Wright. NOSC

What Do the Birds Think? Alfred W. Purdy. MoCV

What do the long years bring us. Retrospection. H. Cordelia Ray. CBWP-3

What Do They Do? Christina Rossetti. *Fr.* Sing-Song. FaPON

What Do They Say. Gary Snyder. NNaP

What do they sing, the last birds. Last Songs. Galway Kinnell. CAPP; VCAP

What do we do when the fanfare ends? Bastille Day. Maxine Cassin. *Fr.* Three Love Poems by a Native. Jaz

What do we know. *(LL)* Pine Tree Tops. Gary Snyder. ArNa; NOBA; PoBeRe; Prf

What do we know of what is behind us? History. Arthur Gregor. TAP

What Do We Plant [When We Plant the Tree]. Henry Abbey. FaPON; OHIP; WBLP

What do we share with the past? Again for Hephaistos, the Last Time. Richard Howard. GLP

What do you call it, bobsled champion. Twentieth-Century Blues. Kenneth Fearing. CMoP

What do you gain, poor Thyrsis, by these tears? Theocritus [*or* Theokritus], *tr. fr. Greek by* Anthony Holden. GrAn

What do you insist on? True Meaning. Anthony Barnett. VaA

What do you paint, when you paint on a wall? I Paint What I See. E. B. White. NBLV; NYBP

What do you say to the mother. The Ring of Irony. Diane Wakoski. NGP

What Do You Say When a Man Tells You, You Have the Softest Skin. Mary Mackey. FF

What do you seek within, O soul, my brother? Introversion. Evelyn Underhill. WGRP

What do you sell, O ye merchants? In the Bazaars of Hyderabad. Sarojini Naidu [*or* Nayadu]. FaPON

What do you take. Bill Manhire. PeNZ

What do you think I saw to-day. The Fairy Cobbler. A. Neil Lyons. BoTP

What do you think? Last night I saw. The Dragon. Mary Mullineaux. BoTP

What Do You Want? John Newlove. NOBC

What does a bird in Cross's air. *Unknown. Fr.* Collection of Hymns . . . of the Moravian Brethren, A. NOEC

What does a Marine feel. Boot Camp Incantation. Martín Espada. UTF

What does he do with them all, the old king. Elegy for Drowned Children. Bruce Dawe. NOBAu

What does he plant who plants a tree? The Heart of the Tree. H. C. Bunner. OHIP

What Does It Matter? Noah Barker. PWR

What does it mean. Gift. Gerald William Barrax. MT

What does it take to make a day? A Day. William Leroy Stidger. PoToHe; SoSe

What does little birdie say? Tennyson. *Fr.* Sea Dreams. BoTP; OxBChV

What does love look like? The Shape of Death. May Swenson. TAP

What does not change/ is the will to change. The Kingfishers. Charles Olson. CMoP; InPS; NAAL-2; NeAP; NOBA; PoM; VCAP

What does not fade? The tower that long had stood. Transience. John Armstrong. *Fr.* Art of Preserving Health, The. NOEC

What does passion know? Passion. Sue May. DT

What does she put four whistles beside heated rugs for? Random Generation of English Sentences; or, The Revenge of the Poets. William Jay Smith. OBAL

What Does the Bee Do? Christina Rossetti. *Fr.* Sing-Song. OxBChV

What does the cracker. Self. Norman Henry, II Pritchard. PoBA

What does the farmer in the spring. Spring Work at the Farm. Thirza Wakley. BoTP

What does the horse give you. Horse. Louise Glück. AnAn; NALW

What Does the Political Scientist Know? Artur Miedzyrzecki, *tr. fr. Polish by* Stanislaw Barańczak *and* Clare Cavanagh. PoSu

What does the storm say? The Ways and the Peoples. Randall Jarrell. PoA

What does the veery say, at dusk in shad-thicket? Code Book Lost. Robert Penn Warren. Poetr

What Does This Mean? Sir Thomas Wyatt. *See* What means [*or* meaneth *or* menethe] this? When I lie [*or* lye] alone.

What Does Your Color Red Look Like? *sels.* Sonja Åkesson. "I know nothing about 'love.' " VBLP

What doest thou here, Elijah? The Ghost of Abel. Blake. ChIV-1

What domination of what darkness dies this hour. The City. "Æ." WGRP

What! dost thou pray that the outgone tide be rolled back on the strand. A Far Cry to Heaven. Edith M. Thomas. WGRP

What doth it serve to see sun's burning face. William Drummond of Hawthornden. EiL

What doth this noise of thoughts within my heart. The Familie. George Herbert. ESCV

What drives me out every morning. The Forget-Me Flower. Wilhelm Müller, *tr. fr. German by* Philip L. Miller. *Fr.* Beautiful Maid of the Mill, The. RiWo

What D'Ye-Call-It, The, *sels.* John Gay. 'Twas When the Seas Were Roaring. HAP

What eagle can beho[u]ld her sunbright[e] eye. Sir John Davies. *Fr.* Gulling[e] Sonnets, The. ESo; NoSic; Scm

What ecstasies her bosom fire! To a Lady on Her Passion for Old China. John Gay. GGP; ImPo; LiTB; SCGP

What else are your *Termes.* Alchemical Ingredients. Ben Jonson. *Fr.* Alchemist, The. CBCK

What else can we do. What Are We Playing At? Andrée Chedid, *tr. fr. French by* Samuel Hazo *and* Mirène Ghossem. BoWoP

What else could we do, for the doors were guarded. Curfew. Paul Éluard, *tr. fr. French by* Quentin Stevenson. BoLoP

What else is there to do? (LL) A Greeting to Lu Hung-Chien. Li Yeh. WPC

What Epilogues are made, for who can tell. Catherine Trotter. *Fr.* Queen Catharine; or, The Ruines of Love. KTR

What ever 'tis, whose beauty here below. The Starre. Henry Vaughan. ESCV

What Every Boy Knows. "Antler." GLP

What eye doth see the heaven but doth admire. Sir John Davies. *Fr.* Orchestra; or, A Poem[e] of Da[u]ncing. NoSic, *abr.*; PeECV; SiPS; SiPSBD

What face, in the water. William Carlos Williams. VGW

What face she put on it, we will not discuss. Conrad Aiken. *Fr.* Time in the Rock [or, Preludes to Definition]. VGW

What fainting hopes are in a lover. (LL) The Primrose. *At. to* Robert Herrick. CBLP; FaBoUs; OBEV; PFP

What Fair Pomp[e]. Thomas Campion. GBL; NoSic; PoEL-2; Prf; SCGP

What fairings will ye that I bring? The Singing Leaves. James Russell Lowell. GN

What fall amounts to is really a cold infusion. The End of Fall. Francis Ponge, *tr. fr. French by* Robert Bly. NU

What falls before us like snow. Moth. Lance Henson. VoR

What falls from the drunken pliers of my nose. Hitler Skeleton Goldplated. William Knott. UL

What field of all the civil wars. Andrew Marvell. *Fr.* Horatian Ode upon Cromwell's [*or* Cromwel's] Return from Ireland, An. EBEV; ESCV; FaBoEH; GeHe; GTBS; GTBS-P; HAP; IIP; InPS; JCP; NOBE; NoP; NOSC; OAEL-1; OBEV; OBWP; OxAEP-1; PoEL-2; SCGP; SeCP; SeCV-1; TFi

What Fifty Said. Robert Frost. NAs

What flew down the chimney. Not the End of the World. Michael Ryan. NAmP90

What flower is my lady like? Of His Lady. *Unknown.* EiL

What for feere of this ferly and of the false Jewes. William Langland. *Fr.* Vision of Piers Plowman, The. EBEV

What Frenzy Has of Late Possess'd the Brain. Sir Samuel Garth. NBLV

What friendship can'st thou boast? what honours claim? Bristol. Richard Savage. FaBoPP

What friendship is, Ardelia, show. Friendship between Ephelia and Ardelia. The Countess of Winchilsea. ECWP; NALW

What from the founder Aesop fell. The Purpose of Fable-writing. Phaedrus, *tr. fr. Latin by* Christopher Smart. AWP

What from this barren being do we reap? Byron. *Fr.* Childe Harold's Pilgrimage. FHYEP, *shorter sel.*

What gentle Ghost, besprent with April deaw. An Elegie on the Lady Jane Pawlet, Marchion: of Winton. Ben Jonson. SeCP

What gifts of speech a man may own. The Sincere Man. Alfred Grant Walton. PoToHe

What gifts shall we bring in worship. Nativity. Craig Powell. NOBAu

What glories would we? Motions of the soul? The Renewal. Theodore Roethke. VGW

What Glorious Vision. *At. to* Thomas Cradock. AH

What Glory's this, my Lord? Should one small Point. Edward Taylor. *Fr.* Preparatory Meditations Before My Approach to the Lord's Supper. EAP

What God gives, and what we take. A Grace for Children. Robert Herrick. OxBChV

What God Hath [*or* Has] Promised! Annie Johnson Flint. BLRP; WBLP

What God Is. Robert Herrick. BeJo; NOSC

What God never sees. *Unknown.* OxNR

What God Used for Eyes Before We Came. William Stafford. PRA

What goes on in the pauses. Torture. Margaret Atwood. PoE

What golden gaine made Higginson remove. Reverend Mr, The. Higginson. Edward Johnson. SCAP

What good is it to me if long ago. Louise Labé, *tr. fr. French by* Willis Barnstone. BoWoP

What Good Poems Are For. Tom Wayman. NoP

What grandeur makes a man seem venerable? Louise Labé, *tr. fr. French by* Willis Barnstone. BoWoP

What Grandma Knew. Edward Field. Poetsp

What great genius invented the waiting room? Waiting Rooms. Howard Nemerov. PoA

What great yoked brutes with briskets low. Crossing the Plains. Joaquin Miller. AnAmPo; GN

What greater torment ever could have been. Lonely Beauty. Samuel Daniel. *Fr.* Complaint of Rosamond, The. CTC

What Greece, when learning flourished, only knew. Dryden. *Fr.* Silent Woman to the University of Oxford, The. NOSC

What Habacuck once spake, mine eyes. Roger Williams. SCAP

What had become of the young shark? The Birth of a Shark. David Wevill. TwCP

What had November done? The Beautiful Ruined Orchard. Daniel Berrigan. FYAP

What had you been thinking about. The Tennis Court Oath. John Ashbery. NoAM; TAP

What hand, what skill can form the artful piece. Advice to a Painter. *Unknown.* APAS

What Happened. Robert Penn Warren. *Fr.* Tale of Time. LCAP

What Happened? John Wieners. PoM

What happened earlier I'm not sure of. Say You Love Me. Molly Peacock. NAmP90

What Happened Here Before. Gary Snyder. NNaP; PoM

What Happened to a Young man in a Place Where He Turned to Water. *Unknown, tr. fr. Apache Indian by* Anselm Hollo. STP

What Happened to Miss Frugle. Brian Patten. OBSP

What happened to the iceman after all? The Iceman. Gordon Challis. PeNZ

What Happens. June Jordan. BPo

What Happens. Robert Long. NAmP90

What Happens. Henrietta O'Neill. UnDi

What Happens in Shakzpeare. Alan Brunton. PeNZ

What happens to a dream deferred. Harlem. Langston Hughes. *Fr.* Lenox Avenue Mural. AiP; AmPP; GLP; HCAP; HeIL; HeIP; HoPM; InPS; NoP; Poetr; PoNe; RaBo; SAmP; (Dream Deferred.) FF; InPK; LiTM; PoBA; PPP; SoSe; (Harlem (A Dream Deferred).) NIP

What happens to the beautiful girls with slender hips and bright round dresses? Hamtramck: The Polish Women. Toi Derricotte. InPS

What happens when the dog sits on a tiger. What Happens. June Jordan. BPo

What Happiness Can Equal Mine. John David. AH

What happiness you gave to me. The Yew-Tree. *Unknown, tr. fr. Welsh by* Geoffrey Grigson. ChTr; GBL

What happy, secret fountain. The Dwelling-Place. Henry Vaughan. GeHe; MeLP; NOSC; PeECV; TrPWD; WGRP

What harm have I done to the stars? Without My Friends the Day Is Dark. Moses ibn Ezra, *tr. fr. Hebrew by* Solomon Solis-Cohen. TrJP

What Harvest Half So Sweet Is, *sels.* Thomas Campion.

What has — / Four pusher-uppers. *Unknown.* RoPo

What has been brought to a finish. Disturbing the Sallies Forth. Clark Coolidge. UL

What has bent you. The Pine at Timber-Line. Harriet Monroe. PoA

What/ has happened. Here. Robert Creeley. NOBA

What has happened in the world? Volcanic Venus. D. H. Lawrence. InPS

What Has Happened to Lulu? Charles Causley. OBSP

What has poor Woman done, that she must be. Aphra Behn. *Fr.* Sir Patient Fancy. WPOW

What Has This Bugbear Death. Lucretius, *tr. by* Dryden. *Fr.* De Rerum Natura (On the Nature of Things). CTC; OBD

What has want to give. Kathleen Raine. WPE

What, hast thou run thy race? Art going down? Of the Going Down of the Sun. Bunyan. CH

What hath man done that man shall not undo. Mercy Pleads for Mankind. Giles Fletcher the Younger. *Fr.* Christ's Victory and Triumph. JCP

What Hath Man Wrought Exclamation Point. Morris Bishop. NYBP

What hatred demands is long suffering and a long fuse. Hatred. Máire Mhac an tSaoi. WoWa

What haunts me is a farmhouse among trees. Landscape with Figures. Frank Ormsby. PBCIP

What have I done for you. England, My England. W. E. Henley. BLPL; MoBrPo; OBEV; PoLF

"What have I done?" said Christine. *Unknown.* PeLi

"What have I earned for all that work," I said. The People. W. B. Yeats. CMoP

What have I made. The Children. Constance Urdang. CoAP; IHMS

What have I to say to you? A Love Song: First Version, 1915. William Carlos Williams. Poetr

What have they done or what left undone. Samuel Butler. *Fr.* Hudibras. FaBoEH

What have they done to Klio what have they done to our Muse. Brian Coffey. *Fr.* Advent. BiHa

What have we done to you, death. Lament for a Brother. Al-Khansa, *tr. fr. Arabic by* Omar S. Pound. ArPe

What Have We Done Today? Nixon Waterman. WBLP

What have we done? What cruel passion moved thee. Dialogue after Enjoyment. Abraham Cowley. BoLoP

What Have We Got. Lemn Sissay. NBrP

What have we swallowed. Love Gone Cold. Lindsay MacRae. DT

What have you got to crow about. Meleager, *tr. fr. Greek by* Kenneth Rexroth. PGA

What have you looked at, Moon. To the Moon. Thomas Hardy. BoNaP; ChTr

What have you more than I, who crave you so? Zora Cross. *Fr.* Love Sonnets. CBAP

What have you seen on the summits, the peaks that plunge their. Charles Brasch. *Fr.* Estate, The. PeNZ

"What have you there?" the great Panjandrum said. The Truant. E. J. Pratt. NOBC; NoP

What! Hayes acquitted! Armstrong's magazine! True and Joyful News. *Unknown.* APAS

What he did with every cent. *(LL)* The Hardship of Accounting. Robert Frost. FaBoCh; FaBoCo; OBAL

What He Said. Allur Nanmullai, *tr. fr. Tamil by* A. K. Ramanujan. PLW

What He Said. Ammuvanar, *tr. fr. Tamil by* A. K. Ramanujan. PLW

What He Said. Catti Natanar, *tr. fr. Tamil by* A. K. Ramanujan. PLW

What He Said. Orerulavanar, *tr. fr. Tamil by* A. K. Ramanujan. PLW

What He Said. Perevin Muruvalar, *tr. fr. Tamil by* A. K. Ramanujan. PLW

What He Said ("As the deer begin to hide.") Peyanar, *tr. fr. Tamil by* A. K. Ramanujan. *Fr.* Nine on Happy Reunion. PLW

What He Said ("As wild oxen bellowed.") Peyanar, *tr. fr. Tamil by* A. K. Ramanujan. *Fr.* Nine on Happy Reunion. PLW

What He Said after a Quarrel, Remembering His Wedding Night. Virrurru Muteyinanar, *tr. fr. Tamil by* A. K. Ramanujan. PLW

What He Said ("Because peacocks moved like you.") Peyanar, *tr. fr. Tamil by* A. K. Ramanujan. *Fr.* Nine on Happy Reunion. PLW

What He Said ("In this time of rain and thunder.") Peyanar, *tr. fr. Tamil by* A. K. Ramanujan. *Fr.* Nine on Happy Reunion. PLW

What He Said ("The red earth.") Peyanar, *tr. fr. Tamil by* A. K. Ramanujan. *Fr.* Nine on Happy Reunion. PLW

What He Said in the Desert. Otalantaiyar, *tr. fr. Tamil by* A. K. Ramanujan. PLW

What He Said to His Charioteer, on His Way Back. Cittalai Cattanar, *tr. fr. Tamil by* A. K. Ramanujan. PLW

What He Said to His Heart, Arguing against Further Ambition and Travel. Ilankiranar, *tr. fr. Tamil by* A. K. Ramanujan. PLW

What He Took. *Unknown.* CoMu

What heart could have thought you? To a Snowflake. Francis Thompson. BoNaP; FaBV; MoAB; MoBrPo; TrGrPo

What heartache — ne'er a hill! From the Flats. Sidney Lanier. AnAmPo; NOBA; OxBA

What heaven-entreated [*or* heaven-besieged heart] is this. To the Noblest and Best of Ladies, the Countess of Denbigh. Richard Crashaw. GeHe; JCP; MeLP
   (Letter from Mr Crashaw to the Countess of Denbigh, Against Irresolution and Delay in Matters of Religion, A.) NOSC
   (Letter to the Countess of Denbigh.) SeCP

What heavy-hoofed coursers the wilderness roam. The Fall of Tecumseh. *Unknown.* PAH

What He(e) Suffered. Ben Jonson. *Fr.* Celebration of Charis in Ten Lyric[k] Peeces (*in pieces*], A. BeJo; OxAEP-1; SeCP

What Hell Is. Heather McHugh. CrSp; PFL

What helps it if of love I sing. Hadewijch, *tr. fr. Dutch by* Frans van Rosevelt. PBWP

What Her Friend Said. Kapilar, *tr. fr. Tamil by* A. K. Ramanujan. PLW

What Her Friend Said Criticizing Him to Give Her Strength. Kuriyiraiyar, *tr. fr. Tamil by* A. K. Ramanujan. PLW

What Her Friend Said to Her, before the Rains. Kapilar, *tr. fr. Tamil by* A. K. Ramanujan. PLW

What Her Friend Said to Her, within the Lover's Hearing. Paranar, *tr. fr. Tamil by* A. K. Ramanujan. PLW

What Her Friend Said to the Foster Mother. Kapilar, *tr. fr. Tamil by* A. K. Ramanujan. PLW

What Her Girl Friend Asked and What She Replied Regarding His Return. *Unknown, tr. fr. Tamil by* A. K. Ramanujan. PLW

What Her Girl Friend Said ("As the cassias blossom.") Peyanar, *tr. fr. Tamil by* A. K. Ramanujan. *Fr.* Nine on Happy Reunion. PLW

What Her Girl Friend Said ("Her eyes lined with kohl.") Peyanar, *tr. fr. Tamil by* A. K. Ramanujan. *Fr.* Nine on Happy Reunion. PLW

What Her Girl Friend Said ("Saying to himself.") Peyanar, *tr. fr. Tamil by* A. K. Ramanujan. *Fr.* Nine on Happy Reunion. PLW

What Her Girl Friend Said ("Your arms are beautiful again.") Peyanar, *tr. fr. Tamil by* A. K. Ramanujan. *Fr.* Nine on Happy Reunion. PLW

What Her Girl Friend Said before the Elopement. Kutavayir Kirattanar, *tr. fr. Tamil by* A. K. Ramanujan. PLW

What Her Girl Friend Said, Consoling Her when She Was Distressed by the Town's Gossip. Uloccanar, *tr. fr. Tamil by* A. K. Ramanujan. PLW

What Her Girl Friend Said on Her Wedding Day. Ammuvanar, *tr. fr. Tamil by* A. K. Ramanujan. PLW

What Her Girl Friend Said, Seeing Her Friend Suffer in Silent Dignity over Her Husband's Infidelity. Kayamanar, *tr. fr. Tamil by* A. K. Ramanujan. PLW

What Her Girl Friend Said, the Lover within Earshot, behind a Fence. Uloccanar, *tr. fr. Tamil by* A. K. Ramanujan. PLW

What Her Girl Friend Said to Her. Kovatattan, *tr. fr. Tamil by* A. K. Ramanujan. PLW

What Her Girl Friend Said to Her. Maturai Marutan Ilanakanar, *tr. fr. Tamil by* A. K. Ramanujan. PLW

What Her Girl Friend Said to Her. Palaipatiya Perunkatunko, *tr. fr. Tamil by* A. K. Ramanujan. PLW

What Her Girl Friend Said to Her Lover on His Return. Kakkai Patiniyar Naccellaiyar, *tr. fr. Tamil by* A. K. Ramanujan. PLW

What Her Girl Friend Said to Him. Ammuvanar, *tr. fr. Tamil by* A. K. Ramanujan. PLW

What Her Girl Friend Said to Him (on Her Behalf) When He Came by Daylight. *Unknown, tr. fr. Tamil by* A. K. Ramanujan. PLW

What Her Girl Friend Said to Him, Trying to Dissuade Him from His Long Journey. *Unknown, tr. fr. Tamil by* A. K. Ramanujan. PLW

What Her Girl Friend Said to Him When He Wanted to Come by Day. Ammuvanar, *tr. fr. Tamil by* A. K. Ramanujan. PLW

What Her Girl Friend Said to the Foster-Mother ("If you think, mother.") Orampokiyar, *tr. fr. Tamil by* A. K. Ramanujan. *Fr.* Five on the Crabs. PLW

What Her Girl Friend Said to the Foster-Mother ("In his fields, mother.") Orampokiyar, *tr. fr. Tamil by* A. K. Ramanujan. *Fr.* Five on the Crabs. PLW

What Her Girl Friend Said when He Sent a Flattering Minstrel on His Behalf. Orampokiyar, *tr. fr. Tamil by* A. K. Ramanujan. PLW

What Her Girl Friend Said, When the Woman Was About to Take Back Her Unfaithful Husband. Orampokiyar, *tr. fr. Tamil by* A. K. Ramanujan. PLW

What Her Girlfriends Said to Her. Okkur Macatti, *tr. fr. Tamil by* A. K. Ramanujan. BoWoP

What Her Mother Said. *Unknown, tr. fr. Tamil by* A. K. Ramanujan. PLW

What heroes from the woodland sprung. Seventy-six. Bryant. PAH

What Hiawatha Probably Did. *Unknown.* NBLV

What hideous noyse was that? John Webster. *Fr.* Duchess of Malfi, The. NAEL-1; PoEL-2

What His Friend Said, Teasing the Man in Love. Milaipperun Kantan, *tr. fr. Tamil by* A. K. Ramanujan. PLW

What ho! my shepherds, sweet it were. A Sylvan Revel. Edward Cracroft Lefroy, *after the Greek of* Theocritus. *Fr.* Echoes from Theocritus. AWP

What honey summons these animalcules? Stings. Sylvia Plath. AnAn; NaP

What Hope Is Here for Modern Rhyme. Tennyson. *Fr.* In Memoriam A. H. H. EBVV, *abr.*; EnVR; MeMBP; OAEL-2, *abr.*; PeECV, *abr.*

What hope of safety for our realm. On Sympathisers with the American Revolution. Charles Wesley. NOCV

What Horace says is. Eheu Fugaces. "Thomas Ingoldsby." FaBoEE; OxBoLi

What horrid sin condemned the teeming Earth. On Tobacco. Charles Cotton. OBSV

What hours I spent of precious time. Poetical Economy. Harry Graham. FaBoCo; Mes

What How? How now? Hath How such hearing found. On How the Cobler. *Unknown.* SCAP

What hue lies in the slit of anger. Outlines. Audre Lorde. GLP

What humour can be so rare. Sister Juana Inés de la Cruz, *tr. fr. Spanish by* Judith Thurman. *Fr.* Satirical Romance, A. PBWP

What hurrying human tides, or day or night! Broadway. Walt Whitman. NAAL-1

What I choose is youse:/ baby. *(LL)* Coon Song. A. R. Ammons. MoP; NOBA

What I did, I won't excuse, except. The Unreal Dwelling: My Years in Volcano. Garrett Kaoru Hongo. OpBo

What I Do. Denise Riley. NBrP

What I Do Is Me. Gerard Manley Hopkins. *See* As Kingfishers Catch Fire [Dragonflies Draw Flame].

What I do mind is going four to not to. *(LL)* Believe me, sir, I'd like to spend whole days. Martial. OBVE

What I do to the grass, does to my thoughts and me. *(LL)* The Mower's Song. Andrew Marvell. CBLP; ESCV; NAEL-1; NOSC; PFP; PoEL-2; PPP; SeCP; SeCV-1

What I Expected [Was]. Stephen Spender. MoAB; MoBrPo; NoAM; NOBE; OxAEP-2

What I fancy, I approve. No Loathsomnesse in Love. Robert Herrick. BeJo; GBL

What I forgot to mention was the desultory. Postscript to an Elegy. Gibbons Ruark. MT

What I get I bring home to you. Wild Strawberries. Helen Dunmore. PWE

What I had never imagined: your return. Brief Encounter. Winfield Townley Scott. GOYP

What I have begun. *(LL)* The Bush Speaks. Ernest G. Moll. NOBAu

What I have from 1956 in one instant at the Holiday. Scene from the Movie Giant. Tino Villanueva. ETG

What I have is an image. Rhody. George Ella Lyon. ETG

What I "have to do" has nothing to do. Last Words. Richard Howard. *Fr.* Ithaca: The Palace at Four A.M. DiPo

What I have written, I cannot unwrite. Ending. Norman Jordan. PoNe

What I Have Written I Have Written. Peter Porter. NOBAu

What I have written I have written. *(LL)* What I Have Written I Have Written. Peter Porter. NOBAu

What I Heard at the Discount Department Store. David Budbill. BAP-89; RaBo; TRP

What I hope (when I hope) is that we'll. To the Dead. Frank Bidart. EOEF

What I, in her, am grievd to want. *(LL)* Though beauty be the mark of praise. Ben Jonson. BeJo; EnRePo; NoP; OBEV

What I Learned from My Mother. Julia Kasdorf. PBCAP

What I Like. Alice Fulton. WeW

What I like about Clive. E. C. Bentley. *Fr.* Clerihews. NOBL (Lord Clive.) MoShBr; PeLV

What I like most is when. Crimes of Passion: The Slasher. Terry Stokes. AmPA

What I Live For. George Linnaeus Banks. BLPA; FaBoBe; WBLP

What I love about dormice is their size. A View of Things. Edwin Morgan. CBCK

What I love best in all the world. Robert Browning. *Fr.* De Gustibus. FHYEP; InPS; OBTV; SCGP (Italy of the South.) FaBoPP

What I mean by too much metaphor and smile. *(LL)* Very like a Whale. Ogden Nash. BLPL; HAP; InPK; InPS; PoLF; TrGrPo

What I meant to say to her as she reached. Feed the Mexican Back into Her. Cherríe Moraga. GLP

What I need is lots of money. Take I, 4:11:58. Philip Whalen. NeAP

What I remember about that day. Eviction. Lucille Clifton. NTCP (1st, The.) InPS

What I remember didn't happen. A Date with Robbe-Grillet. Elaine Equi. PeVV; UTF

What I saw was just one eye. The Bird at Dawn. Harold Monro. BoTP; MoBrPo

What I shall leave thee, none can tell. To His Son [*or* Sonne], Vincent Corbet[t]. Richard Corbett [*or* Corbet]. BeJo; FaBoCh; NOSC; OxAEP-1; OxBChV; TrGrPo

What I Tell Him. Simon J. Ortiz. CDW

What I thought so unusual about today. The Great Pretenderer. Pat Nolan. UL

What I thought was love. The Liar. Amiri Baraka. AmPP; NOBA

What I took in my hand. Robert Creeley. NoP; PoA

What I walked down to the highway. Another Sunday Morning. Carter Revard. VoR

What I wanted. In Weather. Robert Hass. AmPA

What I was doing with my white teeth exposed. The Dog. Gerald Stern. WeW

What I was you called. For My Wife 1936–1974. James Lewisohn. ETG

What I will say today. Lo Que Digo. *Unknown.* AS

What I wished you before, but harder. *(LL)* The Writer. Richard Wilbur. CAPP; HCAP; ImGa; NoAM; OxBC; Poetr; SoSe

What I would speake. *(LL)* The Robin. George Daniel. FaBoRV

What Idiots Lovers Are. Judith Kazantzis. VBLP

What If a Day [*or* a Month *or* a Year]. Thomas Campion. AAS; EBEV; EIL; EnRePo; PrIm

What If a Much of a Which of a Wind. E. E. Cummings. BLPL; ImPo; LiTA; LiTM; MeMAP; MoAmPo; NAAL-2; NOBA; NoP; OxBA; PoA; PoRA; PPP

What if I bade you leave. Those Images. W. B. Yeats. CMoP

What if I do go armed? she said. Arms and the Woman. Dorothea MacKellar. NOBAu

What if jealousy is just a bad dream? Miriam Palmer. NMM

What if outside the dying pine trees sing in the clearing gale. Inside the Cave. Geoffrey Grigson. FaBoPP

What if small birds are peppering the sky. It Is Winter, I Know. Merrill Moore. MoAmPo

What If Some Little Paine the Passage Have. Spenser. *Fr.* Faerie Queene, The. CH

What if the body goes the sense. Image-Nation 3. Robin Blaser. PoM

What if the foot, ordain'd the dust to tread. Pope. *Fr.* Essay on Man, An. FaBoPV

What If the Saint Must Die. John Peck. AH

What if the sun comes out. Boy Remembers in the Field. Raymond Knister. NOBC

What if the ways be stone. City Songs. Mark Van Doren. NYBP

What if there wasn't a metaphor. Stigmata. Patrick Lane. NOBC

What if these long races go on repeating themselves. Written in Dejection near Rome. Robert Bly. NaP

What if they knew nothing, or what they did. Remove the Predicate. Clark Coolidge. UL

What if this present were the world's last night? John Donne. *Fr.* Holy Sonnets. EBEV; ESCV; HeIP; ImPo; InPS; JCP; LiTB; MeLP; NAEL-1; NOCV; NOSC; OxAEP-1; PeECV; PoE; Son; TEP

What if, with my life half over. Id. Harry Clifton. PBCIP

What in our lives is burnt. August 1914. Isaac Rosenberg. EBEV; NOBE; OBWP; OPOP; OxBTC; PAW; PeFWW

What, in the Register of Doom, is writ. Bishop Orders His Tomb in St. Praxed's. Morris Bishop. OBAL

What in the World? Eve Merriam. SiSoPo

What in the world we see. Going Home. Richard Caddel. NBrP

What infants suffer when they breed their teeth. Infant Diseases and Their Treatment. M. Saint-Marthe, *tr. fr. French. Fr.* Paedotrophiae; or, The Art of Bringing Up Children. FaBoUs

What instinct forces man to journey on. The Poet. Amy Lowell. WGRP

What Invisible Rat. Jean-Joseph Rabéarivelo, *tr. fr. French* by Alan Ryder. NegPo, *tr.* by Ellen Conroy Kennedy; TTY

What invisible rat. What Invisible Rat. Jean-Joseph Rabéarivelo, *tr. fr. French* by Alan Ryder. NegPo, *tr.* by Ellen Conroy Kennedy; TTY

What/ irritation of offensively red brick is this. William Carlos Williams. *Fr.* Paterson. MeMAP

What! Irving? thrice welcome, warm heart, and fine brain. Irving. James Russell Lowell. *Fr.* Fable for Critics, A. TAP

What is a blk poem &/or what is it. Food for Thought. Val Ferdinand. NBV

What is a communist? One who hath yearnings. Ebenezer Elliot. NOBVV (On Communists.) NBLV; NOBL

What is a first love worth except to prepare for a second? John Milton Hay. FaBoEE

What is a Friend? I'll tell you. A Friend. *Unknown.* PoToHe

What is a half-truth the lobster declared. The Territory is Not the Map. Jack Spicer. CBNP

What is a Jew in solitude? Yom Kippur 1984. Adrienne Rich. GLP; NoAM

What Is a Jewish Poem? Myra Sklarew. CRP

What is a kiss? Why this, as some approve. A Kiss. Robert Herrick. CaPo

What is a locust? The Locust. *Unknown, tr. fr. Malagasy.* FaPON, *tr.* by Frank Cushing; OBAP, *tr.* by A. Marre and Willard R. Trask; RB, *tr.* by A. Marre and Willard R. Trask (Coyote and the Locust, The.) AWP

What is a modern poet's fate. Thomas Hood. *See* What is a modern Poet's fate?

What is a modern Poet's fate? The Poet's Fate. Thomas Hood. FaBoEE; FiBHP (What is a modern poet's fate.) FaBoEE

What is a poet's love? The Poet's Lot. Oliver Wendell Holmes. PoEL-5

What is a troubadour? *(LL)* The Banjo Player. Fenton Johnson. PoNe

What is a woman that you forsake her. Harp Song of the Dane Women. Kipling. *Fr.* Puck of Pook's Hill. HAP; OBNC; OtMeF; PAW; PoRA

What is a yielded life? The Yielded Life. "W. A. G." BLRP

What is Africa to me. Heritage. Countee Cullen. BPo; FaBV, *abr.*; HeIP; MoAmPo; NAAL-2; NoAM; NoP; PoBA; Poetr; TTY

What is Africa to thee? The Africa Thing. Adam David Miller. NBV

What is all this washing about. Washing. John Drinkwater. FaPON

What is ambition? 'Tis a glorious cheat! Ambition. Nathaniel Parker Willis. OBCA

What is ambition? 'tis unrest, defeat! Ambition. H. Cordelia Ray. AmWP; CBWP-3

What Is an Epigram? Samuel Taylor Coleridge. *See* What is an epigram? a dwarfish whole.

What is an epigram? a dwarfish whole. Samuel Taylor Coleridge. FaBoEE (What Is an Epigram?) NIP

What Is Beauty? Christopher Marlowe. *Fr.* Tamburlaine the Great. ImPo

What is black. Gullfish. Tom Weatherly. *Fr.* Cantos. PoBA

What Is Black? Mary O'Neill. NTCP

What Is Charm? Louisa Carroll Thomas. BLPA

What is credible? January. Anthony Barnett. VaA

What is failure? When the maiden. Failure. H. Cordelia Ray. CBWP-3

"What is funny?" you ask, my child. The Anatomy of Humor. Morris Bishop. NBLV

What Is Good? John Boyle O'Reilly. PoToHe; WBLP

What is green in me. Stepping Westward. Denise Levertov. CAPP; CrSp; NALW; NMM; Poetr; VGW

What Is Happening Now? Hubert Witheford. PeNZ

What is happening to me now that loved faces. Childhood in Jacksonville, Florida. Jane Cooper. TAP

What is he buzzing in my ears? Confessions. Robert Browning. CBLP; ELP; GTBS-P; NOBE; NOBVV

What Is He, This Lordling. William Herebert. ChIV-1; MiEL

What is he, this lordling, that cometh from the fight? What Is He, This Lordling. William Herebert. ChIV-1; MiEL (Knight Stained from Battle, The.) MeEL

What Is Heaven? Philip James Bailey. PWR

What is home without a Bible? Home without a Bible. Charles D. Meigs. WBLP

What is hope? A smiling rainbow. Cui Bono? Thomas Carlyle. WGRP

What Is It? H. E. Wilkinson. BoTP

What is it for, now that dividing neither. A Wall in the Woods: Cummington. Richard Wilbur. BAP-90

What is it, inside them and undeniable. The King's Men. William Heyen. PoA

What is it men in women do require? Blake. *Fr.* Several Questions Answered. OAEL-2

(Question Answered [or A Question Answered], The.) ErPo; FaBoEE; GBL; MeMBP; NoP; OxBM

What is it more eyes doth wear. *Unknown.* GBP

What is it now with me. Fear of Death. John Ashbery. FaBoMo; PlP; TAP

What is it our mammas bewitches. Written for My Son, and Spoken by Him at His First Putting on Breeches. Mary Barber. ECEV; ECWP; NOEC

What is it so transforms the boulevard? Another Spirit Advances. Jules Romains, *tr. fr. French* by Joseph T. Shipley. AWP

What is it? Something sought by everyone? Different Dimensions. Atsumi Ikuko, *tr. fr. Japanese* by Kenneth Rexroth and Ikuko Atsumi. WPJ

What is it that upsets the volcanoes. Pablo Neruda, *tr. fr. Spanish.* TSaS, *tr.* by William O'Daly

What is it to grow old? Growing Old. Matthew Arnold. EnVR; FHYEP; MeMBP; NAEL-2; NOBVV; OAEL-2; PoEL-5

What is it when a woman sleeps, her head bright. Where You Go When She Sleeps. T. R. Hummer. MT

What is it with these people-swallowing streets. All of a Sudden. Teresa de Jesús, *tr. fr. Spanish* by Maria A. Proser, Arlene Scully and James Scully. WPOW

What is it you're mumbling, old Father my Dad? By the Exeter River. Donald Hall. MoBS

What is Life. William Byrd. EnRePo

What is life or worldly pleasure? What is Life. William Byrd. EnRePo

What Is Liquid. Margaret Cavendish, Duchess of Newcastle. FaBoUs

What Is Man? Bible, *O.T.,* paraphrased by Sir Thomas Wyatt. *See* O Lord our Lord, how excellent is thy name.

What Is Man's Body? *Gond Oral Tradition, tr.* by V. Elwin and S. Hivale. WTO

What is our innocence. What Are Years? Marianne Moore. BLPL; CMoP; LiTA; MeMAP; MoAB; MoAmPo; MoP; NoAM; NOBA; OxBA; SoSe; TrGrPo

What Is Our Life? Sir Walter Ralegh. EBEV; EnRePo; FaBoEE; NoSic; OxBSP; SCGP; SiPS; SoSe

What is our life? A play of passion. What Is Our Life? Sir Walter Ralegh. EBEV; EnRePo; FaBoEE; NoSic; OxBSP; SCGP; SiPS; SoSe (All the World's a Stage.) NOBE (On the Life of Man.) NAEL-1; SiPSBD

What is our life on earth? Remembering Min Ch'e. Su Tung-p'o, *tr. fr. Chinese* by Kenneth Rexroth. OHMPC

What is — "Paradise." Emily Dickinson. CMoP

What Is Past. Sir William Davenant. TrGrPo

What Is Pink? Christina Rossetti. *Fr.* Sing-Song. GoJo; OxBChV; SiSoPo

What is pink? a rose is pink. What Is Pink? Christina Rossetti. *Fr.* Sing-Song. GoJo; OxBChV; SiSoPo

What Is Poetry. John Ashbery. LCAP

What Is Poetry. James Scully. FYAP

What is poetry? Is it a mosaic. Amy Lowell. WGRP

What Is Prayer? James Montgomery. BLRP; WGRP

What is reality? Self in 1958. Anne Sexton. HCAP

What Is Repeated, What Abides. Barbara Hendryson. CrSp

What is sin? Town of the Death of Sin. Anne Carson. *Fr.* Life of Towns, The. BAP-90

What is so rare as a day in June? Question and Answer. Samuel Hoffenstein. FiBHP

What is so strange about a tree alone in an open field? Hunting Pheasants in a Cornfield. Robert Bly. TRP

What is song's eternity? Song's Eternity. John Clare. FaBoCh

What Is Terrible. Roy Fuller. PoWW

What is that a-billowing there. Firstfruits in 1812. Wallace Rice. PAH

What is that growling! Screeching! Barking! Spring Cleaning. Phillip William George. VoR

What is that howling, my mother. The World the First Time. Gareth Owen. OBAP

What is the boy now, who has lost his ball. The Ball Poem. John Berryman. CoAP; FF; MoAmPo; NoAM; NOBA; NoP; Poetr

What is the flower that blooms each year. The Christmas Rose. C. Day Lewis. TIRV

What is the head. Some Last Questions. W. S. Merwin. CAPP; HCAP; VCAP

What is the heart of a girl? The Heart of a Girl Is a Wonderful Thing. *Unknown.* BLPA

What is the jewel colour! Hilda Doolittle ("H. D."). *Fr.* Tribute to the Angels. NALW

What is the life. Careers. Amiri Baraka. TRP

What is the loveliest light that Spring. A May-Day carol. Alfred Noyes. PFP

What is the matter, grandmother dear? Grandma's Lost Balance. Sydney Dayre. OBCA

What Is the Matter With Me? *Unknown, tr. fr. Chinese* by Kenneth Rexroth. OHMPC

What is the meaning of this Ideal. W. J. Turner. *Fr.* Seven Days of the Sun, The. OBMV

What is the measure then, the magpie in the field. The Measure. Patrick Lane. NOBC

What is the metre of the dictionary? Dylan Thomas. *Fr.* Altarwise by Owl-Light. CMoP; FaBoMo; LiTM

What is the mirror saying with its O? A Room in the Villa. William Jay Smith. NYBP

What is the misery in one that turns one with gladness. Grace Abounding. A. R. Ammons. HCAP

What is the moral? Who rides may read. The Winners. Kipling. *Fr.* Story of the Gadsbys, The. BLPA; FaPoR
(L'Envoi: "What is the moral? Who rides may read.") MoBrPo; TrGrPo

What is the name of King Ringang's daughter? Beauty Rohtraut. Eduard Friedrich Mörike, *tr. fr. German* by George Meredith. AWP; OBVE

What is the night-bird's tune, wherewith she startles. The New Dodo: Isabrand's Song. Thomas Lovell Beddoes. CBNP

What is the old year? 'Tis a book. The Old Year. Clarence Urmy. PoToHe

What is the opposite of riot. Some Opposites. Richard Wilbur. OBCA

What is the real good? What Is Good? John Boyle O'Reilly. PoToHe; WBLP

What is the rhyme for porringer? Mother Goose. OxNR
(Difficult Rhyme, A.) ReMoGo

What is the song I am singing? The Founts of Song. "Fiona Macleod." WGRP

What is the subject? It looks like a paragraph. Prose. Bernard Welt. EOEF

What is the thing your eyes hold loveliest. The Newlyweds. Cloyd Mann Criswell. PoLF

What Is the Use?, *sels.* Erastus Wolcott Ellsworth.

What is the use of the rule insane. The Solution. Brian Merriman, *tr. by* Arland Ussher. *Fr.* Midnight Court, The. BIrV; NOIV, *tr. by* Thomas Kinsella

What is the voice I hear. To America. Alfred Austin. GN
(Britannia to Columbia.) PAH

What is the word for "death." Flowers for Luis Bunuel. Stuart Z. Perkoff. NeAP

What is the world, and what is life. William Williams. AngWe

What is the world, O soldiers? Napoleon. Walter de la Mare. FaBoCh; FaBoTw; NOBE; OtMeF; RB; Spl

What is the world? tell, Worldling (if thou know it). Mundus Qualis. Joshua Sylvester. FaBoEE

What is there hid in the heart of a rose. Alfred Noyes. CH

What is there in my heart that you should sue. Lachrimae Amantis. Geoffrey Hill. NOCV

What is there left to be said? A. R. D. Fairburn. PeNZ

What is there they will not do to you? The First Test. Susan Fromberg Schaeffer. IHMS

What is this day with two suns in the sky? Quatrain. Jalal al-Din Rumi, *tr. fr. Persian* by John Moyne *and* Coleman Barks. ArLo

What is this flesh and blood compounded of. Allen Tate. *Fr.* Sonnets of the Blood. PoA

What Is This Here? *Unknown.* RoPo

What is this image in the clouded mirror. Image in a Mirror. Mae Winkler Goodman. GoYe

What Is This Knowledge? Sir John Davies. *Fr.* Nosce Teipsum. FaBoRV; NoSic, abr.; SiPS

What is this life if, full of care. Leisure. W. H. Davies. AngWe; ArNa; AWP; BoNaP; BoTP; CH; CoGr; EBEvV; FaBoBe; FaPON; GGP; LiTB; LiTM; MoBrPo; MoShBr; NOBE; NTP; OBEV; OBMV; OtMeF; PoRA; TFi; TrGrPo

What is this life, this active guest. A Solemn Meditation. William Shenstone. NOEC

What is this recompense you'd have from me? From a Woman to a Greedy Lover. Norman Cameron. *Fr.* Three Love Poems. FaBoEE; FaBoTw; GTBS-P

What is this? said God. The obstinacy. Echoes. R. S. Thomas. OxAEP-2

What is this strange and uncouth thing? The Crosse. George Herbert. ESCV

What is this tempest. W. J. Turner. *Fr.* Seven Days of the Sun, The. OBMV

What is this that I can see. Oh! Death. *Unknown.* AmFP

What is this that I have heard? Dawn Has Yet to Ripple In. Melville Cane. MoAmPo

What is this that roareth thus? Motor Bus. Alfred Denis Godley. FaBoCo; NOBL; OtMeF
(On the Motor Bus. FaBoNo; NBLV

What Is This Thing You Earthlings Speak Of. (*LL*) Cuchulainn. Michael O'Loughlin. BiHa; IB; PBCIP

What is this voice I hear. To America. Alfred Austin. GN
(Britannia to Columbia.) PAH

What is this wonderful thing? Brown and everywhere! Looking at a Dry Canadian Thistle Brought In from the Snow. Robert Bly. NNaP

What Is Time? James Marsden. PWR

What Is Tomorrow? Edith Södergran, *tr. fr. Swedish* by David McDuff. VBLP

What is tomorrow? Perhaps not you. What Is Tomorrow? Edith Södergran, *tr. fr. Swedish* by David McDuff. VBLP

What Is Truth?, *sels.* James Harold Manning.

What Is Veal? *Unknown.* FaBoUs

What Is War? J. M. Rose-Troup. NSI

What is weaker than a god? It groans hungry. Rosario Castellanos, *tr. fr. Spanish* by Willis Barnstone. BoWoP

What Is Woman? Mrs. Henry Linden. CBWP-4

What is wrought in the forge of the living and life. Hafiz, *tr. fr. Persian* by Gertrude Lowthian Bell. *Fr.* Odes. AWP; TAL

What is your plaster Doctor? Christmas Rhyme: North Tyrone. *Unknown.* FaBoVe

What is your substance, whereof are you made. Shakespeare. *Fr.* Sonnets. CTC; EBEV; EIL; EnRePo; ImPo; LiTB; NoSic; OAEL-1; OBEV; OxAEP-1; PeHV; SCGP

What is't, fine Grand, makes thee my friendship fly. To Fine Grand. Ben Jonson. JCP

What is't, good prying friend, you say? The Alarm. Hildebrand Jacob. NOEC

What is't you mean, that I am thus approached? The Repulse to Alcander. Sarah Fyge Egerton. ECWP

What It Could Be. Denise Levertov. WoWa

What It Is Like. Gerald Stern. NAmP90

What it may or must become? (*LL*) Imago. Amy Clampitt. VCAP

What it must be like to be an angel. Parents. William Meredith. FYAP

What it showed was always the same. The Night Mirror. John Hollander. NYBP; Prf; VCAP

What it would look like if really there were only. Allen Curnow. *Fr.* Small Room with Large Windows, A. PeNZ

What It's Like Living in My Studio Late in Spring, *sels.* Wen Cheng-ming, *tr. fr. Chinese.*

What Jenner Said on Hearing in Elysium That Complaints Had Been Made of His Having a Statue [in Trafalgar Square]. Shirley Brooks. FaBoEE

What Johnny Told Me. John Ciardi. TLR

What joy hath yon glad wreath of flowers that is. The Garland and the Girdle. Michelangelo, *tr. fr. Italian* by John Addington Symonds. AWP

What joys attend [*or* joy attends] the fisher's life! The Fisher's Life. *Unknown.* ChTr; GBP

What joys! what joys were thine! (*LL*) To the Man-of-War-Bird. Walt Whitman. AmPP; FaBoBe; FM

What jungles he swung out of into the imagination. Gorilla Gorilla. Bruce Dawe. NoAM

What, Kaiser dead? The heavy news. Kaiser Dead. Matthew Arnold. FM

What, keep love in perspective? — that old lie. In Perspective. Robert Graves. OxBSP

What Kin' o' Pants Does the Gambler Wear. *Unknown.* AS

What kind of animal would you get. (*LL*) If You. Robert Creeley. MoP; NeAP; NoAM; NOBA; Poet; SM

What kind of Bacchus are you? By the real. Beer. Julianus, *tr. fr. Greek* by Peter Jay. GrAn

What kind of beast would turn its life into words? Adrienne Rich. *Fr.* Twenty-one Love Poems. GLP

What kind of lover have you made me, mother. Cherríe Moraga. *Fr.* La Dolce Culpa. MDDM

What kind of Mistress He Would Have. Robert Herrick. CaPo; TrGrPo

What kind of walk shall we take today? On Our Way. Eve Merriam. SiSoPo

What lack you, sir? What seek you? What will you buy? Thomas Newbery. *Fr.* Great Merchant, Dives Pragmaticus, Cries His Wares, The. OxBChV

What large, dark hands are those at the window. Love on the Farm. D. H. Lawrence. CBLP; CMoP; ErPo; FaBV; FF; MoAB; MoBrPo; NAEL-2; NoAM; SCGP; TrGrPo

What Larkin bawled to hungry crowds. Inscription for a Headstone. Austin Clarke. BIrV; CIP; IIP

What led to the crassness of Custer. Bill Greenwell. PeLi

What Length of Verse? Sir Philip Sidney. PoE

What lewd, naked and revolting shape is this? Shopping for Meat in Winter. Oscar Williams. LiTA; LiTM

What life can compare with the jolly town-rakes. The Town-Rakes. *At. to* Peter Anthony Motteux. CoMu

What Lips My Lips Have Kissed. Edna St. Vincent Millay. BoLoP; FaBoBl; HeIL; HeIP; HoPM; LiTA; MeMAP; MoAB; MoAmPo; NAAL-2; NIP; PrIm; Son

What little throat. The Blackbird by Belfast Lough. *Unknown, tr. fr. Early Irish by* Frank O'Connor. IIP; PeIV

What lively lad most pleasured me. A Last Confession. W. B. Yeats. BoLoP; CBLP; CMoP; ELP; ErPo; HAP; NIP; OAEL-2

What Love Is. Ella Wheeler Wilcox. PWR

What love is this of thine, that cannot be. Edward Taylor. *Fr.* Preparatory Meditations Before My Approach to the Lord's Supper. AmPP; NOCV; PoEL-3; SCAP

What lovely things. The Scribe. Walter de la Mare. CMoP; EBEvV; FaBoCh; OBMV; TrCP; TrPWD

What made the place a landscape of despair. Claus von Stauffenberg. Thom Gunn. OBWP

What made the porter stare so hard? At Devlin's Siding. Barcroft Henry Boake. CBAP

What makes a city great? Huge piles of stone. The City's Crown. Dudley Foulke. WGRP

What Makes a Happy Life. Martial, *tr. fr. Latin by* Goldwin Smith. AWP

What Makes a Home? *Unknown.* PoToHe

What makes a knave a child of God. Samuel Butler. *Fr.* Hudibras. NOBL; OBSV

What Makes a Nation Great? Alexander Blackburn. WBLP

What makes a plenteous harvest. Virgil, *tr. by* Dryden. *Fr.* Georgics. AWP

What makes all subjects discontent. Samuel Butler. FaBoEE

What makes life worth the living. Giving and Forgiving. Thomas Grant Springer. PoToHe

What makes me disinclined. Pretences. Ibn Rashiq, *tr. fr. Arabic by* A. J. Arberry. TTY

What makes me write my dearest Freind you aske. Hester Wyat. FaBoVe

What makes my bed seem hard, seeing it is soft? Captive of Love. Ovid, *tr. by* Christopher Marlowe. *Fr.* Elegies. AWP

What makes permeable the ghost? The Ghost. Hilary Corke. NYBP

What Makes the Grizzlies Dance. Sandra Alcosser. FoLa

What makes us rove that starlit corridor. Science Fiction. Kingsley Amis. NoAM

What makes you look so black, so glum, so cross? Edward Lear. FaBoNo

What makes your lip so strange? Thomas Middleton. *Fr.* Changeling, The. PoEL-2

What man dost thou dig it for? Shakespeare. *Fr.* Hamlet. DL; NAWM-1

What Man has made of Man? *(LL)* Lines Written in Early Spring. Wordsworth. EnRP; FHYEP; GTBS; GTBS-P; NAEL-2; OAEL-2; PoLF

What man is he, that boasts of fleshly might. Spenser. *Fr.* Faerie Queene, The. FHYEP

What man is he that yearneth. Sophocles, *tr. by* A. E. Housman. *Fr.* Oedipus at Colonus. AWP

What man of ignorance undefiled. Oh Come, Little Children. Phyllis McGinley. FaBV

What man so wise, what earthly wit so ware. Spenser. *Fr.* Faerie Queene, The. FHYEP

What marked the river's flow. "Stephany." NBV

What? Mars his sword? faire Cytherea say. Upon Venus Putting on Mars His Armes. Richard Crashaw. SeCP

What Matter? *Gond Oral Tradition, tr. by* V. Elwin *and* S. Hivale. WTO

What Matters. Janice Mirikitani. ETG

What may be more than my flesh. *(LL)* After the Persian. Louise Bogan. NYBP; PoA

What me betidde this holiday. *(LL)* Ribbe ne rele ne spinne ich ne may. *Unknown.* MiEL

What mean these dreams, and hideous forms that rise. George the Third's Soliloquy. Philip Freneau. EAP; NOBA

What mean these loud aerial cracks I hear? *Unknown. Fr.* Bedlam; a Poem on His Majesty's Happy Escape from His German Dominions. NOEC

What mean these peals from every tower. The Fall of Richmond. Herman Melville. PAH

What mean these showy and these sounding signs. The Feast of Blood. Joseph Fawcett. *Fr.* Art of War, The. NOEC

What mean those Amorous Curles of Jet? In Imitation of Horace. Aphra Behn. KTR; NOSC

What meanes this silence of Harvardine quils. A Supplement. Benjamin Tompson. SCAP

What meanest thou, my fortune. *Unknown.* EnLoPo

What meaneth this, that Christ an hymne did singe. William Alabaster. *Fr.* Divine Meditations. ESCV; Son

What means [*or* meaneth *or* menethe] this? When I lie [*or* lye] alone. Sir Thomas Wyatt. GBL; SiPS; SiPSBD
(What Does This Mean?) MeEL

What means at this unusual hour the light. Sonnet in the Mail Coach. Henry Taylor. TEP

What means this? *(LL)* What means [*or* meaneth *or* menethe] this? When I lie [*or* lye] alone. Sir Thomas Wyatt. GBL; SiPS; SiPSBD

What means this host of advancing. The Advance of Education. Josephine D. Henderson Heard. CBWP-4

What means this new-born child of planets' motion? Eternity's Speech against Time. Fulke Greville. *Fr.* Mustapha. HAP; InvP; JCP; LiTB; NAEL-1; NOBE; OAEL-1; PoEL-1; PPP

What means this stately tablature. To My Noble Kinsman, Thomas Stanley, Esquire, on His Lyric Poems Composed by Master John Gamble. Richard Lovelace. CaPo

What means this strangeness now of late. Song. Sir Robert Ayton. NOSC

What means this vast assemblage here. Dedication Day. Maggie Pogue Johnson. CBWP-4

What means this watery canop' 'bout thy bed. On King Richard the Third, Who Lies Buried under Leicester Bridge. Sir John Suckling. CaPo

What meant our careful parents so to wear, Philippians 1.23. Francis Quarles. ChIV-2

What measure fate to him shall mete. Love Serviceable. Coventry Patmore. *Fr.* Angel in the House, The. EnLoPo

What men are they who haunt these fatal glooms. James Thomson ("B.V."). *Fr.* City of Dreadful Night, The. EBVV; OBNC

What Mérida looked like the first time you were there. Things That Happen to You. Alonzo Gonzales Mó, *tr. fr. Mayan by* Allan F. Burns. STP

What mind, what hunger, first saw this as food. *(LL)* Artichoke. Henry Taylor. MT

What Mr. Robinson Thinks. James Russell Lowell. *Fr.* Biglow Papers, The. AmPP; PAH

What moment in the gradual decay. Pale Fire. Vladimir Nabokov. OBD

What more can I ask? *(LL)* When Hope Comes Back. Gu Cheng. SpMi

What more could I, a young man, want. *(LL)* Eating Alone. Li-Young Lee. TRP; WeW

What more than these I ask'd of Life I am content to have from Death. *(LL)* Wales England Wed. Ernest Rhys. AngWe

What more? Where is the third Calixt. Ballad of the Lords of Old Time. Villon, *tr. fr. French by* Swinburne. AWP; PeVV

What moves that lonely man is not the boom. The Hermit. W. H. Davies. MoBrPo

What must a man do in this house. Blues for the Nightowl. Elton Glaser. PBCAP

What must be studied. The winter trees. Trees. Agnes Nemes Nagy, *tr. fr. Hungarian by* Bruce Berlind. PoSu

What must you do? Writing a Curriculum Vitae. Wislawa Szymborska, *tr. fr. Polish by* Grazyna Drabik *and* Austin Flint. PoSu

What my age and climate held to view. Mark Akenside. EPCY

What My Child Learns of the Sea. Audre Lorde. PoBA

What my friend? Love this! I who have known. Walking with R. B. Evan Jones (b. 1927). PBCV

What mystery pervades a well! Emily Dickinson. NAAL-1

What name do I have for you? Just Walking Around. John Ashbery. NAAL-2

What nedeth these thretning wordes and wasted wynde? Sir Thomas Wyatt, *after the Italian of* Serafino. OBVE

What Need Have I for Memory? Georgia Douglas Johnson. CDC

What need I travel, since I may. Home Travel. Joseph Hall. CBLP

What need Lovers wish for more? *(LL)* Phillis is my only joy. Sir Charles Sedley. EnLoPo; SeCV-2

What need you, being come to sense. September 1913. W. B. Yeats. CMoP; FaBoPV; GTBS-P; HAP; MoP; NAEL-2; NoAM; PeIV; PoRA

What needest thou? a few brief hours of rest. Vain Questioning. Walter de la Mare. OtMeF

What Needeth All This Travail. *Unknown.* ElL

What needs complaints. Comfort to a Youth That Had Lost His Love. Robert Herrick. NOBE; OBEV

What needs my Shakespear[e] for his honoured [*or* honour'd *or* honored] bones. On Shakespeare. Milton. EPCY; HeIL; InvP; MeLP; NAEL-1; NoP; NOSC; PoE; PoRA; SCGP; TrGrPo
(Epitaph on the Admirable Dramatic Poet, W. Shakespeare, An.) FaBoEE

What needs to be fed? On the Nature of Food. Alberta Turner. LCAP

What, never filled? Be thy lips screwed so fast. Isaiah 66.11. Francis Quarles. ChIV-1

What new responsibilities are we hatching now. Green Ice. Vivienne Finch. BrRo

What News. Walter Savage Landor. BoLoP

What next what next what next what next what next. (*LL*) Job. Elizabeth Sewell. ChIV-1

What Night Would It Be? John Ciardi. PDV

What! no more favours? Not a ribbon more. To a Lady That Forbade to Love before Company. Sir John Suckling. CaPo

What no, perdy! (*LL*) What no, Perdy [*or* Perdie]! ye may be sure! Sir Thomas Wyatt. AAS; SiPSBD

What no, Perdy [*or* Perdie]! ye may be sure! Sir Thomas Wyatt. AAS; SiPSBD
(No! Indeed.) MeEL
(What No, Perdy.) PoEL-1

What noble courage must their hearts have fired. Oliver Goldsmith, the Younger. *Fr.* Rising Village, The.
(Lonely Settler, The.) NOBC

What noise of viols is so sweet. Beggars. Francis Davidson. CH

What nothing earthly gives, or can destroy. The Soul's Calm Sunshine. Pope. *Fr.* Essay on Man, An. FaBoRV

What now. Another Poem for Me. Etheridge Knight. NNaP

What now avails to gain a woman's heart. The Mortified Genius. James Graeme. NOEC

What nudity is beautiful as this. Portrait of a Machine. Louis Untermeyer. MoAmPo

What numerous votaries 'neath thy shadowy wing. To the Evening. John Codrington Bampfylde. NOEC

What nymph should I admire or trust. The Question to Lisetta. Matthew Prior. OBEV

What of her glass without her? The blank gray. Without Her. Dante Gabriel Rossetti. *Fr.* House of Life, The. GBL; OBNC; PoEL-5; Son

What of her history when all the traces. The Ghost of My Mother. Matt Simpson. PWE

What of it, that the realms of this epoch. The Animal Howl. "M. J.," *tr. fr. Polish* by A. Glanz-Leyeles. TrJP

What of the faith and fire within us. Thomas Hardy. *See* We be the King's men, hale and hearty.

What of the old chains. Tomorrow Morning. John Harkness. UnDi

What of these verses that I write. Narcissus: To Himself. David Galler. PoA

"What of vile dust?" the preacher said. The Praise of Dust. G. K. Chesteron. MoBrPo; OtMeF

What offspring other men have got. Upon His Verses. Robert Herrick. NAEL-1

What on Earth deserves our Trust? Epitaph on her Son *H. P.* at St. Syth's Church. Katherine Philips. KTR
(Epitaph on Her Son H. P. at St. Syth's Church, where Her Body also Lies Interred.) NOSC

What on earth! I fear and tremble. Darkened in the Soul. Napa, *tr. fr. Eskimo.* WTO

What once Europa was, Nannette is now. (*LL*) Cupid Turned Plowman. Moschus. AWP

What Once I Was. Sir Thomas Wyatt. MeEL

What one art thou, thus in torn weed yclad? Virtue. Nicholas Grimald. SCGP
(Description of Virtue.) NoSic

What [*or* And what] Is So Rare as a Day in June? James Russell Lowell. *Fr.* Vision of Sir Launfal, The. BLPL; FaBoBe; FaPON; ImGa

What others are, to feel, and know myself a Man. (*LL*) Hymn to Adversity. Thomas Gray. EnRP; GTBS; GTBS-P

What others doth discourage and dismay. To His Coy Mistress. Sir Robert Ayton. NOSC

What pain, to wake and miss you! Quite Forsaken. D. H. Lawrence. SCGP

What pangs did he merit — so simple, without misdeed ? Death of a Ram. Sedulius Scottus, *tr. fr. Latin.* NOIV

What! Parted! Not even a kiss? X. A. M. PeLi

What passing-bells for these who die as cattle? Anthem for Doomed Youth. Wilfred Owen. ChTr; ClHu; CMoP; EBEV; FaBoMo; FaBoRV; FaPoB; GTBS-P; HAP; HeIP; HoPM; ImPo; InPK; InPS; LiTM; MoAB; MoBrPo; MoP; NAEL-2; NoAM; NOBE; NoP; OAEL-2; OBEV; OBWP; OxBTC; PlP; PoE; PPP; SCV; Son; SoSe; TFi; TrGrPo; WeW

What peer of France would let him duchess rove. French Fops. John Gay *and* Alexander Pope. *Fr.* Epistle to the Right Honourable William Pulteney, Esq. ECEV

What pen can well report the plight. Another of Seafarers, Describing Evil Fortune. *Unknown.* OxBSS

What Piggy-Wig Found. Enid Blyton. BoTP

What pleases me in my old age. Tune: "Charm of Nien-nu, The." Chu Tun-ju, *tr. fr. Chinese* by Irving Y. Lo. SuSp

What pleasure can this gaudy world afford? Consideratus Considerandus. John Saffin. SCAP

What pleasure have great princes. The Quiet Life. *At. to* William Byrd. EIL; NoSic
(Herdmen, The.) NOBE

What pleasure in such vehement commotion. Boethius, *tr. fr. Latin. Fr.* Consolation of Philosophy, The. MLL, *tr.* by Helen Waddell

What pleasures have great princes? These: to know. The Pleasure of Princes. A. D. Hope. FaBoMA

What plucky sperm invented Mrs. Gale? A New World Symphony. Kit Wright. NBLV; PeLV

What poets feel not, when they make. A Caution to Poets. Matthew Arnold. FaBoUs

What portents, from what distant region, ride. On the Ice Islands Seen Floating in the German Ocean. William Cowper. OAEL-1; PrIm

What potions have I drunk of Siren tears. Shakespeare. *Fr.* Sonnets. OxAEP-1

What Price. Lulu Minerva Schultz. GoYe

What pride by opposition. (*LL*) The Priesthood. George Herbert. ESCV

What Profit? Immanuel di Roma, *tr. fr. Hebrew* by J. Chotzner. TrJP

What profit to Darius of his reign? *Unknown, tr. fr. Latin. Fr.* Carmina Burana. MLL, *tr.* by Helen Waddell

What rage is this? what furor [*or* furour] of what kind [*or* kynd]? Sir Thomas Wyatt. AAS; EnLoPo; SiPS

What ran under the rosebush? Could It Have Been a Shadow? Monica Shannon. FaPON

What reason first imposed thee, gentle name. The Family Name. Charles Lamb. Son

What regiment d'you belong to. Brothers. Giuseppe Ungaretti, *tr. fr. Italian* by Jonathan Griffin. PeFWW

What remains of summer. The Cold. Lance Henson. CDW

What riches have you that you deem me poor? George Santayana. *Fr.* Sonnets. TrGrPo

What Riddle Asked the Sphinx. Archibald MacLeish. HoPM

What Rider Spurs Him from the Darkening East. Edna St. Vincent Millay. TrCP; WPE

What Robin Told. George Cooper. FaPON

What! Roses growing in a meadow. Wild Roses. Mary Effie Lee Newsome. CDC; ShDr

What Rules the World. William Ross Wallace. OHIP

What rumour'd heavens are these. To the Unknown Eros. Coventry Patmore. *Fr.* Unknown Eros, The. PoEL-5

What ruse of vision. The Bear. N. Scott Momaday. CDW; HATNAP

What sacramental hurt that brings. Emily Brontë. Louise Imogen Guiney. AmWP

What sacrifice so great! . A Mother's Love. Josephine D. Henderson Heard. CBWP-4

What savage beast would willfully consent to ride jammed haunch to haunch. Bus Ride. Lenore Kandel. NMM

What Saves Us. Bruce Weigl. NAmP90

What say the Bells of San Blas. The Bells of San Blas. Longfellow. MeMAP; OxBA

What Schoolmasters Say. Martin Seymour-Smith. OxBTC

What scope/ is there where. The Rope. Tania van Zyl. PeSA

What scrap is this, you thrust upon me now? The Count of Senlis at His Toilet. Lord De Tabley. PeVV

What seas did you see. A Conversation. Dylan Thomas. RFM

What seas what shores what grey rocks and what islands. Marina. T. S. Eliot. CMoP; FaBoMo; GTBS-P; HeIP; LiTA; NAEL-2; NOBE; NOCV; PoE; TOF

What Secret Cravings of the Blood. Nelly Sachs, *tr. fr. German* by Michael Hamburger. PoSu

What seems to us for us is true. Perspective. Coventry Patmore. *Fr.* Angel in the House, The. FaBoEE; GBL

What seer is this. Ode on the Twentieth Century. H. Cordelia Ray. CBWP-3

What serious students with their busied brains. Epigram LXVII: Time, the Interpreter. Hugh Crompton. NOSC

What serves for one will serve for t' othèr. (*LL*) Epitaphs [*or* Epitaph] on Two Piping-Bullfinches of Lady Ossory's, Buried under a Rose-Bush in Her Garden. Horace Walpole. FaBoEE; NOEC

What shakes the eye but the invisible? The Decision. Theodore Roethke. CRP; VGW

What shall a Mote up to a Monarch rise? Edward Taylor. *Fr.* Preparatory Meditations Before My Approach to the Lord's Supper. EAP

What shall avail me. The Border. Edwin Muir. Mes

What shall be said between us here. Félise. Swinburne. BeLS

What shall he have that killed the deer? Shakespeare. *Fr.* As You Like It. NoSic
(Song: "What shall he have that kill'd the dear?") CTC

What shall I compare them to. Plum Blossoms on Solitary Hill. Wang An-shih, *tr. fr.* Chinese *by* Jan W. Walls. SuSp

What Shall I Do? Fanny Kemble. *Fr.* Absence. PoToHe

What shall I do? not to be Rich or Great. In Emulation of Mr Cowleys Poem Call'd The Motto. Mary Astell. KTR; NOSC

What shall I do this afternoon? Half Holiday. Olive Enoch. BoTP

What shall I do to be for ever known. The Motto. Abraham Cowley. BeJo; NOSC; SeCP

What shall I do to be just? The Cry of the Age. Hamlin Garland. WGRP

What Shall I Do to Show How Much I Love Her? John Gay. *Fr.* Beggar's Opera, The. OAEL-1; TEP

What shall I do with all the days and hours. What Shall I Do? Fanny Kemble. *Fr.* Absence. PoToHe

What Shall I Give. Gwendolyn Brooks. *Fr.* Womanhood, The. BPo, 2 *sts. only*; PoA, (*complete*); WPE, (1 *and* 2)

What Shall I Give? Edward Thomas. FaBoCh; OxBChV

What Shall I Give My Children? Gwendolyn Brooks. Son

What shall I render thee, Father supreme. The Mother's Sacrifice. Lydia Huntley Sigourney. VPP

What shall I render to thy Name. In Thankfull Remembrance for My Dear Husband's Safe Arrivall Sept. 3, 1662. Anne Bradstreet. TrPWD

What shall I say, because talk I must? The Yellow Flower. William Carlos Williams. HAP

What shall I say, my Deare Deare Lord? Edward Taylor. *Fr.* Preparatory Meditations Before My Approach to the Lord's Supper. EAP

What shall I say, my Lord? With what begin? Edward Taylor. *Fr.* Preparatory Meditations Before My Approach to the Lord's Supper. ChIV-2; HAP

What shall I send my sweet today. A Valentine. Matilda Betham-Edwards. PeHV

What shall I teach in the vivid afternoon. Going to School. Karl Shapiro. TrJP

What shall I tell about my life. My Live Story. Lan Nguyen, *tr. fr. Vietnamese.* TSaS

What shall i wear. 104. Alta. CrSp

What shall I wish thee? New Year's Wishes. Frances Ridley Havergal. BLRP

What shall I wish thee this New Year? A New Year Wish. *Unknown.* BLRP

What shall I your true-love tell. Messages. Francis Thompson. CH; OtMeF

What shall it answer there? (*LL*) Advertisement of a Lost Day. Lydia Huntley Sigourney. WBLP

What Shall it Profit? William Dean Howells.

What shall Presto do for pretty prattle. Swift. Delmore Schwartz. PoA

What! shall that sudden blade. Custer. Edmund Clarence Stedman. PAH

What shall the world do with its children? Romans Angry about the Inner World. Robert Bly. NOBA

What shall uproot a house and bring this care into his eye? (*LL*) October 1. Karl Shapiro. MoAB; MoAmPo; PoA

What shall we add now? He is dead. "Died . . . ." Elizabeth Barrett Browning. NOBVV

What shall we be like when. Seeds. John Oxenham. WGRP

What shall we be, sweet, you and I. These Bones. T. H. Parry-Williams, *tr. fr.* Welsh *by* H. Idris Bell. OBWVE

What shall we count to cool our angry pride? Count Ten. Bonaro W. Overstreet. PoToHe

What shall we do — what shall we think — what shall we say? Conrad Aiken. *Fr.* Preludes for Memnon; or, Preludes to Attitude. FaBoMo

What shall we do for Love these days? Lascelles Abercrombie. *Fr.* Emblems of Love. CH; MoBrPo

What shall we do for timber? Kilcash. *Unknown, tr. fr.* Irish *by* Frank O'Connor. BIrV; IIP; OBMV; PeIV

What shall we know we don't know. Somebody Died. Robert Creeley. LCAP

What Shall We Render. *Unknown.* BLRP

What she and I had between us once, America. John Hollander. *Fr.* Powers of Thirteen. VCAP

What she collects, finally, is pain. (*LL*) The Collector. Raymond Souster. ErPo

What she collects is men. The Collector. Raymond Souster. ErPo

What she for years denied. (*LL*) Advice to a Lover. Thomas Yalden. ECEV

What she remembers. Mother of the Groom. Seamus Heaney. OxBSP

What She Said. Allur Nanmullai, *tr. fr. Tamil by* A. K. Ramanujan. PLW

What She Said. Ammuvanar, *tr. fr. Tamil by* A. K. Ramanujan. PLW

What She Said. Maturai Eruttalan Centamputan, *tr. fr. Tamil by* A. K. Ramanujan. BoLoP

What She Said. Ceyti Valluvan Peruncattan, *tr. fr. Tamil by* A. K. Ramanujan. PLW

What She Said. Kollan Alici, *tr. fr. Tamil by* A. K. Ramanujan. PLW

What She Said. Maturai Ilampalaciriyan Centan Kuttanar, *tr. fr. Tamil by* A. K. Ramanujan. PLW

What She Said. Nannakaiyar, *tr. fr. Tamil by* A. K. Ramanujan. PLW

What She Said. Okkur Macatti, *tr. fr. Tamil by* A. K. Ramanujan. PBWP

What She Said. Palaipatiya Perunkatunko, *tr. fr. Tamil by* A. K. Ramanujan. PLW

What She Said. Paranar, *tr. fr. Tamil by* A. K. Ramanujan. PLW

What She Said. Vayilanrevan, *tr. fr. Tamil by* A. K. Ramanujan. PLW

What She Said. Venkorran, *tr. fr. Tamil by* A. K. Ramanujan. PLW

What She Said about Her Unfaithful, Estranged Husband. Netumpalliyattan, *tr. fr. Tamil by* A. K. Ramanujan. PLW

What She Said ("And all those horses.") Kapilar, *tr. fr. Tamil by* A. K. Ramanujan. PLW

What She Said ('As the lovely new flowers'). Allur Nanmullai, *tr. fr. Tamil by* A. K. Ramanujan. PLW

What She Said ("Bees, six tiny legs and wings all lovely.") Orampokiyar, *tr. fr. Tamil by* A. K. Ramanujan. *Fr.* Five on the Riverside Cane. PLW

What She Said ("Bigger than earth, certainly.") Tevakulattar, *tr. fr. Tamil by* A. K. Ramanujan. PLW

What She Said ("Bird and Beast.") Nannakaiyar, *tr. fr. Tamil by* A. K. Ramanujan. PLW

What She Said ('Forest animals walk there'). Kapilar, *tr. fr. Tamil by* A. K. Ramanujan. PLW

What She Said ("Friend, listen.") Ammuvanar, *tr. fr. Tamil by* A. K. Ramanujan. PLW

What She Said ("Green creepers planted inside the house.") Orampokiyar, *tr. fr. Tamil by* A. K. Ramanujan. *Fr.* Five on the Riverside Cane. PLW

What She Said ("He is from those mountains.") Kapilar, *tr. fr. Tamil by* A. K. Ramanujan. PLW

What She Said Her Lover within Earshot. Kapilar, *tr. fr. Tamil by* A. K. Ramanujan. PLW

What She Said ("Hovering like the heron.") Orampokiyar, *tr. fr. Tamil by* A. K. Ramanujan. *Fr.* Five on the Riverside Cane. PLW

What She Said ("In his fields.") Orampokiyar, *tr. fr. Tamil by* A. K. Ramanujan. *Fr.* Five on the Crabs. PLW

What She Said ("In his place, mother,/ field-crabs cut into the pink.") Orampokiyar, *tr. fr. Tamil by* A. K. Ramanujan. *Fr.* Five on the Crabs. PLW

What She Said ("In his place, mother,/ mud-spattered spotted crabs.") Orampokiyar, *tr. fr. Tamil by* A. K. Ramanujan. *Fr.* Five on the Crabs. PLW

What She Said ("In the full river.") Orampokiyar, *tr. fr. Tamil by* A. K. Ramanujan. *Fr.* Five on the Riverside Cane. PLW

What She Said ("Like the high fanning tufts on swift horses.") Orampokiyar, *tr. fr. Tamil by* A. K. Ramanujan. *Fr.* Five on the Riverside Cane. PLW

What She Said ("My body.") Ammuvanar, *tr. fr. Tamil by* A. K. Ramanujan. PLW

What She Said (" 'O your hair,' he said.") Kapilar, *tr. fr. Tamil by* A. K. Ramanujan. PLW

What She Said ("Only the dim-witted say it's evening.") Milaipperun Kantan, *tr. fr. Tamil by* A. K. Ramanujan. PLW

What She Said ("Only the thief was there, no one else.") Kapilar, *tr. fr. Tamil by* A. K. Ramanujan. PLW

What She Said ("The fishermen who go.") Ammuvanar, *tr. fr. Tamil by* A. K. Ramanujan. PLW

What She Said, Thinking of Him Crossing the Wilderness Alone. Auvaiyar, *tr. fr. Tamil by* A. K. Ramanujan. PLW

What She Said to Her Friend ('The colors on the elephant's body'). Kapilar, *tr. fr. Tamil by* A. K. Ramanujan. PLW

What She Said to Her Friend ("You ask me to forget him.") Kapilar, *tr. fr. Tamil by* A. K. Ramanujan. PLW

What She Said to Her Girl Friend. Ammuvanar, *tr. fr. Tamil by* A. K. Ramanujan. PLW

What She Said to Her Girl Friend. Kapilar, *tr. fr. Tamil by* A. K. Ramanujan. PLW

What She Said to Her Girl Friend. Korran, *tr. fr. Tamil* by A. K. Ramanujan. PLW

What She Said to Her Girl-Friend. Venmanipputi, *tr. fr. Tamil* by A. K. Ramanujan. PBWP

What She Said to Her Girl Friend, after a Tryst at Night (Which Turned Out to Be a Fiasco). Kapilar, *tr. fr. Tamil* by A. K. Ramanujan. PLW

What She Said to Her Girl Friend, and What Her Girl Friend Said in Reply. Uruttiran, *tr. fr. Tamil* by A. K. Ramanujan. PLW

What She Said to Her Girl Friend, Her Foster-Mother within Earshot. Kapilar, *tr. fr. Tamil* by A. K. Ramanujan. PLW

What She Said to Her Girl Friend ("O you, you wear flowers of gold.") Kapilar, *tr. fr. Tamil* by A. K. Ramanujan. PLW

What She Said to Her Girl Friend ("On the tall hill.") Paranar, *tr. fr. Tamil* by A. K. Ramanujan. PLW

What She Said to Her Girl Friend When She Returned from the Hills. Kapilar, *tr. fr. Tamil* by A. K. Ramanujan. PLW

What She Said to Him, after Meeting His Concubine. Cakalacanar, *tr. fr. Tamil* by A. K. Ramanujan. PLW

What Shines in Winter Burns. T. R. Hummer. MT

What Ship Is This?. *At.* to Samuel Hauser. AH

What should be said of him cannot be said. Dante. Michelangelo, *tr. fr. Italian* by Longfellow. AWP

What should I care at all from what my name I take. The Trent Again. Michael Drayton. *Fr.* Polyolbion. FaBoPP

What should I say. Sir Thomas Wyatt. NoSic; SCGP

What should I speak in praise of Surrey's skill. Surrey's Poetic Art. George Turberville. *Fr.* Verse in Praise of Lord Henry Howard, Earl of Surrey. EPCY

What should I tell them? Richard Wilbur. *Fr.* Mind-Reader, The. CRP; LCAP; NAAL-2; NoAM

What should one. The Picture of J. T. in a Prospect of Stone. Charles Tomlinson. PPP

What should [*or* shulde] I say[e]. Sir Thomas Wyatt. NoP; PoEL-1; SiPS; SiPSBD
 (Farewell: "What should I say.") GBL; Mes; NOBE
 (Revocation, A.) OBEV

What should we be without the sexual myth. Men Made out of Words. Wallace Stevens. MeMAP; MoAB; NOBA; OxBSP; TAP; VGW

What should we have taken. Provisions. Margaret Atwood. IHMS

What should we know. Oliver St. John Gogarty. FaBoCh; OBMV; PoRA

What should we see in this artifact? Incredible. A Quilt in the Bennington College Library. Dave Jeddie Smith. NAmP90

What silences we keep, year after year. Too Late. Nora Perry. PoToHe

What sin was mine, sweet, silent boy-god, Sleep. Sleep. Statius, *tr. fr. Latin* by W. H. Fyfe. AWP

What since August, when the sound. Natural History. Richard Howard. TAP

What siren zooming is sounding our coming. The Exiles. W. H. Auden. OxBTC

What sky! And I remember suddenly. Le Tombeau de Frank O'Hara. Art Lange. UL

What slender youth bedewed with liquid odours. I, 5. "What slender youth bedewed with liquid odours" ("Quis multa gracilis.") Horace, *tr. fr. Latin* by Austin Dobson. *Fr.* Odes. OBVE, *tr.* by Milton
 (Another to the Same.) OAEL-1, *tr.* by William Browne; WiR, *tr.* by William Browne
 (Fifth Ode of Horace, The.) EBEV, *tr.* by Milton; EnLoPo, *tr.* by Milton; PoEL-3, *tr.* by Milton
 (Pyrrha, what slender well-shap'd beau.) OBVE, *tr.* by Anthony Horneck
 (Say what slim youth, with moist perfumes.) OBVE, *tr.* by Christopher Smart
 (Tell me, Pyrrha, what fine youth.) OAEL-1, *tr.* by William Browne; WiR, *tr.* by William Browne
 (To a Girl.) WiR, *tr.* by Milton
 (To Pyrrha.) AWP, *tr.* by Milton
 (To whom now, Pyrrha, art thou kind?) OBVE, *tr.* by Abraham Cowley
 (What stripling now thee discomposes.) OBVE, *tr.* by Sir Richard Fanshawe

What smoldering senses in death's sick delay. The Kiss. Dante Gabriel Rossetti. *Fr.* House of Life, The. NOBVV; Son

What so beyond all madness is the elf. Cupid Far Gone. Richard Lovelace. CaPo; OPOP

What! soar'd the old eagle to die at the sun! The Death of Harrison. Nathaniel Parker Willis. PAH

What soft — Cherubic Creatures. Emily Dickinson. AmPP; HAP; MeMAP; MoAB; MoAmPo; NALW; WPE

What solemn sound the ear invades. Mount Vernon. *Unknown.* AmFP

What songs found voice upon those lips. Helen Hunt Jackson. Ina Coolbrith. AmWP

What soon enough we would know? (*LL*) The Bearer of Evil Tidings. Robert Frost. MoP; NoAM; SAmP

What soothes the angry snail? Eine Kleine Snailmusik. May Sarton. NBLV

What sort of a church would our church be. Just like Me. P. W. Sinks. BLRP

What sort of thing is our family wealth? Reading. P'i Jih-hsiu, *tr. fr. Chinese* by William H. Nienhauser. SuSp

What soul hath struck its need of melody. Incompleteness. H. Cordelia Ray. AmWP; CBWP-3

What sound awakened me, I wonder. The Deserter. A. E. Housman. OBMV

What sound awoke me? Dragon Skate. Gladys Cardiff. CDW

What sounds are those, Helvellyn, which are heard. The Fair below Helvellyn. Wordsworth. *Fr.* Prelude [or, Growth of a Poet's Mind], The. EnRP; FaBoPP; HAP, *short sel.*; OAEL-2; PoEL-4, *sl. shorter*

What sower walked over earth. Sunflower. Rolf Jacobsen, *tr. fr. Norwegian* by Robert Bly. NU; RaBo

What sphinx of cement and aluminum bashed open their skulls. Allen Ginsberg. *Fr.* Howl. AmPP; LCAP; NeAP; PoM; SOTW, *abr.*; TAP

What spirit touched the faded lambrequin. The Ilex Tree. Agnes Lee. PoA

What Splendid Rays. Christian Gregor, *tr. fr. German.* AH

What stands 'tween me and her that I adore? Echo Poem. M. Allan. FiBHP

What starts with f and ends with u-c-k? starts. The World of Expectations. Albert Goldbarth. HCAP

What sticks with me is the pit. Moonwalk. John Engels. MAT

What, Still Alive. Hugh Kingsmill. *See* What, still alive at twenty-two.

What, Still Alive at Twenty–Two. Hugh Kingsmill. *See* What, still alive at twenty–two.

What, still alive at twenty–two. Hugh Kingsmill. FaBoCo; NOBL; UV
 (Poem, after A. E. Housman.) FaBoPa
 (What, Still Alive at Twenty–Two.) InPK
 (What, Still Alive.) BXAP; NBLV

What strange effects of Fortune do I prove! Frances Boothby. *Fr.* Marcelia; or, Treacherous Friend, The. KTR

What strange unusual prodigy is here, On the Strange Apparitions at Christ's Death. Henry Colman. ChIV-2

What street is this? Osip Mandelstam, *tr. fr. Russian* by Clarence Brown *and* W. S. Merwin. OBD

What strength! what strife! what rude unrest! Westward Ho! Joaquin Miller. AnAmPo; FaBoBe

What Strikes My Eye. Wang Shih-chieng, *tr. fr. Chinese* by Richard John Lynn. SuSp

What stripling now thee discomposes. Horace. *See* What slender youth bedewed with liquid odours.

What substance had Euridice. Kathleen Raine. NALW

What Sugared Terms. Richard Lynche. *See* What sugred termes, what all-perswading arte.

What sugred termes, what all-perswading arte. Richard Lynche. *Fr.* Diella. AAS
 (What Sugared Terms.) Son

What surety of life have thou, and I? (*LL*) An Epitaph on Master Philip Gray. Ben Jonson. FaBoEE

What sweet relief the showers to thirsty plants we see. A True Love. Nicholas Grimald. EIL; OBEV

What swords and spears, what daggers bright. Frost. W. H. Davies. BoNaP

What taints thy shade — or doth the year decay? Addressed to a Beech Tree. Christian Carstairs. ECWP

What Tait's tête-à-tête ate at 8.8. (*LL*) Archbishop Tait. *Unknown.* ChTr; FaBoNo

What the Birds Said. Whittier. NOBA; PFP

What the blind lost when radio. After the Revolution for Jesus the Associate Professor [*or* a Secular Man] Prepares His Final Remarks. Miller Williams. MT

What the Bones Know. Carolyn Kizer. VBLP

What the Bullet Sang. Bret Harte. GGP; OBEV

What the cats do. The Cats. Weldon Kees. NaP; SoCa

What the Chairman Told Tom. Basil Bunting. OxBTC

What the Choir Sang about the New Bonnet. M. T. Morrison. BLPA

What the Concubine Said When She Heard the Wife Complain about the Concubine's Wiles. Villakaviralinar, *tr. fr. Tamil* by A. K. Ramanujan. PLW

What the day weaves. Thomas A. Clark. *Fr.* Sixteen Sonnets. NBrP

What the Devil Said. James Stephens. CMoP

What the Donkey Saw. U. A. Fanthorpe. OBCP

What the Earth Asked Me. James Wright. NYBP

What the Emanation of Casey Jones Said to the Medium. A. J. M. Smith. MoCV

What the End Is For. Jorie Graham. NAmP90

What the Engines Said. Bret Harte. ImGa

What the Girl Friend Said to the Foster-Mother. Kapilar, *tr. fr. Tamil by* A. K. Ramanujan. PLW

What the goddamn hell are you talking about, boy. How I Wrote It. David Dooley. TRP

What the Goose thinketh. (*LL*) When the Rain Raineth. *Unknown.* GBP; RB

What the Gray Cat Sings. Arthur Guiterman. MoShBr

What the hell am i doing anyway? California. Gerald Locklin. NGP

What the Informant Said to Franz Boas in 1920. *Unknown, tr. fr. Keresan Indian by* Armand Schwerner. STP

What the Intern Saw. Phillis Levin. PFL

What the King Has. Ethel Romig Fuller. PoToHe

What the Light Was Like. Amy Clampitt. FaBoWP

What the Moon Saw. Vachel Lindsay. FaBoEE; OxBSP

What the Motorcycle Said. Mona Van Duyn. NIP

What the Orderly Dog Saw. Ford Madox Ford. CTC

What the Passersby Said to the Lover Eloping with the Girl. Uraiyur Mutukorran, *tr. fr. Tamil by* A. K. Ramanujan. PLW

What the people learn out of lifting and hauling. Carl Sandburg. *Fr.* People, Yes, The. OBAL

What the Rooster Does before Mounting. Cyn Zarco. UL

What the Serpent Said to Adam. Archibald MacLeish. ChIV-1; MeMAP

What the Servants Said to Him, as He Returned Home. Maturaittamilkkuttan Katuvan Mallanar, *tr. fr. Tamil by* A. K. Ramanujan. PLW

What the Sixties Were Really Like. Sam Abrams. UL

What the Sonnet Is. Eugene Lee-Hamilton. HoPM; Son

What the Stone Dreams. James B. Hathaway. GOYP

What the sun burns up of it, the moon puts back. (*LL*) Plague of Dead Sharks. Alan Dugan. LiTM; NoAM

What the swift mind beholds at every turn. (*LL*) Pity Me Not [Because the Light of Day]. Edna St. Vincent Millay. CMoP; FaBoWP; MoAB; MoAmPo; OxBA; TrGrPo

What the Thrush Said. Keats. EBEV; PFP

What the Thrush Says. Queenie Scott-Hopper. BoTP

What the Weather Does. *Unknown.* BoTP

What the wind harried, the fire worried. Deadfall. Martha Keller. GoYe

What the Winds Bring. Edmund Clarence Stedman. AnAmPo

What them fellers does is ART! (*LL*) Art. *Unknown.* BLPA; NBLV

What Then? W. B. Yeats. CMoP

What then does the hunter want here by the millstream? The Hunter. Wilhelm Müller, *tr. fr. German by* Philip L. Miller. *Fr.* Beautiful Maid of the Mill, The. RiWo

What Then Is Love But Mourning? Thomas Campion *and to* Philip Rosseter. EnRePo

What then should happy Britain do? New Year's Day Song. Nahum Tate. FaBoEH

What There Is. Kenneth Patchen. ArLo

What therefore, what ys thyn entent? An Exchange between the Poet and St. Augustine. Petrarch, *tr. fr. Latin by* W. H. Draper. *Fr.* Secretum. OxBLMV

What these can only memorize and mumble. (*LL*) Grandeur of Ghosts. Siegfried Sassoon. MoBrPo; OBMV

What they are doing is turning. Turn (a Poem in 4 Parts). Ken Belford. NOBC

What They Do to You in Distant Places. Marvin Bell. Poetsp

What they eats in Rome. (*LL*) When in Rome. Mari Evans. SoSe

What They Said. Tanure Ojaide. HBAPE

What They Said. *Unknown, tr. fr. German by* Rose Fyleman. SiSoPo

What they undertook to do. Gratitude to the Unknown Instructors. W. B. Yeats. EnlH

What thing did I love that walks the street. The Contemporary Muse. Edgell Rickword. OBSV

What Thing Is Love. George Peele. *Fr.* Hunting of Cupid, The. CBLP; ELP; EnRePo; NOBE

What thing is love? for sure love is a thing. What Thing Is Love. George Peele. *Fr.* Hunting of Cupid, The. CBLP; ELP; EnRePo; NOBE (Love.) EiL; ELP; NOBE

What thing is that, nor felt nor seen. A Riddle: On a Kiss. William Strode. NOSC

What thing shall be held up to woman's beauty? Woman's Beauty. Lascelles Abercrombie. *Fr.* Emblems of Love. MoBrPo

What thing/ should I sing. Dove. Norma Farber. PChr

What things are steadfast? Not the birds. We Manage Most When We Manage Small. Linda Gregg. AmPA

What things have we seen. Beaumont *and* Fletcher *and* John Fletcher. *Fr.* Master Francis Beaumont to Ben Johnson. FaBoEH

What think you of this age now. *Unknown.* APAS

What this mountain means, and the murky dale. William Langland. *Fr.* Vision of Piers Plowman, The. OAEL-1

What Thomas an Buile Said in a Pub. James Stephens. MoAB; MoBrPo; MoP; PoRA; TrGrPo; WGRP

What those four sang. (*LL*) Alexander the Great. *Unknown.* CH

What thou hast done thou hast done; for the heavenly horses are swift. Irrevocable. Mary Wright Plummer. WGRP

What thou lovest well remains. Ezra Pound. *Fr.* Cantos. CMoP; FaBoTw; MoAB; NOBE; OxBA; RaBo

What Thou Lovest Well, Remains American. Richard Hugo. NAAL-2

What though, for showing truth to flatter'd [*or* flattered] state. Sonnet: Written on the Day That Mr. Leigh Hunt Left Prison. Keats. (Written on the Day That Mr. Leigh Hunt Left Prison.) EPCY; Son

What though my penne wax faynt. To Maystres Jane Blenner-Haiset. John Skelton. *Fr.* Garland [*or* Garlande *or* Garlands] of Laurel[l], The. AAS

What, though oblivion in her sable shroud. George Keate. *Fr.* Ancient and Modern Rome. OBTV

What though the music of thy rustic flute. Matthew Arnold. *Fr.* Thyrsis. EPCY; NAEL-2; NOBE; NoP; OBEV; OBNC

What though the rosebuds from my cheek. Departed Youth. Hannah Cowley. ECWP

What though your eyes are stars, your hair be night. To One Black, and Not Very Handsome, Who Expected Commendation. Lord Herbert of Cherbury. NOSC

What thought ye to burn, when ye kindled the pyre. *Unknown, tr. fr. Hebrew. Fr.* Duel with Verses over a Great Man. TrJP

What thoughts I have of you tonight, Walt Whitman. A Supermarket in California. Allen Ginsberg. AmPP; BCF; CoAP; HAP; HCAP; HeIL; HeIP; InPK; InPS; LiTM; NAAL-2; NaP; NeAP; NoAM; NOBA; PoBeRe; PoM; PrIm; SOTW; TAP; TFi; TwCP; UnPo; WeW

What thoughts I have of you tonight, Walt Whitman, for I work late. A Pizza Joint in Cranston. Craig Weeden. BXAP

What tidings of reverent gladness are voiced by the bells that ring. On Easter Morning. Eben E. Rexford. BLRP

What time I see you passing by. *Unknown, tr. fr. Italian by* John Addington Symonds. *Fr.* Popular Songs of Tuscany. AWP

What time the gifted lady took. George Sand. Dorothy Parker. *Fr.* Pig's-Eye View of Literature, A. FiBHP; NALW

What time the Lord drew back the sea. Panama. Amanda T. Jones. PAH

What time the mighty moon was gathering light. Love and Death. Tennyson. OBD

What time the noble Lovewell came. Lovewell's Fight. *Unknown.* PAH

What time the poet hath hymned. Oh, Hollow! Hollow! Hollow! W. S. Gilbert. *Fr.* Patience. FaBoNo

What time the rose of dawn is laid across the lips of night. The Angler's Reveille. Henry van Dyke. *Fr.* Toiling of Felix, The. GN

What time the weary weather-beaten sheep. The Tenth Eclogue. Michael Drayton. *Fr.* Shepherd's Garland, The. JCP

What time the wheat field tinges rusty brown. The Wheat Ripening. John Clare. NTP

What 'tis to serve the great Utopian queen. (*LL*) It was in June the eight and thirtieth day. John Taylor. CBNP; NOSC

What to conceal desire, when every. Delariviere Manley. *Fr.* Royal Mischeif, The. KTR

What to do with a day. The Satisfaction Coal Company. Rita Dove. LCAP

What to Say When You Talk to Yourself. Stephen Knight. CBCK

What to Trust? Shao Yen-hsiang, *tr. fr. Chinese.* LHF, *tr. by* Hualing Nieh

What Tomas Said in a Pub. James Stephens. *See* I saw God! Do you doubt it?

What Tongue Can Her Perfections Tell? Sir Philip Sidney. *Fr.* Arcadia. EnRePo; SiPS; SiPSBD

What torments must the virgin prove. Charlotte Lennox. ECWP

What travellers of matchlesse Venice say. An Elegie Made by Mr. Aurelian Townshend in Remembrance of the Ladie Venetia Digby. Aurelian Townshend. SeCP

What treasure greater than a friend. A Friend. Santob de Carrion. *Fr.* Proverbios Morales. TrJP

What trees are those, where the low clouds infiltrate. Side Window. John James. ImPo; VaA

What trifling coil do we poor mortals keep. Human Life. Matthew Prior. FaBoEE

What triumph moves on the billows so blue? Matthew Gregory Lewis. OBTV

What Ulysses Said to Circe on the Beach of Aeaea. Irving Layton. ErPo

What use to suffer in labor, give birth to children, if she. Diotimus, *tr. fr. Greek by* Barbara Hughes Fowler. *Fr.* Epigrams. HePo

What 'Vaileth [*or* vaileth] truth [*or* trouth]? or by it to take pain [*or* payn]? Sir Thomas Wyatt. AAS
(Rondeau: "What 'vaileth trouth." SiPSBD

What various hindrances we meet. Exhortation to Prayer. William Cowper. NOCV

What Voice at Moth-Hour. Robert Penn Warren. DiPo; ImGa; MT; SM

What voice is this, thou evening gale! Song. Joanna Baillie. WoRP

What voice, what harp, are those we hear. The Minstrel. Goethe, *tr. fr. German by* James Clarence Mangan. AWP

What! want to be buggered, and cry when it's done! Epigram: To Papilus. Martial, *tr. fr. Latin.* PeHV

What Was Ashore, Then. John Berryman. *Fr.* Sonnets. Son

What was he doing, the great god Pan. A Musical Instrument. Elizabeth Barrett Browning. EBEvV; EBVV; FaBoBe; FaPON; NAEL-2; NoP; OAEL-2; OBEV; PoE; Poetr; WPE
(Great God Pan, The.) WiR

What was her beauty in our first estate. She. Richard Wilbur. AmPP

What was his creed? H. N. Fifer. *Fr.* He Lived a Life. PoToHe

What was his name? (*LL*) As I was going o'er London Bridge. Mother Goose. ISE

What was his name? I do not know his name. The Nameless Saints. Edward Everett Hale. WGRP

What was is . . . since 1930. Homecoming. Robert Lowell. CAPP

What was it brought you, Seligenstadter. Memling. Roland Mathias. AngWe

What was called. Custer Lives in Humbolt County. Janet Campbell Hale. VoR

What was it I wonder? The Knife. Richard Tillinghast. MT

What was it like, that country house? Country Villa. Jean Garrigue. TAP

What was it/ that caught in our throats that day. The Greek Room. James W. Thompson. BPo

What was it the Engines said. What the Engines Said. Bret Harte. ImGa

What was it? What was it? Woman as Market. Muriel Rukeyser. NoAM

What was it you remember — the summer mornings. To Any Member of My Generation. George Barker. LiTM; MeMBP; Son

What was most striking about them. Concerning the Dead Women: The Munitions Plant Explosion: June, 1918. Elizabeth Libbey. AmPA

What Was Said. Edward Kleinschmidt. UnDi

What Was Shown. Peter Philpott. VaA

What Was Solomon's Mind? Geoffrey Scott. OBMV

What was that sound we heard. Why Must You Know? John Wheelwright. VGW

What was the first prophetic word that rang. Peace. Edwin Markham. WBLP

What was the name you called me? Evening Waterfall. Carl Sandburg. ImPo

What was the nub of wonder? Was it. Questions of Swimming, 1935. Peter Davison. DiPo

What Was Your Name in the States? *Unknown.* AS

What way does the Wind come? What way does he go? Address to a Child during a Boisterous Winter Evening. Dorothy Wordsworth. NTP; OxBChV; WoRP
(Wind, The.) BoTP

What we are is beyond him utterly. (*LL*) Death Has No Features of His Own. Gwen Harwood. NOBAu

What we below could not see, Winter pass. (*LL*) Thaw. Edward Thomas. ArNa; EBEV; FaBoTw; FM; GTBS-P; MoAB; MoBrPo; NTP; OxAEP-2; OxBSP; OxBTC; Spl

What We Can. Ray A. Young Bear. VoR

What we come round to. Epitaph for the Western Intelligentsia. Richard Allen. NOBAu

What we do best is breed. A Christening. Donald Davie. OxBC

What We Know. Raymond R. Patterson. NBV

What we looked for always remained. The Friendship. Robert Mezey. NaP

What we need now above all is a few hints. Visiting the University. Peter Riley. *Fr.* One Day. VaA

What We Teach at Claflin. L. A. J. Moorer. CBWP-3

What we to-day prize and most fondly cherish. Instability. H. Cordelia Ray. CBWP-3

What we want indeed! He comes in. At the Cafe. Peter Riley. *Fr.* One Day. VaA

What We, When Face to Face. Arthur Hugh Clough. ChIV-2

What we, when face to face we see. What We, When Face to Face. Arthur Hugh Clough. ChIV-2

What weight of ancient witness can prevail. Private Judgement Condemned. Dryden. *Fr.* Hind and the Panther, The. (Confessio Fidei.) NOBE

What well-heeled knuckle-head, straight from the unisex. An Old Malediction. Anthony Hecht, *after* Horace. IHNG; NoAM

What went ye out to see? a shaken reed? John. Jones Very. ChIV-2

What Were They Like? Denise Levertov. HeIP; NIP; OBWP; PAW; VGW; WPE

What were they talking about? Ah yes, the end! Twenty-ninth Canto. Hans Magnus Enzensberger. *Fr.* Sinking of the Titanic, The. PoSu

What were we doing up there. Greenland's History. Sven Holm, *tr. fr. Danish.* TSaS, *tr. by* Paula Hostrup-Jessen

What were we playing? Was it prisoner's base? Running. Richard Wilbur. CoAP

What were you carrying, Pilgrims, Pilgrims? Atlantic Charter: 1942. Francis Brett Young. OtMeF

What were you thinking, a child, when you lay. What Were You Thinking Dear Mother. Robert Penn Warren. *Fr.* Tale of Time. LCAP

What Were You Thinking Dear Mother. Robert Penn Warren. *Fr.* Tale of Time. LCAP

What wert thou, Rome, unbroken, when thy ruin. Rome. Hildebert, *tr. fr. Latin by* Helen Waddell. MLL

What, what, what/ What's the news from Swat? George Thomas Lanigan. FiBHP; NBLV
(Ahkoond of Swat, The.) AnAmPo

What! What!/Go to pot! *Unknown.* ISE

What, why didest thou wink whan thou a wyf toke? *Unknown.* MiEL

What Wild Dawns There Were. Denise Levertov. NOBA

What will become of Hawaii? The Leper. Ka-'ehu, *tr. fr. Hawaiian by* M. K. Pukui *and* A. L. Korn. WTO

What will become of the mice and the rats? (*LL*) Hoddley, poddley, puddle and fogs. *Unknown.* FaBoNo; OxNR

What will happen now? What She Said. Maturai Ilampalaciriyan Centan Kuttanar, *tr. fr. Tamil by* A. K. Ramanujan. PLW

What will it do for him, to have internalized. A Giant Has Swallowed the Earth. Pattiann Rogers. MT

What will our father bring to us. Rondo for the Poet's Children. Jean-Joseph Rabéarivelo, *tr. fr. French by* Ellen Conroy Kennedy. NegPo

What will they give me, when journey's done? Journey's End. Humbert Wolfe. TrJP

What will we do. Poem for Nana. June Jordan. BlSi

What Will We Do for Linen? *Unknown.* GBP; WTO

What will you do with your shovel, Dai. Idris Davies. FaBoEH

What will you lack, sonny, what will you lack. Fall In. Harold Begbie. NSI

What will you ride on? Hey! My Pony! Eleanor Farjeon. FaPON

What winter floods, what showers of spring. Emily Brontë. NOBVV

What winter holiday is this? The Man of Peace. Bliss Carman. OHIP

What wisdom have we that by wisdom all. Relativities. Louis Untermeyer. BXAP

What witchlike spell weaves here its deep design, Anna Hempstead Branch. *Fr.* Sonnets from a Lock Box. NALW

What! without feeling? Don't we make pretense. Two Vast Enjoyments Commemorated. John Danforth. SCAP

What Women Are Not. *Unknown.* MeEL

What Women Are Not. *Unknown.* MeEL; MiEL

What wonder doth in beauty dwell. (*LL*) Against Fulfillment of Desire. *Unknown.* TrGrPo

What wonder, Percy, that with jealous rage. To Percy Shelley: On the Degrading Notions of Deity. Leigh Hunt. Son

What wonders now I have to pen, sir. The Female Husband, Who Had Been Married to Another Female for Twenty-one Years. *Unknown.* CoMu

What wondrous life is this I lead! Andrew Marvell. *Fr.* Garden, The ("How vainly men themselves amaze"). ArNa; AWP; BLPL; BoNaP; CH; ChTr; HAP; InPS; InvP; JCP; LiTB; MeLP; NIP; NOBE; NoP; OAEL-1; PoEL-2; PoLF; PoRA; PPP; SeCP; SeCV-1; TEP; TrGrPo

What Wondrous Love Is This. *At. to* Alex Means. AH, 2 *vers.*

What wondrous pretty things I've seen. Young Master's Account of a Puppet Show. John Marchant. OxBChV

What wonder'rous projects formed the fickle fair? The Nunnery. Anna Williams. ECWP

What Word Did the Greeks have for It? Richard Howard. BAP-91

What word have you, interpreters, of men. Of Heaven Considered as a Tomb. Wallace Stevens. PoA

What words are these have fallen from me. Tennyson. *Fr.* In Memoriam A. H. H. EBEV; EBVV, *abr.*; OAEL-2, *abr.*; PeECV, *abr.*

What words begin with X? John Travers Moore *and* Margaret Moore *and* Margaret Moore. SiSoPo

What Words Have Passed. Milton. *Fr.* Paradise Lost. EPCY; TrCP

What worth to me the seven treasures. An Elegy on the Death of Furuhi. Okura. DL

What would earth do without her blessed boobs. Yes, What? Robert Francis. LCAP

What Would I Do White? June Jordan. NMM

What would I do with these strange tears in a cold night? Strange Tears. Liu Ya-tzu, *tr. fr. Chinese by* Wu-chi Liu. SuSp

What would I do without this world faceless incurious. Samuel Beckett. NoAM; NOIV

What Would I Give? Christina Rossetti. OPOP; OxBSP

What would it be like. A Sacred Grove. Fran Winant. BrRo

What would the world be, once bereft. Wildness. Gerard Manley Hopkins. *Fr.* Inversnaid. EaPr; OtMeF

What would this Man? Now upward will he soar. Pope. *Fr.* Essay on Man, An. HeIP

What Would Tom Paine Do? Edward Sanders. PoBeRe

What would we do in this world of ours. The Dreams Ahead. Edwin Carlile Litsey. PoToHe

What would you buy? *(LL)* Dream-Pedlary. Thomas Lovell Beddoes. BoTP; CH; EnRP; FaBoBe; HAP; LiTB; NOBE; OBEV; OBNC; OtMeF; OxAEP-2; PoEL-4; TrGrPo; WiR

What Would You Fight For? D. H. Lawrence. OxBSP

What would you have? Your gentleness shall force. Shakespeare. *Fr.* As You Like It. OxAEP-1

What would you say. A Dream of Maps. Matthew Sweeney. IB

What wourde is that that chaungeth not. Sir Thomas Wyatt. AAS

What year is this? Who can truthfully say? This Age. Raymond R. Patterson. NBV

What Yo' Gwine to Do When Yo' Lamp Burn Down? *Unknown.* BPo

What you are doing and where you are going. *(LL)* Letter to N. Y. Elizabeth Bishop. ArLo; CAPP; LPA; NoP; TwCP

What, you are stepping westward? Stepping Westward. Wordsworth. CH; EnRP; PoEL-4; SCGP

What you could not see in a face. *(LL)* Everything passes and vanishes. William Allingham. NOBVV

What You Goin' to Do When the Rent Comes 'Round? Andrew B. Sterling. OBAL

What you gwain to do when the meat gives out, my Baby? What Kin' o' Pants Does the Gambler Wear. *Unknown.* AS

What you have heard is true. The Colonel. Carolyn Forché. InPS; OBWP; SoSe

What you hear is not the wind only. *(LL)* Daily Bread. James Ulmer. UTF

What You Need. Kathleen Fraser. AmPA

What you see here is a colorful illusion. She Attempts to Refute the Praises That Truth, Which She Calls Passion, Inscribed on a Portrait of the Poet. Sister Juana Inés de la Cruz, *tr. fr. Spanish.* BoWoP

What You See Is Me. Barbara Gibbs. NYBP

What You Should Know to Be a Poet. Gary Snyder. NNaP; PoM

What you wanted I told you. A Rant. Frank O'Hara. ArLo

What your good leddy costs in coal? . . . I'll burn 'em down to part. *(LL)* McAndrew's Hymn. Kipling. OxBTC

What You're Teaching Me. Ron Schreiber. ETG

What Zimmer Would Be. Paul Zimmer. Poetsp

WhatCHU care. Whitey, Baby. James A. Emanuel. NBV

What'd you get, black boy? Mr. Roosevelt Regrets. Pauli Murray. PoBA

Whate'er Has Been. Sidney Lanier. Son

Whate'er is born of mortal birth. To Tirzah. Blake. *Fr.* Songs of Experience. EnRP; FHYEP; NAEL-2; NOBE; OAEL-2

Whate'er the passion — knowledge, fame, or pelf. Pope. *Fr.* Essay on Man, An. TrGrPo

Whate'er thou art, where'er thy footsteps stray. This, Too, Shall Pass Away. A. L. Alexander. PoToHe

Whate'er thy Countrymen have done. Written in the Beginning of Mezeray's History of France. Matthew Prior. NOBE; PoEL-3

Whatever boon is granted or withheld. *(LL)* So Fair, So Sweet, Withal So Sensitive. Wordsworth. EnRP; NoP; PFP

Whatever brawls disturb the street. Love between Brothers and Sisters. Isaac Watts. FaBoUs

Whatever city or country road. Double Elegy. Michael S. Harper. NoAM

Whatever clime we travel or explore. Evan Evans. *Fr.* Love of Our Country, The. AngWe

Whatever constitutes. The Act of Love. Robert Creeley. HAP

Whatever else be lost among the years. Eternal Values. Grace Noll Crowell. PoToHe

Whatever God's divine/ Decree. To Kiss God's Rod; Occasioned upon a Child's Sickness. Mildmay Fane, 2d Earl of Westmorland. BeJo

Whatever good is naturally done. Sonnet: Of Love, in Honor of His Mistress Becchina. Cecco Angiolieri, da Siena, *tr. fr. Italian by* Dante Gabriel Rossetti. AWP

Whatever Happened? Philip Larkin. Son

Whatever happened to the elephant. Hurrah for Thunder. Christopher Okigbo. HBAPE

Whatever happens with us, your body. Adrienne Rich. *Fr.* Twenty-one Love Poems. GLP; NALW; NoAM

Whatever he was doing, he looks up. Not Working. Henry Taylor. Poetr

Whatever his fortunes or birth. *(LL)* Nobility. Alice Cary. WBLP

Whatever I find if I search will be wrong. The Other. Ruth Fainlight. BrRo

Whatever I said and whatever you said. Husband and Wife. Arthur Guiterman. PoToHe

Whatever i say. *(LL)* Twenty-one years of my life you have been. Lucille Clifton. CrSp; MDDM

Whatever is here, it is. Confessions of the Life Artist. Thom Gunn. CMoP

Whatever Is — Is Best. Ella Wheeler Wilcox. BLPA; PWR

Whatever it is, it must have. American Poetry. Louis Simpson. CAPP; MoP; NoAM; NOBA; TAP

Whatever it is, it's a passion. Love in America. Marianne Moore. AiP; GOA

Whatever it is you're missing, whatever. Call Them Back. Chris Petrakos. GOYP

Whatever it was she had so fiercely fought. The Recognition of Eve. Karl Shapiro. *Fr.* Adam and Eve. ChIV-1; MoAB

Whatever it was: the grains of the glacier caked in the. Adrienne Rich. *Fr.* Shooting Script. FaBoWP; HCAP

Whatever sages say and fools, all's well. *(LL)* Being to Timelessness as It's to Time. E. E. Cummings. HAP; UnAS

Whatever they could be. The Unborn. John Daniel. FoLa

Whatever they said, those ten foot lips pouting across. A Violation. Richard Jackson. NAmP90

Whatever we do, whether we light. Dilemma. David Ignatow. VGW

Whatever went out from your mind. *(LL)* You Never Can Tell. Ella Wheeler Wilcox. BLPA; BLPL; PoToHe

Whatever went wrong, that week, was more than weather. A Hairline Fracture. Amy Clampitt. NoAM

Whatever while the thought comes over me. Dante, *tr. fr. Italian by* Dante Gabriel Rossetti. *Fr.* Vita Nuova, La. AWP

Whatever will rhyme with Summer. Summer. Sir John Betjeman. PeLi

Whatever you can do. Goethe. RaBo

Whatever you have to say, leave. These Days. Charles Olson. RaBo

Whatever You Say Say Nothing. Seamus Heaney. OBWP; OxBC

Whatever you want is yours. The Lay of the Battle of Tombland. Dunstan Thompson. LiTA

Whatever your eye alights on this morning is yours. Years of Indiscretion. John Ashbery. NOBA

Whatever's lost, it first was won. Elizabeth Barrett Browning. *Fr.* De Profundis. TrPWD

Whatever's Merely Wilful. E. E. Cummings. MeMAP

Whatif. Shel Silverstein. OTCP

What'll the Neighbours Say? Sandra Kerr. AIW

What'mmmIdoin'? Martial, *tr. fr. Latin by* Tony Harrison. FaBoBl

What'mmmIdoin'? slurs Lyris, feigning shock. What'mmmIdoin'? Martial, *tr. fr. Latin by* Tony Harrison. FaBoBl

What's a story when there's no one left to listen? The Last Sight of Xencha. Philip Gross. PWE

What's a toad like? Adman into Toad. Frank Polite. UL

What's all this hubbub and yelling. Armistice Day, 1918. Robert Graves. FaBoEH

What's an old man like you doing. Golden Age. Mac Hammond. EOEF

What's become of Waring. Waring. Robert Browning. OtMeF; PoEL-5

What's bought with love. That currency I'll pay. *(LL)* Know what I'm like? Some captain moors his ship. Ausiàs March. STV

What's de Use ob Wukin in de Summer Time at All. Maggie Pogue Johnson. CBWP-4

What's death, more than departure? The dead go. To Castara, Being to Take a Journey. William Habington. NOSC

What's fame? A fancied life in others' breath. Pope. *Fr.* Essay on Man, An. FHYEP

What's filling up the mirror? O, it is not I. The Fat Man in the Mirror. Robert Lowell. PoA

What's Going to Happen to the Tots? Noël Coward. NBLV

What's Good for the Soul Is Good for Sales. Richard Wilbur. NBLV

What's greater, pebble or pond? Orfce More, the Round. Theodore Roethke. ArLo

What's hallowed ground? Has earth a clod. Hallowed Ground. Thomas Campbell. BLPA

What's he that, in yon gilded coach elate. A Remonstrance. John Gerrard. NOEC

What's in a Name? Helen F. More. PAH

What's in a Name? Christina Rossetti. FaBoVe

What's in a name? What's in a name? Fame. Josephine D. Henderson Heard. CBWP-4

What's In It for Me? Edgar A. Guest. PoToHe

What's in the church. *Unknown.* RoPo

What's in the Cupboard? *Unknown.* CH; ChTr; GBP; OxNR

What's in there? *Unknown.* CH; OxNR

What's it like? The Late Train. Theodore Weiss. BTR

What's left but this to say of any war? (*LL*) *Vale* from Carthage. Peter Viereck. ArOW; LiTM; MoAmPo

What's matter but a hardening of the light? (*LL*) Hear the Bird of Day. David Campbell. NOBAu

What's Mo' Temptin' to de Palate? Maggie Pogue Johnson. CBWP-4

What's my sweetheart? — A laundress is she. Jeannette. Otto Julius Bierbaum, *tr. fr. German by* Jethro Bithell. AWP

What's My Thought Like? Thomas Moore. FaBoEE

"What's new?" — What's old? what's anything. S. T. Coleridge Dismisses a Caller from Porlock. Gerard Previn Meyer. GoYe

What's on this May morning in the hills? Ascension Thursday. Saunders Lewis, *tr. fr. Welsh by* Gwyn Morgan. OBWVE

What's poetic. In Defence of Poetry. Mafika Pascal Gwala. PeSAV

What's so urgent about this business you waste your heart on? (*LL*) To Tzŭ-chih: among the 'Flowers.' Li Shang-yin. PLT

What's sweeter than at the end of a summer's day. Thanksgiving. Kenneth Koch. VGW

What's That. Anne Sexton. LCAP

What's that approaching like dust like poverty. Charles Simic. LCAP

What's that cart that nobody sees. Every Day. Norman MacCaig. OBD

What's That Smell in the Kitchen? Marge Piercy. NBLV; NGP; NIP

"What's that that hirples at my side?" Heriot's Ford. Kipling. PoRA

What's that we see from far? the spring of Day. A Nuptial[l] Song, or Epithalamie [or Epithalamy], on Sir Clipseby Crew and His Lady. Robert Herrick. BeJo; CaPo; CBLP; JCP; PoEL-3; SeCP; SeCV-1

What's that you're telling me? The Love Charm. *Unknown, tr. fr. Chippewa Indian by* Jerome K. Rothenberg. STP

What's the balm. Alan Dugan. CAPP; SM

What's the best thing in the world? The Best. Elizabeth Barrett Browning. ArNa; CBCK; OxBSP

(Best Thing in the World, The.) EBVV; NOBVV

What's the greeting for a rajah riding on an elephant? Some Questions to Be Asked of a Rajah, Perhaps by the Associated Press. Preston Newman. FiBHP

What's the hurry? The ship's not sailing till. The Ship's Whistle. Tarapada Ray, *tr. fr. Hindi.* TSaS, *tr. by* Shyamasree Devi *and* P. Lal

What's the ingredience of your Perfume. A Simpler Recipe for Hell-Broth. Lady Jane Cavendish *and* Lady Elizabeth Brackley. CBCK

What's the Life of a Man? *Unknown.* OBET

What's the matter. Dickery Dean. Dennis Lee. TLR

"What's the matter, old chap?" "Well, I came." Joyce Johnson. PeLi

What's the news of the day. Mother Goose. OxNR
(Balloon, The.) ReMoGo

What's the Plural? *Unknown.* FaBoUs

What's the Railroad to Me? Thoreau. PoEL-4; TAP

What's the weather on about? The Weather. Gavin Ewart. OTCP

What's this? A dish for fat lips. The Shape of the Fire. Theodore Roethke. CMoP; LCAP; LiTA; MoAB; VCAP

What's this all about. Monk's Point. Art Lange. Jaz

What's this dull town to me? Robin Adair. Caroline Keppel. FaBoBe

What's this morn's bright eye to me. Morning Hymn. Joseph Beaumont. TrPWD

What's this that with such vigour fills my brest? Ambition. Mary Astell. KTR

What's to be hoped from seeing her again? Elegy. Goethe, *tr. fr. German by* John Frederick Nims. *Fr.* Trilogy of Passion. STV

What's today?/ A Monday? Question. Martin Sorescu, *tr. fr. Romanian by* Michael Hamburger. CBNP

What's under your nose? Immediate distance. Prospects. Tim Longville. VaA

What's up, today, with our lovers? The Lovers Go Fly a Kite. W. D. Snodgrass. NYBP

What's worse than this past century? "Anna Akhmatova," *tr. fr. Russian by* Barbara Einzig. BoWoP

What's wrong with you-zie? Her-zie. Stevie Smith. Mes

What's your name? Pudden Tame. *Unknown.* ChTr; FaBoNo

"What's your name?"/ "Mary Jane." *Unknown.* ISE

Whatso men sayn. Men Only Pretend. *Unknown.* MeEL

Whatsoe'er He bids you — do it! Leave the Miracle to Him. Thomas H. Allan. BLRP

Whatsoever thing I see. Love Dislikes Nothing. Robert Herrick. CBCK

Whatsume'er the failings on his part. Joe Gargery's Epitaph on His Father. Charles Dickens. *Fr.* Great Expectations. FaBoVe

Whaup o' the Reed., *sels.* Will H. Ogilvie.

Whaur are ye gaun. John Hielandman. *Unknown.* GBP

Whaur green abune the banks the links stretch oot. The Planticru. Robert Rendall. OxBS

Whaur yon broken brig hings owre. William Soutar. OxBS

Wheat. Diane Glancy. CRP

Wheat Ripening, The. John Clare. NTP

Wheear 'as tha been sin' ah saw thee? Ilkla Moor. *Unknown.* FaBoPP

Wheel, The. Aimé Césaire, *tr. fr. French by* Clayton Eshleman *and* Denis Kelly. NegPo

Wheel, The. Robert Hayden. BPo

Wheel, The. Julie N. Heifetz. BTR

Wheel, The. Edwin Muir. NoAM

Wheel, The. W. B. Yeats. GTBS-P; Poetr

Wheel is the most beautiful discovery of man and the only one, The. The Wheel. Aimé Césaire, *tr. fr. French by* Clayton Eshleman *and* Denis Kelly. NegPo

Wheel of Fortune, The. Thom Gunn. OxBC

Wheel of Fortune, not the sphere of Love, The. (*LL*) A Lover, upon an Accident Necessitating His Departure, Consults with Reason. Thomas Carew. CaPo

Wheel of the quivering Meat, The. Jack Kerouac. *Fr.* Mexico City Blues. NeAP; PoBeRe; PoM

Wheel Revolves, The. Kenneth Rexroth. NoAM

Wheelbarrow, The. Russell Edson. LCAP

Wheelbarrow. Eleanor Farjeon. FiBHP

Wheelchair Butterfly, The. James Tate. LCAP; NoAM

Wheeler at Santiago. James Lindsay Gordon. PAH

Wheeler's Brigade at Santiago. Wallace Rice. PAH

Wheels jammed and flaming on a metal sea. (*LL*) V-J Day. John Ciardi. ArOW

Wheels line up, pretty right, right, The. Cattle Loading. Gordon Mackay-Warna, *tr. fr. Aborigine by* Georg von Brandenstein. NOBAu

Wheer 'asta beän saw long and meä liggin' 'ere aloän? Northern Farmer: Old Style. Tennyson. EnVR

Wheesht, Wheesht. "Hugh MacDiarmid." ErPo; HAP; InPK; OxAEP-2

Whelming the dwellings of men, and the toils of the slow-/ footed oxen. Charles Kingsley. *Fr.* Andromeda. PeVV

When. Philip Appleman. BXAP

When. Sharon Olds. WoWa

When a Beau Goes In. Gavin Ewart. OBWP; OxBTC

When a Beautiful Woman Gets on the Jutiapa Bus. Belle Waring. NAmP90; PBCAP

When a brass sun staggers above the sky. Tramp. Richard Hughes. MoBrPo

When a brisk gale against the current blows. John Gay. *Fr.* Rural Sports. FM

When a brown person. Flipochinos. Cyn Zarco. UL

When a cat flea bit my scrotum. A Person Is Accidentally Rejuvenated in Old Age. Gavin Ewart. FaBoBl

When a certain great King, whose initial is G. An Ancient Prophecy. Philip Freneau. PAH

When a clatter came. Sounds of the Day. Norman MacCaig. RB

When a daffadill [or daffodil] I see. Divination by a Daffadill [or Daffodil]. Robert Herrick. CaPo; SeCV-1

When a daughter tries suicide. The Risk. Anne Sexton. BoWoP

When a disciple asked of Lu Chü how. The Sage in Unison. Harold Stewart. NOBAu

When a dream is born in you. A Pinch of Salt. Robert Graves. MoBrPo

When a feller hasn't got a cent. Fellowship. *Unknown.* BLPA

When a fellow loves a maiden. La Cucaracha. *Unknown.* AS

When a felon's not engaged in his employment. Policeman's Lot, A [or The]. W. S. Gilbert. *Fr.* Pirates of Penzance, The. NOBL; PeLV; TrGrPo

When a feverish groom in Armenia. Morris Bishop. PeLi

When a Friend Dies. Marge Piercy. HeIP

When a friend said to Leda: "Come on." Peter Alexander. PeLi

When a friend told a typist called Eve. Gordon Harper. PeLi

When a gentleman comes. Winthrop Mackworth Praed. *Fr.* Pledges, by a Ten-pound Householder. FaBoEH

When a goblin you have found. (*LL*) How to Tell Goblins from Elves. Monica Shannon. FaPON

When a green fox looks. Fox. David Campbell. CBAP

When a King Asks for a Chieftain's Daughter. Maturai Marutan Ilanakanar, *tr. fr. Tamil by* A. K. Ramanujan. PLW

When a little water does it? (*LL*) Cleanliness. Charles Lamb *and* Mary Lamb *and* Mary Lamb. OxBChV

When a lover's stiff prick stops your bum? (*LL*) Epigram: To Polycharmus. Martial. PeHV

When a man becomes tired of his life. Song, *Hamlet.* John F. Poole. BXAP

When a man can love no more. Basta! D. H. Lawrence. CBLP

When a man dies. "Anna Akhmatova," *tr. fr. Russian by* Richard McKane. OBD

When a man has grown a body. Simple Truths. William Heyen. BTR

When a Man Has Married a Wife. Blake. ErPo; FaBoEE; FF; OAEL-2

When a man hath no freedom to fight for at home. Byron. EnRP; FaBoEE; NAEL-2; NBLV; PAW; PFP; PoLF; TrGrPo; TRP

  (Stanzas: "When a man hath no freedom to fight for at home.") NoP; OxAEP-2; Poetr

When a man sleeps, often his dream will break. Hugo von Hofmannsthal, *tr. fr. German by* Michael Hamburger. *Fr.* Death and the Fool. OBD

When a Man Turns Homeward. Daniel Whitehead Hicky. PoToHe

When a man turns homeward through the moonfall. When a Man Turns Homeward. Daniel Whitehead Hicky. PoToHe

When a man's too old even to toss off, he. Robert Conquest. PeLi

When a Negro comes in question you may watch the Southern press. The Southern Press. L. A. J. Moorer. CBWP-3

When a new world is born, the old. Rattle. Peter Blue Cloud. HATNAP

When a sighing begins. Chansons d'Automne. Paul Verlaine, *tr. fr. French by* Arthur Symons. AWP

When a statue turns its real gaze. After Plotinus. William Stafford. PoA

When a tree falls in a forest. Bedtime Story. Charles Simic. AnAn

When a twister a-twisting will twist him a twist. John Wallis. FaBoNo, 1 *st.; OxNR, 1 st.*

  (Twister Twisting Twine.) ChTr, 3 *sts.*

When a Woman Blue. *Unknown.* AS

When a Woman Feels Alone. May Sarton. SRLS

"When a woman feels alone, when the room." When a Woman Feels Alone. May Sarton. SRLS

When A Woman Gets Blue. Norman Jordan. NBV

When a yesterday has faded from its page! (*LL*) The Story of Prince Agib. W. S. Gilbert. CBNP; FaBoCo

When Abraham Lincoln was shoveled into the tombs. Cool Tombs. Carl Sandburg. AmPP; BLPL; CMoP; HAP; HeIL; HeIP; MoAB; MoAmPo; MoP; NAAL-2; NoAM; NOBA; OxBSP; PoLF; TAP; TFi; TrGrPo

When Adam Day by Day. A. E. Housman. FiBHP

When Adam delf [*or* dalf]/ and Eve span. *Unknown.* FaBoVe

  (Peasant's Song, The.) FaBoPV, *diff. vers.*

  (Pointless Pride of Man, The.) MeEL

When Adam found his rib was gone. The Lady's-Maid's Song. John Hollander. ErPo; LiTM; TwCP

When Adam Walked in Eden Young. A. E. Housman. ChIV-1

When Adam Was First Created. *Unknown.* OBET

When, after storms that woodlands rue. A Requiem for Soldiers Lost in Ocean Transports. Herman Melville. PoEL-5

When after those, four ages very near. Michael Drayton. *Fr.* To Henry Reynolds, of Poets and Poesy. EPCY

When age hath made me what I am not now. Upon His Picture. Thomas Randolph. BeJo; NOBE

When age once snows upon your heart. (*LL*) Cupid's Call. James Shirley. BeJo; ErPo; NOSC

When air's chill north his noisome frosts shall blow. Winter. Hesiod, *tr. fr. Greek by* George Chapman. *Fr.* Georgics of Heisod, The. NOSC

When Alcuin taught the sons of Charlemagne. The Student's Tale. Longfellow. *Fr.* Tales of a Wayside Inn. AmPP

When Alexander Pope. E. C. Bentley. *Fr.* Clerihews. FiBHP

When Alexander Pope strolled in the city. Mr. Pope. Allen Tate. MoAB; NoAM; NOBA; TwCP; VGW

When Alkibié married. Archilochus, *tr. fr. Greek by* Guy Davenport. GrAn

When all about me memories arise. For My Mother. David Diop, *tr. fr. French by* Ellen Conroy Kennedy. NegPo

When all birds else do of their music fail. Money Makes the Mirth. Robert Herrick. CaPo

When all her robes are gone. (*LL*) My Love in Her Attire. *Unknown.* BLPL; CoGr; FF; GTBS; GTBS-P; HeIP; ImPo; LiTB; NIP; OxBSP; TFi

When All Is Done. Paul Laurence Dunbar. AAP

When all is done and said, in the end thus shall you find. Of a Contented Mind. Thomas, Lord Vaux. EIL; EnRePo

  (Pleasures of Thinking, The.) NoSic

When all is over and you march for home. Spoils. Robert Graves. HAP; Son; WeW

  (Spoils of Love, The.) NYBP

When all is ruin once again. (*LL*) To Be Carved on a Stone at Thoor Ballylee. W. B. Yeats. FaBoEE; IIP; NoAM; NoP

When all is so in peril, and so delicate! (*LL*) Extreme delicacy of this Easter morning, The. May Sarton. EaPr

When all is still within these walls. The Man's Prayer. T. A. Daly. TrPWD

When all mankind are free. (*LL*) John Brown's Prayer. *At. to* Charles Sprague Hall *and to* Thomas Brigham Bishop.

When All My Five and Country Senses See. Dylan Thomas. MoAB; MoBrPo; NoAM; PoA; Son

When all/ My waterfall. Her Time. Theodore Roethke. NAAL-2

When all my words were said. Enough. Digby Mackworth Dolben. EBVV

When all night long a chap remains. The Contemplative Sentry. W. S. Gilbert. *Fr.* Iolanthe. FiBHP

  (Private Willis's Song. IHNG

When all of us wore smaller shoes. Ancient Lights. Austin Clarke. BIrV; CMoP; IPY

When all our hopes are sown on stony ground. A Note of Humility. Arna Bontemps. PoNe

When all the days are hot and long. Swimming. Clinton Scollard. FaPON

When all the others were away at Mass. Seamus Heaney. *Fr.* Clearances. CIP; PBCIP; PNI

When all the rivers turn back again in our time. Wade in the Water. Robert Adamson. FaBoMA

When all the witches were haled to the stake and burned. King Duffus. Sylvia Townsend Warner. FaBoWP

When all the women in the transport. Pigtail. Tadeusz Rózewicz, *tr. fr. Polish by* Adam Czerniawski. PoSu

When All The World Is Young. Charles Kingsley. *See* When all the world is young, lad.

When all the world is young, lad. Young and Old. Charles Kingsley. *Fr.* Water Babies, The. BLPL; EBEV; FaBoBe; FaPoR; ImPo; OxAEP-2; OxBChV; PlP; PoLF

  (When All the World Is Young.) BoTP

When all this All doth pass from age to age. Fulke Greville. *Fr.* Caelica. EBEV; EnRePo; NoSic

"When all this is over," said the swineherd. Swineherd. Eiléan Ní Chuilleanáin. BIrV; CIP; FaBoWP; WPOW

When all was quiet and serene, a storm broke out at the dead. A Riot. Mrs. Henry Linden. CBWP-4

When all within is dark. From Thee to Thee. Solomon ibn Gabirol, *tr. fr. Hebrew by* Israel Abrahams. TrJP

When all your world of Beautie 's gone. (*LL*) To Dianeme. Robert Herrick. BeJo; CaPo; GTBS; GTBS-P; JCP; NOBE; NOSC; OBEV; SeCV-1; TrGrPo

When Alma Gluck. Conversations from Childhood: the Victrola. Joseph Langland. SM

When Alysandyr Our King Was Dede. *Unknown. See* Quhen [*or* Qwhen *or* When] Alexander [*or* Alysandyr] our kynge [*or* King] was dede.

When an amorous youth from Atlantis. C. Vita-Finzi. PeLi

When an obstinate fellow of Fife. Allan M. Laing. PeLi

When and where did you first. Sexual Privacy of Women on Welfare. Pinkie Gordon Lane. BlSi

When any mortal (even the most odd). E. E. Cummings. FaBoEE

When Aphrodite saw the *Aphrodite* of Knidos. *Unknown, tr. fr. Greek by* Peter Jay. GrAn

When approached by a person from Porlock. Richard Leighton Greene. PeLi

When April & dew brings primroses here. An Anecdote of Love. John Clare. NOBVV

When April with Its Sweet Showers. Chaucer. *See* Whan that Aprill[e] with his shoures [*or* shower] soote.

When April with its sweet showers. Chaucer. *See* Whan that Aprill[e] with his shoures [*or* shower] soote.

When are the children all happy and gay? Christmas Times. Maggie Pogue Johnson. CBWP-4

When arms and numbers both have failed. Aguinaldo. Bertrand Shadwell. PAH

When Arthur was homeless and broke. *Unknown.* PeHV

When as her lute is tuned to her voyce. Giles Fletcher the Elder. *Fr.* Licia. ESo

When Faction, in league with the treacherous Gaul. The Lords of the Main. Joseph Stansbury. PAH

When Faction threaten'd Britain's land. The National Savior. *Unknown.* FaBoEH

When fair Columbia was a child. The Daughter's Rebellion. Francis Hopkinson. PAH

When Faith and Love. Milton. *See* When faith and love which parted from thee never.

When faith and love which parted from thee never. Sonnet: On the Religious Memorie of Mrs. Catherine Thomason My Christian Freind Deceas'd Decem. 1646. Milton. ChIV-2
(Sonnet: When faith and love which parted from thee never.
OxAEP-1
(When Faith and Love.) PFP

When faith in God goes, man, the thinker, loses his greatest thought. Have You Lost Faith? *Unknown.* WBLP

When far-spent night persuades each mortal eye. Sir Philip Sidney. *Fr.* Astrophel and Stella. AAS; ESo, *sl. abr.*; GGP; HeIL, *Sonnets, I–CVIII and 11 Songs*; NoSic; PoE; Poetr; SCGP, *Sonnets, I–CVIII and 11 Songs*; SiPS, *Sonnets, I–CVIII and 11 Songs*; SiPSBD, *Sonnets, I–CVIII and 11 Songs*; Son

When Father Carves the Duck. Ernest Vincent Wright. BLPL; FaBV; NTCP; PoLF

When Father Decided He Did Not Love Her Anymore. Lynn Emanuel. NAmP90

When Father goes to town with me to buy my Sunday hat. When Polly Buys a Hat. E. Hill. BoTP

When father takes his spade to dig. The Robin. Laurence Alma-Tadema. BoTP

When Father's airplane stopped. When the Airplane Stopped. Barbara Drake. NGP

When fierce Pizarro's legions flew. The Revenge of America. Joseph Warton. ECEV; OBTV

When fire and drink were a shelter. The Essence Is Not in the Living. Mairtin O Direain, *tr. by* Douglas Sealy *and* Tomás MacSiomóin. BiHa

When First. Edward Thomas. NoAM

When first Apollo got my brain with childe. The Author to His Book. George Alsop. SCAP

When first Eudoxos cut his lovely hair. Euphorion, *tr. fr. Greek by* Alistair Elliot. GrAn

When first, fair mistress, I did see your face. To B. C. Sir John Suckling. CaPo

When first from sea I landed I had a roving mind. The Pride of Kildare. *Unknown.* OBET

When first I came here I had hope. When First. Edward Thomas. NoAM

When first I came to Louisville, some pleasure for to find. The Lily of the West. *Unknown.* AmFP

When first I ended, then I first began. Michael Drayton. *Fr.* Idea. ESo; TrGrPo

When first I ended, then I first begun. Michael Drayton. *Fr.* Idea's Mirrour. TrGrPo

When first I landed in Liverpool I went upon the spree. Off to Sea Once More. *Unknown.* OxBSS

When first I looked on thee, I lost mine eyes. (LL) Samson to His Delilah. Richard Crashaw. ChIV-1; TrGrPo

When first I saw our banner wave. Astraea at the Capitol. Whittier. PAH

When first I saw true beauty, and thy joys. Mount of Olives. Henry Vaughan *and* Thomas Stanley. ESCV; GeHe

When first I saw you in the curious street. German Prisoners. Joseph Lee. NSI

When first I took to cutlass, blunderbuss and gun. The Ballad of O'Bruadir. F. R. Higgins. OBMV

When first I walked here I hobbled. The Seekonk Woods. Galway Kinnell. NoAM

When first I was courtin' sweet Rosie O'Grady. Irish Song (Rosie O'Grady). Noël Coward. NBLV

When first I went a waggoner. The Jolly Waggoner. *Unknown.* OBET

When first in this country a stranger. The Green Mossy Banks of the Lee. *Unknown.* OBET

When first mine eyes beheld your princely name. Owen Tudor to Queen Katherine. Michael Drayton. *Fr.* England's Heroical Epistles. NoSic

When first mine eyes did view and mark. Sir Thomas Wyatt. SiPS; SiPSBD

When first mine infant-ear. Christendom. Thomas Traherne. PoEL-2

When first my lines [or verse] of heav'nly [or heavenly] joy[e]s made mention. Jordan. George Herbert. GeHe; NAEL-1; OAEL-1; OBWVE; PPP; SeCP
(Jordan "When first my lines of heav'nly joy[e]s made mention".) ESCV; NOSC

When first on board of a man-of-war. The Jolly Sailor's True Description of a Man-of-War. *Unknown.* OxBSS

When first the busy, clumsy tongue is stilled. Supersensual. Evelyn Underhill. WGRP

When first the college rolls receive his name. Samuel Johnson. *Fr.* Vanity of Human Wishes, The: The Tenth Satire of Juvenal Imitated. EBEV; ECEV; NOEC; NoP; OAEL-1; OBSV; OxAEP-1; PoEL-3; PrIm; TEP; TFi
(Scholar's Life, The.) NOBE

When first the fiery-mantled sun. Ode to Winter. Thomas Campbell. GTBS; GTBS-P

When first thou didst entice to thee my heart. Affliction. George Herbert. ESCV; FHYEP; GeHe; JCP; LiTB; MeLP; NAEL-1; NOBE; NoP; NOSC; SeCP

When first thou didst even from the grave. Disorder and Frailty. Henry Vaughan. ChIV-1

When first thou on me, Lord, wrought'st thy sweet print. The Ebb and Flow. Edward Taylor. AmPP; SCAP

When first thy eies unveil, give thy soul leave. Rules and Lessons. Henry Vaughan *and* Thomas Stanley. ESCV

When first thy sweet and gracious eye. The Glance. George Herbert. ESCV

When first we met we did not guess. Robert Bridges. OxBSP

When first you sang a song to me. Your Songs. Gwendolyn B. Bennett. CDC

When fishes flew and forests walked. The Donkey. G. K. Chesteron. ChIV-2; CoGr; EBEvV; FaBV; FaPoB; FaPoR; InPK; MoBrPo; OBEV; PoLF; RB; WGRP

When fishes set umbrellas up. Christina Rossetti. *Fr.* Sing-Song. FM

When fivepence a solid meal cannot supply. The Volunteer. *Unknown.* NOEC

When flighting time is on, I go. The Birdcatcher. Ralph Hodgson. MoBrPo

When Flora Had Ourfret the Firth. *Unknown.* NoP; ScCV

When fog come creepin' over Beccles. Molly Fitton. BXAP

When for eternal worlds we steer. Vain World Adieu. *Unknown.* AmFP

When for the thorns with which I long, too long. The Coronet. Andrew Marvell. ESCV; FHYEP; GeHe; MeLP; NAEL-1; NOCV; NoP; NOSC; PoE; SCGP; SeCV-1; TOF

When forehead full of torments hot and red. Chercheuses de Poux, Les. Rimbaud, *tr. by* T. Sturge Moore. *Fr.* Illuminations. AWP

When formed our band, we are all well manned. California. *Unknown.* AS

When fortune, blind goddess, she fled my abode. My Poor Black Bess. *Unknown.* FaBoEH

When fortune's blind goddess had shied my abode. Dick Turpin and Black Bess. *Unknown.* AmFP

When Fortune's shield protects thee, then beware. Fortune's Treachery. Judah Halevi, *tr. fr. Hebrew by* Solomon Solis-Cohen. TrJP

When forty winters shall besiege thy brow. When Forty Winters. Shakespeare. *Fr.* Sonnets. BLPL; FF; HeIP; ImPo; LiTB; NoSic; SCGP; Son; TEP

When foxes eat the last gold grape. Escape. Elinor Wylie. LiTA; MoAmPo

When Francis preached love to the birds. Saint Francis and the Birds. Seamus Heaney. NTP; TIRV

When Francus comes to solace with his whore. In Francum. Sir John Davies. FaBoEE

When Freedom, dressed in bloodstained vest. Ode to Liberty. Thomas Chatterton. *Fr.* Goddwyn. TrGrPo

When Freedom, fair Freedom, her banner display'd. Truxton's Victory. *Unknown.* PAH

When Freedom, from her mountain height. The American Flag. Joseph Rodman Drake. AnAmPo; FaBoBe; GN; PAH; VPP; WBLP

When frequent rains, and gentle show'rs descend. Nathaniel Weekes. *Fr.* Barbados. PBCV

When from afar these mountain tops I view. The Sonnet of the Mountain. Mellin de Saint-Gelais, *tr. fr. French by* Austin Dobson. AWP

When from dark error's subjugation. N. A. Nekrasov, *tr. fr. Russian by* Juliet Soskice. *Fr.* Propos of the Wet Snow, A. NAWM-2

When from my fumbling hand the tired pen falls. The Scribe's Prayer. Robert W. Service. TrPWD

When from the blossoms of the noiseful day. To My Friend. Francis Thompson. PoA

When from the gates of Paradise fair Eve. The Vision of Eve. H. Cordelia Ray. CBWP-3

When from the hush of this cool wood. The Cell. George Rostrevor Hamilton. TrPWD

When from the pallid sky the sun descends. Winter ("When from the pallid sky the sun descends.") James Thomson. *Fr.* Seasons, The. OAEL-1; OxBS

When, from the tower whence I derive love's heaven. Sonnet. *Unknown.* Fr. Zepheria. EIL

When from the Vallais we had turned. Wordsworth. *Fr.* Prelude [or, Growth of a Poet's Mind], The. EnRP; OAEL-2; PoEL-4; TOF

When from the world, I shall be tane. To My Husband. "Eliza." KTR

When frost and dew have caused a hundred plants to wither. In Imitation of T'ao P'eng-tse. Wei Ying-wu, *tr. fr. Chinese by* Irving Y. Lo. SuSp

When frost will not suffer to dike and to hedge. December's Husbandry. Thomas Tusser. *Fr.* Five Hundred Points of Good Husbandry. NoSic

When Gabriel (no blest spirit more kind or fair). Gabriel's Appearance. Abraham Cowley. *Fr.* Davideis. NOSC

When Gaffer be dead for a month or more. Martin Fagg. BXAP

When gardens shone with flowery pride. On a Little Boy's Endeavouring to Catch a Snake. Thomas Foxton. OxBChV

When Gauguin was visiting Fiji. Victor Gray. NOBL

When genial Spring first bears the mating thrush. Albery Allson Whitman. *Fr.* Octoroon, The. AAP

When geometric diagrams and digits. "Novalis," *tr. fr. German by* Robert Bly. NU

When George the King would punish folk. How We Became a Nation. Harriet Prescott Spofford. PAH

When George the Third was reigning a hundred years ago. A Ballad for a Boy. William Johnson Cory. FaPoR; OxBChV

  (Two Captains, The.) FaPoR

When George's Grandmamma was told. George. Hilaire Belloc. FiBHP

When getting my nose in a book. A Study of Reading Habits. Philip Larkin. InPK; NOBL; PPP

When God at first made Man. The Pulley. George Herbert. AWP; ChIV-1; EBEvV; FHYEP; GeHe; GTBS; GTBS-P; HAP; HeIP; ImPo; InPK; InPS; LiTB; Mes; NAEL-1; NOBE; NOCV; NoP; NOSC; OAEL-1; OBEV; OtMeF; OxAEP-1; PPP; PrIm; SCGP; SeCP; SeCV-1; TEP; TFi; TrGrPo

  (Gifts of God, The.) GTBS; GTBS-P

When God created Paradise. The Thing That People Do. James Fenton *and* John Fuller. FaBoBl

When God created thee, one would believe. Lady Mary Wortley Montagu. *Fr.* Verses Addressed to the Imitator of the First Satire of the Second Book of Horace. ECWP

When God Descends with Men to Dwell. Hosea Ballou I. AH

When God, disgusted with man. Crow Blacker than Ever. Ted Hughes. TEP

When God had finished Master Messerin. Sonnet: Of the Making of Master Messerin. Rustico di Filippo, *tr. fr. Italian by* Dante Gabriel Rossetti. AWP

When God Lets My Body Be. E. E. Cummings. MoAB; MoAmPo; NOBA; PFP

When God makes a great Man he intends all others to crush him. Arthur Hugh Clough. *Fr.* Amours de Voyage. NOBVV; OBSV

When God shall sweetning be. (*LL*) God Makes a Path. Roger Williams. PAH; WGRP

When gods had framed the sweet of women's face. (*LL*) Love and Jealousy. Robert Greene. CBLP; EIL

When gods had framed the sweet of women's face. Love and Jealousy. Robert Greene. CBLP; EIL

When God's parachute failed. Religion Back Home. William Stafford. OBAL

When gold was first discovered at Coloma, near the hill. The National Miner. *Unknown.* AmFP

When good King Arthur ruled this [*or* the] land. Mother Goose. FaBoNu; OxNR

  (King Arthur.) NTP

When good may have, as well as bad, their prime! (*LL*) Doth then the world go thus, doth all thus move? William Drummond of Hawthornden. GTBS; GTBS-P

When good St. David, as old writs record. In Honour of St. David's Day. *Unknown.* OBWVE

When Goody O'Grumpity baked a cake. Goody O'Grumpity. Carol Ryrie Brink. FaPON

When Grandmamma fell off the boat. Indifference. Harry Graham. NBLV

When grapes turn. Jalal al-Din Rumi, *tr. fr. Persian by* Robert Bly. EnlH

When Graphicus sat by the baths. Strato, *tr. fr. Greek.* PeHV

When griping grief the heart doth wound. Music's Silver Sound. Shakespeare. *Fr.* Romeo and Juliet. GN

When groping farms are lanterned up. A Country God. Edmund Blunden. MoBrPo

When Gullion died (who knows not Gullion?). Joseph Hall. *Fr.* Virgidemiarum. NoSic

When Gwen heard at last. In Memoriam. W. J. Gruffydd, *tr. fr. Welsh by* R. Gerallt Jones. OBWVE

When,/ Halting in front of it, I look. Hitomaro, *tr. fr. Japanese by* Arthur Waley. *Fr.* Shui Shu. AWP

When hands are joined and head bows in the dark. (*LL*) Penal Law. Austin Clarke. BoLoP; GTBS-P; IPY; NOIV

When, hardly moving, you decorate night's hush. The Waters of Life. Humbert Wolfe. MoBrPo

When harvest is done all thing placed and set. Thomas Tusser. *Fr.* Hundreth Good Poyntes of Husbandry, A. FaBoUs

When have I last looked on. Lines Written in Dejection. W. B. Yeats. NAs

When he breathed his last breath it was he. The Moment of My Father's Death. Sharon Olds. NAmP90; NIP

When he brings home a whale. Naughty Boy. Robert Creeley. HeIP; NoAM; NOBA

When He Came, *sels.* Dorothee Sölle. "He needs you." CrSp

When he came home Mother said he looked. My Father's Martial Art. Stephen Shu Ning Liu. InPK

When he came out, into the world. Born Tying Knots. Samuel Makidemewabe, *tr. fr. Cree Indian by* Howard Norman. STP

When he comes home at night. Wasp Sex Myth (One). Anselm Hollo. PoM

When he comes home from work. Allegory of Death and Night. Frank Stanford. MT

When he comes up to the bedroom. Palladas, *tr. fr. Greek by* Tony Harrison. GrAn

When he did read how did we flock to hear. Thomas Vaughan. *Fr.* On The Death of an Oxford Proctor. AngWe

When he does he will no longer recognize me. (*LL*) The New Wife. Ng Shao. OHMPC

When he got into bed. Damon and Pythias. Robert Creeley. LCAP

When he got out of bed the world had changed. The Drainage. Peter Didsbury. PWE

When he had grown old. (*LL*) The Choirmaster's Burial. Thomas Hardy. PeECV

When He Heard the Owls at Midnight. Longfellow. *Fr.* Song of Hiawatha, The. ArNa; FM

When he is ready he is raised and carried. The Glass King. Eavan Boland. CIP

When he killed the Mudjokivis. George A. Strong. *See* He [*or* When he] killed the noble Mudjokivis.

When he lends any poet about the Town. (*LL*) Session[s] of the Poets, A ("A session was held the other day.") Sir John Suckling. BeJo; SeCV-1

When he lies in the night away from her. The Jealous Lovers. Donald Hall. NYBP

When he married her he said. Thalamos. Peter Kane Dufault. ErPo

When he pressed his lips to my mouth. Steve Kowit. UL

When he pushed his bush of black hair off his brow. Sicilian Cyclamens. D. H. Lawrence. NoAM

When he raised his eyes he'd see peaches rolling all round him over hills and valleys. (*LL*) Chasing the Sun. Jiang He. SpMi

When he raped a young maid in a train. *Unknown.* PeLi

When he said. What She Said. Nannakaiyar, *tr. fr. Tamil by* A. K. Ramanujan. PLW

When he said *Mary,* she did not at once. Contemplations of Mary. Roy McFadden. PNI

When he sailed into the harbor. Korinna, *tr. fr. Greek by* Willis Barnstone. BoWoP

When he saw her. *Unknown, tr. fr. Sanskrit by* John Brough. TOF

When He Says So We Dance in All Directions — Wow! *Unknown, tr. fr. Seneca Indian by* Jerome K. Rothenberg *and* Richard Johnny John. STP

When he sit, he sit on what he ain't got almost. (*LL*) The Frog. *Unknown.* MoShBr; NBLV; NTCP; RB

When He Spoke to Me of Love. M. A. Mokhomo, *tr. fr. Sotho by* Dan Kunene *and* Jack Cope. PeSA

When he the nation's heart had won. The Presidents. L. A. J. Moorer. CBWP-3

When He Thought Himself Contemned. Thomas Howell. EIL

When he understood the power. Cassandra. Cynthia Fuller. NWP

When He was barely five. The Boyhood of Christ. St. Columbanus. NOIV

When he was dead. (*LL*) Old Mother Hubbard. Sarah Catherine Martin. FaBoBe; OxNR; ReMoGo

When he was eight years old he had become. Words and Monsters. Vernon Scannell. OxBC

When he was shot he toppled to the ground. Shot Who? Jim Lane! Merrill Moore. MoAmPo

When he was young, he broke horses. The Passion Drinker. Anita Endrezze-Danielson. VoR

When he went blundering back to God. Of One Self-slain. Charles Hanson Towne. WGRP

When He Who Adores Thee. Thomas Moore. *See* When he who adores thee has left but the name.

When he who adores thee has left but the name. Pro Patria Mori. Thomas Moore. GTBS; GTBS-P; HoPM; OxAEP-2
(When He Who Adores Thee.) HoPM

When he, who, from the scourge of wrong. No Man Knoweth His Sepulchre. Bryant. AnAmPo

When he, who is the unforgiven. The Unforgiven. E. A. Robinson. CMoP

When he whose empire is in clouds saw Hector bent to wage. Hector Arms. Homer, *tr. fr. Greek. Fr.* Iliad, The. NOSC, *tr. by* George Chapman

When He Would Have His Verses Read. Robert Herrick. BeJo; CaPo; NOBE; NOSC; SCGP; SeCV-1

When Heaven in mercy gives thy prayers return. Hezekiah's Display. John Keble. ChIV-1

When Heav'n would kindly set us free. Edward Young. OBF

When Helen first saw wrinkles in her face. Walter Savage Landor. *Fr.* Ianthe. EnLoPo

When Helen Lived. W. B. Yeats. CMoP

When Henri Toussaints. Henri Toussaints. Cheryl Savageau. ETG

When Henry was a baby. Black Henry. Tejumola Ologboni. NBV

When her arms were no longer. From Underneath. Stephen Dunn. FoLa

When her need for you dies. In Her Only Way. Robert Graves. OxBSP

When Hermocrates the Miser lay in bed. Lucilius, *tr. fr. Greek by* Peter Porter. GrAn

When he's got a union wife. (*LL*) Union Maid. Woody Guthrie. SWP

When his bones are as seaweed, when his sweet tongue is parched. The White Rainbow. Starr Nelson. GoYe

When His Excellency Prince Norodom Chantaraingsey. Dead Soldiers. James Fenton. NoAM; OBTV; OBWP

When his hour for death had come. Osceola. Walt Whitman. NAAL-1

When his telephone rings at 3 A.M. The Backward Strut. Robert McDowell. UTF

When hit come ter de question er de female vote. Brother Baptis' on Woman Suffrage. Rosalie Jonas. BlSi

When holy Patrick full of grace. The White Lake. *Unknown, tr. fr. Irish by* Robin Flower. TIRV

When Home We Return. Susanna Blamire. ECWP

When home we return, after youth has been spending. When Home We Return. Susanna Blamire. ECWP

When Hope Comes Back. Gu Cheng, *tr. fr. Chinese by* Donald Finkel *with* Chang Sheng-Tai. SpMi

When Howitzers Began. Hayden Carruth. Poetsp

When I a verse shall make. His Prayer to Ben Jonson [*or* Johnson]. Robert Herrick. BeJo; CaPo; JCP; NAEL-1; NoP; NOSC; OxBoLi; OxBSP; PeLV; SeCV-1; TrGrPo

When I Admire the Greatness. Jacob Steendam, *tr. fr. Dutch.* AH

When I admire the rose. The Rose. Thomas Lodge. *Fr.* Life and Death of William Longbeard, The.
(Fancy, A.) EiL

When I am a sea-flower. Fantasia. Rose Terry Cooke. AmWP

When I am alone. The Fisherman's Wife. Amy Lowell. BoWoP

When I am alone I am happy. Waiting. William Carlos Williams. SAmP

When I am an old woman I shall wear purple. Warning. Jenny Joseph. AIW; FaBoWP; GOYP; OxBTC; PWE

When I Am Dead. Georgia Douglas Johnson. CDC

When I Am Dead. George MacBeth. OxBTC

When I Am Dead. *Unknown.* OxBoLi

When I Am Dead. James Edward Wilson. PoLF

When I am dead, and Doctors know not why. The Damp[e]. John Donne. NOSC; SeCP

When I am dead and over me bright April. I Shall Not Care. Sara Teasdale. MoAmPo; TrGrPo; UnPo

When I am dead and thou wouldst try. *Unknown.* NOSC

When I am dead, even then. Then. Muriel Rukeyser. GLP; LCAP

When I am dead, I hope it may be said. On His Books. Hilaire Belloc. FaBoCo; FaBoEE; MoBrPo; NBLV; OxBoLi; WeW
(Epigram.) OtMeF

When I am dead and I want you to dress me. When I Am Dead. *Unknown.* OxBoLi

When I am dead, my dearest. Christina Rossetti. AWP; BoLoP; CH; CoGr; DL; EBEV; FF; GBL; InPS; MeMBP; NAEL-2; NOBE; NOBVV; NoP; OAEL-2; OBD; OBEV; PlP; Poetr; PoLF; PoRA; SCV; TFi; WPE
(Requiem. OtMeF
(Song: "When I am dead, my dearest.") EBEvV; GGP; OxAEP-2
(When I Am Dead My Dearest.) ELP; LiTB; TrGrPo

When I am dead, no pageant train. Dirge of Alaric the Visigoth. Edward Everett. BeLS

When I am dead, withhold, I pray, your blooming legacy. When I Am Dead. Georgia Douglas Johnson. CDC

When I am dead you'll find it hard. He and She. Eugene Fitch Ware. PoLF

When I am free — I will be free! (*LL*) Southern Africa. Nguno Wakolele. PeSAV

When I am gone. Josephine D. Henderson Heard. AAP; CBWP-4

When I am gone. Ute Mountain. Charles Tomlinson. RB

When I am grown to man's estate. Robert Louis Stevenson.
(Looking Forward.) NBLV; OxBChV

When I am living in the Midlands. The South Country. Hilaire Belloc. MoBrPo; OxAEP-3

When I am no one. (*LL*) Wish for a Young Wife. Theodore Roethke. MoP; NAAL-2; NoAM; NoP; OxBSP; TAP

When I Am Old. Caroline A. B. Mason. BLPA

When I am old. Song: "When I am old." Denis Glover. *Fr.* Sings Harry. PeNZ

When I am old and long turned gray. 2001: The Tennyson/ Hardy Poem. Gavin Ewart. FaBoCo

When I am only fit to go to bed. Resignation. Bliss Carman. AnAmPo

When I am playing by myself. Water Noises. Elizabeth Madox Roberts. BoNaP

When i am quit forgotten. (*LL*) Elizabeth Walters is my name. Elizabeth Walters. FaBoVe

When I am sad and weary. Celia Celia. Adrian Mitchell. FaBoEE

When I am the sky. Denise Levertov. NALW; PoM

When I am very earnestly digging. Pause. Mary Ursula Bethell. PeNZ

When I arrived some clansmen had already come. The Wood-Cutter. Lupenga Mphande. HBAPE

When I ask Daddy. Ask Mummy Ask Daddy. John Agard. OTCP

When I ask what things they fear. Fears of the Eighth Grade. Toi Derricotte. InPS

When I asked for fish in the restaurant facing the Ohio River. Carl Sandburg. *Fr.* Whiffs of the Ohio River at Cincinnati. PoE

When I asked the very old man. Quotations. George Oppen. NNaP

When I awake. I Forget. Yoshihara Sachiko, *tr. fr. Japanese by* Kenneth Rexroth *and* Ikuko Atsumi. WPJ

When I Awake I Am Still with Thee. Harriet Beecher Stowe. *See* Still, Still, with Thee.

When I awake in the early mist. Very Early. Karla Kuskin. PDV

When I Awoke. Raymond R. Patterson. NBV; PoBA

When I awoke this morning. The Blue Animals. Jon Anderson. AmPA; SM

When I awoke with cold. Coffee. J. V. Cunningham. MoAmPo; PrIm; VGW

When I began my love to sow. Husbandry. William Hammond. JCP

When I beheld the poet blind, yet bold. On Mr. Milton's Paradise Lost. Andrew Marvell. EPCY; JCP; NOSC

When I behold a forrest spread. Art above Nature, to Julia. Robert Herrick. BeJo; NOSC

When I behold Becchina in a rage. Sonnet: Of Becchina in a Rage. Cecco Angiolieri, da Siena, *tr. fr. Italian by* Dante Gabriel Rossetti. AWP

When I behold how black, immortal ink. Silet. Ezra Pound. MoAB; MoAmPo; Son

When I behold the havoc and the spoil. Planting. George Wither. *Fr.* Collection of Emblemes, Ancient and Moderne, A. NOSC

When I behold the heavens as in their prime. Anne Bradstreet. *Fr.* Contemplations. AmPP; EAP; PBWP; PoEL-3, *abr.*; SCAP; WPE, *abr.*

When I bethinke me on that speech whyleare. Spenser. *Fr.* Faerie Queene, The. NoSic; OAEL-1

When I bethought me well, under the restless sun. The Earl of Surrey. *Fr.* Paraphrase of Part of the Book of Ecclesiates, A. ChIV-1

When I Blink. Gu Cheng, *tr. fr. Chinese by* Donald Finkel *with* Chang Sheng-Tai. SpMi

When I built upon sand. Foundations. Leopold Staff, *tr. fr. Polish by* Adam Czerniawski. PoSu

When I burned our leaves, a wind from the dark. Looking West. William Stafford. NYBP

When I but hear her sing, I fare. Upon a Rare Voice. Owen Felltham [*or* Feltham]. NOSC

When I but think upon the great dead days. Piere Vidal Old. Ezra Pound. MoAB

When I Buy Pictures. Marianne Moore. OxBA

When I call to you, God. Contact. John F. Deane. TIRV

When I came back, he was gone. My Father's Leaving. Ira Sadoff. AmPA

When I Came from Colchis. W. S. Merwin. VGW

When I came to show you my summer cottage. Summer. Josephine Miles. FaBoWP; WPE

When I can hold a stone within my hand. Rumination. Richard Eberhart. LiTA; LiTM

When I can read my title clear. Ninety-fifth. Isaac Watts. AmFP

When I carefully consider the curious habits of dogs. Meditatio. Ezra Pound. FaBoCh; OBAL

When I catch sight of your fair head. Sonnet. Louise Labé, tr. by Joan Keefe and Richard Terdiman. PBWP

When I chose your name for mine. Lawrence O'Toole. Aidan Carl Mathews. IB

When I come back to my father's house. Galway Kinnell. Fr. Memories of My Father. RaBo

When I come down to sleep death's endless night. My City. James Weldon Johnson. CDC; PoNe

When I come groping back through mists of sleep. Mortal Combat. Countess Alice Fay di Castagnola. GoYe

When I consider everything that grows. Shakespeare. Fr. Sonnets. AWP; BLPL; NAEL-1; NoSic; SCGP; Son; TEP; TrGrPo

When I consider how my life is spent. Reminiscent Reflection. Ogden Nash. FaBoCo

When I Consider How My Light Is Spent. Milton. See When I consider how my light is spent.

When I consider how my light is spent. On His Blindness. Milton. FaPoB; HeIL; InPK; NAEL-1; PoE; Poetr
(On His Blindness. AWP; ChTr; FaBV; GGP; GN; GTBS; HAP; HeIP; ImPo; LiTB; NOBE; OBEV; PoEL-3; PoLF; PoRA; PrIm; SoSe; TFi; TrGrPo; TRP; WeW
(Sonnet: "When I consider how my light is spent.") NOSC
(Sonnet: When I Consider.) ChIV-2
(Sonnet.) EBEvV
(When I Consider How My Light Is Spent.) SCGP

When I consider Life and its few years. Tears. Lizette Woodworth Reese. AmWP; AnAmPo; MoAmPo; WGRP

When I consider men of golden talents. So That's Who I Remind Me Of. Ogden Nash. BLPL; PoLF

When I consider the many hours spent. Lament of a Subwayite. Eugene O'Neill. UV

When I Consider Thy Heavens. Bible, O.T., paraphrased by Sir Thomas Wyatt. Fr. Psalms. AWP; FaPON, sts. 3–5; NAWM-1

When I contemplate o'er me. The Night Serene. Luís de León, tr. fr. Spanish by Thomas Walsh. TrJP

When I couldn't he always discussed things. Action Would Kill It/ A Gamble. Robert Adamson. CBAP; FaBoMA

When I crept over the hill, broken with tears. The Comforters. Dora Sigerson Shorter. CH

When I did wake this morn from sleep. Early Morn. W. H. Davies. CH

When I Die. Fenton Johnson. CDC; PoNe

When I/ die/ I'm sure. The Rebel. Mari Evans. CRP; IHMS; PoBA

When I died, the circulating library. Seth Compton. Edgar Lee Masters. Fr. Spoon River Anthology. LiTA

When I died they washed me out of the turret with a hose. (LL) The Death of the Ball Turret Gunner. Randall Jarrell. ArOW; CAPP; ClHu; CMoP; FF; HAP; HeIP; HoPM; InPK; LCAP; LiTM; MoAmPo; MT; NAAL-2; NAs; NIP; NoAM; NOBA; NoP; OBD; OBWP; OxBA; PoE; Poetr; PoWW; PPP; PrIm; RB; SoSe; TAP; TFi; UnPo; VCAP; VGW

When I do count the clock that tells the time. Shakespeare. Fr. Sonnets. AWP; EIL; EnRePo; HeIP; InPS; NAEL-1; NoP; NoSic; OAEL-1; SCGP; Son; TEP

When I do it, I remember how it was with us. Making Love to Myself. James L. White. GLP

When I dragged the rotten log. Kenneth Rexroth. Fr. Signature of All Things, The. BoNaP; NNaP; NU

When I Drink I Become the Joy of Faggots. Dorothy Allison. GLP

When I drive cab. After Anacreon. Lew Welch. Fr. Taxi Suite. NeAP; PoBeRe; PoM

When I entered the book of myths. The Book of Myths. Joy Harjo. SRLS

When I eye the sun, I do not know. Ode to Two Sisters in the Sun. Nellie Wong. SRLS

When I face north a lost Cree. Returned to Say. William Stafford. NaP

When I faded back to pass. Ties. Dabney Stuart. GrPl

When I fall asleep, and even during sleep. Baudelaire. Delmore Schwartz. TwCP; VGW

When I First Came Here. Edward Thomas. SCGP

When I first came here I had hope. When I First Came Here. Edward Thomas. SCGP

When I first came to live in Japan. The Merchant at Yokohama. Osman Edwards. Fr. Residential Rhymes. OBTV

When I first came to London, I rambled about. The Seeker. Matthew Green. ECEV

When I first learned how to write poetry. Shown to My Son Yü. Lu Yu, tr. fr. Chinese by Irving Y. Lo. SuSp

When I first opened my eyes. Autobiography. Janet Dubé. BrRo

When I first saw a woman after childbirth. Ishtar. Judith Wright. NALW; NoAM

When I first saw America. Poem by a Yellow Woman. Sook Lyol Ryu. WoWa

When I first set foot. Like an Orchid in Deep Muddy Water. Nilene O. A. Foxworth. AIW

When I found where we had crashed, in the snow. He Said. Jean Valentine. TAP

When I gaze at the sun. A Moment Please. Samuel Allen. PoBA

When I gaze upon the sky. Reflection from Sea and Sky. Walter Savage Landor. FaBoEE

When I get home from a day's shopping in a city street. Edna's Hymn. Barry Humphries. NOBAu

When I Get Time. Tom Masson. BLPA

When I get to heaven. Happy Day (or Independence Day). James Cunningham. JB

When I get up in the morning. Getting Up. Lilian McCrea. BoTP

When I go. After Grave Deliberation. Elizabeth Flynn. NBLV

When I go away from you. The Taxi. Amy Lowell. BoWoP; MoAmPo; VBLP

When I go back to earth. The Answer. Sara Teasdale. PoA

When I go musing all alone. The Authors [or Author's] Abstract of Melancholy. Robert Burton. Fr. Anatomy of Melancholy, The. NOSC

When I, Good Friends, Was Called to the Bar. W. S. Gilbert. Fr. Trial by Jury. NAEL-2

When I got home. Baby Lazarus. Jackie Kay. NBrP

When I got to the airport I rushed up to the desk. The Race. Sharon Olds. RaBo

When I grew up I went away to work. Whores. Margaret Walker. NALW

When I grow up, I plan to keep. Plans. Maxine W. Kumin. TLR

When I had firmly answered "No." The Last Ride Together (from Her Point of View). James Kenneth Stephen. BXAP; FaBoCo; UnPo

When I had met my love the twentieth time. Her Merriment. W. H. Davies. EnLoPo

When I had money, money, O! Money. W. H. Davies. OBEV; OBMV

When I Had Need of Him. Samuel Ellsworth Kiser. BLRP

When I had spread it all on linen cloth. The Wife's Tale. Seamus Heaney. CIP; IPY

When I have a house . . . as I sometime may. Vagabond House. Don Blanding. BLPA

When I have a wife at home? (LL) Soldier, Won't You Marry Me? Unknown. AmFP; OxBoLi; PeLV

When I have been dead for several years. Poet's Wish. Valery Larbaud, tr. fr. French by William Jay Smith. GrPl

When I Have Borne in Memory. Wordsworth. EnRP; GTBS; GTBS-P; MeMBP

When I have borne in memory what has tamed. When I Have Borne in Memory. Wordsworth. EnRP; GTBS; GTBS-P; MeMBP
(England, 1802, V.) OBEV

When I have crost the bar. (LL) Crossing the Bar. Tennyson. BLRP; ChIV-2; ClHu; CoGr; DL; EBVV; EBVVPR; FaBoRV; FaBV; FaPoR; FF; HeIP; ImPo; LiTB; NAEL-2; NOBE; NOBVV; NoP; OAEL-2; OBEV; OBNC; PeECV; PlP; PoLF; PoRA; PWR; SoSe; TEP; TFi; TrCP; TrGrPo; WBLP; WGRP

When I have ended, then I see. Laurence Housman. TrPWD

When I Have Fears that I May Cease To Be. Keats. AWP; BLPL; EBEV; EnRP; HAP; HeIP; HoPM; ImPo; InPS; LiTB; NAEL-2; NIP; NoP; OAEL-2; OBEV; OBNC; PoE; PoRA; PrIm; SCGP; Son; TEP; TFi; TrGrPo; UnPo

When I have grown foolish. Peregrine's Sunday Song. Elinor Wylie. NYBP

When I have heard small talk about great men. Grandeur of Ghosts. Siegfried Sassoon. MoBrPo; OBMV

When I have lost my temper I have lost my reason, too. Temper. Unknown. PoToHe

When I have lost the power to feel the pang. Strangeness of Heart. Siegfried Sassoon. TrJP

When I have seen by Time's fell hand defac'd. Shakespeare. Fr. Sonnets. AWP; BLPL; EIL; EnLoPo; EnRePo; HAP; HeIP; ImPo; LiTB; NOBE; NoP; NoSic; OAEL-1; OxAEP-1; PlP; PoE; PoRA; SCGP; Son
(Time and Love, I.) GTBS; GTBS-P

When I have talked for an hour I feel lousy. The Dancers Inherit the Party. Ian Hamilton Finlay. FF

When I Have Time. *Unknown.* PWR

When I hear laughter from a tavern door. Wilfrid Scawen Blunt. *Fr.* Esther [a Young Man's Tragedy]. OBMV; TrGrPo

When I hear the old men. A Song of Greatness. *Unknown, tr. fr. Chippewa Indian.* FaPON; ImGa, *tr. by* Mary Austin

When I hear the song. Heine. RiWo

When I hear you. To the Pianist Bill Evans. Bill Zavatsky. Jaz

When I Hear Your Name. Gloria Fuertes, *tr. fr. Spanish by* Philip Levine *and* Ada Long. VBLP

When I Heard at the Close of the Day. Walt Whitman. AmPP; GBL; NAAL-1; NoAM; OxBA; PoE

When I Heard Dat White Man Say. Zack Gilbert. PoBA

When I Heard the Learn'd Astronomer. Walt Whitman. AmPP; AnAmPo; FF; HAP; MoAmPo; NAAL-1; NoP; OxBA; PAW; Poetr; SoSe; TAP; TrGrPo; WeW

When I heard the terrible news, that Myris was dead. Myris: Alexandria, A.D. 340. C. P. Cavafy, *tr. fr. Greek by* Edmund Keeley *and* Philip Sherrard. AnAn; OBF

When I Held You to My Chest, You Fit. Jack Myers. AmPA

When I hit her on the head, it was good. Herbert White. Frank Bidart. AmPA

When I hug you tight at bedtime. Unspoken. Judith Ortiz Cofer. CrSp

When I in Praise. W. H. Davies. CBLP

When I in praise of babies speak. When I in Praise. W. H. Davies. CBLP

When I languish'd, and wish'd you wou'd something bestow. Mary Pix. *Fr.* Innocent Mistress, The. KTR

When I lay me down to sleep. Insomnia the Gem of the Ocean. John Updike. NBLV

When I Leapt over Tower Bridge. J. C. Squire. UV

When I lie down to sleep dream the Wishing Well it rings. I Am a Victim of Telephone. Allen Ginsberg. NBLV

When I lie where shades of darkness. Fare Well. Walter de la Mare. EBEvV; GTBS-P; NOBE; OBEV

When I live I live in the ancient future. Pushkin Town. Anne Carson. *Fr.* Life of Towns, The. BAP-90

When I lived in Milan the Duomo was thirty years younger. The Duomo. Maria Luisa Spaziani, *tr. fr. Italian by* Beverly Allen. NeIt

When I look at my elder sister now. The Elder Sister. Sharon Olds. NIP

When I look back and in myself behold. On the Instability of Youth. Thomas, Lord Vaux.
(Age Looks Back at Youth.) NoSic

When I look back upon my life nigh spent. George Macdonald. TrPWD

When I look forth at dawning, pool. Nature's Questioning. Thomas Hardy. EnVR; PFP; TEP

When I look in the mirror. Hysteria. Chu Shu-chen, *tr. fr. Chinese by* Kenneth Rexroth. NaP

When I look into a glass. A Thought. W. H. Davies. MoShBr

When I look into your eyes. Heine. RiWo

When I look upon the well-groomed, dark. Anne Playing the Spinet. Clément Marot, *tr. fr. French by* Philip L. Miller. RiWo

When I looked at my poverty. Poverty. Charles Simic. MAT

When I looked into your eyes. Chinoiseries. Amy Lowell. PoRA

When I Lost Slum Life. Sipho Sepamla. PeSAV

When I love (as some have told). A Hymn to the Graces. Robert Herrick. NOSC

When I loved you, I can't but allow. Thomas Moore. EnLoPo; OxBSP

When I Married. John Holmes. *Fr.* Letter to My Mother. ImGa

When I married, I caught up. When I Married. John Holmes. *Fr.* Letter to My Mother. ImGa

When I meet Gustavo and Hilda. Foreigners. Meredith Stricker. LoHo

When I meet the morning beam. The Immortal Part. A. E. Housman. *Fr.* Shropshire Lad, A. FaPoB; MeMBP; MoBrPo; SCGP; SoSe; UnPo

When I meet the skier she is always. Transit. Adrienne Rich. NoP

When I must come to you, O my God, I pray. A Prayer to Go to Paradise with the Donkeys. Jammes Francis, *tr. fr. French by* Richard Wilbur. RB

When I opened your letter. A Thought of Marigolds. Janice Farrar. GoYe

When I parted from my Good. Friedrich von Hausen, *tr. fr. German by* Frederick Goldin. GePo

When i pat this floor. Tapping. Jayne Cortez. Jaz

When I perceive your blond and graceful head. Louise Labé, *tr. fr. French.* BoWoP, *tr. by* Willis Barnstone; PBWP, *tr. by* Joan Keefe *and* Richard Terdiman.

When I Peruse the Conquer'd Fame. Walt Whitman. PoEL-5; SAmP

When I peruse the conquer'd fame of heroes. When I Peruse the Conquer'd Fame. Walt Whitman. PoEL-5; SAmP

When I pictured you. Ollie, Answer Me. Stephen Berg. NaP

When I play on my fiddle in Dooney. The Fiddler of Dooney. W. B. Yeats. EBVV; FaBoCh; NBLV; OxAEP-2

When I, poor Lais, with my crown. Lais to Aphrodite. E. A. Robinson, *after* Plato. FaBoEE

When I pour sake. *Unknown, tr. fr. Japanese by* Kenneth Rexroth *and* Ikuko Atsumi. WPJ

When I put her out, once, by the garbage pail. The Geranium. Theodore Roethke. CoAP; UnPo; WeW

When I put myself out on a saucer. Cannibalism. Diana Chang. WPOW

When I put off the sense in death. The Free Intelligence. Anna Wickham. OBD

When I ran, it rained. Late in the afternoon. Between the Wars. Robert Hass. VCAP

When I ran to snatch the wires off our roof. The Powerline Incarnation. Les A. Murray. CBAP

When I reached fourteen like grey. The Push. Kevin Killian. ETG

When I reached his place. It Was All Very Tidy. Robert Graves. OxBTC; RB

When I Read Shakespeare. D. H. Lawrence. MoP; NoAM; Son

When I Read the Book. Walt Whitman. NAAL-1

When I Recovered from an Illness, *sels.* Li K'ai-hsien, *tr. fr. Chinese by* Jonathan Chaves.

When I remember again. John Skelton. *Fr.* Phyllyp Sparowe [*or* Philip Sparrow]. AAS; PoEL-1
(Sparrow's Dirge, The.) FaBoCh

When I return I search for myself. On Going Home. Marjorie L. Agnew. GoYe

When I returned with drinks and nuts, my friend. The Friend of the Fourth Decade. James Merrill. NYBP

When I revolve in my remembrance. The Epitaph of Sir Griffith ap Rhys. *Unknown.* AngWe

When I ride my bicycle. Different Bicycles. Dorothy W. Baruch. FaPON

When I rise up. Wendell Berry. EaPr

When I rolled three 7's. Situation. Langston Hughes. OBAL

When I run. I Have Ten Legs. Anna Swirszczynska, *tr. fr. Polish.* TSaS, *tr. by* Czeslaw Milosz *and* Leonard Nathan

When I said "You have grown thin." Meeting after Separation. Marula, *tr. fr. Sanskrit by* Tambimuttu *and* G. V. Vaijda. BoWoP

When I sailed out of Baltimore. A Child's Pet. W. H. Davies. CH; CoGr; RB

When I saw my mother's head on the cold pillow. Keine Lazarovitch, 1870-1959. Irving Layton. NIP

When I saw that clumsy crow. Night Crow. Theodore Roethke. HoPM; InPK; OxBSP; VGW

When I saw that the man who stirred the fire. In the Middle of the Party. Carl Dennis. CBNP

When I saw the dark clouds, I wept. The Clouds. Mirabai, *tr. from Medieval Hindi; English version by* Robert Bly. EnIH; NU

When I saw the dark Egyptian stain. The Moment. Sharon Olds. CrSp

When I saw the grapefruit drying, cherries in each center lying. Arrogance Repressed. Sir John Betjeman. FiBHP

When I saw the woman's leg on the floor of the subway train. The Leg in the Subway. Oscar Williams. LiTM

When I saw your head bow, I knew I had beaten you. The Last Word. Peter Davison. InPK

When I see a couple of kids. High Windows. Philip Larkin. FaBoMo; NAEL-2; NoAM

When I See Another's Pain. Mani Leib, *tr. fr. Yiddish by* Joseph Leftwich. TrJP

When I see birches bend to left and right. Birches. Robert Frost. AmPP; CMoP; FaBoVe; FaBV; HeIL; HeIP; ImGa; LiTA; LiTM; MeMAP; MoAB; MoAmPo; MoP; NAAL-2; NoAM; NoP; OxBA; Poetr; PoLF; PoRA; RB; SAmP; SoSe; TAP; TFi; TrGrPo; TRP

When I see blosmes springe. *Unknown.* MiEL

When I see buildings in a town together. Mr. Frost Goes South to Boston. Firman Houghton. UV

When I see carved so clearly on your face. Two Solitudes. Evelyn Ames. GoYe

When I see her sitting by the brook. Life at the Mill. Wilhelm Müller, *tr. fr. German by* Philip L. Miller. *Fr.* Beautiful Maid of the Mill, The. RiWo

When I see how high it is. So Beautiful Is the Tree of Night. Pauline Hanson. TAP

When I see my mother giving away. The Power of My Mother. Sharon Olds. MDDM

When I See on Rood. *Unknown.* OxBSP

When I see some kid from Norway. High Wonders. Naomi Marks. BXAP

When I see the earth ornate and lovely. Veronica Gambara, *tr. fr. Italian by* Brenda Webster. PBWP

When I see the lark a-moving [*or* stir her wings for joy]. The Lark. Bernard de Ventadour, *tr. fr. Provençal*. CTC, *tr. by* Ezra Pound

When I see the next century. A Long and Happy Life. Simon Schuchat. UL

When I/ see you/ climb the walls. Pressure. Anne Waldman. PoM

When I Set Out for Lyonnesse. Thomas Hardy. EBVV; InPS; MoBrPo; OHCV; RB

When I shall be without regret. Epitaph. J. V. Cunningham. InPK

When I show up. *Unknown, tr. fr. Chippewa Indian by* Jerome K. Rothenberg. STP

When I sit by myself at the close of the day. Good Company. *Unknown*. OBET

When I sit in the Churchyard at Stoke. A. M. Sayers. PeLi

When I sit up to bread and milk. At Breakfast. Ida M. Mills. BoTP

When I sold my fake Vermeers to Goering. The Forger. Derek Mahon. SCBI

When I solidly do ponder. Francis Daniel Pastorius. SCAP

When I some antique jar behold. To a Lady. John Gay. OBEV

When I speak now. Volcano. Ivan van Sertima. PBCV

When I spread out my hand here today. Sitting by a Bush in Broad Daylight. Robert Frost. ChIV-1

When I stand in the center of that man's madness. Reflection by a Mailbox. Stanley Kunitz. TrJP

When I stepped homeward to my hill. Home-coming. Léonie Adams. MoAmPo

When I strip,/ stop walking/ and drop into sleep. Anne-Marie Kegels, *tr. fr. French by* Willis Barnstone. BoWoP

When I survey [*or* survay] the bright. "Nox Nocti Indicat Scientiam." William Habington. *Fr.* Castara. BeJo; JCP; MeLP; NOBE; OBEV; SCGP

When I Survey the Wondrous Cross. Isaac Watts. AmFP; FaPoR; WGRP

When I take my girl to the swimming party. The One Girl at the Boys Party. Sharon Olds. InPK

When I taught you. To a Daughter Leaving Home. Linda Pastan. NIP

When I think how far the onion has traveled. The Traveling Onion. Naomi Shihab Nye. MT

When I think of all you've got. A Father's Heart Is Touched. Samuel Hoffenstein. FiBHP

When I think of death. Bop Lyrics. Allen Ginsberg. OBAL

When I think of my fear. The Unblinding. Laurence Lieberman. NYBP

When I think of the hosts of little ones. Mattinata. Mary Effie Lee Newsome. ShDr

When I think of us seated in our separate days. Skydiving. Jim Wayne Miller. ETG

When I think you gone, abruptly. Black Mood. Rosalía de Castro. WeW

When I think you're somewhere yonder. Black Mood. Rosalía de Castro, *tr. fr. Galician by* John Frederick Nims. STV

When I thought of this Duchess affair. *Unknown*. PeLi

When I through all my many poems look. To the Most Virtuous Mistress Pot, Who Many Times Entertained Him. Robert Herrick. CaPo

When I thy singing next shall heare. Againe. Robert Herrick. SeCP

When I too long have looked upon your face. Sonnet. Edna St. Vincent Millay. HeIP

When I/ took my. The Watch. May Swenson. HAP

When I tread the earth, I fear to hurt the ground. Meng Chiao, *tr. by* Stephen Owen. *Fr.* Apricots Die Young. SuSp

When I try to say something about the birds. The Birds. Richard Jones. NAmP90

When I try to skate. Skating. Herbert Asquith. FaPON

When I used to focus on the worries, everybody. Joanne Kyger. UL

When I Vexed You. Robert Browning. *Fr.* Ferishtah's Fancies. OxBSP

When I wake in the early mist. Very Early. Karla Kuskin. PDV

When I wake now it's below ocherous, saw-ridged. Fall River. David Rivard. PBCAP

When I wake up again, when I wake up. The Report. Jon Swan. NYBP

When I walk home through snow or slush. Winter Song. David Daiches. NYBP

When I want to tell of the laughing throne. Old Flag. W. S. Merwin. AnAn

When I was a bachelor bold and young. Bachelor Bold and Young. *Unknown*. AmFP

When I was a bachelor [*or* bach'lor *or* batchelor] I lived all alone [*or* early and young *or* by myself *or* young and gay]. The Foggy, Foggy Dew. *Unknown*. AS; CoMu; ELP; GBP; LiTB; OBET; OxBoLi; PeLV; PlP

When I was a bachelor/ I lived by myself. Mother Goose. ReMoGo

When I was a blonde I. First Corinthians at the Crossroads. Bruce Dawe. NoAM

When I was a boy. The Piper's Progress. Francis Sylvester Mahony. FiBHP

When I was a boy, a relative. A Way to Make a Living. James Wright. NNaP

When I was a boy, and saw bright rows of icicles. Conrad Aiken. *Fr.* Improvisations: Light and Snow. BoNaP

When I was a boy desiring the title of man. George. Dudley Randall. BPo; NoAM

When I was a boy I lived among people. Why I Write about the Holocaust. Gary Pacernick. BTR

When I was a boy I saw the world I was in. Old-Time Childhood in Kentucky. Robert Penn Warren. AiP

When I was a boy, I used to go to bed. The Remorse for Time. Howard Nemerov. Son

When I was a boy they came in blackness. The Lascars. Peter Thomas. AngWe

When I was a chicken. *Unknown*. ISE

When I was a child. Autobiographia Literaria. Frank O'Hara. CAPP; NNaP; NOBA; TTTS

When I was a child. My People. Margery Himel. IHMS

When I was a child. The Truth about My Sister and Me. Anita Endrezze-Danielson. CDW

When I was a child. Why Do You Write about Russia? Louis Simpson. InPS

When I was a child I knew red miners. Childhood. Margaret Walker. IHMS; PBWP; PoBA; Son; WPOW

When I was a child of five winters. Poor Wolf Speaks. Poor Wolf. NU

When I was a chile we used to play. Children's Rhymes. Langston Hughes. BPo; InPS

When I was a girl. Two Gifts. *Unknown, tr. fr. Catalan by* Willis Barnstone. BoWoP

When I was a girl I saw with the old men. You Call That a Ts'ing; a Letter. Jedediah Barrow. BXAP

When I was a good and quick little girl. *Unknown, tr. fr. Pampa Indian by* W. S. Merwin. BoWoP

When I was a greenhorn and young. Charles Kingsley. NOBVV

When I was a kid I froze. The Public Mirror. Richard Katrovas. NAmP90

When I was a kid in summer. Some One Liked Me when I Was Twelve. Peter Orlovsky. GLP

When I Was a King in Babylon. W. E. Henley. VPP

When I was a lad and so was my dad. *Unknown*. OxNR

When I was a lad I served a term. Sir Joseph's Song. W. S. Gilbert. *Fr.* H. M. S. Pinafore. LiTB

(First Lord's Song, The. PeLV

When I Was a Little Boy. *Unknown*. CBNP; OxNR

When I was a little boy/ I had but little wit. *Unknown*. OxNR

When I was a little boy/ I lived by myself. *Unknown*. BoTP; OxNR

When I was a little boy,/ I washed [*or* wash'd] my/ mammy's [*or* Mother's] dishes. When I Was a Little Boy. *Unknown*. CBNP; OxNR

When I was a little boy/ My mammy kept me in. *Unknown*. OxNR

When I was a little girl,/ About seven years old. Mother Goose. OxNR; ReMoGo

When I was a little maid. The Little Maid. Anna Maria Wells. OBCA

When I was a servant in Rosemary Lane. The Servant of Rosemary Lane. *Unknown*. OxBSS

When I was a single girl, I went dressed very fine. Oh, I Wish I Were Single Again. *Unknown*. AmFP

When I was a wee thing. The Kirk of the Birds, Beasts and Fishes. *Unknown*. GBP

When I was a windy boy and a bit. Dylan Thomas. ErPo; OPOP; PPP (Lament. MeMBP

When I was a young girl, I used to seek pleasure. One Morning in May; or, The Young Girl Cut Down in Her Prime. *Unknown*. AmFP

When I Was a Young Maid. *Unknown*. AmFP

When I was a young man I carried a pack. The Band Played Waltzing Matilda. Eric Bogle. OBET

When I was a young man I lived rarely. A Poor Man's Work Is Never Done. *Unknown*. OBET

When I was a youngster I sailed with the rest. Liverpool Girls. *Unknown*. OxBSS

When I was as high as that. A Memory. L. A. G. Strong. FaBoCo; NOBL

When I was at the party. Betty at the Party. *Unknown*. BoTP

When I was born. (*LL*) Wonder. Thomas Traherne. CH; ESCV; GeHe; HAP; ImPo; LiTB; NAEL-1; NoP; PoE; SeCP; SeCV-2; TOF; TrGrPo

When I was born in a world of sin. G. K. Chesterton on His Birth. A. E. Housman. FaBoNo; NBLV

When I was born in the great house on the bank of the sea. Poem of Distant Childhood. Noémia da Sousa, *tr. fr. Portuguese by* Kathleen Weaver *and* Allan Francovich. AIW

When I was born, my mother taped my ears. Youth's Progress. John Updike. FiBHP

When I was born on Amman Hill. The Collier. Vernon Watkins. FaBoTw; OBWVE

When I was born/ they had just gotten. War Baby. William Trowbridge. ArOW

When I was bound apprentice, in famous Lincolnshire. The Lincolnshire Poacher. *Unknown.* CH; FaBoEH; GBP; OxBoLi; PeLV
(Poacher, The.) WiR

When I was bound for London a lady met me there. The Sheffield Apprentice. *Unknown.* OBET
(Sheffield 'Prentice, The,) *diff. version.* AmFP

When I was but thirteen or so. Romance. W. J. Turner. CH; CoGr; EBEvV; GoJo; MoBrPo; NOBAu; NOBE; NTP; OBMV; PlP; PoRA; TrGrPo

When I Was Christened. David McCord. *Fr.* Perambulator Poems, I-VII. OBCA

When I was coming down from the country. The Forgotten City. William Carlos Williams. LiTA

When I was dead, my spirit turned. At Home. Christina Rossetti. OHCV

When I was down beside the sea. At the Seaside. Robert Louis Stevenson. NTCP; OxBChV; TLR; WHSW

When I Was Dying. William Hathaway. UL

When I was eight years old the war broke out. Windward of Hilo. John N. Miller. ArOW

When I was eighteen years of age. McCaffery. *Unknown.* OBET

When I Was Fair and Young. Elizabeth I, Queen of England. CTC; LPA; NIP; NoP; NoSic; NTP; Poetr; PoRA

When I was fair and young and favour graced me. Elizabeth I, Queen of England. *See* When I was fair and young, then favour graced me.

When I was fair and young, then favour graced me. When I Was Fair and Young. Elizabeth I, Queen of England. CTC; LPA; NIP; NoP; NoSic; NTP; Poetr; PoRA
(When I was fair and young and favour graced me.) CTC
(Youth and Cupid.) CBLP

When I was fifteen years of age. Phone Number. Jack Collom. UL

When I was five, we lived in Tesuque. Cherries. Joe Lamb. RaBo

When I was forty the stocktaker came. On My Fortieth Birthday. John Tripp. AngWe; NAs

When I was four my father went to Scotland. The Truth. Randall Jarrell. OxBC

When I was frightened by the spots upon the wall. The Sick-Room. R. A. Simpson. TSaS

When I was Home Last Christmas. Randall Jarrell. MT

When I was in all that wrath? (*LL*) Child Maurice. *Unknown.* ESPB, *B vers.*

When I Was in Bridport. Douglas Oliver. VaA

When I was in the garden. The Queen Bee. Mary K. Robinson. BoTP

When I was just as far as I could walk. The Telephone. Robert Frost. ArLo; ImGa

When I was little, when. The Poplar's Shadow. May Swenson. NYBP

When I was marked for suffering, Love forswore. Cervantes, *tr. fr. Spanish by* Sir Edmund Gosse. AWP

When I was on Night Line. Ego. Philip Booth. TwCP

When I was once in Baltimore. Sheep. W. H. Davies. LiTM; MoBrPo; NTP; RB

When I was One-and-Twenty. A. E. Housman. *Fr.* Shropshire Lad, A. ArLo; CBLP; CMoP; EBEvV; ELP; FaBV; FaPoB; HeIP; ImPo; InPK; LiTB; LiTM; MeMBP; MoAB; MoBrPo; NAEL-2; NoAM; OtMeF; PoE; PoLF; TFi; TrGrPo

When I was one and twenty. The Shropshire Lad's Cousin. Samuel Hoffenstein. BXAP

When I was only five years old. The Wallpaper. Sir Edmund Gosse. Mes

When I was only semen in a gland. James K. Baxter. *Fr.* Pig Island Letters. PeNZ

When I was only six years old. When I Was Six. Zora Cross. FaPON

When I was past such thinking. You Came as a Thought. J. Laughlin. GOYP

When I was Saul, and sat among the cloaks, St. Paul. Thomas Merton. ChIV-2

When I was seven. Growing Up. Harry Behn. PDV

When I was seventeen. Just How Crazy Brenda Is. Melinda Goodman. GLP

When I was seventeen, a man in the Dakar Station. Objets d'Art. Cynthia MacDonald. NMM

When I was sick and lay a-bed. The Land of Counterpane. Robert Louis Stevenson. EBEV; FaBoBe; NBLV; NTCP; OxBChV; PWR; TLR; WHSW

When I was single [*or* a single girl]. I Wish I Was Single Again. *Unknown.* AmFP, *diff. vers.*; AS
(Single Girl, The.) AmFP

When I Was Six. Zora Cross. FaPON

When I Was Small. André de Chénier, *tr. fr. French by* Elizabeth Gerteiny. ErPo

When I was small my mother did my hair. Plaits. Tabitha Tuckett. Mes

When I was still a child. Lesbia Harford. NOBAu

When I was ten my mother, having sold. The Year of the Foxes. David Malouf. FaBoMA; NOBAu

When I was/ thirteen I. Spring. Ruth Whitman. IHMS

When I Was Three. Richard Edwards. Spl

When I was three I had a friend. When I Was Three. Richard Edwards. Spl

When I was told, as Delta children were. Ruby Tells All. Miller Williams. MT

When I Was Twenty. Bliss Carman. AnAmPo

When I was very very. Mama Knows. Sharon Scott. JB

When I was very young. Traveling to Town. Duane Big Eagle. AiP

When I Was Well into Being Savored. Joanne Kyger. PoM

When I was yong, indewd'd with nature's graces. Barnabe Barnes. *Fr.* Parthenophil and Parthenophe. ESo

When I was young. Don Arturo says. Víctor Hernández Cruz. AfAz

When I Was Young. Alun Llywelyn-Williams, *tr. fr. Welsh by* Gwyn Williams. OBWVE

When i was young. Sarah Pelham. FaBoVe

When I was young, a questing child. The Spectator. Evan J. Thomas. AngWe

When I Was Young and Foolish. *Unknown.* AS

When I was young and in my prime. T'ao Ch'ien, *tr. fr. Chinese by* Eugene Eoyang. SuSp

When I was young and in my prime,/ I flourished like a vine. Thyme. *Unknown.* AmFP

When I was young and in my prime,/ I thought I never could marry. Devilish Mary. *Unknown.* AmFP

When I was young and in my prime, my age twenty-two. The Lightning Flash. *Unknown.* AmFP

When I was young and used to wander. Hubert's Museum. Louis Simpson. OxBC

When I was young and wanted to see the sights. On His Queerness. Christopher Isherwood. OxBTC; PeHV

When I was young as you. (*LL*) In Glencullen. J. M. Synge. FM; OBMV

When I was young, I did not fit into the common mold. T'ao Ch'ien, *tr. by* Wu-chi Liu. *Fr.* On Returning to My Garden and Field. SuSp

When I was young I fell in love and got but little good on't. John Clare. EnVR

When I was young, I had a care. Soliloquy. Francis Ledwidge. HoPM

When I was young, I had no sense. The Fiddle. Neil Munro. BoTP

When I was young, I said to Sorrow. Sorrow. Aubrey Thomas De Vere. BLPA; WGRP; WiR

When I was young I scribbled, boasting, on my wall. The Summing-up. Stanley Kunitz. OBAL

When I was young I us'd to wait on Massa and hand him de plate. The Blue-Tail Fly. *Unknown.* GBP

When I was young, I went to school. The One Furrow. R. S. Thomas. HoPM; OxBC

When I was young, love, and in full blossom. Love It Is Pleasing. *Unknown.* OBET

When I was young my heart and head were light. Memory. Siegfried Sassoon. PAW

When I was young my Mom and Dad. The Obsidian Mountain. John Harkness. UnDi

When I was young, my ringlets waved. The Wasp's Song. "Lewis Carroll." FaBoNo

When I was young my teachers were the old. What Fifty Said. Robert Frost. NAs

"When I was young," said Aunt to me. Other Fabrics, Other Mores! Anna Maria Lenngren, *tr. fr. Swedish by* Nadia Christensen *and* Marianne Tiblin. AIW; PBWP

When I was young the days were long. The Flying Wheel. Katharine Tynan. WGRP

When I was young, unapt for use of man. Prayer yo Hymen. *Unknown.* NOSC

When I was young, with sharper sense. A Summer Commentary. Yvor Winters. LiTM

When I was younger. William Carlos Williams. AmPP; OxBA; SAmP

When I watch my two boys, Walter and Robert, at play. I Am as Happy as a Queen on Her Throne. Mrs. Henry Linden. CBWP-4

When I Watch the Living Meet. A. E. Housman. *Fr.* Shropshire Lad, A. CMoP; FaPoB; MoBrPo; NOBVV; NoP; SCGP; TrGrPo

When I watch you. Miss Rosie. Lucille Clifton. AmPA; BlSi; CAPP; NMM; PoBA; Poetr; TwCP

When I water the workers' beer. *(LL)* The Man That Waters the Worker's Beer. Paddy Ryan. SWP

When I went. But I Mean Any Kind of Thief. Judy Grahn. BCF

When I went into my garden, I found. Sister Bertken, *tr. fr. Dutch by* Willis Barnstone. BoWoP

When I went into my room, at mid-morning. Man and Bat. D. H. Lawrence. RB

When I Went Off to Prospect. *Unknown.* AmFP

When I Went Out. Karla Kuskin. NTCP

When I went out to kill myself, I caught. Saint Judas. James Wright. LCAP; NOBA; SM

When I went to bed at night. Through the Porthole. Marjorie Wilson. BoTP

When I went to fight in Saracen country. King Sigurd and King Eystein. Sheenagh Pugh. AngWe

When I went to that house of pleasure. And I Lounged and Lay on Their Beds. C. P. Cavafy, *tr. fr. Greek by* Edmund Keeley *and* Philip Sherrard. FaBoBl

When I Went to the Circus. D. H. Lawrence. CMoP; LiTB; MeMBP; MoP

When I went to the circus that had pitched on the waste lot. When I Went to the Circus. D. H. Lawrence. CMoP; LiTB; MeMBP; MoP

When I wer still a bwoy, an' mother's pride. False Friends-like. William Barnes. NOBVV; OBF

When I were at home wi' my fayther an' mother, I niver had na fun. The Wensleydale Lad. *Unknown.* FaBoPP

When I were just a little lad, right small. Pulling the Chain. Simon Rae. UV

When I woke up this morning I knew there was horror, I. Ice, Ice. Gerald Stern. AnAn

When I Would Die. Josephine D. Henderson Heard. CBWP-4

When I Would Image. George Meredith. NOBVV

When I wrote of the women in their dances and wildness. The Poem As Mask. Muriel Rukeyser. CrSp; NALW

When icicles by silver eaves. Winter Fairyland in Vermont. Francis P. Osgood. WeW

When icicles hang by the wall. Shakespeare. *Fr.* Love's Labour's Lost. AWP; ClHu; FaPON; FF; GN; GoJo; InPK; InPS; LiTB; NAEL-1; NOBE; NoSic; PoRA; PrIm
(Hiems.) FaBoCh
(Merry Note, A.) WiR
(Song: "When icicles hang by the wall.") PoEL-2
(Tu-Whit To-Who.) CH
(Winter.) BoNaP; ChTr; EiL; GTBS; GTBS-P; HAP; ImPo; NIP; OAEL-1; OBEV; SCGP; TEP; TFi; TrGrPo; UnPo; WeW

When idle in a poor Welsh mining valley. Rebel's Progress. Tom Earley. OBWVE

When ignorance possessed the shools. True Knowledge. William Wilkie. *Fr.* Grasshopper and the Glowworm, The. ECEV

When I'm a little older. My Plan. Marchette Chute. FaPON; WHSW

When I'm far out in drink, your musical box. To My Daughter. James Michie. OxBSP

When I'm in bed at night. Noises in the Night. Lilian McCrea. BoTP

When I'm in France, for Frenchmen's sake. The Englishman on the French Stage. Sir Owen Seaman. OBTV

When I'm without you. Nights. Cyn Zarco. UL

When in April the Sweet Showers Fall, *mod. vers. by* Nevill Coghill. Chaucer. *See* Whan that Aprill[e] with his shoures [*or* shower] soote.

When in Banaras. Lepers Cry. Peter Orlovsky. GLP; PoBeRe

When in danger or in doubt. Sound Advice. *Unknown.* FaBoUs; NBLV

When, in Disgrace. Shakespeare. *See* When, in disgrace with fortune and men's eyes.

When, in disgrace with fortune and men's eyes. Shakespeare. *Fr.* Sonnets. AWP; CTC; EBEV; EiL; FaBoRV; FaBV; FaPoB; GBL; HAP; HeIL; HeIP; ImPo; InPK; InPS; InvP; LiTB; NAEL-1; NOBE; NoP; NoSic; OAEL-1; OBEV; OPOP; OxAEP-1; PeHV; PoEL-2; Poetr; SCGP; Son; TFi
(Consolation, A.) GTBS; GTBS-P
(Sonnet: "When, in disgrace with fortune and men's eyes.") WeW
(When, in Disgrace.) PFP

When in her face mine eyes I fix. William Alexander, Earl of Stirling. *Fr.* Aurora. EiL

When in his twenties a poetry's full strength. Duncan. Thom Gunn. BAP-90

When in My Arms. Pushkin, *tr. fr. Russian by* Babette Deutsch. ErPo

When, in my effervescent youth. Who'd Be a Hero (Fictional)? Morris Bishop. FiBHP; OBAL

When, in my fond embraces fast confined. To My Love. "Amorous Lady, The." ECWP

When in My Pilgrimage. *Unknown.* ChIV-2

When in my pilgrimage I reach. When in My Pilgrimage. *Unknown.* ChIV-2

When in my youth I travelled. The Migration of the Grey Squirrels. William Howitt. OxBChV

When in nineteen-thirty-seven, Etta Moten, sweetheart. The Convert. Margaret Danner. BPo

When in Rome. Mari Evans. SoSe

"When, in summer." A Poet's Memory Is Counsel. Kallil Attiraiyanar, *tr. fr. Tamil by* A. K. Ramanujan. PLW

When in the chronicle of wasted time. Shakespeare. *Fr.* Sonnets. AWP; BLPL; CTC; EBEvV; EiL; EnLoPo; EnRePo; FaBoCh; FaBV; ImPo; LiTB; NAEL-1; NOBE; NoP; NoSic; OBEV; OxAEP-1; PoRA; SCGP; Son; TEP; TrGrPo
(To His Love.) GTBS; GTBS-P

When, in the dawn of love and my desire. The Miracle. Allan Dowling. ErPo

When in the east the morning ray. Garden of Appleton House, The ("When in the east the morning ray.") Andrew Marvell. *Fr.* Upon Appleton House, to My Lord Fairfax. NOBE; SeCP; SeCV-1

When in the halcyon days of eld, I was a little tyke. Our Biggest Fish. Eugene Field. AnAmPo

When in the mask of night there shone that cut. Landing on the Moon. May Swenson. TAP

When, in the midst of the thriving alien. Declaration of Independence. Michael Brownstein. UL

When in the mirror of a permanent tear. Elegy on Gordon Barber. Gene Derwood.
(Elegy: "When in the mirror of a permanent tear.") ImPo; LiTA; LiTM

When in the sun the hot red acres smoulder. The Zulu Girl. Roy Campbell. OBMV; OxAEP-2

When Indian sweat was suddenly soaked dry by the sun. Black Ore. René Depestre, *tr. fr. French by* Ellen Conroy Kennedy. NegPo

When infant Reason first exerts her sway. On Education, December 1789. Elizabeth Bentley. WoRP

When Ireland was bloody and leaderless. Gina Berkeley. PeLi

When Isaac watched his father strain back. Abraham's Madness. Bink Noll. ChIV-1

When Israel against Philistia. David and Goliath. Nathaniel Crouch. OxBChV

When Israel Came Forth out of Egypt. Bible, *O.T., paraphrased by* Sir Thomas Wyatt. *See* When Israel went out of Egypt.

When Israel came out of Egypt. Psalm CXIV: A Fountain from Wilderness Stone. Bible, *O.T.* CRP

When Israel, of the Lord beloved. Rebecca's Hymn. Sir Walter Scott. *Fr.* Ivanhoe. EnRP
(When Israel, of the Lord Beloved. ChIV-1)

When Israel, of the Lord Beloved. Sir Walter Scott. *See* When Israel, of the Lord beloved.

When Israel out of Egypt Came. A. E. Housman. ChIV-1; LiTB; MeMBP

When Israel Was in Egypt's Land. *Unknown. See* Go Down, Moses.

When Israel went out of Egypt. Bible, *O.T., paraphrased by* Sir Thomas Wyatt. *Fr.* Psalms.
(Psalm CXIV: "When Israel came from Egypt's coast," *paraphrased by* Christopher Smart.) OBVE
(When Israel Came Forth out of Egypt.) TrJP

When Israel's daughters mourn'd their past offences. Epigram in a Maid of Honour's Prayer-Book. Pope. FaBoEE

When Israel's ruler on the royal bed. Hymn to the Supreme Being. Christopher Smart. ChIV-1

When issuing from the realms of "Shadow Land." To E. O. S. Sarah Helen Whitman. AmWP

When it burns before the harps and freezes behind the easels. Hans Arp, *tr. fr. French by* Harriet Watts. FaBoNo

When it comes to a question of trusting. The Average Man. Margaret E. M. Sangster. WBLP

When it is all over. Lost Moment. Hoyt W. Fuller. PoBA

When it is finally ours, this freedom, this liberty, this beautiful. Frederick Douglass. Robert Hayden. CAPP; GOA; HCAP; NIP; PoBA; PoNe; Son; TTY; VCAP

When it is not yet day. Looking for Mushrooms at Sunrise. W. S. Merwin. NaP; NOBA

When it is past — the golden moment — gone! Lost Opportunities. H. Cordelia Ray. AmWP; CBWP-3

When it makes a man mad all the days of his life? (*LL*) I peeled bits of straw and I got switches too. John Clare. NAEL-2

When it returned, it came again. (*LL*) There was a monkey climbed a tree. *Unknown.* OxNR

When it's cold and raining. Jalal al-Din Rumi, *tr. fr. Persian by* Coleman Barks *and* A. J. Arberry. EnlH

When it's hot. Summer. Frank Asch. NTCP

When it's ninety in the shade. Drive a Tractor. *Unknown.* NBLV

When it's the man I love. *Unknown, tr. fr. Japanese by* Kenneth Rexroth *and* Ikuko Atsumi. WPJ

When it's time. Listening. Aileen Fisher. NTCP

When I've got the blues. *Unknown, tr. fr. Japanese by* Kenneth Rexroth *and* Ikuko Atsumi. WPJ

When J ——— bawls out to the Chair for a Toast. (*LL*) Jinny the Just. Matthew Prior. NOBE; NOEC; OBEV; PoEL-3

When Jack had pulled the oar and the boat was gone. Jackie Tar. *Unknown.* OxBSS

When Jack the King's commander. The Fate of John Burgoyne. *Unknown.* PAH

When Jacob from the land of Canaan down. The Exodus from Egypt. Ezekielos of Alexandria, *tr. fr. Greek by* E. H. Gifford. TrJP

When Jael crept in to see Sisera. Bill Greenwell. PeLi

When James, our great monarch, so wise and discreet. Upon the King's Voyage to Chatham to Make Bulwarks against the Dutch. *Unknown.* APAS

When Januar' wind war blawing cauld. The Lass That Made the Bed for Me. Burns. InvP

When Jemmy the Second, not Jemmy the First. A New Song Entitled the Warming Pan. *Unknown.* CoMu

When Jenny Wren Was Young. *Unknown.* ReMoGo

When Jesus came to Golgotha they hanged Him on a tree. Indifference. G. A. Studdert-Kennedy. TrCP

When Jesus was a little thing. His Mother in Her Hood of Blue. Lizette Woodworth Reese. OHIP

When Jesus was leaving this sin-accursed land. Whoso Gives Freely, Shall Freely Receive! Josephine D. Henderson Heard. CBWP-4

When Jill complains to Jack for want of meat[e]. Upon Jack and Jill: Epigram. Robert Herrick. CaPo; NAEL-1

When John Connu come', he come' wit' style. John Connu Rider. Andrew Salkey. NTP

When John Donne dropped to sleep all around him slept. Elegies. Hugh Maxton. PBCIP

When John Henry was [a little] nothin' but a baby. John Henry. *Unknown.* SWP
   (When John Henry was a little babe.) AmFP; BPo

When Johnny Comes Marching Home. Patrick Sarsfield Gilmore. PAH

When Johnson sought (as Shakespear says) that bourn. Introduction and Anecdotes. "Peter Pindar." *Fr.* Bozzy and Piozzi. PoEL-3

When Jones's Ale Was New. *Unknown.* AmFP

When Joseph was an old man. The Cherry-Tree Carol. *Unknown.* AmFP

When Sir Joshua Reynolds died. Sir Joshua Reynolds. Blake. FaBoCo; FaBoEE; FiBHP; OxBoLi; PeLV

When Judas writes the history of solitude. The Sacrifice. Frank Bidart. GLP; VCAP

When Julius Fabricius, Sub-Prefect of the Weald. The Land. Kipling. CoGr; MoBrPo

When Kavin comes back from the barber. Concerning Kavin. Bliss Carman. AnAmPo

When Keats was at work on *Endymion.* Victor Gray. PeLi

When Klopstock England defied. Blake. OAEL-2

When lads have done with labour. A. E. Housman and a Few Friends. Humbert Wolfe. BXAP; FiBHP; UV

When lads were home from labour. Fancy's Knell. A. E. Housman. FaBoCh; PIP; PoRA

When Lalement and de Brébeuf, brave souls. Brébeuf and His Brethren. F. R. Scott. NOBC

When land is gone and money spent. *Unknown.* OxNR

When last I died [*or* When I dyed last], and, dear[e], I die [*or* dye]. The Legacy [*or* Legacie]. John Donne. SeCP; TrGrPo

When last I heard your nimble fingers play. To Lucia Playing on Her Lute, Another. Samuel Pordage. NOSC

When last mine eyes dislodged from thy beautie. *Unknown. Fr.* Zepheria. ESo

WHEN late, grave Palmer, these thy grafts and flowers. To Thomas Palmer, on His Book 'The Sprite of Trees and Herbs.' Ben Jonson. NoSic

When late I attempted your pity to move. An Expostulation. Isaac Bickerstaffe. FaBoCo; FiBHP

When lately King James, whom our sovereign we call. The Clerical Cabal. *Unknown.* APAS

When Lately Pym Descended Into Hell. William Drummond of Hawthornden. CoGr

When lavish Phoebus pours out melted gold. The Pleasures of Retirement. Edward Benlowes. *Fr.* Theophia. NOSC

When Lazarus came back from the dead. *Unknown.* PeLi

When Lazarus left his charnel-cave. Tennyson. *Fr.* In Memoriam A. H. H. EBVV, *abr.*; FHYEP; OAEL-2, *abr.*; PeECV, *abr.*; TOF

When learning's triumph o'er her barb'rous [*or* barbarous] foes. Prologue [Spoken by Mr. Garrick] [at the Opening of the Theatre in Drury Lane, 1747]. Samuel Johnson. EBEV; EPCY; *ll.* 1–8; NAEL-1; NOEC; NoP; OxAEP-1

When leaves fall and cold winds come. (*LL*) When the Lamp Is Shatter'd. Shelley. CBLP; CH; ImPo; NAEL-2; PPP; TEP; TrGrPo

When leaves, in evenen winds, do vlee. Jay a-Pass'd. William Barnes. NOBVV

When leaving the primrose, bayberry dunes, seaward. The Constant. A. R. Ammons. HAP; WeW

When leaving with your loving in my veins. Late Light. Barbara Bellow Watson. NYBP

When Lemmings migrate, and arrive at a river. Seaside Suicide. Dick King-Smith. OBAP

When Lesbia first I saw so heavenly fair. Lesbia. Congreve. OxBSP

When Letty had scarce pass'd her third glad year. Letty's Globe. Charles Tennyson Turner. NOBVV; OBEV; OHCV; PeVV

When liberty is headlong girl. Liberty. Archibald MacLeish. GOA

When life falls from us like a withered husk. (*LL*) Creed. Mary Ashley Townsend. BLPA; FaBoBe

When Life has borne its harvest from my heart. A Prayer in Late Autumn. Violet Alleyn Storey. TrPWD

When life hath run its largest round. Daniel Webster. Oliver Wendell Holmes. PAH

When like a bud my Julia blows. To Julia under Lock and Key. Sir Owen Seaman. BXAP; FaBoPa

When, like a Running Grave. Dylan Thomas. OAEL-2

When, like all liberal girls and boys. Days Pass: Men Pass. Stephen Vincent Benét. AnAmPo

When, like the early rose. Aileen Aroon. Gerald Griffin. PeIV

When like the rising day. Gerald Griffin. *Fr.* Eileen Aroon. OBEV

When Lilacs Last in the Dooryard Bloom'd. Walt Whitman. *Fr.* Memories of President Lincoln. AmPP; AWP; HAP; LiTA; MeMAP; MoAmPo; NAAL-1; NOBA; NoP; OxBA; PoEL-5; PoRA; PPP; SAmP; TAP; TFi; TrGrPo

When Lil's husband got demobbed, I said. T. S. Eliot. *Fr.* Waste Land, The. AmPP; CMoP; FaBoMo; HAP; LiTA; LiTM; MoAB; MoAmPo; NAs; NAWM-2; NoAM; NOBA; NOBE; NoP; OAEL-2; OxBA; OxBTC; TAP; UnPo

When Lion sends his roaring forth. The Lion. Mary Howitt. FaPON

When little boys grow [*or* grown] patient at last, weary. Death of Little Boys. Allen Tate. LiTA; MoAB

When little Fred went to bed. Little Fred. *Unknown.* ReMoGo

When little girls begin to walk. To My Niece, A.M., with a New Pair of Shoes. *Unknown.* ECWP

When little heads weary have gone to their bed. The Plumppuppets. Christopher Morley. FaPON

When little John Hardy was four years old. John Hardy. *Unknown.* AmFP; FaBoBa

When little people go abroad, wherever they may roam. To Henrietta, on Her Departure for Calais. Thomas Hood. OBTV; OxBChV

When little things would irk me, and I grow. Morning Prayer. *Unknown.* PoToHe

When Liverpool John was just sixteen he went away to sea. Liverpool John. Phil *and* June Colclough *and* June Colclough. OxBSS

When, lo, by break of morning. *Unknown.* NoSic

When London Calls. Victor James Daley. CBAP

When Londons fatal bills were blown abroad. Marlburyes Fate. Benjamin Tompson. SCAP

When, looking on the present face of things. October 1803. Wordsworth. EnRP

When, loosened from the winter's bonds. Princess Nukada. *Fr.* Manyo Shu, Part 4 of 4. PBWP

When Louis came home to the flat. Meet Me in St. Louis, Louis. Andrew B. Sterling. OBAL

When Love Flies In. Walter de la Mare. ArLo

When love is a shimmering curtain. On Diverse Deviations. Maya Angelou. BlSi

When love is gone. (*LL*) The Night Has a Thousand Eyes. Francis William Bourdillon. ArLo; BoLoP; CoGr; OBEV; OxBSP; PoToHe; WBLP

When love is ripe beyond bearing. What He Said. Perevin Muruvalar, *tr. fr. Tamil* by A. K. Ramanujan. PLW

When Love Meets Love. Thomas Edward Brown. UnPo

When love on time and measure makes his ground. False Love. *At. to* John Lilliat. EBEV
(Song: "When love on time and measure makes his ground.") EIL

When love was structured, so was verse — both fit. The Good Old Days. Barbara Fried. NBLV

When love with unconfinèd wings. To Althea, from Prison. Richard Lovelace. AWP; BeJo; BLPA; CaPo; EBEvV; FaBoBe; GBL; GGP; GTBS; GTBS-P; HAP; ImPo; InPS; JCP; LiTB; MeLP; NAEL-1; NOBE; NoP; NOSC; OBEV; PoE; PoRA; SCGP; SeCP; SeCV-1; TEP; TFi; TrGrPo

When Lovely Woman. Phoebe Cary. FaBoBe; UV

When Lovely Woman. Mary Demetriadis. FaBoPa; UV

When lovely woman, prone to folly. *Unknown.* FaBoPa

When lovely woman stoops to folly. Goldsmith. *Fr.* Vicar of Wakefield, The. CoGr; GTBS; GTBS-P; HAP; NoP; PrIm; UnPo
(Song: "When lovely woman stoops to folly.") AWP; BoLoP; EBEvV; FHYEP; NOBE; NOEC; OxAEP-1; TrGrPo
(Stanzas: On Woman.) ELP; PeIV
(When Lovely Woman Stoops to Folly.) SCGP; TFi
(Woman.) ImPo; LiTB; OBEV

When lovely woman stoops to folly. When Lovely Woman. Mary Demetriadis. FaBoPa; UV

When lovely woman stoops to folly and. T. S. Eliot. *Fr.* Waste Land, The. AmPP; CMoP; FaBoMo; HAP; LiTA; LiTM; MoAB; MoAmPo; NAWM-2; NoAM; NOBA; NOBE; NoP; OAEL-2; OxBA; OxBTC; TAP; UnPo; UV

When lovely woman wants a favour. When Lovely Woman. Phoebe Cary. FaBoBe; UV

When love's brief dream is done. Remember. Georgia Douglas Johnson. PoNe

When lyart leaves bestrow the yird. Burns. *Fr.* Jolly Beggars, The. EnRP, *sl. diff. vers.*; NBLV; NOEC; PoEL-4

When Ma Rainey/ Comes to town. Ma Rainey. Sterling A. Brown. Jaz

When Madame Bovary sat up shrieking. Fumetti. Robert Long. NAmP90

When Mahalia Sings. Quandra Prettyman. PoBA

When maidens are young, and in their spring. Aphra Behn. *Fr.* Emperor of the Moon. FF

When maidens such as Hester die. Hester. Charles Lamb. EnRP; GTBS; GTBS-P; OBEV

When maize stands more than ten feet high. Hey, Boys! Up Go We! *Unknown.* NOBAu

When making harmful gunnes, vnfruitfull glasses. A Prophesie When Asses Shall Grow Elephants. Sir John Harington. CBCK

When Malindy Sings. Paul Laurence Dunbar. AAP; PoBA; PoNe

When Mama Came Here as a Gold Panner, *sels.* Jana Harris.
"When mama came here as a gold panner." MDDM

When mama came here as a gold panner. Jana Harris. *Fr.* When Mama Came Here as a Gold Panner. MDDM

When man becomes more faithful to man. Communion II. Tchicaya U Tam'si, *tr. fr. French by* Ellen Conroy Kennedy. NegPo

When man has conquered space. Earth's Bondman. Betty Page Dabney. GoYe

When man in the bush with God may meet? (*LL*) Good-bye. Emerson. AnAmPo; LiTA; MeMAP; PFP; PoToHe; PWR; TAP; WGRP

When man walketh moon. T. Griffiths. BXAP

When many a day had come and fled. James Hogg. *See* Bonnie [*or* Bonny] Kilmeny gaed up the glen.

When many years we'd been apart. Reminiscence. Wallace Irwin. FiBHP; NOBL

When Mary Goes Walking. Patrick R. Chalmers. BoTP

When Mary Rand. Uncle Alfred's Long Jump. Gareth Owen. OBSP

When Mary thro' the Garden Went. Mary Elizabeth Coleridge. BoTP

When May has come, and all around. The Archer. Clinton Scollard. FaPON

When memory's fabled daughter. Notes for a History of Poetry. David Daiches. PoA

When men a dangerous disease did 'scape. To Doctor Empiric[k]. Ben Jonson. FaBoEE; NoP; SeCP

When men are laid away. Inscription for a Graveyard. Yvor Winters. CRP

When men grow old and their balls grow cold. Eskimo Nell. *Unknown.* FaBoBl

When men shall find thy flower [*or* flow'r], thy glory, pass. Samuel Daniel. *Fr.* To Delia. ESo; NAEL-1; NOBE; NoP; NoSic; OBEV; SCGP; Son; TrGrPo
(Sonnet: "When men shall find thy flower, thy glory, pass.") EIL

When men were all asleep the snow came flying. London Snow. Robert Bridges. BoNaP; CH; ChTr; CMoP; EBEV; EBEvV; EBVV; FaBoPP; GTBS-P; LiTB; LiTM; MoAB; MoBrPo; MoP; NoAM; NOBE; NOBVV; OAEL-2; OBNC; OxAEP-2; OxBTC; PoEL-5; TFi; TrGrPo; WiR

When mice with wings can wear a human face. (*LL*) The Bat. Theodore Roethke. GoJo; OBCA; PDV; PYC; SiSoPo; ZA

When Mike stuck a knife in Nancy. The Precinct Station. Louis Simpson. EOEF

When milkweed blows in the pasture. Horse-Chestnut Time. Kaye Starbird. PDV

When Milton sees his "late espoused saint." Confessional Poetry. Tony Harrison. DiPo

When mine eynen misteth. *Unknown.* EBEV
(All too late.) OAEL-1

When mistaken for clover. (*LL*) Third Limick. Ogden Nash. PeLi

When Mr. Apollinax visited the United States. Mr. Apollinax. T. S. Eliot. PoA

When Mr. Croxford. At the St. Louis Institute of Music. Ronald Wallace. GOYP

When Mrs. Gorm (Aunt Eloise). Opportunity. Harry Graham. FaBoCo; PeLV

When Mrs. Taflan Gruffyd Lewis left Dai's flat. What about You? Edward Pygge. BXAP; FaBoPa

When moiling seems at cease. "According to the Mighty Working." Thomas Hardy. CMoP

When moles still had their annual general meetings. Brief Reflection on Cats Growing in Trees. Miroslav Holub, *tr. by* Ewald Osers. CBNP; PWE

When 'mongst the youths you lately came. *Unknown, tr. fr. Greek by* Sydney Oswald. PeHV

When Monmouth the chaste read those impudent lines. An Excellent New Ballad Giving a True Account of the Birth and Conception of a Late Famous Poem Called the Female Nine. Charles Sackville. APAS

When morning came. The Brother. Peter Everwine. FYAP; NNaP

When morning has come, all the chief priests and elders of the people. Bible, *N.T. Fr.* St. Matthew. NAWM-1

When morning is breaking and darkness has fled. We Are Passing Away. Matilda C. Edwards. PWR

When Moses and his people. Just the Same Today. *Unknown.* BLRP; WBLP

When Moses in Horeb struck the rock. On Certain Wits. Howard Nemerov. HCAP; OxBC

When mother died. The Routine Things around the House. Stephen Dunn. NAmP90

When mother divorced you, we were glad. She took it and. The Victims. Sharon Olds. InPS; SoSe

When Mother Reads Aloud. *Unknown.* FaPON; ImGa

When Mother reads aloud, the past. When Mother Reads Aloud. *Unknown.* FaPON; ImGa

When Mother's drinking, the door to my room. Bottled. Jill Breckenridge. LoHo

When mothers weep and fathers richly proud. The Confirmation. Karl Shapiro. ErPo

When mountain rocks and leafy trees. Nature's Lineaments. Robert Graves. FaBoTw; RB

When mountains crumble and rivers all run dry. The Line of Beauty. Arthur O'Shaughnessy. TIRV

When music, heav'nly maid, was young. The Passions, an Ode for [*or* to] Music. William Collins. GTBS; GTBS-P

When my arms wrap you round I press. He Remembers Forgotten Beauty. W. B. Yeats. CTC
(O'Sullivan Rua to Mary Lavell. MeMBP

When my birthday was coming. Little Brother's Secret. Katherine Mansfield. FaPON; NAs

When my blood flows calm as a purling river. Communism. Ella Wheeler Wilcox. AnAmPo

When my breast labors with oppressive care, A Paraphrase of the Latter part of the Sixth Chapter of St. Matthew. James Thomson. ChIV-2

When my brother hogs. Blanket Hog. Paul B. Janeczko. TLR

When my brother Tommy. Two in Bed. Abram Bunn Ross. FaPON; NTCP

When My Desire. Ono no Komachi. VBLP

When my devotions could not pierce. Denial. George Herbert. GeHe; JCP; NAEL-1; NOBE; NoP; OAEL-1
(Deniall.) ESCV; PoEL-2; TOF

When My Dog Died. Freya Littledale. NTCP

When my father died. Between Here and Illinois. Ralph Pomeroy. Poetsp

When my father had been dead a week. White Apples. Donald Hall. TAP

When my flaps peel back, I am seen. Dermis. Anthony McNeill. PBCV

When my grandmother alberta was a girl. Alberta (Factory Poem/Variation 2). Brenda Marie Osbey. UTF

When My Grandmother Died. Sam Cornish. Poetsp

When/ my/ grandmother/ died. When My Grandmother Died. Sam Cornish. Poetsp

When my grandmother left the races with Mr. Hughes. Mr. Hughes. David Campbell. CBAP

When my grandmother was dying. Sorrow. T. R. Hummer. MT

When my Granny was dying. My Granny. Robert Adamson. FaBoMA

When my grave is broke up again[e]. The Relic. John Donne. EiL; EnRePo; FaPoB; FHYEP; GBL; HAP; HeIP; ImPo; LiTB; NOBE; NoP; NOSC; OAEL-1; PoEL-2; PPP; TFi
(Relique, The.) ESCV; MeLP; PoEL-2; SCGP; SeCP; SeCV-1

When my husband. Ten Years and More. Miriam Waddington. NOBC

When my life has enough of love, and my spirit enough of mirth. A Wanderer's Litany. Arthur Stringer. WGRP

When my life was thrifty, thrifty. The Shearing. *Unknown, tr. fr. Welsh by* Glyn Jones. OBWVE

When my little dog is happy. The Tale of a Dog. James H., Jr. Lambert. ZA

When my love becomes/ All-powerful. Ono no Komachi, *tr. fr. Japanese by* Geoffrey Bownas *and* Anthony Thwaite. PBWP

When my love swears [*or* sweares] that she is made of truth. Shakespeare. *Fr.* Sonnets. AWP; EBEV; HeIP; NAEL-1; NoP; NoSic; OAEL-1; OxAEP-1; PlP; PoEL-2; Poetr; PPP; SoSe; TEP; TrGrPo

When my mother died I was very young. Chimney Sweeper, The ("When my mother died I was very young.") Blake. *Fr.* Songs of Innocence. CH; EnRP; FaBoPV; FF; FHYEP; HeIP; InPK; NAEL-1; NAWM-2; NOEC; OAEL-2; OxAEP-2; OxBChV; PoE; Poetr; PPP; SCGP; SoSe; TEP; TFi

When My Poems were Lost. Mazisi Kunene, *tr. fr. Zulu by the author.* PeSAV

When My Sensational Moments Are No More. E. E. Cummings. Son

When my sister came back from Africa. Bill's Story. Mark Doty. PFL

When my son was born, the moon was not bright. Meng Chiao, *tr. by* Stephen Owen. *Fr.* Apricots Die Young. SuSp

When my uncle died I was afraid to cry. My Uncle's Death. Mu Tan, *tr. fr. Chinese.* LHF, *tr. by* Hualing Nieh

When my young brother was killed. War. Joseph Langland. AiP; FF

When Narcissus died the pool of his pleasure changed. The Disciple. Oscar Wilde. OAEL-2

When nature all is sad like me! (*LL*) Again rejoicing Nature sees. Burns. BoNaP

When Nature bids us leave to live, 'tis late. To William Roe. Ben Jonson. NOSC; OAEL-1; SeCV-1

When Nature dreamt of making bores. Epigram: On Sir Roger Phillimore. *Unknown.* FaBoCo; NBLV

When Nature had made all her birds. The Bobolinks. Christopher Pearse Cranch. GN

When Nature heard men thought her old. The Mistress. Sir William Davenant. JCP

When nature once in lustful hot undress. Giantess. Baudelaire, *tr. fr. French.* ErPo, *tr. by* Karl Shapiro; OBVE, *tr. by* Roy Campbell

When nature's God for our offenses died. A Stanza Put on Westminster Hall Gate. *Unknown.* APAS

When Neptune from his billows London spied. Of London Bridge, and the Stupendous Sight, and Structure Thereof. James Howell. ChTr; FaBoPP

When news came that your mother'd. Kin. Michael S. Harper. LCAP

When next we met, she bade me turn. Apostasy. Aus of Kuraiza, *tr. fr. Arabic by* Hartwig Hirschfeld. TrJP

When night comes down on the children's eyes. At Night in the Wood. Nancy M. Hayes. BoTP

When night drifts along the streets of the city. Solitaire. Amy Lowell. MoAmPo

When night first bids the twinkling stars appear. London at Night. John Gay. *Fr.* Trivia; or, The Art of Walking the Streets of London. FaBoPP

When night is come, and all around is still. Safe in His Keeping. Edgar Cooper Mason. BLRP

When night plows the meadows of darkness. Lonely Are the Fields of Sleep. Mary Newton Baldwin. GoYe

When night shadows slipped across the plain, I saw a man. A Nation Wrapped in Stone. Roberta Hill Whiteman. BoWoP; CDW

When night stirred at sea. The Planter's Daughter. Austin Clarke. CIP; OxBTC

When night-time bars me in. Snowdrops. Margiad Evans. OBWVE

When Night's Black Mantle. Mary Sidney Wroth, Countess of Montgomery. *Fr.* Urania. Son; WPE

When no soul walks the softened green. How Shall I Tell You? Carmen Tafolla. ETG

When no streams shall be left but in thine eye. (*LL*) Good Counsel to a Young Maid ("When you the sunburnt pilgrim see.") Thomas Carew. ErPo

When Noah sailed the wet and blue. Noah. Gerda Mayer. OTCP

When North first began. Lord North's Recantation. *Unknown.* PAH

When nothing is happening. How Everything Happens. May Swenson. HAP; RFM

When nothing whereon to lean remains. The Time to Trust. *Unknown.* BLRP

When now & often I begin to grieve. If I Had to Do It All Over Again, I'd Do It All Over You. Nick Totton. VaA

When Oats Were Reaped. Thomas Hardy. OxBTC

When ocean-clouds over inland hills. Misgivings. Herman Melville. NAAL-1; NOBA; OxBA

When o'er the wold the heedless lamb. Thomas Holcroft. NOEC

When Ogden his prosaic verse. On Dr. Samuel Ogden. R. P. Arden. FaBoCo

When Ol' Sis' Judy Pray. James Edwin Campbell. AAP

When old corruption first begun. Blake. *Fr.* Island in the Moon, An. RB (Quid the Cynic's Song.) FaBoNo

When old philosophers wrote the world's birth. A Panegyric on the Author of "Absalom and Achitophel." *Unknown.* APAS

When 'Omer Smote 'Is Bloomin' Lyre. Kipling. OtMeF

When on life's ocean first I spread my sail. On Hearing of the Intention of a Gentleman to Purchase the Poet's Freedom. George Moses Horton. AAP

When on My Bed the Moonlight Falls. Tennyson. *Fr.* In Memoriam A. H. H. EBVV, *abr.*; MeMBP; NoP; OAEL-2, *abr.*; PeECV, *abr.*; SCGP

When on my day of life the night is falling. At Last. Whittier. TrPWD; WGRP

When on my sick bed I languish. A Thought of Death. Thomas Flatman. NOSC

When on my soul in nakedness. The Quiet Pilgrim. Edith M. Thomas. AmWP

When on my time of living I reflect. My Thirty Years. Juan Fransico Manzano, *tr. fr. Spanish by* Oliver Cobarn *and* Ursula Lehrburger. TTY

When on some balmy-breathing night of spring. The Glow-Worm. Charlotte Smith. FM

When on the barn's thatch'd roof is seen. Signs of Christmas. Edwin Lees. OHIP

When, on the bearing mother, death's. Childbirth. Ted Hughes. NAs

When on the earth had settled moral night. The Divine Mission. Alfred Gibbs Campbell. AAP

When on the high bluff discovering. From the North Saskatchewan. Eli W. Mandel. NOBC

When on the Marge of Evening. Louise Imogen Guiney. AmWP

When on this page you look. *Unknown.* RoPo

When once I knew the Lord. Hymn of Sivaite Puritans. *Unknown.* WGRP

When once I rose at morning. Lament for the Woodlands. *Unknown, tr. fr. Irish by* Frank O'Connor. IIP

When once the presence of a friend is gone. Songs Anthome. Lady Jane Cavendish *and* Lady Elizabeth Brackley. *Fr.* Pastorall, A. KTR

When once the scourging prophet, with his cry. The Disused Temple. Norman Cameron. OxBS; OxBTC

When once the sun sinks in the west. Evening Primrose. John Clare. CH; TrGrPo

When one dreams of another. Three Dreams at Chiang-ling. Yüan Chen, *tr. fr. Chinese by* William H. Nienhauser. SuSp

When One Has Lived a Long Time Alone. Galway Kinnell. BAP-90

When One Loves Tensely. Don Marquis. FiBHP; NBLV

When one of the old, little stars doth fall from its place. Sidera Cadentia. Ford Madox Ford. OxBSP

When one or other rambles. Francis Daniel Pastorius. SCAP

When one was on the cursed tree to die. They Gave Him Vinegar and Gall (Matt. 27) and Wine Mingled with Myrrh (Mark 15). Francis Quarles. NOSC

When one's been drunk, the best relief I know. Hangover Cure. Amphis, *tr. fr. Greek.* FaBoUs

When oor lads gaed ower the tap. The Kirk Bell. John Buchan. NSI

When open trucks with German prisoners in them. Wiedersehen. Miller Williams. ArOW; NGP

When Orion straddled his apex of sky. The White Land. Roberta Hill Whiteman. HATNAP

When Orpheus sent down to the regions below. The Power of Music. Thomas Lisle. NOBL; PlP

When seyd was al this miracle, every man. Prologue to Sir Thopas.
Chaucer. *Fr.* Canterbury Tales, The. EnVB
(Whan said was al this miracle, every man.) NAEL-1

When Shakespeare, Jonson, Fletcher ruled the stage. In Defense of Satire.
Sir Carr Scroope. APAS

When shall I master this anxiety. August, Graf von Platen. *Fr.* Sonnets to
Karl Theodore German. PeHV

When shall I see the half-moon sink again. End of Another Home Holiday.
D. H. Lawrence. EBEV; FaBoMo; OxAEP-2

When shall I see the white thorn leaves agen. The Yellowhammer. John
Clare. NOBVV

When Shall My Pilgrimage, Jesus My Saviour, Be Ended?. *At.* to Andrew
Rudman, *tr. fr. Swedish* by Ernest Edwin Ryden. AH

When Shall We All Meet Again?. *Unknown.* AH

When shall we be married. *Unknown.* OxNR

When shall we learn, what should be clear as day. W. H. Auden. LiTA

When shawes beene sheene, and shrads [*or* shradds] fyll [*or* full] fayre.
Robin Hood and Guy of Gisborne. *Unknown.* ESPB

When She a Maiden Slim. Maurice Hewlett. OHIP

When she asked me to keep an eye on her things. Bewley's Oriental Café,
Westmoreland Street. Paul Durcan. CIP

When she begins to comprehend it. *(LL)* To a Child of Quality [Five Years
Old, the Author Supposed Forty]. Matthew Prior. GN; LiTB; NOBE;
NOEC; OBEV; PoEL-3

When she came suddenly in. The Door. Robert Graves. LiTB

When she came to visit me, I turned my face to the wall. Pediatrics. Carol
Muske. PBCAP

When she cannot be sure. Woman Alone. Denise Levertov. WPOW

When she carries food to the table and stoops down. Part of Plenty.
Bernard Spencer. ErPo; GBL; LiTB; LiTM

When She Comes Home. James Whitcomb Riley. AnAmPo; BLPL;
FaBoBe

When she entered his place of work. *(LL)* Stranger, Husband. Thomas
McCarthy. IB

When she fed the/ child. The Feeding. Joel Oppenheimer. NeAP

When she gives a "psychic reading." Crepe de Chine. Tennessee
Williams. NYBP

When she opens her eye this morning. For the Fourth Birthday of My
Daughter. George Barker. NAs

When She Plays upon the Harp or Lute. Moses ibn Ezra, *tr. fr. Hebrew* by
Solomon Solis-Cohen. TrJP

When she rises in the morning. Gloire de Dijon. D. H. Lawrence. CMoP;
ELP; EnLoPo; ErPo; GBL; NoAM

When she sleeps, her soul, I know. Doubts. Rupert Brooke. CH

When she snoozes. Lullaby for Suzanne. Michael Stillman. TLR

When she stopped by, just passing, on her way back from picking up. The
Lover. C. K. Williams. PWE

When she taught her little Lad. *(LL)* The Housewife. Catherine Cate
Coblentz. BLRP; TrPWD

When She Was Born. Robert Tofte. *Fr.* Laura. Son

When she was fourteen, she says. Butterfly. John Tranter. FaBoMA

When She Was Here, Li Bo. Peter Williams. InPK

When she was in her garden. Ann and the Fairy Song. Walter de la
Mare. *Fr.* Child's Day, A. FaBV

When she was little. Poem for Flora. Nikki Giovanni. BPo; CrSp; PoBA

When she was tied to the stake. *(LL)* Lamkin. *Unknown.* ESPB;
FaBoBa; OxBB

When she was young and dancing. Jane Austen at the Window. Patricia
Beer. FaBoWP

When shearing comes, lay down your drums. Whaler's Rhyme. *Unknown.*
NOBAu

When sheep. Sheep. Mike Thaler. ZA

When Silence Divests Me. Henry Birnbaum. GoYe

When silver snow decks Susan's clothes. Blind-Man's Buff. Blake. WiR

When silver snow decks Sylvio's clothes. Song by an Old Shepherd.
Blake. NTP

When, sin-stricken, burdened, and weary. "My Grace Is Sufficient for
Thee." *Unknown.* BLRP

When/ Sir/ Beelzebub. Sir Beelzebub. Edith Sitwell. *Fr.* Façade.
BoWoP; FaBoWP; HoPM; MoAB; MoBrPo; NALW; OxBTC; PrIm
(When Sir Beelzebub.) FaBoMo

When Sisyphus was pushing the stone up the mountain. Sisyphus.
Josephine Miles. NYBP

When ski-ing in the Engadine. Patience. Harry Graham. FiBHP; MoShBr

When skies are low. When Skies are Low and Days are Dark. N. M.
Bodecker. OTCP

When Skies are Low and Days are Dark. N. M. Bodecker. OTCP

When slaves their liberties require. Phillis's Resolution. William Walsh.
OxBSP

When sleep comes down to seal the weary eyes. *(LL)* Ere Sleep Comes
Down to Soothe the Weary Eyes. Paul Laurence Dunbar. CDC; PoNe

When sleeping alone. Hand-Jive. Sandie Castle. UL

When Slow October Changes Color. Umberto Piersanti, *tr. fr. Italian* by
Stephen Sartarelli. NeIt

When sly Jemmy Twitcher had smugged up his face. The Candidate.
Thomas Gray. PPP

When Smoke Stood up from Ludlow. A. E. Housman. *Fr.* Shropshire Lad,
A. FaPoB; MoBrPo; SCGP

When snow like sheep lay in the fold. In Memory of Jane Fraser [*or*
Frazer]. Geoffrey Hill. MoP; NAEL-2; NoAM; OxBTC

When soft Irene like a. Asclepiades, *tr. fr. Greek* by Edward Lucie-Smith.
GrAn

When soft September brings again. Pont-y-Wern. Arthur Hugh Clough.
Fr. Ambarvalia. FaBoPP

When Sol did cast no light. The [Valiant] Seaman's Happy Return [to His
Love]. *Unknown.* ChTr; GBP

When Sol had loosed his weary teams. Juggy's Christening. *Unknown.*
NOEC

When Solomon was reigning in his glory. Solomon and the Bees. John
Godfrey Saxe. GN

When some beloved voice that was to you. Substitution. Elizabeth Barrett
Browning. WGRP

When some beloveds, 'neath whose eyelids lay. Bereavement. Elizabeth
Barrett Browning. WPE

When some boys. Some Boys. Chuck Ortleb. GLP; PeHV

When some great sorrow, like a mighty river. This, Too, Shall [*or* Will]
Pass Away. Lanta Wilson Smith. BLPA

When some proud son of man returns to earth. Inscription on the Monument
of a Newfoundland Dog. Byron. TEP

When somebody as dear as he is dead. Horace, *tr. fr. Latin* by James
Michie. *Fr.* Odes. OBF

When someone brought. The Liberation of Music. Grace Cavalieri. Jaz

When someone hangs up, having said. The Business Life. David Ignatow.
NNaP

When Something Happens. James A. Randall, Jr.. BPo

When somewhere life. Beaver Moon — The Suicide of a Friend. Mary
Oliver. GOYP

When sommer toke in hand the winter to assail. The Earl of Surrey. *See*
When summer took in hand the winter to assail.

When Sorrow walked with me! *(LL)* Along the Road. Robert Browning
Hamilton. BLPA; BLPL

When sorrows had begirt me round. For Deliverance from a Fever. Anne
Bradstreet. NAAL-1; NALW

When Spoon River became a ganglion. Marx the Sign Painter. Edgar Lee
Masters. *Fr.* New Spoon River, The. NoAM; TAP

When Spring came,/ Leaves grew with a green fresh. *Unknown, tr. fr.*
Tlinglit Indian. RFM

When spring comes round, our apple tree. Our Tree. Marchette Chute.
SiSoPo

When spring escapes. Princess Nukada, *tr. fr. Japanese* by Kenneth Rexroth
and Ikuko Atsumi. WPJ

When stags do rut in the Plym. Alan Gibson. BXAP

When starlings cluster. Four Ways of Silence. Ron Schreiber. ETG

When Stars Are Shrouded. "I. T." EiL

When Statesmen gravely say "We must be realistic." W. H. Auden.
FaBoCo

When stealthy age creeps on me unaware. A Litany for Old Age. Una W.
Harsen. TrPWD

When storms arise. Paul Laurence Dunbar. TrPWD

When storms blow loud, 't is sweet to watch at ease. Suave Mari Magno.
Lucretius, *tr. by* W. H. Mallock. *Fr.* De Rerum Natura (On the Nature
of Things). AWP

When stubble-lands were greening, you came among the stooks. The Green
Autumn Stubble. *Unknown, tr. fr. Irish* by Patrick Browne. WTO

When suddenly, he took life by the hand. *(LL)* Abilene. Victoria Kohn.
UTF

When suddenly I am old and start to wear purple. *(LL)* Warning. Jenny
Joseph. AIW; FaBoWP; GOYP; OxBTC; PWE

When Sue Wears Red. Langston Hughes. TTY

When summer ended. Emplumada. Lorna Dee Cervantes. NoAM; PBCAP

When summer smiled, and birds on every spray. Written, Originally
Extempore, on Seeing a Mad Heifer Run through the Village. Elizabeth
Hands. ECWP

When summer strikes Tsukiji. The Missionary at Karnizawa. Osman
Edwards. *Fr.* Residential Rhymes. OBTV

When summer took in hand the winter to assail. The Earl of Surrey. SiPSBD

(Love's Rebel.) SiPS

(When sommer toke in hand the winter to assail.) AAS

When summer's heat hath done his part. Aestas. Joshua Sylvester. NOSC

When summer's in the city. The Ice-Cream Man. Rachel Field. FaPON

When Sun Came to Riverwoman. Leslie Silko. VoR

When Sun Doth Rise. Roger Williams. AH

When sun goes home. Taking Turns. Norma Farber. TLR

When sun, light-handed, sows this Indian water. Aubade: Lake Erie. Thomas Merton. NYBP

When sun the earth least shadow spares. The River Lynher. Richard Carew. *Fr.* Survey of Cornwall. FaBoPP

When Sunday came and old Katis.' Katisje's Patchwork Dress. Pauline Smith. PeSAV

When supper time is almost come. Milking Time. Elizabeth Madox Roberts. FaPON; GoJo; OBCA

When Susanna Jones wears red. When Sue Wears Red. Langston Hughes. TTY

When Susan's work was done, she'd [*or* she would] sit. Old Susan. Walter de la Mare. CMoP; MoBrPo

When swallows come I'm sick with wine. Tune: "Red Embroidered Slippers" — Spring Night. *Unknown, tr. fr. Chinese by* Sherwin S. S. Fu. SuSp

When swallows lay their eggs in snow. Fool's Song. Thomas Holcroft. CBNP; NOEC

When sweet Echo met Narcissus. Echo and Narcissus. Gerda Mayer. PeLV

When swelling buds their od'rous foliage shed. Apple-Culture. John Philips. *Fr.* Cyder. OxAEP-1

When swimming and croquet are in full sway, dolor. Dolor. Josephine Miles. FaBoWP

When sycamore leaves were a-spreadèn. Woak Hill. William Barnes. EnVR

When Sydney and the Bush first met. Sydney and the Bush. Les A. Murray. DiPo

When Tadlow walks the streets the paviours cry. Tadlow. Abel Evans. FaBoCo

When tempest winnowed grain from bran. The Victor of Antietam. Herman Melville. PAH

When that day comes, whose evening sayes I'm gone. His Sailing from Julia. Robert Herrick. PoEL-3

When that humble-headed elder, the sea, gave his wide. End of the Picnic. Francis Webb. NOBAu

When that I was and a little tiny boy. Shakespeare. *Fr.* Twelfth Night. CH; EBEV; EiL; EnRePo; FaBoCh; ImPo; LiTB; NOBE; NoP; NoSic; OAEL-1; PoRA; SCGP; TFi

(Clown's Song.) FaBoBl

(Feste's Song ("When that I was and a little tiny boy").) CBNP; NBLV; OxBoLi

(Song: "When that I was and a little tiny boy.") EBEvV; OxAEP-1; PoEL-2

(Wind and the Rain, The.) WiR

When that my sweet son was thirty winter old. O, My Heart Is Woe. *Unknown.* ChIV-2

When that repentant tears hath cleansed clear from ill. The Earl of Surrey. *Fr.* Paraphrase of Part of the Book of Ecclesiates, A. ChIV-1

When that rich soul which to her heaven is gone. The First Anniversary. John Donne. *Fr.* Anatomy [*or* Anatomie] of the World, An[: The First Anniversary]. NAEL-1; SeCV-1

When that the chill charocco blows. *At. to* Thomas Bonham. *See* Whenas the chill sirocco blowes.

When that the fields put on their gay attire. To the Redbreast. John Codrington Bampfylde. Son

When the African Arts. At Home in Dakar. Margaret Danner. BlSi

When the air is wine and the wind is free. Song of the Queen Bee. E. B. White. NYBP

When the Airplane Stopped. Barbara Drake. NGP

When the alcoholic passed the crucial point. Point of No Return. Robert Graves. BIrV

When the allegorical man came calling. The Inflatable Globe. Theodore Spencer. LiTA; PAW

When the ancient world foundered. Proper Names. Martin Sorescu, *tr. fr. Romanian by* D. J. Enright *and* Ioana Russell-Gebbett. PWE

When the ancients painted swans and tigers. On Seeing a Painting of Plants and Insects by Chü-ning. Mei Yao Ch'en, *tr. fr. Chinese by* Jonathan Chaves. SuSp

When the angry passion gathering in my mother's face I see. The Patter of the Shingle. *Unknown.* BLPA

When the animals come to us. Gary Lawless. EaPr

When the anxious hearts say "Where?" Missing. *Unknown.* WGRP

When the ape. Ay: His Hill. Mutamociyar, *tr. fr. Tamil by* A. K. Ramanujan. PLW

When the ash is before the oak. *Unknown.* FaBoUs

When the Ashes. Jaroslav Seifert, *tr. fr. Czech by* Jeffrey Fiskin *and* Erik Vestville. AnAn

When the Assault Was Intended to the City. Milton. GTBS; GTBS-P; NoP; SCGP; Son

When the Atlantic upsloped itself. Winter Tryst. Mark Van Doren. LiTA

When the autumn winds go wailing. Ungathered Love. Philip Bourke Marston. OBNC

When the autumn's breezes. Mr. Edward Fordham. Mary Weston Fordham. CBWP-2

When the bare branch responds to leaf and light. Spain. Dorothy Livesay. NOBC

When the barn catches fire. The Longing to Be Saved. Maxine W. Kumin. CAPP

When the battle was over. Masses. César Vallejo, *tr. by* Robert Bly. *Fr.* España, Aparta de me Este Caliz. RB

When the bells justle in the tower. A. E. Housman. NOBVV

When the bird flew from the Columbus hull. Jeremiad. Oscar Williams. LiTA

When the birds sang. *Unknown, tr. fr. Spanish by* Willis Barnstone. BoWoP

When the black herds of the rain were grazing. The Lost Heifer. Austin Clarke. BIrV

When the bleak winds of winter. Remember the Poor. Matilda C. Edwards. PWR

When the bombs dropped on us at the end of the war. A Chinaman's Chance. Alex Kuo. UL

When the bones are no longer curious. Overture for Bubble-Gum and Flute. Alistair Paterson. PeNZ

When the bones walk out of me. Never. George Reavey. BIrV

When the brain's black with demonic crisis. The Ferry Pirate. Douglas Oliver. NBrP

When the breaking wavelets pass all sparkling to the sky. Submarines. "Klaxon." NSI

When the breath of twilight blows to flame the misty skies. By the Margin of the Great Deep. "Æ." OBEV; OHCV

When the Bright Consort first stepped out of Han palace. Song of the Radiant Lady. Wang An-shih, *tr. fr. Chinese by* Jan W. Walls. SuSp

When the bright eyes of the day. Day and Night. James Stephens. BoTP

When the British warrior queen. Boadicea; an Ode. William Cowper. BeLS; FaBoEH; FaPoR

When the bronze annals of the oak-tree close. (*LL*) Advice to a Prophet. Richard Wilbur. AmPP; CAPP; FYAP; MAT; MoAmPo; NYBP; OBWP; OxBC; PoE; Poetr; PPP; TwCP; VCAP

When the buds began to burst. The Three Roses. Walter Savage Landor. NAEL-2

When the call comes, be calm. How to Watch Your Brother Die. Michael Lassell. GLP; PFL

When the car spun from the road and your neck broke. Death and the Sun. Derek Mahon. BiHa

When the census is taken, of course. Taking the Census. Charles Robert Thatcher. NOBAu

When the census man called upon Gail. George McWilliam. PeLi

When the Century Dragged. Robert Penn Warren. MoAmPo

When the child's forehead full of red torments. The Lice Seekers. Rimbaud, *tr. by* Kenneth Koch *and* George Guy. *Fr.* Illuminations. SOTW

When the chilled dough of his flesh went in an oven. Marked with D. Tony Harrison. *Fr.* School of Eloquence, The. NAEL-2; NoAM

When the Christ Child Came. Frederic E. Weatherly. OHIP

When the clapper hits the bell? (*LL*) The Bellman's Song. *Unknown.* EBEV; EiL; SCGP

When the clouds are upon the hills. *Unknown.* OxNR

When the clouds' swoln bosoms echo back the shouts of the many and strong. Thomas Hardy. *Fr.* In Tenebris. ChIV-1; CMoP; LiTB; LiTM; MeMBP; NoAM; NOBE; NoP; OxBTC; PrIm

When the cold comes. Where? When? Which? Langston Hughes. BPo

When the cold wind visits you from the corners of the earth. To Li Po. Tu Fu, *tr. fr. Chinese by* Robert Payne. TAL

When the corn's all cut and the bright stalks shine. Corn-Stalk Fiddle, The. Paul Laurence Dunbar. AAP

When the crop is fair in the olive-yard. The Cocooning. Frédéric Mistral, *tr. by* Harriet Waters Preston. *Fr.* Mirèio. AWP

When the crows fly away. My Love. Richard Shelton. GOYP

When the curtain of night, 'tween the dark and the light. Whistling Boy. Nixon Waterman. PoLF

When the dawn comes. *Unknown, tr. by* Arthur Waley. *Fr.* Kokin Shu. AWP

When the day darkens. The Unknown Wind. "Fiona Macleod." BoTP

When the day is stormy, and no sun shines through. A Trust-Song. Eben E. Rexford. BLRP

When the Days Shall Grow Long. Hayyim Nahman Bialik, *tr. fr. Hebrew by* A. M. Klein. TrJP

When the deep-piled winter snow/ melted on her roof. Antipater of Thessalonica, *tr. fr. Greek by* Robin Skelton. GrAn

When the dew is on the grass. *Unknown.* OxNR

When the dogstar is aglow. Garden Calendar. N. M. Bodecker. TLR

When the donkey saw the zebra. *Unknown.* RoPo

When the Dumb Speak. Robert Bly. NOBA

When the dying flame of day. Hymn of the Moravian Nuns of Bethlehem. Longfellow. PAH

When the eager squadrons of day are faint and disbanded. The Cult of the Celtic. Anthony C. Deane. BXAP; NOBL; PeLV

When the earth is turned in spring. The Worm. Ralph Wilhelm Bergengren. FaPON

When the earth with spring returning buds again. To the Nightingale. Fulbert of Chartres, *tr. fr. Latin by* Helen Waddell. MLL

When the echo of the last footstep dies. Eli W. Mandel. MoCV

When the exposed spirit, busy in daytime. Time Exposures. Muriel Rukeyser. PoA

When the Eye of Day Is Shut. A. E. Housman. Mes; NOBVV; OAEL-2

When the Fairies. Edward Dorn. NeAP

When the family upstairs moved away, I awoke in a bed. Furniture. Victor Martinez. AfAz

When the far south glittered. Pilgrimage. Austin Clarke. CIP; IPY; TIRV

When the farmer comes to town. The Farmer. *Unknown.* AS

When the feet of the rain tread a dance on the roofs. Gipsy-Night. Richard Hughes. OBWVE

When the fields catch flower. April. Vidame de Chartres, *tr. fr. French by* Swinburne. AWP

When the fierce north wind with his airy forces. The Day of Judgement [*or* Judgment]; an Ode. Isaac Watts. ECEV; HAP; NOBE; NOEC; NoP; OBEV
 (Day of Judgement, The.) ChIV-2; SCGP

When the fifth month comes. Lady Ise, *tr. fr. Japanese by* Etsuko Terasaki *and* Irma Brandeis. BoWoP

When the film *Tell England* came. A Grand Night. D. J. Enright. NSI

When the Five Prominent Poets. Josephine Jacobsen. TAP

When the flaming lute-thronged angelic door is wide. The Travail of Passion. W. B. Yeats. TrCP

When the floors, the walls, the windows in. Gangue. Edward Kleinschmidt. BAP-90

When the flower droops and the leaf wilts. Lotus. Hsü Wei, *tr. fr. Chinese by* Irving Y. Lo. SuSp

When the flower of the sun, the rose, of Lahore. Imperishable Fragrance. Charles Marie René Leconte de Lisle, *tr. fr. French by* Philip L. Miller. RiWo

When the flowers turn to husks. Cells Breathe in the Emptiness. Galway Kinnell. NaP; VGW

When the flush of a newborn sun fell first on Eden's green and gold. The Conundrum of the Workshops. Kipling. MoBrPo

When the Flyin' Scot. Uncle Henry. W. H. Auden. NOBL; PeHV; PeLV

When the foreman whistled. Field Poem. Gary Soto. PBCAP

When the forests have been destroyed their darkness remains. The Asians Dying. W. S. Merwin. CoAP; HCAP; NaP; NOBA; NYBP; VCAP

When the four quarters shall. Ark Overwhelmed. Jay Macpherson. *Fr.* Ark, The. NOBC

When the French fleet lay. Running the Blockade. Nora Perry. PAH

When the Frost Is on the Punkin. James Whitcomb Riley. AnAmPo; BoNaP; EBEvV; FaBoBe; FaBV; GGP; OBAL; PoLF

When the frost is on the punkin and the fodder's in the shock. (*LL*) When the Frost Is on the Punkin. James Whitcomb Riley. AnAmPo; BoNaP; EBEvV; FaBoBe; FaBV; GGP; OBAL; PoLF

When the full moon comes. Federico García Lorca. *See* When the full moon rises.

When the full moon rises. Song of Black Cubans. Federico García Lorca, *tr. fr. Spanish by* William B. Logan. SOTW
 (Song of the Cuban Blacks.) RaBo, *tr. by* Robert Bly
 (When the full moon comes.) RaBo, *tr. by* Robert Bly

When the game began between them for a jest. Stage Love. Swinburne. PoEL-5

When the gardener has gone this garden. In a Garden. Elizabeth Jennings. NOCV

When the gibbons howl one is sure it's dawn. Journeying by Stream: Following Chin-chu Torrent I Cross the Mountains. Hsieh Ling-yün, *tr. fr. Chinese by* Francis Westbrook. SuSp

When the god, needing something, decided to become a swan. Leda. Rainer Maria Rilke, *tr. fr. German by* Robert Bly. NU; RaBo

When the gold fever raged I was doing very well. The Miner's Lament. *Unknown.* AmFP

When the gong sounds ten in the morning/ and I walk to school by our lane. Vocation. Rabindranath Tagore. FaPON

When the grass grows over me! (*LL*) When the Grass Shall Cover Me. Ina Coolbrith. AmWP

When the Grass Shall Cover Me. Ina Coolbrith. AmWP

When the grass was closely mown. The Dumb Soldier. Robert Louis Stevenson. OxBChV

When the Great Gray Ships Come In. Guy Wetmore Carryl. AnAmPo; FaBoBe; PAH

When the great universe hung nebulous. Egoisme à Deux. Louisa S. Guggenberger. NOBVV

When the green grass rose in the spring. On the Bright Side. Carter Revard. VoR

When the Green Lies over the Earth. Angelina Weld Grimké. CDC; PoNe

When the Green Woods Laugh. Blake. *See* When the green woods laugh with the voice of joy.

When the green woods laugh with the voice of joy. Laughing Song. Blake. *Fr.* Songs of Innocence. BoTP; FHYEP; NAEL-2
 (When the Green Woods Laugh.) CH; EnRP; GoJo; NBLV; OxBChV

When the gunner spoke in his sleep the hut was still. The Gunner. Francis Webb. CBAP; FaBoMA

When the half-body dies its frightful death. Resurrection of the Right Side. Muriel Rukeyser. LCAP

When the heart's feeling. Thomas Moore. OxBSP

When the heat of the summer. A Dragonfly. Eleanor Farjeon. FaPON; PDV

When the heavens with stars are gleaming. For Who? Mary Weston Fordham. CBWP-2

When the herd were watching. William Canton. OHIP
 (Bethlehem.) BoTP

When the hermit made an end. Tennyson. *Fr.* Idylls of the King. PeVV

When the high/ Snows lie worn. Crows. Valerie Worth. ImGa

When the Himalayan peasant meets the he-bear in his pride. The Female of the Species. Kipling. BLPA; FaBoEH, Abr.; OtMeF

When the hounds of spring are on winter's traces. The Hounds of Spring. Swinburne. *Fr.* Atalanta in Calydon. AWP; CTC; EBVV; EnVR; FaBoBe; FaBV; GTBS-P; HAP; LiTB; NAEL-2; NOBE; NoP; OAEL-2; OBEV; PoE; PrIm; SCGP; TEP; TFi; TrGrPo; WeW
 (Chorus: "When the hounds of spring are on winter's traces.") EBVVPR

When the hours of day are numbered. Footsteps of Angels. Longfellow. AnAmPo

When the hurricane unfolds. The Hurricane. Luis Palés Matos, *tr. fr. Spanish by* Alida Malkus. FaPON

When the inmate stirs, the birds retire discreetly. A Bird-Scene at a Rural Dwelling. Thomas Hardy. FM

When the jets crowd close to the house tops. Desperate Message #1 (History). Mark Svenvold. UTF

When the judge with his wife having sport. *Unknown.* PeLi

When the knife slipped into and cut deeply into the fingerpad. History. Donald Hall. BAP-89

When the knight had finished, no one, young or old. Prologue to the Miller's Tale. Chaucer. *Fr.* Canterbury Tales, The. EnVB; NAWM-1

When the Kye Comes Hame. James Hogg. OxBS

When the Lad for Longing Sighs. A. E. Housman. *Fr.* Shropshire Lad, A. FaPoB; MoBrPo

When the Lamp Is Shatter'd. Shelley. CBLP; CH; ImPo; NAEL-2; PPP; TEP; TrGrPo

When the lamp is shattered. When the Lamp Is Shatter'd. Shelley. CBLP; CH; ImPo; NAEL-2; PPP; TEP; TrGrPo
 (Lines: "When the lamp is shattered.") EnRP; FF; MeMBP; NoP; OBEV; OBNC; PoEL-4; SCGP

When the land of El Kanesie awakens. Animism. Birago Diop, *tr. fr. French by* Ellen Conroy Kennedy. NegPo

When the landfolk of Galway converse with a stranger. Undertone. William Bedell Stanford. PeIV

When the last bus leaves, moths stream toward lights. Depot in Rapid City. Roberta Hill Whiteman. BoWoP

When the last Flavius, drunk with fury, tore. Juvenal, *tr. by* William Gifford. *Fr.* Satires. OBVE

When the last newspaper is printed and the ink is faded and dried. Freedom in Peril. "Sagittarius." UV

When the last sea is sailed, when the last shallow['s] charted. D'Avalos' Prayer. John Masefield. TrPWD

When the last star breathes like a rose. Sailors. Louis Simpson. NYBP

When the last voyage is ended. Joseph Lee. OHIP

When the least whistling wind begins to sing. Her Hair. Sir Robert Chester. *Fr.* Love's Martyr. EIL

When the leaves in autumn wither. Autumnus. Joshua Sylvester. EIL

When the Light Falls. Stanley Kunitz. MoAmPo

When the little armadillo. Mexican Serenade. Arthur Guiterman. FiBHP

When the little blue-bird. Let's Do It. Cole Porter. OBAL
(Let's Do It, Let's Fall in Love.) PeLV; UV, *sl. diff. vers.*

When the loneliness of the tomb went down into the marketplace. Mona Sa'udi, *tr. fr. Arabic* by Kamal Boullata. WPOW

When the Lord, Almighty God, came again to His throne. (*LL*) A Dream of the Rood. *At. to* Cynewulf. AnOE; OAEL-1

When the Lord brought back those that returned to Zion. Bible, *O.T., paraphrased* by Sir Thomas Wyatt. *Fr.* Psalms.
(Like unto Them That Dream.) TrJP

When the Lord climbed. *Unknown, tr. fr. Latin* by Helen Waddell. MLL

When the Lord fashioned man, the Lord his God. The Mother. Catulle Mendès, *tr. fr. French* by W. J. Robertson. TrJP

When the lover. The Vow. Galway Kinnell. VCAP

When the man comes home he takes off his hat. A Small Light. Cathy Song. TRP

When the man in the window seat. The Experts. Jack Myers. NAmP90

When the man is busy. Revolution Is One Form of Social Change. Audre Lorde. Poetr

When the manly man goes forth to hold his own on land or sea! (*LL*) The Manly Man. *Unknown.* BLPA; WBLP

When the map blossomed green. Elemental Journey: Anniversary Gift. Alicia Gaspar De Alba. AfAz

When the master lived a king and I a starving hutted slave beneath the lash, and. On Listening to the Spirituals. Lance Jeffers. PoBA

When the master sits at ease. Friend Cato. Anna Wickham. MoBrPo

When the Master was calling the roll. Anseo. Paul Muldoon. CIP; FaBoPV; PNI

When the mind is at peace. Layman P'ang, *tr. fr. Chinese* by Stephen Mitchell. EnIH

When the mind is dark with the multiple shadows of facts. Physiologus. Josephine Miles. BCF

When the Mint Is in the Liquor. Clarence Ousley. PoLF

When the Mississippi Flowed in Indiana. Vachel Lindsay. CMoP

When the mists have rolled in splendor. We Shall Know. *Unknown.* PWR

When the mob swerved. Truth and Consequences. Edward Baugh. PBCV

When the moon appears. My Mother on an Evening in Late Summer. Mark Strand. FYAP

When the moon comes up. The Moon Rises. Federico García Lorca, *tr. fr. Spanish* by William Bryant Logan. SOTW; TTTS

When the Moon Is Full. Elaine Equi. UTF

When the moon shines o'er the corn. The Field Mouse. "Fiona Macleod." FaPON; MoShBr

When the moon was full they came to the water. Moon Fishing. Lisel Mueller. CoAP

When the moon's splendour shines in naked heaven. To His Friend in Absence. Strabo Walafrid, *tr. fr. Latin* by Helen Waddell. PeHV

When the morn was shining clear. (*LL*) Ballad of the Tempest. James Thomas Fields. AnAmPo; BeLS; BLPL; FaBoBe; PoLF

When the morning was waking over the war. Among Those Killed in the Dawn Raid Was a Man Aged a Hundred. Dylan Thomas. Son

When the mouse died at night. The Mouse. Jean Garrigue. TwCP

When the mouse died, there was a sort of pity. Death of a Whale. John Blight. CBAP; OBD

When the mûne was shinin' clearly. (*LL*) A Mile an' a Bittock. Robert Louis Stevenson. NOBVV; OxBS

When the neat white. Duck. Valerie Worth. NTCP

When the Night and Morning Meet. Dora Greenwell. EBVV

When the night her visions is weaving. The Harp of David. "Yehoash," *tr. fr. Yiddish* by Alter Brody. TrJP

When the night is cloudy. In the Hours of Darkness. James Flexner. FaPON

When the night is still and far. The Highway. William Channing Gannett. WGRP

When the nightegale singes. *Unknown.* MiEL

When the nightingale to his mate. Alba ("When the nightingale to his mate.") Ezra Pound, *after the Provençal of* Arnaut Daniel. *Fr.* Langue d'Oc. OBVE; VGW; WeW

When the Norn Mother saw the whirlwind hour. Lincoln, the Man of the People. Edwin Markham. MoAmPo; OHIP; PAH; TrGrPo
(Lincoln the Great Commoner.) GN

When the North wind blows gently. (*LL*) Sprays of frost flowers form. "Ping Hsin." WPC

When the old Cove Creek Dam first was started. The Song of Cove Creek Dam. *Unknown.* AmFP

When the old flaming prophet climbed the sky. On a Virtuous Young Gentlewoman That Died Suddenly. William Cartwright. HAP

When the old, long-preserved wine stands at the repast. Five Arabic Verses in Praise of Wine. *Unknown, tr.* by Hartwig Hirschfeld. TrJP

When the old man died. (*LL*) Grandfather's Clock. Henry Clay Work. BLPA

When the Orient is lit by the great light. Vittoria da Colonna, *tr. fr. Italian* by Brenda Webster. WPOW

When the other children go. The Invisible Playmate. Margaret Widdemer. FaPON

When the outlook is dark, try the uplook. Try the Uplook. *Unknown.* BLRP

When the pale moon hides and the wild wind wails. The Wolf. Georgia Roberts Durston. TLR

When the peach ripens to a rosy bloom. The Morning-Glory. Sarah Helen Whitman. AmWP

When the pen that motto drew. (*LL*) Long neglect has worn away. Emily Brontë. NOBVV

When the pencil undresses for sleep. The Pencil's Dream. Tymoteusz Karpowicz, *tr. fr. Polish* by Czeslaw Milosz.
(Pencil's Sleep, The.) PoSu, *tr.* by Andrzej Busza *and* Bogdan Czaykowski

When the People Arose from Cheese. Duo Duo, *tr. fr. Chinese* by Donald Finkel *with* Li Guohua. SpMi

When the pequi fruit blossomed. A Mehinaku Girl in Seclusion. Cathy Song. OpBo

When the Pilgrims. The First Thanksgiving. Jack Prelutsky. NTCP

When the pills don't work any more. Cole Porter's Son. Gerrit Henry. EOEF

When the pistol muzzle oozing blue vapour. That Moment. Ted Hughes. *Fr.* Crow. FF; PoE; UV

When the place was green with the shaky grass. Where the Lilies Used to Spring. David Gray. OxBS

When the Pleiads were sinking; and he sank with them. (*LL*) Epitaph of Cleonicus. Theocritus [*or* Theokritus]. FaBoEE

When the plunging hoofs were gone. (*LL*) The Listeners. Walter de la Mare. AWP; BLPL; ClHu; CMoP; CoGr; EBEvV; FaPoB; FaPON; GGP; HAP; HeIP; HoPM; ImPo; InPK; InvP; LiTB; LiTM; MoAB; MoBrPo; MoP; NoAM; NOBE; NoP; NTP; OBEV; OBMV; OBSP; OtMeF; OxAEP-2; PIP; Poetr; PoRA; SoSe; TFi; TrGrPo

When the pods went pop on the broom, green broom. A Runnable Stag. John Davidson. CoGr; EBEvV; EBNV; FaPoR; FM; GGP; HAP; MeMBP; OBEV; OxBTC; PrIm; WiR

When the Poet Without Lying Verses in His Heart Returns to His Native Country, *sels.* Rade Drainac, *tr. fr. Serbo-Croatian* by Charles Simic. "Then, the drops were freezing on black branches of ancient ash trees." HSix

When the Portuguese came in. Guerillas. Seamus Deane. BiHa

When the power of Han decayed. The Lamentation. Ts'ai Yen, *tr. fr. Chinese* by Yi-T'ung Wang. SuSp

When the Present has latched its postern behind my tremulous stay. Afterwards. Thomas Hardy. BoNaP; CH; ChTr; CMoP; CoGr; EBEV; FaBoRV; GTBS-P; InPS; LiTB; LiTM; MeMBP; MoAB; MoBrPo; NOBE; NoP; OAEL-2; OBNC; OtMeF; OxAEP-2; PoEL-5; TFi; TOF; TrGrPo

When the priest made his entrance on the altar on the stroke of 10.30. 10.30 AM Mass, June 16, 1985. Paul Durcan. BiHa; CIP

When the prime mover of my many sighs. To Vittoria Colonna. Michelangelo, *tr. fr. Italian* by Longfellow. AWP

When the Prince, who was terribly smit. Joyce Johnson. PeLi

When the procession falls to its knees tomorrow. Mortar Salvos. Jaroslav Seifert, *tr. fr. Czech* by Jeffrey Fiskin *and* Erik Vestville. AnAn

When the Prophet. Stephen Crane. AnAmPo

When the proud fleet that bears the red-cross flag. Wordsworth. *Fr.* Prelude [*or,* Growth of a Poet's Mind], The. EnRP; FaBoPV; OAEL-2

When the proud World does most my world despise. Robert Nichols. *Fr.* Sonnets to Aurelia. OBMV

"When the Pulitzers showered on some dope." Words for Hart Crane. Robert Lowell. CMoP

When the rain an the breeze an the storm an the sun. Quaco Sam. *Unknown.* FaBoVe

When the rain drums loud on the leaf. Resemblance. *Unknown, tr. fr. Hawaiian* by N. B. Emerson. WTO

When the Rain Raineth. *Unknown.* GBP; RB

When the rain smell comes with the wind. (*LL*) Rain smell comes with the wind. Leslie Silko. UnPo; VoR

When the rains began. The Prophetess. Dorothy Livesay. MoCV

When the water fell. Flooded Mind. Norman MacCaig. OxBC

When the water's calm. *Unknown, tr. fr. Chippewa Indian* by Jerome K. Rothenberg. STP

When the waves of trouble roll. Show Me Thyself. Margaret E. M. Sangster. TrPWD

When the weather is rough, said the anxious child. Contemporary Song. Theodore Spencer. LiTA

When the weather suits you not. Try Smiling. *Unknown.* BLPA; PWR; WBLP

When the white feet of the baby beat across the grass. Baby Running Barefoot. D. H. Lawrence. NoP

When the white flame in us is gone. Dust. Rupert Brooke. MoBrPo; OxBTC

When the white fog burns off. The Depths. Denise Levertov. NaP; NU

When the white waters fill the spring embankments. Wild Geese on the Lake. Shen Yüeh, *tr. fr. Chinese* by Richard B. Mather. SuSp

When the white wave of a glory that is hardly I. Sinfonia Domestica. Jean Starr Untermeyer. MoAmPo

When the Wild Goose Finds Food He Calls His Comrades — I Ching. Jan Kemp. PeNZ

When the wind blows. *Unknown.* OxNR

When the wind blows. Wind Song. Lilian Moore. SiSoPo

When the wind blows loud and fearful. The Beggar Boy. Cecil Frances Alexander. OxBChV

When the wind blows, walk not abroad. To the Maids Not to Walk in the Wind. Oliver St. John Gogarty. ErPo

When the wind is asleep and the weather set fair. *Unknown, tr. fr. Anglo-Saxon. Fr.* Phoenix, The. ASW, *tr.* by Kevin Crossley-Holland

When the wind is in the east. Mother Goose. BoTP; CTSV; FaBoUs; FaBoVe; OxNR

When the wind is in the thrift. By the Saltings. Ted Walker. NYBP

When the wind works against us in the dark. Storm Fear. Robert Frost. CMoP; OxBA

When the window glass blows in. Alan Dugan. AnAn

When the Wise Woman is queen. *(LL)* Let Wisdom Wear the Crown: Hymn for Gaia. Elsa Gidlow. SRLS

When the Wise Woman wears the crown. Let Wisdom Wear the Crown: Hymn for Gaia. Elsa Gidlow. SRLS

When the woods are green again. Midsummer Moon. "E. M. G. R." BoTP

When the words rustle no more. Stillness. James Elroy Flecker. CH; GoJo; MoBrPo

When the Work's All Done This Fall. *Unknown.* AS

When the World Ends. Mark Van Doren. GoYe

When the world goes voodoo. Creed. Walter Lowenfels. PoNe

When the world has become a pestilence. Plague. Robert Creeley. PFL

When the World Is Burning. Ebenezer Jones. OBEV

When the world is fast asleep. The Dream-Ship. Eugene Field. AnAmPo

When the world takes over for us. Lear. William Carlos Williams. MeMAP; NAAL-2; NOBA; PoA

When the world vanishes, I will come back. Some Night Again. William Stafford. GOYP

When the World Was in Building. Ford Madox Ford. CTC

When the world's folk, one day of freedom. The Labourer. Iolo Goch, *tr. fr. Welsh* by Gwyn Williams. OBWVE

When the years have died away.' *(LL)* The Poet's Song. Tennyson. EBVV; ELP; EPCY

When the yellow bird's note was almost stopped. Rejoicing at the Arrival of Chi'en Hsiung. Po Chü-i, *tr. fr. Chinese* by Arthur Waley. AWP

When the young Augustus Edward. On the Beach. Charles Stuart Calverley. FiBHP

When the young have grown tired. For Thomas Moore. James Simmons. BiHa; PBCIP

When Thee (O holy sacrificed Lamb). To the Blessed Sacrament. Henry Constable. NoSic

When their eyes opened, it was more than morning. Making Camp. David Wagoner. VCAP

When their time comes they fall. Plums. Gillian Clarke. SCBI

When their vigilance slipped. One Life. Dinah Butler. AIW

When there are animals about, who else. Talking to Animals. Barbara Howes. GrPl

When there are so many we shall have to mourn. In Memory of Sigmund Freud. W. H. Auden. HAP; LiTB; NoAM; OAEL-2; OxBA

When There Is Peace. Austin Dobson. PAH

When There Were Trees. Nancy Willard. FoLa

"When there's no one about in the Quad." *(LL)* Idealism. Ronald Arbuthnott Knox. FaBoCo; NBLV

When these graven lines you see. A Happy Man. Carphyllides, *tr. fr. Greek* by E. A. Robinson. AWP

When these old woods were young. Under the Woods. Edward Thomas. CH

When these were past, thus gan the Titanesse. Mutability. Spenser. *Fr.* Faerie Queene, The. PoEL-1

When they are half-addressed. *(LL)* The Saginaw Song. Theodore Roethke. NBLV; RB

When they arrest you, you say, why me. The Behaviorist. Van K. Brock. ArOW

When they ask your name. Children. Russell Edson. AmPA

When they bare the iron hand. *(LL)* The Martyr. Herman Melville. PoEL-5; TAP; TrGrPo

When they came. Taking Leave. Carol Ganzer. BTR

When they came to that blue harbour. Home. Vincent O'Sullivan. PeNZ

When they can sing no more. *(LL)* Coda. James Tate. AmPA; NYBP

When they confess that they have lost the penial bone. God Bless America. John Fuller. OBSV; PeLV

When they entered through the back door. The Morning They Shot Tony Lopez, Barber and Pusher Who Went Too Far, 1958. Gary Soto. PBCAP

When they found Giotto. Allan M. Laing. FiBHP

When they grab my leg. First Problem. Aimé Césaire, *tr. fr. French* by Ellen Conroy Kennedy. NegPo

When they had won the war. The Inner Part. Louis Simpson. PBCV; RaBo

When they have completed its re-edification. South Parks Road. James Fenton. PeLV

When They Have Lost. C. Day Lewis. MoAB; MoBrPo

When they [or Quhen thai] him fand, and gude [or gud] Wallace him saw. Wallace's Lament for the Graham. Henry the Minstrel. *Fr.* Wallace, The.

(Lament for the Graham.) OxBS

When they in throngs a safe retirement seek. William Diaper, *after the Greek of* Oppian. *Fr.* Halieutica. OBVE

When they killed my mother it made me nervous. The State. Randall Jarrell. LiTM

When they learned 'twas a bull — the great Duke of Buccleuch! *(LL)* The Duke Of Buccleuch. J. A. Phelp. NOBAu

When they love but live no more. *(LL)* Arethusa. Shelley. EnRP; GN; WiR

When they lowered you in the earth. Disappearance. Willis Barnstone. IMW

When they needed a foreign part. Partial Accounts. William Meredith. GLP

When they pass the pink ice cream. *Unknown.* RoPo

When they play like that where everyone is. *Unknown, tr. fr. Tepehua Indian* by Charles Boilès. *Fr.* Tepehua Thought-Songs. STP

When they said Carrickfergus I could hear. The Singer's House. Seamus Heaney. EBEV; IIP

When they said the time to hide was mine. The Rabbit. Elizabeth Madox Roberts. OBCA

When they sailed out of Amsterdam. The Flying Dutchman. Ian D. Colvin. PeSAV

When they saw off Dai Evan's da. Fforestfawr. Kingsley Amis. *Fr.* Evans Country, The. FaBoBl; NOBL

When they saw Patroklos dead. The Horses of Achilles. C. P. Cavafy, *tr. fr. Greek* by Edmund Keeley *and* Philip Sherrard. OBD

When they sd to me this. When. Philip Appleman. BXAP

When they sent the robot camera down. Robot Camera. Robert Johnstone. PNI

When they shook the box, and poured out its chances. For a Daughter Gone Away. William Stafford. AnAn; SV

When they shot Malcolm Little down. At That Moment. Raymond R. Patterson. PoBA

When they stop poems. Today Is a Day of Great Joy. Victor Hernandez Cruz. TTY

When they took us to the shower I saw. Death Camp. Irena Klepfisz. GLP

When they woke me. Coming Back. Joseph Bruchac. CDW

When Thickly Beat the Storms of Life. Gurdon Robins. AH

When thin-strewn memory I look through. Miss Loo. Walter de la Mare. CMoP; OxBTC

When things go wrong, as they sometimes will. Don't Quit. *Unknown.* BLPA

(You Mustn't Quit. PoToHe

When This Blasted War Is Over. *Unknown.* NSI

When This Cruel War Is Over. Charles C. Sawyer. AmFP

When this crystal shall present. To a Lady Upon a Looking-Glass Sent. James Shirley. BeJo

When this fly lived, she used to play. A Fly That Flew into My Mistress's Eye. Thomas Carew. CaPo

When, this incredible thing, the principal of the junior high. Women Who Cook. Anita Skeen. GLP

When this is the thing you put on. Armor. James Dickey. CoAP

When this man, Manes, lived, he was a slave. Anyte. *See* Alive, this man was Manes, a common slave.

When This Old Hat Was New. *Unknown.* OBET

When this troubled life is over, hide Thou me. Hide Thou Me. *Unknown.* AmFP

When this yokel comes maundering. The Plot against the Giant. Wallace Stevens. CMoP; FF; OxBA; SAmP

When thou and I are dead, my dear. Inseparable. Philip Bourke Marston. BoLoP

When thou art dead, and all thy wretched crew? (*LL*) Sonnet: Written on the Day That Mr. Leigh Hunt Left Prison. Keats.

When thou complainst the heat, and feeds the fire. (*LL*) Feed still thy self, thou fondling, with belief. *Unknown.* NoSic

When Thou Did Thinke I Did Not Love. Sir Robert Ayton.

When Thou Didst Think I Did Not Love. Sir Robert Ayton. *See* When Thou Did Thinke I Did Not Love.

When thou dost take this sacred book into thy hand. On the Bible. Thomas Traherne. ChIV-1

When thou hast spent the ling[e]ring day in pleasure and delight. Gascoigne's [*or* Gascoygnes] Good-Night. George Gascoigne. AAS; NOCV; NoSic

When Thou Must Home. Thomas Campion, *after the Latin of* Propertius. AWP; EiL; EnLoPo; EnRePo; NoP; NoSic; OxAEP-1; OxBSP; PoEL-2; PoRA

When thou must home to shades of underground. When Thou Must Home. Thomas Campion, *after the Latin of* Propertius. AWP; EiL; EnLoPo; EnRePo; NoP; NoSic; OxAEP-1; OxBSP; PoEL-2; PoRA (To Shades of Underground.) ChTr

When Thou Passest through the Waters. Henry Crowell. BLRP

"When thou passest through the waters." Passing Through. Annie Johnson Flint. BLRP

When thou, poor[e] excommunicate. To My Inconstant Mistress [*or* Mistris]. Thomas Carew. BeJo; EnLoPo; MeLP; NOBE; SeCV-1; TFi; TrGrPo
(Song: To My Inconstant Mistress.) CaPo; GBL; JCP; NoP; SeCP
(To His Inconstant Mistress.) OBEV

When thou shalt be dispos'd to set me light. Shakespeare. *Fr.* Sonnets. OxAEP-1

When thou taught'st Cambridge and King Edward Greek. (*LL*) On the Detraction Which Followed upon My Writing Certain Treatises. Milton. PoE; Son

When thou thy youth shalt view. To Phryne. Owen Felltham [*or* Feltham]. NOSC

When thou to my true love com'st. Westphalian Song. *Unknown, tr. fr. German by* Samuel Taylor Coleridge. AWP; OBVE

When Thraso meets his friend, he swears by God. Thraso. Samuel Rowlands. NoSic

When thrones shall crumble and moulder to dust. *Unknown.* FaBoEH

When through the North a fire shall rush. Day of Judgement. Henry Vaughan. ChIV-2

When through the Universe with Horrour spread. Urania: The Divine Muse. On the Death of John Dryden, Esq. Lady Sarah Piers. KTR

When through valley and o'er mountain. Lays of Tom-cat Hiddigeigei. Joseph Victor von Scheffel, *tr. by* William Fitzgerald. OFC

When thy beauty appears. Thomas Parnell. OBEV; OxAEP-1

When thy bright beams, my Lord, so strike mine eye. Edward Taylor. *Fr.* Preparatory Meditations Before My Approach to the Lord's Supper. NAAL-1

When Thy Heart with Joy O'erflowing. Theodore Chickering Williams. AH

When Thy King Is a Boy, *sels.* Ed Roberson.
"You black out the sun." PoBA

When time has made you wrinkled, sore and slow. A Long Way After Ronsard. James Simmons. PBCIP

When to assure us on our way. A Rhenish Carol. Robert Finch. NAs, *ad. by* Bernard de la Mannoye

When to Her Lute. Thomas Campion. *See* When to Her Lute Corinna [*or* Corrina] Sings.

When to Her Lute Corinna [*or* Corrina] Sings. Thomas Campion. AAS; BOEP; NAEL-1; NoP; NoSic; OAEL-1; PoE

When, to my deadly [*or* deadlie] pleasure. Sir Philip Sidney. CBLP; EnLoPo; PoEL-1

When to my eyes. Midnight. Henry Vaughan. ChIV-2; ESCV

When to my lone soft bed at eve returning. Povre Ame Amoureuse. Louise Labé, *tr. fr. French by* Robert Bridges. AWP

When to the flowers so beautiful. The Forget-Me-Not. *Unknown.* BoTP

When to the music of Byrd or Tallis. King's College Chapel. Charles Causley. PeECV; TOF

When to the sessions of sweet silent thought. Shakespeare. *Fr.* Sonnets. ArLo; AWP; ClHu; CTC; EBEV; EBEvV; EiL; EnRePo; FaBoRV; FaBV; FaPoB; FF; GBL; HAP; HeIP; ImPo; InPS; LiTB; NAEL-1; NOBE; NoP; NoSic; OAEL-1; OBEV; OxAEP-1; PoE; PoEL-2; PoLF; PoRA; PPP; PrIm; SCGP; TEP; TFi; TrGrPo
(Remembrance. GTBS; GTBS-P

When Tom and Elizabeth took the farm. The Magpies. Denis Glover. NTP; PeNZ

When Tomorrow Is Too Long. Tanure Ojaide. HBAPE

When Toroi Bandi was alive. Toroi Bandi. *Mongol Oral Tradition, tr. by* C. R. Bawden. WTO

When trees did bud, and fields were green. Doun the Burn, Davie. Robert Crawford. ScCV

When trouble comes your soul to try. The Friend Who Just Stands By. B.Y. Williams. PoLF; PoToHe

When trout swim down Great Ormond Street. Conrad Aiken. *Fr.* Priapus and the Pool. NoAM; NOBA

When tunes jigged nimbler than the blood. Song from a Country Fair. Léonie Adams. GoJo; GrPl

When Two Are Parted. Heine, *tr. fr. German by* Louis Untermeyer. AWP

When two Evangelists shall seem to vary. On The Gospel. Francis Quarles. ChIV-2

When two lovers love each other well. Young Bearwell. *Unknown.* ESPB

When two plates of earth scrape along each other. Quake Theory. Sharon Olds. PBCAP

When two strong men stand face to face, though they come from the ends of the earth! (*LL*) The Ballad of East and West. Kipling. EBNV; FaBoBe

When Two Suns Do Appear. Sir Philip Sidney. *Fr.* Arcadia. EnRePo; SiPS; SiPSBD

When two who love are parted. When Two Are Parted. Heine, *tr. fr. German by* Louis Untermeyer. AWP

When Ulysses braved the wine-dark sea. Making the Move. Paul Muldoon. NoAM

When vain desire at last and vain regret. The One Hope. Dante Gabriel Rossetti. *Fr.* House of Life, The. NAEL-2; OAEL-2; PFP

WHEN Venus first did see. Adonis. Theocritus [*or* Theokritus], *tr. fr. Greek.* NoSic

When Venus her Adonis found. The Death of Adonis. Philip Ayres, *after the Greek of* Theocritus. OBVE

When Very was a celibate. Varitalk. Weare Holbrook. NYBP

When Vice triumphant holds her sov'reign sway. Byron. *Fr.* English Bards and Scotch Reviewers. FHYEP

When violets were springing. Words. John Hay. AnAmPo

When walnuts grew in stands like oak. Walnutry. Robert Morgan. MT

When wars and ruined men shall cease. Prayer against Indifference. Joy Davidman. TrPWD

When war's red banner trailed along the sky. Robert G. Shaw. H. Cordelia Ray. AAP; BlSi; CBWP-3; Son

When was it that the particles became. Wallace Stevens. PoA

When Washington has been destroyed. The Destruction of Washington. Reed Whittemore. NGP

When/ Water forgets. Fire. Fazil Hüsnü Daglarca. CRP

When waves invade the yellowing wheat. Composed While under Arrest. M. Y. Lermontov, *tr. fr. Russian by* Max Eastman. AWP

When we are dead, and now no more. To My Ingenuous Friend, R. W. Henry Vaughan. BeJo

When we are dead, some Hunting-boy will pass. The Statue. Hilaire Belloc. OxAEP-2

When we are like two drunken suns. Yvonne Caroutch, *tr. fr. French.* (When we are two drunk suns.) BoWoP, *tr. by* Willis Barnstone *and* Elene Kolb

When We Are Men. Stella Mead. BoTP

When we are old and these rejoicing veins. Edna St. Vincent Millay. ErPo; VGW

When we are shadows watching over shadows. Two Shadows. Elizabeth Spires. DiPo

When we are standing in the parking lot. When. Sharon Olds. WoWa

When we are two drunk suns. Yvonne Caroutch. *See* When we are like two drunken suns.

When we as strangers sought. At an Inn. Thomas Hardy. NOBVV

When we behold. Dahlias. Padraic Colum. GoJo

When we came down from the country, we were strangers to the sea. Down from the Country. John Blight. CBAP

When we carried you, Siân, that winter day. Burial Path. Ruth Bidgood. AngWe

When we come to that dark house. Edith Sitwell. *Fr.* Sleeping Beauty, The. OBMV

When we count out our gold at the end of the day. Service. Georgia Douglas Johnson. CDC

When we dream of what has gone before. Questions of Our Time. Kwesi Brew. PAW

When we enter the unknown. Our Houses. Linda Hogan. CrSp

When we fell apart in the Badlands and lay still. In the Badlands. David Wagoner. UnPo

When we first rade down Ettrick. Ettrick. Lady John Scott. SoSe; WPE

When we fought campaigns (in the long Christmas rains). Many Sisters to Many Brothers. Rose Macaulay. NSI

When we fought the Yankees and annihilation was near. Jubilation T. Cornpone. Johnny Mercer. OBAL

When we get out of the glass bottles of our ego. D. H. Lawrence. EaPr

When We Go Home Again. Daisy Zamora, *tr. fr. Spanish by* Miriam Ellis. WoWa

When we go home again to our old land. When We Go Home Again. Daisy Zamora, *tr. fr. Spanish by* Miriam Ellis. WoWa

When we go out into the fields of learning. Fields of Learning. Josephine Miles. NoAM

When we have come this long way. Anniversary Poem for the Cheyennes Who Fell at Sand Creek. Lance Henson. VoR

When we have thrown off this old suit. The Question Whither. George Meredith. WGRP

When we in kind embracements had agre'd [agreed]. *Unknown. Fr.* Zepheria. AAS; Son

When we laugh in the desert. Desert. Michael Cadnum. PFL

When we lay where Budmouth Beach is. Budmouth Dears. Thomas Hardy. *Fr.* Dynasts, The. CH

When we learn. It Is the Season. Josephine Jacobsen. TAP

When We Looked Back. William Stafford. NYBP

When we loved. Loving. Jane Stembridge. NMM

When we meet them after death we will merge. Post Mortem as Angels. Barry Goldensohn. NAmP90

When we moved here, pulled. An Oregon Message. William Stafford. CoAP

When we, my love, are gone to dust. A Song of Dust. Lord De Tabley. EnLoPo

When we on simple rations sup. Washing the Dishes. Christopher Morley. PoLF

When we parted with you at Geneve. An Epistle to John Walker, Esq. "Eliza." *Fr.* Tour to the Glaciers of Savoy, A. ECWP

When we played in the nursery till seven. Hello There. Brian S. Salome. BXAP

When we reach the field. Celebration: Birth of a Colt. Linda Hogan. HATNAP

When we rested between marches, I read Aristophanes. The Virgin Warrior. Gwendolyn MacEwen. FaBoWP

When we rolled up the three armored vehicles. One Morning We Brought Them Order. Alfred M. Lee. FF

When we sat his mother on her tail, he mouthed her teat. Ted Hughes. *Fr.* Sheep. OBD

When we saw human dignity. Easter 1984. Les A. Murray. ChIV-2

When we shuddered and took into ourselves. The Whole Story. William Stafford. NNaP

When we sigh about our trouble. Good Medicine. *Unknown.* PWR

When we stand on the tops of things. Emily Dickinson. PoE

When we start breaking up in the wet darkness. Consolations of Philosophy. Derek Mahon. BIrV; CIP; SCBI

When We That Now Ha' Childern Wer Childern. William Barnes. NOBVV

When We Two Parted. Byron. BoLoP; CBLP; EBEvV; EnRP; FHYEP; GTBS; GTBS-P; HoPM; NAEL-2; NOBE; NoP; OBEV; OBNC; PIP; PoLF; SCGP; TFi; TrGrPo; UV

When We Two Parted. John C. Desmond. UV

When we were a soft amoeba. Ere You Were Queen of Sheba. Sir Arthur Shipley. FaBoCo

When we were charming *Backfisch.* Friendship. Katherine Mansfield. PeHV

When we were children, clasping hands. But You, My Darling, Should Have Married the Prince. Kathleen Spivack. AmPA; NMM

When we were children old Nurse used to say. The Quiet House. Charlotte Mew. BrRo; EBEV; NALW

When we were farm-boys, years ago. Recollections of "Lalla Rookh." John Townsend Trowbridge. OBAL

When we were first together as lover and beloved. Teaching To Shoot. Valentine Ackland. VBLP

When we were girl and boy together. Ballad of Human Life. Thomas Lovell Beddoes. BeLS

When we were idlers with the loitering rills. To a Friend. Hartley Coleridge. PoLF
(Friendship.) OBEV
(Sonnet: To a Friend.) OBNC

When we were little childer we had a quare wee house. Grace for Light. "Moira O'Neill." TIRV

When we were little, wandering boys. Fratri Dilectissimo. John Buchan. OtMeF

When we were little we could call anything home. *(LL)* Dialogue on Finding Someplace to Live. Lori Storie-Pahlitzsch. LoHo

When we were married eight years. Tryst. Eve Merriam. NMM

When we were silly sisters seven. Fair Mary of Wallington. *Unknown.* ESPB
(Bonny Earl of Livingston, The.) OxBB

When we were small we could call anything home. Dialogue on Finding Someplace to Live. Lori Storie-Pahlitzsch. LoHo

When We Were Very Silly. J. B. Morton. FaBoPa
Sels.
"Hush, hush,/ Nobody cares!"
(Hush, Hush.) UV
Now We Are Sick.
Someone Asked the Publisher. UV
Theobald James.

When we would reach the anguish of the dead. Near an Old Prison. Frances Cornford. OBMV

When weary with the long day's care. To Imagination. Emily Brontë. EnVR

When well we speak, and nothing do that's good. The Chewing of the Cud. Robert Herrick. ChIV-1

When we're done with this embrace. Syndrome. Robert Louthan. PFL

When wert thou born, Desire? Of the Birth and Bringing Up of Desire. Edward de Vere, Earl of Oxford. FaBoEE; NoSic; SCGP

When Wesley died, the Angelic orders. Wesley in Heaven. Thomas Edward Brown. OBNC

When Westwall Downes [*or* Westwell Downs] I gan to tread. On Westwall Downes [*or* On Westwell Downs]. William Strode. FaBoPP; GGP; JCP; NOSC; PoEL-2

When what has helped us has helped us enough. The Place of Backs. W. S. Merwin. HoPM

When what hugs stopping earth than silent is. E. E. Cummings. PoA

When whelmed the altar, priest and creed. Sir William Watson. WGRP

When, when, and whenever death closes our eyelids. Ezra Pound. *Fr.* Homage to Sextus Propertius. MeMAP; MoAB; OBMV; PoA

When whispering strains do softly steal. In Commendation of Music. William Strode. ELP; OBEV

When Whistler's Mother's Picture's frame. Don Marquis. *Fr.* To a Lost Sweetheart. FiBHP

When white people speak of being uptight. The Dancer. Al Young. PoBA

When Wild Confusion Wrecks the Air. Mather Byles. AH

When Will I Be Home? Li Shang-yin, *tr. fr. Chinese by* Kenneth Rexroth. OHMPC

When will I be home? I don't Know. When Will I Be Home? Li Shang-yin, *tr. fr. Chinese by* Kenneth Rexroth. OHMPC

When will I finally become the president's wife? *(LL)* Patriotic Poem. Diane Wakoski. VGW

When will men again. The Leaping Laughers. George Barker. OBMV

When will the bell ring, and end this weariness? Last Lesson of the Afternoon. D. H. Lawrence. NoAM

When will the fountain of my tears be dry? Give Me Leave. "A. W." TrGrPo

When will the stream be aweary of flowing. Nothing Will Die. Tennyson. ArNa

When will you ever, Peace, wild wooddove, shy wings shut. Peace. Gerard Manley Hopkins. ELP; GTBS-P; OxBSP; TrCP

When will you marry me, William. The West-Country Damosel's Complaint. *Unknown.* ESPB

When willing nymphs and swains unite. The Judgement of Tiresias. Hildebrand Jacob. NOEC

When Wilt Thou Save the People? Ebenezer Elliot. *See* When wilt Thou save the people?

When wilt Thou save the people? God Save the People. Ebenezer Elliot. BLPA; WBLP
(When Wilt Thou Save the People?) CoGr; OxAEP-2; SWP

When Wilt Thou Teach the People? D. H. Lawrence. OBSV

When Windesor walles sustain'd my wearied arme. The Earl of Surrey. *See* When Windsor walls sustained [*or* sustain'd] my wearied arm.

When you go away the wind clicks around to the north. When You Go Away. W. S. Merwin. LCAP

When you go away/ you become everything I believe. The Departure. Frank Steele. GOYP

When you go out at early morn. The Serving Maid. A. J. Munby. NOBVV

When you go ten miles away. Viaticum. Pao Yu, *tr. fr. Chinese by* Kenneth Rexroth. OHMPC

When you got up this morning the sun. Wind. Gary Soto. *Fr.* Elements of San Joaquin, The. NoAM; PBCAP

When you ground the lenses and the moons swam free. The Emancipators. Randall Jarrell. PoA

When you grow up, are no more children. Parent to Children. Robert Graves. OxAEP-2

When you had left our pirate fold. A Most Ingenious Paradox. W. S. Gilbert. *Fr.* Pirates of Penzance, The. NAs

When you hark to the voice of the knocker. The Quarrelsome Trio. "L. G." WBLP

When you have bathed in the river. Submission. *Unknown, tr. fr. Siamese by* E. Powys Mathers. ErPo

When you have both. (*LL*) Toads. Philip Larkin. CMoP; NoAM; NOBL; OxAEP-2; OxBTC; PoE; Poetr; SoSe

When You Have Forgotten Sunday: The Love Story. Gwendolyn Brooks. WPOW

When You Have Forgotten Sunday: The Love Story. Gwendolyn Brooks. BPo; FF; WPOW

When you have nothing more to say, just drive. The Peninsula. Seamus Heaney. IIP

When you have/ once had. Self Portrait II. Tove Ditlevsen, *tr. fr. Danish by* Ann Freeman. IMW

When you have tidied all things for the night. Solitude. Harold Monro. MoBrPo; PlP; TrGrPo

When you have wearied of the valiant spires of this country town. Oxford Canal. James Elroy Flecker. OxBTC

When you hear it languishing. The Oxford Voice. D. H. Lawrence. IHNG

When you hear me singing. Rat Song. Margaret Atwood. NIP

When you kiss me, moths flutter in my mouth. Beija-Flor. Diane Ackerman. NIP

When you kneel below me. Celebration. Leonard Cohen. ErPo

When You Laugh. Ingrid Jonker, *tr. fr. Afrikaans by* Elizabeth Jones. WPOW

When you lie with a woman, at least so girls say. Epigram: To Polycharmus. Martial, *tr. fr. Latin.* PeHV

When you look at this memorial. Epitaph from Athens. *Unknown, tr. fr. Greek by* Peter Jay. GrAn

When you look down from the airplane you see lines. Field and Forest. Randall Jarrell. LCAP; VGW

When you look on my grave. *Unknown.* FaBoEE

When you lost touch with lovers' bare skin. John Donne. James Simmons. CIP

When you love, or speak of it. Aphra Behn. BoWoP

When/ you meet me. My Hair. Francisco Alarcon. AfAz

When you move away, you see how much depends. Landscape, Dense with Trees. Ellen Bryant Voigt. MT

When You, My Love, Ascend To Heaven. Paul Johann Ludwig Heyse, *tr. fr. German by* Philip L. Miller. RiWo

When you plunged. The Otter. Seamus Heaney. IPY; NoAM; PNI

When you put on the feet be sure. Dr. Potatohead Talks to Mothers. Judith Johnson Sherwin. MoP

When You Reach the Hilltop the Sky Is on Top of You. Etta Blum. GoYe

When you reach to touch the markings. Indian Rock, Bainbridge Island, Washington. Duane Niatum. CDW

When You Read This Poem. Pinkie Gordon Lane. BlSi

When you remember those days of the past. The Forgotten Majo. Fernando Periquet Y Zuaznabar, *tr. fr. Spanish by* Philip L. Miller. RiWo

When you return as if you had never left. The Return. Matthew Sweeney. IB

When you scuttled the ship, the shore was still in sight. Meditation of a Mariner. Dorothy Auchterlonie. CBAP

When you see a guy reach for stars in the sky. Guys and Dolls. Frank Loesser. OBAL

When you see a monkey up a tree. *Unknown.* RoPo

When you see a ragged urchin. Boys Make Men. *Unknown.* PWR

When you see me. (*LL*) A Form of Women. Robert Creeley. CAPP; NaP

When you see me sitting quietly. On Ageing. Maya Angelou. AIW

When You See Millions of the Mouthless Dead. Charles Hamilton Sorley. OBWP; PAW; PeFWW; PoWW

When you see my gray hair and chin. Anacreon, *tr. fr. Greek by* Sam Hamill. InMo

When you see them. Breath. Mark Strand. HCAP

When you send out invitations, don't ask me. Palladas, *tr. fr. Greek by* Tony Harrison. OBVE

When you set up a mirror on the western side of Easter Island, it runs backward. The Behavior of Mirrors on Easter Island. Julio Cortázar, *tr. by* Paul Blackburn. AnRep

When you show me. Colors for Mama. Barbara Mahone. PoBA

When you sit happy in your own fair house. Alcuin, *tr. fr. Latin by* Helen Waddell. MLL

When you speak of dauntless deeds. The Deed of Lieutenant Miles. Clinton Scollard. PAH

When you stand upon the stump. *Unknown.* RoPo

When you stop to consider. Dog Days. Derek Mahon. SCBI

When you swim in the surf off Seal Rocks, and your family. Family. Josephine Miles. FaBoWP; FYAP; GrPl

When you take off your clothes. In Nakedness. Marnie Pomeroy. ErPo

When You Talk to a Monkey. Rowena Bastin Bennett. SiSoPo

When you the sunburnt pilgrim see. Good Counsel to a Young Maid ("When you the sunburnt pilgrim see.") Thomas Carew. ErPo (Song: Good Counsel to a Young Maid.) CaPo

When you think of the distances. The Distances. W. S. Merwin. NOBA

When you think of the hosts without no. Cautionary Limerick. *Unknown.* FaBoUs; NBLV

When you tilted toward me, arms out. After 37 Years My Mother Apologizes for My Childhood. Sharon Olds. Poetr

When you wake up, in your fourteenth year. Joe Gillon Hypnotizes His Son. Albert Goldbarth. SM

When You Walk. James Stephens. PDV

When you walk in the country, she further confided to him. Henri Michaux, *tr. fr. French by* Richard Ellmann. *Fr.* I Am Writing To You from a Far-Off Country. AnRep

When you walked here. The Dumbfounding. Margaret Avison. NOBC

When you wardance, sometimes you must. Wardance. Phillip William George. VoR

When you watch for. Feather or Fur. John Becker. FaPON

When you wear a cloudy collar and a shirt that isn't white. When Your Pants Begin to Go. Henry Lawson. NOBAu

When you were. For Angela. Zack Gilbert. PoBA

When you were a girl. Woman. Umberto Saba, *tr. fr. Italian by* Thomas G. Bergin. UnAS

When you were a holy priest. Marvellous Grass. Nuala Ni Dhomhnaill, *tr. fr. Irish by* Michael Hartnett. PBCIP

When you were a tadpole and I was a fish. Evolution. Langdon Smith. BeLS; BLPA; FaBoBe

When you were drunk you could always whip Joe Louis. My Right Hand Don't Leave Me No More. Carter Revard. HATNAP

When you were here in wonderful Detroit. Goodbye David Tamunoemi West. Margaret Danner. BPo

When you were not a loafer. (*LL*) Will you sleep forever? Korinna. BoWoP; PBWP, *tr. by* John Dillon

When you were there, and you, and you. Dining-Room Tea. Rupert Brooke. MoBrPo; PFP

When You Will Walk in the Field. Leah Goldberg, *tr. fr. Hebrew by* Simon Halkin. TrJP

When you with Hogh Dutch Heeren dine. Matthew Prior. OBTV

When you woke [up] among them. After Grief. Stanley Plumly. AmPA; LCAP

When you wrap thighs around my head. To Madame * * *. Paul Verlaine, *tr. fr. French by* Alistair Elliot. FaBoBl

When You Write Again. Ingrid Jonker, *tr. fr. Afrikaans by* Jack Cope and William Plomer. PBWP

When you wrote your letter it was April. Response. Mary Ursula Bethell. ArLo; FaBoWP; PeNZ

When Young Hearts Break. Heine, *tr. fr. German by* Louis Untermeyer. AWP

When young I scribbled, boasting, on my wall. The Summing-up. Stanley Kunitz. OBAL

When Young Ladies Get Married. *Unknown.* AmFP

When Young Melissa Sweeps. Nancy Byrd Turner. FaPON; NTCP

When young 'sow wild oats', but when old, grow sage. (*LL*) Gardener's rule applies to youth and age, The. Henry James Byron. FaBoUs; NBLV

When Younglings First. William Byrd. EnRePo

When younglings first on Cupid fix their sight. When Younglings First. William Byrd. EnRePo

When your capitalist boss takes his toll. Dominic Fitzpatrick. PeLi

When Your Cheap Divorce Is Granted. "Orpheus C. Kerr." OBAL

When your client's hopping mad. The Advertising Agency Song. *Unknown.* FaBoUs; NBLV

When your eyes gaze seaward. Golden Moonrise. William Stanley Braithwaite. PoBA

When your eyes shall be closing, your mouth be opening. *Unknown, tr. fr. Gaelic by* Douglas Hyde. WTO

When your hour was rung at last. Rendez-vous Manqué dans la Rue Racine. J. M. Synge. BIrV

When your lips seek my lips they bring. Isolation. Arthur Symons. OxBSP

When Your Pants Begin to Go. Henry Lawson. NOBAu

When you're all alone. (*LL*) John's Song. Joan Aiken. TLR

When You're Away. Samuel Hoffenstein. FiBHP

When you're away I sleep a lot. The Method. J. D. McClatchy. EOEF

When you're doing an escort stunt and the Huns get on your tail. You're Only a PBO. *Unknown.* NSI

When you're lying awake with a dismal headache. Nightmare, [A]. W. S. Gilbert. *Fr.* Iolanthe. NOBL; NoP; NTP; OxBoLi; PoRA (Chancellor's Nightmare, The.) CBNP; FaBoNo (Nightmare, The.) PeLV

When you're out in smart society. Well, Did You Evah? Cole Porter. OBAL

When you're tired and worn at the close of day. Confide In a Friend. *Unknown.* PoToHe

When you're together with her, and you have a good excuse. Juan Ruiz, Archpriest of Hita, *tr. fr. Spanish by* Hubert Creekmore. *Fr.* Book of True Love, The. ErPo

When Youth and Beauty Meet Together. *Unknown.* EIl

When youth and charms have ta'en their wanton flight. Advice to Sophronia. Mary Leapor. ECWP

When Youth Had Led. The Earl of Surrey. EnRePo; SiPS

When youth had led me half the race. When Youth Had Led. The Earl of Surrey. EnRePo; SiPS

When youthful faith hath fled. John Gibson Lockhart. OBEV

When you've just been jugged by an upright judge. They Can't Do That. *Unknown.* WTO

Whenas from cups my Julia sups. Teatime Variations: After Robert Herrick. Peter Titheradge. FaBoPa

Whenas galoshed my Julia goes. Upon Julia's Arctics. Bert Leston Taylor. OBAL

Whenas in furs my Julia goes. Upon Julia's Clothes. E. V. Knox. BXAP; UV

Whenas in Jeans. Paul Dehn. FiBHP

Whenas in perfume Julia went. Herrick's Julia. Helen Smith Bevington. BXAP

Whenas in silks my Julia goes. Upon Julia's Clothes. Robert Herrick. AWP; BeJo; BLPA; CaPo; ChTr; ClHu; EBEV; EnLoPo; FaBV; FF; GBL; GTBS; GTBS-P; HAP; HeIL; HeIP; HoPM; ImPo; InPS; JCP; LiTB; NAEL-1; NBLV; NIP; NOBE; NoP; NOSC; OAEL-1; OBEV; OPOP; OxAEP-1; OxBSP; PeLV; PoE; PoEL-3; Poetr; PPP; SCGP; SeCP; SeCV-1; TEA; TFi; TrGrPo; TRP; TTTS; UV; WeW (When as in silks my Julia goes.) EBEvV

Whenas — methinks that is a pretty way. They Answer Back. "Francis." FiBHP (To His Ever-worshipped Will from W. H.) ErPo

Whenas [*or* When as] man's life, the light of human[e] lust. Fulke Greville. *Fr.* Caelica. LiTB; NoSic; PoEL-1 (Sonnet: "Whenas [*or* When as] man's life, the light of human lust.") NOSC

Whenas [*or* When as] the Rye [Reach to the Chin]. George Peele. *Fr.* Old Wives' [*or* Wife's] Tale, The. CBLP; ELP; EnLoPo; FaBoCh; GBL; InvP; NoP; NoSic; TEP; TFi (Song: "When as [*or* whenas] the rye [*or* rie] reach to the chin.") CBNP; EIl; FaBoVe; OxBoLi; PoEL-2 (Summer Song, A.) NOBE; OBEV

Whenas Queen Anne of great renown. A New Ballad. Arthur Mainwaring. APAS

Whenas the chill sirocco blowes. In Praise of Ale. *At. to* Thomas Bonham. (Pipe and Can II.) OBEV (When as the chill charocco blows.) OBEV (When that the chill charocco blows.) FaBoCh

Whenas the mildest month. The Rose. Thomas Howell. EIl

Whenas to shoot my Julia goes. To Julia in Shooting Togs. Sir Owen Seaman. BXAP

Whence and Whither. Hayyim Nahman Bialik, *tr. fr. Hebrew by* Helena Frank. TrJP

Whence are you, learning's son? The End of Clonmacnois. *Unknown, tr. fr. Irish by* Frank O'Connor. CIP

Whence art thou, thirsty wind. O Thirsty Wind. *Unknown, tr. fr. Hawaiian by* N. B. Emerson. WTO

Whence came this man? As if on the wings. Abraham Lincoln. Samuel Valentine Cole. OHIP

Whence come you, all of you so sorrowful? Sonnet: To Certain Ladies; When Beatrice Was Lamenting Her Father's Death. Dante, *tr. fr. Italian by* Dante Gabriel Rossetti. AWP

Whence comes my love? O heart, disclose! A Sonnet Made on Isabella Markham. John Harington. EIl

Whence comes this rush of wings afar. Carol of the Birds. *Unknown, tr. fr. French.* OHIP

Whence comest thou, Gehazi. Gehazi. Kipling. FaBoEH; FaBoPV; IHNG; OtMeF

Whence did all that fury come? A Stick of Incense. W. B. Yeats. ChIV-2; MeMBP

Whence flee forever a woman and a man. (*LL*) Not with Libations, but with Shouts and Laughter. Edna St. Vincent Millay. MeMAP

Whence Had They Come? W. B. Yeats. BoLoP

Whence let us go to. The Nicest Phantasies Are Shared. Brian Coffey. CIP

Whence my hand is weary with writing. (*LL*) St. Columcille the Scribe. *At. to* St. Columcille Saint Columcille. BIrV, *tr. by* Flann O'Brien

Whence this impatience fluttering in my breast! Urania. Robert Andrews. NOEC

Whenceness of the Which. *Unknown.* UV

Whene'er bitter foe attack thee. Advice to Hotheads. Samuel ben Elhanan Isaac Archevolti, of Padua, *tr. fr. Hebrew by* A. B. Rhine. TrJP

Whene'er I come where ladies are. Love at Large. Coventry Patmore. *Fr.* Angel in the House, The. EBVV, I, ii; NOBVV, I, ii

Whene'er I look into your eyes. I Love But Thee. Heine, *tr. fr. German by* Louis Untermeyer. AWP

Whene'er I see soft hazel eyes. The Lapful of Nuts. Sir Samuel Ferguson. PeIV

Whene'er I take my walks abroad. Praise for Mercies Spiritual and Temporal. Isaac Watts. NOEC

Whene'er the Muse pleases to grace my dull page. Lucretia Davidson. AmWP

Whene'er the old exchange of profit rings. Stay My Steps in Thy Paths, That My Feet Do Not Slide. Francis Quarles. *Fr.* Emblems. NOSC

Whene'er the waist makes too much haste. A Girdle. William Strode. NOSC

Whene'er with haggard eyes I view. Rogero's Song. George Canning , George Ellis, *and* John Hookham Frere. *Fr.* Rovers, The. NOEC (Song by Rogero.) FaBoNo (Song of One Eleven Years in Prison.) FiBHP; PeLV

Whenever a butterfly. A Lesson of Silence. Tymoteusz Karpowicz, *tr. fr. Polish by* Czeslaw Milosz. PoSu

Whenever a fellow called Rex. Limerick. *Unknown.* NOBL

Whenever Auntie moves around. Auntie's Skirts. Robert Louis Stevenson. WHSW

Whenever Chance allows. (*LL*) Kitty and I. W. H. Davies. CBLP

Whenever, Chloe, I begin. Earl of Chesterfield. NOEC

Whenever he got in a fury, a. *Unknown.* PeLi

Whenever he observes me purchasing. Sextus the Usurer. Martial, *tr. fr. Latin by* Kirby Flower Smith. AWP

Whenever I go by there nowadays. The Tavern. E. A. Robinson. AnAmPo

Whenever I Go There. W. S. Merwin. NaP

Whenever I Have. "Furnley Maurice." NOBAu

Whenever I have, in all humility, moved. Whenever I Have. "Furnley Maurice." NOBAu

Whenever I pause. The Noise of the Village. *Unknown, tr. fr. Chippewa Indian by* Frances Densmore. OBVE

Whenever I plunge my arm, like this. Under the Waterfall. Thomas Hardy. BoLoP; CTC; LiTB; NAEL-2

Whenever I see him. Waking in the Dark. Dorothy Livesay. NOBC

Whenever I walk to Suffern along the Erie track. The House with Nobody in It. Joyce Kilmer. BLPA; BLPL

Whenever Mr. Edwards spake. The Theology of Jonathan Edwards. Phyllis McGinley. MoAmPo

Whenever Richard Cory went down town. Richard Cory. E. A. Robinson. AmPP; AnAmPo; CMoP; DL; EBEvV; FF; HAP; ImPo; InPK; LiTA; LiTM; MeMAP; MoAB; MoAmPo; NAAL-2; NOBA; NoP; NTP; OxBA; Poetr; PoLF; PoRA; PrIm; TAP; TFi; TrGrPo

Whenever the moon and stars are set. Windy Nights. Robert Louis Stevenson. BoTP; GoJo; NTP; OTCP; OxBChV; PoRA; SiSoPo

Whenever the wind blows/ I try to question it. Mother of Michitsuna, *tr. fr. Japanese by* Kenneth Rexroth *and* Ikuko Atsumi. WPJ

Whenever troublous hours I find. Happiness amidst Troubles. Immanuel di Roma, *tr. fr. Italian by* J. Chotzner. TrJP

Whenever war is spoken of. The Great War. Vernon Scannell. NSI; OBWP

Whenever you cannot agree. *(LL)* I Wish I Were [*or* Was] Single Again. *Unknown.* AmFP, 2 *vers.*; AS

Whenever you drink all night you make. Martial, *tr. fr. Latin by* James Michie. FaBoEE

Whenever you see the hearse go by. Be Merry. *Unknown.* RB

Whenever you take a step. The Horizon. Kevin Hart. NOBAu

Whenne mine eynen misteth. All Too Late. *Unknown.* EBEV; OAEL-1

Whenneso will wit overstieth. *Unknown.* MiEL

Wher one would be. Sir Edward Dyer. PoEL-1

Where. Walter de la Mare. GoJo; NYBP

Where? Kenneth Patchen. LiTM

Where? A. S. J. Tessimond. OBTV

Where a bullet of sense *ought* to hit. *(LL)* A Pastoral Ballad by John Bull. Thomas Moore. BIrV; OBSV

Where a faithful heart. The Miller and the Brook. Wilhelm Müller, *tr. fr. German by* Philip L. Miller. *Fr.* Beautiful Maid of the Mill, The. RiWo

Where a Roman judged a foreign people. Notre Dame. Osip Mandelstam, *tr. fr. Russian by* James Greene. OBVE

Where a Roman Villa Stood, above Freiburg. Mary Elizabeth Coleridge. OBNC; OBTV

Where a young man lands hatless from the air. *(LL)* "New King Arrives in His Capital by Air . . . " — Daily Newspaper. Sir John Betjeman. OxBoLi

Where all the constellations shine. *(LL)* She Wept, She Railed. Stanley Kunitz. ErPo; VGW

Where all who know may drown. *(LL)* The Man against the Sky. E. A. Robinson. AmPP; CMoP; LiTA; OxBA

Where am I now? And what. A Song in Passing. Yvor Winters. CRP; VGW

Where am I, O awesome friend? Yitzhak Lamdan, *tr. fr. Hebrew by* Simon Halkin. *Fr.* For the Sun Declined. TrJP

Where am I, or how came I here, hath death. On Lazarus Raised From Death. Henry Colman. ChIV-2

Where angel trumpets hail a brighter sun. My Own Hereafter. Eugene Lee-Hamilton. WGRP

Where are all thy beauties now, all hearts enchaining? Thomas Campion. GBL

Where are Elmer, Herman, Bert, Tom and Charley. The Hill. Edgar Lee Masters. *Fr.* Spoon River Anthology. CMoP; FYAP; LiTA; LiTM; NoAM; NOBA; OxBA; TAP

Where are now, in coign or crack. Ballade of England. Louis MacNeice. NYBP

Where are Our Uniforms? *Unknown.* NSI

Where are the bay-leaves, Thestylis, and the charms. The Incantations. Theocritus [*or* Theokritus], *tr. by* Charles Stuart Calverley. *Fr.* Idylls. AWP

Where are the birth-places of the heroes? Alpheios, *tr. fr. Greek by* Edwin Morgan. GrAn

Where are the braves, the faces like autumn fruit. Indian Reservation: Caughnawaga. A. M. Klein. LiTM; NOBC; NoP

Where are the dear domestics, white and black. Familiar Faces, Long Departed. Robert Silliman Hillyer. NYBP

Where are the hands and feet. Give Me My Infant Now. Te-whaka-io-roa, *tr. fr. Maori by* John White. NAs; WTO

Where Are the Hebrew Children? *At. to* Peter Cartwright. AH

Where Are the Men Seized in This Wind of Madness? Alda do Espírito Santo, *tr. fr. Portuguese by* Alan Ryder. TTY; WPOW

Where Are the Ones Who Lived Before?, *mod. English. Unknown. See* Where are those that were before us.

Where are the passions they essayed. Ballade of Dead Actors. W. E. Henley. EBVV; OBMV

Where are the people as beautiful as poems. The Black Angel. Henri Coulette. CoAP; NYBP

Where are the poets, unto whom belong. Possibilities. Longfellow. MeMAP

Where are the ribbons I tie my hair with? Ballade of Lost Objects. Phyllis McGinley. CRP; NBLV; PoRA

Where Are the War Poets? C. Day Lewis. FaBoMo; OBWP; OxBSP; OxBTC; PAW

Where Are the Waters of Childhood? Mark Strand. HCAP; LCAP; VCAP; WeW

Where are the women who, entre deux guerres. Ballad of Ladies Lost and Found. Marilyn Hacker. VCAP

Where are they going, the crowds that pass in the street? Returning to the Port of Authority: A Picaresque. Constance Urdang. PBCAP

Where are they gone, the old familiar faces? The Old Familiar Faces. Charles Lamb. EnRP; FaBoRV

Where are they now, the genteel murderers. Lament for the Murderers. A. D. Hope. FaBoMA

Where are they now, the softly blooming flowers. Irises. Padraic Colum. BoNaP

Where are those that were before us. Ubi Sunt Qui ante Nos Fuerunt? *Unknown, tr. fr. Latin by* George Perkins. NoP; PrIm; WeW
(Where Are the Ones Who Lived Before?,) *mod. English.* HAP
(Where beeth they biforen us weren.) EBEV

Where are we. Bahamas. George Oppen. NYBP

Where are we going? where are we going. Song of Slaves in the Desert. Whittier. OxBA

Where are we to go when this is done? Alfred A. Duckett. PoBA; PoNe

Where are you bound, so fast, so roiled and wild, my beloved brook? Jealousy and Pride. Wilhelm Müller, *tr. fr. German by* Philip L. Miller. *Fr.* Beautiful Maid of the Mill, The. RiWo

"Where are you coming from, Lomey Carter." Old Christmas Morning. Roy Helton. MoAMPo

Where are you damn'd? Christopher Marlowe. *Fr.* Doctor Faustus. NAEL-1; OAEL-1; OBD

Where are you going. *Unknown.* BoTP

Where are you going? asked Manny the Mayor. Jig Tune: Not for Love. Thomas McGrath. VGW

Where Are You Going, Greatheart? John Oxenham. BLPA

Where are you going, Master mine? Whither Away? Mary Elizabeth Coleridge. CH

Where are you going, Mrs. Cat, Country Cat. Elizabeth J. Coatsworth. OFC

Where Are You Going, My Pretty Maid. *Unknown.* NBLV

Where are you going, my spiv, my wide boy. Spiv Song. Royston Ellis. PeHV

Where are you going to, Hywel and Blodwen. Hywel and Blodwen. Idris Davies. AngWe

Where are you going [to], my pretty maid? Mother Goose. OxNR; ReMoGo

Where are you going to-night, to-night. John Evereldown. E. A. Robinson. AnAmPo; CMoP; MeMAP; OxBA

Where are you going? To Scarborough Fair? Scarborough Fair. *Unknown.* OxBoLi; PeLV

Where are you going, you little pig? The Little Piggies. Thomas Hood. BoTP

Where Are You Now Superman? Brian Patten. FF

Where Are You Sleeping To-night, My Lad? John Oxenham. NSI

Where are you teaching a jade girl to blow tunes on your flute? *(LL)* To Judge Han Ch'o at Yang-chou. Tu Mu. PLT

Where are your ancient waves, O river. Home-Coming. Albert Ehrenstein, *tr. fr. German by* Babette Deutsch and Avrahm Yarmolinsky. TrJP

Where are your fabled Doric beauty, the fringe. The Ruins of Corinth. Antipater of Sidon, *tr. fr. Greek by* Peter Jay. GrAn

Where are your heroes, my little black ones. Poem for Black Boys. Nikki Giovanni. BPo

Where are your oranges? The Children's Bells. Eleanor Farjeon. BoTP; CH

Where Art Is a Midwife. Tom Paulin. SCBI

Where art thou gone, light-ankled youth? To Youth. Walter Savage Landor. EnRP

Where art thou, my beloved son. The Affliction of Margaret. Wordsworth. EnRP; GTBS; GTBS-P; PoEL-1

"Where art thou wandering, little child?" The Little Maid and the Cowslips. John Clare. BoTP

Where, at his back, a dome of atoms rose. *(LL)* The Progress of Faust. Karl Shapiro. MoAB; NYBP

Where Balkh amidst the desert stands! *(LL)* "Blood Horse," The. "Barry Cornwall." GN

Where Be You [*or* YE] Going, You [*or* Ye] Devon Maid? Keats. CBLP; ErPo; FHYEP

Where beeth they biforen us weren. Ubi Sunt? *Unknown.* PoE
(Where beth they biforen us weren?) MiEL

Where beeth they biforen us weren. *Unknown. See* Were [*or* Where] beth [*or* beeth] they [that] biforen us weren.

Where beeth they biforen us weren. *Unknown. See* Where are those that were before us.

Where begging hands arch the hot aisles. Shiprock. Lucile Adler. FoLa

Where, behind Keighley, the road. Matthew Arnold. *Fr.* Haworth Churchyard. FaBoPP

Where berries grow. *(LL)* A Berry Feast. Gary Snyder. PoBeRe

Where beth they biforen us weren? *Unknown. See* Where beeth they biforen us weren.

Where beth they biforen us weren. *Unknown. See* Were [*or* Where] beth [*or* beeth] they [*that*] biforen us weren.

Where birds of summer sing. (*LL*) The Little Beach-Bird. Richard Henry Dana. AnAmPo

Where black gusts disarranged. In Whom We Trust. Harry Clifton. IB

Where both he and I are the hunters. (*LL*) My Father's Wedding. Robert Bly. CAPP; InPS; NoAM; RaBo

Where brown children are at play under pollarded willows. Trumpets. Georg Trakl, *tr. fr. German by* David McDuff *and* Jon Silkin. PeFWW

Where Cape Delgado strikes the sea. E. J. Pratt. *Fr.* Cachalot, The. MoCV

Where castles stood & grandeur died. (*LL*) The Flitting. John Clare. FaBoPV; OxAEP-2

Where cider ends there ale begins to reign. The Cambrian Swain. Edward Davies. *Fr.* Chepstow: A Poem. OBWVE

Where clear air blew off the land. York Harbor Morning. George Garrett. MT

Where Cross the Crowded Ways of Life. Frank Mason North. AH

Where Cumbria's mountains in the north arise. James Plumptre. *Fr.* Prologue to "The Lakers; a Comic Opera". NOEC

Where deep in the night I hear a voice. (*LL*) Butcher Shop. Charles Simic. AmPA; InPK; LCAP; NNaP

Where did it roll in from, that sea of light. In Two Fields. Waldo Williams, *tr. fr. Welsh by* Gwyn Jones. OBWVE

Where did the blood come from? On a Line in Sandburg. R. S. Thomas. NAs

Where did the Jewish god go? Harvey Shapiro. BTR

Where did this tiger come from? Ballad of the Ferocious Tiger. Hsü Pen, *tr. fr. Chinese by* Jonathan Chaves. OBAP

Where did you borrow that last sigh. Sir William Berkeley. *Fr.* Lost Lady, The. OxBSP

Where Did You Come From, [Baby Dear?]. George Macdonald. *See* Where did you come from, baby dear?

Where did you come from, baby dear? The Baby. George Macdonald. *Fr.* At the Back of the North Wind. FaPON
(At the Back of the North Wind. VPP
(Where Did You Come From, [Baby Dear?].) BLPA; OxBChV; WHSW

Where dips the rocky highland. The Stolen Child. W. B. Yeats. CMoP; NAEL-2; NoP; OHCV

Where Do School Days End? Josephine D. Henderson Heard. CBWP-4

Where Do the Gipsies Come From? Sir Henry Howarth Bashford. CH; CoGr

Where do the roots go? The Pit. Theodore Roethke. *Fr.* Lost Son, The. HAP; HCAP; LiTM; NAAL-2; VGW

Where do the stars grow, little Garaine? Little Garaine. Sir Gilbert Parker. FaPON

Where Do These Words Come From? Charlotte Pomerantz. SiSoPo

Where do we live? Variations for Two Voices. Roberta Hill Whiteman. HATNAP

Where do you come from, Milord? (*LL*) Homecoming. Ho Ch'e Ch'ang. OHMPC

Where do you go vision without me through my dreams. The Swing over the Calm Source of Our Names. Milorad Pavic, *tr. fr. Serbo-Croatian by* Charles Simic. HSix

Where do you go with your fury. Fury's Field. Cecil Bodker, *tr. fr. Danish by* Nadia Christensen. PBWP

Where do you think I've been to-day? The Pigeon's Story. Jeannie Kirby. BoTP

Where does the stream carry my small face? The Girl Sings to the Stream. Leah Goldberg, *tr. fr. Hebrew by* Ruth Finer Mintz. *Fr.* Songs of the Stream. MHP

Where does this poem come from? Edouard J. Maunick, *tr. fr. French by* Ellen Conroy Kennedy. *Fr.* As Far as Yoruba Land. NegPo

Where Does This Tenderness Come From? Marina Tsvetayeva, *tr. fr. Russian by* Elaine Feinstein. ArLo; VBLP

Where dost [*or* do'st] thou careless[e] lie. An Ode to Himself. Ben Jonson. BeJo; EnRePo; HAP; JCP; LiTB; NOBE; NoP; NOSC; OxAEP-1; PoEL-2; PrIm; SCGP; SeCP; SeCV-1

Where Dunwich Used to Be. Swinburne. *Fr.* By the North Sea. FaBoPP

Where dwell the lovely, wild white womenfolk. The White Women. Mary Elizabeth Coleridge. BrRo; NALW

Where dwells that wish most ardent of the wise? Edward Young. *Fr.* Night Thoughts. OBD

Where-e'er My Flatt'ring Passions Rove. Isaac Watts. NOCV

Where ends our chancel in a vaulted space. The Vicar. George Crabbe. *Fr.* Borough, The. OBSV

Where England's Damon used [*or* us'd] to keep. Pastoral on the King's Death, The; [Written in 1648]. Alexander Brome. NOSC

Where every female delights to give her maiden to her husband. Male & Female Loves in Beulah. Blake. *Fr.* Jerusalem. OBNC

Where everything once was shriek. Columbus of the Alphabet. Eric Nelson. NGP

Where fair Sabrina's wand'ring currents flow. William Somervile. *Fr.* Bowling-Green, The. NOEC

Where Fire Burns. Gladys Cardiff. HATNAP

Where Fishermen Can't Swim. Matthew Sweeney. BiHa

Where foam-white openwork. Waterspout. James Merrill. CAPP

Where foams the fall — a tameless storm. New England's Mountain-child. Frances Sargent Osgood. AmWP

Where folds the central lotus. William Yeats in Limbo. Sidney Keyes. MoBrPo

Where formless shades blindfold the light. (*LL*) The Camera Obscura. John Addington Symonds. NOBVV

Where from the watch towers. Bay Poem. Lance Henson. VoR

Where genius, wit, and humour sleep with Sterne? (*LL*) Epitaph on Laurence Sterne. David Garrick. FaBoEE

Where gentle Thames through stately channels glides. The Playhouse. Joseph Addison. ECEV

Where go the birds when the rain. Jane Heap. PoA

Where Go the Boats? Robert Louis Stevenson. FaBoBe; FaBoCh; GoJo; Mes; NTCP; NTP; OxBChV; PYC; TLR; WHSW

Where goats are slaughtered. Murukan: His Places. Nakkiranar, *tr. fr. Tamil by* A. K. Ramanujan. PLW

Where had I heard this wind before. Bereft. Robert Frost. LiTM; MoAB; MoAmPo; OxBA; SoSe

Where hae ye been a' the day. *Unknown.* OxNR

Where harmless robin dwells with gentle thrush. (*LL*) Happy Were He. Earl of Essex. EIL; NoSic; OxBSP

Where has he of race divine. Chorus of Satyrs, Driving Their Goats. Euripides, *tr. fr. Greek by* Shelley. *Fr.* Cyclops. AWP

Where has spring returned to? Tune: "Pure Serene Music." Huang T'ing-chien, *tr. fr. Chinese by* James J. Y. Liu. SuSp

Where has tenderness gone, he asked the mirror. Delirium in Vera Cruz. Malcolm Lowry. FaBoTw; OxBTC

Where has ti been, maw canny hinny? Captain Bover. *Unknown.* GBP

Where hast been toiling all day, sweetheart. The Child on the Judgment Seat. Elizabeth Rundle Charles. BLPA

Where hast 'te been, ma' canny hinny? Ma Canny Hinny. *Unknown.* FaBoPP; GBP

Where have all the colours gone? The Darkening Garden. *Unknown.* BoTP

Where have these hands been. Musician. Louise Bogan. GoJo; NYBP

Where have they led you, into what disguise. The Kingdom. Jon Swan. NYBP

Where have ye [*or* you] been all the day,/ Billy Boy? *Unknown. See* "Oh, where have you been, Billy boy, Billy boy?"

Where have you been. Banbury Fair. Edith G. Millard. BoTP

"Where have you been all day, Henry my son,/ Where have you been all day, my beloved one?" Henry My Son. *Unknown.* OBET

Where have you been all day, Henry my son,/ Where have you been all day, my pretty one? Green and Yellow. *Unknown.* OBET

Where have you been all the day, Billy boy, Billy boy? *Unknown.* OxNR

Where Have You Been Dear? Karla Kuskin. NTCP

Where have you been, South Wind, this May-day morning? South Wind. Siegfried Sassoon. BoTP

Where have you been this long time. Axle Song. Mairtin O Direain. BiHa

Where Have You Gone? Mari Evans. BPo; PoNe; TTY

Where Have You Gone, Little Boy. Patty L. Harjo. VoR

Where have you gone to, Yesterday. Yesterday. Hugh Chesterman. BoTP

Where have you hidden away. The Spiritual Canticle. St. John of the Cross, *tr. fr. Spanish by* John Frederick Nims. STV

Where he splashed till his heart did laugh. (*LL*) Mercury. Naomi Segal. VBLP

Where he stood and where. Jew. James A. Randall, Jr.. BPo

Where hints of racy sap and gum. Wild Honey. Maurice Thompson. AnAmPo

Where His Lady Keeps His Heart. "A. W." CTC; EIL

Where Hurricane. LeRoy Clarke. PBCV

Where I alone could tell the story. (*LL*) A Date with Robbe-Grillet. Elaine Equi. PeVV; UTF

Where I Came From. Ruth Stone. NAmP90

Where I cling. (*LL*) The Last Leaf. Oliver Wendell Holmes. AmPP; AnAmPo; FaBoBe; FaPON; NAAL-1; PoLF; PWR; WBLP

Where I Come From. Reg Saner. NGP

Where I come from the bright ones. Where I Come From. Reg Saner. NGP

Where I come from we have no snow. Nochebuena. Rosario Caicedo. LoHo

Where I could think of no thoroughfare. Were I in Trouble. Robert Frost. OxBSP

Where I defy, and challenge, all thy utmost love. (*LL*) The Author Apologizes to a Lady for His Being a Little Man. Christopher Smart. BoLoP; CBLP

Where I gaze. Tune: "Jade Butterflies." Liu Yung, *tr. fr. Chinese by* Jerome P. Seaton. SuSp

Where I go are flowers blooming. Les Planches-en-Montagnes. Michael Roberts. OBMV

Where I Hang My Hat. Dick Gallup. UL

Where I Live. Wesley McNair. TRP

Where I shall need no glass. (*LL*) They Are All Gone into the World of Light. Henry Vaughan. ChTr; ESCV; FaBoRV; GeHe; InPS; JCP; NAEL-1; NOBE; NoP; NOSC; OAEL-1; PeECV; PoEL-2; SCGP; SeCP; SeCV-1; TFi

Where I sit is holy. *Unknown.* EaPr

Where I was born. (*LL*) Weight of the world, The. Allen Ginsberg. BCF; PoBeRe

Where icy and bright dungeons lift. Hart Crane. *Fr.* Voyages (I–VI). CMoP; HAP; MeMAP; MoAB; MoAmPo; NoAM; NOBA; NoP; TAP; UnPo

Where ignorant armies clash by night. (*LL*) Dover Beach. Matthew Arnold. AWP; BLPA; ClHu; CoGr; EBVV; EBVVPR; FaBoBe; FaBoPP; FaBoRV; FaBV; FaPoB; FF; GGP; GTBS-P; HAP; HeIP; HoPM; ImPo; InPK; InPS; InvP; LiTB; MAT; NAEL-2; NIP; NOBE; NOBVV; NoP; NU; OAEL-2; OBNC; OPOP; PeVV; PlP; PoE; PoEL-5; PoRA; PPP; Prf; PrIm; SCGP; SCV; TFi; TOF

Where I'll Be Good. Michael Ryan. SM

Where in blind files. Eavan Boland. CIP; IIP; VBLP

Where in dispair I beauty curse. Curse love and all fair faces! (*LL*) Love Is a Secret Feeding Fire. *Unknown.* ArLo; OxBSP

Where in the summer-warm woodlands with the sweet wind. Iphione. Thomas Caulfield Irwin. EnLoPo

Where in what ever-blissfully watered gardens. Rainer Maria Rilke, *tr. by* James Blair Leishman. *Fr.* Sonnets to Orpheus. OBVE
(Where, in whatever happily watered garden, on what trees.) SOTW, *tr. by* Christopher Hawthorne

Where, in whatever happily watered garden, on what trees. Rainer Maria Rilke. *See* Where in what ever-blissfully watered gardens.

Where Innocent Bright-Eyed Daisies Are. Christina Rossetti. Spl

Where is a foot worthy to walk a garden, Jalal al-Din Rumi, *tr. fr. Persian by* Coleman Barks *and* John Moyne. *Fr.* Four Quatrains. RaBo

Where is all the bright company gone. Edith Sitwell. NALW

Where is all, there all should be. (*LL*) The Invitation. George Herbert. ChIV-1; ESCV

Where is another sweet as my sweet. The Letter. Tennyson. TTTS

Where is Becket, the traitor to the king? T. S. Eliot. *Fr.* Murder in the Cathedral. FaBoEH

Where is David? . . . Oh God's people. In Which Roosevelt Is Compared to Saul. Vachel Lindsay. ChIV-1

Where is every piping lad. Dawn of Day. William Browne. *Fr.* Shepherd's Pipe, The. EIL

Where Is He? Mother Goose. OxNR

Where is it now? Look, there it flies in merry sport. The Swallow's Flight. Louis Levy, *tr. fr. Danish by* Martin S. Alwood *and* Sanford Kaufman. TrJP

Where is it, the sad lyre which follows the quick flute? Li Shang-yin, *tr. fr. Chinese by* A. C. Graham. PLT

Where is it Written? Judith Viorst. IHNG

Where is my bay? Bring it, Thestylis. Where are my charms? Theocritus [*or* Theokritus]. *See* Maid, where's my lawrel? Oh my rageing soul!

Where Is My Butterfly Net? David McCord. FiBHP

Where is my Chief, my Master, this bleak night, *mavrone*! O'Hussey's Ode to the Maguire. Eochadh O'Hussey, *tr. fr. Irish by* James Clarence Mangan. NOIV; PeIV
(Ode to the Maguire.) BIrV

Where is my lover and my friend? An Elegiac Ballad. Hannah Cowley. ECWP

Where is my ruined life, and where the fame. Hafiz, *tr. by* Gertrude Lowthian Bell. *Fr.* Odes. AWP; TAL

Where is neither faith nor wonder. (*LL*) Song with Words. James Agee. ChIV-1; MoAmPo

Where is now Elijah's God? A Martyr's Death. Menahem ben Jacob, *tr. fr. Hebrew.* TrJP

Where Is Our Holy Church?. Edwin H. Wilson. AH

Where is Paris and Heleyne? Thomas of Hales. *Fr.* Love-Song, A. ChTr

Where is poor Jesus gone? Jesus. Francis Lauderdale Adams. OxBS

Where is Praxiteles where. Rufinus, *tr. fr. Greek by* Alan Marshfield. GrAn

Where is that holy fire, which verse is said. Sappho to Philaenis. John Donne. FaBoBl

Where is that I wonder? Home. Elaine Feinstein. VBLP

Where is that sugar, Hammond. Early Evening Quarrel. Langston Hughes. SAmP; UnPo

Where is the arbiter of a thousand languages? When My Poems were Lost. Mazisi Kunene, *tr. fr. Zulu by the author.* PeSAV

Where is the arm I well could trust. Address to My Malay Krees. John Leyden. OBTV

Where is the duke my father with his power? Shakespeare. *Fr.* King Richard III. OxAEP-1

Where is the gallant race that rose. Thomas Mercer. *Fr.* Arthur's Seat. OxBS

Where is the grave of Sir Arthur O'Kellyn? The Knight's Tomb. Samuel Taylor Coleridge. EnRP; FaBoCh; GN; MeMBP; RB

Where is the hand to trace. With a Coin from Syracuse. Oliver St. John Gogarty. OBMV

Where is the heart I am calling? Roberto Juarroz. TSaS, *tr. by* W. S. Merwin

Where is the home for me? The Home of Aphrodite. Euripides, *tr. fr. Greek by* Gilbert Murray. *Fr.* Bacchae. AWP

Where is the Jim Crow section. Merry-go-round. Langston Hughes. PoNe (Colored child at carnival:. SAmP

Where is the man who has been tried and found strong and sound? A Degenerate Age. Solomon ibn Gabirol, *tr. fr. Hebrew by* Emma Lazarus. TrJP

Where is the nightingale. Hilda Doolittle ("H. D."). *Fr.* Songs from Cyprus. MoAmPo

Where is the nymph, whose azure eye. Thomas Moore. EnLoPo

Where is the one whose hair was white like the waterfalls? (*LL*) When My Poems were Lost. Mazisi Kunene. PeSAV

Where is the promise of my years. Infelix. Adah Isaacs Menken. AAP; AmWP; CBWP-1

Where is the star of Bethlehem? Christmas 1959 et Cetera. Gerald William Barrax. PChr

Where Is The Sun Today? Allen Grossman. *Fr.* Ether Dome (an Entertainment), The. BAP-91

Where is the sun today? Where has he gone? Where Is The Sun Today? Allen Grossman. *Fr.* Ether Dome (an Entertainment), The. BAP-91

Where is the true man's fatherland? The Fatherland. James Russell Lowell. GN

Where is the word that will fill in for hunger. Guatemala, Your Blood. Alenka Bermudez, *tr. fr. Spanish by* Sara Miles. WoWa

"Where is the world!" cries Young at eighty. Byron. *Fr.* Don Juan. FaBoPV

Where is the world? not about. Merchant Marine. Josephine Miles. TAP; VGW

Where is the world we roved, Ned Bunn? To Ned. Herman Melville. NAAL-1; NOBA; PoEL-5

Where is this stupendous stranger. The Nativity of Our Lord and Saviour Jesus Christ. Christopher Smart. *Fr.* Hymns and Spiritual Songs. EBEV; HAP; NOBE; NOCV; PoEL-3; SCGP
(Christmas Day, *sts.* 6–9.) ChTr; OBCP
(Hymn.) NAs; NOEC

Where is *thy* mate, and where thy nest? (*LL*) Sea-Birds. Elizabeth Akers Allen. FaBoBe

Where Is Your Boy Tonight? *Unknown.* VPP

Where is your famous beauty. Antipater, *tr. fr. Greek by* Kenneth Rexroth. PGA

Where Israel's tents do shine so bright. (*LL*) Mock On, Mock On, Voltaire, Rousseau. Blake. ChIV-1; EnRP; HAP; MeMBP; NAEL-2; NAWM-2; NoP; OAEL-2; OBNC; OxBSP; PeECV; PoE; PoEL-4; PPP; PrIm; SCGP; TFi

Where it is the children go. (*LL*) White Fields. James Stephens. BoNaP; FaPON; MoShBr; OTCP

Where it says snow. Errata. Charles Simic. NNaP

Where it will break at last. (*LL*) The Indian Serenade. Shelley. AWP; BLPL; CBLP; EnRP; HoPM; ImPo; LiTB; MeMBP; OBEV; PlP; RaBo; TrGrPo; TTTS

Where its red bead eyes now stare towards the sun. (*LL*) The Tantanoola Tiger. Max Harris. MoBS

Where Knock Is Open Wide. Theodore Roethke. HAP; VGW

Where laurel hedges hide the coal and coke. Crematorium. Sir John Betjeman. PoA

Where Lie All the Slain. Harry Morris. CRP

Where Lies the Land. Wordsworth. EnRP; MeMBP; OBNC; PoEL-4

Where Lies the Land [to Which the Ship Would Go?]. Arthur Hugh Clough. *Fr.* Songs in Absence. NTP

Where lies the land to which yon ship must go? Where Lies the Land. Wordsworth. EnRP; MeMBP; OBNC; PoEL-4

Where Lies the Truth? Has Man in Wisdom's Creed. Wordsworth. TrCP

Where light is. To a Woman Who Wants Darkness and Time. Gerald William Barrax. PoBA

Where, like a pillow on a bed. The Ecstasy. John Donne. BoLoP; EnRePo; FHYEP; HAP; ImPo; InPS; JCP; LiTB; NAEL-1; NOBE; NoP; OAEL-1; OBEV; PoE; PrIm; TEP; TFi; TOF; TrGrPo

(Extasie, The.) ESCV; CBLP; EnLoPo; MeLP; 09MePo; 09OBS; PoEL-2; SeCP; SeCV-1

Where Lincoln's Inn, wide space, is railed around. John Gay. *Fr.* Trivia; or, The Art of Walking the Streets of London. ECEV

Where Liver Eatin' Johnson lies. Old Trail Town, Cody, Wyoming.sie. John Garmon. BoLoP; EnLoPo; HAP; InPS; JCP; LiTB; MeLP; NOBE; NoP; OAEL-1; OBEV; PoEL-2; PrIm; SeCP; SeCV-1; TEP; TrGrPo

Where long the shadows of the wind had rolled. The Sheaves. E. A. Robinson. AWP; CMoP; FaBV; HAP; ImGa; MoAB; MoAmPo; MoP; NoAM; NOBA; OxBA; Poetr; SoSe; TAP

Where lying on the hearth to bake. *Unknown.* FaBoEH

Where marble stood and fell. Reflection in a Green Arena. Gregory Corso. VGW

Where Martin Luther King could have lived and preached non-violence. (*LL*) The Funeral of Martin Luther King, Jr. Nikki Giovanni. BPo; LPA

Where may the wearied eye repose. Washington. Byron. *Fr.* Ode to Napoleon Buonaparte. OHIP; PAH

Where metalled road invades light thinning air. Sándor Weöres, *tr. fr. Hungarian by* Edwin Morgan. *Fr.* Lost Parasol, The. OBVE

Where might there be a refuge for me. Tell Me, Tell Me. Marianne Moore. LiTM; NYBP

Where mine is. Touch me. This is the body. I Know. (*LL*) What Shines in Winter Burns. T. R. Hummer. MT

Where most she works when we perceive her least. (*LL*) To Wordsworth. Hartley Coleridge. MoP

Where Mountain Lion Lay [or Laid] Down with Deer. Leslie Silko. ImGa; Poetr; TRP; VoR; WPOW

Where murdered Mumford lies. Mumford. Ina M. Porter. PAH

Where my bones will shut up, where I'll be good. (*LL*) Where I'll Be Good. Michael Ryan. SM

Where My Books Go. W. B. Yeats. OBEV

Where my grandmother lived. Number Four. Doughtry Long, Jr.. PoBA

Where my kindred dwell, there I wander. Dawn Boy's Song. *Unknown, tr. fr. Navajo Indian by* Washington Matthews. FaBV

Where Nature such dilemmas could devise. (*LL*) Her Dilemma. Thomas Hardy. EnVR; NOBVV

Where neither King nor shepheard want comes neare. Homer, *tr. by* George Chapman. *Fr.* Odyssey. CTC; NAWM-1

Where not so long ago the breezes stirred. A Fall of Rock. William Plomer. PeSAV

Where Nothing Dwelt but Beasts of Prey. Isaac Watts. AH

Where Now Are the Hebrew Children?. *Unknown.* AH

Where now/ are time and space. Wind Gardens. Louis Untermeyer. BXAP

Where now he roves, by wood or swamp whatever. Proem to "The Kid." Conrad Aiken. *Fr.* Kid, The. MoAB

Where now outside the weary house the pepperina. Old House. Judith Wright. FaBoMA

Where now these mingled ruins lie. Stanzas Occasioned by the Ruins of a Country Inn *or* On the Ruins of a Country Inn. Philip Freneau. AnAmPo; OxBA

Where nowadays the Battery lies. Peter Stuyvesant's New Year's Call. Edmund Clarence Stedman. PAH

Where O Where Is Old Elijah. *Unknown.* AS

Where, Oh Where Are the Hebrew Children? *Unknown.* BLPA

Where on earth. The Question of Time. William Peskett. PNI

Where on the wrinkled stream the willows lean. The Water-Ousel. Mary Webb. CH

Where once my ancestors grubbed for the fern's root. Ancestors. Rowley Habib. PeNZ

Where once Three Graces stood. Callimachus, *tr. fr. Greek by* Sam Hamill. InMo

Where once we danced, where once we sang. An Ancient to Ancients. Thomas Hardy. CMoP; GTBS-P; LiTM; OxBTC; SCGP

Where one needs one's brains all the time. (*LL*) The Lake Isle. Ezra Pound. FaBoCo; FaBoPa; OxBSP; PoA

Where only flowers fret. Aegean. Louis Simpson. GrPl; NYBP

Where or When. Philip Whalen. PoM

Where our dreams will be no more than ashes? (*LL*) Desert. Birago Diop. NegPo

Where oxen do low and apples do grow. Dialogue, between Crab and Gillian. Thomas D'Urfey. *Fr.* Bath; or, The Western Lass, The. NOEC

Where painted women. Landscape. Kevin Faller. PeIV

Where praise already is is the only place Grief. Rainer Maria Rilke, *tr. by* Robert Bly. *Fr.* Sonnets to Orpheus. RaBo

Where racial memories, like snakes. Landscape of Violence. Ralph Nixon Currey. PeSA

Where run your colts at pasture?. White Horses. Kipling. PeVV

Where Runs the River. Francis William Bourdillon. WGRP

Where sea-grass tangles with/ shore-grass. (*LL*) Hermes of the Ways. Hilda Doolittle ("H. D."). LiTA; WPE

Where, selfwrung, selfstrung, sheathe-and shelterless, thóughts agáinst thoughts ín groans grínd. (*LL*) Spelt from Sibyl's Leaves. Gerard Manley Hopkins. CMoP; EnVR; FaBoMo; LiTM; MeMBP; NOBVV; OAEL-2; PrIm; TOF

Where Shall a Sorrow Great. Martin Peerson. EnRePo

Where shall a sorrow great enough be sought. Where Shall a Sorrow Great. Martin Peerson. EnRePo

Where shall Celia fly for shelter. Christopher Smart. EnLoPo

Where shall I gang, my ain true love? The Duke of Athole's Nurse. *Unknown.* ESPB

Where shall I have at mine own will. Sir Thomas Wyatt. SiPS

Where shall I lead the flocks to-day? Where the Flocks Shall Be Led. Adah Isaacs Menken. CBWP-1

Where shall she wait for a kind wind to blow from the South West? (*LL*) Phoenix tail on scented silk, flimsy layer on layer. Li Shang-yin. PLT

Where Shall the Baby's Dimple Be. Josiah Gilbert Holland. BLPA

Where shall the eyes a darkness find. Huw Menai. *Fr.* Back in the Return. OBWVE

Where shall the lover rest. Sir Walter Scott. *Fr.* Marmion. CH, *abr.*; EnRP; GTBS; GTBS-P

(Song: "Where shall the lover rest.') PoEL-4

Where shall we find a Muse like thine, that can. William Cartwright. *Fr.* In the Memory of the Most Worthy Benjamin Jonson. EPCY

Where shall we find Thee — where art Thou, O God? Search. Margaret Widdemer. TrPWD

Where shall we go? The Hounded Lovers. William Carlos Williams. NYBP; TrGrPo

Where shall we go? where shall we go? June Fugue. Thomas W. Shapcott. NOBAu

Where shall we seek for a hero, and where shall we find a story? Crispus Attucks. John Boyle O'Reilly. PAH

Where she lived the close remained the best. The Way a Ghost Dissolves. Richard Hugo. NAAL-2; NoAM; NoP; SM

Where she, of all the plains of Britain that doth bear. Michael Drayton. *Fr.* Polyolbion. NOSC

Where shineth thy spirit, there liberty shineth too! (*LL*) The Irish Peasant to His Mistress. Thomas Moore. TIRV

Where silent, unrefractive whiteness lies. (*LL*) Stories of Snow. P. K. Page. NOBC; NoP; PoA

Where Somnus' temple rises from a ground. Laudanum. *Unknown.* NOEC

Where streetlamps burn. Jessica Drew's Married Son. Tony Flynn. PWE

Where sunless rivers weep. Dream Land. Christina Rossetti. BrRo

Where Sydney Cove her lucid bosom swells. Visit of Hope to Sydney Cove, near Botany-Bay. Erasmus Darwin. ECEV; NOEC; OBTV

Where the acorn tumbles down. The Fieldmouse. Cecil Frances Alexander. OxBChV

Where the afternoon sun blears the city. O My Invisible Estate. Bruce Smith. Son

Where the air is full of sunlight and the flag is full of stars. (*LL*) America for Me. Henry van Dyke. BLPA; BLPL; WBLP

Where the ancients sleep. (*LL*) The Soul of the Black Land. Guy Tirolien. NegPo

Where the bee sucks, there suck I. Where the Bee Sucks. Shakespeare. *Fr.* Tempest, The. AWP; BoTP; CH; CTC; EIL; EnRePo; FaBV; NAEL-1; NBLV; NoP; NoSic; OAEL-1; OBEV; OxBSP; SCGP; TFi; TTTS

(Ariel's Song: "Where the bee sucks, there suck I.") EBEvV; GN; NOBE; PDV

Where the bishop groans to view him. (*LL*) Rich and Poor; or, Saint and Sinner. Thomas Love Peacock. FaBoCo; NOBE; NOBL; OBSV; PeLV

Where the blood pours out the dead come to the feast. (*LL*) In Memoriam. Martin Johnston. NOBAu

Where the blue mountains. Alois Jeitteles, *tr. by* Philip L. Miller. RiWo

Where the buttercups so sweet. The Little Herd-Boy's Song. Robert Buchanan. BoTP

Where the cedar leaf divides the sky. Passage. Hart Crane. CMoP; NOBA; PoE

Where the Cedars. Jacob Glatstein, tr. fr. *Yiddish* by Joseph Leftwich. TrJP

Where the city's ceaseless crowd moves on the livelong day. Sparkles from the Wheel. Walt Whitman. InPS; NAAL-1; SAmP

Where the Corrib river chops through the Claddagh. The Last Galway Hooker. Richard Murphy. IPY; PBCIP

Where the dark primeval forests. Anne Lynch Botta. AmWP

Where the Dead Men Lie. Barcroft Henry Boake. CBAP

Where the dews and the rains of heaven have their fountain. The Battle in the Clouds. William Dean Howells. PAH

Where the dire Circle keeps its station. Cold Ceremony. Hannah More. *Fr. Bas Bleu, The; or, Conversation.* ECWP

Where the Disappeared Would Dance. Martín Espada. ETG

Where the Flocks Shall Be Led. Adah Isaacs Menken. CBWP-1

Where the flowers and trees grow dense. Tune: "Ripples Sifting Sand" — Accompanying My Husband on a Spring Outing to Stone Pavilion. Ku T'ai-ch'ing, tr. fr. *Chinese* by Irving Y. Lo. SuSp

Where the Fu-sang tree grows. Song of Heavenly Ascent. Ts'ao Chih, tr. fr. *Chinese* by Ronald C. Miao. SuSp

Where the good God sits to spangle through. (*LL*) Lady, Lady. Anne Spencer. BlSi; PoBA; ShDr

Where the gully shadows lie. Under the Range. Irene Gough. OBAP

Where the heart reflects. (*LL*) Strains of Sight. Robert Duncan. CMoP; PoE

Where the kings and the slaves and the troubadours rest. (*LL*) Bryan, Bryan, Bryan, Bryan. Vachel Lindsay. CMoP; LiTA; MeMAP; OxBA; OxBoLi

Where the language dreams in derision. Meaning Insomnia. John Hall. VaA

Where the Lilies Used to Spring. David Gray. OxBS

Where the Lilies Were in Flower. Kumattur Kannanar, tr. fr. *Tamil* by A. K. Ramanujan. PLW

Where the living with effort go. The White Ship. Geoffrey Hill. OxBC

Where the lizard ran to its little prey. The Range in the Desert. Randall Jarrell. ArOW; NOBA; PoWW

Where the mighty cliffs are frowning. Rajpoot Rebels. Sir Alfred Comyn Lyall. OBTV

Where the mob gathers, swiftly shoot along. John Gay. *Fr.* Trivia; or, The Art of Walking the Streets of London. OAEL-1 (Pickpockets.) ECEV

Where the Moosatockmaguntic. The Ballad of Hiram Hover. Bayard Taylor. AnAmPo; BXAP; FaBoCo; OBAL

Where the nameless followers sleep. (*LL*) Sheridan at Cedar Creek. Herman Melville. LiTA; PAH

Where the noisy flowers are deepest, a storied building. Tune: "Water Dragon's Chant" — Loathsome Spring. Ch'en Liang, tr. fr. *Chinese* by Hellmut Wilhelm. SuSp

Where the old cow at her leisure chews her cud. (*LL*) Birds' Nests. John Clare. OAEL-2; OxBSP

Where the old trees reign with their forward dark. Provinces. C. D. Wright. LCAP

Where the orange-branches mingle on the sunny garden-side. The Demon of the Mirror. Bayard Taylor. BeLS

Where the path opened. In Duffryn Woods. John Stuart Williams. AngWe

Where the pheasant roosts at night. The Vernal Ague. Philip Freneau. EAP

Where the Picnic Was. Thomas Hardy. OxBTC

Where the pipe ends he had fixed the long trough. Windmill At Mandanthanunguna. Pambardu, tr. fr. *Aborigine* by Georg von Brandenstein. NOBAu

Where the place called morning lies! (*LL*) Will there really be a morning? Emily Dickinson. OBCA

Where — the place of concatenations. Nostoi. Rodolfo Di Biasio, tr. fr. *Italian* by Stephen Sartarelli. NeIt

Where the pools are bright and deep. A Boy's Song. James Hogg. BoTP; CH; CoGr; FaPON; FaPoR; MoShBr; OBEV; OTCP; OxAEP-2; OxBChV; PlP; WiR

Where the quiet-colored [*or* coloured] end of evening smiles. Love among the Ruins. Robert Browning. EnVR; FaBV; FHYEP; HAP; MeMBP; NAEL-2; NOBE; OAEL-2; OBEV; PoEL-5; PrIm; SCGP

Where the racing Wairau slows, homesick for its snowshed. Cloudy Bay. Ellen Duggan. PeNZ

Where the Rainbow Ends. Robert Lowell. HCAP; MoAB; MoAmPo; TrGrPo

Where the Rainbow Ends. Richard Rive. PBA; TTY

Where the rainbow ends. (*LL*) Where the Rainbow Ends. Richard Rive. PBA; TTY

Where the Red Lion flaring o'er the way. A Description of an Author's Bedchamber. Goldsmith. BIrV

Where the red wine-cup floweth, there art thou! Caroline E. Norton. VBLP

Where the remote Bermudas ride. Bermudas. Andrew Marvell. AWP; CH; ChTr; CoGr; ESCV; FaBoCh; FHYEP; GeHe; GN; JCP; NAEL-1; NOBE; NOCV; NoP; NOSC; OBEV; OBTV; PAH; PeECV; PlP; PoE; RB; SCGP; SeCP; SeCV-1; TFi (Song of the Emigrants [in Bermuda].) GTBS; GTBS-P

Where the ripe pears droop heavily. The Wasp. "Fiona Macleod." *Fr.* Transcripts from Nature. FM

Where the road turns to water. Cross Country. Rod Moran. NOBAu

Where the royal Queen Mary went weeping away. (*LL*) The Duke of Grafton. *Unknown.* ChTr; GBP

Where the sally tree went pale in every breeze. Field Work. Seamus Heaney. AnAn; CBLP

Where the sea gulls sleep or indeed where they fly. The Ballet of the Fifth Year. Delmore Schwartz. MoAB; OxBA; TwCP

Where the short-legged Esquimaux. An Arctic Vision. Bret Harte. PAH

Where the Single Men Go in Summer. Nina Bourne. FiBHP

Where the slanting forest eves. To Nature Seekers. Robert W. Chambers. MoShBr

Where the Slow Fig's Purple Sloth. Robert Penn Warren. NoP

Where the slow river. Leda. Hilda Doolittle ("H. D."). NAAL-2

Where the Song Went Where She Went & What Happened When They Met. *Unknown*, tr. fr. *Seneca Indian* by Jerome K. Rothenberg *and* Richard Johnny John. STP

Where the sound of the river streams beyond the border. (*LL*) On the Frontier. Li Ho. PLT

Where the stream ox-bowed. Sap. Robert Minhinnick. AngWe

Where the string. O-Jazz-O. Bob Kaufman. PoBeRe

Where the sturdy ocean breeze. The Ballad of Mr. Cooke. Bret Harte. AnAmPo

Where the Sun Ends. Peter Davison. ChIV-1

Where the sun shines in the street. Feet. Mary Carolyn Davies. WGRP

Where the swan drifts upon a darkening flood. (*LL*) Coole Park and Ballylee, 1931. W. B. Yeats. CMoP; GTBS-P; NoAM; NOIV; OBMV; PPP

Where the tempest whispers, "Pay him!" and I answer, "Nevermore!" (*LL*) The Promissory Note. Bayard Taylor. AnAmPo; BXAP

Where the thistle lifts a purple crown. Daisy. Francis Thompson. AWP; BeLS; FaBV; MoAB; MoBrPo; OBEV; OBNC

Where the waters gently flow. The Song of the Reed Sparrow. *Unknown.* OxBChV

Where the western zun, unclouded. Zun-zet. William Barnes. PoEL-4

Where the wheel of light is turned. Pole Star for This Year. Archibald MacLeish. MeMAP; OxBA

Where the wife is scouring the frying pan. Land of Little Sticks, 1945. James Tate. LCAP

Where the Wild Thyme Blows. Shakespeare. *See* I know a bank where the wild thyme blows.

Where the wild wave, from ocean proudly swelling. Fort Bowyer. Charles L. S. Jones. PAH

Where the wind. Footprints on the Glacier. W. S. Merwin. MoP; NoAM

Where the wind attacks the downs. A Kodak; Tregantle. Horatio Brown. PeHV

Where the young river, from its wild ravine. The Emigrant's Cabin. Thomas Pringle. PeSAV

Where their bright glories shone at first. (*LL*) The Evening Sun. Emily Brontë. CH

Where then shall hope and fear their objects find? An Additional Poem. John Ashbery. FaBoMo

Where then shall Hope and Fear their objects find? The Power of Prayer. Samuel Johnson. *Fr.* Vanity of Human Wishes, The: The Tenth Satire of Juvenal Imitated. EBEV; ECEV; NOBE; NOEC; NoP; OAEL-1; OxAEP-1; PoEL-3; PrIm; TEP; TFi

Where there is personal liking we go. The Hero. Marianne Moore. *Fr.* Part of a Novel, Part of a Poem, Part of a Play. CMoP; NOBA; OxBA; PoA

Where There's a Will There's a Way. Eliza Cook. BLPA

Where There's a Will There's a Way. John Godfrey Saxe. AnAmPo

Where there's one we love to meet us! (*LL*) Home Is Where There Is One to Love Us. Charles Swain. BLPA; BLPL; FaBoBe; PoToHe

Where there's room and bread for the poor. (*LL*) The Orphan Girl. *Unknown.* AmFP; AS

Where they cracked bottles merrily. (*LL*) The Bold Pedlar and Robin Hood. *Unknown.* AmFP; ESPB

Where they once dug for money. The Old Marlborough Road. Thoreau. PoEL-4

Where they tamed the wild Libyan. The Parthenon. John Heath-Stubbs. OBTV

Where They Were. *Unknown.* AS

Where thine earthly part is lying, / Florence Vane. (*LL*) Florence Vane. Philip Pendleton Cooke. AnAmPo

Where this is freedom: free to follow each desire. Freedom. Friedrich von Logau, *tr. fr. German.* GePo, *tr. by* George C. Schoolfield

Where this jolly babe was baptized. (*LL*) Robin Hood and Little John. *Unknown.* AmFP; ESPB

Where thou dwellest, in what grove. The Birds. Blake. CH

Where three eagles cross in the sky. Cabin Site, Christmas Island, N.S. Martin Edmunds. UTF

Where, thy true treasure? Gold says, 'Not in me'. Edward Young. *Fr.* Night Thoughts. OAEL-1

Where thy victory, O Grave? (*LL*) Easter Hymn. Charles Wesley. OHIP

Where tongues were loud and hearts were light. The Ancre at Hamel: Afterwards. Edmund Blunden. PeFWW

Where trees are actual and take no holiday. (*LL*) Robinson. Weldon Kees. MoP; NaP; NYBP

Where turmpets play all night. (*LL*) No Coward's Song. James Elroy Flecker. OxBSP

Where, twining subtile fears with hope. Andrew Marvell. *Fr.* Horatian Ode upon Cromwell's [*or* Cromwel's] Return from Ireland, An. EBEV; ESCV; GeHe; GTBS; GTBS-P; HAP; IIP; InPS; JCP; NOBE; NoP; NOSC; OAEL-1; OBD; OBEV; OBWP; OxAEP-1; PoEL-2; SCGP; SeCP; SeCV-1; TFi

Where two or three were flung together, or fifty. The March 2. Robert Lowell. NoP

Where Unimaginably Bright. Oliver Hale. GoYe

Where unincarnate spirits purely aspire. (*LL*) To George Sand: A Recognition. Elizabeth Barrett Browning. BoWoP; NAEL-2; NALW; TEP

Where Venta's Norman castle still appears. On King Arthur's Round Table, at Winchester. Thomas Warton the Younger. Son

Where virtue's force can cause her to obey. (*LL*) On Fortune. Elizabeth I, Queen of England. PBWP; WPE

Where voices vanish into dream. Elected Silence. Siegfried Sassoon. MoBrPo

Where was it one first heard of the truth? The the. (*LL*) The Rival Curates. W. S. Gilbert. PeLV

Where was Moses when the light went out? *Unknown.* RoPo

Where was you last winter, boys. The Horse Trader's Song. *Unknown.* AmFP

Where wast thou when I laid the foundations of the earth? Bible, *O.T. Fr.* Job. AWP; NAWM-1, *abr.*; PAW, *abr.*

Where We Are. Julia Kasdorf. LoHo

Where We Crashed. Richard Hugo. ArOW

Where we live, the teakettle whistles out. Now. William Stafford. NNaP

Where we made the fire. Where the Picnic Was. Thomas Hardy. OxBTC

Where we went in the boat was a long bay. The Mediterranean. Allen Tate. FaBoMo; GOA; HAP; ImPo; LiTA; LiTM; MoAB; MoAmPo; VGW

Where we were walking in the day's light, seeing. Conrad Aiken. *Fr.* Time in the Rock [*or*, Preludes to Definition]. VGW

Where were the greenhouses going. Big Wind. Theodore Roethke. AmPP; CMoP; GoJo; InvP; NoP; TRP; VGW

Where were we going that. The Drive. Janet Reed McFatter. GrPl

Where were we in that afternoon? And where. Anniversary. Richmond Lattimore. NYBP

Where were you then? A Story. Margaret Avison. MoCV

Where? When? Which? Langston Hughes. BPo

Where, where are now the great reports. Fuimus Fumus. Joshua Sylvester. FaBoEE

Where, where but here have pride and truth. On Hearing That the Students of Our New University Have Joined the Agitation against Immoral Literature. W. B. Yeats. MoP; NoAM

Where will we get married? *Unknown.* RoPo

Where Will You Be? Patricia Parker. GLP

Where will you find this year, Mary. Invitation to Mary. Mairtin O Direain, *tr. fr. Irish by the author.* TIRV

Where wit is over-ruled by will. Desire's Government. "A. W." EiL

Where, without bloodshed, can there be. Long Feud. Louis Untermeyer. MoAmPo

Where you and I pledged our first love so true. (*LL*) Come Hither, My Dear One. John Clare. ELP

Where you arrange them. (*LL*) Jude. Carol Moldaw. UTF

Where you belong! (*LL*) Men at Work. Richard Tipping. NOBAu

Where you do lie beneath. (*LL*) The Brown Girl. *Unknown.* ELP; ESPB, A *and* B *vers.*; OBET

Where You Go When She Sleeps. T. R. Hummer. MT

Where you going?/ (Getting berries. Think I'll try a little farther.). Getting Berries. *Unknown, tr. fr. Bella Bella Indian by* Franz Boas. STP

Where you going?/ (Going to get firewood.). Getting Firewood. *Unknown, tr. fr. Bella Bella Indian by* Franz Boas. STP

Where you have fallen, you stay. On the Wall of a KZ-Lager. János Pilinszky, *tr. fr. Hungarian by* János Csokits *and* Ted Hughes. PoSu

Whereas galoshed my Julia goes. Upon Julia's Arctics. Bert Leston Taylor. NBLV

Whereas, on certain boughs and sprays. The Lawyer's Invocation to Spring. Henry Howard Brownell. PoLF

Whereas the rebels hereabout. Tom Gage's Proclamation. *Unknown.* PAH

Whereat Erewhile I Wept, I Laugh. Robert Greene. *Fr.* Arbasto. EiL

Where'er they met, or parting place has been. (*LL*) Lovers How They Come and Part. Robert Herrick. GBL; OxBoLi; OxBSP; PoEL-3

Where'er thy navy spreads her canvas wings. To the King, on His Navy. Edmund Waller. BeJo

Wherefore and how I am certain, I can hardly tell; but it [*or* is so]. Arthur Hugh Clough. *Fr.* Amours de Voyage. EBVVPR, *canto* II, xiii; NOBVV

Wherefore Hidest Thou Thy Face, and Holdest Me for Thine Enemy [*or* Enemie]? Francis Quarles. *Fr.* Emblems. NOSC

Wherefore, Lucinda, dost aspire. To Miss L. F. on the Occasion of Her Departure for the Continent. J. C. Squire. BXAP

Wherefore peep'st thou, envious day? *Unknown.* GBL

Wherefore the Scars of Christ's Passion Remained in the Body of His Resurrection. Theodulf of Orleans, *tr. fr. Latin by* Helen Waddell. MLL

Wherefore this busy labor without rest? Tuskegee. Leslie Pinckney Hill. PoNe

Where/from/here. 2 B BLK. Val Ferdinand. NBV

Wherein Consists the High Estate. Ebenezer Dayton. AH

Wherein my love had eyes that lighted my delight. (*LL*) O Jealous Night [*or* A Night Piece *or* To Night]. *Unknown.* EiL

Wherein to play your violin with grace. (*LL*) First Fight. Then Fiddle. Gwendolyn Brooks. InPK; NIP; Poetr; PoNe

Wherelings Whenlings. E. E. Cummings. HAP; WeW

Where's an old woman to go when the years. The Riddle. H. E. H. PoToHe

Where's Commander All-a-Tanto? Herman Melville. *Fr.* Bridegroom Dick. PoEL-5

Where's Ho Xuan Huong. Saigon Bar Girls, 1975. Yusef Komunyakaa. MT

Where's the peck of pickled pepper Peter Piper picked? (*LL*) Peter Piper picked a peck of pickled pepper[s]. Mother Goose. FaBoBe; FaPON; OTCP; OxNR; ReMoGo

Where's the poet? show him, show him. Keats. EPCY

Where's the public good in what you write. Palladas, *tr. fr. Greek by* Tony Harrison. GrAn

Where's the Queen of Sheba? Gone. Walter de la Mare. GoJo

Where's the winning without chocolate. The Chocolate Soldiers. Calvin Forbes. MAT

Wheresoe'er I turn mine eyes. God Everywhere. Abraham ibn Ezra, *tr. fr. Hebrew by* D. E. de L. TrJP

Wheresoe'er I turn my view. Lines on Thomas Warton's Poems *or* Lines in Ridicule of Certain Poems Published in 1777. Samuel Johnson. EPCY; FaBoCo; FaBoEE

(Lines Written in Ridicule of Certain Poems.) SCGP

Whereso'er you are, my heart shall truly love you. (*LL*) Were I as Base as Is the Lowly Plain. *At. to* Joshua Sylvester. NoSic; Son

Wheresoever ye fare by frith or by fell. Julians Barnes. *Fr.* Book of Hunting. WPE

Whereto should I express. Henry VIII, King of England. NoSic (To His Lady. CTC; EBEV)

Whereupon told/ That once in the stillness of a summer's noon. Books. Wordsworth. *Fr.* Prelude [*or*, Growth of a Poet's Mind], The. EnRP; OAEL-2

Wherever God erects a house of prayer. Daniel Defoe. *Fr.* True-born Englishman, The. APAS; NOBL; OBSV

Wherever he was,/ with whomever he spoke. Various Masks: Ai Ch'ing. Ai Ch'ing, *tr. fr. Chinese.* LHF, *tr. by* Hualing Nieh

Wherever I am, there's always Pooh. Us Two. A. A. Milne. OxBChV

Wherever I go to find. Pigeons. Bert Meyers. BTR

Wherever in this city, screens flicker. Adrienne Rich. *Fr.* Twenty-one Love Poems. GLP; PeHV

Wherever shadow falls wherever the drowning. Hayden Carruth. *Fr.* Contra Mortem. PoA

Wherever shadow falls wherever the drowning. Contra Mortem. Hayden Carruth. PoA

Wherever we looked the land would hold us up. (*LL*) One Home. William Stafford. CoAP; VGW

Wherever you are is home. Wilfred Pelletier *and* Ted Poole. EaPr

Wherewith free will doth true desert retain. (*LL*) Answer that ye made to me, my dear, The. Sir Thomas Wyatt. SiPS

Whet all your wits and antidote your eyes. The Tragi-Comedy of Titus Oates. *Unknown*. APAS

Whether at doomsday (tell, ye reverend wise). Quaerè. George Farewell. NOEC

Whether day my spirit's yearning. The Thought Eternal. Goethe, *tr. fr. German by* Ludwig Lewisohn. AWP

Whether dinner was pleasant, with the windows lit by gunfire. No Credit. Kenneth Fearing. CMoP

(Whether his mouth be open or shut.) (*LL*) Lines for Cuscuscaraway and Mirza Murad Ali Beg. T. S. Eliot. FiBHP; NBLV; NTP; OBAL; PeLV; UV

Whether I find thee bright with fair. Changeful Beauty. *Unknown, tr. fr. Greek by* Andrew Lang. EnLoPo

Whether I live or fail. (*LL*) V-Letter. Karl Shapiro. NoAM; TrJP

Whether I see you now. *Unknown, tr. fr. Greek by* Sam Hamill. InMo

Whether I sit or lie. Ukihashi, *tr. fr. Japanese by* Kenneth Rexroth *and* Ikuko Atsumi. WPJ; WPOW

Whether it's cold. So Long As There's Weather. Tamara Kitt. SiSoPo

Whether it's sunny or not, it's sure. Poem about Morning. William Meredith. NYBP

Whether Men Do Laugh or Weep. *At. to* Thomas Campion *and to* Philip Rosseter. EnRePo

Whether on Ida's shady brow. To the Muses. Blake. ChTr; EnRP; EPCY; HAP; HeIP; ImPo; LiTB; MeMBP; NAEL-2; NOBE; NOEC; NoP; OAEL-2; OBEV; SCGP; TrGrPo

Whether one paints five Helens. The Ultimate Antientropy. Theodore Weiss. NoAM

Whether or Not. D. H. Lawrence. MoBrPo

Whether outside, around, or in. (*LL*) Fence Wire. James Dickey. NYBP; VGW

Whether that soul which now comes up to you. Hymn to the Saints, and to Marquis Hamilton. John Donne. NOSC

Whether the bees have thoughts we cannot say. The Long Waters. Theodore Roethke. NYBP

Whether the fruitful Nile, or Tyrian shore. John Dryden *and* Nahum Tate. *Fr.* To the Earl of Roscommon, on His Excellent Essay on Translated Verse. EPCY

Whether the graver did by this intend. On the Late Metamorphosis of an Old Picture of Oliver Cromwell's. *Unknown*. APAS

Whether the moorings are invisible. Conversation. John Berryman. LiTA; LiTM

Whether the sensitive plant, or that. Shelley. *Fr.* Sensitive Plant, The. EnRP; FHYEP; OAEL-2

Whether the Turkish new-moon minded be. Sir Philip Sidney. *Fr.* Astrophel and Stella. AAS; GGP; HeIL; NoSic; PoE; Poetr; SCGP, SiPS, SiPSBD.

Whether the weather be fine. Weather. *Unknown*. ImGa; OTCP

Whether the weather be fine, or whether the weather be not. *Unknown*. BoTP

Whether There Is Sorrow in the Demons. John Berryman. LiTM

Whether they cry. Yankees. Reyna Hernández, *tr. fr. Spanish by* Zoe Anglesey. WoWa

Whether they work together or apart. (*LL*) The Tuft of Flowers. Robert Frost. AWP; GoYe; LiTA; MoAB; MoAmPo; NAAL-2; OxBA; PAW

Whether Thou get'st them green, or lets them seed. (*LL*) Upon Wedlock and Death of Children. Edward Taylor. AmPP; EAP; NAAL-1; NoP

Whether to believe them or not. (*LL*) Project for a Cliff Face. John Ciardi. HeIL

Whether to Ceaser he was friend or foe? Upon the Death of G. B. John Cotton. SCAP

Whether to Ceaser hee was friend, or foe. (*LL*) Bacon's Epitaph, Made by His Man. *At. to* John Cotton. PAH; SCAP

Whether to sally and see thee, girl of my dreams. To Meet, or Otherwise. Thomas Hardy. OBNC

Whether to use time, or to kill time, either. Moment. Robert Creeley. CAPP

Whether we climb, whether we plod. Heroism. Lizette Woodworth Reese. AmWP

Whether what we sense of this world. Metonymy as an Approach to a Real World. William Bronk. VGW

Whether White or Black be best. Verses Made Sometime Since upon . . . the Indian Squa. John Josselyn. SCAP

Whether you are a citizen or a stranger coming from elsewhere. Epitaph from Athens. *Unknown, tr. fr. Greek by* Richmond Lattimore. GrAn

Which are the living? We who stride unyielding earth in engine fumes. Three City Cantos. Charles Wagner. GoYe

Which Are You? *Unknown*. PoLF

Which blamed the living man. (*LL*) Growing Old. Matthew Arnold. EnVR; FHYEP; MeMBP; NAEL-2; NOBVV; OAEL-2; PoEL-5

Which burns and moves and kisses us with salt. (*LL*) Night Flower. Geoffrey Lehmann. NOBAu

Which cannot exhale a ship. (*LL*) Night Street. Tuo Ssu. WPC

Which caus'd her thus to send thee out of door. (*LL*) The Author to Her Book. Anne Bradstreet. AmPP; AnAmPo; EAP; InPK; NAAL-1; NALW; NOBA; NoP; OxBA; PoE; Poetr; SCAP; TAP

Which Claus of Innsbruck cast in bronze for me! (*LL*) My Last Duchess. Robert Browning. AWP; BeLS; ClHu; EBNV; EBVV; FaBoPV; FF; FHYEP; GGP; GTBS-P; HAP; HeIL; HeIP; HoPM; ImPo; InPK; InPS; LiTB; MAT; MeMBP; NAEL-2; NIP; NOBE; NOBVV; NoP; OAEL-2; OBNC; OHCV; OtMeF; PeVV; PoE; PoEL-5; Poetr; PoLF; PPP; PrIm; SCGP; SCV; SoSe; TEP; TFi; TrGrPo; TRP

Which come and go. (*LL*) The New Notebook. Maria Banus. AIW; PBWP

Which concludes this very interesting song. (*LL*) Roy Bean. *Unknown*. AnAmPo; BeLS; OBAL

Which cover lightly, gentle earth. (*LL*) On My First Daughter. Ben Jonson. BeJo; EBEV; EnRePo; FaBoEE; HoPM; InPS; JCP; NAEL-1; NOBE; NoP; NOSC; PoE; SeCP; SeCV-1; TEP

Which damp even the topmost blossoms on the tree. (*LL*) Exile. Li Shang-yin. PLT

Which dark green oaks his noontide leisure shields. (*LL*) There is a charm in solitude that cheers. John Clare. NOBVV

Which doesn't belong in this group of three? 7,22,66. Sandra McPherson. AnAn

Which ever so friendly forfeits nothing. (*LL*) L'Agulhas, A Walk. Wilma Stockenström. PeSAV

Which everyone has sat except a man. (*LL*) A Politician. E. E. Cummings. InPK

Which ev'n eternity excludes! (*LL*) Time. George Herbert. NAEL-1; TEP

Which faith had dictated, and angels trod. (*LL*) On Exodus 3: 14: "I am that I am." Matthew Prior. ChIV-1; NOCV

Which false apostates never knew. (*LL*) Broad Is the Road. Isaac Watts. AH; AmFP

Which fashion yearly fades away. (*LL*) December. John Clare. OBCP

Which five hundred did survive? (*LL*) The Test. Emerson. OBAL

Which flows not every day, but ever! (*LL*) When, dearest, I but think on [*or of*] thee. *At. to* Sir John Suckling *and to* Owen Feltham. NoP

Which from afar he bears. (*LL*) The Inward Morning. Thoreau. AmPP; NoP

Which goes with Bridge, and Women and Champagne. (*LL*) On a General Election. Hilaire Belloc. FaBoCo; FaBoEE; NOBE; NOBL; OBSV; OxBTC

Which has no garden or greenery. (*LL*) Kiddushin 4:12. *Unknown*. EaPr

Which hath my heart in keeping. (*LL*) Tan ta ra: cries Mars on bloody rampier. Thomas Weelkes. CBLP

Which he certainly knew you knew, U Nu. (*LL*) Just Dropped In. William Cole. FiBHP; GoJo

Which He from Heaven doth bring. (*LL*) New Prince, New Pomp[e]. Robert Southwell. ELP; ESCV; GN; NOBE; NOCV; NoSic; OHIP; TrCP

Which I gather in a song. (*LL*) The Apology. Emerson. AmPP; AnAmPo

Which I have loved long since, and lost awhile. (*LL*) Lead, Kindly Light. Cardinal Newman. PIP

Which I wish to remark. Plain Language from Truthful James. Bret Harte. AnAmPo; BeLS; BLPA; CTC; EBNV; FaBoBe; NOBL; OBAL; PeLV; UV

(Heathen Chinee, The.) FaBoCo

Which I wish to remark. The Heathen Pass-ee. Arthur Clement Hilton. FaBoCo; NOBL; UV

Which in our winter woodland looks a flower. (*LL*) Dear, near and true — no truer Time himself. Tennyson. OxBSP

Which is I stood and loved you while you slept. (*LL*) A Poem for Emily. Miller Williams. MT; WeW

Which is real. The Indigo Glass in the Grass. Wallace Stevens. PoA

Which is so gladly found. (*LL*) Commentary Applied to Spiritual Things. St. John of the Cross. TOF

Which is the best to hit your taste. Epigram on Two Ladies. Lady Sophia Burrell. ErPo

Which Is the Bow? *Unknown*. GBP

Which is the cosiest voice. Gray Thrums. Clara Doty Bates. OBCA; OFC

Which is the other sex that I possess. (*LL*) Not that miracles are. Janet Gray. VBLP

Which is the strongest thing I know. (*LL*) Parting with Lucasia; a Song. Katherine Philips. CBLP; PeHV

Which is the way to Baby-land? Baby-Land. George Cooper. BoTP

Which is the way to Fairyland. The Way to Fairyland. Eunice Close. BoTP

Which is the way to London Town. *Unknown.* BoTP

Which is the wind that brings the cold? What the Winds Bring. Edmund Clarence Stedman. AnAmPo

Which is, to keep that hid. (*LL*) The Undertaking. John Donne. NAEL-1; NOBE

Which is what. After Love. John Stone. MT

Which is you, old two-in-one? What the Serpent Said to Adam. Archibald MacLeish. ChIV-1; MeMAP

Which knows no pain. (*LL*) My window opens out into the trees. Clarissa Scott Delany. ShDr

Which lacketh will to change his place. (*LL*) For want I will in woe I plain. Sir Thomas Wyatt. SiPS

Which Loved Best? "Joy Allison." WBLP

Which Loved Her Best? "Joy Allison." *See* "I love you, Mother," said little John.

Which made poor Simon whistle. (*LL*) Simple Simon met a pieman. Mother Goose. BoTP; FaBoBe; OxNR; ReMoGo

Which makes dreams materialize. (*LL*) Food is not matter. Edward Espe Brown. EaPr

Which men can neither want, nor well endure. (*LL*) Authority is a disease, and cure. Samuel Butler. FaBoEE

Which my God feels as bloud; but I, as wine. (*LL*) The Agony [*or* Agonie]. George Herbert. ESCV; GeHe

Which nobody can deny. (*LL*) Sweet Meat Has Sour Sauce; or, The Slave-Trader in the Dumps. William Cowper. ECEV; NOEC; OBSV

Which nobody can deny. (*LL*) The Mother Country. Benjamin Franklin. AiP; PAH

Which now the angels sing! (*LL*) It Came upon the Midnight Clear. Edmund Hamilton Sears. AH; FaPON

Which of these statements is true? Tom Joanides. Lloyd Schwartz. EOEF

Which of thy names I take, not only bears. To Sir Horace Vere. Ben Jonson. BeJo

Which of you/ is going to take my body? Song of Starvation. *Unknown*, *tr. fr. Chippewa Indian by* Jerome K. Rothenberg. STP

Which One Is Genuine? Baudelaire, *tr. fr. French by* Robert Bly. RaBo

Which one? Which one? (*LL*) What the Serpent Said to Adam. Archibald MacLeish. ChIV-1; MeMAP

Which one's the mockingbird? Which one's the world? (*LL*) The Mockingbird. Randall Jarrell. NYBP; RFM

Which only breeds your beauty's overthrow. (*LL*) I Saw My Lady Weep. *Unknown.* EIL; ELP; EnLoPo; LiTB; NoSic; TrGrPo

Which out of sight and sound is passing, passing? (*LL*) Ships That Pass in the Night. Paul Laurence Dunbar. AnAmPo; CDC

Which partley assuaged his despair. (*LL*) There was an old man whose despair. Edward Lear. CBNP; FaBoNo

Which river is this. Michael Anania. *Fr.* Riversongs of Arion, The. NoAM

Which Road? William Barnes. NOBVV

Which road, which road did you take. Exaltation. Franz Werfel, *tr. fr. German by* Edith Abercrombie Snow. TrJP

Which sadly annoyed Mistress Towl. (*LL*) Mistress Towl. *Unknown.* FaBoNo

Which screens me from the Western sunlight as I look towards Ch'ang-an. (*LL*) On the Road. Tu Mu. PLT

Which Shall It Be? Ethel Lynn Beers. BLPA

Which Side Are You on? Florence Reese. SWP

Which spent, one death bring to ye both one grave. (*LL*) The Entertainment, or Porch-Verse, at the Marriage of Master Henry Northleigh and the Most Witty Mistress Lettice Yard. Robert Herrick. CaPo

Which the same I am free to maintain. (*LL*) Plain Language from Truthful James. Bret Harte. AnAmPo; BeLS; BLPA; CTC; EBNV; FaBoBe; NOBL; OBAL; PeLV; UV

Which the same I am free to maintain. (*LL*) The Heathen Pass-ee. Arthur Clement Hilton. FaBoCo; NOBL; UV

Which they that know the rest, know more than I. (*LL*) The Answer. George Herbert. FaBoRV; FaBoVe; TEP

Which till their eyes ache, let iron men envy. (*LL*) Song. Thomas Campion. CBLP

Which told her heart was broken. (*LL*) The Maid of Neidpath. Sir Walter Scott. BeLS; EnRP; GTBS; GTBS-P

Which true lovers always admire. (*LL*) Lord Lovel ("Lord Lovel he stood at his castle gate.") *Unknown.* AmFP; AS; BLPA; ESPB, A, B, *and* D *vers.*; FaPON

Which vexed all the folks on the Border. (*LL*) There was an old man on the Border. Edward Lear. EBEV

Which vexed the fat man of Bombay. (*LL*) As a little fat man of Bombay. *Unknown.* OxBChV

Which Washington? Eve Merriam. NTCP

Which we dutifully offer to our mother-land! (*LL*) Utopia Anglicized. W. S. Gilbert. OBSV

Which we held in idea, a little handful. (*LL*) The Horse Chestnut Tree. Richard Eberhart. CMoP; LiTM; MoAB; MoAmPo

Which we saw/ across the winter river. Cathedral 1941. Johannes Bobrowski, *tr. fr. German by* Ruth Mead *and* Matthew Mead. AnRep

Which wine itself enough can do. (*LL*) The Cup. John Oldham. AWP

Which would a gone into the seas and brought proud Ward to me.' (*LL*) Captain Ward and the *Rainbow. Unknown.* ESPB; OBET; OxBSS

Whichway. Ron Welburn. NBV

Whiffs of the Ohio River at Cincinnati, *sels.* Carl Sandburg. "When I asked for fish in the restaurant facing the Ohio River." PoE

Whigmaleerie, A. William Soutar. OxBS

Whig's the first letter of his odious name. An Acrostic on Wharton. *Unknown.* FaBoEH; OBSV

While a child I longed to be staunch in virtue. Passing through My Shih-ning Estate. Hsieh Ling-yün, *tr. fr. Chinese by* Francis Westbrook. SuSp

While a dark root a dark root gripped and bound. (*LL*) A Forked Radish. Jonathan Price. CBLP

While a thousand fine projects are planned ev'ry day. *Unknown.* NOEC

While Adam slept, from him his Eve arose. *Unknown.* FaBoEE

While all the little brown birds sing upon the spray. (*LL*) Cock shall crow, The. Robert Louis Stevenson. TrGrPo

While an intrinsic ardor prompts to write. To the University of Cambridge, in New-England. Phillis Wheatley. AmPP; NAAL-1; TAP

While as I lived no house I had. Upon the Grave of a Beggar. Timothy Kendall. NoSic

While at her bedroom window once. The Keys of Morning. Walter de la Mare. NoP

While billows endless round the beaches die. (*LL*) The Enviable Isles. Herman Melville. FaBoBe

While breaking the big rock. Stone Giant. Joseph Bruchac. CDW

While briers an' woodbines budding green. Epistle to John Lapraik. Burns. EnRP

While bringing Apollo the pick of the Etruscan plunder. Simonides, *tr. fr. Greek by* Peter Jay. GrAn

While Butler, needy wretch, was yet alive. On the Setting Up of Mr. Butler's Monument in Westminster Abbey. Samuel Wesley. InvP; NBLV; NOEC; OBD; OxBSP

While Cecil Snores: Mom Drinks Cold Milk. James Cunningham. JB

While cheeks burn, arms open, eyes shut and lips meet! (*LL*) Now [*or* The Moment Eternal]. Robert Browning. CBLP

While clearing the land, Walter. Horrible Tangents. Victoria Kohn. UTF

While crickets tighten their solitary bolts. Lace. Dean Young. NAmP90

While crossing a field. Out in the Open. Aleksandar Ristovic, *tr. fr. Serbo-Croatian by* Charles Simic. HSix

While death and winter closed the autumn scene. (*LL*) The Closing Scene. Thomas Buchanan Read. AnAmPo

While Delia shines at hurlothrumbo. The Widow and Virgin Sisters. William Broome. ECEV

While Dissecting Frogs in Biology Class Scrut Discovers the Intricacies of the Scooped Neckline in His Lab Partner's Dress. George Roberts. GOYP

While drinking, all at once I saw. The Three Kingdoms of Nature. Gotthold Ephraim Lessing, *tr. fr. German.* NU, *tr. by* Alfred Baskerville

While Dubliner leopold bloom sought solace. Gerard Benson. PeLi

While Eve waited. The Sleep of Adam. John Hejduk. ChIV-1

While far along the eastern sky. After the Fire. Oliver Wendell Holmes. PAH

While fluttering in the bushes. (*LL*) The Green Linnet. Wordsworth. EnRP; GTBS; GTBS-P

While from below all Grub Street rings. (*LL*) The Progress of Poetry. Swift. InvP; NOIV

While gentlefolks strut in their silver and satins. Bartleme Fair. George Alexander Stevens. ELP; NOEC

While God is marching on. (*LL*) The Battle Hymn of the [American] Republic. Julia Ward Howe. AH; AmWP; AnAmPo; BLPA; CH; CoGr; EBEvV; FaBoBe; FaPON; FaPoR; GN; NOBA; NOCV; OBWP;

OHIP; OtMeF; PAH; PWR; SCV; SWP; TAP; TFi; WBLP; WGRP; WPE

While going the road to sweet Athy. Johnny, I Hardly Knew Ye. *Unknown.* BIrV; ELP; FaBoBa; GBP; IIP; OxBoLi; WoWa

While he slept, I poured salt in his ears. Judith Recalls Holofernes. Maura Stanton. AmPA

While Holroyd may boast of her beautiful bottom. On Seeing a Tapestry Chair-Bottom Beautifully Worked by His Daughter for Mrs Holroyd. Richard Owen Cambridge. ECEV

While I am praying. Prayer for a Thief. Phil DuPlessis, *tr. fr. Afrikaans by the author.* PeSAV

While I Am Young. Silas Ballou. AH

While I continue to rave. Violet Star. Philip Lamantia. UL

While I droop here. *(LL)* I Am a Parcel of Vain Strivings Tied. Thoreau. GGP; NoP; PFP; PoEL-4; TAP

While I fled. *(LL)* Intimates. D. H. Lawrence. BoLoP; CBLP; NBLV; OxBSP; RaBo

While I Listen to Thy Voice. Edmund Waller. BeJo

While I recline. The Cotton Boll. Henry Timrod. AmPP

While I sit at the door. Eve. Christina Rossetti. CH; ChIV-1; FM; GTBS-P; MeMBP; NALW; NIP; PoEL-5; Poetr

While I snitch my four hours of sleep. *(LL)* The Bats. Matthew Sweeney. IB

While I so spring, as if I could not fade! *(LL)* The Brecon Beacons and the Black Mountains. Henry Vaughan. FaBoPP

While I stood here, in the open, lost in myself. Milkweed. James Wright. LCAP; NaP; NOBA; NU; RaBo

While I Wait. Vilhelm Andreas Wexels Krag, *tr. fr. Norwegian by* Philip L. Miller. RiWo

While I was building neat. It Is Dangerous to Read Newspapers. Margaret Atwood. CrSp; HeIP; OBWP

While I was cooking dinner. To Ted Hughes. Steve Ellis. PWE

While I watch the Christmas blaze. The Reminder. Thomas Hardy. CMoP; OBCP

While I watch the yellow wheat. Watching the Wheat. John Jones. AngWe

While I'm gone, white mother, kill the fattened oxen. The White and the Black. N. M. Khaketla, *tr. fr. Southern Sotho by* Jack Cope *and* Dan Kunene. PeSA

While in long exile far from you I roam. To Dr. Moore, in Anser to a Poetical Epistle Written by Him in Wales. Helen Maria Williams. ECWP; WoRP

While in the mask of night there shone that cut. Landing on the Moon. May Swenson. TAP

While in the park I sing, the listning deer. At Penshurst. Edmund Waller. BeJo

While it breaks, breaks, breaks on the sheltering bars. *(LL)* The Heart of a Woman. Georgia Douglas Johnson. BlSi; CDC; PoLF; PoNe; ShDr; VBLP

While joy gave clouds the light of stars. The Villain. W. H. Davies. AngWe; MoBrPo; OxBSP; OxBTC

While ladling butter from alternate tubs. On the Historians Freeman and Stubbs. J. E. Thorold Rogers. FaBoEE

While leanest beasts in pastures feed. Supreme Fortune Falls Soonest. Robert Herrick. CaPo

While, Lydia, I was lov'd of thee. III, 9. Dialogue between Horace and Lydia, A ("Donec gratus eram.") Horace, *tr. fr. Latin by* Austin Dobson. *Fr.* Odes. OBVE, *tr. by* Robert Herrick
(Reconciliation: A Modern Version, The.) NBLV, *mod. vers. by* F. P. Adams

While Many a Merry Tale. Samuel Johnson. UV

While maudlin Whigs deplored their Cato's fate. On a Lady Who P-ssed at the Tragedy of Cato. Pope. OxBSP

While mine has grown another beard. *(LL)* Epigram: To Dindymus. Martial. PeHV

While money's a substance, and honour a name? *(LL)* The Song of the Transportationist. *Unknown.* NOBAu

While Morpheus thus doth gently lay. Henry Killigrew. CH

While my father walked through mud. 1905. David Ignatow. BTR

While my hair was still cut straight across my forehead. River Merchant's Wife, The; a Letter. Li Po, *tr. fr. Chinese.* AmPP; AWP; BoLoP; ClHu; FYAP; HAP; HeIP; InPK; InPS; LiTA; LPA, *tr. by* Ezra Pound; MeMAP; MoAB; MoAmPo; MoP; NAAL-2; NIP; NoAM; NOBA; NOBE; NoP; OBMV; OBVE; OxBA; Poetr; PPP; PrIm; RaBo; RB; SOTW; TAP; TFi; TRP; TTTS; TwCP; UnPo; WeW

While neighbouring cities waste the fleeting hours. Anna Seward. *Fr.* Colebrook Dale. NOEC

While Northward the hot sun was sinking o'er the trees. Robert Bridges. FaBoTw; LiTB

While now I lay me down to sleep. Robert Farren. *Fr.* Sleep. TIRV

While now upon the win' do zwell. The Bells ov Alderburnham. William Barnes. EBVV

While ocean thus the latent store bequeaths. Henry Brooke. *Fr.* Universal Beauty. ECEV

While o'er Our Guilty Land, O Lord. Samuel Davies. AH

While o'er the Deep Thy Servants Sail. George Burgess. AH

While one sere leaf, that parting autumn yields. Anna Seward. *Fr.* Sonnets. WoRP

While out of the sea the new land silts beneath the stony mountains. *(LL)* Up in Heaven. Li Ho. PLT

While playing at the woodland's edge. The Terrible Path. Brian Patten. OTCP

While pleasure reigns unrivalled on this shore. Boston in Distress. *Unknown.* NOEC

While rain, with eve in partnership. Beyond the Last Lamp Near Tooting Common. Thomas Hardy. NOBE; OBNC

While round the arméd bands. The Execution of King Charles. Andrew Marvell. PoRA

While rumbling trunks pushed down the hall upstairs. Closing the House. Jim Wayne Miller. MT

While sauntering through the crowded street. Pre-Existence. Paul Hamilton Hayne. AnAmPo

While Shepherds Watched Their Flocks by Night. Margaret Deland. GN

While shepherds watched their flocks by night. "Saki." NSI; UV

While Shepherds Watched [Their Flocks by Night]. Nahum Tate. AmFP, 1 *st.*; GN; NOCV; NOSC; PIP; TIRV; UV, *(Sts.* I *and* II *only)*

While Sherman stood beneath the hottest fire. Before Vicksburg. George Henry Boker. PAH

While side by side the ducks and drakes bath in their crimson coats. *(LL)* The Pool behind Ch'i-an. Tu Mu. PLT

While sitting in my room kind Miss. Dedicated to a Young Lady Representing the Indian Race at Howard University. Alfred Islay Walden. AAP

While snow fell carelessly. The Crack. Denise Levertov. NALW

While snows the window-panes bedim. December. John Clare. OBCP

While snowy nightwinds, blowing bleak. Burncombe Hollow. William Barnes. OBNC

While sober folks, in humble prose. My Last Will. Robert Fergusson. ScCV

While some affect the sun, and some the shade. Robert Blair. *Fr.* Grave, The. EnRP
(Whilst some affect the sun, and some the shade.) NOEC

While some other immigrant. Mother. Rudy Kikel. NGP

While some "rap" over this turmoil. The Rhetoric of Langston Hughes. Margaret Danner. BlSi

While something hummed along the river. From the Sun Itself. Roberta Hill Whiteman. HATNAP

While soon the "garden's flaunting flowers" decay. Sonnet on Reading the Poem upon the Mountain Daisy, by Mr. Burns. Helen Maria Williams. ECWP

While sorrows encompass me round. Death-Bed Song. *Unknown.* AmFP

While Stars of Christmas Shine. Emilie Poulsson. OHIP

While still young,/ I didn't know I was aging. Tune: "Tartar Tune of Eighteen Beats." *Unknown, tr. fr. Chinese by* Sherwin S. S. Fu. SuSp

While strolling through the hills one day. Tannhauser. Newman Levy. OBAL

While summer roses all their glory yield. To the Poppy. Anna Seward. ECWP; WoRP

While sunk in deepest solitude and woe. Sorrow. Laetitia Pilkington. ECWP

While that futile old gentleman dozed. *(LL)* There was an old man who supposed. Edward Lear. NAEL-2; NOBVV; PeLi; Poetr

While that my soul repairs to her devotion. Church Monuments. George Herbert. GeHe; HAP; JCP; NAEL-1; NOCV; NoP; NOSC; OAEL-1; PoE; TRP
(Church-Monuments.) ESCV

While that the sun with his beams hot. The Unfaithful [*or* Faithless] Shepherdess *or* Philon the Shepherd *or* Adieu Love, Untrue Love. *Unknown.* GTBS; GTBS-P
(Adieu Love, Untrue Love.) EIL
(Faithless Shepherdess, The.) OBEV
(Philon the Shepherd.) NOBE

While the air is swimming with insects and children play in the street? *(LL)* The Cottage Hospital. Sir John Betjeman. GTBS-P; MoBrPo; NoAM; NOBE; OBD; PIP; UnPo

While the Billy Boils. David McKee Wright, *tr. fr. Maori by* Margaret Orbell. PeNZ

While the blue noon above us arches. Annihilation. Conrad Aiken. GBL; MoAB; MoAmPo

While the bombers, southward flocking, set Italian cities rocking. Croaked the Eagle: "Nevermore." "Sagittarius." UV

While the Choir Sang. Priscilla Jane Thompson. CBWP-2

While the coarse picture charms his eyes. The Man of Taste. William Parsons. OBTV

While the cobbler mused, there passed his pane. The Great Guest Comes In. Edwin Markham. WBLP

While the Constabulary covered the mob. Summer nineteen sixty nine. Seamus Heaney. CIP

While the corn grows ripe and the apples mellow. (LL) August. Celia Laighton Thaxter. FaPON; ImGa

While the Days Are Going By. George Cooper. BLRP; WBLP

While the dull Fates sit nodding at their loom. Science. Sarah Helen Whitman. AmWP

While the evening here is approaching the mountain paths. Overnight in the Apartment by the River. Tu Fu, tr. fr. Chinese by William Hung. ChTr

While the far farewell music thins and fails. Departure (Southampton Docks: October 1899). Thomas Hardy. Son

While the hum and the hurry. Under a Hat Rim. Carl Sandburg. AnAmPo

While the milder Fates consent. A Lyric to Mirth. Robert Herrick. CaPo

While the noon-lustre o'er the land is spread. M. J. Chapman. Fr. Barbadoes. PBCV

While the pulse in my neck. Desire. Leslie Ullman. NAmP90

While the river banks are quarreling. Agon. Branko Miljkovic, tr. fr. Serbo-Croatian by Charles Simic. HSix

While the south rains, the north. Sled Burial, Dream Ceremony. James Dickey. CAPP

While the sun squats upon the waveless seas. (LL) More Sonnets at Christmas. Allen Tate. LiTA; LiTM

While the Tragedy's afoot. Colophon. Oliver St. John Gogarty. OBMV

While the water-wagon's ringing showers. In the Isle of Dogs. John Davidson. OBNC

While these again have greater still, and greater still,/ and so on. (LL) Great Fleas. Augustus de Morgan. BXAP

While these cold nights freeze me dead. (LL) Shall I Come, Sweet Love. Thomas Campion. AAS; CBLP; EBEV; EIL; EnRePo; GBL; HAP; OxAEP-1; OxBoLi; PoEL-2

While thine forgot lie closed in a tomb. (LL) Spring Bereaved 2. William Drummond of Hawthornden. OBEV

While thirteen moons saw smoothly run. Stanzas Subjoined to the Yearly Bill of Mortality of the Parish of All Saints, Northampton; for the Year 1787. William Cowper. NOCV

While this America settles in the mould of its vulgarity, heavily thickening to empire. Shine, Perishing Republic. Robinson Jeffers. CMoP; FF; LiTA; LiTM; MAT; MoAB; MoP; NAAL-2; NoAM; NOBA; NoP; OxBA; PrIm; TAP; TFi; UnPo; VGW

While this was singing, Ovid young in love. The Ear's Delight. George Chapman. Fr. Ovid's Banquet of Sense. NoSic

While thou hast gode and getest gode. Unknown. MiEL

While Thracians shal with arrowes war, Iaziges with bowe. Ovid, tr. fr. Latin by Thomas Underdowne. Fr. Invective against Ibis. OBVE

While thus he spake, th' Angelic Squadron bright. Milton. Fr. Paradise Lost. EPCY; SCV

While thus he thought, a monst'rous wave up-bore. Homer, tr. by Pope. Fr. Odyssey. NAWM-1; OBVE

While thus I wander'd, step by step led on. Wordsworth. Fr. Prelude [or, Growth of a Poet's Mind], The. EnRP; OAEL-2; OxAEP-2; PoEL-4

While Titian was grinding rose madder. Unknown. NOBL

While upon the journey of life. The Mask. Patty L. Harjo. VoR

While visiting Arundel Castle. Victor Gray. NOBL

While vulgar souls their vulgar love pursue. Cloe to Artimesa. Unknown. ECWP

While walking down a crowded. If I Only Was the Fellow. Will S. Adkin. BLPA

While we are at peace. Albatross. Lele-io-Hoku, tr. fr. Hawaiian by S. H. Elbert and N. Mahoe. WTO

While We Lowly Bow before Thee. Daniel C. Colesworthy. AH

While we shall be merry and sing'. (LL) The Gaberlunzie Man. Unknown. EnSB; OxBB; OxBS

While We Slept. David Wolff. TrJP

While we stood in the dark. Changes. Martha Sansom. UnDi

While we wandered (thus it is I dream!), A. Gray Nights. Ernest Dowson. Son

While we wept idly o'er thy little bier! (LL) Composed on a Journey Homeward; the Author Having Received Intelligence of the Birth of a Son. Samuel Taylor Coleridge. Son

While we were fearing it, it came. Emily Dickinson. MeMAP; PPP

While we were visiting David's grave. Despair. Denise Levertov. NNaP

While with a strong and yet a gentle hand. Edmund Waller. Fr. Panegyric[k] to My Lord Protector, A. JCP; SeCV-1

While with false pride, and narrow jealousy. On the Use of New and Old Words in Poetry. Anna Seward. Son

While with labour assid'ous due pleasure I mix. Verses Written at The Hague. Anno 1696. Matthew Prior. OBTV

While yet the grapes were green, thou didst refuse me. Grapes. Unknown, tr. fr. Greek by Alma Strettell. AWP

While yet the Morning Star. The Unicorn. Ella Young. FaPON

While you clambered up ahead. Climbing Gannett. Roberta Hill Whiteman. HATNAP

While you, my friend, from louring wintry plains. William Julius Mickle. Fr. Almada Hill: An Epistle from Lisbon. OBTV

While you read. The Cat. William Matthews. AmPA; SoCa

While you study as. Patty to Cathy. David Trinidad. BAP-91

While you walk the water's edge. Beach Glass. Amy Clampitt. FaBoWP; NoAM; VCAP

While your great-grandmother and her sons. Separate Parties. Dabney Stuart. NYBP

While you're a white-hot youth, emit the rays. The Star System. Richard Wilbur. NBLV

Whiles someone did chant this lovely lay, The. Spenser. Fr. Faerie Queene, The. OBVE

(Gather the Rose.) EIL

(Song of Bliss.) FF

Whilom, as antique stories tellen us. Spenser. Fr. Faerie Queene, The. EPCY

Whilom ther was dwellynge in my contree. The Friar's Tale. Chaucer. Fr. Canterbury Tales, The. EnVB; PoE

Whil'st Alexis Lay Prest [or Press'd]. Dryden. Fr. Marriage à la Mode. ErPo; FF; PeLV; PrIm

Whilst Echo cries [or eccho cryes], "What shall become of me[e]?" Henry Constable. Fr. Diana. AAS; ESo

Whilst happy I Triumphant stood. On a Juniper-Tree, Cut Down to Make Busks. Aphra Behn. KTR

Whilst human kind/ Throughout the lands lay miserably crushed. Beyond Religion. Lucretius, tr. fr. Latin by William Ellery Leonard. AWP

Whilst I beheld the neck o' th' dove. Patrick Carey. JCP

Whilst in her prime and bloom of years. On a Female Rope-Dancer. Unknown. NOEC

Whilst in peaceful quarters lying. The Battle of Monmouth. "R. H." PAH

Whilst in This World I Stay. Philip Pain. AH

Whilst landmen wander, though controlled. Unknown. OxBSS

Whilst maudlin Whigs deplore their Cato's fate. Nicholas Rowe. ECEV

Whilst my soul's eye beheld no light. A Dialogue betwixt God and the Soul. At. to Sir Henry Wotton. MeLP; PeECV

Whilst on Septimius' panting breast [or brest]. Acme and Septimius. Catullus, tr. by Abraham Cowley. AWP

Whilst on the beach I stood, my courage faint. Written the First Morning of the Author's Bathing at Teignmouth for the Head-Ache. Jane Cave. ECWP

Whilst on thy head I lay my hand. A Spell of Invisibility. At. to Christopher Marlowe. ChTr

Whilst some affect the sun, and some the shade. Robert Blair. See While some affect the sun, and some the shade.

Whilst some the Troiane warres in verse recount. Barnabe Barnes. Fr. Parthenophil and Parthenophe. ESo

Whilst the landmen lies below. (LL) The Seamen's Distress. Unknown. OxBSS

Whilst thirst of praise, and vain desire of fame. The Lady's Resolve. Lady Mary Wortley Montagu. BoWoP; OxBSP

(Resolve, The. ECWP

Whilst thus my pen strives to eternize thee. Michael Drayton. Fr. Idea. AAS; ESo; Son

Whilst Titian was mixing rose madder. Unknown. PeLi

Whilst walking a crowded city street the other day. Just Try to Be the Fellow That Your Mother Thinks You Are. Will S. Adkin. WBLP

Whilst we sing the doleful knell. Ding Dong. Unknown. Fr. Swetnam, the Woman-Hater. EIL

Whilst what I write I do not see. Written in Juice of Lem[m]on. Abraham Cowley. Fr. Mistress, The. SeCP; SeCV-1

Whilst with his falling wings, the courtly dove. Jealousie Is the Rage of a Man. The Countess of Winchilsea. FM

Whil'st with hot scent, the Popish Tory crew. A Hue and Cry after Blood and Murder. Unknown. APAS

Whilst yet to prove. Farewell to Love. John Donne. OAEL-1

Whilst you and I, dilly dilly, keep ourselves warm. (*LL*) Lavender's Blue. *Unknown.* CH; NTP, *diff. vers.*; PYC

Whim of Time, A. Stephen Spender. MoAB; MoBrPo

Whimper of Awakening Passion. Ebenezer Jones. NOBVV

Whins are blythesome on the knowe, The. A New Spring. Albert D. Mackie. OxBS

Whip, The. Robert Creeley. EOEF; MoP; NaP; NeAP; PoE; PoM

Whip-crack of a Union Jack, The. The Boer War. William Plomer. FaBoEH; IHNG

Whip Jamboree. *Unknown.* OxBSS

Whip-the-World. "Hugh MacDiarmid." FaBoVe

Whipping, The. Robert Hayden. GrPl; PoBA; PoE; SoSe

Whipping Cheare. *Unknown.* FaBoBa

Whippoorwill in the Woods, A. Amy Clampitt. BAP-91

Whirl, snow, on the blackbird's chatter. Eager Spring. Gordon Bottomley. MoBrPo

Whirl up, sea. Oread. Hilda Doolittle ("H. D."). AWP; CMoP; GoJo; HeIP; InPS; MoAmPo; MoP; NAAL-2; NALW; NoAM; NOBA; OxBA; Poetr; TAP

Whirl'd off at last, for speech I sought. Coventry Patmore. *Fr.* Angel in the House, The. GBL

Whirled ten years beyond all bounds. Tu Mu, *tr. fr. Chinese by* A. C. Graham. *Fr.* Recalling Former Travels. PLT

Whirlpool, The. *Unknown.* PoToHe

Whirls and stands still: the moon comes: terrain. (*LL*) Terrain. A. R. Ammons. VCAP

Whirlwind. David Rokeah, *tr. fr. Hebrew by* Ruth Finer Mintz. MHP

Whirlwinds. Fily-Dabo Sissoko, *tr. fr. French by* Ellen Conroy Kennedy. NegPo

Whirlwinds/ nearly always. Whirlwinds. Fily-Dabo Sissoko, *tr. fr. French by* Ellen Conroy Kennedy. NegPo

Whiskers Meets Polly. Michael Stillman. TLR

Whiskey on your breath, The. My Papa's Waltz. Theodore Roethke. AnAmPo; CAPP; ClHu; CMoP; FF; HAP; HCAP; HeIL; HeIP; HoPM; InPK; InPS; LCAP; LiTM; MoAB; MoP; NAAL-2; NBLV; NIP; NoAM; NOBA; NoP; NTP; PoE; Poetr; PPP; PrIm; RaBo; SM; TAP; TFi; TRP; VGW

Whisky Frisky. *Unknown.* BoTP

Whisky, frisky,/ Hippity hop. The Squirrel. *Unknown.* FaPON; PDV

Whisky Johnny. *Unknown.* AS

Whisky, Johnny, *vers.* I. *Unknown.* AmFP

Whisper, The. Eugene Gloria. OpBo

Whisper down the bloodstream: it is time, The. (*LL*) The Dependencies. Howard Nemerov. VCAP

Whisper in Agony. Jules Supervielle, *tr. fr. French by* D. J. Enright. OBD

Whisper of yellow globes. Her Lips Are Copper Wire. Jean Toomer. NoAM

Whisper Words of Love to Me. L. A. J. Moorer. CBWP-3

Whisperer, The. James Stephens. WGRP

Whisperer, The. Mark Van Doren. MoAmPo

Whisperin' Bill. Irving Bacheller. PoLF

Whispering ghosts of the west. *Unknown, tr. fr. Maori by* John White. WTO

Whispering like a garden of secrets. (*LL*) Sloops in the Bay. James Tate. AnAn

Whispering to each handhold, "I'll be back." After Arguing against the Contention That Art Must Come from Discontent. William Stafford. NoAM

Whispering Wind. Catherine Braan Layne. PWR

Whisperjet swings wildly, The. In Flight. Jennifer Regan. CrSp

Whispers. Myra Cohn Livingston. PDV

Whispers. Roberta Hill Whiteman. CDW

Whispers of Heavenly Death. Walt Whitman. LiTA

Whispers of Immortality. T. S. Eliot. CMoP; CTC; LiTA; NoAM; NOBA; NoP; OBMV; OxAEP-2

Whist. Eugene Fitch Ware. PoLF

Whistle, The. Charles Murray. OxBS

Whistle Aloud, Too Weedy Wren. Wallace Stevens. *Fr.* Notes toward a Supreme Fiction. LiTA

Whistle, and I'll Come to You, My Lad. Burns. CBLP; OtMeF; OxAEP-2; OxBoLi

Whistle blows, The train moves, The. Patricia Beer. *Fr.* Victorian Trains. FaBoEH

Whistle Column, The. John Haines. AnAn

Whistle, Daughter, Whistle. *Unknown.* AIW; AmFP; ErPo; OBET; OxNR, *shorter vers.*; ReMoGo

Whistle, Daughter, Whistle. *Unknown.* OBET

Whistle fades, dragging freight cars, day coaches and the/ caboose., The. (*LL*) Landscape as Metal and Flowers. Winfield Townley Scott. GoJo

Whistle o'er the Lave o't. Burns. OxBS

Whistle o'er the Lave o't. *Unknown.* GBP

Whistle, The/ of the bright. Belfast Lough. *Unknown, tr. fr. Irish by* John Montague. BIrV

Whistle shrilled, A; the farm hands left the stack. Jack and Jill. Charles Powell. BXAP

Whistles like light in leaves, O light. The Heart Flies Up, Erratic as a Kite. Delmore Schwartz. PoA

Whistling bellows of his furnace, The. Philip of Thessalonica, *tr. fr. Greek by* Edwin Morgan. GrAn

Whistling Boy, The. George Crabbe. TrGrPo

Whistling Boy. Nixon Waterman. PoLF

Whistling girls and crowing hens. *Unknown.* RoPo

Whistling on the inside of your breath and I know well. Meanwhile Cesario Dancing. Helen Kidd. VBLP

Whistling postman swings along, The. The Postman. *Unknown.* FaPON

Whit Monday. John Hewitt. TIRV

Whit Monday. Louis MacNeice. ChIV-1; NYBP; OAEL-2; PeECV

White. Gerald William Barrax. *Fr.* Old Gory, The. NBV

White. Christopher Buckley. NGP

White, a shingled path. Icos. Charles Tomlinson. GTBS-P

White against a ruddy cliff you stand, chalcedony on sard. (*LL*) The Cameo. Edna St. Vincent Millay. FYAP; LiTA; MeMAP; MoAmPo; UnPo; WPE

White an' Blue. William Barnes. GBL; GTBS-P

White and blue, an outspread fan. Environs of Vanholt I. Charles Spear. PeNZ

White and curved as a shell she lies. Discoverer. James Michie. DiPo

White and Red. Edward de Vere, Earl of Oxford.

White and red. Still Life. Francis Sullivan. CRP

White and the Black, The. N. M. Khaketla, *tr. fr. Southern Sotho by* Jack Cope *and* Dan Kunene. PeSA

White Anemone, The, *sels.* "Owen Meredith." "'Tis the white anemone, fashioned so." GN

White Apples. Donald Hall. TAP

White are the streets in this shabbiest. Imagined Arrival. Matthew Sweeney. IB

White as coal-ash pressed. Queen of Heaven Mausoleum. Dennis Schmitz. LCAP

White as crockery. The Sea-Shell. Robert Gray. FaBoMA

White as her hand fair Julia threw. The Snow-Ball. Soame Jenyns. OBVE

White as I can, though not as Thee. (*LL*) The Nymph Complaining for the Death of Her Fawn. Andrew Marvell. CH; ESCV; FM; GeHe; NAEL-1; OAEL-1; OBF, *abr.*; PoEL-2; SeCP; SeCV-1

White as paper a-sail in the air. *Malay Oral Tradition, tr. by* O. Winstedt. WTO

White as snow and snow it isn't. *Unknown.* GBP

White ash amid funereal cypresses. (*LL*) Helen. Hilda Doolittle ("H. D."). AnAmPo; BoWoP; FaBoWP; LiTM; LPA; MoAmPo; NAAL-2; NALW; NoAM; NOBA; NoP; TAP

White Balloon. Maureen Seaton. PFL

White Bear. Joy Harjo. SRLS

White bear slides beneath the ice, A. Twenty-Five. Paul Hoover. *Fr.* Novel, The. BAP-89

White Beauty, The. *Unknown.* MeEL

White Birch. *Unknown, tr. fr. Chinese.* LHF, *tr. by* Hualing Nieh

White Bird, The. Wilfred Watson. MoCV

White bird featherless/ Flew from Paradise. *Unknown.* ChTr; FaBoVe; GBP; OxNR

White bird floats down through the air, A. *Unknown.* ChTr; GBP

White bird of the tempest! O beautiful thing! To a Seagull. Gerald Griffin. TIRV

White Birds, The. W. B. Yeats. UnAS

White Blossom, A. D. H. Lawrence. MoBrPo

White blossom, white, white shell; the Nazarene. Music of Colours — White Blossom. Vernon Watkins. AngWe; LiTM

White Blossoms. Robert Mezey. NaP

White bone-rose, silver thorns. The Brooch. Olga Drucker. BTR

White bones scattered. Crossing the Yellow River: June 12. Yuan Hao-wen, *tr. fr. Chinese by* Stephen West. SuSp

Whi/te boys gone. Val Ferdinand. NBV

White Bracelets. Colleen Thibaudeau. TSaS

White buck come in. Anadarko John. Carroll Arnett. VoR

White Butterflies. Swinburne. FaPON; PDV

White butterfly, A. The Graceful Bastion. William Carlos Williams. NYBP

White caps scudding before the wind. (LL) The Traveler. Ho Hsun. OHMPC

White Captain of my soul, lead on. A Soldier's Prayer. Robert Freeman. TrPWD

White cat, The. Cat Ballerina Assoluta. Emilie Glen. GoYe

White Cat in Moonlight. Douglas Gibson. CRH

White Cat of Trenarren, The. A. L. Rowse. OFC; OxBTC

White Cats. Paul Valéry, tr. fr. French by David Paul. OFC; SoCa

White Cedar Swamp. Steven Bauer. FoLa

White Center. Richard Hugo. NAAL-2; NoP

White chocolate jar full of petals, The. Chez Jane. Frank O'Hara. CoAP; NeAP; NoAM; NOBA; PoA; PoE

White Christmas. W. R. Rodgers. LiTM; MoAB; MoBrPo

White chrysanthemum, The. Mitsune, tr. fr. Japanese by Kenneth Rexroth. PoBeRe

White church on the hill, The. A New England Church. Wilson Agnew Barrett. WGRP

"White City," The. Richard Watson Gilder. PAH

White City, The. Claude McKay. BPo; NoAM; RaBo; TAP

White Cliffs, The, sels. Alice Duer Miller.
English Are Frosty, The. PoLF
I Have Loved England. BLPL; PoLF
"I have seen much to hate here — much to forgive." OtMeF

White clouds, like a belt, wind around the waist of the mountains. Inscribed on a Painting. Shen Chou, tr. fr. Chinese by Daniel Bryant. SuSp

White Clover. Marvin Bell. CAPP; VCAP

White coat worn over a violet waistcoat, A. Elegant Things. Sei Shonagon, tr. fr. Japanese by Ivan Morris. CBCK

White cock in my courtyard. Elegy for a White Cock. Mei Yao Ch'en, tr. fr. Chinese by Jonathan Chaves. SuSp

White cock's tail, The. Ploughing on Sunday. Wallace Stevens. ArNa; FaPON; GoJo; RB; SOTW; TTTS

White Color of Nearness, The, sels. Lan Ling.
"Already yesterday's lips have broken." WPC

White Conduit House. William Woty. NOEC

White coral bells upon a slender stalk. Unknown. PDV

White cormorants shaped like houses stare down at you, The. Party at Hydra. Irving Layton. HeIP

White Cross. Reed Whittemore. ArOW

White cups white. Turkish Love Songs. Unknown, tr. by Reza Baraheni and Zahra-Soltan Shokoohtaezeh. BoWoP

White day, black river. The Predicter of Famine. William Carlos Williams. VGW

White decorators interested in art. Nights of 1964-66: The Old Reliable. Marilyn Hacker. VCAP

White decorators interested in Art. Nights of 1965: the Old Reliable. Marilyn Hacker. PFL

White delightful swan, The. The Dying Swan. Unknown. ChTr

White Devil, The, sels. John Webster.
Call for the Robin-Redbreast and the Wren. ChTr; EBEV; FaBoCh; HAP; NoP; NOSC; OxAEP-1; PoEL-2; PoRA; PrIm; RB; SCGP; TFi
(Cornelia's Song.) TrGrPo
(Dirge, A: "Call for the robin-redbreast and the wren.") EiL; GGP; LiTB; NOBE; OBEV
(Land Dirge, A.) CH; GTBS; GTBS-P
"What, are you drop't?" PoEL-2

White Dou o Truth. The Ineffable Dou. Sydney Goodsir Smith. OxBS

White Dress, The. Marya Zaturenska. MoAmPo

White dusk moved ahead of them. Image of City. Lance Henson. VoR

White Dust, The. W. W. Gibson. MoBrPo

White Dwarf. A. R. Ammons. CAPP

White Earth. Gerald Vizenor. HATNAP

White faces are lit below the high bank, The. Elver Fishers. Ivor Gurney. FaBoPP

White Fields. James Stephens. BoNaP; FaPON; MoShBr; OTCP

White Fisher, The. Unknown. ESPB

White Flag. John Milton Hay. AnAmPo

White flesh quakes to the negro soul, The. The Widow's Jazz. Mina Loy. Jaz

White floating clouds. Unknown. EaPr

White flour, earth-flesh, a cold fleece on the mountain. The Snowfall. Gwerfyl Mechain, tr. fr. Welsh by Kenneth Hurlstone Jackson. OBWVE

White fog lifting & falling on mountain-brow. Wales Visitation. Allen Ginsberg. CAPP; NNaP; NOBA; NYBP; Prf; VCAP

"White folks is white," says Uncle Jim. Uncle Jim. Countee Cullen. NAAL-2

White Foolscap/Book of Cordelia, sels. Susan Howe.
Book of Cordelia. BCF

White founts falling in the courts of the sun. Lepanto. G. K. Chesteron. CoGr; EBEvV, ll. 1–35; EBNV; FaBV; FaPoR; MoBrPo; OBMV; OBNV; OtMeF; RB

White Fox. Elizabeth Alsop Shepard. GoYe

White foxes howl at mountain wind beneath the moon. Ravine on a Cold Evening. Li Ho, tr. fr. Chinese by Maureen Robertson. SuSp

White glare recedes to the Western hills, The. On and On for Ever. Li Ho, tr. fr. Chinese by A. C. Graham. PLT

White Gloves. William Plomer. PeSAV

White Goddess, The. Robert Graves. MeMBP; MoBrPo; NAEL-2; OAEL-2; OPOP

White Guardians of the Universe of Sleep. E. E. Cummings. NYBP

White hair fallen from my father's beard, A. (LL) Heirloom. A. M. Klein. NOBC; TrJP

White-haired Lover., sels. Karl Shapiro.
"I swore to stab the sonnet with my pen." PoA

White-haired woman of winter. Tiva's Tapestry: La Llorona. Linda Hogan. BCF; SRLS

White Hairs. Jamal Isfahani, tr. fr. Persian by Omar S. Pound. ArPe

White hard rock. Silica Carbonate Rock. Fred Berry. NU

White Hare, The. Lilian Bowes-Lyon. OxBTC

White Heliotrope. Arthur Symons. BoLoP; EBEV; PeVV

White herm. Flesh Eggs. Iain Sinclair. VaA

White hill-side is prickled with antlers, The. Knole. C. H. Sisson. NOCV

White Horse, The. W. H. Davies. OxBTC

White Horse, The. D. H. Lawrence. SOTW; TTTS

White Horse, The. Tu Fu, tr. fr. Chinese by Rewi Alley. ChTr

White Horse of Westbury, The. Charles Tennyson Turner. EBEV; PeVV

White Horsemen, with Christ their Captain: for ever He! (LL) Te Martyrum Candidatus. Lionel Johnson. OBMV; TIRV

White Horses. Eleanor Farjeon. PDV

White Horses. Kipling. PeVV

White Horses. Irene F. Pawsey. BoTP

White horses, tails high, rise from the cedar. E Uni Que A The Hi A Tho, Father. Roberta Hill Whiteman. VoR

White-Hot Blizzard, The. Irina Ratushinskaya, tr. fr. Russian by David McDuff. AIW

White-Hot Blizzard, The. Irina Ratushinskaya, tr. fr. Russian by David McDuff. PWE

White-hot midday in the Snake Park, A. In the Snake Park. William Plomer. NYBP; OxBTC

White House, The. Claude McKay. AmPP; NIP; PoBA

White House, A. Rossana Ombres, tr. fr. Italian by Robert McCracken and Pietro Pedace. NeIt

White house in front of the park, A. A White House. Rossana Ombres, tr. fr. Italian by Robert McCracken and Pietro Pedace. NeIt

White Houses. Claude McKay. See Your door is shut against my tightened face.

White houses bank the hill. The Rooftop. Thom Gunn. NoP

White hummocks here are rounded to a thigh. Early Summer Sea-Tryst. Frederick Macartney. CBAP

White ignorant hollow of his face, The. (LL) Father and Son. Stanley Kunitz. CAPP; MoP; Poetr; TwCP

White in the Moon the Long Road Lies. A. E. Housman. Fr. Shropshire Lad, A. AWP; CMoP; ELP; FaPoB; LiTB; MeMBP; NTP

White in the moon the long road lies. White in the Moon the Long Road Lies. A. E. Housman. Fr. Shropshire Lad, A. AWP; CMoP; ELP; FaPoB; LiTB; MeMBP; NTP

White Iris, A. Pauline B. Barrington. PoLF

White is the sail and lonely. A Sail. M. Y. Lermontov, tr. fr. Russian by Max Eastman. AWP

White Island; or, [The] Place of the Blest. Robert Herrick. BeJo; ChTr; JCP; NoP; NOSC; OAEL-1; PFP; TOF; WiR

White Isle of Leuce, The. Sir Herbert Read. FaBoTw

White Knight's Ballad, The. "Lewis Carroll." See I'll tell thee everything I can.

White Knight's Song, The. "Lewis Carroll." See I'll tell thee everything I can.

White Lady has asked me to dance, The. Fourth Dance Poem. Gerald William Barrax. PoBA

White Lake. James Applewhite. MT

White Lake, The. Unknown, tr. fr. Irish by Robin Flower. TIRV

White lambs leap. Through miles of snow. The Fire in the Snow. Vernon Watkins. LiTM

White Land, The. Roberta Hill Whiteman. HATNAP

White Lanterns. David Wojahn. NAmP90

White lather on black soap. Black Soap. Sandra McPherson. VCAP

White Launch. Andrew Crozier. VaA

White, like a spectre seen when night is old. The Taj. H. G. Keene. OBTV

White low sun, low thunderclouds; and back, A. Marina Tsvetayeva, *tr. fr. Russian by* David McDuff *and* Jon Silkin. PeFWW

White Magic; an Ode. William Stanley Braithwaite. PoNe

White man is, The. 12 Gates to the City. Nikki Giovanni. IHMS; PoBA

White man is a tiger at my throat, The. Tiger. Claude McKay. BPo

White man killed my father, The. The Time of Martyrdom. David Diop, *tr. fr. French by* Ellen Conroy Kennedy. NegPo

White Man Pressed the Locks, The. James C. Kilgore. InPK

White-maned, wide-throated, the heavy-shouldered children of the wind. Granite and Cypress. Robinson Jeffers. AmPP

White Man's Burden, The. Kipling. FaBoPV

White mares lashed to the sulky carriages. In Ohio. James Wright. NNaP

White mares of the moon rush along the sky, The. Night Clouds. Amy Lowell. AnAmPo; MoAmPo

White men in Africa. Zebra. Gavin Ewart. OBAP

White men's children spread over the earth. The Riddle. Georgia Douglas Johnson. PoBA

White Mess, A. Anthony Barnett. VaA

White metal tubes contain. Planes Landing. Jamie Grant. NOBAu

White Monster, The. W. H. Davies. LiTB

White moon gleams through scudding/ Clouds, The. Sorrow. Chu Shu-chen, *tr. fr. Chinese by* Kenneth Rexroth. BoWoP; OHMPC

White moon is rising, The. The Moon Is Rising. *Unknown, tr. fr. Chinese by* Robert Payne. TAL

White moon/ shines in the woods, The. Paul Verlaine, *tr. fr. French by* Philip L. Miller. RiWo

White moons like midnight's in the morning sun. Autumn Mushrooms. Kenneth Mackenzie. CBAP

White moth to the closing vine, The. The Gipsy Trail. Kipling. PoRA

White newspaper sky, A. Snow Falling. Gillian Hughes. NTP

White night, the moon an unstrung bow. Two Poems on Night. Tu Fu, *tr. fr. Chinese by* Jan Walls. SuSp

White Notes. Donald Justice. LCAP

White nymph wandering in the woods by night, A. André de Chénier, *tr. fr. French by* Arthur Symons. Fr. Elegies. AWP

White/ of the Northern bird. Drops. Anthony Barnett. VaA

White on White. Maria Luisa Spaziani, *tr. fr. Italian by* Beverly Allen. NeIt

White ones you pluck out. (*LL*) Light Behind the Rain. Michael Longley. CBLP

White, orphaned camel kid, The. *Mongol Oral Tradition, tr. by* C. R. Bawden. WTO

White Owl, The. George Meredith. *Fr.* Love in a Valley. ChTr

White owl in the belfry sits, The. (*LL*) The Owl. Tennyson. BoTP; FaBoCh; FaPON; GoJo; MoShBr

White Oxen. Louis Simpson. NoAM

White Paternoster, The. *Unknown. See* Matthew, Mark, Luke, and John/ Bless the bed that I lie on.

White Peace, The. "Fiona Macleod." FaBoBe

White pebbles jut from the river-stream. In the Hills. Wang Wei, *tr. fr. Chinese by* Robert Payne. TAL

White People. David Henderson. PoBA

White Petticoats. Chana Bloch. CrSp

White phosphorous, white phosphorous. Overheard over S. E. Asia. Denise Levertov. BoWoP

White pine, yellow pine. Southern Pines. John Peale Bishop. GOA

White pinnace on lactic waves, The. Birth by Anesthesia. George Scarbrough. GoYe

White Poetess. Musaemura Bonus Zimunya. PeSAV

White Primit Falls. *Unknown.* ChTr

White Rainbow, The. Starr Nelson. GoYe

White Room, The. Charles Simic. BAP-89

White room that I eat in and write in, The. The Shortest Day. William Dickey. IMW

White Rose, A. John Boyle O'Reilly. OBEV; PeIV

White Rose is a quiet horse. The Four Horses. James Reeves. TLR

White Roses. John Ashbery. TAP

White roses I tried to braid in my hair, The. Yamakawa Tomiko, *tr. fr. Japanese by* Kenneth Rexroth *and* Ikuko Atsumi. WPJ

White rushes on the opposite shore, The. (*LL*) To the Tune "A Branch of Bamboo." Chu Chung-hsien. WPC

White sagebrush desert, The. Noon. O Pioneers! John Peale Bishop. VGW

White Sand, The. Peter Morris. NGP

White sand in the ashtray, The. The White Sand. Peter Morris. NGP

White Season. Frances Frost. FaPON

White Serpent. Nelly Sachs, *tr. fr. German by* Michael Hamburger. BoWoP

White Sheep. W. H. Davies. BoTP

White sheep, white sheep, on a blue hill. *Unknown.* FaBoVe; GBP (Clouds.) SiSoPo

White Ship, The. Geoffrey Hill. OxBC

White Ship, The. Dante Gabriel Rossetti. OBNV

White Ships and the Red, The. Joyce Kilmer. PAH

White Shroud. Allen Ginsberg. PoBeRe

White-sided flowers are thrusting up on the hillside. Hawaii Dantesca. Charles Wright. HCAP; LCAP

White skin shaken like a white snowflake, The. (*LL*) Winter Love. Elizabeth Jennings. BoLoP

White sky, over the hemlocks bowed with snow. The Buck in the Snow. Edna St. Vincent Millay. NALW; PFP

White star! that travellest at old Maggie's pace. Maggie's Star. Charles Tennyson Turner. FM

White stars falling gently. Winter Joys. Dorothy Graddon. BoTP

White sunshine on sweating skulls. Anti-Vietnam War Peace Mobilization. Allen Ginsberg. PoBeRe

White/ sweet/ May/ again. (*LL*) The Locust Tree in Flower. William Carlos Williams. SOTW; Spl; TTTS

White-tailed Hornet, The. Robert Frost. OxBA

White the October air, no snow, easy to breathe. How to Get There. Frank O'Hara. NoP

White Things. Anne Spencer. ShDr

White though ye be, yet, lies, know. How Lillies Came White. Robert Herrick. BeJo; CaPo

White Thought, The. Stevie Smith. Spl

White Tiger, The. R. S. Thomas. AngWe

White to the neck he glides and plunges. Fencing School. John Manifold. CBAP; FaBoMA

White towelling bathrobe, The. La Toilette. Seamus Heaney. CBLP

White Trash. Jim Hall. MT

White tube/ In cephalic vein. Thirteen Things About A Catheter. Edward Kleinschmidt. UnDi

White Venus limpid wandering in the sky. Louise Labé, *tr. fr. French by* Aliki *and* Willis Barnstone. BoWoP

White violet, The. Sea Violet. Hilda Doolittle ("H. D."). NoP

White violets again and lyre orchestras. Philodemus, *tr. fr. Greek by* William Moebius. GrAn

White violets flower. Meleager, *tr. fr. Greek by* Peter Whigham. GrAn

White Witch, The. James Weldon Johnson. CDC

White woman have you heard. Montgomery. Sam Cornish. PoBA; Poetsp

White Women, The. Mary Elizabeth Coleridge. BrRo; NALW

White World. Hilda Doolittle ("H. D."). VBLP

White Zombie. Harrison Fisher. UL

Whitebeard on Videotape. James Merrill. NoP

Whitecaps. Betsy Sholl. CrSp

Whitechapel in Britain. A. N. Stencl. FaBoEH

Whitehall Stairs. Aaron Hill. NOEC

Whiteman Blues, The. Lionel Abrahams. PeSAV

Whiteman blues. (*LL*) The Whiteman Blues. Lionel Abrahams. PeSAV

Whiteness, or Chastity. Joseph Beaumont. NOSC

Whiter/ than the crust. The Wind Sleepers. Hilda Doolittle ("H. D."). WPE

Whites alone upon the jury in a number of the states. Injustice of the Courts. L. A. J. Moorer. CBWP-3

Whitewash. Léon Damas, *tr. fr. French by* Ellen Conroy Kennedy. NegPo

Whitey, Baby. James A. Emanuel. NBV

Whither? Wilhelm Müller, *tr. fr. German by* Philip L. Miller. *Fr.* Beautiful Maid of the Mill, The. AWP, *tr. by* Longfellow; RiWo

Whither Away? Mary Elizabeth Coleridge. CH

Whither away? (*LL*) The Flight of the Birds. Edmund Clarence Stedman. GN

Whither away, Robin. The Flight of the Birds. Edmund Clarence Stedman. GN

Whither away so fast. *Unknown.* NoSic

Whither dost thou hide from the magic of my flute-call? The Snake-Charmer. Sarojini Naidu [*or* Nayadu]. PBWP

Whither? I dread to think — but he is gone. (*LL*) Manfred: A Dramatic Poem. Byron. EnRP; NAEL-2

Whither I kneel or stand or sit in prayer. At Communion. Madeleine L'Engle. TrCP

Whither, 'midst falling dew. To a Waterfowl. Bryant. AmPP; AnAmPo; AWP; BLPL; CH; EAP; FaBoBe; GN; HoPM; ImPo; LiTA; NAAL-1; NOBA; NoP; OxBA; PoEL-4; PoLF; PrIm; PWR; SoSe; TAP; TFi; TrGrPo; WBLP; WGRP

Whither, O city, are your profits and your gilded shrines. Troy. Agathias, tr. fr. Greek by Ezra Pound. GrAn

Whither, O splendid ship, thy white sails crowding. A Passer-by. Robert Bridges. CMoP; EBEvV; ImPo; LiTB; LiTM; MoAB; MoBrPo; OAEL-2; OBEV; OBNC; OxBTC; SCGP; WiR

Whither, O, whither art thou fled. The Search. George Herbert. ESCV; MiEL

Whither, O whither didst thou fly. The Eclipse. Henry Vaughan. OxBSP

Whither, O whither wander I forlorn? Oceana and Britannia. John Ayloffe. APAS

Whither, oh! whither wilt thou wing thy way? Flight of the Spirit. Felicia Dorothea Hemans. Son

Whither, say whither shall I fly. The Frozen Zone; or, Julia Disdainful. Robert Herrick. CaPo

Whither shall I go. At. to John Webster and William Rowley. Fr. Thracian Wonder, The. GBL

Whither I, the fair maiden, flee from Sorrow? Sorrow. Unknown, tr. fr. Russian by W. R. S. Ralston. AWP

Whither So Fast? Unknown. EIL

Whithin a frame, more glorious than the gem. Woman. Frances Sargent Osgood. AmWP

Whitley at Three O'Clock. Jeff Worley. GOYP

Whitman. Larry Levis. Jaz

Whitman at a Grain Depot. James Reiss. AnAn

Whitman in Black. Ted Berrigan. UL

Whitman's Ride for Oregon. Hezekiah Butterworth. PAH

Whitney, you were. Whitney Young. Gwendolyn Brooks. ETG

Whitney Young. Gwendolyn Brooks. ETG

Whitsun Weddings, The. Philip Larkin. FaBoMo; FaPoB; HeIP; MoP; NoAM; NoP; OxAEP-2; OxBM; OxBTC

Whitsunday. George Herbert. GeHe

Whittier. Paul Laurence Dunbar. AnAmPo

Whittier. James Russell Lowell. Fr. Fable for Critics, A. AmPP; NOBA; OxBA

Whittingham Fair. Unknown. GBP

Whittling. John Pierpont. GN

Who. Moyshe-Leyb Halpern, tr. fr. Yiddish by Joseph Leftwich. TrJP

Who? Florence Hoatson. BoTP

Who. Edwin Honig. TAP

Who a Mother Is. Roy W. Watson. PWR

Who alone is Lord and God! (LL) Laus Deo! Whittier. AmPP; PAH

Who Am I? Felice Holman. RFM

Who am I? I am a lady faithful to the ways. Lady of the Ferry Inn. Gwerfyl Mechain, tr. fr. Welsh. BoWoP, tr. by Willis Barnstone

Who am I worthless that you spent such pains. A Prayer for the Self. John Berryman. Fr. Eleven Addresses to the Lord. OxBC; PPP

Who among You Knows the Essence of Garlic? Garrett Kaoru Hongo. InPS

Who Are My People? Rosa Zagnoni Marinoni. BLPA; PoToHe

Who are not sallow, sick, and spare! (LL) The Aesthete to the Rose. Unknown. BXAP

Who are the nobles of the earth. The True Aristocrat. W. Stewart. WBLP

Who are these among you. The Decision. Owen Dodson. PoNe

Who are these from the strange, ineffable places. Arabia. John Meade Falkner. OxBTC

Who are these people at the bridge to meet me? The Bee Meeting. Sylvia Plath. HCAP; InPS; NALW; Poetr; PPP; WPE

Who are these? Why sit they here in twilight? Mental Cases. Wilfred Owen. CMoP; FaBoMo; MeMBP; NoAM; PeFWW; PlP

Who are they. The Passengers. David Antin. NYBP

Who are they now? since the Bathurst ground. From a Republican Grave: Daniel Henry Deniehy, 1828–1865. Philip Mead. NOBAu

Who are they talking to in the big temple? The Temple. C. H. Sisson. OxBTC

Who are they to be in their skin. The Subway Witnesses. Lorenzo Thomas. PoBA

Who are we here? Intra-Political. Margaret Avison. MoCV

Who are we to love. A Footnote to a Gray Bird's Pause. James Cunningham. JB

"Who are we waiting for?" "Soup burnt?" The Feckless Dinner Party. Walter de la Mare. FaBoTw

Who are you? You and I. Tennessee Williams. GLP

Who are you? A dirty old man. Unknown. ISE

Who are you? and, with whom do you sleep here? (LL) On a cold night I came through the cold rain. J. V. Cunningham. HAP; TRP; VCAP

Who are you dusky woman, so ancient hardly human. Ethiopia Saluting the Colors. Walt Whitman. PAH; PoNe

Who are you, listening to me, who are you. Poem for Half White College Students. Amiri Baraka. BPo; TAP; UnPo

Who Are You, Little I. E. E. Cummings. LPA; NYBP

Who are you, Sea Lady. Santorin. James Elroy Flecker. FaBoTw; GoJo; OBMV

Who are you there that from your icy tower. The Astronomers of Mont Blanc. Edgar Bowers. PoA

Who are you to unsettle me? Still Water Tread. Jennifer Rankin. FaBoMA

Who/ Are you/ Who is born. Vision and Prayer. Dylan Thomas. LiTM

Who are you, whose pitiful bones. Leonidas of Tarentum, tr. fr. Greek by Fleur Adcock. GrAn

Who art the love of love, the eternal light of light! (LL) After-Song. Richard Watson Gilder. TrPWD

Who Be Kind To. Allen Ginsberg. NNaP

Who beat you and put you out. Rufinus Domesticus, tr. fr. Greek by Sam Hamill. InMo

Who beckons the green ivy up. The Miracle. Walter de la Mare. LiTB; UnPo

Who bends in garden rows. This Poem Is for Nadine. Paul B. Janeczko. GOYP

Who Bids Us Sing? Rhys Carpenter. WGRP

Who blacks the Boots at the Savoy. (LL) Godolphin Horne. Hilaire Belloc. FaBoCo

Who borrows all your ready cash. A Friend. Marguerite Power. FaBoCo

Who broke the laws of God, and man and metre. (LL) On Peter Robinson. Francis Jeffrey. FaBoCo; FaBoEE; NBLV

Who builds a church within his heart. The Church in the Heart. Morris Abel Beer. PoToHe

Who but the Lord? Langston Hughes. BPo

Who by a life heroic conquers fate. (LL) The Inevitable. Sarah Knowles Bolton. WGRP

Who by low creatures leads to heights of love. (LL) Flush or Faunus. Elizabeth Barrett Browning. FM

Who by Searching Can Find Out God? Eliza Scudder. See I cannot find thee! Still on restless pinion.

Who call violence her way of romance? (LL) A Love Like War. Ruth Asher-Pettipher. VBLP

Who called flowers "mouths"? — these painted lips. Novas. Van K. Brock. MT

"Who called?" I said, and the words. Echo. Walter de la Mare. OBMV

Who called, or what marks we shall leave upon the snow. (LL) The Call. Charlotte Mew. CoGr

Who calls? Welcome Eumenides. Eleanor Ross Taylor. NALW

Who calls her two-faced? Faces, she has three. The Three-faced. Robert Graves. FaBoEE

Who calls? Who calls? Who? For a Mocking Voice. Eleanor Farjeon. CH

Who came whirling out of the North. Of the Scythians. Katha Pollitt. DiPo; InPS; SM

Who can bear/ The wail of a young orphan? Rabbi Yussel Luksh of Chelm. Jacob Glatstein, tr. fr. Yiddish by Nathan Halper. TrJP

Who can believe with common sense. Epigram on Fasting. Swift. OBVE

Who can bring back the magic of that story. The Descent of the Child. Susan Langstaff Mitchell. TIRV

Who can doubt, Rice, to which eternal place. On Mr. Rice the Manciple of Christ Church in Oxford. Richard Corbett [or Corbet]. NOSC

Who can find a virtuous woman? for her price is far above rubies. Bible, O.T. Fr. Proverbs.
(Good Wife, The.) TrGrPo
(Virtuous Woman, The.) TrJP

Who can forget that ne'er forgotten night. On the Nativity of Our Saviour. Thomas Philipott. JCP

Who can grasp for the first time. New Music. Gwen Harwood. CBAP

Who can live in heart so glad. The Merry Country Lad. Nicholas Breton. Fr. Passionate Shepherd, The. EIL; NoSic
(Happy Countryman, The, shorter sel.) CH
(Pastoral: "Who can live in heart so glad.") ELP

Who can remember back to the first poets. The Makers. Howard Nemerov. DiPo; FYAP

Who can review, without a precious loss. The Passion. Ralph Knevet. JCP

Who can say. Tennyson. FaBoCh

Who can say? It is silent now. (LL) What Were They Like? Denise Levertov. HeIP; NIP; OBWP; PAW; VGW; WPE

Who can support the anguish of love? Ibn al-Arabi, tr. fr. Arabic by R. A. Nicholson. AWP

Who Can Tell? Gond Oral Tradition, tr. by V. Elwin and S. Hivale. WTO

Who can tell who was born of what? Doorstep, Lightning, Waif-Dreaming. James Dickey. CAPP

Who can the various city frauds recite. John Gay. Fr. Trivia; or, The Art of Walking the Streets of London. OAEL-1 (Thieves and Whores.) ECEV

Who cannot find some pleasure down below. (LL) The Trucker. Will Dyson. NOBAu

Who cares about the filthy rich. Anacreon, tr. fr. Greek by Sam Hamill. InMo

Who cares if Spring has come? (LL) I Wake Up Alone. Li Shang-yin. OHMPC

Who carved Love/ and placed him by. A Statue of Eros. Zenodotus, tr. fr. Greek by Peter Jay. GrAn

Who claims one needs wine to dispel grief? Tune: "Autumn Waters" — Listening to Rain. Na-lan Hsing-te, tr. fr. Chinese by Bruce Carpenter. SuSp

Who collects the pain. "Stephany." NBV

Who comes? Two Tongue-Pointing (Satirical) Songs. Unknown, tr. fr. Aborigine. NOBAu

Who comes here?/ A grenadier. The Grenadier. Unknown. GBP; OxNR

Who comes only to view the willow's eyebrows? (LL) Willow. Li Shang-yin. PLT

Who comes to-night? We ope the doors in vain. Henry James. Robert Louis Stevenson. OBNC

Who could ask for anything more? (LL) I Got Rhythm. Ira Gershwin. CBLP

Who could dispute his choice. The Net and the Sword. Douglas Le Pan. NOBC

Who could have thought that men and women could feel. Old Paintings on Italian Walls. Kathleen Raine. NYBP

Who could help but long for the gardens of home? (LL) Spring Night in Lo-Yang — Hearing a Flute. Li Po. TTTS

Who could know in advance. Space. Shindo Chie, tr. fr. Japanese by Kenneth Rexroth and Ikuko Atsumi. WJP

Who could remember cause? Both. The Victim. Ellen Bryant Voigt. CrSp

Who counts himself as nobly born. The Nobly Born. Frances E. W. Harper. PWR

Who cries that the days of daring are those that are faded far. Deeds of Valor at Santiago. Clinton Scollard. PAH

Who crieth: "Woe"? who: "Alas"? The Drunkard. Bible, O.T. Fr. Proverbs. TrJP

Who dare complain or be ashamed. Celebrations. Austin Clarke. IPY

Who dare now take and slaughter them. (LL) Battle Song. Shaka, King of the Zulus. PeSAV

Who dat a-knockin' at the door below. What You Goin' to Do When the Rent Comes 'Round? Andrew B. Sterling. OBAL

Who did I write last night? leaning. Trust Me. Jean Valentine. BAP-89

Who did kill Cock Robbin? Mother Goose. See Who Killed Cock Robin.

Who died on the wires, and hung there, one of two. Ivor Gurney. Fr. Silent One, The. NAEL-2; OBD; OBWP; PeFWW; PoWW

Who dissect away the wings and the haggard heart from the dove. (LL) Letter to Alex Comfort. Dannie Abse. FaBoTw; TwCP

Who do what we are born to do. (LL) Tiger. A. D. Hope. OxBC; RB

Who does not love the juniper tree? Juniper. Eileen Duggan. PChr

Who does not love the spring deserves no lovers. Georgian Spring. Roy Campbell. OBSV

Who Does Not Love True Poetry. Henry Clay Hall. PoToHe

Who does not sit in the seat of the scoffer. Blessed Is the Man. Marianne Moore. ChIV-1

Who does not wish ever to judge aright. The Hog, the Sheep and Goat, Carrying to a Fair. The Countess of Winchilsea. ECWP

Who Does the Cold Come Early To? sels. Michizane, tr. fr. Chinese by Burton Watson.

Who doesn't wash her face. (LL) Patience is a virtue. Unknown. ISE; OxNR

Who doth behold my mistress' face. The Fairest of Her Days. Unknown. EIL

Who doth desire that chaste his wife should be. Sir Philip Sidney. Fr. Arcadia. SiPSBD (Advice to the Same.) SiPS

Who doubts? The laws fell down from heaven's height. Joseph Hall. Fr. Virgidemiarum. OBSV, bk. II, III

Who Drags the Fiery Artist Down? Clarence Day. FaBoCo; NBLV

Who dreamed [or dream'd] that beauty passes like a dream? The Rose of the World. W. B. Yeats. CMoP; MoAB; MoBrPo; NAEL-2

Who drives the horses of the sun. The Happiest Heart. John Vance Cheney. WGRP

Who dwelt in [or Pylos] sandie soyle, and [or Arene] the faire. Homer, tr. fr. Greek by George Chapman. Fr. Iliad, The. CBCK

Who eat up a fat goose, but could not digest her. (LL) Epitaph on Dr. Keene. Thomas Gray. FaBoEE

Who else remembers you? (LL) Lines on a Boer War Pin-up Girl Seen in the Falcon Hotel, Bude. Christopher Hope. PeSAV

Who even dead, yet hath his mind entire! Ezra Pound. Fr. Cantos. CMoP; PoE; VGW

Who ever had/ Such a whale of a plan? The Wall of China. Padraic Colum. GrPl

Who ever knew the heavens menace so? Shakespeare. Fr. Julius Caesar. OxAEP-1

Who Ever Loved, That Loved Not at First Sight? Christopher Marlowe. See It lies not in our power to love, or hate.

Who fain would have to be new, tender, quick. (LL) Love Unknown. George Herbert. JCP; Prf

Who fears to speak of Ninety-Eight? The Memory of the Dead. John Kells Ingram. IIP; PeIV

Who feasts tonight? The Fairies Feast. Charles Montague Doughty. CH

Who fed me from her gentle breast. My Mother. Ann Taylor. BLPA; BLPL; OHIP; OxBChV; VPP

Who feels a growing hunger for fair eyes. To Liebig. August, Graf von Platen, tr. fr. German by Reginald Bancroft Cooke. PeHV

Who findeth comfort in the stars and flowers. Thomas Lovell Beddoes. Fr. Death's Jest Book. OBNC

Who fired France for Mary without spot. (LL) Duns Scotus's Oxford. Gerard Manley Hopkins. EBEV; FaBoPP; GTBS-P; MeMBP; NAEL-2; NoAM; OBMV; OxAEP-2; PeECV; PoEL-5

Who first reform'd our stage with justest law[e]s. An Elegy on Ben Jonson. John Cleveland. MeLP

Who flogged you and threw you out. The Slave Girl. Rufinus, tr. fr. Greek by Alan Marshfield. GrAn

Who folds a leafe anone. Unknown. FaBoUs; ISE, diff. vers.

Who Follows in His Train? Reginald Heber. WGRP

Who, for a single glance, gave up her life. (LL) Lot's Wife. "Anna Akhmatova." BoWoP; PBWP

Who forced the Muse to this alliance? On Professor Drennan's Verse. Roy Campbell. GTBS-P

Who framed and fashioned the heavens themselves. (LL) Great Hymn. Ntsikana Gaba. PeSAV

Who gave thee, O Beauty. Ode to Beauty. Emerson. AmPP; PoEL-4

Who gives him the Bath? The New Knighthood. Kipling. UV

Who goes? On the Bus. Mitsuye Yamada. Fr. Camp Notes. WPOW

Who Goes Home? G. K. Chesterton. OtMeF

Who Goes round My Pinfold Wall. Unknown. GBP

Who goes there? hankering, gross, mystical, nude. Walt Whitman. Fr. Song of Myself. AmPP; LiTA; MoAmPo, abr.; NOBA; OxBA; SOTW, (much abr.); TrGrPo

Who goes to join the men of Agincourt. (LL) The Volunteer. Herbert Asquith. OBWP; OtMeF; OxBTC; PAW

Who Goes with Fergus? W. B. Yeats. CMoP; FaBoCh; GoJo; InPK; MoP; NAEL-2; NoAM; NOBE; NOBVV; PeVV; PoE; PoRA; TRP

Who got used to making it through murdered sons. (LL) For de Lawd. Lucille Clifton. IMW; PoBA; TAP; TwCP

Who grace, for zenith had, from which no shadowes grow. Fulke Greville. Fr. Caelica. PoEL-1

Who, gratis, shared my social glass. Thomas Hood. Fr. Lay of Real Life, A. OBF

Who had your God for father, spouse and son? (LL) To Our Blessed Lady. Henry Constable. NoSic

Who half asleep, or waking, does not hear it. The Furnace of Colors. Vernon Watkins. NYBP

Who has but dighted his tricks in a bed. This Is What the Watchbird Sings, Who Perches in the Lovetree. Bruce Boyd. NeAP

Who has ever stopped to think of the divinity of Lamont Cranston? In Memory of Radio. Amiri Baraka. NAAL-2; NeAP; NoP; PoBeRe; Poetr; PoM

Who has gone farthest? for I would go farther. Excelsior. Walt Whitman. SAmP

Who Has Known Heights. Mary Brent Whiteside. BLPA

Who has not found the heaven below. God's Residence. Emily Dickinson. SAmP

Who has not heard of the dauntless Varuna? The Varuna. George Henry Boker. PAH

Who has not heard of the Vale of Cashmere. The Light of the Harem [or Haram]. Thomas Moore. Fr. Lalla Rookh. EnRP; TEP

Who has not thought, when scuffing shells. Lower Forms of Life. Mary Winter. GoYe

Who has not waked to list the busy sounds. London's Summer Morning. Mary Robinson. ECWP; WoRP

Who Has Not Walked upon the Shore. Robert Bridges. SCGP

Who Has Our Redeemer Heard. Stephen Collins Foster. AH

Who Has Seen the Wind? Christina Rossetti. *Fr.* Sing-Song. ArNa; BoTP; FaPON; GoJo; NTCP; NTP; OHCV; PDV; SiSoPo; TLR; WHSW

Who has strangled the tired voice. Appeal. Noémia da Sousa, *tr. fr. Portuguese.* TTY, *tr. by* Dorothy Guedes *and* Philippa Rumsey; WPOW, *tr. by* Alan Ryder

Who has, with most temerity, scaled the heights, the quick or the/ dead? Ghazal: The Quick and The Dead. Edward Kleinschmidt. UnDi

Who has won for once over the world's weight. (*LL*) Juggler. Richard Wilbur. CMoP; LiTM; MoAB; NYBP; TAP

Who hasn't. The Dolphins. Richard Harteis. PFL

Who hast the red pavilion of my heart? An Arab Love-Song. Francis Thompson. AWP; MoAB; MoBrPo; OtMeF

Who Hath a Book. Wilbur D. Nesbit. BLPA

Who hath desired the Sea? — the sight of salt water unbounded. The Sea and the Hills. Kipling. FaBV; OtMeF; SCGP

Who hath gathered the wind in his fists? The Words of Agur. Bible, *O.T. Fr.* Proverbs.

Who hath given man speech? or what hath set therein. Swinburne. *Fr.* Atalanta in Calydon. EnVR; OAEL-2

Who hath herd of such[e] cruelty before: Sir Thomas Wyatt. AAS; SiPS; SiPSBD

Who Hath His Fancy [*or* Fancie] Pleased. Sir Philip Sidney. ElL; EnRePo; PoEL-1

Who hath his Maker's nod. (*LL*) Inspiration. Thoreau. AmPP; BLPL; FaBoBe; NOBA; OxBA

Who hath not sent out ships to sea? The Ship That Went Down. Adah Isaacs Menken. CBWP-1

Who hath that conning by wisdam or prudence. *Unknown.* MiEL

Who Here Can Cast His Eyes Abroad. Abiel Holmes. AH

Who hung like a hero, and never would flinch. (*LL*) Clever Tom Clinch Going to Be Hanged. Swift. CoMu; FaBoBa; NOIV

Who hung these shields here still all shiny. Antipater of Sidon, *tr. fr. Greek by* Tony Harrison. GrAn

Who hunger in the prison of my fear. (*LL*) The Stranger. Jean Garrigue. LiTA; LiTM; NOBA; TwCP

Who hunts so late 'neath evening skies. The Soul-hunter. Julia Ward Howe. AmWP

Who I break my head against. First Claims Poem. Victor Hernandez Cruz. NBV

Who, if I cried out, would hear me among the angels? Rainer Maria Rilke, *tr. fr. German by* Stephen Mitchell. *Fr.* Duino Elegies. NAWM-2

Who in each act that act have done. (*LL*) The Strangers. Jones Very. AnAmPo; OxBA

Who, in his own time, resumed the dark, the straw. (*LL*) The Outlaw. Seamus Heaney. MoP; OxBC

Who in One Lifetime. Muriel Rukeyser. NALW

Who in one lifetime sees all causes lost. Who in One Lifetime. Muriel Rukeyser. NALW

Who, in the brief, incredible northern spring. Let Him Return. Leona Hill. PoToHe

Who, in the dark, has cast the harbor-chain? Putting to Sea. Louise Bogan. LiTM; PoA

Who, in the garden-pony carrying skeps. Horses. Dorothy Wellesley. OBMV; OxBTC

Who, in the public library, one evening after rain. Public Library. Dannie Abse. OxBC

Who in the waters of this reedy lake. Diodorus Zonas, *tr. fr. Greek by* Alistair Elliot. GrAn

Who in him lov'd and sought thy face! (*LL*) The Book. Henry Vaughan. AngWe; GeHe; JCP; SeCV-1

Who invited him in? What was he doing here. The Dirty Little Accuser. Norman Cameron. OxBS

Who is a friend? Who is a foe? Gripe. Lincoln Kirstein. PoWW

Who is a mother some one exclaimed? Who a Mother Is. Roy W. Watson. PWR

Who is, as if he weren't and ne'er had even come. Whoever Has Become All Divine. "Angelus Silesius," *tr. fr. German. Fr.* Cherubical Wanderer, The. GePo, *tr. by* George C. Schoolfield

Who Is at My Window? *Unknown.* ImPo; TrGrPo

Who is but One and True? (*LL*) God gives them sleep on ground, on straw. Roger Williams. SCAP

Who is de prutties' gal you say? My Little Lize. James Martinez. PBCV

Who is divine? This bird. (*LL*) The Blinded Bird. Thomas Hardy. CMoP; LiTM

Who is God. The Questions of Ethne Alba. *Unknown, tr. fr. Irish by* James Carney. PeIV; TIRV

Who is it. The Wind. Kazuko Yamada, *tr. fr. Japanese by* Miyao Ohara *and* D. J. Enright. OBD

Who is it calling by the darkened river. Voices. Walter de la Mare. UnPo

Who is it hides my sandals when I'm trying to get dressed? Late for Breakfast. Mary Dawson. TLR

Who is it runs through the many-storied mansion of myth. Dwarf of Disintegration. Oscar Williams. ImPo; LiTM

Who Is It Talks of Ebony? Manmohan Ghose. OBMV

Who Is It That This Dark Night. Sir Philip Sidney. *Fr.* Astrophel and Stella. AAS; EiL; EnRePo; ESo, *sl. abr.*; GGP; HeIL, *Sonnets, I–CVIII and 11 Songs*; NAEL-1; PoE; PoEL-1; Poetr; SCGP, *Sonnets, I–CVIII and 11 Songs*; SiPS, *Sonnets, I–CVIII and 11 Songs*; SiPSBD, *Sonnets, I–CVIII and 11 Songs*; TEP

Who is like unto thee who teachest knowledge. Hymn of Unity. *Unknown, tr. fr. Hebrew by* H. M. Adler. TrJP

Who is lovelier than she? Alone In Her Beauty. Tu Fu, *tr. fr. Chinese by* Witter Bynner. ArLo

Who Is My Brother? Pinkie Gordon Lane. BlSi

Who is my father in this world, in this house. The Irish Cliffs of Moher. Wallace Stevens, *tr. fr. Spanish.* NOBA; RaBo; TOF; VGW

Who Is My Neighbor? Josephine D. Henderson Heard. CBWP-4

Who is not a stranger still. Stephany Fuller. BPo

Who is quick, quick, quick. The Swallow. Carmen Bernos de Gasztold, *tr. by* Rumer Godden. OBAP

Who is she coming, whom all gaze upon. A Rapture Concerning His Lady. Cavalcanti, *tr. fr. Italian by* Dante Gabriel Rossetti. AWP

Who is she that comes, makyng turn every man's eye. Sonnet [*or* Sonetto] VII. Cavalcanti, *tr. by* Ezra Pound. CTC; OBVE

Who is she whose-feet-go-clattering-the-hard-ground? Choice. Flavien Ranaivo, *tr. fr. French by* Ellen Conroy Kennedy. NegPo

Who Is Silvia [*or* Sylvia]? Shakespeare. *Fr.* Two Gentlemen of Verona, The. BLPL; EiL; EnRePo; FaBoBe; GN; ImPo; LiTB; NoSic; OAEL-1; SCGP; TrGrPo

Who is Silvia? What a shame. Does That Answer Your Question, Mr Shakespeare? Stanley J. Sharpless. PeLV

Who is Silvia? what is she. Who Is Silvia [*or* Sylvia]? Shakespeare. *Fr.* Two Gentlemen of Verona, The. BLPL; EiL; EnRePo; FaBoBe; GN; ImPo; LiTB; NoSic; OAEL-1; SCGP; TrGrPo
(Silvia. OBEV
(Song.) EBEvV

Who is so proud. The Performing Seal. Rachel Field. *Fr.* Circus Garland, A. OBCA

Who is somebody's son, and pride and joy! (*LL*) Somebody's Mother. Mary Dow Brine. BeLS; BLPA; WBLP

Who Is That a-Walking in the Corn? Fenton Johnson. PoNe

Who is that Brahma? What that Soul of Souls. *Unknown, tr. by* Sir Edward Arnold. *Fr.* Bhagavad-Gita, The. TAL

Who is that man with the handshake? Don't you know. The Satirist. Louis MacNeice. IHNG

Who is that student pale and importunate. Student. Josephine Miles. NoP

Who is the East? Emily Dickinson. TTTS
(Yellow Man, Purple Man.) TLR

Who is the happy warrior? Who is he? Character of the Happy Warrior. Wordsworth. EnRP; FaBoBe; LiTB; MeMBP

Who is the mighty master that can trace. To Haydn. Thomas Holcroft. NOEC

Who is the runner in the skies. The Runner in the Skies. James Oppenheim. TrJP

Who Is the Same, Which at My Window Peepes? Spenser. *Fr.* Epithalamion. AAS; BoLoP; EiL; EnRePo; FHYEP; InPS; NAs; NOBE; NoP; NoSic; OAEL-1; OBEV; OxAEP-1; PoEL-1; TEP

Who is this. Peter Damian. *tr. fr. Latin by* Helen Waddell. MLL

Who is this I hear? — Lo, this is I, thine heart. The Dispute of the Heart and Body of François Villon. Villon, *tr. fr. French by* Swinburne. AWP; OBVE

Who is this Man. Genesis XXIV. Arthur Hugh Clough. ChIV-1

Who is this Moses? who made him, we say. A Soliloquy of One of the Spies Left in the Wilderness. Gerard Manley Hopkins. TrCP

Who is this that comes in splendour, coming from the blazing East? The Airy Christ. Stevie Smith. ChIV-2; NOCV

Who is this that cometh from Edom. Vision of the Day of Judgment. Bible, *O.T. Fr.* Isaiah. WGRP

Who is this that darkeneth counsel by words without knowledge? Then the Lord Answered ("Who is this that darkeneth counsel by words without knowledge?") Bible, *O.T. Fr.* Job. AWP; NAWM-1, *abr.*

Who rides so late through the night and the wind? The Erlking. Goethe, *tr. fr. German by* Philip L. Miller. RiWo

Who rideth through the driving rain. The King's Son. Thomas Boyd. OBMV

Who rules the world with iron rod? Tall Hat. Victor James Daley. CBAP

Who said cats have nine lives has told untruth. Homage to Octavian. Joseph Roccasalvo. OFC

Who said November's face was grim? November. Lucy Larcom. AmWP

Who said, "Peacock Pie"? The Song of the Mad Prince. Walter de la Mare. EBEV; FaBoCh; GoJo; MoP; NoAM; NOBE; NTP; OxAEP-2; OxBChV

Who said to the trout. Pisces. R. S. Thomas. OxBC

Who sanctifies. (*LL*) Betony. Mary Mackey. SRLS

Who saw the petals. The Secret Song. Margaret Wise Brown. OBCA; PDV

Who say we no get beauty for Africa. African Beauty. Taiwo Olaleye-Oruene. AIW

Who says that fictions onl[e]y and false hair. Jordan. George Herbert. FHYEP; GeHe; HAP; InPS; JCP; LiTB; MeLP; NAEL-1; NOCV; NoP; NOSC; OAEL-1; PeECV; PoE; PoEL-2; Poetr; PPP; SeCP; TEP; TFi; TrCP

Who says it's cool says wrong. Hollywood Jazz. Lynda Hull. Jaz

Who Says That Drought Was Here? Niyi Osundare. HBAPE

Who says that Giles and Joan at discord be? On Giles and Joan. Ben Jonson. NAEL-1; NOBL; TEP

Who says that sadness can be cast away for long? Tune: "Magpie on the Branch." Feng Yen-ssu, *tr. fr. Chinese by* Daniel Bryant. SuSp

Who says that the dead do not think of us? In Broad Daylight I Dream of My Dead Wife. Mei Yao Ch'en, *tr. fr. Chinese*. OxBM

Who says you're like one of the dog days? Shall I Compare Thee to a Summer's Day? Howard Moss. InPK

Who seeks alway thine honour to preserve. (*LL*) Golden gift that nature did thee give, The. The Earl of Surrey. AAS; SiPS; SiPSBD

Who seeks the way to win renown. In Praise of Seafaring Men, in Hopes [*or* hope] of Good Fortune. Sir Richard Grenville. OBTV; OxBSS

Who seeks wisdom in words. Silences. David Mitchell. PeNZ

Who sees him walk the street, can scarce forbear. Marvellous Martin. Charles Harpur. CBAP

Who sees the cross at Christmas? To See the Cross at Christmas. Roger Cooper. TrCP

Who sees the curve as Robert Fludd saw it. Infield Outfield. Asa Benveniste. NBrP

Who sees, will spew; who smells, be poisoned. (*LL*) A Beautiful Young Nymph Going to Bed. Swift. ECEV; NOEC; OPOP

Who sees you, G, surprises two in one. To Grosphus. Godfrey the Satirist, *tr. fr. Latin*. PeHV

Who/ SELF,/ The World. Job's Epitaph. Joshua Sylvester. ChIV-1

Who sews the body to its sorrow, invisibly. (*LL*) Shéhérazade. Wayne Koestenbaum. UTF

Who Shall Deliver Me? Christina Rossetti. *See* God strengthen me to bear myself.

Who Shall Die. James A. Randall, Jr.. BPo

Who shall doubt, Donne, where [*or* whe'er] I a Poet be[e]. To John Donne. Ben Jonson. BeJo; EPCY; JCP; NoP; SeCP; SeCV-1

Who shall have my fair [*or* faire *or* fayre] lady? My Fair Lady. *Unknown*. EnLoPo; PoEL-1

(Under the Leaves Green. OxBoLi

Who shall invoke when we are gone. Tragic Love. W. J. Turner. OBMV

Who shall speak for the people? Carl Sandburg. *Fr*. People, Yes, The. OxBA

Who shall tell the lady's grief. On the Death of a Cat, a Friend of Mine Aged Ten Years and a Half. Christina Rossetti. OFC; SoCa

Who she was. Back Far Enough, Down Deep Enough. Constance Urdang. PBCAP

Who shot the snake? beat it to death on the road? In Memoriam S. L. Akintola. David Knight. MoCV

Who showed me. To Flossie. William Carlos Williams. SAmP

Who Sleeps by Day and Walks by Night. Thoreau. PoEL-4

Who smoke-snorts toasts o' My Lady Nicotine. Variations on an Air: After Robert Browning. G. K. Chesteron. FaBoPa; NOBL

(Old King Cole. BXAP

Who so late/ at the garden gate. At the Garden Gate. David McCord. FaPON

Who so list to hount, I knowe where is an hynde. Sir Thomas Wyatt. CBLP

Who so valiant to decide? Young Woman at a Window. Mark Van Doren. LiTA

Who sows the seas, or ploughs the easy shore? Woman's Inconstancy. Phineas Fletcher. *Fr*. Sicelides. EIL

Who spurs on the road when day is done. Goethe. *See* O who rides by night thro' the woodland so wild?

Who stands, the crux left of the watershed. The Watershed. W. H. Auden. OAEL-2

Who stands, who always will. (*LL*) The Queen of Wands. Judy Grahn. SRLS

Who steals the common from the goose. (*LL*) On Inclosures. *Unknown*. FaBoCo

Who Stops the Dance? Hsiung-hung, *tr. fr. Chinese by* Kenneth Rexroth *and* Ling Chung. WPC

Who straight, *Your suit is granted*, said, and died. (*LL*) Redemption. George Herbert. ESCV; FF; GeHe; HAP; InPK; InPS; JCP; LiTB; MeLP; NAEL-1; NOBE; NOCV; NoP; NOSC; PeECV; PoE; Poetr; SCGP; SCV; SeCP; SeCV-1; Son; SoSe; TEP; TFi; TrCP; WeW

Who strolls so late, for mugs a bait. French Lisette; a Ballad of Maida Vale. William Plomer. ErPo

"Who stuffed that white owl?" No one spoke in the shop. The Owl-Critic. James Thomas Fields. BLPA; OBAL; WBLP

Who sure intended him to stretch a rope. (*LL*) The Boss. James Russell Lowell. OBAL

Who swept away my gilded fall. The Tree Sings to the Stream. Leah Goldberg, *tr. fr. Hebrew by* Ruth Finer Mintz. *Fr*. Songs of the Stream. MHP

Who take today and jerk it out of joint. Young Africans. Gwendolyn Brooks. NoAM

Who tames the lion now? Lord Alcohol. Thomas Lovell Beddoes. WiR

Who taught him his path to the sea. (*LL*) On the Discoveries of Captain Lewis. Joel Barlow. AmPP; PAH

Who taught me betimes to love working and reading. (*LL*) The Sluggard. Isaac Watts. CH; EBEvV; ECEV; HAP; Mes; MoShBr; NOEC; OxBChV; OxBoLi; PoEL-3; UV, *sh. vers*.; VPP

Who teaches us how to faint? (*LL*) After he stripped off my clothes. Villana. AIW; BoWoP

"Who, tell me, shepherd, owns these rows of plants?" Cometas, *tr. fr. Greek by* Anthony Holden. GrAn

Who telleth a tale of unspeaking death? Shelley. *Fr*. On Death. OBD

Who then made use of the sinister hoe? (*LL*) Kassak. Birago Diop. NegPo

Who then shall but my Pictures Picture be. (*LL*) My Picture. Abraham Cowley. CBLP

Who, then was Cestius. Rome. Thomas Hardy. MoAB

Who thinks of June's first rose to-day? June, 1915. Charlotte Mew. OxAEP-2

Who Thou art I know not. God the Architect. Harry Hibbard Kemp. WGRP

(To God, the Architect. TrPWD

Who thought in high midsummer. Boethius, *tr. fr. Latin*. *Fr*. Consolation of Philosophy, The. MLL, *tr. by* Helen Waddell

Who thought of the lilac? The Lilac. Humbert Wolfe. FaPON

Who to the North, or South, doth set. Observation. Robert Herrick. FaBoUs

Who/ took the dream. Charlie Mehrhoff. EaPr

Who travels [*or* trauels] by the wearie wandring way. Spenser. *Fr*. Faerie Queene, The. OBD; OxAEP-1

Who Walks with Beauty. David Morton. BLPA; FaBoBe

Who wants my jellyfish? The Jellyfish. Ogden Nash. FaPON

Who was a man. (*LL*) Malcolm X. Gwendolyn Brooks. PoBA; TTY

Who was beloved by our Jesus. (*LL*) For Saint John's Day. Luke Wadding. TIRV

Who was born, not of a virgin but a real woman. Jah Son/ Another Way. Kendel Hippolyte. PBCV

Who Was It Came. Daniel Hoffman. CoAP

Who Was It, Tell Me. Heine, *tr. fr. German by* Richard Garnett. TrJP

Who was it that took away my voice? Silence. Bella Akhmadulina, *tr. fr. Russian by* Daniel Halpern. BoWoP

Who was it who held me on her knee? Mother. Josephine D. Henderson Heard. CBWP-4

Who Was Mary Shelley. Lorine Niedecker. PRA

Who was neither ingenious, sober, nor kind. (*LL*) Here lies the body of Richard Hind. Francis Jeffrey. FaBoEE; OxBoLi

Who was responsible for the very first arms deal. Peace. Michael Longley. BiHa; CIP; PBCIP; PNI

Who was St Vincent. (*LL*) St. Vincent's. W. S. Merwin. VCAP

Who was this girl. Looking at Pictures to Be Put Away. Gary Snyder. FF; NNaP

Who wd. cope in this Quick. The Web. Gregory O'Donoghue. BIrV

Who We Are. Daniel Hoffman. BAP-91

Who wears your daughter's face. (*LL*) Invisible Boundaries. Maureen Hurley. LoHo

Who weds a sot to get his cot. *Unknown.* FaBoUs
(Proverbial Advice on Marriage.) NBLV

Who weeps now anywhere in the world. Solemn Hour. Rainer Maria
Rilke, *tr. fr. German by* C. F. MacIntyre. TrJP

Who Were before Me. John Drinkwater. OBMV

Who were the builders? Question not the silence. The Nameless Doon [*or*
Dun]. William Larminie. BIrV; PeIV

"Who were you, shipwrecked stranger?" Leontichos found. Callimachus, *tr.
fr. Greek by* Peter Jay. GrAn

"Who Wert and Art and Evermore Shalt Be." William Channing Gannett.
TrPWD

Who, when asked for a *remedy*, sent them a *rope.* (*LL*) An Ode to the
Framers of the Frame Bill. Byron. CoMu

Who, when he had won all, renounced all, and sought in the bosom of his
family and of nature, retirement, and in the hope of religion,
immortality. (*LL*) Inscription at Mount Vernon. *Unknown.* OHIP

Who? Who? *Unknown.* CH

Who, who and who? The Dark Lord of Savaiki. Alistair Campbell. PeNZ

Who — who — the bride will be? Who? Who? *Unknown.* CH

Who, who will be the next man to entrust his girl to a friend? Ezra Pound.
Fr. Homage to Sextus Propertius. FaBoMo

Who Will Endure. W. H. Auden. FaBoPV

Who will endure. (*LL*) Behold, the Meads. Guillaume de Poitiers. AWP

Who will go drive with Fergus now. Who Goes with Fergus? W. B.
Yeats. CMoP; FaBoCh; GoJo; InPK; MoP; NAEL-2; NoAM; NOBE;
NOBVV; PeVV; PoE; PoRA; TRP

Who will in fairest book of Nature know. Sir Philip Sidney. *Fr.* Astrophel
and Stella. AAS; ESo, *sl. abr.*; GGP; HeIL, *Sonnets,* I–CVIII *and 11
Songs*; InPS; NAEL-1; NoP; NoSic; OAEL-1; PoE; Poetr; SCGP;
Sonnets, I–CVIII *and 11 Songs*; SiPS, *Sonnets,* I–CVIII *and 11 Songs*;
SiPSBD, *Sonnets,* I–CVIII *and 11 Songs*

Who Will Know Us? Gary Soto. AfAz

Who Will Live in Our Houses When We Die? Michael C. Blumenthal.
NoAM

Who will pay for the milk I gave you? Let Me Go. *Gond Oral Tradition,
tr. by* V. Elwin *and* S. Hivale. WTO

Who will remember, passing through this gate. On Passing the New Menin
Gate. Siegfried Sassoon. NAEL-2; NoAM; OBMV; PoWW; Son

Who Will Shoe Your Pretty Little Foot? *Unknown.* AS

Who will show us where. At the Doors. "Der Nistor," *tr. fr. Yiddish by*
Joseph Leftwich. TrJP

Who will take away. Spell against Sorrow. Kathleen Raine. PBWP

Who winds the clumsy flower clock now, I wonder. Heavy Heavy Heavy.
John Malcolm Brinnin. NYBP

Who, with heart in breast, could deny you love? (*LL*) Dear Black Head.
Unknown. BIrV

Who with salt tears this last Farewell did take. (*LL*) Before the Birth of
One of Her Children. Anne Bradstreet. BoWoP; EAP; KTR; MAT;
NAAL-1; NAs; NOBA; OxBM; PeECV; WPE; WPOW

Who with the soldiers was stanch danger-sharer. The Daughter of the
Regiment. Clinton Scollard. PAH

Who with thy leaves shall wipe (at need). To His Book[e] ("Who with thy
leaves . . .") Robert Herrick. FaBoUs; JCP
(Another [to His Book].) NOSC

Who Wot Nowe That Ys Here. *Unknown.* InPS

Who would be/ A mermaid fair. The Mermaid. Tennyson. BoTP, *ll.*
1–14; FaPON; GN

Who would be/ A merman bold. The Merman. Tennyson. BoTP, *ll.*
1–20; FaPON; GN; UV, (*ll.* 1–20)

Who would care to pass his life away. Lotos Eating. Mortimer Collins.
NOBVV

Who would have guessed she didn't have everything. The Leaving. Margot
Fortunato. LoHo

Who would have the day back you saw coming in dreams. The Good
Reason for Our Forgetting. Marie Howe. BAP-89

Who Would Have Thought. Thomas Howell. *Fr.* Lover Deceived Writes to
His Lady, The. EIL

Who would have thought it Sir, actually putting ME in a WRITING! Peter
Reading. FaBoVe

Who would have thought she'd end that way? (*LL*) Mourning Poem for the
Queen of Sunday. Robert Hayden. HCAP; NoAM; NoP; PoBA

Who would I show it to. W. S. Merwin. HCAP

Who Would List. *Unknown, tr. fr. French by* Andrew Lang. *Fr.* Aucassin
and Nicolette. CTC

Who would live in others' breath? Epitaph: Iohannis Sande. Thomas
Bastard. FaBoEE

Who would not be. The Laureate. William Edmonstoune Aytoun. BXAP;
UV

Who would not cut the body from Head. (*LL*) Friend, on This Scaffold
Thomas More Lies Dead. J. V. Cunningham. InPK

Who would not live long. (*LL*) The Shield of Achilles. W. H. Auden.
EBEV; FaBoMo; FaBoPV; GTBS-P; HAP; NAEL-2; NoAM; NOBE;
NOCV; NoP; OxAEP-2; PeECV; PoA; PoE; WeW

Who would not yield to the Lord the word hosanna? (*LL*) Praise the Lord
in your infinite variety all creatures. Ernesto Cardenal. EaPr

Who would the music be. (*LL*) Each More Melodious Note I Hear.
Thoreau. OxBSP

Who would true valour see. Bunyan. *Fr.* Pilgrim's Progress, The. EBEV;
EBEvV
(Pilgrim Song, The.) CoMu; ELP; NOCV
(Pilgrim, The.) BoTP; GN; OtMeF
(Pilgrim's Song, The.) WiR
(To Be a Pilgrim, *sl. diff. vers.*) FaPoR; PlP
(Valiant's Song.) NOSC

Who would want to die defending Firestone Tire. Firestone. David
Rivard. PBCAP

Who would/ who could. Now Ain't That Love? Carolyn M. Rodgers.
BPo

Who would work if he had it to do. (*LL*) An Appeal by Unemployed Ex-
Service Men. *Unknown.* OBET

Who wouldn't want such a bed? Woman Asleep on a Banana Leaf. Katha
Pollitt. InPS

Who wouldn't want to be elsewhere? Taking Sides. Rachel Hadas. UnDi

Who wrote *Who wrote Icon Basilike?* On ["Who Wrote Icon Basilike" by
Dr.] Christopher Wordsworth, Master of Trinity. Benjamin Hall
Kennedy. FaBoCo; FaBoEE

Whoa! but I stagger — too much wine! Argentarius, *tr. fr. Greek by* Sam
Hamill. InMo

Whoa, mule, whoa! *Unknown.* RoPo

Who'd Be a Hero (Fictional)? Morris Bishop. FiBHP; OBAL

Who'd believe me if. The Third Dimension. Denise Levertov. NeAP

Who'd couple with foetus, with handful of sore yell wet, with. The Whore
of Kilpeck. Jeff Nuttall. NBrP

Who'd ever think that Utah would stir the world so much? Marching to
Utah. *Unknown.* AmFP

Whoe'er has gone through London Street. A Butcher. Thomas Hood.
PeLV

Whoe'er he be that to a taste aspires. James Bramston. *Fr.* Man of Taste,
The. NOEC

Whoe'er our stage examines, must excuse. Prologue on the Old Winchester
Playhouse over the Old Butchers' Shambles. Thomas Warton the
Younger. ECEV

Whoe'er [*or* Who e'er *or* Who ere] she[e] be[e]. Wishes to His Supposed
Mistress[e]. Richard Crashaw. BoLoP; EBEV; ImPo; MeLP; NOSC;
OBEV; OxAEP-1; PoEL-2; SeCP; SeCV-1
(Wishes for the Supposed Mistress[e].) GTBS; GTBS-P

Whoe'er sighs most, is cruellest, and hastes the other's death. (*LL*) A
Valediction: Of Weeping. John Donne. EnRePo; ESCV; FHYEP;
HAP; HeIP; InPS; MeLP; NAEL-1; NoP; NOSC; OAEL-1; PoE; SCGP;
SeCP; WeW

Whoe'er this book, if lost, doth find. *Unknown.* FaBoUs

Whoe'er thou art whose path, in summer lies. Mark Akenside. NOEC
(Tragedy of a Shepherd.) ECEV

Whoever coined the phrase *The Body Politic*? Talking to Myself. W. H.
Auden. OBD

Whoever [*or* Who ever] comes to shroud me, do not harm[e]. The
Funeral[l]. John Donne. AWP; BoLoP; EBEV; EnLoPo; EnRePo;
ESCV; HeIP; ImPo; MeLP; NAEL-1; NAWM-1; NoP; OAEL-1; OBEV;
PoEL-2; PoRA; SCGP; SeCP; SeCV-1; TFi

Whoever despises the clitoris despises the penis. The Speed of Darkness.
Muriel Rukeyser. GLP; LCAP

Whoever has a glass roof. Seguidilla of Murcia. Manuel de Falla, *tr. fr.
Spanish by* Philip L. Miller. RiWo

Whoever Has Become All Divine. "Angelus Silesius," *tr. fr. German.* *Fr.*
Cherubical Wanderer, The. GePo, *tr. by* George C. Schoolfield

Whoever has heard of St. Gingo. The New Cecilia. Thomas Lovell
Beddoes. OAEL-2
(Legend of St. Gingulph's Relict, The.) CBNP

Whoever has not choked on a word. Truly. Ingeborg Bachmann, *tr. fr.
German by* Susan L. Cocalis. PoSu, *tr. by* Mark Anderson

Whoever Hath Her Wish, Thou Hast Thy Will. Shakespeare. *Fr.* Sonnets.
NAEL-1; OAEL-1

Whoever hath washed his hands of living. Courage. Sadi, *tr. by* Sir Edwin
Arnold. *Fr.* Gulistan, The. AWP

Whoever hurts my favor with my lady. Heinrich von Veldeke, *tr. fr.
German by* Frederick Goldin. GePo

Whoever it was who brought the first wood and coal. Banking Coal. Jean
Toomer. PoNe

Whoever lives true life, will love true love. The Sweetness of England. Elizabeth Barrett Browning. *Fr.* Aurora Leigh. OxAEP-2

Whoever looks on life will see. James Cawthorn. *Fr.* Wit and Learning. ECEV

Whoever looks round sees Eternity there. (*LL*) Autumn ("Thistledown's flying, The.") John Clare. BoNaP; EnVR; HAP; NU; PoEL-4; WeW

Whoever loves, if he do not propose. Love's Progress. John Donne. *Fr.* Elegies. LiTB; OAEL-1

Whoever passes by my tomb, know. Callimachus, *tr. fr. Greek. Fr.* Epigrams. HePo

Whoever then are you? Whose wretched bones are these. Leonidas of Tarentum, *tr. fr. Greek* by Barbara Hughes Fowler. *Fr.* Epigrams. HePo

Whoever they were, did not arrive. (*LL*) During the Pageant at Medicine Lodge. Charles G. Ballard. VoR

Whoever water drinks, writes wretched poetry. Water and Wine. Friedrich von Logau, *tr. fr. German.* GePo, *tr.* by George C. Schoolfield

Whoever weeps somewhere out in the world. Silent Hour. Rainer Maria Rilke, *tr. fr. German* by Jessie Lemont. AWP

Whoever without money is in love. Of Why He Is Unhanged. Cecco Angiolieri, da Siena, *tr. fr. Italian* by Dante Gabriel Rossetti. (Sonnet: Of Why He Is Unhanged.) AWP

Whoever you are, go out into the evening. Initiation. Rainer Maria Rilke, *tr. fr. German* by C. F. MacIntyre. TrJP

Whoever You Are Holding Me Now in Hand. Walt Whitman. InvP; NAAL-1; PoEL-5

Whoever you are, we too lie in drifts at your feet. (*LL*) As I Ebb'd with the Ocean of Life. Walt Whitman. AmPP; NAAL-1; NOBA; PrIm; TAP

Whole Armour of God, The. Charles Wesley. NOCV

Whole church got hot and vivid, The. The Gift of Tongues. Robert Morgan. MT

Whole day long, under the walking sun, The. The Sleeping Giant. Donald Hall. GoJo; GrPl; NYBP; Poetsp; TwCP

Whole Duty of a Poem, The. Arthur Guiterman. PoToHe

Whole Duty of Children. Robert Louis Stevenson. FaBoUs; NBLV; OxBChV

Whole futures dying in its bleak, marcescent frame. (*LL*) The Chairman's Widow. Thomas McCarthy. IB

Whole heap of nickles and a whole heap of dimes, A. Shout, Little Lulu. *Unknown.* AmFP

Whole idea of sanity is intriguing, The. Greedy Seasons. Eileen Myles. UL

Whole landscape drifted away to the north, The. A Window on the North. R. A. D. Ford. MoCV

Whole landscape flushes on a sudden at a sound, The. (*LL*) The Cuckoo. Gerard Manley Hopkins. MoAB; MoBrPo; OxBSP; RB; TTTS

Whole Lives Missing. Michael Klein. PFL

Whole Mess . . . Almost, The. Gregory Corso. PoBeRe

Whole night long, A. Vigil. Giuseppe Ungaretti, *tr. fr. Italian by* Jonathan Griffin. PeFWW

Whole night through, A. Vigil. Giuseppe Ungaretti, *tr. fr. Italian by* Charles Tomlinson. (Watch, Cima Quattro.) OBD, *tr.* by Patrick Creagh

Whole process is a lie, The. The Ivy Crown. William Carlos Williams. NAAL-2; NoAM; NoP; PrIm

Whole royal family was living in one room at that time, The. The End of a Dynasty. Zbigniew Herbert, *tr. fr. Polish by* Czeslaw Milosz. FaBoPV

Whole Story, The. William Stafford. NNaP

Whole towns shut down. The Late Snow and Lumber Strike of the Summer of Fifty-four. Gary Snyder. NaP

Whole Treasure of All Wordly Bliss, The. Charles, Duc d'Orléans. OxBLMV

Whole villages come. Piarco. Eric Roach. PBCV

Whole weight of history bears down, The. The Awful Mother. Susan Griffin. MDDM

Whole weight of the ocean smashes on rock, The. An Address to the Vacationers at Cape Lookout. William Stafford. NYBP

Whole wide world is ours, The. White World. Hilda Doolittle ("H. D."). VBLP

Whole world, The. Cache la Poudre. James Galvin. AnAn

Whole world here, leavened with madness, swells, The. Ben Jonson. *Fr.* Epistle to a Friend, to Persuade Him to the Wars, An. JCP; TEP

Whole world knows you've never yet given up the secret of where you've hidded your nest, The. (*LL*) A Flock of Guinea Hens Seen from a Car. Eudora Welty. GrPl; NYBP; PrIm

Whole World Now, The. Robert Bridges. *Fr.* Growth of Love, The. Son

Wholesome. William Meredith. TAP

Who'll buy my laces? I've laces to sell! The Lace Pedlar. Catherine A. Morin. BoTP

Who'll have the crumpled pieces of a heart? Laurana's Song. Richard Hovey. AnAmPo

Who'll Help a Fairy? *Unknown.* BoTP

Who'll walk the fields with us to town? Market Day. Mary Webb. CH

Whom first we love, you know, we seldom wed. Changes. "Owen Meredith." PoLF

Whom have We next? (His syntax is. Reckoning. Fay Zwicky. NOBAu

Whom he may call his wares from a pushcart. (*LL*) Fish Crier. Carl Sandburg. OxBA

Whom he thinks he loves. (*LL*) Illiterate. Shadab Vadji. VBLP

Whom I thought I should never see more. (*LL*) The Bailiff's Daughter of Islington. *Unknown.* ESPB; FaBoBa; GN; OBET; OxBB; OxBoLi

Whom Jesus Loved. John Barford. PeHV

Whom shall I marry? *Unknown.* RoPo

Whom Shall One Teach. Bible, *O.T. Fr.* Isaiah. TrJP

Whom the Gods Love. Margaret E. Bruner. PoLF

"Whom the Gods Love die young" I used to quote. Whom the Gods Love. Margaret E. Bruner. PoLF

Whom thus answer'd th' Arch Fiend now undisguis'd. Satan's Guile ("Whom thus answer'd th' Arch Fiend now undisguis'd.") Milton. *Fr.* Paradise Regained [*or* Regain'd]. LiTB

Whom we have found in our beds today, today? (*LL*) To Any Member of My Generation. George Barker. LiTM; MeMBP; Son

Whom when I saw assembled in such wise. Virgil, *tr.* by the Earl of Surrey. *Fr.* Aeneid [*or* Eneados], The. NAWM-1; PoE

Whon men beth muriest at her mele. All Turns into Yesterday. *Unknown.* MeEL

Whoop! the Doodles have broken loose. "Call All." *Unknown.* PAH

Whoopee-Ti-Yi-Yo. *Unknown.* AS; FaPON; ImGa

Whoops!. *Unknown. See* Horse and a flea and three blind mice, A.

Whore of Kilpeck, The. Jeff Nuttall. NBrP

Whore that rides in us abides, The. *Unknown.* SCAP

Whores. Margaret Walker. NALW

Who's In. Elizabeth Fleming. BoTP

Who's in the Next Room? Thomas Hardy. MeMBP; PoEL-5

Who's killed the leaves? Leaves. Ted Hughes. OxBC

Who's making the dream come true! (*LL*) The Thinker. Berton Braley. BLPA; WBLP

Who's Most Afraid of Death? Thou. E. E. Cummings. CMoP; PoE; VGW

Who's That? James Kirkup. OTCP

Who's That A-Knocking? Emile Jacot. BoTP

Who's that crepitating with his knuckledusters on my portico? "Ballocky Bill the Sailor." Gavin Ewart. *Fr.* Variations and Excerpts. FaBoBl

Who's that knocking on the window. Innocent's Song. Charles Causley. GTBS-P; OBCP

Who's that mysterious rider. The Horseman on the Skyline. Henry Lawson. CBAP

Who's that ringing at my door bell? *Unknown.* FaBoCh; OxNR

Who's that ringing at our door-bell? That Little Black Cat. D'Arcy Wentworth Thompson. OFC; OxBChV

Who's that ringing at the front door bell? *Unknown.* BoTP

"Who's that tickling my back?" said the wall. The Tickle Rhyme. Ian Serraillier. NTCP; PYC; Spl

Who's the Dover-based day tripper. A Trifle for Trafalgar Day. Ted Pauker. NOBL

Who's the fool now? (*LL*) Martin to His Man. *Unknown.*

Who's the most important man this country ever knew? Barney Google. Billy Rose. OBAL

Who's the Pretty Girl Milkin' the Cow? *Unknown.* AS

Who's therefore true, because her truth kills mee. (*LL*) Twicknam [*or* Twickenham] Garden. John Donne. EBEV; EnLoPo; ESCV; FaBoPP; MeLP; OPOP; PoE; PoEL-2; SCGP; SeCP; TEP

Who's Who. W. H. Auden. MeMAP; MoAB; MoBrPo; MoP; NoAM; Son

Whose baggage from land to land is despair. Palladas, *tr. fr. Greek by* Frank Kuenstler. GrAn

Whose beauty was my vision! (*LL*) To ——. Winthrop Mackworth Praed. CBLP

Whose blazing forth extinguishes the stars. (*LL*) Boys of Tyre are beautiful, The. Meleager. PeHV

Whose broken window is a cry of art. Boy Breaking Glass. Gwendolyn Brooks. AiP; MoP; NAAL-2; NoAM; NoP

Whose candles light the tulip tree? Tulip Tree. Sacheverell Sitwell. MoBrPo

Whose cherry tree did young George chop? Mingled Yarns. X. J. Kennedy. OBCA

Whose cinders yet with envy they do eat. *(LL)* In the rude age when scyence was not so rife. The Earl of Surrey. AAS

Whose day shall never die in Night. *(LL)* An Epitaph upon Husband and Wife Who Died and Were Buried Together. Richard Crashaw. EBEV; NOBE; OBEV; OxAEP-1; OxBM; TrGrPo

Whose eyes were sleepbound &. Wyatt's Dream. Richard Caddel. NBrP

Whose fire from which I came, has now grown cold? *(LL)* One Flesh. Elizabeth Jennings. AIW; FaBoWP; OxAEP-2; OxBTC; PBWP

Whose fish, fish. *(LL)* Nature's Lineaments. Robert Graves. FaBoTw; RB

Whose freedom is by suff'rance, and at will. William Cowper. *Fr.* Task, The. EnRP

Whose green adventure is to run to seed.y. *(LL)* Remembering the 'Thirties. Donald Davie. FaBoPV; OxBTC

Whose Hand. *Unknown, tr. fr. Hebrew by* Arthur Davis. TrJP

Whose hat was in his hand. *(LL)* I put my hat upon my head. Samuel Johnson. CBNP; NOBL; OxAEP-1; UV

Whose Heart in this Four-footed Thing lies. *(LL)* On the Collar of Mrs. Dingley's Lap-Dog. Swift. FaBoEE; FM

Whose highest 'treason' is but highest love. *(LL)* On the Queen's Return from the Low Countries. William Cartwright. OBEV

Whose is that long white box in the grove, what have they accomplished, why am I cold? *(LL)* The Bee Meeting. Sylvia Plath. HCAP; InPS; NALW; Poetr; PPP; WPE

Whose is that noble dauntless brow? Verses Intended to Be Written below a Noble Earl's Picture. Burns. HoPM

Whose is the river, Excellency, whose the fish. The Geographers. Karl Shapiro. OxBA

Whose is the voice that will not let me rest? Unknown Ideal. Dora Sigerson. IIP

Whose is this horrifying face. Ecce Homo. David Gascoyne. *Fr.* Miserere. ChIV-2; LiTM; OBWP; PeECV

Whose labor is over. *(LL)* The Four Horses. James Reeves. TLR

Whose laughter plays like summer lightning there. *(LL)* Cattle Show. "Hugh MacDiarmid." FaBoMo; HAP; MoBrPo; OBMV; OxBTC

Whose little pigs are these, these, these? *Unknown.* OxNR

Whose love is given over-well. Partial Comfort. Dorothy Parker. FaBoCo; OBAL; OBD

Whose loveth untrewe, his herte is selde seete. *(LL)* Lutel wot it any mon. *Unknown.* MiEL

Whose minds like horse or ox. The Learned Men. Archibald MacLeish. MoAB

Whose modest tresses were bound up for thee! *(LL)* To Spring. Blake. BLPL; BoNaP; BoTP; EnRP; MeMBP; NAEL-2; NOEC; OAEL-2; OBEV; PoEL-4; PoLF; PPP; SCGP; WiR

Whose music is the gladness of the world. *(LL)* O May I Join the Choir Invisible. "George Eliot." OHCV

Whose ne knoweth the strength, power, and might. Venus and Cupide. Sir Thomas More. *Fr.* Pageant Verses. EnRePo

Whose nights are clearer than the days. *(LL)* Upon Visiting His Lady by Moonlight. "A. W." CTC

Whose ribs the laths are, and whose flesh the loam. *(LL)* The Body. Robert Herrick. CaPo

Whose Scene? Ruth Stone. BoWoP

Whose shadow is less given to change than he. *(LL)* Upon His Picture. Thomas Randolph. BeJo; NOBE

Whose songs shall never be heard. *(LL)* Spectral Lovers. John Crowe Ransom. GBL; HeIP

Whose spittle only could restore the blind. *(LL)* Easter-Day. Henry Vaughan. ESCV; PeECV

Whose the hand unloosed Clearista's zone. Meleager, *tr. fr. Greek by* Peter Whigham. GrAn

Whose very beard is flesh, and mouth is horn. *(LL)* On the Cards and Dice. Sir Walter Ralegh. ChIV-2; EnRePo; RB

Whose wild bad father loves you well. *(LL)* A Sympathy, a Welcome. John Berryman. GrPl; NYBP

Whose Window? Alison Brackenbury. DiPo

Whose woods these are I think I know. Stopping by Woods on a Snowy Evening. Robert Frost. AmPP; BoNaP; ClHu; CMoP; CoGr; FaBoCh; FaBV; FaPON; FF; GGP; GoJo; GrPl; HAP; HeIP; HoPM; ImGa; ImPo; InPK; InPS; LiTA; LiTM; MeMAP; MoAB; MoAmPo; MoP; MoShBr; NAAL-2; NIP; NoAM; NOBA; NoP; NTCP; NTP; OBCA; OxBA; PDV; PIP; PoE; Poetr; PoRA; PrIm; PYC; RB; SAmP; SCV; SiSoPo; SoSe; TAP; TFi; TOF; TRP; TTTS

Whose work could this be, Chapman, to refine. To My Worthy and Honoured Friend, Mr George Chapman, On His Translation of Hesiod's *Works and Days*. Ben Jonson. EPCY

Whoso answers my questions. All or Nothing. Bayard Taylor. BXAP

Whoso casteth a stone at the birds frayeth them away. Bible, Apocrypha. *Fr.* Ecclesiasticus. OBF

Whoso discovereth secrets loseth his credit. Bible, Apocrypha. *Fr.* Ecclesiasticus. OBF

Whoso Gives Freely, Shall Freely Receive! Josephine D. Henderson Heard. CBWP-4

Whoso in harvest mindeth to reap. To His Child. William Bullokar. OxBChV

Whoso in love would bear the bell. Ballad[e] of Ladies' Love, Number Two. Villon, *tr. by* John Payne. ErPo

Whoso List to Hunt [I Know Where Is an Hind]. Sir Thomas Wyatt. AAS; BoLoP; EBEV; EnRePo; GBL; HAP; InvP; NAEL-1; NoP; NoSic; OAEL-1; OBVE; PoE; PoEL-1; PrIm; SCGP; SiPSBD; TFi
(Sonnet: "Whoso list to hunt, I know where is an hind." SiPS

Whoso maintains that I am humbled now. Epitaph for a Reviewer. Frances Cornford. OBD

Whoso thou art that passest by this place. An Epitaph of Maister Win Drowned in the Sea. George Turberville. FaBoEE

Whoso to marry a minion wife. A Minion Wife. Nicholas Udall. *Fr.* Ralph Roister Doister. EIL

Whoso walks in solitude. Emerson. *Fr.* Woodnotes II ("As sunbeams stream through liberal space"). NOBA

Whoso Would See This Song of Heavenly Choice. John Wilson. AH

"Who've ye got there?" "Only a dying brother." The Brigade Must Not Know, Sir! *Unknown.* PAH

Whummil Bore, The. *Unknown.* CH; ESPB

Whu's aw thae fflag-poles ffur in Princess Street? Heard in the Cougate. Robert Garioch. OxBTC

Whut do i keer ef de white-folks do 'buse us! Uncle Rube's Defense. Clara Ann Thompson. CBWP-2

Why? Melba Joyce Boyd. BlSi

Why? Stephen Crane. *Fr.* Black Riders, The. MeMAP

Why? Walter de la Mare. FiBHP

Why. M. Y. Lermontov, *tr. fr. Russian by* Philip L. Miller. RiWo

Why? *Unknown, tr. fr. Hebrew. Fr.* Talmud, The. TrJP

Why all that thrusting and shoving when we were twenty? *(LL)* Sing Loud. Li Ho. PLT

Why all the racket, you chattering birds? *Unknown, tr. fr. Greek by* Thomas Meyer. GrAn; PeHV

Why am I a Negro? Oh, why am I black? The Slave's Lament. Massillon Coicou, *tr. fr. French by* Ellen Conroy Kennedy. NegPo

Why am I crying after love? *(LL)* Spring Night. Sara Teasdale. BLPL; FaBoBe; LiTA; MoAmPo

Why am I first in thy so sad regard. Twilight. Robert Frost. AnAmP

Why am I not as they? *(LL)* Lineage. Margaret Walker. BlSi; CrSp; NALW; NMM; PBWP; PoBA

Why and Wherefore set out one day. Metaphysics. Oliver Herford. CBNP

Why anyone bothered. *(LL)* And Was Not Improved. Lerone Bennett, Jr.. PoBA

Why are candles brightly burning. The Christmas Tree. L. A. J. Moorer. CBWP-3

Why Are Daddies So Mean? Jane Chambers. GLP

Why are epics. Note on the Iliad. Raymond Garlick. AngWe

Why are Fire Engines Red? *Unknown.* CBNP

Why are our ancestors. Ancestors. Dudley Randall. BPo

Why are saints so difficult to recognize. Sainthood. Cristoir O'Flynn. TIRV

Why are the public buildings so high? W. H. Auden. FaBoCo

Why are the things that have no death. Irony. Louis Untermeyer. TrJP

Why are these pipples taking their hets off? ? E. E. Cummings. FiBHP

Why are we by all creatures waited on? John Donne. *Fr.* Holy Sonnets. ESCV; JCP; NOCV; PoE; PoEL-2; TrCP

Why are women so energetic? Energetic Women. D. H. Lawrence. InPS

Why are ye wandering aye 'twixt porch and porch. Arcades Ambo. Charles Stuart Calverley. BXAP

Why are you dragged to be stoned? Why? *Unknown, tr. fr. Hebrew. Fr.* Talmud, The. TrJP

Why are your eyes as big as saucers — big as saucers? Man in the Street. Robert Penn Warren. OBAL

Why Art Thou Silent. Speak! Wordsworth. OBEV

Why art thou silent and invisible. To Nobodaddy. Blake. OAEL-2

Why art thou slow, thou rest of trouble, Death. Death Invoked. Philip Massinger. *Fr.* Emperor of the East, The.
(Song.) OxAEP-1

Why be afraid of death, as though your life were breath? Emancipation. Maltbie D. Babcock. BLRP; WBLP
(Death.) WGRP

"Why?" Because all I haply can and do. Why I Am a Liberal. Robert Browning. Son

Why blush, dear girl, pray tell me why? On Seeing a Lady's Garter. *Unknown.* ErPo

Why boast, O arrogant, imperious man. On Mrs. Montagu. Ann Yearsley. ECWP

Why boast we, Glaucus! our extended reign. Homer, *tr.* by Pope. *Fr.* Iliad, The. OBVE

Why boastest thou thyself in mischief, O mighty man? Bible, *O.T.*, *paraphrased by* Sir Thomas Wyatt. *Fr.* Psalms.
(Psalm LII: "Tyrant, why swel'st thou thus," *paraphrased by* the Countess of Pembroke.) OBVE
(Tyrant, why swell'st thou thus.) NoSic, *sect.* LII

Why Brownlee Left. Paul Muldoon. DiPo; PBCIP

Why, by an ingrained habit, elevate. With the Grain. Donald Davie. NoAM

Why call it dead, wi' life a-vled. All Still. William Barnes. NOBVV

Why call the miser miserable? Byron. *Fr.* Don Juan. UnPo

Why, Cambria did I quit thy shore. Edward Williams. *Fr.* Stanzas Written in London in 1773. AngWe

Why came I so untimely forth. To a Very Young Lady. Edmund Waller. SCGP; SeCP; TrGrPo
(To a Girl.) WiR

Why can I think only of you? *(LL)* What Is the Matter With Me? *Unknown.* OHMPC

Why cannot we eat enough for a week. Envying the Pelican. Richard Weber. CIP

Why Can't I Leave You? Ai. AmPA

Why can't we all be like that bird? *(LL)* A Wise Old Owl. Edward Hersey Richards. BLPA; FaBoBe; OxNR; PYC

Why can't you play on *that*? *(LL)* Little Raindrops. *At. to* Ann Hawkshawe *also to* Jane Euphemia Browne. BoTP; OxBChV

Why, Celia, is your spreading waist. Edward Moore. *Fr.* Poet and His Patron, The. ECEV

Why cherish thus the senseless thing? That Glove. Mary E. Tucker. CBWP-1

Why, Chloe, thus squander your prime. A Logical Song. *Unknown.* ErPo

Why climb a mountain? Nanao Sakaki. EaPr

Why come ye hither, stranger, your mind what madness fills? Rifleman's Song at Bennington. Joseph Rodman Drake. PAH

Why Come Ye Not to Court, *sels.* John Skelton.
"Such a prelate, I trow." OBSV
"To tell the truth plainly." FaBoEH

Why confer on us the piercing vision. To Charlotte von Stein. Goethe, *tr. fr. German by* John Frederick Nims. STV

Why, country Pan, sitting still. Anyte, *tr. fr. Greek by* John Heath-Stubbs *and* Carol A. Whiteside. GrAn

Why, cry, cry, again. *(LL)* A Maxim Revised. *Unknown.* BLPA; NBLV; WBLP

Why, Damon, with the forward day. The Dying Man in His Garden. George Sewell. GTBS; GTBS-P

Why did all manly gifts in Webster fail? Emerson. GOA

Why did Hagar weep over Ishmael when he thirsted. Yitzhak Lamdan, *tr. fr. Hebrew by* Ruth Finer Mintz. *Fr.* In the Khamsin. MHP

Why did I laugh tonight? No voice will tell. Keats. TEP

Why did I wrong my judgement so. Upon His Unconstant Mistress. Sir Robert Ayton. NOSC

Why did my parents send me to the schools. Sir John Davies. *Fr.* Of Human Knowledge. ChIV-1

Why did [*or* do] I write? what sin to me unknown. Pope. *Fr.* Epistle to Dr. Arbuthnot. ChTr, *short sel.*; EBEV; EPCY; FHYEP; InPS; NoP; OAEL-1; OxAEP-1; PoE; PoEL-3; TFi; TOF

Why did our blessed Savior please to break. On the Holy Scriptures. Francis Quarles. ChIV-2

Why did the children, Carl Sandburg. *Fr.* People, Yes, The. OBAL

Why did the clerk drag his fingertips. The Great Helmsman. David Woo. OpBo

Why did the sun his beams conceal. The Crucifixion. Mary Weston Fordham. CBWP-2

Why did you choose me for your wife, Joseph? Asenath. Diana Hume George. ChIV-1

Why did you give no hint that night. The Going. Thomas Hardy. CBLP; EBEV; ELP; LiTB; MeMBP; NOBE; OxAEP-2; SCGP; UnPo

Why Did You Go. E. E. Cummings. VGW

Why did you hate to be by yourself. As to Being Alone. James Oppenheim. TrJP

Why did you kiss the girl who cried. What the Earth Asked Me. James Wright. NYBP

Why did you lay there asleep. Fragment from "Clemo Uti — the Water Lilies." Ring Lardner. FiBHP

Why did you melt your waxen man. Sister Helen. Dante Gabriel Rossetti. BeLS

Why did your spirit. Ark Astonished. Jay Macpherson. *Fr.* Ark, The. NOBC

Why didst thou promise such a beauteous day. Shakespeare. *Fr.* Sonnets. HeIP; OxAEP-1

Why disappoint me, distant lights? *(LL)* Only of Myself I Knew How to Tell. Rachel. MHP

Why, disease, dost thou molest. To Sickness. Ben Jonson. BeJo

Why do I avoid the highways. The Guidepost. Wilhelm Müller, *tr. fr. German by* Philip L. Miller. *Fr.* Winter's Journey, The. RiWo

Why do I deny manna to another? Sather Gate Illumination. Allen Ginsberg. NeAP

Why do I imagine that the Creator. Splendid Moments. Alma Villanueva. SRLS

Why do I languish thus, drooping and dull. Dulness. George Herbert. ESCV; MiEL

Why Do I Live? George Linnaeus Banks. *See* I live for those who love me.

Why do I love? go ask the glorious sun. To One That Asked Me Why I Loved J. G. "Ephelia." CBCK; KTR; NOSC; VBLP

Why Do I Love You? *At. to* Roy Croft. *See* I love you,/ Not only for what you are.

Why do I post my love letters. Why Don't You Talk to Me? Alistair Campbell. PeNZ

Why do I sleep amid the snows. Roger Williams. Hezekiah Butterworth. PAH

Why do I use my paper, ink, and pen. Verses Made by a Catholic in Praise of Campion That Was Executed at Tyburn for Treason, As Is Made Known by the Proclamation. *Unknown.* NoSic

Why do I write today? Apology. William Carlos Williams. OxBA; SAmP

Why do my eyes. The Maja's Glance. Fernando Periquet Y Zuaznabar, *tr. fr. Spanish by* Philip L. Miller. RiWo

Why do people sit in darkness as regards the Negro race? The Truth Suppressed. L. A. J. Moorer. CBWP-3

Why do the bells for Christmas ring? Christmas Song. *At. to* Eugene Field. BoTP; OHIP

Why do the Graces now desert the Muse? Walter Savage Landor. FaBoEE

Why do the heathen rage. Bible, *O.T.*, *paraphrased by* Sir Thomas Wyatt. *Fr.* Psalms. NAAL-1, *par. by* Edward Taylor
(Psalm II: "Why do the Gentiles tumult," *(par. by* Milton).) OBVE

Why do the lilies goggle their tongues at me. Grotesque. Amy Lowell. BoWoP

Why do those bell-tones crowd the air? London Birds: a Lollipop. John Heath-Stubbs. *Fr.* Two Wedding Songs. NTP

Why do we grumble because a tree is bent. Variety. *Yoruba Oral Tradition, tr.* by E. Lasebikan. WTO

Why do we labor at the poem. Reasons for Music. Archibald MacLeish. MeMAP

Why Do We Live? Israel Zangwill. TrJP

Why Do We Love. Sir Benjamin Rudyerd. ElL

Why Do We Mourn Departing Friends?. Isaac Watts. AH

Why do we need these goggles to build the dam? Goggles and Telescopes. Pien Chih-lin, *tr. fr. Chinese.* *Fr.* Poems Written at the Construction Site of the Ming Tombs Dam. LHF, *tr.* by Hualing Nieh

Why do we return? Not in the darkened rooms. Roy Fuller. *Fr.* Ghost Voice. OBD

Why do we waste so much time in arguing? Sushi. Paul Muldoon. CIP

Why do [*or doe*] ye weep, sweet babes? To Primroses Filled with Morning Dew. Robert Herrick. SeCV-1

Why do you always fly away? *(LL)* The Lonely Scarecrow. James Kirkup. GrPI; PDV

Why do you cry out, why do I like to hear you. Sound of Breaking. Conrad Aiken. AWP

Why do you dig like long-clawed scavengers. Verlaine. E. A. Robinson. NAAL-2

Why do you dwell so long in clouds. Song to the Masquers. James Shirley. *Fr.* Triumph of Peace, The. OxBSP

Why do you frown on me, you puritans. Petronius Arbiter, *tr. fr. Greek by* Kenneth Rexroth. PGA

Why do you heave apart my stone? Gregory of Nazianzus, Saint, *tr. fr. Greek by* Robin Skelton. GrAn

Why do you hide, O dryads! when we seek. Chant for Reapers. Wilfrid Thorley. OBEV

Why do you lean beside the window, Will? Schoolroom: 158 –. James E. Warren, Jr. GoYe

Why do you lie with your legs ungainly huddled. The Dug-out. Siegfried Sassoon. CH; MoBrPo; NSI; OHIP

Why do you look so gloomy, Naevolus? Juvenal, *tr. fr. Latin. Fr.* Satires. PeHV

Why do you love her? Questions [1]. Donald Hall. FF

Why do you play such dreary music. Radio. Frank O'Hara. PoA

Why do you rack the ore? The cornerstone alone. The Treasure Lies In the Cornerstone. "Angelus Silesius," *tr. fr. German. Fr.* Cherubical Wanderer, The. GePo, *tr. by* George C. Schoolfield

Why do you rush through the field in trains. The Fat White Woman Speaks. G. K. Chesteron. UV

Why do/ or you/ sigh. Post-Coitum Tristesse: A Sonnet. Brad Leithauser. EOEF

Why do you stare at the floor, Chrysilla. Irenaeus Referendarius, *tr. fr. Greek by* Sam Hamill. InMo

Why do you stare at the little box. The Judges of the Little Box. Vasco [*or* Vasko] Popa, *tr. fr. Serbo-Croatian by* Charles Simic. AnRep; HSix

Why do you talk so much. For Robert Frost. Galway Kinnell. NOBA; VGW

Why do/ You thus devise. Susanna and the Elders. Adelaide Crapsey. WPE

Why do you visit me, white moths, so often? Georg Heym, *tr. fr. German by* Christopher Middleton. PeFWW

Why do you wear your hair like a man? After Dilettante Concetti. Henry Duff Traill. BXAP; FaBoCo

Why do you wrap your wisdom in a multitude of words? I Ask My Teachers. Sister Mary Madeleva. *Fr.* Concerning Death. CRP

Why Do You Write about Russia? Louis Simpson. InPS

Why? doan't I pay me car-fare? A Market Basket in the Car. Thomas MacDermot. PBCV

Why doe not all fresh maids appeare. Upon the Death of His Sparrow; an Elegie. Robert Herrick. FM

Why does he keep bruising against me my dead father why still. Sestina with Refrain. Thomas W. Shapcott. CBAP

Why Does It Snow? Laura E. Richards. OBCA

Why does my husband beat me? Poor Me. *Unknown, tr. fr. French by* Richard Beaumont. ErPo

Why does the fire burn high to me. The Last Scab of Hawarth. John Manifold. FaBoMA

Why does the poets abuse us, we that are seamen's poor wives? The Seamen's Wives' Vindication. *Unknown.* OxBSS

Why does the Pygmy. The Third Jungle Book. Ogden Nash. OxBM

Why does the raven cry aloud and no eye pities her? The Lamentation of Enion. Blake. *Fr.* Vala; or The Four Zoas. OBNC

Why does the sea burn? Why do the hills cry? Zaydee. Philip Levine. CAPP; NNaP

Why does the sea moan evermore? By the Sea. Christina Rossetti. BoNaP; NOBVV

Why does the thin grey strand. Sorrow. D. H. Lawrence. CMoP; GTBS-P; OBD; OBMV

Why does the wind so want to be. The Wind. Elizabeth Rendall. BoTP

"Why [*or* Quhy] does [*or* dois] your brand sae [*or* so] drop wi' blude [*or* drap wi bluid]." Edward [*or* Edward, Edward]. *Unknown.* AmFP; CH; ClHu; EBEV; EBEvV; ELP; EnRP; ESPB; FaBoBa; FaPoR; GGP; HAP; HoPM; InPK; InPS; LiTB; Mes; NAEL-1; NOBE; NoP; OBEV; OxBB; OxBS; PoEL-1; PoRA; PrIm; SCGP; SoSe; TFi; TrGrPo; TRP (Why does your brand so drop with blood, Edward, Edward?) CoGr

"Why doesn't somebody buy *me* false ears?" From the Joke Shop. Roy Fuller. OxBC

Why don't I write in the language of air? Mona Sa'udi, *tr. fr. Arabic by* Kamal Boullata. WPOW

Why don't people leave off being lovable. Elemental. D. H. Lawrence. NoP

Why don't we rock the casket here in the moonlight? The Pale Blue Casket. Oliver Pitcher. PoBA; TTY

Why Don't You Talk to Me? Alistair Campbell. PeNZ

Why don't you talk to me? (*LL*) Why Don't You Talk to Me? Alistair Campbell. PeNZ

Why don't you write you never. Dear Reader. Peter Meinke. Poetsp

Why dost not speak? Shakespeare. *Fr.* Coriolanus. OxAEP-1

Why dost thou haste away? Sir Philip Sidney. *Fr.* Arcadia. NoSic; SiPS

Why dost thou hate return instead of love. Lord Herbert of Cherbury. NOSC

Why dost thou shade thy lovely face? O why. To His Mistress. The Earl of Rochester. OBEV

Why dost thou shade thy lovely face? Oh why. Wherefore Hidest Thou Thy Face, and Holdest Me for Thine Enemy [*or* Enemie]? Francis Quarles. *Fr.* Emblems. NOSC

(?.) MeLP; OxAEP-1; TrPWD

Why dost thou so explore. Homer, *tr. by* George Chapman. *Fr.* Iliad, The. OBVE

Why dost thou sound, my dear Aurelian. In Answer of an Elegiacal Letter, Upon the Death of the King of Sweden. Thomas Carew. BeJo

Why doth heaven bear a sun. Barnabe Barnes. *Fr.* Parthenophil and Parthenope. EIL

Why Doubt God's Word? Albert Benjamin Simpson. BLRP

Why drink, why touch you now? If it will be. John Hollander. *Fr.* Sonnets for Roseblush. SM

Why each is striving, from of old. Destiny. Sir Edwin Arnold. NOBVV; OxBSP

Why England is Conservative, *sels.* Alfred Austin. "Let hound and horn in wintry woods and dells." FaBoEH

Why English Is So Hard. *Unknown.* FaBoUs

Why fadest thou in death. Richard Watson Dixon. ChTr

Why Fear to Die? Sir Philip Sidney. *See* Since Nature's works be good, and death doth serve.

Why fearest thou thy outward foe. That Each Thing Is Hurt of Itself. *Unknown.* EIL

Why Flowers Change Color. Robert Herrick. HAP

Why from the danger did mine eyes not start. Sonnet: Of His Pain from a New Love. Cavalcanti, *tr. fr. Italian by* Dante Gabriel Rossetti. AWP

Why God Permits Evil: For Answers to This Question of Interest to Many Write Bible Answers Dept. E-7. Miller Williams. MT; SM

Why has our poetry eschewed. Food and Drink. Louis Untermeyer. MoAmPo

Why has Spring one syllable less. What's in a Name? Christina Rossetti. FaBoVe

Why hast thou breathed, O God, upon my thoughts. Angela Morgan. *Fr.* Poet, The. TrPWD; WGRP

Why Hast Thou Forsaken Me? Chad Walsh. *Fr.* Psalm of Christ, The. TrCP

Why hast thou nothing in thy face? Eros. Robert Bridges. CMoP; LiTB; NOBE; PoEL-5

Why have crowds as magnets drawn. Why We Meet. L. A. J. Moorer. CBWP-3

Why have I locked myself inside. John Hollander. EOEF

Why have such scores of lovely, gifted girls. A Slice of Wedding Cake. Robert Graves. BoLoP; NAEL-2; NOBE; OxBTC; PIP

Why have ye no reuthe on my child? *Unknown.* MiEL (Mary Suffers with Her Son.) MeEL

Why have you come to the shining cliffs. The Knight without a Name. *Unknown.* WiR

Why Have You No Ruth? *Unknown.* OxBSP

Why have you risen, to stand with naked feet. With the Dawn. Thomas Caulfield Irwin. BIrV; EnLoPo

Why, having won her, do I woo? The Married Lover. Coventry Patmore. *Fr.* Angel in the House, The. OBEV; OxAEP-2; TrGrPo

Why He Was There. E. A. Robinson. CMoP; NOBA

Why hoard your maidenhead? There'll not be found. Asclepiades, *tr. fr. Greek by* R. A. Furness. OBD

Why? How? Who is he? (*LL*) Letter from Barcelona, A 1937. Michael O'Loughlin. IB

Why I Am a Liberal. Robert Browning. Son

Why I Am Not a Painter. Frank O'Hara. NeAP; NoAM; NOBA; PoM

Why I Am Not a Painter. Frank O'Hara. CAPP; HCAP; MoP; NeAP; NoAM; NOBA; PoE; Poetr; PoM; VCAP

Why I Didn't Go to Delphi. James Welch. CDW

Why I Like Movies. Patricia Jones. BISi

Why I Like to Go Places: Flagstaff, Arizona — June 1978. Kate Rushin. ETG

Why I Never Answered Your Letter. Nancy Willard. CrSp

Why I Sing the Blues. B. B. King. MAT

Why I tie about thy wrist. The Bracelet: To Julia. Robert Herrick. OBEV; TrGrPo

Why I Voted the Socialist Ticket. Vachel Lindsay. MoAmPo

Why I Write about the Holocaust. Gary Pacernick. BTR

Why I Write Not of Love. Ben Jonson. BeJo; OxBSP

Why, if Becchina's heart were diamond. Sonnet: Of Becchina, the Shoemaker's Daughter. Cecco Angiolieri, da Siena, *tr. fr. Italian by* Dante Gabriel Rossetti. AWP

Why, if this interval of being can be spent serenely. Rainer Maria Rilke, *tr. fr. German by* Stephen Mitchell. *Fr.* Duino Elegies. EnlH; NAWM-2

Why in all the many races of the country where we live. Why Negroes Don't Unite. L. A. J. Moorer. CBWP-3

Why is a pump like Viscount Castlereagh? What's My Thought Like? Thomas Moore. FaBoEE

(Riddle, A. FaBoCo

Why is it. Lover's Meeting. Ray Mathew. CBAP

Why Is It? L. A. J. Moorer. CBWP-3

Why is it me they always sit beside. Conspiracy. Claire Bateman. CrSp

Why is it not enough, to want death's certain peace? Lamentation during His Most Painful Illness. Simon Dach, *tr. fr. German by* Ingrid Waløe-Engel. GePo

Why is it that every moment we are awake we do not weep? (*LL*) Pietà. Allen Afterman. NOBAu

Why is it, when I am in Rome. On Being a Woman. Dorothy Parker. AnAmPo; PoLF

Why is my district death-rate low? Municipal. Kipling. BXAP

Why is my verse so barren of new pride. Shakespeare. *Fr.* Sonnets. EBEV; InvP; NoSic; OxAEP-1

Why is that graceful female here. The Indian's Bride. Edward Coote Pinkney. AnAmPo

Why is the face of the dead so absolute. Stone, Scissors, Paper. Jennifer Strauss. FaBoMA

Why is the floor, Chrysilla. Irenaius, *tr. fr. Greek by* W. G. Shepherd. GrAn

Why is the princess so depressed. Noblesse Oblige. Celeste Turner Wright. Poetsp

Why is the sea-gull flying? (*LL*) A Visit from the Sea. Robert Louis Stevenson. FM; GN

Why/ Is the sky? Questions at Night. Louis Untermeyer. FaPON

Why is the word pretty so underrated? Pretty. Stevie Smith. NAEL-2; NoAM; NoP; TEP

Why is the world beloved, that fals is and vein. Despise the World. *Unknown.* MeEL

Why is your forehead deep-furrowed with care? Call Me Not Back from the Echoless Shore. *Unknown.* BLPA

Why, Jack, how now? I hear strange stories. An Epistle to My Friend J. B. Robert Dodsley. NOEC

Why, kick him out of the army. (*LL*) Captain Jinks. *Unknown.* BLPA

Why lean over the fire, and who is this. In the Secret House. Christopher Middleton. FaBoMo

Why, let the strucken deer go weep. Shakespeare. *Fr.* Hamlet. NAWM-1; NoSic

Why Linger Yet upon the Strand?. Louis FitzGerald Benson. AH

Why listen, even the water is sobbing for something. The Maid's Thought. Robinson Jeffers. ErPo

Why Log Truck Drivers Rise Earlier than Students of Zen. Gary Snyder. NNaP; SOTW

Why look at me like that? Nocturne by Ben Shahn. R. S. Thomas. OxAEP-2

Why looks your Grace so heavily today? Shakespeare. *Fr.* King Richard III. OxAEP-1

Why, Lord ("Why Lord, must something in us.") Mark Van Doren. AH; TrPWD

Why lovest thou so this brittle [*or* brotle] worlde's joy? The Peace of a Good Mind. Sir Thomas More. *Fr.* Twelve Weapons of Spiritual Battle, The. EnRePo; FaBoRV

Why, Madam, must I tell this idle tale? A True Tale. Mary Chandler. ECWP

Why make it doubt — it hurts it so. Emily Dickinson. NALW

Why, man, he doth bestride the narrow world. Portrait of Caesar. Shakespeare. *Fr.* Julius Caesar. TrGrPo

Why, man of morals, tell me why? (*LL*) Drinking. Abraham Cowley, after the Greek of Anacreon. BeJo; BLPL; FF; GGP; NOBE; OBEV; OBVE; OtMeF; OxAEP-1; SeCP; SeCV-1; TrGrPo

Why Mira Can't Go Back to Her Old House. Mirabai, *tr. fr. Medieval Hindi by* Robert Bly. EnlH; NU

Why mourns my beauteous friend, bereft? To Urania. Benjamin Colman. SCAP

Why muse wee thus to see the wheeles run cross. The Town Called Providence, Its Fate. Benjamin Tompson. SCAP

Why must I be hurt? Pain. Elsie Robinson. PoToHe

Why Must You Know? John Wheelwright. VGW

Why must you thrust your loins. Strato, *tr. fr. Greek by* Sam Hamill. InMo

Why My Hair Is Not Gray. Picirantaiyar, *tr. fr. Tamil by* A. K. Ramanujan. PLW

Why My Mother Made Me. Sharon Olds. Poetr

Why Negroes Don't Unite. L. A. J. Moorer. CBWP-3

Why not live sweetly, as in the green trees? (*LL*) I Had a Dove and the Sweet Dove Died. Keats. CH; CoGr; FaPON; FM

Why not mark out the land. Hard Questions. Margaret Tsuda. RFM

Why not merely the despaired of. Cascando. Samuel Beckett. NOIV

Why not? The mouths of the ginger blooms slide open. Chinoiserie. Charles Wright. AmPA

Why now so melancholy, Ben? Leviathan; or, A Hymn to Poor Brother Ben. *Unknown.* APAS

Why of the sheep do you not learn peace? An Answer to the Parson. Blake. FaBoEE; MeMBP; NBLV; OxBoLi

Why only in the spring are roses borne? Lucretius, *tr. fr. Latin. Fr.* De Rerum Natura (On the Nature of Things). KTR, *tr. by* Lucy Hutchingson

Why puts our grand-dame [*or* Grandame] Nature on. On the Unusual Cold and Rainy [*or* Rainie] Weather in the Summer, 1648. Robert Heath. NOSC

Why reclining, interrogating? why myself and all drowsing? To the States. Walt Whitman. CTC; NAAL-1; RaBo

Why rejoice in beauty? What. Reflections. Antoinette Deshoulières, *tr. fr. French by* Yvor Winters. PBWP

Why repeat? I heard you the first time. Carl Sandburg. *Fr.* People, Yes, The. OBAL

Why, Rome was naked once, a bastard smudge. Humble Beginnings. Thomas Lovell Beddoes. NOBVV

Why say the idiot is not. The Locus. Cid Corman. VGW

Why scratch a scratching post when trousers. Vikram Seth. *Fr.* Golden Gate, The. OFC

Why seraphim like lutanists arranged. Evening without Angels. Wallace Stevens. VGW

Why She Moved House. Thomas Hardy. FM

Why She Says No. Ellen Bryant Voigt. FaBoWP

Why Should a Foolish Marriage Vow. Dryden. *Fr.* Marriage à la Mode. CBLP; NAEL-1; NIP; OxBM

Why should I be eaten by love. James A. Randall, Jr.. BPo

Why should I blame her that she filled my days. No Second Troy. W. B. Yeats. CMoP; EnLoPo; GTBS-P; MoP; NAEL-2; NoAM; NOBE; OAEL-2; OxAEP-2; OxBTC; PoEL-5; PPP; TFi; WeW

Why Should I Care for the Men of Thames? Blake. ChTr

Why should I confine myself. Ghetto. Guy Tirolien, *tr. fr. French by* Ellen Conroy Kennedy. NegPo

Why should I find Him here. Christ in the Clay-Pit. Jack R. Clemo. GTBS-P

Why Should I Grieve? Moses ibn Ezra, *tr. fr. Hebrew by* Solomon Solis-Cohen. TrJP

Why should I have raced my boat home from town at dusk? Returning Home at Dusk from Town, on the Fifteenth of the Seventh Month. Shen Chou, *tr. fr. Chinese by* Irving Y. Lo. SuSp

Why should I have returned? Noah's Raven. W. S. Merwin. ChIV-1; HCAP

Why should I heed their railings? What's a prude? A Marriage Prospect. William Hurrell Mallock. NOBVV

Why should I keep holiday. Compensation. Emerson. AmPP; LiTA; MeMAP; NOBA; TAP

Why should I let the toad work. Toads. Philip Larkin. CMoP; NoAM; NOBL; OxAEP-2; OxBTC; PoE; Poetr; SoSe

Why should I longer long to live. Being Forsaken of His Friend He Complaineth. "E. S." EIL

Why Should I Murmur. Hartley Coleridge. Son

Why should I say I see the things I see not. Arthur Hugh Clough. EnVR

Why should I seek for love or study it? Ribh Considers Christian Love Insufficient. W. B. Yeats. RaBo

Why should I seek to ease intense desire. To Tommaso de' Cavalieri. Michelangelo, *tr. fr. Italian by* John Addington Symonds. PeHV

Why Should I Sing in Verse. Samuel Daniel. *Fr.* To Delia. ESo; Son

Why Should I Wander Sadly. Süsskind von Trimberg, *tr. fr. Middle High German.* TrJP

Why should it be *my* loneliness. Tell Me. Langston Hughes. SAmP

Why should my anxious breast repine. Byron. *Fr.* L'Amitié est l'Amour sans Ailes. OBF

Why should my bells, which chime thy praise, when thou. Edward Taylor. *Fr.* Preparatory Meditations Before My Approach to the Lord's Supper. ChIV-2

Why should scribblers discompose. Walter Savage Landor. *See* Why should the scribblers discompose.

Why Should the American Negro Be Proud? Maggie Pogue Johnson. CBWP-4

Why should the living need my oil? Crowds. Vernon Watkins. AngWe

Why should the scribblers discompose. The Scribblers. Walter Savage Landor. FaBoEE; OBSV

   (Why should scribblers discompose. FaBoEE.

Why should this a desert be? Orlando's Rhymes. Shakespeare. *Fr.* As You Like It. CTC

Why should this flower delay so long. The Last Chrysanthemum. Thomas Hardy. CMoP; LiTB; MeMBP

Why should this Negro insolently stride. August. Elinor Wylie. MoAB; MoAmPo

Why should thy look requite so ill. A Paradox. The Earl of Pembroke. EiL

Why Should Vain Mortals Tremble. Nathaniel Niles. AH

Why should we not, as well, desire death. On Death. Francis Quarles. Fr. Divine Fancies. PeECV

Why should we praise them, or revere. Against Seasons. Robert Mezey. NYBP

Why should you believe in magic. Consumed. James Tate. MAT

Why should you [or shouldst thou] swear I am forsworn. The Scrutiny [or Scrutinie]. Richard Lovelace. BeJo; BoLoP; CaPo; ELP; EnLoPo; GBL; MeLP; NoP; SeCP; TrGrPo
(Song: The Scrutiny.) NOSC

Why should you try to crush me? Resentment. Richard Aldington. PeFWW

Why should your face so please me. Edwin Muir. OxBM

Why should your fair eyes with such sovereign grace. Michael Drayton. Fr. Idea. ESo; SCGP

Why, silly Man! so much admirest thou. George Wither. Fr. Collection of Emblemes, Ancient and Moderne, A. SeCV-1

Why sing sadly sad daughter of Pandion. To the Swallow. Pamphilus, tr. fr. Greek by Dennis Schmitz. GrAn

Why Sit'st Thou by That Ruin'd Hall. Sir Walter Scott. Fr. Antiquary, The. EnRP

Why sleeps the pen of Young! the friend profess'd. Lady Bradshaigh. OBF

Why So Many of Them Die. Susan Wallbank. BrRo

Why So Pale and Wan, Fond Lover? Sir John Suckling. Fr. Aglaura. AWP; BeJo; ClHu; ELP; FaBV; HAP; HoPM; NOBE; OBEV; OtMeF; PoE; PoRA; TEP; TrGrPo; UnPo

Why so valiant to decide? Young Woman at a Window. Mark Van Doren. LiTA

Why, Soldiers, Why? At. to James Wolfe. OBET

Why, Some of My Best Friends Are Women. Phyllis McGinley. NMM

Why speak of memory and death. Two Views of Two Ghost Towns. Charles Tomlinson. NoAM

Why speak of the use. Hayden Carruth. VGW

Why stand aghast. He Hath Need of Rest. Josephine D. Henderson Heard. CBWP-4

Why stay we at home now the season is come? The Greenland Voyage; or, The Whale Fisher's Delight. Unknown. OxBSS

Why take time, with so little time left. About Writing Poetry. Sophie Slingeland. LoHo

Why That's Bob Hope. William Hathaway. SM

Why, that's two tree boughs rubbing in the wind. (LL) Mapooram. Aborigine Oral Tradition. NOBAu

Why the Old Woman Limps. Lupenga Mphande. HBAPE

Why the Resurrection Was Revealed to Women. Catharina Regina von Greiffenberg, tr. fr. German by Michael Hamburger. PBWP

Why the Soup Tastes like the Daily News. Marge Piercy. MAT

Why the unbroken spiral, Virtuoso. Apple Peeler. Robert Francis. LCAP

Why the weakness and pallor of your poems? A Rebuttal of Ai Ch'ing. Ting Mang, tr. fr. Chinese. LHF, tr. by Hualing Nieh

Why the Wind Comes. Hirini Melbourne. PeNZ

Why There Are No Cats in the Forest. Simeon Dumdum. TSaS

Why They Waged War. John Peale Bishop. NYBP

Why this desperation to move heaven and earth. Palladas, tr. fr. Greek by Tony Harrison. GrAn

Why this girl has no fear. Carmen. Victor Hernandez Cruz. PoBA

Why, this is hell. How Many Devils Can Dance on the Point. D. J. Enright. AnAn

Why this man gelded Martiall I muse. Raderus. John Donne. PeLV

Why throbs my heart when he appears? The Self-Examination. Unknown. ECWP

Why Tomas Cam Was Grumpy. James Stephens. CMoP

Why vex thy soul that never nations claim thee? A Citizen of — the World. Donald McDonald. PBCV

Why wail you, pretty plover? and what is it that you fear? Happy, The Leper's Bride. Tennyson. CBLP

Why wait we for the torches' lights? Let Us Drink. Alcaeus, tr. fr. Greek by John Hermann Merivale. AWP

Why was a radio sinful? Lord knows. But it was. The Radio under the Bed. Reed Whittemore. NYBP

Why was I born if this ends all. My Song. James Ephriam McGirt. AAP

Why was I made for Love and Love denied to me? (LL) The Blossoming of the Solitary Date-Tree. Samuel Taylor Coleridge. CBLP

Why was it that the thunder voice of fate. Robert Gould Shaw. Paul Laurence Dunbar. Son

Why We Are Late. Josephine Miles. NALW

Why We Meet. L. A. J. Moorer. CBWP-3

Why weep ye by the tide, ladie? Jock of Hazeldean. Sir Walter Scott. BeLS; EnRP; GN; NAEL-2; OxBS; TEP
(Jock o' Hazeldean.) GTBS; GTBS-P

Why weep ye by the tide, ladye? John of Hazelgreen [or Haselgreen]. Unknown. ESPB

Why/ we're just as American. Minority Poem. Wing Tek Lum. BCF

Why were you born when the snow was falling? A Dirge. Christina Rossetti. ChTr; EBVV; NOBVV; SCGP

Why? What are Men? Francis Quarles. Fr. Meditatio. CBCK

Why, who makes much of a miracle? Miracles. Walt Whitman. AnAmPo; PFP; SAmP

Why Why Should I the World Be Minding. Thomas Smith. AiP

Why will Delia thus retire. A Receipt to Cure [or for] the Vapours. Lady Mary Wortley Montagu. ECWP; NOEC; PBWP
(Receipt for the Vapours.) PBWP; PeLV

Why will they never sleep. John Peale Bishop. LiTA; LiTM

Why, William, on that old grey [or gray] stone. Expostulation and Reply. Wordsworth. EnRP; FHYEP; NAEL-2; OAEL-2

Why Would I Want. William J. Harris. PoBA

Why you triple-headed cunt, no wonder you wanted a separation. Sebastian Barker. Fr. On the Rocks. FaBoBl

Whylom [or Whilom] Ther was dwellinge at Oxenford [or Oxenforde]. The Miller's [or Milleres] Tale. Chaucer. Fr. Canterbury Tales, The. EnVB; FaBoBl; NAEL-1; OAEL-1; OxBoLi; PeLV
(Sometime ago there was a rich old codger, mod. vers. by Nevill Coghill.) TEP
(There used to be a rich old oaf who made, mod. vers. by Theodore Morrison.) NAWM-1

Whym Chow. "Michael Field." FM

Why'n't you bring me. To Greet a Letter-Carrier. William Carlos Williams. OBAL; SAmP

Wi' a hundred pipers an' a', an' a.' The Hundred Pipers. Lady Nairne. ScCV

Wi da lentenin days ida first o da Voar. Tuslag. T. A. Robertson. OxBS

Wi' every effort to be fair. A Moolie Besom. "Hugh MacDiarmid." IHNG

Wi' Jock of Hazeldean. (LL) Jock of Hazeldean. Sir Walter Scott. BeLS; EnRP; GN; NAEL-2; OxBS; TEP

Wi October's wind and rain. (LL) The Rooks. Unknown. GBP; OxNR

Wi' patchit brose and ilka pen. Lilt Your Johnnie. Unknown. BXAP

Wi' the truth of his right hand. (LL) Fause Foodrage. Unknown. ESPB

Wich deceased of thier emocion on a past excursion day. (LL) "Wellcome, to the Caves of Artá!" Robert Graves. MeMBP; NBLV; NOBL; NYBP; PeLV

Wichita Vortex Sutra, sels. Allen Ginsberg. PoBeRe
"Face the Nation." NaP

Wicked and the base do compass round, The. Fear Not: For They That Be With Us. Jones Very. ChIV-1

Wicked Clamor, The. Tuvia Rivner, tr. fr. Hebrew by Ruth Finer Mintz. MHP

Wicked clamor, my ear grows deaf, The. The Wicked Clamor. Tuvia Rivner, tr. fr. Hebrew by Ruth Finer Mintz. MHP

Wicked man in the bathroom cupboard., A. (LL) Miss Twye. Gavin Ewart. ErPo; FiBHP; NOBL

Wicked Neighbor, The. "Zelda," tr. fr. Hebrew by Hannah Hoffman. WPOW

Wicked Who Would Do Me Harm, The. Unknown, tr. fr. Gaelic by A. Carmichael. RB

Wickedest Man in Memphis, The. Alex J. Brown. BeLS

Wickedness of Peter Shannon, The. Alden Nowlan. MoCV

Wicker Basket, A. Robert Creeley. CAPP; HAP; MoP; NoAM; NoP; Poetr; SM

Wicket is the harbor and the garden is the shore, The. (LL) Pirate Story. Robert Louis Stevenson. BeLS; FaPON

Widdecombe [or Widdicombe] Fair. Unknown. CH; MoShBr

Wide as this night, old as this night is old and young as it is young. Kenneth Fearing. CMoP

Wide awake and dreaming. Of Calico Cats. Kirsty Seymour-Ure. CRH

Wide Empty Landscape with a Death in the Foreground. N. Scott Momaday. CDW

Wide, ho? Ezra Pound, after the Chinese. OBVE

Wide is our mouth and. Need Is Our Name. Luci Shaw. TrCP

Wide Land, The. A. R. Ammons. TwCP

Wide Mizzoura, The. Unknown. AS

Wide o'er the valley the pennons are fluttering. The Siege of Chapultepec. William Haines Lytle. PAH

Wide open and unguarded stand our gates. Unguarded Gates. Thomas Bailey Aldrich. AnAmPo; PAH

Wide open are the gates of Heaven. The Great Arbiter of Fate. Ch'u Yüan, *tr. fr. Chinese by* Wu-chi Liu. SuSp

Wide Open Are Thy Loving Hands. Bernard of Clairvaux, *tr. fr. Latin by* Charles P. Krauth. AH

Wide sleeves sway. Dancing. Yang Kuei-fei, *tr. fr. Chinese by* Florence Ayscough *and* Amy Lowell. FaPON

Wide Walls. *Unknown.* PoToHe

Wide, Wide World, The. Kipling. *Fr.* In the Neolithic Age. NOBVV; OtMeF

Widening Spell of the Leaves, The. Larry Levis. NAmP90; PBCAP

Widening under my heart. *(LL)* The House That Isn't Mine. Victoria Kohn. UTF

Widest arc of its elliptical turn., The. *(LL)* Achieving Perspective. Pattiann Rogers. MT

Widow. Dorothy Livesay. IMW

Widow, The. Susan Ludvigson. MT

Widow, The. W. S. Merwin. NYBP; UnPo; VGW

Widow, The. Robert Southey. NOEC; UV

Widow, A. Ted Kooser. PBCAP

Widow and Virgin Sisters, The. William Broome. ECEV

Widow at Windsor, The. Kipling. FaBoEH; NAEL-2; NoAM; NoP

Widow bird sate mourning for her love, A. A Widow Bird. Shelley. *Fr.* Charles the First. CoGr; ELP; GTBS; GTBS-P
  (Song, A: "Widow bird sate mourning for her love, A.") MeMBP; NOBE; OBNC; OxBSP; PoEL-4
  (Widow Bird, A.) BoTP; CH; FaPON

Widow Brown's Christmas. John Townsend Trowbridge. BeLS

Widow (conscious that time's on the wing). Stanley J. Sharpless. PeLi

Widow Has Buried Her Second Husband, The. William Dunbar. *Fr.* Tua Mariit Wemen and the Wedo, The. OxBLMV

Widow in Wintertime, A. Carolyn Kizer. CAPP; IMW

Widow kept a favourite cat, A. A Fable of the Widow and Her Cat. Swift. OFC; SoCa

Widow offers her broken tears to an idol, A. Bei Dao, *tr. fr. Chinese by* Donald Finkel *with* Chen Xueliang. SpMi

Widow Speaks, The. William Dunbar. *Fr.* Book of the Two Married Women and the Widow, The. PoEL-1

Widow Teaches Poetry Writing, The. Nell Altizer. IMW

Widow That Keeps the Cock Inn, The. *Unknown.* CoMu

Widow, well met; whither go you today? A Contention betwixt a Wife, a Widow, and a Maid. Sir John Davies. SiPS

Widower. Bible, Apocrypha. OxBM

Widower, The. Kipling. CBLP; OxBM

Widower, The. Royall Tyler. OBAL

Widower in the Country, The. Les A. Murray. DiPo

Widower's Courtship, The. Elizabeth Hands. WoRP

Widows. Louise Glück. NAmP90

Widows. Edgar Lee Masters. MoAmPo

Widow's Curse, The. *Unknown, tr. fr. Irish by* Thomas Kinsella. NOIV

Widow's Hymn, A. George Wither. OBEV

Widow's Jazz, The. Mina Loy. Jaz

Widow's Lament. *Unknown, tr. fr. Chinese by* Arthur Waley. *Fr.* Shih Ching. BoWoP

Widow's Lament in Springtime, The. William Carlos Williams. CMoP; HAP; IMW; LiTM; MoP; NAAL-2; NoAM; NOBA; PFP; PoE; SAmP; SoSe; TAP

Widow's Old Broom, The. *Unknown.* AmFP

Widow's Plot; or, She Got What Was Coming to Her, The. William Plomer. MoP

Widows' Rice. Okkur Macattanar, *tr. fr. Tamil by* A. K. Ramanujan. PLW

Widow's Supper. Mary Jane Moffat. IMW

Widow's Tears, The or, Dirge of Dorcas. Robert Herrick. ChIV-2

Widow's Weeds, A. Walter de la Mare. FaBV

Widow's Yard, The. Isabella Gardner. CAPP; Poetr

Widsith, *sels. Unknown, tr. fr. Anglo-Saxon.* Widsith, the Minstrel. AnOE

Widsith spoke, his word-hoard unlocked. Widsith, the Minstrel. *Unknown, tr. fr. Anglo-Saxon. Fr.* Widsith. AnOE

Widsith, the Minstrel. *Unknown, tr. fr. Anglo-Saxon. Fr.* Widsith. AnOE

Wie langsam kriechet sie dahin. Heine, *tr. fr. German by* Richard Monckton Milnes. AWP

Wiedersehen. Miller Williams. ArOW; NGP

Wife, The. Robert Creeley. VGW

Wife, The. Denise Levertov. ErPo

Wife a-Lost, The. William Barnes. BoLoP; EBVV; ELP; EnLoPo; EnVR; HAP; OBEV; OxBM; SCGP

Wife a-Prais'd, A. William Barnes. EBVV

Wife and all. *(LL)* When I was a little boy/ I lived by myself. *Unknown.* BoTP; OxNR

Wife and servant are the same. To the Ladies. Mary Lee, Lady Chudleigh. ECWP; NALW; NOEC; WPE; WPOW

Wife — at daybreak I shall be, A. Emily Dickinson. AmPP

Wife-Hater, The. *Unknown.* CoMu

Wife in London, A. Thomas Hardy. NOBVV; OBWP

Wife is like a blade of grass, A. Jean-Joseph Rabéarivelo, *tr. fr. French by* Ellen Conroy Kennedy. NegPo

Wife, land of the wave fire. *Unknown, tr. fr. Icelandic by* George Johnston. *Fr.* Saga of Gisli, The. OBVE

Wife of Bath's Prologue, The. Chaucer. *Fr.* Canterbury Tales, The. EnVB; FHYEP; NAEL-1; OAEL-1; OxBoLi, *abr.;* PeLV, *(shorter vers.)*

Wife of Bath's Tale, The. Chaucer. *Fr.* Canterbury Tales, The. EnVB; FHYEP; NAEL-1; OAEL-1

Wife of Flanders, The. G. K. Chesterton. NSI

Wife of Llew, The. Francis Ledwidge. PeIV

Wife of Usher's Well, The. *Unknown.* AmFP; AWP; CH; ChTr; EBEV; EnRP; EnSB; ESPB, A, B, C, *and* D *vers.;* FaBoBa; ImPo, (A *vers.);* LiTB; NAEL-1; NOBE; NoP; OAEL-1; OBEV; OxAEP-1; OxBB; OxBS; PoEL-1; Poetr; PrIm; RB; ScCV; SCGP; TFi; TrGrPo

Wife of Usher's Well, The. *Unknown.* AmFP; ESPB

Wife of Winter's Tale, The. Michael Dennis Browne. SM

Wife Speaks, The. Mary Stanley. PeNZ

"Wife Takes a Child," The. Ellen Bryant Voigt. CrSp; SM

Wife Talks to Herself, A. Stephen Berg. NaP

Wife, there are some points on which we differ from each other. Martial, *tr. fr. Latin.* OxBM

Wife to Husband. Fleur Adcock. PeNZ

Wife to Husband. John Harington. NoSic

Wife was sitting at her reel ae night, A. The Strange Visitor. *Unknown.* ChTr; FaBoCh; GBP

Wife Who Smashed Television Gets Jail. Paul Durcan. CIP

Wife Who Would a Wanton Be, The. *Unknown.* FaBoCo

Wife Wrapt [*or* Wrapped] in Wether's Skin, The. *Unknown.* AmFP; ESPB

Wife Wrapt in Wether's Skin, The. *Unknown.* AmFP; ESPB

Wife's Complaint, The. *Unknown. See* Song I sing of sorrow unceasing, A.

Wife's Complaint, The. *Unknown, tr. fr. Anglo-Saxon by* Michael Alexander. BoLoP

Wife's Lament. *Unknown, tr. fr. Anglo Saxon.* AnOE, *tr. by* Charles W. Kennedy; PBWP, *tr. by* Kemp Malone; PoE, *tr. by* Kemp Malone, WPE

Wife's Tale, The. Seamus Heaney. CIP; IPY

Wig, rouge, honey, wax, teeth. Lucilius, *tr. fr. Greek by* Peter Porter. GrAn

Wiggle waggle went his tail. *(LL)* Niddle Noddle. Mother Goose. OxNR

Wigs and Beards. Robert Graves. NOBL

Wil the Merry Weaver, and Charity the Chamber-Maid; or, A Brisk Encounter between a Youngman and His Love. *Unknown.* CoMu

Wilberforce. Josephine D. Henderson Heard. CBWP-4

Wild, The. Wendell Berry. VGW

Wild air, world-mothering air. The Blessed Virgin Compared to the Air We Breathe. Gerard Manley Hopkins. EaPr; MeMBP; NOBVV; PeVV

Wild animal of the blue ocean. *(LL)* Mbuyazi (Henry Francis Fynn). *Unknown.* PeSAV

Wild as a dingo, fresh as a brumby? *(LL)* A Country Song. Douglas Stewart. NOBAu

Wild as they are, accept them, so were we. Aecclesiae et Reipub. William Strachey. OBTV

Wild Ass. Padraic Colum. MoBrPo

Wild Asters. Ruth Stone. IMW

Wild (at Our First) Beasts Uttered Human Words. E. E. Cummings. FaBoMo; NYBP

Wild Barbaree, The. *Unknown.* AmFP

Wild Bees. James K. Baxter. NoP

Wild Bill Jones. *Unknown.* AmFP

Wild bird filled the morning air, A. The Fowler. W. W. Gibson. NTP

Wild bird singer, sing on. Sand Creek. Charles G. Ballard. UnPo; VoR

Wild bird, whose warble, liquid sweet. Tennyson. *Fr.* In Memoriam A. H. H. EBVV, *abr.;* NoP; OAEL-2, *abr.;* PeECV, *abr.*

Wild birds are flying south. *(LL)* Indian Summer. Wilfred Campbell. NOBC

Wild birds on the roof are bitterly complaining to man, The. Seeking Spring Beyond the city. Su Tung-p'o, *tr. fr. Chinese by* Robert Payne. TAL

Wild Boar and the Ram, The. John Gay. *Fr.* Fables. FM; NOEC

Wild Carthage held her, Rome. A Puritan Lady. Lizette Woodworth Reese. MoAmPo

Wild Cat, The. Iain Crichton Smith. CRH

Wild clefting, you I sing; mountains. Night. Georg Trakl, *tr. fr. German by* David McDuff, Jon Silkin, *and* R. S. Furness. PeFWW

Wild Colloina Boy, The. *Unknown.* AmFP

Wild Colonial Boy, The. *Unknown.* FaBoBa

Wild Common, The. D. H. Lawrence. NoAM

Wild Crab. Mary Ellen Solt. BoWoP

Wild Dog Rose, The. John Montague. BIrV; CIP; IPY; PBCIP; PoE

Wild Dreams of Summer What Is Your Grief. George Barker. OxBTC

Wild ducks/ float with the north wind. Sun Children. Leslie Silko. VoR

Wild Duck's Nest, The. Wordsworth. FM

Wild Eden, *sels.* George Edward Woodberry.

Wild-eyed team with horned and swaying heads, The. The Team. Suzanne Gardinier. CBAP

Wild Flower Man, The. Lu Yu, *tr. fr. Chinese by* Kenneth Rexroth. NaP

Wild Flowers. John Clare. ArNa

Wild flowers and grass grow on. In the Mountain Village. Wang Hung Kung, *tr. fr. Chinese by* Kenneth Rexroth. OHMPC

Wild Flower's Song. Blake. BoTP

Wild Garden, The. Pope. *See* Awake, my St. John! leave all meaner things.

Wild Geese, The. Wendell Berry. TRP

Wild Geese. Elinor Chipp. FaPON

Wild Geese. Mary Oliver. ArNa; EaPr

Wild Geese. Katharine Tynan. IIP

Wild Geese on the Lake. Shen Yüeh, *tr. fr. Chinese by* Richard B. Mather. SuSp

Wild geese returning, The. Tsumori Kunimoto. PDV

Wild geese, wild geese in white flocks. While I Wait. Vilhelm Andreas Wexels Krag, *tr. fr. Norwegian by* Philip L. Miller. RiWo

Wild Goat, The. Claude McKay. CDC

Wild goose, broken-legged on the sandbank. The Boat-pullers. Mei Yao Ch'en, *tr. fr. Chinese by* Jonathan Chaves. SuSp

Wild Goose, Wild Goose. Issa, *tr. fr. Japanese by* Kenneth Rexroth. TTTS

Wild Grapes. Kenneth Slessor. FaBoMA

Wild Gratitude. Edward Hirsch. SoCa

Wild has its skills. Lapsed Meadow. Stanley Plumly. AnAn; FoLa

Wild Honey. Maurice Thompson. AnAmPo

Wild Honey. Francis Webb. NOBAu

Wild Honeysuckle, The. Philip Freneau. AmPP; AnAmPo; BLPL; EAP; LiTA; NAAL-1; NOBA; OxBA; PoEL-4; PoLF; TAP; TrGrPo

Wild Horse. Elder Olson. GrPl

Wild Horses of Assateague Island, The. John Bensko. MT; NGP

Wild Iron. Allen Curnow. NTP; RB

Wild Knight, The. G. K. Chesterton. WGRP

Wild lavender and mint. Travelling. Dick Davis. SCBI

Wild Life Studies., *sels.* James Fenton.
　Of Bison Men. PeLV
　Wild ones. PeLV; SCBI

Wild Light. Lonny Kaneko. ETG

Wild Man Comes to the Monastery, The. *Unknown.* RaBo

Wild midst the teeming buds of opening May. Morning, Rosamonde. Anne Batten Cristall. ECWP

Wild Mushroom, The. Gary Snyder. NoP

Wild Mustard River, The. *Unknown.* AmFP

Wild Nature. Charles Newton. *Fr.* Stanzas. NOEC

Wild Negro Bill. *Unknown.* BPo

Wild Night, A. Julia Ward Howe. AmWP

Wild Night at Treweithan. Gwyn Williams. AngWe

Wild night bitter and vertical. Black Horseman. Branko Miljkovic, *tr. fr. Serbo-Croatian by* Charles Simic. HSix

Wild nights — wild nights! Emily Dickinson. AmPP; CBLP; HeIP; LPA; NAAL-1; NALW; NIP; NoAM; NOBA; NoP; OxBA; PBWP; PFP; Poetr; RaBo; TAP; UnAS; WPE

Wild Oats. Philip Larkin. InPS

Wild Oats. Norman MacCaig. OxBTC

Wild Old Wicked Man, The. W. B. Yeats. CMoP; RaBo

Wild ones. James Fenton. *Fr.* Wild Life Studies. PeLV; SCBI

Wild patience has taken me this far, A. Integrity. Adrienne Rich. CAPP

Wild Peaches. (When the world turns completely upside down.) Elinor Wylie. FaBoWP; LiTA; LiTM; NAAL-2; NALW; OxBA; WPE
　Sels.
　"Down to the Puritan marrow of my bones." BoWoP
　(Puritan Sonnet, IV.) MoAB; MoAmPo; TrGrPo

Wild pigeon of the leaves. Birds. *Unknown, tr. fr. Arabic by* E. Powys Mathers. *Fr.* Thousand and One Nights, The. AWP

Wild Pigs. Ted Kooser. SM

Wild Ride, The, *abr..* Louise Imogen Guiney. AmWP

Wild Rippling Water, The. *Unknown.* FaBoBa

Wild Rose, *abr. William Allingham. GN*

Wild Rose, The. Goethe, *tr. fr. German by* Philip L. Miller. RiWo

Wild Rose of Alloway! my thanks. Burns. Fitz-Greene Halleck. AnAmPo

Wild Roses. Mary Effie Lee Newsome. CDC; ShDr

Wild roved the Indians once. Grand Rapids. Julia A. Moore. OBAL

Wild Shakespeare. James Thomson. *Fr.* Seasons, The. EPCY

Wild Strawberries. Helen Dunmore. PWE

Wild Strawberries. Robert Graves. FaBoCh

Wild Strawberry. Maurice Kenny. HATNAP

Wild Swan: "My attire is noiseless when I tread the earth." Unknown, formerly at. to Cynewulf, *tr. fr. Anglo-Saxon. Fr.* Riddles (Exeter Book). AnOE, *tr. by* Charles W. Kennedy

Wild Swans. Edna St. Vincent Millay. CMoP; MoAmPo; PBWP; UnPo

Wild Swans at Coole, The, *sels.* W. B. Yeats.
　Ego Dominus Tuus. CPCY, abr.
　"Trees are in their autumn beauty, The." ArNa; ChTr; CMoP; FaBoPP; FaBoRV; FM; HeIP; InPS; MoAB; MoBrPo; MoP; NAEL-2; NoAM; NoP; PFP; Poetr; PPP; SCGP; SoSe; SOTW; TEP; TFi; UnPo

Wild Thyme, The. Blake. *Fr.* Milton. WiR

Wild Thyme. Joyce Sambrook. BoTP

Wild to be wreckage forever. *(LL)* Cherrylog Road. James Dickey. CoAP; HAP; HCAP; InPS; MT; NAAL-2; NIP; NYBP; Poetr; PrIm; TwCP; WeW

Wild Turkeys; The Dignity of the Damned. Brigit Pegeen Kelly. NAmP90

Wild was the day; the wintry sea. The Twenty-second of December. Bryant. GN

Wild water-head, what's your reason/ for exalting yourself. A Torrent Cuts Off the Poet's Path. Antiphilus, *tr. fr. Greek by* W. S. Merwin. GrAn

Wild West. Mark Vinz. Poetsp

Wild, wild the storm, and the sea high running. Patrolling Barnegat. Walt Whitman. NoP

Wild wind, chaotic lightning — black clouds are born. Summer Niight. *Unknown, tr. fr. Chinese by* Edward H. Schafer. SuSp

Wild winds weep, The. Mad Song. Blake. EnRP; MeMBP; NAEL-2; NOEC; OAEL-2; PoE; PoEL-4; PrIm; TEP; TrGrPo

Wild with All Regrets, *sels.* Wilfred Owen. SCGP
　"Yes, there's the orderly. He'll change the sheets." PeFWW

Wild Women Blues. Ida Cox. VBLP

Wild women don't have the blues. *(LL)* Wild Women Blues. Ida Cox. VBLP

Wild World. Cat Stevens. UV

Wildcat sits on the rocks, The. The Wild Cat. Iain Crichton Smith. CRH

Wildcat was walking. *Unknown, tr. fr. Navajo Indian by* Jerome K. Rothenberg. STP

Wildebeest, The. June Daly. FaPON

Wilderness, The. Sidney Keyes. LiTB
　Sels.
　"Red rock wilderness, The." OBWP; PoWW

Wilderness, The. Kathleen Raine. BoWoP; WPE

Wilderness. Carl Sandburg. RaBo

Wilderness, The: but otherwise. Esther K. Comes to America: 1931. Jerome Rothenberg. NNaP

Wilderness Gothic. Alfred W. Purdy. HeIP; MoCV; NOBC; NoP

Wilderness Is Tamed, The. Elizabeth J. Coatsworth. *See* Axe has cut the forest down, The.

Wilderness Sacred Wilderness. Philip Lamantia. UL

Wilderness turns up again, The. Travelling. David Chaloner. VaA

Wildernesse and the solitarie place shall be glad for them, The. Bible, O.T. *Fr.* Isaiah. OBVE

Wildflower. Stanley Plumly. AnAn; LCAP

Wildflowers. Richard Howard. NoAM

Wildly-colored girl with her round belly twisted, The. In the Gallery. John Hollander. CBLP

Wildly he wandered on. Shelley. *Fr.* Alastor; or, The Spirit of Solitude. EnRP; OAEL-2; TOF

Wildness. Gerard Manley Hopkins. *Fr.* Inversnaid. EaPr; OtMeF

Wildness of haggard flights. Roussan Camille, *tr. fr. French by* Seth L. Wolitz. TTY

Wildness of your glances pleases me, The. Rama Kam. David Diop, *tr. fr. French* by Ellen Conroy Kennedy. NegPo

Wildness sleeps upon the mountain. The Fisher Cat. Richard Eberhart. GrPl

Wildpeace. Yehuda Amichai, *tr. fr. Hebrew*. TSaS, *tr.* by Chana Bloch

Wildtrack, *sels.* John Wain.
  Lie Easy in Your Secret Cradle. NAs

Wilfred Owen's Photographs. Ted Hughes. FaBoPV; OxBC

Wilful waste brings woeful want. *Unknown.* OxNR

Wilhelm Meister's Apprenticeship, *sels.* Goethe, *tr. fr. German*.
  Mignon. NU
  (Knowest thou the land where bloom the lemon trees.) AWP, *tr.* by James Elroy Flecker
  (You know that land, her lemon groves in bloom?) STV, *tr.* by John Frederick Nims

Wilkes Booth came to Washington, an actor great was he. Booth Killed Lincoln. *Unknown.* AmFP

Will, The. John Donne. CBCK; EBEV; ImPo; LiTB; NoSic

Will. Ella Wheeler Wilcox. BLPA; PoToHe

Will anyone tell me what Minne is? Walther von der Vogelweide, *tr. fr. German* by Frederick Goldin. GePo

Will appear as short as one! *(LL)* On a Fly Drinking out of [*or* from] His Cup. William Oldys. ImPo; OBEV; OxAEP-1; TrGrPo

Will awaits its gradual end, The. *(LL)* Modes of Pleasure. Thom Gunn. PeHV; PPP

Will be changed by the love into sunshine again. *(LL)* Sweet Peril. George Macdonald. BLPA; FaBoBe

Will be content with one? *(LL)* The Poet Loves a Mistress, but Not to Marry. Robert Herrick. CaPo; ErPo

Will be ground by the grinders of Gambart. *(LL)* There is an old he-wolf named Gambart. Dante Gabriel Rossetti. FaBoEE; PeLi

Will be in the aisles and rooms screaming. *(LL)* The Grand Tradition of Western Culture. Julia Stein. LoHo

Will be my home. I can never forget him. *(LL)* Remembering. "Ping Hsin." WPC

Will change to the kind of shock that stunned our prime. *(LL)* Preserving. Roy Fuller. CBLP

Will commit that indiscretion. *(LL)* The Garden. Ezra Pound. AWP; HeIP; LiTA; MoAB; MoAmPo; NIP; NoP; OxBSP; PPP; SOTW; TwCP

Will cover us both. *(LL)* Invitation. *Unknown.* VBLP

Will days, indeed, yet come in forgiveness and grace. When You Will Walk in the Field. Leah Goldberg, *tr. fr. Hebrew* by Simon Halkin. TrJP

Will death take me as sweetly. Interlude. Mary Ann Larkin. LPA

Will dissolves, the heart becomes excited, The. Soliloquy in an Air-Raid. Roy Fuller. PoA

Will dream that hope again, but else would die. *(LL)* The Dream[e]. John Donne. CBLP; EiL; ESCV; InvP; LiTB; MeLP; OAEL-1; OBEV; SeCP; TOF

Will drown the silence. *(LL)* Boundaries. José Emilio Pacheco. STV

Will ever pray. *(LL)* A Petition from the Chain Gang at Newcastle to Captain Furlong the Superintendent. Francis MacNamara. NOBAu

Will find we once had words. *(LL)* About Writing Poetry. Sophie Slingeland. LoHo

Will go on prancing, proud and unafraid. *(LL)* Aunt Jennifer's Tigers. Adrienne Rich. CAPP; FaBoWP; HeIL; HeIP; InPK; NALW; NIP; NoAM; NoP; Poetr; SM; TRP

Will God forever cast us off. Jesse Mercer. AmFP

Will grow to more than this mere grin. *(LL)* The Judgement of God. William Morris. PeVV

Will guide him In. *(LL)* Joy of My Life! While Left Me Here. Henry Vaughan. GeHe; SeCV-1

Will he always love me? Lady Horikawa, *tr. fr. Japanese* by Kenneth Rexroth. BoWoP

Will He No Come Back Again? *Unknown.* OBEV

Will hear the wind sigh through the leaves of a tree. *(LL)* The Farmer of Tilsbury Vale. Wordsworth. EBEV

Will I always be eleven. Untitled. Franz Wright. LCAP

Will I be able to see myself? *(LL)* Proper Distance and Proper Time. Judith Baumel. UTF

Will inherit all his tears. *(LL)* Radio Yerevan. Diana Der Hovanessian. LoHo

Will it last? he says. The Snowflake Which Is Now and Hence Forever. Archibald MacLeish. NoP

Will know the reason why!' *(LL)* The Song of the Western Men. Robert Stephen Hawker. EBEvV; EnRP; FaBoEH; FaPoR; OBNC; PIP; VPP

Will lead my steps aright. *(LL)* To a Waterfowl. Bryant. AmPP; AnAmPo; AWP; BLPL; CH; EAP; FaBoBe; GN; HoPM; ImPo; LiTA; NAAL-1; NOBA; NoP; OxBA; PoEL-4; PoLF; PrIm; PWR; SoSe; TAP; TFi; TrGrPo; WBLP; WGRP

Will lightning strike me if I take. Thoughts of Loved Ones. Margaret Fishback. FiBHP

Will linger, though enjoyed, like joy in memory yet. *(LL)* Stanzas Written in Dejection [–December 1818], near Naples. Shelley. EnRP; FaBV; GTBS; GTBS-P; NAEL-2; NAWM-2; NoP; PoRA; TEP

Will lose my nearest kinsman. *(LL)* Imaginary tremolo. Jean-Joseph Rabéarivelo. NegPo

Will lose the cot and keep the sot. *(LL)* Who weds a sot to get his cot. *Unknown.* FaBoUs

Will, lost in a sea of trouble. Archilochus, *tr. fr. Greek* by Kenneth Rexroth. PGA

Will Love again awake. Muse and Poet. Robert Bridges. OBMV

Will make the whole read human and exact. *(LL)* The Devil's Advice to Story-Tellers. Robert Graves. LiTM; MoP; NAEL-2; NoAM

Will make thee bear. *(LL)* The Kneeling Camel. Anna Temple Whitney. BLPA

Will make your glist'ring gold but more to shine. *(LL)* To sing of wars, of captain[e]s, and of kings. Anne Bradstreet. BoWoP; EAP; NAAL-1; NALW; NOBA; OxBA; PoE; SCAP; TAP; WPE

Will never come back to me. *(LL)* Break, Break, Break. Tennyson. AWP; BLPL; CBLP; CH; ClHu; DL; EBEvV; EnVR; FaBoBe; FaBV; FaPoR; FF; FHYEP; GoJo; GTBS-P; HAP; HeIP; ImPo; LiTB; MeMBP; NAEL-2; NIP; NOBE; NOBVV; NoP; OBNC; OHCV; PIP; PoEL-5; Poetr; PoRA; PrIm; PWR; RB; SoSe; TEP; TFi; TrGrPo; WBLP; WeW

Will night already spread her wings and weave. Night-Thoughts. Solomon ibn Gabirol, *tr. fr. Hebrew* by Emma Lazarus. TrJP

Will no young British bard, on rhyme intent. Edward Davies. *Fr.* Chepstow: A Poem. AngWe; OBWVE

Will not let go. *(LL)* The Face. Lucien Stryk. ArOW

Will not make a fairer creature. *(LL)* The Choice. George Wither. OBEV

Will-o'-the-Wisp, The. Wilhelm Müller, *tr. fr. German* by Philip L. Miller. *Fr.* Winter's Journey, The. RiWo

Will of God be done by us, The. Blessed Be the Holy Will of God. *Unknown, tr. fr. Irish* by Douglas Hyde. TIRV

Will of God we must obey, The. The Death of King Edward VII. *Unknown.* OxBoLi

Will people accept them? Tenzone. Ezra Pound. *Fr.* Contemporania. MeMAP; PoA

Will press the life-drops from the heart. *(LL)* The Slave Auction. Frances E. W. Harper. BPo; PoNe; TTY

Will proffer wave after wave. *(LL)* Cootchie. Elizabeth Bishop. FaBoWP

Will remain when there is no heart to break for it. *(LL)* Credo. Robinson Jeffers. EaPr; MoAB; MoAmPo

Will remember you. *(LL)* Corn Children. Carol Lee Sanchez. SRLS

Will seeing Concan make a dog a lion? Ritual Not Religious. *Unknown, tr. fr. Telugu.* WGRP

Will snarl — and man can never be alone. *(LL)* The Wolves. Allen Tate. LiTA; LiTM; NOBA; OxBA; PoA

Will somebody build me a round house. A Round House. Matthew Sweeney. IB

Will sprawl, now that the heat of day is best. Caliban upon Setebos; or, Natural Theology in the Island. Robert Browning. AWP; EBEV; EnVR; FHYEP; NAEL-2; NOBVV; NoP; OAEL-2; OxAEP-2; PeVV; WGRP

Will Stewart and John. *Unknown.* ESPB

Will still break through. *(LL)* My heart, thinking/ "How beautiful he is." Lady Otomo no Sakanoe. AWP; PBWP

Will tell you how he wrote, and talked, and spit. *(LL)* Doctor Johnson. Soame Jenyns. FaBoEE; OBSV

Will that day hold my heart away from me. *(LL)* One Day. Ray Mathew. NOBAu

Will the fire of the heart and the fire of the mind be one. *(LL)* Heart and Mind. Edith Sitwell. OxBTC; TwCP

Will the lady with locker key 43. Will You Come Out Now? Valerie Sinason. BrRo

Will the man who gets clean love his neighbor? Soap (II). Jerome Rothenberg. NNaP

Will the Real Me Please Stand Up? A. L. Hendricks. PBCV

Will the train never start? Train. Helen Mackay. NSI

Will the Weaver. *Unknown.* AmFP

Will the wolves lie down with the lambs and feed them? The End of Sorrow. Edmond Fleg, *tr. fr. French* by Humbert Wolfe. *Fr.* Wall of Weeping, The. TrJP

Will there never come a season. To R. K. James Kenneth Stephen. BXAP; FaBoCo; FaBoEE; FaBoPa; NBLV; NOBL; OtMeF; PeLV; UV

Will there really be a morning? Emily Dickinson. OBCA (Morning.) FaPON

Will There Yet Come. Leah Goldberg, *tr. fr. Hebrew by* Ruth Finer Mintz. MHP

Will there yet come days of forgiveness and grace. Will There Yet Come. Leah Goldberg, *tr. fr. Hebrew by* Ruth Finer Mintz. MHP

Will They Cry When You're Gone, You Bet. Amiri Baraka. NAAL-2

Will they have children? Will they have more children? Neighbors. James Tate. LCAP

Will they ley adowne." (*LL*) 'Pax vobis," quod the fox. *Unknown.* MiEL

Will they never fade or pass! The Farmer Remembers the Somme. Vance Palmer. NOBAu

Will they occur. Brasília. Sylvia Plath. CAPP

Will they stop. Kenneth Fearing. CMoP

Will to be tickled wants; has got the itch. *Unknown.* FaBoEE

Will to Change, The. Adrienne Rich. NMM

Will wake from sleep and perhaps bark back. (*LL*) Cemetery Nights. Stephen Dobyns. SV

Will wake on its chain to morning. (*LL*) Premeditations. Geoff Page. NOBAu

Will waste, as this flea's death took life from thee. (*LL*) The Flea. John Donne. BLPL; BoLoP; EBEV; ESCV; FF; FM; HoPM; ImPo; InPK; InPS; JCP; LiTB; MAT; NAEL-1; NBLV; NIP; NoSic; OAEL-1; OxAEP-1; PoE; Poetr; SCV; SeCP; SeCV-1; TEP; TFi; TrGrPo

Will we be able to wake ourselves, and act? (*LL*) When the animals come to us. Gary Lawless. EaPr

Will., Will., Hen. Steph. Hen. Dick, John Hen., Eddy Ned, Edward. The Kings and Queens of England. *Unknown.* FaBoUs

Will Ye Na Can Ye Na Let Me Be. *Unknown.* FaBoVe

Will Ye No Come Back Again? Lady Nairne. VBLP

Will ye see what wonders love hath wrought. Sir Thomas Wyatt. SiPS

Will ye that I should sing. A Lady of High Degree. *Unknown*, *tr. fr. French by* Andrew Lang. AWP

Will Yer Write It Down for Me? Henry Lawson. CBAP

Will yet learn to suck a penis. (*LL*) Epigram: To Philaenis. Martial. PeHV

Will you always catch me unaware. To My Mother at 73. Elizabeth Jennings. NAs

Will You Be as Hard? Douglas Hyde, *tr. fr. Irish by* Lady Augusta Gregory. OBMV

Will You Be My Little Wife? Kate Greenaway. MoShBr

Will You Buy a Fine Dog. *Unknown.* CBNP

Will you buy a fine dog with a hole in his head? Will You Buy a Fine Dog. *Unknown.* CBNP

Will You Come? Edward Thomas. CH; GoJo; GrPl

Will you come a boating, my gay old hag. The Gay Old Hag. *Unknown.* BIrV

Will You Come Out Now? Valerie Sinason. BrRo

Will you come to the bower I have shaded for you? Walter Savage Landor. *Fr.* Reply to Lines by Thomas Moore, A. ChTr

Will you come to Turvy Land. Topsy-Turvy Land. Phyllis M. Stone. BoTP

Will you come with me, my Phyllis dear. Wait for the Wagon. *At. to* R. Bishop Buckley. PAH

Will you gang wi' me, Leezie Lindsay. Leezie Lindsay. *Unknown.* FaBoCh

Will you glimmer on the sea? Moonrise. Hilda Doolittle ("H. D."). PoA

Will you have me? A Popular Romance. Kevin Ireland. PeNZ

Will you hear of a bloody battle. The Downfall of Piracy. *At. to* Benjamin Franklin. PAH

Will you heare a tale of Robin Hood. Robin Hood and the Pedlars. *Unknown.* ESPB

Will you leave the hills of Scotland? Highland Mary. Mary Weston Fordham. CBWP-2

Will you lend me your mare to ride but a mile? *Unknown.* OxNR

Will you love me when I'm old. Love. Nilene O. A. Foxworth, *tr. by the author.* AIW

Will You Love Me When I'm Old? *Unknown.* BLPA; BLPL; FaBoBe

Will you make it clear I'm not that sort of boy? (*LL*) They Answer Back. "Francis." FiBHP

Will you marry it, marry it, marry it. (*LL*) The Applicant. Sylvia Plath. MAT; NAAL-2; NaP; NMM; NOBA; TwCP

Will you please rush down and see. To Close. William Carlos Williams. SAmP

Will you seek afar off? you surely come back at last. Walt Whitman. *Fr.* Song for Occupations, A. ChIV-1

Will you sleep forever? Korinna, *tr. fr. Greek by* Willis Barnstone. BoWoP; PBWP, *tr. by* John Dillon

Will you, sometime, who have sought so long, and seek. The Finder Found. Edwin Muir. PoA

Will you take a sprig of hornbeam? Forester's Song. A. E. Coppard. FaPON

Will you take a walk with me. The Clucking Hen. *Unknown.* BoTP

Will you turn a deaf ear. Questioner Who Sits So Sly. W. H. Auden. OxAEP-2

"Will you walk a little faster?" said a [*or* the] whiting to a [*or* the] snail. "Lewis Carroll." *Fr.* Alice's Adventures in Wonderland. NoAM; OxAEP-2

(Lobster Quadrille, The.) BoTP; FaPON; MoShBr; OxBChV; PFP; UV (Mock Turtle's Song, The.) CBNP; ChTr; FaBoNo

"Will you walk into my parlor?" said the Spider to the Fly. The Spider and the Fly. Mary Howitt. BeLS; FaPON; OTCP; OxBChV; PWR; UV; WBLP

Will you wear white, O my dear, O my dear? Jennie Jenkins. *Unknown.* AmFP

Willesden Gree. Jimmy Pearse. UV

Willets, The. May Swenson. WPE

Willi, Home. Jean Valentine. PFL

William I. Eleanor Farjeon. NTP

William and Helen. Sir Walter Scott. EnRP

William and Margaret. David Mallet. NOEC; OxAEP-1

William and Mary. *Unknown.* AmFP

William and Mary,/ George and Anne. *Unknown.* OxNR

William and Phyllis. *Unknown.* OBET

William asked how veal was made. What Is Veal? *Unknown.* FaBoUs

William Blake. James Thomson ("B.V."). EPCY

William Blake (To Frederick Shields, on His Sketch of Blake's Work-room and Death-room, 3 Fountain Court, Strand). Dante Gabriel Rossetti. EPCY

William Brown of Oregon. Joaquin Miller. AnAmPo

William Dewy, Tranter Reuben, Farmer Ledlow late at plough. Friends Beyond. Thomas Hardy. CoGr; EBVV; FaBoRV; FaBoVe; GTBS-P; NOBVV; OBEV

William Gifford. Walter Savage Landor. FaBoEE; GTBS-P

William Hall. *Unknown.* AmFP

William Lisle Bowles. Byron. *Fr.* English Bards and Scotch Reviewers. OBNC

William Lloyd Garrison. Joseph S. Cotter, Sr.. AAP

William Lloyd Garrison. H. Cordelia Ray. CBWP-3

Sir William of Deloraine at the Wizard's Tomb. Sir Walter Scott. *See* If thou would'st view fair Melrose aright.

William of Orange was always worried. Plans. Brendan Kennelly. BiHa

William Oliver maker. Ancestors. Raymond Garlick. AngWe

William P. Frye, The. Jeanne Robert Foster. PAH

William Street. Kenneth Slessor. CBAP

William Taylor. *Unknown.* OBET; OxBSS

William Taylor. *Unknown.* OBET

William the Bastard. "Lakon." FiBHP

William the Conqueror long did reign. England's Sovereigns in Verse. *Unknown.* BLPA

William the Conqueror, ten sixty-six. *Unknown.* FaBoUs; OxNR

William the First was the first of our kings. William I. Eleanor Farjeon. NTP

William the Norman conquers England's state. Lines on Succession of the Kings of England. *Unknown.* FaBoUs

William, the wild round plums are falling. The Dressing Stations. Norman Dubie. AmPA

William Wallace. Francis Lauderdale Adams. OxBS

William was a bashful lover. William Taylor. *Unknown.* OBET; OxBSS

William Was a Royal Lover. *Unknown.* AmFP

William Wordsworth. Sidney Keyes. OxBTC

William Wordsworth (1770-1850). Gavin Ewart. NoAM

William Yeats in Limbo. Sidney Keyes. MoBrPo

Williams: An Essay. Denise Levertov. InPS

Williams Avenue Zionist Church, The. Russia. William Carlos Williams. VGW

Williamstown. Jennifer Rankin. FaBoMA

Willie. *Unknown.* AmFP

Willie and Earl Richard's Daughter, (B *and* C *vers.*). *Unknown.* ESPB

Willie and Earl Richard's Daughter. *Unknown. See* O Willie's large o' limb and lith.

Willie and Lady Maisry. *Unknown.* ESPB, A *and* B *vers.*

Willie and Lady Margerie [*or* Maisry]. *Unknown.* ESPB; OxBB

Willie and Nellie, one evening sat. Willie's and Nellie's Wish. Julia A. Moore. FiBHP

Willie boy, Willie boy, where are you going? *Unknown.* BoTP

Willie Brew'd a Peck o' Maut. Burns. AWP; EnRP; OxBS

Willie Brew'd [*or* Brewed] a Peck o' Maut. Burns. AWP; EnRP; OxBS

Willie had a purple monkey climbing on a yellow stick. In Memoriam. "Max Adeler." FaBoCo

Willie is fair, an Willë's rair. *Unknown. See* Willy's rare, and Willy's fair.

Willie Leonard; or, The Lake of Cold Finn. *Unknown.* AmFP

Willie Macintosh. *Unknown.* ESPB, A *and* B *vers.*; OxBoLi

Willie o Douglas Dale. *Unknown.* ESPB

Willie o [*or of*] Winsbury. *Unknown.* AmFP; ESPB, A *and* D *vers.*

Willie poisoned Auntie's tea. Willie the Poisoner. *Unknown.* NTCP

Willie, take your little drum. Patapan. Bernard de la Monnoye, *tr. fr. French.* PChr

Willie the Poisoner. *Unknown.* NTCP

Willie the Weeper. *Unknown.* BeLS; BLPA; OBAL

Willie was a widow's son. Willie and Lady Maisry. *Unknown.* ESPB, A *and* B *vers.*

Willie, Willie, I'll learn you a wile. Willie's Lyke-Wake. *Unknown.* ESPB

Willie Winkie. William Miller. *See* Wee Willie Winkie rins [*or runs*] through the town.

Willie, with a thirst for gore. Careless Willie. *Unknown.* FaPON

Willie's and Nellie's Wish. Julia A. Moore. FiBHP

Willie's Fatal Visit. *Unknown.* ESPB

Willie's Lady. *Unknown.* ESPB

Willie's Lyke-Wake. *Unknown.* ESPB

Willie's [*or* Willie] has taen him o'er the fame. Willie's Lady. *Unknown.* ESPB

Willing also to be remembered, lost. Peter Riley. *Fr.* Eight Preludes. VaA

Willing Arawak, The. Ethnocide. Howard Fergus. PBCV

Willing Graces to the Gothic pile, The. (LL) Verses on Sir Joshua Reynolds's Painted Window at New College, Oxford. Thomas Warton the Younger. NOEC; PoEL-3

Willing it, my ailment. (LL) No Road. Philip Larkin. CBLP; EBEV; MoBrPo; OxAEP-2

Willing Mistress, The. Aphra Behn. *See* Amyntas Led Me to a Grove.

Willobie His Avisa., *sels.* Henry Willoby. To Avisa. CBLP; ElL

Willoughby liked being Willoughby. The Contentment of Willoughby. Frances Alexander. GoYe

Willow. Richard Watson Dixon. *See* Feathers of the willow, The.

Willow. Li Shang-yin, *tr. fr. Chinese* by A. C. Graham. PLT

Willow. Li Shang-yin, *tr. fr. Chinese* by Eugene Eoyang *and* Irving Y. Lo. SuSp

Willow, The. Tu Fu, *tr. fr. Chinese* by Kenneth Rexroth. NaP

Willow Bend and Weep. Herbert Clark Johnson. PoNe

Willow-Boughs, The. Alexander Block. BoTP

Willow Branch Song. Liu Yu Hsi, *tr. fr. Chinese* by Daniel Bryant. SuSp

Willow Branch Songs, *sels.* Ch'ien Ch'ien-i, *tr. fr. Chinese.* "Crescent moon hangs on the tip of the willows, A." SuSp "Must I lament the time that's gone because I've been cast aside?" SuSp

Willow Branches. Liu Yu Hsi, *tr. fr. Chinese* by Dell R. Hales. SuSp

Willow Catkins. Hsüeh T'ao, *tr. fr. Chinese* by Eric W. Johnson. SuSp

Willow Eyebrows. Chao Luan-luan, *tr. fr. Chinese* by Kenneth Rexroth *and* Ling Chung. WPC

Willow floss in the swift wind races against the Spring Festival. Tune: "Song of River City" — On a Kite. Wu Wei-yeh, *tr. fr. Chinese* by Irving Y. Lo. SuSp

Willow leaves dancing. Eveningsong. Ramona Wilson. VoR

Willow-Man, The. Juliana Horatia Ewing. OxBChV

Willow Poem. William Carlos Williams. NAAL-2

Willow shining, The. The Knowledge of Light. Henry Rago. VGW

Willow-tassels grow in tremors of the spring wind. Lines to Do with Youth. Witter Bynner. PoA

Willow Tree, The. *Unknown.* OBET

Willows, The. Walter Prichard Eaton. FaPON; OHIP

Willows, The. Bret Harte. BXAP

Willows are taking the old river road, The. Old River Road. Blanche Whiting Keysner. GoYe

Willows by the Water Side, The. *Unknown. See* My little breath, under the willows by the water-side we used to sit.

Willows cannot hide a bright moon's sorrow. Heard on a Boat. T'an Yuan-ch'un, *tr. fr. Chinese* by Irving Y. Lo. SuSp

Willows carried a slow sound, The. Repose of Rivers. Hart Crane. AWP; CMoP; LiTM; MeMAP; MoAB; MoAmPo; NOBA; OxBA; PoE

Willows of Massachusetts, The. Denise Levertov. NAAL-2

Willow's shadow straight up. Tune: "Prince of Lan-ling" (*Lan-ling Wang*) — on Willows. Chou Pang-yen, *tr. fr. Chinese* by Irving Y. Lo. SuSp

Willowware Cup. James Merrill. NoP; VCAP

Willowwood ("And now love sang: but his was such a song.") Dante Gabriel Rossetti. *Fr.* House of Life, The. NAEL-2; OAEL-2

Willowwood ("I sat with love upon a woodside well.") Dante Gabriel Rossetti. *Fr.* House of Life, The. NAEL-2; OAEL-2; PoEL-5

Willowwood ("O ye, all ye that walk in Willowwood.") Dante Gabriel Rossetti. *Fr.* House of Life, The. NAEL-2; OAEL-2

Willowwood ("So sang he: and as meeting rose and rose.") Dante Gabriel Rossetti. *Fr.* House of Life, The. NAEL-2; OAEL-2

Will's Love, The. Besmilr Brigham. CrSp; IHMS

Willy boy, Willy boy,/ Where are you going? Mother Goose. OxNR; ReMoGo

Willy Drowned in Yarrow. *Unknown.* GTBS; GTBS-P

Willy, enormous Saskatchewan grizzly. Richard Moore. MAT

Willy Lyons. James Wright. HCAP; NNaP; PoE

Willy the Weeper. *Unknown.* AS; GBP

Willy Wet-Leg. D. H. Lawrence. CMoP; RB

Willy, Willy, Harry, Ste. The Kings and Queens of England. *Unknown.* FaBoUs (Kings and Queens of England after the Conquest, The.) FaBoEH

Willy, Willy Wilkin. Mother Goose. OxNR; ReMoGo

Willy's rare, and Willy's fair. Rare Willie Drowned in Yarrow; or, The Water o Gamrie. *Unknown.* ESPB (Rare Willy.) OxBB (Rare Willy Drowned in Yarrow.) ScCV (Willie is fair, an Willë's rair.) GBP

Wilson and Pilcer and Snack stood before the zoo elephant. Elephants Are Different to Different People. Carl Sandburg. MoAmPo

Wil't please your grace to go along with us? A Quotation from Shakespeare with Slight Improvements. "Lewis Carroll." FaBoNo

Wilt thou forgive that sin where I begun. A Hymn to God the Father. John Donne. AWP; EBEV; EnRePo; HAP; InPK; JCP; LiTB; MeLP; NAEL-1; NOBE; NOSC; OAEL-1; PeECV; PoEL-2; PoRA; SCGP; SCV; SeCP; SeCV-1; SoSe; TFi; TOF; TrGrPo; TrPWD (For Forgiveness.) WGRP

Wilt thou go with me, sweet maid. An Invite to Eternity. John Clare. NAEL-2; NOBVV; OAEL-2; OBNC

Wilt thou hunt the prey for the lion? Bible, *O.T. Fr.* Job. AWP; FM; NAWM-1, *abr.*

Wilt thou love God, as he thee! then digest. John Donne. *Fr.* Holy Sonnets. ESCV; JCP; TrCP

Wilt Thou not visit me? Jones Very. OxBA; TrCP; TrPWD

Wilt thou then serve the Philistines with that gift. Milton. *Fr.* Samson Agonistes. EBEV; FHYEP; OAEL-1; PoEL-3

Wiltshire Downs. Andrew Young. GTBS-P; NTP; OxBTC

Wily Fox, The. Edward Davies, *tr. fr. Welsh* by Joseph P. Clancy. OBWVE

Wily Napoleon Bonaparte, The. Douglas Catley. PeLi

Wily old writer called Maugham, A. Martin Fagg. PeLi

Wimbledon Veteran. Lawrence Sutton. FaBoBl

Win at First and Lose at Last; or, A New Game at Cards. Laurence Price. OxBoLi

Wind, The. Padraic Colum. *See* I Saw the Wind Today.

Wind, The. Dafydd ap Gwilym, *tr. fr. Welsh* by Joseph P. Clancy. OBWVE

Wind. James Fenton. NAEL-2; SCBI

Wind, The. Dorothy Graddon. BoTP

Wind. Ted Hughes. NAEL-2; Poetr

Wind, The. Kazuko Yamada, *tr. fr. Japanese* by Miyao Ohara *and* D. J. Enright. OBD

Wind. *Malay Oral Tradition, tr.* by R. O. Winstedt. WTO

Wind, The. Elizabeth Rendall. BoTP

Wind, The. Christina Rossetti. *See* Who Has Seen the Wind?

Wind. Tim Seibles. NAmP90

Wind. Gary Soto. *Fr.* Elements of San Joaquin, The. NoAM; PBCAP

Wind, The. James Stephens. BoNaP; InPK; MoP; NoAM

Wind, The. Robert Louis Stevenson. BoTP; GN; OHCV

Wind, The. *Unknown.* FaBoCh; GBP; OxNR

Wind, The. Dorothy Wordsworth. *See* What way does the Wind come? What way does he go?

Wind, a rustle of leaves, The. The Edge of Autumn. Michael Anania. NoAM

Wind accounted for all, The. The Scythe. Henry Kanabus. UL

Wind and Absence. Peter Scupham. SCBI

Wind and bamboos strum and speak to each other. Meng Chiao, *tr. fr. Chinese* by A. C. Graham. *Fr.* Autumn Thoughts. PLT

Wind and Glacier Voices. Simon J. Ortiz. HATNAP

Wind and rain see spring off. Tune: "Song of Divination" — On the Plum Tree, after a Poem by Lu Yu. Mao Tse-tung, *tr. fr. Chinese* by Eugene Eoyang. SuSp

Wind is wild tonight, The. *Unknown.* NOIV

Wind it blew, and the ship it flew, The. The Earl o' Quarterdeck. George Macdonald. BeLS

Wind it blew from east to west, The. Get Up and Bar the Door. *Unknown.* AmFP

Wind It Blew up the Railroad Track, The. *Unknown.* AS

Wind keen, the sky high, the gibbons wailing, The. On Climbing the Heights on the Ninth Day of the Ninth Moon. Tu Fu, *tr. fr. Chinese by* Robert Payne. TAL

Wind like an ocean, The. Larry Eigner. PoM

Wind may blow the snow about, The. A Country Boy in Winter. Sarah Orne Jewett. OBCA

Wind meets me at Penistone, The. The Wind at Penistone. Donald Davie. LiTM

Wind mutters thinly on the sagging wire. Prairie Graveyard. Anne Marriott. NOBC

Wind o' the East dark with rain. The Efficient Wife's Complaint. Confucius, *tr. fr. Chinese by* Ezra Pound. *Fr.* Airs of Pei. CTC

Wind of dawning riffles the young furze, The. Drafts for a Quatrain. Edmund Wilson. OBAL

Wind of January, The. Christina Rossetti. BoTP

Wind of old cocoa farms, The. Africa Sky. Kojo Laing. HBAPE

Wind of the Prairie. Grace Clementine Howes. GoYe

Wind of the West, that fans with fragrant wing. To the Western Wind. Judah Halevi, *tr. fr. Hebrew by* Solomon Solis-Cohen. TrJP

Wind on the Corn. Charles Tennyson Turner. EBVV

Wind on the Hills, The. Dora Sigerson Shorter. NOBVV

Wind, One Brilliant Day, The. Antonio Machado Ruiz, *tr. fr. Spanish by* Robert Bly. RaBo

Wind, one brilliant day, called, The. The Wind, One Brilliant Day. Antonio Machado Ruiz, *tr. fr. Spanish by* Robert Bly. RaBo

Wind one morning sprang up from sleep, The. The Wind in a Frolic. William Howitt. MoShBr; OxBChV

Wind, The/ only. Song of the Trees. *Unknown, tr. fr. Chippewa Indian by* Frances Densmore. OBVE

Wind Our Enemy, The, *sels.* Anne Marriott.

Wind over the lake is mild, the moon fair, The. Written at Lakeside Residence. Chiang K'uei, *tr. fr. Chinese by* Chiang Yee. SuSp

Wind piercing, hill bare, hard to find shelter. *Unknown, tr. fr. Welsh by* Joseph P. Clancy. *Fr.* Winter. OBWVE

Wind plays with the weathervane, The. The Weathervane. Wilhelm Müller, *tr. fr. German by* Philip L. Miller. *Fr.* Winter's Journey, The. RiWo

Wind pours down, The. (LL) Ploughing on Sunday. Wallace Stevens. ArNa; FaPON; GoJo; RB; SOTW; TTTS

Wind puffs the rain, The. (LL) The Grave of Little Su. Li Ho. PLT

Wind rattles the moon. (LL) December. Maurice Kenny. HATNAP

Wind rocks the car. Like This Together. Adrienne Rich. VGW

Wind rose cold under our robes, and straw blew loose. The Boy Shepherds' Simile. David Bottoms. MT

Wind sall blaw for evermair, The. (LL) The Twa Corbies. *Unknown.* AWP; CH; CoGr; EBEvV; ELP; EnSB; ESPB; FaBoBa; FaBoCh; GTBS; GTBS-P; HAP; InPK; NoP; OBEV; OxBS; PPP; RB; ScCV; SCGP; UnPo

Wind sang to the cornfields, The. August. Eunice Fallon. BoTP

Wind searching as a sieve of brass. Storm at Sea. *Malay Oral Tradition, tr. by* R. O. Winstedt. WTO

Wind Secrets. Diane Wakoski. AmPA

Wind shakes my window frames. October in the Country: [1983]. James Simmons. BiHa; CIP

Wind shakes the grass. A Melody. Lan Ling, *tr. fr. Chinese by* Kenneth Rexroth *and* Ling Chung. WPC

Wind shall lull us yet, The. From the Antique. Christina Rossetti. EnLoPo

Wind shuffles through the cracked glass and the floorboards rot, The. Snuff Movies. Dermot Bolger. IB

Wind sifts through the curtain. Kuan Han-ch'ing, *tr. by* Jerome P. Seaton. *Fr.* Tune: "Green Jade Flute". SuSp

Wind Sleepers, The. Hilda Doolittle ("H. D."). WPE

Wind Song. Lilian Moore. SiSoPo

Wind Song. Carl Sandburg. MoAB; MoAmPo; MoShBr

Wind Sou'west, The. *Unknown.* AmFP

Wind Sprang Up at Four o'Clock, The. T. S. Eliot. ImPo; LiTB

Wind, stirring in the dark foliage, brings, The. God's Harp. Gustav Falke, *tr. fr. German by* Ludwig Lewisohn. AWP

Wind stood up, and gave a shout, The. The Wind. James Stephens. BoNaP; InPK; MoP; NoAM

Wind stops, The. Spring Ends. Li Ch'ing-chao, *tr. fr. Chinese by* Kenneth Rexroth *and* Ling Chung. WPC

Wind subsides — a fragrance, The. Tune: "Spring at Wu-ling." Li Ch'ing-chao, *tr. fr. Chinese by* Eugene Eoyang. SuSp

Wind Suffers of Blowing, The. Laura Riding. RB

Wind sways the blossoms of the rock orchids, The. Listening-to-the-Rain Studio. Chu Yi-tsun, *tr. fr. Chinese by* Chang Yin-nan *and* Lewis C. Walmsley. SuSp

Wind sways the pines, A. Dirge in Woods. George Meredith. FF; NAEL-2; OBEV; OBNC; OPOP; WiR

Wind takes colour from the trees, The. Winds. Hugh McCrae. CBAP

Wind — tapped like a tired man, The. Emily Dickinson. FaBoVe; Mes; MoAB; MoAmPo; TOF

Wind tapped like a tired man, The. The Wind's Visit. Emily Dickinson. AnAmPo; MeMAP

Wind that rose, A. Emily Dickinson. RB

Wind That Shakes the Rushes, The. John Clare. PoRA

Wind that speeds the bee and plucks the bee-line. Awake! W. R. Rodgers. LiTM

Wind, the Clock, the We, The. Laura Riding. FaBoVe; LiTA

Wind the wind the wind blows high, The. The Wind Blows High. *Unknown.* FaBoVe

Wind Took Up the Northern Things, The. Emily Dickinson. ArNa; SOTW; TTTS

Wind Tossed Dragons. Hsieh Ngao, *tr. fr. Chinese by* Kenneth Rexroth. OHMPC

Wind turned, The. Volitions. A. R. Ammons. CAPP

Wind was a torrent of darkness among the gusty trees, The. The Highwayman. Alfred Noyes. BeLS; EBEvV; EBNV; FaBV; FaPON, *abr.; NTP; OBNV; OBSP; PoLF*

Wind was blowing over the moors, The. Charlotte Brontë. "Susan Coolidge." OBCA

Wind waves the lotoses in the scented palace by the water, The. For the Dancer of the King of Wu. Li Po, *tr. fr. Chinese by* Robert Payne. TAL

Wind whines and whines the shingle. On the Beach at Fontana. James Joyce. MoBrPo; OBMV; PoA; RaBo; RB

Wind whistled loud at the window-pane, The. William Brighty Rands. BoTP

Wind would tear a dead man's shroud. Wind. *Malay Oral Tradition, tr. by* R. O. Winstedt. WTO

Wind/blade cutting in, The. Impressions/of Chicago; for Howlin' Wolf. Quincy Troupe. NBV

Winded, drifting to rest. Fog. Philip Booth. FoLa

Windharp. John Montague. CIP; IIP; PNI

Windhover, The. Gerard Manley Hopkins. ClHu; CMoP; EBEvV; EBVV; EnVR; FaPoB; GTBS-P; HAP; InPK; InPS; InvP; LiTB; LiTM; MeMBP; MoAB; MoBrPo; NAEL-2; NoAM; NOBE; NOBVV; NoP; OAEL-2; OBNC; OxAEP-2; PeECV; PFP; PoE; PoEL-5; Poetr; PoRA; PPP; PrIm; RB; SCGP; SCV; TEP; TFi; TOF; TRP; UnPo

Windigo. Louise Erdrich. NoAM

Windigo. Paulette Jiles. NOBC

Winding around the waters of the world. (LL) The Far Field. Theodore Roethke. NAAL-2; NoAM; NoP; PrIm

Winding Banks of Erne [*or* Adieu to Belashanny], The. William Allingham. PeIV

Winding creek and scattered maple groves, A. Yuan Hao-wen, *tr. by* Stephen West. *Fr.* Random Verses on Mountain Life. SuSp

Winding Up. Derek Walcott. NoAM

Winding way the serpent takes, The. Norembega. Whittier. PAH

Windlass Song. William Allingham. GN

Windless city built on decaying granite, loose ends. Thomas McGrath. *Fr.* Letter to an Imaginary Friend, Part Two. NNaP

Windless northern surge, the sea-gull's scream, The. The Incarnate One. Edwin Muir. PeECV

Windmill, The. Longfellow. MoShBr

Windmill, The. E. V. Lucas. BoTP

Windmill At Mandanthanunguna. Pambardu, *tr. fr. Aborigine by* Georg von Brandenstein. NOBAu

Windmill on the Cape. William Vincent Sieller. GoYe

Window, The. Conrad Aiken. CMoP

Window, The. David Bottoms. NGP

Window, The. Dino Campana, *tr. fr. Italian by* John Frederick Nims. STV

Window, The. Robert Creeley. CAPP; NoAM; NOBA; TAP; VGW

Window, The. Edwin Muir. LiTM

Window-Blind. Denise Levertov. LCAP

Window Boxes ("A window box of pansies.") Eleanor Farjeon. FaPON

Window Cleaner, The. Elizabeth Fleming. BoTP

Window cleaner's life is grand!, A. The Window Cleaner. Elizabeth Fleming. BoTP

Window Dressing. William Peskett. PNI

Window-gazing, at one time or another. Here Live Your Life Out! Robert Graves. FaPoB

Window-Glance, The. Heine, *tr. fr. German* by John Todhunter. AWP

Window in the Cliff, The. Bei Dao, *tr. fr. Chinese* by Donald Finkel *with* Chen Xueliang. SpMi

Window insulates me from the street, The. Maternity Gown. David Holbrook. OxBTC

Window into the ground, A. Skara Brae. Michael Longley. PBCIP

Window Ledge in the Atom Age. E. B. White. NBLV; OBAL

Window of the Tobacco Shop, The. C. P. Cavafy, *tr. fr. Greek* by Edmund Keeley *and* Philip Sherrard. PeHV

Window of the Woman Burning, The. Marge Piercy. SRLS

Window on the North, A. R. A. D. Ford. MoCV

Window, The; or, The Song of the Wrens, *sels.* Tennyson.

Window pales, and by its paltry light, The. Aubade: Donna Anna to Juan, Still Asleep. Richard Howard. PoA

Window remained as before, The. The cold. Telegram. Milo De Angelis, *tr. fr. Italian* by Lawrence Venuti. NeIt

Window Sill, The. The Robert Graves. EnLoPo

Window That Watched the Pru. Anne Sexton. Poetr

Window was made of ice with bears lumbering across it, The. Bad Dream. Louis MacNeice. NoAM

Window window window pane. Summer Shower. David McCord. TLR

Windows, The. George Herbert. ESCV; GeHe; MeLP; NAEL-1; NOCV; NoP; PeECV; PoE; SeCP; SeCV-1; TrCP

Windows. Thomas McCarthy. IB

Windows blurred by the same warm, slow, still rain?, The. (*LL*) Memo. Kenneth Fearing. CMoP; PoE

Windows have their watered silk, The. The Diva's First Song (White's Hotel, London). Karl Kirchwey. BAP-91

Windows in Providence. Aliki Barnstone. BoWoP

Window's length beyond the Pleiades, A. First Snow on an Airfield. John Ciardi. PoA

Windows of Heaven were open wide, The. A Ballad of the Conemaugh Flood. Hardwick Drummond Rawnsley. PAH

Windows of our flat: their shutters. Windows. Thomas McCarthy. IB

Windows of the church are bright, The. Christmas Thoughts, by a Modern Thinker. William Hurrell Mallock. NOBVV

Windows, rapturous windows! (*LL*) Dead Color. Charles Wright. HCAP; LCAP

Winds. Hugh McCrae. CBAP

Winds, The. Thomas Tusser. WiR

Winds, The. *Unknown.* ReMoGo

Winds are bleak, stars are bright. The Victoria Markets Recollected in Tranquility. "Furnley Maurice." NOBAu

Winds are dark passages among the stars, The. Turtle. Peter Blue Cloud. HATNAP

Winds' enclosure, Atlantic's premises, The. The Hebrides. Michael Longley. PBCIP

Wind's Foam. Al Mahmud, *tr. fr. Bengali.* TSaS, *tr.* by Marian Maddern

Winds had hushed at last as by command, The. The Sower. Mathilde Blind. WPE

Wind's in the heart of me, a fire's in my heels, A. A Wanderer's Song. John Masefield. MoAB; MoBrPo

Wind's Lament, The. John Morris-Jones, *tr. fr. Welsh* by Anthony Conran. OBWVE

Wind's might moves along the steep banks, The. The Night. Tu Fu, *tr. fr. Chinese* by Hualing Nieh. LHF

Wind's not blown my plaid awa, The. (*LL*) Lady Isabel and the Elf-Knight [*or* The Elfin Knight]. *Unknown.* CH; FaBoBa; GBP

Winds of Africa. Dorothy S. Obi. WPOW

Winds of Change, The. Charles G. Ballard. VoR

Winds of doctrine blow both ways at once, The. Conrad Aiken. *Fr.* Letter from Li Po, A. VGW

Winds of Fate, The. Ella Wheeler Wilcox. AnAmPo; BLPA; WBLP

Winds of heaven, and learn tranquility, The. (*LL*) Be like a tree in pursuit of your cause. *Unknown.* EaPr

Winds of Orisha, The. Audre Lorde. SRLS

Winds on the stems make them creak like manmade things. Stalin. Robert Lowell. HCAP

Wind's on the wold, The. Inscription for an Old Bed. William Morris. OBEV; WiR

(For the Bed at Kelmscott. FaBoRV; PoEL-5

(Lines for a Bed at Kelmscott Manor.) CH; NTP

Wind's spine is broken, The. Storm Tide on Mejit. *Unknown, tr. fr. Micronesian* by Augustin Kramer *and* Willard Trask. RFM

Winds take up, The. (*LL*) Smell of canyon rain storm. Eric Mottram. NBrP

Winds that drift over the desert. Winds of Africa. Dorothy S. Obi. WPOW

Winds that sweep the southern mountains. Allatoona. *Unknown.* PAH

Winds they did blow, The. The Squirrel. *Unknown.* BoTP; OxNR

Winds through [*or* thro'] the olive trees. Long, Long Ago. *Unknown.* FaPON; OHIP; PChr; PDV

(Christmas Song, A.) BoTP

Wind's Visit, The. Emily Dickinson. AnAmPo; MeMAP

Winds! what have ye gathered from Afric's strand. Christian Settlements in Africa. Lydia Huntley Sigourney. AmWP

Winds, whisper gently whilst she sleeps. Laura Sleeping. Charles Cotton. ELP

Winds; words of the wind; rumor of great walls pierced. Hayden Carruth. *Fr.* Asylum, The. SM

Windsor Castle., *sels.* The Earl of Surrey.
Prisoned in Windsor, He Recounteth His Pleasure There Passed. NAEL-1

Windsor Forest., *sels.* Pope.
"Groves of Eden, vanished now so long, The." OAEL-1
"Here hills and vales, the woodland and the plain." ECEV
"Here too, 'tis sung, of old Diana stray'd." OxAEP-1
Progress. ECEV
"See! from the brake the whirring Pheasant springs." FHYEP; FM; PoEL-3
(Hunting and Fishing.) ECEV
"Thy forests, Windsor! and thy green retreats." NOEC; OxAEP-1

Windstorm. Sun Ching-hsuan, *tr. fr. Chinese. Fr.* Lyrics of the Forest. LHF, *tr.* by Hualing Nieh

Windstorm on the Han River. Ts'ai Ch'i-chiao, *tr. fr. Chinese. Fr.* Han River, The. LHF, *tr.* by Hualing Nieh

Windward of Hilo. John N. Miller. ArOW

Windy Day, A. Winifred Howard. FaPON

Windy evening. Dark Farmhouses. Charles Simic. LCAP

Windy Gap. David Campbell. NTP

Windy Monday. Sylvia Kantaris. PWE

Windy Night, The. Thomas Buchanan Read. GN

Windy Nights. Robert Louis Stevenson. BoTP; GoJo; NTP; OTCP; OxBChV; PoRA; SiSoPo

Wine. Micah Joseph Lebensohn, *tr. fr. Hebrew* by A. M. Klein. TrJP

Wine & bath-house sensualities. *Unknown, tr. fr. Greek* by Tony Harrison. GrAn

Wine and cakes for gentlemen. *Unknown.* OxNR

Wine and Grief. Solomon ibn Gabirol, *tr. fr. Hebrew* by Emma Lazarus. TrJP

Wine and oil gleaming within their heads. Double Ode. Muriel Rukeyser, *tr.* by Edmund Keeley. AnAn

Wine and treacherous proposals. Hedylos, *tr. fr. Greek* by Kenneth Rexroth. PGA

Wine and Water. G. K. Chesteron. *Fr.* Flying Inn, The. ChIV-1; FaBoCo; FiBHP; MoBrPo

Wine and woman and song. Villanelle of the Poet's Road. Ernest Dowson. OBMV; TrGrPo; UnPo

Wine Bowl. Hilda Doolittle ("H. D."). NoP

Wine comes in at the mouth. A Drinking Song. W. B. Yeats. ArLo; BoLoP; OAEL-2; PFP

Wine Cup and Bright Moon. Shen Chou, *tr. fr. Chinese* by Irving Y. Lo. SuSp

Wine cup, you come here. Tune: "Spring in Ch'in's Garden." Hsin Ch'i-chi, *tr. fr. Chinese* by Irving Y. Lo. SuSp

Wine destroyed the Centaur, not just you. Philip V of Macedon. Alcaeus, *tr. fr. Greek* by Alistair Elliot. GrAn

Wine does not reach the earth on Liu Ling's grave. (*LL*) Bring in the Wine. Li Ho. PLT

Wine for our drinking. (*LL*) Come to me from Crete to this holy temple. Sappho. WPOW

Wine, friend, and truth, the proverb says, agree. Theocritus [*or* Theokritus], *tr.* by Thomas Creech. *Fr.* Idylls. PeHV

Wine in the cup is heavy. Lu Chih, *tr.* by Hellmut Wilhelm. *Fr.* Tune: "Pleasure in Front of the Hall". SuSp

Wine is love's test. Asclepiades, *tr. fr. Greek* by Thomas Meyer. GrAn

Wine it is that gives life pleasure. In Praise of Wine. *Unknown, tr. fr. Latin* by Helen Waddell. MLL

Wine-maiden. Midnight Dancer. Langston Hughes. FF

Wine Menagerie, The. Hart Crane. NoAM; NOBA; OxBA; VGW

Wine of Love is music, The. James Thomson ("B.V."). *Fr.* Sunday up the River. OBEV

Wine-Press of Los, The. Blake. *See* This wine-press is call'd war on earth.

Wine presses hard upon spring grief. Tune: "Butterflies Lingering over Flowers." Kung Tzu-chen, *tr. fr. Chinese by* Irving Y. Lo. SuSp

Wine sleeps in casks of Rhine oak. Mittelbergheim. Czeslaw Milosz, *tr. fr. Polish by the author* and Richard Lourie. AnRep

Wine-Songs. Moses ibn Ezra, *tr. fr. Hebrew by* Solomon Solis-Cohen. TrJP
Sels.
Awake, My Soul.
Bring Me the Cup.
Drink, Friends.
Rosy Days Are Numbered, The.

Wine, the red coals, the flaring gas. At the Cavour. Arthur Symons. NOBVV; OxBSP

Wine, the toasts that could not be refused, The. Hedylos, *tr. fr. Greek by* Adrian Wright. GrAn

Wine upon beer, I counsel thee. *Unknown.* FaBoUs

Winemaker's Beat-étude, The. Alfred W. Purdy. MoCV

Wines to Drive Out Melancholy. *Unknown.* CBCK

Wing of Separation, The. Ibn Darraj al-Andalusi, *tr. fr. Arabic by* J. B. Trend. AWP

Wing, or a self-trapping thigh, A. *(LL)* A Fly Caught in a Cobweb. Richard Lovelace. BeJo; CaPo; SeCP

Wing Road. Eamon Grennan. PBCIP

Wing/ torn out of stone. Emblem. Roy Fisher. NBrP

Wingbone of a man's shoulder, The. *(LL)* Super-Brave. Teresa Whitman. LoHo

Winged bull trundles to the wired perimeter, The. C. Day Lewis. *Fr.* Flight to Italy. OxBTC

Winged bulletins issued from frontier outposts. Going Out Through the North Gate of Chi. Pao Chao, *tr. fr. Chinese by* Daniel Bryant. SuSp

Winged Heart, A. Henry Vaughan. *Fr.* Of Life and Death. FaBoRV

Winged in Gold. Euros Bowen, *tr. fr. Welsh by the author.* OBWVE

Wingéd lion on top of that column, The. Notes Made in the Piazza San Marco. May Swenson. CoAP

Winged Man. Stephen Vincent Benét. MoAmPo

Winged Woman. Alma Villanueva. SRLS

Winged woman, feathers. Winged Woman. Alma Villanueva. SRLS

Winged women was saying. Mary's Dream. Lucille Clifton. NALW

Wings. Bible, *O.T., paraphrased by* Sir Thomas Wyatt. *Fr.* Psalms. AWP; FaPON, *ll.* 6–7

Wings, The. Debora Greger. *Fr.* Afterlife, The. BAP-91

Wings. Miroslav Holub, *tr. fr. Czech by* Ian Milner *and* George Theiner. PoSu

Wings, The. Denise Levertov. CAPP; NALW

Wings. *Unknown, tr. fr. Greek by* Barbara Hughes Fowler. HePo

Wings. Judith Wright. CBAP; NOBAu

Wings filmed, the threads of knowledge thicken. The Jam Trap. Charles Tomlinson. MoBrPo

Wings in the Dark. John Gray. NOBVV

Wings of a Wild Goose, The. "Chrystos." GLP

Wings of Time are black and white, The. Compensation. Emerson. AmPP; NOBA

Wings outstretched, a horned owl. Signatures. Daniel Hoffman. VGW

Winifred Waters. William Brighty Rands. OxBChV

Winifreda. *Unknown.* OBEV

Wining at the Eastern Slope tonight. Tune: "Immortal at the River." Su Shih, *tr. fr. Chinese by* Michael E. Workman. SuSp

Wink as they will. Wink most when widows wince. *(LL)* A High-toned Old Christian Woman. Wallace Stevens. CMoP; MoP; NAAL-2; NoAM; NOBA; Poetr; PPP; TAP

Wink at it only with thine eyes. To the Wine Treasurer of the Circuit Mess. Horace Smith *and* James Smith. UV

Winked too much and were afraid of snakes. The Monkeys. Marianne Moore. CMoP; LiTA; MeMAP; NOBA; OxBA

Winkte. Maurice Kenny. GLP

Winner and Waster., *sels. Unknown.*
"Bot then kerpe the king, said, 'Kithe what ye hatten." EnVB

Winners, The. Kipling. *Fr.* Story of the Gadsbys, The. BLPA; FaPoR

Winning of Cales, The. Thomas Deloney. CoMu; OBTV; OxBSS

Winnings. Garrett Kaoru Hongo. OpBo

Winnsboro Cotton Mill Blues, The. *Unknown.* SWP

Wino was eating soup, The. Tornado Soup. A. K. Redwing. VoR

Winsome Torment rose from slumber, rubbed his eyes, and went his way. The Hammam Name. James Elroy Flecker. FaBoBl; PeHV

Sir Winston Churchill advised against suicide. Enigma Variations. David Lehman. NAmP90

Wintah Styles, De. Maggie Pogue Johnson. CBWP-4

Winter. Bella Akhmadulina, *tr. fr. Russian by* Barbara Einzig. BoWoP

Winter. Alexander Barclay. *Fr.* Eclogues. OxBLMV

Winter, *sels.* Robert Bloomfield.
Ploughman's Horse, The. ECEV

Winter. Enid Blyton. BoTP

Winter, *sels.* Charles Cotton.
Winter's Troops. ChTr

Winter. John Davies. AngWe

Winter. Walter de la Mare. ChTr; OAEL-2; OBMV

Winter. Aubrey Thomas De Vere. *Fr.* Year of Sorrow, A. PeIV

Winter. John Lyle Donaghy. BIrV

Winter. Fan Ch'eng-ta, *tr. by* Irving Y. Lo. *Fr.* Seasonal Poems on Fields and Gardens. SuSp

Winter. Hesiod, *tr. fr. Greek by* George Chapman. *Fr.* Georgics of Heisod, The. NOSC

Winter. Richard Hughes. OBMV; OBWVE

Winter. W. D. Landor. BoTP

Winter, The. Morgan Llwyd. *Fr.* 1648. AngWe

Winter. Thomas McCarthy. IB

Winter. Samuel Menashe. GrPl

Winter. Mother Goose. ReMoGo

Winter. Christina Rossetti. BoTP

Winter. Philip Salom. NOBAu

Winter. Shakespeare. *See* When icicles hang by the wall.

Winter. Princess Shikishi, *tr. fr. Japanese by* Hiroaki Sato. PBWP

Winter. Spenser. *Fr.* Faerie Queene, The. GN

Winter. Ruth Stone. BoWoP

Winter. J. M. Synge. NOIV; OBMV; OxBTC

Winter. *Unknown, tr. fr. Irish by* Frank O'Connor. PeIV

Winter, *sels. Unknown, tr. fr. Welsh by* Joseph P. Clancy.
"Wind piercing, hill bare, hard to find shelter." OBWVE

Winter. Sheila Wingfield. EnLoPo

Winter. James Thomson. *Fr.* Seasons, The.

Winter Afternoons in the V & A, Pre-W.W. II. Denise Levertov. CBCK

Winter, and I feel the circles of my world. Robert Polito. BAP-91

Winter and Spring. *Unknown.* BoTP

Winter and Spring have come and gone. In Mourning for His Dead Wife. P'an Yüeh, *tr. fr. Chinese by* Kenneth Rexroth. IMW; OHMPC

Winter and Summer. Stephen Spender. MoAB; MoBrPo

Winter and summer, whatever the weather. The Floor and the Ceiling. William Jay Smith. GoJo; GrPl; OBCA

Winter Anemones. Charles Brasch. *Fr.* Night Cries, Wakari Hospital. PeNZ

Winter Angel. Agnes Nemes Nagy, *tr. fr. Hungarian by* Hugh Maxton. PoSu

Winter,/ at midnight. Weather Nose. Steve Fisher. NGP

Winter at Tomi. Ovid, *tr. fr. Latin by* F. A. Wright. AWP

Winter began with. The Lake of the Woods. Richard Ryan. PBCIP

Winter Billet. Peter Huchel, *tr. fr. German by* Michael Hamburger. PoSu

Winter birds, The. Migration. Pinkie Gordon Lane. BlSi

Winter blows itself out with quick cloud and white. Spring Lambs. David Campbell. *Fr.* Two Songs with Spanish Burdens. FaBoMA

Winter Bouquet. Lewis Turco. EOEF

Winter Burn. Roberta Hill Whiteman. VoR

Winter comes, and under the snow the forest. The Purple Martin. Sun Ching-hsuan, *tr. fr. Chinese. Fr.* Lyrics of the Forest. LHF, *tr. by* Hualing Nieh

Winter comes I walk alone, The. The Winters Spring. John Clare. ArNa; NOBVV

Winter Coming On. Martin Bell, *after the French of* Jules Laforgue. FaBoMo; OBVE; OxBTC

Winter Cricket. John Heath-Stubbs. OBCP

Winter Day. Whittier. *See* Sun that brief December day, The.

Winter Day, A, *sels.* Joanna Baillie.
Morning. ECWP

Winter Daybreak above Vence, A. James Wright. InPS; LCAP; VCAP

Winter Days. Gareth Owen. OBCP

Winter Deepening, The. Richard Wilbur. Son

Winter Downpour. Basho, *tr. fr. Japanese by* Lucien Stryk. ArNa

Winter Drive. James McAuley. PoA

Winter ("Drooping, the labourer-ox.") James Thomson. *Fr.* Seasons, The. FM

Winter: East Anglia. Edmund Blunden. OxBTC

Winter Encounters. Charles Tomlinson. LiTM

Winter Evening ("Just when our drawing-rooms begin to blaze.") William Cowper. *Fr.* Task, The. NOEC

Winter Evening. Walter de la Mare. FaBoRV

Winter Evening. Archibald Lampman. NOBC

Winter Evening Poem. Laura Jensen. LCAP

Winter evening settles down, The. T. S. Eliot. *Fr.* Preludes (I–IV). HeIP; LiTA; MoShBr; NoP; OBMV; Poetr; PPP; SOTW; TwCP; UnPo; VGW; WeW

Winter Fairyland in Vermont. Francis P. Osgood. WeW

Winter fells. Deathward. John Lyle Donaghy. BIrV

Winter Fields. John Clare. EnVR

Winter for a moment takes the mind; the snow. Conrad Aiken. *Fr.* Preludes for Memnon; or, Preludes to Attitude. LiTA; LiTM; OxBA

Winter Galaxy. Charles Heavysege. *See* Stars Are Glittering in the Frosty Sky, The.

Winter Garden. Donald Britton. EOEF

Winter Garden. David Gascoyne. GTBS-P

Winter has a pencil. Pencil and Paint. Eleanor Farjeon. PDV

Winter has at last come. Minamoto no Shigeyuki, *tr. fr. Japanese by* Arthur Waley. *Fr.* Shui Shu. AWP

Winter has come. Haiku (Slightly Overlength). James Laughlin. ArNa

Winter Heavens. George Meredith. NoP

Winter he'll never know — snug in a cozier home. *(LL)* Anacreon's Grave. Goethe. STV

Winter Holding off the Coast of North America. N. Scott Momaday. CDW

Winter Homily on the Calton Hill. Douglas Young. OxBS

Winter Hymn — to the Snow, A. Ebenezer Jones. OBNC

Winter Idyl, A. Whittier. *See* Sun that brief December day, The.

Winter in Durnover Field. Thomas Hardy. MoBrPo

Winter in Étienburgh. Stephen Parker. NYBP

Winter in Lower Canada. Standish O'Grady. *Fr.* Emigrant, The. NOBC

Winter in Minneapolis. Richard Ryan. PBCIP

Winter in Strathearn., sels. John Davidson.

Winter in the country, Southampton, pale horse. Frank O'Hara. Ted Berrigan. UL

Winter in the Fens. John Clare. BoNaP; EnVR

Winter in their cry. *(LL)* Something Told the Wild Geese. Rachel Field. NTCP; OBAP; OBCA; PDV

Winter Intimacies. Andrew Crozier. VaA

Winter is a dreary season. Winter. *Unknown, tr. fr. Irish by* Frank O'Connor. PeIV

Winter is all my year. *(LL)* Idle Verse. Henry Vaughan. MiEL

Winter is almost summer where they grow. *(LL)* Firwood. John Clare. TrGrPo

Winter is cold-hearted. Summer. Christina Rossetti. BoNaP; ELP; PlP

Winter is fallen early. Walter de la Mare. *Fr.* Children of Stare, The. Mes

Winter Is Here. "Katri Vala," *tr. fr. Finnish by* Jaakko A. Ahokas. PBWP

Winter is here with his grouch. *Unknown.* PeLi

Winter is icumen [*or* icummen] in. Ancient Music. Ezra Pound. BXAP; FaBoCo; FaBoPa; FF; HeIL; HeIP; LiTM; NBLV; OBAL; OxBA; PeLV; UV

Winter is passing, and the bells. Spring in the Students' Quarter. Henry Murger, *tr. fr. French by* Andrew Lang. AWP

Winter is past: the light is mild. Paul Verlaine, *tr. fr. French by* Philip L. Miller. RiWo

Winter is the king of showmen. Winter Morning. Ogden Nash. OTCP; TLR

Winter Jacket, The. Sebastian Barry. IB

Winter Joys. Dorothy Graddon. BoTP

Winter Lakes, The. Wilfred Campbell. BoNaP; NOBC

Winter Landscape. John Berryman. LiTA; LiTM; MoAmPo; TwCP

Winter Landscape. Stephen Spender. MoAB; MoBrPo

Winter Landscape with a Girl in Brown Shoes. Sherod Santos. AnAn

Winter Lanscape — Halifax. Douglas Lochhead. NIP

Winter Light. Jon Anderson. AnAn

Winter Longing. Gu Cheng, *tr. fr. Chinese by* Donald Finkel *with* Yi Jinsheng. SpMi

Winter Love, sels. Hilda Doolittle ("H. D.").
"So we were together." FaBoWP

Winter Love. Elizabeth Jennings. BoLoP

Winter Mask. Allen Tate. OxBA; Prf

Winter Memories. Stephen Knight. UnDi

Winter Memories. Thoreau. AmPP; AnAmPo; OxBA

Winter Moon. Langston Hughes. SAmP; SiSoPo

Winter Moon. Maria Luisa Spaziani, *tr. fr. Italian by* Lynne Lawner. PBWP

Winter Morning. Lauris Edmond. PWE

Winter Morning. Frank Flynn. OTCP

Winter Morning. Ogden Nash. OTCP; TLR

Winter Morning. William Jay Smith. BoNaP

Winter Morning, A. James Russell Lowell. *Fr.* Vision of Sir Launfal, The. GN

Winter/ morning./ Snowflakes. Snow Poem. Roger McGough. Spl

Winter morning sunrise, The. Rising in Winter. Hsiao Kang, *tr. fr. Chinese by* Kenneth Rexroth. OHMPC

Winter Morning Walk, The, sels. William Cowper.
"Acquaint thyself with God, if thou wouldst taste." OxAEP-1

Winter must be here, The. What We Can. Ray A. Young Bear. VoR

Winter: My Secret. Christina Rossetti. BrRo; NAEL-2; NOBVV; TEP

Winter my theme confines; whose nitry wind. John Gay. *Fr.* Trivia; or, The Art of Walking the Streets of London. NOEC
(Winter Sports.) ECEV

Winter Night. Louis O. Coxe. NYBP

Winter Night. C. Day Lewis. PoA

Winter Night. Charles Simic. HCAP

Winter Night. Chien Wen-Ti. ArNa

Winter Night. Whittier. *Fr.* Snow-bound; a Winter Idyl [*or* Idyll]. AmPP; GN; NOBA; OxBA; TAP; TrGrPo; WiR

Winter Night. Yüan Mei, *tr. fr. Chinese by* Kenneth Rexroth. OHMPC

Winter Night, A. William Barnes. ChTr; FaBoRV; NOBE; OBNC

Winter Night, A. Priscilla Jane Thompson. CBWP-2

Winter Night, A. James Thomson. *Fr.* Seasons, The. NOBE

Winter night is cold and drear, The. Across the Delaware. Will M. Carleton. PAH

Winter Night: Mount Royal. A. M. Klein. NoAM

Winter Nightfall. Robert Bridges. MoAB; MoBrPo; OBEV; SCGP

Winter Nightfall. J. C. Squire. OxBTC

Winter Nights. Thomas Campion. *See* Now Winter Nights Enlarge.

Winter Noon. Umberto Saba, *tr. fr. Italian by* John Frederick Nims. STV

Winter ("Now, when the cheerless empire of the sky.") James Thomson. *Fr.* Seasons, The. OxBA

Winter Ocean. John Updike. InPK; Poetr

Winter Ode to the Old Men of Lummus Park, Miami, Florida, A. Donald Justice. NGP; WeW

Winter of my infancy being over-past, The. Another Song. Anne Collins. KTR

Winter Offering. D. S. Savage. LiTB

Winter Offerings. Frank Ormsby. PNI

Winter on Black Mingo, sels. *Unknown.*
"Cold, deserted and silent." FiBHP

Winter owl banked just in time to pass, The. Questioning Faces. Robert Frost. GrPl

Winter Paradise. Kathleen Raine. ArNa

Winter Piece, A. Bryant. AmPP; EAP; OxBA

Winter-Piece, A. Ambrose Philips. NOEC; OBTV

Winter-Piece to a Friend Away, A. John Berryman. NOBA

Winter Ploughing. William Everson. NU

Winter Pond. Ben Belitt. NYBP

Winter Portrait. Robert Southey. BoNaP

Winter Quarters. Gwen Harwood. FaBoMA

Winter Rain. Christina Rossetti. BoNaP; WiR

Winter Rains: Cataluña. Philip Levine. NaP

Winter Remembered. John Crowe Ransom. CBLP; HAP; MeMAP; MoAB; NOBA; OxBA; PrIm; UnPo; VGW

Winter Report. Ben Howard. PoA

Winter Scene. Marguerite Young. NU; WPE

Winter seagull, A. Kato Shuson. OBD

Winter Season, A, sels. James Fisher.
"With tramps, and brooms, and stones, a crowd now comes." ScCV

Winter ("See, Winter comes, to rule the varied year.") James Thomson. *Fr.* Seasons, The. NOEC; TEP

Winter Shore, The. Thomas Wade. OAEL-2

Winter Sketches. Charles Reznikoff. PoA

Winter-sky began to frown, The. Stella at Wood-Park. Swift. BIrV

Winter: slippy, drippy, nippy. *(LL)* Spring is showery, flowery, bowery. *Unknown.* FaBoUs

Winter snowes, all covered is the grounde, The. Winter. Alexander Barclay. *Fr.* Eclogues. OxBLMV

Winter Solstice. Peter Blue Cloud. *Fr.* Within the Seasons. HATNAP

Winter Solstice — for Frank. "Asphodel." BrRo

Winter Solstice Poem. Diana Scott. BrRo

Winter Song. David Daiches. NYBP

Winter Song. George Macdonald. NOBVV

Winter Song. Elizabeth Tollet. ECWP; NOEC

Winter Sports. John Gay. *See* Winter my theme confines; whose nitry wind.

Winter Storms, The. Sir William Davenant. *See* Blow! blow! The winds are so hoarse they cannot blow!

Winter Story, A. Matthew Sweeney. IB

Winter Talent, A. Donald Davie. OAEL-2

Winter, the old drover, has brought. Ponies, Twynyrodyn. Meic Stephens. AngWe

Winter They Bombed Pearl Harbor, The. Walter McDonald. ArOW

Winter Time. Robert Louis Stevenson. *Fr.* Child's Garden of Verses, A. EBVV; MoBrPo; OxBChV

Winter time is bleak, the wind. Caoilte. *Unknown, tr. fr. Irish by* Frank O'Connor. PeIV

Winter Tragedy, A. James Thomson. *See* As thus the snows arise, and foul and fierce.

Winter Trees. Sylvia Plath. CAPP; HCAP; LCAP; NMM

Winter trees thrown upwards. Deflowering. Mahmood Jamal. NBrP

Winter Tryst. Mark Van Doren. LiTA

Winter Tuesday, the city pouring fire, A. Coming Home[, Detroit, 1968]. Philip Levine. CAPP

Winter Twilight. Lou Lipsitz. GOYP

Winter Twilight, A. Angelina Weld Grimké. CDC; PoBA; PoNe; ShDr

Winter Twilight, Glowing Black and Gold, The. Delmore Schwartz. NoAM

Winter uses all the blues there are. Blue Winter. Robert Francis. LCAP

Winter Verse for His Sister. William Meredith. NYBP; TAP

Winter Views Serene. George Crabbe. *Fr.* Borough, The. OBNC

Winter Visit, A. Dannie Abse. NoAM

Winter [*or* Wynter] Wakeneth All [*or* Al] My Care. *Unknown.* HAP; MiEL

Winter Walk at Noon, A [*or* The]. William Cowper. *Fr.* Task, The. EnRP; FHYEP; TEP

Winter Walking. Alfred W. Purdy. NoAM

Winter Warfare. Edgell Rickword. OBWP; OxBTC; PAW; PeFWW; PoWW

Winter ("What art thou, frost? and whence are thy keen stores.") James Thomson. *Fr.* Seasons, The. OxBS

Winter ("When from the pallid sky the sun descends.") James Thomson. *Fr.* Seasons, The. OAEL-1; OxBS

Winter will bar the swimmer soon. Swimming Chenango Lake. Charles Tomlinson. FaBoMo; MoP; NoAM

Winter Will Follow. Richard Watson Dixon. *See* Heaving Roses of the Hedge Are Stirred, The.

Winter Winds Cold and Blea. John Clare. GBL; OBNC

Winter Wise. *Unknown.* Spl

Winter with the Gulf Stream. Gerard Manley Hopkins. CMoP; NoAM

Winter without Snow, A. J. D. McClatchy. FYAP

Winter Work. Peter Fallon. CIP; PBCIP

Wintering. Sylvia Plath. NALW; NMM

Winterlong, off La Manche, wind leaning. Gray stones of the gray. Flaubert in Egypt. Robert Penn Warren. NoAM

Wintermusik. Sarah Kirsch, *tr. fr. German by* Wendy Mulford *and* Anthony Vivis. VBLP

Winters at home brought wind. Once in a Lifetime, Snow. Les A. Murray. CBAP

Winters close, springs open, no child stirs, The. John Berryman. *Fr.* Homage to Mistress Bradstreet. NAAL-2; NAs

Winter's Cold. W. R. Rodgers. EnLoPo

Winter's coming on, The. Sanctuary. Dorothy Hewett. CBAP

Winter's Day, A. Joanna Baillie. WoRP

Winter's Fancy, A. Peter Didsbury. PWE

Winter's Frosty Pangs. Henry Vaughan. *Fr.* To His Retired Friend, an Invitation to Brecknock. FaBoRV

Winter's Glance, The. Tomas Tranströmer, *tr. fr. Swedish by* Samuel Charters. AnAn

Winter's Journey, The. Wilhelm Müller, *tr. fr. German by* Philip L. Miller. RiWo

Sels.
By the Stream.
Courage!
Crow, The.
Deluge, The.
Delusion.
Dream of Spring, A.
Frozen Tears.
Good Night.
Gray Head, The.
Guidepost, The.
Hurdy-Gurdy Man, The.
In the Village.
Inn, The.

Last Hope.
Linden Tree, The.
Loneliness.
Mail-Coach, The.
Mock-Suns, The.
Numbness.
Rest.
Retrospect.
Stormy Morning, The.
Weathervane, The.
Will-o'-the-Wisp, The.

Winter's Onset from an Alienated Point of View. Alan Dugan. FF

Winter's Song. *Unknown, tr. fr. Bohemian.* BoTP

Winters Spring, The. John Clare. ArNa; NOBVV

Winter's Tale, The, *sels.* Shakespeare.
"As she liv'd peerless." OxAEP-1
"Give me those flowers there, Dorcas. Reverend sirs." OxAEP-1
"Ha' not you seen, Camillo?" OxBM
"Here's flowers for you." GBL
  Some Flowers o' the Spring ChTr
"I have said/ She 's adulteress; I have said with whom." OxAEP-1
"If you would seek us." OxAEP-1
"Jog On, jog on, the footpath way." FaBoCh; GN; NoSic
  (Merry Heart, A.) EIL; TrGrPo
  (Merry Heart, The.) BoTP
  (Song: "Jog on, jog on, the footpath way.") OxBSP
"Lawn as white as driven snow." NoSic
  (Autolycus as Peddler.) OAEL-1
  (Come Buy! Come Buy!) CBCK; EIL
  (Pedlar, The.) WiR
  (Pedlar's Song, The.) CH
"Shepherdess — / A fair one are you." PoE
"To your owne bents dispose you: you'le be found." FaBoVe
When Daffodils Begin to Peer. ChTr; EIL; FaBoBe; FaBoCh; NoP; NoSic; OxAEP-1; OxBSP; PrIm; SCGP; TFi; UV
  (Autolycus Sings.) NOBE
  (Autolycus's Song ("When daffodils begin to peer").) NOBE; OAEL-1
  (Pedlar's Song, The.) NBLV; OxBoLi; PeLV
  (Song: "When daffodils begin to peer.") PoEL-2

Winter's Tale, A. Robert Patrick Dana. NYBP

Winter's Tale, A. D. H. Lawrence. MoAB; MoBrPo

Winter's Tale, A. Dylan Thomas. CMoP; LiTB; MeMBP

Winter's Tale, A. Andrew Waterman. SCBI

Winter's thunder. *Unknown.* FaBoVe

Winter's Troops. Charles Cotton. *Fr.* Winter. ChTr

Wintertime nighs. Thomas Hardy. *Fr.* In Tenebris. LiTB; MeMBP; NoAM; NOBE; NoP; OAEL-2; PrIm; SCGP

Winterward. William Stafford. SM

Wintry Dawn, *sels.* Meir Wieseltier, *tr. fr. Hebrew by* Warren Bargad *and* Stanley F. Chyet.

Wintry days are with us still, The. Back to the Land. Charles Larcom Graves. NSI

Wintry haw is burning out of season, The. The Haw Lantern. Seamus Heaney. NoAM; PNI

Wintry night, the hearth inhales, A. Remembering Carrigskeewaun. Michael Longley. PBCIP

Winwick, Lancashire. *Unknown.* GBP

Wire. Rod Moran. NOBAu

Wireless. Rodney Bennett. BoTP

Wirikota Wirikota. For the God of Peyote. *Unknown, tr. fr. Huichol Indian by* Jerome K. Rothenberg. STP

Wiring appears to be five years old, The. Richard II. Veronica Forrest-Thomson. VaA

Wisdom. William Cowper. ChIV-1

Wisdom. Phyllis Hanson. GoYe

Wisdom? "Laurence Hope." *See* For This Is Wisdom.

Wisdom. George Sands Johnson. PWR

Wisdom. Hy Sobiloff. VGW

Wisdom. Sara Teasdale. AnAmPo; MoAmPo

Wisdom. W. B. Yeats. TrCP

Wisdom and spirit of the universe! Wordsworth. *Fr.* Prelude [or, Growth of a Poet's Mind], The. CH; EnRP; GN; HAP; NOBE; NoP; NU; OAEL-2; OBNC; OxAEP-2; PoE; SCV

Wisdom found no place where she might dwell. Wisdom's Plight. Bible, Pseudepigrapha. *Fr.* Enoch. TrJP

Wisdom has nothing to do with age. Wisdom. Hy Sobiloff. VGW

Wisdom hath builded her house. The House of Wisdom. Bible, *O.T. Fr.* Proverbs. TrGrPo

Wisdom, innocently the sun rises. Branko Miljkovic, *tr. fr. Serbo-Croatian by* Charles Simic. HSix

Wisdom is better than bread. Nevertheless. Gustav Davidson. GoYe

Wisdom is the finest beauty of a person. *Yoruba Oral Tradition*, tr. by Ulli Beier. WTO

Wisdom is vain, and prophesy. (*LL*) The Conflict of Convictions. Herman Melville. NOBA

Wisdom of æ, The. Thomas McCarthy. PBCIP

Wisdom of Merlyn, The, *sels.* Wilfrid Scawen Blunt.
"Wouldst thou be wise, O Man? At the knees of a woman begin."
OBMV

Wisdom of the Gazelle. George P. Solomos. GoYe

Wisdom of the Streets, The. Gavin Ewart. FaBoBl

Wisdom of the World, The. Siegfried Sassoon. MoBrPo

Wisdom Tooth, The. Jonathan Holden. NAmP90

Wisdom's Plight. Bible, Pseudepigrapha. *Fr.* Enoch. TrJP

Wise, The. Countee Cullen. PoNe

Wise Child, The. Edward Lucie-Smith. PBCV

Wise emblem of our politic [*or* politick] world. The Snail. Richard Lovelace. BeJo; CaPo; OAEL-1
(Snayl, The. PoEL-3

Wise fish digs his silver in, The. Night Catch. Heather McHugh. AmPA

Wise guys, The. Kid Stuff. Frank Horne. PChr; PoBA; PoNe

Wise king dowered with blessings on his throne, The. The Trophy. Edwin Muir. LiTM

Wise Men and Shepherds. Sidney Godolphin. *See* Lord, when the wise men come from far[r].

Wise Men Ask the Children the Way, The. Heine, tr. fr. *German by* Geoffrey Grigson. OBCP

Wise men come here to shit. From a Lavatory Wall. *Unknown*. FaBoEE

Wise men in long white togas come forward during the. Inventions. Miroslav Holub, tr. fr. *Czech by* George Theiner. PoSu

Wise Men of Gotham, The. Thomas Love Peacock. *Fr.* Nightmare Abbey. BXAP; CBNP; FaBoNo

Wise old apple tree in spring, The. Robert Silliman Hillyer. BoNaP

Wise Old Owl, A. Edward Hersey Richards. BLPA; FaBoBe; OxNR; PYC

Wise Owl. Patricia Goedicke. SM

Wise Pallas and the immortal Muses own. (*LL*) Inscription for a Grotto. Mark Akenside. NOEC; PoEL-3

Wise Rochefoucault a maxim writ. Swift. *Fr.* Life and Genuine Character of Dean Swift, The. NOBL

Wise to have gone so early to reward. The Wazir Dandan for Prince Sharkan. *Unknown*, tr. fr. *Arabic by* E. Powys Mathers. *Fr.* Thousand and One Nights, The. AWP

Wise Triangle, A. Vasco [*or* Vasko] Popa, tr. fr. *Serbo-Croatian*. *Fr.* Yawn of Yawns, The. CBNP, tr. by Anne Pennington *and* Charles Simic; CoGr, tr. by Anne Pennington *and* Charles Simic; PoSu, tr. by Anne Pennington

Wise-Unto-Hell Ecclesiast. Past Thinking of Solomon. Francis Thompson. ChIV-1

Wisely a woman prefers to a lover a man who neglects her. Distichs. John Hay. AnAmPo

Wisely and well was it said of him. Addition to Kipling's "The Dead King (Edward VII), 1910." Max Beerbohm. FaBoEE; IHNG

Wisest men that Nature e'er could boast, The. Meditatio Tertia Decima. Francis Quarles. *Fr.* Job Militant. ChIV-1

Wisest of all men lies buried on this spot, The. Sonnet. Daniel Casper von Lohenstein. *Fr.* Arminius. GePo

Wisga. Lew Blockcolski. VoR

Wish, The. Abraham Cowley. *Fr.* Mistress, The. LiTB; NOBE; NoP; NOSC; OBEV; OxAEP-1; SeCV-1; TrGrPo

Wish, A. Matthew Arnold. IHNG

Wish, A. Elizabeth Gould. BoTP

Wish. Lance Henson. CDW

Wish, A. Fanny Kemble. WPE

Wish, A. Laurence David Lerner. FF; OxBTC

Wish, The. Liu Sha-ho, tr. fr. *Chinese*. *Fr.* Family of Plants, A. LHF, tr. by Hualing Nieh

Wish, A. Samuel Rogers. FaPoR; GGP; GTBS; GTBS-P; NOBE; OBEV; OxAEP-2; PlP

Wish, A. J. M. Synge. FaBoEE

Wish, The. Thomas Stanley. AWP

Wish for a Young Wife. Theodore Roethke. MoP; NAAL-2; NoAM; NoP; OxBSP; TAP

Wish for an Overcoat. Alfred Islay Walden. AAP

Wish Foundation, The. Carol Muske. PBCAP

Wish I was in Tennessee. Tennessee. *Unknown*. AmFP

Wish of Manchin of Liath, The. *Unknown*, tr. fr. *Irish by* Kenneth Jackson.

Wish, that of the living whole, The. Tennyson. *Fr.* In Memoriam A. H. H. EBVV, *abr.*; EBVVPR; EnVR; FHYEP; HAP; NoP; OAEL-2, *abr.*; OBNC; PeECV, *abr.*; TOF

"Wish to Be Believed," The. Mona Van Duyn. PoA

Wish to write on petals a message to the clouds of morning. (*LL*) Peonies. Li Shang-yin. PLT

Wishbone, The. Paul Muldoon. CIP; PBCIP

Wished Sunday's come: mirth brightens ev'ry face. White Conduit House. William Woty. NOEC

Wishes. A. C. Child. PoToHe

Wishes. Patty L. Harjo. VoR

Wishes. Georgia Douglas Johnson. ShDr

Wishes. F. Rogers. BoTP

Wishes. Robert Louis Stevenson. OBEV

Wishes. *Unknown*. *See* Said the first little chicken.

Wishes for Her. Denis Devlin. CIP; NOIV

Wishes for My Son. Thomas MacDonagh. TIRV

Wishes for the Supposed Mistress[e]. Richard Crashaw. *See* Whoe'er [*or* Who e'er *or* Who ere] she[e] be[e].

Wishes of an Elderly Man. Sir Walter Alexander Raleigh. FaBoCh; FaBoCo; FaBoEE; FiBHP; NBLV; NOBL; NTP; PeLV

Wishes to His Supposed Mistress[e]. Richard Crashaw. BoLoP; EBEV; ImPo; MeLP; NOSC; OBEV; OxAEP-1; PoEL-2; SeCP; SeCV-1

Wishes. To His (Supposed) Mistresse, *sels.* Richard Crashaw. Specifications for a Perfect Lover. CBCK

Wishful Thinking. Michael C. Blumenthal. HCAP

Wishing. William Allingham. BoTP; FaPON; OHIP; OxBChV

Wishing. John Godfrey Saxe. AnAmPo

Wishing Africa. Marilyn Bowering. NOBC

Wishing Bone Cycle, The, *sels.* Jacob Nibenegenesabe, tr. fr. *Cree Indian by* Howard Norman.
"One time I wanted two moons." STP

Wishing-Caps, The. Kipling. OtMeF

Wishing for roses, I walk through the garden. Summer Garden. "Anna Akhmatova," tr. fr. *Russian by* Stephen Stepanchev. BoWoP

Wishing My Death. *Unknown*. MeEL

Wishing Poem. *Unknown*. NTCP; OxNR; RoPo

Wishing-Well, The. W. W. Gibson. NTP

Wishmakers' Town, *sels.* William Young.

Wispy cuttings lie in rows, The. July in Indiana. Robert Fitzgerald. AiP; NYBP

Wisselton, wasselton, who lives here? Wassailing Song. *Unknown*. OBCP

Wisteria. Philip Levine. ArNa

Wistful,/ they speak of. The People. Robert Creeley. VGW

Wiston Vault. Katherine Philips. NOSC

Wit and Learning., *sels.* James Cawthorn.
"Whoever looks on life will see." ECEV

Wit and Wisdom. Ambrose Philips. OxAEP-1

Wit, transported with enditing, A. A Tale of the Miser and the Poet. The Countess of Winchilsea. ECWP

Wit, Whither Wilt Thou? *Unknown*. EiL

Wit Wonders. *Unknown*. *See* God and Yet a Man, A?

Witch. Patricia Beer. OxBC

Witch, The. Mary Elizabeth Coleridge. BrRo; NALW; OHCV; WPE

Witch, The. Percy H. Ilott. BoTP

Witch, The, *sels.* Thomas Middleton.
"In a maiden-time professed." OxBSP

Witch, The. Santal. RaBo

Witch, The. Robert Southey. WiR

Witch. Jean Tepperman. AIW; NMM

Witch, The. Katharine Tynan. NOBVV

Witch-Bride, The. William Allingham. NOBVV

Witch Burning. Sylvia Plath. CAPP

Witch Doctor. Robert Hayden. MAT; NoAM

Witch Doctor Lady. Nina Simone. Paulette C. White. Jaz

Witch Doctor's Magic Flight, The. Smiler Narautjarri, tr. by Georg von Brandenstein. NOBAu

Witch-elms that counterchange the floor. Tennyson. *Fr.* In Memoriam A. H. H. EBVV, *abr.*; OAEL-2, *abr.*; OBNC; PeECV, *abr.*

Witch flew out on Hallowe'en, The. Oh, Lovely, Lovely, Lovely! *Unknown*. CRH

Witch of Atlas, The, *sels.* Shelley.

Witch of Coös, The. Robert Frost. *Fr.* Two Witches. CMoP; InPS; LiTM; MeMAP; MoAB; MoP; NoAM; NOBA; PoE

Witch of East Seventy-second Street, The. Morris Bishop. NYBP

Witch of Willowby Wood, The. Rowena Bastin Bennett. SiSoPo

Sels.
"There once was a witch of Willowby Wood"
Witch pours the libation, clouds fill the sky, The. Magic Strings. Li Ho, *tr. fr. Chinese* by A. C. Graham. PLT
Witch that came (the withered hag), The. Provide, Provide. Robert Frost. AmPP; ChIV-1; CMoP; HAP; MoAB; MoP; NAAL-2; NoAM; NOBA; NoP; OPOP; PoE; Poetr; PPP; TAP; TFi; TwCP; UnPo; WeW
Witchcraft: New Style. Lascelles Abercrombie. MoBrPo
Witches. Ted Hughes. GoYe
Witches, The. *Unknown. See* Hey-How for Hallowe'en.
Witches and poets co-embrace like fate. Fatales Poetae. Henry Parrot. FaBoEE
Witches' Ballad, The. William Bell Scott. *See* O, I hae come from far away.
Witches' Charm, The. Ben Jonson. *Fr.* Masque of Queens, The. EIL; FaBoCh
Witches' Chasm. Ben Jonson. RB
Witches' Ride, The. Karla Kuskin. PDV; TLR
Witches' Song, The. Ben Jonson. CH
Witches' Spells. Madeleine Edmondson. NTCP
Witches' Wood, The. Mary Elizabeth Coleridge. PBWP
Witch's Ballad, The. William Bell Scott. CoGr; NOBVV; OBEV; PeVV
Witch's Broomstick Spell, The. *Unknown.* ChTr; GBP
Witch's Milking Charm. *Unknown. See* Meare's milk and deer's milk.
Witch's Spell [*or* Witch's Milking Charm], A. *Unknown.* ChTr; GBP
Witch's Work Song, The. T. H. White. FaBoNo
With a China Chamberpot, to the Countess of Hillsborough. Lord Holland. FaBoUs
With a club, Wilma. Fred's Breakfast. David Trinidad. BAP-91
With a Coin from Syracuse. Oliver St. John Gogarty. OBMV
With a cold deep face. (*LL*) The Blizzard. Roger McDonald. NOBAu
With a decent happiness. (*LL*) The Rain. Robert Creeley. CAPP; CoAP; PoE; RaBo; TRP; VGW
With a delusive dream. (*LL*) The Dream. Sir Edward Sherburne. OxBSP
With a fa, la, la. (*LL*) The Challenge. Pope. PoEL-3
With a Fa, la, la, la, la. (*LL*) Song Written at Sea in the First Dutch War (1665), the Night before an Engagement. Charles Sackville. CoMu; EnLoPo; NOBE; OBEV; OBWP; OxAEP-1
With a fate just like mine. (*LL*) Drill Man Blues. George Sizemore. AmFP; WTO
With a fearful shriek, he leaped and fell across the picture — dead. (*LL*) The Face upon [*or* on] the Floor. Hugh Antoine D'Arcy. BeLS; BLPA; FaBoBe; VPP
With a garlande of thornes kene. Christ Complains to Sinners. *Unknown.* MeEL
With a Gasoline can. (*LL*) The Beginning of a Long Poem on Why I Burned the City. Lawrence Benford. TTY
With a gay lady. (*LL*) London Bridge. Mother Goose. CBNP; CH; ChTr; FaBoVe, *diff. vers.*; GBP; OxBoLi; OxNR, *diff. vers.*; ReMoGo
With a Gift of Rings. Robert Graves. GBL
With a glossy rage. Passion. Diane Ward. VBLP
With a Guitar, to Jane. Shelley. EnRP; FHYEP; OAEL-2
With a half-glance upon the sky. Tennyson. *Fr.* Character, A. EBVVPR; Mes
With a handful of weeds I weep in the slanting sun. Boudoir Lament. Yü Hsüan-chi, *tr. by* Geoffrey R. Waters. BoWoP
With a health to each jovial and true-hearted soul. (*LL*) Spanish Ladies. *Unknown.* FaBoCh; OxBSS
With a hey and a heigh and a ho! (*LL*) The Light-hearted Fairy. *Unknown.* BoTP; FaPON
With a hot glide up, then down, his shirts. Ironing Their Clothes. Julia Alvarez. CrSp; VBLP
With a hush in their voices. Country Woman Elegy. Margaret Gibson. CrSp; MT
With a lantern that wouldn't burn. The Draft Horse. Robert Frost. CMoP; HeIP; HoPM; PoE; SAmP; TRP
With a large ax handle tucked in at his waist. A Woodcutter's Ax. P'i Jih-hsiu, *tr. fr. Chinese* by William H. Nienhauser. SuSp
With a Lifting of the Head. "Hugh MacDiarmid." MoBrPo
With a light frost, crouched an outrageous bird. (*LL*) Birdwatchers of America. Anthony Hecht. HoPM; NoAM; NOBA; PPP
With a Little Grin. David Trinidad. BAP-91
With a long stirrup under fern. Craswall. Roland Mathias. OBWVE
With a love a madness for Shelley. I Am 25. Gregory Corso. PoBeRe
With a lucky charm around his throat. Lucilius, *tr. fr. Greek* by Peter Porter. GrAn
With a mind full of Swiss clockmakers. The Innocence of Radium. Lavinia Greenlaw. NWP

With a nice resarvèd sate, says the Shan Van Vocht. (*LL*) Lord Waterford. *Unknown.* ChTr; GBP
With a pale, clear sadness. (*LL*) Autumn. Bella Akhmadulina. BoWoP
With a pale green curly. The Love of Lettuce. Marge Piercy. CAPP
With a pert moustache and a ready candid smile. The Mixer. Louis MacNeice. FaBoTw
With a pint of flour and a sheet of bark. The Limejuice Tub. *Unknown.* NOBAu
With a Presentation Copy of Verses. Martin Bell. PeLV
With a Pressed Flower. James Russell Lowell. AnAmPo
With a pull-through and the .22. Premeditations. Geoff Page. NOBAu
With a pure colour there is little one can do. Morning Glory. Ruth Pitter. FaBoWP
With a pure note he welcomes the evening moon. The Crane. Tu Mu, *tr. fr. Chinese* by John M. Ortinau. SuSp
With a rainbow of silence branching from his lips. (*LL*) Full Fathom Five. A. R. D. Fairburn. PeNZ
With a rank, Arab bloodstain. (*LL*) A Hand of Solo. Thomas Kinsella. CIP; NOIV
With a Rod No Man Alive. Walther von der Vogelweide, *tr. fr. German* by Jethro Bithell. AWP
With a shy pity pouting in the mouth. (*LL*) A la Promenade. Paul Verlaine. AWP; OBVE
With a smiling and a charming little wife. (*LL*) A Shantyman's Life. *Unknown.* AmFP; AS
With a *stake* in his inside! (*LL*) Faithless Nelly Gray. Thomas Hood. BXAP; EnRP; FaBoCo; NOBL; UV, *sh. vers.*
With a thin slice of sky on a hunk of earth. Magic. Aimé Césaire, *tr. fr. French* by Clayton Eshleman *and* Denis Kelly. NegPo
With a very big yawn. Mr. Beetle. Emily Hover. BoTP
With a Violet. John Olaf Paulsen, *tr. fr. Danish* by Philip L. Miller. RiWo
With a violin in the alley grandfather and son disappeared. Beyond Melody. Nathan Alterman, *tr. fr. Hebrew* by Ruth Finer Mintz. MHP
With a wall and a ditch between us, I watched the gate-legged dromedary. The Fruit of the Tree. David Wagoner. NYBP
With a Waterlily. Ibsen, *tr. fr. Norwegian* by Philip L. Miller. RiWo
With a whirl of thought oppressed. The Day of Judgement. Swift. BIrV; ChIV-1; FaBoRV; NOBE; NOEC; OAEL-1; OBSV; PPP; SCGP
With a worthy man. (*LL*) Finally a Love Has Come. Sulpicia. VBLP
With a yellow lantern. Glow-Worms. P. A. Ropes. BoTP
With Acme's and Septimius' life. (*LL*) Acme and Septimius. Catullus. AWP
With afternoon tea-cakes and scones. (*LL*) How to Get On in Society. Sir John Betjeman. NOBL; OBSV; OxBTC; UV
With all a woman's virtues but the pox. Pope. *Fr.* First Satire of the Second Book of Horace, The. OAEL-1; OBSV; PPP
With all a woman's virtues but the pox. Pope. *Fr.* Second Satire of the First Book of Horace Imitated, The. OBSV
With All Deliberate Speed. Don L. Lee. JB
With all its sinful doings, I must say. Italy. Byron. *Fr.* Beppo; a Venetian Story. NOBL, *abr; OBNV, abr; OBSV; PIP*
(Italy versus England. NOBE
With all my heart I am going to work you. (*LL*) O God, my mother, my father, lord of the. Kekchi Maya. EaPr
With all my heart, in truth, and passion strong. The Pride of a Jew. Judah Halevi, *tr. fr. Hebrew* by Israel Cohen. TrJP
With All My Heart, Jehovah, I'll Confess. Henry Ainsworth. AH
With all my will, but much against my heart. Coventry Patmore. *Fr.* Unknown Eros, The. BoLoP; EnLoPo; GTBS-P; NOBE; OBEV; OBNC; PoEL-5; TrGrPo
With all of mankind, towards the light. Yang Lian. EaPr
With all the drifting race of men. Léonie Adams. *Fr.* April Mortality. MoAB; MoAmPo; TrGrPo
With all the heart in my body. Now Jentil Belly Down. *Unknown.* GBP
With all the powres my poor heart hath. The Hymn of Saint Thomas in Adoration of the Blessed Sacrament. Richard Crashaw. (Hymn in Adoration of the Blessed Sacrament.) MeLP
With all the sinister abruptness of. Unhappy Returns. Daryl Hine. PFL
With all these loads of injuries opprest. Dryden. *Fr.* Absalom and Achitophel, Pt. I. EBEV; NoP; OAEL-1; SeCV-2
With an effort Grant swung the great block. Blocking the Pass. Charles Madge. FaBoMo
With an insane. Learning. Earl Simpson. GrPl
With an angry brow and stately tread. The Earthquake of 1886. Josephine D. Henderson Heard. CBWP-4
With Annie gone. For Anne. Leonard Cohen. FF
With anyone to death, comes so far short. Robert Frost. *Fr.* Home Burial. IMW; NAAL-2; OBF; PrIm; SoSe; TAP; TRP

(Temperament.) OBF

With asses' ears, and dirty hands. (*LL*) The Fable of Midas. Swift. APAS

With autumn coming in. Autumn and the Sea. Javier Heraud. TSaS, *tr. by Javier Heraud*

With B. E. F. June 10. Dear Wife. The Letter. Wilfred Owen. OBD

With banked fire to mark the occasion. Family Evening. Daniel Huws. NYBP

With banners and our smiles. Christopher Street Liberation Day, June 28, 1970. Fran Winant. PeHV

With banners furled, the clarions mute. The Night-March. Herman Melville. LiTA

With Bill Pickett at the 101 Ranch. Colleen J. McElroy. NGP

With blackest moss the flower-pots. Mariana. Tennyson. AWP; CBLP; CH; EBVVPR; EnVR; FHYEP; InPS; MeMBP; NAEL-2; NOBE; NoP; OAEL-2; OBEV; OBNC; OxAEP-2; PeVV; PoE; PoEL-5; SCGP; TEP; TFi; TrGrPo; UnPo; WiR

With blameless carriage I lived here. An Epitaph upon a Sober Matron. Robert Herrick. CaPo

With bleeding back, from tyrant's lash. The Fugitive. Priscilla Jane Thompson. CBWP-2

With book in hand to have thy dying day. (*LL*) To Doctor Bale. Barnabe Googe. NoSic

With Bridget and with Nell. (*LL*) A Ballad [*or* Ballade] upon a Wedding. Sir John Suckling. BeJo; CaPo; CoMu; EBEV; EBNV; FaBoBa; InvP; JCP; NoP; OxBM; SeCP; SeCV-1

With bridles in the evening come. (*LL*) At Grass. Philip Larkin. HAP; OxBTC; PlP; RB; WeW

With broken wing they limped across the sky. Reported Missing. John Clifford Bayliss. PoWW

With bruise of lash or stone. (*LL*) Simon the Cyrenian Speaks. Countee Cullen. BPo; ChIV-2; HAP; MoAmPo; TrCP; TTY

With burning fervour. The Crystal. George Barker. LiTM; OBMV

With but foure words, my words, *Thy will be done*. (*LL*) The Crosse. George Herbert. ESCV

With butterflies around their horns. (*LL*) Cows. Peter Kocan. NOBAu

With camel's hair I clothed my skin. Dream. Richard Watson Dixon. EBEV; NOBVV; PeVV; SCGP

With candour I confess my love. *Unknown, tr. fr. Egyptian hieroglyphics by* Ezra Pound *and* Noel Stock. BoWoP

With care in such a world. (*LL*) The Well Rising. William Stafford. NaP; RB

With cheerful mind we yield to men. Frances Gray. FaBoVe

With Child. Genevieve Taggard. AIW; MoAmPo

With Christ above for to be blest. (*LL*) Epitaphium Meum. William Bradford. SCAP

With Christ and All His Shining Train. Thomas Prince. AH

With Christ our head. (*LL*) Farewell to Allen University. Josephine D. Henderson Heard. CBWP-4

With Christopher Smart. Robert Browning. EPCY

With cicada's nymphal skin. The Largess. Richard Eberhart. LiTA

With coat like any mole's, as soft and black. Mole Catcher. Edmund Blunden. OBMV

With Corse at Allatoona. Samuel H. M. Byers. PAH

With Cortez in Mexico. Wilfred Campbell. PAH

With courage seek the kingdom of the dead. The Last Journey. Leonidas of Tarentum, *tr. fr. Greek by* Charles Merivale. AWP; OBD

With courage to endure! (*LL*) The Old Stoic. Emily Brontë. FaPoR; MeMBP; NALW; NOBE; OBEV; OBNC; OxAEP-2; PlP; PoLF; TrGrPo

With crippled Mooimeisjes in the morning. (*LL*) Mooimeisjes. Perceval Gibbon. PeSAV

With Dad gone, Mom and I worked. Adolescence — III. Rita Dove. NoAM

With death doomed to grapple. Epitaph for William Pitt. Byron. FaBoEE

With deathlace tickling my throat. Death-Lace. David Ray. MAT

With deep affection/ And recollection. The Bells of Shandon. Francis Sylvester Mahony. CH; ChTr; GGP; IIP; OBEV; PeIV (Shandon Bells, The. OxAEP-2)

With delicate, mad hands, behind his sordid bars. To One in Bedlam. Ernest Dowson. MoBrPo; OBMV; Son

With Demo I fell in love, of Paphian origins. Philodemus, *tr. fr. Greek by* William Moebius. GrAn

With deportment learnt from samurai films. Glasnevin Cemetery. Michael O'Loughlin. PBCIP

With difficulty persist here and there on earth. (*LL*) Another Epitaph on an Army of Mercenaries. "Hugh MacDiarmid." InPK; MoP; NAEL-2; NoAM; NSI; OBWP; PAW; RB

With difficulty the ship was built. The Critics. Theodore Spencer. NYBP

With Donne, whose muse on dromedary trots. On Donne's Poetry. Samuel Taylor Coleridge. EPCY; InvP; MeMBP; NAEL-2; NoP; OAEL-2; UV

With doubt and dismay you are smitten. Opportunity. Berton Braley. WBLP

With drooping sail and pennant. The White Ships and the Red. Joyce Kilmer. PAH

With each recurrence of this glrious morn. Composed in One of the Valleys of Westmoreland, on Easter Sunday. Wordsworth. ChIV-2

With elbow buried in the downy pillow. Clarimonde. Théophile Gautier, *tr. fr. French by* Lafcadio Hearn. *Fr.* Taches Jaunes, Les. AWP

With elegies, sad songs, and mourning lays. William Drummond of Hawthornden. NOSC

With endless life are crowned. (*LL*) To Live Merrily, and to Trust to Good Verses. Robert Herrick. AWP; BeJo; CaPo; InvP; NOSC; SeCP; SeCV-1

With Esther. Wilfrid Scawen Blunt. *See* He who has once been happy is for aye.

With evening the groom and bride in groundfog. There Should Have Been. Sydney Lea. SM

With ever-yearning love. (*LL*) Die Lotusblume ängstigt. Heine. AWP

With every movement, the soft particles. The Dusting of the Books. Dorothy Hughes. GoYe

With every note/ of the mountain temple. *Unknown, tr. fr. Japanese by* Willis Barnstone. BoWoP

With every rolling stone place me in the breach. Place Me in the Breach. Yehuda Karni, *tr. fr. Hebrew by* Sholom J. Kahn. TrJP

With Eyes at the Back of Our Heads. Denise Levertov. AmPP

With eyes like a lizard. (*LL*) Humanities Lecture. William Stafford. NNaP; NoAM

With fair Ceres, Queen of Grain. Praise of Ceres. Thomas Heywood. *Fr.* Silver Age, The. EIL

With fairest flowers,/ Whilst summer lasts. Shakespeare. *Fr.* Cymbeline. EBEV; RB

With faith I trust in Christ the Lord. Mrs. Saunder's Experience. *Unknown.* AmFP

With falling oars they kept the time. (*LL*) Bermudas. Andrew Marvell. AWP; CH; ChTr; CoGr; ESCV; FaBoCh; FHYEP; GeHe; GN; JCP; NAEL-1; NOBE; NOCV; NoP; NOSC; OBEV; OBTV; PAH; PeECV; PIP; PoE; RB; SCGP; SeCP; SeCV-1; TFi

With farms and villas. (*LL*) Olives and Mountains. Elizabeth Barrett Browning. FaBoPP; OBTV

With favour and fortune fastidiously blest. The Character of Sir Robert Walpole. Swift. FaBoEE; PoE (Two Character Studies.) FaBoEH

With fiery-lashing. Whirlwind. David Rokeah, *tr. fr. Hebrew by* Ruth Finer Mintz. MHP

With fifteen-ninety or sixteen-sixteen. On an Anniversary. J. M. Synge. FaBoEE; NOIV; OBMV; PeIV

With fingers weary and worn. The Song of the Shirt. Thomas Hood. CoGr; EBEvV; EBVV; EnRP; FaPoR; GGP; OHCV; TEP; VPP; WBLP

With flecked feathers and many colors. (*LL*) And I bowed [*or* ich bowede] my body and beheld all about [*or* bihelde al aboute]. William Langland. CTC

With flint in the bosom and guts in the head. (*LL*) The Stars Have Not Dealt Me. A. E. Housman. OxBoLi

With focus sharp as Flemish-painted face. Dome of Sunday, The [*or* A]. Karl Shapiro. CMoP; CoAP; LiTM; MoAB; MoAmPo; NoAM; OxBA

With Fragrant Flowers We Strew the Way. Thomas Watson. *Fr.* Honourable Entertainment Given to the Queen's Majesty in Progress at Elvetham, 1591, The. EIL

With Freedom's Seed. Pushkin, *tr. fr. Russian by* Babette Deutsch. TTY

With ganial foire. Mr. Molony's Account of the Crystal Palace. Thackeray. PeVV

With ganial foire/ Thransfuse me loyre. Mr. Molony's Account of the Great Exhibition. Thackeray. *Fr.* Crystal Palace, The. CBCK

With Garments Flowing. John Clare. GBL

With gingerbread nuts. (*LL*) Tomorrow's the Fair. *Unknown.* GBP

With glass like a bull's eye. Mrs. MacQueen (*or* The Lollie-Shop). Walter de la Mare. BoTP

With God and His Mercy. Carl Olof Rosenius. AH

With God Conversing. Gene Derwood. ImPo; LiTA; LiTM

With gold unfading, WASHINGTON! be thine. (*LL*) To His Excellency, General Washington. Phillis Wheatley. NAAL-1; WPE

With golden reins and jade bridle, a neighing horse. Tune: "Song of a Dandy." Sun Kuang-hsien, *tr. fr. Chinese by* Hellmut Wilhelm. SuSp

With goodbye. (*LL*) Morning. Harry Clifton. IB

With Gorgon's gear and barebill, thongs and fangs. (*LL*) Andromeda. Gerard Manley Hopkins. EBEV; FaBoMo; LiTB; MeMBP; OxAEP-2; SCGP

With leering looks, bullfac'd, and freckled fair. On Jacob Tonson, His Publisher. Dryden. ChTr; FaBoEE; OBSV

With Life and Death I walked when Love appeared. Hymn to Colour. George Meredith. OBNC

With lifted feet, hands still. Going Down Hill on a Bicycle. Henry Charles Beeching. OBEV
(Bicycling Song.) GN

With lightly closed fists and arms partially raised. (LL) The Runner. Walt Whitman. InPK; InPS; SAmP

With Lilacs in My Eye. Lucile Coleman. GoYe

With lions, tigers, leopards, and their kind. (LL) The Greater Cats. V. Sackville-West. CoGr; OBMV; OTCP; Spl

With lips of flame and heart of stone. (LL) Impression du Matin. Oscar Wilde. EBVV; MoBrPo; NAEL-2; NoAM

With little here to do or see. To the Daisy ("With little here to do or see.") Wordsworth. GTBS; GTBS-P
(To the Same Flower.) EnRP

With loitering step and quiet eye. In November. Archibald Lampman. NOBC

With longing I am lad. Unknown. MiEL

With Love among the haycocks. Ralph Hodgson. GoJo

With love exceeding a simple love of the things. Melampus. George Meredith. PoEL-5

With love, upon her bier. (LL) Helen Hunt Jackson. Ina Coolbrith. AmWP

With lovers 'twas of old the fashion. To a Young Lady, with Some Lampreys. John Gay. CBLP; ECEV; FaBoUs; NOEC

With low thunder, with red bushes smooth. Red Rock Ceremonies. Anita Endrezze-Danielson. CDW; VoR

With lullay, lullay, like a child [or childe]. John Skelton. Fr. Garland [or Garlande or Garlands] of Laurel[l], The. InvP; NoSic
(Lullay, Lullay.) ImPo
(Lullay, Lullay, Like a Child.) SCGP
(My Darling Dear, My Daisy Flower.) EnRePo

With maggots and rotten dust and ages of repose. I lie here and plot the agony of resurrection. (LL) Antrim. Robinson Jeffers. BIrV; IIP; NOBA; VGW

With magic in my eyes! (LL) When I Set Out for Lyonnesse. Thomas Hardy. EBVV; InPS; MoBrPo; OHCV; RB

With Mannerly Margery Milk and Ale. (LL) Mannerly Margery Mylk and Ale. John Skelton. AAS; FaBoNo; NAEL-1; NoP

With many a weary step, and many a groan. Homer, tr. fr. Greek by Robert Fitzgerald. Fr. Odyssey. NAWM-1; UV

With marjoram [or margerain] gentle. To Mistress Margery Wentworth. John Skelton. Fr. Garland [or Garlande or Garlands] of Laurel[l], The. EBEV; EnLoPo; EnRePo; NOBE; OAEL-1; OBEV; TrGrPo

With Me My Lover Makes. C. Day Lewis. OBMV

With me, so you call me man. Mo Ghra Thu. Michael Hartnett. PeIV

With me while present, may thy lovely eyes. To Miss Lucy F — —, with a New Watch. George Lyttelton. FaBoUs

With Mercy for the Greedy. Anne Sexton. CAPP; HCAP; TOF; VCAP

With Metaphor. Sarah Wingate Taylor. GoYe

With mighty hand the Holy Lord. The Temptation and Fall of Man. Caedmon, tr. by C. W. Kennedy. Fr. Genesis. AnOE

With modesties enlarged. (LL) Our little kinsmen after rain. Emily Dickinson. FaPON

With Monmouth cap and cutlass by my side. A Long Prologue to a Short Play. Sir Henry Sheeres. APAS

With morning tears thy mournful twilight blesses. (LL) A Letter from a Girl to Her Own Old Age. Alice Meynell. FaBoRV; LiTB; MoBrPo

With Mother Earth. Amen. (LL) Infinite Spirit, when I pray each day. Jennie Frost Butler. EaPr

With much ado you fail to tell. A Critic. Walter Savage Landor. ChTr; FaBoEE

With music strong I come, with my cornets and my drums. Walt Whitman. Fr. Song of Myself. AmPP; LiTA; MoAmPo, abr.; NOBA; OxBA; SOTW, (much abr.); TrGrPo

With my bottle tucked up high away from fumbles. (LL) Zimmer Drunk and Alone, Dreaming of Old Football Games. Paul Zimmer. MAT; PBCAP

With my breath I cut my way through the six forests. Lalleswari, tr. fr. Kashmiri by George Grierson. WPOW, ad. by Deirdre Lashgari

With my hands on my head, what is this here? What Is This Here? Unknown. RoPo

With my heart I worship. St. Thomas Aquinas, tr. fr. Latin by Helen Waddell. MLL

With my looks I am bound to look simple or fast. Magna Est Veritas. Stevie Smith. OxBC

With my name cut into its tail. (LL) Fencing. Anthony Lawrence. NOBAu

With my own hands. (LL) Beneath the Shadow of the Freeway. Lorna Dee Cervantes. BCF; PBCAP

With my red target near the house. (LL) I'm called by the name of a man. Unknown. OxNR

With my teeth. No. Not this pig. (LL) Animals Are Passing from Our Lives. Philip Levine. CAPP; CoAP; NOBA; Poetr; RaBo; SM; TAP

With nerves all shattered and worn. Song of the Sheet. Unknown. BXAP

With nets and kitchen sieves they raid the pond. The Pond. Anthony Thwaite. MAT; NYBP

With never a penny of money. (LL) We Be Soldiers Three. Unknown. ChTr; CoGr; GBP

With new names like Finglas & Ballymun. (LL) Finglas Lilies. Dermot Bolger. IB

With night full of spring and stars we stand. Young Girls. Raymond Souster. HeIP

With night's coming the woodcutter's hut. Night of the Forest. Sun Ching-hsuan, tr. fr. Chinese. Fr. Lyrics of the Forest. LHF, tr. by Hualing Nieh

With noiseless steps good goes its way. The World. Ella Wheeler Wilcox. PWR

With notes as of one who brass is filing. (LL) Spruce and limber yellow-hammer, The. Samuel Taylor Coleridge. FM

With nothing. (LL) Nochebuena. Rosario Caicedo. LoHo

With nothing but the name of a drifter in the blue houses. (LL) Easing My Heart. Tu Mu. PLT

With nothing in our pockets. (LL) Lift-Boy. Robert Graves. NTP; OxAEP-2

With nought to hide or to betray. L'Amitié et l'Amour. John Swanwick Drennan. BIrV

With numberless rich pennons streaming. Unknown. FaBoEH

With oblivion. (LL) Tiny Histories. Mark Svenvold. UTF

With one bold stoke. The Corporal Who Killed Archimedes. Miroslav Holub, tr. fr. Czech by Ian Milner and Jarmila Milner. PoSu; PWE

With one consuming roar along the shingle. Felixstowe; or, The Last of Her Order. Sir John Betjeman. OxBTC

With one finger I followed the grain of the world. (LL) Homegoing. Brigitte Frase. LoHo

With one who safeguards Gwynedd. The Stallion. Tudur Aled, tr. fr. Welsh by Joseph P. Clancy. OBWVE

With only his feeble lantern. Charon's Cosmology. Charles Simic. HCAP; NoP

With Only One Life. Martin Sorescu, tr. fr. Romanian by D. J. Enright and Ioana Russell-Gebbett. PWE

With open ears, and with unfolded arms. (LL) Boldness[e] in Love. Thomas Carew. CaPo; ErPo; SeCV-1

With optimism at the thrill of it. The Departures of Friends in Childhood. Douglas Dunn. OBF

With orange soda and scoops of popcorn. On the Subject of Staying Whole. Tino Villanueva. HCAP

With other women I beheld my love. Ballata: Of His Lady among Other Ladies. Cavalcanti, tr. fr. Italian by Dante Gabriel Rossetti. AWP

With others/ from the neighborhood. Shine. Léon Damas, tr. fr. French by Ellen Conroy Kennedy. NegPo

With paciens thou hast us fed. Farewell! Advent. James Ryman. MeEL

With paste of almonds Syb her hands doth scour[e]. Upon Sybilla. Robert Herrick. CaPo

With patience lows thee quiet and delight. (LL) Barmenissa's Song. Robert Greene. FaBoRV

With peace, let tares and acorns be my food. (LL) The Country-Mouse. Abraham Cowley, after the Latin of Horace. OBVE; SeCP

With peace on earth, good will to men. (LL) Christmas Bells. Longfellow. AH; AnAmPo; BLRP; FaPON; OBCP; PChr, st. 1; WBLP

With perilous stairs/ Between. (LL) The Treehouse. James A. Emanuel. BPo; PoBA

With pinched cheeks hollow and wan. The Outcast. Josephine D. Henderson Heard. CBWP-4

With porcupine locks. The Katzenjammer Kids. James Reaney. MoCV

With proud and tilted chin! (LL) Haven. Donald Jeffrey Hayes. PoNe

With proud thanksgiving, a mother for her children. For the Fallen. Laurence Binyon. CoGr; EBEvV; FaBoEH; NOBE; OBEV; OBWP; OxBTC; PlP

With prune-dark eyes, thick lips, jostling each other. Refugees. Louis MacNeice. LiTB

With reasons for your choice. (LL) O Cuckoo! shall I call thee Bird. F. H. Townsend. UV

With red rosettes. (LL) Rain Forest. Eric Rolls. NOBAu

With reeds and bird-lime from the desert air. On a Fowler. Isidorus, tr. fr. Greek by William Cowper. AWP

With restless step of discontent. Balboa. Nora Perry. PAH

With reverence and submission due. A Petition from the Chain Gang at Newcastle to Captain Furlong the Superintendent. Francis MacNamara. NOBAu

With rhetoric, promising nothing under the sun. (*LL*) Ecclesiastes. Derek Mahon. BIrV; ChIV-1; CIP; PNI

With right all my herte now I you grete. *Unknown*. MiEL

With rue my heart is laden. Samuel Hoffenstein. *Fr*. Mimic Muse, The. NBLV

With Rue My Heart Is Laden. A. E. Housman. *Fr*. Shropshire Lad, A. AWP; BLPL; CMoP; FaPoB; HAP; HeIP; HoPM; ImPo; InPK; LiTB; LiTM; MeMBP; MoAB; MoBrPo; NAEL-2; NoAM; NoP; PoE; Poetr; PrIm; TFi; TrGrPo; UnPo

With sacrifice before the rising morn. Laodamia. Wordsworth. EnRP

With sap running early. Valley Blood. Barry Sternlieb. SM

With Self Dissatisfied. Frederick L. Hosmer. TrPWD

With Serving Still. Sir Thomas Wyatt. EIL; InPK; NoSic; SiPS

With seven matching calfskin cases for his new suits. Home Leave. Barbara Howes. TwCP

With sharpened pen and wit, one tunes his lays. The Praise of New Netherland. Jacob Steendam. PAH

With shimmering shoes of yellow. (*LL*) Sunbeams stream forward, dawn boys, The. *Unknown*. EaPr

With Ships the Sea Was Sprinkled Far and Nigh. Wordsworth. EnRP; SCGP

With shot and shell, like a loosened hell. The Charge at Santiago. William Hamilton Hayne. PAH

With sick and famisht eyes. Longing. George Herbert. ESCV; SeCV-1; UV, *sl. sh. vers.*

With silence and tears. (*LL*) When We Two Parted. Byron. BoLoP; CBLP; EBEvV; EnRP; FHYEP; GTBS; GTBS-P; HoPM; NAEL-2; NOBE; NoP; OBEV; OBNC; PlP; PoLF; SCGP; TFi; TrGrPo; UV

With silent Melancholy. (*LL*) Memory, hither come. Blake. MeMBP; NAEL-2; PoEL-4

With sleep-drunken birds. Safe-Conduct. Ingeborg Bachmann, *tr. fr. German by* Daniel Huws. PoSu

With snort and pant the engine dragged. The Song of the Engine. H. Worsley-Benison. BoTP

With snowy light of moon I cannot you compare. Martin Opitz, *tr. fr. German by* George C. Schoolfield. GePo

With sober pace an heav'enly Maid walks in. Abraham Cowley. *Fr*. Davideis. SeCV-1

With solitude what sorts, that here's not wondrous rife? Michael Drayton. *Fr*. Polyolbion. NOSC

With something of angelic light. (*LL*) She Was a Phantom of Delight. Wordsworth. ArLo; BLPL; EnRP; FaBoBe; FaBV; GTBS; GTBS-P; HeIP; ImPo; LiTB; MeMBP; NoP; OAEL-2; PlP; PoEL-4; PWR; SCGP; TFi; TrGrPo

With songs and honors sounding loud. Edom. Isaac Watts. AmFP

With sorrow here, with wonder on his book. (*LL*) On Ben Jonson. Sidney Godolphin. BeJo; EPCY

With spangles gay and candle light. The Christmas Tree. Isabel de Savitzsky. BoTP

With steadfast heart and true. "Go Forward." "A. R. G." BLRP

With Steve Ovett in Preston Park. Eva Salzman. NWP

With streams, dew, rain. (*LL*) The Flower Pot. David Shimoni. MHP

With such a sound of gently pitying laughter. (*LL*) My Grandmother's Love Letters. Hart Crane. BLPL; CMoP; FaBoBe; InPK; MoAB; NoAM; NOBA; NoP; Poetr

With such a throb does blood. Joy of Knowledge. Isidor Schneider. TrJP

With such compelling cause to grieve. Tennyson. *Fr*. In Memoriam A. H. H. EBVV, *abr*.; OAEL-2, *abr*.; PeECV, *abr*.

With sudden and voracious tooth. The Mansion of Rosamonde. Robert de Bonnières, *tr. fr. French by* Philip L. Miller. RiWo

With sun on his back and sun on his belly. Pig. Paul Éluard, *tr. fr. French by* Kenneth Koch. TTTS

With supping cold plum porridge. (*LL*) Man in the Moon. *Unknown*. CBNP; OxBoLi; OxNR

With sweet surprise, as when one finds a flower. On Finding the Truth. Jones Very. TrCP

With sweetest milk and sugar first. The Nymph and Her Fawn. Andrew Marvell. *Fr*. Nymph Complaining for the Death of Her Faun, The. CH; FaBoCh; FM; HeIP; OAEL-1; PoEL-2; SeCP; SeCV-1 (Girl and Her Fawn, The.) BoTP

With sword unbroken, and with broken heart. (*LL*) Enfant perdu. Heine. AWP

With tall-necked Hesperia and the Medes. A Bridge on the Sangarios. Agathias, *tr. fr. Greek by* Guy Davenport. GrAn

With tearful eye, how frequent have I seen. Mary Latter. *Fr*. Soliloquies on Temporal Indigence. ECWP

With tears thy grief thou dost bemoan. Solomon ibn Gabirol, *tr. fr. Hebrew by* Emma Lazarus. TrJP

With tenderheartedness. I've got this mystic streak in me. (*LL*) Domestic Mysticism. Lucie Brock-Broido. UTF

With Tendrils of Poems. Michael McClure. PoM

With that delight the royal captive's brought. The Lady A. L., My Asylum in a Great Extremity. Richard Lovelace. CaPo

With that he stripped him to the ivory skin. Amorous Neptune. Christopher Marlowe. *Fr*. Hero and Leander. AAS; NOBE; NoP

With that low cunning, which in fools supplies. Character of a Critic. Charles Churchill. *Fr*. Rosciad, The. NOEC

With that more learn'd professor, Ruhnken. (*LL*) Porson's Visit to the Continent. Richard Porson. FaBoCo; FaBoEE

With that, the Wretched Child expires. (*LL*) Henry King, Who Chewed Bits of String, and Was Early Cut Off in Dreadful Agonies. Hilaire Belloc. FaBoNo; FaBoUs; NBLV; OxAEP-2; PeLV

With the Bell. . . . (*LL*) The Canticle of Jack Kerouac. Lawrence Ferlinghetti. PoBeRe

With the blue-dark dome old-starred at night, green boat-lights purring over water, Galilee Shore. Allen Ginsberg. ChIV-2

With the boys busy. Philomena Andronico. William Carlos Williams. FaBoMo

With the breeze and the comfortable shore. (*LL*) The Diver. W. W. Eustace Ross. NOBC

With the bulge and nuzzle to the sea. (*LL*) When God Lets My Body Be. E. E. Cummings. MoAB; MoAmPo; NOBA; PFP

With the colourless tears of Mary Magdalen. (*LL*) Lawrence O'Toole. Aidan Carl Mathews. IB

With the Conchero Dancers, Mission Espada, July. Rosemary Catacalos. AfAz

With the Dawn. Thomas Caulfield Irwin. BIrV; EnLoPo

With the door closed. (*LL*) Hanging Fire. Audre Lorde. NIP; NoAM; NoP; Poetr; TRP

With the early morning tea. The Talking Family. Ruth Pitter. OFC

With the exact length and pace of his father's stride. For a Father. Anthony Cronin. FaBoTw; PeIV

With the exactness of a foreign place. (*LL*) Early Arrival: Sydney. Vivian Smith. NOBAu

With the eye of an anarchist? (*LL*) To Carry the Child. Stevie Smith. MoP; NoAM; NYBP

With the fair Egyptian Queen. (*LL*) Mark Antony. John Cleveland. CBLP

With the festival hour close at hand. King Killi in Combat. Cattantaiyar, *tr. fr. Tamil by* A. K. Ramanujan. PLW

With the fierce rage of winter deep suffused. A Winter Night. James Thomson. *Fr*. Seasons, The. NOBE

With the first gray light of dawn the remnants. Broken Off by the Music. John Yau. EOEF

With the first rains. The Girl Friend Describes the Bull Fight. Uruttiran, *tr. fr. Tamil by* A. K. Ramanujan. PLW

With the gipsies dancing round me. (*LL*) The Gipsy Laddie. *Unknown*. FaBoCh; OxBoLi

With the Grain. Donald Davie. NoAM

With the grave's narrowness, though not its peace. (*LL*) Sick Love. Robert Graves. BoLoP; CMoP; EBEV; GTBS-P; HAP; NOBE; OAEL-2; OxAEP-2

With the green lamp of the spirit. Into the Glacier. John Haines. CoAP; FoLa

With the Green Lute-Ribbon. Wilhelm Müller, *tr. fr. German by* Philip L. Miller. *Fr*. Beautiful Maid of the Mill, The. RiWo

With the heart of a child. (*LL*) I Found Her Out There. Thomas Hardy. CH; CMoP; NoAM; NOBE; OAEL-2; OxAEP-2; PoE; PoEL-5

With the Herring Fishers. "Hugh MacDiarmid." LiTM

With the hooves of a doe. Lenox Avenue. Sidney Alexander. PoNe

With the *it* : to know that I am *it*. (*LL*) Despisals. Muriel Rukeyser. AnAn; NMM; Prf

With the last whippoorwill call of evening. Birmingham. Margaret Walker. PoBA

With the lilt of sunlight in their bones. (*LL*) Hymn to the Sun. Michael Roberts. FaBoCh; OxBTC

With the lost flush of last year's autumn leaves. (*LL*) En Route. Duncan Campbell Scott. NOBC

With the mercury at zero. (*LL*) A More Ancient Mariner. Bliss Carman. AnAmPo; OBAL

With the merry gay coral, ding, ding, a-ding, ding. (*LL*) Dance, Little Baby. *At. to* Mother Goose, *at. to* Mother Goose. ReMoGo

With the Mickey Mouse. The Girl in the Hall. John Stone. MT

With the murmuring sound of rhyme. (*LL*) Birds of Passage. Longfellow. AnAmPo

With the music up high. Snake-Back Solo. Quincy Troupe. BCF

With the nice Caution of a sword between. (*LL*) The Antiplatonic[k]. John Cleveland. CBLP; NOSC; SeCP

With the night half over. Philodemus, *tr. fr. Greek by* William Moebius. GrAn

With the old kindness, the old distinguished grace. Upon a Dying Lady. W. B. Yeats. LiTB; UnPo

With the open eyes of their dead fathers. War. Andrei Voznesensky, *tr. fr. Russian by* William Jay Smith *and* Vera Dunham. RB

With the other husks of summer. (*LL*) The Dragonfly. Louise Bogan. HeIP; Poetr

With the Pawness, lying low,/ Lying low. (*LL*) The Flower-fed Buffaloes. Vachel Lindsay. ChTr; CMoP; FaPON; GoJo; MoAmPo; NOBA; OBAP; OBCA; PoE; RB; RFM; TRP; VGW

With the Quangle Wangle Quee. (*LL*) The Quangle Wangle's Hat. Edward Lear. CBNP; EBEV; PeVV

With the Scotch lords at his feet. (*LL*) Sir Patrick Spens [*or* Spence]. Unknown. AmFP; AWP; BXAP; CH; ClHu, *diff. vers.*; EBEV; ELP; EnRP; EnSB; ESPB; FaBoBa; FaBoCh; FaPoR; FF; GGP; GN; GoJo; HAP; HeIL; HoPM; InPK; InPS; InvP; LiTB; NAEL-1; NIP; NOBE; NoP; OAEL-1; OBEV; OBSP, (*diff. vers.*); OtMeF; OxBB; OxBS; PoE; PoEL-1; PPP; PrIm; RB; ScCV; SCGP; TFi; TrGrPo; UnPo; WeW

With the Shell of a Hermit Crab. James Wright. NoP; SM

With the ship burning in their eyes. Survivors. Alan Ross. PAW

With the shrewd and upright man. Fool and False. Unknown, *tr. fr. Sanskrit by* Arthur Ryder. Fr. Panchatantra, The. AWP

With the slow smokeless burning of decay. (*LL*) The Wood-Pile. Robert Frost. AnAmPo; InPK; LiTA; NAAL-2; NoAM; NoP; SAmP; VGW

With the spring flowers I likewise am. The Bird, the Bird, the Bird. Robert Creeley. Jaz

With the squatter's daughter. (*LL*) Song for the Cattle. David Campbell. NOBAu

With the sweet food she makes. (*LL*) How Doth the Little Busy Bee. Isaac Watts. FaPON; HoPM

With the swinging rainbow on his shoulder. (*LL*) Legend. Judith Wright. NOBAu; NTP; PAW; RB

With the thinking of winter. The Cook. Ray A. Young Bear. CDW

With the tree frogs who live there. (*LL*) In the Mountain Village. Wang Hung Kung. OHMPC

With the vast Sun's impetuous race. (*LL*) On the Infrequency of Celia's Letters. William Hammond. CBLP

With the voices of this land. (*LL*) To Learn How to Speak. Jeremy Cronin. PeSAV

With the want of true grammar, good English, or sense. (*LL*) An Excellent New Ballad Giving a True Account of the Birth and Conception of a Late Famous Poem Called the Female Nine. Charles Sackville. APAS

With the wasp at the innermost heart of a peach. A Scherzo. Dora Greenwell. NOBVV

With Thee a moment! Then what dreams have play! Desire. "Æ." OBMV; TIRV; TrPWD

With thee conversing, I forget all time. Milton. *Fr.* Paradise Lost. EPCY; UV; WiR

(Eve Speaks to Adam.) ArLo; ChTr; GBL

(Eve to Adam.) TrGrPo

With thee, O Master, let me live! (*LL*) O Master, Let Me Walk with Thee. Washington Gladden. AH; PWR; WGRP

With their boxing-glove muzzles. Cattle. Peter Skrzynecki. CBAP

With their eager feet. (*LL*) Case Study. Gayle Kaune. LoHo

With their feet in the earth. Tall Trees. Eileen Mathias. BoTP

With their good will. (*LL*) L'Envoy: To His Book. John Skelton. EnRePo

With their lithe, long, strong legs. Bullfrog. Ted Hughes. NYBP; RFM

With their own personality. (*LL*) Willow Eyebrows. Chao Luan-luan. WPC

With their respective lions. Sea Unicorns and Land Unicorns. Marianne Moore. NALW

With their sealed lips. (*LL*) Islands. Nicholas Hasluck. NOBAu

With their specs on . . . (etc). (*LL*) Maggot Song. Unknown. NOBAu

With their stares others tell me. Handicaps. Bob Henry Baber. ETG

With these green guests around. Who Says That Drought Was Here? Niyi Osundare. HBAPE

With these heaven-assailing spires. New York. "Æ." OBMV

With these poor offerings, a man like thee. (*LL*) To Leigh Hunt, Esq. Keats. EnRP; Son

With thine horses through the sea! (*LL*) A Ballad of the French Fleet. Longfellow. PAH

With this ambiguous earth. Christ in the Universe. Alice Meynell. MoBrPo; NOBE; OxAEP-2

With this, my derisive voice. (*LL*) Seven Sides and Seven Syllables. Edouard J. Maunick. NegPo

With thise maner yiftes the goddesse Rome the princys herte moevid. Rome Araieth Stilico in Vesture of the Consul. Claudian, *tr. fr. Latin by* Osborn Bokenham. *Fr.* De Consulatu Stilichonis. OxBLMV

With throbbings of noontide. (*LL*) I Look into My Glass. Thomas Hardy. EBEV; FaBoTW; HAP; NAEL-2; NOBE; NOBVV; NoP; OxAEP-2; OxBSP; PrIm; SCV; WeW

With thy rugged, ice-girt shore. Alaska. Mary Weston Fordham. AmWP; CBWP-2

With thy small stock, why art thou venturing still. To a Weak Gamester in Poetry. Ben Jonson. JCP

With Timbrels. Bible, Apocrypha. *Fr.* Judith. TrJP

With time/ and space. The Poet the Dreamer. Norman Jordan. NBV

With toilsome steps I pass through life's dull road. Addressed to ———. Lady Mary Wortley Montagu. ECWP

With topsy turvy signs of screamy play. (*LL*) After Tennyson. Edward Lear. FaBoNo

With torches I have wandered the dark poppy world. The Double Axe. Anne Hazlewood-Brady. IHMS

With tramps, and brooms, and stones, a crowd now comes. James Fisher. *Fr.* Winter Season, A. ScCV

With treble vivas and limp hedgerow flags. The Vanquished. Charles Eglington. PeSA

With trembling fingers did we weave. Tennyson. *Fr.* In Memoriam A. H. H. EBVV, *abr.*; FHYEP; OAEL-2, *abr.*; PeECV, *abr.*

With trew love a thousandfold. (*LL*) The One I Love Is Gone Away. Unknown. MeEL

With troubled heart and trembling hand I write. In Memory of My Dear Grandchild [Anne Bradstreet]. Anne Bradstreet. BoWoP; NAAL-1; TrCP

With true adoration shall lisp to Thy praise. (*LL*) The Majesty and Mercy of God. Sir Robert Grant. OHIP; WGRP

With trumpets clap and syphilis. (*LL*) Come, Gaze with Me upon This Dome. E. E. Cummings. NoAM; OxBA

With twenty mortal foes. (*LL*) Let not the sluggish sleep. Unknown. OxBSP

With Two Fair Girls. Unknown, *tr. fr. Greek by* Robert C. MacGregor. ErPo

With two strange fires of equal heat possest. Love and Jealousy. Sir Philip Sidney. *Fr.* Arcadia. SiPS

With two white roses on her breasts. A Brown Girl Dead. Countee Cullen. TAP

With us ther was a doctour of phisik. Chaucer. *Fr.* Canterbury Tales, The. EnVB; FHYEP; NoP; OAEL-1; PPP, *abr.*

With useless venom. (*LL*) In This Murky Tomb. Giussepe Carpani. RiWo

With Usura. Ezra Pound. *Fr.* Cantos. CMoP; LiTM; MeMAP; NAAL-2; NOBA; PoE

With vague attributes, they all wander in here. The Stranger in the Corridor. John Ash. SCBI

With walking sick, with curtseys lame. The Visit. Mary Leapor. ECWP

With walloping tails, the whales off Wales. The Whales off Wales. X. J. Kennedy. OBCA

With what a childish and short-sighted sense. Danger. Helen Hunt Jackson. AmWP

With what a gentle sound. September. H. Cordelia Ray. CBWP-3

With what anguish of mind I remember my childhood. The Old Oaken Bucket. Unknown. BLPA; WBLP

With what attentive courtesy he bent. The Guitarist Tunes Up. Frances Cornford. SoSe

With what attractive charms this goodly frame. Mark Akenside. *Fr.* Pleasures of Imagination, The. EnRP

With what Concern I sat and heard your Play. To My Much Esteemed Friend on Her Play Call'd Fatal-Friendship. Lady Sarah Piers. KTR

With what deep murmurs through time's silent stealth. The Waterfall [*or* Water-Fall]. Henry Vaughan. AngWe; ESCV; FaBoPP; GeHe; MeLP; NAEL-1; NOBE; NOCV; NoP; NOSC; OBWVE; OxAEP-1; PoEL-2; PrIm; SeCV-1; WiR

With what frivolity we have pared them/ Like toenails, clipped them like ends of/ Split hair. (*LL*) Hypocrite Women. Denise Levertov. CAPP; MAT; NALW; NMM; PoM

With what, O Codrus! is thy fancy smit? Edward Young. *Fr.* Love of Fame, the Universal Passion. OBSV

With what sharp checks I in myself am shent. Sir Philip Sidney. *Fr.* Astrophel and Stella. AAS; ESo, *sl. abr.*; GGP; HeIL, *Sonnets, I–CVIII and 11 Songs*; NAEL-1; NoSic; Poetr; SCGP, *Sonnets, I–CVIII and 11 Songs*; SiPS, *Sonnets, I–CVIII and 11 Songs*; SiPSBD, *Sonnets, I–CVIII and 11 Songs*

With what thou gavest me, O Master. Equipment. Paul Laurence Dunbar. TrPWD

With what voice. Spider. Basho, *tr. fr. Japanese.* TTTS

With which I worship thine. *(LL)* I fear thy kisses, gentle maiden. Shelley. GTBS; GTBS-P

With which we were christenèd. *(LL)* As Joseph Was a-Walking [*or* a-Waukin']. *Unknown.* BoTP; OHIP

With wild surprise/ Four great eyes. The Christmas Tree in the Nursery. Richard Watson Gilder. OHIP

With wine and words of love and every vow. Seduced Girl. Hedylos, *tr. fr. Greek by* Louis Untermeyer. BoLoP; ErPo

With wings held close and slim neck bent. Swans. Leonora Speyer. FYAP

With woman's form and woman's tricks. To Miss ――――. Thomas Moore. OxBSP

With words too sad and strange to syllable. *(LL)* Two in August. John Crowe Ransom. AWP; MeMAP; OxBA; PPP

With worms eternally. *(LL)* To the Oaks of Glencree. J. M. Synge. MoBrPo; NOIV; PeIV

With wrinkled hide and great frayed ears. Gunga. Rachel Field. *Fr.* Circus Garland, A. OBCA

With yellow pears and full. Friedrich Hölderlin. *See* With yellow pears leans over.

With yellow pears leans over. Half of Life. Friedrich Hölderlin, *tr. fr. German by* James Blair Leishman. ChTr; OBVE
(With yellow pears and full.) ArNa, *tr. by* John White

With You. Anthony Barnett. VaA

With You. David Diop, *tr. fr. French by* Ellen Conroy Kennedy. NegPo

With you a part of me hath passed away. George Santayana. *Fr.* To W. P. TrGrPo

With you and for you. *(LL)* Plants and Animals in the Garden. Wendy Johnson. EaPr

With you away — despair! Rudaki, *tr. fr. Persian by* Omar S. Pound. ArPe

With you, fair maid. *(LL)* The Fair Maid of Amsterdam. *Unknown.* OxBoLi; PeLV; RB

With you first shown to me. William Barnes. EnLoPo

With you for mast and sail and flag. The Narrow Sea. Robert Graves. FaBoEE; FaBoMo

With you here at Mertu. *Unknown, tr. fr. Egyptian hieroglyphics into Italian by* Boris de Rachewiltz; *English vers. by* Ezra Pound *and* Noel Stock. PBWP

With you I have everything — without you nothing. *(LL)* You Are Alone My Evil and My Good. Louise Labé. VBLP

With you I have refound my name. With You. David Diop, *tr. fr. French by* Ellen Conroy Kennedy. NegPo

With you, I know, my offering will find grace. Ben Jonson. *Fr.* Epistle to Elizabeth, Countess of Rutland. JCP

With your beautiful hair and seemly. *Unknown, tr. fr. Greek by* Kenneth Rexroth. PGA

With your cleansing winds. *(LL)* O our Father, the Sky, hear us. *Unknown.* EaPr

With your clothes on the chair. The Silent Marriage. James Simmons. PWE

With your fair eyes a charming light I see. Love, the Light-Giver [*or* To Tommaso de' Cavalieri]. Michelangelo, *tr. fr. Italian by* John Addington Symonds. AWP; PeHV

With your song of Caty-did. *(LL)* To a Caty-did. Philip Freneau. EAP; TAP

With your wine jars open. Farewell to Pari's Hill. Kapilar, *tr. fr. Tamil by* A. K. Ramanujan. PLW

Withal a meager man was Aaron Stark. Aaron Stark. E. A. Robinson. MeMAP; MoAB; MoAmPo; Son

Withdrawal, The. Robert Lowell. NoP

Withdrawing from the amorous grasses. The Snake. Kenneth Mackenzie. FaBoMA

Withdrawn from layers of upper air, ice-blue and clear. Suburb Hilltop. Richard Moore. NYBP

Withered Flowers. Wilhelm Müller, *tr. fr. German by* Philip L. Miller. *Fr.* Beautiful Maid of the Mill, The. RiWo

Withered flowers fill the courtyard. A Sorrow in the Harem. Wang Ch'ang-ling, *tr. fr. Chinese by* Kenneth Rexroth. OHMPC

Withered grass on the plain. Tune: "Song of Dandy" — Hunting in Autumn. Na-lan Hsing-te, *tr. fr. Chinese by* Bruce Carpenter. SuSp

Withered leaves that drift in Russell Square, The. Drilling in Russell Square. Edward Shanks. OBMV

Withered Rose, A. "Yehoash," *tr. fr. Yiddish by* Isidore Goldstick. TrJP

Withered Tree, A. Han Yü, *tr. fr. Chinese by* A. C. Graham. PLT

Withered vines, old trees, crows at dusk. Tune: "Sky-clear Sand" — Autumn Thoughts. Ma Chih-yüan, *tr. fr. Chinese by* Sherwin S. S. Fu. SuSp

Withering grass knows not its needs. After the Rain. Edward A. Collier. BLRP

Withering plum blossoms by the wayside station. Tune: "Treading on Grass." Ou-yang Hsiu, *tr. fr. Chinese by* An-yan Tang. SuSp

Withering, shrivelling, dancing. Night Street. Tuo Ssu, *tr. fr. Chinese by* Kenneth Rexroth *and* Ling Chung. WPC

Withheld. Ina Coolbrith. AmWP

Within — / The beaten pride. Uncle Tom. Langston Hughes. SAmP

Within a budding grove. Spring: The Lover and the Birds. William Allingham. OBNC

Within a circle of one meter. Nanao Sakaki. EaPr

Within a copse, I met a shepherd-maid. Ballata: Concerning a Shepherd-Maid. Cavalcanti, *tr. fr. Italian by* Dante Gabriel Rossetti. AWP

Within a dark and cheerless hut. The Old Saint's Prayer. Priscilla Jane Thompson. CBWP-2

Within a delicate grey ruin. The Vestal Lady on Brattle. Gregory Corso. Poetr

Within a dream. *(LL)* Vitae Summa Brevis Spem Nos Vetat Incohare Longam. Ernest Dowson. AWP; ChTr; EBVV; FaBoRV; HAP; NOBE; NoP; OBEV; OHCV; OxBSP; PeVV; TFi; TrGrPo; WGRP

Within a garden all alone. Mary, The Mother of Jesus. Ada Belle Gardner. PWR

Within a gloomy dimble she doth dwell. Mother Maudlin the Witch. Ben Jonson. *Fr.* Sad Shepherd, The. ChTr

Within a greenwood sweet of myrtle savour. *Unknown, tr. fr. Italian.* GBL

Within a native hut, ere stirred the dawn. Nativity. Gladys May Casely Hayford. CDC; PBA; TTY

Within a thick and spreading hawthorn bush. The Thrush's Nest. John Clare. BoTP; GoJo

Within an open curled Sea of Gold. A Vision. Lord Herbert of Cherbury. SeCP

Within and around the earth, within and around the hills. Alfonso Ortiz. EaPr

Within Heaven's circle I had not guessed at this. The Flight into Egypt. Peter Quennell. ImPo; LiTB; LiTM

Within her gilded cage confined. The Contrast; the Parrot and the Wren. Wordsworth. FM

Within Her Hair. "E. C." *Fr.* Emaricdulfe. Son

Within her hair Venus and Cupid sport them. Emaricdulfe. "E. C." EIL

Within his office, smiling. The Dove. Victor James Daley. NOBAu

Within King's College Chapel, Cambridge. Wordsworth. *See* Tax not the royal Saint with vain expense.

Within My Breast. Sir Thomas Wyatt. EnRePo

Within my breast I never thought it gain. Within My Breast. Sir Thomas Wyatt. EnRePo

Within my casement came one night. The Dawn of Love. H. Cordelia Ray. BlSi; CBWP-3

Within my garden, rides a bird. Emily Dickinson. AmPP

Within my head, aches the perpetual winter. Winter and Summer. Stephen Spender. MoAB; MoBrPo

Within My Heart. Judah al-Harizi, *tr. fr. Hebrew.* TrJP

Within my heart a stab I felt. En las Internas Entrañas. St. Theresa of Avila, *tr. fr. Spanish by* Father Benedict Zimmerman. WPOW

Within my heart for ever. *(LL)* Constancy. Sir Thomas Wyatt. SiPS

Within my heart Love himself made Heliodora. Meleager, *tr. fr. Greek by* Barbara Hughes Fowler. *Fr.* Epigrams. HePo

Within my house of patterned horn. The Tortoise in Eternity. Elinor Wylie. FaPON

Within one roome, being large and long. Thomas Deloney. *Fr.* Pleasant History of Jack of Newbury, The. FaBoEH

Within our happy castle there dwelt one. Stanzas Written in My Pocket Copy of Thomson's "Castle of Indolence." Wordsworth. EnRP

Within our married miracle. *(LL)* The Trance. Stephen Spender. OxBM

Within that porch, across the way. The Cat. W. H. Davies. CRH; NOBE

Within the Casket of thy Coelick Breast. An Acrostick on Mrs. Winifret Griffin. John Saffin. SCAP

Within the circles of our lives. Wendell Berry. EaPr

Within the Circuit of This Plodding Life. Thoreau. *See* Within the circuit of this plodding life.

Within the circuit of this plodding life. Winter Memories. Thoreau. AmPP; AnAmPo; OxBA
(Within the Circuit of This Plodding Life.) NOBA; PFP

Within the covert of a shady grove. Love Sleeping. Plato, *tr. fr. Greek by* Thomas Stanley. AWP; FaBoEE

Within the Dream You Said. Philip Larkin. InPS

Within the dungeon's noxious gloom. The Cell. John Thelwall. NOEC

Without thought, without remorse, without shame. Walls. C. P. Cavafy, *tr. fr. Modern Greek by* Rae Dalven. TrJP

Without Violence. Pattiann Rogers. SoCa

Without warning their nest. A Call to Action. Ch'iu Chin, *tr. fr. Chinese by* Kenneth Rexroth *and* Ling Chung. PBWP; WPC

Without you. Four, Being a Prayer to the Western Wind. Ken Smith. *Fr.* Tristan Crazy. PWE

Without you and your poetry. *(LL)* Alas! 'Tis Very Sad to Hear. Walter Savage Landor. GTBS-P; WeW

Without you and your poetry. *(LL)* William Gifford. Walter Savage Landor. FaBoEE; GTBS-P

Without You I Am. Diana Der Hovanessian. LoHo

Withouten Time is no erthely thinge. Time and Eternity. Stephen Hawes. *Fr.* Pastime of Pleasure, The. PoEL-1

Withouten you. Little Elegy. Elinor Wylie. IMW

Witlesse gallant, a young wench that woo'd, A. Michael Drayton. *Fr.* Idea. AAS; ESo

Witness. John Montague. CIP

Witness, The. Monique Pasternak. BTR

Witness how it comes to pass. Epitaph in Sirmio. David Morton. PoLF

Witness the man who raved at the wall as he wrote his *questions to Heaven.* *(LL)* Don't Go Out of the Door. Li Ho. PLT

Witness to Death. Richmond Lattimore. VGW

Witnesses, The. X. J. Kennedy. PChr

Witnesses, The. Longfellow. GOA

Witnesses. W. S. Merwin. LCAP

Witnesses, The, *sels.* Clive Sansom. "It was a night in winter." PChr

Wits, The. Sir John Suckling. *See* Session[s] of the Poets, A ("A session was held the other day.")

Wit's Abuse. Anne Wharton. KTR

Wit's an unruly engine, wildly striking. The Church-Porch. George Herbert. OBF

Wit's End Corner. Antoinette Wilson. BLRP

Wit's forge and fire-blast, meaning's press and screw. *(LL)* On Donne's Poetry. Samuel Taylor Coleridge. EPCY; InvP; MeMBP; NAEL-2; NoP; OAEL-2; UV

Wit's Pilgrimage., *sels.* John Davies of Hereford. Some Blaze the Precious Beauties of Their Loves. Son

Wit's queen (if what the poets sing be true). Upon a Girl of Seven Years Old. Pope. OxBSP

Wittgenstein and Engelmann. Gwen Harwood. OBF

Witty as Horatius Flaccus. On Seeing Francis Jeffrey Riding on a Donkey. *At. to* Sydney Smith. FaBoEE

Wives, The. Donald Hall. CoAP

Wives in the Sere. Thomas Hardy. NOBE; NOBVV

Wives of Mafiosi, The. Erica Jong. AmPA

Wives of Spittal, The. *Unknown.* GBP

Wizard of Alderley Edge, The. Peter Coe. OBET

Wizard Oil. *Unknown.* AS

Wizards. Alonzo Gonzales Mó, *tr. fr. Mayan by* Allan F. Burns. STP

Wizard's Funeral, The. Richard Watson Dixon. ELP; NOBVV; PeVV

Wm. Brazier. Robert Graves. NOBL

Wo, his purple an' linen, too. Dives and Laz'us. *Unknown.* TTY

Wo worth the days! The days I spent. A Few Lines to Fill up a Vacant Page. John Danforth. SCAP

Woak Hill. William Barnes. EnVR

Wobbling to his feet, the dumb bull, Copernicus. *(LL)* The First Birth. Rodney Jones. MT

Wobbly Rock. Lew Welch. PoM

Wo'd yee have fresh Cheese and Cream? Fresh Cheese and Cream. Robert Herrick. CBLP

Wodwo. Ted Hughes. CBNP; MoP; NoAM

Woe for the brave ship *Orient!.* The Brave Old Ship, the *Orient.* Robert Traill Spence Lowell. FaBoBe

Woe Is Me! Bible, *O.T. Fr.* Micah. TrJP

Woe is me, my soul says, how bitter is my fate. Rachel Morpurgo, *tr. fr. Hebrew by* Robert Alter. PBWP

Woe is me, my stolen daughters! *(LL)* Gone, gone — sold and gone. Whittier. AWP; PoNe

Woe: lightly to part with one's soul as the sea with its foam! Tarpeia. Louise Imogen Guiney. AmWP

Woe Then to the Gossips. Meinloh von Sevelingen, *tr. fr. German by* J. W. Thomas. GePo

Woe then to the gossips! They show their evil will. Woe Then to the Gossips. Meinloh von Sevelingen, *tr. fr. German by* J. W. Thomas. GePo

Woe, this tumbleweed. A Song of Lament. Ts'ao Chih, *tr. fr. Chinese by* Hans H. Frankel. SuSp

Woe to him by this world enticed. A Child in Prison. Gofraidh Fionn O'Dalaigh. NOIV

Woe to him who slanders women. Gerald Fitzgerald, Earl of Desmond. NOIV

Woe worth thee, woe worth thee, false Scottlande! Earl Bothwell. *Unknown.* ESPB

Woefully Arrayed. *At.* to John Skelton. ChIV-2; ChTr; EnRePo

Woefully arrayed. *(LL)* Woefully Arrayed. *At.* to John Skelton. ChIV-2; ChTr; EnRePo

Woe's me! by dint of all these sighs that come. Dante, *tr. fr. Italian by* Dante Gabriel Rossetti. *Fr.* Vita Nuova, La. AWP

Wofully Araide. *At.* to John Skelton. *See* Woefully Arrayed.

Wofully Araide. *Unknown.* MeEL

Woke up crying the blues. A Day in the Life of a Poet. Quincy Troupe. NBV

Woken, I lay in the arms of my own warmth and listened. First Things First. W. H. Auden. CBLP; NYBP

Woken, we dressed. The Statue. Matthew Sweeney. IB

Wol ze here a wonder thynge. Riddles Wisely Expounded. *Unknown.* ESPB

Wolcum be thu, hevene kyng. Welcome Yule. *Unknown.* CH

Wold Clock, The. William Barnes. FaBoVe

Wold clock's feäce is still in pleäce, The. The Wold Clock. William Barnes. FaBoVe

Wolde God that it were so. *Unknown.* MiEL

Wolf. Peter Blue Cloud. HATNAP; VoR

Wolf, The. Georgia Roberts Durston. TLR

Wolf, The, *sels.* H. Leivick, *tr. fr. Yiddish by* Benjamin *and* Barbara Harshav.

Wolf. Kenneth Rexroth. *Fr.* Bestiary, A. NNaP; OBAL

Wolf also shall dwell with the lamb, The. Bible, *O.T. Fr.* Isaiah. PDV (God's Rule.) FM (Peaceable Kingdom.) FaPON

Wolf-Ancestry. Vasco [*or* Vasko] Popa, *tr. fr. Serbo-Croatian. TSaS, tr. by* Charles Simic

Wolf and the Dog, The. La Fontaine, *tr. fr. French by* Elizur Wright. OBVE

Wolf and the Lambs, The. Ivy O. Eastwick. BoTP

Wolf and the Stork, The. La Fontaine, *tr. fr. French by* Marianne Moore. FM; OBVE

Wolf at the Door. Alma Villanueva. AfAz

Wolf "Aunt". Maurice Kenny. HATNAP

Wolf-Boy. David Malouf. CBAP

Wolf brother, so my old people called you. Malsum. Joseph Bruchac. ETG

"Wolf!" cried my cunning heart. The True Encounter. Edna St. Vincent Millay. OxBSP

Wolf Cry, The. Lew Sarett. FaPON

Wolf is still under the blanket, The. The Sounds That Arrived. Milo De Angelis, *tr. fr. Italian by* Lawrence Venuti. NeIt

Wolf Said to Francis, The. A. G. Rochelle. Mes

Wolf slipped into the supermarket, The. Wolf at the Door. Alma Villanueva. AfAz

Wolf Town. Anne Carson. *Fr.* Life of Towns, The. BAP-90

Wolf tracks/ On the snow. Sacrifice. Maurice Kenny. ETG

Wolfe Tone. Austin Clarke. CIP

Wolfhound. Richard Murphy. *Fr.* Battle of Aughrim, The. NOIV

Wolfpen Creek. James Still. MT

Wolfram's Dirge. Thomas Lovell Beddoes. *See* If thou wilt ease thine heart.

Wolleward and wete-shoed went I forth after. William Langland. *Fr.* Vision of Piers Plowman, The. EnVB, *Passus XVIII*

Wolsey. John Fletcher *and* William Shakespeare. *Fr.* King Henry VIII. FaBoRV

Wolsey, or possibly my John of Gaunt. Santa Claus. Christopher Hassall. OxBTC

Wolsey's Farewell to His Greatness. John Fletcher *and* William Shakespeare. *Fr.* King Henry VIII.

Wolves. Louis MacNeice. NoAM; OxBTC

Wolves, The. Allen Tate. LiTA; LiTM; NOBA; OxBA; PoA

Wolves can outeat anyone. The Wolf and the Stork. La Fontaine, *tr. fr. French by* Marianne Moore. FM; OBVE

Wolves for Company. *Unknown, tr. fr. Irish.* BIrV

Wolves in the Zoo. Howard Nemerov. NoAM

Wolves of evening will be much abroad, The. Runes for an Old Believer. Rolfe Humphries. NYBP

Wolves say to the dogs, The. J. Michael Yates. *Fr.* Great Bear Lake Meditations, The. HoPM

Woman. Eaton Stannard Barrett. TIRV

Woman. Jane Chambers. IHMS

Woman. Nikki Giovanni. HeIL

Woman. Goldsmith. *See* When lovely woman stoops to folly.

Woman. Randall Jarrell. CBLP; NOBA

Woman. Kora Rumiko, *tr. fr. Japanese* by Kenneth Rexroth *and* Ikuko Atsumi. WPJ

Woman. Irving Layton. ErPo

Woman. Elouise Loftin. PoBA

Woman, *sels.* Alexander McLachlan.

Woman. Valente Malangatana, *tr. fr. Portuguese* by Dorothy Guedes *and* Philippa Rumsey. PBA; TTY

Woman. Malangatana Ngwenya, *tr. fr. Portuguese* by Philippa Rumsey. PeSAV

Woman. Frances Sargent Osgood. AmWP

Woman. Magda Portal, *tr. fr. Spanish* by Irene Vegas-Garcia *and* Kathleen Weaver. WPOW

Woman. Carl Rakosi. TAP

Woman. Umberto Saba, *tr. fr. Italian* by Thomas G. Bergin. UnAS

Woman, The. R. S. Thomas. OxBC

Woman. *Unknown, tr.* by H. A. Giles. *Fr.* Shi King. AWP

Woman! Woman. Elolongue Epanya Yondo, *tr. fr. French* by Ellen Conroy Kennedy. NegPo

Woman. Elolongue Epanya Yondo, *tr. fr. French* by Ellen Conroy Kennedy. NegPo

Woman, A. Robert Pinsky. WeW

Woman, a dog and a walnut tree, A. *Unknown.* FaBoUs

Woman, a pleasing but a short-lived flow'r. An Essay on Woman. Mary Leapor. ECWP; NOEC

Woman, A/ sleeps next to me on the earth. Night in the Forest. Galway Kinnell. TAP

Woman Alone. Denise Levertov. WPOW

Woman and Cat. Paul Verlaine, *tr. fr. French* by C. F. MacIntyre. OFC; SoCa

Woman and falcons — they are easily tamed. Der von Kürenberg, *tr. fr. German* by Frederick Goldin. GePo

Woman and Her Dying Warrior, A. Vanparanar, *tr. fr. Tamil* by A. K. Ramanujan. PLW

Woman and Nature., *sels.* Susan Griffin.

Woman and the Aloe, The. Perseus Adams. PeSA

Woman and the Angel, The. Robert W. Service. ChIV-1

Woman and Tree. Robert Graves. ErPo

Woman as Market. Muriel Rukeyser. NoAM

Woman Asleep on a Banana Leaf. Katha Pollitt. InPS

Woman at the Piano. Marya Zaturenska. MoAmPo

Woman at the Washington Zoo, The. Randall Jarrell. CAPP; CoAP; HAP; HCAP; LiTM; OxBC; TAP; TwCP; UnPo; VCAP

Woman at the Washtub, The. Victor James Daley. NOBAu

Woman Back in the Kitchen, The. Nicholas Lloyd Ingraham. PWR

Woman begins to weep, A. *(LL)* Afterimages. Audre Lorde. VCAP

Woman Called Faithless, A. Linda France. NWP

Woman coming down the snowy road, A. Grey Woman. Gladys Cardiff. CDW

Woman could get lost in, A. *(LL)* The Silos. Nancy Paddock. LoHo

Woman dancing with hair. The Window of the Woman Burning. Marge Piercy. SRLS

Woman, Don't Be Troublesome. Augustus Young, *tr. fr. Irish.* CIP; IIP

Woman fears for man, he goes. Abel's Bride. Denise Levertov. FaBoWP; NALW; VGW

Woman Free, *sels.* Elizabeth Wolstenholme-Elmy. "Marriage, which might have been a mateship sweet." BrRo

Woman full of wile. Growing Old. *Unknown, tr. fr. Irish* by Frank O'Connor. ErPo (Autumn.) OBMV

Woman, Gallup, N. M. Karen Swenson. NYBP

Woman Gave Me a Red Star to Wear on My Headband, A. Jimmie Durham. HATNAP

Woman gave me butter now, A. A Present of Butter. Tadhg Dall O'Huiginn, *tr. fr. Irish* by the Earl of Longford. BIrV

Woman grew, with waiting, over-quiet, A. Narrative. Elisabeth Eybers, *tr. fr. Afrikaans by the author.* PeSA; PeSAV

Woman Grows Soon Old, A. Larin Paraske, *tr. fr. Finnish* by Jaakko A. Ahokas. PBWP

Woman Hanging from the Thirteenth Floor Window, The. Joy Harjo. GLP; HATNAP

Woman has given me strength and affluence, A. Manifesto. D. H. Lawrence. CBLP

Woman-Hater, The, *sels.* Beaumont *and* Fletcher *and* John Fletcher. Come, sleep. EIL; ELP

Woman I Am, The. Glen Allen. BLPA

Woman I have never seen before, A. Transit. Richard Wilbur. DiPo; LCAP; NGP

Woman I Mix Men Up, A. Bernadette Mayer. UL

Woman I want, The. No More than Five. Fred Levinson. AmPA

Woman: If you weren't you who would you rather be? Flood. Roger McGough. FF

Woman in childbirth, fainting with cruel pain, A. To a Faithless Friend. Salaan Arrabey, *tr. fr. Somali* by M. Laurence. WTO

Woman in her room is standing at the mirror, The. The Importance of Mirrors. Helga Sandburg. IHMS

Woman in Kitchen. Eavan Boland. BiHa

Woman in Love with a Captive King, A. Nakkannaiyar, *tr. fr. Tamil* by A. K. Ramanujan. PLW

Woman in my class wrote that she is sick, A. Desire. Stephen Dobyns. BAP-91; NAmP90

Woman in My Notebook, The. Lorna Dee Cervantes. WPOW

Woman in Sunshine, The. Wallace Stevens. ArLo

Woman in the, The. Marge Piercy. NMM

Woman in the garden gathers lilacs, A. A. L. Hendricks. *Fr.* D'Où Venons Nous? Que Sommes Nous? Où Allons Nous. PBCV

Woman in the Moon, The. Mary Mackey. SRLS

Woman in the Ordinary, The. Marge Piercy. CrSp

Woman in the shape of a monster, A. Planetarium. Adrienne Rich. CAPP; FaBoWP; HCAP; MoP; NAAL-2; NALW; NIP; NoAM; NOBA; Poetr; VCAP

Woman in the spiked device, The. A Woman's Issue. Margaret Atwood. AIW

Woman inside an enormous sunhat, A. Close-up. Heather McPherson. PeNZ

Woman into Man. Susan Wallbank. AIW

Woman Is a Branchy Tree, A. James Stephens. ErPo

Woman Is a Worthy Thing, A. *Unknown.* FaBoCo; GBP

Woman is aflame. A. Report from Vietnam for International Women's Day. Minerva Salado, *tr. fr. Spanish* by Daniela Gioseffi *with* Enildo Garcia. WoWa

Woman is by aptitude. *Unknown, tr. fr. Welsh* by Gwyn Williams. *Fr.* Against Women. OBWVE

Woman is perfected, The. Edge. Sylvia Plath. FaBoWP; HCAP; NAAL-2; NALW; PoE; TAP; VCAP

Woman is reading a poem on the street, A. The Hug. Tess Gallagher. CrSp

Woman Is Talking to Death, A. Judy Grahn. GLP

Woman is using a handkerchief, The. At the Hammersmith Palais. Alan Riddell. NOBAu

Woman lay dying on a pallet in a gateway, A. The Good Lord Saved Her. Anna Swirszczynska, *tr. fr. Polish* by Magnus J. Krynski *and* Robert A. Maguire. PoSu

Woman leans in, A. Vilna 1938. Shelley Ehrlich. BTR

Woman, let me learn of you. *(LL)* Elizabeth. Sylvia Townsend Warner. MoAB; MoBrPo

Woman like Me, A. Eileen Myles. GLP

Woman Looking Through a Viewmaster. C. D. Wright. LCAP

Woman-love can't touch my heart. *Unknown, tr. fr. Greek* by Thomas Meyer. GrAn

Woman making advances publicly, A. Judith Kazantzis. BrRo

Woman Me. Maya Angelou. BISi; SRLS

Woman monogamous. *(LL)* Hogamous, higamous. William James. OxBM

Woman Mourned by Daughters, A. Adrienne Rich. IHMS; IMW; Poetr

Woman much missed, how you call to me, call to me. The Voice. Thomas Hardy. BoLoP; CBLP; CMoP; EnLoPo; GBL; GTBS-P; HAP; InPS; MoP; NAEL-2; NoAM; NoP; OAEL-2; OBNC; OxAEP-2; PFP; PoE; PoEL-5; Poetr; TFi

Woman named Tomorrow, The. Four Preludes on Playthings of the Wind. Carl Sandburg. CMoP; MoAB; MoAmPo; NOBA

Woman of Exeter, The. *Unknown.* ReMoGo

Woman of the House, The. Richard Murphy. IPY

Woman of Three Cows, The. *Unknown, tr. fr. Irish* by James Clarence Mangan. EnRP; NOIV; PeIV

Woman on the Bridge over the Chicago River, The. Allen Grossman. PRA

Woman one wonderful morning, A. Europa. William Plomer. MoBS

Woman Poem. Nikki Giovanni. BISi; NMM

Woman prepared a mouse for her husband's dinner, A. On the Eating of Mice. Russell Edson.
(Mouse Dinners.) SoSe
(Woman was cooking a mouse for her husband's dinner, A.) SoSe

Woman, rest on my brow your balsam hands. Night of Sine. Léopold Sédar-Senghor, *tr. fr. French.* PBA
(Woman, rest your balsam hands upon my brow.) NegPo, *tr. by* Ellen Conroy Kennedy

Woman, rest your balsam hands upon my brow. Léopold Sédar-Senghor. *See* Woman, rest on my brow your balsam hands.

Woman returns to Auschwitz, A. Kitty Returns to Auschwitz. David Ray. BTR

Woman riding the two mares of her thighs. The Steamboat Whistle. Archibald MacLeish. MeMAP

Woman Seed Player. Roberta Hill Whiteman. HATNAP

Woman Sings of Her Love. *Somali Oral Tradition*, *tr. by* B. W. Andrzejewski *and* I. M. Lewis. WTO

Woman sits in a corner of sun, A. The Survivor. Katherine Gallagher. AIW

Woman sits on her porch. Earle Thompson. HATNAP

Woman Skating. Margaret Atwood. FaBoWP; IHMS

Woman stood up in front of the table. Her sad hands, The. Miniature. Yannis Ritsos, *tr. fr. Greek by* Edmund Keeley. AnRep

Woman takes a small girl's hand, A. 1939. Elaine Terranova. BTR

Woman, tear out thy voice. (*LL*) Nudities. André Spire. AWP; ErPo

Woman That Had More Babies than That, The. Wallace Stevens. LiTA

Woman: that is to say. Of Women. *Unknown*, *tr. fr. Arabic by* E. Powys Mathers. *Fr.* Thousand and One Nights, The. ErPo

Woman Thing, The. Audre Lorde. BlSi; NMM

Woman! thoughtless, giddy creature. The Declaimer. Henry Baker. NOEC

Woman to Child. Judith Wright. MDDM; PBWP; WPE

Woman to Her Lover, A. Christina Walsh. BrRo

Woman to Man. Ai. NoAM

Woman to Man. Judith Wright. CBAP; FaBoMA; WPE

Woman to man, they lie. In Bloemfontein. Alan Ross. BoLoP

Woman travels to Brazil for plastic, A. Tomatoes. Stephen Dobyns. NAmP90

Woman Waits for Me, A. Walt Whitman. ErPo; HeIP; NOBA

Woman Wall. Lin Ling, *tr. fr. Chinese by* Kenneth Rexroth *and* Ling Chung. WPC

Woman wants monogamy. General Review of the Sex Situation. Dorothy Parker. NAAL-2

Woman was cooking a mouse for her husband's dinner, A. Russell Edson. *See* Woman prepared a mouse for her husband's dinner, A.

Woman was old and ragged and gray, The. Somebody's Mother. Mary Dow Brine. BeLS; BLPA; WBLP

Woman watches her husband rubbing his nose, The. Twenty Below. R. A. D. Ford. NOBC

Woman weak and woman mortal, through the spirit's open portal. Streets of Baltimore. *Unknown.* BLPA

Woman went into the same resturant every Tuesday night, A. Sandwiches. David Donnell. NoAM

Woman Who Could Not Live With Her Faulty Heart, The. Margaret Atwood. LCAP

Woman who didn't love me, The. (*LL*) Valentino's Hair. Yvonne Sapia. PeVV; TRP

Woman who has grown old, The. The Crows. Louise Bogan. FaBoWP; NALW

Woman who has nodded to me from her porch, The. Farmwife. Betsy Sholl. CrSp

Woman Who Loved to Cook, The. Erica Jong. TAP

Woman Who Loved Worms, The. Colette Inez. NMM

Woman Who Understands, The. Everard Jack Appleton. PoLF

Woman who writes feels too much, A. The Black Art. Anne Sexton. PoA

Woman with a burning flame, A. Smothered Fires. Georgia Douglas Johnson. BlSi; ShDr

Woman with a Past, A. Wilfrid Scawen Blunt. *Fr.* Love Sonnets of Proteus, The. Son

Woman with broad, rough hands. Woman. Magda Portal, *tr. fr. Spanish by* Irene Vegas-Garcia *and* Kathleen Weaver. WPOW

Woman with Girdle. Anne Sexton. ErPo

Woman with no face walked into the light, A. Homage to Hieronymus Bosch. Thomas MacGreevy. BIrV

Woman with the caught fox. Plea for a Captive. W. S. Merwin. NoAM; NYBP

Woman with the Wild-Grown Hair Relaxes after Another Long Day, The. Nita Penfold. CrSp

Woman, Woman, let us say these things to each other. Conrad Aiken. NYBP

Woman, women/ 1. An adult female person. The Dictionary Is an *His*torian: A Found Political Poem. Judith McCombs. IHMS

Woman working hard and wisely, A. Kassia, *tr. fr. Greek by* Patrick Diehl. WPOW

(Wo)man/ Yes Woman! Sisters. Alma Villanueva. SRLS

Woman, you are afraid of the forest. Maria Wine, *tr. fr. Swedish by* Nadia Christensen. PBWP

Woman, you'll never credit what. The Shepherd's Tale. James Kirkup, *after the French of* Raoul Ponchon. OBCP

Womanhod, wanton, ye want. John Skelton. AAS

Womanhood, The, *sels.* Gwendolyn Brooks.
Children of the Poor, The. PoA, (*complete*); WPE, (1 *and* 2)
What Shall I Give BPo, (2 *sts. only*)
Life for My Child is Simple, and Is Good. LPA
"One wants a Teller in a time like this." WPE
Rites for Cousin Vit, The. BPo; HAP; WeW; WPE
"Stand off, daughter of the dusk,." NALW

Womanisers. John Press. BoLoP; ErPo

Womankind. Gerald Massey. NOBVV

Womanness had formed in a man's hand, A. The Bachelor's Hand. Russell Edson. AnAn

Woman's Answer, A. *At. to* The Earl of Surrey Henry Howard, Earl of Surrey. *See* Girt in my guiltless gown, as I sit here and sew.

Woman's Answer to "The Vampire," A. Felicia Blake. BLPA

Woman's Beauty. Lascelles Abercrombie. *Fr.* Emblems of Love. MoBrPo

Woman's beauty is like a white, A. W. B. Yeats. *Fr.* Only Jealousy of Emer, The. MoAB

Woman's Constancy. John Donne. ESCV; NBLV; NoP; NOSC; SeCV-1

Woman's Constancy. Sir John Suckling. CaPo

Woman's Daughter, The. Dermot Bolger. IB

Woman's deaf, and does not hear, The. (*LL*) On a Certain Lady at Court. Pope. NOBE; NOEC; OBEV; OBF; OxBSP; TrGrPo

Woman's Death-wound, A. Helen Hunt Jackson. AmWP

Woman's Dream, The. Frances Horovitz. BrRo

Woman's face is full of wiles, A. Humphrey Gifford. EIL

Woman's face with Nature's own hand painted, A. Shakespeare. *Fr.* Sonnets. ErPo; HeIP; InvP; NAEL-1; NoSic; OAEL-1; OxAEP-1; PeHV

Woman's Hard Fate. *Unknown.* ECWP

Woman's Inconstancy. Phineas Fletcher. *Fr.* Sicelides. EIL

Woman's Issue, A. Margaret Atwood. AIW

Woman's Labour; an Epistle to Mr. Stephen Duck, The, *sels.* Mary Collier. Washerwoman, The. ECWP; NOEC

Woman's Last Word, A. Robert Browning. BLPA; BLPL; FaBoBe; NAEL-2; TrGrPo

Woman's like the flatt'ring ocean. John Gay. *Fr.* Polly; an Opera. PeLV

Woman's Looks, A. *Unknown.* TrGrPo

Woman's Love. *Unknown.* WBLP

Woman's Love and Life. Adelbert von Chamisso, *tr. fr. German by* Philip L. Miller. RiWo

Woman's Prayer, A. Yehuda Karni, *tr. fr. Hebrew by* Ruth Finer Mintz. MHP

Woman's Question, A. *At. to* Lena Lathrop, *wr. at. to* Elizabeth Barrett Browning. BLPA; PoToHe; WBLP

Woman's Reason, A. Gelett Burgess. FaBoNo

Woman's Shortcomings, A. Elizabeth Barrett Browning. BLPA

Woman's Shortcomings, A, *sels.* Elizabeth Barrett Browning. "Unless you can muse in a crowd all day." PFP

Woman's Song, A. Colleen J. McElroy. BlSi

Woman's Song, about Men, A. *Unknown*, *tr. fr. Eskimo into French by* Paul-Emile Victor; *English vers. by* Armand Schwerner. STP

Woman's Sorrow, A, *sels.* Ho Nansorhon, *tr. fr. Korean by* Peter H. Lee. "Yesterday I fancied I was young." PBWP

Woman's Wish, The. Matthew Prior. FaBoEE

Woman's worth to the world can never be told. Oh Woman, Blessed Woman! Mrs. Henry Linden. CBWP-4

Womanwork. Paula Gunn Allen. SRLS

Womb, The. Apirana Taylor. PeNZ

Womb Song. Susan Fromberg Schaeffer. IHMS

Wombat, The. Ogden Nash. CBNP

Women. Louise Bogan. LiTA; MoAB; MoAmPo; NALW; NoAM; TwCP; VGW; WPE

Women. William Cartwright. BeJo; ErPo

Women. — — Heath. *See* These women all.

Women. Lizette Woodworth Reese. AmWP

Women. Adrienne Rich. NMM; TRP

Women. Yannis Ritsos, *tr. fr. Greek by* Minos Sarras. AnAn

Women. May Swenson. BoWoP; NALW; NMM; Prf

Women. Alice Walker. GOA; WPOW

Women. *Yoruba Oral Tradition, tr. by* Ulli Beier. WTO

Women all/ cause rue. Palladas, *tr. fr. Greek by* Tony Harrison. GrAn

Women all shout after me and mock, The. Palladas, *tr. fr. Greek by* Tony Harrison. GrAn

Women and Men. Hassan Sheikh Mumin, *tr. fr. Somali.* WTO

Women and Roses. Robert Browning. NAEL-2

Women Are Not Gentlemen. Harley Matthews. NOBAu

Women are timid, cower and shrink. Betty Zane. Thomas Dunn English. PAH

Women are walking to town, The. The Rainy Season. Linda Hogan. HATNAP; TRP

Women are within her, smoking angel dust, sipping tea, The. The Administrator. Marilyn Chin. LoHo

Women Are Worthy. *Unknown. See* To onpreise women[e] it were a shame.

Women, as some men say, unconstant be. George Wither. NOSC

Women at the Corners Stand, The. Louis Golding. TrJP

Women at the Market. Angela Figueroa-Aymerich, *tr. fr. Spanish by* Hardie St. Martin. PBWP

Women at the Temple. Herodas, *tr. fr. Greek by* Barbara Hughes Fowler. HePo

Women Bathing at Bergen-Belsen. Enid Shomer. BTR

Women ben full of ragerie. Imitation of Chaucer. Pope. FaBoPa

Women Beware Women., *sels.* Thomas Middleton. "You'll say the gentleman is somewhat simple." OxBM

Women Damned. Baudelaire, *tr. fr. French by* Joanna Richardson. PeHV

Women gather, their dreams, The. Dream of the Hair Burning Smell. Jana Harris. WoWa

Women have loved before as I love now. Edna St. Vincent Millay. HeIP; NALW; PoA

Women have no share in the encampments of this world. Women and Men. Hassan Sheikh Mumin, *tr. fr. Somali.* WTO

Women have no wilderness in them. Women. Louise Bogan. LiTA; MoAB; MoAmPo; NALW; NoAM; TwCP; VGW; WPE

Women he liked, did shovel-bearded Bob. Bob's Lane. Edward Thomas. PoE

Women I Knew, The. Lois Roma-Deeley. LoHo

Women, if we held the oxhide shield. Lament for a Warrior. *Unknown, tr. fr. Sotho by* Dan Kunene *and* Jack Cope. PeSA

Women in black picked up their violins. The Call. Jules Supervielle, *tr. fr. French by* Geoffrey Gardner. NU

Women in Love. Donald Justice. SM

Women in Old Parkas, The. Mary TallMountain. AIW

Women in Vietnam, The. Grace Paley. NMM

Women know how to wait here. Lines for Marking Time. Roberta Hill Whiteman. BoWoP; CDW

Women Men's Shadows. Ben Jonson. *See* Follow a shadow [*or* shaddow], it still flies you.

Women of Dan Dance with Swords in Their Hands to Mark the Time When They Were Warriors, The. Audre Lorde. NAAL-2; NALW; NoAM

Women of Jericho, The. Phyllis McGinley. ChIV-1

Women of my country, black and barefoot girls. Black Island. Charles Pressoir, *tr. fr. French by* Ellen Conroy Kennedy. NegPo

Women of My Land. Frankie Armstrong. BrRo

Women of Rubens, The. Wislawa Szymborska, *tr. fr. Polish by* Magnus F. Krynski. PoSu

Women of Rubens, The. Wislawa Szymborska, *tr. fr. Polish by* Celina Wieniewska. WPOW

Women of the Future. Mary Scott. ECWP

Women of Trachis, *sels.* Sophocles, *tr. fr. Greek by* Ezra Pound. "Kupris bears trophies away." CTC "Torn between griefs, which grief shall I lament." OBVE

Women often seem distant. Women. Yannis Ritsos, *tr. fr. Greek by* Minos Sarras. AnAn

Women on the Road to Pine Gap. Wendy Poussard. AIW

Women Pleased, *sels.* John Fletcher. "Oh [*or* O] fair[e] sweet face, oh [*or* O] eyes celestial[l] bright." PoEL-2 (To His Sleeping Mistress). NOSC

Women reminded him of lilies and roses. Thoughts after Ruskin. Elma Mitchell. FaBoWP

Women sleep, The. Broken Dreams. Hugo Williams. CBLP

Women stone breakers. History Makers. George Campbell. PBCV

Women tease and scold me, The. Palladas, *tr. fr. Greek by* Sam Hamill. InMo

Women that are loved are more than lovable. The Colours of Love. Denis Devlin. IPY; PeIV

Women Transport Corps. *Unknown, tr. fr. Chinese by* Kai-yu Hsu. WPOW

Women Walk. Sam Cornish. ETG

Women walk because. Women Walk. Sam Cornish. ETG

Women were first to catch sight of him, The. The Coming of Raka. N. P. van Wyk Louw, *tr. fr. Afrikaans by* Guy Butler. Fr. Raka. PeSAV

Women,/ What fools we are. Two Strange Worlds. Francesca Yetunde Pereira. PBA

Women Who Cook. Anita Skeen. GLP

Women who do not know me, The. The Women Who Hate Me. Dorothy Allison. GLP

Women Who Hate Me, The. Dorothy Allison. GLP

Women who were mothers told us about it. Portrait of Auntie Blodwen. Elwyn Davies. AngWe

Women, whoever wishes to know my lord. Gaspara Stampa, *tr. fr. Italian by* J. Vitiello. BoWoP

Women Wisdom. Larry Mitchell. GLP

Women with hats like the rear ends of pink ducks. To a Waterfowl. Donald Hall. OBAL

Women, women, love of women. *Unknown.* MiEL

Women, women,/ women, women. A Fixture. May Swenson. NYBP

Women's Degrees. Alfred Denis Godley. NOBL

Women's Jail, The. Miriam Waddington. NOBC

Women's Locker Room. Marilyn Nelson Waniek. Poetr

Women's Marseillaise, The. F. E. M. Macaulay. BrRo

Women's or men's hair waltzed with the wind like. Dusk on the Veranda by Lake Mendota. Chung Ling, *tr. fr. Chinese by* Kenneth Rexroth *and* Ling Chung. WPC

Women's Rondo. *Unknown, tr. fr. Aborigine.* NOBAu

Women's Rule. Friedrich von Logau, *tr. fr. German.* GePo, *tr. by* George C. Schoolfield

Women's Songs. *Unknown, tr. fr. Maori by* Margaret Orbell. PeNZ

Won' you ring, old hammer? Hammer, Ring. *Unknown.* AmFP

Wonder. Thomas Traherne. CH; ESCV; GeHe; HAP; ImPo; LiTB; NAEL-1; NoP; PoE; SeCP; SeCV-2; TOF; TrGrPo

Wonder Clock, The. Katharine Pyle. OBCA *Sels.* Nine o'Clock. One o'Clock. Two o'Clock.

Wonder not if I stay not here. To Master Davenant for Absence. Sir John Suckling. CaPo

Wonder stranger ne'r was known, A. The Suffolk Miracle. *Unknown.* ESPB

Wonderful. Julian S. Cutler. PWR

Wonderful bears that walked my room all night. Bears. Adrienne Rich. NYBP

Wonderful bird is the pelican, A. Dixon Lanier Merritt. PeLi

Wonderful Derby Ram, The. *Unknown.* BoTP

Wonderful Mother, A. Pat O'Reilly. BLPA

Wonderful occupation, A,/ Making songs! The Joy of a Singer. Piuvkaq, *tr. fr. Eskimo.* WTO

Wonderful "One-Hoss Shay," The. Oliver Wendell Holmes. *See* Have you heard of the wonderful one-hoss shay.

Wonderful way is the King's Highway, A. The King's Highway. John Masefield. BLRP

Wonderful workings of the world: wonderful, The. Cut the Grass. A. R. Ammons. CAPP; HAP; Poetr; PPP; TAP; WeW

Wonderful World, The. William Brighty Rands. FaPON

Wondering is a typical pastime of the leisure class. The Ex-Poet. Bill Zavatsky. UL

Wondering, wondering, where we had gone. (*LL*) A Lovely Song for Jackson. V. R. Lang. VBLP

Wonderment of books, The. (*LL*) The Library. Barbara A. Huff. FaPON

Wonders. Lorenzo Thomas. UL

Wonders. *Unknown.* EiL *Sels.* Nine o'Clock. One o'Clock. "Andalusian merchant, that returns, The." FaBoCh

Wonders are many and none is more wonderful that man. Glengormley. Derek Mahon. CIP; IIP

Wonders of Nature. *Unknown.* OTCP

Wonders of Obligation. Roy Fisher. VaA

Wonders of Obligation, *sels.* Roy Fisher. "Near Hartington." NBrP

Wondrous, I grant, and caught from heaven the flame. Literature and Action. Goronva Camlan. AngWe

"Wondrous life!" cried Marvell at Appleton House. Weldon Kees. CoAP; NaP

Wondrous Love. *At.* to Alex Means. *See* What Wondrous Love Is This.

Wondrous the gods, more wondrous are the men. A Compliment to the Ladies. Blake. BXAP

Wondrous the Merge. James Richard Broughton. GLP

Wondrous this masonry wasted by Fate! The Ruin. *Unknown, tr. fr. Anglo-Saxon by* Charles W. Kennedy. AnOE; PrIm

Won't be much consolation. *(LL)* Farewell to Fan Yun at An Ch'eng. Shen Yüeh. OHMPC

Won't bear such a weight of sorrow. *(LL)* To the Tune "Spring at Wu Ling." Li Ch'ing-chao. OHMPC

Won't It Be Strange — ? D. H. Lawrence. MeMBP

Won't it be strange, when the nurse brings the newborn. Won't It Be Strange — ? D. H. Lawrence. MeMBP

Won't you be my chauffeur. Me and My Chauffeur Blues. "Memphis Millie." VBLP

Won't you look out of your window, Mrs. Gill? The Mocking Fairy. Walter de la Mare. MoBrPo; MoShBr

Woo Not the World. Mu'tamid, King of Seville, *tr. fr. Arabic by* Dulcie L. Smith. AWP

Wood. Thomas Hornsby Ferril. PoRA

Wood (and all else) by the sink. Watching Women with Children. Elaine Randell. NBrP

Wood Carols. H. Cordelia Ray. CBWP-3

Wood-chuck. *Unknown. See* How much wood would a woodchuck chuck?

Wood-Cutter, The. Lupenga Mphande. HBAPE

Wood-Cutter's Night Song, The. John Clare. EnRP

Wood-doves are singing along the Perkiomen, The. Thinking of a Relation between the Images of Metaphors. Wallace Stevens. SAmP

Wood Floor Dreams. Lance Henson. VoR

Wood green. Grandfather built it. July 4th. Anne Waldman. UL

Wood House over the Wilia, The. Johannes Bobrowski, *tr. fr. German by* Don Bogen. AnAn

Wood is a good place to find, The. Walking with Lulu in the Wood. Naomi Lazard. NYBP

Wood is bare, The: a river-mist is steeping, The. Robert Bridges. EBVV; IMW

Wood Music. Ethel King. GoYe

Wood of Flowers, The. James Stephens. BoTP; PDV

Wood-Pile, The. Robert Frost. AnAmPo; InPK; LiTA; NAAL-2; NoAM; NoP; SAmP; VGW

Wood shakes in the breeze, The. The Old Tree. Andrew Young. GoJo

Wood So Wild, The. *At.* to Sir Thomas Wyatt. *See* I Must Go Walk[e] the Woods So Wild.

Wood Song. Sara Teasdale. AnAmPo

Wood Song, A. Ralph Hodgson. GoJo

Wood-Swallows, The. "Fiona Macleod." *Fr.* Australian Transcripts. FM

Wood, swollen with mushrooms, The. The Circle. Jean Garrigue. LiTA

Wood, the Weed, the Wag, The. Sir Walter Ralegh. *See* Three Things there be that prosper up apace.

Wood was rather old and dark, The. The Little Boy Lost. Stevie Smith. FaBoTw

Wood Weasel, The. Marianne Moore. CMoP

Wood with bushes broad there was, begrown with bigree boughs, A. Euryalus and Nisus Meet Their Deaths. Virgil, *tr. fr. Latin by* Thomas Phaer. *Fr.* Aeneid [*or* Eneados], The. NAWM-1; NoSic

Woodchucks. Maxine W. Kumin. CAPP; HoPM; NIP; Poetr

Woodchuck's very very fat, The. The Jolly Woodchuck. Marion Edey *and* Dorothy Grider. FaPON; PDV

Woodcutter's Ax, A. P'i Jih-hsiu, *tr. fr. Chinese by* William H. Nienhauser. SuSp

Woodcutter's Wife, The. William Rose Benét. AWP

Wooden belly iron back. *Unknown.* FaBoVe

Wooden Chamber, The. Anne Hébert, *tr. fr. French by* Birgit Swenson. WPOW

Wooden Die, A. Zbigniew Herbert, *tr. fr. Polish by* Czeslaw Milosz *and* Peter Dale Scott. AnRep

Wooden die can be described only from without. A Wooden Die. Zbigniew Herbert, *tr. fr. Polish by* Czeslaw Milosz *and* Peter Dale Scott. AnRep

Wooden Horse then said, The. Jenny Mastoraki, *tr. fr. Modern Greek by* Nikos Germanakos. BoWoP; PBWP

Woodland Mass, The. Dafydd ap Gwilym, *tr. fr. Welsh by* Gwyn Williams. OBWVE

Woodland rivulet, — a Poet's death, A. *(LL)* After Dark Vapours. Keats. EnRP; FaBoRV; TEP

Woodland sprite of the rakish kind, A. A Scandal among the Flowers. Charles S. Taylor. BLPA

Woodlands, The. William Barnes. BoNaP

Woodlark, The. Gerard Manley Hopkins. RB

Woodlot, The. Amy Clampitt. HCAP

Woodlouse. Judith Nicholls. OBAP

Woodman, Spare That Tree. George Pope Morris. AnAmPo; BLPA; FaBoBe; FaPON; OHIP; PWR; VPP; WBLP

Woodniche. Aidan Carl Mathews. PeIV

Woodnotes I ("When the pine tosses its cones.") Emerson. AmPP; NOBA Sels.

"In unplowed Maine he sought the lumberers' gang." MeMAP; TAP

Woodnotes II ("As sunbeams stream through liberal space.") Emerson. NOBA Sels.

"All the forms are fugitive." WGRP

"As the sunbeams stream through liberal space." OHIP

Woodpecker, The. Elizabeth Madox Roberts. FaPON; OBCA; TLR

Woodpecker, The. Joyce Sambrook. BoTP

Woodpecker goes beating a little drum, The. Sleep. Charles Simic. CoAP

Woodpecker pecked out a little round hole, The. The Woodpecker. Elizabeth Madox Roberts. FaPON; OBCA; TLR

Woodpigeons brooding in a sunlit glade. A Winter's Tale. Andrew Waterman. SCBI

Woodrow Wilson. Robinson Jeffers. FaBoPV

Woods, The. Josephine Jacobsen. BAP-91

Woods. Louis MacNeice. IIP

Woods, The. Derek Mahon. NOIV; PBCIP; SCBI

Woods are overhead over everywhere, The. James Cunningham. *Fr.* Narrator's Trance, The. JB

Woods darken, grasses startled by wind. Lu Lun, *tr. by* Ronald C. Miao. *Fr.* Frontier Songs. SuSp

Woods decay, the woods decay and fall, The. Tithonus. Tennyson. EnVR; HAP; ImPo; LiTB; MeMBP; NAEL-2; NAWM-2; NOBE; NOBVV; NoP; OAEL-2; OBNC; PoE; PoEL-5; PPP; SCGP; TEP

Woods harmlesse Shades have only true Delights. *(LL)* Thrice Happy He. William Drummond of Hawthornden. BoNaP

Woods of Arcady are dead, The. The Song of the Happy Shepherd. W. B. Yeats. NoAM

Woods of the horizon, The. Men in the City. Alfonsina Storni, *tr. fr. Spanish.* PBWP, *tr. by* Rachel Benson

Woods shall to me answer and my Eccho ring, The. *(LL)* Epithalamion. Spenser. AAS; BoLoP; EiL; EnRePo; FHYEP; InPS; NOBE; NoP; NoSic; OAEL-1; OBEV; OxAEP-1; PoEL-1; TEP

Woods sleep bathed in shadow, The. Evensong. Paul Gerhardt, *tr. fr. German by* Ingrid Waløe-Engel. GePo

Woodsmen blow their horns, and close the day, The. The Fair in the Woods. Thom Gunn. AnAn

Woodspurge, The. Dante Gabriel Rossetti. *Fr.* House of Life, The. EBEV; ELP; EnVR; GTBS-P; HAP; HeIP; NOBE; NoP; OAEL-2; OBEV; OBNC; PFP; PoEL-5; PrIm; SCGP; TFi; UnPo

Woodspurge has a cup of three, The. *(LL)* The Woodspurge. Dante Gabriel Rossetti. EBEV; ELP; EnVR; GTBS-P; HAP; HeIP; NOBE; NoP; OAEL-2; OBEV; OBNC; PFP; PoEL-5; PrIm; SCGP; TFi; UnPo

Woodtown Manor. John Montague. IPY; PBCIP

Woodworker's Ballad. Herbert Edward Palmer. OBEV

Woody Guthrie Visited by Bob Dylan: Brooklyn State Hospital, New York, 1961. David Wojahn. *Fr.* Mystery Train: A Sequence. PBCAP

Wooed and Married and A'. Alexander Ross. OxBS

Woof of the Sun (Ethereal Gauze). Thoreau. *Fr.* Week on the Concord and Merrimack Rivers, A. TAP

Woof of the sun, ethereal gauze. Woof of the Sun (Ethereal Gauze). Thoreau. *Fr.* Week on the Concord and Merrimack Rivers, A. TAP (Haze.) NoP; PFP

Wooing in a Dream. Nicholas Breton. *See* Shall we go dance the hay? The hay?

Wooing Maid, The. Martin Parker. CoMu

Wooing of Criseide, The, III. Chaucer. *Fr.* Troilus and Criseyde [*or* Criseide]. EnVB; PoEL-1

Wooing of Etain, The. *Unknown, tr. fr. Irish by* John Montague. BIrV

Wooing Rogue, The. *Unknown.* CoMu

Wooing Song. Giles Fletcher the Younger. *Fr.* Christ's Victory and Triumph. EiL; OBEV

Wool-chafed and wet-shoed I went forth after. William Langland. *Fr.* Vision of Piers Plowman, The. NAEL-1

Wool Trade, The. John Dyer. *Fr.* Fleece, The.

Woolly Words. Robert N. Feinstein. NBLV

Woosel cock so black of hue, The. Bottom's Song. Shakespeare. *Fr.* Midsummer Night's Dream, A. CTC

Wooyeo Ball, The. *Unknown.* NOBAu

Word, The. Margaret Avison. MoCV

Words like "I love you" or "Thank you." (*LL*) Long Lines: Youth and Age. Paul Goodman. GLP; PeHV

Words Most Often Mispronouncd in Poetry. Alex Kuo. UL

Words of Agur, The. Bible, *O.T. Fr.* Proverbs.

Words of Finn, The. *Unknown, tr. fr. Old Irish.* ChTr

Words of our day, The. The Same Side of the Canoe. Alda do Espírito Santo, *tr. fr. Portuguese.* PBWP, *tr. by* Allan Francovich *and* Kathleen Weaver

Words of Tayko-mol. William Oandasan. *See* From heart through mind into image.

Words of the All-Wise, The, *sels. Unknown, tr. fr. Icelandic by* W. H. Auden *and* Paul B. Taylor.
"Say, dwarf, for it seems to me." OBVE

Words of the True Poems, The. Walt Whitman. ImGa

Words of the true poems give you more than poems, The. The Words of the True Poems. Walt Whitman. ImGa

Words, one by one. Freedom. Wimal Dissanayake. TSaS

Words say, mispell and mispell your name. Michael Palmer. UL

Words scored upon a bone. Meditation on a Bone. A. D. Hope. NoAM

Words Spoken Alone. Dannie Abse. NYBP

Words Spoken by Pasternak during a Bombing. Bella Akhmadulina, *tr. fr. Russian by* Daniela Gioseffi *with* Sophia Buzevska. WoWa

Words Spoken by Pasternak during a Bombing. Bella Akhmadulina, *tr. fr. Russian by* Jean Valentine *and* Olga Carlisle. BoWoP

Words that pass from lip to lip, The. Speech and Silence. Richard Hovey. AnAmPo

Words to a Song. Agnes Nemes Nagy, *tr. fr. Hungarian by* Bruce Berlind. BoWoP

Words to My Friend. Renée Vivien, *tr. fr. French by* Sandia Belgrade. PeHV

Words were made to prevent us near. (*LL*) My love, if I write a song for you. Veronica Forrest-Thomson. VBLP

Words Wherein Stinging Bees Lurk. Judah Halevi, *tr. fr. Hebrew by* Nina Davis Salaman. TrJP

Words will one day come, The. The Movie Run Backward. Robert Creeley. CAPP

Words Will Resurrect, The. Jorge de Lima, *tr. fr. Portuguese by* John Nist. TTY

Words! Words! Jessie Redmond Fauset. CDC

Words would not have come to write to you. Autumn Wind. Ruth Dallas. *Fr.* Letter to a Chinese Poet. PeNZ

Wordspinning. Olga Kirsch, *tr. fr. Afrikaans by* Jack Cope. PeSA

Wordsworth. Charlotte L. Forten Grimke. AAP

Wordsworth I love, his books are like the fields. To Wordsworth. John Clare. OAEL-2; Son

Wordsworth on Lloyd George. Mary Visick. UV

Wordsworth Reading Chaucer. Wordsworth. *Fr.* Prelude [or, Growth of a Poet's Mind], The. EnRP; EPCY; FaBoPP; HAP; OAEL-2; OxAEP-2, *abr.*

Wordsworth Skates on Esthwaite Water. Wordsworth. *Fr.* Prelude [or, Growth of a Poet's Mind], The. CH; EnRP; FaBoPP; GN; HAP; NOBE; NoP; NU; OAEL-2; OBNC; OxAEP-2; PoE; SCV

Wordsworth to the contrary notwithstanding. In Magic Words. Merrill Moore. Son

Wordsworth Unvisited. Hartley Coleridge. *See* He Lived amidst th' Untrodden Ways.

Wordsworth upon Helvellyn! Let the cloud. On a Portrait of Wordsworth by B. R. Haydon. Elizabeth Barrett Browning. EPCY; HeIP

Wordsworth's Grave. Matthew Arnold. *Fr.* Memorial Verses. EBVVPR; FaBoPP; NAEL-2; OAEL-2

Wordsworth's Grave. Sir William Watson. OBNC

Work, The. Robert Duncan. *Fr.* Dante Études. CAPP

Work. Gyula Illyés, *tr. fr. Hungarian by* William Jay Smith. RaBo

Work. D. H. Lawrence. OBMV

Work. Pushkin, *tr. fr. Russian by* Babette Deutsch *and* Avrahm Yarmolinsky. AWP

Work. Denise Riley. NBrP

Work. J. W. Thompson. PoToHe

Work. (*LL*) Waking up this morning, I see the blue sky. Thich Nhat Hanh. EaPr

Work; a Song of Triumph ("Work!/ Thank God for the might of it.") Angela Morgan. PoLF

Work for Small Men, *sels.* Sam Walter Foss.
"Despise not any man that lives." PoToHe

Work: I am a pal of the world: I came from the wilderness. (*LL*) Wilderness. Carl Sandburg. RaBo

Work?/ I don't have to work. Necessity. Langston Hughes. NOBA; RaBo

Work-in-progress. Mahmood Jamal. NBrP

Work [*or* Worke] is done, The. Young men and maidens, set. Robert Herrick. *Fr.* On Himself[e]. CaPo; SeCP

Work of Artifice, A. Marge Piercy. IHMS; Poetsp

Work of Her That Went, The. Emily Dickinson. MDDM

Work of Love, The. Margaret E. Sangster. BLRP

Work of the sun, not illusion, The. A Slogan Will Not Suffice. Kelvin Corcoran. NBrP

Work on my brain, help every faculty. Mary Pix. *Fr.* Queen Catherine. KTR, *act* I

Work on the railroad. Roll on the Ground. *Unknown.* AmFP

Work-out, The. Geoffrey Movius. MAT

Work out a perfect will. (*LL*) By the Statue of King Charles [*or* I] at Charing Cross. Lionel Johnson. FaBoEH; FaBoRV; MoBrPo; NOBE; OBEV; OBMV; OBNC; PeVV; PoEL-5

Work out. Ten laps. Heartbeats. Melvin Dixon. PFL

Work Rules. John Norton. BCF

Work Song. Raymond Mazisi Kunene, *tr. fr. Zulu by* D. K. Rycroft. WTO

Work Song. Mark Levine. BAP-91

Work-Songs. *Unknown.* PBCV
Sels.
"If me want for go in a Ebo."
"Tink dere is a God in a top."

Work-table, litter, books and standing lamp. Night Sweat. Robert Lowell. NAAL-2; TAP; VGW

Work to Do toward Town. Gary Snyder. VGW

Work while you work. One Thing at a Time. M. A. Stodart. PoToHe

Work without Hope. Samuel Taylor Coleridge. BoNaP; EnRP; MeMBP; NAEL-2; NOBE; NoP; OBEV; OxAEP-2; PFP; Son; TEP

Workaday Morning. Melvin B. Tolson, *tr. fr. Norwegian by* Nadia Christensen. PBWP

Workbox, The. Thomas Hardy. InPK; NAEL-2; UnPo

Workday. Linda Hogan. HATNAP

Worker, The. Gerald Massey. EBVV

Worker, The. Richard W. Thomas. PoBA; PoNe

Worker (We Own Two Houses), The. Charles Fort. NGP

Workers earn it. Money. Richard Armour. NBLV

Workers on the S. P. Line to strike sent out a call, The. Casey Jones. Joe Hill. SWP

Workhouse Boy, The. *Unknown.* GBP

Working. Maxine Scates. PBCAP

Working against Time. David Wagoner. MAT

Working and Waiting. Adah Isaacs Menken. CBWP-1

Working Class. Bertram J. Warr. NOBC

Working Construction. Eric Chock. OpBo

Working girl: child-carrying, sensual, The. I See Cleopatra. Nurunnessa Choudhury, *tr. fr. Bengali by the author* and Paul Joseph Thompson. AIW

Working is another way of praying. Song for Dov Shamir. Dannie Abse. (Song of a Hebrew.) WTO

Working late. Louis Simpson. PBCV

Working Party, A. Siegfried Sassoon. CMoP; PeFWW

Working Song. Buluguru, *tr. fr. Yaoro by* E. A. Worms. CBAP

Working with Mother. Myra Cohn Livingston. · TLR

Working with one eye closed or heads buried. The War Photographers. Frank Ormsby. PNI

Working with Tools. A. R. Ammons. CAPP; TRP

Workman plied his clumsy spade, A. Two Surprises. R. W. McAlpine. PoLF

"Workman, what will you make on the bench today?" Carpenter. George Mackay Brown. OxBC

Works and Days., *sels.* David Campbell.
Harvesting. FaBoMA
Weather. FaBoMA

Works and Days., *sels.* Hesiod, *tr. fr. Greek by* Thomas Cooke.
"Next to my counsels an attention pay." FaBoUs

Works of Art. Elizabeth Jennings. PeECV

Works of God, The. Moses ibn Ezra, *tr. fr. Hebrew by* Solomon Solis-Cohen. TrJP

Works so well. (*LL*) Auto Mobile. A. R. Ammons. FF; OBAL

Works, the days, uh, The. But Not That One. John Ashbery. LCAP

World, The. Robert Creeley. MoP; NaP; VCAP

World, The. Frederick William Faber. PWR

World, The. George Herbert. GeHe; NOSC; SeCV-1

World, The. Kathleen Raine. OxBTC

World, The. William Brighty Rands. *See* Great, wide, beautiful, wonderful World.

World, The. Christina Rossetti. BoWoP; NALW

World, The. Vern Rutsala. Poetsp

World, The. Ella Wheeler Wilcox. PWR

World, The. Wordsworth. *See* World is too much with us; late and soon, The.

World a hunting is, The. William Drummond of Hawthornden. OBD
(Word a Hunt, A.) NOBE

World an Illusion, The. *Unknown.* MeEL

World as Meditation, The. Wallace Stevens. HeIP; LCAP; MoAB; PPP

World Beautiful, The. Milton. *See* Sweet is the breath of Morn, her rising sweet.

World begins with rough and smooth, The. The School for Objects. Paul Hoover. UL

World below the Brine, The. Walt Whitman. ArNa; BoNaP; FM; MAT; NoP; PFP

World, black and white between the wars, The. BW. Aaron Fogel. BAP-89

World changes with every step, The. Homesickness. Eduard Friedrich Mörike, *tr. fr. German by* Philip L. Miller. RiWo

World charged with our beauty. (*LL*) Star & Garter Theater. Dennis Schmitz. LCAP

World Doesn't End, The, *sels.* Charles Simic.
"We were so poor I had to take the place of the." VCAP

World exists beyond the limits of this pane, A. Exile's Letter: After the Failed Revolution. Marilyn Chin. LoHo

World feels dusty, The. Emily Dickinson. MoAmPo
(Flags Vex a Dying Face.) WoWa

World fell into a blood-bath tub!, The. (*LL*) The Saturday Tub. Mary Gilmore. NOBAu

World goes none the lamer, The. A. E. Housman. PeVV

World has held great Heroes, The. The Song of Mr. Toad. Kenneth Grahame. *Fr.* Wind in the Willows, The. CoGr; FaPON; FiBHP; GoJo; NOBL; ZA
(Wind in the Willows, The.) ZA

World has room for the manly man, with the spirit of manly cheer, The. The Manly Man. *Unknown.* BLPA; WBLP

World, haunted by precepts and the Pleiades. (*LL*) On First Looking into Chapman's Hesiod. Peter Porter. NOBAu

World his country, and his God his guide, The. (*LL*) At Dover Cliffs. William Lisle Bowles. EnRP

World Hymn, The. James Gilchrist Lawson. WBLP

World I did not wish to enter, A. A Necessitarian's Epitaph. Thomas Hardy. FaBoEE

World in gloom and splendour passes by, The. To a Millionaire. Archibald Lampman. NOBC

World in its caprice, The. Gossip. Penelope Gilliatt. PRA

World in your hands, love Her, The. (*LL*) The Object. Alma Villanueva. SRLS

World Is a Bundle of Hay, The. Byron. EnRP; FF

World Is a Musician's Cliff House, The. Rodney Hall. *Fr.* Black Bagatelles. CBAP

World is all orange-round, The. The Walking Road. Richard Hughes. OBMV

World is blue spring a yellow, The. What Was Shown. Peter Philpott. VaA

World is but a sorry scene, The. The Crucifixion of Our Blessed Lord. Christopher Smart. ChIV-2

World is charged with the grandeur of God, The. God's Grandeur. Gerard Manley Hopkins. ArNa; AWP; BLPL; ClHu; CMoP; EBVV; EnlH; FF; HAP; ImPo; InPK; InvP; LiTB; LiTM; MoAB; MoBrPo; MoP; NAEL-2; NIP; NoAM; NOBE; NOBVV; NoP; OAEL-2; OBNC; PeVV; PoE; PPP; PrIm; RaBo; SCGP; Son; SoSe; SOTW; TEP; TFi; TrCP; TrGrPo; UnPo; WeW

World is come upon me, I used to keep it a long way off, The. The Deserter. Stevie Smith. FaBoWP

World is dull, the world is blind, The. Welt ist dumm, die Welt ist blind, Die. Heine, *tr. fr. German by* James Thomson. AWP

World Is Everything That Is the Case, The. Derek Mahon. LoHo

World Is Full of Beauty, The. Matilda C. Edwards. PWR

World is full of colour!, The. Colour. Adeline White. BoTP

World Is Full of Elephants, The. Gavin Ewart. OBAP

World is full of gladness, The. Lemon Pie. Edgar A. Guest. OBAL

World is full of mostly invisible things, The. To David, about His Education. Howard Nemerov. HCAP

World is full of those who love to be officials, The. Drinking Wine. Ch'ien Ch'ien-i, *tr. fr. Chinese by* Irving Y. Lo. SuSp

World is full of wistful ones who hoard their souvenirs, The. Ballad of Culinary Frustration. Phyllis McGinley. FiBHP

World is great, The: the birds all fly from me. I Am Lonely. "George Eliot." *Fr.* Spanish Gypsy, The. GN

World is in a mess today, The. Song about Whiskers. P. G. Wodehouse. FiBHP

World Is like a Woman of Folly, The. Moses ibn Ezra, *tr. fr. Hebrew by* Solomon Solis-Cohen. *Fr.* World's Illusion, The. TrJP

World is no more than the Beloved's single face, The. Asadullah Khan Ghalib, *tr. fr. Urdu by* Jane Hirshfield. EnlH

World is,/ not with us enough, The. O Taste and See. Denise Levertov. ChIV-1; CrSp; FoLa; NoP; PBWP; PPP; TAP

World is Rome, The; Carnuntum, on the Danube. Marcus Antoninus Cui Cognomen Erat Aurelius. Burns Singer. OxBS

World is several billion years of age, The. Winter Report. Ben Howard. PoA

World is so full of a number of things, The. Happy Thought. Robert Louis Stevenson. BoTP; FaBoBe; OxBChV; PWR; Spl

World is taking off her clothes, The. X. J. Kennedy. SM

World Is Too Much with Us, The.. Wordsworth. AWP; ChTr; ClHu; CoGr; EBEvV; EnRP; FaPoB; FaPoR; FHYEP; GTBS; GTBS-P; HAP; HeIL; HeIP; HoPM; ImPo; InPK; InPS; LiTB; MAT; MeMBP; NAEL-2; NAWM-2; NOBE; NoP; OAEL-2; OBNC; PIP; PoE; PoEL-4; Poetr; PoLF; PoRA; PPP; PrIm; RaBo; Son; SoSe; TEP; TFi; TrGrPo; TRP; WeW; WGRP
(Sonnet: "This world is too much with us: late and soon.") PWR
(World Is Too Much with Us; Late and Soon, The.) SCGP
(World, The.) OBEV

World Is Too Much with Us; Late and Soon, The. Wordsworth. *See* World is too much with us; late and soon, The.

World is Turned Upside Down, The. *Unknown.* NOSC

World is very flat, The. Night Thought of a Tortoise Suffering from Insomnia on a Lawn. Emile Victor Rieu. FiBHP

World is what you swim in, or dance, it is simple. The Dolphins. Carol Ann Duffy. NBrP

World is wise, for the world is old, The. The World. Frederick William Faber. PWR

World Is with Me, The. Thomas Hood. Son

World Is with Me Just Enough, The. Sam Abrams. UL

World is young today, The. Digby Mackworth Dolben. NOBVV; OBNC

World/ it was long time ago that I first saw you. Remorse Came Slowly. Nishi Junko, *tr. fr. Japanese by* Kenneth Rexroth *and* Ikuko Atsumi. WPJ

World Itself, the Long Poem Foundered, The. John Riley. VaA

World laid low, and the wind blew like a dust, The. *Unknown, tr. fr. Irish by* Thomas Kinsella. NOIV

World Lines. Howard Nemerov. ArOW

World Looks On, The. Louis I. Newman. PoNe

World Needs, the. *Unknown.* PoToHe

World Not Our Rest, The. Maria Frances Cecelia Cowper. ECWP

World of Darkness. Robert Chatain. PoA

World of dew is, The. Issa, *tr. fr. Japanese by* Geoffrey Bownas *and* Anthony Thwaite. OBD

World of Dreams, The. Philip Salom. NOBAu

World of Expectations, The. Albert Goldbarth. HCAP

World of Light, The. Henry Vaughan. *See* They Are All Gone into the World of Light.

World of lunches, conferences behind, A. A Solicitors' World. Evan Jones. FaBoMA

World of Man, speaking. (*LL*) First you must love your body, in games. Lew Welch. EaPr

World of money, promise and disease, A. (*LL*) The Man from Washington. James Welch. CDW; HATNAP; NoAM; RaBo

World of most particular facts, A. Strict and Particular Old Lady. Tim Longville. VaA

World of Simon Raven, The. Peter Porter. PeLV

World Outside, The. Denise Levertov. TRP

World rustles for Esther, The. Lilith Re-Tells Esther's Story. Michelene Wandor. AIW

World-Secret. Hugo von Hofmannsthal, *tr. fr. German by* Charles Wharton Stork. TrJP

World seems smaller, The. That Time in Tangier. Marvin Bell. AnAn

World shall echo with our Lincoln's name, The. (*LL*) Lincoln. H. Cordelia Ray. AmWP; CBWP-3

World should listen then, as I am listening now, The. (*LL*) To a Skylark. Shelley. EBEvV, *sts. 1–3 only*; EnRP; FaBoBe; FaBV; FaPON; FHYEP; GN; GTBS; GTBS-P; HAP; ImPo; InPS; InvP; LiTB; MeMBP; NAEL-2; NoP; OAEL-2; OBEV; OBNC; OxAEP-2; PoLF; SCGP, *sts. 1–3 only*; TEP; TFi, *sts. 1–3 only*; TrGrPo

World-Soul, The. Emerson. PFP

World State, The. G. K. Chesterton. IHNG

World, that all contains, is ever moving, The. Fulke Greville. *Fr.* Caelica. EnRePo; NoSic

World, the Devil, and Tom Paine, The. *Unknown.* AH

World the First Time, The. Gareth Owen. OBAP

World, The (1). Henry Vaughan. AWP; ChIV-2; EBEV; ESCV; FaBV; HAP; ImPo; JCP; LiTB; NAEL-1; NOBE; NOCV; NOSC; OAEL-1; OxAEP-1; PeECV; PoEL-2; PPP; SCGP; SeCP; SeCV-1; TEP; TFi; TrCP; TrGrPo; WGRP

World to Come, A. Bernard Dadié, *tr. fr. French by* Ellen Conroy Kennedy. NegPo

World today is mourning the death of Mother Jones, The. The Death of Mother Jones. *Unknown.* SWP

World Turned Upside Down, The. *Unknown.* PAH

World turns mild, The; democracy, they say. Tempora Mutantur. James Russell Lowell. HAP

World turns round and leaves the sun, The. Eve in My Legend. Denis Devlin. IPY

World turns softly, The. Water. Hilda Conkling. PDV

World under the sky, The. A Gone. Larry Eigner. NeAP

World uprose as a man to find Him, The. At the End of Things. Arthur Edward Waite. WGRP

World vanishes slowly. We all study, The. The Sea Before I Start Dreaming. Branko Miljkovic, *tr. fr. Serbo-Croatian by* Charles Simic. HSix

World War II. Jeni Couzyn. PeSAV

World War II. Edward Field. ArOW; GLP

World War II. Langston Hughes. HCAP

World was everything that was the case?, The. James Merrill. *Fr.* Mirabell: Books of Number. HCAP

World was first a private park, The. The Fisherman. Jay Macpherson. Mes; NOBC

World Was Warm and White When I Was Born. Delmore Schwartz. ArLo

World We Make, The. Alfred Grant Walton. PoToHe

World will burst like an intestine in the sun, The. Passengers. Denis Johnson. SM

World will see thy picture there, The. (*LL*) Secrecy [*or* Secresie] Protested. Thomas Carew. CaPo; SeCP

World will soon break up into small colonies of the saved, The. (*LL*) Those Being Eaten by America. Robert Bly. CoAP; NaP

World Winter. Earle Birney. GrPl

World with all of its thought and action, The. God's Electric Power. Mrs. Henry Linden. CBWP-4

World without Peculiarity. Wallace Stevens. HCAP

World world world world/ and the face grave. Enueg II. Samuel Beckett. NoAM

World,/ world you are wonderful. A Round Song. Rhyll McMaster. CBAP

Worldes bliss ne last no throwe. *Unknown.* MiEL

Worldes blisse, have good day! *Unknown.* CrSp; MiEL

Worldly Wealth. Rowland Watkyns. FaBoEE

Worldly wisdom of the foolish man, The. Francis Quarles. *Fr.* Emblems. ESCV

World's a bubble, and the life of man, The. The Life of Man. Francis Bacon. EIL; GTBS; NoSic
(Life. GTBS-P; OxAEP-1

World's a floor, whose swelling heaps retain, The. Deuteronomy 30.19. Francis Quarles. ChIV-1

World's a Floore, whose swelling heapes retaine, The. Francis Quarles. *Fr.* Emblems. ESCV

World's a popular disease, that reigns, The. Luke 6.25. Francis Quarles. ChIV-2

World's a Sea, The. Francis Quarles. ChTr

World's a stage, The. The light is in one's eyes. Sonnet XXIX. Hilaire Belloc. IHNG

World's a stage, The. The trifling entrance fee. Hilaire Belloc. OxBTC

World's a theater, the earth a stage, The. The Author to His Book[e]. Thomas Heywood. *Fr.* Apology for Actors, An. NOSC

World's a very happy place, The. The World's Music. "Gabriel Setoun." FaBoBe

World's a weary place, The. All thro' the Year. *Unknown.* BLRP

World's a well strung fidle, mans tongue the quill, The. Nathaniel Ward. SCAP

World's an inn, The; and I her guest. On the World. Francis Quarles. HAP

World's and his Hyperion, The (*LL*) In the Glorious Epiphanie of Our Lord God. Richard Crashaw. PoEL-2

Worlds are reconciled, The. (*LL*) A Christmas Hymn. Richard Wilbur. ChIV-2; OBCP; PChr; TrCP

World's Bliss. Alice Notley. UL

World's bright comforter, whose beamsome light, The. God's Virtue. Barnabe Barnes. *Fr.* Divine Century of Spiritual Sonnets, A. NOCV
(Sonnet: "World's bright comforter, whose beamsome light, The.") EIL

World's deceitful, and man's life at best, The. On Mortality. Henry Colman. ChIV-1

World's Desire, The. William Rose Benét. TrPWD

World's gone forward to its latest fair, The. The Moor. Ralph Hodgson. MoBrPo

World's Great Age, The. Shelley. *See* World's great age begins anew, The.

World's great age begins anew, The. Shelley. *Fr.* Hellas. EnRP; HeIP; NAEL-2; PoE; TEP
(Chorus from "Hellas.") AWP
(Chorus: "World's great age begins anew, The.") EBEV; HAP; NOBE; NoP; OAEL-2; PoEL-4
(Hellas.) ChTr; OBEV
(New World, A.) TrGrPo
(World's Great Age, The.) ImPo; MeMBP

World's Greatest Tricycle Rider, The. C. K. Williams. NYBP

World's Illusion, The. *sels.* Moses ibn Ezra, *tr. fr. Hebrew by* Solomon Solis-Cohen. TrJP
All Ye That Go Astray. TrJP
He That Regards the Precious Things of Earth. TrJP
In Vain Earth Decks Herself. TrJP
Promises of the World, The. TrJP
World Is like a Woman of Folly, The. TrJP
Ye Anger Earth. TrJP

World's infection, to be none of it, The. (*LL*) The First Anniversary. John Donne. NAEL-1; SeCV-1

World's Last Unnamed Poem, The. A. K. Redwing. VoR

World's light shines; shine as it will, The. But Men Loved Darkness Rather Than Light. Richard Crashaw. ChIV-2

World's love runs thin, The. To the Tune "The Phoenix Hairpin." T'ang Wan, *tr. fr. Chinese by* Kenneth Rexroth *and* Ling Chung. WPC; WPOW

World's mad business-Eternal Absolution., The. (*LL*) A Sermon on Swift. Austin Clarke. BIrV; IPY

World's Music, The. "Gabriel Setoun." FaBoBe

Worlds on Worlds. Shelley. *See* Worlds on worlds are rolling ever.

Worlds on worlds are rolling ever. Shelley. *Fr.* Hellas. EnRP; NoP; TEP
(Chorus: "Worlds on worlds are rolling ever.") NAEL-2
(Worlds on Worlds.) HeIP

World's pottage, the rat's star., The. (*LL*) With Mercy for the Greedy. Anne Sexton. CAPP; HCAP; TOF; VCAP

World's regeneration may begin, The. (*LL*) Fashion. Ada Cambridge. NOBAu

World's so wide I cannot cross it, The. Fond Affection. *Unknown.* AS

World's unfolded blossom smells of God, The. (*LL*) An Ode after Easter. Francis Thompson. OtMeF

World's Wanderers, The. Shelley. TTTS

World's Way, The. Shakespeare. *See* Tired [*or* Tyr'd, *or* Tir'd] with all these, for restful death I cry.

World's wrong, mother, The. Wyndmere, Windemere. Carol Muske. PBCAP

Worm, The. Ralph Wilhelm Bergengren. FaPON

Worm. Bob Cobbing. NBrP

Worm artist, The. The Earth Worm. Denise Levertov. NOBA

Worm Either Way. D. H. Lawrence. NoAM

Worm Fed on the Heart of Corinth, A. Isaac Rosenberg. OAEL-2; PeFWW; PoWW

Worm unto his love, The: lo, here's fresh store. The Coffin-Worm. Ruth Pitter. MoBrPo

Worm was punished, sir, for early rising!, The. (*LL*) Early Rising. John Godfrey Saxe. AnAmPo; BLPL; PoLF

Worm will make it square, The. (*LL*) The Whaler's Pig. Edwin James Brady. NOBAu

Worms at Heaven's Gate, The. Wallace Stevens. NoAM; OBD

Wormwood. Thomas Kinsella. CIP; PBCIP

'Worn out of virtue, as the time of year,'. David and Bathsheba in the Public Garden. Robert Lowell. ChIV-1

Worn-out voice of the clock breaks on the hour, The. Prize for Good Conduct. Kenneth Allott. OBWP

Worn with life's care, love yet was love. (*LL*) A Marriage Ring. George Crabbe. BoLoP; EnLoP; OBEV; OxBM

Worried Life Blues. *Unknown.* AmFP

Worried Skipper, The. Wallace Irwin. BLPA

Worries. *Unknown.* PoToHe

Worry. *Unknown.* PoToHe

Worry about Money. Kathleen Raine. FaBoTw

Worry — is like a distant hill. Worry. *Unknown.* PoToHe

Worrying, The. Paul Monette. BAP-90

Worrying Fruit. Christina Rossetti. *See* Morning and evening.

Worschippe ye that loveris bene this May. Spring Song of the Birds. James I, King of Scotland. OBEV

Worse. (*LL*) The Lesson. Kathleen Cain. LoHo

Worse for us than the bombs. Famine. Tran Thi Nga *and* Wendy Wilder Larsen, *and* Wendy Wilder Larsen. WoWa

Worsening Situation. John Ashbery. NOBA

Worship, *sels*. William Wilberforce Lord.

Worshi᠈. Robert Whitaker. TrPWD

Worship. Whittier. ChIV-2; NOCV

Worship of Cromm Cruaich, The. *Unknown, tr. fr. Old Irish by* Kuno Meyer. *Fr.* Voyage of Bran, The. TIRV

Worship of virtu is the mede. Carol of St, A George. *Unknown.* MeEL

Worst a coat upon a coat-hager., The. (*LL*) The Apparitions. W. B. Yeats. CMoP; LiTM; TRP

Worst job I ever had was nailing, The. The Feet Man. Philip Dacey. NGP

Worst side of it all, The. White Roses. John Ashbery. TAP

Worth keeping your foot in the door. Respectable House. Anne Stevenson. NALW

Worth patience to regret. (*LL*) Before Parting. Swinburne. CBLP; NOBVV

Worthless Heart, The. Immanuel di Roma, *tr. fr. Hebrew.* TrJP

Worthless man is a leaking wine-jar, A. Lucianus, *tr. fr. Greek by* Edwin Morgan. GrAn

Worthwhile. Ella Wheeler Wilcox. BLPA; EBEvV; PoToHe

Worthy art Thou,/ O Lord, of praise. Deliverance from a Fit of Fainting. Anne Bradstreet. TAP

Worthy kyng, quhen he has seyn, The. Before Bannockburn. John Barbour. *Fr.* Bruce, The. OxBS

Worthy London Prentice, A. The London Prentice. *Unknown.* CoMu

Worthy object: Our Lord's Feet, A. (*LL*) Saint Mary Magdalene. Richard Crashaw. GeHe; MeLP; SeCV-1

Wotton, my little Bere dwells on a hill. Ad Henricum Wottonem. Thomas Bastard. FaBoEE; FaBoPP

Wou' ye hear of William Wallace. Gude Wallace. *Unknown.* ESPB (Sir William Wallace. ScCV

Wou'd you in love succeed, be brisk, be gay. The Advice. Charles Sackville. FaBoUs

Would a circling surface vulture. Mahadevi, *tr. fr. Kannada by* A. K. Ramanujan. BoWoP

Would all did so as well as I! (*LL*) My Mind to Me a Kingdom Is. *Unknown, wr. at. to* Sir Edward Dyer. BLPL; EBEvV; EiL; EnRePo; FaBoBe; GGP; ImPo; LiTB; NOBE; PoEL-1; SCGP; TrGrPo; WGRP

Would-be Critic, The. Mrs. Henry Linden. CBWP-4

Would beat anew a little while, and then no more. (*LL*) And Then No More. Friedrich Rückert. BIrV; BLPA; PeIV

Would but some winged Angel were too late. Omar Khayyám, *tr. fr. Persian by* Edward Fitzgerald. *Fr.* Rubáiyát of Omar Khayyám of Naishápúr, The. AWP; EBVV, *abr.;* FaBoBe; FaBoRV, *abr.;* FaPoR, *abr.;* GGP; HAP, *abr.;* LiTB; NAEL-2; NoP; PoEL-5; PrIm, *abr.;* TrGrPo

Would but the Desert of the Fountain yield. Omar Khayyám, *tr. fr. Persian by* Edward Fitzgerald. *Fr.* Rubáiyát of Omar Khayyám of Naishápúr, The. AWP; EBVV, *abr.;* FaBoBe; FaBoRV, *abr.;* FaPoR, *abr.;* GGP; HAP, *abr.;* LiTB; NAEL-2; NoP; PoEL-5; PrIm, *abr.;* TrGrPo

Would drop Him - Bone by Bone. (*LL*) There is a pain — so utter. Emily Dickinson. BoWoP; NAAL-1; NOBA

Would Edison get the blues if he blew a fuse? Electricity Is Funny! John Currier. GrPl

Would God I in that Golden City were. Edward Taylor. *Fr.* Preparatory Meditations Before My Approach to the Lord's Supper. EAP

Would God that I and my darling. *Unknown, tr. fr. Gaelic by* Frank O'Connor. *Fr.* Beggarman's Song, A. WTO

Would God That It Were Holiday! Thomas Deloney. *Fr.* Gentle Craft, The. EiL

Would have bounced. (*LL*) Zimmer's Last Gig. Paul Zimmer. Jaz

Would he tell us: *Odes* and *Documents* must live to win men? (*LL*) The Book-burning Pit. Lo Yin. SuSp

Would I Be Shrived? John D. Swain. BLPA

Would I could cast a sail on the water. The Collarbone [Collar-Bone] of a Hare. W. B. Yeats. CBNP; NTP; OxAEP-2; OxBTC; RB

Would I had loved him more! (*LL*) The Child's First Grief. Felicia Dorothea Hemans. BLPA

Would I Might Go Far over Sea. Marie de France, *tr. fr. French by* Arthur O'Shaughnessy. AWP; PoRA

Would I might lie like this, without the pain. In Hospital. James Elroy Flecker. OxBTC

Would I might rouse the Lincoln in you all. Lincoln. Vachel Lindsay. *Fr.* Litany of the Heroes. OHIP

Would I were a king of children. The Child-King. Morris Wintchevsky, *tr. fr. Yiddish by* Alter Brody. TrJP

Would I were air that thou with heat opprest. Thomas Stanley. FaBoEE

Would I were chang'd into that golden shower. Sir Arthur Gorges. GBL

Would I were Changed. Barnabe Barnes. *Fr.* Parthenophil and Parthenophe. AAS; ESo; FaBoBl

"Would it had been the man of our wish!" In the Room of the Bride-Elect. Thomas Hardy. *Fr.* Satires of Circumstance. InPK

Would it please you if I strung my tears. The Race Question. Naomi Long Madgett. BPo

Would never let us satiate here. (*LL*) A Farewell. Matthew Arnold. EnVR; MeMBP

Would not have come this far. (*LL*) Spirits, Dancing. Arthur Gregor. NYBP; VGW

Would part with you. (*LL*) Oh Wide and Sad Land. N. P. van Wyk Louw. PeSAV

Would pause with his needle in the air. (*LL*) Illustrious Ancestors. Denise Levertov. AmPP; MoP; NAAL-2; NOBA; VGW

Would pulse with all the life there was within. (*LL*) The Battle. Louis Simpson. ArOW; InPS; OBWP; PBCV; PoWW; PRA

Would stroke that sheep's black nose. (*LL*) A Child's Pet. W. H. Davies. CH; CoGr; RB

Would That All Your Charms Were Painted. Paul Johann Ludwig Heyse, *tr. fr. German by* Philip L. Miller. RiWo

Would that I streamed like water. Like Water down a Slope. Zalman Schneour, *tr. fr. Hebrew by* Harry H. Fein. TrJP

Would That I Were. Arthur Hugh Clough. TrPWD

Would that the structure brave, the manifold music I build. Abt Vogler. Robert Browning. FHYEP; NAEL-2; OAEL-2; TOF; WGRP

Would that there had never been swift ships! Callimachus, *tr. fr. Greek.* *Fr.* Epigrams. HePo

Would the world know how Godfrey lost his breath? Truth Brought to Light, or Murder Will Out. Stephen College. APAS

Would they swept cleaner! To a Shred of Linen. Lydia Huntley Sigourney. AmWP

Would we could coin for thee new words of praise. Washington's Tomb. Ruth Lawrence. OHIP

Would with Thee live, and for thee die. (*LL*) A Dialogue betwixt God and the Soul. *At. to* Sir Henry Wotton. MeLP; PeECV

Would write a letter with/ my scissors mouth. Young Woman's Neo-Aramaic Jewish Persian Blues. Jerome Rothenberg, *after Persian folk poem.* BoWoP

Would you a favourite novel make. A Receipt for Writing a Novel. Mary Alcock. ECWP

Would you be a man in fashion? *Unknown.* NOSC

Would you be an angel. Something of a Departure. Paul Muldoon. PBCIP

Would you be famous and renowned in story. The Advice. *Unknown.* APAS

Would you be preserved from ruin? The Impartial Inspection. *Unknown.* APAS

Would you believe me. A Family. W. S. Merwin. CAPP

Would you believe some-/ one who said he. Dance and Eye Me (Wicked)ly My Breath a Fixed Sphere. Rochelle Owens. NMM

Would you believe, when you this monsieur see. On English Monsieur. Ben Jonson. NBLV; NoP

Would you care for a smoke or a sherry? Mopev. UV

Would you come back if I said the earth. Nadia Tuéni, *tr. fr. French by* Willis Barnstone. BoWoP

Would You Have a Young Virgin? John Gay. *See* If the heart of a man is deprest [*or* depressed] with cares.

Would you have called me a nobody? (*LL*) Somebody. Tennyson. FaBoEE; NOBL

Would You Hear of an Old-Time [*or* Old-Fashioned] Sea fight? Walt Whitman. *Fr.* Song of Myself. AmPP; ImGa, *sect.* XXXV–XXXVI; LiTA; MoAmPo, *abr.;* NOBA; OxBA; SAmP, *sect.* XXXV; SOTW, (*much abr.*)

Would You in Venus' Wars Succeed. *Unknown.* ErPo

Would you know what's soft? I dare. James Shirley. BeJo

Would you, my friend, in little room express. Martial, *tr. fr. Latin by* Elijah Fenton. OBVE

Would you see the little men. The Little Men. Flora Fearne. BoTP

Would you your son should be a sot or dunce. William Cowper. *Fr.* Tirocinium; or, A Review of Schools. OBSV

Wouldn't It Be Funny? Pixie O'Harris. ZA

Wouldn't it be wonderful to come across in cabaret. Unromantic Song. Anthony Brode. FiBHP

Wouldnt think/t look at m. Panther Man. James A. Emanuel. BPo; NBV

"Write me a sonnet. On the spot," said she. Sonnet Right off the Bat. Lope de Vega, *tr. fr. Spanish* by John Frederick Nims. STV

Write not that you content can be. A Colonist in His Garden. William Pember Reeves. IHNG

Write on my grave when I am dead. Katharine Tynan. WGRP

Write on the giddy wind. Write on the stream as it flows. *(LL)* My girl says she'll take no one else as a lover. Catullus. STV

Write this. We have burned all their villages. Sun. Michael Palmer. BAP-89

Write thus uppon my soule: thy Jesue still. *(LL)* O sweete and bitter monuments of paine. William Alabaster. ESCV; Son

"Write to Sardis," saith the Lord, Sardis. William Cowper. ChIV-2

Write to thine eyes? Why, my poor pen. To Fannie. Mary E. Tucker. CBWP-1

Write! Write! Help! Help! Barnabe Barnes. *Fr.* Parthenophil and Parthenophe. Son

Writer, The. Hildebrand Jacob. FaBoCo

Writer, The. Richard Wilbur. CAPP; HCAP; ImGa; NoAM; OxBC; Poetr; SoSe

Writer, attend no schools. The Teacher. Virginia Brady Young. GoYe

"Writer. It's a cul-de-sac, The," you wrote that. Drawings: For John Who Said to Write about True Love. Lorna Dee Cervantes. AfAz

Writers, *sels.* Robert Lowell.

Robert Frost. MoP; NAAL-2; NoAM; Poetr; Son

Writing. William Allingham. NOBVV

Writing. Andrew Motion. DiPo

Writing. Howard Nemerov. NYBP; VCAP

Writing a Curriculum Vitae. Wislawa Szymborska, *tr. fr. Polish* by Grazyna Drabik *and* Austin Flint. PoSu

Writing a letter he said. Buffalo — Isle of Wight Power Cable. Anselm Hollo. PoM

Writing in England Now. Philip O'Connor. OxBTC

Writing in Prison. Ken Smith. NBrP

Writing Letters. Rodney Bennett. BoTP

Writing Poetry in the Back Garden. Chao Yi, *tr. fr. Chinese* by Chang Yin-nan *and* Lewis C. Walmsley. SuSp

Writing poetry needs a mind that's nimble and free. Replying to a Poem by Li T'ien-lin. Yang Wan-li, *tr. fr. Chinese* by Sherwin S. S. Fu. SuSp

Writing these poems!/ Imagine! *(LL)* Autobiographia Literaria. Frank O'Hara. CAPP; NNaP; NOBA; TTTS

Writing through a Text by Chris Mann. John Cage. EOEF

Written a Few Hours before the Birth of a Child. Jane Cave. ECWP

Written after Swimming from Sestos to Abydos. Byron. NAEL-2; NBLV; NoP; OBTV

Written at a Party Where My Lord Gave Away a Thousand Bolts of Silk. Ch'ien T'ao, *tr. fr. Chinese* by Kenneth Rexroth *and* Ling Chung. WPC

Written at [or in] an Inn at Henley. William Shenstone. AWP; NOBE; NOEC; OBEV; OxAEP-1

Written at Cambridge. Charles Lamb. EnRP

Written at Hsiang-kuo Temple on the Occasion of Watching Actors in the Hsing-hsiang Garden of the T'ung-t'ien-chieh Tao-ch'ang. Wang An-shih, *tr. fr. Chinese* by Jan W. Walls. SuSp

Written at Lakeside Residence. Chiang K'uei, *tr. fr. Chinese* by Chiang Yee. SuSp

Written at Mauve Garden: Pine Wind Terrace. Chu Yi-tsun, *tr. fr. Chinese* by Chang Yin-nan *and* Lewis C. Walmsley. SuSp

Written at Sea, in the First Dutch War. Charles Sackville. *See* To all you ladies now at land.

Written at Stonehenge. Thomas Warton the Younger. Son

Written at the White Sulphur Springs. Francis Scott Key. OBAL

Written beneath Hui Mountain, When Tsou Liu-yi Comes by for a Visit. Wang Shih-chieng, *tr. fr. Chinese* by Richard John Lynn. SuSp

Written by Desire of a Lady, on an Angry, Petulant Kitchen-Maid. Jane Cave. ECWP

Written by the Barrow Side, Where She Was Sent to Wash Linen. Ellen Taylor. ECWP

Written December 1790. Anna Seward. Son

Written, Directed by and Starring. James Simmons. PBCIP

Written during My Stay at White Clouds Monastery on West Lake. Su Man-shu, *tr. fr. Chinese* by Wu-chi Liu. SuSp

Written for My Son, and Spoken by Him at His First Putting on Breeches. Mary Barber. ECEV; ECWP; NOEC

Written Forty Miles South of a Spreading City. Robert Bly. NNaP

Written in a Blank Leaf of Dugdale's "Monasticon." Thomas Warton the Younger. *See* Deem not, devoid of elegance, the sage.

Written in a Copy of Swift's Poems, for Wayne Burns. James Wright. NOBA

Written in a Lady's Prayer Book. The Earl of Rochester. BoLoP

Written in a Public Restaurant, *sels.* Israel Efrat, *tr. fr. Hebrew* by Bernhard Frank.

Written in a Thunder Storm July 15th, 1841. John Clare. EnVR

Written in Absence. Alcuin, *tr. fr. Latin* by Helen Waddell. MLL

Written in an Album. Wordsworth. *See* Small service is true service while it lasts.

Written in an Ovid. Matthew Prior. FaBoEE; FaBoUs

Written in Autumn. Thomas Cole. AiP

Written in Behalf of My Wife. Li Po, *tr. fr. Chinese* by Joseph J. Lee. SuSp

Written in Dejection near Rome. Robert Bly. NaP

Written in Early Spring. Wordsworth. *See* I heard a thousand blended notes.

Written in Exile. Kathleen Raine. TrCP; WPE

Written in Her French Psalter. Elizabeth I, Queen of England. PBWP; WPE

Written in Ireland. Mary Alcock. ECWP; NOEC; OBTV

Written in Jest on Elder Stonegate's Eastern Balcony. Liu Tsung-yüan, *tr. fr. Chinese* by Jan W. Walls. SuSp

Written in Juice of Lem[m]on. Abraham Cowley. *Fr.* Mistress, The. SeCP; SeCV-1

Written in London, September, 1802. Wordsworth. FaBoPV; TrGrPo

Written in March. Wordsworth. BoNaP; BoTP; EnRP; FaPON; GoJo; NAEL-2; NTCP; PFP; PYC; SCGP; UnPo

Written in Northampton County Asylum. John Clare. *See* I am: yet what I am none cares or knows.

Written in Pencil in the Sealed Railway-Car. Dan Pagis, *tr. fr. Hebrew* by Stephen Mitchell. OBD

Written in Prison. John Clare. EnVR; OAEL-2

Written in the Album of a Child. Wordsworth. *See* Small service is true service while it lasts.

Written in the Beginning of Mezeray's History of France. Matthew Prior. NOBE; PoEL-3

Written in the Sunset. Hsiung-hung, *tr. fr. Chinese* by Kenneth Rexroth *and* Ling Chung. WPC

Written in Unbridled Repugnance near Sioux Falls, Alabama — April 30, 1974. A. K. Redwing. VoR

Written in Very Early Youth. Wordsworth. EnRP

Written on a Gloomy Day, in Sickness. Susanna Blamire. ECWP

Written on a Leaf. *Unknown, tr. fr. Chinese* by Geoffrey R. Waters. BoWoP

Written on a Looking-Glass. *Unknown.* FaBoEE

Written on a Monastery Wall. Li Shang-yin, *tr. fr. Chinese* by A. C. Graham. PLT

Written on a Wall at Woodstock. Elizabeth I, Queen of England. *See* Oh fortune, [how] thy wresting wavering state.

Written on a Window. Aaron Hill. OxBSP

Written on an Island off the Breton Coast. Saint Venantius Fortunatus, *tr. fr. Latin* by Helen Waddell. PeHV

Written on Beginning Georg Büchner's *Lenz* & While Waiting a Return. John James. VaA

Written on Lake View Tower. P'an Lang, *tr. fr. Chinese* by Jonathan Chaves. SuSp

Written on Seeing Her Two Sons at Play. Henrietta O'Neill. ECWP

Written on Seeing the Flowers, and Remembering My Daughter. Kao Ch'i. DL

Written on the Anniversary of Our Father's Death. Hartley Coleridge. Son

Written on the Day That Mr. Leigh Hunt Left Prison. Keats. *See* What though, for showing truth to flatter'd [or flattered] state.

Written on the Eve of Execution. Chidiock Tichborne. *See* My prime of youth is but a frost of cares.

Written on the Eve of His Execution. James Graham, Marquess of Montrose. *See* Let them bestow on every airt[h] a limb.

Written on the Plain of Thebes. John William Burgon. OBTV

Written on the Thirtieth Day, Ninth Month, Second Year of the Ta-li Reign [767]. Tu Fu, *tr. fr. Chinese* by Irving Y. Lo. SuSp

Written on the Wall at Chang's Hermitage. Tu Fu, *tr. fr. Chinese* by Kenneth Rexroth. EnlH; EOEF; HoPM; NaP

Written on the Wall of Halfway Mountain Temple. Wang An-shih, *tr. fr. Chinese* by Jan W. Walls. SuSp

Written on the Walls of His Dungeon. Luís de León, *tr. fr. Spanish* by Thomas Walsh. TrJP

Written on Whitsun-Monday, 1795. Matilda Betham-Edwards. ECWP

Written, Originally Extempore, on Seeing a Mad Heifer Run through the Village. Elizabeth Hands. ECWP

Written the First Morning of the Author's Bathing at Teignmouth for the Head-Ache. Jane Cave. ECWP

X

Y

Yarn of the *Nancy Bell*, The. W. S. Gilbert. BeLS; BLPA; EBEvV; EBNV; FaBoBe; FaBoCh; FaBoCo; FaBV; HoPM; MoShBr; NOBL; TFi; TrGrPo; UV, sh. vers.

Yarra Park. Anne Elder. FaBoMA

Yarrow counted eight of them. July the First. Robert Currie. Poetsp

Yarrow had to learn it but he loved Young Jacob. Brothers. Robert Currie. Poetsp

Yarrow Unvisited. Wordsworth. EnRP; GTBS; GTBS-P; PoRA

Yarrow Visited. Wordsworth. EnRP; GTBS; GTBS-P

Yasmin. James Elroy Flecker. *See* How splendid in the morning glows.

Yawcob Strauss. Charles Follen Adams. VPP

Yawn of Yawns, The, *sels.* Vasco [*or* Vasko] Popa, *tr. fr. Serbo-Croatian.*
  Forgetful Number. AnRep, *tr. by* Charles Simic; HSix, *tr. by* Charles Simic
  Petrified Echoes. PoSu, *tr. by* Anne Pennington
  Proud Error. AnRep, *tr. by* Charles Simic; HSix, *tr. by* Charles Simic
  Tale About a Tale, The. AnRep, *tr. by* Charles Simic; HSix
  Wise Triangle, A. CBNP, *tr. by* Anne Pennington *and* Charles Simic; CoGr, *tr. by* Anne Pennington *and* Charles Simic; PoSu, *tr. by* Anne Pennington

Yawn of Yawns, The. AnRep, *tr. by* Charles Simic; PoSu, *tr. by* Anne Pennington

Yawn of Yawns, The. Vasco [*or* Vasko] Popa, *tr. fr. Serbo-Croatian. Fr.* Yawn of Yawns, The. AnRep, *tr. by* Charles Simic; PoSu, *tr. by* Anne Pennington

Yawns sobbingly, his head falls back, he sleeps. (*LL*) Pilots, Man Your Planes. Randall Jarrell. MoAB; MoAmPo

Yawp! (*LL*) Home Sweet Home with Variations. H. C. Bunner. BXAP; OBAL

Ydoan/ yunnuhstan. YgUDuh. E. E. Cummings. PeLV

Ye Alps audacious, thro' the heavens that rise. The Hasty Pudding. Joel Barlow. AmPP; EAP; NOBA; OBAL, *abr.;* OxBA; TAP

Ye angells bright, pluck from your wings a quill. Edward Taylor. *Fr.* Preparatory Meditations Before My Approach to the Lord's Supper. ChIV-2; PoEL-3

Ye Anger Earth. Moses ibn Ezra, *tr. fr. Hebrew by* Solomon Solis-Cohen. *Fr.* World's Illusion, The. TrJP

"Ye are the Duke of Athol's nurse." The Duke of Athole's Nurse. *Unknown.* ESPB

Ye are the spirits who preside. Joanna Baillie. *Fr.* Address to the Muses, An. ECWP

Ye are the temples of the Lord. The Exhortation of a Father to His Children. Robert Smith. OxBChV

Ye aye sall be my dearie!' (*LL*) Ca' the Yowes to the Knowes. Isobel Pagan. OBEV; OxAEP-1

Ye ayres and windes, ye elves of hilles. Medea's Incantation. Ovid, *tr. fr. Latin. Fr.* Metamorphoses. AWP, *tr. by* Shakespeare; OBVE, *tr. by* Arthur Golding

Ye banks and braes and streams around. Highland Mary. Burns. AWP; EnRP; GTBS; GTBS-P; OBEV; TrGrPo; WBLP

Ye Banks and Braes [o' Bonnie Doon]. Burns. *See* Ye banks and braes o' Bonnie Doon.

Ye banks and braes o' Bonnie Doon. The Banks of Doon. Burns. BoLoP; GTBS; GTBS-P; NOBE; NOEC; OBEV; PrIm; TrGrPo; WBLP
  (Banks O' Doon, The.) OtMeF; TFi
  (Bonnie Doon.) NoP
  (Ye Banks and Braes [o' Bonnie Doon].) CH; ELP; ScCV
  (Ye Flowery Banks [o' Bonnie].) AWP; EnRP; NAEL-2; PoEL-4; UnPo

Ye be my friends, and so be but few else. (*LL*) Lux my fair falcon, and your fellows all. Sir Thomas Wyatt. AAS; OBF; SiPS

Ye Beauties, Beaux, ye Pleaders at the Bar. *Unknown. Fr.* London Evening Post. FaBoUs

Ye beauties! O how great the sun. On a Bed of Guernsey Lilies. Christopher Smart. NOEC

Ye belles, and ye flirts, and ye pert little things. Song for Ranelagh. William Whitehead. ECEV

Ye [*or* Yee] blushing virgins happy are. To Roses in the Bosom[e] of Castara. William Habington. *Fr.* Castara. BeJo; EnLoPo; MeLP; NOSC; OBEV; SCGP; SeCP

Ye bold British tars, who to glory are free. The *Dolphin's* Return. *Unknown.* OxBSS

Ye brave bold men of 'Cotia. Robens' Promised Land. George Purdom. WTO

Ye brave Columbian bands! a long farewell! On Disbanding the Army. David Humphreys. PAH

Ye brave sons of Freedom, come join in the chorus. The Times. *Unknown.* PAH

Ye Bruthers Dogg. Jon Anderson. NBLV

Ye bubbling springs that gentle music makes. Love's Limit. *Unknown.* TrGrPo

Ye buds of Brutus' land, courageous youths, now play your parts! For Soldiers. Humphrey Gifford. CH; EiL; NoSic

Yᴇ captive souls of blindfold Cyprian's boat. My Love is Past. Thomas Watson. NoSic

Ye cats that at midnight spit love at each other. An Appeal to Cats in the Business of Love. Thomas Flatman. EnLoPo; GBL; HAP

Ye Clerke of Ye Wethere. *Unknown.* BXAP

Ye Clouds! that far above me float and pause. France; an Ode. Samuel Taylor Coleridge. EnRP

Ye Columbians so bold, attend while I sing. Hull's Surrender. *Unknown.* PAH

Ye Commons and Peers. Jack Frenchman's Defeat. Congreve. APAS (Jack Frenchman's Lamentation.) CoMu

Ye coop us up, and tax our bread. Caged Rats. Ebenezer Elliot. EBEV

Ye coopers and hoopers, attend to my ditty. The Cooper o' Dundee. *Unknown.* CoMu

Ye dainty nymphs, that in this blessed brook. Elisa ("Ye dainty nymphs, that in this blessed brook.") Spenser. *Fr.* Shepheardes [*or* Shepeards *or* Shepherd's] Calender, The. NAEL-1; PoEL-1
  (Lay to Eliza, The.) NOBE

Ye distant spires, ye antique towers. Ode on a Distant Prospect of Eton College. Thomas Gray. BLPL; GTBS; GTBS-P; ImPo; LiTB; NAEL-1; NOBE; NOEC; NoP; OAEL-1; OxAEP-1; PoE; PoEL-3; PrIm; SCGP

Ye dogg, O'Toole. Ye Bruthers Dogg. Jon Anderson. NBLV

Ye Dons and ye doctors, ye Provosts and Proctors. Winthrop Mackworth Praed. *Fr.* London University, The. FaBoEH

Ye dorty blackleg miners! (*LL*) The Blackleg Miners. *Unknown.* GBP; OBET

Ye elms that wave on Malvern Hill. Malvern Hill. Herman Melville. AmPP; PAH; TAP

Ye elves of hills, brooks, standing lakes, and groves. Magic. Ovid, *tr. fr. Latin. Fr.* Metamorphoses. AWP, *tr. by* Shakespeare

Ye elves of hill(s), brooks, standing lakes, and groves. Shakespeare. *Fr.* Tempest, The. EBEV; OAEL-1; OxAEP-1; SCV
  (Magic.) AWP

Ye famed physicians of this place. A Lamentable Case. Sir Charles Hanbury Williams. ErPo

Ye few, whose feeling hearts are ne'er estranged. The Canongate Playhouse in Ruins. Robert Fergusson. ScCV

Ye flaming powers, and winged warriors bright, Upon the Circumcision. Milton. ChIV-2

Ye flippering soule. An Address to the Soul Occasioned by a Rain. Edward Taylor. MeMAP; NAAL-1; NOBA; OxBA; PoEL-3

Ye Flowery Banks [o' Bonnie]. Burns. *See* Ye banks and braes o' Bonnie Doon.

Ye fog that creeps there in the uplands. Invocation for a Storm. *Unknown, tr. fr. Hawaiian.* WTO

Ye gallants of Newgate, whose fingers are nice. Newgate's Garland. John Gay. ECEV; FaBoBa; PeLV

Ye gentlemen and ladies fair. The Hunters of Kentucky; or, Half Horse and Half Alligator. Samuel Woodworth. AS; PAH

"Ye gie corn to my horse." Clyde's Water. *Unknown.* ESPB

Ye glorious Jove-born imps how you rejoice. On the Three Children in the Fiery Furnace. Henry Colman. ChIV-1

Ye glowing seraphs, that now breathe above. Friendship in Perfection. Andrew Michael Ramsay. NOEC

Ye Goat-herd Gods. Sir Philip Sidney. *Fr.* Arcadia. HAP; NAEL-1; NOBE; NoP; NoSic; OAEL-1

Ye gods above protect the widow, and with pity look on me. President Parker. *Unknown.* OxBSS

Ye Gods! the raptures of that night! The Enjoyment. *Unknown.* ErPo

Ye golden lamps of heaven, farewell. Philip Doddridge *and* John Logan. ECEV

"Ye graceful peasant-girls and mountain-maids." Ballata: His Talk with Certain Peasant Girls. Franco Sacchetti, *tr. fr. Italian by* Dante Gabriel Rossetti. AWP

Ye green-rob'd Dryads, oft' at dusky eve. The Enthusiast: or, The Lover of Nature. Joseph Warton. NOEC

Ye green-robed Dryads, oft at dusky eve. Joseph Warton. *Fr.* Enthusiast, The; or, The Lover of Nature. ECEV, *ll.* 1–15; EnRP; NOEC; PoEL-3

Ye have been fresh and green. To Meadows. Robert Herrick. AWP; CaPo; CH; JCP; NOBE; NOSC; OBEV
  (To Meddowes.) PoEL-3; SeCP; SeCV-1

"Ye have robbed," said he, "ye have slaughtered and made an end." He Fell among Thieves. Sir Henry Newbolt. EBVV; FaPoR; OBEV; OBWP; OxBTC

Ye have seen a marvel in this town. The Lament for Yellow-haired Donough. *Unknown, tr. fr. Irish by* Frank O'Connor. PeIV

Ye Heavens, Uplift Your Voice. *Unknown.* OHIP

Ye Highlands [*or* hielands] and ye Lawlands [*or* lowlands]. The Bonny Earl of Murray. *Unknown.* ESPB, A *vers.*; FaBoBa; NOSC; OBEV; OxBB; OxBS; PrIm; ScCV; SCGP, A *vers.*

Ye holy Angels bright. Richard Baxter. *Fr.* Psalm of Praise, A. NOCV

Ye Hovering Angels. Emanuel Geibel, *tr. fr. German by* Philip L. Miller. RiWo

Ye humble souls that seek the Lord. Christ's Resurrection and Ascension. Philip Doddridge. NOCV

Ye hypocrites! are these your pranks? Verses Written on a Pane of Glass, on the Occasion of a National Thanksgiving for a Naval Victory. Burns. IHNG
(On Thanksgiving for a National Victory.) ScCV

Ye jolly Yankee gentlemen, who live at home in ease. The C.S.A. Commissioners. *Unknown.* PAH

Ye jovial throng, come join the song. The Battle of Muskingum; or, The Defeat of the Burrites. William Harrison Safford. PAH

Ye know my heart, my lady dear. Sir Thomas Wyatt. SiPS

Ye know on earth, and all ye need to know. (*LL*) Ode on a Grecian Urn. Keats. AWP; ClHu; EBEV; EnRP; FaBoBe; FF; HAP; HeIP; HoPM; ImPo; InPS; LiTB; NAEL-2; NAWM-2; NIP; NOBE; NoP; OAEL-2; OBEV; OBNC; PoE; PoEL-4; PPP; PrIm; SCGP; TEP; TFi; TOF; TrGrPo; UnPo

Ye ladies, walking past me piteous-eyed. Sonnet: To the Same Ladies; With Their Answer. Dante, *tr. fr. Italian by* Dante Gabriel Rossetti. AWP

Ye Little Birds That Sit and Sing. *At. to* Thomas Heywood. *Fr.* Fair Maid of the Exchange, The. ElL

Ye living lamps, by whose dear light. The Mower to the Glow-Worms [*or* Glowworms]. Andrew Marvell. AWP; ELP; FHYEP; GeHe; InvP; NAEL-1; NOBE; NoP; OAEL-1; OxBoLi; PeLV; PPP; SCGP; TFi; TrGrPo
(Mower to the Glo-Worms, The.) CBLP; EnLoPo; ESCV; PoEL-2; SeCP

Ye lords of creation, men you are called. The Lords of Creation. *Unknown.* PoLF

Ye loyal Britons, I pray draw near. The Battle of Shiloh. *Unknown.* AmFP

Ye maggots, feed on Willie's brains. Burns. FaBoEE

Ye Mariners of England. Thomas Campbell. BLPA; EBEvV; EnRP; FaPoR; GN; GTBS; GTBS-P; NOBE; OBEV; OBWP; OxAEP-2; PAW; PlP

Ye mariners of Spain. The Song of the Galley. *Unknown, tr. fr. Spanish by* John Gibson Lockhart. AWP

Ye maun gang to your father, Janet. Fair Janet. *Unknown.* ESPB; OxBB

Ye may simper, blush, and smile. To Cherry-Blossoms. Robert Herrick. SeCV-1

Ye members of Parliament all. The Shash. *Unknown.* APAS

Ye merry hearts that love to play. Win at First and Lose at Last; or, A New Game at Cards. Laurence Price. OxBoLi

Ye mitered fathers of the land. The Sentiments. *Unknown.* APAS

Ye Mongers Aye Need Masks for Cheatrie. Sydney Goodsir Smith. OxBS

Ye morning glories, ring in the gale your bells. The New God. James Oppenheim. WGRP

Ye motions of delight, that through the fields. Imagination, How Impaired and Restored. Wordsworth. *Fr.* Prelude [or, Growth of a Poet's Mind], The. EnRP; OAEL-2; OBNC; PoE; PoEL-4, XII, *abr.*; TOF

Ye mountain valleys, pitifully groan! Lament for Bion. Moschus, *tr. fr. Greek by* George Chapman. AWP
(Sing me "Woe," you glades and Dorian water.) HePo, *tr. by* Barbara Hughes Fowler

Ye nymphs and ye swains that trip over the plains. Black Thing. *Unknown.* CoMu

Ye Nymphs forlorn, who pine away in Shades! From a Marriage Broker's Card, 1776. *Unknown.* FaBoUs

Ye nymphs! if e'er your eyes were red. On the Lamented Death of Mrs. Throckmorton's Bullfinch. William Cowper. NOEC; PPP

Ye nymphs of Solyma! begin the song. Messiah: A Sacred Eclogue in Imitation of Virgil's Pollio. Pope. ChIV-1

Ye old mule, that thinck your self so fayre. Sir Thomas Wyatt. AAS

Ye [*or* you] Goat-herd Gods, [that love the grassy mountains]. Ye Goat-herd Gods. Sir Philip Sidney. *Fr.* Arcadia. HAP; NAEL-1; NOBE; NoP; NoSic; OAEL-1
(Double Sestine [*or* Sestina]. ImPo; LiTB; PoEL-1; SiPSBD

Ye Parliament of England. *Unknown.* AmFP; PAH

Ye paultry underlings of state. On the Irish Club. Swift. OBSV

Ye people of Ireland, both country and city. A New Song of Wood's Halfpence. *At. to* Swift Swift. OxBoLi

Ye people who delight in sin. The Hanging of Sam Archer. *Unknown.* AmFP

Ye pilgrim-folk, advancing pensively. Dante, *tr. fr. Italian by* Dante Gabriel Rossetti. *Fr.* Vita Nuova, La. AWP; CTC

Ye plains, where threefold harvests press the ground. The Passage of the Mountain of St. Gothard. Georgiana Cavendish, Duchess of Devonshire. ECWP

Ye powers above and heavenly poles. On Button the Grave-Maker. *Unknown.* FaBoEE

Ye powers of truth, that bid my soul aspire. On Freedom and Ambition. Goldsmith. *Fr.* Travel[l]er; or, A Prospect of Society, The. NOIV

Ye Protestants of Ulster, I pray you join with me. Lisnagade. *Unknown.* WTO

Ye Realms below the Skies. Hosea Ballou II. AH

Ye sailors bold both great and small. The Fishing Lass of Hakin. Lewis Morris. AngWe

Ye saints who dwell on Europe's shore. The Handcart Song. *Unknown.* AmFP

Ye saw't floueran in my breist. The Mandrake Hert. Sydney Goodsir Smith. OxBS

Ye say they all have passed away. Indian Names. Lydia Huntley Sigourney. FaPON; GOA; OBCA ; PAH; PoLF

Ye Scattered Nations. *Unknown, tr. fr. Latin by* Thomas Cradock. AH

Ye seamen who's a mind to go. A New Song on the *Blandford* Privateer. *Unknown.* OxBSS

Ye seek for that can not be found. (*LL*) Defiled Is My Name Full Sore. *At. to* Anne Boleyn. WPE

Ye shall have rumney and malmesine. Wines to Drive Out Melancholy. *Unknown.* CBCK

Ye shall hear nevermore! (*LL*) Farewells from Paradise. Elizabeth Barrett Browning. OBEV

Ye [*or* You] should stay longer if we durst. Francis Beaumont. *Fr.* Masque of the Inner Temple and Gray's Inne, The. TrGrPo
(Fourth Song, The.) NOSC

Ye silent shades, whose each tree here. To Groves. Robert Herrick. CaPo

Ye single folks all, that adorn this gay table. A Song for the Single Table on New Year's Day. Elizabeth Frances Amherst. ECWP

Ye smarts and belles, whose airs and arts confess. The Vanity of External Accomplishments. Mary Whateley. ECWP

Ye sons of Britain in chorus join and sing. Nelson's Death and Victory. *Unknown.* OxBSS

Ye Sons of Columbia. Thomas Green Fessenden. PAH

Ye Sons of Columbia, who bravely have fought. Adams and Liberty. Robert Treat Paine. PAH

Ye sons of Columbia, your attention I do crave. Fuller and Warren. *At. to* Moses Whitecotton. AmFP; BeLS

Ye sons of earth prepare the plough. The Sower. William Cowper. ChIV-2

Ye sons of Massachusetts, all who love that honored name. The Sudbury Fight. Wallace Rice. PAH

Ye sons of Sedition, how comes it to pass. On the Snake. *Unknown.* PAH

Ye sons of toil, awake to glory! The Marseillaise. Claude Joseph Rouget de Lisle, *tr. by* Charles H. Kerr. WBLP

Ye Sorrowers. Franz Werfel, *tr. fr. German by* Ludwig Lewisohn. *Fr.* Eternal Road, The. TrJP

Ye sorrowing people! who from bondage fly. The Fugitive Slaves. Jones Very. TAP

Ye stoll awaye and durst no more be seene. (*LL*) Admonition to Montgomerie. James I, King of England. GTBS; GTBS-P; OxBS

Ye storm-winds of Autumn. Parting. Matthew Arnold. *Fr.* Switzerland. EnVR

Ye Swains who roam from fair to fair. Would You in Venus' Wars Succeed. *Unknown.* ErPo

Ye sylvan Muses, loftier strains recite. The Birth of the Squire; an Eclogue. John Gay. NAEL-1; NOEC; PoEL-3

Ye tender-hearted people, I pray you lend an ear. Samuel Allen. *Unknown.* AmFP

Ye tender young virgins attend to my lay. Perplexity: A Poem. Elizabeth Hands. WoRP

Ye that have faith to look with fearless eyes. Victory. *Unknown.* WGRP

Ye that passen [*or* pasen] by the weye [*or* weiye]. *Unknown.* MiEL
(Jesus to Those Who Pass By.) MeEL

Ye tourists and travellers, bound to the Rhine. Thomas Hood. OBTV

Ye true lovers bold, come listen unto me. The True Lovers Bold. *Unknown.* AmFP

Ye vales and hills whose beauty hither drew. Wordsworth. *Fr.* Inscription for a Monument in Crosthwaite Church in the Vale of Keswick. EPCY

Ye Virgin Pow'rs defend my heart. Elizabeth Taylor. KTR

Ye walls! sole witnesses of happy sighs. Walter Savage Landor. *Fr.* Ianthe. EnLoPo

Ye Wearie Wayfarer., *sels.* Adam Lindsay Gordon. Chase and the Race, The. OtMeF

Years have gathered grayly, The. In a Eweleaze Near Weatherbury. Thomas Hardy. EnVR

Years have gone, The. It is spring. Andrée Rexroth. Kenneth Rexroth. PrIm; VGW

Years have not damaged your beauty, The. Rufinus Domesticus, *tr. fr. Greek by* Sam Hamill. InMo

Years in the blood keep us naked to the bone, The. The Art of Clay. Duane Niatum. HATNAP

Years I've waited for this. Kite-Flying. Kath McKay. DT

Years Later. Laurence David Lerner. NAs; PeSA

Years Later. Ruth Stone. BoWoP

Years later, they could hardly remember her face. The Dragon Lady's Legacy. Colleen J. McElroy. BCF

Years, many parti-coloured years. Years. Walter Savage Landor. OBEV

Years of Indiscretion. John Ashbery. NOBA

Years of manhood had not tinged, The. Charley du Bignon. Mary E. Tucker. CBWP-1

Years pass on, and overhead, The. His Prime. George Clinton Rowe. *Fr.* Toussaint L'Overture. AAP

Years pile up, but there rides with you still, The. As on a Darkling Plain. Henry Taylor. MT; Poetr

Years ride out from the world like couriers gone to a throne, The. Song of the Riders. Stephen Vincent Benét. *Fr.* John Brown's Body. MoAmPo

Years saw me still Acasto's mansion grace. An Old Cat's Dying Soliloquy. Anna Seward. ECWP; NOEC

Years shaped like the tree trunks. Petrarch. Walter Holland. PFL

Year's Spinning, A. Elizabeth Barrett Browning. NAEL-2

Years they come and go, The. Ad Finem. Heine, *tr. fr. German by* Elizabeth Barrett Browning. AWP

Years they mistook me for you. Dodo. Henry Carlile. Poetsp

Years to come (empty boxcars), The. Time. William Stafford. Son

Years Vanish Like the Morning Dew. Mei Sheng *and* Fu I, *tr. fr. Chinese by* Arthur Waley. IMW

Years, years ago, ere yet my dreams. The Belle of the Ball-Room. Winthrop Mackworth Praed. *Fr.* Every-Day Characters. EnRP; FaBoCo

Yee Shall Not Misse of a Few Lines in Remembrance of Thomas Hooker. Edward Johnson. SCAP

Yee wastefull woods beare witness of my woe. William Smith. *Fr.* Chloris [or the Complaint of the Passionate Despised Shepheard]. ESo

Yeh./ billie. if someone. For Our Lady. Sonia Sanchez. IHMS; VBLP

Yelled Colonel Corporal Punishment at Private Reasons. The Enlisted Man. Robert Graves. IHNG

Yellow. De Leon Harrison. PoBA

Yellow. Kenton Kilmer. GoYe

Yellow. Michael O'Loughlin. IB

Yellow. Charles Wright. AmPA

Yellow and poster-striped the hornet vans. Sensation. Jon Stallworthy. IHNG

Yellow as the cups of gold. "Pat of Butter, A." Sarah Helen Whitman. AmWP

Yellow-belly, yellow-belly, come and take a swim. *Unknown.* OxBoLi

Yellow Bird, The. James W. Thompson. PoBA

Yellow Bird Sings, The. Rabindranath Tagore. *Fr.* Gardener, The. OBMV

Yellow birds flutter through the red maples. A Song of Chin Men District. Hsueh Ch'iung, *tr. fr. Chinese by* Kenneth Rexroth *and* Ling Chung. WPC

Yellow Bittern, The. Cathal Buidhe Mac Giolla Ghunna, *tr. fr. Irish.* NOIV, *tr. by* Thomas Kinsella

Yellow Bittern, The. Cathal Buidhe Mac Giolla Ghunna, *tr. fr. Irish.* BIrV, *tr. by* Thomas MacDonagh; CIP, *tr. by* Tom MacIntyre; NOIV, *tr. by* Thomas Kinsella; PeIV, *tr. by* Tom MacIntyre

Yellow Bittern, The. Tom MacIntyre. PBCIP

Yellow Bittern, The. *Unknown, tr. fr. Irish by* Tom MacIntyre. CIP

Yellow blood on the dunes. Before the Pacific. Blanca Varela, *tr. fr. Spanish by* Willis Barnstone. BoWoP

Yellow butterflies. At. to Koianimptiwa, *tr. fr. Hopi Indian by* Natalie Curtis. AWP; WTO

Yellow canary trilled, A. Jealous Adam. Itsik Manger, *tr. fr. Yiddish by* Jacob Sonntag. TrJP

Yellow chirper, beaks its cage, The. (*LL*) In the Cage. Robert Lowell. FF; NOBA; SM; Son

Yellow chrysanthemums, The. Sequence for a Young Widow Passing. Deborah Munro. IHMS

Yellow cloud rising up from that fighting. *Aborigine Oral Tradition.* WTO

Yellow-coated pomegranate, figs like lizards' necks, A. Philip of Thessalonica, *tr. fr. Greek by* Edwin Morgan. GrAn

Yellow coverlet, A. Rosanna Warren. BAP-91

Yellow dusk: messenger fails to appear. *Unknown, tr. fr. Chinese by* Arthur Waley. OBVE

Yellow Fairy, The. Charlotte Druitt Cole. BoTP

Yellow Fever, The. Lucretia Davidson. AmWP

Yellow Flower, The. William Carlos Williams. HAP

Yellow gold's not precious. Wang Fun-chih, *tr. fr. Chinese by* Eugene Eoyang. SuSp

Yellow Gramophone. Sheila Cussons, *tr. fr. Afrikaans by the author.* PeSAV

Yellow-haired Laddie, The. *Unknown.* GBP

Yellow is for regret, the distal, the second hand. Yellow. Charles Wright. AmPA

Yellow leaf, from the darkness, A. Brooding Grief. D. H. Lawrence. CMoP; IMW; PoE

Yellow leaves do fly from the trees so high, The. The Lamenting Maid. *Unknown.* OBET

Yellow Light. Garrett Kaoru Hongo. InPS; OpBo

Yellow lioness, A. On the Serengeti. Marilyn Watts. OBAP

Yellow-lit [*or* Yellow] Budweiser signs over oaken bars. Uptown. Allen Ginsberg. FF; TwCP

Yellow Man, Purple Man. Emily Dickinson. *See* Who is the East?

Yellow, marked for jealousy. (*LL*) How Marigolds Came Yellow. Robert Herrick. ChTr; TTTS

Yellow november/comes swaying. Rushing. Ray A. Young Bear. CDW

Yellow-oatmeal flowers of the windmill palms. Eden. David Woo. OpBo

Yellow of cancer and nictoine, The. (*LL*) Yellow. Michael O'Loughlin. IB

Yellow Season, The. William Carlos Williams. MoAB; MoAmPo

Yellow Starred. Sister Mary Philip de Camara. BTR

Yellow Sunflower of Szechwan. Chang Yü, *tr. fr. Chinese by* Irving Y. Lo. SuSp

Yellow the bracken. Autumn. Florence Hoatson. BoTP

Yellow Violet, The. Bryant. BLPL; EAP; NAAL-1; PoLF; TAP

Yellowhammer, The. John Clare. NOBVV

Yellowjacket. Peter Blue Cloud. HATNAP

Yeman hadde he, and servaunts namo. Chaucer. *Fr.* Canterbury Tales, The. EnVB; FHYEP; NoP; OAEL-1; PPP, *abr.*

Yen's sorry. A Magpie Rhyme, Northumberland. *Unknown.* GBP

Yeoman of the Guard, *sels.* W. S. Gilbert. Family Fool, The. NBLV "Man who would woo a fair maid, A." FaBoUs

Yere of Our Lord being 1657, The. Needleworks. Adèle Geras. NWP

Yere yernes ful yerne, and yeldes never like, A. The Passage of a Year. *Unknown, tr. fr. Middle English by* Brian Stone. *Fr.* Sir Gawain and the Green Knight. OAEL-1; PoEL-1

Yes. James Joyce. *Fr.* Ulysses. FF

Yes. Brendan Kennelly. CIP

Yes a very important discovery. Robert Southey. *Fr.* Battle of Blenheim, The. OxBM

Yes, all the world must sure agree. Against Marriage to His Mistress. William Walsh. FaBoUs; GGP

Yes, and chilled with fear and despair. (*LL*) Judith of Bethulia. John Crowe Ransom. FaBoMo; FYAP; LiTA; LiTM; MeMAP; NoAM; NOBA

Yes as alike as entirely. To My Father. W. S. Graham. FaBoTw

Yes, Autumn. The leaves yellow and red. The Answer. Stephen Berg. IMW

Yes! Beauty still rebels! Art, I. Alfred Noyes. OBEV

Yes, Breisach, your decrease is profit yet and prize. To Breisach, Taken by That Supremely Celebrated Hero, Bernhard, Duke of Saxony. Georg Rudolph Weckherlin, *tr. fr. German by* George C. Schoolfield. GePo

Yes, But . . . . Theodore Weiss. TAP

Yes, But. James Wright. CAPP

Yes, but look what it's attached to! (*LL*) A Dialogue between the Head and Heart. Gavin Ewart. CBLP

Yes, by golly, when the tide comes in. (*LL*) Yellow-belly, yellow-belly, come and take a swim. *Unknown.* OxBoLi

Yes, Carrey, yes; I know! (*LL*) To Carrey Clavel. Thomas Hardy. CBLP

Yes, contumelious fair, you scorn. The Author Apologizes to a Lady for His Being a Little Man. Christopher Smart. BoLoP; CBLP

Yes, do you remember an inn. Lament for Lost Lodgings. Phyllis McGinley. NYBP

Yes; drive a phaeton and four. (*LL*) On Thomas, Second Earl of Onslow. *Unknown.* FaBoCo

Yes, ducks are valiant things. Frederick William Harvey. *Fr.* Ducks. BoTP

Yes, every poet is a fool. Matthew Prior. FaBoEE (Another.) FaBoCo

Yes, Ezreq had a child — who knows how? Quick little spink. Zamon and the Big Time. Philip Gross. PWE

Yes, faith is a goodly anchor. After the Burial. James Russell Lowell. UnPo

Yes, farewell, farewell forever. Lady Byron's Reply to Lord Byron's "Fare Thee Well." *Unknown.* BLPA

Yes, fickle Cambridge, Perkin's found this true. On the University of Cambridge's Burning the Duke of Monmouth's Picture. George Stepney. APAS

Yes! from mine eyes the tears unbidden start. Distant View of England from the Sea. William Lisle Bowles. EnRP

Yes, from the ingrate heart, the street. The Fugitive. Alice Meynell. NOCV

Yes, gentle Time, thy gradual, healing hand. To Time. Mary Tighe. IMW

Yes, go on! This is plain talk of plainer feelings now. John Hollander. *Fr.* Powers of Thirteen. VCAP

Yes, he said, darling, yes, of course you tried. The Appointment. L. A. G. Strong. OxBTC

Yes, he's got her now. Blues. John Fuller. NOBL

Yes! hope may with my strong desire keep pace. Michelangelo, *tr. by* Wordsworth. OBVE
(Love's Justification.) AWP
(To the Marchesana of Pescara.) CTC

Yes, I Am an African Woman. Nilene O. A. Foxworth. AIW

Yes, I am black! and radiant. Bible, *O.T.*, *tr. by* Marcia Falk. *Fr.* Song of Solomon, The. PBWP

"Yes," I answered you last night. The Lady's "Yes." Elizabeth Barrett Browning. LPA

Yes, I believe He loved them, too. The Young Workman. Mary Dillingham Frear. TrCP

Yes, I Could Love If I Could Find. *Unknown.* ErPo

Yes, I did not plow, I did not sow. Aftergrowth. Rachel, *tr. fr. Hebrew by* Ruth Finer Mintz. MHP

Yes! I forgot. *(LL)* The Last Leaf. Thomas Hardy. CBLP

Yes! I have seen the ancient oak. Felicia Dorothea Hemans. *Fr.* Brereton Omen, The. CTC

Yes I hope that things will work out somehow. *(LL)* The Return of the Proconsul. Zbigniew Herbert. FaBoPV; PoSu

Yes, I know: only the happy man. Bad Time for Poetry. Bertolt Brecht, *tr. fr. German by* John Willett *and* Ralph Manheim. PoSu

Yes, I know what you say. Tempted. Edward Rowland Sill. AnAmPo

Yes, I only got here on my own. On My Own. Philip Levine. FYAP

Yes. I remember Adlestrop. Adlestrop. Edward Thomas. CH; EBEvV; FaBoPP; FaPoB; GGP; GoJo; HAP; LiTB; NAEL-2; NOBE; OBEV; OxBTC; PlP; UV

Yes, I remember that pain precisely. The Blood. Nina Cassian, *tr. fr. Romanian.* WPOW, *tr. by* Laura Schiff

Yes, I remember Willesden Gree. Willesden Gree. Jimmy Pearse. UV

Yes, I said it. Betsy Sholl. *Fr.* Job's Wife. CrSp

Yes, I was only sidesman here when last. Bristol and Clifton. Sir John Betjeman. CMoP

Yes! I Write Verses. Walter Savage Landor. EnRP

Yes, I'd rather hear Heliodora's voice. Meleager, *tr. fr. Greek by* Barbara Hughes Fowler. *Fr.* Epigrams. HePo

Yes I'll treat him good. *(LL)* Me and My Chauffeur Blues. "Memphis Millie." VBLP

Yes: in the sea of life enisled. To Marguerite — Continued. Matthew Arnold. *Fr.* Switzerland. SoSe
(To Marguerite, in Returning a Volume of the Letter of Ortis.) EnVR

Yes, in the summer of 1773. Tom Wedgwood Tells. Brian W. Aldiss. NOBL

Yes, injured Woman! rise, assert thy right! The Rights of Woman. Anna Laetitia Barbauld. ECWP; NOEC; WoRP

Yes, it is there, the city full of music. It Is There. Muriel Rukeyser. WoWa

Yes, It Was the Mountain Echo. Wordsworth. EnRP

Yes, leave it with Him; the lilies all do. Leave It with Him. *Unknown.* BLRP

Yes, let me go. Yon fields are green. Request of a Dying Child. Lydia Huntley Sigourney. OBCA

Yes! let the rich deride, the proud disdain. Goldsmith. *Fr.* Deserted Village, The. BeLS; EnRP; NOEC; NoP; OAEL-1; OBSV; PoEL-3; TEP

Yes, let us speak, with lips confirming. Consolation. William Larminie. *Fr.* Fand. PeIV

Yes, life! though it seems half a death. Fern-life. Lucy Larcom. AmWP

Yes, love, that's why the warning light comes on. Don't. Very Simply Topping Up the Brake Fluid. Simon Armitage. PWE

Yes, Lower to the Level. Frances Sargent Osgood. AmWP

Yes, May and I are friends. After Church. Samuel Alfred Beadle. AAP

Yes, millions beginning to grow. *(LL)* Flower Chorus. Emerson. BoTP

Yes Miss/ Put up your pretty little mouth for a kiss. Admonition to the Muse. Geoffrey Taylor. FaBoEE

Yes, my darling, when life's shadows. In Memoriam. Alphonse Campbell Fordham. Mary Weston Fordham. AAP; CBWP-2

Yes! my Lesbia! let us prove. Catullus, *tr. fr. Latin by* Walter Savage Landor. OBVE

Yes! My son has learned to fall by increments each day. Faith-Falling. Deborah Digges. PFL

Yes, one in a graven silence no birds breaks. *(LL)* Father and Son. F. R. Higgins. BIrV; OBMV

Yes; or pass quick into the skies. *(LL)* A Fragment on Death. Villon. CTC; PeVV

Yes, planet Earth is immune suppressed. Inside His Borrowed Cage. Tommy McClennan. UnDi

"Yes," said the boy, "first come the gum-tree crowds." The Boy who Dreamed the Country Night. Christopher Koch. NOBAu

Yes, sexual intercourse began. Annus Miserabilis. Simon Rae. FaBoBl

Yes sir, no sir. *Unknown.* RoPo

Yes, so be it, though we already knew. The Sinking of the Mendi. S. E. K. Mqhayi, *tr. fr. Xhosa by* C. M. Mcanyangwa *and* Jack Cope. PeSA

Yes, Southey, yes, I to the House of Prayer. A Rebuke to Robert Southey. *Unknown.* ECWP

Yes, stranger! you well may say so. The Wickedest Man in Memphis. Alex J. Brown. BeLS

Yes, Tadeusz Rozewicz, I too. In Praise of Old Women. Marya Fiamengo. WPOW

Yes, take them first, my Father! Let my doves. A Mother's Prayer in Illness. Frances Sargent Osgood. AmWP

Yes! that fair neck, too beautiful by half. Madame d'Albert's Laugh. Clément Marot, *tr. fr. French by* Leigh Hunt. AWP

Yes, that's how I was. Judgment Day. R. S. Thomas. CRP

Yes, the Agency Can Handle That. Kenneth Fearing. WeW

Yes, the candidate's a dodger. The Dodger. *Unknown.* AmFP; GBP

Yes, the Secret Mind Whispers. Al Young. PoBA

Yes, the Town Clerk will see you. In I went. The Town Clerk's Views. Sir John Betjeman. CMoP

Yes, ther, up there, we'll understan. *(LL)* Some Time We'll Understand. Maxwell N. Cornelius. BLRP; WBLP

Yes, there is holy pleasure in thine eye! Admonition to a Traveller. Wordsworth. GTBS; GTBS-P

Yes, there's the orderly. He'll change the sheets. Wilfred Owen. *Fr.* Wild with All Regrets. FePWW

Yes, these are the dog-days, Fortunatus. Under Sirius. W. H. Auden. FaBoMo

Yes, they are alive and can have those colors. A Blessing in Disguise. John Ashbery. PoM

Yes, this is where I stood that day. Ballad of Hector in Hades. Edwin Muir. MoP; NoAM; NOBE

Yes, this is where she lived before she won. Interview. Sara Henderson Hay. OBCA

Yes, this is where the People take tea. *(LL)* In a Chain-Store Cafeteria. Paul Grano. NOBAu

Yes Thou Art Gone. Anne Brontë. OHCV

Yes, thou art gone! and never more. Yes Thou Art Gone. Anne Brontë. OHCV
(Reminiscence, A.) WPE

Yes: though the brine may from the desert deep. Frederick Goddard Tuckerman. *Fr.* Sonnets. HAP

"Yes, 'tis the time," I cried, "impose the chain." On the Benefactions in the Late Frost. Pope. NOEC; OxBSP

Yes to the Earth. "Sibilla Aleramo," *tr. fr. Italian by* Muriel Kittel. WoWa

Yes, true, children will take advantage of. The Little Girl. Nicholas Moore. ErPo

Yes, we are fighting at last, it appears. Arthur Hugh Clough. *Fr.* Amours de Voyage. EBVV; NOBVV; OxAEP-2; PeVV

Yes we did! *(LL)* Martin's Blues. Michael S. Harper. HCAP; PoBA

Yes, we had gone down to the shore. Songs without Words. John Ashbery. NAAL-2

Yes We have No Bananas. Hilton Obenzinger. BCF

Yes, we love this land together. Fatherland Song. Bjøornstjerne Bjøornson, *tr. fr. Norwegian* by William Ellery Leonard. AWP

Yes, we were looking at each other. *(LL)* Looking at Each Other. Muriel Rukeyser. GLP; NNaP; VBLP

Yes, we were looking at each other. Looking at Each Other. Muriel Rukeyser. GLP; NNaP; VBLP

Yes, we'll rally round the flag, boys, we'll rally once again. Battle-Cry of Freedom. George Frederick Root. AnAmPo; FaBoBe; PAH

Yes; we'll wed, my little fay. The Conformers. Thomas Hardy. Mes

Yes, we're all dodging out a way through the world. *(LL)* The Dodger. *Unknown.* AmFP; GBP

Yes, What? Robert Francis. LCAP

Yes. Why do we all, seeing of a soldier, bless him? The Soldier. Gerard Manley Hopkins. MeMBP

Yes, write, if you want to, there's nothing like trying. A Familiar Letter to Several Correspondents. Oliver Wendell Holmes. FaBoUs

Yes, ye have one! *(LL)* Child, is thy father dead? Ebenezer Elliot. FaBoEH

Yes, yes, and there is even a photograph. Meditation on a News Item. John Updike. PeLV

Yes, yes, dear love! I am dead! Resurgam. Adah Isaacs Menken. CBWP-1

Yes, yes, I grant the sons of earth. The Question. James Beattie. FaBoCo

Yes, yes/ it's time. My Spring Thing. Everett Hoagland. BPo

Yes, yes, my boy, there's no mistake. McIlrath of Malate. John Jerome Rooney. PAH

Yes, yes, my dear, I hear you calling! *(LL)* Tristan da Cunha. Ian D. Colvin. PeSAV

Yes yes/ yeah. Brown Skin Girl. Tommy McClennan. FaBoVe

Yes, you did, too! Little Words. Benjamin Keech. PoToHe

Yes, you know it, dear soul. Thanks. Herman von Gilm zu Rosenegg, *tr. fr. German* by Philip L. Miller. RiWo

"Yes," you say, "of course at Christmas". May Sarton. *Fr.* Christmas Letter, 1970. CrSp

Yes, you will do it, silently of course. We Shall Drink to Them That Sleep. Alexander Robertson. NSI

Yes, yours, my love, is the right human face. The Confirmation. Edwin Muir. ArLo; OxBM; OxBS

Yesman is a phonograph alive, A. Song for the Yesman. Li Pai-feng, *tr. fr. Chinese. Fr.* Pearls and Earth. LHF, *tr. by* Hualing Nieh

Yessum, I'm a small farmer. Small Farmer. Jimmy Santiago Baca. ETG

Yesterday. Hugh Chesterman. BoTP

Yesterday. Gu Cheng, *tr. fr. Chinese* by Donald Finkel *with* Li Guohua. SpMi

Yesterday. W. S. Merwin. FYAP; LCAP; RaBo

Yesterday a Euclid took trees. Bright green. Breaking Green. Michael Ondaatje. NOBC

Yesterday all the past. The language of size. Spain 1937. W. H. Auden. FaBoPV; LiTB; NAEL-2; OBWP

Yesterday at ten below. First Winter: Joy. Peggy Shumaker. PBCAP

Yesterday, at the Sessions held in Buckingham. A Case at Sessions. Walter Savage Landor. OBSV

Yesterday Down at the Canal. Frank O'Hara. CAPP

Yesterday, dreamed He was near me. Antonio Machado Ruiz, *tr. fr. Spanish* by John Frederick Nims. STV

Yesterday evening I saw your corpse. Joyce Mansour, *tr. fr. French* by Albert Herzing. WPOW

Yesterday/ God was/ white. The Change. Matabaruka. PBCV

Yesterday He Still Looked in My Eyes. Marina Tsvetayeva, *tr. fr. Russian* by Elaine Feinstein. ArLo

Yesterday He Was Nowhere to Be Found. Ted Hughes. NTP

Yesterday I dined with Demetrius, the boys'/ gymnastics teacher, luckiest of men. The Gymnastics Teacher. Automedon, *tr. fr. Greek* by W. S. Merwin. GrAn

Yesterday I fancied I was young. Ho Nansorhon, *tr. fr. Korean* by Peter H. Lee. Fr. Woman's Sorrow, A. PBWP

Yesterday I found one left. The Survivor. R. S. Thomas. FaBoTw

Yesterday i had a wild thot. hearing james brown on the radio singing *say it.* Alta. CrSp

Yesterday I knew no lullaby. Child of Our Time. Eavan Boland. CIP

Yesterday I planted garlic. James K. Baxter. *Fr.* Jerusalem Sonnets. PeNZ

Yesterday I skipped all day. Tiptoe. Karla Kuskin. PDV

Yesterday I wanted to. For Love. Robert Creeley. NOBA; VCAP

Yesterday I was/ given flowers. Anthology Poem. Petra von Morstein, *tr. by* Rosemarie Waldrop. BoWoP

Yesterday, in a big market, I made seven thousand dollars. Back through the Looking Glass to This Side. John Ciardi. NBLV

Yesterday in drizzling rain. A Tailor Called Sorrow. Betti Alver, *tr. fr. Estonian* by Willis Barnstone *and* Felix Oinas. BoWoP

Yesterday in Oxford Street. Rose Fyleman. PDV

Yesterday Mrs. Friar phoned. "Mr. Ciardi." Suburban. John Ciardi. NBLV

Yesterday my gun exploded. The Perils of Obesity. Harry Graham. FiBHP

Yesterday rain fell in torrents. You Could Say. Robert Mezey. NaP

Yesterday, Rebecca Mason. Truth's the Best. Elizabeth Turner. OxBChV

Yesterday, sitting. Just. Judith Johnson Sherwin. TAP

Yesterday/ some people of this town. What She Said to Her Girl Friend. Ammuvanar, *tr. fr. Tamil* by A. K. Ramanujan. PLW

Yesterday the fields were only gray with scattered snow. A Winter's Tale. D. H. Lawrence. MoAB; MoBrPo

Yesterday the gentle. St. Stephen's Day. Patric Dickinson. OBCP

Yesterday the House was Full of Flies. Geoffrey Summerfield. OTCP

Yesterday the twig was brown and bare. Miracle. Liberty Hyde Bailey. OHIP

Yesterday Vivaldi Visited Me. Alison Brackenbury. SCBI

Yesterday when I'd drunk myself to bed/ with water (neat). Antipater of Thessalonica, *tr. fr. Greek* by Alistair Elliot. GrAn

Yesterday you had a song. An Answer. Perceval Gibbon. PeSAV

Yesterday,/ You were but a thought in our minds. Giovanni Azania. Don Mattera. PeSAV

Yesterday's Illusion *or* Remembering the Thirties. Alun Llywelyn-Williams, *tr. fr. Welsh* by R. Gerallt Jones. OBWVE

Yestreen I had a pint o' wine. Anna. Burns. TrGrPo

Yestreen I stood on Ben Dorain, and paced its dark-/ grey path. On Ben Dorain. Duncan Ban MacIntyre, *tr. fr. Gaelic* by Robert Buchanan. *Fr.* Last Farewell to the Hills.

(Ben Dorain.) ScCV, *tr. by* John Stuart Blackie

Yet a Little While Is the Light With You. Francis Quarles. ChIV-2

Yet a marginal sort of grace. Pastoral Lives. Judith Wright. *Fr.* For a Pastoral Family. FaBoMA

Yet Ah, that Spring should vanish with the Rose! Omar Khayyám, *tr. fr. Persian* by Edward Fitzgerald. *Fr.* Rubáiyát of Omar Khayyám of Naishápúr, The. AWP; EBVV, *abr.;* FaBoBe; FaBoRV, *abr.;* FaPoR, *abr.;* GGP; HAP, *abr.;* LiTB; NAEL-2; NoP; PoEL-5; PrIm, *abr.;* TrGrPo

Yet another great truth I record in my verse. The Viper. Hilaire Belloc. FaBoNo; NoAM

Yet Another Poem about a Dying Child. Janet Frame. PeNZ

Yet burnished by its passage, and still warm. *(LL)* The Harvest Bow. Seamus Heaney. BiHa; NoAM; PBCIP; PNI

Yet but Three? Shakespeare. *Fr.* Midsummer Night's Dream, A. CTC

Yet Chloe [*or* Cloe] sure was formed without a spot. Pope. *Fr.* Moral Essays. ErPo; NAEL-1; NOEC; OAEL-1; OBSV; OxBoLi, *shorter sel.* (Chloe.) AWP; NOBE

Yet couldn't fall out of love, not for the worst you could do. *(LL)* Now my mind's been brought to such a state — and it's your fault. Catullus. STV

Yet count this quest the holiest of thy days. *(LL)* The Quest of the Ideal. H. Cordelia Ray. AmWP; CBWP-3

Yet Dish. Gertrude Stein. SOTW

Yet Do I Marvel. Countee Cullen. BPo; CDC; FF; NAAL-2; NoAM; PoBA; PoNe; Son; TAP; TTY

Yet do not be afraid, yet give no post forlorn. To Himself. Paul Fleming, *tr. fr. German* by George C. Schoolfield. GePo

Yet Each Man Kills the Thing He Loves. Oscar Wilde. *Fr.* Ballad of Reading Gaol, The. BeLS; OBNV; OxAEP-2; TEP; TrGrPo

Yet/ Ere the season died a-cold. Ezra Pound. *Fr.* Cantos. MeMAP

Yet even these ne'er change their love. *(LL)* 'Tis affection but dissembled. Sidney Godolphin. BeJo; JCP

Yet Gentle Will the Griffin Be. Vachel Lindsay. *Fr.* Poems about the Moon. PDV

Yet green eyed golden haired she is not. Judith 2. Patti Smith. VBLP

Yet had his sun not risen; from his lips. The Final Struggle. Louis James Block. *Fr.* New World, The. PAH

Yet Ha'e I Silence Left. "Hugh MacDiarmid." *Fr.* Drunk Man Looks at the Thistle, A. NAEL-2

Yet, hang me, but I love her dearly. *(LL)* Lesbia Forever on Me Rails. Catullus. OBVE

Yet happy he that's robbed of such a theif. *(LL)* Cupid, Dumb Idol. Michael Drayton. EnRePo; ESo

Yet hard/ The travail is for such as bend their minds. *Unknown, tr. by* Sir Edwin Arnold. *Fr.* Bhagavad-Gita, The. TOF

Yet he was there, and all my thirst. And If He Had Been Wrong for Me. Robert Duncan. RaBo

Yet here, Laertes! aboard, aboard, for shame! Shakespeare. *Fr.* Hamlet. EBEvV; NAWM-1

Yet I could think, indeed, the perfect call. Arthur Hugh Clough. *Fr.* Dipsychus. OBNC

Yet I courbed on my knees and cried hire of grace. William Langland. *Fr.* Vision of Piers Plowman, The. EBEV

Yet I go on from day to day, betraying. For Precision. Judith Wright. FaBoMA

Yet if his majesty, our sovereign [*or* soverain] Lord. *Unknown.* FaBoCh; NoP; PIP; PoRA
  (Coming of the King, The.) TrGrPo
  (Guest, The.) OtMeF; TrCP
  (Preparations.) NOBE; OBEV
  (Royal Guest, A.) CH; CoGr

Yet if once we efface the joys of the chase. The Chase and the Race. Adam Lindsay Gordon. *Fr.* Ye Wearie Wayfarer. OtMeF

Yet in spite/ Of pleasure won, and knowledge not withheld. Summer Vacation. Wordsworth. *Fr.* Prelude [*or*, Growth of a Poet's Mind], The. EnRP; OAEL-2; PoEL-4

Yet is day over long. (*LL*) Villanelle of the Poet's Road. Ernest Dowson. OBMV; TrGrPo; UnPo

Yet it is not all immaculate death. Not All Immaculate. Laura Riding. *Fr.* Three Sermons to the Dead. LiTA

Yet it was plain she struggled, and that salt. George Meredith. *Fr.* Modern Love. EnVR

Yet let me flap this bug with gilded wings. Pope. *Fr.* Epistle to Dr. Arbuthnot. ECEV; FHYEP; InPS; NoP; OAEL-1; OxAEP-1; PoE; PoEL-3; TFi

Yet London, empress of the northern clime. Dryden. *Fr.* Annus Mirabilis. NAEL-1; PeECV

Yet love me. (*LL*) A Soldier. Sir John Suckling. PoE; SeCV-1

Yet, love, mere love, is beautiful indeed. Elizabeth Barrett Browning. *Fr.* Sonnets from the Portuguese. CTC; OHCV; OxAEP-2

Yet Love will dream and Faith will trust. Life and Love. Whittier. BLRP

Yet matter must be gravely planned. Robert Lloyd. *Fr.* Poetry Professors, The. ECEV

Yet men and beasts, astonomers will tell. The Element Fire Boasts of the Constellations. Anne Bradstreet. *Fr.* Four Elements, The. CBCK

Yet merry it is, and quiet. (*LL*) The Quiet Life. *At. to* William Byrd. EIl; NoSic

Yet much may be performed, to check the force. Bedford Level. John Dyer. *Fr.* Fleece, The. FaBoPP

Yet never gave it o'er. (*LL*) A Pause of Thought. Christina Rossetti. CoGr; NOBE; OBNC

Yet often I think the king of that country. The Gospel of Labor. Henry van Dyke. WBLP; WGRP

Yet on the other side, faine would he start. Giovanni Battista Marino, *tr. fr. Italian by* Richard Crashaw. *Fr.* Massacre of the Innocents, The. OBVE

Yet once again do I behold the forms. The Voice of the Derwent. Wordsworth. FaBoPP

Yet once again heaven's king, and Earth's great lord. Abraham's Sacrifice of Isaac. Sir John Stradling. NOSC

Yet one more hour, then comes the night. My Drinking Song. Richard Dehmel, *tr. fr. German by* Ludwig Lewisohn. AWP

Yet one smile more, departing, distant sun! November. Bryant. AnAmPo; Son

Yet one thing is behind. John Skelton. *Fr.* Phyllyp Sparowe [*or* Philip Sparrow]. AAS; EPCY; PoEL-1

Yet Ostia boasts of her regeneration. Daniel Defoe. *Fr.* Reformation of Manners. OBSV

Yet out of that I have written these songs. (*LL*) Sometimes with One I Love. Walt Whitman. ArLo; GBL; OxBSP; SAmP

Yet, planter, let humanity prevail. Slaves. James Grainger. *Fr.* Sugar Cane, The. NOEC

Yet reluctant we go. (*LL*) The Old Men. Walter de la Mare. MoAB; MoBrPo

Yet remain an outlaw still! (*LL*) Grizzly. Bret Harte. AnAmPo

Yet still I stand by tilth and filth and praise. (*LL*) Tilth. Robert Graves. FaBoEE; OBSV

Yet still we praise that crocus head,/ April! (*LL*) For City Spring. Stephen Vincent Benét. BXAP; NBLV

Yet surely there are men who have made their art. Ego Dominus Tuus. W. B. Yeats. *Fr.* Wild Swans at Coole, The. EPCY, abr.

Yet that have hearts vexed with unquiet thought. To Spenser. John Hamilton Reynolds. Son

Yet the sign is on her. (*LL*) The Once-over. Paul Blackburn. ErPo; NeAP; PoM

Yet there is no great problem in the world today. "Hugh MacDiarmid." *Fr.* Lament for the Great Music. OxBTC

Yet they grind exceeding small. (*LL*) The Mills of the Gods. *Unknown.* BLPA

Yet think you buy your face, and hire your muse. (*LL*) All praise your face, your verses none abuse. Horace Walpole. FaBoEE

Yet this is you. (*LL*) Portrait d'une Femme. Ezra Pound. CMoP; FF; InPS; MeMAP; MoAB; MoAmPo; MoP; NAAL-2; NoAM; NOBA; NoP; Poetr; PPP; TAP; TwCP

Yet, till it is burned out, you must remain. (*LL*) Genius. Edward Lucas White. WGRP

Yet to the wondrous St. Peter's, and yet to the solemn Rotonda. Ah, That I Were Far Away. Arthur Hugh Clough. *Fr.* Amours de Voyage. NOBVV; OBNC
  (Upon Apennine Slope.) FaBoPP

Yet trusting not in mine, but in His strength alone! (*LL*) First-Day Thoughts. Whittier. AmPP; NoP; TrCP

Yet we were looking away! (*LL*) The Self-Unseeing. Thomas Hardy. EBEV; HAP; MoBrPo; NOBE; NOBVV; OBNC; OxAEP-2; PrIm; RB; WeW

Yet what a gap in the world, the missing white frost-face of that slim yellow mountain lion! (*LL*) Mountain Lion. D. H. Lawrence. FaBoVe; Mes; OBTV; OxBTC; RB; RFM

Yet, when I muse on what life is, I seem. Continued. Matthew Arnold. Son

Yet will I love her till I die. (*LL*) There Is a Lady Sweet and Kind. *At. to* Thomas Ford. CBLP; CH; CoGr; EBEV; EBEvV; EIl; ELP; GBL; HeIP; ImPo; LiTB; NoP; NOSC; OBEV; PIP; TrGrPo

Yet wulde I nat the causer fared amisse. Subject to All Pain. *Unknown.* MeEL

Yet, yet a moment, one dim ray of light. Pope. *Fr.* Dunciad, The. NAEL-1; OAEL-1; PoEL-3

Yeux Glauques. Ezra Pound. *Fr.* Hugh Selwyn Mauberly. (Life and Contacts). AmPP; CMoP; InPS; LiTA; LiTM; MoAmPo; NoAM; NOBA; NoP; TAP

Yevtushenko. Matija Beckovic, *tr. fr. Serbo-Croatian by* Charles Simic. HSix

Yevtushenko. Ted Kooser. NGP

Yevtushenko, Voznesensky and I. A Dream. Charles Tomlinson. OxBC

Yevtushenko, you came to Nebraska. Yevtushenko. Ted Kooser. NGP

Yew-Tree, The. *Unknown, tr. fr. Welsh by* Geoffrey Grigson. ChTr; GBL

Yew-Tree, The. Vernon Watkins. LiTB

Yew Trees. Wordsworth. EnRP; UnPo

Yggdrasill. Paul Muldoon. PBCIP

YgUDuh. E. E. Cummings. PeLV

Yiddish Muses, The. Jacqueline Osherow. UTF

Yiddish Speaking Socialists of the Lower East Side. Edward Sanders. UL

Yield. Ronald Gross. InPK

Yield all, my love; but be withal as coy. Upon A. M. Sir John Suckling. ErPo

Yield./ No Parking. Yield. Ronald Gross. InPK

Yielded Life, The. "W. A. G." BLRP

Yielding clod lulls iron off to sleep. Battlefield. August Stramm, *tr. fr. German by* Michael Hamburger. PeFWW

Yillow, yillow, yillow. Metamorphosis. Wallace Stevens. InPK; VGW

Yippee! she is shooting in the harbor! he is jumping. Blocks. Frank O'Hara. HCAP; LCAP

Yir eyes ur. A Summer's Day. Tom Leonard. NBrP

Yit is God a curteis lord. *Unknown.* MiEL

Yiya wo!/ This land of the Baca. Was It All Worth While? *Zulu Oral Tradition, tr. by* H. Tracey. WTO

Ynne heav'n Godd's mercie synge! (*LL*) Bristowe Tragedie: or, The Dethe of Syr Charles Bawdin. Thomas Chatterton. EnRP; OxBB

Yo-ho-ho and a bottle of rum! (*LL*) Derelict. Young Ewing Allison. BLPA; FaBoBe

Yogi, don't go away. Mirabai, *tr. fr. Hindi by* Willis Barnstone *and* Usha Nilsson. BoWoP

Yogi from far-off Beirut, A. *Unknown.* PeLi

Yohoweyah. When He Says So We Dance in All Directions — Wow! *Unknown, tr. fr. Seneca Indian by* Jerome K. Rothenberg *and* Richard Johnny John. STP

Yoke, The. Kalonymos ben Kalonymos, *tr. fr. Hebrew by* J. Chotzner. *Fr.* Touchstone, The. TrJP

Yoke of Tyranny, The. Sir Philip Sidney. *See* XLVII. "What, have I thus betrayed my liberty?"

Yoke Soft and Dear. John C. Kunze. AH

Yoke uneasy on the ox doth sit, The. Philip Ayres. FaBoEE

Yoko. Thom Gunn. NoAM

Yolanda Meets the Wild Boys. Jessica Hagedorn. OpBo

Yolp, Yolp, Yolp, Yolp. *Unknown.* EIl

Yom HaShoah. Estelle Gershgoren Novak. BTR

Yom Hazikaron. Edmund Pennant. BTR

Yom Kippur. Chana Bloch. CrSp

Yom Kippur. Bradley R. Strahan. BTR

Yom Kippur. Israel Zangwill. TrJP

Yom Kippur 1984. Adrienne Rich. GLP; NoAM

Yome bread and butter and the mermaids' local paper. *(LL)* House-Rules I: Reading. Alistair Elliot. CBLP

Yon cottager who weaves at her own door. Simple Faith. William Cowper. FHYEP

Yon is the laddie lo'ed to daunder far. Lintie in a Cage. Alice V. Stuart. OxBS

Yon Island Carrions Desperate of Their Bones. Shakespeare. *Fr.* King Henry V. RB

Yon laddie wi' the gowdan pow. William Soutar. OxBS

Yon rising Moon that looks for us again. Omar Khayyám, *tr. fr. Persian by* Edward Fitzgerald. *Fr.* Rubáiyát of Omar Khayyám of Naishápúr, The. AWP; EBVV, *abr.;* FaBoBe; FaBoRV, *abr.;* FaPoR, *abr.;* GGP; HAP, *abr.;* LiTB; NAEL-2; NoP; PoEL-5; PrIm, *abr.;* TrGrPo; TRP

Yon spark's a poet, by my troth! The Difference. Tadhg Dall O'Huiginn, *tr. fr. Irish by* Robin Flower. BIrV

Yond cawcrow's way-out. Two More about a Crow, in the Manner of Zukofsky. *Unknown, tr. fr. Seneca Indian by* Jerome K. Rothenberg *and* Richard Johnny John. STP

Yonder. Richard Eberhart. GOA

Yonder. *(LL)* The Leaden Echo and the Golden Echo. Gerard Manley Hopkins. CMoP; FaPoB; GTBS-P; ImPo; LiTB; LiTM; MeMBP; MoAB; MoBrPo; NOBVV; OBMV; OBNC; SOTW

Yonder behold a little purling rill. In Praise of Drainage. Anne Wilson. *Fr.* Teisa, a Descriptive Poem of the River Tees, Its Towns and Antiquities. ECWP

Yonder come Roberta! Tell me how do you know? Midnight Special. *Unknown.* AS

Yonder comes a courteous Knight. The Baffled Knight. *Unknown.* ESPB (Courteous Knight, The.) OxBB, (There Was a Knight [and He Was Young].) CoMu

Yonder comes dat ole Joe Brown. Walky-talky Jenny. *Unknown.* AS

Yonder Comes My Pretty Little Girl. *Unknown.* AS

Yonder comes the dawn. Uru-tu-sendo's Song. *Unknown, tr. fr. Tewa Indian by* H. J. Spinden. WTO

Yonder Comes the High Sheriff. *Unknown.* AS

Yonder great shadow — that blot on the passionate glare of the desert. The Dead of the Wilderness. Hayyim Nahman Bialik, *tr. fr. Hebrew by* Maurice Samuel. AWP

Yonder on the linden tree there sang a merry little bird. Dietmar von Aist, *tr. fr. German by* J. W. Thomas. GePo

Yonder See the Morning Blink. A. E. Housman. CMoP; MoShBr; NOBVV

Yonder stands a pretty fair maiden. No, Sir, No. *Unknown.* AmFP

Yonder they are coming. It Is Mine, This Country Wide. *Unknown.* GOA

Yonder, yonder see the fair rainbow. The Rainbow. *Unknown, tr. fr. Hopi Indian by* Natalie Curtis. WTO

Yonder you weep. Jamila. Nazik al-Mala'ika, *tr. fr. Arabic by* Kamal Boullata. WPOW

Yond's the Cardinall's window: This fortification. John Webster. *Fr.* Duchess of Malfi, The. NAEL-1; PoEL-2

Yong wyf and an harvest-gos, A. *Unknown.* MiEL

Yonnondio. Walt Whitman. NAAL-1

York Harbor Morning. George Garrett. MT

York Play of the Crucifixion, The. *Unknown.* NAEL-1

Yorkshire Wife's Saga. Ruth Pitter. NALW

Yorktown Centennial Lyric. Paul Hamilton Hayne. PAH

Yorunomado sat in. The Black Hat. Clayton Eshleman. VGW

You. Carroll Arnett. VoR

You. Anthony Barnett. VaA

You. Barbara Burford. DT

You. D. H. Lawrence. NoAM

You. Kenneth Rexroth. *Fr.* Bestiary, A. HoPM; OBAL

You! *Unknown.* OBAP

You a gentleman and I up from the grime. December 24 and George McBride Is Dead. Richard Hugo. HoPM

You abandon me, woman, because I am very poor. El Abandonado. *Unknown, tr. by* Frank J. Dobie. AS

You accuse me of sloganeering. To a Foreigner. Mila D. Anguilar. WoWa

You Ain't Nothin' But a Hound Dog. Leiber *and* Stoller *and* Michael E. Stoller. *Fr.* Hound Dog. LPA

You ain't part Indian. Wake-up Niggers. Don L. Lee. PoBA

You All Are Static; I Alone Am Moving. Peter Viereck. LiTA

You alone have become the thought of my thoughts. Thought of My thoughts. Hans Christian Andersen, *tr. fr. Danish by* Philip L. Miller. RiWo

You alone shall hover forever and forever. *(LL)* Request. Nikolaus Lenau. RiWo

You Also, Gaius Valerius Catullus. Archibald MacLeish. NoAM; TAP

You also, our first great. To Whistler, American. Ezra Pound. AiP; NAAL-2; PoA

You always know what to expect. The Country House. Louis Simpson. NOBA

You always read about it. Cinderella. Anne Sexton. HeIP; InPS; NAAL-2

You always sang at break of day. Wolfram von Eschenbach, *tr. fr. German by* Frederick Goldin. GePo

You and I. Henry Alford. BLPA; FaBoBe

You and I. Tennessee Williams. GLP

You and I and Amyas. William Cornish. *See* Knight knocked at the castle gate, The.

You and I and Amyas. Desire. William Cornish. (Latet Anguis.) OBEV

You and I, are we in the same story? A Battle of Wills Disguised. Marge Piercy. HeIP

You and I by this lamp with these. Together. Ludwig Lewisohn. PoToHe; TrJP

You and I, darling, here in the dark. Party. Cynthia Huntington. NAmP90

You and I/ Have so much love. Married Love. Kuan Tao Sheng, *tr. fr. Chinese by* Kenneth Rexroth *and* Ling Chung. OxBM; UnAS; WPC

You and I Saw Hawks Exchanging the Prey. James Wright. NAAL-2; NoAM

You and I will fold the sheets. Folding the Sheets. Rosemary Dobson. *Fr.* Daily Living. FaBoMA; NOBAu

You and I will go to Finegall. *Unknown, tr. fr. Irish by* Thomas Kinsella. NOIV

You and It. Mark Strand. NYBP

You and me. *Unknown, tr. fr. Japanese by* Kenneth Rexroth *and* Ikuko Atsumi. WPJ

You, Andrew Marvell. Archibald MacLeish. AWP; CMoP; FaBV; FYAP; HAP; HeIP; HoPM; LiTA; LiTM; MeMAP; MoAB; MoAmPo; MoP; NAAL-2; NoAM; NOBA; NoP; OxBA; Poetr; PoRA; PPP; PrIm; SoSe; TFi; TrGrPo; TRP; TwCP

You approach me carrying a book. Superballs. Tom Clark. PRA

You are a bee, my flower-lovely. Argentarius, *tr. fr. Greek by* Sam Hamill. InMo

You are a friend then, as I make it out. Ben Jonson Entertains a Man from Stratford. E. A. Robinson. AmPP; MoAB; MoAmPo

You are a generation of yet unbroken channels. *(LL)* Long Person. Gladys Cardiff. CDW

You Are a Jew! Delmore Schwartz. *Fr.* Genesis. TrJP

You are a landscape in the Tale of Terror. For Cora Lightbody, R.N. John Glassco. PoA

You are a lord, an earl, nay more, a man. To the Right Honorable Mildmay, Earl of Westmorland. Robert Herrick. BeJo

You are a mildewed painting. Sprout. Tuo Ssu, *tr. fr. Chinese by* Kenneth Rexroth *and* Ling Chung. WPC

You are a stool pigeon and. Kenneth Rexroth, *after the Latin of* Martial. NNaP; PGA

You are a sunrise. To a Golden-haired Girl in a Louisiana Town. Vachel Lindsay. MoAmPo

You are a traveller to them. Letter from Mama Dot. Fred erick D'Aguiar. PBCV

You are a tried and loyal friend. To My Setter, Scout. Frank H. Seldon. BLPA

You are a tulip seen today. A Meditation for His Mistress[e]. Robert Herrick. CaPo; JCP; NOBE; NOSC; OBEV; SeCP

You are a woman. Another. Ellen Marie Bissert. PeHV

You are all these people. To a Single Shadow without Pity. Sam Cornish. PoBA

You Are Alms. James W. Thompson. PoBA

You Are Alone My Evil and My Good. Louise Labé, *tr. by* Helen R. Lane. VBLP

You are already/ asleep. Touch. Thom Gunn. CMoP

You are as faithless as a Carthaginian. A Satire on an Inconstant Lover. Swift. CBLP

You are as fond of grief as of your child. Shakespeare. *Fr.* King John. IMW

You are as gold. Hilda Doolittle ("H. D."). LiTA; LiTM; MoAmPo

You are barely able to walk. But What I'm Trying to Say Mother Is. Ai. MDDM

You are beautiful. What Ulysses Said to Circe on the Beach of Aeaea. Irving Layton. ErPo

You are beautiful and faded. A Lady. Amy Lowell. AnAmPo; MoAmPo

You are blessëd out of measure. (*LL*) An Assurance. Nicholas Breton. CBLP; SCGP

You are blind like us. Your hurt no man designed. To Germany. Charles Hamilton Sorley. MoBrPo; NSI

You are carrying me, full consciousness, god that has desires. Full Consciousness. Juan Ramón Jiménez, *tr. fr. Spanish by* Robert Bly. NU

You are clear. Garden. Hilda Doolittle ("H. D."). LiTA; NoAM

You are coming to woo me, but not as of yore. Lips That Touch Liquor. George W. Young. NBLV

You are coming toward us. Aunt Laura Moves toward the Open Grave of Her Father. Joseph de Roche. HeIP

You are coming very slowly, why do you delay. My Cobra Girl. *Gond Oral Tradition, tr. by* V. Elwin *and* S. Hivale. WTO

You are desolate, fort of kings. *Unknown.* NOIV

You are disdainful and magnificent. Sonnet to a Negro in Harlem. Helene Johnson. CDC; NIP; ShDr

You Are Distant, You Are Already Leaving. David Constantine. SCBI

You are drowning. How Metaphor Can Save Your Life. Myra Sklarew. CRP

You are eighty years old today, ma. To Mother. Lessie M. Drown. PWR

You are falling asleep and I sit looking at you. After Dark. Adrienne Rich. LCAP; LiTM; VGW

You are famous in my mind. Before the Big Storm. William Stafford. NaP

You are for dreams and slumbers, brother priest. Shakespeare. *Fr.* Troilus and Cressida. OxAEP-1

You are forgetting, I was indeed dead. Lazarus to Christ. David Constantine. PWE

You are fortunate, dear friends, that you can tell. Vidya, *tr. fr. Sanskrit by* Daniel Ingalls. WPOW

You are from my country. Viaticum. Tchicaya U Tam'si, *tr. fr. French by* Ellen Conroy Kennedy. NegPo

You are going far away, far away from poor Jeannette. Jeannette and Jeannot. Charles Jefferys. BLPA

You are going to be hated by the people. To a Russian soldier in Prague. Adrian Mitchell. IHNG

You Are Gorgeous and I'm Coming. Frank O'Hara. NeAP; SM

You Are Happy. Margaret Atwood. TRP

You are here. Minor Things. Heather Ross Miller. MT

You are here now. The Sleeping Fury. Louise Bogan. IHMS; LiTM; NALW

You are holding my sister in your arms. Father and Daughter. Cathy Song. OpBo

You are horizontal. Footpaths Cross in the Rice Field. Lin Ling, *tr. fr. Chinese by* Kenneth Rexroth *and* Ling Chung. WPC

You are horizontal. Footpaths Cross in the Rice Field. "Lin Ling." *Unknown, tr. by* Kenneth Rexroth *and* Ling Chung. PBWP

You are ice and fire. Opal. Amy Lowell. NALW

You are ill and so I lead you away. Alfred W. Purdy. NOBC

You are in love with a country. Where? A. S. J. Tessimond. OBTV

You are in the unlit area of the world. The Source. Andrew Crozier. VaA

You are just the kind of man. Exorcism of the Straight/Man/Demon. Aaron Shurin. GLP

You are less than one-half. The Speaker. Charles G. Ballard. VoR

You are letting her go. Cliona. Catherine Twomey. IIP

You Are Like A Flower. Heine, *tr. fr. German by* Philip L. Miller. RiWo

You are like a god. (*LL*) Cicada. *Unknown.* EaPr

You are like a sun of the tropics. Luxury. Donald Justice. HeIP

You are like an everlasting friendship. Laurel O. Hoye. MDDM

You are like you and I love you. (*LL*) You are like an everlasting friendship. Laurel O. Hoye. MDDM

You are looking now on old Tom Moore. The Days of 'Forty-nine. *Unknown.* PAH

You are lying, O missionary! Raymond Mazisi Kunene, *tr. fr. Zulu by* D. K. Rycroft. WTO

You are mad to mourn alone. Hölderlin Town. Anne Carson. *Fr.* Life of Towns, The. BAP-90

You are made of almost nothing. The Dragonfly. Louise Bogan. HeIP; Poetr

You are Mine said she. (*LL*) May I Feel Said He. E. E. Cummings. BoLoP; ErPo; FF; HeIP; LiTA; NBLV; NOBE; OxBM; PeLV

You are my friend. Lorine Niedecker. VGW

You are my secret coat. You're never dry. Cousin Coat. Sean O'Brien. PWE

You are my stick, my prop. Houseplant. Felicity Napier. BrRo

You are my Sweetheart. The Interpretation of Dreams. Kenneth Koch. PRA

You are [*or* You're] not alone when you are still alone. Michael Drayton. *Fr.* Idea. ESo; PoEL-2; TrGrPo

You are not beautiful, exactly. To Dorothy. Marvin Bell. CAPP; VCAP

You are not here! the quaint witch Memory sees. To Maria Gisborne in England, from Italy. Shelley. *Fr.* Letter to Maria Gisborne. NOBE

You are not merry, brother. Why not laugh. The Prodigal Son. E. A. Robinson. MoAmPo

You are not nearer God than we. Annunciation. Rainer Maria Rilke, *tr. fr. German by* James Blair Leishman. OBVE

You are not wanted. Periphery. Ruth Stone. NALW

You are now/ In London, that great sea. Shelley. *Fr.* Letter to Maria Gisborne. EBEV

You Are Old, Father William. "Lewis Carroll." *See* "You are old, Father William," the young man said,/ "And your nose has a look of surprise."

"You are old, Father William," the young man cried. The Old Man's Comforts and How He Gained Them. Robert Southey. EBEvV; HoPM; OxBChV; UnPo; UV; VPP

'You Are Old, Father William,' the young man said. Father William. "Lewis Carroll." *Fr.* Alice's Adventures in Wonderland. BXAP; CBNP; FaBoCo; FaBoNo; FaBoPa; FaPON; FiBHP; GGP; GoJo; HoPM; LiTB; NOBL; NOBVV; OxBChV; PDV; PoLF; PoRA; TFi; TrGrPo; UnPo

("You Are Old, Father William.") PeLV; PlP; UV

"You are old, Father William," the young man said,/ "And your nose has a look of surprise." Father William. "Lewis Carroll."

(You Are Old, Father William.) CoGr; PlP

"You are old," said the youth, "and your jaws are too weak." "Lewis Carroll." *Fr.* Alice's Adventures in Wonderland. OxBM

You are one of those clear cold creeks. The Creek. Roland Robinson. NOBAu

You are only one of many. One of Many. Stevie Smith. OxBC

You are over there, Father Malloy. Father Malloy. Edgar Lee Masters. *Fr.* Spoon River Anthology. OxBA

You are perishing like the old men. Already your arms are gone. The Chorus Speaks Her Words as She Dances. Linda Gregg. AnAn

You are proof that it can happen. A Tardy Epithalamium for E. and N. Ralph Pomeroy. GLP; PeHV

You are right about it; that wary. Old Tiger. Marianne Moore. AnAn

You are right. In dreams I might well dance. Possession. Marie Ponsot. VGW

You are right. What we call Poetry is the boat. A New Poem. Robert Duncan. NNaP; PoM

You are sad. It is the same with me. (*LL*) Nocturne at Bethesda. Arna Bontemps. CDC; ChIV-2; PoNe

You are singing, little dove. *Unknown.* EaPr

You are small and intense. To a Child Running with Outstretched Arms in Canyon de Chelly. N. Scott Momaday. CDW; HATNAP

You are so small, I. Miss Cho Composes in the Cafeteria. James Tate. SM; WeW

You Are So Tender. Berta Freistadt. DT

You are so witty, profligate, and thin. Epigram on Voltaire. Edward Young. FaBoCo

You are stained, stained/ to perfection. (*LL*) Field Work. Seamus Heaney. AnAn; CBLP

You are such a well-rounded sponge. Sediment. David Ignatow. NYBP

You are that frail decision that devised. Hart Crane. AnAn

You are the baby in the barn. (*LL*) Nick and the Candlestick. Sylvia Plath. CAPP; CoAP; LCAP; NALW; PBWP; Poetr

You are 'the best of cut-throats:'—do not start. Byron. *Fr.* Don Juan. FaBoEH

(On Wellington "You are 'the best of cut-throats' ".) IHNG

You Are the Brave. Raymond R. Patterson. NIP; PoBA

You are the charge of halcyons now, it may be. For the Cenotaph of a Lost Soldier. Theon, *tr. fr. Greek by* Dudley Fitts. GrAn

You are the grain. I Think of Housman Who Said the Poem Is a Morbid Secretion, like a Pearl. Judith Kroll. UnPo

You are the imaginary center of the universe eternity that devours. Horoscope. Rasa Livada, *tr. fr. Serbo-Croatian by* Charles Simic. HSix

You are the last whale. Gary Lawless. EaPr

You are the Maccábee! (*LL*) They Say There Is a Country. Saul Tchernichowsky. MHP

You are the merry men, dwarfs of soul. The Diakka. Gerald Massey. NOBVV

You are the millions, we are multitude. The Scythians. Alexander Blok, *tr. fr. Russian by* Babette Deutsch *and* Avrahm Yarmolinsky. AWP

You are the most beautiful. Martial, *tr. fr. Greek* by Kenneth Rexroth. PGA

You are the notes, and we are the flute. Jalal al-Din Rumi, *tr. fr. Persian* by Robert Bly. EnlH

You are the one. To a Dark Moses. Lucille Clifton. CAPP

You/ are the One who put. Stars in Apple Cores. Luci Shaw. TrCP

You are the problem I propose. The Metaphysical Amorist. J. V. Cunningham. VGW

You are the town and we are the clock. W. H. Auden. *Fr.* Dog beneath the Skin, The. OxBTC

You Are There. Nikki Giovanni. HeIL

You are tired. The Midnight Tennis Match. Thomas Lux. AmPA

You are too splendid for this city street. *(LL)* Sonnet to a Negro in Harlem. Helene Johnson. CDC; NIP; ShDr

You are tranquility. Come To Me. Friedrich Rückert, *tr. fr. German* by Philip L. Miller. RiWo

You are traveling to play basketball. Your team's, In Your Young Dream. Richard Hugo. InPK

"You are wise, Mr. Dodgson," the young child said. Lewis Carroll. Eleanor Farjeon. OxBChV

You are writing a gospel. Your Own Version. Paul Gilbert. BLRP

You arose — I dreamt so last night — and left for. In Memory of My Father: Australia. Joseph Brodsky. BAP-91

You arrived that bad winter. Solstice. Gerald Dawe. PNI

You as then you were. *(LL)* Since. W. H. Auden. CBLP; InPS

You ask. Li Po. EaPr

You ask how it is. I will tell you. Blaen Cwrt. Gillian Clarke. AngWe

You ask how long before I come. Still no date is set. Night Rains: to my Wife up North. Li Shang-yin, *tr. fr. Chinese* by A. C. Graham. PLT

You ask how old am I. Twice Times Then Is Now. Ibn Hazm al-Andalusi, *tr. fr. Persian* by Omar S. Pound. ArPe; OBVE

You Ask Me. Mutabaruka. PBCV

You ask me. To Madame A. V. Pletneff. Karolina Pavlova, *tr. fr. French* by Paul Schmidt. PBWP

You ask me for a song, folks. Cousin Jack Song. *At. to* Charley Tregonning. AmFP

You ask me, girl, why I withdraw my sword. Macedonius, *tr. fr. Greek* by Adrian Wright. GrAn

You ask me how Contempt who claims to sleep. J. V. Cunningham. ErPo; VCAP

You ask me how it is living in exile, friend. Eavesdropper. Breyten Breytenbach, *tr. fr. Afrikaans* by Ernst van Heerden. PeSAV

You ask me how to pray to someone who is not. On Prayer. Czeslaw Milosz, *tr. fr. Polish* by Robert Hass. AnAn

You ask me my name? They got lotsa names. Madarika. Vince Gotera. OpBo

You ask me to be quiet. Forever. Charles-Jean Grandmougin, *tr. fr. French* by Philip L. Miller. *Fr.* Poem of a Day. RiWo

You ask me to forget him. What She Said to Her Friend ("You ask me to forget him.") Kapilar, *tr. fr. Tamil* by A. K. Ramanujan. PLW

You ask me to sing, so I'll sing you a song. The Cranberry Song. Barney Reynolds. AmFP

You ask me *What's love?* — Why, that virtue-fed vapour. Address to Lady ———, Who Asked What the Passion of Love Was? Charles Morris. NOEC

You ask what I have found, and far and wide I go. The Curse of Cromwell. W. B. Yeats. BIrV; IIP

You ask what place I like the best. The Kinkaiders. *Unknown.* AS

You Ask Why. Li Po, *tr. fr. Chinese* by Sam Hamill. ArNa; EnlH

You ask why gold and velvet bind. On a New Duke. *Unknown.* FaBoEE

You ask why I make my home in the mountain forest. You Ask Why. Li Po, *tr. fr. Chinese* by Sam Hamill. ArNa; EnlH

You Ask Why Sometimes I Say Stop. Marge Piercy. CAPP

You asked me to enter the holy cloister. Banishment from Ur. Enheduanna, *tr. fr. Sumerian* by W. W. Hallo *and* J. J. A. van Dijk. BoWoP

You asked me to your baptism, over. A Freethinker's Baptism. Linda Saunders. NWP

You asked us to hear the softest vocable of wind. Lines for Roethke Twenty Years after His Death. Duane Niatum. HATNAP

You at God's altar stand, His minister. Written on an Island off the Breton Coast. Saint Venantius Fortunatus, *tr. fr. Latin* by Helen Waddell. PeHV

You balanced her within a cyclone. Woman Seed Player. Roberta Hill Whiteman. HATNAP

You be the ice cream, I'll be the freezer. *Unknown.* RoPo

You beastly child, I wish you had miscarried. Lightly Bound. Stevie Smith. NALW

You beat your pate, and fancy wit will come. Pope. FaBoEE (To a Blockhead.) NBLV

You beautious ladies, great and small. The Famous Flower of Serving-Men; or, The Lady Turn'd Serving-Man. *Unknown.* ESPB; OBET; OxBB

You became/ In many acts and quiet observances. My Company. Sir Herbert Read. PoWW

You Begin. Margaret Atwood. NOBC; NoP

You believed in your own story. Fairy Tales. Shu Ting, *tr. fr. Chinese* by Donald Finkel *with* Yi Jinsheng. SpMi

You bells in the steeple, ring, ring out your changes. Seven Times Two — Romance. Jean Ingelow. *Fr.* Songs of Seven. GN

You belong to infinity. *(LL)* Belonging. Alla Renee Bozarth. EaPr

You beneath rosebud trees in bloom and they. Eleanor ———. Hayden Carruth. AnAn

You, Benjamin Jones. Jon Dressel. AngWe

You Bet Your Life. Nancy Vieira Couto. PBCAP

You better sure shall live, not evermore. Horace. *See* Receive, dear friend, the truths I teach.

You bible-sharps that thump on tubs. Villon's Good-Night. W. E. Henley. CBNP

You bid me to hold my peace. The Poet to the Birds. Alice Meynell. FM

You bid me write, Sir, I comply. Address to a Bachelor on a Delicate Occasion. Priscilla Pointon. ECWP

You bid my muse not cease to sing. Written to a Near Neighbour in a Tempestuous Night. Henrietta Knight, Lady Luxborough. ECWP

You big black boundin' beggar — for you bruk a British square. *(LL)* Fuzzy-Wuzzy. Kipling. MoBrPo; TrGrPo

You Black Bright Stars. Thomas Morley. EnRePo; NoSic

You black bright stars, that shine while daylight lasteth. You Black Bright Stars. Thomas Morley. EnRePo; NoSic

You/ black man/ made me raw umber. To My Father. Dinah Butler. AIW

You black-maned, horse-haired, long-faced creature. To the Gentlewoman of Llanarth Hall. Evan Thomas, *tr. fr. Welsh* by Gwyn Jones. OBWVE

You black out the sun. Ed Roberson. *Fr.* When Thy King Is a Boy. PoBA

You blame me that I do not write. Letter to a Friend. Jon Stallworthy. NoAM

You Blessed Bowers. *Unknown.* EIL

You blessed shades, which give mee silent rest. Mary Sidney Wroth, Countess of Montgomery. *Fr.* Urania. KTR; WPE

You blew away, feather-brained for beauty. Ducking: After Maupassant. Dave Jeddie Smith. AnAn

You boast about your ancient line. Family Trees. Douglas Malloch. OHIP

You both are modest. So am I. Farewell. *(LL)* An Epistle to Master John Selden. Ben Jonson. BeJo

You bound and made your sport of him, Philistia! Samson Agonistes. Rose Terry Cooke. AmWP

You Brandenburg's support and Prussia's guarantee. On the Entrance of the Castle Bridge. Simon Dach, *tr. fr. German* by George C. Schoolfield. GePo

You brave heroic [*or* heroique] minds. To the Virginian Voyage. Michael Drayton. AiP, *sl. abr.*; EnRePo; FaBoEH, *sl. abr.*; HAP; NAEL-1; NOBE; NOSC; OBEV; PAH; PoEL-2; SCGP, *sl. abr.*; TEP

You bring the only changes to this season. For Nicholas, Born in September. Tod Perry. NYBP

You Britons all of courage bold. A Sea Song. *Unknown.* OxBSS

You brought up something to die. *(LL)* I Met This Guy Who Died. Gregory Corso. NAs; Poetsp

You build it where you will be heard only by chance. The Cabin North of It All. James McMichael. AmPA

You build your harp intime. The Silence. Tomas Mac Siomoin, *tr. fr. Irish* by the author. TIRV

You built the new Court House, Spoon River. Benjamin Franklin Hazard. Edgar Lee Masters. *Fr.* New Spoon River, The. GOA

You built yourself a tower in the wind. Jean-Joseph Rabéarivelo, *tr. fr. French* by Ellen Conroy Kennedy. NegPo

You burst into the world with smiles wide as April. Sleeping with Foxes. Roberta Hill Whiteman. CDW

You but unlock [*or* unlocke], so we each other bless[e]. *(LL)* To a Lady That Desired I Would Love Her. Thomas Carew. BeJo; CaPo; CBLP; MeLP; SCGP; SeCV-1

You buy some flowers for your table. Samuel Hoffenstein. *Fr.* Poems in Praise of Practically Nothing. FiBHP; TrJP

You Call Me by Old Names. Rhina P. Espaillat. LoHo

You call me by old names: how strange. You Call Me by Old Names. Rhina P. Espaillat. LoHo

You Call That a Ts'ing; a Letter. Jedediah Barrow. BXAP

You call that wine? On Beer. Emperor Julian, *tr. fr. Greek* by Kenneth Rexroth. PGA

You called me, but I made no response in that night. On the Death of Young Guerillas. Mazisi Kunene. PAW

You called the blues' loose black belly lover. You Can't Rhumboogie in a Ball and Chain. Alice Fulton. Jaz

You came / to be / in the Month of Malcolm. Circling the Daughter. Etheridge Knight. ETG

You came, and looked and loved the view. Green Sussex. Tennyson. *Fr.* Prologue to General Hamley. FaBoPP

You came. And you did well to come. Sappho, *tr. fr. Greek by* Willis Barnstone. BoWoP

You Came as a Thought. J. Laughlin. GOYP

You came back to us in a dream and we were not here. Come Back. W. S. Merwin. NaP

You came like the dawn. On the Death of a Child. Edward S. Silvera. PoNe

You came to it through wild country, there the sea's voice. The House in the Green Well. John Hall Wheelock. MoAmPo

You Came with Shells. June Jordan. NoAM

You can. Sunrise. Mary Oliver. CrSp

You can always fight the foulest grief. The Five Feet. Edward Sanders. UL

You can be a dancing brontosaurus. No Money in Art. Jim Gustafson. UL

You can be walking along the beach. American Landscape with Clouds & a Zoo. Jon Anderson. AnAn

You can become a shaman. New Indian Medicine. Emma Lee Warrior. HATNAP

You can bring down a house with a sound. Michael Palmer. *Fr.* Six Hermetic Songs. BAP-90

You can call me Herbie Jr. or Ashamah. Unemployment/Monologue. June Jordan. WPOW

You can come to terms with anyone. At the Cave. Artur Miedzyrzecki, *tr. fr. Polish by* Stanisław Barańczak *and* Clare Cavanagh. PoSu

You can decorate your office. The Ultimatum. Ben King. AnAmPo

You can drift through Europe for weeks. Histories. Mary E. O'Donnell. NWP

You can explore your every desire. Antipater of Thessalonica, *tr. fr. Greek by* Sam Hamill. InMo

You can feel the muscles and veins rippling in widening and rising circles. Saying Dante Aloud. James Wright. InPK

You can go back in a clap of blue metal. Southbound. Betty Adcock. MT

You can hang or drown at last. (*LL*) A Short Song of Congratulation [*or* To a Young Heir]. Samuel Johnson. EBEV; ELP; HAP; InPK; InPS; InvP; NOBE; NOEC; NoP; OBSV; OxAEP-1; PeLV; PlP; PoE; PoEL-3; TEP; TFi; UnPo

You Can Have It. Philip Levine. AnAn; CAPP; VCAP

You can hear the silence of it. David Jones. *Fr.* In Parenthesis. FaBoMo

You can love and think, and the Earth cannot! (*LL*) The Wonderful World. William Brighty Rands. FaPON

You can make a tidy leaf-pot out of sarai leaves. Man's Need. *Gond Oral Tradition*, *tr. by* V. Elwin *and* S. Hivale. WTO

You can push. Fourteen Ways of Touching Peter. George MacBeth. CRH

You can see from their faces. Photographs of Pioneer Women. Ruth Dallas. PeNZ

You can see the moon's brightness. Shih Te, *tr. fr. Chinese by* James M. Hargett. SuSp

You can sigh o'er the sad-eyed Armenian. An Appeal to My Countrywomen. Frances E. W. Harper. AmWP; BlSi

You can sing of the maid. The Girl with the Jersey. Ben King. AnAmPo

You can stop me. There's Somethin.' Adam Small, *tr. fr. Afrikaans.* PeSA; PeSAV

You can stroll home after sunset. (*LL*) Tea. Ch'u Ch'uang I. OHMPC

You can take a dog to the keyside, but you can't push him in. The Computer's First Proverbs. Peter Finch. NBrP

You can take a tub with a rub and a scrub in a two-foot tank of tin. Pater's Bathe. Edward Abbott Parry. OxBChV

You can talk about your farms and your Chinaman's charms. The Cowboy's Life Is a Very Dreary Life. *Unknown.* AmFP

You can tell right off what's happening. Roadside Attraction. Mark Vinz. NGP

You cannot cage a field. Lives. Henry Reed. BoNaP; LiTB

You cannot do better than eat them yourselves. (*LL*) Hot cross buns! Hot-cross buns!/ One a penny, two a penny. Mother Goose. BoTP; OxNR; ReMoGo

You Cannot Do This. Gwendolyn MacEwen. FaBoWP

You cannot dream. Things Lovelier. Humbert Wolfe. TrJP

You cannot from the open window invade. The Crow. Rita Boumi-Pappas, *tr. fr. Modern Greek by* Kimon Friar. PBWP

You Cannot Go Down to the Spring. John Shaw Neilson. CBAP

You cannot hope. The British Journalist. Humbert Wolfe. FaBoEE; FiBHP; IHNG; OxBTC

You cannot justly of the Court complain. To a Witty Man of Wealth and Quality; Who, after His Dismissal from Court, Said, He Might Justly Complain of It. William Wycherley. SeCV-2

You cannot miss it, though you shut your eyes. (*LL*) The Last Journey. Leonidas of Tarentum. AWP; OBD

You cannot see mountains and valleys in the clouds. Spyglass Conversations. *Unknown, tr. fr. Tule Indian by* Frances Densmore. STP

You cannot tell the time by the grey light. Interior: Morning. David Chaloner. VaA

You can't beat English lawns. Our final hope. Rolling the Lawn. William Empson. MoBrPo

You can't catch me. *Unknown.* RoPo

You can't ever imagine the Virgin Mary having vulvitis or thrush. Sonnet: Supernatural Beings. Gavin Ewart. Son

You Can't Go to the Moon There's No Trains. Joy Howard. DT

You can't hear it in the house. Geoffrey Lehmann. *Fr.* Ross's Poems. CBAP; FaBoMA

You Can't Rhumboogie in a Ball and Chain. Alice Fulton. Jaz

You can't say it that way any more. And "Ut Pictura Poesis" Is Her Name. John Ashbery. InPS; VCAP

You can't see it or hear it. Spring Breeze. Ho Hsun, *tr. fr. Chinese by* Kenneth Rexroth. OHMPC

You can't take three from two, two is less than three. New Maths. Tom Lehrer. FaBoUs

You can't tell me God would have Heaven. A Malemute Dog. Pat O'Cotter. BLPA

You can't win Love over/ by crying. To Telembrotos. Antipater of Thessalonica, *tr. fr. Greek by* Alistair Elliot. GrAn

You captains and commanders both by land and sea. A Copy of Verses on Jefferys the Seaman. *Unknown.* OxBSS

You captains brave and bold, hear our cries, hear our cries. Captain Kidd. *Unknown.* AmFP

You cathedral, you! Pure astonishment! To Freedom. Agnes Nemes Nagy, *tr. fr. Hungarian by* Bruce Berlind. PoSu

You caught his eye; he could not go. (*LL*) Love ran with me, then walk'd, then sate. Walter Savage Landor. CBLP

You cd just take what. Get It & Feel Good. Ntozake Shange. VBLP

You charm'd me not with that fair face. Dryden. *Fr.* Evening's Love, An. SeCV-2

You choose the life or the life chooses you. Couch Grass. John Hall. VaA

You, City, by two rivers made an isle. Anima Urbis. Edith M. Thomas. AmWP

You claim his poems are garbage. Balderdash! A Poet Defended. Paul Ramsey. InPK

You claim to have brought me back. Treading Water. Tracey Herd. NWP

You clasp the little ball so tightly. For Genevieve. Simeon Dumdum. TSaS

You closed your eyes, crossed your hands. Text, Silk. Novica Tadic, *tr. fr. Serbo-Croatian by* Charles Simic. HSix

You come along . . . tearing your shirt . . . yelling about Jesus. To a Contemporary Bunkshooter. Carl Sandburg. WGRP

You come forth/ the color of a stone cliff. To Insure Survival. Simon J. Ortiz. CDW

You come from a line of. Power. Alma Villanueva. AfAz

You come from the line of a Cola king. Poet's Counsel, A ("You come from the line of a Cola king.") Kovur Kilar, *tr. fr. Tamil by* A. K. Ramanujan. PLW

You come to fetch me from my work tonight. Putting in the Seed. Robert Frost. ErPo; NoAM; OxBA

You come to market — seeking gain, to be sure. Offered to a Man Who Sells Pines. Yü Wu-ling, *tr. fr. Chinese by* Edward H. Schafer. SuSp

You Come to Me. Quincy Troupe. NBV

You coming up as I came down. (*LL*) And No Regrets. Lex Banning. NOBAu

You could be sitting now in a carrel. A Late Aubade. Richard Wilbur. Poetr; SM; SoSe

You could draw a straight line from the heels. Man Lying on a Wall. Michael Longley. PNI

You could hear. Alberta Hunter. Lyn Lifshin. Jaz

You could love here, not the lovely goat. The Milltown Union Bar. Richard Hugo. NoAM

You Could Say. Robert Mezey. NaP

You could sit there with the stains on your shoes. Robert Frost. *Fr.* Home Burial. IMW; NAAL-2; OBD; PrIm; SoSe; TAP; TRP

You go to your church, and I'll go to mine. Your Church and Mine. Phillips H. Lord. BLPA

You gods, teach her some more humanity. (LL) A Divine Mistress. Thomas Carew. BeJo

You gods that have the power. Puerperium. Edmund Waller. JCP

You gods! to fold the charmer in my arms. The Rapture. Henry Baker. NOEC

You golden freedom, both my wish and my desire. Martin Opitz, tr. fr. German by George C. Schoolfield. GePo

You gonna look-out that sky! (LL) Lament for the Drowned Country. Mary Durack. NOBAu

You good folks of Nottingham I would have you draw near. The Red Wig. Unknown. CoMu

You Got to Cross It foh Yohself. Unknown. AS

You govern the locks, You open life. Unknown, tr. fr. Anglo-Saxon. Fr. Christ 1. AnOE; ASW, tr. by Kevin Crossley-Holland

You grow dependent on the weather's moods. Watercolours, Cornwall. Sylvia Kantaris. PWE

You grow impatient while I focus, fiddle. You Have Shown Me a Strange Image, and We Are Strange Prisoners. Jeni Couzyn. PBCAP

You Growing. Milton Acorn. NOBC

You gulp, a frog suddenly on my dinner. You Don't Understand Me. Marge Piercy. NALW

You hack everything down in battle. Lament to the Spirit of War. Enheduanna. WoWa, ad. by Daniela Gioseffi

You had two girls — Baptiste. At the Cedars. Duncan Campbell Scott. NOBC

You had your say. (LL) Talking to Myself. Kiki Dimoula. VBLP

You hailed a cab outside the nondescript. Runaways Café I. Marilyn Hacker. NGP

You Hated Spain. Ted Hughes. OBTV

You have. (LL) Our Past. Anne Waldman. PoBeRe

You have anti-freeze in the car, yes. Christmas Card. Ted Hughes. OBCP

You have been driving for hours. Looking for a Rest Area. Stephen Dunn. AmPa; AnAn

You have been good to me, I give you this. Idolatry. Arna Bontemps. PoNe

You have been my treasure, Rose Pilgrim. Elect. Mary Ursula Bethell. PeNZ

You have beheld a smiling Rose [or rose]. The Lilly in a Christal. Robert Herrick. NAEL-1; NoP; PoEL-3; SeCP
  (Lily in a Crystal, The.) BeJo; NAEL-1; NoP; NOSC; SCGP

You have brought pearly beads. Pearly Beads. Gond Oral Tradition, tr. by V. Elwin and S. Hivale. WTO

You have coats and robes. You Will Die. Unknown, tr. by H. A. Giles. Fr. Shi King. AWP

You have come so far you can imagine nothing further. Jack Anderson. Fr. Field Trips on the Rapid Transit. NGP

You have come your way, I have come my way. Fronleichnam. D. H. Lawrence. GBL

You have consum'd my language, and my pen. Ovid, tr. fr. Latin by Henry Vaughan. Fr. De Ponto. OBVE

You have done nothing but listen to songs. Your Work. Jean-Joseph Rabéarivelo, tr. fr. French by Ellen Conroy Kennedy. NegPo

You have enslaved me with your lovely body. The Apple. Judah Halevi, tr. fr. Hebrew by Robert Mezey. UnAS

You have forgotten me well. (LL) When You Have Forgotten Sunday: The Love Story. Gwendolyn Brooks. BPo; FF; WPOW

You have got it everything for nothing. (LL) I See a Bear. Ted Hughes. NTP

You have heaped my hands with rubies. Odysseus' Song to Calypso. Peter Kane Dufault. ErPo

You have heard, I suppose, of the man in the moon. The Coolie Chinee. Septimus Winner. OBAL

You have heard it said before. A Handle for the Flutist. Odia Ofeimun. HBAPE

You have heard nothing; of course I know you can have heard/ nothing. Arthur Hugh Clough. Fr. Amours de Voyage. EBVVPR, canto V, xi; NOBVV

You have Hera's eyes Melite. Rufinus, tr. fr. Greek by Alan Marshfield. GrAn

You have just come in the door. The Confession. Peter Cooley. AmPA

You have mistook the jest. (LL) The Defiance. Aphra Behn. EnLoPo

You have netted this dawn. The Archaeology of Love. Richard Murphy. EnLoPo

You have not conquered me — it is the surge. Infidelity. Louis Untermeyer. TrJP

You have only to wait, they will find you. Messengers. Louise Glück. AnAn; HCAP; VCAP

You have put your two hands upon me, and your mouth. Betrothed. Louise Bogan. CrSp

You have red toenails, chestnut. Leda and Her Swan. Olga Broumas. PeHV

You have returned. You have returned, my joy. Edward James. Fr. Carmina Amico. PeHV

You Have Shown Me a Strange Image, and We Are Strange Prisoners. Jeni Couzyn. PBCAP

You have spoken your holy command over the city. Inanna and the City of Uruk. Enheduanna, tr. fr. Sumerian. BoWoP, ad. by Aliki and Willis Barnstone

You have taken back the promise. Fidelis. Adelaide Anne Procter. BLPA; FaBoBe

You have the ingredients on hand. Recipe for an Ocean in the Absence of the Sea. Richard Howard. TAP

You Have the Lovers. Leonard Cohen. NOBC

You have to be almost on top of the Mart. New Orleans. Maxine Cassin. Fr. Three Love Poems by a Native. Jaz

You have to inhabit poetry. Making Poetry. Anne Stevenson. DiPo

You have to quit talking. You have to. Quilts. Kathleen Peirce. PBCAP

You have withdrawn. Absence. Elizabeth Knies. GOYP

You have your hat and coat on and she says she will be right down. The Evening Out. Ogden Nash. MoAmPo

You have your language too. The Wellfleet Whale. Stanley Kunitz. CAPP; DiPo; FoLa; NoAM

You have your own place to drink. Hail and beware them, when they come. (LL) A Newly Discovered "Homeric" Hymn. Charles Olson. MoP; NeAP; NoAM; PoM

You have your shadow. Your Shadow. Mark Strand. Fr. Elegy for My Father. HCAP; LCAP; Prf

You have your water and your grain. My Little Birds. Unknown, tr. fr. Arabic by Henrietta Siksek-Su'ad. FaPON

You haven't finished your ape, said mother to father, who had. Ape. Russell Edson. RaBo

You hear them kids over there laugh this old woman? Lament for the Drowned Country. Mary Durack. NOBAu

You Hebrews are too snug in Ur. Joshua at Schechem. Charles Reznikoff. ChIV-1

You held my lotus blossom. To the Tune "Soaring Clouds." Huang O, tr. fr. Chinese by Kenneth Rexroth and Ling Chung. BoWoP; PBWP; WPC; WPOW

You Hide ("You hide in the ostrich egg.") Edith Bruck, tr. fr. Italian by Ruth Feldman and Brian Swann. BoWoP

You hide your face. Lilith to Eve. Michelene Wandor. NBrP

You hit up a faster gait/ Do it now! (LL) Do It Now! Unknown. BLPA; WBLP

You hitched a thousand miles. August on Sourdough, a Visit from Dick Brewer. Gary Snyder. SOTW

You hold a bunch of roses, Rose. Dionysius Sophistes, tr. fr. Greek by Edward Lucie-Smith. GrAn

You hollow-cheeked son. Baboon 2. Unknown, tr. fr. Hottentot. PeSA

You husbandmen and ploughmen, of every degree. The Little Farm; or, The Weary Ploughman. Unknown. CoMu

You I love my dearest life. An Anonymous Satire, 1773. Unknown. CBCK

You imagine that if you were years older. Mrs. Greta Freeport Baxter. Leo Mailman. NGP

You in Anger. James Reeves. OxBTC

You in evening doorways, in half-lit streets. Evening Quiet. Jovan Hristic, tr. fr. Serbo-Croatian by Charles Simic. HSix

You in I'm not talking about. I Want to Breathe. James Laughlin. ArLo

You incongruous old woman of Smyrna! (LL) There was a young person of Smyrna. Edward Lear. OxBoLi; PeLV; TEP

You infant!/ Why do you look at me like that? Therese. Gottfried Keller, tr. fr. German by Philip L. Miller. RiWo

You inquire gracefully of a man sick at heart. Separation from the Torah. Solomon ibn Gabirol, tr. fr. Hebrew by David Goldstein. TOF

You intimidated me. I was thrown into hell without a trial. Denouement. Ruth Stone. BoWoP

You introduced me to my first goddess. In Memoriam Akbar Babool. Wopko Jensma. PeSAV

You invaded my country by accident. Ways of Conquest. Denise Levertov. CAPP

You invite me to a war party. War Party. Eddy Grant. PBCV

You Jane. Carol Ann Duffy. FaBoBl

You judge a woman. To Some Supposed Brothers. Essex Hemphill. GLP

You just punch a hole in the son of a bitch. (LL) Carnation Milk ("Carnation milk is the best in the land.") Unknown. InPK

You keep asking. (*LL*) Looking for a Rest Area. Stephen Dunn. AmPA; AnAn

You keep eating and raising a family. A Suite for Marriage. David Ignatow. NNaP

You keep me waiting in a truck. Twenty-Year Marriage. Ai. BoWoP; NoAM

You keep our love hidden. Love Story. Adrian Henri. UnAS

You killed the Dalmatian puppy. The Dogs. Michael S. Weaver. PBCAP

You kin talk about yer anthems. The Ol'Tunes. Paul Laurence Dunbar. AnAmPo

You Kissed Me. Josephine Slocum Hunt. BLPA; FaBoBe

You kneel and retch and pray. The Lenten Tunnel. Rachel Hadas. PFL; UnDi

You knew, — who knew not Astrophil? On Sir Philip Sidney. Matthew Royden. *Fr.* Elegy, or Friend's Passion for His Astrophil [*or* Astrophel], An. EIL

You knew I was coming for you, little one. Windigo. Louise Erdrich. NoAM

You Know. Jean Garrigue. NYBP; UnPo

You know all the seasons of Fire. (*LL*) The Seasons of Fire. Billy Marshall-Stoneking. NOBAu

You know, dear, that this vicious world. Mrs. Myrick's Lecture. Mary E. Tucker. CBWP-1

You know her hustle. Asking for Ruthie. Judy Grahn. NMM

You know I always loved you. (*LL*) Attack of the Crab Monsters. Lawrence Raab. AmPA; NoP

You know I have a husband. A Faithful Wife. Chang Chi, *tr. fr. Chinese* by Kenneth Rexroth. OHMPC

You know I keep the photograph. War Widow. Kathleen Jamie. PWE

You know/ I know. Alaskan Drinking Song. Dave Morice. EOEF

You know I said to Mark that I'm furious at you. The Quarrel. Diane Di Prima. NMM

You know I'm working Jan, you know. When I Was in Bridport. Douglas Oliver. VaA

You know I've seen a lot of what the world can do. Vile World. Simon Rae. UV

You know I've seen a lot of what the world can do. Wild World. Cat Stevens. UV

You know, Joe, it's a funny thing. Ultimate Equality. Ray Durem. PoNe

"You know," lara says. A Constituency of Dunces. Gerald Locklin. NGP

You know no more than I. (*LL*) Half-moon westers low, my love, The. A. E. Housman. CBLP

You know not how deep was the love your eyes did kindle. Ibn al-Abbar, *tr. fr. Arabic* by A. R. Nykel. PeHV

You know, or you don't know, that great Bacon saith. Byron. *Fr.* Don Juan. NOBL, XIV

You know Saint Wigbald's — yonder nunnery cell. How the Abbey of Saint Werewulf Juxta Slingsby Came by Brother Fabian's Manuscript. Sebastian Evans. PeVV

You know that day at Peach Tree Creek. Logan at Peach Tree Creek. Hamlin Garland. PAH

You know that he is going to die. The Red Dog. Laura Jensen. LCAP

You know that I love you, sweatheart, but every time I come around. *Unknown, tr. fr. Kiowa Indian. Fr.* "49" Songs. STP

You know that land, her lemon groves in bloom? Goethe. *See* Have you been to that country where the gold.

You know that moment in the summer dusk. Dusk. Yannis Ritsos, *tr. fr. Greek* by Paul Merchant. AnRep

You know that old woman. Who Lived in a Shoe? Beatrix Potter. SiSoPo

You know the answer to the last surmise. Sonnet for My Son. Melanie Gordon Barber. GoYe

You Know the Funny Thing Is. Barbara Helfgott Hyett. BTR

You know the hay's in. Hay-Making. Gillian Clarke. AngWe

You know the old woman. The Old Woman. Beatrix Potter. GoJo; NTCP; PDV

You know the place: then. Sappho, *tr. fr. Greek* by Mary Barnard. PBWP

You know the stick patches. Andrew Greig. *Fr.* Len's Poems. PWE

You know the way to heavens doore. (*LL*) Church-Music[k]. George Herbert. ESCV; GeHe; OxBSP; SeCV-1

You know the world how big it is, Southern Africa. Nguno Wakolele. PeSAV

You know there goes a tale. The Modern Jonas. *Unknown.* PAH

You know there is not much. To a Friend Concerning Several Ladies. William Carlos Williams. VGW

You know those rose sherbets. You Know. Jean Garrigue. NYBP; UnPo

You know those windless summer evenings, swollen to stasis. Cigales. Richard Wilbur. NOBA

You know w'at for ees school keep out. Leetla Giorgio Washeenton. T. A. Daly. FaPON

You know we French stormed [*or* storm'd] Ratisbon. Incident of the French Camp. Robert Browning. BeLS; CoGr; FaPoR; GN; OBWP; TrGrPo

You know we must be lonely, you and I. Souls. Paul Wertheimer, *tr. fr. German* by Jethro Bithell. TrJP

You know what it is to be born alone. Baby Tortoise. D. H. Lawrence. CMoP; MeMBP

You ladies all that are in fashion. A New Song called The Curling of the Hair. *Unknown.* CoMu

You landsmen and you seamen bold. The Loss of the *Due Dispatch. Unknown.* AmFP

You laugh, and I must hide the wound. The Negro Laughs Back. Mary Jenness. ShDr

You Laughed and Laughed and Laughed. Gabriel Okara. PBA

You lay a wreath on murdered Lincoln's bier. Abraham Lincoln. Tom Taylor. PAH

You lay in wait. Sappho, *tr. fr. Greek* by Willis Barnstone. BoWoP

You lean on a wire fence, looking across. Somewhere along the Way. Henry Taylor. Poetr

You leaned your body in the doorway. Talkers in a Dream Doorway. Judy Grahn. GLP

You leaped from the white horses. The Distaff. Erinna, *tr. fr. Greek* by Marylin Arthur. WPOW

You learned Lear's *Nonsense Rhymes* by heart, not rote. A Plea to Boys and Girls. Robert Graves. GTBS-P; NAEL-2

You leave dead friends in. Will They Cry When You're Gone, You Bet. Amiri Baraka. NAAL-2

You left behind, Eurymedon, an infant child. Theocritus [*or* Theokritus], *tr. fr. Greek* by Anthony Holden. GrAn

You left me when the weary weight of sorrow. Forgiven. Margaret E. M. Sangster. PoToHe

You left open will never be shut again. (*LL*) Invasion on the Farm. R. S. Thomas. PWE

You let the razor-wound bleed in the warm. Last Days in the Party. Thomas McCarthy. IB

You, Letting the Trees Stand as My Betrayer. Diane Wakoski. MoP

You lie now in many coffins. For Malcolm: After Mecca. Gerald William Barrax. PoBA

You lie, snail-like, on your stomach. Depression. Wendy Cope. FaBoWP

You lights, for which on earth my sight's thirst ne'er is stilled. To the Stars. Andreas Gryphius, *tr. fr. German* by George C. Schoolfield. GePo

You like it under the trees in autumn. The Motive for Metaphor. Wallace Stevens. MoAB; MoAmPo

You like not that French novel? Tell me why. George Meredith. *Fr.* Modern Love. EnVP; NOBVV

You limb of a spider. *Unknown.* ISE

You lit a firebrand. The Floating Candles. Sydney Lea. SM

You little, eager, peeping thing. The Awakening. Angela Morgan. OHIP

You little know the heart that you advise. An Answer to a Lady Advising Me to Retirement. Lady Mary Wortley Montagu. TEP

You, little round-bellied. *Unknown, tr. fr. Greek* by Sam Hamill. InMo

You little stars that live in skies. Fulke Greville. *Fr.* Caelica. ElL; NoP

You live here because there's no other place. So Long Solon. Jack Myers. AmPA

You Live There; I Live Here. Harold Monro. *Fr.* Strange Meetings. Mes

You live under the microscope. Under the Microscope. Slavko Mihalic, *tr. by* Charles Simic. PoSu

You lived and moved among the best society. W. H. Auden. *Fr.* Letter to Lord Byron. OBSV

You lived too near the ghosts. For they were kind. Intimates. Alison Brackenbury. SCBI

You Living Powers. Sir Philip Sidney. *Fr.* Arcadia. SiPSBD

You living powers enclosed in stately shrine. You Living Powers. Sir Philip Sidney. *Fr.* Arcadia. SiPSBD

You, long years; and father, health! (*LL*) To Mistress Anne Cecil, upon Making Her a New Year's Gift, January 1, 1567-8. William Cecil, 1st Baron Burghley. EiL; FaBoEH

You/ Look a while at me. Far and Close. Gu Cheng, *tr. fr. Chinese. TSaS, tr. by* Edward Morin

You look at me. A Drop of Dew. Shmuel Halkin, *tr. fr. Yiddish* by Jacob Sonntag. TrJP

You look at me, a hut or cage contains. Hilda Doolittle ("H. D."). *Fr.* Sagesse. NOCV

You look at me when you're bored with the world. Reassurance. Julia Vinograd. SRLS

You look at me with tender eyes. La Coquette. Rose Terry Cooke. AmWP

You look for prodigies leaning on the sill of storm. The Day of the Statue. Francis Webb. FaBoMA

You look up to heaven in supplication, and hope for grace and mercy. (*LL*) Omnipotence. Johann Ladislaus von Felsö-Eör Pyrker. RiWo

You look upon the air. (*LL*) Late. Louise Bogan. PBWP; VGW

You, love, and I. Counting the Beats. Robert Graves. ELP; GBL; GTBS-P; HAP; LPA; OxAEP-2; OxBTC; WeW

You love not me? (*LL*) A Broken Appointment. Thomas Hardy. GBL; NAEL-2; NoAM; NOBVV; NoP

You love? That's high as you shall go. The Attainment. Coventry Patmore. *Fr*. Angel in the House, The. FaBoEE

You love the roses — so do I. I wish. Roses. "George Eliot." BoTP

You love us when we're heroes, home on leave. Glory of Women. Siegfried Sassoon. NAEL-2; OBWP; OxAEP-2; PAW; PeFWW

You Loved Me. Marina Tsvetayeva, *tr. fr. Russian* by Elaine Feinstein. VBLP

You loved me. And your lies had their own probity. You Loved Me. Marina Tsvetayeva, *tr. fr. Russian* by Elaine Feinstein. VBLP

You loved me for a little. Midsummer. Sydney King Russell. BLPA; FaBoBe

You loved me not at all, but let it go. Edna St. Vincent Millay. VGW

You loved Menophila when you were rich. Argentarius, *tr. fr. Greek* by Fleur Adcock. GrAn

You lower my emotions, sealed in their casket. The Parting. Sara Berkeley. PBCIP

You lumbered along the stadium. My Father's First Baseball Game. Michael S. Weaver. PBCAP

You Made It Rain. Ruby C. Saunders. BISi

You made me blue. Blue. Gerald William Barrax. *Fr*. The Old Gory. NBV

You make bloody bread! (*LL*) High. Philip Lamantia. PoBeRe

You Make Everything Move Me. Jack Skelley. UTF

You make it in your mess-tin by the brazier's rosy gleam. A Pot of Tea. Robert W. Service. NSI; PoWW

'You make me sick!' this, with rancor, vehemence, disgust — again. Kin. C. K. Williams. PWE

You make us want to stay alive, Suzanne. Suzanne. John Logan. CAPP

You, Marc Chagall, should be able to tell us. The Ascensions. William Pillen. BTR; RaBo

You marched off southward with the fire of twenty. Danny. Malcolm Cowley. PoA

You married men, whom Fate hath assign'd. The Merry Cuckold. *Unknown*. CoMu

You Masks of the Masquerade. Gustave Kahn, *tr. fr. French* by Jethro Bithell. TrJP

You, master of delays. Killing No Murder. Sylvia Townsend Warner. MoBrPo

You may be Dirty Dinky. (*LL*) Dinky. Theodore Roethke. OBAL; OBCA; SM

You may be right, divinity. Francis Sullivan. CRP

You may brag about your breakfast foods you eat at break of day. Sausage. Edgar A. Guest. OBAL

You may call, you may call. The Bad Kittens. Elizabeth J. Coatsworth. FaPON; OBCA

You may catch/ a butterfly. Ars Poetica. Linda Pastan. NIP

You may catch all the others, but you wo. (*LL*) The Slithergadee. Shel Silverstein. NBLV

You may for ever tarry. (*LL*) To [the] Virgins, to Make Much of Time. Robert Herrick. AWP; BeJo; BLPA; BoLoP; CaPo; ChTr; ClHu; CoGr; EBEvV; ELP; EnLoPo; ErPo; FaBV; FF; GBL; HAP; HeIP; ImPo; InPK; InPS; JCP; LiTB; NAEL-1; NBLV; NIP; NOBE; NoP; NOSC; OAEL-1; OBEV; OxAEP-1; PoE; PoEL-3; Poetr; PrIm; SCGP; SCV; SeCP; SeCV-1; SoSe; TEP; TFi; TrGrPo; UV

You may get through the world, but 'twill be very slow. People Will Talk. Samuel Dodge. WBLP

You may give over plow, boys. Tommy's Dead. Sydney Thompson Dobell. PeVV

You may have forgot, you were drunk when you dy'd. (*LL*) When Bibo thought fit from the world to retreat. Matthew Prior. FaBoEE

You may have troubles manifold. A Mother's Joy. Ruth Fortney Maxwell. PWR

You may my glories and my state depose. Shakespeare. *Fr*. Richard II. IMW

You may not believe it, for hardly could I. The Pumpkin. Robert Graves. PDV; SiSoPo

You may speak of a grave in a distant land. A Reverie. Mary Weston Fordham. CBWP-2

You may talk about me just as much as you please. Hold the Wind. *Unknown*. GBP; OBD

You may talk about me just as much as you please. Hold the Wind. Villon. OBD

You may talk as you please of the joys of Jamaica. The Song of the Transportationist. *Unknown*. NOBAu

You may talk o' gin and [*or* an'] beer. Gunga Din. Kipling. EBEvV; EBVV; GGP; LiTB; MoBrPo; OBTV; OHCV

You may talk of Columbus's sailing. "Are Ye Right There, Michael?" (A Lay of the Wild West Clare.). William Percy French. WTO

You may tempt the upper classes. Edgar Smith. *Fr*. Heaven Will Protect the Working-Girl. FiBHP

You may want to cut them down. You may want to use a knife. Chrysanthemums. Irene McKinney. PBCAP

You may write me down in history. Still I Rise. Maya Angelou. BISi

"You mean," he said, "a crocodile." (*LL*) The Purist. Ogden Nash. FiBHP; GoJo; MoAmPo; MoShBr; NBLV; OBCA

You meaner beauties of the night. On [*or* To] His Mistress, the Queen of Bohemia. Sir Henry Wotton. CBLP; EIL; ELP; EnLoPo; GBL; HAP; JCP; MeLP; NoP; NOSC; PlP; SCGP; SeCP; TFi; TrGrPo (Elizabeth of Bohemia.) BoLoP; FaBoCh; GTBS; GTBS-P; NOBE; OBEV; OtMeF, *St*. 1 *only*

You meet a man. What Idiots Lovers Are. Judith Kazantzis. VBLP

You meet your friend, your face. Selected Epigrams. Kassia, *tr. fr. Byzantine Greek* by Patrick Diehl. PBWP

You merchant men of Billingsgate, I wonder how you can thrive. Cordial Advice. *Unknown*. OxBSS

You merit more; nor cou'd my Love do less. (*LL*) To My Dear Friend Mr. Congreve [on His Comedy Called "The Double-Dealer"]. Dryden. EBEV; OAEL-1; OxAEP-1; PoEL-3; SeCV-2

You midst gay crowds reside, I, hid in shades. Esther Lewis. *Fr*. Letter to a Lady in London, A. ECWP

You might ask. Battle Scene. Aricil Kilar, *tr. fr. Tamil* by A. K. Ramanujan. PLW

You might be surprised right out the window, whistling dixie on the/ way. (*LL*) Poem for Half White College Students. Amiri Baraka. BPo; TAP; UnPo

You might call this. Old Men on the Courthouse Lawn, Murray, Kentucky. James Galvin. AnAn

You might come here Sunday on a whim. Degrees of Gray in Philipsburg. Richard Hugo. CAPP; CoAP; NAAL-2; NoAM; NoP; TRP; VCAP

You might easy know a doffer. *Unknown*. FaBoVe

You might on a day like this suspect. En Attendant. Tim Longville. VaA

You might suppose it easy. The Boatman. Jay Macpherson. MoCV

You mind things; you'm observant I can see. Minding Things. Paul Hyland. PWE

You modern wits, who call this world a star. To the Same [My Dear Sister, Mrs S.]: The Tears. William Hammond. NOSC

You, Morningtide Star, more are steady-eyed, over the east. Lying Awake. Thomas Hardy. FaBoRV; FaBoVe

You move/ like the sound of pipes. You. Barbara Burford. DT

You must admit the loss of blood, brother. Missing Link. Sean Lucy. BiHa

You must agree that Rubens was a fool. To English Connoisseurs. Blake. OxBoLi

You must be proud, if you'll be wise. (*LL*) To the Ladies. Mary Lee, Lady Chudleigh. ECWP; NALW; NOEC; WPE; WPOW

You must be sad; for though it is to Heaven. To Two Bereaved. Thomas Ashe. NOBVV

You Must Change Your Life. Ken Edwards. NBrP

You must come back, as your grandmother did. Dandelion Greens. Jane Flanders. CrSp

You must do as they do at Hoo. Hoo, Suffolk. *Unknown*. GBP

You must find out, for I don't know. (*LL*) Three Wise Old Women. Elizabeth T. Corbett. BLPA; OBCA; OBSP; OxBChV

You must forgive me, if I've learned to hate! (*LL*) The Slave's Lament. Massillon Coicou. NegPo

You Must Have Been a Sensational Baby. Harold Norse. GLP

You must have been still sleeping, your wife there. The Sacred Hearth. David Gascoyne. FaBoTw

You must have given me up. (*LL*) Kidnaper. Tess Gallagher. AmPA

You Must Know Everything. Allen Grossman. *Fr*. Ether Dome (an Entertainment), The. BAP-91

You must learn how to peel, man. Orange. Barbara Ferland. PBCV

You must learn to make the best of it. (*LL*) You Go to My Head. Elaine Equi. UTF

You must life, get on with your life. (*LL*) What is there left to be said? A. R. D. Fairburn. PeNZ

You must live through the time when everything hurts. The Double Shame. Stephen Spender. LiTB; LiTM

You must not hope to arrive. (*LL*) The Tourist from Syracuse. Donald Justice. CAPP; NoAM; TwCP; VCAP

You must not, said the owl to the capercailzie. The End of ARt. Reiner Kunze, *tr. fr. German by* Michael Hamburger. PoSu

You must not wonder, though you think it strange. For That He Looked Not upon Her. George Gascoigne. ElL; NoP

You must remain very much alone. Presences. Zoé Karélli, *tr. fr. Modern Greek by* Kimon Friar. PBWP

You must remember structures beyond cotton plains. If Blood Is Black Then Spirit Neglects My Unborn Son. Conrad Kent Rivers. PoBA

You must remove your sleepmask, haul it. Sleepmask Dithyrambic. Thomas Lux. PRA

You must stand erect but at your ease, a posture. The Singing Lesson. David Wagoner. NoAM

You must wake and call me early, call me early, mother. Tennyson. *Fr.* May Queen, The. EBEvV

You must wake and call me early, call me early, mother dear. The May Queen. Tennyson. PFP

You Mustn't Quit. *Unknown. See* When things go wrong, as they sometimes will.

You/ my bell-clapper. Christmas Mass for a Little Atheist Jesus. Claude Maillard, *tr. fr. French by* Maxine W. Kumin *and* Judith Kumin. BoWoP

You, my Lord, have tarried long in your journey. Lord of the River Hsiang. Ch'u Yüan, *tr. fr. Chinese by* Wu-chi Liu. SuSp

You My Soul. Friedrich Rückert, *tr. fr. German by* Philip L. Miller. RiWo

You need not be an atom of a poet. (*LL*) It's all a trick, quite easy when you know it. W. W. Skeat. FaBoCo; FiBHP

You need the untranslatable ice to watch. Appendix to the Anniad. Gwendolyn Brooks. BlSi

You neigh and whinny, seeming to invite. Macedonius, *tr. fr. Greek by* Adrian Wright. GrAn

You never attained to Him. If to attain. Via, Veritas, et Vita. Alice Meynell. WGRP

You never bearded more than syllables. Christ-in-the-Woods. Sebastian Barry. IB

You Never Can Tell. Ella Wheeler Wilcox. BLPA; BLPL; PoToHe

You never can tell till you try. (*LL*) There was a young maid who said, "Why." *Unknown.* SoSe

You never claimed to be someone special. She Mends an Ancient Wireless. Paul Durcan. PBCIP

You never could tell what my deaf Uncle Arthur heard. And Don't Be Deaf to the Singing Beyond. Carter Revard. HATNAP

You never get to play it, the rackets. The Badminton at Great Barrington. Michael Benedikt. PRA

You never hear 'the People' now. The People, No. Vicki Raymond. NOBAu

You never know with a doorbell. Doorbells. Rachel Field. FaPON

You never stir, and heaven forbid. The China Cat. Walter de la Mare. OFC; SoCa

You never touch. Yosano Akiko, *tr. fr. Japanese by* Geoffrey Bownas *and* Anthony Thwaite. BoWoP; PBWP

You never will meet such a merchant as I! (*LL*) The Elfin Pedlar. George Darley. BoTP

You, no doubt, have heard the story told of Charleston by the sea? The Crum Appointment. L. A. J. Moorer. CBWP-3

You no give me one wacky you can't pass. Dry River. *Unknown.* FaBoVe

You noble Diggers all, stand up now, stand up now. The Digger's Song. Gerrard Winstanley. FaBoEH; FaBoPV; NOSC

You noble fountain set in peace and joy's design. Concerning the Wolffsbrunnen near Heidelberg. Martin Opitz, *tr. fr. German by* George C. Schoolfield. GePo

You now solicit a few enemy thrusts. D. B. Wyndham Lewis. *Fr.* If So the Man You Are. OBSV

You nurtured grief until that leap. Waiting for Robinson. Roberta Hill Whiteman. HATNAP

You, O Tsui-Xgoa. Hymn to Tsui-Xgoa. *Unknown, tr. fr. Hottentot.* PeSA

You of the same mind, moor-wandering near one. Largo. Paul Celan, *tr. fr. German by* Michael Hamburger. PoSu

You often played. The Musician. Duane Niatum. BCF

You often went to breathe a timeless air. The Scholar. Frances Cornford. BrRo

You, once a belle in Shreveport. Snapshots of a Daughter-in-Law. Adrienne Rich. FaBoWP; HCAP; NAAL-2; NALW; NIP; NMM; NoAM; NoP; Poetr; VCAP

You only come in the tormenting. Suicide. Robert Lowell. PoE

You opened the matchbox. Despair. Aleksandar Ristovic, *tr. fr. Serbo-Croatian by* Charles Simic. HSix

You or I must be he. (*LL*) Hinx! minx!/ The old witch winks! *Unknown.* MAT; OxNR

You ought to know Mr. Mistoffelees! Mr. Mistoffelees. T. S. Eliot. CBNP

You ought to see my blue-eyed Sally. Stay All Night, Stay a Little Longer. *Unknown.* AmFP

You/ Over there/ Beyond the hill. Echo. Mildred Weston. BoNaP

You over there, young man with the guide book red-bound. Home Sweet Home with Variations. H. C. Bunner. BXAP; OBAL

You owe me five shillings. The Bells. *Unknown.* ReMoGo

You owned the surge and swill of water. For Albert Ayler. Victoria McCabe. Jaz

You paint the wild geese as if I could see them crying. For Contemporary Artist Pien Wei-ch'i. Cheng Hsieh, *tr. fr. Chinese by* Irving Y. Lo. SuSp

You pass the tomb of Battus' son, well skilled. Callimachus, *tr. fr. Greek. Fr.* Epigrams. HePo

You plant a border of poppies in my yard, visit. A Partial History of Poppies. Rosemary Catacalos. AfAz

You plant in your son the soul of the desert. (*LL*) Song for Dov Shamir. Dannie Abse. SuSp

You plant like Paul, you water like Apollos. The Rev. Nicholas Noyes to the Rev. Cotton Mather. Nicholas Noyes. SCAP

You planted life, protecting. Discords. Fabio Doplicher, *tr. fr. Italian by* Dana Gioia. NeIt

You play the flute. Longing. *Gond Oral Tradition, tr. by* V. Elwin *and* S. Hivale. WTO

You Playmates of Mine. Rainer Maria Rilke, *tr. fr. German by* Stephen Mitchell. ArLo

You playmates of mine in the scattered parks of the city. You Playmates of Mine. Rainer Maria Rilke, *tr. fr. German by* Stephen Mitchell. ArLo

You plummeting shards of the darkness. To the Swallows of Viterbo. Gibbons Ruark. SM

You poets all, brave Shakespeare, Jonson, Green. *Unknown.* FaBoEH

You poured down like gold,/ Olympian Zeus. Parmenion of Macedon, *tr. fr. Greek by* Peter Jay. GrAn

You praise the firm restraint with which they write. On Some South African Novelists. Roy Campbell. FaBoCo; FaBoEE; GTBS-P; InPK; MoBrPo; NOBL; OxAEP-2; OxBTC; PeLV

You prayer —, you blasphemy, you. Plashes the Fountain. Paul Celan, *tr. fr. German by* Michael Hamburger. OBVE

You prisoners of New South Wales. A Convict's Tour to Hell. Francis MacNamara. NOBAu

You promise heavens free from strife. Mimnermus in Church. William Johnson Cory. CoGr; NOBE; OBEV

You, proud curve-lipped youth, with brown sensitive face. Through the Long Night. Edward Carpenter. *Fr.* Towards Democracy. PeHV

You put your hand on my shoulder. Abdelfatteh. E. A. Lacey. PeHV

You raise me now in song. (*LL*) Silence. Bella Akhmadulina. BoWoP

You rambling boys of Liverpool I'll have you to beware. The Banks of Newfoundland ("You rambling boys of Liverpool I'll have you to beware.") *Unknown.* OxBSS

You read the New York Times. Alfred Corning Clark. Robert Lowell. RB

You, reading over my shoulder, peering beneath. The Reader over My Shoulder. Robert Graves. MeMBP; NAEL-2

You recline that magnificent pair of buttocks. To Kyris. Strato, *tr. fr. Greek by* Teddy Hogge. GrAn; PeHV

You recommend that the motive, in Chapter 8, should be changed. Yes, the Agency Can Handle That. Kenneth Fearing. WeW

You recount old tales of Thebes. Anacreon, *tr. fr. Greek by* Sam Hamill. InMo

You/ Refuse to see. Out. Riots and Rituals. Richard W. Thomas. PoBA

You remember the big Gaston, for whom everyone predicted a bad end? Monsieur Gaston. A. M. Klein. MoCV

You remember the name was Jensen. She seemed old. What Thou Lovest Well, Remains American. Richard Hugo. NAAL-2

You replaced the Douglas firs. You, Letting the Trees Stand as My Betrayer. Diane Wakoski. MoP

You reproach me because each of my stories. Italo Calvino, *tr. fr. Italian. Fr.* Continuous Cities. AnRep, *tr. by* William Weaver

You ride dat horse. Jesus, Won't You Come B'm-By? *Unknown.* AS

You roar over the meadow and roar. Last Days. Richard Hugo. PoA

You ruthless flea, who desecrate my couch. Song of the Flea. Judah al-Harizi, *tr. fr. Hebrew.* TrJP

You, sad Captain, big-knobbed staff of life. The Voyages of Captain Cock. William Jay Smith. ErPo

You said it went all the way. Last Words, 1968. Lance Henson. CDW

You said: My father didn't cry. Ancestral Weight. Alfonsina Storni, *tr. fr. Spanish by* Marti Moody. WPOW

You said my life was meant to run from yours as. Our Past. Anne Waldman. PoBeRe

You said, that October. December at Yase. Gary Snyder. *Fr.* Four Poems for Robin. MoP; NNaP; NoAM; NOBA; NoP; SOTW

You said that your people. To Richard Wright. Conrad Kent Rivers. PoBA

You said to me: But I will be your comrade. Nudities. André Spire, *tr. by* Jethro Bithell. AWP; ErPo

You said to me:/ I shall [*or* would] become your comrade. Nudities. André Spire, *tr. fr. French by* Stanley Burnshaw. TrJP

You said you would kill it this morning. Pheasant. Sylvia Plath. RB

You sail and you seek for the Fortunate Isles. The Fortunate Isles. Joaquin Miller. WGRP

You sang a race from wood and stone to Christ. (*LL*) O Black and Unknown Bards. James Weldon Johnson. BPo; HeIP; PoBA; PoNe; TTY; UnPo

You sang round-dance songs. Liz Sohappy Bahe. CDW

You sat with a bottle of beer. After the Death of an Elder Klallam. Duane Niatum. CDW

You say, as I have often given tongue. To a Poet, Who Would Have Me Praise Certain Bad Poets, Imitators of His and Mine. W. B. Yeats. CTC; FaBoEE

You say, but with no touch of scorn. Tennyson. *Fr.* In Memoriam A. H. H. EBVV, *abr.*; NOCV; OAEL-2, *abr.*; PeECV, *abr.* (Doubt.) WGRP

You say I love not, 'cause I do not play. To His Mistress Objecting to Him neither Toying or Talking. Robert Herrick. FaBV

You say my brow is stern and yet my smile. The Stern Brow. Walter Savage Landor. CBLP

You say my poetry. Complaint to a Court Poet. Rashidi Samarqandi, *tr. fr. Persian by* Omar S. Pound. ArPe

You say that everything is very simple and interesting. Yesterday Down at the Canal. Frank O'Hara. NOBA

You say that I take a good deal upon myself. Monumentum Aere, Etc. Ezra Pound. NOBA

You say that you believe in Democracy for everybody. Everybody but Me. Margaret Goss Burroughs. BlSi

You say the king commands that I appear. Diptych. Velma West Sykes. IHMS

You say there were no people. There Are No People Song. *Navajo Indian Oral Tradition*. TTTS

You say, to me-wards your affection's strong. Love Me Little, Love Me Long. Robert Herrick. BLPA; CaPo; CBLP; EiL; FaBoBe; NoP; SCGP

You say, "Where goest Thou?" I cannot tell. The Poet's Simple Faith. Victor Hugo, *tr. fr. French by* Edward Dowden. WGRP

You Say You Are Holy. Stephen Crane. MeMAP

You say you had a letter from. First Letter From Tamara A. Reiner Kunze, *tr. fr. German by* Ewald Osers. PoSu

You say you "live inside a full-stop." Nichita Stanescu. Brian Turner. PeNZ

You say you love, but with a voice. Keats. CBLP

You say you will leave this place. The City. Michael O'Loughlin. IB

You scarcely move your foot when out of nowhere spring. Voices. Wislawa Szymborska, *tr. fr. Polish by* Magnus F. Krynski. PoSu

You scream, waking from a nightmare. Little Sleep's-Head Sprouting Hair in the Moonlight. Galway Kinnell. LCAP

You seamen bold that have oft withstood. Lady Franklin's Lament for Her Husband. *Unknown*. OxBSS

You seamen bold that plough the ocean. The Ship in Distress. *Unknown*. OxBSS

You see auras, do you not? No? You will. The Reading. David Dooley. BAP-89

You see, he said, the overall simplicity. Patent No. 1. Kay Hargreaves. Mes

You see how, white with snows to the north of us. Horace. *See* To Thaliarchus ("Behold yon mountains.")

You see, I am alive, I am alive. (*LL*) The Delight Song of Tsoai-Talee. N. Scott Momaday. CDW; EaPr; GrPl; InPK

You see, my Lord, I do not wait upon ceremony. T. S. Eliot. *Fr.* Murder in the Cathedral. OBF

You see, my whole life. Woman Poem. Nikki Giovanni. BlSi; NMM

You see, the problem is. Blue like Death. James Welch. CDW

You see the sky now. How to Write a Poem about the Sky. Leslie Silko. NoP

You see the smoke at Kapunda. Song: The Railway Train. *Unknown, tr. by* George Taplin. NOBAu

You see the worst of love, but not the best. Walter Savage Landor. GBL

You see them vanish in their speeding cars. Fugue. Howard Nemerov. TAP

You see these little scars? That's where my wife. Iambic Feet Considered as Honorable Scars. William Meredith. OxBSP; PoA

You see, they have no judgment. The Drowned Children. Louise Glück. HCAP; VCAP

You see this Christmas tree all silver gold? Come Christmas. David McCord. PChr

You see this dog. It was but yesterday. Flush or Faunus. Elizabeth Barrett Browning. FM

You see this pebble-stone? It's a thing I bought. The Cock and the Bull. Charles Stuart Calverley. BXAP; FaBoCo; FaBoNo; FaBoPa

You see this rain. Jenny Joseph. *Fr.* Persephone. PWE

"You see those mothers squabbling there?" In the Cemetery. Thomas Hardy. *Fr.* Satires of Circumstance. InPK; Son

You see what I am: change me, change me! (*LL*) The Woman at the Washington Zoo. Randall Jarrell. CAPP; CoAP; HAP; HCAP; LiTM; OxBC; TAP; TwCP; UnPo; VCAP

You see, where'er you look, on earth but vainness' hour. All Is Vanity. Andreas Gryphius, *tr. fr. German by* George C. Schoolfield. GePo

You seek refuge. The Gift. Greg Delanty. BiHa

You send for her, you tell her to come, you get everything ready. The Impotent Lover. Automedon, *tr. fr. Greek by* W. S. Merwin. GrAn

You send me reams of snowy paper. Leonidas of Alexandria, *tr. fr. Greek by* Robin Skelton. GrAn

You send me your love in a letter. Child and Poet. Swinburne. OHCV

You serve me on plates marked with my grandmother's monogram. At Your Table. Vienna V, 1957. Lisa Ress. BTR

You Serve the Best Wines Always, My Dear Sir. Martial, *tr. fr. Latin by* J. V. Cunningham. InPK

You Shall above All Things Be Glad and Young. E. E. Cummings. NoAM; NOBA; OxBA

You shall be ever pleased, and young maids long. (*LL*) Come Hither, You That Love. John Fletcher. ELP

You shall be true to them, who are false to you. (*LL*) The Indifferent. John Donne. BoLoP; CBLP; ESCV; NAEL-1; NAWM-1; NOSC; SeCV-1; SoSe; TEP

You shall have an apple. For Baby. *Unknown*. ReMoGo

You shall never remain in Thermopylae.' (*LL*) There was an old man of Thermopylae. Edward Lear. EBEV; FaBoNo; NOBL; OxAEP-2; PeLi

You shall not kiss me. (*LL*) Open the Door. *Unknown*. EiL; GBL

You shall not see me now (quoth he), good night. (*LL*) Fool much bit by fleas put out the light, A. Richard Lovelace, *after the Greek of* Lucian. FaBoEE

You shall not vanish into dust today. Funeral. Murray Bennett. GoYe

You shall sleep softly in my arms! (*LL*) Death and the Maiden. Matthias Claudius. RiWo

You Shall Walk in Peace! Martial Sinda, *tr. fr. French by* Ellen Conroy Kennedy. NegPo

You shepherds who wander this lonely mountainside. Leonidas of Tarentum, *tr. fr. Greek by* Fleur Adcock. GrAn

You should be done with blossoming by now. To a Vine-clad Telegraph Pole. Louis Untermeyer. MoAmPo

You should bid me welcome. Walther von der Vogelweide, *tr. fr. German by* Frederick Goldin. GePo

You should entreat trees and rocks. Dogen. EaPr

You should have many lovers. A Very Sad Conversation at Night. Anna Swirszczynska, *tr. fr. Polish by* Czeslaw Milosz *and* Leonard Nathan. PoSu

You should see these musical mice. New Strain. George Starbuck. TwCP

You should try to hear the name. The Name. Jalal al-Din Rumi, *tr. fr. Persian by* Robert Bly. NU (Names.) RaBo

You should understand that I use my body now for everything. At Bickford's. Gerald Stern. CAPP

You shouldn't be afraid of the dark. Lullaby for My Dead Child. Denise Jallais, *tr. fr. French by* Maxine W. Kumin *and* Judith Kumin. BoWoP; IMW

You show me the poems of some woman. Translations. Adrienne Rich. WPOW

You showed your dirty face first in Detroit. To the Eminent Scholar and Meddler. Kofi Awoonor. HBAPE

You shun me, Chloë, wild and shy. To Chloë ("Vitas hinnuleo.") Horace, *tr. fr. Latin by* Austin Dobson. *Fr.* Odes. AWP; OBVE

You sing a hard blues. Bulosan Listens to a Recording of Robert Johnson. Alfred Encarnacion. OpBo

You sit at your high windows, old men. The Old Men. Alexander Javitz. TrJP

You sit behind your coffee. The Quarrel. Karen Swenson. GrPl

You sit down on a hill top, or anywhere high enough for you. *Unknown*, tr. *fr. Chinese*. EaPr

You sit in a chair, touched by nothing, feeling. In Celebration. Mark Strand. NoAM

You sit in the middle of the bed. To a Friend's Child. Aliki Barnstone. BoWoP

You sit in the yard and find. Daily Bread. James Ulmer. UTF

You sit, pray and sing. (*LL*) Within a circle of one meter. Nanao Sakaki. EaPr

You slapped me. For My Torturer, Lieutenant D —. Leila Djabali, tr. *fr. French by* Anita Barrows. WPOW

You slapped my face. Short Poem. William Carlos Williams. SAmP

You sleep at the top of streets. To Waken a Small Person. Donald Justice. NYBP

You sleep here, Daphnis, on the leafy ground. Theocritus [*or* Theokritus], tr. *fr. Greek by* Anthony Holden. GrAn

You sleep in a room with bluegreen curtains. In the Wake of Home. Adrienne Rich. LCAP

You Smile upon Your Friend To-day. A. E. Housman. *Fr. Shropshire Lad, A.* FaPoB; MeMBP

You Smiled, You Spoke, and I Believed. Walter Savage Landor. BoLoP; CBLP; GBL

You son of a bitch. (*LL*) Thou Shalt Not Kill: A Memorial for Dylan Thomas. Kenneth Rexroth. PoBeRe

You sons of England, now listen to my rhymes. Pity Poor Labourers. *Unknown*. OBET

You speak of art. Para un Revolucionario. Lorna Dee Cervantes. Poetr

You speak of whale water. H₂O. Belinda Subraman. NGP

You speed by with your camera and your spear. Interview with a Tourist. Margaret Atwood. IHMS

You spent all summer in cool Kabul. *Unknown*, tr. *fr. Pashto by* Saduddin Shpoon. PBWP

You spotted snakes [with double tongue]. Shakespeare. *Fr. Midsummer Night's Dream, A.* BoTP; InvP; LiTB; NOBE; NoSic; PoRA; SCGP
(Fairies' Lullaby, The.) EIL
(Fairy Land, 2.) OBEV
(Fairy Lullaby.) FaPoN
(Fairy Songs ("You spotted snakes with double tongue.")) TrGrPo
(Lullaby for Titania.) GN

You staged the ultimate coup de grâce. The Lundys Letter. Gerald Dawe. BiHa

You stand against the pillar. Mothers. Kavarpentu, tr. *fr. Tamil by* A. K. Ramanujan. PLW

You stand and hold the post of my small house. Auvaiyar, tr. *fr. Tamil by* George Hart. WPOW

You stand atop your hill. New Hampshire Farm Woman. Rachel Graham. GoYe

You stand behind the old black mare. Why Can't I Leave You? Ai. AmPA

You stand near the window as lights wink. Twenty-third Street Runs into Heaven. Kenneth Patchen. ErPo

You stand over it. The Pitcher. Hsiung-hung, tr. *fr. Chinese by* Kenneth Rexroth *and* Ling Chung. WPC

You start it all. You are lovely. To Women. Richard Hugo. NIP

You stick out your tongue. The Tongue. Pia Tafdrup. TSaS, tr. *by* Monique M. Kennedy *and* Thomas E. Kennedy

You still sometimes sleep. Heron. Stanley Plumly. AmPA

You stood frozen there. To a Japanese Poet. Lucien Stryk. CAPP

You stop to watch the Mandarin ducks. Urban Love Songs. Wing Tek Lum. OpBo

You strange, astonished-looking, angle-faced. To a Fish. Leigh Hunt. *Fr. Fish, the Man, and the Spirit, The.* ChTr; EnRP; FM; GGP; HAP; NBLV; NOBL; NTP; OBEV; PeLV; PoEL-4; SCGP

You, stranger, who only sees us happy and free of care. Hunger. Samik, tr. *fr. Eskimo by* Edward Field. STP

You strike everything down in battle. Inanna and Ishkur. Enheduanna, tr. *fr. Sumerian by* BoWoP, ad. *by* W. W. Hallo *and* J. J. A. van Dijk

You strolled in the open, leisurely and alone. To the Poets in New York. James Wright. NAAL-2

You suit me well, for you can make me laugh. To a Prize Bird. Marianne Moore. ArNa

You sure you aint just feeling sorry for yourself? (*LL*) Margaret Are You Drug. George Starbuck. InPK; MAT

You surprise me, crow. Nigot, tr. *fr. Tlingit Indian by* James Koller. STP

You swear you'll come, you name the time and place. Epigram: To Lygdus. Martial, tr. *fr. Latin*. PeHV

You sweet soft murderess. *Unknown*, tr. *fr. German by* Frederick Goldin. GePo

You take my hand and. Margaret Atwood. HAP

You take off, he takes off, we take off. Clothes. Wislawa Szymborska, tr. *fr. Polish by* Grazyna Drabik *and* Sharon Olds. PoSu

You Take Off Your Jumper. Berta Freistadt. DT

You take the dollar. For One Moment. David Ignatow. NNaP

You talk about your harbor girls. Haul Away, My Rosy. *Unknown*. AmFP

You taught me fear, Momma. Laura Davis. *Fr. Things You Gave Me.* MDDM

You tell me not to long for you. Yosami, tr. *fr. Japanese by* Kenneth Rexroth *and* Ikuko Atsumi. WPJ

You Tell Me to Sit Quiet. A. C. Jordan. PBA

You tell me you're promised a lover. A Letter of Advice. Winthrop Mackworth Praed. NOBL; OxBoLi; PeLV

You Tell on Yourself. *Unknown*. PoToHe

You tell what you are by the friends you seek. You Tell on Yourself. *Unknown*. PoToHe

You tender virgins, fairer than the snow with which you play. Edward May, *after the Latin of* John Parkhurst. FaBoEE

You that a stranger in mid-Rome seek Rome. Rome. J. V. Cunningham, *after the Latin of* Janus Vitalis Panormitanus. OBVE

You that are jealous and have a wife. *Unknown*, tr. *fr. Irish by* Thomas Kinsella. NOIV

You that are sprung of northern stock. To a Calvinist in Bali. Edna St. Vincent Millay. NoAM

You that are weather-wise and pretend to know. Upon a Great Shower of Snow That Fell on May-Day, 1654. Thomas Washbourne. NOCV

You that crossed the ocean old. Ponce de Leon. Edith M. Thomas. PAH

You, that decipher out the fate. Mourning. Andrew Marvell. SeCP

You that do search for euerie purling spring. Sir Philip Sidney. *Fr. Astrophel and Stella.* AAS; ESo, *sl. abr.*; GGP; HeIL, *Sonnets, I–CVIII and 11 Songs*; NAEL-1; NoSic; OAEL-1; OxAEP-1; Poetr; SCGP, *Sonnets, I–CVIII and 11 Songs*; SiPS, *Sonnets, I–CVIII and 11 Songs*; SiPSBD, *Sonnets, I–CVIII and 11 Songs*; Son

You That Have Been Often Invited. *Unknown*. AH

You that have spent the silent night. Gascoigne's Good-Morrow. George Gascoigne. AAS; EnRePo; NOCV; NoSic

You that in love find[e] luck[e] and abundaunce [*or* habundance]. Sir Thomas Wyatt. AAS; SiPS; SiPSBD

You that Jehovah's servants are. Bible, *O.T., paraphrased by* Sir Thomas Wyatt. *Fr. Psalms.* NoSic, *par. by* the Countess of Pembroke

You that know the way. Lemuel's Blessing. W. S. Merwin. NYBP

You That Love England. C. Day Lewis. FaBoMo

You that seek what life is in death. Fulke Greville. *Fr. Caelica.* EnRePo

You that thus wear a modest countenance. Dante, tr. *fr. Italian by* Dante Gabriel Rossetti. *Fr. Vita Nuova, La.* AWP

You that unto your mistress' eyes. Love Deposed. Thomas Stanley. NOSC

You that uphold the world. Pagan Prayer. Alice Brown. WGRP

You that used to ripple so happily. By the Stream. Wilhelm Müller, tr. *fr. German by* Philip L. Miller. *Fr. Winter's Journey, The.* RiWo

You that with allegory's curious frame. Sir Philip Sidney. *Fr. Astrophel and Stella.* AAS; ESo, *sl. abr.*; GGP; HeIL, *Sonnets, I–CVIII and 11 Songs*; NoSic; OAEL-1; Poetr; SCGP, *Sonnets, I–CVIII and 11 Songs*; SiPS, *Sonnets, I–CVIII and 11 Songs*; SiPSBD, *Sonnets, I–CVIII and 11 Songs*

You, the choice minions of the proud-lipped Nine. To Poets. George Darley. Son

You, the crow of the right. Rebuttal of "A Family of Plants." Tien Ch'ien, tr. *fr. Chinese.* LHF, tr. *by* Hualing Nieh

You, the woman; I, the man; this, the world. The Character of Love Seen as a Search for the Lost. Kenneth Patchen. NaP; VGW

You, then, that would the comic laurels wear. Nicolas Boileau-Despéaux, tr. *by* Sir William Soames *and* John Dryden. *Fr. L'Art Poetique.* EPCY

You then vor me meade up your mind. Walken Hwomme at Night. William Barnes. NOBVV

You think Fuseli is not a Great Painter. I'm glad. To Hunt. Blake. OxBoLi

"You think I am dead." Talking in Their Sleep. Edith M. Thomas. BoNaP; OHIP

You think I am your servant but you are wrong. Table Talk. Derek Mahon. DiPo

You think I wrote from love. Song of Bread. Diana Der Hovanessian. WoWa

You think it horrible that lust and rage. The Spur. W. B. Yeats. OxAEP-2; WeW

You think that beard has made you wise. Ammianus, tr. *fr. Greek by* Robin Skelton. GrAn

You were the morning star among the living. Aster ("You were the morning star among the living.") Plato, *tr. fr. Greek* by Peter Jay. PeHV

You were to be the centre of our dream. Nozizwe. Mazisi Kunene, *tr. fr. Zulu by the author.* PeSAV

You Were Wearing. Kenneth Koch. AiP; CoAP; MoP; NIP; NNaP; NoP

You were with me and it wasn't flying, exactly. A Dream as Reported. Virginia Earle. GoYe

You were writing a long poem, yes. Residue of Song. Marvin Bell. AmPA

You were young — but that was scarcely to your credit. Gerald Gould. *Fr.* Monogamy. OxBTC

You were your own and not mine and I had not lost you. *(LL)* Epitaph for a Poet. Homero Aridjis. STV

You weren't even a. To L. Julianne Perry. PoBA

You who are earth, and cannot rise. To the World: the Perfection of Love. William Habington. *Fr.* Castara. BeJo; JCP

You who are so beautiful. The Sun Going Down upon Our Wrath. Denise Levertov, *tr. fr. Japanese.* AIW

You who are still and white. Slain. T. W. H. Crosland. OBWP

You who ask where I find the courage. A Return to the Tree of Time. Vesna Parun, *tr. fr. Croatian* by Vasa D. Mihailovich *and* Ronald Morgan. WPOW

You who can grant, or can refuse, the pow'r. A Sea-Chaplain's Petition to the Lieutenants in the Ward-Room, for the Use of the Quarter-Gallery. "J. T." NOEC

You who come from the old village. Wang Wei, *tr. fr. Chinese* by Robert Payne. TAL

You who descend river by river. Giraffe. *Unknown, tr. fr. Hottentot.* PeSA

  (Thou who descendest river by river.) PeSAV, *tr.* by W. H. I. Bleek

You who desired so much — in vain to ask. To Emily Dickinson. Hart Crane. CMoP; NIP; NoAM; NOBA; NoP; Son; TAP

You Who Dog My Footsteps. Leyb Kvitko, *tr. fr. Yiddish* by Joseph Leftwich. TrJP

You who draw into yourself each depth. The Merciful Shore. Maria Luisa Spaziani, *tr. fr. Italian* by Beverly Allen. NeIt

You who/ fail. Femina. Daphne Marlatt. NOBC

You who give sustenance to your creatures, O God. Prayer for Rain. Sheikh Aquib Abdullahi Jama, *tr. fr. Somali* by B. W. Andrzejewski. WTO

You who go out on schedule. Two Variations. Denise Levertov. NaP

You, who have been so many angels. *(LL)* The Photo That Watches. Carlota Caulfield. LoHo

You who have spoken words in the earth. Reproach to Dead Poets. Archibald MacLeish. NAAL-2

You, who in Cupid's rolls inscribe your name. Ovid, *tr.* by Dryden. *Fr.* Art of Love, The. FaBoUs

You, who inconstancy so constantly can squander. To the Moon. Paul Fleming, *tr. fr. German* by George C. Schoolfield. GePo

You who invoke survival, and condemn. To the Undeceived. Clive Wilmer. SCBI

You who like a boulder stand. The Wildebeest. June Daly. FaPON

You who maddened my heart with love, my Dion! *(LL)* Dion. Plato. GrAn

You who make your escape from the tumult. Hyena. *Unknown, tr. fr. Hottentot.* PeSA

  (Thou who makest thy escape from the tumult!) PeSAV, *tr.* by W. H. I. Bleek

You Who Never Arrived. Rainer Maria Rilke, *tr. fr. German* by Stephen Mitchell. ArLo

You who Occupy Our Land. Manuela Margarido, *tr. fr. Portuguese* by Allan Francovich. WPOW

You who snore with your sleeping wife so near. Tristan Corbière, *tr. fr. French* by Christopher Pilling. *Fr.* Litany of Sleep. OBVE

You who stoop, you who weep. Challenge. David Diop, *tr. fr. French* by Ellen Conroy Kennedy. NegPo

You who visit in turn. Poseidippus, *tr. fr. Greek* by Kenneth Rexroth. PGA

You who walked like a broken old dream. Negro Tramp. David Diop, *tr. fr. French* by Ellen Conroy Kennedy. NegPo

You who were darkness warmed my flesh. Woman to Child. Judith Wright. MDDM; PBWP; WPE

You who were once my friend. Alcaeus, *tr. fr. Greek* by Sam Hamill. InMo

You who will die, watch over your life; don't set sail. Epitaph for Cleonicus. Alexander of Pleuron, *tr. fr. Greek* by W. S. Merwin. GrAn

You who would sorrow even for a token. Reciprocity. Vassar Miller. IHMS; MT

You whom I could not save. Czeslaw Milosz, *tr. fr. Polish by the author.* AnRep

You whom the kings saluted; who refused not. To the Unknown Warrior. G. K. Chesteron. NSI

You will ask how I came to be eavesdropping, in the first place. Confession Overheard in a Subway. Kenneth Fearing. LiTA; LiTM

You Will Be Hearing from Us Shortly. U. A. Fanthorpe. AIW

You will be obscured by a cloud of postures. Nadar. Richard Howard. AnAn

You will carry this suture. Trauma. Brad Leithauser. InPK

You will come into an antique town. Where I Live. Wesley McNair. TRP

You will come, your eyes full of night and of yesterday. Toward Lesbos. Renée Vivien, *tr. fr. French* by Sandia Belgrade. PeHV

You will complain. Small Words. Fiona Hall. NWP

You Will Die. *Unknown, tr.* by H. A. Giles. *Fr.* Shi King. AWP

You Will Forget. Chenjerai Hove. HBAPE

You will get the dark all over you. *(LL)* June Fugue. Thomas W. Shapcott. NOBAu

You will have the road gate open, the front door ajar. In Memory of My Mother. Patrick Kavanagh. ArLo; BIrV

You will hear the drumming hooves. *(LL)* Earth and I Gave You Turquoise. N. Scott Momaday. CDW; HATNAP; UnPo

You Will Know When You Get There. Allen Curnow. PeNZ

You will need. Truganinny. Wendy Rose. HATNAP

You will never be alone, you hear so deep. Assurance. William Stafford. CAPP

You will never meet *another* grizzly bear. *(LL)* Grizzly Bear. Mary Austin. FaPON; GoJo; PDV

You will never want to be anything else. *(LL)* Fix. Michael Dransfield. NOBAu

You will not come. *(LL)* Supper. Alison Fell. VBLP

You will not cry. Gently, gently. Released. Richard Dehmel, *tr. fr. German* by Philip L. Miller. RiWo

You will notice that I do not deny. The Song of the Iron Paul. William Trowbridge. BTR

You will remember the kisses, real or imagined. Resurrection. Kenneth Fearing. CMoP; PoE

You will see Coleridge, he who sits obscure. Shelley. *Fr.* Letter to Maria Gisborne. EPCY

You Will See Your Lord a-Coming. *Unknown.* AH

You will wake, and remember, and understand. *(LL)* Evelyn Hope. Robert Browning. MeMBP; TrGrPo

You wished for a love-letter, Doctor. A Love-letter. Mary E. Tucker. CBWP-1

You with the cross and you without the cross. Niemand. Marie Syrkin. BTR

You with your back to the wall. *(LL)* Orion. Adrienne Rich. MoP; NAAL-2; NIP; NoAM; NoP; Poetr; WPE

You wonder about garbage. Refuse of Our Teeming Shores. Cordelia Candelaria. AfAz

You wonder at that Georgian terrace. Lychees. Medbh McGuckian. PBCIP

You wonder who this is, and why I name. On the Town's Honest Man. Ben Jonson. NOSC

You won't find them in places where society goes. Dandelions. Will D. Stanton. SoSe

You Words. Ingeborg Bachmann, *tr. fr. Hebrew* by Mark Anderson. PoSu

You words, come, after me! You Words. Ingeborg Bachmann, *tr. fr. Hebrew* by Mark Anderson. PoSu

You work in the factory all of your life. Too Old to Work. Joseph Glazer. SWP

You worry me whoever you are. Badman of the Guest Professor. Ishmael Reed. BPo

You Worthless. *Unknown.* FaBoVe

You would have scoffed if we had told you yesterday. To a Child in Death. Charlotte Mew. ChIV-2; MoAB; MoBrPo

You Would Have Understood Me. Paul Verlaine, *tr. fr. French* by Ernest Dowson. BoLoP; MoBrPo; NOBVV

You would have understood me, had you waited. Ernest Dowson. PeVV

You would hoist an old hat on the tines of a fork. A Bat on the Road. Seamus Heaney. PoE

You would know why. *(LL)* Refugee in America. Langston Hughes. GOA

You would lay roses! *(LL)* If You Had Known. Thomas Hardy. FaBoRV; GBL

You would like to go back. You. Anthony Barnett. VaA

You would live with me. *(LL)* If You But Knew. Heinrich Hart. RiWo

You would never shoot smack. Ghost Poem #1. Larry Neal. BCF

You would not have me roar, or crow. (*LL*) After Galen. Oliver St. John Gogarty. FaBoEE; OBMV; PoRA

You would not recognize me. The Tourist from Syracuse. Donald Justice. CAPP; NoAM; TwCP; VCAP

You would not say to children. The Folk Museum. Medbh McGuckian. CIP

You would shrink back/ jump up. July 4, 1984: For Buck. June Jordan. NoAM

You would sleep with the moon. Alternatives. Peter Cooley. AmPA

You would think I'd be a specialist in contemporary. The Put-Down Come On. A. R. Ammons. NoP

You would think the fury of aerial bombardment. The Fury of Aerial Bombardment. Richard Eberhart. ArOW; CMoP; FaBoMo; FF; FYAP; HeIP; HoPM; InPK; LiTA; LiTM; MoP; NIP; NoAM; NoP; OBWP; PoWW; PrIm; RB; TAP; TFi; TwCP; UnPo; VGW

You would think while the hours helped. A Private Person. William Stafford. PRA

You wouldn't believe all this house has cost me. The Flitting. Medbh McGuckian. PBCIP; PNI

You wouldn't do for Australia. (*LL*) Dick Briggs from Australia. Charles Robert Thatcher. NOBAu

You write of goats, I curl. Another Reading. Nicki Jackowska. DT

You write with ease, to shew your breeding. Clio's Protest. Sheridan. FaBoEE

You wrote a poem. Love Poem. Lindsay MacRae. DT

You wrote this from Beirut, two years before. Homage to Faiz Ahmed Faiz. Agha Shahid Ali. OpBo

You X-ari bush. Zebra. *Unknown, tr. fr. Hottentot.* PeSA

You, you are all unloving, loveless, you. The Sea. D. H. Lawrence. BoNaP

You, you caribou. Magic Words for Hunting Caribou. *Unknown, tr. fr. Eskimo by* Jerome K. Rothenberg *and* Johnny John. STP

You. You running across the field. Orpheus and Eurydice. Jean Valentine. FaBoWP; LCAP

You — You — You. (*LL*) Night and Day. Cole Porter. CBLP

You!/ Your head is like a hollow drum. You! *Unknown.* OBAP

You yourself are all the Nine. (*LL*) The Mutual Congratulations of the Poets Anna Seward and Hayley. Richard Porson. FaBoEE; OBSV

You 'Youth' has fallen from its shelf. Killed in Action. Joseph Leftwich. NSI

You'd almost think it was despair. (*LL*) The Combat. Edwin Muir. CMoP; LiTB; Mes; MoBrPo; NOBE

You'd have men's hearts up from the dust. Near Perigord. Ezra Pound. FaBoMo; LiTA; LiTM

You'd know the folly of being comforted. (*LL*) The Folly of Being Comforted. W. B. Yeats. GBL; HeIL; HeIP; NAEL-2

You'd laugh/ If only you knew. To the Woman in the Office. "Kim." DT

You'd like to kiss your little boy but he doesn't want to. Lady on Streetcar. Sandro Penna, *tr. fr. Italian by* John Frederick Nims. STV

You'd scarce expect one of my age. Tall Oaks from Little Acorns Grow. David Everett.
(Boy Reciter, The.) BLPA

You'd start at seven, and then you'd bend your back. Washing the Coins. Douglas Dunn. FaBoPV

You'd think that at 3:00 A.M. L'Elisir d'Amore. Dallas E. Wiebe. MAT

You'l marvel when I tell ye o. Loudon Hill; or, Drumclog. *Unknown.* ESPB

You'll [*or* You'le] ask, perhaps, wherefore I stay. An Excuse of Absence. Thomas Carew. CaPo; SeCP

You'll be my little seven stone missionary! T. S. Eliot. *Fr.* Sweeney Agonistes. UnPo

You'll come a-waltzing Matilda with me! (*LL*) Waltzing Matilda. Andrew Barton Paterson. CBAP; ChTr; GBP

You'll come to our ball; — since we parted. Our Ball. Winthrop Mackworth Praed. *Fr.* Letters from Teignmouth. EnRP

You'll ever give/ Or get. (*LL*) For a Far-out Friend. Gary Snyder. NeAP; PoM

You'll find him if you go to Trenton Falls. (*LL*) Fitz Adam's Story. James Russell Lowell. AmPP

You'll find that I'm the sort. Abner Silver's "Pu-leeze! Mr. Hemingway!" Ring Lardner. OBAL

You'll go on, talking away. Hilda Doolittle ("H. D."). *Fr.* Sigil. AnAn

You'll go to the plaza. Camoes and the Debt. Sophia de Mello Breyner Andresen, *tr. fr. Portuguese by* Willis Barnstone *and* Nelson Cerqueira. BoWoP

You'll have time to grow wise in their company. (*LL*) Dead, they'll burn you up with electricity. Argentarius. PGA

You'll hear me call your name. (*LL*) Should You Go First. Albert K. Rowswell. BLPL; PoLF; PoToHe

You'll know you slept too long. (*LL*) Newsreel. C. Day Lewis. MoAB; MoBrPo

You'll make tea. Just the Two of Us. Tomioka Taeko, *tr. fr. Japanese.* WPOW, *tr. by* Harry *and* Lynn Guest *and* Kajima Shozo

You'll Never Know. Ruby Marion Wray. PWR

You'll never know how far i stand from you. (*LL*) Measure for Measure. Sipho Sepamla. PeSAV

You'll never know *how* good you are. Auto-erotic. *Unknown.* PeLi

You'll say the gentleman is somewhat simple. Thomas Middleton. *Fr.* Women Beware Women. OxBM

You'll see sometime — half. Memorandum. William Stafford. NYBP

You'll show a hat that's white, or a feather! (*LL*) John Burns of Gettysburg. Bret Harte. AnAmPo; OHIP; PAH

You'll wait a long, long time for anything much. On Looking Up by Chance at the Constellations. Robert Frost. CMoP; MeMAP

Young, The. Sebastian Barry. IB

Young Acacia, The. Hayyim Nahman Bialik, *tr. fr. Hebrew by* Helena Frank. TrJP

Young Africans. Gwendolyn Brooks. NoAM

Young Allan. *Unknown.* ESPB

Young Allan. *Unknown.* ESPB

Young American, The. Alexander Hill Everett. VPP

Young Americans. Andrew Greig. PWE

Young and Old. Charles Kingsley. *Fr.* Water Babies, The. BLPL; EBEV; FaBoBe; FaPoR; ImPo; OxAEP-2; OxBChV; PlP; PoLF

Young and old, rejoice. Neidhart von Reuental, *tr. fr. German by* Frederick Goldin. GePo

Young and Radiant, He Is Standing. Allen Eastman Cross. AH

Young [*or* Younge] Andrew. *Unknown.* ESPB; OxBB

Young are quick of speech, The. On Teaching the Young. Yvor Winters. NoAM; NOBA

Young Barnswell. *Unknown.* OBET

Young Bearwell. *Unknown.* ESPB

Young Beichan, (*diff. versions*). *Unknown.* EnSB; ESPB, A *and* C *vers.*; FaBoBa

Young Beichan. *Unknown.* ESPB; FaBoBa

Young Ben he was a nice young man. Faithless Sally Brown. Thomas Hood. NOBL; OBNV
(Sally Brown.) FaBoCo

Young Benjie. *Unknown.* ESPB

Young Benjie. *Unknown.* ESPB; OxBB

Young Birch, A. Robert Frost. BoNaP; LiTA; SAmP

Young Blondes. Gavin Ewart. ErPo

Young bloods come round less often now, The. Horace. *See* Ribald Romeos less and less berattle.

Young bride and groom of Australia, A. *Unknown.* PeLi

Young bull, The. A Young Chieftain. Auvaiyar, *tr. fr. Tamil by* A. K. Ramanujan. PLW

Young Charlottie, or The Frozen Girl. *Unknown.* AmFP; BeLS; BLPA

Young cherry trees, The. April. Linda Pastan. Poetsp

Young Chevalier!, The. (*LL*) Charlie He's My Darling. Burns. CH

Young Chieftain, A. Auvaiyar, *tr. fr. Tamil by* A. K. Ramanujan. PLW

Young child of Diodoros's house, A. Diodoros, *tr. fr. Greek by* W. G. Shepherd. GrAn

Young Colin Clout, a lad of peerless meed. Tuesday; or, the Ditty. John Gay. *Fr.* Shepherd's Week, The. NOEC

Young composer, working that summer at an artist's colony, The. A Story about the Body. Robert Hass. NAmP90; RaBo

Young Cordwainer, The. Robert Graves. MoBS

Young Corydon [*or* Coridon] and Phyllis [*or* Phillis]. On the Happy Corydon and Phyllis. *At.* to Sir Charles Sedley. BoLoP; CoMu; ErPo; FaBoBl

Young Corydon, th'unhappy shepherd swain. The Second Pastoral; or, Alexis. Virgil, *tr. fr. Latin by* Dryden. PeHV

Young couple who lived at "The Laurels," A. W. F. N. Watson. PeLi

Young David: Birmingham, A. Helen Morgan Brooks. PoNe

Young Dead Soldiers, The. Archibald MacLeish. ArOW

Young Democracy., *sels.* Bernard O'Dowd.

Young Dove, The. Moses ibn Ezra, *tr. fr. Hebrew by* Solomon Solis-Cohen. TrJP

Young Drunkards reeling, Bayliffs dogging. A London Street-Scene. Edward Ward. *Fr.* Hudibras Redidivus. CBCK

Young Earl of Essex's Victory over the Emperor of Germany, The. *Unknown.* ESPB; OBET

Young Edward came to Emily his gold all for to show. Edwin in the Lowlands Low. *Unknown.* AmFP

Young Edwin in the Lowlands Low. *Unknown.* OBET

Young Endymion sleeps Endymion's sleep, The. Keats. Longfellow. Son; TAP

Young engine-driver called Hunt, A. Victor Gray. NOBL

Young England's Lament. *Unknown.* FaBoEH

Young eyes leave the volume and stray out, The. History Lesson. Mark Van Doren. NYBP

Young fairy with habits perverse, A. *Unknown.* PeHV

Young Farmer of Leeds, A. *Unknown.* SiSoPo

Young Fellow of King's, The. *Unknown. See* There was a young Fellow of King's.

Young Fellow of Wadham, The. *Unknown. See* There was a young Fellow of Wadham.

Young Fenians, The. Padraic Fallon. BIrV

Young fir is growing, where?, A. Think of It, O Soul. Eduard Friedrich Mörike, *tr. fr. German by* Philip L. Miller. RiWo

Young fir-tree grows, A. Soul, Remember This! Eduard Friedrich Mörike. OBD

Young Fir-Wood, A. Dante Gabriel Rossetti. GN

Young flirt of Ceylon, A. Ogden Nash. PeLi

Young flowers were whispering in melody. Poe. *Fr.* Al Aaraff. NOBA

Young flute player, The. Flute Player. *Gond Oral Tradition, tr. by* V. Elwin *and* S. Hivale. WTO

Young Frederick the Great was a beaut. *Unknown.* PeHV

Young Gal's Blues. Langston Hughes. NAAL-2

Young Girl. Ricarda Huch, *tr. fr. German by* Janine Canan *and* Deirdre Lashgari. WPOW

Young Girl and the Beach, The. Sophia de Mello Breyner Andresen, *tr. fr. Portuguese by* Alexis Levitin. WPOW

Young girl dancing lifts her face, The. The Dancer. W. J. Turner. NOBAu; OBMV

Young girl in remote Samarkand, A. George Seferis, *tr. fr. Greek by* Peter Levi. CBNP

Young girl moves like an ear of grain, A. The Young Girl and the Beach. Sophia de Mello Breyner Andresen, *tr. fr. Portuguese by* Alexis Levitin. WPOW

Young girl of English nativity, A. *Unknown.* PeLi

Young girl stood beside me, The. The Orange Tree. John Shaw Neilson. CBAP; FaBoMA

Young girl who was no good at tennis, A. *Unknown.* PeLi

Young Girl with a Pitcher Full of Water, A. David Wagoner. NoAM

Young Girls. Raymond Souster. HeIP

Young Glass-Stainer, The. Thomas Hardy. CTC

Young Gray Head, The. Caroline Southey. BeLS

Young Harvard man, sweet and tender, A. *Unknown.* PeHV

Young, having risen early, had gone, The. The Guardians. Geoffrey Hill. NoP

Young Hermes, who placed you at the starter's mark? Philip of Thessalonica, *tr. fr. Greek by* Edwin Morgan. GrAn

Young Heroes. Gwendolyn Brooks. BPo

Young Hodge met Mog the miller's maid. Don't Be Foolish Pray. *Unknown.* CoMu

Young homosexuals and hot girls, The. Lone Gentleman. Pablo Neruda, *tr. fr. Spanish by* Clayton Eshleman. ErPo

Young hound howls, A. Unemployment. William Mills. HoPM

Young Housewife, The. William Carlos Williams. HeIP; NAAL-2; NoP; TAP

Young Hunting. *Unknown.* ESPB; OxBB; OxBoLi; FaBoBa

Young Hyllus, why refuse today. A Epigram: Riddle. Martial, *tr. fr. Latin by* Brian Hill. PeHV

Young I am, and yet unskill'd. Song for a Girl. Dryden. ELP; ErPo

Young in Fall I said: the birds. Lorine Niedecker. VGW

Young Irish servant in Drogheda, A. *Unknown.* PeLi

Young Japanese son was in love with a servant boy, The. Dream Data. Robert Duncan. NeAP

Young Jemmy is a lad. England's Darling; or, Great Britain's Joy and Hope on That Noble Prince James, Duke of Monmouth. *Unknown.* CoMu

Young Jockey he courted sweet Mog the Brunette. Mog the Brunette. *Unknown.* CoMu

Young Johnny sails the sea, young Johnny sails the shore. The Green Bed. *Unknown.* AmFP

Young Johnny the miller he courted of late. The Gray Mare. *Unknown.* AmFP

Young Johnstone, (A *vers.*). *Unknown.* ESPB

Young Johnstone ("Young Johnstone and the young Colnel."), (B *vers.*). *Unknown.* ESPB; OxBB

Young Joseph's new coat was real nice. Cyril Mountjoy. PeLi

Young Juan wandered by the glassy brooks. Byron. *Fr.* Don Juan. EPCY

Young knight, what ever that dost armes professe. Spenser. *Fr.* Faerie Queene, The. FHYEP

Young Knowledge. "Robin Hyde." PeNZ

Young Lady From Glitch, A. Tamara Kitt. SiSoPo

Young lady may increase her stock, A. Cillactor, *tr. fr. Greek by* William Moebius. GrAn

Young Lady Named Bright, A. *At. to* Arthur Buller. *See* There was a young lady named [*or* called] Bright.

Young Lady of Exeter, The. *Unknown.* FaBoBl

Young Lady of Lynn, A. *Unknown.* ChTr

Young Lady of Norway, A. Edward Lear. *See* There was a Young Lady of Norway,/ Who casually sat in a doorway.

Young lady, whose life-style the malicious, A. Gavin Ewart. PeLi

Young Lambs. John Clare. TrGrPo

Young Lambs To Sell. *Unknown. See* If I'd as much money/ As I could tell.

Young Lass's Soliloquy, A. Rebekah Carmichael. ECWP

Young Laundryman, The. William Carlos Williams. SAmP

Young Lincoln. Edwin Markham. OHIP

Young Lochinvar. Sir Walter Scott. *See* Oh [*or* O], young Lochinvar is come out of the west.

Young Lochinvar, parody. *Unknown.* FiBHP

Young lords o' the north country, The. Lady Maisry ("The young lords o' the north country.") *Unknown.* ESPB; OxBB

Young Love. Andrew Marvell. OxAEP-1

Young Love lies sleeping. Dream-Love. Christina Rossetti. CH; HAP; PoEL-5

Young man, alone, on the high bridge over the Tagus, A. The High Bridge above the Tagus River at Toledo. William Carlos Williams. CTC

Young man and an aged man of late, A. On a Young Man and an Old Man. Edward May. OxBSP

Young man and maid, pray lend attention. The Silver Dagger. *Unknown.* AmFP

Young Man and the Young Nun, The. Albert D. Mackie. OxBS

Young man by a girl was desired, A. *Unknown.* PeLi

Young man is a pitiful wretch, A. A Song of Parable. *Unknown, tr. fr. Chinese by* Jan W. Walls. SuSp

Young man lately in our Town, A. The Maids Conjuring Book. *Unknown.* CoMu

Young man made for the corner, A. Churning (or Lovemaking): "Young man made for the corner, A." Unknown, formerly at. to Cynewulf, *tr. fr. Anglo-Saxon. Fr.* Riddles (Exeter Book). PeLV, *tr. by* Kevin Crossley-Holland

(Churning or lovemaking: Young man made for the corner, A.) ASW, PcLV *tr. by* Kevin Crossley-Holland

Young man of alien beauty. Muireadach Albanach O'Dalaigh. NOIV

Young Man Thinks of Sons, The. R. A. K. Mason. PeNZ

Young man who lived at Holme Hale, A. Ida Thurtle. PeLi

Young Man Who Loved the Girl Who Took Care of Her Aged Father, The. Greg Kuzma. AmPA

Young Man with a Yellow Hat. Li Ho, *tr. fr. Chinese by* Michael Fish. SuSp

Young man with passions quite gingery, A. *Unknown.* PeLi

Young Man's Epigram on Existence, A. Thomas Hardy. MoP

Young Man's Song, A. William Bell. FaBoTw

Young Martins, The. Andrew Young. FM

Young Mary, loitering once her garden way. Mary and Gabriel. Rupert Brooke. ChIV-2

Young Master's Account of a Puppet Show. John Marchant. OxBChV

Young May Moon, The. Thomas Moore. ELP; EnRP; OBEV; PeLV

Young Men Come Less Often, The — Isn't It So? Horace, *tr. fr. Latin by* Robert Fitzgerald. ErPo

Young men dancing, and the old. Youthful Age. Thomas Stanley, after the Greek of Anacreon. AWP

Young men give ear to me a while. The Maid's Complaint for Want of a Dil Doul. *Unknown.* CoMu

Young men of the world, The. F. S. Flint. PeFWW

Young men who frequent picture palaces. *Unknown.* PeLV

Young men would turn drakes and soon follow after. (*LL*) Hares on the Mountain. *Unknown.* ErPo; OBET

Young Mrs. Snooks was sick of sex. Nursery Rhyme. Kenneth Burke. OBAL

Young Molly Ban. *Unknown.* FaBoBa

Young moon, take my face up yonder. Re-birth. *Unknown, tr. fr. Bushman by* W. H. I. Bleek *and* Jack Cope. PeSA

Young niggers/ die old. Dedication to the Final Confrontation. Lloyd M. Corbin, Jr. PoBA

Young Night Thought. Robert Louis Stevenson. OTCP; PWR

Young Noble at Night's End; a Song. Li Ho, *tr. fr. Chinese by* Maureen Robertson. SuSp

Young Oedipus learned from the Sphinx. Basil Ransome-Davies. PeLi

Young Ones, The. Elizabeth Jennings. OxBTC

Young or Old We Die. Rudaki, *tr. fr. Persian by* Omar S. Pound. ArPe

Young Palmus was a ferryman. Shackley-Hay. *Unknown.* GBP

Young Peggy. *Unknown.* ESPB

Young people all, attention give. Liverpool. *Unknown.* AmFP

Young people, all attention give. Mission. *Unknown.* AmFP

Young People Who Delight in Sin. *Unknown.* AmFP

Young Pilgrim Finds Refuge with the Goatherds, The. Luis de Góngora y Argote, *tr. fr. Spanish by* Edward Meryon Wilson. *Fr.* First Solitude, The. OBVE

Young Poet. Myron O'Higgins. PoBA; PoNe

Young poet Evmenis, The. The First Step. C. P. Cavafy, *tr. fr. Greek by* Edmund Keeley *and* Philip Sherrard. Mes

Young Reynard. George Meredith. HoPM

Young Robin of the plain, erst blithest blade. Snaith Marsh; a Yorkshire Pastoral. 'Ophelia'. ECWP

Young Roger and Dolly. Henry Carey. *See* Young Roger came tapping at Dolly's window.

Young Roger came tapping at Dolly's window. Roger and Dolly. Henry Carey. CBNP; CoMu; NOEC; OxNR, *sl. diff. vers.*

(Young Roger and Dolly.) ReMoGo

Young Ronald. *Unknown.* ESPB

Young Sailor Cut Down in His Prime, The. *Unknown.* OxBSS

Young sapling branches trailed on the ground, The. (*LL*) Late Summer. Theocritus [*or* Theokritus]. EaPr

Young schizophrenic named Struther, A. *Unknown.* PeLi

Young Shepherd Bathing His Feet. Peter Clarke. PBA

Young Snail. Meena Alexander. VBLP

Young Soul. Amiri Baraka. BPo

Young Stock. V. Sackville-West. OxBTC

Young swallows trill their new tune. *Unknown, tr. by* Michael E. Workman. *Fr.* Tzu-yeh Songs of the Four Seasons. SuSp

Young Sycamore. William Carlos Williams. TAP

Young then,/ we were bored already. Eleanor Wilner. ChIV-1

Young things who frequent picture-palaces, The. Limerick. *At. to* Philip Heseltine. NOBL; PeLi

Young Tomcats' Society for Poetic Music. Heine, *tr. fr. German by* Alma Strettell. SoCa

Young Training. Lawrence McGaugh. PoBA

Young Traveller Is Presented to the Goddess Dulness, A. Pope. *Fr.* Dunciad, The. NOEC

Young Una, you were a rose in a garden. Tomas Costello, *tr. fr. Gaelic by* Frank O'Connor. *Fr.* Lament for Una, A. WTO

Young unmarried man, with a good name, A. Byron. *Fr.* Don Juan. NOBL, XII

Young viper grows as it sits, The. *Unknown, tr. by* T. Cope. *Fr.* Shaka, King of the Zulus. PBA; TTY; WTO

Young Warrior, A. Ponmutiyar, *tr. fr. Tamil by* A. K. Ramanujan. PLW

Young Washington. Arthur Guiterman. FaPON; OHIP

Young Waters. *Unknown.* ESPB; OxBB

Young Waters he did dee. (*LL*) Young Waters. *Unknown.* ESPB; OxBB

Young wine ranchers with chew drippings, The. Rhetoric Leads to Cliché. Adrian C. Louis. NAmP90

Young Wife, The. Derek Walcott. DiPo

Young Wife, A. D. H. Lawrence. ELP; MoBrPo

Young Wife's Lament. Brigit Pegeen Kelly. NAmP90

Young will not wear it, The. Kutavayir Kirattanar, *tr. fr. Tamil by* A. K. Ramanujan. PLW

Young Willie stands in his stable door. Clyde's Waters. *Unknown.* OxBB

Young Woman. Howard Nemerov. ErPo

Young Woman at a Window. Mark Van Doren. LiTA

Young Woman from Aenos, The. *Unknown.* OBAL

Young Woman of Beare, The. Austin Clarke. MoP; NoAM

Young Woman's Neo-Aramaic Jewish Persian Blues. Jerome Rothenberg, *after Persian folk poem.* BoWoP

Young women are obsessed with beauty, The. The Clothes Pit. Douglas Dunn. OxBTC

Young women have no orifice that grips. Heterosexual Poem. Strato, *tr. fr. Greek by* Teddy Hogge. GrAn

Young women, they [*or* they'll] run like hares on the mountain. Hares on the Mountain. *Unknown.* ErPo; PeLV

Young Wordsworth's London, The. Wordsworth. *Fr.* Prelude [*or*, Growth of a Poet's Mind], The. EnRP; FaBoPP; HAP, *short sel.*; OAEL-2; PoEL-4, *sl. shorter*

Young Workman, The. Mary Dillingham Frear. TrCP

Younger,/ I felt the dead. Roots. Seamus Deane. PNI

Younger Poet, A. Peter Schjeldahl. PoA

Younger Van Eyck, The. E. C. Bentley. FiBHP

Youngest Daughter, The. Cathy Song. NoAM

Your absence has gone through me. Separation. W. S. Merwin. HAP; NoP

Your abstracted face. (*LL*) To My Father Norman Alone in the Blue Mountains. Jack Lindsay. NOBAu

Your ankle wrapped in iron, yourself encased. Convict. Edward Vincent Swart. PeSAV

Your archival voice. The Music. Everett Hoagland. Jaz

Your are/ Getting free. Thoughts for You (When She Came Back from the Mountains). Ranice Henderson Crosby. NMM

Your arms & legs are shrunken. Recovery. Ron Schreiber. PFL

Your arms are beautiful again. What Her Girl Friend Said ("Your arms are beautiful again.") Peyanar, *tr. fr. Tamil by* A. K. Ramanujan. *Fr.* Nine on Happy Reunion. PLW

Your arms will clasp the gathered grain. The Island. Edwin Muir. OAEL-2

Your ashes will not stir, even on this high ground. In Carrowdore Churchyard. Derek Mahon. CIP; PBCIP; PeIV; PNI

Your attention, ladies and gentlemen, your attention for one moment. The Pilgrim. Nicanor Parra, *tr. fr. Spanish by* W. S. Merwin. AnRep

Your Attention Please. Peter Porter. OBWP; OxBTC; PAW

Your authority returns to you. (*LL*) Within and around the earth, within and around the hills. Alfonso Ortiz. EaPr

Your average tourist: Fifty. 2.3. Casual Wear. James Merrill. NIP

Your baggy lyrics. To a Political Poet. Heine, *tr. fr. German by* Tom Paulin. FaBoPV

Your bards are wearing lotuses. Nettimaiyar, *tr. fr. Tamil by* A. K. Ramanujan. PLW

Your Beauty and My Reason. *Unknown. See* Like two proud armies marching in the field.

Your beauty, ripe, and calm. The Philosopher and the Lover: To a Mistress Dying. Sir William Davenant. OBD

Your beauty, ripe and calm, and fresh. Lover and Philosopher. Sir William Davenant. NOBE; OBEV; Prf

Your bed's got two wrong sides. Your life's all grouse. Long Distance. Tony Harrison. NAEL-2

Your best friend. Kate. Kevin Jeffrey Clarke. PFL

Your best friend is gone. Tomorrow. Mark Strand. GOYP

Your Birthday Comes to Tell Me This. E. E. Cummings. ArLo; NAs

Your Birthday in Wisconsin You Are 140. John Berryman. NAs

Your blessed image. Memory. Joseph Freiherr von Eichendorff, *tr. fr. German by* Philip L. Miller. RiWo

Your blond hair and autumn sweater. Janna. King D. Kuka. VoR

Your blood does not flow, not even a little. A Poem for Diane Wakoski. Ray A. Young Bear. CDW

Your body and you/ in mine. (*LL*) Together. Maxine W. Kumin. BoWoP; NMM

Your body derns. Scunner. "Hugh MacDiarmid." FaBoTw

Your body gleams like copper on the veld. The Fallen Zulu Commander. C. M. Van den Heever, *tr. fr. Afrikaans by* Uys Krige *and* Jack Cope. PeSA

Your body has moved to unstaunchable distance. N. Hugh Seidman. PoA

Your body is a dark wine. Hunger. Kathleen Tankersley Young. ShDr

Your Body Is Stars. Stephen Spender. CBLP; FaBoTw

Your body might have come from the loins of a prince. Moon of the Earth. *Gond Oral Tradition, tr. by* V. Elwin *and* S. Hivale. WTO

Your body to hold, your perfect breasts. Undine. Irving Layton. ErPo

Your bosom's sweet treasures thus ever disclose! To Miss Kitty Phillips. Edward Lovibond. ECEV

Your bottoms are not purple. Horror Comic. Robert Conquest. OxBTC

Your breasts of shining black satin. The Soul of the Black Land. Guy Tirolien, *tr. fr. French by* Ellen Conroy Kennedy. NegPo

Your brother is dead. Dreaming with a Friend. Stephen Berg. NaP

Your bum is a gorgeous basket brimming with fruits and meat. (*LL*) The Peasant Declares His Love. Emile Roumer. ErPo; NegPo; TTY

Your Catullus is depressed, Cornificus. Catullus, *tr. fr. Latin.* PeHV

Your Chase Had a Beast in View. John Peale Bishop. LiTA

Your cheeks flat on the sand. Venus Khoury-Gata, *tr. fr. French by* Willis Barnstone. BoWoP

Your children are not your children. On Children. Kahlil Gibran. *Fr.* Prophet, The. OxBM; PoToHe

Your Church and Mine. Phillips H. Lord. BLPA

Your clear eye is the one absolutely beautiful thing. Child. Sylvia Plath. HCAP; MDDM; PBWP

Your closed eyes bulge like mushrooms. Letter to Kafka. Maura Stanton. AmPA

Your clothes a dark pink heap, a dimming sky. L'Art. Frederick Feirstein. SM

Your clothes of snow and satin and pure blood. The Bed. Karl Shapiro. NYBP

Your comedy I've read, my friend. To a Living Author. *Unknown.* NBLV

Your correspondent must be kidding when he says. Americana IX. *Unknown.* InPS

YOUR coulter cuts the soil that erst was sown. A Poor Ploughman to a Gentleman for Whom He Had Taken a Little Pains. George Turberville. NoSic

Your courtiers scorn we country clowns. A Ballad of the Courtier and the Country Clown. *Unknown.* CoMu

Your dandelions dotting half. Grass Widows. Robert B. Shaw. CRP

Your death has come to me over hundreds of miles away. This Poem Is Dedicated to Brother Andries Raditsela. Nise Malange. PeSAV

Your doctor, Lord. For Dr. and Mrs. Dresser. Margaret Avison. MoCV

Your dog, tranquil and innocent, dozes through. Adrienne Rich. *Fr.* Twenty-one Love Poems. GLP

Your Donkey is better behaved, I trust. (*LL*) The Donkey. Theodore Roethke. GrPl; OBCA

Your door is shut against my tightened face. The White House. Claude McKay. AmPP; NIP; PoBA (White Houses.) PoNe

Your downcast, harlequin, defenceless face. Lynched Negro. Maxwell Bodenheim. PoNe

Your dressing, dancing, gadding, where's the good in? On Ladies' Accomplishments. *Unknown.* FaBoUs

Your dusky shadow at the window lingers. Morning and Evening. Antoni Slonimski, *tr. fr. Polish by* Watson Kirkconnell. TrJP

Your dying was a difficult enterprise. Thom Gunn. GLP

Your ears receive a platter of sound. Walking with Your Eyes Shut. William Stafford. GOYP

Your enemy is not the kind who wears. Poet's Counsel, A ("Your enemy is not the kind who wears.") Kovur Kilar, *tr. fr. Tamil by* A. K. Ramanujan. PLW

Your eyen two will slay me suddenly. Merciless Beauty. Chaucer. *Fr.* Merciles[s] Beaute [*or* Beautée *or* Beauty]. BoLoP; CTC; EBEV; EnLoPo; EnVB, *mod. vers.*; HAP; NAEL-1; NoP; SCGP, *mod. vers.* (Rondel of Merciless Beauty, A, (*mod. vers.* by Louis Untermeyer).) TrGrPo

Your eyes are just. Four-Word Lines. May Swenson. GLP; WPE

Your Eyes Are Mirth. Tom Weatherly. NBV

Your eyes are open. Carious Exposure. Gladys Cardiff. CDW

Your Eyes Have Their Silence. Gerald William Barrax. PoBA

Your eyes, large as Canada, welcome. Nativity: For Two Salvadoran Women, 1986–87. Demetria Martinez. AfAz

Your eyes were ever brown, the colour. On Not Being Your Lover. Medbh McGuckian. PBCIP; PNI

Your eyes, your flowing hair. Auburn. Paul Verlaine, *tr. fr. French by* Lawrence M. Bensky. ErPo

Your face broods from my table, Suicide. John Berryman. *Fr.* Dream Songs. TAP

Your face did not rot. The Lost Pilot. James Tate. ArOW; CoAP; GoJo; NoAM; NoP; OBWP; TwCP; UnPo

Your face fills the sky. Portrait of a Man. Alan Bernheimer. UL

Your face is the face of all the others. The Face of Love. Ingrid Jonker, *tr. fr. Afrikaans by* Jack Cope. PeSA

Your face reveals a down so light. Epigram: To Dindymus. Martial, *tr. fr. Latin by* Brian Hill. PeHV

Your face scrapes my sleep tonight. Letter to Be Disguised as a Gas Bill. Marge Piercy. WPE

Your face, the beauty of a time long past evokes the perfumed robes in faded hues. Léopold Sédar Senghor, *tr. fr. French by* Ellen Conroy Kennedy. *Fr.* Songs for Signare. NegPo

Your face,/so pale now it is blue. David St. John. AmPA

Your faith is in what you hold. Chicago. Lola Ridge. PoA

Your Father Knoweth. *Unknown. See* Precious thought, my Father knoweth.

Your father sits inside. What Hell Is. Heather McHugh. CrSp; PFL

"Your father's gone," my bald headmaster said. The Lesson. Edward Lucie-Smith. IMW; OxBTC; TwCP

Your Father's House. Vincent Buckley. FaBoMA

Your fingers touch me like a bird's wing. The Bird of Endless Time. James Laughlin. WeW

Your fires burnt my forests. The Womb. Apirana Taylor. PeNZ

Your Flag and My Flag. Wilbur D. Nesbit. WBLP

Your flatteries are boring. Bassos, *tr. fr. Greek by* Kenneth Rexroth. PGA

Your foe in war to overrate. Porson on His Majesty's Government. Richard Porson. FaBoCo

Your friend and servant. (*LL*) Epistle to John Lapraik. Burns. EnRP

Your friends come fondly to your living room. Birthday Card for a Psychiatrist. Mona Van Duyn. IHMS

Your friends shall be the tall wind. For a Child. Fannie Stearns Davis. FaPON

Your ghost will walk, you lover of trees. Robert Browning. *Fr.* De Gustibus. FHYEP; InPS; PlP; SCGP

Your grace, and falter on the stony path! (*LL*) Last Days of Alice. Allen Tate. NAAL-2; NOBA; OxBA; UnPo

Your grandfather lived in those. The Trees. Vuyelwa Carlin. NWP

Your hair hovers over the sea with the golden juniper. Your Hair over the Sea. Paul Celan, *tr. fr. German by* Joachim Neugroschel. AnAn

Your Hair over the Sea. Paul Celan, *tr. fr. German by* Joachim Neugroschel. AnAn

Your hand caressing them smooth! (*LL*) Lying here alone. Lady Izumi Shikibu. WeW

Your Hand Full of Hours. Paul Celan, *tr. fr. German by* Michael Hamburger. AnRep; OBVE

Your handkerchief should be blue. Love Song ("Your handkerchief should be blue.") *Unknown, tr. fr. Turkish by* Reza Baraheni and Zahra-Soltan Shokoohtaezeh. BoWoP

Your Hands. Angelina Weld Grimké. CDC; PoBA

Your hands lie open in the long fresh grass. Silent Noon. Dante Gabriel Rossetti. *Fr.* House of Life, The. EnVR; HAP; NAEL-2; NoP; OBNC; PFP; PoEL-5; TrGrPo; UnAS

Your hands made a tent o'er mine eyes. Whimper of Awakening Passion. Ebenezer Jones. NOBVV

Your hands, my dear, adorable. The Chilterns. Rupert Brooke. MoBrPo

Your hands, strewn on the sheets, were my dead leaves. To a Sleeping Friend. Jean Cocteau, *tr. fr. French.* PeHV

Your hands, tiny in all that air, applauding. (*LL*) Broadcast. Philip Larkin. CBLP

Your hat lifts up lightly, says hello, sways in the wind. Tell Me, Love. Ingeborg Bachmann, *tr. fr. German by* Mark Anderson. VBLP

Your hay it is mowed, and your corn is reaped. Harvest Home. Dryden. *Fr.* King Arthur. PrIm (Song: "Your hay it is mow'd, and your corn is reap'd.") SeCV-2

Your health, Master Willow. Contrive me a bat. Tree Party. Louis MacNeice. OxBTC

Your heart trembles in the shadows, like a face. When the Tom-Tom Beats. Jacques Roumain, *tr. fr. French by* Langston Hughes. NegPo

Your heels sound on the steps. The Return. Nika Turbina, *tr. fr. Russian by* Elaine Feinstein and Antonina Bouis. VBLP

Your hour approaching, so (*LL*) Latona cry, Labour. M. Saint-Marthe, *tr. fr. French. Fr.* Paedotrophiae; or, The Art of Bringing Up Children. FaBoUs

Your house is on fire and your children will burn. (*LL*) Ladybug, ladybug, fly away home. *Unknown.* RoPo

Your houseplant is a delicate thing. Why So Many of Them Die. Susan Wallbank. BrRo

Your hulk is like some. Cow. Janet Reed McFatter. GrPl

Your husband will be with us at the treat. To His Mistress. Ovid, *tr. by* Dryden. *Fr.* Amores. BoLoP; ErPo

Your husband, your daughters, your son. (*LL*) The Dream. Irving Feldman. VCAP

Your husband's lying here in the next bed. They Lay Dying Side by Side. Anna Swirszczynska, *tr. fr. Polish by* Magnus J. Krynski and Robert A. Maguire. PoSu

Your kind of night, David, your kind of night. Night Thoughts. Henri Coulette. FYAP

Your kindness is no kindness now. Kindness. Catherine Davis. NYBP

Your kink, Heraclea, is sucking off. Argentarius, *tr. fr. Greek by* Fleur Adcock. GrAn

Your Lad, and My Lad. Randall Parrish. PAH

Your lashes are — longer than anyone's. (*LL*) Where Does This Tenderness Come From? Marina Tsvetayeva. ArLo; VBLP

Your Last Drive. Thomas Hardy. OBNC

Your laughter is like a burst pomegranate. When You Laugh. Ingrid Jonker, *tr. fr. Afrikaans by* Elizabeth Jones. WPOW

Your laundry, like your life, has shrunk. It's No Secret. Medaksé, *tr. fr. Armenian by* Diana Der Hovanessian. VBLP

Your leaves bound up compact and fair. To an Author. Philip Freneau. AmPP; EAP; NOBA; OxBA

Your legs would be pretty, if you had legs. Portrait of a Nun. Bobi Jones, *tr. fr. Welsh by* Joseph P. Clancy. OBWVE

Your letter came. — Glutted the earth and cold. A Winter-Piece to a Friend Away. John Berryman. NOBA

Your letter took only nineteen days. Letter to Corn Island. Linda France. NWP

Your Life. Ron Schreiber. PFL

Your life is a baby not yet born. Maria Luisa Spaziani, *tr. fr. Italian by* Beverly Allen. NeIt

Your life shall never lack a friend. (*LL*) If You Have a Friend. *Unknown.*

Your little dog that barked as I came by. To His Wife, for Striking Her Dog. Sir John Harington. OxBSP

Your little hands. Samuel Hoffenstein. *Fr.* Love-songs, at Once Tender and Informative. FiBHP; NBLV; TrJP

Your Looks So Often Cast. Sir Thomas Wyatt. EnRePo; SiPS

Your love is darkening my star — . Revelation. Edith Södergran, *tr. fr. Swedish by* David McDuff. VBLP

Your love is dead, lady, your love is dead. R. S. Thomas. BoLoP; EnLoPo

Your love lacks joy, your letter says. Coventry Patmore. *Fr.* Victories of Love, The. GBL

(Rain That Fell upon the Height, The.) FaBoRV

Your love turned my body into water. Nur, Empress Jahan, *tr. fr. Persian by* Willis Barnstone. BoWoP

Your love's great realm, my separation measures. (*LL*) Written in Exile. Kathleen Raine. TrCP; WPE

Your lynx-eyes, Asia. "Anna Akhmatova," *tr. fr. Russian by* Stanley Kunitz *and* Max Hayward. BoWoP

Your man, says the Man, will walk into the bar like this — here his. Bloody Hand. Ciaran Carson. PBCIP

Your marvellous songs. (*LL*) For Thomas Moore. James Simmons. BiHa; PBCIP

Your master dead, your life all out of tune. Epitaph for a Dog. Samuel Twardowski, *tr. fr. Polish by* Jerzy Peterkiewicz *and* Burns Singer. OBD

Your memory is leashed into my life. Yahrzeit. Miriam Kessler. BTR

Your midnight ambulances, the first knife-saw. Robert Sheridan Lowell. Robert Lowell. *Fr.* Marriage. NAs

Your midriff sags toward your knees. Woman with Girdle. Anne Sexton. ErPo

Your mind and you are our Sargasso Sea. Portrait d'une Femme. Ezra Pound. CMoP; FF; InPS; MeMAP; MoAB; MoAmPo; MoP; NAAL-2; NoAM; NOBA; NoP; Poetr; PPP; TAP; TwCP

Your mind is light, soon lost for new love. (*LL*) The Unfaithful [*or* Faithless] Shepherdess *or* Philon the Shepherd *or* Adieu Love, Untrue Love. *Unknown.* GTBS; GTBS-P

Your mind lies open like the map of rivers. Five Birds Rise. William Hayward. NYBP

Your Miscellanies do appear. Thomas Spratt. EPCY

Your Mission. Ellen M. Huntington Gates. BLPA; BLRP

Your mistress [*or* mistris], that you follow whores, still taxeth you. A Self[e] Accuser. John Donne. FaBoEE; PeLV

Your moon face. Leaving. Jenny Vuglar. DT

Your Mother. (*LL*) A Letter to a Son. Charles Mungoshi. PeSAV

Your mother hoards flour and sugar. Remembering. Enid Shomer. BTR

Your mother slept through it all. Early Morning Test Light over Nevada, 1955. Robert Vasquez. AfAz

Your mother's often gone. Kay Keeshan Hamod. *Fr.* Transitions. MDDM

Your Mouth Hit Saith. Charles D'Orléans. EnVB

Your mouth hit saith me "Bas me, bas me, sweet." Your Mouth Hit Saith. Charles D'Orléans. EnVB

Your mouth is a pomegranate. Eve to Lilith. Michelene Wandor. NBrP

Your Mouth Says, Kiss Me. Charles, Duc d'Orléans. OxBLMV

Your Name in Arezzo. James Wright. SM

Your name is the Wheel of Progress — a pleasant name indeed. To the Wheel of Progress. Mrs. Henry Linden. CBWP-4

Your Neighbor. H. Howard Biggar. PoToHe

Your neighbor, sir, whose roses you admire. My Neighbor's Reply. *Unknown.* PoToHe

Your new shoes click and slide upon the floor. Evangeline. "Yvonne." *Fr.* Iwilla/Scourge. ETG

Your nurse could only speak Italian. Sailing Home from Rapallo. Robert Lowell. HCAP; TAP

Your old hat hurts me, and those black. Dad. Elaine Feinstein. AIW

Your open palms raised in the air. The Little Boy with His Hands Up. Yala Korwin. BTR

Your other women are well-behaved. The So-and-So's. Sandra Cisneros. ETG

Your overtures overjoy me. Let's Not Think about That. Fran Landesman. DT

Your own hands are lying. (*LL*) Taking Off My Clothes. Carolyn Forché. AmPA; AnAn; NoAM

Your Own Place. Edward Lucie-Smith. PBCV

Your Own Version. Paul Gilbert. BLRP

Your parents don't like me. Farewell, Sweet Mary. *Unknown.* AmFP

Your passion was ever plural, apart. To Thoreau on Rereading Walden. Isabella Gardner. CAPP

Your petals open wet. Lesbian. Paula Jennings. PeHV

Your photo in the newspaper. The hotel. Not in Another Photo. Douglas Oliver. VaA

Your pinks, your tulips live an hour. To the Gardener at Nuneham. Horace Walpole. FaBoEE

Your Place. John Oxenham. BLRP

Your pleasure, Priapus, is the island coast. Maccius, *tr. fr. Greek by* Peter Jay. GrAn

Your poor old friend, what, will you leave him there? (*LL*) Epistle in Form of a Ballad to His Friends. Villon. AWP

Your poore estates, alone. (*LL*) To Meadows. Robert Herrick. AWP; CaPo; CH; JCP; NOBE; NOSC; OBEV

Your Presence. David Diop, *tr. fr. French by* Ulli Beier. PBA

Your price for one more hour? (*LL*) Seventh Day Seventh Month. Kuan Yun She. OHMPC

Your punishment is just, you must confess. To a Gentleman Who Disordered a Lady's Handerchief, and Immediately Cut His Thumb. Elizabeth Teft. ECWP

Your purple rose in your clear sunlight. Nell. Charles Marie René Leconte de Lisle, *tr. fr. French by* Philip L. Miller. RiWo

Your Riches Taught Me Poverty. Emily Dickinson. AnAmPo

Your sands are furrowed. What Her Girl Friend Said to Him. Ammuvanar, *tr. fr. Tamil by* A. K. Ramanujan. PLW

Your Shadow. Kevin Hart. FaBoMA

Your Shadow. Mark Strand. *Fr.* Elegy for My Father. HCAP; LCAP; Prf

Your Shoulders Hold Up the World. Carlos Drummond de Andrade, *tr. fr. Portuguese by* Mark Strand. AnRep

Your shrunken head was bent. The Murder Trial. Perseus Adams. PeSA

Your Sightless Days. Paul Monette. PFL

Your silence is leaning toward judgement. Unanswered Letter. Tess Gallagher. NIP

Your silence today is a pond where drowned things live. Adrienne Rich. *Fr.* Twenty-one Love Poems. GLP

Your sister 's play'd you scorn. (*LL*) The Gay Goshawk [*or* Goss-Hawk]. *At. to* Anna Gordon Brown. ESPB, *A and E vers.*; GN; OxBB; WPE

Your sleep is so profound. Aurora. Timothy Steele. DiPo

Your sleep will be. Caterpillar's Lullaby. Jane Yolen. Spl

Your small embattled eyes dispute a face. On Looking in the Looking Glass. Isabella Gardner. CAPP

Your small hands, precisely equal to my own. Adrienne Rich. *Fr.* Twenty-one Love Poems. GLP; PoE; TRP

Your smile, delicate. Woman Me. Maya Angelou. BlSi; SRLS

Your smile freeze & fly at me. (*LL*) New Year Party. Matthew Sweeney. IB

Your smile that trembles on the edge. Going Off. Tim Longville. VaA

Your smiles are not, as other womens be. To the Lady May. Aurelian Townshend. GBL

Your smiling, or the hope, the thought of it. A Simile for Her Smile. Richard Wilbur. HoPM; InPK

Your son presses against me. The Apple Trees. Louise Glück. HCAP

Your Songs. Gwendolyn B. Bennett. CDC

Your soul is a rare landscape. Moonlight. Paul Verlaine, *tr. fr. French by* Philip L. Miller. RiWo

Your soul is a sealed garden. Clair de Lune. Paul Verlaine, *tr. fr. French by* Arthur Symons. AWP

Your Soul Shines. Alice Walker. MT

Your sound is faultless. For Miles. Gregory Corso. Jaz

Your spouse not laboured-at nor spun. (*LL*) The Habit of Perfection. Gerard Manley Hopkins. ChIV-2; ImPo; LiTB; MeMBP; MoAB; MoBrPo; MoP; NoAM; NoP; OBEV; OBMV; OxAEP-2; Poetr; PoRA; RB; TFi; TrGrPo

Your stones I shall polish into a mirror. Jerusalem. David Rokeah, *tr. fr. Hebrew by* Ruth Finer Mintz. MHP

Your subjects hope, dread Sire. To the King's Most Excellent Majesty. Phillis Wheatley. TAP

Your swag, the camp, the plains all white with frost. (*LL*) The Star-Tribes. *Aborigine Oral Tradition.* NOBAu

Your sweetness of soul was a mystery to me. Hattie Rice Rich. Adrienne Rich. *Fr.* Grandmothers. HCAP; NAAL-2; NoAM

Your tall, fresh faces stand up in snow. My Students Who Stand in Snow. Michael S. Harper. AnAn

Z

Zebra. *Unknown, tr. fr. Hottentot.* PeSA

Zebra, The. *Unknown, tr. fr. Hottentot by* W. H. I. Bleek. PeSAV

Zebra Dun, The. *Unknown.* AmFP

Zebra Stallion. *Unknown, tr. fr. Hottentot.* PeSA

Zebras, The. Roy Campbell. LiTB; MoBrPo; PrIm

Zechariah, *sels.* Bible, *O.T.*
  I Return unto Zion. TrJP
  Open Thy Doors, O Lebanon. AWP

Zeenty, peenty, heathery, mithery. Counting-out Rhyme. *Unknown.* ChTr; GBP

Zeg-Zeg Postcards, The, *sels.* Tony Harrison.
  "Africa — London — Africa." FaBoBl

Zeke. L. A. G. Strong. MoBrPo

Zek'l Weep. *Unknown.* AS

Zelanto, the Fountain of Fame, *sels.* Anthony Munday.

Zella Wheeler! did I evah? The Interrupted Reproof. Priscilla Jane Thompson. CBWP-2

Zen Buddhism and Psychoanalysis/ Psychoanalysis and Zen Buddhism. Jackson MacLow. PoM

Zen mind is unperturbed by the envy of moth-browed beauties, A. Addressed to a Koto-player. Su Man-shu, *tr. fr. Chinese by* Wu-chi Liu. SuSp

Zenonis has a splendid tutor for her son — . Lucilius, *tr. fr. Greek by* Peter Porter. GrAn

Zepheria, *sels. Unknown.*
  "And is it by immutable decree." ESo
  "From the revenew of thine eyes' exchequer." ESo
  "Hoᵥ often hath my pen, mine heart's solicitour." ESo
  "How shall I deck my love in love's habiliment." ESo
  "Illuminating Lamps, ye Orbs christallite." ESo
  Proud in Thy Love. Son
  Sonnet. EiL
  "When last mine eyes dislodged from thy beautie." ESo
  "When we in kind embracements had agre'd [agreed]." AAS; Son

Zephyr. Eugene Fitch Ware. PoLF

Zephyr, kindliest of winds. Dioscorides, *tr. fr. Greek by* Peter Whigham. GrAn

Zépke! Zépke! Monologue of the Crazed Mastodon. Paul Scheerbart. CBNP

Zeppelin Factory, The. Rita Dove. Poetr

Zermatt: To the Matterhorn. Thomas Hardy. OBNC

0°. Elizabeth Spires. DiPo

Zero hour. Waiting yet again. James Merrill. *Fr.* Book of Ephraim, The. HCAP

Zero/ zero/ zero/ the museum of modern art. The Story of the Zeros. Victor Hernandez Cruz. PoBA

Zest of Life, The. Henry van Dyke. *Fr.* Three Best Things, The. WBLP

Zeugma. Christopher Reid. CBLP

Zeus, — by what name soe'er. Hymn to Zeus. Aeschylus, *tr. by* Gilbert Murray. *Fr.* Agamemnon. NAWM-1; WGRP

Zeus,/ Brazen-thunder-hurler. The Faun Sees Snow for the First Time. Richard Aldington. MoBrPo

Zeus isn't such a raving Casanova. Palladas, *tr. fr. Greek by* Tony Harrison. GrAn

Zeus lies in Ceres' bosom. Ezra Pound. *Fr. Cantos.* FaBoMo; MoP; NAAL-2; NoAM; NOBA; VGW

Zeus paid Danaé in gold:/ thus I pay you. Parmenion of Macedon, *tr. fr. Greek by* Peter Jay. GrAn

Zeus was once overheard to shout at Hera. The Weather of Olympus. Robert Graves. FaBoEE

Zeus, whoever Zeus may be, if he. Aeschylus, *tr. fr. Greek by* Peter Levi. TOF

Zhi, zhi, zhi, zhi, zhi, zhi, zhi, zhi. Battle Song. Shaka, King of the Zulus, *tr. fr. Zulu by* Henry Francis Fynn. PeSAV

zi kholmt. *(LL)* A Few Words in the Mother Tongue. Irena Klepfisz. LoHo

Zig-zag bee *zzz* and *zzz*-ing, came, A. The Bee. John Fandel. GoYe

Zilver-Weed, The. William Barnes. EnVR; NOBVV

Zimbabwe. F. D. Sinclair. PeSA

Zimmer and His Turtle Sink the House. Paul Zimmer. Poetsp

Zimmer Drunk and Alone, Dreaming of Old Football Games. Paul Zimmer. MAT; PBCAP

Zimmer Imagines Heaven. Paul Zimmer. PBCAP

Zimmer in Grade School. Paul Zimmer. PBCAP

Zimmer's Head Thudding against the Blackboard. Paul Zimmer. PBCAP

Zimmer's Last Gig. Paul Zimmer. Jaz

Zimmershire Lad, A. Paul Zimmer. SM

Zimri: "Numerous host of dreaming saints succeed." Dryden. *See* Numerous host of dreaming saints succeed, A.

Zimri: "Some of their chiefs were princes of the land." Dryden. *See* Some of their chiefs were princes of the land.

Zimri: The Duke of Buckingham. Dryden. *Fr.* Absalom and Achitophel, Pt. I. NOBE; NoP; OAEL-1; OBSV; SeCV-2

Zinglum, Zanglum, Bolun, Bun. *(LL)* One-ery, two-ery, [*or* ore-ery], ickery, Ann. *Unknown.* FaPON; OxNR

Zinnias. Valerie Worth. NTCP

Zinnias, stout and stiff. Zinnias. Valerie Worth. NTCP

Zion me wan go home. *Unknown.* FaBoVe

Zion, or the City of God. John Newton. *See* Glorious Things of Thee Are Spoken.

Zion, wilt thou not ask if peace's wing. Ode to Zion. Judah Halevi, *tr. fr. Hebrew by* Nina Davis Salaman. TrJP

Zionist Marching Song. Naphtali Herz Imber, *tr. fr. Hebrew by* Israel Zangwill. TrJP

Zion's Sons and Daughters. *Unknown.* AmFP

Zippo lighter, A. Off the Back of a Lorry. Tom Paulin. PBCIP

Zippora Returns to Moses at Rephidim. Rose Drachler. BCF

Zito the Magician. Miroslav Holub, *tr. fr. Czech by* Ian Milner *and* George Theiner. AnRep; PoSu

Zizi's Lament. Gregory Corso. NeAP; VGW

Zobo Bird, The. Frank A. Collymore. GoJo

Zocalo. Michael S. Harper. NBV

Zodiac, The, *sels.* James Dickey.
  "Tenderness, ache on me, and lay your neck." TAP

Zodiac, The. Guillaume de Salluste Du Bartas, *tr. by* Sylvester, Joshua. *Fr.* Divine Weeks and Works, The. NOSC

Zodiac. Eleanor Farjeon. OTCP

Zodiac is changed into a sphere, The. *(LL)* Chosen. W. B. Yeats. BoLoP; CMoP

Zodiac Rhyme, The. *Unknown.* GBP

Zodiac Song, The. John Ruskin. NOBVV

Zoetropes. Bill Manhire. PeNZ

Zoila López. Ana Castillo. AfAz

Zola. E. A. Robinson. OxBA

Zolgotz. *Unknown.* AmFP

Zollicoffer. Henry Lynden Flash. PAH

Zollverein was hardly neutral, The. One recalls. Philatelic Lessons: The German Collection. Lawrence P. Spingarn. NYBP

Zone. Guillaume Apollinaire, *tr. fr. French by* Ron Padgett. SOTW

Zone. Guillaume Apollinaire, *tr. fr. French.* SOTW, *tr. by* Ron Padgett

Zone. Louise Bogan. IMW; WPE

Zone of Death. William Everson. VGW

Zong, A. William Barnes. BoLoP

Zong Belegt Baatar. *Mongol Oral Tradition, tr. by* C. R. Bawden. WTO

Zonnebeke Road, The. Edmund Blunden. OBWP; PeFWW

Zoo, The. Gilbert Sorrentino. NeAP

Zoo, The. Humbert Wolfe. MoShBr

Zoo in the City, The. Sara Van Alstyne Allen. GoYe

Zoo is full of cages and it lies, The. Picture Postcard of a Zoo. Oscar Williams. Son

Zoo Keeper's Wife. Sylvia Plath. VBLP

Zoo Manners. Eileen Mathias. BoTP

Zoo of You, The. Arthur Freeman. ErPo

Zophiël, *sels.* Maria Gowen Brooks.
  Bridal of Helon. AmWP
  Death of Altheëtor. AmWP

Zoroaster Devoutly Questions Ormazd. *At. to* Zoroaster. *See* This I ask Thee — tell it to me truly, Lord!

Zorro Man, A. Maya Angelou. VBLP

Zosimé was a slave in body only. Damaskius, *tr. fr. Greek by* Peter Jay. GrAn

Zouave, The. Peter Cooley. NAmP90

Zounds, gramercy, and rootity-toot! Robin Hood. Phyllis McGinley. *Fr.* Speaking of Television. OBSV

Zounds! how the price went flashing through. Israel Freyer's Bid for Gold. Edmund Clarence Stedman. PAH

Zu fragmentarisch ist Welt und Leben. Heine, *tr. fr. German by* Charles Godfrey Leland. AWP

Zudioska. Aaron Kramer. BTR

Zulu Girl, The. Roy Campbell. OBMV; OxAEP-2

Zum gali gali. *Unknown.* SWP

Zum gali gali gali. Zum Gali Gali. *Unknown.* SWP

Zum Lazarus, *sels.* Heine, *tr. fr. German by* Alistair Elliot.
  "Heavenly fields of Paradise, The." OBD

Zummer Stream. William Barnes. BoNaP

Zun-zet. William Barnes. PoEL-4

Zuni Derivations. *Unknown, tr. fr. Zuni Indian by* Dennis Tedlock. STP

AUTHOR INDEX

*Arabic, Chinese, Korean, and old-style Japanese names in the Author Index are al-
phabetized, following standard practice, in uninverted form. Modern Japanese names,
however, are inverted in the Western manner. Pseudonymous names are enclosed in
quotation marks.*

A

"A., F.P." *See* **Adams, Franklin Pierce.**
A., P. E.
  Limerick: "There we was, and wanting our
    tea."
"A. K." *See* **"K., A."**
"A. R. G." *See* **"G., A. R."**
"A. W." *See* **"W., A."**
"A. W. S." *See* **"S., A. W."**
Aal, Katharyn Machan
  Leda's Sister and the Geese.
Aaron, Jonathan (b. 1941)
  Evidence: from a Reporter's Notebook.
  Voice from Paxos, The.
**Aaron of Lenczicz, Solomon Ephraim ben (d.
  1619)**
  These Things I Do Remember.
Aaronson, Lazarus. *See* **Aaronson, Leonard
  [or Lazarus].**
Aaronson, Leonard [or Lazarus] (b. 1894)
  Homeward Journey, The.
  Pesci Misti.
Abba Arika. *See* **Rab.**
Abbe, George (b. 1911)
  Horizon Thong.
  New York City.
Abbey, Edward
  Benedicto: May your trails be crooked,
    winding, lonesome.
  How strange and wonderful is our home, our
    earth.
Abbey, Henry (1842–1911)
  What Do We Plant [When We Plant the Tree].
Abbott, Clifton (d. 1945)
  Just Keep On.
Abbott, Keith (b. 1944)
  Blue Mason Jars.
  French Desire.
  Good News Bad News.
  Persephone.
  Persephone, 5, Outside.
  To an Old San Francisco Poet.
Abbott, Steve
  Elegy: "First timepieces were encased in
    delicate silver skulls, The."
  Hit by a Space Station.
Abbott, Wenonah Stevens
  Soul's Soliloquy, A.
Abbott, Winston
  Twilight is a time for sharing — and a time for.
Abd al-Hayy, Muhammad (b. 1944)
  Ode of Signs, *Sels.*
Abd-ar-Rahman I
  Palm Tree, The.
Abeita, Louise. *See* **"E-Yeh-Shure."**
Abelard, Peter (1079–1142)
  David's Lament for Jonathan.
  Hymn for the Close of the Week.
Abercrombie, Lascelles (1881–1938)
  All Last Night.
  Emblems of Love, *Sels.*
  Epilogue: "What shall we do for Love these
    days?"

Epitaph: "Sir, you should notice me: I am the
    Man."
Fear, The.
Fools' Adventure, The, *Sels.*
Hope and Despair.
Hymn to Love.
Judith, *Sels.*
Mary and the Bramble.
Sale of Saint Thomas, The, *Sels.*
Seeker, The.
Small Fountains.
Song: "Balkis was in her marble town."
Stream's Song, The.
They say the land is full of apes, which have.
Witchcraft: New Style.
Woman's Beauty.
Abid ibn al-Abras (*fl.* 500–550)
  Arab Chieftain to His Young Wife, An.
  Lament for an Arab Encampment.
Abrahams, Lionel (b. 1928)
  Thresholds of Identity.
  Whiteman Blues, The.
Abrahams, Peter (b. 1919)
  Lonely Road.
  Me, Colored.
  Tell Freedom, *Sels.*
Abrahams, William (b. 1919)
  Séance.
Abrams, Sam (b. 1935)
  Cakewalkman.
  In the Capability.
  Not the Arms Race.
  United States of America We, The.
  What the Sixties Were Really Like.
  World Is with Me Just Enough, The.
Abse, Dannie (b. 1923)
  Angels.
  Brueghel in Naples.
  Cousin Sidney.
  Down the M4.
  Epithalamion: "Singing, today I married my
    white girl."
  Florida.
  In My Fashion.
  In the Theatre.
  Inscription on the Flyleaf of a Bible.
  Letter to Alex Comfort.
  Near the Border of Insanities.
  New Diary, A.
  Not Adlestrop.
  Pathology of Colours.
  Peachstone.
  Poem and Message.
  Public Library.
  Return to Cardiff.
  Snake.
  Social Revolution in England.
  Song for Dov Shamir.
  Tales of Shatz.
  Watching a Cloud.
  Winter Visit, A.
  Words Spoken Alone.
  X-Ray.
Abu Bakr (d. 1116)
  Sword, The.
Abu Dharr (d. 1208)
  Oranges, The.

Abu Dhu'ayb al-Hudhali (d. 649?)
  Lament for Five Sons Lost in a Plague.
Abu Dolama (d. 778)
  Behold My Mother!
  Humorous Verse.
  Traders in Beauty and Delight.
Abu Ishaq al-Ilbin (d. 1967)
  Granada (1000 A.D.).
Abu Khalid, Fawziyya (b. 1955)
  Mother's Inheritance.
Abu-l-Ala al-Maarri
  Aweary Am I.
Abu Nuwas
  Escape, An.
  Rake, The.
Abu Zakariya (d. 1249)
  Bubbling Wine.
Abulafia, Todros Ben Judah
  From Prison.
Abun of Mainz, Simeon ben Isaac, ben. *See*
  Isaac ben Abun of Mainz, Simeon ben.
Abutsu the Nun (d. c.1282)
  Diary of the Waning Moon, The, *Sels.*
  Shore wind is cold on my travel clothes, The.
  Who knows/ that rain in the depth of the ravine.
Acharya, Ananda
  My Faith.
  Realization.
Acholonu, Catherine Obianuju
  Nigeria in the Year 1999.
  Other Forms of Slaughter.
Ackerley, J. R. (1896–1967)
  After the Blitz, 1941.
Ackerly, W. C.
  Prayer of an Unemployed Man.
Ackerman, Diane (b. 1948)
  Beija-Flor.
  Still Life.
  Sweep Me through Your Many-Chambered
    Heart.
Ackland, Valentine (1906–69)
  Teaching To Shoot.
Acorn, Milton (b. 1923)
  Fights, The.
  I've Tasted My Blood.
  Knowing I Live in a Dark Age.
  On Saint-Urbain Street.
  You Growing.
Acosta, Teresa Palma
  My Mother Pieced Quilts.
Acton, Ellen M. V. (b. 1902)
  Exodus from a Renaissance Gallery.
"Ada" (*fl.* c. 1836)
  Lines.
  Lines: "From fair Jamaica's fertile plains."
  Oh, when this earthly tenement.
  To the Memory of J. Horace Kimball.
Adaios of Macedon
  Epigram: "If you see someone beautiful."
  If you see someone beautiful/ hammer it out
    right then.
  John spared his patient labouring ox.
  They say dogs killed you. No, Euripides.
Adair, Ivan
  Real Presence.

Signal Fire, The.
This mountain's secret is the son of Euphorion of Athens.
Wail of Prometheus Bound, The.
Word was given, and, instantaneously, The.
Zeus, whoever Zeus may be, if he.

Aesop (6th century B.C.)
Ass in the Lion's Skin, The ("An ass put on a lion's skin and went").
Mountain in Labor, The.
Shepherd-Boy and the Wolf, The.
Swan and the Goose, The.
Vine and the Goat, The.

Aetolus. See **Alexander of Pleuron.**

Afterman, Allen (b. 1941)
Pietà.
Their Thoughts Cling to Everything They See on the Way.
Van Diemen's Land.

Ag, Linus Suryadi
Dew.

Aganoor Pompilj, Vittoria (1855–1910)
Rain.

Agard, John (b. 1949)
Ask Mummy Ask Daddy.
Don't Call Alligator Long-Mouth till You Cross River.
Half-caste.
Listen Mr Oxford Don.
Lollipop Lady.
New Shoes.
Pan Recipe.
Waiting for Fidel.

Agate, James (1877–1947)
Eumenides at Home, The.

Agathias (536–82)
Astrologer, The.
Beautiful Melite, in the throes of middle age.
Bridge on the Sangarios, A.
House in Byzantium, A.
It is not wine that makes me reel/ Not juice of grape I crave.
Kallirrhoè: A Dedication.
Latrine in a Suburb of Smyrna, A.
Manifesto.
Not Such Your Burden.
On Lot's Wife Turned to Salt.
Partridge.
Plutarch.
Restless and discontent.
Restless and discontent/ I lie awake all night long.
Rhodanthe.
That old crow-beaked hag.
Troy.
You expect, Puss-in-Boots.

Agee, James (1909–55)
Happy Hen, The.
In Heavy Mind.
Lyric: "From now on kill America out of your mind."
Lyrics, *Sels.*
Now stands our love on that still verge of day.
Our doom is in our being. We began.
Permit Me Voyage.
Rapid Transit.
Red Sea.
So it begins. Adam is in his earth.
Song with Words.
Sonnets, *Sels.*
Sunday: Outskirts of Knoxville, Tennessee.
Temperance Note: and Weather Prophecy.
Those former loves wherein our lives have run.
Two Songs on the Economy of Abundance, *Sels.*

Agnew, Edith (b. 1897)
Let me tell to you the story.

Agnew, Joan
Freedom.
Sons of the King.

Agnew, Marjorie L.
On Going Home.

Agosin, Marjorie
Disappeared Woman I.

"**Agricola**" (*fl.* c.1757)
Daventry Wonder, The.

Agustini, Delmira (1886–1914)
Blindness.
From Far Away.

Ai (Florence Anthony) (b. 1947)
Abortion.
Barquisimeto, Venezuela, October 27, 1561.
Buchenwald, 1945.
But What I'm Trying to Say Mother Is.
Child Beater.
Cuba, 1962.
Disregard.
Everything: Eloy, Arizona, 1956.
Gilded Man, The, *Sels.*
Hangman.
He Kept On Burning, *Sels.*
Ice.
Kid, The.
Mexico, 1940.
Mexico, August 20, 1940.
Mother's Tale, The.
Orinoco, 1561, The.
Peru, 1955.
Russia, 1927.
Salome.
Spain, 1929.
Twenty-Year Marriage.
Why Can't I Leave You?
Woman to Man.

Ai Ch'ing (b. 1910)
Chilean Cigarette Pack, The.
Clear mirror of the moon palace, The.
Gamblers, The.
Little Orchids, The.
Old Ash Tree on Ching Hill.
Poet, The.
Reed Pipe, The.
Seaweed, The.
Spirit of Poetry, The.
Translucent Night, The.
Various Masks: Ai Ch'ing.

Ai Shih-te (*fl.* c.17th century)
Human Mind, The.

Aidoo, Christine Ama Ata. See **Ama Ata Aidoo, Christine.**

Aig-Imoukhuede, Frank (b. 1935)
One Wife for One Man.

Aiken, Conrad (1889–1973)
Accomplices, The.
All Lovely Things.
And in the Hanging Gardens.
And in the Human Heart, *Sels.*
Annihilation.
At a Concert of Music.
Bend as the Bow Bends.
Bird flying past my head said previous previous, The.
Blind Date.
But How It Came from Earth.
But no, the familiar symbol, as that the.
Calyx of the Oboe Breaks, The.
Dead Cleopatra lies in a crystal casket.
Dear Uncle Stranger.
Discordants, *Sels.*
Doctors' Row.
Farewell Voyaging World!
Green, Green, and Green Again.
Habeas Corpus Blues, The.
Hatteras Calling.
Herman Melville.
Improvisations: Light and Snow, *Sels.*
It is morning, Senlin says, and in the morning.
Kid, The, *Sels.*
Letter from Li Po, A, *Sels.*
Limerick: "Animula vagula blandula."
Limerick: "It's time to make love. Douse the glim."
Limerick: "On the deck of a ship called the Masm."
Limerick: "Quoth a cow in the marshes of Glynne."
Limerick: "Said a dreadfully literate cat."
Limerick: "Said Isolde to Tristan: "How curious!"

Limerick: "Said Old Father William: "I'm humble."
Limerick: "Scion of Boston society, A."
Limerick: "Sighed a dear little shipboard divinity."
Limerick: "There once was a wicked young minister."
Limerick: "There once was a wonderful wizard."
Limerick: "There was an old mickey called Cassidy."
Lovers, The.
Miracles.
Multitudes Turn in Darkness.
Music I Heard.
Mysticism, but let us have no words.
Nameless Ones, The.
Nuit Blanche: North End.
Obituary.
Prelude VII: "Beloved, let us once more praise the rain."
Prelude XXI: "First note, simple, The; the second note, distinct."
Prelude XLII: "Keep in the heart the journal nature keeps."
Prelude LIII: "Nothing to say? Then we'll say nothing."
Prelude LVII: "One star fell and another as we walked."
Prelude LVI: "Rimbaud and Verlaine, precious pair of poets."
Prelude III: "Sleep: and between the closed eyelids of sleep."
Prelude LII: "Stood, at the closed door."
Prelude XX: "So, in the evening, to the simple cloister."
Prelude XXXIII: "Then came I to the shoreless shore of silence."
Prelude VI: "This is not you? These phrases are not you?"
Prelude XXVIII: "Time has come, the clock says time has come, The."
Prelude II: "Two coffees in the Español, the last."
Prelude XIX: "Watch long enough, and you will see the leaf."
Prelude XXIX: "What shall we do — what shall we think — what shall we say?"
Prelude I: "Winter for a moment takes the mind; the snow."
Prelude: "Woman, Woman, let us say these things to each other."
Prelude XIV: "You went to the verge, you say, and came back safely."
Preludes for Memnon; or, Preludes to Attitude, *Sels.*
Priapus and the Pool, *Sels.*
Proem to "The Kid."
Punch, the Immortal Liar, *Sels.*
Puppet Dreams, The.
Quarrel, The.
Road, The.
Room, The.
Sea Holly.
Senlin; a Biography, *Sels.*
Shaemus.
Snowflake on asphodel, clear ice on rose.
Soldier, The, *Sels.*
Sound of Breaking.
Sounding, The.
South End.
Summer.
Tetélestai.
Things, The.
This Is the Shape of the Leaf.
Three Star Final.
Time in the Rock [or, Preludes to Definition], *Sels.*
Wedding, The.
What face she put on it, we will not discuss.
When I was a boy, and saw bright rows of icicles.
When the Tree Bares.
When trout swim down Great Ormond Street.
Where we were walking in the day's light, seeing.

Al-Qasim al-Shabbi, Abu (1919–34)
In the Shadow of the Valley of Death.
Song of Ecstasy, *Sels.*

Al-Qurtubiyya, 'Aisha bint Ahmad. *See*
'Aisha bint Ahmad al-Qurtubiyya.

Al-Sa'igh, Yusuf
Ants.

Al-Shabbi, Abu al-Qasim. *See* **Al-Qasim Al-Shabbi, Abu.**

Al-Sharqawi, Ali (b. 1948)
Psalm 23 to the Singer's Nectar, *Sels.*

Al-Tirimmah (660?–725)
In the Heart of the Desert.
Lord of the Throne.

Al-Udwani, Ahmad al-Mushari (b. 1923)
Mysterious things within you, The.
Personal Reflections, *Sels.*
Signs, *Sels.*
You I give no name to/ The mysterious things
within you/ are an untrodden bower.
You I give no name to/ The mysterious things
within you/ are fragrance, light and melody.

Alabaster, William
Away, fear, with thy projects, no false fire.
Beehould a cluster to itt selfe a vine.
Divine Meditations, *Sels.*
Divine Sonnet, A.
Exaltatio Humanae Naturae.
Haile gracefull morning of eternall Daye.
Incarnatio Est Maximum Dei Donum [*or*
Donum Dei].
Jesu, thie love within mee is soe maine.
My soule a world is by Contraccion.
Night, the Starless Night of Passion, The.
Now I have found thee, I will ever more.
Now that the midd day heate doth scorch my
shame.
O starry Temple of unvalted space.
O sweete and bitter monuments of paine.
Of the Reed That the Jews Set in Our Saviour's
Hand.
On the Reed of Our Lord's Passion.
Sunne begins uppon my heart to shine, The.
Three sortes of teares doe from myne eies
distraine.
To Christ.
To the Blessed Virgin.
Up to Mount Olivet.
Upon the Crucifix.
Upon the Ensigns of Christ's Crucifying.
Way feare with thy projectes, noe false fyre,
A.
What meaneth this, that Christ an hymne did
singe.
When without tears I looke on Christ, I see.

Alamsaeen
Mosque is the Earth, and as holy it is.

Alarcon, Francisco
In a Neighborhood in Los Angeles.
Letter to America.
My Hair.
Prayer: "I want a god."

Alarcón, Juan Ruiz de (c.1580–1639)
Suspicious Truth, The, *Sels.*

Alattur Killar
Guide to Patrons, A.

Alba, Nanina (1917–68)
Be Daedalus.
For Malcolm X.

Albanez, Franciso
One Who Is at Home, The.

Albert, Heinrich (1604–51)
Musical Pumpkin-Hut.

Albert, Samuel L. (b. 1911)
After a Game of Squash.
Honeymoon.

Alberti, Rafael (b. 1902)
Charlie's Sad Date.
For Aitana.
I went away.
Metamorphosis of the Carnation, *Sels.*

Albiach, Anne-Marie (b. 1937)
And the emphasis.
Availability/ doesn't mean.
Enigma, *Sels.*

État, *Sels.*
For if it's a theme state it.
He accepts the circle, speech and so.
Of the unended in the speed of.
Unspecifiable/ the inexhaustible novel, The.

Albizzi, Niccolò degli (*fl.* 13th century)
Prolonged Sonnet: When the Troops Were
Returning from Milan [*or* When The Troops
Were Returning from Milan].

Albrecht von Johannsdorf (*fl.* 1185–1209)
God's Gifts.
I discovered the sweet lovely lady.
This I know, how love begins to be.

Albright, Mary E.
Let Me Go Back.

Alcaeus (b. c.620 B.C.)
And if the wine leaves him witless.
Come tip a few with me.
Don't wait for the lamplighter.
Fair Protarchus doesn't want to.
Her heart so stricken, Helen.
Hipponax.
I despise love. What weighty God.
I hate Eros. He is loathsome and will not.
I long for the call to council.
Leaving the Peloponnese.
Let Us Drink.
O frail flower.
Philip at Kynoskephalai.
Philip V of Macedon.
Philip of Macedon.
Poet has died, A.
Poverty's the worst savage crime.
So lovely . . . / so tender.
Storm, The.
You who were once my friend.

Alchin, Gordon (Observer RFC) (d. 1947)
Song of the Air, A.

Alcman (*fl.* 7th century B.C.)
Sleep upon the World.

Alcock, Mary (1742?–1798)
Chimney-Sweeper's Complaint, The ("A
chimney-sweepers' boy am I").
Instructions, Supposed to Be Written in Paris,
for the Mob in England.
Modern Manners.
Receipt for Writing a Novel, A.
Written in Ireland.

Alcosser, Sandra
Night on Goat Haunt, A.
What Makes the Grizzlies Dance.

Alcott, Louisa May (1832–88)
Little Kingdom I Possess, A.
Our Little Ghost.

Alcuin (c.735–804)
By these, by these same chains, O Rome.
Come, Make an End.
Dedication to St. Michael.
Epitaph for Paulinus of Aquileia and Arno of
Salzburg.
Epitaph for St. Amand, Bishop of Utrecht.
For His Friends.
In the Refectory.
Inscription in Monastic Refectory.
Lament for the Cuckoo.
Night Prayer, A.
On the Cross ("Adore the lifted standard of the
Cross").
On the Cross ("Here, dying for the world, the
world's life hung").
On the Killing at Lindisfarne.
One goodness ruleth by its single will.
Prayer at Night ("Fountain of light").
Prayer at Night ("He lay with quiet heart").
Sailor rescued from his buffeting, The.
Sequence for Saint Michael, A.
There'll come a time when brother speaks with
brother.
These be great cities, new roofs mounting up.
These days are too full fraught with diverse
dangers.
To Adelhard, Archbishop of Canterbury ("Brief
is our life").
To Adelhard, Archbishop of Canterbury
("Prince-Archbishop").

To Arno of Salzburg.
To Samuel, Bishop of Sens In Time of Dearth.
When you sit happy in your own fair house.
Written in Absence.

Aldan, Daisy (b. 1923)
Stones: Avesbury.

Aldana, Francesco de
Image of God, The.

Alderson, Brian (b. 1930)
Kinder- und Hausmärchen.

Aldington, Richard (1892–1962)
After Two Years.
At the British Museum.
Battlefield.
Evening.
Faun Sees Snow for the First Time, The.
Field Manoeuvres.
Images.
In the Trenches.
Lesbia.
Possession.
Resentment.
Trench Idyll.
Vicarious Atonement.

Aldis, Dorothy (1896–1966)
Blum.
Clown, The.
Everybody Says.
Hiding.
Kick a Little Stone.
Little.
No One Heard Him Call.
On a Snowy Day.
Our Silly Little Sister.
Setting the Table.
Supper for a Lion.

Aldiss, Brian W. (b. 1925)
Frozen Boy, The.
Progression of the Species.
Tom Wedgwood Tells.

Aldrich, Henry (1647–1710)
If all be true that I do think.

Aldrich, Thomas Bailey (1836–1907)
Apparitions.
At a Reading.
Ballad of Baby Bell, The.
Batuschka.
Before the Rain.
Bells at Midnight, The.
By the Potomac.
Fannie.
Fredericksburg.
Guilielmus Rex.
Lady of Castlenoire.
Maple Leaves.
Marjorie's Almanac.
Memory.
Ode, on the Unveiling of the Shaw Memorial
on Boston Common, May 31st, 1897, An.
Tiger-Lilies.
Turkish Legend, A.
Unguarded Gates.
Untimely Thought, An.
When the Sultan Goes to Ispahan.

Alegría, Claribel (b. 1924)
Evasion.
Loneliness and July Ninth.
Search.
Small Country.

Aleichem, Sholom (1859–1916)
Epitaph: "Here lies a simple Jew."
Sleep, My Child.

Aleixandre, Vicente (1898–1984)
My Grandfather's Death.

Alepoudelis, Odysseus. *See* **Elytis, Odysseus.**

Aleqaajik
Great grief came over me.

"Aleramo, Sibilla" (Rina Faccio) (1876–1960)
Yes to the Earth.

Alexander, A. L.
This, Too, Shall Pass Away.

Alexander, Alan (b. 1941)
For Raftery.
Gathering Place, The.

Priapus seeing Kimon with a stand.
Temple of Artemis at Ephesos, The.
That dried-up arse, Lykainis.
Theogenes sent us for Piso's pleasure — .
These are Aristophanes' marvellous plays.
"They pray for children? Let them!" cried
  Polyxo.
To Epicles.
To Telembrotos.
Unlucky Nicanor, quenched by the grey and
  deep.
Watered by the Strymon and great Hellespont.
Water-mill, A.
Waves, the rough surf, swept me on the shore,
  The.
When the deep-piled winter snow/ melted on
  her roof.
Yesterday when I'd drunk myself to bed/ with
  water (neat).
You can explore your every desire.

Antiphanes (c.388 – c.311 B.C.)
Lost Bride, The.
Man's makeshift days would flash past at the
  best.
Piddle-paddling race of critics, rhizome-
  fanciers.
Strange race of critics, A.
When Cytherea slipped her wily sash off.

Antiphilos (fl. late 1st cent. B.C.)
Here is the river Eurotas.

Antiphilus (fl. 1st cent. B.C. – c. 1st cent. A.D.)
Earthquaked, my house collapsed.
Epitaph of a Sailor.
Even then I said.
Gifts to a Lady.
Give me a mattress on the ship's poop some
  day.
Imaginary Dialogue.
On Diogenes the Cynic.
On the Death of the Ferryman, Glaucus.
Quince Preserved through the Winter, Given to
  a Lady, A.
Torrent Cuts Off the Poet's Path, A.

Antistius Vetus (Gaius Antistius Vetus) (fl. c.26
A.D.)
Priapus the Scarecrow.

"Antler" (b. 1946)
Bedrock Mortar Full Moon Illumination.
Discovery of Lake Michigan, The.
I want to lie down in dappled leaf-shade.
Raising My Hand.
To learn how to die cut down a tree.
What Every Boy Knows.

Antokolsky, Pavel Grigoryevich (b. 1896)
Hate!

Antoninus, Brother. *See* **Everson, William.**

Antrobus, John (b. 1933)
Cowboy, The.

Anvari (1126? – 1190?)
Hors de Combat.

Anyiam - St. John, Rita
For Me from You.

Anyte [or Anytes] (fl. 290 B.C.)
Alive, this man was Manes, a common slave.
And you too perished long ago, by a bush with
  matted roots.
Big enough for an ox, the cauldron.
Child Myro made this tomb, The.
Children, billy goat, have put crimson reins,
  The.
Children have put purple, The.
Children have tied you, billy-goat, with bright,
  The.
Cock, A.
Damis set this up, to commemorate.
Dedication: A Spear.
Ease your weary limbs, stranger, under this
  elm — .
Epigrams, *Sels.*
For her locust, nightingale of the fields, and
  her cricket that slept.
I am Hermes. I stand in the crossroads by a
  windy.
I, Hermes, have been set up.
I mourn for Antibia the virgin.

Indeed then, it was your own courage.
Instead of a solemn wedding and marriage-bed.
Kypris keeps this spot.
Look at the horned goat of Dionysus.
Lounge in the shade of the luxuriant laurel's.
No longer, as before, will you wake at dawn
  and flap.
No longer shall I exult in the floating seas and
  arch.
Often on this her daughter's tomb did Cleina
  grieve.
On a Dolphin.
On this her daughter's tomb.
Shepherd's Gift, A.
Sit down in the shade of this fine spreading
  laurel.
This place is the Cyprian's for she has ever the
  fancy.
This tomb Damis built for his courageous
  horse.
Throwing her arms around her father.
To shock-haired Pan and the nymphs who
  protect the cow-byres.
Why, country Pan, sitting still.

Anzaldúa, Gloria (b. 1946)
Interface.
We Call Them Greasers.

Apolebieji, Odeniyi
Salute to the Elephant.

Apollinaire, Guillaume (1880 – 1918)
Calligram, 15 May 1915.
Hat-Tomb.
Heart.
Heart, Crown, and Mirror, *Sels.*
In this mirror I am enclosed.
It's Raining.
Kings who have died.
Little Car, The.
Mirabeau Bridge.
Seal, The.
Shadow.
Sighs of the Gunner from Dakar, The.
Zone.

Apollinaris Sidonius. *See* **Sidonius Apollinaris.**

Apollinarius
If you insult me in my absence.

Apollonides
Beeman Cliton hews/ From the flower fed hive.
Cup clinks out, my friend, The.
Lacking rich acres, thick grape-crops.
Snow, clothing sky & mountain.

Apollonius Rhodius (222 – 181 B.C.)
Argonautica, The.

Appel, Benjamin (b. 1907)
Talker, The.

Appleman, Marjorie (b. 1938)
Melting.

Appleman, Philip (b. 1926)
Amurrika!
Is There a Voice.
It Is Enough.
La Misère.
Maples.
More.
My Friend.
So What.
Try.
When.

Appleton, Everard Jack (1872 – 1931)
Woman Who Understands, The.

Appleton, George
O God, I thank thee.

Applewhite, James (b. 1935)
Barbecue Service.
Bordering Manuscript.
Marriage Portrait.
My Grandfather's Funeral.
To Earth.
White Lake.

Aql, Said (b. 1912)
Book of Roses, The, *Sels.*

Aragon, Louis (1897 – 1982)
Lilacs and the Roses, The.
Mimosas.

Phoenix Reborn from Its Ashes, The.
Tcheliabtraktrostroi Waltz, *Sels.*

Arakida Moritake (1473 – 1549)
Haiku: "Fallen flowers rise."
Haiku: "Falling flower, The."

Aratus (fl. 3d cent. B.C.)
Beneath both the feet of Boötes you may see.
Phaenomena, *Sels.*
Weather Signs.

Arbuthnot, John (1667 – 1735)
Epitaph on Colonel Francis Chartres.
Know Yourself.

Archer, Kate Rennie
Lairdless Place, The.

Archestratus (fl. 4th century B.C.)
Gastrology, *Sels.*
I write these precepts for immortal Greece.
Recipe: Hare.

Archevolti, Samuel ben Elhanan Isaac, of
Padua (fl. 17th century)
Advice to Hotheads.

Archias
Desire, get your bow ready/ and go quietly
  after/ another mark.
Get away from Eros!

Archias of Byzantium (fl. c.120 B.C.)
Not even in death can I.
Sea Dirge.

Archias of Macedon
Hektor of Troy.

Archilochus (c.680 – c.640 B.C.)
Decks awash,/ Mast-top dipping.
I don't give a damn if some Thracian ape strut.
Like Odysseus under the ram.
May he lose his way on the cold sea.
My ash spear is my barley bread.
Sergeant to Enyalios.
This island, garlanded with wild woods.
When Alkibié married.
Will, lost in a sea of trouble.

Arcos, Rene
Dead, The.

Arden, Richard Pepper, Baron Alvanley
(1745 – 1804)
On Dr. Samuel Ogden.

Aretino, Pietro (1492 – 1556)
At the Jesuits' church, the sexton father's
  racked.
Brother Alberto, one hot summer day.
Brother Astolfo sated appetite.
Let's Fuck, Dear Heart.
My Legs Half Round Your Neck.
Put a Finger Up My Arse, You Dear Old Man.
Some More Cases of Love with Solutions, *Sels.*
Stragglers.

Argentarius (Marcus Argentarius) (fl. c.60
B.C.)
About Menophila's morals there are strange
  rumours.
Aristomache loved a drink:/ The old chatterbox
  was fonder.
Blackbird, singing on the highest branch/ Of
  the oak.
Come, Gobrys, there are other gods besides the
  Muses.
Damned bird, why have you ruined my sleep.
Dead, they'll burn you up with electricity.
Dead, you will lie under a yard of earth.
Drunk I observe the golden dance of stars.
Epigram: "Hetero-sex is best for the man of a
  serious turn of mind."
Her perfect naked breast.
Here lie a grasshopper and a/ Cicada.
Here's to Lysidice: pour in ten ladles, boy.
I can't bear to watch your hips.
Isias my love, with your scented breath.
Look at this, golden-horned moon.
Looking and lusting is not love.
Love is not just a function of the eyes.
Melissa means honeybee; yes, you're true.
My name was Pnytagoras; I died by drowning.
Old Story, The.
Once I was reading Hesiod.
Psyllus lies here. Procuring was his trade.

Something has happened to me.
Songs of Sorrow.
To Dennis Brutus.
To the Eminent Scholar and Meddler.
Weaver Bird, The.

Axelrod, David B. (b. 1943)
Once in a While a Protest Poem.

Axelrod, Susan (b. 1944)
Home, The.

Axionicus (*fl.* 4th century B.C.)
Recipe: Sausage.

Ayala, Ramon Perez de (b. 1880)
She Was a Pretty Little Girl.

Ayer, Ethan
Like a Whisper.

Ayer, Jean
Everyday Things.

Ayer, William Ward (d. 1885)
Be Still.

Ayloffe, John (d. 1685)
Britannia and Raleigh.
Marvell's Ghost.
Oceana and Britannia.

Aymerich, Angela Figueroa-. *See* Figueroa-
Aymerich, Angela.

Ayres, Philip (1638–1712)
Cynthia on Horseback.
Death of Adonis, The.
Describes the Place Where Cynthia Is Sporting
Herself.
Epigram on Woman, An.
Ever Present.
Fly, The.
Invites His Nymph to His Cottage.
Invites Poets and Historians to Write in
Cynthia's Praise.
On a Fair Beggar.
On Lydia Distracted.
Yoke uneasy on the ox doth sit, The.

Ayton [*or* **Aytoun**], **Sir Robert (1570–1638)**
Answer, The.
Exercise of Affection, The.
On A Woman's Inconstancy.
On His Mistress.
On Loss.
On Love.
On Platonic Love, to Mistress Cicely Crofts,
Maid of Honour.
On the Prince's Death, to the King.
On the River Tweed.
Rejection, The.
There is none, no none but I.
To His Coy Mistress.
To His Forsaken Mistress.
To Queen Anne on a New Year's Day 1604.
Upon a Diamond Cut in Form[e] of a
Heart . . . Sent in a New Year's [*or* New-
yeares] Gift.
Upon His Unconstant Mistress.
Upon Platonic Love: To Mistress Cicely Crofts,
Maid of Honour.
Upone Tabacco.
Valediction.
When Thou Did Thinke I Did Not Love.
Wrong Not, Sweete Empress of My Heart.

Aytoun, William Edmonstoune [*or*
Edmondstoune] **(1813–65)**
Edinburgh after Flodden, *Sels*.
La Mort d'Arthur.
Laureate, The.
Massacre of the Macpherson, The.
Old Scottish Cavalier, The.
Sonnet to Britain.
Then the Provost he uprose.

Aytoun, William Edmonstoune (1816–1909)
and **Sir Theodore Martin**
Lay of the Lovelorn, The.

A'yunini
Killer, The.

Aziz, Nasima
Home.

B

B., C. K.
American girl in Versailles, An.

B., H. d'A.
Givenchy Field.
No-Man's-Land.

"B., M."
Deportation.

"B., R."
This story's strange, but altogether true.

"B. L. T." *See* **Taylor, Bert Leston.**

Ba, Oumar (b. 1900?)
Drought.

Baba Akiko (b. 1928)
In the autumn when words sound.
Punished in the moment of love.
Since I don't know my mother.

Baba Kuhi of Shiraz (948–1050)
In the market, in the cloister — only God I saw.

Babcock, Donald Campbell (b. 1885)
O God, in Whom the Flow of Days.

Babcock, Maltbie Davenport (1858–1901)
Be Strong.
Emancipation.
Not to Be Ministered To.
School Days.
This Is My Father's World.

Babcock, William Henry (1849–1922)
Bennington.

Baber, Bob Henry
Handicaps.
Richwood.

Baca, Jimmy Santiago (b. 1952)
At Night.
Bells.
Cloudy Day.
Day's Blood.
El Pablo was a bad dude.
Ese Chicano.
Fall.
Green Chile.
I Am Here.
I love the wind.
I Pass La Iglesia.
Main Character.
Pancho, the barrio idiot.
Perfecto Flores.
Small Farmer.
There Are Black.

Bacchylides (b. 450 B.C.)
How white.
Keep to the one path.
Peace on Earth.
This much I know.

Bacheller, Irving (1859–1950)
Whisperin' Bill.

Bachmann, Ingeborg (1926–73)
Autumn Maneuver.
Curriculum Vitae.
Days in White.
Every Day.
Exile.
Firstborn Land, The.
Go, My Thought.
Great Freight, The.
Instructed in love.
No Delicacies.
Out of the corpse-warm vestibule of heaven
steps the sun.
Respite, The.
Safe-Conduct.
Settlement.
Songs in Flight, *Sels*.
Tell Me, Love.
To the Sun.
Truly.
You want the summer lightning, throw the
knives.
You Words.

Backus, Bertha Adams
Then Laugh.

Bacmeister, Rhoda Warner (b. 1893)
Galoshes.

Bacon, Francis (1561–1626)
Life of Man, The.

Bacon, Leonard (1802–81)
Hail, Tranquil Hour of Closing Day.
Pilgrim Fathers, The.
Wake the Song of Jubilee.

Bacon, Leonard (1887–1954)
Flyfisherman in Wartime.
Horatian Variation.

Bacon, Peggy (1895–1987)
Hearth.

Baez, Joan (b. 1941)
Love Song to a Stranger.

Bagg, Robert (b. 1935)
Ronald Wyn.
See That One?
Soft Answers.

Baggesen, Jens (1764–1826)
Childhood.

Baggett, Rebecca
Day Before They Bombed Nagasaki, The.

Bagriana, Elisaveta (b. 1893)
Descendant.

"Bagritzky [*or* **Bagritsky**], **Eduard"** (Eduard
Dzyubin) (1895–1934)
He Tries out the Concords Gently.
My Honeyed Languor.
Piece of Black Bread, A.

Baha Ad-din Zuhayr (d. 1258)
On a Blind Girl.

Baha 'U' Lla'h
Blessed is the spot, and the house.

Bahe, Liz Sohappy (b. 1947)
And What of Me?
Farewell: "You sang round-dance songs."
Grandmother Sleeps.
Once Again.
Printed Words.
Ration Card, The.
Talking Designs.

Bai, Mukta (*fl.* 13th century)
I live where darkness/ is not.

Baildon, Henry Bellyse (1849–1907)
Moth, A.

Bailey, Anthony (b. 1933)
Green and the Black, The.

Bailey, L. W.
Limerick: "There was a young girl from
Uttoxeter."

Bailey, Liberty Hyde (1858–1954)
Miracle.

Bailey, Philip James (1816–1902)
Country Town, A, *Sels*.
We live in deeds, not years; in thoughts, not
breaths.
What Is Heaven?

Bailey, Zoe
Dolphins.

Baillie, Lady Grisel [*or* **Grizel** [*or* **Grisell**]
(1665–1746)
Were Ne [*or* Werena] My Hearts Light [*or*
Heart Licht] I Wad Dye [*or* Dee].
Werena My Heart Licht I Wad Dee.

Baillie, Joanna (1762–1857)
Address to the Muses, An, *Sels*.
Blackcock, The [*or* The Black Cock].
Child to His Sick Grandfather, A.
Disappointment, A.
Evening.
Ghost of Edward.
Hay making.
Hooly and Fairly.
Horse and His Rider, The.
Kitten, The.
Morning.
Mother to Her Waking Infant, A.
Night Scenes of Other Times, *Sels*.
Outlaw's Song, The.
Reverie, A.
Summer Day, A, *Sels*.
Summer's Day, A.
Trysting Bush, The.
Winter Day, A, *Sels*.

Ye are the spirits who preside.

Bain, Andrew Geddes (1797–1864)
Address.
Polyglot Medley.

Bain, Donald
War Poet.

Bainbrigge, Philip
Achilles in Scyros, *Sels.*
Chorus of Scyrian Maidens.

Baird, Martha (1921–1981)
Confidence.

Baker, Austen
There was a young lady named Miller.

Baker, Carlos (b. 1909)
Chinese Mural, A.
Men of Sudbury, The.
On a Landscape of Sestos.
Visit to the Art Gallery, A, *Sels.*

Baker, David (b. 1954)
Ice River.

Baker, Donald W. (b. 1923)
Delinquent Elegy.
Formal Application.

Baker, Dorothy (b. 1907)
Castles in the Sand.
In the Woods.

Baker, Henry (1698–1774)
Declaimer, The.
Love.
Rapture, The.

Baker, Howard (b. 1905)
Ode to the Sea.

Baker, J. G.
My Trundle Bed.

Baker, Julia Aldrich
Mizpah.

Baker, Karle Wilson ("Charlotte Wilson") (b. 1878)
Beauty's Hands Are Cool.
Creeds.
Good Company.
Let Me Grow Lovely.
Ploughman, The.

Baker, Kathleen Leland (b. 1951)
Baby Hilary, Sir Edmund, The.
Honey Moon.

Baker, Thomas (b. 1871)
Electric Telegraph, The.
I dream'd I walk'd in raptures high.
Means of Propulsion for Steam-Ships.
Steam Engine; or, The Power of the Flame, The, *Sels.*
Watt's Improvements to the Steam Engine.

Baker, Tony (b. 1954)
For Geraldine.
Poem: "First day of May Jack."
Storm clouds a smudge of damson.

Balaban, John (b. 1943)
Faith and Practice.
Guard at the Binh Thuy Bridge, The.
Words for My Daughter.

Balbin, Julius
Lament for the Gypsies.
Tonight.

Balbuena, Bernardo de (b. c.1561–1627)
Grandeza Mexicana, *Sels.*

Baldwin, A. W. I.
Ten Little Dicky-Birds.

Baldwin, James (1924–87)
Guilt, Desire and Love.
Le Sporting-Club de Monte Carlo.
Lover's Question, A.

Baldwin, Mary Newton (b. 1903)
Lonely Are the Fields of Sleep.

Baldwin, Michael (b. 1930)
Death on a Live Wire.

Baldwin, Thomas (1753–1825)
From Whence Doth This Union Arise?

Baldwin, William (*fl.* 1547–49)
Christ, My Beloved.
Christ to His Spouse [*or* The Beloved to the Spouse].

Bale, John (1495–1553)
Wassail, Wassail.

Balhurst, W. H.
Unshrinking Faith.

Ballard, Charles G.
During the Pageant at Medicine Lodge.
Grandma Fire.
Memo.
Now the People Have the Light.
Sand Creek.
Speaker, The.
Spirit Craft, The.
Their Cone-like Cabins.
Winds of Change, The.

Ballard, Colin Robert (1868–1941)
Pacific Railway, The.

Ballou, Hosea, I (1771–1852)
Dear Lord, Behold Thy Servants.
In God's Eternity.
When God Descends with Men to Dwell.

Ballou, Hosea, II (1796–1861)
Ye Realms below the Skies.

Ballou, Silas (1753–1837)
Almighty God in Being Was.
While I Am Young.

Balsdon, Dacre (b. 1901)
Endurance Test.

Bamberger, Augustus Wright
Each a Part of All.

Bampfylde, John Codrington (1754–96)
On a Frightful Dream.
On a Wet Summer.
On Hearing That Torture Was Suppressed throughout the Austrian Dominions.
Sonnet: "As when, to one who long hath watched, the morn."
To the Evening.
To the Redbreast.

Bancks, John (1709–51)
Description of London, A.
Fragment: "In Cloe's chamber, she and I."

Bancroft, Charles (1911–69)
Tadoussac.

Bancroft, James Henry (1819–44)
Brother, Though from Yonder Sky.

Bangs, Carol Jane (b. 1949)
Touching Each Other's Surfaces.

Bangs, John Kendrick (1862–1922)
Blind.
Dreadful Fate of Naughty Nate, The.
Hired Man's Way, The.
I Never Knew a Night So Black.
If.
Little Elf, The.
My Dog.
On File.
Philosophy.
Thanksgiving Day.
Today.

Banim, John (1798–1842)
Soggarth Aroon.

Banker, William, Jr.
Battle of Queenstown, The.

Banks, George Linnaeus (1821–81)
What I Live For.

Bannerji, Himani
Paki Go Home.

Bannerman, Frances
Upper Chamber, An.

Banning, Lex (b. 1921)
And No Regrets.
Epitaph for a Scientist.
Romancero.

Bantock, Gavin (b. 1939)
Bard.
Dirge: "Body lies under the ground."
Joy.

Banus, Maria (b. 1914)
Eighteen.
Gift Hour.
New Notebook, The.
Wedding, The.

Banville, Theodore Faullain de (1823–91)
Starry Night.

Baraka, Imamu Amiri (LeRoi Jones) (b. 1934)
After the Ball.
Agony, An. As Now.
Am/Trak.
At the National Black Assembly.
Audubon, Drafted.
Babylon Revisited.
Balboa, the Entertainer.
Ballad of the Morning Streets.
Beautiful Black Women.
Biography.
Black Art.
Black Bourgeoisie.
Black Dada Nihilismus.
Black People!
Bumi.
Cant.
Careers.
Cold Term.
Crow Jane.
Das Kapital.
Dope.
Each Morning.
Epistrophe.
Evil Nigger Waits for Lightnin'.
For Hettie.
Guerrilla Handbook, A.
Hymn for Lanie Poo, *Sels.*
I Substitute for the Dead Lecturer.
In Memory of Radio.
In One Battle.
Incident.
Invention of Comics, The.
It's Nation Time.
Ka 'Ba.
Legacy.
Leroy.
Letter to E. Franklin Frazier.
Liar, The.
Like Rousseau.
Major Bowes' Diary.
New Ark Space.
New Reality Is Better Than a New Movie!, A.
New World, The.
Numbers, Letters.
One Night Stand.
Ostriches and Grandmothers!
Poem for Black Hearts, A.
Poem for Half White College Students.
Poem for Speculative Hipsters, A.
Poem of Destiny, A, *Sels.*
Poem Some People Will Have to Understand, A.
Political Poem.
Politics of Rich Painters, The.
Preface to a Twenty Volume Suicide Note.
Pressures, The.
Red Light.
Return of the Native.
Sacred Chant for the Return of Black Spirit and Power.
Snake Eyes.
Song Form.
SOS.
Study Peace.
Tele/vision.
To a Publisher . . . Cut-out.
Turncoat, The.
W. W.
Way Out West.
We Own the Night.
Will They Cry When You're Gone, You Bet.
Young Soul.

Barakat, Saleem (b. 1951)
Crane, The, *Sels.*
Squirrel, The.

Barba, Sharon (b. 1943)
Dykes in the Garden.

Barbauld, Anna Laetitia (1743–1825)
Corsica, *Sels.*
Life.
Mouse's Petition, The.
Ode to Spring.
On General Paoli and the Corsican Struggle for Liberty.

Autobiography, Chapter XVII: Floating the Big
   Piney.
Autobiography: Last Chapter.
Baii.
Bone Yard.
Camping Out on Rainy Mountain.
Captive Stone, The.
Ex-Deputy Sheriff Remembers the Eastern
   Oklahoma Murderers, An, *Sels.*
Four Things Choctaw, *Sels.*
Halcyon Days.
Heartland.
Isuba.
La Plata, Missouri: Clear November Night.
Last Look at La Plata, Missouri.
Lying in a Yuma Saloon.
Nashoba.
Paiute Ponies.
Red Oak.
Return to La Plata, Missouri.
Season of Loss, A.
Summerfield.
Sunday Dreamer's Guide to Yarrow, Missouri,
   A.
Sweating It Out on Winding Stair Mountain.
These Damned Trees Crouch.
Tracking Rabbits: Night.
Tracking the Siuslaw Man.

Barnes, Jo (b. 1941)
Clinic Day.

Barnes, Julians (*fl.* 15th century)
Book of Hunting, *Sels.*
Time of grease beginneth at Midsummer day.
When we hunt at the roe, then shall ye see
   there.
Wheresoever ye fare by frith or by fell.

Barnes, Kate
Bear Trees, The.
Mare, A.

Barnes, William (1801–86)
All Still.
An' while I went 'ithin a train.
Bachelor, The.
Bells ov Alderburnham, The.
Be'mi'ster.
Best Man in the Vield, The, *Sels.*
Bit o' Sly Coorten, A.
Brisk Wind, A.
Burncombe Hollow.
Childhood.
Clote (Water-Lily), The.
Come!
Common a-Took In, The.
Echo, The.
Evenen in the Village.
Evening, and Maidens.
Fall, The.
False Friends-like.
Geate A-Vallen To, The.
Grammer's Shoes.
Heedless o' My Love.
In the Spring.
Jay a-Pass'd.
Jenny out from Hwome.
Leane, The.
Leaves.
Leaves a-Vallen.
Leeburn Mill.
Light or Sheade.
Lost Little Sister, The.
Lwonesomeness.
Mater Dolorosa.
May, *Sels.*
May Tree, The.
Melhill Feast.
Mother o' blossoms, and ov all.
Musings.
My Love's Guardian Angel.
My Orcha'd in Linden Lea.
Polly Be-en Upzides wi' Tom.
Railroad, The, *Sels.*
Readen ov a Head-Stwone.
Rustic Childhood.
Rwose in the Dark, The.
Sam and Bob.
Sam'el Down vrom Lon'on.

Seasons and Times.
Sheep in the Sheade.
Shellbrook.
Shep'erd Bwoy, The.
Shop o' Meat-Weare.
Sing Again Together.
Slow to Come, Quick a-Gone.
Sonnet: "In every dream thy lovely features
   rise."
Spring, The.
Storm-Wind, The.
Stwonen Steps, The.
Times o' Year.
To Me.
Tokens.
Troubles of the Day.
Turnstile, The.
Uncle an' Aunt.
Vaices That Be Gone, The.
Vield Path, The.
Vierzide Chairs, The.
Walken Hwomme at Night.
When We That Now Ha' Childern Wer
   Childern.
Which Road?
White an' Blue.
Wife a-Lost, The.
Wife a-Prais'd, A.
Wind at the Door, The.
Winter Night, A.
With you first shown to me.
Woak Hill.
Wold Clock, The.
Woodlands, The.
Zilver-Weed, The.
Zong, A.
Zummer Stream.
Zun-zet.

Barnett, Anthony (b. 1941)
After.
Apodal Stride (Cursive).
Blake or Yeats Slept with You.
Book of Mysteries, The.
Crossing.
Death.
Drops.
Far.
Fell.
Flying/ Away and.
Frozen.
Habeas Corpus.
I am abstract.
I Believe You.
I wish you would.
January.
Phrasal.
Quest.
Seventeenth of May, The.
Some Scandal That Has Floated Down from
   Higher Circles.
True Meaning.
White Mess, A.
With You.
You.

Barney, Natalie Clifford (1877–1972)
If You Want Me to Stay with You.

Barnfield [or Barnefield], Richard (1574–1629)
Affectionate Shepherd, The, *Sels.*
Ah no; nor I myselfe: though my pure love.
As it fell upon a day.
But now my Muse toyled with continuall care.
Cherry-lipped Adonis.
Cherry-lipt Adonis in his snowie shape.
Comparison of the Life of Man, A.
Cynthia, *Sels.*
Daphnis to Ganymede.
Here hold this glove (this milk-white cheveril
   glove).
Sighing, and Sadly Sitting by My Love.
Some talk of Ganymede th' Idalian boy.
Sometimes I wish that I his pillow were.
Sonnets, *Sels.*
Sporting at fancie, setting light by love.
Sweet corrall lips, where Nature's treasure lies.
Sweet Thames I honour thee, not for thou art.
Thus was my love, thus was my Ganymed.

To His Friend Master R.L., In Praise of Music
   and Poetry.
Two stars there are in one faire firmament.
Unknown Shepherd's Complaint, The.

Barnstone, Aliki (b. 1956)
Mating the Goats.
To a Friend's Child.
Windows in Providence.

Barnstone, Willis (b. 1927)
Disappearance.
Miklos Radnoti.
Rose of Blue Flesh, The.

Baro, Gene (1924–82)
Cherry.
For Hani, Aged Five, That She Be Better Able
   to Distinguish a Villain.
Street, The.
Travelling Backward.
Under the Boughs.

Barr, Isabel Harriss
Madaket Beach.

Barr, Matthias
Only a Baby Small.

Barras, Leonard
Epitaph for a Sportsman.
Mother Nature's Bloomers.

Barrax, Gerald William (b. 1933)
Black Narcissus.
Blue.
Christmas 1959 et Cetera.
Efficiency Apartment.
For a Black Poet.
For Malcolm: After Mecca.
Fourth Dance Poem.
Gift.
I Had a Terror — Since September.
Old Gory, The, *Sels.*
Red.
Scuba Diver Recovers the Body of a Drowned
   Child, The.
Singer, The.
Spirituals, Gospels.
To a Woman Who Wants Darkness and Time.
Two Figures on Canvas.
White.
Your Eyes Have Their Silence.

**Barreno, Maria Isabella. See Marias, The
Three.**

**Barret, Carlton, and Legon Cogil. See Cogil,
Legon.**

Barret, Eaton Stannard (1786–1920)
Woman.

Barrett, Wilson Agnew (1846–1904)
New England Church, A.

Barrington, Patrick (b. 1908)
I Had a Duck-billed Platypus.

Barrington, Pauline B. (b. 1876)
White Iris, A.

Barrios, Miguel de (1625–1701)
"Daniel and Abigail."

Barrow, Jedediah
You Call That a Ts'ing; a Letter.

Barrows, Anita (b. 1947)
Emigration.
Letter to a Friend in an Unknown Place.
Reflections.

Barry, Michael J. (1817–89)
Hymn of Freedom.

Barry, Noëline
Red-winged Lourie, The.

Barry, Sebastian (b. 1955)
Call.
Cassibus Impositis Venor.
Christ-in-the-Woods.
Ending, An.
February Town, The.
Indian River, The.
Pardon of Assisi, The.
Return, The.
Room of Rhetoric, The.
Ropley District.
Seasonal Aunt, A.
Sketch from the Great Bull Wall.

Cat, The.
Cats.
Correspondences.
Damned Women.
Death of Lovers, The.
Don Juan in Hell.
Élévation.
Epilogue: "With heart at rest I climbed the citadel's."
Giantess [, The].
Harmonie du Soir.
Intimate Associations.
Invitation to a Journey.
Inward Conversation.
Jewels, The.
Landscape.
Le Balcon.
Les Hiboux.
Litany to Satan.
Meditation.
Metamorphoses of the Vampire.
Parfum Exotique.
Peace, Be at Peace, O Thou My Heaviness.
Seven Old Men, The.
Which One Is Genuine?
Women Damned.

Bauer, Steven
White Cedar Swamp.

Baugh, Edward (b. 1936)
Carpenter's Complaint, The.
Colour-Scheme.
Country Dance.
Truth and Consequences.

Baughan, Blanche Edith (1870–1958)
Bush Section, A, *Sels.*
Logs, at the door, by the fence; broadcast over the paddock.
Maui's Fish, *Sels.*
Old Place, The.
Toward the dawn.

Baum, Peter (1869–1916)
Horror.
Psalms of Love.

Baumel, Judith (b. 1956)
Fish Speaking Veneto Dialect.
New York City World's Fairs, 1939 and 1964, The.
Orcio and Fiasco.
Proper Distance and Proper Time.

Bax, Clifford (1886–1962)
Turn Back, O Man.

Baxter, Danu
Goodnight God.

Baxter, Elizabeth
In Your Absence.

Baxter, James Keir (1926–72)
Apple Tree, The.
Autumn Testament, *Sels.*
Ballad of the Stonegut Sugar Works.
Bar Room Conversation.
Bay, The.
Bees that have been hiving above the church pond, The.
Buried Stream, The.
Colin, you can tell my words are crippled now.
Cressida, *Sels.*
Dark Welcome, The.
Dentist's Window, A.
East Coast Journey.
Evidence at the Witch Trials.
Family Photograph 1939, A.
Five Sestinas, *Sels.*
From an old house shaded with macrocarpas.
Haere Ra.
Harry Fat and Uncle Sam.
In the Lecture Room.
Inflammable Woman, The.
Jerusalem Sonnets, *Sels.*
Lament for Barney Flanagan.
Mandrakes for Supper.
New Zealand.
News from a Pacified Area.
Obsequy for Dylan Thomas.
On the Death of Her Body.

Pig Island Letters, *Sels.*
Private Conference of Harry Fat, The.
Prize giving Speech.
Rata blooms explode, the bow-legged tomcat, The.
Rope for Harry Fat, A.
Small grey cloudy louse that nests in my beard, The.
Spider crouching on the ledge above the sink, The.
Spring Song of A Civil Servant.
To a Print of Queen Victoria.
To wish to climb a ladder to the loft.
Virginia Lake.
When I was only semen in a gland.
Wild Bees.
Yesterday I planted garlic.

Baxter, Richard (1615–91)
Now it belongs not to my care.
Psalm of Praise, A, *Sels.*
Ye holy Angels bright.

Baykov, Hala
Café.

Baylebridge, William (Charles William Blocksidge) (1883–1942)
All that I am to Earth Belongs.
Brain, the blood, the busy thews, The.
Choir of spirits on a cloud, A.
God, to get the clay that stayed me.
I worshipped, when my veins were fresh.
Life's Testament, *Sels.*
Love Redeemed, *Sels.*
Quiet moon, immaculate of face, The.
This miracle in me I scan.

Bayliss, John Clifford (b. 1919)
Reported Missing.

Bayly, Thomas Haynes (1797–1839)
Mistletoe Bough, The.
Novel of High Life, A.
Oh, No! We Never Mention Her.
She Wore a Wreath of Roses.

Baynes, A. H.
Limerick: "So obese is my cousin from Hendon."
Limerick: "There was a young girl from a Mission."

Beach, Joseph Warren (b. 1880)
Dropping Your Aitches.
Horatian Ode.

Beach, Seth Curtis (1837–1925)
Mysterious Presence! Source of All.
Thou One in All, Thou All in One.

"Beachcomber". *See* Morton, John Bingham.

Beadle, Samuel Alfred (1857–1932)
After Church.
Lines: "How I love country you have heard."
Lines to Caste.
Words.

Beardsley, Aubrey (1872–98)
Ballad of a Barber, The.
Three Musicians, The.

Beasley, Bruce
Childhood.
Reliquary, The.
Sleeping in Santo Spirito.

Beatrice, [or Beatritz or Beatriz], Countess de Die [or Dia] (*fl.* late 12th century)
Estat ai en greu cossirier.
Handsome friend, charming and kind.
I Must Sing of That.
I sing a song reluctantly.
Lately I've felt a grave concern.
My true love makes me happy.

Beattie, James (1735–1803)
Edwin, The Minstrel.
Epitaph, Intended for Himself.
Epitaph: "Like thee I once have stemm'd the sea of life."
Minstrel, The, *Sels.*
Question, The.
To Mr. Alexander Ross.
Youth of a Poet, The.

Beattie, James Hay (1768–90)
On the Author of the *Treatise of Human Nature.*

Beaumont, Francis (1584–1616)
Masque of the Inner Temple and Gray's Inne, The, *Sels.*
Mr. Francis Beaumont's Letter to Ben Johnson.
Shake off your heavy trance!
True Beauty.
Upon Master Edmund Spenser.
Ye [*or* You] should stay longer if we durst.

Beaumont, Francis *and* **William Basse**
Here's a world of pomp and state.
Lines on the Tombs in Westminster.
On the Tombs in Westminster Abbey, *Sels.*

Beaumont, Francis (1584–1616) *and* **John Fletcher**
Away, Delights.
Bridal Song: "Cynthia, to thy power."
Bridal Song: "Hold back thy hours."
Captain, The, *Sels.*
Come, sleep.
Come, You Whose Loves Are Dead.
Cupid's Revenge, *Sels.*
Jillian of Berry.
Knight of the Burning Pestle, The, *Sels.*
Lay a garland on my hearse.
Letter to Ben Jonson, A.
Lovers Rejoice!
Love's Cure, *Sels.*
Maid's Tragedy, The, *Sels.*
Master Francis Beaumont to Ben Johnson, *Sels.*
Mirth.
Month of May, The.
Nose, nose, jolly red nose.
Song: "Turn, turn thy beauteous face away."
Tell Me Dearest, What is Love?
What things have we seen.
Woman-Hater, The, *Sels.*

Beaumont, Sir John (1583–1627)
Bosworth Field, *Sels.*
Description of Love, A.
Epitaph upon My Dear Brother, Francis Beaumont, An.
Of His Dear Son, Gervase.
Of My Dear Son, Gervase Beaumont, *Sels.*
Richard III's Speech.
To His Late Majesty Concerning the True Form of English Poetry.
Upon a Funeral.

Beaumont, Joseph (1616–99)
Cheat, The.
Garden, The.
Gentle Check, The.
Gnat, The.
Hourglass, The.
Love's Mystery.
Morning Hymn.
Whiteness, or Chastity.

Beauvais, Phyllis (Phyllis Harris)
Furniture.
Outside.
Under Your Voice, among Legends.

Beauveau, Marie-Françoise-Catherine de, Marquise de Boufflers (1711–86)
Air: Sentir avec Ardeur.

Beaver, Bruce (b. 1928)
Entertainer, The.
God knows what was done to you.
I shop in the streets of my hometown with/ my family.
I welcome the anonymity of the middle years.
Lauds and Plaints, *Sels.*
Letters to Live Poets, *Sels.*
Mid-day and a heat haze over all.
Our street is known as the street of widows.
Soft misty rain and a drop of thirty degrees.
Sou'wester whips the day awake, The.
Three anti-depressants and one diuretic a day.
Three images of dying stick in my mind like morbid transfers.
To stand hushed an hour or so.
Today the self-destroying anger.
Walking in late afternoon.

Beccadelli, Antonio. *See* **"Panormitanus."**

Beck, Victor Emanuel (1894–1963)
Sifting.

Becker, Charlotte
Door-Bell, The.
Becker, Edwin (d. 1925)
Mother's Day.
Becker, John
Are You a Marsupial?
Feather or Fur.
Becker, Robin
Bath, The.
Dangers.
Gardener, The.
In Pompano Beach, Florida.
Living in the Barn.
Medical Science.
Story I Like to Tell, The.
Beckett, Samuel (1906–89)
Age is when to a man.
Alba.
Asylum under my tread all this day.
Cascando.
Dieppe.
Echo's Bones, *Sels.*
Enueg I.
Enueg II.
Gnome.
I Would Like My Love to Die.
Malacoda.
My way is in the sand flowing.
Ooftish.
Saint-Lô.
Vladimir's Song.
Vulture, The.
Waiting for Godot, *Sels.*
What would I do without this world faceless
   incurious.
Words and Music, *Sels.*
Beckford, Slim *and* **Sam Blackwood**
Johnny Tek Away Mi Wife.
Beckford, William (1759–1844)
Ode: "To orisons, the midnight bell."
Beckh, Harold (d. 1916)
Soldier's Cigarette, The.
Beckovic, Matija (b. 1939)
If I Knew I'd Bear Myself Proudly.
No One Will Write Poetry.
Two Worlds.
Yevtushenko.
Bécquer, Gustavo Adolfo (1836–70)
They Closed Her Eyes.
Beddo, Frank
Jeff Buckner.
Beddoes, Thomas Lovell (1803–49)
Alpine Spirit's Song.
Another.
Ballad of Human Life.
Bridal Song to Amala.
Bride's Tragedy, The, *Sels.*
Crocodile, A.
Death Sweet.
Death's Jest Book, *Sels.*
Dirge: "Swallow leaves her nest, The."
Dirge Written for a Drama.
Dream-Pedlary.
Drink, Britannia.
Envoi: "Who findeth comfort in the stars and
   flowers."
Fair and bright assembly, A: never strode.
Fantastic Simile, A.
Fragments Intended for the Dramas, *Sels.*
Humble Beginnings.
Hymn: "And many voices marshalled in one
   hymn."
If thou wilt ease thine heart.
Ivory Gate, The, *Sels.*
Lake, A.
Last Man, The, *Sels.*
Lines Written in a Blank Leaf of the
   Prometheus Unbound.
Lord Alcohol.
Mighty Thoughts of an Old World, The.
New Cecilia, The.
New Dodo, The Isabrand's Song.
Old Adam, the Carrion Crow.
Old Ghost, The.
Oviparous Tailor, The.

Phantom-Wooer, The.
Poor Old Pilgrim Misery.
Resurrection Song.
Second Brother, The, *Sels.*
Silenus in Proteus.
Song: "How many times do I love thee, dear?"
Song: "Strew not earth with empty stars."
Song of the Stygian Naiades.
Song on the Water.
Sonnet: To Tartar, a Terrier Beauty.
Squats on a toad-stool under a tree.
Threnody.
To Night.
To Sea.
To Silence.
Torrismond, *Sels.*
We Do Lie beneath the Grass.
"Bede, Cuthbert" (Edward Bradley) (1827–89)
Entrance Exams.
Bede, The Venerable (c.672–c.735)
Bede's Death Song.
Hymn: "Hymn of glory let us sing, A."
Prayer of the Venerable Bede.
**Bedford, Lucy Harrington, Countess of
   Bedford.** *See* **Harington, Lucy, Countess
   of Bedford.**
Beebe, Lucius (1902–66)
Quid Restat.
Beecher, John (1904–80)
I read your testimony and I thought.
To Alexander Meiklejohn, *Sels.*
Beeching, Henry Charles (1859–1919)
First come I. My name is Jowett.
Going Down Hill on a Bicycle.
I am featly-tripping Lee.
Prayers.
Beeching, Henry Charles *and* **John Bowyer
   Nichols**
I am Branson; Nature's laws.
Beedome, Thomas (d. 1641?)
Petition, The.
Question and Answer, The.
To the Noble Sir Francis Drake.
Beer, Christina (b. 1945)
Fox Glove Song.
1974 — The Sounds.
Waiheke 1972 — Rocky Bay.
Beer, Morris Abel (1887?–1936)
Church in the Heart, The.
Beer, Patricia (b. 1924)
Birthday Poem from Venice.
Christmas Carols.
Christmas Eve.
Christmas Tree, The.
Creed of Mr. Nicholas Culpeper.
Dilemma.
Fifth Sense, The.
Gallery Shepherds.
In a Country Museum.
In the Cathedral.
Jane Austen at the Window.
Leaping into the Gulf.
Letter, The.
Lion Hunts.
Middle Age.
Postilion Has Been Struck by Lightning, The.
Return to Sedgemoor.
Victorian Trains, *Sels.*
Waterloo.
Whistle blows, The train moves, The.
Witch.
Beerbohm, Max (1872–1956)
Addition to Kipling's "The Dead King (Edward
   VII), 1910."
After Hilaire Belloc.
Ballade Tragique à Double Refrain.
Brave Rover.
Chorus of a Song That Might Have Been
   Written by Albert Chevalier.
Elegy on Any Lady by George Moore.
Epitaph for G. B. Shaw.
Luncheon, A.
On the Imprint of the First English Edition of
   "The Works of Max Beerbohm."
Police Station Ditties.

Prayer, A.
Road to Zoagli, The.
Same Cottage — But Another Song, of Another
   Season.
Savonarola ("Savonarola looks more grim
   today").
Thomas Hardy and A. E. Housman.
Time, you thief, who love to get.
Vague Lyric by G. M.
Beerbohm, Max *and* **William Rothenstein**
Eli the Thatcher.
Sonnet to the "Most Distinguished Chancellor"
   That Oxford Has Had.
Beer-Hofmann, Richard (1866–1945)
Evil Man, An!
Graf von Charolais, Der, *Sels.*
Jacob's Destiny.
Jacob's Dream, *Sels.*
Beers, Ethel Lynn (1827–79)
All Quiet along the Potomac.
Weighing the Baby.
Which Shall It Be?
Beeton, Douglas Ridley (b. 1929)
Autumn.
Begbie, Harold (1871–1929)
Fall In.
Begbie, Janet
I shouted for blood as I ran, brother.
Behan, Brendan (1923–64)
Repentance.
Behn, Aphra (1640–89)
Abdelazer, *Sels.*
Amyntas Led Me to a Grove.
And Forgive Us Our Trespasses.
Cabal at Nickey Nackey's, The.
Coquette, The.
Defiance, The.
Disappointment, The.
Dream, The.
Dutch Lover, The, *Sels.*
Emperor of the Moon, *Sels.*
Epitaph on the Tombstone of a Child, the Last
   of Seven That Died Before.
In Imitation of Horace.
Letter to a Brother of the Pen in Tribulation,
   A.
Love in fantastic [*or* fantastique] triumph sat
   [*or* sate *or* satt].
Love's Witness.
Lucky Chance, The, *Sels.*
Not to sigh and to be tender.
On *a* Juniper-Tree, Cut Down to Make Busks.
On Her Loving Two Equally.
On Mr. Dryden, Renegade.
Sir Patient Fancy, *Sels.*
Silvio's Complaint: A Song, to a Fine Scotch
   Tune.
Song: "Ah false Amyntas, can that hour."
Song: "All joy to mortals, joy and mirth."
Song: "Curse upon that faithless maid, A."
Song: "How strongly does my passion flow."
Song: "Oh! Love, that stronger art than wine."
Song: "When maidens are young, and in their
   spring."
Song by the Wavering Nymph.
Thousand Martyrs I Have Made, A.
To Alexis in Answer to His Poem against
   Fruition.
To Mrs. W. on Her Excellent Verses.
To the Fair Clarinda, Who Made Love to Me,
   Imagin'd More than Woman.
Voyage to the Isle of Love, A, *Sels.*
What has poor Woman done, that she must be.
When you love, or speak of it.
Behn, Harry (1898–1973)
Christmas Carol: "Angel told Mary, An."
Christmas Morning.
Flowers.
Gnome, The.
Growing Up.
Hallowe'en.
Invitation.
Kite, The.
Mr. Pyme.
New Little Boy, The.

Sipsop's Song.
Smile, The.
Soft Snow.
Some people admire the work of a fool.
Song by an Old Shepherd.
Song: "Fresh from the dewy hill, the merry year."
Song: "Love and harmony combine."
Song: "Memory, hither come."
Song: "My silks and fine array."
Song of Enitharmon.
Song of Liberty, A.
Songs of Experience, *Sels.*
Songs of Innocence, *Sels.*
Spring.
Suction's Anthem.
Sword sang on the barren heath, The.
Take Thy Bliss, O Man.
Thel's Motto.
Then Milton rose up from the heaven of Albion ardorous!
They said this mystery shall never cease.
This wine-press is call'd war on earth.
Thou hearest the nightingale begin the song of spring.
Tiger! [*or* Tyger], The.
To Autumn.
To English Connoisseurs.
To Flaxman.
To forgive enemies Hayley [*or* H.] does pretend.
To God.
To Hunt.
To Morning.
To My Friend Butts I Write.
To Nobodaddy.
To Spring.
To Summer.
To the Evening Star.
To the Muses.
To Tirzah.
To William Hayley.
To Winter.
Truth that's told with bad intent, A.
Vala, Night the Ninth Being the Last Judgment.
Vala; or The Four Zoas, *Sels.*
Vision of Beulah, The ("There is a place where contrarieties are equally true").
Vision of Christ that thou dost see, The.
Visions of the Daughters of Albion.
Visions of the Daughters of Albion, *Sels.*
Visions, *Sels.*
Voice of the Ancient Bard, The.
Voice of the Devil, The.
War Song to Englishmen, A.
Was Jesus Chaste? or did he.
Was Jesus Humble? or did he.
What is it men in women do require?
When a Man Has Married a Wife.
When Klopstock England defied.
When old corruption first begun.
Why Should I Care for the Men of Thames?
Wild Flower's Song.
Wild Thyme, The.
With Happiness Stretch[e]d across the Hills.

Blaker, Margaret
Pippa Passes, But I Can't Get Around This Truck.

Blamire, Susanna (1747–94)
Auld Robin Forbes.
Epistle to Her Friends at Gartmore.
From where dark clouds of curling smoke arise.
I've Gotten a Rock, I've Gotten a Reel.
O Jenny Dear.
Siller Croun, The.
Stoklewath; or, The Cumbrian Village, *Sels.*
Wey, Ned, Man!
When Home We Return.
Written on a Gloomy Day, in Sickness.

Blanchard, Edward Laman (Edward Laman Blanchard) (1804–45)
Ode to the Human Heart.

Blanchard, Ferdinand Q. (1876–1968)
O Child of Lowly Manger Birth,
Word of God, Across the Ages.

Blanco, Alberto (b. 1951)
Horse by Moonlight.
Parakeets, The.

Bland, James A. (1854–1911)
Carry Me Back to Old Virginny.

Bland, Peter (b. 1934)
To a Home-town Conscript Posted Overseas.

Blandiana, Ana (b. 1942)
Couple, The.
Everything.
I need only fall asleep/ to return.

Blanding, Don (1894–1957)
Aloha Oe.
Vagabond House.

Blank, Arapera Hineira (b. 1932)
Yearning, A.

Blankner, Frederika
Remainder.

Blaser, Robin (b. 1925)
4 Part Geometry Lesson, A.
Herons.
Image-Nation 13 (the Telephone).
Image-Nation 3.
Image-Nation (the Poēsis).
Poem: "And when I pay death's duty."
Poem by the Charles River.
Poem: "For years I've heard."
Suddenly.

Blaustein, Rahel. *See* **Rachel [*or* Rahel].**

Blenkhorn, Ada
Heavenly Stranger, The.

Blight, John (b. 1913)
Conflagration.
Coral Reef, The.
Cormorants.
Death of a Whale.
Disarrayed, The.
Down from the Country.
Evolution.
Gate's Open, The.
Letter, The.
Mangrove.
Morgan.
Oyster-Eaters, The.
Pearl Perch.
Tenant at Number 9.

Blind, Mathilde (1841–96)
After-Glow, The.
Dead, The.
Dost thou remember ever, for my sake.
I charge you, O winds of the West, O.
Internal Firesides.
Love in Exile, *Sels.*
On a Forsaken Lark's Nest.
Reapers.
Sower, The.

"Blind, Harry." *See* **Henry the Minstrel.**

Blishen, Edward (b. 1920)
Abroad Thoughts.
Amid the Derringers I Ride.

Bliss, H. W.
Understanding.

Bliss, Philip Paul (1838–76)
Almost Persuaded.

Bliss, William
Limerick: "If no Pain were, how judge we of Pleasure?"

Blitzstein, Marc (1905–64)
Art for Art's Sake.
Cradle Will Rock, The, *Sels.*

Blixen, Karen. *See* **"Dinesen, Isak."**

Bloch, Alice (b. 1947)
Six Years.

Bloch, Anne
Absent Friends.
Dreams.
On Listening to a Bus Conductor.
Pied à Terre.
Separation, *Sels.*

Bloch, Chana (b. 1940)
I and Thou.
In wings and starched.
Magnificat.

Patriarch in black takes, The.
Rising to Meet It.
Sacrifice, The, *Sels.*
Survivors.
White Petticoats.
Yom Kippur.

Bloch, Jean-Richard (1884–1947)
Idea of a Swimmer.

Block, Alexander
Willow-Boughs, The.

Block, Louis James (b. 1851)
Final Struggle, The.
New World, The, *Sels.*

Block, Ron (b. 1925)
Ballade of the Back Road.

Blockcolski, Lew
After the First Frost.
Flicker, The.
Flint Hills, The.
49 Stomp, The.
Indian Love Song.
Langston Hughes.
My Dream.
Peyote Vision.
Playing Pocahontas.
Powwow remnants.
Reservation Special.
Urban Experience, The: Part One.
Urban Experience, The: Part Two.
Wisga.
Woyi, The.

Blocksidge, Charles William. *See* **Baylebridge, William.**

Blodgett, E. D. (b. 1935)
Fossil.
Snails.

Blok, Aleksandr [*or* Alexander] Aleksandrovich (1880–1921)
Black Night./ White snow.
Dances of Death, *Sels.*
Kite, The.
Night, street, a lamp, a chemist's window.
Red Glow in the Sky, A.
Russia.
Scythians, The.
Twelve, The, *Sels.*

Bloom, Valerie (b. 1956)
Longsight Market.
Wat A Rain.
Wha Fe Call I'.

Bloomfield, Robert (1766–1823)
Banks of Wye, The, *Sels.*
Coracle Fishers, The.
Farmer's Boy, The, *Sels.*
Health! I seek thee; dost thou love.
Meandering Wye.
Moonlight . . . Scattered Clouds.
Ploughman's Horse, The.
Shooter's Hill, *Sels.*
Winter, *Sels.*

Bloomgarden, Solomon. *See* **"Yehoash."**

Blount, Annabella (*fl.* 1700–1741)
Cure for Poetry, A.

Blount, Charles (1654–93)
Dialogue between King William and the Late King James on the Banks of the Boyne, A.

Blount, Roy, Jr. (b. 1941)
Against Broccoli.
For the Record.
Gryll's State.

Blue Cloud, Peter (b. 1933)
Autumn Equinox.
Bear: A Totem Dance As Seen by Raven.
Composition.
Coyote Makes the First People.
Coyote Man and the Young Lady.
Crazy Horse Monument.
Death Chant.
Hawk Nailed to a Barn Door.
Oche Iron.
Old Man's Lazy, The.
Rattle.
Spring Equinox.
Summer Solstice.

Sweat Song.
To-ta Ti-om.
Turtle.
Walking through twisted hollow pathways.
Winter Solstice.
Within the Seasons, *Sels.*
Wolf.
Yellowjacket.

Blum, Etta (b. 1908)
When You Reach the Hilltop the Sky Is on Top
of You.

Blumenthal, Michael C. (b. 1949)
Abandoning Your Car in a Snowstorm:
Rosslyn, Virginia.
Back from the Word-Processing Course, I Say
to My Old Typewriter.
Elephants Dying, The.
I Have Lived This Way for Years and Do Not
Wish to Change.
Inventors.
Juliek's Violin.
Litrajure of Everyday Life, The.
Man Lost by a River, A.
No More Kissing — AIDS Everywhere.
Washington Heights, 1959.
Who Will Live in Our Houses When We Die?
Wishful Thinking.

Blumenthal, Walter Hart (1883–1969)
Da Silva Gives the Cue.

Blumgarten, Solomon. *See* **"Yehoash."**
Blumgarten, Solomon. *See* **"Yehoash."**
Blumstein, Rahel. *See* **Rachel [or Rahel].**

Blundell, G. J.
Squire Squint, shooting at a pheasant.

Blunden, Edmund (1896–1974)
Almswomen.
Ancre at Hamel: Afterwards, The.
At the Great Wall of China.
Barn, The.
Come On, My Lucky Lads.
Concert Party: Busseboom.
Cottage at Chigasaki, The.
Country God, A.
Death Mask of John Clare, The.
Departure.
Eastern Tempest.
Escape.
Forefathers.
Giant Puffball, The.
Gouzeaucourt: The Deceitful Calm.
Guard's Mistake, The.
Hurrying Brook, The.
Idlers, The.
In Festubert.
La Quinque Rue.
Late Light.
Lonely Love.
Midnight Skaters, The.
Mole Catcher.
1916 Seen from 1921.
Pike, The.
Poor Man's Pig, The.
Preparations for Victory.
Psalm: "O God, in whom my deepest being
dwells."
Recovery, The.
Reliques, *Sels.*
Report on Experience.
Survival, The.
Third Ypres.
Two Voices.
Vlamertinghe: Passing the Château, July 1917.
Winter: East Anglia.
Zonnebeke Road, The.

Blunt, Wilfrid Scawen (1840–1922)
As to His Choice of Her.
Deeds That Might Have Been, The.
Depreciating Her Beauty.
Esther [a Young Man's Tragedy], *Sels.*
Farewell: "Juliet, farewell. I would not be
forgiven."
Farewell to Juliet ("I see you, Juliet, still, with
your straw hat").
Gibraltar.
He who has once been happy is for aye.

Honour Dishonoured.
I Will Not Tell the Secrets.
In Vinculis, *Sels.*
Love Sonnets of Proteus, The, *Sels.*
Nocturne: "Moon has gone to her rest, The."
Oasis of Sidi Khaled, The.
Old Squire, The.
St. Valentine's Day.
Satan Absolved: a Victorian Mystery, *Sels.*
Smoke of their foul dens, The.
Storm in Summer, A.
When I hear laughter from a tavern door.
Wisdom of Merlyn, The, *Sels.*
Woman with a Past, A.
Wouldst thou be wise, O Man? At the knees of
a woman begin.

Bluwstein, Rahel. *See* **Rachel [or Rahel].**
Bly, Robert (b. 1926)
After Drinking All Night with a Friend, We Go
Out in a Boat at Dawn to See Who Can
Write the Best Poem.
After Long Busyness.
After the Industrial Revolution, All Things
Happen at Once.
After Working.
Afternoon Sleep.
Asian Peace Offers Rejected without
Publication.
At Mid-Ocean.
August Rain.
Awakening.
Breath, The.
Christmas Eve Service at Midnight at St.
Michael's.
Clear Air of October, The.
Come with Me.
Counting Small-boned Bodies.
Danger of Loss, The.
Dead Seal near McClure's Beach, The.
Depression.
Doors Are Closed, The.
Dream of Suffocation, A.
Driving My Parents Home at Christmas.
Driving through Minnesota during the Hanoi
Bombings.
Driving to Town Late to Mail a Letter.
Driving toward the Lac Qui Parle River.
Evening When the Full Moon Rose as the Sun
Set, An.
Evolution from the Fish.
Executive's Death, The.
For My Son, Noah, Ten Years Old.
Great Society, The.
Hatred of Men with Black Hair.
Hearing Men Shout at Night on MacDougal
Street.
Hermit, The.
Hollow Tree, A.
Hunting Pheasants in a Cornfield.
Hurrying Away from the Earth.
In a Mountain Cabin in Norway.
In a Train.
In Rainy September.
Insect Heads.
Johnson's Cabinet Watched by Ants.
Kneeling Down to Look into a Culvert.
Late at Night During a Visit of Friends.
Laziness and Silence.
Leonardo's Secret.
Listening to the Köln Concert.
Looking at a Dead Wren in My Hand.
Looking at a Dry Canadian Thistle Brought In
from the Snow.
Looking at New-fallen Snow from a Train.
Looking at Some Flowers.
Looking into a Face.
Looking into a Tide Pool.
Melancholia.
Mourning Pablo Neruda.
My Father at 85.
My Father's Wedding.
Night.
November Day at McClure's.
Old Boards.
Old dog bends his head listening, The.
Origin of the Praise of God, The.

Passing an Orchard by Train.
Poem against the Rich.
Poem in Three Parts.
Prodigal Son, The.
Puritan on His Honeymoon, The.
Reading in Fall Rain.
Romans Angry about the Inner World.
Schoolcraft's Diary Written on the Missouri:
1830.
Shack Poem.
Silence.
Six Winter Privacy Poems.
Sleet Storm on the Merritt Parkway.
Small Bird's Nest Made of White Reed Fiber,
A.
Snowbanks North of the House.
Snowfall in the Afternoon.
Solitude Late at Night in the Woods.
Such Different Wants.
Surprised by Evening.
Taking the Hands of Someone You Love.
Teeth Mother Naked at Last, The.
Thinking of "The Autumn Fields."
Those Being Eaten by America.
Three Kinds of Pleasures.
Three Presidents.
To President bush at the Start of the Gulf War.
Turning Away from Lies.
Two Choral Stanzas.
Two Translations from Kabir, *Sels.*
Visiting Emily Dickinson's Grave with Robert
Francis.
Waking from Sleep.
Watching Television.
Water under the Earth.
Watering the Horse.
When the Dumb Speak.
Written Forty Miles South of a Spreading City.
Written in Dejection near Rome.

Blyth, Moira
First of all people was Adam, The.

Blyton, Enid (1897–1968)
Fairy Music.
Field-Mouse, The.
What Piggy-Wig Found.
Winter.

Boa, Maria Amalia Fonte. *See* **Fonte Boa,
Maria Amalia.**

Boake, Barcroft Henry (1866–92)
Allegory, An.
At Devlin's Siding.
Digger's Song, The.
Where the Dead Men Lie.

Bobrowski, Johannes (1917–65)
Cathedral 1941.
Childhood.
Kaunas 1941.
Latvian Autumn, The.
Latvian Songs.
Memorial for a Fisherman.
North Russian Town.
On the Jewish Dealer A.S.
Place of Fire.
Spoor in the Sand, The.
Volga Towns, The.
When the Rooms.
Wood House over the Wilia, The.

Boccaccio, Giovanni (1313–75)
Inscription for a Portrait of Dante.
Nymphs of Fiesole, *Sels.*
Of Fiammetta Singing.
Of His Last Sight of Fiammetta.
Of Three Girls and of Their Talk.
Sonnets, *Sels.*
To Dante in Paradise, after Fiammetta's Death.
To One Who Had Censured His Public
Exposition of Dante.

Bock, Frederick (b. 1916)
Big, Fat Summer — and the Lean and Hard.
Desert, The.

Bode, Carl
Requiem: "So. They and I are back from the
outside."

Bode, John E.
To the End.

Bodecker, N. M. (b. 1922)
Cats and Dogs.
First Snowflake.
Garden Calendar.
Hurry, Hurry, Mary Dear!
Miss Bitter.
Mr. 'Gator.
Mr. Slatter.
One Year.
Radish.
Small Rains.
Snowman Sniffles.
When Skies are Low and Days are Dark.

Bodenheim, Maxwell (1893–1954)
Advice to a Forest.
Death.
Lynched Negro.
Negroes.
Poem: "O men, walk on the hills."
Poem to Negro and Whites.
To an Enemy.
Upper Family.

Bodker, Cecil (b. 1927)
Calendar.
Fury's Field.
Self-Portrait.

Boe, Marilyn J.
Sunday Afternoon at the State Hospital.

Boethius (Anicius Manlius Severinus Boethius) (480–524)
Alas, his mind is sunk.
Alas, the ignorance of unhappy men.
All human kind on earth.
Consolation of Philosophy, The, *Sels*.
Happy he whose eyes have view'd.
Happy that first white age! when wee.
Happy, too happy was the world.
Happy Too Much.
He that hath set his headlong heart.
He who has made his reckoning with life.
Heu quam precipiti.
Hither, O captives, hither let you come.
Huc omnes pariter.
New Year's Eve.
O Father, give the spirit power to climb.
O Maker of the starry world.
O thou whose pow'r o'er moving worlds presides.
O Thou whose reason guides the universe.
Songs I wrote when I was young and ardent, The.
Stars hidden by dark clouds.
Then night was shaken from me.
There is no race of men.
This bird was happy once in the high trees.
This concord tempers then the elements.
Though countless as the grains of sand.
What pleasure in such vehement commotion.
Who thought in high midsummer.

Bogan, Louise (1897–1970)
After the Persian.
Alchemist, The.
Animal, Vegetable and Mineral.
Betrothed.
Cartography.
Cassandra.
Come, Break with Time.
Crossed Apple, The.
Crows, The.
Daemon, The.
Decoration.
Didactic Piece.
Dragonfly, The.
Dream, The.
Evening in the Sanitarium.
Frightened Man, The.
Henceforth, from the Mind.
Hypocrite Swift.
I Saw Eternity.
Juan's Song.
Knowledge.
Last Hill in a Vista.
Late.
M., Singing.
Man Alone.
Medusa.

Meeting, The.
Men Loved Wholly beyond Wisdom.
Musician.
Night.
Old Countryside.
Packet of Letters.
Putting to Sea.
Question in a Field.
Roman Fountain.
Several Voices out of a Cloud.
Simple Autumnal.
Single Sonnet.
Sleeping Fury, The.
Song for a Lyre.
Song for the Last Act.
Spirit's Song.
Statue and Birds.
To an Artist, to Take Heart.
To Be Sung on the Water.
To My Brother.
Variation on a Sentence.
Women.
Zone.

Bogin, George (1920–1988)
Abraham.
Pitchipoi.

Bogle, Eric (1822–99)
Band Played Waltzing Matilda, The.
No Man's Land.
Now I'm Easy.

Boileau-Despéaux, Nicolas (1636–1711)
L'Art Poetique, *Sels*.
Waller came last, but was the first whose art.
You, then, that would the comic laurels wear.

Boimwall, Rachel (b. 1913)
Lifelong.

Boker, George Henry (1823–90)
Awaking of the Poetic Faculty, The.
Ballad of New Orleans, The.
Ballad of Sir John Franklin, A.
Battle of Lookout Mountain, The.
Before Vicksburg.
Black Regiment, The.
Countess Laura.
Crossing at Fredericksburg, The.
Cruise of the *Monitor*, The.
Dirge for a Soldier.
God to Thee We Humbly Bow.
Hooker's Across!
Lincoln.
Love Is That Orbit.
On Board the *Cumberland*.
Sonnets, *Sels*.
Upon the Hill before Centreville.
Varuna, The.
Zagonyi.

Bolamba, Antoine-Roger (b. 1913)
Bonguemba.
Esanzo.
In a Storm.

Boland, Eavan (b. 1944)
Achill Woman, The.
Black Lace Fan My Mother Gave Me, The.
Child of Our Time.
Famine Road, The.
From the Painting "Back from Market" by Chardin.
Glass King, The.
I Remember.
In Her Own Image.
Irish Childhood in England, An: 1951.
It's a Woman's World.
Journey, The.
New Territory.
Nocturne.
Ode to Suburbia.
Oral Tradition, The.
Song: "Where in blind files."
War Horse, The.
Woman in Kitchen.

Bolat, Salih (b. 1956)
My Share.

Bold, Alan (b. 1943)
Malfeasance, The.
Special Theory of Relativity, A.

That's Life?

Bold, Henry (1627–83)
Song: "Chloris, forbear a while."
Song: "Fire, fire."

Boleyn, Anne (1507–36)
Defiled Is My Name Full Sore.
Remember me when you do pray.

Boleyn, George (d. 1536)
O Death, Rock Me Asleep.

Bolger, Dermot (b. 1959)
Amsterdam.
Bluebells for Grainne.
Captain of a Space Ship.
Country Girl, The.
Dublin Girl, Mountjoy, 1984.
Finglas Lilies.
Frankenstein in the Markets.
Ghosts in the Ark, The.
Last night in swirling colour we danced again.
Man Who Stepped Out of Feeling, The.
1966.
Scarecrow.
Singer, The.
Snuff Movies.
Stardust Sequence, The, *Sels*.
Woman's Daughter, The.

Bolles, Matthew (1769–1838)
Here, Lord, Retired, I Bow in Prayer.

Bolton, Edmund (1575?–1633?)
As to the blooming prime.
Palinode, A.

Bolton, Frank
Insult before Gift-Giving.

Bolton, Sarah Knowles (1841–1916)
His Monument.
Inevitable, The.
Influence.
Now.

Bonallack, B. G.
That night we blew our guns. We placed a shell.

Bonar, Horatius (1808–90)
Be True [*or* Be True Thyself].
Here, O my Lord, I see Thee face to face.
Length of Days.
Master's Touch, The.
More of Thee.
My Prayer.
This Do in Remembrance of Me, *Sels*.
Thy Way, Not Mine.

Boncho (Nozawa Boncho) (d. 1714)
Abandoned boat, An.
Ash pail has stopped dripping, The.
At an eagle's nest on dead camphor.
At this dilapidated hut.
Blowing wind's companion, A.
Crow wipes its beak on young grass, A.
Dark night: a child begins weeping.
Elongated line of a river, An.
Every bit of water in the paddies.
Fording a stream I stop.
From the porch, in various ways.
I try to call him back.
In a shower, black chopped wood.
In the heat haze a fox.
Meeting Etsujin.
Not a Bird Singing, the Mountain Is All the More Quiet.
Patch of cloud rides the moon tonight, A.
Paulownia tree drops dead leaves, A.
Razor blade rusted overnight, A.
Spring rain isn't even enough, The.
Town smells of things, The.
Twenty-one Hokku, *Sels*.

Bond, Carrie Jacobs (1862–1946)
Perfect Day, A.

Bond, Edward
First World War Poets.
On Our Modern World.

Bond, Harold
Glove, The.

Bond, Julian (b. 1940)
Bishop of Atlanta, The: Ray Charles.
Look at That Gal.

Rotation.

Bone, Edith (1889–1975)
On Myself.

Bone, Florence
Prayer for a Little Home, A.

Bonham, Thomas (d. 1629?)
In Praise of Ale.

Bonitaz Nuño, Rubén (b. 1923)
Smoke.

Bonnières, Robert de (1850–1905)
Former Life, The.
Mansion of Rosamonde, The.

Bontemps, Arna (1902–73)
Black Man Talks of Reaping, A.
Blight.
Close Your Eyes!
Day-Breakers [or Daybreakers], The.
Gethsemane.
God Give to Men ("God give the yellow man").
Golgotha Is a Mountain.
Homing.
Idolatry.
Lancelot.
Length of Moon.
Miracles.
Nocturne at Bethesda.
Nocturne of the Wharves.
Note of Humility, A.
Reconnaissance.
Return, The.
Southern Mansion.
To a Young Girl Leaving the Hill Country.
Tree Design, A.

Boodson, Alison (b. 1925)
Poem: "He lying spilt like water from a bowl."

Booth, Eva Gore-. See Gore-Booth, Eva.

Booth, Philip (b. 1925)
Countershadow, The.
Crossing.
Day the Tide, The.
Deer Isle.
Ego.
First Lesson.
Fog.
Green Song.
Hard Country.
Heron.
How to See Deer.
Jake's Wharf.
Late Spring: Eastport, A.
Marches.
Marin.
Misery of Mechanics, The.
One Man's Wife.
Original Sequence.
Round: "Skunk cabbage, bloodroot."
Seadog and Seal.
Seeing Auden Off.
Stefansson Island.
Stove.
Was a Man.

Boothby, Frances (fl. c. 1669)
Marcelia, The; or, Treacherous Friend, Sels.
Song: "Oh, you powerful Gods, if I must be."
What strange effects of Fortune do I prove!

Boothroyd, John Basil (b. 1910)
And Now.
Holy Order.
Please Excuse Typing.
Sanctuary.

Borawski, Walta (b. 1947)
Cheers, Cheers for Old Cha Cha Ass ("Cheers, cheers for old Patchogue High").
English Was Only a Second Language.
Invisible History.
Talking to Jim.

Borenstein, Emily (b. 1923)
Excavator, The.
I Must Tell the Story.
Shoah, The.

Borges, Jorge Luis (1899–1986)
Afterglow.
Amorous Anticipation.

Ars Poetica.
Dagger, The ("A dagger rests in a drawer").
Hengest Cyning.
Inventory.
Luke 23.
Mirrors of water, mirrors of ebony.
On the Death of Francisco López Merino.
Plainness.
Poem of Quality, Sels.

Borregaard, Ebbe (b. 1933)
Each Found Himself at the End Of . . . .
Some Stories of the Beauty Wapiti.

Borrell, D. E. (b. 1928)
Another Death.

Borson, Roo (b. 1952)
Flowers.
Gray Glove.
Jacaranda.
Talk.

Borthwick, Jane
Light Shining Out of Darkness.

Borum, Poul (b. 1934)
Train is Passing, A.

Bose, Harry
Seven One-Line Poems, Sels.

Bosley, Keith
Bird Sips Water.

Bosman, Herman Charles (1905–51)
Learning Destiny.
Old I Am.
Seed.

Bossidy, John Collins (1860–1928)
Boston.
Boston Toast, A.

Boston, Lucy (1892–1990)
Farewell to a Trappist.

Bostwick, Grace G.
Pep.

Boswell, James (1740–95)
Five winter days at Mannheim shall I be.
Here am I, sitting in a German inn.
Ye who with fortune ever are at strife.

Boswell, Margie B. (1875–1952)
Texas Ranger, The.

Botsford, S. B.
Sonneteering Made Easy.

Botta, Anne Lynch (1815–1891)
Ideal, The.
Ideal Found, The.
Lines: "Nay, read it not, thou wouldst not know."
Lines: "Where the dark primeval forests."
Love.
Milton.
Tarpeia.
To an Astronomer.
To Elizabeth Barrett Browning.
Wounded Vulture, The.

Bottomley, Gordon (b. 1874)
Ah, you have always been a friend to me.
Crier by Night, The, Sels.
Dawn.
Eager Spring.
Eagle Song.
End of the World, The.
King Lear's Wife, Sels.
Louse Crept Out of My Lady's Shift, A.
Suilven and the Eagle, Sels.
To Iron-Founders and Others.

Bottoms, David (b. 1949)
Anniversary, The.
Boy Shepherds' Simile, The.
Desk, The.
Drowned, The.
Face Jugs: Homage to Lanier Meaders.
In a U-Haul North of Damascus.
Sign for My Father, Who Stressed the Bunt.
Smoking in an Open Grave.
Under the Boathouse.
Under the Vulture-Tree.
Window, The.

Bottrall, Ronald (b. 1906)
Darkened Windows.
Icarus.

Mating Answer.

Botwood, Edward
Hot Stuff.

Boufflers, Marie-Françoise-Catherine de Beauveau, Marquise de. See Beauveau, Marie-Françoise-Catherine de, Marquise de Boufflers.

Boumi-Pappas, Rita (b. 1906)
Artemis.
Crow, The.
Krinio.

Boundy, Rex
Virile Christ, A.

Boundzekei-Dongala, Emmanuel
Fantasy under the Moon.

Bourdillon, Francis William (1852–1921)
Ah, happy who have seen Him, whom the world.
Lost God, A, Sels.
Night Has a Thousand Eyes, The.
Where Runs the River.

Bourget, Paul Charles Joseph (1852–1935)
Beautiful Evening.
Romance.

Bourinot, Arthur Stanley (b. 1893)
Legend of Paul Bunyan, A, Sels.
Paul Bunyan.
Snow Anthology.

Bourne, Nina
Where the Single Men Go in Summer.

Bourne, Vincent (1695–1747)
Cricket, The.
Housekeeper, The.
Snail, The.

Bouvé, Thomas Tracy (1815–96)
Shannon and the Chesapeake, The.

Bovshover, Joseph (1872–1916)
To the Laggards.

Bowden, Samuel (1726?–1771?)
Kite, completed thus, is borne along, The.
Paper Kite, The, Sels.

Bowen, Charles Synge Christopher Bowen, Baron (1835–96)
Rain It Raineth, The.

Bowen, Euros (b. 1904)
Blackthorn.
Nettles in May.
Winged in Gold.

Bowen, John Eliot (1858–90)
Man Who Rode to Conemaugh, The.

Bower, John Graham. See "Klaxon."

Bowering, George (b. 1938)
Dobbin.
Envies, The.
Está Muy Caliente.
Grandfather.
Grass, The.
House, The.
I am slowly dying, water evaporating.
In the Forest.
Inside the Tulip.
Moon Shadow.
Pharoah Sanders, in the Flesh.
Summer Solstice, Sels.

Bowering, Marilyn (b. 1949)
Russian Asylum.
Seeing Oloalok.
Wishing Africa.

Bowers, Edgar (b. 1924)
Afternoon at the Beach, An.
Amor Vincit Omnia.
Astronomers of Mont Blanc, The.
Autumn shade is thin, The. Grey leaves lie faint.
Autumn Shade, Sels.
Awakened by some fear, I watch the sky.
Clothes.
Elegy, An: December, 1970.
Fierce and brooding holocaust of faith, The.
I drive home with the books that I will read.
I know a wasted place high in the Alps.
In nameless warmth, sun light in every corner.
Snow and then rain. The roads are wet. A car.

Stoic: for Laura von Courten, The.
Two Poems on the Catholic Bavarians, *Sels.*

Bowes-Lyon, Lilian (1895–1949)
White Hare, The.

Bowie, Walter Russell (1882–1969)
God of the Nations.
O Holy City Seen of John.

Bowles, Paul (1910–86)
Extract.

Bowles, William Lisle (1762–1854)
At Dover Cliffs.
At Tynemouth Priory, after a Tempestuous Voyage.
Distant View of England from the Sea.
Egyptian Tomb, The.
Hope.
In Age.
In Youth.
Milton: On the Busts of Milton, in Youth and Age, *Sels.*
Netley Abbey.
Sonnet: "Evening, as slow thy placid shades descend."
Sonnet: "How sweet the tuneful bells' responsive peal!"
Time and Grief.
To a Friend.
To the River Itchin, near Winton.
Tweed Visited, The.

Bowman, Catherine (b. 1957)
Twins of a Gazelle Which Feed Among the Lilies.

Bowman, Louise Hollingsworth
Quiet Hour, The.

Bowndheri, Ilmi
As Camels Who Have Become Thirsty.

Bowring, Sir John (1510–55)
God Is Love.
In the Cross of Christ I Glory.

Boyd, Bruce (b. 1928)
Sanctuary.
This Is What the Watchbird Sings, Who Perches in the Lovetree.
Venice Recalled.

Boyd, Elizabeth (*fl.* 1727–1745)
On the Death of an Infant of Five Days Old.

Boyd, Mark Alexander (1563–1601)
Fra Bank to Bank, Fra Wood to Wood I Rin.

Boyd, Melba Joyce (b. 1950)
Beer Drops.
Sunflowers and Saturdays.
Why?

"Boyd, Nancy." *See* **Millay, Edna St. Vincent.**

Boyd, Thomas (1898–1935)
King's Son, The.

Boyden, Polly Chase
Mud ("Mud is very nice to feel").

Boye, Karin (1900–1941)
Dedication, A, *Sels.*
I feel your steps in the hall.
Sword, A.

Boyes, Sara (b. 1945)
Bathing.
Breaking Days.
Stars.

Boyle, Kay (b. 1903)
Communication to Nancy Cunard, A.
For James Baldwin.
For Marianne Moore's Birthday.
Monody to the Sound of Zithers.
New Emigration, The.
Poets.
Thunderstorm in South Dakota.
To a Seaman Dead on Land.

Boyle, Virginia Fraser (1863–1938)
Tennessee.

Boynton, H. W. (1869–1947)
Golfer's Rubaiyat, The.

Boyse, Samuel (1708–1749)
On Platonic Love.

Bozarth, Alla Renee
Bakerwoman God.
Belonging.

Blessed be the Creator.

Brabazon, Francis
Victoria Market.

Bracken, Thomas (1843–98)
Not Understood.

Brackenbury, Alison (b. 1953)
By the king's tree I walked afraid.
Castle.
Derby Day: An Exhibition.
House, The.
I am the maid who slept with you.
Intimates.
It could go on for ever so; the giving.
Kingdoms.
March Night.
Medine in Turkey.
Orange of Cloves, An.
Robert Brackenbury.
Strange sea: sudden sea: no thing can be the same.
Trees.
Two dead divers hauled up in their bell, The.
Whose Window?
Yesterday Vivaldi Visited Me.

Brackenridge, Hugh Henry (1748–1816) and Philip Freneau
Eugenio.
Leander.
Rising Glory of America, The, *Sels.*

Bracker, Milton (b. 1909)
P Is for Paleontology.

Brackley, Lady Elizabeth (1626–1663)
On My Boy Henry.
On the Death of My Deare Sister the Countesse of Bridgewater.

Brackley, Lady Elizabeth; and Lady Jane Cavendish. *See* **Cavendish, Lady Jane, and Lady Elizabeth Brackley.**

Bradbury, Ray
Switch on the Night.

Bradford, Gamaliel (1863–1932)
God.

Bradford, William (1589?–1657)
And Truly It Is a Most Glorious Thing.
Epitaphium Meum.
New England's Growth.
Of Boston in New England.
Word to New England, A.

Bradley, Christine E.
Skippets, the Bad One.

Bradley, Edward. *See* **"Bede, Cuthbert."**

Bradley, George (b. 1953)
Great Stone Face.
Of the Knowledge of Good and Evil.

Bradley, Katharine. *See* **"Field, Michael."**

Bradshaigh, Lady
Why sleeps the pen of Young! the friend profess'd.

Bradstreet, Anne (c.1612–1672)
Apology, An.
As Spring the Winter Doth Succeed.
As Weary Pilgrim, Now at Rest.
Author to Her Book, The.
Before the Birth of One of Her Children.
Childhood.
Contemplations, *Sels.*
Deliverance from a Fit of Fainting.
Dialogue between Old England and New, A, *Sels.*
Element Fire Boasts of the Constellations, The.
Flesh and the Spirit, The.
For Deliverance from a Fever.
Four Ages of Man, The, *Sels.*
Four Elements, The, *Sels.*
Four Seasons of the Year, The.
Foure Monarchies, The, *Sels.*
I wist not what to wish, yet sure thought I.
In Honour of That High and Mighty Princess Queen Elizabeth of Happy Memory.
In Memory of My Dear Grandchild [Anne Bradstreet].
In Memory of My Dear Grandchild Elizabeth Bradstreet Who Deceased August, 1665, Being a Year and a Half Old.

In Reference to Her Children, 23 June, 1656 [*or* 1659].
In Thankfull Remembrance for My Dear Husband's Safe Arrivall Sept. 3, 1662.
Letter to Her Husband, A.
Letter to Her Husband, Absent upon Public Employment, A.
Mariner that on smooth waves doth glide, The.
New England.
O Thou Most High Who Rulest All.
O Time the fatal wrack of mortal things.
Of the Four Ages of Man.
Old England.
On My Dear Grandchild Simon Bradstreet, [Who Died on 16 November, 1669, Being But A Month, And One Day Old].
Prologue: "To sing of wars, of captain[e]s, and of kings."
Semiramis.
Shall I then praise the heavens, the trees, the earth.
Silent alone, where none or saw, or heard.
So he that saileth in this world of pleasure.
Some Verses upon the Burning of Our House, July 10th, 1666.
This book by any yet unread.
To Her Father with Some Verses.
To My Dear and Loving Husband.
To the Memory of My Dear and Ever Honored Father Thomas Dudley Esq.
To the Memory of My Dear Daughter in Law, Mrs. Mercy Bradstreet.
Vanity of All Worldly Things, The.
When I behold the heavens as in their prime.

Bradstreet, Samuel (c.1633–1682)
Almanack for the Year of Our Lord, 1657, An.

Brady, Anne Hazlewood-. *See* **Hazlewood-Brady, Anne.**

Brady, Charles A. (b. 1912)
Dimidium Animae Meae.

Brady, Edwin James (1869–1925)
Whaler's Pig, The.

Bragdon, Claude (1866–1946)
Beautiful Necessity, The, *Sels.*

Brainard, E. M.
Compensation.

Brainard, John Gardiner Calkins (1796–1828)
I Saw Two Clouds at Morning.
On the Death of Commodore Oliver H. Perry.
To Thee, O God, the Shepherd Kings.

Braine, Sheila
Mr. Scarecrow.

Braithwaite, William Stanley (1878–1962)
Del Cascar.
Golden Moonrise.
House of Falling Leaves, The.
In a Grave-Yard.
October XXIX, 1795.
Rye Bread.
Scintilla.
To ———.
Watchers, The.
White Magic; an Ode.

Braley, Berton (1882–1966)
Business Is Business.
Do It Now.
Loyalty.
Opportunity.
Prayer: "Lord, let me live like a Regular Man."
Start Where You Stand.
Success!
Thinker, The.

Braley, Ephraim
Canada-I-O ("Come all ye jolly lumbermen and listen to my song").

Bramfit, Sheila
Grandparents.

Bramston, James (1694?–1743)
Art of Politics, The, *Sels.*
Huge commentators grace my learned shelves.
Man of Taste, The, *Sels.*
Time's Changes.
Whoe'er he be that to a taste aspires.

Branch, Anna Hempstead (1875–1937)
I say that words are men and when we spell.

From the Pentlands, *Sels.*
Kirk Bell, The.
On Leave.
Buchan, Tom
Scotland the Wee.
Buchanan, George (1904–89)
Conversations with Strangers.
I Suddenly.
Jill's Death.
Lewis Mumford.
Lyle Donaghy, Poet, 1902-1949.
Revolutionary Revolution.
Song for Straphangers.
Speaker in the Square, A.
Theatrical Venus.
War-and-Peace.
Buchanan, Robert (1841–1901)
Little Herd-Boy's Song, The.
Little Milliner, The.
Starling, The.
Buchanan, Robert Williams (1841–1901)
Blind Linnet, The.
Buck, Byron
Song from a Two-Desk Office.
Buck, John. *See* John Buck.
Buckham, James (b. 1858)
Heart's Proof, The.
Buckham, John Wright (1864–1945)
Hills of God, Break Forth in Singing.
O God, above the Drifting Years.
Buckingham, George Villiers, 2d Duke of (1628–87)
Cabin-Boy, The.
Epitaph upon Thomas, Lord Fairfax, An.
Prayer: "Lord God of the oak and the elm."
Buckland, Frank
Limerick: "That smasher of shams, Bernard Shaw."
Buckley, Christopher (b. 1948)
Sparrows.
White.
Buckley, R. Bishop
Wait for the Wagon.
Buckley, Vincent (1925–88)
Blind School/ Rasps with crying, The.
Death in January.
Ghosts, Places, Stories, Questions.
Golden Builders, *Sels.*
Good Friday and the Present Crucifixion.
How soon will some self-turning.
Internment.
No New Thing.
Parents.
Practising Not Dying.
Rain gusts at the asphalt, The.
Return of a Popular Statesman.
Teaching German Literature.
Your Father's House.
Buckmaster, Charles (1951–72)
Vanzetti.
Buckner, Samuel O.
Do It Right.
Budbill, David
Tommy Again, Finally.
What I Heard at the Discount Department Store.
Budianta, Eka (b. 1956)
Family Portrait.
Bukowski, Charles (b. 1920)
For Jane.
Horsemeat, *Sels.*
My women of the past keep trying to locate me.
Secret, The.
Short Order.
Style.
Sun Wields Mercy, The.
Tragedy of Leaves, The.
Trash Men, The.
20 minutes later.
Vegas.
Wearing the Collar.
Bulcke, Karl (b. 1875)
There Is an Old City.

Bulfinch, Stephen Greenleaf (1809–70)
Hail to the Sabbath Day.
Bulkeley, Peter, the Younger (1643–91)
Like to the Grass That's Green Today.
Bull, Arthur J. (b. 1903)
Eve.
Buller, Arthur (1874–1944)
Limerick: "There was a young lady named [*or* called] Bright."
Limerick: "To her friends, said the Bright one, in chatter."
Bullett, Gerald (b. 1893)
Footnote to Tennyson.
Bullokar, William (c.1520–c.1590)
To His Child.
Buluguru
Working Song.
Bulwer-Lytton, Edward Robert, 1st Earl of Lytton. *See* "Meredith, Owen."
Bumstead, Eudora S. (b. 1860)
Summer Lullaby, A.
Bunan (1602–76)
Die while you're alive.
Bungay, George W. (1818?–1892)
Creeds of the Bells.
Bunin, Ivan (1870–1953)
Flax.
Bunner, Alice Learned (b. c.1860)
Immutabilis.
Separation.
Vingtaine, *Sels.*
Bunner, Henry Cuyler (1855–96)
Behold the Deeds!
Chaperon, The.
Heart of the Tree, The.
Home, *Sels.*
"Home, Sweet Home," with Variations ("As sea-foam blown of the winds, as blossom of brine that is drifted").
"Home, Sweet Home," with Variations ("Brown o' San Juan").
"Home, Sweet Home," with Variations ("Mid pleasures and palaces though we may roam").
One, Two, Three.
Poetry and the Poet.
Shake, Mulleary, and Go-ethe.
Way to Arcady, The.
Bunting, Basil (1900–1985)
As the player's breath warms the fipple the tone clears.
Brag, sweet tenor bull.
Briggflatts [An Autobiography], *Sels.*
Chomei at Toyama.
Coda.
Complaint of the Morpethshire Farmer, The.
Fearfull Symmetry.
Fishermen.
Gin the Goodwife Stint.
Grass caught in willow tells the flood's height.
Light lifts from the water.
Loaded with mail of linked lies.
On the Fly-Leaf of Pound's Cantos.
Orotava Road, The.
Passport Officer, The.
Personal Column.
To Violet [with Prewar Poems].
What the Chairman Told Tom.
Word, The.
Bunyan, John (1628–88)
Author's Apology for His Book, The, *Sels.*
He that is down, needs fear no fall.
My Little Bird.
Of the Boy and Butterfly.
Of the Going Down of the Sun.
Pilgrim's Progress, The, *Sels.*
Time and Eternity.
Upon a Ring of Bells.
Upon the Horse and His Rider.
Upon the Lark and the Fowler.
Upon the [*or* a] Snail.
Upon the Swallow.
Upon the Weathercock.
What danger is the pilgrim in.
When at the first I took my pen in hand.

Who would true valour see.
Burbank, Elevena (b. 1956)
I Danced to the Rumble of the Drum.
Burbidge, Thomas (1816–95)
She Bewitched Me.
Burden, Jean (b. 1914)
Poem before Departure.
Burdette, Robert Jones (1844–1914)
Orphan Born.
"Soldier, Rest!"
Burdick, Arthur J. (b. 1858)
Washington's Birthday.
Burford, Barbara (b. 1945)
Manumission.
Reflections.
Scheherazade.
September Blue.
You.
Burford, William (b. 1927)
Christmas Tree, A.
On the Apparition of Oneself.
Burge, Maureen
Diet, The.
Disillusion.
Burgess, Anthony (b. 1917)
Inspired by the Controversy on the Value or Otherwise of Old English Studies.
Limerick: "Man from the *Washington Post*, A."
Burgess, Gelett (1866–1951)
Ah, Yes, I Wrote the "Purple Cow."
Felicia Ropps.
I seen a dunce of a poet once, a-writin' a little book.
Limerick: "For hours my wife says "Goodbye.""
Limerick: "I wish that my room had a floor."
Low Trick, A.
Nonsense Quatrains.
On Digital Extremities.
On Drawing-Room Amenities.
Protest of the Illiterate, The, *Sels.*
Psycholophon.
Purple Cow, The.
Radical Creed, A.
Sunset, The.
Table Manners.
Trapping fairies in West Virginia.
Woman's Reason, A.
Burgess, George (1809–60)
Harvest Dawn Is Near, The.
While o'er the Deep Thy Servants Sail.
Burghley, William Cecil, 1st Baron (1520–98)
To Mistress Anne Cecil, upon Making Her a New Year's Gift, January 1, 1567-8.
Burgon, John William (1813–88)
Match me such marvel save in Eastern clime.
Pedra.
Petra, *Sels.*
Written on the Plain of Thebes.
Burgos, Julia de (1914–58)
Poem to My Death.
To Julia de Burgos.
Burgoyne, Arthur G. (d. 1914)
"Everybody Works but Father" as W. S. Gilbert Would Have Written It.
Burgunder, Rose
Boy's Place, A.
Burkard, Michael (b. 1947)
Almost to Jesus.
Hotel Tropicana.
Burke, James (1877–1958)
Missionary Hymm.
Burke, Kenneth (b. 1897)
Civil Defense.
Frigate Jones, the Pussyfooter ("Frigate Jones was very slow and fat").
Know Thyself.
Nursery Rhyme.
Burket, Gail Brook (b. 1905)
From Countless Hearts.
So Touch Our Hearts with Loveliness.
Burkholder, Clarence M.
Easter Beatitudes.

Mark the dark rook, on pendent branches hung.
On Jacobinism.
Political Despatch, A.
Progress of Man, The, *Sels.*

**Canning, George (1770–1827), George Ellis,
   and John Hookham Frere**
Rogero's Song.
Rovers, The, *Sels.*

**Canning, George (1770–1827) *and* John
   Hookham Frere**
Friend of Humanity and the Knife Grinder,
   The.
From mental mists to purge a nation's eyes.
Give me the avowed, erect and manly foe.
Inscription: "For one long term, or e'er her trial
   came."
New Morality, *Sels.*

Cannon, David Wadsworth, Jr. (1910–38)
Freedom in Mah Soul.
Western Town.

Cannon, Hughie
Bill Bailey, Won't You Please Come Home.

Cannon, Noah Calwell (1796?–1850)
Ark, The.

Canton, William (1845–1926)
Carol: "When the herd[s] were watching."
Child's Prayer, A.
Day-Dreams.

Cantus, Eleanor Hollister (b. 1908)
Fame.

Canzoneri, Robert (b. 1925)
Two.

Capetanakis, Demetrios (1912–44)
Abel.
Isles of Greece, The.

Capito
Lacking grace/ beauty.

Caprani, Menotti Vincent (b. 1934)
Prizefighter's Prayer, The.

Caragher, Mary E. (b. 1890)
Tree Tag.

**"Carbery, Ethna" (Anna Johnston MacManus)
   (1866–1902)**
King of Ireland's Cairn, The.
Love-Talker, The.
Mea Culpa.
On an Island.

Cardenal, Ernesto (b. 1925)
Bless the Lord, O my soul.
Praise the Lord in your infinite variety all
   creatures.

Cardiff, Gladys (b. 1942)
Candelaria and the Sea Turtle.
Carious Exposure.
Combing.
Dragon Skate.
For His Ring and Watch on the Night Stand.
Grey Woman.
Hunting the Dugong.
Leaves like Fish.
Long Person.
Making Lists.
Swimmer.
Tlanusi' Yi, the Leech Place.
To Frighten a Storm.
Tsa'lagi Council Tree.
Where Fire Burns.

Carducci, Giosuè (1835–1907)
Petrarch.
Primo Vere.
Snowfall.

Carenza (*fl.* c.1150–1350) *and* Iselda
Tenson.

Carew, Jan (b. 1925)
Cliffs at Manzanilla, The.
Faces and Skulls.
Our Home.

Carew, Richard (1555–1620)
River Lynher, The.
Survey of Cornwall, *Sels.*

Carew, Thomas (1589–1639)
Another [Epitaph on the Lady Mary Villiers].
Another [On the Duke of Buckingham].

Ask [or Aske] Me No More Where Jove
   Bestows [or Bestowes].
Boldness[e] in Love.
Celia Bleeding, to the Surgeon.
Comparison, The.
Complement, The.
Deposition from Love, A.
Disdain Returned.
Divine Mistress, A.
Elegy upon the Death of the Dean of [St.]
   Paul's, Dr. John Donne, An, *Sels.*
Epitaph on Maria Wentworth.
Epitaph on the Lady Mary Villiers, An.
Eternity of Love Protested.
Excuse of Absence, An.
Fancy, A.
Fly That Flew into My Mistress's Eye, A.
For a Picture Where a Queen Laments over the
   Tomb of a Slain Knight.
Good Counsel [or Counsell] to a Young Maid.
Hymeneal Song on the Nuptials of the Lady
   Anne Wentworth and the Lord Lovelace, An.
Hymeneall Dialogue, An.
In Answer of an Elegiacal Letter, Upon the
   Death of the King of Sweden.
Ingrateful[l] Beauty Threatened.
Lady's Prayer to Cupid, A.
Looking-Glass, A.
Lover, upon an Accident Necessitating His
   Departure, Consults with Reason, A.
Love's Force.
Maria Wentworth.
Mediocrity in Love Rejected.
Murdring Beautie.
New Year's Sacrifice: To Lucinda, A.
On His Mistress Looking in a Glass.
On Sight of a Gentlewoman's Face in the
   Water.
On the Death of Donne.
On the Marriage of T. K. and C. C., the
   Morning Stormy.
Pastorall Dialogue, A.
Persuasions to Enjoy.
Prayer to the Wind, A.
Psalm 137.
Rapture, A.
Second Rapture, The.
Secrecy [or Secresie] Protested.
Spring, The.
Tinder, The.
To A. L.
To a Lady That Desired I Would Love Her.
To Ben Jonson.
To Her Againe, She Burning in a Feaver.
To Her in Absence; a Ship.
To My Cousin (C.R.) Marrying My Lady (A.).
To My Friend G.N. from Wrest.
To My Inconstant Mistress [or Mistris].
To My Mistress[e] in My Absence.
To My Mistress Sitting by a River's Side; an
   Eddy.
To My Mistris, I Burning in Love.
To My Worthy Friend Master George Sands [or
   Sandys], on His Translation of the Psalms.
To One That Desired To Know My Mistris.
To Saxham.
To T. H., a Lady Resembling My Mistress.
To the King, at His Entrance into Saxham: By
   Master John Crofts.
To the New Year.
To the Reader of Master William Davenant's
   Play, The Wits.
Upon a Mole in Celia's Bosom.
Upon a Ribband [or Ribbon].
Upon Master Walter Montagu's Return from
   Travel.
Upon My Lord Chief Justice's Election of My
   Lady Anne Wentworth for His Mistress.
Upon Some Alterations in My Mistress, after
   My Departure into France.
Willing Prisoner to His Mistress, The.

Carey, Henry (1693?–1743)
Author's Quietus, The.
Drinking-Song, A.
God Save the King.

Lilliputian Ode on Their Majesties' Accession,
   A.
Maid's Husband, The.
Namby-Pamby; or, A Panegyric on the New
   Versification.
Roger and Dolly.
Sally in Our Alley.
Sally Sweetbread.

Carey, Lady Elizabeth (1589–1639)
Chorus: "Those mindes that wholy dote upon
   delight."
Fairest action of our human life, The.
How oft have I with publike voyce runne on?
Mariam, *Sels.*
'Tis not enough for one that is a wife.

Carey, Mary (d. after 1680)
Upon ye Sight of My Abortive Birth.
Wretten by Me at the Death of My 4th Sonne
   and 5th Child Perigrene Payler.
Wretten by Me att the Same Tyme; on the
   Death of My 4th, & Only Child, Robert
   Payler.

Carey, Patrick (c.1623–1657)
And now a fig for the lower house.
Nulla Fides.
To the Tune — "But I Fancy Lovely Nancy."
To the Tune — "Once I Lov'd a Maiden Fair."
Whilst I beheld the neck o' th' dove.

Carey, Steve (b. 1945)
Drysdale and Mantle Whitey Ford and to You.
Lucille.
Methode Champenoise.
Poem.
Sway.
To the Coast Indian.

Carhart, Ann
Saturday Night Worship.

Cariaga, Catalina (b. 1958)
Plantings.

Carkesse, James (*fl.* 1678)
His Petition to Mr. Speaker.
His Rule of Behaviour: If You Are Civil, I Am
   Sober.
On the Doctors' Telling Him that till He Left
   off Making Verses He Was Not Fit to be
   Discharged.

Carleton, Sara King (1886–1967)
Late October.

Carleton, Will M. (1845–1912)
Across the Delaware.
Betsey and I Are Out.
Country Doctor, The.
Cuba to Columbia.
Death-Doomed.
Doctor's Story, The.
Little Black-eyed Rebel, The.
New Church Organ, The.
Over the Hill to the Poor-House.
Prize of the *Margaretta*, The.
Victory-Wreck, The.

Carlile, Henry (b. 1934)
Dodo.
Havana Blues.
Listening to Beethoven on the Oregon Coast.
Spider Reeves.

**Carlin, Francis (James Francis Carlin
   MacDonnell) (1881–1945)**
Plea for Hope.

Carlin, Vuyelwa (b. 1949)
Dragon, The.
Drowned Girl, The.
Exile, The.
Monsters.
Scots Pines.
Spring Fever.
Strange Dolls.
Trees, The.

Carlyle, Thomas (1795–1881)
Cui Bono?
Morning.
Sower's Song, The.
To-Day.
Today.

Carman, Bliss (1861–1929)
Concerning Kavin.

U-24 Anchors off New Orleans.
Castellanos, Rosario (1925–74)
Foreign Woman.
Great fish's eyes never shut, The.
Hecuba's Testament.
O cloud that wants to be the sky's arrow.
Silence Concerning an Ancient Stone.
Useless Day.
What is weaker than a god? It groans hungry.
Casterline, Helen Annis
God Cares.
Castillejo, Cristóbal de (1490–1550)
Some Day, Some Day.
Castillo, Ana (b. 1953)
Marriage of Mutes, A.
Nani Worries about Her Father's Happiness in the Afterlife.
Napa, California.
Seduced by Natassja Kinski.
Ugly Black Dog Named Goya, An.
Zoila López.
Castle, Sandie (b. 1954)
Blake Mistake, The.
Hand-Jive.
Mother's Day.
Casto, Robert Clayton (b. 1932)
Salt Pork, The.
Castro, Rosalía de (1837–85)
Black Mood.
Crickets and locusts, cicadas.
How placidly shine/ The river, the spring, and the sun.
I Was Born at Birth of Blossoms.
Long May.
Now all that sound of laughter, sound of singing.
Plants don't talk, people say.
They say that plants don't talk, nor do.
Castro, Tania Diaz (b. 1939)
Wall, The.
Catacalos, Rosemary
Lesson in "A Waltz for Debby," The.
Measure of Light at the Altar on the Day of the Dead, The.
One Man's Family.
Partial History of Poppies, A.
With the Conchero Dancers, Mission Espada, July.
Catalano, Gary (b. 1947)
Australia.
Jews Speak in Heaven, The.
Cater, Catherine (b. 1917)
Here and Now.
Cather, Willa (1875–47)
Grandmither, Think Not I Forget.
Somewhere, sometime, in an April twilight.
Spanish Johnny.
Catley, Douglas
Limerick: "Boadicea often would goad."
Limerick: "Famed big-hitter in cricket, A."
Limerick: "God brought perfect man to fruition."
Limerick: "Good mechanics are all of one mind."
Limerick: "Lass of curvacious physique, A."
Limerick: "Prostitute living in London, A."
Limerick: "Scribe, to the vulgar inclined, A."
Limerick: "There's a fortunate priest of St. Paul's."
Limerick: "When Pegotty found Barkis was willing."
Limerick: "Wily Napoleon Bonaparte, The."
Catlin, Alan
Pushing Forty.
Catling, B. (b. 1948)
Boschlog: Being a Cartulary from The Ship of Fools.
Cato, Nancy (b. 1917)
Independence.
Cattantaiyar
King Killi in Combat.
Catti Natanar (b. 1940)
What He Said.

Catullus, Caius [or Gaius] Valerius (87–c.54 B.C.)
Acme and Septimius.
Attis.
Carmina, *Sels*.
Come and let us live my deare.
Dearest Ipsitilla.
Death of Lesbia's Bird, The.
Each moment of the long-liv'd day.
Egnatius has fine teeth, and those.
Fabullus I will treat you handsomely.
Fib Detected, A.
Flavius, If Your Girl Friend.
Gellius, what reason can you give why those ruddy lips of yours.
Grief.
Guardian of Helicon, Urania's son.
Her that I love, I hate! "How's that, do you know?" they wonder.
Hymeneal, *Sels*.
Hymn to Diana.
I entrust my all to you, Aurelius.
I have something for you to laugh at, Cato.
I love and hate. Ah! never ask why so!
If I could go on kissing your honeyed eyes.
I'll have you by the short and curly hair.
I'm Placing in Your Hands My Lover and Myself.
Invitation to an Invitation, An.
Jewel of the almost islands and the isles.
Juventius, could you not find in this great crowd of men.
Juventius, my honey, while you played.
Lesbia.
Lesbia Forever on Me Rails.
Lesbia loads me night and day with her curses.
Love and Death.
Miss her, Catullus? don't be so inept to rail.
My girl says she'll take no one else as a lover.
My Lesbia let us love and live.
My mistress sayes she'll marry none but me.
My Woman.
Now my mind's been brought to such a state — and it's your fault.
O poor Catullus, stupid long enough!
Odi et Amo.
Of all our bath-house thieves the cleverest one.
On the Burial of His Brother.
Phyllis Corydon clutched to him.
Sappho.
Sirmio.
Sirmio, thou dearest dear of strands.
So Help Me God.
So let's live — really live! — for love and loving.
Suffenus, whom so well you know [*or* whom you know].
That me alone you lov'd, you once did say.
That no fair woman will, wonder not why.
This racer of the watry plain.
Thou saidst that I alone thy heart cou'd move.
To Himself.
To Naso.
True or False.
Unmuzzle the broad joke.
Unto no body my woman saith she had rather a wife be.
Veranius, my dear friend, the friend worth.
What demented malice, my silly Ravidus.
Yacht, The.
Yes! my Lesbia! let us prove.
Your Catullus is depressed, Cornificus.
"Caudwell, Christopher" (Christopher St. John Sprigg) (1901–37)
Classic Encounter.
Progress of Poetry, The.
Caulfield, Carlota (b. 1953)
Photo That Watches, The.
Causley, Charles (b. 1917)
Angel's Song.
Animals' Carol, The.
Apple-Tree Man, The.
Armistice Day.
At Candlemas.
At Kfar Kana.
At the British War Cemetery, Bayeux.

At the Statue of William the Conqueror, Falaise.
Autobiography.
Balaam.
Ballad for Katharine of Aragon, A.
Ballad of the Bread Man.
Betjeman, 1984.
Bible Story.
By St. Thomas Water.
Chief Petty Officer.
Colonel Fazackerley.
Coming from Evening Church.
Conversation in Gibraltar 1943.
Cowboy Song.
Death of a Poet.
Death of an Aircraft.
Eden Rock.
Envoi: "I am the Prince."
Figgie Hobbin.
For an Ex-Far East Prisoner of War.
Fox Came into my Garden, A.
H. M. S. *Glory* at Sydney.
I Am the Great Sun.
I Saw a Jolly Hunter.
Infant Song.
Innocent's Song.
King's College Chapel.
Legend.
Loss of an Oil Tanker.
Mary's Song.
My Young Man's a Cornishman.
Nursery Rhyme of Innocence and Experience.
Old Mrs. Thing-um-e-bob.
On Being Asked to Write a School Hymn.
On Seeing a Poet of the First World War on the Station at Abbeville.
On the Thirteenth Day of Christmas.
Recruiting Drive.
Sailor's Carol.
Song of Samuel Sweet, The.
Song of the Dying Gunner A.A.1.
Ten Types of Hospital Visitor.
Timothy Winters.
What Has Happened to Lulu?
Caution, Ethel M.
Last Night.
River, The.
To E.J.J.
Cavafy, Constantine P. (1863–1933)
Alexander Jannai.
And I Lounged and Lay on Their Beds.
As Much as You Can.
By the Open Window.
Dareios.
Days of 1896.
First Step, The.
He Asked about the Quality.
Horses of Achilles, The.
In Despair.
In the Evening.
In the Tavernas.
Lovely White Flowers.
Mirror in the Front Hall, The.
Myris: Alexandria, A.D. 340.
Next Table, The.
On Board Ship.
On the Street.
One of the Jews.
Return.
Their Beginning.
To Remain.
Twenty-fifth Year of His Life, The.
Two Young Men, 23 to 24 Years Old.
Waiting for the Barbarians.
Walls.
Window of the Tobacco Shop, The.
Cavalcanti, Guido (1250–1301)
Ballata V: "Light do I see within my Lady's eyes."
Concerning a Shepherd-Maid.
Donna Mi Priegha.
He Compares All Things with His Lady, and Finds Them Wanting.
He Reveals, in a Dialogue, His Increasing Love for Mandetta.
He Speaks of a Third Love of His.
In Exile at Sarzana.

Just Deserts.
Now and Then.
Pact and Impact.
Problem the grass under the saplings, The.
Rain.
Sitting here how do they know where.
Theory.
There is enough for us all.
Today Backwards.
Travelling.
Twice.

Chamberlain, Brenda (1912–71)
Dead Ponies.
Islandman.
Lament: "My man is a bone ringèd with weed."
Song: "Bone-aged is my white horse."

Chamberlain, Karen
Stepping in the Same River.

Chamberlain, Neville
Dear Czecho-Slovakia.

Chamberlain, Richard (1632–98)
To the Much Honoured R. F. Esq.

Chamberlayne, William (1619–1689)
Bad Landlord, The.
Pharonnida, Sels.

Chambers, Jane (1937–83)
Why Are Daddies So Mean?
Woman.

Chambers, Robert William (b. 1865)
"Grey Horse Troop," The.
To Nature Seekers.

Chambre, Alastair
Limerick: "There was a young girl from
Uttoxeter/ Who kept hens, but refused to
have cocks. It a."

Chamisso, Adelbert von (1781–1838)
Fortune-Teller, The.
Soldier, The.
Tragic Story, A.
Woman's Love and Life.

Chan Fang-sheng (fl. c.400)
Sailing Homeward.

Chan-Jan
Man whose mind is rounded out to perfection,
The.

Chandler, Christine
Tree in the Garden, The.

Chandler, Keith
Kett's Rebellion.

Chandler, Mary (1687–1745)
My Own Epitaph.
True Tale, A.

Chandra, G. S. Sharat
Rape of Lucrece Retold.

Chang, Diana (b. 1934)
Cannibalism.
Energy is Eternal Delight.
On Gibson Lane, Sagaponack.

Chang, Edmond Yi-Teh (b. 1965)
After the Storm.
Bamboo Elegy: Two.
Near-Sightedness.

Chang Chi (768–830)
Birds from the Mountains, The.
Faithful Wife, A.
Night at Anchor by Maple Bridge.

Ch'ang Chien (fl. c. 749)
Visit to the Broken Hill Temple, A.

Chang Chih-ho (c. 742–82)
Before dusk on the lake, the moon just full.
Fisherman's Songs, Sels.
Near the rim of Hsi-sai Mountain, white egrets
fly.
Oh, about the joy of owning a crab hut at
Sung-chiang!

Chang Chiu-ling (673–740)
Since You Left.

Chang Heng (78–139)
Bones of Chuang Tzu, The, Sels.
Dead man answered me, The.

Chang Hsien-liang
Great Wind, The.

Chang Hui-yen (1761–1802)
Composed on a Spring Day and Shown to
Yang Tzu-sha, Sels.
Joy at Meeting, Sels.
Year after year, I've missed the season of
flowers.
Young warbler crying through the Festival of
Tombs.

Ch'ang Kuo Fan (fl. 19th cent.)
On His Thirty-Third Birthday.

Chang Ming-ch'uan
Trust Man a Little Bit More.

Chang Shiang-Lua (b. 1939)
Appointment, A.
Wordless Day.

Chang Wên-chi (fl. 9th cent.)
Bamboo Shaded Pool, The.

Chang Wen-t'ao (1764–1814)
Moving to the Cottage of Pine and Bamboo,
Sels.
On Literature, Sels.
Poem without a self is fit only to be excised,
A.
To condone rotten rubbish is to deny the
miraculous.

Chang Yü (1333–85)
Artemisia Tiger, The.
Autumn.
Brewing Tea at Moon Pond.
Butterflies.
Cliff of the Ancient Tomb, The.
Four Poems On the Ch'ung-wu Festival, Sels.
Four Seasons in the Mountains, The, Sels.
His pole and paddle have been with him a long
time.
Hundred-Fold Cord, The.
I close the book in my hands.
Looking at Chrysanthemums.
Moon Window, The.
Painting ("Slowly I walk the gully path,
alone").
Paintings, Sels.
Presented to a Lady within the Palace.
Seven Poems on Living in the Mountains:
Seeing Off, Sels.
"Song of Farewell" in the Tartar Mode.
Spring.
Spring Night.
Summer.
Summer Night at the Pond Pavillion.
Twelve Miscellaneous Poems on the Fang
Garden, Sels.
Winter.
Yellow Sunflower of Szechwan.

Chanler, Isaac (1700–1749)
Awake My Soul, Betimes Awake.
Thrice Welcome First and Best of Days.

Channing, William Ellery (1818–1901)
Poet's Hope, A, Sels.
Prayer: "To Thy continual Presence, in me
wrought."
To live content with small means.

Chao Chih-hsin (1662–1744)
Evening clouds suddenly scatter and peaks
come into view.
Miscellaneous Poems on Mountain Travel, Sels.
Where the summit road twists and turns, I'm
soon to lose my way.

Ch'ao Li-houa [or Chao Li-hua]
Farewell: "My boat goes west, yours east."

Chao Luan-luan (fl. 8th century)
Cloud Hairdress.
Creamy Breasts.
Red Sandalwood Mouth.
Slender Fingers ("Slender, delicate, soft jade").
Willow Eyebrows.

Chao Meng-fu (1254–1322)
Cutstone Pond.
Dragon Mouth Cliff.
Spirit Pool.
Stone Man Peak.
Thunder God Cliff.
Twenty-Eight Poems Inscribed on T'ien-kuan
Mountain, Sels.

Chao Yi (1727–1814)
Best of poetry comes from the destitute, but my
pocket is not yet empty, The.
In Search of Solitude.
On Poetry, Sels.
Poems of Li Po and Tu Fu, passed along by
myriad voices, The.
Rising Early in the Morning.
Spring Sentiments.
Strolling in the Countryside.
Watching an Opera: Impressions, Sels.
World is alive with inspiration to a potter who
turns the wheel, The.
Writing Poetry in the Back Garden.

Chao Ying-tou (fl. 17th century)
Decrees of God, The.

Chapin, Edwin Hubbell (1814–80)
Hark! Hark! with Harps of Gold.
O Thou, Who Didst Ordain the Word.

Chapin, Katherine Garrison (b. 1890)
On a Sea-Grape Leaf.
Portrait in Winter.

Chaplin, Kathleen M.
Merry Little Men.

Chaplin, Ralph
Commonwealth of Toil, The.
Solidarity Forever.

Chapman, Arthur (1873–1935)
Out Where the West Begins ("Out where the
hand-clasp's a little stronger").

Chapman, George (1559?–1634)
And, now gives Time, her states description.
Bridal Song.
Bussy d'Ambois, Sels.
But Dwell in Darkness.
Coronet for His Mistress Philosophy, A, Sels.
Death Described by His True Effects.
Descend, Fair Sun!
Ear's Delight, The.
Epistle Dedicatory to Chapman's Translation of
the Iliad, The, Sels.
Epithalamion Teratos.
Eugenia, Sels.
Euthymiae Raptus; or, The Teares of Peace,
Sels.
Hymn[e] to Our Saviour on the Cross[e], A.
Hymnus in Noctem.
Ile sooth his plots: and strow my hate with
smiles.
In a loose robe of tinsel forth [or tynsell foorth]
she came.
Justice.
Leander to the envious light.
Learning ('So Learned Men in Controversies
Spend').
Love Flows Not from My Liver.
Masque of the Middle Temple and Lincoln's
Inn, The, Sels.
Masque of the Twelve Months, The, Sels.
Muses That Sing Love's Sensual Empery.
New light gives new directions, fortunes new.
Now all the peaceful regents of the night.
Now from Leander's place she rose, and found.
Now shall we see, that nature hath no end.
Ovid's Banquet of Sense, Sels.
Peace Discovers the Poet.
Peace of Death, The.
Poet Questions Peace, The.
Shadow of Night, The, Sels.
Shine Out, Fair Sun, with All Your Heat.
Tragedy of Charles Duke of Byron, The.

Chapman, Jean
Territory.

Chapman, John Alexander (b. 1875)
Gipsy Queen.

Chapman, John Jay (1862–1933)
Lines on the Death of Bismarck.
Song: "Old Farmer Oats and his son Ned."

Chapman, M. J. (b. 1865)
African Dirge.
Barbadoes, Sels.
Still sparkles here the glory of the west.
While the noon-lustre o'er the land is spread.

Chappell, Fred (b. 1936)
Abandoned Schoolhouse on Long Branch.
Cleaning the Well.
Guess Who.
Highest Wind That Ever Blew: Homage to Louis, The.
Lost Carnival, The.
My Father Washes His Hands.
My Grandfather's Church Goes Up.
My Grandmother Washes Her Feet.
My Grandmother Washes Her Vessels.
My Mother Shoots the Breeze.
Narcissus and Echo.
Northwest Airlines.
Rimbaud Fire Letter to Jim Applewhite.
Second Wind.
Skin Flick.
Tiros II.

Chappell, Jeannette (1898?–1976)
Newton to Einstein.

Charlemagne (1631–1700) *and* **Hrabanus Maurus**
Veni Creator Spiritus.

Charles I, King of England
On a Quiet Conscience.

Charles, Duc d'Orléans. *See* **Orléans, Charles, Duc d'.**

Charles, Dorthi (b. 1963)
Concrete Cat.
Getting Dirty.

Charles, Elizabeth Rundle (b. 1828)
Child on the Judgment Seat, The.

Charles, Faustin (b. 1944)
Fireflies.
Omens of the Morning.
Sugar Cane.

Charles, Mary Grant
Flood.

Charles, Robert E.
Roundabout Turn, A.

Charlton, George (b. 1950)
Friday Evenings.
Gateshead Grammar.
Man on a Roof.
Nightshift Workers.

Chartier, Alain (c.1385–c.1433)
I turn you out of doors.
La Belle Dame sans Mercy, *Sels.*
Lady Resists the Lover's Pleas, The.

Chartres, Vidame de (*fl.* 13th century)
April.

Chasin, Helen (b. 1938)
City Pigeons.
Falling Out.
Looking Out.
Mythics.
Photograph at the Cloisters: April 1972.
Poetess Kō Ōgimi, The.
Recovery Room: Lying-in, The.
Word *Plum*, The.

Chatain, Robert
World of Darkness.

Chatt, George (1839–90)
At Elsdon.

Chatterton, Thomas (1752–70)
Aella; a Tragycal Enterlude, *Sels.*
Autumn.
Bristowe Tragedie: or, The Dethe of Syr Charles Bawdin.
Budding floweret blushes at the light [*or* Boddynge flourettes bloshes atte the lyghte], The.
Copernican System, The.
Excelente Balade of Charitie, An.
Goddwyn, *Sels.*
If Wishing for the Mystic Joys of Love.
Last Verses.
Methodist, The.
Mynstrelles Songe: "Angelles bee wrogte to bee of neidher kynde."
Ode to Liberty.
Ode to Miss Hoyland.
Oh! sing unto my roundelay [*or* O! Synge untoe mie roundelaie].

Resignation.
Sentiment.
Sunday: A Fragment Transcribed from a Ms. in Chatterton's Handwriting.

Chaucer, Geoffrey (1340?–1400)
Alas, that I ne had English, rhyme or prose.
And as for me, though that I konne [*or* can] but [*or* my wit be] lyte.
Balade: "Hide [*or* Hyd], Absalon, thy gilte tresses clere."
Balade de Bon Conseill.
Book of the Duchesse, The, *Sels.*
But in the dome of mighty Mars the red.
But, sires o word forgat I in my tale.
Canterbury Tales, The, *Sels.*
Clerk of Oxford, The.
Clerk's Tale, The.
Complaint of Chaucer to His Empty Purse, The.
Complaint of Troilus, The.
Controlling the Tongue.
Cook they hadde with hem for the nones.
Cook's Tale, The.
Courtly Scene and a Sudden Storm, A.
Death and the Three Revellers.
Envoy to Scogan.
Epilogue of the Man of Law's Tale, The.
Fair was this yonge wyf, and therwithal.
Firste stok, fader of gentilesse, The.
Floure and the Leafe, The, *Sels.*
Frankeleyn was in his companye.
Franklin's Prologue, The.
Franklin's Tale, The.
Frere ther was, a wantown and a merye.
Friar's Prologue, The.
Friar's Tale, The.
Gentil maunciple was ther of a Temple, A.
Go, Little Book ("Go, litel book, go litel myn tragedy").
Good Wif [*or* Wyf] was ther of biside [*or* bisyde] Bathe, A.
Haberdasshere and a carpenter.
Hide, Absolon, Thy Gilte Tresses Clere.
If no love is, O God, what fele I so.
If poor (you say) she drains her husband's purse.
In May, that moder is of monthes glade.
Introduction to the Franklin's Prologue, The.
Introduction to the Pardoner's Prologue, The.
Knight's Tale, The.
Knyght [*or* Knight] ther [*or* there] was, and that a worthy man, A.
Lak of Stedfastnesse.
Lat take a cat, and fostre him wel with milk.
Legend of Good Women: Prologue, The, *Sels.*
Letter of Dydo to Eneas, The.
Love Unfeigned, The.
Ma dame, ye ben of all beauté shrine.
Manciple's Tale, The.
Marchant was ther with a forked berd, A.
Merchant's Tale, The.
Merciles[s] Beaute [*or* Beautée *or* Beauty], *Sels.*
Miller was a stout carl, for the nones, The.
Miller's Prologue, The.
Miller's [*or* Milleres] Tale, The.
Monk ther was, a fair for the maistrye [*or* maistrie], A.
Now Welcom[e], Somer [*or* Summer].
Nun's Priest's Prologue, The.
Nun's Priest's Tale, The.
Pardoner's Prologue, The.
Pardoner's Tale, The.
Parlement of Foules, The, *Sels.*
Parson's Prologue, The.
Patient Griselda.
Pite, that I have sought so yore agoo.
Poor Parson, The.
Prioress, The.
Prioress's Tale, The.
Prologue.
Prologue of the Prioress's Tale, The.
Prologue to the Miller's Tale.
Prologue to the Second Nun's Tale, The.
Prologue to Sir Thopas.
Reve was a sclendre colerik man, The.

Sergeant of the Lawe, war and wys, A.
Shipman, The.
Somnour was ther with us in that place, A.
Somtyme the world was so stedfast and stable.
Sorrow of Troilus, The.
Swich fyn hath, lo, this Troilus for love!
Syn I fro Love.
This olde man gan looke in his visage.
This Palamon gain knytte his browes tweye.
This Pardoner had hair as yellow as wax.
This Troilus [*or* Troylus], with blisse [*or* Blysse] of that supprysed [*or* supprised].
Sir Thopas.
Three Rioters, The.
To Adam, His Scribe.
To Rosamond.
To Rosemounde, *Sels.*
Troilus and Criseyde [*or* Criseide], *Sels.*
Whan that Aprill[e] with his shoures [*or* shower] soote.
Whan they unto the paleys were yoemen.
Wife of Bath's Prologue, The.
Wife of Bath's Tale, The.
With him ther was his sone, a young Squyer.
With hym ther was a gentil pardoner.
With hym ther was a plowman, was his brother.
With us ther was a doctour of phisik.
Wooing of Criseide, The, III.
Yeman hadde he, and servaunts namo.

Chaudhari, Kirti (b. 1935)
Inertia.

Chaundler, Christine (1881–1972)
Child's Christmas Carol, A.

Chawner, George F.
Prayer: "Those who love Thee may they find."

Chear, Abraham (d. 1668)
To My Youngest Kinsman, R. L.

Chedid, Andrée (d. 1921)
Future and the Ancestor, The.
What Are We Playing At?

Cheek, Cris
Drawing on the Traditions, *Sels.*
Succulence by implication pinks the eye with condensation, A.

Cheever, George Barrell (1807–90)
Blest Be the Wondrous Grace.
Thy Loving Kindness, Lord, I Sing.

Cheke, Henry (1548–86)
Of Perfect Friendship.

Ch'en Hsiao-keng
Poems of the Hundred Flowers Blooming.

Ch'en Liang (1143–1194)
Tune: "Beautiful Lady Yü, The" — Spring Sorrow.
Tune: "Water Dragon's Chant" — Loathsome Spring.

Ch'en Tao (779–843)
Her Husband Asks Her to Buy a Bolt of Silk.

Ch'en Tzu-ang (661–702)
As the crescent moon is born from the Western Sea.
Impressions of Things Encountered, *Sels.*
Inscription on a Tree atop mount Sacrifice (Ssu Shan) and Sent to Censor Ch'iao.
Kingfishers nest on South Sea islands.
Orchids grow through spring and summer.
Song on Climbing the Gate Tower at Yu-chou, A.

Ch'en Tzu-lung (1608–47)
Ballad of the Little Cart, A.
Parable, A.
Tune: "Telling of Innermost Feelings" — Wandering in Spring.

Ch'en Yu Yi (1090–1138)
Enlightment.
"Immortal at the River" — Ascending a Little Tower at Night.
Journeying to Hsiang-yi.
Sitting on a Rock by Mountain Stream.
Spring Morning.

Cheney, Ednah Dow (1824–1904)
Larger Prayer, The.

Cheney, Elizabeth
Overheard in an Orchard.

To Urania.

Colman, George, the Younger (1762–1836)
Cold blows the blast — the night's obscure.
Maid of the Moor, The; or, The Water-Fiends, *Sels.*
On Sir Nathaniel Wraxall the Historian.
Unfortunate Miss Bailey.

Colman, Henry (*fl.* 1640)
On Lazarus Raised From Death.
On Mortality.
On the Inscription Over the Head of Christ on the Cross.
On the Strange Apparitions at Christ's Death.
On the Three Children in the Fiery Furnace.

Colombo, John Robert (b. 1936)
How They Made the Golem.
Ideal Angels.

Colonna, Vittoria da, Marchesa di Pescara (1490–1547)
As a hungry fledgling, who sees and hears.
As When Some Hungry Fledgling Hears and Sees.
I live on this depraved and lonely cliff.
Like a hungry fledgeling that watches and hears.
O what transparent waves, what a tranquil sea.
When the Orient is lit by the great light.
When the troubled sea swells and surrounds.

Colony, Horatio (1900–1977)
Ghost Pet.

Coltman, Paul
Cissbury Ring.
Hieronymus Bosch, We Can Do It.
Nursery Rhyme 1984.
Troy.

Colton, Arthur Willis (1868–1943)
Harps Hung Up in Babylon.

Colum, Padraic (1881–1972)
After Speaking of One Dead a Long Time.
Book of Kells, The.
Condors.
Cradle Song, A.
Dahlias.
Drover, A.
Fuchsia Hedges in Connacht.
Garland Sunday.
I Saw the Wind Today.
Interior.
Irises.
Monkeys.
No Child.
Old Soldier.
Old Woman of the Roads, An.
Peach Tree with Fruit.
Plower, The.
Poor Scholar of the 'Forties, A.
River-Mates.
She Moved through the Fair.
Wall of China, The.
Wild Ass.

Columba, Saint. *See* Columcille [*or* Columba], Saint.

Columbanus, Saint (*fl.* c.543–615)
Boat Song, A.
Boyhood of Christ, The.

Columcille [*or* Columba], Saint (*fl.* c.521–597)
Clamour of the wind making music.
Farewell to Ireland.
If I owned all of Alba.
Invocation: "My claw is tired of scribing!"
Mary mild, good maiden.
O Son of God, it would be sweet.
On a Dead Scholar, *Sels.*
On some island I long to be.
Prayer to the Virgin.
St. Columcille the Scribe.
Three places most loved I have left.

Colvin, Ian D. (1877–1938)
Flying Dutchman, The.
Tristan da Cunha.

Combs, Tram (b. 1924)
Ars Poetica about Ultimates.
Aware Aware.
Just after Noon with Fierce Shears.

Cometas (*fl.* c.950)
Country Gods.
Phyllis, loving Demophoon.
"Who, tell me, shepherd, owns these rows of plants?"

Comfort, Alex (b. 1920)
After Shakespeare.
After You, Madam.
Atoll in the Mind, The.
Epitaph: "One whom I knew, a student and a poet."
Fear of the Earth.
Haste to the Wedding.
Hoc Est Corpus.
Letter to an American Visitor.
Love Poem: "There is a white mare that my love keeps."
Lovers, The.
Notes for My Son.
Postures of Love, The, *Sels.*
Song for the Heroes.
Song of Lazarus, The, *Sels.*
Sublimation.

Compiuta Donzella (*fl.* c.1205)
To leave the world and serve God.

Concanen, Matthew (1701–49)
Match at Football, A, *Sels.*

Condee, Nancy
In the Late Afternoon.

Conder, Josiah (1789–1855)
Bread of Heaven, on Thee We Feed.
Day by Day the Manna Fell.

Condon, R. D.
Limerick: "Horsewoman of charm at Uttoxeter, A."

Cone, Helen Gray ("Coroebus Green") (1859–1934)
Narcissus in Camden.

Confucius (551–479 B.C.)
Airs of Pei, *Sels.*
Alba.
Aliter.
Baroness Mu Impeded in Her Wish to Help Famine Victims in Wei.
Be kind, good sir, and I'll lift my sark.
"Chkk! chkk!" hopper-grass.
Chou and the South, *Sels.*
Deer Sing, *Sels.*
Efficient Wife's Complaint, The.
Fraternitas.
Hep-Cat Chung, 'ware my town.
In chariot like an hibiscus flower at his side.
In the South be drooping trees.
Marsh bank, lotus rank.
Pedlar.
Sans Equity and sans Poise.
Shao and the South, *Sels.*
So he won't talk to me when we meet?
Songs of Ch'en, *Sels.*
Songs of Cheng, *Sels.*
Songs of T'ang, *Sels.*
Three stars, five stars rise over the hill.
Wei Wind, *Sels.*
Yung Wind, *Sels.*

Congdon, Kirby (b. 1924)
Daredevil.

Congreve, William (1670–1729)
Aisle of a Temple, The.
Doris.
Epilogue: "After our Epilogue this crowd dismisses."
False Though She Be.
Hue and Cry after Fair Amoret, A.
Jack Frenchman's Defeat.
Lesbia.
Love for Love, *Sels.*
Mourning Bride, The, *Sels.*
Music.
Pious Selinda [*or* Celinda].
Prologue: "Of those few fools, who with ill stars are cursed."
Soldier and a Sailor, A.
Song: "See, see, she wakes, Sabina wakes!"
Way of the World, The, *Sels.*

Conkling, Hilda (b. 1910)
Dandelion.
I Am.
Little Papoose.
Little Snail.
Water.

Conn, Stewart (b. 1936)
Driving through Sutherland.
Ferret.
In the Gallery.
Tremors.
Under the Ice.
Visiting Hour.

Connell, Jim
Red Flag, The.

Connellan, Leo
Mommy's Hubby.

Connor, Tony (b. 1930)
Apologue.
Lancashire Winter.
Last of the Poet's Car.

Conoley, Gillian
One, The.

Conolly, John (1794–1866)
Fiddler's Green.

Conolly, John (1794–1866) *and* **Bill Meek**
Grimsby Lads, The.

Conover, Carl
Nude Reclining at Word Processor, in Pastel.

Conquest, Robert (b. 1917)
Appalachian Convalescence.
Excerpt from a Report to the Galactic Council.
Generalities.
Guided Missiles Experimental Range.
Horror Comic.
Lake Success.
Limerick: "My demands upon life are quite modest."
Limerick: "Our existence would be that much grimmer ex-."
Limerick: "Then scorn not the limerick either."
Limerick: "When a man's too old even to toss off, he."
Man and Woman.
Poem in 1944.
Rokeby Venus, The.
Semantic.
747 (London-Chicago).
To Be a Pilgrim.

Conran, Anthony (b. 1931)
Death of a Species.
Elegy for Sir Ifor Williams.
Fledgling.

Constable, Henry (1562–1613)
Dear to my soul! then leave me not forsaken!
Diana, *Sels.*
Hope, like the hyaena [*or* hyena], coming to be old.
Miracle of the world, I never will deny.
Needs must I leave and yet needs must I love.
On the Death of Sir Philip Sidney.
Resolved to Love.
Sonnet: "If ever Sorrow spoke from soul that loves."
Sonnet: "My lady's presence makes the roses red."
To God the Holy Ghost.
To live in hell, and heaven to behold.
To Our Blessed Lady.
To St. John Baptist.
To Saint Margaret.
To Saint Mary Magdalen.
To St. Michael the Archangel.
To St. Peter and St. Paul.
To the Blessed Sacrament.
To the Marquess of Piscat's Soul.
Whilst Echo cries [*or* eccho cryes], "What shall become of me[e]?"

Constable, Henry *and* **Henry Chettle**
Diaphenia.
To His Flocks.

Copenhaver, Laura S. (1868–1940)
Heralds of Christ.

Copland, Robert (*fl.* 1508–47)
High Way to the Spital House, The, *Sels.*
To write of Sol in his exaltation.

Coppard, Alfred Edgar (1878–1957)
Apostate, The.
Epitaph: "Like silver dew are the tears of
  love."
Forester's Song.
Mendacity.
Unfortunate Miller, The.

Copping, Coral E.
Limerick: "Dad waited while Mum bought the
  ham."

Corben, John
Harlech Castle.
In the eggs.
On the Beach.

Corbett, E. R.
Inventor's Wife, The.

Corbett, Elizabeth T. (*fl.* c.1880)
Misspelled Tail, A.
Tail of the See, A.
Three Wise Couples, The.
Three Wise Old Women.

Corbett, Noel Marcus Francis
Sailing of the Fleet, The.

Corbett [*or* Corbet], Richard (1582–1635)
Certain True Woords Spoken Concerning One
  Benet Corbett after Her Death.
Distracted Puritan, The.
Elegy Upon the Death of His Own Father, An.
Epitaph on Dr. Donne, Dean of Paul's, An.
Fairies' Farewell, The, *Sels.*
Farewell rewards and fairies.
Great Tom.
Her Boreale, *Sels.*
Like to the Thundering Tone.
Little lute, when I am gone.
Non Sequitor [*or* Sequitur], A.
On Mr. Rice the Manciple of Christ Church in
  Oxford.
On the Lady Arabella.
Proper New Ballad, Intitled The Fairies'
  Farewell, A.
To His Son [*or* Sonne], Vincent Corbet[t].
Upon Fairford Windows.

Corbière, Edouard Joachim. *See* **Corbière,**
  Tristan.

Corbière, Tristan (Edouard Joachim Corbière)
  (1845–75)
End, The, *Sels.*
Epitaph: "Of many things adulterate."
Litany of Sleep, *Sels.*
To My Mouse-colored Mare.
To the Eternal Feminine.
Well, all these seamen — sailors and skippers —
  they.
You who snore with your sleeping wife so
  near.

Corbin, Alice (Alice Corbin Henderson) (1881–
  1949)
Echoes of Childhood.
Harvest, The.

Corbin, Lloyd M., Jr. (Djangatolum) (b. 1949)
Ali.
Dedication to the Final Confrontation.

Corby, Herbert
Reprisal.

Corcoran, Kelvin (b. 1956)
Apparently in the real past tough men dazzled
  the illiterate tribes.
Man dances with twelve girls, A.
Nobody Thinks Hard Enough for Poetry.
Slogan Will Not Suffice, A.
Volitionist Economics.

Corder, W. (b. 1927?)
Murder of Maria Marten, The.

Cording, Robert
Elegy for John, My Student Dead of AIDS.

Cordle, Edward (1857–1903)
Lizzie and Joe Catch a Thief.
Lizzie and Joe in Court.

Lizzie Discourses on the Small-Pox.

Corinna. *See* **Korinna** [*or* **Corinna**].

Corke, Hilary (b. 1921)
Any Man to His Secretary.
Calm Winter Sleep.
Chair, Dog, and Clock.
Choice, The.
Destroying Angel.
Ghost, The.
November Poppies.
Poem at Equinox.
Storm of Love, A.
Waiting.
Waltz, The.

Corkine, William
My Dearest Mistress.
Shall a Frown.
Sweet Cupid, Ripen Her Desire.

Cormac, King of Cashel (9th cent.)
Instructions of King Cormac.

Corman, Cid (b. 1924)
Call it a louse — I'm.
Container, The.
Deceased.
Desk, The.
I have come far to have found nothing.
La Selva.
Locus, The.
There are things to be said. No doubt.
Three Tiny Songs, *Sels.*
Tortoise, The.

Cormican, P. J. (1858–1945)
True Son of God, Eternal Light.

Corn, Alfred (b. 1943)
Assistances.
Call in the Midst of the Crowd, A, *Sels.*
Darkening Hotel Room.
Deception.
Fire: The People.
Infernal Regions and the Invisible Girl.
Infinity Effect at the Hôtel Soubise.
Naskeag.
Older Men.
One to One.
Remembering Mykenai.

Corneille, Pierre (1606–84)
Psyche.

Cornelius, Maxwell N.
Some Time We'll Understand.

Cornelius, Peter (1824–74)
Christmas Tree, The.

Cornell, Annette Patton
Sailor's Woman.

Cornford, Frances (Darwin) (1886–1960)
All Souls' Night.
At Night.
Autumn Morning at Cambridge.
Childhood.
Coast, The: Norfolk.
Country Bedroom, The.
Daybreak.
Epitaph for a Reviewer.
For M.S. Singing *Fruhlingsglaube* in 1945.
Glimpse, A.
Guitarist Tunes Up, The.
Herd, The.
Hills, The.
In the Backs.
Inscription for a Wayside Spring.
Limerick: "How often and often I wish."
Limerick: "There was a young woman who
  said."
London Despair.
Near an Old Prison.
Night Song.
Parting in Wartime.
Recollection, A.
Scholar, The.
She Warns Him.
Spring Morning.
Summer Beach.
To a Fat Lady Seen from the Train.
Unbeseechable, The.
Village before Sunset.
Wasted Day, A.

Watch, The.
Weekend Stroll.

Cornford, John (1915–36)
Full Moon at Tierz; before the Storming of
  Huesca.
Huesca.
Letter from Aragon, A.

Cornish, Sam (b. 1935)
Black Man, A.
Brother of the Streets.
Death of Dr. King.
Fannie Lou Hamer.
Frederick Douglass.
Harriet in the Promised Land.
Montgomery.
One Eyed Black Man in Nebraska.
Panther.
River, The.
To a Single Shadow without Pity.
When My Grandmother Died.
Women Walk.

Cornish, William (c.1465–c.1523)
Desire.
Pleasure It Is.

"Cornwall, Barry" (Bryan Waller Proctor)
  (1787–1874)
"Blood Horse," The.
Fate of the Oak, The.
For a Fountain.
Hunter's Song, The.
Leveller, The.
Sea, The.

Cornwall, Ursula
Sowing Seeds.

Cornwallis, Kinahan (1839–1917)
Battle of Murfreesboro, The.

Cornwell, Henry Sylvester (1831–86)
Jefferson D.

Corpi, Lucha (b. 1945)
Dark Romance.
Day's Work.
Devil's Daughter, The.
It's Raining.
Mariana.
Marina Mother.
Marina Poems, The, *Sels.*
Marina Virgin.
Nineteen.
She (Marina Distant).

Corrie, Joe (b. 1894)
Image o' God, The.
Miners' Wives.

Corrington, John William (b. 1932)
For a Woodscolt Miscarried.
On the Flesh of Christ.
Second Coming, The.

Corrothers, James David (1869–1917)
Indignation Dinner, An.
Paul Laurence Dunbar.

Corso, Gregory (b. 1930)
Birthplace Revisited.
Body Fished from the Seine.
Bomb.
But I Do Not Need Kindness.
Columbia U Poesy Reading — 1975.
Dialogue — 2 Dollmakers.
Difference of Zoos, A.
Dream of a Baseball Star.
Dreamed Realization, A.
For Miles.
From Another Room.
Hello.
I Am 25.
I Held a Shelley Manuscript.
I Met This Guy Who Died.
In the Fleeting Hand of Time.
Mad Yak, The.
Marriage.
New York City — 1935.
Notes after Blacking Out.
Paranoia in Crete.
Paris.
Poets Hitchhiking on the Highway.
Reflection in a Green Arena.
Requiem for "Bird" Parker.

Seed Journey.
Spontaneous Requiem for the American Indian.
Uccello.
Vestal Lady on Brattle, The.
Vision of Rotterdam.
Waterchew!
Whole Mess . . . Almost, The.
Writ on the Eve of My 32nd Birthday.
Zizi's Lament.

Cortázar, Julio (1914–84)
Behavior of Mirrors on Easter Island, The.
Instructions on How to Wind a Watch.
Instructions on *or rather* Examples of How to
Be Afraid.
Lines of the Hand, The.
Marvelous Pursuits.
Progress and Retrogression.
Theme for a Tapestry.

Cortez, Jayne (b. 1936)
Everything Is Wonderful.
For Real.
For the Poets.
Grinding Vibrato.
I Am New York City.
I See Chano Pozo.
I'm A Worker.
In the Morning.
Initiation.
Into This Time.
Lead.
Lonely Woman.
Mercenaries & Minstrels.
Ogun's Friend.
Orange Chiffon.
Orisha.
Phraseology.
Rising, The.
Rose Solitude.
So Long.
So Many Feathers.
Solo Finger Solo.
Stockpiling.
Suppression.
Tapping.
Under the Edge of February.

Corvo, Baron. *See* **Rolfe, Frederick William.**

Corwin, Norman (b. 1910)
Man unto His Fellow Man.
On a Note of Triumph, *Sels.*

Cory, David (1872–1966)
Miss You.

Cory, William Johnson (1823–92)
Ballad for a Boy, A.
Bride's Song, The.
Dirge: "Naiad, hid beneath the bank."
Eton Boating Song.
Heraclitus.
Hersilia.
Mimnermus in Church.
Poor French Sailor's Scottish Sweetheart, A.
Separation, A.

Coslett, Coslett (1834–1910)
Pole Star, The.

Cossins, A. C.
Limerick: "Modest young maiden of Rennes,
A."

Costello, Tomas
Lament for Una, A, *Sels.*
Young Una, you were a rose in a garden.

Cothi, Lewis Glyn (*fl.* 1447–86)
Lament for Siôn y Glyn.

Cottam, Samuel Elsworth (b. 1863)
To G. R.

Cotter, Joseph Seamon, Sr. (1895–1919)
Algernon Charles Swinburne.
And What Shall You Say?
Answer to Dunbar's "After a Visit."
April Day, An.
Band of Gideon, The.
Book's Creed, The.
Deserter, The.
Dr. Booker T. Washington to the National
Negro Business League.
Don't-Care Negro, The.
Frederick Douglass.

Ned's Psalm of Life for the Negro.
On Hearing James W. Riley Read.
Rain Music.
Sonnet to Negro Soldiers.
Supplication.
Tragedy of Pete, The.
Way-Side Well, The.
William Lloyd Garrison.

Cottle, Joseph (1770–1853)
Industrial Evils.
Malvern Hills, *Sels.*

Cotton, Charles (1630–87)
Alice.
Epitaph on M. H., An.
Evening.
Laura Sleeping.
Litany: "From a ruler that's a curse."
Marg'ret of Humbler Stature by the Head.
Martha Is Not So Tall.
Mary Is Black.
Montrose.
Morning Quatrains, The.
On My Pretty Marten.
On Tobacco.
Resolution in Four Sonnets, of a Poetical
Question Put to Me by a Friend, Concerning
Four Rural Sisters, *Sels.*
Retirement, The.
To Coelia.
To Mr. Izaak Walton, *Sels.*
To Poet Edmund Waller, Occasioned for His
Writing a Panegyric on Oliver Cromwell.
Winter, *Sels.*
Winter's Troops.

Cotton, John (1584–1652)
In Saram.
Pumpkins.
Thankful Acknowledgment of God's
Providence, A.
To My Reverend Dear Brother, M. Samuel
Stone.

Cotton, John (b. 1925)
Old Movies.

Cotton, John (*fl.* 1676)
Bacon's Epitaph, Made by His Man.
Upon the Death of G. B.

Cotton, Nathaniel (1705–80)
Bee, the Ant, and the Sparrow, The.
Contentment.
Early Thoughts of Marriage.
To a Child [of] Five Years Old.

Coulette, Henri (b. 1927)
At the Telephone Club.
Attic, The.
Author to Reader.
Black Angel, The.
Blue-eyed Precinct Worker, The.
Cinema at the Lighthouse.
Correspondence.
Denise: A Letter Never Sent.
Emeritus, n.
Family Goldschmitt, The.
Junk Shop, The.
Night Thoughts.
Phono, at the Boar's Head.
Postscript.
Sickness of Friends, The.
War of the Secret Agents, The, *Sels.*

Coursen, H. R. (b. 1932)
Suburban.

Courthope, William John
Dodoism.
Paradise of Birds, The, *Sels.*

Courtney, Margaret
Be Kind.

Cousens, Mildred (b. 1904)
American Vineyard.

Couto, Nancy Vieira
Living in the La Brea Tar Pits.
Lizzie.
Tea Party.
You Bet Your Life.

Couzyn, Jeni (b. 1942)
Cartography of the Subtle Heart.
Christmas in Africa, *Sels.*

Dawn.
Death in Winter, A.
Message, The.
My Father's Hands.
One autumn afternoon when I was nine.
Way Towards Each Other, The.
World War II.
You Have Shown Me a Strange Image, and We
Are Strange Prisoners.

Coverdale, Miles
Let Go the Whore of Babylon.
Of the Resurrection.
Song of the Virgin Mary, The.

Coward, Noël (1899–1973)
A. Stands for Absolutely Anything.
Any Part of Piggy.
Bar on the Piccola Marina, A.
Boy Actor, The.
Bronxville Darby And Joan.
Children of the Ritz.
Contours.
Convalescence.
Don't Make Fun of the Fair, *Sels.*
Don't make fun of the festival.
He Never Did That to Me.
I Am No Good at Love.
I Wonder What Happened to Him.
Irish Song (Rosie O'Grady).
I've Been to a Marvelous Party.
Let's Do It, *Sels.*
Little Ones' A. B. C., The, *Sels.*
Mad Dogs and Englishmen.
Mr. Irving Berlin.
Mrs Worthingtion, *Sels.*
1901, *Sels.*
Regarding yours, dear Mrs Worthington.
Room with a View, A.
Sail Away, *Sels.*
Stately Homes of England, The.
There Are Bad Times Just around the Corner.
To L. R-M.
To Noël Coward.
What's Going to Happen to the Tots?
When Queen Victoria died.
Words and Music, *Sels.*

Cowdery, Mae V. (b. 1910)
After the Japanese.
Brown Aesthete Speaks, A.
Dusk.
Exultation.
Farewell: "No more/ The feel of your hand."
God Is Kind.
Having Had You.
Heritage.
I Sit and Wait for Beauty.
If I Must Know.
Insatiate.
Interlude.
Lines to a Sophisticate.
Longings.
Of Earth.
Poem . . . For a Lover.
Poplar Tree.
Prayer, A.
Some Hands Are Lovelier.
Want.
Wind Blows, The.

Cowen, Joseph R. (b. 1923)
Recessional for the Class of 1959 of a School
for Delinquent Negro Girls.

Cowley, Abraham (1618–67)
Against Fruition.
Against Hope.
Age.
Beauty.
Change, The.
Cheer Up, My Mates.
Christ's Passion.
Chronicle; a Ballad, The.
Clad All in White.
Country-Mouse, The.
Crown me with roses whilest I live.
David and Jonathan.
Davideis, *Sels.*
Destinie, *Sels.*
Dialogue after Enjoyment.

New Year's Day.
O Heart! the equal poise of love's both parts.
O thou undaunted daughter of desires!
Ode Which was Prefixed to a Prayer Booke Given to a Young Gentlewoman, An.
On a Prayer Book Sent to Mrs. M.R, *Sels*.
On Marriage.
On Mr. G. [*or* George] Herbert's Book[e] Intituled [*or* Entitled] the Temple of Sacred Poems, Sent to a Gentle-woman.
On the Baptized Ethiopian (*or* Aethiopian).
On the Bleeding Wounds of Our Crucified Lord, *Sels*.
On the Blessed Virgin's Bashfulness.
On the Glorious Assumption of Our Blessed Lady.
On the Miracle of Loaves.
On the Miracle of Multiplied Loaves.
On the Water of Our Lord's Baptism.
On the Wounds of Our Crucified Lord.
Out of the Italian; a Song.
Psalm 23.
Saint Mary Magdalene.
Saint Mary Magdalene or the Weeper.
Samson to His Delilah.
She Began to Wash His Feet with Tears and Wipe Them with the Hairs of Her Head.
Shepherds' Hymn, The.
Shepherd's Hymn, The ("We saw Thee in Thy balmy nest").
Song: "Lord, when the sense of Thy sweet grace."
Specifications for a Perfect Lover.
Tear [*or* The Teare], The.
Temperance or the Cheap Physitian upon the Translation of Lessius.
Thou art love's victim; and must die.
To Our Blessed Lord upon the Choice of His Sepulchre.
To Our Lord, upon the Water Made Wine.
To the Infant Martyrs.
To the Name above Every Name, the Name of Jesus, a Hymn.
To the Noblest and Best of Ladies, the Countess of Denbigh.
Two Went Up into the Temple to Pray.
Upon Bishop Andrewes's [*or* Andrewes His] Picture before His Sermons.
Upon Lazarus His Teares.
Upon the Ass That Bore Our Saviour.
Upon the Body of Our Blessed Lord, Naked and Bloody.
Upon the Holy Sepulchre.
Upon the Infant Martyrs.
Upon Venus Putting on Mars His Armes.
Wishes. To His (Supposed) Mistresse, *Sels*.

Crates (*fl.* 450 B.C.)
Time's fingers bend us slowly.

Craveirinha, José (b. 1922)
Man Never Cries, A.
Ode to a Lost Cargo in a Ship Called *Save*.
Poem of the Future Citizen.
Tasty 'Tanjarines' of Inhambane, The.

Crawford, Dan (1869–1926)
Jesus and I.

Crawford, Francis Marion (1854–1929)
New National Hymn.

Crawford, H.
In the Same Boat.

Crawford, Isabella Valancy (1850–87)
Battle, A.
Bite deep and wide, O Axe, the tree.
Camp of Souls, The.
Dark Stag, The.
Gisli, the Chieftain, *Sels*.
Malcolm's Katie, *Sels*.
Said the Canoe.
South Wind laid his moccasins aside, The.

Crawford, Louisa Macartney
Kathleen Mavourneen.

Crawford, Robert (b. 1859)
Doun the Burn, Davie.
My Iambic Pentameter Lines.

Crawford, Roger
Love Song of Tommo Frogley.

Crawford, Tom
Nestucca River Poem.

Crawford, Vesta Pierce (1899–1983)
Pioneer Woman.

Creeley, Robert (b. 1926)
Act of Love, The.
After Lorca.
Again.
Age ("most explicit — ").
Air: "Cat bird singing."
Air: "Love of a woman, The."
All That Is Lovely in Men.
America.
And.
Anger.
As I Was Walking.
Awakening, The.
Ballad of the Despairing Husband.
Bird, the Bird, the Bird, The.
Broken Back Blues.
Business, The.
City, The.
Counterpoint, A.
Crisis, The.
Damon and Pythias.
Death of Venus, The.
Door, The.
End of the Day, The.
Faces, The.
Fancy.
Figures, The.
Finger, The.
Fire, The.
First Rain.
Flower, The.
For Friendship.
For Love.
For My Mother: Genevieve Jules Creeley.
For No Clear Reason.
For the New Year.
For W.C.W.
Form of Women, A.
Gift, The.
Gift of Great Value, A.
Here.
Heroes.
Hill, The.
I Keep to Myself Such Measures.
I Know a Man.
If You.
Immoral Proposition, The.
Innocence, The.
Invoice, The.
Joy.
Just Friends.
Kind of Act Of, The.
Language, The.
Man, The.
Marriage, A.
Mechanic, The.
Memory, The.
Moment.
Moon, The.
Mother's Voice.
Movie Run Backward, The.
Naughty Boy.
Oh No.
Old Song.
On Vacation.
Operation, The.
Outside.
People, The.
Place.
Plague.
Pool, The.
Prayer to Hermes.
Quick-Step.
Rain, The.
Reason, A.
Rescue, The.
Rhythm, The.
Self-Portrait.
She Went to Stay.
Sight, A.
Somebody Died.
Something.

Somewhere.
Song: "Those rivers run from that land."
Song: "What I took in my hand."
Statue, The.
Thinking.
Three Ladies, The.
Time.
Token, A.
Turn, The.
Wait for Me.
Waiting.
Warning, The.
Way, The.
Whip, The.
Wicker Basket, A.
Wife, The.
Window, The.
World, The.

Creelman, Josephine Rice
My Mother.

Cresson, Abigail
Cloak of Laughter.

Crew, Louie (b. 1936)
Gay Psalm from Fort Valley, A.

Crewe, Robert Offley Ashburton Crewe-Milnes, Marquess of (1858–1945)
Harrow and Flanders.

Crinagoras (b. c.70 B.C.)
Back from the west, back from the war, Marcellus.
Dedication of a Torch.
Eartha my mother's name, now earth.
Epigrams, *Sels*.
Epitaph on an Infant.
Forehead without scalp, dry shell without yolk of eye.
Foul sod covers a bad one here.
From the Greek Anthology.
Here are grapes ready to turn to wine.
How long in these empty thermals near the cold.
Left and right, I toss about my bed.
Linguist parrot flicked his flowery wings, The.
Lucky shepherd, if only on the hill.
On the Death of Cleopatra-Selene.
Roses used to bloom in spring.
Sailing to Italy — fitting out/ commissioning — to see the friends.
This longed-for morning here is our sacrifice/ to Zeus the finisher, and Artemis goddess of childbirth.
This silver thing I send you for your birthday.
This wingtip feather from a hook-beaked eagle.
Though of white marble and dressed straight.
Though you are sedentary always, though.
Turn on your left side, back to your right again.
Unhappy men, why do we travel so.
You toss now to the left; you toss now to the right.

Cristall, Anne Batten (b. c.1798)
Blind Man, The.
Evening, Gertrude.
Morning, Rosamonde.
Song: "Through springtime walks, with flowers perfumed."

Criswell, Cloyd Mann (b. 1908)
Newlyweds, The.

Crites, Lucile (b. 1885)
Folks and Me.

"Critics, The" (*fl.* 1960s–1970s)
Grey October.

Croasdell, Ann (b. 1889)
Muffin Man, The.

Crocker, Henry (b. 1845)
Evangelize!

Crocker, T. F. Dillon
To shave, or not to shave? that is the question.

Croft, Julian (b. 1941)
D-Zug.
Graffiti.
Greenhalgh's Pub.

Croft, Roy (1919–77)
Love.

Croly, George (1780?–1860)
Death and Resurrection.
Death of Leonidas, The.
Crompton, Hugh (fl. 1657)
Winifred.
Time, the Interpreter.
Cronin, Anthony (b. 1925)
Apology.
Baudelaire in Brussels.
Elegy for the Nightbound.
For a Father.
Lines for a Painter.
Man Who Went Absent from the Native
    Literature, The.
Middle Years, The.
On the bog road the blackthorn flowers, the
    turf-stacks.
Responsibilities.
R.M.S. *Titanic, Sels.*
Trembling with engines, gulping oil, the river.
Cronin, Jeremy (b. 1949)
Group Photo from Pretoria Local on the
    Occasion of a Fourth Anniversary (Never
    Taken).
Lullaby: "But who killed Johannes, mama
    . . .?"
River That FLows through Our Land, The.
To Learn How to Speak.
Cronwright, Samuel Cron (1863–1936)
Song of the Wagon-whip, A.
Cros, Charles (1842–88)
Smoked Herring, The.
Crosby, Ernest (1856–1907)
"Rebels."
War and Hell.
**Crosby, Fanny (Frances Jane Crosby) (1820–
1915)**
Best of All, The.
Blessed Assurance.
Jesus, Keep Me Near the Cross.
Keep Thou My Way, O Lord.
Unseen.
Crosby, Ranice Henderson (b. 1952)
Poem about a Seashell.
Thoughts for You (When She Came Back from
    the Mountains).
Crosland, T. W. H. (1865–1924)
Slain.
Cross, Allen Eastman (1864–1942)
Gray Hills Taught Me Patience, The.
Though Fatherland Be Vast.
Young and Radiant, He Is Standing.
**Cross, Mary Ann [or Marian] Evans
Lewes.** See **"Eliot, George."**
Cross, Zora (b. 1890)
Elegy on an Australian Schoolboy, *Sels.*
In me there is a vast and lonely place.
Love Sonnets, *Sels.*
What have you more than I, who crave you so?
When I Was Six.
Crossland, John R. (b. 1892)
Water.
Crossley-Holland, Kevin (b. 1941)
Postcards from Kodai.
Crossman, Samuel (1624?–1684)
My Song Is Love Unknown.
Croswell, William (1804–51)
Lord! Lead the Way the Saviour Went.
Crouch, Nathaniel (1632?–1725?)
David and Goliath.
Tower of Babel, The.
Crouch, Stanley (b. 1945)
Albert Ayler: Eulogy for a Decomposed
    Saxophone Player.
Blackie Thinks of His Brothers.
No New Music.
Riding across John Lee's Finger.
Crow, Mary
Fault-Finding.
Going Home.
Crow, Steve (b. 1949)
El Alamein.
Louisiana.

Revival.
Songs, *Sels.*
They say a man dies.
Water Song.
Crowe, William (1745–1829)
Lewesdon Hill, *Sels.*
Up to thy summit, Lewesdon, to the brow.
Crowell, Albert
Joy of Incompleteness, The.
Crowell, Charmaine
Fat Blues.
Crowell, Grace Noll (b. 1877)
Because of Thy Great Bounty.
Common Tasks, The.
Courage to Live.
Definition.
Eternal Values.
I Have Found Such Joy.
I Think That God is Proud.
Poet Prays, The.
Prayer for a Day's Walk.
Quiet Things.
Crowell, Henry
When Thou Passest through the Waters.
Crowley, Aleister (1875–1947)
Lesbian Hell, The.
Crowley, Robert
As I walked alone.
Crowne, John (1640?–1703?)
Calisto, *Sels.*
Song: "Kind lovers, love on."
"Crowquill, Alfred." See **Forrester, Alfred A.**
Croxall, Samuel (1690?–1752)
Sylvia.
Crozier, Andrew
Advance of happiness, The.
Already the ducklings resemble their aunts and
    uncles.
Birds in Sunlight.
Clouds and Windows.
Evaporation of a Dream.
February Evenings.
Fifth Variation.
Forsythia.
Humiliation in Its Disguises.
Life Class, The.
Light in the Air.
Local Colour.
Permanent Wave.
Poem of This Poem.
Rain totally insistent drizzles.
Source, The.
Swoon.
Two Robin Croft.
Utamaro Variations.
Veil Poem, The.
White Launch.
Winter Intimacies.
Crozier, Andrew (b. 1943)
All of your ideas.
All that it should be.
High Zero, *Sels.*
In the time it takes.
Then in the smoke.
Cruceius, Annibal
Fair Ursly, in a merry mood.
Cruickshank, Alfred (c.1880–c.1940)
Convict Song, The.
God or Mammon.
Let Us Be Frank.
Cruickshank, Helen B.
Comfort in Puirtith.
Shy Geordie.
Crum, Lady Erskine
"Good Night," Says the Owl.
Crummy, Biddy
Poem to Be Said on Hearing the Birds Sing, A.
Cruz, Victor Hernandez (b. 1949)
Anonymous.
Carmen.
Confusion.
Don Arturo Says.
Electric Cop, The.

Energy.
First Claims Poem.
Geography of The Trinity Corona.
Going Uptown to Visit Miriam.
Invisibility O.
Listening to the Music of Arsenio Rodríguez Is
    Moving Closer to Knowledge.
Physics of Ochun, The.
Spirits.
Story of the Zeros, The.
Today Is a Day of Great Joy.
Two Guitars.
Urban Dream.
Cruz, Víctor Hernández. See **Hernández
Cruz, Víctor.**
Crystal, Catherine Nomura
Embroidery.
Cudmore, C. D.
Limerick: "Active balls?" said an old man of
    Stoneham."
Cudmore, D. H.
Limerick: "Ascetic art student named Josh,
    An."
Limerick: "Ballistical student named Raffity,
    A."
Limerick: "English professor named Brooks,
    An."
Limerick: "There was a young lady at court."
Cuevish, Lucario
Before They Made Things Be Alive They
    Spoke.
Cullen, Cornelius C.
Battle of Somerset.
Cullen, Countee (1903–46)
Black Majesty.
Brown Boy to Brown Girl.
Brown Girl Dead, A.
Christus Natus Est.
For a Lady I Know.
For a Mouthy Woman.
For a Poet.
For a Virgin Lady.
For Amy Lowell.
For Daughters of Magdalen.
For John Keats, Apostle of Beauty.
For My Grandmother.
For Paul Laurence Dunbar.
Four Epitaphs, *Sels.*
From Life to Love.
From the Dark Tower.
Fruit of the Flower.
Heritage.
I Have a Rendezvous with Life.
Incident.
Judas Iscariot.
Lines to Our Elders.
Litany of the Dark People, The.
Mary, Mother of Christ.
Only the Polished Skeleton.
Protest.
Saturday's Child.
Scottsboro, Too, Is Worth Its Song.
Simon the Cyrenian Speaks.
Tableau.
To Certain Critics.
To John Keats, Poet, at Springtime.
To Lovers of Earth: Fair Warning.
Uncle Jim.
Under the Mistletoe.
Unknown Color, The.
Wise, The.
Yet Do I Marvel.
Youth Sings a Song of Rosebuds.
Cullinan, Patrick (b. 1932)
M. François le Vaillant Recalls His Travels to
    the Interior Parts of Africa.
Cumbie, Richard
New Jersey Turnpike.
Cumbo, Kattie M. (b. 1938)
Black Sister.
Ceremony.
Domestics.
I'm a Dreamer.
Morning after . . . Love, The.
Nocturnal Sounds.

Cumming, Patricia
Caesura.
Spring.

Cummings, David
Emily's Haunted Housman.
From the Brothers Grimm to Sister Sexton to
  Mother Goose; One Transmogrification.
Sweeney, Old and Phthisic, among the
  Hippopotami.

Cummings, Edward Estlin (1894–1962)
All Ignorance Toboggans into Know.
All in Green Went My Love Riding.
All Nearness Pauses, While a Star Can Grow.
All Which Isn't Singing Is Mere Talking.
Always before Your Voice My Soul.
Annie Died the Other Day.
Anyone Lived in a Pretty How Town.
As Freedom Is a Breakfastfood.
As Joe Gould says in.
Being to Timelessness as It's to Time.
Buffalo Bill's.
Buy Me an Ounce and I'll Sell You a Pound.
Cambridge Ladies Who Live in Furnished
  Souls, The.
Chansons Innocentes, Sels.
Come, Gaze with Me upon This Dome.
Darling! Because My Blood Can Sing.
Faithfully Tinying at Twilight Voice.
First of All My Dreams, The.
For prodigal read generous.
Four III.
Gee I Like to Think of Dead.
Goodby Betty, Don't Remember Me.
Great, A.
Greedy the People, The.
He as O, A.
Her Careful Distinct Sex Whose Sharp Lips
  Comb.
Hours Rise Up, The.
How many moments must (amazing each).
I.
I Am a Little Church (No Great Cathedral).
I Am So Glad and Very.
I carry your heart with me (I carry it in).
I Like My Body When It Is With Your Body.
I Sing of Olaf Glad and Big.
I Thank You God for Most This Amazing.
I Was Sitting in McSorley's.
I Will Be.
If Everything Happens That Can't Be Done.
If I Have Made, My Lady, Intricate.
If I Should Sleep with a Lady Called Death.
If in Beginning Twilight.
If There Are Any Heavens [My Mother Will
  (All by Herself) Have].
If (touched by love's own secret) we, like
  homing.
If Up's the Word; and a World Grows Greener.
If You Can't Eat You Got To.
(Im)C-A-T(mo).
IN) all those who got.
In Heavenly Realms of Hellas Dwelt.
In just-/ spring when the world is mud.
In Time of Daffodils(Who Know.
It Is at Moments after I Have Dreamed.
It Is So Long Since My Heart Has Been with
  Yours.
It May Not Always Be So.
It Really Must Be Nice.
It Was a Goodly Co.
Item.
It's Over a (See Just).
L(a.
La Guerre.
Ladies and Gentlemen This Little Girl.
Little joe gould has lost his teeth and doesn't
  know where.
Little tree.
Love is a place.
Maggie and Milly and Molly and May.
Man Who Had Fallen among Thieves, A.
May I Feel Said He.
May My Heart Always.
Me Up at Does.
Melancholy, The.
Mr. U Will Not Be Missed.

Mouse)Won.
My Father Moved through Dooms of Love.
My Love.
My specialty is living said.
My Sweet Old Etcetera.
My Uncle Daniel.
Next to of course god america i.
Nine Birds.
No Man, if Men Are Gods.
No Time Ago.
Nobody Loses All the Time.
Notice the Convulsed Orange Inch of Moon.
Now Comes the Good Rain Farmers Pray for
  (and).
Now Does Our World Descend.
Now is a Ship.
O By the By.
O pr/ gress verily thou art m.
O Sweet Spontaneous.
Old Age Sticks.
One Times One, Sels.
One X.
Out of Midsummer's Blazing Most Not Night.
Paris; This April Sunset Completely Utters.
Pity This Busy Monster, Manunkind.
Plato Told.
Plato Told Him.
Poem, or Beauty Hurts Mr. Vinal.
Politician, A.
Ponder, Darling, These Busted Statues.
Pretty a Day, A.
Purer than Purest Pure.
Q:dwo.
Raise the Shade.
"Right Here the Other Night Something."
R-P-O-P-H-E-S-S-A-G-R.
Salesman Is an It That Stinks Excuse, A.
Season 'Tis, My Lovely Lambs, The.
She Being Brand.
Silence.
Since Feeling Is First.
Slightly before the middle of Congressman
  Pudd.
So Shy Shy Shy(and with a.
Somewhere I Have Never Travelled [, Gladly
  Beyond].
Song: "Thy fingers make early flowers of all
  things."
Sonnet "Wind has blown the rain away and
  blown, A."
Sonnets — Actualities, Sels.
Sonnets — Realities, Sels.
Sonnets — Unrealities, Sels.
Space Being (Don't Forget to Remember)
  Curved.
Spring is like a perhaps hand.
Spring omnipotent goddess thou dost.
Stand with Your Lover on the Ending Earth.
Sunset.
Than (By Yon Sunset's Wintry Glow).
Thanksgiving (1956).
This Is the Garden.
This Little Bride and Groom Are.
Tulips & Chimneys, Sels.
Twenty-seven Bums Give a Prostitute the Once.
Two X.
Up into the Silence the Green.
Way to Hump a Cow Is Not, The.
What a Proud Dreamhorse.
What If a Much of a Which of a Wind.
Whatever's Merely Wilful.
When any mortal (even the most odd).
When faces called flowers float out of the
  ground.
When God Lets My Body Be.
When My Sensational Moments Are No More.
When Serpents Bargain for the Right to
  Squirm.
When the Spent Day Begins to Frail.
When what hugs stopping earth than silent is.
Wherelings Whenlings.
White Guardians of the Universe of Sleep.
Who Are You, Little I.
Who Knows if the Moon's.
Who's Most Afraid of Death? Thou.

Why Did You Go.
Wild (at Our First) Beasts Uttered Human
  Words.
YgUDuh.
You Shall above All Things Be Glad and
  Young.
Your Birthday Comes to Tell Me This.

Cummins, Evelyn Atwater (b. 1891)
I Know Not Where the Road Will Lead.

Cumpian, Carlos (b. 1953)
Above Drudgery.
Coyote Sun.
Survivor, The: Anishinabe Man.

Cuney, Waring (1906–76)
Death Bed, The.
Dust.
I Think I See Him There.
My Lord, What a Morning.
No Images.
O. T.'s Blues.
Radical, The.
Triviality, A.
True Love.

Cunningham, Allan (1784–1842)
Gone Were but the Winter Cold.
Hame, Hame, Hame.
John Grumlie.
Wee, Wee German Lairdie, The.
Wet sheet and a flowing sea, A.

Cunningham, Ed
Limerick: "As the natives got ready to serve."

Cunningham, James (Olumo) (b. 1936)
And birds came crying.
City Rises, The.
Covenant, The.
Footnote to a Gray Bird's Pause, A.
For Cal.
From a Brother Dreaming in the Rye.
Happy Day (or Independence Day).
High-cool/2.
Incidental Pieces to a Walk.
Lee-ers of Hew.
Leg-acy of a Blue Capricorn.
Narrator's Trance, The, Sels.
Plea to My Sister, A.
Rapping Along with Ronda Davis.
St. Julien's Eve.
Slow Riff for Billy.
Solitary Visions of a Kaufmanoid.
Song thumbed down a cruiser for a ride, A.
Street in Kaufman-ville, A.
Tambourine.
There were blood spots on the skirt.
Welcome for Etheridge, A.
While Cecil Snores: Mom Drinks Cold Milk.
Woods are overhead over everywhere, The.

Cunningham, James Vincent (1911–85)
Aged Lover Discourses in the Flat Style, The.
Agnosco Veteris Vestigia Flammae.
All in Due Time.
And Now You're Ready Who While She Was
  Here.
Bride loved old words, and found her pleasure
  marred.
Choice.
Coffee.
Dear Child Whom I Begot.
Envoi: "Hear me, whom I betrayed."
Epigram: "After some years Bohemian came to
  this."
Epigram: "And what is love? Misunderstanding,
  pain."
Epigram: "Dark thoughts are my companions. I
  have wined."
Epigram: "Dear, if unsocial privacies obsess
  me."
Epigram: "Here lies my wife. Eternal peace."
Epigram: "Here lies New Critic who would fox
  us."
Epigram: "Homer was poor. His scholars live at
  ease."
Epigram: "How we desire desire! Joy of
  surcease."
Epigram: "I had gone broke, and got set to
  come back."

Epigram: "I who by day am function of the light."
Epigram: "In whose will is our peace? Thou happiness."
Epigram: "Life flows to death as rivers to the sea."
Epigram: "This is my curse, Pompous, I pray."
Epigram: "Time heals not: it extends a sorrow's scope."
Epigram: "Within this mindless vault."
Epigram: "You ask me how Contempt who claims to sleep."
Epitaph for Someone or Other.
Five Epigrams, *Sels.*
For My Contemporaries.
Friend, on This Scaffold Thomas More Lies Dead.
History of Ideas.
I married in my youth a wife.
In Innocence.
Interview with Doctor Drink.
Lady, of anonymous flesh and face.
Lip was a man who used his head.
Meditation on Statistical Method.
Metaphysical Amorist, The.
Miramar Beach.
Montana Fifty Years Ago.
Montana Pastoral.
Moral Poem, A.
Neaera when I'm there is adamant.
On a cold night I came through the cold rain.
Pope from penance purgatorial, The.
Rome.
Sonnet on a Still Night.
This *Humanist* Whom No Beliefs Constrained.
To a Friend, on Her Examination for the Doctorate in English.
To My Wife.
To What Strangers, What Welcome, *Sels.*
To Whom It May Concern.
Cunningham, John (1729–73)
Epigram: "Member of the modern great, A."
Holiday Gown.
Miller, The.
Morning.
On a Certain Alderman.
Sent to Miss Bell H — — , with a Pair of Buckles.
Cunningham, Julia (b. 1916)
Hymn to Joy.
Cunninghame-Graham, Robert. *See* **Graham, Robert.**
Curnow, Allen (b. 1911)
Canst Thou Draw Out Leviathan with an Hook.
Family Matter, A.
House and Land.
In the interim, how the children should be educated.
Kingfisher's naked arc alight, A.
Lone Kauri Road ("First time I looked seaward, westward").
Moro Assassinato, *Sels.*
Oldest of us burst into tears and cried, The.
Polynesia.
Seven ageing pine tree hide.
Skeleton of the Great Moa in the Canterbury Museum, Christchurch, The.
Small Room with Large Windows, A, *Sels.*
Spectacular Blossom.
Tomb of an Ancestor, *Sels.*
Trees, Effigies, Moving Objects, *Sels.*
Urban Guerrilla, An.
What it would look like if really there were only.
Wild Iron.
You Will Know When You Get There.
Curran, John Philpot (1750–1817)
Deserter's Lamentation, The.
Currey, Ralph Nixon (b. 1907)
Burial Flags.
Children Waking: Indian Hill Station.
Cock-Crow.
Halo.
In Memoriam: Roy Campbell.
Jersey Cattle.
Landscape of Violence.

Marrakech.
Remembering Snow.
Song: "There is no joy in water apart from the sun."
Ultimate Exile IV.
Unseen Fire.
Volubilis, North Africa.
Currie, Robert (b. 1937)
Brothers.
July the First.
Currier, John (1834–1912)
Electricity Is Funny!
Curtis, Christine Turner
Villa Sciarra: Rome.
Curtis, Monica
Limerick: "There were once two young people of taste."
Curtis, Simon (b. 1943)
Satie, at the End of Term.
Curtis, Tony (b. 1946)
Gambit.
Neighbour's Pear Tree.
Spirit of the Place, The.
To My Father.
Curtis, Walt
Skinnydipping on the Molalla River.
Curtright [*or* Curtwright], Wesley (b. 1910)
Close of Day, The.
Heart of the Woods.
Curzon, Colin (b. 1919)
Not Tonight, Josephine.
Curzon, David (b. 1941)
Proverbs 6:6.
Cusack, Cyril (b. 1910)
Cross Talk.
Summer Reflection.
Cushing, William O. (1823–1902)
We Are Watching, We Are Waiting.
Cushman, Ralph Spaulding (b. 1879)
His Presence Came Like Sunrise.
Cussons, Sheila
Barn-yard, The.
1945.
Yellow Gramophone.
Cussrooee, Biddy
My Grief on the Sea.
Cust, Henry (1861–1917)
Non Nobis.
Cutler, Julian S.
Through the Year.
Wonderful.
Cutler, William (1812–89)
One Talent, The.
Cutting, Sewall Sylvester (1813–82)
God of the World, Thy Glories Shine.
Gracious Saviour, We Adore Thee.
Cutts, Lord (1661–1707)
To a Lady, Who Desired Me Not To Be in Love with Her.
Cynddelw Brydydd Mawr (*fl.* 1155–1200)
In Praise of Owain Gwynedd.
Petition for Reconciliation.
Poem on His Death-Bed.
Cynewulf (*fl.* late 7th century)
Anchor: I must fight with the waves whipped up by the wind.
Anchor: "Oft I must strive with wind and wave."
Bellows: O wise man, weigh your words.
Book: Enemey ended my life, deprived me, An.
Book Moth: "A moth ate a word. To me it seemed."
Bread: I'm told a certain object grows.
Chalice: I heard a radiant ring, with no tongue.
Christ 2, *Sels.*
Churning (or Lovemaking): "Young man made for the corner, A."
Coat-of-Mail: Dank earth, wondrously cold, The.
Cock and Hen: I watched a couple of curious creatures.
Constantine's Vision of the Cross.

Creation: Enduring the Creator, He who now guides.
Cuckoo: In former days my father and mother [*or* mother and father].
Dream of the Rood, A.
Elene, *Sels.*
Fates of the Apostles, *Sels.*
Fire: On earth there's a warrior of curious origin.
Fish in River: "My house is not quiet, I am not loud."
Guthlac, *Sels.*
Helena Embarks for Palestine.
Honey-Mead: "I am valued by men, fetched from afar."
Horn: I'm loved by my lord, and his shoulder.
Horn: "Time was when I was weapon and warrior."
House Martins: This wind wafts little creatures.
I have great need that the Saint grant help.
Ice: On the way a miracle: water become bone.
Iceberg: Curious, fair creature came floating on the waves, A.
Jay: I've one mouth but many voices.
Juliana, *Sels.*
Key (or Penis): "Strange thing hangs by man's hip, A."
Leather: I travel by foot, trample the ground.
Lot and his two daughters and their sons: Man sat sozzled with his two wives, A.
Now I pray the man who may love this lay.
One-Eyed Seller of Arrows: Creature came shuffling where there sat, A.
Oyster: Deep sea suckled me, the waves sounded over me.
Pen and four fingers: I watched four fair creatures.
Plough: I keep my snout to the ground; I burrow.
Plow: "My beak is bent downward, I burrow below."
Reed: I sank roots first of all, stood.
Riddle: "I'm a strange creature, for I satisfy women."
Riddles (Exeter Book), *Sels.*
Shield: I'm by nature solitary, scarred by spear.
Shield: "Lonely wanderer, wounded with iron, A."
Soul and Body: I've heard tell of a noble guest.
Storm at Sea: Sometimes I plunge through the press of waves.
Sun and Moon: I saw a strange creature.
Swan, The.
Swan: Silent is my dress when I step across the earth.
Voyage of Life, The.
Weathercock, The: "I puff my breast out, my neck swells."
Wild Swan: "My attire is noiseless when I tread the earth."
Wind: "At times I resort, beyond man's discerning."
Cyrillus
Two-line epigram is perfect, A. Step.

D

"D., H." *See* **Doolittle, Hilda.**
"D., J." (*fl.* c.1595–1655?)
Essay on the Fleet Riding in the Downes, An.
Da Pistoia, Cino. *See* **Cino da Pistoia.**
Da Ponte, Lorenzo (1749–1837)
Capriccio Dramatico, Il, *Sels.*
Don Giovanni, *Sels.*
"Giovinette, Che Fate All'Amore."
To an Artful Theatre Manager.
Dabney, Betty Page (b. 1911)
Earth's Bondman.
Daby, Toolsy (b. 1938)
Labourer, The.
Dabydeen, Cyril (b. 1945)
Fat Men, The.
Fruit, of the Earth.
Rehearsal.

Words and Legacy.

Dabydeen, David (b. 1955)
Coolie Mother.
Coolie Odyssey.
Men and Women.
Slave Song.

Dacey, Florence
Farewell: "I search/ for the straight path."

Dacey, Philip (b. 1939)
Amputee Soldier, The.
Birthday, The.
Feet Man, The.
Form Rejection Letter.
Jack, Afterwards.
Jill, Afterwards.
Obscene Caller, The.
Prisms.
Rondel: "Beautiful snow falls on a bed, A."

Dach, Simon (1605–59)
Bonds of Friendship, The.
Lamentation during His Most Painful Illness.
On the Entrance of the Castle Bridge.
To Be Read above the Castle-Gate, When His Princely Highness Rode in to His Marriage Bed.

Dadié, Bernard (b. 1916)
Dry Your Tears, Africa!
Hands.
I Give You Thanks My God.
I Thank You, Lord.
In Memoriam.
Ode to Africa.
World to Come, A.
Wreath for Africa, A.

Dafydd ab Edmwnd (fl. 1450–80)
Girl's Hair, A.

Dafydd Bach ap Madog Wladaidd (fl. 1340–90)
Christmas Revel, A.

Dafydd Benfras (d. 1257)
From Exile.

Dafydd Nanmor (fl. 1450–90)
Ode to Rhys ap Maredudd of Tywyn.

Dafydd [or David] ap Gwilym (fl. 1340–70)
Cywdd to Morvydd, The.
Girls of Llanbadarn, The.
In Morfudd's Arms.
Rattle Bag, The.
Ruin, The.
Seagull, The.
Wind, The.
Woodland Mass, The.

Daglarca, Fazil Hüsnü (b. 1914)
Fire.
Hollow Echo.
Thought.
Unity.

D'Aguiar, Frederick (b. 1960)
Letter from Mama Dot.
On Duty.

Dahlberg, Edward (1900–1977)
Kansas City West Bottoms.

Daiches, David (b. 1912)
Notes for a History of Poetry.
To Kate, Skating Better than Her Date.
Ulysses' Library.
Winter Song.

Daihaku, Princess
How will you manage.

Dailey, Joel (b. 1953)
Everyone in the World.
Good Night.
Joie de Vivre.
Known.
Meanwhile.
Revving Up la Rêve.

Daini no Sanmi (fl. 10th–11th cent.)
From Mt. Arima/ over the bamboo plains of Ina.

Dainty, Evelyn
Birds on the School Windowsill, The.

Dakin, Laurence (b. 1904)
All night I raced the moon.
How gently sings my soul and whets its wings.

Pyramus and Thisbe, *Sels.*
Song: "Peasant sun went crushing grapes, The."
Tancred, *Sels.*

Dalcour, Pierre
Verse Written in the Album of Mademoiselle.

Dale, Langham (1826–98)
Prejudice against Colour.

Dale, Peter (b. 1938)
Few ever came to help you speak or sell.
Fragments, The, *Sels.*
Rite, The.

Daley, Argentina
On Hearing Peace Has Been Declared.

Daley, Frank (b. 1940)
Piano, The.

Daley, Victor James (1858–1905)
Dove, The.
Lachesis.
Mother Doorstep.
Night, *Sels.*
Tall Hat.
Vision of Sunday in Heaven, A.
When London Calls.
Woman at the Washtub, The.

Dallas, Sir George (1758–1833)
If you my dear mother, had e'er been at sea.
India Guide, The; or, Journal of a Voyage to the East Indies in 1780, *Sels.*
Miss Emily Brittle Sails for India.

Dallas, Ruth (b. 1919)
Autumn Wind.
Clouds on the Sea.
Girl with Pitcher.
In the Giant's Castle.
Letter to a Chinese Poet, *Sels.*
Milking before Dawn.
New Dress, A.
Photographs of Pioneer Women.
Telemachus with a Transistor.

Dalmon, Charles (b. 1862)
Early Morning Meadow Song.
Sussex Legend, A.

Dalton, Henry
Emigrant Ship, The.

Dalton, John (1709–63)
Agape the sooty collier stands.
Descriptive Poem, Addressed to Two Ladies at Their Return from Viewing the Mines, near Whitehaven, A, *Sels.*

Dalven, Rae (b. 1904)
My Father.

Daly, Chris
Extras, The.
No Admittance.

Daly, John Jay (1888–1976)
Toast to the Flag, A.

Daly, June
Wildebeest, The.

Daly, Thomas Augustin (1871–1948)
Boy from Rome, Da.
Leetla Giorgio Washeenton.
Man's Prayer, The.
Mia Carlotta.
Pennsylvania Places.
Sanctum, The.

Damagetus (fl. 3d cent. B.C.)
Epitaph of a Sailor.
In the name of the God of strangers, we beg you.
On the Tomb of Orpheus.

Damas, Léon (b. 1912)
Black Man's Lament, The.
Blues.
Et Cetera.
Hiccups.
Obsession.
Position.
Put Down.
Reality.
Sell Out.
Shine.
Sleepless Night.
So Often.

Their Thing.
There Are Nights.
They Came That Night.
They Came This Evening.
Whitewash.

Damaskius (fl. 6th cent.)
Zosimé was a slave in body only.

Dambroff, Susan
There Were Those.

D'Ambrosio, Vinnie-Marie
Grace of Cynthia's Maidenhood, The.
Grand Commander, 1916, The.
Moon as Medusa.
On the Fifth Anniversary of Bluma Sach's Death.

Damian, Peter (1007–1072)
Paradise.
Who is this.

Damocharis (fl. 6th cent.)
Lead disc composed of black stuff for marking, A.

Dana, Mary Stanley Bunce (1810–83)
O Sing to Me of Heaven.

Dana, Richard Henry (1787–1879)
Immortality.
Little Beach-Bird, The.
Murder of a Spanish Lady by a Pirate.
Pleasure-Boat, The.
Soul, The.

Dana, Robert Patrick (b. 1929)
Winter's Tale, A.

Dance, James (1722–74)
Cricket; an Heroic Poem, *Sels.*
When the returning sun begins to smile.

Dancer, John (fl. 1660–1707)
Variety, The.

Dandridge, Danske Bedinger (b. c.1860)
On the Eve of War.

Dandridge, Ray Garfield (1882–1930)
Time to Die.
Zalka Peetruza.

Danforth, John (1660–1730)
Few Lines to Fill up a Vacant Page, A.
Mercies of the Year, The.
On My Lord Bacon.
Poem upon the Triumphant Translation of . . . Mrs. Anne Eliot, A.
Profit and Loss: An Elegy upon the Decease of Mrs. Mary Gerrish.
Two Vast Enjoyments Commemorated.

Danforth, Samuel (1626–74)
Almanac Verse.
Awake yee westerne nymphs, arise and sing.

Danforth, Samuel, Jr. (1666–1727)
Ad Librum.
Elegy in Memory of the Worshipful Major Thomas Leonard Esq, An.

Daniel, Arnaut (c.1180–1210)
Bel m'es quan lo vens m'alena.
Mot eran dous miei cossir.
Resolute Desire That Enters, The.

Daniel, George (1616–57)
After a Storm, Going a Hawking.
Landscape, The.
One Desiring Me to Read, But Slept It Out, Wakening.
Robin, The.

Daniel, H. J. (1818–89)
In most things I did as my father had done.
My Epitaph.

Daniel, John
Common Ground.
Unborn, The.

Daniel, Robert T. (1773–1840)
Time Will Surely Come, The.

Daniel, Samuel (1562–1619)
And yet I cannot reprehend the flight.
Are they shadows that we see?
Beauty, sweet love, is like the morning dew.
Behold how every man, drawn with delight.
But love whilst that thou mayst be loved again.
But yet in all this interchange of all.
Care-charmer sleep[e], son[ne] of the sable night.

Civil Wars, The, *Sels.*
Cleopatra, *Sels.*
Complaint of Rosamond, The, *Sels.*
Description of Beauty, A, *Sels.*
Early Love.
Enjoy Thy April Now.
Eyes Hide My Love.
Fair is my love, and cruel as she's fair.
Fond man, Musophilus, that thus dost spend.
Had Sorrow Ever Fitter Place.
Hymen's Triumph, *Sels.*
I must not grieve my love, whose eyes would
read.
I once may see when yeares shall wreck my
wrong.
If so it hap, this of-spring of my care.
If this be love, to draw [*or* drawe] a weary [*or*
wearie] breath.
It was upon the twilight of that day.
Let others sing of knights and paladins [*or*
palladines].
Lonely Beauty.
Look, Delia, how we [e]steem the half-blown
rose.
Love Is a Sickness.
Musophilus; or, Defence of All Learning, *Sels.*
My spotless love hovers, with purest wings.
None other fame mine unambitious muse.
O blessed letters, that combine in one.
O fearful, frowning nemesis.
Ode: "Now each creature joys the other."
Place there is, where proudly raised there
stands, A.
Poetry in England.
Read in My Face.
Sacred Religion, mother of form and fear.
Tethy's Festival, *Sels.*
These plaintive verse, the posts [*or* postes] of
my desire.
Thou canst not die whilst any zeal abound.
Time, cruel time, come and subdue that brow.
To Delia, *Sels.*
To the Lady Margaret, Countess [*or* Countesse]
of Cumberland.
Tragedie of Philotas, The, *Sels.*
Ulysses and the Siren [*or* Syren].
When men shall find thy flower [*or* flow'r], thy
glory, pass.
When winter snows upon thy sable hairs.
Why Should I Sing in Verse.
Daniells, Roy (b. 1902)
Journey.
Noah.
So They Went Deeper into the Forest.
Daniels, Jim
Watching My Old House Burn on the News.
Daniels, Kate (b. 1953)
Bathing.
Bus Ride.
Christmas Party.
Ethiopia.
For Miklos Radnóti: 1909-1944.
Not Singing.
Danielson, Anita Endrezze-. *See* **Endrezze-**
Danielson, Anita.
Dann, Jack (b. 1945)
Hospital Songs, *Sels.*
Danner, Margaret (b. 1915)
And through the Caribbean Sea.
At Home in Dakar.
Best Loved of Africa.
Convert, The.
Dance of the Abakweta.
Elevator Man Adheres to Form, The.
Far from Africa: Four Poems, *Sels.*
Garnishing the Aviary.
Goodbye David Tamunoemi West.
Grandson Is a Hoticeberg, A.
Painted Lady, The.
Rhetoric of Langston Hughes, The.
Sadie's Playhouse.
Slave and the Iron Lace, The.
This Is an African Worm.
D'Annunzio, Gabriele (1863-1938)
Dawn Separates the Light from the Shadow,
The.

Shepherds, The.
Dante Alighieri (1265-1321)
All my thoughts always speak to me of Love.
All ye that pass along Love's trodden way.
And now we walked along the solid mire.
As the day stands when the Sun begins to
glow.
At the hour when the heat of the day is
overcome.
At whiles (yea oftentimes) I muse over.
Beyond the sphere which spreads to widest
space.
But you who are so happy here, tell me:.
Canst thou indeed be he that still would sing.
Celestial Pilot, The.
Dark Wood, The.
Day agone, as I rode sullenly, A.
Death, always cruel, Pity's foe in chief.
Divina Commedia, *Sels.*
Earnest to explore within and all around.
Even as the others mock, thou mockest me.
Eyes that weep for pity of the heart, The.
First Canzone of the Convito, The.
For better waters now the little bark.
For certain he hath seen all perfectness.
Gentle thought there is will often start, A.
Glory of Him who moves all things rays forth,
The.
Glory of the great all-mover goes, The.
He Beseeches Death for the Life of Beatrice.
He Will Gaze upon Beatrice.
I felt a spirit of love begin to stir.
Inferno.
Ladies that have intelligence in love.
Like fire-flies that the peasant on the hill.
Love and the gentle heart are one same thing.
Love hath so long possessed me for his own.
Love of God, unutterable and perfect, The.
Love's pallor and the semblance of deep ruth.
Middle of life's journey; I, The.
Mine eyes beheld the blessed pity spring.
My lady carries love within her eyes.
My lady looks so gentle and so pure.
New Love and the Gentle Heart.
Now the hard margin bears us on, while steam.
Of Beatrice de' Portinari, on All Saints' Day.
Of Beauty and Duty.
Of the Lady Pietra degli Scrovigni.
On the 9th of June 1290.
Paradiso.
Pier delle Vigne.
Piercing brightness of the living ray, The.
Purgatorio.
Saints in Glory, The.
Song, 'tis my will that thou do seek out Love.
Sonnet: "Guido, I wish that you and Lapo and
I."
Stay now with me, and listen to my sighs.
That lady of all gentle memories.
That she hath gone to Heaven suddenly.
That sun that breathed love's fire into my
youth.
Then, in the form of a white rose, the host.
This mountain of release is such that the.
Thoughts are broken in my memory, The.
Through me you enter the city of lament.
To Brunetto Latini.
To Certain Ladies; When Beatrice Was
Lamenting Her Father's Death.
To every heart which the sweet pain doth
move.
To Guido Cavalcanti.
To the Lady Pietra degli Scrovigni.
To the Same Ladies; With Their Answer.
To Waning Day, To the Wide Round of
Shadow.
Ugolino.
Very bitter weeping that ye made, The.
Very pitiful lady, very young, A.
Vita Nuova, La, *Sels.*
Weep, Lovers, with Love's very self doth
weep.
Whatever while the thought comes over me.
When the Septentrion of the First Heaven.
Woe's me! by dint of all these sighs that come.
Ye pilgrim-folk, advancing pensively.

You that thus wear a modest countenance.
D'Anvers, Alicia (1688?-1725)
Academia; or The Humours of the University of
Oxford, *Sels.*
I ask'd a young Youth what it mean'd.
Next, who 'as leave to domineer, The.
Now being arrived at his Colledge.
There's some are fat, and some are lean.
To the University.
D'Arcos, Joaquim Paço
Re-encounter.
D'Arcy, Hugh Antoine (1843-1925)
Face upon [*or* on] the Floor, The.
Dard, Khwaja Mir (1720-85)
Tarkib-Bund, *Sels.*
Dare, Joan
Limerick: "Cleric once heard with dismay, A."
Dargan, Olive Tilford (1869-1968)
Rescue.
Darío, Rubén (Félix Rubén García Sarmiento)
(1867-1916)
Alleluya.
Three Kings, The.
To Columbus.
Darley, George (1795-1846)
Dove's Loneliness, The.
Elfin Pedlar, The.
Enchanted Spring, The.
Ethelstan, *Sels.*
Fallen Star, The.
Hundred-gated Thebes.
In Dreamy Swoon.
It Is Not Beauty I Demand.
Lilian's Song.
Mermaidens' Vesper-Hymn, The.
Nepenthe, *Sels.*
O Blest Unfabled Incense Tree.
O'er the Wild Gannet's Bath.
Onward to Far Ida.
Sea-Ritual, The.
Solitary wayfarer!
Song: "Sweet in her green dell the flower of
beauty slumbers."
Speckle-black Toad and freckle-green Frog.
Syren Songs, *Sels.*
Thomas à Becket, a Dramatic Comedy, *Sels.*
To Mie Tirante.
To Poets.
Unicorn, The.
Darnley, Henry Stuart [*or* Stewart], Lord
(1545-67)
Gife Langour.
To the Queen.
Darr, Ann (b. 1920)
About Motion Pictures.
Love Is.
Darring, Walter
Surprised by Me.
Darwin, Erasmus (1731-1802)
Action of Electricity, The.
Action of Invisible Ink, The.
Botanic Garden, The, *Sels.*
Descend, ye hovering sylphs! aerial choirs.
Economy of Vegetation, The, *Sels.*
Eliza.
"How few," the Muse in plaintive accents cries.
Loves of the Plants, The.
Nightmare.
Protection of Plants, The.
Steam Power.
Temple of Nature; or, The Origin of Society,
The, *Sels.*
Visit of Hope to Sydney Cove, near Botany-
Bay.
Darwish, Ali (b. 1944)
Or.
Darwish, Mahmoud (b. 1942)
Beirut, *Sels.*
Diary of a Palestinian Wound, *Sels.*
Earth Scrapes Us.
Poems after Beirut, *Sels.*
Prison Cell, The.
We Move On to a Country.

We Travel like Other People.

Daryush, Elizabeth (1887–1976)
Anger Lay by Me All Night Long.
How on Solemn Fields of Space.
Look, The.
Still-Life.
Subalterns.
Throw Away the Flowers.

Das, Jibauarda
Cat.

Das, Kamala (b. 1934)
House-Builders, The.
Introduction: "I don't know politics but I know the names."

Dasgupta, Manjush (b. 1942)
Companion.

Date, J. C. B.
Limerick: "Though your dreams may seem normal and right."
Limerick: "To Algebra God is inclined."

Dauenhauer, Nora (b. 1927)
Kelp.
Skiing on Russian Christmas.
Tlingit Concrete Poem.
Voices.

Daumer, Georg Friedrich (1800–1875)
How Delightful, O My Queen.
Message, The.
Never Again to Go to You.
We Walked Together.

Davenant [or D'Avenant], Sir William (1606–68)
Christian's Reply to the Philosopher, The, *Sels.*
City Morning, The.
Endimion Porter and Olivia.
For the Lady Olivia Porter; a Present upon a New Year's Day.
Gondibert, *Sels.*
Lark Now Leaves His Watery [or Wat'ry] Nest.
Law against Lovers, The, *Sels.*
Lover and Philosopher.
Mistress, The.
My lodging it is on the cold ground.
O Thou That Sleep'st like Pig in Straw.
Of all the Lombards, by their Trophies knowne.
Philosopher and the Lover: To a Mistress Dying, The.
Praise and Prayer.
Rivals, The, *Sels.*
Soldier Going to the Field, The.
Storm at Sea.
'Tis, in good truth, a most wonderful thing.
To the Queen[e], Entertain[e]d at Night by the Countess[e] of Anglesey.
Under the Willow Shades.
Wake All the Dead.
What Is Past.

D'Avenant, Sir William. *See* **Davenant [or D'Avenant], Sir William.**

Davenport, Mariana B. (b. 1907)
Suspended Moment.

Davenport, Robert (*fl.* 1624–40)
Sacrifice, A.

Davey, Frank (b. 1940)
She'd Say.

David ap Gwilym. *See* **Dafydd [or David] ap Gwilym.**

David ben Meshullam (*fl.* Middle Ages)
Be Not Silent.

David, John (1761–1841)
What Happiness Can Equal Mine.

Davide, Adèle
I Know Things.
My Youngest Daughter Getting Up in the Morning.

Davidman, Joy (b. 1915)
Prayer against Indifference.

Davidson, Francis (b. 1905)
Beggars.

Davidson, Gustav (b. 1895)
Ambushed by Angels.
Nevertheless.

Davidson, John (1857–1909)
Ballad of a Nun, A.
Ballad of Heaven, A.

Ballad of Hell, A.
Battle.
Christmas Eve.
Crystal Palace, The.
Holiday at Hampton Court.
Imagination.
In a Music-Hall.
In Romney Marsh.
In the Isle of Dogs.
Labourer's Wife, A.
London.
New Year's Eve, *Sels.*
Northern Suburb, A.
Outcast, The.
Price, The.
Runnable Stag, A.
Song: "Boat is chafing at our long delay, The."
Summer.
Testament of a Vivisector, The.
Testament of John Davidson, The, *Sels.*
Thirty Bob a Week.
To the New Men.
To the New Women.
To the Street Piano, *Sels.*
Two Dogs.
Unknown, The.
War Song.
Wasp, The.
Winter in Strathearn, *Sels.*

Davidson, Lucretia (1808–1825)
Acrostic, An.
America.
Auction Extraordinary.
Byron.
Fear of Madness, The.
Headache.
Lines: "Whene'er the Muse pleases to grace my dull page."
Sabrina.
Shakespeare.
To My Friend and Patron, M ——— K ———, Esq.
To the Vermont Cadets.
Yellow Fever, The.

Davidson, R. R.
Gravy Train, The.

Davie, Donald (b. 1922)
Across the Bay.
Autumn Imagined.
Barnsley and District.
But this, so feminine?
Christening, A.
Compline.
Devil on Ice.
Forests of Lithuania, The, *Sels.*
Fountain, The.
G. M. B.
Gardens No Emblems.
Hearing Russian Spoken.
Heigh-ho on a Winter Afternoon.
Horae Canonicae, *Sels.*
In California.
Life of Service, The.
Meeting of Cultures, A.
On Bertrand Russell's "Portraits from Memory."
Orpheus.
Ox-Bow.
Prime.
Priory of St. Saviour, Glendalough, The.
Prose for Des Esseintes.
Remembering the 'Thirties.
Rousseau in His Day.
Thanks to Industrial Essex.
Time Passing, Beloved ("Time passing, and the memories of love").
To a Teacher of French.
Wind at Penistone, The.
Winter Talent, A.
With the Grain.
Year 1812, The.

Davies, Alan (b. 1951)
Name, *Sels.*

Davies, Arthur
West Paddocks.

Davies, Dudley G. (1891–1981)
At Branwen's Grave.
Carmarthenshire.

Davies, Edward (1718–89)
Cambrian Swain, The.
Chepstow: A Poem, *Sels.*
Tintern Abbey.
Will no young British bard, on rhyme intent.
Wily Fox, The.

Davies, Elwyn (b. 1912)
Portrait of Auntie Blodwen.

Davies, Frank
Limerick: "Giraffes, yes, even the strongest."

Davies, Gareth Alban (b. 1926)
Dance, The.

Davies, Gloria Evans (b. 1932)
Her Name like the Hours.
Holly Gone.

Davies, Idris (1905–53)
Angry Summer, The ("From Abertillery and Aberdare").
Angry Summer, The ("Mrs. Evans Fach, You Want Butter Again").
Capel Calvin.
Consider Famous Men, Dai Bach.
Do You Remember 1926?
High Summer on the Mountains.
Hywel and Blodwen.
I stood in the ruins of Dowlais.
In Gardens in the Rhondda.
Lay Preacher Ponders, The.
O what can you give me?
Village of Fochriw grunts among the higher hills, The.
What will you do with your shovel, Dai.

Davies, J. Kitchener (1902–52)
Sound of the Wind That Is Blowing, The, *Sels.*
Today,/ there came a breeze thin as the needle of a syringe.

Davies, Sir John (1569–1626)
Affliction.
Amongst the poets Dacus numbered is.
As when the bright[e] Crulean firmament.
Contention between Four Maids Concerning That Which Addeth Most Perfection to That Sex.
Contention Betwixt a Wife, a Widow, and a Maid, A, *Sels.*
Cosmus hath more discoursing in his head.
Dance of Love, The.
Dancing Sea, The.
Dauncing (bright Lady) then began to bee.
Dedication II: "Strongest and the noblest argument, The."
Dedications, I: To His Very Friend, Master Richard Martin.
Dedications, II: To the Prince.
Dedications [of Orchestra], *Sels.*
Epigrams, *Sels.*
Fine youth Ciprius is more terse and neat, The.
Gulling[e] Sonnets, The, *Sels.*
Hardnes[s] of her h[e]art[e] and truth of mine [or myne].
Hymns of Astræa [in Acrostic Verse], *Sels.*
I know my soul hath power to know all things.
If you would know the love which I you bear.
In Francum.
In Fuscum.
In Librum.
In What Manner the Soule Is United to the Body.
Into the mid[d]le temple of my h[e]art[e].
Lover, under burthen of his mistress' love, The.
Maidenhood.
Man.
Mine eye, mine [or myne] ear[e], my will, my wit[t], my h[e]art[e].
Month of September, The.
Muse Reviving, The.
My case is this.
Nosce Teipsum, *Sels.*
Of Astræa.
Of Her Justice.
Of Her Magnanimity.

Lightly stepped a yellow star.
Lightning is a yellow fork, The.
Like rain it sounded till it curved.
Little East of Jordan, A.
Little Madness in the spring, A.
Loss of something ever felt I, A.
Love can do all but raise the dead.
Love is anterior to life.
Love is that later thing than death.
Man may make a Remark, A.
Me From Myself — to Banish.
Mine Enemy Is Growing Old.
Mine — by the right of the white election!
Morns are meeker than they were, The.
Mountain sat upon the plain, The.
Mountains grow unnoticed, The.
Much madness is divinest sense.
Murmur of a bee, The.
My cocoon tightens — Colors tease.
My country need not change her gown.
My friend must be a bird.
My life closed twice before its close.
My life had stood — a loaded gun.
My portion is defeat — today.
My triumph lasted till the drums.
Name of it is "Autumn," The.
Narrow fellow in the grass, A.
Nature — sometimes sears a sapling.
Nature — the Gentlest Mother is.
New feet within my garden go — .
No Passenger was known to flee.
No rack can torture me.
Not any higher stands the Grave.
Not "Revelation" — 'tis — that waits.
Not with a club the heart is broken.
Now I knew I lost her.
Of all the souls that stand create.
Of course I prayed.
Of God we ask one favor.
Of nearness to her sundered things.
Of Paul and Silas it is said.
Oh sumptuous moment.
One blessing had I, than the rest.
One crown that no one seeks.
One dignity delays for all.
One need not be a chamber — to be haunted.
Only news I know, The.
Opinion is a flitting thing.
Our journey had advanced.
Our little kinsmen after rain.
Our lives are Swiss.
Ourselves we do inter with sweet derision.
Ourselves were wed one summer — dear.
Over the fence.
Pain — has an element of blank.
Papa above!
Pass to thy rendezvous of light.
Past is such a curious creature, The.
Pedigree of honey, The.
Perception of an object costs.
Pink, small and punctual.
Poets light but lamps, The.
Precious to me — she still shall be.
Presentiment is that long shadow on the lawn.
Publication — is the auction.
Read, sweet, how others strove.
Rearrange a wife's affection?
"Remember me" implored the Thief!
Remorse is memory awake.
Reportless subjects, to the quick.
Riddle we can guess, The.
Robin is the one, The.
Saddest Noise, the Sweetest Noise, The.
Safe in their alabaster chambers.
Satisfaction — is the agent.
Savior [or Saviour]! I've no one else to tell.
Severer service of myself.
She dealt her pretty words like blades.
She lay as if at play.
She rose to His requirement — dropt.
She sights a bird — she chuckles.
She sweeps with many-colored brooms.
Show is not the show, The.
Sky is low, the clouds are mean, The.
So proud she was to die.

Soft sea washed around the house, A.
Softened by time's consummate plush.
Solemn thing — it was — I said, A.
Some keep the Sabbath [or Sunday] going to
   church.
Some one prepared this mighty show.
Some things that fly there be.
Soul has bandaged moments, The.
Soul selects her own society, The.
Soul's distinct connection, The.
Soul's Superior instants, The.
Sown in dishonor!
Spider holds a silver ball, The.
Spider sewed at night, A.
Split the lark — and you'll find the music.
Spring is the period.
Stars are old, that stood for me, The.
Still — Volcano — Life, A.
Stimulus beyond the Grave, The.
Success is counted sweetest.
Sun and fog contested, The.
Superfluous Were the Sun.
Surgeons must be very careful.
Sweet Mountains — Ye tell Me no lie.
Sweetest heresy received, The.
Tell all the truth but tell it slant.
That it will never come again.
That love is all there is.
There are two Mays.
There came a day at summer's full.
There came a wind like a bugle.
There is a languor of the life.
There is a morn by men unseen.
There is a pain — so utter.
There is no frigate like a book.
There is no silence in the earth — so silent.
There's a certain slant of light.
There's been a death in the opposite house.
These are the days when birds come back.
These strangers, in a foreign world.
They dropped like flakes, they dropped like
   stars.
They might not need me; but they might.
They shut me up in prose.
This consciousness that is aware.
This dirty little heart.
This is my letter to the world.
This quiet dust was gentlemen and ladies.
This was a poet — It is that.
This world is not conclusion.
Those — dying then.
Thought beneath so slight a film, The.
Thought went up my mind today, A.
Through the dark sod — as education.
Through the strait pass of suffering.
Tie the strings to my life, my Lord.
Tint I cannot take is best, The.
'Tis not that dying hurts us so.
'Tis so appalling — it exhilirates.
'Tis so much joy! 'tis so much joy!
Title divine — is mine!
To fight aloud is very brave.
To flee from memory.
To hear an oriole sing.
To know just how He suffered would be dear.
To learn the transport by the pain.
To make a prairie it takes a clover and one
   bee.
To see her is a picture.
Too happy time dissolves itself.
Truth is as old as God.
'Twas just this time, last year, I died.
'Twas like a maelstrom, with a notch.
'Twas warm — at first — like us.
Under the Light, yet under.
Undue significance a starving man attaches.
Until the desert knows.
Victory comes late.
Volcanoes be in Sicily.
Waters chased him as he fled, The.
Way I read a letter's — this, The.
We do not play on graves.
We dream — it is good we are dreaming.
We grow accustomed to the Dark.

We like March — his shoes are purple.
We lose — because we win.
We miss a kinsman more.
We never know how high we are.
We never know we go.
We outgrow love, like other things.
We thirst at first — 'tis nature's act.
Went up a year this evening.
What is — "Paradise."
What mystery pervades a well!
What soft — cherubic creatures.
When we stand on the tops of things.
While we were fearing it, it came.
Who is the East?
Why make it doubt — it hurts it so.
Wife — at daybreak I shall be, A.
Wild nights — wild nights!
Will there really be a morning?
Wind begun to knead the grass, The.
Wind begun to rock the grass, The.
Wind that rose, A.
Wind Took Up the Northern Things, The.
Wind — tapped like a tired man, The.
Within my garden, rides a bird.
Word is dead, A.
Word made flesh is seldom, A.
Work of her that went, The.
World feels dusty, The.
Wounded deer leaps highest, A.
Your riches taught me poverty.

Dickinson, Goldsworthy Lowes (1862–86)
I never asked for more than thou hast given.

Dickinson, Patric (b. 1914)
Advent; a Carol.
St. Stephen's Day.

Dickinson, Peter (b. 1927)
By-Election Idyll.

Didsbury, Peter (b. 1946)
Barn, The.
Drainage, The.
Eikon Basilike.
Hailstone, The.
In Britain.
Jar, The.
Priest in the Sabbath Dawn Addresses His
   Somnolent Mistress, A.
Winter's Fancy, A.

Die, Beatrice, Countess de. *See* **Beatrice, [or
   Beatritz *or* Beatriz], Countess de Die [or
   Dia].**

Diego Padró, José I. de (1899–1975)
Epistolary Briefs to Proclus, *Sels.*

Dienstag, Alan (b. 1929)
Three Women.

Diespecker, Dick (b. 1907)
Between Two Furious Oceans, *Sels.*

Dietmar von Aist (*or* Eist) (*fl.* 12th century)
Bird Was Singing, A.
Gay Summer's Bliss, Good-bye.
How can I hope a wise heart to attain.
Lady Stood, A.
Lady Stood Alone, A.
Parting at Morning.
Yonder on the linden tree there sang a merry
   little bird.

Di Filippo, Rustico (1200?–1270)
Of the Making of Master Messerin.

Digby, John (1580–1655)
Grieve not, dear love, although we often part.

Digges, Deborah
Faith-Falling.
Rock, Scissors, Paper.
To a Milkweed.

Dillard, Annie
Every day is a god, each day is a god.

Dillard, Richard H. W. (b. 1937)
Meditation for a Pickle Suite.
Mullins Farm, The.

Diller, John Irving
Lullaby Town.

Dillon, George (b. 1906)
Hard Lovers, The.
Kind Inn, A.
Dillon, Wentworth, 4th Earl of
Roscommon. *See* **Roscommon, Wentworth**
Dillon, 4th Earl of.
Di Michele, Mary (b. 1949)
Moon and the Salt Flats, The.
Dimitrova, Blaga (b. 1922)
Lullaby for My Mother.
Dimmette, Celia
Apology of the Young Scientists.
Dimoff, John (b. 1931)
West of Chicago.
Dimond, William (b. 1780?)
Mariner's Dream, The.
Di Montecanti, Guerzo (*fl.* **13th century**)
He Is Out of Heart with His Time.
Di Montorio, Antonio (1404–77)
El Ropero.
Dimoula, Kiki (b. 1931)
Talking to Myself.
"Dinesen, Isak" (Karen Blixen) (1885–1962)
Zebra.
Diodoros
Young child of Diodoros's house, A.
Diodorus Zonas (b. 125? B.C.)
Come tawny bees.
For Demeter winnowing, for the Hours who
haunt the furrows.
From the field's plane tree.
Pan Asks about Daphnis.
Pomegranate just splitting, a peach just furry,
A.
Spare the mother of acorns, man. Cut down
some paliurus.
Who in the waters of this reedy lake.
Diogenes Laertius (*fl.* **3d cent. A.D.**)
Nor, by God, shall we neglect.
Tauromancy at Memphis.
Dionysius
No wonder I slipped, being soaked.
Dionysius Sophistes (Dionysius of Andros)
You hold a bunch of roses, Rose.
Diop, Birago (b. 1906)
Animism.
Breaths.
Desert.
Diptych.
Kassak.
Omen.
Spirits.
Those who are dead are never gone.
Viaticum.
Diop, David (1927–60)
Africa.
Challenge.
For a Black Child.
For My Mother.
He Who Has Lost All.
Hours, The.
Listen, Comrades.
Negro Tramp.
Rama Kam.
Suffer, Poor Negro!
Those Who Lost Everything.
Time of Martyrdom, The.
Vultures, The.
With You.
Your Presence.
Diophanes of Myrina
Thief, and triply so! A.
Dioscorides (*fl.* **1st cent. B.C.** *or* **A.D.**)
Call me Polyxena, the wife of Archelaus.
Demaeneta sent eight sons.
Epigrams, *Sels.*
Eros, that bane of men, molded soft as
marrow.
Hiero's former Nurse.
Lamisca, who breathed her last in lamentable
pangs of labor.
They are too much for me.
They drive me mad, those rosy lips, forever
prattling.

Dioscorides (*fl.* **3d cent. B.C.**)
First fruits from her fruitful bed, The.
My downfall: those pink articulate lips.
Thracian page-boy/ mastered, A.
Zephyr, kindliest of winds.
Diotimus (*fl.* **c.250 B.C.**)
Cold Pastoral.
Epigrams, *Sels.*
Homing at dusk — the snow falls on them —
cattle.
Polyaenus' daughter, Scyllis, came to the wide
gates.
What use to suffer in labor, give birth to
children, if she.
Without the Herdsman.
DiPalma, Ray (b. 1943)
Ceremony/ the triumph.
New world/ artful as monkeys, A.
One deep in the dark.
Planh, *Sels.*
Written granite.
DiPasquale, Emanuel (b. 1943)
Rain.
Di Piero, W. S. (b. 1945)
Near Damascus.
Dipoko, Mbella Sonne (b. 1936)
Autobiography.
Di Prima, Diane (b. 1934)
And Will You Hunt the Loba?
April Fool Birthday Poem for Grandpa.
Ave.
Brass Furnace Going Out: Song, after an
Abortion.
Day lay like a pearl on her lap, The.
Dream: The Loba Reveals Herself.
Goodbye Nkrumah.
Her Power Is to Open What Is Shut/ Shut What
Is Open.
In Memory of My First Chapatis.
Jungle, The.
Loba Addresses the Goddess/ or The Poet as
Priestess Addresses the Loba-Goddess, The.
Loba as Kore in the Labyrinth of Her Beauty/
The Loba Seeks the Mother, in the Infinite
Reaches of Night.
Loba Dances, The.
Loba Recovers the Memory of a Mare, The.
Loba, *Sels.*
Love Song of the Loba.
Moon Mattress.
Poet Prays to the Loba, The.
Poetics.
Practice of Magical Evocation, The.
Quarrel, The.
Revolutionary Letter #19.
Ruses: A Coyote Tale, The.
Second Daughter: Li (Brightness), The.
Song for Baby-O, Unborn.
Three Laments.
Di Roma, Immanuel (1261–1330)
Happiness amidst Troubles.
Love.
My Sweet Gazelle!
Paradise.
What Profit?
Worthless Heart, The.
Disch, Thomas M. (b.1940)
Cow of Our Time, A.
Crumbling Infrastructure, The.
Homage to the Carracci.
La, La, La!
Poems.
Rapist's Villanelle, The.
Vowels of Another Language, The.
Dismond, Binga (1891–1956)
At Early Morn.
Status Quo.
Dissanayake, Wimal (b. 1939)
Freedom.
Ditlevsen, Tove (1918–76)
Divorce, *Sels.*
He would/ in the case of a divorce.
It is not easy.
Morning.
Old Folk, The.

Self Portrait II.
Self Portrait 4.
Divakaruni, Chitra (b. 1956)
Brides Come to Yuba City, The.
Childhood.
Indigo.
Outside Pisa.
Yuba City School.
Divine, Charles (b. 1889)
We Met on Roads of Laughter.
Dix, William Chatterton (1837–98)
As with Gladness Men of Old.
Dixon, Henry (1675–1760)
Description of a Good Boy, The.
Dixon, Melvin
80's Miracle Diet, The.
Heartbeats.
One by One.
Tour Guide: La Maison des Esclaves.
Dixon, Richard Watson (1833–1900)
All who have loved, be sure of this from me.
Both Less and More.
By the Sea.
Dawning.
Dream.
Heaving Roses of the Hedge Are Stirred, The.
Judgment of the May, The.
Love's Consolation, *Sels.*
Song: "Feathers of the willow, The."
Song: "Why fadest thou in death."
Spirit Wooed, The.
To Peace.
Unrest.
Wizard's Funeral, The.
Dixon, Ruth G.
Epitome.
Dixon, Sarah (*fl.* **1716–1745**)
Close to Aminta, on the Loss of Her Lover.
Lines Occasioned by the Burning of Some
Letters.
Returned Heart, The.
Slattern, The.
To Strephon.
Verses Left on a Lady's Toilet.
Djabali, Leila (b. 1933)
For My Torturer, Lieutenant D——.
Djangatolum. *See* **Corbin, Lloyd M., Jr.**
Djellaladin Pasha, Mahmud
Song: "If you love God, take your mirror
between your hands and look."
Djurberaui
All You Others, Eat.
Djurdjic, Ljiljana (b. 1946)
Blue Frog Kisses My Sweetheart.
I Carry My Black Sheep Back to Her Herd.
Lucifer.
Unfulfilled Love.
D'Lettuso, Homer
Old Houses.
Dlugas, Tim (d. 1991)
Retrovir.
Doak, Katherine
Before I Slept.
Doane, George Washington (1799–1858)
Bishop Doane on His Dog.
Evening Contemplation.
Fling Out the Banner!
Life Sculpture.
Once More, O Lord.
Thou Art the Way.
Doane, William Croswell (1832–1913)
Ancient of Days.
Modern Baby, The.
Preacher's Mistake, The.
Dobbie, Joan (b. 1946)
My First Memory, Switzerland, Circa 1947.
Things Grow Up out of the Dark.
Dobell, Sydney Thompson (1824–74)
Balder, *Sels.*
Ballad of Keith of Ravelston, The.
Chanted Calendar, A.
Desolate.
He Loves and He Rides Away.

How's My Boy?
Nuptial Eve, A, *Sels.*
Orphan's Song, The.
Perhaps.
Tommy's Dead.
Dobler, Patricia
Field Trip to the Rolling Mill, 1950.
Dobson, Austin (Henry Austin Dobson) (1840–1921)
All passes. Art alone.
Ars Victrix, *Sels.*
Ballad of "Beau Brocade," The.
Ballad of Heroes, A.
Ballad to Queen Elizabeth, A.
Before Sedan.
Child-Musician, The.
City Flower, A.
Clean Hands.
Dora versus Rose.
Fame and Friendship.
Garden Song, A.
In After Days.
Incognita.
Ladies of St. James's, The.
Rose-Leaves, *Sels.*
Urceus Exit.
Virtuoso, A.
When There Is Peace.
Dobson, John (fl. c.1746)
Robin; a Pastoral Elegy.
Dobson, Rosemary (b. 1920)
Being Called For.
Bystander, The.
Child with a Cockatoo.
Country Press.
Daily Living, *Sels.*
Devil and the Angel, The, *Sels.*
Edge, The.
Eutychus.
Fever, The.
Folding the Sheets.
In a Café.
Three Fates, The.
Visiting.
Dobson, Silvia
To the Sphinx.
Dobyns, Stephen (b. 1941)
Cemetery Nights.
Counterparts.
Delicate, Plummeting Bodies, The.
Desire.
Farmyard at Chassy.
Gun, The.
Seeing Off a Friend.
Shaving.
Tomatoes.
Dock, Christopher (d. 1771)
O Children, Would You Cherish?
Dodd, Leonard
Compel Them to Come In.
Dodd, Wayne (b. 1930)
General Mule Poems, The, *Sels.*
Doddridge, Philip (1702–51)
Awake, My Soul!
Christ's Resurrection and Ascension.
Meditations on the Sepulchre in the Garden.
Doddridge, Philip and John Logan
Hymn: "Ye golden lamps of heaven, farewell."
O God of Bethel.
Dodge, Mary Mapes (1831–1905)
Letters at School, The.
Poor Crow!
Stocking Song on Christmas Eve.
That's What We'd Do.
Two Mysteries, The.
Zealless Xylographer, The.
Dodge, Samuel
People Will Talk.
Dodgson, Charles Lutwidge. *See* "Carroll, Lewis."
Dodsley, Robert (1703–64)
Agriculture, *Sels.*
Epistle to My Friend J. B., An.
Method of Preserving Hay from Being Mow-Burnt, or Taking Fire, A.

Progress of Love, The.
Rustic Courtship.
Song: "Man's a poor deluded bubble."
Stolen Kiss, The.
Dodson, Keith A.
Poor Losers.
Dodson, Owen (1914–1983)
Confession Stone, The.
Counterpoint.
Decision, The.
Epitaph for a Negro Woman.
I Break the Sky.
Jonathan's Song.
Mary Passed This Morning.
Poems for My Brother Kenneth, *Sels.*
Rag Doll and Summer Birds.
Six o'Clock.
Sleep late with your dream.
Yardbird's Skull.
Dogen (1200–1253)
On Non-dependence of Mind.
On the Treasury of the True Dharma Eye.
You should entreat trees and rocks.
Dolben, Digby Mackworth (1848–67)
Enough.
He Would Have His Lady Sing.
Homo Factus Est.
Requests.
Sea Song, A.
Song: "World is young today, The."
Strange, All-absorbing Love.
We hurry on, nor passing note.
Domanski, Don (b. 1950)
Deadsong.
Three Songs from the Temple.
Domett, Alfred (1811–77)
Christmas Hymn, A.
It was a wondrous realm beguiled.
Ranolf and Amohia, *Sels.*
Domin, Hilde (b. 1912)
Birthdays.
Domino, Ruth (b. 1908)
Sparrow in the Dust, A.
Donaghy, John Lyle (b. 1902)
Deathward.
Duck.
Glenarm.
Portrait.
Winter.
Donald, Christine M. (b. 1950)
Eye for an Eye, An.
Good Old Body.
I Expect You Think This Huge Dark Coat.
Poor Old Fat Woman.
Thin women woo each other, The.
Donaldson, O. Fred
Grey Wolf.
Donatus, Saint (829–76)
Land Called Scotia, The.
Donne, John (1572–1631)
Air[e] and Angels.
Anatomy [or Anatomie] of the World, An[: The First Anniversary], *Sels.*
And new philosophy calls all in doubt.
Anniversary [or Anniversarie], The.
Annunciation.
Antiquary.
Apparition, The.
As due by many titles I resign[e].
Ascension [or Ascention].
At the round earth's imagined corners, blow.
Autumnal[l], The.
Bait[e], The.
Batter my heart, three person'd [personed] God; for you.
Blossom [or Blossome], The.
Bracelet, The.
Break[e] of Day.
Broken Heart, The.
Burnt Ship, A.
Calm[e], The.
Canonization, The.
Change.
Comparison, The.

Computation, The.
Crucifying.
Damp[e], The.
Dark Churches.
Death, be not proud, though some have called thee.
Dissolution, The.
Doth Not a Tenarif, or Higher Hill.
Dream[e], The.
Ecstasy, The.
Elegies, *Sels.*
Elegy: "Nature's lay idiot [or Ideot], I taught thee to love."
Elegy on Mistress Boulstred.
Epithalamion Made at Lincolnes Inne.
Epithalamion on the Lady Elizabeth and Count Palantine Being Married on St. Valentine's Day, An, *Sels.*
Expiration, The.
Farewell to Love.
Father, The.
Father, part of his double interest.
Fever, A.
First Anniversary, The.
Flea, The.
Funeral[l], The.
God grant thee thine own wish, and grant thee mine.
Going to Bed.
Good Friday [or Goodfriday], 1613. Riding Westward.
Good[-]Morrow, The.
Hail, Bishop Valentine, whose day this is.
Hero and Leander.
His Parting from Her.
His Picture.
Holy Ghost, The.
Holy Sonnets, *Sels.*
Hymn [or Hymne] to Christ, at the Author's Last Going into Germany, A, *Sels.*
Hymn to God the Father, A.
Hymn to the Saints, and to Marquis Hamilton.
Hymne to Christ, at the Author's Last Going into Germany, A.
Hymn[e] to God My God, In My Sickness[e].
I am a little world made cunningly.
I Can Love Both Fair and Brown.
If faithful soules be alike glorifi'd.
If poisonous [or poysonous] mineral[l]s, and if that tree.
Indifferent, The, *Sels.*
It quickned next a toyful Ape, and so.
Jealousy.
Jet Ring Sent, A.
Kind pity [or Kinde pitty] chokes my spleen[e]; brave scorn forbids.
Klockius.
La Corona, *Sels.*
Lame Beggar, A.
Lamentations of Jeremy, For the Most Part According to Tremelius, The.
Lecture upon the Shadow, A.
Legacy [or Legacie], The.
Licentious Person, A.
Litanie, The, *Sels.*
London Street, A.
Lovers' Infiniteness[e].
Love's Alchemy [or Alchemie].
Love's Deity [or Deitie].
Love's Growth.
Love's Progress.
Message, The.
Nativity [or Nativitie].
Nocturnal[l] upon Saint Lucy's [or S. Lucies] Day, Being the Shortest Day, A.
O might those sighes and teares returne againe.
Of My Name in the Window.
Of the Progres[se] of the Soule; the Second Anniversarie, *Sels.*
Of Weeping.
Oh my black[e] soul[e]! now thou art summoned.
On His Mistress [or Mistris].
Our two soules therefore, which are one.
Paradox, The.
Perfume, The.

From Gloucester Out.
Gunslinger, *Sels.*
Hide of My Mother, The.
Home on the Range, February, 1962.
Idle Visitation, An.
La Máquina a Houston.
Los Mineros.
Love Song: "Inside the late nights of last week."
Love Song: "It is deep going from here."
Love Song: "My speech is tinged."
Morning to Remember, A; or, E Pluribus Unum.
On the Debt My Mother Owed to Sears Roebuck.
Oxford, *Sels.*
Poet Lets His Tongue Hang Down, The.
Prolegomenon.
Rick of Green Wood, The.
Song: "So light no one noticed."
Thesis.
Vaquero.
Venceremos.
When the Fairies.
Dorney, Elizabeth
Chemistry of Character, The.
Dornin, Christopher L.
In a Building Named for a Governor.
Dorr, Henry R.
Comrades.
Dorr, Julia Caroline Ripley (1825–1913)
Legend of the Organ-Builder, The.
No More the Thunder of Cannon.
Not Mine.
Dorrance, Dick (b. 1914)
Cockpit in the Clouds.
Dorset, Catherine Ann (1750–1817)
Peacock "At Home," The.
Dos Passos, John (1896–1970)
Crimson Tent.
Doten, Elizabeth (Lizzie) (b. 1829)
God of the Granite and the Rose!
In a Hundred Years.
Reconciliation, *Sels.*
Doty, Mark (b. 1953)
Adonis Theater.
Bill's Story.
Heaven.
Night Ferry.
Tiara.
Turtle, Swan.
Doubiago, Sharon
Appalachian Song.
Mother, *Sels.*
My mother is a poem I'll never be able to write.
Out the window, Colombia, out the window.
Signal Hill.
South America Mi Hija, *Sels.*
Double-face
If there is someone above.
Doudney, Sarah (1843?–1926)
Christian's "Good-Night", The.
Sweet Surprises.
Water Mill, The.
Doughty, Charles Montague (1843–1926)
Bladyn's Song of Cloten.
Dawn in Britain, The, *Sels.*
Fairies Feast, The.
Gauls Sacrifice, The.
Hymn to the Sun.
Roman Officer Writes, A.
Douglas, Lord Alfred Bruce (1870–1945)
Dead Poet, The.
Green River, The.
Impression de Nuit; London.
Prayer: "Often the western wind has sung to me."
Rejected.
To Olive.
To ———, with an Ivory Hand-Glass.
Two Loves.
Douglas, Gawin [or Gavin] (1474?–1522)
Calliope's Nymph Brings the Poet to the Palace to Honour.

Hart's Castle.
King Hart, *Sels.*
Nightmare.
Palace [*or* Palice] of Honor [*or* Honour], The, *Sels.*
Douglas, Keith (1920–44)
Aristocrats.
Behaviour of Fish in an Egyptian Tea Garden.
Cairo Jag.
Deceased, The.
Desert Flowers.
Enfidaville.
Gallantry.
How to Kill.
Knife, The.
Marvel, The.
Offensive, The, *Sels.*
Russians.
Simplify Me When I'm Dead.
Soissons.
Vergissmeinnicht.
Waterloo, *Sels.*
"Douglas, Marian" (Annie Douglas Green Robinson) (1842–1913)
Ant-Hills.
Good Thanksgiving, A.
Snow-Man, The.
Douglas, Norman
Limerick: "There was a young fellow named Skinner."
Limerick: "There was a young lady of Louth."
Douglas, Paul Keens-. *See* **Keens-Douglas, Paul.**
Douglas, William (1672–1748)
Annie Laurie.
Douglass, Frederick (c.1817–1895)
Just God! and these are they.
Narrative of the Life of an American Slave, *Sels.*
Parody, A.
Dove, Olive
Dragon.
Dove, Rita (b. 1952)
Adolescence — I.
Adolescence — II.
Adolescence — III.
Banneker.
Beauty and the Beast.
Cameos.
Canary.
Cane Fields, The.
Courtship.
Daystar.
Dusting.
Elevator Man, 1949.
Event, The.
Fifth Grade Autobiography.
Fish in the Stone, The.
Geometry.
Great Palaces of Versailles, The.
Horse and Tree.
House Slave, The.
Late Notebooks of Albrecht Dürer, The.
Lint.
Nigger Song: An Odyssey.
Ö.
Palace, The.
Parsley, *Sels.*
Persephone, Falling.
Persephone Underground.
Roast Possum.
Satisfaction Coal Company, The.
Secret Garden, The.
Sonnet in Primary Colors.
Sunday Greens.
"Teach Us to Number Our Days."
This Life.
Thomas at the Wheel.
Used.
Weathering Out.
Zeppelin Factory, The.
Dow, Philip (b. 1937)
Air.
Dried Fruit.
Drunk Last Night with Friends, I Go to Work Anyway.

Duck Pond at Mini's Pasture, a Dozen Years Later, The.
Life, The.
Skunk, The.
Suite for Celery and Blind Date.
Sussyissfriin, *Sels.*
Twilight in California.
Dowden, Edward (1843–1913)
Burdens.
Communion.
I found Thee in my heart, O Lord.
In the Cathedral Close.
New Hymns for Solitude, *Sels.*
Seeking God.
Dowden, Elizabeth Dickinson
Adrift.
Dower, E. (*fl.* c.1738)
New River Head, a Fragment, The.
Dowland, John (1562–1626)
Come Away, Come, Sweet Love.
Dear, If You Change.
Flow Not So Fast.
Go, Nightly Cares.
Dowling, Allan (b. 1900)
I Sought with Eager Hand.
Joy of Love, The.
Miracle, The.
Dowling, Bartholomew (1823?–1863)
Revel, The.
Dowling, Basil (b. 1910)
Autumn Scene.
Downie, Freda
Elsdon.
Great-Grandfather.
Her Garden.
Miss Grant.
Starlight.
Dowson, Ernest Christopher (1867–1900)
Autumnal.
Breton Afternoon.
Carthusians.
De Amore, *Sels.*
Dregs.
Epigram: "Because I am idolatrous and have besought."
Exchanges.
Exile.
Extreme Unction.
Flos Lunae.
Garden of Shadow, The.
Gray Nights.
Last Word, A.
Lord over life and all the ways of breath.
Non Sum Qualis Eram Bonae sub Regno Cynarae [*or* Cynara].
O Mors! Quam Amara Est Memoria Tua Homini Pacem Habenti in Substantiis Suis.
Passing of Tennyson, The.
Spleen.
Terre Promise.
To One in Bedlam.
Valediction, A.
Vesperal.
Villanelle of Marguerites.
Villanelle of the Poet's Road.
Vitae Summa Brevis Spem Nos Vetat Incohare Longam.
You would have understood me, had you waited.
Doyle, Sir Francis Hastings (1810–88)
Private of the Buffs; or, The British Soldier in China.
Red Thread of Honour, The.
Doyle, Kirby (1810–88)
Strange.
"Doyle, Lynn" (Leslie Alexander Montgomery) (1873–1961)
Earth.
Good Hands People Know Their Bodies, The.
My Mother in Majorca.
Ulsterman, An.
Drachler, Rose (b. 1911)
Conversation with Rilke about Dragons.
Letter Written in the Year of the Carrying Away to Babylon.

Letters of the Book, The.
Smaragd the Emerald.
Zippora Returns to Moses at Rephidim.

Drainac, Rade (1899–1943)
Classic Verses.
Dreams worn out like small coins taken out of circulation.
Landscape.
Leaf.
My hunger is infinite and my hands always empty.
Opus III, *Sels.*
Then, the drops were freezing on black branches of ancient ash trees.
When the Poet Without Lying Verses in His Heart Returns to His Native Country, *Sels.*

Drake, Barbara (b. 1939)
Mother Said.
When the Airplane Stopped.

Drake, Francis (b. 1650, d. after 1668)
To the Memory of the Learned and Reverend, Mr. Jonathan Mitchell.

Drake, Joseph Rodman (1795–1820)
American Flag, The.
Assembling of the Fays, The.
Bronx.
Culprit Fay, The, *Sels.*
Fairy Dawn.
Fairy in Armor, A.
Fay's Crime, The.
Fay's Departure, The.
Fay's Sentence, The.
If the spray-bead gem be won.
Rifleman's Song at Bennington.
Throne of the Lily-King, The.
To the Defenders of New Orleans.

Drake, Joseph Rodman, *and* **Fitz-Greene Halleck.** *See* **Halleck, Fitz-Greene, and Joseph Rodman Drake.**

Drake, Leah Bodine (b. 1915)
Precarious Ground.

Dransfield, Michael (1948–73)
Bum's Rush.
Epiderm.
Fix.
Geography, *Sels.*
Grandfather, The.
In the forest, in unexplored.
Loft.
Pas de Deux for Lovers.
Pioneer Lane.
Portrait of the Artist as an Old Man.
Presences.
Rainpoem.
Sky ceases. There is only.
That Which We Call a Rose.

Draper, George (b. 1942)
Rink Keeper's Sestina.

Drayson, Phyllis
Blackbird, The.
Hide and Seek.

Drayton, Michael (1563–1631)
And be it said of thee.
And every bird shew'd in his proper kind.
And, now that every thing may in the proper place.
Another to the River Ankor.
As love and I, late harbour'd in one inn.
As other men, so I myself do muse.
Baron's War, The, *Sels.*
By night within my bed, I roamed here and there.
By thine own named town made famous in thy fall.
By this the sun had sucked up the vast deep.
Calling to [my] mind [or minde] since first my love begun.
Chapman the Translator.
Charnwood Forest.
Christopher Marlowe.
Clear [or Cleere] had the day been [or bin] from the dawn [or dawne].
Crier, The.
Cupid, Dumb Idol.

Cupid, I Hate Thee.
David and Goliath, *Sels.*
Deare [or Dear], why should you command [or commaund] me to my rest.
Description of Elizium, The.
Duck, and Mallard first, the falconers onely sport, The.
Dwindling Forest of Arden, The.
Endimion and Phoebe, *Sels.*
Endymion's Convoy.
England's Heroical Epistles, *Sels.*
Eternall and all-working God, which wast.
Evil [or Evill] spirit, your beauty, haunts me still, An.
Fair [or Faire] stood the wind for France.
Fairy Palace, The, *Sels.*
Fen-Men of Lincolnshire's Holland, The.
Fools Gaze at Painted Courts.
Golden sun upon his fiery wheels, The.
Grave moral Spenser after these came on.
Heart, The.
His Defence Against the Idle Critic.
His Remedie for Love.
How Many Paltry, Foolish, Painted Things.
Hundred years the Ark in the building was, A.
I hear some say, this man is not in love.
Idea, *Sels.*
Idea's Mirrour, *Sels.*
If he, from heaven that filched the living fire.
In time the Princess playing with the child.
Into these loves, who but for passion look[e]s.
It was not long e're he perceiv'd the skies.
Legend of Robert, Duke of Normandy, The, *Sels.*
Like an Adventurous Seafarer Am I.
Lincolnshire's Holland Speaks of Her Waterfowl.
Love, in a humour, played the prodigal.
March strongly forth, my Muse, whilst yet the temperate air.
Methinks I See Some Crooked Mimic Jeer.
Moone-Calfe, The, *Sels.*
Moses His Birth and Miracles, *Sels.*
Most Excellent Song Which Was Solomon's, The, *Sels.*
Muses' Elysium [or Elizium], *Sels.*
Neat Marlowe, bathed in the Thepian springs.
Noah's Flood, *Sels.*
Noble Sidney with this last arose, The.
Nothing but no and I, and I and no.
Nymphidia, *Sels.*
Ode Written in the Peak[e], An.
Other Song of the Faithful, for the Mercies of God, An.
Our sacred Muse, of Israel's Singer sings.
Owen Tudor to Queen Katherine.
Owle, The, *Sels.*
Phoebe on Latmus.
Piers Gaveston, *Sels.*
Pigwiggen.
Pigwiggin Arms Himself.
Polyolbion, *Sels.*
Queen Katherine to Owen Tudor.
Roundelay: "Tell me, thou skilful shepherd's swain."
Sacrifice to Apollo, The.
Severn, The.
Shepheard's Daffodil, The.
Shepherd, why creep we in this lowly vein.
Shepherd's Garland, The, *Sels.*
Shepherd's Sirena, The, *Sels.*
Since There's No Help, Come Let Us Kiss and Part.
Skeltoniad, A.
So well I love thee, as without thee I.
Some Atheist or vile Infidel in love.
Song of Jonah in the Whale's Belly, The.
Song of the Faithful, A.
Stay, Speedy Time.
Stay, stay, sweet Time; behold, or ere thou pass.
Stay, Thames, to heare my Song, thou great and famous Flood.
Stonehenge.
Tenth Eclogue, The.
Tenth Nimphall, The.

That noble Chaucer, in those former times.
Then dainty Sandys, that hath to English done.
Then Frome (a nobler flood) the Muses doth implore.
There's nothing grieves me, but that age should haste.
Third Eclogue, The, *Sels.*
This Edward in the Aprill of his age.
This Palace Standeth in the Air.
Three Sorts of Serpents Do Resemble Thee.
To Cupid.
To Henry Reynolds, of Poets and Poesy, *Sels.*
To His Coy Love, A Canzonet.
To His Valentine.
To My Most Dearly-loved Friend, Henry Reynolds, Esquire, of Poets and Poesy.
To nothing fitter can I thee compare.
To the New Yeere [or Year].
To the Virginian Voyage.
Trent, The.
Trent Again, The.
Truce, gentle love, a parley now I crave.
When after those, four ages very near.
When first I ended, then I first began.
Where she, of all the plains of Britain that doth bear.
Whilst thus my pen strives to eternize thee.
Why should your fair eyes with such sovereign grace.
With solitude what sorts, that here's not wondrous rife?
Witlesse gallant, a young wench that woo'd, A.
You are [or You're] not alone when you are still alone.

Drennan, John Swanwick [or Swanick] (1809–93)
Epigram: "Golden casket I designed, A."
Epigram: "Love signed the contract blithe and leal."
L'Amitié et l'Amour.
On the Telescopic Moon.

Drennan, William (1754–1820)
Wake of William Orr, The.

Dresbach, Glenn Ward (1889–1968)
Cave, The.
Last Corn Shock, The.

Dressel, Jon (b. 1931)
Dai, Live.
Drouth, The.
Let's Hear It for Goliath.
You, Benjamin Jones.

Drew, John (b. 1939)
Introduction to Philosophy.
Iqbal's Poem, May 1973.
Lesser Vehicle, The.
Negative Capability.
Nightingale Poem.

Drewry, Carleton (b. 1901)
Evensong.

"Drinan, Adam." *See* **MacLeod, Joseph Gordon.**

Drinkwater, John (1882–1937)
Bird's Nest, The.
Birthright.
Bobby Blue.
Cottage Song.
Deer.
I Want to Know.
Invocation: "As pools beneath stone arches take."
Moonlit Apples.
Morning Thanksgiving.
Petition.
Prayer: "Lord, not for light in darkness do we pray."
Reciprocity.
Snail.
Sun, The.
Sunrise on Rydal Water.
Town Window, A.
Washing.
Who Were before Me.

Driscoll, Jack (b. 1946), Jack Driscoll *and* **Bill Meissner**
Arm Wrestling with My Father.

Driscoll, Louise (b. 1875)
Epitaph: "Here lies the flesh that tried."
God's Pity.
Grace for Gardens.
Hold Fast Your Dreams.
Marigolds.
My garden is a pleasant place.

Driver, C. J. (b. 1941)
Ballad of Hunters, A.
Birthdays.
In Solitary Confinement, Sea Point Police
　Cells.
Letter to Breyten Breytenbach from Hong
　Kong.
To Jann, in Her Absence.

Dromgoole, Will Allen (1865–1943)
Building the Bridge.
Old Ladies.

Dronsfield, John (1900–1951)
Visitation.

Droste-Hülshoff, Annette von (1797–1848)
In the Grass.
Last Day of the Year (New Year's Eve), The.
On the Tower.

Drown, Lessie M.
To Mother.
To-Day.

Drucker, Olga
Brooch, The.

**Drummond, William, of Hawthornden (1585–
　1649)**
Against the King.
Angels, The.
Book, The.
Change Should Breed Change.
Content and Resolute.
Death's Last Will.
Doth then the world go thus, doth all thus
　move?
For a Lady's Summons of Non-Entry.
For the Magdalene.
Forth Feasting, *Sels.*
Hymn of the Fairest Fair, The, *Sels.*
If of the dead save good nought should be said.
In those vast fields of light, ethereal plains.
Iöas' Epitaph.
Ivory, Coral, Gold, The.
Kiss, A.
Kisses Desired.
Madrigal: "Astrea in this time."
Madrigal: "Beauty [or Beautie], and the life,
　The."
Madrigal: "Daedal of my death, A."
Madrigal: "Like the Idalian Queen[e]."
Madrigal: "My thoughts hold mortal[l] strife."
Madrigal: "Poor turtle! thou bemoans."
Madrigal: "This world a hunting is."
Madrigal: "Unhappie [or Unhappy] Light."
Of Phyllis.
On Mary Magdalene.
On Pym.
Phoebus, Arise.
Regrat.
Saint John Baptist.
Sanquhar, whom this earth could scarce
　contain.
Sextain: "Sith gone is my delight and only
　pleasure."
Sextain: "With elegies, sad songs, and
　mourning lays."
Sleep, Silence' Child.
Sonnet: "Alexis, here she stayed; among these
　pines."
Sonnet: "As in a duskie [or dusky] and
　tempestuous night."
Sonnet: "How that vast heaven intitled First is
　rolled."
Sonnet: "I know that all beneath the moon
　decays."
Sonnet: "Lamp of heaven's crystal hall that
　brings the hours."
Sonnet: "My lute, be as thou wast [or wert]
　when thou didst grow."
Sonnet: "Slide soft, fair forth, and make a
　crystal plain."

Sonnet: "Sweet soul, which in the April of thy
　years."
Sonnet: "Triumphing chariots, statues, crowns
　of bay."
Sonnet: "What doth it serve to see sun's
　burning face."
Spring Bereaved.
Spring Bereaved 2.
Stolen Pleasure.
Tell Me No More.
This life, which seems so fair.
Thrice Happy He.
To Chloris.
To Sir William Alexander.
Too Long I Followed.
Translation of the Death of a Sparrow, out of
　Passerat.
Urania, or Spiritual Poems, *Sels.*
What blust'ring noise now interrupts my sleep.
When Lately Pym Descended Into Hell.
World a hunting is, The.

Drummond, William Henry (1854–1907)
Log Jam, The.
Wreck of the *Julie Plante* [or The *Julie
　Plante*], The.

Drummond de Andrade, Carlos (1902–1987)
Dead in Frock Coats, THe.
Dirty Hand, The.
Don't Kill Yourself.
Elephant, The.
Infancy.
Looking for Poetry.
Quadrille.
Souvenir of the Ancient World.
Wandering.
Your Shoulders Hold Up the World.

Dryden, John (1631–1700)
Absalom and Achitophel, Pt. I, *Sels.*
Achitophel: The Earl of Shaftsbury.
After the Pangs of a Desperate Lover.
Ah, Fading Joy.
Ah, How Sweet It Is to Love!
Alexander's Feast; or, The Power of Music [or
　Musique].
All, All of a Piece Throughout.
All for Love, *Sels.*
All human[e] things are subject to decay.
Amboyna; or, The Cruelties of the Dutch to the
　English Merchants, *Sels.*
Amphitryon, *Sels.*
And welcom now (Great Monarch) to your
　own.
Annus Mirabilis, *Sels.*
As, when some treasurer lays down the stick.
Astraea Redux, *Sels.*
Aureng-Zebe, *Sels.*
But gratious [or gracious] God, how well dost
　thou provide.
But if there be a power too just and strong.
Can Life Be a Blessing.
Character of a Good Parson, The.
Charm, A.
Cleomenes, *Sels.*
Conquest of Granada, The, *Sels.*
Cymon and Iphigenia, *Sels.*
Dame, said the Panther, times are mended well.
Damon and Celimena.
Death the Consequence of the Fall.
Diana's Hunting-Song.
Dim, as the borrow'd beams of moon and stars.
Disdain Punished.
Epilogue Spoken by Mrs. Boutell.
Epilogue: "They who have best succeeded on
　the stage."
Epilogue to Nathaniel Lee's "Mithridates", *Sels.*
Epilogue to "Tyrannick Love."
Epitaph on His Wife.
Evening's Love, An, *Sels.*
Farewell, Ungrateful Traitor.
Fife and Drum.
Fire, mean time, walks in a broader gross, The.
Fire of London, The.
From hence began that Plot, the nation's curse.
Harvest Home.
Heroique Stanzas, Consecrated to the Glorious
　Memory of His Most Serene and Renowned

Highnesse, Oliver, Late Lord Protector of
　this Common-Wealth.
Hind and the Panther, The, *Sels.*
In pious times ere [or e'r] priest-craft did
　begin.
In the first rank of these did Zimri stand.
Incantation to Oedipus.
Indian Emperor, The, *Sels.*
Kind Keeper, The, *Sels.*
King Arthur, *Sels.*
Lines Printed under the Engraved Portrait of
　Milton [In Tonson's Folio of the "Paradise
　Lost"].
Love Triumphant, *Sels.*
MacFlecknoe; or, A Satire [or Satyr] upon the
　True-Blue [or -Blew] Protestant Poet T. S,
　Sels.
Marriage à la Mode, *Sels.*
Medal [or Medall], The, *Sels.*
Militia, The.
Milk white Hind, immortal and unchang'd, A.
Momus' Song to Mars.
New London, The.
No, No, Poor Suffering Heart.
No porter guards the passage of your door.
Now on their coasts our conquering navy rides.
Now van to van the foremost squadrons meet.
Now with a general peace the world was blest.
O gracious God, how far have we.
Oak, The.
Ode on the Death of Mr. Henry Purcell, An,
　Sels.
Oedipus, *Sels.*
Of these the false Achitophel was first.
On Jacob Tonson, His Publisher.
One evening, while the cooler shade she
　sought.
Palamon and Arcite, *Sels.*
Parts of the Whole Are We; but God the
　Whole.
Portly prince, and goodly to the sight, A.
Predestination and Free Will.
Presbyterians, The.
Private Judgement Condemned.
Prologue.
Prologue: "As needy gallants in the scriv'ners'
　hands."
Prologue: "Our author by experience finds it
　true."
Prologue: "See my lov'd Britons, see your
　Shakespeare rise."
Prologue to "Love Triumphant."
Prologue to "The Tempest."
Religio Laici, *Sels.*
Secret Love; or, The Maiden Queen, *Sels.*
Secular Masque, The, *Sels.*
Sigismonda and Guiscardo, *Sels.*
Silent Woman to the University of Oxford,
　The, *Sels.*
Some by their friends, more by themselves
　thought wise.
Some of their chiefs were princes of the land.
Song: "Calm was the even, and clear [or cleer]
　was the sky."
Song: "Fair Iris I love, and hourly I die."
Song for a Girl.
Song for St. Cecilia's Day, 1687, A, *Sels.*
Song from the Italian, A.
Song: "I feed a flame within, which so
　torments me."
Song of the Zambra Dance.
Song of Venus.
Song: "Sylvia the fair, in the bloom of fifteen."
Song to a Fair Young Lady, Going Out of the
　Town in the Spring.
Song: "You charm'd me not with that fair
　face."
Sound the trumpet, beat the drum.
Spanish Friar [or Fryar], The, *Sels.*
State of Innocence, The, *Sels.*
Sunk were his eyes, his voice was harsh and
　loud.
Sure there's a lethargy in mighty woe.
Swell'd with our late successes on the foe.
Theodore and Honoria, From Boccace, *Sels.*

This is thy province, this thy wonderous way.
Threnodia Augustalis, *Sels.*
Thus man by his own strength to Heaven would soar.
To His Sacred Majesty, a Panegyrick on His Coronation, 1661, *Sels.*
To My Dear Friend Mr. Congreve [on His Comedy Called "The Double-Dealer"].
To My Friend, Dr. Charleton, on His Learned and Useful Works; and More Particularly This of Stone-Heng, by Him Restored to the True Founders.
To My Honour'd Kinsman, John Driden, of Chesterton, *Sels.*
To the Memory of Mr. Oldham.
To the Pious Memory of the Accomplished [*or* Accomplisht] Young Lady, Mrs. Anne Killigrew, [Excellent in the Two Sister-Arts of Poesie and Painting], *Sels.*
To this the Panther, with a scornful smile.
Troilus and Cressida, *Sels.*
'Twere well your judgments but in plays did range.
Tyrannic Love, *Sels.*
Upon the Death of the Lord Hastings.
Vox Populi.
What Greece, when learning flourished, only knew.
When Athens all the Graecian state did guide.
Whil'st Alexis Lay Prest [*or* Press'd].
Why Should a Foolish Marriage Vow.
With all these loads of injuries opprest.
Yet London, empress of the northern clime.
You've seen a pair of youthful lovers die.
Zimri: The Duke of Buckingham.

Dryden, John (1631–1700) *and* Nahum Tate
Absalom and Achitophel, Pt. II, *Sels.*
Doeg, though without knowing how or why.
Eleonora: A Panegyrical Poem, Dedicated to the Memory of the Late Countess of Abingdon, *Sels.*
Next These, a troop of busy [*or* buisy] spirits press.
Og [and Doeg].
Then wonder not to see this Soul extend.
Thomas Shadwell the Poet.
To make quick way I'll leap o'er heavy blocks.
To the Earl of Roscommon, on His Excellent Essay on Translated Verse, *Sels.*
Whether the fruitful Nile, or Tyrian shore.

Dryden, John *and* Sir Robert Howard. *See* Howard, Sir Robert.

Dryden, Myrtle May
Just Forget.

Du Bartas, Guillaume de Salluste (1544–90)
Divine Weeks and Works, The, *Sels.*
Fifth Day of the First Week, The.
Fourth Day of the First Week, The.
Seventh Day of the First Week, The.
Zodiac, The.

Du Bellay, Joachim (1522–60)
He that has seen a great oak dry and dead.
Hereux Qui, comme Ulysse, A Fait un Beau Voyage.
Heureux Qui, comme Ulysse, A Fait un Beau Voyage.
Hope ye, my verses, that posterity.
Hymn to the Winds.
I saw the bird that can the sun endure.
I Saw the Bird That Dares Behold the Sun.
It Was the Time.
It was the time, when rest, soft sliding downe.
Regrets, *Sels.*
Rome.
Ruins of Rome, *Sels.*
Sonnet to Heavenly Beauty, A.
Thou stranger, which for Rome in Rome here seekest.
Thou that at Rome astonished doth behold.
To His Friend in Elysium.
Visions, *Sels.*
Vow to Heavenly Venus, A.
Who list the Romane greatnes forth to figure.

Du Boccage, Marie-Anne (1710–1802)
Amazons, The, *Sels.*

Du Guillet, Pernette. *See* De [*or* Du] Guillet, Pernette.

Du Maurier, George (1834–96)
Little Work, A.
Music.
Trilby, *Sels.*

Dubé, Janet
Autobiography.
Happily Ever After, from the Story of the Same Name.
No One's Land.
Penelope.
Reflections.
So to Tell the Truth.

Dube, Oswald Basize (b. 1957)
He Was a Man of Jokes outside Office.

Dubie, Norman (b. 1945)
Apocrypha of Jacques Derrida, The.
At Midsummer.
Balalaika.
Czar's Last Christmas Letter: A Barn in the Urals, The.
Diatribe of the Kite, The.
Dressing Stations, The.
Duchess after the Burial, The.
Duchess' Red Shoes, The, *Sels.*
Elegy for Integral Domains, The.
Elegy for Wright & Hugo.
Elegy to the Sioux.
Elizabeth's War with the Christmas Bear.
February; the Boy Breughel.
Fox Who Watched for the Midnight Sun, The.
Funeral, The.
Ganges, The.
Hummingbirds.
In the Dead of the Night.
Killigrew Wood, The.
Lamentations.
Obscure, The.
Of Politics, & Art.
Pastoral: "It all happened so fast. Fenya was in the straight chair."
Radio Sky.
Swann had gone to the estate that afternoon to tell his.
Swann has visited the Duc and Duchess de Guermantes.
Thomas Hardy.
To Michael.
Trakl.
Visit.

Dubois, Lady Dorothea (1728–1774)
Song: "Scholar first my love implored, A."

DuBois, William Edward Burghardt (1868–1963)
Litany of [*or* at] Atlanta, A.
Lord make us mindful of the little things that grow and blossom.
Song of the Smoke, The.

Duché, Jacob (1738–98)
Chilled by the Blasts of Adverse Fate.
Great Lord of All, Whose Work of Love.

Duck, Stephen (1705–56)
On Mites; to a Lady.
Soon as the harvest hath laid bare the plains.
Thresher's Labour, The, *Sels.*

Duckett, Alfred A. (b. 1918)
Portrait Philippines.
Sonnet: "Where are we to go when this is done?"

Dudek, Louis (b. 1918)
Atlantis, *Sels.*
Avant Garde.
Coming Suddenly to the Sea.
Dead, The.
Europe, *Sels.*
Fishing Village.
García Lorca.
Marine Aquarium, The.
News.
Ocean, The.
Provincetown, *Sels.*

Dudley, Thomas (1576–1653)
Verses Found in Thomas Dudley's Pocket after His Death.

Dudley, William E. (b. 1887)
City, Lord, Where Thy Dear Life, The.

Duer, Caroline
International Episode, An.

Duerden, Richard (b. 1927)
Dance with Banderillas.
Moon Is to Blood.
Musica No. 3.

Dufault, Peter Kane (b. 1923)
Black Jess.
First Night, A.
In an Old Orchard.
Letter for Allhallows, A.
Notes on a Girl.
Odysseus' Song to Calypso.
On Aesthetics, More or Less.
Owl.
Possibilities.
Thalamos.
Tour de Force.

Dufferin, Helen Selina Blackwood, Countess of (1807–67)
Countess of Dufferin, The.

Duffield, George, Jr. (1818–88)
Stand Up! Stand Up for Jesus.

Duffy, Carol Ann (b. 1955)
Dolphins, The.
Foreign.
Legend, The.
Telephoning Home.
You Jane.

Duffy, Maureen (b. 1933)
Evesong.
Sonnet: "Afterwards there are dogends in."

Dugan, Alan (b. 1923)
Actual Vision of Morning's Extrusion.
Against a Sickness: To the Female Double Principle God.
Aside.
Decimation before Phraata, The.
Elegy for a Puritan Conscience.
Fabrication of Ancestors.
For Masturbation.
From Heraclitus.
From Rome, for More Public Fountains in New York City.
Funeral Oration for a Mouse.
Glad at the Cold (1955).
How We Heard the Name.
Internal Migration: On Being on Tour.
Last Statement for a Last Oracle.
Let Heroes Account to Love.
Love Song: I and Thou.
Memorial Service for the Invasion Beach Where the Vacation in the Flesh Is Over.
Memories of Verdun.
Mirror Perilous, The.
Monarchs, the butterflies, are commanded, The.
Niagara Falls.
On a Seven-Day Diary.
On Alexander and Aristotle, on a Black-on-Red Greek Plate.
On Being a Householder.
On Don Juan del Norte, Not Don Juan Tenorio del Sur.
On Finding the Tree of Life.
On Hurricane Jackson.
On Leaving Town.
On Trees.
Plague of Dead Sharks.
Poem: "Person who can do, The."
Poem: "What's the balm."
Portrait from the Infantry.
Prayer: "God, I need a job because I need money."
Prison Song.
"Space Is Not Merely a Background for Events, But Possesses an Autonomous Structure." A. Einstein.
Stutterer.
To a Red-headed Do-good Waitress.
Tribute to Kafka for Someone Taken.
Untitled Poem.
Wall, Cave, and Pillar Statements, after Asôka.
What a Circus.

Remembering Lunch.
Removal from Terry Street, A.
Supreme Death.
War Blinded.
Warriors.
Washing the Coins.
Dunn, Gwen
Journey Back to Christmas.
Dunn, Max (b. 1895)
O, Where Were We Before Time Was.
Dunn, Stephen (b. 1939)
At the Smithville Methodist Church.
Choosing to Think of It.
Cleanliness.
Day and Night Handball.
From Underneath.
He/She.
Letting the Puma Go.
Looking for a Rest Area.
On Hearing the Airlines Will Use a
   Psychological Profile to Catch Potential
   Skyjackers.
Poem for People Who Are Understandably Too
   Busy to Read Poetry.
Routine Things around the House, The.
Tangier.
Toward the Verrazano.
Walking the Marshland.
Dunn, Stephen P. (b. 1928)
Bringing It Down.
Dancing with God.
Man Who Closed Shop, The.
Men Talk.
Prayer of the Young Stoic.
Tenderness.
Dunnam, Ouida Smith (b. 1922)
Prayer of a Beginning Teacher.
Dunne, Sean (b. 1956)
Refugees at Cobh.
Throwing the Beads.
Dunton, Theodore Watts-. *See* **Watts-Dunton,**
   Theodore.
Duo Duo
Blood of one entire class . . ., The.
From Death's Point of View.
Gallery.
Night.
Saying Good-bye.
Summer.
When the People Arose from Cheese.
DuPlessis, Phil (b. 1944)
Prayer for a Thief.
DuPlessis, Rachel Blau
Crowbar.
Dupree, Edgar
Light of Faith, The.
Dupuy, J. (d. 1964)
Michael Met a Duck.
Durack, Mary (b. 1913)
Lament for the Drowned Country.
Durand, Oswald (1840–1906)
Black Man's Son, The.
Francie-the-Possessed.
Durcan, Paul (b. 1944)
Around the Corner from Francis Bacon.
Backside to the Wind.
Bewley's Oriental Café, Westmoreland Street.
Birth of a Coachman.
Divorce Referendum, Ireland, 1986, The.
Going Home to Mayo, Winter, 1949.
Hat Factory, The.
Ireland 1972.
Irish Hierarchy Bans Colour Photography.
Jewish Bride, The.
Kilfenora Teaboy, The.
Micheál Mac Liammóir.
Pietà's Over, The.
She Mends an Ancient Wireless.
10.30 AM Mass, June 16, 1985.
Turkish Carpet, The.
Weeping Headstones of the Isaac Becketts,
   The.
Wife Who Smashed Television Gets Jail.
Durell, Ann
Cornish Magic.

Durem, Ray (1915–63)
Award.
Basic.
Friends.
I Know I'm Not Sufficiently Obscure.
Problem in Social Geometry — the Inverted
   Square!
Ultimate Equality.
Vet's Rehabilitation.
D'Urfey [or Durfey], Thomas (1653–1723)
Bath; or, The Western Lass, The, *Sels.*
Chloe Divine.
Crown's far too weighty, The.
Dialogue, between Crab and Gillian.
Fisherman's Song, The.
Fool's Preferment, A, *Sels.*
I'll Sail upon the Dog-Star.
Shepherd Kept Sheep on a Hill So High, A.
Durham, Jimmie (b. 1940)
Columbus Day.
Justiniano Lamé Has Been Killed.
Middle.
Woman Gave Me a Red Star to Wear on My
   Headband, A.
Duris (*fl.* c.3rd cent. B.C.)
Ephesos.
Durrell, Lawrence (b. 1912)
Acropolis.
Adepts, The.
At Epidaurus.
Ballad of the Good Lord Nelson, A.
Ballad of the Oedipus Complex.
Coptic Poem ("A Coptic deputation, going to
   Ethiopia").
Cradle Song: "Curled like a hoop in sleep."
Death of General Uncebunke, The; a Biography
   in Little, *Sels.*
Delos.
Eight Aspects of Melissa, *Sels.*
Epitaph: "Stavro's dead. A truant vine."
Green Coconuts: Rio.
In Arcadia.
In Crisis.
Lesbos.
Levant.
My uncle sleeps in the image of death.
Mythology.
Nemea.
On First Looking into Loeb's Horace.
On Seeming to Presume.
Owed to America.
Paphos.
Poggio.
Salamis.
Sarajevo.
Seferis.
Stoic.
Strip-tease.
Swans.
This Unimportant Morning.
Vega.
Visitations.
Water-Colour of Venice, A.
Durston, Georgia Roberts
Wolf, The.
Duryee, Mary Ballard (1896–1988)
Homestead — Winter Morning.
Dutton, Geoffrey (b. 1922)
Burning Off.
Finished Gentleman, A.
Fish Shop Windows.
Stranded Whales, The.
Time of Waiting.
Dutton, Geoffrey Fraser (b. 1924)
Hazels.
High Flats at Craigston, The.
How Calm the Wild Water.
Idyll: "Engine on the bank, The."
Passage.
Storm.
Duyn, Mona Van. *See* **Van Duyn, Mona.**
Dwight, Timothy (1752–1817)
And now the morn arase, when o'er the plain.
As Down a Lone Valley.
Assault on the Fortress, The.

Columbia.
Conquest of Canaan, The, *Sels.*
Destruction of the Pequods, The.
Flourishing Village, The.
Greenfield Hill, *Sels.*
Here stood Hypocrisy, in sober brown.
I Love Thy Kingdom, Lord.
In scenes of distant death bold Hezron stands.
Prospect, The.
Shall Man, O God of Light.
Sing to the Lord Most High.
Smooth Divine, The.
To the Federal Convention.
Triumph of Infidelity, The, *Sels.*
Dybek, Stuart (b. 1942)
Brass Knuckles.
Cherry.
My Father's Fights.
My Neighborhood.
Dyer, Lady Catherine (*fl.* c.1641)
Epitaph on the Monument of Sir William Dyer
   at Colmworth, 1641.
Sir William Dyer, Knight, *Sels.*
Dyer, Sir Edward (c.1540–1607)
Corydon to His Phyllis.
Fancy, Farewell.
I Would It Were Not As It Is.
Lowest Trees Have Tops, The.
My Mind to Me a Kingdom Is.
Prometheus, when first from heaven high.
Wher one would be.
Dyer, John (1699–1758)
Ah gentle shepherd, thine the lot to tend.
Bedford Level.
Country Walk, The, *Sels.*
English Fog, The.
Enough of Grongar and the shady dales.
Fleece, The, *Sels.*
Grongar Hill, *Sels.*
Happy Workhouse and the Good Effects of
   Industry, The.
How to Shear Sheep.
I am resolved, this charming day.
My Ox Duke.
O may I with myself agree.
To Clio, from Rome.
Treating Sheep Ailments.
Wool Trade, The.
Dylan, Bob (b. 1941)
Ballad of a Thin Man.
Blowin' in the Wind.
Dear Mister Congressman.
Don't Ya Tell Henry.
Hard Rain's A-Gonna Fall, A.
Quinn the Eskimo.
Three Angels.
Times they Are A-Changin', The.
Tiny Montgomery.
Dyment, Clifford (1914–1970)
As a boy with a richness of needs I wandered.
Derbyshire Born, Monmouth Is My Home.
Fox.
From Many a Mangled Truth a War is Won.
Sanctuary.
Dyson, Edward (1865–1931)
Friendly Game of Football, A.
Old Whim Horse, The.
Dyson, Will (1880–1938)
Trucker, The.
Dzyubin, Eduard. *See* **"Bagritzky [or
   Bagritsky], Eduard."**

E

"E." *See* **Fullerton, Mary Elizabeth.**
"E. C." *See* **"C., E."**
"E. H. K." *See* **"K., E. H."**
"E. M. G. R." *See* **"R., E. M. G."**
"E. O. G." *See* **"G., E. O."**
"E. S." *See* **"S., E."**
Eady, Cornelius (b. 1954)
Atomic Prayer.
Jazz Dancer.

Hi-Fashion Girl.
Hope Chest.
Martha Graham.
Think Small.
Vampirella.
When the Moon Is Full.
You Go to My Head.

Eradam, Yusuf (b. 1954)
Brief Note to the Bag Lady, Ma Sister, A.

Eratosthenes
Bacchus, receive my offering, not.
Meditation, Followed by Excellent Advice.

Erdrich, Louise (b. 1954)
Birth of Potchikoo, The.
Butcher's Wife, The.
Captivity.
Death of Potchikoo, The.
Family Reunion.
Francine's Room.
How Potchikoo Got Old.
I Was Sleeping Where the Black Oaks Move.
Indian Boarding School: The Runaways.
Jacklight.
King of Owls, The.
Lady in the Pink Mustang, The.
Love Medicine, A.
Night Sky.
Old Man Potchikoo, *Sels.*
Owls.
Potchikoo Marries.
That Pull from the Left.
Windigo.

Erickson, C. L.
Light in the Window, The.

Erinna (*fl.* 3d century B.C.)
Baucis.
Distaff, The.
Epigrams, *Sels.*
Epitaph on a Betrothed Girl.
I am the grave of Baucis the bride. Passing by.
On the Portrait of a Girl.
Stele and my Sirens and mournful pitcher that hold.

Eristi-Aya (c.1790–1745 B.C.)
Letter to Her Mother, A.

Ernst, John F. (*fl.* late 18th century)
O Jesus Christ, True Light of God.

Erskine, John
Kings and Stars.
Shepherd Speaks, The.

Erskine, Thomas Erskine, 1st Baron (1750–1823)
James Alan Park/ Came naked stark.
On Scott's Poem "The Field of Waterloo."
On Tom Moore's Translation of Anacreon.

Erucius (*fl.* c.30 B.C.)
Even though he lies underground.
Glaukon and Korydon, mountain herdsmen.
How massively, with what a fine stiff rise.
I am Athenian, that was my city.
I, the priest of Rhea, long-haired.
Kleson's goat snorted all night through the dark.
May supple-footed theatre-growing ivy.
Tell me herdsman for the sake of Pan.

Erumai Veliyanar
Horse Did Not Come Back, The.

Erycius of Cyzicus
Demetrius fled the fight in fear.

Escoffery, Gloria (b. 1923)
After the Fall.
Farewell to a Jovial Friend.
No Man's Land.
Twins.

Esdaile, Arundell James Kennedy (1880–1956)
On a War-worker, 1916.

Eshleman, Clayton (b. 1935)
Black Hat, The.
Un Poco Loco.
Very Old Woman, A.

Espada, Martín (b. 1955)
Boot Camp Incantation.
Bully.
Federico's Ghost.

From an Island You Cannot Name.
Jorge the Church Janitor Finally Quits.
La Tumba de Buenaventura Roig.
Latin Night at the Pawnshop.
Manuel Is Quiet Sometimes.
Niggerlips.
Policeman's Ball, The.
Right Hand of a Mexican Farmworker in Somerset County, Maryland, The.
Savior Is Abducted in Puerto Rico, The.
Spanish of Our Out-Loud Dreams, The.
Tiburón.
Trumpets from the Islands of Their Eviction.
Two Mexicanos Lynched in Santa Cruz, California, May 3, 1877.
Voodoo Cucumbers.
Where the Disappeared Would Dance.

Espaillat, Rhina P. (b. 1932)
From the Rain Down.
You Call Me by Old Names.

Espírito Santo, Alda do (b. 1926)
Same Side of the Canoe, The.
Where Are the Men Seized in This Wind of Madness?

Espy, Willard R. (b. 1910)
Gemini Jones.
My TV Came down with a Chill.
Singular Singulars, Peculiar Plurals.

Essenin, Sergei (1895–1925)
Golden Grove, The.

Essex, Edwin (b. 1892)
Loneliness.

Essex, Robert Devereux, 2d Earl of (1567–1601)
Change [Thy Mind since She Doth Change].
Happy Were He.

Esson, Louis (Thomas Louis Buvelot Esson) (1879–1943)
Shearer's Wife, The.

Esson, Thomas Louis Buvelot. *See* **Esson, Louis.**

Eterovic, Ramon Diaz (b. 1956)
Childhood Is the Only Lasting Flower.

E'tesami, Parvin (1910–41)
To His Father on Praising the Honest Life of the Peasant.

Etherege, Sir George (1653–91)
Comical Revenge, The, *Sels.*
Ephelia to Bajazet.
Letter to the Earl of Middleton, A.
Song: "Ladies, though to your conquering eyes."
To a Lady Asking Him How Long He Would Love Her.

Etherege, Sir George *and* **William Walsh**
Imperfect Enjoyment, The.
Rivals.
Song: "If she be not as kind as fair."

Etherege, Sir George *and* **William Walsh.** *See* **Walsh, William.**

Etheridge, Ken (1911–1981)
Annunciation.

Etter, Dave (b. 1928)
Chicken.
Romp.

Eubulus (*fl.* 4th century)
Benefits and Abuse of Alcohol, The.

Euenos (Euenos The Grammarian, Euenos of Askelon) (*fl.* 5th cent. B.C.)
B kw rm.
If hate is painful and if love's a pain.
Vine *v.* Goat.

Euodos
Echo:/ mimic,/ last sip.

Euphorion (b. c.276 B.C.)
Not the wild olive, not the fatal stones.
When first Eudoxos cut his lovely hair.

Euripides (485–406 B.C.)
Alcestis, *Sels.*
Andromache, *Sels.*
Bacchae, *Sels.*
Bellerophon, *Sels.*
Chorus: "And Pergamos,/ City of the Phrygians."

Chorus of Satyrs, Driving Their Goats.
Cyclops, *Sels.*
Hippolytus, *Sels.*
Home of Aphrodite, The.
Iphigenia [*or* Iphigeneia] in Aulis, *Sels.*
Iphigenia in Tauris, *Sels.*
It was everything to me to think well of one man.
Love Song: "One with eyes the fairest."
Medea, *Sels.*
No More, O My Spirit.
O for the Wings of a Dove.
Stranger, if I can save thee, wilt thou bear.
Strength of Fate, The.
This town, now, yes, Mother.
Trojan Women, The, *Sels.*

Euwer, Anthony (1877–1955)
As a Beauty I Am Not a Star.
Limeratomy, The, *Sels.*
Limerick: "Ankle's chief end is exposiery, The."
True Facts of the Case, The.

Evald, Johannes (1743–81)
King Christian.

Evans, Abbie Huston (b. 1881)
Fundament Is Shifted, The.
On the Curve-Edge.

Evans, Abel (1679–1737)
Author's Epitaph, Written by Himself, An.
Keep the commandments, Trapp, and go no further.
On Sir John Vanbrugh [Architect].
Tadlow.

Evans, David Allan (b. 1940)
Bullfrogs.
Neighbors.
Retired Farmer.
Sound of Rain, The.
Story of Lava, The.

Evans, Evan (1731–88)
Hall of Ifor Hael, The.
Love of Our Country, The, *Sels.*
Whatever clime we travel or explore.

Evans, H. A. C.
If Not.
Limerick: "There was a young lady called Clarice."

Evans, Humphrey (b. 1914)
And Again.

Evans, Margiad (1909–58)
Rain.
Resurrection.
Snowdrops.

Evans, Mari E. (b. 1923)
And the Old Women Gathered.
Black Jam for Dr. Negro.
Daufuskie.
How Will You Call Me, Brother.
I Am a Black Woman.
If There Be Sorrow.
Into Blackness Softly.
Limited Aggression.
Man without Food, A.
Marrow of My Bone.
Rebel, The.
Spectrum.
To Mother and Steve.
Vive Noir!
When in Rome.
Where Have You Gone?

Evans, Nathaniel (1742–67)
To Thee, Then, Let All Beings Bend.

Evans, Paul
Blair Peach died with a broken head.
City is a crowded lift, The.
Hail, Garcia, hammer of pigeons.
Infamous Doctrine.
Man points with his umbrella, A.
Mixed with age, she could foresee the future.
Ode to Tennis.
Ode: "Trees have their doubts but we have ours."
Poets detained by Thought Police.
Professor stood still, tall, thin, with stains, The.
Sofa Book, The, *Sels.*

Fairbairns, Zoë
Thing You'll Like Best.
Fairbridge, Kingsley (1885–1924)
Magwere, Who Waits Wondering.
South African Exhibition, 1907.
Fairburn, Arthur Rex Dugard (1904–57)
Album Leaves, *Sels.*
Back Street.
Beggar to Burgher.
Cave, The.
Conversation in the Bush.
Diogenes.
Down on My Luck.
Farewell: "What is there left to be said?"
Full Fathom Five.
I'm Older than You, Please Listen.
Naked Girl Swimming, A.
Possessor, The.
Tapu.
Terms of Appointment.
Fairfax, James Griffyth (1886–1976)
Forest of the Dead, The.
Fairfax, Lord General
Oh let that day from time be blotted quite.
Fairfax, Thomas Fairfax, Baron (1612–1671)
On the Fatal Day January 30, 1648.
Shortness of Life.
Upon the New Building at Appleton.
Falckner, Justus (1672–1723)
Rise, Ye Children.
Falco, Liber (1906–55)
I was Born in Jacinto Vera.
Falconar, Maria (b. 1771?)
Prefatory Epistle, A.
Falconer, E. J.
Cradle Song at Bethlehem.
Doves.
Elephant, The.
Little Finger Game, A.
Marketing.
Falconer, Raymond
No Voice of Man.
Falconer, William (1732–69)
Amid this fearful trance, a thundering sound.
Fair Candia now no more beneath her lee.
Ship Is Lost, The.
Ship Sets Out, The.
Shipwreck, The, *Sels.*
Faleti, Adebayo
Independence.
Falk, Marcia (b. 1946)
At Candlelighting.
Falke, Gustav (1853–1916)
God's Harp.
Strand-Thistle.
Falkland, Elizabeth Cary, Viscountess (d. 1639)
To the Queenes Most Excellent Majestie.
Falkner, John Meade (1858–1922)
After Trinity.
Arabia.
Christmas Day; the Family Sitting.
Epilogue: "Painted autumn overwhelms, The."
Falla, Manuel de
Asturiana.
Jota.
Lullaby: "Sleep, little baby, sleep."
Moorish Cloth, The.
Polo.
Seguidilla of Murcia.
Song: "Because they are traitors, your eyes."
Faller, Kevin (b. 1920)
Landscape.
Fallon, Eunice
August.
Fallon, Padraic (1905–74)
Assumption.
Dardanelles 1916.
Field Observation.
For Paddy Mac.
Head, The.
Hedge Schoolmaster, A.
Kiltartan Legend.
Lakshmi.

Mater Dei.
Odysseus.
Painting of My Father.
Pot Shot.
Weir Bridge.
Young Fenians, The.
Fallon, Peter (b. 1951)
Airs and Graces.
Cardplayers, The.
Herd, The.
Himself.
Meadow, The.
Moons.
My Care.
Spring Song.
Winter Work.
"Falstaff, Jake" (Herman Fetzer) (1899–1935)
Beautiful Sunday.
Fan Ch'eng-ta (1126–1193)
Autumn.
Consoling the Yü Farmers.
Farming Family Invites the Guest to Stay
Overnight, A.
Four Songs in Imitation of Wang Chien, *Sels.*
Late Spring.
Pressing for Tax Payment.
Reeling Silk.
Rejoicing the Spirits.
Seasonal Poems on Fields and Gardens, *Sels.*
Summer.
Winter.
Written While Lying on My Pillow in the
Morning on the Twelfth Day of the Eleventh
Month.
Fan Tseng-hsiang (1846–1931)
Before dawn passing Chiang-k'ou town.
My good wife was born in the Capital.
Random Verses from a Boat, *Sels.*
Within three days we've changed boats twice.
Fan Yun (451–505)
Farewell to Shen Yueh.
Fandel, John (b. 1925)
Bee, The.
Indians.
Fane, Mildmay. *See* **Westmorland, Mildmay**
Fane, 2d Earl of.
Fanshawe, Catherine Maria (1765–1834)
Fragment in Imitation of Wordsworth.
Riddle: "'Twas in heaven pronounced, and
'twas muttered in hell."
Fanshawe, Sir Richard (1608–66)
Fair Golden Age! When milk was th' on[e]ly
food.
Fall, The.
How I forsook/ Elias and Pisa after, and
betook.
Il Pastor Fido, *Sels.*
Learn women all from this housewifery.
Ode on His Majesty's Proclamation.
Of Beauty.
Our beauty is to us that which to men.
Rose, A.
Ten years the world upon him falsely smiled.
Well may that kisse be sweet that's giv'n t' a
sleek.
Fanthorpe, U. A. (b. 1929)
At the Ferry.
BC:AD.
Father in the Railway Buffet.
Growing Up.
Homing In.
Not My Best Side.
Our Dog Chasing Swifts.
Portraits of Tudor Statesmen.
Reindeer Report.
Relief of Myopia, The.
Resuscitation Team.
What the Donkey Saw.
You Will Be Hearing from Us Shortly.
Farber, Norma (1909–84)
Beyond the Tapestries.
Bow Down, Mountain.
Dove.
Hog at the Manger.
How They Brought the Good News by Sea.

Jubilate Herbis.
Ladybug's Christmas.
Manhattan Lullaby.
Spider.
Taking Turns.
Farewell, George (*fl.* c.1733)
Adieu to My Landlady, An.
Country Man, The, *Sels.*
Crunking crane heard high amongst the clouds,
The.
Molly Moor.
Privy-Love for My Landlady.
Quaerè.
There's Life in a Mussel; a Meditation.
To the Archdeacon.
Faricy, Austin (b. 1911)
Through Warmth and Light of Summer Skies.
Farid-uddin Attar (1119–1202)
Conference of the Birds, The, *Sels.*
Dervish wept to feel the violence of, A.
Hallaj's corpse was burnt and when the flame.
In India lives a bird that is unique.
Farjeon, Eleanor (1881–1965)
Advice to a Child.
Bedtime.
Blackfriars.
Blow the Stars Home.
Cat!
Cats.
Children's Bells, The.
Children's Carol, The.
Down! Down!
Dragonfly, A.
Easter Monday.
Flamingo.
Flower-Seller, The ("The flower-seller's fat").
For a Mocking Voice.
For Snow.
Geography.
Golden Cat, The.
Good Night.
Hallowe'en.
Hey! My Pony!
Holly and Mistletoe.
In the Week When Christmas Comes.
Jenny White and Johnny Black.
Keeping Christmas.
Kitten, A.
Lewis Carroll.
Light the Lamps Up, Lamplighter!
Morning has broken like the first morning.
Mrs. Malone.
Mrs. Peck-Pigeon.
Ned.
Night Will Never Stay, The.
Pencil and Paint.
Quarrel, The.
School-Bell.
Sisters.
Tailor.
There Are Big Waves.
There Isn't Time.
Tide in the River, The.
Vegetables.
Wheelbarrow.
White Horses.
William I.
Window Boxes ("A window box of pansies").
Zodiac.
Farley, Henry (*fl.* c.1621)
Bounty of Our Age, The.
Farley, Robert E.
Thinking Happiness.
Farmer, Edward
Little Jim.
Farmer, Harold (b. 1943)
Lost City.
Rhinoceros.
Farnham, Jessie
Garland for a Storyteller.
"Farningham, Marianne" (Mary Ann Hearn)
God Cares.
Last Hymn, The.
Farnsworth, Robert (b. 1929)
Sketch.

Farquhar, George (1678–1707)
Song, A.

Farrar, Janice (b. 1933)
Thought of Marigolds, A.

Farrar, John Chipman (1896–1976)
Brest Left Behind.
Comparison, A.
Parenthood.
Roller Skates.
Time Is Today, The.
Victorian Song.

Farrell, J. R.
Bank Thief, The.

Farrell, Kate (b. 1946)
Double Bubble of Infinity, The.
Thanks to Flowers.

Farren, Robert (Roibéard O'Faracháin) (b. 1909)
Immolation.
Lineage.
Mason, The.
Sleep, *Sels.*
Stable Straw.
While now I lay me down to sleep.

Farrokhzad, Forugh (1935–67)
Born Again.
Couple.
I'm Sad.
In the land of dwarfs.
O Realm Bejewelled.
On Earth.
Once More.
Someone like No One Else.

Fatchen, Max (b. 1920)
I Often Meet a Monster.
It's a Bit Rich.
Night Walk.
Tailpiece.

Fatisha (b. 1940)
From Star to Sun We Are Going.

Fauset, Jessie Redmond (1888–1961)
Dead Fires.
Enigma.
Fragment: "Breath of life imbued those few dim days, The."
La Vie C'est la Vie.
Noblesse Oblige.
Oblivion.
Oriflamme.
Rencontre.
Return, The.
Stars in Alabama.
Touché.
Words! Words!

Fawcett, Brian (b. 1944)
Hand, The.

Fawcett, Edgar (1847–1904)
Fireflies.

Fawcett, Joseph (1758?–1804)
Art of War, The, *Sels.*
Feast of Blood, The.

Fawcett, Susan
Subway.

Fawkes, Francis (1720–77)
Elegy on the Death of Dobbin, the Butterwoman's Horse, An.

Fay, John
Limerick: "Hopeful old fellow called Rousseau, A."

Fazio degli Uberti (1326–60)
Of England, and of Its Marvels.

Fearing, Kenneth (1902–61)
Ad.
American Rhapsody.
Any Man's Advice to His Son.
C Stands for Civilization.
Confession Overheard in a Subway.
Cultural Notes.
Dirge: "1-2-3 was the number he played but today the number came 3-2-1."
Elegy in a Theatrical Warehouse.
End of the Seers' Convention.
Green Light.
Love, 20 Cents the First Quarter Mile.

Lullaby: "Wide as this night, old as this night is old and young as it is young."
Memo.
Minnie and Mrs. Hoyne.
No Credit.
Obituary.
Operative No. 174 Resigns.
Pact.
Pay-off.
People vs. the People, The.
Portrait.
Readings, Forecasts, Personal Guidance.
Requiem: "Will they stop."
Resurrection.
Tomorrow.
Twentieth-Century Blues.
Yes, the Agency Can Handle That.

Fearne, Flora
Little Men, The.

Feinman, Alvin (b. 1929)
November Sunday Morning.

Feinstein, Elaine (b. 1930)
Calliope in the Labour Ward.
Coastline.
Dad.
Home.
June.
Lais.
Magic Apple Tree, The.
Marriage.
Medium, The.
Patience.

Feinstein, Martin (1892–1934)
Burning Bush.

Feinstein, Robert N. (b. 1915)
Woolly Words.

Feinstein, Sascha
Buying Wine.
Monk's Mood.

Feiritear, Piaras (1600–1653)
Lay your weapons down, young lady.

Feirstein, Frederick (b. 1940)
"Grandfather" in Winter.
L'Art.

Feldman, Irving (b. 1928)
All of Us Here, *Sels.*
Death of Vitellozzo Vitelli, The.
Double, The.
Dream, The.
Family History.
Little Lullaby.
My Olson Elegy.
Of Course, We Would Wish.
Old Men, The.
Pripet Marshes, The.
Scene of a Summer Morning.
Simple Outlines, Human Shapes.
Surely They're Just So Large.

Feldman, Ruth (b. 1911)
Survivor.

Feldman, Susan (b. 1950)
How the Invalids Make Love.
Intruder.
Lamentations of an Au Pair Girl.
Sea Legs.

Fell, Alison (b. 1944)
August 6, 1945.
Freeze-frame.
Medusa on Skyros.
Significant Fevers.
Supper.

Felltham [or Feltham], Owen (c.1602–1668)
On a Hopeful Youth.
On the Duke of Buckingham, Slain by Felton, the 23rd August, 1628.
To Phryne.
Upon a Rare Voice.

Feng Yen-ssu (903–960)
Magpie on the Branch.

Fenton, Elijah (1683–1730)
Olivia.

Fenton, Elizabeth (b. 1943)
Masks.
Under the Ladder to Heaven.

Fenton, James *and* **John Fuller**
In a Notebook.
Poem against Catholics.
Size of the Mother Superior, The.
Thing That People Do, The.

Fenton, James (b. 1949)
Cambodia.
Climate of Nut Castanets, A.
Dead Soldiers.
German Requiem, A.
God, A Poem.
Kingfisher's Boxing Gloves, The.
Lollipops of the Pomeranian Baroque.
Of Bison Men.
Pitt-Rivers Museum, Oxford, The, *Sels.*
Skip, The.
Song That Sounds Like This, The.
South Parks Road.
Terminal Moraine, A.
This Octopus Exploits Women.
Wild Life Studies, *Sels.*
Wild ones.
Wind.

Fenyves, Marta
Exile.

Ferdinand, Val
Blues (in Two Parts), The.
Food for Thought.
2 B BLK.
White boys gone.

Ferebe, George (*fl.* 1593–1613)
Houseless Downs, The.
Shepherds' Song, Sung before Queen Anne, on the Wiltshire Downs, 11 June 1613, The, *Sels.*

Fergus, Howard (b. 1937)
Ethnocide.
Forecast.
Lament for Maurice Bishop.

Ferguson, James (1842–c.1910)
Auld Daddy Darkness.

Ferguson, Sir Samuel (1810–86)
Aideen's Grave.
At the Polo-Ground.
Burial of King Cormac, The.
Fairy Thorn, The.
Forging of the Anchor, The.
Lament for the Death of Thomas Davis.
Lapful of Nuts, The.
Lark in the Clear Air, The.
Vengeance of the Welshmen of Tirawley, The.

Fergusson, Robert (1750–74)
Ah that sweet period of revolving time.
Braid Claith.
Called Oysters.
Canongate Playhouse in Ruins, The.
Daft Days, The.
Drinking Song.
Elegy on the Death of Scots Music.
Epigram on a Lawyer's Desiring One of the Tribe to Look with Respect to a Gibbet.
Ghaists; a Kirk-yard Eclogue, The.
Hallow-Fair.
Leith Races, *Sels.*
My Last Will.
My Winsome Dear.
Ode to the Gowdspink.
On Seeing a Butterfly in the Street.
On the Death of Mr. Thomas Lancashire, Comedian.
Rising of the Session, The.
Saturday's Expedition, A, *Sels.*
Sow of Feeling, The.

Ferland, Barbara (b. 1919)
Ave Maria.
Expect No Turbulence.
Orange.

Ferlinghetti, Lawrence (b. 1919)
Away above a Harborful.
Away above a harborful.
Canticle of Jack Kerouac, The.
Christ Climbed Down.
Coney Island of the Mind, A, *Sels.*
Constantly risking absurdity.
Crazy/ to be alive in such a strange.

Movie Actors Scribbling Letters Very Fast in Crucial Scenes.
Now Snow Descends.
Of History More Like Myth.
Old Haven.
Primer of Plato.
Remember That Country.
Shore.
Song for "Buvez les Vins du Postillion" — Advt.
Stranger, The.
Unicorn and the Lady, The.
You Know.

Garrison, Wendell Phillips (b. 1840)
Afternoon.
Evening.
Post-Meridian, Sels.

Garrison, William Lloyd (1805–79)
Freedom for the Mind.

Garrison, Winfred Ernest (b. 1874)
Thy Sea So Great ("Thy sea, O God, so great").

Garrison, Theodosia Pickering (1874–1944)
Closed Door, The.
Ilicet.
Memorial Day.
Poplars, The.
Prayer: "Let me work and be glad."
Shade.
Shepherd Who Stayed, The.
Stains.
Torch, The.

Garstin, Crosbie (1887–1930)
Chemin Des Dames.
Nocturne: "Red flame flowers bloom and die, The."

Garston, Edward John Langford (b. 1893)
To the Rats.

Garth, Sir Samuel (1661–1719)
As bold Mirmillo the grey dawn descries.
Dispensary, The, Sels.
How impotent a deity am I!
Oft has this planet rolled around the sun.
This wight all mercenary projects tries.
What Frenzy Has of Late Possess'd the Brain.

Garvey, Marcus (1887–1940)
Centenary's Day.
Keep Cool.

Gascoigne, George (1539–77)
Adventures of Master F. I., The, Sels.
All were too little for the merchant's hand.
And every year a world my will did deem.
And if I did, what then?
Arraignment of a Lover, The.
Before mine eye to feed my greedy will.
Common speech is, spendd and God will send, The.
Conference among ourselves we called, A.
Constancy of a Lover, The.
Councell Given to Master Bartholmew Withipoll.
De Profundis, Sels.
Divorce of a Lover, The ("Divorce me nowe good death").
Farewell with a Mischeife.
Fie, Pleasure, Fie!
For That He Looked Not upon Her.
For why? the gaines doth seldome quitte the charge.
From depth of dole wherein my soul doth dwell.
Fruits of War, The, Sels.
Gascoigne's Good-Morrow.
Gascoigne's [or Gascoygnes] Good-Night.
Gascoigne's Memories, Sels.
Gascoigne's Woodmanship.
Gloze upon This Text, Dominus iis opus habet, A.
Green Knight's Farewell to Fancy, The.
I Could Not though I Would.
In haste poste haste, when first my wandering [or wandring] mind[e].
Inscription in a Garden.
Looks of a Lover Enamoured, The.
Lullaby [or Lullabie] of a Lover, The.

Magnum Vectigal Parsimonia.
No haste but good, where wisdome makes the waye.
Of All the Birds That I Do Know.
Praise of Philip Sparrow, The, Sels.
Skies gan scowl, o'ercast with misty clouds, The.
Sonet Written in Prayse of the Browne Beautie, A.
Steele Glas, The.
Straunge [or Strange] Passion of a Lover, A.
To prink me up and make me higher placed.
Vain excess of flattering fortune's gifts, The.

Gascoyne, David
De Profundis.
Ecce Homo.
Elegy: "Friend, whose unnatural early death."
Eve.
Ex Nihilo.
Landscape.
Miserere, Sels.
Orpheus in the Underworld.
Patmos.
Sacred Hearth, The.
Salvador Dali.
Tenebrae.
Tough Generation, A.
Uncertain Battle, The.
Unsagacious Animal, An.
Wartime Dawn, A.
Winter Garden.

Gashe, Marina
Village, The.

Gaspar De Alba, Alicia
Elemental Journey: Anniversary Gift.

Gasztold, Carmen Bernos de
Camel, The.
Gazelle, The.
Noah's Prayer.
Prayer of the Cat, The.
Prayer of the Donkey, The.
Prayer of the Goldfish, The.
Prayer of the Little Ducks, The.
Prayer of the Mouse, The.
Prayer of the Old Horse, The.
Swallow, The.

Gates, Beatrix (b. 1949)
Deadly Weapon.

Gates, Ellen M. Huntington (1835–1920)
Home of the Soul.
Sleep Sweet.
Your Mission.

Gatsos, Nikos (b. 1914)
Black Sun, The.
Evening at Colonos.
Four Songs, Sels.
Myrtle Tree, The.
We Who Are Left.

Gatty, Sir Alfred Scott (1847–1918)
Three Little Pigs, The.

Gault, A. J. (1818–1903) and Dill Armor Smith
Twenty Years Ago.

Gauradas
Dear Echo, do me a favour; it's somewhat . . . Some what?

Gautier, Théophile (1811–72)
Absence.
Art.
Clarimonde.
Infidelity.
Phantom of the Rose, The.
Posthumous Coquetry.
Taches Jaunes, Les, Sels.

Gaxe
I wonder what eagle did to him.

Gay, John (1685–1732)
About in London.
Achilles, Sels.
Acis and Galatea, Sels.
Air.
Air: "Fox may steal your hens, sir, A."
Air: "O ruddier than the cherry!"
Air: "Since laws were made for ev'ry degree."

Ballad: "Of all the girls that e'er were seen."
Beggar's Opera, The, Sels.
Birth of the Squire; an Eclogue, The.
Butterfly and the Snail, The.
Council of Horses, The.
Damon and Cupid.
Employments of Life, The.
Epistle to the Right Honourable William Pulteney, Esq.
Experienced men, inured to city ways.
Fable XXI: The Rat-catcher and Cats.
Fables, Sels.
Highwaymen, The.
Honour plays a bubble's part.
I rage, I melt, I burn.
If clothed in black you tread the busy town.
If the heart of a man is deprest [or depressed] with cares.
I'm like a skiff on the ocean tost.
Last May-day fair I search'd to find a snail.
Let due civilities be strictly paid.
Lion and the Cub, The.
London at Night.
Love in Her Eyes.
Mr. Pope's Welcome from Greece.
Molly Mog; or, The Fair Maid of the Inn.
Mother, the Nurse, and the Fairy, The.
My Own Epitaph.
New Song of New Similies, A.
Newgate's Garland.
O Polly, you might have toy'd and kist.
Ode for the New Year, An.
On a Miscellany of Poems, Sels.
Packington's Pound.
Painter Who Pleased Nobody and Everybody, The.
Poet and the Rose, The.
Polly; an Opera, Sels.
Receipt for Stewing Veal, A.
Rural Sports, Sels.
She who hath felt a real pain.
Shepherd's Week, The, Sels.
Soldier, think before you marry.
Song: "Before the barn-door crowing."
Song: "Can love be controlled by advice?"
Song: "If any wench Venus's girdle wear."
Song: "Thus when the swallow, seeking prey."
Song: "Were I laid on Greenland's coast."
Sweet William's Farewell to Black-eyed [or ey'd] Susan.
Think of dress in every light.
Thoughtless wits shall frequent forfeits pay, The.
Three children sliding on the ice.
Thursday; or, The Spell.
Thus I stand like the Turk, with his doxies around.
'Tis woman that seduces all mankind!
To a Lady.
To a Lady on Her Passion for Old China.
To a Young Lady, with Some Lampreys.
To My Ingenious and Worthy Friend William Lowndes, Esq.
Trivia; or, The Art of Walking the Streets of London, Sels.
Tuesday; or, the Ditty.
'Twas When the Seas Were Roaring.
Wednesday; or, The Dumps.
What D'Ye-Call-It, The, Sels.
What Shall I Do to Show How Much I Love Her?
When a brisk gale against the current blows.
When Pope's harmonious Muse with pleasure roves.
Where Lincoln's Inn, wide space, is railed around.
Where the mob gathers, swiftly shoot along.
Who can the various city frauds recite.
Wild Boar and the Ram, The.
Winter my theme confines; whose nitry wind.
Woman's like the flatt'ring ocean.
Youth's the Season.

Gay, John, and Alexander Pope
Epistle to the Right Honourable William Pulteney, Esq, Sels.
French Fops.

Mary Gulliver to Captain Lemuel Gulliver.
Toilette, The.

Gbadamosi, Gabriel (b. 1961)
Death of the Polar Explorers.
Flying Home.
No Blacks, No Irish, *Sels.*
Padraic's Point.
Reading, The.
Sango, *Sels.*
Sango's son came down to the river.
Scene 6 The Boat Passage.
Sewing-Box, The.

Gearold Iarla Mac Gearailt. *See* **Desmond, Gerald Fitzgerald, 4th Earl of.**

Gebirtig, Mordecai (1877–1942)
Waiting for Death.

Geddes, Alexander (1737–1802)
Epistle to the President of the Scottish Society of Antiquaries: On Being Chosen a Correspondent Member.

Geddes, Gary (b. 1940)
Inheritors, The.
Transubstantiation.

Geibel, Emanuel (1815–1884)
Ye Hovering Angels.

Geilt, Suibne (*fl.* 12th century)
Starry frost descends, The.

Geisel, Theodore Seuss. *See* "**Seuss, Dr.**"

Gellert, Christian Fürchtegott (1715–69)
Nature's Praise of God.

Gellert, Leon (b. 1892)
Before Action.
House-Mates.

Genet, Jean (1910–86)
Man Sentenced to Death, The, *Sels.*
Murderers of the wall wrap themselves in sunrise, The.

Gensei (1623–68)
Poem without a Category.

Gensler, Kinereth
For Nelly Sachs.

Gentry, Jane
Aunt Lucy.

Geoghegan, Arthur G. 1810–89
After Aughrim.

Geoghegan, J. B. (1815–89)
Down in a Coal Mine.

Georgakas, Dan (b. 1938)
Acrobat from Xanadu disdained all nets, The.

George, Chief Dan
Beauty of the trees, The.

George, Diana Hume (b. 1948)
Asenath.

George, Glenda (b. 1951)
Quasi Quasi . . . as If Repeated.

George, Marguerite (b. 1898)
Prisoner.

George, Phillip William (Phil George)
America's Wounded Knee.
Battle Won Is Lost.
Favorite Grandson Braid.
First Grade.
Moon of Huckleberries.
Morning Vigil.
Name Giveaway.
Old Man, the Sweat Lodge.
Prelude to Memorial Song: 100 Years Later.
Spokane Falls.
Spring Cleaning.
Spruce.
Sunflower Moccasins.
Visit, The.
Wardance.
Wardance Soup.

George, Stefan (1868–1933)
Invocation and Prelude.
Jahr der Seele, Das, *Sels.*
Lord of the Isle, The.
Lyre Player, The.
No way too long — no path too steep.
Rapture.
Stanzas Concerning Love.

Georges, Esther Valck
Alley Cat.

Gerard, Gertrude
In Arabia.

Geras, Adèle (b. 1944)
Needleworks.

Gergely, Agnes (b. 1933)
Crazed Man in Concentration Camp.

Gerhardt, Paul (1607–76)
Courage.
Evensong.
Go out in this dear summertide.
O sacred head, now wounded.

Gerondi, Abraham (*fl.* 13th century)
Hymn for the Eve of the New Year.

Gerrard, John (*fl.* c.1769)
Remonstrance, A.

Gershwin, Ira (1896–1983)
Blah, Blah, Blah.
Embraceable You.
I Got Rhythm.
It Ain't Neccessarily So.
'S Wonderful.

Gerstler, Amy (b. 1956)
Direct Address.

Gethyn, Ieuan
Shilling in the Armpit, The.

Getsi, Lucia Cordell
Oradour-sur-Glane. Silence.

Gezelle, Guido (1830–99)
To the Sun from a Flower.

Ghalib, Asadullah Khan (1797–1869)
Colors of tulips and roses are not the same, The.
Even at prayer, our eyes look inward.
For the raindrop, joy is in entering the river.
Let the ascetics sing of the garden of Paradise.
World is no more than the Beloved's single face, The.

Ghigna, Charles (b. 1946)
Untold Truth about Hank, The.

Ghiselin, Brewster (b. 1903)
Catch, The.
Credo.
Headland.
Rattler, Alert.
Rattlesnake.
Song at San Carlos Bay.
To the South.

Ghose, Manmohan (1869–1924)
Who Is It Talks of Ebony?

Ghose, Zulfikar (b. 1935)
Rise of Shivaji, The.

Gibbon, Monk (b. 1896)
French Peasants.
Poetry of Gerard Manley Hopkins, The.
Prayer of the Arab Physician, The.
Salt.

Gibbon, Perceval (1878–1926)
Answer, An.
Mooimeisjes.

Gibbons, James Sloan (1810–92)
Three Hundred Thousand More.

Gibbons, Orlando (1583–1625)
Silver Swan, The.

Gibbons, Reginald (b. 1947)
Hoppy.

Gibbs, Barbara
What You See Is Me.

Gibbs, C. Armstrong
Limerick: "Serious young lady from Welwyn, A."

Gibbs, Jessie Wiseman
If We Believed in God.

Gibbs, Margaret E.
On the Banisters.
Song of the Bath, The.

Gibran, Kahlil (1883–1931)
Crime and Punishment.
Love One Another.
Of Love.
On Children.

On Work.
Prophet, The, *Sels.*
Then Almitra spoke, saying, We would ask now of Death.

Gibson, Alan (1856–1922)
When stags do rut in the Plym.

Gibson, Barbara (b. 1930)
After the Quarrel.

Gibson, Douglas
January.
White Cat in Moonlight.

Gibson, Margaret (b. 1944)
Country Woman Elegy.
Doing Nothing.
Invisible Work.
October Elegy.
Onion, The.
Today snow sparks the air like mica — the sun's.
Unborn Child Elegy, *Sels.*

Gibson, Morgan (b. 1929)
Beyond the Presidency.

Gibson, Walker (b. 1919)
Advice to Travelers.
Blues for an Old Blue.
Essay on Lunch.
In Memory of the Circus Ship *Euzkera.*
Killer Too, The.
Soliloquy in a Motel.

Gibson, Wilfrid Wilson (1878–1962)
All Being Well.
Ambulance Train.
Breakfast.
Drove-Road, The.
Flannan Isle.
Fowler, The.
Geraniums.
Henry Turnbull.
Ice, The.
Inspiration.
Lament: "We who are left, how shall we look again."
Long Tom.
Luck.
Messages, The.
Michael's Song.
Old Skinflint.
Parrot, The.
Parrots, The.
Prelude: "As one, at midnight, wakened by the call."
Question, The.
Retreat.
Ridge, The: 1919.
Sight.
Skye, *Sels.*
Stone, The.
Trooposhp: Mid-Atlantic.
White Dust, The.
Wishing-Well, The.

Gibson, William (1826–87)
Circe.

Gidlow, Elsa (b. 1898)
Chains of Fire, *Sels.*
Creed for Free Women, A.
For the Goddess Too Well Known.
I know myself linked by chains of fire.
Invocation to Sappho.
Let Wisdom Wear the Crown: Hymn for Gaia.

Gifford, Humphrey [or Humfrey] (*fl.* c.1580)
For Soldiers.
In the Praise of Music.
Song: "Woman's face is full of wiles, A."

Gilbart, Thomas (*fl.* c. 1583)
Delcaration of the Death of John Lewes, A.

Gilbert, Bernard (b. 1882)
If The War Keeps On.

Gilbert, Celia (b. 1932)
Circles.
Midwives, The.

Gilbert, Christopher (b. 1950)
Backyard, The.
Beginning by Example, *Sels.*
Blue.

Ye Wearie Wayfarer, *Sels*.

Gordon, Don (b. 1902)
Kimono, The.

Gordon, J. (1865–1901)
To Amy.

Gordon, James Lindsay (1860?–1904)
Wheeler at Santiago.

Gordon, Judah Leib (1830–92)
Simhat Torah.

Gordon, Mary (d. 1942?)
Unwanted, The.

Gore-Booth, Eva (1870–1926)
Crucifixion.
Heretic's Pilgrimage, A.

Gorey, Edward (b. 1925)
Gift was delivered to Laura, A.
Limerick: "As tourists inspected the apse."
Limerick: "Babe, with a cry brief and dismal, The."
Limerick: "Dowager Duchess of Spout, The."
Limerick: "Each night father fills me with dread."
Limerick: "From Number Nine, Penwiper Mews."
Limerick: "From the bathing machine came a din."
Limerick: "Headstrong young lady of Ealing, A."
Limerick: "Incautious young woman named Venn, An."
Limerick: "Lady, who signs herself "Vexed," A."
Limerick: "There was a young woman named Plunnery."
Limerick: "To his club-footed child said Lord Stipple."
Listing Attic, The, *Sels*.
Some Harvard men, stalwart and hairy.
Utter Zoo Alphabet, The.

Gorges, Sir Arthur (1577–1625)
Desportes, *Sels*.
Henceforth I will not set my love.
Her [or hir] face her [or hir] tongue [or tong] her [or hir] wit.
She that holds me under the laws of love.
Tell me, my heart, how wilt thou do.
Would I were chang'd into that golden shower.

Gorham, Sarah
My Car Slides Off the Road.

Goring, J. H.
Home.

Gormley, Queen of Ireland (*fl.* 13th century)
Gormley's Laments, *Sels*.
I have loved thirty by three.

Gorton, Samuel (c.1592–1677)
Serpent with a voyce, so slie and fine, The.

Go-Shirakawa, Emperor (1127–92)
Ryojin Hisho, *Sels*.

Gosse, Sir Edmund William (1849–1928)
Lying in the Grass.
On Yes Tor.
Revelation.
Wallpaper, The.

Gotera, Vince (b. 1952)
Dance of the Letters.
Gambling.
Hot Club de France Reprise on MTV.
Madarika.

Gotlieb, Phyllis (b. 1926)
Cocker of Snooks, A.
Death's Head.
Late Gothic.
This One's on Me.
Three-handed Fugue.

Goto Miyoko (b. 1898)
Gay colors flow.
I listen to the pulse of a life/ different from mine.

Gottfried von Strassburg (*fl.* 13th century)
Tristan und Isolt.

Gottheil, Gustav (1827–1903)
Come, O Sabbath Day.

Gottlieb, Ann (b. 1946)
Lady Luck.

Götz, Johann Nikolaus (1721–81)
First Rondeau: After a French Poet of the Fourteenth Century.
Second Rondeau.

Gough, Irene
Under the Range.

Gould, Alan (b. 1949)
Galaxies.
Ice.
Pearls.

Gould, E. E.
Tadpole, The.

Gould, Elizabeth (b. 1904)
Grace and Thanksgiving.
Midsummer Night.
Mincemeat.
Mistress Comfort.
My New Rabbit.
Red in Autumn.
Shining Things.
Slumber in Spring.
Such a Blustery Day!
Washing-Up Song, The.
Wish, A.

Gould, Gerald (1885–1936)
Child's Song.
Happy Tree, The.
Monogamy, *Sels*.
This is the horror that, night after night.
You were young — but that was scarcely to your credit.

Gould, Hannah Flagg (1789–1865)
Day of God! Thou Blessed Day.
Dying Child's Request, The.
Frost, The.
Spider, The.

Goulder, Dave
January Man.
Long and Lonely Winter, The.

Gourghenian, Shushanig (1876–1927)
Desire.

Gouri, Chaim. *See* Guri [*or* Gouri], Haim [*or* Chaim *or* Khayim].

Gourmont, Remy de (1858–1915)
Hair.

Gove, Jim
Meditating at Olema.

Govinda, Lama
To see the greatness of a mountain, one must keep one's distance.

Gowar, Mick (b. 1951)
Annabell and the Witches.
Christmas Thank You's.

Gower, John (1325–1408)
Address to the King, An, *Sels*.
Among these othre of Slouthes kinde.
Confessio Amantis, *Sels*.
O worthi noble kyng, Henry the ferthe.
Parting of Venus and Old Age, The.

Gozzano, Guido (1883–1916)
Most Beautiful, The.

Graddon, Dorothy
Fairy Dream, A.
North Wind, The.
Travelling.
Wind, The.
Winter Joys.

Grade, Chaim (b. 1910)
Sodom.
To Life I Said Yes.

Graeme, James (1721–66)
Mortified Genius, The.

Grafflin, Margaret Johnston
To My Son.

Grafton, Richard (d. 1527)
Thirty days hath November.

Graham, A. M.
Aconite, The.

Graham, D. L. (1944–70)
Soul.
Tony Get the Boys.
West Ridge Is Menthol-Cool, The.

Graham, Harry ("Col. D. Streamer") (1874–1936)
Aunt Eliza.
Auntie, did you feel no pain.
Battue of Berlin, The, *Sels*.
Bob was bathing in the Bay.
Breakfast.
Cockney of the North, The.
Compensation.
Englishman's Home, The.
Father, chancing to chastise.
Gourmand, The.
I had written to Aunt Maud.
Indifference.
It was a winter's morning.
L'Enfant Glacé.
Lord Gorbals.
My First Love.
Necessity.
O'er the rugged mountain's brow.
Opportunity.
Patience.
Perils of Obesity, The.
Philip, foozling with his cheek.
Poetical Economy.
Some Ruthless Rhymes, *Sels*.
Stern parent, The.
Tender-Heartedness.
"There's been an accident!" they said.

Graham, James, Marquess of Montrose. *See* Montrose, James Graham, Marquess of.

Graham, Jorie (b. 1951)
At Luca Signorelli's Resurrection of the Body.
Geese, The.
History.
Masaccio's Expulsion.
Mind.
My Garden, My Daylight.
Orpheus and Eurydice.
Over and Over Stitch.
Phase after History, The.
Salmon.
San Sepolcro.
Two Paintings by Gustav Klimt.
Wanting a Child.
What the End Is For.

Graham, Rachel (b. 1895)
New Hampshire Farm Woman.

Graham, Robert (Robert Cunninghame-Graham) (1735–99)
If Doughty Deeds ("If daughty deeds my lady pleases.")

Graham, Rudy Bee (b. 1947)
Memorandum.

Graham, Virginia (b. 1912)
Disillusionment.

Graham, William Sydney (1918–86)
Almost I, yes, I hear.
Beast in the Space, The.
Children of Greenock, The.
Constructed Space, The.
Dark Dialogues, The, *Sels*.
I Leave This at Your Ear.
Johann Joachim Quantz's Five Lessons.
Language Ah Now You Have Me.
Letter V.
Letter VI.
Listen. Put on Morning.
Many without Elegy.
Note to the Difficult One, A.
Now in the third voice.
Thermal Stair, The.
To My Father.

Grahame, James (1859–1932)
Birds of Scotland, The, *Sels*.

Grahame, Kenneth (1859–1932)
Ducks' Ditty.
Song of Mr. Toad, The.
Villagers all, this frosty tide.
Wind in the Willows, The, *Sels*.

Grahn, Judy (b. 1940)
Asking for Ruthie.
But I Mean Any Kind of Thief.
Carol, in the Park, Chewing on Straws.
Common Woman, The, *Sels*.

White Goddess, The.
Wigs and Beards.
Wild Strawberries.
Window Sill, The.
With a Gift of Rings.
With Her Lips Only.
Wm. Brazier.
Woman and Tree.
Wreath, The.
Young Cordwainer, The.

Gray, Sir Alexander (1882–1968)
Sir Halewyn.
On a Cat Aging.
Scotland.

Gray, Darrell (1945–86)
Foreplay of the Alphabet.
Moving.
Ode to Food.
20th Century, The.

Gray, David (1838–61)
Golden Wedding, The.
In the Shadows, *Sels.*
My Epitaph.
Sonnet I: "If it must be; if it must be, O God!"
Sonnet: "October's gold is dim — the forests rot."
Where the Lilies Used to Spring.

Gray, Frances
With cheerful mind we yield to men.

Gray, Janet (b. 1948)
However heavy the walls of love, or well shored, they.
Not that miracles are.

Gray, John (1866–1934)
Barber, The.
Battledore.
Flying Fish, The.
Flying Fish, The, *Sels.*
Gazelles and Unicorn.
Les Demoiselles de Sauve.
Long Road, The, *Sels.*
Lord, If Thou Art Not Present.
Mishka.
Night Nurse Goes Her Round, The.
Odiham.
Of the birds that fly in the farthest sea.
On the South Coast of Cornwall.
Poem: "Geranium, houseleek, laid in oblong beds."
Spleen.
They say, in other days.
Tobias and the Angel.
Vines, The.
Wings in the Dark.

Gray, Robert (b. 1945)
Curriculum Vitae.
5 Poems.
Flames and Dangling Wire.
Journey: the North Coast.
Kangaroo, A.
Landscape.
North Coast Town.
Sea-Shell, The.
Single Principle of Forms, The.
Sketch of the Harbour.

Gray, Stephen (b. 1941)
Apollo Café.
Girl with Doves.
Girl with Long Dark Hair.
Hottentot Venus.

Gray, Thomas (1716–71)
Bard, The, *Sels.*
Behold, where Dryden's less presumptuous car.
Boast of heraldry, the pomp of pow'r, The.
Candidate, The.
Curfew tolls the knell of parting day, The.
Curse upon Edward, The.
Death of Hoel, The.
Descent of Odin, The.
Elegy Written in a Country Churchyard, *Sels.*
Epitaph: "Here rests his head upon the lap of earth."
Epitaph on Dr. Keene.
Epitaph on Dr. Keene's Wife.
Far from the sun and summer gale.

Fatal Sisters, The.
Fragment: "There pipes the wood-lark, and the song thrush there."
Hymn to Adversity.
In climes beyond the solar road.
Nor second he, that rode sublime.
Now the golden morn aloft.
Ode on a Distant Prospect of Eton College.
Ode on [*or* On] the Death of a Favourite [*or* Favorite] Cat, Drowned in a Tub [*or* Bowl] of Gold Fishes.
Ode on the Pleasure Arising from Vicissitude, *Sels.*
Ode on the Spring, An.
Oh lyre divine, what daring spirit.
On Dr. Keene, Bishop of Chester.
On Lord Holland's Seat near Margate, Kent.
Progress of Poesy, The, *Sels.*
Ruin seize thee, ruthless King!.
Satire upon the Heads.
Sonnet on the Death of Mr. Richard West.
Stanzas to Mr. Bentley.
Tophet.
Triumphs of Owen, The.

Gray, Victor (b. 1926)
All the World's a Stage.
Limerick: "Charlotte Brontë said, 'Wow, sister! What a man!' "
Limerick: "Example of Kant's sterling wit, An."
Limerick: "First chap to fuck little Sophie, The."
Limerick: "I was thrilled when I went to the Zoo."
Limerick: "It's a pity that Casabianca."
Limerick: "Sir John Shagbag (Conservative, Nore)."
Limerick: "Meanwhile, back home at the ranch."
Limerick: "Oedipus said to the Sphinx."
Limerick: "Old East End worker called Jock, An."
Limerick: "One midnight, old D. G. Rossetti."
Limerick: "One morning old Wilfrid Scawen Blunt."
Limerick: "Postmaster-General cried: 'Arsehole!', The."
Limerick: "Rebuke by the Bishop of London, A."
Limerick: "Said a famous old writer called Fender."
Limerick: "Said a gloomy young fellow called Fart."
Limerick: "Said Arnold to Arthur Hugh Clough."
Limerick: "Said Tennyson: 'Yes, *Locksley Hall*'s."
Limerick: "Said the famous philosopher, Russell."
Limerick: "Taxi-cab whore out at Iver, A."
Limerick: "There was a young fellow called Crouch."
Limerick: "There was a young fellow called Shit."
Limerick: "There was a young girl of Mauritius."
Limerick: "There was an old man of Lugano."
Limerick: "When Gauguin was visiting Fiji."
Limerick: "When Keats was at work on *Endymion*."
Limerick: "When our dean took a pious young spinster."
Limerick: "While visiting Arundel Castle."
Limerick: "Young engine-driver called Hunt, A."

Gray, William B. (1891–1977)
She Is More to Be Pitied than Censured.

Grayson, Caroline
After.

Greacen, Robert (b. 1920)
Bird, The.
Captain Fox.
Carnival at the River.
Father and Son.
St. Andrew's Day.
Summer Day, A.

Ten New Commandments.

Greeff, Adele (b. 1911)
Sonnet XI: "Is God invisible? This very room."

Green, Ber (1901–1989)
Martyrs Are Calling, The.

Green, Brenda Heloise
New England Is New England Is New England.

"Green, Coroebus." *See* Cone, Helen Gray.

Green, F. Pratt (b. 1903)
Old Couple, The.

Green, Jane
Songs of Divorce.

Green, Joseph (1706–80)
Permit Us, Lord, to Consecrate.

Green, Kensall
His fame endures; we shall not quite forget.
Sad day this for Alexander, A.

Green, Matthew (1696–1737)
But now more serious let me grow.
First know, my friend, I do not mean.
Forced by soft violence of prayer.
In Praise of Water-Gruel.
On Barclay's Apology for the Quakers.
Seeker, The.
Sometimes I dress, with women sit.
Sparrow and Diamond, The.
Spleen, The, *Sels.*
To cure the mind's wrong bias, Spleen.
When by its magic lantern Spleen.

Green, Melissa (b. 1954)
Consolation of Boethius, The.
More than novelty crooked its finger — silent, austere.

Greenaway, Kate (1846–1901)
Boat Sails Away, The.
Five Little Sisters Walking in a Row.
Happy Child, A.
In go-cart so tiny.
Little Jumping Girls, The.
Little Wind.
Ring-a-Ring.
Will You Be My Little Wife?

Greenberg, Barbara L. (b. 1932)
Faithful Wife, The.

Greenberg, Samuel (1893–1917)
Blank Book Letter, The.
Conduct.
Essentials.
Glass Bubbles, The.
I Cannot Believe That I Am of Wind.
Immortality.
Killing.
Soul's Kiss.
Spirituality.
To Dear Daniel.

Greenberg, Uri Zvi (1896–81)
At Your Feet, Jerusalem.
By the Waters of the Sava.
In the Covenant's Radiance.
In the Kingdom of the Cross, *Sels.*
Jerusalem, *Sels.*
Jerusalem the Dismembered.
Lord! You Saved Me from Ur-Germany as I Fled.
Mephisto, *Sels.*
Naming Souls.
Penny for You, A.
We Were Not Likened to Dogs among the Gentiles.

Greene, Albert Gorton (1802–68)
Baron's Last Banquet, The.
Old Grimes.

Greene, Alice (1858–1920)
Four Roads, The.

Greene, Angela
Cézanne.
Encounter.
Recipe.
Sand.
Seal Off Clogherhead, The.
Terrorist's Wife.

Greene, Carl H. (b. 1945)
Excuse, The.
Realist, The.

Something Old, Something New.
Greene, Richard Leighton (1904–83)
Limerick: "When approached by a person from Porlock."
Song to Imogen [in Basic English].
Greene, Robert (1558?–1592)
Ah Were She Pitiful.
Arbasto, *Sels.*
Barmenissa's Song.
Coridon and Phillis.
Description of Sir Geoffrey Chaucer, The.
Description of the Shepherd and His Wife, The.
Doron's Description of Samela.
Doron's Jigge.
Eurymachus's Fancy.
Fair Is My Love.
Farewell to Folly, *Sels.*
Fie, Fie on Blind Fancy!
Francesco's Fortunes, *Sels.*
Greene's Farewell to Folly, *Sels.*
Greene's Groatsworth of Wit, *Sels.*
Greene's Mourning Garment, *Sels.*
Greene's Vision, *Sels.*
Hexametra Alexis in Laudem Rosamundi.
Ideals.
Love and Jealousy.
Maesia's Song.
Menaphon, *Sels.*
Never Too Late, *Sels.*
Night Visitor, A.
Of His Mistress.
Palinode, A.
Palmer, The.
Palmer's Ode, The.
Pandosto, *Sels.*
Penitent Palmer's Ode, The.
Perimedes [*or* Perimedes, the Blacksmith], *Sels.*
Philomela, the Lady Fitzwater's Nightingale, *Sels.*
Sephestia's Song to Her Child[e].
Shepherd's Wife's Song, The.
Sitting by a river['s] side.
Song: "Sweet are the thoughts that savour of content."
Tullie's Love, *Sels.*
Whereat Erewhile I Wept, I Laugh.
Greenfield, Eloise (b. 1929)
Moochie ("Moochie likes to keep on playing").
Greenfield, Freddie (b. 1929)
Oh God Forbid.
Greenfield, Marjorie H.
Things I Like.
Greening, John (b. 1954)
I Still Would Plant My Apple Tree.
Lists of Coventry, The.
London Plane, The.
Sweet Chestnut.
Greenlaw, Lavinia (b. 1962)
Anchorage.
Chapel Snake, The.
Death of a Butcher, The.
Gift of Life, The.
He Wanted Someone to Cook Chicken.
Hurting Small Animals.
Innocence of Radium, The.
North.
Off the Map.
Sex, Politics, and Religion.
Greenwell, Bill
Christopher Robin Changes Guard with Dylan Thomas.
King Ethelred the Unready.
Limerick: "By Loch Ness they can toss, like confetti."
Limerick: "Filthy young fellow called Lawrence, A."
Limerick: "For his Campbell's Soup screen-prints, society's."
Limerick: "Glib little beer-buff from Troon, A."
Limerick: "In Genesis, Adam's the winner."
Limerick: "No, listen, there's this albatross."
Limerick: "Pop's tops!"
Limerick: "Reason we're asked to endure, The."
Limerick: "Shelley's death — was it really his wish."

Limerick: "There was a young lady of Ulva/ Who drunkenly said: 'What a hulva'."
Limerick: "Watt's dream was the cream of steam engines."
Limerick: "What led to the crassness of Custer."
Limerick: "When Jael crept in to see Sisera."
That rebellious rodent called Jerry.
Greenwell, Dora (1812–82)
Content.
Picture, A.
Saturday Review, The.
Scherzo, A.
Sun-Flower, The.
When the Night and Morning Meet.
Greenwood, Dr. ——
Epitaph — on the Wife of Dr. Greenwood.
"Greenwood, Grace" (Sarah Jane Clarke Lippincott) (1823–1904)
Illumination for Victories in Mexico.
Greer, Adrienne (b. 1965)
Constantly.
Greger, Debora (b. 1949)
Afterlife of Things, The.
Afterlife, The, *Sels.*
In Violet.
Light Dress, The.
Next Act, The.
Of.
Patches of Sky.
Snapshot, A.
Wings, The.
Gregerson, Linda (b. 1950)
Safe.
Gregg, Linda (b. 1942)
Beckett Kit, The.
Chorus Speaks Her Words as She Dances, The.
Dark Thing Inside the Day, A.
Girl I Call Alma, The.
Lilith.
Not Saying Much.
Sigismundo.
Taken By Each Thing.
War, The.
We Manage Most When We Manage Small.
Gregh, Fernand (1873–1960)
Doubt.
Gregor, Arthur (b. 1923)
Enough.
Gentle Lamb.
History.
Irreconcilables.
Late Last Night.
Likeness, The.
Lyric: "Embodiment of what, The."
Poem: "So many pigeons at Columbus."
Spirits, Dancing.
Two Shapes.
Unalterables.
Gregor, Christian (1723–89)
What Splendid Rays.
Gregory, Carole C. (b. 1945)
Freedom Song for the Black Woman, A.
Greater Friendship Baptist Church, The.
Love Letter.
Revelation.
Gregory, Horace (1898–1982)
And of Columbus.
Ask no return for love that's given.
Chorus for Survival, *Sels.*
Death and Empedocles 444 B.C.
Elegy and Flame.
For You, My Son.
Longface Mahoney Discusses Heaven.
On a Celtic Mask by Henry Moore.
Passion of M'Phail, The, *Sels.*
Poems for My Daughter.
Postman's Bell Is Answered Everywhere, The.
Rehearsal, The.
They Found Him Sitting in a Chair.
They Were All like Geniuses.
This Is the Place to Wait.
To the Last Wedding Guest.
Valediction to My Contemporaries.

Gregory, Leona
Silence, an Eloquent Applause.
Gregory, Mrs. Horace. *See* **Zaturenska, Marya Alexandrovna.**
Gregory of Nazianzus, Saint (c.330–90)
Leave my tomb. Employ your pick.
On Naucratius, Brother of St. Basil.
Why do you heave apart my stone?
Gregory the Great, Saint (540–604)
Behold, the Shade of Night Is Now Receding.
Morning Hymn.
Greiffenberg, Catharina Regina von (1633–94)
Concerning the Fruit-bringing Autumn Season.
On the Ineffable Inspiration of the Holy Spirit.
Spring Joy Praising God.
Why the Resurrection Was Revealed to Women.
Zealous Admonition to Praise.
Greig, Andrew
"Finest summer I remember" Old George says.
I watch my tracers arc and seed.
I went to visit Tim last night. He's a.
Interlude on Mustagh Tower.
Len's Poems, *Sels.*
Men on Ice, *Sels.*
Still.
You know the stick patches.
Young Americans.
Greig, Desmond A. (b. 1926)
On a Scooter.
To a Flea in a Glass of Water.
Gréki, Anna (1931–67)
Before Your Waking.
Future is for tomorrow, The.
Grenelle, Lisa (b. 1900)
Duel in the Park.
Grenfell, Joyce (1910–79)
Joyce: By Herself and Her Friends.
Grenfell, Julian (1888–1915)
Into Battle.
To a Black Greyhound.
Grenier, Robert (b. 1941)
For Windows.
Of life days like.
Prewar Late October Sea Breeze.
Sequence/ 28 Separate Poems, A, *Sels.*
Snow covers the slopes, covers the slopes.
Spring.
Wrath to Sadness.
Yah gee.
Grennan, Eamon (b. 1941)
Conjunctions.
Facts of Life, Ballymoney.
Incident.
Lizards in Sardinia.
Men Roofing.
Soul Music: The Derry Air.
Sunday Morning Through Binoculars.
Wing Road.
Grenville, George, Baron Lansdowne. *See* **Granville [or Grenville], George, Baron Lansdowne.**
Grenville, R. H.
Pawnshop Window.
Praise.
Grenville, Sir Richard (1542–91)
In Praise of Seafaring Men, in Hopes [*or* hope] of Good Fortune.
Gresham, Walter S.
Crowded Ways of Life.
Greville, Fanny (Frances) Macartney (c. 1727–1789)
I ask no kind return of love.
Miss F[— —]ny M[— —]t[— —]y to Miss P[— —]y B[— —]s.
Prayer for Indifference, A, *Sels.*
Greville, Fulke, 1st Baron Brooke (1554–1628)
Absence, the noble truce.
All my senses, like beacon's flame.
Away with these self-loving lads.
Caelica, *Sels.*
Caelica, I overnight was finely used.
Caelica, when I did see you every day.

Grossman
Holy Ghost Hospital.
I Fell in Love.
O Wonderous Universe!
Someone Lies On A Path.
What Do I Love?
Where Is The Sun Today?
Woman on the Bridge over the Chicago River, The.
You Must Know Everything.

Grossman, Reuben (1905–74)
Therefore, We Thank Thee, God.

Groth, Klaus (1819–99)
Like Melodies.
O That I Knew the Way Back.

Grove, Matthew (fl. c.1587)
In Praise of His Lady.
Pelops and Hippodamia, Sels.

Groves, Paul
Housewife Hooker.
Humming Bird.
Making Love to Marilyn Monroe.

Gruber, Abraham L.
My Neighbor's Roses.

Gruber, Johann A. (1694–1763)
Love That's Pure, Itself Disdaining.

Grudin, Louis (b. 1899)
Dust on Spring Street.

Grue, Lee Meitzen
Billie Pierce's Jazz Funeral.
Jazzmen.

Gruffudd ab yr Ynad Coch (fl. c.1280)
Lament for Llywelyn ap Gruffudd.

Gruffydd, Owen (1643–1730)
Men That Once Were, The, Sels.
Old, old/ To live on, wretched to behold.

Gruffydd, Peter (b. 1935)
Digging Soil.
Slate Quay: Felinheli.

Gruffydd, W. J. (1881–1954)
Gwladys Rhys.
In Memoriam.
This Poor Man.

Grumbach, Argula von (1492–1554)
Answer in Verse for Someone Studying in Ingolst, An, Sels.
Argula's Answer.
Verses against Argula.

Grundtvig, Nicolai Frederik Severin (1783–1872)
I Know a Flower So Fair and Fine.

Gruppe, Otto Friedrich (1806–76)
Maiden Speaks, The.

Gryphius, Andreas (1616–64)
All Is Vanity.
Evening.
Human Misery.
Midnight.
On the Birth of Jesus.
Solitude.
Tears of the Fatherland, Anno Domini 1636.
To Himself.
To the Stars.

Gu Cheng (b. 1956)
Ark.
Autumn.
Black-and-White Sketches.
Capital "I."
Crack, A.
Dream Garden.
Far and Close.
Headstrong Boy, A.
Image.
Parting.
Rebel Camp in the Hindu Kush.
When Hope Comes Back.
When I Blink.
Winter Longing.
Yesterday.

Guarini, Giovanni Battista (1537–1612)
Claim to Love.
Faithful Shepherd, The, Sels.
Spring.
Thus saith my Chloris bright.

Guérin, Charles (1873–1904)
Partings.

Guernsey, Bruce (b. 1944)
Louis B. Russell.

Guest, Barbara (b. 1920)
Direction.
Green Revolutions.
Luminous, The.
Parachutes, My Love, Could Carry Us Higher.
Parade's End.
Piazzas.
Poem: "Disturbing to have a person."
Red Lilies.
River Road Studio.
Santa Fe Trail.
Sunday Evening.
20.

Guest, Edgar Albert (1881–1959)
Becoming a Dad.
Equipment.
Friend's Greeting, A.
Grace at Evening.
Home.
It Couldn't Be Done.
Kindly Neighbor, The.
Lemon Pie.
Lord, Make a Regular Man out of Me.
Myself.
Out Fishin'.
Sausage.
What's In It for Me?

Guevara, Pablo (b. 1930)
Civil Marriage, Sels.

Guggenberger, Louisa S. (b. 1945)
Afternoon.
Am I to Lose You?
Egoisme à Deux.
Love and Language.
Twilight.

Guidacci, Margherita (b. 1921)
All Saints' Day, Sels.
At Night.
Cain and Abel.

Guido delle Colonne. See **Delle Colonne, Guido.**

Guillaume de Lorris (d. c.1240) and Jean de Meun
Garden of Amour, The.
Romance [or Romaunt] of the Rose, The, Sels.
Short space my feet had traversed ere.

Guillaume de Poitiers (fl. 11th century)
Behold, the Meads.
Count William's Escapade.

Guillén, Nicolás (b. 1904)
Bars.
Dead Soldier.
Guadalupe, W.I.
Proposition.
Sightseers in a Courtyard.

Guillet, Pernette de. See **De [or Du] Guillet, Pernette.**

Guiney, Louise Imogen (1861–1920)
Astræa.
Borderlands.
Deo Optimo Maximo.
Emily Brontë.
John Brown; a Paradox.
Kings, The.
Knight Errant, The.
Monochrome.
Open, Time.
Outdoor Litany, An.
Pascal.
Planting the Poplar.
Romans in Dorset.
Sanctuary.
Talisman, A.
Tarpeia.
W. H.
When on the Marge of Evening.
Wild Ride, The.

Guinicelli, Guido (fl. 13th century)
He Perceives His Rashness in Love, but Has No Choice.

He Will Praise His Lady.
Of Moderation and Tolerance.
Of the Gentle Heart.

Guinness, Bryan
By Loch Etive.

Guiterman, Arthur (1871–1943)
Ain't Nature Commonplace!
Alibi.
Ancient History.
Anthologistics.
Bears.
Blessing on Little Boys.
Brief Essay on Man.
Call to the Colors, The.
Consolation.
Daniel Boone.
Everything in Its Place.
Haarlem Heights.
Habits of the Hippopotamus.
He Leads Us Still.
Heredity.
House Blessing.
Husband and Wife.
In Praise of Llamas.
In the Hospital.
Local Note.
Mavrone.
Mexican Serenade.
Of Certain Irish Fairies.
Of Courtesy.
Of Tact.
Offer, An.
On the Vanity of Earthly Greatness.
Oregon Trail, The.
Quivíra.
Rush of the Oregon, The.
School Days in New Amsterdam.
Scribe's Prayer, The.
Sea-Chill.
Song of Hate for Eels.
Storming of Stony Point, The.
Strictly Germ-proof.
What the Gray Cat Sings.
Whole Duty of a Poem, The.
Young Washington.

Gulick, Alida Carey
On Waking.

Gullans, Charles (b. 1929)
Satyr.

Gumilev, Nikolai Stepanovich (1886–1921)
Giraffe, The, Sels.
Listen:/ There roams, far away, by the waters of Clead.

Gunn, Louise D. (b. 1906)
Conversation with Rain.

Gunn, Thom (b. 1919)
Allegory of the Wolf Boy, The.
Apartment Cats.
As Expected.
Autobiography.
Autumn Chapter in a Novel.
Baby Song.
Back to Life.
Beautician, The.
Black Jackets.
Breakfast.
Byrnies, The.
Cafeteria in Boston.
Carnal Knowledge.
Cat and the Wind, The.
Cherry Tree, The.
Claus von Stauffenberg.
Confessions of the Life Artist.
Considering the Snail.
Courage, a Tale.
Das Liebesleben.
Discovery of the Pacific, The.
Donahue's Sister.
Duncan.
Elegy on the Dust.
Encolpius.
Expression.
Fair in the Woods, The.
Faustus Triumphant.
Fever.

H

Hamilton, Bobb (b. 1928)
Poem to a Nigger Cop.
Hamilton, Cicely (1872–1952)
March of the Women, The.
Hamilton, Elizabeth (1758–1816)
My Ain Fireside.
Hamilton, George Rostrevor ("George Rostrevor") (1888–1967)
Cell, The.
Don's Holiday.
Exchange.
Exile.
No Occupation.
Old Ox, The.
On a Distant Prospect of an Absconding Bookmaker.
On a Statue of Sir Arthur Sullivan.
Schoolmaster.
To the Greek Anthologists.
Hamilton, Harold
School of Sorrow, The.
Hamilton, Horace (b. 1911)
Before Dawn.
Hamilton, John (b. 1947)
Cold Blows the Wind.
Hamilton, Marion Ethel (b. 1881)
Bird at Night.
Hamilton, Robert Browning (b. 1938)
Along the Road.
Hammerstein, Oscar II (1895–1960)
Kansas City.
Money Isn't Everything!
There Is Nothin' like a Dame.
Hammial, Philip (b. 1937)
Russians Breathing.
Hammon, Jupiter (1720?–1806?)
Address to Miss Phillis Wheatley, An, *Sels.*
Evening Thought, An.
O come you pious youth! adore.
Hammond, Geraldine (b. 1909)
Encounter.
Hammond, Mac (b. 1926)
Golden Age.
In Memory of V. R. Lang.
Hammond, William (b. 1614?)
Delay.
Husbandry.
Mutual Love.
On the Infrequency of Celia's Letters.
On the Same [Death of My Dear Brother, Mr. H.S., Drowned]: The Boat.
To Her Questioning His Estate.
To His Scornful Mistress.
To the Same [My Dear Sister, Mrs S.]: The Tears.
Hamod, Kay Keeshan
Transitions, *Sels.*
Your mother's often gone.
Hampl, Patricia (b. 1946)
Resort, *Sels.*
Hampson, Norman
Assault Convoy.
Hampton, Susan (b. 1949)
Crafty Butcher, The.
Fire Station's Delight, The.
Han Ts'ui-p'in (fl. 9th cent.)
Poem Written on a Floating Red Leaf, A.
Han Wo (fl. 902)
Sent to a Ch'an Master.
Han Yü (786–824)
Amongst the Cliffs.
Autumn Thoughts, *Sels.*
Demoted I Arrive at Lan-t'ien Pass and Show This Poem to My Brother's Grandson Han Hsiang.
Don't shoo the morning flies away.
Evening: for Chang Chi and Chou K'uang.
Fine weather since yesterday.
Frosty wind harries the *wu-t'ung*, A.
Gazing as I climbed a high peak.
Girl from Flower Mountain, The.
Leaves fall turning turning to the ground.
Mornings the sparrow twitters seeking food.

My ceramic lake in dawn, water settled clear.
North of the great lake of K'un-ming,
Occasional Poem ("Ancient annals strewn left and right").
Officer at the Rapids, The.
Old men are like little boys.
Poem on Losing One's Teeth.
Pond in a Bowl, The.
Pond in a Jardiniere, A, *Sels.*
Pond shine and sky glow, blue matching blue.
Sentiments at Autumn.
South Mountains, The, *Sels.*
This morning I can't seem to get out of bed.
To the Wooden Hermit.
When white dew descends on the hundred grasses.
Withered Tree, A.
Hanaford, Phoebe A. (1829–1921)
Cast Thy Bread upon the Waters.
Ha-Nagid, Samuel (993–1055)
I Look Up to the Sky.
Proverbs.
Hanan, Deborah
On Watching *Heritage: Civilization and the Jews.*
Handcox, John, and Lee Hays
Roll the Union on.
Handke, Peter (b. 1942)
Wrong Way Round, The.
Handley, Helen
Deer Hunt, Salt Lake Valley.
Hands, Elizabeth (fl. c. 1789)
Favourite Swain, The.
Lob's Courtship.
On an Unsociable Family.
Perplexity: A Poem.
Poem on the Supposition of an Advertisement, A; Appearing in a Morning Paper, of the Publication of a Volume of Poems, by a Servant-Maid.
Poem on the Supposition of the Book Having Been Published and Read, A.
Widower's Courtship, The.
Written, Originally Extempore, on Seeing a Mad Heifer Run through the Village.
Hands, Rina
Chatterton.
Handy, M. P.
Only a Little Thing.
Handy, William Christopher (1873–1958)
St. Louis Blues.
Hanes, Leigh (b. 1894)
Old Fence Post.
Hanh, Thich Nhat
As we are together, praying for peace, let us be truly with each other.
Do not say that I'll depart tomorrow.
Earth brings us into life.
I entrust myself to earth.
Looking at Your Empty Plate.
Waking up this morning, I see the blue sky.
Waking up this morning, I smile.
Water flows from high in the mountains.
Water flows over these hands.
Hanim, Leylâ (d. 1847)
Let's get going.
Hanim, Nigâr (1862–1918)
Tell Me Again.
Hankin, St. John Emile Clavering (1869–1909)
Soul-Severance.
Hanlon, Guy
They Told Me, Heraclitus.
Hann, Isaac (1690–1778)
After Reading the Life of Mrs. Catherine Stubbs in Isaac Ambrose's "War with the Devils."
Hannay, Patrick (d. 1629?)
Philomela, the Nightingale, *Sels.*
Hanney, G. W.
Limerick: "Wanting children a couple once sat."
Hanscombe, Gillian Eve
Five Lovesick Poems, *Sels.*
From her grave.

Jezebel: Her Progress, *Sels.*
Men made myths.
Hanscombe, Gillian Eve and Suniti Namjoshi
All the Words.
Christ How My Circumspect Heart.
I Moved in My House.
Measure.
Hansen, Chadwick (b. 1926)
Creator of Infinities.
Hansen, Joseph
Dakota: Five Times Six.
Loved One, The.
Red Suspenders, Boxes of Cigars.
Han-shan (c. 700–c. 780)
Clambering up the Cold Mountain path.
Clouds and mountains all tangled together up to the blue sky.
Man lives his life in a dust bowl.
My home was at Cold Mountain from the start.
Parrots dwell in the west country.
Swine gobble dead men's flesh.
There is a poetaster named Wang.
Hanson, Amos
Schooner *Fred Dunbar*, The.
Trip to the Grand Banks, A.
Hanson, Kenneth O. (b. 1922)
Before the Storm.
Lighting the Night Sky.
Take It from Me.
West Lake.
Hanson, Pauline (b. 1917)
And I Am Old to Know.
From Creature to Ghost.
So Beautiful Is the Tree of Night.
Hanson, Phyllis
Wisdom.
Hanzlik, Josef (b. 1938)
Clap Your Hands for Herod.
Harasymowicz, Jerzy (b. 1933)
Green Lowland of Pianos, A.
Harata Tangikuku (c.1860–1875)
Invalid's Song.
Harbaugh, Henry
Aloe Plant, The.
Jesus, I Live to Thee.
Harbaugh, Thomas Chalmers (1817–67)
Trouble in the "Amen Corner."
Harchik, Annette Bialik
Earrings.
Hard, Walter
Medical Aid.
Hardenberg, Friedrich von. *See* "**Novalis.**"
Harding, George (d. 1816)
Reply to a Creditor.
Harding, Mike
Christmas 1914.
Harding, Samuel (fl. 1640)
Noblest bodies are but gilded clay.
Hardison, O. B., Jr. (b. 1928)
Marina.
Small Talk in a Garden.
Stella Maris.
Hardt, Ernst (1876–47)
Specter, The.
Hardwick, Natalie (b. c. 1975)
Other Side, The.
Hardy, Elizabeth Clark (1794–1854)
Some Time at Eve.
Hardy, Elizabeth Stanton
Echo.
Hardy, Jane L. (1828–1915)
Lincoln.
Hardy, John Edward (b. 1922)
Voyeur.
Hardy, Thomas (1840–1928)
According to the Mighty Working.
After a Journey.
After the Fair.
After the Visit.
Afternoon Service at Mellstock.
Afterwards.
Agnosto Theo (To an Unknown God).

Harford, Lesbia (1891–1927)
Beauty and Terror.
Experience.
Poem: "I'm like all lovers, wanting love to be."
Poem: "Sometimes I wish that I were Helen-fair."
Poem: "When I was still a child."

Hargreaves, Kay (b. 1951)
Patent No. 1.

Haring, Phyllis (b. 1919)
Earth Asks and Receives Rain, The.
Foetus.
Forbidden, The.
Jungle.
Overture to Strangers.
Twin.

Harington, Henry (1727–1816)
Abbey Church at Bath, The.

Harington, John (fl. 1550)
Elegy Wrote in the Tower, 1554.
Groom of the Chamber's Religion in King Henry the Eighth's Time, A.
Husband to Wife.
I See My Plaint.
Sir John Raynsford's Confession.
Of the Wars in Ireland.
Sonnet Made on Isabella Markham, A.
Sonnet Written upon My Lord Admiral Seymour, A.
To His Mother.
Wife to Husband.

Harington [or Harrington], Sir John (1561–1612)
Against an Old Lecher.
Author, of His Own Fortune, The.
Author to His Wife, of a Woman's Eloquence, The.
Epigrams, Sels.
Fair, Rich, and Young.
Health Counsel.
Of a Faire Woman: Translated out of Casaneus His Catalogus Gloriae Mundi.
Of a Zealous Lady.
Of an Heroical Answer of a Great Roman Lady to Her Husband.
Of Treason.
Prophesie When Asses Shall Grow Elephants, A.
To His Wife, for Striking Her Dog.

Harington, Lucy, Countess of Bedford (d. 1627)
Elegy: "Death be not proud, thy hand gave not this blow."

Harjo, Joy (b. 1951)
Anchorage.
Blue Elliptic.
Book of Myths, The.
Eagle Poem.
Early Morning Woman.
For Alva Benson, and for Those Who Have Learned to Speak.
Grace.
Healing Animal.
I Give You Back.
New Orleans.
Nine Below.
Petroglyph.
Remember.
Resurrection.
Santa Fe.
She Had Some Horses.
Transformations.
White Bear.
Woman Hanging from the Thirteenth Floor Window, The.

Harjo, Patty L. ("Ya-Ka-Nes") (b. 1947)
Death.
Mask, The.
Taos Winter.
To an Indian Poet.
Where Have You Gone, Little Boy.
Wishes.

Harkness, Edward (b. 1947)
Man in the Recreation Room, The.

Harkness, John
AIDS and the Art of Living.
Domination of Black.
New Song on the Birth of the Prince of Wales, A.
Obsidian Mountain, The.
Retinitis.
Tomorrow Morning.
Umbrellas for the Wind.

Harlow, Michael (b. 1937)
Anima Has a Predilection, The.
Poem Then, for Love, Sels.
Vlaminck's Tie, the Persistent Imaginal.

Harmon, William (b. 1938)
Bureaucratic Limerick ("The Bureau of Labor Statistics").
Dawn Horse, A.

Harney, Ben (1872–1938)
Mister Johnson.
You've Been a Good Old Wagon, but You've Done Broke Down.

Harney, W. E. (1895–1903)
West of Alice.

Harper, Frances Ellen Watkins (1825–1911)
Appeal to My Countrywomen, An.
Artist, The.
Aunt Chloe's Politics.
Burdens of All, The.
Bury Me in a Free Land.
Crocuses, The.
Death of Moses, The.
Deliverance.
Double Standard, A.
Eliza Harris.
Flight into Midian.
Go Work in My Vineyard.
God Bless Our Native Land.
Grain of Sand, A.
He "Had Not Where to Lay His Head."
Learning to Read.
Let the Light Enter.
Mission of the Flowers, The.
Moses: A Story of the Nile, Sels.
Night of Death, The.
Nobly Born, The.
Nothing and Something.
Present Age, The.
President Lincoln's Proclamation of Freedom.
Pure in Heart Shall See God, The.
Ragged Stocking, The.
Refiner's Gold, The.
Renewal of Strength.
Revel, The.
Save the Boys.
She's Free!
Sir, We Would See Jesus.
Slave Auction, The.
Songs for the People.
Sparrow's Fall, The.
Thank God for Little Children.
Then and Now.
To the Union Savers of Cleveland.
Vashti.

Harper, Gordon
Limerick: "When a friend told a typist called Eve."

Harper, Michael S. (b. 1938)
American History.
Barricades.
"Bird Lives": Charles Parker [in St. Louis].
Black Study.
Blue Ruth: America.
Borning Room, The.
Buck.
Cannon Arrested.
Clan Meeting: Births and Nations: A Blood Song.
Come Back Blues.
Dance of the Elephants, The.
Dear John, Dear Coltrane.
Deathwatch.
Debridement.
Double Elegy.
Effendi.
Elvin's Blues.

For Bud.
Grandfather.
Guerrilla-Cong, The.
Healing Song.
Here Where Coltrane Is.
High Modes: Vision as Ritual: Confirmation.
Homage to the New World.
I Want a Witness.
Jazz Station.
John Gibson's Bat.
Kin.
Landfill.
Last Affair: Bessie's Blues Song.
Lecturing on the Theme of Motherhood.
Makin' Jump Shots.
Martin's Blues.
Militance of a Photograph in the Passbook of a Bantu under Detention, The.
Mother Speaks: The Algiers Motel Incident, Detroit, A.
My Students Who Stand in Snow.
New Season.
Newletter from My Mother.
Nightmare Begins Responsibility.
Photographs: A Vision of Massacre.
Poetry Concert.
Reuben, Reuben.
Sandra: At the Beaver Trap.
Tongue-tied in Black and White.
We Assume: On the Death of Our Son, Reuben Masai Harper.
Zocalo.

Harpur, Charles (1813–68)
Basket Of Summer Fruit, A.
Bush Justice.
Coast View, A, Sels.
Creek of the Four Graves, The, Sels.
Dead city walls may pen us in, but still.
Flight of Wild Ducks, A.
I verse a settler's tale of olden times.
Marvellous Martin.
Temple of Infamy, The, Sels.
Tower of the Dream, The, Sels.
Wellington.

Harr, Barbara (b. 1937)
Walking through a Cornfield in the Middle of Winter I Stumble over a Cow Pie and Think of the Sixties Press.

Harries, E. Howard (1876–1961)
Bone Prison, The.

"Harriet Annie"
Death of Gaudentis.

Harrigan, Edward (1845–1911)
My Dad's Dinner Pail.

Harriman, Dorothy
Cat on the Porch at Dusk.

Harrington, Sir John. *See* **Harington [or Harrington], Sir John.**

Harris, Benjamin (c.1640–1720)
Account of the Cruelty of the Papists, An.
God save the King, that King that sav'd the land.
Of the French Kings Nativity.

Harris, Claire (b. 1937)
Framed.
Policeman Cleared in Jaywalking Case.

Harris, Jana (b. 1947)
Beneath the Pole of Proud Raven.
Dream of the Hair Burning Smell.
Norma at the A&W Drive-In.
We Fish Our Lives Out.
When Mama Came Here as a Gold Panner, Sels.

Harris, Joel Chandler (1848–1908)
My Honey, My Love.
Uncle Remus and His Friends, Sels.

Harris, June Brown
Home.

Harris, Marguerite (1899–1978)
My Sun-killed Tree.

Harris, Max (b. 1921)
Martin Buber in the Pub.
Message from a Cross.
Tantanoola Tiger, The.

Harris, Milly
October 1936.

Harris, Norman (b. 1918)
Fable: "There is an inevitability."

Harris, Phyllis. *See* **Beauvais, Phyllis.**

Harris, Robert (b. 1951)
Isaiah by Kerosene Lantern Light.
Sydney.

Harris, Sydney Justin (1917–86)
I Come to Bury Caesar.

Harris, William J. (b. 1942)
Daddy Poem, A.
For Bill Hawkins, a Black Militant.
Grandfather Poem, A.
My baby/ loves flowers.
Practical Concerns.
We Live in a Cage.
Why Would I Want.

Harris, Wilson (b. 1921)
Charcoal.
Laocoön.

Harrison, De Leon (b. 1941)
Collage for Richard Davis — Two Short Forms, A.
Room, The.
Seed of Nimrod, The.
Some Days/ Out Walking Above.
Yellow.

Harrison, Florence (b. 1884)
Faerie Fair, The.
Summer Day, A.

Harrison, Gregory (b. 1928)
Distracted the Mother Said to Her Boy.

Harrison, James [*or* Jim] (b. 1937)
After the Anonymous Swedish.
Helen.
Leda's Version.
Locations.
Penelope.
Poem: "Form is the woods: the beast."
Returning at Night.
Returning to Earth, *Sels.*
Sketch for a Job Application Blank.
Sound.
Suite to Fathers.
Walking.

Harrison, Tony (b. 1937)
Africa — London — Africa.
Art & Extinction, *Sels.*
Birds of America, The: John James Audubon.
Birds of America, The; Weeki Wachee.
Book Ends.
Brazil.
Breaking the Chain.
Call of Nature, The.
Classics Society.
Confessional Poetry.
Continuous.
Dark Times.
Durham.
Five.
Hands, The.
Heredity.
History Classes.
"I've done my bits of mindless aggro too."
Killing Time.
Kumquat for John Keats, A.
Lines to My Grandfathers.
Long Distance.
Looking Up.
Loving Memory.
Marked with D.
Me Tarzan.
Morning After, The.
National Trust.
Nuptial Torches, The.
On Not Being Milton.
Prague Spring.
Queen's English, The.
Remains.
School of Eloquence, The, *Sels.*
Self Justification.
Sentences, *Sels.*
Songs of the PWD Man, The.

Standards in Hopeful Anticipation of the Bicentenery of the National Emblem of the United States of America.
Still.
T'ark.
Thomas Campey and the Copernican System.
Timer.
Turns.
Zeg-Zeg Postcards, The, *Sels.*

Harrison, William (1685–1713)
In Praise of Laudanum.

Harry, J. S. (b. 1939)
Honesty-Stones.

Harsen, Una W. (b. 1888)
Litany for Old Age, A.
Prayer before Meat.

Hart, Elizabeth Anna (1822–88)
Mother Tabbyskins.

Hart, Heinrich (1855–1906)
If You But Knew.

Hart, Howard (b. 1927)
Ben Webster and a Lady.
Sonny Greer.

Hart, Kevin (b. 1954)
Come Back.
Dream of France, A.
Flemington Racecourse.
Horizon, The.
Members of the Orchestra, The.
Midsummer.
Real World, The.
This Day.
Your Shadow.

Hart, Lorenz (1895–1943)
Blue Room, The.
Lady Is a Tramp, The.
Manhattan.
Most Beautiful Girl in the World, The.
Mountain Greenery.

Hart-Smith, William (b. 1911)
Altamira.
Ambrosia.
Bathymeter.
Birth.
Boomerang.
Christopher Columbus, *Sels.*
Cipangu.
Comes Fog and Mist.
Departure.
Fishing.
Galahs.
Golden Pheasant.
Inca Tupac Upanqui, The.
Observation.
Space.
Waterspout, The.

Harte, Bret (Francis Bret Harte) (1836–1902)
Aged Stranger, The.
Arctic Vision, An.
Ballad of Mr. Cooke, The.
Ballad of the Emeu, The.
Caldwell of Springfield.
Chicago.
Chiquita.
Colenso Rhymes for Orthodox Children.
Coyote.
Dickens in Camp.
Dow's Flat.
Further Language from Truthful James.
Greyport Legend, A.
Grizzly.
Guild's Signal.
Her Letter.
His Answer to "Her Letter."
How Are You, Sanitary?
Jessie.
Jim.
John Burns of Gettysburg.
Mrs. Judge Jenkins (Being the Only Genuine Sequel to "Maud Muller").
Plain Language from Truthful James.
Ramon.
Reveille, The.
Sanitary Message, A.
Schemmelfennig.

Second Review of the Grand Army, A.
Society upon the Stanislaus, The.
Stage-Driver's Story, The.
Tale of a Pony, The.
What the Bullet Sang.
What the Engines Said.
Willows, The.

Harte, Walter (1709–74)
Above all flattery, all thirst of gain.
Enchanted Region; or, Mistaken Pleasures, The.
Essay on Satire, Particularly on The Dunciad, An, *Sels.*
In Albion then, with equal lustre bright.
Mock-Epic Satire.
What burlesque could, was by that genius done.

Harteis, Richard (b. 1946)
Dolphins, The.
Grace of Animals, The.
Star Trek III.

Hartford, John (b. 1937)
Poor Old Prurient Interest Blues, The.

Hartigan, Anne (b. 1932)
Advent.
Brazen Image.
No Easy Harbour.
St. Bridget's Cross.
Salt.

Hartigan, Patrick Joseph ("John O'Brien") (1879–1952)
Field of the Cloth of Gold, The.

Hartman, Charles O. (b. 1949)
Double Mock Sonnet.
Inflation.
Little Song, A.

Hartman, Mary R.
Life's Made up of Little Things.

Hartmann von Aue (1170–1215)
I go, with your good grace, lords and kinsmen.
I said I would always live for her.
None Is Happy.
Often a friend will greet me thus.

Hartnett, Michael (b. 1911)
All That Is Left.
All the Death-Room Needs.
All the Same, It Would Make You Laugh.
Death of an Irishwoman.
Domestic Scene.
Enamoured of the Miniscule.
Farewell to English, A, *Sels.*
For My Grandmother, Bridget Halpin.
Gaelic is the conscience of our leaders.
Half afraid to break a promise.
Hartnett, the poet, might as well be dead.
I Have Heard Them Knock.
Lament for Tadhg Cronin's Children.
Last Vision of Eoghan Rua Ó Súilleabháin, The.
Mo Ghra Thu.
Person as Dreamer: We Talk about the Future, The.
Pity the Man Who English Lacks.
Possibility That Has Been Overlooked Is the Future, The.
Purge, The, *Sels.*
Retreat of Ita Cagney, The.
Small Farm, A.
Sonnet: "I saw magic on a green country road."
There will be a Talking.
Visit to Castletown House, A.
Wounded Otter, The.

Hartsough, Lewis (1828–1919)
Come, Friends and Neighbors, Come.
Let Me Go Where Saints Are Going.

Harvey, Anthony
Old Man at the Window, The.

Harvey, Christopher (1597–1663)
Church Festivals.
Synagogue, The, *Sels.*
What Church is this? Christ's Church. Who builds it?

Harvey, Frederick William (1888–1957)
Ducks, *Sels.*
November.
Yes, ducks are valiant things.

Miles Keogh's Horse.
Not in Dumb Resignation.
Pledge at Spunky Point, The.
Religion and Doctrine.
What is a first love worth except to prepare for
    a second?
White Flag, The.
Hay, Sara Henderson (1906–87)
Bottle Should Be Plainly Labeled "Poison."
Christmas, the Year One, A.D.
Daily Manna, The.
For a Dead Kitten.
Interview.
Prayer in April.
Hayakawa, Samuel Ichiye (b. 1906)
To One Elect.
Hayashi Fumiko (1904–1951)
Lord Buddha, The.
Hayati, Bibi (d. 1853)
Before there was a trace of this world of men.
Hayden, Robert Earl (1913–80)
Aunt Jemima of the Ocean Waves.
Bahá'u'lláh in the Garden of Ridwan.
Ballad of Nat Turner, The.
Ballad of Remembrance, A.
Ballad of Sue Ellen Westerfield, The.
Beginnings, *Sels.*
Belsen, Day of Liberation.
Bone-Flower Elegy.
Diver, The.
Double Feature.
Dream, The.
El-Hajj Malik El-Shabazz.
For a Young Artist.
Frederick Douglass.
From the Corpse Woodpiles, from the Ashes.
Full Moon.
Homage to the Empress of the Blues.
In the Mourning Time.
Incense of the Lucky Virgin.
Letter from Phillis Wheatley, A.
Locus.
Middle Passage.
Monet's "Waterlilies."
Mourning Poem for the Queen of Sunday.
"Mystery Boy Looks for Kin in Nashville."
Night, Death, Mississippi.
Night-blooming Cereus, The.
O Daedalus, Fly Away Home.
On Lookout Mountain.
Paul Laurence Dunbar.
Perseus.
Plague of Starlings, A.
Prisoners, The.
Runagate Runagate.
Soledad.
Sphinx.
Stars, *Sels.*
Sub Specie Aeternitatis.
Summertime and the Living.
Tattooed Man, The.
Those Winter Sundays.
Tour 5.
Wheel, The.
Whipping, The.
Witch Doctor.
Words in the Mourning Time, *Sels.*
Hayes, Alfred (1911–85)
Angel, The.
Death of the Craneman, The.
Epistle to the Gentiles.
Joe Hill.
Nice Part of Town, A.
Slaughter-House, The.
Hayes, Daniel (*fl.* 18th cent.)
Poem Dedicated to Mrs. Blennerhasset, the
    Only Female Member of the Limerick Hell
    Fire Club, A.
Hayes, Donald Jeffrey (b. 1904)
After All.
Alien.
Appoggiatura.
Auf Wiedersehen.
Benediction.
Confession.

Haven.
Inscription: "He wrote upon his heart."
Night.
Nocturne: "Softly blow lightly."
Poet.
Prescience.
"Hayes, Evelyn." *See* Bethell, Mary Ursula.
Hayes, J. Milton (1884–1940)
Green Eye of the Yellow God, The.
Hayes, Nancy M.
At Night in the Wood.
Shiny Little House, The.
**Hayford, Gladys May Casely (Aquah Laluah)
(1904–50)**
Baby Cobina.
Nativity.
Palm Wine Seller, The.
Rainy Season Love Song.
Serving Girl, The.
Shadow of Darkness.
Hayford, James (b. 1913)
Mason's Trick.
Haygarth, William (*fl.* early 19th century)
Genius of Greece! thou livest, though thy
    domes.
Greece, *Sels.*
Mournful is the remembrance which awakes.
Hayiaku
Funeral Song.
Hayley, William (1745–1820)
Apart, and on the sacred hill retired.
Essay on Epic Poetry, An, *Sels.*
To Mr. William Long, On His Recovery from
    a Dangerous Illness, 1785.
To Mrs. Smith, Occasioned by the First of Her
    Sonnets.
Hayman, Jane
Murdered Girl Is Found on a Bridge, The.
Hayman, Robert (1579?–1631?)
Mad Answer of a Madman, A.
Of the Great and Famous . . . Sir Francis
    Drake, and of My Little-Little Selfe.
Owen's Bracelet.
Owen's Epigrams, *Sels.*
Pleasant Life in Newfoundland, The.
Saturn's Three Sons.
Hayne, Paul Hamilton (1830–86)
Battle of Charleston Harbor, The.
Beyond the Potomac.
Butler's Proclamation.
Charleston.
In Harbor.
Little while (my life is almost set!), A.
Love Scorns Degrees.
Macdonald's Raid.
Mocking Bird, The.
Mountain of the lovers, The, *Sels.*
Pre-Existence.
Rose and the Thorn, The.
South Carolina to the States of the North.
Stricken South to the North, The.
True Heaven, The.
Vicksburg.
Yorktown Centennial Lyric.
Hayne, William Hamilton (1856–1929)
Charge at Santiago, The.
Haynes, Carol
Any Wife or Husband.
Haynes, David (b. 1957)
Mediatrix.
Hays, Edward
Autumn Psalm of Contentment.
Hays, Lee. *See* Handcox, John, *and* Lee Hays.
Hays, Will S. (1837–1909)
O'Grady's Goat.
Hayward, Charles W. (1866–1950)
King George V.
Hayward, William (b. 1906)
Five Birds Rise.
Hazard, Caroline (1856–1945)
Great Swamp Fight, The.
Hazeley, Iyamide
Beloved.
You're So Far Away.

Hazlewood-Brady, Anne
Closer First to Earth.
Double Axe, The.
Hazo, Samuel (b. 1928)
After the Hurricane.
Between You and Me.
Skycoast.
To a Blind Student Who Taught Me to See.
Head, Sir Henry (1861–1940)
Destroyers.
Headly, Henry (1765–1788)
Child of the potent spell and nimble eye.
Invocation to Melancholy, An, *Sels.*
Healy, Eloise Klein
Like a Wick, I Thought, a Woman.
Moon on the Porch.
Healy, Ian (b. 1919)
Poems from the Coalfields, *Sels.*
Heaney, Seamus (b. 1939)
Alphabets.
Anahorish.
And yes, my friend, we, too.
Ash Plant, The.
At a Potato Digging.
Barn, The.
Bat on the Road, A.
Be literal a moment. Recollect.
Black water. White waves. Furrows
    snowcapped.
Blackberry-picking.
Bog Queen.
Bogland.
Broagh.
Cana Revisited.
Casualty.
Clearances, *Sels.*
Constable Calls, A.
Cool that came off sheets just off the line, The.
Crossings, *Sels.*
Death of a Naturalist.
Digging.
Docker.
Drink of Water, A.
Exposure, *Sels.*
Fear of affection made her affect.
Field Work.
Follower.
Forge, The.
From the Canton of Expectation.
Funeral Rites.
Gifts of Rain.
Girls Bathing, Galway 1965.
Glanmore Sonnets, *Sels.*
Guttural Muse, The.
Harvest Bow, The.
Haw Lantern, The.
Hazel Stick for Catherine Ann, A.
I dreamt we slept in a moss in Donegal.
I had come to the edge of the water.
I stirred wet sand and gathered myself.
I thought of walking round and round a space.
In Memoriam Francis Ledwidge.
In the last minutes he said more to her.
Iron Spike.
Kinship.
La Toilette.
Leavings.
Like a convalescent, I took the hand.
Limbo.
Mid-Term Break.
Mossbawn Sunlight.
Mossbawn: Two Poems in Dedication, *Sels.*
Mother.
Mother of the Groom.
Mud Vision, The.
My brain dried like spread turf, my stomach.
New Song, A.
North.
Not an avenue and not a bower.
On St. Brigid's Day the new life could be
    entered.
Other Side, The.
Otter, The.
Outlaw, The.
Oysters.
Peacock's Feather, A.

Hedges, Doris (b. 1900)
Prayer: "O God of goodness, forwardness, and fulness."

Hedley, Leslie Woolf
Chant for All the People on Earth.

Hedylos (fl. 270? B.C.)
Dedication to Aphrodite, A.
From dawn to dark, and back from dark to dawn.
Let's drink up: with wine, what original.
Musical Wine-Jar, A.
Our prize fish is done!
Seduced Girl.
Wine and treacherous proposals.
Wine, the toasts that could not be refused, The.

Heffernan, Michael (b. 1942)
Colloquy of Silences, A.
Daffodils.
Living Room.
Naked War.
Putting On My Shoes I Hear the Floor Cry Out beneath Me.
Reading Aquinas.
Sunday Service.
Table, The.

Heffernan, William (b. 1937)
Kathaleen Ny-Houlahan [or Kathleen-Ni-Houlahan].

Hegemon (fl. c. 370 B.C.)
Thermopylai.

Hegesippus (fl. 300 B.C.)
Hang that day with black, that night, sinister, moonless.

Heginbothom, Ottiwell (1744–68)
Great God, let all my tuneful pow'rs.

Heguri, Lady
Thousand years, you said, A.

Heidbreder, Robert
Copycat.

Heide, Florence Parry (b. 1919)
Rocks.

Heifetz, Julie N.
Blue Parakeet, The.
Harry Lenga.
Wheel, The.

Heifetz-Tussman, Malka (b. 1896)
Mount Gilboa.
Thou Shalt Not.

Heikel, Karen Alice. *See* **"Vala, Katri."**

Heine, Heinrich (1797–1856)
Ad Finem.
And if the flowers knew, the little ones.
And When I Lamented.
Anniversary.
Anno 1829.
Atlas.
Auf meiner Herzliebsten Äugelein.
Azra, The.
Best Religion, The.
Beware of Kittens.
Boy loves a girl, A.
Broad Sea Sparkled, The.
By the Waters of Babylon.
Coffin, The.
Dear Maiden.
Dearest Friend, Thou Art in Love.
Death is the Cool Night.
Die blauen Veilchen der Äugelein.
Die Lotusblume ängstigt.
Du bist wie eine Blume.
Ein Fichtenbaum steht einsam.
Enfant perdu.
Epilogue: "Like the stalks of wheat in the fields."
Es fällt ein Stern herunter.
Es Stehen Unbeweglich.
Evening Twilight.
Every night in my dreams I see you.
Farewell: "Linden blossomed, the nightingale sang, The."
Fresco-Sonnets to Christian Sethe.
From my tears spring up.
Grenadiers, The.
Heavenly fields of Paradise, The.

Hebrew Melodies, *Sels.*
Heimkehr, Die, *Sels.*
Homeward Bound, *Sels.*
I, a Most Wretched Atlas.
I bear no grudge, even though my heart may break.
I cried in my dream.
I Love But Thee.
I Met by Chance.
I Wept as I Lay Dreaming.
I will dip my soul.
Ich Weiss Nicht Was Soll es Bedeuten.
If, Jerusalem, I Ever Should Forget Thee.
I'm Black and Blue.
Im Traum sah ich ein Männchen klein und putzig.
In the bright summer morning.
It's Going Out.
Lassie, What Mair Wad You Hae?
Lorelei [, The].
Lotus Flower, The.
Love's Résumé.
Mädchen mit dem rothen Mündchen.
Maiden Lies in Her Chamber, A.
Mein Herz, Mein Herz Ist Traurig.
Mein Liebchen, wir sassen zusammen.
Message, The.
Mir träumte von einem Königskind.
Mir träumte wieder der alte Traum.
Mond ist aufgegangen, Der.
Morning After, The.
Mortal, Sneer Not at the Devil.
Mutilated choir boys, The.
My child, we were two children.
My Double.
My Songs Are Poisoned ("My songs, they say, are poisoned").
New Jewish Hospital at Hamburg, The.
Night by the Sea, A.
North Sea, The, *Sels.*
Oh Lovely Fishermaiden.
Old evil songs, The.
On Wings of Song.
Out Of My Great Afflictions.
Out of the old fairy tales.
Poet's Love.
Princess Sabbath.
Proem: "Out of my own great woe."
Rhine, the beautiful river, The.
Rose, die Lilie, die Taube, die Sonne, Die.
Rose, the lily, the dove, the sun, The.
Sag', wo ist dein schönes Liebchen.
Sea Hath Its Pearls, The.
Shadow-Love.
Shepherd Boy, The.
Solomon.
Song: "There stands a lonely pine-tree."
Songs to Seraphine, *Sels.*
Sonnet to My Mother, A.
Storm, The.
Tannhäuser, *Sels.*
Tell me where thy lovely love is.
There is playing of flutes and fiddles.
This delightful young man.
This mad carnival of loving.
Thou Hast Diamonds.
Three Holy Kings from Morgenland.
To a Political Poet.
To Angélique, *Sels.*
To Edom.
To My Mother.
Twilight.
Voyage, The.
Warum sind denn die Rosen so blass.
Waves Gleam in the Sunshine, The.
We Cared for Each Other.
Weavers.
Welt ist dumm, die Welt ist blind, Die.
When I hear the song.
When I look into your eyes.
When Two Are Parted.
When Young Hearts Break.
Who Was It, Tell Me.
Wie langsam kriecht sie dahin.
Window-Glance, The.
Wise Men Ask the Children the Way, The.

You Are Like A Flower.
Young Tomcats' Society for Poetic Music.
Zu fragmentarisch ist Welt und Leben.
Zum Lazarus, *Sels.*

Heinrich von Morungen (d. 1222)
Alas, shall I not see again.
I believe there is no one alive who weeps for my sorrow.
I heard on the meadow.
It has gone with me as with a child.
Legacy, The.
Many a man gets bewitched by the elves.

Heinrich von Rugge (fl. 12th century)
He That Loves a Rosy Cheek.

Heinrich von Veldeke (1140?–1210?)
In April when the flowers spring.
Tristan had no choice.
Whoever hurts my favor with my lady.

Hejduk, John
Sleep of Adam, The.

Hejinian, Lyn (b. 1941)
Agreement swerves.
Angels, it seems, don't always know.
Imagine observing ones fear.
Nostalgia is the elixir drained.
Sun is just appearing, The.

Helburn, Theresa (1887?–1959)
Mother.

Heller, Binem (b. 1943)
Pesach Has Come to the Ghetto Again.

Helm, Erica (b. 1954)
Creation Songs of Eurynome, The, *Sels.*
Egg of the Universe Hatches All Things, The.
Eurynome Banishes Ophion and Completes Creation.
Eurynome Births the Egg of the Universe.
Eurynome Creates Her Consort Ophion.
Eurynome Divides Chaos.

Helmer, Charles D.
Battle of Oriskany, The.

Helmore, Thomas (1811–90)
Christmas Carol: "Christ was born on Christmas day."

Helton, Roy (b. 1886)
Lonesome Water.
Old Christmas Morning.

Helwig, David (b. 1938)
Considerations.
Dead Weasel, A.
Drunken Poem.
For Edward Hicks.
Lot.
Words from Hell.

Hemans, Felicia Dorothea (1793–1835)
Agony in the Garden, The.
Brereton Omen, The, *Sels.*
Casabianca.
Child's First Grief, The.
Corinne at the Capitol.
Dirge: "Calm on the bosom of thy God."
Flight of the Spirit.
Graves of a Household, The.
Homes of England, The.
Hour of Death, The.
Hymn for Christmas.
Landing of the Pilgrim Fathers [in New England], The.
Prayer: "Father in Heaven! from whom the simplest flower."
Sabbath Sonnet.
Siege of Valencia, The, *Sels.*
To the Poet Wordsworth.
Yes! I have seen the ancient oak.

Hemingway, Ernest (1899–1961)
Champs d'Honneur.
Chapter Heading.
Earnest Liberal's Lament, The.
Neo-Thomist Poem.
Valentine.

Hemminger, Graham Lee (1896–1949)
Tobacco ("Tobacco is a dirty weed").

Hemp, Christine E.
To Build a Poem.

Hemphill, Essex (b. 1957)
Cordon Negro.
Family Jewels.
Isn't It Funny?
To Some Supposed Brothers.
Hemphrey, Malcolm
Lanes in Summer.
Hempseed, Isabell
Rufty and Tufty.
Hemschemeyer, Judith (b. 1935)
First Love.
I Remember the Room Was Filled with Light.
My Mother's Death.
Painters, The.
This Love.
Hemsley, Stuart (b. 1905)
S.P.C.A. Sermon.
Henchman, Richard (c.1655–1725)
In Consort to Wednesday, Jan. 1st. 1701.
Vox Oppressi, to the Lady Phipps.
Henderson, Alice Corbin. *See* **Corbin, Alice.**
Henderson, Daniel (1851–1906)
Road to France, The.
Henderson, David (b. 1943)
Do Nothing till You Hear from Me.
Documentary on Airplane Glue, A.
Downtown-Boy Uptown.
Keep on Pushing.
Louisiana Weekly #4, The.
Sketches of Harlem.
They Are Killing All the Young Men.
Walk with de Mayor of Harlem.
White People.
Henderson, E. H.
March Wind, The.
Henderson, Hamish (b. 1919)
End of a Campaign.
First Elegy for the Dead in Cyrenaica.
Flyting o' Life and Daith, The.
We Show You That Death as a Dancer.
"Henderson, Paul" (Ruth France) (1913–67)
Shag Rock.
Henderson, Peggy (b. 1949)
Serpent Muses, The.
Hendricks, A. L. (b. 1922)
Boundary.
D'Où Venons Nous? Que Sommes Nous? Où
Allons Nous, *Sels.*
Hot Summer Sunday.
I touch jig-saw fragments.
Looking out toward the stars.
Migrant, The.
Recollections of the Sun.
Will the Real Me Please Stand Up?
Woman in the garden gathers lilacs, A.
Hendry, Hamish (*fl.* c.1897)
Silver Bells.
Silver Road, The.
Upside-Down World, The.
Hendry, J. F. (b. 1912)
Constant North, The.
Hendryson, Barbara
Prayer for a Tenspeed Heart.
What Is Repeated, What Abides.
Henkell, Karl (1864–1929)
Rest, My Soul.
Henley, Samuel (1740–1815)
Verses Addressed to a Friend, Just Leaving a
Favourite Ernest.
Henley, William Ernest (1849–1903)
All in a Garden Green.
Apparition.
Ballade Made in the Hot Weather.
Ballade of Dead Actors.
Before.
Blackbird, The.
Bowl of Roses, A.
Discharged.
Echoes, *Sels.*
England, My England.
From a Window in Princes Street.
Home *or* Falmouth.
I am the reaper.

In Hospital, *Sels.*
Invictus.
Largo e mesto.
London Voluntaries, *Sels.*
Madam Life's a Piece in Bloom.
Margaritæ Sorori, [I. M.].
Moral, The.
On the Way to Kew.
Out of Tune.
Romance.
Rondel: "Beside the idle summer sea."
Sands Are Alive With Sunshine, The.
Scherzando.
Since Those We Love and Those We Hate.
Street Scene.
Suicide.
To My Mother.
To Robert Louis Stevenson.
Villon's Good-Night.
Villon's Straight Tip to All Cross Coves.
Waiting.
We'll Go No More a-Roving.
When I Was a King in Babylon.
Hennamma (*fl.* late 17th century)
Wasn't your mother a woman?
Hennell, Thomas (1903–45)
Mermaiden, A.
Queen Anne's Musicians.
Shepherd and Shepherdess.
Henri, Adrian (b. 1932)
Adrian Henri's Talking after Christmas Blues.
Love Story.
Mrs. Albion You've Got a Lovely Daughter.
Henri, Raymond (d. 1927?)
Bridge from Brooklyn, The, *Sels.*
Chartres.
Duomo, Milan.
View of the Cathedral, *Sels.*
Henry VIII, King of England (1491–1547)
Love Ever Green.
Pastime with good company.
Whereto should I express.
Henry, Gerrit (b. 1950)
Cole Porter's Son.
Henry, James (1798–1876)
Another and another and another.
My Stearine Candles.
Old Man.
Once on a time a thousand different men.
Out of the Frying Pan into the Fire.
Pain.
Two hundred men and eighteen killed.
Very Old Man.
"Henry, O." *See* **"O. Henry."**
Henry, William
Verses.
Henry the Minstrel ("Blind Harry") (*fl.*
c.1470–c.1492)
Burning of the Barns of Ayr, The.
Description of Wallace, A.
Out off the south thai saw quhar at the queyn.
Wallace, The, *Sels.*
Wallace's Lament for the Graham.
Sir William Wallace, *Sels.*
Henryson, Robert (c.1425–c.1506)
Assembly of the Gods, The.
Cresseid's Complaint against Fortune.
I mend the fyre and beikit me about.
Lion Calls All the Beasts to His Parliment.
Lipper folk to Cresseid than can draw, The.
Prayer against the Plague, A.
Preiching of the Swallow, The.
Robin [*or* Robene] and Makyne.
Taill of the Foxe, That Begylit the Wolf, in the
Schadow of the Mone, The.
Taill of the Wolf and the Wedder, The.
Taille of the Sone and Air of the Foxe, The,
Sels.
Tale of the Upland Mouse and the Burgess
Mouse, The.
Testament of Cresseid, The, *Sels.*
Henson, Lance (b. 1944)
After a Summer Fire.
Among Hawks.

Anniversary Poem for the Cheyennes Who Fell
at Sand Creek.
At Chadwicks Bar and Grill.
Bay Poem.
Between Rivers and Seas.
Buffalo Blood.
Cold, The.
Comanche Ghost Dance: An Impression.
Coyote Fragments.
Crazy Horse: The Last Morning.
Curtain.
Dawn in January.
Day Song.
Flock.
Grandfather.
I Am Singing the Cold Rain.
Image of City.
In January.
Last Words, 1968.
Moon at Three A.M.
Moth.
Near Twelve Mile Point.
North.
Old Man Told Me.
Old Story.
Other.
Our Smoke Has Gone Four Ways.
Poem for Carroll, Descendant of Chiefs.
Rain.
Scattered Leaves.
Sitting Alone in Tulsa Three A.M.
Sitting Outside in Early Morning.
Sketches near Youngstown Ohio.
Sleep Watch.
Snake River.
Solitary.
Splitting Wood Near Morris, Oklahoma on
Robbie and Lesa McMurtry's Farm.
Sundown at Darlington 1878.
Travels with the Band-Aid Army.
Warrior Nation Trilogy.
We Are a People.
Wish.
Wood Floor Dreams.
Henson, Pauline (b. 1914)
On the Edge of the Copper Pit.
Henze, Helen Rowe (b. 1899)
Etruscan Warrior's Head.
Hepburn, Thomas Nicoll. *See* **"Setoun,**
Gabriel."
Heppenstall, Rayner (1911–81)
Actaeon.
Heraclitus of Halicarnassus (*fl.* c.240 B.C.)
Soil is freshly dug, the half-faded wreaths of
leaves, The.
Heraud, Javier (1942–63)
Autumn and the Sea.
Earth Poems, *Sels.*
Herbert, Sir Alan Patrick (1890–1971)
After the Battle.
At the Theater.
Beaucourt Revisited.
Chameleon, The.
Cookers, The: A Song of the Transport.
Dead-Mule Tree: A Song of Wisdom.
General inspecting the trenches, The.
German Graves, The.
Hattage.
He Didn't Oughter.
I Can't Think What He Sees in Her.
I Like Them Fluffy.
Inst., Ult., and Prox.
I've Got the Giggles Today.
Less Nonsense.
Lines for a Worthy Person Who Has Drifted by
Accident into a Chelsea Revel.
Mr. Churchill.
Racing-Man, The.
Saturday Night.
Stop, Science — Stop!
To a Junior Waiter.
Triangular Legs.
Herbert, Audrey
Limerick: "All his life, Mr. George Bernard
Shaw."

Wele, herying and worshipe be to Crist [*or*
   Christ] that dere us [*or* ous] boughte.
What Is He, This Lordling.

Heredia, José-Maria de (1842–1905)
Flute; a Pastoral, The.
Laborer, The.

Herford, Oliver (1863–1935)
Bashful Earthquake, The, *Sels.*
Bunny Romance, A.
Cat, The.
Child's Natural History, *Sels.*
Chimpanzee, The.
Crocodile, The.
Dog, The.
Elf and the Dormouse, The.
Eve.
Fall of J. W. Beane, The.
I Heard a Bird Sing.
Japanesque.
Last Violet, The.
Metaphysics.
More Animals, *Sels.*
Musical Lion, The.
Penguin, A.
Platypus, The.
Smile of the Goat, The.
Smile of the Walrus, The.
Some Geese.
Stairs.

"Hermes, Paul." *See* **Thayer, William Roscoe.**

Hermocreon (*fl.* 3d? cent. B.C.)
Inscription on a Statue.
Nymphs of the surface, whom Hermokreon
   gave.

Hernandez Cruz, Victor. *See* **Cruz, Victor
   Hernandez.**

Hernández, Miguel (1910–42)
War.

Hernández, Reyna (b. 1962)
Yankees.

Hernton, Calvin C. (b. 1932)
D Blues.
Distant Drum, The.
Fall Down.
Jitterbugging in the Streets.
Madhouse.

Herodas (*fl.* 3d cent. B.C.)
Friends in Private.
Procuress, The.
Schoolmaster, The.
Women at the Temple.

Herodicus (*fl.* 2d cent. B.C.)
Out of Hellas if you please, Aristarchean
   pedants.

Herrera, Juan Felipe
Boy of Seventeen, The.
Earth Chorus.
Foreign Inhabitant.
Pyramid of Supplications.
These Words Are Synonymous, Now.
Velvet Baroque/Act.
Water Girl.

Herrick, Robert (1591–1674)
Againe.
All Things Decay and Die.
Amber Bead, The.
Ambition.
Anacreontic.
Anacreontic Verse.
Another.
Another Charm for Stables.
Another to Bring In the Witch.
Another to the Maids.
Apparition of His Mistress[e] Calling Him to
   Elizium [*or* Elysium], The.
Apron of Flowers, The.
Argument of His Book, The.
Art above Nature, to Julia.
Ass, The.
Bad Season Makes the Poet Sad, The.
Barley-Break; or, Last in Hell.
Beggar to Mab, the Fairy [*or* Fairie] Queen,
   The.
Bell-Man [*or* Bellman], The.
Body, The.

Born[e] I was to meet with ages.
Bracelet: To Julia, The.
Bubble; a Song, The.
Calling, and Correcting.
Canticle to Apollo, A.
Captived Bee; or, The Little Filcher, The.
Ceremonies for Candlemas[se] Eve.
Ceremonies for Christmas[se], *Sels.*
Ceremony upon Candlemas Eve.
Changes to Corinna, The.
Charm, A.
Charm me asleep, and melt me so.
Charme, or an Allay for Love, A.
Charmes.
Cheat of Cupid; or, The Ungentle Guest, The.
Cherry-ripe.
Chewing of the Cud, The.
Chop-Cherry.
Christmas Caroll Sung to the King in the
   Presence at White-Hall, A, *Sels.*
Christmas Eve — Another Ceremony.
Clothes Do but Cheat and Cozen Us.
Comfort to a Youth That Had Lost His Love.
Coming of Good Luck, The.
Conjuration, to Electra, A.
Corinna's Going a-Maying.
Country Life: To His Brother, Master Thomas
   Herrick, A.
Country Life, to the Honored Mr. Endymion
   Porter, The.
Crosses.
Cruel Maid, The.
Crutches.
Curse, The; a Song.
Darling of the world is come, The.
Dean-bourn, a Rude River in Devon, by Which
   Sometimes He Lived ("Dean-bourn, farewell;
   I never look to see").
Definition of Beauty, The.
Delight in Disorder.
Departure of the Good Daemon, The.
Dew Sat on Julia's Hair.
Dirge of Jephthah's Daughter, The.
Dirge upon the Death of the Right Valiant
   Lord, Bernard Stuart, A.
Discontents in Devon.
Distrust.
Divination by a Daffadill [*or* Daffodil].
Dreams.
End of His Work, The.
Entertainment, or Porch-Verse, at the Marriage
   of Master Henry Northleigh and the Most
   Witty Mistress Lettice Yard, The.
Epitaph upon a Child, An.
Epitaph upon a Sober Matron, An.
Epitaph upon a Virgin, An.
Epithalamy to Sir Thomas Southwell and His
   Lady, An.
Eternity.
Eye, The.
Fair Days; or, Dawns Deceitful.
Fairies, The.
Fairy Temple; or, Oberon's Chapel, The.
Fame.
Fame Makes Us Forward.
Farewell Frost; or, Welcome the Spring.
Four Sweet Months, The.
Four Things Make Us Happy Here.
Fresh Cheese and Cream.
Frolic, A.
Frozen Zone; or, Julia Disdainful, The.
Funeral Rites of the Rose, The.
God to Be First Served.
God's Mercy.
Good Christians.
Good Friday: Rex Tragicus; or, Christ Going to
   His Cross.
Good Men Afflicted Most.
Good-Night, or Blessing, The.
Grace for a Child.
Grace for Children, A.
Hag, The.
Her Legs.
Here a pretty baby lies.
Here down my wearied limbs I'll lay.
His Age, Dedicated to His Peculiar Friend,

Master John Wickes, under the Name of
   Posthumus.
His Cavalier.
His Charge to Julia at His Death.
His Content in the Country.
His Creed.
His Desire.
His Ejaculation to God.
His Farewell to Sack.
His Grange, or Private Wealth.
His Hope or Sheet-Anchor.
His Lachrimae or Mirth, Turn'd to Mourning.
His Litany to the Holy Spirit.
His Offering, With the Rest, At the Sepulcher.
His Own Epitaph.
His Poetry His Pillar.
His Prayer for Absolution.
His Prayer to Ben Jonson [*or* Johnson].
His Request to Julia.
His Return to London.
His Sailing from Julia.
His Saviour's Words, Going to the Cross.
His Tears to Thamesis[*or* Thamasis].
His Winding-Sheet.
Hock-Cart, or Harvest Home, The.
Hour-Glass, The.
How Lillies Came White.
How Marigolds Came Yellow.
How Roses Came Red.
How Violets Came Blue.
Hymn to Bacchus, A.
Hymn to Love, An.
Hymn to the Graces, A.
I Call and I Call ("I call, I call. Who do ye
   call?")
I fear no earthly powers.
I will no longer kiss.
I'll write no more of love, but now repent.
Impossibilities to His Friend.
In the Dark None Dainty.
Instead of Neat Inclosures.
Invitation, The.
Julia's Petticoat.
Kiss, A.
Kisses Loathesome.
Kissing and Bussing.
Let me not live, if I not love.
Life Is the Body's Light.
Lilly in a Christal, The.
Long and Lazy.
Love Dislikes Nothing.
Love Me Little, Love Me Long.
Love What It Is.
Lovers How They Come and Part.
Lyric to Mirth, A.
Lyric[k] for Legacies.
Mad Maid's Song, The.
Man's Dying-Place Uncertain.
Matins, or Morning Prayer.
Maypole, The.
Meddow Verse; or, Aniversary to Mistris
   Bridget Lowman, The.
Meditation for His Mistress[e], A.
Mercy and Love.
Mirth.
Moderation.
Money Gets the Mastery.
Money Makes the Mirth.
Mount of the Muses, The.
Music.
My Ben!
Neutrality Loathsome.
New-Year's Gift Sent to Sir Simeon Steward,
   A.
New-Yeeres Gift, or Circumcisions Song, Sung
   to the King in the Presence at White Hall,
   The.
Night-Piece [*or* Nightpiece], to Julia, The.
No Coming to God without Christ.
No Difference in the Dark.
No Loathsomnesse in Love.
No Lock against Lechery.
Not Every Day Fit for Verse.
Not to Love.
Nothing New.
Nuptial[l] Song, or Epithalamie [*or*

Eia, with handbells, jews' harps, risible.
Funeral Music, *Sels*.
Gasholders, russet among fields.
Genesis.
Guardians, The.
He adored the desk, its brown-oak inlaid with ebony.
Hymns to Our Lady of Chartres, *Sels*.
I was invested in mother-earth, the crypt of roots.
Idylls of the King.
Imaginative Life, The.
In Memory of Jane Fraser [*or* Frazer].
In Piam Memoriam.
King of the perennial holly-groves, the riven sandstone.
Lachrimae, *Sels*.
Lachrimae Amantis.
Lachrimae Verae.
Laurel Axe, The.
Mad are predators, The. Too often lately they harbor.
Masque of Blackness, The.
Mercian Hymns, *Sels*.
Merlin.
My little son, when you could command marvels.
Mystery of the Charity of Charles Péguy, The, *Sels*.
Not as we are but as we must appear.
Not strangeness, but strange likeness.
On the morning of the crowning we chorused our remission from school.
Orpheus and Eurydice.
Ovid in the Third Reich.
Pentecost Castle, The.
Pet-name, a common name. Best-selling brand, curt, A.
Picture of a Nativity.
Prayer to the Sun, A.
Pre-Raphaelite Notebook, A.
Princes of Mercia were badger and raven, The.
Processes of generation; deeds of settlement.
Quaint Mazes.
Requiem for the Plantagenet Kings.
September Song.
Short History of British India, A.
So much for the elves' wergild, the true governance.
Song from Armenia, A.
Strange church smelled a bit 'high,' of censers, The.
Their spades grafted through the variably-resistant.
Trim the lamp; polish the lens; draw, one by one, rare coins.
Turtle Dove, The.
Two Chorale-Preludes.
Veni Coronaberis.
We ran across the meadow scabbed with the cow-dung.
White Ship, The.
Wreaths.
Hill, Hyacinthe (b. 1920)
Old Emily.
Hill, Joe (1879–1914)
Casey Jones.
Preacher and the Slave, The.
Hill, Leona
Let Him Return.
Hill, Leslie Pinckney (1880–1960)
So Quietly.
Teacher, The.
Tuskegee.
Hill, Roberta. *See* **Whiteman, Roberta Hill.**
Hill, Selima (b. 1945)
Below Hekla.
Crossing the Desert in a Pram.
Looking for Camels.
Ram, The.
Voice in the Garden, A.
Hille, Peter (1854–1904)
Beauty.
Maiden, The.
Hillel, Omer (b. 1926)
Sun.

Hillhouse, Augustus Lucas (1792–1859)
Trembling before Thine Awful Throne.
Hillhouse, James Abraham (1789–1841)
Hadad, *Sels*.
Hillman, Brenda (b. c.1945)
No Greener Pastures.
Hillyer, Robert Silliman (1895–1961)
As One Who Bears beneath His Neighbor's Roof.
Assassination, The.
Bats, The.
Eppur Si Muove?
Eternal Return, The.
Familiar Faces, Long Departed.
Hills turn hugely in their sleep, The.
Ivory Tower, The.
Letter to Robert Frost, A.
Lullaby: "Long canoe, The."
Moo!
Nocturne: "If the deep wood is haunted."
Over Bright Summer Seas.
Pastoral: "So soft in the hemlock wood."
Pastoral: "Wise old apple tree in spring, The."
Prothalamion, *Sels*.
Relic, The.
Thought in Time, A.
Hilton, Arthur Clement (1851–77)
Ding Dong.
Heathen Pass-ee, The.
Limerick: "There was a young critic of King's."
Limerick: "There was a young genius of Queens'."
Limerick: "There was a young gourmand of John's."
Limerick: "There was an old fellow of Trinity."
Octopus.
Vulture and the Husbandman, The.
Hilton, David (b. 1938)
Blind Saxophonist Dies.
Melmac Year, The.
Hilton, John (d. 1657)
Madrigal: "My mistress frowns when she should play."
Hilton, L. M.
Have Courage, My Boy, to Say No!
Hilton, Roger (1911–75)
Demands.
Himel, Margery
My People.
Himmell, Sophie (1896?–1966)
In the Month of Green Fire.
Hind bint Utba (*fl.* early 7th century)
Fury against the Moslems at Uhud.
Tambourine song for Soldiers Going into Battle.
Hind bint Uthatha (*fl.* early 7th century)
To a Hero Dead at al-Safra.
Hindley, Charles (d. 1893)
Mother Shipton's Prophecies.
Hine, Daryl (b. 1936)
Begging the Question.
Bewilderment at the Entrance of the Fat Boy into Eden, A.
Destruction of Sodom, The.
Doppelganger, The.
Fabulary Satire IV.
For the friendships of youth are more instant.
Here is another poem in a picture.
March, *Sels*.
Once when I was coming from art class they surprised me.
Plain Fare.
Point Grey.
Si Monumentum Requiris.
Survivors, The.
Trompe L'Oeil.
Trout, The.
Under the Hill.
Unhappy Returns.
Vowel Movements.
Wasp, The.
Wave, The.

Hines, Nellie Womack
Home.
Hines, P. R.
My Garden.
Hinkson, Katharine Tynan. *See* **Tynan, Katharine.**
Hioki no Ko-okima
On the shore of Nawa.
Hippius, Zinaida (1869–1945)
Grey Frock, A.
L'Imprévisibilité.
Hippolyte, Kendel (b. 1952)
Jah Son/ Another Way.
Hirsch, Edward (b. 1950)
After the Last Practice.
And Who Will Look Upon Our Testimony.
Art Pepper.
At Kresge's Diner in Stonefalls, Arkansas.
Fast Break.
For the Sleepwalkers.
Leningrad (1941–1943).
My Father's Back.
Paul Celan: A Grave and Mysterious Sentence.
Short Lexicon of Torture in the Eighties, A.
Wild Gratitude.
Hirshbein, Peretz (b. 1880)
Captive.
I Shall Weep.
Stars Fade.
Hirshfield, Jane
To Drink.
Hitchcock, George
Figures in a Ruined Ballroom.
May All Earth Be Clothed in Light.
Three Found Poems.
Three Portraits.
Hitomaro (Kakinomoto no Hitomaro) (*fl.* c.700)
Bay of Tsunu, The.
For my sister's sake.
May the men who are born.
My thoughts are with a boat.
O boy cutting grass.
On the moor of Kasuga.
This morning I will not.
When,/ Halting in front of it, I look.
Hittan of Tayyi
Hamasah, *Sels*.
His Children.
Ho, Lady (*fl.* c. 300 B.C.)
Song of Magpies, A.
Ho Ch'e Ch'ang (659–744)
Homecoming.
Ho Chi Minh
On the Way.
Ho Hsun (d. 527)
Spring Breeze.
Traveler, The.
Ho Nansorhon (1563–1603)
Woman's Sorrow, A, *Sels*.
Yesterday I fancied I was young.
Ho Shuang-ch'ing (*fl.* 18th cent.)
To the Tune "A Watered Silk Dress."
To the Tune "Washing Silk in the Stream."
Ho Xuan Huong (*fl.* late 18th century)
Buddhist Priest, A.
Carved on an Areca Nut.
Jackfruit, The.
Hoagland, Everett (b. 1942)
Anti-Semanticist, The.
It's a Terrible Thing!
Jamming.
Love Child — a Black Aesthetic.
Music, The.
My Spring Thing.
Hoagland, Tony
One Season.
Poem for Men Only.
Sweet Rain.
Hoare, Florence
Pedlar Jim.
Hoare, Prince (1755–1834)
Arethusa, The.

Hoatson, Florence
Autumn.
Bird Bath, The.
Who?

Hoban, Russell (b. 1925)
Egg Thoughts.
Friendly Cinnamon Bun, The.
Jigsaw Puzzle.
Old Man Ocean.
Tin Frog, The.

Hoberman, Mary Ann (b. 1930)
Brother.
Bugs, *Sels.*
Cockroach.
Combinations.
Fireflies.
Folk Who Live in Backward Town, The.
Foxes.
Let's Dress Up.

Hobsbaum, Philip (b. 1932)
Lesson in Love, A.

Hobson, Geary (b. 1941)
Central Highlands, Viet Nam, 1968.

Hobson, Katherine Thayer (1889–1982)
Duality.

Hoccleve [or Occleve], Thomas (1370?–1450?)
Admirer's Lament of Chaucer, An.
After that hervest inned had his sheves.
Balade and Roundel to Master Somer.
Complaint, The, *Sels.*
Cupid Defends Women.
De Regimine Principum, *Sels.*
Description of His Ugly Lady, A.
Hoccleve Remembers His Madness.
Hoccleve's Complaint, *Sels.*
Lament for Chaucer.
Letter of Cupid, The, *Sels.*
O maister deere and fader reverent!
Prologue: "Musing upon the restless bisinesse."
Regement of Princes, *Sels.*

Hochman, Sandra (b. 1936)
Couple, The.
Eyes of Flesh, The.
Goldfish Wife, The.
Postscript.

Hodeir, Andre
By salt and by mercury.
Outside the Capsule, *Sels.*

Hodes, Aubrey (b. 1927)
Jew Walks in Westminster Abbey, A.

Hodgdon, Florence B.
How Can I Smile?

Hodge, Arthur J. (fl. late 19th century)
Five Were Foolish.

Hodges, Cyril (1915–1974)
Naturalised.

Hodges, Elizabeth (b. 1943)
Persimmons and Plums.

Hodgins, Philip (b. 1959)
Making Hay.
Self-Pity.

Hodgkinson, T.
Sand of Palestine, The.

Hodgson, A. B. L.
In Memoriam.

Hodgson, Ralph (c.1871–1962)
After.
Bells of Heaven, The.
Birdcatcher, The.
Bull, The.
Dust thou art, but dust carefully.
Eve.
Flying Scrolls, *Sels.*
Ghoul Care.
Gipsy Girl, The.
Great Auk's Ghost, The.
Hammers, The.
House across the Way, The.
Hymn to Moloch.
Late, Last Rook, The.
Moor, The.
Movement, she explained, would bring poetry
   to the rich, The.
Mystery, The.

Reason Has Moons.
Silver Wedding.
Song of Honor [*or* Honour], The.
Song: "With Love among the haycocks."
Stupidity Street.
Time.
Time, You Old Gypsy Man.
Wood Song, A.

Hodgson, William Noel (1893–1916)
Before Action.

Hodza, Aaron (1924–83)
Slighted Wife, The.

Hoey, George (1885–1955)
Asleep at the Switch.

Hoffenstein, Samuel (1890–1947)
As the Crow Flies, Let Him Fly, *Sels.*
Babies Haven't Any Hair.
Bird, The.
Birdie McReynolds.
Breathes there a man with hide so tough.
Come, live with me and be my love.
Dry.
Early bird may catch the worm, The.
Father's Heart Is Touched, A.
I Burned My Candle at Both Ends.
I'd rather listen to a flute.
If you love me, as I love you.
Invocation: "Come, lovely Muse, desert for
   me."
Invocation, *Sels.*
Love-songs, at Once Tender and Informative,
   Sels.
Lullaby: "Sleep, my little baby, sleep."
Makes the Little Ones Dizzy.
Mimic Muse, The, *Sels.*
Miss Millay Says Something Too.
Mr. Vachel Lindsay Discovers Radio.
Nothing from a straight line swerves.
Of all the birds that sing and fly.
Only the wholesomest foods you eat.
Poem Intended to Incite the Utmost Depression,
   A.
Poems in Praise of Practically Nothing, *Sels.*
Question and Answer.
Sheep.
Shropshire Lad's Cousin, The.
Songs about Life and Brighter Things Yet,
   Sels.
Unequal Distribution.
When You're Away.
With rue my heart is laden.
You buy some flowers for your table.
Your little hands.

Hoffman, Balthasar (1686–1775)
Be Glorified Eternally.

Hoffman, Charles Fenno (1806–88)
Monterey.

Hoffman, Daniel Gerard (b. 1923)
As I Was Going to Saint Ives.
Ballad of No Proper Man.
Center of Attention, The.
City of Satisfactions, The.
È, the Feasting Florentines.
Exploration.
First Flight.
In the Days of Rin-Tin-Tin.
Inviolable.
Lines Written near Linton, on Exmoor.
Seals in Penobscot Bay, The.
Signatures.
Three Jovial Gentlemen.
Who Was It Came.
Who We Are.

Hoffman, O. S.
Five Best Doctors, The.

Hoffman, Phoebe W. (b. 1894)
Pedro.

Hoffman, Richard
From a Front Window.
Sweat.

Hoffman, Sydney
Limerick: "No Portuguese Lady is Nautical."

Hoffman, William M. (b. 1939)
Screw Spring.

Hoffmann, Heinrich (1809–94)
Story of Augustus, Who Would Not Have Any
   Soup, The.
Story of Fidgety Philip, The.
Story of Johnny Head-in-Air, The.

Hofman, Michael
First Night.

Hofmann, Michael (b. 1957)
Austrians After Sadowa (1866), The.
Boys' Own.
C. & W.
Ecologue.
Fürth I. Wald.
Myopia in Rupert Brooke Country.
Nights in the Iron Hotel.
1967–1971.

Hofmannsthal, Hugo von (1874–1929)
Ballad of the Outer Life.
Death and the Fool, *Sels.*
Many Indeed Must Perish in the Keel.
Ship's Cook, a Captive Sings, The.
Stanzas on Mutability.
Travel Song.
Two, The.
Two of Them, The.
Venetian Night, A.
Vision, A.
When a man sleeps, often his dream will break.
World-Secret.

Hofmannswaldau, Christian Hofmann von
Beauty's Transitoriness.
Description of Perfect Beauty.
He Loves in Vain.
So sweet, so golden.

**Hofshteyn [or Hofstein], Dovid [or David]
(1889–1952)**
My Thread.
On Winter Evenings; 1912, *Sels.*

Hogan, Linda (b. 1947)
All Winter.
Avalanche, The.
Black Hills Survival Gathering, 1980.
Celebration: Birth of a Colt.
Desert.
Eclipse II.
Elk Song.
First Light.
Gamble.
It Must Be.
Man in the Moon.
Morning: The World in the Lake.
New Apartment, Minneapolis, The.
Night and Day.
November.
Other Side, The.
Our Houses.
Planting a Cedar.
Rainy Season, The.
Scorpion.
Seeing through the Sun.
Thought, A.
Tiva's Tapestry: La Llorona.
To Light.
Truth Is, The.
Turning.
Workday.

Hogan, Michael (b. 1943)
Spring.

**Hogg, James ("The Ettrick Shepherd") (1770–
1835)**
Boy's Song, A.
Flying Tailor, The.
Isabelle.
James Rigg.
Kilmeny.
Lock the Door, Lariston.
McLean's Welcome.
Nor for the crabbed state-creed, wayward
   wight.
Queen's Wake, The, *Sels.*
Skylark, The.
To The Right Honourable Lord Byron, *Sels.*
Village of Balmaquhapple, The.
Walsinghame's Song.
When the Kye Comes Hame.

Hogg, Robert (b. 1942)
Little Falls.

Hoggra, Robert
Poem: "In its going down, the moon."

Holan, Vladimir (1905–80)
Between.
But.
Chicken, The.
Epoch.
Glimpsed.
How?
Mother.
Old Priest, The.
Reminiscence.
Resurrection.
You're Thinking of Children.

Holbrook, David (b. 1923)
Coming Home from Abroad.
Day in France, A.
Drought.
Maternity Gown.

Holbrook, Weare
Varitalk.

Holcroft, Thomas (1745–1809)
Dying Prostitute, The; an Elegy.
Fool's Song.
Gaffer Gray.
On Shakespeare and Voltaire.
Seasons, The.
Song: "When o'er the wold the heedless lamb."
To Haydn.

Holden, Jonathan (b. 1941)
Against Paradise.
Alone.
American Boyhood, An.
Dancing School.
Driving through Coal Country in Pennsylvania.
First Kiss.
Full Moon, Rising.
Seventeen.
Tumbleweed.
Wisdom Tooth, The.

Holden, Molly (b. 1927)
Giant Decorative Dahlias.
Hare.
Photograph of Haymaker, 1890.
Seaman, 1941.

Holden, Oliver (1765–1844)
How Sweet Is the Language of Love.
Weeping Sinner, Dry Your Tears.
Within These Doors Assembled Now.

Holden, Stephen (b. 1939)
In Praise of Antonioni.

Holder, C. S.
King's Wood, The.

Hölderlin, Friedrich (1770–1843)
All the fruit is ripe, plunged in fire, cooked.
Bread and Wine, Sels.
Half of Life.
Oh friend, we arrived too late.
Ripe, Being Plunged into Fire.
Sanctimonious Poets, The.
To the Fates.

Holland, Henry Fox, 1st Baron (1705–74)
With a China Chamberpot, to the Countess of Hillsborough.

Holland, Hugh (1569–1635)
Epitaph on Prince Henry.
Owen Tudor.
Upon the Lines and Life of the Famous Scenic Poet, Master William Shakespeare.

Holland, Josiah Gilbert (1819–81)
Bitter-sweet, Sels.
Christmas Carol: "There's a song in the air!"
God, Give Us Men!
Gradatim.
Hymn: "For Summer's bloom and Autumn's blight."
Mistress of the Manse, The, Sels.
Song of Doubt, A.
Song of Faith, A.
To My Dog "Blanco."
Where Shall the Baby's Dimple Be.

Holland, Kevin Crossley-. See Crossley-Holland, Kevin.

Holland, Norah M. (1876–1925)
Little Dog-Angel, A.

Holland, Sir Richard (c.1420–c.1485)
Buke of the Howlat, The, Sels.
Roye Robert the Bruss the rayke he avowit, The.

Holland, Walter
Petrarch.

Hollander, John (b. 1929)
Adam's Task.
After the midwinter marriages — the bride of snow.
Appearance and Reality.
Back to Town.
Breadth. Circle. Desert. Monarch. Month. Wisdom.
Curse, The.
Danish Wit.
Disagreements.
Flears, The.
Great Bear, The.
Hall of Ocean Life.
Helicon.
Heliogabalus.
Historical Reflections.
In the Gallery.
Jefferson Valley.
Kinneret.
Kitty and Bug.
Lady at the Castle, The.
Lady's-Maid's Song, The.
Last Words.
Like some ill-fated butterfly, the literalists.
Lion Named Passion, A.
Mad Potter, The.
Movie-Going.
Night Mirror, The.
Ninth of July, The.
No Foundation.
Non Sum Qualis Eram in Bona Urbe Nordica Illa.
Old Guitar, The.
Old-Fashioned Song, An.
Paysage Moralisé.
Powers of Thirteen, Sels.
Refrains.
Russian Soul II, The.
See-Saw, The.
Skeleton Key.
Slepynge Long in Greet Quiete Is Eek a Greet Norice to Leccherie.
So we came at last to meet, after the lights were out.
Some Walks with You.
Sonnets for Roseblush, Sels.
State of Nature, A.
Sunday Evenings.
Swan and Shadow.
There was an end to hearts and rhymes.
These two tales I tell of myself and the life I led.
To the Lady Portrayed by Margaret Dumont.
Under Cancer.
Violet.
What she and I had between us once, America.
Why drink, why touch you now? If it will be.
Why have I locked myself inside.
Yes, go on! This is plain talk of plainer feelings now.

Hollander, Martha
Back in the Twilight Zone.
Detective Examines the Body, The.
Ogata Kōrin on His Field of Irises.

Hollander, Robert (b. 1933)
You Too? Me Too — Why Not? Soda Pop.

Holley, Horace (b. 1887)
Hill, The.

Hollis, Mark (b. 1908)
Careless Talk.
'Twixt Cup and Lip.

Hollo, Anselm (b. 1934)
Amazing Grace.
Anthropology.
Aubade: "Night's ride's over."
Behaviorally.
Big Dog.
Buffalo — Isle of Wight Power Cable.
Discovery of LSD a True Story, The.
If.
In the Land of Art.
Language, The.
Le Jazz Hot.
Lecture.
Manifest Destiny.
No Complaints.
Out of the "Kalevala", Sels.
Rain.
Terrorist Smiles, The.
That Old Sauna High.
T.V. (1).
T.V. (2).
Wasp Sex Myth (One).
Wasp Sex Myth (Two).

Holloway, Geoffrey
Grown-ups.

Holloway, John Wesley (b. 1865)
Miss Melerlee.

Holloway, Lucy Ariel Williams (b. 1905)
Northboun'.

Holly, Joseph Cephas (1825–55)
Our Family Tree.
Patriot's Lament, The.
This Is a Fatherland to Me.
Wreath of Holly, A.

Holm, Bill
Advice.

Holm, Sven (b. 1940)
Greenland's History.

Holman, Bob (b. 948)
One Flight Up.

Holman, Felice (b. 1919)
Clock, The.
I Can Fly.
Supermarket.
Who Am I?

Holman, Jesse L. (1783–1842)
Lord, in Thy Presence Here.

Holman, M. Carl (b. 1919)
And on This Shore.
Letter across Doubt and Distance.
Mr. Z.
Notes for a Movie Script.
Picnic: the Liberated.
Song: "Dressed up in my melancholy."

Holmes, Abiel (1763–1837)
To Thee, O God.
Who Here Can Cast His Eyes Abroad.

Holmes, Georgiana Klingle. See "Klingle, George."

Holmes, Janet
Pastoral: "I don't know much about sheep, don't know."

Holmes, John (1904–62)
At a Country Fair.
Boy Reading.
Evening Meal in the Twentieth Century.
Good Night! Good Night!
Herself.
Letter to My Mother, Sels.
Map of My Country, A.
Maybe for Love.
Metaphor for My Son.
Misery.
Peace Is the Mind's Old Wilderness.
Poetry Defined.
Portrait: My Wife.
Rhyme of Rain.
Somerset Dam for Supper, The.
Thrifty Elephant, The.
When I Married.

Holmes, John Haynes (1879–1964)
God of the Nations, Near and Far.
Hymn: "Great Spirit of the speeding spheres."
Hymn: "Thou God of all, whose presence dwells."
O'er Continent and Ocean.
Voice of God Is Calling, The.

Holmes, Oliver Wendell (1809–94)
Additional Verses to Hail Columbia.
Aestivation [an Unpublished Poem, by My Late Latin Tutor].
After the Fire.
Angel of Peace, Thou Hast Wandered Too Long.
Angel-Thief, The.
Autocrat of the Breakfast Table, The, *Sels.*
Ballad of the Boston Tea-Party, A.
Ballad of the Oysterman, The.
Boys, The.
Broomstick Train, The, *Sels.*
Brother Jonathan's Lament for Sister Caroline.
Cacoëthes Scribendi.
Chambered Nautilus, The.
Contentment.
Daily Trials.
Daniel Webster.
Deacon's Masterpiece, The; or, The Wonderful "One-Hoss Shay."
Dorchester Giant, The.
Dorothy Q.
Familiar Letter to Several Correspondents, A.
Grandmother's Story of Bunker-Hill Battle.
Height of the Ridiculous, The.
Iron Gate, The, *Sels.*
It chanced to be our washing day.
Last Leaf, The.
Lexington.
Limerick [or An Eggstravagance or Henry Ward Beecher].
Look out! Look out, boys! Clear the track!
Lord of All Being, Throned Afar.
Many Things.
My Aunt.
O Love Divine, That Stooped to Share.
Ode for a Social Meeting.
Old Ironsides.
Old Man Dreams, The.
On the Death of President Garfield.
Our Father! While Our Hearts Unlearn.
Parody on "A Psalm of Life", A.
Poem: "Father of all! in Death's relentless claim."
Poem for the Meeting of the American Medical Association, A.
Poet at the Breakfast Table, The, *Sels.*
Poet's Lot, The.
Professor at the Breakfast Table, The, *Sels.*
Programme, *Sels.*
Reflections of a Proud Pedestrian.
Sea Dialogue, A.
September Gale, The, *Sels.*
Sherman's in Savannah.
Sun and Shadow.
To an Insect.
Turn my pages, — never mind.
Union and Liberty.
Welcome to the Nations.
Holmes, Ruth
No Thoroughfare.
Holmes, Timothy (b. 1936)
Deep.
Room for All.
Holmes, W. F.
Old Brown Horse, The.
Holmes, W. K.
Dream Ship, The.
Holst, Henriëtte Roland-. *See* **Roland-Holst, Henriëtte.**
Holt, Jane (*fl.* 1701–1717)
To Mr. Wren, My Valentine Six Year Old.
Holtby, Mary
Answer to a Kind Enquiry.
Dawn Chorus.
Limerick: "Said Mars when entangled with Venus."
Limerick: "There once was a lass of Shalott."
Limerick: "There once was monarch called Harry."
Sister Swallow to Swinburne.
Hölty, Ludwig Heinrich Christoph (1748–76)
Harvest Song.
Love Song: "More pleasing sounds the song of the birds."

May Night, The.
To the Nightingale.
Holub, Miroslav (b. 1923)
Achilles and the Tortoise.
Biodrama.
Boy's Head, A.
Brief Reflection on Accuracy.
Brief Reflection on Cats Growing in Trees.
Brief Thoughts on cats Growing on Trees.
Brief Thoughts on Cracks.
Brief Thoughts on Floods.
Bullfight.
Cinderella.
Conversation with a Poet.
Corporal Who Killed Archimedes, The.
Death in the Evening.
Distant Howling.
End of the World, The.
Fairy Tale.
Five Minutes after the Air Raid.
Fly, The.
Forest, The.
Great and Strong.
Half a Hedgehog.
Helping Hand, A.
History Lesson, A.
How to Paint a Perfect Christmas.
In the Miscroscope.
Interferon.
Inventions.
Jewish Cemetery at Olsany, Kafka's Grave, April, Sunny Weather, The.
Lesson, THe.
Man Cursing the Sea.
Napoleon.
Silence.
Suffering.
Swans in Flight.
Wings.
Zito the Magician.
Holyday, Barten (1593–1661)
Bogs, purgatory, wolves and ease, by fame.
Clay, sand, and rock, seem of a diff'rent birth.
Pride cannot see itself by mid-day light.
Song: "O harmless feast."
Technogamia, *Sels.*
Holz, Arno (1863–1929)
Buddha.
Leave-Taking, A.
On a mountain of sugar-candy.
Phantasus, *Sels.*
Roses Red.
"Home, Cecil." *See* **Webster, Augusta Davies.**
Homer (*fl.* before 700 B.C.)
Achilles with wild fury in his heart.
Ajax the swift swerv'd never from the side.
Alike he thwarts the hospitable end.
All grave old men, and souldiers they had bene, but for age.
And as in winter time when Jove his cold-sharpe javelines throwes.
And as when with the West-wind's flawes the sea thrusts up her waves.
And now Eurynome had bath'd the king.
And now his well-known bow the master bore.
And now man-slaughtering Pallas took in hand.
And now the Queene of women had intent.
And now was Paris come/ From his high towres.
And when they came together in one place.
Andromache's Lament for Hector.
Andromache's Lamentation.
As when an architect some palace wall.
As when devouring flames some forest seize.
As when of frequent bees.
As when the winds, ascending by degrees.
Ascend my shoulders, firmly keep thy seat.
At her departure his disdain return'd.
At this th' impatient hero sowrly smil'd.
Battle of the Frogs and Mice, The, *Sels.*
Big with great purposes and proud, they sat.
Bright-footed Thetis did the sphere aspire.
But ere sterne conflict mixt both strengths, faire Paris stept before.
But now, no longer deaf to honour's call.
Catalogue of the Ships, The.

Cave we found, but vacant all within, The.
Downe to the king's most bright-kept baths they went.
Embodied close, the lab'ring Grecian train.
Fierce they drove on, impatient to destroy.
For my part, I'le not meddle with the cause.
Frail as the leaves that quiver on the sprays.
From her bed's high and odoriferous roome.
From Phylace, and from the flow'ry fields.
Gardens of Alcinous, The.
Ghost of Patroclus, The.
God who mounts the winged winds, The.
He ended, nor the Argicide refus'd.
He spake, to whom I, answ'ring, thus replied.
Hector Arms.
Hector's Defiance.
Helen's Lamentation.
His hand came out of the east.
Homer and the Brazen Head of Rumour.
Homer's Gift of Fame.
Hornets occasionally build their nests near roads.
Iliad, The, *Sels.*
Just then, forgetful of the strict command.
Like leaves on trees the race of man is found.
Meanwhile the troops beneath Patroclus' care.
Mighty wave rush'd o'er him as he spoke, A.
Neptune Goes to the Greeks.
New Coasts and Poseidon's Son.
Nor lingered Paris in the lofty house.
Nor long the trench or lofty walls oppose.
Now front to front the hostile armies stand.
Now gently winding up the fair ascent.
Now side by side, with like unweary'd care.
Now to dispose the dead, the care remains.
Now toils the Heroe; trees on trees o'erthrown.
Now when the solemn rites of pray'r were past.
Now, when twelve days complete had run their race.
Nymph turnd home, The. He fell to felling downe.
Odyssey, *Sels.*
Oileus by his brother's side stood close.
Priam and Achilles.
Proposition and Invocation.
Sarpedon's Speech.
She thus; when I had great desire to prove.
Shield of Achilles, The.
So saying, light-foot Iris passed away.
Son of Enops, Thestor next he smote, The.
Their ardour kindless all the Grecian pow'rs.
Their ground they stil made good.
Then first he form'd th' immense and solid shield.
Then rising in his rage above the shores.
There grew two olives, closest of the grove.
There sate the seniors of the Trojan Race.
This said, he reacht to take his sonne.
This spoke, a huge wave tooke him by the head.
Thus at the panting dove a falcon flies.
Thus charg'd he; nor Argicides denied.
Thus to Glaucus spake/ Divine Sarpedon.
To the Earle of Somerge.
Trembling the spectres glide, and plaintive vent.
Trojans Outside the Walls, The.
Troops exulting sate in order round, The.
Twelve herds of oxen, no less flockes of sheepe.
Ulysses Insults over the Cyclops.
Ulysses Invokes the Dead.
Ulysses Leaves the Nymph Calypso.
Unweary'd watch their list'ning leaders keep, Th'.
Where neither King nor shepheard want comes neare.
While thus he thought, a monst'rous wave up-bore.
Who dwelt in [or Pylos] sandie soyle, and [or Arene] the faire.
Why boast we, Glaucus! our extended reign.
Why dost thou so explore.
With many a weary step, and many a groan.
Wrath of Peleus son, O muse, resound, The.
Youth there was, Elpenor was he nam'd, A.

Homer-Dixon, Homera
New Year, The.
Homfray, Francis (*fl.* **c. 1817**)
Thoughts on Happiness.
Hone, William
Bath, The.
Honestus (*fl.* **A.D. 40**)
I would never marry a young girl or an old woman.
Requirements ("Not too old, and not too young").
Thebes.
Very day one son was drowned, The.
Honeywood, St. John (1763–98)
Radical Song of 1786, A.
Hongo, Garrett Kaoru (b. 1951)
Four Chinatown Figures.
Legend, The.
Mendocino Rose.
Pier, The.
Roots.
Something Whispered in the *Shakuhachi*.
Underworld, The.
Unreal Dwelling: My Years in Volcano, The.
Who Among You Knows the Essence of Garlic?
Winnings.
Yellow Light.
Honig, Edwin (b. 1919)
Being Somebody.
Bodega, Goodbye.
1925.
November through a Giant Copper Beech.
Now, My Usefullness Over.
Tête-à-Tête.
Through You.
To Restore a Dead Child, *Sels*.
Walt Whitman.
Who.
Hood, E. P. (d. 1885)
God, Who Hath Made the Daisies.
Hood, Thomas (1799–1845)
Address to Mr. Cross, of Exeter 'Change, on the Death of the Elephant.
Athol Brose.
Autumn.
Bed-time.
Born in wealth and wealthily nursed.
Bridge of Sighs, The.
Butcher, A.
Carelesse Nurse Mayd, The.
Centipede along the threshold crept, The.
Death of Leander, The.
Death-Bed, The.
Domestic Asides; or, Truth in Parentheses.
Domestic Poems, *Sels*.
Dream Fairy, The.
Dream of Eugene Aram [the Murderer], The.
Dust to Dust.
Epicurean Reminiscences of a Sentimentalist.
Epigram: "When would-be suicides in purpose fail."
Fair Ines.
Fairy's Reply to Saturn, The.
Faithless Nelly Gray.
Faithless Sally Brown.
False Poets and True.
Farewell, Life.
Flying Visit, A.
Friendly Address, A.
Gold.
Good Night.
Green Dryad's Plea, The.
Haunted House, The, *Sels*.
Her Accident.
Her Christening.
Her Death.
Her Education.
Her Precious Leg.
Hero and Leander, *Sels*.
I Remember, I Remember.
Irish Schoolmaster, The.
It Was Not in the Winter.
Lament of Toby the Learned Pig, The.
Lay of Real Life, A, *Sels*.

Little Piggies, The.
Love.
Lullaby, O, Lullaby.
Mary's Ghost.
Melodies of Time, The.
Miss Kilmansegg and Her Precious Leg, *Sels*.
No!
Nocturnal Sketch, A.
Ode on a Distant Prospect of Clapham Academy.
Ode to the Cameleopard.
On a Royal Demise.
On the Death of the Giraffe.
Our Village — by a Villager.
Parental Ode to My Son, Aged Three Years and Five Months, A.
Plea of the Midsummer Fairies, The, *Sels*.
Poet's Fate, The.
Poor dear dead have been laid out in vain, The.
Quadrupedremian Song, A.
Reflection, A.
Ruth.
Sally Simpkin's Lament [or John Jones's Kit-Cat-astrophe].
Scylla's Lament.
Sea of Death, The.
Shakespeare: The Fairies' Advocate.
She Is Far from the Land.
Silence.
Song of the Shirt, The.
Song of the Shirt, The, *Sels*.
Sonnet: "It is not death, that sometime in a sigh."
Sonnet to Vauxhall.
Sonnet Written in Keats's *Endymion*.
Stars Are with the Voyager, The.
Sun Was Slumbering in the West, The.
Tim Turpin.
To ——: "I gaze upon a city."
To Henrietta, on Her Departure for Calais.
To Minerva.
Two Swans, The.
Water Lady, The.
What Different Dooms Our Birthdays Bring!
Who, gratis, shared my social glass.
World Is with Me, The.
Ye tourists and travellers, bound to the Rhine.
Hood, Tom (Thomas Hood, Jr.) (1835–74)
Ballad of the Basking Shark, The.
Confounded Nonsense.
How Singular.
Muddled Metaphors.
Ravings.
Sunset in the Sea.
Hooey, M. J. Slim
I have come to terms with the future.
Hook, Theodore (1788–1841)
Cautionary Verses to Youth of Both Sexes.
Hooker, Jeremy (b. 1941)
As a Thousand Years.
Behind the Lights.
Brynbeidog.
Dragons in the Snow.
From a Pill-Box on the Solent.
Gull on a Post.
Landscape of the Daylight Moon.
On Saint David's Day.
Pitts Deep.
Rice Grass.
Soft Days After Snow.
Take a long view from Mynydd Bach.
Wind Blew Once.
Hookes, N. (1628–1712)
To Amanda Walking in the Garden.
Hooley, Teresa
War Film, A.
Hooper, Ellen S. (1812–48)
Duty.
Hooper, Lucy Hamilton (1835–93)
Three Loves.
Hooper, Peter (b. 1919)
Pencilled by the Rain.
Hooton, Earnest Albert (1887–1954)
Ode to a Dental Hygienist.

Hooton, Harry (1908–1961)
Sweet Disorder in the Dress, A.
Hoover, Paul (b. 1946)
Desire.
Long History of the Short Poem.
Novel, The, *Sels*.
Ode to the Protestant Poets.
Poems We Can Understand.
School for Objects, The.
Trumpet Voluntary.
Twenty-Five.
Hope, Alec Derwent (b. 1907)
Advice to Young Ladies.
As Well as They Can ("As well as it can, the hooked fish while it dies").
Ascent into Hell.
Australia.
Bed, The.
Beware of Ruins.
Blason, A.
Bounce to Pope.
Brides, The.
Chorale: "Often had I found her fair."
Circe.
Coasts of Cerigo, The.
Commination, A.
Death of the Bird, The.
Double Looking Glass, The.
Dunciad Minor, *Sels*.
E Questo il Nido in Che la Mia Fenice?
Easter Hymn.
Elegy: "Madam, no more! The time has come to eat."
Faustus.
Female Principle, The.
Gateway, The.
Hay Fever.
House of God, The.
Imperial Adam.
Inscription for a War.
Lament for the Murderers.
Letter to David Campbell on the Birthday of W. B. Yeats, 1965, A.
Lingam and the Yoni, The.
Lot and His Daughters I.
Lot and His Daughters II.
Loving Kind.
Martyrdom of St. Theresa, The.
Meditation on a Bone.
Moschus Moschiferus.
Now Muse assist me, aptly to describe.
Observation Car.
On an Engraving by Casserius.
On Shakespeare Critics.
Parabola.
Paradise Saved.
Pleasure of Princes, The.
Prometheus Unbound.
School Of Night, The.
Tiger.
Hope, Allan. See Mutabaruka.
Hope, Christopher (b. 1944)
Flight of the White South Africans, The.
Lines on a Boer War Pin-up Girl Seen in the Falcon Hotel, Bude.
Hope, Francis (b. 1938)
Peeping Tom.
Hope, James Barron (1829–87)
John Smith's Approach to Jamestown.
"Hope, Laurence" (Adela Florence Cory Nicolson) (1815–1904)
Carpe Diem.
For This Is Wisdom.
In the Early, Pearly Morning, *Sels*.
Kashmiri Song.
Teak Forest, The, *Sels*.
Youth.
Hope, T.
Death Again.
Hopes, David Brendon (b. 1953)
Lament for Turlough O'Carolan.
Hopkins, Ellice
Life in Death.
Hopkins, Gerard Manley (1844–89)
Alchemist in the City, The.

Lancer.
Last Poems, *Sels*.
Laws of God, the Laws of Man, The.
Lent Lily, The.
Loitering With a Vacant Eye.
Look Not in My Eyes, for Fear.
Loveliest of Trees [the Cherry Now].
March.
Mill-stream, now that noises cease, The.
My dreams are of a field afar.
New Mistress, The.
Night Is Freezing Fast, The.
Now Dreary Dawns the Eastern Light.
Now hollow fires burn out to black.
O Billows Bounding Far.
O Have You Caught the Tiger?
Oh, See How Thick the Goldcup Flowers.
Oh stay at home, my lad, and plough.
Oh, When I Was in Love with You.
Oh Who Is That Young Sinner with the
   Handcuffs on His Wrists?
Olive, The.
On Moonlit Heath and Lonesome Bank.
On the idle hill of summer.
On Wenlock Edge the Wood's in Trouble.
Oracles, The.
Others, I Am Not the First.
Parta Quies.
Purple William or The Liar's Doom.
Rain, it streams on stone and hillock, The.
Rainy Pleiads Wester, The.
Recruit, The.
Reveille.
Revolution.
Shades of Night, The.
Shake hands, we shall never be friends, all's
   over.
Shot? So Quick, So Clean an Ending?
Shropshire Lad, A, *Sels*.
Sigh that heaves the grasses, The.
Sinner's Rue.
Sloe was lost in flower, The.
Soldier from the Wars Returning.
Some can gaze and not be sick.
Stars Have Not Dealt Me, The.
Stars, I Have Seen Them Fall.
Street Sounds to the Soldiers' Tread, The.
Strong Love.
Tell Me Not Here [It Needs Not Saying].
Terence, This Is Stupid Stuff.
They Say My Verse Is Sad: No Wonder.
Think no more, lad; laugh, be jolly.
This Time of Year a Twelvemonth Past.
'Tis spring; come out to ramble.
To an Athlete Dying Young.
To Stand Up Straight.
True Lover, The.
Wake Not for the World-heard Thunder.
We'll to the Woods No More.
Welsh Marches, The.
Wenlock Edge (" 'Tis time, I think; by
   Wenlock town").
When Adam Day by Day.
When Adam Walked in Eden Young.
When I was One-and-Twenty.
When I Watch the Living Meet.
When Israel out of Egypt Came.
When Smoke Stood up from Ludlow.
When the bells justle in the tower.
When the Eye of Day Is Shut.
When the Lad for Longing Sighs.
White in the Moon the Long Road Lies.
With Rue My Heart Is Laden.
World goes none the lamer, The.
Yonder See the Morning Blink.
You Smile upon Your Friend To-day.

Housman, Laurence (1865–1959)
All Fellows, *Sels*.
Continuing City, The.
Dear love, when with a two-fold mind.
Dedication: "When I have ended, then I see."
Gardener, The.
Spikenard.

Houston, Douglas (b. 1947)
Devotions.
Horst Wessel on Alcatraz.

To the Management.
Houston, Libby (b. 1941)
House, A.
Judging Lear.
Old Woman and the Sandwiches, The.
Post-War.
Scales.
Story of Canobie Dick, The.
Houston, Peyton (b. 1910)
Canzone: "Love, which is least sure and most
   dared, the pure, keen."
Doll, The.
Quick Gold, Slant Blue, Sharp Scarlet, The.
Sonnet Variations, *Sels*.
Time's Mirror.
Houston, Virginia A.
Class Room.
Ecstasy.
Hovanessian, Diana Der
Anniversary Poem, The.
Armenian Looking at Newsphotos of the
   Cambodian Deathwatch, An.
At Mt. Auburn Cemetery.
Poultry.
Radio Yerevan.
Rain.
Song of Bread.
Without You I Am.
Hovanessian, Diana Der. *See* **Hovanessian,
   Diana Der.**
Hove, Chenjerai
Child's Parliment.
Country Life.
Lost Bird.
Migratory Bird ("One day he perched. . .")
Other Syllabus, The.
Red Hills of Home.
You Will Forget.
Hovell, Jim
Landscape with Tanks.
**Hovell-Thurlow, Edward, 2d Baron Thurlow
   (1781–1829)**
May.
Hover, Emily
Mr. Beetle.
Hovey, Richard (1864–1900)
Barney McGee.
Battle of Manila, The.
Birth of Galahad, The, *Sels*.
Call of the Bugles, The.
Distillation.
Eleazar Wheelock.
Evening on the Potomac.
Immanence.
In a Silence.
Isabel.
Kavin Again.
Laurana's Song.
More Songs from Vagabondia, *Sels*.
Premonition.
Sea Gypsy, The.
Secrets.
Speech and Silence.
Taliesin, *Sels*.
Three of a Kind.
Transcendence.
Unmanifest Destiny.
Vagabondia.
Word of the Lord from Havana, The.
**Howard, Anne, Duchess of Arundel (1557–
   1630)**
Good Shepherd's Sorrow for the Death of His
   Beloved Son, The.
Howard, Ben (b. 1944)
Diver, The.
Lynx.
Winter Report.
Howard, Dorothy S. (b. 1921)
Birkett's Eagle.
Howard, Frances Minturn
Heron in Swamp.
Narcissus in a Cocktail Glass.
Sampler from Haworth.
Howard, Joy
Casablanca Time Again.

Vanilla Sugar; or, Verse for a "Hallmark"
   Greeting Card.
You Can't Go to the Moon There's No Trains.
Howard, Leonard (1699?–1764)
Humours of the King's Bench Prison, a Ballad,
   The.
Howard, Richard (b. 1929)
Again for Hephaistos, the Last Time.
At the Monument to Pierre Louÿs.
Aubade: Donna Anna to Juan, Still Asleep.
Author of *Christine*, The.
Bonnard; a Novel.
Comedy of Art: Henri de Toulouse Lautrec,
   The.
Compulsive Qualifications, *Sels*.
Crepuscular.
Far Cry after a Close Call, A.
Gaiety, *Sels*.
Giovanni da Fiesole on the Sublime; or, Fra
   Angelico's "Last Judgment."
Ithaca: The Palace at Four A.M., *Sels*.
Landed: A Valentine.
Last Words.
Nadar.
Natural History.
On Arrival.
On Tour.
Oystering.
Personal Values.
Queer's Song.
Recipe for an Ocean in the Absence of the Sea.
Richard, may I ask a question? What is an
   episteme?
Richard, what will it be like when you ask the
   questions?
Saturday Morning.
Secular Games.
209 Canal.
Venetian Interior, 1889.
Victor Vanquished, The.
What Word Did the Greeks have for It?
Wildflowers.
**Howard, Sir Robert (1626–98) *and* John
   Dryden**
Indian Queen, The, *Sels*.
Poor mortals that are clogged with earth below.
To the Unconstant Cynthia.
Howard, Winifred (d. 1909)
Windy Day, A.
Howard-Jones, Stuart (1904–74)
Hibernia.
Howarth, B. L.
Brown paper worn next to the skin.
Howcroft, Wilbur G.
Personable Porcupine, The.
Howe, Fanny (b. 1940)
But I, Too, Want to Be a Poet.
Nursery, The.
Howe, George
Sun-Witch to the Sun, The.
Howe, Joseph (1804–73)
Acadia, *Sels*.
Howe, Julia Ward (1819–1910)
Battle Hymn of the [American] Republic, The.
Decoration Day.
J. A. G.
Kosmos.
Middle Age.
Mother's Day Proclamation of 1870.
New Sculptor, A.
Our Country.
Pardon.
Parricide.
Robert E. Lee.
Rough Sketch, The.
Save the Old South!
Soul-hunter, The.
Spring-blossoms.
Tea-party, The.
Telegrams, The.
Thought for Washing Day, A.
Wedding, The.
Wild Night, A.
Howe, Marie (b. 1950)
Death, the Last Visit.

Ishikawa Takuboku (1885–1920)
Act like a wizard.
All I'd wanted was to get on a train.
As if my thoughts were secretly listened to.
By accident I broke a rice bowl.
By the eastern sea.
Calling out the station name as if singing.
Chin buried in the collar of my overcoat.
Come to think of it.
Coming in front of a mirror store.
Cover myself with the quilt.
Die for a thing like that?
Even while pillowing her lap.
Everyone's/ heading in the same direction.
For fun I carried mother on my back.
For thinking somehow tomorrow will bring
    something good.
Forty-seven Tanka in Three Lines, *Sels.*
Heart felt/ as if being sucked into a very dark
    hole.
I believe in the coming of a new tomorrow, I
    say.
I get anxious to die, at times.
I got out and for about five blocks.
I look at my dirty hands.
I push the door and step out.
I said those words casually.
I scolded my child.
It rains,/ and the people of my house look
    depressed.
Let down, I stood in the hall.
Like a weak-minded scout.
Little man I always see on the streetcar, The.
Name known, but no relations or kin in this
    place.
No better than the ordinary in talent.
Nurse's hand taking my pulse, The.
Old letters!/ I was on such familiar terms.
On the sand of a sandhill.
On the way, a whim, I changed my mind.
Parted, I came away and years have passed.
Sadness of the lifeless sand.
Somehow,/ I feel there are more people than I
    expect.
Taking off my gloves, my hands stop.
That creepy feeling you have.
That kiss from the past.
Those days I didn't even notice.
Though I close my eyes.
Uneventfully/ and pleasantly I go on putting on
    weight.
Useless letter, long, yet to be finished, A.
Vague sadness, A.
Water spurting out of a pump, The.
When was it?
Wishing someone would.

Ish-Kishor, Sulamith
War.

Ishpriya
O Lord.
O Lord,/ One tiny bit of water rests on the
    palm of my hand.
Sandhya.

Isidorus (d. 450?)
My name is Eteocles. The sea seduced me from
    my farm.
Now Endymion dedicates/ his cold bed's failure
    to the moon.
On a Fowler.

Isler, Elizabeth
Little Things, The.

Issa (Kobayashi Issa) (1763–1827)
Among the fleeing silverfish.
Another round of farting.
Awakened by a horse's fart, I see a firefly in
    the air.
Awakened by someone gnashing his teeth.
Beautiful — the sky.
Big cat teases a butterfly, A.
Blossom drops, and that, A.
Buddha's Birthday: April 8, 1819.
Buddha's Death Day: February 15, 1815.
Butterfly comes and takes a butterfly, A.
By a clump of grass.
Cold night: I keep a vigil.
Departing wild geese.

Door-latch rusted, A.
Dragonflies' resting place.
Falling leaves, making no sound.
Firefly: a frog opens his mouth a bit.
Flying out from.
For a fresh start.
Forty-four Hokku, *Sels.*
Frog keeps still, A.
Frog looks at me, A.
Frogs play hide-and-seek.
From a brat's sleeve.
Great sky splendidly darkens, The.
Heaven's River.
Huge firefly, undulating, A.
I know, I know it.
I let the sparrows play.
In the autumn wind a beggar.
In the cherry blossom's shade.
I've survived, I've survived.
Just one mosquito raises a fuss.
Kitten twirls around, A.
Laconic crow flies by, A.
Lending a branch of his antlers.
Lying on the ground, I pick young herbs.
Man pulling radishes, The.
Mosquito larva plays alone, A.
Mother, A.
Mountain mist: a horse-dung cleaner.
Must be a good day.
On a potato leaf, by a dewdrop, a snail.
On the heavily loaded bull's head.
One person.
Only one guy and.
Oraga Haru, *Sels.*
Pissing and trembling.
Shrike call takes a persimmon thief, A.
Snow.
Snow gone, the village fills up.
Snowy day: the temple hall's.
Sparrow goes in and out of jail, A.
Sparrows' friendship breaks up.
Through a long night.
Wild geese gone, the cove looks cleared.
Wild Goose, Wild Goose.
Willow tickles awake, A.
World of dew is, The.
Wren, The.

Issahakian, Avedik (1875–1957)
Mirage, The.

Issaia, Nana (b. 1934)
Dream.
Sacrifice.

Ita, Saint (480–570)
Jesukin.

Ivanov, Vyacheslav Ivanovich (1866–1949)
Holy Rose, The.

Iverson, Lucille
Outrage.

Ives, George (1867–1950)
Message, A.
Once.

Izumi Shikibu, Lady (c. 974–c. 1030)
After the Death of Her Daughter in Child-birth.
Another cruel letter today.
As the rains of spring.
At the Sutra Chanting of Her Dead Daughter.
Aware that your body cannot follow.
Breaking off rock azaleas.
Dew that formed remains, The.
Don't tell people how it was.
Down the mountain into the path of darkness.
Elegies for Her Daughter, Ko-Shikibu ("That
    she may know I love her and miss her").
Elegies for Prince Atsumichi ("Because I do not
    know where you are").
Elegies for Prince Atsumichi ("Clearly he
    would notice: in my eyes").
Elegies for Prince Atsumichi ("Dead people
    come to visit tonight").
Elegies for Prince Atsumichi ("Discard
    myself — just the thought is bitter").
Elegies for Prince Atsumichi ("I miss your
    voice as you talked to me").
Elegies for Prince Atsumichi ("I wish I could
    see you like this snow").

Elegies for Prince Atsumichi ("It would console
    me to see you").
Elegies for Prince Atsumichi ("No dreams
    through the night").
Elegies for Prince Atsumichi ("One body, but
    heart shattered into a thousand pieces").
Elegies for Prince Atsumichi ("Though my
    heart isn't a summer field").
Elegies for Prince Atsumichi ("You are gone,
    and I have nothing unhappy to remember").
Even my pillow, not knowing, won't talk.
Fifty-one Tanka, *Sels.*
From darkness/ I go onto the road/ of darkness.
From Prince Atsumichi ("I tell myself not to
    doubt you").
From that first night.
Harbor plovers calling to their friends.
Having waited for this one for this.
Here in this world/ I won't live.
I go out of darkness/ Onto a road of darkness.
I left my hills.
I look around: because charcoal firing warms
    the air.
I want to see and be seen by you.
I wish you would come.
If I should forget you because of this
    unhappiness.
If you have no time.
If you love me.
If you'd left me unhappy and hadn't come.
In Reply ("Don't keep your heart from
    resenting me").
In Reply ("I don't think you are like everyone
    else").
In the dusk the path.
It is the time of rain and snow.
Less troublesome than unforgettable.
Looking at My Grandchildren.
Lost in thought — even the firefly from the
    marsh.
Loving you, my heart may shatter.
Lying here alone.
Moon above the clouds doesn't look like the
    moon, The.
Never could I think/ Our love a worldly
    commonplace.
No soothing time for someone who thinks of
    blossoms.
No wonder you're grieved this morning.
On nights when hail/ falls noisily.
On spring fields there was only snow.
On this winter night.
Orange leaves are gone.
Out of the darkness/ on a dark path.
Pillow that knows all, The.
Plum fragrance startles me again and again.
Recklessly/ I cast myself away.
Since that night/ I cannot know myself.
Someone else/ looked at the sky.
There's no color called love in this world.
To a Man I Met Only Briefly.
To a Man Who Left Me Early in My Life.
To a Man Who Said, "You've forgotten me."
To a Sage in Harima.
To Someone, when I Was Distressed.
Today again, quietly and leisurely I make my
    ablutions.
Tonight, as hail falls on bamboo leaves.
Unaware of my black hair in disorder.
Watching the moon.
We retain the flowers in mind as we pass.
When you broke from me.
Which is worse, to love someone far away.
Which is worse, to miss someone dead.
Which should I think shouldn't exist in this
    world.
You left, the mist lingered by the hedge.
You rose with eastern clouds and left.
You told me it was/ because of me.
You wear the face.

J

Day at the Farm, A.

Kaplinski, Jaan (b. 1941)
Once I got a postcard from the Fiji Islands.
Kappiyarrukkappiyanar
Harvest of War.
Karélli, Zoé (b. 1901)
Exhumation.
Presences.
Karibo, Minji
Superstition.
Kariuki, Joseph E. (b. 1931)
New Life.
Karni, Yehuda (1884–1949)
Place Me in the Breach.
Put Me into the Breach.
Woman's Prayer, A.
Károlyi, Amy (b. 1909)
Third House, The, *Sels.*
Karp, Vickie
Elegy: "Light on the table so capable of
 leaving."
Elegy, *Sels.*
Getting Dressed in the Dark.
Glass.
Goodbye.
Police Sift New Clues in Search for Beauty.
Tulips: A Selected History.
Karpowicz, Tymoteusz (b. 1921)
Dog Which Barked Itself Out, The.
Hunting.
Lesson of Silence, A.
Love.
Pencil's Dream, The.
Rifle, The.
Silence.
Kartun, D.
Limerick: "There was a young girl of Uttoxeter/
 Who noticed that men waved their cocks at
 her."
Kasa no Iratsume (*fl.* 8th century)
Evening comes and sorrow crowds my mind.
Gods of heaven are irrational, The.
I dreamed I held/ A sword against my flesh.
I love and fear him.
To love somebody/ Who doesn't love you.
To love someone/ Who does not return that
 love.
When evening comes.
Kaschnitz, Marie Luise (1901–74)
Humility.
Resurrection.
Return to Frankfurt, *Sels.*
Kasdaglis, Lina (b. 1928)
Traffic Lights.
Kasdorf, Julia
Dying with Amish Uncles.
Green Market, New York.
Leftover Blessings.
Mennonites.
Uncle.
Vesta's Father.
What I Learned from My Mother.
When Our Women Go Crazy.
Where We Are.
Kasenduaxtc
Throw him into the river.
Kasischke, Laura
For Malka Who Lived Three Days Dying.
Kasmuneh (*fl.* 12th–13th century)
Overripe Fruit.
Timid Gazelle, The.
Kassia (*fl.* 9th century)
Epigram: "Poverty? wealth? seek neither."
Epigram: "Wealth covers sin — the poor."
Epigram: "Woman working hard and wisely,
 A."
Lord, this woman who fell into many sins.
Selected Epigrams.
Sticheron for Matins, Wednesday of Holy
 Week.
Kästner, Erich (1899–1924)
Moral Taxi Ride, The.
Ragoût Fin de Siècle (with Reference to Certain
 Cafés).

Kataiyan Kannanar
In Praise of a Cremation Ground.
Katda
My wife went away, left me.
Katene-Horvath, Hera (b. 1912)
In Days Gone By.
Kato Kyotai (1732–92)
Cold night/ pasania nuts rolling down.
Column of mosquitoes, A.
Day ending/ and again it starts.
Daybreak/ whales trumpet.
Falling leaves/ fall and pile up.
Leaves falling/ on top of the smoke.
Melting snow/ among deep mountains clouded
 over.
Nights when the muddy river.
Observing as I go along.
On her way, the little nun.
Quivering/ in the heat waves.
Sixteen Hokku, *Sels.*
Start of winter.
Sun has set, The.
Waves are hot, The.
Winter shut in — / a single fly.
Kato Shuson (b. 1905)
Winter seagull, A.
Katrovas, Richard (b. 1953)
Beating, The.
Dog and a Boy, A.
Elegy for My Mother.
My Friends the Pigeons.
Public Mirror, The.
Katuvan Ilaveyinanar
Tirumal.
Katz, Dori (b. 1939)
Line-up.
Return, The.
Katzin, Olga. *See* "Sagittarius."
Kaufman, Bob (b. 1925)
African Dream.
Afterwards, They Shall Dance.
Bagel Shop Jazz.
Battle Report.
Benediction.
Blues Note.
Cincophrenicpoet.
Cocoa Morning.
Falling.
Geneology.
Heavy Water Blues.
I Have Folded My Sorrows.
Jazz Chick.
Mingus.
O-Jazz-O.
On.
Patriotic Ode on the Fourteenth Anniversary of
 the Persecution of Charlie Chaplin.
Round about Midnight.
To My Son Parker, Asleep in the Next Room.
Unholy Missions.
Walking Parker Home.
War Memoir.
Kaufman, Herbert
This Is Your Hour.
Kaufman, Shirley (b. 1923)
Abishag.
Always She Moves from Me.
Apples.
Beetle on the Shasta Daylight.
Dream of Completion, The.
He's learning to shoot.
His Wife.
I Hear You.
I see bodies in the morning kneel.
Looking at Henry Moore's Elephant Skull
 Etchings in Jerusalem during the War.
Mothers, Daughters.
Nechama.
Room.
There are caverns/ under our feet.
Watts, *Sels.*
We are going down a long slide.
Kaune, Gayle
Case Study.

Kavanagh, P. J. (b. 1931)
Birthday.
Praying.
Temperance Billiards Rooms, The.
Kavanagh, Patrick (1905–69)
Advent.
Ante-natal Dream.
April, and no one able to calculate.
Art McCooey.
Bluebells for Love.
Canal Bank Walk.
Candida ("Candida is one today").
Christmas Childhood, A, *Sels.*
Clay is the word and clay is the flesh.
Come Dance with Kitty Stobling.
Dear Folks.
Epic.
Father Mat, *Sels.*
Gold Watch.
Great Hunger, The, *Sels.*
He gave himself another year.
Health and wealth and love he too dreamed of
 in May.
Hospital, The.
I Had a Future.
I May Reap.
If Ever You Go to Dublin Town.
In a meadow/ Beside the chapel three boys
 were playing football.
In Memory of My Mother.
Inniskeen Road: July Evening.
Innocence.
Intimate Parnassus.
Is.
Kerr's Ass.
Leave Them Alone.
Lecture Hall.
Lines Written on a Seat on the Grand Canal,
 Dublin.
Long Garden, The.
Lough Derg.
Maguire is not afraid of death, the Church will
 light him a candle.
Memory of Brother Michael.
Memory of my Father.
My father played the melodion.
October.
On an apple-ripe September morning.
On Looking into E. V. Rieu's Homer.
One, The.
Peace.
Pegasus.
Ploughman.
Poor Paddy Maguire, a fourteen-hour day.
Prelude: "Give us another poem, he said."
Question to Life.
Sanctity.
Self-slaved, The.
Shancoduff.
Spraying the Potatoes.
Stony Grey Soil.
Tarry Flynn, *Sels.*
Tinker's Wife.
To Hell with Commonsense.
To the Man after the Harrow.
Kavarpentu
Mothers.
Kawai Chigetsu-ni (1632–1736)
Cats making love in the temple.
Grasshoppers/ Chirping in the sleeves.
"Kay"
Christmas Verse, A.
Kay, Jackie (b. 1961)
Angela Davis.
Baby Lazarus.
Bette Davis.
Diary of Days for Adjoa.
Generations, *Sels.*
Mother Poem (two), The.
Peony.
Sun went out just like that, The.
Telling Part, The.
That Distance Apart.
Visit, The.
Kaya Shirao
About the time I miss someone.

Guide to the Symphony.
Henry James at Newport.
Homage to Arthur Waley.
January.
June 1940.
La Vita Nuova.
1926.
Patient Is Rallying, The.
Problems of a Journalist.
Relating to Robinson.
River Song.
Robinson.
Robinson at Home.
Round: " 'Wondrous life!' cried Marvell at
    Appleton House."
Saratoga Ending.
Small Prayer.
Smiles of the Bathers, The.
There was a French writer named Sartre.
Wet Thursday.

Keesing, Nancy (b. 1923)
Queer Thing, A.
Reverie of a Mum.

Kefala, Antigone
Saturday Night.

Kegels, Anne-Marie (b. 1912)
I write to make you suffer.
Nocturnal Heart.
When I strip,/ stop walking/ and drop into
    sleep.

Kein, Sybil
Jazz.

Keiter, Anne
Past Love.

Keith, Bernard
Essay on Meter.

Keith, Joseph Joel
Definitions.
In the First House.

Keithley, George (b. 1935)
Donner Party, The, *Sels.*

Kell, Richard (b. 1927)
Spring Night.

Keller, Gottfried (1819–90)
Therese.

Keller, Helen (1880–1968)
In the Garden of the Lord.

Keller, Martha (b. 1902)
Deadfall.
Mountain Meadows.

Kelly, Blanche Mary (1881–1966)
Mirror, The.
Omniscience.

Kelly, Brigit Pegeen
Silver Lake.
Those Who Wrestle with the Angel for Us.
Wild Turkeys; The Dignity of the Damned.
Young Wife's Lament.

Kelly, David
Counting a Decade.

Kelly, Dennis (b. 1943)
Chicken.

Kelly, Isabella (c. 1759–1857)
To an Unborn Infant.

Kelly, Jenifer
If You Go Softly.

Kelly, Robert (b. 1934)
Book of Persephone, The, *Sels.*
Dance, The.
Earth is a woman who imagines us. She sings.
Flower for the New Year, A.
Fourth Ode to Persephone.
Glade, The.
Last Light.
Ninth Matter: Shape.
Persephone is the woman buried.
Poem for Easter.
Prefix.
Re: Snow Jobs/ We Have Got.
Second Ode to Persephone.
Sound, The.
Tenth Matter: Story.
Third Ode to Persephone.

Versions.

Kelly, Roy (b. 1949)
Death, Don't Be Boring.
Ode to a Nightingale.

Kelly, Walt (b. 1913)
Boston Charlie.
How Low Is the Lowing Herd.

Kelpius, Johannes (1673?–1708)
I Love My Jesus Quite Alone.

Kelso, Ian
Busy Old Fool.

Kemal Khojandi (d. 1401?)
One Final Fling.

Kemble, Frances Anne (Fanny) (1809–93)
Absence, *Sels.*
Faith.
To Shakespeare.
What Shall I Do?
Wish, A.

Kemp, Harry Hibbard (1883–1960)
God the Architect.
He Did Not Know.
Hummingbird [*or* Humming Bird], The.
Prayer: "I kneel not now to pray that Thou."
Seaman's Confession of Faith, A.

Kemp, Jan (b. 1949)
Letter to the Immigration Officer.
Poem: "Puriri moth's wing, A."
"When the Wild Goose Finds Food He Calls
    His Comrades" — *I Ching.*

Ken, Thomas (1637–1711)
Evening Hymn, An.
Glory to Thee, My God, This Night.
Morning Hymn.

Kendall, Henry Clarence (1839–82)
Bell-Birds.
Beyond Kerguelen.
Christmas Creek.
Last of His Tribe, The.
Mooni.
Orara.

**Kendall, John Kaye ("Dum-Dum") (1869–
1952)**
My Last Illusion.

Kendall, Laura E.
Evening Prayer, An.

Kendall, Timothy (*fl.* 1577)
Desire of Dominion.
Difference Between a King and a Tyrant, The.
Of a Good Prince and an Evil.
Tyrant in Sleep, Naught Differeth from a
    Common Man, A.
Upon the Grave of a Beggar.

Kendon, Frank
Looker-On, The.

Kennedy, Benjamin Hall (1804–89)
Memorial Lines on the Gender of Latin
    Substantives.
On ["Who Wrote Icon Basilike" by Dr.]
    Christopher Wordsworth, Master of Trinity.
Roman Calendar, The.

Kennedy, Edwin O. (b. 1900)
Prayer for Charity, A.

Kennedy, G. A. Studdert-. *See* **Studdert-
Kennedy, Geoffrey Anketell.**

Kennedy, Gerta
Chesapeake.

Kennedy, James (1793–1827)
Chased from my calling to this hackneyed
    trade.
Exile's Reveries, The, *Sels.*

Kennedy, Mary
Indolent Gardener, The.
Unfortunate Mole, The.

Kennedy, Susan
Dancing with the Dog.

Kennedy, Walter (c.1460–c.1508)
Honour with Age.

Kennedy, X. J. (b. 1929)
Aged Wino's Counsel to a Young Man on the
    Brink of Marriage, The.
Ars Poetica.
Artificer.

At a Low Mass for Two Hot-Rodders.
Bee.
Birth Report.
Brats.
Bulsh, *Sels.*
Bulsh in the desert prays, and camels bawl.
Cross Ties.
Different Door, A.
Down in Dallas.
Driving Cross-Country.
Edgar's Story, *Sels.*
Epitaph for a Postal Clerk.
Father and Mother.
First Confession.
For Jed.
From Emily Dickinson in Southern California.
Golgotha.
Great-great Grandma, Don't Sleep in Your
    Treehouse Tonight.
Hangover Mass.
In a Prominent Bar in Secaucus [One Day].
Japanese Beetles.
Joshua.
Keep a Hand on Your Dream.
Last Child.
Last Lines.
Last Lines on a Wrestler.
Little Elegy.
Loose Woman.
Medusa.
Mingled Yarns.
Mother's Nerves.
Nothing in Heaven Functions as It Ought.
Nude Descending a Staircase.
On a Child Who Lived One Minute.
On the Proposed Seizure of Twelve Graves in a
    Colonial Cemetery.
One Winter Night in August.
Rondel: "World is taking off her clothes, The."
Self-Exposed, The.
Snapshots, *Sels.*
Snicketty Snacketty Sneeze.
Terse Elegy for J.V. Cunningham.
To an Angry God.
To Dorothy on Her Exclusion from the
    Guinness Book of World Records.
Whales off Wales, The.
Witnesses, The.

Kennelly, Brendan (b. 1936)
Bread.
Dream of a Black Fox.
Example, An.
Glimpse of Starlings, A.
Horsechestnuts.
Horse's Head, The.
In the Sea.
Island, The.
Limerick Train, The.
Manager, Perhaps?
Master.
My Dark Fathers.
Nails.
Pilgrim, The.
Plans.
Poem from a Three Year Old.
Position of Praise, The.
Proof.
Rebecca Hill.
Running Battle, A.
Swimmer, The.
Thatcher, The.
Visitor, The.
Wound, A.
Yes.

Kenner, Peggy Susberry (b. 1937)
Black Taffy.
Comments.
Image in the Mirror.
No Bargains Today.

Kennet of the Dene, 1st Baron. *See* **Young,
Edward Hilton, 1st Baron Kennet of the
Dene.**

Kenney, Richard (b. 1948)
Encantadas, The, *Sels.*
Evolution of the Flightless Bird, The.
Hours of the Day, The, *Sels.*

Koller, James (b. 1936)
I Have Cut an Eagle.
My paw is holy.
O Dirty Bird Yr Gizzard's Too Big & Full of
   Sand.
Some Magic.
Unreal Song of the Old, The.

Kolmar, Gertrud (1894–1943?)
Murder.
Out of the Darkness.
Paris.

Komey, Ellis Ayitey (1927–72)
Oblivion.

Komunyakaa, Yusef (b. 1947)
Blackberries.
Elegy for Thelonious.
Facing It.
February in Sydney.
Ia Drang Valley.
Landscape for the Disappeared.
My Father's Loveletters.
Saigon Bar Girls, 1975.
Sunday Afternoons.
Temples of Smoke.
Venus's-flytraps.
We Never Know.

Konek, Carol (b. 1934)
Daring.

Konishi Raizan. *See* **Raizan.**

Konopnicka, Maria (1842–1910)
Vision, A.

Kooser, Ted (b. 1939)
Abandoned Farmhouse.
Anniversary.
At Midnight.
At the End of the Weekend.
At the Office Early.
Beer Bottle.
Buffalo Skull, A.
Camera.
Central.
Child's Grave Marker, A.
First Snow.
Flying at Night.
For a Friend.
How to make Rhubarb Wine.
In January, 1962.
In the Basement of the Goodwill Store.
Myrtle.
Porch Swing in September.
Selecting a Reader.
Self-Portrait at Thirty-Nine.
Shooting a Farmhouse.
Very Old, The.
Widow, A.
Wild Pigs.
Year's End.
Yevtushenko.

Kopelke, Kendra (b. 1957)
Eager Street.

Kopp, Karl
Incident.

Kora Rumiko (b. 1932)
Woman.

Korelitz, Jean Hanff (b. 1961)
Brund.
Dream of Scorpions, A.
Spawn.

Korinna [or Corinna] (fl. c.500? B.C.)
Although I was her pupil,/ even I reproach
   Myrtis.
I blame Myrtis.
I come tonight to sing you songs.
I disapprove even of eloquent/ Myrtis.
I Korinna am here to sing the courage.
Kithairon sang of cunning Kronos.
Sehnsucht; or, What You Will.
Terpsichore looks kindly on me.
To the white-mantled maidens.
When he sailed into the harbor.
Will you sleep forever?

Korn, Rachel [or Rokhl] (1898–1982)
Keep Hidden from Me ("Keep from me all that
   I might comprehend!")

Koroneu
Funeral Eva.

Korran
What She Said to Her Girl Friend.

Körte, Sister Mary Norbert (b. 1934)
Cat, The.
Ghost Poem Five.
Rain to River to The Sea.
This Room of Trees & Moving Earth/ This
   Room Where No One Knows How Sky
   Begins.

Korwin, Yala
Little Boy with His Hands Up, The.
Passover Night 1942.

Kosovic, Ante (1882–1958)
Ah Dalmatia, if only I could send word of your
   dear sons.

Kostelanetz, Richard (b. 1940)
Concentric.
Disintegration.
Stringfive.
Stringfour.

Kovatattan
What Her Girl Friend Said to Her.

Kovner, Abba (b. 1918)
My Sister.

Kovur Kilar
Poet's Counsel, A ("You come from the line of
   a Cola king").
Poet's Counsel, A ("Your enemy is not the
   kind who wears").

Kowit, Steve (b. 1938)
Hate Mail.
It Was Your Song.
Josephine's Garden.
Renewal.
Swell Idea, A.
That smudge of mascara by your mouth.
When he pressed his lips to my mouth.

Koziol, Urszula (b. 1935)
Alarum.

Kräftner, Hertha (1928–51)
I idolize you with litanies.
Litanies, Sels.
You, pushed-in window in terribly beautiful
   countries!
You stony angel over the pain.

Krag, Vilhelm Andreas Wexels (1871–1933)
Bird Cried, A.
I Shall Have a Sweetheart.
While I Wait.

Kramer, Aaron (b. 1921)
They've lost it, lost it.
Westminster Synagogue.
Zudioska.

Kramer, Edgar Daniel
Sequence.

Krapf, Norbert (b. 1943)
Name of a Place, The.

Kraus, Karl (1874–1936)
Express Train.
On the Threshold.

Krauss, Ruth (b. 1901)
Beginning on Paper.
Snow Melting.

Kraut, Rochelle (b. 1952)
My Makeup.
No Regret.
Sheep.
We Laughed.

Kreiter-Kurylo, Carolyn
Leaving a Country Behind.

Kremer, Pem
Epiphany.

Kretzmer, Herbert
Limerick: "Kinky young girl from Uttoxeter,
   A."

Kreymborg, Alfred (1883–1966)
Life.
To W. C. W. M. D.

Kriebel, Casper (fl. mid–18th century)
Now Sleep My Little Child So Dear.

Krige, Uys (b. 1910)
Distant View.
Encounter.
Farm Gate.
Soldier, The.
Swallows over the Camp.
Taking of the Koppie, The.

Kriloff, Ivan Andreevich (1768–1844)
Peasant and the Sheep, The.

Krishnamurti, M. (b. 1912)
Spirit's Odyssey, The.

Krishnasami, Christine M.
Beside a stone three.

Kristensen, Tom (1893–1974)
Grass.

Krmpotic, Vesna (b. 1932)
December Forest, A.

Kroetsch, Robert (b. 1927)
Stone Hammer Poem.

Kroll, Judith (b. 1943)
Dick and Jane.
I Think of Housman Who Said the Poem Is a
   Morbid Secretion, like a Pearl.
Not Thinking of America.
Sestina: "Is this the object."

Krolow, Karl
Open Shutter, The.

Kruchenykh, Aleksei (1886–1968)
Battle of India and Europe.
Heights.

Kruger, Dorothy
Dark Dreaming.

Kruger, Fania (b. 1893)
Passover Eve.

Krysl, Marilyn
Grandmother.

Kshetrayya (fl. 17th century)
Dancing-Girl's Song.

Ku Hsiung (fl. c.928)
Tune: "Telling of Innermost Feelings."

Ku K'uang (725–814)
On the River.
Sonny.
Upon a Brook.
Written upon Returning to the Mountains.

Ku T'ai-ch'ing (1799–1876?)
Tune: "Partridge Sky" — Puppet Theater.
Tune: "Phoenix Hairpin" — Crab Apple.
Tune: "Ripples Sifting Sand" — Accompanying
   My Husband on a Spring Outing to Stone
   Pavilion.

Kuan Han-ch'ing (c. 1220–c. 1300)
Fear, as I see the spring go.
"Four Pieces of Jade" — Idle Leisure.
"Green Jade Flute", Sels.
Grief: I've grieved as a solitary phoenix
   grieves.
Heaven in the South, earth Northward.
"Intoxication in the East Wind", Sels.
Lightly she turns back her long red sleeves.
Snow powder, flowery.
"Song of Great Virtue" — Spring.
"Song of Great Virtue" — Winter, Sels.
"Sprig of Flowers, A" — Not Bowing to Old
   Age.
This autumn scene is worthy of the brush.
Toot once, strum once.
Wind sifts through the curtain.

Kuan P'an-p'an (fl. 8th–9th cent.)
Mourning.

Kuan Tao Sheng (1262–1319)
Married Love.

Kuan Yun She (fl. 13th cent.)
Seventh Day Seventh Month.

Kuan Yun-shih (1286–1324))
"Butterflies."
"Chilly East Wind."
"Coda."
"Going Up Small Pavilion."
"Happy Events Approaching."
Medley of Southern and Northern Tunes —
   Scenic Tour of West Lake, Sels.
"Moth Fluttering Against Lamp."

Lalleswari (*fl.* **late 14th century**)
Good repute is water carried in a sieve.
I set forth hopeful — cotton-blossom Lal.
With my breath I cut my way through the six forests.

La Loca
Adventures on the Isle of Adolescence, *Sels*.
Hello, animal sacrifice hotline?

Laluah, Aqua
Lullaby: "Close your sleepy eyes, or the pale moonlight will steal you."

Laluah, Aquah.   *See* **Hayford, Gladys May Casely.**

Lamantia, Philip (**b. 1927**)
Fud at Foster's.
Hermetic Bird.
High.
I Have Given Fair Warning.
Irrational.
Man Is in Pain.
Morning Light Song.
Night Is a Space of White Marble, The.
She Speaks the Morning's Filigree.
Surrealism in the Middle Ages.
Terror Conduction.
There Is This Distance between Me and What I See.
Violet Star.
Wilderness Sacred Wilderness.

Lamarre, Hazel Washington
Time and Tide.

Lamartine, Alphonse Marie Louis de (**1790–1869**)
Cedars of Lebanon, The.

Lamb, Charles (**1775–1834**)
As When a Child.
Childhood Fled.
David in the Cave of Adullam.
Family Name, The.
Farewell to Tobacco, A.
Free Thoughts on Several Eminent Composers.
Going or Gone.
Hester.
Hypochondriacus.
Io! Paean! Io! sing.
Lines Written during the Time of the Spy System.
Methinks How Dainty Sweet It Were.
Nonsense Verses.
Old Familiar Faces, The.
On an Infant Dying as Soon as Born.
Salome.
To John Lamb, Esq.: Of the South-Sea House.
Triumph of the Whale, The, *Sels*.
Written at Cambridge.

Lamb, Charles, *and* **Mary Lamb** (**1765–1847**)
Anger.
Boy and the Snake, The.
Choosing a Name.
Cleanliness.
Envy.
Feigned Courage.
First Tooth, The.
Going into Breeches.

Lamb, Joe
Cherries.

Lamb, Mary (**1765–1847**)
Parental Recollections.
Two Boys, The.

Lambert, James H., Jr.
Tale of a Dog, The.

"Lambert, Louis."   *See* **Gilmore, Patrick Sarsfield.**

Lamdan, Yitzhak (**1899–1954**)
Distant soughing of pine forests caresses my ear, The.
For the Sun Declined, *Sels*.
How little of God's grace caresses you, Massadah.
In the Khamsin, *Sels*.
Israel.
Massada, *Sels*.
On roads beyond the camp the Khamsin struck me.

Where am I, O awesome friend?
Why did Hagar weep over Ishmael when he thirsted.

Lame Deer, John
I'm an Indian.
Listen to the air.

Lampman, Archibald (**1861–99**)
City of the End of Things, The.
Heat.
In November.
Prayer: "O Earth, O dewy mother, breathe on us."
Solitude.
Thunderstorm, A.
To a Millionaire.
Winter Evening.

Lamport, Felicia (**b. 1916**)
Eggomania.
Mother, Mother, Are You All There?
Poll Star.

Lampson, Frederick Locker-.   *See* **Locker-Lampson, Frederick.**

Lancaster, Osbert (**b. 1908**)
Afternoons with Baedeker, *Sels*.
Eireann.
English.
French.
Italian.
Manhattan.

Lancaster, Sarah
Come on, my fellow pilgrims, come.

Landesman, Fran (**b. 1927**)
I Quite Like Men.
Let's Not Think about That.

Landon, Letitia Elizabeth (**"L. E. L."**)
Little Shroud, The.

Landor, W. D.
Winter.

Landor, Walter Savage (**1775–1864**)
Above all gifts we most should prize.
Absence.
Age.
Alas! 'Tis Very Sad to Hear.
Alciphron and Leucippe.
Art thou afraid the adorer's prayer.
Before a Saint's Picture.
Behold, O Aspasia! I Send You Verses.
Bourbons.
Called Proud.
Case at Sessions, A.
Chatting on deck was Dryden too.
Citation and Examination of William Shakespeare, The, *Sels*.
Corinna, from Athens, to Tanagra.
Cowley's Style.
Cowper.
Critic, A.
Darling Shell, where hast thou been.
Dead Marten, The.
Death of Artemidora, The.
Death of the Day.
Death Stands above Me.
Defiance.
Dirce.
Distribution of Honours for Literature.
Do You Remember Me?
Does it become a girl so wise.
Dragon-Fly, The.
Duke of York's Statue, The.
Dull Is My Verse.
Epigrams must be curt, nor seem.
Exhausted now her sighs, and dry her tears.
Fiesolan Idyl, A.
For an Epitaph at Fiesole.
Foreign Ruler, A.
From you, Ianthe, little troubles pass.
Garden at Heidelberg.
Gebir, *Sels*.
Georges, The.
God Scatters Beauty.
Graceful Acacia.
Had We Two Met.
Hamadryad, The.
Have I, this moment, led thee from the beach.
He lighted with his golden lamp on high.

Heart's Abysses, The.
Hearts-Ease.
Hellenics, The, *Sels*.
Here lies Landor.
How often, when life's summer day.
How to Read Me.
I Know Not Whether I Am Proud.
I Strove With None.
Ianthe, *Sels*.
Ianthe! you resolve [*or* are called] to cross the sea!
Idle Words.
Interlude.
Iphigeneia and Agamemnon.
Ireland Never Was Contented.
Is it no dream that I am he.
Izaac Walton, Cotton, and William Oldways.
Keats.
La Promessa Sposa.
Last Fruit Off an Old Tree, The, *Sels*.
Lately Our Poets.
Listen, mad girl! for giving ear.
Love and Age.
Love ran with me, then walk'd, then sate.
Loves who many years held all my mind, The.
Maid's Lament, The.
Memory.
Mild is the parting year, and sweet.
Mimnermus Incert.
Mother, I Cannot Mind My Wheel.
My hopes retire; my wishes as before.
Neither in idleness consume thy days.
No charm can stay, no medicine can assuage.
No, thou hast never griev'd but I griev'd too.
O fond, but fickle and untrue.
O friends! who have accompanied thus far.
O Friendship! Friendship! the shell of Aphrodite.
On Catullus.
On Himself.
On Man.
On Music.
On Seeing a Hair of Lucretia Borgia.
On the Death of M. D'Ossoli and His Wife, Margaret Fuller.
On the Heights.
On the Hellenics.
On the smooth brow and clustering hair.
Our youth was happy: why repine.
Past ruin'd [*or* ruined] Ilion Helen lives.
Perfidious, The.
Pericles and Aspasia, *Sels*.
Pigmies and Cranes.
Place where soon I think to lie, The.
Plays.
Poem: "I cannot tell, not I, why she."
Poet! I like not mealy fruit; give me.
Progress of Evening.
Proud word you never spoke, but you will speak.
Pyrrha! your smiles are gleams of sun.
Quarrelsome Bishop, A.
Reflection from Sea and Sky.
Remain, Ah Not in Youth Alone.
Reply to Lines by Thomas Moore, A, *Sels*.
Reproof of Thanks.
Retired this hour from wondering crowds.
Rose Aylmer.
Scentless laurel a broad leaf displays, The.
Scribblers, The.
Sensible Girl's Reply to Moore's, A.
Shakespeare, The.
Silent, you say, I'm grown of late.
So Then, I Feel Not Deeply!
Some of Wordsworth.
Stern Brow, The.
Tamar's Wrestling.
Ten thousand flakes about my window blow.
Ternissa! You Are Fled.
There Are Sweet Flowers.
There are two miseries in human life.
Thou hast not rais'd, Ianthe, such desire.
Three Roses, The.
To a Spaniel.
To Age.
To My Child Carlino.

Leconte de Lisle, Charles Marie René (1818–94)
Hialmar Speaks to the Raven.
Imperishable Fragrance.
Lydia.
Nell.
Phidylé.
Roses of Ispahan, The.

LeCron, Helen Cowles
Little Charlie Chipmunk.

Ledgister, Fragano (b. 1956)
Cities Have Fallen, The.
On Parade.

Ledoux, Louis V. (1880–1948)
Slumber Song.

Ledwidge, Francis (1891–1917)
Coming Poet, The.
Dream of Artemis, A, *Sels.*
Fear, A.
God, whose kindly hand doth sow.
God's Remembrance.
Herons, The.
Ireland.
June.
Lament for the Poets: 1916.
Lament for Thomas MacDonagh.
My Mother.
Soliloquy.
Twilight in Middle March, A.
Wife of Llew, The.

Lee, Agnes (1868–1939)
Ilex Tree, The.
Motherhood.

Lee, Alfred M. ("Al") (b. 1932)
Among Sharks.
Beside My Grandmother.
Far Side of Introspection, The.
Karl Marx.
Lie, The.
One Morning We Brought Them Order.
Poem for the Year Twenty Twenty.
Weathering the Depths.

"Lee, Andy" (W. W. Delaney)
Crazy Song on the Air of "Dixie."

Lee, Arthur (1740–90)
Prophecy, A.

Lee, Dennis (b. 1939)
Billy Batter.
Civil Elegies, *Sels.*
Coat, The.
Coming of Teddy Bears, The.
Dickery Dean.
Dimpleton the Simpleton.
Gods, The.
I Eat Kids Yum Yum!
Last Cry of the Damp Fly, The.
Often I sit in the sun and brooding over the city, always.
You Too Lie down.

Lee, Don L. (Haki R. Madhubuti) (b. 1942)
African Poems, *Sels.*
Afterword: For Gwen Brooks, An.
Assassination.
Awareness.
Back Again, Home.
Big Momma.
But He Was Cool; or, He Even Stopped for Green Lights.
Change Is Not Always Progress.
Change-up.
Communication in Whi-te.
Empty Warriors.
Judy-One.
Man Thinking about Woman.
Men and Birth: the Unexplainable.
Mixed Sketches.
Mwilu/ or Poem for the Living.
One Sided Shoot-out.
Poem for a Poet, A.
Poem to Complement Other Poems, A.
Positives for Sterling Plumpp.
Primitive, The.
Re-act for Action ("Re-act to Animals").
Self-Hatred of Don L. Lee, The.
To Be Quicker.

Wake-up Niggers.
We Walk the Way of the New World.
With All Deliberate Speed.

Lee, J. H.
Limerick: "Man from Maputo and so on, A."

Lee, John Robert (b. 1948)
Kite.
Return.
Third World Snapshots.

Lee, Joseph (1862–1937?)
German Prisoners.
Requiem: "When the last voyage is ended."

Lee, Joyce (b. 1913)
Firebell for Peace.
My Father's Country.

Lee, Laurie (b. 1914)
Boy in Ice.
Christmas Landscape.
Day of These Days.
Edge of Day, The.
Field of Autumn.
Home from Abroad.
Invasion Summer.
Long Summer.
Long War, The.
Milkmaid.
Moment of War, A.
My Many-Coated Man.
Sunken Evening [in Trafalgar Square].

Lee, Li-Young (b. 1957)
Between Seasons.
City in Which I Love You, The.
Cleaving, The.
Eating Alone.
From Blossoms.
Gift, The.
I Ask My Mother to Sing.
Persimmons.
Story, A.
This Room and Everything in It.
Visions and Interpetations.
Weight of Sweetness, The.

Lee, Nathaniel (1653–93)
Nathaniel Lee to Sir Roger L'Estrange.
Take it as earnest of a faith renewed.
To the Unkown Author of *Absalom and Achitophel, Sels.*

Lee, Sang-hua
Does Spring Come to a Lost Land?

Lee-Hamilton, Eugene (1845–1907)
Among the Firs.
Henry I to the Sea.
Idle Charon.
Imaginary Sonnets, *Sels.*
Ipsissimus.
Luca Signorelli to His Son.
Luther to a Bluebottle Fly.
My Own Hereafter.
Noon's Dream-Song.
Snail's Derby, A.
Sunken Gold.
To My Tortoise Chronos.
What the Sonnet Is.

Lees, Edwin (1800–1877)
Signs of Christmas.

Le Fanu, Joseph Sheridan (1814–73)
Beatrice, *Sels.*
Hymn: "Hush! oh ye billows."

Lefcowitz, Barbara F. (b. 1935)
Emily Dickinson's Sestina for Molly Bloom.

Lefroy, Edward Cracroft (1855–91)
Cleonicos.
Echoes from Theocritus, *Sels.*
Epitaph of Eusthenes, The.
Flute of Daphnis, The.
Grave of Hipponax, The.
Monument of Cleita, The.
Sacred Grove, A.
Sylvan Revel, A.
Thyrsis.

Leftwich, Joseph (1892–1983)
Killed in Action.
Tailor, The.

Le Gallienne, Richard (1866–1947)
After the War.
Ballad of London, A.
Beatus Vir.
Easter Hymn, An.
May Is Building Her House.
Melton Mowbray Pork Pie, A.
Prayer: "Out of the deeps I cry to thee, O God!"
Second Crucifixion, The.
Song: "She's somewhere in the sunlight strong."

LeGear, Laura Lourene
Unbridled Now.

Léger, Alexis Saint-Léger. *See* "**Perse, St.-John.**"

Lehman, David (b. 1948)
Amnesia.
Enigma Variations.
Fear.
Fear and Trembling.
For David Shapiro.
Operation Memory.
Perfidia.
Spontaneous Combustion.
Towards the Vanishing Point.

Lehmann, Geoffrey (b. 1940)
Auntie Bridge and Uncle Pat.
Driving through thick bush.
I Was Born at a Place of Pines.
Music Is Unevennesses.
My Father's a Still Day.
Night Flower.
Pigs, The.
Poem for Maurice O'Shea, A.
Pope Alexander VI.
Ross's Poems, *Sels.*
Saving the Harvest.
Some musical intervals survive.
Some of Our Koorawatha Saints.
Song for Past Midnight.
There Are Some Lusty Voices Singing.
You can't hear it in the house.

Lehmann, John (1907–87)
Ballad of Banners (1944), The.
This Excellent Machine.

Lehmann, R. P. M.
Limerick: "There was a young girl of Bahari."

Lehrer, Tom (b. 1928)
Alma.
Elements, The.
I Wanna Go Back to Dixie.
New Maths.

Leib [or Leyb], Mani (1883–1953)
Door and Window Bolted Fast.
Hush, Hush.
When I See Another's Pain.

Leiber, Jerry, and Michael E. Stoller
Hound Dog, *Sels.*
You Ain't Nothin' But a Hound Dog.

Leifer, Jay (b. 1954)
Six-forty-two Farm Commune Struggle Poem.

Leigh, Barbara
Limerick: "There was an old Member called Bevan."

Leigh, F., and L. Murray. *See* **Murray, L.**

Leigh, Helen (fl. 1788, d. c. 1795))
Lady and the Doctor, The.
Natural Child, The.

Leigh, Henry Sambrooke (1837–83)
Only Seven.
Rhymes (?).
Saragossa.
'Twas Ever Thus.
Twins, The.

Leigh, Richard (1649?–1728)
Greatness in Little.
On a Fair Lady, Looking in the Glass.
Thus Lovely Sleep.

Leigh-Fermor, Patrick (b. 1915)
Greek Archipelagoes.

Leighton, Louise
Earthly Illusion.

Pontoon-Bridge Miracle, The.
Potatoes' Dance, The.
Rain.
Simon Legree — a Negro Sermon.
Sorceress, The!
Spider and the Ghost of the Fly, The.
To a Golden-haired Girl in a Louisiana Town.
Traveler, The.
Two Old Crows.
Unpardonable Sin, The.
What the Moon Saw.
When the Mississippi Flowed in Indiana.
Why I Voted the Socialist Ticket.
Yet Gentle Will the Griffin Be.

Lingg, Herman von (1820–1905)
Song: "Each night I sleep more lightly."

Linik, Abraham
Thief, The.

Link, Carolyn Wilson
Elements.

Link, Gordden (b. 1907)
Artist and Ape.

Link, Lenore M.
Holding Hands.

Linton, William James (*fl.* c.1851)
Bob Thin; or, the Poorhouse Fugitive, *Sels.*
Epicurean.
Spring and Autumn.

Liotta, P. H. (b. 1956)
Story I Can't Tell, The.

Lipkin, Jean (b. 1926)
Credo.
Father.
Pre Domina.

Lippincott, Sarah Jane Clarke. *See*
"Greenwood, Grace."

Lipsitz, Lou (b. 1938)
Bedtime Story.
Prospect Beach.
Thaw in the City.
Winter Twilight.

Lipton, James (b. 1946)
Misericordia!

Liptrot, David
Condor, The.

Lisboa, Henriqueta
Minor Elegy.

Lisle, Thomas (1709–67)
Letter from Smyrna to His Sisters at Crux-
Easton, 1733.
Power of Music, The.

Lissauer, Ernst
Chant of Hate against England, A.
Hymn of Hate against England, A, *Sels.*

List, Amedie Eva
Mon that wist for raine, The.

Lister, Elizabeth H.
Limerick: "Don't thee think, Zurrr, I be zo
amazin'."
Limerick: "I consider I really am through."

Lister, Richard Percival (b. 1914)
At the Ship.
Bone China.
Gemlike Flame, The.
Human Races, The.
Lament of an Idle Demon.
Revolutionaries, The.
Tale of Jorkyns and Gertie, The; or, Vice
Rewarded.
Time Passes.

Litchfield, Grace Denio (1849–1946)
Good-By.

Litherland, S. J.
Debt Problem, The.
Long Interval, The.
Synagogue in Samarkand, A.
Wake, The.

Lithgow, William (1582?–1645)
Painted whore, the mask of deadly sin, A.
Still this, still that I would! all I surmise.

Litsey, Edwin Carlile
Dreams Ahead, The.

Little, Geraldine Clinton
Meditation after Hearing the Richard Yardumian
Mass, "Come, Creator Spirit."

Little, Janet (1759–1813)
Given to a Lady Who Asked Me to Write a
Poem.

Little, Katharine Day (b. 1889)
Hazlitt Sups.

Little, Lessie Jones
My Yellow Straw Hat.

Little Billee
Limerick: "Devil, who plays a deep part, The."
Limerick: "Devil's no longer a myth, The."
Limerick: "Said an elderly Bishop called
Greville."
Limerick: "There was a young lady of Nîmes."

Littlebird, Harold (Harold Bird) (b. 1951)
After the Pow-Wow, *Sels.*
Alone Is the Hunter.
Coming Home in March.
Could I Say I Touched You.
For Drum Hadley.
For the Girls 'cause They Know.
For Tom Numkena, Hopi/ Spokane.
Gaa-a-Muna, a Mountain Flower.
Hummingbird.
If You Can Hear My Hooves.
In a Double Rainbow.
Mother/ Deer/ Lady.
Oh but It Was Good.
Old Moke.
Pennsylvania Winter Indian 1974.
Wrap Me in Blankets of Momentary Winds.

LittleCoon. *See* **Oliver, Louis.**

Littledale, Freya
When My Dog Died.

Littlefield, Hazel (b. 1889)
Not for Its Own Sake.

Littlefield, Milton S. (1864–1934)
Come, O Lord, Like Morning Sunlight.
O Son of Man, Thou Madest Known.

Littleton, Edward (1698?–1734)
Spider, The.

Littlewort, Dorothy
Prayer of a Teacher.

Littman, Jeffery
Limerick: "O Great Queen Whom I Idolize."

Littman, S.
Limerick: "There was a young lady of Nantes."

Litvinoff, Emanuel (b. 1915)
If I Forget Thee.

Liu, Bea
Mother.

Liu Ch'ang-ch'ing (710?–785?)
At an Inn in Yü-kan.
Encountering a Snowstorm, I Stay with the
Recluse of Mount Hibiscus.
Listening to the Washblock in the Moonlight.
Replying to a Poem by the Monk Ling-yi at the
New Spring.
Saying Goodby to the Monk Ling-ch'e.
Sent to the Taoist of Dragon Mountain, Hsü
Fa-leng.
Snow on Lotus Mountain.

Liu Ch'e (157–87 B.C.)
Autumn Wind, The.

Liu Chih (c. 1280–c. 1335)
Tune: "Decorous and Pretty" — Respectfully
Offered to Circuit Inspector Kao.

Liu Chun (430–464)
In Imitation of Hsü Kan ("Since You Went
Away").

Liu E (1857–1909)
Academics? Politics? I've nothing to do with
them!
Beautiful women — we've vowed to be lovers!
Cotton blankets left in the cold.
Last year, with jade hands, you offered cups of
tea.
My thoughts flow in streams around this tower.
"Next year you must come again."
On the Fifteenth Day of the Eighth Month,
Sels.

On the Twenty-fourth: Improvisations, *Sels.*
Poems for Yukiko of Tamba, *Sels.*

Liu K'o-chuang (1187–1269)
Ten Poems Recording Things that Happened at
the Ye, *Sels.*

Liu Pang (256–195 B.C.)
Song of the Great Wind.

Liu Sha-ho
Ash Tree on Ching Hill, The.
Cactus.
Evening View at the Western Palace.
Family of Plants, A, *Sels.*
Goldfish, The.
Ivy.
Plum.
Poisonous Mushroom.
Poplar.
Two Poems of Peking, *Sels.*
Wish, The.

Liu, Stephen Shu Ning (b. 1930)
Chung Shin.
Homecoming for April.
My Father's Martial Art.

Liu Tsung-yüan (773–819)
Arriving at North Pond by Stupid Brook on a
Morning Walk after the Rain.
Beyond the bamboo fence, cooking fire and
smoke.
By an ancient road, abundant thistle plants.
Drinking at Night in the Western Pavilion of
the Fa-hua Temple.
Farmers, *Sels.*
Feeling Old Age.
Meditation Hall.
On Covering the Bones of Chang Chin, the
Hired Man.
Viewing Mountains with His Reverence Hao
Ch'u: To My Friends and Relatives in the
Capital.
Written in Jest on Elder Stonegate's Eastern
Balcony.

Liu Ya-tzu (1887–1958)
Beyond the stream at Seta stretches an endless
view.
By Flower-and-Moon Pavilion, I stay my
carriage.
Cataracts flying down a thousand fathoms roll
up a raging billow.
Dragons and Snakes.
Filled with Emotions on the Moon-ferrying
Bridge at Arashiyama.
For Guests after Their Visit.
Miscellaneous Poems on Lake Biwa, *Sels.*
On Hearing the News of the Japanese
Surrender.
On the Second Day of the Fifth Month —
Written after Drink.
Overjoyed at Soviet Russia's Entry into the
War.
Strange Tears.
To a Friend, Using the Same Rhymes of a
Peom He Sent Me.

Liu Yu Hsi (772–842)
Bamboo Branch Song, *Sels.*
Chin-ling.
Coming Again to Heng-yang, I Mourn for Liu
Tsung-yüan.
Drinking with Friends amongst the Blooming
Peonies.
Gorges of Wu are hoary and im in the season
of mist and rain, The.
Looking at My Knife-hilt Ring, a Song.
Song of Spring Replying to a Poem by Po Chü-
yi, A.
Sorrowing for the Past at Western Pass
Mountain.
To the Tune "Glittering Sword Hilts."
Tune: "Ripples Sifting Sand."
Up in the hills are bank on bank of blossoming
peach and plum trees.
Willow Branch Song.
Willow Branches.

Liu Yung (*fl.* c.1034)
Tune: "Chrysanthemums Fresh."
Tune: "Eight Beats of a Kan-chou Song."

Tune: "Jade Butterflies."
Tune: "Midnight Music."
Tune: "Prelude to Allure Goddesses."
Tune: "Wanderings of a Youth."

Livada, Rasa (b. 1948)
Horoscope.

Livesay, Dorothy (b. 1909)
Children's Letters, The.
Eve.
Fantasia.
Green Rain.
Leader, The.
Prophetess, The.
Serenade for Strings.
Spain.
Three Emily's, The.
Uninvited, The.
Waking in the Dark.
Widow.
Without Benefit of Tape.

Livingston, Edna (b. 1897)
Question, A.

Livingston, Myra Cohn (b. 1926)
Car Wash.
Dark, The.
Doll.
Father.
For a Bird.
German Shepherd.
Grunion.
Invitation.
Lemonade Stand.
Mill Valley.
Mrs. Spider.
Night, The.
October Magic.
Rain.
Tape, The.
Time for Building, A.
12 October.
Whispers.
Working with Mother.

Livingstone, Dinah
Desire.
In Perfect Time.
Night Prayers.
Praise.

Livingstone, Douglas (b. 1932)
Bad Run at King's Rest.
Bateleur.
Evasion, An.
On Clouds.
One Time.
Peace Delegate.
Piece of Earth, A.
Sleep of My Lions, The.
Sunstrike.
To a Dead Elephant.
Vanderdecken.
Vulture.

Lizzie. *See* Doten, Elizabeth.

Llawdden (*fl.* c.1460)
No Place Like Home.

Llewellyn, Kate (b. 1940)
Colonel.
Finished.

Lloyd, D. H.
Bible Bob Responds to a Jesus Honker.

Lloyd, David (1597–1633)
Legend of Captain Jones, The, *Sels.*
'Twas well the wars were done before.

Lloyd, Evan (1734–1776)
Helen like the Rose.
Methodist, The, *Sels.*
Portrait of a Bishop.
Powers of the Pen, The, *Sels.*
Religion and the Lower Classes.
Sons of War sometimes are known, The.

Lloyd, Hilary Sametz
Unveiling.

Lloyd, John (1797–1875)
Kingfisher, The.
Thoughts of Boyhood.

Lloyd, Ludovic (*fl.* 1573–1610)
Flee, stately Juno, Samos fro.
Sidanen, *Sels.*

Lloyd, Robert (1733–64)
Acting, dear Thornton, its perfection draws.
Actor, The, *Sels.*
Cit's Country Box, The.
Familiar Epistle to J. B. Esq., A, *Sels.*
Mark yon round parson, fat and sleek.
Old England has not lost her prayer.
On Rhyme, *Sels.*
Poetry Professors, The, *Sels.*
Public Schools.
Sent to a Lady, with a Seal.
Shakespeare; an Epistle to David Garrick, Esq,
    Sels.
Some, Milton-mad (an affectation).
True Genius.
Yet matter must be gravely planned.

Lluellyn [*or* Lluelyn], Martin (1616–82)
To Mistress M. A.

Llwyd, Huw (c.1568–1630)
Fox's Counsel, The.

Llwyd, John Plummer Derwent (1861–1933)
Vestal Virgin, The, *Sels.*

Llwyd, Morgan (1619–1659)
Awake, O Lord, Awake Thy Saints.
Charles, the last king of Britain, *Sels.*
Come Wisdome Sweet.
Excuse, The.
Harvest, The.
Law was ever above kings, The.
1648, *Sels.*
Spring, The.
Summer, The.
Winter, The.

Llwyd, Richard (1752–1835)
Beaumaris Bay, *Sels.*
Here, still sequestered, Penmon's sacred dome.

Llywarch the Aged
Hearth of Urien, The.

Llywelyn ab y Moel (d. 1440)
Battle of Waun Gaseg, The.

Llywelyn Goch ap Meurig Hen (*fl.* 1360–90)
Lament for Lleucu Llwyd.

Llywelyn-Williams, Alun (b. 1913)
In Berlin, August 1945: Lehrte Bahnhof.
Pont y Caniedydd.
When I Was Young.
Yesterday's Illusion *or* Remembering the
    Thirties.

Lo Yin (833–909)
Book-burning Pit, The.
Sent to the Ch'an Master Wu-hsiang.
Thinking of the Way Home, a Song.

Lochhead, Douglas (b. 1922)
Winter Lanscape — Halifax.

Lochhead, Liz (b. 1947)
Abortion, An.
Mirror's Song.
Sundaysong.
Tam Lin's Lady.

Locke, Lawrence
Animal Pictures.
Leaving Mendota, 1956.
River.

Locke, Mary (*fl.* 1786–1816)
Sonnet: "I hate the Spring in parti-coloured
    vest."
Sonnet: "'Tis dead of night; storms rend the
    troubled air."

Locker-Lampson, Frederick (1821–95)
Loulou and Her Cat.
Mr. Placid's Flirtation.
Old Oak Tree at Hatfield Broadoak, The.
Our Photograph[s].
Terrible Infant, A.

Lockhart, John Gibson (1794–1854)
Lines: "When youthful faith hath fled."
Wandering Knight's Song, The.

Locklin, Gerald (b. 1941)
California.
Constituency of Dunces, A.
Since You Seem Intent.

Lockman, John (1698–1771)

Penitent Nun, The.

Lockwood, Margo (b. 1939)
December Eclipse.
Victorian Grandmother.

Lockyer, Milton
Dark Mountains.

Lodge, Edith (1908–71)
Song of the Hill.

Lodge, Thomas (1558?–1625)
Devoide of reason, thrale to foolish ire.
Earth, Late Choked with Showers, The.
Faire art thou Phillis, I, so faire (sweet mayd).
Fancy, A.
For Pity, Pretty Eyes, Surcease.
I would in rich and golden coloured raine.
Life and Death of William Longbeard, The,
    Sels.
Long hath my sufferance labored to in force.
Love Guards [*or* Guides] the Roses of Thy
    Lips.
Love's Witchery.
Margarite of America, A, *Sels.*
Montanus' Sonnet.
My Mistress.
No Stars Her Eyes.
O Pleasing Thoughts.
Ode: "Now I find thy looks were feigned."
Phillis ("My Phillis hath the morning sun").
Phyllis, *Sels.*
Pluck the Fruit and Taste the Pleasure.
Robert, Second Duke of Normandy, *Sels.*
Rosalind's [*or* Rosalynd's] Madrigal[l].
Rosaline.
Rosalynde; or Euphues' Golden Legacy, *Sels.*
Rose, The.
Scilla's Metamorphosis, *Sels.*
Sonnet: "O shady vales, O fair enriched
    meads."

Lodge, Thomas, *and* **Robert Greene**
Animal Weather-Forecasting.
Beauty, Alas, Where Wast Thou Born.
Shepherd's Sorrow, Being Disdained in Love,
    The.

Loesser, Frank (1910–69)
Guys and Dolls.

Loewinsohn, Ron (b. 1937)
Against the Silences to Come.
Insomniac Poem.
Mrs. Loewinsohn &c.
My Sons.
Pastoral: "Death./ The death of a million."
Stillness of the Poem, The.
Thing Made Real, The.

Loftin, Elouise (b. 1950)
Virginia.
Weeksville Women.
Woman.

Lofting, Hugh (1886–1947)
Mister Beers.
Picnic.

Loftis, N. J. (b. 1943)
Spiked cadillacs with silver teeth.

Logan, John (1748–88)
Braes of Yarrow, The.

Logan, John (1923–1971?)
Avocado.
Believe It.
Century Piece for Poor Heine, A.
Chicago Scene.
Cycle for Mother Cabrini, A, *Sels.*
Death of Southwell, The, *Sels.*
Experiment That Failed, The.
For My Daughter.
Happening on Aegina.
He told the crowd "The devils."
Lines for a Young Wanderer in Mexico.
Love Poem: "Last night you would not come."
Mallard's Going, The.
Nude Kneeling in Sand.
On the Death of Keats.
Picnic, The.
Poem in Progress, *Sels.*
Rescue, The.
Saint, who overlaps.
San Francisco Poem.

Further adventure of Skinny Marcus.
Gently, so as not to rouse/ His skinny girl.
Here I am launching my Second Book of Epigrams.
Hermogenes is rather short.
HIS GRATEFUL OPPONENTS SET UP THIS STATUE OF APIS THE BOXER.
I'm round at Heliodorus' place.
It's said you take a long time over a bath.
Lazy Marcus once dreamed.
Lean Gaius, who was thinner than a straw.
Lifted by a little breeze.
Light-fingered Dio takes after the God of Thieves.
Lysimachus' cushion caught Antiochus' eye.
Marcus in the armed hoplites' race.
Mean old Hermon.
My Dad was worried about his brother.
Olympicus, the welter-weight.
Olympikos, with your ugly face.
On an Old Woman.
On Kriton the Miser.
Orator Flaccus can commit solecisms.
Poor Calpurnius, the most Schweikian soldier in the land.
Recent earthquake, A.
Some say you dye your hair, Nikylla.
That poet is best.
There's one Grammarian I know.
They whisper of you, Nicole.
Tiny Erotion, borne away/ By a gnat had this to say.
Treasure.
Well, Menestratus, you ask me what I think.
When Hermocrates the Miser lay in bed.
Wig, rouge, honey, wax, teeth.
With a lucky charm around his throat.
Zenonis has a splendid tutor for her son.

Lucretius (Titus Lucretius Carus) (94–55 B.C.)
Address to Venus.
Against the Fear of Death.
Argument of the Fourth Booke, The.
Beyond Religion.
Child is like a sailor cast up by the sea, The.
Concerning the Nature of Love.
De Rerum Natura (On the Nature of Things), *Sels.*
Delight of humane kind, and gods above.
If all this world had no original.
No Single Thing Abides.
Nor will ingenious women, free from pride.
Now since the members of the world we view.
Suave Mari Magno.
What Has This Bugbear Death.
Why only in the spring are roses borne?

Lucy, Sean (b. 1931)
Friday Evening.
Longshore Intellectual.
Missing Link.
Senior Members.
Supervising Examinations.
These Six.

Ludlow, Fitz Hugh (1836–90)
Socrates Snooks.
Too Late.

Ludlum, William (d. 1949)
Business Man's Prayer, A.
Radio Religion, The.

Ludvigson, Susan Bartels (b. 1942)
Jeanne d'Arc.
Love at Cooter's Carpet, Fort Lawn, S.C.
Man Arrested in Hacking Death Tells Police He Mistook Mother-in-Law for Raccoon.
Paris Aubade.
Punishment, The.
Some Notes on Courage.
Widow, The.

Lui Chi (1311–75)
Poet Thinks, A.

Lum, Wing Tek
At a Chinaman's Grave.
It's Something Our Family Has Always Done.
Minority Poem.
Picture of My Mother's Family, A.
Riding the North Point Ferry.

To a Poet Who Says He's Stopped Writing (Temporarily).
To Li Po.
To My Father.
Urban Love Songs.

Lummis, Charles Fletcher (1859–1928)
John Charles Frémont.
Poe-'em of Passion, A.

Lumumba, Patrice Emery (1926–51)
Dawn in the Heart of Africa.

Lupellus
Limerick: "Solipsist with triplets said, A: Though."

Luria, Isaac (1534–72)
Sabbath of Rest, A.

Luria, Yaacov
There Is One Synagogue Extant in Kiev.

Lushington, Franklin (d. 1855)
No More Words.

Luswat
Shaman Song.

Luther, Martin (1483–1546)
All Hail, Thou Noble Guest.
Ane Sang of the Birth of Christ, with the Tune of Baw Lula Low.
Away in a Manger.
Ein feste Burg ist unser Gott.
From Depths of Woe I Cry to You.
From Heaven Above to Earth I Come.
From Heaven High I Come to You.
In the Very Midst of Life.
Mighty Fortress Is Our God, A.

Luton, Mildred
Mouse Ate the Bait, The.

Luttrell, Henry (1765?–1851)
O death, thy certainty is such.
On a Man Run Over by an Omnibus.

Lutz, Gertrude May (b. 1899)
Prisoner of War.

Lux, Thomas (b. 1946)
All the Slaves.
Barn Fire.
Elegy for Frank Stanford.
Farmers.
Flying Noises.
Graveyard by the Sea.
History and Abstraction.
If You See This Man.
Lament City.
Man Asleep in a Child's Bed.
Midnight Tennis Match, The.
Milkman and His Son, The.
My Grandmother's Funeral.
Sleepmask Dithyrambic.
Solo Native.
Tarantulas on the Lifebuoy.
There Were Some Summers.
This Is a Poem for the Fathers and for Michael Ryan.
Time.

Luxborough, Henrietta Knight, Lady. *See* **Knight, Henrietta, Lady Luxborough.**

Luzzatto, Isaac (*fl.* 16th century)
Death, Thou Hast Seized Me.

Luzzatto, Moses Hayyim, of Padua (1707–47)
Chorus: "All ye that handle harp and viol."
Unto the Upright Praise, *Sels.*

Lyall, Sir Alfred Comyn (1835–1911)
Badminton.
Meditations of a Hindu Prince.
Night in the Red Sea, A.
Rajpoot Rebels.
Studies at Delhi, 1876, *Sels.*

Lydgate, John (1370?–1451?)
Balade Simple.
Boy Serving at Table, The.
Court of Sapience, *Sels.*
Devotions of the Fowls, *Sels.*
Duplicity of Women, The.
Fall of Princes, The, *Sels.*
Henry before Agincourt: October 25, 1415.
Lament: "Farewell Mercy, farewell thy piteous grace."
Letter of Compleynt of Canace, The.

Lover's New Year's Gift, A.
Lyarde.
On the Departing of Thomas Chaucer.
Siege of Thebes, The, *Sels.*
To the King on his Coronation.
Transient as a Rose.
Vox Ultima Crucis.
When brighte Phoebus passed was the Ram.

Lydston, Donna R.
Family, The.

Lyle, K. Curtis (b.1944)
Lacrimas or There Is a Need to Scream.
Sometimes I Go to Camarillo and Sit in the Lounge.
Songs for the Cisco Kid; or, Singing for the Face.
Songs for the Cisco Kid; or, Singing: Song #2.

Lyly, John (1553–1606)
Alexander and Campaspe, *Sels.*
Cupid and my Campaspe played [*or* playd].
Cupid's Indictment.
Endimion, *Sels.*
Endymion, *Sels.*
Galathea, *Sels.*
'Las, how long shall I.
Midas, *Sels.*
Mother Bombie, *Sels.*
My Daphne's hair is twisted gold.
O cruel Love! on thee I lay.
O Cupid! Monarch over Kings.
O! [*or* Oh] for a bowl of fat canary.
Pan's Syrinx was a girl[e] indeed.
Pinch him, pinch him black and blue.
Sapho and Phao, *Sels.*
Sing to Apollo, God of Day.
Stand! Who goes there?
Trico's Song.
Vulcan's Song.

Lyly, John, *and* **Thomas Ravenscroft**
By the Moon ("By the moon we sport and play").
Elves' Dance, The.
Mayde's Metamorphosis, The, *Sels.*

Lynch, Annette (b. 1922)
Bridgework.
Gratitude.

Lynch, Charles (b. 1943)
If We Cannot Live People as People.
Memo.

Lynch, Janice M.
Friend asks why I swim, A.
Sixty-four Caprices for a Long-Distance Swimmer: Notes on Swimming 100 Miles, *Sels.*

Lynch, Thomas Toke (1818–71)
Lift Up Your Heads, Rejoice!
Thousand Years Have Come, A.

Lynche, Richard (*fl.* 1596–1601)
But thou my deere sweet-sounding lute be still.
Diella, *Sels.*
Love's Despair.
Soon as the Azure-colored Gates.
What sugred termes, what all-perswading arte.

Lynde, Benjamin (1666–1745)
Lines Descriptive of Thomson's Island.

Lyndsay, Sir David. *See* **Lindsay [*or* Lyndsay], Sir David.**

Lynn, Elizabeth Cook-. *See* **Cook-Lynn, Elizabeth.**

Lyon, George Ella (b. 1949)
Birth.
Cousin Ella Goes to Town.
Foot-Washing, The.
Inventing Sin.
My Grandfather in Search of Moonshine.
Rhody.
Salvation.
Testimony, A.
Visit, A.

Lyon, P. H. B. (b. 1893)
Envoi: "Earth puts her colours by."

Lyon, Roger H.
Keep On Praying.

Lyons, A. Neil (1880–1940)
Fairy Cobbler, The.

Stranger, Husband.
Toast.
Windows.
Winter.
Wisdom of Æ, The.
Word "Silk", The.

McCartney, Mabel E.
Refuge.

MacCathmhaoil, Seosamh. *See* **Campbell, Joseph.**

Maccius
I swore, love, by your/ dominion, to rest.
Philistion's a hard bitch:/ in her book "penniless lover."
Your pleasure, Priapus, is the island coast.

McClane, Kenneth
At the Bridge with Rufus.

McClatchy, J. D. (b. 1945)
At a Reading.
Essay on Friendship, An.
Fog.
Landing, The.
Method, The.
Pleasure of Ruins, The.
Wells River.
Winter without Snow, A.

McClaurin, Irma (b. 1945)
I, Woman.
Mask, The.
To a Gone Era.

McClellan, George Marion (b. 1860)
Daybreak.
Feet of Judas, The.
Hydromel and Rue.
January Dandelion, A.
Lines to Mount Glen.
Love Is a Flame.
September Night, A.
Sun Went down in Beauty, The.
To Theodore.

McClennan, Tommy
Brown Skin Girl.
Inside His Borrowed Cage.
Les Plaisirs.
My True Desire.

McCloskey, Mark (b. 1938)
Too Dark.

McClure, Michael (b. 1932)
Aelf-Scin, The.
Breech, The.
Canticle.
Clear — the senses bright — sitting in the black chair — Rocker.
Death of Kin Chuen Louie, The.
Flowers of Politics, I, The.
Flowers of Politics, II, The.
For Artaud.
For the Death of 100 Whales.
Gesture the gesture the gesture the gesture, The.
Hymn to St. Geryon, *Sels.*
It's Nation Time.
List, The.
Mad Sonnet 1.
Ode for Soft Voice.
Peyote Poem, *Sels.*
Point Lobos: Animism.
Rug, The.
Song: "I Work with the shape."
Watching the Stolen Rose.
With Tendrils of Poems.

MacColl, Dugald Sutherland (1859–1948)
Miners' Response, The.

MacColl, Ewan (b. 1915)
Dove, The.
First Time Ever I Saw Your Face, The.
Freeborn Man.
Shoals of Herring, The.

Mac Coisdealbhaigh, Tomas ("Laider") (*fl.* mid–17th century)
Una Bhan.

McCombs, Judith (b. 1939)
Dictionary Is an *His*torian: A Found Political Poem, The.

Mac Con Brettan, Bláthmac (*fl.* 8th century)
I call you with honest words.
Poem to Mary, A, *Sels.*

MacConglinne (*fl.* 12th century)
Vision of MacConglinne, The.

Mac Con Midhe, Giolla Brighde (*fl.* mid–13th century)
Defence of Poetry, A.

McCord, David (b. 1897)
Ascot Waistcoat.
At the Garden Gate.
Axolotl, The.
Baccalaureate.
Blessed Lord, What It Is to Be Young.
Books Fall Open.
Christmas Package, A, *Sels.*
Cocoon.
Come Christmas.
Conversation.
Crickets.
Crows, The.
Crows.
Epitaph on a Waiter.
Every Time I Climb a Tree.
Fisherman, The.
Gloss.
Glowworm.
Go Fly a Saucer, *Sels.*
Grasshopper, The.
Hex on the Mexican X, A.
History of Education.
I Want You to Meet.
I've seen one flying saucer. Only when.
Jamboree, *Sels.*
Kite.
Lacquer Liquor Locker, The.
Mantis.
Mr. Bidery's Spidery Garden.
Mr. Macklin's Jack O'Lantern ("Mr. Macklin takes his knife").
My stocking's where.
New Chitons for Old Gods, *Sels.*
Perambulator Poems, I-VII, *Sels.*
Pickety fence, The.
Plane Geometer.
Rainbow, The.
Rhyme for ham? A. Jam.
Singular Indeed.
Snowflakes.
Song of the Train.
Summer Shower.
That broken star.
This Is My Rock.
To a Certain Most Certainly Certain Critic.
Walnut Tree, The.
When I Was Christened.
Where Is My Butterfly Net?

McCorkle, James (b. 1954)
Showing Us the Fields.

McCrae, George Gordon (1833–1927)
Mamba the Bright-eyed, *Sels.*

McCrae, Hugh Raymond (1876–1958)
Mimshi Maiden, The.
Song of the Rain.
Winds.

McCrae, John (1872–1918)
Anxious Dead, The.
In Flanders Fields.

McCray, Chirlane (b. 1908)
I Used to Think.

McCrea, Lilian
Boots and Shoes.
Getting Up.
My Toys.
Noises in the Night.
Pussy-Cat and Puppy-Dog.
Rain.
Wash-Day.

McCreery, John Luckey (1835–1906)
There Is No Death.

McCuaig, Ronald (b. 1908)
Au Tombeau de Mon Père.
Betty by the Sea.
Music in the Air.

Recitative: "Farmer's son is good and mad, The."

Mac Cuarta, Seamas Dall (1650–1733)
Houses of Corr an Chait are cold, The.

McDaniel, Wilma Elizabeth
Calendars.
Definition.
Night Treasures.
Note Slipped under a Door.
U.F.W. Pickets on Old Highway 99.

MacDermot, Thomas (1870–1933)
Cuba.
Dark foreboding haunts me lest I die, A.
Market Basket in the Car, A.
San Gloria, *Sels.*

"MacDiarmid, Hugh" (Christopher Murray Grieve) (1892–1978)
Allelauder.
Another Epitaph on an Army of Mercenaries.
At My Father's Grave.
Bagpipe Music.
Bonnie Broukit Bairn, The.
Bracken Hills in Autumn.
British Leftish Poetry, 1930-40.
By Wauchopeside.
Cattle Show.
Cloudburst and Soaring Moon.
Cophetua.
Crowdieknowe.
Crystals like Blood.
Dae what ye wull ye canna parry.
Dead Liebknecht, The.
Drunk Man Looks at the Thistle, A, *Sels.*
Eemis-Stane, The.
Empty Vessel.
Facing the Chair.
Farewell to Dostoevski.
Farmer's Death.
Fleggit Bride, The.
Glen of Silence, The.
Glog-Hole, The.
Great Wheel, The.
I Heard Christ Sing.
In Memoriam James Joyce, *Sels.*
In the Children's Hospital.
In the Fall.
In the Pantry.
Innumerable Christ, The.
It was Landor who first said.
Judge Commits Suicide, A.
Lament for the Great Music, *Sels.*
Light of Life, The.
Love.
Moolie Besom, A.
Moonlight among the Pines.
Moonstruck.
Nuts in May.
O Wha's the Bride?
Old Wife in High Spirits.
On the Ocean Floor.
On the Oxford Book of Victorian Verse.
On the Right.
One of the Principal Causes of War.
Parley of Beasts.
Parrot Cry, The.
Perfect.
Prayer for a Second Flood.
Reflections in a Slum.
Rhymes for the Times.
Robber, The.
Royal Stag, The.
Royal Wedding Gifts.
Sauchs in the Reuch Heuch Hauch, The.
Scotland Small?
Scunner.
Second Hymn to Lenin.
Sic Transit Gloria Scotia.
Skeleton of the Future, The.
Spanish War, The.
Storm-Cock's Song, The.
Sunny Gale.
To a Sea Eagle.
Two Parents, The.
Under the Greenwood Tree.
Up to Date.
Watergaw, The.

Après-midi d'un Faune, L', *Sels*.
Glazier, The.
Proud of my music, let me often make.
Saint, The.
Sea-Wind.
Sigh.

Mallet, David (1705–1765)
First that broke silence was good old Ben, The.
Of Verbal Criticism, *Sels*.
Pride of his own, and wonder of his age.
Through all thy various *Winter, full are found*.
To Mr. Thomson, on His Publishing the
Second Edition of His Poem Called Winter,
Sels.
William and Margaret.

Mallet, David and James Thomson. *See*
Thomson, James.

"Malley, Ern" (James McAuley and Harold
Stewart) (1917–76)
Dürer; Innsbruck, 1495.

Malley, Jean
Words do not grow on the landscape.

Malloch, Douglas (1877–1938)
Ain't It [*or* It's] Fine Today.
Be the Best of Whatever You Are.
Family Trees.

Mallock, William Hurrell (1849–1923)
Brussels and Oxford.
Christmas Thoughts, by a Modern Thinker.
Marriage Prospect, A.
Softly the Evening.

"Malone, Carroll." *See* McBurney, William
B.

Malone, Walter (1866–1915)
Opportunity.

Malouf, David (b. 1934)
Asphodel.
An Die Musik.
Early Discoveries.
Guide to the Perplexed.
Off the Map.
Reading Horace outside Sydney: 1970.
Snow.
This Day, under My Hand.
Wolf-Boy.
Year of the Foxes, The.

Manaka, Matsemela (b. 1956)
Chorus: "Babylon, I did not come to you for
the sake of coming."
Chorus: "In the name of the people."
Pula, *Sels*.

Manchán, Saint (d. 665)
Manchán's Prayer.

Mandel, Eli W. (b. 1922)
Envoi: "My country is not a country."
Four Songs from the Book of Samuel.
From the North Saskatchewan.
Houdini.
Madwomen of the Plaza de Mayo, The.
Minotaur Poems, *Sels*.
My father was always out in the garage.
On the 25th Anniversary of the Liberation of
Auschwitz.
Song: "When the echo of the last footstep
dies."

Mandela, Zindzi (b. 1959)
My Country.

Mandelbaum, Harriet
Deus "Sex" Machina.

Mandelstam, Osip Emilyevich (1891–1938)
Age, The.
Ariosto.
Armenia, *Sels*.
Arteries Juicy with Blood.
Azure and Clay.
Batyushkov.
Feodosia.
From Prison.
I Was Washing Outside in the Darkness.
Leningrad.
Lines Concerning the Unknown Soldier, *Sels*.
Mounds of Human Heads Are Wandering into
the Distance.
Not yet dead, not yet alone.

Notre Dame.
On a board of raspberry and pure gold.
Petropolis.
Phaedra.
Shy speechless sound, The.
Stalin Epigram, The.
Stanzas: "I don't want to pay down the last
penny of my soul."
Take from my palms, to soothe your heart.
What street is this?

Mander, John (b. 1932)
As It Was.

Mandeville, Bernard (1670–1733)
On Honour.

Mang Ke
After the Night.
Fallen Tree, A.
Old Age.
Sorrows.
These Days.

Mangan, Gerald (b. 1951)
Glasgow 1956.
Scotland the Ghost.
Waiting for the Storm.

Mangan, James Clarence (1803–49)
Gone in the Wind.
Hymn for Pentecost.
Karamanian Exile, The.
Kinkora.
Lament for the Princes of Tyrone [*or* Tir-
Owen] and Tyrconnel [*or* Tirconnell], A.
Lover's Farewell, The.
Nameless One, The.
One Mystery, The.
Rest Only in the Grave.
St. Patrick's Hymn before Tara.
Shapes and Signs.
Siberia.
Song from the Coptic, A.
Time of the Barmecides, The.
To Amine.
To Joseph Brenan.
To Sultan Murad II.
To the Ingleezee Khafir, Calling Himself Djan
Bool Djenkinzun.
Twenty Golden Years Ago.
Vision of Connaught in the Thirteenth Century,
A.

Manger, Itsik [*or* Itzik *or* Itzig] (1901–69)
Adam and Eve.
Autumn.
I Am the Autumn.
Jealous Adam.
Mother Sarah's Lullaby ("Mother Sarah rocks
the cradle").

Mangoaela, Z. D. (1883–1963)
Boast of Masopha.

Manhire, Bill (b. 1946)
Children.
Contemplation of the Heavens.
Late Victorian Girl, The.
On Originality.
Prayer: "What do you take."
Selenologist, The.
Trees, The.
Zoetropes.

Manifold, John Streeter (1915–85)
Assignation with a Somnambulist.
Bunyip and the Whistling Kettle, The.
Defensive Position.
Deserter, The.
Fencing School.
Fife Tune.
For Comrade Katharine.
Garcia Lorca Murdered in Granada.
Griesly Wife, The.
Last Scab of Hawarth, The.
L'Embarquement pour Cythère.
Makhno's Philosophers.
Making Contact.
Night Piece.
Sirens, The.
Tomb of Lt. John Learmonth, A.I.F., The.

Manitongquat
Hear, O Humankind, the prayer of my heart.

Manley, Delariviere (1670–1724)
Epilogue: "Our Poet tells me I am very pretty."
Lost Lover, The, *Sels*.
Prologue: "Criticks, ye are grown so much
unkind of late."
Prologue: "First Adventurer for her fame I
stand, The."
Royal Mischeif, The, *Sels*.
Song: "Ah Dangerous Swain, tell me no more."
To the Author of Agnes de Castro.
What to conceal desire, when every.

Manley, Frank
Dead Letters.

Mann, Chris (b. 1948)
Comrades Marathon, The.
Poet's Progress, The.

Manner, Eeva-Liisa (b. 1921)
Cambrian, *Sels*.
If they wanted freedom.
Lunar Games, The.
To move over shifting borders.
Turn the page of stone and there.

Manning, Frederic (1882–1935)
Face (Guillemont), The.
Grotesque.
Leaves.
Trenches, The.

Manning, James Harold (1897–1924)
What Is Truth? *Sels*.

Manning, Nichola
Three Cars.

Manning, Robert. *See* Mannyng, Robert.

Manning-Sanders, Ruth (b. 1895)
Come Wary One.
Old City, The.

Mannyng, Robert (1288–1338)
Dancers of Colbek, The.
Handling Sin, *Sels*.
Praise of Women.

Mansel, William Lort (1753–1820)
Sun's Perpendicular Rays, The.

Mansfield, Katherine (1888–1923)
Friendship.
Little Brother's Secret.

Mansfield, Margery Swett (d. 1937)
Blessing Mrs. Larkin.

Mansfield, Richard (1857–1907)
Eagle's Song, The.

Mansour, Joyce (b. 1928)
Embrace the Blade.
Last night I saw your corpse.
North Express.
Seated on her bed legs spread open.
Sun in Capricorn, The.
Yesterday evening I saw your corpse.

Mansour, Khairi (b. 1945)
Nightwatch, *Sels*.

Mansur, Abul Kasim. *See* Firdausi.

Manville, Marion (b. 1859)
Lee's Parole.
Surrender of New Orleans, The.

Manwell, Juana. *See* Owl Woman.

Manyase, L. T. (b. 1915)
Mother Crab and Her Family, The.
Vusumzi's Song.

Manzano, Juan Fransico (1797–1854)
My Thirty Years.

Mao Tse-tung (1893–1976)
Chinese Ballad.
Day of Chung Yang, The.
"Deva-like Barbarian" — Ta-po-ti.
"Full River Red" — A Reply to Kuo Mo-jo.
Midstream.
Spring in Ch'in's Garden ("Alone I stand").
"Remembering the Lady of Ch'in" — Loushan
Pass.
"Song of Divination" — On the Plum Tree, after
a Poem by Lu Yu.
"Song of Picking Mulberry" Double-Ninth
Festival.
"Spring in Ch'in's Garden" ("Northern
landscape").
"Charm of Nien-nu, The" — Kunlun Mountains.

Mapanje, Jack A.
After Wiriyamu Village Massacre by Protuguese.
Another Fools' Day Touches Down: Shush.
Baobab Fruit Picking; or, Development in Monkey Bay.
Cheerful Girls at Smiller's Bar, The.
From Florrie Abraham Witness, *December 1972.*
Glory Be to Chingwe's Hole.
Making Our Clowns Martyrs.
Messages.
On African Writing.
Steve Biko is Dead.
These Too Are Our Elders.
We Wondered about the Mellow Peaches.

Mapes, Edith L.
Oh, If They Only Knew!

Mar, Laureen (b. 1953)
My Mother, Who Came from China, Where She Never Saw Snow.

Mar, Yekhi'el [or Yehiel] (1921–69)
Handfuls of Wind.

Marais, Eugène (1871–1936)
Dance of the Rain, The.
Deep River.
Heart-of-the-Daybreak.
Here We have No Firm Dwelling-Place.
Radio Cradle-song.
Sorceress, The.

Maran, René (1887–1960)
Human Soul.
Silence.
Tropicals.

Marbod of Rennnes (1035–1123)
Enemy in the Fortress, The.
Epitaph for Bruno of Angers.
Hymn of the Magdalen.
I Give You No Greeting.
Meditation among Trees.
Now must I mend my manners.
Of the Resurrection of the Body.
Prayer to God the Father.

Marcabrun (*fl.* 12th century)
At the Fountain.

Marcela de Carpio de San Felix, Sister (*fl.* 16th century)
Amor Mysticus.

March, Ausiàs (1397?–1459)
As someone on his back for months of illness.
Day's in dread of losing her bright features, The.
Know what I'm like? Some captain moors his ship.
Let others hail the holidays with laughter.
Much as a man who takes delight in dreaming.
Not so with me as with the little page.
Out scouting for sound counsels? How to prosper?

March, Caeia (b. 1946)
Ms World.

Marchant, John (*fl.* c.1751)
Little Miss and Her Parrot.
Young Master's Account of a Puppet Show.

Marchbank, Isobel
Sinn Fein: Ourselves Alone.

Marckant, John (*fl.* 16th century)
O Lord, Turn Not Away Thy Face.

Marcus, Morton (b. 1936)
Look Closely.

Mardale, W. R. (*fl.* c.1853)
Pop Goes the Weasel!

Margarido, Manuela (b. 1926)
You Who Occupy Our Land.

Margolis, Silvia (b. 1900)
Never Ask Me Why.

Marguerite de Navarre (1492–1549)
Autant En Emporte le Vent.
Smell of death is so powerful, The.

Mariah, Paul (b. 1937)
Brothers Grief, The.
Christmas 1962.
Quarry/ Rock.

Marianus
In this bath Cypris once was bathed by Love, her son.

Marias, Eugène
Desert Lark, The.

Marias, The Three (Maria Isabella Barreno *and* Maria Teresa Horta *and* Maria Velho da Costa) (c.1939)
Saddle and Cell.

Marie de France (c.1155–1189)
Chartivel, *Sels.*
Goat's-Leaf.
Hath any loved you well, down there.
Honeysuckle (Chevrefoil).
Lay of the Honeysuckle, The.
Love Is a Wound Within the Body.
Nightingale, The.
Two Lovers, The.
Would I Might Go Far over Sea.

Marino, Giovanni Battista (1569–1625)
Fading Beauty.
Lips and Eyes.
Madrigal: "Love now no fire hath left him."
Massacre of the Innocents, The, *Sels.*
Sospetto d'Herode.
Strage degli innocenti, La, *Sels.*
Yet on the other side, faine would he start.

Marinoni, Rosa Zagnoni (1888?–1970)
At Sunrise.
For a New Home.
Who Are My People?

Marion, Jeff Daniel
At the Wayside.

Marippittiyar
Charmer Turned Ascetic, A.
Hunter Once, Now an Ascetic, A.

Mark, Rickman
Snow in Town.

Markham, E. A. (b. 1939)
Don't Talk to Me about Bread.
Grandfather's Sermon and Michael Smith.
Late Return.
Old Thought for a New Couple, An.
Rewrite.
Towards the End of a Century.

Markham, Edwin (1852–1940)
Avengers, The.
Christ of the Andes, The, *Sels.*
Creed, A.
Forgotten Man, The.
Great Guest Comes In, The.
Guard of the Sepulcher, A.
How the Great Guest Came.
Joy of the Morning.
Lincoln, the Man of the People, *Sels.*
Man with the Hoe, The.
O Christ of Olivet, you hushed the wars.
Outwitted.
Peace.
Poet, The.
Prayer: "Teach me, Father, how to go."
Preparedness.
Revelation.
Right Kind of People, The.
Shine on Me, Secret Splendor.
Song to a Tree.
Task That Is Given to You, The.
There Is a High Place.
Third Wonder, The.
Victory in Defeat.
Young Lincoln.

Markham, Gervase (1568–1637)
Fragment: "I walked [or walk'd] along a stream for pureness rare."

Markish, Perets [or Peretz] (1895–1952)
After you, the killed of the Ukraine.
Mound, The, *Sels.*
No! Heavenly tallow, don't lick my gummy beards.
To a Jewish Dancer, *Sels.*
We Reached Out Far.

Markman, Stephanie
And/ Mother Why Did You Tell Me.
Rime of the Ancient Feminist, The, *Sels.*

They lived out in a women's house.

Marks, Naomi
Come Live with Me.
High Wonders.

Marks, S. J. (b. 1939)
How.

Marlatt, Daphne (b. 1942)
Femina.
Imagine: A Town.
Long Time Coming.
Steveston, *Sels.*

Marlatt, Earl Bowman (1892–1976)
Spirit of Life, in This New Dawn.
Through the Dark the Dreamers Came.

Marley, Bob (1945–89)
Trenchtown Rock.

Marlowe, Christopher (1564–93)
Ah, fair Zenocrate, divine Zenocrate.
Ah, Faustus,/ Now hast thou but one bare hour [or hower] to live.
Amorous Leander, beautiful and young.
Amorous Neptune.
And now the sun that through the horizon peeps.
And Ride in Triumph through Persepolis.
Beauty.
Bloody Conquests of Mighty Tamburlaine, The.
By this, Leander, being near the land.
Doctor Faustus, *Sels.*
Edward the Second, *Sels.*
Her veil was artificial flowers and leaves.
Hero and Leander, *Sels.*
Hero Feels the Shaft of Love.
I Have an Orchard.
In winter woe befell me.
It lies not in our power to love, or hate.
Jew of Malta, The, *Sels.*
Leander's Return.
Love at First Sight.
Mine Argosy from Alexandria.
Nature That Framed Us of Four Elements.
Now Clear the Triple Region of the Air.
Now, lusty lords now, not by chance of war.
O none but gods have power their love to hide.
On Hellespont, guilty of true love's blood.
Passionate Shepherd to His Love, The.
So on she goes, and in her idle flight.
Spell of Invisibility, A.
Tamburlaine the Great, *Sels.*
To Entertain Divine Zenocrate.
Tragedy of Dido, The, *Sels.*
Virgins, in vain you labour to prevent.
Was This the Face.
What Is Beauty?
Where are you damn'd?

Marot, Clément (1495–1544)
Anne Playing the Spinet.
Friar Lubin.
Love-Lesson, A.
Madame d'Albert's Laugh.
Posy Ring, The.

Marquis, Don (Donald Robert Marquis) (1878–1937)
Archy and Mehitabel, *Sels.*
Archy at the Zoo.
Archy Confesses.
Archy, the Cockroach, Speaks.
Archys Life of Mehitabel, *Sels.*
Ballade of the Under Side.
Certain Maxims of Archy, *Sels.*
Cheerio My Deario.
God-Maker, Man, The.
Grotesques, *Sels.*
Hen and the Oriole, The.
I oft stand in the snow at dawn.
I once heard the survivors.
Jokesmith's Vacation, The.
Limerick: "It needn't have ribaldry's taint."
Limerick: "There was a young fellow named Sydney."
Mehitabel and Her Kittens.
Mehitabel Tries Companionate Marriage.
No Social Stuff for Mehitabel.
Noah an' Jonah an' Cap'n John Smith.
Old Trouper, The.

Only Thy Dust.
Reverie.
Song of Mehitabel, The.
Time time said old King Tut.
To a Lost Sweetheart, Sels.
Tom-Cat, The.
Wail of Archy, The.
Warty Bliggens, the Toad.
Was it fancy, sweet nurse.
When One Loves Tensely.
When Whistler's Mother's Picture's frame.

Marr, Barbara (b. 1923)
Prayer: "Lord, make me sensitive to the sight."

Marriot, John (1893–1977)
On John Donne's Book of Poems.

Marriott, Anne (b. 1913)
As You Come In.
Beaver Pond.
Prairie Graveyard.
Wind Our Enemy, The, Sels.

Marryat, Frederick (1792–1848)
Captain Stood on the Carronade, The.
Snarleyyow; or, The Dog Fiend, Sels.

Mars, Ann (Annalita Marsigli)
Shadow.

Marsden, James (1908–73)
What Is Time?

Marsh, Daniel L. (1880–1968)
Greatest Person in the Universe, The.

Marsh, E. L.
Magic Piper, The.

Marshall, Archibald (1866–1934)
Limerick: "There was a young man of
Devizes."

Marshall, Austin John
Dancing at Whitsun.

Marshall, Edward (b. 1932)
Leave the Word Alone.

Marshall, Emily (b. c. 1978)
Friendship.

Marshall, Jack (b. 1937)
Arabian Nights.
Corroding Air, The.
F.
Hitchhiker.

Marshall, Lenore G. (1897–1971)
Invented a Person.

Marshall, Marjorie
Autumn.
Desire.
Night's Protégé.
Nostalgia.
To a Dark Dancer.

Marshall, Tom (b. 1938)
Interior Monologue 666.
Politics.
Summer.

Marshall, William E. (1859–1923)
Brookfield, Sels.

Marshall-Stoneking, Billy (b. 1947)
Passage.
Seasons of Fire, The.

Marsigli, Annalita. See Mars, Ann.

Marson, Una (1905–65)
Brown Baby Blues.
Gettin de Spirit.
Kinky Hair Blues.
Politeness.
Repose.
To Wed or Not to Wed.

Marston, John (1575–1634)
Cynic Satire, A.
Humours.
I cannot sleepe, my eyes ill neighbouring lids.
Malcontent, The, Sels.
Metamorphosis of Pygmalion's Image, The,
Sels.
O gracious gods, take compassion.
Satires, Sels.
Scourge of Villainy [or Villanie], The, Sels.
Song: "Delicious beauty that doth lie."
Song: "O Love, how strangely sweet."
To Detraction I Present My Poesie.

Marston, Philip Bourke (1850–87)
After.
Inseparable.
Not Thou but I.
Old Churchyard of Bonchurch, The.
Speechless [upon the Marriage of Two Deaf
and Dumb Persons].
Too Late.
Ungathered Love.

Marthe, M. Saint-. See Saint-Marthe, M.
Martí, José (1853–95)
I am a sincere man.
I grow a white rose.
Simple Verses, Sels.
Two Countries.

**Martial (Marcus Valerius Martialis) (c.40–
c.104)**
Advantages of Learning, The.
Believe me, sir, I'd like to spend whole days.
Bought Locks.
Country Pleasures.
Critics.
Dasius, chucker-out/ at the Turkish Baths.
De Coenatione Micae.
Don't pay any attention.
Either get out of my house or conform to my
tastes, woman.
Epigram: "Charm of my life, my dearest care."
Epigram: "Give me a boy whose tender skin."
Epigram: "Me Polytimus vexes and provokes."
Epigram: "Milo's from home; and, Milo being
gone."
Epigram: "My better half, why turn a peevish
scold."
Epigram: "Wife, there are some points on
which we differ from each other."
Epitaph for Erotion.
Erotion.
Erotion rests here, in the.
For Erotion's Grave.
Garland of roses, whether you come.
Go, Happy Rose.
Happy Life, A.
Hinted Wish, A.
His Tool was Large.
I Am Not Made of Fragile Elm.
I send you a lock of hair.
Laid with papyrus to catch fire.
Lentinus! thou dost nought but fume, and fret.
Likeness, The.
Lycoris darling, once I burned for you.
Martial [or Marshall or My Friend], the
thing[e]s that do [or for to] attain [or
attayne].
Near Neighbors.
Near the Vipsanian columns where the
aqueduct.
On a Slanderer.
On Bassa.
On Hedylus.
On the Death of a Young and Favorite Slave.
Post-Obits and the Poets.
Prithee die and set me free.
Procrastination.
Roman Presents.
Roman Thank-You Letter, A.
Sextus the Usurer.
Since your marriage you have lost the look.
Temperament.
Thais, why do you call me old.
Things that make the happier life, are these,
The.
To Charinus, a Catamite.
To Cloe.
To Dindymus.
To His Book[e].
To Julius.
To Labienus.
To Lygdus.
To Papirus.
To Philaenis.
To Phoebus.
To Polycharmus.
To Sextus.
Verses on Blenheim.

To Everlasting Oblivion.
We're at the Bath-house.
What a host you are, Mancinus.
What Makes a Happy Life.
What'mmmIdoin'?
Whenever you drink all night you make.
Would you, my friend, in little room express.
You are the most beautiful.
You Serve the Best Wines Always, My Dear
Sir.
You've Told Me, Maro.

Martin, C. D. (b. 1943)
God's Goodness.

Martin, Charles (b. 1942)
Leaving Buffalo.
Sharks at the New York Aquarium.
Signs.

"Martin, David" (Ludwig Detsinyi) (b. 1915)
Dreams in German.

Martin, Egbert (1859–1887)
National Anthem.
Trade.

Martin, Herbert (b. 1933)
Antigone I.
Antigone VI.
Lines: "Singularly and in pairs the decade has
been ripped by bullets."
Negro Soldier's Viet Nam Diary, A.

Martin, John
God's Dark.

Martin, Philip (b. 1931)
Nursing Home.
Tongues.

Martin, Sarah Catherine (1768–1826)
Old Mother Hubbard.

Martin, Sir Theodore (1816–1909)
I met a cracksman coming down the Strand.
Thieves' Anthology, The, Sels.

**Martin, Sir Theodore. See Aytoun, William
Edmonstoune.**

Martin, William
Apple Orchard in the Spring, An.

Martinez, Demetria
Chimayo.
Crossing Over.
Nativity: For Two Salvadoran Women, 1986–
87.
Salvadoran Woman's Lament.

Martinez, Dionisio D.
Three or Four Shades of Blues ("Stress of
Gijón, The").
Three or Four Shades of Blues ("These days in
Europe").

Martinez, James (c.1860–c.1945)
Dis Time No Stan' Like befo' Time.
My Little Lize.

Martinez, Maurice (b. 1934)
Suburbia.

Martinez, Victor
All Is Well.
Furniture.
Ledger, The.
Shoes.
Some Things Left Unsaid.

Martinson, Harry Edmund (b. 1904)
Cable Ship, The.
Cotton.
Dusk in the Country.
Earthworm, The.
On the Congo.
Sea Wind, The.

Martos, Marco (b. 1942)
Casa Nuestra, Sels.

Marty, Sid (b. 1944)
In the Dome Car of the "Canadian."

Martyrov, Leonid
In the Land Where Tanks.

Marula (fl. c.1156)
Meeting after Separation.

Marutanilanakanar
Hunchback and the Dwarf, The.

Marvell, Andrew (1621–78)
After Floods on the Wharfe.
After two sittings, now our Lady State.

Wanderer's Song, A.
West Wind, The.

Masham, Damaris, Lady (1659–1708)
When deaths cold hand shall close my eyes.

Mason, Caroline Atherton Briggs (1823–90)
President Lincoln's Grave.
When I Am Old.

Mason, Edgar Cooper
Safe in His Keeping.
Satisfied.

Mason, Herbert
Gilgamesh, *Sels.*
I asked unanswerable questions a child asks.

Mason, Madeline (b. 1913)
Janus.

Mason, Mason Jordan
Big Man.
In War.
Last Impression of New York.
Pen Hy Cane ("Pen Hyrogliphic Cane").
Pico della Mirandola.
Things of the Spirit.

Mason, Ronald Allison Kells
Be Swift O Sun.
Body of John.
Ecce Homunculus.
Footnote to John II: 4.
Judas Iscariot.
Latter-day Geography Lesson.
Old Memories of Earth.
On the Swag.
Prelude: "This short straight sword."
Sonnet of Brotherhood.
Spark's Farewell to Its Clay, The.
Young Man Thinks of Sons, The.

Mason, Ronald (b. 1912)
Self-Congratulatory Ode on Mr. Auden's
Election to the Professorship of Poetry at
Oxford.

Mason, William (1725–97)
English Garden, The, *Sels.*
How to Build a Ha-ha.
Nor, Shenstone, thou/ Shalt pass withou thy
meed, thou son of peace!
Ode to Memory, *Sels.*
Rise, hallowed Milton! rise, and say.
Thomas Gray's View of Nature.

Massey, Gerald (1828–1907)
All's Right with the World.
As proper mode of quenching legal lust.
Desolate.
Diakka, The.
His Banner over Me.
Little Willie.
O, Lay Thy Hand in Mine, Dear!
Robin Burns, *Sels.*
Womankind.
Worker, The.

Massimi, Petronilla Paolini (1663–1726)
Unbind Your Angered Tresses, *Sels.*

Massinger, Philip (1583–1640)
Death Invoked.
Emperor of the East, The, *Sels.*
Maid of Honour, The, *Sels.*
Men May Talk of Country-Christmasses.
Renegado, The, *Sels.*

**Masson, Tom (Thomas Lansing Masson)
(1866–1934)**
Enough.
He Took Her.
My Poker Girl.
Tragedy, A.
When I Get Time.

Masters, Edgar Lee (1869–1950)
Aaron Hatfield.
Amanda Barker.
Anne Rutledge.
Arlo Will.
Benjamin Franklin Hazard.
Business Reverses.
Carl Hamblin.
Cassius Hueffer.
Chase Henry.
Circuit Judge, The.

Daisy Fraser.
Davis Matlock.
Dora Williams.
Earth keeps some vibration going, The.
Editor Whedon.
Edmund Pollard.
Elliott Hawkins.
Elsa Wertman.
English Thornton.
Father Malloy.
Franklin James.
Hamilton Greene.
Henry C. Calhoun.
Herman Altman.
Hill, The.
In Memory of Bryan Lathrop.
Jacob Godbey.
Jonathan Houghton.
Jonathan Swift Somers.
Judge Somers.
Keats to Fanny Brawne.
Knowlt Hoheimer.
Lost Orchard, The.
Lucinda Matlock.
Marx the Sign Painter.
Meredith Phyfe.
Mind Flying Afar.
My Dog Ponto.
New Spoon River, The, *Sels.*
New World, The, *Sels.*
Ollie McGee.
Petit, the Poet.
Rutherford McDowell.
Scholfield Huxley.
Seth Compton.
Silence.
Spoon River Anthology, *Sels.*
Spooniad, The.
Supplication.
Thing Is Sex, Ben, The.
Tomorrow Is My Birthday, *Sels.*
Unknown Soldiers.
Village Atheist, The.
Wedding Feast, The.
Week-End by the Sea.
Widows.

Masters, Marcia Lee (b. 1910)
At My Mother's Bedside.
Country Ways.
Impressions of My Father, *Sels.*

Masterson, Dan
Bloodline.

Mastin, Florence Ripley (b. 1896)
Return to Spring.

Mastoraki, Jenny (b. 1949)
Crusaders knew the Holy Places, The.
Death of a Warrior, The.
Prometheus.
Then they paraded Pompey's urn.
Vandals, The.
Wooden Horse then said, The.

Matabaruka
Change, The.

Mataira, Katerina Te Hei Koko (b. 1932)
Restoring the Ancestral House.

Matchett, William H. (b. 1923)
Head Couples.
Water Ouzel.

Mathema, N. C. G. (b. 1949)
Maze of Blood, A.

Mather, Cotton (1663–1728)
Epitaph: "Dummer the shepherd sacrific'd."
Eternal God, How They're Increased.
Go then, my dove, but now no longer mine.
I Lift My Eyes Up to the Hills.
My Heart, How Very Hard It's Grown.
O Glorious Christ of God; I live.
Vigilantius, or a Servant of the Lord Found
Ready.
When the Seed of Thy Word Is Cast.

Mather, Joseph (1737–1804)
File-Hewer's Lamentation, The.
God Save Great Thomas Paine.

Matheson, George (1842–1906)
Christian Freedom.

O Love That Wilt Not Let Me Go.

Matheus, John Frederick (1887–1983)
Requiem: "She wears, my beloved, a rose upon
her head."

Mathew, Ray (b. 1929)
Good Thing, A.
Lover's Meeting.
One Day.
Poem in Time of Winter.
Seeing St. James's.
Wynyard Sailor.

Mathews, Aidan Carl (b. 1956)
Adam's Commentary After the Fall.
At the Wailing Wall.
Caedmon.
Cave Painter.
Chronicle.
Death of Irish, The.
Descartes at Daybreak.
Elegy for a Five Year Old.
Handbook for Revolutionaries.
How Words Meet to Make a Poem.
Interiors.
Keeping Pacific Time.
Landing, A.
Lawrence O'Toole.
Letter Following.
Library, The.
Minding Ruth.
Passages.
Persons Unknown.
Perspectives.
Process.
Returning to Kilcoole.
River's Elegy, The.
Severances.
Spectrum.
To a Child.
Two Months Married.
Woodniche.

Mathews, Esther
Song: "I can't be talkin' of love, dear."

Mathews, Harry (b. 1930)
ABC From the Store.
Condition of Desire.
Condo Auction.
Histoire.
Plaque, *Sels.*

Mathias, Eileen
All in Red.
Go Out.
In the Wood.
Just Jumbo.
Little Things.
My Hut.
Sea Fairies.
Tall Trees.
Zoo Manners.

Mathias, Roland (b. 1915)
Brechfa Chapel.
Craswall.
Departure in Middle Age.
Flooded Valley, The.
Sir Gelli to R.S.
God Is.
Laus Deo.
Memling.
Porth Cwyfan.
Testament.
Tide-Reach, *Sels.*

Mathieu, Lois
Counting Sheep by Night.

Mathis, Cleopatra (b. 1942)
Elegy for the Other.
Getting Out.

Mathison, Thomas (d. 1754)
Goff; an Heroi-comical Poem, The, *Sels.*
Victory on the Last Green.

Matos, Luis Palés (1898–1959)
Hurricane, The.

Matshoba, Mtutuzeli (b. 1950)
Mantatee Horde, The.

Matsumoto Koyu-Ni (*fl.* late 18th cent.)
At Ichiyiama/ Boating on Lake Nio.

Matsuo Basho. *See* **Basho.**

Mattam, Donald (b. 1909)
In a Town Garden.
Table Talk.

Mattera, Don (b. 1935)
Day They Came for Our House, The.
Giovanni Azania.

Matthews, Alice Clear
Of the Mathematician.

Matthews, Dorothea
Lynching, The.

Matthews, Harley (b. 1889)
Women Are Not Gentlemen.

Matthews, Marc (b. 1937)
Guyana not Ghana.

Matthews, Tom (b. 1945)
Cowboy Film.
Even the Whales.
Happy Arabia.
Private But Sulphurous.
Robert Sat.

Matthews, William (b. 1942)
Airline Breakfast, An.
Alice Zeno Talking, and Her Son George Lewis
    the Jazz Clarinetist in Attendance.
Blues for John Coltrane, Dead at 41.
Bmp Bmp.
Bud Powell, Paris, 1959.
Cat, The.
Civilization and Its Discontents.
Coleman Hawkins (d. 1969), RIP.
Directions.
In Memory of the Utah Stars.
Listening to Lester Young.
Merida, 1969.
Mood Indigo.
Nabokov's Death.
New.
Oh Yes.
Praise.
Psychopathology of Everyday Life, The.
Spring Snow.
Unrelenting Flood.
Waking at Dusk from a Nap.

Matthison, Friedrich von (1761–1831)
Adelaide.

Maturai Ilampalaciriyan Centan Kuttanar
What She Said.

Maturai Marutan Ilanakanar
What Her Girl Friend Said to Her.
When a King Asks for a Chieftain's Daughter.

Maturai Velacan
Peace Poem.

Maturaipputan Ilanakanar
Mothers.

Maturaittamilkkuttan Katuvan Mallanar
What the Servants Said to Him, as He Returned
    Home.

Matveyeva, Novella (b. 1934)
Eggplants Have Pins and Needles, The.

Maughan, Henry Neville
Husband of Poverty, The, *Sels.*
Song: "There was a Knight of Bethlehem."

Maughan, Jill (b. 1958)
Flames.
Long shadows.
Remembering.
Small Death, A.

Maunick, Edouard J. (b. 1931)
Accept from me not silence.
And I have chosen the sea as no man's land.
As Far as Yoruba Land, *Sels.*
Enter in the circle.
For there is an African virtue of the tree.
I am from everywhere.
I have mentioned it by name.
I have understood nothing.
I made the motions of the sacred place.
Letter to Ellen Conroy Kennedy.
Ofatedo/ seek it out upon the skin of Africa.
Point no scornful finger at Yoruba Land.
Seven Sides and Seven Syllables.
Speaking of Gethsemane in Yoruba Land.

This is where the warrior from Ibokun came.
This Strange Calculation of Roots.
Trees were forbidden me, The.
Where does this poem come from?

Maura, Sister (b. 1915)
Creation of Light, The.
Each Day.

"Maurice, Furnley" (Frank Wilmot) (1881–1942)
Echoes of Wheels.
Victoria Markets Recollected in Tranquility,
    The.
Whenever I Have.

Maurice, Thomas (1754–1824)
Epistle to the Right Hon. Charles James Fox,
    An, *Sels.*
How cursed that country, how severe its doom.

Mavimbela
My money! O, my money!

Maxson, Gloria A.
Baker.
Dead, The.
Epitaphs, *Sels.*
Golfer.
Living, The.
Miser.
Two Guitars, *Sels.*

Maxton, Hugh (b. 1947)
At the Protestant Museum.
Cernunnos.
Deutschland.
Elegies.
Ode.
Urgent Letter, An.
Waking.

Maxwell, Glyn (b. 1962)
Tale of the Mayor's Son.

Maxwell, James Clerk (1831–79)
Rigid Body Sings.

Maxwell, Ruth Fortney
Mother's Joy, A.

Maxwell-Hall, Agnes (b. 1894)
Jamaica Market.

May, Derwent (b. 1930)
"A Midsummer Night's Dream" in Regent's
    Park.
Child in the 80's, A.

May, Edward (*fl.* c.1633)
Five Things White.
On a Young Man and an Old Man.
To a Covetous Churl.
To Barba.
To Her Love.
You tender virgins, fairer than the snow with
    which you play.

May, John (b. 1932)
Six Things for Christmas.

May, Julia Harris (1833–1912)
Day by Day.

May, Sue (b. 1955)
Double Bass.
Haircut.
House.
Mildmay Grove.
Passion.
Photograph.

Maya, Kekchi
O God, my mother, my father, lord of the.

Mayakovsky, Vladimir Vladimirovich (1893–1930)
Cloud in Trousers, A.
Last Statement.
Our March.
Past One O'Clock.

Mayer, Bernadette (b. 1945)
Booze Turns Men into Women.
Complete Introductory Lectures on Poetry, The.
Essay.
Eve of Easter.
It Was Miss Scarlet with the Candlestick in the
    Billiard Room.
Kamikaze.
Laundry and School Epigrams.

Sonnet: "Everyone makes love to their bereft &
    go."
Tragic Condition of the Statue of Liberty, The.
Warren Phinney.
Woman I Mix Men Up, A.

Mayer, Gerda (b. 1927)
Ballad: "Knight went down to the river's rim,
    A."
Bilberries.
Chopin's Minute Waltz.
Count Carrots.
Crunch, The.
Dandelions.
Drip Drip or Not Bloody Likely.
Echo and Narcissus.
15th March 1939.
529 1983.
Her Friend Flo.
Noah.
Nocturne.
Old Mrs. Lazibones.
Old Wife Speaks, The.
Poor Mrs. Prior.
Small Park in East Germany: 1969.
Song: "Does the policeman sleep with his boots
    on."
There'll Be No Better.

Mayer, Hansjörg (b. 1943)
Oil.

Mayhall, Jane (b. 1921)
City Sparrow.
For the Market.
Human Animal, The.
Marshes, The.

Mayle, Bessie
Night is like an avalanche.
Skylines/ Are marking me in today.

Maynard, Theodore (1890–1956)
Faith's Difficulty.

Mayne, Jasper (1604–72)
Time.
To the Memory of Ben Johnson, *Sels.*

Mayne, John (1759–1836)
Logan Braes.

Mayne, Seymour (b. 1944)
Before Passover.
Roots.

Mayo, Edward Leslie (b. 1904)
Anglo-Saxon.
Diver, The.
El Greco.
Poem for Gerard.
Poet Who Talks to Himself, The.
Questioners, The.
Word of Water, The.

Mayröcker, Friederike (b. 1924)
Patron of Flawless Serpent Beauty.

Maze, Mack
If you see my mother, partner, tell her pray for
    me.

Mazhar, Farhad (b. 1946)
On My Birthday.

Mazur, Gail (b. 1937)
Family Plot, October.
May, Home after a Year Away.
Phonic.
Spring Planting.

Mbiti, John S.
Litany for Rain, A.
Snake Song, The.

Mbuyazi. *See* **Fynn, Henry Francis.**

Meacham, Harry M. (b. 1901)
On Hearing a Symphony of Beethoven.
To a Young Poet.

Mead, Jane (b. 1958)
Concerning That Prayer I Cannot Make.

Mead, Margaret (1901–78)
Misericordia.
That I Not Be a Restless Ghost, *Sels.*

Mead, Philip (b. 1953)
From a Republican Grave: Daniel Henry
    Deniehy, 1828–1865.
Man and the Tree, The.

Miller, Joaquin (Cincinnatus Heine [or Hiner] Miller) (1841–1913)
Alaska.
At the Grave of Walker.
Bravest Battle, The.
Byron, Sels.
Columbus.
Crossing the Plains.
Cuba Libre.
Defense of the Alamo, The.
For Those Who Fail.
Fortunate Isles, The.
In Men Whom Men Condemn as Ill.
Mothers of Men, The.
Rejoice.
Resurge San Francisco.
San Francisco.
That Gentle Man from Boston Town.
That Texan Cattle Man.
Washington by the Delaware.
Westward Ho!
William Brown of Oregon.
Miller, John N. (b. 1933)
Windward of Hilo.
Miller, Madeleine Sweeny (b. 1890)
How Far to Bethlehem?
Miller, Mary Britton (1883–1975)
Cat.
Foal.
Houses.
Miller, May (b. 1918)
Gift from Kenya.
Not That Far.
Scream, The.
Miller, Peter (b. 1920)
Capture of Edwin Alonzo Boyd, The.
Prevention of Stacy Miller, The.
Miller, Russell
Limerick: " 'If you dream,' said the eminent Freud."
Miller, Ruth (b. 1919)
Birds.
Cover my eyes with your palm.
Cycle, Sels.
Dropped leaf, The.
It Is Better to Be Together.
Long Since Last.
Mantis.
Penguin on the Beach.
Plankton.
Sterkfontein.
To eat pain like bread is a condition.
Miller, Thomas (1807–74)
Evening.
Summer Morning, Sels.
Watercress Seller, The.
Miller, Vassar (b. 1924)
Adam's Footprint.
At a Child's Baptism.
Beat Poem by an Academic Poet.
Beside a Deathbed.
Bird in the Hand, A.
Bout with Burning.
Christmas Mourning.
Defense Rests.
Dirge in Jazz Time.
Final Hunger, The.
Judas.
Lord, hush this ego as one stops a bell.
Love Song for the Future.
Love's Bitten Tongue, Sels.
On Approaching My Birthday.
Quarry, The.
Reciprocity.
Slump.
Spinster's Lullaby.
Trimming the Sails.
Without Ceremony.
Miller, William (1810–72)
Wee Willie Winkie rins [or runs] through the town.
Millett, William (b. 1925)
I Am Ham Melanite.
Milligan, Alice (1866–1953)
House of the Apple-Trees, The.

Milligan, Spike (b. 1918)
Cat Will Rhyme with Hat.
Christmas 1970.
Limerick: "Man who was asked out to dinner, A."
My Sister Laura.
Pygmy Elephant.
Thousand Hairy Savages, A.
Millikin, Richard Alfred (1764–1815)
Groves of Blarney, The.
Mills, Elizabeth Randall-. *See* **Randall-Mills, Elizabeth.**
Mills, Ida M.
At Breakfast.
In Days Gone By.
Mills, William (b. 1935)
Motel.
Necessity of Falling, The.
Pity.
Rituals along the Arkansas.
Unemployment.
Mills, William G.
Arise, O Glorious Zion.
Millward, Pamela
Just as the Small Waves Came Where No Waves Were.
Milne, Alan Alexander (1882–1956)
At the Zoo.
Buckingham Palace.
Disobedience.
Four Friends, The.
From a Full Heart.
Furry Bear.
Gold Braid.
Halfway Down.
Hoppity.
Hush! Hush! Whisper who dares!
King's Breakfast, The.
Lines Written by a Bear of Very Little Brain.
Miss James.
Missing.
More It Snows, The.
Politeness.
Puppy and I.
Three Foxes, The.
Us Two.
Vespers, Sels.
Milne, Angela. *See* **"Ande."**
Milne, Ewart (b. 1903)
Ballad for an Orphan.
Diamond Cut Diamond.
Martyred Earth, The.
Vanessa Vanessa.
Milner, B. E.
Christmas Night.
Milner-Brown, A. L.
Who Knows?
Milnes, Richard Monckton, 1st Baron Houghton (1809–85)
Burden of Egypt, The, Sels.
Columbus and the Mayflower.
Corfou.
England and America, 1863.
Good Night and Good Morning.
Ionian Islands, The, Sels.
Lady Moon.
Men of Old, The.
Our Mother Tongue.
Tranquil above the rapids, rocks, and shoals.
Sir Walter Scott at the Tomb of the Stuarts in St. Peter's.
Milns, William (1761–1801?)
Federal Constitution, The.
Milosz, Czeslaw (b. 1911)
Ars Poetica?
Between her and me there was a table.
Bobo, a nasty boy, was changed into a fly.
Bobo's Metamorphosis, Sels.
By the Peonies.
Cabeza, if anyone knew all about civilization, it was you.
Cafe.
Consciousness ("Consciousness enclosed in itself every separate birch").

Dedication: "You whom I could not save."
Elegy for N. N.
Esse.
Faith.
Fall, The.
Felicitous Life, A.
I liked him as he did not look for an ideal object.
If I had to tell what the world is for me.
Into the Tree.
Magic Mountain, A.
Master, The.
Mittelbergheim.
My Faithful Mother Tongue.
My-ness.
On Prayer.
On the Other Side.
Paulina, her room behind the servants' quarters.
Poet at Seventy.
Poor Christian Looks at the Ghetto, A.
Proof.
Rivers.
Song on the End of the World, A.
They are so persistent, that give them a few stones.
Throughout Our Lands, Sels.
To Raja Rao.
To Robinson Jeffers.
With their chins high, girls come back from the tennis courts.
Milton, John (1608–74)
About them frisking played.
Adam the goodliest man of men since born.
All Is Best.
And God said, let the waters generate.
Arcades, Sels.
As thus he spake, each bird and beast behold.
As when of old some orator renowed.
Ascent of Species.
At a Solemn Music [or Musick], Sels.
At a Vacation Exercise [in the College], Sels.
At once on th' eastern cliff of paradise.
At thy nativity a glorious quire.
Ay me! whilst thee the shores and sounding seas.
Banquet, The.
Be it so, for I submit; his doom is fair.
Beneath him with new wonder now he views.
Birds their quire apply; airs, vernal airs, The.
Blest pair of Sirens, pledges of Heaven's joy.
Blindness of Samson, The.
Brandish't sword of God before them blaz'd, The.
But peaceful was the night.
But see here comes thy reverend Sire.
But what is strength without a double share.
Chastity ("I Mean That Too, But Yet a Hidden Strength").
Come, come, no time for lamentation now.
Comus; a Masque Presented at Ludlow Castle, Sels.
Comus's Praise of Nature.
Creation of the Animals, The.
Descend from Heav'n [or heaven], Urania, by that name.
Descended, Adam to the bower where Eve.
Dungeon horrible, on all sides round, A.
Echo.
Egypt, divided by the river Nile.
Feast and noon grew high, and Sacrifice, The.
Fiend/ Saw undelighted all delight, all kind, The.
Flood, The.
For man to tell how human life began.
Forthwith the sounds and seas, each creek and bay.
Hail, holy light, ofspring [or offspring] of Heav'n [or heaven] first born.
Hail native language, that by sinews weak.
Hail wedded love, mysterious law, true source.
Half yet remains unsung, but narrower bound.
Happy rural seat of various view, A.
Haste thee, nymph, and bring with thee.
He ended, and they both descend the hill.
He ended; and thus Adam last replied.

Montgomerie, Alexander (1540?–1610?)
About ane bank, where birdis on bewis.
Away Vane World.
Cherry and the Slae, The, *Sels.*
Description of Tyme, A.
Night Is Near [*or* Neir] Gone, The.
Solsequium, The.
Tender Snow, of Granis Soft & Quhyt, The.
To Henry Constable and Henry Keir.
To His Maistres [*or* Mistress].
To R. Hudson.

Montgomerie, William (b. 1904)
Author Unknown.
Elegy for William Soutar.
Epitaph: "My brother is skull and skeleton now."
Glasgow Street.
Is there no vision in a lovely place?
Kinfauns Castle, *Sels.*

Montgomery, James (1771–1854)
Daisy, The, *Sels.*
Field Flower, A.
Indian Mother about to Destroy Her Child, An.
Inspiration, The.
Lust of Gold, The.
Nativity.
West Indies, The, *Sels.*
What Is Prayer?

Montgomery, John (b. 1919)
Snowmelt from Yesteryears.

Montgomery, M. T.
United Steelworkers Are We.

Montgomery, U. M.
Grey Brother.

Montoya, José (b. 1932)
Rough Time in th' Barrio.

Montrose, James Graham, Marquess of (1612–1650)
His Metrical Vow.
My Dear and Only Love, *Sels.*
On Himself, upon Hearing What Was His Sentence.
Touch, The.

Montross, Percy
Oh, My Darling Clementine.

"Monty Python"
All Things dull and Ugly.

Moody, Elizabeth (d. 1814)
Dr. Johnson's Ghost.
Housewife's Prayer on the Morning Preceding a Fete, The.
Sappho Burns Her Books and Cultivates the Culinary Arts.
To a Gentleman Who Invited Me to Go A-Fishing.

Moody, Minnie Hite
Say This of Horses.

Moody, William Vaughn (1869–1910)
Departure, The.
Faded Pictures.
Fire-Bringer, The, *Sels.*
Gloucester Moors, *Sels.*
Harmonics.
I Stood within the Heart of God.
Menagerie, The.
Ode in Time of Hesitation, An, *Sels.*
On a Soldier Fallen in the Philippines.
On the River.
This earth is not the steadfast place.

Moomey, Diana Lee
Again did the.

Mooney, Stephen (b. 1937)
Water Color.

Moor, George
Eternale Footeman's Tale, The.

Moore, Alan (b. 1960)
Girls' School.

Moore, Bertha
Child's Thought, A.

Moore, Clement Clarke (1779–1863)
Lord of Life, All Praise Excelling.
Visit from St. Nicholas, A.

Moore, Edward (1712–57)
Goose and the Swans, The, *Sels.*
Nun, The.

Poet and His Patron, The, *Sels.*
Song III: "As Phyllis the gay, at the break of the day."
To the Right Hon. Henry Pelham.
Why, Celia, is your spreading waist.

Moore, Egbert ("Lord Beginner")
Victory Calypso, Lord's 1950.

Moore, George (1852–1933)
Sonnet: "Idly she yawned, and threw her heavy hair."

Moore, Honor (b. 1945)
First Time: 1950.
Memoir.
Mourning Pictures, *Sels.*

Moore, John Travers (b. 1908) *and* **Margaret Moore**
Certainly, Carrie, cut the cake.
In winter when it's/ Zero.
Kettle's for the kitchen, A.
R is for ribbon.
What words begin with X?

Moore, Julia A. (1847–1920)
And now, kind friends, what I have wrote.
Ashtabula Disaster, The.
Departed Friend, A.
Grand Rapids.
Little Libbie.
Sketch of Lord Byron's Life.
Willie's and Nellie's Wish.

Moore, Lilian (b. 1909)
Bedtime Story.
Dragon Smoke.
In the Fog.
Listen!
Night Creature.
No One.
Sometimes.
To a Red Kite.
Until I Saw the Sea.
Wind Song.

Moore, Margaret. *See* **Moore, John Travers.**

Moore, Marianne (1887–1972)
Animals Sick of the Plague, The.
Arctic Ox, The.
Arthur Mitchell.
At Rest in the Blast.
Baseball and Writing.
Bird-witted.
Black Earth.
Blessed Is the Man.
Buffalo, The.
Carriage from Sweden, A.
Charity Overcoming Envy.
Critics and Connoisseurs.
Dream.
Egyptian Pulled Glass Bottle in the Shape of a Fish, An.
England.
Enough.
Face, A.
Fish, The.
Four Quartz Crystal Clocks.
Frigate Pelican, The.
Glory.
Granite and Steel.
Grave, A.
He "Digesteth Harde Yron."
Hero, The.
His Shield.
Hometown Piece for Messrs. Alston and Reese.
I May, I Might, I Must.
In Distrust of Merits.
In the Days of Prismatic Colour.
In the Public Garden.
In This Age of Hard Trying, Nonchalance Is Good And.
Jellyfish, A.
Jerboa, The, *Sels.*
Keeping Their World Large.
Labors of Hercules, The.
Leonardo Da Vinci's.
Lion in Love, The.
Love in America.
Marriage.
Mind, Intractable Thing, The.

Mind Is an Enchanting Thing, The.
Monkeys, The.
Nevertheless.
New York.
Nine Nectarines and Other Porcelain.
No Swan So Fine.
O to Be a Dragon.
Old Amusement Park.
Old Tiger.
Pangolin, The.
Paper Nautilus, The.
Part of a Novel, Part of a Poem, Part of a Play, *Sels.*
Past Is the Present, The.
People's Surroundings.
Peter.
Pigeons.
Poetry.
Rigorists.
Roman had an, A/ artist, a freedman.
Roses Only.
Saint Nicholas.
St. Valentine.
Sea Unicorns and Land Unicorns.
See in the Midst of Fair Leaves.
Silence.
Snakes, Mongooses, Snake-Charmers and the Like.
Sojourn in the Whale.
Spenser's Ireland.
Steeple-Jack, The.
Student, The.
Talisman, A.
Tell Me, Tell Me.
That Harp You Play So Well.
Then the Ermine.
Those Various Scalpels.
To a Chameleon.
To a Prize Bird.
To a Snail.
To a Steam Roller.
To Military Progress.
To Victor Hugo of My Crow Pluto.
Tom Fool at Jamaica.
W. S. Landor.
Walking-Sticks and Paperweights and Watermarks.
What Are Years?
When I Buy Pictures.
Wood Weasel, The.

Moore, Maurice
To the Peacock of France.

Moore, Merrill (1903–57)
And to the Young Men.
Book of How, The.
Domestic: Climax.
How She Resolved to Act.
In Magic Words.
It Is Winter, I Know.
Noise That Time Makes, The.
Old Men and Old Women Going Home on the Street Car.
Pandora and the Moon.
Shot Who? Jim Lane!
Transfusion.
Undergraduate.
Unknown Man in the Morgue.
Village Noon; Mid-Day Bells.
Warning to One.

Moore, Nicholas (b. 1918)
Fivesucked the features of my girl by glory.
Fred Apollus at Fava's.
Incidents in Playfair House.
Little Girl, The.
Love.

Moore, Richard (b. 1927)
Friends.
It Took TV to Civilize Our Village.
Suburb Hilltop.
Though the New Teacher Is a Trifle Odd.
Unable, Father, Still, to Disavow.
Visitors, The.
Willy, enormous Saskatchewan grizzly.
Word from the Hills, *Sels.*

Moore, Rosalie (b. 1910)
Catalogue, *Sels.*

Moore, Thomas (1779–1852)
After dreaming some hours of the land of Cockaigne.
And is there then no earthly place.
Argument, An.
At length, my Lord, I have the bliss.
At the Mid Hour of Night.
Believe Me, If All Those Endearing Young Charms.
Cherries, The; a Parable.
Come, Ye Disconsolate.
Copy of an Intercepted Despatch from His Excellency Don Strepitoso Diabolo.
Dear Harp of My Country.
Did Not.
Echo.
Epitaph on Robert Southey.
Epitaph on Tuft-Hunter.
Fly to the desert, fly with me.
Fragment of a Character.
From Miss Biddy Fudge to Miss Dorothy ———.
Fudge Family in Paris, The, *Sels.*
Fum and Hum, the Two Birds of Royalty.
Garden Song, A.
Glory of God in Creation, The.
Go Where Glory Waits Thee.
Golden Hour, The.
Hark! the Vesper Hymn Is Stealing.
Harp That Once through Tara's Halls, The.
How Oft Has the Banshee Cried.
I pray you, let us roam no more.
I Saw from the Beach.
I Wish I Was by That Dim Lake.
Ill Omens.
Irish Antiquities.
Irish Peasant to His Mistress, The.
Joke Versified, A.
Journey Onwards, The.
Kiss, The.
Lake of the Dismal Swamp, The.
Lalla Rookh, *Sels.*
Let Erin Remember the Days of Old.
Light of the Harem [*or* Haram], The.
Lines on the Death of Mr P — R — C — V — L.
Long, Long Be My Heart with Such Memories Filled.
Love's Young Dream.
Lying.
Meeting of the Waters, The.
Minstrel Boy, The.
Nay, tempt me not to love again.
Nonsense.
Odes to Nea, *Sels.*
Of All the Men.
Oft, in the Stilly Night.
Oh! blame not the bard, if he fly to the bowers.
Oh, Breathe Not His Name!
Oh, Come to Me When Daylight Sets.
Oh! ever thus from childhood's hour.
Oh, Thou! Who Dry'st the Mourner's Tear.
Oh! where's the slave so lowly.
On a Squinting Poetess.
Pastoral Ballad by John Bull, A.
Peri's Lament for Hinda, The.
Petition of the Orangemen of Ireland, The.
Pro Patria Mori.
Rhymes on the Road, *Sels.*
Scene from a Play, Acted at Oxford, Called "Matriculation."
She Is Far from the Land.
Song: "When the heart's feeling."
Song: "Where is the nymph, whose azure eye."
Song of Fionnuala, The.
Song of the Evil Spirit of the Woods.
Sound the Loud Timbrel.
Sweet Innisfallen.
Take Back the Virgin Page.
Temple to Friendship, A.
Thee, Thee, Only Thee.
They May Rail at This Life.
This Life Is All Chequer'd with Pleasures and Woes.
Thy Heaven.
Time I've Lost in Wooing, The.

'Tis the Last Rose of Summer.
To ———: "When I loved you, I can't but allow."
To Ladies' Eyes.
To Miss ———.
To My Mother.
To Sir Hudson Lowe.
Tory Pledges.
Venetian Air.
Weep, Children of Israel.
What's My Thought Like?
Young May Moon, The.

Moore, Thomas Sturge (1870–1944)
Beautiful Meals.
Daughter of Admetus, A.
Duet, A.
Dying Swan, The.
Event, The.
Gazelles, The.
Kindness.
Lubber Breeze.
On Harting Down.
Response to Rimbaud's Later Manner.
Sent from Egypt with a Fair Robe of Tissue to a Sicilian Vinedresser.
Variation on Ronsard.

Moore, Todd
After Work.

Moorer, Lizelia Augusta Jenkins
Accompanying a Gift ("From thy patient, who while here").
Accompanying a Gift ("One whose love will never end").
Africa.
Benefits of Sorrow.
Bible, The.
Birthday Wishes to a Husband.
Birthday Wishes to a Minister of the Gospel.
Birthday Wishes to a Physician.
Christmas Eve.
Christmas Tree, The.
Circle, The.
Claflin's Alumni.
Crum Appointment, The.
Dedication Day Poem.
Dialogue, A.
Door of Hope, The.
Duty, or Truth at Work.
Easter; or, Spring-Time.
Emancipation Day.
Eutawville Lynching, The.
Hallowe'en.
Immortality.
In Memoriam of E. B. Clark.
Injustice of the Courts.
Jim Crow Cars.
Legal Mouse, A.
Lela's Charms.
Lines to a Graduate.
Loyalty to the Flag.
Lynching.
Misunderstood.
Mountain Tops.
Must Be Freed.
Negro Ballot, The.
Negro Heroines.
Negro Schools, The.
Notable Dinner, A.
Peonage System, The.
Pharaohs of Today, The.
Prejudice.
Presidents, The.
Price of Disrespect, The.
Refining Fire.
Retribution.
Russia's Resentment.
Social Glass, The.
Social Life, The.
Song of the Angels.
Southern Press, The.
Southern Pulpit, The.
Southern Work of Dr. and Mrs. L. M. Dunton.
Sympathy.
Thanksgiving.
Tree of Knowledge, The.
Truth Suppressed, The.

Voice of the Negro, The.
What We Teach at Claflin.
Whisper Words of Love to Me.
Why Is It?
Why Negroes Don't Unite.
Why We Meet.

Moos, Lotte
Black Shawl, The.
Sisters?
Spendthrifts.

Mopev
Limerick: "There was a young girl with a hernia."
Would you care for a smoke or a sherry?

Mora, Pat
Arte Popular.
Gentle Communion.
Rituals.
Señora X No More.
Sonrisas.

Moraes, Dom (b. 1938)
Santa Claus.

Moraff, Barbara (b. 1940)
Let us suppose the mind.

Moraga, Cherríe (b. 1952)
Feed the Mexican Back into Her.
For You, Mamá.
La Dolce Culpa, *Sels.*
Poema Como Valentin (or a San Francisco Love Poem).
What kind of lover have you made me, mother.

Morales, Rosario
Crow's wings not feet — pinions.
Old, *Sels.*
Skin/ practicing to be old.

Moran, Michael ("Zozimus")
Pharao's Daughter.

Moran, Rod (b. 1952)
Cross Country.
Wire.

Morante, Elsa (b. 1918)
Sunday Evening.

Mordaunt, Charles, Earl of Peterborough (1658–1735)
I Said to My Heart.

Mordaunt, Thomas Osbert (1730–1809)
Sound, Sound the Clarion.
Verses Written during the War, 1756–1763, *Sels.*

Mordecai, Pamela (b. 1942)
For Eyes to Bless You.
Shooting the Horses.
Tell Me.

Mordecai ben Isaac (*fl.* 13th–14th century)
Fair Thou Art.
Rock of My Salvation.

More, Hannah (1745–1833)
Bas Bleu, The; or, Conversation, *Sels.*
Cold Ceremony.
Come, neighbour, take a walk with me.
Epilogue: "Child! we must quit these visionary scenes."
Gin-Shop, The; A Peep into Prison, *Sels.*
Hackney Coachman, The; Or, The Way to Get a Good Fare.
Inscription in a Beautiful Retreat Called Fairy Bower.
Patient Joe; or, The Newcastle Collier.
Perish th' illiberal thought which would debase.
Riddle: "I'm a strange contradiction; I'm new, and I'm old."
Riot; or, Half a Loaf Is Better than No Bread, The.
Search after Happiness, The, *Sels.*
Sensibility; a Poetical Epistle, *Sels.*
Slavery.
Slavery, a Poem, *Sels.*
Solitude.
Sweet Sensibility! thou soothing power.

More, Helen F.
What's in a Name?

More, Henry (1614–87)
Argument of Democritus Platonissans, or the Infinitie of Worlds, The.

Contrition.
Psychozoia, or, the Life of the Soul, *Sels*.

More, Sir Thomas (Saint Thomas More)
(1478–1535)
Age.
Death.
Eleventh Property, The.
Eternal Reward, Eternal Pain.
Eternity.
Fame.
First Property, The.
He struts about.
I am called Childhood. In Play is all my mind.
Manhood.
Mery Gest How a Sergeaunt Wolde Lerne to
Be A Frere, A.
Mine high estate, power and auctority.
Pageant Verses, *Sels*.
Peace of a Good Mind, The.
Rueful Lamentation on the Death of Queen
Elizabeth, A.
Seventh Property, The.
Things, good Lord, that we pray for, give,
The.
This life a Dream and Shadow.
Time.
Twelve Weapons of Spiritual Battle, The, *Sels*.
Venus and Cupide.

Morejón, Nancy (b. 1944)
Black Woman.
Central Park Some People (3 P.M.).
I Love My Master.
Mother.
Reason for Poetry, The.
Richard Brought His Flute.
To a Boy.

Moreland, John Richard
Birch Trees.
Faith.

Moreland, Wayne (b. 1948)
Sunday Morning.

Moreton, J. B. (*fl*. 18th century)
Ballad: "Altho' a slave me is born and bred."

Morfin, Guadalupe (b. 1953)
Paper Doll.

Morgan, Albert (b. 1908)
Union Man.

Morgan, Angela (1874–1957)
Awakening, The.
Choice.
God Prays.
God the Artist.
Poet, The, *Sels*.
Reality.
Thanksgiving.
Today.
Why hast thou breathed, O God, upon my
thoughts.
Work; a Song of Triumph ("Work!/ Thank God
for the might of it").

Morgan, Edwin (b. 1920)
Canedolia.
Computer's First Christmas Card, The.
First Men on Mercury, The.
Hyena.
In the Snack-Bar.
Instamatic.
Second Life, The.
Siesta of a Hungarian Snake.
Soho.
Strawberries.
To Hugh MacDiarmid.
View of Things, A.

Morgan, Elizabeth (b. 1947)
Caravati's Junkyard.

Morgan, Frederick (b. 1922)
February 11, 1977.
I Remember the Sea When I Was Six.
I Saw My Darling.
Night Skater, The.
1904.

Morgan, James Appleton (1845–1928)
Malum Opus.

Morgan, Jean (b. 1922)
Misogynist, The.

Morgan, John (1827–1903)
My Welsh Home.

Morgan, Robert (b. 1920)
Blood Donor.
Shadow Valley.

Morgan, Robert (b. 1944)
Chant Royal.
Death Crown.
Gift of Tongues, The.
Grandma's Bureau.
Hollow, The.
Mountain Bride.
Passenger Pigeons.
Stretching.
Walnutry.

Morgan, Robin (b. 1941)
And blessed be the women who get you
through.
And this is the fragrance, almost forgotten.
As it was in the beginning.
Blessed be my brain.
Ceremony, A, *Sels*.
Hallowing of Hell, The, *Sels*.
Invisible Woman, The.
Lesbian Poem.
Little heart, little heart.
Network of the Imaginary Mother, The, *Sels*.
On the Watergate Women.
Pedestrian Woman, The.
Self, The.
Survival.
Two Gretels, The.
We will grow old, and older.

Morgan, Sydney, Lady Morgan (1783–1859)
Kate Kearney.

Morgan-Browne, L. E.
Purple, White and Green, The.

Morganwg, Iolo. *See* **Williams, Edward.**

Morgenstern, Christian (1871–1914)
Aesthete Weasel, The.
Delayed Action.
Fish's Nightsong.
Funnels, The.
Great Lalula, The.
Hen, The.
Knee, The.
Knee on Its Own, The.
Korf's Clock.
Midnightmouse, The.
Moonsheep, The.
Nosobame, The.
On the Planet of Flies.
Palmstroem in Animal Costume.
Pearl-Hen, The.
Philosophy Is Born.
Picket Fence, The.
Police Inquiry, The.
Rabbi, The.
Salmon, The.

Morgridge, Harriet S. (*fl*. 19th century)
Mother Goose Sonnets, *Sels*.

Moriarty, Laura (b. 1952)
La Malinche.

Morice, Dave (b. 1946)
Alaskan Drinking Song.

Mörike [*or* Möricke], Eduard Friedrich (1804–
75)
Beauty Rohtraut.
Early Morning.
For the New Year.
Forsaken Girl, The.
Homesickness.
Insatiable Love.
It Is He.
It's Spring.
Mousetrap Incantation.
On An Old Painting.
Parting.
Prayer: "Lord, as thou wilt, bestow."
Prayer: "Lord, send what Thou wilt."
Prisoner, The.
Secrecy.
Sleeping Christchild.
Soul, Remember This!
Think of It, O Soul.

To an Aeolian Harp.
Tramping.
Weyla's Song.

Morin, Catherine A.
High June.
Lace Pedlar, The.

Morin, Maud
Bachelors' Buttons.
Shower and Sunshine.

Moritake. *See* **Arakida Moritake.**

Moritz, A. F. (b. 1947)
Protracted Episode.

Moritz, Yunna Petrovna (b. 1937)
Recollections.

Morley, Christopher (1890–1957)
Animal Crackers.
At the Dog Show.
Dial Call.
Elegy Written in a Country Coal-Bin.
Forever Ambrosia.
Gospel of Mr. Pepys, The.
In Honour of Taffy Topaz.
Nursery Rhymes for the Tender-hearted, *Sels*.
Pennsylvania Deutsch.
Plumpuppets, The.
Public Beach (Long Island Sound).
Secret Laughter.
Song for a Little House.
To a Post-Office Inkwell.
Trees, The.
Washing the Dishes.

Morley, Hilda (b. 1916)
December.

Morley, I. D. M.
Limerick: "Far beyond all the girls of Pirelli."

Morley, Judith
By what miracle.

Morley, Thomas
In Nets of Golden Wires.
Ladies, You See time Flieth.
No, No, Nigella!
Sing We and Chant It.
You Black Bright Stars.

Moronelli da Fiorenza, Pier (*fl*. 13th century)
Bitter Song to His Lady, A.

Morpurgo, Rachel [*or* Rahel] (1790–1871)
Song: "Ah, vale of woe, of gloom and darkness
moulded."
Sonnet: "My soul surcharged with grief now
loud complains."
Woe is me, my soul says, how bitter is my
fate.

Morpurgo, Rahel. *See* **Morpurgo, Rachel [*or***
Rahel].

Morris, Betty (b. 1948)
"Poet from Cheltenham Spa, A."

Morris, Brian (b. 1930)
Dinas Emrys.

Morris, Charles (1745–1838)
Address to Lady ——, Who Asked What the
Passion of Love Was?
But mark what he did.
Country and Town.

Morris, George Hornell
Sailor's Prayer, A.

Morris, George Pope (1802–64)
Main-Truck; or, A Leap for Life, The.
My Mother's Bible.
Pocahontas.
Retort, The.
Woodman, Spare That Tree.

Morris, Harry (b. 1924)
Because Thou Did'st Give.
Girod Street Cemetery: New Orleans.
Maine Lake at Night.
Where Lie All the Slain.

Morris, Herbert (b. 1928)
Newport, 1930.
Road, The.
Spanish Blue.
This Alice.

Morris, Ida Goldsmith
Give to the Living.

Twelve pears hanging high.
Two Comical Folk.
Two legs sat upon three legs.
Ungrateful Jenny.
Up at Piccadilly oh!
Wash the dishes, wipe the dishes.
What are little boys made of, made of?
What is the rhyme for porringer?
What's the news of the day.
When good King Arthur ruled this [or the] land.
When I was a bachelor/ I lived by myself.
When I was a little girl,/ About seven years old.
When the wind is in the east.
Where are you going [to], my pretty maid?
Where Is He?
Who Killed Cock Robin.
Willy boy, Willy boy,/ Where are you going?
Willy, Willy Wilkin.
Winter.

Motherwell, William (1797–1935)
Cavalier's Song, The.
Sing On, Blithe Bird.

Mothibi, Chief
Speech.

Motion, Andrew (b. 1952)
Anne Frank Huis.
Dying Race, A.
Human Geography.
Leaving Belfast.
No News from the Old Country.
One Life.
These Days.
Writing.

Mott, Elaine
Last Visa for Palestine, The.
On the Wings of the Wind.

Mott, Michael (b. 1930)
Islanders, Inlanders.

Motteux, Peter Anthony (Pierre Antoine) (1660–1718)
Town-Rakes, The.

Mottram, Eric
Brief Novel (3).
Peace Project (5).
Smell of canyon rain storm.

Moulton, Louise Chandler (Ellen Louise Chandler) (1835–1908)
At End.
Shall I Complain.

Moultrie, John (1799–1874)
Forget Thee?
Violets.

Mounsey, Messenger (1693–1788)
Here lie my old bones: my vexation now ends.

Mountjoy, Cyril
Limerick: "Gay soccer spectator from Wix, A."
Limerick: "Psychic researcher's elation, A."
Limerick: "Slow-footed stockman called Beales, A."
Limerick: "Victoria was bitterly short."
Limerick: "Young Joseph's new coat was real nice."

Mousley, James P. (b. 1937)
Prayer: "God of light and blossom."

Movius, Geoffrey (b. 1940)
Work-out, The.

Mowrer, Paul Scott (b. 1887)
Mozart's Grave.

Moyer, Linda Lancione
Listen.

Moyles, Lois
Report from California.
Tale Told by a Head, A.
Thomas in the Fields.

Mozart, Wolfgang Amadeus (1756–91)
Kanonentext.

Mozeen, Thomas (d. 1768)
Bedlamite, The.
Kilruddery Hunt, The.

Mozley, Abigail (b. 1947)
Summer I Taught English to the French, The.

Mphahlele, Ezekiel (b. 1919)
Exile in Nigeria.

Mphande, Lupenga (b. 1947)
Why the Old Woman Limps.
Wood-Cutter, The.

Mqhayi, S. E. K. (1875–1945)
Black Army, The.
Pleiades, The.
Sinking of the Mendi, The.

Mririda n'Ait Attik
Azouou.
God Hasn't Made Room.
Like Smoke.
Mririda.

Msham, Mwana Kupona (c.1810–1860)
Daughter, take this amulet.
Poem to Her Daughter, *Sels.*

Mtshali, Mbuyiseni Oswald (b. 1940)
Day We Buried Our Bully, The.
Farewell to My Scooter.
Removal of Our Village, KwaBhanya, The.
Shepherd and His Flock, The.

Mu Tan (b. 1917)
Funeral Ode.
Let Ninety-Nine Schools of Thought Contend.
My Uncle's Death.
Political Studies Class, The.

Mudie, Ian (1911–76)
This Land.

Mueller, Brian (b. c. 1974)
Kissing.

Mueller, Ilze
Another Time Track.
Invisibility Poem: Lesbian.
Night Shift at the Fruit Cannery.

Mueller, Jack
Death Jazz: A Review.

Mueller, Lisel (b. 1924)
Alive Together.
Blind Leading the Blind, The.
Historical Museum, Manitoulin Island.
January Afternoon, with Billie Holiday.
Lonesome Dream, The.
Merce Cunningham and the Birds.
Mermaid, The.
Monet Refuses the Operation.
Moon Fishing.
Palindrome.
Reading the Brothers Grimm to Jenny.

Mueller, Melinda (b. 20th cent.)
Teratology.

Muhammad al-Fayiz (b. 1938)
Sailor's Memoirs.

Mühlenberg, William Augustus (1796–1877)
Fulfillment.
I Would Not Live Alway.
Like Noah's Weary Dove.
Saviour, Who Thy Flock Art Feeding.

Muir, Edwin (1887–1959)
Abraham.
Absent, The.
Animals, The.
Annunciation, The.
Ballad of Hector in Hades.
Ballad of the Flood.
Bird, The.
Birthday, A.
Border, The.
Breaking, The.
Bridge of Dread, The.
Brothers, The.
Castle, The.
Child Dying, The.
Childhood.
Cloud, The.
Combat, The.
Confirmation, The.
Debtor, The.
Enchanted Knight, The.
Face, The.
Fathers, The.
Finder Found, The.
For Ann Scott-Moncrieff.
Gate, The.

Good Man in Hell, The.
Good Town, The.
Grove, The.
Horses.
Horses, The ("Barely a twelvemonth after").
Human Fold, The.
In Love for Long.
Incarnate One, The.
Interrogation, The.
Island, The.
Labyrinth, The.
Love's Remorse.
Mary Stuart.
Merlin.
Myth, The.
Mythical Journey, The.
Oedipus.
One Foot in Eden.
Prize, The.
Recurrence, The.
Refugees, The.
Return, The ("The doors flapped open in Ulysses' house").
Return, The ("The veteran Greeks came home").
Rider Victory, The.
River, The.
Road, The.
Robert the Bruce.
Salem, Massachusetts.
Scotland 1941.
Scotland's Winter.
Song: "Why should your face so please me."
Suburban Dreams.
Sunset.
Then.
Three Mirrors, The.
Too Much.
Town Betrayed, The.
Transfiguration, The.
Trophy, The.
Troy.
Usurpers, The.
Voyage, The.
Wayside Station, The.
Wheel, The.
Window, The.

Muir, Henry D. (b. 1870)
Soldier's Grave, The.

Muir, John (1838–1914)
From garden to garden, ridge to ridge.

Muireadhach Albannach (c. 1180–1220)
Prayer: "I praise Thee, Christ, that on Thy breast."

Mukai Kyorai (1651–1704)
Close of day.
Coming, coming!
Cuckoo sings/ at right angles, The.
Deep in the family shrine.
Distant sailboat never quite, A.
Every boatman in.
Fall breezes/ time to try out the.
Full sail, reefed sail.
He doesn't seem.
How to tell.
In this heat.
On the Death of His Younger Sister.
Poem of Parting.
Point of rock.
Rocky shore/ flocks of plovers.
So hot the melons.
That mountain I crossed.
Too dark to tell the gate.
Twenty Hokku, *Sels.*
Waters of the lake, The.
What's this?/ wearing a long sword.

Mukhopadhyay, Vijaya (b. 1937)
At the Ferry.
Wanting to Move.

Mukpo, C. T.
In protecting the earth, we found good pine needles and harsh.

Mukta Bai (*fl.* 13th century)
Although he has no form.

Muldoon, Paul (b. 1951)
Aisling.

Shower, *Sels.*
Smell of Coal Smoke, The.
Stars of the holiday step out all over the sky, The.
Sydney and the Bush.
There is a glow in the kitchen window now.
Valet, a Pillar, a Cloudburst of Water, A.
Walking to the Cattle Place, *Sels.*
Weights.
Widower in the Country, The.
Murray, Michele (1934–74)
Dance Poem, *Sels.*
I am giving you the dark birds of night.
My mother talked of breakfast or laundry.
Poem of Two, *Sels.*
Poem to My Grandmother in Her Death.
Murray, Patrick J. (b. 1911)
God's Little Angel.
Murray, Paul (b. 1947)
Rain.
Murray, Pauli (b. 1910)
Dark Testament.
Death of a Friend.
For Mack C. Parker.
Harlem Riot, 1943.
Inquietude.
Mr. Roosevelt Regrets.
Ruth.
Song: "Because I know deep in my own heart."
Without Name.
Murray, Raymond (b. 1938)
Carmelite.
Murray, Robert Fuller (1863–94)
Andrew M'Crie.
Wasted Day, The.
Murray, Rona (b. 1924)
Lizard, The.
Murry, Ann (b. c. 1755, d. after 1816)
Familiar Epistle, A.
Tête à Tête; or, Fashionable Pair: an Eclogue, The.
Mus, David
Conserves.
Joy of Cooking, The, *Sels.*
Musgrave, Susan (b. 1951)
Burial of the Dog.
I Am Not a Conspiracy Everything Is Not Paranoid.
Judas Goat, The.
Returning to the Town Where We Used to Live.
Salad Days.
Musinsky, Gerald
Drawing the Blinds.
Muske, Carol (b. 1945)
Applause.
August, Los Angeles, Lullaby.
Child with Six Fingers.
Eulogy, The.
Found.
Hyena.
Intensive Care.
Pediatrics.
Rice.
Swansong.
Wish Foundation, The.
Wyndmere, Windemere.
Musset, Alfred de (1810–57)
Juana.
Souvenir.
Mutabaruka (Allan Hope) (b. 1952)
Free Up de Lan, White Man.
Revolutionary Poets.
You Ask Me.
Mu'tamid, King of Seville (1040–95)
Tears of the World.
Woo Not the World.
Mutamociyar
Ay: A Gift of Elephants.
Ay: His Hill.
Mutanabbi (915–65)
Shame Kept My Tears Away.
Mutswairo, Solomon (b. 1924)
My Birds.

Muuse, 'Abdillaahi
Elder's Reproof to his Wife, An.
Muzahim al-Ugaili (*fl.* 700)
Earth Outside, The.
Mycall, John (d. 1833)
Our States, O Lord.
Myers, Frederic William Henry (1843–1901)
Inner Light, The.
Prayer: "O for one minute hark what we are saying!"
Saint Paul, *Sels.*
Myers, Jack (b. 1941)
Apprentice Painter, The.
Experts, The.
Have a Nice Day.
Jake Addresses the World from the Garden.
Mirror for the Barnyard.
Not Thinking of Himself.
So Long Solon.
Visitation Rites.
When I Held You to My Chest, You Fit.
Myhill, Kevin
They Dared Him.
Myles, Eileen (b. 1949)
At Last.
Dawn.
Greedy Seasons.
Medium Poem.
My Cheap Lifestyle.
On the Death of Robert Lowell.
Poetry Reading.
Woman like Me, A.
Mylonas, Eva (b. 1936)
Holidays.
Myoe (1173–1232)
Because fog engulfs.
Bright bright!/ bright bright bright!
Floating cloud, A.
How they sting!
Night deepening.
Set now,/ and I too will go below.
Shining moon, A.
Ten Tanka, *Sels.*
Under the pines.
While I, with no guide.
Winter moon.
Myrinos
"L" may stand for fifty, Lais.
Time topples Statyllios like a doddery oak.

N

Na-lan Hsing-te (1655–85)
"Autumn Waters" — Listening to Rain.
"Big String of Words, A" — The Great Wall.
"Butterflies Lingering over Flowers" — Leaving the Border.
"Immortal at the River" — Winter Willow.
"Partridge Sky" — Parting Sorrows.
"Remembering the Lady of Ch'in — At the Mouth of Dragon Pool.
"Remembering the Prince."
"Song of Dandy" — Hunting in Autumn.
Nabbes, Thomas (1605?–1641)
Microcosmus, *Sels.*
Song: "Beauty no more the subject be."
Song: "What a dainty life the milkmaid leads!"
Nabokov, Vladimir (1899–1977)
Ballad of Longwood Glen, The.
Evening of Russian Poetry, An.
Lines Written in Oregon.
Literary Dinner, A.
Ode to a Model.
On Discovering a Butterfly.
Pale Fire.
Rain.
Room, The.
Nachman of Bratslav
Grant me the ability to be alone.
Nadaud, Gustave (1820–93)
Carcassonne.
Nadir, Moishe (Yitzhok Reis) (1885–1943)
Adjectives.

Nadson, Semion Yakovlevich (1862–87)
Brother, The.
Nagase Kiyoko (b. 1906)
Mother.
Nagy, Agnes Nemes (b. 1922)
Bird.
Geyser, The.
Ghost, The.
I Carried Statues.
Lazarus.
Pinetree.
Scene, The.
Simile.
Storm.
To a Poet.
To Freedom.
Trees.
Winter Angel.
Words to a Song.
Nahman of Bratzlav, Rabbi (1770–1811)
Annul Wars.
Heart of the World, The.
Nahum (*fl.* c.1300)
Spring Song.
Naidu [*or* Nayadu], Sarojini (1879–1949)
Cradle Song: "From groves of spice."
In the Bazaars of Hyderabad.
Snake-Charmer, The.
Naiman, Adeline
Jennie Lubell is In a Nursing Home in Provincetown, *Sels.*
My mother has died, but I visit her weekly.
Nairne, Carolina Oliphant, Baroness (1766–1845)
Caller Herrin'.
Charlie is my Darling.
Hundred Pipers, The.
Laird o' Cockpen, The.
Land o' the Leal, The.
Will Ye No Come Back Again?
Naisby, T. H. (1931–1989)
Reflections on Hillsborough in Memoriam.
Naito Joso (1630–75)
Below the boulder where I sit.
Blackening the offing.
Both fields and mountains.
Bottom of loneliness, The.
Colder than the snow.
Dragonfly catches a fly, A.
Fifteen Hokku, *Sels.*
From my sleeve a katydid.
I run into fireflies.
Ill in Bed.
I've just come up.
Just seen the bottom of the water.
On the boulder at the bottom.
Thinking I'm after them.
Waiting on Basho as He Lay Ill.
White beach: a dog barks.
Wolves' voices harmonize.
Najara, Israel (1555–1628)
God of the World.
Loved of My Soul.
Nájera, Manuel Gutiérrez. *See* Gutiérrez Nájera, Manuel.
Najlis, Michele (b. 1946)
They Followed Us into the Night.
Nakajima Soin (1780–1856)
Before Gion Shrine, determined to drive away poverty.
Miscellaneous Songs of the Four Seasons East of the Kamo, *Sels.*
No more light from second-story lamps.
Nakamura Chio (b. 1913)
Diary without Dates, A.
Nakamura Teijo (b. 1900)
Season of changing clothes, The.
Nakasuk
Great Farter, The.
Gull, it is said, The.
Invisible Men, The.
Invocation: "Land earth-root."
Magic Words to Feel Better.

Twenty-seven Hokku, *Sels.*
Under how many layers of fallen leaves.
Useless acquaintances increase.
Visiting My Wife's Grave.
When Mother Died.
White peonies about to collapse.
Wild cat steps over kudzu vines, A.

Natsume Soseki (1867–1916)
Over the wintry.

Naudé, Adèle (b. 1910)
Africa.
From a Venetian Sequence.
Idiot, The.
Portrait.
Unpossessed, The.

Nauen, Elinor (b. 1952)
History of the Human Body/ Winfield's Infield
  Hit/ The Lassitude of the Infinite, The.
If I Ever Grow Old: Grim and Gleeful
  Resolutions.
Maine.
3 More Things.

Naylor, James Ball (1860–1945)
King David and King Solomon.

"Nayo." *See* Watkins, Nayo-Barbara.

Ndebele, Njabulo S. (b. 1948)
Revolution of the Aged, The.

Ndlovu, Thembinkosi
Elegy for the Dead of Soweto.

Neal, Larry (b. 1937)
Can I Tell You This Story, Or Will You Send
  Me through All Kinds of Changes?
Don't Say Goodbye to the Porkpie Hat.
Ghost Poem #1.
Harlem Gallery: From the Inside.
James Powell on Imagination.
Lady's Days.
Life, The: Hoodoo Hollerin' Bebop Ghosts.
Malcolm X — an Autobiography.
Middle Passage and After, The.

Neale, John Mason (1818–66)
Hymn for Easter Morn.
Oh, Give Us Back the Days of Old!

Neaves, Lord (1800–1876)
Let Us All Be Unhappy on Sunday.

Negri, Ada (1870–1945)
Make Way!
Mists.
Night.

Neidhart von Reuental (*fl.* 13th century)
On the Mountain.
"Sing, my golden cock, I'll give thee grain!"
Summer, now we must live without your sweet
  weather.
There is pain in my heart.
"Young and old, rejoice."

Neihardt, John G. (1881–1973)
Easter, 1923.
Envoi: "Oh, seek me not within a tomb."
One more rendezvous.
Prayer for Pain.
Song of Jed Smith, The, *Sels.*

Neill, Isabel
October.

Neilson, Francis (b. 1867)
Eugenio Pacelli.

Neilson, John Shaw (1872–1942)
Colour Yourself for a Man.
Crane Is My Neighbor, The.
Flowers in the Ward.
In the Street.
May.
Orange Tree, The.
Schoolgirls Hastening.
Soldier Is Home, The.
Stony Town.
Sun Is Up, The.
Sundowner, The.
Take Down the Fiddle, Karl!
To the Red Lory.
You Cannot Go Down to the Spring.

Nekrasov, Nikolai Alekseyevich (1821–77)
A Propos of the Wet Snow, *Sels.*
Capitals Are Rocked, The.

Frost, the Red-nosed, *Sels.*
Reflections by a Main Entrance, *Sels.*
When from dark error's subjugation.

Nelms, Sheryl L.
Into Fish.

Nelson, Alice Moore Dunbar-. *See* Dunbar-
Nelson, Alice Moore.

Nelson, David (1793–1844)
My Days are Gliding Swiftly By.

Nelson, Eric (1944–85)
Columbus of the Alphabet.
Everywhere Pregnant Women Appear.

Nelson, Frank Carleton
Human Heart, The.

Nelson, Howard
Cows near the Graveyard, The.
My Father Went to Funerals.

Nelson, Lynn. *See* Waniek, Marilyn Nelson.

Nelson, Paula (b. 1897)
House, The.

Nelson, Starr
White Rainbow, The.

Nelson, Willie (b. 1933)
Heaven and Hell.

Nemerov, Howard (b. 1920)
Amateurs of Heaven, The.
Angel and Stone.
At a Country Hotel.
Author to His Body on Their Fifteenth
  Birthday, 29.ii.80, The.
Backward Look, The.
Because You Asked about the Line between
  Prose and Poetry.
Blue Swallows, The.
Boom!
Brainstorm.
Brief Journey West, The.
Cabinet of Seeds Displayed, A.
Carol.
Casting.
Companions, The.
Death of God, The.
Dependencies, The.
Dial Tone, The.
Dialogue.
Dragonfly, The.
Dying Garden, The.
Easter.
Elegy for a Nature Poet.
Epigrams, I-IX.
Eve.
Extract from Memoirs.
Fable of the War, A.
Faith, The.
Found Poem.
Fugue.
Ginkgoes in Fall.
"Good-bye," said the river, "I'm going
  downstream."
Goose Fish, The.
Grace to Be Said at the Supermarket.
Gyroscope.
Historical Judas, The.
History of a Literary Movement.
Holding the Mirror Up to Nature.
Human Things.
I Only Am Escaped Alone to Tell Thee.
Icehouse in Summer, The.
IFF.
Insomnia I.
Landscape with Self-Portrait.
Learning by Doing.
Learning the Trees.
Life Cycle of Common Man.
Lot Later.
Make Love Not War.
Makers, The.
Manners.
Mapmaker on His Art, The.
Marriage of Heaven and Earth, The.
May Day Dancing, The.
Metamorphoses.
Money.
More Joy in Heaven.
Mousemeal.

Mud Turtle, The.
Murder of William Remington, The.
Mystery Story.
Negro Cemetery Next to a White One, A.
Night Operations, Coastal Command RAF.
Old Picture, An.
On Being Asked for a Peace Poem.
On Certain Wits.
Ozymandias II.
Phoenix, The.
Picture, A.
Primer of the Daily Round, A.
Reading Pornography in Old Age.
Redeployment.
Reflexions on the Seizure of the Suez, and on a
  Proposal to Line the Banks of That Canal
  with Bill.
Remorse for Time, The.
Santa Claus.
Scales of the Eyes, The.
September, the First Day of School.
Sigmund Freud.
Snowflakes.
Sparrow in the Zoo, The.
Speculation.
Spell before Winter, A.
Storm Windows.
Style.
Sunday at the End of Summer.
Sweeper of Ways, The.
Tapestry, The.
Thirtieth Anniversary Report of the Class of
  '41.
To D——, Dead by Her Own Hand.
To David, about His Education.
To the Rulers.
Town Dump, The.
Translation.
Trees.
Truth.
Vacuum, The.
View, The.
View from an Attic Window, The.
Waiting Rooms.
War in the Air, The.
Way of Life, A.
Western Approaches, The.
Wolves in the Zoo.
World Lines.
Writing.
Young Woman.

Nepo, Mark
I Wake from a Dream of Killing Hitler.

Nerber, John (1915?–1968)
Castaway.

**Neruda, Pablo (Neftalí Ricardo Reyes Basualto)
(1904–73)**
Body of a Woman.
Burial in the East.
Cat.
Drunk as drunk on turpentine.
Elephant, *Sels.*
Enigmas.
Fickle One, The.
Funeral in the East.
Gross innocent.
Keeping Quiet.
Lone Gentleman.
Materia Nupcial.
Melancholy inside Families.
Ode to My Socks.
Ode to Salt.
Ode to the Watermelon.
Our Child.
Stolen Branch, The.
To the Foot from Its Child.
Tonight I Can Write the Saddest Lines.
United Fruit Co, The.
Walking Around.
What is it that upsets the volcanoes.

**Nerval, Gérard de (Gérard Labrunie) (1808–
55)**
Delfica.
Golden Lines.
Grandmother, The.
Old Tune, An.

Howling Wolf (1850-1927) Cheyenne.
Indian Rock, Bainbridge Island, Washington.
Lines for Roethke Twenty Years after His
    Death.
Maggie.
Musician, The.
No One Remembers [Abandoning] the Village
    of White Fir.
Novelty Shop, The.
Old Woman Awaiting the Greyhound Bus.
On Hearing the Marsh Bird's Water Cry.
On Leaving Baltimore.
On Visiting My Son, Port Angeles,
    Washington.
Pieces.
Prisoners at Fort Marion: 1875-1878.
Reality of Autumn, The.
Slow Dancer That No One Hears but You.
Snowy Owl near Ocean Shores ("Snowy owl,
    storm cast from the arctic tundra").
Spider.
To Your Question.
Traveler, The.
Warrior Artists of the Southern Plains, *Sels.*

Niazi, Munir (b. 1928)
Dream of Paradise in the Shadow of War, A.

Nibenegenesabe, Jacob
One time I wanted two moons.
Wishing Bone Cycle, The, *Sels.*

Niblett, Peter
Tiger, The.

Nicaenetus (*fl.* 3d cent. B.C.)
Not in the city, Philoterus.
Speaks Bito's tomb to whomsoever reads.

Nicander (*fl.* 2d century B.C.)
Recipe: Gourds.

Nicarchos
Sweet Nicarete, who served Athene's shuttle.

Nicarchus of Alexandria (*fl.* 1st cent. A.D.)
Agelaus was kind to Acestorides.
All great events have harbingers.
Another doctor story. Our G.P., Marcus.
Diodorus the hunchback/ Went to Socles the
    quack.
Have you heard the latest miser story.
I like a lot of woman, full grown.
I like a woman built on ample lines.
If blocked, a fart can kill a man.
It's true I will die. So what do I care.
Law should have ear-plugs, not bandaged eyes,
    The.
Listen! The night-raven's song.
Little Diodoros is so skinny.
Nicole may have been a beauty long ago.
Niconoë has just inched past her prime.
No man's forever fully satisfied.
One deaf man went to law with.
Path of glory leads but to the grave, The.
Phido the miser's crying.
Single stench two winds have parted, A.
Take note who stoop.

Nichol, B. P. (b. 1944)
Gorg, a Detective Story.
Two Words; a Wedding.

Nicholl, Louise Townsend (1890–1981)
Cigar Smoke, Sunday, after Dinner.
Creation.
Cruse, The.

Nicholl, Theodore (1902–1973)
His Friend's Last Battle.

Nicholls, Judith
Journey.
Mary Celeste.
Orang-utan.
Season Song.
Storytime.
Whalesong.
Woodlouse.

Nichols, Carrie May
Boomerang, The.

Nichols, Grace (b. 1950)
Ala.
Alligator.
Caribbean Woman Prayer.

Grease.
Hi De Buckras Hi!
I Go to Meet Him.
Iguana Memory.
In My Name.
Invitation.
Lizard.
Loveact.
Old Magic.
Skin-Teeth.
Waterpot.
Without Song.

**Nichols, John Bowyer and Henry Charles
    Beeching.** *See* **Beeching, Henry Charles.**

Nichols, Kevin
Feast of Stephen, The.

Nichols, Robert (1893–1944)
Aurelia.
Before I woke I knew her gone.
Burial in Flanders, The.
But piteous things we are — when I am gone.
Come, let us sigh a requiem over love.
Comrades: an Episode.
Don Juan's Address to the Sunset.
Fisbo, *Sels.*
Flower of Flame, The, *Sels.*
Full Heart, The.
Harlot's Catch.
Moon behind High Tranquil Leaves, The.
Our Dead.
Secret Garden, The.
Sonnets to Aurelia, *Sels.*
Sprig of Lime, The.
Talking of Ezra Pound and long-dead pantos.
Though to your life apparent stain attach.
To D'Annunzio: Lines from the Sea.
When the proud World does most my world
    despise.

Nicholson, John (1790–1843)
On a Calm Summer's Night.

Nicholson, John Gambril (1866–1931)
Chaplet of Southernwood, A, *Sels.*
I love him wisely if I love him well.

Nicholson, L.
Bubbles.

Nicholson, Norman (1914–87)
Blackberry, The.
Caedmon.
Carol: "Mary laid her Child among."
Carol for the Last Christmas Eve.
Cleator Moor.
Cowper's Tame Hare.
Early March.
Glacier.
Michaelmas.
On the Closing of Millom Ironworks.
Ravenglass Railway Station, Cumberland.
Rockferns.
Shepherds' Carol.
Song at Night.
To a Child before Birth.
Weather Ear.

Nicias (c.470–413 B.C.)
Fountain at the Tomb, The.
I, Hermes, guard Cyllene's wooded slopes.
Spring blossoms, honey-bee, in the colours you
    parade.

Nicochares (*fl.* c.400 B.C.)
Hangover Cure.

Nicol, Abioseh (b. 1924)
African Easter.
Meaning of Africa, The.

Nicolson, Adela Florence Cory. *See* **"Hope,
    Laurence."**

Nicolson, Veronica
Limerick: "I once took my girl to Southend."

Nicophon (*fl.* c.400 B.C.)
Beware of Figs.

Niedecker, Lorine (b. 1903)
As praiseworthy/ the power of breathing.
For best work.
HJ, *Sels.*
Lake Superior.
My mother saw the green tree toad.

Old man who seined.
Old mother turns blue and from us.
Smile/ to see the lake.
Who Was Mary Shelley.
You are my friend.
Young in Fall I said: the birds.

Nieh Sheng-ch'iung (*fl.* 11th cent.)
Farewell to Li.

Nietzche, Vincente Rodríguez (b. 1942)
Mural, *Sels.*

Nietzsche, Friedrich Wilhelm (1844–1900)
Solitary, The.
Star Morals.

Niger, Paul (1917–62)
Initiations, *Sels.*
What?/ a rhythm.

Nightingale, Madeleine (b. 1879)
Apple Rhyme, The.
Caravan, The.
Scissor-Man, The.

Nigot
You surprise me, crow.

Nihoniho, Tuta
Government!

Nikitin, Ivan Savvich (1824–77)
Night in a Village, A.

Niles, John Jacob (1892–1980)
In All the Magic of Christmas-Tide.

Niles, Nathaniel (1741–1828)
Why Should Vain Mortals Tremble.

Nimmo, Kurt
All the Women in Suburbia.

Nims, Bonnie
On a Cold Autumn Day.

Nims, John Frederick (b. 1913)
Agamemnon before Troy.
Clock without Hands.
Conclusion: "If what began (look far and wide)
    will end."
Contemplation.
Love and Death.
Love Poem: "My clumsiest dear, whose hands
    shipwreck vases."
Parting: 1940.
Tide Turning.

Nishi Junko
Remorse Came Slowly.
Revolution.

Nitschmann, Anna (1715–60)
This Flock So Small.

Niyazi [or Niazi], Salah (b. 1935)
Thinker, The, *Sels.*

Nizami Arudi (*fl.* 1110)
Calling the Doctor (1000 A.D.).

No Ch'ŏn-myŭng (1813–57)
Cricket.
Deer.

Noailles, Anna de (1876–1933)
Image.
Poem on Azure.

Noble, Fay Lewis
Prayer for Song.

Noel, Henry (d. 1597) and William Strode
Beauty Extoll'd.

Noel, Thomas (1799–1861)
Old Winter.
Pauper's Drive, The.

"Nogar, Rui" (b. 1933)
Poem of the Conscripted Warrior.

Noguere, Suzanne (b. 1947)
Pervigilium Veneris.

Noho-mai-te-Rangi (*fl.* c.18th century)
Lullaby: "O my son, born on a winter's morn."
Song for Te Hauapu.

Nolan, James (b. 1947)
Jazz Poem for the Girl Who Cried Wolf.
Presenting Eustacia Beauchaud: Ward 3.

Nolan, Pat (b. 1943)
Doubt.
Exercise ("Get loaded").
Exercise ("Just as I stood up").
Great Pretenderer, The.

Celestial Evening, October 1967.
Cole's Island.
Colored pictures.
Colored pictures/ of all things to eat: dirty.
Death of Europe, The.
Distances, The.
I, Maximus of Gloucester, to You ("By ear, she sd").
I, Maximus of Gloucester, to You ("Off-shore, by islands hidden in the blood").
In Cold Hell, in Thicket.
Kingfishers, The.
Knowing All Ways, Including the Transposition of Continents.
La Chute.
La Préface.
Later Note on Letter 15, A.
Librarian, The.
Lordly and Isolate Satyrs, The.
Maximus from Dogtown-II.
Maximus Poems, The, Sels.
Maximus, to Gloucester, Letter 19.
Maximus, to Gloucester, Letter 27.
Maximus, to Gloucester, Letter 2.
Maximus, to Gloucester, Sunday, July 19.
Maximus, to Himself.
Merce of Egypt.
Moon Is the Number 18, The.
Moonset, Gloucester, December 1, 1957, 1:58 A.M.
Newly Discovered "Homeric" Hymn, A.
Perfume / of Flowers!, The.
Praises, The.
Ring Of, The.
Songs of Maximus.
These Days.
This morning of the small snow.
Variations Done for Gerald Van de Wiele.

Olson, Elder (1909–1992)
Ballad of the Scarecrow Christ.
Childe Roland, etc.
In Defense of Superficiality.
Knight, with Umbrella.
Reflections on Mirrors.
Wild Horse.

Olson, Ernst W. (1870–1958)
God of Peace, in Peace Preserve Us.

Olson, Ted (b. 1899)
Hawk's Way.
Things That Endure.

Olumo. See **Cunningham, James.**

Om Ui-Gil (fl. 17th cent.)
Sitting at Night.

O'Malley, D. J.
Tenderfoot, The.

Omar b. Abi Rabi'a (d. 720)
Damsel, The.

Omar Khayyám (d. 1123)
Ah Love! could you and I with Him conspire.
Ah, with the grape my fading life provide.
And when like her, oh Sákí, you shall pass.
Awake! for morning in the bowl of night.
Book of verses underneath the bough, A.
Come, fill the cup, and in the fire of spring.
For some we loved, the loveliest and the best.
Here with a Loaf of Bread beneath the Bough.
'How sweet is mortal Sovranty!' — think some.
I sometimes think that never blows so red.
Iram indeed is gone with all his rose.
Moving Finger writes; and, having writ, The.
Myself when young did eagerly frequent.
Oh, come with old Khayyam and leave the Wise.
Rubáiyát of Omar Khayyám of Naishápúr, The, Sels.
Some for the Glories of This World; and some.
They say the lion and the lizard keep.
Think, in this batter'd caravanserai.
Wake! for the sun, who scattered [or scatter'd] into flight.
Would but some winged Angel ere too late.
Would but the Desert of the Fountain yield.
Yet Ah, that Spring should vanish with the Rose!

Yon rising Moon that looks for us again.

Ombres, Rossana (b. 1931)
Afternoon Hours.
Ballad of Noah's Daughter.
Embalmer.
Ensnaring Flower of Psalms.
Excursion to Ravenna of a Young Girl with Her Parents, Sels.
Flower Ensnarer of Psalms.
Meadow Bug.
Morning Hours.
Strange Adventure.
Twelve.
White House, A.

Ome Shushiki (1668–1725)
Be careful! Be careful!

Onakatomi Yoshinobu. See **Yoshinobu.**

Ondaatje, Michael (b. 1943)
Biography.
Breaking Green.
Burning Hills.
Cinnamon Peeler, The.
Dog in San Francisco, A.
Elizabeth.
Gold and Black.
House Divided, A.
Inner Tube.
Letters & Other Worlds.
Light.
Notes for the Legend of Salad Woman.
Sweet Like a Crow.
To a Sad Daughter.
Walking to Bellrock.

Onderdonk, Henry Ustic (1789–1858)
On Zion and on Lebanon.
Spirit in Our Hearts, The.
Though I Should Seek.

Oneil, Henrietta (1758–93)
Ode to the Poppy.

Onitsura (Uejima Onitsura) (1661–1738)
At the Opening of Chikubu's Collection of Haikai.
Bright Moon: after an Illness.
Cooling Off in the Evening.
Early Autumn.
Fir stands sveltely under the moon, A.
Gargoyle spits out a sparrow to a peach tree, A.
I poured water in the basin.
I think the May rains.
In spring they croak.
In the mist something's visible.
Late spring.
Leaving Itami in Early February.
Monk Kudo Asked Me, "What's Your Haikai Eye Like?"
Night Grew Late in Kuzuha Village in Hirakata, The.
On My Way Home.
Profusely in confusion.
Remembering with Feeling.
Spring day: a sparrow sand-bathing in my garden.
Spring water's visible here and there, The.
Thirteenth Year of Genroku [1700], the Year My Boy Toshiaki Died, The.
Twenty-three Hokku, Sels.
Under flying sweetfish clouds flow in a stream.
Water bird, looking heavy, floats, A.
Why are some icicles long, some short?

Ono, Yoko (b. 1933)
Let Me Count the Ways.

Ono no Komachi (834–80)
Although I come to you constantly.
Color of the flowers, The/ has faded.
Colors of the flowers fade, The.
Doesn't he realize/ that I am not.
Doesn't he realize/ that I am not/ like the swaying kelp.
He does not come.
I fell asleep thinking of him.
If it were real/ Perhaps I'd understand it.
In the daytime.
No moon, no chance to meet.
Seeing the Moonlight.

Since I've felt this pain.
So lonely am I.
Thing which fades, A.
This night of no moon.
When My Desire.
When my love becomes/ All-powerful.
Without changing color.

Ono no Takamura (802–52)
Did I ever think.

Ono no Yoshiki
My love/ Is like the grasses.

Onuora, Oku (Orlando Wong) (b. 1952)
Last Night.
Pressure Drop.
Reflection in Red.

Oodgeroo Noonuccal. See **Walker, Kath.**

"Ophelia" (fl. mid–18th century)
Snaith Marsh; a Yorkshire Pastoral.

Opie, Amelia Alderson (1769–1853)
Orphan Boy's Tale, The.

Opitz, Martin (1597–1639)
Ah Dearest, let us haste us.
Concerning the Wolffsbrunnen near Heidelberg.
I'll lay this halfway me, which we the body name.
To This Book.
With snowy light of moon I cannot you compare.
You golden freedom, both my wish and my desire.

Opoku, Andrew Amankwa (b. 1912)
River Afram.

Oppen, George (b. 1908)
Bahamas.
Book of Job and a Draft of a Poem to Praise the Paths of the Living, The.
Building of the Skyscraper, The.
Exodus.
Five Poems about Poetry, Sels.
Forms of Love, The.
From Virgil.
Gesture, The.
It Is Difficult Now to Speak of Poetry.
Of Being Numerous, Sels.
Of Being Numerous #24.
Population.
Psalm: "In the small beauty of the forest."
Quotations.
Sara in Her Father's Arms.
Some San Francisco Poems.

Oppenheim, James (1882–1932)
Action.
As to Being Alone.
Bread and Roses.
Death.
Future, The.
Handful of Dust, A.
Hebrews.
New God, The.
Runner in the Skies, The.
Slave, The.

Oppenheimer, Joel (b. 1930)
Bath, The.
Blue Funk.
Bus Trip, The.
Father Poem.
Feeding, The.
Innocent Breasts, The.
Leave It to Me Blues.
Love Bit, The.
Mare Nostrum.
Mother Poem.
Undefined Tenderness, An.

Opperman, D. J. (b. 1914)
Christmas Carol: "Three outas from the [High] bleak Karoo."
Fable: "Under a dung-cake."
Fable of the Speckled Cow.
Water Whirligigs.

Orampokiyar
Five on the Crabs, Sels.
Five on the Riverside Cane, Sels.
What Her Girl Friend Said to the Foster-Mother ("If you think, mother").

What Her Girl Friend Said to the Foster-Mother ("In his fields, mother").
What Her Girl Friend Said when He Sent a Flattering Minstrel on His Behalf.
What Her Girl Friend Said, When the Woman Was About to Take Back Her Unfaithful Husband.
What She Said ("Bees, six tiny legs and wings all lovely").
What She Said ("Green creepers planted inside the house").
What She Said ("Hovering like the heron").
What She Said ("In his fields").
What She Said ("In his place, mother,/ field-crabs cut into the pink").
What She Said ("In his place, mother,/ mud-spattered spotted crabs").
What She Said ("In the full river").
What She Said ("Like the high fanning tufts on swift horses").

Orente, Rose J. (b. 1919)
Master City, The.

Orerulavanar
Relations.
What He Said.

"Orestes" (fl. c.1796)
Sonnet to Opium; Celebrating Its Virtues, A.

Orfalea, Gregory
Poacher, The.

"Orinda." *See* Philips, Katherine.

Orléans, Charles, Duc d' (1391–1465)
Alas, Death.
Alons au bois le may cueillir.
Come, Death — My Lady Is Dead.
Dieu Qu'il la Fait.
Go, Sad Complaint.
Honure, joy, helthe, and plesaunce.
In the Forest of Noyous Heaviness.
Mistress without Compare, A.
My Ghostly Father, I me confess.
Oft in My Thought.
Rondel: "Strengthen, my Love, this castle of my heart."
Smiling mouth and laughing eyn grey, The.
Spring.
Wanton Eye.
Well, Wanton Eye.
Whole Treasure of All Wordly Bliss, The.
Your Mouth Says, Kiss Me.

Orlen, Steve [or Stephen] (b. 1942)
Aga Khan, The.
Big Friend of the Stones.
Biplane, The.
Bridge of Sighs, The.

Orlovitz, Gil (1918–55)
Art of the Sonnet, *Sels.*
Night comes. Day runs for its life into my eyes.

Orlovsky, Peter (b. 1933)
Lepers Cry.
Second Poem.
Some One Liked Me when I Was Twelve.

Ormerod, V. R.
Limerick: "In dealing with time it is found."
Limerick: "Night's bible-black darkness prevails."
Limerick: "There was a young student called Fred."

Ormond, John (b. 1923)
Ancient Monuments.
At His Father's Grave.
Cathedral Builders.
Certain Questions for Monsieur Renoir.
Definition of a Waterfall.
Design for a Quilt.
Key, The.
Lament for a Leg.
My Grandfather and His Apple-Tree.
To a Nun.

Ormsby, Eric (b. 1941)
My Mother in Old Age.

Ormsby, Frank (b. 1947)
Apples, Normandy, 1944.
At the Jaffé Memorial Fountain, Botanic Gardens.

Day in August, A.
Home.
Interim.
Landscape with Figures.
Moving In.
My Careful Life.
Northern Spring, A, *Sels.*
Ornaments.
Padre, The.
School Hockey Team in Amsterdam, The.
Soldier Bathing.
Some of us stayed forever, under the lough.
Spot the Ball.
Survivors.
Under the Stairs.
War Photographers, The.
Winter Offerings.

Orozco, Olga (b. 1920)
Sphinxes Inclined to Be.

Orpingalik
In a Time of Sickness.
My Breath.

Orr, Bob (b. 1949)
Here.
Parable.

Orr, Elaine
In This Motherless Geography.

Orr, Gregory (b. 1947)
Adolescence.
After a Death.
All Morning.
Concerning the Stone.
Doll, The.
Gathering the Bones Together.
Like Any Other Man.
Love Poem: "Black biplane crashes into [or through] the window, The."
Poem: "This life like no other."
Song of the Invisible Corpse in the Field.
Sweater, The.
"Transients Welcome."
Two Lines from the Brothers Grimm.

Orr, Rosie
Moonpoem.

Orrery, Robert Boyle, 1st Earl of (1621–79)
On Christmas Day.

Orrick, John
Little Things.

Ortiz, Alfonso
Within and around the earth, within and around the hills.

Ortiz, Simon J. (b. 1941)
Bend in the River.
Bony.
Canyon de Chelly.
Creation, According to Coyote, The.
Dry Root in a Wash.
Forming Child Poems.
Four Bird Songs.
From Sand Creek, *Sels.*
My Father's Song.
Pretty Woman, A.
Returned from California.
San Diego Poem, A.
Serenity in Stones, The.
Spreading Wings on Wind.
Story of How a Wall Stands, A.
Survival This Way.
Telling about Coyote.
To Insure Survival.
Waiting for You to Come By.
Watching Salmon Jump.
Watching You.
What I Tell Him.
Wind and Glacier Voices.

Ortiz de Montellano, Ana Luisa
Space Between, The.

Ortleb, Chuck (b. 1950)
Metaphor as Illness.
Militerotics.
On Finding Out that the One You Slept with the Night Before Was Murdered the Next Day.
Some Boys.

Oruene, Taiwo Olaleye-. *See* Olaleye-Oruene, Taiwo.

Orwell, George (Eric Blair) (1903–50)
As One Non-Combatant to Another.
Dressed man and a naked man, A.
Italian soldier shook my hand, The.
Lesser Evil, The.
Oh You Young Men.
On Money.

Osadebay, Dennis C. (b. 1911)
African Trader's Complaint, The.

Osaki Hosai. *See* Hosai.

Osbey, Brenda Marie (b. 1951)
Alberta (Factory Poem/Variation 2).
Desperate Circumstance, Dangerous Woman, *Sels.*
In These Houses of Swift Easy Women.
Memory.
Portrait.
Wastrel-Woman Poem, The.

Osborn, Laughton (c.1809–1878)
Death of General Pike, The.

Osborn, Mary I.
Every Day.
My Playmate.
Swing, The.

Osborn, Selleck (c.1782–1826)
Modest Wit, A.

Osborne, Louis Shreve (b. 1923)
Riding Down from Bangor.

Osgood, Frances Sargent (1811–50)
Ah! Woman Still.
Caprice.
Celeste Dancing.
Child Playing with a Watch, The.
Cocoa-nut Tree, The.
Daisy's Mistake, The.
Ellen Learning to Walk.
Exile's Lament, The.
Flight of Fancy, A.
Forgive and Forget.
Had We But Met.
He Bade Me Be Happy.
I Turned From the Monitor.
Mother's Prayer in Illness, A.
New England's Mountain-child.
On a Dead Poet.
Statue to Pygmalion, The.
Woman.
Yes, Lower to the Level.

Osgood, Francis P. (b. 1910)
Winter Fairyland in Vermont.

Osgood, Kate Putnam (1841–1910)
Driving Home the Cows.

Osherow, Jacqueline
Looking for Angels in New York.
Sonnet: "He is like a cloud that for an instant."
Yiddish Muses, The.

Oshima Ryota. *See* Ryota.

"Ossian." *See* Macpherson, James.

Ostriker, Alicia (b. 1937)
Anxiety about Dying.
Everywoman Her Own Theology.
Extraterrestrial.
Happy Birthday.
I Brood about Some Concepts, for Example.
In the Twenty-Fifth Year of Marriage, It Goes On.
Meditation in Seven Days, A.
Pure Products of America, The.
Story of Joshua.

Osundare, Niyi (b. 1947)
Excursion.
Eyeful Glances.
Frantic as a prentice poet.
Goree.
Maddening moon, A.
Moon is an exile, The.
Moonsongs, *Sels.*
Our Earth Will Not Die.
We called the statue.
Who Says That Drought Was Here?

Oswald von Wolkenstein (1377–1445)
O Margie, Marge, Dear Margaret.

We Thank Thee.
We Thank Thee, Lord.
Where Are You Going, Greatheart?
Where Are You Sleeping To-night, My Lad?
With hearts responsive.
Your Place.

Oxlie, Mary, of Morpeth (*fl.* c.1656)
To William Drummond of Hawthornden.

Ozer, Kemal (b. 1935)
At the Beach.

P

"P., F. B."
O Mother Dear, Jerusalem.

Pace, Charles Nelson (1877–1954)
Cross, The.

Pacernick [*or* Pacernik], **Gary** (b. 1941)
Why I Write about the Holocaust.

Pacheco, José Emilio (b. 1939)
Boundaries.
On the Fragile Labyrinth.
Song to Be Written on a Wave.

Pack, Richardson (1682–1728)
Epistle from a Half-Pay Officer in the Country
    to His Friend in London, An.

Pack, Robert (b. 1929)
Adam on His Way Home.
Birthday.
Boat, The.
Cleaning the Fish.
Departing Words to a Son.
Don't Sit under the Apple Tree with Anyone
    Else but Me.
Everything Is Possible.
Frog Prince, The.
In a Field.
Pack Rat, The.
Raking Leaves.
Waiting.
Watchers.

Packard, Frederick (1794–1867)
Balearic Idyll.

Pacosz, Christina
Seed Is the Light of the Earth, The.

Paddock, Nancy
Alien.
Epiphany.
Original Mind.
Silos, The.

Padel, Ruth
Watercourse.

Padeshah Khatun (*fl.* 14th century)
Sovereign Queen.

Padgett, Ron (b. 1942)
Big Bluejay Composition.
Butterfly, The.
Chocolate Milk.
Electric Eel, The.
4:50 and dark.
Giraffe, The.
High Heels.
I call you on.
In literature and song.
Louisiana Perch.
Love Poem.
Ode to Bohemians.
Poema Del Dity 2.
Sonnet: "Lights in daytime indoors make
    outside."
Three Animals, *Sels.*
3 Little Poems, *Sels.*
Voice.

Padhi, Bibhu (b. 1951)
Poem for My Son.
Small Wants.

Padró, José I. de Diego. *See* **Diego Padró,
    José I. de.**

Paech, Neil
Parrots.

Pagan, Isobel (1740–1821)
Ca' the Yowes to the Knowes.

Page, G. K.
Kaleidoscope.

Page, Geoff (b. 1940)
Country Nun.
Grit.
Inscription at Villers-Bretonneux.
Premeditations.

Page, Patricia K. (b. 1916)
After Rain.
Arras.
Brazilian Fazenda.
Deaf-Mute in the Pear Tree.
Element.
Evening Dance of the Grey Flies.
Images of Angels.
Man with One Small Hand.
Permanent Tourists, The.
Photos of a Salt Mine.
Puppets.
Schizophrenic.
Snowman, The.
Stenographers, The.
Stories of Snow.
Suffering.
T-Bar.
Typists.
War Lord in the Early Evening.

Page, Thomas Nelson (1853–1922)
Dragon of the Seas, The.

Pagis, Dan (b. 1930)
Autobiography.
Draft of a Reparations Agreement.
End of the Questionnaire.
I am already quite scarce. For years [*or* now].
In the Laboratory.
Instructions for Crossing the Border.
Roll-Call In the Concentration Camp.
Scrawled in Pencil in a Sealed Car.
Story, The.
Testimony.
Written in Pencil in the Sealed Railway-Car.

Pagnucci, Gianfranco (b. 1940)
Death of an Elephant, The.

"Pai Wei" (b. 1902)
Madrid.

Pain, Barry (1864–1928)
Army of the Dead, The.
Poets at Tea, The, *Sels.*
Ride a Cock Horse.

Pain, D. W.
Limerick: "Modern young curate called Hyde,
    A."

Pain, Philip (d. 1668?)
Meditation 8.
Meditation 9.
Meditation 10.
Meditation 29.
Meditation 62.
Meditations for August 1, 1666.
Meditations for July 19, 1666.
Meditations for July 25, 1666.
Meditations for July 26, 1666, *Sels.*
Porch, The.
Whilst in This World I Stay.

Paine, Albert Bigelow (1861–1937)
Cooky-Nut Trees, The.
Dancing Bear, The.
Hills of Rest, The.
Mis' Smith.

Paine, Robert Treat (1773–1811)
Adams and Liberty.

Paine, Thomas (1737–1809)
Liberty Tree.

Paino, Frankie
For David.
Horse Latitudes.
Truth, The.

Painter, Charlotte
Elegy for Jack Moffat.

Palagyi, Louis (b. 1866)
Aimless.

Palaipatiya Perunkatunko
What Her Girl Friend Said to Her.
What She Said.

Palea (b. 1852)
Piano at Evening.

Palen, Jennie M.
Early Dutch.

Paley, Grace (b. 1922)
One day when I was a child, long ago.
Sad Children's Song, The.
That Year.
Women in Vietnam, The.

Paley Francescato, Martha (b. 1934)
Semen.

Palgrave, Francis Turner (1824–97)
City of God, The.
Creçy.
Eutopia.
Linnet in November, The.
Trafalgar.

Palladas [*or* Pallades] (360–430)
Blacksmith's quite a logical man, The.
Born crying, and after crying, die.
Born naked. Buried naked. So why fuss?
By what right do they call Zeus a lover?
Cuckolded husbands have no certain sign.
Death feeds us up, keeps an eye on our weight.
Don't fash yourself, man! Don't complain.
Each new daybreak we are born again.
Fate didn't hustle Gessius to his death.
God rot the guts and the guts' indulgences.
God's philosophical and so can wait.
Grammar commences with a 5-line curse.
Grammarian's daughter, The.
He, cursed with an ugly wife.
Hope! Fortune! Je m'en fous!
"I know all," you say; of incompleteness, you
    have enough.
I was promised a horse but what I got instead.
Ignorant man does well to shut his trap, The.
Ignorant of all logic and all law.
It's no great step for a poor man to the grave.
Just look at them, the shameless well-to-do.
Let this life of worry.
Life's a performance. Either join in.
Life's an ocean crossing where winds howl.
Lifetime's teaching grammar come to this, A.
Loving the rituals that keep men close.
Lyf So Short, The.
Man stole fire, and Zeus created flame.
Maurus.
Meditation.
Mein Breast, mein Corset und mein Legs.
Mere ants and gnats and trivia with stings.
Monks.
Murderer & Sarapis, The.
Poor devil that I am, being so attacked.
Poor little donkey! It's no joke.
Racing, reckoning fingers flick.
Sad and great evil is the expectation of death,
    A.
So, Mister Moneybags, you're loaded? So?
Thanks for the haggis. Could you really spare.
Theft of fire, The. Man's worst bargain yet.
Think of your conception, you'll soon forget.
This is all the life there is.
This is my mule, a poor long-suffering hack.
This Life a Theater.
Totting up the takings, quick Death can/ reckon
    much faster than the businessman.
We Greeks have fallen on evil.
When he comes up to the bedroom.
When you send out invitations, don't ask me.
Where's the public good in what you write.
Whose baggage from land to land is despair.
Why this desperation to move heaven and
    earth.
Women all/ cause rue.
Women all shout after me and mock, The.
Women tease and scold me, The.
Zeus isn't such a raving Casanova.

Pallottini, Renata
Message.

Palmer, Alice Freeman (1855–1902)
Communion Hymn, A.
On a Gloomy Easter.

Palmer, E. Harriet (1840–82)
Parterre, The.

Palmer, Herbert Edward (b. 1880)
Aunt Zillah Speaks.
Ishmael.
Rock Pilgrim.
Woodworker's Ballad.
Wounded Hawk, The.

Palmer, John F. (b. c.1870)
Band Played On, The.

Palmer, John Williamson (1825–1906)
Fight at [the] San Jacinto, The.
Maryland Battalion, The.
Ned Braddock.
Reid at Fayal.
Stonewall Jackson's Way.
Theodosia Burr: The Wrecker's Story.

Palmer, Michael (b. 1943)
At the fever of tongues.
Barely anything to say, everything said. But
you break.
Body in fog and the tongue, The.
Desire was a quotation from someone.
How did we measure.
I have answers to all of your questions.
She says, you are the negative.
Six Hermetic Songs, Sels.
Sun.
There were nine grand pianos in my father's
house.
View from an Apartment.
Words say, mispell and mispell your name.
You can bring down a house with a sound.

Palmer, Miriam (b. 1878?)
Raccoon Poem.
Vierge Ouvrante.
What if jealousy is just a bad dream?

Palmer, Opal
Flying to Ireland.
Wasting Time.

Palmer, Ray (1808–87)
Jesus, These Eyes Have Never Seen.
Lord, My Weak Thought in Vain Would
Climb.
My Faith Looks Up to Thee.

Palmer, Samuel (1805–81)
Shoreham: Twilight Time.

Palmer, T. H. (1782–1861)
Try, Try Again.

Palmer, Vance (1885–1959)
Farmer Remembers the Somme, The.
Snake, The.

Palmer, Winthrop
Arlington Cemetery Looking toward the
Capitol.

Palquera, Shem-Tob ben Joseph (1225–90)
Adapt Thyself.
Mouth and the Ears, The.

Paman, Clement (fl. c.1660)
On Christmas Day to My Heart.

Pambardu
Windmill At Mandanthanunguna.

Pamphilus
To the Swallow.

Pan, Lady. See Pan Chieh-yü.

Panatattu
True Knowledge.
Unity of God, The.

Pan Chao (48–117?)
Needle and Thread.

Pan Chieh-yü (fl. 1st cent. B.C.)
Present from the Emperor's New Concubine, A.
Song of Grief, A.

P'an Lang (d. 1009)
"Song of the Wine Spring."
Written on Lake View Tower.

"Panormitanus" (Antonio Beccadelli)
Epitaph on Pegasus, a Limping Gay.
This Quintus, Corydon, for whom you lust.

Pantiyan Arivutai Nampi
Children.

"Pantycelyn." See Williams, William.

P'an Yüeh (d. 300)
In Mourning for His Dead Wife.

Pao Chao (414–66)
Going Out Through the North Gate of Chi.
Have you not seen the grasses on the
riverbank?
In Imitation of Ancient-style Poetry.
Presented as a Farewell to Secretary Fu.
Water spilled on level ground.
Weary Road, The, Sels.

Pao Ling-hui (fl. 5th cent.)
After One of the 19 Famous Han Poems.

Pao Yu (fl. 5th cent.)
Viaticum.

Pape, Greg (b. 1947)
Birds of Detroit.
Dinner on the Miami River.
For Rosa Yen, Who Lived Here.
In Line at the Supermarket.
Indian Ruins along Rio de Flag.
La Llorona.
Mercado.
Minotaur Next Door, The.
October.
Storm Pattern.
Street Music.

Paramore, Edward E., Jr. (1895–1956)
Ballad of Yukon Jake, The.

Paranar
What Her Friend Said to Her, within the
Lover's Hearing.
What She Said.
What She Said to Her Girl Friend ("On the tall
hill").

Paraone, Tiwai
Chant to Io.

Paraske, Larin (1833–1904)
My Little Love Lies on the Ground.
Sad Is the Seagull.
Woman Grows Soon Old, A.

Pari, the daughter of
That Month.

Park, Mok-wol
Hills Surround Me.

Park, Roswell (1807–69)
Jesus Spreads His Banner o'er Us.

Parke, Walter (b. 1845)
His Mother-in-Law.

Parker, Alan Michael
Mud.

Parker, C. J.
Old soak from Stoke, An.

Parker, Dorothy (1893–1967)
Alfred, Lord Tennyson.
Bohemia.
Certain Lady, A.
Chant for Dark Hours.
Comment.
D. G. Rossetti.
De Profundis.
Experience.
Flaw in Paganism, The.
General Review of the Sex Situation.
George Sand.
Godmother.
Harriet Beecher Stowe.
Indian Summer.
Inventory.
Little Old Lady in Lavender Silk, The.
Lives and Times of John Keats, Percy Bysshe
Shelley, and George Gordon Noel, Lord
Byron, The.
News Item.
Observation.
On Being a Woman.
One Perfect Rose.
Oscar Wilde.
Partial Comfort.
Penelope.
Pictures in the Smoke.
Pig's-Eye View of Literature, A, Sels.
Résumé.
Sanctuary.
Social Note.
Some Beautiful Letters, Sels.
Song of One of the Girls.

Theory.
Thomas Carlyle.
Unfortunate Coincidence.
Walter Savage Landor.

Parker, Edwin Pond (1836–1925)
Master, No Offering.

Parker, Sir Gilbert (1862–1932)
Little Garaine.
Reunited.

Parker, Henry Adams
Apple Blossoms.

Parker, Lizbeth
Girl My Age, A.

Parker, Martin (c.1600–c.1656)
Description of a Strange (and Miraculous) Fish,
A.
Keep a Good Tongue in Your Head.
King Enjoys His Own Again, The.
Maunding Soldier; or, The Fruits of Warre Is
Beggery, The.
Sailors [or Saylors] for My Money.
Wooing Maid, The.

Parker, Patricia (b. 1944)
From the Cavities of Bones.
I Followed a Path.
My Brother.
Prologue from "Legacy."
There Is a Woman in This Town.
Where Will You Be?

Parker, Stephen (b. 1939?)
Winter in Étienburgh.

Parker, Theodore (1810–60)
Higher Good, The.
Way, the Truth, and the Life, The.

Parkes, Francis Ernest Kobina (b. 1932)
Apocalypse.
Blind Steersmen.
Three Phases of Africa.

Parkwood, Rose
Garden, The.

**"Parley, Peter." See Goodrich, Samuel
Griswold.**

Parmenion of Macedon
For a little gold, Zeus bought Danae.
Gutsy bugs grabbed grub from me till
disgusted, The.
Protection of a cheap coat suffices, The.
Statue of Nemesis at Rhamnus, The.
Thermopylai.
You poured down like gold,/ Olympian Zeus.
Zeus paid Danaé in gold:/ thus I pay you.

Parnell, Fanny (1854–1883)
After Death.

Parnell, Thomas (1679–1718)
Elegy, to an Old Beauty, An.
Essay on the Different Styles of Poetry, The,
Sels.
From the black beach and broad expanse of
sea.
Here all the passions, for their greater sway.
Hezekiah, Sels.
How deep yon azure dyes the sky!
How flame the glories of Belinda's hair.
Hymn to Contentment, A.
Night Piece on Death, Sels.
On Bishop Burnet's Being Set on Fire in His
Closet.
Riddle: "Upon a bed of humble clay."
Song: "When thy beauty appears."
To Mr. Pope, Sels.
Up yonder hill, behold how sadly slow.

Parone, Edward
Morning Track, The.

Parr, Joyce
Limerick: "There was an old sage of New
Delhi."

Parra, Nicanor (b. 1914)
I Move the Meeting Be Adjourned.
I Take Back Everything I've Said.
Journey Through Hell.
Litany of the Little Bourgeois.
Manifesto, Sels.
Piano Solo.
Pilgrim, The.

Paz, Octavio (b. 1914)
Friendship.
Girl.
Here.
Hurry.
Landscape.
Letter to Two Strangers.
Marvels of the Will.
Natural Being.
Obsidian Butterfly.
Old Poem.
Pause.
Solo for Two Voices.
Street, The.
Touch.
Tree Within, A.
Vrindaban.

Peabody, Josephine Preston (1874–1922)
Hymn: "Dear Lord, Whose serving-maiden."
Song of a Shepherd Boy at Bethlehem.
To a Dog.

Peach, Arthur Wallace (b. 1886)
Mosaic Worker, The.

Peacham, Henry (c.1576–c.1643)
Nuptial Hymn.
Period of Mourning, The, *Sels.*

Peacock, Molly (b. 1947)
Among Tall Buildings.
Breach of Or, The.
Commands of Love.
Don't Think Governments End the World.
How I Had to Act.
Just about Asleep Together.
Mental France.
Say You Love Me.
She Lays ("She lays each beautifully mooned finger").
Subway Vespers.
Surge, The.

Peacock, Thomas Love (1785–1866)
Andonis, My Daughter.
Border Ballad, A.
Chorus: "If I drink water while this doth last."
Crocket [*or* Crotchet] Castle, *Sels.*
Earth Song.
Even while he sung Sir Proteus rose.
Fear.
For the Children.
For the Slender Beech and the Sapling Oak.
Grave of Love, The.
Greatness.
Gryll Grange, *Sels.*
Headlong Hall, *Sels.*
In His Last Binn Sir Peter Lies.
In Respect of the Elderly.
Letter from School, A.
Love and Age.
Maid Marian, *Sels.*
Margaret Love Peacock, for Her Tombstone, 1826.
Melincourt, *Sels.*
Misfortunes of Elphin, The, *Sels.*
Newark Abbey.
Nightmare Abbey, *Sels.*
Over, Over.
Poor Johnny looked exceeding blue.
Priest and the Mulberry-Tree, The.
Sir Proteus, a Satirical Ballad, *Sels.*
Rich and Poor; or, Saint and Sinner.
Robin Hood and the Grey Friars.
Six Eagles.
Song by Mr. Cypress.
Song of the Four Winds, The.
Sun-Dial, The.
Ten thousand thousand fathoms down.
War Song of Dinas Vawr, The.
Wise Men of Gotham, The.

Peake, Mervyn Laurence (1911–68)
Conceit.
Frivolous Cake, The.
It Makes a Change.
My Uncle Paul of Pimlico.
Sensitive, Seldom and Sad.

Pearce, Ellen (b. 1946)
Orange Tree, The.

Turtle's Belly, The.

Pearce, Norman V.
Blind.

Pearl, Robert
Mourning Song.

Pearse, Jimmy
As he stood in their shop, Mr. Boosey.
Willesden Gree.

Pearse, Mark Guy (1842–1930)
Don't Trouble Trouble.
Facing the New Year.

Pearse, Padraic (1880–1916)
Christmas 1915.
Fool, The.
I Am Ireland.
Ideal.
Mother, The.
Prayer to Mother Mary.
Rebel, The.
Renunciation.

Pearson, Jean
Daily Prayer, A, *Sels.*
We ate no flesh in Eden, but afterwards.

Pearson, Mrs., *and* Richard Scrafton. *See* **Sharpe, Richard Scrafton.**

Pease, Deborah
Geography Lesson.

Peck, John (b. 1941)
Bracelet, The.
Cider and Vesalius.
Colophon for Lan-t'ing Hsiu-hsi.
Here Is a Song.
In Front of a Japanese Photograph.
October Cycle.
Ringers, The.
Rowing Early.
Spring Festival on the River, The.
Watcher, The.
What If the Saint Must Die.

Peck, Samuel Minturn (b. 1854)
Autumn's Mirth.
Kiss in the Rain, A.

Pedrick, Jean (b. 1922)
Carefully.
Inlet, The.
Redlight.

Pedroso, Regino
Opinions of the New Student.

Peele, George (1559–96)
And Who Has Seen a Fair Alluring Face.
Arraignment of Paris, The, *Sels.*
Bethsabe's Song.
David and [Fair] Bethsabe, *Sels.*
Dirge: "Welladay, welladay, poor Colin, thou art going to the ground."
Fair and Fair.
Fair Maiden.
Gently Dip.
Harvester's Song.
His Golden Lock[e]s [Time Hath to Silver Turned].
Hunting of Cupid, The, *Sels.*
O Gentle Love.
Oenone's Complaint.
Old Wives' [*or* Wife's] Tale, The, *Sels.*
Polyhymnia, *Sels.*
Song: "Lo! here we come a-reaping, a-reaping."
Spell, A.
Spread, table, spread.
Then proudly shocks amid the martial throng.
Three merry men, and three merry men.
Voice [Speaks] from the Well, A.
What Thing Is Love.
Whenas [*or* When as] the Rye [Reach to the Chin].

Peerson, Martin
Since Just Disdain.
Spring of Joy Is Dry, The.
Where Shall a Sorrow Great.

Peirce, Kathleen
Alcoholic's Son at Ten, The.
Farmers.
Near Burning.
Need Increasing Itself by Rounds.

Quilts.

Pelham, Sarah
Chuck: A Reminiscence.
Titian: Assumption (Detail).
When i was young.

Pelletier, Wilfred *and* Ted Poole
Wherever you are is home.

Peloubet, Maurice E.
Eternal Kinship, The.

Pembroke, Mary Sidney Herbert, Countess of (1562–1621)
Antonius, *Sels.*
Dedicatory poem: To the Angel Spirit of the Most Excellent Sir Philip Sidney.
Dialogue between two shepherds, Thenot and Piers, in praise of ASTRÆA.
From the depth of grief.
If Ever Hapless Woman Had a Cause.
Inhabitants of heavenly land.
Laudate Dominum.
"O Lord God of My Salvation.
Of Death.
Psalm CXLVII: "Praise ye the Lord."
Psalms of David, The, *Sels.*
To the Thrice-Sacred Queen Elizabeth.

Pembroke, William Herbert, Earl of (1580–1630)
Disdain Me Still.
Paradox, A.
Song: "Soules joy, now I am gone."

Pender, Lydia
Flying Foxes.

Penfold, Merimeri (b. 1824)
Land Laws, The.
Tamaki of a Hundred Lovers.

Penfold, Nita
Woman with the Wild-Grown Hair Relaxes after Another Long Day, The.

P'eng Sun-yü (1631–1700)
From withered trees we gather the silkworm floss.
Mooring in the Evening at Plum Village, *Sels.*
Mounted on a mule, to ford the shallow stream.
North-of-the-River Rhymes, *Sels.*

Penha, Abraham A. Lopez-. *See* **Lopez-Penha, Abraham A.**

Peniarth Poet, The (*fl.* after 1484)
Drinking Song, A, *Sels.*
Loke that none of you departe.

Penkethman, John (*fl.* c.1630)
Schoolmaster's Precepts, A.
Some Boys.

Penna, Sandro (1906–77)
Lady on Streetcar.

Pennant, Edmund (b. 1917)
Lost Explorer.
Thoughts under the Giant Sequoia.
Yom Hazikaron.

Pennecuik, Alexander (d. 1730)
Below fair Peebles, on the river's side.
Marriage betwixt Scrape, Monarch of the Maunders, and Blobberlips, Queen of the Gypsies, A, *Sels.*

Pennell, Henry Cholmondeley. *See* **Cholmondeley-Pennell, Henry.**

Penny, Anne (1731–1784)
Odes Sung in Commemoration of the Marine Society, *Sels.*
Sung at Table by the Same Choir.
Sung by a Choir of Boys Marching Round the Room.

Penny, Rob (b. 1940)
And We Conquered.
Be Cool, Baby.
I Remember How She Sang.
Real People Loves One Another, The.

Penny, W. E.
Town of Nogood, The.

Penrose, Roland (1900–1984)
Road Is Wider than Long, The, *Sels.*

Penrose, Thomas (1742–79)
Helmets; a Fragment, The.

Percival, James Gates (1795–1856)
Apostrophe to the Island of Cuba.
Coral Grove, The.
May.
To Senaca Lake.

Percy, William (1575–1648)
Coelia, Sels.
Judged by my goddess' doom to endless pain.
Relent, my dear yet unkind Coelia.
Sonnet: "It shall be said [or sayd] I died [or dy'de] for Coelia."

Percy, William Alexander (1885–1942)
Epilogue: "Giver of bliss and pain, of song and prayer."
Farmers.
Hymn to the Sun.
Page's Road Song, A.
They Cast Their Nets in Galilee.

Pereira, Francesca Yetunde (b. 1933)
Burden, The.
Mother Dark.
Paradox, The.
Two Strange Worlds.

Perelman, Bob (b. 1947)
Chronic Meanings.
Movie.

Péret, Benjamin (1899–1959)
Little Song of the Maimed.

Peretz [or Perets], Isaac Leibush [or Yitskhok Leybush] (1852?–1915)
All through the Stranger's Wood.
Believe Not.
Eternal Sabbath.
Hope and Faith.
In the Silent Night.
Little People.
Three Seamstresses, The.

Perevin Muruvalar
Elegy: "He has held."
What He Said.

Perez, Tony
Brownout.
Volunteer Worker.

Perez de Ayala, Ramon. *See Ayala, Ramon Perez de.*

Periquet Y Zuaznabar, Fernando (1873–1940)
Discreet Majo, The.
Forgotten Majo, The.
Love and Hate.
Maja's Glance, The.
Piteous Maja, The ("Oh cruel death").
Piteous Maja, The ("Of that loving majo").
Piteous Maja, The ("Oh majo of my life").
Timid Majo, The.
Walk, A.

Perkins, Emily Swan (1866–1941)
Thou Art, O God, the God of Might.

Perkins, Louis Saunders
Genius.

Perkins, Lucy Alice
"Laborers Together with God."

Perkins, Silas H.
Common Road, The.

Perkoff, Stuart Z. (1930–74)
Feasts of Death, Feasts of Love.
Flowers for Luis Bunuel.
Recluses, The.

Perlberg, Mark (b. 1929)
Hiroshige.

Pernath, Hugues C. (1931–75)
Index, Sels.

Perrine, Laurence (b. 1915)
Janus.

Perronet, Edward (1725–92)
All Hail the Power of Jesus' Name.

Perry, Gordon (b. 1909)
Aids for Latin.
Great Lakes of Canada, The.

Perry, Grace (b. 1927)
Time of Turtles.

Perry, Julianne (b. 1952)
No Dawns.
To L.

Perry, Lilla Cabot (1848–1933)
As It Was.
As She Feared It Would Be.
Meeting after Long Absence, Sels.

Perry, Nora (1831–76)
Balboa.
Coming of Spring, The.
Next Year.
Running the Blockade.
Too Late.

Perry, Thomas (fl. c.1772–c.1775)
Antarctic Muse, The.

Perry, Tod (b. 1931)
For Nicholas, Born in September.

Perryman, Kevin (b. 1950)
Improvisation (Eching).

"Perse, St.-John" (Alexis Saint-Léger Léger) (1887–1975)
Anabasis, Sels.
Birds, Sels.
Exile, Sels.
Snows, Sels.
Such is the way of the world.

Perses (fl. 316 B.C.)
Artemis.
Death came before Marriage, Philaenion.
Lucina, Care.
Mnasylla, the daughter you lament.
Time & prayer fitting, I, the god.

Persius (Aulus Persius Flaccus) (A.D. 34–62)
Prologue to the First Satire.
Satires, Sels.

Peruncittiranar
Bard's Family, A.

Perunkunrur Kilar
Parade, A.

Peseroff, Joyce
Hardness Scale, The.

Peskett, William (b. 1952)
Bottles in the Zoological Museum.
From Belfast to Suffolk.
Inheritors, The.
Question of Time, The.
Star and Sea.
Window Dressing.

Pessoa, Fernando (1888–1935)
Ascent of Vasco da Gama, The.
Blighter, The.
I Am Tired.
If, after I Die.
If They Want Me To Be a Mystic, Fine. So I'm a Mystic.
Portuguese Sea, The.
Salutation to Walt Whitman.
Tobacco Shop.

Pestel [or Pestell], Thomas (1585–1667)
On Tobacco.
Song: "Silly boy, there is no cause."

Petchenik, Kenneth
Limerick: "There was a young faggot called Willy."

"Peter"
Bus, The.
Poetry.
Saint Wears a Halo, The.
Speed Track, The.

Peters, Lenrie (b. 1932)
After They Put Down Their Overalls.
Home Coming.
I am asking about the way ahead.
Isatou died.
Remember They Say.

Peters, Robert (b. 1924)
Arrival, New York Harbor.
Blessing a Bride and Groom; a Wedding Night Poem.
Blood Countess, The, Sels.
Buying a Record.
Crazy Bill to the Bishop.
Darkling Chicken, The.
Feathered Friends.
Final Soliloquy on a Randy Rooster (in a Key of Yellow).
Hollywood Boulevard Cemetery.

I, Lessimus, of Salt Lake City.
Meeting Mick Jagger.
Melon-Slaughterer; or, A Sick Man's Praise for a Well Woman.
Miscarriage.
Reflecting on the Aging-Process.
Song for a Son.
Sow's Head, The.
Study in Aesthetics, A.

Petersen, Donald (b. 1928)
Walking along the Hudson.

Peterson, Henry (1818–91)
Death of Lyon, The.
O gallant brothers of the generous South.
Ode for Decoration Day, Sels.

Peterson, Nancy
Search, The.

Peterson, Peter (b. 1926)
On First Looking into Chapman's Homer II.

Petrakos, Chris
Call Them Back.

Petrarch (Francesco Petrarca) (1304–74)
Alas! So All Things Now Do Hold Their Peace.
Bicause I have the still kept fro lyes and blame.
Blest be the day, and blest the month and year.
Canzone: "So feeble is the thread that doth the burden stay."
Ever myn happe is slack and slo in commyng.
Exchange between the Poet and St. Augustine, An.
Eyes that drew from me such fervent praise, The.
First day she passed up and down through the Heavens, The.
Go, grieving rimes of mine, to that hard stone.
Great is my envy of you, earth, in your greed.
Heart on the Hill, The.
How Oft Have I My Dere and Cruell Foo.
How the Lover Perisheth in His Delight, As the Fly in the Fire.
I find no peace and all my war[r] is done.
I saw a Phoenix in the Wood Alone.
I saw the tracks of angels in the earth.
If It Be Destined.
In the years of her age the most beautiful.
In Wintry Midnight, o'er a Stormy Main.
It was the morning of that blessed day.
Love, That Doth Reign [or Raine] and Live within My Thought.
Mine old dear enemy, my froward master.
My flowery and green age was passing away.
My Galley ("My galley charged with forgetfulness").
Secretum, Sels.
Set me whereas the sun doth parch the green [or sonne dothe perche the grene].
She used to let her golden hair fly free.
Signs of Love.
Sonnets to Laura, Sels.
That gallant lady, gloriously bright.
That night which did the dreadful hap ensue.
To Laura in Life.
Triumph of Death, Sels.
Triumphs.
Visions, The.
What a grudge I am bearing the earth.

Petrie, Paul (b. 1936)
Church of San Antonio de la Florida, The.
Dream, The.
Enigma Variations, The.
Murderer, The.
Not Seeing Is Believing.
Old Pro's Lament, The.
Phases of Darkness, The.

Petröczi, Kata Szidónia (1662–1708)
Swift Floods.

Petronius Arbiter (Caius Petronius Arbiter) (d. A.D. 66)
Doing, a Filthy Pleasure Is, and Short.
Encouragement to Exile.
Fate brought three men to birth.
Fornication is a filthy business.
From the high Alpine pass.

Stay, Nymph.
Wake, Sleepy Thyrsis.

Pilkington, Laetitia (1712?–1750)
Memory, a Poem.
Song: "Lying is an occupation."
Sorrow.

Pillen [or Pillin], William (1910–1985)
Ascensions, The.
Farewell to Europe.
Miserere.
Requirement, The.
Terrified Meadows, The.

Pilling, Christopher (b. 1936)
Adoration of the Magi, The.

Pinar, Florencia del (b. c.1460)
Another Song of the Same Woman, to Some
Partridges, Sent to Her Alive.

Pindar (c.518–c.438 B.C.)
Lament.
Nemean Odes, *Sels*.
Ode on Theoxenos.

"Pindar, Peter" (John Wolcot) (1738–1819)
Apple Dumplings and a King, The.
Bozzy and Piozzi, *Sels*.
Epigram.
George III and the Sailor.
George III Visits Whitbread's Brewery.
Instructions to a Celebrated Laureat, *Sels*.
Introduction and Anecdotes.
Mr. Whitebead's Brewhouse, *Sels*.
Now majesty into a pump so deep.
Ode: "That I have often been in love, deep
love."
Ode to a Country Hoyden.
On a Stone Thrown at a Very Great Man, But
Which Missed Him.
On George III.
Resignation; an Ode to the Journeyman
Shoemakers, *Sels*.
Royal Tour, The.
Royal Tour, and Weymouth Amusements, The,
Sels.
Sons of Saint Crispin, 'tis in vain!
Sorrows of Sunday; an Elegy, The, *Sels*.
Susan, the constant slave to mop and broom.
To a Fly, Taken out of a Bowl of Punch.

Pine, John C.
Survivor, The.

"Ping Hsin" (Hsieh Wang-ying) (b. 1902)
Bright moon.
Builder of Continents, The.
Commonplace puddle, The.
Falling Star, The.
Fishing boats have returned, The!
For the Record.
In shaping the snow into blossoms.
Multitudinous Stars, *Sels*.
O, Lord/ If in life eternal.
Oh little island.
Orphan beat of my heart, The.
Remembering.
Rose of Heaven, The.
Sprays of frost flowers form.
Spring Waters, *Sels*.
Stars, The, *Sels*.
These fragmented verses.
Three Poems, *Sels*.
Trellis of sticks, A.
Void only.

Pinkney, Dorothy Cowles (b. 1904)
Dame Liberty Reports from Travel.

Pinkney, Edward Coote [or Coate] (1802–28)
Health, A.
Indian's Bride, The.
Memory.
Serenade: "Look out upon the stars, my love."
Votive Song.

Pinsky, Robert (b. 1940)
At Pleasure Bay.
Dionysus as Psychiatrist.
Doctor Frolic.
Dying.
Essay on Psychiatrists, *Sels*.
Explanation of America, An, *Sels*.
Figured Wheel, The.

Hearts, The.
History of My Heart.
Icicles.
Invocation.
Late Child.
Living, The.
Mad, The.
Memorial.
New Saddhus, The.
Peroration, Concerning Genius.
Pilgrimage.
Poem about People.
Proposition.
Prostate Operation.
Questions, The.
Ralegh's Prizes.
Senior Poet.
Serpent Knowledge.
Shirt.
Some Terms.
Song of Reasons.
Superb Lily, The.
Their Patients.
Their Philistinism Considered.
Their Seriousness, with Further Comparisons.
Their Speech, Compared with Wisdom and
Poetry.
Three on Luck, *Sels*.
Volume, The.
Want Bone, The.
Woman, A.

Pinto, Floria Herrero (b. 1943)
Coils the Robot.

Pinto, Vivian de Sola (1895–1969)
At Piccadilly Circus.

Pinytos (fl. 1st cent. A.D.)
Epitaph: Sappho.

Piper, Edwin Ford (1871–1939)
Church, The.

Piper, Linda (b. 1949)
Missionaries in the Jungle.
Sweet Ethel.

Piron, Alexis (1689–1773)
Here lies Piron — a man of no position.
My Epitaph.

Pise, Constantine (1801–66)
Let the Deep Organ Swell.

Pitcher, Oliver (b. 1923)
Pale Blue Casket, The.
Salute.

Pitchford, Kenneth (b. 1930)
Good for Nothing Man, *Sels*.
Lobotomy.
104 Boulevard Saint-Germain.
Pickup in Tony's Hashhouse.
Queen, The.
Surgery.

Pitkin, Anne
Blue Morning Glory.

Pitman, Hassall
Limerick: "Cynical sage with a kink, A."

Pitt, Christopher (1699–1748)
Fable of the Young Man and His Cat, The.
On the Masquerades.
'Tis true what famed Pythagoras maintained.
To Mr. Pope, on His Translation of Homer's
Iliad, *Sels*.

Pitt, William (1759–1806)
Sailor's Consolation, The.

Pitter, Ruth (b. 1897)
Bat, The.
But for Lust.
Coffin-Worm, The.
Dun-Colour [or Dun-Color].
Eternal Image, The.
For Sleep, or Death.
Hen under Bay-Tree.
Irish Patriarch, The.
Lost Tribe, The.
Matron-Cat's Song, The.
Military Harpist, The.
Mister the Blitzkit.
Morning Glory.
Old Nelly's Birthday.

Old Woman Speaks of the Moon, An.
Sparrow's Skull, The.
Swan Bathing, The.
Talking Family, The.
Task, The.
Three Cheers for the Black, White and Blue.
Time's Fool.
Unicorn, The.
Viper, The.
Yorkshire Wife's Saga.

Pittis, William (1674–1724)
Battle Royal between Dr. Sherlock, Dr. South,
and Dr. Burnet, The.

Pitt-Kethley, Fiona
God made the sex-shop keeper.
Limerick: "Platinum blonde, Goldilocks, A."
Limerick: "There was a young boy, Jack
Horner."
Limerick: "Two playwrights called Beaumont
and Fletcher."

Piuvkaq [or Pluvkag]
It Is Hard to Catch Trout.
Joy of a Singer, The.
Mocking Song against Qaqortingneq.

Pix, Mary (1666–c. 1709)
Deceiver Deceived, The, *Sels*.
Innocent Mistress, The, *Sels*.
Prologue: "Deceiv'd Deceiver, and Imposter
cheated!"
Queen Catherine, *Sels*.
Song by Mrs. P —, A: "When I languish'd,
and wish'd you wou'd something bestow."
Song: "Fairest Nymph that ever bless'd our
Shore."
Spanish Wives, The, *Sels*.
To Mrs. Manley, upon Her Tragedy Call'd The
Royal Mischief.
Work on my brain, help every faculty.

Pixner, Stef (b. 1945)
Day in the Life, A.
Near Death.

Pizarnik, Alejandra (1936–1972)
Signs.

"Placido" (1809–44)
Farewell to My Mother.
Prayer to God.

Plaiwon
Limerick: "I once knew a spinster of Staines."

Planché, James Robinson (1796–1880)
Ching a Ring.
Love, You've Been a Villain.

Plantier, Thérèse (b. 1911)
Doors.
Overdue Balance Sheet.

Plarr, Victor (1863–1929)
Epitaphium Citharistriae.
Of Change of Opinions.
Shadows.

**Platen, August, Graf von (Karl August Georg
Maximilian, Graf von Platen-Hallermünde)
(1796–1835)**
How shall I still mankind's good will retrieve.
Sonnets to Karl Theodore German, *Sels*.
To Bülow.
To Liebig.
To Rotenham.
To Schmidlein.
When shall I master this anxiety.

Plath, Sylvia (1932–63)
All the Dead Dears.
Amnesiac.
Among the Narcissi.
Applicant, The.
Ariel.
Arrival of the Bee Box, The.
Babysitters, The.
Balloons.
Barren Woman.
Bed Book, The, *Sels*.
Bee Meeting, The.
Beekeeper's Daughter, The.
Berck-Plage, *Sels*.
Black Rook in Rainy Weather.
Blackberrying.

On a Moonlit Night, Sent to my Brothers and Sisters.
On an Ancient Tomb East of the Village.
On Being Sixty.
Painting Bamboo, a Song.
Parrot.
People of Tao-chou, The.
Planting Bamboos.
Planting Flowers on the Eastern Embankment.
P'u — Hua Fei Hua.
Reading the Collected Works of Li Po and Tu Fu: A Colophon.
Red Cuckatoo, The.
Red Embroidered Carpet.
Rejoicing at the Arrival of Chi'en Hsiung.
Remembering Golden Bells.
"Ripples Sifting Sand," *Sels.*
Seeing Hsia Chan off by River.
Sitting at Night.
Song of the pines.
Song of the Rear Palace.
Starting Early from the Ch'u-ch'êng Inn.
Temple, The.
There'll be a day when dust flies at the bottom of the sea.
To Li Chien.
To the Distant One.
Traveler's Moon, A.
Visiting the Hermit Cheng.
Watching the Wheat-Reapers.

Pocock, Guy Noel (1880–1955)
Years Ahead.

Poe, Edgar Allan (1809–49)
Al Aaraff, *Sels.*
Annabel Lee.
Assignation, The, *Sels.*
Bells, The.
City in the Sea *or* The Doomed City, The.
Coliseum, The.
Conqueror Worm, The.
Dream within a Dream, A, *Sels.*
Dream-Land.
Dreams, *Sels.*
Eldorado.
Enigma, An.
Fairyland.
Fall of the House of Usher, The, *Sels.*
For Annie.
From Childhood's Hour.
Happiest Day, the Happiest Hour, The.
Haunted Palace, The.
I stand amid the roar.
Israfel.
Lake, The.
Lenore.
Ligeia, *Sels.*
Oh! that my young life were a lasting dream!
Raven, The.
Romance.
Sleeper, The.
Song from "Al Aaraaf."
Song: "Young flowers were whispering in melody."
Sonnet — Science.
Sonnet — Silence.
Sonnet to Science.
To Helen.
To My Mother.
To One in Paradise.
To Science.
Ulalume.
Valley of Unrest, The.

Pointon, Priscilla (c. 1740–1801)
Address to a Bachelor on a Delicate Occasion.
In a post-coach and four, with postillions as fine.
Letter to a Sister, Giving an Account of the Author's Wedding-Day, *Sels.*
On Her Blindness.
To the Critics, *Sels.*

Polglaze, Pascoe
There's a cut-price whore.

Polite, Frank (b. 1934)
Adman into Toad.
Empty at the Heart of Things.
Imitations Based on the American.

In My Black Book.
Japanese Consulate, The.
Mine.
Politian. *See* **Poliziano, Angelo [*or* Andrea].**
Polito, Robert
Evidence.
Winter, and I feel the circles of my world.
Poliziano, Angelo [*or* Andrea] (Politian) (1454–94)
He who knows not what thing is Paradise.
I found myself one day all, all alone.
I went a roaming, maidens, one bright day.
Three Ballate, *Sels.*
Unto the Breach.
Pollak, Felix (b. 1909)
Another transparent skin has grown.
Dream, The.
Finger, The, *Sels.*
First the light cracked.
Her voice enters the room.
I dream of the finger of the statue.
I look out of my window at night.
I may pass through once more next month.
I wake to the sound of rain.
Tunnel Visions, *Sels.*
Pollard, Josephine
Price of a Drink.
Pollitt, Katha (b. 1949)
Ballet Blanc.
Composition in Black and White.
Night Subway.
Of the Scythians.
Onion.
Small Comfort.
Turning Thirty.
Two Fish.
Woman Asleep on a Banana Leaf.
Polwhele, Richard (1760–1838)
Influence of Local Attachment, The, *Sels.*
Visit to the Author's Paternal Seat, A.
Pomerantz, Charlotte (b. 1930)
Lulu, Lulu, I've a Lilo.
Where Do These Words Come From?
Pomeroy, Marnie (b. 1932)
Ground Hog Day.
In Nakedness.
Pomeroy, Ralph (b. 1926)
Between Here and Illinois.
High Wind at the Battery.
Leather Bar, The.
River's End.
Snow.
Tardy Epithalamium for E. and N., A.
To Janet.
Pomfret, John (1767–1802)
Choice, The, *Sels.*
That life may be more comfortable yet.
Pomfret, Richard
July Wakes.
Pommy-Vega, Janine (b. 1942)
Rites of the Eastern Star.
Voices, The.
Pompeius (d. 33 A.D.)
Even if I am only more dust.
Lais, who was a lovely flower.
Pompili, Vittoria Aganoor (1855–1910)
Fear.
Finally.
Ponciano, Angelo de
Empties Coming Back.
Ponge, Francis (1899–1988)
Delights of the Door, The.
End of Fall, The.
Horse, The.
Oyster, The ("The oyster, about as large as a medium-sized stone").
Pebble, The.
Pleasures of the Door, The.
Trees Lose Parts of Themselves Inside a Circle of Fog.
Water.
Poniewaz, Jeff
Whale Wisdom Peace Illumination.
Ponika, Kohine Whakarua (b. 1920)
Call Together.

Song of Yearning, A.
Ponmutiyar
Mother's List of Duties, A.
Young Warrior, A.
Ponsot, Marie (b. 1922)
Communion of Saints: The Poor Bastard under the Bridge.
Multipara: Gravida 5.
Nursing: Mother, *Sels.*
Possession.
Subject.
To the Age's Insanities.
Tranquilized, she speaks or does not speak.
"Pontiff"
Rime of the Gentle Pacifist, The.
Pook, John (b. 1942)
English Lesson.
In Chapel.
Weekend at Home.
Poole, John F. (1786?–1872)
No Irish Need Apply.
Song, *Hamlet.*
Poole, Richard (b. 1945)
Dark, The.
Poole, Ted. *See* **Pelletier, Wilfred.**
Poore, Jo
Mother, Father, God, Universal Power.
Popa, Vasco [*or* Vasko] (b. 1922)
Admirers of the Little Box, The.
Adventure of the Quartz Pebble, The.
Ashes.
Battle on the Blackbird's Field, The.
Be Seeing You.
Before Play.
Before the Game.
Benefactors of the Little Box, The.
Besieged Serenity, *Sels.*
Blackbird's Field, The, *Sels.*
Burning Shewolf.
Craftsmen of the Little Box, The.
Dream of the Quartz Pebble, The.
Echo.
Echo Turned to Stone.
Enemies of the Little Box, The.
Far Within Us, *Sels.*
Forgetful Number.
Games, *Sels.*
He.
Heart of the Quartz Pebble, The.
Hide-and-Seek.
Hunter.
In the Village of My Forefathers.
Journey.
Judges of the Little Box, The.
Last News about the Little Box.
Life of St Sava, The.
Little Box, The.
Look that is that uninvited.
Love of the Quartz Pebble, The.
Nail, The.
Owners of the Little Box, The.
Petrified Echoes.
Pig.
Prisoners of the Little Box, The.
Proud Error.
Quartz Pebble, The, *Sels.*
Raw Flesh, *Sels.*
Rose Thieves, The.
Secret of the Quartz Pebble, The.
Seed, The.
St Sava's Forge.
St Sava's Journey.
St Sava's Spring, *Sels.*
Stargazer's Legacy, The.
Story of a Story, The.
Streets of your glances, The.
Tale About a Tale, The.
Tenants of the Little Box, The.
These are your lips.
Time Swept Up.
Two Quartz Pebbles.
Victims of the Little Box, The.
Wise Triangle, A.
Wolf-Ancestry.
Yawn of Yawns, The, *Sels.*

Primas of Orleans, Hugh (1094–1160)
Lament for Troy.
Primrose, Lady Diana (*fl.* **c.1630)**
Chain of Pearl, A, *Sels.*
First Pearle, The: Religion.
Fourth Pearl, The: Temperance.
Sixth Pearle, The: Justice.
Prince, Frank Templeton (b. 1912)
Babiaantje, The.
Memoirs in Oxford, *Sels.*
Old Age of Michelangelo, The.
Question, The.
Soldiers Bathing.
Somewhere in Mauriac a girl.
To a Friend on His Marriage.
Token, The.
Wind in the Tree, The.
Prince, John Critchley (*fl.* **c.1841)**
Poet's Sabbath, The, *Sels.*
Prince, Thomas (1687–1758)
Give Ear, O God, to My Loud Cry.
O Lord, Bow Down Thine Ear.
With Christ and All His Shining Train.
Pringle, Thomas (1789–1834)
Caffer Commando, The.
Desolate Valley, The.
Emigrant's Cabin, The.
Ghona Widow's Lullaby, The.
Hottentot, The.
Lion-Hunt, The.
Prior, Matthew (1664–1721)
Advice to the Painter.
Against Modesty in Love.
Alma; or, The Progress of the Mind, *Sels.*
Another True Maid.
Answer to Cloe [*or* Chloe] Jealous.
But, Greatest *Anna*! while Thy Arms pursue.
Chameleon, The.
Chaste Florimel.
Democritus and Heraclitus.
Divine Blacksmith, The.
Dutch Proverb, A.
Earning a Dinner.
English Ballad, on the Taking of Namur by the
King of Great Britain, 1695, An.
Enigma.
Epigram: "Thy nags (the leanest things alive)."
Epigram: "To John I ow'd great obligation."
Epigram: "Tom's sickness did his morals
mend."
Epigram: "When Bibo thought fit from the
world to retreat."
Epigram: "Yes, every poet is a fool."
Epitaph: "Interred [*or* Interr'd] beneath this
marble stone."
Epitaph: "Meek Francis lies here, friend,
without stop or stay."
Epitaph on True, Her Majesty's Dog, An.
Fable: "In Aesop's tales an honest wretch we
find."
Fatal Love.
Fix thy corporeal, and internal eye.
For My Own Monument.
Great Bacchus: From the Greek.
Hans Carvel.
Human Life.
In Britain's isles, as Heylyn notes.
In Imitation of Anacreon.
Insatiable Priest, The.
Jinny the Just.
Lady Who Offers Her Looking-Glass to Venus,
The.
Les Estreines.
Letter to the Honourable Lady Miss Margaret
Cavendish Holles-Harley, A.
Lover's Anger, A.
Mercury and Cupid.
Nonpareil.
Ode Humbly Inscrib'd to the Queen, A, *Sels.*
Ode: "Merchant, to secure his treasure, The."
Oft have I said, the praise of doing well.
On Exodus 3: 14: "I am that I am."
On Himself.
On My Birthday, July 21.
Orange, The.
Paraphrase from the French, A.

Pass we the ills, which each man feels or
dreads.
Phillis's [*or* Phyllis's] Age.
Pleasure: The Second Book of Solomon on the
Vanity of the World, *Sels.*
Question to Lisetta, The.
Quid Sit Futurum Cras Fuge Quaerere.
Reasonable Affliction, A.
Remedy Worse than the Disease, The.
Simile, A.
Solomon on the Vanity of the World, *Sels.*
To a Child of Quality [Five Years Old, the
Author Supposed Forty].
To a Child of Quality of Five Years Old, the
Author Supposed Forty.
To a Lady: She Refusing to Continue a Dispute
with Me, and Leaving Me in the Argument.
To a Young Gentlemen in Love; a Tale.
Town Mouse and the Country Mouse, The.
True Maid, A.
Turtle and the Sparrow, The, *Sels.*
Verses Written at The Hague. Anno 1696.
When you with Hogh Dutch Heeren dine.
Woman's Wish, The.
Written in an Ovid.
Written in the Beginning of Mezeray's History
of France.
Pritam, Amrita (b. 1919)
Annunciation, The.
Daily Wages.
Pritchard, Norman Henry, II
Aswelay.
Gyre's Galax.
Self.
Signs, The.
Probyn, May
"Is It Nothing to You?"
Procter, Adelaide Anne (1825–64)
Cleansing Fires.
Envy.
Fidelis.
Lost Chord, The.
One by One.
Per Pacem ad Lucem.
Present, The.
Thankfulness.
Proctor, Bryan Waller. *See* **"Cornwall,
Barry."**
Proctor, Edna Dean (b. 1838)
Brooklyn Bridge, The.
Captive's Hymn, The.
Columbia's Emblem.
Columbus Dying.
John Brown.
Lost War-Sloop, The.
Sa-cá-ga-we-a.
Proctor, Thomas (*fl.* **c.1578)**
Proper Sonnet, How Time Consumeth All
Earthly Things, A.
Respice Finem.
Prokosch, Frederic (b. 1908)
Conspirators, The.
Festival, The.
Gothic Dusk, The.
**Propertius (Sextus Propertius) (c.54 B.C.–A.D.
c.2)**
Ah Woe Is Me.
Elegies, *Sels.*
Hylas.
Revenge to Come.
Stab me with sword, or poison strong.
Prospere, Susan (b. 1946)
Into the Open.
Passion.
Sub Rosa.
"Prout, Father". *See* **Mahony, Francis
Sylvester.**
Provins, Marguerite Burnat-. *See* **Burnat-
Provins, Marguerite.**
**Prudentius (Prudentius Aurelius Clemens)
(348–c. 410)**
At Cock-crow.
Come from the confines of the sunset world.
Easter Eve.

For the Kindling of the Light on Easter Eve.
Hymn for Morning.
Prudhomme, René François Armand Sully-.
See **Sully-Prudhomme, René François
Armand.**
Prynne, J. H.
Again in the Black Cloud.
Against Hurt.
As It Were an Attendant.
At the onset of the single life.
Bee Target on His Shoulder, The.
Common Gain, Reverted, The.
Concerning Quality, Again.
Dream of Retained Colour, A.
Es Lebe Der König.
First Notes on Daylight.
From End to End.
Frost and Snow, Falling.
Get out of this, dainty blood in.
Ideal Star-Fighter, The.
If There Is a Stationmaster at Stamford S.D.
Hardly Sp.
Limit spark under water, A.
Love.
Love in the Air.
Of Movement towards a Natural Place.
One Way at Any Time.
Shadow Songs.
Sketch for a Financial Theory of the Self.
So the seeds are cut, loose and like.
They brought up some tale about white fox.
Thoughts on the Esterházy Court Uniform.
Treatment in the Field.
Prys, Edmwnd (1544–1623)
Welsh Ballad, A.
Prys, Thomas (c.1564–1639)
Poem to Show the Trouble That Befell Him
When He Was at Sea, A.
Prys-Jones, A. G. (b. 1888)
Cors-y-Gwaed: Fenland of Blood.
Day Which Endures Not, A.
Henry Morgan's March on Panama.
Limerick: "Artist who lived in St. Ives, An."
Limerick: "There was a young man of
Porthcawl."
Ploughman, The: In Welsh Uplands.
St. Govan.
Unfortunate Occurrence at Cwm-Cadno.
Ptolemy (Claudius Ptolemaeus) (*fl.* **121–151)**
Mortal though I be, yea ephemeral, if but a
moment.
Star-Gazing.
Pudjipangu
Aeroplane.
Pudney, John (1909–77)
For Johnny.
Missing.
On Seeing My Birthplace from a Jet Aircraft.
Stiles.
Pugh, Sheenagh (b. 1950)
Coming into Their Own.
King Billy on the Walls.
King Sigurd and King Eystein.
Shoni Onions.
Pugliesi, Giacomino (*fl.* **13th century)**
Of His Dead Lady.
Of His Lady in Absence.
Pulci, Luigi (1432–84)
Morgante Maggiore, Il, *Sels.*
Prophecy.
Pullen, Eugene Henry (1832–99)
"Now I Lay Me Down to Sleep."
Now I wake and see the light.
Pulsford, Doris
Limerick: "Budding young playwright named
Coward, A."
Pulsifer, Susan Nichols
Sounding Fog, The.
Punkanuttiraiyar
Mothers.
**Purcell, Victor William Williams
Saunders.** *See* **"Buttle, Myra."**
Purdom, George
Robens' Promised Land.

Purdy, Alfred Wellington (b. 1919)
Alive or Not.
Cariboo Horses, The.
Country North of Belleville, The.
Dead Poet, The.
Dead Seal.
Evergreen Cemetery.
Lament for the Dorsets.
Love at Roblin Lake.
Madwoman on the Train, The.
Night Song for a Woman.
Poem: "You are ill and so I lead you away."
Rattlesnake, The.
Remains of an Indian Village.
Spinning.
Trees at the Arctic Circle.
What Do the Birds Think?
Wilderness Gothic.
Winemaker's Beat-étude, The.
Winter Walking.

Purdy, James
Brooklyn Branding Parlors, The.
I Have Told You Your Hands Are Salt.
Solitary in Brooklyn.

Purohit, Swami (1882–1936?)
I Know That I Am a Great Sinner.
Miracle Indeed, A.
Shall I Do This.

Pushkin, Aleksandr Sergeyevich (1799–1851)
Autumn.
Captive, The.
Entering Moscow.
Evgeny Onegin, Sels.
Fountain at Tzarskoye Selo, The.
Gloomy Day Is Ended, The.
I Loved You, Even Now I May Confess.
I Loved You Once.
Message to Siberia.
No, Never Think.
O Do Not Sing.
Prophet, The.
She's Gazing at You So Tenderly.
Sweet boy, gentle boy.
When in My Arms.
With Freedom's Seed.
Work.

Putnam, Howard Phelps (Phelps Putnam) (1874–1948)
Ballad of a Strange Thing.
Hasbrouck and the Rose.
Romeo and Juliet.

Puttenham, George (1529–90)
Cruel You Be.

Puttkamer, Baroness von. See "Madelaine, Marie."

Pye, Henry James (1745–1813)
Aerophorion, Sels.
Air Balloon, The.

Pygge, Edward
Crow Resting.
Notes for a Revised Sonnet.
Notes for a Sonnet.
Occam's Razor Starts in Massachusetts.
Revised Notes for a Sonnet.
Shantih shantih shantih.
Wasted Land, The.
What about You?

Pyke, B. K.
Blacksmith.

Pyle, Katharine (1863–1938)
August.
Circus Parade, The.
Clever Peter and the Ogress.
Nine o'Clock.
One o'Clock.
Toys Talk of the World, The.
Two o'Clock.
Waking.
Wonder Clock, The, Sels.

Pyrker, Johann Ladislaus von Felsö-Eör (1773–1847)
Omnipotence.

Pyrlaeus, Johann C. (1713–85)
Jesu, Come on Board.

Q

"Q". See Quiller-Couch, Sir Arthur Thomas.

Qabbani, Nizar (b. 1923)
Actors, The, Sels.
June war is over, The.
Notes on the Book of Defeat, Sels.
Painting with Words, Sels.
Stage is burned, The.
When a helmet becomes God in heaven.
When ideas, when thought itself.

Qabula, Alfred Temba (b. 1942)
Migrant's Lament: A Song.

Qaqatcguk
I keep dreaming I'm dead.

Qarshe, Cabdullaahi
Colonialism ("The colonialist governments").

Qorratu'l-Ayn (1814–52)
Cupbearer, O victorious Falcon, come!
He the Beloved, Sels.

Quarles, Francis (1592–1644)
Are all such off'rings, as are crusht, and bruis'd.
Argalus and Parthenia, Sels.
At length, by flight, I over-went the Pack.
Be Sad, My Heart.
Before a Pack of deep-mouth'd Lusts I flee.
Behold thy darling, which thy lustfull care.
Best-Beloved, The.
Born in Winter.
Can he be fair that withers at a blast.
Come then, my soule, approach this royall Burse.
Crucified.
David's Epitaph on Jonathan.
Deuteronomy 30.19.
Divine Fancies, The, Sels.
Emblems, Sels.
Epigram: "My soul, sit thou a patient looker-on."
Epigram: "My soul, thy love is dear: 'twas thought a good."
Forbear, fond taper: what thou seek'st, is fire.
Galatians 6.14.
Good-Night, A.
Great All in All, that art my rest, my home.
Hieroglyphics of the Life of Man, Sels.
High Perfections of Our Transitory Days, The.
Hos Ego Versiculos.
How shall my tongue expresse that hallow'd fire.
If lust should chase my soule, made swift by fright.
Isaiah 66.11.
Job Militant, Sels.
Let Grace conduct thee to the paths of peace.
Like to the Arctic Needle.
Luke 6.25.
Matthew 9.12.
Meditatio, Sels.
Meditatio Septima.
Meditatio Tertia Decima.
My Beloved Is Mine, and I Am His; He Feedeth among the Lillies.
My soul, what's lighter than a feather? Wind.
My Soule is like a Bird; my Flesh, the Cage.
Nahum 2.10.
Not as the thirsty soyle desires soft showres.
Of St Stephen.
On a Feast.
On Balaam's Ass.
On Change of Weathers.
On Death.
On Dinah.
On God's Favour.
On God's Law.
On Jacob's Purchase.
On Judas Iscariot.
On Our Saviour's Passion.
On Saul and David.
On Sin.
On the Babel-Builders.
On the Cuckoo.
On The Gospel.
On the Holy Scriptures.

On the Life of Man.
On the Needle of a Sundial.
On the Ploughman [or Plough-Man].
On the Two Great Floods.
On the World.
On Those That Deserve It.
On Zacchaeus [or Zacheus].
On Zacheus [or Zacchaeus].
Our God and soldiers we alike adore.
Pentelogia, Sels.
Philippians 1.23.
Psalm 119.37.
Purified Soul, The.
Stay My Steps in Thy Paths, That My Feet Do Not Slide.
They Gave Him Vinegar and Gall (Matt. 27) and Wine Mingled with Myrrh (Mark 15).
This furnisht Ark presents the greedy view.
Upon the Day of Our Saviour's Nativity.
Wherefore Hidest Thou Thy Face, and Holdest Me for Thine Enemy [or Enemie]?
Why? What are Men?
Worldly wisdome of the foolish man, The.
World's a Floore, whose swelling heapes retaine, The.
World's a Sea, The.
Yet a Little While Is the Light With You.

Queneau, Raymond (1903–76)
Conch.

Quennell, Peter (b. 1905)
Divers, The.
Flight into Egypt, The.
Hero Entombed I.
Leviathan, Sels.
Music met Leviathan returning, A.
Procne.

Questel, Victor (1949–82)
This Island Mopsy.
Tom.

Quevedo y Villegas, Francisco de (1580–1645)
Death Warnings.

Quick, Richard (b. 1944)
Reagan, The.

Quickenden, Beatrice (1902–67)
Hail, Oh Hail to the King.

Quiller-Couch, Sir Arthur Thomas ("Q") (1863–1944)
Doom Ferry.
Lady Jane.
Lion is the [or a] beast to fight, The.
Planted Heel, The.

Quillet, Claude (1602–61)
Beneath those parts, where stretching to its bound.
Best Time for Conception, The.
Callipaedia; or, The Art of Getting Beautiful Children, Sels.
How to Conceive Boys.

Quinn, Roderic (1867–1949)
Fisher, The.

Quinones, Lolly (1934–1979)
February.

Quinonez, Naomi
America's Wailing Wall.
Hesitations.
My Shattered Sister.
People of the Harvest.

Quint, Beverly
View, A.

Quintana, Leroy V.
After Her Husband Died, Doña Carlota Was So Alone.
Grandfather Never Wrote a Will.
Grandmother's Father Was Killed by Some Tejanos.
Granizo.

Quintana Pigno, Antionia
December's Picture.
La Jornada.
Vicente.

Quintus Horatius Flaccus. See Horace.

Quirino, Giovanni (fl. c.1300)
To Dante Alighieri (He Commends the Work of Dante's Life).

Quirk, Cathleen (b. 1944)
Another Night on the Porch Swing.

R

"R., E. M. G."
Midsummer Moon.
"R. B." See "B., R."
"R. H." See "H., R."
Raab, Lawrence (b. 1946)
Assassin's Fatal Error, The.
Attack of the Crab Monsters.
Pastoral: "Today in Peru, this first day of summer."
This Day.
Visiting the Oracle.
Voices Answering Back: The Vampires.
Rab (Abba Arika) (fl. 3d century)
Kingdom of God, The.
Rabbitt, Thomas (b. 1943)
Bernadette Murphy, 1943-1955.
Blue Lights.
Coon Hunt.
For Thomas Stearns Eliot on the Occasion of His One Hundredth Birthday.
Gargoyle.
Old Sipsey Valley Road, The.
Power of Faith, The.
Rabéarivelo [or Rebéarivelo], Jean-Joseph (1901–1937)
Cactus.
Close by, to the north, there were two oranges.
Here is.
Here She Stands.
Imaginary tremolo.
May I come in? May I come in?
One day some young poet.
Reading.
Rondo for the Poet's Children.
Slowly/ like a crippled cow.
There you are.
Three Dawns.
What Invisible Rat.
Wife is like a blade of grass, A.
You built yourself a tower in the wind.
You delude yourself.
Your Work.
Rabelais, François (c.1494–1553)
Antidoted Fanfreluches: or, a Galimatia of Extravagant Conceits Found in an Ancient Monument, The.
Epistemon's Visit to Elysium.
Games of Gargantua, The.
Gargantua and Pantagruel, Sels.
Inscription above the Entrance to the Abbey of Theleme.
Shrovetide's Countenance.
Rabémanganjara, Jacques (b. 1913)
In hermetic enclosure.
Lamba, Sels.
Lament: "Blue, so blue that eye of sky."
Song: "Isle!/ Island of the syllables of flame!"
Rabi'a al-Adawiyya (Rabi'a the Mystic) (712–801)
My Lord/ if I worship Thee from fear of Hell.
Stars are shining/ the eyes of men are closed.
Two ways I love Thee, selfishly.
Rabi'a bint Isma'il of Syria (d. 755)
Sufi Quatrain.
Rabi'a of Balkh (fl. 10th century)
My wish for you/ that God should make your love.
Rabi'a the Mystic. See Al-Adawiyya, Rabi'a.
Rabinowitz, Anna
Sappho Comments on an Exhibition of Expressionist Landscapes.
Rachel [or Rahel] (Rahel Blumstein [or Blaustein or Bluwstein]) (1890–1931)
Aftergrowth.
Barren.
Dawn.
Here on Earth.

His Wife.
Jonathan.
Kinnereth.
Only of Myself I Knew How to Tell.
To My Country.
Racine, Jean (1639–99)
Athalie, Sels.
Bérénice, Sels.
Berenice Enumerates the Triumph of Titus, Sels.
God whose goodness filleth every clime, The.
Phaedra.
Time for tremblin's past, I've Titus' love, The.
Radcliffe, Alexander (fl. 1669–96)
As Concerning Man.
Radcliffe, Ann (1764–1823)
Night.
Song of a Spirit.
Sonnet: "Now the bat circles on the breeze of eve."
Stanzas: "How smooth that lake expands its ample breast!"
Radford, Dollie (Mrs. Ernest Radford) (b. 1858)
Soliloquy of a Maiden Aunt.
Radford, Ernest (b. 1853)
Upon Julia.
Radnóti, Miklós (1909–44)
I Hid You.
Postcard (Found on His body after He Was Killed by the Nazis).
Rae, Simon (b. 1952)
Annus Miserabilis.
Pulling the Chain.
Vile World.
Rafat, Tawfiq (b. 1927)
Medal, The.
Raftery [or Raifteiri], Anthony [or Antoine] (1784–1835)
I Am Raftery [or Raferty].
I am Raifteiri, the poet, full of courage and love.
Lass from Bally-na-Lee, The.
Mary Hynes.
Rago, Henry (1915–69)
Childhood Painting Lesson.
Coming of Dusk upon a Village in Haiti, The.
Green Afternoon, The.
Knowledge of Light, The.
Monster, The.
Summer Countries, The.
Rahel. See Rachel [or Rahel].
Raifteiri, Antoine. See Raftery [or Raifteiri], Anthony [or Antoine].
"Raile, Arthur Lyon" (Edward Perry Warren) (1860–1928)
Waning of Love, The.
"Raimar, Freimund." See Rückert, Friedrich.
Raine, Craig (b. 1944)
Anno Domini, Sels.
Arsehole.
Attempt at Jealousy, An.
Birth.
City Gent.
Dandelions.
Gardener, The.
In Modern Dress.
Martian Sends a Postcard Home, A.
Nature Study.
Onion, Memory, The.
Plain Song.
Sexual Couplets.
Raine, Kathleen Jessie (b. 1908)
Air.
Beinn Naomh, Sels.
By the River Eden.
Daisies of Florence.
Death, I repent.
Easter Poem.
Eileann Chanaidh, Sels.
Envoi: "Take of me what is not my own."
Envoi: "What has want to give."
Eudaimon.
From a place I came.

Heirloom.
Human Form Divine, The.
I Used to Watch You, Sleeping.
Images.
In Time.
Instrument, The.
Isis Wanderer.
Kore in Hades.
Lachesis.
Last Things.
Love Poem: "Yours is the face that the earth turns to me."
Message from Home.
My Mother's Birthday, Sels.
Natura Naturans.
Old Paintings on Italian Walls.
On its way I see.
Puer Aeternus.
Pythoness, The.
Question and Answer.
Rock, Sels.
Rose.
Scala Coeli.
Spell against Sorrow.
Spell of Creation.
Statues.
Still Pool, The.
Summit, The.
To My Mountain.
"Tu Non Se' in Terra, Si Come Tu Credi."
Two Invocations of Death, Sels.
Water, Sels.
What substance had Euridice.
Wilderness, The.
Winter Paradise.
World, The.
Worry about Money.
Written in Exile.
Raine, Thomas
Fourpence a Day.
Rainey, Gertrude ("Ma" Rainey) (1886–1939)
Don't Fish in My Sea.
Rainsford, Christina
Shadbush.
Rai San'yo (1781–1832)
Eastern hills — dense and lush.
I attend her palanquin a hundred miles.
I chastise the bones of an old villain of a thousand years ago.
I put away my book, chin in hand, alone.
Landscape Vignettes, Sels.
Mount Yoshino, Sels.
On flowered paths, squeaks of flying squirrels.
Out the gate I meet a friend.
Random Thoughts on the Writing of History, Sels.
Reading Books, Sels.
Shortly after I Married, I Had to Go into Mourning, Sels.
Songs of Satsuma, Sels.
Ten thousand heaps of fragrant snow fallen in the dust.
Twenty-seven Quatrains Discussing Poetry, Sels.
Twenty-some years and I've finished my book.
Raizan (Konishi Raizan) (1654–1716)
Blossoms bloom, I don't wanna die, but this illness.
Both have whiskers — I mean, the cat's wife, too.
Green, green, the young herbs are green in the snowy field.
How many autumns? unable to soothe myself.
I hug myself and again it's hard to breathe.
I pluck, I pluck and throw away spring grasses.
I turn to look: cold in the evening dusk, mountain cherries.
Mosquitoes came in, and while the two.
Spring dream — that I don't go mad is what I resent, A.
Spring rain falls, unknown to the cow's eyes.
Spring rain: I put my foot out of the footwarmer.
Spring wind: over the river bank comes a bull's voice.
Thirteen Hokku, Sels.

White fish graphically move in the water's
color.

Rákos, Sándor (b. 1921)
Bear Song, *Sels.*
To the Animal Lover.
To the Bear.
To the Hunter.

Rakosi, Carl (b. 1903)
Exercises in Scriptural Writing, *Sels.*
Florida.
Founding of New Hampshire, The.
In a Warm Bath.
Israel.
Medium IV: Sights, The.
Memoirs, The.
Sandlewood comes to my mind.
Services.
Woman.

Ralegh, Sir Walter (1552?–1618)
Advice, The.
Another of the Same.
As You Came from the Holy Land, *Sels.*
But true love is a durable fire.
Commendatory Verses to Edmund Spenser's
Fairy Queen, *Sels.*
Conceit Begotten by the Eyes.
Epitaph on Sir Philip Sidney.
Epitaph on the Earl of Leicester.
Even Such Is Time.
Excuse, The.
Farewell to False Love, A.
Farewell to the Court.
Fortune Hath Taken Away.
His Petition to Queen Anne of Denmark
(1618).
If Cynthia Be a Queen.
In Commendation of George Gascoigne's Steel
Glass.
Lie, The.
Like to an Hermit Poor.
Likes to a hermit poor in place obscure.
My Body in the Walls Captived.
My day's delight[s], my springtime joys
for[e]done.
My Woe Must Ever Last.
Nature, That Washed [or Washt] Her Hands in
Milk[e].
Now We Have Present Made.
Nymph's Reply to the Shepherd, The.
Ocean's Love to Cynthia, The, *Sels.*
On Dulcina.
On the Cards and Dice.
On the Snuff of a Candle.
Passionate Man's Pilgrimage, The.
Passions are liken'd best to floods and streams.
Poem Put into My Lady Laiton's Pocket, A.
Praised be Diana's fair and harmless light.
Silent Lover, The, *Sels.*
Sufficeth it to you [or yow] my joys [or joyes]
interred.
Sun [or Sunne] may set and rise, The.
Sweet Unsure.
Three Things [or Thinges] There Be[e] That
Prosper All [or Up] Apace.
To His Love When He Had Obtained Her.
To His Mistress.
To the Translator of Lucan [or Lucan's
Pharsalia, 1614].
Vision upon This Conceit of the Faerie [or
Fairy] Queene [or Queen], A.
What Is Our Life?

**Ralegh, Sir Walter (1552?–1618) and to
George Clifford**
My thoughts are winged with hopes.

Raleigh, Sir Walter Alexander (1861–1922)
Wishes of an Elderly Man.

"Ramal, Walter". See De la Mare, Walter.

Ramanujan, A. K. (b. 1929)
Hindoo: He Doesn't Hurt a Fly or a Spider
Either, The.
Last of the Princes, The.
Small-scale Reflections on a Great House.
Some Indian Uses of History on a Rainy Day.

Ramke, Bin (b. 1947)
Cats of Balthus, The.

Georgia.
Nostalgia.
Victory Drive, near Fort Benning, Georgia.

Ramler, Karl Wilhelm (1725–98)
Yearning for Winter.

Ramsay, Allan (1686–1758)
An Thou Were My Ain Thing.
Carle He Came o'er the Croft, The.
Chamaeleon, The.
Elegy on Lucky Wood in the Canongate, May
1717.
Epigram: "Lasses, like nuts at bottom brown."
Epigram: "Now, Priam's Son, thou may'st be
mute."
Gentle Shepherd, The, *Sels.*
Genty Tibby and Sonsy Nelly.
Lass of Patie's Mill, The.
Lass with a Lump of Land.
Leith Races.
Lucky Spence's Last Advice.
My Peggy is a young thing.
Ode to Mr. F — [or Mr. Forbes].
Poet's Wish, The; an Ode.
Polwart on the Green.
Prologue Spoken by Mr. Anthony Alston,
1726.
Twa Books, The.
Up in the Air.

Ramsay, Andrew Michael (1686–1743)
Friendship in Perfection.

Ramsey, Hettye Rayburn
Home and Mother.
Mother.

Ramsey, Jarold (b. 1937)
Hand-Shadows.
Ontogeny.
Tally Stick, The.

Ramsey, Paul (b. 1924)
Angels, The.
Consolations.
Exiles, The.
Hours, The.
Images for the Gospel of Christ.
Modern Theologian, A.
On Words and Concepts and Things.
Poet Defended, A.
Three Epigrams, *Sels.*

Ranaivo, Flavien (b. 1914)
Carry Me.
Choice.
Distress.
Humped Ox, The.
Love Song: "Do not love me, my friend."
Old Merina Theme.
Song of a Common Lover.

Randall, Belle (b. 1940)
City Hall.
Hundred Ways of Playing Solitaire, A, *Sels.*
Mabel Woo.
Playing at Cards.

Randall, Deborah (b. 1957)
Danda with a Dead Fish.
Finney's Bar.
My Roaring Boy.
Nightwatchman.

Randall, Dudley (b. 1914)
Abu.
Analysands.
Ancestors.
Bag Woman.
Ballad of Birmingham.
Black Poet, White Critic.
Blackberry Sweet.
Booker T. and W. E. B.
Different Image, A.
George.
Hail, Dionysos.
Idiot, The.
Intellectuals, The.
Legacy: My South.
Melting Pot, The.
Memorial Wreath.
Old Witheringon.
On Getting a Natural.
Pacific Epitaphs.

Poet Is Not a Jukebox, A.
Primitives.
Profile on the Pillow, The.
Rite, The.
Roses and Revolutions.
Southern Road, The.
Souvenirs.
To the Mercy Killers.
Vacant Lot.

Randall, James A., Jr. (b. 1938)
Don't Ask Me Who I Am.
Execution.
Jew.
When Something Happens.
Who Shall Die.
Why should I be eaten by love.

Randall, James Ryder (1839–1908)
John Pelham.
My Maryland.

Randall, Julia (b. 1923)
Adam Says See, *Sels.*
For a Homecoming.
How shall we walk naked when.
Miracles.
Rockland.
To William Wordsworth from Virginia.

Randall, Margaret (b. 1936)
Ever Notice How It Is with Women?
Memory says Yes.
Under Attack.

Randall-Mills, Elizabeth (b. 1906)
Crossing the County Line.

Randell, Deborah (b. 1957)
Ballygrand Widow.

Randell, Elaine (b. 1951)
Watching Women with Children.

Randlev, Karen
Progress.
Sound of Drums, The.

Randolph, Innes (1837–87)
Rebel, The.

Randolph, Thomas (1605–35)
Answer to Mr. Ben Jonson's Ode, to Persuade
Him Not to Leave the Stage, An.
Come from Thy Palace.
Conceited Pedlar, The, *Sels.*
Devout Lover, A.
Eclogue to Mr. Johnson, An, *Sels.*
Gratulatory to Mr. Ben Johnson for His
Adopting of Him to Be His Son, A.
He Lives Long Who Lives Well.
In Praise of Women in General.
Love, give me leave to serve thee, and be
wise.
Mask for Lydia, A.
Milkmaid's Epithalamium, The.
Ode to Mr. Anthony Stafford to Hasten Him
into the Country, An.
On a Maid [or Maide] of Honour Seen by a
Scholar in Somerset Garden.
On Sir Robert Cotton the Antiquary.
On the Death of a Nightingale.
Parley with His Empty Purse, A.
Phyllis.
Poet, The.
Song: "Music, thou queen of souls, get up and
string."
This definition poetry doth fit.
Upon His Picture.
Upon Love Fondly Refused [or Refus'd] for
Conscience's Sake.
Upon the Loss[e] of His Little Finger.

**Rands, William Brighty ("Matthew Browne")
(1823–80)**
Cat of Cats, The.
Dream of a Boy Who Lived at Nine Elms,
The.
Dream of a Girl Who Lived at Sevenoaks, The.
Drummer-Boy and the Shepherdess, The
("Drummer-boy, drummer-boy, where is your
drum?")
Gipsy Jane.
Godfrey Gordon Gustavus Gore.
Lullaby: "Wind whistled loud at the window-
pane, The."

Invocation to the Muse.
January.
July.
June.
Life.
Life's Boundary.
Limitations.
Lincoln.
Lines Written on a Farewell View of the
    Franconia Mountains at Twilight.
Listening Nydia.
Little Fay's Thanksgiving.
Longfellow.
Lost Opportunities.
Love's Vista.
Maid of Ehrenthal, The.
March.
May.
May's Invocation after a Tardy Spring.
Messengers, The.
Midnight.
Mignon.
Mildred's Doves.
Milton.
Mist Maiden, The.
Musidora's Vision.
My Easter Dove.
My Spirit's Complement.
Nature's Minor Chords.
Nature's Uplifting.
Niobe.
Noonday Thought.
Noontide.
November.
O Restless Heart, Be Still!
Ocean Musing, An.
October.
Ode on the Twentieth Century.
On a Nook Called Fairyland.
On the Concord River.
On the Picture of a Child.
On the rapids of the St. Lawrence.
Our Task.
Pastoral: "Annette came through the meadows."
Perfect Orchestra, The.
Picture, A.
Poet's Ideal, The.
Poet's Ministrants, The.
Prayer: "O Christ, who in Gethsemane."
Quebec.
Quest of the Ideal, The.
Questioning.
Raphael.
Recompensed?
Repose.
Retrospection.
Reunited.
Reverie.
Rhyme of the Antique Forest.
Robert G. Shaw.
Sculptor's Vision, The.
Sea Cadences.
Self-Mastery.
September.
Shadow and Sunrise.
Shakespeare.
Siren Bird, The.
Sky Picture.
Snow Song.
Song: "O sweet, sad, singing river."
Soul Incense.
Soul's Courts, The.
Star Song.
Starlight Thought.
Sunrise.
Sunrise Thought.
Sunset.
Sunset Picture.
Sunset Thought.
Thought at Walden, A.
Thought of Lake Ontario, A.
Tireles Sculptor, The.
To Laura.
To My Father.
To My Mother.
Toussaint L'Ouverture.

Triple Benison, The.
Two Musicians, The.
Venus of Milo, The.
Verses to my Heart's-Sister.
Vision of Eve, The.
Vision of Moonlight, A.
Voices of the Rain.
Wendell Phillips.
William Lloyd Garrison.
Wood Carols.

Ray, Maude Louise
My Task.

Ray, Tarapada
My Great Grand Uncle.
Ship's Whistle, The.

Raymond, Richard C. (d. 1980)
And Nothing Moved.

Raymond, Vicki (b. 1949)
Extinguish, One by One.
People, No, The.
Reculver Bay.

Read, Sir Herbert (1893–1968)
Beata l'Alma.
Cranach.
End of a War, The.
Falcon and the Dove, The.
Happy Warrior, The.
Mutations of the Phoenix, *Sels*.
My Company.
1945.
Phoenix, bird of terrible pride.
Short Poem for Armistice Day, A.
Sic et Non.
Summer Rain.
To a Conscript of 1940.
White Isle of Leuce, The.

Read, Thomas Buchanan (1822–72)
Angler, The.
Attack, The.
Blennerhassett's Island.
Brave at Home, The.
Closing Scene, The.
Drifting.
Eagle and Vulture, The.
New Pastoral, The, *Sels*.
Rising, The.
Sheridan's Ride.
Valley Forge.
Wagoner of the Alleghanies, The, *Sels*.
Windy Night, The.

Read, Vail (b. 1909)
This New Day.

Reading, Peter
Carte Postale.
Who would have thought it Sir, actually putting
    ME in a WRITING!

Reading, Peter (b. 1946)
Ballad: "I'll tell you a story/ concerning John
    and Joan."
Camping Provencial. Notices: (1).
Correspondence.
Travelogue, *Sels*.
Tryst.

Realf, Richard (1834–78)
Defence of Lawrence, The.
Word, The.

Reaney, James (b. 1926)
Baby, The.
Branwell's Sestina.
Granny Crack.
Katzenjammer Kids, The.
Le Tombeau de Pierre Falcon.
Lost Child, The.
Oracular Portcullis, The.
School Globe, The.
Sequence in Four Keys, A, *Sels*.
Suit of Nettles, A, *Sels*.
To the Avon River above Stratford, Canada.
Upper Canadian, The.

Reap, Norah
Numbers.

Reason, Charles Lewis (1818–93)
Freedom, *Sels*.
O Freedom! Freedom! O! how oft.

Spirit Voice, The; or Liberty Call to the
    Disfranchised (State of New York).

Reavey, George (1907–76)
Bridge of Heraclitus, The.
Never.

Rebéarivelo, Jean-Joseph. *See* Rabéarivelo [*or*
    Rebéarivelo], Jean-Joseph.

Rechter, Judith (b. 1937)
Fay Wray to the King.

Reckord, Margaret
Ama Credo.
Journey, The.
Miss Geeta.

Rector, Liam (b. 1949)
Showing.

Redgrove, Peter (b. 1932)
Christiana.
Corposant.
Curiosity-Shop, The.
Design.
Dog Prospectus.
Eggs, The.
For No Good Reason.
Ghostly Father, The.
Idea of Entropy at Maenporth Beach, The.
Intimate Supper.
Light Hotel.
Million, The.
Minerals of Cornwall, Stones of Cornwall.
Red Indian Corpse.
Required of You This Night.
Secretary, The.
Serious Readers.
Visible Baby, The.

Redi, Francesco (1626–98)
Bacchus in Tuscany, *Sels*.
Bacchus's Opinion of Wine, and Other
    Beverages.
Creation of My Lady, The.

Redmond, Eugene B. (b. 1937)
Definition of Nature.
Epigrams for My Father, *Sels*.
Fatherlore: papa-rites, daddyhood.
45–degree hat, Bulldurham butt bailing from
    lips.
Gods in Vietnam.
Parapoetics.
Spearo's Blues (or: Ode to a Grecian Yearn).
Stone-story. The story of stone, brokenbricks.
Sun-son. Stonebone. Blackblitz.
Wanderer across waters.

Redshaw, Thomas Dillon (b. 1944)
Voice from Danang.

Redwing, A. K. (b. 1948)
Agent of Love.
Blue Jeaned Rock Queen in Search of
    Happiness on a Blind Thursday at 1/3 Speed
    and Crying, A.
Chrome Babies Eating Chocolate Snowmen in
    the Moonlight.
Cosmic Eye.
Hoofer, The.
Lost Mohican Visits Hell's Kitchen, A.
Sitting Bull's Will versus the Sioux Treaty of
    1868 and Monty Hall.
Tornado Soup.
Two Hookers.
World's Last Unnamed Poem, The.
Written in Unbridled Repugnance near Sioux
    Falls, Alabama – April 30, 1974.

Reed, Douglas
Hand that blew the sacred fire has failed, The.

Reed, Edward Bliss (1872–1940)
Poplars.

Reed, Henry (1914–86)
Auction Sale, The.
Chard Whitlow.
Judging Distances.
Lessons of the War, *Sels*.
Lives.
Naming of Parts.
Sailor's Harbor.
Unarmed Combat.
Wall, The.

Lice Seekers, The.
My mouth is often joined against his mouth.
Napoleon after Sedan.
Ophelia.
Poets Seven Years Old.
Poster of Our Dazzling Victory at Saarbrucken,
A.
Royalty.
Season in Hell, A, *Sels.*
Sensation.
Sleeper in the Valley, The.
Sleeper in the Valley, The.
Song of the Highest Tower.
Strolling Player, The.
To the French of the Second Empire.
Tortured Heart, The.
Vowels.

Rimos of Majorca, Moses (1406–30)
Elegy (for Himself).

Rinckhart, Martin (1586–1649)
Now Thank We All Our God.

Ringelnatz, Joachim
Ambition.

Rioff, Suzanne Berger (b. 1944)
Cycles, Cycles.
Seduction, The.

Ríos, Alberto A. (b. c.1952)
At Kino Viejo, Mexico.
Dream of Husbands, A.
Good Lunch of Oceans, The.
I Held His Name.
I Would Visit Him in the Corner.
Incident at Imuris.
Inquietude of a Particular Matter, The.
Island of the Three Marias.
Juan Rulfo Moved Away.
Lost on Septemter Trail, 1967, *Sels.*
Madre Soffa.
Man Then Suddenly Stops Moving, A.
Man Who Became Old, The.
Nani.
Purpose of Altar Boys, The.
Saints, and Their Care.
Singing the Internationale.
There Was a Roof over Our Heads.
True Story of the Pins.

Risi, Nelo (b. 1920)
Elementary Thoughts, *Sels.*
Loud voices are needed.
To deny what we know.
Variations on White, *Sels.*

Risley, Richard Vorhees (1874–1904)
Dewey in Manila Bay.

Rist, Johann (1607–67)
Eternity, Thou Thunderous Word, *Sels.*
She Boasts of Her Constancy.

Ristovic, Aleksandar (b. 1933)
About Death and Other Things.
Dead Leaves.
Despair.
Flirting with a Pig.
Gingerbread Heart.
Law, The.
Maids.
Monastic Outhouse.
Old Motif.
Out in the Open.
Outhouse.
Time of fools is coming.

Ritchie, Elisavietta (b. 1932)
Sorting Laundry.

Ritsos, Yannis (b. 1909)
Alone with His Work.
Approximately.
Augmentation of the Unknown.
Beauty.
Disfigurement.
Dusk.
Final Hour.
Healing.
Insignificant Needs.
Marpessa's Choice.
Meaning of Simplicity, The.
Miniature.
Our Land.

Penelope's Despair.
Philomela.
Poet's Place, The.
Putting Out the Lamp.
Women.

Rittenhouse, Jessie Belle (1869–1948)
My Wage.

Ritter, Margaret Tod (b. 1893)
Faith, I Wish I Were a Leprechaun.

Rivard, David
Earth to Tell of the Beasts.
Fall River.
Firestone.
How It Will Always Seem.
Later History.
Naive Invocation.
1966.
One Too Many Mornings.
Summons.
Torque.

Rive, Richard (b. 1931)
Where the Rainbow Ends.

Rivera, Louis Reyes
I Care about Whichever Word.

Rivers, Conrad Kent (1933–68)
Death of a Negro Poet, The.
Four Sheets to the Wind and a One-Way Ticket
to France.
If Blood Is Black Then Spirit Neglects My
Unborn Son.
In Defense of Black Poets.
Mourning Letter from Paris, A.
On the Death of William Edward Burghardt Du
Bois by African Moonlight and Forgotten
Shores.
Prelude: "Night and the hood."
Still Voice of Harlem, The.
To Richard Wright.
Train Runs Late to Harlem, The.
Watts.

Rivner, Tuvia (b. 1924)
Fire in the Stone, The.
Lullaby: "Nocturnal, my panther, has eyes that
spark, The."
Sunflower.
Wicked Clamor, The.

Roach, Eric (1915–74)
At Guaracara Park.
Love Overgrows a Rock.
Piarco.

Robbins, Howard Chandler (1876–1952)
And Have the Bright Immensities.
Put Forth, O God, Thy Spirit's Might.
Sabbath Day Was By, The.
Saviour, Whose Love Is Like the Sun.
Spirit from Whom Our Lives Proceed.

Robbins, Martin (b. 1931)
Cantor's Dream before the High Holy Days, A.
Chicago Scene (1952, 1969).
On Seeing a Torn Out Coin Telephone.

Robbins, Richard
Change to One-Way after Repaving, The.
Vandal.

Roberson, Ed (b. 1939)
Blue Horses.
Eclipse.
18,000 Feet.
Four Lines of a Black Love Letter Between
Teachers.
If the Black Frog Will Not Ring.
Mayday.
Othello Jones Dresses for Dinner.
Poll.
Seventh Son.
When Thy King Is a Boy, *Sels.*
You black out the sun.

Robert II, King of France (970–1031)
Strength, Love, Light.

Roberts, Cecil (b. 1892)
Prayer for a Pilot.

Roberts, Sir Charles G. D. (1860–1943)
Ballad of Manila Bay, A.
Brook in February, The.
Brooklyn Bridge.

Herring Weir, The.
Ice.
In Apia Bay.
Mowing, The.
Pea-Fields, The.
Potato Harvest, The.
Skater, The.
Songs of the Common Day, *Sels.*
Tantramar Revisited, The.

Roberts, Daniel C. (1841–1907)
God of Our Fathers, Whose Almighty Hand.

Roberts, David ("Dewi Havhesp") (1831–84)
Beloved, The.

Roberts, Dorothy (b. 1907)
Cold.
Dazzle.

Roberts, Elizabeth Madox (1885–1941)
Big Brother.
Butterbean Tent, The.
Christmas Morning.
Circus, The.
Cold Fear.
Cornfield, The.
Father's Story.
Firefly.
Hens, The.
Milking Time.
Mr. Wells.
Mumps.
Orpheus.
People, The.
Rabbit, The.
Sky, The.
Strange Tree.
Stranger.
Water Noises.
Woodpecker, The.

Roberts, G. D. (1860–1943)
Old Morgan.

Roberts, George (b. 1943)
Lament: "My old red Schwinn had a carrier
over the back fender."
While Dissecting Frogs in Biology Class Scrut
Discovers the Intricacies of the Scooped
Neckline in His Lab Partner's Dress.

Roberts, Jack (b. 1960)
New Reforms, The.

Roberts, Len
Ten Below.

Roberts, Lynette
Poem from Llanybri.

Roberts, Mary M. (1877–1959)
Little Pudding.

Roberts, Michael (1902–48)
"Already," Said My Host.
H. M. S. *Hero.*
Hymn to the Sun.
In the Flowering Season.
Les Planches-en-Montagnes.
Midnight.
St. Gervais.
St. Ursanne.

Roberts, Michele (b. 1949)
After My Grandmother's Death.
Demeter Grieving.
Madwoman at Rodmell.
Magnificat.
Out of Chaos Out of Order Out.
Rite de Passage.
Sibyl's Song, The.

Roberts, Nigel (b. 1941)
After / the Moratorium Reading.
Gull's Flight, The.

Roberts, Teresa Noelle
Apotheosis of the Kitchen Goddess II.

Roberts, Theodore Goodridge (1877–1953)
Blue Heron, The.
Maid, The.

Roberts, Ursula. *See* Miles, Susan.

Roberts, Walter Adolphe (1886–1962)
Maroon Girl, The.
On a Monument to Martí.
Peacocks.
San Francisco.

Song: "Give me leave to rail at you."
Song: "Leave this gaudy gilded stage."
Song: "Love a woman? You're [or Y'are] an ass."
Song: "My dear mistress has a heart."
Song of a Young Lady to Her Ancient Lover, A.
Song to Cloris, A.
Tired with the noisome follies of the age.
To Chuse a Friend, but Never Marry.
To His Mistress.
To Love and Nature all their rights restore.
To My More Than Meritorious Wife.
Tunbridge Wells.
Upon Drinking in a Bowl.
Upon [His] Leaving His Mistress.
Upon Nothing.
Very Heroical Epistle in Answer to Ephelia, A.
Waller, by nature for the bays designed.
Were I, who to my cost already am.
Written in a Lady's Prayer Book.

Rock, Madeleine Caron
He Is the Lonely Greateness.

Rockwell, Levi (*fl.* c.1853)
From a Connecticut Newspaper.

Rodd, Sheila Desirée Savory. *See* Flynn, Desirée.

Rode, Helge (1870–1937)
Snow.

Rodefer, Stephen (b. 1940)
Codex.
Pretext.

Roderick, John M.
Passage.

Rodgers, Carolyn M. (b. 1942)
And While We Are Waiting.
Breakthrough.
For H. W. Fuller.
In This House, There Shall Be No Idols.
Jazz.
Jesus Was Crucified or: It Must Be Deep.
Look at My Face, a Collage.
Masquerade.
Me, in Kulu Se and Karma.
Missing Beat.
Newark, for Now (68).
Now Ain't That Love?
One.
Phoenix.
Poem for Some Black Women.
Poem/ Ditty-Bop.
Proclamation/ From Sleep, Arise.
Rebolushinary X-mas.
Remember Times for Sandy.
Setting/ Slow Drag.
Somebody Call.
Testimony.
U Name This One.
Voodoo on the Un-Assing of Janis Joplin.
We Dance Like Ella Riffs.
What Color Is Lonely.
Yuh Lookin Good.

Rodgers, William Robert (1909–69)
Apollo and Daphne.
Awake!
Beagles.
Carol: "Deep in the fading leaves of night."
Christ Walking on the Water.
Directions to a Rebel.
Field Day.
Home Thoughts from Abroad.
Irish Lake, An.
It was a lovely night.
Lent.
Life's Circumnavigators.
Lovers, The.
Neither Here nor There.
Net, The.
Paired Lives.
Party, The.
Raider, The.
Resurrection: An Easter Sequence, *Sels.*
Scapegoat.
Sing, Brothers, Sing!
Snow.

Stormy Day.
Stormy Night.
Summer Holidays.
Summer Journey.
Swan, The.
War-Time.
White Christmas.
Winter's Cold.
Words.

Roditi, Edouard (b. 1910)
Night Prayer of Glückel of Hameln, The.

Rodman, Frances (b. 1934?)
Spring Cricket.

Rodman, Selden (b. 1909)
Daphne.
Harpers Ferry.
Norris Dam.
On a Picture by Pippin, Called "The Den."
Time of Day.

Rodman, Thomas P. (*fl.* c.1833)
Battle of Bennington, The.

Rodríguez, Aleida (b. 1953)
Epiphany.
Island of the Living, The.

Rodriguez, Judith (b. 1936)
At the Nature-Strip.
Eskimo Occasion.
Handloom, The.
How Come the Truck-Loads?
Lifetime Devoted to Literature, A.
New York Sonnet.
Rebeca in a Mirror.

Rodriguez, Luis J.
Blast Furnace, The.
Every Breath a Prayer.
Juchitán.
Tomatoes.

Rodriguez, Magdalena de
June 10.

Roe, Barbara
Into Concrete Mixer Throw.

Roe, Sir Thomas (1581–1644)
On Gustavus Adolphus, King of Sweden.

Roethke, Theodore (1908–63)
Academic.
All Morning.
Bat, The.
Big Wind.
Bound.
Bring the Day!
Child on Top of a Greenhouse.
Coming of the Cold, The.
Cow, The.
Cuttings ("Sticks-in-a-drowse droop over sugary loam").
Cuttings ("This urge, wrestle, resurrection of dry sticks").
Decision, The.
Dinky.
Dolor.
Donkey, The.
Dream, The.
Elegy for Jane.
Far Field, The.
Field of Light, A.
First Meditation.
Flight, The.
Follies of Adam, The.
For an Amorous Lady.
Forcing House.
Four for Sir John Davies.
Frau Bauman, Frau Schmidt, and Frau Schwartze.
Geranium, The.
Gibber, The.
Give Way, Ye Gates.
Heard in a Violent Ward.
Her Longing.
Her Time.
Heron, The.
Hippo, The.
I Knew a Woman [Lovely in Her Bones].
I thirst by day. I watch by night.
I'm Here.
In a Dark Time, *Sels.*

In a dark time, the eye begins to see.
In Evening Air.
Infirmity.
It Was Beginning Winter.
Journey to the Interior.
Judge Not.
Kitty-Cat Bird, The.
Lady and the Bear, The.
Light Breather, A.
Light Listened.
Lizard, The.
Long Live the Weeds.
Long Waters, The.
Lost Son, The, *Sels.*
Marrow, The.
Meadow Mouse, The.
Meditation at Oyster River.
Meditations of an Old Woman, *Sels.*
Mid-Country Blow.
Minimal, The.
Mips and ma the mooly moo.
Mistake, The.
Moment, The.
Moss-gathering.
My Papa's Waltz.
Night Crow.
Night Journey.
North American Sequence.
Old Florist.
Once More, the Round.
Open House.
Orchids.
Pit, The.
Praise to the End!, *Sels.*
Prayer before Study.
Prayer: "If I must of my senses lose."
Premonition, The.
Reckoning, The.
Renewal, The.
Reply, The.
Return, The.
Right Thing, The.
Root Cellar.
Rose, The.
Rouse for Stevens, The.
Running Lightly over Spongy Ground.
Saginaw Song, The.
Second Shadow.
Sensualists, The.
Sequel, The.
Shape of the Fire, The.
She.
Sloth, The.
Small, The.
Snake.
Song for the Squeeze-Box.
Swan, The.
They Sing.
Thing, The.
Three Epigrams, *Sels.*
Transplanting.
Visitant, The.
Voice, The.
Waking, The.
Waking ("I strolled across/ An open field"), The.
Weed Puller.
Whale, The.
What Can I Tell My Bones?
Where Knock Is Open Wide.
Wish for a Young Wife.
Words for the Wind.

Rogers, Del Marie
Desert.

Rogers, Elymas Payson (1815–61)
Covetous Nebraskaites, The.
Law! what is law? The wise and sage.
Poem on the Fugitive Slave Law, A, *Sels.*
Repeal of the Missouri Compromise Considered, The, *Sels.*

Rogers, F.
Wishes.

Rogers, George (1805–46)
As Gentle Dews Distill.

Mrs. Francis Ellen Harper.
Reason Why, The.
Toussaint L'Overture, *Sels.*
We Are Rising.
Rowe, Henry (1754–1819)
Moon.
Sun.
Rowe, James Wilton (1865–1933)
Lake Chemo.
Rowe, Nicholas (1674–1718)
Epigram: "Whilst maudlin Whigs deplore their Cato's fate."
Rowland, J. R. (b. 1925)
Canberra in April.
London.
Traveller, A.
Rowlands, Samuel (1570?–1630?)
Boreas.
Melancholy Knight, The, *Sels.*
Poetaster, The.
Prologue: "Under the shadow of the gloomy night."
Sir Eglamour.
Sir Revel.
Thraso.
Rowlandson, Thomas (1756–1827)
Epitaph on a Willing Girl.
Rowley, William *and* **John Fletcher.** *See* **Fletcher, John.**
Rowley, William *and* **John Webster.** *See* **Webster, John.**
Rowley, William *and* **Thomas Middleton.** *See* **Middleton, Thomas.**
Rowse, Alfred Leslie (b. 1903)
White Cat of Trenarren, The.
Rowswell, Albert K.
Should You Go First.
Royde-Smith, Naomi (d. 1964)
Horse, The.
Royden, Matthew (*fl.* 1580–1622)
Elegy, or Friend's Passion for His Astrophil [*or* Astrophel], An, *Sels.*
On Sir Philip Sidney.
Royle, Edwin Milton (1862–1942)
Doan't You Be What You Ain't.
Rózewicz, Tadeusz (b. 1921)
Busy with Many Jobs.
Fight With An Angel.
I See Madmen.
In the Middle of Life.
Lament: "I turn to you high priests."
Larva, The.
Massacre of the Innocents.
Memory of a Dream from the Year 1963.
Pigtail.
Poem of Pathos.
Posthumous Rehabilitation.
Proofs.
She Looked At the Sun.
Sketch for a Modern Love Poem, A.
Survivor, The.
To the Heart.
Transformations.
Warning.
Ruark, Gibbons (b. 1941)
Basil.
Finding the Pistol.
For a Suicide, a Little Early Morning Music.
Lament: "One sore thing is the way."
Larkin.
Lost Letter to James Wright, with Thanks for a Map of Fano.
Muse's Answer, The.
Postscript to an Elegy.
Rose Growing into the House, The.
Sleeping Out with My Father.
To the Swallows of Viterbo.
Visitor, The.
Watching You Sleep under Monet's Water Lilies.
Rubadiri, James David (b. 1930)
Stanley Meets Mutesa.
Rubin, Larry (b. 1930)
Addict, The.
Brother, The.

Brother-in-Law, The.
Dinner at the Mongoloid's.
Exile, The.
Houses of Emily Dickinson, The.
Lesson, The.
Manual, The.
Nazi in the Dock, at Sixty, The.
Rubin, Ron
Limerick: "I'm getting deep lines on my forehead."
Limerick: "I'm glad pigs can't fly," said young Sellers."
Limerick: "There was a trombonist called Herb."
Limerick: "There was a young Japanese geisha."
Limerick: "There was an old drunk called Hieronymus."
Limerick: "There was an old drunkard of Devon."
Limerick: "There was an old Welshman called Morgan."
Limerick: "Vain old Professor of Greek, A."
Rückert, Friedrich ("Freimund Raimar") (1788–1866)
And Then No More.
Barbarossa.
Come To Me.
Reasons for Laughter and Crying.
Songs on the Death of Children, *Sels.*
Sun is soon to rise as bright, The.
You My Soul.
Rudaki (870?–c.940)
Came to me.
Quatrain: "With you away — despair!"
Young or Old We Die.
Ruddock, Margot
Autumn, Crystal Eye.
Child Compassion, The.
I Take Thee Life.
Love Song: "Though to think/ Rejoiceth me."
O Holy Water.
Spirit, Silken Thread.
Take Away.
Rudman, Andrew (d. 1708)
When Shall My Pilgrimage, Jesus My Saviour, Be Ended?
Rudman, Mark (b. 1948)
Nerves.
Shoebox, The.
Rudnik, Raphael (b. 1933)
Lady in the Barbershop, The.
Penny Trumpet.
Rudyerd, Sir Benjamin (1572–1658)
Why Do We Love.
Ruebner, Tuvia (b. 1924)
Among Iron Fragments.
Rueckert, Friedrich
Ride round the Parapet, The.
Ruff, "Whistling Bill"
Delia Holmes ("Delia, Delia, why didn't you run?")
Ruffilli, Paolo (b. 1949)
Malaria.
Personal Mirror.
Ruffin, Paul (b. 1941)
Grandma Chooses Her Plot at the County Cemetery.
Hotel Fire: New Orleans.
Rufinus (*fl.* 150–400)
Amymone.
Did I not say we grow old.
Epigram: "Boy-mad no longer."
Europa's kiss/ even if.
Faint Heart.
Her eyes are gold.
Here Rhodoklea/ is a garland.
I do not enjoy.
I hate an easy woman.
I have armoured my feelings.
If girls were nice.
In Spite.
Lay neither the scrawny.
Leaving the Boys Behind.

Let us wash each other's body.
Letter from Ephesos.
Melissias.
Pallas and/ golden-shoed Hera.
Prodike.
Requirements ("Not too chary, not too fast.")
Requirements ("Not too lean, and not too fat").
Rhodope is so stuck up/ because of her beauty.
Rhodope, Melite and Rhodoklea/ contested.
Silvertoed virgin, A.
Slave Girl, The.
So it's hullo now.
Waterfront Girls, The.
Where is Praxiteles where.
You have Hera's eyes Melite.
Rufinus Domesticus (*fl.* c.550)
Ah, Melissa, where's your famous golden beauty.
Andante, ma Non Assai.
Dear God, I didn't know that Cytherea was bathing.
Epigrams, *Sels.*
Europa kisses sweetly.
Her foot sparkled like silver.
How can any man throw out.
How could I have known.
I wove this garland, Rodokleia.
Kiss from Her, A.
Lamplighter, if you can't set two equally.
Lover's Posy, The.
Melissias denies her love, but her body screams.
Rhodoclea, I send you this wreath which I wove with my own hands.
Silver-footed girl was bathing, letting the water, The.
Time has not quenched your beauty. Much of your bygone prime.
We who find no joy in celebrity.
Were that woman's postcoital charms.
When Pallas and golden-sandaled Hera saw Maeonis.
Who beat you and put you out.
Years have not damaged your beauty, The.
Ruggieri, Helen
Forked Tongue.
Ohio Is the Iroquois Word for Beautiful.
Unspoken World.
Ruiz, Antonio Machado. *See* **Machado Ruiz, Antonio.**
Ruiz, Juan, Archpriest of Hita (*fl.* c.1343)
Book of True Love, The, *Sels.*
Praise of Little Women.
When you're together with her, and you have a good excuse.
Rukeyser, Muriel (1913–80)
Ajanta.
Alloy.
Along History.
Ballad of Orange and Grape.
Believing in Those Inexorable Laws.
Birth of Venus, The.
Boy with His Hair Cut Short.
Boys of These Men Full Speed.
Ceiling Unlimited.
Children, the Sandbar, That Summer.
Children's Elegy.
Columbus.
Darkness Music.
Despisals.
Don Baty, the Draft Register.
Double Ode.
Easter Eve.
Effort at Speech between Two People.
Eighth Elegy, *Sels.*
Endless.
Even During War.
Eyes of Night-Time.
Fields Where We Slept.
Gauley Bridge.
George Robinson: Blues.
Gibbs, *Sels.*
Holy Family.
It Is There.
Käthe Kollwitz.
Leg in a Plaster Cast, A.

Letter to the Front, *Sels.*
Looking at Each Other.
Madboy's Song.
Meeting, The.
Mrs. Walpurga.
More Clues.
More of a Corpse than a Woman.
Motive.
Myth.
Night Feeding.
Nine Poems for the Unborn Child, *Sels.*
No one ever walking this our only earth.
Now Green, Now Burning.
Nuns in the Wind.
On the Death of Her Mother.
Paper Anniversary.
Place at Albert Bay, The.
Poem: "I lived in the first century of world wars."
Poem As Mask, The.
Poem Out of Childhood.
Power of Suicide, The.
Question, The.
Reading Time: 1 Minute 26 Seconds.
Resurrection of the Right Side.
Rondel: "Now that I am fifty-six."
Rune.
St. Roach.
Seventh Avenue.
Soul and Body of John Brown, The.
Speaking Tree, The.
Speed of Darkness, The.
Tenth Elegy. Elegy in Joy, *Sels.*
Then.
Then I Saw What the Calling Was.
They Came to Me and Said, "There Is a Child."
This Morning.
This Place in the Ways.
Time Exposures.
To be a Jew in the twentieth century.
Trial, The.
Waiting for Icarus.
Who in One Lifetime.
Woman as Market.

Rumaker, Michael (b. 1932)
Fairies Are Dancing All Over the World, The.

Rumens, Carol (b. 1944)
Easter Garland, An.
Geography Lesson.
Green Windows.
In the Cloud of Unknowing.
Leningrad Romance.
Limerick: "Ancient biologist, Heine, An."
Persephone in Armenia.
Vocation.

Runcie, John (1864–1939)
Slumber Song of the Gardens, A.

Runeberg, Johann Ludvig (1804–77)
Maiden Came from the Tryst, The.

Runyon, Damon (Alfred Damon Runyon) (1884–1946)
Song of Panama, A.

Ruse-Glason, Kate
Loop.

Rushin, Kate (b. 1951)
Black Back-Ups, The.
Bridge Poem, The.
Why I Like to Go Places: Flagstaff, Arizona — June 1978.

Rushton, Edward (1756–1814)
Human Debasement; a Fragment.

Ruskin, John (1817–1900)
La Madonna dell' Acqua.
My Dog Dash.
Needless Alarm, The.
There is religion in everything around us.
Trust Thou Thy Love.
Zodiac Song, The.

Russ, Virginia (b. 1916)
Shape of Autumn, The.

Russell, Bertrand
Limerick: "There was a young girl of Shanghai."

Russell, Charles E. (1860–1941)
Fleet at Santiago, The.

Russell, Ethel Green (b. 1890)
Letter from the Vieux Carre.

Russell, G. J.
It Might Have Been Worse.

Russell, George William. *See* "Æ."

Russell, Irwin (1853–99)
Christmas Night in the Quarters, *Sels.*
Fust Banjo, De.

Russell, Norman H. (b. 1921)
Indian School.

Russell, Sydney King (b. 1897)
Death Was a Woman.
Midsummer.
Phyllis.

Russell, Thomas (1762–88)
Names and Order of the Books of the Old Testament, The.
Sonnet: Suppos'd to Be Written at Lemnos.
To Oxford.
To the Spider.

Rutilius (*fl.* c.416)
Roma.

Rutsala, Vern (b. 1934)
New House, The.
Northwest Passage.
War of the Worlds, The.
Washrags.
Words.
World, The.

Rutter, Joseph (*fl.* 1635)
Epithalamium: "Hymen, god of marriage bed."

Rutter, Owen (Klip-Klip) (1889–1944)
In this war the Hun has brought us.
Rumour.
Salonika Campaign.
Song of Tiadatha, The, *Sels.*
Trenches.

Ryan, Abram Joseph (Father Ryan) (1839–86)
Better than Gold.
Conquered Banner, The.
Thought, A.

Ryan, Gig (b. 1956)
Too Bad.

Ryan, John C. (b. c. 1960)
Pawntickets.

Ryan, Michael (b. 1946)
Barren Poem.
Consider a Move.
Letter from an Institution: III.
My Dreams by Henry James.
Not the End of the World.
Prothalamion.
Speaking.
Switchblade.
This Is a Poem for the Dead.
TV Room at the Children's Hospice.
Where I'll Be Good.

Ryan, Paddy
Man That Waters the Worker's Beer, The.

Ryan, Richard (b. 1949)
At the End.
Deafness.
El Dorado.
Father of Famine.
From My Lai the Thunder Went West.
God the Father.
Ireland.
Lake of the Woods, The.
O, Saw Ye the Lass.
Wet Night, A.
Winter in Minneapolis.

Ryden, Ernest Edwin (1886–1981)
Twilight Shadows round Me Fall, The.

Rye, Anthony
Redbreast, The.

Ryman, James (*fl.* late 15th century)
Farewele Advent; Cristemas [*or* Christemas] is cum [*or* come].
Farewell! Advent.
Now the Most High Is Born.

Rymer, Thomas (1641–1713)
To ——: "Let those with cost deck their ill-fashioned clay."

Rymkiewicz, Jaroslaw Marek (b. 1934)
Spinoza Was a Bee.

Ryojin Hisho (*fl.* c.1179?)
May the man who gained my trust yet did not come.

Ryokan (1758–1831)
First Days of Spring.
How Can We Ever Lose Interest in Life?
In all ten directions of the universe.
To lazy to be ambitious.

Ryota (Oshima Ryota) (1718–87)
No one spoke.
They look/ like newlyweds.

Ryou, Kyongjoo Hong (b. 1959)
Jasmine.

S

"S., A. W." (1825–1861?)
Life That Counts, The.

"S., E." (*fl.* c.1576)
Being Forsaken of His Friend He Complaineth.

"S., J. H."
New Year's Wish, A.

"S. C. McK." *See* "McK., S. C."

Saadi. *See* Sadi [*or* Saadi].

Saba, Umberto (1883–1957)
Winter Noon.
Woman.

Sabin, Edwin L. (1870–1952)
Easter.

Sabina, María (b. 1894)
Ah, Jesu Kri.
Chants, The, *Sels.*
Shaman.

Saboly, Nicolas (1614–75)
Boots and Saddles.
Bring a Torch, Jeanette, Isabella.
Shepherd Boys, The.

Sabti, Kamal (b. 1958)
Jungles, *Sels.*

Sacchetti, Franco (1335–1400?)
His Talk with Certain Peasant Girls.
On a Wet Day.

Sachs, Hans (1494–1576)
Fair Melody: To Be Sung by Good Christians, A.

Sachs, Nelly (1891–1969)
Above the rocking heads of the mothers.
Already Embraced by the Arm of Heavenly Solace.
Awakening — / Voices of birds.
But Perhaps.
Chorus of the Dead.
Chorus of the Rescued.
Chorus of the Unborn.
Dead Child Speaks, A.
If I Only Knew.
In flight in escape.
In the blue distance.
Landscape of Screams.
Last one, The/ to die here.
Line Like.
Machines of War.
O My Mother.
Oblivion! Skin.
Vainly ("Vainly/the epistles burn").
We Mothers.
What Secret Cravings of the Blood.
White Serpent.

Sackville, Charles, 6th Earl of Dorset (1688–1706)
À Madame, Madame B, Beauté Sexagenaire.
Advice, The ("Wou'd you in love succeed, be brisk, be gay").
Curs'd be those dull, unpointed, dogg'rel rhymes.
Dorinda's sparkling wit, and eyes.

Soup.
Southern Pacific.
Splinter.
Spring Grass.
Summer Stars.
Sunset from Omaha Hotel Window.
Sunsets.
Ten Definitions of Poetry.
There Are Different Gardens.
They All Want to Play Hamlet.
They have yarns.
Three Spring Notations on Bipeds.
Threes.
To a Contemporary Bunkshooter.
Under a Hat Rim.
Upstream.
Washington Monument by Night.
We Must Be Polite.
What the people learn out of lifting and
    hauling.
When I asked for fish in the restaurant facing
    the Ohio River.
Whiffs of the Ohio River at Cincinnati, *Sels.*
Who shall speak for the people?
Why did the children.
Why repeat? I heard you the first time.
Wilderness.
Wind Song.

Sandburg, Helga (b. 1918)
Importance of Mirrors, The.

Sandeen, Ernest (b. 1908)
Late Twentieth-Century Prayer, A.
Nearing Winter.
Plaint of Flowers, A.
Poète Manqué.
They Are Wicked.
Way Down, The.

Sanders, Donald T. (b. 1944)
Love Tells Us Who We Are.
Poem for Shane on Her Brother's Birthday.

Sanders, Edward (b. 1939)
Chain, The.
Cutting Prow, The.
Five Feet, The.
Flower from Robert Kennedy's Grave, A.
Fugs, The.
Holy Was Demeter Walking th' Corn Furrow.
Hymn to Archilochus.
Leaves of Heaven, The.
Pindar's Revenge.
Poem From Jail, *Sels.*
Redeem Zion!
What Would Tom Paine Do?
Yiddish Speaking Socialists of the Lower East
    Side.

Sanders, Ruth Manning-. *See* Manning-
    Sanders, Ruth.

Sanders, Sue (b. 1947)
We Are Welcome.

Sandford, James (*fl.* c.1576)
Of Love.

Sandler, Luada
Gift, The.
Scene from Shoah, A.

Sandstrom, Flora
Stately Lady, The.

Sandy, Stephen (b. 1934)
Ballad of Mary Baldwin, The.
Declension.
Et Quid Amabo Nisi Quod Aenigma Est.
Hunter's Moon.
Second Law, The.

Sandys, Edwin (1561–1629)
In Pilgrim Life Our Rest.

Sandys, George (c.1577–1644)
Again when all the radiant sons of light.
Bounty of Jehovah Praise, The.
Judah in Exile Wanders.
O Blest Estate, Blest from Above.
"O Father, I acknowledge, " Job replied.
Paraphrase on the Psalms of David, *Sels.*
Paraphrase Upon Job, A, *Sels.*
Psalm XXIII: "Lord my shepherd, me His
    sheep, The."

Saner, Reg (b. 1931)
Aspen Oktoberfest.
Fifth Season, The.
Waiting Out Rain, Sheltered by Overhang.
Where I Come From.

Sanetomo (Minamoto no Sanetomo) (1192–
    1219)
As evening comes.
As the warrior reaches up.
Bamboo frond, The.
Bitter sight — / I watch and my tears.
Boneset, why are you blooming.
By Hakone Road/ I cross over.
Fabrics swirled in a thousand.
Grown over with straggly saw grass.
Gull-haunted,/ the windblown shore of Susaki.
I didn't mean/ to recall the past.
I open the pine door.
If only the world.
In the rockbound pool.
Is it always so bleak a sight?
Leaves of the small oaks, The.
Long-drawn-out autumn, The.
Sleet rattles on the leaves.
So cold the night.
This world — / call it an image.
Though a time come.
Too much/ at one time.
Twenty-four Tanka, *Sels.*
Waves of the great sea, The.
When the wild goose.
You erect pagodas.

Sanford, Christy Sheffield
Dreams of Snakes, Chocolate and Men.
Romance of Citrus, The.
Romance of Imprinting, The.
Scattered Fog.
Traveling through Ports That Begin with "M."

Sangster, Charles (1822–93)
Our life is like a forest, where the sun.
Pleasant Memories, *Sels.*
St. Lawrence and the Saguenay, *Sels.*
Sonnets Written in the Orillia Woods, *Sels.*
Thousand Islands, The.

Sangster, Margaret Elizabeth (b. 1894)
Blind Man, The.
Mother's Prayer, A.
Prayer for Faith, A.
Security.
Work of Love, The.

Sangster, Margaret Elizabeth Munson (1898–
    1912)
At Sunset.
Average Man, The.
Forgiven.
Oh, face to face with trouble.
Our Own.
Patience with the Living.
Show Me Thyself.
Thanksgiving.
They Never Quite Leave Us.
Within the Veil.

Sanguineti, Edoardo (b. 1930)
Erotopaegnia, *Sels.*
Laborintus, *Sels.*
Purgatory of Hell, *Sels.*

Sannazaro, Jacopo (Actius Sincerus
    Sannazarius) (1458–1530)
Like to these unmesurable montayns.

Sanpu (1647–1732)
May rains!

Sansom, Clive (1910–81)
Dustman, The.
Harvest Mouse.
Innkeeper's Wife, The.
It was a night in winter.
Ladybird.
Me — Pirate.
Milkman, The.
Postman, The.
Snowflakes.
Witnesses, The, *Sels.*

Sansom, Martha (1690–1736)
Changes.
Crayons.

Death is Abstract.
Haunted.
I Am the Loveless.
I Sat Through a Distant Autumn.
Invitation from a Country Cottage, The.
Isolation.
It was not that I lost direction.
Lost Monday.
Maze of Decades, A.
Meal, The.
Saturday Night.
Song: "Foolish eyes, thy streams give over."
Storm, The.
Sunday March.
To Cleon's Eyes.

Sant, Andrew (b. 1950)
Homage to the Canal People.
Soundwaves.

Sant' Angelo, Bartolomeo di (*fl.* 13th century)
He Jests Concerning His Poverty.

Santal
Witch, The.

Sant'Ana, Gloria de
African Day.

Santayana, George (1863–1952)
After Grey Vigils.
Among the Myriad Voices of the Spring.
As in the midst of battle there is room.
Cape Cod.
Deem not, because you see me in the press.
Dreamt I today the dream of yesternight.
Have I the heart to wander on the earth.
I sought on earth a garden of delight.
I Would I Might Forget That I Am I.
Mightier Storms than This.
Minuet on Reaching the Age of Fifty, A.
O Martyred Spirit.
O world, thou choosest not the better part!
On the Death of a Metaphysician.
Perfect love is nourished by despair, A.
Sonnets, *Sels.*
Sorrow.
Sweet Are the Days.
There May Be Chaos Still.
'Tis Love That Moveth the Celestial Spheres.
To W. P, *Sels.*
What riches have you that you deem me poor?
With you a part of me hath passed away.

Santob de Carrion (*fl.* 14th century)
Consejos y Documentos al Rey Dom Pedro,
    Sels.
Jewish Poet Counsels a King, A.

Santos, Benilda S.
Atong.
Atong and His Goodbye.

Santos, Christian (b. 1941)
They Carried Their Truth to the Ditch where
    They Were Thrown.

Santos, Sherod (b. 1949)
Air Base at Châteauroux, France, The.
Breakdown, The.
Early morning, a woman sits up in bed.
First Child, Born Out of Breach in Mid-May.
I Bent to Touch a Damp Cloth to Your Mouth.
Inspiration.
Late November.
Madame Orchidée.
Married Love.
Nineteen Fifty-five.
Sheltering Ground, The, *Sels.*
Terra Incognita.
Weeks, maybe months, have passed and just.
Winter Landscape with a Girl in Brown Shoes.

Sanuki, Lady (*fl.* early 13th century)
Like a great rock, far out at sea.

Sapia, Yvonne (b. 1946)
Valentino's Hair.

Sappho (*fl.* c.612 B.C.)
About the cool water.
Achtung.
All the stars turn away their faces.
All the while, believe me, I prayed.
Alone.
Already old age is wrinkling my.
Andromache's Wedding.

Wha Is Perfyte.

Scott, Alexander (b. 1920)
Calvinist Sang.
Problems.

Scott, Bob
Limerick: "Sky's are a pitiful lot, The."
Limerick: "There was a young girl from Uttoxeter/ Who out on a date with two Jocks at a."
Limerick: "There was an old Doctor called Coué."

Scott, Clement (1841–1904)
Story of a Stowaway, The.

Scott, David (b. 1947)
Churchyard under Snow.
Flanking Sheep in Mosedale.
Hopkins Enters the Roman Catholic Church.
Kirkwall Auction Mart.
Letters from Baron Von Hügel to a Niece.
Locking the Church.
Scattering Ashes.
Surplice, The.

Scott, Dennis (b. 1939)
Epitaph: "They hanged him on a clement morning, swung."
For the Last Time, Fire.
Grampa.
Homecoming.
Mouth.
Uncle Time.
Version.

Scott, Diana (b. 1947)
Lucy Taking Birth.
Prayer for the Little Daughter between Death and Burial.
Winter Solstice Poem.

Scott, Duncan Campbell (1862–1947)
At Gull Lake; August, 1810.
At the Cedars.
En Route.
Fallen, The.
Forsaken, The.
On the Way to the Mission.

Scott, Elizabeth (1708–76)
Now Let Our Hearts Their Glory Wake.
See How the Rising Sun.

Scott, Francis Reginald (1899–1985)
Bangkok.
Bonne Entente.
Brébeuf and His Brethren.
Canadian Authors Meet, The.
Lakeshore.
Laurentian Shield.
Night Club.
W. L. M. K.

Scott, Frederick George (1861–1944)
Requiescant.
Unnamed Lake, The.

Scott, Geoffrey (1884–1924)
All Our Joy Is Enough.
Frutta di Mare.
Hector, the captain bronzed, from simple fight.
Skaian Gate, The, *Sels.*
What Was Solomon's Mind?

Scott, Herbert (b. 1931)
Morning, Milking.

Scott, Johnie (b. 1946)
American Dream, The, *Sels.*

Scott, Lady John (1810–1900)
Ettrick.

Scott, Margaret (b. 1934)
Portrait of a Married Couple.

Scott, Mary (1752?–1793)
Women of the Future.

Scott, Peter Dale (b. 1929)
Argenteuil County.
Loon's Egg, The.

Scott, Robert Balgarnie Young (1899–1987)
O Day of God, Draw Nigh.

Scott, Sharon (b. 1951)
Between Me and Anyone Who Can Understand.
Come On Home.
Discovering.

Fisk is/ a/ negroid/ institution.
For Both of Us at Fisk.
Just Taking Note.
Little More about the Brothers and Sisters, A.
Mama Knows.
Oh — Yeah!
Okay.
On My Stand.
Our Lives.
Sharon Will Be No/Where on Nobody's Best-selling List.
Sometimes/ the poems.

Scott, Tom (b. 1918)
Real Muse, The.

Scott, W. N. (b. 1923)
Bundaberg Rum.

Scott, Sir Walter (1771–1832)
Alice Brand.
Allen-a-Dale.
And What though Winter Will Pinch Severe.
Annot Lyle's Song.
Antiquary, The, *Sels.*
Battle, The ("But as they left the dark'ning heath").
Battle, The ("By this, though deep the evening fell").
Battle, The ("Not far advanc'd was morning day").
Bonny [*or* Bonnie] Dundee.
Border Ballad.
Breathes There the [*or* a] Man [with Soul So Dead].
Bride of Lammermoor, The, *Sels.*
Brignall Banks.
Challenge.
Chase, The.
Christmas in England.
Coronach.
Datur Hora Quieti.
Doom of Devorgoil, The, *Sels.*
Dreary Change, The.
Edinburgh from the Pentland Hills.
Ettrick Forest in November.
Eve of Saint John, The.
Father's Notes of Woe, A.
Fire, The.
Flowers and Trees.
For though, with men of high degree.
Friday.
Gallant Ship, The.
Gathering, The.
Gin by Pailfuls.
Guy Mannering, *Sels.*
Hail to the Chief Who in Triumph Advances.
Harold the Dauntless, *Sels.*
Harp of the North, Farewell! The Hills Grow Dark.
Heap on more wood! — the wind is chill.
Heart of Midlothian, The, *Sels.*
Hellvellyn.
Hie Away, Hie Away.
Hour with Thee, An.
Hunting Song.
Hymn to the Virgin.
Ivanhoe, *Sels.*
Jock of Hazeldean.
Lady of the Lake, The, *Sels.*
Lay of the Last Minstrel, The, *Sels.*
Legend of Montrose, The, *Sels.*
Lochinvar.
Love.
Lucy Ashton's Song.
Lullaby of an Infant Chief.
MacGregor's Gathering.
Maid of Neidpath, The.
Man the Enemy of Man.
Marmion, *Sels.*
Marmion and Douglas.
Melrose Abbey.
Minstrel, The.
Minstrel Responds to Flattery, The.
Monastery, The, *Sels.*
Nativity Chant, The.
Nelson, Pitt, Fox.
Now, yield thee, or by Him who made.
O Caledonia!

Old Mortality, *Sels.*
On Having Piles.
Oyster, The.
Peveril of the Peak, *Sels.*
Pibroch of Donuil Dhu.
Pirate, The, *Sels.*
Proud Maisie ("Proud Maisie is in the wood").
Quentin Durward, *Sels.*
Rebecca's Hymn.
Red Harlaw.
Rokeby, *Sels.*
Rosabelle.
Saint Cloud.
Serenade.
Soldier Rest! [Thy Warfare O'er].
Song of Albert Graeme.
Song of the Reim-Kennar, The.
Speak not of niceness, when there's chance of wreck.
Tis Merry in Greenwood.
To a Lock of Hair.
To an Oak Tree.
To-Day I Leave Mrs. Brown's Lodgings.
Toils Are Pitched, The.
Twist Ye, Twine Ye! Even So.
Violet, The.
Sir Walter Scott's Tribute.
Wasted, Weary, Wherefore Stay.
Waverley, *Sels.*
Weary Lot Is Thine, A.
Western Waves of Ebbing Day, The.
Where shall the lover rest.
Why Sit'st Thou by That Ruin'd Hall.
William and Helen.
Youth! Thou Wear'st to Manhood Now.

Scott, William Bell (1811–90)
Death.
Music.
Rhyme of the Sun-Dial, A.
Robin, The.
Witch's Ballad, The.

Scott, Winfield Townley (1910–68)
Annual Legend.
Biography for Traman, *Sels.*
Brief Encounter.
First Reader, The.
Five for the Grace of Man.
Grant Wood's American Landscape.
Ivory Bed, The.
Landscape as Metal and Flowers.
Let us record/ The evenings when we were innocents of twenty.
May 1506 (Christopher Columbus Speaking).
Mr. Whittier.
Mrs. Severin.
O Lyric Love.
Sonnet XV: "This is the way we say it in our time."
Swedish Angel.
Two.
U. S. Sailor with the Japanese Skull, The.
Uses of Poetry.
Watch Hill.
Wax.

Scott-Hopper, Queenie
Amy Elizabeth Ermyntrude Annie.
My Party.
Very Nearly.
What the Thrush Says.

Scott of Amwell, John (1730–83)
Amoebaean Eclogues, *Sels.*
How to Fertilize Soil.
Ode: "I hate that drum's discordant sound."
Written After Reading Some Modern Love-Verses.

Scovell, Edith Jay (b. 1907)
After Midsummer.
Alone.
Betrothal, A.
Boy Fishing, The.
Days Drawing In.
First Year, The, *Sels.*
In a Wood.
Love's Immaturity.
Marriage and Death.
Swan's Feet, The.

Thine eyes I love, and they, as pitying me.
This day is called the Feast of Crispian.
This England.
This England never did, nor never shall.
This new and gorgeous garment, majesty.
This quarry cries on havoc. O proud Death.
This royal throne of kings, this scepter'd isle.
This she? no, this is Diomed's Cressida.
This Spring of Love.
Those Hours, That With Gentle Work Did Frame.
Those Lips That Love's Own Hand Did Make.
Those petty [or pretty] wrongs that liberty commits.
Thou God of This Great Vast, Rebuke These Surges.
Thou hast a sister by the mother's side.
Thou, Nature, art my goddess; to thy law.
Thrice the Brinded Cat Hath Mewed.
Through the Forest Have I Gone.
Through the House.
Thus have I shunned the fire for fear of burning.
Thus Is This Cheek the Map of Days Outworn.
Thus with imagin'd wing our swift scene flies.
Thy Bosom Is Endeared With All Hearts.
Thy glass will show thee how thy beauties wear.
Time, thou anticipat'st my dread exploits.
Time's Glory.
Timon of Athens, *Sels.*
Timon's Epitaph.
Tired [*or* Tyr'd, *or* Tir'd] with all these, for restful death I cry.
'Tis better to be vile than vile esteem'd.
'Tis but thy name that is my enemy.
'Tis one thing to be tempted, Escalus.
To be, or not to be, that is the question.
To Gild Refinèd Gold.
To me, fair[e] friend, you never can be old.
To your owne bents dispose you: you'le be found.
To-morrow, and to-morrow, and to-morrow.
Troilus and Cressida, *Sels.*
True, I talk of dreams.
Twelfth Night, *Sels.*
Two Gentlemen of Verona, The, *Sels.*
Two Loves I Have of Comfort and Despair.
Two truths are told.
Tyrannous and bloody act is done, The.
Ulysses Advises Achilles.
Under the greenwood tree.
Under your pardon. You must note besides.
Up and Down.
Venus and Adonis, *Sels.*
Villanious and Abominable Falstaff.
Violet Bank, A.
Warr'st thou 'gainst Athens?
Was it the proud full sail of his great verse.
We few, we happy few, we band of brothers.
We were as twinned lambs that did frisk i' the sun.
Weary with toil, I haste me to my bed.
Wedding is great Juno's crown.
Were't aught to me I bore the canopy.
What! are my deeds forgot?
What ceremony else?
What is your substance, whereof are you made.
What man dare, I dare.
What man dost thou dig it for?
What potions have I drunk of Siren tears.
What shall he have that killed the deer?
What would you have? Your gentleness shall force.
What you do still betters what is done.
What's he that wishes so?
When beggars die there are no comets seen.
When Daffodils Begin to Peer.
When Forty Winters.
When I consider everything that grows.
When I do count the clock that tells the time.
When I have seen by Time's fell hand defac'd.
When icicles hang by the wall.
When, in disgrace with fortune and men's eyes.
When in the chronicle of wasted time.

When my love swears [*or* sweares] that she is made of truth.
When thou shalt be dispos'd to set me light.
When to the sessions of sweet silent thought.
Whence is that knocking?
Where is the duke my father with his power?
Where the Bee Sucks.
While you here do snoring lie.
Who ever knew the heavens menace so?
Who Is Silvia [*or* Sylvia]?
Who made thee then a bloody minister.
Whoever Hath Her Wish, Thou Hast Thy Will.
Why didst thou promise such a beauteous day.
Why dost not speak?
Why is my verse so barren of new pride.
Why, let the strucken deer go weep.
Why looks your Grace so heavily today?
Why, man, he doth bestride the narrow world.
Why, there's no remedy. 'Tis the curse of service.
Why, why is this?
Winter's not gone yet if the wild geese fly that way.
Winter's Tale, The, *Sels.*
With fairest flowers,/ Whilst summer lasts.
Woman's face with Nature's own hand painted, A.
Ye elves of hill(s), brooks, standing lakes, and groves.
Yet better thus, and known to be contemned.
Yet but Three?
Yet here, Laertes! aboard, aboard, for shame!
Yon Island Carrions Desperate of Their Bones.
Yon king's to me like to my father's picture.
You are as fond of grief as of your child.
You are for dreams and slumbers, brother priest.
You do look, my son, in a mov'd sort.
You may my glories and my state depose.
You spotted snakes [with double tongue].

Shakespeare, William *and* **John Fletcher.** *See* **Fletcher, John.**

Shalom, Shin (b. 1904)
All's Not That Simple.
At Evening when Flicker.
Drink Wonder.
Guard Me, Oh God.
In the World's Heart Burns a Torch of Fire.
Stoker, The.
Suddenly We Will Wake.
They That Sow at Night.

Shange, Ntozake (b. 1948)
Ancestral Messengers/Composition 11.
At 4:30 AM/ she rose.
Dark Phrases.
For Colored Girls Who Have Considered Suicide When the Rainbow Is Enuf, *Sels.*
Frank Albert and Viola Benzena Owens.
Get It & Feel Good.
I Sat Up One Night.
Nappy Edges (A Cross Country Sojourn).
No More Love Poems #1.
Sechita Had Heard These Things.
Somebody almost walked off wid alla my stuff.

Shanks, Edward (1892–1953)
Boats at Night.
Drilling in Russell Square.
Going In to Dinner.
Halt, The.
High Germany.
Sleeping Heroes.
Storm, The.
To the Unknown Light.

Shanly, Charles Dawson (1811–75)
Civil War.

Shannon, Monica (d. 1965?)
Could It Have Been a Shadow?
Country Trucks.
How to Tell Goblins from Elves.
Only My Opinion.
Our Hired Man (And His Daughter, Too).
Tree Toad, The ("The tree Toad is a creature neat").

Shao Fei-fei (*fl.* 17th cent.)
Letter, A.

Shao Yen-hsiang (b. c. 1933)
Chia Kuei-hsiang.
Song of Rubber.
Time Speaks.
What to Trust?

Shapcott, Jo (b. 1953)
Electroplating the Baby.
Lies.
Photograph: Sheepshearing.
Surrealists' Summer Convention Came to Our City, The.

Shapcott, Thomas William (b. 1935)
Autumn.
Bicycle Rider, The.
Flying Fox.
June Fugue.
Litanies of Julia Pastrana (1832-1860), The.
Near the School for Handicapped Children.
Piano Pieces, *Sels.*
Schoenberg Op. 11.
Sestina with Refrain.
Webern.

Shapiro, Alan (b. 1952)
Familiar Story.

Shapiro, Arnold L.
I Speak, I Say, I Talk.

Shapiro, David (b. 1947)
About This Course.
Canticle.
For Victims.
From Malay.
In a Blind Garden.
Lord I Sleep and I Sleep.
Lost Golf Ball, The.
Memory of the Present.
Seasons, The.
Sonnet: "Ice over time."

Shapiro, Gregg
Tattoo.

Shapiro, Harvey (b. 1924)
Auschwitz.
Ditty: "Where did the Jewish god go?"
Feast of the Ram's Horn.
Happiness of 6 A.M.
Heart, The.
Mountain, Fire, Thornbush.
National Cold Storage Company.
Provincetown, Mass.

Shapiro, Karl (b. 1913)
Adam and Eve, *Sels.*
After the War.
All Tropic Places Smell of Mold.
Alphabet, The.
Aubade: "What dawn is it?"
Auto Wreck.
Bed, The.
Boy-Man.
Buick.
California Winter, *Sels.*
Christmas Eve.
Confirmation, The.
Conscientious Objector, The.
Cut Flower, A.
D. C.
Dirty Word, The.
Dome of Sunday, The [*or* A].
Drug Store.
Elegy for a Dead Soldier, *Sels.*
Elegy for Two Banjos.
Exile.
First Time, The.
Fly, The.
Fox Hole.
Garage Sale.
Geographers, The.
Girls Working in Banks.
Going to School.
Haircut.
Hollywood.
Homecoming.
Hospital.
Human Nature.
I sing the simplest flower.
I swore to stab the sonnet with my pen.
In India.

Siegel, Eli (b. 1902)
All the Smoke.
Fare Thee Well.
Siegel, Robert (b. 1839)
Ego.
Siegrist, Mary
League of Nations, The.
Sieller, William Vincent (b. 1917)
Windmill on the Cape.
Sigerson, Dora (1866–1918)
Unknown Ideal.
Sigerson, George (1839–1925)
My Own Cáilin Donn.
Sigourney, Lydia Huntley (1791–1865)
Advertisement of a Lost Day.
Blessed Comforter Divine.
Bubble, The.
California.
Christian Settlements in Africa.
Columbus.
Death of a Young Lady at the Retreat for the
Insane.
Death of an Infant.
Female Education.
Funeral of Mazeen.
God Save the Plough.
Indian Names.
Laborers of Christ! Arise.
Meeting of the Susquehanna with the
Lackawanna.
Mother of Washington, The.
Mother's Sacrifice, The.
Onward, Onward, Men of Heaven.
Request of a Dying Child.
Sick Child, The.
Stars, The.
Suttee, The.
To a Shred of Linen.
To the First Slave Ship.
We Praise Thee, If One Rescued Soul.
Sigüenza y Góngora, Carlos de (1645–1700)
Eastern Evangelic Planet, Sels.
Sikelianos, Angelos [or Anghelos] (1884–1951)
Doric.
Silabhattarika (fl. before 11th century)
He who stole my virginity/ is the same man.
My husband is the same who took my
maidenhead.
Wanton, Sels.
Silbert, Layle
Enemy, The.
Silcock, Ruth
Limerick: "Hibiscus is flaming and frillier."
Limerick: "In the rain in a yard in Cessnock."
Limerick: "Land of blue skies, and sunlight,
A."
Limerick: "There's an emerald frog down the
loo."
Pioneer Village.
Silgardo, Melanie (b. 1956)
Length of an Arm, The.
Silkin, Jon (b. 1930)
Caring for Animals.
Death of a Son.
Lilies of the Valley.
Space in the Air, A.
Silko, Leslie Marmon (b. 1948)
Alaskan Mountain Poem #1.
Deer Song.
Four Mountain Wolves.
Hawk and Snake.
Horses at Valley Store.
How to Write a Poem about the Sky.
In Cold Storm Light.
Indian Song: Survival.
Invention of White People, The.
It Was a Long Time Before.
Long Time Ago.
Love Poem: "Rain smell comes with the wind."
Poem for Ben Barney.
Poem for Myself and Mei: Abortion.
Prayer to the Pacific.
Preparations.
Slim Man Canyon.

Sun Children.
Time We Climbed Snake Mountain, The.
Toe'osh; a Laguna Coyote Story.
When Sun Came to Riverwoman.
Where Mountain Lion Lay [or Laid] Down
with Deer.
Sill, Edward Rowland (1841–87)
Baker's Duzzen uv Wize Sawz, A.
Coup de Grace, The.
Crickets in the Fields, The.
Dead President, The.
Deserter, The.
Eve's Daughter.
Fool's Prayer, The, Sels.
For the Gifts of the Spirit.
Force.
Life.
Lost Love.
Opportunity.
Philosopher, The.
Prayer for Peace, A.
Space.
Tempted.
Things that Will Not Die, The.
'Tis not by guilt the onward sweep.
To a Maid Demure.
Sillè, Nicasius de (b. 1610)
God Set Us Here.
Sillitoe, Alan (b. 1928)
Picture of Loot.
Silvera, Edward S. (1906–37)
Forgotten Dreams.
Jungle Taste.
On the Death of a Child.
South Street.
Silvers, Frances
Frankie Silvers.
Silverstein, Shel (Shelley) (b. 1932)
Beware, My Child.
Clarence ("Clarence Lee from Tennessee").
Dirtiest Man in the World, The.
Friendship.
Hug o' War.
Jimmy Jet and His TV Set.
Lazy People, The.
Longmobile.
Nobody.
Oh Did You Hear?
One Inch Tall.
Rock 'n' roll Band.
Sarah Cynthia Sylvia Stout Would Not Take the
Garbage Out.
Slithergadee, The.
Tree House.
Whatif.
Silvestre, Paul Armand (1837–1901)
Autumn.
Dawn.
Secret, The.
Simcox, George Augustus (1841–1905)
Love's Votary.
Simias of Rhodes. *See* **Simmias [or Simias] of
Rhodes.**
Simic, Charles (b. 1938)
Animal Acts.
Apocrypha.
Ballad: "What's that approaching like dust like
poverty."
Bedtime Story.
Begotten of the Spleen.
Bestiary for the Fingers of My Right Hand.
Bird, The.
Breasts.
Brooms.
Butcher Shop.
Charon's Cosmology.
Classic Ballroom Dances.
Cold, The.
Concerning My Neighbors, the Hittites.
Country Fair.
Dark Farmhouses.
Drawing the Triangle.
Elementary Cosmogony.
Empire of Dreams.
Errata.

Eyes Fastened with Pins.
Fear.
Fork.
Garden of Earthly Delights, The.
Great Infirmities.
Harsh Climate.
Healer, The.
Hearing Steps.
Hunger.
Initiate, The.
Landscape with Crutches, A.
Lesson, The.
Marvels of the City, The.
My Shoes.
Nothing.
Old Couple.
Old Mountain Road.
Partial Explanation, The.
Pastoral: "I came to a field."
Poem: "Every morning I forget how it is."
Poem without a Title.
Poverty.
Prodigy.
Promises of Leniency and Forgiveness.
Psalm: "Old ones to the side."
Shelley.
Shirt.
Sleep.
Soup, The.
Spoon, The.
Stone.
Story, The.
Strictly Bucolic.
Strictly for Posterity.
System, The.
Tapestry.
Theory, A.
Unintelligible Terms.
Wall, A.
Watch Repair.
Watermelons.
We were so poor I had to take the place of the.
White Room, The.
Winter Night.
World Doesn't End, The, Sels.
Simmerman, Jim (b. 1952)
Child's Grave, Hale County, Alabama.
Simmias [or Simias] of Rhodes (fl. c.300 B.C.)
At the Tomb of Sophokles.
Decoy Partridge, A.
Simmias of Thebes (fl. 5th century B.C.)
To Prote.
Simmons, James (b. 1933)
After Eden.
Archæologist, The.
Art and Reality.
Birthday Poem, A.
Cavalier Lyric.
Claudy.
Didn't He Ramble.
Drowning Puppies.
Eden.
End of the Affair, The.
Experience.
Fear Test: Integrity of Heroes.
For Imelda.
For Thomas Moore.
From the Irish.
Goodbye, Sally.
Honeymoon, The.
Influence of Natural Objects, The.
John Donne.
Join Me in Celebrating.
Long Way After Ronsard, A.
Lullaby for Rachael.
Me and the World.
October in the Country: [1983].
One of the Boys.
Outward Bound.
Playing with Fire.
Pleasant Joys of Brotherhood, The.
Reformer to His Father, A.
Rogation Day: Portrush.
Silent Marriage, The.
Sonnet for the Class of '58.
Speech for the Clown, A.

Swift fleet the billowy clouds along the sky.
Thirty-eight.
To Sleep.
To Spring.
To the Moon.
Smith, Cicely Fox
Admiral Dugout.
Smith, Dave Jeddie (b. 1942)
Ancestor, The.
Antipastoral Memory of One Summer, An.
Bats.
Championship Fight.
Chopping Wood.
Cleaning a Fish.
Collector of the Sun, The.
Cooking Eggs.
Cuba Night.
Cumberland Station.
Desks.
Dome Poem.
Drag Race.
Ducking: After Maupassant.
Elegy in an Abandoned Boatyard.
Hawktree.
Hole, Where Once in Passion We Swam.
Lake Drummond Dream.
Leafless Trees, Chickahominy Swamp.
Looking for the Melungeon.
Mending Crab Pots.
Old Whore Speaks to a Young Poet, The.
On a Field Trip at Fredericksburg.
Pink Slip at Tool & Dye.
Pulling a Pig's Tail.
Quilt in the Bennington College Library, A.
Rain Forest.
Reading the Books Our Children Have Written.
Roundhouse Voices, The.
Sailing the Back River.
Sea Owl.
Smithfield Ham.
Snapshot of a Crab-Picker among Barrels
   Spilling Over, Apparently at the End of Her
   Shift.
Snow Owl.
Tire Hangs in the Woods, The.
Smith, Dexter (*fl.* c.1876?)
Our National Banner.
Smith, Edgar (1857–1938)
Heaven Will Protect the Working-Girl, *Sels.*
You may tempt the upper classes.
Smith, Elizabeth Oakes (1806–93)
Annihilation.
Atheism, *Sels.*
Bard, The.
Dream, The.
Faith.
Incident, An.
Inscription: "Sweet Eva! shall I send thee
   forth."
Ode to Sappho.
Poet, The.
Reason.
Sinless Child, The, *Sels.*
Strength from the Hills.
To the Hudson.
Unattained, The.
Smith, Eunice (*fl.* late 18th century)
Dear Brethren, Are Your Harps in Tune?
Dear Happy Souls.
Smith, Florence (1845–71)
Song: "How pleasant it is that always."
Smith, Francis J. (b. 1920)
First Prelude.
Smith, George (1713–76)
Country Lovers; or, Isaac and Marget Going to
   Town, on a Summer's Morning, The.
Smith, Gwen A.
Off We Go to Market.
Smith, Harry Bache (1860–1936)
Armorer's Song, The.
My Angeline.
Smith, Horace [or Horatio] (1779–1849)
Bit of Colour, A.
Evening; an Elegy.
Gouty Merchant and the Stranger, The.

On a Stupendous Leg of Granite, Discovered
   Standing by Itself in the Deserts of Egypt,
   with the Inscription Inserted Below.
Tale of Drury Lane, A.
Smith, Horace (1775–1839) *and* **James Smith**
Macbeth.
To the Wine Treasurer of the Circuit Mess.
Smith, Horatio. *See* **Smith, Horace [or Horatio].**
Smith, Iain Crichton (b. 1928)
All day the kookaburra is laughing.
Australia, *Sels.*
Culloden and After.
Deer on the High Hills — a Meditation, *Sels.*
For Angus MacLeod.
For My Mother.
John Knox.
Life, A, *Sels.*
None is the Same as Another.
Nose, The.
Old Woman.
Wild Cat, The.
Smith, J.
Unseaworthy Ship, The.
Smith, J. Moyr (*fl.* c.1887)
Four and Twenty Merulae.
She Lost Her Sheep.
Smith, James (1775–1839)
On the American Rivers.
Playhouse Musings.
Smith, James (1775–1839) *and* **Sir George Rose**
Conversation in Craven Street, Strand.
Smith, James *and* **Horace Smith.** *See* **Smith, Horace.**
Smith, Jessie Welborn
Sew a Pocket.
Smith, Joan Jobe
Heartthrobs.
Hollow Cost.
Me and My Mother's Morphine.
Smith, John (1580–1631)
In the Due Honor of the Author Master Robert
   Norton.
John Smith of His Friend Master John Taylor.
Sea Marke.
Smith, John (1662–1717)
Solitary Canto to Chloris the Disdainful, A.
Smith, John (b. 1934)
First, Goodbye.
Smith, Kay (b. 1911)
Annunciation.
Footnote to the Lord's Prayer, *Sels.*
Heaven which art in Heaven Our Father in
   Heaven.
Smith, Ken (b. 1938)
After Mr. Mayhew's Visit.
As It Happens, *Sels.*
Beginning again and again.
Being the Third Song of Urias.
Bodies.
Bogart in the Dumb Waiter.
Botanic Garden Oath, The.
Eli's Poem.
Encounter at St. Martin's.
Family Group.
Four, Being a Prayer to the Western Wind.
Fox Running, *Sels.*
In Silvertown, Chasing the Dragon.
In the Flats, flat voices.
Jack's Postcards.
Living with the Boss.
Night Whispers, The.
Old Business: The Drowned Bride.
Remembered City, The.
Snobby Roberts' Message.
Tristan Crazy, *Sels.*
Writing in Prison.
Smith, Langdon (1858–1908)
Evolution.
Smith, Lanta Wilson
This, Too, Shall [*or* Will] Pass Away.
Smith, Laurence
Christmas Tree.
Skeleton House.

Smith, Lewis Worthington (1866–1947)
News from Yorktown.
Smith, Lucy (1869–1939)
Face of Poverty.
Smith, Margoret
Cataract.
Smith, Marion Couthouy (1853–1931)
King of the Belgians.
Star, The.
Smith, Mary Brainerd (1871–1952)
Poor for Our Sakes.
Smith, Mary Carter (b. 1924)
Clubwoman.
Jungle.
Smith, Mary Lonnberg (d. 1939?)
Cartwheels.
Smith, May Riley (1842–1927)
God's Plans.
If We Knew.
My Life Is a Bowl.
My Uninvited Guest.
Scatter Seeds of Kindness.
Sometime.
Smith, Michael (1954–83)
Asleep in the City.
Black Bud.
Chimes.
City.
Fall.
From the Chinese.
I an I Alone; or Goliath.
In Prison.
Mitching.
Stopping to Take Notes.
Visit to the Village, A.
Smith, Naomi Royde-. *See* **Royde-Smith, Naomi.**
Smith, Patti (b. 1946)
Judith 2.
Smith, Pauline (1882–1959)
Katisje's Patchwork Dress.
Smith, Ray (b. 1915)
Apple, The.
Smith, Robert (d. 1555)
Exhortation of a Father to His Children, The.
Smith, Samuel Francis (1808–95)
America.
As Flows the Rapid River.
Down to the Sacred Wave.
Morning Light Is Breaking, The.
Softly Fades the Twilight Ray.
Tree-planting.
Smith, Samuel J. (1771–1835)
Arise, My Soul! With Rapture Rise!
Smith, Stevie (1902–71)
Admire Cranmer!
After-Thought, The.
Airy Christ, The.
Ambassador, The.
Angel Boley.
Anger's Freeing Power.
At School.
Away, Melancholy.
Be Off!
Bereaved Swan, The.
Bog-Face.
Celtic Fringe, The.
Celts, The.
Childe Rolandine.
Cold as no love, and wild with all negation.
Commuted Sentence, The.
Correspondence between Mr. Harrison in
   Newcastle and Mr. Sholto Peach Harrison in
   Hull.
Dear Female Heart.
Death Sentence, The.
Dedicated Dancing Bull and the Water Maid,
   The, *Sels.*
Deserter, The.
Distractions and the Human Crowd.
Drugs Made Pauline Vague.
Edmonton, thy cemetery.
Egocentric.
English, The.

Oh, Sing to God.
Praise of New Netherland, The.
When I Admire the Greatness.

Steere, Richard (1643–1721)
Earth Felicities, Heavens Allowances.
Monumental Memorial of Marine Mercy, A.
On a Sea-Storm nigh the Coast.
Poem upon the Caelestial Embassy, A.

Steese, Edward (1902–81)
Tenth Reunion.

Stein, Dona Luongo
Searching for Schüpfen.

Stein, Gertrude (1874–1946)
Before the Flowers of Friendship Faded Faded, *Sels.*
Blue Coat, A.
Cézanne.
Colored Hats.
Dog, A.
Four Saints in Three Acts, *Sels.*
Full well I know that she is there.
George Hugnet.
How do you like what you have.
How I wish I were able to say what I think.
I Am Rose.
I love my love with a v.
Ladies' Voices.
More.
New Cup and Saucer, A.
Nothing Elegant.
Petticoat, A.
Piano, A.
Pigeons on the grass alas.
Portraits and Repetition, *Sels.*
Red Roses.
Sacred.
She is that kind of a wife. She can see.
Sonatina Followed by Another, A, *Sels.*
Sound, A.
Stanzas in Meditation, *Sels.*
Susie Asado.
Tender Buttons, *Sels.*
Umbrella, An.
Valentine to Sherwood Anderson, A.
Very Valentine, A.
Water Raining.
Yet Dish.

Stein, Julia
Grand Tradition of Western Culture, The.

Stein, Kurt M.
Morning Song.
Vor a Gauguin Picture zu Singen.

Stein, Rose M. (d. 1938)
Lines to Mother.

Steinbarg, Eliezer (1880–1932)
Terrible Thought, A.

Steinberg, Jakov [or Jacob] (1887–1947)
Heart, The.

Steiner, George
Samurai Who Tried to Kill All the Roosters in Japan, A.

Steingesser, Martin
Three, The.

Steinman, D. B. (1886–1960)
Blueprint.

Steinmar (fl. late 13th cent.)
Farmhand lay all hidden, A.
Since She Gives So Little Pay.

Stembridge, Jane (b. 1936)
City.
Loving.
Mrs. Hamer.

Stencl, A. N. (b. 1897)
Whitechapel in Britain.

Stennett, Samuel (1728–95)
Promised Land, The.

Stephanou, Lydia (b. 1922)
"Case of Assault," A.

"Stephany"
I have spent my life.
It is again.
Moving deep.
What marked the river's flow.

Who collects the pain.

Stephen, James Kenneth (1859–92)
After the Golden Wedding, *Sels.*
Drinking Song.
England and America, *Sels.*
Grievance, A.
In the Backs.
Last Ride Together (from Her Point of View), The.
On a Parisian Boulevard.
On a Rhine Steamer.
Remonstrance, A.
Senex to Matt. Prior.
She's not a faultless woman; no!
Sincere Flattery of R. B.
Sincere Flattery of W. W. (Americanus).
Sonnet: "Two voices are there: one is of the deep."
Thought, A.
To R. K.
Two Epigrams, *Sels.*

Stephens, Brunton (1835–1902)
Gentle Anarchist, The.

Stephens, Harry
Night-herding Song.

Stephens, James (1880–1950)
And It Was Windy Weather.
Blue Blood.
Cage, The.
Canal Bank, The.
Christmas at Freelands.
Crest Jewel, The.
Daisies, The.
Danny Murphy.
Dark Wings.
Day and Night.
Deirdre.
Donnybrook.
Evening.
Fifteen Acres, The.
Glass of Beer, A.
Goat Paths, The.
Good and Bad.
Hate.
In the Night.
In the Poppy Field.
In Waste Places.
Lake, The.
Little Things.
Main-Deep, The.
Night, The.
Odell.
Outcast, The.
Red-haired Man's Wife, The.
Rivals, The.
Road, The.
Seumas Beg.
Shell, The.
Snare, The.
Sweet Apple.
Theme.
To the Four Courts, Please.
Twins, The.
Voice of God, The.
Watcher, The.
What the Devil Said.
What Thomas an Buile Said in a Pub.
When You Walk.
Whisperer, The.
White Fields.
Why Tomas Cam Was Grumpy.
Wind, The.
Woman Is a Branchy Tree, A.
Wood of Flowers, The.

Stephens, Meic (b. 1938)
Elegy for Llywelyn Humphries.
Elegy for Mr. Lewis (Welsh).
Hooters.
Ponies, Twynyrodyn.

Stephens, Michael (b. 1946)
Good Ship, The.
Mom's Homecooked Trees.

Stephenson, John (1808–86)
If angels sung a Savior's birth.

Stepney, George
On the University of Cambridge's Burning the Duke of Monmouth's Picture.

Sterling, Andrew B. (1874–1955)
Meet Me in St. Louis, Louis.
Under the Anheuser Bush.
What You Goin' to Do When the Rent Comes 'Round?

Sterling, George (1869–1926)
Omnia Exeunt in Mysterium.
Pumas.

Sterling, John (1806–44)
Alfred the Harper.
Louis XV.

Stern, Gerald (b. c.1925)
Adler.
At Bickford's.
Baja.
Bull-roarer, The.
Cemetery of Orange Trees in Crete, The.
Dancing, The.
Days of 1978.
Dog, The.
Expulsion, The.
Founder, The.
Fritz.
Ground Hog Lock.
I Remember Galileo.
Ice, Ice.
In Carpenter's Woods.
Kissing Stieglitz Goodbye.
Lord, Forgive a Spirit.
Morning Harvest.
Pick and Poke.
Power of Maples, The.
Romance.
Romania, Romania.
Saving My Skin from Burning.
Shirt Poem, The.
Soap.
Song: "There's nothing in this gardenous world more delightly."
Straus Park.
There Is Wind, There Are Matches.
War against the Jews, The.
Weeping and Wailing.
What It Is Like.

Sternberg, Jacob (b. 1890)
Little Birds.

Sternhold, Thomas (c.1500–1549)
I Lift My Heart to Thee.
Lord Descended from Above, The.
My Shepherd Is the Living Lord.

Sternlieb, Barry (b. 1947)
Valley Blood.

Stetler, Charles B.
Hit in the Head.
Man of Action, A.
To John Garfield, for Whom the Postman Only Rang Once.

Stevens, Cat
Wild World.

Stevens, George Alexander (1710–84)
Bartleme Fair.
Pastoral: "By the side of a green stagnate pool."
Repentance.
Simple Pastoral, A.

Stevens, George W. (1866–1926)
Organist, The.

Stevens, Wallace (1879–1955)
And for what, except for you, do I feel love?
Anecdote of the Jar.
Anecdote of the Prince of Peacocks.
Angel Surrounded by Paysans.
Anglais Mort a Florence.
Annual Gaiety.
Arrival at the Waldorf.
Ascetic Trove of Responsive Fact, The.
Asides on the Oboe.
Auroras of Autumn, The, *Sels.*
Autumn Refrain.
Bantams in Pine-Woods.
Begin, ephebe, by perceiving the idea.
Beginning, The.

Bethou me, said sparrow, to the crackled blade.
Bouquet of Belle Scavoir.
Brave Man, The.
Candle, a Saint, The.
Comedian as the Letter C, The.
Connoisseur of Chaos.
Continual Conversation with a Silent Man.
Contrary Theses (I).
Course of a Particular, The.
Credences of Summer.
Crude Foyer.
Cuisine Bourgeoise.
Curtains in the House of the Metaphysician, The.
Dance of the Macabre Mice.
Death of a Soldier, The.
Debris of Life and Mind.
Depression before Spring.
Disillusionment of Ten o'Clock.
Domination of Black.
Dry Loaf.
Dwarf, The.
Earthy Anecdote.
Emperor of Ice-Cream, The.
Esthétique du Mal, Sels.
Evening without Angels.
Everything Juts Up in Europe.
Extract from Addresses to the Academy of Fine Ideas, An.
Farewell to an idea . . . A cabin stands.
Farewell to an idea . . . The mother's face.
Farewell to Florida.
Final Soliloquy of the Interior Paramour.
First idea was not our own, The. Adam.
Flyer's Fall.
Gallant Château.
Girl in a Nightgown.
Glass of Water, The.
God is Good. It Is a Beautiful Night.
Good Man Has No Shape, The.
Gray Room.
Gray Stones and Gray Pigeons.
Great Statue of the General Du Puy, The.
Greenest Continent, The, Sels.
Gubbinal.
He was at Naples writing letters home.
Hibiscus on the Sleeping Shores.
High poetry and low.
High-toned Old Christian Woman, A.
Holiday in Reality.
Homunculus et la Belle Étoile.
House Was Quiet and the World Was Calm, The.
How red the rose that is the soldier's wound.
I cannot bring a world quite round.
I feel an apparition.
Idea of Order at Key West, The.
Idiom of the Hero.
In the Carolinas.
Indigo Glass in the Grass, The.
Irish Cliffs of Moher, The.
Is there an imagination that sits enthroned.
It feels good as it is without the giant.
It is a theatre floating through the clouds.
John Smith and His Son, John Smith.
Large Red Man Reading.
Le Monocle de Mon Oncle.
Less and Less Human, O Savage Spirit.
Life is a bitter aspic. We are not.
Life Is Motion.
Lunar Paraphrase.
Major abstraction is the idea of man, The.
Man bent over his guitar, The.
Man on the Dump, The.
Man with the Blue Guitar, The, Sels.
Martial Cadenza.
Men Made out of Words.
Metamorphosis.
Metaphor as Degeneration.
Metaphors of a Magnifico.
Mrs. Alfred Uruguay.
Montrachet — le — Jardin, Sels.
Motive for Metaphor, The.
Mountains Covered With Cats, Sels.
New England Verses, Sels.
Night-Wind of August, The.

No Possum, No Sop, No Taters.
Not Ideas about the Thing but the Thing Itself.
Notes toward a Supreme Fiction, Sels.
Nuances of a Theme by Williams.
Of Heaven Considered as a Tomb.
Of Mere Being.
Of Modern Poetry.
Of the Manner of Addressing Clouds.
Old Lutheran Bells at Home, The.
On an Old Horn.
On the Adequacy of Landscape.
On the Road Home.
Ordinary Women, The.
Our Stars Come from Ireland.
Owl in the Sarcophagus, The.
Paltry Nude Starts on a Spring Voyage, The.
Parochial Theme.
Peter Quince at the Clavier.
Plain Sense of Things, The.
Planet on the Table, The.
Pleasures of Merely Circulating, The.
Plot against the Giant, The.
Ploughing on Sunday.
Poem That Took the Place of a Mountain, The.
Poems of Our Climate, The.
Poetry Is a Destructive Force.
Postcard from the Volcano, A.
Prejudice against the Past, The.
President Ordains the Bee to Be, The.
Primitive like an Orb, A.
Puella Parvula.
Quiet Normal Life, A.
Rabbit as King of the Ghosts, A.
Reader, The.
Reality Is an Activity of the Most August Imagination.
River of Rivers in Connecticut, The.
Room on a Garden, A.
Sad Strains of a Gay Waltz.
Sea Surface Full of Clouds.
Sense of the Sleight-of-Hand Man, The.
Sick Man, The.
Snow Man, The.
So-and-So Reclining on Her Couch.
Soldier, There Is a War between the Mind.
Song of Fixed Accord.
Souls of Women at Night, The.
Study of Two Pears.
Sun, in clownish yellow, but not a clown, The.
Sunday Morning.
Table Talk.
Tattoo.
Tea at the Palaz of Hoon.
These locusts by day, these crickets by night.
Thinking of a Relation between the Images of Metaphors.
Thirteen Ways of Looking at a Blackbird.
This is where the serpent lives, the bodiless.
This Solitude of Cataracts.
To an Old Philosopher in Rome.
To the One of Fictive Music.
Tom-tom, c'est moi. The blue guitar.
Too Commodious.
Tune beyond us as we are, A.
Two Figures in Dense Violet Light.
Two Things of Opposite Natures Seem to Depend.
Ultimate Poem Is Abstract, The.
Unhappy people in a happy world, An.
Vacancy in the Park.
Valley Candle.
When was it that the particles became.
Whistle Aloud, Too Weedy Wren.
Woman in Sunshine, The.
Woman That Had More Babies than That, The.
World as Meditation, The.
World without Peculiarity, The.
Worms at Heaven's Gate, The.

Stevenson, Anne (b. 1933)
By the Boat House, Oxford.
Correspondences, Sels.
Daughter's Difficulties as a Wife, A: Mrs. Reuben Chandler to Her Mother in New Orleans.
Demolition, The.
Epitaph for a Good Mouser.

Fiction-Makers, The.
From an Asylum; Kathy Chattle to Her Mother, Ruth Arbeiter.
Gales.
Giving Rabbit to My Cat Bonnie.
Himalayan Balsam.
Larousse Gastronomique.
Love Letter, A: Ruth Arbeiter to Major Paul Maxwell.
Making Poetry.
Marriage, The.
Price, The.
Re-reading Jane.
Respectable House.
Sous-Entendu.
Suburb, The.
Suicide.
Television.
Utah.
Victory, The.

Stevenson, Burton Egbert (1872–1962)
Henry Hudson's Quest.
Peace Message, The.
Stevenson, Candace Thurber (1883?–1968)
Public Library.
Stevenson, James (b. 1929)
Gallant Fighting "Joe," The.
Stevenson, Matthew (fl. 1654–85)
Elegy upon Old Freeman, An, Sels.
Here in this homely cabinet.
Stevenson, Robert Louis (1850–94)
Alcaics; to H. F. B.
Armies in the Fire.
As with heaped bees at hiving time.
At the Seaside.
Auntie's Skirts.
Autumn Fires.
Bed in Summer.
Block City.
Blows the Wind Today.
Bright is the ring of words.
Brilliant kernel of the night, The.
Browning.
Canoe Speaks, The, Sels.
Celestial Surgeon, The.
Child's Garden of Verses, A, Sels.
Child's Thought, A.
Christmas at Sea.
Christmas Prayer, A.
Christmas Sermon, A, Sels.
Cow, The.
Ditty: "Cock shall crow, The."
Dumb Soldier, The.
Escape at Bedtime.
Evensong.
Fair Isle at Sea — thy lovely name.
Farewell to the Farm.
Far-Farers, The.
Flowers, The.
Foreign Children.
Foreign Lands.
Fragment: "Thou strainest through the mountain fern."
From a Railway Carriage.
Good and Bad Children.
Good Boy, A.
Good Play, A.
Happy Thought.
Henry James.
Home No More Home to Me.
House Beautiful, The.
I Am a Hunchback.
I saw red evening through the rain.
If This Were Faith.
Ille Terrarum.
In autumn when the woods are red.
In the Highlands.
In the States.
It's an overcome sooth for age an' youth.
Lamplighter, The.
Land of Counterpane, The.
Land of Nod, The.
Land of Story-Books, The.
Last night we had a thunderstorm in style.
Light-Keeper, The, Sels.
Limerick: "There was an old man of the Cape."

Under the Baby Blanket.
Waking from a Nap on the Beach.
Watch, The.
Water Picture.
Willets, The.
Women.
Swett, Herbert B.
Gathering, The.
Swett, Susan Hartley (d. 1967)
July.
Swift, Joan (b. 1926)
Line-up, The.
Oxygen.
Swift, Jonathan (1667–1745)
A E I O U.
All human race would fain be wits.
As I strole the city, oft I.
Baucis and Philemon; Imitated from the Eighth
  Book of Ovid.
Beautiful Young Nymph Going to Bed, A.
Behold the fatal day arrive!
Bubble, The.
Cassinus and Peter.
Character of Sir Robert Walpole, The.
Clever Tom Clinch Going to Be Hanged.
Daphne.
Day of Judgement, The.
Day will come, when't shall be said, The.
Description of a City Shower, A.
Description of the Morning, A.
Dick, a Maggot.
Directions for Making a Birth-Day Song, *Sels.*
Doctors tender of their fame, The.
Epigram: "As Thomas was cudgell'd [*or*
  cudgel'd] one day by his wife."
Epigram on Fasting.
Epigram on Scolding.
Excellent New Song, Being the Intended
  Speech of a Famous Orator against Peace,
  An.
Excellent New Song on a Seditious Pamphlet,
  An.
Excellent New Song upon His Grace Our Good
  Lord Archbishop of Dublin, An.
Fable of Midas, The.
Fable of the Widow and Her Cat, A.
Fool, to put up four crosses at your door.
Gentle Echo on Woman, A.
Hail, happy Pope, whose generous mind.
Here shift the scene, to represent.
Herrings.
Hobbes clearly proves that every creature.
Holyhead, Sept. 25th, 1727.
I Walk Before no Man (Composed While
  Asleep).
In Sickness Written Soon after the Author's
  Coming to Live in Ireland, upon the Queen's
  Death, October 1714.
Inscription for the Sign of *The Jolly Barber,*
  with a Razor in One Hand, and a Pot of
  Beer in the Other, *Sels.*
Ireland.
Lady's Dressing Room, The.
Legion Club, The, *Sels.*
Libel on the Reverend Dr. Delany, A, *Sels.*
Life and Character of Dean Swift, The, *Sels.*
Life and Genuine Character of Dean Swift,
  The, *Sels.*
Mary the Cook-Maid's Letter to Dr. Sheridan.
Mollis Abuti.
My female friends, whose tender hearts.
New Song of Wood's Halfpence, A.
No doubt he well invented, nobly felt.
Now Curll his shop from rubbish drains.
On a Curate's Complaint of Hard Duty.
On Bankers.
On Dreams.
On His Own Deafness.
On Irish Memebers of Parliament.
On Poetry; a Rhapsody, *Sels.*
On Reading Dr Young's Satires, Called *The
  Universal Passion,* by Which He Means
  Pride.
On the Astrologer and Almanac Maker, John
  Partridge.
On the Collar of Mrs. Dingley's Lap-Dog.

On the Irish Club.
On the Vowels — a Riddle.
Onyons.
Oysters.
Parson's Case, The, *Sels.*
Perhaps I may allow, the Dean.
Phyllis; or, The Progress of Love.
Place of the Damn'd [*or* Damned], The.
Power of Time, The.
Progress of Poetry, The.
Prometheus.
Roam not from pole to pole, but enter here.
Run Upon the Bankers, The, *Sels.*
Satire on an Inconstant Lover, A.
Satirical Elegy on the Death of a Late Famous
  General, A.
Stella at Wood-Park.
Stella's Birth-day, 1718/19.
Stella's Birthday, 1721 ("All travelers at first
  incline").
Stella's Birthday, 1725.
Stella's Birthday; March 13, 1726/27.
Suppose me dead; and then suppose.
Thy curate's place, thy fruitful wife.
Time is not remote when I, The.
To Form a Just and Finish'd Piece.
To Stella.
To the Earl of Oxford, Late Lord Treasurer.
To Their Excellencies the Lords Justices of
  Ireland, the Humble Petition of Frances
  Harris, Who Must Starve, and Die a Maid if
  It Miscarries.
True and Faithful Inventory of the Goods
  Belonging to Dr. Swift, Vicar of Laracor, A;
  upon Lending His House to the Bishop of
  Meath, till His Palace Was Rebuilt.
Twelve Articles.
Verses for Fruitwomen, *Sels.*
Verses Occasioned by the Sudden Drying Up of
  St. Patrick's Well, *Sels.*
Verses on the Death of Doctor Swift
  [D.S.P.D., Occasioned by Reading a Maxim
  in Rochefoucauld], *Sels.*
Verses Said to Be Written on the Union.
Verses Written upon Windows.
Virtue conceal'd within our breast.
Virtues of Sid Hamet, the Magician's Rod,
  The.
Wise Rochefoucault a maxim writ.
Wretched Ierne! with what grief I see.

Swinburne, Algernon Charles (1837–1909)
After Death.
Aholibah.
Atalanta in Calydon, *Sels.*
August.
Ave atque Vale.
Baby's feet, like sea-shells pink, A.
Ballad of François Villon, A.
Before Parting.
Before Sunset.
Before the Beginning of Years.
Before the Mirror, *Sels.*
Ben Jonson.
By the North Sea, *Sels.*
Child and Poet.
Child's Laughter, A.
Chorus: "Who hath given man speech? or what
  hath set therein."
Christmas Antiphones, *Sels.*
Christopher Marlowe.
Cleopatra.
Come into the orchard, Anne.
Dialogue, A.
Dolores, *Sels.*
Duriesdyke.
Erotion.
Étude Réaliste, *Sels.*
Evening by the Sea.
Evening on the Broads.
Faustine.
Félise.
Forsaken Garden, A.
From too much love of living.
Garden of Cymodoce, The, *Sels.*
Garden of Proserpine, The, *Sels.*
Glad, but not flush'd with gladness.

Hendecasyllabics.
Heptalogia, The, *Sels.*
Hermaphroditus.
Hertha.
Hesperia.
Higher Pantheism in a Nutshell, The.
Hope and Fear.
Hounds of Spring, The.
Hymn to Proserpine.
I Will Go Back to the Great Sweet Mother.
Ilicet.
In Memory of Walter Savage Landor.
In the Orchard.
Interpreters, The.
Itylus.
John Jones.
John Webster.
King Mark, Tristram, and Palamede.
Lake of Gaube, The.
Land that is lonelier than ruin, A.
Leave-taking, A.
Leper, The.
Limerick: "There was a young girl of
  Aberystwyth."
Limerick: "There was a young lady of Norway/
  Who hung by her toes in a doorway."
Limerick: "There was a young man of Cape
  Horn."
Love and Sleep.
Love at Sea.
Maiden, and mistress of the months and stars.
Match, A.
Nephelidia.
O lips full of lust and of laughter.
On Arthur Hugh Clough.
On the Russian Persecution of the Jews.
Oscar Wilde.
Poeta Loquitur.
Proserpine.
Rondel: "Kissing her hair, I sat against her
  feet."
Sapphics.
Sark.
Satia Te Sanguine.
Shakespeare.
Song: "Love laid his sleepless head."
Sonnet for a Picture.
Sonnets of English Dramatic Poets, *Sels.*
Stage Love.
Suffolk.
Sundew, The.
Super Flumina Babylonis.
Swan Song.
Swimming.
Thank your engines.
Thou whose birth on earth.
To a Cat.
Tristram of Lyonesse, *Sels.*
Triumph of Time, The, *Sels.*
Unhappy Revenge, The, *Sels.*
Watchman, What of the Night?
What is that death they boast but a frail
  pageant.
Where Dunwich Used to Be.
White Butterflies.
Swirszczynska, Anna (1909–84)
Good Lord Saved Her, The.
Greatest Love, The.
Happy as a Dog's Tail.
He Is Gone.
He Was Lucky.
I Have Ten Legs.
Parting.
Terminally Ill.
They Lay Dying Side by Side.
Very Sad Conversation at Night, A.
Visit, A.
We Are Going to Shoot at the Heart.
Sykes, Arthur A.
Splendid Bankrupt, The.
Sykes, Velma West (b. 1892)
Diptych.
Sylvester, Joshua (1561–1618)
Aestas.
Autumnus.
Beware Fair Maide.

October 21st, 9 P.M. (Autumn She Don't Waste no Time!).
Poquito Allá.

Taft, Margo (b. 1950)
I have been my arm.

Tagami, Jeff (b. 1954)
Mussel Rock/Lowtide — Santa Cruz, California 1959.
Song of Pajaro.
Tobera.

Tagami Kikusha-Ni (1752–1826)
Wind From Mt. Fuji, The.

Taggard, Genevieve (1894–1948)
American Farm, 1934.
Dilemma of the Elm.
Doomsday Morning.
Enamel Girl, The.
Geraniums, The.
In the Tail of the Scorpion.
Little Girl with Bands on Her Teeth, The.
Millions of Strawberries.
Poem to Explain Everything about a Certain Day in Vermont, A.
Solar Myth.
Song for Unbound Hair.
Squirrel near Library.
Train: Abstraction.
Try Topic.
With Child.

Taggart, John
Coming Forth by Day.

Tagliabue, John (b. 1923)
Bare Arms of Trees, The.
I Sought All Over the World.
Maine Vastly Covered with Much Snow.
Unseen Deer, An.

Tagore, Rabindranath (1861–1941)
Autumn.
Day after Day.
Deliverance is not for me in renunciation.
Echo always mocks the sound, The.
Epigrams, *Sels*.
Gardener, The, *Sels*.
Gitanjali, *Sels*.
Have you not heard his silent steps?
He it is, the innermost one, who awakens my being with his deep hidden touches.
Here is thy footstool and there rest thy feet.
Home, The.
I ask for a moment's indulgence to sit by Thy side.
I Have Got My Leave.
I know not from what distant time thou art ever coming nearer to meet me.
If It Is Not My Portion.
In the Dusky Path of a Dream.
Journey Nears the Road-End, The.
Leave this chanting and singing and telling of beads.
Light, My Light, the World-Filling Light.
My Song.
On the Slope of the Desolate River.
Paper Boats.
Thou Art the Sky.
Unending Love.
Vocation.
Yellow Bird Sings, The.

Tahureau, Jacques (1527–55)
Moonlight.
Shadows of His Lady.

Taigi (Tan Taigi) (1709–71)
Angry, is he, a wasp drinking water.
At daybreak when plovers call.
Autumn night: I question.
Beautiful sunlight has come.
Cold moon — the sound of the bridge.
Eyes open, I listen to spring.
I feel someone dying of an illness.
I lie down, I get up.
I peer into quietness.
I swept and ended up not sweeping.
In the waves rolling in.
Kyuko and I Stayed at Rittei's.
Long night: I wake up, A.
Many mosquitoes bloated with blood.

Near a fence, young, small grasses.
Other end of this long bridge, The.
Rat has dropped into the water jar, A.
Servant, taking leave, A.
Shower: on a raft the pole, A.
Sound of casting a net downstream.
Sound of the rain, The.
Spring night: I frighten a woman, A.
Stream's clear: five inches, The.
Tree-searing wind: wrinkles of age.
Twenty-nine Hokku, *Sels*.
Village child with spring grass, A.
Warbler: leaves hiding it.
Water of a shallow river, The.
Way it walks, the snail, The.
With a faint scent of river.

Tai Piao-yüan (1244–1310)
Following His Rhymes and Answering the Poems of My Friend Next Door, *Sels*.

Tai Shu-lun (732–789)
Accidental Meeting with an Old Friend While Traveling at Night, An.
Living in the Mountains.
Wang Chao-chün.

Tait, William J. (b. 1918)
Gallow Hill.

Takada Toshiko (b. 1916)
Seacoast at Mera, The.

Takahashi Mutsuo (b. 1934)
Ode in 1,000 Lines, *Sels*.

Takahashi Shinkichi (b. 1901)
Birth.
Fish.
Snail ("The snail crawls over blackness").
Sparrow in Winter.

Takai Kito. *See* Kito.

Takako Uchino Lento (b. 1941)
Glass.

Takakuwa Ranko. *See* Ranko.

Takamura Kotaro (1883–1956)
Brief History of Imbecility, A, *Sels*.
Cooperative Council.
Day of Pearl Harbor, The.
Sculpting in the Imperial Presence.

Takenaka Iku (b. 1904)
Stars at Night.

Takiguchi Masako (b. 1918)
Blue Horse.
Slaughterhouse.

Talal, Marilynn
Being Children.
For Our Dead.

Talbot, Charles Remington. *See* "Brownjohn, John."

Talbot, Kirkham
Limerick: "King Henry the Eighth was a Tudor."

Talbot, Norman (b. 1936)
Ballad of Old Women & of How They Are Constrained To Simulate Youth In Order To Avoid Shocking the Young.

Talcott, William
Boogie Board.

Talfourd, Sir Thomas N.
Friend, A.

Taliesin (fl. c.550)
Battle of Argoed Llwyfain, The.
Death Song for Owain ab Urien.
Song to the Wind, A.

Tall, Grace Cornell
Needle, The.

Tallet, José Zacarías (b. 1983)
Rumba.

Tallis
Limerick: "Conclusion I reach at the Tate, The."

TallMountain, Mary
Matmiya.
Peeling Pippins.
There Is No Word for Goodbye.
Women in Old Parkas, The.

Talpalar, Morris
True Happiness.

Tamekane (Kyōgoku Tamekane) (1254–1332)
Twenty-three Tanka, *Sels*.

Tam'si, Tchicaya U (b. 1931)
Bad Blood.
Brush Fire.
Communion II.
Debout, *Sels*.
Fragile, *Sels*.
Headline to Summarize a Passion.
Here is the stream again under the rainbow.
I am no longer master of my tears.
Mat to Weave, A.
Promenade, The.
Scorner, The.
Sea Nocturne.
Viaticum.

Tanfield, Lady Elizabeth (fl. 1565–1628)
Here shadow[e] lie.

T'ang Hsien-tsu (1550–1616)
Twenty-two Quatrains on Receiving the Obituary Notice for my Son Shih-Chü, *Sels*.

Tangikuku, Harata. *See* Harata Tangikuku.

Tangikuku, Hine
Song of Sickness, A.

T'ang Wan (fl. 12th century)
To the Tune "The Phoenix Hairpin."

T'ang Yen-ch'ien (fl. c. 880)
Walk in the Country, A.

T'ang Yin (1470–1523)
Among red leaves and green mountains, white clouds fly.
Inscribed on a Painting.
Inscribed on a Painting of a Cock.
Miscellaneous Feelings, *Sels*.
Mountain pavilion is silent — few people visit me here, The.
Nature has endowed her with complete charm.
On a Painting of a Woman Shown Half-Length, *Sels*.
Pines and cedars, a hundred feet of green, clinging to the earth.
Poems Inscribed on Paintings, *Sels*.
Rainstorm Has Dragged on for Ten Days Now, A, *Sels*.
Spring — River — Flower — Moon — Night, *Sels*.
Who used his masterful brush to paint this romantic beauty?
Wind sighs in the reeds — autumn on the rustic shore, The.

Taniguchi Buson. *See* Buson.

Tanikawa Shuntaro (b. 1931)
I see a woman/ I see my wife.
I see a woman/ it's a woman who was my lover.
On Destiny.
Picnic to the Earth.
Spring.
Two Portraits, *Sels*.

Tannahill, Robert (1774–1810)
Midges Dance aboon the Burn, The.
O! Are Ye Sleepin [or Sleeping], Maggie?

Tan Taigi. *See* Taigi.

Tan Ying (b. 1943)
Drinking the Wind.

T'an Yuan-ch'un (1588–1631)
Heard on a Boat.

T'ao Ch'ien [or T'ao Yuan-ming] (365–427)
Autumn chrysanthemums have beautiful color.
Bank to bank, the stream is wide.
Begging for Food.
Bright blossoms seldom last long.
Bright sun lights out over the western bank.
By and by, the seasons come and go.
Drinking Wine, *Sels*.
Fall chrysanthemums have beautiful colors.
Green pine grows in eastern garden, A.
I built my hut in a place where people live.
I plant beans at the foot of the southern hill.
I Return to the Place I Was Born.
In Praise of Poor Scholars.
In the morning and at night.
Long I Have Loved to Stroll.
Long time ago, A.

Lord, art thou at the table head above.
Meditation Eight.
Methinks I spy Almighty holding in.
Mine Heart's a Park or Chase of Sins.
My Blessed Lord, how doth thy Beautious
   Spouse.
My gracious Lord, I would thee glory doe.
My Lord, my life, can envy ever bee.
My shattred phancy stole away from mee.
My sin! my sin, my God, these cursed dregs.
Oh! Golden Rose! Oh. Glittering Lilly White.
Oh! Good, good, good, my Lord. What more
   love yet.
Oh leaden heeld. Lord, give, forgive I pray.
Oh! that I allwayes breath'd in such an aire.
Oh that I was the Bird of Paradise!
Oh! what a thing is man? Lord, who am I?
Orator from Rhetorick gardens picks, The.
Our Insufficiency to Praise God Suitably for
   His Mercy.
Outward Man Accused, The.
Preface, The.
Preface: "Infinity, when all things it beheld."
Preparatory Meditations Before My Approach to
   the Lord's Supper, Sels.
Prologue: "Lord, can a crumb of dust the earth
   outweigh."
Should I with Silver Tooles Delve through the
   Hill.
Soul's Groan to Christ for Succo[u]r, The.
State, a state, oh! dungeon state indeed, A.
Still I complain; I am complaining still.
Stupendious love! all saints astonishment.
Thou Art the Tree of Life.
Thy grace, dear Lord's my golden wrack I
   find.
Thy human frame, my glorious Lord, I spy.
Unclean, unclean: my Lord, undone, all vile.
Upon a Spider Catching a Fly.
Upon a Wasp Chilled [or Child] with Cold.
Upon Wedlock and Death of Children.
View, all ye eyes above, this sight which
   flings.
What Glory's this, my Lord? Should one small
   Point.
What love is this of thine, that cannot be.
What shall a Mote up to a Monarch rise?
What shall I say, my Deare Deare Lord?
What shall I say, my Lord? With what begin?
When thy bright beams, my Lord, so strike
   mine eye.
Why should my bells, which chime thy praise,
   when thou.
Would God I in that Golden City were.
Ye angells bright, pluck from your wings a
   quill.

Taylor, Eleanor Ross (b. 1920)
Harvest, 1925.
In the Churchyard.
Welcome Eumenides.

Taylor, Elizabeth (fl. c. 1680)
Ode: "Ah poor Olinda never boast."
Song: "Strephon has fashion, wit and youth."
Song: "Ye Virgin Pow'rs defend my heart."
To Mertill Who Desired Her to Speak to
   Clorinda of His Love.

Taylor, Ellen (fl. c. 1792)
Written by the Barrow Side, Where She Was
   Sent to Wash Linen.

Taylor, Eric Clough
Catmint.

Taylor, Geoffrey (1900–1957)
Admonition to the Muse.
Cruel, Clever Cat.
English Liberal.
Epitaph: "Nor practising virtue nor committing
   crime."
Gentlemen.

Taylor, George Lansing (1835–1903)
Dare to Do Right.

Taylor, Hannah
Virtue alone can never die, but lives to.

Taylor, Sir Henry (1800–1886)
Airing Linen.
Artichoke.

As on a Darkling Plain.
At the Swings.
Breakings.
Country Curate, The.
Depressed by the Death of the Horse That He
   Bought from Robert Bly.
Elena's Song.
Flying Change, The.
Getting at the Root of the Matter.
In Orbit.
J. V. Cunningham Gets Hung Up on a Dirty,
   of All Things, Joke.
Miss Creighton.
Not Working.
Philip van Artevelde, Sels.
Projectile Point, Circa 2500 B.C.
Riding a One-eyed Horse.
Riding Lesson.
Robert Bly Says Something Too.
Somewhere along the Way.
Sonnet in the Mail Coach.
Speech.
Taking to the Woods.
Two Husbands.
View from a Cab, The.
Way It Sometimes Is, The.

Taylor, James Bayard (1825–78)
To G. H. B.

Taylor, Jane (1783–1824)
Disappointment, The.
Field Daisy, The.
Gleaner, The.
Greedy Richard.
I Like Little Pussy.
Pigs, The.
Recreation.
Star, The.
Tell me, mamma, if I must die.
Two Little Kittens.
Violet, The.

Taylor, Jeremy (1613–67)
My Soul Doth Pant towards Thee.

Taylor, John (1580–1653)
About my circle, I a Posie have.
Epigram, A Supposed Construction.
Epigram: "Fair Beatrice tucks her coat up
   somewhat high."
Epigram: "Look how yon lecher's legs are worn
   away."
Epigram: "Lusty wench as nimble as an eel,
   A."
Epigram: "There chanced to meet together in an
   inn."
Epitaph in the Bermuda Tongue, Which Must
   Be Pronounced With the Accent of the
   Grunting of a Hog.
Epitaph in the Utopian Tongue.
Sir Gregory Nonsense's News from No Place,
   Sels.
I come from Bohem, yet no news I bring.
It was in June the eight and thirtieth day.
Libra, September.
O for a rope of Onions from Saint Omers.
Odcomb's Complaint, Sels.
Prague is a famous, ancient, kingly seat.
Sonnet: "Sweet semi-circled Cynthia played at
   maw."
Taylor's Arithmetic from One to Twelve, Sels.
Taylor's Travels from London to Prague, Sels.
10 Commandments, are the Law Divine.
Trumpet of Liberty, The.
Virgo, August.

Taylor, Joseph Russell (1868–1933)
Breath on the Oat.

Taylor, Richard
Limerick: "Sexy young student once toyed, A."

Taylor, Rockie D. See Ologboni, Tejumola.

Taylor, Rod (b. 1947)
Dakota: October, 1822, Hunkpapa Warrior.

Taylor, Sarah Wingate (b. 1906)
With Metaphor.

Taylor, Tom (1817–80)
Abraham Lincoln.

Taylor, William (1765–1836)
Vision, The.

Tchaikovsky, Peter Ilich (1840–93)
Legend, A.

**Tchernichowsky [or Tchernichovsky], Saul [or
Shaul] (1875–1943)**
Before the Statue of Apollo.
Bells, The.
Dance of Saul with the Prophets, The.
Death of Tammuz, The.
Grave in Ukraine, A.
I Believe.
I have been to my God like the iris and the
   anemone.
Images of a faded world possessed me, I
   cannot flee!
Levivot.
Or the image-kingdom's idol of the past
   generation.
They Say There Is a Country.
This Be Our Revenge.
To Ashtaroth and Bel.
To the Sun, Sels.

Tchicaya U Tam'si. See U'Tamsi, Felix
   TchiKaya.

Te Aomuhurangi Te Maaka (b. 1927)
Go Down, O Sun, Out from the Motu River.
Haka: Hinemotu.

Te Apakura, Irihapeti Rangi
Reply to a Marriage Proposal.

Te Heuheu Tukino
Lament for Te Heuheu Herea.

Te-whaka-io-roa
Give Me My Infant Now.

Te Whetu (fl. c.1880)
Sound of My Sneezing Nose, The.

Teasdale, Sara (1884–1933)
Answer, The.
Appraisal.
April.
August Night.
Autumn on the Beaches.
Barter.
Crystal Gazer, The.
Epitaph: "Serene descent, as a red leaf's
   descending."
Falling Star, The.
February Twilight.
Full Moon; Santa Barbara.
Grace before Sleep.
I Am Not Yours.
I Have Loved Hours at Sea.
I Shall Not Care.
Immortal.
Inn of Earth, The.
Long Hill, The.
Mastery.
May Day.
Moonlight.
Morning Song.
Night.
Night Song at Amalfi.
On the South Downs.
Philosopher, The.
Prayer: "Until I lose my soul and lie."
September Midnight.
Solitary, The.
Song: "Let it be forgotten, as a flower is
   forgotten."
Song Making.
Spring in War-Time.
Spring Night.
Stars.
There Will Come Soft Rains.
Understanding.
Water-Lilies.
What Do I Care.
Wisdom.
Wood Song.

Tecumseh (1768–1813)
When you arise in the morning.

Teft, Elizabeth (fl. 1741–1747)
On Learning.
On Snuff-Taking.
On Viewing Herself in a Glass.
To a Gentleman Who Disordered a Lady's

Handerchief, and Immediately Cut His Thumb.

Tegnér, Esaias (1782–1846)
Frithiof's Farewell.
Frithiof's Homestead.
Frithiof's Saga, *Sels.*

Teika (Fujiwara no Teika) (1162–1241)
About people, no, I don't know how they feel.
Above a clear, penetrating wind.
Above the wind the starlight is clear.
Against the cherries on the hazy hilltop.
As a warbler flits from one plum twig to another.
As far away as distant China.
As I look around, I see a weir of waves.
As I look out, there are neither blossoms nor crimson leaves.
As I look, the moon has moved West.
As I pick young herbs for you.
As I searched for cherry blossoms.
As it begins to dawn, I almost take for daybreak.
As soon as it blows, autumn grass and trees wither.
As winds blow over white dewdrops.
At the rising, climbing, southern limit there are clouds.
Autumn gone, the past distant in the great sky.
Autumn has come; crimson leaves have fallen.
Autumn wind is and is not as of old, The.
Autumn's come — The year's half gone.
Away from the direction of falling blossoms.
Because limits are set.
Because my home village is close to Mount Yoshino.
Bitter — that I should not have decayed.
Building a Sano boat-bridge.
Bush clovers must have shed their flowers.
Carried overhead and wished upon.
Cherries bloom on distant hills.
Cherry blossoms must have opened.
Cicada voices rising continually, far away.
Cloud, a reminder of my lover, The.
Coming to an end and leaving the moon as a keepsake.
Compendium of Good Tanka, A, *Sels.*
Crimson leaves flow in Tatsuta River.
Dew at the tip of a leaf.
Dew on my sleeves, The.
Dew, scatter if you will.
Didn't we make a vow.
Do not let it be known.
Dozing, thoughts interminable in paths of dream.
Drawn by the memory of your face I turn to look.
Dream broken by the sound of a mallet.
Eighty-four Tanka, *Sels.*
Even her heart again a stranger's.
Even in a remote place eightfold heaps.
Evening voices of cicadas, The.
Everyone else has changed to a flowery robe.
Fading, desolate: at the autumn coloring.
Faintly, in the dawn moonlight.
Floating bridge of dreams this spring night, The.
Flower's color has passed, The.
For the one I await the path must have ended.
From now on may it go on falling.
From tomorrow, who will visit.
Frost has touched the bamboo grass.
Great sky hazy with scents of plum blossoms, The.
Had I expected this?
He does not come, but I wait.
Here again, another useless sign of the floating world.
Hint at the hilltop of the moon, A.
How can I forget? — spring hazes lost.
How many autumns have I passed.
I lifted her hair strand by strand.
I remember, I burn brushwood.
I suffer enough, now it would all be the same.
I will return and look on Matsushima once again.
Ice on my laid-out sleeve still frozen, The.

If by chance someone asks.
If I can't twist my thread with yours.
If I must, I'll have to pick them haphazardly.
If only I had my phantom to send to you.
If you do not come, must I sleep alone.
In a winter-seared forest.
In Akishino is it raining on the villages.
In May rain, the smoke from the seaweed.
In May rains the water, the waves.
In my birthplace, the garden and the hedges.
In the autumn paddies, the roof mats for the makeshift.
In the evening my thoughts go toward the end of the clouds.
In the past too, hearts have separated from hearts.
In Yatano Field the reeds have turned color.
Is it because autumn dew has collected.
Its dark green — what if it should be unable to resist.
It's the start of spring, they say.
Izumi River: like the bubbles on a pole.
Just because you said, "I'll come right away."
Lamplight in the window at slow dawn, A.
Light of the moon that crosses the Plain of Heaven, The.
Like a mountain stream whose rapids are blocked.
Like some ailing leaf.
Like the foam on the ever-flowing Thinking River.
Like the white dewdrop that forms at the leaf-tip.
Like tinkling gems, neither dewdrops nor tears stay.
Like trees buried in the shallows of Natori River.
Lodging in a hut where the Naniwa men burn reeds.
Loneliness has no special color.
Loneliness is more intense with frost than with snow.
Long as the foot-wearying mountain.
Look, this must be love that fills the sky!
Looking at it, just thinking about it.
Looking at the moon, I feel sad.
Lovely rock buried under the seaweed, A.
Lush emerald the summer color becomes.
Missives, fleeting, my lover's only trace.
Mists above the crimson leaves.
More melancholy than the bright moon.
My love affair is like the clumps of bush clover.
My thought grows like rock azaleas.
My thoughts, useless dreams in midair.
Neglectful, I have not died of love.
Negligently the day opens before I have time to sleep.
No shade for halting the horse to shake my sleeves.
Not like an ordinary cloud.
Not many days have passed.
Now, today, I'll lose myself.
On a spring day when boundless light.
On his way home, he may be watching this.
On Mount Moru where both white dew.
On my way home at dusk.
On the sea god's plain the waves and the sky merge.
On this trip I couldn't come with offerings.
One who's unkind is like you, The.
Only one or two nights since winter came.
Orange flowers scatter in a village.
Parting from you, I go to Inaba.
People of the hundred-acre palace, The.
Pity, how the dew must spill from grass leaves.
Plain of Heaven, think of it, The.
Plum blossoms are hard to make out.
Princess Tatsuta's headband loosened.
Rampant rank reed, to repress it I try.
Regarding my infants as friends from old days.
Relished as cooler than usual tonight.
Retaining the colors of snow and moon.
Rippling, a wind from the Bay of Grebes.
Rising sun casts the same light, The.
Scent of the plum blossoms, The.

Since our parting when the moon at dawn looked unfriendly.
Since the mountain cherries began to bloom.
Since the sparse bush clover began to flower.
Snow falling in quantities and the valley deep, The.
So far apart our meetings.
So light the sleeves of this cicada-wing robe.
Somehow my heart settles on the hill's rim.
Sound of pine winds and their color are one, The.
Spring passed, and summer it seems has come.
Stalling ox, shuffling, swirls up dust, A.
Straw mattress: the Bridge Princess of Uji.
Suddenly darkening, the sky beyond my eaves.
Take it as a pledge: a dewdrop on a lotus leaf.
Tears of wild geese crying, The.
They become fragrant, and the Spring ends.
Thinking of the past I wake.
Those early-rice paddies by the hill.
Though false rumors pop up as at a fair.
Though the space may be short.
Through a rift in evening rainclouds.
Throughout the land, blossoms are in their prime.
To my hut overgrown with burdocks.
Tomorrow I'll come again to this wild path.
Traveler's sleeves fluttered by an autumn wind, A.
Troubled throughout the year.
Turning and turning, these summer days, to my regret.
Unable to settle through the long unending night.
Under a willow by the road.
Under the lamplight that grows feeble.
Under the lower leaves of hydrangea fireflies cluster.
Unexpectedly cool, in summer clothes.
Unheard of even in the age of mighty gods.
Wakeful for last year's call that I loved.
Weir that winds have made in a mountain stream, The.
Well into the distance young leaves of grass undulate.
What should I do? If only I had a hut.
When day breaks, must I go over the mountain ridge apart.
When evening falls, the autumn wind rustles.
When I hear deep in the mountains.
When there's love as unrecognized as a lily.
While we bring to dawn the flower and the moon.
White chrysanthemums they've set up at Fukiage.
Wild geese departing, their wings in white clouds, The.
Wild geese lured by the autumn wind.
Will I see it again.
Wind passes, the mirror of blossoms clouds, A.
With no more fragrance, the *sakaki*, its voice.
Woods again holing up for winter, under snow.
Would the moon ever tell us to grieve.
Yearning for the moon hazy.
Years and months, The.
You, weary of the waves rolling into autumn.
Your Majesty's reign will never end.

Teilhard de Chardin, Pierre (1881–1955)
Blessed be you, harsh matter, barren soil, stubborn rock.

Teish, Luisah
All that I have comes from my Mother!

"Tekahionwake." *See* **Johnson, Emily Pauline.**

Te Kooti Rikirangi (c.1830–1893)
Song of Instruction, A.

Telemaque, Harold Milton (b. 1911)
Adina.

Telesilla (*fl.* 5th century)
O Artemis and your virgin girls.

Telestes (*fl.* c.401 B.C.)
It was a Phrygian king.
It was a Phrygian, Pelops.

Telfer, James (1800–1862)
Goblin's Song, The.

Teller, Judah [*or* Judd] Leib (1912–72)
Flood.

Prologue to General Hamley, *Sels*.
Revenge, The, Sels.
Ring out, Wild Bells (To the Wild Sky).
Risest thou thus, dim dawn, again.
Rivulet crossing my ground.
Rizpah.
Robby, git down wi'tha, wilt tha?
Rose, but one, none other rose had I, A.
Sad Hesper o'er the buried sun.
Sadness.
Sailor Boy, The.
St. Agnes' Eve.
St. Simeon Stylites.
Scorned, to be scorned by one that I scorn.
Sea Dreams, *Sels*.
See What a Lovely Shell.
She came to the village church.
Sick, am I sick of a jealous dread?
Sisters, The.
Sleep, Ellen Aubrey, sleep, and dream of me.
Sleeping House, The.
So all day long the noise of battle rolled.
"So careful of the type?" but no.
So dark a mind within me dwells.
Somebody.
Song at the Ruin'd Inn.
Song of Love and Death, The.
Song: "Who can say."
Sonnet: "She took the dappled partridge flecked [*or* fleckt] with blood."
Spinster's Sweet-Arts, The, *Sels*.
Spirit Haunts the Year's Last Hours, A.
Splendor falls on castle walls, The.
Stormed at with shot and shell.
Strange, that I felt so gay.
Strong Son of God (Immortal Love).
Sweet after showers, ambrosial air.
Sweet and Low [Sweet and Low].
Talking Oak, The, *Sels*.
Tears, Idle Tears.
Tears of the widower, when he sees.
That which we dare invoke to bless.
Then loudly cried the bold Sir Bedivere.
Then rose the King and moved his host by night.
Then saw they how there hove a dusky barge.
There Is None like Her.
There Is Sweet Music Here.
There lay she all her length and kiss'd his feet.
There Rolls the Deep.
This lump of earth has left his estate.
Thou comest, much wept for: such a breeze.
Throstle, The.
Thy voice is heard through rolling drums.
Thy voice is on the rolling air.
Till now the doubtful dusk reveal'd.
Time draws near the birth of Christ, The.
'Tis well, 'tis something; we may stand.
Tithonus.
To Christopher North.
To E. Fitzgerald.
To sleep I give my powers away.
To the Rev. F. D. Maurice, *Sels*.
To Virgil [*or* Vergil].
To-night the Winds Begin.
Tonight ungathered let us leave.
Tristram's Song.
Two Voices, The.
Ulysses.
Unwatch'd [*or* unwatched], the garden bough shall sway.
Vastness.
Vision of Sin, The, *Sels*.
Vivien's Song ("But now the wholesome music of the wood").
Voice by the Cedar Tree, A.
Voyage of Maeldune, The.
Sir Walter Vivian's House.
We leave the well-beloved place.
What Hope Is Here for Modern Rhyme.
What words are these have fallen from me.
When Lazarus left his charnel-cave.
When on My Bed the Moonlight Falls.
When rosy plumelets tuft the larch.
When the hermit made an end.
Wild bird, whose warble, liquid sweet.

Window, The; or, The Song of the Wrens, *Sels*.
Wish, that of the living whole, The.
Witch-elms that counterchange the floor.
With a half-glance upon the sky.
With such compelling cause to grieve.
With trembling fingers did we weave.
You must wake and call me early, call me early, mother.
You say, but with no touch of scorn.

Tennyson, Frederick (1807–98)
Glory of Nature, The.
Holy Tide, The.
Old Age.
Skylark, The.

Tennyson-Turner, Charles. *See* **Turner, Charles Tennyson.**

Tepperman, Jean (b. 1945)
Going through Changes.
Witch.

Te Puea Herangi (1884–1952)
Remain, Rata.

Teresa, Saint, of Avila. *See* **Theresa [*or* Teresa], Saint, of Avila.**

Terracina, Laura (1519–77)
Discourse on the Principle in All the Cantos, The, *Sels*.

Terranova, Elaine
1939.

Terrell, Myra Burnham (b. 1897)
Theodosia Burr.

Terry, Ellen (1847–1928)
No Funeral Gloom.

Terry, Lucy (1730–1821)
Bar's Fight, August 28, 1746.

Terry, Uriah
Wyoming Massacre, The.

Tessimond, Arthur Seymour John (1902–62)
Cats No Less Liquid Than Their Shadows.
England.
Heaven.
Jamaican Bus Ride.
Postscript to a Pettiness.
Where?

Tevakulattar
What She Said ("Bigger than earth, certainly").

Thackeray, William Makepeace (1811–63)
At the Zoo.
Ballad of Bouillabaisse, The, *Sels*.
Cane-bottomed [*or* Cane-bottom'd] Chair, The.
Crystal Palace, The, *Sels*.
Damages, Two Hundred Pounds.
Dr. Birch and His Young Friends, *Sels*.
Due of the Dead, The.
End of the Play, The.
Foreign Literature.
George I — Star of Brunswick.
George III.
George IV.
Georges, The, *Sels*.
King Canute, *Sels*.
King Canute was weary-hearted; he had reigned for years a score.
King of Brentford, The.
King of Brentford's Testament *abr*, The.
Little Billee.
Mr. Molony's Account of the Crystal Palace.
Mr. Molony's Account of the Great Exhibition.
Peg of Limavaddy.
Pocahontas, *Sels*.
Sorrows of Werther, The.
Speculators, The.
This Bouillabaisse a noble dish is.
Wearied arm, and broken sword.

Thaler, Mike
Hyena, The.
Sheep.

Thallus (*fl*. 1st cent. A.D.)
Now the green plane-tree hides the lovers, hides the lovers'/ rites.

Tharp, H. M.
Finger Folk.

Thatcher, Charles Robert (1831–82)
Dick Briggs from Australia.
Moggy's Wedding.

Taking the Census.
Thatcher, Thomas (1620–78)
Love Letter to Elizabeth Thatcher, A.
Thaxter, Celia Laighton (1835–94)
Alone.
August.
Cruise of the *Mystery*, The.
Favorite Flower, The.
Flowers for the Brave.
Imprisoned.
Jack Frost.
Land-locked.
Little Gustava.
Minute-Guns, The.
Modjeska.
Nikolina.
On Easter Day.
S. E.
Sandpiper, The.
Schumann's Sonata in A Minor.
Submission.
Thayer, Ernest Lawrence (1863–1940)
Casey at the Bat.
Thayer, Louis E. (1870–1966)
Hang to Your Grit!
Little Child's Faith, The.
Thayer, Mary Dixon (b. 1896)
Prayer: "God, is it sinful if I feel."
Thayer, William Roscoe ("Paul Hermes") (1859–1923)
Last Hunt, The.
Theaitetos (*fl*. 6th cent.)
Already the field, fair with leaves, in her fruitful bringing to birth.
Krantor.
Thelwall, John (1764–1834)
Cell, The.
Day of my double birth, if such the year.
Lines Written at Bridgewater, 27 July 1797, *Sels*.
Theocritus [*or* Theokritus] (c.310–c.250 B.C.)
Adonis.
Along that footpath, shepherd, past the oaks.
Amorous shepherd lov'd a charming boy, An.
And so an easier life our Cyclops drew.
Countryman's Wooing, A.
Damoetas and Daphnis.
Daphnis the fair-skinned, who plays country songs.
Death of Daphnis, The.
Enchantment, The.
Epitaph of Cleonicus.
Epitaph of Hipponax.
Eunica scorned [*or* skornde] me, when her I would have sweetly kissed [*or* kist].
Fishermen, The.
Gorgo and Praxinoa.
Harvest-Home.
Herdsmen, The.
Hylas.
Idylls, *Sels*.
Incantations, The.
Late Summer.
Little Heracles.
Look on this statue, traveller; look well.
O NICIAS, there is no other remedy for love.
Ortho's Epitaph.
Shepherd Paris bore the Spartan bride, The.
Take, friend, Orthon of Syracuse' advice.
This bank makes welcome citizen and foreigner.
This is the grave of Eusthenes the wise.
Those dew-moist roses and that bushy thyme.
What do you gain, poor Thyrsis, by these tears?
Wine, friend, and truth, the proverb says, agree.
Words are Doric, Doric too the man, The.
You left behind, Eurymedon, an infant child.
You sleep here, Daphnis, on the leafy ground.
Theodoridas (*fl*. 3d cent. B.C.)
I am the tomb of a shipwrecked man. Sail on.
Roused by November seas, wrecked on Italian rocks.
To the triple goddess of Amarynthus.

To a Snowflake.
To My Friend.
To Olivia.
To the Dead Cardinal of Westminster.
Tokens, The.
We Poets Speak.
Thompson, Frank
London, 1940.
Thompson, Irene (b. 1919)
Caravans.
Country Child, The.
Feet.
Holiday Train, The.
Penny Wish, A.
Rainy Nights.
Secret Places.
Swinging.
Town Child, The.
Welcome to Spring.
Thompson, J. W.
Work.
Thompson, James W. (b. 1936)
Constant Labor, A.
Greek Room, The.
Plight, The.
Spawn of Slums, The.
Yellow Bird, The.
You Are Alms.
Thompson, John (1907–68)
Bread Hot from the Oven, The.
Homecoming.
Now You Have Burned.
Onion, The.
Thompson, John, Jr. (b. 1918)
Love for Patsy, A.
Thompson, John Randolph (b. 1838)
Lee to the Rear.
Obsequies of Stuart.
Thompson, John Reuben (1823–73)
Burial of Latané, The.
Music in Camp.
On to Richmond.
Thompson, Larry (b. 1950)
Black Is Best.
Thompson, Leslie (d. 1955)
There Are So Many Ways of Going Places.
Thompson, Maurice (1844–1901)
Ballad of Chickamauga, The.
Lincoln's Grave, Sels.
Wild Honey.
Thompson, Priscilla Jane (b. 1882)
Address to Ethiopia.
Adieu, Adieu, Forever.
Adown the Heights of Ages.
After the Quarrel.
Afternoon Gossip, An.
Alberta.
Athelstane.
Autumn ("List to the sad wind, drearily moaning").
Autumn ("Sun shines bright, but sadly, The").
Christmas Ghost, A.
Common Occurrence, A.
Consumptive, The.
David and Goliath.
Death and Resurrection.
Domestic Storm, A.
Emancipation.
Evelyn.
Examination, The.
Favorite Slave's Story, The.
Freedom at McNealy's.
Fugitive, The.
Glimpses of Infancy.
Happy Pair, A.
Home Greeting, A.
Husband's Return, The.
Hymn: "Lord, within thy fold I be."
In the Valley.
Inner Realm, The.
Insulted.
Interrupted Reproof, The.
Just How It Happened.
Kindly Deed, A.
King's Favorites, The.

Knight of My Maiden Love.
Lines on a Dead Girl.
Lines to an Old School-House.
Lines to Emma.
Little Wren, A.
Muse's Favor, The.
My Father's Story.
Oh, Whence Comes the Gladness?
Old Freedman, The.
Old Saint's Prayer, The.
Old Year, The.
Prayer: "Oh, Lord! I lift my heart."
Precious Pearl, The.
Raphael.
Snail's Lesson, The.
Snow-Flakes, The.
Soft Black Eyes.
Song of the Moon.
Song: "Oh, foully slighted Ethiope maid!"
Southern Scene, A.
They Are the Same.
Thwarted.
To a Deceased Friend.
To a Little Colored Boy.
To the New Year.
Tribute to the Bride and Groom, A.
Turncoat, The.
Uncle Ike's Holiday.
Uncle Jimmie's Yarn.
Unromantic Awakening, An.
Valentine, A.
Vineyard of My Beloved, The.
While the Choir Sang.
Winter Night, A.
Thompson, Samuel (1766–1816)
April.
To a Hedgehog.
Thompson, Ted
Limerick: "Having rid Hamelin town of its vermin."
Thompson, Will Henry (1848–1918)
High Tide at Gettysburg, The.
Thompson, William (1712?–1766?)
Happy Life, The.
Next, in a low-browed cave, a little hell.
Sickness, Sels.
Thomson, Charles
On the Low Status of Masturbation.
Thomson, James (1700–1748)
All–intellectual eye, our solar round.
And what, my thoughtless sons, should fire you more.
As rising from the vegetable World.
Castle of Indolence, The, Sels.
Even *Light itself*, which every thing displays.
Flushed by the spirit of the genial year.
For ever, Fortune, wilt thou prove.
Happy Britannia!
His was the treasure of two thousand years.
How sweet and innocent are country sports.
Hymn on Solitude.
Hymn on the Seasons, A.
In lowly dale, fast by a river's side.
Keener tempests come, The: and fuming dun.
Lisy's Parting with Her Cat.
Masque of Alfred, The, Sels.
Nor shall my verse that elder bard forget.
Of a Country Life, Sels.
On the Death of a Particular Friend.
On the Death of Mr. William Aikman the Painter, Sels.
Paraphrase of the Latter part of the Sixth Chapter of St. Matthew, A.
Seasons, The, Sels.
Should I my steps turn to the rural seat.
Sometimes the pencil, in cool airy halls.
Song: "One day the god of fond desire."
Spring.
Spring ("Behold yon breathing prospect bids the muse").
Spring Flowers.
Still let me pierce into the midnight depth.
Summer.
Summer ("Home from his morning task the swain retreats").

'Tis done! Dread Winter spreads his latest glooms.
'Tis raging noon; and vertical, the sun.
To the Memory of Sir Isaac Newton, Sels.
When Britain first at Heaven's command,
Wild Shakespeare.
Winter.
Winter ("As thus the snows arise, and foul and fierce").
Winter ("Drooping, the labourer-ox").
Winter Night, A.
Winter ("Now, when the cheerless empire of the sky").
Winter ("See, Winter comes, to rule the varied year").
Winter ("What art thou, frost? and whence are thy keen stores").
Winter ("When from the pallid sky the sun descends").
Thomson, James (1700–1748) and David Mallet
Alfred, A Masque, Sels.
On Beauety, Sels.
Rule, Britannia!
This happy place with all delights abounds.
Thomson, James ("B.V." or "Bysshe Vanolis") (1834–82)
Although lamps burn along the silent streets.
Anear the centre of that northern crest.
Art, Sels.
As I came through the desert thus it was.
As We Rush, As We Rush in the Train.
City is of Night, The; perchance of Death.
City of Dreadful Night, The, Sels.
Gifts.
He stood alone within the spacious square.
How your eyes dazzle down into my soul!
I wandered in a suburb of the north.
In a Christian Churchyard.
In the Room.
Large glooms were gathered in the mighty fane.
Mighty river flowing dark and deep, The.
Mr. MacCall at Cleveland Hall.
Once in a Saintly Passion.
Proem: "Lo, thus, as prostrate, "In the dust I write."
Shelley, Sels.
Singing is sweet; but be sure of this.
Sunday at Hampstead, Sels.
Sunday up the River, Sels.
This is the Heath of Hampstead.
Voice of right amidst a world gone wrong, A.
Was it hundreds of years ago, my love.
What men are they who haunt these fatal glooms.
William Blake.
Wine of Love is music, The.
Thomson, Mary A. (1834–1923)
O King of Saints, We Give Thee Praise and Glory.
O Sion, Haste, Thy Mission High Fulfilling.
Thomson, Veronica Forrest. See Forrest-Thomson, Veronica.
Thoreau, Henry David (1817–62)
Among the Worst of Men That Ever Lived.
At Midnight's Hour I Raised My Head.
Between the Traveller and the Setting Sun.
Each More Melodious Note I Hear.
Epitaph on the World.
Fisher's Boy, The.
For Though the Eaves [or Caves] Were Rabbeted [or Rabbited].
Forever in My Dream and in My Morning Thought.
Great Friend.
Great God, I Ask Thee for No Meaner Pelf.
I Am a Parcel of Vain Strivings Tied.
I Am the Little Irish Boy.
I Was Born upon Thy Bank, River.
I Was Made Erect and Lone.
If with light head erect I sing.
I'm Thankful That My Life Doth Not Deceive.
Indeed Indeed, I Cannot Tell.
Inspiration, Sels.
Inward Morning, The.
It Is No Dream of Mine.
Lately, Alas, I Knew a Gentle Boy.

From behind the Bars, *Sels.*
From the Diary of — —.
My mother's phantom hovers here.
Turberville, George (c.1540–c.1610)
Epitaph of Maister Win Drowned in the Sea,
An.
Lover Abused Renounceth Love, The, *Sels.*
Lover to the Thames of London, to Favour [*or*
Favor] His Lady Passing Thereon, The.
Lover Whose Mistress Feared a Mouse, The.
Of Drunkenness.
Of One That Had a Great Nose.
Poor Ploughman to a Gentleman for Whom He
Had Taken a Little Pains, A.
Surrey's Poetic Art.
That He Findeth Others as Fair, but Not So
Faithful as His Friend.
To an Old Gentlewoman That Painted Her
Face.
To His Friend P. of Courting, Traveling,
Dicing, and Tennis.
To His Friend, Promising That Though Her
Beauty Fade, Yet His Love Shall Last.
To His Ring, Given to His Lady, Wherein Was
Graven This Verse, "My Heart Is Yours."
To Parker.
To Spencer.
Unable by Long and Hard Travel to Banish
Love, Returns Her Friend.
Verse in Praise of Lord Henry Howard, Earl of
Surrey, *Sels.*
Was never day came on my head.
Turbina, Nika (b. 1924)
Return, The.
Turbyfill, Mark
Benediction.
Turco, Lewis (b. 1934)
Bordello, *Sels.*
Depot, The.
Ordinary Evening in Cleveland, An.
Rick De Travaille.
Simon Judson.
Wind Carol, The.
Winter Bouquet.
Turei, Mohi
Ruaumoko — the Earthquake God.
Turnbull, Gael (b. 1928)
Residues: Thronging the Heart.
They Have Taken.
Turner, Alberta (b. 1921)
Drift.
Fourth Wish.
In Love with Wholes.
Making Old Bones.
On the Nature of Food.
Small Animal.
Three Easters.
Water Eased of Its Cliffs by Falling.
Turner, Brian (b. 1944)
Coming Home.
Nichita Stanescu.
Responses to Montale.
Turner, Charles Tennyson (1808–79)
Artist on Penmaenmawr, The.
Bee-Wisp, The.
Brilliant Day, A.
Buoy-Bell, The.
Cader Idris at Sunset.
Calvus to a Fly.
Country Dance, A.
Cowper's Three Hares.
Drowned Spaniel, The.
From Harvest to January.
Gout and Wings.
Great Britain Through the Ice: Or, Premature
Patriotism.
Julius Caesar and the Honey-Bee.
Letty's Globe.
Lion's Skeleton, The.
Maggie's Star.
Minnie and Her Dove.
Needles' Lighthouse from Keyhaven,
Hampshire, The.
Old Ruralities: A Regret.
Old Stephen.

On a Vase of Gold-Fish.
On Finding a Small Fly Crushed in a Book.
On Seeing a Little Child Spin a Coin of
Alexander the Great.
On Shooting a Swallow in Early Youth.
On Some Humming-Birds in a Glass Cage.
On the Eclipse of the Moon of October 1865.
Quiet Tide near Ardossan, The.
Rose and Cushie.
Seaside: In and Out of the Season, The.
Steam Threshing-Machine, The.
Summer Night in the Beehive, A.
To a "Tenting" Boy.
Vacant Cage, The.
White Horse of Westbury, The.
Wind on the Corn.
Turner, Darwin T. (b. 1931)
To Vanity.
Turner, Doris (b. 1930)
Fragment Reflection I.
Reckoning A.M. Thursday.
Turner, Elizabeth (1755–1846)
Bird's Nest, The.
Canary, The.
How to Write a Letter.
Truth's the Best.
Two Little Miss Lloyds, The.
Turner, Godfrey (*fl.* c.1878)
Journal of Society, The.
Tattle.
Turner, Nancy Byrd (b. 1880)
Death Is a Door.
First Thanksgiving of All.
Let Us Have Peace.
Lincoln.
Pop Corn Song, A.
Washington.
When Young Melissa Sweeps.
Turner, S. C.
Limerick: "Youth and a maiden from
Costessey, A."
Turner, Steve (b. 1951)
Christmas Is Really for the Children.
Turner, Walter James (1889–1946)
Beneath a thundery glaze.
Dancer, The.
Dian, Isis, Artemis, whate'er thy name.
Ecstasy.
Epithalamium: "Can the lover share his soul."
Giraffe and Tree.
Hymn to Her Unknown.
I had watched the ascension and decline of the
moon.
I have seen mannequins.
If God kept a terrarium.
In Time like Glass.
India.
Life and Death.
Lion, The.
Love-song: "Beautiful, delicate bright gazelle,
The."
Marriage.
Men Fade Like Rocks.
Music of a Tree, The.
Navigators, The.
Reflection.
Robber, The.
Romance.
Seven Days of the Sun, The, *Sels.*
Silence.
Soldiers in a Small Camp.
Song: "Lovely hill-torrents are."
Spirits walking everywhere.
Sun, The.
Talking with Soldiers.
This is the last time.
Tragic Love.
What is the meaning of this Ideal.
What is this tempest.
Word Made Flesh, The.
Turner, William (*fl.* 1612)
Turners Dish of Lentten Stuffe or A
Galymaufery.
Turner, William Price (b. 1927)
Alien.

Coronary Thrombosis.
University Curriculum.
Turtiainen, Arvo (1904–80)
Ballad of Herman's Rose, *Sels.*
Finally I understood Rose's death.
Helsinki.
There where the Kulo Saari bridge.
Where could I find the words.
Tusiani, Joseph
Anticipation.
Rest O Sun I Cannot.
Tusser, Thomas (c.1524–1580)
Advice of Housewives.
December's Husbandry.
Five Hundred Points of Good Husbandry, *Sels.*
Hundreth Good Poyntes of Husbandry, A, *Sels.*
Upon the Author's First Seven Years' Service.
When harvest is done all thing placed and set.
Winds, The.
Tussman, Malka Heifetz-. *See* Heifetz-
Tussman, Malka.
Tuttle, Stella Weston (b. 1907)
Quickening, The.
Tuwhare, Hone (b. 1922)
Friend.
Heemi.
Monologue.
No Ordinary Sun.
Ron Mason.
Song in Praise of a Favourite Humming-Top,
A.
Talk with My Cousin Alone, A.
Tuwim, Julian [*or* Juljan] (Juljah) (1894–1953)
Prayer: "I pray Thee O Lord."
Pursuit.
There Is No Country.
**"Twain, Mark" (Samuel Langhorne Clemens)
(1835–1910)**
Adventures of Huckleberry Finn, The, *Sels.*
Aged Pilot Man, The.
Emmeline Grangerford's "Ode to Stephen
Dowling Bots, Dec'd."
Epitaph Placed on His Daughter's Tomb.
He Done His Level Best.
Home without a Cat, A.
Imitation of Julia A. Moore.
Limerick: "Man hired by John Smith and Co.,
A."
Twardowski, Samuel (1600–1660)
Epitaph for a Dog.
Tweedy, Henry Hallam (1868–1953)
Eternal God, Whose Power Upholds.
O Gracious Father of Mankind.
Twichell, Chase (b. 1950)
Chanel No. 5.
Condom Tree, The.
Physics.
Revenge.
Shades of Grand Central, The.
Six Belons.
Twiss, Horace (1786/87–1849)
Fashion.
Our Parodies are Ended.
Patriot's Progress, The.
Twomey, Catherine (b. c.1960)
Cliona.
Tylee, Edward Sydney
Outward Bound.
Tyler, Inez M.
Call to Pentecost, A.
Tyler, Parker (1907–74)
Anthology of Nouns.
Nijinsky.
Tyler, Royall (1757–1826)
Anacreontic to Flip.
Gambling.
Hail to the Joyous Day.
Independence Day.
Love Song: "By the fierce flames of love I'm
in a sad taking."
Original Epitaph on a Drunkard.
Widower, The.
Tymnes (*fl.* 2d century B.C.)
Dear little bird, the Graces' favourite.
Don't let it matter much, Philaenis.

Epigrams, *Sels.*
Eumelos had a Maltese dog.
Maltese Dog, A.
Stone says that it covers here the white dog,
  The.
Tynan, Katharine (Katharine Tynan Hinkson)
  (1861–1931)
Doves, The.
Epitaph: "Write on my grave when I am dead."
Farewell: "Not soon shall I forget — a sheet."
Flying Wheel, The.
Holy Family.
In Time of Need.
Leaves.
Lux in Tenebris.
Making of Birds, The.
Man of the House, The.
Mater Dei.
Nightingale, The.
Of an Orchard.
Passiontide Communion.
Pink Almond.
Sheep and Lambs.
Slow Spring.
Vision, The.
Wild Geese.
Witch, The.
Tyutchev, Fyodor [*or* Feodor] Ivanovich (1803–
  73)
As Ocean's Stream.
At Vshchizh.
Last Love.
Spring; a Formal Ode.
Spring Waters.
Tzara, Tristan (1896–1963)
Approximate Man, The, *Sels.*
Tzu Yeh (*fl.* **3d–4th century)**
Bare branches tremble, The.
I am the North Pole.
I cannot sleep.
I had not fastened my sash over my gown.
It is night again.

U

Uahupirapi, Dina
Imagination.
Uberti, Fazio degli (1320–60)
His Portrait of His Lady, Angiola of Verona.
Uceda, Julia (b. 1925)
Time Reminded Me.
2976.
Udal, Nicholas. *See* Udall [*or* Udal], Nicholas.
Udall, L. G.
Limerick: "Each Lon was a notable man."
Limerick: "Pulmonary tuberculosis."
Udall [*or* Udal], Nicholas (1305–56)
I Mun Be Married a Sunday.
Minion Wife, A.
Ralph Roister Doister, *Sels.*
Uejima Onitsura. *See* Onitsura.
Ugaas, Raage
Like the yu'ub wood tied to gelded camels
  that are running away.
Uhland, Ludwig (Johann Ludwig Uhland)
  (1787–1862)
Blacksmith, The.
Castle by the Sea, The.
Durand of Blonden.
Hostess' Daughter, The.
Ichabod! The Glory Has Departed.
In a Lovely Garden Walking.
Leaf, A.
Luck of Edenhall, The.
Spirits Everywhere.
Sunday.
Ujejski, Kornel (1823–97)
Polish Eagle, The.
Ukihashi (*fl.* **late 17th century)**
Whether I sit or lie.
Ukon, Lady (*fl.* **10th cent.)**
I am forgotten now.

Ullman, Leslie (b. 1947)
Dawn Feeding.
Desire.
Dreams by No One's Daughter.
Living Near the Plaza of Thieves.
Mauve.
Running.
Ullmann, Liv (b. 1938)
Changing, *Sels.*
Ulloa, Yolanda (b. 1948)
Ita.
Short Biography of a Washerwoman.
Ulmer, James (b. 1942)
Crabbing for Blue-claws.
Daily Bread.
From a Box of Old Photographs.
These Nights.
Uloccanar
What Her Girl Friend Said, Consoling Her
  when She Was Distressed by the Town's
  Gossip.
What Her Girl Friend Said, the Lover within
  Earshot, behind a Fence.
Ulrich, Anton (1633–1714)
Dying Song.
Underhill, Evelyn (1875–1941)
Introversion.
Supersensual.
Theophany.
Underwood, Wilbur (b. 1876)
Cattle of His Hand, The.
To the Brave Soul.
Ungar, Lynn
Common Prayer.
Ungaretti, Giuseppe (1888–1970)
Agony.
Brothers.
I Am a Creature.
Italy.
No More Crying Out.
Rivers.
San Martino del Carso.
Vigil.
You Were Broken.
Unger, Barbara
Pillar of Flame.
Untermeyer, Jean Starr (1886–1970)
Autumn.
Country of No Lack.
Dew on a Dusty Heart.
False Enchantment.
High Tide.
Lake Song.
Last Plea.
Passionate Sword, The.
Sinfonia Domestica.
Sung on a Sunny Morning.
Untermeyer, Louis (1885–1977)
Archibald MacLeish Suspends the Five Little
  Pigs.
At the Bottom of the Well.
Caliban in the Coal Mines.
Dance of Dust, The.
Dark Chamber, The.
Edgar A. Guest Considers "The Good Old
  Woman Who Lived in a Shoe" and the Good
  Old Truths Simultaneously.
Edna St. Vincent Millay Exhorts Little Boy
  Blue.
End of the Comedy.
Feuerzauber.
Food and Drink.
Glad Day.
Goliath and David.
Infidelity.
Irony.
John Masefield Relates the Story of Tom, Tom,
  the Piper's Son.
Koheleth.
Last Words before Winter.
Long Feud.
Mother Goose Up-to-Date, *Sels.*
On Hearing Prokofieff's Grotesque for Two
  Bassoons, Concertina and Snare-Drums.
Portrait of a Machine.

Prayer.
Prayer for This House.
Prayer: "God, though [*or* although] this life is
  but a wraith."
Questions at Night.
Relativities.
Repentance.
Sagging Bough, The.
Song Tournament: New Style.
Swimmers, *Sels.*
To a Vine-clad Telegraph Pole.
Wallflower to a Moonbeam.
Walter de la Mare Tells the Listener about Jack
  and Jill.
Wind Gardens.
Unwin, Richard
Limerick: "My beard's overcrowded. Now
  that."
Updike, John (b. 1932)
Agatha Christie and Beatrix Potter.
Amish, The.
August.
Bendix.
Child's Calendar, A, *Sels.*
Dea ex Machina.
Dog's Death.
Dutch Cleanser.
Ex-Basketball Player.
February 22.
From a Cheerful Alphabet.
Great Scarf of Birds, The.
I Like to Sing Also.
I Missed His Book, I Read His Name.
Insomnia the Gem of the Ocean.
January.
Love Sonnet.
May.
Meditation on a News Item.
Minority Report.
Mosquito.
Movie House.
Naked Ape, The.
Note to the Previous Tenants.
October.
Ode: "I'm going to write a novel, hey."
Party Knee.
Player Piano.
Recital.
Seagulls.
Seven Stanzas at Easter.
Short Days, The.
Some Frenchmen.
Sunflower.
Telephone Poles.
There was an old poop from Poughkeepsie.
3 A.M.
Touch of Spring.
Touchy old gent from Cohasset, A.
Two Limericks after Lear, *Sels.*
Upon Learning That a Bird Exists Called the
  Turnstone.
Upon Shaving Off One's Beard.
V. B. Nimble, V. B. Quick ("V. B.
  Wigglesworth wakes at noon").
Vow.
Winter Ocean.
Youth's Progress.
Upham, Thomas Cogswell (1799–1872)
Fear Not, Poor Weary One.
Song of the Pilgrims.
Upson, Arthur W. (1887–1908)
Failures.
Upton, Lee
Water Gardening.
Uraiyur Mutukorran
What the Passersby Said to the Lover Eloping
  with the Girl.
Urchard, T. (1611–60)
Truly Rich, The.
Urdang, Constance (b. 1922)
All Around Us.
At Frank 'n' Helen's.
Back Far Enough, Down Deep Enough.
Birth of Venus.
Children, The.

Wild West.

Violi, Paul (b. 1944)
At the Corner of Muck and Myer.
Index.
Outside Baby Moon's.
Whalefeathers.

Viorst, Judith (b. 1931)
Mother Doesn't Want a Dog.
Night Fun.
Where is it Written?

Virgil [or Vergil] (Publius Vergilius Maro) (70–19 B.C.)
Aeneas Sees Italy.
Aeneid [or Eneados], The, Sels.
Affrayit, I glistnyt of sleip, and stert on feit.
Amyd the wod his modir met thame tway.
And now Aeneas charges straight at Turnus.
And now we gan draw near unto the gate.
And oft the owle with rufull song complaind.
And Turnus than, quhar he at erth dyd ly.
Arms, and the man I sing, who forc'd by fate.
As, sum tyme, dois the curser stert and ryn.
As this convine and ordinance was mayd.
As when a fragment, from a mountain torn.
Attentively he heard us, while we spoke.
Batellis [or Batalis] and the man I will descrive.
Belive Eneas membris schuk for cald.
Bot now the haisty, egir, and wild Dido.
But lo, Polites, one of Priam's sons.
But now the wounded queen with heavy care.
But trembling Dido eagerly now bent.
Care of Bees, The.
Come is the ending day, Troy's hour is come.
Corydon and Thyrsis.
Dear Sister, my resentment had not been.
Destruction of Troy, The.
Eclogues, Sels.
Eneas wonderit the greitnes of Cartaige.
Euryalus and Nisus Meet Their Deaths.
Exulting in his strength, he seems to dare.
For Thee, Little Boy.
Georgics, Sels.
Gravid Mares, The.
Greeks' chieftains, all irked with the war, The.
Heaven, the earth, and all the liquid main [or mayne], The.
Hesperia the Grecians call the place.
How hard a fate enthrals the wretched maid.
In the main sea the isle of Crete doth lie.
It was the time when, granted from the gods.
It was then night: the sound[e] and quiet sleep [or slepe].
Loe! formest of a rout that followd him.
Loud report through Lybian cities goes, The.
Lycidas and Moeris.
Messiah, The.
Now manhood and garbroyls I chaunt.
O boys, O strong of heart in vain.
Observe the daily circle of the sun.
Onto the hallowit steid bryng in, thai cry.
Polyphemus.
Prelude: "What makes a plenteous harvest."
Prince, with wonder, sees the stately tow'rs, The.
Prologue to Book VII, The.
Queen Dido Rides Out Hunting.
Quhen thou art careit to that cuntree.
Second Pastoral; or, Alexis, The.
Shepherd's Gratitude, The.
Sixth Book of the Aeneis, The.
There Charon stands, who rules the dreary coast.
They wished [or whisted] all, with fixèd face attent.
Thir riveris and thir watteris kepit war.
Thus fell the King, whom yet surviv'd the state.
To my prowd foe thus, sister, humblie saye.
Wee leave Creete Country; and our sayls unwrapped uphoysing.
Whom when I saw assembled in such wise.

Virgilio, Nicholas
Into the blinding sun.

Virrurru Muteyinanar
What He Said after a Quarrel, Remembering His Wedding Night.

Virtue, Vivian (b. 1911)
Hour, The.
Waifs.

Visick, Mary
Wordsworth on Lloyd George.

Vita-Finzi, C.
Limerick: "Her husband was hors de combat."
Limerick: "Lecherous young Lilliputian, A."
Limerick: "Some people may think I'm a bit la-di."
Limerick: "Three scribblers whose names end in Bert."
Limerick: "Unperson from West Oceania, An."
Limerick: "When an amorous youth from Atlantis."

Vittorelli, Jacopo (1749–1803)
On a Nun.

Vivian, Mary
Four Scarlet Berries.
Snowdrops.

Vivien, Renée (1877–1909)
Pillory, The.
Toward Lesbos.
Words to My Friend.

Vizenor, Gerald (b. 1934)
Anishinabe Grandmothers.
Family Photograph.
February Park.
Haiku: "August heat."
Indians at the Guthrie.
North to Milwaukee.
Raising the Flag.
Seasons in Santa Fe.
Seven Woodland Crows.
Shaman Breaks.
Surrendered Names.
Thumbing Old Magazines.
Tropisms on John Berryman.
Tyranny of Moths.
Unhappy Diary Days.
White Earth.

Voigt, Ellen Bryant (b. 1943)
At the Movie: Virginia, 1956.
Bat, The.
Blue Ridge.
Dancing with Poets.
Daughter.
Delilah.
Farm Wife.
Farmer, The.
Feast Day, Sels.
Feast of the Assumption of the Virgin, The.
For My Husband.
For My Mother.
January.
Jug Brook.
Landscape, Dense with Trees.
Last Class, The.
Letter from Vermont.
Lotus Flowers, The.
O mild Christ.
Rescue.
Spire, The.
Sweet Everlasting.
Tropics.
Victim, The.
Why She Says No.
Wife Takes a Child, The.
Year's End.

Voiture, Vincent (1597–1648)
Rondeau: "Lord, I'm done for: now Margot."

Vollmoeller, Karl Gustav (b. 1878)
Nocturne in G Minor.

Voltaire (François, Marie Arouet) (1694–1778)
Lisbon Earthquake, The, Sels.
Moralist still obstinate replies, The.

Von Trimberg, Süsskind (c.1250–1300)
Power of Thought, The.
Virtuous Wife, The.
Why Should I Wander Sadly.

Vories, William M. (b. 1880)
Let There Be Light.

Voss, Fred
Edgy.
Lingo.

Stud, The.

Voznesensky, Andrei (b. 1933)
Bicycles.
Darkmotherscream.
Dead Still.
I Am Goya.
Somewhere a man puts on his shorts.
War.

"Vrepont, Brian" (B.A. Trubridge) (1882–1955)
Bomber, The.

Vriesland, Victor van (b. 1891)
Ars Poetica.

Vuco, Aleksandar (1897–1985)
Cyril aand Methodius, Sels.

Vuglar, Jenny (b. 1954)
Leaving.

W

"W., A." (fl. c.1586)
Desire's Government.
Dispraise of Love, and Lovers' Follies.
Give Me Leave.
Hopeless Desire Soon Withers and Dies.
In Praise of a Beggar's Life.
In Praise of the Sun.
To Time.
Upon Visiting His Lady by Moonlight.
Where His Lady Keeps His Heart.

"W., C. A."
To have it out or not? that is the question.

"W., J. J." (fl. c.1888)
Brotherhood.

"W.A.G." See "G., W. A."

"W. J." See "J., W."

W ——, Miss (fl. 18th century)
Gentleman's Study, in Answer to The Lady's Dressing-Room, The.

Wabnitz, William S. (b. 1890)
Hinds of Kerry, The.

Wachtel, Chuck (b. 1950)
Answer, The.
Horror Story Written for the Cover of a Matchbook, A.
Paragraph Made Up of Seven Sentences Which Have Entered My Memory, A.
Sirventes against the Management of the Mammoth Supermarket in Toulouse, A.

Waddell, Helen (1889–1965)
But we, whose sands run low.
December nights are frosts and stars.
Dim grey wastes of the silent hills.
Earth Said to Death.
Hitler Speaks.
I Shall Not Go to Heaven When I Die.
I stood within the empty House of Youth.
New York City.

Waddell, P. Hately (1817–91)
David and Goliath.
Psalm XXIII.

Wadding [or Waddinge], Luke (1588–1657)
Christmas Day [Is Come].
For Christmas Day.
For Innocents' Day.
For Saint John's Day.
For Saint Stephen's Day.
For Twelfth Day.
On the Circumcision: New Year's Day.

Waddington, Miriam (b. 1917)
Advice to the Young.
Catalpa Tree.
Icons.
My Lessons in the Jail.
Old Women of Toronto.
Season's Lovers, The.
Ten Years and More.
Women's Jail, The.

Wade, Barrie
Goldfish.
Truth.

Wade, Blanche Elizabeth (d. 1928)
Song of the Christmas Tree, The.

When the tide ebbed in the Ch'in-huai, autumn after spring.
Written beneath Hui Mountain, When Tsou Liu-yi Comes By for a Visit.

Wang T'ing-hsiang (1474–1544)
I am a man of Chiang-nan.
I pluck *heng*-herbs at the Chin-ling riverside.
Miscellaneous Poems on Spirit-Valley Temple, *Sels*.
Pagoda of Master Chih, The.
Song of Wu-ch'eng, *Sels*.
Songs of Chiang-nan, *Sels*.
Traveling by Boat, *Sels*.
Wall Painting by Wu Wei, A.

Wang Ts'an (177–217)
Joining the Army: A Song.
Land of the Ching tribes is not my home, The.
Occasional Verse.
Seven Poems of Lament, *Sels*.
Seven Sorrows, *Sels*.
This frontier post brings me sorrow.
Tribes of Ching — that's not my home.
Western Capital in lawless disorder, The.
Western Capital is in turmoil, The.

Wang Wei (*fl.* 17th century)
After Long Rain.
Autumn.
Autumn Twilight in the Mountains.
Bamboo Mile Lodge.
Bird and Waterfall Music.
Birdsong Brook.
Cold Mountain, The.
Deep in the Mountain Wilderness.
Deer Fence.
Departure.
Enjoying Coolness.
Farms at Wei River, The.
In the Hills.
Joys of the Country: Seven Poems, *Sels*.
Meng-ch'eng Hollow.
Morning.
On Returning to Sung Mountain.
Red Peonies.
Seeing Someone Off.
Seeking a Mooring.
Song for Wei City, A.
Suffering from Heat.
Thinking of My Brother in Shantung on the Ninth Day of the Ninth Moon.
To Subprefect Chang.
Twenty Views of Wang-ch'uan, *Sels*.
Twilight Comes.
Verses: "You who come from the old village."
Walking at Leisure.

Wang Yu (c. 764–c. 835)
Palace Poem.
Song of Autumn Night.
Song of Spring Journeying.

Wang Yü-ch'eng (954–1001)
Journeying to the Village.
Random Thoughts Written in Spring.
Song of the Crow Pecking at My Scarred Donkey.

Waniek, Marilyn Nelson (b. 1946)
Balance.
Chosen.
It's All in Your Head.
Lonely Eagles.
Star-fix.
Women's Locker Room.

Wanley, Nathaniel (1634–80)
Instead of Incense (Blessed Lord) if wee.
Royal [*or* Royall] Presents, *Sels*.

Wantling, William (b. 1933)
Plea for Workmen's Compensation, A.

Warburton, N. J.
Snake on D. H. Lawrence, The.

Warburton, R. E. Egerton (1804–91)
Past and Present.

Ward, Diane (b. 1956)
Passion.

Ward, Edward (1667–1731)
Ballad on the Taxes, A.
Dialogue between a Squeamish Cotting

Mechanic and His Sluttish Wife, in the Kitchen.
Extravagant Drunkard's Wish, The.
Hudibras Redidivus, *Sels*.
Journey to Hell, A; or, A Visit Paid to the Devil, *Sels*.
London Street-Scene, A.
Nuptial Dialogues, *Sels*.
Parish Poor-Officers, The.

Ward, Elizabeth Stuart Phelps (Elizabeth Stuart Phelps) (1844–1911)
Conemaugh.
Generous Creed, A.
Message, A.

Ward, J. P. (b. 1937)
Every Single Night.
To Get Clear.
Unusual View of the Town.

Ward, Jerry W., Jr. (b. 1943)
Jazz to Jackson to John.

Ward, John
Come, Sable Night.

Ward, May Williams (b. 1915)
Wet Summer.

Ward, Nathaniel (1578–1652)
Mercury shew'd Apollo, Bartas Book.
Mr. Ward of Anagrams Thus.
Poetry's a gift wherein but few excell.
World's a well strung fidle, mans tongue the quill, The.

Ware, Eugene Fitch ("Ironquill") (1841–1911)
Ballad in "G," A.
He and She.
Manila.
Whist.
Zephyr.

Ware, Henry, Jr. (1794–1843)
Great God, the Followers of Thy Son.
Lift Your Glad Voices in Triumph on High.

Warfield, Catherine Anne (1816–77)
Beauregard.
Manassas.

Waring, Anna L. (1823–1950)
My Times Are in Thy Hand.

Waring, Belle
Baby Random.
Back to Catfish.
Breeze in Translation.
Nothing Happened.
Our Lady of the Laundromat.
Refuge at the One Step Down.
Reprieve on the Stoop.
Tip, The.
When a Beautiful Woman Gets on the Jutiapa Bus.

Waring, H. C.
Quite the Cheese.

Warne, Candice (b. 1945)
Blackbird Sestina.

Warner, Anna Bartlett ("Amy Lothrop") (1827–1915)
Jesus Loves Me, This I Know.
One More Day's Work for Jesus.
We Would See Jesus.

Warner, Eva
Irony of God.

Warner, Francis
Epithalamium: "This girl all in white is my crystal of light."

Warner, Rex (b. 1905)
Chough.
Palm Trees.

Warner, Sylvia Townsend (1893–1978)
Absence, The.
After He Had Gone.
Alarum, The.
Benicasim.
Building in Stone.
Country Thought.
Drawing You, Heavy With Sleep.
Elizabeth.
Epitaph: "Her grieving parents cradled here."
Epitaph: "I, an unwedded wandering dame."

Epitaph: "I, Richard Kent, beneath these stones."
Epitaph: "John Bird, a laborer, lies here."
Gloriana Dying.
Graveyard in Norfolk.
Green Valley, The.
Killing No Murder.
King Duffus.
Mr. Gradgrind's Country.
Modo and Alciphron.
Nelly Trim.
Rival, The.
Sad Green.
Sailor, The.
Song from the Bride of Smithfield.
Song: "She has left me, my pretty."
Triumph of Sensibility.
Under the Sudden Blue.

Warner, William (1558?–1609)
Albion's England, *Sels*.
My Mistress.
Tale of the Beginning of Friars and Cloisterers, A.

Warr, Bertram J. (1917–43)
Working Class.

Warren, Edward Perry. *See* "Raile, Arthur Lyon."

Warren, Hamilton (b. 1898)
Requiem: "Let the mountains stand forth!"

Warren, James E., Jr. (b. 1908)
Schoolroom: 158–.

Warren, Joseph (1740–75)
Free America.

Warren, Mrs. Mercy (1728–1814)
Limerick: "Maiden at college called Breeze, A."
Massachusetts Song of Liberty.

Warren, Robert Penn (1905–1989)
American Portrait: Old Style.
Answer Yes or No.
Aubade for Hope.
Audubon, *Sels*.
Ballad of Billie Potts, The.
Bearded Oaks.
Between the Boxcars, *Sels*.
Birth of Love.
Boyhood in Tobacco Country.
Boy's Will, Joyful Labor without Pay, and Harvest Home, *Sels*.
Code Book Lost.
Colder Fire.
Country Burying (1919).
Covered Bridge.
Debate: Question, Quarry, Dream.
Deciduous Spring.
Dragon Country: To Jacob Boehme.
Dragon-Tree.
Dream, Dump-Heap, and Civilization.
Evening Hawk.
Evening Hour.
Fall Comes in Back-Country Vermont.
First Moment of Autumn Recognized.
Flaubert in Egypt.
Founding Fathers, Nineteenth-Century Style.
Function of Blizzard.
Garden, The.
Gold Glade.
Heart of Autumn.
Heart of the Backlog.
Heat Lightning.
History among the Rocks.
History during Nocturnal Snowfall.
I Can't Even Remember the Name.
In Time's concatenation and/ Carnal conventicle.
Insomnia.
Interim, The.
Kentucky Mountain Farm, *Sels*.
Last Laugh.
Last Meeting.
Letter from a Coward to a Hero.
Letter of a Mother.
Letter to a Friend.
Limited, The.
Little Girl Wakes Early.

Watson, Nancy Dingman
Grasshopper Green.
Watson, Robert (b. 1925)
Blue Whale, The.
Watson, Rosamund Marriott ("Graham R. Tomson"; "R. Armytage") (1863–1911)
Ave atque Vale.
To My Cat.
Watson, Roy W. (b. 1926)
View on Death, A.
Who a Mother Is.
Watson, Thomas (c.1557–1592)
Come, Gentle Death!
Go Idle Lines.
Hecatompathia; or, Passionate Century of Love, Sels.
Here Lieth Love.
I Saw the Object.
My Love is Past.
Some that reporte great Alexanders life.
Speake gentle heart, where is thy dwelling place?
Tears of Fancy, The, Sels.
Time.
With Fragrant Flowers We Strew the Way.
Watson, W. F. N.
Hicche-Hykeres Tale, The.
Limerick: "Couple there was in Blefuscu, A."
Limerick: "Dear Albert, of Saxe-Coburg-Gotha."
Limerick: "Fellow from far Erewhon, A."
Limerick: "Feminine mouth in Utopia, The."
Limerick: "Few things to desire can so prod us."
Limerick: "Lady from Vanity Fair, A."
Limerick: "There was a young lady of Lundy."
Limerick: "Young couple who lived at 'The Laurels'," A."
Watson, Wilfred (b. 1911)
Canticle of Darkness.
Emily Carr.
Invocation: "Appear, O Mother, was the perpetual cry."
Lines: I Praise God's Mankind in an Old Woman.
O My Poor Darling.
White Bird, The.
Watson, Sir William (1858–1935)
Church Today, The.
Domine Quo Vadis?
Epigram: "When whelmed the altar, priest and creed."
Epitaph: "His friends he loved. His direst earthly foes."
God-seeking.
Hope of the World, The.
If I had never known your face at all.
Love.
Ode in May.
Poet, The.
Song: "April, April,/ Laugh thy girlish laughter."
Sonnets to Miranda, Sels.
Sovereign Poet, The.
To Lord Tennyson.
Two Epigrams, Sels.
Unknown God, The.
Wordsworth's Grave.
Watt, T. S. (b. 1935)
From My Rural Pen.
Watt, W. W. (b. 1909)
Summer Song.
Watteau, Otto
Limerick: "'Oh, halt!'" cried Virginia, "'Enough!'"
Watterman, Catharine H. (1812–97)
Come unto Me, When Shadows Darkly Gather.
Wattles, Willard Austin (1888?–1950)
Pisgah.
Watts, Alaric Alexander (1797–1864)
Austrian Army, An.
Watts, Isaac (1674–1748)
Adventurous Muse, The.
Adventurous Muse, The, Sels.
Almighty Maker God!

Broad Is the Road.
Christ hath a garden walled around.
Church the Garden of Christ, The.
Comparison and Complaint, The.
Cradle Hymn, A.
Day of Judgement [or Judgment]; an Ode, The.
Early, my God, without delay.
Edom.
Few Happy Matches.
Flying Fowl, and Creeping Things, Praise Ye the Lord.
For the Lord's Day Evening.
Give me the Muse whose generous force.
Great God, attend while Zion sings.
Hosanna to Christ.
How Doth the Little Busy Bee.
How long, dear Savior, O how long.
Hurry of the Spirits, in a Fever and Nervous Disorders, The.
Incomprehensible, The.
Innocent Play.
Jesus Shall Reign Where'er the Sun.
Kind Deeds.
Law Given at Sinai, The.
Look on Him Whom They Pierced, and Mourn.
Love between Brothers and Sisters.
Miracles at the Birth of Christ.
Ninetieth Psalm, The.
Ninety-fifth.
O God, Our Help in Ages Past.
Our God, Our Help in Ages Past.
Our Saviour's Golden Rule.
Passion and Exaltation of Christ, The.
Praise for Mercies Spiritual and Temporal.
Shortness and Misery of Life, The.
Sincere Praise, Sels.
Sluggard, The.
Spare Us, O Lord, Aloud We Pray.
Submission to Afflictive Providences.
Sweet Muse, Descend.
There is a land of pure delight.
Through every age, eternal God.
When I Survey the Wondrous Cross.
Where Nothing Dwelt but Beasts of Prey.
Where-e'er My Flatt'ring Passions Rove.
Why Do We Mourn Departing Friends?
Watts, Marilyn
On the Serengeti.
Watts-Dunton, Theodore (1832–1914)
Coleridge.
Waugh, Alec (1898–1981)
From Albert to Bapaume.
Wavell, Archibald Percival Wavell, 1st Earl (1883–1950)
Sonnet for the Madonna of the Cherries.
Wayman, Tom (b. 1945)
Another Poem about the Madness of Women.
Chilean Elegies, The: 5. Interior, The.
Picketing Supermarkets.
Wayman in Love.
What Good Poems Are For.
Wayne, Jane O. (b. 1938)
Looking Both Ways.
Weare, Meshech (1713–86)
Blasted Herb, The.
Weatherly, Frederic Edward (1848–1929)
Holy City, The.
When the Christ Child Came.
Weatherly, Tom (b. 1942)
Arroyo.
Autobiography.
Barre Lizzy hates.
Blatherskite.
Blues for Franks Wooten.
Canto 7: First Thesis.
Cantos, Sels.
Cobalt.
Coon Fire.
First Monday Scottsboro Alabama.
First Thesis.
Gullfish.
Imperial Thumbprint.
Mud Water Shango.
Poetics.
Times.

Your Eyes Are Mirth.
Weaver, Helen
Almighty God, who are mother and father to us all.
O our Mother the Earth, blessed is our name.
Weaver, Michael S.
Beginnings.
Dogs, The.
Message on Cape Cod, The.
Missing Patriarch, The.
My Father's First Baseball Game.
My Father's Geography.
Webb, Charles
Dr. Invisible and Mr. Hide.
Webb, Charles Henry ("John Paul") (fl. c.1678)
At the Ball!
Autumn Leaves.
Webb, Francis (1925–73)
Airliner.
Dawn Wind on the Islands.
Day of the Statue, The.
Death at Winson Green, A.
Drum for Ben Boyd, A, Sels.
End of the Picnic.
For My Grandfather.
Gunner, The.
Leichhardt in Theatre, Sels.
Morgan's Country.
Nessun Dorma.
Sea, The.
This Runner.
Towards the Land of the Composer.
Vlamingh and Rottnest Island.
Ward Two.
Wild Honey.
Webb, Frederick G.
Dash for the Colors, The.
Webb, Harri (b. 1920)
Abbey Cwmhir.
Cywydd o Fawl.
Epil y Filiast.
Nightingales, The.
Stone Face, The.
Synopsis of the Great Welsh Novel.
Thanks in Winter.
Webb, Mary (1881–1927)
Foxgloves.
Green Rain.
Market Day.
Secret Joy, The.
Water-Ousel, The.
Webb, Phyllis (b. 1927)
Days of the Unicorns, The.
Imperfect Sestina.
Kropotkin Poems, The, Sels.
Poetics against the Angel of Death.
Propositions.
Spots of Blood.
Syllables disintegrate ingrate alphabets.
Time of Man, The.
To Friends Who Have Also Considered Suicide.
Webb, Tessa Sweazy (b. 1886)
Bright Abandon.
Webb, Thomas Henry Basil (b. 1935)
Ancient Prayer, An.
Webbe, Charles (fl. c.1678)
Against Indifference.
Weber, Mark
Hite Marina, Lake Powell.
Weber, Richard (b. 1932)
Elizabeth in Italy.
Envying the Pelican.
In Memoriam I, Elizabeth at Twenty.
Lady & Gentleman.
Poet's Day, The.
Primer for Schoolchildren, A.
Visit to Bridge House, A.
Webster, Augusta Davies ("Cecil Home") (1837–94)
Castaway, A, Sels.
Circe, Sels.
Medea in Athens, Sels.
Oh smooth adder/ who with fanged kisses changedst my natural blood.

Pine, The.
Sun drops luridly into the west, The.
Well, well, I know the wise ones talk and talk.

Webster, H. D. L.
Lorena.

Webster, John (c.1580–1638)
All the flowers of the spring.
Call for the Robin-Redbreast and the Wren.
Devil's Law Case, The, *Sels.*
Duchess of Malfi, The, *Sels.*
Hark, Now Everything Is Still.
I am come to make thy tomb.
Lady Jane Grey, *Sels.*
Madman's Song, The.
O that it were possible we might.
Thus like a nun, not like a princess born.
What, are you drop't?
What death?
What hideous noyse was that?
White Devil, The, *Sels.*
Yond's the Cardinall's window: This
   fortification.

**Webster, John (c.1580–1638) and William
   Rowley**
Art Thou Gone in Haste?
Love Is a Law.
Thracian Wonder, The, *Sels.*
Whither shall I go.

Webster, Mary Morison
Gallipoli.
Grass.
I Set Aside.
Illi Morituri.
Marriage of Pocahontas, The.
Ox, The.
Quiet of the Dead, The.
Secret, The.

Webster, W. J.
Prick a maiden nether holly.
To His Coy Mistress.

Weckherlin, Georg Rudolph (1584–1653)
Concerning the King of Sweden.
Love Is Life and Death.
She Is the Greatest Wealth.
To Breisach, Taken by That Supremely
   Celebrated Hero, Bernhard, Duke of Saxony.
To Germany.

Wedde, Ian (b. 1946)
And this is where.
Angel, *Sels.*
Beggar at the Gate, The.
By day and also by night and you are.
Diesel trucks past the Scrovegni chapel.
Earthly: Sonnets for Carlos, *Sels.*
Hardon ("Get One Today").
I imagine the womb as a honeycomb.
If thy wife is small bend down to her and.
King Solomon Vistas.
Losing the Straight Way, *Sels.*
Power Transformer.
That autumn day suddenly broken into.
Those Others.

Wedgefarth, W. Dayton
Bum.
Mother in gladness, Mother in sorrow.
Mother's Hands.

Weeden, Craig
Pizza Joint in Cranston, A.

Weeden, Lula Lowe (b. 1918)
Dance.
Have You Seen It.
Little Dandelion, The.
Me Alone.
Robin Red Breast.
Stream, The.

Weekes, Nathaniel (b. c.1730)
Barbados, *Sels.*
Virtues of the cane must now be sung, The.
When frequent rains, and gentle show'rs
   descend.

Weeks, James Eyre (b. 1719?)
On the Great Fog in London, December 1762.

Weeks, Robert Lewis
Appalachian Front.

Weelkes, Thomas (*fl.* c.1600)
Fara Diddle Dyno.
Gods Have Heard My Vows, The.
Madrigal: "Ay me, alas, heigh ho, heigh ho!"
Tan ta ra: cries Mars on bloody rampier.

Weever, John (1576–1632)
De Se.

Wegner, Bettina
Enemy, The.

Wei, Lady (*fl.* late 11th–12th cent.)
To the Tune "The Bodhisattva's Barbaric
   Headdress."

Wei Chuang (836–910)
"Deva-like Barbarian."
Lament of the Lady of Ch'in, The.
"Sand of Silk-washing Stream."
Spoken to Pines and Bamboos.

Weigel, James, Jr. (b. 1937)
Egg grew human, The.
I should quit this craft.
Mouth should launch words gracefully, A.
Out of my sleeves ten bones protrude.
Testaments, *Sels.*
Translated once.

Weigl, Bruce (b. 1949)
Anna's Grace.
Black Hose, The.
Confusion of Planes We Must Wander in Sleep,
   The.
Meditation at Pearl Street.
Snowy Egret.
They Name Heaven.
What Saves Us.

Weil, James L. (b. 1929)
At a Loss.

Weil, Simone (1909–43)
Random Thoughts on the Love of God, *Sels.*

Weiman, Andrew (b. 1956)
Andy-Diana DNA Letter.

Wein, Jules Alan
Genesis.

Weinberger, Florence
Dancing Dog, The.
Survivor.

Weinerman, Chester (d. 1991)
AIDS-Related Complex.

Weiners, John (b. 1934)
Poem for the Insane, A.

Weingarten, Roger (b. 1945)
Blue Bog Children.
Ethan Boldt.
Father Hunger and Son.
Four Seasons of His Discontent.
From the Temple of Longing.
Her Apron through the Trees.
Jungle Gliders.
These Obituaries of Rattlesnakes Being Eaten
   by the Hogs.

Weinstein, Berish. *See* **Vaynshteyn, Berysh.**

Weise, Christian (1642–1708)
Upon the Birth of a Young and Highly Desired
   Son.

Weiser, Conrad (1696–1760)
Jehovah, Lord and Majesty.

Weislitz, Vera
Roses and the Grave.

Weismiller, Edward (b. 1915)
To the Woman in Bond Street Station.

Weiss, Neil (b. 1914)
Word, The.

Weiss, Theodore (b. 1916)
Another and Another and.
As You Like It.
Barracks Apt. 14.
Clothes Maketh the Man.
Dab of Color, A.
Death of Fathers, The.
Egyptian Passage, An.
Everlasting Once, An.
Every Second Thought, *Sels.*
Fire at Alexandria, The.
Grey and dankish thing, A.
Last Day and the First, The.

Late Train, The.
Letter from the Pygmies, A.
Life of . . . , The.
Moral, The.
Off to Patagonia.
Pair of Shoes, A.
Preface: "Sonja Henie, the young girl."
Ten Little Rembrandts.
To Forget Me.
Ultimate Antientropy, The.
Web, The.
Yes, But . . . .

Weisslitz, E. F.
Baldpate Pond.

Wei Ying-wu (b. 736)
Crossing the Lang-yeh Mountain with a Friend.
In Imitation of T'ao P'eng-tse.
Longing in My Heart.
Moon is full, the autumn nights grow longer,
   The.
On Dewdrop.
On Sound.
"Song of Flirtatious Laughter."

Wei Yüan (1794–1857)
Ah-fu-jung, ah-fu-jung!
Plant the flower farms.
Song of Chiang-nan, *Sels.*

Welburn, Ron (b. 1944)
And universals/ are not that world.
Avoidances.
Black is beautiful.
Cecil County.
Condition Blue/ Dress.
Eulogy for Populations.
It is overdue time.
Lyrics shimmy like.
Put u red-eye in.
Tu/ cson's of blackmens/.
Whichway.

Welby, Amelia B. (1819–52)
Twilight at Sea.

Welch, Don
Poet in Residence at a Country School.
Spade Scharnweber.
We Used to Play.

Welch, James (b. 1940)
Across to the Peloponnese.
Arizona Highways.
Blue like Death.
Christmas Comes to Moccasin Flat.
Day after Chasing Porcupines.
Directions to the Nomad.
D-Y Bar.
Going to Remake This World.
Grandma's Man.
Harlem, Montana; Just Off the Reservation.
In My First Hard Springtime.
In My Lifetime.
Lady in a Distant Face.
Magic Fox.
Man from Washington, The.
Never Give a Bum an Even Break.
Only Bar in Dixon, The.
Plea to Those Who Matter.
Please Forward.
Renegade Wants Words, The.
Snow Country Weavers.
Surviving.
Thanksgiving at Snake Butte.
Verifying the Dead.
Visit.
Why I Didn't Go to Delphi.

Welch, Lew (b. 1920)
After Anacreon.
Basic Con, The.
Chicago Poem.
Few things that grow here poison us.
First you must love your body, in games.
Gentle Goddess.
I Saw Myself.
Image, As In a Hexagram, The.
Not Yet 40, My Beard is Already White.
Religion is Revelation.
Sausalito,/ Little Willow.
Song of the Turkey Buzzard.

Step out onto the Planet.
Taxi Suite, *Sels.*
Wobbly Rock.
Welch, Marie De L. (b. 1905)
Prelude to Commencement.
Welch, Myra Brooks
Touch of the Master's Hand, The.
Welch, Noel
Anne and the Peacock.
Weldon, Charles
Poem of the Universe, The.
Welish, Marjorie (b. 1944)
Careers.
Picture Collection.
Servant in Literature, The.
Street Cries.
Welles, Winifred (1893–1939)
Cruciform.
Dogs and Weather.
Man with a Little Pleated Piano, A.
Old Ellen Sullivan.
Starfish.
Stocking Fairy.
**Wellesley, Dorothy, Duchess of Wellington
(1891–1956)**
As Lambs into the Pen.
Asian Desert.
Camels in Persia.
Deserted House, *Sels.*
Epilogue: "He is not dead nor liveth."
Fire.
First Flight.
Fishing.
Horses.
Lenin, *Sels.*
Lighthouses.
Lost Lane.
Matrix, *Sels.*
Morning After, The.
So I came down the steps to Lenin.
Spiritual, the carnal, are one, The.
Wells, Amos Russel (1862–1935)
Ambitious Ant, The.
Considerate Crocodile, The.
Inn That Missed Its Chance, The.
Length of Life, The.
Mothers — and Others.
Wells, Anna Maria (1795–1868)
Cow-Boy's Song, The.
Little Maid, The.
Wells, Carolyn (1862–1942)
Alone.
Baker's Dozen of Wild Beasts, A, *Sels.*
Bath-Bunny, The.
Canner, Exceedingly Canny, A.
Corn-Pone-y, The.
Cream-Puffin, The.
Diversions of the Re-Echo Club.
Dresscessional, A.
Grandiloquent Goat, The.
How To Tell the Wild Animals.
Limerick: "There was a young person called
Tate."
Limerick: "Tutor who tooted a flute, A."
Marvel, A.
Mince-Python, The.
Overworked Elocutionist, An.
Oyster-Crabs.
Poster Girl, The.
Puzzled.
To a Baked Fish.
Universal Favorite, The.
Wells, Faith
More than We Ask.
Wells, H. G.
Limerick: "Mr. Wells of the big cerebellum."
Limerick: "Our novels get longa and longa."
Wells, Marcus Morris (1815–95)
Holy Spirit, Faithful Guide.
Wells, Nigel (b. 1944)
Dumps, The.
Easter with Horses.
Owl Wives.
Quince.

So Spring.
Up.
Wells, Robert (b. 1947)
After Haymaking.
At Licenza.
Attributes, The.
Axehandle, The.
Breakfast.
Colonist, The.
Derelict Landscape.
For Pasolini.
Further on Down.
Gran Sasso.
Hero, The.
His Thirst.
Knot, The.
Median Palace.
Shape of Air.
Vendemmia.
Wells, Rollin J. (b. 1848)
Growing Old [or Growing Older].
Welsh, Anne (b. 1922)
Between Seasons.
Many Birds.
Sharpeville Inquiry.
That Way.
Waterfall.
Welshimer, Helen
Dusk.
Welsted, Leonard (1688–1747)
Invitation, The.
Welt, Bernard (b. 1952)
Prose.
Welte, Lou Ann (b. 1923)
Those Last, Late Hours of Christmas Eve.
Welty, Eudora (b. 1909)
Flock of Guinea Hens Seen from a Car, A.
Wenberi
Wenberi's Song.
Wen Cheng-ming (1470–1559)
Chung-i Temple, The, *Sels.*
Improvised on Horseback to Say Good-bye to
Those Who Are Seeing Me Off, *Sels.*
Inscribed on a Painting: Cultivating Leisure,
Sels.
Lines Written on New Year's Day, *Sels.*
My Son's One-Year Test: Improvised, *Sels.*
What It's Like Living in My Studio Late in
Spring, *Sels.*
Wendt, Ingrid (b. 1944)
Newest Banana Plant Leaf, The.
Personal Poem.
Wen-Ti, Chien (6th cent.)
Winter Night.
Wen T'ing-shih (1856–1904)
I diligently concoct my elixir in a crucible of
Himalayan bamboo.
Miscellaneous Verses on Living in the
Mountains, *Sels.*
Out of the floodgate of stone, just closed, a
three-foot cataract.
Wen T'ing-yün (812–72)
Crossing South of Li-chou, A.
"Dreaming of the South."
Early Autumn in the Mountains.
Early Walk on Shang Mountain, An.
Fishing Trapping Song, A.
In the Mountains as Autumn Begins.
"Lotus-leaf Cup."
"Pacifying the Western Barbarians."
Passing a Ruined Palace.
"River Messages."
Song of Chang Ching-yüan Picking Lotus
Flowers, A.
Song of Distant Waters, A.
Song of Wildfire, A.
"Southern Song, A."
Spring Day in the Countryside, A.
"Telling of Innermost Feelings."
Wen Yi-tuo (1898–1946)
Confession, The.
Wentworth, William Charles (1790–1872)
Australasia, *Sels.*

Wenzig, Josef (1807–76)
Going to My Sweetheart.
Of Eternal Love.
Weöres, Sándor (b. 1913)
Lost Parasol, The, *Sels.*
Monkeyland.
Where metalled road invades light thinning air.
Werfel, Franz (1890–1945)
Eternal Road, The, *Sels.*
Exaltation.
For I Have Done a Good and Kindly Deed.
Litany of the Rooms of the Dead.
Loneliness.
Song of Life, A.
Strangers Are We All upon the Earth.
Teach Us to Mark This, God.
To a Lark in War-Time.
Ye Sorrowers.
Wergeland, Henrik Arnold Thaulov (1808–45)
Wall-Flower, The.
Werner, Martina (b. 1929)
Monogram 4.
Monogram 23.
Monogram 29.
Wertheimer, Paul (1874–1948)
Souls.
Wescott, Glenway (b. 1901)
Poet at Night-Fall, The.
Summer Ending, The.
Wesley, Cecil Cobb
As Night Comes On.
Wesley, Charles (1707–88)
Ah! Lovely Appearance of Death!
Come, Thou Almighty King.
During His Courtship.
Easter Hymn.
Father, How Wide Thy Glories Shine.
For His Wife, on Her Birthday.
Free Grace.
Gentle Jesus Meek and Mild.
He Shook off the Beast.
Horrible Decree, The, *Sels.*
Hymn: "O thou who camest from above."
Incarnation, The.
Jesus, Lover of My Soul.
Love Divine, All Loves Excelling.
Morning Hymn.
N T.
O Thou Eternal Victim Slain.
On Sympathisers with the American Revolution.
On the Death of His Son.
On Worldly Prelates.
Sinners, abhor the Fiend.
Whole Armour of God, The.
Wrestling Jacob.
Wesley, John (1703–91)
Hymn: "Thou hidden love of God, whose
height."
Wesley, Samuel (1691–1739)
Anacreontic, on Parting with a Little Child.
Epitaph: "Here lie I, once a witty fair."
Monument, The.
On the Setting Up of Mr. Butler's Monument
in Westminster Abbey.
Pindaric on the Grunting of a Hog, A.
West, Arthur Graeme
Night Patrol, The.
West, Colin
Crocodile Or Alligator?
West, Don (1909–54)
My South.
West, Gilbert (1703–1756)
Lives there on Earth to whom I am unknown.
Triumphs of the Gout, The, *Sels.*
West, Jane (1758–1852)
Married, poor soul! your empire's over.
To a Friend on her Marriage, *Sels.*
To the Hon. Mrs. C———e.
West, Jessamyn
Song of the Settlers.
West, Robert A. (1809–65)
Come, Let Us Tune Our Loftiest Song.

West, Victoria Mary Sackville. *See* Sackville-
West, Victoria Mary.
Westcott, G. C.
Gobbolino, the Witch's Cat.
Western, Daniel
Sacred Songs IV.
Westmorland, Mildmay Fane, 2d Earl of
(1602–65)
Dedication of My First Son, A.
Happy Life, A.
How to Ride Out a Storm.
In Obitum Ben. Jons.
In Praise of Fidelia.
Man Leavens the Batch.
My Carol.
My Close-Committee.
My Country Audit.
My Observation at Sea.
Occasioned by Seeing a Walk of Bay Trees.
Reveille Matin, or Good Morrow to a Friend.
Shamed by the Creature.
To Kiss God's Rod; Occasioned upon a Child's
Sickness.
To Retiredness.
Upon the Times.
Weston, Mildred (b. 1900)
Bleat of Protest.
Cider Song.
Echo.
Hat Bar.
To a Lady Holding the Floor.
Westrup, J. M. (1904–75)
Best of All.
Flying.
Furry Home, The.
Growing Rhyme, A.
My Little House.
Poor Snail, The.
Vision Clear, The.
Westwood, Thomas (1814–88)
Little Bell.
Mine Host of "The Golden Apple."
Motionless sat the shadow at the helm.
Night of Spring.
Quest of the Sancgreall, The, *Sels.*
Wetea *and* Tu-kehu. *See* Tu-kehu.
Wever, Robert (*fl.* c.1550)
In a herber [*or* a harbour *or* an arbour] green
[*or* grene], asleep [*or* aslepe] whereas [*or*
where as *or* where] I lay.
Lusty Juventus, *Sels.*
Wevill, David (b. 1935)
Birth of a Shark, The.
Body of a Rook.
In Love.
Irish Hotel.
Monsoon.
Snow.
Spiders.
Wexionius, Olof (1656–1690?)
On the Death of a Pious Lady.
Wexler, Irving (b. 1918)
Elegy for My Father, *Sels.*
Weyburn, Ruby. *See* Tobias, Ruby Weyburn.
Whalen, Philip (b. 1923)
Denunciation; or, Unfrock'd Again.
Dim View of Berkeley in the Spring, A.
For C.
For Kai Snyder.
Further Notice.
Life in the City: In Memoriam Edward Gibbon.
Literary Life in the Golden West.
Martyrdom of Two Pagans.
Plus Ça Change . . .
Same Old Jazz, The.
Sourdough Mountain Lookout.
Take I, 4:11:58.
Technicalities for Jack Spicer.
10:X:57, 45 Years Since the Fall of the Ch'ing
Dynasty.
To the Muse.
25:I:68.
2 Variations: All About Love.
Where or When.

Whalley, George (b. 1915)
Affair of Honour.
Wharton, Anne (1659–1685)
Elegy on the Earl of Rochester.
Penelope this slow Epistle sends.
Penelope to Ulysses, *Sels.*
Wit's Abuse.
Wharton, Thomas Wharton, 1st Marquess of
(1648–1715)
Lilli Burlero [*or* Lilliburlero].
Wharton, William H. (b. 1925)
Ben Milam.
Whateley, Mary (1738–1825)
Ode to Truth.
On the Author's Husband Desiring Her to Write
Some Verses.
Power of Destiny, The.
Vanity of External Accomplishments, The.
Whately, Richard, Archbishop (1787–1863)
There Is a Place in Distant Seas.
Wheatley, John (d. 1830)
Cape of Storms, The.
Wheatley, Phillis (c.1753–1784)
Hymn to the Evening, An.
Hymn to the Morning, An.
Liberty and Peace, *Sels.*
Lo! Freedom comes. Th' prescient Muse
foretold.
No more, America, in mournful strain.
On Being Brought from Africa to America.
On Imagination.
On the Death of the Rev. Mr. George
Whitefield.
On Virtue.
Should You, My Lord.
Thoughts on the Works of Providence.
To a Gentleman and Lady on the Death of the
Lady's Brother and Sister, and a Child of the
Name Avis, Aged One Year.
To a Lady on the Death of Her Husband.
To His Excellency, General Washington.
To S.M., a Young African Painter, on Seeing
His Works.
To the King's Most Excellent Majesty.
To the Right Honourable William, Earl of
Dartmouth, *Sels.*
To the University of Cambridge, in New-
England.
Wheeler, Charles Enoch (b. 1909)
Adjuration.
Tumult.
Wheeler, Ruth Winant
Prayer for Shut-Ins.
Wheeler, Susan (b. 1955)
Lasting Influence.
Wheelock, C. Webster (b. 1939)
Divorcee.
Wheelock, John Hall (1886–1978)
Afternoon: Amagansett Beach.
Amagansett Beach Revisited.
Beethoven.
Black Panther, The.
Dear Men and Women.
Divine Insect, The.
Earth ("Grasshopper, your fairy song").
Earth ("Planet doesn't explode, A").
Elegy: "Gnu up at the zoo, The."
Exile from God.
Far Land, The.
Gardener, The.
Hippopotamothalamion.
Holy Poet, I have heard.
House in the Green Well, The.
Love and Liberation.
Night Thoughts in Age.
Nirvana.
Random Reflections on a Summer Evening.
Silence.
Slow Summer Twilight.
Sunday Evening in the Common.
Thanks from Earth to Heaven, *Sels.*
This Quiet Dust.
Triumph of Love.
Wheelock, Lucy (1859–1946)
Song of the Lilies, The.

Wheelwright, John (1897–1940)
Abel.
Bread-Word Giver.
Canal Street.
Father.
Fish Food.
Forty Days, *Sels.*
Live, Evil Veil.
Second Ascension of Christ, The.
There Is No Opera like "Lohengrin."
Train Ride.
Why Must You Know?
Whetstone, George (1544?–1587)
Give Me My Work.
Whinery, Verna
This Day is Thine.
Whisenand, Emma Bridge
Open Your Eyes.
Whistler, Laurence (b. 1912)
Form of Epitaph, A.
Portrait in the Guards, A.
Whitaker, Robert (1863–1944)
Out-of-Doors.
Worship.
Whitbread, Thomas (b. 1931)
CCC, The ("CCC campers near West
Cummington").
Pool, A.
To My Fellow-Mariners, March, '53.
White, Adeline
Autumn Morning.
Christmas Party, The.
Colour.
Over the Fields.
White, Edward Lucas (1865–1934)
Genius.
White, Elwyn Brooks (1899–1985)
Classic Waits for Me, A.
Commuter.
Critic.
Definitions, *Sels.*
Fashions in Dogs.
I Paint What I See.
Listener's Guide to the Birds, A.
Marble-Top.
Natural History.
Red Cow Is Dead, The.
Song of the Queen Bee.
Window Ledge in the Atom Age.
White, Gilbert (1720–93)
Naturalist's Summer-Evening Walk, The.
On the Dark, Still, Dry, Warm Weather
Occasionally Happening in the Winter
Months.
White, Henry Kirke (1785–1806)
Clifton Grove, *Sels.*
Lo! in the West, fast fades the ling'ring light.
Man's Littleness in Presence of the Stars.
To an Early Primrose.
White, J. P. (b. 1940)
In Ecclesiastes I Read.
White, James L. (1936–81)
Making Love to Myself.
White, John (b. 1958)
Softly.
White, Joseph Blanco (1775–1841)
Black Is a Soul.
To Night.
White, Paulette C.
Nina Simone.
White, Richard Edward (b. 1944)
Discovery of San Francisco Bay.
White, Terence Hanbury (1906–64)
To Myself, after Forty Years.
Witch's Work Song, The.
White, William Allen (1868–1944)
Rhyme of the Dream-Maker Man, A.
White-arm
Child listen/ I am singing.
Whitecotton, Moses
Fuller and Warren.
Whitehead, Charles (1804–62)
Lamp, The.

I Sit and Look Out.
I swear the earth shall surely be complete to him or.
I think I could turn and live awhile with animals.
I understand the large hearts of heroes.
In Paths Untrodden.
In the swamp in secluded recesses.
Joy, Shipmate, Joy!
Justified Mother of Men, The.
Last Invocation, The.
Little one sleeps in its cradle, The.
Long I Thought That Knowledge Alone Would Suffice.
Long, Too Long America.
Mannahatta.
Man's body at auction, A.
March in the Ranks Hard-Prest, and the Road Unknown, A.
Me Imperturbe.
Memories of President Lincoln, Sels.
Miracles.
Muse in the New World, The.
My Picture-Gallery.
My 71st Year.
My signs are a rain-proof coat, good shoes, a staff cut from the woods.
Native Moments.
Night on the Prairies.
Noiseless Patient Spider, A.
Now I will do nothing but listen.
O Captain! My Captain!
O Hymen! O Hymenee!
O Living Always, Always Dying.
O my body! I dare not desert the likes of you in other men and women, nor the likes of the parts of you.
Old Ireland.
Old War-Dreams.
On the Beach at Night.
On the Beach at Night Alone.
Once I Pass'd through a Populous City.
One's-Self I Sing.
Orange Buds by Mail from Florida.
Osceola.
Out of the Cradle Endlessly Rocking.
Oxen that rattle the yoke and chain or halt in the leafy shade.
Ox-Tamer, The.
Passage to India.
Passage to India, Sels.
Patrolling Barnegat.
Pensive, on Her Dead Gazing, I Heard the Mother of All.
Pioneers! O Pioneers!
Place Where a Great City Stands, The.
Poet, The.
Poets to Come.
Prayer of Columbus, Sels.
Pure contralto sings in the organloft, The.
Reconciliation.
Recorders Ages Hence.
Respondez!
Rounded Catalogue Divine Complete, The.
Runaway Slave, The.
Runner, The.
Scented Herbage of My Breast.
Shut Not Your Doors.
Sight in Camp [in the Daybreak Gray and Dim], A.
Singer in the Prison, The.
Sleepers, The.
Sometimes with One I Love.
Song for All Seas, All Ships.
Song for Occupations, A, Sels.
Song of Myself, Sels.
Song of the Broad-Ax [or Broad-Axe], Sels.
Song of the Exposition, Sels.
Song of the Open Road, Sels.
Song of the Redwood-Tree.
Sparkles from the Wheel.
Spirit Whose Work Is Done.
Spontaneous Me.
Spotted hawk swoops by and accuses me, The.
Swiftly Arose.
Thanks in Old Age.

There Was a Child Went Forth.
There Was a Child Went Forth, Sels.
This Compost.
This is the female form.
Thou knowest my years entire, my life.
To a Common Prostitute.
To a Locomotive in Winter.
To a President.
To a Stranger.
To Him That Was Crucified.
To Old Age.
To Soar in Freedom and in Fullness of Power.
To the Garden the World.
To the Man-of-War-Bird.
To the Pending Year.
To the States.
To Think of Time.
Torch, The.
Trickle Drops.
Trippers and askers surround me.
Twenty-eight young men bathe by the shore.
Unseen Buds.
Untold Want, The.
Vigil Strange I Kept on the Field One Night.
Wallabout Martyrs, The.
Walt Whitman.
Walt Whitman, a kosmos, of Manhattan the son.
Warble for Lilac Time.
We are nature, long have we been absent, but now we return.
We Two Boys Together Clinging.
When I Heard at the Close of the Day.
When I Heard the Learn'd Astronomer.
When I Peruse the Conquer'd Fame.
When I Read the Book.
When Lilacs Last in the Dooryard Bloom'd.
Whispers of Heavenly Death.
Who goes there? hankering, gross, mystical, nude.
Whoever You Are Holding Me Now in Hand.
Will you seek afar off? you surely come back at last.
With music strong I come, with my cornets and my drums.
Woman Waits for Me, A.
Words of the True Poems, The.
World below the Brine, The.
Would You Hear of an Old-Time [or Old-Fashioned] Sea fight?
Wound-Dresser, The.
Wounded Person, The.
Yonnondio.

Whitmell, Lucy
Christ in Flanders.

Whitney, Adeline D. T. (1824–1906)
Peace.

Whitney, Anna Temple
Kneeling Camel, The.

Whitney, Geffrey (1548?–1601?)
Content.

Whitney, Isabella (fl. c.1567–c.1573)
Do not account that for thine own.
Gold savours well, though it be got.
In loving, each one hath free choice.
Little gold in law will make, A.
Manner of Her Will and What She Left to London and to All Those in It, at Her Departing, The, Sels.
Present day we cannot spend, The.
Seek not man to please, for that.
Such poor folk as to law do go.
Sweet Nosegay, A, or Pleasant Posy, Sels.

Whittaker, Frederick (d. 1963)
Custer's Last Charge.

Whittemore, Elizabeth
My Friends Are Little Lamps to Me.

Whittemore, Reed (b. 1919)
Abbreviated Interviews with a Few Disgruntled Literary Celebrities.
Black Cross.
Clamming.
Day with the Foreign Legion, A.
Departure, The.
Destruction of Washington, The.

Losses, The.
Only the Dead.
Party, The.
Projection, A.
Radio under the Bed, The.
Recall.
Still Life.
Storm from the East, A.
Tarantula, The.
Thinking of Tents.
White Cross.

Whittier, John Greenleaf (1807–92)
Abraham Davenport.
Adjustment.
All souls that struggle and aspire.
All's Well.
Among the Hills, Sels.
Amy Wentworth.
And Thou, O Lord! by whom are seen.
Andrew Rykman's Prayer, Sels.
Angel of Patience, The.
Angels of Buena Vista, The.
Astraea at the Capitol.
At Last.
At Port Royal, Sels.
Barbara Frietchie.
Barefoot Boy, The, Sels.
Bartholdi Statue, The.
Battle Autumn of 1862, The.
Blessings on thee, little man.
Book Our Mothers Read, The.
Brewing of Soma, The, Sels.
Brown of Ossawatomie.
Burial of Barber.
Cable Hymn, The.
Call of the Christian, The.
Cassandra Southwick.
Centennial Hymn.
Chicago.
Cities of the Plain, The.
Clerical Oppressors.
Conductor Bradley.
Corn-Song, The.
Crisis, The.
Dead Feast of the Kol-Folk, The.
Dear Lord and Father of Mankind.
Dedication: "I would the gift I offer here."
Eternal Goodness, The, Sels.
Ezekiel.
Farewell: "Gone, gone — sold and gone."
First-Day Thoughts.
For an Autumn Festival, Sels.
For Righteousness' Sake.
Forgiveness.
Godspeed.
Harvest Hymn.
Haschish, The.
Help.
Henchman, The.
Hunters of Men, The.
Hymn from the French of Lamartine, Sels.
I know not what the future hath.
Ichabod.
Immortal Love, Forever Full.
In Earthen Vessels.
In School-Days.
Inscription: "Eagle, stooping from yon snow-blown peaks, The."
John Underhill.
Kallundborg Church.
Kansas Emigrants, The.
King Solomon and the Ants.
King's Missive, The.
Laus Deo!
Le Marais du Cygne.
Lexington.
Life and Love.
Lost Occasion, The.
Make my mortal dreams come true.
Maud Muller.
Maud Muller, Sels.
Miriam, Sels.
Mother.
My Playmate.
My Triumph.
My Trust, Sels.

Philadelphia: 1978.
Shame.
Spit.
Tar.
Then the Brother of the Wind.
They Warned Him Then They Threw Him
   Away.
World's Greatest Tricycle Rider, The.

Williams, Daniel (1927–72)
We Are the Cenotaphs.

Williams, Edward (Iolo Morganwg) (1747–
1826)
Happy Farmer, The, *Sels.*
I live on my farm in a beautiful vale.
Poet's Arbour in the Birchwood, The.
Stanzas Written in London in 1773, *Sels.*
Why, Cambria did I quit thy shore.

Williams, Edward W. (1863–91)
At Harper's Ferry Just Before the Attack.

Williams, Eliseus (1867–1926)
Heather Flowers.

Williams, Emmett (b. 1925)
Like Attracts Like.

Williams, Evan Gwyn (b. 1938)
Day Trip.

Williams, Evelyn M. (d. 1959)
Chestnut Buds.

Williams, Frederick (b. 1947)
Eighties, De.

Williams, George. *See Awoonor, Kofi.*

Williams, Gwyn (b. 1904)
Aspects of Now, *Sels.*
City Under Snow.
Pelagius.
Saint Ursula of Llangwyryfon.
Today has it all, sunshine.
Wild Night at Treweithan.

Williams, Helen Maria (1761?–1827)
Elegy on a Young Thrush Which Escaped from
   the Writer's Hand.
On the Death of the Rev. Dr. Kippis.
Song, A.
Sonnet on Reading the Poem upon the
   Mountain Daisy, by Mr. Burns.
Sonnet to Hope.
To Dr. Moore, in Anser to a Poetical Epistle
   Written by Him in Wales.
To Mrs. K ——, On Her Sending Me an
   English Christmas Plum-Cake at Paris.
To the Curlew.

Williams, Herbert (b. 1932)
Like Father.
Old Tongue, The.

Williams, Hugo (b. 1947)
Aborigine.
Broken Dreams.
Butcher, The.
Calling Your Name in the Zoo, *Sels.*
Elaine.
Girl.
Gladys.
Kirsten.
Love-Life.
Noelle.
Some Kisses from *The Kama Sutra.*
Sure.
Them.
Toilet.
Tracy & Co.

Williams, John (1664–1729)
Some Contemplations of the Poor, and Desolate
   State of the Church at Deerfield.

Williams, John (1761–1818)
Matrimony.
On Reading Aloud My Early Poems.

Williams, John Hartley (b. 1942)
Ephraim Destiny's Perfectly Utter Darkness,
   Sels.
I scalped a lie.

Williams, John Lloyd (d. 1945)
Naming of Private Parts.

Williams, John Stuart (b. 1920)
In Duffryn Woods.
River Walk.

Williams, Jonathan (b. 1929)
Adhesive Autopsy of Walt Whitman, The.
A.L.B. (1917–1978).
Anthropophagites See a Sign on NC Highway
   177 That Looks like Heaven, The.
Bitch-Kitty, The.
Distances to the Friend, The.
Farmer Beresford, on Nobility in Langstrothdale
   Chase.
Fast Ball.
Fourteen-Year-Old Samuel Palmer's Watercolor
   Notations for the Sketch "A Lane at Thanet,"
   The.
Hermit Cackleberry Brown, on Human Vanity,
   The.
Honey Lamb, The.
Little Tumescence, A.
Mahler, *Sels.*
Mrs. Sadie Grindstaff, Weaver and Factotum.
Ovid, Meet a Metamorphodite.
Ride in a Blue Chevy from Alum Cave Trail to
   Newfound Gap, A.
Shepherd.
Switch Blade, The; or, John's Other Wife.
Symphony No. 3, in D Minor.
Those Troublesome Disguises.
Three Sayings from Highlands, North Carolina.
Uncle Iv Surveys His Domain from His
   Rocker.
Vulnerary, A.

Williams, Kim (1924?–1986)
Requiem for a River.

Williams, Lucy (b. 1893)
Origin of the Skagit Indians, The.

Williams, Max
Empty House, The.

Williams, Miller (b. 1930)
After the Revolution for Jesus the Associate
   Professor [*or* a Secular Man] Prepares His
   Final Remarks.
Aging Actress Sees Herself a Starlet on the
   Late Show, The.
Caterpillar, The.
Firebreathers at the Café Deux Magots, The.
For Victor Jara.
Love and How It Becomes Important in Our
   Day to Day Lives.
Love Poem: "Six o'clock and/ the sun
   rises . . . ."
On a Photograph of My Mother at Seventeen.
On the Symbolic Consideration of Hands and
   the Significance of Death.
Poem for Emily, A.
Rubaiyat for Sue Ella Tucker.
Ruby Tells All.
Thinking about Bill, Dead of AIDS.
Why God Permits Evil: For Answers to This
   Question of Interest to Many Write Bible
   Answers Dept. E-7.
Wiedersehen.

Williams, Oscar (b. 1900)
Borrower of Salt, The.
By Fiat of Adoration.
Dwarf of Disintegration.
Golden Fleece, The.
I Sing an Old Song.
Jeremiad.
Last Supper, The.
Leg in the Subway, The.
Man Coming toward You, The.
Milk at the Bottom of the Sea.
Mirage, The.
On the Death of an Acquaintance.
Picture Postcard of a Zoo.
Praying Mantis Visits a Penthouse, The ("The
   praying mantis with its length of straw").
Seesaw, The.
Shopping for Meat in Winter.
Spring.
Spritely Dead, The.
Variations on a Theme, *Sels.*

Williams, Patrick (b. 1950)
Baby in the House, A.
In the Dark.
Lost Seed.
Passing Through.

Rhapsody on Main Street.
Trails.

Williams, Peter (b. 1937)
When She Was Here, Li Bo.

Williams, Rhydwen (b. 1916)
Baboon, The.

Williams, Robert (1830–77)
On a Woman.

Williams, Roger (c.1603–1683)
Adulteries, murthers, robberies, thefts.
Boast not proud English, of thy birth and
   blood.
Course bread and water's most their fare.
Courteous pagan shall condemn[e], The.
God gives them sleep on ground, on straw.
God Makes a Path.
How busie are the sonnes of men?
I have heard ingenuous Indians say.
If Birds That neither Sow nor Reap.
Indians count of men as dogs, The.
Indians prize not English gold, The.
Mans restlese soule hath restlesse eyes and
   ears.
One step twix't me and death, (twas Davids
   speech).
Our English gamesters scorne to stake.
Pagans wild confesse the bonds, The.
They see Gods wonders that are call'd.
Truth is a native, naked beauty; but.
What Habacuck once spake, mine eyes.
When Sun Doth Rise.

Williams, Sarah (1837–68)
Deep Sea Soundings.
Is It True?
Old Astronomer to His Pupil, The.

Williams, Sherley Anne (b. 1944)
Any Woman's Blues.
Driving Wheel.
Empress Brand Trim, The: Ruby Reminisces.
House of Desire, The.
I never thought to see us.
I Sing This Song for Our Mothers: Ruise.
1 Poem 2 Voices A Song.
Peacock Poems, The, *Sels.*
Say Hello to John.

Williams, Shirley
If He Let Us Go Now.
Killing of the Birds, The.

Williams, Taliesin (1787–1847)
Cardiff Castle, *Sels.*
Tourist, as he views the place, The.

Williams, Tennessee (1914–83)
Carrousel Tune.
Crepe de Chine.
Gold Tooth Blues.
Kitchen Door Blues.
Life Story.
My Love Was Light.
Sugar in the Cane.
You and I.

Williams, Theodore Chickering (1855–1915)
Hast Thou Heard It, O My Brother.
My Country, to Thy Shore.
When Thy Heart with Joy O'erflowing.

Williams, Trevor (b. 1921)
Girl I Took to the Cocktail Party, The.

Williams, Waldo (1904–72)
Daffodil.
In Two Fields.
Summer Cloud, A.

Williams, William ("Pantycelyn") (1717–91)
Guide Me, O Thou Great Jehovah.
Hymn: "Now the shadow flee and vanish."
Hymn: "What is the world, and what is life."
I Gaze across the Distant Hills.
Marriage in Eden, A.
View of Christ's Kingdom, A, *Sels.*

Williams, William Carlos (1883–1963)
Act, The.
Apology.
Approach to a City.
Approaching death.
Après le Bain.
Arrival.

Z

"Z., Z."
Here lies a poet — where's the great surprise!

Zabel, Morton Dauwen (b. 1901)
Journal to Stella.

Zable, Jeffrey A. Z.
To the End.

Zabolotsky, Nikolai Alekseevich (1903–58)
Face of the Horse, The.
Thistle.
Walk, A.

Zach, Natan (b. 1930)
Against Parting.
Be Attentive.
Be Careful.
Greater Courage.
King Solomon's Camel.

Zaidi, Mustafa (1930–70)
Life!/ I came to your door like a beggar.
Lights were drowned in fog, The.
Renewal, *Sels.*

Zaimof, Gueni (b. 1922)
Star Obscure, The.

Zamora, Daisy (b. 1959)
Song of Hope.
When We Go Home Again.

Zangwill, Israel (1864–1926)
At the Worst, *Sels.*
At the Zoo.
Death's Transfiguration.
Despair and Hope.
Dreams.
Evolution.
In the City.
In the Morgue.
Inexhaustible.
Israel.
Jehovah.
Might Is Right.
Moses and Jesus.
Oliver Singing.
Seder-Night.
Sundered.
Tabernacle Thought, A.
Theodor Herzl.
To a Pretty Girl.
Vanitas Vanitatum.
Vision.
Why Do We Live?
Yom Kippur.

Zaranka, William
Conceit upon the Feet.
Continuation of *The Cook's Tale*, The.
Cropdusting, The.
Cry of the Child, The.
High-toned Old Fascist Gentleman, A.
In the Ladies' Room at the Bus Terminal.
Lovers' Debouchment.
Memories of Aunt Maria-Martha.
Ode: "Mistah Berrybones, you daid?"
Parachuting Thoor Ballylee.
Peruke of Poets.
Quicksands.
Ragout.
Robert Frost's Left-leaning *Trespassers Will Be Shot* Sign.

Zarathustra. *See* **Zoroaster.**

Zarco, Cyn (b. 1950)
Air.
Cocktails.
Emergency Poem 1973.
Flipochinos.
In Memory of Forgetting.
Nights.
Poem in Nueva York.
Saxophonetyx.

What the Rooster Does before Mounting.

Zaret, Hy
It Could Be a Wonderful World.

Zarin, Cynthia (b. 1959)
Near and Dear, The.
Pears Soap.
Swordfish Tooth, The.

Zaturenska, Marya Alexandrovna (Mrs. Horace Gregory) (1902–82)
Bird and the Muse.
Daisy, The.
Descent of the Vulture, The.
Head of Medusa.
Lovers, The.
Tempest, The.
Variations on a Theme by George Herbert.
White Dress, The.
Woman at the Piano.

Zavatsky, Bill (b. 1943)
Bald.
Elegy: "Music your hands are no longer here to make."
Ex-Poet, The.
Testament.
To the Pianist Bill Evans.

Zeb-un-Nissa, Princess (1638–1702)
Though I am Laila of the Persian romance.

Zeidner, Lisa (b. 1955)
Still.

Zeigler, L. L.
Misconceptions.
Snack, The.

Zeitlin, Aaron (1899–1974)
Dream about an Aged Humorist, A.

"Zelda" (Zelda Schneurson) (b. 1914)
Wicked Neighbor, The.

Zeldis, Chayyim (b. 1927)
Holy Ones, the Young Ones, The.

Zelk, Zoltán (b. 1906)
Petrified Minute.
Salt and Memory.

Zengetsu (833–912)
Twenty-four Poems of Living in the Mountains, *Sels.*

Zenodotus (b. c.325 B.C.)
Statue of Eros, A.

Zepeda, Rafael
Burrito.
Cowboys and Indians.
Wreckers, The.

Zerbe, Evelyn Arcad
In Memory of My Arab Grandmother.

Zesen, Philipp von (1619–89)
Evening Song.
To the Superhuman Adelmund, When She Would Undo the Kiss Already Done.

Zhang, Zhimin
Between Battles.

Zierlin, Israel. *See* **Tiempo, César.**

Zieroth, Dale (b. 1946)
Baptism.
Beautiful Woman.
Hunters of the Deer, The.

Ziety, Ann
O.K.

Zimmer, Paul (b. 1934)
Apple Blight.
Day Zimmer Lost Religion, The.
Duke Ellington Dream, The.
Eisenhower Years, The.
Great Bird of Love [over the Kingdoms], The.
Julian Barely Misses Zimmer's Brains.
Lord Fluting Dreams of America on the Eve of His Departure from Liverpool.
Phineas Within and Without.
Rollo's Miracle.

Visit from Alphonse, A.
What Zimmer Would Be.
Zimmer and His Turtle Sink the House.
Zimmer Drunk and Alone, Dreaming of Old Football Games.
Zimmer Imagines Heaven.
Zimmer in Grade School.
Zimmer's Head Thudding against the Blackboard.
Zimmer's Last Gig.
Zimmershire Lad, A.

Zimunya, Musaemura Bonus
After the Massacre.
Arrivants.
Kisimiso.
White Poetess.

Zinnes, Harriet
Wounds.

Zinzendorf, Nikolaus [or Nicolaus] Ludwig, Graf von (1700–1760)
For Us No Night Can Be Happier.
Jesu, to Thee My Heart I Bow.
On Earth There Is a Lamb So Small.
Slain Lamb of God.

Zivančević, Nina
Duende.
Florence.
Kindergarten Curse.
Poem with a Tilde in the Title, A.

Zolotow, Charlotte (b. 1915)
Riddle: "Once when I was very scared."

Zolynas, Al (b. 1945)
Man Who Had Singing Fits, The.

Zonas (*fl.* 90 B.C.)
Make my cup with clay.
Pass me the sweet earthenware jug.

Zoroaster (*fl.* 7th century B.C.)
Sacred Book, The.

"Zozimus." *See* **Moran, Michael.**

Zuccalmaglio, Anton Wilhelm Florentin von (1803–69)
Serenade in Vain, A.

Zucker, David
Entrance to the Old Cracow Ghetto.

Zuckmayer, Carl (b. 1896)
My Death.

Zukofsky, Louis (1904–78)
"A" (1–12), *Sels.*
"A 4" ("Giant sparkler,/ Lights of the river.")
"A 11" ("River that must turn full after I stop dying").
Blue light is the night harbor-slip.
Cars Once Steel and Green, Now Old.
1892-1941.
For you I have emptied the meaning.
Green Leaf that will outlast the winter.
I walk in the old street.
In Arizona.
It's hard to see but think of a sea.
Like Grandpa Paul/ The water is all of my mind.
Lines of this new song are nothing, The.
Non Ti Fidar.
Not much more than being.
Of Dying Beauty.
29 Poems, *Sels.*
Ways, The.

Zuma, Nongejeni (1870–1942)
Praises of Field-marshal J. C. Smuts, The.

Zweig, Stefan (1881–1942)
Chosen of God.
Flowering Without End.
Jeremiah, *Sels.*

Zwicky, Fay (b. 1933)
Bat.
Dreams.
Reckoning.
Summer Pogrom.
To a Sea-Horse.

SUBJECT INDEX

Entries in the Subject Index contain one or more of the following types of information: first, poems are listed that fall within the particular subject category (for example, **Ghosts***); second, in many cases anthologies are listed that in whole or in part focus on the subject in question; third, anthologies that are mainly translations into English are listed under their appropriate countries or languages; fourth, there may be cross-references to related subjects.*

The categories here range from specific (for example, persons) to general (for example, abstractions such as **Loneliness***). Some categories, such as* **Love** *are so broad that we have used them only to list anthologies.*

A

Aaron
Aaron. Herbert

Abandonment
Abandoned, The. Alterman
Airly Beacon. Kingsley
Cooking Eggs. Smith
Crossing Over. Martinez
Cumnor Hall. Mickle
Death of the Kapowsin Tavern. Hugo
Frozen Boy, The. Aldiss
Havana Blues. Carlile
House on 15th S.W., The. Hugo
I Dreamt You Went. Freistadt
John Kinsella's Lament for Mrs. Mary
  Moore. Yeats
Lady of Miracles. Cassian
Montana Ranch Abandoned. Hugo
Mother Doorstep. Daley
Only When My Heart Freezes. Nowlan
Out of her womb of pain my mother spat
  me. Lorde
Presences. Justice
Rubaiyat for Sue Ella Tucker. Williams
Speaking of Loss. Clifton
Valley Blood. Sternlieb

Abbey Theatre, Dublin
At The Abbey Theatre (Imitated from
  Ronsard). Yeats
Old Woman, Outside the Abbey Theater,
  An. Strong

Abbeys. *See* **Monasteries.**

Abel. *See* **Cain and Abel.**

Abelard and Heloise
Eloisa to Abelard. Pope
Sic et Non. Read

Aberdeen, Scotland
To Aberdein. Dunbar

Abishag
Abishag. Kaufman
Abishag. Spire

Abolitionists
Abolitionist Hymn, The. *Unknown*
At Harper's Ferry Just Before the
  Attack. Williams
Douglass. Dunbar
Runagate Runagate. Hayden
To W. L. G. on Reading His "Chosen
  Queen." Forten

Aborigines
Aborigine. Williams
Bora Ring. Wright
Lament for the Drowned Country. Durack
We Are Going. Walker

Abortion
Abortion. Ai
Abortion, The. Sexton

Blackout Sonnets. Larkin
Brass Furnace Going Out: Song, after an
  Abortion. Di Prima
Cold Front, A. Williams
Epitaph on a Child Killed by Procured
  Abortion. *Unknown*
Inquest, The. Davies
Lost Baby Poem, The. Clifton
Moral Tale, A. Woddis
Mother, The. Brooks
Sabbath of Mutual Respect, The. Piercy
Ten Years Ago. Moeller
Today snow sparks the air like mica — the
  sun's. Gibson

Abraham
Abraham. Muir
Abraham. Schwartz
Abraham and Isaac. Lasker-Schüler
Abraham to kill him. Dickinson
Abraham's Madness. Noll
Abraham's Sacrifice of Isaac. Stradling
Faith. Smart
Harlot's Catch. Nichols
In wings and starched. Bloch
Parable of the Old Man and the Young,
  The. Owen
Patriarch in black takes, The. Bloch

Absalom
Dispraise of Absalom, The. *Unknown*

Absence
Absence. Gautier
Absence. *At.* to Hoskyns
Absence. Jago
Absence. Knies
Absence. McKay
Absence. Mew
Absence, The. Warner
Alone. De la Mare
Ballade: "Tell me where, in what country,
  where." Villon
Banks of Claudy, The. *Unknown*
By Faith Not Sight. McHugh
Can You Imagine. Miedzyrzecki
"Coming" is an empty word, "going" leaves no
  trace. Li Shang-yin
Coming was an empty promise, you have gone,
  and left no footprint. Li Shang-yin
Curtains. Stone
Daisy, The. Tennyson
Day writhes in an immense crater, The. James
Deepening shadows bring on sorrow,
  The. Hsü Kan
Drifting clouds, distant and vast, The. Hsü
  Kan
Elegy for a Five Year Old. Mathews
Elinda's [*or* Ellinda's] Glove. Lovelace
Ellen Taylor. *Unknown*
Filling the Gap. Inada

For Anne. Cohen
Found and Lost. Long
From the Temple of Longing. Weingarten
Girl I Left behind Me, The. *Unknown*
Good ladies, ye [or you] that have your
  pleasure in exile. Surrey
Green is the grass on riverbanks. *Unknown*
Here Today Here Tomorrow. Chaloner
Horse on the Wall. Southwick
Hours Ago, 1973. McCarthy
Humiliation in Its Disguises. Crozier
Hush. St. John
I Live Not Where I Love. *Unknown*
I ne have joy, pleasauns, nor
  comfort. *Unknown*
Ideal, The. Botta
If care do cause men cry, why do not I
  complain. Surrey
If I Had but Two Little Wings. Coleridge
In Imitation of Ancient Songs. Li Po
In Imitation of Hsü Kan ("Since You Went
  Away"). Liu Chun
In the courtyard is a marvelous tree. *Unknown*
In Your Absence. Baxter
Keeping Pacific Time. Mathews
Lady on Streetcar. Penna
Lady Prayeth the Return of Her Lover Abiding
  on the Seas, The. *Unknown*
Lamenting Maid, The. *Unknown*
Lass A-Laundering. *Unknown*
Late Light. Blunden
Letter Following. Mathews
Like as the culver on the bared
  bough. Spenser
Listening to the Washblock in the
  Moonlight. Liu Ch'ang-ch'ing
Lost Bird. Hove
Love-Letter One. *Unknown*
Love-Letter Two. *Unknown*
Lying down in my father's grey dressing
  gown. Oliver
Lying here alone. Izumi Shikibu
Lyric: "Absence, alas,/ Causeth me
  pass." Wyatt
Many Years. Bei Dao
Mirror of Matsuyama, The. Hashimoto
Missing You. Shu Ting
Never the Time and the Place. Browning
Now and Then. Chaloner
On a Moonlit Night, Sent to my Brothers and
  Sisters. Po Chü-i
On the bank of Lake Rouge a chestnut steed
  treads proudly. Su Man-shu
Ostella forth of Town: To My Heart. Tatham
Out of Sight, Out of Mind. Googe
"Pacifying the Western Barbarians." Wen
  T'ing-yün
Parrot. Po Chü-i
Parted by death, we swallow remorse. Tu Fu

Panther Man. Emanuel
Philip V of Macedon. Alcaeus
Zolgotz. *Unknown*
Asses. *See* Donkeys.
Assyrians
Destruction of Sennacherib, The. Byron
Astaire, Fred
Dream with Fred Astaire. Berkson
Astarte
To Ashtaroth and Bel. Tchernichowsky
Astrea (mythology)
Wit's Abuse. Wharton
Astrology
Astrologer's Song, An. Kipling
Horoscope. Salzman
Love's Horoscope. Crashaw
Zodiac Rhyme, The. *Unknown*
Astronauts
Problems. Scott
Projection, A. Whittemore
So long. Dickey
Astronomy and Astronomers
Astronomer's Journal, An. Shore
Astronomers of Mont Blanc, The. Bowers
Blue Glass. Adcock
Copernican System, The. Chatterton
Ex-Queen among the Astronomers,
The. Adcock
Gemini Jones. Espy
Greenwich Observatory. Keyes
Old Astronomer to His Pupil, The. Williams
Planetarium. Rich
Showing Us the Fields. McCorkle
Stargazer, The. *Unknown*
That Night They All Gathered on the Highest
Tower. Hristic
To an Astronomer. Botta
When I Heard the Learn'd
Astronomer. Whitman
Atalanta
Atalanta in Calydon. Swinburne
Atheism
At the Smithville Methodist Church. Dunn
Impercipient, The. Hardy
Athena. *See* Minerva.
Athens, Greece
Look once more ere we leave this specular
Mount. Milton
Spring Wind, A. Spencer
Athletes
Ex-Basketball Player. Updike
Morning Athletes. Piercy
Runner, The. Whitman
To an Athlete Dying Young. Housman
With Steve Ovett in Preston Park. Salzman
Atlanta, Georgia
Atlanta Exposition Ode. Fordham
Litany of [*or at*] Atlanta, A. DuBois
Atlantic Charter
Atlantic Charter: 1942. Young
Atlantic Ocean
Atlantic. Scupham
Castaway, The. Cowper
Crossing the Atlantic. Sexton
Goree. Osundare
How Cyrus Laid the Cable. Saxe
Seaweed. Longfellow
Atlantis
Atlantis. Constantine
Atomic Bomb
Actual Vision of Morning's Extrusion. Dugan
At the Bomb Testing Site. Stafford
August 6, 1945. Fell
Bath, The. Hahn
Creation. Trinity Site, New Mexico. 5:30 A.M.,
July 16th, 1945. Saenz
Day I Once Dreamed, The. Arrowsmith
Earth ("Planet doesn't explode,
A"). Wheelock
Flesh. Levy
Gathered at the River. Levertov
Ghosts, Fire, Water. Kirkup
Hibakusha's Letter (1955), The. Mura

Hiding Place. Armour
Hieronymus Bosch, We Can Do It. Coltman
In the Year 1945 an Original Child Was
Born. Merton
Kimono, The. Gordon
Monuments of Hiroshima, The. Enright
On a Japanese Beach. Cassian
Poem for a Chorus. Cartier
They Dared Him. Myhill
U. S. 1946 King's X. Frost
See also **Hiroshima, Japan; Nuclear War.**
Atsumichi, Prince
Elegies for Prince Atsumichi ("Because I do not
know where you are"). Izumi Shikibu
Elegies for Prince Atsumichi ("Clearly he
would notice: in my eyes"). Izumi Shikibu
Elegies for Prince Atsumichi ("Dead people
come to visit tonight"). Izumi Shikibu
Elegies for Prince Atsumichi ("Discard
myself — just the thought is bitter"). Izumi
Shikibu
Elegies for Prince Atsumichi ("I miss your
voice as you talked to me"). Izumi Shikibu
Elegies for Prince Atsumichi ("I wish I could
see you like this snow"). Izumi Shikibu
Elegies for Prince Atsumichi ("It would console
me to see you"). Izumi Shikibu
Elegies for Prince Atsumichi ("No dreams
through the night"). Izumi Shikibu
Elegies for Prince Atsumichi ("One body, but
heart shattered into a thousand
pieces"). Izumi Shikibu
Elegies for Prince Atsumichi ("Though my
heart isn't a summer field"). Izumi Shikibu
Elegies for Prince Atsumichi ("You are gone,
and I have nothing unhappy to
remember"). Izumi Shikibu
Atterbury, Francis, Bishop of Rochester
Epitaph: "Meek Francis lies here, friend,
without stop or stay." Prior
Attics
Attic, The. Coulette
In the Attic. Justice
Inventory. Borges
Up There. Auden
Auctions
Auction Sale, The. Reed
Auction Sale — Household
Furnishings. DeLeeuw
Bags of Meat. Hardy
Kirkwall Auction Mart. Scott
To Henry Wright of Mobberley, Esq. on
Buying the Picture of Father
Malebranche. Byrom
Auden, Wystan Hugh
Auden at Milwaukee. Spender
Auden's Funeral. Spender
In Memory of W. H. Auden. Slavitt
Just a Smack at Auden. Empson
Seeing Auden Off. Booth
Self-Congratulatory Ode on Mr. Auden's
Election to the Professorship of Poetry at
Oxford. Mason
To Auden on His Fiftieth. Eberhart
To Wystan Auden. Grigson
Audubon, John James
Birds of America: John James Audubon,
The. Harrison
Aughrim, Battle of (1691)
After Aughrim. Geoghegan
After Aughrim. Lawless
Deep red bogs divided. Murphy
Green Martyrs. Murphy
Rapparees. Murphy
Wolfhound. Murphy
August
August. Clare
August. García Lorca
August. Ray
August. San Geminiano
August. Swinburne
August. Thaxter
August. Wylie
August Midnight, An. Hardy
August Sleepwalker, The. Bei Dao

Day-Dreams. Canton
Mid-August at Sourdough Mountain
Lookout. Snyder
Poem for August — or for My Birthday. Monk
Augustine, Saint
Saint Augustine. Plunkett
Auks
Great Auk's Ghost, The. Hodgson
Aunt Jemima
Aunt Jemima of the Ocean Waves. Hayden
Aunts
Aga Khan, The. Orlen
Aunt Jennifer's Tigers. Rich
Aunts and Nieces or Time and
Space. Housman
Cherry. Dybek
Family Turn, A. Stafford
Introduction to Some Poems, An. Stafford
My Aunt. Holmes
Photo of Emily, The. Ferlinghetti
Satin Doll. Wojahn
Seasonal Aunt, A. Barry
Sister Ev. Hall
To Aunt Rose. Ginsberg
Tunnel, The. Parra
Auschwitz, Poland
Auschwitz #1. Van Loen
Auschwitz #5. Van Loen
Auschwitz #6. Van Loen
Bramble. Kaminsky
Harry Lenga. Heifetz
On the 25th Anniversary of the Liberation of
Auschwitz. Mandel
Passover at Auschwitz. Josephs
Saving the Children. Singer
Unforgettable. Pawlak
Your Attention Please. Porter
Australia
As a Man Walks. Simpson
At Cooloolah. Wright
Australia. Catalano
Australia. Hope
Australia 1970. Wright
Botany Bay. Freeth
Death of Morgan, The. *Unknown*
Early Arrival: Sydney. Smith
Edna's Hymn. Humphries
First of the Emigrants, The. *Unknown*
Gravy Train, The. Davidson
H. M. S. *Glory* at Sydney. Causley
Hail South Australia! *Unknown*
Hot Day In Sydney, A. *Unknown*
Now I'm Easy. Bogle
Rhiannon. Jones
Short Time. Ewart
Summer Christmas in Australia, A. Sladen
Sydney. Harris
Sydney Cove, 1788. Porter
Terra Australis. McAuley
Terra Australis. Stewart
Visit of Hope to Sydney Cove, near Botany-
Bay. Darwin
We who are called Australians have no
country. Ingamells
Wild Colonial Boy, The. *Unknown*
Collins Book of Australian Poetry, The
(CBAP). Rodney Hall, comp.
Faber Book of Modern Australian Verse, The
(FaBoMA). Vincent Buckley, ed.
New Oxford Book of Australian Verse
(NOBAu). Les Murray, comp.
Authorship and Authors
Absolute and Abitofhell. Knox
After Dilettante Concetti. Traill
Argument of His Book, The. Herrick
Author to Her Book, The. Bradstreet
Boatman, The. Macpherson
Burning Hills. Ondaatje
Cacoëthes Scribendi. Holmes
Canadian Authors Meet, The. Scott
For the Young Who Want To. Piercy
George Crabbe. Robinson
Hamlet's Soliloquy Imitated. Jago
I Have Approached. Paton
Ladies and gents, you are here
assembled. Joyce

Buddha and Buddhism
Buddha at Kamakura. Kipling
Buddha in Glory. Rilke
Buddha's Birthday: April 8, 1819. Issa
Further Advantages of Learning. Rexroth
I entrust myself to earth. Hanh
Lesser Vehicle, The. Drew
Lord Buddha, The. Hayashi Fumiko
Man whose mind is rounded out to perfection,
  The. Chan-Jan
Proofs of Buddha's Existence. *Unknown*
We venerate the Three Treasures. *Unknown*
Written on the Wall of Halfway Mountain
  Temple. Wang An-shih
You should entreat trees and rocks. Dogen
You sit down on a hill top, or anywhere high
  enough for you. *Unknown*
Buffalo Bill (William Frederick Cody)
Buffalo Bill's. Cummings
Buffaloes
Bison, The. Belloc
Bone Yard. Barnes
Buffalo. Eglington
Buffalo, The. Moore
Buffalo. *Unknown*
Buffalo Country. Paterson
Buffalo Dusk. Sandburg
Buffalo Skinners, The. *Unknown*
Flower-fed Buffaloes, The. Lindsay
Ghosts of the Buffaloes, The. Lindsay
I Rise, I Rise. *Unknown*
I thought I saw buffalo. *Unknown*
Song: "Hear me, ye smokeless skies and grass-
  green earth." Mair
Song of the Red & Green Buffalo,
  A. *Unknown*
Trail beside the River Platte, The. Heyen
Bugles and Buglers
Call of the Bugles, The. Hovey
Danny Deever. Kipling
Buildings and Builders
About an Excavation. Reznikoff
Blue Taj, The. Berssenbrugge
Building. Snyder
Cathedral Builders. Ormond
Dome Poem. Smith
Foundations. Staff
I and Thou. Dugan
Midst the fair range of buildings which, new-
  reared. Keate
Scaffolding. Heaney
Bukowski, Charles
You Don't Know What Love Is. Carver
Bull Run, Battles of (1861, 1862)
Battle of Bull Run, The. *Unknown*
Manassas. Warfield
March into Virginia, The. Melville
Our Left. Ticknor
Run from Manassas Junction, The. *Unknown*
Upon the Hill before Centreville. Boker
Bullets
What the Bullet Sang. Harte
Bullfights and Bullfighters
Bullard's Song, The. *Unknown*
Bullfight. Holub
Death Invited. Swenson
Girl Friend Describes the Bull Fight,
  The. Uruttiran
Goring, The. Plath
Lament for Ignacio Sánchez Mejías. García
  Lorca
Matadors, The. Jacobsen
Bulls
Bull, The. Hodgson
Bull, The. Sackville-West
Bull, The. Williams
Bull, The. Wright
Bull Calf, The. Layton
Bull Moses, The. Hughes
Bullfight. Holub
Duke Of Buccleuch, The. Phelp
Hoosen Johnny. *Unknown*
Magnificent Bull, The. *Dinka Oral Tradition*
Outlaw, The. Heaney
Spilled from a tree-searing wind. Shiba
  Sonome

Three Tall Men, The. *Unknown*
Two Bulls, The. *Unknown*
Bundling
New Bundling Song, A. *Unknown*
Bunke, Tamara ("Ita")
Ita. Ulloa
Bunker Hill, Battle of (1775)
Bunker Hill. Calvert
Bunker's Hill, or the Soldier's
  Lamentation. Freeth
Bunyan, John
Of John Bunyan's Life. James
Bureaucracy and Bureaucrats
Anteroom: Geneva. Devlin
Bureau 2. Miles
Departmental. Frost
Frigate Jones, the Pussyfooter ("Frigate Jones
  was very slow and fat"). Burke
Pass Office Song. *Unknown*
Unknown Citizen, The. Auden
Burglars
Burglar Bill. "Anstey"
Burial
Antigone. Malancioui
Box Comes Home, A. Ciardi
Burial. Vaughan
Burial Detail. Hudgins
Burial Flags. Currey
Call for the Robin-Redbreast and the
  Wren. Webster
Earth Buried. Mackenzie
Etchings. Chichetto
Etruscan Tombs. Robinson
Excavator, The. Borenstein
Exhumation. Karélli
Foul sod covers a bad one here. Crinagoras
Give me one small smothering of
  earth. Leonidas of Tarentum
Hearse Song, The. *Unknown*
Here it's rose-time again, chick-peas in
  season. Philodemus
I Am Asking You to Come Back
  Home. Carson
I Found Her Out There. Hardy
If of the dead save good nought should be
  said. Drummond
Mummy of a Lady Named Jemutesonekh XXI
  Dynasty. James
On Covering the Bones of Chang Chin, the
  Hired Man. Liu Tsung-yüan
Sea Burial. Ciardi
Sled Burial, Dream Ceremony. Dickey
Though of white marble and dressed
  straight. Crinagoras
Tumba de Buenaventura Roig, La. Espada
Upon Prue, His Maid. Herrick
Urn for Burial, An. *Unknown*
When the deep-piled winter snow/ melted on
  her roof. Antipater of Thessalonica
Why do you heave apart my stone? Gregory
  of Nazianzus, Saint
See also **Cemeteries; Funerals; Graves.**
Burke, Edmund
Here lies our good Edmund, whose genius was
  such. Goldsmith
Burma
Mandalay. Kipling
Burne-Jones, Edward
For "The Wine of Circe" by Edward Burne-
  Jones. Rossetti
Burns, Robert
At the Grave of Burns. Wordsworth
Burns. Halleck
Had We Two Met. Landor
Sonnet on Reading the Poem upon the
  Mountain Daisy, by Mr. Burns. Williams
Burr, Aaron
Aaron Burr's Wooing. Stedman
To Aaron Burr, under Trial for High
  Treason. Morton
Burr, Theodosia
Theodosia Burr. Terrell
Theodosia Burr: The Wrecker's Story. Palmer

Burros. *See* **Donkeys.**
Bus Terminals
In the Baggage Room at Greyhound. Ginsberg
Buses
B's the Bus. McGinley
Bus, The. Cohen
Bus Ride. Kandel
Bus Ride. Robinson
Lady on a Bus. Lohmann
Last Bus, The. Knox
Late Bus (After a Series of Hold-Ups). Atkins
Sleep Bus, The. Barton
Business and Businessmen
Accountant in His Bath, The ("The accountant
  dried his imperfect back"). Mitchell
Any Man to His Secretary. Corke
Between a Contractor and His Wife. *Unknown*
Business Is Business. Braley
Declasse Memory. O'Loughlin
Dirge: "1-2-3 was the number he played but
  today the number came 3-2-1." Fearing
Endurance Test. Balsdon
Every Day There Are New Memow. Jones
Executive. Betjeman
My Brother, Beautiful Shinault, That
  Goat. Huddle
See also **Accounting and Accountants;
  Advertising; Banking and Bankers;
  Capitalism; Commerce; Financiers.**
Butchering and Butchers
Bags of Meat. Hardy
Bull-roarer, The. Stern
Butcher, A. Hood
Butcher Shop. Simic
Cleaving, The. Lee
Crafty Butcher, The. Hampton
Cutting up an Ox. Chuang Tzu
Fifth Hell, The. Rothenberg
Guys of the Volye. Vaynshteyn
Hi-tiddley-i-ti, brown bread! *Unknown*
Leicester Chambermaid, The. *Unknown*
My father owns the butcher shop. *Unknown*
On a Pig's Head. Tomlinson
Psychonaut Sonnets: Jones, The. Goldbarth
Reuben Bright. Robinson
Slaughterhouse. Takiguchi Masako
Stockyard, The. Squire
Butler, Samuel (1612-80)
English Liberal. Taylor
On Butler who can think without
  rage. Oldham
Butter
Butter Charm. *Unknown*
Pendydd. Amis
Buttercups
Buttercup, A. *Unknown*
Buttercups. Thorley
Buttercups. *Unknown*
Buttercups and Daisies. Howitt
Butterflies
Against the morning glories. Kikaku
Blue-Butterfly Day. Frost
Butterflies. Chang Yü
Butterflies darting. Saigyo
Butterfly, The. Fuller
Butterfly, The. Hawker
Butterfly, The. Kolatkar
Butterfly. Lawrence
Butterfly, The. Padgett
Butterfly, The. Rose
Butterfly. Smith
Butterfly and the Snail, The. Gay
Butterfly comes unasked a butterfly, A. Issa
Butterfly dying right in front, A. Natsume
  Seibi
Butterfly: now in front. Chiyojo
Butterfly on Rock. Layton
Butterfly settles on the neckplate, A. Buson
Butterfly Song. *Unknown*
Butterfly: what's it dreaming of. Chiyojo
By its own wind, a small butterfly. Chiyojo
Coming out of the privy. Buson
Corn-grinding Song. *Unknown*
Dandelion: from time to time. Chiyojo
Dead Butterfly, The. Levertov

Buzzards (continued)

Evening dusk: flying in the middle. Kikaku
Example, The. Davies
Flying Crooked. Graves
From time to time, a butterfly. Chiyojo
Graceful Bastion, The. Williams
Haiku: "Falling flower, The." Arakida
   Moritake
Haiku: "Fluttering, fluttering." Masaoka Shiki
Hoofer, The. Redwing
I was round and small like a pearl. *Unknown*
In the Garden. Majumdar
King of Yellow Butterflies, The. Lindsay
Ode to a Butterfly. Higginson
Of the Boy and Butterfly. Bunyan
On Discovering a Butterfly. Nabokov
On Seeing a Butterfly in the Street. Fergusson
Only butterflies fly in the field. Basho
Purple butterflies/ fly at night through my
   dreams. Yosano Akiko
Roots and Branches. Duncan
Settled on a temple bell and asleep. Buson
Sleep of the Painted Ladies, The. Willard
Sleeping butterfly. Kikaku
They look/ like newlyweds. Ryota
To a Butterfly. Davies
To a Butterfly. Wordsworth
True Story of the Pins. Ríos
Tuft of Flowers, The. Frost
Unconscious Came a Beauty. Swenson
Wings. Wright

Buzzards
Pondy Woods. Warren
Song of the Turkey Buzzard. Welch
See also **Vultures.**

Byelorussia
Byelorussia. Kulbak

Byrd, Mary Furman Weston
Mrs. Mary Furman Weston Byrd. Fordham

Byron, George Gordon Noel Byron, 6th Baron
Another Letter to Lord Byron. Slavitt
Byron. Coogler
Byron. Davidson
Byron Recollected at Bologna. Rogers
Byron's Oak at Newstead Abbey. Fortune
Fashion changes! Maidens do not wear,
   The. Lang
He is now at rest. Rogers
Inscribed on Byron's Poetic Works. Su Man-
   shu
Lives and Times of John Keats, Percy Bysshe
   Shelley, and George Gordon Noel, Lord
   Byron, The. Parker
Lord Byron. Clare
Nor for the crabbed state-creed, wayward
   wight. Hogg
On This Day I Complete My Thirty-sixth
   Year. Byron
Sea Replies to Byron, The. Chesterton
Sketch of Lord Byron's Life. Moore
Sonnet to Byron. Shelley
To Lord Byron. Keats
Very like a Whale. Nash
When Byron's eyes were shut in
   death. Arnold
You lived and moved among the best
   society. Auden

Byzantium
Byzantium. Yeats
Sailing to Byzantium. Yeats

C

Cabbages
Cabbage. Norman

Cactus
Night-blooming Cereus, The. Hayden

Cadavers. *See* **Corpses.**

Cadiz, Spain, Battle of (1596)
Winning of Cales, The. Deloney

Cads
Rain It Raineth, The. Bowen

Caedmon
Caedmon. Levertov
Caedmon. Nicholson

Caesar, Julius
Friends, Romans, countrymen, lend me your
   ears. Shakespeare
Julius Caesar. *Unknown*
Julius Caesar made a law. *Unknown*
Julius Caesar said with a smile. *Unknown*
To Clement Edmonds, on His *Caesar's
   Commentaries* Observed, and
   Translated. Jonson

Cafés
Apollo Café. Gray
At the Cafe. Riley
In a Café. Dobson

Cain and Abel
Abel. Capetanakis
Abel. Wheelwright
Autobiography. Pagis
Cain and Abel. Guidacci
Ghost of Abel, The. Blake
My Answer. Adamo
Oh! thou dead/ And everlasting witness! whose
   unsinking. Byron

Cakes
After the Party. Wise
On My Birthday. Mazhar
To Mrs. K———, On Her Sending Me an
   English Christmas Plum-Cake at
   Paris. Williams

Caliban
Caliban upon Setebos; or, Natural Theology in
   the Island. Browning

California
Across the Bay. Davie
Barnsley and District. Davie
Beauty and Sadness. Song
Before the Stuff Comes Down. Snyder
Blue Ridge. Voigt
Burning the Small Dead. Snyder
California. Locklin
California Dreaming. Wright
California Hills in August. Gioia
California Oaks, The. Winters
California Phrasebook, The. Schmitz
Californians, The. Spencer
Carmel Point. Jeffers
Circumambulation of Mt. Tamalpais. Hoyem
City [San Francisco]. Hughes
Clouds of Evening. Jeffers
Como lo Siento. Cervantes
Elements of San Joaquin, The. Soto
Freeway 280. Cervantes
Hay for the Horses. Snyder
In Montecito. Jarrell
Letter from Vermont. Voigt
Lights among Redwood. Gunn
Mendocino Rose. Hongo
Mission Bay. Koethe
Napa, California. Castillo
Report from California. Moyles
Sleep in the Mojave Desert. Plath
Smudging. Wakoski
Song of the Redwood-Tree. Whitman
Walking Down the Road. Rich
Yugoslav Cemetery. Wright

Calligraphy
Leaf From a French Bible (circa
   1270). Scupham

Calliope (muse)
To Calliope. Graves

Calm
He That Is Slow to Anger. Bible, *O.T.*
Hermit, The. "Æ"
I Saw Two Clouds at Morning. Brainard
Keep Cool. Garvey

Calvary. *See* **Crucifixion, The.**

Calves
Birth of Rainbow. Hughes
Bridestones. Hughes
First Birth, The. Jones
I Would Like You for a Comrade. Parry
March Calf, A. Hughes
Teaching a Dumb Calf. Hughes
Two-headed Calf, The. Gilpin
What Is Veal? *Unknown*

Calvinism
Holy Willie's Prayer. Burns
Latest Decalogue, The. Clough
McAndrew's Hymn. Kipling
Mr. Edwards and the Spider. Lowell

Calypso (mythology)
Calypso's Island. MacLeish
Forever Ambrosia. Morley
Ulysses Leaves the Nymph Calypso. Homer

Calypso Music
Calypsomania. Brode

Camaraderie
Assurance. Stafford
Embarkation, 1942. Jarmain
Rumors of liberation. We could not believe
   it. Eberhart
See also **Friendship.**

Cambodia and Cambodians
Armenian Looking at Newsphotos of the
   Cambodian Deathwatch, An. Hovanessian
Cambodia. Fenton
Dead Soldiers. Fenton
Sun. Palmer

Cambridge, England
Autumn Morning at Cambridge. Cornford
Cambridge and the Cam. Fletcher
Hic Vir, Hic Est. Calverley
In the Backs. Cornford
Inside of King's College Chapel,
   Cambridge. Wordsworth
Residence at Cambridge. Wordsworth
Written at Cambridge. Lamb

Cambridge, Massachusetts
Professor Kelleher and the Charles
   River. O'Grady
See also **Harvard University.**

Cambridge University
Autumn Morning at Cambridge. Cornford
Inside of King's College Chapel,
   Cambridge. Wordsworth
On the University of Cambridge's Burning the
   Duke of Monmouth's Picture. Stepney
Semantic Limerick According to Dr. Johnson's
   Dictionary (Edition of 1765), The. Ewart
Semantic Limerick According to the Shorter
   Oxford English Dictionary (1933),
   The. Ewart

Cambridgeshire, England
Bedford Level. Dyer
Old Vicarage, Grantchester, The. Brooke

Camden, William
To William Camden. Jonson

Camden, New Jersey
Narcissus in Camden. Cone

Camellias
Camellia drops and spills, A. Buson
Into the darkness of an old well. Buson

Camelot
Lady of Shalott, The. Tennyson

Camels
Camel. Akhyaliyya
Camel, The. Gasztold
Camel, The. Nash
Camels in Persia. Wellesley
Fruit of the Tree, The. Wagoner
How to Tell a Camel. Lewis
In the North. Kung Liu
Song of the Camel, The. Carryl

Cameras
Camera. Kooser
See also **Photography and Photographers.**

Camões, Luis de
Camoes and the Debt. Andresen
Luis de Camões. Campbell

Campbell, Roy
In Memoriam: Roy Campbell. Currey

Camping
August on Sourdough, a Visit from Dick
   Brewer. Snyder
Campfire Extinguished. Roseliep
Camping Provencial. Notices: (1). Reading
Making Camp. Wagoner
Night in the Forest. Kinnell
Oh, Lovely Rock. Jeffers

Dentures
Poet's Farewell to His Teeth, The. Dickey
Denver, Colorado
Waltz against the Mountains. Ferril
Department Stores
Fixture, A. Swenson
Hi-Fashion Girl. Equi
Deportation
Three. Teller
Depression (economic). *See* **Great Depression.**
Depression (psychological). *See* **Melancholy;**
Mental Illness.
Descartes, René
Theological. Fadiman
Deserts
Burial Flags. Currey
Death in the Desert, A. Tomlinson
Desert Shipwreck. Jordan
Drifting Sands and a Caravan. Langworthy
Eden. Woo
Leaving Sonora. Ali
My Car Slides Off the Road. Gorham
Negev. Rokeah
Ozymandias [*or* Ozymandias of Egypt *or*
Sonnet: Ozymandias]. Shelley
Simoom, The. Tupper
Sleep in the Mojave Desert. Plath
Sustenance, The. Gonzáles
Desire
Abstinence Sows Sand All Over. Blake
All my senses, like beacon's flame. Greville
All Things Insensible. Young
As Your Eyes Are Blue. Harwood
Assurance, An. Breton
At Mid-Ocean. Bly
Beloved,/ What does it take to put a house in
order? Mager
Big Meal. Sinclair
Bitto gives to Athena. Antipater of Sidon
Blossom. Oliver
Blue Crêpe. Benveniste
Blueberry Man. Bergman
Body's Speech, The. *Unknown*
Bookmaking. Alvarez
Borderlands. Guiney
But, fair Iëmpsar (wife of Potiphar). Sylvester
By Loch Etive. Guinness
Canzone: "So feeble is the thread that doth the
burden stay." Petrarch
Come Back. Hart
Come, come, my companion. *Unknown*
Complete innocence, A. James
Conversations in Crisis. Lorde
Courtship. Strand
"Courtyard Full of Fragrance." Ch'in Kuan
Cruel, you pull away too soon your lips whenas
you kiss me. *Unknown*
Dark Night, The. John of the Cross
Dawning of the Day, The. Walsh
Delay. Hammond
Desire. "Æ"
Desire. Cornish
Desire. Dobyns
Desire. Fagan
Desire. Gourghenian
Desire. Ullman
Desire is a witch. Day Lewis
Desire Is Dead. Lawrence
Desires. Bensley
Desperate Message #3 (Desire). Svenvold
Didyme waved her wand at me. Asclepiades
Do You Remember That Night? *Unknown*
Duende. Zivančević
Dusk on the Veranda by Lake
Mendota. Chung Ling
Ecstasy. Houston
El Beso. Grimké
Epigram: "Sometime I fled the fire that me
brent." Wyatt
Fallen Leaves. Shu Ting
Far from kingdoms. Cavalli
Filling her compact and delicious
body. Berryman
Fire and Ice. Frost
First Love. Clare

For My Husband. Voigt
Genty Tibby and Sonsy Nelly. Ramsay
Good time of the year, The. Bernard de
Ventadour
Grasshopper Is a Burden. Lawrence
Growing Together. Oates
Hares on the Mountain. *Unknown*
Hide, Absolon, Thy Gilte Tresses
Clere. Chaucer
High on the upper, outermost bough. Sappho
Honestly I'd as soon be dead! Sappho
House. May
Hunger. Young
Hungry. Glatt
Hymn to Love, An. Herrick
I Go to Meet Him. Nichols
I had just gone to bed. Petronius Arbiter
I Knew a Woman [Lovely in Her
Bones]. Roethke
I love thee for thy fickleness. *Unknown*
I turn you out of doors. Chartier
If Pythias has a customer. Poseidippus
If Thou Wilt Mighty Be. Wyatt
In Her Own Image. Boland
In Imitation of Horace. Behn
In the Badlands of Desire. Goldberg
In the time it takes. Crozier
Insatiableness. Traherne
It Really Is the Heart. Riley
"Joy in Spring's Coming" — Seven
Songs. *Unknown*
Judith 2. Smith
Kaddish. Ginsberg
Know what I'm like? Some captain moors his
ship. March
Lady, those cherries plenty. *Unknown*
Lively lark stretched forth her wing, The. De
Vere
Long Lines: Youth and Age. Goodman
Love. Baker
Love. Prynne
Love in the Air. Prynne
Lover, The. Schoultz
Lover that Durst Not Speak to His M[istress],
A. Shirley
Love-Song, A. *Unknown*
Lyric: "For want of will in woe I
plain." Wyatt
Lyric: "It burneth yet, alas, my heart's
desire." Wyatt
Manifesto. Lawrence
Man's Requirements, A. Browning
Mary Hynes. Raftery
Meanwhile Cesario Dancing. Kidd
Mistress, The. Williams
Moving Occupations, The. Koestenbaum
My Afternoon. Adamson
My Lover Will Soon Be Here. *Unknown*
My Past. Cooper
My True Desire. McClennan
Night Gives Us the Next Day. Pratt
Nightwatchman. Randall
Not Long Ago. D'Orléans
O! From what power hast thou this powerful
might. Shakespeare
O Swallow, Swallow. Tennyson
Object, The. Villanueva
Office Friendships. Ewart
Older Men. Corn
On Being a Poet in Sierra Leone. Cheney-
Coker
On Platonic Love, to Mistress Cicely Crofts,
Maid of Honour. Ayton
On Spadina Avenue. Grosholz
On the Eve of Our Mutually Assured
Destruction. Wright
Or whether doth in my mind, being crowned
with you. Shakespeare
Oranges Are Ripe, The. Bei Dao
Palmer's Ode, The. Greene
Passion. Ward
Phalanstery. Ladányi
Phoebus Farewell. Sidney
Phoebus farewell, a sweeter saint I
serve. Sidney

"Pleasure of Returning to the Fields: A
Prelude." Huang T'ing-chien
Poem: "I don't know as I get what D.H.
Lawrence is driving at." O'Hara
Poema Como Valentin (or a San Francisco
Love Poem). Moraga
"Rapt with Wine, Loudly Singing; Joy in
Spring's Coming." Kuan Yun-shih
Rapture, The. Baker
Re-forming the Crystal. Rich
Relish. Algarin
Renunciation. Pearse
Resolute Desire That Enters, The. Daniel
Runaways Café I. Hacker
Sea at Evening, The. Laird
Sex, as they harshly call it. Rich
Shall I come, if I swim? wide are the waves,
you see. Campion
She Loves. Broumas
Since fortune's wrath envieth the
wealth. Surrey
Since That the Stormy Rage. Sidney
Sleeping Beauty. Broumas
Sleepwalkers' Ballad. García Lorca
So unwarely was never no man caught. Wyatt
Some People's Dreams Pay All Their
Bills. Ratushinskaya
Something of a Departure. Muldoon
Song: "Weight of the world, The." Ginsberg
"Song of Picking Mulberry." Li Ch'ing-chao
Sonnet: "If amorous faith in heart
unfeigned." Wyatt
Sonnet: "In Cyprus springs, whereas dame
Venus dwelt." Surrey
Story I Like to Tell, The. Becker
Success ("If you want a thing bad
enough"). Braley
Tell Me, Love. Bachmann
Tenderness. Dunn
This Dark Longing. Kantaris
This Song Is Dedicated to the One Eye
Love. Totton
To a Lady, Who Desired Me Not To Be in
Love with Her. Cutts
To Drink. Hirshfield
To His Mistress. Stewart
To the Fair Clarinda, Who Made Love to Me,
Imagin'd More than Woman. Behn
Tom. Schuyler
Too dearly had I bought my green and youthful
years. Surrey
Turkish Bakery, The. *Unknown*
Urban Love Songs. Lum
Want Bone, The. Pinsky
Want of You, The. Grimké
What a Man Needs. Seth
What is it men in women do require? Blake
What They Said. Ojaide
When My Desire. Ono no Komachi
White Rose, A. O'Reilly
Wondrous the Merge. Broughton
"Wu-t'ung Leaves" — Written in Jest at a
Banquet. Lu Chih
Yes! hope may with my strong desire keep
pace. Michelangelo Buonarroti
You Must Have Been a Sensational
Baby. Norse
You recount old tales of Thebes. Anacreon
You say you love, but with a voice. Keats
Zealots of Yearning. Rokeah
See also **Erotic Love; Lust.**
Desks
Desks. Smith
My desk, most loyal friend. Tsvetayeva
Desolation
Adrian Henri's Talking after Christmas
Blues. Henri
Ha'nacker Hill. Belloc
Hand That Signed the Paper [Felled a City],
The. Thomas
Last Visit. Finch
Looking for Camels. Hill
Neglect. Williams
No Voice of Man. Falconer
Remembrance. Brontë
Reservoirs. Thomas

Yes to the Earth. "Aleramo"
You Can't Go to the Moon There's No
   Trains. Howard
You Were Broken. Ungaretti

Earthquakes
Before They Made Things Be Alive They
   Spoke. Cuevish
California Crack, The. Coleman
Crack in the Wall Holds Flowers. Miller
Earth Tremor in Lugano. Kirkup
Earthquake. Ford
Earthquake of 1886, The. Heard
Earthquaked, my house collapsed. Antiphilus
English Earthquake, The. Salzman
Fifties, The. Rose
Lines Written Near San Francisco. Simpson
On Catania and Syracuse Swallowed Up by an
   Earthquake, from the Italian of
   Filicaja. Seward
Pyramid of Supplications. Herrera
Quake Theory. Olds
Ruaumoko — the Earthquake God. Turei
Santa Barbara Earthquake, The. *Unknown*
Then earthquakes, nature's agonizing
   pangs. Grainger

Easter
African Easter. Nicol
Alleluia! Christ Is Risen Today. Hopkins
Christ Is Risen! Dugan
Christmas Is Really for the Children. Turner
Composed in One of the Valleys of
   Westmoreland, on Easter
   Sunday. Wordsworth
Day of Resurrection, The. John of Damascus
Easter ("Rise, heart, thy Lord is
   risen"). Herbert
Easter. Kilmer
Easter. Sabin
Easter. Saenz
Easter. Sisson
Easter Beatitudes. Burkholder
Easter Carol. Lovejoy
Easter Carol. Ray
Easter Chick, An. Wakley
Easter-Day. Vaughan
Easter Day. Wilde
Easter Eve. Prudentius
Easter Hymn. Hope
Easter Hymn. Housman
Easter Hymn. Vaughan
Easter Hymn. Wesley
Easter Light, The. Thompson
Easter Monday. Farjeon
Easter Monday. Rossetti
Easter Morn. Heard
Easter Morning. Ammons
Easter Night. Meynell
Easter, 1923. Neihardt
Easter; or, Spring-Time. Moorer
Easter Poem. Raine
Easter Praise. Bennett
Easter Wings. Herbert
Easter with Horses. Wells
Extreme delicacy of this Easter morning,
   The. Sarton
For the Kindling of the Light on Easter
   Eve. Prudentius
God Send Easter. Clifton
If Easter Be Not True. Barstow
Legend of the Easter Eggs, The. O'Brien
Morning, Noon, And. Truax
Most glorious lord of life that on this
   day. Spenser
On Easter Day. Thaxter
On Easter Morning. Rexford
Rejoice, Let Alleluias Ring. Schaefer
Resurrection, The. Brooks
Rhyme for Remembering the Date of
   Easter. Richardson
Seven Stanzas at Easter. Updike
That Nature Is a Heraclitean Fire and of the
   Comfort of the Resurrection. Hopkins
Three Easters. Turner
Well Pleaseth Me the Sweet Time of
   Easter. Bertrans de Born
When Mary thro' the Garden Went. Coleridge

Easter Island
Behavior of Mirrors on Easter Island,
   The. Cortázar
Easter Rebellion (1916)
Easter, 1916. Yeats
Lament for the Poets: 1916. Ledwidge
Lament for Thomas MacDonagh. Ledwidge
Rose Tree, The. Yeats
Veterans, The. MacDonagh
Eatherly, Claude R.
Song about Major Eatherly, A. Wain
Eating
All life is your own. Starhawk
All that I have comes from my Mother! Teish
Beautiful Meals. Moore
Frugal Repasts. Hull
Inviting a Friend to Supper. Jonson
Life would be an easy matter. Waterman
My friends, let us give thanks for
   Wonder. Shapiro
Oberon's Feast. Herrick
Soul Food. Mirikitani
When Father Carves the Duck. Wright
See also **Food; Gluttony and Gluttons.**
Eating Disorders
Ellen West. Bidart
Echo Lake, New Hampshire
Echo Reverie. Ray
Echo (mythology)
Echo's Complaint. Ray
See also **Narcissus (mythology).**
Echoes
Echo, The. Barnes
Echo. Clark
Echo. De la Mare
Echo. Popa
Echo. Saxe
Echo. Sidney
Echo. Weston
Echo Turned to Stone. Popa
Echoes. Lazarus
Gentle Echo on Woman, A. Swift
Eclipses
December Eclipse. Lockwood
Moon Eclipse Exorcism. *Unknown*
Total Eclipse. Rosen
Ecology
All the Smoke. Siegel
Baby Ten Months Old Looks at the Public
   Domain, A. Stafford
Binsey Poplars (Felled 1879). Hopkins
Bungaloid Growth. Ellis
Dead Seal. Purdy
Flower-fed Buffaloes, The. Lindsay
For All. Snyder
For the marvelous grace of Your Creation — .
   Unknown
Gathered at the River. Levertov
Great Spirit. *Unknown*
Great Spirit, whose dry lands thirst, help us to
   find. *Unknown*
Hard Questions. Tsuda
Hymn to Moloch. Hodgson
I have come to terms with the future. Hooey
Inversnaid. Hopkins
Little Things. Stephens
Martyred Earth, The. Milne
Moss-gathering. Roethke
Mother Earth; Her Whales. Snyder
Mystic River. Ciardi
Only the winds of spring. Franklin
Plans for Altering the River. Hugo
Poplar Field, The. Cowper
Quid Restat. Beebe
Requiem for a River. Williams
Smokey the Bear Sutra. Snyder
Song of Cove Creek Dam, The. *Unknown*
Statement on Our Higher Education. Ransom
Stranded Whales, The. Dutton
War against the Trees, The. Kunitz
We have forgotten who we are. *Unknown*
We join with the earth and with each
   other. *Unknown*
When There Were Trees. Willard
Why the Soup Tastes like the Daily
   News. Piercy

Woodman, Spare That Tree. Morris
Working against Time. Wagoner
News of the Universe (NU). Robert Bly,
   comp.
See also **Pollution.**
Eden
Adam Lay yBounden [*or* I-
   bounden]. *Unknown*
Alas, that ever that speche was
   spoken. *Unknown*
Apple, The. Smith
Brazen Image. Hartigan
Corruption. Vaughan
Descended, Adam to the bower where
   Eve. Milton
Eve Names the Animals. Donnelly
Fall, The. Rochester
Garden, The. Beaumont
Garden, The. Very
Lord God Planted a Garden, The. Gurney
Man the Monarch. Leapor
Naming of the Beasts, The. Sparshott
Occupations of Hell. Milton
Of all the Trees that in the Garden
   grew. Sutcliffe
On its way I see. Raine
One Foot in Eden. Muir
Paradise. Milton
Paradise Re-entered. Lawrence
Rose of Eden, The. Phillips
So spake our Mother Eve, and Adam
   heard. Milton
Spring. Hopkins
Tempter Disarmed, The. Milton
Theology. Hughes
Tree, The. Auchterlonie
What Words Have Passed. Milton
When Adam Walked in Eden
   Young. Housman
See also **Adam and Eve.**
Edinburgh, Scotland
Daft Days, The. Fergusson
To the Merchantis of Edinburgh. Dunbar
Editors
Editor Whedon. Masters
Education
Advance of Education, The. Heard
As Joe Gould says in. Cummings
Campus on the Hill, The. Snodgrass
Clerk of Oxford, The. Chaucer
Degrees. Bartlett
Elementary School Classroom in a Slum,
   An. Spender
Female Education. Sigourney
Government Quarters. Clifton
History of Education. McCord
Intention to Escape from Him. Millay
Lines to a Don. Belloc
Little Black Boy's Prayer, A. Tirolien
Little learning is a dangerous thing, A. Pope
On Education, December 1789. Bentley
On Having Been an Experimental Sacred Cow
   for Four Years, and a Token African on
   Faculty. Awoonor
On Learning. Teft
On the Prospect of Planting Arts and Learning
   in America. Berkeley
Poem: "In the earnest path of duty." Forten
Prize giving Speech. Baxter
Rain. Nye
Supervising Examinations. Lucy
Sweeper of Ways, The. Nemerov
These Words Are Synonymous, Now. Herrera
Through the Dark Sod — as
   Education. Dickinson
To Cyriack Skinner ("Cyriack, whose
   grandsire"). Milton
To David, about His Education. Nemerov
University Examinations in Egypt. Enright
Women. Walker
Would you your son should be a sot or
   dunce. Cowper
See also **Colleges and Universities;**
   Scholarship and Scholars; Students;
   Teaching and Teachers.

Praise to the emptiness that blanks out existence. Existence. Jalal al-Din Rumi
Tangier. Dunn
Waiting. Cooper

Emus
Emu Shot. Tjinapirrgarri

Enclosures. *See* **Inclosure Movement.**

End of the World
Advice to a Prophet. Wilbur
End of the World, The. Bottomley
End of the World, The. MacLeish
Epitaph Ending in And, The. Stafford
Everyone Knows the World Is Ending. Fulton
Fire and Ice. Frost
Fundamental Project of Technology, The. Kinnell
LMFBR. Snyder
Once by the Pacific. Frost
Song on the End of the World, A. Milosz
What If a Much of a Which of a Wind. Cummings
When I Awoke. Patterson
See also **Judgment Day.**

Endangered Species
Moschus Moschiferus. Hope

Endurance
See also **Fortitude.**

Endymion
Endymion [a Poetic Romance]. Keats
I Envy Not Endymion. Stirling
Oh, sleep forever in the Latmian cave. Millay
Phoebe on Latmus. Drayton

Enemies
Enemy, The. Wegner
Loving My Enemies. Kamienska
Man He Killed, The. Hardy
Reconciliation. Whitman
Rivals, The. Epstein
War and Hell. Crosby

Energy Crisis
Elegy Written in a Country Coal-Bin. Morley

England
Above the Medway. Munby
Adlestrop. Thomas
Adore November's sacred seventeenth day. Kyffin
And Did Those Feet in Ancient Time. Blake
Ave Imperatrix! Wilde
Bonis Avibus. Oliver
British Church, The. Herbert
British [*or* Brittish] Church, The. Vaughan
By the River Eden. Raine
Channel Crossing. Barker
Chant of Hate against England, A. Lissauer
Christmas. Betjeman
Classics Society. Harrison
Corrymeela. "O'Neill"
Crystal Palace, The. Davidson
Dialogue Between Old England and New, A; Concerning Their Present Troubles, Anno, 1642. Bradstreet
Distant View of England from the Sea. Bowles
Drink, Britannia. Beddoes
Durham. Harrison
Effeminate Englishmen. Cowper
Elegy in a Country Churchyard. Chesterton
England. Kipling
England. Salter
England. Tessimond
England. *Unknown*
England, My England. Henley
England's Heart. Tupper
England's Sovereigns in Verse. *Unknown*
England's Standard. Macaulay
English Are So Nice!, The. Lawrence
English Earthquake, The. Salzman
English Fog, The. Dyer
English Succession, The. *Unknown*
English War, The. Sayers
Farewell to England. *Unknown*
Fields from Islington to Marybone, The. Blake
Fleadh Cheoil. Hutchinson
Foot of the tower, The. An angle where the darkness. Kinsella

Free Parliament Litany, A. *Unknown*
George III. Lowell
Glory of the Garden, The. Kipling
God Hath Sent Me to Sea for Pearls. Smart
Good Old Harry. James
Ha'nacker Mill. Belloc
Happy Britannica. Thomson
Happy is England! I could be content. Keats
His Petition to Queen Anne of Denmark (1618). Ralegh
Home Thoughts from Abroad. Browning
Home Thoughts, from the Sea. Browning
Homes of England, The. Hemans
Homing In. Fanthorpe
Hope. *Unknown*
How Sleep the Brave. Collins
I Don't Want to Be a Soldier. *Unknown*
I Have Loved England. Miller
I have seen much to hate here — much to forgive. Miller
In Praise of Drainage. Wilson
In the middle silences of this night's course the blackthorn. Jones
In Westminster Abbey. Betjeman
International Hymn. Huntington
Italy. Byron
John of Gaunt Speaks. Shakespeare
Land, The. Kipling
Land of Hope and Glory. Benson
Last Buccaneer, The. Kingsley
Laurel Axe, The. Hill
Leavings. Heaney
London, 1802 ("Milton! thou should'st be living at this hour"). Wordsworth
Matlock Bath. Betjeman
Mercian Hymns. Hill
Mr. Molony's Account of the Crystal Palace. Thackeray
Mock Song, A. Lovelace
MCMXIV. Larkin
North, The. Higgins
O England, Country of My Heart's Desire. Lucas
O My Mother Isle! ("Not yet enslaved, not wholly vile"). Coleridge
Old England. Bradstreet
Old Vicarage, Grantchester, The. Brooke
On a Political Prisoner. Yeats
On This Island. Auden
Once more unto the breach, dear friends, once more. Shakespeare
Princely Ditty in Praise of the English Rose, A. Deloney
Properties of the Shires of England, The. *Unknown*
Puck's Song. Kipling
Ravenglass Railway Station, Cumberland. Nicholson
Red Flag, The. Connell
Return, The. Kipling
Rhymed Mnemonic of the Forty Counties of England. Monat
Rhyming Prophecy for a New Year. Cooper
Sir Richard's Song. Kipling
Rolling English Road, The. Chesterton
Rule, Britannia! Thomson
Shires, The. *Unknown*
Soldier, The. Brooke
Song for England, A. Salkey
Song of Sherwood, A. Noyes
Song to the Men of England. Shelley
Sonnet: "England! the time is come when thou shouldst wean." Wordsworth
South Country, The. Belloc
Summer in England, 1914. Meynell
Sung at Table by the Same Choir. Penny
Sweetness of England, The. Browning
This Is England. Binyon
To Nye Bevan Despite His Change of Heart. Mitchell
To thee — rude warrior, who, we once admired. Centlivre
Town Clerk's Views, The. Betjeman
Ulster. Kipling
Utopia Anglicized. Gilbert
Whack Fol the Diddle. Kearney

While with a strong and yet a gentle hand. Waller
Writing in England Now. O'Connor
You That Love England. Day Lewis
See also **Civil Wars, English.**

England, Church of. *See* **Church of England.**

English, The
Also scripture saithe, woo be to that regyon. *Unknown*
Ancient and Modern. Scammell
Anvil, The. Kipling
Ballad for an Orphan. Milne
Bonne Entente. Scott
Britannia's Baby. Lawrence
British Journalist, The. Wolfe
Don't make fun of the festival. Coward
England. Tessimond
England Expects. Nash
England's Heart. Tupper
English, The. Smith
English, The. *Unknown*
English Are Frosty, The. Miller
Englishman, The. Cook
Englishman on the French Stage, The. Seaman
Epilogue to an Empire 1600-1900. Stallworthy
Everybody's mad about ya. *Unknown*
Fears in Solitude. Coleridge
For the Rain It Raineth Every Day. Graves
He rais'd no Money, for he paid in land. Defoe
Here must I tell the praise. *Unknown*
How Beastly the Bourgeois Is. Lawrence
How? "Providence", and yet a Scottish crew? Cleveland
In pious times ere [*or* e'r] priest-craft did begin. Dryden
Jacobite's Epitaph, A. Macaulay
Jobson's Amen. Kipling
John of Gaunt's Dying Speech. Shakespeare
Just such a happy Change, our Nation finds. Defoe
Lament for Yellow-haired Donough, The. *Unknown*
Last Lines. O'Rahilly
Let hound and horn in wintry woods and dells. Austin
London Subverted by the Furies. Cowley
Mad Dogs and Englishmen. Coward
Mr. Churchill. Herbert
My Opinion. Sackville
Neutral British Gentleman, The. "Kerr"
New Year's Day Song. Tate
Observations in a Cornish Teashop. Rexroth
Oh let that day from time be blotted quite. Fairfax
Oh You Young Men. Orwell
Old England Forever and Do It No More. *Unknown*
Our gracious Queen. Deloney
Protest against the Ballot. Wordsworth
Sad day this for Alexander, A. Green
Secret People, The. Chesterton
Soldier, The. Brooke
Solitary Travel. MacNeice
Song to the Men of England. Shelley
State of the Nation, The. *Unknown*
True-Born Englishman, The. Defoe
True Englishman, A. *Unknown*
Two Englishmen. Stewart
We Can't Be Too Careful. Lawrence
Wherever God erects a house of prayer. Defoe
Why Should I Care for the Men of Thames? Blake
World Is a Bundle of Hay, The. Byron
Ye Mariners of England. Campbell

English Channel
Channel Crossing. Barker
Outlanders, The. Glaze

Envy
School for Satire, The. Burrell
See also **Jealousy.**

Epic Poetry
Critics say that epics have died out, The. Browning
Epic. Kavanagh

Faith Healers
Faith Healing. Larkin
Faithfulness. *See* **Fidelity.**
Falcons
Epigram: "Lux my fair falcon, and your fellows all." Wyatt
Falcon, The. Lovelace
Falcon and the Dove, The. Read
Falcons, The. Merwin
I trained me a falcon, for more than a year. *Unknown*
Lover Compareth Himself to the Painful Falconer, The. *Unknown*
My Mother Would Be a Falconress. Duncan
Timor Mortis. *Unknown*
Windhover, The. Hopkins
Falkland, Lucius Cary, Viscount
Falkland at Newbury, 1643. Conway
Fall. *See* **Autumn.**
Fame
After Publication of Under the Volcano. Lowry
Consider Famous Men, Dai Bach. Davies
Contemporary. Flexner
Elegy: "Crying from exile, I." Hacker
Fame. Cantus
Fame. Cary
Fame. Emerson
Fame. Heard
Fame. Mew
Fame. More
Fame Makes Us Forward. Herrick
Glory and Enduring Fame. Simms
I'm Nobody! Who are you? Dickinson
In an Album. Lowell
Let us now praise famous men. Bible, Apocrypha
Love of praise, howe'er concealed by art, The. Young
Motto, The. Cowley
On Fame. Juvenal
Ozymandias [*or* Ozymandias of Egypt *or* Sonnet: Ozymandias]. Shelley
Provide, Provide. Frost
Resolve, The. Chudleigh
Stanzas Written on the Road between Florence and Pisa. Byron
There is a tall long-sided dame. Butler
Three things there be in man's opinion dear[e]. Greville
True and False Glory ("To whom our Saviour calmly thus reply'd"). Milton
Wish, A. Kemble
See also **Greatness.**
Family
Abiku. Clark Bekedereme
Animal House, The. Brechin
At Last. Montague
Brown Circle. Glück
Cracked Portraits. Ali
Death of a Lady. Clark Bekedereme
Did This Happen to Your Mother? Walker
Drink of Spring, A. Ennis
Family Is All There Is, The. Rogers
Family Portrait. Budianta
Family Procession, A. Clark Bekedereme
Family Reunion. Kumin
Father and Son. Kunitz
Father, Mother, Son. McAuley
Fifth Grade Autobiography. Dove
For man is between the pinchers while his soul is shaping and purifying. Smart
For Two Who Slipped Away Almost Entirely. Walker
Fording the River. Deane
From the Suburbs. Glück
Funeral Rites. Heaney
Girl threw an apple to a cloud, A. *Unknown*
Glasnevin Cemetery. O'Loughlin
Holy Family. Cooley
Housewife. Schaeffer
Idleness. Lu Yu
In the Village of My Forefathers. Popa
In vain I gather up these stars from the ground. Meng Chiao
Invitation. Livingston

It's Something Our Family Has Always Done. Lum
Joshua Clark. Kenny
Just to Be Needed. Eversley
Letter Following. Mathews
Light. Ondaatje
Lychees. McGuckian
Meal, The. Sansom
On a Moonlit Night, Sent to my Brothers and Sisters. Po Chü-i
On the Night of the Fifteenth Day of the First Month I Go Out and Return. Mei Yao Ch'en
Order of the Dead, The. Clark Bekedereme
Our Family Tree. Holly
Parrot. Po Chü-i
People Next Door, The. Simpson
Picnic. Wong
Picture of My Mother's Family, A. Lum
Pigeons. Longville
Poem about Faith, A. Norris
Quoof. Muldoon
Retrieval System, The. Kumin
Sisters. Clifton
Smokey's Getting Old. Hagedorn
Time of lamentation and curses is passing, The. Lorde
To My Father. Lum
War, The. Parun
When I tread the earth, I fear to hurt the ground. Meng Chiao
White Shroud. Ginsberg
Widows. Glück
Family Life
Abandonment, The. McNair
Amazons. Glück
And the Scream. Berg
Animal Crackers. Morley
Ave Maria. O'Hara
Be Kind. Courtney
Beneath the Shadow of the Freeway. Cervantes
Brown Family, The. Thibaudeau
Childhood. Stanton
Country Letter. Clare
Dandelion Greens. Flanders
Emerald, The. Merrill
Epitaph: "My grandmother, dying, thought my." Longville
Every Town a Home Town. Kaniyan Punkunran
Eyes, the Blood, The. Meltzer
Family. MacCaig
Family Court. Nash
Family Life. *Unknown*
Family Pictures. Morris
Family Turn, A. Stafford
Fifties, The. McDowell
Folded Flock, The. Meynell
From a Childhood. Rilke
Funnel. Sexton
Good Times. Clifton
Grandmother, The. Tennyson
Green Family, The. Thibaudeau
Handful of Pebbles, Mouthful of Stones. Hughes
"Have you got a sister?" *Unknown*
House on Buder Street, The. Gildner
I went to my father's garden. *Unknown*
Ice Cream. Wild
Idea of Ancestry, The. Knight
In the Park. Harwood
In the Wake of Home. Rich
In this house (in a dying orchard). Atwood
Ironing Their Clothes. Alvarez
Island on Sunday Afternoons, The. Larkin
Lament: "Listen, children:/ Your father is dead." Millay
Long Island Springs. Moss
Looking for a Country under Its Original Name. McElroy
Love between Brothers and Sisters. Watts
Love Should Grow Up like a Wild Iris in the Fields. Griffin
Loveact. Nichols
Mothers, Daughters. Kaufman

Muse of Distance, The. Williamson
My Father in the Night Commanding No. Simpson
Nails. Gildner
Nikki-Rosa. Giovanni
O mild Christ. Voigt
Obon: Festival of the Dead. Yamada
Old Man Dreams, The. Holmes
On an Unsociable Family. Hands
Physical Universe. Simpson
Piggy-back. Hughes
Prayer for Broken Little Families, A. Storey
Provincial Adolescence, A. Foley
Relations. Orerulanavar
Rescued Year, The. Stafford
Rural Idyll. Toms
Search, The. Peterson
Somerset Dam for Supper, The. Holmes
Sunday Morning. Jenkins
Super-Brave. Whitman
Talking Family, The. Pitter
Those Winter Sundays. Hayden
Verandahs. Brissenden
Victim, The. Voigt
What Hell Is. McHugh
When Father Carves the Duck. Wright
When I was a chicken. *Unknown*
Why I Never Answered Your Letter. Willard
Woman Mourned by Daughters, A. Rich
Famine
Cold Weather Proverb. Graves
Epigram: "In doubtful breast whilst motherly Pity." Wyatt
Famine. Tran Thi Nga
Famine Year, The. Wilde
Father of Famine. Ryan
Few Sirens, A. Walker
Hunger. Binyon
In Time of Famine. Jackson
Maguire is not afraid of death, the Church will light him a candle. Kavanagh
New from Ethiopia and the Sudan, The. Clark Bekedereme
Fancy. *See* **Imagination.**
Fans
Eagle-Feather Fan, The. Momaday
In Passing. Jonas
Japanese Fan. Kirkup
Present from the Emperor's New Concubine, A. Pan
To a Lady, with a Present of a Fan. *At. to* Brandling
Fantasies
Doctor Type. Koestenbaum
Fantasia. Cooke
Heartthrobs. Smith
Making Love to Marilyn Monroe. Groves
Man and Superman. Self
May Queen, The. Tennyson
On Thinking of Photographing My Fantasies. Wong
Pat of Butter, A. Whitman
Perfection Eludes Us. Seidel
Pitman's Lovesong, A. *Unknown*
Venus in Concrete. O'Loughlin
You must wake and call me early, call me early, mother. Tennyson
Farewell
"Crows Crying at Nighit." Li Yü
Farewell of an Old Man. Tu Fu
Farewell to a Friend. Hsüeh T'ao
First Farewell to J. G. "Ephelia"
Good Night! Good Night! Holmes
Grass on Ancient Plain, a Song of Farewell. Po Chü-i
He Bade Me Be Happy. Osgood
I Say Goodby to Fan An-ch'eng. Shen Yüeh
"Joy at Meeting." Li Yü
"Partridge Sky" — Parting Sorrows. Na-lan Hsing-te
Passion too deep seems like none. Tu Mu
Saying Farewell to Magistrate Ch'en Ta-yu. Lin Hung
Seeing Meng Hao-jan Off to Kuang-ling. Li Po
Seeing Someone Off. Wang Wei

Sowing Seeds. Cornwall
Spring Arithmetic. *Unknown*
Summer Garden. "Akhmatova"
Their Lonely Betters. Auden
This Poem Is for Nadine. Janeczko
Time and the Garden. Winters
Transplanting. Roethke
Villa d'Este Gardens. Sassoon
Warning of Winter. Bethell
Watching gardeners label their plants. Aitken
What You're Teaching Me. Schreiber
When I was young, I did not fit into the common mold. T'ao Ch'ien
Who Loves a Garden. Jones
Widow's Weeds, A. De la Mare

Gardner, John
Notes for an Elegy: for John Gardner. Pastan

Garfield, James Abram
At the President's Grave. Gilder
Bells at Midnight, The. Aldrich
Charles Guiteau. *Unknown*
On the Death of President Garfield. Holmes
President Garfield. Longfellow

Gargoyles
Gargoyle. Rabbitt
Gargoyle. Sandburg
Gargoyle. Shaw

Garlic
Counterblast against Garlic, A. Horace
Garlic. Foster
Ode to Garlic. Stafford

Garrick, David
Prologue [Spoken by Mr. Garrick] [at the Opening of the Theatre in Drury-Lane, 1747]. Johnson

Garrison, William Lloyd
To William Lloyd Garrison. Whittier
William Lloyd Garrison. Ray

Garters
On a Pair of Garters. Davies

Gasoline Stations
Filling Station. Bishop

Gauguin, Paul
Vor a Gauguin Picture zu Singen. Stein

Gaveston, Piers
This Edward in the Aprill of his age. Drayton

Gawaine, Sir
Sir Gawaine and the Green Knight. Winters
This kyng lay at Camylot upon Krystmasse. *Unknown*

Gazelles
Gazelle, The. Gasztold
Gazelle Calf, The. Lawrence
Gazelles, The. Moore

Geese
About Geese. Li Shang-yin
As banked clouds. Saigyo
As the first spring mists appear. Ise
Boat-pullers, The. Mei Yao Ch'en
Cackle, cackle, Mother Goose. *Unknown*
Complaint of the Wild Goose. *Unknown*
Departing wild geese. Issa
Early Geese. Tu Mu
Fox and the Goose, The. *Unknown*
Goose. Braun
Heart of Autumn. Warren
Last Scene in the First Act. Piercy
Late at Night. Stafford
Lilies, The. Braun
Lone Wild Goose, A. Lu Kuei-meng
Old Grey Goose, The. *Unknown*
"Pax vobis," quod the fox. *Unknown*
Poem about Poems about Vietnam, A. Stallworthy
Postcard from the Garden. Piercy
Something Told the Wild Geese. Field
Stepping in the Same River. Chamberlain
Swan and the Goose, The. Aesop
Their high pitched baying. Levertov
Three grey geese in a green field grazing. *Unknown*
To a Goose [or Gosse]. Southey
We hearing them. Shunzei
When the Rain Raineth. *Unknown*

When the wild goose. Sanetomo
Wild Geese, The. Berry
Wild Geese. Chipp
Wild Geese. Tynan
Wild geese departing, The. Saigyo
Wild geese departing, their wings in white clouds, The. Teika
Wild geese gone, the cove looks cleared. Issa
Wild geese leave no trace in the citadel of water, The. Shikishi
Wild geese lured by the autumn wind. Teika
Wild geese returning, The. Tsumori Kunimoto
Wild Goose, Wild Goose. Issa

Gems
Laurentia. McGuckian
Mine Argosy from Alexandria. Marlowe
Mineral Rejoicings. Smart
Scientists find universe awash in tiny diamonds. Ellis
Smaragd the Emerald. Drachler
Stars in Sand. Slater
Stone Diary, A. Lowther

Generals
Bold General Wolfe. *Unknown*
Bury the Great Horse. Garman
General, The. Sassoon
General Elliott, The. Graves
Nightline: An Interview with the General. Wallace

Generosity
Elegy: "He has held." Perevin Muruvalar
Kari Sober. Kapilar
Sunbeams. Trainin
This World Lives Because. Ilam Peruvaluti Urban. Davies

Genetics and Genetic Engineering
Progression of the Species. Aldiss
See also **Evolution.**

Geneva, Switzerland
Geneva. Reid

Genius
Ben Jonson Entertains a Man from Stratford. Robinson
Genius. Menken
Mortified Genius, The. Graeme
On Hearing James W. Riley Read. Cotter

Gentians
Bavarian Gentians. Lawrence
Fringed Gentians. Lowell
God made a little gentian. Dickinson
To the Fringed Gentian. Bryant

Geodes
Geode, the troll's melon. Merrill

Geography and Geographers
Geography. Chesterton
Geography. Farjeon

Geology
Goodnight. Ciardi
Minerals of Cornwall, Stones of Cornwall. Redgrove
Precambrian [or Pre-Cambrian] Shield, The. Pratt
What Happened Here Before. Snyder

Geometry
Geometry. Dove
See also **Euclid.**

George I, King of England
Epigram: "King George, observing with judicious eyes." Trapp
Epigram: "King to Oxford sent a troop of horse, The." Browne
On George I. *Unknown*
Pasquin to the Queen's Statue at St. Paul's. Shippen
Wee, Wee German Lairdie, The. Cunningham

George II, King of England
Lilliputian Ode on Their Majesties' Accession, A. Carey
What mean these loud aerial cracks I hear? *Unknown*

George III, King of England
George III. Lowell
George III Visits Whitbread's Brewery. "Pindar"

Lilliputian Ode on Their Majesties' Accession, A. Carey
On George III. "Pindar"
Saint Peter sat by the celestial gate. Byron
Slow-worm from my orchard seeking me, The. Wainwright

George IV, King of England
Epitaph on the Late King of the Sandwich Isles. Praed
More On George IV. *Unknown*
On George IV. *Unknown*

George V, King of England
King George V. Hayward
"New King Arrives in His Capital by Air . . . " — Daily Newspaper. Betjeman

George VI, King of England
Praises of King George VI. Ngani

Georgia
Childhood. Beasley
Daufuskie. Evans
Georgia Dusk. Toomer
In a U-Haul North of Damascus. Bottoms
In the Marble Quarry. Dickey
Marching through Georgia. Work
Purpose of Altar Boys, The. Ríos
Refugee. Madgett
Robert Whitmore. Davis
Song of the Chattahoochee. Lanier

Geraniums
Geranium, The. Roethke
Geraniums. Gibson
Red Geranium and Godly Mignonette. Lawrence
Red Geraniums. Clark

German Verse
German Poetry from the Beginning to 1750 (GePo). Ingrid Walsoe-Engel, ed.

Germans, The
Riddle: "From Belsen a crate of gold teeth." Heyen

Germany
Bingen on the Rhine. Norton
Booty from the German War. Logau
Deutschland. Maxton
Die Gedanken Sind Frei. *Unknown*
Dreams in German. "Martin"
German Language, The. Logau
High Germany. Shanks
In Freiburg Station. Brooke
In Saxony. Levine
Mittelbergheim. Milosz
No Offence. Enright
Nuremberg. Longfellow
On a German Tour. Porson
Over the Wall: Berlin, May 1975. Sisson
Pictures of the Rhine. Meredith
Small Park in East Germany: 1969. Mayer
Song of the Cape of Good Hope. Schubart
To Germany. Sorley
To Germany. Weckherlin
Walk in Würzburg, A. Plomer
Ye tourists and travellers, bound to the Rhine. Hood

Germs
Germ, The. Nash
Some Little Bug. Atwell

Geronimo
Geronimo. McGaffey

Gethsemane
Agony in the Garden, The. Hemans
Christs Sleeping Friends. Southwell
Sinnes Heavie Loade. Southwell
Sory beverech [or beverech] it is, and sore it is abought [or abouth], A. *Unknown*

Gettysburg, Battle of (1863)
Battle of Gettysburg, The. Benét
Dickens in Camp. Harte
Gettysburg. Roche
Gettysburg. Stedman
High Tide at Gettysburg, The. Thompson
John Burns of Gettysburg. Harte
Lincoln at Gettysburg. Taylor
Sanitary Message, A. Harte

Ghana
Cornfields in Accra. Ama Ata Aidoo

Moon of Mind against the Wooden Louver,
  The. Broumas
Not Singing. Daniels
Notes for the Chart in 306. Nash
Old Men's Ward. Dean
Operation, The. Snodgrass
Pediatrics. Muske
Plague and Hospice. Clifton
Rescue the Dead. Ignatow
Room 3366, Bed 1. Knight
St. Vincent's. Merwin
Scarecrow. Bolger
Second Law, The. Sandy
Staff. Engman
Still Life. Gunn
Stones, The. Plath
Sunday at the State Hospital. Ignatow
Surgical Ward: Men. Graves
Teddy Bear, A. Knight
Transfusion. Moore
Tubes. Hall
Tulips. Plath
University Hospital, Boston. Oliver
Unknown Girl in the Maternity Ward. Sexton
Visit to a Hospital. Chace
Visitors Laugh at Locksmiths or, Hospital
  Doors Haven't Got Locks Anyhow. Nash
Wait. Steele
Ward Two. Webb
What the Intern Saw. Levin
Wings, The. Greger

Hotels
At a Summer Hotel. Gardner
At the Algonquin. Moss
At the End of the Affair. Kumin
Birmingham. McGough
Black Man, 13th Floor. Emanuel
Conversation Piece. Graves
Dolgelley Hotel, The. Hughes
Finn's Wishes. O'Grady
Irish Hotel. Wevill
Lament for Lost Lodgings. McGinley
Stirling's Hotel. *Unknown*
Strand Hotel, Rosslare, The. Liddy
Uphill [*or* Up-Hill]. Rossetti
Written at [*or in*] an Inn at Henley. Shenstone
See also **Motels.**

Hottentots
Hottentot, The. Pringle

Houdini, Harry
Houdini. Mandel

Hourglasses
Hour-Glass, The. Herrick
Hourglass [*or* The Houre-Glasse], The ("Do but
  consider this small dust"). Jonson

House Painting
Painters, The. Hemschemeyer

Housekeeping
Housewife, The. Coblentz
Huswifery. Taylor
I Like Housecleaning. Thompson
When Young Melissa Sweeps. Turner
See also **Housewives.**

Houses
After Reading in a Letter Proposals for
  Building a Cottage. Clare
Beginnings. Weaver
Crack is moving down the wall, The. Kees
Deserted House, The. Coleridge
Deserted House, The. Reese
Directive. Frost
Domicilium. Hardy
Dream House. Newell
Empty House, The. Spender
Empty House, The. Williams
Fire. Carpenter
Floating Houses. Wojahn
Floor and the Ceiling, The. Smith
Gregory's House. Huddle
Ground for the Floor. *Unknown*
Home. Feinstein
House, The. Bowering
House. Browning
House, The. Minhinnick
House, The. Nelson

House, The. Van Zyl
House, The. Williams
House Blessing. Guiterman
House Made of Rain, The. Nye
House of Pride, The. Dawson
House on the Hill, The. Robinson
House Remembered, The. Ní Chuilleanáin
House to let, enquire within. *Unknown*
House with Nobody in It, The. Kilmer
Houses. Fisher
I and Thou. Dugan
I built my house, I built my walls. *Unknown*
I know some lonely houses off the
  road. Dickinson
I Like Housecleaning. Thompson
I Walked Past a House Where I Lived
  Once. Amichai
Interiors. Mathews
Invites His Nymph to His Cottage. Ayres
Invocation: "Silent, about-to-be-parted-from
  house." Levertov
Jeronimo's House. Bishop
Mending the Adobe. Carruth
My house, I say. But hark to the sunny
  doves. Stevenson
My Little House. Westrup
Naming the House. Lauterbach
New House, The. Thomas
O Blessèd House, That Cheerfully
  Receiveth. Spitta
O Thou Whose Gracious Presence
  Blest. Benson
Old Houses. D'Lettuso
Old Houses. Romano
Old Houses of Flanders, The. Ford
Old Mansion. Ransom
Old Woman of the Roads, An. Colum
On a Picture of Your House. Jones
On Lord Holland's Seat near Margate,
  Kent. Gray
On the Hall at Stowey. Tomlinson
One bright September morning in. *Unknown*
Point Shirley. Plath
Prayer for This House. Untermeyer
Quebec Farmhouse. Glassco
Round House, A. Sweeney
Sestina for the House. Wallace
Setting the Table. Aldis
Shooting a Farmhouse. Kooser
Shoplifter, The. Sweeney
Song for a Little House. Morley
Split Level. Sweeney
Stately Homes of England, The. Coward
Thanksgiving to God for His House,
  A. Herrick
To Saxham. Carew
To the New Owner. Reynolds
Vagabond House. Blanding
Welcome House, The. O'Donnell
Wide Walls. *Unknown*
World, The. Herbert
See also **Home.**

Housewives
Affections Must Not. Riley
Divine Office of the Kitchen, The. Hallack
Farmer's Bride, The. Mew
Gone Is the Sleepgiver. Shuttle
Household Dilemma. Gilligan
Housewife, The. Coblentz
Hurry, Hurry, Mary Dear! Bodecker
Letter from a Far Country. Clarke
Life Is a Toil. *Unknown*
Lysidice, I'm anxious to find out the
  meaning. Antipater of Sidon
Marks. Pastan
My Love. *Unknown*
Next Day. Jarrell
Satire on the Town Ladies. Maitland
Suburban Wife's Song. Hutchinson
Woman in Kitchen. Boland
Young Housewife, The. Williams
See also **Housekeeping.**

Housman, Alfred Edward
Another Epitaph on an Army of
  Mercenaries. "MacDiarmid"
Mr. Housman's Message. Pound

Hudson, Henry
Henry Hudson's Quest. Stevenson
Hudson Bay
Empty Threat, An. Frost
Hudson River
Egyptian Passage, An. Weiss
Lordly Hudson, The. Goodman
Mouth of the Hudson, The. Lowell
Hughes, Langston
Do Nothing till You Hear from
  Me. Henderson
For Langston Hughes. Knight
Langston Hughes. Blockcolski
Reading Walt Whitman. Forbes
Rhetoric of Langston Hughes, The. Danner
Hughes, Ted
Policeman's Lot, A. Cope
Huguenots
Psalm: "While Northward the hot sun was
  sinking o'er the trees." Bridges
Human Folly
Whate'er the passion — knowledge, fame, or
  pelf. Pope
Human Race. *See* **Mankind.**
Humility
Ambition. Astell
Bran, a chaff, a very barley [y]awn,
  A. Taylor
Charity. Bensley
Clod and the Pebble, The. Blake
Cock's crow means profit, The. Tseng Jui
Composed at Sunset at the Dunes of Ho-
  yen. Ts'en Shen
Contrition. Knevet
Eating Shepherd's-purse. Mei Yao Ch'en
Grass hovel filled with wind and dust. Wang
  Fun-chih
Happiest Heart, The. Cheney
He that is down, needs fear no fall. Bunyan
House by the Side of the Road, The. Foss
Humble Heart, A. Norris
Humility. Herbert
I love thee for thy fickleness. *Unknown*
If. Kipling
In Emulation of Mr Cowleys Poem Call'd The
  Motto. Astell
Joseph in Carcere. Hubert
Near Damascus. Di Piero
Oaks and Squirrels. Porter
Out of Horace. Wright
Paraphrase. Johnson
Paraphrase Upon Part of the CXXXIX Psalm,
  A. Stanley
"Partridge Sky" — Written at the Po-shan
  Monastery. Hsin Ch'i-chi
Proverbs 6:6. Curzon
Psalm 119.37. Quarles
Recessional. Kipling
Resolve, The. Chudleigh
Rochester Extempore. Rochester
"Sand of Silk-washing Stream." Wang Kuo-
  wei
"Sheep on Mountain Slope." Ch'iao Chi
"Slow Chant." Ma Chih-yüan
State, a state, oh! dungeon state indeed,
  A. Taylor
Step out onto the Planet. Welch
That fellow rides a big horse. Wang Fun-chih
To Show How Humble. *Unknown*
Violet, The. Taylor
We who prayed and wept. Berry
When that repentant tears hath cleansed clear
  from ill. Surrey

Hummingbirds
Container, The. Corman
Humming Bird. Groves
Humming Bird, The. Kemp
Humming-Bird. Lawrence
Humming-Bird, The. Tucker
Hummingbird. Littlebird
Hummingbird: a Seduction, The. Rogers
Hummingbirds. Dubie
Murmurers, The. Jacobsen
Vision. Eberhart

Hymns

Hymn Tunes, The. Lucie-Smith
American Hymns Old and New (AH). Albert
   Christ-Janer, Charles W. Hughes, *and*
   Carleton Sprague Smith, eds.

Hypocrisy

Address to the Unco Guid, or the Rigidly
   Righteous. Burns
American Heartbreak. Hughes
At dinner, she is hostess, I am host. Meredith
Beard-wagging stick-waving beggarman Cynic,
   A. Lucianus
Better to live as a rogue and a bum. Mahsati
Confessor, The. Belli
Double Standard, A. Harper
Epistle from Mrs. Yonge to Her
   Husband. Montagu
Ethics for Everyman. Woddis
Holy Willie's Prayer. Burns
Hue and Cry after Fair Amoret, A. Congreve
Hyena. *Unknown*
Hypocrisy will serve as well. Butler
Hypocrite Women. Levertov
Latest Decalogue, The. Clough
Look, No Hands. Hutchinson
"May Grace be with you all" said the
   bishop. *Unknown*
Next to of course god america i. Cummings
On the Town's Honest Man. Jonson
Soliloquy of the Spanish Cloister. Browning
Stanzas: "In this vain, busy world, where the
   good and the gay." Robinson
Tommy. Kipling
We Wear the Mask. Dunbar

I

Ibn Ezra, Moses

On Parting with Moses ibn Ezra. Halevi

Ibsen, Henrik

Fox Who Watched for the Midnight Sun,
   The. Dubie

Icarus

Brueghel in Naples. Abse
Daedalus. Ovid
Icarus. Iremonger
Icarus. Spender
Landscape with the Fall of Icarus. Williams
Musée des Beaux Arts. Auden
Waiting for Icarus. Rukeyser
Winged Man. Benét

Ice

Break-up, The. Klein
Fire and Ice. Frost
Ice. De la Mare
Ice. Roberts
Ice River. Baker
Image of the frozen lake, The. Fontanella
Sleet. MacCaig

Ice Cream

Good Humor Man, The. McGinley
I scream/ You scream. *Unknown*
Ice-Cream Man, The. Field
Tableau at Twilight. Nash
When they pass the pink ice cream. *Unknown*

Ice Hockey

Rink Keeper's Sestina. Draper

Ice-Skating. *See* **Skating and Skaters.**

Icebergs

Berg, The. Melville
Convergence of the Twain (Lines on the Loss
   of the *Titanic*), The. Hardy
Icebergs. Michaux
Imaginary Iceberg, The. Bishop
On the Ice Islands Seen Floating in the German
   Ocean. Cowper

Iceland

Gunnar's Howe above the House at
   Lithend. Morris
Iceland First Seen. Morris
Journey to Iceland. Auden
Journey to Iceland. Auden
Letter to Graham and Anna. MacNeice

Icicles

Icicles. Pinsky
To an Icicle. Dickinson
Why are some icicles long, some
   short? Onitsura

Idaho

Idaho. *Unknown*
Way Out in Idaho. *Unknown*

Identity Crisis

After Love. Kumin
Agony, An. As Now. Baraka
Being Somebody. Honig
Cousin Ella Goes to Town. Lyon
Exits and Entrances. Madgett
I Am Not I. Jiménez
My Son. Stone
Not Thinking of Himself. Myers
Self-Dependence. Arnold
Twins, The. Stephens
Woman at the Washington Zoo, The. Jarrell

Idleness

Breakfast in Bed (Influenza in War-
   time). McDonald
Lament of a Slug-a-Bed's Wife. Smith
Sluggard, The. Watts
See also **Sloth.**

Idolatry

Iconoclast, The. Cooke
Idols. Burton
Manicheans did no idols make, The. Greville
Three things there be in man's opinion
   dear[e]. Greville
Worship of Cromm Cruaich, The. *Unknown*

Ignorance

Poet of Ignorance, The. Sexton

Iguanas

Mid-Noon in January. "Macleod"

Illegitimacy

Brown Baby Blues. Marson
Elsa Wertman. Masters
Girl's Lamentation, The. Allingham
Natural Child, The. Leigh
Poet's Welcome to His Love-begotten
   Daughter, A. Burns
Practical Woman, A. Hardy
Unknown Girl in the Maternity Ward. Sexton

Illinois

Blues for Bessie. O'Higgins
El-a-noy. *Unknown*
First Song. Kinnell
Lovers of the Poor, The. Brooks
Making Chicago. Schmitz
Planting Trout in the Chicago River. Schmitz

Illiteracy

Harriet in the Promised Land. Cornish
Illiterate, The. Meredith
Reading Lesson, The. Murphy
Sarah Byng Who Could Not Read and Was
   Tossed into a Thorny Hedge by a Bull. A
   Cautionary Tale. Belloc
Señora X No More. Mora

Illness

Adieu, Farewell, Earth's Bliss[e]. Nashe
Ah! why from me art thou for ever
   flown. Cave
Airing Cupboard. Walton
Almost to Jesus. Burkard
Among the Narcissi. Plath
Anastasia McLaughlin. Paulin
Annie ate jam. *Unknown*
Answer to a Kind Enquiry. Holtby
Assistances. Corn
Blossoms bloom, I don't wanna die, but this
   illness. Raizan
Bout with Burning. Miller
But, O immortals! What had I to plead. Smart
Caroline Pink, she fell down the
   sink. *Unknown*
Charm me asleep, and melt me so. Herrick
Child to His Sick Grandfather, A. Baillie
City/Country. Wyat
Commands of Love. Peacock
Composed While Ill. Basho
Convalescence. McAuley
Daughter's House, A. Richman

Day in August, A. Ormsby
Death Is. Sinclair
Derailment: A Delirium. Chimombo
Dialogue between the Soul and [the] Body,
   A. Marvell
Diarrhea Sestina. Kleinschmidt
Each Day. Maura
80's Miracle Diet, The. Dixon
Enticing Lane, The. Hewitt
Entreaty. Fitzgerald
Evans. Thomas
Faith-Falling. Digges
Far Cry after a Close Call, A. Howard
Fear of Madness, The. Davidson
Felix Randal. Hopkins
Flat One, A. Snodgrass
For Deliverance from a Fever. Bradstreet
Foreign Element, The. Johnson
France. Dunn
Gifts, The. Austin
Good Timing. Ebbecke
Greeting to Lu Hung-Chien, A. Li Yeh
Haiku: "This year/ I took sick with the
   peonies." Masaoka Shiki
Half-Life, A. Cole
Have You Anything to Say in Your
   Defense? Vallejo
Healing. Lawrence
Heartbeats. Dixon
His Illness. Ibn Gabirol
Household Remedies. *Unknown*
Hymn to My God in a Night of My Late
   Sickness[e], A. Wotton
I Have Told You Your Hands Are Salt. Purdy
In a Time of Sickness. Orpingalik
In Memoriam. Rich
In Sickness Written Soon after the Author's
   Coming to Live in Ireland, upon the Queen's
   Death, October 1714. Swift
In the Waiting Room. Bergman
Infirmity. Roethke
Invalid's Song. Harata Tangikuku
Isolation. Sansom
Judgment, The. Spivack
Land of Counterpane, The. Stevenson
Lenten Tunnel, The. Hadas
Letters from a Father. Van Duyn
Librarian, The. Olson
Look, our Spaniard's yawning. Machado Ruiz
Madam and the Wrong Visitor. Hughes
Mama Rosanna's Last Bead-Clack. Speer
Me and My Mother's Morphine. Smith
Medicine. Walker
Menace of the Sick. Breytenbach
Missing, The. Gunn
Moon of Mind Against the Wooden Louver,
   The. Broumas
Mother's Prayer in Illness, A. Osgood
Night Nurse Gets Her Round, The. Gray
999 Call. Bartlett
Nine times the sun his yearly course had
   run. Thomas
Notes for the Chart in 306. Nash
Nurse's hand taking my pulse, The. Ishikawa
   Takuboku
Of One Dying. Owens
Old Gardens Are Not Relevant. O'Donnell
One by One. Dixon
Other Syllabus, The. Hove
Personal Values. Howard
Plague and Hospice. Clifton
Pneumoconiosis. Bush
Poem: "You are ill and so I lead you
   away." Purdy
Retrovir. Dlugas
Saturday Night. Sansom
Scar, The. Hewitt
Sick Child, The. Sigourney
Sick-room, The. Lowell
Singer, The. Bolger
Sisters. McPherson
Song of Sickness, A. Tangikuku
Song of the Darkness. Bricuth
Sparrow. *Unknown*
Star Trek III. Harteis
Still Life. Gunn

To an Oak Tree. Scott
To the Oaks of Glencree. Synge
Yardley Oak. Cowper

Oases
Ease your weary limbs, stranger, under this
  elm —. Anyte
Green, Green Is El Aghir. Cameron
I, Hermes, have been set up. Anyte
Needles of the lofty pine, The. *Unknown*
Oasis of Sidi Khaled, The. Blunt
On a Statue of Pan. *Unknown*
Sit down in the shade of this fine spreading
  laurel. Anyte
See also **Deserts.**

Oates, Joyce Carol
When she lived near St. Lawrence. Cole

Oates, Titus
Ballad upon the Popish Plot, A. Gadbury
Panegyric upon Oates, A. Duke
Tragi-Comedy of Titus Oates, The. *Unknown*

Obesity
Dogs. Longville
Fat Blues. Crowell
Fat Boy's Dream, The. McCann
Fat Men, The. Dabydeen
Good Old Body. Donald
Heavy As Ever. Longville
Invitation. Nichols
Perils of Obesity, The. Graham
Syn I fro Love. Chaucer
Whistle, Daughter, Whistle. *Unknown*
Zimmershire Lad, A. Zimmer

Obscenity
Gentleman's Study, in Answer to The Lady's
  Dressing-Room, The. W ——
On First Looking into Krafft-Ebing's
  *Psychopathosexualis [or Psychopathia
  Sexualis].* Gogarty
See also **Pornography.**

Observatories
Greenwich Observatory. Keyes
See also **Astronomy and Astronomers.**

Obsessions
Circe. Ewart
Food of Love. Kizer
If I Had to Do It All Over Again, I'd Do It All
  Over You. Totton
Incantation, The. Kirsch
Julian of Norwich. Jamie
Juliet. Belloc
Little-Bitty Man. Storni
Love: First Version, 1915, A. Williams
Lovesong: "He loved her and she loved
  him." Hughes
Now my mind's been brought to such a state —
  and it's your fault. Catullus
Obsession. Damas
Process of time worketh such wonder. Wyatt
When I Hear Your Name. Fuertes
When — presto — turf and trees are
  green. Bernard de Ventadour

Occult, The
Crossroads, The. Moldaw
Diehard. Moffett
Séance. King
Spell for Sleeping, A. Reid
Suddenly you feel a touch. Michaux

Occupations
Foreplay of the Alphabet. Gray
My Share. Bolat
No Money in Art. Gustafson
Vocation. Tagore

Ocean. *See* **Sea.**

O'Connor, Flannery
Flannery O'Connor. Walters

O'Connor, Rory
They are the spit of virtue now. Clarke

October
Especially When the October Wind. Thomas
In the Month of Green Fire. Himmell
Late October. Carleton
Now Blue October. Nathan
October. Fordham
October. Frost

October. Kavanagh
October. Ray
October. Rossetti
October. Schuyler
October. Thomas
October. Updike
October Elegy. Gibson
October Is Here. Linden
October Journey. Walker
October's Bright Blue Weather. Jackson
October's Party. Cooper
Poem in October. Thomas
Tregardock. Betjeman
Vagabond Song, A. Carman
When Slow October Changes Color. Piersanti

Octopuses
Octopus. Hilton
Octopus, The. Merrill
Octopus, The. Nash
Octopus. Worth

Odysseus. *See* **Ulysses.**

Oedipus
Antigone and Oedipus. Ray
Incantation to Oedipus. Dryden
Myth. Rukeyser
Oedipus. Blackburn
Oedipus. Muir
When Athens all the Graecian state did
  guide. Dryden

Oenone
Oenone's Complaint. Peele

Offa, King of Mercia
Princes of Mercia were badger and raven,
  The. Hill

Office Workers
Any Man to His Secretary. Corke
Back Again, Home. Lee
Dolor. Roethke
Office Friendships. Ewart
Report, The. Swan
Return to Work, The. Williams
Song from a Two-Desk Office. Buck
Stenographers, The. Page
What Grandma Knew. Field
See also **Clerks; Secretaries.**

Officers, Military
Base Details. Sassoon
From a Young Woman to an Old Officer Who
  Courted Her. Amherst
In Memoriam[, Private D.
  Sutherland]. Mackintosh

Ogres
Ogres and Pygmies. Graves
See also **Monsters; Trolls.**

O'Hara, Frank
Frank O'Hara. Berrigan

Ohio
At the Executed Murderer's Grave. Wright
Autumn Begins in Martins Ferry,
  Ohio. Wright
Beautiful Ohio. Wright
By the Beautiful Ohio. LaBombard
Founders of Ohio, The. Venable
In Response to a Rumor That the Oldest
  Whorehouse in Wheeling, West Virginia, Has
  Been Condemned. Wright
Ohioan Pastoral. Wright
Produce. Allbery
To the Union Savers of Cleveland. Harper
Yes, But. Wright

Ohio River
When I asked for fish in the restaurant facing
  the Ohio River. Sandburg

Oisin
History. Liddy
Praise of Fionn, The. *Unknown*
Wanderings of Oisin, The. Yeats

Okinawa, Japan
Picture of Okinawa, A. Schmitz

Oklahoma
Captive Stone, The. Barnes
Driving into Enid. Van Walleghen
Starving to Death on a Government
  Claim. *Unknown*

Old Age
Acre of Grass, An. Yeats
Advice to the Old Beaux. Sedley
After Touch. Clausen
Age. Jones
Age. Landor
Age. More
Age in Prospect. Jeffers
Aged Fisherman. Bynner
Aged Lover Renounceth Love, The. Vaux
Ago. Jennings
Alas! 'Tis Very Sad to Hear. Landor
Almswomen. Blunden
Already old age is wrinkling my. Sappho
Ancient to Ancients, An. Hardy
Annuity, The. Outram
Apology. Niatum
April Inventory. Snodgrass
Are you Content? Yeats
As I grow old, and weaker grow my
  eyes. Yüan Mei
At home I loved to wear old clothes. Wang
  Chien
At the Doors. "Der Nistor"
Aunt Lucy. Gentry
Auspex. Lowell
Autumn finds me old and poorer. Meng Chiao
Autumnus. Sylvester
Ballad of Old Women & of How They Are
  Constrained To Simulate Youth In Order To
  Avoid Shocking the Young. Talbot
Baucis and Philemon. Hoskins
Bean Eaters, The. Brooks
Bedtime Story, A. Mezey
Bee Dice Game, The. Barton
Before my back was bent I was
  eloquent. *Unknown*
Belly Dancer in the Nursing Home,
  The. Wallace
Bent. Carter
Black and glossy as a bee and curled was my
  hair. Ambapali
Blue Springs, Georgia. Young
Body of John. Mason
Bones of the lonely-wretched spend no quiet
  nights. Meng Chiao
Both Less and More. Dixon
Boys, The. Holmes
Cassibus Impositis Venor. Barry
Centenarian's Story, The. Whitman
Chaperon, The. Bunner
Chard Whitlow. Reed
Chasing the Sun. Jiang He
Childhood. Cornford
City Pigeons. Chasin
Come On in, the Senility Is Fine. Nash
Comfort. Widdemer
Coming of Wisdom with Time, The. Yeats
Complaint of the Grandparents. Justice
Costa Geriatrica. Sharpless
Cowboy Film. Matthews
Crows, The. Bogan
Cup clinks out, my friend, The. Apollonides
Daguerreotype Taken in Old Age. Atwood
Danny Murphy. Stephens
Dear Men and Women. Wheelock
Death Invoked. Massinger
Did I not say we grow old. Rufinus
Disturb me not, oh bouyant youths! *Unknown*
Do Not Go Gentle into That Good
  Night. Thomas
Dust to Dust. De la Mare
Each Bird Walking. Gallagher
Elderly Discontented Women. Lawrence
Emancipation. *Unknown*
Envy the Old. Van Doren
Epicurean. Linton
Fall. Smith
Farewell of an Old Man. Tu Fu
Father. Lipkin
Father William. "Carroll"
Fear of Death. Ashbery
Feeling Old Age. Liu Tsung-yüan
Felicitous Life, A. Milosz
First Meditation. Roethke
Flying Wheel, The. Tynan

Q

When Thou Did Thinke I Did Not
  Love. Ayton
Words! Words! Fauset
See also **Anger.**

Quarries
Green Slates. Hardy
Rockferns. Nicholson

Quebec (province), Canada
Bonne Entente. Scott
Indian Reservation: Caughnawaga. Klein
On Autumn Lake. Ashbery
Quebec Farmhouse. Glassco
Wednesday at North Hatley. Gustafson

Quebec (city), Canada
Brave Wolfe. *Unknown*
Houses Burning; Quebec. Anderson
Quebec. Ray

Queen Anne's Lace
Queen Anne's Lace. Newton
Queen-Ann's-Lace. Williams

Queens
Alas! Poor Queen. Angus
Australian Dream, The. Campbell
But, Greatest *Anna*! while Thy Arms
  pursue. Prior
Courting the Faerie Queen. Newcastle
English Queen, The. Lawson
Esther. Jackson
Everybody's mad about ya. *Unknown*
His Petition to Queen Anne of Denmark
  (1618). Ralegh
Memoir of a Queen. Jackson
New Year Gift to the Queen Mary When She
  First Came Home, 1562, A. Scott
Our gracious Queen. Deloney
Queen Mother to New Queen. Graves
Queen Nefertiti. *Unknown*
Queen of the Nile, The. Smith
Queen, Queen Caroline. *Unknown*
Queens. Synge
To His Mistress. Ralegh
You poets all, brave Shakespeare, Jonson,
  Green. *Unknown*
See also individual names of queens (e.g.,
  Elizabeth I, Queen of England).

Questions
After. Barnett
And what *do* we love anyway (here I am
  coming up to). Riley
Another Fools' Day Touches Down:
  Shush. Mapanje
At the Door. Merriam
Catechism. Sholl
Civilization and Its Discontents. Matthews
Diagonal Is Diagonal, The. Oliver
I have lived on the lip. Jalal al-Din Rumi
Old Age. Mang Ke
Police Inquiry, The. Morgenstern
Question, The. Auden
Questioners, The. Mayo
Questions. *Unknown*
South Mount Soaring High. Shih Ching
Spirit Appeared to Me, A. Melville
Vain Questioning. De la Mare
What is it that upsets the volcanoes. Neruda
Whichway. Welburn
Why? De la Mare

Quests
Credo. Gale
Desire. "Æ"
I found Thee in my heart, O Lord. Dowden
If There Had Anywhere Appeared. Trench
Lord, If Thou Art Not Present. Gray
Loving Mad Tom. *Unknown*
O Thou/ God of all long desirous
  roaming. Brooke
O Thou who bidst the torrent flow. Whittier
Odysseus. Guri
Prayer: "Bear with me, Master, when I turn
  from Thee." Pierce
Pursuit. Warren
Quest, The. Scudder
Rev'rend Father stood inculcating,
  The. Camões
Search. Widdemer

Seeker in the Night, A. Coates
Sight and Insight. Slater
Tipperary. O'Grady
To Tarshish. Halkin
To-Morrow. Lope de Vega Carpio
World's Desire, The. Benét

Quilts
Design for a Quilt. Ormond
In a Country Museum. Beer
My Mother Pieced Quilts. Acosta
Patchwork Quilt, The. Fleming
Quilt, The. Newsome
Quilt in the Bennington College Library,
  A. Smith
Quilt Song. Vinz
Quilts. Peirce
Spare Quilt, The. Bishop

Quince Trees and Quinces
As for the Quince. Ni Dhomhnaill
Quince Preserved through the Winter, Given to
  a Lady, A. Antiphilus

Quivira
Quivíra. Guiterman

Quotidian
Epistle to Her Friends at Gartmore. Blamire
I Have Found Such Joy. Crowell
Little Things. *Unknown*
Wishes. Child

Qur'an
Even from earthly love thy face avert
  not. Jami

R

Ra. *See* **Amon Ra.**
Rabbis
Baal Shem Tov. Klein
Bratzlav Rabbi to His Scribe, The. Glatstein
Rabbi, The. Morgenstern
Rabbi Yom-Tob of Mayence Petitions His
  God. Klein
White Petticoats. Bloch

Rabbits
Big Rabbit goes to see his baby. *Unknown*
Bunny Rabbit. *Unknown*
Giving Rabbit to My Cat Bonnie. Stevenson
Hares at Play. Clare
My New Rabbit. Gould
Myxomatosis. Larkin
Rabbit, The. Cassian
Rabbit, The. King
Rabbit, The. Roberts
Rabbit. Robinson
Rabbit, The. *Unknown*
Rabbit Story, The. Edson
Rabbit's Advice, The. Jennings
Skippets, the Bad One. Bradley
Snare, The. Stephens
Song of the Rabbits outside the Tavern,
  The. Coatsworth
Thorny. Cole
Timid Bunnies. Kirby
Topsy-Turvy Land. Stone
White Season. Frost
See also **Hares.**

Raccoons
Diary of a Raccoon. Bennett
Mill Valley. Livingston
Raccoon, The. Johnson
Raccoon. Rexroth
Raccoon on the Road. Brennan
Raccoon Poem. Palmer
Raccoons. Fisher

Rachel
At the Tomb of Rachel. "Yehoash"

Racial Prejudice
American History. Harper
American Memory of Africa, An. Awoonor
Backlash Blues, The. Hughes
Ballad of Rudolph Reed, The. Brooks
Birmingham Sunday. Hughes
Black Poet, White Critic. Randall
Bronzeville Woman in a Red Hat. Brooks

Children's Rhymes. Hughes
Cloud Unfolding, The. Trejo
Communication to Nancy Cunard, A. Boyle
Cordon Negro. Hemphill
Creation, According to Coyote, The. Ortiz
Crispus Attucks McCoy. Brown
Cross. Hughes
Daddy Poem, A. Harris
Dance for Militant Dilettantes, A. Young
Defeat. Bynner
Dream Boogie. Hughes
Everybody but Me. Burroughs
Family Jewels. Hemphill
Grandfather. Harper
Gulf, The. Walcott
Half-caste. Agard
Harlem, Montana; Just Off the
  Reservation. Welch
Hatred of Men with Black Hair. Bly
I am no longer master of my tears. Tam'si
I Fight Back. Allen
In Bloemfontein. Ross
In re Solomon Warshawer. Klein
Incident. Cullen
Island. Hughes
It is true — / I've always loved. Walker
Justiniano Lamé Has Been Killed. Durham
Kinky Hair Blues. Marson
Little Black Boy, The. Blake
Little White Schoolhouse Blues. Lennon
Lover's Question, A. Baldwin
Mat to Weave, A. Tam'si
Melting Pot, The. Randall
Merry-go-round. Hughes
Moment Please, A. Allen
Monangamba. Jacinto
Montgomery. Cornish
1974. Hacker
No Irish Need Apply. Poole
Oh God Forbid. Greenfield
Old Lem. Brown
On Knowing the Difference Between Prejudice,
  Discrimination, and Oppression. Leonard
On Seeing Two Brown Boys in a Catholic
  Church. Horne
Parasitosis. Davis
Poem about My Rights. Jordan
Poem for the Young White Man Who Asked
  Me How I, an Intelligent, Well-read Person,
  Could Believe in the War between
  Races. Cervantes
Politeness. Marson
Power. Lorde
Prejudice. Johnson
Prejudice against Colour. Dale
Riot. Brooks
Runaway Slave at Pilgrim's Point,
  The. Browning
Searching. Cobb
Sleepless Night. Damas
So Often. Damas
Southern Cop. Brown
Status Quo. Dismond
Tableau. Cullen
Telephone Conversation. Soyinka
There's Somethin'. Small
Tiger. McKay
Time of Martyrdom, The. Diop
Tripart. Jones
Ultimate Equality. Durem
Upstairs Downstairs. Allen
Vietnam #4. Major
We Call Them Greasers. Anzaldúa
Where? When? Which? Hughes
White and the Black, The. Khaketla
White House, The. McKay
Whitewash. Damas
With All Deliberate Speed. Lee
With the Herring Fishers. "MacDiarmid"
See also **Apartheid.**

Racing. *See* **Automobile Racing; Crew Racing;
  Horse Racing; Track Athletics.**

Racism
Ajax' Conclusion. Coffin
Alabama Bus. Hairston

South African War

Penguin Book of Southern African Verse, The (PeSAV). Stephen Gray, ed.

South African War. *See* **Boer War.**

South America. *See* **Peru.**

South Carolina

Battle of Charleston Harbor, The. Hayne
Brother Jonathan's Lament for Sister
  Caroline. Holmes
Carolina. Timrod
Charleston. Gilder
Charleston. Hayne
Charleston. Timrod
Crum Appointment, The. Moorer
Ode: "Sleep sweetly in your humble
  graves." Timrod
South Carolina to the States of the
  North. Hayne

South Sea Islands

Fun with Fishing. Tietjens

South Wind

Awake! Bible, *O.T.*
Moon's the North Wind's Cooky,
  The. Lindsay
South Wind laid his moccasins aside,
  The. Crawford

Southern Cross, The (constellation)

Southern Cross. Melville

Southey, Robert

Dedication: "Bob Southey! You're a poet —
  poet-laureate." Byron
Rebuke to Robert Southey, A. *Unknown*

Soy Sauce

Soy Sauce. Snyder

Space and Space Travel

Achieving Perspective. Rogers
Apollo 8. Berryman
Autoincineration of the Right Stuff. Argüelles
Autosonic Door. Thompson
Canopus. Taylor
Christmas 1959 et Cetera. Barrax
First Walk on the Moon. Swenson
Moon Landing. Auden
Moonwalk. Engels
On Shooting Particles beyond the
  World. Eberhart
Package for Another World. Sharah
Tiros II. Chappell
Walk on the Moon. Momaday

Spain

And I remember Spain. MacNeice
Feller I Know, A. Austin
García Lorca: A Photograph of the Granada
  Cemetery, 1966. Levis
Here's another Spaniard! Welcome! Machado
  Ruiz
Lost Fan, Hotel Californian, Fresno,
  1923. Levis
Madrid. Wright
On the Banks of the Duero. Machado Ruiz
On the Right. "MacDiarmid"
Plaça Santiago, The. "Eliot"
Poem for Garcia Lorca. Woodcock
Port Bou. Spender
Quit now the town, and with a journeying
  dream. "Eliot"
Recollections of a Day's Journey in
  Spain. Southey
Spain. Symons
You Hated Spain. Hughes

Spanish-American Verse. *See* **Hispanic Verse.**

Spanish-American War

Breath on the Oat. Taylor
Deeds of Valor at Santiago. Scollard
Dewey at Manila. Johnson
On a Soldier Fallen in the Philippines. Moody
Unmanifest Destiny. Hovey

Spanish Armada

Armada, The. Macaulay
Armada, 1588, The. Wilson
Joyful [*or* Joyfull] New Ballad, A. Deloney
Sailor's Only Delight, The. *Unknown*
Sir Francis Drake; or, Eighty-eight. *Unknown*

Spanish Civil War. *See* **Civil War, Spanish.**

Spanish Succession, War of the

Battle of Blenheim, The. Southey

But O, my Muse, what numbers wilt thou
  find. Addison
Word's gone out, and now they spread the
  main, The. Defoe
See also **Blenheim, Battle of (1704).**

Spankings

Whipping, The. Hayden

Sparrows

Because You Asked about the Line between
  Prose and Poetry. Nemerov
Bee, the Ant, and the Sparrow, The. Cotton
Breakfast. Williams
Cat and the Two Sparrows, The. De la
  Fontaine
City Sparrow. Mayhall
Dead Sparrow, The. Cartwright
Did You Ever Hear an English Sparrow
  Sing? Johnston
Disaster, The. Savage
Haiku: "I know the footsteps of the
  sparrow." Hosai
Haiku: "Sparrows all at once are gone,
  The." Hosai
Hedge-Sparrows and House-Sparrows. Fuller
I let the sparrows play. Issa
Icehouse in Summer, The. Nemerov
Little cock sparrow sat on a tree, A. *Unknown*
Mr. and Mrs. Spikky Sparrow. Lear
Song of the Reed Sparrow, The. *Unknown*
Sparrow, The. Williams
Sparrow and Diamond, The. Green
Sparrow goes in and out of jail, A. Issa
Sparrow in the Zoo, The. Nemerov
Sparrow in Winter. Takahashi Shinkichi
Sparrows. Buckley
Sparrows' Chorus, The. Jennings
Sparrow's Fall, The. Harper
Sparrow's Feather, A. Barker
Sparrows' friendship breaks up. Issa
Spring day: a sparrow sand-bathing in my
  garden. Onitsura
Upon the Death of His Sparrow; an
  Elegie. Herrick

Sparta, Greece

Death of Leonidas, The. Croly
Demaeneta sent eight sons. Dioscorides
Demetrius fled the fight in fear. Erycius of
  Cyzicus
On the Spartan Dead at
  Thermopylae. Simonides
On the Tomb of the Spartan Dead at
  Thermopylae. *Unknown*
To the Lacedemonians. Tate

Spas

Tunbridge Wells. Rochester

Speech

Effort at Speech between Two
  People. Rukeyser
Overworked Elocutionist, An. Wells
See also **Screams; Talk.**

Spelling

I before E. *Unknown*
Jack Jelf. *Unknown*
Persimmons. Lee
Principal and Principle. *Unknown*

Spenser, Edmund ("Colin Clout")

Gentle Spenser. Wordsworth
Grave moral Spenser after these came
  on. Drayton
In trellised shed with clustering roses
  gay. Wordsworth
Master. Kennelly
Muse of my Spenser, who so well could
  sing. Crabbe
Spenser! a jealous honourer of thine. Keats
Sweet Spenser, sweetest bard; yet not more
  sweet. Southey
To Spenser. Reynolds
To the Most Excellent and Learned Shepherd,
  Colin Clout. Smith
Upon Master Edmund Spenser. Beaumont
Vision upon This Conceit of the Faerie [*or*
  Fairy] Queene [*or* Queen], A. Ralegh

Sphinx

Mouth of the Wolf. Stewart

Myth. Rukeyser
Sphinx, The. Emerson

Spiders

Arachne. Empson
Broken, The. Merwin
Christmas Spider, The. Richards
Design. Frost
Discoveries in Arizona. Wright
Geese, The. Graham
I Would Visit Him in the Corner. Ríos
Image, The. Fuller
In White. Frost
Incey Wincey Spider. *Unknown*
Mr. Edwards and the Spider. Lowell
Mrs. Spider. Livingston
Natural History. White
Noiseless Patient Spider, A. Whitman
Parson's Pleasure. Higgs
Slowly/ like a crippled cow. Rabéarivelo
Spider. Basho
Spider, The. Eberhart
Spider. Farber
Spider, The. Littleton
Spider, The. Vallejo
Spider and the Fly, The. Howitt
Spider and the Ghost of the Fly, The. Lindsay
Spider holds a silver ball, The. Dickinson
Study of a Spider, The. De Tabley
To a Spider. Southey
To the Spider. Russell
To the Spider in the Crevice behind the Toilet
  Door. Sutherland
Upon a Spider Catching a Fly. Taylor

Spies

Childhood of a Spy. Davis
On Spies. Jonson
Perfidia. Lehman

Spinning and Spinners

Factory Workers' Song. *Unknown*
My Mother Spinning. Olds
You might easy know a doffer. *Unknown*

Spinsters

Eleanor Rigby. Lennon
I'll Marry Not at All. *Unknown*
Leftover Blessings. Kasdorf
Lizzie. Couto
Mezzo Cammin. Moffett
Miss Gee. Auden
My Aunt. Holmes
My Mother's Sister. Day Lewis
O Jenny Dear. Blamire
Old Ladies, The. Ellis
Old Maid's Song. *Unknown*
Some Foreign Letters. Sexton
Spinster. Plath
Spinster's Lullaby. Miller
Three Sisters. De la Mare
Tunnel, The. Parra
Upon Himself. Herrick

Spiritualists

Plain Song. Raine

Spirituals

Go Down, Moses. *Unknown*
Negro Spiritual. Trott
Negro Spirituals. Benét
O Black and Unknown Bards. Johnson
Swing Low, Sweet Chariot. *Unknown*

Spittoons

Brass Spittoons. Hughes

Sports

First Practice. Gildner
Frisbee. Humphries
On the Ambivalence of Male Contact
  Sports. Ewart
Owdham Footbo'. Wrigley
We Used to Play. Welch
Where fair Sabrina's wand'ring currents
  flow. Somervile
With tramps, and brooms, and stones, a crowd
  now comes. Fisher
See also **Athletes; Games; names of
  individual sports.**

Spring

Abishag. Fichman
After Dark Vapours. Keats

Stars around the luminous moon — how soon
   they. Sappho
Stars at Night. Takenaka Iku
Stars, I Have Seen Them Fall. Housman
Stars in Apple Cores. Shaw
Stars of the superior class. Smart
Stars over the Dordogne. Plath
Summer Stars. Sandburg
Suns in a skein, the uncut stones of
   night. Fuller
Taking Turns. Farber
To Himself. Gryphius
To the Evening Star. Blake
To the Evening Star. Campbell
Traveling Star. Simovic
Twilight. Menashe
Waiting Both. Hardy
When I Heard the Learn'd
   Astronomer. Whitman
When Sun Doth Rise. Williams
Winter Heavens. Meredith
Wishing Poem. *Unknown*
You Black Bright Stars. Morley
See also **Astronomy and Astronomers;**
   Astrophysics; Constellations; Sky.
Statistics
Meditation on Statistical Method. Cunningham
Statue of Liberty. *See* **Liberty, Statue of.**
Statues
After Plotinus. Stafford
Archaic Torso of Apollo. Rilke
By the Statue of King Charles [or I] at Charing
   Cross. Johnson
Christmas Eve under Hooker's Statue. Lowell
Colossus, The. Plath
Duke of York's Statue, The. Landor
Figures, The. Creeley
Founder, The. Stern
Frozen Hero, The. Vance
Green Mountain Boy. Smyth
Haiku: "Carved into Buddha's form." Hosai
I Carried Statues. Nagy
Marble Statuette Harpist. Allen
On a Statue of Sir Arthur Sullivan. Hamilton
Ozymandias [or Ozymandias of Egypt or
   Sonnet: Ozymandias]. Shelley
Rider Victory, The. Muir
Spanish Lions, The. McGinley
Statue, The. Creeley
Statue, The. Roseveare
Statue, The. Sweeney
Statues. Raine
Statues, The. Yeats
Venus of Milo, The. Ray
Steak
Thoughts of Loved Ones. Fishback
Steam Baths. *See* **Baths and Bathing.**
Steam Rollers
To a Steam Roller. Moore
Steam Shovels
Steam Shovel, The. Bennett
Steam Shovel. Malam
Steamers. *See* **Ships and Shipbuilding.**
Steel
Bar of steel — it is only, A. Sandburg
My Father's Garden. Wagoner
Prayers of Steel. Sandburg
Smoke and Steel. Sandburg
See also **Iron.**
Steel Bands
Pans at Carnival. Beissel
Steeples
Steeple-Jack, The. Moore
To a Solitary Disciple. Williams
Steers. *See* **Oxen.**
Stein, Gertrude
They Don't Speak English in Paris. Nash
Stenographers
Stenographers, The. Page
See also **Scribes; Secretaries.**
Stephen, Saint
Feast o' Saint [or St.] Stephen, The. Sawyer
Feast of Stephen, The. Nichols
Good King Wenceslas. *Unknown*

St. Stephen's Day. Dickinson
Upon Stephen Stoned. Suckling
Sterne, Laurence
Epitaph on Laurence Sterne. Garrick
Stevedores. *See* **Longshoremen.**
Stevens, Wallace
So Long? Stevens. Berryman
Stevenson, Robert Louis
Apparition. Henley
Kidnapped. Bible, Apocrypha
Stockmen
Man from Snowy River, The. Paterson
Sick Stockrider, The. Gordon
Stoicism
It might be lonelier. Dickinson
Old Stoic, The. Brontë
Stoic. Durrell
Stonecutters
To the Stone-Cutters. Jeffers
Stonehenge, England
In Love, at Stonehenge. Patmore
Salisbury Plain and Stonehenge. Wordsworth
Seven Wonders of England, The. Sidney
Stonehenge. Drayton
To My Friend, Dr. Charleton, on His Learned
   and Useful Works; and More Particularly
   This of Stone-Heng, by Him Restored to the
   True Founders. Dryden
Written at Stonehenge. Warton
Stones and Rocks
Apologia pro Vita Sua. Ammons
Birth of a Stone. Kim
Black Pebble, The. Reeves
Black Rock of Kiltearn. Young
Crystals like Blood. "MacDiarmid"
Cutting Edge, The. Levine
How happy is the little stone. Dickinson
I've Got a Home in That Rock. Patterson
Mason, The. Farren
Minerals of Cornwall, Stones of
   Cornwall. Redgrove
Naskeag. Corn
Palace of Rocks, The. Yuan Chieh
Path among the Stones, The. Kinnell
Pebble, The. Ponge
Phenomenology of Stones, The. McCarthy
Rock Climbing. Cooper
Serenity in Stones, The. Ortiz
Shiprock. Adler
Silica Carbonate Rock. Berry
Standing Stone. Bidgood
Stone, The. Blackburn
Stone. Justice
Stone. Simic
Stone, The. Vaughan
Symbolum. Goethe
Tergvinder's Stone. Merwin
This Is My Rock. McCord
Thyme Flowering among Rocks. Wilbur
To the Stone-Cutters. Jeffers
Token. Bielski
Stonington, Battle of
Battle of Stonington on the Seaboard of
   Connecticut, The. Freneau
Stony Point, Battle of (1779)
Storming of Stony Point, The. Guiterman
Wayne at Stony Point. Scollard
Storms
After the Music. Riley
Approach of the Storm, The. *Unknown*
Ballad of the Tempest. Fields
Beginning to Squall. Swenson
Black Cloud, The. Davies
Brainstorm. Nemerov
City-Storm. Monro
Eastern Tempest. Blunden
Epitaph Ending in And, The. Stafford
Equinox, The. Heyward
Far off brough, A. *Unknown*
Fifties, The. Rose
First Things First. Auden
First Winter Storm. Everson
Found in a Storm. Stafford
Gale in April. Jeffers
Golden Hour, The. Moore

Hailstone, The. Didsbury
Hatteras Calling. Aiken
History. McGrath
Hurricane, The. Freneau
If Only I Knew the Truth, I Swear I Would
   Act on It. Goodman
In Cold Storm Light. Silko
Island, The. Kennelly
It. Snyder
It sounded as if the streets were
   running. Dickinson
Late Light. Blunden
Late Summer Storm. Churches
Lengthening Days. *Unknown*
Lightning. Oliver
Little Exercise at 4. A.M. Bishop
Lord Ullin's Daughter. Campbell
Low Barometer. Bridges
Mightier Storms than This. Santayana
On a Sea-Storm nigh the Coast. Steere
Room for All. Holmes
Safe. Walker
Sheltering Places. Dawe
Snow! Hail! Lower! Lightning!
   Thunder! Asclepiades
Snow Storm, The. Fordham
Snow-Storm, The. Emerson
Spring Storm. Miller
Storm. Dutton
Storm, The. Herbert
Storm. McGough
Storm, The. Patmore
Storm, The. Shanks
Storm, The. Wallace
Storm. Wright
Storm and Calm: Sent from Embden to M.
   Edw. Ma. and M. Tho. Ly., The. Murford
Storm and the Calm, The. De Arguijo
Storm at Sea. Davenant
Storm at Sea. *Unknown*
Storm Cone, The. Kipling
Storm Fear. Frost
Storm from the East, A. Whittemore
Storm in April, A. Wilbur
Storm in Summer, A. Blunt
Storm is over, the land hushes to rest,
   The. Bridges
Storm Warning. Moss
Storm Warnings. Rich
Storm Windows. Nemerov
Stormy Morning, The. Müller
Stormy Night in Autumn. Chu Shu-chen
Sudden storms that heave me to and fro,
   The. Surrey
Summer Night. *Unknown*
Tempest, The. Smith
Tempest, The. *Unknown*
Tempest, The. Zaturenska
That Is All I Heard. "Yehoash"
Thunder mutters louder and more loud,
   The. Clare
Thunderstorm, A. Lampman
Thunderstorm. Mitchell
Thunderstorm in Town, A. Hardy
Tornado. Stafford
Waiting for the Storm. Mangan
West Palm Beach Storm, The. *Unknown*
Wet Night, A. Ryan
Wild Night, A. Howe
Wind. Hughes
Wind begun to knead the grass,
   The. Dickinson
Wind begun to rock the grass, The. Dickinson
Wind Took Up the Northern Things,
   The. Dickinson
Windy Gap. Campbell
See also **Blizzards.**
Story Poems
Best Loved Story Poems (BeLS). Walter E.
   Thwing, ed.
Everyman Book of Narrative Verse, The
   (EBNV). David Herbert, ed.
Modern Ballads and Story Poems
   (MoBS). Charles Causley, ed.
Oxford Book of Narrative Verse, The
   (OBNV). Iona Opie *and* Peter Opie, eds.

House on the Hill, The. Robinson
It is the pain, it is the pain, endures. Empson
Missing Dates. Empson
Obsessions. Levertov
One Art. Bishop
Runes for an Old Believer. Humphries
Unknown, The. Davidson
Villanelle of Marguerites. Dowson
Waking, The. Roethke
Want Bone, The. Pinsky
Women in Love. Justice

Villon, François
Ballad of François Villon, A. Swinburne
Ballade which Villon Made. MacDonagh

Vilna, Poland
Like Groping Fingers. Sutskever
Secret Town, The. Sutskever
Vilna 1938. Ehrlich
We Survive! Glick

Vinci, Leonardo da. See Leonardo da Vinci.

Vines
Tapestry Trees. Morris
Vine, The. Sun Ching-hsuan

Vinland
Story of Vinland, The. Lanier

Violence
Alley, The. Cervantes
Arms and the Man. Butler
Be punctual then to know. Unknown
Beating, The. Stanford
Because the Wind Remembers. Chipasula
Beginnings. Weaver
Bloody Sire, The. Jeffers
Book of Invader. Sinclair
Club, The. Yamada
Crusader. McGough
Danny. Synge
Dogs. Longville
Dusk. Chipasula
For the Record. Lorde
Geneology. Kaufman
Ghost of My Mother, The. Simpson
Great Palaces of Versailles, The. Dove
He Was Lucky. Swirszczynska
Kristallnacht. Sinclair
Legend, The. Hongo
Militerotics. Ortleb
Missing Patriarch, The. Weaver
New Speaker. Berry
Other Forms of Slaughter. Acholonu
Robben Island Sequence. Brutus
Say You Love Me. Peacock
Slade's Invective. Sinclair
Snowy Egret. Weigl
Street Fight. Monro
Talking of Sharp Things. Chipasula
This Morning. Rukeyser
Tywater. Wilbur
Unlocking the Doors. Breckenridge
Yesterday. Gu Cheng

Violets
Coming by a mountain path. Basho
How Violets Came Blue. Herrick
Not content, the violets have dyed. Shiba Sonome
On a Violet in Her Breast. Stanley
Sea Violet. Doolittle
Sonnet: "I had no thought of violets of late." Dunbar-Nelson
Sweet Violets. Unknown
To Violets. Herrick
Violet, The. Goethe
Violet, The. Taylor
Violets. Moultrie
Violets. Ropes
Violets. Unknown
Violets have withered. Shiba Sonome
Yellow Violet, The. Bryant

Violins
My Fiddle. Riley
Out-of-the-Body Travel. Plumly
Touch of the Master's Hand, The. Welch

Virgin Islands
Beauties of Santa Cruz, The. Freneau
Skin Diving in the Virgins. Brinnin

Virgins, The. Walcott

Virgin Mary. See Mary, the Virgin.

Virginia
As Toilsome I Wander'd Virginia's Woods. Whitman
Carry Me Back to Old Virginny. Bland
Farewell: "Gone, gone — sold and gone." Whittier
Jamestown. Jarrell
Leafless Trees, Chickahominy Swamp. Smith
Life-long, Poor Browning. Spencer
Low Fields and Light. Merwin
Monticello. Sarton
On a Field Trip at Fredericksburg. Smith
Snowy Egret. Weigl
Springfield, Virginia. Rouse
To the Virginian Voyage. Drayton
Virginia. Eliot
Virginians of the Valley, The. Ticknor

Virginity
Advice to Lovers. Armstrong
Alas How Long ("Alas how long shall I and my maidenhead lie"). Unknown
Beware Fair Maide. At. to Sylvester
Blow Away the Morning Dew. Unknown
Bride: Maidenhood, Maidenhood. Sappho
Broomfield Hill, The. Unknown
Chastity ("I Mean That Too, But Yet a Hidden Strength"). Milton
Deflowering. Jamal
Dialogue after Enjoyment. Cowley
Epitaph of a Girl. Unknown
Epithalamium: "Hymen, god of marriage bed." Rutter
Honour. Cowley
How hard a fate enthrals the wretched maid. Virgil
In Bertram's Garden. Justice
In Praise of Virginity. Hroswitha
Inscription on a Chemise. Unknown
Like to a ring without a finger. Unknown
My Little Love Lies on the Ground. Paraske
O Wha's the Bride? "MacDiarmid"
On the Marriage of a Virgin. Thomas
She Being Brand. Cummings
Something Old, Something New. Greene
Song: "Where shall Celia fly for shelter." Smart
Tarpeia. Guiney
To Mistress M. A. Lluellyn [or Lluelyn]
True Maid, A. Prior
Twa Magicians, The. Unknown
Virgin, The. Jackson
Virgin Life, A. Barker
Virgo, August. Taylor
What are you saving it for? Asclepiades
Whistle, Daughter, Whistle. Unknown
Whiteness, or Chastity. Beaumont

Virtue
Blessed Is the Man. Moore
Loyal Woman's No, A. Larcom
Sonnet: "'Tis dead of night; storms rend the troubled air." Locke
To you I dedicate this work of grace. Lanier
Twin-born. Wilcox
Under this plaque I lie, the famous woman. Unknown
Virtue. Herbert
Virtue alone can never die. but lives to. Taylor

Viruses
First Photos of Flu Virus. Witt

Vishnu
Gita Govinda, The. Jayadeva
Hymn to Tirumal (Visnu). Kirantaiyar

Vision
Another transparent skin has grown. Pollak
First the light cracked. Pollak
Her voice enters the room. Pollak
I wake to the sound of rain. Pollak

Visiting and Visitors
Door-Bell, The. Becker
Doorbells. Field
Guest, The. "Akhmatova"
I know a washerwoman, she knows me. Unknown

Invitation. Unknown
Last Supper. Sweeney
Some One. De la Mare
Tête à Tête; or, Fashionable Pair: an Eclogue, The. Murry
Visit. Ammons
Visit, The. Leapor
Visit the Sick. Metcalfe

Vivaldi, Antonio
Vivaldi. Schwartz

Vocations. See Occupations.

Vogler, Georg Joseph
Abt Vogler. Browning

Voices
London ("I wander through each chartered street"). Blake
Successful Summer, A. Schubert
Tone of Voice, The. Unknown
Upon Julia's Voice. Herrick
Voices. Dauenhauer
What Voice at Moth-Hour. Warren
See also Screams; Speech; Talk.

Volcanoes
But lo! The reaking surface of the vale. Singleton
Crusoe in England. Bishop
Listening Nydia. Ray
Loo-wit. Rose
On Mayon Volcano. Lewis
Peace. Lawrence
Romance. Turner
Soufrière. Salkey
Then earthquakes, nature's agonizing pangs. Grainger
Volcano. Van Sertima
Volcanoes. Akhmadulina
Volcanoes be in Sicily. Dickinson

Voltaire, François Marie Arouet de
Mock On, Mock On, Voltaire, Rousseau. Blake
Voltaire at Ferney. Auden

Voodoo
Country Graveyard. Pressoir
Francie-the-Possessed. Durand
Voodoo. Laleau
Women's Locker Room. Waniek

Voting and Voters
Deliverance. Harper
Juchitán. Rodriguez
Negro Ballot, The. Moorer
Poll. Roberson
Vote for Lunn. Unknown
Vote, vote, vote for (Billy Martin). Unknown
See also Woman Suffrage.

Vowels
A E I O U. Swift
On the Vowels — a Riddle. Swift

Voyages
Christmas at Sea. Stevenson
Crossing the Atlantic. Sexton
First Night at Sea. Berryman
Helena Embarks for Palestine. Cynewulf
Ice. Gould
North Ship, The. Larkin
Pat Cloherty's Version of The Maisie. Murphy
St. Andrew's Voyage to Mermedonia. Unknown
Seafarer, The. Unknown
To the Virginian Voyage. Drayton
Voyage. Gardinier
What triumph moves on the billows so blue? Lewis

Voyeurism
Close under here, I watched two lovers once. "Hyde"
Fiend, The. Dickey
Girl in a Window, A. Wright
Mary Pary Pinder. Unknown
Outhouse. Ristovic
Peeper, The. Davison
Peeping Tom. Hope
Voyeur. Hardy

Vulcan
Execration upon Vulcan, An. Jonson
Shield of Achilles, The. Auden

Z